Jonangeliz Alvarez Rodriguez
P9-DHS-260

THE *American Heritage*®

DESK DICTIONARY AND THESAURUS

Houghton Mifflin Harcourt

Boston • New York

Words are included in this dictionary on the basis of their usage. Words that are known to have current trademark registrations are shown with an initial capital and are also identified as trademarks. No investigation has been made of common-law trademark rights in any word, because such investigation is impracticable. The inclusion of any word in this dictionary is not, however, an expression of the publisher's opinion as to whether or not it is subject to proprietary rights. Indeed, no definition in this dictionary is to be regarded as affecting the validity of any trademark.

Visit our websites: hmhco.com *and* ahdictionary.com

ISBN: 978-0-544-17618-8

Library of Congress Cataloging-in-Publication Data

The American Heritage desk dictionary and thesaurus.
p. cm.
ISBN-13: 978-0-618-59261-6
ISBN-10: 0-618-59261-X
1. English language--United States--Dictionaries. 2. English language--United States--Synonyms and antonyms. 3. English language--Dictionaries. 4. English language--Synonyms and antonyms. I. Title: Desk dictionary and thesaurus. II. Houghton Mifflin Company.
PE2835.A47 2005
423--dc22

2005012406

Manufactured in the United States of America

3 4 5 6 7 8 9 10 - EB - 19 18 17 16 15

EDITORIAL AND PRODUCTION STAFF

TABLE OF CONTENTS

GUIDE TO THE DICTIONARY AND THESAURUS

This Dictionary and Thesaurus is designed for ease of use and convenience. Each page is split into two sections: the top portion of each page is a dictionary, and the bottom portion is a thesaurus. The following guide explains the conventions used in presenting the information that is contained in the Dictionary and Thesaurus, enabling you to find and understand that information quickly and easily.

Guide to the Dictionary Portion

Main Entries. Entries are listed in alphabetical order without taking into account spaces or hyphens. Two or more entries with identical spellings but different origins are distinguished by superscript numbers. For example: **ground**^{1}, **ground**^{2}, **groundbreaking, ground floor, groundhog, groundless**. A boldface guideword at the top of each even-numbered page shows the first main dictionary entry on that page, and a boldface guideword at the top of each odd-numbered page shows the last main dictionary entry on that page. Thus **balk** and **bankrupt** and all of the entries that fall alphabetically between them are entered and defined on pages 58 and 59. Entry words of more than one syllable are divided by centered dots. Syllable dots are omitted for parts of compound words that are also main entries in the Dictionary; for example, see **consumer goods** (p. 163).

Variant Forms. If a word has two or more different spellings, the definition appears at the spelling that is most frequently used. The variant spellings are shown in boldface type after the main entry. The word "or" separates two forms that are used with approximately equal frequency; "also" introduces a variant that is less frequent. Variant forms are listed separately when they fall more than ten entries away from the main entry.

Pronunciations. Pronunciations appear in parentheses after boldface entry words. If a word has more than one pronunciation, the first pronunciation is usually more common than the other, but often they are equally common. The pronunciation symbols used in this Dictionary are shown on page xii.

Inflected Forms. Inflected forms regarded as being irregular or those offering possible spelling problems are entered in boldface type, often in shortened form. Pronunciations are given only if they differ significantly from the base form of the word:

good (go͝od) ▸ *adj.* **bet·ter** (bĕt′ər), **best** (bĕst). 1. Being ...

com·pute (kəm-pyo͞ot′) ▸ *v.* **–put·ed, –put·ing.** 1. To ...

ax·is (ăk′sĭs) ▸ *n., pl.* **ax·es** (ăk′sēz′). 1. A ...

The inflected forms of verbs are given in the following order: past tense, past participle (if it differs from the past tense), and present participle. Irregular inflected forms are listed separately when they fall more than ten entries away from the main entry.

Verbs. Verbal definitions indicate transitivity or intransitivity by their wording. In the following examples, **bloom** is defined intransitively and **shuck** transitively:

bloom (blo͞om) ... ▸ *v.* 1. To bear flowers.

shuck (shŭk) ... ▸ *v.* 1. To remove the husk or shell from.

Parentheses are used in certain transitive definitions to indicate a usual or typical direct object:

de·clas·si·fy (dē-klăs′ə-fī′) ▸ *v.* To remove official security classification from (a document).

Parentheses are also used around a final preposition to indicate that a verb can be used either transitively or intransitively in that sense:

> **kink** (kĭngk) ▸ *n.* 1. A tight curl ... ▸ *v.* To form a kink (in).

Labels. The following labels, set in italics, indicate that an entry word or a definition is limited to a particular level or style of usage: *Nonstandard* is applied to forms and usages that educated speakers and writers consider unacceptable (e.g., **ain't**); *Informal* indicates a term whose acceptability is limited to conversation and informal writing (e.g., **enthuse**); *Slang* indicates a style of language that is distinguished by a striving for rhetorical effect through the use of extravagant, often facetious coinages or figures of speech (e.g., **boffo**); and *Offensive* is reserved for words and expressions considered insulting and derogatory. Other, usually abbreviated labels, such as *Geol.* and *Electron.*, identify the special area of knowledge to which an entry word of a definition applies, while such labels as *Scots* and *Chiefly Brit.* identify an entry as a form that is used chiefly in another part of the English-speaking world.

Undefined Forms. At the end of many entries additional boldface words appear without definitions. They are closely and clearly related in basic meaning to the entry word but may have different grammatical functions.

Abbreviations. Common abbreviations used in this Dictionary and Thesaurus, such as *adj.*, *pl.*, *var.*, and *e.g.*, are main entries. A list of the abbreviations used in this book can also be found on pages x–xi.

Guide to the Thesaurus Portion

Entry Order. Headwords are listed alphabetically in boldface type and are followed by an italic part-of-speech label. If a headword has more than one part of speech, each additional part of speech appears boldface and indented within the same entry. Phrasal verbs (two-word verbs consisting of a verb and an adverb or preposition) are listed in alphabetical order, also boldface and indented, directly under the base verbs:

> **smile** *n.* A facial expression marked by an upward curving of the lips ▸ grin, simper, smirk. [*Compare* SNEER.]
> **smile** *v.* To curve the lips upward in expressing amusement, pleasure, or happiness ▸ beam, grin, simper, smirk. ***Idioms:*** break into a smile, crack (*or* flash *or* give) a smile.
> **smile on** or **upon** *v.* To lend supportive approval to ▸ countenance, encourage, favor. [*Compare* APPROVE, SUPPORT.]

Synonym Lists. Synonyms are presented in lists following the definition to which they belong; they are introduced by the symbol ▸.

> **absent-minded** *adj.* So lost in thought as to be unable to remember or attend to things ▸ absent, abstracted, bemused, distracted, distrait, faraway, forgetful, inattentive, lost, oblivious, preoccupied, scatter-brained. *Slang:* spaced-out, spacy. ***Idioms:*** a million miles away, gathering wool, lost (*or* off) in space, out of it. [*Compare* CARELESS, DETACHED, DREAMY, NEGLIGENT.]

Most of the synonyms in a list are also entered individually at their own alphabetical place in the Thesaurus as cross-references. Many words appear in more than one synonym list, and so are cross-referenced to more than one main entry.

> **forgetful** *adj.* —*See* ABSENT-MINDED, CARELESS.

Note that many of the entries in the Thesaurus contain both main-entry lists, which are generally grouped first in the entry, and cross-references, which follow the senses listed under a part of speech and are introduced by *See also*:

> **blink** *v.* To open and close one or both eyes rapidly ▸ bat, flutter, nictitate, twinkle, wink. —*See also* GLITTER, RENEGE, SURRENDER (1).
> **blink at** *v.* To pretend not to see ▸ connive at, disregard, ignore, overlook, pass over, wink at. ***Idioms:*** be blind to, close (*or* shut) one's eyes to, let go (*or* pass), look the other way, make allowances for, sweep under the rug, turn a blind eye (*or* deaf ear) to.
> **blink** *n.* A brief closing of the eyes ▸ bat, flutter, nictitation, wink. —*See also* FLASH (1), FLASH (2).

Senses and Definitions. The main entries in this Thesaurus are organized into defined senses, as in a dictionary. Each sense begins with a brief definition that identifies the central meaning shared by the entry word and its synonyms. If an entry has more than one sense for any part of speech, the senses are numbered. Numbering begins again, if needed, for each new part of speech. In the entry for **breach**, the noun has two numbered senses; the verb has only one sense and is unnumbered:

> **breach** *n.* **1.** An act of breaking a law or of nonfulfillment of an obligation ▸ contravention, delinquency, dereliction, infraction, infringement, malfeasance, nonfeasance, negligence, transgression, trespass, violation. [*Compare* CRIME.] **2.** An interruption in friendly relations ▸ alienation, break, breakdown, collapse, disaffection, estrangement, falling out, fissure, rent, rift, rupture, schism, split. [*Compare* ARGUMENT.] —*See also* CRACK (2).
> **breach** *v.* To make a hole or other opening in ▸ break (through), gap, hole, perforate, pierce, punch (through), puncture. *Slang:* bust (through). [*Compare* CUT.] —*See also* VIOLATE (1).

When an entry with only one part of speech has a single sense that is a cross-reference, the definition is omitted as unnecessary. The definition for such a sense will be found at the main entry to which the cross-reference points:

> **boaster** *n.* —*See* BRAGGART.
>
> **braggart** *v.* One given to boasting ▸ blusterer, boaster, brag, braggadocio, bragger, swaggerer, vaunter. *Informal:* blowhard. *Slang:* blower, windbag. [*Compare* EGOIST, SHOW-OFF.]
> **braggart** *adj.* —*See* BOASTFUL.

Cross-References. There are three distinct types of cross-references between synonym lists. A cross-reference introduced by the word *See* leads from a *cross-reference entry* to the full *main-entry list*, as described above. If the word you have looked up contains a *See* cross-reference, you know that you will find the complete list of synonyms for that sense, including all labeled terms and idioms, at the entry to which the cross-reference points.

A second kind of cross-reference leads from a cross-reference entry with multiple senses to a main entry elsewhere in the alphabetical list. These are the *See also* cross-references listed at the end of an entry and described above.

A third kind of cross-reference, enclosed in brackets and introduced by the word *Compare*, leads from a synonym list at a main entry to one or more other, closely related main entries elsewhere in the Thesaurus. If you have already found the right synonym for your purpose, you may not choose to follow a *Compare* cross-reference. However, if you want to consider other synonyms with similar but somewhat different meanings, the *Compare* cross-references will help you broaden your search:

> **anchor** *n.* A device for supporting or holding in place ▸ brake, dowel, grapnel, kedge, mooring, wedge. [*Compare* BOND, CORD, FASTENER, NAIL.] —*See also* PRESS.
> **anchor** *v.* —*See* FASTEN.
>
> **nail** *v.* —*See* CAPTURE, FASTEN, HIT.
> **nail** *n.* A bolt or shaft that is hammered or drilled in place and is used to support or hold together ▸ bolt, peg, pin, rivet, screw, spike, stud, tack. [*Compare* ANCHOR, CORD, FASTENER.]

Labels. All words requiring status labels are clearly tagged at the boldface entry word and in synonym lists. The usage labels *Informal* and *Slang* indicate levels of usage and styles of expression that may not be appropriate in all contexts. *Informal* generally applies to those words that are commonly used in the spoken language and in ordinary writing but that may not be appropriate in formal or official contexts. The word *buddy*, for example, carries an *Informal* label in the synonym list at **friend**. *Slang*, on the other hand, is a style of language characteristic of very casual speech. The *Slang* label appears at words and special senses of words that have an exceptionally vivid, humorous, irreverent, or sarcastic flavor. For example, at the synonym list at **eat**, the word *chow down* is labeled *Slang*.

The dialect label *Chiefly Regional* indicates that a term is indigenous to one or more geographic areas within the United States. For example, the words *chaw*, a synonym of **chew**, and *poorly*, a synonym of **sick**, are labeled *Chiefly Regional* because they are more commonly used in some parts of the country than in others.

ABBREVIATIONS USED IN THIS DICTIONARY AND THESAURUS

abbr.	abbreviation	E	east, eastern
A.D.	anno Domini	Eccles.	Ecclesiastical
adj.	adjective	Ecol.	Ecology
adv.	adverb	Econ.	Economics
Amer.	American	e.g.	for example
Anat.	Anatomy	Elect.	Electricity
Anthro.	Anthropology	Electron.	Electronics
Archit.	Architecture	esp.	especially
approx.	approximately	fl.	flourished
Astron.	Astronomy	ft	foot, feet
b.	born	gen.	generally
B.C.	before Christ	Geol.	Geology
Biol.	Biology	Gk. Myth.	Greek Mythology
Bot.	Botany	Gram.	Grammar
Brit.	British	in.	inch(es)
Bus.	Business	indef. art.	indefinite article
c.	circa	indic.	indicative
Cap.	capital	interj.	interjection
Chem.	Chemistry	I.	Island
cm	centimeter(s)	Is.	Islands
comp.	comparative	km	kilometer(s)
Comp. Sci.	Computer Science	kph	kilometers per hour
conj.	conjunction	Lat.	Latin
d.	died	Ling.	Linguistics
DC	District of Columbia	m	meter(s)
def. art.	definite article	Math.	Mathematics

ABBREVIATIONS USED IN THIS DICTIONARY AND THESAURUS (continued)

Medic.	Medicine	pref.	prefix
Metall.	Metallurgy	prep.	preposition
Meteorol.	Meteorology	prob.	probably
mph	miles per hour	pron.	pronoun
Mt.	Mountain, Mount	pr.part.	present participle
Mts.	Mountains	pr.t.	present tense
Mus.	Music	Psychol.	Psychology
Myth.	Mythology	p.t.	past tense
N	north, northern	R.	River
n.	noun	Rom. Cath. Ch.	Roman Catholic Church
Naut.	Nautical	Rom. Myth.	Roman Mythology
NE	northeast, northeastern	S	south, southern
NW	northwest, northwestern	SE	southeast, southeastern
orig.	originally	sing.	singular
p.	past	St.	Saint
Pathol.	Pathology	suff.	suffix
pers.	person	superl.	superlative
Philos.	Philosophy	SW	southwest, southwestern
Phys.	Physics	US	United States
Physiol.	Physiology	usu.	usually
pl.	plural	v.	verb
pl.n.	plural noun	var.	variant
Pop.	population	W	west, western
p.part.	past participle	Zool.	Zoology
pr.	present		

PRONUNCIATION KEY

ă	pat	th	thin
ā	pay	*th*	this
âr	care	ŭ	cut
ä	father	ûr	urge, term, firm, word, heard
är	car	v	valve
b	bib	w	with
ch	church	y	yes
d	deed, milled	z	zebra, xylem
ĕ	pet	zh	vision, pleasure, garage
ē	be, bee	ə	about, item, edible, gallon, circus
f	fife, phase, rough		
g	gag		
h	hat		
hw	which		
ĭ	pit		
ī	pie, by		
îr	dear, deer, pier		
j	judge		
k	kick, cat, pique		
l	lid, needle		
m	mum		
n	no, sudden		
ng	thing		
ŏ	pot		
ō	toe		
ô	caught, paw		
ôr	core		
oi	noise, boy		
o͝o	took		
o͝or	lure		
o͞o	boot		
ou	out		
p	pop		
r	roar		
s	sauce		
sh	ship, dish		
t	tight, stopped		

Foreign

œ	French	feu
	German	schön
ü	French	tu
KH	German	ich
	Scottish	loch
N	French	bon

The symbol (ə) is called *schwa*. It represents a vowel with the weakest level of stress in a word. The schwa sound varies slightly according to the vowel it represents or the sounds around it.

Stress is the relative degree of emphasis with which a word's syllables are spoken. An unmarked syllable has the weakest stress in the word. The strongest, or primary, stress is indicated with a bold mark (**′**). A lighter mark (′) indicates a secondary level of stress. The stress mark follows the syllable it applies to. Words of one syllable have no stress mark, because there is no other stress level that the syllable is compared to.

THE *American Heritage*®

DESK DICTIONARY AND THESAURUS

A

a[1] or **A** (ā) ▸ *n., pl.* **a's** or **A's** also **as** or **As**. 1. The 1st letter of the English alphabet. 2. The 1st in a series. 3. The best in quality or rank. 4. *Mus.* The 6th tone in the scale of C major. 5. **A** A type of blood in the ABO system.

a[2] (ə; ā *when stressed*) ▸ *indef.art.* 1. One: *a region; a person.* 2. Any: *not a drop to drink.*

a[3] (ə) ▸ *prep.* Per: *once a day.*

a[4] ▸ *abbr.* acceleration

A ▸ *abbr.* 1. alto 2. ampere 3. or **Å** angstrom 4. area

a. ▸ *abbr.* 1. acre 2. adjective 3. answer

a–[1] or **an–** ▸ *pref.* Without; not: *amoral.*

a–[2] ▸ *pref.* 1. On; in: *abed.* 2. In the direction of: *astern.* 3. In a specified state: *aflutter.*

aard·vark (ärd′värk′) ▸ *n.* A burrowing African mammal having large ears, a long tubular snout, and strong digging claws.

Aar·on (âr′ən, ăr′-) ▸ In the Bible, the elder brother of Moses.

AB[1] (ā′bē′) ▸ *n.* A type of blood in the ABO system.

AB[2] ▸ *abbr.* Alberta

ab– ▸ *pref.* Away from: *aboral.*

a·back (ə-băk′) ▸ *adv.* By surprise: *I was taken aback by her retort.*

ab·a·cus (ăb′ə-kəs, ə-băk′əs) ▸ *n., pl.* **-cus·es** or **-ci** (ăb′ə-sī′, ə-băk′ī′). A manual computing device consisting of a frame holding parallel rods strung with movable counters.

a·baft (ə-băft′) *Naut.* ▸ *adv.* Toward the stern. ▸ *prep.* Toward the stern from.

ab·a·lo·ne (ăb′ə-lō′nē) ▸ *n.* A large, edible marine gastropod having an ear-shaped shell.

a·ban·don (ə-băn′dən) ▸ *v.* 1. To forsake; desert. 2. To give up completely: *abandoned the ship.* 3. To quit: *abandoned the search.* ▸ *n.* A complete surrender to feeling or impulse. **—a·ban′don·ment** *n.*

a·ban·doned (ə-băn′dənd) ▸ *adj.* 1. Deserted; forsaken. 2. Recklessly unrestrained.

a·base (ə-bās′) ▸ *v.* **a·based, a·bas·ing.** To humble or degrade. **—a·base′ment** *n.*

a·bash (ə-băsh′) ▸ *v.* To make ashamed; disconcert. **—a·bash′ment** *n.*

a·bate (ə-bāt′) ▸ *v.* **a·bat·ed, a·bat·ing.** 1. To reduce in amount, degree, or intensity; lessen. 2. *Law* To make void. **—a·bate′ment** *n.*

ab·at·toir (ăb′ə-twär′) ▸ *n.* A slaughterhouse.

ab·ba·cy (ăb′ə-sē) ▸ *n., pl.* **-cies.** The office, term, or jurisdiction of an abbot.

ab·bess (ăb′ĭs) ▸ *n.* The superior of a convent.

ab·bey (ăb′ē) ▸ *n., pl.* **-beys.** 1. A monastery supervised by an abbot. 2. A convent supervised by an abbess. 3. A church that is or once was part of a monastery or convent.

ab·bot (ăb′ət) ▸ *n.* The superior of a monastery.

abbr. or **abbrev.** ▸ *abbr.* abbreviation

ab·bre·vi·ate (ə-brē′vē-āt′) ▸ *v.* **-at·ed, -at·ing.** To make shorter. **—ab·bre′vi·a′tor** *n.*

ab·bre·vi·a·tion (ə-brē′vē-ā′shən) ▸ *n.* 1. The act or product of shortening. 2. A shortened form of a word or phrase, such as *Tex.* for *Texas.*

ABC (ā′bē-sē′) ▸ *n.* often **ABCs** 1. The alphabet: *learned her ABCs.* 2. The rudiments of reading and writing.

ab·di·cate (ăb′dĭ-kāt′) ▸ *v.* **-cat·ed, -cat·ing.** To relinquish (power or responsibility) formally. **—ab′di·ca′tion** *n.* **—ab′di·ca′tor** *n.*

ab·do·men (ăb′də-mən, ăb-dō′-) ▸ *n.* 1. The part of the body that lies between the thorax and the pelvis; belly. 2. The posterior segment of the body in arthropods. **—ab·dom′i·nal** (ăb-dŏm′ə-nəl) *adj.* **—ab·dom′i·nal·ly** *adv.*

ab·duct (ăb-dŭkt′) ▸ *v.* To carry off by force; kidnap. **—ab·duc′tion** *n.* **—ab·duc′tor** *n.*

a·beam (ə-bēm′) ▸ *adv.* At right angles to the keel of a ship.

a·bed (ə-bĕd′) ▸ *adv.* In bed.

A·bel (ā′bəl) ▸ In the Bible, the son of Adam and Eve; slain by Cain.

Ab·e·na·ki (ä′bə-nä′kē, ăb′ə-năk′ē) or **Ab·na·ki** (äb-nä′kē, ăb-) ▸ *n., pl.* **-ki** or **-kis.** 1. A member of a group of Native American peoples of N New England and S Quebec. 2. The Algonquian language of the Abenaki.

THESAURUS

aback *adv.* Without adequate preparation ▸ short, unawarely, unawares. *Idioms:* by surprise, off guard, without notice.

abandon *v.* 1. To give up or leave completely ▸ abdicate, cast aside, cede, demit, desert, forfeit, forgo, forsake, forswear, hand over, lay aside, lay down, leave, maroon, quit, quitclaim, relinquish, render, renounce, resign, sacrifice, surrender, throw over, waive, yield. *Idioms:* back out on, leave in the lurch, run out on, walk out on. [*Compare* DEFECT, DISCARD, EMPTY.] 2. To cease trying to continue ▸ break off, desist, discontinue, give up, leave off, quit, remit, stop. *Informal:* knock off, swear off. *Slang:* lay off. *Idioms:* call it a day, call it quits, have done with, throw in the towel (*or* sponge). [*Compare* STOP.] 3. To yield oneself unrestrainedly, as to an impulse ▸ deliver, relinquish, surrender. *Idiom:* give oneself up (*or* over). *—See also* DROP (4).

abandon *n.* 1. A complete surrender of inhibition ▸ abandonment, incontinence, unrestraint, wantonness, wildness. [*Compare* ENTHUSIASM, EASE, FREEDOM.] 2. A careless, often reckless regard for consequences ▸ blitheness, carelessness, heedlessness, thoughtlessness. [*Compare* TEMERITY.]

abandoned *adj.* 1. Having been given up and left alone ▸ bereft, derelict, deserted, desolate, forlorn, forsaken, jilted, lorn, marooned, outcast, rejected, relinquished. *Idioms:* left holding the bag, left in the lurch, out in the cold, out on a limb. [*Compare* EMPTY, LONELY, UNRESERVED.] 2. Lacking in moral restraint ▸ dissipated, dissolute, fast, licentious, profligate, rakish, unbridled, unconstrained, uncontrolled, ungoverned, uninhibited, unrestrained, wanton, wild. [*Compare* CORRUPT, UNSCRUPULOUS.]

abandonment *n.* 1. A giving up of a possession, claim, or right ▸ abdication, quitclaim, relinquishment, renunciation, resignation, sacrifice, surrender, waiver. 2. The act of forsaking ▸ dereliction, desertion. *—See also* ABANDON (1), DEFECTION.

abase *v.* *—See* DEBASE, DISGRACE, HUMBLE.

abasement *n.* *—See* DEGRADATION (1).

abash *v.* *—See* EMBARRASS.

abashment *n.* *—See* EMBARRASSMENT.

abate *v.* *—See* DECREASE, DEDUCT, SUBSIDE.

abatement *n.* *—See* DECREASE, DEDUCTION (1), WANING.

abbé *n.* *—See* CLERIC.

abbot *n.* *—See* CLERIC.

abbreviate *v.* *—See* SHORTEN.

abdicate *v.* *—See* ABANDON (1).

abdication *n.* *—See* ABANDONMENT (1).

abduct *v.* To seize and detain a person unlawfully ▸ kidnap, snatch, spirit away, take hostage. [*Compare* SEIZE, STEAL.]

abecedarian *n.* *—See* BEGINNER.

ab·er·ra·tion (ăb′ə-rā′shən) ▸ *n.* **1.** A deviation from the normal, proper, or expected course. **2.** A defect of focus, such as blurring in an image. **—ab′er·rant** (ăb′ər-ənt, ă-bĕr′-) *adj.*

a·bet (ə-bĕt′) ▸ *v.* **a·bet·ted, a·bet·ting.** To encourage or assist, esp. in wrongdoing. **—a·bet′ment** *n.* **—a·bet′tor, a·bet′ter** *n.*

a·bey·ance (ə-bā′əns) ▸ *n.* The condition of being temporarily set aside; suspension.

ab·hor (ăb-hôr′) ▸ *v.* **-horred, -hor·ring.** To regard with loathing; detest. **—ab·hor′rer** *n.*

ab·hor·rence (ăb-hôr′əns, -hŏr′-) ▸ *n.* A feeling of repugnance or loathing. **—ab·hor′rent** *adj.* **—ab·hor′rent·ly** *adv.*

a·bide (ə-bīd′) ▸ *v.* **a·bode** (ə-bōd′) or **a·bid·ed, a·bid·ing. 1.** To put up with; tolerate. **2.** To remain; endure. **3.** To dwell; reside. ***—idiom:* abide by** To comply with: *abide by the rules.* **—a·bid′er** *n.*

a·bid·ing (ə-bī′dĭng) ▸ *adj.* Lasting; enduring.

a·bil·i·ty (ə-bĭl′ĭ-tē) ▸ *n., pl.* **-ties. 1.** The power to do something. **2.** A skill or talent.

ab·ject (ăb′jĕkt′) ▸ *adj.* **1.** Contemptible; despicable: *abject cowardice.* **2.** Miserable; wretched: *abject poverty.* **—ab′ject′ly** *adv.* **—ab·ject′ness, ab·jec′tion** *n.*

ab·jure (ăb-jo͝or′) ▸ *v.* **-jured, -jur·ing. 1.** To renounce under oath. **2.** To recant solemnly; repudiate. **3.** To give up; abstain from. **—ab′ju·ra′tion** *n.*

ab·la·tion (ă-blā′shən) ▸ *n.* **1.** Amputation of a body part. **2.** Reduction or dissipation, as by melting.

ab·la·tive (ăb′lə-tĭv) ▸ *adj.* Of or being a grammatical case indicating separation, direction away from, and sometimes manner or agency. ▸ *n.* The ablative case.

a·blaze (ə-blāz′) ▸ *adj.* **1.** Being on fire; blazing. **2.** Bright with color. **—a·blaze′** *adv.*

a·ble (ā′bəl) ▸ *adj.* **a·bler, a·blest. 1.** Having sufficient ability or resources. **2.** Highly capable or talented. **—a′bly** (ā′blē) *adv.*

–able or **–ible** ▸ *suff.* **1.** Susceptible, capable, or worthy of (an action): *debatable.* **2.** Inclined or given to: *changeable.*

a·ble-bod·ied (ā′bəl-bŏd′ēd) ▸ *adj.* Physically strong and healthy.

able-bodied seaman ▸ *n.* A merchant seaman certified for all seaman's duties.

a·bloom (ə-blo͞om′) ▸ *adj.* Being in bloom.

ab·lu·tion (ă-blo͞o′shən) ▸ *n.* A washing or cleansing of the body, esp. in a ritual manner.

ABM (ā′bē-ĕm′) ▸ *n.* See **antiballistic missile.**

Ab·na·ki (ăb-nä′kē, ăb-) ▸ *n.* Var. of **Abenaki.**

ab·ne·ga·tion (ăb′nĭ-gā′shən) ▸ *n.* Self-denial; renunciation.

ab·nor·mal (ăb-nôr′məl) ▸ *adj.* Not typical or normal; deviant. **—ab′nor·mal′i·ty** (ăb′nôr-măl′ĭ-tē) *n.* **—ab·nor′mal·ly** *adv.*

abnormal psychology ▸ *n.* The study of mental and emotional disorders or of mental phenomena such as altered levels of consciousness.

a·board (ə-bôrd′) ▸ *adv.* On or onto a passenger vehicle, such as a ship, train, or aircraft. ▸ *prep.* On board of; on; in.

a·bode (ə-bōd′) ▸ *v.* P.t. and p.part of **abide.** ▸ *n.* A dwelling place; home.

a·bol·ish (ə-bŏl′ĭsh) ▸ *v.* To do away with; annul. **—a·bol′ish·er** *n.* **—a·bol′ish·ment** *n.*

ab·o·li·tion (ăb′ə-lĭsh′ən) ▸ *n.* **1.** The act of abolishing. **2.** Abolishment of slavery.

ab·o·li·tion·ism (ăb′ə-lĭsh′ə-nĭz′əm) ▸ *n.* Advocacy of the abolition of slavery. **—ab′o·li′tion·ist** *n.*

A-bomb (ā′bŏm′) ▸ *n.* See **atom bomb** 1.

a·bom·i·na·ble (ə-bŏm′ə-nə-bəl) ▸ *adj.* Utterly detestable; loathsome. **—a·bom′i·na·bly** *adv.*

abominable snowman ▸ *n.* A hairy humanlike animal supposedly inhabiting the snows of the high Himalaya Mountains.

a·bom·i·nate (ə-bŏm′ə-nāt′) ▸ *v.* **-nat·ed, -nat·ing.** To detest thoroughly; abhor. **—a·bom′i·na′tion** *n.* **—a·bom′i·na′tor** *n.*

ab·o·rig·i·nal (ăb′ə-rĭj′ə-nəl) ▸ *adj.* **1.** Existing from the beginning. **2.** Of or relating to aborigines. **3.** often **Aboriginal** Relating to any of the indigenous peoples of Australia. ▸ *n.* An aborigine. **—ab′o·rig′i·nal·ly** *adv.*

ab·o·rig·i·ne (ăb′ə-rĭj′ə-nē) ▸ *n.* **1.** A member of the earliest known population of a region. **2.** often **Aborigine** A member of any of the indigenous peoples of Australia.

a·born·ing (ə-bôr′nĭng) ▸ *adv.* While coming into being or getting under way.

a·bort (ə-bôrt′) ▸ *v.* **1a.** To cause the abortion of (a fetus or embryo). **b.** To terminate (a pregnancy) by inducing abortion. **2.** To miscarry. **3.** To terminate before completion: *abort a takeoff.* ▸ *n.* The act of terminating before completion. **—a·bor′tive** *adj.*

a·bor·ti·fa·cient (ə-bôr′tə-fā′shənt) ▸ *adj.* Causing abortion. **—a·bor′ti·fa′cient** *n.*

a·bor·tion (ə-bôr′shən) ▸ *n.* **1.** Induced termination of pregnancy and expulsion of an embryo or fetus before it is viable. **2.** A miscarriage. **—a·bor′tion·ist** *n.*

ABO system (ā′bē′ō′) ▸ *n.* A system of classifying blood into four major groups, A, B, AB, and O, used in determining blood compatibility in transfusions.

a·bound (ə-bound′) ▸ *v.* **1.** To be great in number or amount. **2.** To be fully supplied; teem.

a·bout (ə-bout′) ▸ *adv.* **1.** Approximately. **2.** Almost. **3.** To a reversed position: *Turned about.* **4.** All around. **5.** In the

THESAURUS

aberrance or **aberrancy** *n.* —*See* ABNORMALITY.

aberrant *adj.* —*See* ABNORMAL, ERRANT (2).

aberration *n.* —*See* ABNORMALITY, DEVIATION.

abet *v.* —*See* HELP, PROMOTE (2).

abetment *n.* —*See* HELP.

abettor or **abetter** *n.* —*See* ACCESSORY, ASSISTANT.

abeyance *n.* The condition of being temporarily inactive ▸ dormancy, intermission, latency, quiescence, suspension, remission. [*Compare* BREAK, REST[1].]

abeyant *adj.* —*See* LATENT.

abhor *v.* —*See* HATE.

abhorrence *n.* —*See* DESPISAL, DISGUST, HATE (1), HATE (2).

abhorrent *adj.* —*See* OFFENSIVE (1).

abide *v.* —*See* ENDURE (1), ENDURE (2), LIVE[1], REMAIN.

abide by *v.* —*See* FOLLOW (4).

abiding *adj.* —*See* CONTINUING.

ability *n.* **1.** Natural or acquired skill or talent ▸ adeptness, art, command, craft, expertise, expertness, knack, mastery, proficiency, skill, technique. *Informal:* know-how, savvy. [*Compare* DEXTERITY, TALENT.] **2.** Physical, mental, financial, or legal power to perform ▸ capability, capacity, competence, competency, faculty, might. [*Compare* ENERGY, POWER.]

abjuration *n.* —*See* RETRACTION.

abjure *v.* —*See* BREAK (5), RETRACT (1).

ablaze *adj.* —*See* BURNING.

able *adj.* Having sufficient ability or resources ▸ capable, competent, good, skilled, skillful. [*Compare* DEXTEROUS, EXPERT, GIFTED, QUALIFIED.]

able-bodied *adj.* —*See* HEALTHY, LUSTY.

ablution *n.* —*See* PURIFICATION (2).

abnegate *v.* —*See* DENY.

abnegation *n.* —*See* DENIAL (1).

abnormal *adj.* Departing from the normal or typical ▸ aberrant, anomalistic, anomalous, atypic, atypical, deviant, divergent, irregular, preternatural, unnatural. [*Compare* ECCENTRIC, UNUSUAL.]

abnormality *n.* The condition of being abnormal ▸ aberrance, aberrancy, aberration, anomaly, atypicality, deviance, deviancy, deviation, exception, irregularity, oddity, preternaturalness, unnaturalness. [*Compare* DEFECT, DEFORMITY, DIFFERENCE, ECCENTRICITY.]

abnormally *adv.* —*See* UNUSUALLY.

abode *n.* —*See* HOME (1).

abolish *v.* To put an end to ▸ abrogate, annihilate, annul, cancel, extinguish, invalidate, negate, nullify, set aside, vitiate, void. *Informal:* ax. [*Compare* CANCEL, ELIMINATE, STOP, SUPPRESS.] —*See also* ANNIHILATE.

abolition or **abolishment** *n.* An often formal act of putting an end to ▸ abrogation, annihilation, annulment, cancellation, defeasance, invalidation, negation, nullification, voidance. [*Compare* ANNIHILATION, REPEAL.]

abominable *adj.* —*See* DAMNED, OFFENSIVE (1).

abominate *v.* —*See* DESPISE, HATE.

abomination *n.* —*See* HATE (1), HATE (2).

aboriginal *adj.* —*See* DOMESTIC (3), INDIGENOUS.

abound *v.* —*See* TEEM[1].

about *adv.* —*See* APPROXIMATELY, BACKWARD.

vicinity. ▸ *prep.* **1.** On all sides of. **2.** In the vicinity of. **3.** Relating to; concerning. **4.** On the point of: *about to go.*

a·bout-face (ə-bout′fās′) ▸ *n.* A sudden change to the opposite direction, attitude, or viewpoint. **—a·bout′-face′** *v.*

a·bove (ə-bŭv′) ▸ *adv.* **1.** On high; overhead. **2.** In or to a higher place. **3.** In an earlier part of a text. ▸ *prep.* **1.** Over or higher than. **2.** Superior to: *put principles above expediency.* ▸ *n.* An earlier part of a given text. ▸ *adj.* Appearing earlier in the same text.

above all ▸ *adv.* Exceeding all other factors in importance.

a·bove·board (ə-bŭv′bôrd′) ▸ *adv. & adj.* Without deceit or trickery.

ab·ra·ca·dab·ra (ăb′rə-kə-dăb′rə) ▸ *n.* **1.** A magical charm believed to ward off disease or disaster. **2.** Gibberish.

a·brade (ə-brād′) ▸ *v.* **a·brad·ed, a·brad·ing. 1.** To wear away by friction; erode. **2.** To be abrasive; irritate. **—a·bra′sion** (ə-brā′zhən) *n.*

A·bra·ham (ā′brə-hăm′) ▸ In the Bible, the first patriarch and progenitor of the Hebrew people.

a·bra·sive (ə-brā′sĭv, -zĭv) ▸ *adj.* **1.** Causing abrasion. **2.** Harsh or irritating in manner. ▸ *n.* A substance that abrades. **—a·bra′sive·ly** *adv.* **—a·bra′sive·ness** *n.*

a·breast (ə-brĕst′) ▸ *adv.* **1.** Side by side. **2.** Up to date with: *abreast of developments.*

a·bridge (ə-brĭj′) ▸ *v.* **a·bridged, a·bridg·ing. 1.** To reduce the length of (a text); condense. **2.** To cut short; curtail. **—a·bridg′ment, a·bridge′ment** *n.*

a·broad (ə-brôd′) ▸ *adv. & adj.* **1.** In or to a foreign country, esp. overseas. **2.** Away from home. **3.** In wide circulation; at large.

ab·ro·gate (ăb′rə-gāt′) ▸ *v.* **-gat·ed, -gat·ing.** To abolish or annul, esp. by authority. **—ab′ro·ga′tion** *n.*

a·brupt (ə-brŭpt′) ▸ *adj.* **1.** Unexpectedly sudden. **2.** Curt; brusque: *an abrupt retort.* **3.** Jerky; disconnected. **4.** Steeply inclined. **—a·brupt′ly** *adv.* **—a·brupt′ness** *n.*

ab·scess (ăb′sĕs′) ▸ *n.* A collection of pus surrounded by an inflamed area. ▸ *v.* To form an abscess.

ab·scis·sa (ăb-sĭs′ə) ▸ *n., pl.* **-scis·sas** or **-scis·sae** (-sĭs′ē). *Symbol* **x** The coordinate representing the position of a point along a line perpendicular to the *y*-axis in a plane Cartesian coordinate system.

ab·scis·sion (ăb-sĭzh′ən) ▸ *n.* The shedding of leaves, flowers, or fruits.

ab·scond (ăb-skŏnd′) ▸ *v.* To leave secretly and hide, often in order to avoid the law. **—ab·scond′er** *n.*

ab·sence (ăb′səns) ▸ *n.* **1.** The state or a period of being away. **2.** Lack; nonexistence: *an absence of leadership.*

ab·sent (ăb′sənt) ▸ *adj.* **1.** Not present. **2.** Not existent; lacking. **3.** Absent-minded; inattentive: *an absent nod.* ▸ *v.* (ăb-sĕnt′) To keep (oneself) away. ▸ *prep.* Without. **—ab′sent·ly** *adv.*

ab·sen·tee (ăb′sən-tē′) ▸ *n.* One that is absent. ▸ *adj.* Not in residence: *absentee landlords.*

absentee ballot ▸ *n.* A ballot mailed in advance by a voter unable to go to the polls.

ab·sen·tee·ism (ăb′sən-tē′ĭz′əm) ▸ *n.* Habitual absence, esp. from work or duty.

ab·sent-mind·ed (ăb′sənt-mīn′dĭd) ▸ *adj.* **1.** Lost in thought; preoccupied. **2.** Inattentive; forgetful. **—ab′sent-mind′ed·ly** *adv.* **—ab′sent-mind′ed·ness** *n.*

ab·sinthe also **ab·sinth** (ăb′sĭnth) ▸ *n.* A strong, bitter liqueur flavored with wormwood.

ab·so·lute (ăb′sə-lo͞ot′) ▸ *adj.* **1.** Perfect in quality or nature; complete. **2.** Not mixed; pure. **3a.** Not limited by restrictions or exceptions: *absolute trust; absolute power.* **b.** Total; utter: *absolute silence.* **4.** Certain; positive: *absolute proof.* **5.** *Phys.* **a.** Relating to measurements or units of measurement derived from fundamental units of length, mass, and time. **b.** Relating to a temperature scale whose zero is absolute zero. ▸ *n.* Something that is absolute. **—ab′so·lute′ly** *adv.* **—ab′so·lute′ness** *n.*

absolute pitch ▸ *n.* **1.** The precise pitch of an isolated tone as established by its rate of vibration. **2.** *Mus.* The ability to identify any pitch heard or sing any pitch named.

absolute value ▸ *n.* The numerical value of a real number without regard to its sign.

absolute zero ▸ *n.* The theoretical temperature at which substances possess no thermal energy, equal to –273.15°C, or –459.67°F.

ab·so·lu·tion (ăb′sə-lo͞o′shən) ▸ *n.* **1.** The act of absolving. **2.** The formal remission of sin imparted by a priest, as in the sacrament of penance.

ab·so·lut·ism (ăb′sə-lo͞o′tĭz′əm) ▸ *n.* A form of government in which all power is vested in a single ruler or other authority. **—ab′so·lut′ist** *n.* **—ab′so·lu·tis′tic** *adj.*

ab·solve (əb-zŏlv′, -sŏlv′) ▸ *v.* **-solved, -solv·ing. 1.** To pronounce clear of guilt or blame. **2.** To relieve of a requirement or obligation. **3.** To grant absolution to. **—ab·solv′a·ble** *adj.* **—ab·solv′er** *n.*

THESAURUS

about-face *v.* To turn sharply around ▸ double (back), reverse. ***Idiom:*** turn on one's heels.

about-face *n.* —*See* REVERSAL (1).

aboveboard *adj.* —*See* FRANK, HONEST.

abracadabra *n.* —*See* GIBBERISH, SPELL².

abrade *v.* —*See* CHAFE, ERODE, SCRAPE (1).

abrasion *n.* A mark or shallow cut made by contact with an object ▸ scrape, scratch, scuff, striation. [*Compare* CUT, FURROW.]

abrasive *adj.* —*See* ROUGH (1).

abrasiveness *n.* —*See* IRREGULARITY.

abridge *v.* —*See* SHORTEN.

abridgment *n.* —*See* SYNOPSIS.

abrogate *v.* —*See* ABOLISH.

abrogation *n.* —*See* ABOLITION.

abrupt *adj.* **1.** Rudely informal ▸ bald, bluff, blunt, brief, brusque, crusty, curt, gruff, short, short-spoken. [*Compare* IMPUDENT, RUDE.] **2.** Unexpectedly sudden ▸ hurried, precipitant, precipitate, sharp, sudden, unannounced. ***Idioms:*** from out of nowhere (*or* the blue), without warning. [*Compare* QUICK, RASH¹.] —*See also* STEEP¹ (1).

abscond *v.* —*See* ESCAPE (1).

abscond with *v.* —*See* STEAL.

absence *n.* **1.** Failure to be present ▸ cut, nonappearance, nonattendance, truancy, truantry. *Informal:* hooky. [*Compare* EMPTINESS, NOTHINGNESS.] **2.** The condition of lacking something ▸ dearth, lack, want. [*Compare* NEED, SHORTAGE.]

absent *adj.* Not present ▸ away, elsewhere, gone, missing, nonattendant, nonexistent, off, out, truant. ***Idioms:*** AWOL, gone fishing, playing hooky. [*Compare* EMPTY.] —*See also* ABSENT-MINDED.

absent-minded *adj.* So lost in thought as to be unable to remember or attend to things ▸ absent, abstracted, bemused, distracted, distrait, faraway, forgetful, inattentive, lost, oblivious, preoccupied, scatterbrained. *Slang:* spaced-out, spacy. ***Idioms:*** a million miles away, gathering wool, lost (*or* off) in space, out of it. [*Compare* CARELESS, DETACHED, DREAMY, NEGLIGENT.]

absent-mindedness *n.* —*See* TRANCE.

absolute *adj.* Having and exercising complete political power and control ▸ absolutistic, arbitrary, autarchic, autarchical, autocratic, autocratical, despotic, dictatorial, monocratic, totalitarian, tyrannic, tyrannical, tyrannous. [*Compare* INFLUENTIAL, POWERFUL, STRONG.] —*See also* DEFINITE (3), IMPLICIT (2), PERFECT, PURE, UNCONDITIONAL, UTTER².

absolutely *adv.* Without question ▸ categorically, certainly, definitely, doubtless, doubtlessly, indubitably, positively, surely, undoubtedly, unquestionably. ***Idioms:*** beyond (*or* without) a doubt, beyond the shadow of a doubt. [*Compare* CONSIDERABLY, REALLY, UNUSUALLY, VERY.] —*See also* COMPLETELY (1), YES.

absolution *n.* —*See* EXCULPATION, FORGIVENESS.

absolutism *n.* **1.** A political doctrine advocating the principle of absolute rule ▸ authoritarianism, autocracy, despotism, dictatorship, totalitarianism. [*Compare* SUBJUGATION.] **2.** A government in which all power is vested in a single leader or party ▸ autarchy, autocracy, despotism, dictatorship, monocracy, one-party rule, tyranny.

absolutistic *adj.* —*See* ABSOLUTE.

absolve *v.* —*See* CLEAR (3), EXCUSE (1).

ab·sorb (əb-sôrb′, -zôrb′) ▸ *v.* **1.** To take (something) in through or as through pores or interstices. **2.** To occupy completely; engross. **3.** *Phys.* To retain (e.g., sound) wholly, without reflection or transmission. **4.** To assimilate into a larger whole. **5.** To take on: *absorb a cost.* **—ab·sorb′a·ble** *adj.* **—ab·sorb′er** *n.* **—ab·sorb′ing·ly** *adv.*

ab·sor·bent (əb-sôr′bənt, -zôr′-) ▸ *adj.* Capable of absorbing. **—ab·sor′ben·cy** *n.* **—ab·sor′bent** *n.*

ab·sorp·tion (əb-sôrp′shən, -zôrp′-) ▸ *n.* **1.** The act or process of absorbing. **2.** A state of mental concentration. **—ab·sorp′tive** (-tĭv) *adj.* **—ab′sorp·tiv′i·ty** *n.*

ab·stain (ăb-stān′) ▸ *v.* To refrain from something by one's own choice. **—ab·stain′er** *n.*

ab·ste·mi·ous (ăb-stē′mē-əs) ▸ *adj.* Exercising self-restraint in appetites or behavior. **—ab·ste′mi·ous·ly** *adv.* **—ab·ste′mi·ous·ness** *n.*

ab·sten·tion (ăb-stĕn′shən) ▸ *n.* The act or habit of abstaining.

ab·sti·nence (ăb′stə-nəns) ▸ *n.* **1.** Deliberate self-restraint. **2a.** Abstention from alcoholic beverages. **b.** Abstention from sexual activity; continence. **—ab′sti·nent** *adj.*

ab·stract (ăb-străkt′, ăb′străkt′) ▸ *adj.* **1.** Considered apart from concrete existence: *an abstract concept.* **2.** Not applied or practical. **3.** Difficult to understand; abstruse. **4.** Considered without reference to a specific instance. **5.** Having an artistic content that depends on intrinsic form rather than on pictorial representation: *abstract painting.* ▸ *n.* (ăb′străkt′) **1.** A summary or condensation. **2.** Something abstract. ▸ *v.* (ăb-străkt′) **1.** To take away; remove. **2.** To steal; filch. **3.** (ăb′străkt′) To summarize. **—ab·stract′er** *n.* **—ab·stract′ly** *adv.* **—ab·stract′ness** *n.*

ab·stract·ed (ăb-străk′tĭd) ▸ *adj.* **1.** Removed; apart. **2.** Lost in thought; preoccupied. **—ab·stract′ed·ly** *adv.*

ab·strac·tion (ăb-străk′shən) ▸ *n.* **1a.** The act or process of abstracting. **b.** An abstract idea or term. **2.** Preoccupation; absent-mindedness. **3.** An abstract work of art.

ab·struse (ăb-stro͞os′) ▸ *adj.* Difficult to understand. **—ab·struse′ly** *adv.* **—ab·struse′ness** *n.*

ab·surd (əb-sûrd′, -zûrd′) ▸ *adj.* **1.** Ridiculously incongruous or nonsensical. **2.** Devoid of meaning, value, or purpose. **—ab·surd′i·ty, ab·surd′ness** *n.* **—ab·surd′ly** *adv.*

a·bun·dant (ə-bŭn′dənt) ▸ *adj.* **1.** Richly supplied. **2.** Abounding with. **—a·bun′dance** *n.* **—a·bun′dant·ly** *adv.*

a·buse (ə-byo͞oz′) ▸ *v.* **a·bused, a·bus·ing. 1.** To use wrongly or improperly. **2.** To hurt or injure by maltreatment. **3.** To rape or molest. **4.** To insult; revile. ▸ *n.* (ə-byo͞os′) **1.** Misuse: *drug abuse.* **2.** Physical maltreatment. **3.** Insulting or coarse language. **—a·bus′er** *n.* **—a·bu′sive** *adj.* **—a·bu′sive·ly** *adv.*

a·but (ə-bŭt′) ▸ *v.* **a·but·ted, a·but·ting. 1.** To have a common boundary; lie adjacent. **2.** To border upon. **—a·but′ter** *n.*

a·but·ment (ə-bŭt′mənt) ▸ *n.* **1.** The act of abutting. **2.** Something that abuts. **3.** A supporting structure, as at the end of a bridge.

a·bysm (ə-bĭz′əm) ▸ *n.* An abyss.

a·bys·mal (ə-bĭz′məl) ▸ *adj.* **1.** Very profound; limitless. **2.** Very bad: *an abysmal performance.* **—a·bys′mal·ly** *adv.*

a·byss (ə-bĭs′) ▸ *n.* **1.** An immeasurably deep chasm, depth, or void. **2a.** The primeval chaos. **b.** Hell.

Ab·ys·sin·i·a (ăb′ĭ-sĭn′ē-ə) ▸ See **Ethiopia. —Ab′ys·sin′i·an** *adj. & n.*

Ac ▸ The symbol for the element **actinium.**

AC ▸ *abbr.* alternating current

a·ca·cia (ə-kā′shə) ▸ *n.* **1.** Any of various often spiny trees or shrubs having feathery leaves and heads or spikes of small flowers. **2.** See **gum arabic.**

ac·a·deme (ăk′ə-dēm′) ▸ *n.* **1.** Academia. **2.** A scholar, esp. a pedant.

ac·a·de·mi·a (ăk′ə-dē′mē-ə) ▸ *n.* The academic life or environment.

ac·a·dem·ic (ăk′ə-dĕm′ĭk) ▸ *adj.* **1.** Of or relating to a school or college. **2a.** Liberal or classical rather than technical or vocational. **b.** Relating to scholarly performance: *a student's academic average.* **3.** Scholarly to the point of triviality. **4.** Excessively abstract. ▸ *n.* A member of a college or university faculty. **—ac′a·dem′i·cal·ly** *adv.*

ac·a·de·mi·cian (ăk′ə-də-mĭsh′ən, ə-kăd′ə-) ▸ *n.* **1.** An academic. **2.** A member of an academy or learned society.

ac·a·dem·i·cism (ăk′ə-dĕm′ĭ-sĭz′əm) also **a·cad·e·mism** (ə-kăd′ə-mĭz′əm) ▸ *n.* Traditional formalism, esp. when reflected in art.

ac·a·dem·ics (ăk′ə-dĕm′ĭks) ▸ *n. (takes pl. v.)* College or university studies.

a·cad·e·my (ə-kăd′ə-mē) ▸ *n., pl.* **-mies. 1.** A school for special instruction. **2.** A secondary or college-preparatory school, esp. a private one. **3a.** Academia. **b.** A society of scholars, scientists, or artists.

A·ca·di·a (ə-kā′dē-ə) ▸ A region and former French colony of E Canada and E ME. **—A·ca′di·an** *adj. & n.*

THESAURUS

absorb *v.* **1.** To occupy the attention of ▸ consume, employ, engage, engross, immerse, involve, monopolize, occupy, preoccupy, tie up. [*Compare* CHARM, GRIP.] **2.** To take in and incorporate, especially mentally ▸ assimilate, digest, drink in, grasp, imbibe, incorporate, learn, sponge up, take up. *Informal:* soak up. [*Compare* KNOW, UNDERSTAND.] *—See also* DRINK (3).

absorbed *adj.* *—See* BUSY (1), RAPT.

absorbent or **absorptive** *adj.* Having a capacity or tendency to absorb or soak up ▸ assimilative, bibulous, imbibing, permeable, retentive, spongy.

absorption *n.* **1.** The process of absorbing and incorporating ▸ assimilation, digestion, incorporation, intake, osmosis. [*Compare* MASTERY.] **2.** Total occupation of the attention or of the mind ▸ engagement, engrossment, enthrallment, immersion, involvement, preoccupation, prepossession.

absquatulate *v.* *—See* ESCAPE (1).

abstain *v.* *—See* REFRAIN.

abstain from *v.* *—See* AVOID.

abstemious *adj.* *—See* TEMPERATE (2).

abstemiousness *n.* *—See* MODERATION.

abstinence *n.* *—See* TEMPERANCE (1), TEMPERANCE (2).

abstinent *adj.* *—See* ASCETIC.

abstract *adj.* *—See* DEEP (2), THEORETICAL (1), THEORETICAL (2).

abstract *n.* *—See* SYNOPSIS.

abstract *v.* *—See* DETACH, REVIEW (1).

abstracted *adj.* *—See* ABSENT-MINDED.

abstraction *n.* *—See* DETACHMENT (1), TRANCE.

abstruse *adj.* *—See* AMBIGUOUS (1), DEEP (2), OBSCURE (1).

absurd *adj.* *—See* FOOLISH.

absurdity *n.* *—See* FOOLISHNESS, SCREAM (2).

abundance *n.* A great deal ▸ bounty, mass, mountain, much, plenty, plethora, profusion, wealth, world. *Informal:* barrel, heap, lot, mess, pack, peck, pile. [*Compare* EXCESS, FLOOD.] *—See also* PLENTY.

abundant *adj.* *—See* GENEROUS (2).

abundantly *adv.* *—See* CONSIDERABLY.

abuse *v.* **1.** To treat wrongfully or harmfully ▸ exploit, ill-treat, ill-use, impose on (*or* upon), maltreat, mishandle, mistreat, misuse, oppress, persecute, use, victimize, wrong. *Idioms:* kick around, knock about (*or* around), take advantage of, treat like dirt. [*Compare* INJURE, INSULT, VIOLATE.] **2.** To use improperly ▸ exploit, misapply, misappropriate, mishandle, mistreat, misuse, pervert. *—See also* REVILE.

abuse *n.* **1.** Improper use or handling ▸ ill-usage, misapplication, misappropriation, mishandling, misuse, perversion. [*Compare* DEGRADATION.] **2.** Physically harmful treatment ▸ ill-treatment, maltreatment, mishandling, mistreatment, misusage. *—See also* VITUPERATION.

abusive *adj.* Of, relating to, or characterized by verbal abuse ▸ contumelious, invective, opprobrious, scurrilous, sharp-tongued, vituperative. [*Compare* DISDAINFUL, IMPUDENT.]

abut *v.* *—See* ADJOIN.

abutting *adj.* *—See* ADJOINING.

abysm *n.* *—See* DEEP.

abysmal *adj.* Open wide ▸ abyssal, cavernous, gaping, yawning. [*Compare* BROAD, OPEN.] *—See also* DEEP (1), TERRIBLE.

abyss *n.* *—See* DEEP.

academic *adj.* *—See* DIDACTIC, EDUCATIONAL (1), PEDANTIC, THEORETICAL (1).

a·can·thus (ə-kăn′thəs) ▸ *n., pl.* **-thus·es** or **-thi** (-thī′). 1. Any of various Mediterranean shrubs with large, segmented, thistlelike leaves. 2. *Archit.* A design patterned after acanthus leaves.

a cap·pel·la (ä′ kə-pĕl′ə) ▸ *adv. Mus.* Without instrumental accompaniment.

Ac·a·pul·co (ăk′ə-po͞ol′kō, ä′kä-po͞ol′-) ▸ A city of S Mexico on the Pacific.

ac·cede (ăk-sēd′) ▸ *v.* **-ced·ed, -ced·ing.** 1. To give one's consent; agree. 2. To come into an office or dignity: *accede to the throne.* **—ac·ced′ence** *n.*

ac·cel·er·an·do (ä-chĕl′ə-rän′dō) ▸ *adv. & adj. Mus.* Gradually accelerating in tempo.

ac·cel·er·ate (ăk-sĕl′ə-rāt′) ▸ *v.* **-at·ed, -at·ing.** 1. To make or become faster. 2. To cause to occur sooner than expected. **—ac·cel′er·a′tion** *n.* **—ac·cel′er·a′tive** *adj.*

ac·cel·er·a·tor (ăk-sĕl′ə-rā′tər) ▸ *n.* 1. A device, esp. the gas pedal of a motor vehicle, for increasing speed. 2. *Phys.* A device, such as a cyclotron, that accelerates charged subatomic particles or nuclei to high energies.

ac·cel·er·om·e·ter (ăk-sĕl′ə-rŏm′ĭ-tər) ▸ *n.* An instrument used to measure acceleration.

ac·cent (ăk′sĕnt′) ▸ *n.* 1. Vocal emphasis given to a particular syllable, word, or phrase. 2. A characteristic manner of speech or pronunciation: *a British accent.* 3. A mark placed over a letter to indicate vocal stress or phonetic quality: *an acute accent.* 4. Rhythmical stress in a line of verse. 5. A distinctive quality, as of decorative style. 6. Particular importance or interest. ▸ *v.* To stress or emphasize.

ac·cen·tu·ate (ăk-sĕn′cho͞o-āt′) ▸ *v.* **-at·ed, -at·ing.** To stress; accent.

ac·cept ▸ *v.* 1. To receive willingly. 2. To admit to a group or place. 3. To regard as proper or true: *accept a new theory.* 4. To answer affirmatively: *accept an invitation.* 5. To consent to pay, as by a signed agreement.

ac·cept·a·ble (ăk-sĕp′tə-bəl) ▸ *adj.* Adequate; satisfactory. **—ac·cept′a·bil′i·ty** *n.* **—ac·cept′a·bly** *adv.*

ac·cep·tance (ăk-sĕp′təns) ▸ *n.* 1. The act or process of accepting. 2. The state of being accepted or acceptable. 3. A formal agreement to pay a draft or bill of exchange.

ac·cep·ta·tion (ăk′sĕp-tā′shən) ▸ *n.* The usual meaning, as of a word or expression.

ac·cept·ed (ăk-sĕp′tĭd) ▸ *adj.* Widely encountered, used, or recognized.

ac·cep·tor (ăk-sĕp′tər) ▸ *n. Chem.* The atom that contributes no electrons to a covalent bond.

ac·cess (ăk′sĕs) ▸ *n.* 1. A means of approaching or entering; passage. 2. The right to enter or make use of: *has access to classified material.* 3. An outburst: *an access of rage.* ▸ *v.* To obtain access to.

ac·ces·si·ble (ăk-sĕs′ə-bəl) ▸ *adj.* Easily approached, entered, or obtained. **—ac·ces′si·bil′i·ty, ac·ces′si·ble·ness** *n.* **—ac·ces′si·bly** *adv.*

ac·ces·sion (ăk-sĕsh′ən) ▸ *n.* 1. The attainment of a dignity or rank. 2a. Something acquired or added. b. An increase by means of something added. **—ac·ces′sion·al** *adj.*

ac·ces·so·ry (ăk-sĕs′ə-rē) ▸ *n., pl.* **-ries.** 1a. A supplementary item; adjunct. b. Something nonessential but desirable. 2. *Law* One who though absent aids or assists in the commission of a crime. ▸ *adj.* Supplementary; adjunct.

ac·ci·dent (ăk′sĭ-dənt) ▸ *n.* 1a. An unexpected, undesirable event. b. An unforeseen incident. 2. Chance; fortuity: *discovered the secret by accident.* 3. *Logic* An attribute that is not essential to the nature of something.

ac·ci·den·tal (ăk′sĭ-dĕn′tl) ▸ *adj.* 1. Occurring unexpectedly, unintentionally, or by chance. 2. Incidental. ▸ *n. Mus.* A sharp, flat, or natural not indicated in the key signature. **—ac′ci·den′tal·ly** *adv.*

ac·claim (ə-klām′) ▸ *v.* To praise openly and enthusiastically; applaud. ▸ *n.* Enthusiastic applause; acclamation. **—ac·claim′er** *n.*

ac·cla·ma·tion (ăk′lə-mā′shən) ▸ *n.* 1. A show of enthusiastic approval. 2. An oral vote, esp. a vote of approval taken without formal ballot. **—ac·clam′a·to′ry** (ə-klăm′ə-tôr′ē) *adj.*

ac·cli·mate (ăk′lə-māt′) ▸ *v.* **-mat·ed, -mat·ing.** To make or become accustomed to a new environment or situation; adapt. **—ac′cli·ma′tion** *n.*

ac·cli·ma·tize (ə-klī′mə-tīz′) ▸ *v.* **-tized, -tiz·ing.** To acclimate. **—ac·cli′ma·ti·za′tion** *n.*

ac·cliv·i·ty (ə-klĭv′ĭ-tē) ▸ *n., pl.* **-ties.** An upward slope.

THESAURUS

accede *v.* —*See* ASSENT.

accelerate *v.* —*See* SPEED.

accent *n.* Special attention given to something considered important ▸ accentuation, emphasis, stress, weight. [*Compare* IMPORTANCE, NOTICE.] —*See also* TONE (2).

accent or **accentuate** *v.* —*See* EMPHASIZE.

accentuation *n.* Special attention given to something considered important ▸ accent, emphasis, stress, weight. [*Compare* IMPORTANCE, NOTICE.]

accept *v.* 1. To receive something offered willingly and gladly ▸ embrace, take (up), welcome. ***Idioms:*** receive with open arms, take (*or* fold) to one's bosom. [*Compare* ACQUIRE, TAKE.] 2. To admit to one's possession, presence, or awareness ▸ have, receive, take. [*Compare* ABSORB.] 3. To allow admittance, as to a group ▸ admit, intromit, let in, receive, take in. ***Idioms:*** welcome aboard (*or* on board), take (*or* welcome) into the fold. [*Compare* PERMIT.] —*See also* ASSENT, BELIEVE (1), ENDURE (1), UNDERSTAND (1).

acceptable *adj.* 1. Worthy of being accepted or allowed ▸ admissible, allowable, permissible, unobjectionable, unexceptionable. *Slang:* kosher. 2. Adequate to satisfy a need, requirement, or standard ▸ adequate, all right, average, common, decent, fair, fairish, goodish, moderate, modest, palatable, passable, popular, reasonable, respectable, satisfactory, sufficient, tolerable. *Informal:* OK, tidy. [*Compare* APPROPRIATE.]

acceptance *n.* 1. The act of accepting or adopting ▸ acquiescence, adoption, agreement, assent, consent, embracement, espousal, nod, yes. *Informal:* OK. ***Idiom:*** stamp (*or* seal) of approval. [*Compare* CONFIRMATION, PERMISSION.] 2. Favorable reception or regard ▸ acknowledgement, approbation, approval, credit, esteem, favor, recognition, regard, welcome. [*Compare* PRAISE.] —*See also* PATIENCE.

acceptant *adj.* —*See* RECEPTIVE.

acceptation *n.* —*See* MEANING.

accepted *adj.* Generally approved or agreed upon ▸ admitted, conventional, customary, established, orthodox, received, recognized, sanctioned, time-honored, traditional. [*Compare* COMMON, ORDINARY.]

accepting *adj.* —*See* PATIENT.

access *n.* —*See* ADMISSION, OUTBURST.

access *v.* To gain entry into a computer network or database ▸ enter, log in (*or* on). *Idioms:* gain access (*or* admittance *or* entry), get connected.

accessible *adj.* Easily approached ▸ approachable, responsive, welcoming. —*See also* CONVENIENT (2), OPEN (4).

accession *n.* —*See* ADDITION (1).

accessory *n.* One who assists a lawbreaker in a wrongful or criminal act ▸ abettor, accomplice, confederate, conspirator. *Idiom:* partner in crime. —*See also* ATTACHMENT.

accessory *adj.* —*See* AUXILIARY (1).

accident *n.* An unexpected and usually undesirable event ▸ casualty, contretemps, misadventure, mischance, misfortune, mishap, reversal, setback. [*Compare* COLLISION, DISASTER.] —*See also* CHANCE (1), CHANCE (2), CRASH (2).

accidental *adj.* Occurring unexpectedly ▸ adventitious, casual, chance, contingent, fluky, fortuitous, inadvertent, incidental, odd, serendipitous, unanticipated, unexpected, unintended, unplanned. [*Compare* CHANCE, RANDOM.] —*See also* UNINTENTIONAL.

acclaim *v.* —*See* HONOR (1), PRAISE (1).

acclaim or **acclamation** *n.* —*See* PRAISE (1).

acclamatory *adj.* —*See* COMPLIMENTARY (1).

acclimate or **acclimatize** *v.* —*See* ADAPT, HARDEN (1).

acclimated or **acclimatized** *adj.* —*See* ACCUSTOMED (1).

acclimation or **acclimatization** *n.* —*See* ADAPTATION.

acclivity *n.* —*See* ASCENT (2).

ac·co·lade (ăk′ə-lād′, -läd′) ▸ *n.* 1. High praise. 2. A special acknowledgment or award.
ac·com·mo·date (ə-kŏm′ə-dāt′) ▸ *v.* **-dat·ed, -dat·ing.** 1. To do a favor for. 2. To provide or allow for: *accommodate the needs of both groups.* 3. To hold or contain comfortably. 4. To make suitable; adjust. 5. To settle; reconcile.
ac·com·mo·dat·ing (ə-kŏm′ə-dā′tĭng) ▸ *adj.* Helpful and obliging. **—ac·com′mo·dat′ing·ly** *adv.*
ac·com·mo·da·tion (ə-kŏm′ə-dā′shən) ▸ *n.* 1. The act of accommodating or the state of being accommodated. 2. Something that meets a need. 3. **accommodations** Room and board; lodgings.
ac·com·pa·ni·ment (ə-kŭm′pə-nē-mənt, ə-kŭmp′nē-) ▸ *n.* 1. *Mus.* A part that supports another, often solo, part. 2. Something that accompanies or complements.
ac·com·pa·nist (ə-kŭm′pə-nĭst, ə-kŭmp′nĭst) ▸ *n. Mus.* One who plays or sings an accompaniment.
ac·com·pa·ny (ə-kŭm′pə-nē, ə-kŭmp′nē) ▸ *v.* **-nied, -ny·ing.** 1. To go with as a companion. 2. To add to; supplement. 3. To occur with. 4. *Mus.* To perform an accompaniment to.
ac·com·plice (ə-kŏm′plĭs) ▸ *n.* One who aids or abets a lawbreaker in a criminal act.
ac·com·plish (ə-kŏm′plĭsh) ▸ *v.* 1. To succeed in doing; achieve. 2. To finish; complete. **—ac·com′plish·er** *n.*
ac·com·plished (ə-kŏm′plĭsht) ▸ *adj.* 1. Skilled; expert: *an accomplished pianist.* 2. Definite: *an accomplished fact.*
ac·com·plish·ment (ə-kŏm′plĭsh-mənt) ▸ *n.* 1. The act of accomplishing or state of being accomplished. 2. Something completed successfully; achievement. 3. An acquired skill. 4. Social poise and grace.
ac·cord (ə-kôrd′) ▸ *v.* 1. To cause to conform or agree. 2. To grant or bestow. 3. To be in agreement or harmony. ▸ *n.* 1. Agreement; harmony. 2. A settlement or understanding, esp. between nations. 3. Free or spontaneous choice: *signed up on my own accord.*
ac·cor·dance (ə-kôr′dns) ▸ *n.* Agreement: *in accordance with your instructions.*
ac·cord·ing·ly (ə-kôr′dĭng-lē) ▸ *adv.* 1. In accordance; correspondingly. 2. So; consequently.
ac·cord·ing to (ə-kôr′dĭng) ▸ *prep.* 1. As stated or indicated by: *according to law.* 2. In keeping with: *according to custom.*
ac·cor·di·on (ə-kôr′dē-ən) ▸ *n.* A portable musical instrument with a small keyboard and free metal reeds that sound when air is forced past them by pleated bellows. **—ac·cor′di·on·ist** *n.*
ac·cost (ə-kôst′, -kŏst′) ▸ *v.* To approach and speak to in an aggressive or hostile manner.
ac·count (ə-kount′) ▸ *n.* 1a. A narrative or record of events. b. A set of reasons; explanation. 2a. A business arrangement, as with a bank or store, in which money is kept, exchanged, or owed. b. A detailed record, esp. of financial transactions. 3. Worth or importance. 4. Profit; advantage: *turned her skills to good account.* ▸ *v.* To consider as being; regard. ***—phrasal verb:* account for** To provide or constitute a reason for; explain. ***—idioms:* on account of** Because of. **take into account** To take into consideration.
ac·count·a·ble (ə-koun′tə-bəl) ▸ *adj.* Responsible; answerable. **—ac·count′a·bil′i·ty, ac·count′a·ble·ness** *n.* **—ac·count′a·bly** *adv.*
ac·coun·tant (ə-koun′tənt) ▸ *n.* One trained in accounting. **—ac·coun′tan·cy** *n.*
ac·count·ing (ə-koun′tĭng) ▸ *n.* The bookkeeping methods involved in recording business transactions and preparing the financial statements of a business.
ac·cou·ter or **ac·cou·tre** (ə-ko͞o′tər) ▸ *v.* **-tered, -ter·ing** or **-tred, -tre·ing.** To outfit and equip, as for military duty. **—ac·cou′ter·ments** *n.*
ac·cred·it (ə-krĕd′ĭt) ▸ *v.* 1. To attribute to; credit. 2. To supply with credentials. 3. To certify as meeting a prescribed standard. **—ac·cred′i·ta′tion** *n.*
ac·cre·tion (ə-krē′shən) ▸ *n.* 1. Growth or increase in size by gradual addition. 2. The result of such growth or increase. **—ac·cre′tion·ar′y, ac·cre′tive** *adj.*
ac·crue (ə-kro͞o′) ▸ *v.* **-crued, -cru·ing.** 1. To come to one as a gain: *benefits that accrue from scientific research.* 2. To increase or accumulate over time: *interest accruing in a bank account.* **—ac·cru′al** *n.*
ac·cul·tur·a·tion (ə-kŭl′chə-rā′shən) ▸ *n.* The modification of the culture of a group or individual by contact with a different culture. **—ac·cul′tur·ate′** *v.*
ac·cu·mu·late (ə-kyo͞om′yə-lāt′) ▸ *v.* **-lat·ed, -lat·ing.** To

THESAURUS

accolade *n.* A memento received as a symbol of excellence or victory ▸ award, cup, prize, trophy. *—See also* COMPLIMENT, DISTINCTION (2), PRAISE (1), REWARD.
accolade *v.* *—See* PRAISE (1).
accommodate *v.* To have the room or capacity for ▸ contain, hold. *—See also* ADAPT, COMPROMISE, HARMONIZE (1), LODGE, OBLIGE (1).
accommodating *adj.* *—See* OBLIGING.
accommodation *n.* *—See* ADAPTATION, COMPROMISE.
accommodations *n.* Steps taken in preparation for an undertaking ▸ arrangements, plans, preparations, provisions.
accompaniment *n.* *—See* CONCOMITANT, ENHANCEMENT.
accompanist *n.* *—See* CONCOMITANT.
accompany *v.* To be with or go with ▸ attend, chaperon, companion, company, convoy, escort. ***Idioms:*** go hand in hand with, hang around (*or* out) with, hang out with, tag along with. [*Compare* GUIDE.] *—See also* SUPPLEMENT.
accompanying *adj.* *—See* CONCURRENT.
accomplice *n.* *—See* ACCESSORY.
accomplish *v.* To obtain a goal or objective by effort ▸ achieve, arrive at, attain, come to, fulfill, gain, get to, reach, realize. *Informal:* hit on. *Slang:* score. ***Idiom:*** bring to pass. [*Compare* FULFILL.] *—See also* EFFECT, PERFORM (1).
accomplished *adj.* Proficient as a result of practice and study ▸ finished, polished, practiced. [*Compare* ABLE, EXPERT.]
accomplishment *n.* Something that is completed or attained successfully ▸ achievement, acquirement, acquisition, arrival, attainment, coup, deed, effort, endeavor, exploit, feat, masterstroke, realization, success, successfulness, triumph, tour de force. [*Compare* CONQUEST, GOAL.] *—See also* FULFILLMENT (1).
accord *v.* To let have as a favor, prerogative, or privilege ▸ award, concede, give, grant, vouchsafe. [*Compare* YIELD.] *—See also* AGREE (1), AGREE (2), CONFER (2).
accord *n.* *—See* AGREEMENT (1), AGREEMENT (2), HARMONY (1), TREATY.
accordance *n.* *—See* AGREEMENT (2), CONFERMENT.
accordant *adj.* *—See* AGREEABLE, UNANIMOUS.
accost *v.* To approach for the purpose of speech ▸ greet, hail, salute. [*Compare* ENCOUNTER, INTERRUPT, WELCOME.]
accouchement *n.* *—See* BIRTH (1).
account *n.* 1. A statement of causes or motives ▸ explanation, justification, rationale, rationalization, reason. [*Compare* ANSWER, APOLOGY, BELIEF.] 2. A precise list of fees or charges ▸ bill, check, invoice, reckoning, statement, tally. *Informal:* damage, tab. 3. A measure of those qualities that determine merit, desirability, usefulness, or importance ▸ valuation, value, worth. [*Compare* COST, IMPORTANCE.] *—See also* ESTEEM, STORY (1), USE (2).
account *v.* *—See* REGARD.
account for *v.* To offer reasons for or a cause of ▸ explain, justify, rationalize. [*Compare* CLARIFY, RESOLVE.]
accountability *n.* *—See* RESPONSIBILITY.
accountable *adj.* *—See* EXPLAINABLE, LIABLE (1).
accouter or **accoutre** *v.* *—See* FURNISH.
accouterments or **accoutrements** *n.* *—See* OUTFIT.
accredit *v.* *—See* ATTRIBUTE, AUTHORIZE, CONFIRM (3).
accreditation *n.* *—See* CONFIRMATION (1).
accretion *n.* *—See* BUILDUP (2).
accrue *v.* *—See* ACCUMULATE.
acculturate *v.* To fit for companionship with others, especially in attitude or manners ▸ civilize, humanize, socialize.
acculturation *n.* *—See* ADAPTATION.
accumulate *v.* To bring together so as to increase in mass or number ▸ accrue, agglomerate, aggregate, amass,

gather or pile up; amass. **—ac·cu′mu·la′tion** *n.* **—ac·cu′mu·la′tor** *n.*

ac·cu·ra·cy (ăk′yər-ə-sē) ▸ *n.* 1. Conformity to fact. 2. Precision; exactness.

ac·cu·rate (ăk′yər-ĭt) ▸ *adj.* 1. Conforming exactly to fact; errorless. 2. Capable of providing a correct reading or measurement: *an accurate scale.* **—ac′cu·rate·ly** *adv.* **—ac′cu·rate·ness** *n.*

ac·curs·ed (ə-kûr′sĭd, ə-kûrst′) also **ac·curst** (ə-kûrst′) ▸ *adj.* 1. Abominable; odious: *this accursed mud.* 2. Being under a curse; doomed. **—ac·curs′ed·ly** *adv.*

ac·cu·sa·tive (ə-kyo͞o′zə-tĭv) ▸ *adj.* Of or relating to the case of a noun, pronoun, adjective, or participle that is the direct object of a verb or the object of certain prepositions. ▸ *n.* The accusative case.

ac·cuse (ə-kyo͞oz′) ▸ *v.* **-cused, -cus·ing.** 1. To charge with an error or offense. 2. To bring charges against. **—ac′cu·sa′tion** (ăk′yo͞o-zā′shən) *n.* **—ac·cus′er** *n.* **—ac·cus′ing·ly** *adv.*

ac·cused (ə-kyo͞ozd′) ▸ *n.* The defendant or defendants in a criminal case.

ac·cus·tom (ə-kŭs′təm) ▸ *v.* **-tomed, -tom·ing.** 1. To familiarize, as by habit or frequent use: *accustom oneself to working late.* 2. To adjust; adapt.

ac·cus·tomed (ə-kŭs′təmd) ▸ *adj.* 1. Usual; customary. 2. Being in the habit of: *I am accustomed to sleeping late.*

ace (ās) ▸ *n.* 1. A playing card, die, or domino having one spot or pip. 2. In racket games, a serve that one's opponent fails to return. 3. A fighter pilot who has destroyed five or more enemy aircraft. 4. An expert in a given field. ▸ *adj.* Top-notch; first-rate. ▸ *v.* **aced, ac·ing.** 1. To serve an ace against. 2. *Slang* To triumph over; defeat. ***—idioms:* ace in the hole** A hidden advantage. **within an ace of** Very near to.

a·cer·bic (ə-sûr′bĭk) also **a·cerb** (ə-sûrb′) ▸ *adj.* Acid or biting, as in taste, manner, or tone. **—a·cer′bi·cal·ly** *adv.*

a·cer·bi·ty (ə-sûr′bĭ-tē) ▸ *n., pl.* **-ties.** Bitterness, acidness.

a·cet·a·min·o·phen (ə-sē′tə-mĭn′ə-fən) ▸ *n.* A crystalline compound, $C_8H_9NO_2$, used in medicine to relieve pain and fever.

ac·e·tate (ăs′ĭ-tāt′) ▸ *n.* 1. A salt or ester of acetic acid. 2. Cellulose acetate or a product, esp. fibers, derived from it.

a·ce·tic (ə-sē′tĭk) ▸ *adj.* Of, relating to, or containing acetic acid or vinegar.

acetic acid ▸ *n.* A clear, colorless organic acid, CH_3COOH, with a distinctive pungent odor, that is the chief acid of vinegar.

ac·e·tone (ăs′ĭ-tōn′) ▸ *n.* A colorless, volatile, highly flammable liquid, CH_3COCH_3, used as an organic solvent.

a·ce·tyl·cho·line (ə-sēt′l-kō′lēn′) ▸ *n.* A white crystalline compound, $C_7H_{17}NO_3$, that mediates transmission of nerve impulses across synapses.

a·cet·y·lene (ə-sĕt′l-ēn′, -ən) ▸ *n.* A colorless, highly flammable or explosive gas, C_2H_2, used for metal welding and cutting.

a·ce·tyl·sal·i·cyl·ic acid (ə-sēt′l-săl′ĭ-sĭl′ĭk) ▸ *n.* See **aspirin** 1.

ache (āk) ▸ *v.* **ached, ach·ing.** 1. To suffer a dull, sustained pain. 2. To yearn painfully. ▸ *n.* 1. A dull, steady pain. 2. A longing or yearning. **—ach′y** *adj.*

a·chene (ā-kēn′) ▸ *n.* A small, dry, one-seeded fruit with a thin wall.

a·chieve (ə-chēv′) ▸ *v.* **a·chieved, a·chiev·ing.** 1. To perform successfully; accomplish: *achieve a task.* 2. To attain with effort: *achieve fame.* **—a·chiev′a·ble** *adj.* **—a·chiev′er** *n.*

a·chieve·ment (ə-chēv′mənt) ▸ *n.* 1. The act of achieving. 2. Something accomplished successfully.

A·chil·les (ə-kĭl′ēz) ▸ *n.* *Gk. Myth.* The hero of Homer's *Iliad,* who slew Hector.

Achilles' heel ▸ *n.* A seemingly small but fatal weakness.

Achilles tendon ▸ *n.* The large tendon connecting the heel bone to the calf muscle.

ach·ro·mat·ic (ăk′rə-măt′ĭk) ▸ *adj.* 1. Designating a color, such as black or white, that has no hue. 2. Refracting light without spectral color separation. **—ach′ro·mat′i·cal·ly** *adv.* **—a·chro′ma·tism** (ā-krō′mə-tĭz′əm) *n.*

ac·id (ăs′ĭd) ▸ *n.* 1. *Chem.* Any of a large class of sour-tasting substances whose aqueous solutions turn blue litmus red and react with bases, alkalis, or certain metals to form salts. 2. A sour-tasting substance. 3. *Slang* See **LSD.** ▸ *adj.* 1. *Chem.* a. Of an acid. b. Having a high concentration of acid. 2. Having a sour taste. 3. Biting; sarcastic: *an acid wit.* **—a·cid′ic** (ə-sĭd′ĭk) *adj.* **—a·cid′i·ty** *n.* **—ac′id·ly** *adv.* **—ac′id·ness** *n.*

a·cid·i·fy (ə-sĭd′ə-fī′) ▸ *v.* **-fied, -fy·ing.** To make or become acid. **—a·cid′i·fi·ca′tion** *n.* **—a·cid′i·fi′er** *n.*

THESAURUS

assemble, build up, collect, cumulate, garner, gather, hive, heap up, mass, pile up, roll up. [*Compare* ASSEMBLE, INCREASE, SAVE.]

accumulation *n.* 1. A quantity accumulated ▸ aggregation, amassment, assemblage, buildup, collection, congeries, cumulation, gathering, mass. [*Compare* HEAP.] 2. The act of accumulating ▸ agglomeration, buildup, conglomeration. [*Compare* INCREASE.] *—See also* BUILDUP (2), DEPOSIT (2).

accumulative *adj.* Increasing, as in force, by successive additions ▸ additive, cumulative.

accuracy or **accurateness** *n.* Freedom from error ▸ correctness, definitude, exactitude, exactness, meticulousness, preciseness, precision, rightness. *—See also* VERACITY.

accurate *adj.* Conforming exactly to fact ▸ actual, correct, errorless, exact, factual, faithful, precise, right, rigorous, true, veracious, veridical. *Idioms:* on the button (*or* money *or* nose), spot on. [*Compare* LITERAL, PERFECT, SURE.] *—See also* CAREFUL (2).

accursed *adj.* *—See* DAMNED.

accusation *n.* A charging of someone with a misdeed ▸ arraignment, crimination, charge, denouncement, denunciation, finger-pointing, impeachment, imputation, incrimination, inculpation, indictment, recrimination.

accusatorial or **accusatory** *adj.* Containing, relating to, or involving an accusation ▸ denunciative, denunciatory, incriminating, incriminatory, inculpatory. [*Compare* INSINUATING.]

accuse *v.* To make an accusation against ▸ arraign, blame, charge, denounce, impeach, incriminate, inculpate, indict, tax, recriminate. *Slang:* finger. *Idioms:* hang (*or* pin) something on, point the finger at, put the finger on. [*Compare* IMPLICATE.]

accused *n.* A person against whom an action is brought ▸ defendant, respondent.

accuser *n.* 1. One that accuses ▸ arraigner, denouncer, indicter, recriminator. 2. One that makes a formal complaint, especially in court ▸ claimant, complainant, plaintiff.

accustom *v.* To make familiar through constant practice, use, or habit ▸ condition, familiarize, habituate, inure, wont. [*Compare* ADAPT.]

accustomed *adj.* 1. Adapted to the existing environment and conditions ▸ acclimated, acclimatized, adapted, conditioned, hardened, inured, seasoned, toughened. 2. Subject to a pattern or habit of behavior ▸ chronic, habitual, routine. 3. In the habit ▸ habituated, used, wont. *—See also* COMMON (1).

ace *n.* A key resource to be used at an opportune moment ▸ trump, trump card. *Informal:* clincher. *Idiom:* ace in the hole. *—See also* EXPERT.

ace *adj.* *—See* EXCELLENT.

ace *v.* *—See* DEFEAT.

acerbic *adj.* *—See* BITING, BITTER (1), SOUR.

acerbity *n.* *—See* SARCASM.

acetous *adj.* *—See* SOUR.

ache *v.* To experience or express compassion ▸ commiserate, condole, feel, sympathize. *Idioms:* be (*or* feel) sorry, have one's heart ache (*or* bleed) for someone, have one's heart go out to someone. [*Compare* COMFORT, PITY.] *—See also* DESIRE, HURT (2).

ache *n.* *—See* PAIN.

achievable *adj.* *—See* POSSIBLE.

achieve *v.* *—See* ACCOMPLISH, EFFECT, PERFORM (1).

achievement *n.* *—See* ACCOMPLISHMENT.

aching or **achy** *adj.* *—See* PAINFUL.

acicula *n.* *—See* POINT (1).

acicular or **aciculate** or **aciculated** *adj.* *—See* POINTED.

acid or **acidic** *adj.* *—See* BITING, SOUR.

acidity *n.* *—See* SARCASM.

ac·i·do·sis (ăs'ĭ-dō'sĭs) ▸ *n.* An abnormal increase in the acidity of the body's fluids. **—ac'i·dot'ic** (-dŏt'ĭk) *adj.*
acid rain ▸ *n.* Rain having an abnormally high acidity as a result of interactions with atmospheric pollutants.
acid test ▸ *n.* A decisive or critical test.
a·cid·u·late (ə-sĭj'ə-lāt') ▸ *v.* **-lat·ed, -lat·ing.** To make or become slightly acid.
a·cid·u·lous (ə-sĭj'ə-ləs) ▸ *adj.* Slightly sour in taste or in manner.
ac·knowl·edge (ăk-nŏl'ĭj) ▸ *v.* **-edged, -edg·ing. 1a.** To admit the existence, reality, or truth of. **b.** To recognize as being valid. **2a.** To express recognition of: *acknowledge a friend's smile.* **b.** To express thanks or gratitude for. **3.** To report the receipt of. **—ac·knowl'edge·a·ble** *adj.* **—ac·knowl'edg·ment, ac·knowl'edge·ment** *n.*
ac·me (ăk'mē) ▸ *n.* The highest point, as of perfection.
ac·ne (ăk'nē) ▸ *n.* An inflammatory disease of the oil glands and hair follicles of the skin, marked by pimples, esp. on the face. **—ac'ned** *adj.*
ac·o·lyte (ăk'ə-līt') ▸ *n.* **1.** One who assists the celebrant in the performance of liturgical rites. **2.** A devoted follower.
A·con·ca·gua (ăk'ən-kä'gwə, ä'kən-) ▸ A mountain, about 7,025.4 m (23,034 ft), in the Andes of W Argentina; highest peak of the Western Hemisphere.
ac·o·nite (ăk'ə-nīt') ▸ *n.* **1.** Any of various usu. poisonous plants with hooded flowers. **2.** The dried roots of these plants, used as a source of drugs.
a·corn (ā'kôrn', -kərn) ▸ *n.* The fruit of an oak, consisting of a nut set in a woody, cuplike base.
acorn squash ▸ *n.* A type of squash that is shaped somewhat like an acorn with a ridged rind and yellow to orange flesh.
a·cous·tic (ə-ko͞o'stĭk) also **a·cous·ti·cal** (-stĭ-kəl) ▸ *adj.* **1.** Of or relating to sound, the sense of hearing, or the science of sound. **2.** Designed to aid in hearing. **3.** *Mus.* Not electronically produced or modified: *an acoustic guitar.* **—a·cous'ti·cal·ly** *adv.*
a·cous·tics (ə-ko͞o'stĭks) ▸ *n.* **1.** *(takes sing. v.)* The scientific study of sound. **2.** *(takes pl. v.)* The total effect of sound, esp. as produced in an enclosed space.
ac·quaint (ə-kwānt') ▸ *v.* To make familiar: *acquainted myself with the controls.*
ac·quain·tance (ə-kwān'təns) ▸ *n.* **1.** Knowledge of a person less intimate than friendship. **2.** A person whom one knows. **3.** Personal knowledge or information. **—ac·quain'tance·ship'** *n.*
ac·qui·esce (ăk'wē-ĕs') ▸ *v.* **-esced, -esc·ing.** To consent or comply without protest. **—ac'qui·es'cence** *n.* **—ac'qui·es'cent** *adj.* **—ac'qui·es'cent·ly** *adv.*
ac·quire (ə-kwīr') ▸ *v.* **-quired, -quir·ing. 1.** To gain possession of. **2.** To get by one's own efforts: *acquire proficiency in math.* **—ac·quir'a·ble** *adj.* **—ac·quire'ment** *n.*
ac·quired (ə-kwīrd') ▸ *adj.* **1.** Developing after birth; not congenital. **2.** Caused by exposure to something. **3.** Gained by one's own efforts.
acquired immune deficiency syndrome ▸ *n.* AIDS.
ac·qui·si·tion (ăk'wĭ-zĭsh'ən) ▸ *n.* **1.** The act of acquiring. **2.** Something acquired.
ac·quis·i·tive (ə-kwĭz'ĭ-tĭv) ▸ *adj.* Eager to gain and possess; grasping. **—ac·quis'i·tive·ly** *adv.* **—ac·quis'i·tive·ness** *n.*
ac·quit (ə-kwĭt') ▸ *v.* **-quit·ted, -quit·ting. 1.** *Law* To free from a charge or accusation. **2.** To discharge from a duty. **3.** To conduct (oneself) in a specified manner. **—ac·quit'tal** *n.*
a·cre (ā'kər) ▸ *n.* See **measurement** in Appendix.
a·cre·age (ā'kər-ĭj) ▸ *n.* Land area in acres.
ac·rid (ăk'rĭd) ▸ *adj.* **1.** Unpleasantly sharp or bitter to the taste or smell. **2.** Caustic in language or tone. **—a·crid'i·ty** (ə-krĭd'ĭ-tē), **ac'rid·ness** *n.* **—ac'rid·ly** *adv.*
ac·ri·mo·ny (ăk'rə-mō'nē) ▸ *n.* Bitter, ill-natured animosity, esp. in speech or behavior. **—ac'ri·mo'ni·ous** *adj.*
acro– or **acr–** ▸ *pref.* **1.** Height; summit: *acrophobia.* **2.** Beginning: *acronym.*
ac·ro·bat (ăk'rə-băt') ▸ *n.* One skilled in feats of agility in gymnastics. **—ac'ro·bat'ic** *adj.* **—ac'ro·bat'i·cal·ly** *adv.*
ac·ro·bat·ics (ăk'rə-băt'ĭks) ▸ *n.* *(takes sing. or pl. v.)* **1.** The gymnastic moves of an acrobat. **2.** A display of spectacular agility: *vocal acrobatics.*
ac·ro·nym (ăk'rə-nĭm') ▸ *n.* A word formed from the initial letters of a name, such as *AIDS* for *a*cquired *i*mmune *d*eficiency *s*yndrome. **—ac'ro·nym'ic, a·cron'y·mous** (ə-krŏn'ə-məs) *adj.*
ac·ro·pho·bi·a (ăk'rə-fō'bē-ə) ▸ *n.* An abnormal fear of high places.
a·crop·o·lis (ə-krŏp'ə-lĭs) ▸ *n.* The fortified height or citadel of an ancient Greek city.
a·cross (ə-krôs', -krŏs') ▸ *prep.* On, at, to, or from the other side of. ▸ *adv.* **1.** From one side to the other: *The footbridge swayed when I ran across.* **2.** Crosswise; crossed.
a·cross-the-board (ə-krôs'*th*ə-bôrd', ə-krŏs'-) ▸ *adj.* **1.** Including all categories or members. **2.** *Sports & Games* Combining win, place, or show in one bet.
a·cros·tic (ə-krô'stĭk, -krŏs'tĭk) ▸ *n.* A poem or series of lines in which certain letters, usu. the first in each line, form a name, motto, or message when read in sequence. **—a·cros'tic** *adj.*
a·cryl·ic (ə-krĭl'ĭk) ▸ *n.* **1.** An acrylic resin. **2.** A paint containing acrylic resin. **3.** An acrylic fiber. **—a·cryl'ic** *adj.*
acrylic fiber ▸ *n.* Any of numerous synthetic fibers used in sweaters, knits, and carpets.
acrylic resin ▸ *n.* Any of numerous thermoplastics used to produce paints, synthetic rubbers, and lightweight plastics.
act (ăkt) ▸ *n.* **1.** The process of doing something. **2.** Something done; a deed. **3.** *Law* A statute, decree, or enactment. **4.** A formal written record of transactions. **5.** One of the major divisions of a play or opera. **6.** A manifestation of insincerity; pose: *put on an act.* ▸ *v.* **1.** To perform in a dramatic role. **2.**

THESAURUS

acidulous *adj.* *—See* SOUR.
acknowledge *v.* **1.** To admit to the reality or truth of ▸ admit, avow, concede, confess, grant, own (up). *Slang:* fess up. *Chiefly Regional:* allow. [*Compare* ASSENT.] **2.** To express recognition of ▸ admit, recognize. [*Compare* CONFIRM.]
acknowledgment *n.* **1.** The act of admitting to something ▸ admission, avowal, concession, confession, recognition. *Idiom:* owning up. **2.** Favorable notice, as of an achievement ▸ credit, recognition. *—See also* ACCEPTANCE (2), APPRECIATION.
acme *n.* *—See* CLIMAX.
acolyte *n.* *—See* DEVOTEE.
acquaint *v.* To make known socially ▸ familiarize, introduce, present. *—See also* INFORM (1).
acquaintance *n.* Personal knowledge derived from participation or observation ▸ conversance, experience, familiarity. [*Compare* AWARENESS.]
acquainted *adj.* Having good knowledge of something ▸ conversant, familiar, schooled, versant, versed. *Idiom:* up on. [*Compare* ACCUSTOMED.] *—See also* INFORMED.
acquiesce *v.* *—See* ASSENT, SURRENDER (1).
acquiescence *n.* *—See* ACCEPTANCE (1), OBEDIENCE.
acquiescent *adj.* *—See* OBEDIENT, PASSIVE, WILLING.
acquirable *adj.* *—See* AVAILABLE.
acquire *v.* *—See* DEVELOP (1), GET (1), LEARN (1).
acquirement *n.* *—See* ACCOMPLISHMENT.
acquisition *n.* *—See* ACCOMPLISHMENT, ADDITION (1).
acquisitive *adj.* *—See* CURIOUS (2), GREEDY.
acquisitiveness *n.* *—See* GREED.
acquit *v.* *—See* ACT (1), CLEAR (3).
acquittal *n.* *—See* EXCULPATION.
acreage *n.* *—See* LAND, LOT (1).
acres *n.* *—See* LAND.
acrid *adj.* *—See* BITING, BITTER (1).
acridity *n.* *—See* SARCASM.
acrimonious *adj.* *—See* RESENTFUL.
acrimony *n.* *—See* RESENTMENT.
across *adj.* *—See* TRANSVERSE.
act *n.* **1.** Something done ▸ action, deed, doing, performance, thing, work. [*Compare* ACCOMPLISHMENT.] **2.** A display of insincere behavior ▸ acting, affectation, disguise, dissemblance, dissimulation, masquerade, pretense, sham, show, simulation. [*Compare* AFFECTATION, FAÇADE, POSE.] **3.** A short theatrical piece within a larger production ▸ sketch, skit. [*Compare* SATIRE.] *—See also* BIT[1] (4), LAW (2).

To behave; conduct oneself. **3.** To seem to be. **4.** To carry out an action. **5.** To substitute for another. **6.** To produce an effect. ***—phrasal verb:* act up** **1.** To misbehave. **2.** To malfunction. ***—idiom:* get (one's) act together** *Slang* To get organized.

ACTH (ā′sē′tē-āch′) ▸ *n.* A hormone that stimulates the secretion of cortisone and other hormones by the adrenal cortex.

ac·tin (ăk′tĭn) ▸ *n.* A muscle protein that acts with myosin to produce muscle contraction.

act·ing (ăk′tĭng) ▸ *adj.* Temporarily assuming the duties or authority of another. ▸ *n.* The occupation of or performance as an actor or actress.

ac·ti·nide (ăk′tə-nīd′) ▸ *n.* Any of a series of chemically similar radioactive elements with atomic numbers ranging from 89 (actinium) through 103 (lawrencium).

ac·ti·nism (ăk′tə-nĭz′əm) ▸ *n.* The intrinsic property in radiation that produces photochemical activity. **—ac·tin′ic** (-tĭn′ĭk) *adj.*

ac·tin·i·um (ăk-tĭn′ē-əm) ▸ *n. Symbol* **Ac** A radioactive metallic element found in uranium ores and used as a source of alpha rays. At. no. 89.

ac·ti·no·my·cin (ăk′tə-nō-mī′sĭn) ▸ *n.* Any of various red, often toxic antibiotics obtained from soil bacteria.

ac·tion (ăk′shən) ▸ *n.* **1.** The state or process of acting or doing. **2.** Something done; a deed or act. **3.** A movement or a series of movements. **4.** Manner of movement: *a gearshift with smooth action.* **5.** Habitual or vigorous activity; energy. **6.** often **actions** Behavior or conduct. **7.** The operating parts of a mechanism. **8.** The plot of a story or play. **9.** A lawsuit. **10.** Combat. **11.** Important or exciting work or activity.

ac·tion·a·ble (ăk′shə-nə-bəl) ▸ *adj.* Giving cause for legal action: *an actionable statement.* **—ac′tion·a·bly** *adv.*

ac·ti·vate (ăk′tə-vāt′) ▸ *v.* **-vat·ed, -vat·ing. 1.** To make active. **2.** To organize or create (e.g., a military unit). **3.** To treat (sewage) with aeration and bacteria. **4.** *Phys.* To make radioactive. **—ac′ti·va′tion** *n.* **—ac′ti·va′tor** *n.*

ac·tive (ăk′tĭv) ▸ *adj.* **1.** Being in motion. **2.** Capable of functioning; working. **3.** Disposed to make changes. **4.** Engaged in activity; participating. **5.** Being in action; not passive: *an active volcano.* **6a.** Energetic; lively. **b.** Requiring physical exertion: *active sports.* **7.** *Gram.* Of or being a verb form or voice used to indicate that the subject of the sentence is performing or causing the action. **—ac′tive·ly** *adv.* **—ac′tive·ness** *n.*

ac·tiv·ism (ăk′tə-vĭz′əm) ▸ *n.* A theory or practice based on often militant action to oppose or support a social or political end. **—ac′tiv·ist** *adj. & n.* **—ac·tiv·ist′ic** *adj.*

ac·tiv·i·ty (ăk-tĭv′ĭ-tē) ▸ *n., pl.* **-ties. 1.** The state of being active. **2.** Energetic action; liveliness. **3a.** A pursuit or pastime. **b.** An educational procedure to stimulate learning through actual experience.

act of God ▸ *n.* An unforeseeable manifestation of the forces of nature beyond human intervention, such as a tornado or flood.

ac·tor (ăk′tər) ▸ *n.* **1.** A theatrical performer. **2.** A participant. **3.** *Law* One, such as an administrator, who acts for another.

ac·tress (ăk′trĭs) ▸ *n.* A woman who is an actor.

Acts of the Apostles (ăkts) ▸ *pl.n. (takes sing. v.)* See **Bible** table in Appendix.

ac·tu·al (ăk′cho͞o-əl) ▸ *adj.* **1.** Existing in fact; real. **2.** Existing or acting at the present moment; current. **—ac′tu·al·ly** *adv.*

ac·tu·al·i·ty (ăk′cho͞o-ăl′ĭ-tē) ▸ *n., pl.* **-ties.** The state or fact of being actual; reality.

ac·tu·al·ize (ăk′cho͞o-ə-līz′) ▸ *v.* **-ized, -iz·ing.** To realize in action. **—ac′tu·al·i·za′tion** *n.*

ac·tu·ar·y (ăk′cho͞o-ĕr′ē) ▸ *n., pl.* **-ies.** A statistician who computes insurance risks and premiums. **—ac′tu·ar′i·al** (-âr′ē-əl) *adj.*

ac·tu·ate (ăk′cho͞o-āt′) ▸ *v.* **-at·ed, -at·ing.** To put into motion or action. **—ac′tu·a′tion** *n.* **—ac′tu·a′tor** *n.*

a·cu·i·ty (ə-kyo͞o′ĭ-tē) ▸ *n.* Acuteness of vision or perception; keenness.

ac·u·men (ăk′yə-mən, ə-kyo͞o′-) ▸ *n.* Accuracy and keenness of judgment or insight.

ac·u·pres·sure (ăk′yə-prĕsh′ər) ▸ *n.* See **shiatsu.**

ac·u·punc·ture (ăk′yo͝o-pŭngk′chər) ▸ *n.* A Chinese medical procedure in which specific body areas are pierced with fine needles for pain relief or other therapeutic purposes. **—ac′u·punc′ture** *v.* **—ac′u·punc′tur·ist** *n.*

a·cute (ə-kyo͞ot′) ▸ *adj.* **1.** Having a sharp point. **2.** Keenly perceptive or discerning. **3.** Sensitive. **4.** Crucial: *an acute lack of research funds.* **5.** Extremely sharp or severe: *acute pain.* **6.** *Medic.* Having a rapid onset and following a short but severe course: *acute disease.* **7.** *Geometry* Designating angles less than 90°. **—a·cute′ly** *adv.* **—a·cute′ness** *n.*

acute accent ▸ *n.* A mark (´) indicating: **a.** Stress of a syllable. **b.** Metrical stress in poetry. **c.** Sound quality or quantity.

acute care ▸ *n.* Short-term medical treatment, usu. in a hospital, for acute illness or injury.

a·cy·clo·vir (ā-sī′klō-vîr) ▸ *n.* A drug used topically to treat herpes simplex infections.

ad (ăd) ▸ *n.* An advertisement.

A.D. ▸ *abbr.* often **A.D.** anno Domini

ad– ▸ *pref.* Toward; to; near: *adrenal.*

ad·age (ăd′ĭj) ▸ *n.* A short proverb; saying.

a·da·gio (ə-dä′jō, -jē-ō′) ▸ *adv. & adj. Mus.* In a slow tempo.

Ad·am (ăd′əm) ▸ In the Bible, the first man and the husband of Eve.

THESAURUS

act *v.* **1.** To conduct oneself in a specified way ▸ acquit, bear, behave, carry, comport, demean, deport, do, handle, quit. [*Compare* APPEAR.] **2.** To behave insincerely or take on as a false appearance ▸ affect, assume, counterfeit, dissemble, dissimulate, fabricate, fake, feign, play-act, pose, pretend, put on, sham, simulate. *Idioms:* make believe, put on an act. [*Compare* DISGUISE, FAKE.] **3.** To play the part of ▸ do, dramatize, enact, impersonate, perform, play, play-act, portray, represent. *—See also* FUNCTION, STAGE.

act on *v.* *—See* INFLUENCE.

act up *v.* *—See* MALFUNCTION, MISBEHAVE.

acting *n.* The art and occupation of an actor ▸ dramatics, stage, theater, theatrics. *—See also* ACT (2).

acting *adj.* *—See* TEMPORARY (1).

action *n.* *—See* ACT (1), BATTLE, BEHAVIOR (1), LAWSUIT, MOTION, PLOT (1).

activate *v.* To set in motion ▸ actuate, spark, start, turn on. [*Compare* ENERGIZE, PROVOKE.] *—See also* MOBILIZE.

active *adj.* In action or full operation ▸ alive, functioning, going, humming, operating, operative, running, ticking, working. *Slang:* purring. *Idioms:* going full blast (*or* force *or* tilt), in high gear. [*Compare* BUSY.] *—See also* ENERGETIC.

activity *n.* Energetic physical action ▸ exercise, exertion, workout. [*Compare* ENERGY.] *—See also* AGITATION (3), MOTION.

actor or **actress** *n.* A theatrical performer ▸ player, thespian, trouper. [*Compare* FAKE, LEAD, MIMIC.] *—See also* PARTICIPANT.

actual *adj.* Occurring or existing in act or fact ▸ existent, extant, real, true. [*Compare* PHYSICAL.] *—See also* ACCURATE, AUTHENTIC (1).

actuality *n.* Something that is demonstrated to exist or is known to have existed ▸ event, fact, phenomenon, reality. *Idiom:* hard (*or* cold *or* plain) fact. [*Compare* INFORMATION.] *—See also* CERTAINTY, EXISTENCE.

actualization *n.* The condition of being in full force or operation ▸ being, effect, force, realization. [*Compare* EXERCISE.]

actualize *v.* To make real or actual ▸ bring about, make happen, materialize, realize. *Idioms:* bring to pass, carry (*or* put) into effect. [*Compare* EFFECT, PRODUCE.]

actually *adv.* In point of fact ▸ as a matter of fact, indeed, in fact, really. *—See also* NOW (1), REALLY.

actuate *v.* To set in motion ▸ activate, start, turn on. [*Compare* ENERGIZE, PROVOKE.] *—See also* USE.

acumen *n.* *—See* DISCERNMENT.

acuminate *adj.* *—See* POINTED.

acumination *n.* *—See* POINT (1).

acute *adj.* *—See* CLEVER (1), CRITICAL (2), HIGH (3), POINTED, SHARP (3), URGENT (1).

acutely *adv.* *—See* VERY.

acuteness *n.* *—See* DISCRIMINATION (1).

adage *n.* *—See* PROVERB.

ad·a·mant (ăd′ə-mənt) ▸ *adj.* Impervious to pleas or reason; unyielding. ▸ *n.* A legendary stone of impenetrable hardness.

Ad·ams, **Abigail Smith** (1744–1818) ▸ First Lady of the US (1797–1801) and noted correspondent.

Adams, **John** (1735–1826) ▸ The first Vice President (1789–97) and second President (1797–1801) of the US.

Adams, **John Quincy** (1767–1848) ▸ The sixth US President (1825–29).

Adam's apple ▸ *n.* The slight projection at the front of the throat formed by the largest cartilage of the larynx.

a·dapt (ə-dăpt′) ▸ *v.* To make or become suitable for a specific use. **—a·dapt′a·bil′i·ty** *n.* **—a·dapt′a·ble** *adj.* **—a·dapt′a·ble·ness** *n.*

ad·ap·ta·tion (ăd′ăp-tā′shən) ▸ *n.* **1a.** The act or process of adapting. **b.** The state of being adapted. **2.** A composition recast into a new form: *The play is an adaptation of a short novel.* **3.** *Biol.* An alteration or adjustment by which a species or individual improves its condition in relationship to its environment. **—ad′ap·ta′tion·al** *adj.*

a·dapt·er also **a·dap·tor** (ə-dăp′tər) ▸ *n.* One that adapts, such as a device used to effect compatibility between different parts of a system or apparatus.

a·dap·tive (ə-dăp′tĭv) ▸ *adj.* Capable of adapting or of being adapted: *an adaptive nature.* **—a·dap′tive·ness** *n.*

A·dar (ä-där′) ▸ *n.* A month of the Jewish calendar.

Adar She·ni (shā-nē′) ▸ *n.* An intercalary month in the Jewish calendar.

add (ăd) ▸ *v.* **1.** To combine (e.g., a column of figures) to form a sum. **2.** To join so as to increase in size, quantity, quality, or scope: *added 12 inches to the deck.* **3.** To say or write further. ***—phrasal verb:*** **add up** To be reasonable or plausible: *an excuse that didn't add up.* ***—idiom:*** **add up to** To constitute; mean. **—add′a·ble, add′i·ble** *adj.*

ad·dend (ăd′ĕnd′) ▸ *n.* Any of a set of numbers to be added.

ad·den·dum (ə-dĕn′dəm) ▸ *n., pl.* **-da** (-də). Something added or to be added, esp. a supplement to a book.

add·er[1] (ăd′ər) ▸ *n.* One that adds, esp. a device that performs arithmetic addition.

ad·der[2] (ăd′ər) ▸ *n.* **1.** See **viper** 1. **2.** Any of several nonvenomous snakes, such as the milk snake of North America, popularly believed to be harmful.

ad·dict (ə-dĭkt′) ▸ *v.* **1.** To give (oneself) habitually or compulsively: *We were addicted to gambling.* **2.** To cause to become compulsively and physiologically dependent on a habit-forming substance. ▸ *n.* (ăd′ĭkt) One who is addicted, as to narcotics. **—ad·dic′tion** *n.* **—ad·dic′tive** *adj.*

add-in (ăd′ĭn′) ▸ *n.* **1.** Something designed for use in conjunction with another. **2.** *Comp. Sci.* A software program that extends the capabilities of an existing application.

Ad·dis Ab·a·ba (ăd′ĭs ăb′ə-bə, ä′dĭs ä′bə-bä′) ▸ The capital of Ethiopia, in the central part.

ad·di·tion (ə-dĭsh′ən) ▸ *n.* **1.** The act or process of adding. **2.** Something added, such as a room to a building. ***—idiom:*** **in addition** Also; as well as. **—ad·di′tion·al** *adj.* **—ad·di′tion·al·ly** *adv.*

ad·di·tive (ăd′ĭ-tĭv) ▸ *n.* A substance added in small amounts to something else to improve or strengthen it. ▸ *adj.* Relating to addition.

ad·dle (ăd′l) ▸ *v.* **-dled, -dling.** **1.** To make or become confused. **2.** To become rotten; spoil.

add-on (ăd′ŏn′, -ôn′) ▸ *n.* **1.** One thing added as a supplement to another. **2.** *Comp. Sci.* **a.** See **add-in** 2. **b.** A hardware device added to a computer to increase its capabilities.

ad·dress (ə-drĕs′) ▸ *v.* **1.** To speak to. **2.** To direct to the attention of. **3.** To mark with a destination. **4.** To direct one's efforts or attention to. ▸ *n.* **1.** A formal spoken or written communication. **2.** (*also* ăd′rĕs′) The directions on a deliverable item indicating destination. **3.** (*also* ăd′rĕs′) The location at which an organization or person may be found. **4.** (*also* ăd′rĕs′) *Comp. Sci.* **a.** A number assigned to a specific memory location. **b.** A name or character sequence that designates an e-mail account or website.

ad·dress·ee (ăd′rĕ-sē′, ə-drĕs′ē′) ▸ *n.* The one to whom something is addressed.

ad·duce (ə-do͞os′, -dyo͞os′) ▸ *v.* **-duced, -duc·ing.** To cite as an example or means of proof in an argument. **—ad·duce′a·ble, ad·duc′i·ble** *adj.*

-ade ▸ *suff.* A sweetened beverage of: *lemonade.*

ad·e·nine (ăd′n-ēn′, -ĭn) ▸ *n.* A purine base, $C_5H_5N_5$, that is a constituent of DNA and RNA.

ad·e·noid (ăd′n-oid′) ▸ *n.* A lymphoid tissue growth in the nose above the throat. Often used in the plural. **—ad′e·noid′** *adj.*

ad·e·noi·dal (ăd′n-oid′l) ▸ *adj.* **1.** Of the adenoids. **2.** Nasal; stuffy: *an adenoidal voice.*

a·dept (ə-dĕpt′) ▸ *adj.* Very skilled; expert. **—ad′ept′** (ăd′ĕpt′) *n.* **—a·dept′ly** *adv.*

ad·e·quate (ăd′ĭ-kwĭt) ▸ *adj.* **1.** Sufficient to satisfy a requirement. **2.** Barely satisfactory. **—ad′e·qua·cy** (-kwə-sē) *n.* **—ad′e·quate·ly** *adv.*

ad·here (ăd-hîr′) ▸ *v.* **-hered, -her·ing.** **1.** To stick fast, as by suction or glue. **2.** To be a devoted follower. **3.** To carry something out without deviation: *We will adhere to*

THESAURUS

adamant *adj.* —*See* STUBBORN (1).

adapt *v.* To make or become suitable to a particular situation or use ▸ acclimate, acclimatize, accommodate, adjust, conform, fashion, fit, remodel, shape, suit, tailor. *Idioms:* get used to, learn to live with (*or* accept). [*Compare* CHANGE, CONVERT.]

adaptable *adj.* Capable of adapting or being adapted ▸ adaptive, adjustable, elastic, flexible, malleable, pliable, pliant, supple, versatile. [*Compare* CHANGEABLE, OBEDIENT.]

adaptation *n.* The act or process of adapting ▸ acclimation, acclimatization, accommodation, acculturation, adaption, adjustment, conditioning, conformation. [*Compare* CHANGE.] —*See also* VARIATION.

adapted *adj.* —*See* ACCUSTOMED (1).

adaption *n.* —*See* ADAPTATION.

adaptive *adj.* —*See* ADAPTABLE.

add *v.* To combine numbers to form a sum ▸ add up, cast, foot (up), sum (up), tot (up), total, totalize. [*Compare* CALCULATE, COUNT.] —*See also* ATTACH (2).

add up *v.* —*See* AMOUNT.

added *adj.* —*See* ADDITIONAL.

addendum *n.* —*See* ADDITION (1).

addiction *n.* Compulsive physiological and psychological need for a habit-forming substance ▸ craving, compulsion, dependence, drug abuse, enslavement, fixation, substance abuse. [*Compare* CUSTOM.]

addition *n.* **1.** Something tending to augment something else ▸ accession, acquisition, addendum, augmentation. [*Compare* ATTACHMENT.] **2.** The act or process of adding ▸ summation, sums, totalization. [*Compare* CALCULATION.] —*See also* EXTENSION (2).

additional *adj.* Being an addition ▸ added, extra, fresh, further, more, new, other, supplemental, supplementary. [*Compare* AUXILIARY.]

additionally *adv.* In addition ▸ also, besides, further, furthermore, likewise, more, moreover, still, too, yet. *Idioms:* as well, for good measure, not to mention, on top of, to boot, to say nothing of.

additive *adj.* Increasing, as in force, by successive additions ▸ accumulative, cumulative.

additive-free *adj.* —*See* NATURAL (1).

addle *v.* —*See* CONFUSE (1).

addled or **addlepated** *adj.* —*See* CONFUSED (1).

add-on *n.* —*See* ENHANCEMENT, EXTENSION (2).

address *v.* **1.** To talk to an audience formally ▸ lecture, prelect, sermonize, speak. [*Compare* CONVERSE[1].] **2.** To bring an appeal or request to the attention of ▸ appeal, apply, approach, petition. [*Compare* APPEAL, REQUEST.] **3.** To mark a written communication with its destination ▸ direct, superscribe. [*Compare* TICKET.] —*See also* APPLY (1), DEAL (1), SEND (1).

address *n.* —*See* BEARING (1), HOME (1), SPEECH (2), TACT.

addresses *n.* —*See* ADVANCES.

adduce *v.* —*See* CITE.

adept *adj.* —*See* EXPERT.

adept *n.* —*See* EXPERT.

adeptness *n.* —*See* ABILITY (1).

adequacy *n.* An adequate quantity ▸ enough, sufficiency.

adequate *adj.* —*See* ACCEPTABLE (2), SUFFICIENT.

adhere *v.* —*See* BOND, FOLLOW (4).

adherence *n.* —*See* BOND (3).

adherent *n.* —*See* DEVOTEE, FOLLOWER.

our plan. **—ad·her′ence** *n.* **—ad·her′ent** *adj.* & *n.*

ad·he·sion (ăd-hē′zhən) ▸ *n.* **1.** The act or state of adhering. **2.** Attachment or devotion; loyalty. **3.** *Medic.* A condition in which normally separate bodily tissues grow together.

ad·he·sive (ăd-hē′sĭv, -zĭv) ▸ *adj.* **1.** Tending to adhere; sticky. **2.** Gummed so as to adhere. **—ad·he′sive** *n.* **—ad·he′sive·ly** *adv.* **—ad·he′sive·ness** *n.*

ad hoc (ăd hŏk′, hōk′) ▸ *adv.* For only the specific case or situation at hand. ▸ *adj.* Improvised; impromptu.

ad hom·i·nem (ăd hŏm′ə-nĕm′) ▸ *adj.* Attacking an opponent's character to avoid discussing the issues. **—ad hom′i·nem′** *adv.*

a·dieu (ə-dyo͞o′, -do͞o′) ▸ *interj.* Used to express farewell. ▸ *n., pl.* **a·dieus** or **a·dieux** (ə-dyo͞oz′, -do͞oz′). A farewell.

ad in·fi·ni·tum (ăd ĭn′fə-nī′təm) ▸ *adv.* & *adj.* To infinity; having no end.

ad·i·os (ăd′ē-ōs′, ä′dē-) ▸ *interj.* Used to express farewell.

ad·i·pose (ăd′ə-pōs′) ▸ *adj.* Relating to animal fat; fatty.

Ad·i·ron·dack Mountains (ăd′ə-rŏn′dăk′) ▸ A group of mountains in NE NY rising to about 1,630 m (5,344 ft).

adj. ▸ *abbr.* adjective

ad·ja·cent (ə-jā′sənt) ▸ *adj.* **1.** Close to; lying near: *adjacent cities.* **2.** Next to; adjoining: *adjacent garden plots.* **—ad·ja′cen·cy** *n.*

ad·jec·tive (ăj′ĭk-tĭv) ▸ *n.* The part of speech that modifies a noun or other substantive by limiting, qualifying, or specifying. **—ad′jec·ti′val** (-tī′vəl) *adj.* **—ad′jec·ti′val·ly** *adv.*

ad·join (ə-join′) ▸ *v.* **1.** To be next to. **2.** To attach.

ad·journ (ə-jûrn′) ▸ *v.* **1.** To suspend until a later time. **2.** To move from one place to another: *After the meal we adjourned to the living room.* **—ad·journ′ment** *n.*

ad·judge (ə-jŭj′) ▸ *v.* **-judged, -judg·ing.** **1.** To determine or award by law. **2.** To regard; deem: *was adjudged incompetent.*

ad·ju·di·cate (ə-jo͞o′dĭ-kāt′) ▸ *v.* **-cat·ed, -cat·ing.** To hear and settle (a case) by judicial procedure. **—ad·ju′di·ca′tion** *n.* **—ad·ju′di·ca′tive** *adj.* **—ad·ju′di·ca′tor** *n.*

ad·junct (ăj′ŭngkt′) ▸ *n.* One attached to another in a dependent or subordinate position. **—ad·junc′tive** *adj.*

ad·jure (ə-jo͝or′) ▸ *v.* **-jured, -jur·ing.** **1.** To command or enjoin solemnly, as under oath. **2.** To appeal to or entreat earnestly. **—ad′ju·ra′tion** (ăj′ə-rā′shən) *n.*

ad·just (ə-jŭst′) ▸ *v.* **1.** To change so as to match or fit. **2.** To bring into proper relationship. **3.** To adapt or conform, as to new conditions. **4.** To settle (an insurance claim). **—ad·just′a·ble** *adj.* **—ad·just′er, ad·jus′tor** *n.* **—ad·just′ment** *n.*

ad·ju·tant (ăj′ə-tənt) ▸ *n.* **1.** A staff officer who helps a commanding officer with administration. **2.** An assistant. **—ad′ju·tan·cy** *n.*

ad lib (ăd lĭb′) ▸ *adv.* In an unrestrained manner; spontaneously.

ad-lib (ăd-lĭb′) ▸ *v.* **-libbed, -lib·bing.** To improvise and deliver extemporaneously. ▸ *n.* (ăd′lĭb′) Words, music, or actions uttered or performed extemporaneously. **—ad′-lib′** *adj.* **—ad-lib′ber** *n.*

ad·min·is·ter (ăd-mĭn′ĭ-stər) ▸ *v.* **1.** To direct; manage. **2a.** To give or apply in a formal way: *administer the last rites.* **b.** To apply as a remedy: *administer a sedative.* **3.** To mete out; dispense: *administer justice.* **4.** To tender (an oath). **—ad·min′is·trant** *adj.* & *n.*

ad·min·is·tra·tion (ăd-mĭn′ĭ-strā′shən) ▸ *n.* **1.** The act of administering. **2.** Management, esp. of business affairs. **3.** The activity of a sovereign state in the exercise of its powers or duties. **4.** often **Administration** The executive branch of a government. **5.** Those who manage an institution. **—ad·min′is·tra′tive** (-strā′tĭv, -strə-) *adj.* **—ad·min′is·tra′tive·ly** *adv.*

ad·min·is·tra·tor (ăd-mĭn′ĭ-strā′tər) ▸ *n.* **1.** One who administers. **2.** One appointed to manage an estate.

ad·mi·ra·ble (ăd′mər-ə-bəl) ▸ *adj.* Deserving admiration. **—ad′mi·ra·bly** *adv.*

ad·mi·ral (ăd′mər-əl) ▸ *n.* **1.** The commander in chief of a fleet. **2.** A rank, as in the US Navy, above vice admiral and below fleet admiral.

ad·mi·ral·ty (ăd′mər-əl-tē) ▸ *n., pl.* **-ties.** **1a.** A court exercising jurisdiction over all maritime cases. **b.** Maritime law. **2. Admiralty** The department of the British government that once had control over all naval affairs.

ad·mire (ăd-mīr′) ▸ *v.* **-mired, -mir·ing.** **1.** To regard with pleasure, wonder, and approval. **2.** To esteem or respect. **3.** *Archaic* To marvel at. **—ad′mi·ra′tion** (ăd′mə rā′shən) *n.* **—ad·mir′er** *n.* **—ad·mir′ing·ly** *adv.*

ad·mis·si·ble (ăd-mĭs′ə-bəl) ▸ *adj.* **1.** That can be accepted; allowable: *admissible evidence.* **2.** Worthy of admission. **—ad·mis′si·bil′i·ty, ad·mis′si·ble·ness** *n.*

ad·mis·sion (ăd-mĭsh′ən) ▸ *n.* **1.** The act of admitting. **2.**

THESAURUS

adherents *n.* The steadfast believers in a faith or cause ▸ congregation, faithful, fold. [*Compare* FOLLOWER, ASSEMBLY.]

adhesion *n.* *—See* BOND (3).

adhesive *adj.* *—See* STICKY (1).

ad hoc *adj.* *—See* TEMPORARY (2).

adieu *n.* *—See* DEPARTURE.

ad interim *adj.* *—See* TEMPORARY (1).

adipose *adj.* *—See* FATTY.

adjacent *adj.* *—See* ADJOINING, CLOSE (1).

adjoin *v.* To be contiguous or next to ▸ abut, border, bound, butt, flank, impinge, join, meet, neighbor, touch, verge. [*Compare* BORDER.] *—See also* ATTACH (1).

adjoining *adj.* Sharing a common boundary ▸ abutting, adjacent, bordering, conjoining, conterminous, contiguous, neighboring, next.

adjourn *v.* *—See* DEFER[1].

adjournment *n.* *—See* DELAY (1).

adjudicate or **adjudge** *v.* *—See* JUDGE.

adjudication *n.* *—See* RULING.

adjunct *n.* *—See* ATTACHMENT.

adjure *v.* *—See* APPEAL (1), COMMAND (1).

adjust *v.* To alter for proper or accurate functioning ▸ align, attune, calibrate, fine-tune, fix, modulate, regulate, set, temper, tweak, tune (up). [*Compare* FIX, TINKER.] *—See also* ADAPT.

adjustable *adj.* *—See* ADAPTABLE.

adjustment *n.* *—See* ADAPTATION.

adjutant *n.* *—See* ASSISTANT.

ad-lib *v.* *—See* IMPROVISE (1).

ad-lib *n.* Something improvised ▸ extemporization, impromptu, improvisation. [*Compare* MAKESHIFT.]

ad-lib *adj.* *—See* EXTEMPORANEOUS.

admeasure *v.* *—See* DISTRIBUTE.

admeasurement *n.* *—See* DISTRIBUTION (1).

administer *v.* **1.** To have charge of the affairs of others ▸ administrate, captain, control, dictate, direct, dominate, govern, head, lead, manage, reign, rule, run. *Idioms:* be at the helm, be in the driver's seat, hold sway over, hold the reins. [*Compare* COMMAND, SUPERVISE.] **2.** To oversee the provision or execution of ▸ administrate, carry out, dispense, execute. [*Compare* CONDUCT.] **3.** To provide as a remedy ▸ apply, dispense, dose, give, medicate, prescribe, treat, vaccinate. *Informal:* doctor. [*Compare* CURE, DRESS, DRUG.] **4.** To mete out by means of some action ▸ deal, deliver, give.

administrable *adj.* Capable of being governed ▸ controllable, governable, manageable, rulable. [*Compare* LOYAL, OBEDIENT.]

administrant *n.* *—See* EXECUTIVE.

administrate *v.* *—See* ADMINISTER (1), ADMINISTER (2).

administration *n.* *—See* EXERCISE (1), GOVERNMENT (1), GOVERNMENT (2), MANAGEMENT.

administrative *adj.* Of, for, or relating to administration or administrators ▸ directorial, executive, governmental, managerial, ministerial, organizational, supervisory.

administrator *n.* *—See* EXECUTIVE.

admirable *adj.* Deserving honor, respect, or admiration ▸ commendable, creditable, deserving, estimable, exemplary, honorable, laudable, meritorious, praiseworthy, reputable, respectable, venerable, worthy. [*Compare* CHOICE, EXCELLENT, HONEST, MARVELOUS.]

admiration *n.* *—See* ESTEEM.

admire *v.* To have a feeling of great awe and rapt admiration ▸ marvel, wonder. *Idiom:* be agog (*or* agape *or* awestruck). [*Compare* GAZE, STAGGER.] *—See also* VALUE.

admirer *n.* *—See* BEAU (1), FAN[2].

admissible *adj.* *—See* ACCEPTABLE (1).

admission *n.* The act of admitting or

Right to enter; access. **3.** The price required for entering; entrance fee. **4.** A confession, as of having committed a crime. **—ad·mis′sive** (-mĭs′ĭv) *adj.*

ad·mit (ăd-mĭt′) ► *v.* **-mit·ted, -mit·ting.** **1.** To permit to enter. **2.** To serve as a means of entrance. **3.** To have room for; accommodate. **4.** To allow; permit. **5.** To acknowledge; confess. **6.** To grant as true or valid; concede.

ad·mit·tance (ăd-mĭt′ns) ► *n.* **1.** The act of admitting. **2a.** Permission to enter. **b.** Right of entry.

ad·mit·ted·ly (ăd-mĭt′ĭd-lē) ► *adv.* By general admission; confessedly.

ad·mix·ture (ăd-mĭks′chər) ► *n.* **1.** The act of mixing. **2.** A mixture. **3.** Something added in mixing. **—ad·mix′** *v.*

ad·mon·ish (ăd-mŏn′ĭsh) ► *v.* **1.** To reprove gently but earnestly. **2.** To warn; caution. **3.** To remind of an obligation. **—ad·mon′ish·ment, ad′mo·ni′tion** (ăd′mə-nĭsh′ən) *n.*

ad·mon·i·to·ry (ăd-mŏn′ĭ-tôr′ē) ► *adj.* Showing admonition.

ad nau·se·am (ăd nô′zē-əm) ► *adv.* To a disgusting or absurd degree.

a·do (ə-do͞o′) ► *n.* Bustle; fuss; bother.

a·do·be (ə-dō′bē) ► *n.* **1.** A sun-dried, unburned brick of clay and straw. **2.** A structure built of adobe brick.

ad·o·les·cence (ăd′l-ĕs′əns) ► *n.* The period of physical and psychological development from the onset of puberty to maturity. **—ad′o·les′cent** *adj. & n.*

A·don·is (ə-dŏn′ĭs, -dō′nĭs) ► *n.* **1.** *Gk. Myth.* A beautiful young man loved by Aphrodite. **2.** often **adonis** A handsome young man.

a·dopt (ə-dŏpt′) ► *v.* **1.** To take (a child) into one's family through legal means and raise as one's own. **2.** To take and follow (a course of action) by choice or assent. **3.** To take up and make one's own. **—a·dopt′a·ble** *adj.* **—a·dopt′er** *n.* **—a·dop′tion** *n.*

a·dop·tee (ə-dŏp′tē) ► *n.* One, such as a child, that is or has been adopted.

a·dop·tive (ə-dŏp′tĭv) ► *adj.* **1.** Of or relating to adoption. **2.** Related by adoption. **—a·dop′tive·ly** *adv.*

a·dor·a·ble (ə-dôr′ə-bəl) ► *adj.* **1.** Delightful, lovable, and charming. **2.** Worthy of adoration. **—a·dor′a·bly** *adv.*

a·dore (ə-dôr′) ► *v.* **a·dored, a·dor·ing.** **1.** To worship as divine. **2.** To regard with deep, often rapturous love. **3.** To like very much. **—ad·o·ra′tion** (ăd′ə-rā′shən) *n.* **—a·dor′er** *n.* **—a·dor′ing·ly** *adv.*

a·dorn (ə-dôrn′) ► *v.* **1.** To lend beauty to; enhance. **2.** To decorate; embellish. **—a·dorn′ment** *n.*

ad·re·nal (ə-drē′nəl) ► *adj.* **1.** At, near, or on the kidneys. **2.** Of or relating to the adrenal glands or their secretions.

adrenal gland ► *n.* Either of two small endocrine glands, one located above each kidney.

a·dren·a·line (ə-drĕn′ə-lĭn) ► *n.* See **epinephrine** 1.

A·dri·at·ic Sea (ā′drē-ăt′ĭk) ► An arm of the Mediterranean between Italy and the Balkan Peninsula.

a·drift (ə-drĭft′) ► *adv. & adj.* **1.** Drifting or floating freely; not anchored. **2.** Without direction or purpose.

a·droit (ə-droit′) ► *adj.* **1.** Dexterous; deft. **2.** Proficient under pressing conditions. **—a·droit′ly** *adv.* **—a·droit′ness** *n.*

ad·sorb (ăd-sôrb′, -zôrb′) ► *v.* To take up and hold (liquid or gas) on the surface of a solid. **—ad·sorb′a·ble** *adj.* **—ad·sorp′tion** (-sôrp′shən, -zôrp′-) *n.* **—ad·sorp′tive** *adj.*

ad·u·late (ăj′ə-lāt′) ► *v.* **-lat·ed, -lat·ing.** To praise or admire excessively; fawn on. **—ad′u·la′tion** *n.* **—ad′u·la·to′ry** (-lə-tôr′ē) *adj.*

a·dult (ə-dŭlt′, ăd′ŭlt) ► *n.* One that has attained maturity or legal age. ► *adj.* **1.** Fully developed; mature. **2.** For or befitting adults: *adult education.* **—a·dult′hood′** *n.*

a·dul·ter·ate (ə-dŭl′tə-rāt′) ► *v.* **-at·ed, -at·ing.** To make impure by adding improper or inferior ingredients. **—a·dul′ter·ant** *adj. & n.* **—a·dul′ter·a′tion** *n.* **—a·dul′ter·a′tor** *n.*

a·dul·ter·y (ə-dŭl′tə-rē, -trē) ► *n., pl.* **-ies.** Voluntary sexual intercourse between a married person and a partner other than the lawful spouse. **—a·dul′ter·er** *n.* **—a·dul′ter·ess** (-trĭs, -tər-ĭs) *n.* **—a·dul′ter·ous** *adj.*

ad·um·brate (ăd′əm-brāt′, ə-dŭm′-) ► *v.* **-brat·ed, -brat·ing.** **1.** To give a sketchy outline of. **2.** To foreshadow. **3.** To disclose partially. **—ad′um·bra′tion** *n.*

adv. ► *abbr.* adverb

ad·vance (ăd-văns′) ► *v.* **-vanced, -vanc·ing.** **1.** To move or bring forward. **2.** To put forward; suggest. **3a.** To aid the progress of. **b.** To make progress; proceed. **4.** To raise or rise in rank, amount, or value. **5.** To cause to occur sooner. **6.** To pay (money or interest) before due. **7.** To lend, esp. on credit. ► *n.* **1.** The act or process of moving or going forward. **2.** Improvement; progress. **3.** An increase of price or value. **4.** **advances** Opening approaches made to secure acquaintance, favor, or an agreement. **5.** Payment of money before due. ► *adj.* **1.** Made or given ahead of time: *an advance payment.* **2.**

THESAURUS

the state of being admitted ► access, admittance, entrance, entrée, entry, ingress, introduction, intromission. [*Compare* ACCEPTANCE, PERMISSION.] *—See also* ACKNOWLEDGMENT (1).

admit *v.* To express recognition of ► acknowledge, recognize. [*Compare* CONFIRM.] *—See also* ACCEPT (3), ACKNOWLEDGE (1), PERMIT (3).

admittance *n.* *—See* ADMISSION.

admitted *adj.* *—See* ACCEPTED.

admix *v.* *—See* MIX (1).

admixture *n.* *—See* MIXTURE.

admonish *v.* *—See* CHASTISE, WARN.

admonishing *adj.* Giving warning ► admonitory, cautionary, monitory, warning.

admonition or **admonishment** *n.* *—See* REBUKE, WARNING.

admonitory *adj.* Giving warning ► admonishing, cautionary, monitory, warning.

ado *n.* *—See* AGITATION (3).

adolescence *n.* *—See* YOUTH (1).

adolescent *n.* *—See* TEENAGER.

adolescent *adj.* *—See* CHILDISH.

adopt *v.* To take, as another's idea, and make one's own ► appropriate, assume, embrace, espouse, take on, take up. [*Compare* ACT, SEIZE.] *—See also* CONFIRM (3), PASS (6).

adoption *n.* *—See* ACCEPTANCE (1), CONFIRMATION (1), EXERCISE (1).

adorable *adj.* *—See* DELIGHTFUL.

adoration *n.* The act of adoring, especially reverently ► idolization, reverence, veneration, worship. [*Compare* HONOR, PRAISE.] *—See also* DEVOTION, LOVE (1).

adore *v.* **1.** To feel deep devoted love for ► love, worship. *Idioms:* be soft (*or* stuck *or* sweet on, place (*or* put) on a pedestal, worship the ground someone walks on. **2.** To like or enjoy enthusiastically ► be big on, be crazy about, be hot on, be into, be keen on, be mad about, be nuts about, be wild about, delight (in), dote on (*or* upon), love. *Slang:* eat up, get off on. *—See also* LIKE[1], REVERE.

adorn *v.* **1.** To furnish with decorations ► bedeck, bejewel, deck (out), decorate, dress (up), embellish, emblazon, festoon, garnish, gild, ornament, trim. *Slang:* doll up, gussy up. **2.** To endow with beauty and elegance by way of a notable addition ► beautify, embellish, enhance, grace, set off.

adornment *n.* Something that adorns ► decoration, embellishment, garnishment, garniture, ornament, ornamentation, trim, trimming.

adrift *adj.* *—See* LOST (1).

adroit *adj.* *—See* DEXTEROUS.

adroitness *n.* *—See* DEXTERITY.

adscititious *adj.* Not part of the real or essential nature of a thing ► adventitious, incidental, inessential, supervenient. [*Compare* IRRELEVANT, UNNECESSARY.]

adulate *v.* *—See* FLATTER (1).

adulation *n.* *—See* FLATTERY.

adulator *n.* *—See* SYCOPHANT.

adult *adj.* *—See* MATURE.

adulterant *n.* *—See* CONTAMINANT.

adulterate *v.* *—See* CONTAMINATE, DILUTE.

adulterated *adj.* *—See* IMPURE (2).

adulteration *n.* *—See* CONTAMINATION.

adulterator *n.* *—See* CONTAMINANT.

adulterer *n.* *—See* PHILANDERER.

adumbrate *v.* *—See* DRAFT (1), FORESHADOW, OBSCURE, SHADE (2).

advance *v.* **1.** To cause to move forward or upward, as toward a goal ► drive, forward, foster, further, promote, propel, push. [*Compare* DRIVE, IMPROVE.] **2.** To move forward ► come (along), get along, march, move (up), press (on), proceed, progress, push (on). [*Compare* PLUNGE.] *—See also* LEND, OFFER (1), PROMOTE (1), PROPOSE, RISE (3).

advance *n.* Forward movement ► advancement, furtherance, headway, march, procession, progress, progres-

Going before or in front. *—idioms:* **in advance** Ahead of time; beforehand. **in advance of** Ahead of. **—ad·vanc′er** *n.*

ad·vanced (ăd-vănst′) ▸ *adj.* **1.** Highly developed or complex. **2.** At a higher level than others: *an advanced text in physics.* **3.** Progressive: *advanced teaching methods.* **4.** Far along in course or time: *an advanced stage of illness.*

ad·vance·ment (ăd-văns′mənt) ▸ *n.* **1.** The act of advancing. **2.** Development; progress: *the advancement of knowledge.* **3.** A promotion.

ad·van·tage (ăd-văn′tĭj) ▸ *n.* **1.** A beneficial factor or combination of factors. **2.** Benefit or profit; gain. **3.** A relatively favorable position. **4.** The first point scored in tennis after deuce. ▸ *v.* **-taged, -tag·ing.** To afford profit or gain to; benefit. *—idiom:* **take advantage of 1.** To put to good use. **2.** To exploit. **—ad·van·ta′geous** (-văn-tā′jəs) *adj.* **—ad′van·ta′geous·ly** *adv.*

ad·vent (ăd′vĕnt′) ▸ *n.* **1.** The coming or arrival, esp. of something important: *the advent of the computer.* **2.** also **Advent a.** The period of preparation for Christmas, beginning on the fourth Sunday before Christmas. **b.** *Christianity* The coming or birth of Jesus.

ad·ven·ti·tious (ăd′vĕn-tĭsh′əs) ▸ *adj.* Not inherent but added extrinsically. **—ad′ven·ti′tious·ly** *adv.*

ad·ven·ture (ăd-vĕn′chər) ▸ *n.* **1a.** An enterprise of a hazardous nature. **b.** An undertaking of a questionable nature, esp. intervention in another state's affairs. **2.** An unusual or exciting experience. **3.** A business venture. ▸ *v.* **-tured, -tur·ing. 1.** To hazard or risk. **2.** To take risks.

ad·ven·tur·er (ăd-vĕn′chər-ər) ▸ *n.* **1.** One that seeks adventure. **2.** A soldier of fortune. **3.** A financial speculator. **4.** One who attempts to gain wealth and social position by unscrupulous means.

ad·ven·ture·some (ăd-vĕn′chər-səm) ▸ *adj.* Daring.

ad·ven·tur·ess (ăd-vĕn′chər-ĭs) ▸ *n.* A woman who seeks social and financial advancement by unscrupulous means.

ad·ven·tur·ous (ăd-vĕn′chər-əs) ▸ *adj.* **1.** Inclined to undertake new and daring enterprises. **2.** Hazardous; risky. **—ad·ven′tur·ous·ly** *adv.* **—ad·ven′tur·ous·ness** *n.*

ad·verb (ăd′vûrb) ▸ *n.* The part of speech that modifies a verb, an adjective, or another adverb. **—ad·ver′bi·al** *adj.* **—ad·ver′bi·al·ly** *adv.*

ad·ver·sar·i·al (ăd′vər-sâr′ē-əl) ▸ *adj.* Characteristic of an adversary; antagonistic.

ad·ver·sar·y (ăd′vər-sĕr′ē) ▸ *n., pl.* **-ies.** An opponent; enemy.

ad·verse (ăd-vûrs′, ăd′vûrs′) ▸ *adj.* **1.** Acting or serving to oppose; antagonistic: *adverse criticism.* **2.** Harmful or unfavorable: *adverse circumstances.* **—ad·verse′ly** *adv.*

ad·ver·si·ty (ăd-vûr′sĭ-tē) ▸ *n., pl.* **-ties. 1.** Great hardship or affliction; misfortune. **2.** A calamitous event.

ad·vert (ăd-vûrt′) ▸ *v.* To call attention; refer: *advert to a problem.*

ad·ver·tise (ăd′vər-tīz′) ▸ *v.* **-tised, -tis·ing. 1.** To make public announcement of, esp. to promote sales: *advertise a new product.* **2.** To make known. **3.** To warn or notify. **—ad′ver·tis′er** *n.*

ad·ver·tise·ment (ăd′vər-tīz′mənt, ăd-vûr′tĭs-, -tĭz-) ▸ *n.* **1.** The act of advertising. **2.** A notice designed to attract public attention or patronage.

ad·ver·tis·ing (ăd′vər-tī′zĭng) ▸ *n.* **1.** The business of designing, preparing, and disseminating advertisements. **2.** Advertisements collectively.

ad·vice (ăd-vīs′) ▸ *n.* Opinion about a course of action; counsel.

ad·vis·a·ble (ăd-vī′zə-bəl) ▸ *adj.* Worthy of being recommended or suggested; prudent. **—ad·vis′a·bil′i·ty** *n.* **—ad·vis′a·bly** *adv.*

ad·vise (ăd-vīz′) ▸ *v.* **-vis·ed, -vis·ing. 1.** To offer advice to; counsel. **2.** To recommend; suggest: *advised patience.* **3.** To inform; notify. **—ad·vis′er, ad·vi′sor** *n.*

ad·vis·ed·ly (ăd-vī′zĭd-lē) ▸ *adv.* With careful consideration; deliberately.

ad·vise·ment (ăd-vīz′mənt) ▸ *n.* Careful consideration.

ad·vi·so·ry (ăd-vī′zə-rē) ▸ *adj.* **1.** Empowered to advise: *an*

THESAURUS

sion, stride. [*Compare* ACCOMPLISHMENT, PROGRESS.] *—See also* INCREASE (2).

advance *adj.* Going before ▸ antecedent, anterior, earlier, precedent, preceding, previous, prior.

advanced *adj.* *—See* COMPLEX (1), OLD (2), PROGRESSIVE (1).

advancement *n.* A progression upward in rank ▸ elevation, jump, preferment, promotion, raise, rise, upgrade. [*Compare* INCREASE.] *—See also* ADVANCE, DEVELOPMENT, IMPROVEMENT (1), PROGRESS.

advances *n.* Personal approach to gain acquaintance, favor, or an agreement ▸ addresses, approach, attentions, moves, overture, proposition. [*Compare* FEELER, OFFER.]

advantage *n.* **1.** A factor conducive to superiority and success ▸ handicap, head start, odds, start, toehold, vantage. *Informal:* jump. **2.** Something beneficial ▸ avail, benefit, blessing, boon, favor, gain, profit. [*Compare* HELP, LUCK, PATRONAGE.] **3.** A dominating position, as in a conflict ▸ better, bulge, draw, drop, edge, leverage, superiority, upper hand, vantage, whip hand. *Informal:* inside track, jump, leg up. *—See also* INTEREST (1), USE (2).

advantage *v.* *—See* PROFIT (2).

advantageous *adj.* *—See* BENEFICIAL, PROFITABLE.

advantages *n.* *—See* AMENITIES (1).

advent *n.* The act of arriving ▸ appearance, arrival, coming. [*Compare* ENTRANCE[1].]

adventitious *adj.* Not part of the real or essential nature of a thing ▸ adscititious, incidental, inessential, supervenient. [*Compare* IRRELEVANT, UNNECESSARY.] *—See also* ACCIDENTAL.

adventure *n.* An exciting or unusual undertaking ▸ emprise, enterprise, escapade, experience, odyssey, venture. [*Compare* FEAT, JOURNEY, TRIP.]

adventure *v.* *—See* GAMBLE (2), VENTURE.

adventurer *n.* **1.** One who seeks adventure ▸ daredevil, quester, venturer. [*Compare* BUILDER.] **2.** A freelance fighter ▸ mercenary, soldier of fortune. [*Compare* FIGHTER, SOLDIER.] **3.** One who speculates for quick profits ▸ gambler, speculator, operator.

adventuresome *adj.* *—See* ADVENTUROUS.

adventuresomeness *n.* *—See* DARING.

adventurous *adj.* Taking or willing to take risks ▸ adventuresome, audacious, bold, daredevil, daring, enterprising, venturesome, venturous. [*Compare* BRAVE, RASH[1].] *—See also* DANGEROUS.

adventurousness *n.* *—See* DARING.

adversarial *adj.* *—See* OPPOSING.

adversary *n.* *—See* OPPONENT.

adverse *adj.* Not encouraging life or growth ▸ hostile, inhospitable, unfavorable. [*Compare* SEVERE.] *—See also* HARMFUL, OPPOSING, UNFAVORABLE (1).

adversity *n.* *—See* MISFORTUNE.

advert *v.* *—See* REFER (1).

advertise *v.* *—See* ANNOUNCE, PROMOTE (3).

advertisement *n.* *—See* PUBLICITY.

advertising *n.* The act or profession of promoting something, as a product ▸ ballyhooing, billing, promoting, promotion, publicity, publicizing. *Informal:* plugging. *—See also* PUBLICITY.

advice *n.* An opinion as to a decision or course of action ▸ counsel, direction, guidance, pointer, recommendation, suggestion, tip. *Idiom:* word to the wise. [*Compare* COMMAND, DELIBERATION, WARNING.] *—See also* NEWS.

advisable *adj.* Worth doing, especially for practical reasons ▸ best, desirable, expedient, politic, practicable, recommendable, well, wisest. [*Compare* APPROPRIATE, SENSIBLE.]

advise *v.* To give recommendations to someone about a decision or course of action ▸ counsel, direct, guide, recommend, steer. *Informal:* mentor. *Idiom:* give a piece of advice. [*Compare* GUIDE, PROPOSE, WARN.] *—See also* CONFER (1), INFORM (1).

advised *adj.* *—See* DELIBERATE (2), INFORMED.

advisement *n.* Careful thought ▸ consideration, deliberation, study. [*Compare* ATTENTION, EXAMINATION, SCRUTINY.]

adviser or **advisor** *n.* One who advises another ▸ consultant, counselor, guide, guru, mentor. [*Compare* ASSISTANT, EXPERT, LAWYER.]

advisory *adj.* Giving advice ▸ consultative, consultatory, consulting, consultive, counseling, recommendatory. [*Compare* CAUTIONARY, EDUCATIONAL.]

advisory *n.* A report giving informa-

advisory committee. **2.** Containing advice, esp. a warning. ▸ *n., pl.* **-ries.** A report giving information, esp. a warning.

ad·vo·ca·cy (ăd′və-kə-sē) ▸ *n.* The act of arguing in favor of something, such as a cause, idea, or policy.

ad·vo·cate (ăd′və-kāt′) ▸ *v.* **-cat·ed, -cat·ing.** To speak, plead, or argue in favor of. ▸ *n.* (-kĭt, -kāt′) **1.** One that argues for a cause. **2.** One that pleads in another's behalf. **3.** A lawyer. **—ad′vo·ca′tor** *n.*

adz or **adze** (ădz) ▸ *n.* An axlike tool with a curved blade at right angles to the handle that is used for dressing wood.

Ae·ge·an Sea (ĭ-jē′ən) ▸ An arm of the Mediterranean off SE Europe between Greece and Turkey.

ae·gis also **e·gis** (ē′jĭs) ▸ *n.* **1.** Protection. **2.** Sponsorship; patronage. **3.** *Gk. Myth.* The shield of Zeus, later an attribute of Athena.

Ae·ne·as (ĭ-nē′əs) ▸ *n.* *Gk. & Rom. Myth.* Trojan hero and ancestor of the Romans.

ae·on (ē′ŏn′, ē′ən) ▸ *n.* Var. of **eon.**

aer·ate (âr′āt) ▸ *v.* **-at·ed, -at·ing.** **1.** To charge (liquid) with a gas, esp. with carbon dioxide. **2.** To expose to fresh air for purification. **3.** To oxygenate (blood) by respiration. **—aer·a′tion** *n.* **—aer′a′tor** *n.*

aer·i·al (âr′ē-əl) ▸ *adj.* **1.** Of, in, or caused by the air. **2.** Lofty. **3.** Airy. **4.** Of, for, or by means of aircraft: *aerial photography.* **5.** *Bot.* Growing above the ground or water: *aerial roots.* ▸ *n.* A radio antenna, esp. one extending into the air.

aer·i·al·ist (âr′ē-ə-lĭst) ▸ *n.* An acrobat who performs in the air, as on a trapeze.

aer·ie or **aer·y** also **ey·rie** (âr′ē, îr′ē) ▸ *n., pl.* **-ies.** A nest, as of an eagle, built on a high place.

aero– or **aer–** ▸ *pref.* **1.** Air; atmosphere: *aeropause.* **2.** Aviation: *aeronautics.*

aer·o·bat·ics (âr′ə-băt′ĭks) ▸ *n.* *(takes sing. or pl. v.)* The performance of stunts by an airplane.

aer·obe (âr′ōb′) ▸ *n.* An organism, such as a bacterium, requiring oxygen to live.

aer·o·bic (â-rō′bĭk) ▸ *adj.* **1.** Occurring or living only in the presence of oxygen. **2.** Relating to aerobics. **—aer·o′bi·cal·ly** *adv.*

aer·o·bics (â-rō′bĭks) ▸ *n.* *(takes sing. or pl. v.)* An exercise regimen designed to strengthen the cardiovascular system.

aer·o·dy·nam·ic (âr′ō-dī-năm′ĭk) also **aer·o·dy·nam·i·cal** (-ĭ-kəl) ▸ *adj.* **1.** Of or relating to aerodynamics. **2.** Styled with rounded edges to reduce wind drag. **—aer′o·dy·nam′i·cal·ly** *adv.*

aer·o·dy·nam·ics (âr′ō-dī-năm′ĭks) ▸ *n.* *(takes sing. v.)* The dynamics of bodies moving relative to gases, esp. the interaction of moving objects with the atmosphere.

aer·om·e·ter (â-rŏm′ĭ-tər) ▸ *n.* An instrument for determining the weight and density of a gas.

aer·o·naut (âr′ə-nôt′) ▸ *n.* A pilot or navigator of a lighter-than-air craft, such as a balloon.

aer·o·nau·tics (âr′ə-nô′tĭks) ▸ *n.* *(takes sing. v.)* **1.** The design and construction of aircraft. **2.** Aircraft navigation. **—aer′o·nau′tic, aer′o·nau′ti·cal** *adj.*

aer·o·pause (âr′ō-pôz′) ▸ *n.* The region of the atmosphere above which aircraft cannot fly.

aer·o·plane (âr′ə-plān′) ▸ *n.* *Chiefly Brit.* Var. of **airplane.**

aer·o·pon·ics (âr′ə-pŏn′ĭks) ▸ *n.* *(takes sing. v.)* A technique for growing plants without soil by misting the roots with nutrient-laden water.

aer·o·sol (âr′ə-sôl′, -sŏl′) ▸ *n.* **1.** A gaseous suspension of fine solid or liquid particles. **2.** A substance packaged under pressure for release as a spray of fine particles.

aer·o·space (âr′ō-spās′) ▸ *adj.* **1.** Relating to Earth's atmosphere and the space beyond. **2.** Relating to the science or technology of flight. **—aer′o·space′** *n.*

aer·y (âr′ē, îr′ē) ▸ *n.* Var. of **aerie.**

Aes·chy·lus (ĕs′kə-ləs, ē′skə-) (525–456 B.C.) ▸ Greek tragic dramatist. **—Aes′chy·le′an** (-lē′ən) *adj.*

Ae·sop (ē′səp, -sŏp′) (6th cent. B.C.) ▸ Greek storyteller. **—Ae·so′pi·an** (ē-sō′pē-ən), **Ae·sop′ic** (-sŏp′ĭk) *adj.*

aes·the·sia (ĕs-thē′zhə) ▸ *n.* Var. of **esthesia.**

aes·thete or **es·thete** (ĕs′thēt) ▸ *n.* One who cultivates a superior sensitivity to beauty, esp. in art.

aes·thet·ic or **es·thet·ic** (ĕs-thĕt′ĭk) ▸ *adj.* **1.** Relating to aesthetics. **2.** Of or concerning the appreciation of beauty. **3.** Artistic: *The play was an aesthetic success.* ▸ *n.* A guiding principle in matters of artistic beauty. **—aes·thet′i·cal·ly** *adv.*

aes·thet·i·cism or **es·thet·i·cism** (ĕs-thĕt′ĭ-sĭz′əm) ▸ *n.* **1.** Devotion to the beautiful. **2.** The doctrine that beauty is the basic principle from which all others are derived.

aes·thet·ics or **es·thet·ics** (ĕs-thĕt′ĭks) ▸ *n.* *(takes sing. v.)* The branch of philosophy that deals with the nature and expression of beauty, as in the fine arts.

aes·ti·vate (ĕs′tə-vāt′) ▸ *v.* Var. of **estivate.**

a·far (ə-fär′) ▸ *adv.* From, at, or to a great distance: *traveled afar.*

af·fa·ble (ăf′ə-bəl) ▸ *adj.* Easy and pleasant to speak to; amiable. **—af′fa·bil′i·ty** *n.* **—af′fa·bly** *adv.*

af·fair (ə-fâr′) ▸ *n.* **1.** Something done or to be done. **2. affairs** Matters of personal or professional business. **3a.** An occurrence; event. **b.** A social function. **4.** A matter of personal concern. **5.** A sexual relationship between two people who are not married to each other.

af·fect[1] (ə-fĕkt′) ▸ *v.* **1.** To influence or change. **2.** To touch the emotions of. ▸ *n.* (ăf′ĕkt′) Feeling or emotion, esp. as expressed physically.

af·fect[2] (ə-fĕkt′) ▸ *v.* **1.** To put on a false or pretentious show of: *affected a British accent.* **2.** To fancy; like: *affects dramatic clothes.*

af·fec·ta·tion (ăf′ĕk-tā′shən) ▸ *n.* **1.** A show; pretense. **2.** Behavior that is assumed rather than natural.

af·fect·ed (ə-fĕk′tĭd) ▸ *adj.* **1.** Assumed or simulated to impress others. **2.** Mannered; artificial. **—af·fect′ed·ly** *adv.*

af·fect·ing (ə-fĕk′tĭng) ▸ *adj.* Inspiring strong emotion; moving. **—af·fect′ing·ly** *adv.*

af·fec·tion (ə-fĕk′shən) ▸ *n.* A tender feeling toward another; fondness. **—af·fec′tion·ate** (-shə-nĭt) *adj.* **—af·fec′tion·ate·ly** *adv.*

THESAURUS

tion ▸ bulletin, notice. [*Compare* REPORT, WARNING.]

advocacy *n.* —*See* PATRONAGE (1).

advocate *n.* One that argues for or defends a cause ▸ booster, champion, defender, promoter, proponent, supporter, upholder, vindicator. [*Compare* LAWYER, PATRON, SPONSOR.] —*See also* REPRESENTATIVE.

advocate *v.* —*See* SUPPORT (1).

aegis *n.* —*See* PATRONAGE (1).

aeon *n.* *See* EON.

aerate *v.* To expose to circulating air ▸ air, freshen, ventilate, wind.

aerial *adj.* Of or relating to air ▸ airy, atmospheric, pneumatic. —*See also* HIGH (1).

aesthetic or **esthetic** *adj.* Relating to or appreciative of the arts ▸ artistic, creative. *Informal:* artsy, arty. —*See also* CULTURAL.

affability *n.* —*See* AMIABILITY.

affable *adj.* Characterized by kindness and warm, unaffected courtesy ▸ courteous, gracious, hospitable. [*Compare* ATTENTIVE, COURTEOUS.] —*See also* AMIABLE.

affair *n.* **1.** Something that concerns or involves one personally ▸ business, concern, interest, lookout. **2.** Something to be done, considered, or dealt with ▸ business, matter, thing. [*Compare* BUSINESS, PROBLEM, TASK.] —*See also* LOVE (3), PARTY.

affect[1] *v.* —*See* INFLUENCE, MOVE (1).

affect *n.* —*See* EMOTION.

affect[2] *v.* —*See* ACT (2).

affectation *n.* Behavior that is assumed rather than natural ▸ affectedness, air, airs, artificiality, mannerism, pose, pretense, simulation, theatricism. [*Compare* FAÇADE, POSTURE.] —*See also* ACT (2).

affected *adj.* —*See* ARTIFICIAL (2), CONCERNED.

affectedness *n.* —*See* AFFECTATION.

affecting *adj.* Exciting a deep, usually somber response ▸ heart-rending, impressive, moving, poignant, stirring, touching. [*Compare* PITIFUL.]

affection *n.* —*See* EMOTION, LOVE (1).

affectional or **affective** *adj.* Relating to, arising from, or appealing to the emotions ▸ emotional, emotive.

affectionate *adj.* Feeling or expressing fond feelings or affection ▸ caring, devoted, doting, fond, loving, tender.

af·fec·tive (ə-fĕk′tĭv) ▸ *adj. Psychol.* Influenced by or resulting from the emotions: *affective disorders.*

af·fer·ent (ăf′ər-ənt) ▸ *adj.* Carrying inward to a central organ or section.

af·fi·ance (ə-fī′əns) ▸ *v.* **-anced, -anc·ing.** To pledge to marry; betroth.

af·fi·da·vit (ăf′ĭ-dā′vĭt) ▸ *n.* A written declaration made under oath before an authorized officer.

af·fil·i·ate (ə-fĭl′ē-āt′) ▸ *v.* **-at·ed, -at·ing.** To accept as a member, associate, or branch. ▸ *n.* (-ē-ĭt, -āt′) An associate or subordinate member: *network affiliates.* **—af·fil′i·a′tion** *n.*

af·fin·i·ty (ə-fĭn′ĭ tē) ▸ *n., pl.* **-ties. 1.** A natural attraction or feeling of kinship. **2.** Relationship by marriage. **3.** An inherent similarity.

af·firm (ə-fûrm′) ▸ *v.* **1.** To declare firmly; maintain to be true. **2.** To declare support for or belief in. **3.** To rule (a court decision) to have been correct. **—af·firm′a·ble** *adj.* **—af·fir′mant** *adj. & n.* **—af′fir·ma′tion** (ăf′ər-mā′shən) *n.*

af·fir·ma·tive (ə-fûr′mə-tĭv) ▸ *adj.* **1.** Giving assent; confirming. **2.** Positive; optimistic: *an affirmative outlook.* ▸ *n.* **1.** A word or statement of assent. **2.** The side in a debate that upholds the proposition. **—af·fir′ma·tive·ly** *adv.*

affirmative action ▸ *n.* A policy that seeks to redress past discrimination by ensuring equal opportunity, as in education and employment.

af·fix (ə-fĭks′) ▸ *v.* **1.** To secure; attach. **2.** To add or append. ▸ *n.* (ăf′ĭks′) **1.** Something affixed. **2.** A word element, such as a prefix or suffix, that is attached to a base, stem, or root.

af·fla·tus (ə-flā′təs) ▸ *n.* **1.** A strong creative impulse. **2.** Divine inspiration.

af·flict (ə-flĭkt′) ▸ *v.* To inflict grievous suffering on. **—af·flic′tive** *adj.*

af·flic·tion (ə-flĭk′shən) ▸ *n.* **1.** A condition of distress. **2.** A cause of distress.

af·flu·ence (ăf′lo͞o-əns) ▸ *n.* **1.** Wealth; prosperity. **2.** A great quantity; abundance.

af·flu·ent (ăf′lo͞o-ənt) ▸ *adj.* **1.** Wealthy. **2.** Plentiful; abundant. ▸ *n.* A stream; tributary. **—af′flu·ent·ly** *adv.*

af·ford (ə-fôrd′) ▸ *v.* **1.** To have the financial means for. **2.** To be able to spare or give up. **3.** To provide: *a tree that affords ample shade.* **—af·ford′a·bil′i·ty** *n.* **—af·ford′a·ble** *adj.* **—af·ford′a·bly** *adv.*

af·for·est (ə-fôr′ĭst, -fŏr′-) ▸ *v.* To convert (open land) into a forest by planting trees. **—af·for′es·ta′tion** *n.*

af·fray (ə-frā′) ▸ *n.* A noisy quarrel or brawl.

af·front (ə-frŭnt′) ▸ *v.* **1.** To insult intentionally. **2.** To confront. ▸ *n.* An insult.

Af·ghan (ăf′găn′) ▸ *n.* **1.** A native or inhabitant of Afghanistan. **2.** See **Pashto. 3. afghan** A coverlet knitted or crocheted in geometric designs. **4.** An Afghan hound. **—Af′ghan** *adj.*

Afghan hound ▸ *n.* A large slender hunting dog having long hair and drooping ears.

af·ghan·i (ăf-găn′ē, -gä′nē) ▸ *n.* See **currency** table in Appendix.

Af·ghan·i·stan (ăf-găn′ĭ-stăn′) ▸ A landlocked country of SW-central Asia E of Iran.

a·fi·cio·na·do (ə-fĭsh′ē-ə-nä′dō) ▸ *n., pl.* **-dos.** A fan; devotee.

a·field (ə-fēld′) ▸ *adv.* **1.** Off the usual or desired track. **2.** Away from one's usual environment. **3.** To or on a field.

a·fire (ə-fīr′) ▸ *adv. & adj.* On fire.

a·flame (ə-flām′) ▸ *adv. & adj.* On fire.

af·la·tox·in (ăf′lə-tŏk′sĭn) ▸ *n.* A toxic compound that is produced by certain molds and contaminates stored food.

a·float (ə-flōt′) ▸ *adv. & adj.* **1.** Floating. **2.** At sea. **3.** Awash; flooded. **4.** Financially sound.

a·flut·ter (ə-flŭt′ər) ▸ *adj.* **1.** Fluttering: *with flags aflutter.* **2.** Nervous and excited.

a·foot (ə-fo͝ot′) ▸ *adv. & adj.* **1.** On foot. **2.** In progress: *plans afoot to resign.*

a·fore·men·tioned (ə-fôr′mĕn′shənd) ▸ *adj.* Mentioned previously.

a·fore·said (ə-fôr′sĕd′) ▸ *adj.* Spoken of earlier.

a·fore·thought (ə-fôr′thôt′) ▸ *adj.* Premeditated: *malice aforethought.*

a for·ti·o·ri (ä fôr′tē-ôr′ē, ā) ▸ *adv.* For a stronger reason. Used of a conclusion logically more certain than another.

a·foul of (ə-foul′) ▸ *prep.* In or into collision, entanglement, or conflict with.

a·fraid (ə-frād′) ▸ *adj.* **1.** Filled with fear. **2.** Averse; opposed: *not afraid of hard work.* **3.** Regretful: *I'm afraid you're wrong.*

A-frame (ā′frām′) ▸ *n.* A structure with steeply angled sides in the shape of the letter A.

a·fresh (ə-frĕsh′) ▸ *adv.* Once more; anew; again: *start afresh.*

Af·ri·ca (ăf′rĭ-kə) ▸ The second-largest continent, S of Europe between the Atlantic and Indian oceans.

Af·ri·can (ăf′rĭ-kən) ▸ *adj.* Of or relating to Africa or its peoples, languages, or cultures. ▸ *n.* **1.** A native or inhabitant of Africa. **2.** A person of African descent.

Af·ri·ca·na (ăf′rĭ-kä′nə, -kăn′ə, -kā′nə) ▸ *n. (takes pl. v.)* Materials relating to the history or culture of African peoples.

African American ▸ *n.* A Black American of African ancestry. **—Af′ri·can-A·mer′i·can** *adj.*

African violet ▸ *n.* Any of various East African plants having showy violet, pink, or white flowers and grown as house plants.

Af·ri·kaans (ăf′rĭ-käns′, -känz′) ▸ *n.* A language that developed from 17th-cent. Dutch and is an official language of South Africa.

Af·ri·ka·ner (ăf′rĭ-kä′nər) ▸ *n.* A South African descended from Dutch settlers, esp. one who speaks Afrikaans.

Af·ro (ăf′rō) ▸ *n., pl.* **-ros.** A rounded, thick, tightly curled hair style. ▸ *adj.* African in style or origin.

Afro– ▸ *pref.* African: *Afro-Asiatic.*

Af·ro-A·mer·i·can (ăf′rō-ə-mĕr′ĭ-kən) ▸ *n.* An African American. **—Af′ro-A·mer′i·can** *adj.*

Af·ro-A·si·at·ic (ăf′rō-ā′zhē-ăt′ĭk, -zē-) ▸ *n.* A family of languages spoken in N Africa and SW Asia. **—Af′ro-A′si·at′ic** *adj.*

Af·ro·cen·tric (ăf′rō-sĕn′trĭk) ▸ *adj.* Centered or focused on Africa or African peoples. **—Af′ro·cen′trism** *n.*

THESAURUS

affectivity *n.* —*See* EMOTION.

affectless *adj.* —*See* EXPRESSIONLESS.

affianced *adj.* —*See* ENGAGED.

affidavit *n.* A formal declaration of truth or fact given under oath ▸ deposition, testimony, witness.

affiliate *v.* —*See* ASSOCIATE (1), PASS (6).

affiliate *n.* —*See* ASSOCIATE (1), BRANCH (3).

affiliation *n.* —*See* ASSOCIATION (1).

affinity *n.* —*See* INCLINATION (1), LIKENESS (1).

affirm *v.* —*See* ASSERT, CONFIRM (1), CONFIRM (3).

affirmation *n.* —*See* ASSERTION, CONFIRMATION (1).

affirmative *adj.* —*See* FAVORABLE (2).

affirmative *adv.* —*See* YES.

affix *v.* —*See* ATTACH (1), ATTACH (2), FIX (3).

afflict *v.* To cause great pain or suffering to ▸ agonize, excruciate, kill, pain, plague, rack, scourge, smite, strike, torment, torture, wound. [*Compare* DISTRESS, HURT, TRAUMATIZE.]

afflicted *adj.* —*See* MISERABLE.

affliction *n.* —*See* BURDEN[1] (1), CURSE (3), DISTRESS, SICKNESS, TRIAL (1).

afflictive *adj.* —*See* PAINFUL.

affluence *n.* —*See* WEALTH.

affluent *adj.* —*See* RICH (1).

afford *v.* —*See* OFFER (2).

affray *n.* —*See* FIGHT (1).

affright *v.* —*See* FRIGHTEN.

affright *n.* —*See* FEAR.

affront *v.* —*See* INSULT, OFFEND (1).

affront *n.* —*See* DISRESPECT, INDIGNITY.

afghan *n.* WRAP.

aficionado *n.* —*See* FAN[2].

afield *adv.* Not in the right way or on the proper course ▸ amiss, astray, awry, wrong.

afire or **aflame** *adj.* —*See* BURNING.

a fortiori *adv.* —*See* EVEN (2).

afraid *adj.* Filled with fear or terror ▸ aghast, alarmed, apprehensive, fearful, fearsome, frightened, funky, horrified, panicky, panic-stricken, petrified, scared, terrified, timid, timorous, tremulous. *Informal:* spooked. *Slang:* chicken. *Idioms:* frightened (*or* scared) to death, scared stiff. [*Compare* FEARFUL.]

afresh *adv.* —*See* ANEW.

aft (ăft) ▸ *adv. & adj.* At, in, or toward a ship's stern or the rear of an aircraft.

af·ter (ăf′tər) ▸ *prep.* **1.** Behind in place or order. **2.** In pursuit of. **3.** Concerning: *asked after you.* **4.** At a later time than. **5.** In the style of: *satires after Horace.* **6.** With the same name as. ▸ *adv.* **1.** Behind. **2.** Afterward: *forever after.* ▸ *adj.* **1.** Later: *in after years.* **2.** *Naut.* Nearer the stern. ▸ *conj.* Following the time that.

after all (ăf′tər-ôl′) ▸ *adv.* **1.** In spite of everything. **2.** Ultimately.

af·ter·birth (ăf′tər-bûrth′) ▸ *n.* The placenta and fetal membranes expelled from the uterus following childbirth.

af·ter·burn·er (ăf′tər-bûr′nər) ▸ *n.* A device for augmenting jet engine thrust by burning additional fuel with the hot exhaust gases.

af·ter·ef·fect (ăf′tər-ĭ-fĕkt′) ▸ *n.* A delayed or prolonged response to a stimulus.

af·ter·glow (ăf′tər-glō′) ▸ *n.* **1.** The light emitted after removal of a source of energy. **2.** A lingering pleasantness.

af·ter-hours (ăf′tər-ourz′) ▸ *adj.* Occurring or operating after the usual closing time.

af·ter·im·age (ăf′tər-ĭm′ĭj) ▸ *n.* A visual image persisting after the visual stimulus has ceased.

af·ter·life (ăf′tər-līf′) ▸ *n.* A life or existence after death.

af·ter·math (ăf′tər-măth′) ▸ *n.* **1.** A consequence, esp. of a disaster or misfortune. **2.** A second crop in the same season.

af·ter·noon (ăf′tər-no͞on′) ▸ *n.* The part of day from noon until sunset.

af·ter·school (ăf′tər-sko͞ol′) ▸ *adj.* Of or being a program providing care for children following school classes.

af·ter·shave (ăf′tər-shāv′) ▸ *n.* A usu. fragrant lotion for use after shaving.

af·ter·shock (ăf′tər-shŏk′) ▸ *n.* **1.** A quake of lesser magnitude following a large earthquake. **2.** A subsequent shock or trauma.

af·ter·taste (ăf′tər-tāst′) ▸ *n.* **1.** A taste remaining after the original stimulus is gone. **2.** A lingering emotion or feeling.

af·ter·thought (ăf′tər-thôt′) ▸ *n.* An idea that occurs to one after an event or decision.

af·ter·ward (ăf′tər-wərd) also **af·ter·wards** (-wərdz) ▸ *adv.* At a later time; subsequently.

af·ter·word (ăf′tər-wûrd′) ▸ *n.* See **epilogue** 2.

af·ter·world (ăf′tər-wûrld′) ▸ *n.* A world believed to exist for those in the afterlife.

Ag ▸ The symbol for the element **silver**.

a·gain (ə-gĕn′) ▸ *adv.* **1.** Once more; anew. **2.** To a previous place, position, or state: *never went back again.* **3.** Furthermore. **4.** On the other hand.

a·gainst (ə-gĕnst′) ▸ *prep.* **1.** In a direction opposite to. **2.** So as to hit or touch: *waves dashing against the shore.* **3.** Resting or pressing on: *leaned against the tree.* **4.** In opposition to. **5.** Contrary to: *against all advice.* **6.** As a safeguard from: *protection against the cold.*

Ag·a·mem·non (ăg′ə-mĕm′nŏn′) ▸ *n.* *Gk. Myth.* King of Mycenae and leader of the Greeks in the Trojan War.

a·gape[1] (ə-gāp′, ə-găp′) ▸ *adv. & adj.* **1.** With the mouth wide open, as in wonder. **2.** Wide open.

a·ga·pe[2] (ä-gä′pā, ä′gə-pā′) ▸ *n.* Love as revealed in Jesus, seen as spiritual and selfless.

a·gar (ā′gär′, ä′gär′) also **a·gar-a·gar** (ā′gär-ā′gär′, ä′gär-ä′-) ▸ *n.* A gelatinous material prepared from certain saltwater algae and used in bacterial culture media and for thickening foods.

ag·ate (ăg′ĭt) ▸ *n.* **1.** A variety of chalcedony with colored bands. **2.** A marble made of agate or a glass imitation.

a·ga·ve (ə-gä′vē, ə-gā′-) ▸ *n.* Any of various tropical American plants with tough sword-shaped leaves.

age (āj) ▸ *n.* **1.** The length of time that one has existed. **2.** The time of life when a person can assume certain civil and personal rights and responsibilities: *under age; of age.* **3.** A stage of life. **4.** Old age: *hair white with age.* **5.** often **Age a.** A distinctive period in human history. **b.** A period in the history of the earth: *the Ice Age.* **6. ages** *Informal* A long time: *left ages ago.* ▸ *v.* **aged, ag·ing. 1.** To grow older or more mature. **2.** To bring or come to a desired ripeness.

-age ▸ *suff.* **1.** Collection; mass: *sewerage.* **2.** Relationship; connection: *parentage.* **3.** Condition; state: *vagabondage.* **4a.** An action: *blockage.* **b.** Result of an action: *breakage.* **5.** Residence or place of: *vicarage.* **6.** Charge or fee: *dockage.*

ag·ed (ā′jĭd) ▸ *adj.* **1.** Advanced in years; old. **2.** (ājd) Of the age of: *aged three.* **3.** (ājd) Of a desired ripeness or maturity: *aged cheese.* ▸ *n.* Elderly people. Used with *the.*

age·ism also **ag·ism** (ā′jĭz′əm) ▸ *n.* Discrimination based on age, esp. against the elderly. **—age′ist** *adj. & n.*

age·less (āj′lĭs) ▸ *adj.* **1.** Seeming never to grow old. **2.** Existing forever; eternal. **—age′less·ly** *adv.* **—age′less·ness** *n.*

a·gen·cy (ā′jən-sē) ▸ *n., pl.* **-cies. 1.** Action; operation. **2.** A mode of acting; means. **3.** A business or service acting for others: *an employment agency.* **4.** An administrative division of a government.

a·gen·da (ə-jĕn′də) ▸ *n., pl.* **-das.** A list or program of things to be done or considered.

a·gent (ā′jənt) ▸ *n.* **1.** One that acts or has the power to act. **2.** One that acts for or represents another: *an insurance agent.* **3.** A means of doing something; instrument. **4.** Something that causes a change: *a chemical agent.* **5.** A member of a government agency. **6.** A spy.

Agent Orange ▸ *n.* A herbicide used in the Vietnam War to defoliate areas of forest.

a·gent pro·vo·ca·teur (ă-zhäN′ prô-vô′kä-tœr′) ▸ *n., pl.* **a·gents pro·vo·ca·teurs** (ă-zhäN′ prô-vô′kä-tœr′). One who infiltrates an organization in order to incite its members to commit illegal acts.

age-old (āj′ōld′) ▸ *adj.* Very old.

ag·er·a·tum (ăj′ə-rā′təm) ▸ *n.* Any of a genus of tropical New World plants having showy colorful flower heads.

ag·gie (ăg′ē) ▸ *n.* *Games* A playing marble.

ag·glom·er·ate (ə-glŏm′ə-rāt′) ▸ *v.* **-at·ed, -at·ing.** To gather into a rounded mass. ▸ *n.* (-ər-ĭt) A jumbled mass; heap. **—ag·glom′er·a′tion** *n.*

ag·glu·ti·nate (ə-glo͞ot′n-āt′) ▸ *v.* **-nat·ed, -nat·ing. 1.** To join; adhere. **2.** To cause (red blood cells or bacteria) to clump together. **—ag·glu′ti·na′tion** *n.* **—ag·glu′ti·na′tive** *adj.*

THESAURUS

after *adv.* —*See* LATER.

after *adj.* Following something else in time ▸ later, posterior, subsequent, ulterior. [*Compare* FOLLOWING.]

afterlife *n.* —*See* IMMORTALITY.

aftermath *n.* —*See* EFFECT (1).

aftermost *adj.* —*See* LAST[1] (2).

afterward or **afterwards** *adv.* —*See* LATER.

afterworld *n.* —*See* ETERNITY (2).

again *adv.* —*See* ANEW.

against *adj.* —*See* INDISPOSED.

agape *adj.* —*See* OPEN (1).

age *n.* **1.** Old age ▸ agedness, elderliness, maturity, old age, senectitude, senescence, seniority, years. [*Compare* SENILITY.] **2.** A particular time notable for its distinctive characteristics ▸ day, epoch, era, period, time, times.

age *v.* To grow old ▸ get along, get on. *Idiom:* advance in years. —*See also* MATURE.

aged *adj.* Brought to full flavor and richness by aging ▸ mellow, ripe. [*Compare* MATURE.] —*See also* OLD (2).

agedness *n.* —*See* AGE (1).

ageism *n.* Discrimination based on age ▸ discrimination, intolerance, prejudice. [*Compare* HATE.]

ageless *adj.* Existing unchanged forever ▸ eternal, timeless. [*Compare* CONTINUAL, ENDLESS.] —*See also* VINTAGE.

agency *n.* —*See* AGENT, BRANCH (3).

agenda *n.* —*See* LIST[1], PROGRAM (1).

agent *n.* That by which something is done or caused ▸ agency, channel, instrument, instrumentality, intermediary, means, mechanism, medium, organ. [*Compare* GO-BETWEEN, REPRESENTATIVE.] —*See also* SPY.

age-old *adj.* —*See* OLD (1).

ages *n.* A long time ▸ blue moon, eon, eternity, forever, long, years. *Idioms:* dog's age, coon's age, donkey's years, forever and a day, forever and ever, a month (*or* week) of Sundays.

agglomerate *v.* —*See* ACCUMULATE.

agglomeration *n.* The act of accumulating ▸ accumulation, buildup, conglomeration. —*See also* HEAP (1).

ag·gran·dize (ə-grăn′dīz′, ăg′rən-) ▸ *v.* **-dized, -diz·ing.** To make greater; increase. **—ag·gran′dize·ment** (ə-grăn′dĭz-mənt, -dīz′-) *n.*

ag·gra·vate (ăg′rə-vāt′) ▸ *v.* **-vat·ed, -vat·ing. 1.** To make worse or more troublesome. **2.** To exasperate; provoke. **—ag′gra·vat′ing·ly** *adv.* **—ag′gra·va′tion** *n.* **—ag′gra·va′tor** *n.*

ag·gre·gate (ăg′rĭ-gĭt) ▸ *adj.* Amounting to a whole; total. ▸ *n.* A whole considered with respect to its constituent parts. ▸ *v.* (-gāt′) **-gat·ed, -gat·ing.** To gather into a mass or whole. **—ag′gre·ga′tion** *n.* **—ag′gre·ga′tive** *adj.*

ag·gres·sion (ə-grĕsh′ən) ▸ *n.* **1.** The initiation of unprovoked hostilities. **2.** The launching of attacks. **3.** Hostile behavior.

ag·gres·sive (ə-grĕs′ĭv) ▸ *adj.* **1.** Inclined to hostile behavior. **2.** Bold and enterprising: *an aggressive young executive.* **3.** Intense or harsh, as in color. **—ag·gres′sive·ly** *adv.* **—ag·gres′sive·ness** *n.* **—ag·gres′sor** *n.*

ag·grieve (ə-grēv′) ▸ *v.* **-grieved, -griev·ing. 1.** To distress; afflict. **2.** To injure; wrong.

ag·grieved (ə-grēvd′) ▸ *adj.* **1.** Distressed; afflicted. **2.** Treated wrongly or unjustly.

a·ghast (ə-găst′) ▸ *adj.* Struck by terror or amazement.

ag·ile (ăj′əl, -īl′) ▸ *adj.* **1.** Quick, light, and easy in movement; nimble. **2.** Mentally alert. **—ag′ile·ly** *adv.* **—a·gil′i·ty** (ə-jĭl′ĭ-tē), **ag′ile·ness** *n.*

ag·ing (ā′jĭng) ▸ *n.* The process of growing old or maturing.

ag·ism (ā′jĭz′əm) ▸ *n.* Var. of **ageism.**

ag·i·tate (ăj′ĭ-tāt′) ▸ *v.* **-tat·ed, -tat·ing. 1.** To move with violence or sudden force. **2.** To upset; disturb. **3.** To stir up public interest in a cause. **—ag′i·tat′ed·ly** *adv.* **—ag′i·ta′tion** *n.*

ag·i·ta·tor (ăj′ĭ-tā′tər) ▸ *n.* **1.** One who agitates, esp. in political struggles. **2.** An apparatus that shakes or stirs, as in a washing machine.

a·gleam (ə-glēm′) ▸ *adv.* & *adj.* Brightly shining.

a·glit·ter (ə-glĭt′ər) ▸ *adv.* & *adj.* Glittering; sparkling.

a·glow (ə-glō′) ▸ *adv.* & *adj.* Glowing.

ag·nos·tic (ăg-nŏs′tĭk) ▸ *n.* **1.** One who believes that there can be no proof of the existence of God but does not deny the possibility. **2.** One who is doubtful or noncommital about something. **—ag·nos′tic** *adj.* **—ag·nos′ti·cism** (-tĭ-sĭz′əm) *n.*

Ag·nus De·i (ăg′nəs dē′ī′, än′yo͞os dā′ē) ▸ *n.* **1.** Lamb of God; an emblem of Jesus; Jesus. **2a.** A liturgical prayer. **b.** A musical setting for this prayer.

a·go (ə-gō′) ▸ *adv.* & *adj.* **1.** Gone by; past: *two years ago.* **2.** In the past: *It happened ages ago.*

a·gog (ə-gŏg′) ▸ *adv.* & *adj.* Full of eager excitement.

ag·o·nist (ăg′ə-nĭst) ▸ *n.* A contracting muscle that is counteracted by the antagonist.

ag·o·nize (ăg′ə-nīz′) ▸ *v.* **-nized, -niz·ing. 1.** To suffer or cause to suffer great anguish. **2.** To make a great effort; struggle. **—ag′o·niz′ing·ly** *adv.*

ag·o·ny (ăg′ə-nē) ▸ *n., pl.* **-nies. 1.** Intense physical or mental pain. **2.** The struggle that precedes death. **3.** An intense emotion: *an agony of doubt.*

ag·o·ra (ăg′ər-ə) ▸ *n., pl.* **-o·rae** (ə-rē′) or **-o·ras.** A place of congregation, esp. an ancient Greek marketplace.

ag·o·ra·pho·bi·a (ăg′ər-ə-fō′bē-ə) ▸ *n.* An abnormal fear of open or public places. **—ag′o·ra·pho′bic** (-fō′bĭk, -fŏb′ĭk) *adj.* & *n.*

a·grar·i·an (ə-grâr′ē-ən) ▸ *adj.* **1.** Relating to land and its ownership. **2.** Relating to agriculture. ▸ *n.* One who favors equitable distribution of land.

a·grar·i·an·ism (ə-grâr′ē-ə-nĭz′əm) ▸ *n.* A movement for equitable distribution of land and for agrarian reform.

a·gree (ə-grē′) ▸ *v.* **1.** To grant consent; accede. **2.** To come into or be in accord. **3.** To be of one opinion; concur. **4.** To come to an understanding or to terms. **5.** To be in correspondence: *The copy agrees with the original.* **6.** To be pleasing or healthful: *Spicy food does not agree with me.* **7.** *Gram.* To correspond in gender, number, case, or person.

a·gree·a·ble (ə-grē′ə-bəl) ▸ *adj.* **1.** To one's liking; pleasing. **2.** Suitable; conformable. **3.** Ready to consent or

THESAURUS

aggrandize *v.* —*See* EXAGGERATE, EXALT, INCREASE.

aggrandizement *n.* —*See* EXALTATION, INCREASE (1).

aggravate *v.* —*See* ANNOY, INTENSIFY.

aggravation *n.* —*See* ANNOYANCE (1), ANNOYANCE (2).

aggregate *n.* —*See* TOTAL, WHOLE.

aggregate *v.* —*See* ACCUMULATE, AMOUNT.

aggregation *n.* —*See* ACCUMULATION (1).

aggress *v.* —*See* ATTACK (1).

aggression *n.* Hostile or warlike behavior or attitude ▸ aggressiveness, bellicoseness, bellicosity, belligerence, combativeness, contentiousness, hostility, militance, pugnaciousness, pugnacity, saber-rattling, truculence, truculency, warmongering. [*Compare* HATE.] —*See also* ATTACK.

aggressive *adj.* Inclined to act in a way that shows hostility or an eagerness to fight ▸ bellicose, belligerent, combative, contentious, hawkish, hostile, militant, pugnacious, quarrelsome, scrappy, truculent, warlike, warmongering. —*See also* ASSERTIVE.

aggressiveness *n.* —*See* AGGRESSION.

aggressor *n.* One who starts a hostile action ▸ assailant, assailer, assaulter, attacker, provoker. [*Compare* OPPONENT.]

aggrieve *v.* —*See* DISTRESS.

aghast *adj.* —*See* AFRAID.

agile *adj.* —*See* DEXTEROUS.

agility or **agileness** *n.* The quality or state of being agile ▸ deftness, dexterity, dexterousness, nimbleness, quickness, spryness, swiftness. [*Compare* ENERGY, HASTE.]

aging *adj.* —*See* OLD (2).

agitate *v.* **1.** To cause to move to and fro violently ▸ churn, convulse, rock, shake, whip, worry. [*Compare* DISORDER, DISTURB, UPSET.] **2.** To impair or destroy the composure of ▸ bewilder, bother, discompose, disorient, disquiet, distract, disturb, flurry, fluster, jar, perturb, rock, ruffle, shake (up), toss, unsettle, upset. *Informal:* rattle, throw (off). ***Idiom:*** throw out of kilter (*or* whack). [*Compare* CONFUSE, DISTRESS, NONPLUS.] —*See also* AROUSE.

agitated *adj.* Marked by unrest or disturbance ▸ convulsed, disturbed, flustered, stormy, tempestuous, tumultuous, turbulent, restless, unsettled. *Idioms:* all shook up, all worked up, in a ferment (*or* spin *or* state *or* stir). [*Compare* CONFUSED, DISORDERLY, UNRULY.] —*See also* ANXIOUS.

agitating *adj.* —*See* DISTURBING.

agitation *n.* **1.** A condition of being agitated or disturbed; a confused or emotional situation ▸ commotion, convulsion, disorder, disturbance, ferment, helter-skelter, ruckus, scene, stir, Sturm und Drang, tempest, tumult, turbulence, turmoil, unrest, uproar. *Informal:* flap, to-do. *Slang:* hoo-ha, stink. [*Compare* DISORDER, DISPLAY, RESTLESSNESS.] **2.** A state of discomposure ▸ disconcertment, dither, fluster, flutter, hurry-scurry, perturbation, tumult, turmoil, twitter, upset. *Informal:* lather, stew. *Slang:* tizzy. [*Compare* ANXIETY, CONFUSION, WORRY.] **3.** Agitated, excited movement and activity ▸ ado, bustle, commotion, excitement, flurry, fuss, stir, whirl, whirlpool. *Informal:* state.

agitator *n.* One who agitates, especially politically ▸ firebrand, fomenter, incendiary, inciter, instigator, malcontent, rabble-rouser, troublemaker. [*Compare* AGGRESSOR, EXTREMIST.]

agnate *adj.* —*See* KINDRED.

agnostic *n.* —*See* SKEPTIC.

ago *adj.* —*See* PAST.

agog *adj.* —*See* EAGER.

agonize *v.* —*See* AFFLICT, BROOD.

agonizing *adj.* —*See* TORMENTING.

agony *n.* —*See* DISTRESS.

agrarian *adj.* —*See* COUNTRY.

agree *v.* **1.** To be compatible, suitable, or in correspondence ▸ accord, belong, check, chime, comport, conform, consist, correspond, dovetail, fit, go (together), harmonize, match (up), square, tally. *Informal:* jibe. [*Compare* SUIT.] **2.** To come to an understanding or to terms ▸ accord, coincide, concur, get together, harmonize. *Idioms:* be of one mind, see eye to eye. —*See also* ASSENT.

agreeability *n.* —*See* AMIABILITY.

agreeable *adj.* In keeping with one's

submit. **—a·gree′a·ble·ness** *n.* **—a·gree′a·bly** *adv.*

a·gree·ment (ə-grē′mənt) ▸ *n.* **1.** Harmony of opinion; accord. **2.** An arrangement between parties regarding a method of action; a covenant. **3.** *Law.* A compact that is properly executed and legally binding. **4.** *Gram.* Correspondence in gender, number, case, or person between words.

ag·ri·busi·ness (ăg′rə-bĭz′nĭs) ▸ *n.* Farming as a large-scale business operation.

ag·ri·cul·ture (ăg′rĭ-kŭl′chər) ▸ *n.* The cultivation of the soil and raising of livestock; farming. **—ag′ri·cul′tur·al** *adj.* **—ag′ri·cul′tur·al·ly** *adv.* **—ag′ri·cul′tur·ist, ag′ri·cul′tur·al·ist** *n.*

a·gron·o·my (ə-grŏn′ə-mē) ▸ *n.* Application of soil and plant sciences to farming. **—ag′ro·nom′ic** (ăg′rə-nŏm′ĭk), **ag′ro·nom′i·cal** *adj.* **—a·gron′o·mist** *n.*

a·ground (ə-ground′) ▸ *adv. & adj.* Stranded on a shore, reef, or in shallow water.

a·gue (ā′gyo͞o) ▸ *n.* A fever with alternating chills and sweating, esp. associated with malaria. **—a′gu·ish** *adj.*

ah (ä) ▸ *interj.* Used to express various emotions, such as satisfaction, surprise, delight, dislike, or pain.

a·ha (ä-hä′) ▸ *interj.* Used to express surprise, pleasure, or triumph.

a·head (ə-hĕd′) ▸ *adv.* **1.** At or to the front. **2a.** In advance; before: *Pay ahead.* **b.** In or into the future: *planned ahead.* **3.** Forward: *The train moved ahead slowly.* **—*idioms:* be ahead** To be winning or in a superior position. **get ahead** To attain success.

a·hem (ə-hĕm′) ▸ *interj.* Used to attract attention or to express doubt or warning.

–aholic ▸ *suff.* One that is compulsively in need of: *workaholic.*

a·hoy (ə-hoi′) ▸ *interj. Naut.* Used to hail a ship or person or to attract attention.

AI ▸ *abbr.* artificial intelligence

aid (ād) ▸ *v.* To help; support. ▸ *n.* **1.** Assistance. **2a.** An assistant. **b.** A device that assists: *visual aids such as slides.* **—aid′er** *n.*

aide (ād) ▸ *n.* **1.** An aide-de-camp. **2.** A helper.

aide-de-camp (ād′dĭ-kămp′) ▸ *n., pl.* **aides-de-camp.** A military or naval officer acting as an assistant to a superior officer.

AIDS (ādz) ▸ *n.* A severe immunological disorder caused by the retrovirus HIV, resulting in an increased susceptibility to opportunistic infections and to certain rare cancers.

ai·grette or **ai·gret** (ā-grĕt′, ā′grĕt′) ▸ *n.* An ornamental tuft of plumes, esp. the tail feathers of an egret.

ai·ki·do (ī′kē-dō′, ī-kē′dō) ▸ *n.* A Japanese art of self-defense that employs holds, locks, and principles of nonresistance.

ail (āl) ▸ *v.* **1.** To feel ill or have pain. **2.** To make ill or cause pain.

ai·lan·thus (ā-lăn′thəs) ▸ *n.* Any of several Asian trees, esp. the tree-of-heaven.

ai·le·ron (ā′lə-rŏn′) ▸ *n.* A movable flap on the wings of an airplane that controls rolling and banking.

ail·ment (āl′mənt) ▸ *n.* A mild illness.

aim (ām) ▸ *v.* **1.** To direct (e.g., a weapon or remark) toward an intended target. **2.** To determine a course: *aim for a better life.* **3.** To propose to do something; intend. ▸ *n.* **1a.** The act of aiming. **b.** Skill at hitting a target: *a good aim.* **2.** The line of fire of an aimed weapon. **3.** A purpose or intention.

aim·less (ām′lĭs) ▸ *adj.* Without direction or purpose. **—aim′less·ly** *adv.* **—aim′less·ness** *n.*

ain't (ānt) ▸ *Nonstandard* **1.** Am not. **2.** Used also as a contraction for *are not, is not, has not,* and *have not.*

Ai·nu (ī′no͞o) ▸ *n., pl.* **Ainu** or **-nus. 1.** A member of an indigenous people inhabiting the northernmost islands of Japan. **2.** The language of the Ainu.

air (âr) ▸ *n.* **1a.** A colorless, odorless, tasteless, gaseous mixture, mainly nitrogen (78%) and oxygen (21%). **b.** The earth's atmosphere. **c.** The atmosphere in an enclosure. **2.** The sky; firmament. **3.** A breeze or wind. **4.** Aircraft: *send troops by air.* **5.** Airwaves. **6.** A characteristic impression; aura: *an air of mystery.* **7.** Personal bearing or manner. **8. airs** An affected pose. **9.** *Mus.* A melody or tune. ▸ *v.* **1.** To expose to air; ventilate. **2.** To give public utterance to. **3.** To broadcast on television or radio. **—*idioms:* in the air** Abroad; prevalent: *Excitement was in the air.* **on** (or **off**) **the air** Being (or not being) broadcast on radio or television. **up in the air** Not yet decided; uncertain.

air bag ▸ *n.* An automotive passive restraint that inflates upon collision and prevents passengers from pitching forward.

air·borne (âr′bôrn′) ▸ *adj.* **1.** Carried by or through the air. **2.** In flight; flying.

air brake ▸ *n.* A brake, esp. on a motor vehicle, that is operated by compressed air.

air·brush (âr′brŭsh′) ▸ *n.* An atomizer using compressed air to spray a liquid, such as paint, on a surface. **—air′brush** *v.*

air·bus or **air bus** (âr′bŭs′) ▸ *n.* A commercial passenger jet used for short trips.

air conditioner ▸ *n.* An apparatus for lowering the temperature of an enclosed space. **—air′-con·di′tion** *v.* **—air conditioning** *n.*

air·craft (âr′krăft′) ▸ *n., pl.* **aircraft.** A machine, such as an airplane or helicopter, capable of atmospheric flight.

aircraft carrier ▸ *n.* A large naval vessel designed as a mobile air base.

air-cush·ion vehicle (âr′ko͝osh′ən) ▸ *n.* A usu. propeller-driven vehicle for traveling over land or water on a cushion of air.

THESAURUS

needs or expectations ▸ accordant, compatible, concordant, conformable, congenial, congruous, consistent, consonant, correspondent, corresponding, harmonious. [*Compare* FIT[1], SIMILAR.] *—See also* AMIABLE, FAVORABLE (2), OBLIGING, PLEASANT, WILLING.

agreeableness *n.* *—See* AMIABILITY.

agreed *adv.* *—See* YES.

agreeing *adj.* *—See* UNANIMOUS.

agreement *n.* **1.** An often written acceptance of terms between parties ▸ accord, arrangement, bargain, bond, charter, compact, contract, convention, covenant, deal, pact, understanding. [*Compare* COMPROMISE.] **2.** The act or state of agreeing or conforming ▸ accord, accordance, concord, concordance, chime, concert, conformance, conformation, conformity, congruence, congruity, consensus, consonance, correspondence, harmonization, harmony, keeping, rapport, tune, unanimity, unanimousness, unison, unity. *Idiom:* meeting of the minds. [*Compare* UNDERSTANDING.] *—See also* ACCEPTANCE (1), TREATY.

ahead *adv.* *—See* EARLY, FORWARD.

aid *n.* *—See* ASSISTANT, HELP, RELIEF (2).

aid *v.* *—See* HELP, OBLIGE (1).

aide *n.* *—See* ASSISTANT.

ail *v.* *—See* WORRY.

ailing *adj.* *—See* SICK (1).

ailment *n.* *—See* DISEASE, SICKNESS.

aim *v.* **1.** To direct something, such as a weapon or a remark, often toward a target ▸ cast, direct, head, lay, level, point, set, train, turn, zero in. [*Compare* GUIDE.] **2.** To strive toward a goal ▸ aspire, seek. *Idioms:* go (*or* grab) for the brass ring, keep one's eyes on the prize, set one's sights on. *—See also* BEAR (5), INTEND.

aim *n.* *—See* INTENTION, THRUST.

aimless *adj.* Without aim, purpose, or intent ▸ desultory, directionless, errant, pointless, purposeless, rambling, rudderless, wandering, undirected. [*Compare* ERRATIC, FUTILE, RANDOM.]

air *n.* **1.** The gaseous mixture enveloping the earth ▸ atmosphere, ether. **2.** The celestial regions as seen from the earth ▸ firmament, heavens, sky. *Idiom:* wild blue yonder. **3.** A general impression produced by a predominant quality or characteristic ▸ ambiance, atmosphere, aura, feel, feeling, mood, smell, tone. *Slang:* vibe, vibration. [*Compare* ENVIRONMENT, SHADE.] *—See also* AFFECTATION, BEARING (1), MELODY, WIND[1].

air *v.* **1.** To expose to circulating air ▸ aerate, freshen, ventilate, wind. **2.** To utter publicly ▸ disclose, divulge, express, put, state, vent, ventilate, voice. *Idiom:* come out with. [*Compare* ANNOUNCE, SAY.]

air·drome (âr′drōm′) ▸ *n.* An airport.
air·drop (âr′drŏp′) ▸ *n.* A delivery, as of supplies, by parachute from aircraft. **—air′drop′** *v.*
Aire·dale (âr′dāl′) ▸ *n.* A large terrier with a wiry tan coat marked with black.
air·fare (âr′fâr′) ▸ *n.* Fare for travel by aircraft.
air·field (âr′fēld′) ▸ *n.* **1.** A runway or landing strip. **2.** An airport.
air·foil (âr′foil′) ▸ *n.* An aircraft part or surface, such as a wing, that controls stability, direction, lift, thrust, or propulsion.
air force ▸ *n.* The aviation branch of a country's armed forces.
air gun ▸ *n.* A gun discharged by compressed air.
air lane ▸ *n.* A regular route of travel for aircraft.
air·lift (âr′lĭft′) ▸ *n.* A system of transportation by aircraft when surface routes are blocked. **—air′lift′** *v.*
air·line (âr′līn′) ▸ *n.* **1.** A system for scheduled air transport. **2.** A business providing such a system.
air·lin·er (âr′lī′nər) ▸ *n.* A large passenger airplane.
air lock ▸ *n.* An airtight chamber, usu. located between two regions of unequal pressure, in which air pressure can be regulated.
air·mail (âr′māl′) ▸ *v.* To send (e.g., a letter) by air. ▸ *n.* **air mail** also **airmail 1.** The system of conveying mail by aircraft. **2.** Mail conveyed by aircraft. **—air′mail′** *adj.*
air·man (âr′mən) ▸ *n.* **1.** Any of the three lowest ranks in the US Air Force. **2.** An aviator.
air mass ▸ *n.* A large body of air with only small horizontal variations of temperature, pressure, and moisture.
air mile ▸ *n.* A nautical mile.
air·plane (âr′plān′) ▸ *n.* A self-propelled winged vehicle heavier than air and capable of flight.
air·play (âr′plā′) ▸ *n.* The broadcasting of a recording by a radio station.
air·port (âr′pôrt′) ▸ *n.* A facility where aircraft can take off and land, with accommodations for passengers and cargo.
air·pow·er or **air power** (âr′pou′ər) ▸ *n.* The strategic strength of a country's air force.
air raid ▸ *n.* An attack by military aircraft.
air rifle ▸ *n.* A low-powered rifle, such as a BB gun, that uses manually compressed air to fire small pellets.
air sac ▸ *n.* See **alveolus** 2.
air·ship (âr′shĭp′) ▸ *n.* A self-propelled lighter-than-air craft with directional control surfaces; dirigible.
air·sick (âr′sĭk′) ▸ *adj.* Suffering nausea from the motion of air flight. **—air′sick′ness** *n.*
air·space or **air space** (âr′spās′) ▸ *n.* The portion of the atmosphere above a particular land area, esp. above a nation.
air speed ▸ *n.* The speed of an aircraft relative to the air.
air·strip (âr′strĭp′) ▸ *n.* See **landing strip.**
air·tight (âr′tīt′) ▸ *adj.* **1.** Impermeable by air. **2.** Solid; sound: *an airtight excuse.*
air·time (âr′tīm′) ▸ *n.* **1.** The time that a radio or television station is broadcasting. **2.** The scheduled time of a broadcast.
air-to-air (âr′tə-âr′) ▸ *adj.* Operating or fired between aircraft in flight: *air-to-air missiles.*
air-to-sur·face (âr′tə-sûr′fĭs) ▸ *adj.* Operating or fired from aircraft to ground targets or installations: *air-to-surface communications.*
air·wave (âr′wāv′) ▸ *n.* The medium for transmitting radio and television signals. Often used in the plural.
air·way (âr′wā′) ▸ *n.* **1.** A passageway or shaft in which air circulates. **2a.** See **air lane. b.** See **airline** 2.
air·wor·thy (âr′wûr′thē) ▸ *adj.* **-thi·er, -thi·est.** Fit to fly. **—air′wor′thi·ness** *n.*
air·y (âr′ē) ▸ *adj.* **-i·er, -i·est. 1.** Of or like air. **2.** High in the air; lofty. **3.** Open to the air. **4.** Immaterial; unreal. **5.** Speculative and impractical. **6.** Displaying lofty nonchalance. **7.** Light-hearted; gay. **—air′i·ly** *adv.* **—air′i·ness** *n.*
aisle (īl) ▸ *n.* **1.** A passageway between rows of seats, as in a theater or airplane. **2.** A part of a church separated from the nave by a row of pillars or columns. **3.** A passageway for inside traffic, as in a store.
a·jar (ə-jär′) ▸ *adv. & adj.* Partially opened: *left the door ajar.*
AK ▸ *abbr.* Alaska
AKA ▸ *abbr.* also known as
a·kim·bo (ə-kĭm′bō) ▸ *adv. & adj.* With hands on hips and elbows bowed outward.
a·kin (ə-kĭn′) ▸ *adj.* **1.** Of the same kin; related by blood. **2.** Similar in quality or character; analogous. **3.** *Ling.* Cognate.
Ak·ka·di·an (ə-kā′dē-ən) ▸ *n.* The Semitic language of Mesopotamia. **—Ak·ka′di·an** *adj.*
Al ▸ The symbol for the element **aluminum.**
AL ▸ *abbr.* Alabama
-al[1] ▸ *suff.* Of, relating to, or characterized by: *parental.*
-al[2] ▸ *suff.* Action; process: *retrieval.*
a·la (ā′lə) ▸ *n., pl.* **a·lae** (ā′lē). A winglike structure or part.
Ala. ▸ *abbr.* Alabama
à la also **a la** (ä′ lä, ä′ lə) ▸ *prep.* In the style or manner of: *a poem à la Ogden Nash.*
Al·a·bam·a (ăl′ə-băm′ə) ▸ A state of the SE US. Cap. Montgomery. **—Al′a·ba′mi·an** (-bā′mē-ən), **Al′a·bam′an** *adj. & n.*
al·a·bas·ter (ăl′ə-băs′tər) ▸ *n.* **1.** A translucent white or tinted gypsum used esp. for carving. **2.** A translucent, often banded variety of calcite.
à la carte also **a la carte** (ä′lə kärt′) ▸ *adv. & adj.* With a separate price for each item on the menu.
a·lac·ri·ty (ə-lăk′rĭ-tē) ▸ *n.* **1.** Cheerful willingness; eagerness. **2.** Speed or quickness. **—a·lac′ri·tous** *adj.*
Al·a·mo (ăl′ə-mō′) ▸ A mission in San Antonio, TX; besieged and taken by Mexico (1836) during the Texas Revolution.
à la mode (ä′lə mōd′) ▸ *adj.* **1.** In the prevailing fashion. **2.** Served with ice cream: *apple pie à la mode.*
a·larm (ə-lärm′) ▸ *n.* **1.** A sudden feeling of fear. **2.** A warning of danger. **3.** A device that signals a warning. **4.** The sounding mechanism of an alarm clock. **5.** A call to arms. ▸ *v.* **1.** To frighten. **2.** To warn. **—a·larm′ing·ly** *adv.*
a·larm·ist (ə-lär′mĭst) ▸ *n.* One who needlessly alarms others. **—a·larm′ism** *n.*
a·las (ə-lăs′) ▸ *interj.* Used to express sorrow, regret, or grief.
A·las·ka (ə-lăs′kə) ▸ A state of the US in extreme NW North America. Cap. Juneau. **—A·las′kan** *adj. & n.*
Alaska Native ▸ *n.* A member of any of the aboriginal people of Alaska, including Native American and Eskimo peoples.

THESAURUS

airing *n.* A show that is aired on television or radio ▸ broadcast, program. *—See also* EXPRESSION (1).
airless *adj.* **1.** Lacking fresh air ▸ close, stale, stifling, stuffy, suffocating, unventilated. [*Compare* MOLDY.] **2.** Lacking movement of air ▸ breathless, breezeless, stagnant, still, windless. *Idiom:* dead (*or* flat) calm. [*Compare* STILL.]
airs *n.* *—See* AFFECTATION.
airy *adj.* **1.** Of or relating to air ▸ aerial, atmospheric, pneumatic. **2.** Having little weight; not heavy ▸ fluffy, light, lightweight, weightless. *Idiom:* light as air (*or* a feather). [*Compare* IMMATERIAL.] **3.** Exposed to or characterized by the presence of freely circulating air or wind ▸ blowy, breezy, gusty, ventilated, windblown, windswept, windy. *—See also* HIGH (1), LIGHTHEARTED, SHEER[2].
ajar *adj.* *—See* OPEN (1).
akin *adj.* *—See* KINDRED, LIKE[2].
alabaster *adj.* *—See* FAIR[1] (3).
alacrity *n.* *—See* HASTE (1).
à la mode *adj.* *—See* FASHIONABLE.
alarm *n.* A signal that warns of imminent danger ▸ alarum, alert, heads up, high sign, red flag, warning. [*Compare* OMEN.] *—See also* FEAR.
alarm *v.* *—See* DISMAY, FRIGHTEN, WARN.
alarmed *adj.* *—See* AFRAID.
alarming *adj.* *—See* FEARFUL.
alarmist *n.* One who needlessly alarms others ▸ Chicken Little, panicmonger, scaremonger. *Idiom:* one who cries wolf. [*Compare* PESSIMIST.]

alb (ălb) ▸ *n.* A long white linen robe worn by a priest at Mass.

al·ba·core (ăl′bə-kôr′) ▸ *n., pl.* **al·ba·core** or **-cores.** A large marine fish that is a major source of canned tuna.

Al·ba·ni·a (ăl-bā′nē-ə, -bān′yə) ▸ A country of SE Europe on the Adriatic Sea.

Al·ba·ni·an (ăl-bā′nē-ən, -bān′yən) ▸ *n.* **1.** A native or inhabitant of Albania. **2.** The Indo-European language of the Albanians. **—Al·ba′ni·an** *adj.*

Al·ba·ny (ôl′bə-nē) ▸ The capital of NY, in the E part on the Hudson R.

al·ba·tross (ăl′bə-trôs′, -trŏs′) ▸ *n., pl.* **-tross** or **-tross·es. 1.** Any of several large web-footed sea birds. **2.** A constant, worrisome burden.

al·be·do (ăl-bē′dō) ▸ *n., pl.* **-dos. 1.** The reflecting power of a surface, as of a planet. **2.** The white tissue inside a citrus fruit rind.

al·be·it (ôl-bē′ĭt, ăl-) ▸ *conj.* Even though; although.

Al·ber·ta (ăl-bûr′tə) ▸ A province of W Canada between British Columbia and Saskatchewan. Cap. Edmonton. **—Al·ber′tan** *adj. & n.*

al·bi·no (ăl-bī′nō) ▸ *n., pl.* **-nos.** A person or animal lacking normal pigmentation, esp. one having abnormally white skin, white hair, and pink eyes. **—al′bi·nism** (ăl′bə-nĭz′əm) *n.*

al·bum (ăl′bəm) ▸ *n.* **1.** A book or binder with blank pages for stamps, photographs, or autographs. **2a.** A set of phonograph records in one binding. **b.** A recording of different musical pieces, esp. a long-playing phonograph record.

al·bu·men (ăl-byo͞o′mən) ▸ *n.* **1.** The white of an egg, mainly albumin dissolved in water. **2.** See **albumin.**

al·bu·min (ăl-byo͞o′mĭn) ▸ *n.* A class of proteins found in egg white, blood serum, milk, and many other animal and plant tissues. **—al·bu′mi·nous** *adj.*

Al·ca·traz (ăl′kə-trăz′) ▸ A rocky island of W CA in San Francisco Bay; site of a prison until 1963.

al·caz·ar (ăl-kăz′ər, ăl′kə-zär′) ▸ *n.* A Spanish palace or fortress.

al·che·my (ăl′kə-mē) ▸ *n.* **1.** A medieval chemical philosophy concerned primarily with the transmutation of base metals into gold. **2.** A seemingly magical power. **—al·chem′i·cal** (ăl-kĕm′-ĭ-kəl), **al·chem′ic** *adj.* **—al′chem·ist** *n.*

al·co·hol (ăl′kə-hôl′, -hŏl′) ▸ *n.* **1.** A colorless flammable liquid, C_2H_5OH, obtained by fermentation of sugars and starches and used as a solvent, in drugs, and in intoxicating beverages; ethanol. **2.** Intoxicating liquor containing alcohol. **3.** Any of a series of organic compounds with the general formula $C_nH_{2n+1}OH$.

al·co·hol·ic (ăl′kə-hô′lĭk, -hŏl′ĭk) ▸ *adj.* **1.** Of, containing, or resulting from alcohol. **2.** Suffering from alcoholism. ▸ *n.* A person who suffers from alcoholism.

al·co·hol·ism (ăl′kə-hô-lĭz′əm, -hŏ-) ▸ *n.* **1.** The compulsive consumption of alcoholic beverages. **2.** A chronic pathological condition caused by this.

Al·cott (ôl′kət, -kŏt), **Louisa May** (1832–88) ▸ Amer. writer and reformer.

al·cove (ăl′kōv′) ▸ *n.* A small recessed or partly enclosed extension of a room.

al·de·hyde (ăl′də-hīd′) ▸ *n.* Any of a class of highly reactive organic chemical compounds obtained by oxidation of alcohols.

al·der (ôl′dər) ▸ *n.* A deciduous shrub or tree having toothed leaves and tiny fruits in woody, conelike catkins.

al·der·man (ôl′dər-mən) ▸ *n.* A member of a municipal legislative body.

ale (āl) ▸ *n.* A fermented, bitter alcoholic beverage similar to beer.

a·le·a·to·ry (ā′lē-ə-tôr′ē) ▸ *adj.* **1.** Dependent on chance. **2.** Relating to gambling.

a·lee (ə-lē′) ▸ *adv. Naut.* Away from the wind.

a·lem·bic (ə-lĕm′bĭk) ▸ *n.* An apparatus formerly used for distilling.

a·lert (ə-lûrt′) ▸ *adj.* **1.** Vigilantly attentive; watchful. **2.** Mentally perceptive; quick. **3.** Brisk or lively. ▸ *n.* **1.** A signal that warns of attack or danger. **2.** A period of watchfulness or preparation for action. ▸ *v.* To notify of approaching danger; warn. ***—idiom:* on the alert** Watchful for danger or opportunity. **—a·lert′ness** *n.*

A·leut (ə-lo͞ot′, ăl′ē-o͞ot′) ▸ *n., pl.* **Aleut** or **A·leuts. 1.** A member of a Native American people inhabiting the Aleutian Islands and coastal areas of SW Alaska. **2.** The language of the Aleut, related to Eskimo. **—A·leu′tian** (ə-lo͞o′shən) *adj. & n.*

Aleutian Islands ▸ A chain of volcanic islands of SW AK curving about 1,931 km (1,200 mi) W from the Alaska Peninsula and separating the Bering Sea from the Pacific.

Al·ex·an·der III (ăl′ĭg-zăn′dər) "Alexander the Great" (356–323 B.C.) ▸ King of Macedonia (336–323) and conqueror of Asia Minor, Syria, Egypt, Babylonia, and Persia.

Al·ex·an·dri·an (ăl′ĭg-zăn′drē-ən) ▸ *adj.* **1.** Relating to Alexander the Great. **2.** Relating to Alexandria, Egypt. **3.** Relating to a learned school of Hellenistic literature, science, and philosophy at Alexandria in the last three centuries B.C.

al·ex·an·drine (ăl′ĭg-zăn′drĭn) ▸ *n.* **1.** A line of English verse composed in iambic hexameter. **2.** A line of French verse consisting of 12 syllables.

a·lex·i·a (ə-lĕk′sē-ə) ▸ *n.* Loss of the ability to read, usu. caused by brain lesions.

al·fal·fa (ăl-făl′fə) ▸ *n.* A cloverlike perennial herb widely cultivated for forage.

al·fres·co (ăl-frĕs′kō) ▸ *adv. & adj.* In the fresh air; outdoors.

al·ga (ăl′gə) ▸ *n., pl.* **-gae** (-jē). Any of various chiefly aquatic photosynthetic organisms, ranging from single-celled forms to the giant kelp. **—al′gal** *adj.*

al·ge·bra (ăl′jə-brə) ▸ *n.* A branch of mathematics in which symbols represent numbers or members of a specified set and express general relations that hold for all members in the set. **—al′ge·bra′ic** (-brā′ĭk) *adj.*

Al·ge·ri·a (ăl-jîr′ē-ə) ▸ A country of NW Africa on the Mediterranean Sea E of Morocco and W of Tunisia and Libya. **—Al·ge′ri·an** *adj. & n.*

-algia ▸ *suff.* Pain: *neuralgia.*

Al·giers (ăl-jîrz′) ▸ The capital of Algeria, in the N.

Al·gon·qui·an (ăl-gŏng′kwē-ən, -kē-ən) also **Al·gon·ki·an** (-kē-ən) ▸ *n., pl.* **-an** or **-ans. 1.** A family of North American Indian languages spoken or formerly spoken in an area from Labrador to the Carolinas between the Atlantic coast and the Rocky Mountains. **2.** A member of a people speaking an Algonquian language. **—Al·gon′qui·an** *adj.*

Al·gon·quin (ăl-gŏng′kwĭn, -kĭn) also **Al·gon·kin** (-kĭn) ▸ *n., pl.* **-quin** or **-quins** also **-kin** or **-kins. 1.** A member of any of various Native American peoples inhabiting the Ottawa R. valley of Quebec and Ontario. **2.** Any of the varieties of Ojibwa spoken by these peoples.

al·go·rithm (ăl′gə-rĭth′əm) ▸ *n.* A step-by-step problem-solving procedure. **—al′go·rith′mic** *adj.*

a·li·as (ā′lē-əs) ▸ *n.* An assumed name. ▸ *adv.* Also known as; otherwise.

al·i·bi (ăl′ə-bī′) ▸ *n., pl.* **-bis. 1.** *Law* A form of defense whereby a defendant attempts to prove that he or she was elsewhere when the crime was committed. **2.** *Informal* An excuse.

a·li·en (ā′lē-ən, āl′yən) ▸ *adj.* **1.** Owing political allegiance

THESAURUS

alcoholic *adj.* —*See* HARD (3).
alcoholic *n.* —*See* DRUNKARD.

alehouse *n.* —*See* BAR (2).

alert *adj.* Vigilantly attentive ▸ attentive, bright-eyed, heedful, intent, observant, open-eyed, regardful, vigilant, wakeful, wary, watchful, wide-awake. *Idioms:* all ears (*or* eyes), on guard, on one's toes, on the ball, on the lookout, on the qui vive. [*Compare* AWARE, WARY.] —*See also* CLEVER (1).
alert *n.* —*See* ALARM.
alert *v.* —*See* WARN.

alertness *n.* The condition of being alert ▸ caution, vigilance, wakefulness, wariness, watchfulness. [*Compare* CARE.]

alibi *n.* —*See* EXCUSE (1).

alien *adj.* Not part of the essential nature of a thing ▸ foreign, extraneous,

to another country; foreign. **2.** Belonging to a very different place or society. **3.** Dissimilar or opposed: *ideas alien to her nature.* ▸ *n.* **1.** An unnaturalized foreign resident of a country. **2.** A person from a very different group or place. **3.** An outsider. **4.** A creature from outer space.

al·ien·a·ble (āl′yə-nə-bəl, ā′lē-ə-) ▸ *adj. Law* Transferrable to the ownership of another. **—al′ien·a·bil′i·ty** *n.*

al·ien·ate (āl′yə-nāt′, ā′lē-ə-) ▸ *v.* **-at·ed, -at·ing. 1.** To make unfriendly or hostile; estrange. **2.** *Law* To transfer (property) to the ownership of another. **—al′ien·a′tor** *n.*

al·ien·a·tion (āl′yə-nā′shən, ā′lē-ə-) ▸ *n.* **1.** The act of alienating or the condition of being alienated. **2.** *Psychol.* A state of estrangement esp. between the self and the objective world.

al·ien·ist (āl′yə-nĭst, ā′lē-ə-) ▸ *n. Law* A psychiatrist accepted by a court of law as an expert.

a·light[1] (ə-līt′) ▸ *v.* **a·light·ed** or **a·lit** (ə-lĭt′), **a·light·ing. 1.** To come down and settle, as after flight. **2.** To dismount.

a·light[2] (ə-līt′) ▸ *adj.* **1.** Burning; lighted. **2.** Illuminated. **—a·light′** *adv.*

a·lign also **a·line** (ə-līn′) ▸ *v.* **a·ligned, a·lign·ing** also **a·lined, a·lin·ing. 1.** To arrange or be arranged in a straight line. **2.** To adjust (e.g., parts of a mechanism) to produce a proper orientation. **3.** To ally (oneself) with one side of an argument or cause. **—a·lign′ment** *n.*

a·like (ə-līk′) ▸ *adj.* Having close resemblance; similar. ▸ *adv.* In the same manner or to the same degree. **—a·like′ness** *n.*

al·i·ment (ăl′ə-mənt) ▸ *n.* **1.** Nourishment. **2.** Support.

al·i·men·ta·ry (ăl′ə-mĕn′tə-rē, -trē) ▸ *adj.* **1.** Relating to food, nutrition, or digestion. **2.** Providing nourishment.

alimentary canal ▸ *n.* The mucous membrane-lined tube of the digestive system that extends from the mouth to the anus and includes the pharynx, esophagus, stomach, and intestines.

al·i·mo·ny (ăl′ə-mō′nē) ▸ *n., pl.* **-nies.** *Law* An allowance for support usu. made under court order to a divorced person by the former spouse.

al·i·phat·ic (ăl′ə-făt′ĭk) ▸ *adj.* Relating to a group of organic chemical compounds in which the carbon atoms are linked in open chains.

al·i·quot (ăl′ĭ-kwŏt′) *Math.* ▸ *adj.* Relating to an exact divisor or factor, esp. of an integer. ▸ *n.* An aliquot part.

a·lit (ə-lĭt′) ▸ *v.* P.t. and p.part. of **alight**[1].

a·live (ə-līv′) ▸ *adj.* **1.** Having life; living. **2.** In existence or operation. **3.** Full of living things. **4.** Animated; lively. ***—idiom:*** **alive to** Aware of; alert to. **—a·live′ness** *n.*

a·liz·a·rin (ə-lĭz′ər-ĭn) ▸ *n.* An orange-red crystalline compound, $C_{14}H_6O_2(OH)_2$, used in dyes.

al·ka·li (ăl′kə-lī′) ▸ *n., pl.* **-lis** or **-lies. 1.** A carbonate or hydroxide of an alkali metal, the aqueous solution of which is basic in reactions. **2.** Any of various soluble mineral salts found in natural water and arid soils.

alkali metal ▸ *n.* Any of a group of highly reactive metallic elements, including lithium, sodium, potassium, rubidium, cesium, and francium.

al·ka·line (ăl′kə-lĭn, -līn′) ▸ *adj.* **1.** Relating to or containing an alkali. **2.** Having a pH greater than 7. **—al′ka·lin′i·ty** (-lĭn′ĭ-tē) *n.*

al·ka·line-earth metal (ăl′kə-lĭn-ûrth′, -līn′-) ▸ *n.* Any of a group of metallic elements, esp. calcium, strontium, magnesium, and barium, but usu. including beryllium and radium.

al·ka·lize (ăl′kə-līz′) also **al·ka·lin·ize** (-lə-nīz′) ▸ *v.* **-lized, -liz·ing** also **-ized, -iz·ing.** To make alkaline or become an alkali. **—al′ka·li·za′tion** *n.*

al·ka·loid (ăl′kə-loid′) ▸ *n.* Any of various organic compounds containing nitrogen, occurring in many vascular plants, and including nicotine, quinine, cocaine, and caffeine. **—al′ka·loi′dal** *adj.*

al·ka·lo·sis (ăl′kə-lō′sĭs) ▸ *n.* Abnormally high alkalinity of the blood and body fluids.

al·kyd (ăl′kĭd) ▸ *n.* A widely used durable synthetic resin.

all (ôl) ▸ *adj.* **1.** Being the total number, amount, or quantity. **2.** Constituting or being the total. **3.** The utmost possible. **4.** Every: *all kinds of trouble.* **5.** Any whatsoever. ▸ *n.* Everything one has: *They gave their all.* ▸ *pron.* **1.** The total number; totality: *All the kittens are black.* **2.** Everyone; everything: *justice for all.* ▸ *adv.* **1.** Wholly; completely: *directions that were all wrong.* **2.** Each; apiece: *a score of five all.* **3.** So much: *I am all the better for that experience.* ***—idioms:*** **all along** From the beginning. **all but** Nearly; almost: *all but crying with relief.* **all in** Tired; exhausted. **all in all** Everything considered. **be all** *Informal* To say: *He's all, "Why did you do that?"*

Al·lah (ăl′ə, ä′lə) ▸ *n.* God, esp. in Islam.

all-A·mer·i·can (ôl′ə-mĕr′ĭ-kən) ▸ *adj.* **1.** Representative of the people of the US; typically American. **2.** *Sports* Chosen as the best amateur in the US at a particular position or event. **3.** Composed entirely of Americans or American materials. **—All′-A·mer′i·can** *n.*

all-a·round (ôl′ə-round′) also **all-round** (ôl′round′) ▸ *adj.* **1.** Comprehensive: *a good all-around education.* **2.** Versatile: *an all-around athlete.*

al·lay (ə-lā′) ▸ *v.* **1.** To lessen or relieve. **2.** To calm or pacify.

all clear ▸ *n.* A signal, usu. by siren, that an air raid is over or a danger has passed.

al·lege (ə-lĕj′) ▸ *v.* **-leged, -leg·ing. 1.** To assert to be true, usu. without offering proof. **2.** To cite as a plea or excuse. **—al′le·ga′tion** (ăl′ĭ-gā′shən) *n.* **—al·lege′a·ble** *adj.* **—al·leg′er** *n.*

al·leged (ə-lĕjd′, ə-lĕj′ĭd) ▸ *adj.* Not proved; supposed. **—al·leg′ed·ly** (ə-lĕj′ĭd-lē) *adv.*

Al·le·ghe·ny Mountains (ăl′ĭ-gā′nē) also **Al·le·ghe·nies** (-nēz) ▸ A range forming the W part of the Appalachian Mts. and extending from N PA to SW VA.

Allegheny River ▸ A river rising in N-central PA and flowing about 523 km (325 mi) to Pittsburgh, where it forms the Ohio R.

al·le·giance (ə-lē′jəns) ▸ *n.* Loyalty or the obligation of loyalty, as to a nation, sovereign, or cause.

al·le·go·ry (ăl′ĭ-gôr′ē) ▸ *n., pl.* **-ries. 1.** The use of characters or events to represent ideas or principles in a story, play, or picture. **2.** A story, play, or picture in which such representation occurs. **—al′le·gor′ic, al′le·gor′i·cal** *adj.* **—al′le·gor′i·cal·ly** *adv.* **—al′le·go′rist** *n.*

al·le·gret·to (ăl′ĭ-grĕt′ō) ▸ *adv. & adj. Mus.* In a moderately quick tempo.

al·le·gro (ə-lĕg′rō, ə-lā′grō) ▸ *adv. & adj. Mus.* In a quick, lively tempo.

al·lele (ə-lēl′) ▸ *n.* One member of a pair or series of genes

THESAURUS

extrinsic. [*Compare* IRRELEVANT.] *—See also* FOREIGN (1).

alien *n.* *—See* FOREIGNER.

alienate *v.* *—See* ESTRANGE, ISOLATE (1).

alienation *n.* *—See* BREACH (2), GRANT, ISOLATION.

alight[1] *v.* To come ashore from a seacraft ▸ debark, disembark, land, light. *—See also* LAND (2).

alight on or **upon** *v.* *—See* ENCOUNTER (1).

alight[2] *adj.* *—See* BURNING.

align *v.* *—See* ADJUST, ALLY, EQUALIZE, EVEN, LINE.

alignment *v.* *—See* ARRANGEMENT (1).

alike *adj.* *—See* LIKE[2].

alikeness *n.* *—See* LIKENESS (1).

aliment *n.* *—See* FOOD.

alimentary *adj.* *—See* NUTRITIOUS.

alimentation *n.* *—See* LIVING.

alimony *n.* *—See* LIVING.

alive *adj.* Having or exhibiting existence or life ▸ animate, animated, around, breathing, existent, existing, extant, live, living, subsisting, vital. *Idioms:* alive and kicking, among the living. [*Compare* LIVELY.] *—See also* ACTIVE, AWARE, BUSY (2).

alky *n.* *—See* DRUNKARD.

all *adj.* *—See* COMPLETE (1).

all *n.* *—See* WHOLE.

all *adv.* *—See* COMPLETELY (1).

all-around *adj.* *—See* GENERAL (2), VERSATILE.

allay *v.* *—See* PACIFY, RELIEVE (1).

allegation *n.* *—See* ASSERTION.

allege *v.* *—See* ASSERT.

alleged *adj.* *—See* SUPPOSED.

allegiance *n.* *—See* FIDELITY.

allegiant *adj.* *—See* FAITHFUL.

allegorize *v.* *—See* EMBODY (1).

allegory *n.* *—See* EMBODIMENT.

that occupy a specific position on a specific chromosome. **—al·le′lic** (-lē′lĭk, -lĕl′ĭk) *adj.*

al·le·lop·a·thy (ə-lē-lŏp′ə-thē, ăl′ə-) ▸ *n.* The inhibition of growth in one plant by chemicals produced by another plant. **—al·le′lo·path′ic** (-lē′lə-păth′ĭk, -lĕl′ə-) *adj.*

al·le·lu·ia (ăl′ə-lo͞o′yə) ▸ *interj.* Hallelujah.

Al·len (ăl′ən), **Ethan** (1738–89) ▸ Amer. Revolutionary soldier.

Allen wrench ▸ *n.* A wrench used to secure screws threaded in hexagonally shaped nuts.

al·ler·gen (ăl′ər-jən) ▸ *n.* A substance that causes an allergy. **—al′ler·gen′ic** (-jĕn′ĭk) *adj.*

al·ler·gist (ăl′ər-jĭst) ▸ *n.* A physician specializing in treating allergies.

al·ler·gy (ăl′ər-jē) ▸ *n., pl.* **-gies**. An abnormally high sensitivity to certain substances, such as pollens, foods, or microorganisms. **—al·ler′gic** (ə-lûr′jĭk) *adj.*

al·le·vi·ate (ə-lē′vē-āt′) ▸ *v.* **-at·ed, -at·ing**. To make more bearable. **—al·le′vi·a′tion** *n.*

al·ley (ăl′ē) ▸ *n., pl.* **-leys**. **1.** A narrow street or passageway between or behind buildings. **2.** A straight, narrow course or track. ***—idiom:* up (one's) alley** Compatible with one's interests or qualifications.

al·ley·way (ăl′ē-wā′) ▸ *n.* A narrow passage between buildings.

al·li·ance (ə-lī′əns) ▸ *n.* **1a.** A close, formal association of nations or other groups. **b.** A formal agreement establishing such an association. **2.** A connection based on kinship, marriage, or common interest. **3.** Close similarity in nature or type.

al·lied (ə-līd′, ăl′īd′) ▸ *adj.* **1.** Joined in an alliance. **2.** Of a similar nature; related: *city planning and allied studies.*

al·li·ga·tor (ăl′ĭ-gā′tər) ▸ *n.* **1.** A large amphibious reptile having sharp teeth, powerful jaws, and a broader, shorter snout than the related crocodile. **2.** Leather made from the hide of one of these reptiles.

alligator pear ▸ *n.* See **avocado**.

all-im·por·tant (ôl′ĭm-pôr′tnt) ▸ *adj.* Of the greatest importance; crucial.

al·lit·er·a·tion (ə-lĭt′ə-rā′shən) ▸ *n.* The repetition of the same consonant sounds or of different vowel sounds at the beginning of words or in stressed syllables, as in *"When to the sessions of sweet silent thought"* (Shakespeare). **—al·lit′er·ate** *v.* **—al·lit′er·a′tive** *adj.* **—al·lit′er·a·tive·ly** *adv.*

allo– ▸ *pref.* Other; different: *allophone.*

al·lo·cate (ăl′ə-kāt′) ▸ *v.* **-cat·ed, -cat·ing**. **1.** To set apart; designate. **2.** To distribute; allot. **—al′lo·ca·ble** (-kə-bəl) *adj.* **—al′lo·ca′tion** *n.*

al·lo·morph (ăl′ə-môrf′) ▸ *n.* Any of the variant forms of a morpheme. **—al′lo·mor′phic** *adj.* **—al′lo·mor′phism** *n.*

al·lo·phone (ăl′ə-fōn′) ▸ *n.* A predictable phonetic variant of a phoneme. **—al′lo·phon′ic** (-fŏn′ĭk) *adj.*

al·lot (ə-lŏt′) ▸ *v.* **-lot·ted, -lot·ting**. **1.** To parcel out; distribute by lot. **2.** To assign as a portion; allocate. **—al·lot′ment** *n.* **—al·lot′ter** *n.*

al·lot·ro·py (ə-lŏt′rə-pē) ▸ *n.* The existence, esp. in the solid state, of two or more crystalline or molecular structural forms of an element. **—al′lo·trope** (ăl′ə-trōp′) *n.* **—al′lo·trop′ic** (-trŏp′ĭk, -trō′pĭk), **al′lo·trop′i·cal** *adj.*

all-out (ôl′out′) ▸ *adj.* Wholehearted: *an all-out sprint.*

all over ▸ *adv.* **1.** Over the whole area. **2.** Everywhere. **3.** In all respects. **—all′-o′ver** *adj.*

al·low (ə-lou′) ▸ *v.* **1.** To let do or happen; permit. **2.** To permit to have. **3.** To make provision for. **4.** To grant as a discount. **5.** *Regional* To admit; grant: *I allowed as how he was right.* ***—phrasal verbs:* allow for** To make a provision for: *allow for bad weather.* **allow of** To admit: *a poem allowing of several interpretations.* **—al·low′a·ble** *adj.* **—al·low′a·bly** *adv.*

al·low·ance (ə-lou′əns) ▸ *n.* **1.** The act of allowing or an amount allowed. **2.** Something, such as money, given at regular intervals or for a specific purpose. **3.** A price reduction. **4.** A consideration for circumstances: *an allowance for breakage.*

al·low·ed·ly (ə-lou′ĭd-lē) ▸ *adv.* By general admission; admittedly.

al·loy (ăl′oi′, ə-loi′) ▸ *n.* **1.** A homogeneous mixture of two or more metals. **2.** Something added that lowers value or purity. **—al·loy′** *v.*

all-pur·pose (ôl′pûr′pəs) ▸ *adj.* Having many uses.

all right ▸ *adj.* **1.** In satisfactory order. **2.** Correct. **3.** Average; mediocre. ▸ *adv.* **1.** In a satisfactory way; adequately. **2.** Very well; yes. **3.** Without a doubt.

all-round (ôl′round′) ▸ *adj.* Var. of **all-around**.

All Saints' Day ▸ *n.* Nov. 1, a Christian feast honoring all the saints.

All Souls' Day ▸ *n.* *Rom. Cath. Ch.* Nov. 2, the day on which prayers are offered for the souls in purgatory.

all·spice (ôl′spīs′) ▸ *n.* The dried, nearly ripe berries of a tropical American evergreen tree, used as a spice.

all-star (ôl′stär′) ▸ *adj.* Made up wholly of star performers.

all-time (ôl′tīm′) ▸ *adj.* Unsurpassed by any others: *an all-time broad jump record.*

all told ▸ *adv.* With everything considered; in all: *All told, we won 100 games.*

al·lude (ə-lo͞od′) ▸ *v.* **-lud·ed, -lud·ing**. To make an indirect reference. **—al·lu′sion** (-lo͞o′zhən) *n.* **—al·lu′sive** (-sĭv) *adj.*

al·lure (ə-lo͝or′) ▸ *v.* **-lured, -lur·ing**. To attract with something desirable; entice. ▸ *n.* The power to attract; enticement. **—al·lure′ment** *n.* **—al·lur′ing·ly** *adv.*

al·lu·vi·on (ə-lo͞o′vē-ən) ▸ *n.* **1.** See **alluvium**. **2.** The flow of water against a shore or bank.

al·lu·vi·um (ə-lo͞o′vē-əm) ▸ *n., pl.* **-vi·ums** or **-vi·a** (-vē-ə). Sediment deposited by flowing water, as in a river bed. **—al·lu′vi·al** *adj.*

al·ly (ə-lī′, ăl′ī) ▸ *v.* **-lied, -ly·ing**. **1.** To unite in a formal re-

THESAURUS

alleviate *v.* —*See* RELIEVE (1).

alleviation *n.* —*See* RELIEF (1).

alley *n.* —*See* WAY (2).

alliance *n.* An association for a common cause or interest ▸ bloc, cartel, coalition, combination, combine, confederacy, confederation, consortium, faction, federation, league, monopoly, organization, party, pool, ring, syndicate, trust, union. [*Compare* ASSEMBLY, BAND², FORCE, UNION.] —*See also* ASSOCIATION (1).

allied *adj.* Closely connected by or as if by a treaty ▸ aligned, confederated, federated, unified. —*See also* KINDRED.

all-inclusive *adj.* —*See* DETAILED, GENERAL (2).

allocate *v.* —*See* APPROPRIATE, DISTRIBUTE.

allocation *n.* —*See* ALLOTMENT, DISTRIBUTION (1).

allocution *n.* —*See* SPEECH (2).

allot *v.* —*See* APPROPRIATE, DISTRIBUTE.

allotment *n.* That which is allotted ▸ allocation, allowance, apportionment, distribution, division, dole, lot, measure, part, portion, quantum, quota, ration, share, split. *Informal:* cut. *Slang:* divvy. [*Compare* CUT.] —*See also* ARRANGEMENT (1), DISTRIBUTION (1).

all-out *adj.* —*See* INTENSE, UTTER².

all-overs *n.* —*See* JITTERS.

allow *v.* —*See* ACKNOWLEDGE (1), DISTRIBUTE, PERMIT (1), PERMIT (2), PERMIT (3).

allowable *adj.* —*See* ACCEPTABLE (1).

allowance *n.* —*See* ALLOTMENT, PERMISSION.

alloy *n.* —*See* MIXTURE.
 alloy *v.* —*See* MIX (1).

alloyed *adj.* —*See* IMPURE (2).

all-purpose *adj.* —*See* VERSATILE.

all right *adj.* —*See* ACCEPTABLE (2), HEALTHY.
 all right *adv.* —*See* YES.

all-right *adj.* —*See* GOOD (1).

all-round *adj.* —*See* GENERAL (2), VERSATILE.

all the same *adv.* —*See* STILL (1).

allude to *v.* —*See* HINT, REFER (1).

allure *v.* —*See* ATTRACT, SEDUCE.
 allure *n.* —*See* ATTRACTION.

allurement *n.* —*See* ATTRACTION, LURE (1).

allurer *n.* —*See* SEDUCER (1).

alluring *adj.* —*See* DESIRABLE, SEDUCTIVE.

allusion *n.* —*See* HINT (2).

allusive *adj.* Tending to bring a memory, mood, or image, for example, subtly or indirectly to mind ▸ connotative, evocative, impressionistic, reminiscent, suggestive. [*Compare* DESIGNATIVE, SYMBOLIC.]

alluvion *n.* —*See* FLOOD.

alluvium *n.* —*See* DEPOSIT (2).

ally *v.* To be formally associated, as by treaty ▸ align, confederate, federate, league. *Idioms:* band together,

lationship, as by treaty or contract. **2.** To join with another or others out of mutual interest. ▸ *n., pl.* **-lies.** One allied with another, esp. by treaty or contract.

al·ma ma·ter or **Al·ma Ma·ter** (ăl′mə mä′tər, ăl′mə) ▸ *n.* **1.** The school that one has attended. **2.** The anthem of a school or college.

al·ma·nac (ôl′mə-năk′, ăl′-) ▸ *n.* An annual publication in calendar form with weather forecasts, astronomical information, tide tables, and other information.

al·might·y (ôl-mī′tē) ▸ *adj.* Omnipotent; all-powerful. **—al·might′i·ly** *adv.*

al·mond (ä′mənd, ăl′-, ôl′-, ăm′ənd) ▸ *n.* **1.** A deciduous tree having pink flowers and leathery fruits. **2.** The kernel of this tree, eaten or used for flavoring.

al·most (ôl′mōst′, ôl-mōst′) ▸ *adv.* Slightly short of; not quite.

alms (ämz) ▸ *pl.n.* Money or goods given as charity to the poor.

alms·house (ämz′hous′) ▸ *n.* A poorhouse.

al·oe (ăl′ō) ▸ *n.* **1.** Any of various chiefly African plants having rosettes of succulent, often spiny-margined leaves. **2. aloes** *(takes sing. v.)* A laxative obtained from the juice of a certain aloe.

aloe ver·a (vĕr′ə, vîr′ə) ▸ *n.* **1.** An aloe native to the Mediterranean region. **2.** The gel obtained from its leaves, widely used in cosmetics.

a·loft (ə-lôft′, -lŏft′) ▸ *adv.* **1.** In or into a high place. **2.** *Naut.* At or toward the upper rigging.

a·lo·ha (ə-lō′ə, ä-lō′hä′) ▸ *interj.* Used as a greeting or farewell.

a·lone (ə-lōn′) ▸ *adj.* **1.** Apart from others; solitary. **2.** Without anyone or anything else; only. **3.** Separate from all others of the same class. **4.** Without equal; unique. **—a·lone′** *adv.* **—a·lone′ness** *n.*

a·long (ə-lông′, -lŏng′) ▸ *prep.* **1.** Over the length of. **2.** On a course parallel and close to. **3.** In accordance with: *The committee split along party lines.* ▸ *adv.* **1.** Forward; onward: *moving along.* **2.** As a companion: *Bring your friend along.* **3.** In accompaniment; together. **4.** With one; at hand: *had my camera along.* **5.** *Informal* Advanced to some degree: *getting along in years.*

a·long·shore (ə-lông′shôr′, -lŏng′-) ▸ *adv.* Along, near, or by the shore.

a·long·side (ə-lông′sīd′, -lŏng′-) ▸ *adv.* Along, near, at, or to the side. ▸ *prep.* By the side of; side by side with.

a·loof (ə-lo͞of′) ▸ *adj.* Distant or reserved in manner or social relations. ▸ *adv.* Apart. **—a·loof′ly** *adv.* **—a·loof′ness** *n.*

al·o·pe·cia (ăl′ə-pē′shə, -shē-ə) ▸ *n.* Loss of hair, esp. as a result of disease.

a·loud (ə-loud′) ▸ *adv.* **1.** Using the voice; orally: *Read this passage aloud.* **2.** In a loud tone; loudly: *crying aloud for help.*

alp (ălp) ▸ *n.* A high mountain.

al·pac·a (ăl-păk′ə) ▸ *n., pl.* **-a** or **-as. 1.** A domesticated South American mammal related to the llama and having fine long wool. **2a.** The silky wool of this mammal. **b.** Cloth made from alpaca.

al·pen·horn (ăl′pən-hôrn′) ▸ *n.* A long curved wooden horn used by herders in the Alps to call cows to pasture.

al·pha (ăl′fə) ▸ *n.* The 1st letter of the Greek alphabet.

al·pha·bet (ăl′fə-bĕt′) ▸ *n.* **1.** The letters of a language, arranged in a customary order. **2.** The basic principles; rudiments.

al·pha·bet·i·cal (ăl′fə-bĕt′ĭ-kəl) also **al·pha·bet·ic** (-bĕt′ĭk) ▸ *adj.* **1.** Arranged in the customary order of the letters of a language. **2.** Relating to or expressed by an alphabet. **—al′pha·bet′i·cal·ly** *adv.*

al·pha·bet·ize (ăl′fə-bĭ-tīz′) ▸ *v.* **-ized, -iz·ing.** To arrange in alphabetical order. **—al′pha·bet′i·za′tion** *n.* **—al′pha·bet·iz′er** *n.*

al·pha·nu·mer·ic (ăl′fə-no͞o-mĕr′ĭk, -nyo͞o-) also **al·pha·mer·ic** (-fə-mĕr′ĭk) ▸ *adj.* Consisting of both letters and numbers.

alpha particle ▸ *n.* A positively charged particle, indistinguishable from a helium atom nucleus, consisting of two protons and two neutrons.

alpha ray ▸ *n.* A stream of alpha particles.

al·pine (ăl′pīn′) ▸ *adj.* **1. Alpine** Relating to the Alps or their inhabitants. **2.** Of or relating to high mountains.

Alps (ălps) ▸ A mountain system of S-central Europe.

al·read·y (ôl-rĕd′ē) ▸ *adv.* **1.** By this or a specified time; before: *It was already dark at 5:00.* **2.** So soon: *Are you going already?*

al·right (ôl-rīt′) ▸ *adv.* *Nonstandard* All right.

Al·sa·tian (ăl-sā′shən) ▸ *n.* **1.** A native or inhabitant of Alsace, France. **2.** *Chiefly Brit.* A German shepherd.

al·so (ôl′sō) ▸ *adv.* **1.** In addition; besides. **2.** Likewise; too. ▸ *conj.* And in addition.

al·so-ran (ôl′sō-răn′) ▸ *n.* **1.** A horse that does not win, place, or show in a race. **2.** A loser in a competition.

alt. ▸ *abbr.* **1.** alternate **2.** altitude

Alta. ▸ *abbr.* Alberta

Al·ta·ic (ăl-tā′ĭk) ▸ *n.* A language family of Europe and Asia that includes the Turkic, Tungusic, and Mongolian subfamilies. ▸ *adj.* **1.** Of or relating to the Altai Mountains. **2.** Of or relating to Altaic.

al·tar (ôl′tər) ▸ *n.* An elevated place or structure before or upon which religious ceremonies may be performed.

al·tar·piece (ôl′tər-pēs′) ▸ *n.* A piece of artwork, such as a painting or carving, that is placed above and behind an altar.

al·ter (ôl′tər) ▸ *v.* **1.** To change; modify. **2.** To adjust (a garment) for a better fit. **3.** To castrate or spay (an animal). **—al′ter·a·ble** *adj.* **—al′ter·a′tion** *n.*

al·ter·cate (ôl′tər-kāt′) ▸ *v.* **-cat·ed, -cat·ing.** To argue or dispute vehemently. **—al′ter·ca′tion** *n.*

alter ego ▸ *n.* **1.** Another side of oneself. **2.** An intimate friend.

al·ter·nate (ôl′tər-nāt′, ăl′-) ▸ *v.* **-nat·ed, -nat·ing. 1.** To perform or occur in successive turns. **2.** To pass back and forth from one state, action, or place to another. ▸ *adj.* (-nĭt) **1.** Happening or following in turns. **2.** Designating or relating to every other one of a series. **3.** Substitute: *an alternate plan.* ▸ *n.* (-nĭt) **1.** A substitute. **2.** An alternative. **—al′ter·nate·ly** *adv.* **—al′ter·na′tion** *n.*

al·ter·nat·ing current (ôl′tər-nā′tĭng, ăl′-) ▸ *n.* An electric current that reverses direction at regular intervals.

al·ter·na·tive (ôl-tûr′nə-tĭv, ăl-) ▸ *n.* **1.** The choice between two or more exclusive possibilities. **2.** One of these possibilities. ▸ *adj.* **1.** Allowing or necessitating a choice between two or more things. **2.** Existing outside convention: *an alternative lifestyle.* **—al·ter′na·tive·ly** *adv.*

alternative medicine ▸ *n.* Any of various health care practices that do not follow generally accepted medical methods.

alternative school ▸ *n.* A school that is nontraditional, esp. in ideals or curriculum.

al·ter·na·tor (ôl′tər-nā′tər, ăl′-) ▸ *n.* An electric generator that produces alternating current.

THESAURUS

join forces, team up. [*Compare* COMBINE.] *—See also* ASSOCIATE (1).

ally *n.* *—See* ASSOCIATE (1).

almost *adv.* *—See* APPROXIMATELY.

alms *n.* *—See* DONATION.

almsman or **almswoman** *n.* *—See* BEGGAR (1).

aloha *interjection* *—See* HELLO.

alone *adv.* Without the presence or aid of another ▸ single-handedly, singly, solely, solitarily, solo. *Idioms:* by oneself, all by one's lonesome. [*Compare* SEPARATELY.] *—See also* SOLELY.

alone *adj.* *—See* SOLITARY, UNIQUE.

aloneness *n.* *—See* SOLITUDE.

aloof *adj.* *—See* COOL, DETACHED (1).

aloofness *n.* *—See* APATHY, DETACHMENT (2), INHOSPITALITY.

already *adv.* *—See* EARLIER (1).

also *adv.* *—See* ADDITIONALLY.

alter *v.* *—See* CHANGE (1), CHANGE (2), DISTORT, STERILIZE (2).

alterable *adj.* *—See* CHANGEABLE (1).

alteration *n.* *—See* CHANGE (1), VARIATION.

altercate *v.* *—See* ARGUE (1).

altercation *n.* *—See* ARGUMENT.

alter ego *n.* *—See* FRIEND.

alternate *v.* To take turns ▸ interchange, rotate, shift.

alternate *n.* *—See* SUBSTITUTE.

alternation *n.* Occurrence in successive turns ▸ interchange, rotation, shift.

alternative *n.* *—See* CHOICE, VARIATION.

al·though also **al·tho** (ôl-*thō*′) ▸ *conj.* Regardless of the fact that; even though.
al·tim·e·ter (ăl-tĭm′ĭ-tər) ▸ *n.* An instrument for determining elevation. **—al·tim′e·try** *n.*
al·ti·tude (ăl′tĭ-to͞od′, -tyo͞od′) ▸ *n.* **1.** The height of a thing above a reference level, esp. above sea level. **2.** A high region. **3.** The angular height of a celestial object above the horizon. **4.** The perpendicular distance from the base of a geometric figure to the opposite vertex, parallel side, or parallel surface. **—al′ti·tu′di·nal** *adj.*
al·to (ăl′tō) ▸ *n., pl.* **-tos** *Mus.* **1.** A low female singing voice; contralto. **2.** The range between soprano and tenor. **3.** A singer, voice, or instrument having this range.
al·to·geth·er (ôl′tə-gĕ*th*′ər) ▸ *adv.* **1.** Entirely. **2.** With all included or counted: *Altogether the bill came to $30.* **3.** On the whole.
al·tru·ism (ăl′tro͞o-ĭz′əm) ▸ *n.* Unselfish concern for the welfare of others; selflessness. **—al′tru·ist** *n.* **—al′tru·is′tic** *adj.* **—al′tru·is′ti·cal·ly** *adv.*
al·um (ăl′əm) ▸ *n.* Any of various double sulfates of a trivalent metal and a univalent metal, esp. aluminum potassium sulfate, used as hardeners and purifiers.
a·lu·mi·na (ə-lo͞o′mə-nə) ▸ *n.* Any of several forms of aluminum oxide, Al_2O_3, occurring naturally as corundum, in bauxite, and with various impurities as ruby, sapphire, and emery.
al·u·min·i·um (ăl′yə-mĭn′ē-əm) ▸ *n.* *Chiefly Brit.* Var. of **aluminum.**
a·lu·mi·nize (ə-lo͞o′mə-nīz′) ▸ *v.* **-nized, -niz·ing.** To coat or cover with aluminum.
a·lu·mi·nous (ə-lo͞o′mə-nəs) ▸ *adj.* Relating to or containing aluminum or alum.
a·lu·mi·num (ə-lo͞o′mə-nəm) ▸ *n.* *Symbol* **Al** A silvery-white, ductile metallic element used to form many hard, light, corrosion-resistant alloys. At. no. 13.
a·lum·na (ə-lŭm′nə) ▸ *n., pl.* **-nae** (-nē′). A female graduate of a school, college, or university.
a·lum·nus (ə-lŭm′nəs) ▸ *n., pl.* **-ni** (-nī′). A male graduate of a school, college, or university.
al·ve·o·lus (ăl-vē′ə-ləs) ▸ *n., pl.* **-li** (-lī′). **1.** A tooth socket in the jawbone. **2.** A tiny, capillary-rich sac in the lungs where the exchange of oxygen and carbon dioxide takes place.
al·ways (ôl′wāz, -wĭz) ▸ *adv.* **1.** At all times; invariably. **2.** For all time; forever. **3.** At any time; in any event.
a·lys·sum (ə-lĭs′əm) ▸ *n.* **1.** See **sweet alyssum**. **2.** A Mediterranean weed or ornamental having white or yellow flowers.
Alz·hei·mer's disease (älts′hī-mərz, ălts′-) ▸ *n.* A disease marked by progressive loss of mental capacity.
am (ăm) ▸ *v.* 1st pers. sing. pr. indic. of **be.**
Am ▸ The symbol for the element **americium.**
AM ▸ *abbr.* amplitude modulation
A.M. also **a.m.** ▸ *abbr.* ante meridiem
a·mal·gam (ə-măl′gəm) ▸ *n.* **1.** An alloy of mercury with other metals, as with tin or silver. **2.** A combination of diverse elements.
a·mal·ga·mate (ə-măl′gə-māt′) ▸ *v.* **-mat·ed, -mat·ing.** To form into an integrated whole; unite. **—a·mal′ga·ma′tion** *n.*
a·man·u·en·sis (ə-măn′yo͞o-ĕn′sĭs) ▸ *n., pl.* **-ses** (-sēz). A secretary.
am·a·ranth (ăm′ə-rănth′) ▸ *n.* **1.** Any of various annuals having dense clusters of tiny flowers. **2.** An imaginary flower that never fades. **—am′a·ran′thine** *adj.*
am·a·ryl·lis (ăm′ə-rĭl′ĭs) ▸ *n.* A tropical American bulbous plant grown as an ornamental for its large lilylike flowers.
a·mass (ə-măs′) ▸ *v.* To accumulate. **—a·mass′ment** *n.*
am·a·teur (ăm′ə-tûr′, -cho͝or′, -tyo͝or′) ▸ *n.* **1.** One who engages in an activity or study as a pastime and not as a profession. **2.** One lacking expertise. **—am′a·teur′ish** *adj.* **—am′a·teur′ish·ly** *adv.* **—am′a·teur·ism** *n.*
am·a·to·ry (ăm′ə-tôr′ē) ▸ *adj.* Relating to love, esp. sexual love.
a·maze (ə-māz′) ▸ *v.* **a·mazed, a·maz·ing.** To affect with great wonder; astonish. **—a·maz′ed·ly** (-mā′zĭd-lē) *adv.* **—a·maze′ment** *n.* **—a·maz′ing·ly** *adv.*
Am·a·zon (ăm′ə-zŏn′) ▸ *n.* **1.** *Gk. Myth.* A member of a nation of women warriors. **2.** often **amazon** A tall, aggressive, strong-willed woman.
Am·a·zo·ni·a (ăm′ə-zō′nē-ə) ▸ The vast basin of the Amazon R. in N South America.
Am·a·zo·ni·an (ăm′ə-zō′nē-ən) ▸ *adj.* **1.** Relating to the Amazon R. or to Amazonia. **2.** Relating to an Amazon.
Amazon River ▸ The world's second-longest river, flowing about 6,275 km (3,900 mi) from N Peru across N Brazil to a wide delta on the Atlantic.
am·bas·sa·dor (ăm-băs′ə-dər) ▸ *n.* A diplomat of the highest rank accredited as representative in residence by one government to another. **—am·bas′sa·do′ri·al** (-dôr′ē-əl) *adj.* **—am·bas′sa·dor·ship′** *n.*
am·ber (ăm′bər) ▸ *n.* **1.** A hard, translucent, brownish-yellow fossil resin, used esp. for making jewelry. **2.** A brownish yellow. **—am′ber** *adj.*
am·ber·gris (ăm′bər-grĭs′, -grēs′) ▸ *n.* A waxy, grayish substance formed in the intestines of sperm whales and used in perfumes.
ambi– ▸ *pref.* Both: *ambivalence.*
am·bi·ance also **am·bi·ence** (ăm′bē-əns) ▸ *n.* The special atmosphere of a particular environment.
am·bi·dex·trous (ăm′bĭ-dĕk′strəs) ▸ *adj.* **1.** Able to use both hands with equal facility. **2.** Unusually skillful; adroit. **—am′bi·dex·ter′i·ty** (-stĕr′ĭ-tē) *n.* **—am′bi·dex′trous·ly** *adv.*
am·bi·ent (ăm′bē-ənt) ▸ *adj.* Surrounding; encircling.
am·big·u·ous (ăm-bĭg′yo͞o-əs) ▸ *adj.* **1.** Open to more than one interpretation. **2.** Doubtful or uncertain. **—am′bi·gu′i·ty** (-bĭ-gyo͞o′ĭ-tē) *n.* **—am′big′u·ous·ly** *adv.*
am·bit (ăm′bĭt) ▸ *n.* **1.** An external boundary; circuit. **2.** Sphere or scope.

THESAURUS

altitude *n.* The distance of something from a given level ▸ elevation, height, loftiness, tallness. [*Compare* ASCENT.]
alto *adj.* —*See* LOW (1).
altogether *adv.* —*See* COMPLETELY (1).
altruism *n.* —*See* BENEVOLENCE.
altruistic *adj.* Of or concerned with charity ▸ benevolent, charitable, eleemosynary, philanthropic. —*See also* BENEVOLENT (1).
always *adv.* —*See* FOREVER.
amalgam or **amalgamation** *n.* —*See* MIXTURE.
amalgamate *v.* —*See* ASSOCIATE (1), MIX (1).
amaranthine *adj.* —*See* ENDLESS (2).
amass *v.* —*See* ACCUMULATE.
amassment *n.* —*See* ACCUMULATION (1).
amateur *n.* One lacking professional skill and ease in a pursuit ▸ dabbler, dilettante, layperson, nonprofessional, smatterer, uninitiate. *Informal:* duffer. [*Compare* BEGINNER, FAN[1].]
amateurish *adj.* Lacking the required professional skill ▸ crude, dilettante, dilettantish, inexpert, nonprofessional, unprofessional, unskilled, unskillful. [*Compare* INEFFICIENT, UNSKILLFUL.]
amativeness *n.* —*See* DESIRE (2), LOVE (2).
amatory *adj.* —*See* EROTIC.
amaze *v.* —*See* SURPRISE.
  amaze *n.* —*See* WONDER (1).
amazement *n.* —*See* WONDER (1).
amazing *adj.* —*See* ASTONISHING.
ambassador *n.* —*See* REPRESENTATIVE.
ambiance or **ambience** *n.* —*See* AIR (3), ENVIRONMENT (2).
ambiguity *n.* An expression or term liable to more than one interpretation ▸ double-entendre, equivocality, equivocation, equivoque, tergiversation. —*See also* EQUIVOCATION, VAGUENESS.
ambiguous *adj.* **1.** Lacking certainty or clarity ▸ abstruse, borderline, chancy, clouded, cryptic, doubtful, dubious, dubitable, enigmatic, equivocal, inconclusive, indecisive, indeterminate, obscure, perplexing, problematic, questionable, recondite, uncertain, unclear, unsure, woolly. *Informal:* iffy. *Idioms:* at issue, in doubt, in question, up in the air. [*Compare* INDEFINITE, UNCLEAR.] **2.** Liable to more than one interpretation ▸ ambivalent, cloudy, double-edged, equivocal, inexplicit, nebulous, obscure, two-edged, uncertain, unclear, vague.
ambiguousness *n.* —*See* VAGUENESS.
ambit *n.* —*See* CIRCUMFERENCE, RANGE (1).

am·bi·tion (ăm-bĭsh′ən) ▸ *n.* **1.** A strong desire to achieve something. **2.** The object or goal desired.

am·bi·tious (ăm-bĭsh′əs) ▸ *adj.* **1.** Full of or motivated by ambition. **2.** Challenging: *an ambitious schedule.* **—am·bi′tious·ly** *adv.* **—am·bi′tious·ness** *n.*

am·biv·a·lence (ăm-bĭv′ə-ləns) ▸ *n.* The coexistence of opposing feelings toward a person, object, or idea. **—am·biv′a·lent** *adj.* **—am·biv′a·lent·ly** *adv.*

am·ble (ăm′bəl) ▸ *v.* **-bled, -bling.** To walk slowly or leisurely; stroll. **—am′ble** *n.* **—am′bler** *n.*

am·bro·sia (ăm-brō′zhə) ▸ *n.* **1.** *Gk. & Rom. Myth.* The food of the gods. **2.** Something with a delicious flavor or fragrance. **—am·bro′sial** *adj.*

am·bu·lance (ăm′byə-ləns) ▸ *n.* A specially equipped vehicle used to transport the sick or injured.

am·bu·lant (ăm′byə-lənt) ▸ *adj.* Moving or walking about.

am·bu·la·to·ry (ăm′byə-lə-tôr′ē) ▸ *adj.* **1.** Relating to or adapted for walking. **2.** Capable of walking; not bedridden: *an ambulatory patient.* **3.** Moving about. ▸ *n., pl.* **-ries.** A covered place for walking, as in a cloister.

am·bus·cade (ăm′bə-skād′) ▸ *n.* An ambush. ▸ *v.* **-cad·ed, -cad·ing.** To attack suddenly from a concealed place.

am·bush (ăm′bo͝osh) ▸ *n.* **1.** The act of lying in wait to attack by surprise. **2.** A sudden attack made from a concealed position. ▸ *v.* To attack from a concealed position. **—am′bush′er** *n.*

a·me·ba (ə-mē′bə) ▸ *n.* Var. of **amoeba.**

a·me·lio·rate (ə-mēl′yə-rāt′) ▸ *v.* **-rat·ed, -rat·ing.** To make or become better; improve. **—a·me′lio·ra′tion** *n.*

a·men (ā-mĕn′, ä-) ▸ *interj.* Used at the end of a prayer or to express approval.

a·me·na·ble (ə-mē′nə-bəl, -mĕn′ə-) ▸ *adj.* **1.** Obedient; compliant. **2.** Responsible; accountable. **—a·me′na·bly** *adv.*

a·mend (ə-mĕnd′) ▸ *v.* **1.** To improve. **2.** To remove the errors in; correct. **3.** To alter (e.g., a law) formally by adding, deleting, or rephrasing.

a·mend·ment (ə-mĕnd′mənt) ▸ *n.* **1.** Improvement. **2.** Correction. **3a.** Formal revision, as of a bill or constitution. **b.** A statement of such a revision: *The 19th Amendment gave women the right to vote.*

a·mends (ə-mĕndz′) ▸ *pl.n. (takes sing. or pl. v.)* Recompense for grievance or injury.

a·men·i·ty (ə-mĕn′ĭ-tē, -mē′nĭ-) ▸ *n., pl.* **-ties.** **1.** Pleasantness; agreeableness. **2.** Something that contributes to comfort. **3.** A feature that increases attractiveness or value. **4. amenities** Social courtesies; pleasantries.

a·men·or·rhe·a or **a·men·or·rhoe·a** (ā-mĕn′ə-rē′ə) ▸ *n.* Abnormal suppression or absence of menstruation. **—a·men′or·rhe′ic** *adj.*

Amer. ▸ *abbr.* **1.** America **2.** American

Am·er·a·sian (ăm′ə-rā′zhən, -shən) ▸ *n.* A person of American and Asian descent. **—Am′er·a′sian** *adj.*

a·merce (ə-mûrs′) ▸ *v.* **a·merced, a·merc·ing.** To punish, esp. by a fine imposed arbitrarily by the court.

A·mer·i·ca (ə-mĕr′ĭ-kə) ▸ **1.** The United States. **2.** Also **the Americas** The landmasses and islands of North America, Central America, and South America.

A·mer·i·can (ə-mĕr′ĭ-kən) ▸ *adj.* **1.** Of or relating to the US. **2.** Of or relating to America or the Americas. ▸ *n.* **1.** A citizen of the US. **2.** A native or inhabitant of America or the Americas.

A·mer·i·ca·na (ə-mĕr′ə-kä′nə, -kăn′ə, -kā′nə) ▸ *n. (takes sing. or pl. v.)* Materials relating to American history, folklore, or geography.

American English ▸ *n.* The English language as used in the US.

American Indian ▸ *n.* See **Native American.**

A·mer·i·can·ism (ə-mĕr′ĭ-kə-nĭz′əm) ▸ *n.* **1.** A custom or trait originating in the US. **2.** A word, phrase, or idiom characteristic of American English.

A·mer·i·can·ize (ə-mĕr′ĭ-kə-nīz′) ▸ *v.* **-ized, -iz·ing.** **1.** To make or become American, as in culture or method. **2.** To bring under American control. **—A·mer′i·can·i·za′tion** *n.*

American plan ▸ *n.* A system of hotel management in which a guest pays a fixed daily rate for room and meals.

American Samoa ▸ An unincorp. territory of the US in the S Pacific NE of Fiji.

American Sign Language ▸ *n.* An American system of communication for the hearing-impaired that uses manual signs.

American Spanish ▸ *n.* The Spanish language as used in the Western Hemisphere.

am·er·i·ci·um (ăm′ə-rĭsh′ē-əm) ▸ *n. Symbol* **Am** A white metallic radioactive element used as a radiation source in research. At. no. 95.

Am·er·in·di·an (ăm′ə-rĭn′dē-ən) also **Am·er·ind** (ăm′ə-rĭnd′) ▸ *n.* See **Native American.** **—Am′er·in′di·an, Am′er·ind′** *adj.*

am·e·thyst (ăm′ə-thĭst) ▸ *n.* **1.** A purple or violet variety of transparent quartz or corundum used as a gemstone. **2.** A moderate to grayish purple. **—am′e·thys′tine** (-thĭs′tĭn, -tīn′) *adj.*

Am·har·ic (ăm-hăr′ĭk, äm-hä′rĭk) ▸ *n.* A Semitic language, the official language of Ethiopia.

a·mi·a·ble (ā′mē-ə-bəl) ▸ *adj.* Friendly; good-natured. **—a′mi·a·bil′i·ty, a′mi·a·ble·ness** *n.* **—a′mi·a·bly** *adv.*

am·i·ca·ble (ăm′ĭ-kə-bəl) ▸ *adj.* Friendly; peaceable. **—am′i·ca·bil′i·ty** *n.* **—am′i·ca·bly** *adv.*

a·mid (ə-mĭd′) also **a·midst** (ə-mĭdst′) ▸ *prep.* Surrounded by; in the middle of.

THESAURUS

ambition *n.* A strong desire to achieve something ▸ ambitiousness, aspiration, emulation. [*Compare* DRIVE, ENTHUSIASM, THIRST.] *—See also* DREAM (3), INTENTION.

ambitious *adj.* Full of ambition ▸ aspiring, desirous, determined, driven, emulous, enterprising, highflying, hustling, overambitious. *Idioms:* on the fast track, on the make. [*Compare* ASSERTIVE, DILIGENT.]

ambitiousness *n.* A strong desire to achieve something ▸ ambition, aspiration, emulation. [*Compare* DRIVE, ENTHUSIASM, THIRST.]

ambivalent *adj.* *—See* AMBIGUOUS (2), DOUBTFUL (2).

amble *v.* *—See* STROLL.

amble *n.* *—See* WALK (1).

ambrosial *adj.* *—See* DELICIOUS.

ambulance chaser *n.* *—See* LAWYER.

ambulate *v.* *—See* WALK.

ambuscade *v.* *—See* AMBUSH.

ambuscade *n.* An attack or stratagem for capturing or tricking an unsuspecting person ▸ ambush, trap. [*Compare* DECEIT, TRICK.]

ambush *v.* To attack suddenly and without warning ▸ ambuscade, bushwhack, raid, surprise, waylay. *Idioms:* lay (*or* set) a trap for, lie in wait for. [*Compare* ATTACK, CATCH.] *—See also* LURK.

ambush *n.* An attack or stratagem for capturing or tricking an unsuspecting person ▸ ambuscade, trap. [*Compare* DECEIT, TRICK.]

ameliorate *v.* *—See* IMPROVE.

amelioration *n.* *—See* IMPROVEMENT (1), PROGRESS.

amenability or **amenableness** *n.* *—See* OBEDIENCE, OPENNESS, RESPONSIBILITY.

amenable *adj.* *—See* LIABLE (1), OBEDIENT, RECEPTIVE, WILLING.

amend *v.* *—See* CORRECT (1), IMPROVE, REVISE.

amendatory *adj.* *—See* CORRECTIVE.

amendment *n.* *—See* IMPROVEMENT (1), REVISION.

amends *n.* *—See* COMPENSATION.

amenities *n.* **1.** Anything that increases physical comfort ▸ advantages, comforts, conveniences, facilities, resources, services. **2.** Social courtesies ▸ civility, courteousness, courtesy, graciousness, pleasantry, politeness, proprieties, urbanity. [*Compare* AMIABILITY, MANNERS, TACT.]

amenity *n.* *—See* AMIABILITY.

amerce *v.* To impose a fine on ▸ fine, mulct, penalize. [*Compare* PUNISH.]

amercement *n.* A sum of money levied as punishment for an offense ▸ fine, mulct, penalty. [*Compare* PUNISHMENT.]

amiability or **amiableness** *n.* The quality of being pleasant and friendly ▸ affability, agreeability, agreeableness, amenity, congeniality, congenialness, cordiality, cordialness, friendliness, geniality, genialness, kindness, pleasantness, sociability, sociableness, sweetness, warmth. [*Compare* AMENITY, BENEVOLENCE.]

amiable or **amicable** *adj.* Pleasant and friendly in disposition ▸ affable, agreeable, approachable, companionable, congenial, cordial, friendly, genial, good-natured, good-tempered, likable, neighborly, pleasant, sociable, sweet, warm, warm-hearted. [*Compare* BENEVOLENT, OBLIGING, SOCIAL.]

a·mid·ships (ə-mĭd′shĭps′) also **a·mid·ship** (-shĭp′) ▸ *adv.* *Naut.* Midway between the bow and the stern.
a·mi·go (ə-mē′gō) ▸ *n., pl.* **-gos.** A friend.
a·mine (ə-mēn′, ăm′ēn) ▸ *n.* Any of a group of organic compounds derived from ammonia by replacing one or more hydrogen atoms by a hydrocarbon radical.
a·mi·no acid (ə-mē′nō, ăm′ə-nō′) ▸ *n.* Any of a class of organic compounds, esp. any of the 20 compounds that form proteins.
A·mish (ä′mĭsh, ăm′ĭsh) ▸ *n.* A member of an Anabaptist sect that settled primarily in SE Pennsylvania in the late 17th cent. **—A′mish** *adj.*
a·miss (ə-mĭs′) ▸ *adj.* **1.** Out of proper order. **2.** Not in perfect shape; faulty. ▸ *adv.* In a defective, unfortunate, or mistaken way.
am·i·ty (ăm′ĭ-tē) ▸ *n., pl.* **-ties.** Peaceful relations, as between nations.
am·me·ter (ăm′mē′tər) ▸ *n.* An instrument that measures electric current.
am·mo (ăm′ō) ▸ *n.* *Informal* Ammunition.
am·mo·nia (ə-mōn′yə) ▸ *n.* **1.** A colorless, pungent gas, NH_3, used to manufacture fertilizers and a wide variety of nitrogen-containing chemicals. **2.** See **ammonium hydroxide.**
am·mo·ni·um (ə-mō′nē-əm) ▸ *n.* The chemical ion NH_4^+.
ammonium chloride ▸ *n.* A white crystalline compound, NH_4Cl, used in dry cells and as an expectorant.
ammonium hydroxide ▸ *n.* A basic, aqueous solution of ammonia, NH_4OH, used as a household cleanser and in other products.
am·mu·ni·tion (ăm′yə-nĭsh′ən) ▸ *n.* **1.** Projectiles that can be fired from guns or otherwise propelled. **2.** Explosive or destructive materials used in war. **3.** A means of offense or defense.
am·ne·sia (ăm-nē′zhə) ▸ *n.* Loss of memory. **—am·ne′si·ac′** (-zē-ăk′, -zhē-ăk′), **am·ne′sic** (-zĭk, -sĭk) *n. & adj.*
am·nes·ty (ăm′nĭ-stē) ▸ *n., pl.* **-ties.** A general pardon, esp. for political offenses. **—am′nes·ty** *v.*
am·ni·o·cen·te·sis (ăm′nē-ō-sĕn-tē′sĭs) ▸ *n., pl.* **-ses** (-sēz). A procedure in which a small sample of fluid is drawn out of the uterus, then analyzed to determine genetic abnormalities in, or the sex of, a fetus.
am·ni·on (ăm′nē-ən) ▸ *n., pl.* **-ni·ons** or **-ni·a** (-nē-ə). A membranous sac filled with a serous fluid that encloses the embryo or fetus of a mammal, bird, or reptile. **—am′ni·ot′ic** (-ŏt′ĭk), **am′ni·on′ic** (-ŏn′ĭk) *adj.*
a·moe·ba also **a·me·ba** (ə-mē′bə) ▸ *n., pl.* **-bas** or **-bae** (-bē). A protozoan occurring in water, soil, or as a parasite and consisting essentially of an indefinitely shaped mass of protoplasm. **—a·moe′bic** *adj.*
a·mok (ə-mŭk′, ə-mŏk′) ▸ *adv.* Var. of **amuck.**
a·mong (ə-mŭng′) also **a·mongst** (ə-mŭngst′) ▸ *prep.* **1.** In the midst of; surrounded by. **2.** In the group or class of. **3.** With portions to each of: *Distribute this among you.* **4.** Each with the other.
a·mon·til·la·do (ə-mŏn′tl-ä′dō) ▸ *n., pl.* **-dos.** A pale dry sherry.
a·mor·al (ā-môr′əl, -mŏr′-) ▸ *adj.* **1.** Neither moral nor immoral. **2.** Lacking moral sensibility; not caring about right and wrong. **—a·mor′al·ism** *n.* **—a′mo·ral′i·ty** (ā′mô-răl′ĭ-tē, -mə-) *n.* **—a·mor′al·ly** *adv.*
am·o·rous (ăm′ər-əs) ▸ *adj.* **1.** Strongly disposed to love, esp. sexual love. **2.** Showing or expressing love. **—am′or·ous·ly** *adv.* **—am′or·ous·ness** *n.*
a·mor·phous (ə-môr′fəs) ▸ *adj.* **1.** Lacking definite organization or form. **2.** Of no particular type; anomalous. **3.** *Chem.* Lacking distinct crystalline structure.
am·or·tize (ăm′ər-tīz′, ə-môr′-) ▸ *v.* **-tized, -tiz·ing.** To liquidate (a debt) by installment payments. **—am′or·tiz′a·ble** *adj.* **—am′or·ti·za′tion** *n.*
A·mos (ā′məs) ▸ *n.* *Bible* **1.** A Hebrew prophet of the 8th cent. B.C. **2.** See **Bible** table in Appendix.
a·mount (ə-mount′) ▸ *n.* **1.** The total quantity or number. **2.** A principal plus its interest, as in a loan. ▸ *v.* **1.** To add up in number. **2.** To add up in effect. **3.** To be equivalent.
a·mour (ə-mo͝or′) ▸ *n.* A love affair, esp. an illicit one.
a·mour-pro·pre (ä-mo͝or-prôp′rə) ▸ *n.* Self-respect.
a·mox·i·cil·lin (ə-mŏk′sĭ-sĭl′ĭn) ▸ *n.* A type of penicillin having antibacterial properties similar to ampicillin.
amp (ămp) ▸ *n.* **1.** An ampere. **2.** An amplifier, esp. one used to amplify music.
am·per·age (ăm′pər-ĭj, ăm′pîr′-) ▸ *n.* The strength of an electric current expressed in amperes.
am·pere (ăm′pîr′) ▸ *n.* A unit of electric current strength, equal to a flow of one coulomb per second.
am·per·sand (ăm′pər-sănd′) ▸ *n.* The character (&) representing the word *and.*
am·phet·a·mine (ăm-fĕt′ə-mēn′, -mĭn) ▸ *n.* A colorless, volatile liquid, $C_9H_{13}N$, or one of its derivatives, used primarily as a central nervous system stimulant.
am·phib·i·an (ăm-fĭb′ē-ən) ▸ *n.* **1.** A vertebrate that hatches as an aquatic larva with gills, then transforms into an adult having air-breathing lungs. **2.** An aircraft that can take off and land on land or water. **3.** A vehicle that can operate on land and in water.
am·phib·i·ous (ăm-fĭb′ē-əs) ▸ *adj.* **1.** Able to live on land and in water. **2.** Able to operate on land and in water.
am·phi·bole (ăm′fə-bōl′) ▸ *n.* Any of a group of silicate minerals containing various combinations of sodium, calcium, magnesium, iron, and aluminum. **—am′phi·bol′ic** (-bŏl′ĭk) *adj.*
am·phi·the·a·ter (ăm′fə-thē′ə-tər) ▸ *n.* A round structure having tiers of seats rising gradually outward from a central arena.
am·pho·ra (ăm′fər-ə) ▸ *n., pl.* **-pho·rae** (-fə-rē′) or **-pho·ras.** A two-handled jar with a narrow neck used by the ancient Greeks and Romans.
am·pi·cil·lin (ăm′pĭ-sĭl′ĭn) ▸ *n.* A type of penicillin having a broad antibacterial spectrum and used to treat a variety of infections.
am·ple (ăm′pəl) ▸ *adj.* **-pler, -plest.** **1.** Large in size or extent. **2.** Large in degree or quantity. **3.** Sufficient for a purpose. **—am′ple·ness** *n.* **—am′ply** *adv.*
am·pli·fi·er (ăm′plə-fī′ər) ▸ *n.* **1.** One that amplifies. **2.** A device that produces amplification of an electrical signal.
am·pli·fy (ăm′plə-fī′) ▸ *v.* **-fied, -fy·ing.** **1.** To make greater; increase. **2.** To add to; make complete. **3.** To exaggerate. **4.** To increase the magnitude of a variable quantity, esp. of voltage, power, or current. **—am′pli·fi·ca′tion** *n.*
am·pli·tude (ăm′plĭ-to͞od′, -tyo͞od′) ▸ *n.* **1.** Largeness; magnitude. **2.** Fullness; copiousness. **3.** *Phys.* The maximum absolute value of a periodically varying quantity.
amplitude modulation ▸ *n.* The encoding of a carrier wave by variation of its amplitude in accordance with an input signal.
am·poule also **am·pule** (ăm′po͞ol, -pyo͞ol) ▸ *n.* A small sealed vial used as a container for a hypodermic injection solution.
am·pu·tate (ăm′pyo͞o-tāt′) ▸ *v.* **-tat·ed, -tat·ing.** To cut off (a part of the body), esp. by surgery. **—am′pu·ta′tion** *n.* **—am′pu·ta′tor** *n.*

THESAURUS

amigo *n.* —*See* FRIEND.
amiss *adj.* Having a defect or defects ▸ defective, blemished, faulty, flawed, imperfect. [*Compare* SHABBY, TRICK.] —*See also* CONFUSED (2).
amiss *adv.* Not in the right way or on the proper course ▸ afield, astray, awry, wrong.
amity *n.* —*See* FRIENDSHIP.
amnesty *n.* —*See* FORGIVENESS.
amoral *adj.* —*See* UNSCRUPULOUS.
amorist *n.* —*See* GALLANT.
amorous *adj.* —*See* EROTIC, LASCIVIOUS.
amorousness *n.* —*See* EROTICISM, LOVE (2).
amorphous *adj.* —*See* SHAPELESS.
amount *v.* To come to in number or quantity ▸ add up, aggregate, come, number, reach, run, sum up, total (up). —*See also* EQUAL (1).
amount *n.* —*See* IMPORT, QUANTITY (3), TOTAL.
amour *n.* —*See* LOVE (3).
amour-propre *n.* —*See* EGOTISM, PRIDE.
ample *adj.* Having plenty of room ▸ capacious, commodious, roomy, spacious. [*Compare* BIG.] —*See also* BROAD (1), FULL (3), GENEROUS (2), SUFFICIENT.
amplification *n.* —*See* INCREASE (1).
amplify *v.* —*See* BROADEN, ELABORATE, ELEVATE (2), INCREASE.
amplitude *n.* —*See* BULK (1), SIZE (2).
amply *adv.* —*See* CONSIDERABLY.
amputate *v.* —*See* CRIPPLE.

am·pu·tee (ăm′pyo͞o-tē′) ▸ *n.* A person who has had one or more limbs amputated.

Am·ster·dam (ăm′stər-dăm′) ▸ The constitutional capital of the Netherlands, in the W part.

a·muck (ə-mŭk′) also **a·mok** (ə-mŭk′, ə-mŏk′) ▸ *adv.* **1.** In a frenzy to do violence or kill: *rioters running amuck.* **2.** In a jumbled or confused state: *The plans went amuck.*

am·u·let (ăm′yə-lĭt) ▸ *n.* An object worn, esp. around the neck, as a charm against evil or injury.

a·muse (ə-myo͞oz′) ▸ *v.* **a·mused, a·mus·ing. 1.** To occupy in an entertaining fashion. **2.** To cause to laugh. **—a·mus′a·ble** *adj.* **—a·muse′ment** *n.*

am·y·lase (ăm′ə-lās′) ▸ *n.* Any of a group of enzymes that convert starch to sugar.

an (ən; ăn *when stressed*) ▸ *indef.art.* The form of *a* used before words beginning with a vowel or with an unpronounced *h*: *an elephant; an hour.*

an– ▸ *pref.* Var. of **a–**[1].

–an ▸ *suff.* **1.** Of or resembling: *Korean.* **2.** One relating to or characterized by: *librarian.*

ana– ▸ *pref.* Upward; up: *anabolism.*

–ana or **–iana** ▸ *suff.* A collection of items relating to a specified person or place: *Americana.*

An·a·bap·tist (ăn′ə-băp′tĭst) ▸ *n.* A member of a radical Protestant movement of the 16th-cent. Reformation. **—An′a·bap′tism** *n.*

a·nab·o·lism (ə-năb′ə-lĭz′əm) ▸ *n.* Metabolic activity in which complex substances are synthesized from simpler substances. **—an′a·bol′ic** (ăn′ə-bŏl′ĭk) *adj.*

a·nach·ro·nism (ə-năk′rə-nĭz′əm) ▸ *n.* **1.** Representation of something as existing or happening outside its historical order. **2.** One that is out of its proper or chronological order. **—a·nach′ro·nis′tic, a·nach′ro·nous** (-nəs) *adj.* **—a·nach′ro·nis′ti·cal·ly, a·nach′ro·nous·ly** *adv.*

an·a·con·da (ăn′ə-kŏn′də) ▸ *n.* A large nonvenomous snake of tropical South America that suffocates its prey in its coils.

an·aer·obe (ăn′ə-rōb′, ăn-âr′ōb′) ▸ *n.* An organism, such as a bacterium, that can live in the absence of atmospheric oxygen. **—an′aer·o′bic** *adj.* **—an′aer·o′bi·cal·ly** *adv.*

an·aes·the·sia (ăn′ĭs-thē′zhə) ▸ *n.* Var. of **anesthesia.**

an·a·gram (ăn′ə-grăm′) ▸ *n.* A word formed by reordering the letters of another word, such as *satin* to *stain.*

a·nal (ā′nəl) ▸ *adj.* **1.** Of or near the anus. **2.** Relating to the second stage of psychosexual development in psychoanalytic theory. **—a′nal·ly** *adv.*

an·al·ge·si·a (ăn′əl-jē′zē-ə, -zhə) ▸ *n.* A deadening of the sense of pain without loss of consciousness.

an·al·ge·sic (ăn′əl-jē′zĭk, -sĭk) ▸ *n.* A medication that reduces or eliminates pain. **—an′al·ge′sic** *adj.*

a·nal·o·gous (ə-năl′ə-gəs) ▸ *adj.* **1.** Similar or alike in such a way as to permit the drawing of an analogy. **2.** *Biol.* Similar in function but not in structure and evolutionary origin. **—a·nal′o·gous·ly** *adv.*

an·a·logue also **an·a·log** (ăn′ə-lôg′, -lŏg′) ▸ *n.* Something that is analogous. ▸ *adj.* often **analog** Of or relating to the representation of data by measurable physical variables: *an analog computer.*

a·nal·o·gy (ə-năl′ə-jē) ▸ *n., pl.* **-gies. 1a.** Similarity in some respects between things otherwise dissimilar. **b.** A comparison based on such similarity. **2.** *Biol.* Correspondence in function between organs of dissimilar evolution. **3.** An inference that if two things are alike in some respects they must be alike in others.

a·nal·y·sis (ə-năl′ĭ-sĭs) ▸ *n., pl.* **-ses** (-sēz′). **1.** The separation of a whole into its parts for study. **2.** A statement of the results of such a separation or study. **3.** Psychoanalysis. **4.** Systems analysis. **—an′a·lyst** (ăn′ə-lĭst) *n.*

an·a·lyt·ic (ăn′ə-lĭt′ĭk) or **an·a·lyt·i·cal** (-ĭ-kəl) ▸ *adj.* **1.** Relating to analysis. **2.** Reasoning or acting from a perception of the parts and interrelations of a subject. **3.** Expert in or using analysis, esp. in thinking. **—an′a·lyt′i·cal·ly** *adv.*

an·a·lyze (ăn′ə-līz′) ▸ *v.* **-lyzed, -lyz·ing. 1.** To make an analysis of. **2.** To psychoanalyze.

an·a·pest (ăn′ə-pĕst′) ▸ *n.* A metrical foot composed of two short syllables followed by one long one. **—an′a·pes′tic** *adj.*

an·ar·chism (ăn′ər-kĭz′əm) ▸ *n.* **1.** The theory that all forms of government are oppressive and should be abolished. **2.** Terrorism against the state. **—an′ar·chist** *n.* **—an′ar·chis′tic** *adj.*

an·ar·chy (ăn′ər-kē) ▸ *n., pl.* **-chies. 1.** Absence of governmental authority or law. **2.** Disorder and confusion. **—an·ar′chic** (ăn-är′kĭk), **an·ar′chi·cal** *adj.* **—an·ar′chi·cal·ly** *adv.*

A·na·sa·zi (ä′nə-sä′zē) ▸ *n., pl.* **-zi** or **-zis.** A member of a former Native American people of the SW US whose descendants are considered to include the present-day Pueblo peoples.

a·nath·e·ma (ə-năth′ə-mə) ▸ *n., pl.* **-mas. 1.** A formal ecclesiastical ban or excommunication. **2.** One that is greatly reviled or shunned.

An·a·to·li·a (ăn′ə-tō′lē-ə, -tōl′yə) ▸ The Asian part of Turkey; usu. considered synonymous with Asia Minor.

An·a·to·li·an (ăn′ə-tō′lē-ən) ▸ *n.* **1.** A native or inhabitant of Anatolia. **2.** An extinct group of Indo-European languages of ancient Anatolia, including Hittite. **—An′a·to′li·an** *adj.*

a·nat·o·mize (ə-năt′ə-mīz′) ▸ *v.* **-mized, -miz·ing. 1.** To dissect (an organism) for study. **2.** To analyze.

a·nat·o·my (ə-năt′ə-mē) ▸ *n., pl.* **-mies. 1.** The structure of an organism or organ. **2.** The science of the structure of organisms and their parts. **3.** A detailed analysis. **—an′a·tom′ic** (ăn′ə-tŏm′ĭk), **an′a·tom′i·cal** *adj.* **—an′a·tom′i·cal·ly** *adv.* **—a·nat′o·mist** *n.*

–ance ▸ *suff.* **1.** State or condition: *repentance.* **2.** Action: *utterance.*

an·ces·tor (ăn′sĕs′tər) ▸ *n.* **1.** A person from whom one is remotely descended; forebear. **2.** A forerunner or predecessor. **3.** *Biol.* The organism from which later kinds evolved. **—an·ces′tral** *adj.* **—an·ces′tral·ly** *adv.*

an·ces·try (ăn′sĕs′trē) ▸ *n., pl.* **-tries. 1.** Descent or lineage. **2.** Ancestors collectively.

THESAURUS

amuck *adj.* Out of control ▸ runaway, unbridled, uncontrolled. *Idioms:* out of hand, running wild. [*Compare* ABANDONED, LOOSE.]

amulet *n.* —*See* CHARM.

amuse *v.* To occupy in an agreeable or pleasing way ▸ charm, cheer, divert, entertain, recreate, regale. [*Compare* ABSORB, CHEER.] —*See also* DELIGHT (1).

amusement *n.* Something that amuses, entertains, or pleases ▸ delight, disport, distraction, diversion, enjoyment, entertainment, fun, hobby, pastime, play, pleasure, recreation, sport, treat. *Slang:* jollies, kicks. [*Compare* GAIETY.]

amusing *adj.* —*See* DELIGHTFUL, FUNNY (1), PLEASANT.

analogize *v.* —*See* LIKEN.

analogous *adj.* —*See* LIKE[2].

analogue *n.* —*See* PARALLEL.

analogy *n.* —*See* LIKENESS (1), PARALLEL.

analysis *n.* The separation of a whole into its parts for study ▸ anatomization, anatomy, breakdown, dissection, reduction, subdivision. —*See also* EXAMINATION (1), EXAMINATION (2), LOGIC.

analytical or **analytic** *adj.* —*See* LOGICAL (1).

analyze *v.* To separate into parts for study ▸ anatomize, break down, dissect, reduce, resolve, subdivide, take apart. —*See also* EXAMINE (1).

anarchy *n.* —*See* DISORDER (2), LICENSE (2).

anathema *n.* —*See* CURSE (1), HATE (2).

anathematize *v.* To invoke evil upon ▸ curse, damn, hex, imprecate. [*Compare* CHARM.]

anatomize *v.* —*See* ANALYZE.

anatomy or **anatomization** *n.* —*See* ANALYSIS.

ancestor *n.* **1.** A person from whom one is descended ▸ antecedent, ascendant, father, forebear, forefather, foremother, mother, parent, primogenitor, progenitor. **2.** One that precedes, as in time ▸ antecedent, forerunner, precursor, predecessor, progenitor, prototype.

ancestral *adj.* Of or from one's ancestors ▸ familial, genealogical, hereditary, inherited, patrimonial.

ancestry *n.* One's ancestors or their character or one's ancestral derivation ▸ birth, blood, bloodline, descent, derivation, extraction, family, family tree, genealogy, line, lineage, origin, parentage, pedigree, race, roots, seed, stock. [*Compare* KIN, PROGENY.]

an·chor (ăngʹkər) ▸ *n.* **1.** A heavy object attached to a vessel and cast overboard to keep the vessel in place. **2.** A source of security or stability. **3.** *Sports* An athlete who runs the last stage of a relay race. **4.** An anchorperson. ▸ *v.* **1.** To hold fast by or as if by an anchor. **2.** *Sports* To serve as an anchor for (a team). **3.** To narrate or coordinate (a newscast).

an·chor·age (ăngʹkər-ĭj) ▸ *n.* A place for anchoring ships.

an·cho·rite (ăngʹkə-rīt′) ▸ *n.* A religious hermit.

an·chor·man (ăngʹkər-măn′) ▸ *n.* **1.** A man who anchors a newscast. **2.** See **anchor** 3.

an·chor·per·son (ăngʹkər-pûr′sən) ▸ *n.* An anchorman or anchorwoman.

an·chor·wom·an (ăngʹkər-wo͝om′ən) ▸ *n.* A woman who anchors a newscast.

an·cho·vy (ănʹchō′vē) ▸ *n., pl.* **-vy** or **-vies.** A small, edible, herringlike marine fish.

an·cien ré·gime (äN-syăNʹ rā-zhēmʹ) ▸ *n.* **1.** The political and social system that existed in France before the Revolution of 1789. **2.** A former or outmoded sociopolitical system.

an·cient (ānʹshənt) ▸ *adj.* **1.** Of great age; very old. **2.** Relating to times long past, esp. before the fall of Rome (A.D. 476). ▸ *n.* **1.** A very old person. **2. ancients** The peoples of classical antiquity. **—anʹcient·ly** *adv.*

an·cil·lar·y (ănʹsə-lĕr′ē) ▸ *adj.* **1.** Subordinate. **2.** Auxiliary; helping.

-ancy ▸ *suff.* Condition or quality: *buoyancy.*

and (ənd, ən; ănd *when stressed*) ▸ *conj.* **1.** Together with or along with; as well as. **2.** Added to; plus.

An·da·lu·sia (ăn′də-lo͞oʹzhə, -zhē-ə) ▸ A region of S Spain on the Mediterranean. **—An′da·luʹsian** *adj. & n.*

an·dan·te (än-dänʹtā) ▸ *adv. & adj. Mus.* In a moderately slow tempo.

an·dan·ti·no (än′dän-tēʹnō) ▸ *adv. & adj. Mus.* In a tempo slightly faster or slower than andante.

An·der·sen (ănʹdər-sən), **Hans Christian** (1805–75) ▸ Danish writer.

An·des (ănʹdēz) ▸ A mountain system of W South America extending from Venezuela to Tierra del Fuego. **—Anʹde·an** *adj. & n.*

and·i·ron (ăndʹī′ərn) ▸ *n.* One of a pair of metal supports for logs in a fireplace.

and/or (ăndʹôrʹ) ▸ *conj.* Used to indicate that either or both of the items connected by it are involved.

An·dor·ra (ăn-dôrʹə, -dŏrʹə) ▸ A tiny country of SW Europe between France and Spain in the E Pyrenees. **—An·dorʹran** *adj. & n.*

andro– or **andr–** ▸ *pref.* Male; masculine: *androgen.*

an·dro·gen (ănʹdrə-jən) ▸ *n.* A hormone that controls and maintains masculine characteristics. **—an′dro·genʹic** (-jĕnʹĭk) *adj.*

an·drog·y·nous (ăn-drŏjʹə-nəs) ▸ *adj.* **1.** *Biol.* Having both female and male characteristics; hermaphroditic. **2.** Being neither distinguishably masculine nor feminine. **—an·drogʹy·nous·ly** *adv.* **—an·drogʹy·ny** *n.*

an·droid (ănʹdroid′) ▸ *n.* An automaton created from biological materials and resembling a human. **—anʹdroid** *adj.*

–andry ▸ *suff.* Kind or number of husbands: *polyandry.*

–ane ▸ *suff.* A saturated hydrocarbon: *propane.*

an·ec·dote (ănʹĭk-dōt′) ▸ *n.* A short account of an interesting or humorous incident. **—an′ec·dotʹal** *adj.*

an·e·cho·ic (ăn′ĕ-kōʹĭk) ▸ *adj.* Neither having nor producing echoes.

a·ne·mi·a (ə-nēʹmē-ə) ▸ *n.* A pathological deficiency in the oxygen-carrying component of the blood. **—a·neʹmic** *adj.*

an·e·mom·e·ter (ăn′ə-mŏmʹĭ-tər) ▸ *n.* An instrument for measuring wind force and velocity.

a·nem·o·ne (ə-nĕmʹə-nē) ▸ *n.* **1.** A perennial plant having lobed leaves and large flowers with showy sepals. **2.** The sea anemone.

a·nent (ə-nĕntʹ) ▸ *prep.* Regarding; concerning.

an·er·oid barometer (ănʹə-roid′) ▸ *n.* A barometer in which variations of atmospheric pressure are indicated by the relative bulges of a thin elastic metal disk covering a partially evacuated chamber.

an·es·the·sia also **an·aes·the·sia** (ăn′ĭs-thēʹzhə) ▸ *n.* Total or partial loss of physical sensation caused by disease or an anesthetic.

an·es·the·si·ol·o·gy also **an·aes·the·si·ol·o·gy** (ăn′ĭs-thē′zē-ŏlʹə-jē) ▸ *n.* The medical study and application of anesthetics. **—an′es·the′si·olʹo·gist** *n.*

an·es·thet·ic also **an·aes·thet·ic** (ăn′ĭs-thĕtʹĭk) ▸ *adj.* Causing anesthesia. ▸ *n.* An agent or substance that induces anesthesia. **—an′es·thetʹi·cal·ly** *adv.*

a·nes·the·tize also **a·naes·the·tize** (ə-nĕsʹthĭ-tīz′) ▸ *v.* **-tized, -tiz·ing.** To induce anesthesia in. **—an·esʹthe·tist** *n.* **—an·es′the·ti·zaʹtion** *n.*

an·eu·rysm also **an·eu·rism** (ănʹyə-rĭz′əm) ▸ *n.* A pathological, blood-filled dilatation of a blood vessel.

a·new (ə-no͞oʹ, -nyo͞oʹ) ▸ *adv.* **1.** Once more; again. **2.** In a new and different way.

an·gel (ānʹjəl) ▸ *n.* **1a.** A usu. benevolent celestial being that acts as an intermediary between heaven and earth. **b.** *Christianity* An angel of the lowest order. **2.** A good, kind person. **3.** *Informal* A financial backer of an enterprise, esp. a dramatic production. **—an·gelʹic** (ăn-jĕlʹĭk), **an·gelʹi·cal** *adj.*

Angel Fall or **Falls** ▸ A waterfall, about 980 m (3,212 ft), in SE Venezuela.

an·gel·fish (ānʹjəl-fĭsh′) ▸ *n., pl.* **-fish** or **-fish·es.** A brightly colored tropical fish having a laterally compressed body.

an·gel·i·ca (ăn-jĕlʹĭ-kə) ▸ *n.* An herb in the parsley family, whose roots and fruits are used in flavoring.

an·ger (ăngʹgər) ▸ *n.* A strong feeling of displeasure, resentment, or hostility. ▸ *v.* To make or become angry.

an·gi·na (ăn-jīʹnə) ▸ *n.* **1.** Angina pectoris. **2.** A condition in which spasmodic attacks of suffocating pain occur.

angina pec·to·ris (pĕkʹtər-ĭs) ▸ *n.* Severe paroxysmal pain in the chest associated with an insufficient supply of blood to the heart.

THESAURUS

anchor *n.* A device for supporting or holding in place ▸ brake, dowel, grapnel, kedge, mooring, wedge. [*Compare* BOND, CORD, FASTENER, NAIL.] *—See also* PRESS.
  anchor *v.* *—See* FASTEN.

anchorage *n.* *—See* HARBOR.

anchorman or **anchorwoman** *n.* *—See* PRESS.

ancient *adj.* *—See* EARLY (1), OLD (1).
  ancient *n.* *—See* SENIOR (2).

ancient history *n.* *—See* ANTIQUITY.

ancillary *adj.* *—See* AUXILIARY (1).

androgynous *n.* Being neither distinguishably masculine nor feminine ▸ degendered, epicene, genderless, gender-neutral, gender-nonspecific, sexless, ungendered. [*Compare* EFFEMINATE, MASCULINE.]

androgyny *n.* The quality of being androgynous ▸ epicenism, genderneutrality, sexlessness. [*Compare* EFFEMINACY, MASCULINITY.]

anecdote *n.* *—See* YARN.

anemic *adj.* *—See* PALE (2), SICK (1).

anesthetic *adj.* *—See* CALLOUS.

anesthetize *v.* *—See* DRUG (1).

anew *adv.* Once more ▸ afresh, again, once again, over again. ***Idiom:*** from the beginning (*or* start *or* top).

anfractuous *adj.* *—See* INDIRECT (1), WINDING.

angel *n.* *—See* INNOCENT (1), PATRON, RESCUER, SPONSOR.

angelic or **angelical** *adj.* *—See* INNOCENT (1).

anger *n.* A strong feeling of displeasure or hostility ▸ animosity, choler, fury, furor, indignation, irateness, ire, outrage, rage, resentment, wrath, wrathfulness. *Informal:* dander. [*Compare* ENMITY, HATE, ANNOYANCE.]

anger *v.* **1.** To cause to feel or show anger ▸ burn (up), enrage, exasperate, incense, infuriate, irritate, madden, provoke, rile. *Informal:* tee off, tick off. *Slang:* piss off, p.o. ***Idioms:*** bend out of shape, get one's dander up, get on one's nerves, make one hot under the collar, make one's blood boil, make one's fur fly, put one's back up, rub one the wrong way. [*Compare* ANNOY, OFFEND.] **2.** To be or become angry ▸ blow up, boil over, bristle, burn, explode, flare up, foam, fume, rage, seethe, storm. *Informal:* steam. ***Idioms:*** blow a fuse, blow a gasket, blow one's stack (*or* top), breathe fire, fly off the handle, foam (*or* froth) at the mouth, get hot under the collar, have a cow, hit the ceiling (*or* roof), lose one's temper, see red, throw a fit. [*Compare* BOIL.] *—See also* OFFEND (1).

an·gi·o·gram (ăn′jē-ə-grăm′) ▸ *n.* An x-ray of the blood vessels, used in diagnosis of the cardiovascular system.
an·gi·o·plas·ty (ăn′jē-ə-plăs′tē) ▸ *n., pl.* **-ties.** A surgical procedure that uses a catheter fitted with an inflatable tip to clear blocked arteries.
an·gi·o·sperm (ăn′jē-ə-spûrm′) ▸ *n.* A seed-bearing plant whose ovules are enclosed in an ovary; a flowering plant.
an·gle[1] (ăng′gəl) ▸ *v.* **-gled, -gling.** **1.** To fish with a hook and line. **2.** To try to get something by using schemes or tricks. **—an′gler** *n.*
an·gle[2] (ăng′gəl) ▸ *n.* **1.** *Math.* **a.** The figure formed by two lines diverging from a common point. **b.** The figure formed by two planes diverging from a common line. **c.** The space between such lines or surfaces. **2.** A corner, as of a building. **3a.** The place or direction from which an object is seen. **b.** A point of view. **4.** *Slang* A devious method; scheme. ▸ *v.* **-gled, -gling.** **1.** To move or turn at an angle. **2.** *Informal* To impart a biased point of view to.
An·gle (ăng′gəl) ▸ *n.* A member of a Germanic people that migrated to England from S Jutland in the 5th cent. A.D. and formed part of the Anglo-Saxon peoples.
an·gle·worm (ăng′gəl-wûrm′) ▸ *n.* An earthworm used as bait in fishing.
An·gli·can (ăng′glĭ-kən) ▸ *adj.* Relating to the Church of England or to the churches in communion with it. **—An′gli·can** *n.* **—An′gli·can·ism** *n.*
An·gli·cism (ăng′glĭ-sĭz′əm) ▸ *n.* A word, phrase, or idiom peculiar to the English language, esp. as spoken in England.
An·gli·cize (ăng′glĭ-sīz′) ▸ *v.* **-cized, -ciz·ing.** To make or become English. **—An′gli·ci·za′tion** *n.*
An·glo (ăng′glō) ▸ *n., pl.* **-glos.** An English-speaking person, esp. a white North American. **—An′glo** *adj.*
Anglo– ▸ *pref.* England; English: *Anglophile.*
An·glo-A·mer·i·can (ăng′glō-ə-mĕr′ĭ-kən) ▸ *n.* An American of English ancestry. ▸ *adj.* Relating to England and the US.
An·glo-Nor·man (ăng′glō-nôr′mən) ▸ *n.* **1.** A Norman settler in England after 1066. **2.** The dialect of Old French used by the Anglo-Normans. **—An′glo-Nor′man** *adj.*
An·glo·phile (ăng′glə-fīl′) also **An·glo·phil** (-fĭl) ▸ *n.* One who admires England and its culture. **—An′glo·phil′i·a** (-fĭl′ē-ə) *n.*
An·glo·phobe (ăng′glə-fōb′) ▸ *n.* One who dislikes England or its culture. **—An′glo·pho′bi·a** *n.* **—An′glo·pho′bic** *adj.*
An·glo·phone (ăn′glə-fōn′) ▸ *n.* An English-speaking person, esp. in a region of linguistic diversity.
An·glo-Sax·on (ăng′glō-săk′sən) ▸ *n.* **1.** A member of one of the Germanic peoples who migrated to Britain in the 5th and 6th cent. **2.** See **Old English.** **3.** A person of English ancestry. **—An′glo-Sax′on** *adj.*
An·go·la (ăng-gō′lə, ăn-) ▸ A country of SW Africa bordering on the Atlantic Ocean. **—An·go′lan** *adj. & n.*
An·go·ra (ăng-gôr′ə) ▸ *n.* **1.** A cat, goat, or rabbit with long silky hair. **2.** often **angora** A yarn or fabric made from the hair of the Angora goat or rabbit.
an·gry (ăng′grē) ▸ *adj.* **-gri·er, -gri·est.** **1.** Feeling or showing anger. **2.** Resulting from anger: *an angry silence.* **3.** Having a menacing aspect; threatening: *angry clouds.* **4.** Inflamed and painful.
angst (ängkst) ▸ *n.* A feeling of anxiety or apprehension.
ang·strom or **ång·strom** (ăng′strəm) ▸ *n.* A unit of length equal to one hundred-millionth (10^{-8}) of a centimeter.
An·guil·la (ăng-gwĭl′ə, ăn-) ▸ An island of the British West Indies in the N Leeward Is.
an·guish (ăng′gwĭsh) ▸ *n.* Agonizing physical or mental pain; torment. ▸ *v.* To cause or suffer anguish.
an·gu·lar (ăng′gyə-lər) ▸ *adj.* **1.** Having an angle or angles. **2.** Measured by an angle. **3.** Bony and lean; gaunt. **—an′gu·lar′i·ty** (-lăr′ĭ-tē) *n.* **—an′gu·lar·ly** *adv.*
an·hy·dride (ăn-hī′drīd′) ▸ *n.* A chemical compound formed from another by the removal of water.
an·hy·drous (ăn-hī′drəs) ▸ *adj.* Without water.
an·i·line also **an·i·lin** (ăn′ə-lĭn) ▸ *n.* A colorless, oily, poisonous benzene derivative, $C_6H_5NH_2$, that is used in rubber, dyes, resins, pharmaceuticals, and varnishes. **—an′i·line** *adj.*
an·i·mad·vert (ăn′ə-măd-vûrt′) ▸ *v.* To comment critically, usu. with disapproval. **—an′i·mad·ver′sion** *n.*
an·i·mal (ăn′ə-məl) ▸ *n.* **1.** An organism of the kingdom Animalia, differing from plants in certain typical characteristics such as capacity for locomotion. **2.** An animal organism other than a human. **3.** A brutish person. ▸ *adj.* **1.** Of or relating to animals. **2.** Relating to the physical as distinct from the spiritual nature of people: *animal instincts.*
an·i·mal·cule (ăn′ə-măl′kyo͞ol) ▸ *n.* A microscopic animal organism.
animal husbandry ▸ *n.* The care and breeding of domestic animals.
animal rights ▸ *pl.n.* The rights to humane treatment claimed on behalf of animals.
an·i·mate (ăn′ə-māt′) ▸ *v.* **-mat·ed, -mat·ing.** **1.** To give life to. **2.** To impart interest to. **3.** To fill with spirit. **4.** To produce (e.g., a cartoon) with the illusion of motion. ▸ *adj.* (ăn′ə-mĭt) **1.** Possessing life; living. **2.** Relating to animal life.
an·i·mat·ed (ăn′ə-mā′tĭd) ▸ *adj.* **1.** Spirited; lively. **2.** Designed so as to appear alive and moving. **—an′i·mat′ed·ly** *adv.*
animated cartoon ▸ *n.* A motion picture or television film consisting of a series of drawings, objects, or computer graphics photographed sequentially to simulate motion.
a·ni·ma·to (ä′nē-mä′tō) ▸ *adv. & adj. Mus.* In an animated or lively manner.
an·i·ma·tor (ăn′ə-mā′tər) ▸ *n.* One that animates, esp. an artist or technician who produces animated cartoons.
an·i·me (ăn′ə-mā′) ▸ *n.* A style of animation marked by colorful art, futuristic settings, and violence.
an·i·mism (ăn′ə-mĭz′əm) ▸ *n.* The belief that natural phenomena or inanimate objects possess spirits. **—an′i·mist** *n.* **—an′i·mis′tic** *adj.*
an·i·mos·i·ty (ăn′ə-mŏs′ĭ-tē) ▸ *n., pl.* **-ties.** Bitter hostility or open enmity.
an·i·mus (ăn′ə-məs) ▸ *n.* **1.** An attitude; disposition. **2.** Animosity.
an·i·on (ăn′ī′ən) ▸ *n.* A negatively charged ion, esp. one that migrates to an anode. **—an′i·on′ic** (-ŏn′ĭk) *adj.* **—an′i·on′i·cal·ly** *adv.*
an·ise (ăn′ĭs) ▸ *n.* **1.** An annual aromatic Mediterranean herb in the parsley family used as flavoring. **2.** Anise seed.
anise seed or **an·i·seed** (ăn′ĭ-sēd′) ▸ *n.* The seedlike fruit of the anise.
an·i·sette (ăn′ĭ-sĕt′, -zĕt′) ▸ *n.* A liqueur flavored with anise.
An·jou (ăn′zho͞o, -jo͞o) ▸ *n.* A variety of pear.

THESAURUS

angle[1] *v.* —*See* FISH (1).
angle[2] *n.* —*See* BEND, VIEWPOINT, WRINKLE (2).
angle *v.* —*See* BEND (2), BIAS (2), SWERVE.
angry *adj.* Feeling or showing anger ▸ annoyed, boiling, choleric, cross, enraged, exacerbated, fuming, furious, huffy, incensed, indignant, inflamed, infuriated, irate, ireful, irritated, livid, mad, nettled, peeved, rabid, raging, seething, vexed, wrathful. *Informal:* sore. *Slang:* het up. *Idioms:* at the boiling point, bent out of shape, fit to be tied, foaming (*or* frothing) at the mouth, hot under the collar, in a rage (*or* temper), in a towering rage, seeing red, up in arms.
angst *n.* —*See* ANXIETY (1).
anguish *n.* —*See* DISTRESS, GRIEF.
anguish *v.* —*See* DISTRESS, GRIEVE.
anguishing *adj.* —*See* TORMENTING.
angular *adj.* —*See* THIN (1).
anhydrous *adj.* —*See* DRY (1).
anima *n.* —*See* SPIRIT (2).
animal *adj.* —*See* SENSUAL (2).
animalism or **animality** *n.* —*See* SENSUALITY (1).
animalize *v.* —*See* CORRUPT.
animate *v.* **1.** To make alive ▸ enliven, quicken, vitalize, vivify. [*Compare* ENERGIZE, PROVOKE.] **2.** To make lively or animated ▸ brighten, enliven, light (up), perk up. —*See also* ELATE, ENCOURAGE (1), FIRE (1).
animate *adj.* —*See* ALIVE.
animated *adj.* —*See* ALIVE, CHEERFUL, LIVELY.
animating *adj.* —*See* INVIGORATING.
animation *n.* —*See* ELATION, ENERGY, SPIRIT (1).
animosity *n.* —*See* ANGER, ENMITY.
animus *n.* —*See* ENMITY.

An·ka·ra (ăng′kər-ə, äng′-) ▸ The capital of Turkey, in the W-central part.

ankh (ăngk) ▸ *n.* A cross shaped like a T with a loop at the top.

an·kle (ăng′kəl) ▸ *n.* **1.** The joint between the foot and the leg. **2.** The slender section of the leg above the foot.

an·kle·bone (ăng′kəl-bōn′) ▸ *n.* See **talus.**

an·klet (ăng′klĭt) ▸ *n.* **1.** An ornament worn around the ankle. **2.** A sock that reaches just above the ankle.

an·nals (ăn′əlz) ▸ *pl.n.* **1.** A chronological record of the events of successive years. **2.** A descriptive account or record; history. **3.** A periodical journal in which the records and reports of a learned field are compiled. **—an′nal·ist** *n.* **—an′nal·is′tic** *adj.*

An·nap·o·lis (ə-năp′ə-lĭs) ▸ The capital of MD, in the central part on an inlet of Chesapeake Bay SSE of Baltimore.

an·neal (ə-nēl′) ▸ *v.* **1.** To heat (glass or metal) and slowly cool it to toughen and reduce brittleness. **2.** To strengthen or harden.

an·ne·lid (ăn′ə-lĭd) ▸ *n.* Any of various worms with cylindrical segmented bodies, including the earthworm and leech.

an·nex (ə-nĕks′) ▸ *v.* **1.** To add, esp. to a larger thing. **2.** To incorporate (territory) into a larger existing political unit. ▸ *n.* (ăn′ĕks′) A building near or added on to a larger one. **—an′nex·a′tion** *n.* **—an′nex·a′tion·ist** *n.*

an·ni·hi·late (ə-nī′ə-lāt′) ▸ *v.* **-lat·ed, -lat·ing.** To destroy completely. **—an·ni′hi·la′tion** *n.*

an·ni·ver·sa·ry (ăn′ə-vûr′sə-rē) ▸ *n., pl.* **-ries.** The annually recurring date of a past event.

an·no Dom·i·ni (ăn′ō dŏm′ə-nī′, -nē) ▸ *adv.* In a specified year of the Christian era.

an·no·tate (ăn′ō-tāt′) ▸ *v.* **-tat·ed, -tat·ing.** To furnish (a literary work) with critical commentary or explanatory notes. **—an′no·ta′tion** *n.* **—an′no·ta′tive** *adj.* **—an′no·ta′tor** *n.*

an·nounce (ə-nouns′) ▸ *v.* **-nounced, -nounc·ing. 1.** To make known publicly. **2.** To proclaim the arrival of. **3.** To serve as an announcer (for). **—an·nounce′ment** *n.*

an·nounc·er (ə-noun′sər) ▸ *n.* One who announces, esp. a radio or television employee who provides program continuity and delivers announcements or commentaries.

an·noy (ə-noi′) ▸ *v.* To bother or irritate. **—an·noy′ing·ly** *adv.*

an·noy·ance (ə-noi′əns) ▸ *n.* **1.** The act of annoying or the state of being annoyed. **2.** A cause of vexation; nuisance.

an·nu·al (ăn′yo͞o-əl) ▸ *adj.* **1.** Recurring or done every year; yearly. **2.** Determined by a year: *an annual income.* **3.** *Bot.* Living or growing for only one year or season. ▸ *n.* **1.** A periodical published yearly; yearbook. **2.** *Bot.* An annual plant. **—an′nu·al·ly** *adv.*

annual ring ▸ *n.* The layer of wood, esp. in a tree, formed during a single year.

an·nu·i·tant (ə-no͞o′ĭ-tənt, -nyo͞o′-) ▸ *n.* One that receives an annuity.

an·nu·i·ty (ə-no͞o′ĭ-tē, -nyo͞o′-) ▸ *n., pl.* **-ties. 1.** The annual payment of an allowance or income. **2.** An investment on which one receives fixed payments for a lifetime or for a specified period.

an·nul (ə-nŭl′) ▸ *v.* **-nulled, -nul·ling.** To declare invalid, as a marriage or a law; nullify. **—an·nul′ment** *n.*

an·nu·lar (ăn′yə-lər) ▸ *adj.* Ring-shaped.

an·nu·lus (ăn′yə-ləs) ▸ *n., pl.* **-lus·es** or **-li** (-lī′). A ringlike figure, part, structure, or marking.

an·nun·ci·ate (ə-nŭn′sē-āt′) ▸ *v.* **-at·ed, -at·ing.** To announce; proclaim.

an·nun·ci·a·tion (ə-nŭn′sē-ā′shən) ▸ *n.* **1.** The act of announcing. **2.** An announcement; proclamation. **3. Annunciation** *Christianity* The angel Gabriel's announcement to the Virgin Mary of the Incarnation.

an·ode (ăn′ōd′) ▸ *n.* A positively charged electrode.

an·o·dize (ăn′ə-dīz′) ▸ *v.* **-dized, -diz·ing.** To coat (a metal) electrolytically with an oxide.

an·o·dyne (ăn′ə-dīn′) ▸ *n.* **1.** A medicine that relieves pain. **2.** A source of comfort. **—an′o·dyne** *adj.*

a·noint (ə-noint′) ▸ *v.* **1.** To apply oil or ointment to, esp. in a religious ceremony. **2.** To choose by or as if by divine intervention. **—a·noint′ment** *n.*

a·no·le (ə-nō′lē) ▸ *n.* Any of a genus of tropical American lizards having the ability to change color.

a·nom·a·ly (ə-nŏm′ə-lē) ▸ *n., pl.* **-lies. 1.** Deviation from the normal order, form, or rule. **2.** One that is peculiar, abnormal, or difficult to classify. **—a·nom′a·lis′tic** (-lĭs′tĭk) *adj.* **—a·nom′a·lous** *adj.*

a·non (ə-nŏn′) ▸ *adv. Archaic* At once; forthwith.

anon. ▸ *abbr.* anonymous

a·non·y·mous (ə-nŏn′ə-məs) ▸ *adj.* Having an unknown or unacknowledged name, authorship, or agency. **—an′o·nym′i·ty** (ăn′ə-nĭm′ĭ-tē) *n.* **—a·non′y·mous·ly** *adv.*

a·noph·e·les (ə-nŏf′ə-lēz′) ▸ *n.* A mosquito that transmits malaria to humans.

an·o·rak (ăn′ə-răk′) ▸ *n.* A parka.

an·o·rec·tic (ăn′ə-rĕk′tĭk) ▸ *adj.* **1.** Marked by or causing loss of appetite. **2.** Of or afflicted with anorexia nervosa. **—an′o·rec′tic** *n.*

an·o·rex·i·a (ăn′ə-rĕk′sē-ə) ▸ *n.* **1.** Loss of appetite, esp. as a result of disease. **2.** Anorexia nervosa.

anorexia ner·vo·sa (nûr-vō′sə) ▸ *n.* A psychophysiological disorder usu. occurring in teenage women that is marked

THESAURUS

annals *n.* A chronological record of past events ▸ archive, chronicle, historical record, history. [*Compare* STORY.]

annex *v.* *—See* ATTACH (2).

annex *n.* *—See* EXTENSION (2).

annihilate *v.* To destroy all traces of ▸ abolish, blot out, clear, eradicate, erase, expunge, exterminate, extinguish, extirpate, kill, liquidate, obliterate, remove, root (out *or* up), rub out, snuff out, stamp out, uproot, wipe out. *Idioms:* do away with, make an end of, put an end to, put to bed. [*Compare* ABOLISH, OVERWHELM.] *—See also* ABOLISH, DESTROY (1), MASSACRE.

annihilation *n.* Utter destruction ▸ eradication, extermination, extinction, extinguishment, extirpation, liquidation, obliteration. [*Compare* DEFEAT.] *—See also* ABOLITION, DESTRUCTION.

annotation *n.* *—See* COMMENTARY.

announce *v.* To bring to public notice or make known publicly ▸ advertise, annunciate, blaze, blazon, broadcast, bruit, declare, herald, noise (about *or* around), proclaim, promulgate, propagate, publish, trumpet. *Idioms:* issue a statement, make public (*or* known), spread the word. [*Compare* GOSSIP, REVEAL, SPREAD.] *—See also* PROCLAIM.

announcement *n.* The act of announcing ▸ annunciation, broadcasting, communication, declaration, notification, proclamation, promulgation, publication. *—See also* MESSAGE.

annoy *v.* To trouble the nerves or peace of mind of, especially by repeated vexations ▸ aggravate, bother, bug, chafe, disturb, exasperate, fret, gall, get (to), irk, irritate, molest, nettle, peeve, pester, provoke, put out, rankle, rile, ruffle, vex. *Idioms:* drive one bananas (*or* crazy *or* nuts), drive one up a wall, get in one's hair, get on one's nerves, get under one's skin, try one's patience. [*Compare* AGITATE, DISTRESS, INSULT.] *—See also* HARASS, OFFEND (1).

annoyance *n.* **1.** The act of annoying or the state of being annoyed ▸ aggravation, bother, botheration, bothering, exasperation, harassment, irritation, pestering, provocation, vexation. [*Compare* DISTRESS.] **2.** Something that annoys ▸ aggravation, besetment, bother, irritant, irritation, nuisance, pain, peeve, pest, plague, thorn, torment, trial, vexation. *Informal:* hassle, headache. *Idioms:* pain in the neck (*or* butt), thorn in one's side.

annoyed *adj.* *—See* ANGRY.

annoying *adj.* *—See* DISTURBING.

annul *v.* *—See* ABOLISH, CANCEL (1).

annular *adj.* *—See* ROUND (1).

annulment *n.* *—See* ABOLITION.

annulus *n.* *—See* CIRCLE (1).

annunciate *v.* *—See* ANNOUNCE.

annunciation *n.* *—See* ANNOUNCEMENT, MESSAGE.

anoint *v.* *—See* OIL.

anointed *adj.* *—See* DIVINE (2).

anomalous or **anomalistic** *adj.* *—See* ABNORMAL.

anomaly *n.* *—See* ABNORMALITY.

anonymity *n.* *—See* OBSCURITY.

anonymous *adj.* Having an unknown or withheld authorship or agency ▸ nameless, unacknowledged, uncredited, unidentified, unknown, unnamed, unsigned. [*Compare* OBSCURE.]

anorak *n.* *—See* COAT (1).

by an abnormal fear of becoming obese.
an·o·rex·ic (ăn′ə-rĕk′sĭk) ▸ *adj.* **1.** Afflicted with anorexia nervosa. **2.** Anorectic. **—an′o·rex′ic** *n.*
an·oth·er (ə-nŭth′ər) ▸ *adj.* **1.** One more; an additional: *another cup of coffee.* **2.** Different: *tried another method.* **3.** Some other: *costumes from another era.* ▸ *pron.* **1.** An additional or different one. **2.** One of an undetermined number.
an·swer (ăn′sər) ▸ *n.* **1.** A spoken or written reply, as to a question. **2.** A solution, as to a problem. **3.** An act in response. ▸ *v.* **1.** To reply (to). **2.** To be liable or accountable. **3.** To suffice. **4.** To correspond (to); match. **—an′swer·a·ble** *adj.* **—an′swer·a·bly** *adv.*
an·swer·ing machine (ăn′sər-ĭng) ▸ *n.* An electronic device for answering one's telephone and recording callers' messages.
ant (ănt) ▸ *n.* Any of various social insects usu. having wings only in the males and fertile females and living in complexly organized colonies.
ant– ▸ *pref.* Var. of **anti–.**
–ant ▸ *suff.* **1a.** Performing or promoting an action: *conversant.* **b.** In a state or condition: *expectant.* **2.** One that performs or promotes an action: *stimulant.*
ant·ac·id (ănt-ăs′ĭd) ▸ *adj.* Counteracting acidity, esp. of the stomach. ▸ *n.* A substance, such as sodium bicarbonate, that neutralizes acid.
an·tag·o·nism (ăn-tăg′ə-nĭz′əm) ▸ *n.* **1.** Hostility; enmity. **2.** The condition of being an opposing force.
an·tag·o·nist (ăn-tăg′ə-nĭst) ▸ *n.* **1.** One who opposes; adversary. **2.** The principal character in opposition to the protagonist or hero of a narrative or drama. **3.** *Physiol.* A muscle that counteracts the action of another muscle, the agonist. **—an·tag′o·nis′tic** *adj.* **—an·tag′o·nis′ti·cal·ly** *adv.*
an·tag·o·nize (ăn-tăg′ə-nīz′) ▸ *v.* **-nized, -niz·ing.** To incur the dislike of.
Ant·arc·ti·ca (ănt-ärk′tĭ-kə, -är′tĭ-) ▸ An ice-covered continent asymmetrically centered on the South Pole. **—Ant·arc′tic** *adj.*
Antarctic Circle ▸ The parallel of latitude (approx. 66°33′ S) that separates the South Temperate and South Frigid zones.
Antarctic Ocean ▸ The waters surrounding Antarctica, actually the S extensions of the Atlantic, Pacific, and Indian oceans.
An·tar·es (ăn-târ′ēz, -tăr′-) ▸ *n.* The brightest star in the constellation Scorpio.
an·te (ăn′tē) ▸ *n.* **1.** The stake each poker player puts into the pool before receiving a hand or before receiving new cards. **2.** A price to be paid, esp. as one's share. ▸ *v.* **-ted** or **-teed, -te·ing. 1.** To put up (one's stake) in poker. **2.** To pay (one's share).
ante– ▸ *pref.* **1.** Earlier: *antedate.* **2.** In front of: *anteroom.*
ant·eat·er (ănt′ē′tər) ▸ *n.* Any of several tropical American mammals that lack teeth and feed on ants and termites.
an·te·bel·lum (ăn′tē-bĕl′əm) ▸ *adj.* Of the period before the American Civil War.
an·te·ce·dent (ăn′tĭ-sēd′nt) ▸ *adj.* Going before; preceding. ▸ *n.* **1.** One that precedes. **2.** A preceding occurrence or cause. **3. antecedents** One's ancestors. **4.** *Gram.* The word, phrase, or clause to which a pronoun refers. **—an′te·cede′** *v.* **—an′te·ce′dence** *n.*
an·te·cham·ber (ăn′tē-chām′bər) ▸ *n.* An anteroom.
an·te·date (ăn′tĭ-dāt′) ▸ *v.* **-dat·ed, -dat·ing. 1.** To precede in time. **2.** To give a date earlier than the actual one.
an·te·di·lu·vi·an (ăn′tĭ-də-lo͞o′vē-ən) ▸ *adj.* **1.** Extremely old and antiquated. **2.** *Bible* Occurring before the Flood. **—an′te·di·lu′vi·an** *n.*
an·te·lope (ăn′tl-ōp′) ▸ *n., pl.* **-lope** or **-lopes. 1.** Any of various swift-running ruminant mammals of Africa and Asia, having long horns and a slender build. **2.** The pronghorn.
an·te me·rid·i·em (ăn′tē mə-rĭd′ē-əm) ▸ *adv. & adj.* Before noon.
an·ten·na (ăn-tĕn′ə) ▸ *n., pl.* **-ten·nae** (-tĕn′ē). **1.** One of the paired, flexible sensory organs on the head of an insect, myriapod, or crustacean. **2.** *pl.* **-nas.** An apparatus for sending or receiving electromagnetic waves.
an·te·pe·nult (ăn′tē-pē′nŭlt′) ▸ *n.* The third syllable from the end in a word, such as *te* in *antepenult.*
an·te·ri·or (ăn-tîr′ē-ər) ▸ *adj.* **1.** Placed before or in front. **2.** Prior in time.
an·te·room (ăn′tē-ro͞om′, -ro͝om′) ▸ *n.* An outer room that opens into another room, often used as a waiting room.
an·them (ăn′thəm) ▸ *n.* **1.** A hymn of praise or loyalty. **2.** A sacred choral composition.
an·ther (ăn′thər) ▸ *n.* The pollen-bearing part of the stamen.
ant·hill (ănt′hĭl′) ▸ *n.* A mound of earth formed by ants or termites in digging a nest.
an·thol·o·gy (ăn-thŏl′ə-jē) ▸ *n., pl.* **-gies.** A collection of selected writings. **—an·thol′o·gist** *n.* **—an·thol′o·gize′** *v.*
An·tho·ny (ăn′thə-nē) Saint (A.D. 250?–350?) ▸ Egyptian ascetic monk considered the founder of Christian monasticism.
Anthony, Susan Brownell (1820–1906) ▸ Amer. feminist leader and suffragist.
an·thra·cite (ăn′thrə-sīt′) ▸ *n.* A dense shiny coal that has a high carbon content. **—an′thra·cit′ic** (-sĭt′ĭk) *adj.*
an·thrax (ăn′thrăks′) ▸ *n.* An infectious, usu. fatal bacterial disease esp. of cattle and sheep, marked by skin ulcers and transmissible to humans.
anthropo– ▸ *pref.* Human: *anthropoid.*
an·thro·po·cen·tric (ăn′thrə-pə-sĕn′trĭk) ▸ *adj.* Interpreting reality in terms of human values and experience. **—an′thro·po·cen′trism** *n.*
an·thro·poid (ăn′thrə-poid′) ▸ *adj.* Resembling a human, as the great apes. ▸ *n.* A great ape, such as a gorilla.
an·thro·pol·o·gy (ăn′thrə-pŏl′ə-jē) ▸ *n.* The scientific study of the origin, culture, and development of humans. **—an′thro·po·log′i·cal** (-pə-lŏj′ĭ-kəl), **an′thro·po·log′ic** (-ĭk) *adj.* **—an′thro·pol′o·gist** *n.*
an·thro·po·mor·phism (ăn′thrə-pə-môr′fĭz′əm) ▸ *n.* Attribution of human characteristics to animals, inanimate objects, or natural phenomena. **—an′thro·po·mor′phic** *adj.* **—an′thro·po·mor′phize** *v.*
an·ti (ăn′tī, -tē) ▸ *n., pl.* **-tis.** One who is opposed. **—an′ti** *adj. & prep.*
anti– or **ant–** ▸ *pref.* **1a.** Opposite: *antiparticle.* **b.** Opposed to: *antinuclear.* **c.** Counteracting: *antibody.* **2.** Inverse: *antilogarithm.*
an·ti·a·bor·tion (ăn′tē-ə-bôr′shən, ăn′tī-) ▸ *adj.* Opposed to abortion. **—an′ti·a·bor′tion·ist** *n.*
an·ti·bal·lis·tic missile (ăn′tĭ-bə-lĭs′tĭk, ăn′tī-) ▸ *n.* A defensive missile designed to intercept and destroy a ballistic missile in flight.
an·ti·bi·ot·ic (ăn′tĭ-bī-ŏt′ĭk, ăn′tī-) ▸ *n.* A substance, such as penicillin or streptomycin, that destroys or inhibits the growth of microorganisms and is widely used to treat infectious diseases. **—an′ti·bi·ot′ic** *adj.*

THESAURUS

answer *v.* To speak or act in response, as to a question ▸ field, rejoin, reply, respond, retort, return, riposte. [*Compare* ACKNOWLEDGE.] *—See also* SATISFY (1), SOLVE (1).
answer *n.* **1.** Something spoken or written in return, as to a question or demand ▸ comeback, rejoinder, repartee, reply, response, return, retort, riposte. **2.** A solution, as to a problem ▸ determination, explanation, key, resolution, result, solution. [*Compare* DISCOVERY.]
answerability *n.* *—See* RESPONSIBILITY.
answerable *adj.* *—See* LIABLE (1).
antagonism *n.* *—See* ENMITY, OPPOSITION (1).
antagonist *n.* *—See* OPPONENT.
antagonistic *adj.* *—See* CONTRARY, OPPOSING, UNFAVORABLE (1).
antagonize *v.* *—See* ESTRANGE.
ante *n.* *—See* BET.
ante *v.* *—See* CONTRIBUTE (1).
antecede *v.* *—See* PRECEDE.
antecedence *n.* *—See* PRECEDENCE.
antecedent *adj.* *—See* ADVANCE, PAST.
antecedent *n.* That which produces an effect ▸ cause, determinant, occasion, reason. [*Compare* IMPACT, ORIGIN, STIMULUS.] *—See also* ANCESTOR (1), ANCESTOR (2).
antedate *v.* *—See* PRECEDE.
antediluvian *adj.* *—See* EARLY (1), OLD (1).
anterior *adj.* *—See* ADVANCE, PAST.
anthropic *adj.* *—See* HUMAN.
anthropoid *adj.* *—See* HUMAN, HUMANLIKE.
anthropomorphic or **anthropomorphous** *adj.* *—See* HUMANLIKE.

an·ti·bod·y (ăn′tĭ-bŏd′ē) ▸ *n.* A protein produced in the blood as an immune response to a specific antigen.
an·tic (ăn′tĭk) ▸ *n.* A ludicrous act or gesture. **—an′tic** *adj.*
an·ti·christ (ăn′tĭ-krīst′, ăn′tī-) ▸ *n.* **1.** An enemy of Christ. **2. Antichrist** *Bible* The antagonist expected to oppose Christ in the last days. **3.** A false Christ.
an·tic·i·pate (ăn-tĭs′ə-pāt′) ▸ *v.* **-pat·ed, -pat·ing. 1.** To foresee. **2.** To look forward to; expect. **3.** To act in advance to prevent; forestall. **—an·tic′i·pa′tion** *n.* **—an·tic′i·pa′tor** *n.* **—an·tic′i·pa·to′ry** (-pə-tôr′ē) *adj.*
an·ti·cler·i·cal (ăn′tē-klĕr′ĭ-kəl, ăn′tī-) ▸ *adj.* Opposed to the influence of the church in public life. **—an′ti·cler′i·cal·ism** *n.*
an·ti·cli·max (ăn′tē-klī′măks′, ăn′tī-) ▸ *n.* **1.** A decline viewed in disappointing contrast to previous events. **2.** Something commonplace that concludes a series of significant events. **—an′ti·cli·mac′tic** *adj.*
an·ti·cy·clone (ăn′tē-sī′klōn′, ăn′tī-) ▸ *n.* A system of winds spiraling outward from a high-pressure center. **—an′ti·cy·clon′ic** (-klŏn′ĭk) *adj.*
an·ti·de·pres·sant (ăn′tē-dĭ-prĕs′ənt, ăn′tī-) ▸ *n.* A drug used to treat mental depression. **—an′ti·de·pres′sive** *adj.*
an·ti·dote (ăn′tĭ-dōt′) ▸ *n.* **1.** An agent that counteracts a poison. **2.** Something that relieves or counteracts. **—an′ti·dot′al** *adj.*
An·tie·tam (ăn-tē′təm) ▸ A creek of N-central MD emptying into the Potomac R.; site of a Civil War battle (1862).
an·ti·freeze (ăn′tĭ-frēz′) ▸ *n.* A substance, such as ethylene glycol, mixed with another liquid to lower its freezing point.
an·ti·gen (ăn′tĭ-jən) ▸ *n.* A substance, such as a toxin, bacterium, or foreign cell, that when introduced into the body stimulates the production of an antibody. **—an′ti·gen′ic** (-jĕn′ĭk) *adj.* **—an′ti·ge·nic′i·ty** (-jə-nĭs′ĭ-tē) *n.*
An·ti·gua and Barbuda (ăn-tē′gə) ▸ A country in the N Leeward Is. of the Caribbean Sea, comprising the islands of **Antigua**, Barbuda, and Redonda. **—An·ti′guan** *adj. & n.*
an·ti·he·ro also **an·ti·he·ro** (ăn′tē-hîr′ō, ăn′tī-) ▸ *n., pl.* **-roes.** A fictional or dramatic character lacking traditional heroic qualities. **—an′ti·her·o′ic** (-hĭ-rō′ĭk) *adj.*
an·ti·her·o·ine or **an·ti-her·o·ine** (ăn′tē-hĕr′ō-ĭn, ăn′tī-) ▸ *n.* A woman protagonist who lacks traditional heroic qualities or who acts counter to traditional expectations of women.
an·ti·his·ta·mine (ăn′tē-hĭs′tə-mēn′, -mĭn) ▸ *n.* A drug used to counteract the physiological effects of histamine production in allergic reactions and colds. **—an′ti·his′ta·min′ic** (-mĭn′ĭk) *adj.*
an·ti·knock (ăn′tĭ-nŏk′) ▸ *n.* A substance added to gasoline to reduce engine knock.
An·til·les (ăn-tĭl′ēz) ▸ The islands of the West Indies except for the Bahamas, separating the Caribbean Sea from the Atlantic and divided into the **Greater Antilles** to the N and the **Lesser Antilles** to the E.
an·ti·lock (ăn′tē-lŏk′, ăn′tī-) ▸ *adj.* Of or being a motor vehicle braking system in which wheel speeds are electronically adjusted to prevent locking.
an·ti·log (ăn′tē-lôg′, -lŏg′, ăn′tī-) ▸ *n.* An antilogarithm.
an·ti·log·a·rithm (ăn′tē-lô′gə-rĭ*th*′əm, -lŏg′ə-, ăn′tī-) ▸ *n.* The number for which a given logarithm stands; e.g., where log *x* equals *y*, then *x* is the antilogarithm of *y*.
an·ti·ma·cas·sar (ăn′tē-mə-kăs′ər) ▸ *n.* A protective covering for the backs of chairs and sofas.
an·ti·mat·ter (ăn′tĭ-măt′ər, ăn′tī-) ▸ *n.* A hypothetical form of matter that is identical to physical matter with the exception that it is composed of antiparticles.
an·ti·mo·ny (ăn′tə-mō′nē) ▸ *n. Symbol* **Sb** A metallic element used in a wide variety of alloys, esp. with lead in battery plates, and in paints, semiconductors, and ceramics. At. no. 51.
an·ti·neu·tron (ăn′tē-no͞o′trŏn′, -nyo͞o′-, ăn′tī-) ▸ *n.* The antiparticle of the neutron.
an·ti·nov·el (ăn′tē-nŏv′əl, ăn′tī-) ▸ *n.* A fictional work that lacks traditional elements of the novel, such as coherent plot structure or realistic character development.
an·ti·nu·cle·ar (ăn′tē-no͞o′klē-ər, -nyo͞o′-, ăn′tī-) ▸ *adj.* Opposing the production or use of nuclear power or nuclear weaponry.
an·ti·ox·i·dant (ăn′tē-ŏk′sĭ-dənt, ăn′tī-) ▸ *n.* **1.** A substance that inhibits oxidation. **2.** A substance, such as vitamin E, thought to protect body cells from the damaging effects of oxidation.
an·ti·par·ti·cle (ăn′tē-pär′tĭ-kəl, ăn′tī-) ▸ *n.* A subatomic particle, such as a positron or antiproton, having the same mass, lifetime, and spin as the particle to which it corresponds but having the opposite electric charge and magnetic properties.
an·ti·pas·to (än′tē-päs′tō) ▸ *n., pl.* **-tos** or **-ti** (-tē). An appetizer usu. of assorted meats, cheeses, and vegetables.
an·tip·a·thy (ăn-tĭp′ə-thē) ▸ *n., pl.* **-thies. 1.** A strong aversion or repugnance. **2.** An object of aversion. **—an·tip′a·thet′ic** (-thĕt′ĭk), **an·tip′a·thet′i·cal** *adj.*
an·ti·per·son·nel (ăn′tē-pûr′sə-nĕl′, ăn′tī-) ▸ *adj.* Designed to cause death or injury rather than material damage.
an·ti·per·spi·rant (ăn′tē-pûr′spər-ənt, ăn′tī-) ▸ *n.* A preparation applied to the skin to decrease perspiration.
an·ti·phon (ăn′tə-fŏn′) ▸ *n.* A devotional composition sung responsively as part of a liturgy. **—an·tiph′o·nal** (-tĭf′ə-nəl) *adj.*
an·tiph·o·ny (ăn-tĭf′ə-nē) ▸ *n., pl.* **-nies. 1.** Responsive or antiphonal singing. **2.** An exchange, as of ideas or opinions.
an·ti·pode (ăn′tĭ-pōd′) ▸ *n.* A direct opposite. **—an·tip′o·dal** (-tĭp′ə-dəl) *adj.*
an·tip·o·des (ăn-tĭp′ə-dēz′) ▸ *pl.n.* **1.** Two places on diametrically opposite sides of the earth. **2.** *(takes sing. or pl. v.)* One that is the exact opposite of another.
an·ti·pope (ăn′tĭ-pōp′) ▸ *n.* One claiming to be pope in opposition to the one chosen by church law.
an·ti·pro·ton (ăn′tē-prō′tŏn′, ăn′tī-) ▸ *n.* The antiparticle of the proton.
an·ti·psy·chot·ic (ăn′tē-sī-kŏt′ĭk, ăn′tī-) ▸ *adj.* Counteracting the symptoms of psychotic disorders.
an·ti·py·ret·ic (ăn′tē-pī-rĕt′ĭk, ăn′tī-) ▸ *adj.* Reducing fever. ▸ *n.* A medication that reduces fever. **—an′ti·py·re′sis** (-rē′sĭs) *n.*
an·ti·quar·i·an (ăn′tĭ-kwâr′ē-ən) ▸ *adj.* **1.** Relating to the study or collecting of antiquities. **2.** Dealing in old or rare books. **—an′ti·quar′i·an** *adj. & n.*
an·ti·quar·y (ăn′tĭ-kwĕr′ē) ▸ *n., pl.* **-ies.** One who collects or deals in antiquities.
an·ti·quate (ăn′tĭ-kwāt′) ▸ *v.* **-quat·ed, -quat·ing.** To make obsolete. **—an′ti·qua′tion** *n.*
an·tique (ăn-tēk′) ▸ *adj.* **1.** Belonging to or made in an earlier period. **2.** Belonging to ancient times, esp. ancient Greece or Rome. ▸ *n.* An object considered valuable because of its age and artistry. ▸ *v.* **-tiqued, -tiqu·ing.** To give the appearance of an antique to. **—an·tique′ly** *adv.* **—an·tique′ness** *n.*
an·tiq·ui·ty (ăn-tĭk′wĭ-tē) ▸ *n., pl.* **-ties. 1.** Ancient times, esp. those before the Middle Ages. **2.** The quality of being old or ancient: *a carving of great antiquity.* **3.** often **antiquities** Something dating from ancient times.

THESAURUS

antic *n.* —*See* PRANK[1].
antic *adj.* —*See* ECCENTRIC.
anticipant *adj.* —*See* EXPECTANT.
anticipate *v.* —*See* EXPECT (1), FORESEE, PREVENT.
anticipated *adj.* —*See* DUE (2).
anticipation *n.* **1.** The condition of looking forward to something, especially with eagerness ▸ expectance, expectancy, expectation, hopefulness. *Idiom:* high hopes. [*Compare* DESIRE.] **2.** Something that is expected ▸ expectation, likelihood, promise, prospect. [*Compare* CHANCE, THEORY.]
anticipatory or **anticipative** *adj.* —*See* EXPECTANT.
anticlimax *n.* —*See* DISAPPOINTMENT (2).
antidotal *adj.* —*See* CURATIVE.
antidote *n.* —*See* CURE.
antipathetic *adj.* —*See* OFFENSIVE (1), OPPOSING.
antipathy *n.* —*See* ENMITY, HATE (1).
antipode *n.* —*See* OPPOSITE.
antipodean or **antipodal** *adj.* —*See* OPPOSITE.
antiquated *adj.* —*See* OLD-FASHIONED, OLD (1).
antique *adj.* —*See* OLD-FASHIONED, OLD (1), VINTAGE.
antiquity *n.* Ancient times ▸ ancient history, distant past, prehistory, protohistory, time immemorial, time out of mind. *Idiom:* mists of time. [*Compare* PAST.]

an·ti·re·jec·tion (ăn′tē-rĭ-jĕk′shən, ăn′tī-) ▸ *adj.* Preventing rejection of a transplanted tissue or organ.

an·ti·sat·el·lite (ăn′tē-săt′l-īt, ăn′tī-) ▸ *adj.* Directed against enemy satellites.

an·ti-Sem·ite (ăn′tē-sĕm′īt′, ăn′tī-) ▸ *n.* One who is prejudiced against Jews. **—an′ti-Se·mit′ic** (-sə-mĭt′ĭk) *adj.* **—an′ti-Sem′i·tism** (-sĕm′ĭ-tĭz′əm) *n.*

an·ti·sep·sis (ăn′tĭ-sĕp′sĭs) ▸ *n.* Destruction of disease-causing microorganisms to prevent infection.

an·ti·sep·tic (ăn′tĭ-sĕp′tĭk) ▸ *adj.* **1.** Relating to or producing antisepsis. **2.** Thoroughly clean; aseptic. **—an′ti·sep′tic** *n.* **—an′ti·sep′ti·cal·ly** *adv.*

an·ti·se·rum (ăn′tĭ-sîr′əm) ▸ *n., pl.* **-se·rums** or **-se·ra** (-sîr′ə). Serum containing antibodies that are specific for one or more antigens.

an·ti·smok·ing (ăn′tē-smō′kĭng, ăn′tī-) ▸ *adj.* Opposed to or prohibiting the smoking of tobacco, esp. in public.

an·ti·so·cial (ăn′tē-sō′shəl, ăn′tī-) ▸ *adj.* **1.** Shunning others; not sociable. **2.** Hostile to the established social order. **—an′ti·so′cial·ly** *adv.*

an·ti·theft (ăn′tē-thĕft′, ăn′tī-) ▸ *adj.* Designed to prevent theft.

an·tith·e·sis (ăn-tĭth′ĭ-sĭs) ▸ *n., pl.* **-ses** (-sēz′). **1.** Direct contrast; opposition. **2.** The direct opposite. **3.** The juxtaposition of contrasting ideas in parallel grammatical structures. **—an′ti·thet′i·cal** (ăn′tĭ-thĕt′ĭ-kəl), **an′ti·thet′ic** *adj.*

an·ti·tox·in (ăn′tē-tŏk′sĭn) ▸ *n.* An antibody formed in response to and capable of neutralizing a specific biological toxin.

an·ti·trust (ăn′tē-trŭst′, ăn′tī-) ▸ *adj.* Opposing or regulating business monopolies, such as trusts or cartels.

an·ti·tus·sive (ăn′tē-tŭs′ĭv, ăn′tī-) ▸ *adj.* Relieving or suppressing coughing. **—an′ti·tus′sive** *n.*

an·ti·vi·ral (ăn′tē-vī′rəl, ăn′tī-) ▸ *adj.* **1.** Destroying or inhibiting viral growth and reproduction. **2.** *Comp. Sci.* Designed to inactivate a virus.

an·ti·vi·rus (ăn′tē-vī′rəs, ăn′tī-) ▸ *n.* An antiviral software program.

ant·ler (ănt′lər) ▸ *n.* One of a pair of branched bony growths on the head of a deer. **—ant′lered** *adj.*

ant lion ▸ *n.* **1.** An insect which at maturity resembles a dragonfly. **2.** The large-jawed larva of the ant lion, which digs holes to trap ants for food.

an·to·nym (ăn′tə-nĭm′) ▸ *n.* A word meaning the opposite of another word. **—an′to·nym′ic** *adj.* **—an·ton′y·mous** (ăn-tŏn′ə-məs) *adj.* **—an·ton′y·my** *n.*

ant·sy (ănt′sē) ▸ *adj.* **-si·er, -si·est.** *Slang* Restless or fidgety.

a·nus (ā′nəs) ▸ *n., pl.* **a·nus·es.** The excretory opening at the lower end of the alimentary canal.

an·vil (ăn′vĭl) ▸ *n.* **1.** A heavy block of iron or steel with a smooth flat top on which metals are shaped by hammering. **2.** *Anat.* See **incus.**

anx·i·e·ty (ăng-zī′ĭ-tē) ▸ *n., pl.* **-ties.** **1.** A state or cause of uneasiness and apprehension; worry. **2.** *Psychiat.* Intense fear resulting from the anticipation of a threatening event.

anx·ious (ăngk′shəs, ăng′-) ▸ *adj.* **1.** Uneasy and apprehensive; worried. **2.** *Informal* Eager; desirous: *was anxious to see the new show.* **—anx′ious·ly** *adv.* **—anx′ious·ness** *n.*

an·y (ĕn′ē) ▸ *adj.* One, some, every, or all without specification: *Take any book you want. Are there any messages for me? Any child would love that.* ▸ *pron. (takes sing. or pl. v.)* Any one or more persons, things, or quantities. ▸ *adv.* To any degree; at all: *didn't feel any better.*

an·y·bod·y (ĕn′ē-bŏd′ē, -bŭd′ē) ▸ *pron.* Anyone. ▸ *n.* An important person: *Everybody who is anybody was there.*

an·y·how (ĕn′ē-hou′) ▸ *adv.* **1.** In whatever way or manner. **2.** Haphazardly. **3a.** In any case; at least. **b.** Nevertheless.

an·y·more (ĕn′ē-môr′) ▸ *adv.* **1a.** Any longer; still: *Do they make this model anymore?* **b.** From now on: *promised not to quarrel anymore.* **2.** *Regional* Nowadays.

an·y·one (ĕn′ē-wŭn′, -wən) ▸ *pron.* Any person.

an·y·place (ĕn′ē-plās′) ▸ *adv.* To, in, or at any place; anywhere.

an·y·thing (ĕn′ē-thĭng′) ▸ *pron.* Any object or matter at all. ***—idiom:*** **anything but** By no means: *anything but happy to do it.*

an·y·time (ĕn′ē-tīm′) ▸ *adv.* At any time.

an·y·way (ĕn′ē-wā′) ▸ *adv.* **1.** In any manner whatever. **2.** Nevertheless: *It was raining but they played the game anyway.*

an·y·where (ĕn′ē-hwâr′, -wâr′) ▸ *adv.* **1.** To, in, or at any place. **2.** To any extent at all.

A-one also **A-1** (ā′wŭn′) ▸ *adj.* *Informal* First-class; excellent.

a·or·ta (ā-ôr′tə) ▸ *n., pl.* **-tas** or **-tae** (-tē). The main trunk of the systemic arteries, carrying blood to all bodily organs except the lungs. **—a·or′tal, a·or′tic** *adj.*

a·ou·dad (ä′o͞o-dăd′, ou′dăd′) ▸ *n.* A wild sheep of N Africa.

a·pace (ə-pās′) ▸ *adv.* At a rapid pace; swiftly.

A·pach·e (ə-păch′ē) ▸ *n., pl.* **-e** or **-es.** **1.** A member of a Native American people of the SW US and N Mexico, now mainly in Arizona, New Mexico, and Oklahoma. **2.** Any of the Athabaskan languages of the Apache.

a·part (ə-pärt′) ▸ *adv.* **1.** Separately or at a distance in place, position, or time. **2.** In or into pieces: *split apart.* **3.** One from another: *I can't tell the twins apart.* **—a·part′ness** *n.*

a·part·heid (ə-pärt′hīt′, -hāt′) ▸ *n.* A formerly official policy of racial segregation practiced in the Republic of South Africa.

a·part·ment (ə-pärt′mənt) ▸ *n.* **1.** A room or suite designed as a residence. **2.** An apartment building.

apartment building ▸ *n.* A building divided into apartments.

ap·a·thy (ăp′ə-thē) ▸ *n.* **1.** Lack of interest or concern, esp. in important matters. **2.** Lack of emotion; impassiveness. **—ap′a·thet′ic** (-thĕt′ĭk) *adj.* **—ap′a·thet′i·cal·ly** *adv.*

a·pat·o·saur (ə-păt′ə-sôr′) or **a·pat·o·sau·rus** (ə-păt′ə-sôr′əs) ▸ *n.* A large herbivorous dinosaur of the Jurassic Period.

ape (āp) ▸ *n.* **1a.** A large tailless Old World primate such as the chimpanzee, gorilla, gibbon, and orangutan. **b.** A monkey. **2.** A mimic. **3.** *Informal* A clumsy person. ▸ *v.* **aped, ap·ing.** To mimic.

THESAURUS

antiseptic *adj.* —*See* CLEAN (1), STERILE (1).

antiseptic *n.* —*See* PURIFIER.

antithesis *n.* —*See* OPPOSITE, OPPOSITION (1).

antithetical *adj.* —*See* OPPOSITE.

antonym *n.* —*See* OPPOSITE.

antonymic or **antonymous** *adj.* —*See* OPPOSITE.

antsy *adj.* —*See* EDGY.

anxiety *n.* **1.** A troubled or anxious state of mind ▸ angst, anxiousness, apprehension, care, concern, concernment, disquiet, disquietude, distress, nervousness, stress, solicitude, unease, uneasiness, worriment, worry. [*Compare* AGITATION, FEAR, RESTLESSNESS.] **2.** An exaggerated concern ▸ complex, neurosis, phobia. *Informal:* hang-up. [*Compare* OBSESSION.]

anxious *adj.* In a state of anxiety, uneasiness, or emotional distress ▸ agitated, apprehensive, concerned, distraught, distressed, disturbed, impatient, nervous, overcome, overwrought, rattled, shaken, shaken-up, solicitous, stressed, troubled, uneasy, unnerved, unsettled, upset, worried. *Informal:* stressed-out. *Slang:* het up. *Idioms:* ill at ease, on tenterhooks. [*Compare* AFRAID, EAGER, EDGY.]

anxiousness *n.* —*See* ANXIETY (1).

anyway *adv.* —*See* STILL (1).

A-one or **A-1** *adj.* —*See* EXCELLENT.

apace *adv.* —*See* FAST.

apart *adv.* —*See* SEPARATELY.

apart *adj.* —*See* SOLITARY.

apartment *n.* An often rented living space in a building ▸ condominium, co-op, efficiency, flat, loft, pied-à-terre, rental, suite, studio, walk-up. *Informal:* condo.

apathetic *adj.* Lacking interest ▸ blasé, detached, disinterested, impassive, incurious, indifferent, lethargic, listless, phlegmatic, supine, unconcerned, uninterested, unresponsive. [*Compare* COLD, COOL, LANGUID.]

apathy *n.* Lack of emotion or interest ▸ aloofness, callousness, coldness, coolness, detachment, disinterest, impassiveness, impassivity, incuriosity, incuriousness, indifference, insensibility, insensibleness, insouciance, lassitude, lethargy, listlessness, nonchalance, phlegm, stolidity, stolidness, unconcern, uninterest, unresponsiveness.

ape *v.* —*See* IMITATE.

ape *n.* —*See* MIMIC, OAF.

Ap·en·nines (ăp′ə-nīnz′) ▸ A mountain system extending from NW Italy S to the Strait of Messina.
a·pé·ri·tif (ä-pĕr′ĭ-tēf′) ▸ *n.* An alcoholic drink taken as an appetizer.
ap·er·ture (ăp′ər-chər) ▸ *n.* **1.** An opening, such as a hole or slit. **2.** A usu. adjustable opening in an optical instrument, such as a camera, that limits the amount of light passing through a lens. **—ap′er·tur′al** *adj.*
a·pex (ā′pĕks) ▸ *n., pl.* **-es** or **a·pi·ces** (ā′pĭ-sēz′, ăp′ĭ-). The highest point; peak.
a·pha·sia (ə-fā′zhə) ▸ *n.* Partial or total loss of the ability to speak or comprehend spoken or written language, resulting from brain damage. **—a·pha′si·ac′** (-zē-ăk′) *n.* **—a·pha′sic** (-zĭk, -sĭk) *adj. & n.*
a·phe·li·on (ə-fē′lē-ən, ə-fēl′yən) ▸ *n., pl.* **-li·a** (-lē-ə). The point on the orbit of a celestial body that is farthest from the sun.
a·phid (ā′fĭd, ăf′ĭd) ▸ *n.* Any of various small, soft-bodied insects that feed by sucking sap from plants.
aph·o·rism (ăf′ə-rĭz′əm) ▸ *n.* **1.** A maxim; adage. **2.** A brief statement of a principle. **—aph′o·rist** *n.* **—aph′o·ris′tic** *adj.*
aph·ro·di·si·ac (ăf′rə-dē′zē-ăk′, -dĭz′ē-) ▸ *adj.* Arousing or intensifying sexual desire. ▸ *n.* An aphrodisiac food or drug.
Aph·ro·di·te (ăf′rə-dī′tē) ▸ *n. Gk. Myth.* The goddess of love and beauty.
a·pi·ar·y (ā′pē-ĕr′ē) ▸ *n., pl.* **-ies.** A place where bees are raised for their honey. **—a′pi·a·rist** (-ə-rĭst) *n.*
a·pi·ces (ā′pĭ-sēz′, ăp′ĭ-) ▸ *n.* Pl. of **apex.**
a·pi·cul·ture (ā′pĭ-kŭl′chər) ▸ *n.* The raising of bees. **—a′pi·cul′tur·al** *adj.* **—a′pi·cul′tur·ist** *n.*
a·piece (ə-pēs′) ▸ *adv.* To or for each one.
a·plomb (ə-plŏm′, ə-plŭm′) ▸ *n.* Self-confidence; poise.
ap·ne·a (ăp′nē-ə, ăp-nē′ə) ▸ *n.* Temporary absence or cessation of breathing.
APO ▸ *abbr.* Army Post Office
a·poc·a·lypse (ə-pŏk′ə-lĭps′) ▸ *n.* **1. Apocalypse** *Bible* The Book of Revelation. **2.** Great devastation; doom. **—a·poc′a·lyp′tic, a·poc′a·lyp′ti·cal** *adj.* **—a·poc′a·lyp′ti·cal·ly** *adv.*
A·poc·ry·pha (ə-pŏk′rə-fə) ▸ *n. (takes sing. or pl. v.)* **1.** *Bible* The 14 books of the Septuagint included in the Vulgate but considered uncanonical by some. See **Bible** table in Appendix. **2. apocrypha** Writings of questionable authenticity.
a·poc·ry·phal (ə-pŏk′rə-fəl) ▸ *adj.* **1.** Of questionable authorship or authenticity. **2.** Erroneous; fictitious. **3. Apocryphal** *Bible* Of the Apocrypha. **—a·poc′ry·phal·ly** *adv.*
ap·o·gee (ăp′ə-jē) ▸ *n.* **1.** The point in the orbit of the moon or of an artificial satellite most distant from the center of the earth. **2.** The farthest or highest point; apex.
a·po·lit·i·cal (ā′pə-lĭt′ĭ-kəl) ▸ *adj.* **1.** Having no interest in politics. **2.** Politically unimportant. **—a′po·lit′i·cal·ly** *adv.*
A·pol·lo (ə-pŏl′ō) ▸ *n.* **1.** *Gk. Myth.* The god of prophecy, music, medicine, and poetry. **2. apollo** *pl.* **-los.** A beautiful young man.
a·pol·o·get·ic (ə-pŏl′ə-jĕt′ĭk) also **a·pol·o·get·i·cal** (-ĭ-kəl) ▸ *adj.* Making an apology. ▸ *n.* A formal defense or apology. **—a·pol′o·get′i·cal·ly** *adv.*
ap·o·lo·gi·a (ăp′ə-lō′jē-ə, -jə) ▸ *n.* A formal defense or justification. **—a·pol′o·gist** (ə-pŏl′ə-jĭst) *n.*
a·pol·o·gize (ə-pŏl′ə-jīz′) ▸ *v.* **-gized, -giz·ing. 1.** To make an apology. **2.** To make a formal defense or justification.
a·pol·o·gy (ə-pŏl′ə-jē) ▸ *n., pl.* **-gies. 1.** A statement expressing regret or asking pardon for a fault or offense. **2.** A formal justification or defense. **3.** An inferior substitute.
ap·o·plex·y (ăp′ə-plĕk′sē) ▸ *n.* **1.** Sudden impairment of neurological function, esp. resulting from a cerebral hemorrhage; stroke. **2.** A fit of extreme anger; rage. **—ap′o·plec′tic** *adj.* **—ap′o·plec′ti·cal·ly** *adv.*
a·pos·ta·sy (ə-pŏs′tə-sē) ▸ *n., pl.* **-sies.** Abandonment of one's religious faith, political party, or cause. **—a·pos′tate** (-tāt′) *n. & adj.* **—a·pos′ta·tize** (-tə-tīz′) *v.*
a pos·te·ri·o·ri (ä′ pŏ-stîr′ē-ôr′ē, ā′) ▸ *adj.* Reasoning from particular facts to general principles; empirical.
a·pos·tle (ə-pŏs′əl) ▸ *n.* **1. Apostle** One of the 12 disciples chosen by Jesus to preach the gospel. **2.** One who pioneers a cause.
ap·os·tol·ic (ăp′ə-stŏl′ĭk) ▸ *adj.* **1.** Relating to an apostle. **2.** Relating to the teaching of the 12 Apostles. **3.** Papal.
a·pos·tro·phe[1] (ə-pŏs′trə-fē) ▸ *n.* The sign (') used to indicate omission of a letter or letters from a word, the possessive case, and the plurals of numbers, letters, and abbreviations.
a·pos·tro·phe[2] (ə-pŏs′trə-fē) ▸ *n.* A rhetorical device in which a speaker or writer addresses an absent person, an abstraction, or an inanimate object. **—ap′os·troph′ic** (ăp′ə-strŏf′ĭk) *adj.* **—a·pos′tro·phize** *v.*
a·poth·e·car·ies' measure (ə-pŏth′ĭ-kĕr′ēz) ▸ *n.* A system of liquid volume measure used in pharmacy.
apothecaries' weight ▸ *n.* A system of weights used in pharmacy and based on an ounce equal to 480 grains and a pound equal to 12 ounces.
a·poth·e·car·y (ə-pŏth′ĭ-kĕr′ē) ▸ *n., pl.* **-ies. 1.** A druggist; pharmacist. **2.** See **pharmacy** 2.
ap·o·thegm (ăp′ə-thĕm′) ▸ *n.* A proverb; maxim. **—ap′o·theg·mat′ic** (-thĕg-măt′ĭk) *adj.*
ap·o·them (ăp′ə-thĕm′) ▸ *n.* The perpendicular distance from the center of a regular polygon to any of its sides.
a·poth·e·o·sis (ə-pŏth′ē-ō′sĭs, ăp′ə-thē′ə-sĭs) ▸ *n., pl.* **-ses** (-sēz′). **1.** Exaltation to divine rank or stature; deification. **2.** An exalted or glorified example. **—a·poth′e·o·size′** *v.*
Ap·pa·la·chi·a (ăp′ə-lā′chē-ə, -chə, -lăch′ē-ə, -lăch′ə) ▸ A region of the E US including the Appalachian Mts.
Ap·pa·la·chi·an Mountains (ăp′ə-lā′chē-ən, -chən, -lăch′ē-ən, -lăch′ən) ▸ A mountain system of E North America extending SW from E Canada to central AL.
ap·pall (ə-pôl′) ▸ *v.* To fill with horror or dismay. **—ap·pall′ing·ly** *adv.*
ap·pa·loo·sa (ăp′ə-lo͞o′sə) ▸ *n.* A horse having a spotted rump.
ap·pa·rat·us (ăp′ə-răt′əs, -rā′təs) ▸ *n., pl.* **-us** or **-us·es. 1a.** The means by which a function or task is performed. **b.** A political organization or movement. **2a.** A machine or machinery. **b.** A group of materials or devices used for a particular purpose: *dental apparatus.* **3.** A system.
ap·par·el (ə-păr′əl) ▸ *n.* Clothing, esp. outer garments. ▸ *v.* **-eled, -el·ing** or **-elled, -el·ling.** To clothe or dress.
ap·par·ent (ə-păr′ənt, -pâr′-) ▸ *adj.* **1.** Readily seen; visible. **2.** Readily understood; obvious. **3.** Appearing as

THESAURUS

apéritif *n.* —*See* APPETIZER.
aperture *n.* —*See* HOLE (2).
apex *n.* —*See* CLIMAX, POINT (1).
aphonic *adj.* —*See* MUTE.
aphorism *n.* —*See* PROVERB.
aphoristic *adj.* —*See* PITHY.
aphrodisiac *adj.* —*See* EROTIC.
aping *n.* —*See* MIMICRY.
apish *adj.* —*See* IMITATIVE (1).
aplomb *n.* —*See* BALANCE (2), CONFIDENCE.
apocalypse *n.* —*See* REVELATION.
apocalypticist *n.* —*See* PESSIMIST (2).
apocryphal *adj.* —*See* FALSE, MYTHICAL.
apogee *n.* —*See* CLIMAX.
apologetic *adj.* —*See* SORRY.
apologia *n.* —*See* APOLOGY (1).
apologize *v.* —*See* DEFEND (2).
apology *n.* **1.** A statement that justifies or defends something, such as a past action or policy ▸ apologetic, apologia, defense, justification, plea, vindication. [*Compare* EXPLANATION.] **2.** A statement of acknowledgment expressing regret or asking pardon ▸ excuse, mea culpa, regrets. [*Compare* ACKNOWLEDGMENT.]
apoplexy *n.* —*See* SEIZURE (1).
apostasy *n.* —*See* DEFECTION.
apostate *n.* —*See* DEFECTOR.
apostatize *v.* —*See* DEFECT.
apostle *n.* A person doing religious or charitable work in a foreign country ▸ evangelist, missionary, missioner. [*Compare* CLERIC, REPRESENTATIVE.]
apothegm *n.* —*See* PROVERB.
apotheosis *n.* —*See* EXALTATION.
apotheosize *v.* —*See* EXALT.
appall *v.* —*See* DISGUST, DISMAY.
appalling *adj.* —*See* FEARFUL, GHASTLY (1), OUTRAGEOUS, TERRIBLE.
apparatus *n.* Something attached as a permanent part of something else ▸ fitting, fixture, installation. [*Compare* ATTACHMENT.] —*See also* DEVICE (1), GADGET, OUTFIT.
apparel *n.* —*See* DRESS (1).
apparel *v.* —*See* DRESS (1).
apparent *adj.* **1.** Readily seen, perceived, or understood ▸ clear, clear-

such but not necessarily so. **—ap·par′ent·ly** *adv.* **—ap·par′ent·ness** *n.*

ap·pa·ri·tion (ăp′ə-rĭsh′ən) ▸ *n.* **1.** A ghost. **2.** A sudden or unusual sight. **—ap′pa·ri′tion·al** *adj.*

ap·peal (ə-pēl′) ▸ *n.* **1.** An earnest request. **2.** An application to a higher authority: *an appeal to reason.* **3.** *Law* **a.** The transfer of a case from a lower to a higher court for a new hearing. **b.** A request for a new hearing. **4.** The power of attracting interest: *a city with appeal for tourists.* ▸ *v.* **1.** To make an earnest request, as for help. **2.** To have recourse. **3.** *Law* To make or apply for an appeal. **4.** To be attractive. **—ap·peal′a·ble** *adj.* **—ap·peal′er** *n.* **—ap·peal′ing·ly** *adv.*

ap·pear (ə-pîr′) ▸ *v.* **1.** To become visible. **2.** To come into existence. **3.** To seem. **4.** To seem likely. **5.** To come before the public. **6.** *Law* To present oneself before a court.

ap·pear·ance (ə-pîr′əns) ▸ *n.* **1.** The act of appearing. **2.** Outward aspect: *an untidy appearance.* **3.** A pretense.

ap·pease (ə-pēz′) ▸ *v.* **-peased, -peas·ing. 1.** To satisfy or relieve. **2.** To pacify (an enemy) by granting concessions. **—ap·peas′a·ble** *adj.* **—ap·pease′ment** *n.* **—ap·peas′er** *n.*

ap·pel·lant (ə-pĕl′ənt) ▸ *adj.* Appellate. ▸ *n.* One who appeals a court decision.

ap·pel·late (ə-pĕl′ĭt) ▸ *adj.* Empowered to hear judicial appeals.

ap·pel·la·tion (ăp′ə-lā′shən) ▸ *n.* A name or title.

ap·pend (ə-pĕnd′) ▸ *v.* **1.** To add as a supplement. **2.** To attach.

ap·pend·age (ə-pĕn′dĭj) ▸ *n.* **1.** Something attached to a larger entity. **2.** *Biol.* A subordinate external body part or organ, such as an arm or tail.

ap·pen·dec·to·my (ăp′ən-dĕk′tə-mē) ▸ *n., pl.* **-mies.** Surgical removal of the vermiform appendix.

ap·pen·di·ci·tis (ə-pĕn′dĭ-sī′tĭs) ▸ *n.* Inflammation of the vermiform appendix.

ap·pen·dix (ə-pĕn′dĭks) ▸ *n., pl.* **-dix·es** or **-di·ces** (-dĭ-sēz′). **1.** Supplementary material at the end of a book. **2.** *Anat.* The vermiform appendix.

ap·per·tain (ăp′ər-tān′) ▸ *v.* To belong as a part.

ap·pe·tite (ăp′ĭ-tīt′) ▸ *n.* **1.** A desire for food or drink. **2.** A strong wish or urge. **—ap′pe·ti′tive** *adj.*

ap·pe·tiz·er (ăp′ĭ-tī′zər) ▸ *n.* A food or drink served before a meal.

ap·pe·tiz·ing (ăp′ĭ-tī′zĭng) ▸ *adj.* Stimulating the appetite. **—ap′pe·tiz′ing·ly** *adv.*

ap·plaud (ə-plôd′) ▸ *v.* To express approval (of), esp. by clapping hands. **—ap·plaud′a·ble** *adj.* **—ap·plaud′er** *n.*

ap·plause (ə-plôz′) ▸ *n.* Approval expressed esp. by the clapping of hands.

ap·ple (ăp′əl) ▸ *n.* **1.** A deciduous tree having alternate white or pink flowers. **2.** The firm, edible, usu. rounded fruit of this tree. ***—idiom:* apple of (one's) eye** One that is treasured: *Her grandson is the apple of her eye.*

ap·ple·jack (ăp′əl-jăk′) ▸ *n.* Brandy distilled from hard cider.

ap·ple·sauce (ăp′əl-sôs′) ▸ *n.* **1.** Apples stewed to a pulp. **2.** *Slang* Nonsense.

ap·plet (ăp′lĭt) ▸ *n.* A computer application with limited features and memory requirements.

ap·pli·ance (ə-plī′əns) ▸ *n.* A device, esp. one operated by gas or electricity, designed for household use.

ap·pli·ca·ble (ăp′lĭ-kə-bəl, ə-plĭk′ə-) ▸ *adj.* That can be applied; appropriate. **—ap′pli·ca·bil′i·ty** *n.* **—ap′pli·ca·bly** *adv.*

ap·pli·cant (ăp′lĭ-kənt) ▸ *n.* One who applies.

ap·pli·ca·tion (ăp′lĭ-kā′shən) ▸ *n.* **1.** The act of applying. **2.** Something applied. **3.** The act of putting something to a special use. **4.** The capacity of being usable; relevance. **5.** Close attention; diligence: *shows application to her work.* **6a.** A request, as for employment. **b.** The form on which such a request is made. **7.** *Comp. Sci.* A computer program with a user interface. ▸ *adj.* also **applications** *Comp. Sci.* Of or being a program designed for a specific task.

ap·pli·ca·tor (ăp′lĭ-kā′tər) ▸ *n.* An instrument for applying something, such as glue.

ap·plied (ə-plīd′) ▸ *adj.* Put into practice; used: *applied physics.*

ap·pli·qué (ăp′lĭ-kā′) ▸ *n.* A decoration, as in needlework, cut from one material and applied to the surface of another. **—ap′pli·qué′** *v.*

THESAURUS

cut, conspicuous, crystal clear, distinct, evident, glaring, manifest, marked, noticeable, observable, obvious, patent, plain, pronounced, self-evident, unmistakable, visible. [*Compare* DEFINITE, PERCEPTIBLE, SHARP.] **2.** Appearing as such but not necessarily so ▸ external, ostensible, ostensive, outward, seeming, superficial. [*Compare* PROBABLE.]

apparently *adv.* On the surface ▸ evidently, externally, ostensibly, ostensively, outwardly, seemingly, superficially. *Idioms:* as far as one can tell (*or* see), on the face of it, to all appearances.

apparition *n.* *—See* APPEARANCE (2), GHOST.

appeal *v.* **1.** To make an earnest or urgent request ▸ adjure, ask (for), beg, beseech, crave, entreat, implore, petition, plead, pray, request, seek, solicit, sue, supplicate. **2.** To bring an appeal or request to the attention of ▸ address, apply, approach, petition. [*Compare* REQUEST.] *—See also* ATTRACT.

appeal for *v.* *—See* DEMAND (1).

appeal *n.* An earnest or urgent request ▸ application, entreaty, imploration, imploring, importunity, petition, plea, prayer, requisition, supplication. [*Compare* QUESTION.] *—See also* ATTRACTION, DEMAND (1).

appealer *n.* One that asks a higher authority for something, as a favor or redress ▸ appellant, petitioner, suitor.

appealing *adj.* *—See* ATTRACTIVE.

appear *v.* **1.** To come into view ▸ come out, emerge, issue, loom, materialize, show (up), turn up. *Idioms:* come to light, make (*or* put in) an appearance, meet the eye. **2.** To give the impression of being ▸ feel, look, seem, sound. *Idioms:* have all the earmarks of being, give the idea (*or* impression) of being, strike one as being. [*Compare* RESEMBLE.] *—See also* BEGIN.

appearance *n.* **1.** The way something or someone looks ▸ aspect, guise, look, looks, features, mien, semblance, stamp, visage. [*Compare* FACE.] **2.** The act of coming into sight ▸ apparition, emergence, manifestation, materialization, turning up. *Idiom:* coming into view. **3.** The act of arriving ▸ advent, arrival, coming. [*Compare* ENTRANCE[1].] **4.** The character projected or given by someone to the public ▸ image, impression. [*Compare* FAÇADE.]

appease *v.* *—See* PACIFY, SATISFY (2).

appellant *n.* One that asks a higher authority for something, as a favor or redress ▸ appealer, petitioner, suitor.

appellation or **appellative** *n.* *—See* NAME (1).

append *v.* *—See* ATTACH (1), ATTACH (2).

appendage *n.* *—See* ATTACHMENT.

appertain *v.* *—See* APPLY (2).

appetence or **appetency** *n.* *—See* DESIRE (1).

appetite *n.* A desire for food or drink ▸ hunger, ravenousness, stomach, taste, thirst. *Idioms:* a stomach for, the munchies. [*Compare* VORACITY.] *—See also* DESIRE (1), DESIRE (2).

appetizer *n.* A food or drink served before a meal ▸ amuse bouche, apéritif, hors d'oeuvre, starter, tapa. [*Compare* REFRESHMENT.]

appetizing *adj.* *—See* DELICIOUS.

applaud *v.* To express approval audibly, as by clapping ▸ cheer, clap, root. *Idioms:* give a big hand (*or* welcome), give an ovation, give someone a hand, put one's hands together. *—See also* PRAISE (1).

applause *n.* Approval expressed by clapping ▸ hand, ovation, plaudit. *Idiom:* round of applause. *—See also* PRAISE (1).

apple-polish *v.* *—See* FAWN.

apple-polisher *n.* *—See* SYCOPHANT.

apple-polishing *n.* *—See* FLATTERY.

applesauce *n.* *—See* NONSENSE.

appliance *n.* *—See* DEVICE (1).

applicability *n.* *—See* RELEVANCE.

applicable *adj.* *—See* RELEVANT, USABLE.

applicant *n.* A person who applies for or seeks something, such as a job or position ▸ aspirant, candidate, hopeful, petitioner, seeker. [*Compare* COMPETITOR.]

application *n.* A document used in applying, as for a job ▸ form, paper, sheet. *—See also* APPEAL, DILIGENCE, DUTY (2), EXERCISE (1), RELEVANCE.

ap·ply (ə-plī′) ▸ *v.* **-plied, -ply·ing. 1.** To bring into contact with something. **2.** To adapt for a special use. **3.** To put into action: *applied the brakes.* **4.** To devote (oneself or one's efforts) to something. **5.** To be relevant. **6.** To request or seek assistance, employment or admission.

ap·point (ə-point′) ▸ *v.* **1.** To select for an office or position. **2.** To fix or set by authority. **3.** To furnish; equip.

ap·point·ee (ə-poin′tē′, ăp′oin-) ▸ *n.* One who is appointed to an office or position.

ap·poin·tive (ə-poin′tĭv) ▸ *adj.* Relating to or filled by appointment: *an appointive office.*

ap·point·ment (ə-point′mənt) ▸ *n.* **1.** The act of appointing. **2.** The office or position to which one has been appointed. **3.** An arrangement for a meeting. **4. appointments** Furnishings; equipment.

Ap·po·mat·tox (ăp′ə-măt′əks) ▸ A town of S-central VA E of Lynchburg; site of Confederate surrender that ended the Civil War (1865).

ap·por·tion (ə-pôr′shən) ▸ *v.* To divide and assign by a plan; allot. **—ap·por′tion·ment** *n.*

ap·po·site (ăp′ə-zĭt) ▸ *adj.* Appropriate; relevant. **—ap′po·site·ly** *adv.*

ap·po·si·tion (ăp′ə-zĭsh′ən) ▸ *n.* **1.** *Gram.* A construction in which a noun or noun phrase is placed with another as an explanatory equivalent, e.g., *Copley* and *the painter* in *The painter Copley was born in Boston.* **2.** Placement side by side. **—ap′po·si′tion·al** *adj.*

ap·pos·i·tive (ə-pŏz′ĭ-tĭv) ▸ *adj.* Being in apposition. **—ap·pos′i·tive** *n.*

ap·praise (ə-prāz′) ▸ *v.* **-praised, -prais·ing.** To evaluate, esp. in an official capacity. **—ap·prais′a·ble** *adj.* **—ap·prais′al** *n.* **—ap·praise′ment** *n.* **—ap·prais′er** *n.*

ap·pre·cia·ble (ə-prē′shə-bəl) ▸ *adj.* Possible to estimate, measure, or perceive. **—ap·pre′cia·bly** *adv.*

ap·pre·ci·ate (ə-prē′shē-āt′) ▸ *v.* **-at·ed, -at·ing. 1.** To recognize the quality or magnitude of. **2.** To be fully aware of; realize. **3.** To be thankful for. **4.** To increase in value. **—ap·pre′ci·a′tion** *n.* **—ap·pre′ci·a′tor** *n.*

ap·pre·cia·tive (ə-prē′shə-tĭv, -shē-ā′tĭv) ▸ *adj.* Capable of or showing appreciation. **—ap·pre′cia·tive·ly** *adv.*

ap·pre·hend (ăp′rĭ-hĕnd′) ▸ *v.* **1.** To arrest. **2.** To understand. **3.** To perceive. **4.** To anticipate with anxiety; dread. **—ap′pre·hen′sion** *n.*

ap·pre·hen·sive (ăp′rĭ-hĕn′sĭv) ▸ *adj.* Fearful about the future. **—ap′pre·hen′sive·ly** *adv.*

ap·pren·tice (ə-prĕn′tĭs) ▸ *n.* **1.** One learning a trade under a skilled master. **2.** A beginner. ▸ *v.* **-ticed, -tic·ing.** To place or take on as an apprentice. **—ap·pren′tice·ship′** *n.*

ap·prise (ə-prīz′) ▸ *v.* **-prised, -pris·ing.** To give notice to; inform.

ap·proach (ə-prōch′) ▸ *v.* **1.** To come near or nearer (to). **2.** To come close to, as in appearance; approximate. **3.** To make a proposal or overtures to. **4.** To begin to deal with: *approached the task with dread.* ▸ *n.* **1.** The act of approaching. **2.** A fairly close resemblance. **3.** A means of reaching something; access. **—ap·proach′a·ble** *adj.*

ap·pro·ba·tion (ăp′rə-bā′shən) ▸ *n.* Approval; praise.

ap·pro·pri·ate (ə-prō′prē-ĭt) ▸ *adj.* Suited to a particular condition or use; fitting. ▸ *v.* (-āt′) **-at·ed, -at·ing. 1.** To set apart for a specific use. **2.** To take possession of, often without permission. **—ap·pro′pri·ate·ly** *adv.* **—ap·pro′pri·ate·ness** *n.* **—ap·pro′pri·a′tor** *n.*

ap·pro·pri·a·tion (ə-prō′prē-ā′shən) ▸ *n.* **1.** The act of appropriating. **2.** Something appropriated, esp. public funds set aside for a specific purpose.

ap·prov·al (ə-pro͞o′vəl) ▸ *n.* **1.** The act of approving. **2.** Approbation; sanction. **3.** Favorable regard. ***—idiom:* on approval** For inspection by a customer with no obligation to buy.

ap·prove (ə-pro͞ov′) ▸ *v.* **-proved, -prov·ing. 1a.** To consider

THESAURUS

apply *v.* **1.** To devote oneself or one's efforts ▸ address, bend, buckle down, concentrate, dedicate, devote, direct, exert, focus, give, turn. ***Idiom:*** keep one's nose to the grindstone. [*Compare* COMMIT, ENGAGE.] **2.** To be pertinent ▸ appertain, bear on (*or* upon), concern, pertain, refer, relate. ***Idioms:*** have a bearing on, have to do with. **3.** To bring an appeal or request to the attention of ▸ address, appeal, approach, petition. [*Compare* APPEAL, REQUEST.] **4.** To ask for employment, acceptance, or admission ▸ petition, put in. *—See also* ADMINISTER (3), RESORT, USE.

appoint *v.* To select for an office or position ▸ assign, designate, elect, make, name, nominate, tap. [*Compare* AUTHORIZE, CHOOSE.] *—See also* FURNISH.

appointment *n.* The act of appointing to an office or position ▸ assignment, designation, election, installation, naming, nomination. [*Compare* CONFIRMATION.] *—See also* ENGAGEMENT (1), POSITION (3).

apportion *v.* *—See* DISTRIBUTE.

apportionment *n.* *—See* DISTRIBUTION (1).

apposite *adj.* *—See* RELEVANT.

appositeness *n.* *—See* RELEVANCE.

appraisal or **appraisement** *n.* *—See* ESTIMATE (1).

appraise *v.* *—See* ESTIMATE (1), TEST (1).

appreciable *adj.* *—See* PERCEPTIBLE, UNDERSTANDABLE.

appreciate *v.* *—See* ENJOY, VALUE.

appreciation *n.* A being grateful ▸ acknowledgment, gratefulness, gratitude, indebtedness, thankfulness, thanks. *—See also* ESTEEM.

appreciative *adj.* Showing or feeling gratitude ▸ grateful, thankful. [*Compare* OBLIGED.]

apprehend *v.* *—See* ARREST, KNOW (1), PERCEIVE, UNDERSTAND (1).

apprehensible *adj.* *—See* UNDERSTANDABLE.

apprehension *n.* Intellectual hold ▸ comprehension, grasp, grip, hold, understanding. [*Compare* KNOWLEDGE.] *—See also* ANXIETY (1), ARREST, FEAR.

apprehensive *adj.* *—See* AFRAID, ANXIOUS.

apprentice *n.* *—See* BEGINNER, STUDENT.

apprise *v.* *—See* INFORM (1).

approach *v.* **1.** To come near in space or time ▸ close in on, converge on, gain on, near. ***Idioms:*** be around the corner, close the gap, come close to, come within spitting distance, draw near to (*or* nigh), stare one in the face. **2.** To bring an appeal or request to the attention of ▸ address, appeal, apply, petition. [*Compare* APPEAL, REQUEST.] *—See also* RIVAL, START (1).

approach *n.* **1.** A method used for making, doing, or accomplishing something ▸ attack, blueprint, course, design, game plan, idea, layout, line, means, modus operandi, plan, procedure, process, project, schema, scheme, strategy, tack, tactic, technique. ***Idiom:*** course of action. [*Compare* LINE, WAY.] **2.** The act or fact of coming near ▸ coming, convergence, imminence, nearness. [*Compare* ADVANCE, APPEARANCE.] *—See also* ADVANCES.

approachable *adj.* Easily approached ▸ accessible, responsive, welcoming. [*Compare* CONVENIENT.] *—See also* AMIABLE.

approaching *adj.* In the relatively near future ▸ coming, due, forthcoming, upcoming. ***Idioms:*** around the corner, on the horizon. [*Compare* CLOSE.] *—See also* IMMINENT.

approaching *adv.* *—See* APPROXIMATELY.

approbate *v.* *—See* PERMIT (2).

approbation *n.* *—See* ACCEPTANCE (2), PERMISSION, PRAISE (1).

approbatory *adj.* *—See* COMPLIMENTARY (1).

appropriate *adj.* Suitable for a particular person, condition, occasion, or place ▸ apt, becoming, befitting, comely, comme il faut, correct, decent, decorous, de rigueur, felicitous, fit, fitting, nice, proper, right, respectable, seemly, tailor-made. ***Idiom:*** cut out for. [*Compare* BENEFICIAL, OPPORTUNE, RELEVANT.] *—See also* CONVENIENT (1), JUST.

appropriate *v.* To set aside or apart for a specified purpose ▸ allocate, allot, assign, budget, designate, earmark, set apart, set aside. [*Compare* DISTRIBUTE.] *—See also* ADOPT, PLAGIARIZE, SEIZE (1).

appropriation *n.* Money or other resources granted for a particular purpose ▸ budget, grant, subsidy, subvention. *—See also* SEIZURE (2).

approval *n.* *—See* ACCEPTANCE (2), CONFIRMATION (1), PERMISSION.

approve *v.* To be favorably disposed toward ▸ countenance, favor, hold with. *Informal:* go for. ***Idioms:*** be in favor of, take kindly to, think highly

right or good. **b.** To express approval. **2.** To consent to formally; authorize.

ap·prox·i·mate (ə-prŏk′sə-mĭt) ▸ *adj.* **1.** Almost exact or correct. **2.** Very similar. ▸ *v.* (-māt′) **-mat·ed, -mat·ing.** To come close to; be nearly the same as. **—ap·prox′i·mate·ly** *adv.* **—ap·prox′i·ma′tion** *n.*

ap·pur·te·nance (ə-pûr′tn-əns) ▸ *n.* **1.** Something added to a more important thing; appendage. **2. appurtenances** Equipment used for a specific task. **—ap·pur′te·nant** *adj.*

Apr. ▸ *abbr.* April

a·pri·cot (ăp′rĭ-kŏt′, ā′prĭ-) ▸ *n.* **1.** A deciduous tree having clusters of white flowers. **2.** Its edible, yellow-orange, peachlike fruit.

A·pril (ā′prəl) ▸ *n.* The 4th month of the Gregorian calendar.

April Fools' Day ▸ *n.* Apr. 1, marked by the playing of practical jokes.

a pri·o·ri (ä′ prē-ôr′ē) ▸ *adj.* **1.** From a known or assumed cause to a necessarily related effect; deductive. **2.** Based on theory rather than on experiment. **—a′ pri·o′ri** *adv.*

a·pron (ā′prən) ▸ *n.* **1.** A garment worn over the front of the body to protect clothing. **2.** The paved strip around airport hangars and terminal buildings. **3.** The part of a theater stage in front of the curtain.

ap·ro·pos (ăp′rə-pō′) ▸ *adj.* Appropriate; pertinent. ▸ *adv.* **1.** Appropriately; opportunely. **2.** Incidentally. ▸ *prep.* With regard to.

apropos of ▸ *prep.* Speaking of.

apse (ăps) ▸ *n.* A semicircular or polygonal, usu. domed projection of a church. **—ap′si·dal** (ăp′sĭ-dəl) *adj.*

ap·sis (ăp′sĭs) ▸ *n., pl.* **-si·des** (-sĭ-dēz′). The nearest or farthest orbital point of a celestial body from a center of attraction.

apt (ăpt) ▸ *adj.* **1.** Exactly suitable; appropriate. **2.** Liable; likely: *The river is apt to flood in spring.* **3.** Quick to learn or understand: *an apt student.* **—apt′ly** *adv.* **—apt′ness** *n.*

apt. ▸ *abbr.* apartment

ap·ti·tude (ăp′tĭ-to͞od′, -tyo͞od′) ▸ *n.* **1.** A natural ability; talent. **2.** Quickness in learning. **3.** Suitability.

aq·ua (ăk′wə, ä′kwə) ▸ *n., pl.* **aq·uae** (ăk′wē, ä′kwī′) or **aq·uas.** **1.** Water. **2.** An aqueous solution. **3.** A light blue-green to green-blue. **—aq′ua** *adj.*

aq·ua·cul·ture (ăk′wə-kŭl′chər, ä′kwə-) ▸ *n.* The cultivation of fish or shellfish for food. **—aq′ua·cul′tur·ist** *n.*

aq·ua·ma·rine (ăk′wə-mə-rēn′, ä′kwə-) ▸ *n.* **1.** A transparent blue-green beryl, used as a gemstone. **2.** A pale to light greenish blue.

aq·ua·naut (ăk′wə-nôt′, ä′kwə-) ▸ *n.* One who works in scientific research conducted in underwater installations.

aq·ua·plane (ăk′wə-plān′, ä′kwə-) ▸ *n.* A board pulled over the water by a motorboat and ridden by a person standing up. **—aq′ua·plane′** *v.*

aqua re·gi·a (rē′jē-ə) ▸ *n.* A corrosive, fuming mixture of hydrochloric and nitric acids, used for testing metals and dissolving platinum and gold.

a·quar·i·um (ə-kwâr′ē-əm) ▸ *n., pl.* **-i·ums** or **-i·a** (-ē-ə). **1.** A water-filled enclosure in which living aquatic animals and plants are kept. **2.** A place for the public exhibition of live aquatic animals and plants.

A·quar·i·us (ə-kwâr′ē-əs) ▸ *n.* **1.** A constellation in the equatorial region of the Southern Hemisphere. **2.** The 11th sign of the zodiac. **—A·quar′i·an** *adj. & n.*

a·quat·ic (ə-kwăt′ĭk, ə-kwŏt′-) ▸ *adj.* **1.** Living or growing in, on, or near the water. **2.** Taking place in or on the water: *an aquatic sport.* **—a·quat′i·cal·ly** *adv.*

aq·ua·tint (ăk′wə-tĭnt′, ä′kwə-) ▸ *n.* **1.** A process of etching capable of producing tonal variations in the resulting print. **2.** An etching so made.

a·qua·vit (ä′kwə-vēt′) ▸ *n.* A strong clear liquor flavored with caraway seed.

aqua vi·tae (vī′tē) ▸ *n.* A strong liquor such as brandy.

aq·ue·duct (ăk′wĭ-dŭkt′) ▸ *n.* **1.** A conduit for transporting water from a remote source. **2.** A bridgelike structure supporting a conduit or canal passing over a river or low ground.

a·que·ous (ā′kwē-əs, ăk′wē-) ▸ *adj.* Relating to, containing, or dissolved in water; watery.

aqueous humor ▸ *n.* *Anat.* The clear, watery fluid in the chamber of the eye between the cornea and the lens.

aq·ui·fer (ăk′wə-fər, ä′kwə-) ▸ *n.* An underground layer of earth, gravel, or porous stone that yields water.

aq·ui·line (ăk′wə-līn′, -lĭn) ▸ *adj.* **1.** Of or like an eagle. **2.** Curved like an eagle's beak: *an aquiline nose.*

A·qui·nas (ə-kwī′nəs), Saint **Thomas** (1225–74) ▸ Italian Dominican theologian.

Ar ▸ The symbol for the element **argon.**

AR ▸ *abbr.* Arkansas

–ar ▸ *suff.* Of, relating to, or resembling: *polar.*

Ar·ab (ăr′əb) ▸ *n.* **1.** A member of a Semitic people of Arabia whose language and Islamic religion spread widely throughout the Middle East and N Africa from the 7th cent. **2.** A member of an Arabic-speaking people. **—Ar′ab** *adj.*

ar·a·besque (ăr′ə-bĕsk′) ▸ *n.* **1.** A complex design of interwined floral, foliate, and geometric figures. **2.** A short, whimsical composition esp. for the piano.

A·ra·bi·a (ə-rā′bē-ə) also **A·ra·bi·an Peninsula** (-bē-ən) ▸ A peninsula of SW Asia between the Red Sea and the Persian Gulf. **—A·ra′bi·an** *adj. & n.*

Arabian Desert ▸ A desert of E Egypt between the Nile Valley and the Red Sea.

Arabian Sea ▸ The NW part of the Indian Ocean between Arabia and western India.

Ar·a·bic (ăr′ə-bĭk) ▸ *adj.* Of or relating to Arabia, the Arabs, their language, or their culture. ▸ *n.* The Semitic language of the Arabs, spoken throughout the Middle East and parts of North Africa.

Arabic numeral ▸ *n.* One of the numerical symbols 1, 2, 3, 4, 5, 6, 7, 8, 9, or 0.

ar·a·ble (ăr′ə-bəl) ▸ *adj.* Fit for cultivation. **—ar′a·bil′i·ty** *n.*

a·rach·nid (ə-răk′nĭd) ▸ *n.* Any of various eight-legged arthropods such as spiders, scorpions, mites, and ticks. **—a·rach′ni·dan** *adj. & n.*

Ar·al Sea (ăr′əl) ▸ An inland sea between S Kazakhstan and NW Uzbekistan.

Ar·a·ma·ic (ăr′ə-mā′ĭk) ▸ *n.* A Semitic language widely used throughout SW Asia from the 7th cent. B.C. to the 7th cent. A.D. **—Ar′a·ma′ic** *adj.*

A·rap·a·ho (ə-răp′ə-hō′) ▸ *n., pl.* **-ho** or **-hos.** **1.** A member of a Native American people formerly of E Colorado and SE Wyoming, now in Oklahoma and Wyoming. **2.** Their Algonquian language.

Ar·a·rat (ăr′ə-răt′), **Mount** ▸ A massif of extreme E Turkey; traditional resting place of Noah's ark.

Ar·a·wak (ăr′ə-wäk′) ▸ *n., pl.* **-wak** or **-waks.** **1.** A member of an American Indian people formerly inhabiting parts of the West Indies, now chiefly in NE South America. **2.** The Arawakan language of the Arawak.

Ar·a·wa·kan (ăr′ə-wä′kən) ▸ *n., pl.* **-kan** or **-kans.** **1.** A family of South American Indian languages spoken in the Amazon Basin, NE South America, and formerly the Greater Antilles. **2.** A member of an Arawakan-speaking people. **—Ar′a·wa′kan** *adj.*

ar·bi·ter (är′bĭ-tər) ▸ *n.* One having the power to judge or decide.

ar·bi·trage (är′bĭ-träzh′) ▸ *n.* The purchase of securities on one market for resale on another to profit from a price

THESAURUS

(*or* well) of. [*Compare* ASSENT, VALUE.] —*See also* CONFIRM (3), PERMIT (2).

approving *adj.* —*See* FAVORABLE (2).

approximate *v.* —*See* ESTIMATE (2), RIVAL.

approximate *adj.* —*See* LOOSE (3).

approximately *adv.* Near to in quantity or amount ▸ about, almost, approaching, around, circa, nearly, practically, roughly, some. *Idioms:* for all practical purposes, for the most part, give or take a little, in all (*or* everything) but name, in the ballpark (*or* neighborhood) of, on the order of, pretty much. [*Compare* FAIRLY, USUALLY.]

approximation *n.* —*See* ESTIMATE (2).

appurtenance *n.* —*See* ATTACHMENT.

apropos *adj.* —*See* RELEVANT.

apt *adj.* —*See* APPROPRIATE, INCLINED.

aptitude *n.* —*See* INTELLIGENCE, TALENT.

aptness *n.* —*See* TALENT.

aquiver *adj.* —*See* TREMULOUS.

arbiter *n.* —*See* JUDGE (2).

discrepancy. **—ar′bi·trage′** *v.* **—ar′bi·tra·geur′** *n.*

ar·bit·ra·ment (är-bĭt′rə-mənt) ▸ *n.* **1.** The act of arbitrating. **2.** The judgment of an arbiter.

ar·bi·trar·y (är′bĭ-trĕr′ē) ▸ *adj.* **1.** Determined by chance, whim, or impulse. **2.** Not limited by law; despotic. **—ar′bi·trar′i·ly** (-trâr′ə-lē) *adv.* **—ar′bi·trar′i·ness** *n.*

ar·bi·trate (är′bĭ-trāt′) ▸ *v.* **-trat·ed, -trat·ing.** **1.** To judge or decide as an arbitrator. **2.** To submit (a dispute) to settlement by arbitration. **3.** To serve as an arbitrator. **—ar′bi·tra′tion** *n.*

ar·bi·tra·tor (är′bĭ-trā′tər) ▸ *n.* A person chosen to settle a dispute.

ar·bor (är′bər) ▸ *n.* A shady resting place in a garden or park.

ar·bo·re·al (är-bôr′ē-əl) ▸ *adj.* **1.** Of or like a tree. **2.** Living in trees.

ar·bo·re·tum (är′bə-rē′təm) ▸ *n., pl.* **-tums** or **-ta** (-tə). A place for the study and exhibition of trees.

ar·bor·vi·tae also **ar·bor vi·tae** (är′bər-vī′tē) ▸ *n.* Any of several evergreen trees having scalelike leaves and small cones.

ar·bo·vi·rus (är′bə-vī′rəs) ▸ *n.* Any of a large group of viruses that cause encephalitis and yellow fever.

ar·bu·tus (är-byo͞o′təs) ▸ *n.* The trailing arbutus.

arc (ärk) ▸ *n.* **1.** Something shaped like a curve or an arch. **2.** *Math.* A segment of a circle. **3.** A luminous electric discharge, as when a current jumps a gap between two electrodes. ▸ *v.* **arced** (ärkt), **arc·ing** (är′kĭng). To move in or form an arc.

ARC (ärk) ▸ *n.* A combination of symptoms first considered to be a precursor to AIDS, but now thought of as a milder form of the disease.

ar·cade (är-kād′) ▸ *n.* **1.** A series of arches supported by columns. **2.** A roofed passageway, esp. one with shops on one or both sides. **3.** A commercial establishment featuring rows of coin-operated games.

ar·ca·na (är-kā′nə) ▸ *pl.n.* Specialized knowledge or detail that is mysterious to the average person.

ar·cane (är-kān′) ▸ *adj.* Known to only a few; esoteric.

arch[1] (ärch) ▸ *n.* **1.** A structure forming the curved, pointed, or flat upper edge of an open space and supporting the weight above it. **2.** A structure, such as a monument, shaped like an inverted U. **3.** Something curved like an arch. ▸ *v.* **1.** To provide with an arch. **2.** To form or cause to form an arch. **—arched** *adj.*

arch[2] (ärch) ▸ *adj.* **1.** Chief; principal: *their arch foe.* **2.** Mischievous: *an arch glance.* **—arch′ly** *adv.* **—arch′ness** *n.*

arch– ▸ *pref.* **1.** Chief; highest: *archbishop.* **2.** Extreme: *archconservative.*

–arch ▸ *suff.* Ruler; leader: *matriarch.*

ar·chae·ol·o·gy or **ar·che·ol·o·gy** (är′kē-ŏl′ə-jē) ▸ *n.* The systematic study of past human life and culture by the examination of remaining material evidence. **—ar′chae·o·log′i·cal** (-ə-lŏj′ĭ-kəl), **ar′chae·o·log′ic** *adj.* **—ar′chae·ol′o·gist** *n.*

ar·cha·ic (är-kā′ĭk) ▸ *adj.* **1.** Belonging to an earlier time. **2.** No longer current; antiquated. **3.** Relating to words and language once in regular use but now rare and suggestive of an earlier style or period. **—ar·cha′i·cal·ly** *adv.*

ar·cha·ism (är′kē-ĭz′əm, -kā-) ▸ *n.* An archaic word, phrase, or style. **—ar′cha·ist** *n.*

arch·an·gel (ärk′ān′jəl) ▸ *n.* An angel of the next to the lowest order.

arch·bish·op (ärch-bĭsh′əp) ▸ *n.* A bishop of the highest rank. **—arch·bish′op·ric** *n.*

arch·dea·con (ärch-dē′kən) ▸ *n.* A church official, as in the Anglican Church, in charge of temporal and other affairs in a diocese. **—arch·dea′con·ate** (-kə-nĭt) *n.*

arch·di·o·cese (ärch-dī′ə-sĭs, -sēs′, -sēz′) ▸ *n.* The district under an archbishop's jurisdiction. **—arch′di·oc′e·san** (-ŏs′ĭ-sən) *adj.*

arch·duch·ess (ärch-dŭch′ĭs) ▸ *n.* A royal princess, esp. of imperial Austria.

arch·duke (ärch-do͝ok′, -dyo͝ok′) ▸ *n.* A royal prince, esp. of imperial Austria.

arch·en·e·my (ärch-ĕn′ə-mē) ▸ *n.* A principal enemy.

ar·che·ol·o·gy (är′kē-ŏl′ə-jē) ▸ *n.* Var. of **archaeology.**

arch·er (är′chər) ▸ *n.* One who shoots with a bow and arrow. **—arch′er·y** *n.*

ar·che·type (är′kĭ-tīp′) ▸ *n.* **1.** An original model or type after which other similar things are patterned; prototype. **2.** An ideal example of a type. **—ar′che·typ′al** (-tī′pəl), **ar′che·typ′ic** (-tĭp′ĭk), **ar′che·typ′i·cal** *adj.*

arch·fiend (ärch-fēnd′) ▸ *n.* **1.** A principal fiend. **2. Archfiend** Satan.

ar·chi·e·pis·co·pal (är′kē-ĭ-pĭs′kə-pəl) ▸ *adj.* Relating to an archbishop.

ar·chi·man·drite (är′kə-măn′drīt′) ▸ *n. Eastern Orthodox Ch.* A cleric ranking below a bishop.

Ar·chi·me·des (är′kə-mē′dēz) (287?–212 B.C.) ▸ Greek mathematician, engineer, and physicist. **—Ar′chi·me′de·an** *adj.*

ar·chi·pel·a·go (är′kə-pĕl′ə-gō′) ▸ *n., pl.* **-goes** or **-gos.** **1.** A large group of islands. **2.** A sea containing a large group of islands. **—ar′chi·pe·lag′ic** (-pə-lăj′ĭk) *adj.*

ar·chi·tect (är′kĭ-tĕkt′) ▸ *n.* **1.** One who designs and supervises the construction of buildings. **2.** One that plans or devises.

ar·chi·tec·ton·ics (är′kĭ-tĕk-tŏn′ĭks) ▸ *n. (takes sing. v.)* **1.** The science of architecture. **2.** Structural design, as in a musical work. **—ar′chi·tec·ton′ic** *adj.*

ar·chi·tec·ture (är′kĭ-tĕk′chər) ▸ *n.* **1.** The art and science of designing and erecting buildings. **2.** A style and method of design and construction: *Byzantine architecture.* **—ar′chi·tec′tur·al** *adj.*

ar·chi·trave (är′kĭ-trāv′) ▸ *n.* **1.** In classical architecture, the lowest part of an entablature, resting on top of a column. **2.** The molding around a door or window.

ar·chive (är′kīv′) ▸ *n.* **1.** often **archives** Public records of historical interest. **2.** A place for storing archives. **3.** *Comp. Sci.* **a.** A storage area, usu. on magnetic tape, for files not in active use. **b.** A file containing data compressed for ease of storage or transfer. **—ar·chi′val** *adj.* **—ar′chive** *v.*

ar·chi·vist (är′kə-vĭst, -kī′-) ▸ *n.* One who is in charge of archives.

arch·ri·val (ärch′rī′vəl) ▸ *n.* A principal rival.

arch·way (ärch′wā′) ▸ *n.* **1.** A passageway under an arch. **2.** An arch over a passageway.

–archy ▸ *suff.* Rule; government: *oligarchy.*

arc lamp ▸ *n.* An electric light in which a current traverses a gas between two incandescent electrodes.

arc·tic (ärk′tĭk, är′tĭk) ▸ *adj.* Extremely cold; frigid.

Arctic ▸ A region between the North Pole and the N timberlines of North America and Eurasia. **—Arctic** *adj.*

Arctic Archipelago ▸ A group of islands of Northwest Terrs., Canada, in the Arctic between North America and Greenland.

Arctic Circle ▸ The parallel of latitude (approx. 66°33' N)

THESAURUS

arbitrary *adj.* Based on individual judgment or discretion ▸ discretionary, judgmental, personal, subjective, unscientific. [*Compare* RANDOM.] *—See also* ABSOLUTE, CAPRICIOUS.

arbitrate *v.* To intervene between disputants in order to bring about an agreement ▸ mediate, moderate. [*Compare* CONFER.] *—See also* JUDGE.

arbitration *n.* *—See* COMPROMISE.

arbitrator *n.* *—See* JUDGE (2).

arc *v.* *—See* BEND (1).

arc *n.* *—See* BEND.

arcadian *adj.* Charmingly simple and carefree ▸ idyllic, pastoral. [*Compare* FRESH, STILL.] *—See also* COUNTRY.

arcane *adj.* *—See* MYSTERIOUS, OBSCURE (1).

arced *adj.* *—See* BENT.

arch[1] *v.* *—See* BEND (1), STOOP.

arch *n.* *—See* BEND.

arch[2] *adj.* *—See* MISCHIEVOUS.

archaic *adj.* *—See* OLD (1), OLD-FASHIONED.

arched *adj.* *—See* BENT.

archenemy *n.* *—See* OPPONENT.

archetypal or **archetypical** *adj.* *—See* IDEAL, ORIGINAL, TYPICAL.

archetype *n.* *—See* EPITOME, ORIGINAL.

archfiend *n.* *—See* FIEND.

architect *n.* *—See* ORIGINATOR.

archive *n.* A chronological record of past events ▸ annals, chronicle, historical record, history. [*Compare* STORY.] *—See also* DEPOSITORY.

arciform *adj.* *—See* BENT.

arctic *adj.* *—See* COLD (1).

that separates the North Temperate and North Frigid zones.
Arctic Ocean ▸ The waters around the North Pole between North America and Eurasia.
-ard or **-art** ▸ *suff.* One who habitually or excessively is in a certain state or performs a certain action: *drunkard.*
ar·dent (är′dnt) ▸ *adj.* **1.** Characterized by warmth of feeling; passionate. **2a.** Burning; fiery. **b.** Glowing; shining. **—ar′den·cy** *n.* **—ar′dent·ly** *adv.*
ar·dor (är′dər) ▸ *n.* **1.** Fiery intensity of feeling. **2.** Intense heat.
ar·du·ous (är′jo͞o-əs) ▸ *adj.* **1.** Strenuous; difficult. **2.** Full of hardships. **—ar′du·ous·ly** *adv.*
are[1] (är) ▸ *v.* 2nd pers. sing. and pl. and 1st and 3rd pers. pl. pr. indic. of **be.**
are[2] (âr, är) ▸ *n.* A unit of area equal to 100 square meters.
ar·e·a (âr′ē-ə) ▸ *n.* **1.** A portion of the space on a surface; region. **2.** A distinct part or section: *a storage area.* **3.** A division of experience or knowledge; field. **4.** *Math.* The extent of a planar region or of the surface of a solid.
area code ▸ *n.* A number used to distinguish broad geographic areas of telephone service, esp. a 3-digit number used in the US, Canada, and the Caribbean.
ar·e·a·way (âr′ē-ə-wā′) ▸ *n.* A small sunken area allowing access or light and air to basement doors or windows.
a·re·na (ə-rē′nə) ▸ *n.* **1.** A building for the presentation of sports events and spectacles. **2.** A sphere of activity: *the political arena.*
arena theater ▸ *n.* A theater in which the stage is at the center of the auditorium.
aren't (ärnt, är′ənt) ▸ Are not.
Ar·es (âr′ēz) ▸ *n.* *Gk. Myth.* The god of war.
Ar·gen·ti·na (är′jən-tē′nə) ▸ A country of SE South America E of Chile extending to S Tierra del Fuego, an island it shares with Chile. **—Ar′gen·tine′** (-tēn′, -tīn′), **Ar′gen·tin′e·an** (-tĭn′ē-ən) *adj. & n.*
ar·gon (är′gŏn′) ▸ *n.* *Symbol* **Ar** A colorless, odorless, inert gaseous element constituting approx. one percent of Earth's atmosphere and used in electric light bulbs, fluorescent tubes, and welding. At. no. 18.
ar·go·sy (är′gə-sē) ▸ *n., pl.* **-sies. 1.** A large merchant ship. **2.** A fleet of ships.
ar·got (är′gō, -gət) ▸ *n.* The specialized vocabulary of a group: *thieves' argot.*
ar·gu·a·ble (är′gyo͞o-ə-bəl) ▸ *adj.* **1.** Open to argument. **2.** Defensible in argument; plausible. **—ar′gu·a·bly** *adv.*
ar·gue (är′gyo͞o) ▸ *v.* **-gued, -gu·ing. 1.** To put forth reasons for or against; debate. **2.** To maintain by reasoning; contend. **3.** To give evidence of. **4.** To quarrel; dispute. **—ar′gu·er** *n.*
ar·gu·ment (är′gyə-mənt) ▸ *n.* **1.** A discussion of differing points of view; debate. **2.** A quarrel; dispute. **3a.** A course of reasoning aimed at demonstrating truth or falsehood. **b.** A persuasive reason: *The low rates are an argument for buying now.*
ar·gu·men·ta·tion (är′gyə-mĕn-tā′shən) ▸ *n.* The presentation and elaboration of an argument.
ar·gu·men·ta·tive (är′gyə-mĕn′tə-tĭv) ▸ *adj.* **1.** Given to arguing; disputatious. **2.** Of or marked by argument.
ar·gyle also **ar·gyll** (är′gīl′) ▸ *n.* **1.** A knitting pattern of varicolored, diamond-shaped areas on a solid background. **2.** A sock knit in this pattern.
a·ri·a (ä′rē-ə) ▸ *n.* A solo vocal piece with instrumental accompaniment, as in an opera.
-arian ▸ *suff.* Believer in; advocate of: *utilitarian.*
a·ri·a·ry (ä′rē-ä′rē) ▸ *n., pl.* **-ries.** See **currency** table in Appendix.
ar·id (ăr′ĭd) ▸ *adj.* **1.** Lacking in rainfall; dry. **2.** Lifeless; dull. **—a·rid′i·ty** (ə-rĭd′ĭ-tē), **ar′id·ness** *n.*
Ar·ies (âr′ēz, âr′ē-ēz′) ▸ *n.* **1.** A constellation in the Northern Hemisphere. **2.** The 1st sign of the zodiac.
a·right (ə-rīt′) ▸ *adv.* Properly; correctly.
ar·il (ăr′əl) ▸ *n.* A fleshy, usu. brightly colored cover of a seed.
a·rise (ə-rīz′) ▸ *v.* **a·rose** (ə-rōz′), **a·ris·en** (ə-rĭz′ən), **a·ris·ing. 1.** To get up: *arose from my chair.* **2.** To awaken and get up: *arose at dawn.* **3.** To move upward; ascend. **4.** To originate. **5.** To result or proceed.
ar·is·toc·ra·cy (ăr′ĭ-stŏk′rə-sē) ▸ *n., pl.* **-cies. 1.** A hereditary ruling class. **2.** Government by the nobility or by a privileged upper class. **3.** A group or class considered superior to others. **—a·ris′to·crat′** (ə-rĭs′tə-krăt′, ăr′ĭs-) *n.* **—a·ris′to·crat′ic** *adj.*
Ar·is·toph·a·nes (ăr′ĭ-stŏf′ə-nēz) (448?–388? B.C.) ▸ Athenian playwright.
Ar·is·tot·le (ăr′ĭ-stŏt′l) (384–322 B.C.) ▸ Greek philosopher.
a·rith·me·tic (ə-rĭth′mĭ-tĭk) ▸ *n.* The mathematics of integers, rational numbers, real numbers, or complex numbers under addition, subtraction, multiplication, and division. **—ar′ith·met′i·cal·ly** *adv.*
arithmetic mean ▸ *n.* The value obtained by dividing the sum of a set of quantities by the number of quantities in the set.
-arium ▸ *suff.* A place or device containing or associated with: *planetarium.*
Ariz. ▸ *abbr.* Arizona
Ar·i·zo·na (ăr′ĭ-zō′nə) ▸ A state of the SW US on the Mexican border. Cap. Phoenix. **—Ar′i·zo′nan** *adj. & n.*
ark (ärk) ▸ *n.* **1.** often **Ark** *Bible* The chest containing the Ten Commandments, carried by the Hebrews during their desert wanderings. **2.** often **Ark** *Judaism* The Holy Ark. **3.** *Bible* The boat built by Noah for the Flood. **4.** A shelter or refuge.
Ark. ▸ *abbr.* Arkansas
Ar·kan·sas (är′kən-sô′) ▸ A state of the S-central US. Cap. Little Rock. **—Ar·kan′san** (-kăn′zən) *adj. & n.*

THESAURUS

ardent *adj.* —*See* EAGER, ENTHUSIASTIC, HOT (1), PASSIONATE.
ardor *n.* —*See* ENTHUSIASM (1), LOVE (2), PASSION.
ardorless *adj.* —*See* FRIGID.
arduous *adj.* —*See* BURDENSOME, DIFFICULT (1), ROUGH (3).
arduously *adv.* —*See* HARD (2).
area *n.* **1.** A sphere of activity, experience, study, or interest ▸ arena, bailiwick, circle, department, domain, field, orbit, province, realm, scene, subject, terrain, territory, world. *Slang:* bag, turf. [*Compare* BRANCH, RANGE.] **2.** A part of the earth's surface ▸ belt, district, locality, neighborhood, quarter, region, section, sector, tract, zone. *Informal:* neck of the woods. [*Compare* FIELD, TERRITORY.] —*See also* LOCALITY, NEIGHBORHOOD (1), SIZE (1).
arena *n.* —*See* AREA (1).
argot *n.* —*See* DIALECT, LANGUAGE (2).
arguable *adj.* —*See* DEBATABLE.
argue *v.* **1.** To engage in a quarrel ▸ altercate, bicker, brawl, broil, caterwaul, contend, dispute, fall out, feud, fight, quarrel, quibble, row, spar, spat, squabble, tiff, wrangle. *Informal:* hassle, tangle. *Idioms:* be at loggerheads, cross swords, have a brush with, have it out, have words, lock horns, mix it up. [*Compare* CONFLICT, CONTEST, HAGGLE.] **2.** To put forth reasons for or against something, often excitedly ▸ contend, debate, dispute, moot, plead. *Idioms:* make a case for, put up an argument. [*Compare* APPEAL, ASSERT.] —*See also* ASSERT, DISCUSS, INDICATE (1).
argue into *v.* —*See* PERSUADE.
argument *n.* A discussion, often heated, in which a difference of opinion is expressed ▸ altercation, bicker, clash, contention, controversy, debate, difficulty, disagreement, dispute, falling out, feud, fight, fireworks, fracas, fuss, misunderstanding, polemic, quarrel, row, run-in, set-to, spat, squabble, tiff, words, wrangle. *Informal:* hassle, rhubarb, tangle. *Idiom:* war of words. [*Compare* CONFLICT, DELIBERATION, UPROAR.] —*See also* LOGIC, OBJECTION, REASON (1), SUBJECT.
argumentative *adj.* Given to or characterized by arguing ▸ cantankerous, combative, contentious, disagreeable, disputatious, eristic, factious, feisty, hotheaded, litigious, polemic, polemical, quarrelsome, scrappy. *Idiom:* having a chip on one's shoulder. [*Compare* AGGRESSIVE, ILL-TEMPERED.]
aria *n.* —*See* MELODY.
arid *adj.* —*See* DRY (2), DULL (1).
arise *v.* —*See* BEGIN, RISE (1), RISE (2), STAND (1), STEM.
aristocracy *n.* —*See* SOCIETY (1).
aristocratic *adj.* —*See* NOBLE.
arithmetic *n.* Arithmetic calculations ▸ computation, figures, numbers. [*Compare* ADDITION, CALCULATION.]
ark *n.* —*See* COVER (1).

arm¹ (ärm) ▸ *n.* **1.** An upper limb of the human body. **2.** A part similar to a human arm. **3.** A narrow extension: *an arm of the sea.* **4.** An administrative or functional branch. **—*idiom:* with open arms** In a warm, friendly manner. **—armed** *adj.*

arm² (ärm) ▸ *n.* **1.** A weapon. **2.** A branch of a military force. **3. arms a.** Warfare: *a call to arms.* **b.** Military service. **4. arms** Heraldic bearings or insignia. ▸ *v.* **1.** To equip with weapons. **2.** To prepare for or as if for war. **3.** To prepare (a weapon) for use. **—*idiom:* up in arms** Angry; indignant. **—armed** *adj.*

ar·ma·da (är-mä′də, -mā′-) ▸ *n.* A fleet of warships.

ar·ma·dil·lo (är′mə-dĭl′ō) ▸ *n., pl.* **-los.** A burrowing mammal of South America and S North America having bony, armorlike plates.

Ar·ma·ged·don (är′mə-gĕd′n) ▸ *n.* **1.** *Bible* The scene of a final battle between the forces of good and evil. **2.** A catastrophic confrontation.

ar·ma·ment (är′mə-mənt) ▸ *n.* **1.** The weapons and supplies of a military unit. **2.** often **armaments** All the military forces and equipment of a country.

ar·ma·ture (är′mə-cho͝or′, -chər) ▸ *n.* **1.** *Elect.* **a.** The rotating part of a dynamo, consisting of copper wire wound around an iron core. **b.** The moving part of an electromagnetic device such as a relay, buzzer, or loudspeaker. **c.** A piece of soft iron connecting the poles of a magnet. **2.** *Biol.* A protective covering or part. **3.** A supporting framework.

arm·chair (ärm′châr′) ▸ *n.* A chair with sides to support the arms or elbows.

armed forces ▸ *pl.n.* The military forces of a country.

Ar·me·ni·a (är-mē′nē-ə, -mēn′yə) ▸ A country of Asia Minor S of Georgia.

Ar·me·ni·an (är-mē′nē-ən, -mēn′yən) ▸ *n.* **1a.** A native or inhabitant of Armenia. **b.** A person of Armenian ancestry. **2.** The Indo-European language of the Armenians. **—Ar·me′ni·an** *adj.*

arm·ful (ärm′fo͝ol′) ▸ *n.* The amount that an arm or arms can hold.

arm·hole (ärm′hōl′) ▸ *n.* An opening in a garment for an arm.

ar·mi·stice (är′mĭ-stĭs) ▸ *n.* A temporary cessation of fighting by mutual consent; truce.

arm·let (ärm′lĭt) ▸ *n.* A band worn esp. on the upper arm for ornament or identification.

ar·moire (ärm-wär′) ▸ *n.* A large, often ornate cabinet or wardrobe.

ar·mor (är′mər) ▸ *n.* **1.** A protective or defensive covering for the body. **2a.** Metal plates covering a military vehicle or ship. **b.** The armored vehicles of an army. ▸ *v.* To cover with armor. **—ar′mored** *adj.*

ar·mo·ri·al (är-môr′ē-əl) ▸ *adj.* Of or relating to heraldry or heraldic arms.

ar·mor·y (är′mə-rē) ▸ *n., pl.* **-ies. 1.** A storehouse for arms and military equipment. **2.** An arms factory.

arm·pit (ärm′pĭt′) ▸ *n.* The hollow under the upper part of the arm at the shoulder.

arm·rest (ärm′rĕst′) ▸ *n.* A support for the arm.

Arm·strong (ärm′strông′), **Louis.** "Satchmo" (1900–71) ▸ Amer. jazz musician.

arm-twist (ärm′twĭst′) ▸ *v. Informal* To use pressure to persuade or to gain support.

ar·my (är′mē) ▸ *n., pl.* **-mies. 1a.** A large body of people organized for warfare. **b.** often **Army** The entire military land forces of a country. **2.** A large group of people organized for a cause. **3.** A multitude.

army ant ▸ *n.* Any of various rapacious tropical ants that move in swarms and subsist on other insects.

ar·ni·ca (är′nĭ-kə) ▸ *n.* **1.** A perennial herb having yellow flowers. **2.** A tincture of dried arnica flower heads used for bruises and sprains.

Ar·nold (är′nəld), **Benedict** (1741–1801) ▸ Amer. Revolutionary general and traitor.

a·ro·ma (ə-rō′mə) ▸ *n.* **1.** A quality that can be perceived by the olfactory sense. **2.** A usu. pleasant characteristic odor, as of a plant, spice, or food. **—ar′o·mat′ic** (ăr′ə-măt′ĭk) *adj.*

a·rose (ə-rōz′) ▸ *v.* P.t. of **arise.**

a·round (ə-round′) ▸ *adv.* **1a.** On or to all sides: *toys lying around.* **b.** In all directions. **2.** In a circle. **3.** In circumference. **4.** In succession. **5.** In the opposite direction: *wheeled around.* **6.** From one place to another: *wander around.* **7.** Nearby. **8.** Approximately: *weighed around 30 pounds.* ▸ *prep.* **1.** On all sides of. **2a.** About the circumference of. **b.** So as to encircle or surround. **3a.** Here and there within: *walked around the city.* **b.** Near. **4.** On or to the farther side of: *around the corner.* **5.** So as to bypass or avoid. **6.** Approximately at: *left around seven.*

a·rouse (ə-rouz′) ▸ *v.* **a·roused, a·rous·ing. 1.** To awaken from or as if from sleep. **2.** To stir up; excite: *aroused her curiosity.* **—a·rous′al** *n.*

ar·peg·gi·o (är-pĕj′ē-ō′, -pĕj′ō) ▸ *n., pl.* **-os. 1.** The playing of the tones of a chord in rapid succession rather than simultaneously. **2.** A chord played or sung in this manner.

ar·raign (ə-rān′) ▸ *v.* **1.** To call (an accused person) before a court to answer a charge. **2.** To denounce. **—ar·raign′ment** *n.*

ar·range (ə-rānj′) ▸ *v.* **-ranged, -rang·ing. 1.** To put into a specific order or relation. **2.** To plan: *arrange a picnic.* **3.** To agree about; settle. **4.** To reset (music) for other instruments or voices. **—ar·range′ment** *n.* **—ar·rang′er** *n.*

ar·rant (ăr′ənt) ▸ *adj.* Utter; thoroughgoing: *an arrant fool.*

ar·ras (ăr′əs) ▸ *n.* **1.** A tapestry. **2.** A curtain or wall hanging.

ar·ray (ə-rā′) ▸ *v.* **1.** To place in an orderly arrangement. **2.** To dress in finery; adorn. ▸ *n.* **1.** An orderly arrangement. **2.** An impressively large number. **3.** Splendid attire; finery. **4.** *Math.* An arrangement of quantities in rows and columns. **5.** *Comp. Sci.* An arrangement of memory elements in one or more planes.

THESAURUS

arm *n.* —*See* BRANCH (1), BRANCH (3), EXTENSION (2).
  arm *v.* —*See* GIRD.

armada *n.* A group of warships operating under one command ▸ fleet, flotilla.

armistice *n.* —*See* TRUCE.

armpit *n.* —*See* PIT[1].

army *n.* —*See* CROWD.

aroma *n.* **1.** The quality of something that may be perceived by the olfactory sense ▸ odor, scent, smell. [*Compare* FRAGRANCE, STENCH.] **2.** A distinctive yet intangible quality ▸ atmosphere, flavor, savor, smack. [*Compare* QUALITY.] —*See also* FRAGRANCE.

aromatic *adj.* —*See* FRAGRANT, SPICY.

aromatize *v.* To fill with a pleasant odor ▸ perfume, scent.

around *adv.* —*See* APPROXIMATELY, BACKWARD.
  around *adj.* —*See* ALIVE.

around-the-clock *adj.* —*See* CONTINUAL.

arouse *v.* To induce or elicit a reaction or emotion ▸ agitate, awake, awaken, kindle, raise, rouse, stir (up), waken. [*Compare* PROVOKE.] —*See also* FIRE (1), WAKE[1].

arraign *v.* —*See* ACCUSE.

arraigner *n.* A person who accuses ▸ accuser, denouncer, indicter, recriminator.

arraignment *n.* —*See* ACCUSATION.

arrange *v.* **1.** To put into a deliberate order ▸ array, codify, collocate, deploy, dispose, marshal, methodize, order, organize, range, regiment, regulate, sort, systemize, systematize. [*Compare* CLASSIFY, LINE.] **2.** To plan the details or arrangements of ▸ blueprint, lay out, map (out), organize, plan, prepare, schedule, set out (*or* up), work out. *Idiom:* get (*or* put) into shape. [*Compare* DESIGN, DRAFT.] —*See also* COMPROMISE, HARMONIZE (2), SETTLE (1), SETTLE (2).

arrangement *n.* **1.** The act or condition of being arranged ▸ alignment, allotment, assortment, categorization, classification, codification, deployment, disposal, disposition, distribution, format, formation, grouping, harmonization, layout, lineup, orchestration, order, ordering, organization, positioning, ranking, sequence, setup. **2.** The way in which one is placed or arranged ▸ attitude, pose, position, posture. —*See also* AGREEMENT (1), COMPROMISE, SYSTEM.

arrangements *n.* Steps taken in preparation for an undertaking ▸ accommodations, plans, preparations, provisions.

arrant *adj.* —*See* UTTER[2].

array *v.* —*See* ARRANGE (1), DRESS UP.
  array *n.* An impressive or ostentatious exhibition ▸ display, manifestation, pageant, panoply, parade, pomp, show, spectacle. —*See also* ATTIRE, GROUP.

ar·rears (ə-rîrz′) ▸ *pl.n.* **1.** An overdue debt. **2.** The state of being behind in fulfilling obligations: *an account in arrears.* **—ar·rear′age** *n.*

ar·rest (ə-rĕst′) ▸ *v.* **1.** To stop; check. **2.** To seize and hold by legal authority. **3.** To capture; engage: *arrested my attention.* ▸ *n.* **1.** The act of stopping or the condition of being stopped. **2a.** The act of detaining in legal custody. **b.** The state of being so detained: *under arrest.* **—ar·rest′er, ar·res′tor** *n.*

ar·rest·ing (ə-rĕs′tĭng) ▸ *adj.* Attracting and holding the attention; striking.

ar·rhyth·mi·a (ə-rĭth′mē-ə) ▸ *n.* An irregularity in the force or rhythm of the heartbeat.

ar·ri·val (ə-rī′vəl) ▸ *n.* **1.** The act of arriving. **2.** One that arrives or has arrived.

ar·rive (ə-rīv′) ▸ *v.* **-rived, -riv·ing. 1.** To reach a destination. **2.** To come eventually: *The day of reckoning has arrived.* **3.** To achieve success or recognition.

ar·ro·gant (ăr′ə-gənt) ▸ *adj.* Unpleasantly or disdainfully self-important; haughty. **—ar′ro·gance** *n.* **—ar′ro·gant·ly** *adv.*

ar·ro·gate (ăr′ə-gāt′) ▸ *v.* **-gat·ed, -gat·ing.** To take or claim for oneself without right. **—ar′ro·ga′tion** *n.* **—ar′ro·ga′tive** *adj.*

ar·row (ăr′ō) ▸ *n.* **1.** A straight thin shaft with a pointed head and often stabilizing feathers, meant to be shot from a bow. **2.** Something, such as a directional symbol, shaped like an arrow.

ar·row·head (ăr′ō-hĕd′) ▸ *n.* The pointed, removable striking tip of an arrow.

ar·row·root (ăr′ō-ro͞ot′, -ro͝ot′) ▸ *n.* **1.** An edible starch obtained from the rhizomes of a tropical American plant. **2.** This plant or its rhizome.

ar·roy·o (ə-roi′ō) ▸ *n., pl.* **-os.** A deep gully cut by an intermittent stream.

ar·se·nal (är′sə-nəl) ▸ *n.* **1.** A place for the storage, manufacture, or repair of arms and ammunition. **2.** A stock or supply, esp. of weapons.

ar·se·nic (är′sə-nĭk) ▸ *n. Symbol* **As** A highly poisonous metallic element used in insecticides, weed killers, solid-state doping agents, and various alloys. At. no. 33.

ar·son (är′sən) ▸ *n.* The crime of willfully setting fire to buildings or other property. **—ar′son·ist** *n.*

art[1] (ärt) ▸ *n.* **1a.** Creative or imaginative activity, esp. the expressive arrangement of elements within a medium. **b.** Works, such as paintings or poetry, resulting from such activity. **2.** A branch of artistic activity, such as musical composition, using a special medium and technique. **3.** The aesthetic values of an artist. **4.** Any of various disciplines, such as the humanities, that do not rely on the scientific method. **5.** A craft or trade and its methods. **6.** Contrivance; cunning. **7.** A practical skill; knack.

art[2] (ərt; ärt *when stressed*) ▸ *v. Archaic* 2nd pers. sing. pr. indic. of **be**.

-art ▸ *suff.* Var. of **-ard.**

art dec·o (dĕk′ō) ▸ *n.* A decorative style of the period 1925–40, marked by geometric designs and bold colors.

ar·te·fact (är′tə-făkt′) ▸ *n.* Var. of **artifact.**

Ar·te·mis (är′tə-mĭs) ▸ *n. Gk. Myth.* The virgin goddess of the hunt and the moon.

ar·te·ri·o·scle·ro·sis (är-tîr′ē-ō-sklə-rō′sĭs) ▸ *n.* A chronic disease in which thickening and hardening of the arterial walls impair blood circulation. **—ar·te′ri·o·scle·rot′ic** (-rŏt′ĭk) *adj.*

ar·ter·y (är′tə-rē) ▸ *n., pl.* **-ies. 1.** Any of a branching system of muscular tubes that carry blood away from the heart. **2.** A major transportation route into which local routes flow. **—ar·te′ri·al** (-tîr′ē-əl) *adj.*

ar·te·sian well (är-tē′zhən) ▸ *n.* A deep well in which water rises to the surface by internal hydrostatic pressure.

art·ful (ärt′fəl) ▸ *adj.* **1.** Exhibiting art or skill. **2.** Deceitful; cunning; crafty. **—art′ful·ly** *adv.* **—art′ful·ness** *n.*

ar·thri·tis (är-thrī′tĭs) ▸ *n.* Inflammation of a joint or joints. **—ar·thrit′ic** (-thrĭt′ĭk) *adj.*

arthro– or **arthr–** ▸ *pref.* Joint: *arthropod.*

ar·thro·pod (är′thrə-pŏd′) ▸ *n.* Any of numerous invertebrates, including the insects, crustaceans, and arachnids, characterized by an exoskeleton, a segmented body, and paired, jointed limbs.

ar·thros·co·py (är-thrŏs′kə-pē) ▸ *n., pl.* **-pies.** Endoscopic examination of a joint, such as the knee. **—ar′thro·scop′ic** (-skŏp′ĭk) *adj.*

Ar·thur (är′thər) ▸ *n.* A legendary British hero, said to have been king of the Britons in the 6th cent. A.D. who held court at Camelot. **—Ar·thu′ri·an** (-tho͝or′ē-ən) *adj.*

Arthur, Chester Alan (1829–86) ▸ The 21st US President (1881–85).

ar·ti·choke (är′tĭ-chōk′) ▸ *n.* **1.** A thistlelike plant having large heads of bluish flowers. **2.** The edible, unopened flower head of this plant.

ar·ti·cle (är′tĭ-kəl) ▸ *n.* **1.** An individual element of a class; item. **2.** A section in a written document. **3.** A nonfictional composition or essay in a publication. **4.** *Gram.* Any of a class of words, such as *a* or *the,* used to signal nouns and to specify their application.

ar·tic·u·lar (är-tĭk′yə-lər) ▸ *adj.* Of a joint or joints.

ar·tic·u·late (är-tĭk′yə-lĭt) ▸ *adj.* **1.** Endowed with speech. **2.** Composed of meaningful syllables or words. **3.** Using or characterized by clear, expressive language. **4.** *Anat.* Jointed. ▸ *v.* (är-tĭk′yə-lāt′) **-lat·ed, -lat·ing. 1.** To pronounce distinctly; enunciate. **2.** To utter (a speech sound). **3.** To express in words. **4.** To fit together; unify.

THESAURUS

arrears or **arrearage** *n.* —*See* DEBT (1), DEBT (2).

arrest *v.* To take into custody as a prisoner ▸ apprehend, seize. *Informal:* nab, pick up. *Slang:* bust, collar, cuff, haul up, pinch, pull in, run in. *Idiom:* take charge (*or* hold) of. [*Compare* CATCH, TAKE.] —*See also* GRIP, STOP (2).

arrest *n.* A seizing and holding by law ▸ apprehension, seizure. *Slang:* bust, collar, pickup, pinch. [*Compare* CATCH.] —*See also* DETENTION.

arresting *adj.* —*See* NOTICEABLE.

arrival *n.* **1.** The act of arriving ▸ advent, appearance, coming. [*Compare* ENTRANCE[1].] **2.** One that arrives ▸ comer, newcomer, visitor. [*Compare* ADDITION, COMPANY.] —*See also* ACCOMPLISHMENT.

arrive *v.* **1.** To come to a particular place ▸ breeze in, check in, come, drop in, get in, make it, pop in, pull in, reach, roll in (*or* up), show up, turn up. *Slang:* blow in. ***Idioms:*** arrive (*or* come) onto the scene, make (*or* put in) an appearance, make the scene. **2.** To gain success ▸ get ahead, get on, rise, succeed. *Idioms:* go far, go places, make good, make it. —*See also* HAPPEN (1).

arrive at *v.* —*See* ACCOMPLISH.

arrogance *n.* The quality of being arrogant ▸ braggodocio, disdainfulness, haughtiness, hauteur, hubris, insolence, loftiness, lordliness, overbearingness, pomposity, pompousness, presumption, pride, pridefulness, priggishness, proudness, self-importance, self-satisfaction, smugness, superciliousness, superiority. [*Compare* EGOTISM, IMPUDENCE.]

arrogant *adj.* Overly convinced of one's own superiority and importance ▸ disdainful, haughty, high-and-mighty, hubristic, insolent, lofty, lordly, overbearing, overweening, prideful, priggish, proud, self-important, self-satisfied, smug, supercilious, superior. *Informal:* high-hat, snooty, swell-headed. ***Idioms:*** full of oneself, on one's high horse. [*Compare* DICTATORIAL, EGOTISTIC, POMPOUS, SNOBBISH.]

arrogate *v.* —*See* SEIZE (1).

arrogation *n.* —*See* SEIZURE (2).

art *n.* Deceitful cleverness ▸ artfulness, artifice, cleverness, craft, craftiness, cunning, deceitfulness, deviousness, disingenuousness, foxiness, guile, shrewdness, slyness, wiliness. [*Compare* DECEIT, DISHONESTY, STEALTH.] —*See also* ABILITY (1), BUSINESS (2).

artery *n.* —*See* VESSEL (2).

artful *adj.* Deceitfully clever ▸ calculating, crafty, cunning, designing, double-dealing, foxy, guileful, scheming, sharp, shrewd, sly, tricky, wily. [*Compare* SHREWD, STEALTHY, UNDERHAND.] —*See also* DEXTEROUS.

artfulness *n.* —*See* ART.

article *n.* —*See* ELEMENT (2), ITEM, OBJECT (1).

article of faith *n.* —*See* DOCTRINE.

articulacy or **articulateness** *n.* —*See* ELOQUENCE.

articulate *adj.* —*See* ELOQUENT, ORAL.

articulate *v.* —*See* COMBINE (1), PRONOUNCE, SAY.

articulation *n.* —*See* EXPRESSION (1), VOICING.

5. *Anat.* To unite by or form a joint. **—ar·tic′u·late·ly** *adv.* **—ar·tic′u·late·ness, ar·tic′u·la′tion** *n.* **—ar·tic′u·la′tor** *n.*

ar·ti·fact also **ar·te·fact** (är′tə-făkt′) ▸ *n.* An object, such as a tool, made by human craft.

ar·ti·fice (är′tə-fĭs) ▸ *n.* **1.** A crafty expedient; stratagem. **2.** Deception; trickery. **3.** Cleverness; ingenuity.

ar·ti·fi·cial (är′tə-fĭsh′əl) ▸ *adj.* **1.** Made by humans rather than occurring in nature. **2.** Made in imitation of something natural. **3.** Not genuine: *an artificial smile.* **—ar′ti·fi′ci·al′i·ty** (-ē-ăl′ĭ-tē) *n.* **—ar′ti·fi′cial·ly** *adv.*

artificial insemination ▸ *n.* Introduction of semen into the vagina or uterus without sexual contact.

artificial intelligence ▸ *n.* The ability of a computer to perform activities normally thought to require intelligence.

artificial life ▸ *n.* The simulation of biological phenomena through computer models, robotics, or biochemistry.

artificial respiration ▸ *n.* A procedure to restore respiration in a person who has stopped breathing by forcing air into and out of the lungs in a rhythmic fashion.

ar·til·ler·y (är-tĭl′ə-rē) ▸ *n.* **1.** Large-caliber weapons, such as cannon, operated by crews. **2.** Troops armed with artillery.

ar·ti·san (är′tĭ-zən, -sən) ▸ *n.* A skilled manual worker. **—ar′ti·san·ship′** *n.*

art·ist (är′tĭst) ▸ *n.* **1.** One who practices any of the fine or performing arts, as painting or music. **2.** One whose work shows skill. **—ar·tis′tic** *adj.* **—ar·tis′ti·cal·ly** *adv.*

ar·tiste (är-tēst′) ▸ *n.* A public performer, esp. a singer or dancer.

art·ist·ry (är′tĭ-strē) ▸ *n.* Artistic ability, quality, or craft.

art·less (ärt′lĭs) ▸ *adj.* **1.** Without cunning; guileless. **2.** Simple; natural. **3.** Lacking art; crude. **—art′less·ly** *adv.* **—art′less·ness** *n.*

artsy ▸ *adj.* **-sier, -siest.** Var. of **arty.**

art·y (är′tē) or **art·sy** (ärt′sē) ▸ *adj.* **-i·er, -i·est** or **-si·er, -si·est.** *Informal* Affectedly artistic. **—art′i·ly** *adv.* **—art′i·ness** *n.*

A·ru·ba (ə-ro͞o′bə) ▸ An island and autonomous territory of the Netherlands in the Lesser Antilles N of the Venezuela coast.

a·ru·gu·la (ə-ro͞o′gə-lə) ▸ *n.* See **rocket**[2].

ar·um (ăr′əm, âr′-) ▸ *n.* Any of several Old World plants having arrowhead-shaped leaves.

–ary ▸ *suff.* Of or relating to: *reactionary.*

Ar·y·an (âr′ē-ən, ăr′-) ▸ *n.* **1.** See **Indo-Iranian. 2.** A member of the people who spoke Proto-Indo-European. **3.** A member of a people speaking an Indo-European language. **4.** In Nazism, a non-Jewish Caucasian, esp. one of Nordic type. **—Ar′y·an** *adj.*

as (ăz; əz *when unstressed*) ▸ *adv.* **1.** To the same extent or degree; equally. **2.** For instance: *large carnivores, as the bear or lion.* ▸ *conj.* **1.** To the same degree or quantity that: *as sweet as sugar.* **2.** In the same way that: *Think as I think.* **3.** At the same time that; while. **4.** Since; because. **5.** Though: *Trite as it sounds, it's true.* **6.** *Informal* That: *I don't know as I can.* ▸ *pron.* That; which; who: *I received the same grade as you did.* ▸ *prep.* **1.** In the role, capacity, or function of: *acting as a mediator.* **2.** In a manner similar to; the same as. **—*idioms:* as is** *Informal* Just the way it is. **as it were** In a manner of speaking.

As ▸ The symbol for the element **arsenic.**

as·a·fet·i·da (ăs′ə-fĕt′ĭ-də) ▸ *n.* A brownish, bitter, foul-smelling resin.

ASAP ▸ *abbr.* as soon as possible

as·bes·tos (ăs-bĕs′təs, ăz-) ▸ *n.* An incombustible, chemical-resistant, fibrous mineral used for fireproofing and electrical insulation.

as·bes·to·sis (ăs′bĕs-tō′sĭs, ăz′-) ▸ *n.* A progressive lung disease caused by prolonged inhalation of asbestos particles.

as·cend (ə-sĕnd′) ▸ *v.* **1a.** To go or move upward; rise. **b.** To climb: *ascend the stairs.* **2.** To succeed to; occupy: *ascended the throne.*

as·cen·dan·cy also **as·cen·den·cy** (ə-sĕn′dən-sē) ▸ *n.* Decisive advantage; domination.

as·cen·dant also **as·cen·dent** (ə-sĕn′dənt) ▸ *adj.* **1.** Inclining or moving upward. **2.** Dominant; superior. ▸ *n.* The position or state of being dominant.

as·cen·sion (ə-sĕn′shən) ▸ *n.* **1.** The act or process of ascending. **2. Ascension** *Christianity* The bodily rising of Jesus into heaven on the 40th day after his Resurrection.

as·cent (ə-sĕnt′) ▸ *n.* **1.** The act of rising upward. **2.** An upward slope.

as·cer·tain (ăs′ər-tān′) ▸ *v.* To discover through investigation. **—as′cer·tain′a·ble** *adj.*

as·cet·ic (ə-sĕt′ĭk) ▸ *n.* One who leads a life of austerity, esp. for religious reasons. **—as·cet′ic** *adj.* **—as·cet′i·cism** (-ĭ-sĭz′əm) *n.*

a·scor·bic acid (ə-skôr′bĭk) ▸ *n.* A vitamin, $C_6H_8O_6$, found in citrus fruits and leafy green vegetables and used to prevent scurvy; vitamin C.

as·cot (ăs′kət) ▸ *n.* A broad scarf knotted so that its ends are laid flat upon each other.

as·cribe (ə-skrīb′) ▸ *v.* **-cribed, -crib·ing.** To attribute to a specified cause, source, or origin. **—as·crib′a·ble** *adj.* **—as·crip′tion** (-skrĭp′shən) *n.*

–ase ▸ *suff.* Enzyme: *amylase.*

a·sep·tic (ə-sĕp′tĭk, ā-) ▸ *adj.* Free of pathogenic microorganisms. **—a·sep′sis** *n.*

a·sex·u·al (ā-sĕk′sho͞o-əl) ▸ *adj.* **1.** Having no sex or sex organs; sexless. **2.** Not involving sex organs or the union of sex cells. **3.** Lacking interest in or desire for sex. **—a·sex′u·al·ly** *adv.*

as for ▸ *prep.* With regard to.

ash[1] (ăsh) ▸ *n.* **1.** The grayish-white to black powdery residue of combustion. **2.** *Geol.* Pulverized particulate matter ejected by volcanic eruption. **3. ashes** Ruins. **4. ashes** Human remains, esp. after cremation.

ash[2] (ăsh) ▸ *n.* **1.** A deciduous ornamental or timber tree. **2.** The strong elastic wood of this tree.

THESAURUS

artifice *n.* —*See* ART, TRICK (1).

artificial *adj.* **1.** Made by humans, often in imitation of something else ▸ ersatz, imitation, manmade, manufactured, mock, pretend, simulated, synthetic. *Informal:* pretend. [*Compare* COUNTERFEIT, FAKE.] **2.** Not genuine or sincere ▸ affected, contrived, feigned, insincere, phony, pretended, stagy, studied. *Slang:* phony-baloney. [*Compare* POMPOUS.]

artificiality *n.* —*See* AFFECTATION, INSINCERITY.

artisan *n.* —*See* MAKER.

artistic *adj.* Relating to or appreciative of the arts ▸ aesthetic, creative. *Informal:* artsy, arty. —*See also* INVENTIVE.

artless *adj.* Free from guile, cunning, or deceit ▸ guileless, ingenuous, innocent, naive, natural, simple, unaffected, unsophisticated, unstudied, unworldly. [*Compare* FRANK, GENUINE, INNOCENT.] —*See also* RUSTIC.

artlessness *n.* The absence of guile, cunning, or deceit ▸ guilelessness, ingenuousness, innocence, naiveté, naturalness, simpleness, simplicity, unsophistication, unworldliness. [*Compare* HONESTY.]

arty or **artsy** *adj.* **1.** *Informal* Relating to or appreciative of the arts ▸ aesthetic, artistic, creative. **2.** *Informal* Pretentiously artistic ▸ *Informal:* artsy-craftsy.

as *conj.* —*See* BECAUSE.

ascend *v.* To move upward along a surface or slope ▸ clamber, climb, go up, mount, scale, scramble. —*See also* RISE (2), RISE (3).

ascendance or **ascendancy** *n.* —*See* DOMINANCE.

ascendant *adj.* —*See* DOMINANT (1).
ascendant *n.* —*See* ANCESTOR (1).

ascension *n.* —*See* ASCENT (1).

ascent *n.* **1.** The act of rising or moving upward ▸ ascension, climb, climbing, lift, mounting, rise, rising. [*Compare* INCREASE.] **2.** An upward path or surface ▸ acclivity, grade, gradient, inclined plane, rise, slant, slope. [*Compare* ELEVATION, HILL.]

ascertain *v.* —*See* DISCERN, DISCOVER.

ascertainment *n.* —*See* DISCOVERY.

ascetic *adj.* Renouncing material comforts and pleasures ▸ abstinent, austere, monkish, puritan, puritanical, self-denying. [*Compare* MEAGER, TEMPERATE.]

ascribe *v.* —*See* ATTRIBUTE, FIX (3).

aseptic *adj.* —*See* DULL (1), STERILE (1).

asepticism *n.* —*See* DULLNESS.

ashen or **ashy** *adj.* —*See* PALE (1).

ashes *n.* The substance of the body, especially after decay or cremation ▸ clay, cremains, dust, remains.

a·shamed (ə-shāmd′) ▸ *adj.* **1.** Feeling shame. **2.** Feeling inferior or embarrassed. **3.** Reluctant through fear of shame: *ashamed to tell.* **—a·sham′ed·ly** (-shā′mĭd-lē) *adv.*

A·shan·ti (ə-shăn′tē, ə-shän′-) ▸ *n., pl.* **-ti** or **-tis. 1.** A member of a people of central Ghana. **2.** The Twi language of the Ashanti.

ash·en (ăsh′ən) ▸ *adj.* **1.** Consisting of ashes. **2.** Resembling ashes, esp. in color; pale.

Ash·ke·naz·i (äsh′kə-nä′zē) ▸ *n., pl.* **-naz·im** (-năz′ĭm, -nä′zĭm). A usu. Yiddish-speaking Jew of E and central Europe.

ash·lar (ăsh′lər) ▸ *n.* **1.** A squared block of building stone. **2.** Masonry of such stones.

a·shore (ə-shôr′) ▸ *adv.* To or on the shore.

ash·ram (äsh′rəm) ▸ *n.* A residence of a Hindu religious community and its guru.

ash·tray (ăsh′trā′) ▸ *n.* A receptacle for tobacco ashes and cigarette butts.

Ash Wednesday ▸ *n.* The 7th Wednesday before Easter and the 1st day of Lent.

ash·y (ăsh′ē) ▸ *adj.* **-i·er, -i·est. 1.** Of or covered with ashes. **2.** Ashen; pale.

A·sia (ā′zhə, -shə) ▸ The largest continent, occupying the E part of the Eurasian landmass and its adjacent islands and separated from Europe by the Ural Mts.

Asia Minor ▸ A peninsula of W Asia between the Black and Mediterranean seas.

A·sian (ā′zhən, -shən) ▸ *adj.* Of or relating to Asia or its peoples, languages, or cultures. ▸ *n.* **1.** A native or inhabitant of Asia. **2.** A person of Asian descent.

Asian American ▸ *n.* A US citizen or resident of Asian descent. **—A′sian-A·mer′i·can** *adj.*

A·si·at·ic (ā′zhē-ăt′ĭk, -shē-, -zē-) ▸ *adj.* Asian. ▸ *n. Often Offensive* An Asian.

a·side (ə-sīd′) ▸ *adv.* **1.** To one side. **2.** Out of one's thoughts or mind. **3.** Apart. **4.** In reserve; away. ▸ *n.* Dialogue supposedly not heard by the other actors in a play.

aside from ▸ *prep.* Excluding; except for.

as·i·nine (ăs′ə-nīn′) ▸ *adj.* Stupid; silly.

ask (ăsk) ▸ *v.* **1.** To put a question to. **2.** To seek an answer to. **3.** To inquire. **4.** To request. **5.** To expect or demand. **6.** To invite.

a·skance (ə-skăns′) ▸ *adv.* **1.** With disapproval or distrust. **2.** With a sideways glance; obliquely.

a·skew (ə-skyo͞o′) ▸ *adv. & adj.* To one side; awry.

ASL ▸ *abbr.* American Sign Language

a·slant (ə-slănt′) ▸ *adv. & adj.* Obliquely.

a·sleep (ə-slēp′) ▸ *adj.* **1.** Sleeping. **2.** Inactive; dormant. **3.** Numb. **—a·sleep′** *adv.*

a·so·cial (ā-sō′shəl) ▸ *adj.* **1.** Averse to the society of others. **2.** Unwilling to conform to normal social behavior; antisocial.

as of ▸ *prep.* On; at: *payable as of May 1.*

asp (ăsp) ▸ *n.* Any of several venomous African or Eurasian snakes.

as·par·a·gus (ə-spăr′ə-gəs) ▸ *n.* A plant having leaflike stems, scalelike leaves, and edible young shoots.

as·pect (ăs′pĕkt) ▸ *n.* **1.** An appearance; air. **2.** An element; facet. **3.** A position facing a given direction. **4.** *Gram.* A category of the verb designating the duration or type of action.

as·pen (ăs′pən) ▸ *n.* A poplar tree having leaves that flutter readily in even a light breeze.

as·per·i·ty (ă-spĕr′ĭ-tē) ▸ *n.* **1.** Roughness; harshness. **2.** Ill temper.

as·per·sion (ə-spûr′zhən, -shən) ▸ *n.* A slanderous remark.

as·phalt (ăs′fôlt′) ▸ *n.* A brownish-black solid or semisolid mixture of bitumens used in paving, roofing, and waterproofing. **—as·phal′tic** *adj.*

as·pho·del (ăs′fə-dĕl′) ▸ *n.* A Mediterranean plant having clusters of white, pink, or yellow flowers.

as·phyx·i·a (ăs-fĭk′sē-ə) ▸ *n.* Lack of oxygen accompanied by an increase of carbon dioxide in the blood, leading to unconsciousness or death.

as·phyx·i·ate (ăs-fĭk′sē-āt′) ▸ *v.* **-at·ed, -at·ing.** To suffocate; smother. **—as·phyx′i·a′tion** *n.* **—as·phyx′i·a′tor** *n.*

as·pic (ăs′pĭk) ▸ *n.* A clear jelly made of meat, fish, or vegetable stock and gelatin.

as·pi·dis·tra (ăs′pĭ-dĭs′trə) ▸ *n.* A popular houseplant having large evergreen leaves.

as·pi·rant (ăs′pər-ənt, ə-spīr′-) ▸ *n.* One who aspires, as to advancement.

as·pi·rate (ăs′pə-rāt′) ▸ *v.* **-rat·ed, -rat·ing. 1.** *Ling.* To pronounce (e.g., a vowel) with the release of breath associated with English *h,* as in *he.* **2.** To inhale. **3.** *Medic.* To remove with a suction device. **—as′pi·rate** (-pər-ĭt) *n.*

as·pi·ra·tion (ăs′pə-rā′shən) ▸ *n.* **1a.** A desire for achievement. **b.** An object of such desire. **2.** The removal of fluids or gases from the body by suction. **3.** The pronunciation of an aspirated speech sound.

as·pi·ra·tor (ăs′pə-rā′tər) ▸ *n.* A device for removing substances, such as mucus or serum, from a body cavity by suction.

as·pire (ə-spīr′) ▸ *v.* **-pired, -pir·ing.** To have a great ambition; desire. **—as·pir′er** *n.* **—as·pir′ing·ly** *adv.*

as·pi·rin (ăs′pər-ĭn, -prĭn) ▸ *n.* **1.** A white crystalline compound derived from salicylic acid and used to relieve pain and reduce fever and inflammation. **2.** A tablet of aspirin.

ass (ăs) ▸ *n.* **1.** Any of several hoofed, long-eared mammals resembling and closely related to the horse. **2.** A vain, silly, or stupid person.

as·sail (ə-sāl′) ▸ *v.* To attack violently. **—as·sail′a·ble** *adj.* **—as·sail′ant** *n.* **—as·sail′er** *n.*

as·sas·sin (ə-săs′ĭn) ▸ *n.* A murderer, esp. of a prominent person.

as·sas·si·nate (ə-săs′ə-nāt′) ▸ *v.* **-nat·ed, -nat·ing. 1.** To murder by surprise attack, as for political reasons. **2.** To destroy (a rival's character). **—as·sas′si·na′tion** *n.*

as·sault (ə-sôlt′) ▸ *n.* **1.** A violent physical or verbal attack. **2.** An unlawful threat or attempt to do bodily injury to another. **3.** The crime of rape. **—as·sault′** *v.* **—as·sault′er** *n.* **—as·saul′tive** *adj.*

assault and battery ▸ *n. Law* A physical assault involving bodily injury to another.

assault weapon ▸ *n.* An infantry weapon designed for individual use.

as·say (ăs′ā′, ă-sā′) ▸ *n.* Qualitative or quantitative analysis

THESAURUS

aside *n.* —*See* COMMENT, DIGRESSION.

asinine *adj.* —*See* FOOLISH.

ask *v.* **1.** To put a question to someone ▸ cross-examine, examine, **inquire,** interrogate, query, question, quiz, pump. *Informal:* grill. ***Idiom:*** give someone the third degree. **2.** To seek an answer to a question ▸ pose, put, raise. [*Compare* SAY.] **3.** To request that someone take part in or be present at a particular occasion ▸ bid, invite, summon. ***Idioms:*** extend an invitation to, request the presence of. [*Compare* REQUEST.] —*See also* APPEAL (1), DEMAND (2).

askance *adv.* —*See* SKEPTICALLY.

asleep *adj.* —*See* DEAD (1), DEAD (2), SLEEPING.

aspect *n.* —*See* APPEARANCE (1), EXPRESSION (4), FACE (3), VIEWPOINT.

asperity *n.* —*See* DIFFICULTY.

asperse *v.* —*See* MALIGN.

aspersion *n.* —*See* INDIGNITY, LIBEL.

asphyxiate *v.* —*See* CHOKE.

aspirant *n.* One who aspires ▸ aspirer, dreamer, hopeful, seeker. *Informal:* wannabe. —*See also* APPLICANT.

aspiration *n.* A strong desire to achieve something ▸ ambition, ambitiousness, emulation. [*Compare* DRIVE, ENTHUSIASM, THIRST.] —*See also* DREAM (3).

aspire *v.* To strive toward a goal ▸ aim, seek. ***Idioms:*** go (*or* grab) for the brass ring, keep one's eyes on the prize, set one's sights on. —*See also* DESIRE.

aspiring *adj.* —*See* AMBITIOUS.

ass *n.* —*See* FOOL.

assail *v.* —*See* ATTACK (1), BEAT (1), REVILE.

assailability *n.* —*See* EXPOSURE.

assailable *adj.* —*See* VULNERABLE.

assailant or **assailer** *n.* —*See* AGGRESSOR.

assailment *n.* —*See* ATTACK.

assassin *n.* —*See* MURDERER.

assassinate *v.* —*See* MURDER.

assassination *n.* —*See* MURDER.

assault *n.* —*See* ATTACK.

assault *v.* To compel another to participate in or submit to a sexual act ▸ force, molest, rape, ravish, violate. —*See also* ATTACK (1), BEAT (1).

assaulter *n.* —*See* AGGRESSOR.

assay *v.* —*See* ATTEMPT, ESTIMATE (1), TEST (1).

of a substance, esp. of an ore or drug. ▸ *v.* (ă-sā′, ăs′ā′) **1.** To subject to or undergo an assay. **2.** To evaluate; assess. **3.** To attempt. **—as·say′a·ble** *adj.* **—as·say′er** *n.*

as·sem·blage (ə-sĕm′blĭj) ▸ *n.* **1.** The act of assembling or the state of being assembled. **2.** A collection of persons or things. **3.** A fitting together of parts, as in a machine. **4.** An art work consisting of an arrangement of miscellaneous objects, such as pieces of metal, cloth, and string.

as·sem·ble (ə-sĕm′bəl) ▸ *v.* **-bled, -bling. 1.** To bring or gather together. **2.** To fit together the parts of.

as·sem·bler (ə-sĕm′blər) ▸ *n.* **1.** One that assembles. **2.** A program that produces executable machine code from symbolic assembly language.

as·sem·bly (ə-sĕm′blē) ▸ *n., pl.* **-blies. 1.** The act of assembling or the state of being assembled. **2.** A group of persons gathered together for a common purpose. **3. Assembly** The lower house of a legislature. **4a.** The putting together of parts to make a product. **b.** A set of parts so assembled. **5.** *Comp. Sci.* The automatic translation of symbolic code into machine code.

assembly line ▸ *n.* An arrangement of workers and tools in which the product passes from operation to operation until completed.

as·sent (ə-sĕnt′) ▸ *v.* To agree; concur. **—as·sent′** *n.* **—as·sent′er, as·sen′tor** *n.*

as·sert (ə-sûrt′) ▸ *v.* **1.** To state positively; affirm. **2.** To defend or maintain. **3.** To put (oneself) forward boldly or forcefully. **—as·ser′tive** *adj.* **—as·ser′tive·ly** *adv.* **—as·ser′tive·ness** *n.*

as·ser·tion (ə-sûr′shən) ▸ *n.* A positive, often unsupported declaration.

as·sess (ə-sĕs′) ▸ *v.* **1.** To evaluate, esp. for taxation. **2.** To set the amount of (a tax or fine). **3.** To charge with a tax or fine. **4.** To make a judgment about. **—as·sess′a·ble** *adj.* **—as·sess′ment** *n.* **—as·ses′sor** *n.*

as·set (ăs′ĕt′) ▸ *n.* **1.** A useful or valuable quality, person, or thing. **2. assets** All properties, such as cash or stock, that may cover the liabilities of a person or business.

as·sev·er·ate (ə-sĕv′ə-rāt′) ▸ *v.* **-at·ed, -at·ing.** To declare positively; assert. **—as·sev′er·a′tion** *n.*

as·sid·u·ous (ə-sĭj′o͞o-əs) ▸ *adj.* Constant in application or attention; diligent. **—as′si·du′i·ty** (ăs′ĭ-do͞o′ĭ-tē, -dyo͞o′-) *n.* **—as·sid′u·ous·ly** *adv.* **—as·sid′u·ous·ness** *n.*

as·sign (ə-sīn′) ▸ *v.* **1.** To specify; designate. **2.** To select for a duty; appoint. **3.** To give out as a task; allot. **4.** To ascribe; attribute. **5.** *Law* To transfer (e.g., property) from one to another. **—as·sign′a·bil′i·ty** *n.* **—as·sign′a·ble** *adj.* **—as·sign′er** *n.*

as·sig·na·tion (ăs′ĭg-nā′shən) ▸ *n.* An appointment for a meeting between lovers.

as·sign·ment (ə-sīn′mənt) ▸ *n.* **1.** The act of assigning. **2.** Something assigned.

as·sim·i·late (ə-sĭm′ə-lāt′) ▸ *v.* **-lat·ed, -lat·ing. 1.** To take in, digest, and transform (food) into living tissue. **2.** To take in and understand. **3.** To make or become similar. **—as·sim′i·la·ble** (-lə-bəl) *adj.* **—as·sim′i·la′·tion** *n.* **—as·sim′i·la′tor** *n.*

As·sin·i·boin (ə-sĭn′ə-boin′) ▸ *n., pl.* **-boin** or **-boins. 1.** A member of a Native American people of N Montana and adjacent regions of Canada. **2.** Their Siouan language.

as·sist (ə-sĭst′) ▸ *v.* To help; support. ▸ *n.* An act of giving aid; help. **—as·sis′tance** *n.*

as·sis·tant (ə-sĭs′tənt) ▸ *n.* One that assists; helper. **—as·sis′tant** *adj.*

as·sist·ed living (ə-sĭs′tĭd) ▸ *n.* A living arrangement in which people with special needs reside in a facility that provides help with everyday tasks.

assisted suicide ▸ *n.* Suicide accomplished with the aid of another person, esp. a physician.

as·size (ə-sīz′) ▸ *n.* **1.** A session or a decree of a court. **2. assizes** One of the periodic court sessions formerly held in the counties of England and Wales.

as·so·ci·ate (ə-sō′shē-āt′, -sē-) ▸ *v.* **-at·ed, -at·ing. 1.** To join or connect in a relationship. **2.** To connect in the mind or imagination. ▸ *n.* (-ĭt, -āt′) **1.** A partner; col-

THESAURUS

assay *n.* —*See* TEST (1).

assemblage *n.* —*See* ACCUMULATION (1), ASSEMBLY.

assemble *v.* To come, bring, or call together ▸ call, cluster, collect, congregate, convene, convoke, forgather, gather, get together, group, muster, round up, send for, summon. [*Compare* MOBILIZE.] —*See also* ACCUMULATE, MAKE.

assembler *n.* —*See* MAKER.

assembly *n.* A number of persons who have come or been gathered together ▸ assemblage, body, company, conclave, conference, congregation, congress, convention, convocation, council, crowd, forum, galaxy, gathering, group, meeting, muster, rally, troop. *Informal:* get-together. [*Compare* ATTENDANCE, BAND², CROWD, FORCE.] —*See also* CONVENTION.

assent *v.* To respond affirmatively; receive with agreement or compliance ▸ accede, accept, acquiesce, agree, concur, consent, nod, subscribe, yes. [*Compare* ACKNOWLEDGE, AGREE, APPROVE, PERMIT.]

assent *n.* —*See* ACCEPTANCE (1), PERMISSION.

assenting *adj.* —*See* FAVORABLE (2), UNANIMOUS.

assert *v.* To put into words positively and with conviction ▸ affirm, allege, argue, asseverate, aver, avouch, avow, claim, contend, declare, enounce, enunciate, hold, insist, maintain, profess, say, state, swear. *Idiom:* have it. [*Compare* ANNOUNCE, CONFIRM, STIPULATE, SUPPORT.] —*See also* CLAIM.

assertion *n.* The act of asserting positively or something so asserted ▸ affirmation, allegation, asseveration, averment, avowal, claim, contention, declaration, profession, statement. [*Compare* ANNOUNCEMENT, ASSUMPTION.]

assertive *adj.* Bold or confident in assertion ▸ aggressive, emphatic, forceful, insistent, in-your-face. *Informal:* go-ahead. [*Compare* DEFINITE, DICTATORIAL, FRANK.]

assess *v.* To establish and apply as compulsory ▸ exact, impose, levy, put. —*See also* ESTIMATE (1).

assessed *adj.* —*See* CALCULATED.

assessment *n.* —*See* ESTIMATE (1), TAX.

assessor *n.* —*See* CRITIC (1).

asset *n.* —*See* SPY, VIRTUE.

assets *n.* —*See* CAPITAL (1), RESOURCES.

asseverate *v.* —*See* ASSERT.

asseveration *n.* —*See* ASSERTION.

assiduity or **assiduousness** *n.* —*See* DILIGENCE.

assiduous *adj.* —*See* DILIGENT.

assign *v.* To appoint and send to a particular place ▸ post, set, station. [*Compare* POSITION.] —*See also* APPOINT, APPROPRIATE, ATTRIBUTE, DISTRIBUTE, FIX (3), TRANSFER (1).

assignation *n.* —*See* ENGAGEMENT (1).

assignment *n.* —*See* APPOINTMENT, DISTRIBUTION (1), GRANT, TASK (1).

assimilate *v.* —*See* ABSORB (2), LIKEN.

assimilation *n.* —*See* ABSORPTION (1).

assimilative *adj.* —*See* ABSORBENT.

assist *v.* —*See* HELP, OBLIGE (1).

assist *n.* —*See* HELP.

assistance *n.* —*See* HELP.

assistant *n.* A person who assists someone else, especially a person who assumes some of the duties of a superior ▸ abettor, adjutant, aid, aide, attendant, auxiliary, coadjutant, coadjutor, deputy, help, helper, lieutenant, reliever, second, succorer. *Slang:* gofer. *Idioms:* man (*or* girl) Friday, right-hand man (*or* woman), second in command. [*Compare* ASSOCIATE, FOLLOWER, MINOR, SUBORDINATE.]

assistant *adj.* —*See* AUXILIARY (1).

assize *n.* —*See* LAW (2).

associate *v.* **1.** To unite or be united in a relationship ▸ amalgamate, affiliate, ally, bind, combine, conjoin, connect, federate, incorporate, join, link, relate. [*Compare* BAND², COMBINE.] **2.** To be with as a companion ▸ be friendly, be intimate, consort, fall in with, fraternize, hang around, hobnob, pal (around), run (around), take up with, troop. *Slang:* hang out. *Idioms:* have relations, keep company, rub elbows (*or* shoulders). **3.** To come or bring together in one's mind or imagination ▸ bracket, connect, correlate, couple, identify, link. [*Compare* EQUAL, LIKEN.]

associate *n.* **1.** One who is united in a relationship with another ▸ affiliate, ally, cohort, colleague, compatriot, confederate, copartner, fellow, partner. [*Compare* PEER².] **2.** One who shares interests or activities with another ▸ chum, companion, comrade, crony, fellow, mate. *Informal:* bud, buddy, pal. *Slang:* sidekick. *Idiom:* partner in crime. [*Compare*

league. 2. A companion; comrade. ▸ *adj.* (-ĭt, -āt′) Joined in equal or nearly equal status.

as·so·ci·a·tion (ə-sō′sē-ā′shən, -shē-) ▸ *n.* **1.** The act of associating or the state of being associated. **2.** An organized body of people; society. **—as·so′ci·a′tion·al** *adj.*

association football ▸ *n. Chiefly Brit.* Soccer.

as·so·ci·a·tive (ə-sō′shə-tĭv, -sē-ə-tĭv, -shē-ā′tĭv, -sē-) ▸ *adj.* **1.** Of or causing association. **2.** *Math.* Independent of the grouping of elements. **—as·so′ci·a′tive·ly** *adv.*

as·so·nance (ăs′ə-nəns) ▸ *n.* Resemblance esp. of the vowel sounds in words. **—as′so·nant** *adj.* & *n.* **—as′so·nan′tal** (-năn′tl) *adj.*

as·sort (ə-sôrt′) ▸ *v.* To separate into groups according to kind; classify. **—as·sor′ta·tive** *adj.* **—as·sort′er** *n.*

as·sort·ed (ə-sôr′tĭd) ▸ *adj.* Of different kinds; various: *assorted sizes.*

as·sort·ment (ə-sôrt′mənt) ▸ *n.* **1.** The act of assorting. **2.** A collection of various kinds; variety.

asst. ▸ *abbr.* assistant

as·suage (ə-swāj′) ▸ *v.* **-suaged, -suag·ing. 1.** To make less severe; ease. **2.** To satisfy or appease.

as·sume (ə-so͞om′) ▸ *v.* **-sumed, -sum·ing. 1.** To take upon oneself. **2.** To take on; adopt. **3.** To pretend; feign. **4.** To take for granted; suppose. **—as·sum′a·ble** *adj.* **—as·sum′a·bly** *adv.*

as·sumed (ə-so͞omd′) ▸ *adj.* **1.** Feigned; pretended. **2.** Taken for granted; supposed. **—as·sum′ed·ly** (-so͞o′mĭd-lē) *adv.*

as·sum·ing (ə-so͞o′mĭng) ▸ *adj.* Presumptuous; arrogant. ▸ *conj.* Supposing.

as·sump·tion (ə-sŭmp′shən) ▸ *n.* **1.** The act of assuming. **2.** A statement accepted as true without proof; supposition. **3. Assumption** *Christianity* The bodily taking up of the Virgin Mary into heaven after her death.

as·sur·ance (ə-sho͝or′əns) ▸ *n.* **1.** The act of assuring. **2.** Freedom from doubt; certainty. **3.** Self-confidence. **4.** *Chiefly Brit.* Insurance, esp. life insurance.

as·sure (ə-sho͝or′) ▸ *v.* **-sured, -sur·ing. 1.** To inform positively. **2.** To cause to feel sure. **3.** To make certain; ensure. **4.** *Chiefly Brit.* To insure, as against loss. **—as·sur′er** *n.*

as·sured (ə-sho͝ord′) ▸ *adj.* **1.** Certain; guaranteed. **2.** Confident; sure. **—as·sur′ed·ly** (-ĭd-lē) *adv.* **—as·sur′ed·ness** *n.*

As·syr·i·a (ə-sîr′ē-ə) ▸ An ancient empire and civilization of W Asia in the upper valley of the Tigris R.

As·syr·i·an (ə-sîr′ē-ən) ▸ *adj.* Of or relating to Assyria. ▸ *n.* **1.** A native or inhabitant of Assyria. **2.** See **Akkadian** 2.

as·ta·tine (ăs′tə-tēn′, -tĭn) ▸ *n. Symbol* **At** A highly unstable radioactive element used in medicine as a radioactive tracer.

as·ter (ăs′tər) ▸ *n.* Any of various plants having daisylike flower heads with white, pink, or violet rays and a usu. yellow disk.

as·ter·isk (ăs′tə-rĭsk′) ▸ *n.* A star-shaped figure (*) that is used in printing to indicate an omission or a reference to a footnote.

a·stern (ə-stûrn′) ▸ *adv.* & *adj.* **1.** Behind a vessel. **2.** At or to the stern of a vessel.

as·ter·oid (ăs′tə-roid′) ▸ *n.* Any of numerous small celestial bodies that revolve around the sun chiefly between Mars and Jupiter.

asth·ma (ăz′mə, ăs′-) ▸ *n.* A respiratory disease, often arising from allergies, marked by labored breathing, chest constriction, and coughing. **—asth·mat′ic** (-măt′ĭk) *adj.* & *n.*

a·stig·ma·tism (ə-stĭg′mə-tĭz′əm) ▸ *n.* A refractive defect of a lens, esp. of the eye, that prevents focusing of sharp, distinct images. **—as′tig·mat′ic** (ăs′tĭg-măt′ĭk) *adj.* & *n.*

a·stir (ə-stûr′) ▸ *adj.* Moving about.

a·ston·ish (ə-stŏn′ĭsh) ▸ *v.* To fill with sudden wonder or amazement. **—a·ston′ish·ing·ly** *adv.* **—a·ston′ish·ment** *n.*

a·stound (ə-stound′) ▸ *v.* To astonish and bewilder. **—a·stound′ing** *adj.* **—a·stound′ing·ly** *adv.*

a·strad·dle (ə-străd′l) ▸ *adv.* & *prep.* Astride.

as·tral (ăs′trəl) ▸ *adj.* Of, relating to, or resembling the stars.

a·stray (ə-strā′) ▸ *adv.* **1.** Away from the correct direction or route. **2.** Into wrong or evil ways. **—a·stray′** *adj.*

a·stride (ə-strīd′) ▸ *adv.* & *prep.* With a leg on each side (of).

as·trin·gent (ə-strĭn′jənt) ▸ *adj.* **1.** *Medic.* Tending to draw together or constrict living tissues; styptic. **2.** Sharp; harsh: *astringent remarks.* ▸ *n.* An astringent agent or drug. **—as·trin′gen·cy** *n.* **—as·trin′gent·ly** *adv.*

astro– or **astr–** ▸ *pref.* **1.** Star: *astrophysics.* **2.** Outer space: *astronaut.*

as·tro·labe (ăs′trə-lāb′) ▸ *n.* A medieval instrument used to determine the altitude of a celestial body.

as·trol·o·gy (ə-strŏl′ə-jē) ▸ *n.* The study of the positions and aspects of celestial bodies with a view to predicting their influence on human affairs. **—as·trol′o·ger** *n.* **—as′tro·log′i·cal** (ăs′trə-lŏj′ĭ-kəl), **as′tro·log′ic** *adj.* **—as′tro·log′i·cal·ly** *adv.*

as·tro·naut (ăs′trə-nôt′) ▸ *n.* A person trained to pilot or otherwise participate in the flight of a spacecraft.

as·tro·nau·tics (ăs′trə-nô′tĭks) ▸ *n. (takes sing. or pl. v.)* The science and technology of space flight. **—as′tro·nau′tic, as′tro·nau′ti·cal** *adj.* **—as′tro·nau′ti·cal·ly** *adv.*

as·tro·nom·i·cal (ăs′trə-nŏm′ĭ-kəl) also **as·tro·nom·ic** (-nŏm′ĭk) ▸ *adj.* **1.** Of or relating to astronomy. **2.** Colossal; immense. **—as′tro·nom′i·cal·ly** *adv.*

astronomical unit ▸ *n.* A unit of length equal to the mean distance from Earth to the sun, approx. 150 million km (93 million mi).

as·tron·o·my (ə-strŏn′ə-mē) ▸ *n.* The scientific study of the positions, distribution, motion, and composition of celestial bodies. **—as·tron′o·mer** *n.*

THESAURUS

FRIEND.] *—See also* CONCOMITANT.

association *n.* **1.** The state of being associated ▸ affiliation, alliance, combination, conjunction, connection, cooperation, partnership. [*Compare* FRIENDSHIP, RELATION.] **2.** Something, such as a feeling or idea, associated with a specific person or thing ▸ connection, connotation, impression, suggestion. *—See also* CONFERENCE (2), UNION (1).

assort *v.* *—See* CLASSIFY.

assorted *adj.* *—See* VARIOUS.

assortment *n.* A collection of various things ▸ conglomeration, gallimaufry, hodgepodge, jumble, medley, mélange, miscellany, mishmash, mixed bag, mixture, olio, patchwork, potpourri, salmagundi, variety. *Slang:* grab bag. [*Compare* COMBINATION, MIXTURE, ODDS AND ENDS.] *—See also* ARRANGEMENT (1).

assuage *v.* *—See* PACIFY, RELIEVE (1).

assuagement *n.* *—See* RELIEF (1).

assume *v.* To take upon oneself ▸ incur, shoulder, tackle, take on, take over, undertake. [*Compare* ENDURE, TAKE.] *—See also* ACT (2), ADOPT, DON, SEIZE (1), SUPPOSE (1).

assumed *adj.* Being fictitious and not real, as a name ▸ made-up, pretended, pseudonymous. [*Compare* FALSE, FICTITIOUS.]

assuming *adj.* *—See* IMPUDENT.

assumption *n.* Something taken to be true without proof ▸ axiom, assertion, given, lemma, postulate, postulation, premise, presumption, presupposition, speculation, supposition. [*Compare* ASSERTION, THEORY.] *—See also* IMPUDENCE, SEIZURE (2).

assumptive *adj.* *—See* IMPUDENT, PRESUMPTIVE.

assurance *n.* *—See* CONFIDENCE, OPTIMISM, PROMISE (1), SAFETY, SURENESS.

assure *v.* *—See* CONVINCE, GUARANTEE (2).

assured *adj.* *—See* CONFIDENT, OPTIMISTIC, SURE (1).

assuredly *adv.* *—See* YES.

assuredness *n.* *—See* DECISION (2), SURENESS.

astir *adj.* *—See* BUSY (2).

astonish *v.* *—See* SURPRISE.

astonishing *adj.* So remarkable as to be difficult to believe ▸ amazing, astounding, awe-inspiring, dumbfounding, fabulous, fantastic, flabbergasting, incredible, marvelous, miraculous, overwhelming, phenomenal, prodigious, staggering, stunning, stupendous, unbelievable, wonderful, wondrous. *Informal:* mind-blowing, mind-boggling. [*Compare* EXCEPTIONAL, RARE.]

astonishment *n.* *—See* MARVEL, WONDER (1).

astound *v.* *—See* SURPRISE.

astounding *adj.* *—See* ASTONISHING.

astray *adv.* Not in the right way or on the proper course ▸ afield, amiss, awry, wrong.

astray *adj.* *—See* LOST (1).

astringent *adj.* *—See* BITING.

astronomical *adj.* *—See* ENORMOUS, HEAVENLY (2).

as·tro·phys·ics (ăs′trō-fĭz′ĭks) ▸ *n.* *(takes sing. v.)* The branch of astronomy that deals with the physics of stellar phenomena. **—as′tro·phys′i·cal** *adj.* **—as′tro·phys′i·cist** (-fĭz′ĭ-sĭst) *n.*

As·tro·Turf (ăs′trō-tûrf′) ▸ A trademark for an artificial grasslike ground covering.

as·tute (ə-sto͞ot′, ə-styo͞ot′) ▸ *adj.* Having or showing keen judgment; shrewd. **—as·tute′ly** *adv.* **—as·tute′ness** *n.*

a·sun·der (ə-sŭn′dər) ▸ *adv.* 1. Into separate parts, pieces, or groups. 2. Apart in position or direction.

as well as ▸ *conj.* And in addition: *big as well as strong.* ▸ *prep.* In addition to.

a·sy·lum (ə-sī′ləm) ▸ *n.* 1. An institution for the care of ill or needy people, esp. those with mental impairments. 2. A place of safety; refuge. 3. Protection granted by a government to a political refugee from another country.

a·sym·met·ri·cal (ā′sĭ-mĕt′rĭ-kəl) also **a·sym·met·ric** (-rĭk) ▸ *adj.* Not symmetrical. **—a′sym·met′ri·cal·ly** *adv.* **—a·sym′me·try** *n.*

a·symp·to·mat·ic (ā′sĭmp-tə-măt′ĭk) ▸ *adj.* Neither causing nor exhibiting symptoms of disease. **—a′symp·to·mat′i·cal·ly** *adv.*

as·ymp·tote (ăs′ĭm-tōt′, -ĭmp-) ▸ *n.* A line whose distance to a given curve tends to zero. **—as′ymp·tot′ic** (-tŏt′ĭk), **as′ymp·tot′i·cal** *adj.*

at (ăt; ət *when unstressed*) ▸ *prep.* 1. In or near the position or area occupied by: *at the market; at the top of the page.* 2. To or toward the direction or goal of: *looked at them; worked at the task.* 3. In the state or condition of: *at peace.* 4. In the activity or field of: *good at math; at work.* 5. On, near, or by the time or age of: *at three o'clock.* 6. Because of: *rejoice at a victory.*

At ▸ The symbol for the element **astatine.**

at·a·vism (ăt′ə-vĭz′əm) ▸ *n.* The reappearance of a characteristic in an organism after several generations of absence. **—at′a·vis′tic** *adj.* **—at′a·vis′ti·cal·ly** *adv.*

ate (āt) ▸ *v.* P.t. of **eat.**

-ate[1] ▸ *suff.* 1a. Having: *nervate.* b. Characterized by: *affectionate.* c. Resembling: *palmate.* 2. Rank; office: *pastorate.* 3. To act upon in a specified manner: *acidulate.* 4. Product of an action or process: *distillate.*

-ate[2] ▸ *suff.* 1. A derivative of a specified chemical compound or element: *silicate.* 2. A salt or ester of a specified acid: *acetate.*

at·el·ier (ăt′l-yā′) ▸ *n.* A workshop or studio, esp. for an artist.

Ath·a·bas·kan or **Ath·a·bas·can** (ăth′ə-băs′kən) also **Ath·a·pas·can** (-păs′-) ▸ *n.* 1. A group of related Native American languages including Navajo, Apache, and languages of NW Canada. 2. A member of an Athabaskan-speaking people.

a·the·ism (ā′thē-ĭz′əm) ▸ *n.* Disbelief in or denial of the existence of God. **—a′the·ist** *n.* **—a′the·is′tic** *adj.*

A·the·na (ə-thē′nə) also **A·the·ne** (-nē) ▸ *n.* *Gk. Myth.* The goddess of wisdom, the practical arts, and warfare.

ath·e·nae·um also **ath·e·ne·um** (ăth′ə-nē′əm) ▸ *n.* 1. An institution for the promotion of learning. 2. A library.

Ath·ens (ăth′ənz) ▸ The capital of Greece, in the E part near the Saronic Gulf; reached the height of its power and cultural achievements in the 5th cent. B.C. **—A·the′ni·an** (ə-thē′nē-ən) *adj.* & *n.*

ath·er·o·scle·ro·sis (ăth′ə-rō-sklə-rō′sĭs) ▸ *n.* A form of arteriosclerosis in which plaque containing cholesterol and lipids is deposited on the inner walls of the arteries.

a·thirst (ə-thûrst′) ▸ *adj.* Strongly desirous; eager: *athirst for freedom.*

ath·lete (ăth′lēt′) ▸ *n.* One who participates esp. in competitive sports.

ath·lete's foot (ăth′lēts) ▸ *n.* A contagious fungal infection of the skin usu. affecting the feet, characterized by itching, blisters, cracking, and scaling.

ath·let·ic (ăth-lĕt′ĭk) ▸ *adj.* 1. Of or for athletics or athletes. 2. Physically strong. **—ath·let′i·cal·ly** *adv.* **—ath·let′i·cism** (-lĕt′ĭ-sĭz′əm) *n.*

ath·let·ics (ăth-lĕt′ĭks) ▸ *n.* *(takes sing. or pl. v.)* 1. Athletic activities. 2. A system of training and practice for such activities.

athletic supporter ▸ *n.* An elastic support for the male genitals, worn esp. during sports.

a·thwart (ə-thwôrt′) ▸ *adv.* From side to side; crosswise. ▸ *prep.* 1. From one side to the other of; across. 2. Contrary to.

a·tilt (ə-tĭlt′) ▸ *adv.* & *adj.* In a tilted position.

-ation ▸ *suff.* 1a. Action or process: *strangulation.* b. The result of an action or process: *acculturation.* 2. State, condition, or quality of: *moderation.*

-ative ▸ *suff.* Relating to or characterized by: *talkative.*

At·lan·ta (ăt-lăn′tə) ▸ The capital of GA, in the NW part.

At·lan·tic Ocean (ăt-lăn′tĭk) ▸ The second-largest ocean, divided into the **North Atlantic** and the **South Atlantic** and extending from the Arctic in the N to the Antarctic in the S between the Americas and Europe and Africa.

At·lan·tis (ăt-lăn′tĭs) ▸ *n.* A legendary sunken island in the Atlantic Ocean W of Gibraltar.

at·las (ăt′ləs) ▸ *n.* A book or bound collection of maps.

Atlas ▸ *n.* *Gk. Myth.* A Titan condemned by Zeus to hold up the heavens.

ATM ▸ *abbr.* automated teller machine

at·mos·phere (ăt′mə-sfîr′) ▸ *n.* 1. The mixture of gases that surrounds a celestial body, esp. Earth, and is held by the force of gravity. 2. *Phys.* A unit of pressure equal to the air pressure at sea level. 3. The air or climate of a place: *the dry atmosphere of the desert.* 4. A dominant tone or attitude: *an atmosphere of distrust.* **—at′mos·pher′ic** (-sfĕr′ĭk) *adj.* **—at′mos·pher′i·cal·ly** *adv.*

at·mos·pher·ics (ăt′mə-sfĕr′ĭks) ▸ *n.* *(takes sing. v.)* Radio interference produced by electromagnetic radiation from natural phenomena.

at. no. ▸ *abbr.* atomic number

a·toll (ăt′ôl′, -ŏl′, ā′tôl′, ā′tŏl′) ▸ *n.* A ringlike coral island or chain of islets that encloses a lagoon.

at·om (ăt′əm) ▸ *n.* 1. An extremely small part, quantity, or amount. 2. A unit of matter, the smallest unit of an element, having all the characteristics of that element and consisting of a dense, positively charged nucleus surrounded by a system of electrons.

atom bomb ▸ *n.* 1. An explosive weapon of great destructive power derived from the rapid release of energy in the fission of heavy atomic nuclei. 2. A nuclear weapon.

a·tom·ic (ə-tŏm′ĭk) ▸ *adj.* 1. Of or relating to an atom. 2. Of or employing nuclear energy: *an atomic submarine.* 3. Very small; infinitesimal. **—a·tom′i·cal·ly** *adv.*

atomic bomb ▸ *n.* See **atom bomb** 1.

atomic energy ▸ *n.* See **nuclear energy.**

atomic number ▸ *n.* The number of protons in an atomic nucleus.

atomic weight ▸ *n.* The average mass of an atom of an element, usu. given relative to carbon 12, which is assigned a mass of 12.

at·om·ize (ăt′ə-mīz′) ▸ *v.* **-ized, -iz·ing.** 1. To reduce to fine

THESAURUS

astute *adj.* —*See* DISCRIMINATING, SHREWD.

astuteness *n.* —*See* DISCERNMENT, DISCRIMINATION (1).

asylum *n.* —*See* COVER (1), HOME (3), REFUGE (1).

asymmetric or **asymmetrical** *adj.* —*See* IRREGULAR.

asymmetry *n.* —*See* IRREGULARITY.

atelier *n.* An artist's workspace ▸ studio, workroom, workshop.

atheism *n.* Lack of belief in God ▸ disbelief, faithlessness, godlessness, impiety, irreligion, unbelief.

atheist *n.* One who does not believe in God ▸ heathen, infidel, nonbeliever, pagan.

atheistic *adj.* Not believing in God ▸ disbelieving, faithless, godless, impious, irreligious, ungodly. [*Compare* DOUBTFUL.]

athirst *adj.* —*See* EAGER.

athletic *adj.* —*See* MUSCULAR.

atmosphere *n.* 1. The gaseous mixture enveloping the earth ▸ air, ether. 2. A distinctive yet intangible quality ▸ aroma, flavor, savor, smack. [*Compare* QUALITY.] —*See also* AIR (3), ENVIRONMENT (2).

atmospheric *adj.* Of or relating to air ▸ aerial, airy, pneumatic.

atomize *v.* —*See* CRUSH (2), DISINTEGRATE.

or minute particles, as in a spray. **2.** To fragment; disintegrate. **—at′om·i·za′tion** *n.*
at·om·iz·er (ăt′ə-mī′zər) ▸ *n.* A device for producing a fine spray of a liquid.
atom smasher ▸ *n.* See **accelerator** 2.
a·ton·al (ā-tōn′əl) ▸ *adj. Mus.* Lacking a traditional key or tonality. **—a′to·nal′i·ty** (-tō-năl′ĭ-tē) *n.* **—a·ton′al·ly** *adv.*
a·tone (ə-tōn′) ▸ *v.* **a·toned, a·ton·ing.** To make amends (for). **—a·ton′er** *n.*
a·tone·ment (ə-tōn′mənt) ▸ *n.* Reparation made for an injury, wrong, or sin.
a·top (ə-tŏp′) ▸ *adv.* To, on, or at the top. ▸ *prep.* On top of. **—a·top′** *adj.*
–ator ▸ *suff.* One that acts in a specified manner: *radiator.*
–atory ▸ *suff.* **1a.** Of or relating to: *reconciliatory.* **b.** Tending to: *derogatory.* **2.** One that is connected with: *observatory.*
ATP (ā′tē′pē′) ▸ *n.* A nucleotide that supplies energy to cells.
a·tri·um (ā′trē-əm) ▸ *n., pl.* **a·tri·a** (ā′trē-ə) or **-ums. 1a.** A usu. skylighted central area in a building, esp. a public building. **b.** An open central court in an ancient Roman house. **2.** A body cavity or chamber, esp. either of the upper chambers of the heart; auricle.
a·tro·cious (ə-trō′shəs) ▸ *adj.* **1.** Extremely evil, savage, or cruel: *an atrocious crime.* **2.** Exceptionally bad; abominable: *atrocious decor.* **—a·tro′cious·ly** *adv.* **—a·tro′cious·ness** *n.*
a·troc·i·ty (ə-trŏs′ĭ-tē) ▸ *n., pl.* **-ties. 1.** Atrocious state, quality, or behavior. **2.** An appalling act or object. **3.** An act of vicious cruelty, esp. the killing of unarmed people.
at·ro·phy (ăt′rə-fē) ▸ *n., pl.* **-phies.** A wasting or shrinking of a bodily organ, tissue, or part. ▸ *v.* **-phied, -phy·ing.** To waste or cause to waste away. **—a·troph′ic** (ā-trŏf′ĭk) *adj.*
at·ro·pine (ăt′rə-pēn′, -pĭn) also **at·ro·pin** (-pĭn) ▸ *n.* A poisonous, bitter, crystalline alkaloid, $C_{17}H_{23}NO_3$, obtained from belladonna and used to dilate the pupil of the eye.
at·tach (ə-tăch′) ▸ *v.* **1.** To fasten or become fastened; connect. **2.** To bind by ties of affection or loyalty. **3.** To affix or append: *attached her signature to the contract.* **4.** To seize by legal writ. **—at·tach′a·ble** *adj.*
at·ta·ché (ăt′ə-shā′, ă-tă-) ▸ *n.* One who is assigned to a diplomatic mission to serve in a particular capacity: *a cultural attaché.*
attaché case ▸ *n.* A slim briefcase with flat sides and hinges.
at·tach·ment (ə-tăch′mənt) ▸ *n.* **1.** The act of attaching or the condition of being attached. **2.** Something, such as a tie or band, that attaches one thing to another. **3.** A bond of affection or loyalty. **4.** A supplementary part, as of an appliance; accessory. **5.** *Law* **a.** Legal seizure of property or a person. **b.** The writ ordering this.
at·tack (ə-tăk′) ▸ *v.* **1.** To set upon with violent force. **2.** To criticize strongly. **3.** To start work on with vigor. **4.** To affect harmfully: *a disease that attacked the nervous system.* ▸ *n.* **1.** The act of attacking; assault. **2.** An expression of strong or hostile criticism. **3.** The onset of a disease, esp. a chronic disease. **—at·tack′er** *n.*
at·tain (ə-tān′) ▸ *v.* **1.** To accomplish; achieve. **2.** To arrive at. **—at·tain′a·bil′i·ty** *n.* **—at·tain′a·ble** *adj.* **—at·tain′ment** *n.*
at·tain·der (ə-tān′dər) ▸ *n.* Formerly, the loss of all civil rights by a person sentenced for a capital offense.
at·taint (ə-tānt′) ▸ *v.* To pass a sentence of attainder against.
at·tar (ăt′ər) ▸ *n.* A fragrant oil obtained from flowers.
at·tempt (ə-tĕmpt′) ▸ *v.* To make an effort to do, perform, or achieve; try. ▸ *n.* **1.** An effort; try. **2.** An attack; assault: *an attempt on someone's life.* **—at·tempt′a·ble** *adj.*
at·tend (ə-tĕnd′) ▸ *v.* **1.** To be present (at). **2.** To accompany. **3.** To take care (of). **4.** To take charge of; manage. **5.** To pay attention (to); heed.
at·ten·dance (ə-tĕn′dəns) ▸ *n.* **1.** The act of attending. **2.** The number of persons present.
at·ten·dant (ə-tĕn′dənt) ▸ *n.* **1.** One who attends or waits on another. **2.** One who is present. **3.** An accompanying circumstance; consequence. ▸ *adj.* Accompanying; consequent: *attendant conditions.*
at·ten·tion (ə-tĕn′shən) ▸ *n.* **1.** Concentration of the mental powers upon an object. **2.** Observant consideration; notice. **3.** Courtesy or consideration: *attention to a guest's comfort.* **4. attentions** Acts of courtesy and consideration, esp. by a suitor. **5.** An erect military posture assumed on command. **—at·ten′tive** *adj.* **—at·ten′tive·ly** *adv.* **—at·ten′tive·ness** *n.*
attention deficit disorder ▸ *n.* A syndrome, usu. diagnosed in childhood, marked by persistent impulsiveness and inattention, with or without hyperactivity.
attention deficit hyperactivity disorder ▸ *n.* Attention

THESAURUS

atone *n.* *—See* PURIFY (1).
atonement *n.* The act of making amends ▸ expiation, penance, reconciliation, reparation. [*Compare* COMPENSATION, PURIFICATION.]
atrium *n.* *—See* COURT (1).
atrocious *adj.* *—See* OFFENSIVE (1), OUTRAGEOUS, TORMENTING.
atrociousness *n.* *—See* OUTRAGEOUSNESS.
atrocity *n.* *—See* OUTRAGE, OUTRAGEOUSNESS.
atrophy *n.* *—See* DETERIORATION (1).
atrophy *v.* *—See* DETERIORATE.
attach *v.* **1.** To join one thing to another ▸ adjoin, append, affix, clamp, clip, connect, couple, fasten, fuse, fix, moor, secure. [*Compare* BOND, COMBINE, JOIN.] **2.** To add as a supplement or an appendix ▸ add (on), affix, annex, append, subjoin.
attachment *n.* A subordinate element that is added to another entity ▸ accessory, add-on, adjunct, appendage, appurtenance, supplement. [*Compare* ADDITION.] *—See also* BOND (3), LOVE (1).
attack *v.* **1.** To set upon with violent force ▸ aggress, assail, assault, beset, bombard, charge, fall on (*or* upon), go at, have at, march against, rush, sail into, storm, strike. *Informal:* light into, pitch into. *Slang:* lay into, tear into. *Idioms:* gang up on, have a go at, let have it, open up on. [*Compare* AMBUSH, CONTEND, RAID.] **2.** To start work on vigorously ▸ dive into, go at, plunge into, set to work, tackle, wade in (*or* into). *Idioms:* get a move on, get cracking (*or* moving), hop to it, look lively, roll up one's sleeves. [*Compare* START.]
attack *n.* The act of attacking ▸ aggression, assailment, assault, attempt, drive, offense, offensive, onrush, onset, onslaught, storming, strike. [*Compare* ADVANCE, CHARGE, SIEGE.] *—See also* APPROACH (1), SEIZURE (1).
attackable *adj.* *—See* VULNERABLE.
attacker *n.* *—See* AGGRESSOR.
attain *v.* *—See* ACCOMPLISH, GET (1).
attainable *adj.* *—See* AVAILABLE, POSSIBLE.
attainment *n.* A quality that makes a person suitable for a particular position or task ▸ credential, endowment, qualification, skill. *—See also* ACCOMPLISHMENT, FULFILLMENT (1).
attempt *v.* To make an attempt to do or make ▸ assay, endeavor, essay, seek, strive, struggle, try (for). *Informal:* shoot for (*or* at). *Idioms:* give a whirl, go to all lengths, have a go at, have (*or* make *or* take) a shot at, have a try at, make a grab (*or* stab) at, take a crack at, try one's hand at, have (*or* take) a whack at. [*Compare* ASPIRE, PRESUME, START.]
attempt *n.* A trying to do or make something ▸ bid, crack, effort, endeavor, essay, go, offer, stab, trial, try, undertaking. *Informal:* shot, whirl. *Slang:* take. [*Compare* EFFORT.] *—See also* ATTACK.
attend *v.* **1.** To occur as a consequence ▸ ensue, follow, result. [*Compare* STEM.] **2.** To work and care for ▸ do for, minister to, serve, wait on (*or* upon). [*Compare* HELP, WORK.] **3.** To make an effort to hear something ▸ hark, hearken, heed, listen. *Idioms:* be all ears, give (*or* lend) an ear. *—See also* ACCOMPANY, HEAR, TEND[2].
attendance *n.* The condition or fact of being present ▸ occurrence, presence. [*Compare* EXISTENCE.]
attendant *n.* *—See* ASSISTANT, CONCOMITANT.
attendant *adj.* *—See* CONCURRENT.
attending *adj.* *—See* CONCURRENT, FOLLOWING (2).
attention *n.* Concentration of the mental powers on something ▸ attentiveness, concentration, consideration, contemplation, heedfulness, intentness, preoccupation, regardfulness. [*Compare* ALERTNESS, CARE, DILIGENCE.] *—See also* NOTICE (1).

deficit disorder with hyperactivity.

at·ten·u·ate (ə-tĕn′yo͞o-āt′) ▸ *v.* **-at·ed, -at·ing. 1.** To make or become thin or small. **2.** To weaken. **3.** To rarefy or dilute. **—at·ten′u·a′tion** *n.*

at·test (ə-tĕst′) ▸ *v.* **1.** To affirm to be correct, true, or genuine, esp. by affixing one's signature as witness. **2.** To supply evidence of: *actions that attested their bravery.* **3.** To bear witness: *attested to their good faith.* **—at′tes·ta′tion** (ăt′ĕs-tā′shən) *n.* **—at·test′er, at·tes′tor** *n.*

at·tic (ăt′ĭk) ▸ *n.* A story or room directly below the roof of a building, esp. a house.

Attic ▸ *adj.* **1.** Of ancient Attica or Athens. **2.** Pure and simple: *Attic prose.* ▸ *n.* A dialect of ancient Greek.

At·ti·la (ăt′l-ə, ə-tĭl′ə) (A.D. 406?–453) ▸ King of the Huns (433?–453).

at·tire (ə-tīr′) ▸ *v.* **-tired, -tir·ing.** To dress or clothe. ▸ *n.* Clothing or array; apparel.

at·ti·tude (ăt′ĭ-to͞od′, -tyo͞od′) ▸ *n.* **1.** A position of the body or manner of carrying oneself: *stood in a belligerent attitude.* **2.** A state of mind or a feeling; disposition: *an attitude of friendliness.* **3.** The orientation of an aircraft's axes esp. with respect to the horizon. **4.** The orientation of a spacecraft relative to its direction of motion. **5.** A position in which a ballet dancer stands on one leg with the other raised and bent at the knee. **—at′ti·tu′di·nal** *adj.*

attn. ▸ *abbr.* attention

at·tor·ney (ə-tûr′nē) ▸ *n., pl.* **-neys.** A person, esp. a lawyer, legally appointed or empowered to act as another's agent. **—at·tor′ney·ship′** *n.*

attorney at law ▸ *n., pl.* **attorneys at law.** An attorney.

attorney general ▸ *n., pl.* **attorneys general** or **attorney generals.** The chief law officer and counsel of a state or nation's government.

at·tract (ə-trăkt′) ▸ *v.* **1.** To cause to draw near or adhere. **2.** To arouse the interest, admiration, or attention of. **—at·tract′a·ble** *adj.* **—at·trac′tive** *adj.* **—at·trac′tive·ness** *n.*

at·trac·tion (ə-trăk′shən) ▸ *n.* **1.** The act or power of attracting. **2.** Allure; charm. **3.** A feature or characteristic that attracts. **4.** A public spectacle or entertainment.

at·trib·ute (ə-trĭb′yo͞ot) ▸ *v.* **-ut·ed, -ut·ing.** To regard or assign as a particular cause, source, or agent; ascribe. ▸ *n.* **at·tri·bute** (ăt′rə-byo͞ot′) **1.** A distinctive feature of or object associated with someone or something. **2.** *Gram.* An attributive. **—at·trib′ut·a·ble** *adj.* **—at·trib′ut·er, at·trib′u·tor** *n.* **—at′tri·bu′tion** (ăt′rə-byo͞o′shən) *n.*

at·trib·u·tive (ə-trĭb′yə-tĭv) ▸ *n.* A word or word group, such as an adjective, that is adjacent to the noun it modifies without a linking verb; e.g., *pale* in *the pale moon.* ▸ *adj.* **1.** Of or being an attributive. **2.** Of or like an attribute. **—at·trib′u·tive·ly** *adv.*

at·trit (ə-trĭt′) ▸ *v.* **-trit·ted, -trit·ting. 1.** To lose (e.g., personnel) by attrition. **2.** To destroy or kill (e.g., troops).

at·tri·tion (ə-trĭsh′ən) ▸ *n.* **1.** A rubbing away or wearing down by friction. **2.** A gradual diminution in number or strength because of constant stress: *a war of attrition.* **3.** A gradual, natural reduction in membership or personnel, as through resignation or death.

At·tucks (ăt′əks), **Crispus** (1723?–70) ▸ Amer. patriot; killed in the Boston Massacre.

at·tune (ə-to͞on′, -tyo͞on′) ▸ *v.* **-tuned, -tun·ing. 1.** To bring into harmony. **2.** To tune.

Atty. ▸ *abbr.* attorney

Atty. Gen. ▸ *abbr.* Attorney General

at. wt. ▸ *abbr.* atomic weight

a·typ·i·cal (ā-tĭp′ĭ-kəl) ▸ *adj.* Not typical; unusual or irregular. **—a·typ′i·cal·ly** *adv.*

Au ▸ The symbol for the element **gold**.

au·burn (ô′bərn) ▸ *n.* A reddish brown. **—au′burn** *adj.*

au cou·rant (ō′ ko͞o-räɴ′) ▸ *adj.* **1.** Up-to-date. **2.** Knowledgeable.

auc·tion (ôk′shən) ▸ *n.* A public sale in which property or items of merchandise are sold to the highest bidder. ▸ *v.* To sell at or by an auction. **—auc′tion·eer′** (-shə-nîr′) *n. & v.*

au·da·cious (ô-dā′shəs) ▸ *adj.* **1.** Fearlessly daring. **2.** Arrogantly insolent; impudent. **—au·da′cious·ly** *adv.* **—au·da′cious·ness** *n.* **—au·dac′i·ty** (-dăs′ĭ-tē) *n.*

au·di·al (ô′dē-əl) ▸ *adj.* Of or relating to the sense of hearing; aural.

au·di·ble (ô′də-bəl) ▸ *adj.* That is or can be heard. **—au′di·bil′i·ty** *n.* **—au′di·bly** *adv.*

au·di·ence (ô′dē-əns) ▸ *n.* **1.** A gathering of spectators or listeners. **2.** All those reached by printed matter or a radio or television broadcast. **3.** A formal hearing or conference: *a papal audience.* **4.** An opportunity to be heard.

THESAURUS

attentions *n.* —*See* ADVANCES.

attentive *adj.* Full of polite concern for the well-being of others ▸ considerate, courteous, gallant, neighborly, polite, regardful, respectful, solicitous, thoughtful. [*Compare* BENEVOLENT, FRIENDLY.] —*See also* ALERT.

attentiveness *n.* —*See* ATTENTION, CONSIDERATION (1).

attenuate *v.* To become diffuse ▸ rarefy, thin. —*See also* DILUTE, ENERVATE.

attenuate or **attenuated** *adj.* Marked by great diffusion of component particles ▸ rare, rarefied, thin.

attenuation *n.* —*See* DEBILITATION.

attest *v.* —*See* CERTIFY, CONFIRM (1), INDICATE (1), TESTIFY.

attestant or **attester** or **attestor** *n.* One who testifies, especially in court ▸ deponent, testifier, witness.

attestation *n.* —*See* CONFIRMATION (2).

attire *n.* Showy and elaborate clothing or apparel ▸ array, finery, frippery, regalia. *Slang:* get-up, glad-rags, Sunday best. ***Idiom:*** go-to-meeting clothes. —*See also* DRESS (1).

attire *v.* —*See* DRESS UP, DRESS (1).

attitude *n.* **1.** A general cast of mind with regard to something ▸ feeling, sentiment. [*Compare* IDEA.] **2.** The way in which one is placed or arranged ▸ arrangement, pose, position, posture. —*See also* POSTURE (1), POSTURE (2).

attitudinize *v.* —*See* IMPERSONATE, POSE (1).

attorney *n.* —*See* LAWYER.

attract *v.* To direct or impel to oneself by some quality or action ▸ allure, appeal, draw, entice, lure, magnetize, take. *Informal:* pull. ***Idioms:*** catch one's eye, pique one's interest. [*Compare* CHARM.] —*See also* GRIP.

attraction *n.* The power or quality of attracting ▸ allure, allurement, appeal, attractiveness, call, captivation, charisma, charm, draw, enchantment, enticement, fascination, glamour, gravitation, lure, magnetism, witchery. *Informal:* pull. —*See also* LURE (1).

attractive *adj.* Pleasing to the eye or mind ▸ appealing, bewitching, captivating, charismatic, charming, cute, desirable, enchanting, engaging, enticing, fascinating, fetching, glamorous, graceful, lovely, magic, magical, magnetic, pretty, sweet, taking, tempting, well-favored, winning, winsome. [*Compare* DELIGHTFUL, SEDUCTIVE.] —*See also* BEAUTIFUL, BECOMING.

attractiveness *n.* —*See* ATTRACTION.

attribute *v.* To regard as belonging to or resulting from another ▸ accredit, ascribe, assign, charge, credit, refer. [*Compare* ACCUSE.] —*See also* FIX (3).

attribute *n.* An object or expression associated with and serving to identify something else ▸ emblem, metaphor, signifier, symbol, token. [*Compare* EXPRESSION, SIGN, TERM.] —*See also* QUALITY (1).

attrition *n.* —*See* PENITENCE.

attune *v.* —*See* ADJUST, HARMONIZE (1).

atypical or **atypic** *adj.* —*See* ABNORMAL, UNUSUAL.

atypically *adv.* —*See* UNUSUALLY.

au courant *adj.* —*See* CONTEMPORARY (2).

auction *n.* —*See* DEAL (1).

audacious *adj.* —*See* ADVENTUROUS, BRAVE, IMPUDENT.

audacity or **audaciousness** *n.* —*See* DARING, IMPUDENCE.

audience *n.* **1.** The body of persons who admire a public personality, especially an entertainer ▸ following, public. [*Compare* FAN[2].] **2.** A chance to be heard ▸ audition, hearing, listen. ***Idiom:*** one's day in court. **3.** Someone who sees something occur ▸ eyewitness, seer, viewer, witness.

au·di·o (ô′dē-ō′) ▸ *adj.* 1. Of or relating to audible sound. 2. Of the broadcasting or reception of sound. 3. Of the high-fidelity reproduction of sound. ▸ *n., pl.* **-di·os.** 1. The audio part of television or motion-picture equipment. 2. The broadcasting, reception, or reproduction of sound. 3. Audible sound.
audio– ▸ *pref.* 1. Hearing: *audiology.* 2. Sound: *audiophile.*
audio book ▸ *n.* A recorded reading of a book reproduced in cassette or CD form.
au·di·o·cas·sette (ô′dē-ō-kə-sĕt′) ▸ *n.* A cassette containing audiotape.
audio frequency ▸ *n.* A range of frequencies, usu. from 15 hertz to 20,000 hertz, characteristic of signals audible to the normal human ear.
au·di·ol·o·gy (ô′dē-ŏl′ə-jē) ▸ *n.* The study of hearing, esp. hearing defects and their treatment. **—au′di·o·log′i·cal** (-ə-lŏj′ĭ-kəl) *adj.* **—au′di·ol′o·gist** *n.*
au·di·o·phile (ô′dē-ə-fīl′) ▸ *n.* One who has an ardent interest in high-fidelity sound reproduction.
au·di·o·tape (ô′dē-ō-tāp′) ▸ *n.* A magnetic tape recording of sound made for later playback. ▸ *v.* **-taped, -tap·ing.** To record (sound) on magnetic tape.
au·di·o-vis·u·al (ô′dē-ō-vĭzh′o͞o-əl) ▸ *adj.* Both audible and visible. ▸ *n.* Educational material (e.g., a language film) in audible and visible form.
au·dit (ô′dĭt) ▸ *n.* A formal examination or verification of financial accounts. ▸ *v.* 1. To formally examine or correct the financial accounts of: *audit a tax return.* 2. To attend (a college course) without receiving academic credit.
au·di·tion (ô-dĭsh′ən) ▸ *n.* A hearing, esp. a trial performance of an actor, dancer, or musician, to obtain a particular role or position. ▸ *v.* 1. To take part in an audition. 2. To evaluate (a performer) in an audition.
au·di·tor (ô′dĭ-tər) ▸ *n.* 1. One who audits accounts. 2. One who audits a college course. 3. One who hears; listener.
au·di·to·ri·um (ô′dĭ-tôr′ē-əm) ▸ *n.* 1. A large room to accommodate an audience. 2. A building for public gatherings or entertainments.
au·di·to·ry (ô′dĭ-tôr′ē) ▸ *adj.* Of or relating to the sense, the organs, or the experience of hearing.
auf Wie·der·seh·en (ouf vē′dər-zā′ən) ▸ *interj.* Farewell.
Aug. ▸ *abbr.* August
au·ger (ô′gər) ▸ *n.* A tool for boring holes in wood, ice, or the earth.
aught¹ also **ought** (ôt) ▸ *pron.* Anything whatever.
aught² also **ought** (ôt) ▸ *n.* 1. A cipher; zero. 2. *Archaic* Nothing.
aug·ment (ôg-mĕnt′) ▸ *v.* To make or become greater in size, extent, or quantity; increase. **—aug′men·ta′tion** *n.*
au gra·tin (ō grät′n, grăt′n) ▸ *adj.* Baked with a topping of bread crumbs and sometimes butter and grated cheese.
au·gur (ô′gər) ▸ *n.* A seer; soothsayer. ▸ *v.* 1. To predict, esp. from signs or omens. 2. To serve as a sign or omen (of).
au·gu·ry (ô′gyə-rē) ▸ *n., pl.* **-ries.** 1. The art or practice of auguring. 2. An omen.
au·gust (ô-gŭst′) ▸ *adj.* 1. Inspiring awe, reverence, or admiration; majestic. 2. Venerable. **—au·gust′ly** *adv.* **—au·gust′ness** *n.*
August ▸ *n.* The 8th month of the Gregorian calendar.
Au·gus·ta (ô-gŭs′tə, ə-) ▸ The capital of ME, in the SW part NNE of Portland.
Au·gus·tine (ô′gə-stēn′, ô-gŭs′tĭn) Saint (A.D. 354–430) ▸ Early Christian church father and philosopher.
Au·gus·tus (ô-gŭs′təs) Orig. **Oc·ta·vi·an** (ŏk-tā′vē-ən) (63 B.C. – A.D. 14) ▸ 1st emperor of Rome (27 B.C. – A.D. 14); defeated Mark Antony and Cleopatra in 31 B.C.
au jus (ō zho͞os′, zhü′) ▸ *adj.* Served with the natural juices or gravy.
auk (ôk) ▸ *n.* A diving sea bird of northern regions, having a chunky body, short wings, and webbed feet.
auld lang syne (ôld′ lăng zīn′, sīn′) ▸ *n.* The good old days long past.
aunt (ănt, änt) ▸ *n.* 1. The sister of one's father or mother. 2. The wife of one's uncle.
au pair (ô pâr′) ▸ *n.* A young foreigner who works for a family for room and board and in order to learn the language.
au·ra (ôr′ə) ▸ *n., pl.* **-ras** or **-rae** (ôr′ē). 1. An invisible breath or emanation. 2. A distinctive quality that seems to surround a person or thing; atmosphere.
au·ral¹ (ôr′əl) ▸ *adj.* Of or perceived by the ear. **—au′ral·ly** *adv.*
au·ral² (ôr′əl) ▸ *adj.* Of or relating to an aura.
au·re·ole (ôr′ē-ōl′) also **au·re·o·la** (ô-rē′ə-lə) ▸ *n.* 1. A halo. 2. See **corona** 1.
au re·voir (ō′ rə-vwär′) ▸ *interj.* Farewell.
au·ri·cle (ôr′ĭ-kəl) ▸ *n.* 1. *Anat.* a. The outer projecting portion of the ear. b. See **atrium** 2. 2. *Biol.* An earlobe-shaped part or appendage. **—au′ri·cled** (-kəld) *adj.*
au·ric·u·lar (ô-rĭk′yə-lər) ▸ *adj.* 1. Aural. 2. Received by or spoken into the ear. 3. Shaped like an ear or earlobe. 4. Of or relating to an auricle of the heart.
au·ro·ra (ə-rôr′ə) ▸ *n.* 1. Aurora borealis. 2. Aurora australis. 3. The dawn. **—au·ro′ral** *adj.*
Aurora ▸ *n. Rom. Myth.* The goddess of the dawn.
aurora aus·tra·lis (ô-strā′lĭs) ▸ *n.* A luminous phenomenon of southern regions that corresponds to the aurora borealis; southern lights.
aurora bo·re·al·is (bôr′ē-ăl′ĭs) ▸ *n.* Luminous bands or streamers in the night skies of northern regions, likely caused by charged particles entering the earth's magnetic field; northern lights.
aus·cul·ta·tion (ô′skəl-tā′shən) ▸ *n.* Diagnostic monitoring of the sounds made by internal bodily organs.
aus·pice (ô′spĭs) ▸ *n., pl.* **aus·pi·ces** (ô′spĭ-sĭz, -sēz′). 1. also **auspices** Protection or support; patronage. 2. A sign, portent, or omen.
aus·pi·cious (ô-spĭsh′əs) ▸ *adj.* 1. Favorable; propitious. 2. Successful; prosperous. **—aus·pi′cious·ly** *adv.*
Aus·ten (ô′stən), **Jane** (1775–1817) ▸ British writer.
aus·tere (ô-stîr′) ▸ *adj.* **-ter·er, -ter·est.** 1. Severe or stern; somber: *an austere Puritan minister.* 2. Strict or severe in discipline; ascetic: *a nomad's austere life.* 3. Without adornment; bare: *austere living quarters.* **—aus·tere′ly** *adv.* **—aus·ter′i·ty** (-stĕr′ĭ-tē).
Aus·tin (ô′stən, ŏs′tən) ▸ The capital of TX, in the S-central part.
aus·tral (ô′strəl) ▸ *adj.* Southern.
Aus·tral·a·sia (ô′strə-lā′zhə, -shə) ▸ 1. The islands of the S Pacific, including Australia, New Zealand, and New Guinea. 2. Oceania. **—Aus′tral·a′sian** *adj.* & *n.*
Aus·tra·lia (ô-strāl′yə) ▸ 1. The world's smallest continent, SE of Asia between the Pacific and Indian Oceans. 2. A commonwealth comprising the continent of Australia, the island state of Tasmania, two external territories, and several dependencies.
Aus·tra·lian (ô-strāl′yən) ▸ *adj.* Of or relating to Australia. ▸ *n.* 1. A native or inhabitant of Australia. 2a. A member

THESAURUS

audit *n.* —*See* EXAMINATION (1).
audit *v.* —*See* EXAMINE (1).
audition *n.* 1. A chance to be heard ▸ audience, hearing, listen. ***Idiom:*** one's day in court. 2. The sense or faculty by which sound is perceived ▸ ear, hearing.
augment *v.* —*See* GAIN (1), INCREASE, SUPPLEMENT.
augment *n.* —*See* INCREASE (1).
augmentation *n.* —*See* ADDITION (1), INCREASE (1).
augur *v.* —*See* FORESHADOW, PROPHESY.
augur *n.* —*See* PROPHET.
augural *adj.* —*See* PROPHETIC.
augury *n.* —*See* MAGIC (1), OMEN, PROPHECY.
august *adj.* —*See* EXALTED, GRAND.
au naturel *adj.* —*See* NUDE.
aura *n.* —*See* AIR (3).
aureate *adj.* —*See* ORATORICAL.
aurora *n.* —*See* DAWN.
auspex *n.* —*See* PROPHET.
auspices *n.* —*See* PATRONAGE (1).
auspicious *adj.* —*See* FAVORABLE (1), OPPORTUNE.
austere *adj.* —*See* ASCETIC, BARE (1), BLEAK (1).
austerity *n.* —*See* SEVERITY.

of an aboriginal people of Australia. **b.** Any of the aboriginal languages of Australia.

Aus·tra·loid (ô′strə-loid′) ▸ *adj. Anthro.* Of or being a human racial classification distinguished by dark skin and dark curly hair and including peoples indigenous to Australia and parts of SE Asia. **—Aus′tra·loid′** *n.*

Aus·tri·a (ô′strē-ə) ▸ A landlocked country of central Europe W of Czech Republic and Hungary. **—Aus′tri·an** *adj. & n.*

Aus·tro-A·si·at·ic (ô′strō-ā′zhē-ăt′ĭk, -shē-, -zē-) ▸ *n.* A family of languages of SE Asia once dominant in NE India and Indochina. **—Aus′tro-A′si·at′ic** *adj.*

Aus·tro·ne·sia (ô′strō-nē′zhə, -shə) ▸ The islands of the Pacific, including Indonesia, Melanesia, Micronesia, and Polynesia.

Aus·tro·ne·sian (ô′strō-nē′zhən, -shən) ▸ *adj.* Of or relating to Austronesia or its peoples, languages, or cultures. ▸ *n.* A family of languages that includes the Indonesian, Malay, Melanesian, Micronesian, and Polynesian subfamilies.

aut– ▸ *pref.* Var. of **auto–**.

au·tar·chy (ô′tär′kē) ▸ *n., pl.* **-chies.** Autocracy. **—au′tarch** *n.* **—au·tar′chic** *adj.*

au·then·tic (ô-thĕn′tĭk) ▸ *adj.* **1.** Worthy of trust, reliance, or belief. **2.** Having a claimed and verifiable origin or authorship. **—au·then′ti·cal·ly** *adv.* **—au′then·tic′i·ty** (-tĭs′ĭ-tē) *n.*

au·then·ti·cate (ô-thĕn′tĭ-kāt′) ▸ *v.* **-cat·ed, -cat·ing.** To prove or establish as being genuine. **—au·then′ti·ca′tion** *n.*

au·thor (ô′thər) ▸ *n.* **1a.** The writer of a literary work. **b.** One who writes as a profession. **2.** One who originates or creates something. **—au′thor** *v.* **—au·thor′i·al** (ô-thôr′ē-əl, -thŏr′-) *adj.* **—au′thor·ship′** *n.*

au·thor·i·tar·i·an (ə-thôr′ĭ-târ′ē-ən, -thŏr′-, ô-) ▸ *adj.* Of, characterized by or favoring absolute obedience to authority. **—au·thor′i·tar′i·an** *n.* **—au·thor′i·tar′i·an·ism** *n.*

au·thor·i·ta·tive (ə-thôr′ĭ-tā′tĭv, -thŏr′-, ô-) ▸ *adj.* **1.** Having or arising from proper authority; official. **2.** Having or showing expert knowledge. **—au·thor′i·ta′tive·ly** *adv.* **—au·thor′i·ta′tive·ness** *n.*

au·thor·i·ty (ə-thôr′ĭ-tē, -thŏr′-, ô-) ▸ *n., pl.* **-ties. 1a.** The right and power to enforce laws, exact obedience, command, determine, or judge. **b.** One that is invested with this right and power, esp. a government or government official. **2.** Authorization. **3a.** One that is an accepted source of expert information. **b.** A citation from such a source. **4.** Firm self-assurance; confidence.

au·thor·i·za·tion (ô′thər-ĭ-zā′shən) ▸ *n.* **1.** The act of authorizing. **2.** Something that authorizes.

au·thor·ize (ô′thə-rīz′) ▸ *v.* **-ized, -iz·ing. 1.** To grant authority or power to. **2.** To give permission for; sanction. **3.** To justify.

au·tism (ô′tĭz′əm) ▸ *n.* A pervasive developmental disorder characterized by severe deficits in social interaction and communication, by an extremely limited range of activities and interests, and often by the presence of repetitive, stereotyped behaviors. **—au·tis′tic** (-tĭs′-tĭk) *adj. & n.*

au·to (ô′tō) ▸ *n., pl.* **-tos.** An automobile.

auto– or **aut–** ▸ *pref.* **1.** Self; same: *autobiography.* **2.** Automatic: *autopilot.*

au·to·bahn (ô′tə-bän′, ou′tō-) ▸ *n.* An expressway in Germany.

au·to·bi·og·ra·phy (ô′tō-bī-ŏg′rə-fē) ▸ *n., pl.* **-phies.** The biography of a person written by that person. **—au′to·bi·og′ra·pher** *n.* **—au′to·bi′o·graph′ic** (-bī′ə-grăf′ĭk), **au′to·bi′o·graph′i·cal** *adj.*

au·toch·tho·nous (ô-tŏk′thə-nəs) ▸ *adj.* Originating where found; indigenous; native.

au·toc·ra·cy (ô-tŏk′rə-sē) ▸ *n., pl.* **-cies.** Government by a single person having unlimited power. **—au′to·crat′** *n.* **—au′to·crat′ic, au′to·crat′i·cal** *adj.*

au·to·di·dact (ô′tō-dī′dăkt′) ▸ *n.* One who is self-taught. **—au′to·di·dac′tic** *adj.*

au·to·graph (ô′tə-grăf′) ▸ *n.* **1.** A person's own signature or handwriting. **2.** A manuscript in the author's handwriting. ▸ *v.* To write one's signature on; sign.

au·to·im·mune (ô′tō-ĭ-myo͞on′) ▸ *adj.* Of or relating to an immune response by the body against one of its own tissues or types of cells. **—au′to·im·mu′ni·ty** *n.*

au·to·mate (ô′tə-māt′) ▸ *v.* **-mat·ed, -mat·ing. 1.** To convert to automatic operation. **2.** To operate by automation.

automated teller machine ▸ *n.* An electronic machine in a public place that is connected to a bank's data system and is activated by a customer to obtain specified banking services, esp. deposits and cash withdrawals.

au·to·mat·ic (ô′tə-măt′ĭk) ▸ *adj.* **1.** Acting or operating with little or no external influence or control. **2.** Involuntary; reflex. **3.** Responding or behaving in a mechanical way. **4.** Capable of firing continuously until ammunition is exhausted. ▸ *n.* A machine or device, esp. a firearm, that is automatic. **—au′to·mat′i·cal·ly** *adv.*

automatic pilot ▸ *n.* A navigational mechanism, as on an aircraft, that automatically maintains a preset course; autopilot.

automatic teller machine ▸ *n.* See **automated teller machine.**

au·to·ma·tion (ô′tə-mā′shən) ▸ *n.* **1.** The automatic operation or control of equipment, a process, or a system. **2.** The techniques and equipment that are used to achieve automatic operation or control. **3.** The condition of

THESAURUS

autarchic or **autarchical** *adj.* —*See* ABSOLUTE.

autarchist *n.* —*See* DICTATOR.

autarchy *n.* —*See* ABSOLUTISM (2).

authentic *adj.* **1.** Not counterfeit or copied ▸ actual, bona fide, certified, confirmed, genuine, good, indubitable, legitimate, original, proved, real, tested, true, undoubted, unquestionable, verified, veritable. *Slang:* legit, kosher. *Idioms:* honest to goodness, for real, real live, sure enough, the real McCoy, the real thing, true to life. [*Compare* ACTUAL, CERTAIN.] **2.** Worthy of belief, as because of precision or faithfulness to an original ▸ authoritative, convincing, credible, faithful, true, trustworthy, valid. [*Compare* ACCURATE, DEFINITIVE, DEPENDABLE.]

authenticate *v.* —*See* CONFIRM (1), PROVE.

authentication *n.* —*See* CONFIRMATION (2).

authenticity *n.* —*See* VERACITY.

author *n.* —*See* ORIGINATOR.

author *v.* —*See* PUBLISH (2).

authoritarian *adj.* Characterized by or favoring absolute obedience to authority ▸ autocratic, despotic, dictatorial, totalitarian, tyrannic, tyrannical. [*Compare* ABSOLUTE.] —*See also* DICTATORIAL.

authoritarian *n.* One who imposes or favors absolute obedience to authority ▸ autocrat, despot, dictator, martinet, totalitarian, tyrant. —*See also* DICTATOR.

authoritarianism *n.* —*See* ABSOLUTISM (1), TYRANNY.

authoritative *adj.* **1.** Having or arising from authority ▸ conclusive, formal, imperial, official, ruling, sanctioned, standard, supreme. [*Compare* ADMINISTRATIVE.] **2.** Exercising authority ▸ commanding, dominant, lordly, masterful. —*See also* AUTHENTIC (2), DEFINITIVE.

authority *n.* The right and power to command, decide, rule, or judge ▸ carte blanche, command, control, domination, dominion, jurisdiction, mandate, mastery, might, omnipotence, power, prerogative, rule, sovereignty, superiority, supremacy, sway. *Informal:* muscle, say-so. —*See also* DOMINANCE, EXPERT, PERMISSION.

authorization *n.* —*See* PERMISSION.

authorize *v.* To give authority to ▸ accredit, commission, empower, enable, entitle, license, qualify. [*Compare* APPOINT, ELECT, LEGALIZE.] —*See also* PERMIT (2).

autochthonous *adj.* —*See* DOMESTIC (3), INDIGENOUS.

autocracy *n.* —*See* ABSOLUTISM (1), ABSOLUTISM (2), TYRANNY.

autocrat *n.* —*See* AUTHORITARIAN, DICTATOR.

autograph *v.* —*See* SIGN.

automatic *adj.* —*See* PERFUNCTORY, SPONTANEOUS.

being automatically controlled or operated.
au·tom·a·tism (ô-tŏm′ə-tĭz′əm) ▸ *n.* The state, quality, or action of being automatic.
au·tom·a·tize (ô-tŏm′ə-tīz′) ▸ *v.* **-tized, -tiz·ing.** To make automatic. **—au·tom′a·ti·za′tion** *n.*
au·tom·a·ton (ô-tŏm′ə-tən, -tŏn′) ▸ *n., pl.* **-tons** or **-ta** (-tə). **1.** An automatic machine or mechanism, esp. a robot. **2.** One that behaves or responds in an automatic or mechanical way.
au·to·mo·bile (ô′tə-mō-bēl′, -mō′bēl′) ▸ *n.* A self-propelled land vehicle, esp. a four-wheeled passenger car powered by an internal-combustion engine.
au·to·mo·tive (ô′tə-mō′tĭv) ▸ *adj.* **1.** Moving by itself; self-propelled. **2.** Of or relating to self-propelled vehicles, esp. automobiles.
au·to·nom·ic nervous system (ô′tə-nŏm′ĭk) ▸ *n.* The part of the vertebrate nervous system that regulates involuntary action, as of the intestines, heart, and glands.
au·ton·o·mous (ô-tŏn′ə-məs) ▸ *adj.* **1.** Not controlled by others; independent. **2.** Self-governing. **—au·ton′o·my** *n.*
au·to·pi·lot (ô′tō-pī′lət) ▸ *n.* Automatic pilot.
au·top·sy (ô′tŏp′sē, ô′təp-) ▸ *n., pl.* **-sies.** Examination of a dead body to find the cause of death; postmortem. **—au′top′sist** *n.*
au·to·some (ô′tə-sōm′) ▸ *n.* A chromosome that is not a sex chromosome.
au·to·sug·ges·tion (ô′tō-səg-jĕs′chən) ▸ *n. Psychol.* The process by which a person induces self-acceptance of an opinion, belief, or plan of action.
au·to·troph (ô′tə-trŏf′, -trōf′) ▸ *n.* An organism capable of synthesizing its own food from inorganic substances. **—au′to·troph′ic** *adj.*
au·tumn (ô′təm) ▸ *n.* **1.** The season between summer and winter; fall. **2.** A period of maturity verging on decline. **—au·tum′nal** (-tŭm′nəl) *adj.*
aux. ▸ *abbr.* **1.** auxiliary **2.** auxiliary verb
aux·il·ia·ry (ôg-zĭl′yə-rē, -zĭl′ə-rē) ▸ *adj.* **1.** Giving assistance or support; helping. **2.** Subsidiary; supplementary. **3.** Held in or used as a reserve. ▸ *n., pl.* **-ries. 1.** One that acts in a supporting capacity. **2.** An auxiliary verb.
auxiliary verb ▸ *n.* A verb, such as *have, can,* or *will,* that comes first in a verb phrase and helps form the mood, voice, aspect, and tense of the main verb.
aux·in (ôk′sĭn) ▸ *n.* Any of several plant growth hormones.
Av (äv, ôv) ▸ *n.* A month of the Jewish calendar.
Av. ▸ *abbr.* avenue
a·vail (ə-vāl′) ▸ *v.* To be of use or advantage (to); help. ▸ *n.* Use, benefit, or advantage: *labored to no avail.*
a·vail·a·ble (ə-vā′lə-bəl) ▸ *adj.* **1.** At hand; accessible. **2.** Capable of being used or gotten; obtainable. **—a·vail′a·bil′i·ty** *n.*
av·a·lanche (ăv′ə-lănch′) ▸ *n.* **1.** A slide of a large mass, as of snow or rock, down a mountainside. **2.** A massive amount: *an avalanche of mail.*
a·vant-garde (ä′vänt-gärd′, ăv′änt-) ▸ *n.* A group active in the invention and application of new techniques in a given field, esp. in the arts. **—a′vant-garde′** *adj.*
av·a·rice (ăv′ə-rĭs) ▸ *n.* Extreme desire for wealth; greed. **—av′a·ri′cious** (-ə-rĭsh′əs) *adj.*
a·vast (ə-văst′) ▸ *interj. Naut.* Used as a command to stop or desist.
av·a·tar (ăv′ə-tär′) ▸ *n.* **1.** *Hinduism* One that is regarded as an incarnation, esp. of Vishnu. **2.** An embodiment or exemplar; archetype.
a·vaunt (ə-vônt′, ə-vänt′) ▸ *adv.* Hence; away.
Ave. ▸ *abbr.* avenue
a·venge (ə-vĕnj′) ▸ *v.* **a·venged, a·veng·ing. 1.** To take revenge for: *avenge a murder.* **2.** To take vengeance on behalf of: *avenged his father.* **—a·veng′er** *n.*
av·e·nue (ăv′ə-no͞o′, -nyo͞o′) ▸ *n.* **1.** A wide street or thoroughfare. **2.** A means of access, approach, or achievement.
a·ver (ə-vûr′) ▸ *v.* **a·verred, a·ver·ring.** To assert positively; declare. **—a·ver′ment** *n.*
av·er·age (ăv′ər-ĭj, ăv′rĭj) ▸ *n.* **1a.** A number that typifies a set of numbers of which it is a function. **b.** See **arithmetic mean. 2.** A relative level, proportion, or degree that indicates position or achievement. ▸ *adj.* **1.** Of or constituting a mathematical average. **2.** Intermediate between extremes, as on a scale. **3.** Usual; ordinary: *a poll of average people.* ▸ *v.* **-aged, -ag·ing. 1.** To calculate the average of. **2.** To do or have an average of: *averaged ten pages an hour.* **3.** To distribute proportionately.
a·verse (ə-vûrs′) ▸ *adj.* Strongly disinclined; reluctant. **—a·verse′ly** *adv.*
a·ver·sion (ə-vûr′zhən, -shən) ▸ *n.* **1.** A fixed, intense dislike; repugnance. **2.** One that is intensely disliked and avoided.
a·vert (ə-vûrt′) ▸ *v.* **1.** To turn away: *avert one's eyes.* **2.** To ward off; prevent. **—a·vert′i·ble, a·vert′a·ble** *adj.*
a·vi·an (ā′vē-ən) ▸ *adj.* Of or characteristic of birds.
a·vi·ar·y (ā′vē-ĕr′ē) ▸ *n., pl.* **-ies.** A large enclosure for holding birds, as in a zoo.
a·vi·a·tion (ā′vē-ā′shən, ăv′ē-) ▸ *n.* **1.** The operation of aircraft. **2.** The design, development, and production of aircraft.
a·vi·a·tor (ā′vē-ā′tər, ăv′ē-) ▸ *n.* One who operates an aircraft; pilot.
a·vi·a·trix (ā′vē-ā′trĭks, ăv′ē-) ▸ *n.* A woman who operates an aircraft.
av·id (ăv′ĭd) ▸ *adj.* **1.** Having an ardent desire or craving; eager: *avid for adventure.* **2.** Passionate; enthusiastic: *an avid sports fan.* **—a·vid′i·ty** (ə-vĭd′ĭ-tē) **—av′id·ly** *adv.*

THESAURUS

autonomous *adj.* —*See* FREE (1), INDEPENDENT (1).
autonomy *n.* —*See* FREEDOM, INDEPENDENCE.
auxiliary *adj.* **1.** Giving or able to give help or support ▸ accessory, aiding, ancillary, assistant, assisting, collateral, contributory, cooperating, helping, subsidiary, supporting, supportive. [*Compare* [illegible]] **2.** Used or held in reserve ▸ backup, emergency, reserve, secondary, standby, supplemental, supplementary. [*Compare* ADDITIONAL.]
auxiliary *n.* —*See* ASSISTANT.
avail *v.* —*See* PROFIT (2).
avail *n.* —*See* ADVANTAGE (2), USE (2).
available *adj.* Capable of being obtained or used ▸ acquirable, attainable, gettable, obtainable, procurable. *Idioms:* at (*or* on) hand, at one's disposal, on tap, to be had, within reach. [*Compare* CONVENIENT, OPEN, UNOCCUPIED.] —*See also* SINGLE.
avant-garde *n.* —*See* FOREFRONT.
avant-garde *adj.* —*See* PROGRESSIVE (1).
avarice or **avariciousness** *n.* —*See* GREED.
avaricious *adj.* —*See* GREEDY.
avenge *v.* To exact revenge for or [illegible] get, pay back, pay off, redress, repay, requite, vindicate. *Informal:* fix. *Idioms:* even the score, get back at, get even with, give a taste of one's own medicine, pay back in kind (*or* in one's own coin), pay off old scores, settle a score, settle (*or* square) accounts, take an eye for an eye. [*Compare* PUNISH, RETALIATE.]
avenging *adj.* —*See* VINDICTIVE.
avenue *n.* —*See* WAY (2).
aver *v.* —*See* ASSERT.
average *adj.* Relating to or occupying a middle position on a scale of evaluation ▸ fair, indifferent, mediocre, medium, middling, tolerable. —*See also* ACCEPTABLE (2), COMMON (1), ORDINARY.
average *n.* Something, as a type, number, quantity, or degree, that represents a midpoint between extremes ▸ mean, median, medium, midpoint, norm, par. [*Compare* CENTER.] —*See also* USUAL.
averageness *n.* —*See* USUALNESS.
averment *n.* —*See* ASSERTION.
averse *adj.* —*See* INDISPOSED.
averseness *n.* —*See* INDISPOSITION.
aversion *n.* —*See* HATE (1), HATE (2), INDISPOSITION, OPPOSITION (1).
avert *v.* —*See* PREVENT, TURN (2).
aviator *n.* A person who flies an airplane ▸ flier, pilot. *Slang:* flyboy.
avid *adj.* —*See* EAGER, GREEDY, VORACIOUS.
avidity or **avidness** *n.* —*See* GREED, VORACITY.

a·vi·on·ics (ā′vē-ŏn′ĭks, ăv′ē-) ▸ *n.* *(takes sing. v.)* The science and technology of electronics as applied to aeronautics and astronautics. **—a′vi·on′ic** *adj.*

av·o·ca·do (ăv′ə-kä′dō, ä′və-) ▸ *n., pl.* **-dos.** **1.** A tropical American tree having pear-shaped fruit with leathery skin and yellowish-green flesh. **2.** The edible fruit of this tree.

av·o·ca·tion (ăv′ō-kā′shən) ▸ *n.* An activity taken up in addition to one's regular work, usu. for enjoyment; hobby. **—av′o·ca′tion·al** *adj.*

av·o·cet (ăv′ə-sĕt′) ▸ *n.* A long-legged shore bird with a long slender beak.

A·vo·ga·dro's number (ä′vō-gä′drōz) ▸ *n.* The number of atoms or molecules in a mole, approx. 6.02×10^{23}.

a·void (ə-void′) ▸ *v.* **1.** To stay clear of; evade; shun. **2.** To keep from happening; prevent. **3.** To refrain from. **—a·void′a·ble** *adj.* **—a·void′a·bly** *adv.* **—a·void′ance** *n.* **—a·void′er** *n.*

av·oir·du·pois weight (ăv′ər-də-poiz′) ▸ *n.* A system of weights and measures based on one pound containing 16 ounces or 7,000 grains and equal to 453.59 grams.

a·vouch (ə-vouch′) ▸ *v.* **1.** To affirm. **2.** To vouch for.

a·vow (ə-vou′) ▸ *v.* **1.** To acknowledge openly; confess: *avow guilt.* **2.** To assert: *avowed the words to be true.* **—a·vow′al** *n.* **—a·vowed′** *adj.* **—a·vow′ed·ly** (-ĭd-lē) *adv.*

a·vun·cu·lar (ə-vŭng′kyə-lər) ▸ *adj.* Of or like an uncle.

a·wait (ə-wāt′) ▸ *v.* **1.** To wait (for). **2.** To be in store (for): *Success awaits him. A busy day awaits.*

a·wake (ə-wāk′) ▸ *v.* **a·woke** (ə-wōk′) or **a·waked, a·waked** or **a·wok·en** (ə-wō′kən), **a·wak·ing. 1.** To rouse or become roused from sleep. **2.** To excite. **3.** To stir up (e.g., desire). **4.** To become aware: *awoke to reality.* ▸ *adj.* **1.** Not asleep. **2.** Vigilant; alert.

a·wak·en (ə-wā′kən) ▸ *v.* To awake. **—a·wak′en·ing** *adj. & n.*

a·ward (ə-wôrd′) ▸ *v.* **1.** To grant or declare as merited or due: *awarded damages to the plaintiff.* **2.** To bestow for performance or quality: *award a prize to the victor.* ▸ *n.* **1.** Something awarded; prize. **2.** A decision, as by a judge or arbitrator.

a·ware (ə-wâr′) ▸ *adj.* Having knowledge or cognizance; mindful. **—a·ware′ness** *n.*

a·wash (ə-wŏsh′, -wôsh′) ▸ *adj. & adv.* **1.** Level with or washed by waves. **2.** Flooded. **3.** Afloat.

a·way (ə-wā′) ▸ *adv.* **1.** From a particular thing or place: *ran away from the lion.* **2.** At or to a distance in space or time: *away off on the horizon.* **3.** In or to a different place or direction: *glanced away.* **4.** Out of existence: *music fading away.* **5.** From one's presence or possession: *gave the tickets away.* **6.** Continuously; steadily: *worked away.* **7.** At will; freely: *Fire away!* ▸ *adj.* **1.** Absent: *The neighbors are away.* **2.** Distant, as in space or time: *miles away.* **3.** Played on an opponent's home grounds: *an away game.*

awe (ô) ▸ *n.* **1.** A mixed emotion of reverence, dread, and wonder. **2.** Respect tinged with fear. ▸ *v.* **awed, aw·ing.** To inspire or fill with awe.

a·weigh (ə-wā′) ▸ *adj.* Hanging clear of the bottom. Used of an anchor.

awe·some (ô′səm) ▸ *adj.* **1.** Inspiring awe. **2.** Expressing awe. **3.** *Slang* Superb; outstanding. **—awe′some·ly** *adv.* **—awe′some·ness** *n.*

awe·struck (ô′strŭk′) also **awe·strick·en** (-strĭk′ən) ▸ *adj.* Full of awe.

aw·ful (ô′fəl) ▸ *adj.* **1.** Very bad or unpleasant; terrible. **2.** Commanding, inspiring, or filled with awe. **3.** Great: *an awful burden.* **—aw′ful·ly** *adv.* **—aw′ful·ness** *n.*

a·while (ə-hwīl′, ə-wīl′) ▸ *adv.* For a short time.

awk·ward (ôk′wərd) ▸ *adj.* **1.** Lacking grace or dexterity; clumsy or ungainly. **2.** Hard to handle or manage; unwieldy: *an awkward bundle.* **3.** Uncomfortable; inconvenient: *an awkward pose; an awkward time.* **4.** Causing embarrassment: *an awkward remark.* **—awk′ward·ly** *adv.* **—awk′ward·ness** *n.*

awl (ôl) ▸ *n.* A pointed tool for making holes, as in wood or leather.

awn (ôn) ▸ *n.* A slender bristle on the spikelets of many grasses. **—awned** *adj.*

awn·ing (ô′nĭng) ▸ *n.* A canvas rooflike structure, as over a window or storefront, that is used to provide shade or shelter.

a·woke (ə-wōk′) ▸ *v.* P.t. of **awake.**

a·wok·en (ə-wō′kən) ▸ *v.* P.part. of **awake.**

AWOL (ā′wôl′) ▸ *adj. & adv.* Absent without leave. ▸ *n.* A person who is absent without leave, esp. from military service.

a·wry (ə-rī′) ▸ *adv.* **1.** Askew. **2.** Wrong; amiss. **—a·wry′** *adj.*

ax or **axe** (ăks) ▸ *n., pl.* **ax·es** (ăk′sĭz). **1.** A chopping tool with a bladed head mounted on a handle. **2.** *Informal* A sudden termination, as of employment. ▸ *v.* **axed, ax·ing. 1.** To use an ax on in order to chop or fell. **2.** To remove ruthlessly or suddenly. ***—idiom:*** **ax to grind** A selfish or subjective aim: *claimed disinterest but had an ax to grind.*

ax·i·al (ăk′sē-əl) ▸ *adj.* **1.** Of, relating to, or forming an axis. **2.** Located on, around, or along an axis. **—ax′i·al·ly** *adv.*

THESAURUS

avocation *n.* —*See* BUSINESS (2).

avoid *v.* To keep away from ▸ abstain from, burke, bypass, circumvent, dodge, duck, elude, escape, eschew, evade, get around, lay off, refrain from, shun, stay off. *Idioms:* fight shy of, give a wide berth to, have no truck with, keep at arm's length, keep (*or* stay *or* steer) clear of, keep one's distance from, let well enough alone. [*Compare* EVADE, SKIRT.]

avoidance *n.* —*See* ESCAPE (2).

avoirdupois *n.* —*See* HEAVINESS.

avouch *v.* —*See* ASSERT, CONFIRM (1).

avow *v.* —*See* ACKNOWLEDGE (1), ASSERT.

avowal *n.* —*See* ACKNOWLEDGMENT (1), ASSERTION.

await *v.* —*See* EXPECT (1), LURK.

awaiting *adj.* —*See* EXPECTANT.

awake *adj.* Not in a state of sleep or unable to sleep ▸ unsleeping, wakeful, wide-awake. *Idiom:* tossing and turning. [*Compare* RESTLESS.] —*See also* AWARE.

awake or **awaken** *v.* —*See* AROUSE, WAKE[1].

award *v.* **1.** To let have as a favor, prerogative, or privilege ▸ accord, concede, give, grant, vouchsafe. [*Compare* YIELD.] **2.** To bestow a reward on ▸ guerdon, honor, reward. —*See also* CONFER (2), DONATE, GIFT.

award *n.* A memento received as a symbol of excellence or victory ▸ accolade, cup, prize, trophy. [*Compare* MEDAL.] —*See also* DISTINCTION (2), DONATION, REWARD.

aware *adj.* Marked by comprehension, cognizance, and perception ▸ alive, awake, cognizant, sensible, sentient, wise. *Informal:* with-it. *Slang:* hip. *Idioms:* in the know (*or* swim), on to, up on. [*Compare* ALERT, INFORMED, SENSITIVE.]

awareness *n.* The condition of being aware ▸ cognizance, consciousness, mindfulness, perception, realization, recognition, sense. [*Compare* ALERTNESS.]

awash *adj.* —*See* FULL (1).

away *adj.* —*See* ABSENT.

awe *n.* —*See* WONDER (1).

awe *v.* —*See* SURPRISE.

awe-inspiring *adj.* —*See* ASTONISHING, GRAND.

awesome *adj.* —*See* EXCELLENT, EXCEPTIONAL, GRAND.

awful *adj.* —*See* TERRIBLE.

awful *adv.* —*See* VERY.

awfully *adv.* —*See* VERY.

awkward *adj.* **1.** Lacking dexterity and grace in physical movement ▸ butterfingered, cloddish, clumsy, gawky, graceless, inept, lubberly, lumpish, maladroit, stumbling, uncoordinated, ungainly, ungraceful. *Slang:* klutzy. *Idioms:* all thumbs, having two left feet. **2.** Difficult to handle or manage ▸ bulky, clumsy, ungainly, unhandy, unmanageable, unwieldy. [*Compare* HEAVY, UNRULY.] **3.** Characterized by embarrassment and discomfort ▸ constrained, embarrassed, embarrassing, self-conscious, uncomfortable, uneasy. *Idiom:* ill at ease. [*Compare* DELICATE, UNPLEASANT.] —*See also* UNFORTUNATE (2), UNSKILLFUL.

awry *adv.* Not in the right way or on the proper course ▸ afield, amiss, astray, wrong.

ax *n.* —*See* DISMISSAL.

ax *v.* —*See* ABOLISH, DISMISS (1).

axial *adj.* —*See* CENTRAL.

ax·il·la (ăk-sĭl′ə) ▸ *n., pl.* **-il·lae** (-sĭl′ē). **1.** The armpit. **2.** An analogous structure, as under a bird's wing.

ax·i·om (ăk′sē-əm) ▸ *n.* **1.** A self-evident or universally recognized truth; maxim. **2.** A principle that is accepted as true without proof; postulate. **—ax′i·o·mat′ic** *adj.*

ax·is (ăk′sĭs) ▸ *n., pl.* **ax·es** (ăk′sēz′). **1.** A straight line about which an object rotates or can be conceived to rotate. **2.** *Math.* **a.** A line, ray, or line segment with respect to which a figure or object is symmetric. **b.** A reference line from which distances or angles are measured in a coordinate system. **3.** A center line to which parts of a structure or body may be referred. **4.** *Bot.* The main stem or central part about which plant parts, as branches, are arranged. **5.** An alliance of powers, such as nations, to promote mutual interests.

ax·le (ăk′səl) ▸ *n.* A supporting shaft on which a wheel or a set of wheels revolves.

ax·le·tree (ăk′səl-trē′) ▸ *n.* A crossbar, as on a cart, with terminal spindles on which the wheels revolve.

ax·on (ăk′sŏn′) ▸ *n.* The usu. long process of a nerve cell that conducts impulses away from the body of the nerve cell.

a·ya·tol·lah (ī′ə-tō′lə) ▸ *n. Islam* A Shiite leader having religious and administrative authority.

aye[1] also **ay** (ī) ▸ *n.* An affirmative vote or voter. ▸ *adv.* Yes; yea.

aye[2] also **ay** (ā) ▸ *adv.* Always; ever: *for aye.*

Ay·ma·ra (ī′mä-rä′, ī′mə-) ▸ *n., pl.* **-ra** or **-ras**. **1.** A member of a South American Indian people inhabiting parts of highland Bolivia and Peru. **2.** Their Aymaran language.

Ay·ma·ran (ī′mä-rän′) ▸ *n.* A group of South American Indian languages, the most important being Aymara. **—Ay′ma·ran′** *adj.*

AZ ▸ *abbr.* Arizona

a·zal·ea (ə-zāl′yə) ▸ *n.* Any of a genus of shrubs cultivated for their showy, variously colored flowers.

A·zer·bai·jan (ăz′ər-bī-jän′, ä′zər-) ▸ A country of Transcaucasia N of Iran, formerly a kingdom that extended into NW Iran. **—A′zer·bai·ja′ni** *adj. & n.*

az·i·muth (ăz′ə-məth) ▸ *n.* The horizontal angular distance from a reference direction, usu. measured clockwise from due north, to the point where a vertical circle through a celestial body intersects the horizon.

A·zores (ā′zôrz, ə-zôrz′) ▸ A group of Portuguese volcanic islands in the N Atlantic about 1,448 km (900 mi) W of mainland Portugal.

AZT (ā′zē-tē′) ▸ *n.* An antiviral drug that inhibits replication of the AIDS virus.

Az·tec (ăz′tĕk′) ▸ *n.* **1.** A member of an American Indian people of central Mexico whose empire was at its height at the time of the Spanish conquest in the early 16th cent. **2.** The Nahuatl language of the Aztecs. **—Az′tec′**, **Az′tec′an** *adj.*

az·ure (ăzh′ər) ▸ *n.* A light purplish blue. **—az′ure** *adj.*

THESAURUS

axiom *n.* —*See* ASSUMPTION, LAW (3), MORAL, PROVERB.

axis *n.* —*See* CENTER (3).

aye *n.* An affirmative vote or an affirmative voter ▸ yea, yes.

aye *adv.* —*See* YES.

B

b or **B** (bē) ▸ *n., pl.* **b's** or **B's** also **bs** or **Bs**. **1.** The 2nd letter of the English alphabet. **2.** The 2nd in a series. **3.** The second best in quality or rank. **4.** *Mus.* The 7th tone in the scale of C major. **5. B** A type of blood in the ABO system.

B[1] ▸ The symbol for the element **boron**.

B[2] ▸ *abbr.* **1.** base **2.** *Mus.* bass **3.** bishop (chess)

b. ▸ *abbr.* born

B. ▸ *abbr.* bay

Ba ▸ The symbol for the element **barium**.

BA ▸ *abbr.* Bachelor of Arts

baa (bă, bä) ▸ *v.* **baaed, baa·ing**. To make a bleating sound, as a sheep or goat. **—baa** *n.*

Ba·al (bā′əl) ▸ *n., pl.* **-als** or **-al·im** (-ə-lĭm). Any of various fertility and nature gods of the ancient Semitic peoples.

Bab·bitt (băb′ĭt) ▸ *n.* A smug, provincial member of the American middle class. **—Bab′bitt·ry** *n.*

bab·ble (băb′əl) ▸ *v.* **-bled, -bling**. **1.** To utter meaningless words or sounds. **2.** To talk foolishly; chatter. **3.** To make a continuous low, murmuring sound. **—bab′ble** *n.* **—bab′bler** *n.*

babe (bāb) ▸ *n.* **1.** A baby. **2.** An innocent or naive person. **3.** *Slang* A woman.

ba·bel (băb′əl, bā′bəl) ▸ *n.* A confusion of sounds or voices.

Ba·bel (bā′bəl, băb′əl) ▸ In the Bible, a city (now thought to be Babylon) in Shinar.

ba·boon (bă-bo͞on′) ▸ *n.* **1.** Any of several large African and Asian monkeys having an elongated, doglike muzzle. **2.** *Slang* A lout; oaf.

ba·bush·ka (bə-bo͝osh′kə) ▸ *n.* A woman's head scarf, folded triangularly and tied under the chin.

ba·by (bā′bē) ▸ *n., pl.* **-bies**. **1a.** A very young child; infant. **b.** The youngest member of a family or group. **c.** A very young animal. **2.** One who behaves in an infantile way. **3.** *Slang* A girl or young woman. **4.** *Slang* An object of personal concern: *The project is your baby.* ▸ *v.* **-bied, -by·ing**. To treat overindulgently; pamper. **—ba′by·hood′** *n.* **—ba′by·ish** *adj.*

baby boom ▸ *n.* A sudden, large increase in the birthrate, esp. the one in the US after World War II. **—ba′by-boom′** *adj.* **—ba′by-boom′er** *n.*

Bab·y·lon (băb′ə-lən, -lŏn′) ▸ The capital of ancient Babylonia, on the Euphrates R.

Bab·y·lo·ni·a (băb′ə-lō′nē-ə) ▸ An ancient empire of Mesopotamia in the Euphrates R. valley.

Bab·y·lo·ni·an (băb′ə-lō′nē-ən) ▸ *adj.* Of Babylonia or Babylon. ▸ *n.* **1.** A native or inhabitant of Babylon or Babylonia. **2.** The form of Akkadian used in Babylonia.

ba·by's breath (bā′bēz) ▸ *n.* A plant having panicles of numerous small white flowers.

ba·by-sit (bā′bē-sĭt′) ▸ *v.* To take care of a child or children, as when the parents are away. **—baby sitter** *n.*

bac·ca·lau·re·ate (băk′ə-lôr′ē-ĭt) ▸ *n.* **1.** See **bachelor's degree**. **2.** A farewell address delivered to a graduating class.

bac·ca·rat (bä′kə-rä′, băk′ə-) ▸ *n.* A card game in which the objective is to hold cards totaling closest to nine.

bac·cha·nal (băk′ə-năl′, -näl′) ▸ *n.* **1.** A drunken or riotous celebration. **2.** A reveler.

Bac·cha·na·lia (băk′ə-nāl′yə, -nā′lē-ə) ▸ *n.* **1.** The ancient Roman festival in honor of Bacchus. **2. bacchanalia** A drunken festivity. **—Bac′cha·na′lian** *adj. & n.*

Bac·chus (băk′əs) ▸ *n. Gk. & Rom. Myth.* See **Dionysus**. **—Bac′chic** *adj.*

Bach (bäкн, bäk), **Johann Sebastian** (1685–1750) ▸ German composer and organist.

bach·e·lor (băch′ə-lər, băch′lər) ▸ *n.* **1.** An unmarried man. **2.** A person who holds a bachelor's degree. **—bach′e·lor·hood′, bach′e·lor·dom** *n.*

bach·e·lor's button (băch′ə-lərz, băch′lərz) ▸ *n.* See **cornflower**.

bachelor's degree ▸ *n.* A college or university degree signifying completion of the undergraduate curriculum.

ba·cil·lus (bə-sĭl′əs) ▸ *n., pl.* **-cil·li** (-sĭl′ī′). Any of various rod-shaped aerobic bacteria. **—bac′il·lar′y** (băs′ə-lĕr′ē), **ba·cil′lar** *adj.*

bac·i·tra·cin (băs′ĭ-trā′sĭn) ▸ *n.* An antibiotic obtained from bacteria and used in the topical treatment of certain bacterial infections.

back (băk) ▸ *n.* **1a.** The part of the vertebrate body nearest or along the spine. **b.** The upper or dorsal region in invertebrates. **2a.** The backbone or spine. **b.** A part that supports or fits the human back: *the back of a chair.* **3.** The part farthest from or behind the front; the rear. **4.** The reverse side. **5.** *Sports* A player who takes a position behind the frontline. ▸ *v.* **1.** To move or cause to move backward.

THESAURUS

babble *v.* To talk rapidly, incoherently, or indistinctly ▸ blather, burble, chatter, gabble, gibber, jabber, jibber-jabber, prate, prattle, rant, rave. [*Compare* SPEAK, STAMMER.] *—See also* BURBLE, CHATTER (1).

babble *n.* Empty or foolish talk ▸ blarney, blather, blatherskite, double talk, drivel, gabble, gibberish, gobbledygook, jabber, jabberwocky, jargon, jibber-jabber, nonsense, prate, prattle, twaddle. *Slang:* hot air. [*Compare* NONSENSE.] *—See also* BURBLE, CHATTER.

babe *n.* *—See* BABY (1), BEAUTY, DARLING (1), INNOCENT (2).

babel *n.* *—See* NOISE (1).

baby *n.* **1.** A very young child ▸ babe, babe in arms, bambino, cherub, infant, neonate, newborn, nursling, papoose, toddler, tot. *Informal:* preemie. *Idiom:* bundle of joy. **2.** A childish or pampered person ▸ crybaby, milksop, milquetoast, mollycoddle, namby-pamby. *Informal:* softy. *Slang:* cream puff. *Idiom:* mama's boy (*or* girl). [*Compare* WEAKLING.] *—See also* DARLING (1).

baby *v.* To treat indulgently ▸ cater (to), coddle, cosset, humor, indulge, mollycoddle, overindulge, pamper, spoil. [*Compare* ADORE, DEFER[2].]

babyish *adj.* Of or like a baby ▸ cherubic, childlike, infantile, infantine. *Informal:* kidlike. [*Compare* INNOCENT.] *—See also* CHILDISH.

baby-sit *v.* *—See* TEND[2].

back *n.* The part farthest from the front ▸ back end, back side, end, hind end, rear, stern, tag end, tail, tail end.

back *v.* **1.** To move in a reverse direction ▸ back away (*or* off), backpedal, backtrack, back up, fall back, retreat, retrocede, retrograde, retrogress, reverse. *Idiom:* retrace one's steps. [*Compare* FLINCH, RECEDE, RETREAT.] **2.** To present evidence in support of ▸ back up, bolster, buttress, corroborate, substantiate, support, sustain, vouch (for). [*Compare* PROVE.] **3.** To act as a patron to ▸ patronize, sponsor, support. [*Compare* DONATE.] *—See also* CONFIRM (1), FINANCE, SUPPORT (1).

back away or **off** *v.* *—See* BACK (1).

back down or **away** or **out** *v.* *—See* RENEGE.

back down or **off** *v.* *—See* WEAKEN.

back up *v.* *—See* BACK (1).

back *adj.* Located in the rear ▸ hind, hinder, hindmost, hindermost, posterior, rear, rearward. *—See also* REMOTE (1).

back *adv.* *—See* BACKWARD.

2. To support or sustain: *back a political cause.* **3.** To bet on. **4.** To form the back or backing of. ***—phrasal verbs:*** **back down** To withdraw, as from a confrontation. **back off** To retreat, as from a position or commitment. **back out** To withdraw from something before completion. **back up 1.** To accumulate in a clogged state. **2.** To assist, support, or corroborate. **3.** *Comp. Sci.* To make a backup of. ▸ *adj.* **1.** At the rear. **2.** Distant; remote. **3.** Of a past date; not current: *a back issue of a periodical.* **4.** In arrears: *back pay.* **5.** Operating or directed backward. ▸ *adv.* **1.** To or toward the rear; backward. **2.** To or toward a former place, state, or time. **3.** In reserve or concealment. **4.** In check: *Barriers held the crowd back.* **5.** In reply or return. **—back′less** *adj.*

back·ache (băk′āk′) ▸ *n.* Discomfort or a pain in the region of the back or spine.

back·beat (băk′bēt′) ▸ *n.* A loud, steady beat characteristic of rock music.

back·bite (băk′bīt′) ▸ *v.* To speak spitefully or slanderously about a person who is not present. **—back′bit′er** *n.*

back·board (băk′bôrd′) ▸ *n.* **1.** A board placed under or behind something to provide support. **2.** *Basketball* The elevated board from which the basket projects.

back·bone (băk′bōn′) ▸ *n.* **1.** The vertebrate spine. **2.** A main support: *the backbone of a policy.* **3.** Strength of character.

back·break·ing (băk′brā′kĭng) ▸ *adj.* Demanding great exertion; arduous.

back·court (băk′kôrt′) ▸ *n. Sports* The part of a court farthest from the net, goal, or front wall.

back·date (băk′dāt′) ▸ *v.* To supply (e.g., a check) with a date earlier than the actual date.

back·door (băk′dôr′) ▸ *adj.* Secret or surreptitious; clandestine.

back·drop (băk′drŏp′) ▸ *n.* **1.** A painted curtain hung at the back of a stage set. **2.** A setting; background.

back·er (băk′ər) ▸ *n.* One that backs a person, group, or enterprise: *a financial backer.*

back·field (băk′fēld′) ▸ *n.* **1.** *Football* The players stationed behind the line of scrimmage. **2.** The primarily defensive players in soccer, field hockey, and Rugby.

back·fire (băk′fīr′) ▸ *n.* **1.** An explosion of prematurely ignited fuel or of unburned exhaust in an engine. **2.** A fire started to extinguish or control a larger fire. ▸ *v.* **1.** To explode in a backfire. **2.** To produce an unexpected, undesired result.

back-for·ma·tion (băk′fôr-mā′shən) ▸ *n.* **1.** A new word created by removing an actual or supposed affix from an already existing word, as *laze* from *lazy.* **2.** This process.

back·gam·mon (băk′găm′ən) ▸ *n.* A board game for two persons, with moves determined by throws of dice.

back·ground (băk′ground′) ▸ *n.* **1.** The area or surface against which something is seen or depicted. **2.** A setting or context. **3.** A state of relative obscurity. **4.** The circumstances leading up to an event. **5.** One's total experience, training, and education. **6.** Sound or radiation present at a relatively constant low level.

back·hand (băk′hănd′) ▸ *n.* **1.** *Sports* A stroke, as of a racket, made with the back of the hand facing outward and the arm moving forward. **2.** Handwriting having letters that slant to the left. ▸ *adj.* Backhanded. **—back′hand′** *v. & adv.*

back·hand·ed (băk′hăn′dĭd) ▸ *adj.* **1.** *Sports* Backhand. **2.** Oblique or roundabout: *a backhanded compliment.* **—back′hand′ed·ly** *adv.* **—back′hand′ed·ness** *n.*

back·hoe (băk′hō′) ▸ *n.* An excavator with a boom that is drawn backward to the machine.

back·ing (băk′ĭng) ▸ *n.* **1.** Something forming a back: *the backing of a carpet.* **2a.** Support or aid. **b.** Approval or endorsement.

back·lash (băk′lăsh′) ▸ *n.* **1.** A sudden or violent backward whipping motion. **2.** A hostile reaction, esp. to a social or political movement. **—back′lash′** *v.*

back·light (băk′līt′) ▸ *v.* To light (a subject or scene) from behind. **—back′light′** *n.*

back·log (băk′lôg′, -lŏg′) ▸ *n.* **1.** A reserve supply or source. **2.** An accumulation, esp. of unfinished work or unfilled orders.

back·pack (băk′păk′) ▸ *n.* **1.** A knapsack, often on a lightweight frame, that is worn on the back. **2.** An apparatus designed to be used while carried on the back. ▸ *v.* To hike with a backpack. **—back′pack′er** *n.*

back·ped·al (băk′pĕd′l) ▸ *v.* **1.** To pedal backward, as in braking. **2.** To back off.

back·rest (băk′rĕst′) ▸ *n.* A rest or support for the back.

back seat ▸ *n.* **1.** A seat in the back, esp. of a vehicle. **2.** A subordinate position.

back-seat driver (băk′sēt′) ▸ *n.* One who gives unsolicited direction or advice.

back·side (băk′sīd′) ▸ *n. Informal* The buttocks.

back·slash (băk′slăsh′) ▸ *n.* A backward virgule (\).

back·slide (băk′slīd′) ▸ *v.* To revert esp. to sin or bad habits. **—back′slid′er** *n.*

back·space (băk′spās′) ▸ *v.* To move the cursor on a computer screen or the carriage of a typewriter back one or more spaces. ▸ *n.* The key used for backspacing.

back·spin (băk′spĭn′) ▸ *n.* A spin that tends to slow, stop, or reverse the linear motion of an object, esp. of a ball.

back·stage (băk′stāj′) ▸ *adv.* **1.** In or toward the area behind the performing space in a theater. **2.** In secret; privately.

back·stairs (băk′stârz′) ▸ *adj.* Furtively carried on; clandestine: *backstairs gossip.*

back·stop (băk′stŏp′) ▸ *n.* **1.** A screen or fence used to stop a ball from going beyond the playing area. **2.** *Baseball* A catcher.

back·stretch (băk′strĕch′) ▸ *n.* The part of an oval racecourse farthest from the spectators and opposite the homestretch.

back·stroke (băk′strōk′) ▸ *n.* **1.** A swimming stroke executed with the swimmer lying face up in the water. **2.** A backhanded stroke. **—back′stroke′** *v.*

back·swept (băk′swĕpt′) ▸ *adj.* Brushed or angled backward: *a backswept hairstyle.*

back talk ▸ *n.* Insolent or impudent retorts.

back·track (băk′trăk′) ▸ *v.* **1.** To retrace one's route. **2.** To reverse one's position.

back·up (băk′ŭp′) ▸ *n.* **1a.** A reserve or substitute. **b.** *Comp. Sci.* A copy of a program or file stored separately from the original. **2a.** Support or backing. **b.** *Mus.* A background accompaniment. **3.** An overflow or accumulation caused by clogging. ▸ *adj.* Auxiliary; standby.

back·ward (băk′wərd) ▸ *adj.* **1.** Directed or facing toward the back. **2.** Reversed. **3.** Unwilling; reluctant. **4.** Behind

THESAURUS

backbite *v.* —*See* MALIGN.

backbone *n.* —*See* COURAGE.

backbreaking *adj.* —*See* BURDENSOME.

backcountry *n.* —*See* COUNTRY.

backdrop *n.* —*See* SCENE (1), SCENE (2).

backer *n.* —*See* PATRON, SPONSOR.

backfire *v.* To produce an unexpected and undesired result ▸ boomerang. *Idiom:* blow up in one's face. [*Compare* FAIL.] —*See also* EXPLODE (1).

background *n.* —*See* HISTORY (2), SCENE (2).

backhanded *adj.* —*See* INDIRECT (1).

backing *n.* —*See* CAPITAL (1), CONFIRMATION (2), ENDORSEMENT, PATRONAGE (1).

backlog *n.* —*See* HOARD.

backpack *v.* To travel about or journey on foot ▸ hike, march, tramp, trek. [*Compare* JOURNEY, WALK.]

backpack *n.* —*See* PACK (1).

backpedal *v.* —*See* BACK (1), RENEGE.

backset *n.* A change from better to worse ▸ reversal, reverse, setback. [*Compare* MISFORTUNE, RELAPSE.]

backside *n.* —*See* BUTTOCKS.

backslide *v.* —*See* RELAPSE.

backslide or **backsliding** *n.* —*See* RELAPSE.

backstairs *adj.* —*See* SECRET (1).

back talk *n.* Insolent talk ▸ mouth. *Informal:* lip, sass. [*Compare* IMPUDENCE.]

back-to-back *adj.* —*See* CONSECUTIVE.

backtrack *v.* —*See* BACK (1).

backup *adj.* —*See* AUXILIARY (2).

backward *adj.* **1.** Having only a limited ability to learn and understand ▸ dense, dull, feeble-minded, half-witted, simple, simple-minded, slow, slow-witted, thick-witted, weak-minded. *Informal:*

in progress or development. ▸ *adv.* or **back·wards** (-wərdz) 1. To or toward the back. 2. With the back leading. 3. In a reverse manner. 4. Toward a worse or less advanced condition. —*idiom:* **bend (or lean) over backward** To do one's utmost. —**back′ward·ly** *adv.* —**back′ward·ness** *n.*

back·wash (băk′wŏsh′, -wôsh′) ▸ *n.* 1. A backward flow. 2. An aftermath.

back·wa·ter (băk′wô′tər, -wŏt′ər) ▸ *n.* 1. Water that stagnates or flows backward, as at the edge of a current. 2. A backward or isolated place.

back·woods (băk′wo͝odz′) ▸ *pl.n.* *(takes sing. or pl. v.)* 1. Heavily wooded, thinly settled areas. 2. An isolated and uncultured place. —**back′woods′man** *n.*

ba·con (bā′kən) ▸ *n.* The salted and smoked meat from the back and sides of a pig.

Bacon, Francis (1561–1626) ▸ English philosopher, essayist, and politician.

Bacon, Roger (1214?–92) ▸ English friar, scientist, and philosopher.

bac·te·ri·a (băk-tîr′ē-ə) ▸ *n.* Pl. of **bacterium**.

bac·te·ri·cide (băk-tîr′ĭ-sīd′) ▸ *n.* An agent that kills bacteria. —**bac·te′ri·cid′al** *adj.*

bac·te·ri·ol·o·gy (băk-tîr′ē-ŏl′ə-jē) ▸ *n.* The scientific study of bacteria. —**bac·te′ri·o·log′i·cal** *adj.* —**bac·te′ri·ol′o·gist** *n.*

bac·te·ri·o·phage (băk-tîr′ē-ə-fāj′) ▸ *n.* A virus that destroys certain bacteria.

bac·te·ri·um (băk-tîr′ē-əm) ▸ *n., pl.* **-te·ri·a** (-tîr′ē-ə). Any of numerous unicellular microorganisms existing in several typical shapes and variously associated with processes of putrefaction, fermentation, and causation of infectious disease in plants or animals. —**bac·te′ri·al** *adj.* —**bac·te′ri·al·ly** *adv.*

bad (băd) ▸ *adj.* **worse** (wûrs), **worst** (wûrst). 1. Of inferior quality; poor. 2. Evil; sinful. 3. Ill-behaved. 4. Unpleasant or disturbing: *bad news.* 5. Unfavorable: *a bad review.* 6. Not fresh; spoiled. 7. Detrimental: *bad habits.* 8. Defective. 9. Severe; intense: *a bad cold.* 10. Being in poor health or condition. 11. Sorry; regretful. ▸ *n.* Something bad: *Take the good with the bad.* ▸ *adv. Informal* Badly. —**bad′ly** *adv.* —**bad′ness** *n.*

bad blood ▸ *n.* Enmity or bitterness between persons or groups.

bade (băd, bād) ▸ *v.* P.t. of **bid**.

badge (băj) ▸ *n.* A device or emblem worn as an insignia of rank, office, or honor.

badg·er (băj′ər) ▸ *n.* A carnivorous burrowing mammal with long front claws and a heavy grizzled coat. ▸ *v.* To harry or pester persistently.

bad·i·nage (băd′n-äzh′) ▸ *n.* Light, playful banter.

Bad·lands also **Bad Lands** (băd′lăndz′) ▸ A heavily eroded arid region of SW SD and NW NE.

bad·min·ton (băd′mĭn′tən) ▸ *n.* A sport that is played by volleying a shuttlecock with long-handled rackets over a high net.

bad·mouth (băd′mouth′, -mouth′) ▸ *v. Slang* To criticize or disparage, often spitefully.

Baf·fin Bay (băf′ĭn) ▸ An ice-clogged body of water between NE Canada and Greenland.

Baffin Island ▸ An island of E Nunavut, Canada, W of Greenland.

baf·fle (băf′əl) ▸ *v.* **-fled, -fling.** 1. To confuse (someone) in a way that frustrates or prevents further action from being taken. 2. To impede. ▸ *n.* A barrier designed to check or regulate the flow of a liquid, gas, sound, or light. —**baf′fle·ment** *n.*

bag (băg) ▸ *n.* 1a. A nonrigid container, as of paper, plastic, or leather. b. A handbag; purse. c. A suitcase. 2. An object that resembles a pouch. 3. An amount of game taken at one time. 4. *Baseball* A base. 5. *Slang* An area of interest or skill: *Cooking is not my bag.* ▸ *v.* **bagged, bag·ging.** 1. To put into a bag. 2a. To hang loosely. b. To bulge out. 3. To capture or kill as game. —*idiom:* **in the bag** Assured of a successful outcome. —**bag′ful** *n.*

bag·a·telle (băg′ə-tĕl′) ▸ *n.* 1. A trifle. 2. A short piece of music.

ba·gel (bā′gəl) ▸ *n.* A ring-shaped roll with a tough chewy texture.

bag·gage (băg′ĭj) ▸ *n.* 1. The bags and belongings of a traveler. 2. The movable supplies of an army.

bag·gy (băg′ē) ▸ *adj.* **-gi·er, -gi·est.** Bulging or hanging loosely: *baggy trousers.* —**bag′gi·ly** *adv.* —**bag′gi·ness** *n.*

Bagh·dad or **Bag·dad** (băg′dăd′) ▸ The capital of Iraq, in the center on the Tigris R.

bag·pipe (băg′pīp′) ▸ *n.* often **bagpipes** A wind instrument having an inflatable bag, a double-reed melody pipe, and one or more drone pipes. —**bag′pipe′** *v.* —**bag′pip′er** *n.*

ba·guette (bă-gĕt′) ▸ *n.* 1. A gem cut in a narrow rectangle. 2. A narrow loaf of French bread.

Ba·ha·mas (bə-hä′məz, -hā′-) also **Ba·ha·ma Islands** (-mə) ▸ An island country in the Atlantic E of FL and Cuba. —**Ba·ha′mi·an** (-hā′mē-ən, -hä′-), **Ba·ha′man** *adj. & n.*

Bah·rain or **Bah·rein** (bä-rān′) ▸ An island country in the Persian Gulf between Qatar and Saudi Arabia. —**Bah·rain′i** *adj. & n.*

baht (bät) ▸ *n., pl.* **bahts** or **baht.** See **currency** table in Appendix.

Bai·kal (bī-kôl′, -kŏl′), **Lake** ▸ A deep lake of S-central Russia.

bail[1] (bāl) ▸ *n.* 1. Security, usu. money, supplied as a guar-

THESAURUS

soft. *Slang:* dim, dimwitted. *Idioms:* not playing with a full deck, soft in the head. [*Compare* STUPID.] 2. Behind others in progress or development ▸ lagging, underdeveloped, undeveloped. 3. Moving or directed toward the rear ▸ rearward, retrograde, retrogressive. 4. Clinging to obsolete ideas ▸ reactionary, unprogressive. [*Compare* CONSERVATIVE.] —*See also* DEPRESSED (2), IGNORANT (2), SHY[1].

backward *adv.* Toward the back ▸ about, around, back, backwards, rearward.

backwardness *n.* —*See* IGNORANCE (1), SHYNESS.

backwards *adv.* —*See* BACKWARD.

backwoods *n.* A dense growth of trees and underbrush covering an area ▸ forest, timberland, woodland, woods. [*Compare* WILDERNESS.] —*See also* COUNTRY.

bacterium *n.* —*See* GERM (1).

bad *adj.* 1. Of low or lower quality ▸ bum, coarse, common, dissatisfactory, inadequate, inferior, low-grade, low-quality, mean, mediocre, poor, second-class, second-rate, shabby, subpar, substandard, unsatisfactory. *Slang:* bush-league. *Idioms:* below par, not up to scratch (*or* snuff). [*Compare* DEFECTIVE, SHABBY, SHODDY, TERRIBLE.] 2. Marred by decay ▸ decayed, flyblown, foul, overripe, putrescent, putrid, rancid, rotten, spoiled, worm-eaten, wormy. [*Compare* FILTHY, MOLDY, OFFENSIVE.] —*See also* EVIL, FATEFUL (1), HARMFUL, UNPLEASANT, UNRULY.

bad *n.* Whatever is destructive or harmful ▸ badness, evil, ill, worse. [*Compare* HARM.]

badge *n.* —*See* DECORATION, SIGN (1).

badger *v.* —*See* HARASS.

badinage *n.* —*See* RIBBING.

badlands *n.* —*See* DESERT[1].

badmouth *v.* —*See* BELITTLE, MALIGN.

bad name *n.* —*See* DISGRACE.

badness *n.* Whatever is destructive or harmful ▸ bad, evil, ill, wrong. [*Compare* HARM.]

bad odor *n.* —*See* DISGRACE.

bad-tempered *adj.* —*See* ILL-TEMPERED.

baffle *v.* To put at a loss as to what to say or do ▸ confound, mystify, nonplus, perplex. *Informal:* flummox, stick, stump, throw. *Slang:* beat. [*Compare* CONFUSE, EMBARRASS.]

baffle *n.* —*See* BRAKE.

baffled *adj.* —*See* CONFUSED (1).

bafflement *n.* —*See* DAZE.

bag *n.* A flexible container for carrying items ▸ pouch, sack, tote (bag). *Chiefly Regional:* croker sack, crocus sack, gunnysack, poke, tow bag, tow sack. —*See also* AREA (1), FORTE, PURSE, SUITCASE.

bag *v.* —*See* BULGE, CAPTURE, CATCH (1), GET (1).

baggage *n.* —*See* SLUT.

bag lady *n.* —*See* PAUPER.

bail[1] *n.* One who posts bond ▸ bailsman, bondsman. —*See also* PAWN[1].

bail[2] *v.* —*See* DIP (2).

bail out *v.* To catapult oneself from a disabled aircraft ▸ eject, jump. —*See also* ESCAPE (1).

antee that an arrested person will appear for trial. 2. Release from imprisonment obtained by bail. ▸ *v.* To secure the release of by paying bail. ***—phrasal verb:* bail out** *Informal* To extricate from trouble. **—bail′er** *n.*

bail² (bāl) ▸ *v.* 1. To remove (water) from a boat by dipping with a container. 2. To empty (a boat) by bailing. ***—phrasal verb:* bail out** 1. To parachute from an aircraft. 2. To abandon a project or enterprise. **—bail′er** *n.*

bail³ (bāl) ▸ *n.* The arched, hooplike handle of a container, such as a pail.

bail·ee (bā-lē′) ▸ *n.* A person to whom property is bailed.

bail·iff (bā′lĭf) ▸ *n.* 1. A court attendant with duties such as the maintenance of order during a trial. 2. An official who assists a British sheriff by executing writs and arrests. 3. *Chiefly Brit.* An overseer of an estate.

bail·i·wick (bā′lə-wĭk′) ▸ *n.* 1. One's specific area of interest, skill, or authority. 2. The office or district of a bailiff.

bail·or (bā′lər, bā-lôr′) ▸ *n.* One who bails property to another.

bails·man (bālz′mən) ▸ *n.* One who provides bail or security for another.

bait (bāt) ▸ *n.* 1. Food or other lure used to catch fish or trap animals. 2. An enticement; lure. ▸ *v.* 1. To place bait in (a trap) or on (a fishhook). 2. To entice; lure. 3. To set dogs upon (a chained animal) for sport. 4. To torment, esp. with criticism or ridicule. 5. To tease. **—bait′er** *n.*

bait and switch ▸ *n.* A sales tactic in which a bargain-priced item is used to attract customers who are then encouraged to purchase a more expensive similar item.

baize (bāz) ▸ *n.* A thick feltlike cloth used chiefly to cover gaming tables.

Ba·ja California (bä′hä). Also **Lower California** ▸ A peninsula of W Mexico extending SSE between the Pacific and the Gulf of California.

bake (bāk) ▸ *v.* **baked, bak·ing.** 1. To cook (food) with dry heat, esp. in an oven. 2. To harden or dry in or as if in an oven: *bake bricks.* ▸ *n.* 1. The act or process of baking. 2. A social gathering at which food is baked and served. **—bak′er** *n.*

bak·er's dozen (bā′kərz) ▸ *n.* A group of 13.

bak·er·y (bā′kə-rē) ▸ *n., pl.* **-ies.** A place where products such as bread, cake, and pastries are baked or sold.

bak·ing powder (bā′kĭng) ▸ *n.* A mixture of baking soda, starch, and an acidic compound such as cream of tartar, used as a leavening agent in baking.

baking soda ▸ *n.* A white crystalline compound, $NaHCO_3$, used esp. in baking powder, effervescent beverages, pharmaceuticals, and fire extinguishers.

ba·kla·va (bä′klə-vä′) ▸ *n.* A dessert made of paper-thin layers of pastry, chopped nuts, and honey.

bak·sheesh (băk′shēsh′, băk-shēsh′) ▸ *n., pl.* **-sheesh.** A gratuity or tip in certain Near Eastern countries.

bal·a·lai·ka (băl′ə-lī′kə) ▸ *n.* A musical instrument with a triangular body, fretted neck, and three strings.

bal·ance (băl′əns) ▸ *n.* 1. A weighing device, esp. one consisting of a rigid beam suspended at its center and brought into equilibrium by adding known weights at one end while the unknown weight hangs from the other. 2a. A state of equilibrium. b. An influence or force tending to produce equilibrium. 3. Emotional stability. 4. A harmonious arrangement or proportion of parts. 5. *Accounting* a. Equality of totals in the debit and credit sides of an account. b. A difference between such totals. 6. Something left over; remainder. 7. *Math.* Equality of symbolic quantities on each side of an equation. ▸ *v.* **-anced, -anc·ing.** 1. To weigh in or as if in a balance. 2. To bring into or be in a state of equilibrium. 3. To counterbalance. 4. *Accounting* To compute the difference between the debits and credits of (an account). ***—idioms:* in the balance** With the result or outcome still uncertain. **on balance** Taking everything into consideration.

balance beam ▸ *n.* A horizontal raised beam used in gymnastics for balancing exercises.

balance sheet ▸ *n.* A statement of the assets and liabilities of a business or institution.

balance wheel ▸ *n.* A wheel that regulates rate of mechanical movement, as in a watch.

bal·bo·a (băl-bō′ə) ▸ *n.* See **currency** table in Appendix.

Balboa, Vasco Núñez de (1475–1517) ▸ Spanish explorer.

bal·co·ny (băl′kə-nē) ▸ *n., pl.* **-nies.** 1. A platform that projects from the wall of a building and is surrounded by a railing. 2. A gallery that projects over the main floor in a theater or auditorium.

bald (bôld) ▸ *adj.* **-er, -est.** 1. Lacking hair on the head. 2. Lacking a natural or usual covering; bare. 3. *Zool.* Having white feathers or markings on the head. 4. Plain; blunt: *the bald truth.* **—bald′ly** *adv.* **—bald′ness** *n.*

bal·da·chin (bôl′də-kĭn, băl′-) also **bal·da·chi·no** (băl′də-kē′nō) ▸ *n., pl.* **-chins** also **-chi·nos.** A canopy over an altar, throne, or dais.

bald eagle ▸ *n.* A North American eagle with a dark body and white head and tail.

bal·der·dash (bôl′dər-dăsh′) ▸ *n.* Nonsense.

bald-faced (bôld′fāst′) ▸ *adj.* Blatant; brazen: *a bald-faced lie.*

bal·dric (bôl′drĭk) ▸ *n.* A belt worn across the chest to support a sword or bugle.

bale (bāl) ▸ *n.* A large, tightly bound package of raw or finished material. ▸ *v.* **baled, bal·ing.** To bind in bales. **—bal′er** *n.*

ba·leen (bə-lēn′) ▸ *n.* See **whalebone** 1.

bale·ful (bāl′fəl) ▸ *adj.* 1. Portending evil; ominous. 2. Malignant in intent or effect. **—bale′ful·ly** *adv.* **—bale′ful·ness** *n.*

Ba·li (bä′lē) ▸ An island of S Indonesia in the Lesser Sundas E of Java.

Ba·li·nese (bä′lə-nēz′, -nēs′) ▸ *n., pl.* **-nese.** 1. A native or inhabitant of Bali. 2. The Indonesian language of Bali. **—Ba′li·nese′** *adj.*

THESAURUS

bailiwick *n.* —*See* AREA (1).

bailsman *n.* One who posts bond ▸ bail, bondsman.

bait *n.* Something that leads one into danger or entrapment ▸ decoy, lure. [*Compare* TRAP, TRICK.] —*See also* LURE (1).

bait *v.* To arouse hope or desire without affording satisfaction ▸ tantalize, tease. *Idiom:* make one's mouth water. [*Compare* CHARM, FLIRT.] —*See also* HARASS.

bake *v.* —*See* BURN (3), COOK.

baked *adj.* —*See* DRUGGED.

baker *n.* A person who prepares food for eating ▸ chef, cook, culinary artist.

baking *adj.* —*See* HOT (1).

balance *n.* 1. A stable state of opposing forces ▸ counterpoise, equilibrium, equipoise, poise, stasis. [*Compare* EQUIVALENCE, STABILITY.] 2. A stable emotional state ▸ aplomb, collectedness, composure, coolness, equanimity, imperturbability, imperturbableness, levelheadedness, nonchalance, poise, sang-froid, self-possession, steadiness, unflappability. *Slang:* cool. [*Compare* CALM, RESERVE.] 3. Satisfying arrangement that is marked by even distribution of elements, as in a design ▸ harmony, proportion, symmetry. [*Compare* AGREEMENT.] 4. A remaining part ▸ leavings, leftover, leftovers, pickings, remainder, remains, remnant, residue, rest. [*Compare* END, SURPLUS, TRACE.]

balance *v.* 1. To put in balance ▸ counterbalance, equalize, even (out), level (off), poise, stabilize, steady. [*Compare* EQUALIZE.] 2. To act as an equalizing force to ▸ compensate, counteract, counterbalance, counterpoise, countervail, make up, offset, oppose, set off. [*Compare* HARMONIZE.] 3. To rest on a narrow or insecure surface ▸ perch, poise, roost, teeter. [*Compare* SWAY.] —*See also* CANCEL (2), COMPARE.

balanced *adj.* 1. Neither favorable nor unfavorable ▸ even, fifty-fifty, nip and tuck. 2. Characterized by or displaying symmetry, especially correspondence in scale or measure ▸ proportional, proportionate, regular, symmetric, symmetrical. [*Compare* EVEN, PARALLEL.] 3. Having components that are pleasingly combined ▸ concordant, congruous, harmonious, symmetrical. [*Compare* PLEASANT.] —*See also* FAIR¹ (1), SENSIBLE.

bald *adj.* —*See* ABRUPT (1), BARE (1), BARE (3).

balderdash *n.* —*See* NONSENSE.

bald-faced *adj.* —*See* IMPUDENT.

baleful *adj.* —*See* FATEFUL (1).

balk (bôk) ► *v.* **1.** To stop short and refuse to go on. **2.** To refuse to proceed, as out of doubt or moral principle. **3.** *Baseball* To make an illegal motion before pitching, entitling any base runner to advance. ► *n.* **1.** A hindrance, check, or defeat. **2.** *Baseball* An act of balking. **—balk′er** *n.* **—balk′y** *adj.*

Bal·kan Mountains (bôl′kən) also **Bal·kans** (-kənz) ► A mountain system of SE Europe extending about 563 km (350 mi) from E Serbia through central Bulgaria to the Black Sea.

Balkan Peninsula also **Balkans** ► A peninsula of SE Europe bounded by the Black Sea, the Sea of Marmara, and the Aegean, Mediterranean, Ionian, and Adriatic seas. **—Bal′kan** *adj.*

ball[1] (bôl) ► *n.* **1.** A spherical or almost spherical object or body. **2a.** Any of various round or rounded objects used in sports and games. **b.** A game played with such an object. **c.** A pitched baseball that does not pass through the strike zone and is not swung at by the batter. **3.** A usu. round projectile. **4.** A rounded part or protuberance: *the ball of the foot.* ► *v.* To form or become formed into a ball. ***—phrasal verb:*** **ball up** To confuse; bungle. ***—idiom:*** **on the ball** *Informal* Alert or efficient.

ball[2] (bôl) ► *n.* **1.** A formal gathering for social dancing. **2.** *Slang* An extremely enjoyable time or experience: *had a ball on our vacation.*

bal·lad (băl′əd) ► *n.* **1a.** A narrative poem, often of folk origin and intended to be sung, consisting of simple stanzas and usu. having a refrain. **b.** The music for such a poem. **2.** A slow, usu. romantic song. **—bal′lad·eer′** *n.* **—bal′lad·ry** *n.*

bal·last (băl′əst) ► *n.* **1.** Heavy material placed in the hold of a ship or the gondola of a balloon to enhance stability. **2.** Coarse gravel or crushed rock laid to form a roadbed. ► *v.* To provide with ballast.

ball bearing ► *n.* **1.** A friction-reducing bearing, as for a rotating shaft, in which the moving and stationary parts are separated by hard metal balls revolving freely in a lubricated track. **2.** A hard ball that is used in such a bearing.

bal·le·ri·na (băl′ə-rē′nə) ► *n.* A principal woman dancer in a ballet company.

bal·let (bă-lā′, băl′ā′) ► *n.* **1.** A classical dance form characterized by elaborate formal technique. **2.** A choreographed theatrical presentation danced to a musical accompaniment. **3.** A company that performs ballet.

bal·let·o·mane (bă-lĕt′ə-mān′) ► *n.* An admirer of ballet.

ball game ► *n.* **1.** A game or sport played with a ball. **2.** *Slang* **a.** A highly competitive situation. **b.** A particular set of circumstances.

ballistic missile ► *n.* A projectile that assumes a free-falling trajectory after an internally guided, self-powered ascent.

bal·lis·tics (bə-lĭs′tĭks) ► *n.* *(takes sing. v.)* **1.** The study of the dynamics or flight characteristics of projectiles. **2a.** The study of the functioning of firearms. **b.** The study of the firing, flight, and effects of ammunition. **—bal·lis′tic** *adj.* **—bal·lis′ti·cal·ly** *adv.*

bal·loon (bə-lo͞on′) ► *n.* **1a.** A flexible bag inflated with a gas, such as helium, that causes it to rise in the atmosphere. **b.** Such a bag capable of lifting and transporting a gondola or other load. **2.** An inflatable toy rubber bag. **3.** An outline containing the words or thoughts of a cartoon character. ► *v.* **1.** To ride in a balloon. **2.** To expand or cause to expand like a balloon. **3.** To increase rapidly. **—bal·loon′ist** *n.*

bal·lot (băl′ət) ► *n.* **1.** A paper or card used to cast or register a vote. **2.** The act or method of voting. **3.** A list of candidates for office. **4.** The total of all votes cast in an election. **5.** The right to vote; franchise. ► *v.* To cast a ballot.

ball·park (bôl′pärk′) ► *n.* **1.** A park or stadium in which ball games are played. **2.** *Slang* The approximately proper range, as of an estimate. **—ball′park′** *adj.*

ball·point pen (bôl′point′) ► *n.* A pen having a small, freely revolving ball as its writing point.

ball·room (bôl′ro͝om′, -ro͞om′) ► *n.* A large room for dancing.

bal·ly·hoo (băl′ē-ho͞o′) ► *n., pl.* **-hoos. 1.** Sensational promotion or publicity. **2.** Clamor; uproar. ► *v.* To promote by sensational methods.

balm (bäm) ► *n.* **1.** Any of several aromatic plants, esp. one used as a seasoning or for tea. **2.** An aromatic salve or oil. **3.** Something that soothes, heals, or comforts.

balm·y (bä′mē) ► *adj.* **-i·er, -i·est. 1.** Having the quality or fragrance of balm. **2.** Mild and pleasant: *a balmy breeze.* **3.** *Slang* Eccentric or crazy. **—balm′i·ly** *adv.* **—balm′i·ness** *n.*

ba·lo·ney[1] (bə-lō′nē) ► *n.* Var. of **bologna.**

ba·lo·ney[2] (bə-lō′nē) ► *n.* *Slang* Nonsense.

bal·sa (bôl′sə) ► *n.* **1.** A tropical American tree having very light, soft, buoyant wood. **2.** The wood of this tree.

bal·sam (bôl′səm) ► *n.* **1.** An aromatic resin obtained from various trees or plants. **2.** A tree, esp. the balsam fir, yielding balsam. **3.** See **jewelweed.**

balsam fir ► *n.* A North American evergreen tree that yields pulpwood and is widely used as a Christmas tree.

Balt (bôlt) ► *n.* A member of a Baltic-speaking people.

Bal·tic (bôl′tĭk) ► *adj.* **1.** Of the Baltic Sea, the Baltic States, or a Baltic-speaking people. **2.** Of the branch of Indo-European that includes Latvian and Lithuanian. ► *n.* The Baltic language branch.

Baltic Sea ► An arm of the Atlantic in N Europe.

Baltic States ► Estonia, Latvia, and Lithuania, on the E coast of the Baltic Sea.

Bal·ti·more (bôl′tə-môr′) ► A city of N MD on an arm of Chesapeake Bay NE of Washington DC.

bal·us·ter (băl′ə-stər) ► *n.* One of the upright supports of a handrail.

bal·us·trade (băl′ə-strād′) ► *n.* A handrail and the row of balusters or posts that support it.

Bal·zac (bôl′zăk′, bäl-zäk′), **Honoré de** (1799–1850) ► French writer.

bam·boo (băm-bo͞o′) ► *n., pl.* **-boos. 1.** Any of various tall, usu. woody, temperate or tropical grasses. **2.** The hard hollow stems of any of these grasses, used in construction and crafts.

bam·boo·zle (băm-bo͞o′zəl) ► *v.* **-zled, -zling.** *Informal* To trick or deceive; hoodwink. **—bam·boo′zle·ment** *n.*

ban (băn) ► *v.* **banned, ban·ning.** To prohibit, esp. by official decree. ► *n.* **1.** A condemnation by church officials. **2.** A prohibition imposed by law or official decree. **3.** A curse.

ba·nal (bə-năl′, bā′nəl, bə-näl′) ► *adj.* Completely ordinary and commonplace; trite. **—ba·nal′i·ty** (-năl′ĭ-tē) *n.* **—ba·nal′ly** *adv.*

ba·nan·a (bə-năn′ə) ► *n.* **1.** Any of several treelike tropical or subtropical plants having large leaves and hanging clusters of edible fruit. **2.** The elongated fruit of these plants, having yellowish to reddish skin and white pulpy flesh.

THESAURUS

balk *v.* —*See* FRUSTRATE.

balky *adj.* —*See* CONTRARY.

ball *n.* An object that is spherical in shape ► globe, orb, sphere, spheroid. [*Compare* CIRCLE, DROP.] —*See also* DANCE.

ballad *n.* —*See* SONG.

balloon *v.* To increase or expand suddenly, rapidly, or without control ► explode, mushroom, snowball. [*Compare* INCREASE.] —*See also* BULGE, SWELL.

ballot *v.* To cast a vote ► poll, vote. *Idioms:* exercise one's civic duty, go to the polls.

ballot *n.* A list of candidates proposed or endorsed by a political party ► lineup, ticket, slate.

balloter *n.* One who votes ► elector, voter.

ball up *v.* —*See* BOTCH, CONFUSE (3).

ballyhoo *n.* —*See* PUBLICITY.

ballyhoo *v.* —*See* PROMOTE (3).

balm *n.* —*See* OINTMENT.

balminess *n.* —*See* FOOLISHNESS.

balmy *adj.* Free from extremes in temperature ► clement, mild, moderate, temperate. [*Compare* PLEASANT.] —*See also* FOOLISH, GENTLE (2).

baloney *n.* —*See* NONSENSE.

bambino *n.* —*See* BABY (1).

bamboozle *v.* —*See* DECEIVE.

ban *v.* —*See* CENSOR (2), EXCLUDE, FORBID.

ban *n.* —*See* CURSE (1), FORBIDDANCE.

banal *adj.* —*See* TRITE.

banality *n.* —*See* CLICHÉ, INSIPIDITY.

bananas *adj.* —*See* INSANE.

band¹ (bănd) ▸ *n.* **1.** A thin strip of flexible material used to encircle and bind together. **2.** A strip or stripe of a contrasting color or material. **3.** A simple ring, esp. a wedding ring. **4.** *Phys.* A range or interval, esp. of radio wavelengths or frequencies. ▸ *v.* **1.** To bind with or as if with a band. **2.** To tag (e.g., birds) with a band.

band² (bănd) ▸ *n.* **1.** A group of people or animals. **2.** A group of musicians who perform together. ▸ *v.* To assemble or unite in a group: *band together for safety.*

band·age (băn′dĭj) ▸ *n.* A strip of material used to protect or support a wound or other injury. ▸ *v.* **-aged, -ag·ing.** To apply a bandage to.

Band-Aid (bănd′ād′) ▸ A trademark for an adhesive bandage with a gauze pad in the center, used to protect minor wounds.

ban·dan·na or **ban·dan·a** (băn-dăn′ə) ▸ *n.* A large handkerchief, usu. patterned and brightly colored.

band·box (bănd′bŏks′) ▸ *n.* A rounded box used to hold small articles of apparel.

ban·di·coot (băn′dĭ-ko͞ot′) ▸ *n.* **1.** A large rat of SE Asia. **2.** A ratlike Australian marsupial.

ban·dit (băn′dĭt) ▸ *n.* A robber, esp. one who is armed. **—ban′dit·ry** *n.*

ban·do·leer or **ban·do·lier** (băn′də-lîr′) ▸ *n.* A military belt for carrying cartridges that is worn across the chest.

band saw ▸ *n.* A power saw having a toothed metal band driven around pulleys.

band·stand (bănd′stănd′) ▸ *n.* A platform for a band or orchestra, often roofed when outdoors.

band·wag·on (bănd′wăg′ən) ▸ *n.* **1.** A decorated wagon used to transport musicians in a parade. **2.** *Informal* A cause or party that attracts increasing numbers of adherents.

band·width (bănd′wĭdth′, -wĭth′) ▸ *n.* *Comp. Sci.* The amount of data that can be passed along a communications channel in a given period of time.

ban·dy (băn′dē) ▸ *v.* **-died, -dy·ing. 1.** To toss back and forth. **2.** To discuss in a casual or frivolous manner. ▸ *adj.* Bowed in an outward curve: *bandy legs.*

bane (bān) ▸ *n.* **1.** Fatal injury or ruin. **2.** A cause of death or ruin. **3.** A deadly poison. **—bane′ful** *adj.*

bang¹ (băng) ▸ *n.* **1.** A sudden loud noise, blow, or thump. **2.** *Slang* A sense of excitement; thrill. ▸ *v.* **1.** To hit noisily; bump. **2.** To handle noisily or violently. **3.** To make a loud, explosive noise. ▸ *adv.* Exactly; precisely: *hit bang on the target.*

bang² (băng) ▸ *n.* often **bangs** Hair cut straight across the forehead.

Bang·kok (băng′kŏk′) ▸ The capital of Thailand, in the SW.

Bang·la·desh (băng′glə-dĕsh′, băng′-) ▸ A country of S Asia between India and Myanmar on the Bay of Bengal. **—Bang′la·desh′i** *adj. & n.*

ban·gle (băng′gəl) ▸ *n.* **1.** A hooplike bracelet or anklet. **2.** A hanging ornament.

bang-up (băng′ŭp′) ▸ *adj. Informal* Very good; excellent.

ban·ian (băn′yən) ▸ *n.* Var. of **banyan.**

ban·ish (băn′ĭsh) ▸ *v.* **1.** To force to leave a country or place by official decree; exile. **2.** To drive away; expel. **—ban′ish·ment** *n.*

ban·is·ter also **ban·nis·ter** (băn′ĭ-stər) ▸ *n.* **1.** A handrail, esp. on a staircase. **2.** A baluster.

ban·jo (băn′jō) ▸ *n., pl.* **-jos** or **-joes** *Mus.* A usu. fretted stringed instrument having a hollow circular body with a stretched diaphragm of vellum. **—ban′jo·ist** *n.*

bank¹ (băngk) ▸ *n.* **1.** A piled-up mass, as of snow or clouds. **2.** A steep natural incline. **3.** An artificial embankment. **4.** often **banks** The slope of land adjoining a body of water, esp. a river, lake, or channel. **5.** often **banks** A large elevated area of a sea floor. **6.** Lateral tilting, as of an aircraft or vehicle in turning. ▸ *v.* **1.** To border or protect with a bank. **2.** To pile up; amass. **3.** To cover (a fire) with ashes or fuel for continued low burning. **4.** To construct with a slope rising to the outside edge. **5.** To tilt (e.g., an aircraft) in turning.

bank² (băngk) ▸ *n.* **1a.** A business establishment authorized to perform financial transactions, such as receiving or lending money. **b.** The offices in which a bank is located. **2.** The funds held by a dealer or banker in some gambling games. **3.** A supply for future or emergency use: *a blood bank.* **4.** A place of storage: *a computer's memory bank.* ▸ *v.* **1.** To deposit in a bank. **2.** To transact business with a bank. **3.** To operate a bank. ***—phrasal verb:* bank on** To count on; rely on. **—bank′a·ble** *adj.* **—bank′er** *n.* **—bank′ing** *n.*

bank³ (băngk) ▸ *n.* **1.** A set of similar things arranged in a row: *a bank of elevators.* **2.** *Naut.* A bench for rowers or a row of oars in a galley. ▸ *v.* To arrange in a row.

bank·book (băngk′bo͝ok′) ▸ *n.* A booklet held by a depositor in which deposits and withdrawals are entered by the bank; passbook.

bank·card (băngk′kärd′) ▸ *n.* A card issued by a bank, used for receiving credit or for operating an automated teller machine.

bank holiday ▸ *n.* A day on which banks are legally closed.

bank note ▸ *n.* A note issued by an authorized bank payable to the bearer on demand and acceptable as money.

bank·roll (băngk′rōl′) ▸ *n.* **1.** A roll of paper money. **2.** *Informal* One's ready cash. ▸ *v.* *Informal* To underwrite the expense of.

bank·rupt (băngk′rŭpt′, -rəpt) ▸ *n.* A debtor that is judged legally insolvent and whose remaining property is then administered for the creditors or is distributed among them. ▸ *adj.* **1a.** Having been legally declared insolvent. **b.** Financially ruined; impoverished. **2.** Lacking in quality

THESAURUS

band¹ *n.* A long narrow piece, as of material ▸ bandeau, belt, cincture, cinch, fillet, girdle, riband, ribbon, sash, strap, strip, stripe, strop, swatch, swath, tape. *—See also* CIRCLE (1), STRIPE.

band *v.* *—See* ENCIRCLE, STREAK.

band² *n.* A group of people acting together in a shared activity ▸ cohort, company, corps, party, troop, troupe, unit. [*Compare* ALLIANCE, ASSEMBLY, FORCE, UNION.] *—See also* GANG, GROUP.

band *v.* To form a united group ▸ combine, come together, flock (together), gang (together), group, join (together), league, unite. ***Idiom:*** join forces. [*Compare* ALLY, ASSEMBLE, ASSOCIATE, COMBINE.]

bandage *v.* *—See* DRESS (2).

bandeau *n.* *—See* BAND¹.

banderole *n.* *—See* FLAG¹.

bandit *n.* *—See* THIEF.

bandsman *n.* *—See* PLAYER (2).

bandy *v.* *—See* DISCUSS, EXCHANGE.

bane *n.* *—See* CURSE (3), DESTRUCTION, POISON, RUIN (1).

baneful *adj.* *—See* HARMFUL.

bang *v.* To strike together or handle noisily ▸ clang, clap, clash, crack, crash, ding, knock, rap, slam, smack, smash, thump, thwack, whack. [*Compare* HIT, SLAP, THUD.] *—See also* BEAT (1), BLAST (1), CRACK (2).

bang up *v.* *—See* BATTER.

bang *n.* A forceful movement causing a loud noise ▸ crash, slam, smash, wham. *—See also* BLAST (1), BLOW², CRACK (1), THRILL.

bang *adv.* *—See* DIRECTLY (3).

banish *v.* To force to leave a country or place by official decree ▸ deport, exile, expatriate, expel, extradite, ostracize, transport. [*Compare* EJECT, EXCLUDE, FORBID.] *—See also* DISMISS (2), DISMISS (3).

banishment *n.* *—See* EXILE.

bank¹ *n.* *—See* HEAP (1).

bank *v.* *—See* HEAP (1).

bank² *v.* To place money in an account ▸ deposit, invest, lay away, salt away. *Informal:* sock away. [*Compare* CONSERVE, SAVE.]

bank on or **upon** *v.* *—See* DEPEND ON (1).

bank *n.* *—See* DEPOSITORY.

bankable *adj.* *—See* PROFITABLE.

banking *n.* The management of money ▸ finance, investment, money management.

bankroll *v.* *—See* FINANCE.

bankroll *n.* *—See* CAPITAL (1).

bankrupt *v.* *—See* DESTROY (1), RUIN.

bankrupt *n.* *—See* PAUPER.

bankrupt *adj.* *—See* EMPTY (2), POOR.

or resources; depleted. ▸ *v.* To cause to become financially bankrupt. **—bank′rupt·cy** *n.*

ban·ner (băn′ər) ▸ *n.* 1. A piece of cloth attached to a staff and used as a standard by a monarch, military commander, or knight. 2. A flag. 3. A headline spanning the width of a newspaper page. ▸ *adj.* Outstanding: *a banner crop.*

ban·nis·ter (băn′ĭ-stər) ▸ *n.* Var. of **banister.**

ban·nock (băn′ək) ▸ *n.* A flat, usu. unleavened bread made of oatmeal or barley flour.

banns (bănz) ▸ *pl.n.* An announcement, esp. in a church, of an intended marriage.

ban·quet (băng′kwĭt) ▸ *n.* 1. An elaborate, sumptuous feast. 2. A ceremonial dinner honoring a particular guest or occasion. ▸ *v.* To honor at or partake of a banquet. **—ban′quet·er** *n.*

ban·quette (băng-kĕt′) ▸ *n.* 1. A platform lining a trench or parapet for soldiers when firing. 2. A long upholstered bench along a wall.

ban·shee (băn′shē) ▸ *n.* A female spirit in Gaelic folklore believed to presage a death in a family by wailing.

ban·tam (băn′təm) ▸ *n.* 1. Any of various breeds of small domestic fowl. 2. A small but aggressive person. ▸ *adj.* 1. Diminutive; small. 2. Aggressive and spirited.

ban·tam·weight (băn′təm-wāt′) ▸ *n.* A boxer weighing from 113 to 118 lbs., between a flyweight and a featherweight.

ban·ter (băn′tər) ▸ *n.* Good-humored, playful conversation. ▸ *v.* To exchange playful or teasing remarks.

Ban·tu (băn′tōō) ▸ *n., pl.* **-tu** or **-tus.** 1. A large group of related languages spoken in central, E-central, and S Africa, including Swahili, Zulu, and Xhosa. 2. A member of a Bantu-speaking people. **—Ban′tu** *adj.*

ban·yan also **ban·ian** (băn′yən) ▸ *n.* A tropical fig tree having many aerial roots that descend from the branches and develop new trunks.

ban·zai (bän-zī′) ▸ *n.* A Japanese battle cry or patriotic cheer.

ba·o·bab (bā′ō-băb′, bä′-) ▸ *n.* A tropical African tree with large, hard-shelled hanging fruits and a short swollen trunk that stores water.

bap·tism (băp′tĭz′əm) ▸ *n.* 1. A Christian sacrament of spiritual rebirth marked by the symbolic use of water. 2. A ceremony or an experience by which one is purified, given a name, or initiated. **—bap·tis′mal** *adj.*

Bap·tist (băp′tĭst) ▸ *n.* 1. A member of an evangelical Protestant church that practices voluntary adult baptism. 2. **baptist** One that baptizes. **—Bap′tist** *adj.*

bap·tis·ter·y also **bap·tis·try** (băp′tĭ-strē) ▸ *n., pl.* **-ies** also **-tries.** 1. A part of a church or a separate building used for baptizing. 2. A font used for baptism.

bap·tize (băp-tīz′, băp′tīz′) ▸ *v.* **-tized, -tiz·ing.** 1. To administer baptism (to). 2a. To cleanse or purify. b. To initiate. 3. To give a first or Christian name to; christen. **—bap·tiz′er** *n.*

bar (bär) ▸ *n.* 1. A relatively long, straight, rigid piece of solid material. 2. A solid oblong block of a substance, such as soap, candy, or gold. 3. An obstacle. 4. A narrow marking, as a stripe or band. 5. *Law* The nullification or prevention of a claim or action. 6. The railing in a courtroom in front of which the judges, lawyers, and defendants sit. 7. *Law* a. Attorneys considered as a group. b. The legal profession. 8. *Mus.* A vertical line drawn through a staff to mark off a measure. 9a. A counter at which food and esp. drinks are served: *an oyster bar.* b. A place having such a counter. 10. Var. of **barre.** ▸ *v.* **barred, bar·ring.** 1. To fasten securely with a bar. 2. To shut in or out with or as if with bars. 3. To obstruct. 4a. To forbid; prohibit. b. To exclude. 5. To mark with stripes or bands. ▸ *prep.* Except for; excluding: *my best performance, bar none.*

barb (bärb) ▸ *n.* 1. A sharp backward-pointing projection, as on an arrow or fishhook. 2. A cutting remark. 3. A parallel filament projecting from the main shaft of a feather. 4. *Bot.* A hooked bristle or hairlike projection. 5. See **barbel.** ▸ *v.* To provide with a barb. **—barbed** *adj.*

Bar·ba·dos (bär-bā′dōs′, -dōz′) ▸ An island country of the E West Indies. **—Bar·ba′di·an** *adj. & n.*

bar·bar·i·an (bär-bâr′ē-ən) ▸ *n.* 1. A member of a people considered by others to have a primitive civilization. 2. A savage, brutal, or cruel person. 3. An insensitive, uncultured person. **—bar·bar′i·an** *adj.* **—bar·bar′i·an·ism** *n.*

bar·bar·ic (bär-băr′ĭk) ▸ *adj.* 1. Of or typical of barbarians. 2. Marked by crudeness in taste, style, or manner.

bar·ba·rism (bär′bə-rĭz′əm) ▸ *n.* 1. An act or custom marked by brutality or crudity. 2. The use of words or expressions considered incorrect or unacceptable.

bar·ba·rous (bär′bər-əs) ▸ *adj.* 1. Primitive in culture and customs. 2. Lacking refinement; coarse. 3. Marked by savagery; brutal; cruel. 4. Marked by the use of barbarisms in language. **—bar′ba·rize′** *v.* **—bar′ba·rous·ly** *adv.* **—bar′ba·rous·ness, bar·bar′i·ty** (-băr′ĭ-tē) *n.*

Bar·ba·ry (bär′bə-rē, -brē) ▸ A region of N Africa on the Mediterranean coast between Egypt and the Atlantic.

Barbary Coast ▸ The Mediterranean coastal area of Barbary.

bar·be·cue (bär′bĭ-kyōō′) ▸ *n.* 1. A grill, pit, or outdoor fireplace for roasting meat. 2. Meat roasted over an open fire. 3. A social gathering, usu. held outdoors, at which food is cooked over an open fire. ▸ *v.* **-cued, -cu·ing.** To roast (meat or seafood) over an open fire.

barbed wire ▸ *n.* Twisted strands of fence wire with barbs at regular intervals.

bar·bel (bär′bəl) ▸ *n.* One of the whiskerlike feelers of certain fishes, such as catfishes.

bar·bell (bär′bĕl′) ▸ *n.* A bar with weights at each end, lifted for sport or exercise.

bar·ber (bär′bər) ▸ *n.* One whose business is to cut hair and to shave or trim beards. ▸ *v.* To cut the hair or beard (of).

bar·ber·ry (bär′bĕr′ē) ▸ *n.* Any of various often spiny shrubs having small reddish or blackish berries.

bar·ber·shop (bär′bər-shŏp′) ▸ *n.* The place of business of a barber. ▸ *adj.* Relating to sentimental songs sung in four-part harmony.

bar·bi·tal (bär′bĭ-tôl′, -tăl′) ▸ *n.* A barbiturate, $C_8H_{12}N_2O_3$, used as a sedative.

bar·bi·tu·rate (bär-bĭch′ər-ĭt, -ə-rāt′, -ə-wĭt) ▸ *n.* Any of a group of barbituric acid derivatives used as sedatives or hypnotics.

bar·bi·tu·ric acid (bär′bĭ-tŏŏr′ĭk, -tyŏŏr′-) ▸ *n.* An organic acid, $C_4H_4O_3N_2$, used in the manufacture of barbiturates.

THESAURUS

bankruptcy *n.* The condition of being financially insolvent ▸ failure, insolvency, ruin, ruination. [*Compare* POVERTY.]

banned *adj.* —*See* FORBIDDEN.

banner *n.* —*See* FLAG[1].

banner *adj.* —*See* EXCELLENT.

banneret *n.* —*See* FLAG[1].

banquet *n.* A large, elaborately prepared meal ▸ feast, junket. *Informal:* feed, spread.

bantam *adj.* —*See* LITTLE.

banter *n.* —*See* RIBBING.

banter *v.* —*See* JOKE (2).

baptize *v.* —*See* NAME (1).

bar *n.* 1. Something that blocks entry or passage ▸ barricade, barrier, block, blockage, bottleneck, clog, dam, encumbrance, hindrance, hurdle, impediment, obstacle, obstruction, snag, sticking point, stop, stumbling block, wall. [*Compare* CATCH, DISADVANTAGE.] 2. A public establishment that sells alcoholic drinks and often food, often from a counter ▸ alehouse, cocktail lounge, inn, lounge, nightclub, pub, public house, roadhouse, saloon, tavern, wine bar. *Informal:* juke joint, watering hole. —*See also* COURT (2), FASTENER, ROD, STRIPE.

bar *v.* —*See* ENCLOSE (1), EXCLUDE, FORBID, OBSTRUCT, STREAK.

barb *n.* —*See* CRACK (3), SPIKE.

barbarian *n.* —*See* BOOR, FIEND.

barbarian *adj.* —*See* COARSE (1), UNCIVILIZED.

barbaric *adj.* —*See* COARSE (1), UNCIVILIZED.

barbarism *n.* —*See* CORRUPTION (3).

barbarity *n.* —*See* CRUELTY, OUTRAGE.

barbarous *adj.* —*See* CRUEL, UNCIVILIZED.

barbecue *v.* —*See* COOK.

barbed *adj.* —*See* THORNY (1).

Bar·bu·da (bär-bo͞o′də) ▸ An island of Antigua and Barbuda in the West Indies N of Antigua. **—Bar·bu′dan** *adj. & n.*

barb·wire (bärb′wīr′) ▸ *n.* Barbed wire.

Bar·ce·lo·na (bär′sə-lō′nə) ▸ A city of NE Spain on the Mediterranean Sea.

bar code ▸ *n.* A series of vertical bars of varying widths printed on consumer product packages and used esp. for inventory control.

bard (bärd) ▸ *n.* **1.** One of an ancient Celtic order of singing narrative poets. **2.** A poet, esp. an exalted national poet. **—bard′ic** *adj.*

bare (bâr) ▸ *adj.* **bar·er, bar·est. 1.** Lacking the usual or appropriate covering or clothing; naked. **2.** Exposed to view. **3.** Lacking the usual furnishings, equipment, or decoration. **4.** Having no addition or qualification: *the bare facts.* **5.** Just sufficient: *the bare necessities.* ▸ *v.* **bared, bar·ing.** To make bare; reveal. **—bare′ness** *n.*

bare·back (bâr′băk′) ▸ *adj.* Using no saddle: *a bareback rider.* **—bare′back′** *adv.*

bare·faced (bâr′fāst′) ▸ *adj.* **1.** Having no covering or beard on the face. **2.** Shameless; brazen: *a barefaced lie.* **—bare′fac′ed·ly** (-fā′sĭd-lē, -fāst′lē) *adv.*

bare·foot (bâr′fo͝ot′) also **bare·foot·ed** (-fo͝ot′ĭd) ▸ *adj.* Wearing nothing on the feet. **—bare′foot** *adv.*

bare·hand·ed (bâr′hăn′dĭd) ▸ *adj.* Having no covering on the hands. **—bare′hand′ed** *adv.*

bare·head·ed (bâr′hĕd′ĭd) ▸ *adj.* Having no covering on the head. **—bare′head′ed** *adv.*

bare·leg·ged (bâr′lĕg′ĭd, -lĕgd′) ▸ *adj.* Having the legs uncovered. **—bare′leg′ged** *adv.*

bare·ly (bâr′lē) ▸ *adv.* **1.** By a very little; hardly. **2.** Sparsely; sparely: *a barely furnished room.*

barf (bärf) ▸ *v. Slang* To vomit. **—barf** *n.*

bar·fly (bär′flī′) ▸ *n. Slang* One who frequents drinking establishments.

bar·gain (bär′gĭn) ▸ *n.* **1.** An agreement between parties fixing obligations that each promises to carry out. **2a.** An agreement establishing the terms of a sale or exchange of goods or services. **b.** The property acquired or services rendered as a result of such an agreement. **3.** Something offered or acquired at a price advantageous to the buyer. ▸ *v.* **1.** To negotiate the terms of a sale, exchange, or other agreement. **2.** To arrive at an agreement. **3.** To exchange; trade. ***—phrasal verb:* bargain for** To count on; expect. ***—idiom:* into (or in) the bargain** More than what is expected. **—bar′gain·er** *n.*

barge (bärj) ▸ *n.* **1.** A long, large, usu. flat-bottomed boat for transporting freight. **2.** A large open pleasure boat used for parties. **3.** A powerboat reserved for the use of an admiral. ▸ *v.* **barged, barg·ing. 1.** To carry by barge. **2.** To move about clumsily. **3.** To intrude.

bar graph ▸ *n.* A graph consisting of parallel, usu. vertical bars or rectangles with lengths proportional to specified quantities.

bar·ite (bâr′īt, băr′-) ▸ *n.* A crystalline mineral that is the chief source of barium compounds.

bar·i·tone (băr′ĭ-tōn′) ▸ *n.* **1.** A male singer or voice with a range higher than a bass and lower than a tenor. **2.** A wind instrument with a similar range.

bar·i·um (bâr′ē-əm, băr′-) ▸ *n. Symbol* **Ba** A soft, silvery-white metal used to deoxidize copper and in various alloys. At. no. 56.

bark[1] (bärk) ▸ *n.* The harsh, abrupt sound uttered by a dog. ▸ *v.* **1.** To utter a bark. **2.** To speak sharply; snap. ***—idiom:* bark up the wrong tree** To misdirect one's efforts.

bark[2] (bärk) ▸ *n.* The tough outer covering of the stems and roots of trees and other woody plants. ▸ *v.* **1.** To remove bark from. **2.** To scrape; skin: *barked my shin.*

bark[3] also **barque** (bärk) ▸ *n.* **1.** A sailing ship with from three to five masts. **2.** A boat, esp. a small sailing vessel.

bar·keep·er (bär′kē′pər) also **bar·keep** (-kēp′) ▸ *n.* **1.** One who owns or runs a bar. **2.** See **bartender.**

bark·er (bär′kər) ▸ *n.* **1.** One that barks. **2.** One who stands at the entrance to a show, as at a carnival, and solicits customers with a loud colorful sales spiel.

bar·ley (bär′lē) ▸ *n.* A cereal grass that bears grain used as food, livestock feed, and for malt production.

bar·maid (bär′mād′) ▸ *n.* A woman who serves drinks in a bar.

bar·man (bär′mən) ▸ *n.* A man who serves drinks in a bar.

bar mitz·vah or **bar miz·vah** (bär mĭts′və) ▸ *n.* **1.** A 13-year-old Jewish boy, considered an adult and responsible for his moral and religious duties. **2.** The ceremony that confirms a boy as a bar mitzvah.

barn (bärn) ▸ *n.* A large farm building used for storing farm products and sheltering livestock.

bar·na·cle (bär′nə-kəl) ▸ *n.* A small, hard-shelled crustacean that attaches itself to submerged surfaces.

barn owl ▸ *n.* An owl with a white, heart-shaped face, often nesting in barns.

barn·storm (bärn′stôrm′) ▸ *v.* **1.** To travel about making political speeches, giving lectures, or presenting plays. **2.** To tour as a stunt flyer. **—barn′storm′er** *n.*

Bar·num (bär′nəm), **P(hineas) T(aylor)** (1810–91) ▸ Amer. circus impresario.

barn·yard (bärn′yärd′) ▸ *n.* The area surrounding a barn, often enclosed by a fence.

bar·o·graph (băr′ə-grăf′) ▸ *n.* A recording barometer. **—bar′o·graph′ic** *adj.*

ba·rom·e·ter (bə-rŏm′ĭ-tər) ▸ *n.* **1.** An instrument for measuring atmospheric pressure, used esp. in weather forecasting. **2.** An indicator of change. **—bar′o·met′ric** (băr′ə-mĕt′rĭk), **bar′o·met′ri·cal** *adj.* **—ba·rom′e·try** *n.*

bar·on (băr′ən) ▸ *n.* **1a.** A British or Japanese nobleman of the lowest rank. **b.** A nobleman of continental Europe, ranked variously in different countries. **2.** One having great power in a specified field. **—bar′on·age** *n.* **—ba·ro′ni·al** (bə-rō′nē-əl) *adj.* **—bar′o·ny** *n.*

bar·on·ess (băr′ə-nĭs) ▸ *n.* **1.** The wife or widow of a baron. **2.** A woman holding a baronial title.

bar·on·et (băr′ə-nĭt, băr′ə-nĕt′) ▸ *n.* A man holding a British hereditary title reserved for commoners. **—bar′on·et·cy** *n.*

bar·on·et·ess (băr′ə-nĭ-tĭs, băr′ə-nĕt′ĭs) ▸ *n.* A woman holding a British hereditary title reserved for commoners.

ba·roque (bə-rōk′) ▸ *adj.* **1.** also **Baroque a.** Of an artistic style current in Europe from the early 17th to mid-18th cent. typified by bold, curving forms and elaborate ornamentation. **b.** Of a musical style current in Europe from about 1600 to 1750, marked by strict forms and elaborate

THESAURUS

bard *n.* —*See* POET.

bare *adj.* **1.** Without addition, decoration, or qualification ▸ austere, bald, bare-bones, classic, dry, plain, plain-Jane, plain vanilla, severe, simple, spare, spartan, stark, unadorned, undecorated, unvarnished, vanilla. [*Compare* RUSTIC.] **2.** Just sufficient ▸ mere, scant, scanty. [*Compare* INSUFFICIENT, MEAGER.] **3.** Without the usual covering ▸ bald, barren, hairless, leafless, naked, nude. [*Compare* OPEN.] —*See also* EMPTY (1), NUDE.

bare *v.* To remove the clothing or covering from ▸ denude, disrobe, divest, expose, flay, peel, strip, unclothe, uncover, undress. [*Compare* SKIN.] —*See also* REVEAL.

bare-bones *adj.* —*See* BARE (1).

barefaced *adj.* —*See* IMPUDENT.

barely *adv.* By a very little; almost not ▸ hardly, just, scarce, scarcely. *Idiom* by the skin of one's teeth. [*Compare* APPROXIMATELY, MERELY, ONLY.]

bareness *n.* —*See* EMPTINESS (2), NUDITY.

barf *v.* —*See* VOMIT.

bargain *n.* Something offered or bought at a low price ▸ find. *Informal:* buy, deal. *Slang:* steal. —*See also* AGREEMENT (1), DEAL (1).

bargain *v.* —*See* CONTRACT (1), HAGGLE.

bargain for or **on** *v.* —*See* EXPECT (1).

bargain-basement *adj.* —*See* CHEAP.

barge in *v.* —*See* INTERRUPT (2), INTRUDE.

bark *v.* —*See* CRACK (2), SNAP (3).

bark *n.* —*See* CRACK (1).

barm *n.* —*See* FOAM.

barmy *adj.* —*See* FOAMY.

barnyard *adj.* —*See* OBSCENE.

baronial *adj.* —*See* GRAND.

baroque *adj.* —*See* COMPLEX (1), ORNATE.

ornamentation. 2a. Highly intricate or ornate. b. Grotesque; bizarre. **—ba·roque′ly** *adv.* **—ba·roque′** *n.*

barque (bärk) ▸ *n.* Var. of **bark**[3].

bar·rack (băr′ək) ▸ *v.* To house (e.g., soldiers) in quarters. ▸ *n.* often **bar·racks** (băr′əks) A building or group of buildings used to house military personnel.

bar·ra·cu·da (băr′ə-ko͞o′də) ▸ *n., pl.* **-da** or **-das**. A narrow-bodied, chiefly tropical marine fish with very sharp fang-like teeth.

bar·rage (bə-räzh′) ▸ *n.* 1. A heavy curtain of artillery or missile fire. 2. An overwhelming outpouring: *a barrage of criticism.* ▸ *v.* **-raged, -rag·ing**. To direct a barrage at.

bar·ra·try (băr′ə-trē) ▸ *n., pl.* **-tries**. 1. *Law* The offense of instigating quarrels or groundless lawsuits. 2. An unlawful breach of duty on the part of a ship's master or crew resulting in injury to the ship's owner. 3. Sale or purchase of positions in church or state.

barre also **bar** (bär) ▸ *n.* 1. In ballet, a horizontal rail used as a support in exercises. 2. *Mus.* A technique in which a finger is laid across a fingerboard to stop several strings at once.

bar·rel (băr′əl) ▸ *n.* 1. A large cask usu. made of curved wooden staves bound with hoops and having a flat top and bottom. 2a. The long tube of a firearm. b. A cylindrical machine part. 3. *Informal* A great deal: *a barrel of fun.* 4. See **measurement** table in Appendix. ▸ *v.* **-reled, -rel·ing** or **-relled, -rel·ling**. 1. To put or pack in a barrel. 2. To move at a high speed.

barrel organ ▸ *n.* A mechanical instrument on which a tune is played by a revolving cylinder turned by a hand crank.

barrel roll ▸ *n.* A flight maneuver in which an aircraft makes a complete rotation on its longitudinal axis.

bar·ren (băr′ən) ▸ *adj.* 1a. Not producing offspring. b. Incapable of producing offspring; sterile. 2. Lacking vegetation. 3. Unproductive of results. 4. Devoid; lacking: *writing barren of insight.* ▸ *n.* often **barrens** A tract of unproductive land. **—bar′ren·ness** *n.*

bar·rette (bə-rĕt′) ▸ *n.* A hair clasp.

bar·ri·cade (băr′ĭ-kād′, băr′ĭ-kād′) ▸ *n.* A makeshift barrier or fortification set up across a route of access. ▸ *v.* **-cad·ed, -cad·ing**. To block or confine with a barricade.

bar·ri·er (băr′ē-ər) ▸ *n.* 1. A structure, such as a fence, built to bar passage. 2. Something immaterial that impedes. 3. A boundary or limit.

barrier island ▸ *n.* A long narrow island running parallel to the mainland.

barrier reef ▸ *n.* A long narrow ridge of coral parallel to a coastline and separated from it by a lagoon too deep for coral growth.

bar·ring (bär′ĭng) ▸ *prep.* Apart from the occurrence of; excepting.

bar·ri·o (bä′rē-ō′) ▸ *n., pl.* **-os**. A chiefly Spanish-speaking neighborhood in a US city.

bar·ris·ter (băr′ĭ-stər) ▸ *n. Chiefly Brit.* A lawyer who argues cases in the superior courts.

bar·room (bär′ro͞om′, -ro͝om′) ▸ *n.* A place where alcoholic beverages are sold at a bar.

bar·row[1] (băr′ō) ▸ *n.* 1. A flat rectangular tray or cart with handles at each end. 2. A wheelbarrow.

bar·row[2] (băr′ō) ▸ *n.* A large mound of earth or stones placed over a burial site.

bar·tend·er (bär′tĕn′dər) ▸ *n.* One who serves alcoholic drinks at a bar; barkeeper.

bar·ter (bär′tər) ▸ *v.* To trade (goods or services) without using money. **—bar′ter** *n.* **—bar′ter·er** *n.*

Bar·ton (bär′tn), **Clara** (1821–1912) ▸ Amer. founder of the American Red Cross (1881).

Bar·uch (bâr′ək, bə-ro͞ok′) ▸ *n.* See **Bible** table in Appendix.

bar·y·on (băr′ē-ŏn′) ▸ *n.* Any of a family of subatomic particles, including protons and neutrons, that are composed of three quarks.

bas·al (bā′səl, -zəl) ▸ *adj.* 1. Of, located at, or forming a base. 2. Of primary importance; basic. **—bas′al·ly** *adv.*

basal metabolism ▸ *n.* The minimum amount of energy required to maintain vital functions in an organism at complete rest.

ba·salt (bə-sôlt′, bā′sôlt′) ▸ *n.* A hard, dense, dark volcanic rock. **—ba·sal′tic** *adj.*

base[1] (bās) ▸ *n.* 1. The lowest or bottom part. 2. A foundation. 3. The fundamental principle of a system or theory; basis. 4. A chief constituent: *a paint with an oil base.* 5. The fact, observation, or premise from which a reasoning process is begun. 6a. *Games* A starting point, safety area, or goal. b. *Baseball* Any one of the four corners of an infield marked by a bag or plate. 7. A center of organization, supply, or activity; headquarters. 8a. A fortified center of operations. b. A supply center for a large force of military personnel. 9. *Ling.* A morpheme regarded as a form to which affixes or other bases may be added. 10. *Math.* The number that is raised to various powers to generate the principal counting units of a number system. 11. A line used as a reference for measurement or computations. 12. *Chem.* a. Any of a large class of compounds, including the hydroxides and oxides of metals, having a bitter taste, a slippery solution, the ability to turn litmus blue, and the ability to react with acids to form salts. b. A molecular or ionic substance capable of combining with a proton to form a new substance. ▸ *adj.* Forming or serving as a base. ▸ *v.* **based, bas·ing**. 1. To form or assign a base for. 2. To find a basis for; establish. ***—idiom:* off base** Badly mistaken.

base[2] (bās) ▸ *adj.* **bas·er, bas·est**. 1. Morally bad; contemptible. 2. Lowly; menial. 3. Inferior in value or quality. 4. Containing inferior substances: *a base metal.* **—base′ly** *adv.* **—base′ness** *n.*

base·ball (bās′bôl′) ▸ *n.* 1. A game played with a bat and ball by two teams of nine players, each team playing al-

THESAURUS

barracks *n.* Usually temporary living accommodations ▸ lodgings, rooms, quarters. *Slang:* crash-pad. [*Compare* APARTMENT, HOME.]

barrage *n.* A concentrated outpouring, as of missiles, words, or blows ▸ bombardment, broadside, burst, cannonade, crossfire, discharge, fire, flak, fusillade, hail, rain, salvo, shower, storm, volley. [*Compare* ATTACK, BLAST, FLOOD.]

barrage *v.* To direct a concentrated outpouring at ▸ blitz, bomb, bombard, cannonade, fusillade, pelt, pepper, shell, shower. [*Compare* ATTACK, OVERWHELM.]

barred *adj.* —*See* FORBIDDEN.

barrel *n.* —*See* ABUNDANCE, VAT.

barrel *v.* —*See* RUSH.

barren *adj.* 1. Unable to produce offspring ▸ childless, impotent, infertile, sterile, unfruitful. 2. Unable to support vegetation or crops ▸ dead, desert, desolate, infertile, lifeless, sterile, unfruitful, unproductive, waste. [*Compare* BLEAK, DRY.] —*See also* BARE (3), EMPTY (1), EMPTY (2), FUTILE.

barren *n.* —*See* DESERT[1].

barrenness *n.* —*See* EMPTINESS (2), FUTILITY, NOTHINGNESS (2), STERILITY (2).

barrens *n.* —*See* DESERT[1].

barricade *n.* —*See* BAR (1), BULWARK, DEFENSE.

barricade *v.* —*See* OBSTRUCT.

barrier *n.* A solid structure that separates one area from another ▸ partition, screen, wall. [*Compare* BORDER.] —*See also* BAR (1).

barter *n.* —*See* CHANGE (2), DEAL (1).

barter *v.* —*See* CHANGE (3).

basal *adj.* —*See* CONSTITUTIONAL, ELEMENTARY, RADICAL.

base[1] *n.* 1. A center of organization, supply, or activity ▸ camp, command post, complex, depot, headquarters, home, home base, home office, installation, post, station. [*Compare* CENTER.] 2. The lowest or supporting part or structure ▸ basis, bed, bottom, cornerstone, foot, footing, foundation, ground, groundwork, pedestal, seat, stand, substratum, substructure, underpinning. [*Compare* STAGE, SUPPORT.] —*See also* BASIS (1), THEME (1).

base *v.* To provide a basis for ▸ build, construct, establish, found, ground, model, predicate, rest, root, undergird, underpin. [*Compare* DEPEND, SUPPORT.] —*See also* POSITION.

base[2] *adj.* —*See* SHODDY, SORDID.

ternately in the field and at bat, the players at bat having to run a course of four bases laid out in a diamond pattern in order to score. 2. The hard ball used in this game.

base·board (bās′bôrd′) ▸ *n.* A molding that conceals the joint between an interior wall and the floor.

base·born (bās′bôrn′) ▸ *adj.* 1. Ignoble; contemptible. 2a. Born of unwed parents; illegitimate. b. Of humble birth.

base hit ▸ *n.* *Baseball* A hit by which the batter reaches base safely.

base·less (bās′lĭs) ▸ *adj.* Having no basis or foundation in fact; unfounded.

base line ▸ *n.* 1. A line serving as a basis, as for measurement or comparison. 2. *Baseball* An area within which a base runner must stay when running between bases. 3. *Sports* The boundary line at either end of a court, as in badminton or tennis.

base·man (bās′mən) ▸ *n.* *Baseball* A player assigned to first, second, or third base.

base·ment (bās′mənt) ▸ *n.* 1. The substructure or foundation of a building. 2. The lowest story of a building, usu. below ground.

ba·sen·ji (bə-sĕn′jē) ▸ *n.* A dog having a short smooth coat and lacking a bark.

base on balls ▸ *n.* *Baseball* The advance of a batter to first base after four pitches that are balls.

ba·ses (bā′sēz′) ▸ *n.* Pl. of **basis**.

bash (băsh) ▸ *v.* 1. To strike with a heavy crushing blow. 2. *Informal* To criticize (another) harshly. ▸ *n.* 1. *Informal* A heavy crushing blow. 2. *Slang* A party. **—bash′er** *n.*

bash·ful (băsh′fəl) ▸ *adj.* Shy and self-conscious. **—bash′ful·ly** *adv.* **—bash′ful·ness** *n.*

ba·sic (bā′sĭk) ▸ *adj.* 1. Of or forming a base; fundamental. 2. First and necessary beyond all else. 3. *Chem.* a. Of, producing, or resulting from a base. b. Containing a base, esp. in excess of acid. c. Containing oxide or hydroxide anions. Used of a salt. ▸ *n.* A fundamental element or entity: *the basics of math.* **—ba′si·cal·ly** *adv.* **—ba·sic′i·ty** (-sĭs′ĭ-tē) *n.*

BA·SIC (bā′sĭk) ▸ *n.* A simple programming language.

bas·il (băz′əl, bā′zəl) ▸ *n.* An Old World aromatic herb with leaves used as seasoning.

ba·sil·i·ca (bə-sĭl′ĭ-kə) ▸ *n.* 1a. A public building of ancient Rome, used as a courtroom or assembly hall. b. A Christian church building having a nave with a semicircular apse. 2. *Rom. Cath. Ch.* A church accorded certain privileges by the pope.

bas·i·lisk (băs′ə-lĭsk′, băz′-) ▸ *n.* 1. A legendary serpent with lethal breath and glance. 2. Any of various crested tropical American lizards that can run on the hind legs.

ba·sin (bā′sĭn) ▸ *n.* 1. An open, shallow, usu. round container used esp. for holding liquids. 2. A washbowl; sink. 3a. An artificially enclosed area of a river or harbor. b. A small enclosed or partly enclosed body of water. 4. A region drained by a single river system. 5. A bowl-shaped depression in the surface of the land or ocean floor. **—ba′sin·al** *adj.*

ba·sis (bā′sĭs) ▸ *n., pl.* **-ses** (-sēz′). 1. A foundation upon which something rests. 2. The chief constituent. 3. A fundamental principle.

bask (băsk) ▸ *v.* 1. To expose oneself to pleasant warmth. 2. To take great satisfaction: *basked in the teacher's praise.*

bas·ket (băs′kĭt) ▸ *n.* 1. A container made of interwoven material. 2. A usu. open gondola on a hot-air balloon. 3. *Basketball* A metal hoop from which an open-bottomed circular net is suspended, serving as a goal.

bas·ket·ball (băs′kĭt-bôl′) ▸ *n.* 1. A game played between two teams of five players each, the object being to throw an inflated ball through an elevated basket on the opponent's side of the rectangular court. 2. The ball for this game.

basket case ▸ *n.* *Informal* One that is in a completely hopeless or useless condition.

bas·ket·ry (băs′kĭ-trē) ▸ *n.* 1. The craft of making baskets. 2. Baskets collectively.

bas mitz·vah (bäs mĭts′və) ▸ *n.* Var. of **bat mitzvah.**

Basque (băsk) ▸ *n.* 1. A member of a people of unknown origin inhabiting the W Pyrenees and the Bay of Biscay in France and Spain. 2. The language of the Basques, of no known linguistic affiliation. **—Basque** *adj.*

Bas·ra (bäs′rə, bŭs′-) ▸ A city of SE Iraq.

bas-re·lief (bä′rĭ-lēf′) ▸ *n.* See **low relief.**

bass¹ (băs) ▸ *n., pl.* **bass** or **-es**. Any of several freshwater or marine food and game fishes.

bass² (bās) ▸ *n.* 1. A low-pitched tone. 2. The tones in the lowest register of an instrument. 3a. The lowest singing voice of a man. b. The tonal range characteristic of a bass. c. A singer or voice having this range. d. An instrument, esp. a double bass or bass guitar, having this range. **—bass** *adj.*

bass clef (bās) ▸ *n.* *Mus.* A symbol that is centered on the fourth line from the bottom of a staff to indicate F below middle C.

basset hound (băs′ĭt) ▸ *n.* A short-haired dog with a long body, short legs, and drooping ears.

bas·si·net (băs′ə-nĕt′) ▸ *n.* An oblong basketlike bed for an infant.

bass·ist (bā′sĭst) ▸ *n.* One who plays a bass instrument, esp. a double bass or bass guitar.

bas·so (băs′ō, bä′sō) ▸ *n., pl.* **-sos** or **-si** (-sē). A bass singer, esp. an operatic bass.

bas·soon (bə-so͞on′, bă-) ▸ *n.* A low-pitched double-reed woodwind instrument having a long wooden body. **—bas·soon′ist** *n.*

bass viol (bās) ▸ *n.* See **double bass.**

bass·wood (băs′wo͝od′) ▸ *n.* 1. See **linden.** 2. The soft wood of a linden.

bast (băst) ▸ *n.* Fibrous plant material used to make cordage and textiles.

bas·tard (băs′tərd) ▸ *n.* 1. An illegitimate child. 2. *Slang* A mean person. ▸ *adj.* 1. Illegitimate. 2. Not genuine; spurious. **—bas′tard·ly** *adj.* **—bas′tard·y** *n.*

bas·tard·ize (băs′tər-dīz′) ▸ *v.* **-ized, -iz·ing.** To lower in quality or character; debase. **—bas′tard·i·za′tion** *n.*

baste¹ (bāst) ▸ *v.* **bast·ed, bast·ing.** To sew temporarily with large running stitches.

baste² (bāst) ▸ *v.* **bast·ed, bast·ing.** To moisten (e.g., meat) periodically with a liquid while cooking. **—bast′er** *n.*

THESAURUS

baseborn *adj.* —*See* ILLEGITIMATE, LOWLY (1).

baseless *adj.* Having no basis in fact ▸ groundless, idle, meritless, unfounded, unproved, unwarranted. [*Compare* EMPTY, FALSE.]

baselessly *adv.* Without basis or foundation in fact ▸ groundlessly, unwarrantedly, unfoundedly.

baseness *n.* —*See* CORRUPTION (2).

bash *v.* —*See* HIT, SLAM (1).

bash *n.* —*See* BLAST (3), BLOW², PARTY.

bashful *adj.* —*See* SHY¹.

bashfulness *n.* —*See* SHYNESS.

basic *adj.* —*See* ELEMENTAL, ELEMENTARY, ESSENTIAL (2), RADICAL.

basic *n.* —*See* ELEMENT (1).

basically *adv.* —*See* ESSENTIALLY.

basin *n.* The region drained by a river system ▸ drainage basin, watershed. —*See also* DEPRESSION (1), VAT.

basis *n.* 1. An underlying support, as for an argument, action, or belief ▸ base, cornerstone, footing, foundation, fundamental, ground, grounds, groundwork, keystone, root, rudiment, underpinning. [*Compare* CAUSE, ORIGIN, SUPPORT.] 2. A justifying fact or consideration ▸ foundation, justification, reason, warrant. [*Compare* ACCOUNT, APOLOGY.] 3. An established position from which to operate or deal with others ▸ footing, standing, status, terms. [*Compare* PLACE.] —*See also* BASE¹ (2).

bask *v.* —*See* LUXURIATE.

basket *n.* 1. A container made of interwoven material ▸ creel, hamper, pannier. [*Compare* CONTAINER.] 2. The contents of a basket ▸ basketful, bushel. 3. The goal in the game of basketball ▸ bucket, field goal, hoop, net, swish, swisher.

bass *adj.* —*See* LOW (1).

bastard *adj.* —*See* ILLEGITIMATE.

bastardize *v.* —*See* CORRUPT.

baste *v.* —*See* BEAT (1).

baste³ (bāst) ▸ *v.* **bast·ed, bast·ing.** 1. To beat vigorously; thrash. 2. To lambaste.

Bas·tille Day (bă-stēl′) ▸ *n.* Jul. 14, observed in France to commemorate the storming of the Bastille prison in 1789.

bas·tion (băs′chən, -tē-ən) ▸ *n.* 1. A projecting part of a fortification. 2. A bulwark; stronghold.

bat¹ (băt) ▸ *n.* 1. A stout wooden stick; cudgel. 2. A blow, as with a stick. 3. *Sports* a. A rounded, tapered, usu. wooden club used to hit the ball in baseball. b. A flat-sided club used in cricket. c. A racket, as in table tennis. ▸ *v.* **bat·ted, bat·ting.** 1. To hit with or as if with a bat. 2. *Sports* a. To be the batter or batsman in baseball or cricket. b. To have (a certain batting average). 3. *Informal* To discuss: *bat an idea around.* **—*idioms:* at bat** Taking one's turn at hitting a pitched or bowled ball in baseball or cricket. **go to bat for** To support or defend. **off the bat** Immediately.

bat² (băt) ▸ *n.* Any of various nocturnal flying mammals having membranous wings.

bat³ (băt) ▸ *v.* **bat·ted, bat·ting.** To flutter (e.g., one's eyes).

bat⁴ (băt) ▸ *n. Slang* A binge; spree.

batch (băch) ▸ *n.* 1. An amount prepared or produced at one time. 2. A group of persons or things. 3. *Comp. Sci.* A set of data to be processed in a single program run. **—batch** *v.*

bate (bāt) ▸ *v.* **bat·ed, bat·ing.** To lessen the force of; moderate.

ba·teau (bă-tō′) ▸ *n., pl.* **-teaux** (-tōz′). A light, flat-bottomed boat.

bath (băth) ▸ *n., pl.* **baths** (bă*th*z, băths). 1a. The act of soaking or cleansing the body, as in water or steam. b. The water used for bathing. 2a. A bathtub. b. A bathroom. 3. A building equipped for bathing. 4. often **baths** A spa. 5. A liquid in which something is dipped or soaked in processing.

bathe (bā*th*) ▸ *v.* **bathed, bath·ing.** 1a. To take a bath. b. To give a bath to. 2. To go swimming. 3. To wash or wet. 4. To treat by applying a liquid. 5. To suffuse, as with light. **—bath′er** *n.*

bath·house (băth′hous′) ▸ *n.* 1. A building with facilities for bathing. 2. A building with dressing rooms for swimmers.

bath·ing suit (bā′*th*ĭng) ▸ *n.* A swimsuit.

ba·thos (bā′thŏs′, -thôs′) ▸ *n.* 1. A ludicrously abrupt transition in style from the exalted to the commonplace. 2. Grossly sentimental pathos. **—ba·thet′ic** (bə-thĕt′ĭk) *adj.*

bath·robe (băth′rōb′) ▸ *n.* A loose-fitting robe worn before and after bathing and for lounging.

bath·room (băth′ro͞om′, -ro͝om′) ▸ *n.* A room equipped with a bathtub or shower and usu. a sink and toilet.

bath salts ▸ *pl.n.* Perfumed crystals for softening the water in a bathtub.

bath·tub (băth′tŭb′) ▸ *n.* A tub or fixture for bathing.

bath·y·scaph (băth′ĭ-skăf′) also **bath·y·scaphe** (-skăf′, -skāf′) ▸ *n.* A free-diving deep-sea research vessel with a crewed observation capsule.

bath·y·sphere (băth′ĭ-sfîr′) ▸ *n.* A crewed spherical deep-diving chamber lowered by cable.

ba·tik (bə-tēk′, băt′ĭk) ▸ *n.* 1. A method of dyeing fabric by applying a design in removable wax. 2. Fabric so dyed.

ba·tiste (bə-tēst′, bă-) ▸ *n.* A fine, plain-woven fabric.

bat mitz·vah (bät mĭts′və) or **bas mitz·vah** (bäs) ▸ *n.* 1. In Conservative and Reform Judaism, a Jewish girl of 12 or 13 years of age, considered an adult and responsible for her moral and religious duties. 2. The ceremony that confirms a girl as a bat mitzvah.

ba·ton (bə-tŏn′, băt′n) ▸ *n.* 1. *Mus.* A slender rod used by a conductor to direct an orchestra. 2. A hollow metal rod with heavy rubber tips twirled by a drum major or majorette. 3. The hollow cylinder passed to each member of a relay team.

Bat·on Rouge (băt′n ro͞ozh′) ▸ The capital of LA, in the SE-central part.

bats (băts) ▸ *adj. Slang* Crazy; insane.

bats·man (băts′mən) ▸ *n.* The player at bat in cricket and baseball.

bat·tal·ion (bə-tăl′yən) ▸ *n.* 1. An army unit typically consisting of a headquarters and two or more companies or batteries. 2. A large body of organized troops.

bat·ten (băt′n) ▸ *n.* A flexible wooden strip used esp. in flattening a sail or securing a hatch. ▸ *v.* To furnish or secure with battens: *batten down the hatches.*

bat·ter¹ (băt′ər) ▸ *v.* 1. To hit repeatedly with heavy blows. 2. To damage. 3. To inflict continuing physical injuries on, esp. within a family or marital relationship.

bat·ter² (băt′ər) ▸ *n.* The player at bat in baseball and cricket.

bat·ter³ (băt′ər) ▸ *n.* A beaten mixture, as of flour, milk, and eggs, used in cooking.

bat·ter·ing ram (băt′ər-ĭng) ▸ *n.* A heavy beam used in ancient warfare to batter down walls and gates.

bat·ter·y (băt′ə-rē) ▸ *n., pl.* **-ies.** 1a. The act of battering. b. The unlawful beating of a person. 2a. An emplacement for artillery. b. A set of heavy guns, as on a warship. 3a. An array: *a battery of tests.* b. An impressive body or group. 4. The percussion section of an orchestra. 5. *Elect.* A cell or group of connected cells that produces direct current, usu. by converting chemical to electrical energy.

bat·ting (băt′ĭng) ▸ *n.* Fiber wadded into rolls or sheets, as for lining quilts.

batting average ▸ *n. Baseball* The ratio of a batter's hits to the number of times at bat.

bat·tle (băt′l) ▸ *n.* 1a. An encounter between opposing forces. b. Armed fighting; combat. 2a. A protracted struggle. b. An intense competition. ▸ *v.* **-tled, -tling.** 1. To engage in or as if in battle. 2. To fight against. **—bat′tler** *n.*

bat·tle-ax or **bat·tle-axe** (băt′l-ăks′) ▸ *n.* A broad heavy ax formerly used as a weapon.

battle cry ▸ *n.* 1. A rallying cry uttered in combat. 2. A militant slogan.

bat·tle·field (băt′l-fēld′) ▸ *n.* 1. An area where a battle is fought. 2. A sphere of conflict.

bat·tle·front (băt′l-frŭnt′) ▸ *n.* The area where opponents meet in battle.

bat·tle·ground (băt′l-ground′) ▸ *n.* A battlefield.

bat·tle·ment (băt′l-mənt) ▸ *n.* A parapet built on top of a wall, with notched indentations for decoration or defense.

battle royal ▸ *n., pl.* **battles royal.** 1. An all-out fight. 2. A battle with many combatants.

bat·tle·ship (băt′l-shĭp′) ▸ *n.* Any of the largest, most heavily armed and armored class of warships.

bat·ty (băt′ē) ▸ *adj.* **-ti·er, -ti·est.** *Slang* Crazy.

THESAURUS

bastion *n.* —*See* BULWARK, FORT.

bat¹ *v.* —*See* BLINK.

bat *n.* —*See* BLINK.

bat² *n.* —*See* BENDER.

batch *n.* —*See* GROUP.

bate *v.* —*See* SUBSIDE.

bathe *v.* 1. To make moist ▸ dampen, moisten, wash, wet. 2. To flow against or along ▸ lap, lave, lip, wash. [*Compare* FLOW.] —*See also* CLEAN (1).

bathetic *adj.* —*See* SENTIMENTAL.

bathos *n.* —*See* SENTIMENTALITY.

baton *n.* —*See* STICK (1).

batten *v.* To make a large profit ▸ cash in, profit. *Slang:* clean up. *Idioms:* make a killing, make out like a bandit. —*See also* PROSPER.

batter *v.* To injure or damage, as by abuse or heavy wear ▸ bang up, knock about (*or* around), maim, mangle, manhandle, maul, mutilate, ravage, rough up, scuff, work over. *Idiom:* play (*or* wreak) havoc (on *or* with). [*Compare* ABUSE, DAMAGE, DEFORM.] —*See also* BEAT (1).

battle *n.* An encounter between opposing military forces ▸ action, belligerency, brush, clash, combat, conflict, confrontation, encounter, engagement, hostilities, skirmish, sortie, strife, struggle, war, warfare. [*Compare* COMPETITION, CONFLICT, FIGHT.] —*See also* COMPETITION (1).

battle *v.* —*See* CONTEND.

battle-ax or **battle-axe** *n.* —*See* SCOLD, WITCH (2).

battle cry *n.* —*See* CRY (2).

batty *adj.* —*See* INSANE.

bau·ble (bôʹbəl) ▸ *n.* A trinket.

baud (bôd) ▸ *n.* *Comp. Sci.* A unit of speed in data transmission equal to one bit per second.

Baude·laire (bōd-lârʹ), **Charles Pierre** (1821–67) ▸ French writer, translator, and critic.

baux·ite (bôkʹsītʹ) ▸ *n.* The principal ore of aluminum, composed mainly of hydrous aluminum oxides and aluminum hydroxides.

Ba·var·i·a (bə-vârʹē-ə) ▸ A region of S Germany. **—Ba·varʹi·an** *adj. & n.*

bawd (bôd) ▸ *n.* 1. A woman who keeps a brothel. 2. A prostitute.

bawd·y (bôʹdē) ▸ *adj.* **-i·er, -i·est.** 1. Humorously indecent; risqué. 2. Vulgar; lewd. **—bawdʹi·ly** *adv.* **—bawdʹi·ness** *n.*

bawl (bôl) ▸ *v.* 1. To sob loudly; wail. 2. To cry out loudly; bellow. ***—phrasal verb:*** **bawl out** *Informal* To scold loudly or harshly.

bay[1] (bā) ▸ *n.* A body of water partially enclosed by land but with a wide outlet to the sea.

bay[2] (bā) ▸ *n.* 1. A part of a building marked off by vertical elements, such as columns. 2a. A bay window. b. An opening or recess in a wall. 3. A section or compartment set off for a specific purpose: *a cargo bay.*

bay[3] (bā) ▸ *adj.* Reddish-brown. ▸ *n.* 1. A reddish brown. 2. A reddish-brown animal, esp. a horse.

bay[4] (bā) ▸ *n.* A deep prolonged bark, as of a hound. ***—idioms:*** **at bay** Held at a safe distance: *kept trouble at bay.* **to bay** Cornered by and facing pursuers: *bring quarry to bay.* **—bay** *v.*

bay[5] (bā) ▸ *n.* 1. See **laurel** 1. 2. A tree or shrub with aromatic foliage similar to the laurel.

bay·ber·ry (bāʹbĕrʹē) ▸ *n.* 1. An aromatic shrub bearing waxy, fragrant, berrylike fruit. 2. The fruit of this shrub.

bay leaf ▸ *n.* The dried aromatic leaf of the laurel, used as a seasoning.

bay·o·net (bāʹə-nĭt, -nĕtʹ, bāʹə-nĕtʹ) ▸ *n.* A blade adapted to fit the muzzle of a rifle. ▸ *v.* **-net·ed, -net·ing** or **-net·ted, -net·ting.** To stab with a bayonet.

bay·ou (bīʹo͞o, bīʹō) ▸ *n.* A marshy creek or small river tributary to a larger body of water.

bay window ▸ *n.* A large window or series of windows projecting from a building and forming an alcove within.

ba·zaar also **ba·zar** (bə-zärʹ) ▸ *n.* 1. A market consisting of a street lined with shops and stalls, esp. in the Middle East. 2. A fair or sale esp. for charity.

ba·zoo·ka (bə-zo͞oʹkə) ▸ *n.* A shoulder-held, tube-shaped weapon for firing armor-piercing rockets at short range.

BB[1] (bēʹbē) ▸ *n.* A small size of lead pellet used in air rifles.

BB[2] ▸ *abbr.* base on balls

BBS ▸ *abbr.* *Comp. Sci.* bulletin board system

B.C. ▸ *abbr.* 1. also **B.C.** before Christ 2. or **BC** British Columbia

B cell ▸ *n.* A lymphocyte in the immune system responsible for the production of antibodies.

be (bē) ▸ *v.* *1st and 3rd pers. sing. p. indic.* **was** (wŭz, wŏz; wəz *when unstressed*) *2nd pers. sing. and pl. and 1st and 3rd pers. pl. p. indic.* **were** (wûr) *p. subjunctive,* **were** *p.part.* **been** (bĭn) *pr.part.* **be·ing** (bēʹĭng) *1st pers. sing. pr. indic.* **am** (ăm) *2nd pers. sing. and pl. and 1st and 3rd pers. pl. pr. indic.* **are** (är) *3rd pers. sing. pr. indic.* **is** (ĭz) *pr. subjunctive,* **be.** 1. To exist: *I think, therefore I am.* 2a. To occupy a specified position: *The food is on the table.* b. To remain undisturbed or untouched: *Let the dog be.* 3. To take place; occur. 4. To go or come: *Have you ever been to Japan?* 5. Used as a copula linking a subject and a predicate nominative, adjective, or pronoun, as: a. To equal in identity: *All athletes are hard workers.* b. To signify; symbolize: *A is excellent, C is passing.* c. To belong to a specified class or group: *The human being is a primate.* d. To have or show a specified quality or characteristic: *She is smart.* 6. To belong; befall: *Woe is me.* 7. *Informal* Used in combination with *all* or *like* to introduce quotations. ▸ *aux.* 1. Used with the past participle of a transitive verb to form the passive voice: *The election is held annually.* 2. Used with the present participle of a verb to express a continuing action: *We are working to improve housing conditions.* 3. Used with the infinitive of a verb to express intention, obligation, or future action: *She was to call before she left.* 4. *Archaic* Used with the past participle of certain intransitive verbs to form the perfect tense: *He is gone to a better place.*

Be ▸ The symbol for the element **beryllium.**

be– ▸ *pref.* 1. To make; cause to become: *benumb.* 2a. To cover with: *befog.* b. On; over: *bedaub.* 3. Used as an intensive: *belabor.* 4. About: *bewail.* 5. To remove: *behead.*

beach (bēch) ▸ *n.* The shore of a body of water, esp. when sandy or pebbly. ▸ *v.* To haul or run ashore.

beach buggy ▸ *n.* See **dune buggy.**

beach·comb·er (bēchʹkōʹmər) ▸ *n.* One who scavenges along beaches.

beach·head (bēchʹhĕdʹ) ▸ *n.* 1. A position on an enemy shoreline captured by troops in advance of an invading force. 2. A first achievement that opens the way; foothold.

bea·con (bēʹkən) ▸ *n.* 1. A lighthouse. 2. A radio transmitter that emits a guidance signal for aircraft. 3. A source of guidance. 4. A signal fire.

bead (bēd) ▸ *n.* 1a. A small piece of material pierced for stringing. b. **beads** A necklace made of beads. c. **beads** A rosary. 2. A small round object, as: a. A drop of moisture. b. A knoblike forward sight on a firearm. ▸ *v.* To decorate with or collect into beads. ***—idiom:*** **draw** (or **get**) **a bead on** To take careful aim at.

bea·dle (bēdʹl) ▸ *n.* A former minor parish official in an English church.

bead·y (bēʹdē) ▸ *adj.* **-i·er, -i·est.** Small, round, and shiny: *beady eyes.*

bea·gle (bēʹgəl) ▸ *n.* A small hound with drooping ears and a smooth white, black, and tan coat.

beak (bēk) ▸ *n.* 1. The horny projecting mandibles of a bird; bill. 2. A similar part or structure.

beak·er (bēʹkər) ▸ *n.* 1. A wide glass cylinder with a pouring lip, used as a laboratory container. 2. A wide-mouthed drinking cup.

beam (bēm) ▸ *n.* 1. A large timber or squared-off log used as a horizontal support in construction. 2a. The maximum breadth of a ship. b. The side of a ship. 3. A horizontal bar. 4a. A ray of light. b. A concentrated stream of particles, waves, or signals. ▸ *v.* 1. To radiate; shine. 2. To emit or transmit (e.g., a signal). 3. To smile expansively. ***—idiom:*** **on the beam** 1. Following a radio beam, as an aircraft. 2. On the right track.

bean (bēn) ▸ *n.* 1a. Any of various twining plants with edible pods and seeds. b. A seed or pod of a bean plant. 2.

THESAURUS

bauble *n.* —*See* NOVELTY (3).

bawd *n.* —*See* HARLOT.

bawdiness *n.* —*See* OBSCENITY (1).

bawdry *n.* —*See* OBSCENITY (2).

bawdy *adj.* —*See* OBSCENE.

bawl *v.* To cry loudly, as an upset baby does ▸ caterwaul, holler, howl, squall, wail, yowl. [*Compare* SCREAM.] —*See also* CRY, SHOUT.

bawl out *v.* —*See* CHASTISE.

bawl *n.* —*See* ROAR.

bawling *n.* —*See* CRY (1).

bay[1] *n.* A body of water partly enclosed by land but having a wide outlet to the sea ▸ bight, gulf, sound. [*Compare* CHANNEL, HARBOR, INLET.]

bay[2] *n.* —*See* HOWL.

bay *v.* —*See* HOWL.

bayonet *v.* —*See* CUT (1).

bazaar *n.* —*See* EXHIBITION.

be *v.* —*See* EXIST.

be into *v.* —*See* ENJOY.

bead *n.* —*See* DROP (1).

beak *n.* The horny projection forming a bird's jaws ▸ bill, mandible, nib. —*See also* NOSE (1).

beam *n.* 1. A narrow line of light or other radiant energy ▸ finger, ray, shaft, stream. 2. A sturdy horizontal structural support ▸ crossbeam, crosstie, girder, I-beam, joist, lintel, rafter, tie beam, timber, trestle, viga. [*Compare* COLUMN, SUPPORT.]

beam *v.* To emit a bright light ▸ blaze, burn, gleam, glow, incandesce, radiate, shine. [*Compare* GLARE, GLITTER, ILLUMINATE.] —*See also* SMILE.

beamy *adj.* —*See* BRIGHT.

bean *n.* —*See* HEAD (1).

Any of various plants related to or suggestive of beans. 3. *Slang* The head. ▸ *v. Slang* To hit on the head. *—idioms:* **full of beans** 1. Energetic; frisky. 2. Badly mistaken. **spill the beans** To disclose a secret.

bean·bag (bēnʹbăgʹ) ▸ *n.* A small bag filled with dried beans and thrown in games.

bean ball ▸ *n. Baseball* A pitch aimed at the batter's head.

bean curd ▸ *n.* Tofu.

bean·ie (bēʹnē) ▸ *n.* A small brimless cap.

bean·o (bēʹnō) ▸ *n., pl.* **-os.** A form of bingo.

bean sprouts ▸ *pl.n.* The tender, edible seedlings of certain beans, esp. the mung bean.

bear[1] (bâr) ▸ *v.* **bore** (bôr), **borne** (bôrn) or **born** (bôrn), **bear·ing.** 1. To hold up; support. 2. To carry on one's person. 3. To harbor: *bear a grudge.* 4. To transmit; relate: *bearing glad tidings.* 5. To have or exhibit. 6. To conduct: *bore herself with dignity.* 7. To be accountable for; assume: *bearing heavy responsibilities.* 8. To endure: *couldn't bear the pain.* 9a. To warrant: *This case bears investigation.* b. To have relevance; apply. 10. *p.part* **born.** To give birth to. 11. To yield: *bear flowers.* 12. To exert pressure or influence. 13. To offer; render: *bear witness.* 14. To proceed in a specified direction: *bear left.* *—phrasal verbs:* **bear down** 1. To weigh on; overwhelm. 2. To exert oneself. **bear out** To prove right; confirm. **bear up** To endure. **bear with** To be tolerant of or toward. *—idiom:* **bear in mind** To remember. **—bearʹa·ble** *adj.* **—bearʹa·bly** *adv.*

bear[2] (bâr) ▸ *n.* 1. Any of various large, usu. omnivorous mammals having a shaggy coat and short tail. 2. A clumsy or grouchy person. 3. One that sells securities or commodities in expectation of falling prices. **—bearʹish** *adj.*

beard (bîrd) ▸ *n.* 1. The hair on a man's chin, cheeks, and throat. 2. A hairy or hairlike growth, as on certain animals and plants. ▸ *v.* To confront boldly. **—beardʹed** *adj.*

bear·er (bârʹər) ▸ *n.* 1. One that bears. 2. One that holds a check or note for payment.

bear hug ▸ *n.* A rough, tight hug.

bear·ing (bârʹĭng) ▸ *n.* 1. Deportment; demeanor. 2. A device that supports, guides, and reduces the friction of motion between fixed and moving machine parts. 3. Something that supports weight. 4. Direction, esp. angular direction measured using geographical or celestial reference lines. 5. often **bearings** Awareness of one's position relative to one's surroundings. 6. Relevant relationship: *That has no bearing on our work.* 7. A heraldic emblem.

béar·naise sauce (bâr-nāzʹ, bāʹär-, -ər-) ▸ *n.* A sauce of egg yolk, butter, shallots, tarragon, and chervil.

bear·skin (bârʹskĭnʹ) ▸ *n.* 1. A bear pelt. 2. A tall military hat made of black fur.

beast (bēst) ▸ *n.* 1. An animal, esp. a large four-footed mammal. 2. Animal nature. 3. A brutal person.

beast·ly (bēstʹlē) ▸ *adj.* **-li·er, -li·est.** 1. Of or like a beast; bestial. 2. Very disagreeable; nasty: *beastly behavior.* **—beastʹli·ness** *n.*

beat (bēt) ▸ *v.* **beat, beat·en** (bētʹn) or **beat, beat·ing.** 1a. To strike repeatedly; pound. b. To punish by hitting. 2. To flap, esp. wings. 3. To sound by striking: *beat a drum.* 4a. To shape by blows; forge. b. To make by trampling: *beat a path.* 5. To mix rapidly: *beat eggs.* 6. To pulsate; throb. 7. To defeat. 8. *Informal* To be better than: *Riding beats walking.* 9. *Slang* To baffle: *It beats me.* 10. *Informal* a. To circumvent: *beat the traffic.* b. To arrive or finish before (another). *—phrasal verb:* **beat off** To drive away. ▸ *n.* 1. A stroke or blow. 2. A pulsation; throb. 3. A rhythmic stress or stress pattern, as in meter or verse. 4. An area regularly covered, as by a reporter or police officer. ▸ *adj.* 1. *Informal* Worn-out; fatigued. 2. Of or being a beatnik. *—idioms:* **beat around** (or **about**) **the bush** To fail to confront a subject directly. **beat it** *Slang* To leave hurriedly. **beat the bushes** To make an exhaustive search. **—beatʹer** *n.*

be·a·tif·ic (bēʹə-tĭfʹĭk) ▸ *adj.* Showing exalted joy or bliss: *a beatific smile.* **—beʹa·tifʹi·cal·ly** *adv.*

be·at·i·fy (bē-ătʹə-fīʹ) ▸ *v.* **-fied, -fy·ing.** 1. To make blessedly happy. 2. *Rom. Cath. Ch.* To proclaim (a deceased person) to be one of the blessed. **—be·atʹi·fi·caʹtion** *n.*

be·at·i·tude (bē-ătʹĭ-to͞odʹ, -tyo͞odʹ) ▸ *n.* Supreme blessedness.

beat·nik (bētʹnĭk) ▸ *n.* A member of a group or movement esp. of the 1950s stressing nonconformity to social and cultural mores.

THESAURUS

bear *v.* 1. To hold the weight of ▸ carry, hold (up), shoulder, support, sustain, uphold. 2. To keep steadily in mind ▸ cherish, entertain, harbor, nourish, nurse. [*Compare* PONDER, THINK.] 3. To have as a visible characteristic ▸ carry, display, exhibit, have, possess, wear. [*Compare* DISPLAY, SHOW.] 4. To give birth to ▸ bring forth, deliver, have. *Chiefly Regional:* birth. *Idiom:* be brought abed (*or* to bed) of. 5. To proceed in a specified direction ▸ aim, go, head, make, set out, start out, strike out, turn. *Informal:* light out. [*Compare* GO, START, TURN.] *—See also* ACT (1), BRING (1), CARRY (1), CARRY (2), ENDURE (1), PRODUCE (1), PUSH (1).

bear on or **upon** *v.* *—See* APPLY (2).

bear out *v.* *—See* CONFIRM (1), PROVE.

bear up *v.* To withstand stress or difficulty ▸ endure, hold up, stand up. *Idioms:* bite the bullet, grin and bear it, keep a stiff upper lip, make the best of it, take one's medicine, take it (lying down). [*Compare* CARRY ON, ENDURE.]

bearable *adj.* Capable of being tolerated ▸ endurable, sufferable, supportable, tolerable.

beard *v.* *—See* DEFY (1).

bearer *n.* *—See* MESSENGER.

bearing *n.* 1. Behavior that reveals one's personality or state of mind ▸ address, air, demeanor, manner, mien, poise, presence, style. [*Compare* APPEARANCE, BEHAVIOR, POSTURE.] 2. The compass direction in which a ship or aircraft moves ▸ course, heading, vector. [*Compare* DIRECTION.] 3. One's place and direction relative to one's surroundings ▸ bearings, location, orientation, position, situation, whereabouts. *—See also* IMPACT, RELEVANCE.

beast *n.* *—See* FIEND.

beastly or **beastlike** *adj.* Similar to a beast in behavior ▸ bestial, brutish. [*Compare* CRUEL, SAVAGE, UNCIVILIZED.]

beat *v.* 1. To hit heavily and repeatedly ▸ assail, assault, bang, baste, batter, belabor, bludgeon, buffet, club, cudgel, drub, flail, hammer, maul, pelt, pound, pummel, smash, thrash, thresh, whale. *Informal:* lambaste, lather, thump. *Slang:* clobber. *Idioms:* knock the daylights (*or* stuffing *or* tar) out of, rain blows on, tan someone's hide. [*Compare* BATTER, HIT, SLAP.] 2. To punish with blows or lashes ▸ birch, cane, flagellate, flay, flog, hide, horsewhip, lash, scourge, strap, thrash, whip. *Informal:* trim. *Slang:* lay into, lick. 3. To shape, break, or flatten with repeated blows ▸ forge, hammer, pound, stamp. [*Compare* EVEN.] 4. To indicate time or rhythm ▸ count, tap (out). *Idioms:* keep time, mark time. 5. To make rhythmic contractions, sounds, or movements ▸ drum, flutter, hammer, palpitate, pound, pulsate, pulse, tap, throb, thump, tick. 6. To combine or process ingredients by stirring ▸ blend, cream, fold (in), mix, stir, whip, whisk. [*Compare* COMBINE, MIX.] *—See also* BAFFLE, DECEIVE, DEFEAT, FLAP (1), SURPASS.

beat down *v.* *—See* BREAK (2), GLARE (2).

beat off *v.* *—See* REPEL.

beat *n.* 1. A stroke or blow that produces a sound ▸ bump, clunk, knock, pound, rap, smack, thud, thump, whack. [*Compare* BLOW[2].] 2. An area regularly covered, as by a policeman or reporter ▸ circuit, round, rounds, route, territory. [*Compare* CIRCLE.] 3. A rhythmic contraction or sound ▸ drumbeat, palpitation, pounding, pulsation, pulse, throb, throbbing, tick, ticktock. *—See also* RHYTHM.

beat *adj.* *—See* TIRED (1).

beatification *n.* *—See* EXALTATION.

beating *n.* A punishment dealt with blows or lashes ▸ caning, flagellation, flaying, flogging, hiding, lashing, pounding, thrashing, whipping. *Informal:* trimming. *Slang:* licking. *—See also* DEFEAT.

beatitude *n.* *—See* HAPPINESS, HOLINESS.

beat-up (bĕt′ŭp′) ▸ *adj. Slang* Damaged or worn through neglect or heavy use.
beau (bō) ▸ *n., pl.* **beaus** or **beaux** (bōz). 1. A suitor. 2. A dandy; fop.
beau geste (bō zhĕst′) ▸ *n., pl.* **beaux gestes** or **beau gestes** (bō zhĕst′). 1. A gracious gesture. 2. A gesture noble in form but meaningless in substance.
beau i·de·al (bō′ ī-dē′əl) ▸ *n., pl.* **beau ideals**. An ideal type or model.
beau monde (bō mŏnd′, môNd′) ▸ *n., pl.* **beaux mondes** (bō môNd′) or **beau mondes** (bō mŏndz′). Fashionable society.
beau·te·ous (byo͞o′tē-əs) ▸ *adj.* Beautiful. **—beau′te·ous·ly** *adv.*
beau·ti·cian (byo͞o-tĭsh′ən) ▸ *n.* One skilled in giving cosmetic treatments.
beau·ti·ful (byo͞o′tə-fəl) ▸ *adj.* Having beauty. **—beau′ti·ful·ly** *adv.*
beau·ti·fy (byo͞o′tə-fī′) ▸ *v.* **-fied, -fy·ing**. To make or become beautiful. **—beau′ti·fi·ca′tion** *n.* **—beau′ti·fi′er** *n.*
beau·ty (byo͞o′tē) ▸ *n., pl.* **-ties**. 1. A quality that pleases or delights the senses or mind. 2. One that is beautiful. 3. An outstanding example.
beauty parlor ▸ *n.* An establishment providing women with such services as hair treatment, manicures, and facials.
Beau·voir (bō-vwär′), **Simone de** (1908–86) ▸ French writer, existentialist, and feminist.
beaux (bōz) ▸ *n.* Pl. of **beau**.
beaux-arts (bō-zär′, -zärt′) ▸ *pl.n.* The fine arts.
bea·ver (bē′vər) ▸ *n.* 1. A large aquatic rodent having thick brown fur, webbed hind feet, a broad flat tail, and sharp incisors adapted for felling trees to build dams. 2. The fur of a beaver.
bea·ver·board (bē′vər-bôrd′) ▸ *n.* A wallboard of compressed wood pulp.
be·bop (bē′bŏp′) ▸ *n. Mus.* Bop.
be·calm (bĭ-käm′) ▸ *v.* To render (e.g., a ship) motionless for lack of wind.
be·cause (bĭ-kôz′, -kŭz′) ▸ *conj.* For the reason that; since.
beck (bĕk) ▸ *n.* A summons. ***—idiom:* at (one's) beck and call** Ready to comply with any wish or command.
Beck·et (bĕk′ĭt), Saint **Thomas à** (1118?–70) ▸ English Roman Catholic martyr.
beck·on (bĕk′ən) ▸ *v.* 1. To summon by nodding or waving. 2. To be inviting or enticing (to); attract.
be·cloud (bĭ-kloud′) ▸ *v.* To obscure.
be·come (bĭ-kŭm′) ▸ *v.* **be·came** (-kām′), **-come, -com·ing**. 1. To grow or come to be. 2. To be suitable to. ***—phrasal verb:* become of** To be the fate of: *What will become of us?*
be·com·ing (bĭ-kŭm′ĭng) ▸ *adj.* 1. Appropriate or suitable. 2. Pleasing or attractive. **—be·com′ing·ly** *adv.*
bed (bĕd) ▸ *n.* 1. A place for sleeping, esp. a piece of furniture that frames or supports a mattress. 2. A small plot of cultivated land: *a flower bed.* 3. The bottom of a body of water, such as a stream. 4. A supporting or underlying part; foundation. 5. *Geol.* **a.** A large layer of rock or earth extending horizontally; stratum. **b.** A deposit, as of ore. ▸ *v.* **bed·ded, bed·ding**. 1. To furnish with a bed or sleeping quarters. 2. To put, send, or go to bed. 3. To plant in a prepared plot of soil. 4. To lay flat or arrange in layers. 5. To embed.
be·daub (bĭ-dôb′) ▸ *v.* To smear; soil.
be·daz·zle (bĭ-dăz′əl) ▸ *v.* **-zled, -zling**. 1. To dazzle so completely as to confuse or blind. 2. To enchant. **—be·daz′zle·ment** *n.*
bed·bug (bĕd′bŭg′) ▸ *n.* A wingless, blood-sucking insect that infests dwellings and bedding.
bed·clothes (bĕd′klōz′, -klōthz′) ▸ *pl.n.* Coverings ordinarily used on a bed.
bed·ding (bĕd′ĭng) ▸ *n.* 1. Bedclothes. 2. Material, esp. straw, on which animals sleep. 3. A foundation.
Bede (bēd) (673?–735) ▸ Anglo-Saxon theologian and historian.
be·deck (bĭ-dĕk′) ▸ *v.* To adorn or ornament.
be·dev·il (bĭ-dĕv′əl) ▸ *v.* **-iled, -il·ing** or **-illed, -il·ling**. 1. To torment; harass. 2. To worry, annoy, or frustrate. **—be·dev′il·ment** *n.*
be·dew (bĭ-do͞o′, -dyo͞o′) ▸ *v.* To wet with or as if with dew.
bed·fel·low (bĕd′fĕl′ō) ▸ *n.* 1. One with whom a bed is shared. 2. An often temporary associate, as for convenience.
bed·lam (bĕd′ləm) ▸ *n.* 1. A place of noisy uproar and confusion. 2. An insane asylum.
Bed·ou·in also **Bed·u·in** (bĕd′o͞o-ĭn, bĕd′wĭn) ▸ *n., pl.* **-in** or **-ins**. An Arab of any of the nomadic tribes of the Arabian, Syrian, Nubian, or Sahara deserts.
bed·pan (bĕd′păn′) ▸ *n.* A receptacle used as a toilet by a bedridden person.
bed·post (bĕd′pōst′) ▸ *n.* A vertical post at the corner of a bed.
be·drag·gled (bĭ-drăg′əld) ▸ *adj.* Wet, limp, or soiled, as by being dragged through mud.
bed·rid·den (bĕd′rĭd′n) ▸ *adj.* Confined to bed, esp. because of illness or infirmity.
bed·rock (bĕd′rŏk′) ▸ *n.* 1. The solid rock that underlies the loose surface material of the earth. 2a. Fundamental principles; foundation. b. The lowest point; bottom.
bed·roll (bĕd′rōl′) ▸ *n.* A portable roll of bedding used esp. for sleeping outdoors.
bed·room (bĕd′ro͞om′, -ro͝om′) ▸ *n.* A room in which to sleep.
bed·side (bĕd′sīd′) ▸ *n.* The space alongside a bed, esp. of a sick person. **—bed′side′** *adj.*
bed·sore (bĕd′sôr′) ▸ *n.* A pressure-induced ulceration of the skin occurring during long confinement to bed.
bed·spread (bĕd′sprĕd′) ▸ *n.* A usu. decorative covering for a bed.
bed·stead (bĕd′stĕd′) ▸ *n.* The frame supporting a bed.
bed·time (bĕd′tīm′) ▸ *n.* The time at which one goes to bed.

THESAURUS

beau *n.* 1. A man who courts a woman ▸ admirer, courter, suitor, swain, wooer. [*Compare* GALLANT.] 2. A man who is vain about his clothes ▸ coxcomb, dandy, fop, peacock, swell. *—See also* BOYFRIEND.
beau ideal *n.* *—See* MODEL.
beautiful *adj.* Having qualities that delight the eye ▸ attractive, beauteous, comely, exquisite, fair, good-looking, gorgeous, handsome, lovely, pretty, pulchritudinous, ravishing, sightly, statuesque, stunning. *Idiom:* easy on the eyes. [*Compare* ATTRACTIVE, SEDUCTIVE.]
beautify *v.* To endow with beauty and elegance ▸ embellish, enhance, grace, set off. [*Compare* ADORN.]
beauty *n.* A person regarded as physically attractive ▸ Adonis (for a man), belle (for a woman), dreamboat, eyeful, goddess (for a woman), lovely, stunner, Venus (for a woman), vision. *Slang:* babe, dish, doll, fox, hotty, hunk (for a man), knockout, looker, stud (for a man). *—See also* VIRTUE.
becalm *v.* *—See* PACIFY.
because *conj.* For the reason that ▸ as, for, inasmuch as, seeing as, since. *Idioms:* on account of the fact that, in consequence of the fact that, in view of the fact that.
because of *preposition* By the cause of ▸ as a result of, by reason of, by virtue of, due to, in consequence of, in view of, on account of, owing to, through.
beckon *v.* *—See* GESTURE.
becloud *v.* *—See* OBSCURE.
become *v.* 1. To come to be ▸ change (to *or* into), come (to be), develop (into), get (to be), grow (to be), turn (to *or* into), wax. 2. To look good on or with ▸ enhance, flatter, suit. *Idiom:* put in the best light. *—See also* SUIT (1).
becoming *adj.* Pleasingly suited to the wearer ▸ attractive, fetching, flattering, perfect, well suited. [*Compare* ATTRACTIVE.] *—See also* APPROPRIATE.
bed *v.* *—See* LODGE, RETIRE (1).
bed *n.* *—See* BASE[1] (2).
bedaub *v.* *—See* DIRTY, SMEAR.
bedaze *v.* *—See* DAZE (1).
bedazzle *v.* To confuse with bright light ▸ blind, daze, dazzle.
bedeck *v.* *—See* ADORN (1), DRESS UP.
bedevil *v.* *—See* HARASS.
bedim *v.* *—See* OBSCURE.
bedraggled *adj.* *—See* SHABBY.
bedtime *n.* *—See* NIGHT.

Bed·u·in (bĕd′o͞o-ĭn, bĕd′wĭn) ▸ *n.* Var. of **Bedouin.**

bee (bē) ▸ *n.* 1. Any of several winged, hairy-bodied, usu. stinging insects that gather nectar and pollen from which some species produce honey. 2. A social gathering where people work together or compete. ***—idiom:* a bee in (one's) bonnet** A persistent notion, esp. an idea that keeps one angry or upset.

beech (bēch) ▸ *n.* A deciduous tree having smooth gray bark, edible nuts, and strong heavy wood.

beech·nut (bēch′nŭt′) ▸ *n.* The small, three-angled nut of a beech tree.

beef (bēf) ▸ *n., pl.* **beeves** (bēvz) or **beef. 1a.** A full-grown steer, bull, ox, or cow, esp. one intended for use as meat. **b.** The flesh of a slaughtered steer, bull, ox, or cow. 2. *Informal* Human muscle; brawn. 3. *pl.* **beefs.** *Slang* A complaint. ▸ *v.* To complain. ***—phrasal verb:* beef up** To build up; reinforce.

beef·a·lo (bē′fə-lō′) ▸ *n., pl.* **-lo** or **-los** or **-loes.** A hybrid that results from a cross between the American buffalo, or bison, and beef cattle.

beef·eat·er (bēf′ē′tər) ▸ *n.* A yeoman of the British monarch's royal guard.

beef·y (bē′fē) ▸ *adj.* **-i·er, -i·est.** Muscular in build; brawny. **—beef′i·ness** *n.*

bee·hive (bē′hīv′) ▸ *n.* 1. A hive for bees. 2. A place teeming with activity.

bee·keep·er (bē′kē′pər) ▸ *n.* One who raises or tends bees. **—bee′keep·ing** *n.*

bee·line (bē′līn′) ▸ *n.* A fast straight course.

Be·el·ze·bub (bē-ĕl′zə-bŭb′) ▸ *n.* The Devil.

been (bĭn) ▸ *v.* P.part. of **be.**

beep (bēp) ▸ *n.* A sound or signal, as from a horn or electronic device. **—beep** *v.*

beep·er (bē′pər) ▸ *n.* 1. One that beeps. 2. A portable electronic paging device that emits a beeping signal.

beer (bîr) ▸ *n.* 1. An alcoholic beverage brewed from malt and hops. 2. Any of various carbonated beverages made from roots and plants. **—beer′y** *adj.*

bees·wax (bēz′wăks′) ▸ *n.* The wax secreted by honeybees for making honeycombs and used in candles, crayons, and polishes.

beet (bēt) ▸ *n.* 1. A cultivated plant with a fleshy, usu. dark-red edible root. 2. The sugar beet.

Bee·tho·ven (bā′tō′vən), **Ludwig van** (1770–1827) ▸ German composer.

bee·tle[1] (bēt′l) ▸ *n.* Any of numerous insects with horny forewings that protect the membranous hind wings when at rest.

bee·tle[2] (bēt′l) ▸ *adj.* Jutting; overhanging: *beetle brows.* ▸ *v.* **-tled, -tling.** To jut.

beeves (bēvz) ▸ *n.* Pl. of **beef.**

be·fall (bĭ-fôl′) ▸ *v.* **-fell** (-fĕl′), **-fall·en** (-fô′lən), **-fall·ing.** 1. To come to pass; happen. 2. To happen to.

be·fit (bĭ-fĭt′) ▸ *v.* **-fit·ted, -fit·ting.** To be suitable to or appropriate for.

be·fog (bĭ-fôg′, -fŏg′) ▸ *v.* **-fogged, -fog·ging.** 1. To fog. 2. To confuse; muddle.

be·fore (bĭ-fôr′) ▸ *adv.* 1. Earlier in time; previously. 2. In front; ahead. ▸ *prep.* 1. Prior to. 2. In front of. 3. In store for; awaiting. 4. Into or in the presence of. 5. Under the consideration of: *the case before the court.* 6. In a position superior to: *She comes before him in rank.* ▸ *conj.* 1. In advance of the time when: *See me before you leave.* 2. Rather than; sooner than: *I will die before I will betray you.*

before Christ ▸ *adv.* In a specified year of the pre-Christian area.

be·fore·hand (bĭ-fôr′hănd′) ▸ *adv. & adj.* In advance; early.

be·foul (bĭ-foul′) ▸ *v.* To make dirty; soil.

be·friend (bĭ-frĕnd′) ▸ *v.* To act as a friend to.

be·fud·dle (bĭ-fŭd′l) ▸ *v.* **-dled, -dling.** 1. To confuse or muddle; perplex. 2. To stupefy.

beg (bĕg) ▸ *v.* **begged, beg·ging.** 1. To ask for (alms or charity). 2. To entreat. 3. To evade; dodge: *begged the question.* ***—phrasal verb:* beg off** To ask to be excused from something.

be·get (bĭ-gĕt′) ▸ *v.* **-got** (-gŏt′), **-got·ten** (-gŏt′n) or **-got, -get·ting.** 1. To father; sire. 2. To cause; produce.

beg·gar (bĕg′ər) ▸ *n.* 1. One who solicits alms for a living. 2. A pauper. ▸ *v.* 1. To impoverish. 2. To exceed the limits of: *beauty that beggars description.* **—beg′gar·ly** *adj.* **—beg′gar·y** *n.*

be·gin (bĭ-gĭn′) ▸ *v.* **-gan** (-găn′), **-gun** (-gŭn′), **-gin·ning.** 1. To commence or start. 2. To come into being. **—be·gin′ner** *n.*

be·gin·ning (bĭ-gĭn′ĭng) ▸ *n.* 1. The act or process of bringing or being brought into being; start. 2. The time when something begins or is begun. 3. The place where something begins or is begun. 4. A source; origin. 5. The first part. 6. often **beginnings** An early or rudimentary phase.

be·gone (bĭ-gôn′, -gŏn′) ▸ *interj.* Used chiefly to express dismissal.

be·go·nia (bĭ-gōn′yə) ▸ *n.* Any of various plants cultivated for their brightly colored leaves and flowers.

be·grime (bĭ-grīm′) ▸ *v.* **-grimed, -grim·ing.** To smear or grime with or as if with dirt.

be·grudge (bĭ-grŭj′) ▸ *v.* **-grudged, -grudg·ing.** 1. To envy. 2. To give with reluctance. **—be·grudg′ing·ly** *adv.*

THESAURUS

beef *n.* —*See* BRAWN, COMPLAINT.
beef *v.* —*See* COMPLAIN.
beef up *v.* —*See* INCREASE.

beefy *adj.* —*See* MUSCULAR.

beetle *v.* —*See* BULGE.

befall *v.* To take place by chance ▸ betide, chance, hap, happen. —*See also* HAPPEN (1).

befit *v.* —*See* JUSTIFY (2), SUIT (1).

befitting *adj.* —*See* APPROPRIATE, CONVENIENT (1).

befog *v.* —*See* OBSCURE.

before *adv.* Until then ▸ beforehand, earlier. —*See also* EARLIER (1), EARLIER (2).

beforehand *adv.* Until then ▸ before, earlier. —*See also* EARLIER (1), EARLY.

befoul *v.* —*See* DENIGRATE, DIRTY.

befuddle *v.* —*See* CONFUSE (1), DRUG (2).

befuddlement *n.* —*See* DAZE.

beg *v.* To ask for as charity; solicit money or favors ▸ bum, cadge. *Informal:* panhandle. *Slang:* mooch, scrounge. *Idioms:* hit someone up for, pass the cup (*or* hat), touch someone for. [*Compare* FREELOAD.] —*See also* APPEAL (1), DEMAND (2).

beget *v.* To be the biological father of ▸ father, get, sire. —*See also* BREED.

begetter *n.* —*See* FATHER, ORIGINATOR.

beggar *n.* 1. One who begs habitually or for a living ▸ almsman, almswoman, cadger, mendicant. *Informal:* panhandler. *Slang:* bummer, mooch, moocher. [*Compare* PARASITE.] 2. One who humbly entreats ▸ petitioner, prayer, suitor, suppliant, supplicant. —*See also* PAUPER.

beggarly *adj.* —*See* POOR.

beggary *n.* The condition of being a beggar ▸ mendicancy, mendicity. —*See also* POVERTY.

begin *v.* To come into being ▸ appear, arise, commence, crop up, dawn, emerge, originate, start. *Idioms:* raise (one's) head, see the light of day. [*Compare* CAUSE, STEM.] —*See also* START (1).

beginner *n.* One who is just starting to learn or do something ▸ abecedarian, apprentice, cub, fledgling, freshman, greenhorn, initiate, learner, neophyte, newcomer, novice, novitiate, tenderfoot, tyro. *Slang:* newbie, rookie. [*Compare* AMATEUR.]

beginning *n.* The act or process of bringing or being brought into existence ▸ commencement, conception, inauguration, inception, incipience, incipiency, initiation, introduction, invention, launch, leadoff, opening, origination, start. *Informal:* kickoff. [*Compare* FOUNDATION.] —*See also* BIRTH (2), ORIGIN.
beginning *adj.* Of or occurring at the start of something ▸ early, inaugural, inceptive, incipient, initial, initiatory, introductory, leadoff, opening, starting. [*Compare* FIRST, INTRODUCTORY.] —*See also* ELEMENTARY.

begird *v.* —*See* ENCIRCLE.

begrime *v.* —*See* DIRTY.

begrudge *v.* ▸ covet, envy, grudge.

begrudging *adj.* —*See* ENVIOUS.

be·guile (bĭ-gīl′) ▸ *v.* **-guiled, -guil·ing.** **1.** To deceive by guile. **2.** To distract; divert. **3.** To pass (time) pleasantly. **4.** To amuse or delight. **—be·guile′ment** *n.*

be·gum (bā′gəm, bē′-) ▸ *n.* A Muslim woman of rank.

be·half (bĭ-hăf′, -häf′) ▸ *n.* Interest, support, or benefit. ***—idioms:*** **in behalf of** For the benefit of. **on behalf of** As the agent of.

be·have (bĭ-hāv′) ▸ *v.* **-haved, -hav·ing.** **1a.** To conduct oneself in a specified way. **b.** To conduct oneself in a proper way. **2.** To act, react, function, or perform in a particular way.

be·hav·ior (bĭ-hāv′yər) ▸ *n.* **1.** The manner in which one behaves. **2.** The actions or reactions of persons or things under given circumstances. **—be·hav′ior·al** *adj.*

behavioral science ▸ *n.* A scientific discipline, such as sociology, anthropology, or psychology, that deals with the study of human behavior.

be·hav·ior·ism (bĭ-hāv′yə-rĭz′əm) ▸ *n.* A school of psychology that studies observable and quantifiable aspects of behavior but excludes subjective phenomena. **—be·hav′ior·ist** *n.* **—be·hav′ior·is′tic** *adj.*

be·head (bĭ-hĕd′) ▸ *v.* To decapitate.

be·he·moth (bĭ-hē′məth, bē′ə-məth) ▸ *n.* **1.** Something enormous in size or power. **2.** A huge animal described in the Bible.

be·hest (bĭ-hĕst′) ▸ *n.* **1.** An authoritative command. **2.** An urgent request.

be·hind (bĭ-hīnd′) ▸ *adv.* **1.** In, to, or toward the rear. **2.** In a place or condition that has been passed or left: *I left my gloves behind.* **3.** In arrears; late. **4.** In or into an inferior position: *fell behind in class.* **5.** Slow: *My watch is running behind.* ▸ *prep.* **1.** At the back or in the rear of. **2.** On the farther or other side of. **3.** In a former place, time, or situation. **4.** Later than: *behind schedule.* **5.** Below, as in rank or ability: *behind us in technology.* **6a.** Concealed by: *hatred behind a smile.* **b.** Underlying: *Behind your action is greed.* **7.** In support of. ▸ *n. Informal* The buttocks.

be·hind·hand (bĭ-hīnd′hănd′) ▸ *adj.* **1.** Being in arrears. **2.** Being behind time; slow. **—be·hind′hand′** *adv.*

be·hold (bĭ-hōld′) ▸ *v.* **-held** (-hĕld′), **-hold·ing.** **1.** To look upon; gaze at. **2.** Used in the imperative to direct attention. **—be·hold′er** *n.*

be·hold·en (bĭ-hōl′dən) ▸ *adj.* Obliged or indebted, as from gratitude.

be·hoove (bĭ-ho͞ov′) ▸ *v.* **-hooved, -hoov·ing.** To be necessary or proper for: *It behooves you at least to try.*

beige (bāzh) ▸ *n.* A light grayish or yellowish brown. **—beige** *adj.*

Bei·jing (bā′jĭng′) also **Pe·king** (pē′kĭng′, pā′-) ▸ The capital of China, in the NE.

be·ing (bē′ĭng) ▸ *n.* **1.** The state or quality of existing. **2a.** A person. **b.** One that exists or has a life. **3.** One's essential nature.

Bei·rut (bā-ro͞ot′) ▸ The capital of Lebanon, in the W part on the Mediterranean.

be·la·bor (bĭ-lā′bər) ▸ *v.* **1.** To attack with blows. **2.** To harp on.

Bel·a·rus (bĕl′ə-ro͞os′, byĕl′-) ▸ A country of E Europe E of Poland.

be·lat·ed (bĭ-lā′tĭd) ▸ *adj.* Done or sent too late; delayed; tardy. **—be·lat′ed·ly** *adv.* **—be·lat′ed·ness** *n.*

be·lay (bĭ-lā′) ▸ *v.* **1.** *Naut.* To secure or make fast (e.g., a rope). **2.** To secure (a mountain climber) at the end of a rope. **3.** To stop: *Belay there!*

be·lay·ing pin (bĭ-lā′ĭng) ▸ *n.* A pin fitted in the rail of a boat for securing running gear.

belch (bĕlch) ▸ *v.* **1.** To expel gas noisily from the stomach through the mouth. **2.** To gush forth violently. **—belch** *n.*

bel·dam or **bel·dame** (bĕl′dəm, -dăm) ▸ *n.* An old woman.

be·lea·guer (bĭ-lē′gər) ▸ *v.* **1.** To harass; beset. **2.** To surround with troops.

Bel·fast (bĕl′făst′, bĕl-făst′) ▸ The capital of Northern Ireland, in the E part.

bel·fry (bĕl′frē) ▸ *n., pl.* **-fries.** **1.** A bell tower, esp. one attached to a building. **2.** The part of a tower or steeple in which bells are hung.

Bel·gium (bĕl′jəm) ▸ A country of NW Europe on the North Sea. **—Bel′gian** *adj. & n.*

Bel·grade (bĕl′grād′, -gräd′) ▸ The capital of Serbia.

be·lie (bĭ-lī′) ▸ *v.* **-lied, -ly·ing.** **1.** To misrepresent or disguise. **2.** To show to be false. **3.** To be counter to; contradict.

be·lief (bĭ-lēf′) ▸ *n.* **1.** Trust or confidence. **2.** A conviction or opinion. **3.** Something believed or accepted as true, esp. a tenet or body of tenets.

be·liev·a·ble (bĭ-lē′və-bəl) ▸ *adj.* Capable of eliciting belief or trust. **—be·liev′a·bil′i·ty** *n.*

be·lieve (bĭ-lēv′) ▸ *v.* **-lieved, -liev·ing.** **1.** To accept as true or real. **2.** To credit with veracity: *I believe you.* **3.** To have confidence (in); trust: *I believe in you. I believe the ruby to be genuine.* **4.** To expect or suppose; think. **5.** To have firm faith. **—be·liev′er** *n.*

THESAURUS

beguile *v.* —*See* CHARM (1), DECEIVE.

beguiling *adj.* —*See* SEDUCTIVE.

behave *v.* —*See* ACT (1), FUNCTION.

behavior *n.* **1.** The manner in which one behaves ▸ action, actions, comportment, conduct, deportment, form, manner, style, way, ways. [*Compare* BEARING, CUSTOM, MANNERS.] **2.** The way in which something functions ▸ functioning, operation, performance, reaction, working, workings.

behemoth *n.* —*See* GIANT.

behemoth *adj.* —*See* ENORMOUS.

behest *n.* —*See* COMMAND (1), DEMAND (1).

behind *adv.* So as to fall behind schedule ▸ behindhand, late, slow. *Idiom:* behind time. —*See also* LATE.

behind *n.* —*See* BUTTOCKS.

behindhand *adj.* —*See* LATE (1).

behold *v.* —*See* SEE (1).

beholden *adj.* —*See* OBLIGED (1).

beholder *n.* —*See* WATCHER (1).

being *n.* The condition of being in full force or operation ▸ actualization, effect, force, realization. [*Compare* EXERCISE.] —*See also* ESSENCE, EXISTENCE, HUMAN BEING, THING (1).

bejewel *v.* —*See* ADORN (1).

belabor *v.* To discuss at great or excessive length ▸ dwell on, harp on, labor. *Idiom:* run into the ground. [*Compare* ELABORATE, EXAGGERATE.] —*See also* BEAT (1).

belated *adj.* —*See* LATE (1).

belatedly *adv.* —*See* LATE.

belatedness *n.* The quality or condition of not being on time ▸ lateness, slowness, tardiness, unpunctuality.

belay *v.* —*See* STOP (2).

belch *v.* —*See* ERUPT.

beldam or **beldame** *n.* —*See* WITCH (2).

beleaguer *v.* —*See* BESIEGE, HARASS.

beleaguerment *n.* A prolonged encirclement of an objective by hostile troops ▸ besiegement, blockade, investment, siege. [*Compare* ATTACK.]

belie *v.* —*See* DISTORT, REFUTE.

belief *n.* **1.** Something believed or thought to be true ▸ conviction, estimate, estimation, feeling, idea, judgment, mind, notion, opinion, persuasion, position, sentiment, view. [*Compare* ASSUMPTION, DEDUCTION, POSTURE, VIEWPOINT.] **2.** Mental acceptance of the truth or actuality of something ▸ credence, credit, faith. —*See also* DOCTRINE, TRUST.

believability *n.* —*See* VERISIMILITUDE.

believable *adj.* Worthy of being believed ▸ credible, creditable, plausible, reasonable, valid. [*Compare* CONVINCING, SOUND[2].]

believe *v.* **1.** To regard something as true or real ▸ accept. *Slang:* buy, swallow. *Idioms:* have no doubt about, feel certain (*or* sure) of, take for granted. **2.** To have confidence in the truthfulness of ▸ credit, trust. *Idioms:* give credence to, have faith (*or* trust *or* confidence) in, take at one's word. [*Compare* DEPEND ON.] **3.** To have an opinion ▸ conceive, consider, deem, hold, opine, think. *Informal:* figure, judge. *Idioms:* be convinced, be of the opinion. [*Compare* GUESS, INFER, SUPPOSE.] **4.** To view in a certain way ▸ feel, hold, sense, think. [*Compare* PERCEIVE, REGARD.]

believe in *v.* —*See* DEPEND ON (1).

believer *n.* —*See* DEVOTEE, FOLLOWER.

be·lit·tle (bĭ-lĭt′l) ▸ *v.* **-tled, -tling.** To speak of as small or unimportant; disparage. **—be·lit′tle·ment** *n.* **—be·lit′tler** *n.*

Be·lize (bə-lēz′) ▸ A country of Central America on the Caribbean Sea.

bell (bĕl) ▸ *n.* **1.** A hollow metal instrument, usu. cup-shaped with a flared opening, that emits a metallic tone when struck. **2.** Something shaped like bell. **3.** *Naut.* **a.** A stroke on a bell to mark the hour. **b.** The time thus marked. ▸ *v.* To put a bell on.

Bell, Alexander Graham (1847–1922) ▸ Scottish-born Amer. inventor of the telephone.

bel·la·don·na (bĕl′ə-dŏn′ə) ▸ *n.* **1.** A poisonous plant with purplish-brown flowers and glossy black berries. **2.** A medicinal drug derived from this plant.

bell-bot·tom (bĕl′bŏt′əm) ▸ *adj.* Having legs that flare at the bottom: *bell-bottom pants.*

bell·boy (bĕl′boi′) ▸ *n.* A bellhop.

bell curve ▸ *n.* A curve symmetrical about the mean, used to show statistical probability in the distribution of measurements.

belle (bĕl) ▸ *n.* An attractive and admired girl or woman.

belles-let·tres (bĕl-lĕt′rə) ▸ *pl.n.* *(takes sing. v.)* Literature regarded for its artistic value rather than for its content.

bell·flow·er (bĕl′flou′ər) ▸ *n.* Any of various plants with bell-shaped bluish flowers.

bell·hop (bĕl′hŏp′) ▸ *n.* A hotel porter.

bel·li·cose (bĕl′ĭ-kōs′) ▸ *adj.* Warlike in manner; pugnacious; belligerent. **—bel′li·cos′i·ty** (-kŏs′ĭ-tē) *n.*

bel·lig·er·ent (bə-lĭj′ər-ənt) ▸ *adj.* **1.** Eager to fight; aggressively hostile. **2.** Engaged in warfare. ▸ *n.* One that is engaged in war. **—bel·lig′er·ence, bel·lig′er·en·cy** *n.* **—bel·lig′er·ent·ly** *adv.*

bell jar ▸ *n.* A bell-shaped glass vessel used esp. to establish a controlled atmosphere in scientific experiments.

bel·low (bĕl′ō) ▸ *v.* **1.** To roar in the manner of a bull. **2.** To utter or cry out in a deep loud voice. **—bel′low** *n.*

bel·lows (bĕl′ōz, -əz) ▸ *pl.n.* *(takes sing. or pl. v.)* An apparatus for directing a strong current of air, as for increasing the draft to a fire.

bell pepper ▸ *n.* A pepper plant cultivated for its edible, bell-shaped fruit.

bell·weth·er (bĕl′wĕ*th*′ər) ▸ *n.* One that is a leader or a leading indicator of future trends.

bel·ly (bĕl′ē) ▸ *n., pl.* **-lies. 1.** See **abdomen** 1. **2.** The underside of the body of an animal. **3.** *Informal* The stomach. **4.** A part that protrudes. ▸ *v.* **-lied, -ly·ing.** To protrude.

bel·ly·ache (bĕl′ē-āk′) ▸ *n.* **1.** Pain in the abdomen. **2.** *Slang* A whining complaint. ▸ *v.* *Slang* To complain in a whining manner.

bel·ly·but·ton (bĕl′ē-bŭt′n) ▸ *n.* *Informal* The navel; umbilicus.

belly dance ▸ *n.* A dance in which the performer makes sinuous movements of the belly. **—bel′ly-dance′** *v.* **—belly dancer** *n.*

belly flop ▸ *n.* *Informal* A dive in which the front of the body hits flat against the surface of the water.

bel·ly·ful (bĕl′ē-fo͝ol′) ▸ *n.* *Informal* An undesirable or unendurable amount.

belly laugh ▸ *n.* A deep laugh.

bel·ly-up (bĕl′ē-ŭp′) ▸ *adj.* *Informal* Bankrupt.

be·long (bĭ-lông′, -lŏng′) ▸ *v.* **1.** To have a proper or suitable place. **2.** To be a member of a group. **3.** To be owned by someone. **4.** To be a part of or in natural association with something.

be·long·ing (bĭ-lông′ĭng, -lŏng′-) ▸ *n.* **1.** often **belongings** Personal possessions. **2.** Close, secure relationship: *a sense of belonging.*

Be·lo·rus·sia (bĕl′ō-rŭsh′ə, byĕl′-) ▸ See **Belarus.**

be·lov·ed (bĭ-lŭv′ĭd, -lŭvd′) ▸ *adj.* Dearly loved. **—be·lov′ed** *n.*

be·low (bĭ-lō′) ▸ *adv.* **1.** In or to a lower place or level; beneath. **2.** Later in a text: *See below.* **3.** On earth. ▸ *prep.* **1.** Lower than; under. **2.** Inferior to.

belt (bĕlt) ▸ *n.* **1.** A flexible, ornamental, or supportive band, as of leather or cloth, worn around the waist. **2.** A safety belt. **3.** A continuous moving band used in mechanics to transfer motion or to convey materials. **4.** A band of tough reinforcing material beneath the tread of a tire. **5.** A geographic region that is distinctive in a specific way. **6.** *Slang* A powerful blow; wallop. **7.** *Slang* A drink of hard liquor. ▸ *v.* **1.** To encircle; gird. **2.** To attach with a belt. **3.** *Slang* To strike forcefully; punch. **4.** *Slang* To sing loudly. **5.** *Slang* To swig (liquor). ***—idioms:*** **below the belt** Against the rules; unfairly. **tighten (one's) belt** To exercise frugality. **under (one's) belt** In one's possession or experience.

belt-tight·en·ing (bĕlt′-tīt′n-ĭng) ▸ *n.* A reduction in spending; frugality.

belt·way (bĕlt′wā′) ▸ *n.* **1.** A highway that skirts an urban area. **2. Beltway** The political establishment of Washington DC.

be·lu·ga (bə-lo͞o′gə) ▸ *n.* **1.** See **white whale. 2.** A large white sturgeon whose roe is used for caviar.

be·moan (bĭ-mōn′) ▸ *v.* **1.** To mourn over; lament. **2.** To express pity or grief for.

be·muse (bĭ-myo͞oz′) ▸ *v.* **-mused, -mus·ing. 1.** To cause to be bewildered. **2.** To absorb; preoccupy. **—be·muse′ment** *n.*

bench (bĕnch) ▸ *n.* **1.** A long seat, often without a back, for two or more persons. **2.** *Law* **a.** The judge's seat in a court. **b.** The office or position of a judge. **c.** often **Bench** The court or judges composing a court. **3.** A worktable. **4.** *Sports* **a.** The place where team players sit when not playing. **b.** The reserve players on a team. ▸ *v.* **1.** To seat on a bench. **2.** *Sports* To remove (a player) from a game.

bench·mark (bĕnch′märk′) ▸ *n.* **1.** A standard by which something can be judged. **2.** often **bench mark** A surveyor's mark made on a stationary object and used as a reference point.

bench·warm·er (bĕnch′wôr′mər) ▸ *n.* *Sports* A substitute player.

bench warrant ▸ *n.* A warrant issued by a judge or court ordering the apprehension of an offender.

THESAURUS

belittle *v.* To represent or speak of as small or insignificant ▸ decry, denigrate, deprecate, depreciate, derogate, discount, disparage, downgrade, minimize, run down, slight, talk down. *Informal:* badmouth, pooh-pooh. *Slang:* put down. *Idiom:* make light (*or* little) of. [*Compare* DENIGRATE, HUMBLE, RIDICULE, SNUB.]

belittlement *n.* The act or an instance of belittling ▸ denigration, deprecation, depreciation, derogation, detraction, disparagement, minimization.

belittling *adj.* *—See* DISPARAGING.

bell *v.* *—See* RING².

belle *n.* *—See* BEAUTY.

bellicose *adj.* *—See* AGGRESSIVE, MILITARY (1).

bellicosity or **bellicoseness** *n.* *—See* AGGRESSION, FIGHT (2).

belligerence *n.* *—See* AGGRESSION, FIGHT (2).

belligerency *n.* *—See* BATTLE, FIGHT (2).

belligerent *adj.* Engaged in warfare ▸ clashing, combatant, fighting, hostile, militant, warring. *Idioms:* at war, under arms. [*Compare* MILITARY.] *—See also* AGGRESSIVE.

belligerent *n.* One who engages in a combat or struggle ▸ combatant, fighter, soldier, warrior. [*Compare* AGGRESSOR, SOLDIER.]

bellow *v.* *—See* SHOUT.

bellow *n.* *—See* ROAR, SHOUT.

belly *v.* *—See* BULGE.

bellyache *v.* *—See* COMPLAIN.

bellyache *n.* *—See* COMPLAINT.

bellyacher *n.* *—See* GROUCH.

belong *v.* *—See* AGREE (1).

belongings *n.* *—See* EFFECTS, HOLDINGS.

beloved *adj.* *—See* DARLING.

beloved *n.* *—See* DARLING (1).

belowground *adj.* *—See* UNDERGROUND.

belt *n.* *—See* AREA (2), BAND¹, BLOW², DRINK (2), DROP (4), TERRITORY.

belt *v.* *—See* DRINK (1), ENCIRCLE, HIT.

bemire *v.* *—See* DIRTY.

bemoan *v.* *—See* DEPLORE (1), GRIEVE.

bemuse *v.* *—See* DAZE (1).

bemused *adj.* *—See* ABSENT-MINDED, CONFUSED (1).

bemusement *n.* *—See* TRANCE.

benchmark *n.* *—See* STANDARD.

bend (bĕnd) ▸ *v.* **bent** (bĕnt), **bend·ing.** 1. To tighten: *bend a bow.* 2. To curve or cause to curve. 3. To stoop. 4. To turn or deflect. 5a. To render submissive; subdue. b. To yield; submit. 6. To concentrate. 7. *Naut.* To fasten. ▸ *n.* 1. The act of bending or the state of being bent. 2. Something bent; a curve or crook. 3. **bends** *(takes sing. or pl. v.)* A manifestation of decompression sickness.

bend·er (bĕn′dər) ▸ *n.* 1. One that bends. 2. *Slang* A drinking spree.

be·neath (bĭ-nēth′) ▸ *adv.* 1. In a lower place; below. 2. Underneath. ▸ *prep.* 1. Lower than; under. 2. Unworthy of.

Ben·e·dict XVI (bĕn′ĭ-dĭkt′) (b. 1927) ▸ Pope (2005–2013).

ben·e·dic·tion (bĕn′ĭ-dĭk′shən) ▸ *n.* 1. A blessing. 2. An invocation of divine blessing, usu. at the end of a church service.

ben·e·fac·tion (bĕn′ə-făk′shən, bĕn′ə-făk′-) ▸ *n.* 1. The act of conferring a benefit. 2. A charitable gift or deed.

ben·e·fac·tor (bĕn′ə-făk′tər) ▸ *n.* One that gives aid, esp. financial aid.

ben·e·fac·tress (bĕn′ə-făk′trĭs) ▸ *n.* A woman who gives aid, esp. financial aid.

ben·e·fice (bĕn′ə-fĭs) ▸ *n.* A church office endowed with fixed assets that provide a living.

be·nef·i·cence (bə-nĕf′ĭ-səns) ▸ *n.* 1. The quality of being kind or charitable. 2. A charitable act or gift. **—be·nef′i·cent** *adj.*

ben·e·fi·cial (bĕn′ə-fĭsh′əl) ▸ *adj.* Producing a favorable result; advantageous. **—ben′e·fi′cial·ly** *adv.*

ben·e·fi·ci·ar·y (bĕn′ə-fĭsh′ē-ĕr′ē, -fĭsh′ə-rē) ▸ *n., pl.* **-ies.** One that receives a benefit, as funds or property from an insurance policy or will. **—ben′e·fi′ci·ar′y** *adj.*

ben·e·fit (bĕn′ə-fĭt) ▸ *n.* 1a. An advantage. b. A help; aid. 2. A payment made or an entitlement available in accordance with a wage agreement, insurance policy, or public assistance program. 3. A fund-raising public entertainment. ▸ *v.* 1. To be helpful or advantageous to. 2. To derive benefit; profit.

be·nev·o·lence (bə-nĕv′ə-ləns) ▸ *n.* 1. An inclination to do kind or charitable acts. 2. A kindly or charitable act.

be·nev·o·lent (bə-nĕv′ə-lənt) ▸ *adj.* 1. Having or showing benevolence. 2. Organized to benefit charity. **—be·nev′o·lent·ly** *adv.*

Ben·gal (bĕn-gôl′, bĕng-) ▸ A region of E India and Bangladesh on the **Bay of Bengal**, an arm of the Indian Ocean between India and Myanmar.

Ben·ga·li (bĕn-gô′lē, bĕng-) ▸ *n.* 1. A native or inhabitant of Bengal. 2. The modern Indic language of W Bengal and Bangladesh. **—Ben·ga′li** *adj.*

be·night·ed (bĭ-nī′tĭd) ▸ *adj.* Ignorant; unenlightened. **—be·night′ed·ness** *n.*

be·nign (bĭ-nīn′) ▸ *adj.* 1. Showing kindness, gentleness, and mildness. 2. Favorable. 3. *Pathol.* Not malignant. **—be·nign′ly** *adv.*

be·nig·nant (bĭ-nĭg′nənt) ▸ *adj.* Kind and gracious. **—be·nig′nant·ly** *adv.*

Be·nin (bə-nĭn′, bĕ-nēn′) ▸ A country of W Africa.

bent (bĕnt) ▸ *v.* P.t. and p.part. of **bend.** ▸ *adj.* 1. Not being straight or even; crooked. 2. Determined to take a course of action. 3. *Chiefly Brit.* Corrupt; dishonest. ▸ *n.* A tendency, disposition, or inclination: *a strong bent for studying science.*

be·numb (bĭ-nŭm′) ▸ *v.* 1. To numb, esp. by cold. 2. To stupefy.

ben·zene (bĕn′zēn′, bĕn-zēn′) ▸ *n.* A clear flammable liquid, C_6H_6, derived from petroleum and used in products such as insecticides and motor fuels.

ben·zine (bĕn′zēn′, bĕn-zēn′) ▸ *n.* A flammable liquid mixture of petroleum fractions, used in cleaning and as a motor fuel.

benzo– or **benz–** ▸ *pref.* Benzene; benzoic acid: *benzoate.*

ben·zo·ate (bĕn′zō-āt′) ▸ *n.* A salt or ester of benzoic acid.

ben·zo·ic acid (bĕn-zō′ĭk) ▸ *n.* A crystalline acid, $C_7H_6O_2$, used as a food preservative and germicide and in the manufacture of dyes.

ben·zo·in (bĕn′zō-ĭn, -zoin′) ▸ *n.* A balsamic resin obtained from certain tropical Asian trees and used in perfumery and medicine.

ben·zol (bĕn′zôl′, -zōl′, -zŏl′) ▸ *n.* See **benzene.**

be·queath (bĭ-kwēth′, -kwēth′) ▸ *v.* 1. *Law* To leave or give (property) by will. 2. To hand down. **—be·queath′al, be·queath′ment** *n.*

THESAURUS

bend *v.* 1. To deviate or cause to deviate from a straight line in a smooth, continuous manner ▸ arc, arch, bow, crook, curve, hook, loop, round, turn. [*Compare* WAVE, WIND[2].] 2. To move or cause to move in a bent or angular direction ▸ angle, deflect, flex, refract, reflect, turn, warp. [*Compare* GLANCE, SWERVE.] 3. To curve or yield under pressure ▸ bow, buckle, give, kink, sag, warp. [*Compare* CAVE IN, DEFORM.] *—See also* APPLY (1), DISTORT, STOOP.

bend *n.* Something bent or curved ▸ angle, arc, arch, bow, crescent, crook, curvature, curve, flexure, fold, hairpin, hook, horseshoe, oxbow, round, turn, turning, U-turn. [*Compare* CURL.]

bendability *n.* *—See* FLEXIBILITY (1).

bendable *adj.* *—See* MALLEABLE.

bender *n.* *Slang* A drinking bout ▸ bacchanal, bacchanalia, binge, brannigan, carousal, carouse, drunk, spree. *Slang:* bat, beer blast, booze, jag, souse, tear, toot. [*Compare* BINGE, BLAST.]

bending *adj.* *—See* BENT.

benediction *n.* 1. A short prayer said at meals ▸ blessing, grace, thanks, thanksgiving. [*Compare* PRAYER[1].] 2. The act of praying ▸ invocation, prayer, supplication. [*Compare* APPEAL.]

benefaction *n.* *—See* DONATION, FAVOR (1).

benefactor or **benefactress** *n.* *—See* DONOR, PATRON.

benefic *adj.* *—See* BENEFICIAL.

beneficence *n.* *—See* BENEVOLENCE, DONATION, FAVOR (1).

beneficent *adj.* *—See* BENEFICIAL, BENEVOLENT (1).

beneficial *adj.* Affording benefit or advantage ▸ advantageous, benefic, beneficent, benignant, constructive, contributive, favorable, fruitful, good, helpful, profitable, propitious, toward, salubrious, salutary, useful, valuable, worthwhile. [*Compare* EFFECTIVE.]

benefit *n.* *—See* ADVANTAGE (2), INTEREST (1), USE (2).

benefit *v.* To derive advantage ▸ capitalize, gain, profit. *Idiom:* do well. *—See also* PROFIT (2).

benevolence *n.* Kindly, charitable interest in others ▸ altruism, beneficence, benignancy, benignity, charitableness, charity, goodwill, grace, humanity, kindheartedness, kindliness, kindness, philanthropy. *Idiom:* the goodness (*or* kindness) of one's heart. [*Compare* AMIABILITY, CONSIDERATION, GENEROSITY.] *—See also* FAVOR (1).

benevolent *adj.* 1. Characterized by kindness and concern for others ▸ altruistic, beneficent, benign, benignant, good, goodhearted, helpful, kind, kindhearted, kindly. [*Compare* AMIABLE, GENEROUS, HUMANITARIAN, SELFLESS.] 2. Of or concerned with charity ▸ altruistic, charitable, eleemosynary, philanthropic.

benighted *adj.* *—See* IGNORANT (2).

benightedness *n.* *—See* IGNORANCE (1).

benign *adj.* *—See* BENEVOLENT (1), FAVORABLE (1), HARMLESS.

benignancy *n.* *—See* BENEVOLENCE.

benignant *adj.* *—See* BENEFICIAL, BENEVOLENT (1).

benignity *n.* *—See* BENEVOLENCE, FAVOR (1).

bent *adj.* Deviating from a straight line ▸ angled, arced, arched, arciform, bending, bowed, crooked, curled, curved, curvilinear, curving, doubled, flexed, folded, hooked, looped, recurved, rounded, warped. [*Compare* CURLY.] *—See also* INTENT.

bent *n.* *—See* DISPOSITION, INCLINATION (1), TALENT.

benumb *v.* *—See* DAZE (1), DEADEN, PARALYZE.

benumbed *adj.* *—See* DEAD (2).

bequeath *v.* To convey something from one generation to the next ▸ hand down, hand on, pass (along *or* on), transmit. *—See also* DONATE, LEAVE[1] (1).

be·quest (bĭ-kwĕst′) ▸ *n.* **1.** The act of bequeathing. **2.** Something bequeathed; legacy.

be·rate (bĭ-rāt′) ▸ *v.* **-rat·ed, -rat·ing.** To scold angrily and at length.

Ber·ber (bûr′bər) ▸ *n.* **1.** A member of a North African people living in settled or nomadic tribes from Morocco to Egypt. **2.** Any of their Afro-Asiatic languages.

ber·ceuse (bĕr-sœz′) ▸ *n., pl.* **-ceuses** (-sœz′) *Mus.* **1.** A lullaby. **2.** A soothing composition similar to a lullaby.

be·reave (bĭ-rēv′) ▸ *v.* **-reaved** or **-reft** (-rĕft′), **-reav·ing.** To leave desolate or alone, esp. by death. **—be·reave′ment** *n.*

be·reaved (bĭ-rēvd′) ▸ *adj.* Suffering the loss of a loved one. ▸ *n.* One who is or those who are bereaved.

be·reft (bĭ-rĕft′) ▸ *v.* P.t. and p.part of **bereave.** ▸ *adj.* **1.** Lacking or deprived of something: *bereft of dignity.* **2.** Bereaved.

be·ret (bə-rā′) ▸ *n.* A round, brimless cloth cap often worn to one side.

ber·i·ber·i (bĕr′ē-bĕr′ē) ▸ *n.* A thiamine-deficiency disease characterized by neurological symptoms, cardiovascular abnormalities, and edema.

Ber·ing (bîr′ĭng, bâr′-), **Vitus** (1681–1741) ▸ Danish navigator and explorer.

Bering Sea ▸ A northward extension of the Pacific between Siberia and AK, connected with the Arctic Ocean by the **Bering Strait.**

ber·ke·li·um (bər-kē′lē-əm, bûrk′lē-əm) ▸ *n. Symbol* **Bk** A synthetic radioactive element. At. no. 97.

Ber·lin (bər-lĭn′) ▸ The capital of Germany, in the NE part; formerly divided into **East Berlin** and **West Berlin** (1945–90).

Berlin, Irving (1888–1989) ▸ Russian-born Amer. songwriter.

berm (bûrm) ▸ *n.* **1.** A raised bank or path, as along a roadway or canal. **2.** A protective mound or bank of earth.

Ber·mu·da (bər-myo͞o′də) ▸ A self-governing British colony comprising about 300 islands in the Atlantic SE of Cape Hatteras. **—Ber·mu′di·an, Ber·mu′dan** *adj. & n.*

Bermuda onion ▸ *n.* A large mild onion.

Bermuda shorts ▸ *pl.n.* Short pants that end slightly above the knee.

Ber·noul·li effect (bər-no͞o′lē) ▸ *n.* The phenomenon of internal pressure reduction with increased stream velocity in a fluid.

ber·ry (bĕr′ē) ▸ *n., pl.* **-ries.** **1.** *Bot.* A fruit derived from a single ovary and having the whole wall fleshy, such as the grape or tomato. **2.** A small, juicy, many-seeded fruit, such as a blackberry. ▸ *v.* **-ried, -ry·ing.** To hunt for or gather berries.

ber·serk (bər-sûrk′, -zûrk′) ▸ *adj.* **1.** Destructively violent. **2.** Crazed; deranged. **—ber·serk′** *adv.*

berth (bûrth) ▸ *n.* **1.** Sufficient space for a ship to maneuver. **2.** A space for a ship to dock or anchor. **3.** Employment, esp. on a ship. **4a.** A built-in bed, as on a ship or train. **b.** A place to sleep or stay; accommodations. **5.** A space where a vehicle can be parked, as for loading. ▸ *v.* To bring (a ship) to a berth. ***—idiom:*** **a wide berth** Ample space or distance to avoid any trouble.

ber·yl (bĕr′əl) ▸ *n.* A hard glassy mineral, essentially $Be_3Al_2Si_6O_{18}$, the chief source of beryllium and used as a gem. **—ber′yl·line** (-ə-lĭn, -līn′) *adj.*

be·ryl·li·um (bə-rĭl′ē-əm) ▸ *n. Symbol* **Be** A high-melting, lightweight, corrosion-resistant, rigid, steel-gray metallic element used as a moderator in nuclear reactors and in sturdy light alloys. At. no. 4.

be·seech (bĭ-sēch′) ▸ *v.* **-sought** (-sôt′) or **-seeched, -seech·ing.** To request urgently; implore.

be·seem (bĭ-sēm′) ▸ *v. Archaic* To befit.

be·set (bĭ-sĕt′) ▸ *v.* **-set, -set·ting.** **1.** To attack from all sides. **2.** To trouble persistently; harass.

be·side (bĭ-sīd′) ▸ *prep.* **1.** Next to. **2.** In comparison with. **3.** In addition to. **4.** Except for. **5.** Not relevant to: *beside the point.* ***—idiom:*** **beside (oneself)** Extremely agitated or excited.

be·sides (bĭ-sīdz′) ▸ *adv.* **1.** In addition; also. **2.** Moreover; furthermore. **3.** Otherwise; else. ▸ *prep.* **1.** In addition to. **2.** Except for.

be·siege (bĭ-sēj′) ▸ *v.* **-sieged, -sieg·ing.** **1.** To surround with hostile forces. **2.** To crowd around; hem in. **3.** To harass or importune, as with requests. **—be·sieg′er** *n.*

be·smear (bĭ-smîr′) ▸ *v.* To smear.

be·smirch (bĭ-smûrch′) ▸ *v.* **1.** To stain; sully. **2.** To make dirty; soil. **—be·smirch′er** *n.*

be·sot (bĭ-sŏt′) ▸ *v.* **-sot·ted, -sot·ting.** To muddle or stupefy, as with liquor or infatuation.

be·spat·ter (bĭ-spăt′ər) ▸ *v.* To spatter with or as if with mud.

be·speak (bĭ-spēk′) ▸ *v.* **-spoke** (-spōk′), **-spo·ken** (-spō′kən) or **-spoke, -speak·ing.** **1.** To be or give a sign of; indicate. **2.** To engage, hire, or order in advance. **3.** To foretell.

be·sprin·kle (bĭ-sprĭng′kəl) ▸ *v.* **-kled, -kling.** To sprinkle.

Bes·sa·ra·bi·a (bĕs′ə-rā′bē-ə) ▸ A region of Moldova and W Ukraine. **—Bes′sa·ra′bi·an** *adj. & n.*

Bes·se·mer process (bĕs′ə-mər) ▸ *n.* A method for making steel by blasting compressed air through molten iron to burn out excess carbon and impurities.

best (bĕst) ▸ *adj.* Superl. of **good.** **1.** Surpassing all others in quality. **2.** Most satisfactory or desirable: *the best solution.* **3.** Greatest; most: *the best part of an hour.* ▸ *adv.* Superl. of **well²**. **1.** Most creditably or advantageously. **2.** To the greatest degree or extent; most. ▸ *n.* **1.** One that surpasses all others. **2.** The best part, moment, or value: *Let's get the best out of life.* **3.** The optimum condition or quality: *look your best.* **4.** One's best clothing. **5.** The best effort one can make. **6.** One's regards: *Give them my best.* ▸ *v.* To surpass; beat. ***—idioms:*** **at best** **1.** Interpreted most favorably: *no more than 40 people at best.* **2.** Under the most favorable conditions: *runs 20 miles per hour at best.* **for the best** For the ultimate good. **get the best of** To outdo or outwit.

bes·tial (bĕs′chəl, bēs′-) ▸ *adj.* **1.** Beastlike. **2.** Marked by

THESAURUS

bequest *n.* Something bestowed voluntarily ▸ gift, present, presentation. *Slang:* freebie. [*Compare* GRANT.] *—See also* DONATION.

berate *v.* To reprimand loudly or harshly ▸ bawl out, rate. *Informal:* tell off. *Idioms:* give hell to, give it to. *—See also* CHASTISE.

berating *n.* *—See* TIRADE.

bereft *adj.* *—See* ABANDONED (1), EMPTY (2).

berth *n.* *—See* POSITION (3).

berth *v.* *—See* LODGE.

beseech *v.* *—See* APPEAL (1).

beset *v.* *—See* ATTACK (1), BESIEGE, HARASS, SURROUND.

besetment *n.* *—See* ANNOYANCE (2).

besides *adv.* *—See* ADDITIONALLY.

besiege *v.* To surround with hostile troops ▸ beleaguer, beset, blockade, invest, siege. *Idiom:* lay siege to. [*Compare* ATTACK, SURROUND.] *—See also* ENCLOSE (2), HARASS.

besiegement *n.* *—See* SIEGE.

besmear *v.* *—See* DENIGRATE, SMEAR.

besmirch *v.* *—See* DENIGRATE, DIRTY, DISGRACE.

besoil *v.* *—See* DIRTY.

besot *v.* *—See* DRUG (2).

besotted *adj.* *—See* DRUNK, INFATUATED.

bespatter *v.* *—See* DENIGRATE, DIRTY, SPLASH (1), STAIN.

bespeak *v.* *—See* BOOK, INDICATE (1).

bespeckle *v.* *—See* SPECKLE.

bespoke *adj.* *—See* CUSTOM.

bespoken *adj.* *—See* ENGAGED.

besprinkle *v.* *—See* SPECKLE, SPRINKLE.

best *adj.* **1.** Surpassing all others in quality, achievement, or desirability ▸ finest, first, foremost, greatest, highest, leading, nicest, optimal, optimum, preeminent, superlative, supreme, top, unsurpassed. [*Compare* CHOICE, EXCEPTIONAL, PRIMARY, UNIQUE.] **2.** Much more than half ▸ better, biggest, greater, larger, largest, most. *—See also* ADVISABLE.

best *n.* **1.** The finest or most preferable part of something ▸ choice, cream, crème de la crème, elite, flower, pick, prize, top. *Idioms:* cream of the crop, pick of the bunch (*or* crop *or* litter), top of the line, top of the heap. **2.** Friendly greetings ▸ regards, respects.

best *v.* *—See* DEFEAT, SURPASS.

bestain *v.* *—See* STAIN.

bestial *adj.* Similar to a beast in behavior ▸ beastlike, beastly, brutish. [*Compare* CRUEL, SAVAGE, UNCIVILIZED.]

brutality or depravity. **—bes′ti·al′i·ty** (-chē-ăl′ĭ-tē) *n.* **—bes′tial·ly** *adv.*

bes·ti·ar·y (bĕs′chē-ĕr′ē, bēs′-) ▸ *n., pl.* **-ies.** A medieval collection of stories providing descriptions of real and fabulous animals along with moral interpretation of their behavior.

be·stir (bĭ-stûr′) ▸ *v.* **-stirred, -stir·ring.** To cause to become active; rouse.

best man ▸ *n.* A bridegroom's chief attendant.

be·stow (bĭ-stō′) ▸ *v.* To present as a gift or honor; confer. **—be·stow′al** *n.*

be·strew (bĭ-strōō′) ▸ *v.* **-strewed, -strewed** or **-strewn** (-strōōn′), **-strew·ing.** To strew.

be·stride (bĭ-strīd′) ▸ *v.* **-strode** (-strōd′), **-strid·den** (-strĭd′n), **-strid·ing.** To sit or stand astride; straddle.

best·sell·er (bĕst′sĕl′ər) ▸ *n.* A product, such as a book, that is among those sold in the largest numbers.

bet (bĕt) ▸ *n.* **1.** A wager. **2.** The amount or object risked in a wager; stake. **3.** One on which a stake is or can be placed. **4.** A considered plan or option: *Your best bet is to make reservations.* ▸ *v.* **bet** or **bet·ted, bet·ting. 1.** To stake (e.g., an amount) in a bet. **2.** To make a bet (with). ***—idiom:* you bet** *Informal* Of course.

be·ta (bā′tə, bē′-) ▸ *n.* The 2nd letter of the Greek alphabet.

be·take (bĭ-tāk′) ▸ *v.* **-took** (-tŏŏk′), **-tak·en** (-tā′kən), **-tak·ing.** To cause (oneself) to go.

beta particle ▸ *n.* A high-speed electron or positron, esp. from radioactive decay.

beta ray ▸ *n.* A stream of beta particles, esp. of electrons.

beta rhythm also **beta wave** ▸ *n.* A pattern of electrical oscillations occurring in the brain at a frequency of 13 to 30 hertz when a person is awake and alert.

be·ta·tron (bā′tə-trŏn′, bē′-) ▸ *n.* A fixed-radius magnetic induction electron accelerator.

be·tel (bēt′l) ▸ *n.* A climbing or trailing Asian shrub having usu. ovate leaves used to wrap betel nuts.

Be·tel·geuse (bēt′l-jōōz′, bĕt′l-jœz′) ▸ *n.* A bright-red variable star in the constellation Orion.

betel nut ▸ *n.* The seed of the betel palm, chewed with betel leaves, lime, and flavorings as a mild stimulant.

betel palm ▸ *n.* A tropical Asian feather-leaved palm cultivated for its seeds.

bête noire (bĕt nwär′) ▸ *n.* One that is an object of intense dislike or aversion.

be·think (bĭ-thĭngk′) ▸ *v.* **-thought** (-thôt′), **-think·ing.** To remind (oneself).

Beth·le·hem (bĕth′lĭ-hĕm′, -lē-əm) ▸ A town in the West Bank S of Jerusalem; traditional birthplace of Jesus.

be·tide (bĭ-tīd′) ▸ *v.* **-tid·ed, -tid·ing.** To happen (to); befall.

be·times (bĭ-tīmz′) ▸ *adv.* In good time; early.

be·to·ken (bĭ-tō′kən) ▸ *v.* To give a sign or portent of.

be·took (bĭ-tŏŏk′) ▸ *v.* P.t. of **betake.**

be·tray (bĭ-trā′) ▸ *v.* **1.** To commit treason against; be a traitor to. **2.** To be false or disloyal to. **3.** To make known unintentionally. **4.** To show; reveal. **5.** To lead astray; deceive. **—be·tray′al** *n.* **—be·tray′er** *n.*

be·troth (bĭ-trōth′, -trôth′) ▸ *v.* To promise or engage to marry. **—be·troth′al** *n.*

be·trothed (bĭ-trōthd′, -trôtht′) ▸ *n.* The person to whom one is engaged to be married.

bet·ter (bĕt′ər) ▸ *adj.* Comp. of **good. 1.** Greater in excellence or higher in quality. **2.** More appropriate, useful, or desirable. **3.** Greater or larger: *the better part of an hour.* **4.** Healthier than before. ▸ *adv.* Comp. of **well**[2]. **1.** In a more excellent way. **2.** To a greater extent or degree. **3.** To greater use or advantage. **4.** More: *better than a year.* ▸ *n.* **1.** One that is better in excellence or quality. **2.** A superior, as in standing. ▸ *v.* **1.** To make or become better; improve. **2.** To surpass or exceed. ***—idioms:* better off** In a wealthier or better condition. **for the better** Resulting in improvement. **had better** Ought to. **think better of** To change one's mind about.

bet·ter·ment (bĕt′ər-mənt) ▸ *n.* An improvement, often financially or educationally.

bet·tor also **bet·ter** (bĕt′ər) ▸ *n.* One that bets.

be·tween (bĭ-twēn′) ▸ *prep.* **1.** In or through the position or interval separating: *between the trees; between 11 and 12 o'clock.* **2.** Associating in a reciprocal relationship: *an agreement between workers and management.* **3a.** By the combined effort or effect of: *Between them they succeeded.* **b.** In the combined ownership of: *They had only a few dollars between them.* **4.** From one or another of: *choose between us.* ▸ *adv.* In an intermediate space, position, or time. ***—idiom:* between you and me** In the strictest confidence.

be·twixt (bĭ-twĭkst′) ▸ *adv. & prep.* Between. ***—idiom:* betwixt and between** In an intermediate position.

bev·el (bĕv′əl) ▸ *n.* **1.** The angle or inclination of a line or surface that meets another at any angle but 90°. **2.** A rule with an adjustable arm used to measure or draw angles or to fix a surface at an angle. ▸ *v.* **-eled, -el·ing** or **-elled, -el·ling. 1.** To cut at a bevel. **2.** To be inclined; slant.

bev·er·age (bĕv′ər-ĭj, bĕv′rĭj) ▸ *n.* Any one of various liquids for drinking, usu. excluding water.

bev·y (bĕv′ē) ▸ *n., pl.* **-ies. 1.** A group of animals or birds, esp. quail. **2.** A group or assemblage.

be·wail (bĭ-wāl′) ▸ *v.* To express sorrow (about); lament.

THESAURUS

bestiality *n.* —*See* CORRUPTION (1), CRUELTY.

bestialize *v.* —*See* CORRUPT.

bestow *v.* —*See* CONFER (2), DONATE, LODGE.

bestowal or **bestowment** *n.* —*See* CONFERMENT.

bestride *v.* To sit or stand with a leg on each side of ▸ straddle, stride.

bet *n.* Something risked on an uncertain outcome ▸ ante, kitty, pool, pot, stake, stakes, venture, wager. —*See also* GAMBLE.

bet *v.* To make a bet ▸ gamble, game, lay, play, wager. *Idioms:* ante (*or* pony) up, feed the pot (*or* kitty), lay odds (*or* a wager), put money on something, put one's money where one's mouth is, put up or shut up, show the color of one's money. —*See also* EXPECT (1), GAMBLE (2).

bête noire *n.* —*See* HATE (2).

bethink *v.* —*See* REMEMBER (1).

betide *v.* To take place by chance ▸ befall, chance, hap, happen. —*See also* HAPPEN (1).

betimes *adv.* —*See* EARLY, INTERMITTENTLY.

betoken *v.* —*See* FORESHADOW, INDICATE (1).

betray *v.* **1.** To be treacherous to ▸ cross up, double-cross, turn in. *Informal:* knife. *Slang:* rat (on *or* out), sell out. *Idioms:* play someone false, sell down the river, stab in the back. [*Compare* ABANDON, DISAPPOINT, INFORM.] **2.** To disclose in a breach of confidence ▸ blab, divulge, expose, give away, let out, reveal, tell, uncover, unveil. *Informal:* leak, spill. *Idioms:* let slip, let the cat out of the bag, spill the beans, tell all. [*Compare* REVEAL.] —*See also* DECEIVE.

betrayal *n.* An act of betraying ▸ backstabbing, double cross, double-dealing, treachery. *Slang:* sellout. [*Compare* TREASON.] —*See also* FAITHLESSNESS.

betrayer *n.* One who betrays ▸ Benedict Arnold, double-crosser, double-dealer, Judas, quisling, snake, traitor. *Slang:* rat. *Idiom:* snake in the grass. [*Compare* CREEP, INFORMER, DEFECTOR.]

betroth *v.* —*See* PLEDGE (1).

betrothal *n.* The act or condition of being pledged to marry ▸ engagement, espousal, troth.

betrothed *adj.* —*See* ENGAGED.

betrothed *n.* —*See* INTENDED.

better[1] *adj.* Of greater excellence than another ▸ finer, nicer, preferable, superior, worthier. —*See also* BEST (2).

better *adv.* To a greater extent ▸ more. *Idioms:* more fully, to a greater degree.

better *n.* One who stands above another in rank ▸ elder, senior, superior. *Informal:* higher-up. [*Compare* CHIEF.] —*See also* ADVANTAGE (3).

better *v.* —*See* IMPROVE, SURPASS.

better[2] *n.* *See* BETTOR.

better half *n.* —*See* SPOUSE.

betterment *n.* —*See* IMPROVEMENT (1), PROGRESS.

bettor or **better** *n.* —*See* GAMBLER (1).

between *adj.* —*See* MIDDLE.

beveled *adj.* —*See* OBLIQUE.

beverage *n.* —*See* DRINK (1).

bevy *n.* —*See* FLOCK, GROUP.

bewail *v.* —*See* DEPLORE (1), GRIEVE.

be·ware (bĭ-wâr′) ▸ *v.* **-wared, -war·ing.** To be on guard (against); be cautious (of).

be·wil·der (bĭ-wĭl′dər) ▸ *v.* To confuse or befuddle, esp. with numerous conflicting situations, objects, or statements. **—be·wil′der·ment** *n.*

be·witch (bĭ-wĭch′) ▸ *v.* **1.** To place under one's power by or as if by magic; cast a spell over. **2.** To captivate completely; entrance. **—be·witch′ing·ly** *adv.* **—be·witch′ment** *n.*

bey (bā) ▸ *n.* **1.** A provincial governor in the Ottoman Empire. **2.** A ruler of the former kingdom of Tunis.

be·yond (bē-ŏnd′, bĭ-yŏnd′) ▸ *prep.* **1.** On the far side of; past. **2.** Later than; after. **3.** Past the understanding, reach, or scope of. **4.** To a degree or amount greater than. **5.** In addition to.

bez·el (bĕz′əl) ▸ *n.* **1.** A slanting edge on a cutting tool. **2.** The faceted portion of a cut gem.

Bh ▸ The symbol for the element **bohrium.**

BHT (bē′āch-tē′) ▸ *n.* A crystalline phenolic antioxidant, $C_{15}H_{24}O$, that is used to preserve fats and oils, esp. in foods.

Bhu·tan (bo͞o-tăn′, -tän′) ▸ A country of central Asia in the E Himalayas. **—Bhu′tan·ese′** *adj. & n.*

Bi ▸ The symbol for the element **bismuth.**

bi– or **bin–** ▸ *pref.* **1.** Two; twice: *bipolar.* **2.** Occurring twice during: *biweekly.*

bi·an·nu·al (bī-ăn′yo͞o-əl) ▸ *adj.* Semiannual. **—bi·an′nu·al·ly** *adv.*

bi·as (bī′əs) ▸ *n.* **1.** A line going diagonally across the grain of fabric. **2.** A preference or inclination that inhibits impartiality; prejudice. ▸ *adj.* Slanting or diagonal; oblique. ▸ *v.* **-ased, -as·ing** or **-assed, -as·sing.** To cause to have a bias; prejudice.

bi·ath·lon (bī-ăth′lən, -lŏn′) ▸ *n.* An athletic competition that combines events in cross-country skiing and rifle shooting.

bib (bĭb) ▸ *n.* A cloth or plastic napkin secured under the chin and worn esp. by children to protect clothing while eating.

bi·be·lot (bē′bə-lō′, bē-blō′) ▸ *n.* A small decorative object.

Bi·ble (bī′bəl) ▸ *n.* **1a.** The sacred book of Christianity, which includes the Old Testament and the New Testament. **b.** The sacred book of Judaism, consisting of the Torah, the Prophets, and the Writings. See **Bible** table in Appendix on page 842. **2.** often **bible** A book considered authoritative in its field: *the bible of Chinese cooking.* **—Bib′li·cal** (bĭb′lĭ-kəl) *adj.* **—Bib′li·cal·ly** *adv.*

biblio– ▸ *pref.* Book: *bibliophile.*

bib·li·og·ra·phy (bĭb′lē-ŏg′rə-fē) ▸ *n., pl.* **-phies. 1.** A list of the works of a specific author or publisher. **2.** A list of writings relating to a given subject. **3.** The description and identification of the editions, dates of issue, authorship, and typography of books or other written material. **—bib′li·og′ra·pher** *n.* **—bib′li·o·graph′i·cal** (-ə-grăf′ĭ-kəl), **bib′li·o·graph′ic** *adj.*

bib·li·o·phile (bĭb′lē-ə-fīl′) ▸ *n.* A lover or connoisseur of books.

bib·u·lous (bĭb′yə-ləs) ▸ *adj.* Given to convivial, often excessive alcoholic drinking. **—bib′u·lous·ly** *adv.*

bi·cam·er·al (bī-kăm′ər-əl) ▸ *adj.* Composed of two legislative branches. **—bi·cam′er·al·ism** *n.*

bi·car·bon·ate (bī-kär′bə-nāt′, -nĭt) ▸ *n.* The radical group HCO_3 or a compound, such as sodium bicarbonate, containing it.

bicarbonate of soda ▸ *n.* See **baking soda.**

bi·cen·ten·a·ry (bī′sĕn-tĕn′ə-rē, bī-sĕn′tə-nĕr′ē) ▸ *n., pl.* **-ries.** A bicentennial. **—bi′cen·ten′a·ry** *adj.*

bi·cen·ten·ni·al (bī′sĕn-tĕn′ē-əl) ▸ *n.* A 200th anniversary or its celebration; bicentenary. **—bi′cen·ten′ni·al** *adj.*

bi·ceps (bī′sĕps′) ▸ *n., pl.* **-ceps** or **-ceps·es** (-sĕp′sĭz). A muscle with two points of origin, esp. the large muscle at the front of the upper arm.

bick·er (bĭk′ər) ▸ *v.* To engage in a petty quarrel; squabble. ▸ *n.* A petty quarrel; squabble.

bi·con·cave (bī′kŏn-kāv′, bī-kŏn′kāv′) ▸ *adj.* Concave on both sides or surfaces. **—bi′con·cav′i·ty** (-kăv′ĭ-tē) *n.*

bi·con·vex (bī′kŏn-vĕks′, bī-kŏn′vĕks′) ▸ *adj.* Convex on both sides or surfaces. **—bi′con·vex′i·ty** (-vĕk′sĭ-tē) *n.*

bi·cus·pid (bī-kŭs′pĭd) ▸ *adj.* Having two points or cusps. ▸ *n.* A bicuspid tooth, esp. a premolar.

bi·cy·cle (bī′sĭk′əl, -sĭ-kəl) ▸ *n.* A vehicle consisting of a metal frame mounted on two wire-spoked wheels and having a seat, handlebars for steering, brakes, and pedals. ▸ *v.* **-cled, -cling.** To ride or travel on a bicycle. **—bi′cy·cler, bi′cy·clist** *n.*

bid (bĭd) ▸ *v.* **bade** (băd, bād) or **bid, bid·den** (bĭd′n) or **bid, bid·ding. 1.** To command; direct. **2.** To utter (a greeting or salutation). **3.** To invite to attend; summon. **4.** *p.t. and p.part.* **bid. a.** To offer to pay or accept a specified price. **b.** To offer as a price. **c.** To state one's intention to take (tricks of a certain number or suit) in card games. ▸ *n.* **1a.** An offer of a price. **b.** The amount offered. **2.** An invitation. **3a.** The act of bidding in card games. **b.** The number of tricks declared. **c.** A player's turn to bid. **4.** An earnest effort to gain something. **—bid′der** *n.*

bid·da·ble (bĭd′ə-bəl) ▸ *adj.* **1.** Capable of being bid. **2.** Obedient; docile.

bid·dy (bĭd′ē) ▸ *n., pl.* **-dies.** A hen.

bide (bīd) ▸ *v.* **bid·ed** or **bode** (bōd), **bid·ed, bid·ing. 1.** To remain; stay. **2.** To wait; tarry. **3.** *p.t.* **bided.**To await.

bi·det (bē-dā′) ▸ *n.* A fixture similar in design to a toilet, used for bathing the genitals and posterior parts of the body.

bi·en·ni·al (bī-ĕn′ē-əl) ▸ *adj.* **1.** Lasting or living for two years. **2.** Happening every second year. **3.** *Bot.* Having a life cycle that normally takes two growing seasons. **—bi·en′ni·al** *n.* **—bi·en′ni·al·ly** *adv.*

bier (bîr) ▸ *n.* A stand on which a corpse or a coffin is placed before burial.

bi·fo·cal (bī-fō′kəl, bī′fō′-) ▸ *adj.* **1.** Having two different focal lengths. **2.** Having one section that corrects for distant vision and another that corrects for near vision, as an eyeglass lens. ▸ *pl.n.* **bi·fo·cals** Eyeglasses with bifocal lenses.

bi·fur·cate (bī′fər-kāt′, bī-fûr′-) ▸ *v.* **-cat·ed, -cat·ing.** To divide

THESAURUS

beware *v.* To be careful ▸ look out, mind, watch out. ***Idioms:*** be on guard, be on the lookout, keep an eye peeled, take care (*or* heed).

bewilder *v.* *—See* AGITATE (2), CONFUSE (1), DAZE (1).

bewildered *adj.* *—See* CONFUSED (1).

bewilderedness *n.* *—See* DAZE.

bewilderment *n.* *—See* COMPLEXITY, DAZE.

bewitch *v.* *—See* CHARM (1), CHARM (2).

bewitching *adj.* *—See* ATTRACTIVE, MAGIC, SEDUCTIVE.

bias *v.* **1.** To cause to have a prejudiced view ▸ jaundice, prejudice, prepossess, turn (against), warp. [*Compare* INDOCTRINATE, INFLUENCE.] **2.** To alter or present material so as to favor a particular viewpoint ▸ doctor, fiddle (with), massage, skew, slant, tailor. *Informal:* angle. [*Compare* DISTORT.]

bias *n.* An inclination for or against that inhibits impartial judgment ▸ one-sidedness, partiality, partisanship, preconception, prejudice, prepossession, slant, tendentiousness. *—See also* INCLINATION (1).

bias *adj.* *—See* OBLIQUE.

biased *adj.* Exhibiting bias ▸ discriminatory, one-sided, opinionated, partial, partisan, preconceived, predisposed, prejudiced, prejudicial, prepossessed, skewed, slanted, tendentious. [*Compare* INTOLERANT, NARROW, UNFAIR.] *—See also* OBLIQUE.

bibelot *n.* *—See* NOVELTY (3).

bibulous *adj.* *—See* ABSORBENT, DRUNK.

bicker *v.* *—See* ARGUE (1).

bicker *n.* *—See* ARGUMENT.

bid *v.* **1.** To request that someone take part in or be present at a particular occasion ▸ ask, invite, summon. ***Idioms:*** extend an invitation to, request the presence of. [*Compare* APPEAL, REQUEST.] **2.** To make an offer of ▸ offer. *Informal:* go. *—See also* COMMAND (1), COMPETE.

bid *n.* A spoken or written request for someone to take part or be present ▸ call, invitation, summons. *Informal:* invite. [*Compare* REQUEST.] *—See also* ATTEMPT, OFFER.

biddable *adj.* *—See* OBEDIENT.

bidding *n.* *—See* COMMAND (1).

biddy *n.* *—See* WITCH (2).

bide *v.* *—See* ENDURE (2), REMAIN.

biff *v.* *—See* HIT.

biff *n.* *—See* BLOW[2].

biform *adj.* *—See* DOUBLE (2).

bifurcate *v.* *—See* BRANCH.

or separate into two parts or branches. **—bi′fur·ca′tion** *n.*

big (bĭg) ▸ *adj.* **big·ger, big·gest. 1.** Of considerable size, number, quantity, or extent. **2.** Grown-up; adult. **3.** Pregnant: *big with child.* **4.** Of great significance: *a big decision.* **5.** *Informal* Self-important; cocky. ▸ *adv.* **1.** In a self-important or boastful way. **2.** *Informal* With great success. ***—idiom:* big on** Enthusiastic about; partial to. **—big′gish** *adj.* **—big′ness** *n.*

big·a·my (bĭg′ə-mē) ▸ *n., pl.* **-mies.** *Law* The criminal offense of marrying one person while still legally married to another. **—big′a·mist** *n.* **—big′a·mous** *adj.*

big bang theory ▸ *n.* A cosmological theory holding that the universe originated approx. 20 billion years ago from the violent explosion of a small point source of extremely high density and temperature.

big brother also **Big Brother** ▸ *n.* An omnipresent, seemingly benevolent figure representing the oppressive control over individuals exerted by an authoritarian government.

Big Dipper ▸ *n.* A cluster of seven stars in the constellation Ursa Major forming a dipper-shaped configuration.

Big·foot (bĭg′fo͝ot′) ▸ *n.* A very large, hairy, humanlike creature purported to inhabit the Pacific Northwest and Canada; Sasquatch.

big game ▸ *n.* Large animals or fish hunted or caught for sport. **—big′-game′** *adj.*

big-heart·ed (bĭg′här′tĭd) ▸ *adj.* Generous; kind.

big·horn (bĭg′hôrn′) ▸ *n., pl.* **-horn** or **-horns.** A wild sheep of the mountains of W North America, the male of which has massive, curved horns.

bight (bīt) ▸ *n.* **1.** A loop in a rope. **2a.** A bend or curve, esp. in a shoreline. **b.** A wide bay formed by a bight.

big·mouth (bĭg′mouth′) ▸ *n.* *Slang* A loud-mouthed or gossipy person.

big-name (bĭg′nām′) ▸ *adj.* *Informal* Widely acclaimed; famous. **—big name** *n.*

big·ot (bĭg′ət) ▸ *n.* One who is intolerant esp. in matters of religion, race, or politics. **—big′ot·ed** *adj.* **—big′ot·ry** *n.*

big shot ▸ *n.* *Slang* An important or influential person. **—big′shot′, big′-shot′** *adj.*

big-tick·et (bĭg′tĭk′ĭt) ▸ *adj.* *Informal* Having a high price or cost: *big-ticket items.*

big time ▸ *n.* *Informal* The highest level of attainment in a competitive field or profession. **—big′-time′** *adj.*

big top ▸ *n.* **1.** The main tent of a circus. **2.** The circus.

big·wig (bĭg′wĭg′) ▸ *n.* *Slang* A big shot.

bike (bīk) ▸ *n.* **1.** A bicycle. **2.** A motorcycle. **3.** A motorbike. **—bike** *v.*

bik·er (bī′kər) ▸ *n.* **1.** One who rides a bicycle or motorbike. **2.** A motorcyclist, esp. a member of a motorcycle gang.

bi·ki·ni (bĭ-kē′nē) ▸ *n.* **1.** A woman's brief, close-fitting two-piece bathing suit. **2.** A man's brief bathing trunks.

Bikini ▸ An atoll of the Marshall Is. in the W-central Pacific.

bi·lat·er·al (bī-lăt′ər-əl) ▸ *adj.* **1.** Having or formed of two sides; two-sided. **2.** Affecting or undertaken by two sides equally. **—bi·lat′er·al·ly** *adv.*

bile (bīl) ▸ *n.* **1.** A bitter greenish-yellow fluid that is secreted by the liver and aids in the digestion and absorption of fats. **2.** Ill temper; irascibility. **—bil′i·ar′y** (bĭl′ē-ĕr′ē) *adj.*

bilge (bĭlj) ▸ *n.* **1.** The lowest inner part of a ship's hull. **2.** Bilge water. **3.** *Slang* Nonsense.

bilge water ▸ *n.* **1.** Water that collects and stagnates in a ship's bilge. **2.** *Slang* Nonsense.

bi·lin·gual (bī-lĭng′gwəl) ▸ *adj.* Expressed in or able to speak or use two languages. **—bi·lin′gual·ism** *n.* **—bi·lin′gual·ly** *adv.*

bil·ious (bĭl′yəs) ▸ *adj.* **1.** Of or containing bile. **2.** Characterized by or experiencing gastric distress caused by a disorder of the liver or gallbladder. **3.** Irascible. **—bil′ious·ly** *adv.* **—bil′ious·ness** *n.*

bilk (bĭlk) ▸ *v.* To defraud, cheat, or swindle. **—bilk′er** *n.*

bill[1] (bĭl) ▸ *n.* **1.** A statement of charges for goods or services. **2.** A list of particulars, such as a theater program or menu. **3.** The entertainment offered by a theater. **4.** A public notice, such as an advertising poster. **5.** A piece of legal paper money. **6.** A bill of exchange. **7a.** A draft of a law presented for approval to a legislative body. **b.** The law enacted from such a draft. **8.** *Law* A document containing a formal statement of a case, complaint, or petition. ▸ *v.* **1.** To present a statement of costs or charges to. **2.** To enter on a bill. **3.** To advertise by public notice. **—bill′a·ble** *adj.*

bill[2] (bĭl) ▸ *n.* **1.** The horny part of the jaws of a bird; beak. **2.** A beaklike mouth part, as of a turtle. **3.** The visor of a cap. ▸ *v.* To touch beaks together.

bill·board (bĭl′bôrd′) ▸ *n.* A structure for the public display of advertisements.

bil·let (bĭl′ĭt) ▸ *n.* **1a.** Lodging for troops. **b.** A written order directing that such lodging be provided. **2.** A position of employment; job. ▸ *v.* To assign quarters to by billet.

bil·let-doux (bĭl′ā-do͞o′) ▸ *n., pl.* **bil·lets-doux** (bĭl′ā-do͞oz′). A love letter.

bill·fold (bĭl′fōld′) ▸ *n.* A wallet.

bil·liards (bĭl′yərdz) ▸ *pl.n.* *(takes sing. v.)* A game played on a rectangular cloth-covered table, in which a cue is used to hit three small, hard balls against one another or the raised cushioned sides of the table.

bill·ing (bĭl′ĭng) ▸ *n.* The relative importance of performers as indicated by their listing on programs or advertisements: *top billing.*

bil·lings·gate (bĭl′ĭngz-gāt′, -gĭt) ▸ *n.* Foul, abusive language.

bil·lion (bĭl′yən) ▸ *n.* **1.** The cardinal number equal to 10^9. **2.** *Chiefly Brit.* The cardinal number equal to 10^{12}. **—bil′lion** *adj. & pron.*

THESAURUS

big *adj.* Above average in amount, size, or scope ▸ biggish, considerable, extensive, good, goodly, great, healthy, king-size, large, large-scale, largish, outsize, queen-size, respectable, significant, sizable, substantial. *Informal:* tidy. [*Compare* BULKY, ENORMOUS, GRAND.] *—See also* GENEROUS (1), IMPORTANT, MATURE, PREGNANT (1).

Big Brother *n.* *—See* DICTATOR.

biggest *adj.* *—See* BEST (2).

biggish *adj.* *—See* BIG.

big gun *n.* *—See* DIGNITARY.

big head or **bigheadedness** *n.* *—See* EGOTISM.

bigheaded *adj.* *—See* EGOTISTIC (1).

big-hearted *adj.* *—See* GENEROUS (1).

big-heartedness *n.* *—See* GENEROSITY.

big house *n.* *—See* JAIL.

bight *n.* A body of water partly enclosed by land but having a wide outlet to the sea ▸ bay, gulf, sound. [*Compare* CHANNEL, HARBOR, INLET.]

big-league *adj.* *Informal* Being among the leaders in one's field ▸ big-name, blue-chip, celebrity, leading, major, major-league. *Informal:* big-time, heavyweight. [*Compare* FAMOUS, IMPORTANT, PRIMARY.]

big name *n.* *—See* CELEBRITY, DIGNITARY.

bigness *n.* *—See* SIZE (2).

bigoted *adj.* *—See* INTOLERANT (1).

bigotry *n.* Irrational suspicion or hatred of a particular group, race, or religion ▸ discrimination, intolerance, prejudice. [*Compare* HATE.]

big shot *n.* *—See* DIGNITARY.

big-ticket *adj.* *—See* COSTLY.

bigtime or **big-time** *adj.* *—See* BIG-LEAGUE, IMPORTANT.

big-timer *n.* *—See* DIGNITARY.

big wheel *n.* *—See* BOSS, DIGNITARY.

bigwig *n.* *—See* DIGNITARY.

bile *n.* *—See* TEMPER (1).

bilge *n.* *—See* NONSENSE.

biliousness *n.* *—See* TEMPER (1).

bilk *v.* *—See* CHEAT (1).

bilk *n.* *—See* CHEAT (2).

bill[1] *v.* To present with a request or demand for payment ▸ charge, dun, invoice, solicit.

bill *n.* *—See* ACCOUNT (2), LAW (2), PROGRAM (2), SIGN (2).

bill[2] *n.* **1.** The horny projection forming a bird's jaws ▸ beak, mandible, nib. **2.** The projecting rim on the front of a cap ▸ brim, eyeshade, peak, visor.

billboard *n.* *—See* SIGN (2).

billet *n.* *—See* POSITION (3).

billet *v.* *—See* LODGE.

billingsgate *n.* *—See* VITUPERATION.

billion *n.* *—See* HEAP (2).

bil·lion·aire (bĭl′yə-nâr′) ▸ *n.* One whose wealth equals at least a billion dollars, pounds, or the equivalent in other currency.
bil·lionth (bĭl′yənth) ▸ *n.* **1.** The ordinal number matching the number billion in a series. **2.** One of a billion equal parts. **—bil′lionth** *adj. & adv.*
bill of exchange ▸ *n.* A written order directing that a specified sum of money be paid to a specified person.
bill of fare ▸ *n.* A menu.
bill of goods ▸ *n.* **1.** A consignment of items for sale. **2.** *Informal* A dishonest or misleading promise or offer.
bill of lading ▸ *n.* A document listing and acknowledging receipt of goods for transport.
bill of rights ▸ *n.* **1.** A formal summary of the rights of a group of people: *a consumer bill of rights.* **2. Bill of Rights** The first ten amendments to the US Constitution.
bill of sale ▸ *n.* A document that attests a transfer of personal property.
bil·low (bĭl′ō) ▸ *n.* **1.** A large wave of water. **2.** A great swell or surge, as of smoke or windblown fabric. ▸ *v.* **1.** To surge or roll in billows. **2.** To swell or cause to swell in billows. **—bil′low·y** *adj.*
bil·ly (bĭl′ē) ▸ *n., pl.* **-lies.** A billy club.
billy club ▸ *n.* A short wooden club, esp. a police officer's.
billy goat ▸ *n. Informal* A male goat.
bi·me·tal·lic (bī′mə-tăl′ĭk) ▸ *adj.* **1.** Consisting of two metals. **2.** Of, based on, or using the principles of bimetallism.
bi·met·al·lism (bī-mĕt′l-ĭz′əm) ▸ *n.* The use of both gold and silver in a fixed ratio of value as a monetary standard.
bi·mod·al (bī-mōd′l) ▸ *adj.* Having two distinct modes or forms. **—bi′mo·dal′i·ty** *n.*
bi·month·ly (bī-mŭnth′lē) ▸ *adj.* **1.** Happening every two months. **2.** Happening twice a month; semimonthly. ▸ *n., pl.* **-lies.** A bimonthly publication. **—bi·month′ly** *adv.*
bin (bĭn) ▸ *n.* A container or enclosed space for storage.
bin– ▸ *pref.* Var. of **bi–.**
bi·na·ry (bī′nə-rē) ▸ *adj.* **1.** Having two distinct parts or components. **2.** Of a number system having 2 as its base. **—bi′na·ry** *n.*
binary digit ▸ *n.* Either of the digits 0 or 1, used in the binary number system.
binary number system ▸ *n.* A method of representing numbers, using the digits 0 and 1, in which successive units are powers of 2.
binary star ▸ *n.* A system consisting of two stars orbiting about a common center of mass and often appearing as a single object.
bin·au·ral (bī-nôr′əl, bĭn-ôr′-) ▸ *adj.* **1.** Of or hearing with two ears. **2.** Relating to sound transmission from two sources, which may vary acoustically to give a stereophonic effect. **—bin·au′ral·ly** *adv.*
bind (bīnd) ▸ *v.* **bound** (bound), **bind·ing. 1.** To tie or encircle with or as with a rope or cord. **2.** To bandage. **3.** To hold or restrain. **4.** To compel or obligate. **5.** To place under legal obligation by contract or oath. **6.** To cohere or cause to cohere in a mass. **7.** To enclose and fasten (e.g., a book) between covers. **8.** To reinforce or ornament with an edge or border. **9.** To constipate. **10.** To be tight and uncomfortable. **11.** To be compelling or unifying: *the ties that bind.* ▸ *n.* **1.** Something that binds. **2.** *Informal* A difficult or restrictive situation. **—bind′er** *n.*
bind·er·y (bīn′də-rē) ▸ *n., pl.* **-ies.** A place where books are bound.
bind·ing (bīn′dĭng) ▸ *n.* Something that binds, as: **a.** The cover that holds together the pages of a book. **b.** A strip sewn along an edge. **c.** Fastenings on a ski for securing the boot. ▸ *adj.* **1.** Serving to bind. **2.** Commanding adherence to an obligation or commitment: *binding arbitration.*
binge (bĭnj) ▸ *n.* **1.** A drunken spree. **2.** A period of uncontrolled self-indulgence. ▸ *v.* **binged, bing·ing** or **binge·ing.** To be or go on a binge.
bin·go (bĭng′gō) ▸ *n.* A game of chance in which players place markers on a pattern of numbered squares according to numbers drawn by a caller. ▸ *interj.* Used to express occurrence or completion.
bin·na·cle (bĭn′ə-kəl) ▸ *n. Naut.* A case near the helm that supports a ship's compass.
bin·oc·u·lar (bə-nŏk′yə-lər, bī-) ▸ *adj.* Of or involving both eyes at the same time: *binocular vision.* ▸ *n.* often **binoculars** A binocular optical device, such as field glasses.
bi·no·mi·al (bī-nō′mē-əl) ▸ *adj.* Consisting of or relating to two names or terms. ▸ *n.* **1.** *Math.* A polynomial with two terms. **2.** A taxonomic plant or animal name consisting of two terms. **—bi·no′mi·al·ly** *adv.*
bi·o (bī′ō) ▸ *n., pl.* **-os.** *Informal* A biography.
bio– ▸ *pref.* Life; living organism: *biochemistry.*
bi·o·chem·is·try (bī′ō-kĕm′ĭ-strē) ▸ *n.* The study of the chemical substances and vital processes occurring in living organisms. **—bi′o·chem′i·cal** (-ĭ-kəl) *adj. & n.* **—bi′o·chem′i·cal·ly** *adv.* **—bi′o·chem′ist** *n.*
bi·o·con·ver·sion (bī′ō-kən-vûr′zhən, -shən) ▸ *n.* The conversion of organic materials into usable products or energy by biological means.
bi·o·de·grad·a·ble (bī′ō-dĭ-grā′də-bəl) ▸ *adj.* Capable of being decomposed by natural biological processes. **—bi′o·de·grad′a·bil′i·ty** *n.* **—bi′o·deg′ra·da′tion** (-dĕg′rə-dā′shən) *n.* **—bi′o·de·grade′** *v.*
bi·o·di·ver·si·ty (bī′ō-dĭ-vûr′sĭ-tē) ▸ *n.* The number and variety of organisms found in a specified geographic region or environment.
bi·o·feed·back (bī′ō-fēd′băk′) ▸ *n.* The technique of using monitoring devices to learn about an involuntary bodily function, such as blood pressure, in order to gain some voluntary control over that function.
bi·o·gas (bī′ō-găs′) ▸ *n.* A mixture of methane and carbon dioxide produced by bacterial degradation of organic matter and used as a fuel.
bi·o·gen·ic (bī′ō-jĕn′ĭk) ▸ *adj.* **1.** Produced by living organisms or biological processes. **2.** Necessary for the maintenance of life.
bi·o·ge·og·ra·phy (bī′ō-jē-ŏg′rə-fē) ▸ *n.* The biological study of the geographic distribution of plants and animals.
bi·og·ra·phy (bī-ŏg′rə-fē) ▸ *n., pl.* **-phies. 1.** An account of a person's life written or produced by someone else. **2.** Biographies collectively, esp. when regarded as a literary form. **—bi·og′ra·pher** *n.* **—bi′o·graph′i·cal** (bī′ə-grăf′ĭ-kəl), **bi′o·graph′ic** *adj.*
bi·o·log·i·cal (bī′ə-lŏj′ĭ-kəl) also **bi·o·log·ic** ▸ *adj.* **1.** Of or relating to biology. **2.** Related by blood: *the child's biological parents.* **—bi′o·log′i·cal·ly** *adv.*
biological clock ▸ *n.* **1.** A mechanism in organisms that controls the periodic occurrence of functions or activities, such as metabolic change or photosynthesis. **2.** The span of a woman's fertility, from puberty to menopause.
biological warfare ▸ *n.* Warfare in which disease-producing microorganisms and bacteria are used to cause death or injury to humans, animals, or plants.
bi·ol·o·gy (bī-ŏl′ə-jē) ▸ *n.* **1.** The science of life and of living organisms. **2.** The life processes of a particular group or category of living organisms. **—bi·ol′o·gist** *n.*
bi·o·mass (bī′ō-măs′) ▸ *n.* **1.** The total mass of living matter within a given unit of environmental area. **2.** Plant material, vegetation, or agricultural waste used as a fuel.
bi·ome (bī′ōm′) ▸ *n.* A major regional biotic community, such as a grassland or desert.
bi·o·med·i·cine (bī′ō-mĕd′ĭ-sĭn) ▸ *n.* The study of medicine as it relates to all biological systems. **—bi′o·med′i·cal** (-ĭ-kəl) *adj.*

THESAURUS

binary *adj.* —*See* DOUBLE (2).
bind *v.* To make fast or firmly fixed, as by means of a cord or rope ▸ fasten, knot, secure, tie (up). —*See also* ASSOCIATE (1), COMMIT (2), DRESS (2), FASTEN.
bind *n.* —*See* PREDICAMENT, PROBLEM.
binder *n.* —*See* FASTENER.
binding *n.* —*See* BOND (2), FASTENER.
bine *n.* —*See* SHOOT.
binge *n.* A period of uncontrolled self-indulgence ▸ debauch, fling, orgy, rampage, riot, saturnalia, splurge, spree. *Slang:* jag. [*Compare* BLAST.] —*See also* BENDER.
biome *n.* —*See* ENVIRONMENT (3).

bi·on·ic (bī-ŏn′ĭk) ▸ *adj.* **1.** Having anatomical structures that are replaced or enhanced esp. by electronic components. **2.** Superhuman.

bi·o·phys·ics (bī′ō-fĭz′ĭks) ▸ *n.* *(takes sing. v.)* The physics of biological processes. **—bi′o·phys′i·cal** *adj.* **—bi′o·phys′i·cist** *n.*

bi·op·sy (bī′ŏp′sē) ▸ *n., pl.* **-sies.** The removal and examination of a sample of tissue from a living body for medical diagnosis.

bi·o·re·me·di·a·tion (bī′ō-rĭ-mē′dē-ā′shən) ▸ *n.* The use of biological agents, such as bacteria or plants, to decontaminate polluted soil or water.

bi·o·rhythm (bī′ō-rĭth′əm) ▸ *n.* An innate, cyclical biological process or function.

–biosis ▸ *suff.* A way of living: *symbiosis.*

bi·o·sphere (bī′ə-sfîr′) ▸ *n.* The part of the earth and its atmosphere in which living organisms exist.

bi·o·ta (bī-ō′tə) ▸ *n.* The combined flora and fauna of a region.

bi·o·tech·nol·o·gy (bī′ō-tĕk-nŏl′ə-jē) ▸ *n.* **1.** The use of microorganisms or biological substances to perform industrial or manufacturing processes. **2.** See **ergonomics.** **—bi′o·tech′no·log′i·cal** (-nə-lŏj′ĭ-kəl) *adj.*

bi·ot·ic (bī-ŏt′ĭk) ▸ *adj.* **1.** Of life or living organisms. **2.** Produced by living organisms.

bi·o·tin (bī′ə-tĭn) ▸ *n.* A crystalline vitamin of the vitamin B complex, found esp. in liver, egg yolk, milk, and yeast.

bi·par·ti·san (bī-pär′tĭ-zən, -sən) ▸ *adj.* Of, consisting of, or supported by members of two parties, esp. two major political parties. **—bi·par′ti·san·ship′** *n.*

bi·par·tite (bī-pär′tīt′) ▸ *adj.* **1.** Having or consisting of two parts. **2a.** Having two corresponding parts, one for each party: *a bipartite contract.* **b.** Having two participants: *a bipartite agreement.*

bi·ped (bī′pĕd′) ▸ *n.* An animal with two feet. ▸ *adj.* also **bi·ped·al** (bī-pĕd′l) Having two feet; two-footed.

bi·plane (bī′plān′) ▸ *n.* An airplane having two pairs of wings fixed at different levels, esp. one above and one below the fuselage.

bi·po·lar (bī-pō′lər) ▸ *adj.* **1.** Of or having two poles. **2.** Having two opposing sides or systems. **3.** *Psychiat.* Of or having a disorder marked by alternating episodes of mania and depression. **—bi′po·lar′i·ty** (-lăr′ĭ-tē) *n.*

bi·ra·cial (bī-rā′shəl) ▸ *adj.* **1.** Of or consisting of members of two races. **2.** Having parents of two different races. **—bi·ra′cial·ism** *n.*

birch (bûrch) ▸ *n.* **1a.** Any of various deciduous trees with bark that separates from the wood in sheets. **b.** The hard wood of a birch. **2.** A birch rod used for whipping. ▸ *v.* To whip with a birch.

bird (bûrd) ▸ *n.* **1.** A warm-blooded, egg-laying, feathered vertebrate with forelimbs modified to form wings. **2.** *Slang* A person: *a sly old bird.* ***—idiom:*** **for the birds** Objectionable or worthless.

bird·bath (bûrd′băth′, -bäth′) ▸ *n.* A water basin for birds to drink from and bathe in.

bird·er (bûr′dər) ▸ *n.* **1.** A bird watcher. **2a.** A breeder of birds. **b.** A hunter of birds.

bird·house (bûrd′hous′) ▸ *n.* **1.** A box made as a nesting place for birds. **2.** An aviary.

bird·ie (bûr′dē) ▸ *n.* **1.** One stroke under par for a hole in golf. **2.** See **shuttlecock.** **—bird′ie** *v.*

bird·lime (bûrd′līm′) ▸ *n.* A sticky substance that is smeared on branches or twigs to capture small birds.

bird of paradise ▸ *n., pl.* **birds of paradise.** **1.** Any of various New Guinean birds usu. having brilliant plumage and long tail feathers in the male. **2.** A plant having showy orange and blue flowers.

bird's-eye (bûrdz′ī′) ▸ *adj.* Marked with a spot or spots resembling a bird's eye.

bird·shot (bûrd′shŏt′) ▸ *n.* A small lead shot for shotgun shells.

bi·ret·ta (bə-rĕt′ə) ▸ *n.* A stiff square cap worn esp. by the Roman Catholic clergy.

birr (bîr) ▸ *n., pl.* **birr** or **birrs.** See **currency** table in Appendix.

birth (bûrth) ▸ *n.* **1a.** The fact of being born. **b.** The act of bearing young. **2.** Origin or ancestry: *of Iraqi birth.* **3.** A beginning or commencement. ▸ *v.* **1.** *Regional* To deliver (a baby). **2.** To bear (a child).

birth canal ▸ *n.* The passage from the uterus through the cervix, vagina, and vulva.

birth control ▸ *n.* Voluntary control of the number of children conceived, esp. by use of contraceptive techniques.

birth·day (bûrth′dā′) ▸ *n.* The day or anniversary of one's birth.

birth defect ▸ *n.* A physiological abnormality present at the time of birth, esp. as a result of faulty development, heredity, or injury.

birth family ▸ *n.* A family consisting of one's biological, as opposed to adoptive, parents and their offspring.

birth·mark (bûrth′märk′) ▸ *n.* A mole or blemish present on the skin from birth.

birth parent ▸ *n.* A biological parent.

birth·place (bûrth′plās′) ▸ *n.* The place where someone is born or something originates.

birth·rate (bûrth′rāt′) ▸ *n.* The ratio of live births to total population in a specified community or area over a specified period.

birth·right (bûrth′rīt′) ▸ *n.* A right, possession, or privilege that is one's due by birth.

birth·stone (bûrth′stōn′) ▸ *n.* A gemstone associated with the specific month of a person's birth.

bis·cuit (bĭs′kĭt) ▸ *n.* **1.** A small cake of bread leavened with baking powder or soda. **2.** *Chiefly Brit.* **a.** A thin crisp cracker. **b.** A cookie. **3.** A pale brown.

bi·sect (bī′sĕkt′, bī-sĕkt′) ▸ *v.* **1.** To cut or divide into two parts, esp. two equal parts. **2.** To split; fork. **—bi·sec′tion** *n.* **—bi′sec′tor** *n.*

bi·sex·u·al (bī-sĕk′shōō-əl) ▸ *adj.* **1.** Of or relating to both sexes. **2.** Having both male and female organs. **3.** Of or having a sexual orientation to persons of either sex. **—bi·sex′u·al** *n.* **—bi′sex·u·al′i·ty** (-ăl′ĭ-tē) *n.* **—bi·sex′u·al·ly** *adv.*

bish·op (bĭsh′əp) ▸ *n.* **1.** A high-ranking Christian cleric, usu. in charge of a diocese. **2.** *Games* A chess piece that can move diagonally across any number of free spaces.

bish·op·ric (bĭsh′ə-prĭk) ▸ *n.* The office, rank, or diocese of a bishop.

Bis·marck (bĭz′märk′) ▸ The capital of ND, in the S-central part.

Bismarck, Prince **Otto Eduard Leopold von.** "the Iron Chancellor" (1815–98) ▸ Creator and first chancellor of the German Empire (1871–90).

Bismarck Archipelago ▸ A group of volcanic islands and islets of Papua New Guinea in the SW Pacific.

bis·muth (bĭz′məth) ▸ *n.* *Symbol* **Bi** A white, crystalline, brittle metallic element used in low-melting alloys. At. no. 83.

bi·son (bī′sən, -zən) ▸ *n.* A bovine mammal of W North America, having a shaggy mane and massive head with short curved horns; buffalo.

bisque (bĭsk) ▸ *n.* **1.** A cream soup made esp. from meat or seafood. **2.** Ice cream mixed with crushed macaroons or nuts.

bis·tro (bē′strō, bĭs′trō) ▸ *n., pl.* **-tros.** **1.** A small bar, tavern, or nightclub. **2.** A small informal restaurant.

bit[1] (bĭt) ▸ *n.* **1.** A small portion, degree, or amount. **2.** A

THESAURUS

biosphere *n.* *—See* ENVIRONMENT (3).

bird *n.* *—See* HISS (2).

bird *v.* *—See* HISS (2).

birdbrained *adj.* *—See* GIDDY (2), STUPID.

bird-dog *v.* *—See* FOLLOW (3).

birth *n.* **1.** The act or process of bringing forth young ▸ accouchement, birthing, childbearing, childbirth, delivery, labor, lying-in, nativity, parturition, travail. **2.** The initial stage of a developmental process ▸ beginning, commencement, dawn, embarkation, genesis, inception, nascence, nascency, onset, opening, origin, outset, spring, start. *—See also* ANCESTRY, NOBILITY.

birth *v.* *—See* BEAR (4).

birthing *n.* *—See* BIRTH (1).

birthplace *n.* *—See* ORIGIN.

birthright *n.* Any special privilege accorded a firstborn ▸ heritage, inheritance, legacy, patrimony. *—See also* RIGHT.

bishop *n.* *—See* CLERIC.

bit[1] *n.* **1.** A tiny amount ▸ crumb, dab, dash, dot, dram, drop, fragment, grain,

moment. 3. An entertainment routine; act. 4. A particular kind of action or behavior: *got tired of the macho bit.* 5. *Informal* An amount equal to ⅛ of a dollar. ***—idioms:* a bit** Somewhat: *a bit warm.* **bit by bit** Gradually.

bit² (bĭt) ▸ *n.* 1. The sharp part of a tool, such as the cutting edge of an ax. 2. A pointed and threaded tool for drilling and boring that is secured in a brace, bitstock, or drill press. 3. The metal mouthpiece of a horse's bridle.

bit³ (bĭt) ▸ *n. Comp. Sci.* A fundamental unit of information having just two possible values, as either of the binary digits 0 or 1.

bitch (bĭch) ▸ *n.* 1. A female canine animal, esp. a dog. 2. *Offensive Slang* A spiteful or overbearing woman. 3. *Slang* A complaint. 4. *Slang* Something very unpleasant or difficult. ▸ *v. Slang* To complain. **—bitch′y** *adj.*

bite (bīt) ▸ *v.* **bit** (bĭt), **bit·ten** (bĭt′n) or **bit, bit·ing.** 1. To cut, grip, or tear with or as if with the teeth. 2. To pierce the skin of with or as if with fangs. 3. To cut into with or as if with a sharp instrument. 4. To corrode. 5. To take or swallow bait. ▸ *n.* 1. The act of biting. 2. A skin wound or puncture produced by biting. 3a. A stinging or smarting sensation. b. An incisive, penetrating quality. 4a. A mouthful. b. *Informal* A light meal or snack. 5. The act of taking bait. 6. The angle at which the upper and lower teeth meet; occlusion. ***—idioms:* bite the bullet** *Slang* To face a painful situation bravely and stoically. **bite the dust** *Slang* To fall dead, esp. in combat. **—bit′er** *n.*

bite·wing (bīt′wĭng′) ▸ *n.* A dental x-ray film with a central projection on which the teeth can close.

bit·ing (bī′tĭng) ▸ *adj.* 1. Causing a stinging sensation. 2. Incisive; penetrating.

bit map ▸ *n. Comp. Sci.* A set of bits representing a graphic image, with each bit or group of bits corresponding to a pixel in the image. **—bit′-mapped′** *adj.*

bit·ter (bĭt′ər) ▸ *adj.* **-er, -est.** 1. Having or being a taste that is sharp and unpleasant. 2. Causing sharp pain to the body or great discomfort to the mind: *a bitter wind; bitter sorrow.* 3. Proceeding from or exhibiting strong animosity. 4. Having or marked by resentment or disappointment: *bitter feelings.* ▸ *adv.* In an intense or harsh way; bitterly: *a bitter cold night.* ▸ *n.* **bitters** A bitter, usu. alcoholic liquid that is made with herbs or roots and is used in cocktails or as a tonic. **—bit′ter·ly** *adv.* **—bit′ter·ness** *n.*

bit·tern (bĭt′ərn) ▸ *n.* A wading bird having mottled brownish plumage and a deep booming cry.

bit·ter·sweet (bĭt′ər-swēt′) ▸ *n.* 1. A woody vine having small, round, yellow-orange fruits that split open to expose red seeds. 2. See **bittersweet nightshade.** ▸ *adj.* 1. Bitter and sweet at the same time. 2. Producing or expressing a mixture of pain and pleasure.

bit·ty (bĭt′ē) ▸ *adj.* **-ti·er, -ti·est.** *Informal* Tiny. **—bit·ti·ness** *n.*

bi·tu·men (bĭ-to͞o′mən, -tyo͞o′-, bī-) ▸ *n.* Any of various flammable mixtures of hydrocarbons and other substances that are constituents of asphalt and tar.

bi·tu·mi·nous (bĭ-to͞o′mə-nəs, -tyo͞o′-, bī-) ▸ *adj.* Like or containing bitumen.

bituminous coal ▸ *n.* A mineral coal with a high percentage of volatile matter that burns with a smoky yellow flame; soft coal.

bi·va·lent (bī-vā′lənt) ▸ *adj. Chem.* Divalent.

bi·valve (bī′vălv′) ▸ *n.* A mollusk, such as an oyster or clam, that has a shell consisting of two hinged valves. **—bi′valve′** *adj.*

biv·ou·ac (bĭv′o͞o-ăk′, bĭv′wăk′) ▸ *n.* A temporary encampment, esp. one made by soldiers. ▸ *v.* **-acked, -ack·ing.** To camp in a bivouac.

bi·week·ly (bī-wēk′lē) ▸ *adj.* 1. Happening every two weeks. 2. Happening twice a week; semiweekly. ▸ *n., pl.* **-lies.** A publication issued every two weeks. **—bi·week′ly** *adv.*

bi·year·ly (bī-yîr′lē) ▸ *adj.* 1. Happening every two years. 2. Happening twice a year; semiyearly. **—bi·year′ly** *adv.*

bi·zarre (bĭ-zär′) ▸ *adj.* Strikingly unconventional in style or appearance; odd. **—bi·zarre′ly** *adv.*

Bk ▸ The symbol for the element **berkelium.**

blab (blăb) ▸ *v.* **blabbed, blab·bing.** 1. To reveal (secret matters) esp. through careless talk. 2. To chatter indiscreetly. **—blab** *n.*

blab·ber (blăb′ər) ▸ *v.* To chatter; blab. **—blab′ber** *n.*

blab·ber·mouth (blăb′ər-mouth′) ▸ *n. Informal* A gossip or chatterbox.

black (blăk) ▸ *adj.* **-er, -est.** 1. Being of the color black. 2. Without light: *a black, moonless night.* 3. often **Black** a. Of or belonging to a racial group having brown to black skin, esp. one of African origin. b. African-American. 4. Soiled, as from soot; dirty. 5. Evil; wicked: *black deeds.* 6. Depressing; gloomy. 7. Angry; sullen. 8. Marked by morbid or grimly satiric humor: *a black comedy.* ▸ *n.* 1. The achromatic color of maximum darkness; the color of objects that absorb nearly all light of all visible wavelengths. 2. Absence of light; darkness. 3. Something colored black, esp. clothing worn for mourning. 4. often **Black** a. A member of a racial group having brown to black skin. b. An African American. ▸ *v.* To make or become black. ***—phrasal verb:* black out** 1. To lose consciousness or memory temporarily. 2. To produce or cause a blackout. ***—idiom:* in the black** On the credit side of a ledger. **—black′ish** *adj.* **—black′ly** *adv.* **—black′ness** *n.*

black-and-blue (blăk′ən-blo͞o′) ▸ *adj.* Discolored from bruising.

THESAURUS

iota, jot, little, minim, mite, modicum, molecule, morsel, nip, ort, ounce, particle, pinch, scrap, scruple, shard, shred, smidgen, snip, snippet, speck, tad, tittle, trifle, whit. [*Compare* FLAKE, PART, SHADE.] 2. A small portion of food ▸ bite, crumb, dollop, morsel, mouthful, piece, scrap, slice, sliver, swallow, taste, tidbit. [*Compare* DROP.] 3. A rather short period ▸ interval, space, spell, time, while. [*Compare* FLASH.] 4. *Informal* A characteristic behavior or performance ▸ act. *Slang:* number, routine, shtick. —*See also* ITEM.

bit² *n.* —*See* BRAKE.

bit *v.* —*See* RESTRAIN.

bitch *v.* —*See* COMPLAIN.

bitch *n.* —*See* COMPLAINT.

bitchy *adj.* —*See* MALEVOLENT.

bite *v.* —*See* CHEW, ERODE, HURT (2).

bite *n.* —*See* BIT¹ (2), EDGE, REFRESHMENT.

biting *adj.* So sharp as to cause mental pain ▸ acerbic, acid, acidic, acrid, astringent, catty, caustic, corrosive, cutting, harsh, mordacious, mordant, pungent, scathing, scorching, searing, sharp, sharp-tongued, slashing, stinging, trenchant, truculent, venomous, vitriolic, waspish, withering. [*Compare* ILL-TEMPERED, RESENTFUL, SARCASTIC.] —*See also* SHARP (3).

bits and pieces *n.* —*See* ODDS AND ENDS.

bitter *adj.* 1. Having a sharp, unpleasant, alkaline taste or smell ▸ acerbic, acrid, brackish, briny, harsh, pungent. [*Compare* SOUR.] 2. Painfully intense ▸ brutal, cruel, hard, harsh, penetrating, punishing, racking, relentless, rigorous, rough, severe, stinging, tough. [*Compare* BLEAK, INTENSE, SHARP.] 3. Difficult to accept or bear ▸ disagreeable, distasteful, galling, indigestible, painful, unpalatable, unpleasant. [*Compare* DISTURBING, UNBEARABLE, VEXATIOUS.] —*See also* RESENTFUL.

bitterness *n.* —*See* RESENTMENT, SARCASM.

bizarre *adj.* Conceived or done with no reference to reality or common sense ▸ antic, fantastic, fantastical, far-fetched, grotesque. —*See also* ECCENTRIC, EXOTIC.

bizarrely *adv.* —*See* UNUSUALLY.

blab *v.* —*See* BETRAY (2), CHATTER (1), GOSSIP.

blab *n.* —*See* CHATTER, GOSSIP (2).

blabber *v.* —*See* CHATTER (1).

blabber *n.* —*See* CHATTER.

blabby *adj.* Inclined to gossip ▸ gossipy, talebearing, taletelling.

black *adj.* 1. Of the darkest color ▸ blue-black, coal-black, ebon, ebony, inky, jet, jet-black, jetty, onyx, pitch-black, pitchy, raven, sable, sooty. 2. Having little or no light ▸ dark, inky, lightless, moonless, pitch-dark, starless, sunless, unlit. *Idiom:* as black as pitch. [*Compare* SHADY.] —*See also* DARK (2), DIRTY, EVIL, GLOOMY, MALEVOLENT.

black *v.* —*See* DIRTY.

black out *v.* —*See* CENSOR (2), FAINT.

black and white ▸ *n.* **1.** Writing or print. **2.** A visual medium, such as photography, using black and white, and sometimes values of gray. **—black′-and-white′** *adj.*

black·ball (blăk′bôl′) ▸ *n.* **1.** A negative vote, esp. one that blocks the admission of an applicant to an organization. **2.** A small black ball used as a negative ballot. ▸ *v.* **1.** To vote against (e.g., an applicant). **2.** To ostracize.

black bear ▸ *n.* The common North American bear, having a black or dark brown coat.

black belt ▸ *n.* **1.** The rank of expert in a martial art such as judo or karate. **2.** The black sash that symbolizes this rank.

black·ber·ry (blăk′bĕr′ē) ▸ *n.* **1.** Any of various shrubs having usu. prickly, canelike stems and black or purplish edible fruit. **2.** The fruit of these plants.

black·bird (blăk′bûrd′) ▸ *n.* Any of various birds, such as the grackle or cowbird, having predominantly black plumage.

black·board (blăk′bôrd′) ▸ *n.* A smooth panel for writing on with chalk.

black·bod·y (blăk′bŏd′ē) ▸ *n.* A theoretically perfect absorber of all incident radiation.

black box ▸ *n.* **1.** A usu. electronic device with known performance characteristics but unknown constituents and means of operation. **2.** See **flight recorder.**

Black Death ▸ *n.* A form of bubonic plague pandemic in Europe and Asia in the 14th cent.

black·en (blăk′ən) ▸ *v.* **1.** To make or become black. **2.** To defame. **—black′en·er** *n.*

black eye ▸ *n.* **1.** Bruised discoloration of the skin around the eye. **2.** A dishonored reputation.

black-eyed Su·san (blăk′īd′ so͞o′zən) ▸ *n.* A plant having daisylike flowers with orange-yellow rays and dark brown centers.

black·face (blăk′fās′) ▸ *n.* Makeup for a conventionalized comic travesty of Black people, esp. in a minstrel show.

black·fish (blăk′fĭsh′) ▸ *n.* See **pilot whale.**

Black·foot (blăk′fo͝ot′) ▸ *n., pl.* **-foot** or **-feet. 1.** A member of a Native American confederacy of three tribes inhabiting the N Great Plains from central Alberta to NW Montana. **2.** Their Algonquian language.

Black Forest ▸ A mountainous region of SW Germany.

black·guard (blăg′ərd, -ärd′) ▸ *n.* A thoroughly unprincipled person; scoundrel.

Black Hawk (1767–1838) ▸ Sauk leader in the Black Hawk War (1832).

black·head (blăk′hĕd′) ▸ *n.* A plug of dried fatty matter that clogs a pore in the skin and is blackened at the surface.

Black Hills ▸ A group of mountains of SW SD and NE WY.

black hole ▸ *n.* An area of space-time with a gravitational field so intense that nothing can escape, not even light.

black·jack (blăk′jăk′) ▸ *n.* **1.** A small leather-covered bludgeon with a short flexible shaft. **2.** A card game in which the object is to accumulate cards with a higher count than that of the dealer but not exceeding 21.

black light ▸ *n.* Invisible ultraviolet or infrared radiation.

black·list (blăk′lĭst′) ▸ *n.* A list of disapproved persons or organizations. ▸ *v.* To place on a blacklist.

black lung ▸ *n.* A lung disease caused by the long-term inhalation of coal dust.

black magic ▸ *n.* Magic practiced for evil purposes or in league with evil spirits.

black·mail (blăk′māl′) ▸ *n.* **1.** Extortion by the threat of exposing something criminal or discreditable. **2.** Something extorted by blackmail. **—black′mail′** *v.* **—black′mail′er** *n.*

black market ▸ *n.* The illegal buying or selling of goods or currency. **—black′-mar′ket·er, black′-mar′ket·eer′** *n.*

black·out (blăk′out′) ▸ *n.* **1.** The concealment or extinguishment of lights that might be visible to enemy aircraft during an air raid. **2.** Lack of illumination caused by an electrical power failure. **3.** A temporary loss of memory or consciousness. **4a.** A suppression, as of news, by censorship. **b.** Restriction of local telecasting of a sports event.

black pepper ▸ *n.* **1.** A peppercorn. **2.** A pungent spice made from ground peppercorns.

Black Power ▸ *n.* A movement among Black Americans to achieve equality through Black political and cultural institutions.

Black Sea ▸ An inland sea between Europe and Asia.

black sheep ▸ *n.* A member of a family or group who is considered undesirable or disgraceful.

black·smith (blăk′smĭth′) ▸ *n.* One who forges and shapes iron with an anvil and hammer.

black·snake (blăk′snāk′) ▸ *n.* Any of various dark-colored, chiefly nonvenomous snakes.

black·thorn (blăk′thôrn′) ▸ *n.* A thorny Eurasian shrub with white flowers and bluish-black, plumlike fruits used as a flavoring.

black·top (blăk′tŏp′) ▸ *n.* A bituminous material, such as asphalt, used to pave roads.

black widow ▸ *n.* A black spider, the female of which has red markings and produces extremely toxic venom.

blad·der (blăd′ər) ▸ *n. Anat.* Any of various distensible membranous sacs, such as the urinary bladder or the swim bladder, found in most animals and that serve as receptacles for fluid or gas.

blade (blād) ▸ *n.* **1.** The flat-edged cutting part of a sharpened weapon or tool. **2.** A dashing youth. **3.** A flat thin part or structure similar to a blade: *the blade of an oar; a blade of grass.* ▸ *v.* **blad·ed, blad·ing.** To skate on in-line skates. **—blad′ed** *adj.*

blain (blān) ▸ *n.* A skin swelling or sore.

Blair (blâr), **Anthony Charles Lynton.** "Tony" (b. 1953) ▸ British prime minister (1997–2007).

blam·a·ble also **blame·a·ble** (blā′mə-bəl) ▸ *adj.* Deserving blame; culpable. **—blam′a·bly** *adv.*

blame (blām) ▸ *v.* **blamed, blam·ing. 1.** To hold responsible. **2.** To find fault with; censure. ▸ *n.* **1.** Responsibility for a fault or error; culpability. **2.** Censure, as for a fault; condemnation. **—blame′less** *adj.*

blame·wor·thy (blām′wûr′thē) ▸ *adj.* Deserving blame. **—blame′wor′thi·ness** *n.*

Blanc (blăngk, bläɴ), **Mont** ▸ The highest peak of the Alps, rising to 4,810.2 m (15,771 ft) in SE France on the Italian border.

blanch (blănch) ▸ *v.* **1.** To bleach. **2.** To make or become pale or white. **3.** To scald (food) briefly, as before freezing.

blanc·mange (blə-mänj′, -mäɴzh′) ▸ *n.* A flavored, sweet milk pudding.

bland (blănd) ▸ *adj.* **-er, -est. 1.** Characterized by a moderate, unperturbed, or tranquil quality. **2.** Not irritating; soothing: *a bland diet.* **3.** Lacking a distinctive character; dull and insipid. **—bland′ly** *adv.* **—bland′ness** *n.*

blan·dish (blăn′dĭsh) ▸ *v.* To coax by flattery or wheedling; cajole. **—blan′dish·ment** *n.*

THESAURUS

blackball *v.* —*See* EXCLUDE, VETO.

blacken *v.* —*See* DENIGRATE, DIRTY.

black eye *n.* A bruise surrounding the eye ▸ *Informal:* mouse. *Slang:* shiner. [*Compare* BRUISE.] —*See also* STAIN.

blackleg *n.* —*See* CHEAT (2).

blacklist *v.* —*See* EXCLUDE.

blackmail *v.* —*See* EXTORT.

blackout *n.* ▸ faint, fainting spell, swoon, syncope.

black-tie *adj.* —*See* FORMAL.

blade *n.* The cutting part of a sharp instrument ▸ edge, knife blade, knife-edge, razor, razorblade.

blah *adj.* —*See* BORING, DEPRESSED (1), DULL (1).

blamable *adj.* —*See* BLAMEWORTHY.

blame *n.* Responsibility for an error or crime ▸ blameworthiness, culpability, fault, guilt, onus. *Slang:* rap. [*Compare* BURDEN[1], ERROR, RESPONSIBILITY.] —*See also* CRITICISM.

blame *v.* —*See* ACCUSE, CRITICIZE (1), FIX (3).

blamed *adj.* —*See* DAMNED.

blameful *adj.* —*See* BLAMEWORTHY.

blameless *adj.* —*See* EXEMPLARY, INNOCENT (2).

blameworthy *adj.* Deserving blame ▸ blamable, blameful, censurable, culpable, guilty, red-handed, reprehensible. *Idioms:* at fault, in error (*or* the wrong), to blame. [*Compare* LIABLE.]

blanch *v.* —*See* COOK, PALE.

bland *adj.* Without definite or distinctive characteristics ▸ colorless, indistinctive, neutral. [*Compare* BORING.] —*See also* FLAT (2), INSIPID, ORDINARY.

blandish *v.* —*See* COAX, FLATTER (1).

blandishment *n.* —*See* FLATTERY.

blandness *n.* —*See* DULLNESS, INSIPIDITY.

blank (blăngk) ▸ *adj.* **-er, -est.** 1a. Devoid of writing, images, or marks. b. Containing no information: *a blank diskette.* 2. Not completed or filled in. 3. Not having received final processing: *a blank key.* 4. Lacking thought, impression, or expression; vacant: *a blank mind.* 5. Appearing dazed or confused; bewildered: *a blank stare.* 6. Absolute; complete: *a blank refusal.* ▸ *n.* 1. An empty space or place; void. 2a. A space to be filled in on a document. b. A document with such spaces. 3. An unfinished manufactured article ready for final processing: *a key blank.* 4. A gun cartridge with a powder charge but no bullet. ▸ *v.* 1. To remove, as from view; obliterate. 2. *Sports* To prevent (an opponent) from scoring. 3. To become abstracted: *My mind blanked out for a few seconds.* **—blank′ly** *adv.* **—blank′ness** *n.*

blank check ▸ *n.* 1. A signed check without the amount filled in. 2. Total freedom of action.

blan·ket (blăng′kĭt) ▸ *n.* 1. A piece of woven material used as a covering. 2. A layer that covers or encloses. ▸ *adj.* Applying to all conditions, instances, or members: *a blanket insurance policy.* ▸ *v.* To cover with or as if with a blanket.

blank verse ▸ *n.* Unrhymed verse, esp. in iambic pentameter.

blare (blâr) ▸ *v.* **blared, blar·ing.** To sound or cause to sound loudly and stridently. **—blare** *n.*

blar·ney (blär′nē) ▸ *n.* Smooth, flattering talk.

bla·sé (blä-zā′) ▸ *adj.* 1. Uninterested or bored. 2. Very sophisticated.

blas·pheme (blăs-fēm′, blăs′fēm′) ▸ *v.* **-phemed, -phem·ing.** To speak of (God or a sacred entity) in an irreverent, impious manner. **—blas·phem′er** *n.* **—blas′phe·mous** *adj.* **—blas′phe·mous·ly** *adv.* **—blas′phe·my** *n.*

blast (blăst) ▸ *n.* 1. A strong gust of wind. 2. A forcible stream of air, gas, or steam from an opening. 3. A sudden loud sound, as of a whistle or trumpet. 4. An explosion, as of dynamite or a bomb. 5. Any of various plant diseases; blight. 6. A powerful hit, blow, or shot. 7. A violent verbal assault. 8. *Slang* A highly exciting or pleasurable experience. ▸ *v.* 1. To explode. 2. To sound loudly; blare. 3. To hit with great force. 4. To have a harmful or destructive effect (on). 5. To criticize vigorously. 6. To shoot. ***—phrasal verb:*** **blast off** To take off, as a rocket or space vehicle. ***—idiom:*** **full blast** At full speed, volume, or capacity. **—blast′er** *n.*

blast furnace ▸ *n.* A furnace in which combustion is intensified by a blast of air.

blast-off (blăst′ôf′, -ŏf′) ▸ *n.* The launch, esp. of a rocket or space vehicle.

bla·tant (blāt′nt) ▸ *adj.* 1. Unpleasantly loud and noisy. 2. Offensively conspicuous or undisguised: *a blatant lie.* **—bla′tan·cy** *n.* **—bla′tant·ly** *adv.*

blath·er (blăth′ər) ▸ *v.* To talk foolishly or nonsensically. **—blath′er** *n.* **—blath′er·er** *n.*

blaze[1] (blāz) ▸ *n.* 1a. A brilliant burst of fire; flame. b. A destructive fire. 2. A bright, direct, or steady light: *the blaze of the desert sun.* 3. A brilliant, striking display: *a blaze of color.* 4. A sudden outburst, as of activity or emotion. 5. **blazes** Used as an intensive: *Where in blazes are my keys?* ▸ *v.* **blazed, blaz·ing.** 1. To burn or shine brightly. 2. To show strong emotion. 3. To shoot rapidly and continuously.

blaze[2] (blāz) ▸ *n.* 1. A white or light-colored spot on the face of an animal. 2. A mark cut or painted on a tree to indicate a trail. ▸ *v.* **blazed, blaz·ing.** To indicate (a trail) by marking trees with blazes.

blaz·er (blā′zər) ▸ *n.* An informal sports jacket.

bla·zon (blā′zən) ▸ *v.* 1. To adorn or embellish with or as if with a coat of arms. 2. To display ostentatiously. ▸ *n.* A coat of arms. **—bla′zon·ry** *n.*

bleach (blēch) ▸ *v.* To make or become white or colorless. ▸ *n.* A chemical agent used for bleaching.

bleach·ers (blē′chərz) ▸ *pl.n.* An outdoor grandstand for seating spectators.

bleak (blēk) ▸ *adj.* **-er, -est.** 1. Dreary and somber; depressing: *a bleak prognosis.* 2. Cold; raw: *bleak winds.* 3. Exposed to the elements; barren. **—bleak′ly** *adv.* **—bleak′ness** *n.*

blear (blîr) ▸ *v.* 1. To blur or redden (the eyes) with or as if with tears. 2. To dim or obscure; blur. ▸ *adj.* Indistinct. **—blear′i·ly** *adv.* **—blear′i·ness** *n.* **—blear′y** *adj.*

bleat (blēt) ▸ *n.* 1. The characteristic cry of a goat, sheep, or calf. 2. A sound similar to this cry. **—bleat** *v.*

bleed (blēd) ▸ *v.* **bled** (blĕd), **bleed·ing.** 1a. To emit or lose blood. b. To extract blood from. 2. To feel sympathetic grief or anguish: *My heart bleeds for you.* 3. To exude or extract a fluid such as sap (from). 4. To extort money from. 5. To run together, as dyes on wet cloth or paper. 6. To draw or drain liquid or gaseous contents from: *bleed the pipes.*

bleed·er (blē′dər) ▸ *n.* One that bleeds freely, esp. a hemophiliac.

bleed·ing heart (blē′dĭng) ▸ *n.* 1. A garden plant having arching pink heart-shaped flowers. 2. One who is excessively sympathetic toward others.

bleep (blēp) ▸ *n.* A brief high-pitched electronic sound. ▸ *v.* 1. To emit a bleep or bleeps. 2. To edit out (spoken material) from a broadcast or recording, esp. by replacing with bleeps.

THESAURUS

blank *adj.* —*See* EMPTY (1), EXPRESSIONLESS, VACANT.

blanket *n.* —*See* COAT (2).

blanket *v.* —*See* COVER (1).

blanket *adj.* —*See* GENERAL (1).

blankness *n.* —*See* EMPTINESS (1), EMPTINESS (2), NOTHINGNESS (2).

blare *v.* —*See* SHOUT.

blaring *adj.* —*See* LOUD.

blarney *n.* —*See* BABBLE, FLATTERY.

blasé *adj.* —*See* APATHETIC.

blaspheme *v.* To use profane, obscene, or impious language ▸ curse, damn, swear. *Informal:* cuss. —*See also* REVILE.

blasphemous *adj.* Showing irreverence and contempt for something sacred ▸ impious, profane, sacrilegious.

blasphemy *n.* —*See* SACRILEGE, SWEARWORD.

blast *n.* 1. An explosive noise ▸ bang, boom, crash, crump, reverberation, rumble, roar, sonic boom, thunder. [*Compare* CLASH, CRACK, NOISE.] 2. A violent release of confined energy ▸ blowout, blowup, burst, detonation, discharge, eruption, explosion, flare-up, fulmination. [*Compare* BARRAGE.] 3. *Slang* A big, exuberant party ▸ celebration, shindig, shindy. *Informal:* to-do, wingding. *Slang:* bash, blowout. [*Compare* BENDER, BINGE.] —*See also* WIND[1].

blast *v.* 1. To make an explosive noise ▸ bang, boom, crash, roar, rumble, thunder. [*Compare* CRACK.] 2. To spoil or destroy ▸ blight, corrode, corrupt, dash, nip, scorch, shrivel, wither. [*Compare* DESTROY, RUIN.] 3. To discharge a gun or firearm ▸ blast away, fire (away *or* off), pop (off), shoot (away *or* off). *Idioms:* go bang-bang, open fire, take a shot (*or* potshot). —*See also* EXPLODE (1), SLAM (1).

blasted *adj.* —*See* BLEAK (1), DAMNED.

blatancy *n.* —*See* IMPUDENCE.

blatant *adj.* —*See* IMPUDENT, OBVIOUS, VOCIFEROUS.

blather *n.* —*See* BABBLE, NONSENSE.

blather *v.* —*See* BABBLE.

blatherskite *n.* —*See* BABBLE.

blaze[1] *n.* 1. The visible signs of combustion ▸ conflagration, fire, flame, flare-up. 2. An intense blinding light ▸ dazzle, flare, glare.

blaze *v.* —*See* BEAM, BURN (2), GLARE (2).

blaze[2] *v.* —*See* ANNOUNCE.

blazing *adj.* —*See* BRILLIANT, BURNING, PASSIONATE.

blazon *v.* —*See* ANNOUNCE.

bleach *v.* —*See* PALE.

bleak *adj.* 1. Marked by cold and unpleasant conditions ▸ austere, blasted, dour, exposed, forbidding, foul, grim, hard, harsh, inclement, nasty, raw, severe, stark, unsheltered, windswept. [*Compare* BARREN, BITTER, LONELY.] 2. Offering very little encouragement ▸ dark, depressing, dim, discouraging, dismal, downbeat, gloomy, inauspicious, pessimistic, unencouraging, unpromising, unpropitious. [*Compare* DOUBTFUL, UNFAVORABLE.] —*See also* GLOOMY.

blear *v.* —*See* OBSCURE.

blear *adj.* —*See* UNCLEAR.

bleary *adj.* —*See* TIRED (1), UNCLEAR.

bleed *v.* —*See* DRAIN (1), OOZE.

bleep *v.* —*See* CENSOR (1).

blem·ish (blĕm′ĭsh) ► *v.* To mar, spoil, or impair by a flaw. ► *n.* A flaw or defect.
blench (blĕnch) ► *v.* To draw back, as from fear; flinch.
blend (blĕnd) ► *v.* **blend·ed** or **blent** (blĕnt), **blend·ing**. **1.** To make or form a uniform mixture. **2.** To combine (varieties or grades) to obtain a new mixture: *blend whiskeys.* **3.** To become merged into one; unite. **4.** To create a harmonious effect or result: *colors that blend well.* ► *n.* **1.** Something blended: *a blend of coffee and chicory.* **2.** *Ling.* A word produced by combining parts of other words, as *smog* from *smoke* and *fog.*
blend·er (blĕn′dər) ► *n.* One that blends, esp. an appliance for chopping, mixing, or liquefying foods.
bless (blĕs) ► *v.* **blessed** or **blest** (blĕst), **bless·ing**. **1.** To make holy by religious rite; sanctify. **2.** To make the sign of the cross over. **3.** To invoke divine favor upon. **4.** To honor as holy; glorify: *Bless the Lord.* **5.** To confer well-being or prosperity upon. **6.** To endow, as with talent.
bless·ed (blĕs′ĭd) ► *adj.* **1.** Worthy of worship; holy. **2.** Enjoying happiness; fortunate. **3.** Bringing happiness or pleasure. **4.** Used as an intensive: *I don't have a blessed dime.* **—bless′ed·ly** *adv.* **—bless′ed·ness** *n.*
bless·ing (blĕs′ĭng) ► *n.* **1.** The act or ceremony of one who blesses. **2.** A short prayer said at a meal; grace. **3.** Something promoting or contributing to happiness, well-being, or prosperity; boon. **4.** Approbation; approval: *This plan has my blessing.*
blew[1] (blo͞o) ► *v.* P.t. of **blow[1]**.
blew[2] (blo͞o) ► *v.* P.t. of **blow[3]**.
blight (blīt) ► *n.* **1.** A plant disease caused esp. by a bacterium, fungus, or virus. **2.** An adverse environmental condition, such as air pollution. **3.** Something that impairs growth or withers hopes. ► *v.* **1.** To affect with blight. **2.** To ruin. **3.** To frustrate.
blimp (blĭmp) ► *n.* A nonrigid, buoyant airship.
blind (blīnd) ► *adj.* **-er, -est.** **1a.** Sightless. **b.** Greatly impaired in vision. **2.** Of or for sightless persons. **3.** Performed by instruments and without the use of sight: *blind navigation.* **4.** Unable or unwilling to perceive or understand: *blind to a child's faults.* **5.** Not based on reason or evidence: *blind faith.* **6.** Hidden or screened from sight: *a blind seam; a blind intersection.* **7.** Closed at one end: *a blind passage.* **8.** Having no opening: *a blind wall.* ► *n.* **1.** Something, such as a window shade, that shuts out light. **2.** A shelter for concealing hunters. **3.** A subterfuge. ► *adv.* **1.** Without seeing; blindly. **2.** Used as an intensive: *Thieves robbed us blind.* ► *v.* **1.** To deprive of sight. **2.** To dazzle. **3.** To deprive of perception, insight, or reason: *Prejudice blinded them.* **—blind′ly** *adv.* **—blind′ness** *n.*
blind date ► *n.* **1.** A social engagement between two persons who have not previously met. **2.** Either of the persons participating in such a date.
blind·ers (blīn′dərz) ► *pl.n.* A pair of leather flaps attached to a horse's bridle to curtail side vision.
blind·fold (blīnd′fōld′) ► *v.* **1.** To cover the eyes of with or as if with a bandage to prevent seeing. **2.** To mislead or delude. **—blind′fold′** *n.* **—blind′fold′ed** *adj.*
blind side ► *n.* **1.** The side on which one's peripheral vision is obstructed. **2.** The side away from which one is directing one's attention.
blind-side (blīnd′sīd′) ► *v.* **1.** To hit or attack on the blind side. **2.** To take unawares, esp. with harmful results.
blind spot ► *n.* **1.** The small, optically insensitive region of the eye where the optic nerve enters the retina. **2.** A subject about which one is ignorant or prejudiced.
blink (blĭngk) ► *v.* **1.** To close and open (one or both eyes) rapidly. **2.** To flash on and off. **3.** To look with feigned ignorance: *blink at corruption.* ► *n.* **1.** A brief closing of the eyes. **2.** A flash of light; twinkle. ***—idiom:*** **on the blink** Out of working order.
blink·er (blĭng′kər) ► *n.* **1.** One that blinks, esp. a light that conveys a signal. **2. blinkers** See **blinders**.
blintz (blĭnts) ► *n.* A thin rolled pancake usu. filled with cottage cheese and often served with sour cream.
blip (blĭp) ► *n.* **1.** A spot of light on a radar or sonar screen. **2.** A high-pitched electronic sound; bleep. ► *v.* **blipped, blip·ping**. To bleep.
bliss (blĭs) ► *n.* **1.** Extreme happiness; ecstasy. **2.** Religious ecstasy; spiritual joy. **—bliss′ful** *adj.* **—bliss′ful·ly** *adv.*
blis·ter (blĭs′tər) ► *n.* **1.** A local swelling of the skin that contains watery fluid and is caused by burning or irritation. **2.** Something resembling a blister, such as a raised plastic bubble. **—blis′ter** *v.* **—blis′ter·y** *adj.*
blis·ter·ing (blĭs′tər-ĭng) ► *adj.* **1.** Intensely hot. **2.** Harsh; severe: *blistering criticism.* **3.** Very rapid: *a blistering pace.*
blister pack ► *n.* A form of packaging in which the merchandise is sealed into a transparent plastic blister.
blithe (blīth, blīth) ► *adj.* **blith·er, blith·est**. Carefree and lighthearted. **—blithe′ly** *adv.* **—blithe′ness** *n.*
blith·er (blĭth′ər) ► *v.* To blather.
blithe·some (blīth′səm, blīth′-) ► *adj.* Cheerful; merry. **—blithe′some·ly** *adv.* **—blith′some·ness** *n.*
blitz (blĭts) ► *n.* **1a.** A blitzkrieg. **b.** A heavy aerial bombardment. **2.** An intense campaign: *a media blitz.* **3.** *Football* A rushing of the quarterback by the defensive team, esp. in a passing situation. **—blitz** *v.*
blitz·krieg (blĭts′krēg′) ► *n.* A swift, sudden military offensive, usu. by combined air and land forces.
bliz·zard (blĭz′ərd) ► *n.* A very heavy snowstorm with high winds.

THESAURUS

blemish *v.* —*See* DAMAGE, DEFORM.
blemish *n.* —*See* DEFECT, DEFORMITY, STAIN.
blemished *adj.* Having a defect or defects ► amiss, defective, faulty, flawed, imperfect. [*Compare* SHABBY, TRICK.]
blench *v.* —*See* FLINCH.
blend *v.* —*See* BEAT (6), HARMONIZE (2), MIX (1).
blend *n.* —*See* HARMONY (1), MIXTURE.
bless *v.* To make sacred by a religious rite ► consecrate, hallow, sanctify. [*Compare* EXALT.] —*See also* DEVOTE.
blessed *adj.* —*See* DAMNED, HOLY.
blessedness *n.* —*See* HAPPINESS, HOLINESS.
blessing *n.* A short prayer said at meals ► benediction, grace, thanks, thanksgiving. [*Compare* PRAYER[1].] —*See also* ADVANTAGE (2), ENDORSEMENT.
blight *v.* —*See* BLAST (2), DECAY.
blight *n.* —*See* DECAY.
blind *adj.* **1.** Having little or no sight ► blinded, dim-sighted, eyeless, legally blind, sightless, stone-blind, unseeing, unsighted, visionless, visually impaired. **2.** Concealed from view ► hidden, secluded, screened, secret. *Idioms:* out of sight, out of view. [*Compare* HIDDEN.] **3.** Unwilling or unable to perceive ► dull, insensible, obtuse, purblind, uncomprehending, undiscerning, unnoticing, unperceptive, unseeing. [*Compare* IGNORANT.] —*See also* DRUNK.
blind *v.* To confuse with bright light ► bedazzle, daze, dazzle.
blind alley *n.* A course leading nowhere ► cul-de-sac, dead end.
blindness *n.* The condition of not being able to see ► legal blindness, sightlessness, visual impairment.
blink *v.* To open and close one or both eyes rapidly ► bat, flutter, nictitate, twinkle, wink. —*See also* GLITTER, RENEGE, SURRENDER (1).
blink at *v.* To pretend not to see ► connive at, disregard, ignore, overlook, pass over, wink at. *Idioms:* be blind to, close (*or* shut) one's eyes to, let go (*or* pass), look the other way, make allowances for, sweep under the rug, turn a blind eye (*or* deaf ear) to.
blink *n.* A brief closing of the eyes ► bat, flutter, nictitation, wink. —*See also* FLASH (1), FLASH (2).
bliss *n.* —*See* DELIGHT, HAPPINESS, HEAVEN.
blissful *adj.* —*See* DELIGHTFUL.
blister *v.* —*See* SLAM (1).
blister *n.* —*See* BURN, WELT.
blistering *adj.* —*See* HOT (1).
blithe *adj.* —*See* CARELESS, LIGHTHEARTED.
blitheness *n.* A careless, often reckless regard for consequences ► abandon, carelessness, heedlessness, thoughtlessness. [*Compare* TEMERITY.] —*See also* MERRIMENT (1).
blithesome *adj.* —*See* CHEERFUL.
blithesomeness *n.* —*See* MERRIMENT (1).
blitz *n.* —*See* CHARGE (1).
blitz *v.* —*See* BARRAGE.
blitzkrieg *n.* —*See* CHARGE (1).

bloat (blōt) ▸ *v.* To make or become swollen or inflated, as with liquid or gas.

blob (blŏb) ▸ *n.* **1.** A soft formless mass: *a blob of wax.* **2.** A splotch of color. ▸ *v.* **blobbed, blob·bing.** To splotch.

bloc (blŏk) ▸ *n.* A group of nations, parties, or persons united by common interests.

block (blŏk) ▸ *n.* **1.** A solid piece of a hard substance, such as wood or stone, having one or more flat sides. **2.** A stand from which articles are displayed at an auction. **3.** A pulley or a system of pulleys set in a casing. **4.** A set of like items, such as tickets or shares of stock, sold or handled as a unit. **5a.** A section of a city or town bounded on each side by consecutive streets. **b.** A segment of a street bounded by consecutive cross streets. **6.** The act of obstructing. **7.** Something that obstructs; obstacle; hindrance. **8.** *Sports* An act of bodily obstruction. **9.** *Medic.* Interruption, esp. obstruction, of a neural, digestive, or other physiological function. **10.** *Psychol.* Sudden cessation of speech or a thought process without an immediate observable cause. **11.** *Slang* The human head. ▸ *v.* **1.** To support, strengthen, or retain in place by means of a block. **2.** To shape or form with or on a block: *block a hat.* **3a.** To stop or impede the passage of: *block traffic.* **b.** To shut out from view: *a curtain blocking the stage.* **4.** To indicate broadly; sketch: *block out a plan of action.* **5.** *Sports* To obstruct by physical interference. **6.** *Medic.* To interrupt the proper functioning of (a physiological process). **7.** *Psychol.* To fail to remember. **—*idiom:* on the block** Up for sale. **—block′age** *n.* **—block′er** *n.*

block·ade (blŏ-kād′) ▸ *n.* **1.** The hostile isolation of a nation, city, or harbor so as to prevent traffic and commerce. **2.** The forces used in a blockade. ▸ *v.* **-ad·ed, -ad·ing.** To set up a blockade against.

block and tackle ▸ *n.* An apparatus of pulley blocks and ropes or cables used for hauling and hoisting.

block·bust·er (blŏk′bŭs′tər) ▸ *n.* **1.** Something, such as a film, that achieves enormous success. **2.** A high-explosive bomb used for demolition purposes.

block·bust·ing (blŏk′bŭs′tĭng) ▸ *n.* *Informal* The practice of persuading homeowners to sell quickly, usu. at a loss, by appealing to the fear that encroaching minority groups will cause property values to decline.

block·head (blŏk′hĕd′) ▸ *n.* A stupid person.

block·house (blŏk′hous′) ▸ *n.* **1.** A wooden or concrete fortification. **2.** A heavily reinforced building from which the launching of missiles or space vehicles is observed.

bloke (blōk) ▸ *n.* *Chiefly Brit.* A man.

blond also **blonde** (blŏnd) ▸ *adj.* **blond·er, blond·est. 1.** Having light or fair hair and skin. **2.** Of a flaxen or golden color: *blond hair.* ▸ *n.* **1.** A blond person. **2.** A light yellowish brown. **—blond′ish** *adj.* **—blond′ness** *n.*

blood (blŭd) ▸ *n.* **1a.** The fluid consisting of plasma, blood cells, and platelets that is circulated by the heart in vertebrates, carrying oxygen and nutrients to and waste materials away from all body tissues. **b.** A functionally similar fluid in an invertebrate. **2.** A vital force; lifeblood. **3.** Bloodshed; murder. **4.** Temperament or disposition: *hot blood; sporting blood.* **5.** Kinship: *related by blood.* **6.** National or racial ancestry. **7.** Membership; personnel: *new blood in the organization.* **8.** A dandy. **—*idiom:* in cold blood** Deliberately and dispassionately. **—blood′less** *adj.*

blood bank ▸ *n.* A place where whole blood or plasma is stored for use in transfusion.

blood·bath (blŭd′băth′, -bäth′) ▸ *n.* A massacre.

blood count ▸ *n.* A test in which the cells in a blood sample are classified and counted.

blood·cur·dling (blŭd′kûrd′lĭng) ▸ *adj.* Causing great horror; terrifying.

blood·ed (blŭd′ĭd) ▸ *adj.* **1.** Having blood or a temperament of a specified kind: *a cold-blooded reptile.* **2.** Thoroughbred: *blooded horses.*

blood group ▸ *n.* Any of several genetically determined classes of human blood that are based on the presence or absence of certain antigens.

blood·hound (blŭd′hound′) ▸ *n.* A hound with drooping ears, sagging jowls, and a keen sense of smell, used in tracking.

blood·let·ting (blŭd′lĕt′ĭng) ▸ *n.* **1.** Bloodshed. **2.** Phlebotomy.

blood·line (blŭd′līn′) ▸ *n.* Direct line of descent; pedigree.

blood poisoning ▸ *n.* **1.** See **septicemia**. **2.** See **toxemia**.

blood pressure ▸ *n.* The pressure exerted by the blood against the walls of the blood vessels, esp. the arteries.

blood·shed (blŭd′shĕd′) ▸ *n.* The injury or killing of humans.

blood·shot (blŭd′shŏt′) ▸ *adj.* Red and inflamed from congested blood vessels: *bloodshot eyes.*

blood·stain (blŭd′stān′) ▸ *n.* A discoloration caused by blood. **—blood′stained′** *adj.*

blood·stream (blŭd′strēm′) ▸ *n.* The blood flowing through a circulatory system.

blood·suck·er (blŭd′sŭk′ər) ▸ *n.* **1.** An animal, such as a leech, that sucks blood. **2.** An extortionist. **—blood′suck′ing** *adj.*

blood·thirst·y (blŭd′thûr′stē) ▸ *adj.* Eager for bloodshed. **—blood′thirst′i·ly** *adv.* **—blood′thirst′i·ness** *n.*

blood vessel ▸ *n.* An elastic tubular channel, such as an artery, vein, or capillary, through which blood circulates.

blood·y (blŭd′ē) ▸ *adj.* **-i·er, -i·est. 1.** Of, emitting, or stained with blood. **2.** Causing or marked by bloodshed: *a bloody fight.* **3.** Used as an intensive: *a bloody fool.* ▸ *adv.* Used as an intensive: *bloody well right.* ▸ *v.* **-ied, -y·ing.** To stain with or as if with blood. **—blood′i·ly** *adv.* **—blood′i·ness** *n.*

bloody mary also **Bloody Mary** ▸ *n.* A drink made with vodka and tomato juice.

bloom (bloom) ▸ *n.* **1.** The flower of a plant. **2a.** The condition or time of flowering: *a rose in bloom.* **b.** A time of vigor, freshness, and beauty; prime. **3.** A fresh, rosy complexion. **4.** A powdery coating on some fruits or leaves. **5.** A dense growth of plankton. ▸ *v.* **1.** To bear flowers. **2.** To shine with health and vigor; glow. **3.** To grow or flourish.

THESAURUS

bloat *v.* —*See* SWELL.

bloc *n.* An association for a common cause or interest ▸ coalition, league, organization. [*Compare* ASSOCIATION.] —*See also* PUBLIC (1).

block *v.* To cut off from sight ▸ block out, blot (out), conceal, curtain, hide, obscure, obstruct, screen, shroud, shut off (*or* out). [*Compare* DISGUISE, HIDE[1], WRAP.] —*See also* FILL (2), OBSTRUCT, VETO.

block in or **out** *v.* —*See* DRAFT (1).

block *n.* —*See* BAR (1), HEAD (1).

blockade *n.* A prolonged encirclement of an objective by hostile troops ▸ beleaguerment, besiegement, investment, siege. [*Compare* ATTACK.]

blockade *v.* —*See* BESIEGE, OBSTRUCT.

blockage *n.* —*See* BAR (1).

blockhead *n.* —*See* DULLARD.

blockheaded *adj.* —*See* STUPID.

blocky *adj.* —*See* BULKY (1), STOCKY.

blond or **blonde** *adj.* —*See* FAIR[1] (2).

blood *n.* —*See* ANCESTRY, MURDER, NOBILITY.

bloodbath *n.* —*See* MASSACRE.

bloodcurdling *adj.* —*See* HORRIBLE.

bloodless *adj.* —*See* CALLOUS, PALE (1), PALE (2).

bloodletting *n.* —*See* MASSACRE.

bloodline *n.* —*See* ANCESTRY.

bloodshed *n.* —*See* MASSACRE.

bloodstain *v.* To cover with blood ▸ bloody, ensanguine, incarnadine.

bloodsucker *n.* —*See* PARASITE.

bloodsucking *adj.* —*See* PARASITIC.

bloodthirsty *adj.* —*See* MURDEROUS.

blood vessel *n.* —*See* VESSEL (2).

bloody *adj.* Of or covered with blood ▸ bleeding, blood-soaked, bloodstained, gory, hemorrhaging. [*Compare* GHASTLY.] —*See also* DAMNED, MURDEROUS.

bloody *v.* To cover with blood ▸ bloodstain, ensanguine, incarnadine.

bloody-minded *adj.* —*See* MURDEROUS.

bloom[1] *n.* **1.** A time of vigor, youth, or peak condition ▸ blossom, efflorescence, florescence, flower, flush, heyday, prime, salad days. **2.** A fresh rosy complexion ▸ blush, color, flush, glow. [*Compare* COLOR, COMPLEXION.] —*See also* FLOWER.

bloom *v.* **1.** To bear flowers ▸ blossom, blow, bud (out), burgeon, effloresce, flower, open (up *or* out). *Idiom:* burst into flower (*or* bloom). **2.** To grow rapidly ▸ blossom, flourish, thrive. [*Compare* INCREASE.]

bloom[2] *n.* —*See* ROD.

Bloom·er (blo͞o′mər), **Amelia Jenks** (1818–94) ▸ Amer. social reformer.

bloom·ers (blo͞o′mərz) ▸ *pl.n.* Women's wide loose pants or underpants gathered at the knee.

bloop·er (blo͞o′pər) ▸ *n.* **1.** *Informal* An embarrassing mistake; faux pas. **2.** *Baseball* A short, weakly hit fly ball.

blos·som (blŏs′əm) ▸ *n.* **1.** A flower or cluster of flowers. **2.** The condition or time of flowering: *peach trees in blossom.* **3.** A period or condition of maximum development. ▸ *v.* **1.** To flower; bloom. **2.** To develop; flourish.

blot (blŏt) ▸ *n.* **1.** A spot or stain: *a blot of ink.* **2.** A moral blemish; disgrace. ▸ *v.* **blot·ted, blot·ting. 1.** To spot or stain. **2.** To bring moral disgrace to. **3.** To obliterate; cancel. **4.** To make obscure; hide. **5.** To soak up or dry with absorbent material. **6.** To make a blot. **7.** To become blotted.

blotch (blŏch) ▸ *n.* **1.** A spot or blot; splotch. **2.** A discoloration on the skin; blemish. **—blotch** *v.* **—blotch′i·ness** *n.* **—blotch′y** *adj.*

blot·ter (blŏt′ər) ▸ *n.* **1.** A piece of blotting paper. **2.** A book containing daily records of occurrences: *a police blotter.*

blot·ting paper (blŏt′ĭng) ▸ *n.* Absorbent paper used to dry a surface or soak up excess ink.

blouse (blous, blouz) ▸ *n.* **1.** A loosely fitting shirtlike garment. **2.** The jacket of certain US armed forces uniforms. ▸ *v.* **bloused, blous·ing.** To hang loosely.

blow[1] (blō) ▸ *v.* **blew** (blo͞o), **blown** (blōn), **blow·ing. 1.** To be in a state of motion, as air or wind. **2a.** To be carried by the wind: *Her hat blew away.* **b.** To cause to move by means of a current of air. **3.** To drive a current of air upon, in, or through. **4a.** To expel a current of air, as from a bellows. **b.** To expel (air), as from the mouth. **c.** To clear by forcing air through: *blow one's nose.* **5.** To sound by expelling a current of air: *blow a trumpet.* **6.** To pant. **7a.** To burst suddenly: *The tire blew.* **b.** To cause to explode. **8.** To melt (a fuse). **9.** To spout. Used of a whale. **10.** To shape (e.g., glass) by forcing air through at the end of a pipe. **11.** *Slang* To spend (money) freely. **12.** To handle ineptly. **13.** To depart. ***—phrasal verbs:*** **blow out 1.** To extinguish or be extinguished by blowing. **2.** To fail, as an electrical apparatus. **blow over 1.** To subside; wane. **2.** To be forgotten. **blow up 1.** To come into being: *A storm blew up.* **2.** To fill with air; inflate. **3.** To enlarge (a photographic image or print). **4.** To explode. **5.** To lose one's temper. ▸ *n.* **1.** The act of blowing. **2a.** A blast of air or wind. **b.** A storm. ***—idioms:*** **blow off steam** To give release to one's anger or other pent-up emotion. **blow (one's) mind** *Slang* To amaze or shock. **blow (one's) top** *Informal* To lose one's temper. **—blow′er** *n.*

blow[2] (blō) ▸ *n.* **1.** A sudden hard stroke or hit, as with the fist or an object. **2.** An unexpected shock or calamity. **3.** A sudden attack.

blow[3] (blō) ▸ *n.* A mass of blossoms: *peach blow.* ▸ *v.* **blew** (blo͞o), **blown** (blōn), **blow·ing.** To bloom or cause to bloom.

blow-by-blow (blō′-bī-blō′) ▸ *adj.* Describing in great detail.

blow-dry (blō′drī′) ▸ *v.* To dry or style (hair) with a handheld dryer. **—blow dryer** *n.*

blow·fly (blō′flī′) ▸ *n.* A fly that deposits its eggs in carrion or open sores.

blow·gun (blō′gŭn′) ▸ *n.* A long narrow pipe through which darts may be blown.

blow·hard (blō′härd′) ▸ *n.* *Informal* A boaster or braggart.

blow·hole (blō′hōl′) ▸ *n.* An opening on the head of a cetacean for breathing.

blow·out (blō′out′) ▸ *n.* **1.** A sudden bursting, as of an automobile tire. **2.** A sudden escape of a confined gas or liquid, as from a well. **3.** *Slang* A large boisterous party.

blow·torch (blō′tôrch′) ▸ *n.* A portable burner that mixes gas and oxygen to produce a flame hot enough to melt soft metals.

blow·up (blō′ŭp′) ▸ *n.* **1.** An explosion. **2.** A violent outburst of temper. **3.** A photographic enlargement.

blow·y (blō′ē) ▸ *adj.* **-i·er, -i·est.** Windy or breezy.

blow·zy also **blow·sy** (blou′zē) ▸ *adj.* **-zi·er, -zi·est** also **-si·er, -si·est.** Disheveled and frowzy.

blub·ber[1] (blŭb′ər) ▸ *v.* To weep and sob noisily. ▸ *n.* A loud sobbing.

blub·ber[2] (blŭb′ər) ▸ *n.* **1.** The fat of whales, seals, and other marine mammals, from which an oil is obtained. **2.** Excessive body fat. **—blub′ber·y** *adj.*

bludg·eon (blŭj′ən) ▸ *n.* A short heavy club, usu. of wood, that is thicker or loaded at one end. ▸ *v.* **1.** To hit with or as with a bludgeon. **2.** To threaten or bully.

blue (blo͞o) ▸ *n.* **1a.** Any of a group of colors whose hue is that of a clear daytime sky. **b.** The hue of the visible spectrum lying between green and indigo. **2a.** The sky. **b.** The sea. ▸ *adj.* **blu·er, blu·est. 1.** Of the color blue. **2.** Having a gray or purplish color, as from cold or bruising. **3.** Downhearted or low; gloomy. **4.** Puritanical; strict. **5.** Indecent; risqué: *a blue joke.* ▸ *v.* **blued, blu·ing.** To make or become blue. ***—idiom:*** **out of the blue 1.** From an unforeseen source. **2.** At a completely unexpected time. **—blue′ness** *n.* **—blu′ish, blue′ish** *adj.*

blue baby ▸ *n.* An infant born with bluish skin from inadequate oxygenation of its blood.

blue·bell (blo͞o′bĕl′) ▸ *n.* Any of several plants having blue bell-shaped flowers.

blue·ber·ry (blo͞o′bĕr′ē) ▸ *n.* **1.** Any of numerous plants having edible blue-black berries. **2.** The fruit of a blueberry.

blue·bird (blo͞o′bûrd′) ▸ *n.* A North American songbird having blue plumage and usu. a rust-colored breast in the male.

blue blood ▸ *n.* **1.** Noble or aristocratic descent. **2.** A member of the aristocracy. **—blue′-blood′ed** *adj.*

blue·bon·net (blo͞o′bŏn′ĭt) ▸ *n.* A plant with compound leaves and light blue flowers.

blue·bot·tle (blo͞o′bŏt′l) ▸ *n.* Any of several flies that have a bright metallic-blue body.

blue cheese ▸ *n.* A semisoft tangy cheese streaked with a greenish-blue mold.

blue chip ▸ *n.* **1.** A stock highly valued for its long record of steady earnings. **2.** A valuable property. **—blue′-chip′** *adj.*

THESAURUS

bloomer *n.* —*See* BLUNDER.

blooming *adj.* —*See* RUDDY.

blooper *n.* —*See* BLUNDER.

blossom *n.* —*See* BLOOM[1] (1), FLOWER.

blossom *v.* To grow rapidly ▸ bloom, flourish, thrive. [*Compare* INCREASE.] —*See also* BLOOM[1] (1).

blot *n.* —*See* SMEAR, STAIN.

blot *v.* —*See* BLOCK, CANCEL (1), DENIGRATE, DISGRACE.

blot out *v.* —*See* ANNIHILATE.

blotch *n.* —*See* SMEAR.

blotch *v.* —*See* STAIN.

blotto *adj.* —*See* DRUNK.

blow[1] *v.* **1.** To be in a state of motion, as air or wind ▸ bluster, breathe, freshen, gust, puff, rise, stir, sweep. ***Idiom:*** come (*or* kick *or* spring) up. **2.** To move in or on the wind ▸ drift, flap, float, flutter, fly, sail, stream, waft, wave. **3.** To come open or fly apart suddenly and violently, as from internal pressure ▸ blow out, burst, explode, pop. *Slang:* bust. **4.** To manifest strong winds and precipitation ▸ blow up, set in, squall, storm. [*Compare* RAIN.] —*See also* BOAST, BOTCH, EXPLODE (1), GO (1), PANT, TREAT (2), WASTE.

blow in *v.* —*See* ARRIVE (1).

blow up *v.* —*See* ANGER (2), INCREASE, SWELL.

blow *n.* —*See* BOAST, STORM, WIND[1].

blow[2] *n.* A sudden heavy stroke ▸ bang, bonk, buffet, bust, chop, clout, crack, hit, jab, lick, pound, punch, slug, sock, stroke, swat, swing, swipe, thump, thwack, welt, whack, wham, whop. *Informal:* bash, biff, bop, clip, wallop. *Slang:* belt, conk, haymaker, knuckle sandwich, paste, roundhouse. [*Compare* SLAP.] —*See also* SHOCK[1].

blow[3] *v.* —*See* BLOOM[1] (1).

blow-by-blow *adj.* —*See* DETAILED.

blower or **blowhard** *n.* —*See* BRAGGART.

blowout *n.* —*See* BLAST (2), BLAST (3), DEFEAT.

blowup *n.* —*See* BLAST (2), OUTBURST.

blowy *adj.* —*See* AIRY (3).

blubber[1] *v.* —*See* CRY.

blubber[2] *n.* Adipose tissue ▸ fat, lard, suet, tallow. [*Compare* OIL.]

blubbering *n.* —*See* CRY (1).

bludgeon *v.* —*See* BEAT (1), INTIMIDATE.

blue *adj.* —*See* DEPRESSED (1), GLOOMY, RACY, SORROWFUL.

blue blood *n.* —*See* NOBILITY, SOCIETY (1).

blue-blooded *adj.* —*See* NOBLE.

blue-chip *adj.* —*See* BIG-LEAGUE.

bluecoat *n.* —*See* POLICE OFFICER.

blue-col·lar (blo͞o′kŏl′ər) ▸ *adj.* Of or relating to wage earners whose jobs involve skilled or semiskilled manual labor.
blue·fish (blo͞o′fĭsh′) ▸ *n.* A food and game fish of temperate and tropical waters.
blue·gill (blo͞o′gĭl′) ▸ *n.* A common edible sunfish of North American lakes and streams.
blue·grass (blo͞o′grăs′) ▸ *n.* **1.** A usu. bluish lawn and pasture grass. **2.** A type of lively folk music originating in the S US, typically played on banjos, guitars, and fiddles.
blue·ing (blo͞o′ĭng) ▸ *n.* Var. of **bluing.**
blue jay ▸ *n.* A North American jay having a crested head, predominantly blue plumage, and a harsh noisy cry.
blue jeans ▸ *pl.n.* Clothes, esp. pants, made of blue denim.
blue law ▸ *n.* A law designed to regulate Sunday activities.
blue moon ▸ *n.* *Informal* A relatively long period of time: *once in a blue moon.*
Blue Nile ▸ A river of NE Africa flowing about 1,609 km (1,000 mi) from NW Ethiopia to Sudan. At Khartoum it merges with the White Nile to form the Nile R. proper.
blue·nose (blo͞o′nōz′) ▸ *n.* A puritanical person.
blue-pen·cil (blo͞o′pĕn′səl) ▸ *v.* To edit with or as if with a blue pencil.
blue·print (blo͞o′prĭnt′) ▸ *n.* **1.** A photographic reproduction, as of architectural plans, rendered as white lines on a blue background. **2.** A detailed plan of action. **—blue′print′** *v.*
blue ribbon ▸ *n.* The first prize in a competition. **—blue′-rib′bon** *adj.*
blues (blo͞oz) ▸ *pl.n.* *(takes sing. or pl. v.)* **1.** A state of depression or melancholy. **2.** A style of music evolved from southern African-American secular songs and usu. marked by a syncopated 4/4 rhythm, flatted thirds and sevenths, and a 12-bar structure. **—blues′man** *n.* **—blues′y** *adj.*
blue·stock·ing (blo͞o′stŏk′ĭng) ▸ *n.* A woman with strong scholarly or literary interests.
blu·ets (blo͞o′ĭts) ▸ *pl.n.* *(takes sing. or pl. v.)* A low-growing plant having blue flowers with yellow centers.
blue whale ▸ *n.* A very large baleen whale having a bluish-gray back, yellow underparts, and several ventral throat grooves.
bluff[1] (blŭf) ▸ *v.* To mislead or intimidate, esp. by a false display of confidence. ▸ *n.* **1.** The act or practice of bluffing. **2.** One that bluffs. **—bluff′er** *n.*
bluff[2] (blŭf) ▸ *n.* A steep headland, riverbank, or cliff. ▸ *adj.* **-er, -est.** Rough and blunt but not unkind in manner. **—bluff′ly** *adv.* **—bluff′ness** *n.*
blu·ing also **blue·ing** (blo͞o′ĭng) ▸ *n.* **1.** A coloring agent used to counteract the yellowing of laundered fabrics. **2.** A rinsing agent used with gray hair.
blun·der (blŭn′dər) ▸ *n.* A usu. serious mistake caused by ignorance, confusion, or foolishness. ▸ *v.* **1.** To move clumsily or blindly. **2.** To make a stupid, usu. serious error. **—blun′der·er** *n.* **—blun′der·ing·ly** *adv.*
blun·der·buss (blŭn′dər-bŭs′) ▸ *n.* A short musket with a wide muzzle for scattering shot at close range.
blunt (blŭnt) ▸ *adj.* **-er, -est. 1.** Having a dull edge or end. **2.** Abrupt and frank in speech and manner; brusque. ▸ *v.* **1.** To make or become blunt. **2.** To make less effective; weaken. **—blunt′ly** *adv.* **—blunt′ness** *n.*
blur (blûr) ▸ *v.* **blurred, blur·ring. 1.** To make or become indistinct. **2.** To smear or stain. **3.** To lessen the perception of; dim. ▸ *n.* **1.** A smear or smudge. **2.** Something indistinct to sight or mind. **—blur′ry** *adj.*
blurb (blûrb) ▸ *n.* A brief favorable publicity notice, as on a book jacket.
blurt (blûrt) ▸ *v.* To say suddenly and impulsively: *blurt a confession.*
blush (blŭsh) ▸ *v.* **1.** To become red in the face, esp. from modesty, embarrassment, or shame; flush. **2.** To become red or rosy. **3.** To feel embarrassed or ashamed about something. **—blush** *n.*
blush·er (blŭsh′ər) or **blush** (blŭsh) ▸ *n.* Facial makeup used esp. on the cheeks to give a red or rosy tint.
blus·ter (blŭs′tər) ▸ *v.* **1.** To blow in loud violent gusts, as wind in a storm. **2.** To speak in a noisy, arrogant, or bullying manner. **—blus′ter** *n.* **—blus′ter·er** *n.* **—blus′ter·y** *adj.*
Blvd. ▸ *abbr.* boulevard
bo·a (bō′ə) ▸ *n.* **1.** Any of various large, nonvenomous tropical snakes, including the python, anaconda, and boa constrictor, that coil around and suffocate their prey. **2.** A long scarf made of soft fluffy material, such as fur or feathers.
boa constrictor ▸ *n.* A large boa of tropical America having brown markings.
boar (bôr) ▸ *n.* **1.** An uncastrated male pig. **2.** A wild pig.
board (bôrd) ▸ *n.* **1.** A flat length of sawed lumber; plank. **2.** A flat piece of wood or similar material adapted for a special use. **3.** A flat surface on which a game is played. **4. boards** A theater stage. **5a.** A table, esp. one set for serving food. **b.** Food or meals considered as a whole: *board and lodging.* **6.** A table at which official meetings are held. **7.** An organized body of administrators. **8.** A circuit board. **9.** The side of a ship. ▸ *v.* **1.** To cover or close with boards: *board up a broken window.* **2.** To provide with or receive food and lodging for a charge. **3.** To enter or go aboard (a ship, train, or plane). **4.** To come alongside (a ship). ***—idiom:*** **On board 1.** Aboard. **2.** On the job. **—board′er** *n.*
board foot ▸ *n., pl.* **board feet.** A unit of cubic measure for lumber, equal to one foot square by one inch thick.
board·ing house also **board·ing·house** (bôr′dĭng-hous′) ▸ *n.* A house where paying guests are provided with meals and lodging.
boarding school ▸ *n.* A school where pupils are provided with meals and lodging.
board·walk (bôrd′wôk′) ▸ *n.* A promenade, esp. of planks, along a beach.
boast (bōst) ▸ *v.* **1.** To talk in a self-admiring way. **2.** To talk about or speak with excessive pride. **3.** To possess or own (a desirable feature). ▸ *n.* **1.** An instance of bragging. **2.** A

THESAURUS

blue moon *n.* —*See* AGES.
bluenose *n.* —*See* PRUDE.
bluenosed *adj.* —*See* PRUDISH.
blue-pencil *v.* —*See* CENSOR (1).
blueprint *n.* —*See* APPROACH (1), DRAFT (1).
blueprint *v.* —*See* ARRANGE (2), DESIGN (1), DESIGN (2).
blue-ribbon *adj.* —*See* EXCELLENT.
blues *n.* —*See* DEPRESSION (2).
bluff *v.* —*See* DECEIVE.
bluff *adj.* —*See* ABRUPT (1).
blunder *v.* To move heavily or clumsily ▸ bumble, clump, flounder, galumph, hulk, lumber, lump, lurch, stump, stumble. [*Compare* STAGGER, STUMBLE.] —*See also* BOTCH, ERR, MUDDLE.
blunder *n.* A stupid, clumsy mistake ▸ bobble, bungle, faux pas, foozle, fumble, muff, solecism, stumble. *Informal:* blooper, boner, boo-boo, fluff, no-no. *Slang:* bloomer, clinker, goof, howler. [*Compare* MESS, ERROR.]
blunderer *n.* A clumsy, inept person ▸ botcher, bungler, dub, foozler, lubber. *Informal:* sad sack. *Slang:* klutz, screwup. *Idiom:* bull in a china shop. [*Compare* BOOR, OAF.]
blunt *adj.* —*See* ABRUPT (1), DULL (3).
blunt *v.* —*See* DEADEN, DULL.
blur *v.* —*See* DRUG (2), OBSCURE.
blurry *adj.* —*See* UNCLEAR.
blurt *v.* —*See* EXCLAIM.
blush *v.* To become red in the face ▸ color, crimson, flush, glow, mantle, redden. *Idioms:* go red (*or* crimson *or* scarlet), turn red as a beet.
blush *n.* A fresh rosy complexion ▸ bloom, color, flush, glow. [*Compare* COLOR, COMPLEXION.]
bluster *v.* —*See* BLOW[1] (1), BOAST, SHOUT.
bluster *n.* —*See* ROAR.
blustery *adj.* —*See* ROUGH (2).
board *v.* To go aboard a means of transport ▸ catch, take. *Informal:* hop. —*See also* LODGE.
boards *n.* —*See* STAGE (1).
boast *v.* To talk with excessive pride ▸ bluster, brag, crow, gasconade, puff (up), swagger, swell (up), vaunt. *Informal:* blow. *Idioms:* blow one's own horn (*or* trumpet), pat oneself on the back, shoot off one's mouth (*or* face), sing one's own praises, talk big. [*Compare* EXAGGERATE, EXULT, STRUT.] —*See also* COMMAND (2).
boast *n.* Boastful talk or behavior ▸ boasting, brag, braggadocio, bragging, bravado, fanfaronade, gasconade, vaunt. *Informal:* blow, fish story. *Slang:* gas. [*Compare* BOMBAST.]
boaster *n.* —*See* BRAGGART.

source of pride. **—boast′er** *n.* **—boast′ful** *adj.* **—boast′ful·ly** *adv.* **—boast′ful·ness** *n.*

boat (bōt) ▸ *n.* 1a. A relatively small, usu. open water craft. b. A ship or submarine. 2. A dish shaped like a boat: *a sauce boat.* ▸ *v.* To travel or transport by boat. —*idiom:* **in the same boat** In the same situation. **—boat′ing** *n.* **—boat′er** *n.*

boat·swain also **bo's'n** or **bos'n** or **bo·sun** (bō′sən) ▸ *n.* A warrant officer or petty officer in charge of a ship's rigging, anchors, cables, and deck crew.

bob[1] (bŏb) ▸ *v.* **bobbed, bob·bing.** To move or cause to move up and down. ▸ *n.* A quick jerky movement.

bob[2] (bŏb) ▸ *n.* 1. A small, knoblike pendent object. 2. A fishing float. 3. A woman's or child's short haircut. 4. The docked tail of a horse. ▸ *v.* **bobbed, bob·bing.** To cut short or reshape: *bobbed her hair.*

bob[3] (bŏb) ▸ *n., pl.* **bob** *Chiefly Brit.* A shilling.

bob·bin (bŏb′ĭn) ▸ *n.* A spool for thread, as on a sewing machine.

bob·ble (bŏb′əl) ▸ *v.* **-bled, -bling.** 1. To bob up and down. 2. To fumble (e.g., a ball) momentarily. **—bob′ble** *n.*

bob·by (bŏb′ē) ▸ *n., pl.* **-bies.** *Chiefly Brit.* A police officer.

bobby pin ▸ *n.* A small metal hair clip with the ends pressed tightly together.

bobby socks also **bobby sox** ▸ *pl.n. Informal* Ankle socks.

bob·by·sox·er (bŏb′ē-sŏk′sər) ▸ *n. Informal* A teenage girl.

bob·cat (bŏb′kăt′) ▸ *n.* A wild cat of North America, having spotted reddish-brown fur, tufted ears, and a short tail.

bob·o·link (bŏb′ə-lĭngk′) ▸ *n.* An American migratory songbird.

bob·sled (bŏb′slĕd′) ▸ *n.* 1. A long racing sled with a steering mechanism controlling the front runners. 2. A long sled made of two sleds joined in tandem. **—bob′sled′** *v.*

bob·tail (bŏb′tāl′) ▸ *n.* 1. A short tail or one that has been cut short. 2. An animal, esp. a horse, having a bobtail. **—bob′tailed′** *adj.*

bob·white (bŏb-hwīt′, -wīt′) ▸ *n.* A small North American quail.

bock beer (bŏk) ▸ *n.* A dark, usu. springtime beer.

bod (bŏd) ▸ *n. Slang* The human body.

bode[1] (bōd) ▸ *v.* **bod·ed, bod·ing.** To be an omen of.

bode[2] (bōd) ▸ *v.* P.t. of **bide.**

bo·de·ga (bō-dā′gə) ▸ *n.* A small grocery store specializing in products from Latin America.

bod·ice (bŏd′ĭs) ▸ *n.* The fitted upper part of a dress.

bod·i·less (bŏd′ē-lĭs) ▸ *adj.* Having no body, form, or substance: *bodiless fears.*

bod·i·ly (bŏd′l-ē) ▸ *adj.* 1. Of, relating to, or belonging to the body. 2. Physical: *bodily welfare.* ▸ *adv.* 1. In person. 2. As a complete physical entity: *lifted bodily from his chair.*

bod·kin (bŏd′kĭn) ▸ *n.* 1. An awl for piercing fabric or leather. 2. A blunt needle for pulling ribbon through loops or a hem. 3. A dagger.

bod·y (bŏd′ē) ▸ *n., pl.* **-ies.** 1a. The entire material or physical structure of an organism, esp. of a human or animal. b. A corpse or carcass. 2. The trunk or torso. 3a. A person. b. A group of individuals regarded as an entity: *a governing body.* 4. A collection of related things: *a body of information.* 5. The main or central part, as of a vehicle, document, or musical instrument. 6. A well-defined object, mass, or collection of material: *a body of water.* 7. Consistency of substance, as in paint, textiles, or wine. **—bod′ied** *adj.*

body bag ▸ *n.* A zippered bag, usu. of rubber, for transporting a human corpse.

bod·y·board (bŏd′ē-bôrd′) ▸ *n.* A short surfboard with one straight end, usu. ridden on one's chest. **—bod′y·board′** *v.*

bod·y·build·ing (bŏd′ē-bĭl′dĭng) ▸ *n.* The process of developing the musculature of the body through diet and physical exercise, esp. for competitive exhibition. **—bod′y·build′er** *n.*

body count ▸ *n.* A count of individual bodies, as those killed in combat operations.

body English ▸ *n.* The tendency of a person to try to influence the movement of a propelled object, such as a ball, by twisting his or her body toward the desired goal.

bod·y·guard (bŏd′ē-gärd′) ▸ *n.* A person or group of persons, usu. armed, responsible for protecting another or others.

body language ▸ *n.* The gestures, postures, and facial expressions by which a person communicates nonverbally with others.

body politic ▸ *n.* The aggregate people of a politically organized nation or state.

body shop ▸ *n.* A garage where the bodies of automotive vehicles are repaired.

body stocking ▸ *n.* A tight-fitting, usu. one-piece garment that covers the torso and sometimes the arms and legs.

body suit ▸ *n.* A tight-fitting one-piece garment for the torso.

bod·y·surf (bŏd′ē-sûrf′) ▸ *v.* To ride waves to shore without a surfboard.

bod·y·work (bŏd′ē-wûrk′) ▸ *n.* 1. The body of a motor vehicle. 2. The manufacturing or repairing of motor vehicle bodies.

Boer (bôr, bŏŏr) ▸ *n.* A Dutch colonist or descendant of a Dutch colonist in South Africa.

bof·fo (bŏf′ō) ▸ *adj. Slang* Extremely successful; great.

bog (bôg, bŏg) ▸ *n.* An area of soft, naturally waterlogged ground. ▸ *v.* **bogged, bog·ging.** To hinder or be hindered: *bogged down in the mud; bogged me down with details.* **—bog′gy** *adj.*

bo·gey (bō′gē) ▸ *n.* also **bo·gy** or **bo·gie** *pl.* **-geys** also **-gies.** 1. (*also* bŏŏg′ē, bōō′gē) An evil or mischievous spirit; hobgoblin. 2. One golf stroke over par on a hole. 3. *Slang* An unidentified flying aircraft. ▸ *v.* **-geyed, -gey·ing.** To shoot (a hole in golf) one stroke over par.

bo·gey·man or **bo·gy·man** also **boog·ey·man** (bŏŏg′ē-măn′, bō′gē-, bōō′gē-) ▸ *n.* A terrifying specter; hobgoblin.

bog·gle (bŏg′əl) ▸ *v.* **-gled, -gling.** 1. To hesitate or shy away as if in fear or doubt. 2. To overwhelm with astonishment: *boggles the mind.*

Bo·go·tá (bō′gə-tä′) ▸ The capital of Colombia, in the central part on a high plain in the E Andes.

bo·gus (bō′gəs) ▸ *adj.* Counterfeit or fake.

Bo·he·mi·a (bō-hē′mē-ə) ▸ A historical region and former kingdom of W Czech Republic. **—Bo·he′mi·an** *adj. & n.*

bo·he·mi·an (bō-hē′mē-ən) ▸ *n.* A person with artistic interests who disregards conventional standards of behavior. **—bo·he′mi·an** *adj.* **—bo·he′mi·an·ism** *n.*

Bohr (bôr), **Niels Henrik David** (1885–1962) ▸ Danish physicist; 1922 Nobel.

bohr·i·um (bôr′ē-əm) ▸ *n. Symbol* **Bh** A synthetic radioactive element. At. no. 107.

boil[1] (boil) ▸ *v.* 1a. To vaporize (a liquid) by applying heat.

THESAURUS

boastful *adj.* Characterized by or given to boasting ▸ blustering, bombastic, braggart, cocky, puffed up, swollen, vaunting. *Idiom:* full of gas (*or* hot air). [*Compare* ARROGANT, EGOTISTIC, POMPOUS.]

boat *n.* A conveyance that travels over water ▸ bark, barque, craft, ship, vessel, watercraft.

boatman *n.* —*See* SAILOR.

bob *v.* —*See* BOW[1] (1), FLOAT (1).

bode *v.* —*See* FORESHADOW, THREATEN (1).

bodiless *adj.* —*See* IMMATERIAL.

bodily *adj.* Of or relating to the body ▸ corporal, corporeal, fleshly, incarnate, mortal, personal, physical, somatic. [*Compare* PERCEPTIBLE, PHYSICAL, REAL.]

body *n.* 1. The human body excluding the head and limbs ▸ midsection, torso, trunk. 2. The physical frame of a dead person or animal ▸ bones, cadaver, carcass, corpse, mummy, relics, remains. *Slang:* stiff. —*See also* ASSEMBLY, CONSTITUTION, FORCE (3), GROUP, HUMAN BEING, OBJECT (1), QUANTITY (3), SYSTEM.

body forth *v.* —*See* EMBODY (1).

body politic *n.* —*See* STATE (1).

boff or **boffo** or **boffola** *n.* —*See* HIT.

bog *n.* —*See* SWAMP.

bog *v.* —*See* HINDER.

bog down *v.* —*See* HINDER.

bogey or **bogeyman** *n.* —*See* GHOST.

boggle *v.* —*See* BOTCH, STAGGER (2).

bogle *n.* —*See* GHOST.

bogus *adj.* —*See* COUNTERFEIT.

boil *v.* To be in a state of turmoil or

b. To bring to or reach the boiling point. 2. To cook or clean by boiling. 3. To be in a state of agitation; seethe: *a river boiling over the rocks*. 4. To be greatly excited, as by rage. *—phrasal verbs:* **boil down** 1. To reduce in bulk or size by boiling. 2. To summarize. **boil over** To lose one's temper. ▸ *n.* The condition or act of boiling.

boil[2] (boil) ▸ *n.* A painful, pus-filled inflammation of the skin usu. caused by bacterial infection.

boil·er (boi′lər) ▸ *n.* 1. An enclosed vessel in which water is heated and circulated, as either hot water or steam, for heating or power. 2. A container for boiling liquids.

boil·er-room (boi′lər-ro͞om′, -ro͝om′) ▸ *adj. Informal* Of or involving often illegal, high-pressure telephone sales tactics.

boil·ing point (boi′lĭng) ▸ *n.* 1. The temperature at which a liquid boils at a fixed pressure, esp. under standard atmospheric conditions. 2. *Informal* The point at which one loses one's temper.

Boi·se (boi′sē, -zē) ▸ The capital of ID, in the SW part on the **Boise River**, about 257 km (160 mi).

bois·ter·ous (boi′stər-əs, -strəs) ▸ *adj.* 1. Rough and stormy. 2. Loud, noisy, and unrestrained. **—bois′ter·ous·ly** *adv.* **—bois′ter·ous·ness** *n.*

bok choy (bŏk′ choi′) ▸ *n.* A cabbagelike Chinese vegetable.

bo·la (bō′lə) also **bo·las** (-ləs) ▸ *n.* A rope with round weights attached, used esp. in South America to catch cattle or game by entangling their legs.

bold (bōld) ▸ *adj.* **-er, -est.** 1. Fearless and daring; courageous. 2. Requiring or exhibiting courage and bravery. 3. Unduly forward and brazen. 4. Clear and distinct to the eye. 5. *Print.* Boldface. **—bold′ly** *adv.* **—bold′ness** *n.*

bold·face (bōld′fās′) ▸ *n. Print.* Type with thick, heavy lines. **—bold′face′, bold′faced′** *adj.*

bole (bōl) ▸ *n.* A tree trunk.

bo·le·ro (bō-lâr′ō, bə-) ▸ *n., pl.* **-ros.** 1. A very short jacket worn open in the front. 2a. A Spanish dance in triple meter. b. The music for this dance.

bo·li·var (bō-lē′vär, bŏl′ə-vər) ▸ *n., pl.* **bo·li·vars** or **bo·li·va·res** (bō-lē′vä-rĕs′). See **currency** table in Appendix.

Bo·liv·i·a (bə-lĭv′ē-ə, bō-) ▸ A landlocked country of W-central South America. **—Bo·liv′i·an** *adj. & n.*

bo·li·vi·a·no (bə-lĭv′ē-ä′nō, bō-) ▸ *n., pl.* **-nos.** See **currency** table in Appendix.

boll (bōl) ▸ *n.* The seedpod esp. of cotton and flax.

boll weevil ▸ *n.* A small, grayish, long-snouted beetle that lays its eggs in cotton buds and bolls, causing great damage.

bo·lo·gna (bə-lō′nē, -nə, -nyə) also **ba·lo·ney** or **bo·lo·ney** (-nē) ▸ *n.* A large smoked sausage made of mixed meats, such as beef, pork, and veal.

Bol·she·vik (bōl′shə-vĭk′, bŏl′-) ▸ *n., pl.* **-viks** or **-vi·ki** (-vē′kē). 1. A member of the radical Marxist party that seized power in Russia (1917–22). 2. A Communist. **—Bol′she·vik′** *adj.* **—Bol′she·vism** *n.* **—Bol′she·vist** *adj. & n.*

bol·ster (bōl′stər) ▸ *n.* A long narrow pillow or cushion. ▸ *v.* 1. To support with or as if with a bolster. 2. To buoy up; reinforce: *bolstered their morale.*

bolt[1] (bōlt) ▸ *n.* 1. A sliding bar used to fasten a door or gate. 2. A metal bar in a lock that is extended or withdrawn by turning the key. 3. A threaded pin or rod with a head at one end, used with a mated nut to hold things together. 4. A flash of lightning; thunderbolt. 5. A sudden movement toward or away; dash. 6. A large roll of cloth. ▸ *v.* 1. To secure or lock with or as if with a bolt. 2. To eat hurriedly; gulp. 3. To desert (a political party). 4. To move or spring suddenly. 5. To run away.

bolt[2] (bōlt) ▸ *v.* To sift (e.g., flour) through a sieve.

bo·lus (bō′ləs) ▸ *n., pl.* **-lus·es.** 1. A small round mass. 2. A large, round, usu. soft pill or tablet.

bomb (bŏm) ▸ *n.* 1a. An explosive weapon detonated esp. by impact or a timing mechanism. b. A nuclear weapon. Used with *the*. 2. A weapon detonated to release smoke or gas. 3. A container that ejects a spray, foam, or gas under pressure. 4. *Slang* A dismal failure. ▸ *v.* 1. To attack or damage with bombs. 2. *Slang* To fail miserably.

bom·bard (bŏm-bärd′) ▸ *v.* 1. To attack with bombs, explosive shells, or missiles. 2. To assail persistently, as with requests. 3. To irradiate (an atom). **—bom·bard′ment** *n.*

bom·bar·dier (bŏm′bər-dîr′) ▸ *n.* The member of a combat aircraft crew who operates the bombing equipment.

bom·bast (bŏm′băst′) ▸ *n.* Grandiloquent, pompous speech or writing. **—bom·bas′tic** *adj.*

Bom·bay (bŏm-bā′) ▸ See **Mumbai.**

bom·ba·zine (bŏm′bə-zēn′) ▸ *n.* A fine twilled fabric often dyed black.

bombed (bŏmd) ▸ *adj. Slang* Drunk.

bomb·er (bŏm′ər) ▸ *n.* 1. A combat aircraft designed to carry and drop bombs. 2. One who bombs.

bomb·shell (bŏm′shĕl′) ▸ *n.* 1. An explosive bomb. 2. A shocking surprise.

bomb·sight (bŏm′sīt′) ▸ *n.* A device in a combat aircraft for aiming a bomb.

bo·na fide (bō′nə fīd′, fī′dē, bŏn′ə) ▸ *adj.* 1. Made or carried out in good faith; sincere: *a bona fide offer.* 2. Authentic; genuine: *a bona fide Rembrandt.*

bo·nan·za (bə-năn′zə) ▸ *n.* 1. A rich mine or vein of ore. 2. A source of great wealth or prosperity.

bon·bon (bŏn′bŏn′) ▸ *n.* A coated candy with a creamy center.

bond (bŏnd) ▸ *n.* 1. Something that binds, ties, or fastens things together. 2. often **bonds** Confinement in prison; captivity. 3. A uniting force or tie; link: *the familial bond.* 4. A binding agreement; covenant. 5. A promise or obligation by which one is bound. 6. A union or cohesion between two or more parts. 7. A chemical bond. 8. *Law* a. A sum of money paid as bail or surety. b. A bail bondsman. 9. A certificate of debt issued by a government or corporation guaranteeing payment of the original investment plus interest by a specified future date. 10. The condition of storing goods in a warehouse until the taxes or duties owed on them are paid. 11. An insurance contract that guarantees payment to an employer for financial loss

THESAURUS

excitement ▸ bubble, burn, churn, effervesce, ferment, froth, percolate, seethe, simmer, smolder. *—See also* ANGER (2), BURN (3), COOK.

boil away *v.* *—See* EVAPORATE.

boil down *v.* To reduce in complexity or scope ▸ pare (down), simplify, streamline. ***Idiom:*** reduce to the basics (*or* essentials *or* bare bones). [*Compare* EXPLAIN.] *—See also* SHORTEN.

boil *n.* *—See* WELT.

boilerplate *n.* Written material used to fill space in a publication ▸ filler. [*Compare* ITEM.]

boiling *adj.* *—See* HOT (1).

boisterous *adj.* *—See* VOCIFEROUS.

bold *adj.* *—See* ADVENTUROUS, BRAVE, IMPUDENT, NOTICEABLE, STEEP[1] (1).

boldfaced *adj.* *—See* IMPUDENT.

boldness *n.* *—See* DARING, IMPUDENCE.

bollix up *v.* *—See* BOTCH.

bolster *v.* *—See* BACK (2), DEFEND (2), SUPPORT (2).

bolt *v.* To move suddenly and involuntarily ▸ jump, start. [*Compare* BUMP, JERK.] *—See also* FASTEN, GULP, RUN (2), RUSH.

bolt *n.* A sudden and involuntary movement ▸ jump, start, startle. [*Compare* JERK, RECOIL.] *—See also* NAIL.

bomb *n.* *—See* FAILURE (1).

bomb *v.* *—See* BARRAGE, FAIL (1).

bombard *v.* *—See* ATTACK (1), BARRAGE.

bombardment *n.* *—See* BARRAGE.

bombast *n.* Pretentious, pompous speech or writing ▸ claptrap, fire and brimstone, fustian, grandiloquence, magniloquence, orotundity, rant, turgidity. [*Compare* GIBBERISH, NONSENSE, ORATORY.]

bombastic *adj.* *—See* BOASTFUL, ORATORICAL.

bombed *adj.* *—See* DRUNK.

bombshell *n.* *—See* SHOCK[1].

bona fide *adj.* *—See* AUTHENTIC (1).

bond *n.* 1. Something that physically confines the legs or arms ▸ ball and chain, chains, fetter, handcuffs, hobble, irons, leg irons, manacle, restraint, shackle, straitjacket, trammel. [*Compare* BRAKE, RESTRAINT.] 2. That which unites or binds ▸ binding, cinch, girth, hitch, holdfast, knot, ligament, ligature, link, nexus, splice, tie, vinculum, yoke. [*Compare* BAND[1], JOINT.] 3. The close physical union of two objects ▸ adherence, adhesion, attachment, cohesion. *—See also* AGREEMENT (1), CORD, PAWN[1].

bond *v.* To form a tight bond ▸ ad-

or theft by an employee. **12.** Bond paper. ▸ *v.* **1.** To mortgage or place a guaranteed bond on. **2.** To furnish bond or surety for. **3.** To place (e.g., an employee) under bond or guarantee. **4.** To join securely, as with glue. **5.** To form a close nurturing relationship.

bond·age (bŏn′dĭj) ▸ *n.* The condition of a slave or serf; servitude.

bond·man (bŏnd′mən) ▸ *n.* A male bondservant.

bond paper ▸ *n.* A superior grade of white paper made wholly or in part from rag pulp.

bond·ser·vant (bŏnd′sûr′vənt) ▸ *n.* **1.** A person obligated to service without wages. **2.** A slave or serf.

bonds·man (bŏndz′mən) ▸ *n.* **1.** One who provides bond or surety for another. **2.** A male bondservant.

bond·wom·an (bŏnd′wŏŏm′ən) ▸ *n.* A woman bondservant.

bone (bōn) ▸ *n.* **1a.** The dense, semirigid, porous, calcified tissue forming the skeleton of most vertebrates. **b.** A skeletal structure made of this material. **2.** An animal material, such as whalebone, resembling bone. **3.** Something made of bone or similar material. ▸ *v.* **boned, bon·ing. 1.** To remove the bones from. **2.** *Informal* To study intensely, usu. at the last minute: *boned up on the chemical elements.* ***—idioms:*** **bone of contention** The subject of dispute. **bone to pick** Grounds for a complaint or dispute. **—bone′less** *adj.* **—bon′i·ness** *n.* **—bon′y, bon′ey** *adj.*

bone·black also **bone black** (bōn′blăk′) ▸ *n.* A black material made by roasting animal bones and used esp. as a pigment.

bone-dry (bōn′drī′) ▸ *adj.* Completely dry.

bone meal ▸ *n.* Crushed and coarsely ground bones used as fertilizer and animal feed.

bon·er (bō′nər) ▸ *n. Informal* A blunder.

bon·fire (bŏn′fīr′) ▸ *n.* A large outdoor fire.

bong (bŏng, bông) ▸ *n.* A deep ringing sound, as of a bell. **—bong** *v.*

bon·go[1] (bŏng′gō, bông′-) ▸ *n., pl.* **-gos.** A large reddish-brown antelope of central Africa, having white stripes and spirally twisted horns.

bon·go[2] (bŏng′gō, bông′-) ▸ *n., pl.* **-gos** or **-goes.** One of a pair of connected tuned drums played by beating with the hands.

bon·ho·mie (bŏn′ə-mē′) ▸ *n.* A pleasant and affable disposition; geniality.

bo·ni·to (bə-nē′tō) ▸ *n., pl.* **-to** or **-tos.** Any of several marine food and game fishes related to and resembling the tuna.

bon mot (bôɴ mō′) ▸ *n., pl.* **bons mots** (bôɴ mō′, mōz′). A witticism.

bon·net (bŏn′ĭt) ▸ *n.* **1.** A hat held in place by ribbons tied under the chin, esp. one worn by women and children. **2.** *Chiefly Brit.* The hood of an automobile.

bon·ny also **bon·nie** (bŏn′ē) ▸ *adj.* **-ni·er, -ni·est** *Scots.* **1.** Physically attractive or appealing; pretty. **2.** Excellent.

bo·no·bo (bə-nō′bō) ▸ *n., pl.* **-bos.** A small anthropoid ape of W-central Africa having more arboreal habits than the closely related chimpanzee.

bon·sai (bŏn-sī′, bŏn′sī′, -zī′) ▸ *n., pl.* **-sai.** A dwarfed, ornamentally shaped tree grown in a shallow pot.

bo·nus (bō′nəs) ▸ *n., pl.* **-es.** Something given or paid in addition to what is usual or expected.

bon vi·vant (bôɴ′ vē-väɴ′) ▸ *n., pl.* **bons vi·vants** (bôɴ′ vē-väɴ′). One who enjoys good living.

bon voy·age (bôɴ′ vwä-yäzh′) ▸ *interj.* Used to express farewell and good wishes to a departing traveler.

boo (bo͞o) ▸ *n., pl.* **boos.** A sound uttered to show contempt, scorn, or disapproval or to frighten or startle. **—boo** *v.*

boob (bo͞ob) ▸ *n. Slang* A stupid or foolish person; dolt.

boo·by (bo͞o′bē) ▸ *n., pl.* **-bies. 1.** A stupid person. **2.** Any of several tropical sea birds related to the gannets.

booby prize ▸ *n.* An award for the lowest score in a game or contest.

booby trap ▸ *n.* **1.** A concealed, often explosive device triggered when a harmless-looking object is touched. **2.** A situation that catches one off guard; pitfall. **—boo′by-trap′** *v.*

boo·dle (bo͞od′l) ▸ *n. Slang* **1a.** Money, esp. counterfeit money. **b.** Money accepted as a bribe. **2.** Stolen goods; swag.

boog·ey·man (bo͝og′ē-măn′, bā′gē-, bo͞o′gē-) ▸ *n. Slang* Var. of **bogeyman.**

boog·ie-woog·ie (bo͝og′ē-wo͝og′ē, bo͞o′gē-wo͞o′gē) ▸ *n.* A style of blues piano playing marked by an up-tempo rhythm and a repeated melodic pattern in the bass.

book (bo͝ok) ▸ *n.* **1.** A set of written, printed, or blank pages fastened along one side and encased between protective covers. **2a.** A printed or written literary work. **b.** A main division of a larger printed or written work. **3.** A volume in which financial transactions are recorded. **4. Book** The Bible. **5.** A packet of similar items bound together: *a book of matches.* **6.** A record of bets placed on a race. ▸ *v.* **1.** To reserve or schedule, as by listing in a book. **2.** To record charges against on a police blotter. ***—idiom:*** **like a book** Thoroughly; completely.

book·case (bo͝ok′kās′) ▸ *n.* A piece of furniture with shelves for holding books.

book·end (bo͝ok′ĕnd′) ▸ *n.* A prop used to keep a row of books upright.

book·ie (bo͝ok′ē) ▸ *n.* See **bookmaker** 2.

book·ing (bo͝ok′ĭng) ▸ *n.* A scheduled engagement, as for a performance.

book·ish (bo͝ok′ĭsh) ▸ *adj.* **1.** Fond of books; studious. **2.** Dull.

book·keep·ing (bo͝ok′kē′pĭng) ▸ *n.* The recording of the accounts and transactions of a business. **—book′keep′er** *n.*

book·let (bo͝ok′lĭt) ▸ *n.* A small bound book or pamphlet.

book·mak·er (bo͝ok′mā′kər) ▸ *n.* **1.** One who prints or publishes books. **2.** One who accepts and pays off bets, as on a horserace; bookie. **—book′mak′ing** *n.*

book·mark (bo͝ok′märk′) ▸ *n.* An object placed between book pages to mark one's place.

book·plate (bo͝ok′plāt′) ▸ *n.* A label bearing the owner's name pasted inside a book.

book·worm (bo͝ok′wûrm′) ▸ *n.* **1.** One who spends much time reading or studying. **2.** Any of various insects, esp. silverfish, that infest books and feed on the bindings.

Bool·e·an (bo͞o′lē-ən) ▸ *adj.* Of or relating to an algebraic system used in symbolic logic and in logic circuits in computer science.

boom[1] (bo͞om) ▸ *v.* **1.** To make a deep resonant sound. **2.** To flourish rapidly or vigorously. ▸ *n.* **1.** A booming sound. **2.** A sudden increase, as in growth, wealth, or popularity.

THESAURUS

here, cleave, cling, cohere, stick. *Idioms:* hold tight (*or* fast), stick (*or* cling) tight, stick like glue (*or* a bur). [*Compare* ATTACH.] *—See also* PAWN[1].

bondage *n.* *—See* SLAVERY.

bondservant *n.* *—See* SLAVE.

bondsman *n.* One who posts bond ▸ bail, bailsman.

bone-dry *adj.* *—See* DRY (1).

boneheaded *n.* *—See* STUPID.

boneheadedness *n.* *—See* STUPIDITY.

boner *n.* *—See* BLUNDER.

bone up *v. Informal* To apply one's mind to the acquisition of knowledge, especially when pressed for time ▸ lucubrate, study. *Informal:* cram, grind. *Idioms:* burn the midnight oil, hit the books. [*Compare* EXAMINE.]

bong *v.* *—See* RING[2].

bonk *n.* *—See* BLOW[2].

bonkers *adj.* *—See* INSANE.

bonny *adj.* *—See* GOOD (1).

bonus *n.* *—See* REWARD.

bony *adj.* *—See* THIN (1).

boo *v.* *—See* HISS (2).

boob *n.* *—See* DULLARD, FOOL.

boobishness *n.* *—See* FOOLISHNESS.

booby trap *n.* *—See* TRAP (1).

boodle *n.* *—See* BRIBE, PLUNDER.

boogie *v.* *—See* DANCE.

book *n.* A printed and bound work ▸ booklet, edition, hardcover, paperback, tome, volume. [*Compare* PUBLICATION.] *—See also* SCRIPT (2).

book *v.* To cause to be set aside, as for one's use, in advance ▸ arrange for, bespeak, engage, reserve. [*Compare* HIRE, LEASE.] *—See also* LIST[1].

booking *n.* A commitment, as for a performance by an entertainer ▸ date, engagement. *Slang:* gig.

bookish *adj.* Devoted to study or reading ▸ scholarly, studious. [*Compare* EDUCATED, INTELLECTUAL, LEARNED.] *—See also* PEDANTIC.

boom *v.* *—See* BLAST (1), PROSPER, RUMBLE (1).

boom *n.* *—See* BLAST (1).

boom² (bo͞om) ▸ *n.* **1.** A long spar extending from a mast to hold or extend the bottom of a sail. **2.** A long pole extending upward at an angle from the mast of a derrick to support or guide objects being lifted. **3a.** A chain of floating logs enclosing other free-floating logs. **b.** A floating barrier used to contain an oil spill. **4.** A long movable arm used to maneuver a microphone.

boom box ▸ *n. Slang* A portable audio system capable of high volume.

boo·mer·ang (bo͞o′mə-răng′) ▸ *n.* **1.** A flat, curved, usu. wooden missile configured so that when hurled it returns to the thrower. **2.** A statement or course of action that backfires. ▸ *v.* To have an opposite effect; backfire.

boon¹ (bo͞on) ▸ *n.* Something beneficial; blessing.

boon² (bo͞on) ▸ *adj.* Convivial; jolly: *a boon companion to all.*

boon·docks (bo͞on′dŏks′) ▸ *pl.n. Slang* **1.** A jungle. **2.** Rural country; hinterland.

boon·dog·gle (bo͞on′dô′gəl, -dŏg′əl) ▸ *n. Informal* Unnecessary, wasteful, and often counterproductive work. **—boon′dog′gle** *v.*

Boone (bo͞on), **Daniel** (1734–1820) ▸ Amer. frontier settler and folk hero.

boor (bo͝or) ▸ *n.* A crude person with rude, clumsy manners. **—boor′ish** *adj.* **—boor′ish·ly** *adv.* **—boor′ish·ness** *n.*

boost (bo͞ost) ▸ *v.* **1.** To lift by or as if by pushing up from behind or below. **2.** To increase; raise. **3.** To promote vigorously; aid. ▸ *n.* **1.** A push upward or ahead. **2.** An increase.

boost·er (bo͞o′stər) ▸ *n.* **1.** A device for increasing power or effectiveness. **2.** A promoter. **3.** A rocket that provides the main thrust for the launch of a missile or space vehicle. **4.** A booster shot.

booster shot ▸ *n.* A supplementary dose of a vaccine to sustain the immune response.

boot¹ (bo͞ot) ▸ *n.* **1.** Footgear covering the foot and part of the leg. **2.** A protective covering or sheath. **3.** *Chiefly Brit.* An automobile trunk. **4a.** A kick. **b.** *Slang* A dismissal, esp. from a job. **5.** A marine or navy recruit. **6.** The starting or restarting of a computer. ▸ *v.* **1.** To put boots on. **2.** To kick. **3.** *Slang* To discharge; dismiss. **4.** *Comp. Sci.* To start (a computer) by loading an operating system from a disk.

boot² (bo͞ot) ▸ *v.* To be of help; avail. ▸ *n. Regional* See **lagniappe.** ***—idiom:*** **to boot** In addition.

boot·black (bo͞ot′blăk′) ▸ *n.* One who polishes shoes for a living.

boot camp ▸ *n.* A training camp for military recruits.

boo·tee also **boo·tie** (bo͞o′tē) ▸ *n.* A soft, usu. knitted shoe for a baby.

booth (bo͞oth) ▸ *n., pl.* **booths** (bo͞o*th*z, bo͞oths). **1.** A small enclosed compartment; box: *a ticket booth.* **2.** A dining area in a restaurant having seats whose high backs serve as partitions. **3.** A small stall for the sale of goods.

Booth ▸ Family of reformers, including **William** (1829–1912) and his wife, **Catherine Mumford Booth** (1829–90), founders of the Salvation Army (1878).

Booth, John Wilkes (1838–65) ▸ Amer. assassin of Abraham Lincoln.

boot·leg (bo͞ot′lĕg′) ▸ *v.* **-legged, -leg·ging.** To make, sell, or transport illegally, as liquor or record albums. **—boot′leg′** *n. & adj.* **—boot′leg′ger** *n.*

boot·less (bo͞ot′lĭs) ▸ *adj.* Useless. **—boot′less·ness** *n.*

boot·lick (bo͞ot′lĭk′) ▸ *v.* To behave in a servile manner. **—boot′lick′er** *n.*

boot·strap (bo͞ot′străp′) ▸ *n.* A loop sewn at the top rear of a boot to help in pulling it on. ***—idiom:*** **by one's (own) bootstraps** By one's own effort.

boo·ty (bo͞o′tē) ▸ *n., pl.* **-ties. 1.** Plunder taken from an enemy in war. **2.** Seized or stolen goods.

booze (bo͞oz) *Slang* ▸ *n.* Hard liquor. ▸ *v.* **boozed, booz·ing.** To drink alcoholic beverages excessively. **—booz′er** *n.* **—booz′y** *adj.*

bop¹ (bŏp) *Informal* ▸ *v.* **bopped, bop·ping.** To hit or strike. ▸ *n.* A blow; punch.

bop² (bŏp) ▸ *n.* A style of jazz marked by rhythmic and harmonic complexity and improvised solo performances. ▸ *v.* **bopped, bop·ping. 1.** To dance to bop. **2.** *Slang* To go: *bopped off to the movies.* **—bop′per** *n.*

bo·rate (bôr′āt′) ▸ *n.* A salt of boric acid.

bo·rax (bôr′ăks′, -əks) ▸ *n.* A sodium borate used in detergents and in making glass and ceramics.

Bor·deaux (bôr-dō′) ▸ *n., pl.* **Bor·deaux** (bôr-dō′, -dōz′). A red or white wine from the region around Bordeaux, France.

bor·del·lo (bôr-dĕl′ō) ▸ *n., pl.* **-los.** A house of prostitution.

bor·der (bôr′dər) ▸ *n.* **1.** A part that forms the outer edge of something. **2.** A political or geographic boundary. ▸ *v.* **1.** To put a border on. **2.** To share a border with; be next to. **3.** To be almost like; approach: *an act that borders on heroism.*

bor·der·land (bôr′dər-lănd′) ▸ *n.* **1.** Land on or near a border. **2.** An indeterminate area.

bor·der·line (bôr′dər-līn′) ▸ *n.* **1.** A boundary. **2.** An indefinite area between two qualities or conditions. ▸ *adj.* **1.** Verging on a given condition: *borderline poverty.* **2.** Uncertain; dubious: *borderline qualifications.*

Border States ▸ The slave states of DE, MD, VA, KY, and MO adjacent to the free states during the Civil War.

bore¹ (bôr) ▸ *v.* **bored, bor·ing. 1.** To make a hole in or through with or as if with a drill. **2.** To form (e.g., a tun-

THESAURUS

boomerang *v.* To produce an unexpected and undesired result ▸ backfire, boomerang. ***Idiom:*** blow up in one's face. [*Compare* FAIL.]

booming *adj.* —*See* FLOURISHING, LOUD.

boomy *adj.* —*See* FLOURISHING.

boon¹ *n.* —*See* ADVANTAGE (2).

boon² *adj.* —*See* CHEERFUL.

boondocks or **boonies** *n.* —*See* COUNTRY.

boor *n.* An unrefined, rude person ▸ barbarian, cad, chuff, churl, Philistine, troglodyte, vulgarian, yahoo. *Informal:* caveman, slob. [*Compare* BLUNDERER, CLODHOPPER, OAF.]

boorish *adj.* —*See* COARSE (1).

boost *v.* To increase in amount ▸ hike, jack (up), jump, raise, up. [*Compare* INCREASE.] —*See also* ELEVATE (1), HELP, INCREASE, PROMOTE (3), STEAL.

boost *n.* —*See* ENCOURAGEMENT, INCREASE (2), INCREASE (1), LIFT.

booster *n.* —*See* ADVOCATE.

boot *n.* —*See* DISMISSAL, EJECTION, THRILL.

boot *v.* —*See* DISMISS (1), EJECT (1), VOMIT.

booth *n.* A small, often makeshift structure for the display and sale of goods ▸ counter, stand, stall. [*Compare* STORE.]

bootleg *v.* —*See* SMUGGLE.

bootlegger *n.* A person who engages in smuggling ▸ contrabandist, runner, smuggler. *Slang:* mule.

bootless *adj.* —*See* FUTILE.

bootlessness *n.* —*See* FUTILITY.

bootlick *v.* —*See* FAWN.

bootlicker *n.* —*See* SYCOPHANT.

booty *n.* —*See* PLUNDER.

booze *n.* —*See* BENDER.

booze *v.* —*See* DRINK (2).

boozed or **boozy** *adj.* —*See* DRUNK.

boozehound or **boozer** *n.* —*See* DRUNKARD.

bop *v.* —*See* HIT.

bop *n.* —*See* BLOW².

border *n.* **1.** A line or area where something ends or abruptly changes ▸ brim, brink, curb, edge, edging, fringe, hem, limit, lip, margin, perimeter, periphery, rim, threshold, verge. [*Compare* CIRCUMFERENCE.] **2.** The line or area separating geopolitical units ▸ borderland, borderline, boundary, frontier, march, marchland. [*Compare* LIMIT, OUTSKIRTS.]

border *v.* To put or form a border on ▸ bound, edge, fringe, margin, rim, skirt, verge. —*See also* ADJOIN.

border on or **upon** *v.* —*See* RIVAL.

bordering *adj.* —*See* ADJOINING.

borderland *n.* —*See* BORDER (2).

borderline *n.* —*See* BORDER (2).

borderline *adj.* —*See* AMBIGUOUS (1).

bore¹ *v.* —*See* CUT (1), DIG.

bore² *v.* To make weary with dullness or tedium ▸ fatigue, stultify, tire, weary. ***Idioms:*** bore out of one's mind, bore to death (*or* distraction *or* tears), put to sleep. [*Compare* ANNOY, TIRE.]

bore *n.* —*See* DRIP (2).

nel) by drilling, digging, or burrowing. ▸ *n.* **1.** A hole or passage made by or as if by drilling. **2.** The interior diameter of a hole, tube, or cylinder. **3.** The caliber of a firearm. **4.** A drilling tool. **—bor′er** *n.*

bore[2] (bôr) ▸ *v.* **bored, bor·ing.** To make weary by being dull, repetitive, or tedious. ▸ *n.* One that is boring.

bore[3] (bôr) ▸ *v.* P.t. of **bear**[1].

bo·re·al (bôr′ē-əl) ▸ *adj.* Northern.

bore·dom (bôr′dəm) ▸ *n.* The condition of being bored; ennui.

Bor·gia (bôr′jə, -zhə) ▸ Italian family, including **Cesare** (1475?–1507), a religious and political leader, and **Lucrezia** (1489–1519), a patron of the arts.

bo·ric acid (bôr′ĭk) ▸ *n.* A white or colorless crystalline compound, H_3BO_3, used esp. as an antiseptic and preservative.

born (bôrn) ▸ *v.* P.part. of **bear**[1]. ▸ *adj.* **1.** Brought into life by birth. **2.** Having a natural talent: *a born artist.* **3.** Resulting or coming from: *wisdom born of experience.*

borne (bôrn) ▸ *v.* P.part. of **bear**[1].

Bor·ne·o (bôr′nē-ō′) ▸ An island of the W Pacific in the Malay Archipelago between the Sulu and Java seas. **—Bor′ne·an** *adj.*

bo·ron (bôr′ŏn′) ▸ *n.* *Symbol* **B** A soft, brown, amorphous or crystalline nonmetallic element used in flares, nuclear reactor control elements, abrasives, and hard metallic alloys. At. no. 5.

bor·ough (bûr′ō, bŭr′-ō) ▸ *n.* **1.** A self-governing incorporated town in some US states. **2.** One of the five administrative units of New York City. **3.** A civil division of Alaska equivalent to a county. **4.** *Chiefly Brit.* **a.** A town having a municipal corporation. **b.** A town that sends a representative to Parliament.

bor·row (bŏr′ō, bôr′ō) ▸ *v.* **1.** To obtain or receive (something) on loan with the intent to return it. **2.** To adopt or use as one's own. **—bor′row·er** *n.*

bor·row·ing (bŏr′ō-ĭng, bôr′-) ▸ *n.* Something borrowed, especially a word borrowed from one language for use in another.

borscht also **borsht** (bôrsht) ▸ *n.* A beet soup served hot or cold, usu. with sour cream.

bor·zoi (bôr′zoi′) ▸ *n.* A tall slender dog having a narrow pointed head and silky coat.

bosh (bŏsh) ▸ *n.* *Informal* Nonsense. **—bosh** *interj.*

bo's'n or **bos'n** (bō′sən) ▸ *n.* Vars. of boatswain.

Bos·ni·a (bŏz′nē-ə) ▸ The N part of Bosnia and Herzegovina. **—Bos′ni·an** *adj. & n.*

Bosnia and Herzegovina or **Bos·ni·a-Her·ze·go·vi·na** (bŏz′nē-ə-hĕrt′sə-gō′vē-nə, -gō-vē′-, hûrt′-) ▸ A country of the NW Balkan Peninsula W of Serbia.

bos·om (bo͝oz′əm, bo͞o′zəm) ▸ *n.* **1a.** The human chest. **b.** A woman's breast or breasts. **2.** The part of a garment covering the chest. **3.** The heart or center: *the bosom of our family.* ▸ *adj.* Intimate: *a bosom friend.*

Bos·po·rus (bŏs′pər-əs) ▸ A narrow strait separating European and Asian Turkey and joining the Black Sea with the Sea of Marmara.

boss[1] (bôs, bŏs) ▸ *n.* **1.** An employer or supervisor. **2.** A politician who controls a political party or machine. ▸ *v.* **1.** To supervise or control. **2.** To give orders to, esp. in a domineering manner. **—boss′y** *adj.*

boss[2] (bôs, bŏs) ▸ *n.* A knoblike ornament. ▸ *v.* To emboss.

Bos·ton (bô′stən, bŏs′tən) ▸ The capital of MA, in the E part. **—Bos·to′ni·an** (bô-stō′nē-ən, bŏs-) *adj. & n.*

bo·sun (bō′sən) ▸ *n.* Var. of **boatswain.**

bot (bŏt) ▸ *n.* A software program that imitates human behavior, as by querying search engines.

bot·a·ny (bŏt′n-ē) ▸ *n.* The science or study of plants. **—bo·tan′i·cal** (bə-tăn′ĭ-kəl), **bo·tan′ic** *adj.* **—bot′a·nist** *n.*

botch (bŏch) ▸ *v.* **1.** To ruin through clumsiness. **2.** To repair clumsily. **—botch** *n.* **—botch′er** *n.* **—botch′i·ly** *adv.* **—botch′y** *adj.*

both (bōth) ▸ *adj.* One and the other; of or being two in conjunction: *Both guests are here.* ▸ *pron.* The one and the other: *Both were tall.* ▸ *conj.* Used with *and* to indicate that each of two things in a coordinated phrase or clause is included: *Both on and off.*

both·er (bŏ*th*′ər) ▸ *v.* **1.** To disturb, annoy, or anger, esp. by minor irritations. **2.** To trouble or concern oneself. ▸ *n.* A cause or state of disturbance. ▸ *interj.* Used to express annoyance. **—both′er·some** (-səm) *adj.*

Bot·swa·na (bŏt-swä′nə) ▸ A landlocked country of S-central Africa.

bot·tle (bŏt′l) ▸ *n.* **1.** A receptacle having a narrow neck, usu. no handles, and a mouth that can be plugged, corked, or capped. **2.** *Informal* Intoxicating liquor. ▸ *v.* **-tled, -tling.** **1.** To place in a bottle. **2.** To restrain: *bottled up my emotions.* **—bot′tle·ful′** *n.* **—bot′tler** *n.*

bot·tle·neck (bŏt′l-nĕk′) ▸ *n.* **1.** A narrow or obstructed section, as of a highway or pipeline, where movement is slowed down. **2.** A hindrance to progress or production.

bot·tom (bŏt′əm) ▸ *n.* **1.** The deepest or lowest part: *the bottom of a well; the bottom of the page.* **2.** The underside. **3.** The supporting part; base. **4.** The basic underlying quality; essence. **5.** The solid surface under a body of water. **6.** often **bottoms** Low-lying land adjacent to a river. **7.** *Informal* The buttocks. ***—idiom:* at bottom** Basically. **—bot′tom·less** *adj.*

bot·tom·land (bŏt′əm-lănd′) ▸ *n.* See **bottom** 6.

bottom line ▸ *n.* **1.** The lowest line in a financial statement that shows net income or loss. **2.** The final result or statement; upshot. **3.** The main or essential point.

bot·u·lism (bŏch′ə-lĭz′əm) ▸ *n.* A severe, sometimes fatal

THESAURUS

boreal *adj.* —*See* COLD (1).

boredom *n.* The condition of being bored ▸ ennui, listlessness, tediousness, tedium. *Informal:* blahs, doldrums. [*Compare* APATHY, DULLNESS, MONOTONY.]

boring *adj.* Arousing no interest or curiosity ▸ deadly, drear, dreary, dry, dull, humdrum, irksome, monotonous, stuffy, tedious, tiresome, uninteresting, unvaried, wearful, wearisome, weary. *Informal:* blah, ho-hum. *Slang:* draggy. [*Compare* DULL, INSIPID, TRITE.] —*See also* ORDINARY.

borough *adj.* —*See* CITY.

borrow *v.* —*See* PLAGIARIZE.

bosom *n.* The seat of a person's innermost emotions and feelings ▸ breast, heart, soul. *Idioms:* the bottom (*or* cockles) of one's heart, one's heart of hearts.

bosom *adj.* —*See* INTIMATE[1] (1).

boss *n.* Someone who directs and supervises workers ▸ director, foreman, foreperson, forewoman, head, manager, overseer, superintendent, superior, supervisor, taskmaster, taskmistress. *Informal:* straw boss. *Slang:* big cheese, big wheel, chief. [*Compare* EXECUTIVE.] —*See also* CHIEF.

boss *v.* To command in an arrogant manner ▸ dictate, dominate, domineer, order, rule, tyrannize. *Idioms:* boss around, lord it over, throw one's weight around. [*Compare* COMMAND.] —*See also* SUPERVISE.

boss *adj.* —*See* EXCELLENT.

bossy *adj.* —*See* DICTATORIAL.

botch *v.* To ruin through clumsiness or ineptness ▸ ball up, blunder, boggle, bungle, butcher, foul up, fumble, gum up, mangle, mess up, mishandle, mismanage, muddle, muff, spoil, wreck. *Informal:* bollix up, flub, muck up. *Slang:* blow, goof up, louse up, screw up, snafu. *Idiom:* make a mess (*or* muck *or* hash) of. [*Compare* DAMAGE, DESTROY.]

botch *n.* —*See* MESS (1).

botcher *n.* —*See* BLUNDERER.

bother *n.* Needless trouble or annoyance ▸ botheration, fuss, pother, red tape, rigmarole. *Informal:* hassle, headache. [*Compare* AGITATION, INCONVENIENCE.] —*See also* ANNOYANCE (1), ANNOYANCE (2).

bother *v.* —*See* AGITATE (2), ANNOY, HURT (3), WORRY.

botheration *n.* —*See* ANNOYANCE (1), BOTHER.

bothering *n.* —*See* ANNOYANCE (1).

bothersome *adj.* —*See* DISTURBING.

bottleneck *n.* —*See* BAR (1).

bottle up *adj.* —*See* REPRESS.

bottom *n.* **1.** A side or surface that is below or under ▸ underneath, underpart, underside, undersurface. **2.** A very low or lowest level, position, or degree ▸ low, minimum, nadir, rock bottom. —*See also* BASE[1] (2), BUTTOCKS, CENTER (3).

bottom *adj.* Opposite to or farthest from the top ▸ lowermost, lowest, nethermost, undermost.

food poisoning caused by bacteria that grow in improperly canned foods.

bou·doir (bo͞o′dwär′, -dwôr′) ▸ *n.* A woman's private room.

bouf·fant (bo͞o-fänt′) ▸ *adj.* Puffed-out; full: *a bouffant hair style.*

bou·gain·vil·le·a (bo͞o′gən-vĭl′ē-ə, -vĭl′yə) ▸ *n.* A woody tropical shrub or vine with variously colored petallike bracts attached to the flowers.

bough (bou) ▸ *n.* A tree branch, esp. a large or main branch.

bought (bôt) ▸ *v.* P.t. and p.part. of **buy**.

bouil·la·baisse (bo͞o′yə-bās′, bo͞ol′yə-bās′) ▸ *n.* A stew made of several kinds of fish and shellfish.

bouil·lon (bo͝ol′yŏn′, -yən) ▸ *n.* A clear thin meat broth.

boul·der (bōl′dər) ▸ *n.* A large rounded mass of rock.

boul·e·vard (bo͝ol′ə-värd′, bo͞o′lə-) ▸ *n.* **1.** A broad city street, often tree-lined and landscaped. **2.** *Regional* See **median strip**.

bounce (bouns) ▸ *v.* **bounced, bounc·ing. 1.** To rebound or cause to rebound after having struck an object or surface. **2.** To move jerkily; bump: *The car bounced over the potholes.* **3.** To recover quickly: *bounced back to good health.* **4.** To bound; spring. **5.** *Informal* To be sent back by a bank as valueless: *a check that bounced.* ▸ *n.* **1.** A bound or rebound. **2.** A spring or leap. **3.** The capacity to rebound. **4.** Spirit; liveliness. **—bounc′i·ly** *adv.* **—bounc′y** *adj.*

bounc·er (boun′sər) ▸ *n.* *Slang* A person employed to expel disorderly persons from a public place, esp. a bar.

bounc·ing (boun′sĭng) ▸ *adj.* Vigorous; healthy: *a bouncing baby.*

bound¹ (bound) ▸ *v.* **1.** To leap or spring. **2.** To move by leaping. **3.** To bounce or rebound. ▸ *n.* **1.** A leap; jump. **2.** A rebound; bounce.

bound² (bound) ▸ *n.* **1.** often **bounds** A boundary; limit. **2. bounds** The territory on or within a boundary. ▸ *v.* **1.** To limit or confine. **2.** To constitute the limit of. **3.** To demarcate.

bound³ (bound) ▸ *v.* P.t. and p.part. of **bind**. ▸ *adj.* **1.** Confined by or as if by bonds. **2.** Being under legal or moral obligation. **3.** Equipped with a cover or binding. **4.** Certain: *We're bound to be late.*

bound⁴ (bound) ▸ *adj.* On the way: *bound for home.*

bound·a·ry (boun′də-rē, -drē) ▸ *n., pl.* **-ries.** Something that indicates a border or limit.

bound·en (boun′dən) ▸ *adj.* Obligatory: *their bounden duty.*

bound·er (boun′dər) ▸ *n.* *Chiefly Brit.* A cad.

bound·less (bound′lĭs) ▸ *adj.* Being without limits. **—bound′less·ly** *adv.* **—bound′less·ness** *n.*

boun·te·ous (boun′tē-əs) ▸ *adj.* **1.** Giving generously. **2.** Copiously given; plentiful. **—boun′te·ous·ly** *adv.*

boun·ti·ful (boun′tə-fəl) ▸ *adj.* **1.** Giving generously. **2.** Marked by abundance; plentiful. **—boun′ti·ful·ly** *adv.*

boun·ty (boun′tē) ▸ *n., pl.* **-ties. 1.** Liberality in giving: *a patron's bounty.* **2.** Something given liberally. **3.** A reward or inducement, esp. one given by a government for performing a service, such as killing predatory animals.

bou·quet (bō-kā′, bo͞o-) ▸ *n.* **1.** A cluster of flowers. **2.** A pleasant fragrance, esp. of a wine.

bour·bon (bûr′bən) ▸ *n.* A whiskey distilled from a fermented mash of corn, malt, and rye.

bour·geois (bo͝or-zhwä′, bo͝or′zhwä′) ▸ *n., pl.* **-geois. 1.** One belonging to the middle class. **2.** In Marxist theory, a capitalist. ▸ *adj.* **1.** Of or typical of the middle class. **2.** Preoccupied with respectability and material values.

bour·geoi·sie (bo͝or′zhwä-zē′) ▸ *n.* **1.** The middle class. **2.** In Marxist theory, the social group opposed to the proletariat.

bout (bout) ▸ *n.* **1.** A contest; match: *a wrestling bout.* **2.** A period of time spent in a particular way; spell: *a bout of the flu.*

bou·tique (bo͞o-tēk′) ▸ *n.* A small retail shop that specializes in gifts, fashionable items, or food.

bou·ton·niere (bo͞o′tə-nîr′, -tən-yâr′) ▸ *n.* A flower worn in a buttonhole.

bo·vine (bō′vīn′, -vēn′) ▸ *adj.* **1.** Of or resembling an ox or cow. **2.** Dull and stolid. **—bo′vine′** *n.*

bow¹ (bou) ▸ *n.* The front section of a ship or boat.

bow² (bou) ▸ *v.* **1.** To bend the body, head, or knee in order to express greeting, consent, courtesy, or veneration. **2.** To acquiesce; submit. ***—phrasal verb:* bow out** To remove oneself; withdraw. ▸ *n.* An act of bowing, as in respect.

bow³ (bō) ▸ *n.* **1.** A curve or arch. **2.** A weapon consisting of a curved, flexible strip of wood, strung taut from end to end and used to launch arrows. **3.** *Mus.* A rod strung with horsehair, used in playing the violin and related instruments. **4.** A knot usu. having two loops and two ends, as a bowknot. **5.** A rainbow. ▸ *v.* **1.** To bend into a bow. **2.** *Mus.* To play (a stringed instrument) with a bow.

bowd·ler·ize (bōd′lə-rīz′, boud′-) ▸ *v.* **-ized, -iz·ing.** To expurgate (e.g., a book) prudishly. **—bowd′ler·i·za′tion** *n.*

bow·el (bou′əl, boul) ▸ *n.* **1a.** often **bowels** The intestine. **b.** A division of the intestine: *the large bowel.* **2. bowels** The interior of something: *in the bowels of the ship.*

bow·er (bou′ər) ▸ *n.* A shaded, leafy recess.

bow·ie knife (bō′ē, bo͞o′ē) ▸ *n.* A long, single-edged steel hunting knife.

bow·knot (bō′nŏt′) ▸ *n.* **1.** A knot with large, decorative loops. **2.** A bowtie.

bowl¹ (bōl) ▸ *n.* **1a.** A rounded hollow vessel for food or fluids. **b.** The contents of such a vessel. **2.** A curved hollow part, as of a spoon or pipe. **3.** A bowl-shaped structure or edifice, such as a stadium.

THESAURUS

boulevard *n.* *—See* WAY (2).

bounce *v.* To reverse direction after striking something ▸ bounce back, rebound, reflect, snap back, spring back. [*Compare* BEND, GLANCE.] *—See also* BOUND¹, BUMP, DISMISS (1), EJECT (1).

bounce back *v.* *—See* ECHO, RECOVER (2).

bounce *n.* **1.** A bouncing movement ▸ bound, hop, rebound. **2.** The ability to recover quickly from depression or discouragement ▸ buoyancy, elasticity, flexibility, resilience, resiliency. *—See also* BOUND¹ (2), DISMISSAL, EJECTION, FLEXIBILITY (1), SPIRIT (1).

bouncy *adj.* *—See* LIVELY.

bound¹ *v.* To move in a lively way ▸ bounce, hop, jump, leap, skip, skitter, spring, trip. [*Compare* GAMBOL.]

bound *n.* A sudden lively movement ▸ bounce, hop, jump, leap, skip, spring. *—See also* BOUNCE (1).

bound² *v.* *—See* ADJOIN, BORDER, DETERMINE, LIMIT.

bound *n.* *—See* LIMITS.

bound³ *adj.* *—See* OBLIGED (2).

boundary *n.* *—See* BORDER (2).

boundless *adj.* *—See* ENDLESS (1), INCALCULABLE.

boundlessness *n.* *—See* INFINITY (1).

bounds *n.* *—See* LIMITS.

bounteous *adj.* *—See* GENEROUS (2).

bounteousness *n.* *—See* GENEROSITY, PLENTY.

bountiful *adj.* *—See* GENEROUS (1), GENEROUS (2).

bountifulness *n.* *—See* GENEROSITY, PLENTY.

bounty *n.* *—See* ABUNDANCE, GENEROSITY, REWARD.

bouquet *n.* A cluster or arrangement of cut flowers or foliage set out or worn for display ▸ boutonniere, corsage, garland, lei, nosegay, posy, wreath. [*Compare* FLOWER.] *—See also* FRAGRANCE.

bout *n.* *—See* COMPETITION (2), TURN (1).

boutique *n.* A retail establishment where merchandise is sold ▸ emporium, outlet, shop, store.

bow¹ *v.* **1.** To incline the head or body, as in greeting, consent, courtesy, submission, or worship ▸ bob, curtsy, genuflect, kneel, kowtow, nod, salaam. **2.** To conform to the will or judgment of another ▸ defer, submit, yield. *Idioms:* give ground, give way. [*Compare* HUMOR.] *—See also* STOOP, SUCCUMB, SURRENDER (1).

bow *n.* An inclination of the head or body, as in greeting, consent, courtesy, submission, or worship ▸ curtsy, genuflection, kowtow, nod, obeisance, salaam.

bow² *v.* *—See* BEND (1), BEND (3).

bow *n.* *—See* BEND.

bow³ *n.* *—See* FRONT.

bowdlerize *v.* *—See* CENSOR (1).

bowed *adj.* *—See* BENT.

bowels *n.* *—See* VISCERA.

bowl *v.* *—See* THROW.

bowl over *v.* *—See* STAGGER (2).

bowl *n.* *—See* THROW.

bowl[2] (bōl) ► *n.* **1.** A large solid ball rolled in certain games. **2.** A roll of the ball in bowling. ► *v.* **1.** To play the game of bowling. **2.** To roll a ball in bowling. ***—phrasal verb:* bowl over** **1.** To astound. **2.** To knock over.

bow·leg·ged (bō′lĕg′ĭd, -lĕgd′) ► *adj.* Having legs that curve outward at the knees.

bowl·er[1] (bō′lər) ► *n.* One who bowls.

bowl·er[2] (bō′lər) ► *n.* A derby hat.

bow·line (bō′lĭn, -līn′) ► *n.* A knot forming a loop that does not slip.

bowl·ing (bō′lĭng) ► *n.* **1a.** A game played by rolling a heavy ball down a wooden alley in order to knock down a triangular group of ten pins; tenpins. **b.** A similar game, such as duckpins. **2.** A game played on a bowling green by rolling a wooden ball as close as possible to a target ball.

bowling alley ► *n.* **1.** A level wooden lane used in bowling. **2.** A place containing such lanes.

bowling green ► *n.* A level grassy area for bowling.

bow·man (bō′mən) ► *n.* An archer.

bow·sprit (bou′sprĭt′, bō′-) ► *n.* A spar extending forward from the bow of a sailing ship.

bow·string (bō′strĭng′) ► *n.* The cord attached to both ends of an archer's bow.

bow tie (bō) ► *n.* A short necktie tied in a bowknot close to the collar.

box[1] (bŏks) ► *n.* **1a.** A container, usu. rectangular and often with a lid. **b.** The amount or quantity a box can hold. **2.** A square or rectangle. **3.** A separated seating compartment, as in a theater. **4.** A booth: *a sentry box.* **5.** A perplexing situation. ► *v.* **1.** To place in or as if in a box. **2.** To restrict to a narrow scope or position: *boxed in by new rules.* **—box′ful′** *n.* **—box′y** *adj.*

box[2] (bŏks) ► *n.* A slap or blow with the hand or fist. ► *v.* **1.** To hit with the hand or fist. **2.** To take part in a boxing match.

box[3] (bŏks) ► *n., pl.* **box** or **box·es.** An evergreen shrub or tree having hard yellowish wood, widely grown as a hedge.

box·car (bŏks′kär′) ► *n.* A fully enclosed railroad car used to transport freight.

box·er[1] (bŏk′sər) ► *n. Sports* One who boxes, esp. professionally.

box·er[2] (bŏk′sər) ► *n.* A medium-sized, short-haired dog having a short, square-jawed muzzle.

box·ing (bŏk′sĭng) ► *n.* The sport of fighting with the fists.

box office ► *n.* A booth, as in a theater, where tickets are sold. **—box′-of′fice** *adj.*

box·wood (bŏks′wŏŏd′) ► *n.* **1.** The box shrub or tree. **2.** The hard wood of the box.

boy (boi) ► *n.* A male child or youth. ► *interj.* Used to express mild elation or disgust. **—boy′hood′** *n.* **—boy′ish** *adj.* **—boy′ish·ly** *adv.* **—boy′ish·ness** *n.*

boy·cott (boi′kŏt′) ► *v.* To abstain from buying or dealing with as a protest. **—boy′cott′** *n.*

boy·friend (boi′frĕnd′) ► *n.* **1.** A favored male companion or sweetheart. **2.** A male friend.

Boy Scout ► *n.* A member of a worldwide organization of young men and boys, founded for character development, citizenship training, and outdoor skills.

boy·sen·ber·ry (boi′zən-bĕr′ē) ► *n.* **1.** A prickly bramble derived from a W North American blackberry. **2.** The edible wine-red fruit of this plant.

Br ► The symbol for the element **bromine.**

bra (brä) ► *n.* A brassiere.

brace (brās) ► *n.* **1.** A clamp. **2.** A device, such as a beam in a building, that steadies or supports a weight. **3. braces** *Chiefly Brit.* Suspenders. **4.** An orthopedic appliance used to support a bodily part. **5.** often **braces** A dental appliance of bands and wires that is fixed to the teeth to correct irregular alignment. **6.** A cranklike handle for securing and turning a bit. **7.** A symbol, { or }, used to enclose written or printed lines that are considered a unit. ► *v.* **braced, brac·ing. 1.** To support, strengthen, or hold steady. **2.** To prepare for a struggle, impact, or danger. **3.** To fill with energy; stimulate.

brace·let (brās′lĭt) ► *n.* An ornamental band or chain worn around the wrist or arm.

bra·chi·o·saur (brā′kē-ə-sôr′, brăk′ē-) or **bra·chi·o·sau·rus** (brā′kē-ə-sôr′əs, brăk′ē-) ► *n.* A massive, herbaceous dinosaur of the Jurassic and Cretaceous periods, having forelegs longer than the hind legs.

brack·en (brăk′ən) ► *n.* A widespread weedy fern having large triangular fronds, tough stems, and often forming dense thickets.

brack·et (brăk′ĭt) ► *n.* **1.** An L-shaped fixture, one arm of which is fastened to a vertical surface, the other projecting to support a shelf or other weight. **2.** A shelf supported by brackets. **3.** One of a pair of marks, [ ], used to enclose written or printed material. **4.** A classification or grouping, esp. by income, within a sequence of numbers or grades. **—brack′et** *v.*

brack·ish (brăk′ĭsh) ► *adj.* Containing a mixture of seawater and fresh water. **—brack′ish·ness** *n.*

bract (brăkt) ► *n.* A leaflike plant part located just below a flower, flower stalk, or flower cluster.

brad (brăd) ► *n.* A thin wire nail with a small head. **—brad** *v.*

brag (brăg) ► *v.* **bragged, brag·ging.** To talk or assert boastfully. **—brag** *n.* **—brag′ger** *n.*

brag·ga·do·ci·o (brăg′ə-dō′sē-ō′, -shē-ō′) ► *n., pl.* **-os. 1.** A braggart. **2a.** Empty or pretentious bragging. **b.** A swaggering, cocky manner.

brag·gart (brăg′ərt) ► *n.* One given to empty boasting; bragger.

Brahe (brä, brä′hē), **Tycho** (1546–1601) ► Danish astronomer.

Brah·ma (brä′mə) ► *n.* **1.** *Hinduism* The creator god, conceived chiefly as a member of the triad including also Vishnu and Shiva. **2.** Var. of **Brahman** 2.

Brah·man (brä′mən) also **Brah·min** (-mĭn) ► *n.* **1.** A member of the highest of the four major castes of traditional Indian society, responsible for officiating at religious rites and studying and teaching the Vedas. **2.** also **Brah·ma** (-mə) One of a breed of domestic cattle bred from stock originating in India, having a hump between the shoulders.

Brah·man·ism (brä′mə-nĭz′əm) also **Brah·min·ism** (-mĭ-) ► *n. Hinduism* **1.** The religion of ancient India as reflected in the Vedas. **2.** The social and religious system of Hindus, esp. of Brahmins, based on a caste structure. **—Brah′man·ist** *n.*

Brah·ma·pu·tra (brä′mə-pŏŏ′trə) ► A river of S Asia rising in SW Xizang (Tibet) and flowing about 2,896 km (1,800 mi) to join the Ganges R.

Brah·min (brä′mĭn) ► *n.* **1.** Var. of **Brahman. 2.** A member

THESAURUS

box[1] *n.* —*See* [illegible], PREDICAMENT.

box *v.* —*See* ENCLOSE (1).

box[2] *v.* —*See* HIT, SLAP.

box *n.* —*See* SLAP.

boxer *n.* A contestant in a boxing match ► fighter, prizefighter, pugilist. [*Compare* FIGHTER.]

box office *n.* The amount of money that is collected as admission, especially to a sporting event ► gate, receipts, take.

boy *n.* A young male person ► boychild, lad, stripling, youth. *Informal:* junior, son. *Slang:* homeboy, little shaver, nip- [illegible] [*Compare* CHILD.] —*See also* FEL- LOW.

boycott *v.* —*See* EXCLUDE.

boyfriend *n.* A man who is a woman's romantic partner ► beau, inamorato. *Informal:* fellow, main man. *Slang:* old man. [*Compare* DARLING, LOVER.]

bozo *n.* —*See* FOOL.

brace *v.* —*See* GIRD, SUPPORT (2), TENSE.

brace *n.* —*See* COUPLE, SUPPORT.

bracer *n.* —*See* TONIC.

bracing *adj.* —*See* INVIGORATING.

bracket *n.* —*See* CLASS (2), SUPPORT.

bracket *v.* —*See* [illegible], SUPPORT (2).

brackish *adj.* Containing salt ► briny, saline, salty. —*See also* BITTER (1).

brag *v.* —*See* BOAST.

brag *n.* —*See* BOAST, BRAGGART.

braggadocio *n.* —*See* ARROGANCE, BOAST, BRAGGART.

braggart *n.* One given to boasting ► blusterer, boaster, brag, braggadocio, bragger, swaggerer, vaunter. *Informal:* blowhard. *Slang:* blower, windbag. [*Compare* EGOTIST, SHOWOFF.]

braggart *adj.* —*See* BOASTFUL.

of a cultural and social elite: *a Boston Brahmin.* **—Brah·min′ic** (-mĭn′ĭk) *adj.*

Brahms (brämz), **Johannes** (1833–97) ▸ German composer. **—Brahms′i·an** *adj.*

braid (brād) ▸ *v.* **1.** To interweave strands or lengths of. **2.** To make by weaving strands together. **3.** To decorate or edge with an interwoven trim. ▸ *n.* **1.** A braided segment or length, as of hair, fabric, or fiber. **2.** Ornamental cord or ribbon, used esp. for decorating or edging fabrics. **—braid′er** *n.*

Braille or **braille** (brāl) ▸ *n.* A system of writing and printing for visually impaired people, in which raised dots represent letters and numerals.

Braille, Louis (1809–52) ▸ French inventor of a writing system for the blind (1829).

brain (brān) ▸ *n.* **1a.** The portion of the vertebrate central nervous system, enclosed within the cranium and composed of gray matter and white matter, that is the primary center for the regulation and control of bodily activities, the receiving and interpreting of sensory impulses, and the exercising of thought and emotion. **b.** A functionally similar portion of the invertebrate nervous system. **2.** often **brains** Intellectual power; intelligence. **3.** A highly intelligent person. ▸ *v. Slang* **1.** To smash in the skull of. **2.** To hit on the head. ***—idioms:*** **on the brain** Obsessively in mind. **pick (someone's) brain** To explore another's ideas through questioning. **—brain′i·ness** *n.* **—brain′less** *adj.* **—brain′less·ness** *n.* **—brain′y** *adj.*

brain·child (brān′chīld′) ▸ *n.* An original idea, plan, or creation.

brain death ▸ *n.* Irreversible brain damage and loss of brain function, as evidenced by cessation of activity of the central nervous system. **—brain′-dead′** (brān′dĕd′) *adj.*

brain·pow·er (brān′pou′ər) ▸ *n.* Intellectual capacity.

brain·storm (brān′stôrm′) ▸ *n.* A sudden clever plan or idea. ▸ *v.* To attempt to solve a problem by a method in which the members of a group spontaneously propose ideas and solutions. **—brain′storm′ing** *n.*

brain·wash·ing (brān′wŏsh′ĭng, -wô′shĭng) ▸ *n.* Intensive, forcible indoctrination aimed at replacing a person's basic convictions with an alternative set of fixed beliefs. **—brain′-wash′** *v.*

brain wave ▸ *n.* A rhythmic fluctuation of electric potential between parts of the brain, as seen on an electroencephalogram.

braise (brāz) ▸ *v.* **braised, brais·ing.** To brown in fat and then simmer in a small quantity of liquid in a covered container.

brake[1] (brāk) ▸ *n.* A device for slowing or stopping motion, as of a vehicle, esp. by contact friction. ▸ *v.* **braked, brak·ing. 1.** To reduce the speed of with or as if with a brake. **2.** To operate or apply a brake.

brake[2] (brāk) ▸ *n.* Any of several ferns, esp. bracken.

brake[3] (brāk) ▸ *n.* A densely overgrown area; thicket.

brake·man (brāk′mən) ▸ *n.* A railroad employee who assists the conductor and checks on the operation of a train's brakes.

bram·ble (brăm′bəl) ▸ *n.* A prickly plant or shrub, esp. the blackberry or raspberry. **—bram′bly** *adj.*

bran (brăn) ▸ *n.* The outer husks of cereal grain removed during the process of milling and used for dietary fiber.

branch (brănch) ▸ *n.* **1a.** A secondary woody stem growing from the trunk, main stem, or limb of a tree or shrub. **b.** A similar structure or part. **2.** Something that resembles a branch of a tree, as the tine of a deer's antlers. **3.** A limited part of a larger or more complex unit or system. **4.** A division of a family or tribe. **5.** A tributary of a river. ▸ *v.* **1.** To divide or spread out in branches. **2.** To enlarge one's scope: *branch out into new fields.* **—branched** *adj.*

brand (brănd) ▸ *n.* **1a.** A trademark or distinctive name identifying a product or manufacturer. **b.** A product line so identified. **c.** A distinctive kind. **2.** A mark indicating ownership, burned on the hide of an animal. **3.** A mark formerly burned into the flesh of criminals. **4.** A mark of disgrace. **5.** A branding iron. **6.** A piece of burning wood. ▸ *v.* **1.** To mark with or as if with a brand. **2.** To stigmatize.

brand·ing iron (brăn′dĭng) ▸ *n.* An iron that is heated and used for branding.

bran·dish (brăn′dĭsh) ▸ *v.* **1.** To wave or flourish (e.g., a weapon) menacingly. **2.** To display ostentatiously.

brand name ▸ *n.* See **trade name** 1. **—brand′-name′** *adj.*

brand-new (brănd′no͞o′, -nyo͞o′) ▸ *adj.* Being fresh and unused; completely new.

bran·dy (brăn′dē) ▸ *n., pl.* **-dies.** An alcoholic liquor distilled from wine or fermented fruit juice. **—bran′dy** *v.*

Brant (brănt), **Joseph** (1742–1807) ▸ Mohawk leader.

brash (brăsh) ▸ *adj.* **-er, -est. 1.** Hasty and unthinking; rash. **2.** Bold; impudent. **—brash′ly** *adv.* **—brash′ness** *n.*

Bra·sí·lia (brə-zĭl′yə) ▸ The capital of Brazil, in the central plateau NW of Rio de Janeiro.

brass (brăs) ▸ *n.* **1a.** A yellowish alloy of copper and zinc. **b.** Objects made of brass. **2.** often **brasses** *Mus.* The brass instruments of an orchestra or band. **3.** *Informal* Bold self-assurance; effrontery. **4.** *Slang* High-ranking military officers. **—brass′y** *adj.*

bras·se·rie (brăs′ə-rē′) ▸ *n.* A bar serving food as well as alcoholic beverages.

brass hat ▸ *n. Slang* One of high rank or position, esp. a high-ranking military officer.

bras·siere (brə-zîr′) ▸ *n.* A woman's undergarment that supports the breasts.

THESAURUS

braid *v.* *—See* WEAVE.

braid *n.* *—See* WEB.

brain *n.* The seat of the faculty of intelligence and reason ▸ head, mind. *Informal:* gray matter. [*Compare* IMAGINATION.] *—See also* MIND (2).

braincase *n.* ▸ brainpan, cranium, skull. [*Compare* HEAD.]

brainchild *n.* *—See* INVENTION (2).

brainless *adj.* *—See* FOOLISH, MINDLESS, STUPID.

brainlessness *n.* *—See* STUPIDITY.

brainpan *n.* The bony framework of the head ▸ braincase, cranium, skull. [*Compare* HEAD.]

brainpower or **brains** *n.* *—See* INTELLIGENCE.

brainsick *adj.* *—See* INSANE.

brainsickness *n.* *—See* INSANITY.

brainstorm *n.* A sudden exciting thought ▸ inspiration, bright idea. *Informal:* brain wave. [*Compare* IDEA.]

brainstorming *n.* *—See* THOUGHT.

brainwash *v.* *—See* INDOCTRINATE (2).

brainwashing *n.* *—See* PROPAGANDA.

brain wave *n.* *Informal* A sudden exciting thought ▸ brainstorm, bright idea, inspiration. [*Compare* IDEA.]

brainwork *n.* *—See* THOUGHT.

brainy *adj.* *—See* INTELLIGENT.

braise *v.* *—See* COOK.

brake *n.* A device for slowing or stopping motion ▸ baffle, bit, bridle, checkrein, curb, damper, drag, leash, rein, restraint, snaffle. [*Compare* BOND, RESTRAINT.] *—See also* ANCHOR.

brake *v.* *—See* RESTRAIN.

brambly *adj.* *—See* THORNY (1).

branch *n.* **1.** Something resembling or analogous to a tree branch ▸ arm, division, extension, fork, offshoot, ramification, subdivision, tributary. [*Compare* DIVISION.] **2.** An area of academic study that is part of a larger body of learning ▸ discipline, field, specialty. [*Compare* AREA.] **3.** An administrative unit, as of government or a company ▸ affiliate, agency, arm, bureau, chapter, department, division, office, organ, section, wing. *—See also* BROOK[1], STICK (1).

branch *v.* To separate into branches or branchlike parts ▸ bifurcate, branch out (*or* off), diverge, diversify, divide, fork, part, radiate, ramify, split, subdivide. [*Compare* DEVIATE, SCATTER.]

brand *n.* *—See* KIND[2], MARK (1).

brand *v.* To cause to feel embarrassment, dishonor, and often guilt ▸ mortify, reproach, shame, stigmatize. *Idioms:* put to shame, put to the blush. [*Compare* BELITTLE, DENIGRATE, EMBARRASS, HUMBLE.] *—See also* MARK (1).

brandish *v.* To wield boldly and dramatically ▸ flourish, sweep, wave. [*Compare* HANDLE.] *—See also* DISPLAY.

brand-new *adj.* *—See* NEW.

brannigan *n.* *—See* BENDER.

brash *adj.* *—See* IMPUDENT, RASH[1], TACTLESS.

brashness *n.* *—See* IMPUDENCE, TEMERITY.

brass *n.* *—See* IMPUDENCE.

brassbound *adj.* *—See* STUBBORN (1).

brass hat *n.* *—See* CHIEF.

brass ring *n.* *Slang* A person or thing

brass tacks ▸ *pl.n. Informal* Essential facts; basics: *getting down to brass tacks.*

brat (brăt) ▸ *n.* A spoiled or ill-mannered child. **—brat′ty** *adj.*

bra·va·do (brə-vä′dō) ▸ *n., pl.* **-dos** or **-does.** **1.** Defiant or swaggering behavior. **2.** A false show of bravery.

brave (brāv) ▸ *adj.* **brav·er, brav·est.** **1.** Possessing or displaying courage; valiant. **2.** Making a fine display; splendid. **3.** Excellent; great. ▸ *n.* A Native American warrior. ▸ *v.* **braved, brav·ing.** **1.** To undergo or face courageously. **2.** To challenge; dare. **—brave′ly** *adv.* **—brave′ness** *n.*

brav·er·y (brā′və-rē, brāv′rē) ▸ *n.* Courage.

bra·vo (brä′vō, brä-vō′) ▸ *interj.* Used to express approval, esp. of a performance. ▸ *n., pl.* **-vos.** A cry of "bravo."

bra·vu·ra (brə-vo͝or′ə, -vyo͝or′ə) ▸ *n.* **1.** *Mus.* Brilliant technique or style in performance. **2.** A showy manner or display.

brawl (brôl) ▸ *n.* A noisy quarrel or fight. **—brawl** *v.* **—brawl′er** *n.*

brawn (brôn) ▸ *n.* **1.** Solid and well-developed muscles. **2.** Muscular strength.

brawn·y (brô′nē) ▸ *adj.* **-i·er, -i·est.** Well-muscled; strong.

bray (brā) ▸ *v.* To utter the loud harsh cry of a donkey. **—bray** *n.*

braze (brāz) ▸ *v.* **brazed, braz·ing.** To solder together using a solder with a high melting point. **—braz′er** *n.*

bra·zen (brā′zən) ▸ *adj.* **1.** Rudely bold; insolent. **2.** Having a loud harsh sound. **3.** Made of or resembling brass. ▸ *v.* To face with bold self-assurance: *brazened out the crisis.* **—bra′zen·ly** *adv.* **—bra′zen·ness** *n.*

bra·zier[1] (brā′zhər) ▸ *n.* One who works in brass.

bra·zier[2] (brā′zhər) ▸ *n.* A metal pan for holding burning coals or charcoal.

Bra·zil (brə-zĭl′) ▸ A country of central and E South America. **—Bra·zil′i·an** *adj. & n.*

Brazil nut ▸ *n.* The hard-shelled edible seed of a South American tree.

breach (brēch) ▸ *n.* **1.** An opening, tear, or rupture, esp. in a solid structure. **2.** A violation or infraction, as of a law or obligation. **3.** A disruption of friendly relations. **4.** A leap of a whale from the water. **—breach** *v.*

bread (brĕd) ▸ *n.* **1.** A staple food made chiefly from moistened, usu. leavened flour or meal kneaded and baked. **2.** Food in general, regarded as necessary to sustain life. **3a.** Livelihood: *earn one's bread.* **b.** *Slang* Money. ▸ *v.* To coat with bread crumbs before cooking.

bread·bas·ket (brĕd′băs′kĭt) ▸ *n.* An abundant grain-producing region.

bread·board (brĕd′bôrd′) ▸ *n.* **1.** A slicing board. **2.** An experimental model, esp. of an electronic circuit.

bread·fruit (brĕd′fro͞ot′) ▸ *n.* **1.** A Malaysian timber tree having large round yellowish fruits. **2.** The edible fruit of this tree, having a breadlike texture when cooked.

bread·stuff (brĕd′stŭf′) ▸ *n.* **1.** Bread in any form. **2.** Flour or grain used in making bread.

breadth (brĕdth) ▸ *n.* **1.** The measure or dimension from side to side; width. **2a.** Wide range or scope. **b.** Tolerance; broadmindedness: *a jurist of great breadth and wisdom.*

bread·win·ner (brĕd′wĭn′ər) ▸ *n.* A person whose earnings are the primary source of support for one's dependents.

break (brāk) ▸ *v.* **broke** (brōk), **bro·ken** (brō′kən), **break·ing.** **1a.** To separate into or reduce to pieces by sudden force. **b.** To crack without separating into pieces. **2.** To make or become unusable or inoperative. **3.** To give way; collapse. **4.** To force or make a way into, through, or out of. **5.** To pierce the surface of. **6.** To disrupt the uniformity or continuity of: *break ranks.* **7.** To make or become known or noticed, esp. suddenly: *break a story.* **8.** To begin or emerge suddenly: *break into bloom.* **9.** To change suddenly: *broke to the left.* **10.** To surpass, outdo, or overcome: *broke the record.* **11.** To ruin or destroy, as in spirit or health. **12.** To reduce in rank. **13.** To lessen in force or effect: *break a fall.* **14.** To fail to conform (to); violate: *break a law.* ***—phrasal verbs:*** **break down** To undergo a breakdown. **break in** **1.** To train. **2.** To enter forcibly or illegally. **3.** To interrupt. **break off** **1.** To separate or become separated. **2.** To stop suddenly. **break out** **1.** To develop suddenly. **2.** To erupt. **3.** To escape, as from prison. ▸ *n.* **1.** The act or an occurrence of breaking. **2.** The result of breaking, as a crack or separation. **3.** An emergence. **4.** A disruption in continuity. **5.** A sudden or marked change. **6.** A violation: *a security break.* **7.** A stroke of luck. ***—idioms:*** **break bread** To eat together. **break even** To

THESAURUS

worth catching ▸ *Informal:* catch, plum, prize. [*Compare* TREASURE.]

brass-tacks *adj.* *—See* PITHY.

brassy *adj.* *—See* IMPUDENT.

brat *n.* *—See* URCHIN.

brattle *v.* To make or cause to make a succession of short, sharp sounds ▸ chatter, clack, clank, clatter, rattle. [*Compare* KNOCK, SHAKE.]

bravado *n.* *—See* BOAST.

brave *adj.* Having or showing courage ▸ audacious, bold, courageous, dashing, dauntless, doughty, fearless, fortitudinous, gallant, game, gritty, hardy, heroic, intrepid, mettlesome, nervy, plucky, spirited, stout, stouthearted, unafraid, undaunted, unflinching, valiant, valorous. *Informal:* spunky. *Slang:* gutsy, gutty. *Regional:* bodacious. [*Compare* ADVENTUROUS, RASH[1].]

brave *v.* *—See* DEFY (1), VENTURE.

bravery *n.* *—See* COURAGE.

brawl *n.* *—See* FIGHT (1).

brawl *v.* To exchange blows with another person ▸ fight. *Slang:* rumble. *Idioms:* duke it out, mix it up, slug it out. [*Compare* WRESTLE.] *—See also* ARGUE (1).

brawn *n.* Solid and well-developed muscles ▸ bulk, muscle, muscularity, physique. *Informal:* beef. [*Compare* CONSTITUTION.] *—See also* STRENGTH.

brawny *adj.* *—See* MUSCULAR.

bray *v.* *—See* CRUSH (2).

brazen or **brazenfaced** *adj.* *—See* IMPUDENT.

brazenness *n.* *—See* IMPUDENCE.

breach *n.* **1.** An act of breaking a law or of nonfulfillment of an obligation ▸ contravention, delinquency, dereliction, infraction, infringement, malfeasance, nonfeasance, negligence, transgression, trespass, violation. [*Compare* CRIME.] **2.** An interruption in friendly relations ▸ alienation, break, breakdown, collapse, disaffection, estrangement, falling out, fissure, rent, rift, rupture, schism, split. [*Compare* ARGUMENT.] *—See also* CRACK (2).

breach *v.* To make a hole or other opening in ▸ break (through), gap, hole, perforate, pierce, punch (through), puncture. *Slang:* bust (through). [*Compare* CUT.] *—See also* VIOLATE (1).

bread *n.* *—See* FOOD, LIVING, MONEY (1).

bread and butter *n.* *—See* LIVING.

breadth *n.* The extent of something from side to side ▸ broadness, expanse, wideness, width. [*Compare* DISTANCE.]

break *v.* **1.** To crack or split into two or more fragments by means of force or strain ▸ crack (apart *or* open), fracture, rift, rive, shatter, shiver, smash, splinter, sunder. *Idioms:* break (*or* crack) asunder, break in two, smash to bits (*or* pieces *or* smithereens). [*Compare* BURST, CRUSH, DESTROY, DISINTEGRATE.] **2.** To severely impair someone's spirit, health, or will ▸ beat down, crush, destroy, overwhelm, ruin, shatter. **3.** To give way mentally and emotionally ▸ break down, collapse, crack, crumble, crumple, fall, fold, snap. **4.** To be made public ▸ come out, get out, out, transpire. *Informal:* leak (out). *Idiom:* come to light (*or* notice). [*Compare* AIR, ANNOUNCE, APPEAR.] **5.** To discontinue (a habit, for example) ▸ abjure, cut out, forswear, give up, leave off, renounce, stop. *Informal:* swear off. *Slang:* kick. [*Compare* ABANDON.] **6.** To interrupt regular activity for a short period ▸ recess. *Informal:* knock off. *Idioms:* take a break, take a breather, take five (*or* ten). [*Compare* REST[1].] *—See also* BREACH, COLLAPSE (1), COMMUNICATE (1), CRACK (1), DECIPHER, DEMOTE, DISOBEY, DIVIDE, GENTLE, MALFUNCTION, PENETRATE, RUIN, VIOLATE (1).

break apart *v.* *—See* DISINTEGRATE, DIVIDE.

break away *v.* To withdraw from an association or federation ▸ pull out,

have neither losses or gains. **break new ground** To advance beyond previous achievements. **—break′a·ble** *adj. & n.*

break·age (brā′kĭj) ▸ *n.* 1. The act of breaking. 2. A quantity broken. 3a. Loss as a result of breaking. b. A commercial allowance for loss or damage.

break·down (brāk′doun′) ▸ *n.* 1a. The act or process of failing to function. b. The condition resulting from this. 2. A collapse in physical or mental health. 3. An analysis, outline, or summary consisting of itemized data or essentials. 4. Disintegration or decomposition into parts or elements.

break·er (brā′kər) ▸ *n.* 1. One that breaks. 2. *Elect.* A circuit breaker. 3. A wave that breaks into foam, esp. against a shoreline.

break·fast (brĕk′fəst) ▸ *n.* The first meal of the day. **—break′fast** *v.*

break·front (brāk′frŭnt′) ▸ *n.* A cabinet or bookcase having a central section projecting farther forward than the end sections.

break·neck (brāk′nĕk′) ▸ *adj.* 1. Dangerously fast. 2. Hazardous: *a breakneck curve.*

break·out (brāk′out′) ▸ *n.* A forceful emergence from a restrictive condition.

break·through (brāk′thrōō′) ▸ *n.* 1. An act of overcoming or penetrating an obstacle or restriction. 2. A major success that permits further progress, as in technology.

break·up (brāk′ŭp′) ▸ *n.* 1. A division, dispersal, or disintegration. 2. The discontinuance of a relationship.

break·wa·ter (brāk′wô′tər, -wŏt′ər) ▸ *n.* A barrier that protects a harbor or shore from the full impact of waves.

bream (brēm, brĭm) ▸ *n., pl.* **bream** or **breams**. A freshwater fish having a flattened body and silvery scales.

breast (brĕst) ▸ *n.* 1. The mammary gland, esp. of the human female. 2. The upper front of the human body from the neck to the abdomen. 3. The seat of affection and emotion. ▸ *v.* To meet or confront boldly.

breast·bone (brĕst′bōn′) ▸ *n.* See **sternum**.

breast-feed (brĕst′fēd′) ▸ *v.* To suckle.

breast·plate (brĕst′plāt′) ▸ *n.* A piece of armor that covers the breast.

breast·stroke (brĕst′strōk′) ▸ *n.* A swimming stroke performed face down with the arms sweeping back to the sides while kicking.

breast·work (brĕst′wûrk′) ▸ *n.* A temporary, quickly constructed fortification, usually breast-high.

breath (brĕth) ▸ *n.* 1. The air inhaled and exhaled in respiration. 2. The act or process of breathing; respiration. 3. The ability to breathe. 4. A slight breeze. 5. A trace or suggestion. 6. A whisper. ***—idiom:*** **out of breath** Breathing with difficulty; gasping. **—breath′less** *adj.* **—breath′less·ly** *adv.* **—breath′y** *adj.*

breathe (brēth) ▸ *v.* **breathed, breath·ing.** 1. To inhale and exhale air. 2. To be alive; live. 3. To pause to rest. 4. To utter quietly; whisper. ***—idiom:*** **breathe down (someone's) neck** To threaten or annoy by proximity. **—breath′a·ble** *adj.*

breath·er (brē′thər) ▸ *n.* 1. One that breathes. 2. *Informal* A short rest period.

breath·tak·ing (brĕth′tā′kĭng) ▸ *adj.* Inspiring awe. **—breath′tak′ing·ly** *adv.*

breech (brēch) ▸ *n.* 1. The buttocks. 2. **breech·es** (brĭch′ĭz) a. Knee-length trousers. b. *Informal* Trousers. 3. The part of a firearm behind the barrel.

breech·cloth (brēch′klôth′, -klŏth′) ▸ *n.* A loincloth.

breed (brēd) ▸ *v.* **bred** (brĕd), **breed·ing.** 1a. To produce (offspring). b. To reproduce. 2. To bring about; engender. 3. To raise or mate animals. 4. To rear or train; bring up. ▸ *n.* 1. A genetic strain, esp. one developed and maintained by controlled propagation. 2. A kind; sort.

breed·er (brē′dər) ▸ *n.* 1. One who breeds animals or plants. 2. A source or cause.

breeder reactor ▸ *n.* A nuclear reactor that produces as well as consumes fissionable material.

breed·ing (brē′dĭng) ▸ *n.* 1. One's line of descent; ancestry. 2. Training in the proper forms of social and personal conduct.

breeze (brēz) ▸ *n.* 1. A light gentle wind. 2. *Informal* Something, such as a task, that is easy to do. ▸ *v.* **breezed, breez·ing.** *Informal* To progress swiftly and effortlessly. **—breez′i·ly** *adv.* **—breez′i·ness** *n.* **—breez′y** *adj.*

breeze·way (brēz′wā′) ▸ *n.* A roofed, open-sided passageway connecting two structures, such as a house and garage.

breth·ren (brĕth′rən) ▸ *n.* Pl. of **brother** 2.

Bret·on (brĕt′n) ▸ *n.* 1. A native or inhabitant of Brittany. 2. The Celtic language of Brittany. **—Bret′on** *adj.*

breve (brĕv, brēv) ▸ *n.* 1. A symbol (˘) placed over a vowel to show that it has a short sound. 2. *Mus.* A note equivalent to two whole notes.

THESAURUS

secede, splinter (off), withdraw. *Informal:* split (away). [*Compare* QUIT.]

break down *v.* To take something apart ▸ disassemble, dismantle, take down. *—See also* ANALYZE, DECAY, DESTROY (1), DISINTEGRATE, MALFUNCTION.

break in *v.* To enter forcibly or illegally ▸ burglarize, invade, trespass. [*Compare* ROB, STEAL.] *—See also* DOMESTICATE, INTERRUPT (2).

break off *v.* To bring an activity or relationship to an end suddenly ▸ cease, discontinue, interrupt, suspend, terminate. *—See also* ABANDON (2), SEPARATE (1).

break out *v.* To become manifest suddenly and in full force ▸ be triggered (*or* sparked *or* touched off), burst (forth *or* out), erupt, explode, flare (up), irrupt. *—See also* ESCAPE (1).

break up *v.* *—See* DISINTEGRATE, DIVIDE, LAUGH, SCATTER (2), SEPARATE (1).

break *n.* A cessation of continuity or regularity ▸ discontinuance, discontinuation, discontinuity, disruption, interruption, pause, suspension. [*Compare* STOP.] *—See also* BREACH (2), CRACK (2), ESCAPE (1), GAP (2), OPPORTUNITY, REST[1] (1).

breakable *adj.* *—See* FRAGILE.

breakage *n.* *—See* DAMAGE.

breakdown *n.* 1. A sudden sharp decline in mental, emotional, or physical health ▸ collapse. *Informal:* crackup. [*Compare* INFIRMITY.] 2. A cessation of proper functioning ▸ collapse, failure, malfunction, outage. *—See also* ANALYSIS, BREACH (2), COLLAPSE (2), DECAY.

breaker *n.* *—See* WAVE.

break-in *n.* The act of entering a building or room with the intent to commit theft ▸ breaking and entering, burglary, forced entry, trespass. [*Compare* LARCENY.]

breakneck *adj.* *—See* FAST (1).

breakout *n.* *—See* ERUPTION, ESCAPE (1).

breast *n.* The seat of a person's innermost emotions and feelings ▸ bosom, heart, soul. ***Idioms:*** the bottom (*or* cockles) of one's heart, one's heart of hearts.

breastwork *n.* *—See* BULWARK.

breath *n.* The act or process of breathing ▸ exhalation, expiration, inhalation, inspiration, respiration, suspiration, wind. *—See also* BREEZE (1), SHADE (2), SPIRIT (2).

breathe *v.* 1. To take a breath or breaths ▸ breathe in (*or* out), exhale, expire, inhale, inspire, respire, suspire. ***Idiom:*** draw breath. [*Compare* PANT.] 2. To tell in confidence ▸ confide, share, unbosom, whisper. [*Compare* COMMUNICATE, REVEAL, SAY.] *—See also* BLOW[1] (1), EXIST.

breather *n.* *—See* REST[1] (1).

breathing *adj.* *—See* ALIVE.

breathless *adj.* *—See* AIRLESS (2).

breech *n.* *—See* BUTTOCKS.

breed *v.* To give life to; have offspring ▸ beget, engender, father, hatch, increase, multiply, parent, procreate, proliferate, propagate, reproduce, spawn. [*Compare* PRODUCE.] *—See also* GROW.

breed *n.* *—See* KIND[2].

breeding *n.* Training in the proper forms of social and personal conduct ▸ education, upbringing. [*Compare* COURTESY, MANNERS.] *—See also* CULTURE (3), REPRODUCTION.

breeze *n.* 1. A gentle wind ▸ breath, cat's-paw, draft, eddy, puff, whiff, zephyr. [*Compare* WIND[1].] 2. *Informal* An easily accomplished task ▸ cakewalk, child's play, cinch, picnic, pushover, snap, walkaway, walkover. *Slang:* duck soup. ***Idioms:*** piece of cake, walk in the park. [*Compare* RUNAWAY.]

breeze *v.* *Informal* To progress quickly and effortlessly ▸ coast, sail, skate, zip. *Informal* romp, waltz.

breezeless *adj.* *—See* AIRLESS (2).

breezy *adj.* *—See* AIRY (3), LIVELY.

bre·vi·ar·y (brē′vē-ĕr′ē, brĕv′ē-) ▸ *n., pl.* **-ies.** A book containing the hymns, offices, and prayers for the canonical hours.
brev·i·ty (brĕv′ĭ-tē) ▸ *n.* **1.** Briefness of duration. **2.** Concise expression; terseness.
brew (bro͞o) ▸ *v.* **1.** To make (ale or beer) from malt and hops by infusion, boiling, and fermentation. **2.** To make (a beverage) by boiling or steeping. **3.** To be imminent: *Trouble's brewing.* **—brew** *n.* **—brew′er** *n.* **—brew′er·y** *n.*
Brezh·nev (brĕzh′nĕf), **Leonid Ilyich** (1906–82) ▸ Soviet political leader.
bri·ar[1] also **bri·er** (brī′ər) ▸ *n.* **1.** A Mediterranean shrub whose woody roots are used to make tobacco pipes. **2.** A pipe made from this root.
bri·ar[2] (brī′ər) ▸ *n.* Var. of **brier**[1].
bribe (brīb) ▸ *n.* Something, such as money or a favor, offered or given to induce or influence a person to act dishonestly. ▸ *v.* **bribed, brib·ing. 1.** To give, offer, or promise a bribe (to). **2.** To gain influence over or corrupt by a bribe. **—brib′a·ble** *adj.* **—brib′er·y** *n.*
bric-a-brac (brĭk′ə-brăk′) ▸ *n.* Small objects usu. displayed as ornaments.
brick (brĭk) ▸ *n., pl.* **bricks** or **brick. 1.** A molded rectangular block of clay baked until hard and used as a building and paving material. **2.** An object shaped like a brick: *a brick of cheese.* ▸ *v.* To construct, line, or pave with bricks.
brick-and-mor·tar (brĭk′ənd-môr′tər) ▸ *adj.* Serving consumers in a physical facility rather than providing remote, esp. online, services.
brick·bat (brĭk′băt′) ▸ *n.* **1.** A piece of brick, esp. when thrown. **2.** A critical remark.
brick·lay·er (brĭk′lā′ər) ▸ *n.* A person skilled in building with bricks. **—brick′lay′ing** *n.*
bri·dal (brīd′l) ▸ *n.* A wedding. **—bri′dal** *adj.*
bride (brīd) ▸ *n.* A woman recently married or about to be married.
bride·groom (brīd′gro͞om′, -gro͝om′) ▸ *n.* A man who is about to be married or has recently been married.
brides·maid (brīdz′mād′) ▸ *n.* A woman who attends the bride at a wedding.
bridge[1] (brĭj) ▸ *n.* **1.** A structure spanning and providing passage over an obstacle. **2.** The upper bony ridge of the human nose. **3.** A fixed or removable replacement for missing natural teeth. **4.** *Mus.* A thin, upright piece of wood in some stringed instruments that supports the strings above the sounding board. **5.** A crosswise platform or enclosed area above the main deck of a ship from which the ship is controlled. ▸ *v.* **bridged, bridg·ing. 1.** To build a bridge over. **2.** To cross by or as if by a bridge. **—bridge′a·ble** *adj.*
bridge[2] (brĭj) ▸ *n.* Any of several card games usu. for four people, derived from whist.
bridge·head (brĭj′hĕd′) ▸ *n.* A forward position seized by advancing troops in enemy territory as a foothold for further advance.
bridge·work (brĭj′wûrk′) ▸ *n.* A dental bridge or bridges used to replace missing teeth.
bri·dle (brīd′l) ▸ *n.* **1.** The harness fitted about a horse's head, used to restrain or guide. **2.** A curb or check. ▸ *v.* **-dled, -dling. 1.** To put a bridle on. **2.** To control or restrain with or as if with a bridle. **3.** To show anger: *bridled at the remark.*
brief (brēf) ▸ *adj.* **-er, -est. 1.** Short in duration or extent. **2.** Succinct; concise. ▸ *n.* **1.** A short or condensed statement, esp. of a legal case or argument. **2. briefs** Short, tight-fitting underpants. ▸ *v.* To give a briefing to. **—brief′ly** *adv.* **—brief′ness** *n.*
brief·case (brēf′kās′) ▸ *n.* A portable, often flat case, used esp. for carrying papers.
brief·ing (brē′fĭng) ▸ *n.* **1.** The act of giving or receiving concise preparatory instructions or information. **2.** The information itself.
bri·er[1] also **bri·ar** (brī′ər) ▸ *n.* Any of several prickly plants, such as certain rosebushes. **—bri′er·y** *adj.*
bri·er[2] (brī′ər) ▸ *n.* Var. of **briar**[1].
brig (brĭg) ▸ *n.* **1.** A two-masted square-rigged sailing ship. **2.** A prison on board a US Navy or Coast Guard vessel.
bri·gade (brĭ-gād′) ▸ *n.* **1.** A military unit consisting of a variable number of combat battalions, with supporting units and services. **2.** A group organized for a specific task: *a fire brigade.*
brig·a·dier general (brĭg′ə-dîr′) ▸ *n., pl.* **brigadier generals.** A rank, as in the US Army, above colonel and below major general.
brig·and (brĭg′ənd) ▸ *n.* A bandit, esp. one of an outlaw band. **—brig′and·age** (-ən-dĭj) *n.*
brig·an·tine (brĭg′ən-tēn′) ▸ *n.* A two-masted square-rigged sailing ship having a fore-and-aft mainsail.
bright (brīt) ▸ *adj.* **-er, -est. 1.** Emitting or reflecting light; shining. **2.** Brilliant in color; vivid. **3.** Glorious; splendid. **4.** Happy; cheerful. **5.** Clever; intelligent. **—bright′ly** *adv.* **—bright′ness** *n.*
bright·en (brīt′n) ▸ *v.* To make or become bright or brighter. **—bright′en·er** *n.*
bril·liant (brĭl′yənt) ▸ *adj.* **1.** Full of light; shining brightly. **2.** Bright and vivid in color. **3.** Glorious; magnificent. **4.** Highly intelligent: *a brilliant mind.* ▸ *n.* A precious gem, esp. a diamond, cut with numerous facets. **—bril′liance, bril′lian·cy** *n.* **—bril′liant·ly** *adv.*
bril·lian·tine (brĭl′yən-tēn′) ▸ *n.* An oily, perfumed hairdressing.
brim (brĭm) ▸ *n.* **1.** The rim or uppermost edge of a cup or other vessel. **2.** A projecting rim, as on a hat. ▸ *v.* **brimmed, brim·ming. 1.** To be full to the brim. **2.** To overflow. **—brim′ful′** *adj.*
brim·stone (brĭm′stōn′) ▸ *n.* Sulfur.
brin·dled (brĭn′dld) ▸ *adj.* Tawny or grayish with streaks or spots of a darker color.

THESAURUS

brew *n.* —*See* COMBINATION, DRINK (1).
brew *v.* —*See* THREATEN (2).
brewing *adj.* —*See* IMMINENT.
bribe *n.* Money or a favor given as an inducement to dishonest behavior ▸ fix, graft, payola, soap, sop. *Informal:* hush money, payoff. *Slang:* boodle, grease, kickback, protection.
bribe *v.* To give or promise a bribe to ▸ buy (off), corrupt, fix, suborn. *Informal:* pay off. *Idioms:* cross someone's palm, grease someone's palm (*or* hand), take care of.
bric-a-brac *n.* —*See* NOVELTY (3).
bridal *n.* —*See* WEDDING.
bridle *n.* —*See* BRAKE.
bridle *v.* —*See* RESTRAIN.
bridled *adj.* —*See* RESTRICTED.
brief *adj.* Expressed in few words ▸ abbreviated, abridged, compendious, compressed, concise, condensed, crisp, curt, laconic, lean, short, succinct, summary, terse, thumbnail, trenchant. [*Compare* PITHY.] —*See also* ABRUPT (1), QUICK, TRANSITORY.
brief *n.* —*See* MESSAGE, SYNOPSIS.
briery *adj.* —*See* THORNY (1).
brig *n.* —*See* JAIL.
brigade *n.* —*See* DETACHMENT (3).
brigand *n.* —*See* THIEF.
bright *adj.* Giving off or reflecting much light ▸ beaming, beamy, brilliant, effulgent, fulgent, glowing, incandescent, irradiant, lambent, lucent, luminescent, luminous, lustrous, radiant, refulgent, shining, shiny. [*Compare* BRILLIANT, GLOSSY, SPARKLING.] —*See also* CHEERFUL, CLEAR (2), CLEVER (1), COLORFUL (1), FAVORABLE (1), INTELLIGENT.
brighten *v.* To make lively or animated ▸ animate, enliven, light (up), perk up. —*See also* CLEAR (1).
bright-eyed *adj.* —*See* ALERT.
bright idea *adj.* A sudden exciting thought ▸ brainstorm, inspiration. *Informal:* brain wave. [*Compare* IDEA.]
brilliance *n.* **1.** Exceptional brightness and clarity ▸ brilliancy, effulgence, fire, luminosity, radiance. **2.** Liveliness and vivacity of imagination ▸ brilliancy, fire, genius, inspiration. [*Compare* INTELLIGENCE, INVENTION.] —*See also* GLITTER (2), GLORY.
brilliant *adj.* Extremely or harshly bright ▸ blazing, blinding, dazzling, glaring, glary, pulsing, throbbing. [*Compare* SPARKLING.] —*See also* BRIGHT, FAVORABLE (1), GLORIOUS, GLOSSY, INTELLIGENT.
brim *n.* —*See* BILL[2] (2), BORDER (1), LIMIT (1).
brimful or **brimming** *adj.* —*See* FULL (1).

brine (brīn) ▸ *n.* **1.** Water saturated with salt. **2.** The ocean. **—brin′i·ness** *n.* **—brin′y** *adj.*
bring (brĭng) ▸ *v.* **brought** (brôt), **bring·ing.** **1.** To take with oneself to a place. **2.** To lead or force into a specified state or condition: *bring water to a boil; brought the meeting to a close.* **3.** To persuade; induce. **4.** To cause; produce. **5.** To sell for. ***—phrasal verbs:* bring about** To cause to happen. **bring down** To cause to fall or collapse. **bring forth** To produce. **bring off** To accomplish successfully. **bring on** To result in; cause. **bring out** **1.** To reveal or expose. **2.** To produce or publish. **bring to** To cause to recover consciousness. **bring up** **1.** To rear as a parent. **2.** To mention. **—bring′er** *n.*
brink (brĭngk) ▸ *n.* **1.** The upper edge of a steep place. **2.** The verge of something.
brink·man·ship (brĭngk′mən-shĭp′) also **brinks·man·ship** (brĭngks′-) ▸ *n.* A policy aimed at pushing a dangerous situation to the limit so that an opponent will concede.
bri·o (brē′ō) ▸ *n.* Vigor; vivacity.
bri·oche (brē-ôsh′, -ōsh′) ▸ *n.* A soft roll made from a dough of yeast, butter, and eggs.
bri·quette also **bri·quet** (brĭ-kĕt′) ▸ *n.* A block of compressed coal dust, charcoal, or sawdust, used for fuel and kindling.
bris (brĭs) ▸ *n., pl.* **bris·es.** *Judaism* The rite of male circumcision.
brisk (brĭsk) ▸ *adj.* **-er, -est.** **1.** Marked by speed, liveliness, and vigor; energetic. **2.** Stimulating and invigorating. **—brisk′ly** *adv.* **—brisk′ness** *n.*
bris·ket (brĭs′kĭt) ▸ *n.* **1.** The chest of an animal. **2.** The ribs and meat taken from the brisket.
bris·ling (brĭz′lĭng, brĭs′-) ▸ *n.* See **sprat** 1.
bris·tle (brĭs′əl) ▸ *n.* A stiff coarse hair. ▸ *v.* **-tled, -tling.** **1.** To stand or erect stiffly on end like bristles. **2.** To raise the bristles stiffly. **3.** To react in an angry or offended manner. **4.** To abound with or as with bristles: *The path bristled with thorns.* **—bris′tly** *adj.*
Brit (brĭt) ▸ *n.* *Informal* A British person.
Brit·ain[1] (brĭt′n) ▸ The island of Great Britain.
Brit·ain[2] (brĭt′n) ▸ See **United Kingdom.**
Bri·tan·nic (brĭ-tăn′ĭk) ▸ *adj.* British.
britch·es (brĭch′ĭz) ▸ *pl.n.* Breeches.
Brit·i·cism (brĭt′ĭ-sĭz′əm) ▸ *n.* A word, phrase, or idiom peculiar to British English.
Brit·ish (brĭt′ĭsh) ▸ *adj.* **1.** Of or relating to Great Britain. **2.** Of or relating to the ancient Britons. ▸ *n.* **1.** The people of Great Britain. **2.** British English. **3.** The Celtic language of the ancient Britons.
British Columbia ▸ A province of W Canada bordering on the Pacific Ocean. Cap. Victoria.
British Commonwealth ▸ See **Commonwealth of Nations.**
British English ▸ *n.* The English language as used in England.
British Isles ▸ A group of islands off the NW coast of Europe comprising Great Britain, Ireland, and adjacent smaller islands.
British thermal unit ▸ *n.* Formerly, the quantity of heat required to raise the temperature of one pound of water by 1°F; now defined as 1,055.06 joules.
British Virgin Islands ▸ A British colony in the E Caribbean E of Puerto Rico and the US Virgin Is.
British West Indies ▸ The islands of the West Indies formerly under British control, including Jamaica, Barbados, Trinidad and Tobago, and the Bahamas.
Brit·on (brĭt′n) ▸ *n.* **1.** A native or inhabitant of Great Britain. **2.** One of a Celtic people inhabiting ancient Britain at the time of the Roman invasion.
Brit·ta·ny (brĭt′n-ē) ▸ A historical region and former province of NW France on a peninsula between the English Channel and the Bay of Biscay.
brit·tle (brĭt′l) ▸ *adj.* **-tler, -tlest.** Likely to break, snap, or crack; fragile. **—brit′tle·ness** *n.*
Bro. ▸ *abbr.* *Eccles.* brother
broach (brōch) ▸ *v.* **1.** To bring up (a subject) for discussion or debate. **2.** To pierce in order to draw off liquid. ▸ *n.* **1.** A tapered, serrated tool used to shape or enlarge a hole. **2.** A gimlet for tapping casks. **—broach′er** *n.*
broad (brôd) ▸ *adj.* **-er, -est.** **1.** Wide in extent from side to side. **2.** Large in expanse; spacious. **3.** Full; open: *broad daylight.* **4.** Covering a wide scope; general. **5.** Liberal; tolerant. **6.** Main; essential. **7.** Plain and clear; obvious: *gave us a broad hint to leave.* **—broad′ly** *adv.* **—broad′ness** *n.*
broad·band (brôd′bănd′) ▸ *adj.* **1.** Of or having a wide band of electromagnetic frequencies. **2.** Relating to the use of multiple channels to transmit multiple pieces of data at the same time.
broad bean ▸ *n.* **1.** An annual Old World plant in the pea family. **2.** The edible seed or thick green pod of this plant.
broad·cast (brôd′kăst′) ▸ *v.* **-cast** or **-cast·ed, -cast·ing.** **1a.** To transmit by radio or television. **b.** To be on the air. **2.** To make known over a wide area. **3.** To sow (seed) widely, esp. by hand. ▸ *n.* **1.** Transmission of a radio or television program or signal. **2.** A radio or television program. **—broad′cast′er** *n.*
broad·cloth (brôd′klôth′, -klŏth′) ▸ *n.* **1.** A fine textured woolen cloth with a glossy texture. **2.** A closely woven silk, cotton, or synthetic fabric.
broad·en (brôd′n) ▸ *v.* To make or become broad or broader. **—broad′en·er** *n.*
broad jump ▸ *n.* *Sports* See **long jump.**
broad·loom (brôd′lo͞om′) ▸ *adj.* Woven on a wide loom: *a broadloom carpet.*
broad-mind·ed (brôd′mīn′dĭd) ▸ *adj.* Having or marked by tolerant or liberal views. **—broad′-mind′ed·ness** *n.*
broad·side (brôd′sīd′) ▸ *n.* **1.** The side of a ship above the water line. **2.** The simultaneous discharge of all the guns on one side of a warship. **3.** A forceful verbal attack. ▸ *adv.* With the side turned to a given object. ▸ *v.* **-sid·ed, -sid·ing.** To collide with full on the side.
broad-spec·trum (brôd′spĕk′trəm) ▸ *adj.* Widely applicable or effective: *a broad-spectrum antibiotic.*

THESAURUS

bring *v.* **1.** To cause to come along with oneself ▸ bear, carry, convey, fetch, take (along), transport. [*Compare* CARRY.] **2.** To achieve a certain price ▸ bring in, fetch, get, go for, realize, sell for. *—See also* CAUSE.
bring about *v.* *—See* CAUSE, EFFECT.
bring around or **round** *v.* *—See* CONVINCE, PERSUADE, REVIVE (2).
bring down *v.* *—See* OVERTHROW.
bring forth *v.* *—See* BEAR (4), PRODUCE (1).
bring in *v.* *—See* RETURN (3).
bring off *v.* *—See* EFFECT.
bring on *v.* *—See* CAUSE.
bring out *v.* *—See* PUBLISH (1).
bring up *v.* To take care of and educate a child ▸ foster, parent, raise, rear. [*Compare* NURTURE.] *—See also* BROACH, REFER (1).
brink *n.* *—See* BORDER (1).
briny *adj.* Containing salt ▸ brackish, saline, salty. *—See also* BITTER (1), MARINE (1).
briny *n.* *—See* OCEAN.
brio *n.* *—See* SPIRIT (1).
brisk *adj.* *—See* ENERGETIC, FAST (1).
bristle *v.* *—See* ANGER (2), TEEM[1].
bristly *adj.* *—See* HAIRY, THORNY (1).
brittle *adj.* *—See* FRAGILE.
broach *v.* To put forward a topic for discussion ▸ bring up, introduce, moot, put forth, raise. [*Compare* NAME, PROPOSE, REFER.]
broad *adj.* **1.** Of large extent or expanse ▸ ample, expansive, extended, extensive, outspread, outstretched, spacious, spread out, wide. [*Compare* WIDESPREAD.] **2.** Spread out over a large area ▸ far-flung, widespread. *—See also* BROAD-MINDED, GENERAL (2), LOOSE (3), OBSCENE, OBVIOUS.
broadcast *v.* *—See* ANNOUNCE, PLANT.
broadcast *n.* A show that is aired on television or radio ▸ airing, program.
broaden *v.* To make or become broader or more comprehensive ▸ amplify, dilate, distend, enlarge, expand, extend, spread (out), widen. [*Compare* INCREASE, LENGTHEN, SPREAD.]
broadening *n.* *—See* EXPANSION.
broad-minded *adj.* Not narrow or intolerant; respectful of others' views ▸ accepting, broad, humanistic, liberal, open-minded, progressive, tolerant. [*Compare* FAIR[1], LIBERAL, TOLERANT.]
broadness *n.* The extent of something from side to side ▸ breadth, expanse, wideness, width. [*Compare* DISTANCE.]
broadside *n.* *—See* BARRAGE.
broad-spectrum *adj.* *—See* GENERAL (2).

broad·sword (brôd′sôrd′) ▸ *n.* A sword with a wide, usu. two-edged blade.

broad·tail (brôd′tāl′) ▸ *n.* **1.** See **karakul**. **2.** The flat, glossy, wavy pelt of a prematurely born karakul sheep.

Broad·way (brôd′wā′) ▸ The principal theater and amusement district of New York City, on the West Side of midtown Manhattan.

bro·cade (brō-kād′) ▸ *n.* A heavy fabric interwoven with a rich, raised design. **–bro·cade′** *v.*

broc·co·li (brŏk′ə-lē) ▸ *n.* A plant with densely clustered green flower buds and stalks, eaten as a vegetable.

bro·chette (brō-shĕt′) ▸ *n.* A skewer.

bro·chure (brō-shŏŏr′) ▸ *n.* A pamphlet, often containing promotional material.

bro·gan (brō′gən) ▸ *n.* A heavy ankle-high shoe.

brogue[1] (brōg) ▸ *n.* A strong oxford shoe.

brogue[2] (brōg) ▸ *n.* A strong dialectal accent, esp. an Irish accent.

broil (broil) ▸ *v.* **1.** To cook by direct radiant heat. **2.** To expose or be exposed to great heat. **–broil** *n.*

broil·er (broi′lər) ▸ *n.* **1.** One that broils, esp. a small oven or the part of a stove used for broiling food. **2.** A tender young chicken suitable for broiling.

broke (brōk) ▸ *v.* P.t. of **break**. ▸ *adj. Informal* Lacking funds.

bro·ken (brō′kən) ▸ *v.* P.part. of **break**. ▸ *adj.* **1.** Shattered; fractured. **2.** Having been violated: *a broken promise.* **3.** Not continuous. **4.** Spoken imperfectly: *broken English.* **5.** Subdued totally; tamed or humbled. **6.** Not functioning; out of order. **–bro′ken·ly** *adv.*

bro·ken-down (brō′kən-doun′) ▸ *adj.* **1.** Out of working order. **2.** In poor condition.

bro·ken·heart·ed (brō′kən-här′tĭd) ▸ *adj.* Grievously sad or despairing.

bro·ker (brō′kər) ▸ *n.* One that acts as an agent and negotiates contracts, purchases, or sales in return for a fee or commission. ▸ *v.* To arrange or manage: *broker an agreement.*

bro·ker·age (brō′kər-ĭj) ▸ *n.* **1.** The business of a broker. **2.** A fee or commission paid to a broker.

bro·me·li·ad (brō-mē′lē-ăd′) ▸ *n.* Any of various mostly epiphytic tropical American plants usu. having long, stiff leaves and colorful flowers.

bro·mide (brō′mīd′) ▸ *n.* **1a.** A chemical compound of bromine with another element, such as silver. **b.** Potassium bromide. **2.** A platitude. **–bro·mid′ic** (-mĭd′ĭk) *adj.*

bro·mine (brō′mēn) ▸ *n. Symbol* **Br** A heavy, volatile, corrosive, reddish-brown, nonmetallic liquid element used in gasoline antiknock mixtures, fumigants, dyes, and photographic chemicals. At. no. 35.

bron·chi·al (brŏng′kē-əl) ▸ *adj.* Of or relating to either bronchus or their extensions.

bron·chi·tis (brŏn-kī′tĭs, brŏng-) ▸ *n.* Inflammation of the mucous membrane of the bronchial tubes. **–bron·chit′ic** (-kĭt′ĭk) *adj.*

bron·cho·pul·mo·nar·y (brŏng′kō-pŏŏl′mə-nĕr′ē, -pŭl′-) ▸ *adj.* Relating to the bronchi and the lungs.

bron·chus (brŏng′kəs) ▸ *n., pl.* **-chi** (-kī′, -kē′). Either of two main branches of the trachea, leading directly to the lungs.

bron·co (brŏng′kō) ▸ *n., pl.* **-cos**. A wild horse of W North America.

bron·co·bust·er (brŏng′kō-bŭs′tər) ▸ *n.* One who breaks wild horses to the saddle.

Bron·të (brŏn′tē) ▸ Family of British novelists and poets, including **Charlotte** (1816–55), **Emily** (1818–48), and **Anne** (1820–49).

bron·to·saur (brŏn′tə-sôr′) or **bron·to·sau·rus** (brŏn′tə-sôr′əs) ▸ *n.* An apatosaur.

Bronx (brŏngks) ▸ A borough of New York City in SE NY on the mainland N of Manhattan.

bronze (brŏnz) ▸ *n.* **1.** Any of various alloys consisting chiefly of copper and tin. **2.** A work of art made of bronze. **3.** A yellowish to olive brown. ▸ *v.* **bronzed, bronz·ing.** To give the color or appearance of bronze to. **–bronze** *adj.*

Bronze Age ▸ *n.* A period of human culture between the Stone Age and the Iron Age, characterized by weapons and implements made of bronze.

brooch (brōch, brŏŏch) ▸ *n.* A decorative pin or clasp.

brood (brŏŏd) ▸ *n.* The young of certain animals, esp. a group of young birds or fowl hatched at one time. ▸ *v.* **1.** To sit on in order to hatch. **2.** To think deeply or worry anxiously. **–brood′er** *n.* **–brood′ing·ly** *adv.*

brook[1] (brŏŏk) ▸ *n.* A small stream; creek.

brook[2] (brŏŏk) ▸ *v.* To put up with; tolerate.

Brook·lyn (brŏŏk′lĭn) ▸ A borough of New York City in SE NY on W Long I.

brook trout ▸ *n.* A freshwater game fish of E North America.

broom (brŏŏm, brŏŏm) ▸ *n.* **1.** A bunch of twigs, straw, or bristles bound together, attached to a stick or handle, and used for sweeping. **2.** Any of various Mediterranean shrubs having compound leaves and usu. bright yellow flowers.

bros. ▸ *abbr.* brothers

broth (brôth, brŏth) ▸ *n., pl.* **broths** (brôths, brŏths, brô*thz*, brŏ*thz*). **1.** The water in which meat, fish, or vegetables have been boiled; stock. **2.** A thin clear soup made with stock.

broth·el (brŏth′əl, brô′thəl) ▸ *n.* A house of prostitution.

broth·er (brŭ*th*′ər) ▸ *n.* **1.** A male having one or both parents in common with another person. **2.** *pl.* **-ers** or **breth·ren** (brĕ*th*′rən). One sharing a common ancestry or allegiance with another, esp.: **a.** A kinsman. **b.** A close male friend. **c.** A fellow African-American male. **3.** A member of a Christian men's religious order who is not a priest. **–broth′er·li·ness** *n.* **–broth′er·ly** *adj.*

broth·er·hood (brŭ*th*′ər-hŏŏd′) ▸ *n.* **1.** The state or relationship of being brothers. **2.** Fellowship. **3.** An association of men united for common purposes. **4.** All the members of a profession or trade.

broth·er-in-law (brŭ*th*′ər-ĭn-lô′) ▸ *n., pl.* **broth·ers-in-law** (-ərz-). **1.** The brother of one's husband or wife. **2.** The husband of one's sister. **3.** The husband of the sister of one's husband or wife.

brougham (brŏŏm, brŏŏ′əm, brōm) ▸ *n.* **1.** A closed four-wheeled carriage with an open driver's seat in front. **2.** An automobile with an open driver's seat.

brought (brôt) ▸ *v.* P.t. and p.part. of **bring**.

brou·ha·ha (brŏŏ′hä-hä′) ▸ *n.* An uproar.

brow (brou) ▸ *n.* **1a.** The ridge over the eyes. **b.** The eyebrow. **c.** The forehead. **2.** The projecting upper edge of a steep place.

brow·beat (brou′bēt′) ▸ *v.* To intimidate with an overbearing manner; bully.

brown (broun) ▸ *n.* Any of a group of colors between red and yellow in hue. ▸ *v.* **1.** To make or become brown. **2.** To cook until brown. **–brown** *adj.* **–brown′ish** *adj.* **–brown′ness** *n.*

THESAURUS

Brobdingnagian *adj.* —*See* ENORMOUS.

broil[1] *n.* —*See* BURN (3), COOK.

broil[2] *v.* —*See* ARGUE (1).

broiling *adj.* —*See* HOT (1).

broke *adj.* —*See* POOR.

broken-down *adj.* —*See* SHABBY.

brokenhearted *adj.* —*See* DEPRESSED (1).

broker *n.* —*See* GO-BETWEEN.

bromide *n.* —*See* CLICHÉ.

bromidic *adj.* —*See* TRITE.

Bronx cheer *n.* —*See* HISS (2).

Bronx cheer *v.* —*See* HISS (2).

brood *v.* To focus the attention on something moodily and at length ▸ agonize, dwell, fret, fuss, mope, worry. *Informal:* stew. *Idiom:* eat one's heart out. [*Compare* PONDER, SULK.]

brood *n.* The offspring, as of an animal or bird, for example, that are the result of one breeding season ▸ litter, spawn, young. —*See also* FLOCK, PROGENY.

brook[1] *n.* A small stream ▸ arroyo, bayou, bourne, creek, feeder, rill, rivulet, runnel, tributary, watercourse. *Chiefly Regional:* branch, kill, run.

brook[2] *v.* —*See* ENDURE (1).

brother *n.* —*See* FRIEND.

brotherhood *n.* —*See* COMPANY (3).

brouhaha *n.* —*See* DISORDER (2), SENSATION (2), VOCIFERATION.

browbeat *v.* —*See* INTIMIDATE.

browbeater *n.* —*See* BULLY.

brown *adj.* —*See* DARK (2).

brown *v.* —*See* COOK.

Brown, John (1800–59) ▸ Amer. abolitionist.
brown bear ▸ *n.* Any of several large bears of W North America and N Eurasia, such as the grizzly and Kodiak bears.
brown dwarf ▸ *n.* A starlike celestial body that does not emit light because it is too small to ignite internal nuclear fusion.
brown·field (broun′fēld′) ▸ *n.* An abandoned, usu. contaminated commercial property that has potential for redevelopment.
brown·ie (brou′nē) ▸ *n.* 1. **Brownie** A junior member of the Girl Scouts. 2. A bar of moist, usu. chocolate cake often with nuts. 3. A small helpful elf in folklore.
Brown·ing (brou′nĭng), **Elizabeth Barrett** (1806–61) ▸ British poet.
brown·out (broun′out′) ▸ *n.* A reduction or cutback in electric power.
brown rice ▸ *n.* Unpolished rice that retains the germ and outer layers.
brown·stone (broun′stōn′) ▸ *n.* 1. A brownish-red sandstone. 2. A house built or faced with brownstone.
brown sugar ▸ *n.* Unrefined or incompletely refined sugar that still retains some molasses.
browse (brouz) ▸ *v.* **browsed, brows·ing.** 1. To inspect leisurely or casually. 2. To look for information on the World Wide Web. 3. To feed on leaves, young shoots, and other vegetation; graze. **—browse** *n.*
brows·er (brou′zər) ▸ *n.* 1. One that browses. 2. A computer program that accesses and displays data from the Internet or other networks.
bru·in (bro͞o′ĭn) ▸ *n.* A bear.
bruise (bro͞oz) ▸ *v.* **bruised, bruis·ing.** 1a. To injure (body tissue) without breaking the skin. b. To suffer such injury. 2. To damage (plant tissue), as by abrasion. 3. To pound; crush. 4. To hurt or offend. ▸ *n.* 1. A bruised area, often marked by discoloration. 2. A hurt, as to one's feelings.
bruis·er (bro͞o′zər) ▸ *n. Informal* A large, powerfully built person.
bruit (bro͞ot) ▸ *v.* To spread news of; repeat.
brunch (brŭnch) ▸ *n.* A meal eaten late in the morning combining breakfast and lunch.
Bru·nei (bro͞o-nī′) ▸ A sultanate of NW Borneo on the South China Sea.
bru·net (bro͞o-nĕt′) ▸ *adj.* 1. Of a dark complexion or coloring. 2. Having dark or brown hair or eyes. ▸ *n.* A person with dark or brown hair.
bru·nette (bro͞o-nĕt′) ▸ *n.* A girl or woman with dark or brown hair. **—bru·nette′** *adj.*
brunt (brŭnt) ▸ *n.* The main impact or force, as of an attack or blow.
brush[1] (brŭsh) ▸ *n.* 1. A device consisting of bristles fastened into a handle, used in scrubbing, polishing, grooming the hair, or painting. 2. A light touch in passing; graze. 3. A bushy tail, as of a fox. 4. A sliding connection completing a circuit between a fixed and a moving conductor. 5. A brushoff. ▸ *v.* 1. To use a brush (on). 2. To apply or remove with or as if with motions of a brush. 3. To dismiss abruptly: *brushed the matter aside.* 4. To touch lightly in passing; graze. ***—phrasal verb:* brush up** 1. To refresh one's memory. 2. To renew a skill.
brush[2] (brŭsh) ▸ *n.* 1. A dense growth of bushes or shrubs. 2. Cut or broken branches. **—brush′y** *adj.*
brush[3] (brŭsh) ▸ *n.* A brief, often alarming encounter.
brush·off (brŭsh′ôf′, -ŏf′) ▸ *n.* An abrupt dismissal or snub.
brusque (brŭsk) ▸ *adj.* Abrupt and curt in manner or speech. **—brusque′ly** *adv.* **—brusque′ness** *n.*
Brus·sels (brŭs′əlz) ▸ The capital of Belgium, in the central part.
Brussels sprouts ▸ *pl.n. (takes sing. or pl. v.)* The edible buds of a variety of cabbage, eaten as a vegetable.
bru·tal (bro͞ot′l) ▸ *adj.* 1. Extremely ruthless or cruel. 2. Crude or unfeeling. 3. Harsh; unrelenting: *a brutal winter.* **—bru·tal′i·ty** (-tal′ĭtē) *n.* **—bru′tal·ly** *adv.*
bru·tal·ize (bro͞ot′l-īz′) ▸ *v.* **-ized, -iz·ing.** 1. To make brutal. 2. To treat in a brutal manner. **—bru′tal·i·za′tion** *n.*
brute (bro͞ot) ▸ *n.* 1. An animal; beast. 2. A brutal person. ▸ *adj.* 1. Of or relating to beasts. 2a. Entirely physical: *brute force.* b. Lacking reason or intelligence: *a brute impulse.* **—brut′ish** *adj.* **—brut′ish·ly** *adv.* **—brut′ish·ness** *n.*
Bru·tus (bro͞o′təs), **Marcus Junius** (85?–42 B.C.) ▸ Roman politician and general.
Bryan (brī′ən), **William Jennings** (1860–1925) ▸ Amer. lawyer and politician.
BS ▸ *abbr.* Bachelor of Science
BTU or **Btu** ▸ *abbr.* British thermal unit
bub·ble (bŭb′əl) ▸ *n.* 1. A thin, usu. spherical or hemispherical film of liquid filled with air or gas. 2. A globular body of air or gas formed within a liquid. 3a. An illusion. b. A speculative scheme that comes to nothing. 4. A usu. transparent glass or plastic dome. ▸ *v.* **-bled, -bling.** To form or give off bubbles. **—bub′bly** *adj.*
bub·ble·gum also **bubble gum** (bŭb′əl-gŭm′) ▸ *n.* Chewing gum that can be blown into bubbles.
bubble top ▸ *n.* A transparent glass or plastic dome, as over a swimming pool or open car.
bu·bo (bo͞o′bō, byo͞o′-) ▸ *n., pl.* **-boes.** An inflamed swelling of a lymph node, esp. near the armpit or groin.
bu·bon·ic plague (bo͞o-bŏn′ĭk, byo͞o-) ▸ *n.* A contagious, often fatal epidemic disease caused by bacteria transmitted by fleas from an infected host, esp. a rat, and characterized by chills, fever, vomiting, diarrhea, and buboes.
buc·ca·neer (bŭk′ə-nîr′) ▸ *n.* A pirate.
Bu·chan·an (byo͞o-kăn′ən, bə-), **James** (1791–1868) ▸ The 15th US President (1857–61).
Bu·cha·rest (bo͞o′kə-rĕst′, byo͞o′-) ▸ The capital of Romania, in the SE part on a tributary of the Danube R.
buck[1] (bŭk) ▸ *n.* 1. The adult male of some animals, such as the deer or rabbit. 2. A robust or high-spirited young man. ▸ *v.* 1a. To leap upward arching the back, as a horse or mule. b. To throw (a rider or burden) by bucking. 2. To butt (against). 3. To make sudden jerky movements; jolt. 4. To resist stubbornly. 5. *Informal* To strive with determination: *bucking for a promotion.* ***—phrasal verb:* buck up** To raise (one's) spirits; hearten. ▸ *adj.* Of the lowest rank: *a buck private.* **—buck′er** *n.*
buck[2] (bŭk) ▸ *n. Informal* A dollar.

THESAURUS

brownnose *v.* —*See* FAWN.
brownnose or **brownnoser** *n.* —*See* SYCOPHANT.
brown study *n.* —*See* TRANCE.
browse *v.* 1. To look through reading matter casually ▸ dip into, flip through, glance at (*or* over *or* through), leaf (through), look through (*or* over), riffle (through), run through, scan, skim, thumb (through). *Idiom:* pass (*or* run) one's eyes over. [*Compare* EXAMINE.] 2. To feed on vegetation ▸ crop, forage, graze, nibble (at), pasture. [*Compare* CHEW.]
bruise *n.* An injury that does not break the skin ▸ black-and-blue mark, contusion. [*Compare* BLACK EYE, HARM.]
bruise *v.* To make a bruise or bruises on ▸ contuse. *Idiom:* beat (*or* leave) black-and-blue. [*Compare* HURT.]
bruiser *n.* —*See* THUG.
bruit *v.* —*See* ANNOUNCE.
brume *n.* —*See* HAZE.
brunet *adj.* —*See* DARK (2).
brush[1] *n.* Light and momentary contact with another person or thing ▸ flick, graze, kiss, rub, skim. —*See also* BATTLE.
brush *v.* To make light, gentle, and momentary contact with, as in passing ▸ flick, graze, kiss, rub, rub against, rub along, shave, skim. [*Compare* CARESS, RUB, TOUCH.]
brush[2] *n.* A dense growth of shrubs ▸ brake, brushwood, bushes, canebrake, chaparral, scrub, shrubbery, thicket, underbrush, undergrowth.
brusque *adj.* —*See* ABRUPT (1).
brutal *adj.* —*See* BITTER (2), CRUEL.
brutality *n.* —*See* CRUELTY.
brutalize *v.* —*See* CORRUPT.
brute *n.* —*See* FIEND.
brutish *adj.* —*See* BESTIAL, UNCIVILIZED.
bubble *n.* —*See* BURBLE, DREAM (2).
bubble *v.* —*See* BOIL, BURBLE, FOAM.
bubbly *adj.* —*See* LIVELY.
buck *v.* —*See* CONTEST, DEFY (1).
buck up *v.* —*See* ENCOURAGE (2).

buck·board (bŭk′bôrd′) ▸ *n.* A four-wheeled open carriage with the seat attached to a flexible board.
buck·et (bŭk′ĭt) ▸ *n.* **1a.** A cylindrical vessel used for holding or carrying liquids or solids; pail. **b.** The amount that a bucket can hold. **2.** A receptacle, such as the scoop of a power shovel, used to gather and convey material.
bucket seat ▸ *n.* A single, usu. low seat with a contoured back, as in some cars.
buck·eye (bŭk′ī′) ▸ *n.* Any of various North American trees or shrubs having erect flower clusters and large, shiny brown seeds.
buck·le (bŭk′əl) ▸ *n.* **1.** A clasp, esp. a frame with a movable tongue, for fastening two ends, as of straps or a belt. **2.** An ornament that resembles a buckle. **3.** A bend or bulge. ▸ *v.* **-led, -ling. 1.** To fasten or become fastened with a buckle. **2.** To bend, warp, or crumple under pressure or heat. **3.** To give way; collapse. **4.** To give in; succumb. ***—phrasal verbs:*** **buckle down** To begin working hard. **buckle up** To use a safety belt, esp. in an automobile.
buck·ler (bŭk′lər) ▸ *n.* A small round shield.
buck·ram (bŭk′rəm) ▸ *n.* A coarse cotton fabric heavily stiffened with glue, used for lining garments and in bookbinding.
buck·saw (bŭk′sô′) ▸ *n.* A woodcutting saw, usu. in an H-shaped frame.
buck·shot (bŭk′shŏt′) ▸ *n.* A large lead shot for shotgun shells, used esp. in hunting big game.
buck·skin (bŭk′skĭn′) ▸ *n.* **1.** A soft, grayish-yellow leather made from deerskin or sheepskin. **2. buckskins** Clothing made from buckskin.
buck·tooth (bŭk′to͝oth′) ▸ *n.* A prominent, projecting upper front tooth. **—buck′toothed′** (-to͝otht′) *adj.*
buck·wheat (bŭk′hwēt′, -wēt′) ▸ *n.* **1.** A plant having small, seedlike, triangular fruits. **2.** The edible fruits of this plant, often ground into flour.
bu·col·ic (byo͞o-kŏl′ĭk) ▸ *adj.* Rustic; pastoral. **—bu·col′i·cal·ly** *adv.*
bud (bŭd) ▸ *n.* **1.** A small, protuberant plant structure containing an undeveloped shoot, leaf, or flower. **2.** An asexual reproductive structure, as in yeast or a hydra, that resembles a bud. **3.** One that is not yet fully developed. ▸ *v.* **bud·ded, bud·ding. 1.** To put forth or cause to put forth buds. **2.** To develop from or as if from a bud.
Bu·da·pest (bo͞o′də-pĕst′, -pĕsht′) ▸ The capital of Hungary, in the N-central part on the Danube R.
Bud·dha (bo͞o′də, bo͝od′ə) (563?–483? B.C.) ▸ Indian mystic and founder of Buddhism.
Bud·dhism (bo͞o′dĭz′əm, bo͝od′ĭz′-) ▸ *n.* A religion founded on the teachings of Buddha, esp. that enlightenment obtained through right conduct and meditation releases one from suffering. **—Bud′dhist** *adj. & n.*
bud·ding (bŭd′ĭng) ▸ *n.* Asexual reproduction in which an outgrowth forms on the parent organism and detaches to produce a new individual.
bud·dy (bŭd′ē) ▸ *n., pl.* **-dies.** *Informal* A good friend.
buddy system ▸ *n.* An arrangement in which persons are paired, as for mutual safety or assistance.
budge (bŭj) ▸ *v.* **budged, budg·ing. 1.** To move or cause to move slightly. **2.** To alter a position or attitude.
budg·er·i·gar (bŭj′ə-rē-gär′, bŭj′ə-rē′-) ▸ *n.* A small parakeet bred in green, yellow, or blue plumage.
budg·et (bŭj′ĭt) ▸ *n.* **1.** An itemized summary of probable expenditures and income for a given period. **2.** The sum of money allocated for a particular purpose or period of time. ▸ *v.* **1.** To make a budget. **2.** To plan in advance the expenditure of. **3.** To enter or account for in a budget. **—budg′et·ar′y** (-ĭ-tĕr′ē) *adj.*
budg·ie (bŭj′ē) ▸ *n.* *Informal* A budgerigar.
Bue·nos Ai·res (bwā′nəs âr′ēz, bwĕ′nōs ī′rĕs) ▸ The capital of Argentina, in the E part on the Río de la Plata.
buff[1] (bŭf) ▸ *n.* **1.** A soft, thick, undyed leather made chiefly from the skins of buffalo, elk, or oxen. **2.** A yellowish tan. **3.** A piece of soft material used for polishing. ▸ *adj.* Of the color buff. ▸ *v.* To polish or shine with a buff.
buff[2] (bŭf) ▸ *n.* *Informal* One who is enthusiastic and knowledgeable about a particular subject.
buf·fa·lo (bŭf′ə-lō′) ▸ *n., pl.* **-lo** or **-loes** or **-los. 1.** Any of several oxlike Old World mammals, such as the water buffalo. **2.** The North American bison. ▸ *v.* To intimidate or bewilder.
Buffalo Bill ▸ See **William Frederick Cody.**
buffalo wing ▸ *n.* A fried chicken wing served with a spicy sauce and blue cheese dressing.
buff·er[1] (bŭf′ər) ▸ *n.* One that shines or polishes, esp. a soft cloth or a machine with a moving head.
buff·er[2] (bŭf′ər) ▸ *n.* **1.** Something that lessens, absorbs, or protects against the shock of an impact. **2.** Something that separates potentially antagonistic entities. **3.** *Chem.* A substance that minimizes change in the acidity of a solution when an acid or base is added to the solution. **4.** *Comp. Sci.* A device or area used to store data temporarily. **—buf′fer** *v.*
buffer zone ▸ *n.* A neutral area between hostile forces that serves to prevent conflict.
buf·fet[1] (bə-fā′, bo͞o-) ▸ *n.* **1.** A large sideboard. **2.** A counter, as in a restaurant, for serving refreshments. **3.** A meal at which guests serve themselves from dishes displayed on a table.
buf·fet[2] (bŭf′ĭt) ▸ *n.* A blow or cuff with or as if with the hand. ▸ *v.* To hit or strike against, esp. repeatedly. **—buf′fet·er** *n.*
buf·foon (bə-fo͞on′) ▸ *n.* A clown; jester. **—buf·foon′er·y** *n.*
bug (bŭg) ▸ *n.* **1.** Any of various often harmful insects such as the bedbug, louse, and chinch bug. **2.** Any insect or similar organism. **3.** A disease-producing microorganism; germ. **4.** A mechanical, electrical, or other defect, as in a system, design, or computer code. **5.** An enthusiast; buff. **6.** An electronic listening device, such as a wiretap, used in surveillance. ▸ *v.* **bugged, bug·ging. 1.** To annoy; pester. **2.** To equip (e.g., a room) with a bug. **3.** To bulge out. Used of the eyes. **—bug′ger** *n.*
bug·a·boo (bŭg′ə-bo͞o′) ▸ *n., pl.* **-boos.** An object of obsessive, usu. exaggerated fear or anxiety.
bug·bear (bŭg′bâr′) ▸ *n.* A bugaboo.
bug-eyed (bŭg′īd′) ▸ *adj.* Agog.
bug·gy[1] (bŭg′ē) ▸ *n., pl.* **-gies.** A small, light, usu. four-wheeled carriage.
bug·gy[2] (bŭg′ē) ▸ *adj.* **-gi·er, -gi·est. 1.** Infested with bugs. **2.** *Slang* Crazy.
bu·gle (byo͞o′gəl) ▸ *n.* A trumpetlike musical instrument lacking keys or valves. **—bu′gle** *v.* **—bu′gler** *n.*
build (bĭld) ▸ *v.* **built** (bĭlt), **build·ing. 1.** To make by combining parts; construct. **2.** To fashion; create. **3.** To add

THESAURUS

bucket *v.* —*See* RUSH.
bucket *n.* —*See* BASKET (1).
buckle *v.* To fall in ▸ cave in, collapse, crumple, give, go. *Idiom:* give way. [*Compare* FALL.] —*See also* BEND (3), FASTEN, SUCCUMB.
buckle down *v.* —*See* APPLY (1).
buckle *n.* —*See* FASTENER.
buckram *adj.* Rigidly constrained or formal; lacking grace and spontaneity ▸ starchy, stiff, stilted, wooden. [*Compare* COOL, FORCED, PRUDISH.]
bucolic *adj.* —*See* COUNTRY.
bud[1] *n.* —*See* GERM (2).
bud *v.* —*See* BLOOM[1] (1).
bud[2] *n.* —*See* FRIEND.
buddy *n.* —*See* ASSOCIATE (2), FRIEND.
budge *v.* To move or cause to move slightly ▸ move, shift, stir.
budget *n.* Money or other resources granted for a particular purpose ▸ appropriation, grant, subsidy, subvention. —*See also* OVERHEAD, QUANTITY (3).
budget *v.* —*See* APPROPRIATE.
budget *adj.* —*See* CHEAP.
buff[1] *v.* —*See* GLOSS[1].
buff *adj.* —*See* MUSCULAR.
buff[2] *n.* —*See* FAN[2].
buffet *n.* —*See* BLOW[2].
buffet *v.* —*See* BEAT (1).
buffoon *n.* —*See* FOOL.
bug *n.* —*See* DEFECT, FAN[2], GERM (1), SICKNESS.
bug *v.* To monitor telephone calls with a concealed device connected to the circuit ▸ tap, wiretap. —*See also* ANNOY.
bugbear *n.* —*See* HATE (2).
buggy *adj.* —*See* INSANE.
build *v.* To make or form a structure ▸ carpenter, construct, erect, frame, knock together, put up, raise, rear. —*See also* BASE[1], INCREASE, MAKE.
build in *v.* To construct as an integral part ▸ include, incorporate, integrate.

gradually to: *build support; build up strength.* 4. To establish a basis for. ***—phrasal verb:* build up** To develop or increase in stages or by degrees. ▸ *n.* Physical makeup; physique. **—build′er** *n.*

build·ing (bĭl′dĭng) ▸ *n.* 1. A structure; edifice. 2. The act or art of constructing.

build-up (bĭld′ŭp′) ▸ *n.* 1. The act of amassing or increasing. 2. Widely favorable publicity, esp. by a systematic campaign.

built-in (bĭlt′ĭn′) ▸ *adj.* 1. Constructed as part of a larger unit; not detachable. 2. Forming a permanent element or quality; inherent.

bulb (bŭlb) ▸ *n.* 1. *Bot.* A short, modified underground stem, such as that of the onion or tulip, that contains stored food for the shoot within. 2. A rounded projection or part. 3. A light bulb. **—bul′bous** *adj.*

Bul·gar (bŭl′gär′, bo͝ol′-) ▸ *n.* See **Bulgarian** 1.

Bul·gar·i·a (bŭl-gâr′ē-ə, bo͝ol-) ▸ A country of SE Europe on the Black Sea.

Bul·gar·i·an (bŭl-gâr′ē-ən, bo͝ol-) ▸ *n.* 1. A native or inhabitant of Bulgaria; Bulgar. 2. The Slavic language of the Bulgarians. **—Bul·gar′i·an** *adj.*

bulge (bŭlj) ▸ *n.* A protruding part; swelling. ▸ *v.* **bulged, bulg·ing.** To swell or cause to swell outward. **—bulg′i·ness** *n.* **—bulg′y** *adj.*

bul·gur also **bul·ghur** (bo͝ol-go͝or′, bŭl′gər) ▸ *n.* Cracked wheat grains, often used in Middle Eastern dishes.

bu·li·mi·a (bo͞o-lē′mē-ə, -lĭm′ē-, byo͞o-) ▸ *n.* An eating disorder esp. of young women that is marked by episodic binge eating and subsequent feelings of guilt and by measures to prevent weight gain, such as self-induced vomiting. **—bu·li′mic** *adj. & n.*

bulk (bŭlk) ▸ *n.* 1. Size, mass, or volume, esp. when very large. 2. The major portion of something. 3. See **fiber** 6. ▸ *v.* To be or appear massive in size or importance; loom. ***—idiom:* in bulk** Unpacked; loose. **—bulk′i·ly** *adj.* **—bulk′i·ness** *n.* **—bulk′y** *adj.*

bulk·head (bŭlk′hĕd′) ▸ *n.* 1a. One of the upright partitions dividing a ship into compartments. b. A partition in an aircraft or spacecraft. 2. A retaining wall in a mine or along a waterfront.

bull[1] (bo͝ol) ▸ *n.* 1a. An adult male bovine mammal. b. The uncastrated adult male of domestic cattle. c. The male of certain other animals, such as the alligator, elephant, or moose. 2. One who buys commodities or securities in anticipation of a rise in prices. 3. *Slang* A police officer. 4. *Slang* Empty talk; nonsense. ▸ *adj.* 1. Male. 2. Large and strong. 3. Characterized by rising prices: *a bull market.* **—bull′ish** *adj.* **—bull′ish·ly** *adv.* **—bull′ish·ness** *n.*

bull[2] (bo͝ol) ▸ *n.* An official document issued by the pope.

bull·dog (bo͝ol′dôg′, -dŏg′) ▸ *n.* A short-haired dog having a large head, strong square jaws, and a stocky body. ▸ *adj.* Stubborn. ▸ *v.* **-dogged, -dog·ging.** To throw (a calf or steer) by seizing its horns and twisting its neck.

bull·doze (bo͝ol′dōz′) ▸ *v.* **-dozed, -doz·ing.** 1. To clear, dig up, or move with a bulldozer. 2. To bully.

bull·doz·er (bo͝ol′dō′zər) ▸ *n.* A heavy, driver-operated machine for clearing and grading land, usu. having continuous treads and a broad hydraulic blade in front.

bul·let (bo͝ol′ĭt) ▸ *n.* 1. A usu. metal projectile that is expelled from a firearm. 2. *Print.* A heavy dot (•) used for highlighting. **—bul′let·proof** *adj.*

bul·le·tin (bo͝ol′ĭ-tn, -tĭn) ▸ *n.* 1. A printed or broadcast statement on a matter of public interest. 2. A periodical, esp. one published by an organization or society.

bulletin board ▸ *n.* 1. A board, usu. mounted on a wall, on which notices are posted. 2. *Comp. Sci.* A system for sending or reading electronic messages of general interest.

bull·fight (bo͝ol′fīt′) ▸ *n.* A public spectacle, esp. in Spain, Portugal, and parts of Latin America, in which a matador engages and usu. kills a fighting bull. **—bull′fight′er** *n.*

bull·finch (bo͝ol′fĭnch′) ▸ *n.* A European bird having a short thick bill and a red breast.

bull·frog (bo͝ol′frôg′, -frŏg′) ▸ *n.* A large frog having a deep resonant croak.

bull·head (bo͝ol′hĕd′) ▸ *n.* A North American freshwater catfish.

bull·head·ed (bo͝ol′hĕd′ĭd) ▸ *adj.* Very stubborn; headstrong. **—bull′head′ed·ly** *adv.* **—bull′head′ed·ness** *n.*

bull·horn (bo͝ol′hôrn′) ▸ *n.* An electric megaphone used esp. to amplify the voice.

bul·lion (bo͝ol′yən) ▸ *n.* Gold or silver bars, ingots, or plates.

bul·lock (bo͝ol′ək) ▸ *n.* A steer or young bull.

bull·pen (bo͝ol′pĕn′) ▸ *n.* *Baseball* An area where relief pitchers warm up.

Bull Run ▸ A small stream of NE VA SW of Washington DC; site of two Civil War battles (Jul. 21, 1861, and Aug. 29–30, 1862).

bull session ▸ *n.* *Informal* An informal group discussion.

bull's-eye (bo͝olz′ī′) ▸ *n.* 1. The small central circle on a target. 2. A shot that hits this circle. 3. A direct hit.

bull·whip (bo͝ol′hwĭp′, -wĭp′) ▸ *n.* A long plaited rawhide whip with a knotted end.

bul·ly (bo͝ol′ē) ▸ *n., pl.* **-lies.** One who is habitually cruel to smaller or weaker people. ▸ *v.* **-lied, -ly·ing.** To behave like a bully (toward). ▸ *adj.* Excellent; splendid. ▸ *interj.* Used to express approval.

bul·rush (bo͝ol′rŭsh′) ▸ *n.* Any of various grasslike marsh plants.

bul·wark (bo͝ol′wərk, -wôrk′, bŭl′-) ▸ *n.* 1. A wall or embankment raised as a defensive fortification. 2. Something serving as a defense or safeguard.

bum (bŭm) ▸ *n.* 1. A tramp; vagrant. 2. One who seeks to

THESAURUS

build up *v.* *—See* ACCUMULATE, GAIN (1), INCREASE, PROMOTE (3).

build *n.* *—See* CONSTITUTION.

builder *n.* A person or business that builds or constructs something ▸ carpenter, constructor, contractor, erector, mason. [*Compare* MAKER.] *—See also* DEVELOPER.

building *n.* Something built, especially for human use ▸ construction, edifice, erection, pile, structure.

building block *n.* *—See* PART (1).

buildup *n.* 1. The act of accumulating ▸ accumulation, agglomeration, conglomeration. 2. The result or product of building up ▸ accretion, accumulation, development, enlargement, growth, multiplication, proliferation, sprawl, spread. *—See also* ACCUMULATION (1), INCREASE (1), PUBLICITY.

built-in *adj.* Serving as a nondetachable part of a larger unit ▸ component, constituent, incorporated, integral. *—See also* CONSTITUTIONAL.

bulge *v.* To curve outward past the normal or usual limit ▸ bag, balloon, beetle, belly, jut, overhang, pouch, project, protrude, protuberate, stand out, stick out. *—See also* SWELL.

bulge *n.* *—See* ADVANTAGE (3), PROJECTION.

bulk *n.* 1. Great amount or dimension ▸ amplitude, magnitude, mass, size, volume. 2. The greatest part or portion ▸ mass, preponderance, preponderancy, weight. [*Compare* CENTER.] *—See also* BRAWN, QUANTITY (3).

bulky *adj.* 1. Of large, often awkward size and weight ▸ blockish, blocky, cumbersome, cumbrous, heavy, hefty, lumpish, lumpy, massive, oversize, oversized, ponderous, voluminous. [*Compare* BIG, HEAVY.] 2. Having a large body, especially in girth ▸ full-figured, heavy, hefty, hulking, hulky, husky, plus-sized, stout, sturdy. [*Compare* FAT, MUSCULAR, STOCKY.] *—See also* AWKWARD (2).

bull *n.* *—See* NONSENSE, POLICE OFFICER.

bulldoze *v.* *—See* INTIMIDATE, MUSCLE.

bulldozer *n.* *—See* BULLY.

bulletin *n.* A report giving information ▸ advisory, notice. [*Compare* REPORT, WARNING.] *—See also* ITEM, MESSAGE.

bullheaded *adj.* *—See* STUBBORN (1).

bullheadedness *n.* *—See* STUBBORNNESS.

bull session *n.* *—See* CONVERSATION.

bully *n.* One who is habitually cruel to smaller or weaker people ▸ browbeater, bulldozer, hector, intimidator, persecutor, tease, tormentor. [*Compare* TOUGH.]

bully *v.* *—See* INTIMIDATE.

bulwark *n.* A structure used as a defense against an attack ▸ barricade, bastion, breastwork, earthwork, parapet, rampart. [*Compare* BASE[1], FORT.]

bum[1] *n.* *—See* PAUPER, WASTREL (2).

bum *v.* *—See* BEG, IDLE (1).

bum out *v.* *—See* DEPRESS.

live off others. ▸ *v.* **bummed, bum·ming.** 1. To live or acquire by begging and scavenging. 2. To loaf. ▸ *adj.* 1. Inferior; worthless. 2. Disabled; malfunctioning. 3. Unfavorable or unfair.

bum·ble (bŭm′bəl) ▸ *v.* **-bled, -bling.** To speak, behave, or proceed in a faltering or clumsy manner. **—bum′bler** *n.*

bum·ble·bee (bŭm′bəl-bē′) ▸ *n.* Any of various large, hairy, social bees that nest underground.

bump (bŭmp) ▸ *v.* 1. To strike or collide (with). 2. To knock: *bumped my knee on the table.* 3. To jolt; jerk. 4. To displace; oust. ***—phrasal verbs:* bump into** To meet by chance. **bump off** *Slang* To murder. ▸ *n.* 1. A blow, collision, or jolt. 2. A slight swelling or lump. **—bump′i·ness** *n.* **—bump′y** *adj.*

bump·er[1] (bŭm′pər) ▸ *n.* A horizontal bar attached to either end of a motor vehicle to absorb the impact in a collision.

bump·er[2] (bŭm′pər) ▸ *n.* A drinking vessel filled to the brim. ▸ *adj.* Unusually abundant or full: *a bumper crop.*

bump·kin (bŭmp′kĭn, bŭm′-) ▸ *n.* An awkward, unsophisticated person.

bump·tious (bŭmp′shəs) ▸ *adj.* Crudely or loudly assertive; pushy. **—bump′tious·ly** *adv.*

bun (bŭn) ▸ *n.* 1. A small bread roll, often sweetened. 2. A roll of hair worn at the back of the head.

bunch (bŭnch) ▸ *n.* A group, cluster, or clump. **—bunch** *v.* **—bunch′y** *adj.*

bun·co (bŭng′kō) ▸ *n., pl.* **-cos.** *Informal* A confidence game; swindle. **—bun′co** *v.*

bun·dle (bŭn′dl) ▸ *n.* 1. A group of objects held together, as by tying or wrapping; package. 2. *Informal* A large sum of money. ▸ *v.* **-dled, -dling.** 1. To tie, wrap, fold, or otherwise gather together. 2. To dress warmly.

bundt cake (bŭnt, bo͝ont) ▸ *n.* A ring-shaped cake with fluted sides, baked in a mold.

bung (bŭng) ▸ *n.* A stopper for a bunghole. **—bung** *v.*

bun·ga·low (bŭng′gə-lō′) ▸ *n.* A small house or cottage usu. of one story.

bun·gee cord (bŭn′jē′) ▸ *n.* An elasticized rubber cord used to fasten, bear weight, or absorb shock.

bungee jumping ▸ *n.* The sport of jumping from a great height while attached to a bungee cord.

bung·hole (bŭng′hōl′) ▸ *n.* The hole in a cask, keg, or barrel through which liquid is poured in or drained out.

bun·gle (bŭng′gəl) ▸ *v.* **-gled, -gling.** To work, manage, or act ineptly or inefficiently. **—bun′gle** *n.* **—bun′gler** *n.*

bun·ion (bŭn′yən) ▸ *n.* A painful, inflamed swelling of the bursa at the first joint of the big toe.

bunk[1] (bŭngk) ▸ *n.* 1. A narrow built-in bed. 2. A bunk bed. 3. A place for sleeping. **—bunk** *v.*

bunk[2] (bŭngk) ▸ *n.* Empty talk; nonsense.

bunk bed ▸ *n.* A double-decker bed.

bun·ker (bŭng′kər) ▸ *n.* 1. A bin or tank esp. for fuel storage, as on a ship. 2a. An underground fortification. b. A reinforced chamber or observation post. 3. A sand trap on a golf course.

Bunker Hill ▸ A hill of Charlestown, MA, near the site of the first major Revolutionary War battle (Jun. 17, 1775).

bunk·house (bŭngk′hous′) ▸ *n.* Sleeping quarters on a ranch or in a camp.

bun·ny (bŭn′ē) ▸ *n., pl.* **-nies.** A rabbit, esp. a young one.

Bun·sen burner (bŭn′sən) ▸ *n.* A small, adjustable gas-burning laboratory burner.

bunt (bŭnt) ▸ *v.* 1. *Baseball* To bat (a pitched ball) by tapping it lightly so that the ball rolls slowly in front of the infielders. 2. To butt with the head. **—bunt** *n.* **—bunt′er** *n.*

bunt·ing[1] (bŭn′tĭng) ▸ *n.* 1. A light cloth used for making flags. 2. Flags collectively. 3. Long colored strips of cloth or material used esp. for festive decoration.

bunt·ing[2] (bŭn′tĭng) ▸ *n.* Any of various birds having short, cone-shaped bills.

buoy (bo͞o′ē, boi) ▸ *n.* 1. A float, often having a bell or light, moored in water as a warning of danger or as a marker for a channel. 2. A life buoy. ▸ *v.* 1. To keep afloat or aloft. 2. To hearten or inspire.

buoy·an·cy (boi′ən-sē, bo͞o′yən-) ▸ *n.* 1a. The tendency to float in a liquid or to rise in a gas. b. The upward force a fluid exerts on an object less dense than itself. 2. Ability to recover quickly from setbacks. 3. Cheerfulness. **—buoy′ant** *adj.*

bur[1] also **burr** (bûr) ▸ *n.* 1. A rough, prickly husk surrounding the seeds or fruits of certain plants. 2. A rotary cutting tool designed to be attached to a drill.

bur[2] (bûr) ▸ *n. & v.* Var. of **burr**[2].

bur·den[1] (bûr′dn) ▸ *n.* 1. Something that is carried. 2. Something that is emotionally difficult to bear. 3. A responsibility or duty. ▸ *v.* 1. To weigh down; oppress. 2. To load or overload. **—bur′den·some** *adj.*

bur·den[2] (bûr′dn) ▸ *n.* 1. A principal or recurring idea; theme. 2. *Mus.* A chorus or refrain.

bur·dock (bûr′dŏk′) ▸ *n.* A weedy plant having purplish flowers surrounded by prickly bracts.

bu·reau (byo͝or′ō) ▸ *n., pl.* **-reaus** or **-reaux** (-ōz). 1. A chest of drawers. 2a. A government department or a subdivision

THESAURUS

bum *adj.* —*See* BAD (1).

bum[2] *n.* —*See* BUTTOCKS.

bumble[1] *v.* —*See* BLUNDER, MUDDLE.

bumble[2] *v.* —*See* HUM.

bumble *n.* —*See* HUM.

bumbling *adj.* —*See* UNSKILLFUL.

bummer *n. Slang* A great disappointment or regrettable fact ▸ crime, pity, shame. *Idiom:* a crying shame. —*See also* BEGGAR (1), KILLJOY.

bump *v.* To proceed with sudden, abrupt movements ▸ bounce, jar, jerk, jiggle, jolt, jounce, lurch, rattle. [*Compare* SHAKE.] —*See also* COLLIDE, DEMOTE, EJECT (1).

bump into *v.* —*See* ENCOUNTER (1).

bump off *v.* —*See* MURDER.

bump *n.* 1. An unevenness or elevation on a surface ▸ burl, excrescence, gnarl, growth, hump, knob, knot, lump, node, nodule, nub, outgrowth, protuberance. [*Compare* PROJECTION.] 2. A small raised area of skin, as from a blow or sting ▸ bunch, knot, lump, swelling. *Informal:* boo-boo. *Slang:* goose egg. [*Compare* WELT.] —*See also* BEAT (1), COLLISION, HILL.

bumpiness *n.* —*See* IRREGULARITY.

bumpkin *n.* —*See* CLODHOPPER.

bumpy *adj.* —*See* ROUGH (1).

bunch *n.* —*See* BUMP (2), CIRCLE (3), GROUP, HEAP (2), QUANTITY (2).

bundle *n.* —*See* FORTUNE, GROUP, PACKAGE.

bundle *v.* —*See* WRAP (1).

bundle up *v.* To put on warm clothes ▸ wrap, wrap up.

bung *n.* —*See* PLUG.

bungle *v.* —*See* BOTCH, MUDDLE.

bungle *n.* —*See* BLUNDER.

bungler *n.* —*See* BLUNDERER.

bungling *adj.* —*See* INEFFICIENT, UNSKILLFUL.

bunk[1] *v.* —*See* LODGE.

bunk[2] or **bunkum** *n.* —*See* NONSENSE.

buns *n.* —*See* BUTTOCKS.

Bunyanesque *adj.* —*See* ENORMOUS.

buoy *v.* —*See* ELATE, SUPPORT (2).

buoyancy *n.* The ability to recover quickly from depression or discouragement ▸ bounce, elasticity, flexibility, resilience, resiliency.

buoyant *adj.* —*See* LIGHTHEARTED.

burble *v.* To flow with or make a soft liquid sound ▸ babble, bubble, gurgle, lap, murmur, purl, ripple. [*Compare* TRICKLE, WASH.] —*See also* BABBLE.

burble *n.* A soft liquid sound ▸ babble, bubble, gurgle, lap, murmur, purl, ripple.

burden[1] *n.* 1. A source of persistent worry or hardship ▸ affliction, albatross, cross, drag, drain, millstone, onus, strain, tax, trial, tribulation, weight. *Informal:* headache, pain. *Idioms:* royal headache (*or* pain), weight (*or* load) on one's mind. [*Compare* CARE, CURSE, DIFFICULTY.] 2. Something carried or transported ▸ ballast, cargo, encumbrance, freight, haul, lading, load, weight. —*See also* DUTY (1).

burden *v.* To weigh down or place a heavy load on ▸ charge, cumber, encumber, freight, lade, load, oppress, saddle, strain, tax, try, weight. [*Compare* FILL, HINDER.]

burden[2] *n.* —*See* IMPORT, THRUST.

burdensome *adj.* Requiring great bodily, mental, or spiritual strength ▸ arduous, backbreaking, crushing, formidable, grinding, grueling, heavy, laborious, onerous, oppressive, overpowering, overtaxing, rigorous, rough, severe, taxing, toilsome, tough, trying, weighty. [*Compare* DIFFICULT.] —*See also* DISTURBING.

bureau *n.* —*See* BRANCH (3).

of a department. **b.** An office or business that performs a specific duty: *a travel bureau.*

bu·reauc·ra·cy (byo͞o-rŏk′rə-sē) ▸ *n., pl.* **-cies. 1a.** Administration of a government chiefly through bureaus and departments staffed with nonelected officials. **b.** The departments and their officials as a group. **2.** An unwieldy administrative system. **—bu′reau·crat′** (byo͝or′ə-krăt′) *n.* **—bu′reau·crat′ic** *adj.* **—bu′reau·crat′i·cal·ly** *adv.*

bu·rette also **bu·ret** (byo͞o-rĕt′) ▸ *n.* A glass tube with fine gradations and a stopcock at the bottom, used esp. for accurate fluid dispensing.

burg (bûrg) ▸ *n. Informal* A city or town.

bur·geon (bûr′jən) ▸ *v.* **1a.** To put forth new buds, leaves, or greenery; sprout. **b.** To begin to grow or blossom. **2.** To grow and flourish.

burg·er (bûr′gər) ▸ *n.* **1.** A hamburger. **2.** A sandwich with a nonbeef patty as a filling: *a crab burger.*

bur·gess (bûr′jĭs) ▸ *n.* A freeman, citizen, or representative of an English borough.

burgh (bûrg) ▸ *n.* A chartered town or borough in Scotland.

burgh·er (bûr′gər) ▸ *n.* A solid citizen; bourgeois.

bur·glar (bûr′glər) ▸ *n.* One who commits burglary; housebreaker. **—bur′glar·ize** *v.* **—bur′glar·proof′** *adj.* **—bur′gla·ry** *n.*

bur·gle (bûr′gəl) ▸ *v.* **-gled, -gling.** To commit burglary (on).

bur·go·mas·ter (bûr′gə-măs′tər) ▸ *n.* The principal magistrate of some European cities.

Bur·gun·dy[1] (bûr′gən-dē) also **Bour·gogne** (bo͝or-gôn′yə) ▸ A historical region and former province of E France.

Bur·gun·dy[2] (bûr′gən-dē) ▸ *n., pl.* **-dies. 1.** Any of various red or white wines produced in Burgundy, France. **2. burgundy** A dark purplish red.

bur·i·al (bĕr′ē-əl) ▸ *n.* The act or process of burying.

Bur·ki·na Fa·so (bər-kē′nə fä′sō). Formerly **Upper Volta** ▸ A landlocked country of W Africa.

burl (bûrl) ▸ *n.* A large rounded outgrowth on a tree.

bur·lap (bûr′lăp′) ▸ *n.* A coarse cloth made of jute, flax, or hemp.

bur·lesque (bər-lĕsk′) ▸ *n.* **1.** A ludicrous or mocking imitation. **2.** Vaudeville entertainment characterized by ribald comedy and display of nudity. ▸ *v.* **-lesqued, -lesqu·ing.** To imitate mockingly.

bur·ly (bûr′lē) ▸ *adj.* **-li·er, -li·est.** Heavy and strong. **—bur′li·ness** *n.*

Bur·ma (bûr′mə) ▸ See **Myanmar.**

Bur·mese (bər-mēz′, -mēs′) ▸ *n., pl.* **Burmese. 1.** also **Bur·man** (bûr′mən) A native or inhabitant of Myanmar. **2.** The Sino-Tibetan language of Myanmar. **—Bur·mese′, Bur′man** *adj.*

burn (bûrn) ▸ *v.* **burned** or **burnt** (bûrnt), **burn·ing. 1a.** To undergo or cause to undergo combustion. **b.** To destroy or be destroyed with fire. **2.** To consume or use as a fuel: *a furnace that burns coal.* **3.** To damage or be damaged by fire, heat, radiation, electricity, or a caustic agent. **4.** To execute, esp. by electrocution. **5.** To make or produce by fire or heat: *burn a hole in the rug.* **6.** To impart a sensation of intense heat to: *The chili burned my mouth.* **7.** To make or become very angry. **8.** To emit heat or light by or as if by fire. **9.** To feel or look hot. ***—phrasal verbs:* burn out 1.** To stop burning from lack of fuel. **2.** To wear out or fail, esp. because of heat. **3.** To become exhausted from long-term stress. **burn up** To make or become very angry. ▸ *n.* **1.** An injury produced by fire, heat, radiation, electricity, or a caustic agent. **2.** A sunburn or windburn. **3.** *Aerospace* A firing of a rocket. ***—idioms:* burn (one's) bridges** To eliminate the possibility of return or retreat. **to burn** In great amounts: *They had money to burn.*

burned-out (bûrnd′out′) or **burnt-out** (bûrnt′-) ▸ *adj.* Worn out or exhausted, esp. as a result of long-term stress.

burn·er (bûr′nər) ▸ *n.* **1.** One that burns, esp.: **a.** A device, as in a furnace, that is lighted to produce a flame. **b.** A device on a stovetop that produces heat. **2.** A unit, such as a furnace, in which fuel is burned.

bur·nish (bûr′nĭsh) ▸ *v.* To polish by or as if by rubbing. ▸ *n.* A glossy finish; luster.

bur·nous also **bur·noose** (bər-no͞os′) ▸ *n.* A hooded cloak worn esp. by Arabs.

burn·out (bûrn′out′) ▸ *n.* **1.** A failure in a device caused by excessive heat or friction. **2.** Termination of rocket or jet-engine operation due to fuel exhaustion or shutoff. **3a.** Exhaustion, esp. from long-term stress. **b.** One who is burned out.

Burns (bûrnz), **Robert** (1759–96) ▸ Scottish poet.

Burn·side (bûrn′sīd′), **Ambrose Everett** (1824–81) ▸ Amer. general and politician.

burnt (bûrnt) ▸ *v.* P.t. and p.part of **burn.**

burp (bûrp) ▸ *n.* A belch. ▸ *v.* **1.** To belch. **2.** To cause (a baby) to belch.

bur·qa (bo͝or′kə) ▸ *n.* A loose outer garment worn by Muslim women that covers the head and face and sometimes the entire body.

burr[1] (bûr) ▸ *n.* **1.** A rough edge remaining esp. on metal after it has been cast or cut. **2.** Var. of **bur**[1]. ▸ *v.* **1.** To form a burr on. **2.** To remove burrs from.

burr[2] also **bur** (bûr) ▸ *n.* **1.** A trilling of the letter *r,* as in Scottish speech. **2.** A buzzing or whirring sound. **—burr** *v.*

Burr, Aaron (1756–1836) ▸ US Vice President (1801–05).

bur·ri·to (bo͞o-rē′tō, bə-) ▸ *n., pl.* **-tos.** A flour tortilla wrapped around a filling, as of beef, beans, or cheese.

bur·ro (bûr′ō, bo͝or′ō, bŭr′ō) ▸ *n., pl.* **-ros.** A small donkey, esp. one used as a pack animal.

bur·row (bûr′ō, bŭr′ō) ▸ *n.* A hole or tunnel dug in the ground by an animal for habitation or refuge. ▸ *v.* **1.** To dig a burrow. **2.** To move or progress by or as if by tunneling. **—bur′row·er** *n.*

bur·sa (bûr′sə) ▸ *n., pl.* **-sae** (-sē) or **-sas.** A saclike body cavity, esp. one located between moving structures. **—bur′sal** *adj.*

bur·sar (bûr′sər, -sär′) ▸ *n.* A treasurer, as at a college. **—bur′sa·ry** *n.*

bur·si·tis (bər-sī′tĭs) ▸ *n.* Inflammation of a bursa, esp. in the shoulder, elbow, or knee.

THESAURUS

bureaucratic *adj.* —*See* GOVERNMENTAL.

burg *n.* —*See* CITY.

burgeon *v.* —*See* BLOOM[1] (1), INCREASE.

burgess or **burgher** *n.* —*See* CITIZEN.

burglar *n.* —*See* THIEF.

burglarize *v.* To enter forcibly or illegally ▸ break in, invade, trespass. [*Compare* STEAL.] —*See also* ROB.

burglary *n.* The act of entering a building or room with the intent to commit theft ▸ break-in, breaking and entering, forced entry, trespass. —*See also* LARCENY.

burial *n.* An act of placing a body in a grave or tomb ▸ burying, entombment, inhumation, interment, sepulture. [*Compare* FUNERAL.]

buried *adj.* —*See* HIDDEN (1), ULTERIOR (1), UNDERGROUND.

burke *v.* —*See* AVOID, REPRESS.

burlesque *n.* —*See* SATIRE.

burlesque *v.* —*See* IMITATE.

burly *adj.* —*See* MUSCULAR.

burn *v.* **1.** To undergo or cause to undergo damage by fire ▸ burn down (*or* up), carbonize, incinerate, char, scorch, sear, singe. *Slang:* torch. *Idioms:* burn to a crisp, go up in flames (*or* smoke), reduce to ashes (*or* cinders). **2.** To undergo combustion; be on fire ▸ blaze, crackle, combust, flame, flare, hiss, roar. [*Compare* SMOLDER.] **3.** To feel or look hot ▸ bake, boil, broil, burn up, roast, steam, swelter. *Idiom:* be on fire. **4.** To cause to become sore or inflamed ▸ inflame, irritate, sting. —*See also* ANGER (1), ANGER (2), BEAM, BOIL, CHEAT (1), DECEIVE, HURT (2).

burn off *v.* —*See* EVAPORATE.

burn out *v.* —*See* TIRE (2).

burn *n.* Damage that results from burning ▸ blister, char, scorch, sear, singe. —*See also* CHEAT (1), PAIN.

burning *adj.* On fire ▸ ablaze, afire, aflame, alight, blazing, conflagrant, fiery, flaming. *Idioms:* in a blaze, in flames. —*See also* HOT (1), PASSIONATE, URGENT (1).

burnish *v.* —*See* GLOSS[1].

burnish *n.* —*See* GLOSS[1].

burnout *n.* —*See* EXHAUSTION.

burr *n.* —*See* HUM.

burr *v.* —*See* HUM.

burrow *n.* A place used as an animal's dwelling ▸ den, hole, lair. [*Compare* CAVE.]

burrow *v.* —*See* DIG.

burst (bûrst) ▸ *v.* **burst, burst·ing.** 1a. To come open or fly apart suddenly, esp. from internal pressure. b. To break, shatter, or explode. 2. To be full to the breaking point. 3. To emerge or arrive suddenly: *burst out of the door.* 4. To give sudden utterance or expression: *burst out laughing.* ▸ *n.* 1. A sudden outbreak or explosion. 2. The result of bursting. 3. An abrupt increase: *a burst of speed.*

Bu·run·di (bo͝o-ro͞on′dē, -ro͞on′-) ▸ A country of E-central Africa with a coastline on Lake Tanganyika. **—Bu·run′di·an** *adj. & n.*

bur·y (bĕr′ē) ▸ *v.* **-ied, -y·ing.** 1. To place in the ground: *bury a bone.* 2. To place (a corpse) in a grave or tomb. 3. To embed deeply; sink. 4. To conceal; hide. 5. To absorb: *I'm buried in work.* 6. To abandon: *buried their quarrel.* **—*idiom:* bury the hatchet** To stop fighting.

bus (bŭs) ▸ *n., pl.* **bus·es** or **bus·ses.** 1. A long motor vehicle for carrying passengers. 2. A circuit that connects a computer's major components. ▸ *v.* **bused, bus·ing** or **bussed, bus·sing.** 1. To transport or travel in a bus. 2. To clear (dishes) in a restaurant.

bus·boy (bŭs′boi′) ▸ *n.* A restaurant employee who clears dishes and sets tables.

bus·by (bŭz′bē) ▸ *n., pl.* **-bies.** A tall, full-dress fur hat worn in certain regiments of the British army.

bush (bo͝osh) ▸ *n.* 1. A low shrub with many branches. 2a. Land covered with dense vegetation or undergrowth. b. Land remote from settlement. 3. A shaggy mass, as of hair. ▸ *v.* To grow or branch out like a bush. ▸ *adj. Slang* Bush-league. **—bush′i·ness** *n.* **—bush′y** *adj.*

Bush, George Herbert Walker (b. 1924) ▸ The 41st US President (1989–93).

Bush, George Walker (b. 1946) ▸ The 43rd US President (2001–09).

bushed (bo͝osht) ▸ *adj. Informal* Exhausted.

bush·el (bo͝osh′əl) ▸ *n.* 1. See **measurement** table in Appendix. 2. A container with the capacity of a bushel. 3. *Informal* A large amount.

bush·ing (bo͝osh′ĭng) ▸ *n.* A cylindrical metal lining used to constrain, guide, or reduce friction.

bush-league (bo͝osh′lēg′) ▸ *adj. Slang* Second-rate.

Bush·man (bo͝osh′mən) ▸ *n.* See **San.**

bush·mas·ter (bo͝osh′măs′tər) ▸ *n.* A large venomous snake of tropical America.

bush·whack (bo͝osh′hwăk′, -wăk′) ▸ *v.* 1. To travel through dense growth by cutting away bushes and branches. 2. To ambush. **—bush′whack′er** *n.*

busi·ness (bĭz′nĭs) ▸ *n.* 1. The occupation in which a person is engaged. 2. Commercial, industrial, or professional dealings. 3. A commercial establishment. 4. Volume of commercial trade: *Business had fallen off.* 5. Patronage: *took my business elsewhere.* 6. One's concern or interest. 7. Serious work: *got down to business.* 8. An affair or matter. 9. An incidental action performed by an actor on the stage, as to fill a pause. 10. *Informal* Verbal abuse; scolding: *gave me the business for being late.* **—busi′ness·per′son** *n.*

business card ▸ *n.* A small card printed with a person's name and business affiliation.

busi·ness·like (bĭz′nĭs-līk′) ▸ *adj.* 1. Methodical and systematic. 2. Unemotional.

busi·ness·man (bĭz′nĭs-măn′) ▸ *n.* A man engaged in business.

busi·ness·wom·an (bĭz′nĭs-wo͝om′ən) ▸ *n.* A woman engaged in business.

bus·ing or **bus·sing** (bŭs′ĭng) ▸ *n.* The transportation of children by bus to schools outside their neighborhoods, esp. to achieve racial integration.

bus·kin (bŭs′kĭn) ▸ *n.* 1. A laced half boot worn by actors of Greek and Roman tragedies. 2. Tragedy.

bus·man's holiday (bŭs′mənz) ▸ *n. Informal* A vacation during which one engages in activity similar to one's usual work.

buss (bŭs) ▸ *v.* To kiss. ▸ *n.* A kiss.

bus·ses (bŭs′ĭz) ▸ *n.* Pl. of **bus.**

bust[1] (bŭst) ▸ *n.* 1. A sculpture representing a person's head, shoulders, and upper chest. 2. A woman's bosom.

bust[2] (bŭst) ▸ *v.* 1. *Slang* a. To burst or break. b. To render or become inoperable. 2. To break up: *bust the gang.* 3. To break (a horse). 4. To bankrupt. 5. *Slang* To reduce in rank. 6. To hit; punch. 7. *Slang* a. To arrest. b. To make a raid on. ▸ *n.* 1. A failure; flop. 2. A widespread financial depression. 3. A punch. 4. A spree. 5. *Slang* A raid or arrest.

bus·tle[1] (bŭs′əl) ▸ *v.* **-tled, -tling.** To move energetically and busily. ▸ *n.* A commotion; stir.

bus·tle[2] (bŭs′əl) ▸ *n.* A frame or pad formerly worn under the back of a woman's skirt to add fullness.

bus·y (bĭz′ē) ▸ *adj.* **-i·er, -i·est.** 1. Engaged in work or activity. 2. Full of activity: *a busy morning.* 3. Meddlesome; prying. 4. Being in use, as a telephone line. 5. Cluttered with detail: *a busy design.* ▸ *v.* **-ied, -y·ing.** To make busy. **—bus′i·ly** *adv.* **—bus′y·ness** *n.*

bus·y·bod·y (bĭz′ē-bŏd′ē) ▸ *n.* A meddlesome person.

bus·y·work (bĭz′ē-wûrk′) ▸ *n.* Activity that takes up time but does not necessarily yield productive results.

but (bŭt; bət *when unstressed*) ▸ *conj.* 1. On the contrary. 2. Contrary to expectation; yet. 3. Except; save. 4. Except that: *would have come but I had to work.* 5. *Informal* Without the result that: *It never rains but it pours.* 6. *Informal* That. Often used after a negative: *no doubt but we'll win.* 7. That . . . not. Used after a negative or question:

THESAURUS

burst *v.* To break open or fly apart suddenly, as from internal pressure ▸ blow (out), explode, pop, rupture. *Slang:* bust. ***Idiom:*** give way. *—See also* BREAK OUT, EXPLODE (1).

burst out *v.* *—See* EXCLAIM.

burst *n.* *—See* BARRAGE, BLAST (2), ERUPTION, OUTBURST.

bursting *adj.* *—See* EAGER, FULL (1).

bury *v.* To place a corpse in or as if in a grave ▸ entomb, inhume, inter, lay, sepulcher. ***Idiom:*** lay (*or* put) to rest. *—See also* HIDE[1].

bush *n.* *—See* WILDERNESS.

bushed *adj.* *—See* TIRED (1).

bushel *n.* The contents of a basket ▸ basket, basketful. *—See also* HEAP (2).

bush-league *adj.* *—See* BAD (1), MINOR (1).

bushwhack *v.* *—See* AMBUSH.

business *n.* 1. Commercial, industrial, or professional activity in general ▸ commerce, enterprise, industry, trade, trading, traffic. 2. Activity pursued as a livelihood ▸ art, avocation, calling, career, craft, employment, handicraft, job, line, métier, occupation, practice, profession, pursuit, specialty, trade, vocation, walk of life, work. *Slang:* dodge, racket. [*Compare* POSITION.] 3. Something to be done, considered, or dealt with ▸ affair, matter, thing. [*Compare* PROBLEM, TASK.] 4. Something that concerns or involves one personally ▸ affair, concern, interest, lookout. *—See also* ABILITY (1), COMPANY (1), PATRONAGE (2).

businesslike *adj.* *—See* SERIOUS (1).

businessperson *n.* *—See* DEALER.

buss *v.* *—See* KISS.

buss *n.* *—See* KISS.

bust[1] *v. Slang* To come open or fly apart suddenly and violently, as from internal pressure ▸ blow (out), burst, explode, pop. *—See also* ARREST, BREACH, DEMOTE, GENTLE, HIT, MALFUNCTION, RUIN.

bust *n.* *—See* ARREST, BLOW[2], DISAPPOINTMENT (2), FAILURE (1).

bust[2] *n.* *—See* SCULPTURE.

busted *adj.* *—See* POOR.

bustle *v.* *—See* RUSH.

bustle *n.* *—See* AGITATION (3).

bustling *adj.* *—See* BUSY (2).

busy *adj.* 1. Involved in activity or work ▸ absorbed, at work, employed, engaged, occupied, taken up (with), working. ***Idiom:*** in the middle (of). [*Compare* RAPT.] 2. Full of lively activity ▸ alive, astir, bustling, crawling, hectic, humming, restless, swarming, teeming. *Informal:* hopping. [*Compare* ACTIVE, FRANTIC.] 3. Excessively filled with detail ▸ cluttered, crowded, fussy, overloaded. [*Compare* DETAILED, ELABORATE, ORNATE.] *—See also* CURIOUS (1).

busy *v.* To make busy ▸ employ, engage, occupy. [*Compare* ABSORB, INVOLVE.]

busybody *n.* A person who meddles or pries into the affairs of others ▸ interloper, meddler, quidnunc. *Informal:* kibitzer. *Slang:* buttinsky, nosy parker, yenta. [*Compare* GOSSIP, SNOOP.]

but *adv.* Nothing more than ▸ just, merely, only, simply. [*Compare* BARELY, SOLELY.]

There never is a tax law but someone opposes it. 8. *Informal* Than: *no sooner arrived but they had to go.* ▸ *prep.* Except: *no one but us.* ▸ *adv.* Merely; only: *lasted but a moment.*

bu·ta·di·ene (byo͞o′tə-dī′ēn′, -dī-ēn′) ▸ *n.* A gaseous hydrocarbon, C_4H_6, obtained from butane and used in making synthetic rubber.

bu·tane (byo͞o′tān′) ▸ *n.* Either of two isomers of a gaseous hydrocarbon, C_4H_{10}, produced from petroleum and used as a household fuel.

butch·er (bo͝och′ər) ▸ *n.* **1a.** One who slaughters and dresses animals for food. **b.** One who sells meats. **2.** A cruel or wanton killer. ▸ *v.* **1.** To slaughter or prepare (animals). **2.** To kill brutally or indiscriminately. **3.** To botch; bungle: *butchered the language.* **—butch′er·er** *n.* **—butch′er·y** *n.*

bu·te·o (byo͞o′tē-ō′) ▸ *n., pl.* **-os.** Any of various broad-winged, soaring hawks.

but·ler (bŭt′lər) ▸ *n.* The head servant in a household, usu. in charge of food service.

butt[1] (bŭt) ▸ *v.* To hit with the head or horns. ***—phrasal verb:*** **butt in** To interfere or meddle in other people's affairs. ▸ *n.* A push or blow with the head or horns.

butt[2] (bŭt) ▸ *v.* To join or be joined end to end; abut. **—butt** *n.*

butt[3] (bŭt) ▸ *n.* An object of ridicule: *the butt of their jokes.*

butt[4] (bŭt) ▸ *n.* **1.** The larger or thicker end: *the butt of a rifle.* **2a.** An unburned end, as of a cigarette. **b.** *Informal* A cigarette. **3.** A short or broken remnant; stub. **4.** *Informal* The buttocks.

butt[5] (bŭt) ▸ *n.* A large cask.

butte (byo͞ot) ▸ *n.* A flat-topped hill that rises abruptly from the surrounding area.

but·ter (bŭt′ər) ▸ *n.* **1.** A soft yellowish fatty food churned from milk or cream. **2.** Any of various substances similar to butter. ▸ *v.* To put butter on or in. ***—phrasal verb:*** **butter up** To flatter. **—but′ter·y** *adj.*

but·ter·cup (bŭt′ər-kŭp′) ▸ *n.* Any of numerous plants with usu. glossy yellow flowers.

but·ter·fat (bŭt′ər-făt′) ▸ *n.* The natural fat of milk from which butter is made.

but·ter·fin·gers (bŭt′ər-fĭng′gərz) ▸ *pl.n.* *(takes sing. v.)* A person who tends to drop things. **—but′ter·fin′gered** *adj.*

but·ter·fish (bŭt′ər-fĭsh′) ▸ *n.* An Atlantic marine food fish having a flattened body.

but·ter·fly (bŭt′ər-flī′) ▸ *n.* **1.** Any of an order of insects having slender bodies and four broad, usu. colorful wings. **2.** The butterfly stroke. **3.** **butterflies** A feeling of unease caused esp. by fearful anticipation.

butterfly stroke ▸ *n.* A swimming stroke in which both arms are drawn upward and forward with a simultaneous kick.

but·ter·milk (bŭt′ər-mĭlk′) ▸ *n.* The sour liquid remaining after butterfat is removed from whole milk or cream by churning.

but·ter·nut (bŭt′ər-nŭt′) ▸ *n.* **1.** An E North American walnut having light brown wood and a nut enclosed in an egg-shaped husk. **2.** The edible, oily nut of this tree. **3.** A brownish dye obtained from the husks of the butternut.

but·ter·scotch (bŭt′ər-skŏch′) ▸ *n.* A syrup, candy, or flavoring made by melting butter and brown sugar.

but·tock (bŭt′ək) ▸ *n.* **1.** Either of the two rounded prominences posterior to the hips. **2.** **buttocks** The rear pelvic area of the body.

but·ton (bŭt′n) ▸ *n.* **1.** An often disk-shaped fastener on a garment, designed to fit through a buttonhole or loop. **2.** An object resembling a button, such as a push-button switch or a round flat pin. **3.** *Comp. Sci.* A defined area within an interface that one clicks to select a command. ▸ *v.* To fasten or be fastened with buttons. ***—idiom:*** **on the button** Exactly.

but·ton-down (bŭt′n-doun′) ▸ *adj.* **1.** Having the ends of the collar fastened down by buttons. **2.** Conservative.

but·ton·hole (bŭt′n-hōl′) ▸ *n.* A small slit in a garment or cloth for fastening a button. ▸ *v.* **-holed, -hol·ing.** To hold or detain (a person) in conversation.

but·tress (bŭt′rĭs) ▸ *n.* **1.** A structure, usu. brick or stone, built against a wall for support. **2.** Something that serves to support or reinforce. ▸ *v.* To support with or as if with a buttress: *buttress a wall; buttress an argument.*

bu·tyl (byo͞ot′l) ▸ *n.* A hydrocarbon radical, C_4H_9.

bux·om (bŭk′səm) ▸ *adj.* **1.** Healthily plump. **2.** Full-bosomed.

buy (bī) ▸ *v.* **bought** (bôt), **buy·ing.** **1.** To acquire in exchange for money; purchase. **2.** To be capable of purchasing: *the best that money can buy.* **3.** To acquire by sacrifice, exchange, or trade: *buy love with favors.* **4.** To bribe. **5.** *Slang* To accept; believe: *didn't buy my lame excuse.* ***—phrasal verbs:*** **buy off** To bribe. **buy out** To purchase the entire stock, business rights, or interests of. **buy up** To purchase all that is available of. ▸ *n.* **1.** Something bought. **2.** *Informal* A bargain. **—buy′er** *n.*

buy·out (bī′out′) ▸ *n.* **1.** The purchase of the entire holdings of an owner. **2.** The purchase of a company or business.

buzz (bŭz) ▸ *v.* **1.** To make a low droning or vibrating sound like that of a bee. **2.** To talk excitedly in low tones. **3.** To hum; bustle. **4.** To signal with a buzzer. **5.** *Informal* To fly low over: *buzzed the control tower.* **6.** To telephone: *Buzz me later.* ***—phrasal verb:*** **buzz off** *Informal* To go away. ▸ *n.* **1.** A vibrating, humming, or droning sound. **2.** A low murmur. **3.** A telephone call. **4.** *Slang* Pleasant intoxication.

buz·zard (bŭz′ərd) ▸ *n.* **1.** Any of various North American vultures. **2.** *Chiefly Brit.* A broad-winged hawk.

buzz·er (bŭz′ər) ▸ *n.* An electric signaling device that makes a buzzing sound.

buzz saw ▸ *n.* See **circular saw.**

buzz·word (bŭz′wûrd′) ▸ *n.* A word or phrase connected with a specialized field that is used esp. to impress laypersons.

by (bī) ▸ *prep.* **1.** Next to. **2.** With the use of; through. **3.** Up to and beyond; past. **4.** During: *sleeping by day.* **5.** Not later than: *by 5:30 P.M.* **6a.** In the amount of: *letters by the thousands.* **b.** To the extent of: *shorter by two inches.* **7a.** According to: *played by the rules.* **b.** With respect to: *siblings by blood.* **8.** In the name of: *swore by the Bible.* **9.** Through the agency or action of: *killed by a bullet.* **10.** In succession to; after: *one by one.* **11a.** Used in multiplication and division: *4 by 6 is 24.* **b.** Used with measurements: *a room 12 by 18 feet.* **c.** Used with compass directions: *south by southeast.* ▸ *adv.* **1.** On hand; nearby: *Stand by.* **2.** Aside; away: *Put it by for later.* **3.** Up to, alongside, and past: *raced by.* **4.** Into the past: *as years go by.* ***—idiom:*** **by and by** In a while.

by– ▸ *pref.* **1.** By: *bygone.* **2.** Secondary: *byway.*

by-and-by (bī′ən-bī′) ▸ *n.* Some future time or occasion.

THESAURUS

butcher *n.* —*See* MURDERER.

butcher *v.* —*See* BOTCH, MASSACRE.

butchery *n.* —*See* MASSACRE.

butt[1] *v.* —*See* ADJOIN, DRIVE (2), PUSH (1).

butt in *v.* —*See* MEDDLE.

butt *n.* —*See* PUSH.

butt[2] *n.* **1.** One that is fired at, attacked, or abused ▸ mark, target. **2.** An object of amusement or laughter ▸ jest, joke, laughingstock, mockery. *Idiom:* figure of fun. [*Compare* FOOL.] —*See also* DUPE, OBJECT (2).

butt[3] *n.* —*See* BUTTOCKS, END (3).

butte *n.* —*See* HILL.

butter up *v.* —*See* FLATTER (1).

buttery *adj.* —*See* FLATTERING.

buttinsky *n.* —*See* BUSYBODY.

buttocks *n.* The part of the body on which one sits ▸ breech, derrière, fundament, hindquarters, posterior, rump, seat. *Informal:* backside, behind, bottom, bum, butt, hind end, rear, rear end. *Slang:* booty, buns, can, duff, fanny, heinie, kiester, tail, tush, tushy.

button-down or **buttoned-down** *adj.* —*See* CONVENTIONAL.

buttress *n.* —*See* SUPPORT.

buttress *v.* —*See* BACK (2), SUPPORT (2).

buxom *adj.* —*See* SHAPELY.

buy *v.* To acquire in exchange for money ▸ pay for, purchase. *Slang:* score. [*Compare* GET, SPEND.] —*See also* BELIEVE (1), BRIBE.

buy *n.* **1.** Something that is bought or capable of being bought ▸ purchase. [*Compare* EFFECTS.] **2.** *Informal* Something offered or bought at a low price ▸ bargain, find. *Informal:* deal. *Slang:* steal.

buyer *n.* —*See* CONSUMER.

buzz *v.* —*See* HUM, TELEPHONE.

buzz *n.* A telephone communication ▸ call, ring. —*See also* HUM, THRILL.

by-and-by *n.* Time that is yet to be ▸ future, futurity, hereafter, tomorrow.

by and large ▸ *adv.* For the most part.
bye[1] also **by** (bī) ▸ *n.* **1.** A side issue. **2.** *Sports* The position of one who draws no opponent for a round in a tournament and so advances to the next round. ***—idiom:* by the bye** By the way; incidentally.
bye[2] (bī) ▸ *interj.* Used to express farewell.
bye-bye (bī′bī′, bī-bī′) ▸ *interj.* Used to express farewell.
by·gone (bī′gôn′, -gŏn′) ▸ *adj.* Gone by; past: *bygone days.* ▸ *n.* One, esp. a grievance, that is past: *Let bygones be bygones.*
by·law (bī′lô′) ▸ *n.* **1.** A law or rule governing the internal affairs of an organization. **2.** A secondary law.
by·line also **by-line** (bī′līn′) ▸ *n.* A line at the head of a newspaper or magazine article carrying the writer's name. **—by′lin′er** *n.*
by·pass also **by-pass** (bī′păs′) ▸ *n.* **1.** A highway that passes around an obstructed or congested area. **2.** A means of circumvention. **3.** *Elect.* See **shunt** 3. **4.** *Medic.* **a.** An alternative passage created surgically to divert the flow of blood or other bodily fluid. **b.** A surgical procedure to create a bypass. ▸ *v.* **1.** To avoid (an obstacle) by using a bypass. **2.** To ignore: *bypass the rules.*
by-path (bī′păth′, -päth′) ▸ *n.* An indirect or rarely used path.
by-play (bī′plā′) ▸ *n.* Theatrical action or speech taking place on stage while the main action proceeds.
by·prod·uct or **by-prod·uct** (bī′prŏd′əkt) ▸ *n.* **1.** Something that is produced in the making of something else. **2.** A side effect.
By·ron (bī′rən), **George Gordon** Sixth Baron Byron of Rochdale (1788–1824) ▸ British poet. **—By·ron′ic** (bī-rŏn′ĭk) *adj.*
by·stand·er (bī′stăn′dər) ▸ *n.* One who is present at an event without participating.
byte (bīt) ▸ *n.* A sequence of adjacent bits, usu. eight, operated on as a unit by a computer.
by·way (bī′wā′) ▸ *n.* **1.** A side road. **2.** A secondary or arcane field of study.
by·word also **by-word** (bī′wûrd′) ▸ *n.* **1a.** A proverb. **b.** An often-used word or phrase. **2.** One that represents a type, class, or quality: *Einstein is a byword for genius.*
Byz·an·tine (bĭz′ən-tēn′, -tīn′, bĭ-zăn′tĭn) ▸ *adj.* **1.** Relating to Byzantium or the Byzantine Empire. **2.** Of the richly decorative artistic or architectural style developed in the Byzantine Empire. **3.** Of the Eastern Orthodox Church or the rites performed in it. **4.** often **byzantine** **a.** Marked by intrigue; devious. **b.** Highly complex; intricate: *a byzantine tax law.* ▸ *n.* A native or inhabitant of Byzantium.

THESAURUS

Idiom: time to come. [*Compare* APPROACH, POSSIBILITY.]
bygone *adj.* *—See* OLD (1), PAST.
bylaw *n.* *—See* LAW (1).
bypass *n.* *—See* ESCAPE (2).
bypass *v.* *—See* AVOID, SKIRT.
bypast *adj.* *—See* PAST.
byproduct *n.* *—See* DERIVATIVE.
bystander *n.* *—See* WATCHER (1).
byword *n.* *—See* PROVERB.
byzantine *adj.* *—See* COMPLEX (1).

C

c[1] or **C** (sē) ► *n., pl.* **c's** or **C's** also **cs** or **Cs. 1.** The 3rd letter of the English alphabet. **2.** The 3rd in a series. **3.** The third best in quality or rank. **4.** *Mus.* The 1st tone in the scale of C major.

c[2] ► *abbr.* **1.** carat **2.** also **C** constant **3.** cubic

C[1] ► **1.** The symbol for the element **carbon** 1. **2.** also **c** The symbol for the Roman numeral 100. **3.** The symbol for **capacitance** 1, 2.

C[2] ► *abbr.* **1.** Celsius **2.** centigrade **3.** consonant

c. ► *abbr.* **1.** cent **2.** circa **3.** copyright **4.** cup

ca ► *abbr.* circa

Ca ► The symbol for the element **calcium.**

CA ► *abbr.* California

cab (kăb) ► *n.* **1.** A taxicab. **2.** The enclosed compartment for the operator or driver of a heavy vehicle or machine.

ca·bal (kə-băl′, -bäl′) ► *n.* **1.** A conspiratorial group. **2.** A secret plot.

cab·a·la (kăb′ə-lə, kə-bä′-) ► *n.* Var. of **kabbalah.**

ca·ban·a also **ca·ba·ña** (kə-băn′ə, -băn′yə) ► *n.* A shelter esp. on a beach, used as a bathhouse.

cab·a·ret (kăb′ə-rā′) ► *n.* **1.** A restaurant or nightclub providing live entertainment. **2.** The floor show in a cabaret.

cab·bage (kăb′ĭj) ► *n.* A vegetable of the mustard family, having a large round head of tightly overlapping green to purplish leaves. **—cab′bag·y** *adj.*

cab·by or **cab·bie** (kăb′ē) ► *n., pl.* **-bies.** A cab driver.

cab·in (kăb′ĭn) ► *n.* **1.** A small, roughly built house. **2.** A room in a ship used as living quarters. **3.** The enclosed space in an aircraft or spacecraft for the crew, passengers, or cargo.

cabin class ► *n.* A class of accommodations on some passenger ships, lower than first class and higher than tourist class.

cabin cruiser ► *n.* A powerboat with a cabin.

cab·i·net (kăb′ə-nĭt) ► *n.* **1.** An upright case or cupboard with shelves, drawers, or compartments for the safekeeping or display of objects. **2.** The box that houses a computer's main components. **3.** often **Cabinet** A body of persons appointed by a head of state or a prime minister to head the executive departments of the government and to act as official advisers. **4.** *Regional* See **milk shake.**

cab·i·net·mak·er (kăb′ə-nĭt-mā′kər) ► *n.* An artisan who makes fine articles of wooden furniture. **—cab′i·net·mak′ing** *n.*

cab·i·net·work (kăb′ə-nĭt-wûrk′) ► *n.* Finished furniture made by a cabinetmaker.

cabin fever ► *n.* Uneasiness resulting from confinement to a limited space or routine.

ca·ble (kā′bəl) ► *n.* **1.** A strong, large-diameter steel or fiber rope. **2.** *Elect.* A bound or sheathed group of mutually insulated conductors. **3.** A cablegram. **4.** Cable television. ► *v.* **-bled, -bling.** To send a cablegram (to).

cable car ► *n.* A vehicle that is moved along a route by an endless cable.

ca·ble·cast (kā′bəl-kăst′) ► *n.* A telecast by cable television. **—ca′ble·cast′** *v.*

ca·ble·gram (kā′bəl-grăm′) ► *n.* A telegram sent by submarine cable.

cable television ► *n.* A television distribution system in which station signals received by a central antenna are delivered by cable to the receivers of subscribers.

ca·ble·vi·sion (kā′bəl-vĭzh′ən) ► *n.* See **cable television.**

cab·o·chon (kăb′ə-shŏn′) ► *n.* A highly polished, convex-cut, unfaceted gem.

ca·boo·dle (kə-bo͞od′l) ► *n.* *Informal* The lot, group, or bunch: *donated the whole caboodle.*

ca·boose (kə-bo͞os′) ► *n.* The last car on a freight train, having kitchen and sleeping facilities for the train crew.

cab·ri·o·let (kăb′rē-ə-lā′) ► *n.* **1.** A two-wheeled, one-horse carriage with a folding top. **2.** A convertible coupe.

ca·ca·o (kə-kä′ō, -kā′ō) ► *n., pl.* **-os. 1.** An evergreen tropical American tree having ribbed, reddish-brown fruits. **2.** The seed of this plant, used in making chocolate, cocoa, and cocoa butter.

cach·a·lot (kăsh′ə-lŏt′, -lō′) ► *n.* See **sperm whale.**

cache (kăsh) ► *n.* **1.** A hiding place for storing provisions. **2.** A place for concealing valuables. **3.** The goods or valuables hidden in a cache. ► *v.* **cached, cach·ing.** To hide or store in a cache.

ca·chet (kă-shā′) ► *n.* **1.** A mark or quality of distinction, individuality, or authenticity. **2.** A seal on a document.

cack·le (kăk′əl) ► *v.* **-led, -ling. 1.** To make the shrill cry characteristic of a hen after laying an egg. **2.** To laugh or talk in a shrill manner. ► *n.* **1.** The act or sound of cackling. **2.** Shrill laughter. **—cack′ler** *n.*

ca·coph·o·ny (kə-kŏf′ə-nē) ► *n., pl.* **-nies.** Jarring, discordant sound; dissonance. **—ca·coph′o·nous** *adj.*

cac·tus (kăk′təs) ► *n., pl.* **-ti** (-tī′) or **-tus·es.** Any of various fleshy-stemmed, spiny, usu. leafless plants native to arid regions of the New World.

cad (kăd) ► *n.* A man of unprincipled behavior, esp. toward women. **—cad′dish** *adj.* **—cad′dish·ly** *adv.* **—cad′dish·ness** *n.*

ca·dav·er (kə-dăv′ər) ► *n.* A dead body, esp. one intended for dissection.

ca·dav·er·ous (kə-dăv′ər-əs) ► *adj.* **1.** Suggestive of death; corpselike. **2.** Pale and gaunt. **—ca·dav′er·ous·ness** *n.*

cad·die also **cad·dy** (kăd′ē) ► *n., pl.* **-dies.** One hired to attend a golfer, esp. by carrying the clubs. ► *v.* **-died, -dy·ing.** To serve as a caddie.

Cad·do·an (kăd′ō-ən) ► *n.* A family of Native American languages of the E Great Plains from the Dakotas to Oklahoma, Texas, and Louisiana.

cad·dy (kăd′ē) ► *n., pl.* **-dies.** A small container, esp. for tea.

ca·dence (kād′ns) ► *n.* **1.** Balanced, rhythmic flow, as of poetry. **2.** The beat of movement, as in marching. **3.** Vocal inflection or modulation. **4.** *Mus.* A progression of chords moving to a harmonic close or sense of resolution.

ca·den·cy (kād′n-sē) ► *n., pl.* **-cies.** Cadence.

ca·den·za (kə-dĕn′zə) ► *n.* *Mus.* **1.** An ornamental melodic flourish, as in an aria. **2.** An extended virtuosic section for the soloist usu. near the end of a concerto movement.

ca·det (kə-dĕt′) ► *n.* **1.** A student at a military school who is training to be an officer. **2.** A younger son or brother.

THESAURUS

cabal *n.* —*See* PLOT (2).
  cabal *v.* —*See* PLOT (2).
cabalistic *adj.* —*See* MYSTERIOUS, OBSCURE (1).
cabbage *n.* —*See* MONEY (1).
cabin *n.* —*See* HUT.
cable *n.* —*See* CORD.
cache *n.* —*See* DEPOSITORY, HOARD.
  cache *v.* To have or put in a customary place ► keep, put, store. —*See also* HIDE[1].
cachinnate *v.* —*See* LAUGH.
cachinnation *n.* —*See* LAUGH.
cackle *v.* —*See* LAUGH.
  cackle *n.* —*See* LAUGH.
cacophonous or **cacophonic** or **cacophonical** *adj.* —*See* INHARMONIOUS (2).
cacophony *n.* —*See* NOISE (1).
cad *n.* —*See* BOOR.
cadaver *n.* —*See* BODY (2).
cadaverous *adj.* —*See* GHASTLY (2), HAGGARD, PALE (1).
cadence *n.* —*See* RHYTHM.
cadenced *adj.* —*See* RHYTHMICAL.
cadency *n.* —*See* RHYTHM.

cadge (kăj) ▸ *v.* **cadged, cadg·ing.** To beg or get by begging. **—cadg′er** *n.*

cad·mi·um (kăd′mē-əm) ▸ *n. Symbol* **Cd** A soft, bluish-white metallic element used in low-friction alloys, solders, dental amalgams, and nickel-cadmium storage batteries. At. no. 48. **—cad′mic** (-mĭk) *adj.*

cad·re (kä′drā, -drə, kăd′rē) ▸ *n.* **1.** A nucleus of trained personnel around which a larger organization can be built. **2a.** A tightly knit group, esp. of political activists. **b.** A member of such a group.

ca·du·ce·us (kə-do͞o′sē-əs, -shəs, -dyo͞o′-) ▸ *n., pl.* **-ce·i** (-sē-ī′). **1.** *Gk. Myth.* A winged staff with two serpents twined around it, carried by Hermes. **2.** This staff used as the symbol of the medical profession.

cae·cum (sē′kəm) ▸ *n.* Var. of **cecum.**

cae·sar also **Cae·sar** (sē′zər) ▸ *n.* **1.** Used as a title for Roman emperors. **2.** A dictator or autocrat.

Caesar, Julius. Gaius Julius Caesar (100–44 B.C.) ▸ Roman political and military leader and historian. **—Cae·sar′e·an, Cae·sar′i·an** (sĭ-zâr′ē-ən) *adj.*

cae·sar·e·an or **cae·sar·i·an** (sĭ-zâr′ē-ən) ▸ *adj. & n.* Vars. of **cesarean.**

cae·si·um (sē′zē-əm) ▸ *n.* Var. of **cesium.**

cae·su·ra also **ce·su·ra** (sĭ-zho͝or′ə, -zo͝or′ə) ▸ *n., pl.* **-su·ras** or **-su·rae** (-zho͝or′ē, -zo͝or′ē). A pause in a line of verse dictated by sense or speech rhythm rather than by metrics.

ca·fé also **ca·fe** (kă-fā′, kə-) ▸ *n.* A coffee house, restaurant, or bar.

ca·fé au lait (kă-fā′ ō lā′) ▸ *n.* **1.** Coffee with hot milk. **2.** A light yellowish brown.

caf·e·te·ri·a (kăf′ĭ-tîr′ē-ə) ▸ *n.* **1.** A restaurant in which customers are served at a counter and carry their meals on trays to tables. **2.** A dining area, as at a school, where meals may be purchased or brought from home.

caf·feine also **caf·fein** (kă-fēn′, kăf′ēn′, kăf′ē-ĭn) ▸ *n.* A bitter white alkaloid, $C_8H_{10}N_4O_2$, often derived from tea or coffee and used chiefly as a mild stimulant. **—caf′fein·at′ed** (kăf′ə-nā′tĭd) *adj.*

caf·tan or **kaf·tan** (kăf′tăn′, -tən, kăf-tăn′) ▸ *n.* A full-length sleeved garment worn chiefly in the Near East.

cage (kāj) ▸ *n.* **1.** A barred or grated enclosure for confining birds or animals. **2.** A similar enclosure or structure. **3.** An elevator car. **4a.** *Baseball* A wire backstop used in batting practice. **b.** A hockey or soccer goal. **c.** *Basketball* The basket. ▸ *v.* **caged, cag·ing.** To put in or as if in a cage.

ca·gey also **ca·gy** (kā′jē) ▸ *adj.* **-gi·er, -gi·est. 1.** Wary; careful. **2.** Crafty; shrewd. **—ca′gi·ly** *adv.* **—ca′gi·ness** *n.*

ca·hoots (kə-ho͞ots′) ▸ *pl.n. Informal* Secret partnership: *in cahoots with organized crime.*

cai·man also **cay·man** (kā′mən) ▸ *n., pl.* **-mans.** Any of various tropical American reptiles resembling and closely related to the alligators.

Cain (kān) ▸ In the Bible, the eldest son of Adam and Eve; murdered Abel.

cairn (kârn) ▸ *n.* A mound of stones erected as a memorial or marker.

Cai·ro (kī′rō) ▸ The capital of Egypt, in the NE part on the Nile R.

cais·son (kā′sŏn′, -sən) ▸ *n.* **1.** A watertight structure within which construction work is carried on under water. **2.** See **camel** 2. **3a.** A horse-drawn vehicle formerly used to carry artillery ammunition. **b.** A large ammunition box.

caisson disease ▸ *n.* See **decompression sickness.**

cai·tiff (kā′tĭf) ▸ *n.* A despicable coward. **—cai′tiff** *adj.*

ca·jole (kə-jōl′) ▸ *v.* **-joled, -jol·ing.** To wheedle. **—ca·jol′er** *n.* **—ca·jol′er·y** *n.* **—ca·jol′ing·ly** *adv.*

Ca·jun (kā′jən) ▸ *n.* A member of a group of people in S Louisiana descended from French colonists exiled from Acadia in the 18th cent. **—Ca′jun** *adj.*

cake (kāk) ▸ *n.* **1.** A sweet baked food typically made of flour, liquid, and eggs. **2.** A flat mass of baked or fried batter. **3.** A flat mass of chopped food; patty. **4.** A shaped mass, as of soap or ice. **5.** A coat or crust. ▸ *v.* **caked, cak·ing.** To coat; encrust: *hands caked with mud.*

Cal. or **Calif.** ▸ *abbr.* California

cal·a·bash (kăl′ə-băsh′) ▸ *n.* **1.** An annual vine having large hard-shelled gourds. **2.** A tropical American tree bearing hard-shelled, gourdlike fruits. **3.** The fruit of a calabash, often dried and hollowed for use as a utensil.

cal·a·boose (kăl′ə-bo͞os′) ▸ *n. Slang* A jail.

cal·a·mine (kăl′ə-mīn′, -mĭn) ▸ *n.* A pink powder of zinc oxide with a small amount of ferric oxide, used in skin lotions.

ca·lam·i·ty (kə-lăm′ĭ-tē) ▸ *n., pl.* **-ties. 1.** A disaster. **2.** Dire distress. **—ca·lam′i·tous** *adj.*

cal·car·e·ous (kăl-kâr′ē-əs) ▸ *adj.* Composed of or containing calcium carbonate, calcium, or limestone.

cal·ces (kăl′sēz′) ▸ *n.* Pl. of **calx.**

calci– or **calc–** ▸ *pref.* Calcium: *calciferous.*

cal·cif·er·ous (kăl-sĭf′ər-əs) ▸ *adj.* Of or containing calcium or calcium carbonate.

cal·ci·fy (kăl′sə-fī′) ▸ *v.* **-fied, -fy·ing.** To make or become calcareous. **—cal′ci·fi·ca′tion** *n.*

cal·ci·mine (kăl′sə-mīn′) ▸ *n.* A white or tinted liquid containing zinc oxide, water, and glue, used as a wash for walls and ceilings. **—cal′ci·mine′** *v.*

cal·cine (kăl-sīn′, kăl′sīn′) ▸ *v.* **-cined, -cin·ing.** To heat (a substance) to a high temperature but below the melting or fusing point, causing loss of moisture, reduction, or oxidation. **—cal′ci·na′tion** (-sə-nā′shən) *n.*

cal·cite (kăl′sīt′) ▸ *n.* A common crystalline form of natural calcium carbonate. **—cal·cit′ic** (-sĭt′ĭk) *adj.*

cal·ci·um (kăl′sē-əm) ▸ *n. Symbol* **Ca** A silvery metallic element that occurs in bone, shells, limestone, and gypsum and forms compounds used to make plaster, quicklime, cement, and metallurgic and electronic materials. At. no. 20.

calcium carbonate ▸ *n.* A colorless or white crystalline compound, $CaCO_3$, occurring naturally as chalk, limestone, and marble, and used in commercial chalk, medicines, and dentifrices.

calcium chloride ▸ *n.* A white deliquescent compound, $CaCl_2$, used chiefly as a drying agent, refrigerant, and preservative and for controlling dust and ice on roads.

calcium hydroxide ▸ *n.* A soft white powder, $Ca(OH)_2$, used in making mortar, cements, calcium salts, paints, and petrochemicals.

calcium oxide ▸ *n.* A white, caustic, lumpy powder, CaO, used as a refractory, as a flux, in making steel, paper, and glass, and in waste treatment and insecticides.

cal·cu·late (kăl′kyə-lāt′) ▸ *v.* **-lat·ed, -lat·ing. 1.** To compute mathematically. **2.** To estimate; reckon. **3.** To intend: *a choice calculated to please.* **4.** *Regional* **a.** To suppose; guess. **b.** To depend; rely. **—cal′cu·la·ble** *adj.* **—cal′cu·la′tive** *adj.*

cal·cu·lat·ed (kăl′kyə-lā′tĭd) ▸ *adj.* Undertaken after careful forethought: *a calculated risk.* **—cal′cu·lat′ed·ly** *adv.*

cal·cu·lat·ing (kăl′kyə-lā′tĭng) ▸ *adj.* **1.** Shrewd; crafty. **2.** Coldly scheming.

THESAURUS

cadge *v.* —*See* BEG.

cadger *n.* —*See* BEGGAR (1).

caducity *n.* The condition of being senile ▸ anecdotage, anility, dotage, sanility. [*Compare* AGE.]

cage *v.* —*See* ENCLOSE (1).

cage *n.* An enclosure for confining an animal or bird ▸ coop, cote, crate, hutch, kennel, pound, run, stall. [*Compare* PEN[2].]

cagey *adj.* —*See* SHREWD.

caitiff *adj.* —*See* COWARDLY.

caitiff *n.* —*See* COWARD.

cajole *v.* —*See* COAX.

cake *v.* —*See* HARDEN (2).

cake *n.* —*See* LUMP[1].

cakewalk *n.* —*See* RUNAWAY (1).

calaboose *n.* —*See* JAIL.

calamitous *adj.* —*See* DISASTROUS.

calamity *n.* —*See* DISASTER.

calculate *v.* To ascertain by mathematics ▸ cast, cipher, compute, figure, reckon. *Idioms:* crunch numbers, do the math (*or* numbers). [*Compare* ADD, COUNT, MEASURE.] —*See also* ESTIMATE (1).

calculated *adj.* Planned, weighed, or estimated in advance ▸ assessed, considered, contrived, deliberate, designed, devised, figured, formulated, intentional, predetermined, premeditated, schemed. —*See also* DELIBERATE (2).

calculating *adj.* Coldly planning to achieve selfish aims ▸ conniving, designing, manipulative, scheming. —*See also* ARTFUL.

cal·cu·la·tion (kăl′kyə-lā′shən) ▸ *n.* **1a.** The act, process, or result of calculating. **b.** A probable estimate. **2.** Careful, often cunning forethought.
cal·cu·la·tor (kăl′kyə-lā′tər) ▸ *n.* **1.** One who calculates. **2.** An electronic or mechanical device for the performance of mathematical computations.
cal·cu·lus (kăl′kyə-ləs) ▸ *n., pl.* **-li** (-lī′) or **-lus·es. 1.** *Pathol.* An abnormal mineral concretion in the body, as in the gallbladder or kidney; stone. **2.** *Dentistry* Tartar. **3.** *Math.* The mathematics of limits, instantaneous rates of change, and finding areas and volumes.
Cal·cut·ta (kăl-kŭt′ə) ▸ See **Kolkata.**
cal·de·ra (kăl-dâr′ə, -dîr′ə, kôl-) ▸ *n.* A large crater formed by volcanic processes.
cal·dron (kôl′drən) ▸ *n.* Var. of **cauldron.**
cal·en·dar (kăl′ən-dər) ▸ *n.* **1.** Any of various systems of reckoning the length and divisions of a year. See **calendar** table in Appendix on page 843. **2.** A table showing the months, weeks, and days of a year. **3.** A chronological list. ▸ *v.* To enter in a calendar. **—ca·len′dri·cal** (kə-lĕn′drĭ-kəl), **ca·len′dric** *adj.*
cal·en·der (kăl′ən-dər) ▸ *n.* A machine in which paper or cloth is made smooth and glossy by being pressed through rollers. **—cal′en·der** *v.*
cal·ends (kăl′əndz, kā′ləndz) ▸ *n., pl.* **-ends.** The first day of the month in the ancient Roman calendar.
calf[1] (kăf) ▸ *n., pl.* **calves** (kăvz). **1a.** A young cow or bull. **b.** The young of certain other mammals, such as the elephant or whale. **2.** Calfskin.
calf[2] (kăf) ▸ *n., pl.* **calves** (kăvz). The fleshy muscular back of the human leg between the knee and ankle.
calf·skin (kăf′skĭn′) ▸ *n.* Fine leather made from the hide of a calf.
Cal·ga·ry (kăl′gə-rē) ▸ A city of S Alberta, Canada, S of Edmonton.
cal·i·ber (kăl′ə-bər) ▸ *n.* **1a.** The diameter of the inside of a round cylinder, esp. the bore of a firearm. **b.** The diameter of a bullet or projectile. **2.** Degree of worth; quality: *a school of high caliber.*
cal·i·brate (kăl′ə-brāt′) ▸ *v.* **-brat·ed, -brat·ing. 1.** To check or adjust the graduations of (a quantitative measuring instrument). **2.** To determine the caliber of. **3.** To make fine corrections in. **—cal′i·bra′tion** *n.*
cal·i·bre (kăl′ə-bər) ▸ *n. Chiefly Brit.* Var. of **caliber.**
cal·i·co (kăl′ĭ-kō′) ▸ *n., pl.* **-coes** or **-cos. 1.** A coarse, brightly printed cloth. **2.** A cat having a white coat mottled with red and black. **—cal′i·co** *adj.*
Cal·i·for·nia (kăl′ĭ-fôr′nyə, -fôr′nē-ə) ▸ A state of the W US on the Pacific. Cap. Sacramento. **—Cal′i·for′nian** *adj. & n.*
California, Gulf of ▸ An arm of the Pacific in NW Mexico separating Baja California from the mainland.
California condor ▸ *n.* A very large, nearly extinct vulture of S California.
California poppy ▸ *n.* A plant of W North America having showy, often orange or yellow flowers.
cal·i·for·ni·um (kăl′ə-fôr′nē-əm) ▸ *n. Symbol* **Cf** A radioactive element produced synthetically from curium. At. no. 98.
cal·i·per also **cal·li·per** (kăl′ə-pər) ▸ *n.* **1.** often **calipers** An instrument consisting of two curved hinged legs, used to measure thickness and distances. **2.** A vernier caliper.
ca·liph also **ca·lif** (kā′lĭf, kăl′ĭf) ▸ *n.* A leader of an Islamic polity, regarded as a successor of Muhammad. **—ca′liph·ate′** (-fāt′, -fĭt) *n.*
cal·is·then·ics (kăl′ĭs-thĕn′ĭks) ▸ *n. (takes pl. v.)* Gymnastic exercises designed to develop muscular tone and promote physical well-being. **—cal′is·then′ic** *adj.*
calk (kôk) ▸ *v.* Var. of **caulk.**
call (kôl) ▸ *v.* **called, call·ing. 1.** To cry or utter loudly or clearly. **2.** To summon. **3.** To telephone. **4.** To name; designate: *Don't call me a liar.* **5.** To consider; estimate: *Would you call him an expert?* **6.** To pay a brief visit. **7.** To demand payment of (a loan or bond issue). **8.** *Sports* **a.** To stop or postpone (a game), as for bad weather. **b.** To declare as an umpire or referee: *call a runner out.* **9.** To indicate accurately in advance: *call the outcome of an election.* ***—phrasal verbs:*** **call down** To reprimand. **call for 1.** To stop for: *I'll call for you on my way home.* **2.** To warrant. **call forth** To evoke. **call in 1.** To take out of circulation: *calling in silver dollars.* **2.** To summon for assistance or consultation. **call off 1.** To cancel or postpone. **2.** To restrain: *Call off your dogs!* **call out** To cause to assemble; summon. **call up 1.** To summon to military service. **2.** To bring to mind: *call up old times.* **call upon 1.** To order; require: *I call upon you to tell the truth.* **2.** To make a demand or appeal on. ▸ *n.* **1.** A loud cry; shout. **2.** The characteristic cry of an animal. **3.** A telephone communication. **4.** Demand; occasion: *There's no call for haste.* **5.** A short visit. **6.** A summons or invitation. **7.** A strong urge or prompting. **8.** *Sports* A decision made by an umpire or referee. **9.** A demand for payment, as of a debt. ***—idioms:*** **call it a day** *Informal* To stop one's work for the day; quit. **call it quits** *Informal* To leave off; quit. **call the shots** *Informal* To be in charge. **call to mind** To remind of. **on call 1.** Available when summoned. **2.** Payable on demand. **—call′er** *n.*
cal·la lily (kăl′ə) ▸ *n.* Any of several ornamental plants cultivated for their showy, usu. white or yellow spathes.
caller ID ▸ *n.* A telephone service that displays an incoming caller's name and telephone number.
cal·lig·ra·phy (kə-lĭg′rə-fē) ▸ *n.* The art of fine handwriting. **—cal·lig′ra·pher, cal·lig′ra·phist** *n.* **—cal′li·graph′ic** (kăl′ĭ-grăf′ĭk) *adj.*
call-in (kôl′ĭn′) ▸ *adj.* Inviting listeners or viewers to participate in a program by means of broadcasted telephone calls.
call·ing (kô′lĭng) ▸ *n.* **1.** An inner urge; strong impulse. **2.** An occupation; vocation.
calling card ▸ *n.* **1.** An engraved card bearing one's full name. **2.** A phone card.
cal·li·o·pe (kə-lī′ə-pē′, kăl′ē-ōp′) ▸ *n.* A musical instrument fitted with steam whistles, played from a keyboard.
cal·li·per (kăl′ə-pər) ▸ *n.* Var. of **caliper.**
call letters ▸ *pl.n.* The identifying code letters or numbers of a radio or television station.
call loan ▸ *n.* A loan repayable on demand at any time.
call number ▸ *n.* A number used in libraries to classify a book and indicate its location on the shelves.
cal·los·i·ty (kə-lŏs′ĭ-tē) ▸ *n., pl.* **-ties. 1.** The condition of being calloused. **2.** Hardheartedness; insensitivity. **3.** See **callus.**
cal·lous (kăl′əs) ▸ *adj.* **1.** Having calluses; toughened. **2.**

THESAURUS

calculation *n.* The act, process, or result of calculating ▸ cast, computation, figuring, reckoning. *—See also* CAUTION.
calendar *n.* *—See* PROGRAM (1).
calendar *v.* To enter on a schedule ▸ docket, program, slate, schedule. [*Compare* LIST[1].]
calender *v.* *—See* PRESS (2).
caliber *n.* Degree of excellence ▸ class, grade, quality. [*Compare* DEGREE.] *—See also* MERIT.
calibrate *v.* *—See* ADJUST.
call *v.* To describe with a word or term ▸ characterize, denominate, designate, label, name, style, tag, term, title. [*Compare* DESCRIBE.] *—See also* ASSEMBLE, NAME (1), PREDICT, SHOUT, TELEPHONE, VISIT.
call down *v.* *—See* CHASTISE.
call for *v.* *—See* DEMAND (1), DEMAND (2), JUSTIFY (2).
call forth *v.* *—See* EVOKE.
call off *v.* To decide not to continue ▸ cancel. *Slang:* scrap, scratch, scrub. [*Compare* DEFER[1], DROP.]
call up *v.* *—See* IMAGINE, MOBILIZE.
call *n.* **1.** A telephone communication ▸ buzz, ring. **2.** A spoken or written request for someone to take part or be present ▸ bid, invitation, summons. *Informal:* invite. [*Compare* REQUEST.] *—See also* ATTRACTION, CAUSE (2), DEMAND (1), SHOUT, VISIT (1).
caller *n.* A person or persons visiting one ▸ company, guest, visitant, visitor.
call girl *n.* *—See* HARLOT.
calligraphic *adj.* Of or relating to representation by means of writing ▸ graphic, scriptural, written.
calligraphy *n.* *—See* SCRIPT (1).
calling *n.* An inner urge to pursue an activity or perform a service ▸ mission, vocation. [*Compare* DREAM, DUTY, FATE.] *—See also* BUSINESS (2).
callous *adj.* Lacking compassion or mercy ▸ anesthetic, bloodless, cold-blooded, cold-hearted, compassionless,

Insensitive: *a callous indifference to suffering.* ▸ *v.* To make or become callous. **—cal′lous·ly** *adv.* **—cal′lous·ness** *n.*

cal·low (kăl′ō) ▸ *adj.* Lacking experience; immature: *a callow youth.* **—cal′low·ness** *n.*

call-up (kôl′ŭp′) ▸ *n.* The summoning of reserve military personnel to active service.

cal·lus (kăl′əs) ▸ *n., pl.* **-lus·es.** A localized thickening and enlargement of the horny layer of the skin. **—cal′lus** *v.*

call waiting ▸ *n.* A telephone service that alerts someone using the phone to an incoming call and allows switching between calls.

calm (käm) ▸ *adj.* **-er, -est. 1.** Nearly or completely motionless; undisturbed: *calm seas.* **2.** Not excited or agitated; composed: *a calm voice.* ▸ *n.* **1.** An absence of motion; stillness. **2.** Serenity; peace. ▸ *v.* To make or become calm. **—calm′ly** *adv.* **—calm′ness** *n.*

calm·a·tive (kä′mə-tĭv, kăl′mə-) ▸ *adj.* Having sedative properties. ▸ *n.* A sedative.

cal·o·mel (kăl′ə-mĕl′, -məl) ▸ *n.* A usu. white tasteless compound, Hg_2Cl_2, used as a purgative and insecticide.

ca·lor·ic (kə-lôr′ĭk, -lŏr′-) ▸ *adj.* **1.** Of or relating to heat. **2.** Of or relating to calories.

cal·o·rie (kăl′ə-rē) ▸ *n.* **1.** A unit of heat equal to the amount of heat required to raise the temperature of 1 gram of water by 1°C at 1 atmosphere pressure; small calorie. **2a.** A unit of heat equal to the amount of heat required to raise the temperature of 1 kilogram of water by 1°C at 1 atmosphere pressure; large calorie. **b.** A unit of energy-producing potential equal to this amount of heat that is contained in food.

cal·o·rif·ic (kăl′ə-rĭf′ĭk) ▸ *adj.* Of or generating heat or calories.

cal·o·rim·e·ter (kăl′ə-rĭm′ĭ-tər) ▸ *n.* An apparatus for measuring the heat generated by a chemical reaction or change of state.

cal·u·met (kăl′yə-mĕt′, kăl′yə-mĕt′) ▸ *n.* A long-stemmed ceremonial tobacco pipe used by certain Native American peoples.

ca·lum·ni·ate (kə-lŭm′nē-āt′) ▸ *v.* **-at·ed, -at·ing.** To slander or malign. **—ca·lum′ni·a′tion** *n.* **—ca·lum′ni·a′tor** *n.*

cal·um·ny (kăl′əm-nē) ▸ *n., pl.* **-nies. 1.** A false statement maliciously made to injure another's reputation. **2.** The utterance of maliciously false statements; slander. **—ca·lum′ni·ous** (kə-lŭm′nē-əs) *adj.* **—ca·lum′ni·ous·ly** *adv.*

Cal·va·ry (kăl′və-rē) also **Gol·go·tha** (gŏl′gə-thə, gŏl-gŏth′ə) ▸ A hill outside ancient Jerusalem where Jesus was crucified.

calve (kăv) ▸ *v.* **calved, calv·ing. 1.** To give birth to a calf. **2.** To break at an edge. Used of a glacier.

calves[1] (kăvz) ▸ *n.* Pl. of **calf**[1].

calves[2] (kăvz) ▸ *n.* Pl. of **calf**[2].

Cal·vin (kăl′vĭn), **John** (1509–64) ▸ French-born Swiss theologian. **—Cal′vin·ism′** *n.* **—Cal′vin·ist** *adj. & n.*

calx (kălks) ▸ *n., pl.* **-es** or **cal·ces** (kăl′sēz′). The residue left after a mineral or metal has been calcined.

Ca·lyp·so or **ca·lyp·so** (kə-lĭp′sō) ▸ *n., pl.* **-sos** also **-soes.** A type of West Indian music with improvised lyrics on topical or broadly humorous subjects. **—Ca·lyp·so′ni·an** (kə-lĭp-sō′nē-ən, kăl′ĭp-) *n.*

ca·lyx (kā′lĭks, kăl′ĭks) ▸ *n., pl.* **-es** or **ca·ly·ces** (kā′lĭ-sēz′, kăl′ĭ-). The sepals of a flower that together form a cuplike base.

cal·zo·ne (kăl-zō′nē, -zōn′) ▸ *n.* A baked turnover filled with vegetables, meat, or cheese.

cam (kăm) ▸ *n.* A multiply curved wheel mounted on a rotating shaft, used to produce reciprocating motion.

ca·ma·ra·der·ie (kä′mə-rä′də-rē, kăm′ə-răd′ə-) ▸ *n.* Spirited goodwill among friends.

cam·ber (kăm′bər) ▸ *n.* **1.** A slightly arched surface, as of a road. **2.** A setting of automobile wheels in which they are closer together at the bottom than at the top. **—cam′ber** *v.*

cam·bi·um (kăm′bē-əm) ▸ *n.* A layer of soft growing tissue in a plant body that develops into new bark and new wood and produces the annual rings.

Cam·bo·di·a (kăm-bō′dē-ə) ▸ A country of SE Asia. **—Cam·bo′di·an** *adj. & n.*

Cam·bri·an (kăm′brē-ən) *Geol.* ▸ *adj.* Of or being the 1st and oldest period of the Paleozoic Era, marked by an abundance of marine invertebrates. ▸ *n.* The Cambrian Period.

cam·bric (kām′brĭk) ▸ *n.* A fine white linen or cotton fabric.

cambric tea ▸ *n.* A hot drink made from milk, sugar, water, and usually a small amount of tea.

cam·cord·er (kăm′kôr′dər) ▸ *n.* A camera that records video on a storage device.

came (kām) ▸ *v.* P.t. of **come.**

cam·el (kăm′əl) ▸ *n.* **1.** A humped, long-necked ruminant mammal domesticated in Old World desert regions as a beast of burden. **2.** A hollow, watertight device used to raise sunken objects.

cam·el·hair (kăm′əl-hâr′) also **cam·el's hair** (kăm′əlz) ▸ *n.* **1.** The soft fine hair of the camel or a substitute for it. **2.** A soft, heavy, usu. light tan cloth, made chiefly of camelhair.

ca·mel·lia (kə-mēl′yə) ▸ *n.* Any of a genus of evergreen Asian shrubs having showy, usu. red, white, or pink roselike flowers.

Cam·e·lot (kăm′ə-lŏt′) ▸ *n.* **1.** The legendary site of King Arthur's court. **2.** A place or time of idealized beauty, peacefulness, and enlightenment.

cam·e·o (kăm′ē-ō′) ▸ *n., pl.* **-os. 1.** A gem or medallion with a design cut in raised relief, usu. of a contrasting color. **2.** A brief appearance of a prominent actor, as in a single scene.

cam·er·a (kăm′ər-ə, kăm′rə) ▸ *n.* A usu. portable device containing a light-sensitive surface that records images through a lens.

cam·er·a·man (kăm′ər-ə-măn′, kăm′rə-) ▸ *n.* A man who operates a movie or television camera.

cam·er·a·wom·an (kăm′ər-ə-wŏŏm′ən, kăm′rə-) ▸ *n.* A woman who operates a movie or television camera.

Cam·e·roon (kăm′ə-rōōn′) also **Came·roun** (käm-rōōn′) ▸ A country of W-central Africa on the Atlantic Ocean.

cam·i·sole (kăm′ĭ-sōl′) ▸ *n.* A woman's sleeveless undergarment or shirt with narrow straps.

cam·o·mile (kăm′ə-mīl′, -mēl′) ▸ *n.* Var. of **chamomile.**

cam·ou·flage (kăm′ə-fläzh′, -fläj′) ▸ *n.* A means of concealment or a disguise that creates the effect of being part of the natural surroundings. ▸ *v.* **-flaged, -flag·ing. 1.** To conceal by camouflage. **2.** To mask. **—cam′ou·flag′er** *n.*

camp[1] (kămp) ▸ *n.* **1a.** A place of temporary residence or shelter, as for soldiers or travelers. **b.** The shelters, such as tents or cabins, at such a place. **2.** A usu. rural place offering organized recreation or instruction: *a girls' summer camp.* **3.** A group sharing a common cause or opinion. ▸ *v.* To set up or live in a camp.

camp[2] (kămp) ▸ *n.* An affectation, esp. for humor's sake, of manners commonly thought to be vulgar or banal. ▸ *adj.* Deliberately artificial, vulgar, or banal. ▸ *v.* To act in a camp manner. **—camp′y** *adj.*

cam·paign (kăm-pān′) ▸ *n.* **1.** A series of military operations undertaken to achieve a large-scale objective during

THESAURUS

hard, hard-boiled, hardened, hard-hearted, heartless, insensate, insensible, insensitive, merciless, obdurate, pitiless, remorseless, soulless, stonyhearted, thick-skinned, uncaring, uncompassionate, unfeeling, unmerciful, unpitying, unsympathetic, untouched. *Idiom:* hard (*or* tough) as nails. [*Compare* COLD, SEVERE.]

call to arms or **call to battle** *n.* —*See* CRY (2).

calm *adj.* Not excited or agitated ▸ collected, composed, cool, coolheaded, detached, easygoing, even, even-tempered, imperturbable, mellow, nonchalant, peaceful, placid, poised, possessed, serene, tranquil, unflappable, unruffled. *Idiom:* cool as a cucumber. —*See also* STILL.

calm *n.* Lack of emotional agitation ▸ calmness, peace, peacefulness, placidity, placidness, quietude, repose, serenity, tranquillity. *Idiom:* peace of mind. [*Compare* BALANCE.] —*See also* STILLNESS.

calm *v.* —*See* PACIFY.

calmness *n.* —*See* CALM, STILLNESS.

calumniate *v.* —*See* MALIGN.

calumniation *n.* —*See* LIBEL.

calumnious *adj.* —*See* LIBELOUS.

calumny *n.* —*See* LIBEL.

camaraderie *n.* —*See* COMPANY (3), FRIENDSHIP.

camouflage *v.* —*See* CONCEAL, DISGUISE.

camp *n.* —*See* BASE[1] (1).

campaign *n.* —*See* DRIVE (1).

a war. 2. An organized operation to accomplish a purpose: *an ad campaign; a political campaign.* ▸ *v.* To engage in a campaign. **—cam·paign′er** *n.*

cam·pa·ni·le (kăm′pə-nē′lē) ▸ *n.* An often freestanding bell tower.

camp·er (kăm′pər) ▸ *n.* **1.** One who camps or attends a camp. **2.** A motor vehicle equipped, as with a rear compartment or attached trailer, for sleeping and housekeeping, used for recreational travel.

camp·fire (kămp′fīr′) ▸ *n.* **1.** An outdoor fire in a camp, used for cooking or warmth. **2.** A meeting held around such a fire.

camp·ground (kămp′ground′) ▸ *n.* An area for camping, esp. one containing individual campsites.

cam·phor (kăm′fər) ▸ *n.* A natural aromatic compound used in the manufacture of film and plastics and as an external medicinal preparation. **—cam′phor·at′ed** (-fə-rā′tĭd) *adj.*

camp meeting ▸ *n.* An evangelistic gathering held in a tent or outdoors.

camp·site (kămp′sīt′) ▸ *n.* An area used or suitable for setting up a camp.

cam·pus (kăm′pəs) ▸ *n., pl.* **-pus·es.** The grounds of a school, college, university, or hospital.

cam·shaft (kăm′shăft′) ▸ *n.* An engine shaft fitted with a cam or cams.

Ca·mus (kä-mo͞o′, -mü′), **Albert** (1913–60) ▸ French writer and philosopher; 1957 Nobel.

can[1] (kăn; kən *when unstressed*) ▸ *aux.v., P.t.* **could** (ko͝od). **1.** Used to indicate: **a.** Physical or mental ability: *I can carry both suitcases.* **b.** Possession of a power, right, or privilege: *The President can veto bills.* **c.** Possession of a capability or skill: *I can tune a piano.* **2.** Used to indicate: **a.** Possibility or probability: *I wonder if I could be sick.* **b.** That which is permitted, as by conscience or feelings: *I can hardly blame you for laughing.* **3.** Used to request or grant permission.

can[2] (kăn) ▸ *n.* **1.** A metal container: *a garbage can.* **2a.** An airtight storage container, usu. made of tin-coated iron and used esp. for foods. **b.** The contents of a can. **3.** *Slang* A jail. **4.** *Slang* A toilet. ▸ *v.* **canned, can·ning. 1.** To seal in a can or jar; preserve. **2.** *Slang* To dismiss; fire. **3.** *Slang* To put a stop to: *Can the chatter.* **—can′ner** *n.*

Ca·naan (kā′nən) ▸ An ancient region made up of Palestine or the part of it between the Jordan R. and the Mediterranean. **—Ca′naan·ite′** *adj. & n.*

Can·a·da (kăn′ə-də) ▸ A country of N North America. **—Ca·na′di·an** (kə-nā′dē-ən) *adj. & n.*

Canada Day ▸ *n.* July 1, observed in Canada in commemoration of the formation of the Dominion in 1867.

Canada goose or **Canadian goose** ▸ *n.* A common wild goose of North America, having grayish plumage, a black neck and head, and a white throat patch.

Canadian French ▸ *n.* The French language as used in Canada.

ca·naille (kə-nī′, -nāl′) ▸ *n.* The common people.

ca·nal (kə-năl′) ▸ *n.* **1.** An artificial waterway used for travel, shipping, or irrigation. **2.** *Anat.* A tube or duct. **—can′al·i·za′tion** (kăn′ə-lĭ-zā′shən) *n.* **—can′al·ize′** *v.*

Canal Zone also **Panama Canal Zone** ▸ A strip of land across the Isthmus of Panama, formerly administered by the US for the operation of the Panama Canal.

can·a·pé (kăn′ə-pā′, -pē) ▸ *n.* A cracker or small piece of bread topped with a spread.

ca·nard (kə-närd′) ▸ *n.* An unfounded or false, deliberately misleading story.

ca·nar·y (kə-nâr′ē) ▸ *n., pl.* **-ies. 1.** A small, greenish to yellow finch long bred as a cage bird. **2.** A sweet white wine. **3.** A light to vivid yellow.

Canary Islands ▸ A group of Spanish islands in the Atlantic off the NW coast of Africa.

ca·nas·ta (kə-năs′tə) ▸ *n.* A card game related to rummy and requiring two decks of cards.

Ca·nav·er·al (kə-năv′ər-əl, -năv′rəl), **Cape** ▸ A sandy promontory extending into the Atlantic on the E-central coast of FL.

Can·ber·ra (kăn′bər-ə, -bĕr′ə) ▸ The capital of Australia, in the SE part.

can·can (kăn′kăn′) ▸ *n.* An exuberant exhibition dance marked by high kicking.

can·cel (kăn′səl) ▸ *v.* **-celed, -cel·ing** also **-celled, -cel·ling. 1.** To cross out with lines or other markings. **2.** To annul or invalidate. **3.** To mark or perforate (e.g., a postage stamp or check) to insure against further use. **4.** To counteract; offset. **5.** *Math.* **a.** To remove (a common factor) from the numerator and denominator of a fractional expression. **b.** To remove (a common factor or term) from both sides of an equation or inequality. **—can′cel·a·ble** *adj.* **—can′cel·er** *n.* **—can′cel·la′tion** *n.*

can·cer (kăn′sər) ▸ *n.* **1a.** A malignant tumor that tends to invade surrounding tissue and spread to new body sites. **b.** The pathological condition characterized by such growths. **2.** A pernicious, spreading evil. **—can′cer·ous** (-sər-əs) *adj.*

Can·cer (kăn′sər) ▸ *n.* **1.** A constellation in the Northern Hemisphere. **2.** The 4th sign of the zodiac.

can·del·a (kăn-dĕl′ə) ▸ *n.* A unit of luminous intensity equal to 1/60 of the luminous intensity per square cm of a blackbody radiating at the temperature of 2,046°K.

can·de·la·bra (kăn′dl-ä′brə, -ăb′rə, -ā′brə) ▸ *n.* A candelabrum.

can·de·la·brum (kăn′dl-ä′brəm, -ăb′rəm, -ā′brəm) ▸ *n., pl.* **-bra** (-brə) or **-brums.** A large decorative candlestick having several arms or branches.

can·des·cence (kăn-dĕs′əns) ▸ *n.* The state of being white hot; incandescence. **—can·des′cent** *adj.*

can·did (kăn′dĭd) ▸ *adj.* **1.** Free from prejudice; impartial. **2.** Direct and frank; straightforward: *my candid opinion.* **3.** Not posed or rehearsed: *a candid snapshot.* **—can′did·ly** *adv.* **—can′did·ness** *n.*

can·di·date (kăn′dĭ-dāt′, -dĭt) ▸ *n.* A person who seeks or is nominated for an office, prize, or honor. **—can′di·da·cy** (-də-sē), **can′di·da·ture′** (-də-cho͝or′, -chər) *n.*

can·dle (kăn′dl) ▸ *n.* **1.** A solid, usu. cylindrical mass of tallow, wax, or other fatty substance with an embedded wick that is burned to provide light. **2.** See **candela.** ▸ *v.* **-dled, -dling.** To examine (an egg) in front of a bright light. **—can′dler** *n.*

can·dle·light (kăn′dl-līt′) ▸ *n.* **1.** Illumination from a candle or candles. **2.** Dusk; twilight.

can·dle·pin (kăn′dl-pĭn′) ▸ *n.* A slender bowling pin used with a smaller ball in a variation of the game of tenpins.

can·dle·pow·er (kăn′dl-pou′ər) ▸ *n.* Luminous intensity expressed in candelas.

can·dle·stick (kăn′dl-stĭk′) ▸ *n.* A holder with a cup or spike for a candle.

can·dor (kăn′dər) ▸ *n.* Frankness or sincerity of expression.

can·dy (kăn′dē) ▸ *n., pl.* **-dies.** A sweet confection made with sugar and often with fruits or nuts. ▸ *v.* **-died, -dying.** To cook, preserve, saturate, or coat with sugar or syrup.

candy striper ▸ *n.* A usu. young volunteer worker in a hospital.

can·dy·tuft (kăn′dē-tŭft′) ▸ *n.* Any of several plants with white, pink, red, or purple flowers.

cane (kān) ▸ *n.* **1a.** A slender, strong but often flexible stem, as of certain bamboos or reeds. **b.** A plant with

THESAURUS

campestral *adj.* —*See* COUNTRY.
campiness *n.* —*See* THEATRICALISM.
can *n.* —*See* BUTTOCKS, JAIL.
can *v.* —*See* DISMISS (1), PRESERVE (1).
canal *n.* —*See* VESSEL (2), WAY (2).
canard *n.* —*See* LIE[2].
cancel *v.* **1.** To cross out or remove ▸ annul, blot (out), cross (off *or* out), delete, efface, erase, expunge, obliterate, rub (out), scratch (out *or* off), strike (out *or* off), undo, vacate, wipe (out), x (out). [*Compare* DROP, LIFT.] **2.** To make ineffective by applying an opposite force or amount ▸ balance, compensate, counteract, counterbalance, counterpoise, countervail, negate, neutralize, nullify, offset, outweigh, redeem, set off. [*Compare* ABOLISH, BALANCE.] **3.** To decide not to continue ▸ call off. *Slang:* scrap, scratch, scrub. [*Compare* DEFER, DROP.] —*See also* ABOLISH.
cancellation *n.* —*See* ABOLITION, ERASURE.
candid *adj.* —*See* FRANK.
candidate *n.* —*See* APPLICANT, COMER (2).
candidness *n.* —*See* HONESTY.
candy *v.* —*See* SWEETEN.
cane *n.* —*See* STICK (2).

such a stem. c. Interwoven strips of such stems, esp. rattan. 2. Sugar cane. 3. A walking stick or similar rod. ► *v.* **caned, can·ing.** 1. To make or repair with cane. 2. To hit or beat with a rod. **—can′er** *n.*

cane·brake (kān′brāk′) ► *n.* A dense thicket of cane.

cane sugar ► *n.* Sucrose obtained from sugar cane.

ca·nine (kā′nīn) ► *adj.* 1. Of or belonging to the family of carnivorous mammals that includes dogs, jackals, foxes, and wolves. 2. Of or being one of the pointed conical teeth between the incisors and bicuspids. ► *n.* 1. A canine animal, esp. a dog. 2. A canine tooth; cuspid.

Ca·nis Major (kā′nĭs, kăn′ĭs) ► *n.* A constellation in the Southern Hemisphere containing the star Sirius.

Canis Minor ► *n.* A constellation in the Southern Hemisphere.

can·is·ter (kăn′ĭ-stər) ► *n.* 1. A usu. metal box or can used for holding dry foodstuffs. 2. A metal cylinder packed with shot that are scattered when the cylinder is fired.

can·ker (kăng′kər) ► *n.* Ulceration of the mouth and lips. **—can′ker·ous** *adj.*

canker sore ► *n.* A small painful ulcer or sore, usu. of the mouth.

can·na (kăn′ə) ► *n.* Any of various tropical plants having large, showy red or yellow flowers.

can·na·bis (kăn′ə-bĭs) ► *n.* 1. A tall Asian plant having alternate leaves and tough bast fibers. 2. The dried flowers and leaves of the cannabis, from which mildly euphoriant and intoxicating drugs, such as marijuana, are prepared.

canned (kănd) ► *adj.* 1. Preserved and sealed in an airtight can or jar. 2. *Informal* Recorded or taped: *canned laughter.*

can·ner·y (kăn′ə-rē) ► *n., pl.* **-ies.** A factory where meat, fish, vegetables, fruit, or other foods are canned.

can·ni·bal (kăn′ə-bəl) ► *n.* 1. A person who eats the flesh of other humans. 2. An animal that feeds on others of its own kind. **—can′ni·bal·ism** *n.* **—can′ni·bal·is′tic** *adj.*

can·ni·bal·ize (kăn′ə-bə-līz′) ► *v.* **-ized, -iz·ing.** To remove serviceable parts from (e.g., damaged vehicles) for use in the repair of other equipment of the same kind. **—can′ni·bal·i·za′tion** *n.*

can·no·li (kə-nō′lē, kă-) ► *n.* A fried pastry roll with a sweet creamy filling.

can·non (kăn′ən) ► *n., pl.* **-non** or **-nons.** A large mounted weapon, such as a gun or howitzer, that fires heavy projectiles. **—can′non·eer′** *n.*

can·non·ade (kăn′ə-nād′) ► *n.* An extended discharge of artillery. **—can′non·ade′** *v.*

can·non·ball (kăn′ən-bôl′) ► *n.* 1. A round projectile fired from a cannon. 2. Something, such as a fast train, moving with great speed. **—can′non·ball′** *v.*

can·not (kăn′ŏt, kə-nŏt′, kă-) ► *aux.v.* The negative form of **can**[1].

can·nu·la (kăn′yə-lə) ► *n., pl.* **-las** or **-lae** (-lē′). A flexible tube inserted into a body cavity or vessel to drain fluid or administer a medication.

can·ny (kăn′ē) ► *adj.* **-ni·er, -ni·est.** 1. Careful and shrewd. 2. Thrifty; frugal. **—can′ni·ly** *adv.* **—can′ni·ness** *n.*

ca·noe (kə-no͞o′) ► *n.* A light slender boat that has pointed ends and is propelled by paddles. ► *v.* **-noed, -noe·ing.** To carry or travel by canoe. **—ca·noe′ist** *n.*

ca·no·la (kə-nō′lə) ► *n.* An oil made from rape seeds, high in monounsaturated fatty acids.

can·on[1] (kăn′ən) ► *n.* 1. A code of laws established by a church council. 2. An accepted standard. 3. The books of the Bible officially accepted by a Christian church. 4. *Mus.* A round.

can·on[2] (kăn′ən) ► *n.* A member of the clergy serving in a cathedral or collegiate church.

ca·ñon (kăn′yən) ► *n.* Var. of **canyon.**

ca·non·i·cal (kə-nŏn′ĭ-kəl) also **ca·non·ic** (-ĭk) ► *adj.* 1. Of or according to canon law. 2. Conforming to standard or orthodox rules. **—ca·non′i·cal·ly** *adv.* **—can′on·ic′i·ty** (kăn′ə-nĭs′ĭ-tē) *n.*

canonical hours ► *pl.n.* 1. The times of day at which canon law prescribes certain prayers to be recited. 2. The prayers recited.

can·on·ize (kăn′ə-nīz′) ► *v.* **-ized, -iz·ing.** 1. To declare (a deceased person) a saint. 2. To exalt; glorify. **—can′on·i·za′tion** *n.*

canon law ► *n.* The body of official rules governing a church or other religious denomination.

can·o·py (kăn′ə-pē) ► *n., pl.* **-pies.** 1. A usu. cloth covering suspended over a throne or bed or held aloft on poles, as over a monarch. 2. *Archit.* An ornamental rooflike structure. 3. An awning over a walkway or door. 4. *Ecol.* The uppermost layer in a forest, formed by the crowns of the trees. 5. A transparent enclosure over an aircraft cockpit. **—can′o·py** *v.*

canst (kănst) ► *aux.v.* *Archaic* 2nd pers. sing. pr.t. of **can**[1].

cant[1] (kănt) ► *n.* 1. Angular deviation from a vertical or horizontal plane or surface. 2. A slanted or oblique surface. 3. A thrust or motion that tilts something. ► *v.* To slant or tilt.

cant[2] (kănt) ► *n.* 1. Insincere speech full of platitudes or pious expressions. 2. The special vocabulary peculiar to the members of a group. 3. Whining or singsong speech, such as that of beggars. ► *v.* 1. To speak sententiously. 2. To whine or plead. **—cant′ing·ly** *adv.*

can't (kănt) ► Cannot.

can·ta·bi·le (kän-tä′bĭ-lā′) ► *adv.* *Mus.* In a smooth, lyrical, flowing style. **—can·ta′bi·le′** *adj. & n.*

can·ta·loupe also **can·ta·loup** (kăn′tl-ōp′) ► *n.* A melon with a ribbed, rough rind and orange flesh.

can·tan·ker·ous (kăn-tăng′kər-əs) ► *adj.* Ill-tempered and quarrelsome. **—can·tan′ker·ous·ly** *adv.* **—can·tan′ker·ous·ness** *n.*

can·ta·ta (kən-tä′tə) ► *n.* *Mus.* An often sacred composition comprising recitatives, arias, and choruses.

can·teen (kăn-tēn′) ► *n.* 1a. A snack bar or small cafeteria. b. A store for on-base military personnel. 2. An institutional recreation hall or social club. 3. A temporary or mobile eating place, esp. one set up in an emergency. 4. A flask for carrying drinking water. 5. A soldier's mess kit.

can·ter (kăn′tər) ► *n.* A smooth gait, esp. of a horse, slower than a gallop but faster than a trot. **—can′ter** *v.*

Can·ter·bur·y (kăn′tər-bĕr′ē, -brē, -tə-) ► A borough of SE England ESE of London; site of Canterbury Cathedral.

can·thus (kăn′thəs) ► *n., pl.* **-thi** (-thī′). The angle formed by the meeting of the upper and lower eyelids at either side of the eye.

can·ti·cle (kăn′tĭ-kəl) ► *n.* A liturgical chant.

can·ti·le·ver (kăn′tl-ē′vər, -ĕv′ər) ► *n.* A projecting structure, such as a beam, that is supported at one end and carries a load at the other. **—can′ti·le′ver** *v.*

can·ti·na (kăn-tē′nə) ► *n.* *Regional* A bar that serves liquor.

can·tle (kăn′tl) ► *n.* The raised rear part of a saddle.

can·to (kăn′tō) ► *n., pl.* **-tos.** One of the principal divisions of a long poem.

can·ton (kăn′tən, -tŏn′) ► *n.* A small territorial division of a country, esp. one of the states of Switzerland. **—can′ton·al** *adj.*

Can·ton (kăn′tŏn, kăn′tŏn′) ► See **Guangzhou.**

can·ton·ment (kăn-tōn′mənt, -tŏn′-) ► *n.* 1. Temporary quarters for troops. 2. Assignment of troops to temporary quarters.

can·tor (kăn′tər) ► *n.* 1. The official who leads the congregation in the musical part of a Jewish religious service. 2. The person who leads a church choir or congregation in singing. **—can·to′ri·al** (kăn-tôr′ē-əl, -tŏr′-) *adj.*

can·vas (kăn′vəs) ► *n.* 1. A heavy, closely woven fabric of cotton, hemp, or flax, used for tents and sails. 2. A piece of such fabric on which a painting is executed. 3. Sails.

THESAURUS

cane *v.* *—See* BEAT (2).

canker *n.* *—See* POISON.

canker *v.* *—See* CORRUPT, POISON.

cannonade *v.* *—See* BARRAGE.

cannonade *n.* *—See* BARRAGE.

canny *adj.* *—See* ECONOMICAL, SHREWD.

can of worms *n.* *—See* PROBLEM.

canon *n.* *—See* DOCTRINE, LAW (1).

canonical *adj.* *—See* CONVENTIONAL.

canonization *n.* *—See* EXALTATION.

canoodle *v.* *—See* CARESS.

cant[1] *n.* *—See* INCLINATION (2).

cant *v.* *—See* INCLINE.

cant[2] *n.* *—See* DIALECT, LANGUAGE (2).

cantankerous *adj.* *—See* ARGUMENTATIVE, ILL-TEMPERED.

cantankerousness *n.* *—See* TEMPER (1).

canter *v.* *—See* RUN (1).

canter *n.* *—See* RUN (1).

4. The floor of a boxing ring or wrestling ring.

can·vas·back (kăn′vəs-băk′) ▸ *n.* A North American duck having a reddish-brown head and neck and a whitish back.

can·vass (kăn′vəs) ▸ *v.* **1.** To scrutinize. **2a.** To go through (a region) in order to solicit votes or orders. **b.** To conduct a survey. ▸ *n.* **1.** An examination or discussion. **2.** A solicitation of votes, sales, orders, or opinions. **—can′vass·er** *n.*

can·yon also **ca·ñon** (kăn′yən) ▸ *n.* A narrow chasm with steep cliff walls.

cap (kăp) ▸ *n.* **1.** A usu. soft and close-fitting head covering, with or without a visor. **2.** A protective cover or seal, esp. one that closes off an end or tip: *a bottle cap.* **3.** An upper limit; ceiling. **4a.** A percussion cap. **b.** A small explosive charge enclosed in paper for use in a toy gun. ▸ *v.* **capped, cap·ping. 1.** To cover or seal with a cap. **2.** To lie on top of: *hills capped with snow.* **3.** To set an upper limit on. **—*idiom:* cap in hand** Respectfully or humbly; unpretentiously.

ca·pa·ble (kā′pə-bəl) ▸ *adj.* **1.** Having ability; competent. **2.** Having the potential: *capable of violence.* **—ca′pa·bil′i·ty** *n.* **—ca′pa·bly** *adv.*

ca·pa·cious (kə-pā′shəs) ▸ *adj.* Able to hold a large amount; roomy. **—ca·pa′cious·ly** *adv.* **—ca·pa′cious·ness** *n.*

ca·pac·i·tance (kə-păs′ĭ-təns) ▸ *n.* *Symbol* **C 1.** The ratio of charge to potential on an isolated conductor. **2.** The ratio of the electric charge on one of a pair of conductors to the potential difference between them. **3.** The property of a circuit element that permits it to store charge. **—ca·pac′i·tive** *adj.*

ca·pac·i·tate (kə-păs′ĭ-tāt′) ▸ *v.* **-tat·ed, -tat·ing.** To render fit; enable.

ca·pac·i·tor (kə-păs′ĭ-tər) ▸ *n.* An electric circuit element used to store charge temporarily, consisting in general of two metallic plates separated by a dielectric.

ca·pac·i·ty (kə-păs′ĭ-tē) ▸ *n., pl.* **-ties. 1.** The ability to receive, hold, or absorb. **2.** The maximum amount that can be contained. **3.** The maximum or optimum amount that can be produced. **4.** The ability to learn or retain knowledge. **5.** The quality of being suitable for or receptive to specified treatment: *the capacity of elastic to be stretched.* **6.** Position; role: *in your capacity as sales manager.* **7.** *Elect.* Capacitance. ▸ *adj.* As large or numerous as possible: *a capacity crowd.*

ca·par·i·son (kə-păr′ĭ-sən) ▸ *n.* An ornamental covering for a horse. **—ca·par′i·son** *v.*

cape[1] (kāp) ▸ *n.* A sleeveless garment often tied at the throat and worn hanging over the shoulders.

cape[2] (kāp) ▸ *n.* A headland projecting into a body of water.

Cape buffalo ▸ *n.* A large African buffalo having massive downward-curving horns.

ca·per[1] (kā′pər) ▸ *n.* **1.** A playful leap or hop. **2.** A wild escapade. **3.** *Slang* An illegal enterprise, esp. one involving theft. ▸ *v.* To leap or frisk about.

ca·per[2] (kā′pər) ▸ *n.* The pickled flower bud of a Mediterranean shrub, used as a pungent condiment.

Cape Town or **Cape·town** (kāp′toun′) ▸ The legislative capital of South Africa, in the extreme SW.

Cape Verde (vûrd) ▸ An island country of the Atlantic W of Senegal.

cap·il·lar·i·ty (kăp′ə-lăr′ĭ-tē) ▸ *n., pl.* **-ties.** The interaction between contacting surfaces of a liquid and a solid that distorts the liquid surface from a planar shape.

cap·il·lar·y (kăp′ə-lĕr′ē) ▸ *adj.* **1.** Of or resembling a hair; fine and slender. **2.** Having a very small internal diameter: *a capillary tube.* **3.** *Anat.* Of the capillaries. **4.** Of capillarity. ▸ *n., pl.* **-ies. 1.** One of the minute blood vessels that connect the arteries and veins. **2.** A tube with a very small internal diameter.

capillary attraction ▸ *n.* The force that causes a liquid to be raised against a vertical surface, as water is in a clean glass tube.

cap·i·tal[1] (kăp′ĭ-tl) ▸ *n.* **1.** A town or city that is the official seat of government in a political entity. **2.** Wealth in the form of money or property. **3.** The net worth of a business. **4.** Capital stock. **5.** Capitalists considered as a group or class. **6.** An asset or advantage. **7.** A capital letter. ▸ *adj.* **1.** First and foremost; principal. **2.** First-rate; excellent: *a capital idea.* **3.** Of or being a political capital. **4.** Extremely serious: *a capital blunder.* **5.** Involving or punishable by death: *a capital offense.* **6.** Of or relating to financial assets, esp. those that add to the net worth of a business. **7.** Of or being a capital letter.

cap·i·tal[2] (kăp′ĭ-tl) ▸ *n.* *Archit.* The top part of a pillar or column.

capital gain ▸ *n.* The amount by which the sale of a capital asset exceeds the original cost.

cap·i·tal·ism (kăp′ĭ-tl-ĭz′əm) ▸ *n.* An economic system in which the means of production and distribution are privately or corporately owned and development is proportionate to the accumulation and reinvestment of profits gained in a free market.

cap·i·tal·ist (kăp′ĭ-tl-ĭst) ▸ *n.* **1.** A supporter of capitalism. **2.** An investor of capital in business. **3.** A person of great wealth. **—cap′i·tal·is′tic** *adj.*

cap·i·tal·ize (kăp′ĭ-tl-īz′) ▸ *v.* **-ized, -iz·ing. 1.** To convert into capital. **2.** To supply with capital. **3a.** To print in capital letters. **b.** To begin (a word) with a capital letter. **4.** To turn something to one's advantage: *capitalize on another's error.* **—cap′i·tal·i·za′tion** *n.*

capital letter ▸ *n.* A letter written or printed in a size larger than and often in a form differing from its corresponding lowercase letter; uppercase letter.

cap·i·tal·ly (kăp′ĭ-tl-ē) ▸ *adv.* Excellently.

capital punishment ▸ *n.* The death penalty.

capital stock ▸ *n.* **1.** The total amount of stock authorized for issue by a corporation. **2.** The total value of the permanently invested capital of a corporation.

cap·i·ta·tion (kăp′ĭ-tā′shən) ▸ *n.* A poll tax.

cap·i·tol (kăp′ĭ-tl) ▸ *n.* **1.** The building in which a legislature meets. **2. Capitol** The building in Washington DC where the US Congress meets.

ca·pit·u·late (kə-pĭch′ə-lāt′) ▸ *v.* **-lat·ed, -lat·ing. 1.** To surrender under specified conditions. **2.** To give up all resistance; acquiesce. **—ca·pit′u·la′tion** *n.*

cap·let (kăp′lĭt) ▸ *n.* A coated capsule-shaped medicine tablet intended to be tamper-resistant.

ca·po[1] (kā′pō) ▸ *n., pl.* **-pos.** A small movable bar placed

THESAURUS

canvass *n.* A gathering of information or opinion from a variety of sources or individuals ▸ count, poll, survey.

canyon *n.* —*See* VALLEY.

cap *n.* Something that covers, especially to prevent contents from spilling ▸ cover, covering, lid, top. [*Compare* PLUG.] —*See also* CLIMAX, LIMIT (1).

cap *v.* To put a topping on ▸ crest, crown, tip, top, top off. —*See also* CLIMAX, COVER (1).

capability *n.* —*See* ABILITY (2).

capable *adj.* —*See* ABLE.

capacious *adj.* Having plenty of room ▸ ample, commodious, roomy, spacious. [*Compare* BIG, BROAD.] —*See also* FULL (3).

capacity *n.* The ability or power to seize or attain ▸ compass, grasp, range, reach, scope. [*Compare* INFLUENCE.] —*See also* ABILITY (2).

caper *n.* —*See* PRANK[1].

caper *v.* —*See* GAMBOL.

capillary *n.* —*See* VESSEL (2).

capital *n.* **1.** Money or property used to produce more wealth ▸ assets, backing, capitalization, financing, funding, grubstake, principal, resources, risk capital, stake, venture capital. *Informal:* bankroll. [*Compare* FUNDS, GRANT, MONEY.] **2.** The monetary resources of a government, organization, or individual ▸ finances, funds, money, moneys. —*See also* RESOURCES.

capital *adj.* —*See* EXCELLENT, PRIMARY (1).

capitalist *n.* One who is occupied with or expert in large-scale financial affairs ▸ financier. *Informal:* moneyman.

capitalization *n.* —*See* CAPITAL (1).

capitalize *v.* —*See* BENEFIT, FINANCE.

capitulate *v.* —*See* SUCCUMB, SURRENDER (1).

capitulation *n.* The act of submitting or surrendering to the power of another ▸ giving up, submission, surrender. [*Compare* OBEDIENCE.]

across the fingerboard of a guitar to raise the pitch of all the strings uniformly.

ca·po² (kä′pō, kăp′ō) ▸ *n., pl.* **-pos.** The head of a branch of an organized crime syndicate.

ca·pon (kā′pŏn′, -pən) ▸ *n.* A castrated rooster raised for food.

cap·puc·ci·no (kăp′ə-chē′nō, kä′pə-) ▸ *n., pl.* **-nos.** Espresso coffee with steamed milk or cream.

ca·pric·cio (kə-prē′chō, -chē-ō′) ▸ *n., pl.* **-cios** *Mus.* An instrumental work with an improvisatory style and a free form.

ca·price (kə-prēs′) ▸ *n.* 1a. An impulsive change of mind. b. An inclination to change one's mind impulsively. 2. *Mus.* A capriccio.

ca·pri·cious (kə-prĭsh′əs, -prē′shəs) ▸ *adj.* Impulsive and unpredictable. **—ca·pri′cious·ly** *adv.* **—ca·pri′cious·ness** *n.*

Cap·ri·corn (kăp′rĭ-kôrn′) ▸ *n.* 1. A constellation in the Southern Hemisphere. 2. The 10th sign of the zodiac.

cap·ri·ole (kăp′rē-ōl′) ▸ *n.* An upward leap made by a trained horse without going forward.

cap·si·cum (kăp′sĭ-kəm) ▸ *n.* Any of a genus of tropical American pepper plants having pungent fruit used as a condiment.

cap·sid (kăp′sĭd) ▸ *n.* The protein shell of a virus particle.

cap·size (kăp′sīz′, kăp-sīz′) ▸ *v.* **-sized, -siz·ing.** To overturn or cause to overturn. Used of a boat.

cap·stan (kăp′stən, -stăn′) ▸ *n.* 1. *Naut.* A vertical spool-shaped revolving cylinder for hoisting weights by winding in a cable. 2. A small cylindrical shaft used to drive magnetic tape at a constant speed in a tape recorder.

cap·stone (kăp′stōn′) ▸ *n.* 1. The top stone of a structure or wall. 2. The crowning achievement; acme.

cap·su·late (kăp′sə-lāt′, -lĭt, -syo͞o-) also **cap·su·lat·ed** (-lā′tĭd) ▸ *adj.* Enclosed in or formed into a capsule. **—cap′su·la′tion** *n.*

cap·sule (kăp′səl, -so͞ol) ▸ *n.* 1. A small soluble container, usu. of gelatin, that encloses a dose of oral medicine or vitamins. 2. A fibrous, membranous, or fatty sheath that encloses a bodily organ or part. 3. A seed case that dries and splits open. 4. A pressurized compartment of an aircraft or spacecraft. ▸ *adj.* 1. Condensed; brief. 2. Very small; compact. **—cap′su·lar** *adj.*

cap·sul·ize (kăp′sə-līz′, -syo͞o-) ▸ *v.* **-ized, -iz·ing.** To condense or summarize.

cap·tain (kăp′tən) ▸ *n.* 1. One who commands, leads, or guides. 2. The officer in command of a ship, aircraft, or spacecraft. 3a. A rank, as in the US Army, above first lieutenant and below major. b. A rank, as in the US Navy, above commander and below commodore. 4. A leading figure: *a captain of industry.* ▸ *v.* To command or direct. **—cap′tain·cy** *n.* **—cap′tain·ship′** *n.*

cap·tion (kăp′shən) ▸ *n.* 1. A short legend or description accompanying an illustration. 2. A series of words superimposed on the bottom of television or motion picture frames. 3. A title, as of a document or article. ▸ *v.* To furnish a caption for.

cap·tious (kăp′shəs) ▸ *adj.* 1. Inclined to find fault; critical. 2. Intended to entrap or confuse. **—cap′tious·ly** *adv.* **—cap′tious·ness** *n.*

cap·ti·vate (kăp′tə-vāt′) ▸ *v.* **-vat·ed, -vat·ing.** To attract and hold by charm, beauty, or excellence. **—cap′ti·va′tion** *n.* **—cap′ti·va′tor** *n.*

cap·tive (kăp′tĭv) ▸ *n.* 1. A prisoner. 2. One held in the grip of a strong emotion. ▸ *adj.* 1. Held as prisoner. 2. Kept under restraint or control: *captive birds; a captive nation.* 3. Restrained by circumstances that prevent free choice: *a captive audience.* 4. Enraptured. **—cap·tiv′i·ty** *n.*

cap·tor (kăp′tər, -tôr′) ▸ *n.* One who captures.

cap·ture (kăp′chər) ▸ *v.* **-tured, -tur·ing.** 1. To take captive; seize. 2. To gain possession or control of. 3. To attract and hold: *capture the imagination.* 4. To preserve in lasting form. ▸ *n.* 1. The act of capturing; seizure. 2. One that is seized, caught, or won.

cap·u·chin (kăp′yə-chĭn, -shĭn, kə-pyo͞o′-) ▸ *n.* 1. **Capuchin** A monk belonging to an independent order of Franciscans. 2. Any of several long-tailed tropical American monkeys.

car (kär) ▸ *n.* 1. An automobile. 2. A conveyance with wheels that runs along tracks: *a railroad car.* 3. A boxlike enclosure for passengers on a conveyance: *an elevator car.*

Ca·ra·cas (kə-rä′kəs) ▸ The capital of Venezuela, in the N part near the Caribbean coast.

ca·rafe (kə-răf′) ▸ *n.* A glass or metal bottle, often with a flared lip, used for serving water or wine.

car·a·mel (kăr′ə-məl, -mĕl′, kär′məl) ▸ *n.* 1. A smooth chewy candy made with sugar, butter, cream or milk, and flavoring. 2. Burnt sugar, used for coloring and sweetening foods.

car·a·pace (kăr′ə-pās′) ▸ *n.* *Zool.* A hard outer covering, such as the upper shell of a turtle.

car·at (kăr′ət) ▸ *n.* 1. A unit of weight for precious stones, equal to 200 mg. 2. Var. of **karat.**

car·a·van (kăr′ə-văn′) ▸ *n.* 1. A company of travelers journeying together, esp. across a desert. 2. A single file of vehicles or pack animals. 3. A van.

car·a·van·sa·ry (kăr′ə-văn′sə-rē) also **car·a·van·se·rai** (-rī′) ▸ *n., pl.* **-ries** also **-rais.** An inn built around a large court for accommodating caravans in central or western Asia.

car·a·vel or **car·a·velle** (kăr′ə-vĕl′) ▸ *n.* A small, light sailing ship used by the Spanish and Portuguese in the 15th and 16th cent.

car·a·way (kăr′ə-wā′) ▸ *n.* A plant with pungent, aromatic, seedlike fruit used in cooking and flavoring.

car·bide (kär′bīd′) ▸ *n.* A binary compound of carbon and a more electropositive element.

car·bine (kär′bēn′, -bīn′) ▸ *n.* A lightweight rifle with a short barrel.

carbo– or **carb–** ▸ *pref.* Carbon: *carbohydrate.*

car·bo·hy·drate (kär′bō-hī′drāt′) ▸ *n.* Any of a group of photosynthetically produced organic compounds that includes sugars, starches, celluloses, and gums and serves as a major energy source in the diet.

car·bol·ic acid (kär-bŏl′ĭk) ▸ *n.* See **phenol.**

car·bon (kär′bən) ▸ *n.* 1. *Symbol* **C** A naturally abundant nonmetallic element that occurs in many inorganic and in all organic compounds, exists freely as graphite and diamond, and is capable of chemical self-bonding to form an enormous number of chemically, biologically, and commercially important molecules. At. no. 6. 2a. A sheet of carbon paper. b. A carbon copy. **—car′bon·ize** *v.* **—car′bon·ous** *adj.*

carbon 14 ▸ *n.* A naturally radioactive carbon isotope with atomic mass 14 and half-life 5,730 years, used in carbon dating.

car·bo·na·ceous (kär′bə-nā′shəs) ▸ *adj.* Of, consisting of, or yielding carbon.

car·bon·ate (kär′bə-nāt′) ▸ *v.* **-at·ed, -at·ing.** To charge (e.g., a beverage) with carbon dioxide gas. ▸ *n.* (-nāt′, -nĭt) A salt or ester of carbonic acid. **—car′bon·a′tion** *n.*

carbon black ▸ *n.* A finely divided form of carbon derived from the incomplete combustion of hydrocarbons and used principally in rubber, inks, paints, and polishes.

carbon copy ▸ *n.* 1. A duplicate, as of a letter, made by using carbon paper. 2. One that closely resembles another.

carbon dating ▸ *n.* See **radiocarbon dating.**

carbon dioxide ▸ *n.* A colorless, odorless, incombustible gas, CO_2, formed during respiration, combustion, and organic decomposition.

car·bon·ic acid (kär-bŏn′ĭk) ▸ *n.* A weak, unstable acid, H_2CO_3, present in solutions of carbon dioxide in water.

Car·bon·if·er·ous (kär′bə-nĭf′ər-əs) ▸ *adj.* 1. *Geol.* Of or

THESAURUS

caprice *n.* —*See* FANCY.

capricious *adj.* Marked by whim or impulse ▸ arbitrary, changeable, erratic, fickle, flighty, freakish, impulsive, inconsistent, inconstant, mercurial, shifty, temperamental, ticklish, uncertain, unpredictable, unstable, unsteady, vagrant, variable, volatile, wayward, whimsical. [*Compare* CHANGEABLE, SPONTANEOUS.]

capsize *v.* —*See* OVERTURN.

capsized *adj.* —*See* UPSIDE-DOWN.

captain *n.* The person in charge of a ship ▸ commander, shipmaster, skipper. —*See also* CHIEF.

captain *v.* —*See* ADMINISTER (1).

captious *adj.* —*See* CRITICAL (1).

captivate *v.* —*See* CHARM (1), GRIP.

capture *v.* To obtain possession or control of ▸ catch, gain, get, net, secure, take, win. *Informal:* bag. *Slang:* cop, nail. [*Compare* ARREST, GET, SEIZE.] —*See also* GRIP, OCCUPY (2).

capture *n.* —*See* CATCH (1).

carbon copy *n.* —*See* COPY (1).

being a division of the Paleozoic Era comprising the Mississippian and Pennsylvanian periods and marked by the deposition of plant remains that later hardened into coal. 2. **carboniferous** Producing or containing carbon or coal. ▸ *n.* The Carboniferous Period.

carbon monoxide ▸ *n.* A colorless, odorless, highly poisonous gas, CO, formed by the incomplete combustion of carbon.

carbon paper ▸ *n.* Thin paper coated with a dark waxy pigment, placed between blank sheets so that writing on the top sheet is copied onto the bottom sheet.

carbon tet·ra·chlo·ride (tĕt′rə-klôr′īd′) ▸ *n.* A poisonous, nonflammable, colorless liquid, CCl_4, used as a solvent.

Car·bo·run·dum (kär′bə-rŭn′dəm) ▸ A trademark for a silicon carbide abrasive.

car·boy (kär′boi′) ▸ *n.* A large bottle, usu. encased in a protective covering and used to hold corrosive liquids.

car·bun·cle (kär′bŭng′kəl) ▸ *n.* **1.** A painful, localized, pus-producing bacterial infection of the skin. **2.** A deep-red garnet. **—car·bun′cu·lar** (-kyə-lər) *adj.*

car·bu·ret (kär′bə-rāt′, -rĕt′, -byə-) ▸ *v.* **-ret·ed, -ret·ing** or **-ret·ted, -ret·ting.** To mix (air or a gas) with volatile hydrocarbons so as to increase available fuel energy. **—car·bu·re′tion** *n.*

car·bu·re·tor (kär′bə-rā′tər, -byə-) ▸ *n.* A device used in internal-combustion engines to produce an explosive mixture of vaporized fuel and air.

car·bu·rize (kär′bə-rīz′, -byə-) ▸ *v.* **-rized, -riz·ing. 1.** To treat, combine, or impregnate with carbon. **2.** To carburet. **—car′bu·ri·za′tion** *n.*

car·cass (kär′kəs) ▸ *n.* A dead body, esp. of an animal.

car·cin·o·gen (kär-sĭn′ə-jən, kär′sə-nə-jĕn′) ▸ *n.* A cancer-causing substance or agent. **—car′ci·no·gen′e·sis** *n.* **—car′cin·o·gen′ic** *adj.*

car·ci·no·ma (kär′sə-nō′mə) ▸ *n., pl.* **-mas** or **-ma·ta** (-mə-tə). A malignant tumor derived from epithelial tissue. **—car′ci·nom′a·tous** (-nŏm′ə-təs, -nō′mə-) *adj.*

car coat ▸ *n.* A three-quarter-length overcoat.

card[1] (kärd) ▸ *n.* **1.** A flat, usu. rectangular piece of stiff paper, cardboard, or plastic, esp.: **a.** One of a set of playing cards. **b.** A greeting card. **c.** A post card. **d.** A business card. **e.** A credit card. **2. cards** *(takes sing. or pl. v.)* A game using playing cards. **3.** A circuit board. **4.** A program, esp. for a sports event. **5.** *Informal* An eccentrically amusing person. ▸ *v.* **1.** To furnish with or attach to a card. **2.** To list (something) on a card; catalog. **3.** To check the identification of, esp. in order to verify legal age. ***—idioms:*** **card up (one's) sleeve** A secret resource or plan held in reserve. **in the cards** Likely or certain to happen. **put (or lay) (one's) cards on the table** To reveal frankly and clearly, as one's motives.

card[2] (kärd) ▸ *n.* A wire-toothed brush used to disentangle textile fibers. **—card** *v.* **—card′er** *n.*

car·da·mom (kär′də-məm) or **car·da·mon** (-mən) ▸ *n.* **1.** A tropical Asian plant having capsular fruits whose aromatic seeds are used as a spice or condiment. **2.** The seed of this plant.

card·board (kärd′bôrd′) ▸ *n.* A thick stiff material made of pressed paper pulp or pasted sheets of paper. ▸ *adj.* **1.** Made of cardboard. **2.** Flimsy; insubstantial.

card-car·ry·ing (kärd′kăr′ē-ĭng) ▸ *adj.* **1.** Being an enrolled member of an organization, esp. the Communist Party. **2.** Avidly devoted to a group or cause.

card catalog ▸ *n.* An alphabetical listing, esp. of books in a library, made with a separate card for each item.

car·di·ac (kär′dē-ăk′) ▸ *adj.* Of or near the heart.

cardiac arrest ▸ *n.* Sudden cessation of heartbeat and cardiac function, resulting in the loss of effective circulation.

cardiac massage ▸ *n.* A resuscitative procedure employing rhythmic compression of the chest and heart, as after cardiac arrest.

Car·diff (kär′dĭf) ▸ The capital of Wales, in the SE part on Bristol Channel.

car·di·gan (kär′dĭ-gən) ▸ *n.* A sweater or knitted jacket that opens down the front.

car·di·nal (kär′dn-əl, kärd′nəl) ▸ *adj.* **1.** Of foremost importance; paramount. **2.** Dark to deep or vivid red. ▸ *n.* **1.** *Rom. Cath. Ch.* A high church official, ranking just below the pope. **2.** A North American finch having a crested head, a short thick bill, and bright red plumage in the male.

car·di·nal·ate (kär′dn-ə-lĭt, -lāt′, kärd′nə-) ▸ *n. Rom. Cath. Ch.* The position, rank, dignity, or term of a cardinal.

cardinal number ▸ *n.* A number, such as 3 or 11 or 412, used in counting to indicate quantity but not order.

cardinal point ▸ *n.* One of the four principal directions on a compass: north, south, east, or west.

cardio– or **cardi–** ▸ *pref.* Heart: *cardiovascular.*

car·di·o·gram (kär′dē-ə-grăm′) ▸ *n.* **1.** The curve traced by a cardiograph, used in the diagnosis of heart disorders. **2.** See **electrocardiogram.**

car·di·o·graph (kär′dē-ə-grăf′) ▸ *n.* **1.** An instrument used to record graphically the mechanical movements of the heart. **2.** See **electrocardiograph. —car′di·og′ra·phy** (-ŏg′rə-fē) *n.*

car·di·ol·o·gy (kär′dē-ŏl′ə-jē) ▸ *n.* The study of the structure, functioning, and disorders of the heart. **—car′di·ol′o·gist** *n.*

car·di·o·pul·mo·nar·y (kär′dē-ō-po͝ol′mə-nĕr′ē, -pŭl′-) ▸ *adj.* Of or involving the heart and lungs.

cardiopulmonary resuscitation ▸ *n.* A procedure used after cardiac arrest in which cardiac massage, artificial respiration, and drugs are used to restore circulation.

car·di·o·vas·cu·lar (kär′dē-ō-văs′kyə-lər) ▸ *adj.* Of or involving the heart and the blood vessels.

card·sharp (kärd′shärp′) ▸ *n.* An expert in cheating at cards. **—card′sharp′ing** *n.*

care (kâr) ▸ *n.* **1.** A burdened state of mind; worry. **2.** Mental suffering; grief. **3.** An object or source of attention or solicitude. **4.** Caution: *handle with care.* **5.** Charge or supervision: *in the care of a nurse.* **6.** Assistance or treatment: *emergency care.* ▸ *v.* **cared, car·ing. 1.** To be concerned or interested. **2.** To provide assistance or supervision. **3.** To object or mind.

ca·reen (kə-rēn′) ▸ *v.* **1.** To rush headlong or carelessly; career. **2.** To cause (a ship) to lean to one side; tilt. **—ca·reen′er** *n.*

ca·reer (kə-rîr′) ▸ *n.* **1.** A chosen pursuit; profession or occupation. **2.** The general progress in one's working or professional life. ▸ *v.* To move or run at full speed; rush.

care·free (kâr′frē′) ▸ *adj.* Free of worries and responsibilities.

care·ful (kâr′fəl) ▸ *adj.* **1.** Attentive to potential danger, error, or harm; cautious. **2.** Thorough and painstaking; conscientious. **—care′ful·ly** *adv.* **—care′ful·ness** *n.*

care·giv·er (kâr′gĭv′ər) ▸ *n.* **1.** One, such as a nurse or social worker, who assists in the treatment of an illness or disability. **2.** One who attends to the needs of a child or dependent adult. **—care′giv′ing** *adj. & n.*

care·less (kâr′lĭs) ▸ *adj.* **1.** Inattentive; negligent. **2.** Marked by or resulting from lack of thought. **3.** Incon-

THESAURUS

carcass *n.* *—See* BODY (2).

card *n.* *—See* CHARACTER (5), JOKER, PROGRAM (2).

cardinal *adj.* *—See* PRIMARY (1).

cardsharp *n.* *—See* CHEAT (2).

care *n.* **1.** Cautious attentiveness ▸ carefulness, caution, gingerliness, heed, heedfulness, mindfulness, regard, wariness, watchfulness. [*Compare* DILIGENCE, PRUDENCE.] **2.** The function of watching, guarding, or overseeing ▸ charge, custody, guardianship, keeping, protection, safeguard, safekeeping, superintendence, supervision, trust, tutelage, ward. [*Compare* CONSERVATION, PATRONAGE.] **3.** A cause of distress or anxiety ▸ concern, stressor, trouble, worry. [*Compare* ANXIETY, BURDEN[1].] *—See also* ANXIETY (1), CAUTION, THOROUGHNESS, TREATMENT.

care *v.* To have an objection ▸ mind, object.

care for *v.* *—See* ENJOY, TEND[2].

careen *v.* *—See* STAGGER (1).

career *n.* *—See* BUSINESS (2), HISTORY (2).

carefree *adj.* *—See* LIGHTHEARTED.

careful *adj.* **1.** Cautiously attentive ▸ conscious, heedful, mindful, observant, regardful, watchful. **2.** Marked by attentiveness to every detail ▸ accurate, fastidious, fussy, meticulous, painstaking, punctilious, scrupulous, solicitous. [*Compare* DELIBERATE, DETAILED, THOROUGH.] *—See also* CONSERVATIVE (2), WARY.

carefulness *n.* *—See* CARE (1), CAUTION, THOROUGHNESS.

careless *adj.* Lacking concern, attention,

siderate: *a careless remark.* **4.** Free from cares; cheerful. **—care′less·ly** *adv.* **—care′less·ness** *n.*

ca·ress (kə-rĕs′) ▸ *n.* A gentle touch or gesture of fondness. ▸ *v.* To touch or stroke fondly. **—ca·ress′er** *n.*

car·et (kăr′ĭt) ▸ *n.* A proofreading symbol (^) used to indicate where something is to be inserted in a line of printed or written matter.

care·tak·er (kâr′tā′kər) ▸ *n.* One employed to look after or take charge of goods, property, or a person; custodian.

care·worn (kâr′wôrn′) ▸ *adj.* Showing the effects of worry or care.

car·fare (kär′fâr′) ▸ *n.* The fare charged a passenger, as on a streetcar or bus.

car·go (kär′gō) ▸ *n., pl.* **-goes** or **-gos.** The freight carried by a ship, aircraft, or other vehicle.

car·hop (kär′hŏp′) ▸ *n.* One who waits on customers at a drive-in restaurant.

Car·ib (kăr′ĭb) ▸ *n., pl.* **-ib** or **-ibs. 1.** A member of a group of American Indian peoples of N South America, the Lesser Antilles, and the E coast of Central America. **2.** Any of the languages of the Carib.

Car·i·ban (kăr′ə-bən, kə rē′bən) ▸ *n.* A language family comprising the Carib languages.

Car·ib·be·an Sea (kăr′ə-bē′ən, kə-rĭb′ē-ən) ▸ An arm of the W Atlantic bounded by the coasts of Central and South America and the West Indies. **—Car′ib·be′an** *adj.*

car·i·bou (kăr′ə-bo͞o′) ▸ *n., pl.* **-bou** or **-bous.** Any of several large reindeer native to N North America.

car·i·ca·ture (kăr′ĭ-kə-cho͝or′, -chər) ▸ *n.* **1.** A representation, esp. pictorial, in which the subject's distinctive features or peculiarities are exaggerated for comic or grotesque effect. **2.** A mockery; farce. ▸ *v.* **-tured, -tur·ing.** To represent or imitate in a caricature. **—car′i·ca·tur′ist** *n.*

car·ies (kâr′ēz) ▸ *n., pl.* **-ies.** Decay of a bone or tooth.

car·il·lon (kăr′ə-lŏn′, -lən) ▸ *n.* A stationary set of bells hung in a tower and usu. played from a keyboard. **—car′il·lon′** *v.*

car·ing (kâr′ĭng) ▸ *adj.* Feeling and exhibiting concern and empathy for others.

car·load (kär′lōd′) ▸ *n.* The quantity that a car, esp. a railroad car, can hold.

car·min·a·tive (kär-mĭn′ə-tĭv, kär′mə-nā′-) ▸ *adj.* Inducing expulsion of intestinal gas. ▸ *n.* A carminative drug or agent.

car·mine (kär′mĭn, -mīn′) ▸ *n.* A strong to vivid red. **—car′mine** *adj.*

car·nage (kär′nĭj) ▸ *n.* Massive slaughter or bloodshed.

car·nal (kär′nəl) ▸ *adj.* **1.** Relating to the physical and esp. sexual appetites. **2.** Not spiritual; worldly or earthly: *the carnal world.* **—car·nal′i·ty** (-năl′ĭ-tē) *n.* **—car′nal·ly** *adv.*

car·na·tion (kär-nā′shən) ▸ *n.* A plant cultivated for its fragrant flowers with fringed petals.

car·nau·ba (kär-nô′bə, -nou′-, -no͞o′-) ▸ *n.* **1.** A Brazilian palm tree. **2.** A hard wax obtained from its leaves, used esp. in polishes and floor waxes.

Car·ne·gie (kär′nə-gē, kär-nā′gē, -nĕg′ē), **Andrew** (1835–1919) ▸ Scottish-born Amer. industrialist and philanthropist.

car·nel·ian (kär-nēl′yən) ▸ *n.* A reddish variety of clear chalcedony.

car·ni·val (kär′nə-vəl) ▸ *n.* **1.** A festival marked by merrymaking and feasting just before Lent. **2.** A traveling amusement show. **3.** A festival or revel: *the winter carnival.*

car·ni·vore (kär′nə-vôr′) ▸ *n.* A flesh-eating animal, esp. one of a group including dogs, cats, and bears.

car·niv·o·rous (kär-nĭv′ər-əs) ▸ *adj.* **1.** Of or relating to carnivores. **2.** Predatory. **—car·niv′o·rous·ly** *adv.* **—car·niv′o·rous·ness** *n.*

car·ny also **car·ney** (kär′nē) ▸ *n., pl.* **-nies** also **-neys.** *Informal* **1.** A carnival. **2.** One who works with a carnival.

car·ob (kăr′əb) ▸ *n.* **1.** A Mediterranean evergreen tree having large leathery pods. **2.** A chocolatelike powder made from the seeds and pods of the carob.

car·ol (kăr′əl) ▸ *n.* A song of praise or joy, esp. for Christmas. **—car′ol** *v.* **—car′ol·er** *n.*

Car·o·line Islands (kăr′ə-līn′, -lĭn) ▸ An archipelago of the W Pacific E of the Philippines.

car·om (kăr′əm) ▸ *n.* **1.** A collision followed by a rebound. **2.** A shot in billiards in which the cue ball successively strikes two other balls. ▸ *v.* **1.** To collide with and rebound. **2.** To make a carom in billiards.

car·o·tene (kăr′ə-tēn′) ▸ *n.* An orange-yellow pigment found in plants such as carrots and squash and converted to vitamin A in the liver.

ca·rot·id (kə-rŏt′ĭd) ▸ *n.* Either of the two major arteries, one on each side of the neck, that carry blood to the head.

ca·rouse (kə-rouz′) ▸ *n.* Boisterous, drunken merrymaking. ▸ *v.* **-roused, -rous·ing. 1.** To engage in drunken revelry. **2.** To drink excessively. **—ca·rous′al** *n.* **—ca·rous′er** *n.*

car·ou·sel or **car·rou·sel** (kăr′ə-sĕl′, -zĕl′) ▸ *n.* **1.** A merry-go-round. **2.** A circular conveyor on which objects are displayed or rotated.

carp[1] (kärp) ▸ *v.* To find fault and complain fretfully. **—carp′er** *n.*

carp[2] (kärp) ▸ *n., pl.* **carp** or **carps.** An edible freshwater fish, often bred commercially.

-carp ▸ *suff.* Fruit; fruitlike structure: *mesocarp.*

car·pal (kär′pəl) ▸ *adj.* Of or near the carpus. ▸ *n.* A bone of the carpus.

carpal tunnel syndrome ▸ *n.* A condition marked by pain and numbing in the hand, caused by compression of a nerve in the wrist.

Car·pa·thi·an Mountains (kär-pā′thē-ən) ▸ A mountain system of central Europe in Slovakia, S Poland, W Ukraine, and NE Romania.

car·pel (kär′pəl) ▸ *n.* One of the structural units of a pistil, representing a modified ovule-bearing leaf.

car·pen·ter (kär′pən-tər) ▸ *n.* A skilled worker who makes, finishes, and repairs wooden objects and structures. **—car′pen·ter** *v.* **—car′pen·try** *n.*

car·pet (kär′pĭt) ▸ *n.* A heavy, usu. woven or piled covering for a floor. ▸ *v.* To cover with or as if with a carpet. ***—idiom:* on the carpet** In a position of being reprimanded by one in authority.

car·pet·bag (kär′pĭt-băg′) ▸ *n.* A traveling bag made of carpet fabric.

car·pet·bag·ger (kär′pĭt-băg′ər) ▸ *n.* A Northerner who went to the South after the Civil War for political or financial advantage. **—car′pet·bag′ger·y** *n.*

carpet beetle ▸ *n.* Any of various small beetles having larvae that are injurious to fabrics.

car·pet-bomb (kär′pĭt-bŏm′) ▸ *v.* To bomb in a close pattern over a large target area.

THESAURUS

or regard ▸ blithe, feckless, forgetful, heedless, inadvertent, inattentive, inobservant, irresponsible, insouciant, mindless, nonchalant, reckless, thoughtless, unconcerned, unheeding, unmindful, unthinking. [*Compare* APATHETIC, LIGHTHEARTED, NEGLIGENT, RASH.] *—See also* MESSY (1).

carelessness *n.* A careless, often reckless disregard for consequences ▸ abandon, blitheness, heedlessness, thoughtlessness. [*Compare* TEMERITY.]

caress *v.* To touch or handle affectionately ▸ cuddle, fondle, pat, pet, stroke. *Informal:* canoodle. [*Compare* NECK, SNUGGLE.]

caretaker *n.* One who is legally responsible for the care and management of the person or property of an incompetent or a minor ▸ conservator, custodian, guardian, keeper. [*Compare* REPRESENTATIVE.]

careworn *adj.* *—See* HAGGARD.

cargo *n.* *—See* BURDEN[1] (2).

caricature *n.* *—See* MOCKERY (2), SATIRE.

caricature *v.* *—See* IMITATE.

caring *adj.* *—See* AFFECTIONATE.

carnage *n.* *—See* MASSACRE.

carnal *adj.* *—See* SENSUAL (2).

carnality *n.* *—See* SENSUALITY (1).

carnival *n.* *—See* CELEBRATION (1).

carol *v.* *—See* SING.

carol *n.* *—See* SONG.

carom *v.* *—See* GLANCE (1).

carousal or **carouse** *n.* *—See* BENDER.

carp *v.* *—See* COMPLAIN, QUIBBLE.

carp at *v.* *—See* CRITICIZE (1), NAG.

carp *n.* *—See* COMPLAINT.

carper *n.* *—See* CRITIC (2).

carpet *v.* *—See* COVER (1).

car pool ► *n.* **1.** An arrangement whereby several commuters travel together in one vehicle and share the costs. **2.** A group participating in a car pool. **—car′-pool′** *v.*

car·port (kär′pôrt′) ► *n.* An open-sided shelter for an automobile formed by a roof projecting from a building.

car·pus (kär′pəs) ► *n., pl.* **-pi** (-pī′). The wrist or its bones.

car·ra·geen also **car·ra·gheen** (kăr′ə-gēn′) ► *n.* See **Irish moss.**

car·ra·geen·an also **car·ra·geen·in** (kăr′ə-gē′nən) ► *n.* A colloid derived esp. from Irish moss and used as a thickener, stabilizer, and emulsifier.

car·rel also **car·rell** (kăr′əl) ► *n.* A partially partitioned nook near the stacks in a library, used for private study.

car·riage (kăr′ĭj) ► *n.* **1.** A wheeled vehicle, esp. a four-wheeled horse-drawn passenger vehicle. **2.** A baby carriage. **3.** A wheeled support or frame. **4.** A machine part for holding or shifting another part. **5a.** The act of transporting or carrying. **b.** (kăr′ē-ĭj) The charge for transporting. **6.** Posture; bearing.

carriage trade ► *n.* Wealthy patrons or customers, as of a store.

car·ri·er (kăr′ē-ər) ► *n.* **1.** One that carries or conveys. **2.** One that transports passengers or goods. **3.** *Medic.* An immune organism that transmits a pathogen to others. **4.** *Genet.* An individual that carries one gene for a particular recessive trait. **5.** An aircraft carrier.

carrier pigeon ► *n.* A homing pigeon, esp. one trained to carry messages.

carrier wave ► *n.* An electromagnetic wave that can be modulated to transmit sound or images.

car·ri·on (kăr′ē-ən) ► *n.* Dead and decaying flesh.

Car·roll (kăr′əl), **Lewis** ► See **Charles Lutwidge Dodgson.**

car·rot (kăr′ət) ► *n.* **1.** A plant widely cultivated for its edible taproot. **2.** Its fleshy orange root, eaten as a vegetable. **3.** A reward or inducement.

car·rot-and-stick (kăr′ət-ən-stĭk′) ► *adj.* Combining a promised reward with a threatened penalty.

car·rou·sel (kăr′ə-sĕl′, -zĕl′) ► *n.* Var. of **carousel.**

car·ry (kăr′ē) ► *v.* **-ried, -ry·ing. 1.** To hold while moving; bear. **2.** To convey or transport. **3.** To have on one's person: *carry cash.* **4.** To support the weight of. **5.** To hold (e.g., the head or body) in a certain way. **6.** To conduct (oneself) in a certain way. **7.** To have as a consequence: *The job carries a heavy workload.* **8.** To support (one that is weaker). **9.** To keep in one's accounts as a debtor. **10.** To offer for sale or keep in stock. **11.** To seize or capture. **12.** To win most of the votes in. **13.** To secure the adoption of (e.g., a bill or amendment). **14.** To print or broadcast. ***—phrasal verbs:* carry away** To move or excite greatly. **carry forward** *Accounting* To transfer (an entry) to the next column or book. **carry off 1.** To cause the death of. **2.** To handle (e.g., a situation) successfully. **carry on 1.** To conduct; maintain. **2.** To engage in: *carry on a love affair.* **3.** To continue without halting: *carry on in the face of disaster.* **carry out 1.** To put into practice. **2.** To follow or obey. **carry over 1.** *Accounting* To transfer (an account) to the next column or book. **2.** To continue at or retain for a later time. **carry through 1.** To accomplish; complete. **2.** To enable to endure; sustain. ► *n., pl.* **-ries. 1.** An act of carrying. **2.** The range of a gun or projectile.

car·ry·all (kăr′ē-ôl′) ► *n.* A large receptacle, such as a bag, basket, or pocketbook.

car·ry·on (kăr′ē-ŏn′) ► *adj.* Small enough to be carried aboard an airplane by a passenger: *carryon luggage.* **—car′ry·on′** *n.*

car·ry·out (kăr′ē-out′) ► *adj.* Takeout.

car·sick (kär′sĭk′) ► *adj.* Nauseated by vehicular travel. **—car′sick′ness** *n.*

Car·son (kär′sən), **Christopher.** "Kit" (1809–68) ► Amer. frontier settler.

Carson, Rachel Louise (1907–64) ► Amer. environmentalist and writer.

Carson City ► The capital of NV, in the W part near the CA border.

cart (kärt) ► *n.* **1.** A small wheeled vehicle typically pushed by hand: *a shopping cart.* **2.** A two-wheeled vehicle drawn by an animal. **3.** A light motorized vehicle: *a golf cart.* ► *v.* **1.** To convey in a cart or truck: *cart away garbage.* **2.** To convey laboriously or remove unceremoniously. **—cart′er** *n.*

cart·age (kär′tĭj) ► *n.* **1.** Transportation by cart or truck. **2.** The cost of cartage.

carte blanche (kärt blänsh′, blänch′, blănch′) ► *n.* Unrestricted authority.

car·tel (kär-tĕl′) ► *n.* A monopolistic combination of independent business organizations.

Car·ter (kär′tər), **James Earl, Jr.** "Jimmy" (b. 1924) ► The 39th US President (1977–81).

Car·te·sian coordinate (kär-tē′zhən) ► *n.* A member of the set of numbers that locates a point in a Cartesian coordinate system.

Cartesian coordinate system ► *n.* A coordinate system in which the coordinates of a point are its distances from a set of perpendicular lines that intersect at an origin, such as two lines in a plane or three in space.

Car·thage (kär′thĭj) ► An ancient city and state of N Africa on the Bay of Tunis NE of modern Tunis. **—Car′tha·gin′i·an** (-thə-jĭn′ē-ən) *adj. & n.*

car·ti·lage (kär′tl-ĭj) ► *n.* A tough white fibrous connective tissue found in various parts of the body, such as the joints, outer ear, and larynx. **—car′ti·lag′i·nous** (-ăj′ə-nəs) *adj.*

car·tog·ra·phy (kär-tŏg′rə-fē) ► *n.* The making of maps or charts. **—car·tog′ra·pher** *n.* **—car′to·graph′ic** (-tə-grăf′ĭk) *adj.*

car·ton (kär′tn) ► *n.* **1.** A container made from cardboard or coated paper. **2.** The contents of a carton.

car·toon (kär-to͞on′) ► *n.* **1.** A humorous or satirical drawing, often with a caption. **2.** A preliminary full-scale sketch, as for a fresco. **3.** An animated cartoon. **4.** A comic strip. **—car·toon′** *v.* **—car·toon′ist** *n.*

car·tridge (kär′trĭj) ► *n.* **1a.** A cylindrical, usu. metal casing containing the primer and powder of small arms ammunition. **b.** Such a casing fitted with a bullet. **2.** A small modular unit designed to be inserted into a larger piece of equipment: *an ink cartridge; a cartridge of film.* **3.** A magnetic tape cassette.

cart·wheel (kärt′hwēl′, -wēl′) ► *n.* A handspring in which the body turns over sideways with the arms and legs extended.

Ca·ru·so (kə-ro͞o′sō, -zō), **Enrico** (1873–1921) ► Italian operatic tenor.

carve (kärv) ► *v.* **carved, carv·ing. 1.** To divide into pieces by cutting; slice. **2.** To disjoint, slice, and serve (meat or poultry). **3.** To make or form by or as if by cutting. **—carv′er** *n.*

Car·ver (kär′vər), **George Washington** (1864?–1943) ► Amer. botanist and educator.

carv·ing (kär′vĭng) ► *n.* **1.** The cutting of material such as

THESAURUS

carping *adj.* —*See* CRITICAL (1).

carriage *n.* —*See* POSTURE (1), TRANSPORTATION.

carrier *n.* —*See* MESSENGER.

carrot *n.* —*See* LURE (1).

carry *v.* **1.** To move while supporting ► bear, cart, convey, haul, lug, pack, transport. *Informal:* tote. *Slang:* schlep. [*Compare* SEND.] **2.** To hold on one's person ► bear, have, possess. *Informal:* pack. [*Compare* HOLD.] **3.** To have as a condition or a consequence ► entail, involve. **4.** To have for sale ► deal (in), keep, offer, stock. [*Compare* SELL.] —*See also* ACT (1), BEAR (1), BEAR (3), BRING (1), COMMUNICATE (1), COMMUNICATE (2), CONDUCT (3), EXTEND (1), PASS (6).

carry away *v.* —*See* ENRAPTURE.

carry off *v.* —*See* KILL[1], STEAL.

carry on *v.* To engage in (a war or campaign, for example) ► carry out, conduct, wage. [*Compare* OPPOSE.] —*See also* CONDUCT (1), ENDURE (1), MISBEHAVE, PARTICIPATE, RAVE.

carry out *v.* **1.** To engage in (a war or campaign, for example) ► carry on, conduct, wage. [*Compare* OPPOSE.] **2.** To be responsible for or guilty of an error or crime ► commit, do, perpetrate. *Informal:* pull off. [*Compare* PERFORM.] —*See also* ADMINISTER (2), EFFECT, ENFORCE, FOLLOW (4).

carry through *v.* —*See* EFFECT.

cart *v.* —*See* CARRY (1).

carte blanche *n.* —*See* AUTHORITY.

cartel *n.* ► bloc, coalition, organization. [*Compare* ASSOCIATION.]

carton *n.* —*See* PACKAGE.

carve *v.* —*See* CUT (2), ENGRAVE (1).

carving *n.* —*See* SCULPTURE.

stone or wood to form a figure or design. **2.** A figure or design so formed.

car·y·at·id (kăr′ē-ăt′ĭd) ▸ *n., pl.* **-ids** or **-i·des** (-ĭ-dēz′) *Archit.* A supporting column sculptured in the form of a woman.

ca·sa·ba (kə-sä′bə) ▸ *n.* A melon having a yellow rind and sweet whitish flesh.

Cas·a·blan·ca (kăs′ə-blăng′kə, kä′sə-blăng′kə) ▸ A city of NW Morocco on the Atlantic SSW of Tangier.

Cas·a·no·va de Sein·galt (kăs′ə-nō′və də săN-gält′), **Giovanni Jacopo** (1725–98) ▸ Italian adventurer and writer.

cas·cade (kăs-kād′) ▸ *n.* **1.** A waterfall or series of small waterfalls. **2.** A fall of material, such as lace. **3.** A succession of stages, operations, or units. ▸ *v.* **-cad·ed, -cad·ing.** To fall in a cascade.

cas·car·a (kă-skăr′ə) ▸ *n.* A tree of NW North America, the dried bark of which is used as a laxative.

case[1] (kās) ▸ *n.* **1.** An instance of something; example. **2a.** An occurrence of a disease, disorder, or injury. **b.** A person or group being treated, assisted, or studied, as by a physician, attorney, or social worker. **3.** A set of circumstances or state of affairs; situation. **4.** A question or problem; matter. **5.** *Law* An action or suit or just grounds for an action. **6.** A persuasive argument, demonstration, or justification. **7.** *Ling.* An inflectional pattern or form of nouns, pronouns, and adjectives to express syntactic functions in a sentence. ▸ *v.* **cased, cas·ing.** *Informal* To examine (e.g., a place) carefully, as in planning a crime. ***—idioms:*** **in any case** Regardless of what has occurred or will occur. **in case** If it happens that; if. **in case of** If there should happen to be.

case[2] (kās) ▸ *n.* **1.** A container or receptacle. **2.** A decorative or protective covering. **3.** A set or pair: *a case of pistols.* **4.** The frame of a window, door, or stairway. **5.** A shallow tray with compartments for storing printing type. ▸ *v.* **cased, cas·ing.** To put into or cover with a case.

case history ▸ *n.* A record of the facts affecting the development or condition of a person or group under treatment or study.

ca·sein (kā′sēn′, -sē-ĭn) ▸ *n.* A white, tasteless, odorless milk protein, used to make plastics, adhesives, paints, and foods.

case·load (kās′lōd′) ▸ *n.* The number of cases handled in a given period, as by an attorney or social services agency.

case·ment (kās′mənt) ▸ *n.* **1.** A window sash that opens outward by means of hinges. **2.** A window with casements.

case study ▸ *n.* A detailed analysis of a person or group, esp. as a model of medical, psychiatric, or social phenomena.

case·work (kās′wûrk′) ▸ *n.* Social work dealing with the needs of a particular case. **—case′work′er** *n.*

cash (kăsh) ▸ *n.* **1.** Money in the form of bills or coins; currency. **2.** Immediate payment for goods or services in currency. ▸ *v.* To exchange for or convert into ready money.

cash·ew (kăsh′o͞o, kə-sho͞o′) ▸ *n.* **1.** A tropical American tree bearing edible nutlike seeds. **2.** The kidney-shaped nut or seed of the cashew.

cash·ier[1] (kă-shîr′) ▸ *n.* **1.** The officer of a bank or business concern in charge of paying and receiving money. **2.** A store employee who handles cash transactions with customers.

ca·shier[2] (kă-shîr′) ▸ *v.* To dismiss in disgrace from a position of responsibility.

ca·shier's check (kă-shîrz′) ▸ *n.* A check drawn by a bank on its own funds and signed by the bank's cashier.

cash machine ▸ *n.* See **automated teller machine.**

cash·mere (kăzh′mîr′, kăsh′-) ▸ *n.* **1.** Fine wool from an Asian goat. **2.** A soft fabric made from cashmere.

Cash·mere (kăsh′mîr′, kăsh-mîr′) ▸ See **Kashmir.**

cash register ▸ *n.* A machine that tabulates the amount of sales transactions and makes a permanent and cumulative record of them.

cas·ing (kā′sĭng) ▸ *n.* An outer cover; case.

ca·si·no (kə-sē′nō) ▸ *n., pl.* **-nos.** A public room or building for gambling and other entertainment.

cask (kăsk) ▸ *n.* **1.** A barrel of any size. **2.** The amount a cask holds.

cas·ket (kăs′kĭt) ▸ *n.* **1.** A small case or chest, as for jewels. **2.** A coffin.

Cas·pi·an Sea (kăs′pē-ən) ▸ A saline lake between SE Europe and W Asia.

casque (kăsk) ▸ *n.* A helmet. **—casqued** (kăskt) *adj.*

Cas·san·dra (kə-săn′drə) ▸ *n.* **1.** *Gk. Myth.* A Trojan prophetess fated by Apollo never to be believed. **2.** One that utters unheeded prophecies.

cas·sa·va (kə-sä′və) ▸ *n.* A tropical American plant grown for its tuberous starchy root, a staple food and the source of tapioca.

cas·se·role (kăs′ə-rōl′) ▸ *n.* **1.** A dish, usu. of earthenware, glass, or cast iron, in which food is baked and served. **2.** Food baked and served in a casserole.

cas·sette (kə-sĕt′, kă-) ▸ *n.* A cartridge for holding and winding magnetic tape, photographic film, or typewriter ribbon.

cassette deck ▸ *n.* A tape deck designed for recording or playing audiocassettes.

cas·sia (kăsh′ə) ▸ *n.* **1.** Any of a genus of chiefly tropical trees or shrubs having usu. yellow flowers and long pods. **2.** A tropical Asian evergreen tree having cinnamonlike bark.

Cas·si·o·pe·ia (kăs′ē-ə-pē′ə) ▸ *n.* A W-shaped constellation in the Northern Hemisphere.

cas·sit·er·ite (kə-sĭt′ə-rīt′) ▸ *n.* A yellow, brown, or black mineral, SnO_2, that is an important tin ore.

cas·sock (kăs′ək) ▸ *n.* An ankle-length garment worn by the clergy.

cas·so·war·y (kăs′ə-wĕr′ē) ▸ *n., pl.* **-ies.** A large flightless bird of Australia and New Guinea with brightly colored wattles.

cast (kăst) ▸ *v.* **cast, cast·ing. 1.** To throw or fling. **2.** To shed or discard; molt. **3.** To deposit or indicate (a ballot or vote). **4.** To turn or direct: *cast a glance at me.* **5a.** To choose actors for. **b.** To assign a role to. **6.** To form (e.g., liquid metal) by molding. **7.** To add up (a column of figures); compute. ▸ *n.* **1.** A throw. **2.** A throw of dice. **3.** Something, such as molted skin, that is shed or thrown off. **4.** A mold. **5.** A rigid dressing, usu. made of gauze and plaster of Paris, used to immobilize an injured body part. **6.** Outward appearance; look. **7.** The actors in a theatrical presentation. **8.** A slight trace of color; tinge.

cas·ta·nets (kăs′tə-nĕts′) ▸ *pl.n.* A percussion instrument consisting of a pair of ivory or hardwood shells held in the hand and clapped together with the fingers.

cast·a·way (kăst′ə-wā′) ▸ *adj.* **1.** Cast adrift or ashore; shipwrecked. **2.** Thrown away; discarded. **—cast′a·way′** *n.*

caste (kăst) ▸ *n.* **1.** Any of the hereditary social classes of traditional Hindu society, stratified according to Hindu ritual purity. **2a.** A social class separated from others by distinctions of hereditary rank, profession, or wealth. **b.** Social position or status.

cast·er (kăs′tər) ▸ *n.* **1.** One that casts. **2.** also **castor** A small wheel on a swivel, attached to the underside of a heavy object to make it easier to move. **3.** also **castor** A

THESAURUS

Casanova *n.* *—See* GALLANT, PHILANDERER.

cascade *v.* *—See* FLOW (2).

cascade *n.* *—See* FLOW.

case *n.* *—See* CHARACTER (5), CONDITION (1), EXAMPLE (1), FRAME, LAWSUIT, PROBLEM, REASON (1), SUBJECT, WRAPPER.

case *v.* *—See* EXAMINE (1).

caseharden *v.* *—See* HARDEN (1).

cash *n.* *—See* MONEY (1).

cash in *v.* To make a large profit ▸ batten, profit. *Slang:* clean up. *Idioms:* make a killing, make out like a bandit.

cashier *v.* *—See* DISMISS (1).

casing *n.* *—See* FRAME, WRAPPER.

cask *n.* *—See* VAT.

Cassandra *n.* *—See* PESSIMIST (2).

cast *v.* *—See* ADD, AIM (1), CALCULATE, CHOOSE (1), DESIGN (1), FISH (1), SHED[1] (1), THROW.

cast about or **around** *v.* *—See* SEEK (1).

cast aside *v.* *—See* ABANDON (1).

cast down *v.* *—See* LOWER[2].

cast out *v.* *—See* DISMISS (3), DISMISS (3).

cast *n.* **1.** A hollow device for shaping a fluid or plastic substance ▸ form, matrix, mold. **2.** The act, process, or result of calculating ▸ calculation, computation, figuring, reckoning. *—See also* CHANCE (2), COLOR (1), EXPRESSION (4), FORM (1), INCLINATION (1), KIND[2], SCULPTURE, THROW.

caste *n.* *—See* CLASS (2).

small bottle or cruet that is used for condiments.

cas·ti·gate (kăs′tĭ-gāt′) ▸ *v.* **-gat·ed, -gat·ing.** To chastise or criticize severely. **—cas′ti·ga′tion** *n.*

Cas·tile (kăs-tēl′) ▸ A region and former kingdom of central and N Spain.

Cas·til·ian (kă-stĭl′yən) ▸ *n.* 1. A native or inhabitant of Castille. 2. The Spanish dialect of Castille. **—Cas·til′ian** *adj.*

cast·ing (kăs′tĭng) ▸ *n.* 1. Something cast in a mold. 2. Something cast off or out.

cast iron ▸ *n.* A hard, brittle nonmalleable iron-carbon alloy containing 2 to 4.5% carbon, 0.5 to 3% silicon. **—cast′-i′ron** *adj.*

cast-i·ron plant (kăst′ī′ərn) ▸ *n.* See **aspidistra.**

cas·tle (kăs′əl) ▸ *n.* 1. A large fortified building or group of buildings. 2. A large imposing building. 3. *Games* See **rook**[2].

cast·off (kăst′ôf′, -ŏf′) ▸ *n.* One that has been discarded. **—cast′off** *adj.*

cas·tor (kăs′tər) ▸ *n.* Var. of **caster** 2, 3.

castor oil ▸ *n.* An oil extracted from the seeds of a tropical plant and used as a laxative and industrially as a lubricant.

cas·trate (kăs′trāt′) ▸ *v.* **-trat·ed, -trat·ing.** To remove the testicles or ovaries of. **—cas′trat·er, cas′tra·tor** *n.* **—cas·tra′tion** *n.*

Cas·tro (kăs′trō), **Fidel** (b. 1927) ▸ Cuban revolutionary leader.

ca·su·al (kăzh′o͞o-əl) ▸ *adj.* 1. Occurring by chance. 2a. Irregular; occasional. b. Unpremeditated; offhand: *a casual remark.* 3a. Informal or relaxed. b. Suited for informal wear or use. 4. Not thorough; superficial. 5. Nonchalant. **—ca′su·al·ly** *adv.* **—ca′su·al·ness** *n.*

ca·su·al·ty (kăzh′o͞o-əl-tē) ▸ *n., pl.* **-ties.** 1. A disastrous accident. 2. One injured or killed in an accident. 3. One injured, killed, captured, or missing in military action.

ca·su·ist·ry (kăzh′o͞o-ĭ-strē) ▸ *n.* Specious or overly subtle reasoning intended to rationalize or mislead. **—ca′su·ist** *n.* **—ca′su·is′tic** *adj.*

cat (kăt) ▸ *n.* 1a. A small carnivorous mammal domesticated as a catcher of rats and mice and as a pet. b. An animal related to the cat, including the lion, tiger, and leopard. 2. *Slang* A person, esp. a man.

ca·tab·o·lism (kə-tăb′ə-lĭz′əm) ▸ *n.* Metabolic activity in which complex substances are broken down into simpler substances. **—cat′a·bol′ic** (kăt′ə-bŏl′ĭk) *adj.*

cat·a·clysm (kăt′ə-klĭz′əm) ▸ *n.* A violent and sudden, usu. destructive upheaval. **—cat′a·clys′mic, cat′a·clys′mal** *adj.*

cat·a·comb (kăt′ə-kōm′) ▸ *n.* often **catacombs** An underground chamber with recesses for graves.

cat·a·falque (kăt′ə-fălk′, -fôlk′) ▸ *n.* A decorated platform on which a coffin rests in state during a funeral.

Cat·a·lan (kăt′l-ăn′) ▸ *n.* 1. A native or inhabitant of Catalonia. 2. The Romance language of Catalonia. **—Cat′a·lan′** *adj.*

cat·a·lep·sy (kăt′l-ĕp′sē) ▸ *n., pl.* **-sies** *Pathol.* Muscular rigidity, lack of awareness of environment, and lack of response to external stimuli. **—cat′a·lep′tic** *adj.*

cat·a·log or **cat·a·logue** (kăt′l-ôg′, -ŏg′) ▸ *n.* 1. An itemized, often descriptive list. 2. A publication containing a catalog. 3. A card catalog. ▸ *v.* **-loged, -log·ing** or **-logued, -logu·ing.** To list in or make a catalog. **—cat′a·log′er, cat′a·logu′er** *n.*

Cat·a·lo·nia (kăt′l-ōn′yə) ▸ A region of NE Spain bordering on France and the Mediterranean. **—Cat′a·lo′nian** *adj. & n.*

ca·tal·pa (kə-tăl′pə, -tôl′-) ▸ *n.* A North American tree having large heart-shaped leaves, showy white flower clusters, and long slender pods.

ca·tal·y·sis (kə-tăl′ĭ-sĭs) ▸ *n., pl.* **-ses** (-sēz′). The action of a catalyst, esp. an increase in the rate of a chemical reaction. **—cat′a·lyt′ic** (kăt′l-ĭt′ĭk) *adj.* **—cat′a·lyt′i·cal·ly** *adv.*

cat·a·lyst (kăt′l-ĭst) ▸ *n.* 1. *Chem.* A substance that modifies and esp. increases the rate of a reaction without being consumed in the process. 2. An agent of change.

catalytic converter ▸ *n.* A device for reducing carbon monoxide and hydrocarbon pollutants in automobile exhaust.

cat·a·lyze (kăt′l-īz′) ▸ *v.* **-lyzed, -lyz·ing.** To modify the rate of (a chemical reaction) by catalysis. **—cat′a·lyz′er** *n.*

cat·a·ma·ran (kăt′ə-mə-răn′) ▸ *n.* A boat, esp. a light sailboat, with two parallel hulls or floats.

cat·a·mount (kăt′ə-mount′) ▸ *n.* See **mountain lion.**

cat·a·pult (kăt′ə-pŭlt′, -po͝olt′) ▸ *n.* 1. An ancient military machine for hurling large missiles. 2. A mechanism for launching aircraft from the deck of a carrier. **—cat′a·pult′** *v.*

cat·a·ract (kăt′ə-răkt′) ▸ *n.* 1. A large waterfall. 2. A downpour. 3. Opacity of the lens or capsule of the eye, causing partial or total blindness.

ca·tarrh (kə-tär′) ▸ *n.* Inflammation of mucous membranes, esp. of the nose and throat. **—ca·tarrh′al** *adj.*

ca·tas·tro·phe (kə-tăs′trə-fē) ▸ *n.* A great, often sudden calamity; disaster. **—cat′a·stroph′ic** (kăt′ə-strŏf′ĭk) *adj.* **—cat′a·stroph′i·cal·ly** *adv.*

cat·a·to·ni·a (kăt′ə-tō′nē-ə) ▸ *n.* An abnormal condition most often associated with schizophrenia and variously marked by stupor, mania, and either rigidity or extreme flexibility of the limbs. **—cat′a·ton′ic** (-tŏn′ĭk) *adj. & n.* **—cat′a·ton′i·cal·ly** *adv.*

Ca·taw·ba (kə-tô′bə) ▸ *n., pl.* **-ba** or **-bas.** 1. A member of a Native American people now located in W South Carolina. 2. The Siouan language of the Catawba.

cat·bird (kăt′bûrd′) ▸ *n.* A dark gray North American songbird with a mewing call.

cat·call (kăt′kôl′) ▸ *n.* A shrill call or cry of derision or disapproval. **—cat′call′** *v.*

catch (kăch, kĕch) ▸ *v.* **caught** (kôt), **catch·ing.** 1. To capture, esp. after a chase. 2. To snare or trap. 3. To discover or come upon unexpectedly or accidentally. 4. To take hold of or apprehend suddenly; grasp. 5. To snatch; grab. 6a. To intercept or overtake. b. To get to in time: *catch a plane.* 7. To become or cause to become held, entangled, or fastened. 8. To hold up; delay. 9. To become subject to or contract, as by contagion. 10. To apprehend or grasp mentally. 11. *Informal* To go to see: *caught the late show.* ***—phrasal verbs:*** **catch on** 1. To understand or perceive. 2. To become popular. **catch up** 1. To come up from behind; overtake. 2. To bring up to date: *caught up on my reading.* ▸ *n.* 1. The act of catching. 2. Something that catches, esp. a device for fastening or for checking motion. 3a. Something caught. b. *Informal* One worth catching. 4. A game of throwing and catching a ball. 5. *Informal* An unsuspected drawback. ***—idioms:*** **catch fire** 1.

THESAURUS

castigate *v.* —*See* CHASTISE, PUNISH.

castigation *n.* —*See* PUNISHMENT.

castle in the air *n.* —*See* DREAM (2).

castrate *v.* —*See* CRIPPLE, STERILIZE (2).

casual *adj.* —*See* ACCIDENTAL, EASYGOING, EVERYDAY.

casualness *n.* —*See* EASE (1).

casualty *n.* A loss of life, or one who has lost life, usually as a result of accident, disaster, or war ▸ death, fatality, kill, loss. —*See also* ACCIDENT, VICTIM.

casuistry *n.* —*See* FALLACY (2).

catachresis *n.* —*See* CORRUPTION (3).

cataclysm *n.* —*See* DISASTER, REVOLUTION (2).

cataclysmic *adj.* —*See* DISASTROUS.

catacomb *n.* —*See* GRAVE[1].

catalog *n.* —*See* LIST[1], PROGRAM (1), PROGRAM (2).

catalog *v.* —*See* CLASSIFY, LIST[1].

catalyst *n.* An agent that stimulates or precipitates a reaction or change ▸ ferment, leaven, leavening, reactant, yeast. —*See also* STIMULUS.

cataract *n.* —*See* FLOOD.

catastrophe *n.* —*See* COLLAPSE (2), DISASTER.

catastrophic *adj.* —*See* DISASTROUS.

catcall *n.* —*See* HISS (2).

catcall *v.* —*See* HISS (2).

catch *v.* 1. To gain control of or an advantage over by or as if by trapping ▸ bag, enmesh, ensnare, ensnarl, entangle, entrap, net, snare, tangle, trammel, trap, web. *Informal:* hook. [*Compare* SEIZE, TAKE.] 2. To get hold of something moving ▸ clutch, grab, seize, snag, snatch. *Informal:* nab. *Idiom:* lay hands on. [*Compare* GRASP.] 3. To become stuck or entangled ▸ fix, hook, lodge, snag, stick. [*Compare* FIX.] 4. To have a sudden overwhelming effect on ▸ seize, strike, take. [*Compare* MOVE.] 5. To go aboard a means of transport ▸ board, take. *Informal:* hop. 6. *Informal* To succeed in communicating with ▸ contact, reach. *Informal:* get. *Idioms:* catch up with, get hold of, get in touch with, get through to, get

To ignite. 2. To gain sudden popularity. **catch (one's) breath** To pause or rest briefly.

Catch-22 (kăch′twĕn-tē-to͞o′, kĕch′-) ▸ *n.* A situation in which a desired outcome is impossible to attain because of a set of inherently contradictory rules or conditions.

catch·all (kăch′ôl′, kĕch′-) ▸ *n.* A receptacle or storage area for odds and ends.

catch·er (kăch′ər, kĕch′-) ▸ *n.* One that catches, esp. the baseball player positioned behind home plate.

catch·ing (kăch′ĭng, kĕch′-) ▸ *adj.* 1. Infectious or contagious. 2. Attractive; alluring.

catch·up (kăch′əp, kĕch′-) ▸ *n.* Var. of **ketchup.**

catch·word (kăch′wûrd′, kĕch′-) ▸ *n.* A well-known word or phrase, esp. one that exemplifies a notion, class, or quality.

catch·y (kăch′ē, kĕch′ē) ▸ *adj.* **-i·er, -i·est.** 1. Easily remembered: *a catchy tune.* 2. Tricky; deceptive. **—catch′i·ness** *n.*

cat·e·chism (kăt′ĭ-kĭz′əm) ▸ *n.* A book giving a brief summary of the basic principles of Christianity in question-and-answer form. **—cat′e·chist** *n.* **—cat′e·chize′** *v.*

cat·e·chu·men (kăt′ĭ-kyo͞o′mən) ▸ *n.* One who is being taught the principles of Christianity.

cat·e·gor·i·cal (kăt′ĭ-gôr′ĭ-kəl, -gŏr′-) also **cat·e·gor·ic** (-ĭk) ▸ *adj.* 1. Being without exception or qualification; absolute. 2. Of or included in a category. **—cat′e·gor′i·cal·ly** *adv.*

cat·e·go·rize (kăt′ĭ-gə-rīz′) ▸ *v.* **-rized, -riz·ing.** To put into categories. **—cat′e·go·riz′a·ble** *adj.* **—cat′e·go·ri·za′tion** *n.*

cat·e·go·ry (kăt′ĭ-gôr′ē) ▸ *n., pl.* **-ries.** A specifically defined division in a system of classification; class.

ca·ter (kā′tər) ▸ *v.* 1. To provide food and service (for). 2. To be attentive or solicitous: *catered to our needs.* **—ca′ter·er** *n.*

cat·er·cor·nered (kăt′ər-kôr′nərd, kăt′ē-) also **cat·ty-cor·nered** (kăt′ē-kôr′nərd) or **cat·ty-cor·ner** (-nər) ▸ *adj.* Diagonal. ▸ *adv.* Diagonally.

cat·er·pil·lar (kăt′ər-pĭl′ər, kăt′ə-) ▸ *n.* The wormlike, often hairy larva of a butterfly or moth.

cat·er·waul (kăt′ər-wôl′) ▸ *v.* To make a discordant sound or shriek. **—cat′er·waul′** *n.*

cat·fish (kăt′fĭsh′) ▸ *n.* Any of numerous scaleless fishes with whiskerlike feelers near the mouth.

cat·gut (kăt′gŭt′) ▸ *n.* A tough cord made from the dried intestines of certain animals.

ca·thar·sis (kə-thär′sĭs) ▸ *n., pl.* **-ses** (-sēz). 1. *Medic.* Purgation, esp. for the digestive system. 2. A purging of the emotions as a result of experiencing esp. a dramatic work of art.

ca·thar·tic (kə-thär′tĭk) ▸ *adj.* Inducing catharsis; purgative. ▸ *n.* A purgative.

ca·the·dral (kə-thē′drəl) ▸ *n.* The principal church of a bishop's diocese.

Cath·e·rine II (kăth′ər-ĭn, kăth′rĭn). "Catherine the Great" (1729–96) ▸ Empress of Russia (1762–96).

cath·e·ter (kăth′ĭ-tər) ▸ *n.* A hollow flexible tube for insertion into a bodily channel to allow the passage of fluids or to distend a passageway.

cath·ode (kăth′ōd′) ▸ *n.* 1. A negatively charged electrode. 2. The positively charged terminal of a primary cell or storage battery. **—ca·thod′ic** (kă-thŏd′ĭk) *adj.*

cath·ode-ray tube (kăth′ōd-rā′) ▸ *n.* A vacuum tube in which a hot cathode emits electrons that are accelerated and focused on a phosphorescent screen.

cath·o·lic (kăth′ə-lĭk, kăth′lĭk) ▸ *adj.* 1. Universal; general. 2. **Catholic** Of or involving the Roman Catholic Church or Catholics. ▸ *n.* **Catholic** A member of the Roman Catholic Church. **—ca·thol′i·cal·ly** (kə-thŏl′ĭk-lē) *adv.* **—cath′o·lic′i·ty** (-ə-lĭs′ĭ-tē) *n.*

Ca·thol·i·cism (kə-thŏl′ĭ-sĭz′əm) ▸ *n.* The faith, doctrine, system, and practice of the Roman Catholic Church.

cat·i·on (kăt′ī′ən) ▸ *n.* An ion or group of ions having a positive charge and characteristically moving toward a negative electrode in electrolysis. **—cat′i·on′ic** (-ŏn′ĭk) *adj.*

cat·kin (kăt′kĭn) ▸ *n.* A dense, often drooping cluster of scalelike flowers found in willows, birches, and oaks.

cat·nap (kăt′năp′) ▸ *n.* A short nap; light sleep. **—cat′nap′** *v.*

cat·nip (kăt′nĭp′) ▸ *n.* An aromatic plant to which cats are strongly attracted.

cat-o'-nine-tails (kăt′ə-nīn′tālz′) ▸ *n., pl.* **cat-o'-nine-tails.** A flogging whip consisting of nine knotted cords fastened to a handle.

CAT scanner (kăt) ▸ *n.* A device that produces cross-sectional views of an internal body structure using computerized axial tomography. **—CAT scan** *n.*

cat's cradle (kăts) ▸ *n.* A game in which an intricately looped string is transferred from the hands of one player to another.

cat's-eye (kăts′ī′) ▸ *n.* A semiprecious gem displaying a band of reflected light that shifts position as the gem is turned.

Cats·kill Mountains (kăt′skĭl′) ▸ A range of the Appalachian Mts. in SE NY.

cat's-paw also **cats·paw** (kăts′pô′) ▸ *n.* A person used by another as a dupe or tool.

cat·sup (kăt′səp, kăch′əp, kĕch′-) ▸ *n.* Var. of **ketchup.**

cat·tail (kăt′tāl′) ▸ *n.* A tall-stemmed marsh plant having long straplike leaves and a dense brown cylindrical head.

cat·tle (kăt′l) ▸ *pl.n.* Bovine mammals such as cows, steers, bulls, and oxen, often raised for meat and dairy products. **—cat′tle·man** *n.*

cat·ty (kăt′ē) ▸ *adj.* **-ti·er, -ti·est.** Slyly malicious. **—cat′ti·ly** *adv.* **—cat′ti·ness** *n.*

cat·ty-cor·nered (kăt′ē-kôr′nərd) or **cat·ty-cor·ner** (-nər) ▸ *adj. & adv.* Vars. of **cater-cornered.**

cat·walk (kăt′wôk′) ▸ *n.* A narrow, often elevated walkway, as on the sides of a bridge.

Cau·ca·sian (kô-kā′zhən) ▸ *adj.* 1. *Anthro.* Of or being a human racial classification traditionally distinguished by very light to brown skin color and including peoples indigenous to Europe, N Africa, W Asia, and India. 2. Of the Caucasus. ▸ *n.* 1. *Anthro.* A member of the Caucasian racial classification. 2. A native or inhabitant of the Caucasus.

Cau·ca·soid (kô′kə-soid′) ▸ *adj.* *Anthro.* Of or relating to the Caucasian racial classification. **—Cau′ca·soid′** *n.*

Cau·ca·sus (kô′kə-səs) also **Cau·ca·sia** (kô-kā′zhə, -shə) ▸ A region between the Black and Caspian seas that includes Russia, Georgia, Azerbaijan, and Armenia.

THESAURUS

to, make contact with. *—See also* CAPTURE, CONTRACT (2), FASTEN, HIT, SEE (1), UNDERSTAND (1).

catch up *v.* To come up even with another ▸ overtake, pull alongside, pull even. [*Compare* APPROACH, EQUALIZE.] *—See also* INVOLVE (1).

catch *n.* 1. The act of catching, especially a sudden taking and holding ▸ capture, clutch, grab, seizure, snatch. [*Compare* ARREST, HOLD.] 2. *Informal* A person or thing worth catching ▸ plum, prize. *Slang:* brass ring. 3. *Informal* A tricky or unsuspected condition ▸ hitch, rub, snag. [*Compare* BAR, DISADVANTAGE, TRICK.] *—See also* FASTENER, TREASURE.

catching *adj.* *—See* CONTAGIOUS.

catechism or **catechization** *n.* *—See* TEST (2).

catechize *v.* To subject to a test of knowledge or skill ▸ examine, quiz, test. [*Compare* ASK.] *—See also* INDOCTRINATE (1).

categorical *adj.* *—See* DEFINITE (1).

categorically *adv.* *—See* ABSOLUTELY.

categorization *n.* *—See* ARRANGEMENT (1).

categorize *v.* *—See* CLASSIFY.

category *n.* *—See* CLASS (1).

cater *v.* 1. To comply with the wishes or ideas of another ▸ cater to, gratify, humor, indulge. [*Compare* DEFER[2].] 2. To place food and beverages before someone ▸ serve, wait on (*or* upon). [*Compare* GIVE, DISTRIBUTE.] *—See also* BABY.

caterwaul *v.* *—See* ARGUE (1), BAWL.

caterwaul *n.* *—See* NOISE (1).

catharsis *n.* *—See* PURIFICATION (1), PURIFICATION (2).

cathartic *adj.* *—See* ELIMINATIVE.

cathartic *n.* *—See* PURIFIER.

catholic *adj.* *—See* UNIVERSAL (1).

catholicon *n.* Something believed to cure all human disorders ▸ cure-all, elixir, panacea. [*Compare* CURE.]

catlike *adj.* *—See* STEALTHY.

catnap *n.* *—See* NAP.

catnap *v.* *—See* NAP.

cat's cradle *n.* *—See* TANGLE.

cat's-paw *n.* *—See* DUPE, PAWN[2].

catty *adj.* *—See* BITING.

Caucasus Mountains ▸ A range extending from the N to the SE in the Caucasus.
cau·cus (kô′kəs) ▸ *n., pl.* **-cus·es** or **-cus·ses**. **1.** A meeting of the local members of a political party esp. to select delegates to a convention. **2.** A group within a legislative body seeking to represent a specific interest or policy. **—cau′cus** *v.*
cau·dal (kôd′l) ▸ *adj.* Of, at, or near the tail or hind parts; posterior.
cau·dil·lo (kô-dēl′yō, -dē′yō) ▸ *n., pl.* **-los**. A leader or chief, esp. a military dictator.
caught (kôt) ▸ *v.* P.t. and p.part. of **catch**.
caul (kôl) ▸ *n.* A portion of the amnion, esp. when it covers the head of a fetus at birth.
caul·dron also **cal·dron** (kôl′drən) ▸ *n.* **1.** A large kettle or vat. **2.** A situation of seething unrest.
cau·li·flow·er (kô′lĭ-flou′ər, kŏl′ĭ-) ▸ *n.* A plant related to the cabbage and broccoli and having a whitish undeveloped flower with a large edible head.
cauliflower ear ▸ *n.* An ear swollen and deformed by repeated blows.
caulk also **calk** (kôk) ▸ *v.* **1.** To make (e.g., pipes) watertight or airtight by sealing. **2.** To make (a boat) watertight by packing seams with oakum or tar. ▸ *n.* Caulking. **—caulk′er** *n.*
caulk·ing (kô′kĭng) ▸ *n.* A usu. impermeable substance used to caulk or seal.
caus·al (kô′zəl) ▸ *adj.* Of, constituting, or expressing a cause. **—cau·sal′i·ty** (-zăl′ĭ-tē) *n.* **—caus′al·ly** *adv.*
cau·sa·tion (kô-zā′shən) ▸ *n.* **1.** The act or process of causing. **2.** A causal agency.
cause (kôz) ▸ *n.* **1.** The one, such as a person, event, or condition, responsible for an action or result. **2.** A reason; motive. **3.** A goal or principle. **4a.** A ground for legal action. **b.** A lawsuit. ▸ *v.* **caused, caus·ing**. To be the cause of; bring about. **—cause′less** *adj.*
cause cé·lè·bre (kōz′ sā-lĕb′rə) ▸ *n., pl.* **causes cé·lè·bres** (kōz′ sā-lĕb′rə). **1.** An issue arousing widespread controversy or heated debate. **2.** A celebrated legal case.
cause·way (kôz′wā′) ▸ *n.* A raised roadway across water or marshland.
caus·tic (kô′stĭk) ▸ *adj.* **1.** Capable of burning, corroding, or dissolving by chemical action. **2.** Sarcastic; biting. ▸ *n.* A caustic substance.
cau·ter·ize (kô′tə-rīz′) ▸ *v.* **-ized, -iz·ing**. To burn or sear so as to stop bleeding and prevent infection. **—cau′ter·i·za′tion** *n.*
cau·tion (kô′shən) ▸ *n.* **1.** Careful forethought to avoid danger or harm. **2.** A warning or admonition. ▸ *v.* To warn. **—cau′tion·ar′y** *adj.*
cau·tious (kô′shəs) ▸ *adj.* Showing or practicing caution; careful. **—cau′tious·ly** *adv.* **—cau′tious·ness** *n.*
cav·al·cade (kăv′əl-kād′, kăv′əl-kād′) ▸ *n.* **1.** A procession of riders or horse-drawn carriages. **2.** A ceremonial procession.
cav·a·lier (kăv′ə-lîr′) ▸ *n.* **1.** A gallant gentleman. **2.** A mounted soldier; knight. **3. Cavalier** A supporter of Charles I of England. ▸ *adj.* **1.** Haughty; disdainful. **2.** Carefree and nonchalant; jaunty. **—cav′a·lier′ly** *adv.*
cav·al·ry (kăv′əl-rē) ▸ *n., pl.* **-ries**. Troops trained to fight on horseback or in light armored vehicles. **—cav′al·ry·man** *n.*
cave (kāv) ▸ *n.* A hollow or natural passage under or into the earth with an opening to the surface. ▸ *v.* **caved, cav·ing**. **1.** To fall in; collapse. **2.** To capitulate; yield: *caved in to their demands.* **3.** To explore caves. **—cav′er** *n.*
ca·ve·at (kăv′ē-ăt′, kä′vē-ät′) ▸ *n.* A warning or caution.
cave-in (kāv′ĭn′) ▸ *n.* A collapse, as of a tunnel or structure.
cave·man (kāv′măn′) ▸ *n.* A prehistoric human who lived in caves.
cav·ern (kăv′ərn) ▸ *n.* A large cave. **—cav′ern·ous** *adj.*
cav·i·ar also **cav·i·are** (kăv′ē-är′, kä′vē-) ▸ *n.* The roe of a large fish, esp. a sturgeon, salted and eaten as a delicacy.
cav·il (kăv′əl) ▸ *v.* **-iled, -il·ing** also **-illed, -il·ling**. To find fault unnecessarily. **—cav′il** *n.* **—cav′il·er** *n.*
cav·i·ty (kăv′ĭ-tē) ▸ *n., pl.* **-ties**. **1.** A hollow or hole. **2.** A hollow area within the body: *the abdominal cavity.* **3.** A pitted area in a tooth caused by decay.
ca·vort (kə-vôrt′) ▸ *v.* To leap about; caper.
caw (kô) ▸ *n.* The hoarse raucous sound of a crow or similar bird. **—caw** *v.*
cay (kē, kā) ▸ *n.* A small low island of coral or sand; key.
cay·enne pepper (kī-ĕn′, kā-) ▸ *n.* A condiment made from the fruit of a pungent variety of capsicum pepper.
cay·man (kā′mən) ▸ *n.* Var. of **caiman**.
Cay·man Islands (kā-măn′, kā′mən) ▸ A British-administered group of three islands in the Caribbean Sea NW of Jamaica.
Ca·yu·ga (kā-yōō′gə, kī-) ▸ *n., pl.* **-ga** or **-gas**. **1.** A member of a Native American people formerly of W-central New York, now living in W New York, Wisconsin, and Oklahoma. **2.** Their Iroquoian language.
cay·use (kī-yōōs′, kī′yōōs′) ▸ *n.* A horse, esp. an Indian pony of the Pacific Northwest.
Cayuse ▸ *n., pl.* **-use** or **-us·es**. **1.** A member of a Native American people of NE Oregon and SE Washington. **2.** Their language.
cc ▸ *abbr.* **1.** carbon copy **2.** cubic centimeter
Cd ▸ The symbol for the element **cadmium**.
CD ▸ *abbr.* **1.** also **C/D** certificate of deposit **2.** compact disk
CD-ROM (sē′dē′rŏm′) ▸ *n.* A compact disk that functions as read-only memory.
Ce ▸ The symbol for the element **cerium**.
cease (sēs) ▸ *v.* **ceased, ceas·ing**. To bring or come to an end.
cease-fire (sēs′fīr′) ▸ *n.* **1.** An order to stop firing. **2.** Suspension of hostilities; truce.
cease·less (sēs′lĭs) ▸ *adj.* Never ending. **—cease′less·ly** *adv.* **—cease′less·ness** *n.*
ce·cum also **cae·cum** (sē′kəm) ▸ *n., pl.* **-ca** (-kə). The large blind pouch forming the beginning of the large intestine. **—ce′cal** *adj.* **—ce′cal·ly** *adv.*
ce·dar (sē′dər) ▸ *n.* Any of a genus of evergreen trees having large erect cones and aromatic, usu. reddish wood.
cede (sēd) ▸ *v.* **ced·ed, ced·ing**. **1.** To surrender possession of, esp. by treaty. **2.** To yield or grant.

THESAURUS

caulking *n.* —*See* FILLER (1).
cause *n.* **1.** That which produces an effect ▸ antecedent, determinant, occasion, reason. [*Compare* IMPACT, ORIGIN, STIMULUS.] **2.** A basis for an action or a decision ▸ call, grounds, justification, mainspring, motivation, motive, necessity, occasion, reason, spring, wherefore, why. ***Idiom:*** why and wherefore. [*Compare* ACCOUNT, BASIS.] **3.** A goal served with great or uncompromising dedication ▸ crusade, holy war, jihad. [*Compare* DRIVE.] —*See also* LAWSUIT.
cause *v.* To be the cause of ▸ bring, bring about, bring on, effect, effectuate, generate, induce, ingenerate, inspire, lead to, make, occasion, precipitate, prompt, provoke, result in, secure, set off, stir (up), touch off, trigger. ***Idioms:*** bring to pass (*or* effect), give rise to. [*Compare* BEGIN, DEVELOP, PRODUCE, START.]
caustic *adj.* —*See* BITING.
causticity *n.* —*See* SARCASM.
caution *n.* Careful forethought to avoid harm or risk ▸ calculation, care, carefulness, chariness, gingerliness, precaution, wariness. —*See also* ALERTNESS, CARE (1), PRUDENCE, WARNING.
caution *v.* —*See* WARN.
cautionary *adj.* Giving warning ▸ admonishing, admonitory, monitory, warning.
cautious *adj.* —*See* CONSERVATIVE (2), DELIBERATE (3), WARY.
cave or **cavern** *n.* A hollow beneath the earth's surface ▸ dugout, grotto, tunnel. [*Compare* HOLE.]
cave in *v.* —*See* BUCKLE, COLLAPSE (1).
caveat *n.* —*See* EXAMPLE (2), WARNING.
cavernous *adj.* Open wide ▸ abysmal, abyssal, gaping, yawning. [*Compare* BROAD, OPEN.] —*See also* HOLLOW (2).
cavil *v.* —*See* QUIBBLE.
caviler *n.* —*See* CRITIC (2).
caviling *n.* —*See* QUIBBLING.
cavity *n.* —*See* DEPRESSION (1), HOLE (1).
cavort *v.* —*See* GAMBOL.
cease *v.* To bring an activity or relationship to an end suddenly ▸ break off, discontinue, interrupt, suspend, terminate. —*See also* DISAPPEAR (2), LAPSE, STOP (2), STOP (1).
cease-fire *n.* —*See* TRUCE.
ceaseless *adj.* —*See* CONTINUAL, ENDLESS (2).
ceaselessness *n.* —*See* ENDLESSNESS.
cede *v.* —*See* ABANDON (1), TRANSFER (1).

ce·di (sä′dē) ▸ *n., pl.* **ce·dis.** See **currency** table in Appendix.

ce·dil·la (sĭ-dĭl′ə) ▸ *n.* A mark (¸) that is placed beneath the letter *c,* as in *façade,* to indicate that the letter is to be pronounced (s).

cei·ba (sā′bə) ▸ *n.* The silk-cotton tree.

ceil·ing (sē′lĭng) ▸ *n.* **1.** The upper interior surface of a room. **2.** An upper limit: *wage and price ceilings.* **3.** The highest altitude under particular weather conditions from which the ground is visible.

Cel·e·bes (sĕl′ə-bēz′, sə-lē′bēz′) ▸ See **Sulawesi.**

cel·e·brate (sĕl′ə-brāt′) ▸ *v.* **-brat·ed, -brat·ing. 1.** To observe (a day or event) with ceremonies of respect, festivity, or rejoicing. **2.** To perform (a religious ceremony). **3.** To extol or praise. **—cel′e·brant** *n.* **—cel′e·bra′tion** *n.* **—cel′e·bra′tor** *n.* **—cel′e·bra·to′ry** (sĕl′ə-brə-tôr′ē, sə-lĕb′rə-) *adj.*

cel·e·brat·ed (sĕl′ə-brā′tĭd) ▸ *adj.* Known and praised widely.

ce·leb·ri·ty (sə-lĕb′rĭ-tē) ▸ *n., pl.* **-ties. 1.** A famous person. **2.** Renown; fame. **—ce·leb′ri·ty·hood′** *n.*

ce·ler·i·ty (sə-lĕr′ĭ-tē) ▸ *n.* Swiftness; speed.

cel·er·y (sĕl′ə-rē) ▸ *n.* A plant having edible roots, leafstalks, leaves, and seedlike fruits.

ce·les·ta (sə-lĕs′tə) also **ce·leste** (-lĕst′) ▸ *n.* A keyboard instrument with metal plates struck by hammers.

ce·les·tial (sə-lĕs′chəl) ▸ *adj.* **1.** Of or relating to the sky or the heavens. **2.** Of or suggestive of heaven; heavenly.

celestial equator ▸ *n.* A great circle on the celestial sphere in the same plane as the earth's equator.

celestial navigation ▸ *n.* Navigation based on the positions of celestial bodies.

celestial sphere ▸ *n.* An imaginary sphere of infinite extent with the earth at its center.

cel·i·bate (sĕl′ə-bĭt) ▸ *adj.* **1.** Abstaining from sexual intercourse, esp. by reason of religious vows. **2.** Unmarried. **—cel′i·ba·cy** (-bə-sē) *n.* **—cel′i·bate** *n.*

cell (sĕl) ▸ *n.* **1.** A narrow confining room, as in a prison or convent. **2.** A small enclosed space, as in a honeycomb. **3.** A rectangular box on a spreadsheet where a column and a row intersect. **4.** *Biol.* The smallest structural unit of an organism that is capable of independent functioning, consisting of one or more nuclei, cytoplasm, and various organelles, all surrounded by a semipermeable membrane. **5.** The smallest organizational unit esp. of a revolutionary political party. **6.** *Elect.* **a.** A single unit for electrolysis or conversion of chemical into electric energy, usu. consisting of a container with electrodes and an electrolyte. **b.** A unit that converts radiant energy into electric energy.

cel·lar (sĕl′ər) ▸ *n.* **1.** An underground room usu. beneath a building. **2.** A stock of wines.

cell·block (sĕl′blŏk′) ▸ *n.* A group of cells that make up a unit of a prison.

cell·mate (sĕl′māt′) ▸ *n.* One with whom a cell is shared, esp. in a prison.

cel·lo (chĕl′ō) ▸ *n., pl.* **-los** *Mus.* An instrument of the violin family, pitched lower than the viola but higher than the double bass. **—cel′list** *n.*

cel·lo·phane (sĕl′ə-fān′) ▸ *n.* A thin, flexible, transparent cellulose material used as a moistureproof wrapping.

cell phone ▸ *n.* A cellular telephone.

cel·lu·lar (sĕl′yə-lər) ▸ *adj.* **1.** Of or resembling a cell. **2.** Consisting of cells.

cellular telephone ▸ *n.* A mobile radiotelephone that uses a network of transmitters to connect to regular telephone lines.

cel·lu·lite (sĕl′yə-līt′, -lēt′) ▸ *n.* A fatty deposit causing dimpled skin as around the thighs.

cel·lu·loid (sĕl′yə-loid′) ▸ *n.* A colorless flammable material made from nitrocellulose and camphor, used to make photographic film.

cel·lu·lose (sĕl′yə-lōs′, -lōz′) ▸ *n.* A complex carbohydrate, $(C_6H_{10}O_5)_n$, the main constituent of the cell wall in most plants, used in the manufacture of paper, textiles, and explosives. **—cel′lu·lo′sic** *adj.*

cellulose acetate ▸ *n.* A cellulose resin used in lacquers and photographic film.

Cel·si·us (sĕl′sē-əs, -shəs) ▸ *adj.* Of or according to a temperature scale that registers the freezing point of water as 0° and the boiling point as 100° under normal atmospheric pressure.

Celt (kĕlt, sĕlt) ▸ *n.* **1.** One of an ancient people of central and W Europe, esp. a Briton or Gaul. **2.** A speaker of a Celtic language.

Celt·ic (kĕl′tĭk, sĕl′-) ▸ *n.* A subfamily of the Indo-European language family that includes Welsh, Irish Gaelic, Scottish Gaelic, Breton, and Gaulish. ▸ *adj.* Of or relating to the Celts or the Celtic languages.

ce·ment (sĭ-mĕnt′) ▸ *n.* **1.** A building material made by grinding calcined limestone and clay to a fine powder, which can be mixed with water and poured to set as a solid mass or used as an ingredient in making mortar or concrete. **2.** A substance that hardens to act as an adhesive; glue. **3.** Var. of **cementum.** ▸ *v.* **1.** To bind with or as if with cement. **2.** To cover or coat with cement.

cement mixer ▸ *n.* A machine, often mounted on a truck, having a revolving drum in which cement, sand, gravel, and water are combined into concrete.

ce·men·tum (sĭ-mĕn′təm) also **ce·ment** (-mĕnt′) ▸ *n.* A bonelike substance covering the root of a tooth.

cem·e·ter·y (sĕm′ĭ-tĕr′ē) ▸ *n., pl.* **-ies.** A place for burying the dead; graveyard.

–cene ▸ *suff.* Recent: *Oligocene, Pleistocene.*

cen·o·taph (sĕn′ə-tăf′) ▸ *n.* A monument to commemorate a dead person whose remains lie elsewhere.

Ce·no·zo·ic (sĕn′ə-zō′ĭk, sē′nə-) ▸ *adj.* Of or being the 4th and most recent geologic era, including the Tertiary and Quaternary periods and marked by the formation of modern continents and the diversification of mammals, birds, and plants. ▸ *n.* The Cenozoic Era.

cen·ser (sĕn′sər) ▸ *n.* A vessel in which incense is burned, esp. during religious services.

cen·sor (sĕn′sər) ▸ *n.* **1.** One authorized to examine books, films, or other material and remove or suppress what is considered objectionable. **2.** A Roman official responsible for supervising the census. ▸ *v.* To examine and expurgate. **—cen·so′ri·al** (sĕn-sôr′ē-əl) *adj.*

THESAURUS

ceiling *n.* —*See* LIMIT (1).

celebrate *v.* **1.** To mark a day or an event with ceremonies of respect, festivity, or rejoicing ▸ commemorate, keep, observe, solemnize. [*Compare* SANCTIFY.] **2.** To show joyful satisfaction in an event, especially by merrymaking ▸ feast, party, rejoice, revel. *Idioms:* beat the drum, have a ball, jump for joy, kick up one's heels, kill the fatted calf, let one's hair down, live it up, make merry, paint the town red, whoop it up. [*Compare* EXULT, REJOICE, REVEL.] —*See also* HONOR (1).

celebrated *adj.* —*See* FAMOUS.

celebration *n.* **1.** A joyous or festive occasion ▸ carnival, festival, festivity, fete, fiesta, holiday, jubilee, red-letter day, revel, revels. **2.** The act of observing a day or an event with ceremonies ▸ commemoration, keeping, observance, solemnity, solemnization. [*Compare* CEREMONY, MEMORIAL.] **3.** The act of showing joyful satisfaction in an event ▸ festivity, jollification, jubilation, merrymaking, pageantry, rejoicing, revelry. —*See also* BLAST (3), MERRIMENT (2), PARTY, PRAISE (1).

celebratory *adj.* —*See* MERRY.

celebrity *n.* A famous person ▸ figure, hero, heroine, idol, legend, lion, luminary, name, notable, personage, personality, star, superstar. *Informal:* big name. [*Compare* DIGNITARY.] —*See also* FAME.

celerity *n.* —*See* HASTE (1).

celestial *adj.* —*See* DIVINE (1), HEAVENLY (1), HEAVENLY (2).

celibacy *n.* —*See* CHASTITY.

celibate *adj.* —*See* CHASTE.

cement *v.* —*See* HARDEN (2).

censor *v.* **1.** To examine and remove objectionable or improper material from a publication or broadcast ▸ bowdlerize, cut, edit, expurgate, sanitize, screen. *Informal:* bleep, blue-pencil, red-pencil. [*Compare* EXAMINE.] **2.** To keep from being published or transmitted ▸ ban, black out, hush, hush up, kill, silence, stifle, suppress, withhold. *Idioms:* keep a lid on, put a lid on. [*Compare* FORBID, REPRESS, SILENCE.]

cen·so·ri·ous (sĕn-sôr′ē-əs) ▸ *adj.* Tending to censure; critical. **—cen·so′ri·ous·ly** *adv.*
cen·sor·ship (sĕn′sər-shĭp′) ▸ *n.* **1.** The act or process of censoring. **2.** The office of a Roman censor.
cen·sure (sĕn′shər) ▸ *n.* **1.** An expression of disapproval, blame, or criticism. **2.** An official rebuke. ▸ *v.* **-sured, -sur·ing.** To criticize severely; blame. **—cen′sur·a·ble** *adj.*
cen·sus (sĕn′səs) ▸ *n.* A periodic official population count.
cent (sĕnt) ▸ *n.* **1.** A monetary unit equal to 1/100 of the US dollar. **2.** A monetary unit equal to 1/100 of various standard monetary units.
cen·taur (sĕn′tôr′) ▸ *n. Gk. Myth.* One of a race of monsters having the head, arms, and trunk of a man and the body and legs of a horse.
cen·ta·vo (sĕn-tä′vō) ▸ *n., pl.* **cen·ta·vos. 1.** A former subunit of Portuguese currency, equal to 1/100 of an escudo. **2.** A similar unit used in various Central and South American countries.
cen·te·nar·i·an (sĕn′tə-nâr′ē-ən) ▸ *n.* One that is 100 years or older. **—cen′te·nar′i·an** *adj.*
cen·ten·a·ry (sĕn-tĕn′ə-rē, sĕn′tə-nĕr′ē) ▸ *n., pl.* **-ries.** A centennial. **—cen·ten′a·ry** *adj.*
cen·ten·ni·al (sĕn-tĕn′ē-əl) ▸ *n.* A 100th anniversary. **—cen·ten′ni·al** *adj.*
cen·ter (sĕn′tər) ▸ *n.* **1.** A point equidistant from the sides or outer boundaries of something; middle. **2a.** A point equidistant from the vertices of a regular polygon. **b.** A point equidistant from all points on the circumference of a circle or on the surface of a sphere. **3.** A point around which something revolves; axis. **4.** A place of concentrated activity, service, or influence: *a medical center.* **5.** One occupying a middle position. **6.** A political group with views midway between the right and the left. **7.** *Sports* A player who holds a middle position. ▸ *v.* **1.** To place in, on, or at the center. **2.** To have a center; focus.
cen·ter·board (sĕn′tər-bôrd′) ▸ *n.* A movable keel in a sailboat that can be pivoted upward, as in shallow water.
center field ▸ *n. Baseball* The middle third of the outfield, behind second base. **—center fielder** *n.*
cen·ter·fold (sĕn′tər-fōld′) ▸ *n.* A magazine center spread, esp. an oversize feature that folds out.
center of mass ▸ *n., pl.* **centers of mass.** The point in a system at which its mass may be considered to be concentrated.
cen·ter·piece (sĕn′tər-pēs′) ▸ *n.* **1.** A decorative arrangement placed at the center of a table. **2.** The most important feature.
cen·tes·i·mal (sĕn-tĕs′ə-məl) ▸ *adj.* Relating to or divided into hundredths. **—cen·tes′i·mal·ly** *adv.*
centi– ▸ *pref.* **1.** One hundredth part (10^{-2}): *centiliter.* **2.** One hundred: *centipede.*
cen·ti·grade (sĕn′tĭ-grād′) ▸ *adj.* Celsius.
cen·ti·gram (sĕn′tĭ-grăm′) ▸ *n.* See **measurement** table in Appendix.
cen·ti·li·ter (sĕn′tə-lē′tər) ▸ *n.* See **measurement** table in Appendix.
cen·time (sän′tēm′, säN-tēm′) ▸ *n.* **1.** A former subunit of the currency of France, Belgium, and Luxembourg, equal to 1/100 of a franc. **2.** A monetary unit equal to 1/100 of the standard unit in Algeria, Morocco, Switzerland, and various other countries.
cen·ti·me·ter (sĕn′tə-mē′tər) ▸ *n.* See **measurement** table in Appendix.
cen·ti·pede (sĕn′tə-pēd′) ▸ *n.* A wormlike arthropod having many legs and body segments.
cen·tral (sĕn′trəl) ▸ *adj.* **1.** At, in, near, or being the center. **2.** Key; essential: *the central topic of a story.* **3.** Easily reached from many places: *a central location for the new grocery store.* **—cen·tral′i·ty** (-trăl′ĭ-tē) *n.* **—cen′tral·ly** *adv.*
Central African Republic ▸ A country of central Africa.
Central America ▸ A region of S North America extending from the S border of Mexico to the N border of Colombia. **—Central American** *adj. & n.*
cen·tral·ize (sĕn′trə-līz′) ▸ *v.* **-ized, -iz·ing.** To bring or come to a center or under a central authority. **—cen′tral·i·za′tion** *n.*
central nervous system ▸ *n.* The portion of the vertebrate nervous system consisting of the brain and spinal cord.
central processing unit ▸ *n.* The part of a computer that interprets and executes instructions.
cen·tre (sĕn′tər) ▸ *n. & v. Chiefly Brit.* Var. of **center.**
cen·trif·u·gal (sĕn-trĭf′yə-gəl, -trĭf′ə-) ▸ *adj.* **1.** Moving or directed away from a center or axis. **2.** Operated by means of centrifugal force. **—cen·trif′u·gal·ly** *adv.*
centrifugal force ▸ *n.* The apparent force, equal and opposite to the centripetal force, drawing a rotating body away from the center of rotation, caused by the inertia of the body.
cen·tri·fuge (sĕn′trə-fyo͞oj′) ▸ *n.* A compartment spun about a central axis to separate contained materials of different densities or to simulate gravity with centrifugal force.
cen·trip·e·tal (sĕn-trĭp′ĭ-tl) ▸ *adj.* **1.** Moving or directed toward a center or axis. **2.** Operated by means of centripetal force. **—cen·trip′e·tal·ly** *adv.*
centripetal force ▸ *n.* The component of force acting on a body in curvilinear motion that is directed toward the center of curvature or axis of rotation.
cen·trism (sĕn′trĭz′əm) ▸ *n.* The political philosophy of avoiding the extremes of right and left by taking a moderate position. **—cen′trist** *adj. & n.*
centro– or **centr–** or **centri–** ▸ *pref.* Center: *centrism.*
cen·tu·ri·on (sĕn-to͝or′ē-ən, -tyo͝or′-) ▸ *n.* The commander of a century in the ancient Roman army.
cen·tu·ry (sĕn′chə-rē) ▸ *n., pl.* **-ries. 1.** A period of 100 years. **2.** A unit of the ancient Roman army orig. consisting of 100 men.
ce·phal·ic (sə-făl′ĭk) ▸ *adj.* Of or relating to the head.
ceph·a·lo·pod (sĕf′ə-lə-pŏd′) ▸ *n.* Any of various marine mollusks, such as the octopus or squid, having a large head, many arms or tentacles, and usu. an ink sac for protection or defense.
ce·ram·ic (sə-răm′ĭk) ▸ *n.* **1.** Any of various hard, brittle, heat-resistant and corrosion-resistant materials made by firing clay or other nonmetallic minerals. **2a.** An object made of ceramic. **b. ceramics** *(takes sing. v.)* The art of making objects of ceramic, esp. from fired clay. **—ce·ram′ic** *adj.* **—ce·ram′ist** *n.*
ce·re·al (sîr′ē-əl) ▸ *n.* **1.** A grass such as wheat, oats, or corn, whose starchy grains are used as food. **2.** A food prepared from such grains.
cer·e·bel·lum (sĕr′ə-bĕl′əm) ▸ *n., pl.* **-lums** or **-bel·la** (-bĕl′ə). The structure of the brain responsible for control of voluntary muscular movement. **—cer′e·bel′lar** *adj.*
cer·e·bral (sĕr′ə-brəl, sə-rē′-) ▸ *adj.* **1.** Of the brain or cerebrum. **2.** Intellectual rather than emotional. **—cer·e′bral·ly** *adv.*
cerebral cortex ▸ *n.* The outer layer of gray matter that covers the two parts of the cerebrum, largely responsible for higher nervous functions.
cerebral palsy ▸ *n.* A disorder usu. caused by brain damage at or before birth and marked by muscular impairment and often poor coordination.
cer·e·brum (sĕr′ə-brəm, sə-rē′-) ▸ *n., pl.* **-brums** or **-bra** (-brə).

THESAURUS

censorious *adj.* —*See* CRITICAL (1).
censurable *adj.* —*See* BLAMEWORTHY.
censure *n.* —*See* CRITICISM.
censure *v.* —*See* CHASTISE, CRITICIZE (1), DEPLORE (1).
censurer *n.* —*See* CRITIC (2).
center *n.* **1.** A place of concentrated activity, influence, or importance ▸ focus, headquarters, heart, hotbed, hub, locus, seat. **2.** A point or area equidistant from all sides of something ▸ median, middle, midpoint, midst, navel, omphalos. **3.** A point of origin or crucial factor ▸ axis, bottom, core, cynosure, focus, heart, hub, nave, nucleus, pivot, quick, root. [*Compare* CRISIS, GERM.] —*See also* HEART (1).
center *v.* —*See* CONCENTRATE.
center *adj.* —*See* CENTRAL.
central *adj.* At, in, near, or being the center ▸ axial, center, centric, equidistant, focal, inmost, innermost, medial, median, mid, middle, middlemost, midmost, nuclear. [*Compare* CONVENIENT.] —*See also* MIDDLE, PRIMARY (1).
centric *adj.* —*See* CENTRAL.
cerebral *adj.* —*See* INTELLECTUAL, MENTAL.
cerebrate *v.* —*See* THINK (1).
cerebration *n.* —*See* THOUGHT.

The large rounded structure of the brain occupying most of the cranial cavity and divided into two cerebral hemispheres.

cere·cloth (sîr′klôth′, -klŏth′) ▸ *n.* Cloth coated with wax, formerly used for wrapping the dead.

cer·e·ment (sĕr′ə-mənt, sîr′mənt) ▸ *n.* **1.** Cerecloth. **2.** often **cerements** A burial garment.

cer·e·mo·ni·al (sĕr′ə-mō′nē-əl) ▸ *adj.* Of or characterized by ceremony. ▸ *n.* **1.** A set of ceremonies for a specific occasion; ritual. **2.** A ceremony. **—cer′e·mo′ni·al·ly** *adv.*

cer·e·mo·ni·ous (sĕr′ə-mō′nē-əs) ▸ *adj.* **1.** Strictly observant of ceremony or etiquette; punctilious. **2.** Characterized by ceremony; formal. **—cer′e·mo′ni·ous·ly** *adv.*

cer·e·mo·ny (sĕr′ə-mō′nē) ▸ *n., pl.* **-nies. 1.** A formal act performed as prescribed by ritual, custom, or etiquette. **2.** A conventional social gesture or courtesy: *the ceremony of shaking hands.* **3.** Strict observance of formalities or etiquette.

Ce·res (sîr′ēz) ▸ *n. Rom. Myth.* The goddess of agriculture.

ce·re·us (sîr′ē-əs) ▸ *n.* Any of a genus of cactus that includes the saguaro and several night-blooming species.

ce·rise (sə-rēs′, -rēz′) ▸ *n.* A purplish red.

ce·ri·um (sîr′ē-əm) ▸ *n. Symbol* **Ce** A lustrous, iron-gray, malleable metallic element, used in various metallurgical and nuclear applications. At. no. 58.

cer·tain (sûr′tn) ▸ *adj.* **1.** Definite; fixed. **2.** Sure to come or happen. **3.** Established beyond doubt. **4.** Having no doubt; confident. **5.** Not identified but assumed to be known: *a certain teacher.* **6.** Limited: *to a certain degree.* ▸ *pron.* An indefinite number; some. **—cer′tain·ly** *adv.*

cer·tain·ty (sûr′tn-tē) ▸ *n., pl.* **-ties. 1.** The fact, quality, or state of being certain. **2.** Something that is clearly established.

cer·tif·i·cate (sər-tĭf′ĭ-kĭt) ▸ *n.* **1.** A document testifying to the truth of something. **2.** A document certifying completion of requirements, as of a course of study. **3.** A document certifying ownership.

cer·ti·fi·ca·tion (sûr′tə-fĭ-kā′shən) ▸ *n.* **1a.** The act of certifying. **b.** The state or condition of being certified. **2.** A certified statement.

cer·ti·fied check (sûr′tə-fīd′) ▸ *n.* A check guaranteed by a bank to be covered by sufficient funds on deposit.

certified public accountant ▸ *n.* An accountant certified by a state examining board as having met the state's legal requirements.

cer·ti·fy (sûr′tə-fī′) ▸ *v.* **1. -fied, -fy·ing.** To confirm formally as true, accurate, or genuine. **2.** To acknowledge on (a check) that the maker has sufficient funds on deposit for payment. **3.** To issue a certificate to. **4.** To declare legally insane. **—cer′ti·fi′a·ble** *adj.* **—cer′ti·fi′a·bly** *adv.* **—cer′ti·fi′er** *n.*

cer·ti·tude (sûr′tĭ-to͞od′, -tyo͞od′) ▸ *n.* The state of being certain.

ce·ru·le·an (sə-ro͞o′lē-ən) ▸ *adj.* Azure; sky-blue.

ce·ru·men (sə-ro͞o′mən) ▸ *n.* See **earwax. —ce·ru′mi·nous** *adj.*

Cer·van·tes Sa·a·ve·dra (sər-văn′tēz sä′ə-vä′drə), **Miguel de** (1547–1616) ▸ Spanish writer.

cer·vi·cal (sûr′vĭ-kəl) ▸ *adj.* Of or relating to a neck or cervix.

cer·vix (sûr′vĭks) ▸ *n., pl.* **-vix·es** or **-vi·ces** (-vĭ-sēz′, sər-vī′sēz). **1.** The neck. **2.** A neck-shaped anatomical structure, such as the outer end of the uterus.

ce·sar·e·an also **cae·sar·e·an** or **cae·sar·i·an** or **ce·sar·i·an** (sĭ-zâr′ē-ən) ▸ *n.* A cesarean section. **—ce·sar′e·an** *adj.*

cesarean section ▸ *n.* A surgical incision through the abdominal wall and uterus to deliver a fetus.

ce·si·um also **cae·si·um** (sē′zē-əm) ▸ *n. Symbol* **Cs** A soft, silvery-white, highly electropositive metallic element, used in photoelectric cells. At. no. 55.

ces·sa·tion (sĕ-sā′shən) ▸ *n.* A ceasing; halt.

ces·sion (sĕsh′ən) ▸ *n.* A ceding or surrendering, as of territory to another country by treaty.

cess·pool (sĕs′po͞ol′) ▸ *n.* A covered hole or pit for receiving drainage, waste, or sewage.

ce·su·ra (sĭ-zho͝or′ə, -zo͝or′ə) ▸ *n.* Var. of **caesura.**

ce·ta·cean (sĭ-tā′shən) ▸ *n.* Any of a group of aquatic, chiefly marine mammals that includes the whales, dolphins, and porpoises. **—ce·ta′cean, ce·ta′ceous** *adj.*

Cey·lon (sĭ-lŏn′, sā-) ▸ See **Sri Lanka. —Cey′lo·nese′** (-nēz′, -nēs′) *adj. & n.*

Cf ▸ The symbol for the element **californium.**

cg ▸ *abbr.* centigram

Cha·blis (shă-blē′, shä-, shăb′lē) ▸ *n.* A very dry white Burgundy wine.

cha-cha (chä′chä) ▸ *n.* A rhythmic ballroom dance that originated in Latin America. **—cha′-cha** *v.*

Chad (chăd) ▸ A country of N-central Africa. **—Chad′i·an** *adj. & n.*

Chad·ic (chăd′ĭk) ▸ *n.* A branch of the Afro-Asiatic language family.

cha·dor (chä-dôr′) ▸ *n.* A loose, usu. black robe worn by Muslim women that covers the body and most of the face.

chafe (chāf) ▸ *v.* **chafed, chaf·ing. 1.** To make or become worn or sore by rubbing. **2.** To annoy; vex. **3.** To heat or warm by rubbing.

chaff[1] (chăf) ▸ *n.* **1.** Grain husks, as of wheat, removed during threshing. **2.** Trivial or worthless matter.

chaff[2] (chăf) ▸ *v.* To tease good-naturedly. **—chaff** *n.*

chaf·finch (chăf′ĭnch) ▸ *n.* A small European songbird.

chaf·ing dish (chā′fĭng) ▸ *n.* A pan mounted above a heating device, used to cook food at the table.

cha·grin (shə-grĭn′) ▸ *n.* A feeling of embarrassment, humiliation, or annoyance. ▸ *v.* To cause to feel chagrin.

chain (chān) ▸ *n.* **1.** A connected, flexible series of links. **2. chains a.** Bonds, fetters, or shackles. **b.** Bondage. **3.** A series of related things. **4.** A number of commercial establishments under common ownership. **5.** A range of mountains. **6a.** An instrument used in surveying, consisting of 100 linked pieces of iron or steel. **b.** A unit of

THESAURUS

ceremonial *adj.* —*See* RITUAL.
ceremonial *n.* —*See* CEREMONY (1).

ceremonious *adj.* Fond of or given to ceremony ▸ conventional, courtly, dignified, formal, official, punctilious, solemn, stately. [*Compare* GRACIOUS, PRUDISH, SERIOUS.] —*See also* RITUAL.

ceremoniousness *n.* —*See* CEREMONY (2).

ceremony *n.* **1.** A formal act or set of acts prescribed by ritual ▸ ceremonial, custom, liturgy, observance, office, ordinance, rite, ritual, service, solemnity, tradition. **2.** Strict observance of social conventions ▸ ceremoniousness, etiquette, form, formality, protocol, punctiliousness. [*Compare* CUSTOM, MANNERS.] —*See also* RITUAL.

certain *adj.* **1.** Bound to happen ▸ ineluctable, inescapable, inevitable, irresistible, necessary, sure, unavoidable. *Idioms:* in the cards, sure as shooting. [*Compare* FATED, IRREVOCABLE, SET[1].] **2.** Established beyond a doubt ▸ conclusive, decisive, hard, inarguable, incontestable, incontrovertible, indisputable, indubitable, irrefutable, positive, sure, unassailable, undeniable, undisputable, unquestionable, unquestioned. [*Compare* AUTHENTIC, DECIDED, IMPLICIT.] —*See also* DEFINITE (3), SEVERAL, SURE (1), SURE (2).

certainly *adv.* —*See* ABSOLUTELY.

certainty *n.* The quality of being actual or factual ▸ actuality, cinch, fact, reality, sure thing, truth. *Idioms:* matter of fact, the case. —*See also* SURENESS.

certification *n.* An assumption of responsibility, as one given by a manufacturer, for the quality, worth, or durability of a product ▸ guarantee, guaranty, surety, warrant, warranty. —*See also* CONFIRMATION (1).

certify *v.* To confirm formally as true, accurate, or genuine ▸ attest, swear (to), testify, verify, witness. *Idiom:* bear witness. [*Compare* PROVE.] —*See also* CONFIRM (3), GUARANTEE (1).

certitude *n.* —*See* CONFIDENCE, SURENESS.

cessation *n.* —*See* END (1), STOP (1), STOP (3).

cesspool or **cesspit** *n.* —*See* PIT[1].

chachka *n.* —*See* NOVELTY (3).

chafe *v.* To make the skin raw by friction ▸ abrade, excoriate, fret, irritate, gall, rub. [*Compare* SCRAPE.] —*See also* ANNOY.

chaff *v.* —*See* JOKE (2).
chaff *n.* —*See* RIBBING.

chagrin *n.* —*See* EMBARRASSMENT.
chagrin *v.* —*See* EMBARRASS, OFFEND (1).

chain *n.* —*See* CORD, SERIES.
chain *v.* —*See* FASTEN, HAMPER[1].

length equal to 100 links, or 66 ft (20.1 m). ▸ *v.* 1. To bind or make fast with a chain. 2. To fetter.
chain gang ▸ *n.* A group of convicts chained together, esp. for outdoor labor.
chain mail ▸ *n.* Flexible armor made of joined metal links or scales.
chain reaction ▸ *n.* 1. A series of events in which each induces or influences the next. 2. *Phys.* A multistage nuclear reaction, esp. a self-sustaining series of fissions in which the release of neutrons from the splitting of one atom leads to the splitting of others. 3. *Chem.* A series of reactions in which one product of a reacting set is a reactant in the following set. **—chain′-re·act′** *v.*
chain saw ▸ *n.* A portable power saw with teeth linked in an endless chain.
chain-smoke (chān′smōk′) ▸ *v.* To smoke (e.g., cigarettes) in close succession. **—chain smoker** *n.*
chain store ▸ *n.* One of a number of retail stores under the same ownership and dealing in the same merchandise.
chair (châr) ▸ *n.* 1. A seat with a back, designed to accommodate one person. 2a. A seat of office, authority, or dignity, such as that of a bishop, chairperson, or professor. b. One who holds such a chair. 3. *Slang* The electric chair. ▸ *v.* To preside over as chairperson.
chair lift ▸ *n.* A mechanized, cable-suspended chair assembly used to transport people up or down a mountain slope.
chair·man (châr′mən) ▸ *n.* The presiding officer of a meeting, committee, or board. **—chair′man·ship′** *n.*
chair·per·son (châr′pûr′sən) ▸ *n.* A chairman or chairwoman.
chair·wom·an (châr′wo͝om′ən) ▸ *n.* A woman presiding officer of a meeting, committee, or board.
chaise (shāz) ▸ *n.* 1. A two-wheeled, horse-drawn carriage with a collapsible hood. 2. A post chaise.
chaise longue (lông′) ▸ *n., pl.* **chaise longues** (lông′). A reclining chair with a lengthened seat to support the outstretched legs.
chal·ced·o·ny (kăl-sĕd′n-ē) ▸ *n., pl.* **-nies.** A translucent milky or grayish quartz.
cha·let (shă-lā′, shăl′ā) ▸ *n.* 1. A wooden dwelling with a sloping roof and overhanging eaves, common in Alpine regions. 2. The hut of an Alpine herder.
chal·ice (chăl′ĭs) ▸ *n.* 1. A cup or goblet. 2. A cup for the consecrated wine of the Eucharist.
chalk (chôk) ▸ *n.* 1. A soft compact calcite, $CaCO_3$, derived chiefly from fossil seashells. 2. A piece of chalk used for marking on a surface such as a blackboard. ▸ *v.* To mark, draw, or write with chalk. ***—phrasal verb:*** **chalk up** 1. To earn or score. 2. To credit: *Chalk that up to experience.* **—chalk′y** *adj.*
chalk·board (chôk′bôrd′) ▸ *n.* A blackboard.
chal·lenge (chăl′ənj) ▸ *n.* 1. A call to engage in a contest, fight, or competition. 2. A demand for an explanation. 3. A sentry's call for identification. 4. A formal objection, esp. to the qualifications of a juror or voter. ▸ *v.* **-lenged, -leng·ing.** 1a. To call to engage in a contest. b. To invite with defiance; dare. 2. To call into question; dispute. 3. To order to halt and be identified. 4. To take formal objection to (a juror or voter). 5. To summon to action or effort; stimulate. **—chal′leng·er** *n.*
chal·lenged (chăl′ənjd) ▸ *adj.* 1. Having a disability or impairment. 2. Deficient or lacking: *ethically challenged.*
chal·leng·ing (chăl′ən-jĭng) ▸ *adj.* Calling for full use of one's abilities or resources.
chal·lis (shăl′ē) ▸ *n.* A lightweight, usu. printed fabric of wool, cotton, or rayon.
cham·ber (chām′bər) ▸ *n.* 1. A room, esp. a bedroom. 2. **chambers** A judge's office. 3. A hall, esp. for the meetings of a legislative or other assembly. 4. A legislative, judicial, or deliberative body. 5. An enclosed space; a compartment or cavity. 6. A compartment in a firearm that holds the cartridge. **—cham′bered** *adj.*
cham·ber·lain (chām′bər-lĭn) ▸ *n.* 1a. A chief steward. b. A high-ranking official in a royal court. 2. A treasurer.
cham·ber·maid (chām′bər-mād′) ▸ *n.* A maid who cleans bedrooms, as in a hotel.
chamber music ▸ *n.* Music, as for a trio or quartet, appropriate for performance in a small concert hall.
chamber of commerce ▸ *n.* An association of businesses for the promotion of commercial interests in the community.
cham·bray (shăm′brā′) ▸ *n.* A fine, lightweight fabric woven with white threads across a colored warp.
cha·me·leon (kə-mēl′yən, -mē′lē-ən) ▸ *n.* 1. Any of various tropical Old World lizards capable of changing color. 2. See **anole.** 3. A changeable person.
cham·fer (chăm′fər) ▸ *v.* 1. To cut off the edge or corner of; bevel. 2. To cut a groove in; flute. **—cham′fer** *n.*
cham·ois (shăm′ē) ▸ *n., pl.* **cham·ois** (shăm′ēz). 1. A goat antelope of mountainous regions of Europe. 2. also **cham·my** or **sham·my** (shăm′ē) *pl.* **-mies.** a. A soft leather made from the hide of a chamois. b. A piece of such leather used esp. as a polishing cloth.
cham·o·mile or **cam·o·mile** (kăm′ə-mīl′, -mēl′) ▸ *n.* An aromatic plant having daisylike white flower heads that are used for herbal tea and in flavorings.
champ[1] (chămp) ▸ *v.* To chew upon noisily. ***—idiom:*** **champ at the bit** To show impatience at being delayed.
champ[2] (chămp) ▸ *n.* *Informal* A champion.
cham·pagne (shăm-pān′) ▸ *n.* A sparkling white wine orig. produced in Champagne.
Cham·pagne (shăm-pān′, shäɴ-pän′yə) ▸ A region and former province of NE France.
cham·pi·on (chăm′pē-ən) ▸ *n.* 1. One that holds first place or wins first prize in a contest. 2. An ardent defender or supporter of a cause or another person. ▸ *v.* To fight for, defend, or support as a champion.
cham·pi·on·ship (chăm′pē-ən-shĭp′) ▸ *n.* 1. The position or title of a champion. 2. Defense or support. 3. A competition held to determine a champion.
Cham·plain (shăm-plān′), **Lake** ▸ A lake of NE NY, NW VT, and S Quebec, Canada.
chance (chăns) ▸ *n.* 1a. The unknown and unpredictable element in happenings that seems to have no assignable cause. b. This element viewed as a cause of events; luck. 2. often **chances** The likelihood of something happening; probability. 3. An accidental or unpredictable event. 4. An opportunity. 5. A risk or hazard. 6. A raffle or lottery ticket. ▸ *v.* **chanced, chanc·ing.** 1. To come about by chance. 2. To risk; hazard. ***—phrasal verb:*** **chance on** To find accidentally; happen upon.
chan·cel (chăn′səl) ▸ *n.* The space around the altar of a

THESAURUS

chains *n.* —*See* BOND (1).
chalet *n.* —*See* VILLA.
challenge *n.* An act of taunting another to do something bold or rash ▸ dare, gauntlet, provocation. —*See also* DEFIANCE (1), OBJECTION.
challenge *v.* To call on another to do something bold ▸ dare, defy. *Idiom:* throw down the gauntlet. —*See also* CLAIM, CONTEST, DEFY (1), OBJECT, RIVAL.
challenger *n.* —*See* COMPETITOR.
challenging *adj.* —*See* DIFFICULT (1).
champ *v.* —*See* CHEW.
champ *n.* —*See* WINNER.
champion *adj.* —*See* EXCELLENT, VICTORIOUS.
champion *v.* —*See* SUPPORT (1).
champion *n.* A person revered especially for noble courage ▸ hero, heroine, paladin. *Idiom:* knight in shining armor. —*See also* ADVOCATE, WINNER.
championship *n.* —*See* PATRONAGE (1).
chance *n.* 1. An unexpected random event ▸ accident, fluke, fortuity, hap, happenchance, happenstance, hazard. [*Compare* EVENT.] 2. The random, unintended, or unpredictable element of an event or the force regarded as the cause of such an event ▸ accident, cast, coincidence, contingency, fortuitousness, fortuity, fortune, hap, hazard, lottery, luck, serendipity. *Idiom:* luck of the draw. [*Compare* FATE, GAMBLE.] 3. The likeliness of a given event occurring ▸ likelihood, odds, possibility, probability, prospects. —*See also* OPPORTUNITY, RISK.
chance *v.* To take place by chance ▸ befall, betide, hap, happen. —*See also* GAMBLE (2), VENTURE.
chance on or **upon** *v.* —*See* ENCOUNTER (1).
chance *adj.* —*See* ACCIDENTAL, RANDOM.

church for the clergy and often the choir.

chan·cel·ler·y or **chan·cel·lor·y** (chăn′sə-lə-rē, -slə-rē) ▸ *n., pl.* **-ies.** **1.** The rank or position of a chancellor. **2.** The office of an embassy or consulate.

chan·cel·lor (chăn′sə-lər, -slər) ▸ *n.* **1.** The chief minister of state in some countries. **2.** The head of a university. **3.** *Law* The presiding judge of a court of equity. **—chan′cel·lor·ship′** *n.*

chan·cer·y (chăn′sə-rē) ▸ *n., pl.* **-ies.** **1.** *Law* **a.** A court with jurisdiction in equity. **b.** An office of archives. **2.** The office of a chancellor.

chan·cre (shăng′kər) ▸ *n.* A dull red, hard, insensitive lesion that is the first sign of syphilis. **—chan′crous** (-krəs) *adj.*

chanc·y (chăn′sē) ▸ *adj.* **-i·er, -i·est.** Uncertain as to outcome; risky.

chan·de·lier (shăn′də-lîr′) ▸ *n.* A branched lighting fixture holding bulbs or candles, usu. suspended from a ceiling.

chan·dler (chănd′lər) ▸ *n.* **1.** One that makes or sells candles. **2.** A dealer in specified goods: *a ship chandler.* **—chan′dler·y** (chănd′lə-rē) *n.*

change (chānj) ▸ *v.* **changed, chang·ing.** **1.** To be or cause to be different; alter. **2.** To interchange. **3.** To exchange for or replace with another. **4.** To transfer from (one conveyance) to another: *change planes.* **5.** To give or receive an equivalent sum of money in lower denominations or in foreign currency. **6.** To put fresh clothes or coverings on. ▸ *n.* **1.** The act or result of changing. **2.** A fresh set of clothing. **3a.** Money of smaller denomination changed for money of higher denomination. **b.** The balance of money returned when an amount given is more than what is due. **c.** Coins. **—change′a·bil′i·ty, change′a·ble·ness** *n.* **—change′a·ble** *adj.* **—change′less** *adj.* **—chang′er** *n.*

change·ling (chānj′lĭng) ▸ *n.* A child secretly exchanged for another.

change of life ▸ *n.* Menopause.

change·o·ver (chānj′ō′vər) ▸ *n.* A conversion, as from one system to another.

Chang Jiang (chăng′ jyăng′) or **Yang·tze River** (yăng′sē′, -tsē′) ▸ The longest river of China and of Asia, flowing about 5,551 km (3,450 mi) from Xizang (Tibet) to the East China Sea.

chan·nel (chăn′əl) ▸ *n.* **1.** The bed of a stream or river. **2.** The deeper part of a river or harbor, esp. a navigable passage. **3.** A strait. **4.** A trench, furrow, or groove. **5.** A tubular passage. **6.** A means of passage. **7.** often **channels** Official routes of communication. **8.** A specified frequency band for the transmission and reception of electromagnetic signals. **9.** A site on a network where online conversations are held in real time. ▸ *v.* **-neled, -nel·ing** also **-nelled, -nel·ling.** **1.** To make or form channels in. **2.** To direct along a channel or path. **—chan′nel·i·za′tion** *n.* **—chan′nel·ize′** *v.*

Channel Islands ▸ A group of British islands in the English Channel off the coast of Normandy, France.

chan·son (shäɴ-sôɴ′) ▸ *n.* A song, esp. a French one.

chant (chănt) ▸ *n.* **1a.** A series of syllables sung on the same note or a limited range of notes. **b.** A canticle sung thus. **2.** A monotonous rhythmic call or shout. ▸ *v.* **1.** To sing (a chant). **2.** To celebrate in song. **3.** To utter (e.g., a slogan) in the manner of a chant. **—chant′er** *n.*

chan·teuse (shäɴ-tœz′) ▸ *n.* A woman singer, esp. in a nightclub.

chan·tey (shăn′tē, chăn′-) ▸ *n., pl.* **-teys.** A song sailors sing to the rhythm of their work.

chan·ti·cleer (chăn′tĭ-klîr′, shăn′-) ▸ *n.* A rooster.

Cha·nu·kah (ᴋʜä′nə-kə, hä′-) ▸ *n.* Var. of **Hanukkah.**

cha·os (kā′ŏs′) ▸ *n.* **1.** Great disorder or confusion. **2.** **Chaos** The disordered state held to have existed before the ordered universe. **—cha·ot′ic** *adj.* **—cha·ot′i·cal·ly** *adv.*

chap¹ (chăp) ▸ *v.* **chapped, chap·ping.** To split or roughen (the skin), esp. from cold or exposure.

chap² (chăp) ▸ *n.* *Informal* A man or boy; fellow.

chap·ar·ral (shăp′ə-răl′) ▸ *n.* A dense thicket of shrubs.

chap·el (chăp′əl) ▸ *n.* **1.** A place of worship that is smaller than and subordinate to a church, esp. in a prison, college, or hospital. **2.** A place of worship for those not belonging to an established church. **3.** The services held at a chapel.

chap·er·on or **chap·er·one** (shăp′ə-rōn′) ▸ *n.* **1.** A person, esp. an older or married woman, who accompanies and supervises young unmarried people. **2.** An older person who attends and supervises a social gathering for young people. ▸ *v.* **-oned, -on·ing.** To act as chaperon to or for.

chap·lain (chăp′lĭn) ▸ *n.* A member of the clergy attached to a chapel, legislative assembly, or military unit. **—chap′lain·cy, chap′lain·ship′** *n.*

chap·let (chăp′lĭt) ▸ *n.* **1.** A wreath for the head. **2.** *Rom. Cath. Ch.* A rosary having beads for five decades. **3.** A string of beads.

chap·man (chăp′mən) ▸ *n.* *Chiefly Brit.* A peddler.

chaps (chăps, shăps) ▸ *pl.n.* Heavy leather trousers without a seat, worn by horseback riders to protect their legs.

chap·ter (chăp′tər) ▸ *n.* **1.** A main division of a book. **2.** A local branch of a club or fraternity. **3.** An assembly of members, as of a religious order.

char¹ (chär) ▸ *v.* **charred, char·ring.** **1.** To scorch or become scorched. **2.** To reduce or be reduced to carbon or charcoal by incomplete combustion.

char² (chär) ▸ *n., pl.* **char** or **chars.** Any of several fishes related to the trout.

char³ (chär) *Chiefly Brit.* ▸ *n.* A charwoman. ▸ *v.* **charred, char·ring.** To work as a charwoman.

THESAURUS

chancy *adj.* *—See* AMBIGUOUS (1), DANGEROUS.

change *v.* **1.** To make different ▸ alter, modify, mutate, shade, shake up, spice up, turn, vary. [*Compare* ADAPT, RENEW, REVISE, REVOLUTIONIZE.] **2.** To become different ▸ alter, change over, develop, evolve, fluctuate, modify, mutate, shift, turn, vacillate, vary. [*Compare* CONVERT.] **3.** To give up in return for something else ▸ barter, commute, exchange, interchange, shift, substitute, switch, trade, transpose. *Informal:* swap. [*Compare* RECIPROCATE.]

change *n.* **1.** The process or result of making or becoming different ▸ alteration, development, evolution, fluctuation, modification, mutation, permutation, shift, variation, vicissitude. [*Compare* ADAPTATION, RENEWAL.] **2.** The act of exchanging or substituting ▸ barter, commutation, exchange, interchange, reciprocation, reciprocity, shift, substitution, switch, trade, transposition. *Informal:* swap. *—See also* CONVERSION (1), TRANSITION.

changeable *adj.* **1.** Capable of or liable to change ▸ alterable, commutative, convertible, fluctuant, fluid, inconstant, kaleidoscopic, labile, modifiable, mutable, permutable, reversible, transformable, transmutable, uncertain, unsettled, unstable, unsteady, variable, variant, varying. [*Compare* MALLEABLE.] **2.** Changing easily, as in expression ▸ fluid, mobile, plastic. [*Compare* UNSTABLE.] *—See also* CAPRICIOUS.

changeless *adj.* *—See* UNCHANGING.

changelessness *n.* The condition of being without change or variation ▸ consistency, constancy, evenness, firmness, fixedness, flatness, immutability, invariableness, invariance, permanence, regularity, sameness, steadiness, unchangingness, unfailingness, uniformity. [*Compare* CONTINUATION, ENDLESSNESS.]

change of heart *n.* *—See* REVERSAL (1).

changeover *n.* *—See* CONVERSION (1).

channel *v.* *—See* CONCENTRATE, CONDUCT (3).

channel *n.* A narrow body of water, usually connecting two larger bodies ▸ narrows, neck, reach, strait. [*Compare* BAY¹, HARBOR, INLET.] *—See also* AGENT, FURROW, WAY (2).

chant *v.* *—See* SING.

chaos *n.* *—See* DISORDER (1), DISORDER (2), DISORDERLINESS.

chaotic *adj.* *—See* CONFUSED (2).

chap *n.* *—See* FELLOW.

chaperon or **chaperone** *v.* *—See* ACCOMPANY.

chaperon or **chaperone** *n.* A guide or companion whose purpose is to ensure propriety or restrict activity ▸ companion, escort. [*Compare* GUIDE.]

chaplain *n.* *—See* CLERIC.

chapter *n.* A particular subdivision of a written work ▸ part, passage, section, segment. *—See also* BRANCH (3).

char *v.* *—See* BURN (1).

char *n.* *—See* BURN.

char·ac·ter (kăr′ək-tər) ► *n.* **1.** The qualities that distinguish one person from another. **2.** A distinguishing feature or attribute. **3.** *Genet.* A structure, function, or attribute determined by a gene or group of genes. **4.** Moral or ethical strength. **5.** Reputation. **6.** An eccentric person. **7.** A person portrayed in a drama or novel. **8.** A symbol in a writing system. **9.** *Comp. Sci.* **a.** A symbol, such as a letter or number, that expresses information. **b.** The code that represents such a symbol.

char·ac·ter·is·tic (kăr′ək-tə-rĭs′tĭk) ► *adj.* Distinctive; typical. ► *n.* A distinguishing attribute. **—char′ac·ter·is′ti·cal·ly** *adv.*

char·ac·ter·ize (kăr′ək-tə-rīz′) ► *v.* **-ized, -iz·ing. 1.** To describe the qualities of. **2.** To be a distinctive trait or mark of. **—char′ac·ter·iz′er** *n.* **—char′ac·ter·i·za′tion** *n.*

cha·rade (shə-rād′) ► *n.* **1. charades** *(takes sing. or pl. v.)* A game in which words or phrases are represented in pantomime until guessed by the other players. **2.** A pretense; sham.

char·broil (chär′broil′) ► *v.* To broil over charcoal: *charbroil a steak.*

char·coal (chär′kōl′) ► *n.* **1.** A black, porous, carbonaceous material produced by the destructive distillation of wood and used as a fuel, filter, and absorbent. **2.** A drawing pencil made from charcoal. **3.** A dark gray.

chard (chärd) ► *n.* Swiss chard.

charge (chärj) ► *v.* **charged, charg·ing. 1.** To impose a duty or responsibility on. **2.** To set as a price. **3.** To demand payment from. **4.** To purchase on credit. **5a.** To load or fill. **b.** To saturate: *an atmosphere charged with tension.* **6.** To instruct or command authoritatively. **7.** To accuse or blame. **8.** To attack violently. **9.** *Elect.* **a.** To cause formation of a net electric charge on or in (a conductor). **b.** To energize (a storage battery). ► *n.* **1.** Price; cost. **2a.** A burden; load. **b.** The quantity that a container or apparatus can hold. **3.** A quantity of explosive to be set off at one time. **4.** A duty or responsibility. **5.** One entrusted to another's care. **6a.** Supervision; management. **b.** Care; custody: *a child put in my charge.* **7.** A command or injunction. **8.** An accusation or indictment. **9.** A rushing, forceful attack. **10.** A debt in an account. **11.** *Symbol* **q** *Phys.* **a.** The intrinsic property of matter responsible for all electric phenomena, occurring in two forms arbitrarily designated *negative* and *positive.* **b.** A measure of this property. **12.** *Informal* A feeling of pleasant excitement; thrill.

charge account ► *n.* A credit arrangement in which a customer receives purchased goods or services before paying for them.

charge card ► *n.* See **credit card.**

char·gé d'af·faires (shär-zhā′ də-fâr′, dä-) ► *n., pl.* **char·gés d'affaires** (-zhā′, -zhāz′). A diplomat who temporarily substitutes for an absent ambassador or minister.

charg·er (chär′jər) ► *n.* **1.** One that charges, such as a device that charges storage batteries. **2.** A horse trained for battle.

char·i·ot (chăr′ē-ət) ► *n.* An ancient horse-drawn two-wheeled vehicle used in war, races, and processions. **—char′i·o·teer′** *n.*

cha·ris·ma (kə-rĭz′mə) ► *n.* A personal quality attributed to those who arouse fervent popular devotion and enthusiasm.

char·is·mat·ic (kăr′ĭz-măt′ĭk) ► *adj.* **1.** Of or relating to charisma. **2.** Of or being a type of Christianity that emphasizes personal religious experience and divinely inspired powers. ► *n.* A member of a Christian charismatic group.

char·i·ta·ble (chăr′ĭ-tə-bəl) ► *adj.* **1.** Generous to the needy. **2.** Tolerant in judging others. **3.** Of or for charity. **—char′i·ta·bly** *adv.*

char·i·ty (chăr′ĭ-tē) ► *n., pl.* **-ties. 1.** Help or relief given to the poor. **2.** An organization or fund that helps the needy. **3.** Benevolence toward others. **4.** Forbearance in judging others. **5.** often **Charity** *Christianity* Love directed first toward God but also toward oneself and one's neighbors.

char·la·tan (shär′lə-tən) ► *n.* A person who makes elaborate and fraudulent claims to skill or knowledge. **—char′la·tan·ism, char′la·tan·ry** *n.*

Char·le·magne (shär′lə-mān′). Also called Charles I or **"Charles the Great"** (742?–814) ► King of the Franks (768–814); emperor of the West (800–814).

Charles (chärlz). Prince of Wales (b. 1948) ► Prince of Wales (since 1969).

Charles·ton[1] (chärl′stən) ► The capital of WV, in the W-central part.

Charles·ton[2] (chärl′stən) ► *n.* A fast ballroom dance popular in the 1920s.

char·ley horse (chär′lē) ► *n.* *Informal* A muscle cramp.

Char·lotte·town (shär′lət-toun′) ► The capital of Prince Edward I., Canada, on the S coast.

charm (chärm) ► *n.* **1.** The quality of pleasing or delighting. **2.** A small ornament worn on a bracelet. **3.** An item worn for its supposed magical benefit; amulet. **4.** An action or formula thought to have magical power. ► *v.* **1.** To

THESAURUS

character *n.* **1.** The combination of emotional, intellectual, and moral qualities that distinguishes an individual ► complexion, disposition, makeup, nature, personality, temperament. [*Compare* DISPOSITION, IDENTITY, PSYCHOLOGY.] **2.** Moral or ethical strength ► fiber, honesty, honor, integrity, principle, probity, uprightness. [*Compare* GOOD.] **3.** A statement attesting to personal qualifications, character, and dependability ► recommendation, reference, testimonial. [*Compare* ENDORSEMENT.] **4.** Public estimation of someone ► name, report, reputation, repute. *Informal:* rep. [*Compare* IMAGE, STATUS.] **5.** One who is appealingly odd or curious ► eccentric, oddity, original. *Informal:* card, case, oddball. *Slang:* flake. [*Compare* CRACKPOT.] **6.** One portrayed in fiction or drama ► part, persona, personage, role. **7.** A conventional mark used in a writing system ► figure, letter, mark, sign, symbol. *—See also* DIGNITARY, QUALITY (1).

character assassination *n.* *—See* LIBEL.

characteristic *adj.* *—See* SPECIAL.

characteristic *n.* *—See* QUALITY (1).

characterization *n.* *—See* REPRESENTATION.

characterize *v.* *—See* CALL, DISTINGUISH (2), REPRESENT (2).

charade *n.* *—See* FAÇADE (2).

charbroil *v.* *—See* COOK.

charge *v.* **1.** To cause to be filled, as with a particular mood or tone ► fill, imbue, impregnate, permeate, pervade, saturate, suffuse, transfuse. [*Compare* STEEP[2].] **2.** To place a trust upon ► entrust, trust. [*Compare* AUTHORIZE.] **3.** To put explosive material into a weapon ► load, prime, ready. *—See also* ACCUSE, ATTACK (1), ATTRIBUTE, BILL[1], BURDEN[1], COMMAND (1), COMMIT (2), FILL (1).

charge in *v.* *—See* INTRUDE.

charge with *v.* *—See* IMPOSE ON.

charge *n.* **1.** A swift advance or attack ► blitz, blitzkrieg, onslaught, raid, rush. [*Compare* ATTACK, INVASION.] **2.** A person who relies on another person for support ► dependent, ward. *—See also* ACCUSATION, CARE (2), COMMAND (1), COST (1), DETENTION, DUTY (1), KICK, MANAGEMENT, MISSION (1), TOLL[1] (1).

chariness *n.* *—See* CAUTION.

charisma *n.* *—See* ATTRACTION.

charitable *adj.* Of or concerned with charity ► altruistic, benevolent, eleemosynary, philanthropic. [*Compare* BENEVOLENT.] *—See also* HUMANITARIAN, TOLERANT.

charitableness *n.* *—See* BENEVOLENCE, TOLERANCE.

charity *n.* *—See* BENEVOLENCE, DONATION, MERCY, TOLERANCE.

charlatan *n.* *—See* FAKE.

charm *v.* **1.** To please greatly or irresistibly ► beguile, bewitch, captivate, enchant, entrance, fascinate, win over. [*Compare* DELIGHT, SEDUCE.] **2.** To act upon with or as if with magic ► bewitch, enchant, ensorcell, enthrall, entrance, hypnotize, mesmerize, spell, spellbind, vamp, voodoo, witch. [*Compare* ENRAPTURE.] *—See also* AMUSE.

charm *n.* A small object worn or kept for its supposed magical power ► amulet, fetish, grigri, juju, mascot, mojo, obeah, periapt, phylactery,

attract or delight greatly. **2.** To cast or seem to cast a spell on; bewitch. **—charm′er** *n.* **—charm′ing·ly** *adv.*

char·nel house (chär′nəl) ▸ *n.* **1.** A repository for the bones or bodies of the dead. **2.** A scene of great carnage or loss of life.

Char·on (kâr′ən) ▸ *n. Gk. Myth.* The ferryman of Hades.

chart (chärt) ▸ *n.* **1.** A map. **2.** A sheet presenting information in the form of graphs or tables. ▸ *v.* **1.** To make a chart of. **2.** To plan.

char·ter (chär′tər) ▸ *n.* **1.** A document issued by a government authority, creating a corporation and defining its privileges and purposes. **2.** A document outlining the organization of a corporate body. **3.** An authorization from an organization to establish a local chapter. **4a.** A contract to lease a vessel. **b.** The hiring of an aircraft, vessel, or other vehicle. ▸ *v.* **1.** To grant a charter to. **2.** To hire or lease by charter.

charter member ▸ *n.* An original member of an organization.

charter school ▸ *n.* An independent public school, often with a distinct curriculum and educational philosophy.

char·treuse (shär-tro͞oz′) ▸ *n.* A strong greenish yellow to yellow green.

char·wom·an (chär′wo͝om′ən) ▸ *n.* A cleaning woman.

char·y (châr′ē) ▸ *adj.* **-i·er, -i·est.** **1.** Very cautious. **2.** Not giving freely; sparing. **—char′i·ly** *adv.* **—char′i·ness** *n.*

chase[1] (chās) ▸ *v.* **chased, chas·ing.** **1.** To follow rapidly in order to catch; pursue. **2.** To hunt. **3.** To put to flight: *chased the dog away.* ▸ *n.* **1.** The act of chasing. **2.** The hunting of game.

chase[2] (chās) ▸ *n.* **1.** A groove cut in an object; slot. **2.** A trench or channel for drainpipes or wiring. ▸ *v.* **chased, chas·ing.** To decorate (metal) by engraving or embossing.

chas·er (chā′sər) ▸ *n.* **1.** One that chases. **2.** *Informal* A drink of beer or water taken after hard liquor.

chasm (kăz′əm) ▸ *n.* **1.** A deep opening in the earth; gorge. **2.** A great disparity, as of opinion or interests.

Chas·sid (KHä′sĭd, KHô′-, hä′-) ▸ *n.* Var. of **Hasid.** **—Chas·si′dic** *adj.* **—Chas·si′dism** *n.*

chas·sis (shăs′ē, chăs′ē) ▸ *n., pl.* **chas·sis** (-ēz). **1.** The rectangular steel frame that holds the body and motor of an automotive vehicle. **2.** The landing gear of an aircraft. **3.** The framework to which the components of a radio, television, or other electronic equipment are attached.

chaste (chāst) ▸ *adj.* **chast·er, chast·est.** **1.** Morally pure; modest. **2.** Abstaining from illicit sexual acts or thoughts. **3.** Simple in design or style; austere. **—chaste′ly** *adv.* **—chaste′ness** *n.* **—chas′ti·ty** (chăs′tĭ-tē) *n.*

chas·ten (chā′sən) ▸ *v.* **1.** To correct by punishment or reproof. **2.** To restrain; subdue. **—chas′ten·er** *n.*

chas·tise (chăs-tīz′, chăs′tīz′) ▸ *v.* **-tised, -tis·ing.** **1.** To punish, as by beating. **2.** To criticize severely. **—chas·tise′ment** *n.* **—chas·tis′er** *n.*

chas·u·ble (chăz′ə-bəl, chăzh′-, chăs′-) ▸ *n.* A long sleeveless vestment worn over the alb by a priest at Mass.

chat (chăt) ▸ *v.* **chat·ted, chat·ting.** **1.** To converse in an easy manner. **2.** To converse in real time over a computer network. ▸ *n.* **1.** An informal conversation. **2.** Any of several birds with a chattering call. **—chat′ti·ness** *n.* **—chat′ty** *adj.*

cha·teau also **châ·teau** (shă-tō′) ▸ *n., pl.* **-teaus** or **-teaux** (-tōz′). **1.** A French castle. **2.** A large country house.

chat·room (chăt′ro͞om′, -ro͝om′) ▸ *n.* A site on a computer network where online conversations are held in real time.

chat·tel (chăt′l) ▸ *n.* **1.** *Law* An article of personal, movable property. **2.** A slave.

chat·ter (chăt′ər) ▸ *v.* **1.** To talk rapidly and incessantly on trivial subjects. **2.** To utter inarticulate speechlike sounds. **3.** To click quickly and repeatedly, as the teeth from cold. **—chat′ter** *n.*

chat·ter·box (chăt′ər-bŏks′) ▸ *n.* An extremely talkative person.

Chau·cer (chô′sər), **Geoffrey** (1340?–1400) ▸ English poet.

chauf·feur (shō′fər, shō-fûr′) ▸ *n.* One employed to drive an automobile. **—chauf′feur** *v.*

chau·vin·ism (shō′və-nĭz′əm) ▸ *n.* **1.** Fanatical patriotism. **2.** Prejudiced belief in the superiority of one's own group. **—chau′vin·ist** *n.* **—chau′vin·is′tic** *adj.* **—chau′vin·is′ti·cal·ly** *adv.*

cheap (chēp) ▸ *adj.* **-er, -est.** **1.** Inexpensive. **2.** Charging low prices. **3.** Achieved with little effort. **4.** Of little value. **5.** Of poor quality; inferior. **6.** Vulgar or contemptible. **7.** Stingy. ▸ *adv.* **-er, -est.** Inexpensively: *got the new car cheap.* **—cheap′ly** *adv.* **—cheap′ness** *n.*

cheap·en (chē′pən) ▸ *v.* **1.** To make or become cheap. **2.** To debase or degrade.

cheap shot ▸ *n.* An unfair verbal attack on a vulnerable target.

cheap·skate (chēp′skāt′) ▸ *n. Slang* A miser.

cheat (chēt) ▸ *v.* **1.** To deceive by trickery; swindle. **2.** To

THESAURUS

talisman. [*Compare* MAGIC.] *—See also* ATTRACTION, SPELL[2].

charmer *n.* *—See* SEDUCER (1).

charming *adj.* *—See* ATTRACTIVE, DELIGHTFUL.

chart *n.* An orderly columnar display of data ▸ table, tabulation. [*Compare* LIST[1].]

chart *v.* *—See* DESIGN (1), PLOT (1).

charter *v.* To engage the temporary use of something for a fee ▸ hire, lease, rent. [*Compare* LEASE.]

charter *n.* *—See* AGREEMENT (1), LAW (1).

chary *adj.* *—See* ECONOMICAL, WARY.

chase *v.* *—See* COURT (2), DRIVE (3), FOLLOW (3), HUNT, PURSUE (1).

chase *n.* The following of another in an attempt to overtake and capture ▸ hot pursuit, hunt, pursuit.

chasm *n.* *—See* DEEP, GAP (1).

chaste *adj.* Morally beyond reproach, especially in sexual conduct ▸ celibate, continent, decent, modest, moral, pure, virgin, virginal, virtuous. *Idiom:* pure as the driven snow. [*Compare* INNOCENT.]

chasten *v.* To castigate for the purpose of improving ▸ chide, correct. *—See also* CHASTISE.

chastise *v.* To criticize for a fault or an offense ▸ admonish, berate, call down, castigate, censure, chasten, chide, dress down, jump (on *or* all over), lecture, objurgate, rap, rebuke, reprimand, reproach, reprove, scold, tax, upbraid. *Informal:* bawl out, lambaste, tell off. *Slang:* chew out. ***Idioms:*** blow up at, bring (*or* call *or* take) to task, call on the carpet, give hell to, give it to, haul over the coals, jump down someone's throat, lay someone out in lavender, let someone have it, rake over the coals. [*Compare* CRITICIZE, REVILE, SLAM.] *—See also* PUNISH.

chastisement *n.* *—See* PUNISHMENT.

chastity *n.* The condition of being chaste ▸ celibacy, decency, innocence, modesty, morality, purity, virginity, virtue, virtuousness.

chat *v.* *—See* CONVERSE[1].

chat *n.* *—See* CHATTER, CONVERSATION.

chattel *n.* *—See* EFFECTS, SLAVE.

chatter *v.* **1.** To talk rapidly and incessantly on trivial matters ▸ babble, blab, blabber, chitchat, clack, drivel, jabber, natter, palaver, patter, prate, prattle, rattle (on), run on, tattle. *Informal:* go on, ramble (on), spiel, yammer. *Slang:* chin wag, gab, gas, jaw, yak. ***Idioms:*** bend someone's ear, run off at the mouth, shoot the breeze (*or* bull). [*Compare* SPEAK.] **2.** To make or cause to make a succession of short, sharp sounds ▸ brattle, clack, clank, clatter, rattle. [*Compare* KNOCK, SHAKE.] *—See also* BABBLE, GOSSIP.

chatter *n.* Incessant and usually inconsequential talk ▸ babble, blab, blabber, chat, chitchat, clack, drivel, jabber, palaver, patter, prate, prattle, small talk, tattle. *Informal:* yammer. *Slang:* gab, gas, yak. [*Compare* SPEECH.]

chatty *adj.* *—See* CONVERSATIONAL, TALKATIVE.

chauffeur *n.* A person who operates a motor vehicle ▸ driver, motorist, operator.

chauffeur *v.* *—See* DRIVE (1).

chaw *n.* *—See* CHEW.

cheap *adj.* Low in price ▸ bargain-basement, budget, dirt-cheap, economy, frugal, inexpensive, low, low-cost, low-priced. *Idiom:* for a song. [*Compare* MEAGER.] *—See also* SHODDY, STINGY.

cheapen *v.* *—See* DEBASE, DEPRECIATE.

cheapskate *n.* *—See* MISER.

cheat *v.* **1.** To get money or something else from someone by deceitful trickery ▸ bilk, burn, cozen, defraud, fleece,

act dishonestly. **3.** To elude; escape: *cheat death.* **4.** To be sexually unfaithful. ▸ *n.* **1.** A fraud or swindle. **2.** One that cheats; swindler. **—cheat′er** *n.* **—cheat′ing·ly** *adv.*

Chech·en (chĕch′ən) ▸ *n.* **1.** A native or inhabitant of Chechnya. **2.** The Caucasian language of the Chechens.

Chech·nya (chĕch′nē-ə, chĕch-nyä′) ▸ A region of SW Russia in the N Caucasus bordering on Georgia.

check (chĕk) ▸ *n.* **1.** A curb or restraint. **2.** An abrupt stop or halt. **3.** An instance of inspecting or testing. **4.** A standard for inspecting or evaluating. **5.** A mark to show verification. **6.** A slip for identification: *a baggage check.* **7.** A bill at a restaurant or bar. **8.** A written order to a bank to pay an amount from funds on deposit. **9a.** A pattern of small squares. **b.** A fabric patterned with squares. **10.** *Games* A move in chess that directly attacks an opponent's king. **11.** *Sports* The act of checking in ice hockey. ▸ *v.* **1.** To arrest the motion of abruptly. **2.** To curb; restrain. **3.** To inspect, as to determine accuracy or quality: *check the brakes.* **4.** To verify: *check a spelling in the dictionary.* **5.** To put a check mark on. **6.** To deposit for temporary safekeeping: *check one's coat.* **7.** *Sports* To block or impede (an opposing player with the puck) in ice hockey by using one's body or one's stick. ***—phrasal verbs:*** **check in** To register, as at a hotel. **check out 1.** To settle one's bill and leave, as from a hotel. **2.** To withdraw (an item) after recording the withdrawal: *check out books.* **3.** To pay for purchases, as at a supermarket. **—check′a·ble** *adj.*

check·book (chĕk′bo͝ok′) ▸ *n.* A book containing blank checks issued by a bank.

check·er (chĕk′ər) ▸ *n.* **1a.** One that checks. **b.** One who receives items for temporary safekeeping: *a baggage checker.* **2.** *Games* **a. checkers** *(takes sing. v.)* A game played on a checkerboard by two players, each using 12 pieces. **b.** One of the round flat pieces used in this game. ▸ *v.* To mark with a checked or squared pattern.

check·er·board (chĕk′ər-bôrd′) ▸ *n.* A board on which chess and checkers are played, divided into 64 squares of two alternating colors.

check·ered (chĕk′ərd) ▸ *adj.* **1.** Divided into squares. **2.** Having light and dark patches. **3.** Marked by great changes in fortune: *a checkered career.*

check·ing account (chĕk′ĭng) ▸ *n.* A bank account against which checks may be written drawing from amounts on deposit.

check·mate (chĕk′māt′) ▸ *v.* **-mat·ed, -mat·ing. 1.** To attack (a chess opponent's king) in such a manner that no escape or defense is possible, thus ending the game. **2.** To defeat completely. **—check′mate′** *n.*

check·out (chĕk′out′) ▸ *n.* **1.** The act, time, or place of checking out, as at a hotel, library, or supermarket. **2.** A test, as of a machine, for proper functioning. **3.** An investigation.

check·point (chĕk′point′) ▸ *n.* A place where surface traffic is stopped for inspection.

check·rein (chĕk′rān′) ▸ *n.* A short rein that extends from a horse's bit to the saddle to keep the horse from lowering its head.

check·room (chĕk′ro͞om′, -ro͝om′) ▸ *n.* A place where items, such as hats or packages, can be stored temporarily.

check·up (chĕk′ŭp′) ▸ *n.* **1.** An examination or inspection. **2.** A physical examination.

Ched·dar also **ched·dar** (chĕd′ər) ▸ *n.* Any of several types of smooth hard cheese varying in flavor from mild to extra sharp.

cheek (chēk) ▸ *n.* **1.** The fleshy part of either side of the face below the eye and between the nose and ear. **2.** Either of the buttocks. **3.** Impertinence. ***—idiom:*** **cheek by jowl** Close together.

cheek·bone (chēk′bōn′) ▸ *n.* A small bone forming the prominence of the cheek.

cheek·y (chē′kē) ▸ *adj.* **-i·er, -i·est.** Impertinent. **—cheek′i·ly** *adv.* **—cheek′i·ness** *n.*

cheep (chēp) ▸ *n.* A faint shrill sound like that of a young bird. ▸ *v.* To chirp.

cheer (chîr) ▸ *n.* **1.** Gaiety or joy. **2.** A source of happiness or comfort. **3.** A shout of encouragement or congratulation. ▸ *v.* **1.** To make or become happier. **2.** To encourage with cheers. **3.** To salute or acclaim with cheers. **4.** To shout cheers. **—cheer′y** *adj.* **—cheer′less** *adj.* **—cheer′i·ly** *adv.* **—cheer′i·ness** *n.*

cheer·ful (chîr′fəl) ▸ *adj.* **1.** In good spirits. **2.** Promoting cheer. **—cheer′ful·ly** *adv.* **—cheer′ful·ness** *n.*

cheer·lead·er (chîr′lē′dər) ▸ *n.* One who leads the cheering of spectators, as at a sports contest.

cheers (chîrz) ▸ *interj.* Used as a toast.

cheese (chēz) ▸ *n.* A solid food prepared from the pressed curd of milk.

cheese·burg·er (chēz′bûr′gər) ▸ *n.* A hamburger topped with melted cheese.

cheese·cake (chēz′kāk′) ▸ *n.* **1.** A cake made of cottage or cream cheese, eggs, milk, and sugar. **2.** *Informal* Photographs of minimally attired women.

cheese·cloth (chēz′klôth′, -klŏth′) ▸ *n.* A coarse, loosely woven cotton gauze.

chees·y (chē′zē) ▸ *adj.* **-i·er, -i·est. 1.** Containing or resembling cheese. **2.** *Informal* Of poor quality; shoddy. **—chees′i·ness** *n.*

chee·tah (chē′tə) ▸ *n.* A long-legged, swift-running spotted wild cat of Africa and SW Asia.

chef (shĕf) ▸ *n.* A cook, esp. a chief cook.

THESAURUS

game, gull, hoax, mulct, overcharge, rook, swindle, victimize. *Informal:* chisel, flimflam, shortchange, take, trim. *Slang:* clip, con, diddle, do, gouge, nick, rip off, scalp, scam, skin, soak, stick, sting. *Idioms:* load the dice, stack the cards (*or* deck), take someone for a ride, take someone to the cleaners. [*Compare* DECEIVE, PIRATE, STEAL.] **2.** To be sexually unfaithful to another ▸ philander. *Informal:* fool around, mess around, play around. *Slang:* two-time. *—See also* DECEIVE.

cheat *n.* **1.** An act of cheating ▸ burn, deceit, fraud, hoax, humbug, masquerade, swindle, victimization. *Informal:* flimflam. *Slang:* con, grift, scam, sting. **2.** A person who cheats ▸ bilk, blackleg, cardsharp, cheater, cozener, deceiver, defrauder, dodger, knave, masquerader, rook, sharper, swindler, trickster, victimizer. *Informal:* chiseler, crook, flimflammer. *Slang:* diddler, grifter, scammer, shill. [*Compare* FAKE.]

cheater *n.* *—See* CHEAT (2), PHILANDERER.

check *n.* *—See* ACCOUNT (2), EXAMINATION (1), RESTRAINT, STOP (1).

check *v.* *—See* AGREE (1), EXAMINE (1), FRUSTRATE, REPEL, RESTRAIN, STOP (2), STOP (1), TEST (1).

check in *v.* *—See* ARRIVE (1).

check out *v.* *—See* DIE.

checked *adj.* *—See* RESTRICTED.

checklist *n.* *—See* LIST[1].

checkmate *v.* *—See* DEFEAT, FRUSTRATE.

checkmate *n.* *—See* DEFEAT.

checkup *n.* *—See* EXAMINATION (1), EXAMINATION (2).

cheek or **cheekiness** *n.* *—See* IMPUDENCE.

cheeky *adj.* *—See* DISRESPECTFUL, IMPUDENT.

cheer *n.* *—See* HAPPINESS, PRAISE (1).

cheer *v.* To express approval audibly, as by clapping ▸ applaud, clap, root. *Idioms:* give a big hand (*or* welcome), give an ovation, give someone a hand, put one's hands together. *—See also* AMUSE, DELIGHT (1), ENCOURAGE (1), ENCOURAGE (2), PRAISE (1).

cheerful *adj.* Being in or showing good spirits ▸ animated, blithesome, boon, bright, cheery, chipper, convivial, exhilarated, gay, glad, gleeful, happy, jocund, jolly, jovial, joyful, lighthearted, merry, mirthful, sunny. *Idiom:* on top of the world. [*Compare* LIGHTHEARTED, LIVELY.] *—See also* MERRY, OPTIMISTIC.

cheerfulness *n.* *—See* HAPPINESS, OPTIMISM.

cheering *adj.* *—See* ENCOURAGING.

cheerless *adj.* *—See* GLOOMY, SORROWFUL.

cheery *adj.* *—See* CHEERFUL, MERRY.

cheesy *adj.* *—See* SHODDY.

chef *n.* A person who prepares food for eating ▸ baker, cook, culinary artist.

chef-d'oeu·vre (shā-dœ′vrə, -dûrv′) ▸ *n., pl.* **chefs-d'oeuvre** (shā-). A masterpiece.
chef's salad (shĕfs) ▸ *n.* A tossed green salad usu. with raw vegetables, hard-boiled eggs, and julienne strips of cheese and meat.
chem·i·cal (kĕm′ĭ-kəl) ▸ *adj.* **1.** Of or relating to chemistry. **2.** Involving or produced by chemicals. ▸ *n.* A substance produced by or used in a chemical process. **—chem′i·cal·ly** *adv.*
chemical bond ▸ *n.* Any of several forces or mechanisms, esp. the ionic bond, covalent bond, and metallic bond, by which atoms or ions are bound in a molecule or crystal.
chemical dependency ▸ *n.* A physical and psychological habituation to a mood- or mind-altering drug, such as alcohol or cocaine.
chemical engineering ▸ *n.* The technology of large-scale chemical production. **—chemical engineer** *n.*
chemical warfare ▸ *n.* Warfare involving poisons, contaminants, and irritants.
chem·i·lu·mi·nes·cence (kĕm′ə-lo͞o′mə-nĕs′əns) ▸ *n.* Emission of light as a result of a chemical reaction at environmental temperatures. **—chem′i·lu′mi·nes′cent** *adj.*
che·mise (shə-mēz′) ▸ *n.* **1.** A woman's loose, shirtlike undergarment. **2.** A dress that hangs straight from the shoulders.
chem·ist (kĕm′ĭst) ▸ *n.* **1.** A scientist specializing in chemistry. **2.** *Chiefly Brit.* A pharmacist.
chem·is·try (kĕm′ĭ-strē) ▸ *n., pl.* **-tries. 1.** The science of the composition, structure, properties, and reactions of matter, esp. of atomic and molecular systems. **2.** The composition, structure, properties, and reactions of a substance. **3.** The interrelation of elements in a complex entity. **4.** Mutual attraction; rapport.
che·mo (kē′mō, kĕm′ō) ▸ *n. Informal* Chemotherapy.
chemo– or **chemi–** or **chem–** ▸ *pref.* Chemicals; chemical: *chemurgy.*
che·mo·re·cep·tion (kē′mō-rĭ-sĕp′shən, kĕm′ō-) ▸ *n.* The response of a sense organ to a chemical stimulus. **—che′mo·re·cep′tive** *adj.* **—che′mo·re′cep·tiv′i·ty** *n.* **—che′mo·re·cep′tor** *n.*
che·mo·syn·the·sis (kē′mō-sĭn′thĭ-sĭs, kĕm′ō-) ▸ *n.* Synthesis of carbohydrate from carbon dioxide and water using energy from a chemical reaction rather than from light. **—che′mo·syn·thet′ic** *adj.*
che·mo·ther·a·py (kē′mō-thĕr′ə-pē, kĕm′ō-) ▸ *n.* The treatment of cancer and other diseases using specific chemical agents or drugs. **—che′mo·ther′a·peu′tic** *adj.* **—che′mo·ther′a·pist** *n.*
chem·ur·gy (kĕm′ər-jē, kĭ-mûr′-) ▸ *n.* The development of new industrial chemical products from organic raw materials, esp. from those of agricultural origin. **—che·mur′gic, che·mur′gi·cal** *adj.*
che·nille (shə-nēl′) ▸ *n.* **1.** A soft tufted cord of silk, cotton, or worsted. **2.** Fabric made of this cord.
Chen·nai (chə-nī′) Formerly **Ma·dras** (mə-drăs′, -dräs′) ▸ A city of SE India on the Bay of Bengal.
cheque (chĕk) ▸ *n. Chiefly Brit.* Var. of **check.**
cheq·uer (chĕk′ər) ▸ *n. Chiefly Brit.* Var. of **checker.**
cher·ish (chĕr′ĭsh) ▸ *v.* To treat with affection; hold dear.
Cher·no·byl (chər-nō′bəl) ▸ A city of N-central Ukraine NNW of Kiev; site of a nuclear power plant accident (Apr. 16, 1986).
Cher·o·kee (chĕr′ə-kē′, chĕr′ə-kē′) ▸ *n., pl.* **-kee** or **-kees. 1.** A member of a Native American people formerly of the S Appalachians, now living in NE Oklahoma and W North Carolina. **2.** Their Iroquoian language.
che·root (shə-ro͞ot′) ▸ *n.* A cigar with square-cut ends.
cher·ry (chĕr′ē) ▸ *n., pl.* **-ries. 1.** Any of several trees or shrubs having pink or white flowers and small juicy drupes. **2.** The yellow, red, or blackish fruit of any of these plants. **3.** The wood of a cherry tree. **4.** A strong red to purplish red.
cherry tomato ▸ *n.* A variety of tomato having red to yellow, cherry-sized fruits.
chert (chûrt) ▸ *n.* A variety of silica containing microcrystalline quartz.
cher·ub (chĕr′əb) ▸ *n.* **1.** *pl.* **cher·u·bim** (chĕr′ə-bĭm′, -yə-bĭm′). One of the 2nd order of angels. **2.** *pl.* **cher·ubs.** A small angel, portrayed as a winged child with a chubby, rosy face. **—che·ru′bic** (chə-ro͞o′bĭk) *adj.*
cher·vil (chûr′vəl) ▸ *n.* A Eurasian herb with parsleylike leaves used as a seasoning or garnish.
Ches·a·peake Bay (chĕs′ə-pēk′) ▸ An inlet of the Atlantic separating the Delmarva Peninsula from mainland MD and VA.
chess (chĕs) ▸ *n.* A board game for two players, each beginning with 16 pieces, with the objective of checkmating the opposing king.
chess·board (chĕs′bôrd′) ▸ *n.* A board with 64 squares, used in playing chess.
chess·man (chĕs′măn′, -mən) ▸ *n.* One of the pieces used in chess.
chest (chĕst) ▸ *n.* **1.** The part of the body between the neck and the abdomen. **2a.** A sturdy box with a lid, used for storage. **b.** A small closet or cabinet: *a medicine chest.* **3.** A bureau; dresser.
ches·ter·field (chĕs′tər-fēld′) ▸ *n.* An overcoat with a velvet collar.
chest·nut (chĕs′nŭt′, -nət) ▸ *n.* **1.** Any of several deciduous trees having nuts enclosed in a prickly husk. **2.** The often edible nut of these trees. **3.** The wood of a chestnut tree. **4.** A deep reddish brown. **5.** A stale joke or story.
chev·a·lier (shĕv′ə-lîr′) ▸ *n.* **1.** A member of certain orders of knighthood or merit. **2.** A French nobleman of the lowest rank.
Chev·i·ot (shĕv′ē-ət, chĕv′-) ▸ *n.* **1.** A hornless sheep with short thick wool. **2.** also **cheviot** A woolen fabric with a coarse twill weave.
chev·ron (shĕv′rən) ▸ *n.* A badge or insignia consisting of stripes meeting at an angle, worn on the sleeve of a military or police uniform to indicate rank, merit, or length of service.
chew (cho͞o) ▸ *v.* **1.** To grind and crush with the teeth. **2.** To ponder: *chew a problem over.* ***—phrasal verb:* chew out** *Slang* To scold. ▸ *n.* **1.** The act of chewing. **2.** Something chewed. ***—idiom:* chew the fat** *Slang* To talk in a leisurely way. **—chew′a·ble** *adj.* **—chew′er** *n.*
chew·ing gum (cho͞o′ĭng) ▸ *n.* A sweetened, flavored preparation for chewing, usu. made of chicle.
chew·y (cho͞o′ē) ▸ *adj.* **-i·er, -i·est.** Needing much chewing. **—chew′i·ness** *n.*
Chey·enne[1] (shī-ĕn′, -ăn′) ▸ *n., pl.* **-enne** or **-ennes. 1.** A member of a Native American people of the W Great Plains, now living in Montana and Oklahoma. **2.** The Algonquian language of the Cheyenne.
Chey·enne[2] (shī-ăn′, -ĕn′) ▸ The capital of WY, in the SE part.
chi[1] (kī) ▸ *n.* The 22nd letter of the Greek alphabet.
chi[2] (chē) ▸ *n.* The vital force believed in Taoism and other Chinese thought to be inherent in all things.
chi·a·ro·scu·ro (kē-är′ə-sko͝or′ō, -skyo͝or′ō) ▸ *n.* The technique of using light and shade in pictorial representation. **—chi·a′ro·scu′rist** *n.*
chic (shēk) ▸ *adj.* **chic·er, chic·est.** Stylish. **—chic** *n.* **—chic′ly** *adv.* **—chic′ness** *n.*
Chi·ca·go (shĭ-kä′gō, -kô′-) ▸ A city of NE IL on Lake Michigan. **—Chi·ca′go·an** *n.*
Chi·ca·na (chĭ-kä′nə, shĭ-) ▸ *n.* A Mexican-American woman or girl.

THESAURUS

chef-d'oeuvre *n.* An outstanding and ingenious work ▸ magnum opus, masterpiece, masterwork. [*Compare* ACCOMPLISHMENT, COMPOSITION, TREASURE.]
chemical-free *adj.* *—See* NATURAL (1).
cherish *v.* To care enough to keep someone in mind ▸ remember, think about, think of. *—See also* BEAR (2), VALUE.
cherub *n.* *—See* BABY (1), INNOCENT (1).
cherubic *adj.* *—See* BABYISH.
chew *v.* To seize and grind with the teeth ▸ bite, champ, chomp, chump, crump, crunch, gnash, gnaw, masticate, munch, nibble, ruminate. *Chiefly Regional:* chaw. [*Compare* BROWSE, EAT.]
chew out *v.* *—See* CHASTISE.
chew on or **over** *v.* *—See* PONDER.
chic *adj.* *—See* EXCLUSIVE (3), FASHIONABLE.
chic *n.* *—See* ELEGANCE.

chi·can·er·y (shĭ-kā′nə-rē, chĭ-) ▸ *n., pl.* **-ies. 1.** Deception by trickery or sophistry. **2.** A trick; subterfuge.

Chi·ca·no (chĭ-kä′nō, shĭ-) ▸ *n., pl.* **-nos.** A Mexican American. **—Chi·ca′no** *adj.*

chi·chi (shē′shē) ▸ *adj.* **-chi·er, -chi·est.** Ostentatiously stylish.

chick (chĭk) ▸ *n.* **1.** A young chicken. **2.** Any young bird. **3.** *Slang* A young woman.

chick·a·dee (chĭk′ə-dē′) ▸ *n.* A small, gray, dark-crowned North American bird.

Chick·a·saw (chĭk′ə-sô′) ▸ *n., pl.* **-saw** or **-saws. 1.** A member of a Native American people formerly of NE Mississippi and NW Alabama, now living in Oklahoma. **2.** The Muskogean language of the Chickasaw.

chick·en (chĭk′ən) ▸ *n.* **1.** The common domestic fowl or its young. **2.** The flesh of this fowl. **3.** *Slang* A coward. ▸ *adj. Slang* Afraid; cowardly. ▸ *v. Slang* To act in a cowardly manner: *chickened out at the last moment.*

chicken feed ▸ *n. Slang* A trifling amount of money.

chick·en-heart·ed (chĭk′ən-här′tĭd) ▸ *adj.* Cowardly. **—chick′en·heart′ed·ness** *n.*

chick·en-liv·ered (chĭk′ən-lĭv′ərd) ▸ *adj.* Cowardly; timid.

chick·en·pox or **chicken pox** (chĭk′ən-pŏks′) ▸ *n.* A contagious viral disease, primarily of children, characterized by skin eruptions and slight fever.

chicken wire ▸ *n.* A light-gauge galvanized wire fencing usu. of hexagonal mesh.

chick·pea (chĭk′pē′) ▸ *n.* **1.** An Old World plant cultivated for its edible pealike seeds. **2.** A seed of this plant.

chick·weed (chĭk′wēd′) ▸ *n.* A low weedy plant with small white flowers.

chic·le (chĭk′əl, chē′klĕ) ▸ *n.* The coagulated milky juice of a tropical American tree, used as the principal ingredient of chewing gum.

chic·o·ry (chĭk′ə-rē) ▸ *n., pl.* **-ries. 1.** A plant having blue daisylike flowers and leaves used as salad. **2.** The roasted ground roots of this plant, used as a coffee admixture or substitute.

chide (chīd) ▸ *v.* **chid·ed** or **chid** (chĭd), **chid·ed** or **chid** or **chid·den** (chĭd′n), **chid·ing.** To scold mildly; reprimand. **—chid′er** *n.* **—chid′ing·ly** *adv.*

chief (chēf) ▸ *n.* **1.** One who is highest in rank or authority. **2.** often **Chief a.** A chief petty officer. **b.** The chief engineer of a ship. ▸ *adj.* **1.** Highest in rank or authority. **2.** Most important. **—chief′ly** *adj. & adv.*

chief justice also **Chief Justice** ▸ *n.* The presiding judge of a high court having several judges, esp. the US Supreme Court.

chief master sergeant ▸ *n.* The highest noncommissioned rank in the US Air Force.

chief of staff ▸ *n., pl.* **chiefs of staff. 1.** often **Chief of Staff** The ranking officer of the US Army, Navy, or Air Force, responsible to the secretary of his or her branch and to the President. **2.** The senior military staff officer at the division level or higher.

chief of state ▸ *n., pl.* **chiefs of state.** The formal head of a nation, distinct from the head of the government.

chief petty officer ▸ *n.* **1.** A rank, as in the US Navy, below senior chief petty officer. **2.** One holding this rank.

chief·tain (chēf′tən) ▸ *n.* The leader esp. of a clan or tribe.

chif·fon (shĭ-fŏn′, shĭf′ŏn′) ▸ *n.* A fabric of sheer silk or rayon.

chif·fo·nier (shĭf′ə-nîr′) ▸ *n.* A narrow, high chest of drawers.

chig·ger (chĭg′ər) ▸ *n.* **1.** A parasitic mite larva that lodges on the skin and whose bite causes severe itching. **2.** See **chigoe** 1.

chi·gnon (shēn-yŏn′, shēn′yŏn′) ▸ *n.* A roll of hair worn esp. at the nape of the neck.

chig·oe (chĭg′ō, chē′gō) ▸ *n.* **1.** A small tropical flea, the fertilized female of which burrows under the skin and causes intense irritation and sores. **2.** See **chigger** 1.

Chi·hua·hua (chĭ-wä′wä, -wə) ▸ *n.* A very small dog having pointed ears and a short smooth coat.

chil·blain (chĭl′blān′) ▸ *n.* An inflammation of the hands, feet, or ears, due to exposure to moist cold.

child (chīld) ▸ *n., pl.* **chil·dren** (chĭl′drən). **1.** A person between birth and puberty. **2.** An immature person. **3.** A son or daughter; offspring. **—child′hood′** *n.* **—child′less** *adj.* **—child′like′** *adj.*

child·bear·ing (chīld′bâr′ĭng) ▸ *n.* Pregnancy and childbirth. **—child′bear′ing** *adj.*

child·birth (chīld′bûrth′) ▸ *n.* Parturition.

child-care or **child·care** (chīld′kâr′) ▸ *adj.* Of or providing care for children, esp. preschoolers. **—child′care′** *n.*

child·ish (chīl′dĭsh) ▸ *adj.* **1.** Of or suitable for a child. **2.** Immature in behavior. **—child′ish·ly** *adv.* **—child′ish·ness** *n.*

child·proof (chīld′pro͞of′) ▸ *adj.* Designed to resist tampering by young children.

chil·dren (chĭl′drən) ▸ *n.* Pl. of **child.**

child's play (chīldz) ▸ *n.* **1.** Something very easy to do. **2.** A trivial matter.

Chil·e (chĭl′ē, chē′lĕ) ▸ A country of SW South America with a long Pacific coastline. **—Chil′e·an** *adj. & n.*

chil·i (chĭl′ē) also **chil·e** or **chil·li** ▸ *n., pl.* **-ies** also **-es** or **-lis. 1.** The pungent pod of several varieties of capsicum pepper, used esp. as a flavoring in cooking. **2.** A spicy stew of meat or beans (or both) and usu. tomatoes.

chil·i·bur·ger (chĭl′ē-bûr′gər) ▸ *n.* A hamburger covered with chili con carne.

chil·i·dog (chĭl′ē-dôg′, -dŏg′) ▸ *n.* A hot dog covered with chili con carne.

chili sauce ▸ *n.* A spiced sauce made with chilies and tomatoes.

chill (chĭl) ▸ *n.* **1.** A moderate but penetrating cold. **2.** A cold or clammy sensation, as from fever or fear, often accompanied by shivering and pallor. **3.** A dampening of enthusiasm or spirit. ▸ *adj.* Chilly. ▸ *v.* **1.** To make or become cold. **2.** To dispirit. **3.** *Slang* To calm down or relax. Often used with *out.* **—chill′ness** *n.*

chill·y (chĭl′ē) ▸ *adj.* **-i·er, -i·est. 1.** Cold enough to cause shivering. **2.** Seized with cold; shivering. **3.** Cool; unfriendly. **—chill′i·ness** *n.*

chime (chīm) ▸ *n.* **1.** often **chimes** A set of tuned bells used as a musical instrument. **2.** The sound produced by or as if by a bell or bells. ▸ *v.* **chimed, chim·ing. 1.** To sound with a harmonious ring when struck. **2.** To agree; harmonize. **3.**

THESAURUS

chicanery *n.* —*See* DISHONESTY (2).

chichi *adj.* —*See* EXCLUSIVE (3).

chick *n.* —*See* GIRL.

chicken *n.* —*See* COWARD.

chicken *adj.* —*See* AFRAID, COWARDLY.

chicken feed *n.* —*See* PEANUTS.

chickenhearted or **chicken-livered** *adj.* —*See* COWARDLY.

chickenheartedness *n.* —*See* COWARDICE.

chide *v.* To castigate for the purpose of improving ▸ chasten, correct. —*See also* CHASTISE.

chief *n.* One who governs or leads ▸ boss, captain, chieftain, commander, director, elder, emir, emperor, general, governor, head, headman, hierarch, king, kingpin, leader, lord, majesty, master, monarch, overlord, potentate, prince, queen, ringleader, ruler, sachem, sagamore, sheik, sovereign, suzerain. *Slang:* brass hat, honcho. *Idiom:* cock of the block (*or* walk). [*Compare* DICTATOR.] —*See also* BOSS.

chief *adj.* —*See* DOMINANT (1), PRIMARY (1).

chieftain *n.* —*See* CHIEF.

child *n.* **1.** A young person between birth and puberty ▸ innocent, juvenile, moppet, preadolescent, preteen, tot, whelp, youngster. *Informal:* kid, young'un. [*Compare* BABY.] **2.** One who is not yet legally of age ▸ juvenile, minor, underage person. [*Compare* YOUTH.] —*See also* INNOCENT (2), PROGENY.

childbearing *n.* —*See* BIRTH (1).

childbirth *n.* —*See* BIRTH (1).

childhood *n.* The stage of life between birth and puberty ▸ innocence, early years, preadolescence, prepubescence. [*Compare* YOUTH.]

childish *adj.* Of or characteristic of a child, especially in immaturity ▸ adolescent, babyish, childlike, immature, infantile, juvenile, puerile, sophomoric. [*Compare* FOOLISH.]

childless *adj.* —*See* BARREN (1).

childlike *adj.* —*See* BABYISH, CHILDISH.

child's play *n.* —*See* BREEZE (2).

chill *n.* —*See* COLD.

chill *adj.* —*See* COLD (1), COOL.

chill out *v.* —*See* REST[1] (1).

chilliness *n.* —*See* COLD.

chilly *adj.* —*See* COLD (1), COOL.

chime *v.* —*See* AGREE (1), RING[2].

To signal by chiming: *The clock chimed noon.* **—phrasal verb: chime in** To interrupt, as in a conversation. **—chim′er** *n.*

Chi·me·ra (kī-mîr′ə, kĭ-) ► *n.* **1.** *Gk. Myth.* A fire-breathing she-monster usu. represented as a composite of a lion, goat, and serpent. **2. chimera** An impossible or foolish fantasy.

chi·mer·i·cal (kī-mĕr′ĭ-kəl, -mîr′-, kĭ-) ► *adj.* **1.** Imaginary; unreal. **2.** Given to unrealistic fantasies. **—chi·mer′i·cal·ly** *adv.*

chim·ney (chĭm′nē) ► *n., pl.* **-neys. 1.** A usu. vertical passage through which smoke and gases escape from a fire or furnace. **2.** A glass tube for enclosing the flame of a lamp.

chim·ney·piece (chĭm′nē-pēs′) ► *n.* **1.** The mantel of a fireplace. **2.** A decoration over a fireplace.

chimney pot ► *n.* A short pipe placed on the top of a chimney to improve the draft.

chimney sweep ► *n.* A worker employed to clean soot from chimneys.

chimney swift ► *n.* A small swallowlike New World bird that often nests in chimneys.

chimp (chĭmp) ► *n. Informal* A chimpanzee.

chim·pan·zee (chĭm′păn-zē′, chĭm-păn′zē) ► *n.* A gregarious anthropoid ape of tropical Africa, having long dark hair.

chin (chĭn) ► *n.* The central forward portion of the lower jaw. ► *v.* **chinned, chin·ning.** To pull (oneself) up with the arms while grasping an overhead horizontal bar until the chin is level with the bar.

chi·na (chī′nə) ► *n.* **1.** High-quality porcelain or ceramic ware. **2.** Porcelain or earthenware used for the table.

China ► A country of E Asia.

China, Republic of ► See **Taiwan.**

China Sea ► The W part of the Pacific extending from S Japan to the Malay Peninsula.

chinch (chĭnch) ► *n. Regional* See **bedbug.**

chinch bug ► *n.* A small black and white insect that is destructive to grains and grasses.

chin·chil·la (chĭn-chĭl′ə) ► *n.* **1a.** A squirrellike South American rodent having soft, pale-gray fur. **b.** The fur of this animal. **2.** A thick wool cloth used for overcoats.

chine (chīn) ► *n.* **1a.** The backbone or spine, esp. of an animal. **b.** A cut of meat containing part of the backbone. **2.** A ridge or crest.

Chi·nese (chī-nēz′, -nēs′) ► *adj.* Of or relating to China or its peoples, languages, or cultures. ► *n., pl.* **-nese. 1a.** A native or inhabitant of China. **b.** A person of Chinese ancestry. **c.** See **Han. 2a.** A branch of the Sino-Tibetan language family that consists of the various dialects spoken by the Chinese people. **b.** Any of these dialects.

Chinese cabbage ► *n.* A plant related to the common cabbage, having an elongated head of overlapping, crinkled edible leaves.

Chinese checkers ► *pl.n. (takes sing. or pl. v.)* A game played with marbles on a board shaped like a six-pointed star.

Chinese lantern ► *n.* A decorative collapsible lantern of thin, brightly colored paper.

Chinese puzzle ► *n.* **1.** A very intricate puzzle. **2.** Something very difficult or complex.

chink[1] (chĭngk) ► *n.* A narrow opening, such as a crack or fissure. ► *v.* To fill cracks or chinks in.

chink[2] (chĭngk) ► *n.* A slight clinking sound. ► *v.* To make a chink.

chi·no (chē′nō, shē′-) ► *n., pl.* **-nos. 1.** A coarse twilled cotton fabric. **2.** often **chinos** Trousers made of chino.

chi·nook (shĭ-no͝ok′, chĭ-) ► *n.* **1.** A moist warm marine wind in the Pacific NW. **2.** A warm dry wind of the E Rocky Mountains.

Chinook ► *n., pl.* **-nook** or **-nooks. 1.** A member of any of various Chinookan-speaking peoples of the Columbia River valley in Washington and Oregon. **2.** Any of their Chinookan languages.

Chi·nook·an (shĭ-no͝ok′ən, chĭ-) ► *n.* A Native American language family of Washington and Oregon. **—Chi·nook′an** *adj.*

Chinook Jargon ► *n.* A pidgin language combining words from Native American languages, French, and English, formerly used as a lingua franca in the Pacific Northwest.

Chinook salmon ► *n.* A very large, commercially valuable salmon of N Pacific waters.

chin·qua·pin (chĭng′kə-pĭn′) ► *n.* **1.** Any of several deciduous shrubs or small trees related to the chestnut. **2.** A large evergreen tree of the Pacific Northwest. **3.** The nut of a chinquapin.

chintz (chĭnts) ► *n.* A printed and glazed cotton fabric, usu. of bright colors.

chintz·y (chĭnt′sē) ► *adj.* **-i·er, -i·est. 1.** Gaudy or cheap; trashy. **2.** Stingy; miserly.

chin-up (chĭn′ŭp′) ► *n.* The act of chinning oneself, practiced esp. as a fitness exercise.

chip (chĭp) ► *n.* **1.** A small broken or cut off piece, as of wood, stone, or glass. **2.** A crack or flaw caused by the removal of such a piece. **3a.** A coinlike disk used as a counter, as in poker. **b. chips** *Slang* Money. **4a.** *Electron.* A minute slice of a semiconducting material, such as silicon, processed to have specified electrical characteristics, esp. before it is developed into an electronic component or integrated circuit; microchip. **b.** An integrated circuit. **5a.** often **chips** A thin, usu. fried slice of food: *a potato chip.* **b. chips** *Chiefly Brit.* French fries. **6.** *Sports* A chip shot. ► *v.* **chipped, chip·ping.** To break, chop, or cut a small piece from. **—phrasal verb: chip in** To contribute. **—idioms: chip off the old block** A child who closely resembles his or her parent. **chip on (one's) shoulder** A habitually hostile attitude. **—chip′per** *n.*

Chip·e·wy·an (chĭp′ə-wī′ən) ► *n., pl.* **-an** or **-ans. 1.** A member of a Native American people of N-central Canada. **2.** The Athabaskan language of the Chipewyan.

chip·munk (chĭp′mŭngk′) ► *n.* Any of several small terrestrial squirrels having a striped back.

chipped beef (chĭpt) ► *n.* Dried beef smoked and sliced very thin.

chip·per (chĭp′ər) ► *adj.* In lively spirits; cheerful.

Chip·pe·wa (chĭp′ə-wô′, -wä′, -wā′) ► *n., pl.* **-wa** or **-was.** See **Ojibwa.**

chiro– ► *pref.* Hand: *chiropractic.*

chi·ro·man·cy (kī′rə-măn′sē) ► *n.* Palmistry. **—chi′ro·man′cer** *n.*

chi·rop·o·dy (kĭ-rŏp′ə-dē, shĭ-) ► *n.* See **podiatry. —chi·rop′o·dist** *n.*

chi·ro·prac·tic (kī′rə-prăk′tĭk) ► *n.* A system of therapy typically involving manipulation of the spinal column and other bodily structures. **—chi′ro·prac′tor** *n.*

chirp (chûrp) ► *n.* A short, high-pitched sound, such as that made by a small bird or insect. **—chirp** *v.*

chis·el (chĭz′əl) ► *n.* A metal tool with a sharp beveled edge, used to cut and shape stone, wood, or metal. ► *v.* **-eled, -el·ing** or **-elled, -el·ling. 1.** To shape or cut with a chisel. **2.** *Informal* To swindle or obtain by swindling; cheat. **—chis′el·er** *n.*

chit[1] (chĭt) ► *n.* A voucher for an amount owed for food and drink.

chit[2] (chĭt) ► *n.* **1.** A child. **2.** A saucy girl or young woman.

chit·chat (chĭt′chăt′) ► *n.* Casual conversation. **—chit′chat′** *v.*

chi·tin (kīt′n) ► *n.* A tough protective substance that is the principal component of crustacean shells and insect exoskeletons. **—chi′tin·ous** *adj.*

chi·ton (kīt′n, kī′tŏn′) ► *n.* **1.** Any of a class of marine mollusks that live on rocks and have shells with eight overlapping calcareous plates. **2.** A tunic worn by men and women in ancient Greece.

chit·ter·lings also **chit·lins** or **chit·lings** (chĭt′lĭnz) ► *pl.n.* The small intestines of pigs, cooked as food.

chiv·al·ry (shĭv′əl-rē) ► *n., pl.* **-ries. 1.** The medieval system

THESAURUS

chime in *v.* —*See* INTERRUPT (2).
chime *n.* —*See* AGREEMENT (2).
chimera *n.* —*See* DREAM (2).
chimeric or **chimerical** *adj.* —*See* ILLUSIVE, IMAGINARY.
chink *n.* —*See* CRACK (2).
chintzy *adj.* —*See* GAUDY.
chin wag *v.* —*See* CHATTER (1).
chip *n.* —*See* FLAKE.
chip *v.* —*See* FLAKE.
chip in *v.* —*See* CONTRIBUTE (1), CONTRIBUTE (2), INTERRUPT (2).
chipper *adj.* —*See* CHEERFUL, LIVELY.
chisel *v.* —*See* CHEAT (1), ENGRAVE (1).
chiseler *n.* —*See* CHEAT (2).
chitchat *n.* —*See* CHATTER.
chitchat *v.* —*See* CHATTER (1).
chivalric *adj.* —*See* GALLANT.
chivalrous *adj.* —*See* GALLANT, GRACIOUS (2).
chivalry or **chivalrousness** *n.* Respect-

of knighthood. **2a.** Qualities, such as bravery, honor, and gallantry toward women, idealized by knighthood. **b.** A gallant or courteous act. **—chiv′al·rous, chi·val′ric** *adj.*

chive (chīv) ► *n.* often **chives** A plant with grasslike onion-flavored leaves used as seasoning.

chla·myd·i·a (klə-mĭd′ē-ə) ► *n., pl.* **-i·ae** (-ē-ē′). **1.** Any of various spherical microorganisms pathogenic to humans and other animals. **2.** Any of several often asymptomatic sexually transmitted diseases caused by one of these microorganisms.

chlo·ral (klôr′əl) ► *n.* A colorless oily liquid used to manufacture DDT and chloral hydrate.

chloral hydrate ► *n.* A colorless crystalline compound, $CCl_3CH(OH)_2$, used medicinally as a sedative and hypnotic.

chlo·rate (klôr′āt′) ► *n.* The inorganic group ClO_3 or a compound containing it.

chlor·dane (klôr′dān′) also **chlor·dan** (-dăn′) ► *n.* A colorless, odorless, viscous liquid, $C_{10}H_6Cl_8$, used as an insecticide.

chlo·rel·la (klə-rĕl′ə) ► *n.* Any of a genus of unicellular green algae often used in studies of photosynthesis.

chlo·ric acid (klôr′ĭk) ► *n.* A strongly oxidizing unstable acid, $HClO_3{\cdot}7H_2O$.

chlo·ride (klôr′īd′) ► *n.* A binary compound of chlorine. **—chlo·rid′ic** (klə-rĭd′ĭk) *adj.*

chlo·ri·nate (klôr′ə-nāt′) ► *v.* **-nat·ed, -nat·ing.** To treat or combine with chlorine or a chlorine compound. **—chlo′ri·na′tion** *n.* **—chlo′ri·na′tor** *n.*

chlo·rine (klôr′ēn′, -ĭn) ► *n. Symbol* **Cl** A highly reactive, poisonous greenish-yellow gaseous element used to purify water, as a disinfectant and bleaching agent, and in the manufacture of many compounds. At. no. 17.

chloro– or **chlor–** ► *pref.* **1.** Green: *chlorophyll.* **2.** Chlorine: *chloroform.*

chlo·ro·fluor·o·car·bon (klôr′ō-flo͝or′ō-kär′bən, -flôr′-) ► *n.* Any of various gaseous compounds of carbon, hydrogen, chlorine, and fluorine, once used widely as aerosol propellants and refrigerants, now believed to cause depletion of the atmospheric ozone layer.

chlo·ro·form (klôr′ə-fôrm′) ► *n.* A clear colorless liquid, $CHCl_3$, used in refrigerants, propellants, and resins, as a solvent, and sometimes as an anesthetic. ► *v.* To anesthetize or kill with chloroform.

chlo·ro·phyll (klôr′ə-fĭl) ► *n.* Any of a group of green pigments essential in photosynthesis.

chlo·ro·plast (klôr′ə-plăst′) ► *n.* A chlorophyll-containing plastid found in algal and green plant cells.

chlor·tet·ra·cy·cline (klôr′tĕt-rə-sī′klēn′, -klĭn) ► *n.* An antibiotic obtained from a soil bacterium.

chock (chŏk) ► *n.* A block or wedge placed under something else, such as a wheel, to keep it from moving. ► *v.* To secure by a chock.

chock-a-block or **chock·a·block** (chŏk′ə-blŏk′) ► *adj.* Squeezed together; jammed.

chock-full or **chock·full** (chŏk′fo͝ol′) ► *adj.* As full as possible.

choc·o·late (chô′kə-lĭt, chôk′lĭt, chŏk′-) ► *n.* **1.** Fermented, roasted, and ground cacao seeds, often sweetened. **2.** A candy or beverage made from chocolate. **—choc′o·late** *adj.*

Choc·taw (chŏk′tô) ► *n., pl.* **-taw** or **-taws. 1.** A member of a Native American people formerly of S Mississippi and SW Alabama, now living in Mississippi and Oklahoma. **2.** The Muskogean language of the Choctaw.

choice (chois) ► *n.* **1.** The act of choosing; selection. **2.** The power, right, or liberty to choose. **3.** One that is chosen. **4.** A number or variety from which to choose. **5.** The best part. ► *adj.* **choic·er, choic·est. 1.** Of very fine quality. **2.** Selected with care. **—choice′ness** *n.*

choir (kwīr) ► *n.* **1.** An organized company of singers, esp. one singing in a church. **2.** The part of a church used by a choir. **3.** A group of similar orchestral instruments.

choke (chōk) ► *v.* **choked, chok·ing. 1a.** To have difficulty in breathing, swallowing, or speaking. **b.** To cause to choke, as by constricting or obstructing the windpipe. **2.** To check or repress forcibly. **3.** To block up or obstruct; clog. **4.** To reduce the air intake of (a carburetor), thereby enriching the fuel mixture. **5.** To fail to perform effectively because of nervous tension. ***—phrasal verb:*** **choke up** To be unable to speak because of strong emotion. ► *n.* **1.** The act or sound of choking. **2.** A device used in choking a carburetor.

choke collar ► *n.* A chain collar that tightens like a noose when the leash is pulled, used in canine obedience training.

chok·er (chō′kər) ► *n.* **1.** One that chokes. **2.** A tight-fitting necklace.

chol·er (kŏl′ər, kō′lər) ► *n.* Anger; irritability.

chol·er·a (kŏl′ər-ə) ► *n.* An infectious, often fatal epidemic disease characterized by profuse watery diarrhea, vomiting, muscle cramps, and severe dehydration.

chol·er·ic (kŏl′ə-rĭk, kə-lĕr′ĭk) ► *adj.* Easily angered; bad-tempered; irritable.

cho·les·ter·ol (kə-lĕs′tə-rôl′, -rōl′) ► *n.* A white crystalline substance, $C_{27}H_{45}OH$, found in animal tissues and various foods, that is normally synthesized by the liver and is thought to be a factor in atherosclerosis.

chol·la (choi′ə) ► *n.* Any of a genus of spiny, shrubby or treelike cacti having cylindrical, often detachable stem segments.

chomp (chŏmp) ► *v.* To chew or bite on noisily or repeatedly.

choose (cho͞oz) ► *v.* **chose** (chōz), **cho·sen** (chō′zən), **choos·ing. 1.** To decide on and pick out; select. **2.** To prefer above others. **—choos′er** *n.*

choos·y also **choos·ey** (cho͞o′zē) ► *adj.* **-i·er, -i·est.** Highly selective. **—choos′i·ness** *n.*

chop[1] (chŏp) ► *v.* **chopped, chop·ping. 1a.** To cut by striking with a heavy sharp tool. **b.** To mince. **2.** *Sports* To hit with a short, swift downward stroke. ► *n.* **1a.** A swift, short, cutting blow or stroke. **b.** *Sports* A short downward stroke. **2.** A cut of meat, usu. taken from the rib, shoulder, or loin and containing a bone. **3.** A short irregular motion of waves.

chop[2] (chŏp) ► *n.* **1.** An official stamp or permit in the Far East. **2.** Quality; class.

chop·house (chŏp′hous′) ► *n.* A restaurant that specializes in steaks and chops.

Cho·pin (shō′păn′, shō-păn′), **Frédéric François** (1810–49) ► Polish-born French composer and pianist.

chop·per (chŏp′ər) ► *n. Informal* **1.** A helicopter. **2. choppers** Teeth or dentures. **3.** A usu. customized motorcycle.

chop·ping block (chŏp′ĭng) ► *n.* A wooden block on which food or wood is chopped.

THESAURUS

ful attention, especially toward women ► gallantry. [*Compare* CONSIDERATION, COURTESY.]

chock-full or **chock-a-block** *adj.* *—See* FULL (1).

choice *n.* The act, power, or right of choosing ► alternative, decision, discretion, election, free will, option, pick, preference, selection, volition. *Informal:* druthers. [*Compare* VOICE, WILL.] *—See also* BEST (1), ELECT.

choice *adj.* **1.** Of fine quality ► exceptional, fine, first-class, first-rate, high-grade, premium, prime, select, sterling, superior, top-drawer, top-grade, top-of-the-line. [*Compare* BEST, EXCELLENT, EXCEPTIONAL.] **2.** Singled out in preference ► chosen, elect, exclusive, select. [*Compare* FAVORITE.] *—See also* DELICATE (1).

choke *v.* To stop breathing or to stop the breathing of ► asphyxiate, gag, smother, stifle, strangle, strangulate, suffocate, throttle. *—See also* FAIL (1), FILL (2), OBSTRUCT, REPRESS, SUPPRESS.

choke off *v.* *—See* SUPPRESS.

choke *n.* *—See* PLUG.

choked *adj.* *—See* OVERCROWDED.

choler *n.* *—See* ANGER.

choleric *adj.* *—See* ANGRY, TESTY.

chomp *v.* *—See* CHEW.

choose *v.* **1.** To make a choice from a number of alternatives ► cast, cull, decide (on), elect, go with, opt (for), pick (out), select, single (out), take, vote (for), weigh, will. **2.** To have an inclination to ► desire, like, please, prefer, want, will, wish. ***Idioms:*** have a mind, see fit.

choosy *adj.* *—See* FUSSY.

chop *v.* *—See* CUT (3).

chop down *v.* *—See* DROP (3).

chop *n.* *—See* BLOW[2].

choppiness *n.* *—See* IRREGULARITY.

chop·py (chŏp′ē) ► *adj.* **-pi·er, -pi·est.** 1. Having many small waves. 2. Marked by abrupt starts and stops. **—chop′pi·ly** *adv.*
chops (chŏps) ► *pl.n.* The jaws, cheeks, or jowls.
chop·stick (chŏp′stĭk′) ► *n.* One of a pair of slender sticks used as an eating utensil chiefly in Asian countries.
chop su·ey (so͞o′ē) ► *n.* A Chinese-American dish consisting of small pieces of meat or chicken cooked with bean sprouts and other vegetables and served with rice.
cho·ral (kôr′əl) ► *adj. Mus.* Of or for a chorus or choir. **—cho′ral·ly** *adv.*
cho·rale also **cho·ral** (kə-răl′, -räl′) ► *n.* 1. A harmonized hymn. 2. A chorus or choir.
chord[1] (kôrd) *Mus.* ► *n.* A combination of three or more pitches sounded simultaneously. ► *v.* To play chords on: *chord a guitar.*
chord[2] (kôrd) ► *n.* 1. A line segment that joins two points on a curve. 2. *Anat.* Var. of **cord** 3. 3. An emotional feeling or response: *a sympathetic chord.*
chore (chôr) ► *n.* 1. **chores** Daily or routine domestic tasks. 2. An unpleasant task.
cho·re·a (kô-rē′ə, kō-, kə-) ► *n.* A nervous disorder, esp. of children, marked by uncontrollable movements, esp. of the arms, legs, and face.
cho·re·og·ra·phy (kôr′ē-ŏg′rə-fē) ► *n.* The art of creating and arranging dances or ballets. **—cho′re·o·graph′** (kôr′ē-ə-grăf′) *v.* **—cho′re·og′ra·pher** *n.* **—cho′re·o·graph′ic** *adj.*
cho·ris·ter (kôr′ĭ-stər, kŏr′-) ► *n.* A singer in a choir.
cho·ri·zo (chə-rē′zō, -sō) ► *n.* A spicy pork sausage seasoned esp. with garlic.
cho·roid (kôr′oid′) or **cho·ri·oid** (kôr′ē-oid′) ► *n.* The vascular coat of the eye between the sclera and retina.
chor·tle (chôr′tl) ► *n.* A snorting, joyful laugh or chuckle. **—chor′tle** *v.* **—chor′tler** *n.*
cho·rus (kôr′əs) ► *n., pl.* **-rus·es.** 1. *Mus.* **a.** A composition written for a large number of singers. **b.** A body of singers who perform choral compositions. **c.** A line or group of lines repeated at intervals in a song. 2. A body of vocalists and dancers who support the leading performers in operas, musical comedies, and revues. 3. A group of persons who speak or recite together, esp. in a play. 4. A simultaneous utterance by many voices. **—cho′rus** *v.*
chose (chōz) ► *v.* P.t. of **choose.**
cho·sen (chō′zən) ► *v.* P.part. of **choose.** ► *adj.* Selected from or preferred above others.
chow[1] (chou) ► *n.* A heavy-set dog having a usu. reddish-brown coat and a blue-black tongue.
chow[2] (chou) *Slang* ► *n.* Food. ► *v.* To eat: *chowed down on pizza.*
chow·der (chou′dər) ► *n.* 1. A thick seafood soup often with a milk base. 2. A similar soup: *corn chowder.*
chow mein (chou′ mān′) ► *n.* A Chinese-American dish consisting of various stewed vegetables and meat served over fried noodles.
Chré·tien (krā-tyăɴ′), **Jean** (b. 1934) ► Canadian prime minister (1993–2003).
chrism (krĭz′əm) ► *n.* Consecrated oil and balsam that is used for anointing, esp. in baptism and confirmation. **—chris′mal** *adj.*
Christ (krīst) ► *n.* 1. The Messiah, as foretold by the prophets of the Heb. Scriptures. 2. *Christianity* Jesus. **—Christ′like′** *adj.* **—Christ′ly** *adj.*
chris·ten (krĭs′ən) ► *v.* **1a.** To baptize into a Christian church. **b.** To give a name to at baptism. 2. To name and dedicate ceremonially: *christen a ship.* **—chris′ten·ing** *n.*
Chris·ten·dom (krĭs′ən-dəm) ► *n.* 1. Christians collectively. 2. The Christian world.
Chris·tian (krĭs′chən) ► *adj.* 1. Professing belief in Christianity. 2. Of or derived from Jesus's teachings. 3. Of Christianity or its adherents. ► *n.* An adherent of Christianity. **—Chris′tian·ize′** *v.*
Christian era ► *n.* The period beginning with the birth of Jesus.
chris·ti·an·i·a (krĭs′tē-ăn′ē-ə, -ä′nē-ə, krĭs′chē-) ► *n.* A christie.
Chris·ti·an·i·ty (krĭs′chē-ăn′ĭ-tē, krĭs′tē-) ► *n.* 1. The Christian religion, founded on the life and teachings of Jesus. 2. Christendom. 3. The state or fact of being a Christian.
Christian name ► *n.* A name given at birth or baptism.
Christian Science ► *n.* The church and the religious system founded by Mary Baker Eddy, emphasizing healing through spiritual means. **—Christian Scientist** *n.*
chris·tie or **chris·ty** (krĭs′tē) ► *n., pl.* **-ties.** A ski turn in which the skis are kept parallel.
Christ·mas (krĭs′məs) ► *n.* A Christian feast commemorating the birth of Jesus, celebrated on Dec. 25.
Christ·mas·tide (krĭs′məs-tīd′) ► *n.* The season of Christmas.
Christmas tree ► *n.* An evergreen or artificial tree decorated during the Christmas season.
Chris·to·pher (krĭs′tə-fər) Saint (fl. 3rd cent. A.D.) ► Legendary Christian martyr.
chro·mat·ic (krō-măt′ĭk) ► *adj.* 1. Relating to colors or color. 2. *Mus.* Proceeding by half tones: *a chromatic scale.* **—chro·mat′i·cal·ly** *adv.* **—chro·mat′i·cism** *n.*
chrome (krōm) ► *n.* 1. Chromium or a chromium alloy. 2. Something plated with a chrome.
chro·mi·um (krō′mē-əm) ► *n. Symbol* **Cr** A lustrous, hard, steel-gray metallic element used to harden steel alloys, to produce stainless steels, and in corrosion-resistant platings. At. no. 24.
chromo– or **chrom–** ► *pref.* Color: *chromosome.*
chro·mo·some (krō′mə-sōm′) ► *n.* A linear strand of DNA and associated proteins in the nucleus of animal and plant cells that carries the genes determining heredity. **—chro′mo·so′mal** *adj.*
chron·ic (krŏn′ĭk) ► *adj.* 1. Of long duration; continuing or lingering: *chronic money problems; chronic colitis.* 2. Firmly established by habit: *a chronic liar.* **—chron′i·cal·ly** *adv.*
chronic fatigue syndrome ► *n.* A syndrome marked by debilitating fatigue and flulike symptoms.
chron·i·cle (krŏn′ĭ-kəl) ► *n.* 1. A chronological account of historical events. 2. **Chronicles** *(takes sing. v.)* See **Bible** table in Appendix. ► *v.* **chron·i·cled, chron·i·cling.** To record in or in the form of a chronicle.
chrono– or **chron–** ► *pref.* Time: *chronometer.*
chron·o·log·i·cal (krŏn′ə-lŏj′ĭ-kəl, krō′nə-) also **chron·o·log·ic** (-lŏj′ĭk) ► *adj.* 1. Arranged in order of time of occurrence. 2. Relating to or in accordance with chronology. **—chron′o·log′i·cal·ly** *adv.*
chro·nol·o·gy (krə-nŏl′ə-jē) ► *n., pl.* **-gies.** 1. The determination of dates and sequence of events. 2. The arrangement of events in time. 3. A chronological list or table. **—chro·nol′o·gist** *n.*
chro·nom·e·ter (krə-nŏm′ĭ-tər) ► *n.* An exceptionally precise timepiece.
chrys·a·lis (krĭs′ə-lĭs) ► *n.* A pupa, esp. of a moth or butterfly, enclosed in a firm case or cocoon.
chry·san·the·mum (krĭ-săn′thə-məm, -zăn′-) ► *n.* Any of a genus of plants cultivated for their showy flower heads.
chub (chŭb) ► *n., pl.* **chub** or **chubs.** 1. Any of a family of freshwater fishes related to the carps and minnows. 2. Any of several North American food fishes.
chub·by (chŭb′ē) ► *adj.* **-bi·er, -bi·est.** Rounded and plump. **—chub′bi·ly** *adv.* **—chub′bi·ness** *n.*

THESAURUS

chops *n.* —*See* MOUTH (1).
chore *n.* —*See* TASK (1), TASK (2).
chortle *v.* —*See* LAUGH.
  chortle *n.* —*See* LAUGH.
chosen *adj.* Singled out in preference ► choice, elect, exclusive, select. [*Compare* EXCELLENT, FAVORITE.]
  chosen *n.* —*See* ELECT.
chow *n.* —*See* FOOD.
  chow down *v.* —*See* EAT (1).
christen *v.* —*See* NAME (1).
chronic *adj.* 1. Subject to a disease or habit for a long time ► confirmed, habitual, habituated, inveterate. [*Compare* STUBBORN.] 2. Of long duration ► continuing, lingering, persistent, prolonged, protracted. [*Compare* CONFIRMED, CONTINUING.] 3. Subject to a habit or pattern of behavior ► accustomed, habitual, routine.
chronicle *n.* A chronological record of past events ► annals, archive, chronicle, historical record. —*See also* STORY (1).
  chronicle *v.* —*See* LIST[1].
chronological *adj.* —*See* CONSECUTIVE.
chubby *adj.* —*See* FAT (1).

chuck[1] (chŭk) ► *v.* 1. To pat or squeeze playfully, esp. under the chin. 2a. To throw or toss. b. *Informal* To throw out; discard. —**chuck** *n.*

chuck[2] (chŭk) ► *n.* 1. A cut of beef extending from the neck to the ribs. 2. A clamp that holds a tool or the material being worked, as in a drill or lathe.

chuck·hole (chŭk′hōl′) ► *n.* See **pothole.**

chuck·le (chŭk′əl) ► *v.* **-led, -ling.** To laugh quietly. ► *n.* A quiet laugh of mild amusement.

chuck wagon ► *n.* A wagon equipped with food and cooking utensils, as on a ranch.

chug[1] (chŭg) ► *n.* A brief dull explosive sound made by or as if by a laboring engine. ► *v.* **chugged, chug·ging.** 1. To make chugs. 2. To move at a steady speed.

chug[2] (chŭg) ► *v. Slang* To chugalug.

chug·a·lug (chŭg′ə-lŭg′) ► *v.* **-lugged, -lug·ging.** *Slang* To swallow (a liquid) without pausing.

chuk·ka (chŭk′ə) ► *n.* An ankle-length, usu. suede leather boot.

chuk·ker also **chuk·kar** (chŭk′ər) ► *n.* A period of play, lasting 7 ½ minutes, in a polo match.

chum[1] (chŭm) ► *n.* An intimate friend. ► *v.* **chummed, chum·ming.** To spend time with a friend.

chum[2] (chŭm) ► *n.* Bait, esp. oily fish, ground up and scattered on the water.

Chu·mash (cho͞o′măsh) ► *n., pl.* **-mash** or **-mash·es.** A member of a Hokan-speaking Native American people of S California.

chum·my (chŭm′ē) ► *adj.* **-mi·er, -mi·est.** Intimate; friendly. —**chum′mi·ly** *adv.* —**chum′mi·ness** *n.*

chump (chŭmp) ► *n.* A dupe.

chunk (chŭngk) ► *n.* 1. A thick mass or piece. 2. *Informal* A substantial amount.

chunk·y (chŭng′kē) ► *adj.* **-i·er, -i·est.** Short and thick; stocky. —**chunk′i·ness** *n.*

church (chûrch) ► *n.* 1. A building for public, esp. Christian worship. 2. often **Church** All Christians regarded as a spiritual body. 3. A congregation. 4. A religious service. 5. The clergy. 6. Ecclesiastical power: *the separation of church and state.*

church·go·er (chûrch′gō′ər) ► *n.* One who attends church. —**church′go′ing** *adj. & n.*

Chur·chill (chûr′chĭl′, chûrch′hĭl′), Sir **Winston Leonard Spenser** (1874–1965) ► British prime minister (1940–45 and 1951–55) and writer; 1953 Nobel Prize for literature.

church key ► *n.* A can or bottle opener having a usu. triangular head.

church·man (chûrch′mən) ► *n.* 1. A clergyman. 2. A man who is a member of a church.

Church of Christ, Scientist ► *n.* See **Christian Science.**

Church of England ► *n.* The Anglican church as established in England and headed by the Archbishop of Canterbury.

Church of Jesus Christ of Latter-day Saints ► *n.* See **Mormon Church.**

church·war·den (chûrch′wôr′dn) ► *n.* A lay officer who handles the secular affairs of an Anglican or Episcopal church.

church·wom·an (chûrch′wo͝om′ən) ► *n.* 1. A clergywoman. 2. A woman who is a member of a church.

church·yard (chûrch′yärd′) ► *n.* A yard adjacent to a church, esp. a cemetery.

churl (chûrl) ► *n.* A rude, surly person. —**churl′ish** *adj.* —**churl′ish·ness** *n.*

churn (chûrn) ► *n.* A vessel or device in which cream or milk is agitated to make butter. ► *v.* 1a. To agitate or stir (milk or cream) in a churn. b. To make (butter) by churning. 2. To shake or stir vigorously. —***phrasal verb:*** **churn out** To produce in an abundant and automatic manner: *churns out four novels a year.*

chute (sho͞ot) ► *n.* 1. An inclined trough or passage through or down which things may pass. 2. A parachute.

chut·ney (chŭt′nē) ► *n.* A pungent relish made of fruits, spices, and herbs.

chutz·pah (ᴋʜo͝ot′spə, ho͝ot′-) ► *n.* Utter nerve; gall.

Chuuk Islands (cho͞ok) or **Truk Islands** (trŭk, tro͝ok) ► An island group of the W Pacific in the central Caroline Is.

CIA ► *abbr.* Central Intelligence Agency

ciao (chou) ► *interj.* Used to express greeting or farewell.

ci·bo·ri·um (sĭ-bôr′ē-əm) ► *n., pl.* **-bo·ri·a** (-bôr′ē-ə). 1. A vaulted canopy over an altar. 2. A covered receptacle for the consecrated wafers of the Eucharist.

ci·ca·da (sĭ-kā′də, -kä′-) ► *n., pl.* **-das** or **-dae** (-dē′). A large insect with membranous wings and in the male a pair of organs that produce a shrill drone.

cic·a·trix (sĭk′ə-trĭks′, sĭ-kā′trĭks) ► *n., pl.* **-tri·ces** (-trī′sēz, -trī-sēz′). A scar. —**cic′a·tri′cial** (-trĭsh′əl) *adj.*

Cic·e·ro (sĭs′ə-rō′), **Marcus Tullius** (106–43 B.C.) ► Roman political leader and orator.

–cide ► *suff.* 1. Killer: *pesticide.* 2. Act of killing: *genocide.*

ci·der (sī′dər) ► *n.* The juice pressed esp. from apples, used as a beverage or to make vinegar.

ci·gar (sĭ-gär′) ► *n.* A compact roll of tobacco leaves prepared for smoking.

cig·a·rette also **cig·a·ret** (sĭg′ə-rĕt′, sĭg′ə-rĕt′) ► *n.* A small roll of finely cut tobacco for smoking, usu. enclosed in a wrapper of thin paper.

ci·lan·tro (sĭ-lăn′trō) ► *n.* See **coriander** 2.

cil·i·a (sĭl′ē-ə) ► *n.* Pl. of **cilium.**

cil·i·ar·y (sĭl′ē-ĕr′ē) ► *adj.* Of or resembling cilia.

cil·i·ate (sĭl′ē-ĭt, -āt′) ► *adj.* Ciliated. ► *n.* Any of a class of protozoans characterized by numerous cilia.

cil·i·at·ed (sĭl′ē-ā′tĭd) ► *adj.* Having cilia.

cil·i·um (sĭl′ē-əm) ► *n., pl.* **-i·a** (-ē-ə). 1. A microscopic hairlike process extending from a cell or unicellular organism and capable of rhythmical motion. 2. An eyelash.

cinch (sĭnch) ► *n.* 1. A girth for holding a pack or saddle in place. 2. A firm grip. 3. Something easy to accomplish. 4. A sure thing; certainty. —**cinch** *v.*

cin·cho·na (sĭng-kō′nə, sĭn-chō′-) ► *n.* 1. Any of a genus of South American trees whose bark yields quinine and other medicinal alkaloids. 2. The dried bark of a cinchona.

Cin·cin·na·ti (sĭn′sə-năt′ē, -năt′ə) ► A city of SW OH on the Ohio R.

cinc·ture (sĭngk′chər) ► *n.* A belt or sash; girdle. —**cinc′ture** *v.*

cin·der (sĭn′dər) ► *n.* 1a. A burned substance that is not reduced to ashes but cannot be burned further. b. A glowing coal. 2. **cinders** Ashes. 3. **cinders** *Geol.* See **scoria** 1. 4. *Metall.* See **scoria** 2. —**cin′der·y** *adj.*

cinder block ► *n.* A usu. hollow building block made with concrete and coal cinders.

cin·e·ma (sĭn′ə-mə) ► *n.* 1a. A film or movie. b. A movie theater. 2a. Films or movies collectively. b. The film or movie industry. 3. The art of making films; filmmaking. —**cin′e·mat′ic** (-măt′ĭk) *adj.* —**cin′e·mat′i·cal·ly** *adv.*

cin·e·ma·tize (sĭn′ə-mə-tīz′) ► *v.* **-tized, -tiz·ing.** To adapt (e.g., a novel or play) for film or movies. —**cin′e·mat′i·za′tion** *n.*

THESAURUS

chuck *v.* —*See* DISCARD, EJECT (1), THROW, VOMIT.
chuck *n.* —*See* THROW.
chuck-full *adj. See* CHOCK-FULL.
chuckle *v.* —*See* LAUGH.
chuckle *n.* —*See* LAUGH.
chuff *n.* —*See* BOOR.
chug or **chugalug** *v.* —*See* DRINK (2).
chum *n.* —*See* ASSOCIATE (2), FRIEND.
chumminess *n.* —*See* FRIENDSHIP.
chummy *adj.* —*See* INTIMATE[1] (1).
chump[1] *n.* —*See* DRIP (2), DULLARD.
chump[2] *v.* —*See* CHEW.
chunk *n.* —*See* LUMP[1].
chunky *adj.* —*See* STOCKY.
church *adj.* Of or relating to a church or to an established religion ► churchly, ecclesiastical, religious, spiritual. [*Compare* CLERICAL, DIVINE, HOLY, RITUAL.]
churchman or **churchwoman** *n.* —*See* CLERIC.
churl *n.* —*See* BOOR, MISER.
churlish *adj.* —*See* COARSE (1), ILL-TEMPERED.
churn *v.* —*See* AGITATE (1), BOIL.
chutzpah or **hutzpah** *n.* —*See* IMPUDENCE.
cinch *n.* —*See* BAND[1], BREEZE (2), CERTAINTY.
cinch *v.* —*See* GUARANTEE (2).
cincture *n.* —*See* BAND[1].
cincture *v.* —*See* ENCIRCLE.

cin·e·ma·tog·ra·phy (sĭn′ə-mə-tŏg′rə-fē) ► *n.* The art or technique of movie photography. **—cin′e·ma·tog′ra·pher** *n.* **—cin′e·mat′o·graph′ic** (-măt′ə-grăf′ĭk) *adj.*

ci·né·ma vé·ri·té (sē′nā-mä′ vā′rē-tā′) ► *n.* Documentary filmmaking that stresses unbiased realism.

cin·e·rar·i·a (sĭn′ə-râr′ē-ə) ► *n.* Any of several tropical plants cultivated as house plants for their showy, daisylike flowers.

cin·e·rar·i·um (sĭn′ə-râr′ē-əm) ► *n., pl.* **-i·a** (-ē-ə). A place for keeping the ashes of a cremated body. **—cin′er·ar′y** (sĭn′ə-rĕr′ē) *adj.*

cin·na·bar (sĭn′ə-bär′) ► *n.* **1.** A heavy reddish compound, HgS, that is the principal ore of mercury. **2.** See **vermilion** 2.

cin·na·mon (sĭn′ə-mən) ► *n.* **1.** The aromatic reddish or yellowish-brown bark of certain tropical Asian trees, dried and often ground for use as a spice. **2.** A light reddish brown. **—cin′na·mon** *adj.*

ci·pher (sī′fər) ► *n.* **1.** The mathematical symbol (0) denoting absence of quantity; zero. **2.** An Arabic numeral or figure. **3.** A nonentity. **4a.** A system of secret writing in which units of plain text are substituted according to a predetermined key. **b.** The key to a cipher. **c.** A message in cipher. ► *v.* To compute arithmetically.

cir·ca (sûr′kə) ► *prep.* About: *born circa 1900.*

cir·ca·di·an (sər-kā′dē-ən, -kăd′ē-, sûr′kə-dī′ən, -dē′-) ► *adj. Biol.* Of or exhibiting approx. 24-hour periodicity.

cir·cle (sûr′kəl) ► *n.* **1.** A plane curve everywhere equidistant from a given fixed point, the center. **2.** A planar region bounded by a circle. **3.** Something shaped like a circle. **4.** A group of people sharing an interest or activity. **5.** A sphere of influence or interest. ► *v.* **-cled, -cling. 1.** To make a circle around. **2.** To move in a circle (around).

cir·clet (sûr′klĭt) ► *n.* A small circle.

cir·cuit (sûr′kĭt) ► *n.* **1a.** A closed, usu. circular line around an area. **b.** The region enclosed by such a line. **2.** A closed path or route. **3a.** A closed path followed by an electric current. **b.** A configuration of electrically or electromagnetically connected components or devices. **4a.** A regular or accustomed course from place to place, as that of a salesperson. **b.** The area or district thus covered, esp. a territory served by a circuit court. ► *v.* To make a circuit (of).

circuit board ► *n. Comp. Sci.* An insulated board on which interconnected circuits and components such as microchips are mounted or etched.

circuit breaker ► *n.* An automatic switch that interrupts an overloaded electric circuit.

circuit court ► *n.* A state court that holds sessions periodically at several different places within a judicial district.

cir·cu·i·tous (sər-kyo͞o′ĭ-təs) ► *adj.* Being or taking a roundabout course. **—cir·cu′i·tous·ly** *adv.* **—cir·cu′i·ty, cir·cu′i·tous·ness** *n.*

cir·cuit·ry (sûr′kĭ-trē) ► *n., pl.* **-ries. 1.** The design of or a detailed plan for an electric circuit. **2.** Electric circuits collectively.

cir·cu·lar (sûr′kyə-lər) ► *adj.* **1.** Of or relating to a circle. **2a.** Shaped like a circle; round. **b.** Moving in or forming a circle. **3.** Circuitous. **4.** Self-referential: *circular reasoning.* ► *n.* A printed advertisement or notice for mass distribution. **—cir′cu·lar′i·ty** (-lăr′ĭ-tē) *n.* **—cir′cu·lar·ly** *adv.*

circular saw ► *n.* A power saw consisting of a toothed disk rotated at high speed.

cir·cu·late ► *v.* **-lat·ed, -lat·ing. 1.** To move in or flow through a circle or circuit. **2.** To move around, as from person to person or place to place. **3.** To move or cause to move, as air. **4.** To disseminate. **—cir′cu·la′tive** *adj.* **—cir′cu·la′tor** *n.* **—cir′cu·la·to′ry** (-lə-tôr′ē) *adj.*

cir·cu·la·tion (sûr′kyə-lā′shən) ► *n.* **1.** Movement in a circle or circuit. **2.** The movement of blood through bodily vessels as a result of the heart's pumping action. **3.** The passing of something, such as money, from place to place or person to person. **4a.** The distribution of printed material, esp. newspapers or magazines. **b.** The number of copies sold or distributed.

circulatory system ► *n.* The heart, blood vessels, and lymphatic system of the body.

circum– ► *pref.* Around; about: *circumlunar.*

cir·cum·cise (sûr′kəm-sīz′) ► *v.* **-cised, -cis·ing. 1.** To remove the prepuce of (a male). **2.** To remove a part of the clitoris of (a female). **—cir′cum·ci′sion** (-sĭzh′ən) *n.*

cir·cum·fer·ence (sər-kŭm′fər-əns) ► *n.* **1.** The boundary line of a circle. **2a.** The boundary line of a figure, area, or object. **b.** The length of such a boundary. **—cir·cum′fer·en′tial** (-fə-rĕn′shəl) *adj.*

cir·cum·flex (sûr′kəm-flĕks′) ► *n.* Any of several marks, especially (ˆ), used over a vowel to indicate quality of pronunciation.

cir·cum·lo·cu·tion (sûr′kəm-lō-kyo͞o′shən) ► *n.* **1.** The use of wordy and indirect language. **2.** A roundabout expression.

cir·cum·lu·nar (sûr′kəm-lo͞o′nər) ► *adj.* Revolving about or surrounding the moon.

cir·cum·nav·i·gate (sûr′kəm-năv′ĭ-gāt′) ► *v.* **-gat·ed, -gat·ing.** To go or proceed completely around: *circumnavigating the earth.* **—cir′cum·nav′i·ga′tion** *n.*

cir·cum·po·lar (sûr′kəm-pō′lər) ► *adj.* Located or found in one of the polar regions.

cir·cum·scribe (sûr′kəm-skrīb′) ► *v.* **-scribed, -scrib·ing. 1.** To draw a line around. **2.** To confine within bounds; restrict. **3.** To enclose (a polygon or polyhedron) within a configuration of lines, curves, or surfaces so that every vertex of the enclosed object touches the enclosing configuration. **—cir′cum·scrip′tion** (-skrĭp′shən) *n.*

cir·cum·so·lar (sûr′kəm-sō′lər) ► *adj.* Revolving around or surrounding the sun.

cir·cum·spect (sûr′kəm-spĕkt′) ► *adj.* Heedful of potential consequences; prudent. **—cir′cum·spec′tion** *n.* **—cir′cum·spect′ly** *adv.*

cir·cum·stance (sûr′kəm-stăns′) ► *n.* **1.** A condition or fact attending an event and having some bearing on it. **2.**

THESAURUS

cinerarium *n.* —*See* GRAVE[1].

cipher *n.* —*See* NONENTITY.

cipher *v.* —*See* CALCULATE.

circa *adv.* —*See* APPROXIMATELY.

circle *n.* **1.** A round closed plane shape or figure ► annulus, band, circlet, cirque, circuit, crown, disk, gyre, halo, hoop, ring, round, roundlet, wheel, wreath, zodiac. [*Compare* BALL, CIRCUMFERENCE, LOOP.] **2.** A course, process, or journey that ends where it began or repeats itself ► circuit, cycle, orbit, round, tour, turn. **3.** A small group of friends or associates ► clique, coterie, crew, crowd, group, in-group, set. *Informal:* bunch, gang. [*Compare* CROWD, GROUP.] —*See also* AREA (1), RANGE (1), REVOLUTION (1).

circle *v.* —*See* ENCIRCLE, SURROUND, TURN (1).

circlet *n.* —*See* CIRCLE (1).

circuit *n.* —*See* BEAT (2), CIRCLE (1), CIRCLE (2), CIRCUMFERENCE, CONFERENCE (2), JOURNEY, LOOP, REVOLUTION (1).

circuitous *adj.* —*See* INDIRECT (1).

circular *adj.* —*See* INDIRECT (1), ROUND (1).

circular *n.* An announcement distributed on paper to a large number of people ► flier, handbill, leaflet, notice.

circulate *v.* To become known far and wide ► get around, go around, spread, travel. *Idiom:* go (*or* make) the rounds. —*See also* FLOW (1), SPREAD (2).

circulation *n.* —*See* DISTRIBUTION (2), PUBLICATION (1), REVOLUTION (1).

circumference *n.* A line around a closed figure or area ► ambit, circuit, compass, perimeter, periphery. [*Compare* BORDER, CIRCLE, LIMITS.]

circumlocution *n.* —*See* WORDINESS.

circumlocutionary *adj.* —*See* WORDY (1).

circumlocutory *adj.* —*See* INDIRECT (1), WORDY (1).

circumnavigate *v.* —*See* ENCIRCLE, SKIRT.

circumscribe *v.* —*See* DETERMINE, ENCIRCLE, LIMIT.

circumscribed *adj.* —*See* RESTRICTED.

circumscription *n.* —*See* RESTRAINT, RESTRICTION.

circumspect *adj.* —*See* DELIBERATE (3), WARY.

circumspection *n.* —*See* PRUDENCE.

circumstance *n.* **1.** Something that takes place ► episode, event, experience, happening, incident, occasion, occurrence, thing. [*Compare* EVENT.] **2.** One of the conditions or facts at-

often **circumstances** The sum of determining factors beyond willful control. 3. **circumstances** Financial status or means. 4. Formal display; ceremony: *pomp and circumstance.* —*idioms:* **under no circumstances** Never. **under** (or **in**) **the circumstances** Given these conditions.
cir·cum·stan·tial (sûr′kəm-stăn′shəl) ▸ *adj.* 1. Of or dependent on circumstances. 2. Of minor import; incidental. 3. Complete and particular. —**cir′cum·stan′tial·ly** *adv.*
circumstantial evidence ▸ *n.* Evidence not bearing directly on the fact in dispute but on various attendant circumstances from which the judge or jury might infer the occurrence of the fact in dispute.
cir·cum·stan·ti·ate (sûr′kəm-stăn′shē-āt′) ▸ *v.* **-at·ed, -at·ing.** To give detailed proof or description of. —**cir′cum·stan′ti·a′tion** *n.*
cir·cum·ter·res·tri·al (sûr′kəm-tə-rĕs′trē-əl) ▸ *adj.* Revolving around or surrounding the earth.
cir·cum·vent (sûr′kəm-vĕnt′) ▸ *v.* 1. To entrap or overcome by ingenuity. 2. To avoid or get around: *circumvent a regulation.* —**cir′cum·ven′tion** *n.* —**cir′cum·ven′tive** *adj.*
cir·cus (sûr′kəs) ▸ *n.* 1a. A public entertainment consisting typically of a variety of performances by acrobats, clowns, and trained animals. b. A traveling company that performs such entertainments, often under a tent. 2. *Informal* A humorous or rowdy time or event. —**cir′cus·y** *adj.*
cirque (sûrk) ▸ *n.* A steep hollow, often containing a small lake, at the upper end of a mountain valley.
cir·rho·sis (sĭ-rō′sĭs) ▸ *n.* A chronic, sometimes fatal liver disease caused esp. by alcohol abuse or hepatitis. —**cir·rhot′ic** (-rŏt′ĭk) *adj.*
cir·ro·cu·mu·lus (sîr′ō-kyo͞om′yə-ləs) ▸ *n.* A high-altitude cloud composed of a series of small, regularly arranged cloudlets in the form of ripples or grains.
cir·ro·strat·us (sîr′ō-străt′əs, -strā′təs) ▸ *n.* A high-altitude, thin hazy cloud or cloud cover, often producing a halo effect.
cir·rus (sîr′əs) ▸ *n., pl.* **cir·ri** (sîr′ī′). A high-altitude cloud composed of thin, usu. white fleecy bands or patches.
cis·tern (sĭs′tərn) ▸ *n.* A receptacle for holding water, esp. a tank for catching and storing rainwater.
cit·a·del (sĭt′ə-dəl, -dĕl′) ▸ *n.* 1. A fortress in a commanding position in or near a city. 2. A stronghold.
cite (sīt) ▸ *v.* **cit·ed, cit·ing.** 1. To quote as an authority or example. 2. To mention as support, illustration, or proof. 3. To commend officially for meritorious action, esp. in military service. 4. To summon before a court of law. —**ci·ta′tion** *n.*
cit·i·fy (sĭt′ĭ-fī′) ▸ *v.* **-fied, -fy·ing.** 1. To make urban. 2. To impart the styles and manners of a city to. —**cit′i·fi·ca′tion** *n.* —**cit′i·fied′** *adj.*
cit·i·zen (sĭt′ĭ-zən) ▸ *n.* 1. A person owing loyalty to and entitled by birth or naturalization to the protection of a state or nation. 2. A resident of a city or town. —**cit′i·zen·ly** *adj.*
cit·i·zen·ry (sĭt′ĭ-zən-rē) ▸ *n., pl.* **-ries.** Citizens collectively.
cit·i·zens band (sĭt′ĭ-zənz) ▸ *n.* A radio-frequency band officially allocated for private use by individuals.
cit·i·zen·ship (sĭt′ĭ-zən-shĭp′) ▸ *n.* The status of a citizen with its duties, rights, and privileges.
cit·rate (sĭt′rāt′) ▸ *n.* A salt or ester of citric acid.
cit·ric acid (sĭt′rĭk) ▸ *n.* A colorless acid derived from citrus and pineapple juices and used in flavorings and metal polishes.
ci·trine (sĭ-trēn′, sĭt′rēn′) ▸ *n.* 1. A pale yellow quartz resembling topaz. 2. A light yellow. —**ci·trine′** *adj.*
cit·ron (sĭt′rən) ▸ *n.* 1. A thorny evergreen shrub with large, lemonlike fruits. 2. Its fruit, whose rind is often candied and used in confections.
cit·ro·nel·la (sĭt′rə-nĕl′ə) ▸ *n.* A pale yellow aromatic oil obtained from a tropical Asian grass and used in perfumery, insect repellents, and flavorings.
cit·rus (sĭt′rəs) ▸ *n., pl.* **-rus** or **-rus·es.** Any of various evergreen shrubs or trees such as the grapefruit, lemon, or orange, bearing juicy edible fruits with an aromatic rind.
cit·y (sĭt′ē) ▸ *n., pl.* **-ies.** 1. A town of significant size and importance. 2. An incorporated US municipality with definite boundaries and legal powers set forth in a state charter. 3. The inhabitants of a city as a group.
city council ▸ *n.* The governing body of a city.
city hall ▸ *n.* 1. The building housing the administrative offices of a municipal government. 2. A municipal government.
cit·y-state (sĭt′ē-stāt′) ▸ *n.* A sovereign state consisting of an independent city and its surrounding territory.
civ·et (sĭv′ĭt) ▸ *n.* 1. A catlike mammal of Africa and Asia that secretes a musky fluid. 2. This fluid, used in perfumery.
civ·ic (sĭv′ĭk) ▸ *adj.* Of a city, a citizen, or citizenship.
civ·ics (sĭv′ĭks) ▸ *n.* *(takes sing. v.)* The study of civic affairs and the rights and duties of citizens.
civ·ies (sĭv′ēz) ▸ *pl.n.* *Slang* Var. of **civvies.**
civ·il (sĭv′əl) ▸ *adj.* 1. Of or relating to a citizen or citizens. 2. Of ordinary community life as distinguished from the military or the ecclesiastical. 3. Civilized. 4. Not rude; polite. —**civ′il·ly** *adv.*
civil defense ▸ *n.* Emergency measures to be taken by organized civilian volunteers for protection of life and property in the event of natural disaster or enemy attack.
civil disobedience ▸ *n.* Refusal to obey civil laws in an effort to induce change in governmental policy or legislation, characterized by nonviolent means.
civil engineer ▸ *n.* An engineer trained in the design and construction of public works, as bridges or dams. —**civil engineering** *n.*
ci·vil·ian (sĭ-vĭl′yən) ▸ *n.* A person following the pursuits of civil or nonmilitary life. —**ci·vil′ian** *adj.*
ci·vil·i·ty (sĭ-vĭl′ĭ-tē) ▸ *n., pl.* **-ties.** 1. Politeness; courtesy. 2. A courteous act.
civ·i·li·za·tion (sĭv′ə-lĭ-zā′shən) ▸ *n.* 1. An advanced state of cultural and material development in human society, marked by political and social complexity and progress in the arts and sciences. 2. The culture developed by a particular society or epoch. 3. Cultural refinement. 4. Modern society with its conveniences.
civ·i·lize (sĭv′ə-līz′) ▸ *v.* **-lized, -liz·ing.** 1. To raise (a society) to an advanced stage of development. 2. To educate in manners; sophisticate. —**civ′i·liz′er** *n.*

THESAURUS

tending an event and having some bearing on it ▸ condition, detail, fact, factor, particular. [*Compare* ELEMENT, QUALITY.] —*See also* EVENT (1).
circumstances *n.* —*See* CONDITIONS.
circumstantial *adj.* —*See* DETAILED, GRACIOUS (2).
circumstantiate *v.* —*See* PROVE.
circumstantiation *n.* —*See* CONFIRMATION (2).
circumvent *v.* —*See* AVOID, SKIRT.
circumvention *n.* —*See* ESCAPE (2).
circumvolution *n.* —*See* REVOLUTION (1).
circumvolve *v.* —*See* TURN (1).
cirque *n.* —*See* CIRCLE (1).
cistern *n.* —*See* VAT.
citadel *n.* —*See* FORT.
citation *n.* A written or printed notification of a legal infraction ▸ ticket. —*See also* DISTINCTION (2), REFERENCE (1).
cite *v.* To bring forward as proof or support ▸ adduce, invoke, lay, present, produce. [*Compare* OFFER.] —*See also* NAME (2), NAME (1).
citizen *n.* A person owing loyalty to and entitled to the protection of a given state ▸ burgess, burgher, freeman, national, subject, taxpayer. [*Compare* INHABITANT.]
city *n.* A large and important town ▸ borough, megalopolis, metropolis, municipality. *Informal:* burg, town. [*Compare* VILLAGE.]
city *adj.* Of, in, or belonging to a city ▸ civic, local, metropolitan, municipal, urban.
civic *adj.* —*See* CITY, POPULAR.
civil *adj.* —*See* COURTEOUS (1), POPULAR, PROFANE (2).
civility *n.* —*See* AMENITIES (2), COURTESY.
civilization *n.* The total product of human creativity and intellect ▸ culture, Kultur, society. —*See also* CULTURE (2), CULTURE (3).
civilize *v.* To fit for companionship with others, especially in attitude or manners ▸ acculturate, humanize, socialize.

civil law ▸ *n.* The body of laws dealing with the rights of private citizens.
civil liberties ▸ *pl.n.* Fundamental individual rights, such as freedom of speech and religion, protected by legal guarantee.
civil rights ▸ *pl.n.* The rights belonging to an individual by virtue of citizenship, esp. the rights to due process, equal protection of the laws, and freedom from discrimination. **—civil rights, civ′il-rights′** *adj.*
civil service ▸ *n.* Those branches of public service that are not legislative, judicial, or military. **—civil servant** *n.*
civil war ▸ *n.* **1.** A war between factions or regions of the same country. **2. Civil War** The war between the Union and the Confederacy from 1861 to 1865.
civ·vies also **civ·ies** (sĭv′ēz) ▸ *pl.n. Slang* Civilian clothes.
cl ▸ *abbr.* centiliter
Cl ▸ The symbol for the element **chlorine.**
clab·ber (klăb′ər) ▸ *n.* Sour curdled milk. ▸ *v.* To curdle.
clack (klăk) ▸ *v.* **1.** To make or cause to make a sharp sound, as by the collision of hard surfaces. **2.** To chatter. ▸ *n.* A clacking sound. **—clack′er** *n.*
clad[1] (klăd) ▸ *v.* **clad, clad·ding.** To cover (a metal) with a bonded metal coating.
clad[2] (klăd) ▸ *v.* P.t. and p.part of **clothe.**
clad·dagh (klä′də) ▸ *n.* A ring formed of two hands clasping a crowned heart.
claim (klām) ▸ *v.* **1.** To ask for as one's due: *claim a reward.* **2.** To state to be true; assert. **3.** To call for: *problems that claim her attention.* ▸ *n.* **1.** A demand for something as one's due. **2.** A title or right. **3.** Something claimed formally or legally. **4.** A statement of something as a fact. ***—idiom:* lay claim to** To assert one's right to. **—claim′a·ble** *adj.*
claim·ant (klā′mənt) ▸ *n.* One making a claim.
clair·voy·ance (klâr-voi′əns) ▸ *n.* The supposed power to see objects or events that cannot be perceived by the senses. **—clair·voy′ant** *adj. & n.*
clam (klăm) ▸ *n.* **1.** Any of a class of bivalve mollusks, many of which are edible. **2.** *Slang* A dollar. ▸ *v.* **clammed, clam·ming.** To hunt for clams. ***—phrasal verb:* clam up** *Informal* To refuse to talk. **—clam′mer** *n.*
clam·bake (klăm′bāk′) ▸ *n.* A picnic where clams, corn, and other foods are baked in layers on hot stones covered with seaweed.
clam·ber (klăm′bər, klăm′ər) ▸ *v.* To climb with difficulty, esp. on all fours; scramble. **—clam′ber·er** *n.*
clam·my (klăm′ē) ▸ *adj.* **-mi·er, -mi·est.** Disagreeably moist, sticky, and usu. cold. **—clam′mi·ness** *n.*
clam·or (klăm′ər) ▸ *n.* **1.** A loud outcry; hubbub. **2.** A vehement outcry or protest. **—clam′or** *v.* **—clam′or·ous** *adj.*
clamp (klămp) ▸ *n.* Any of various devices used to join, grip, support, or compress mechanical or structural parts. ▸ *v.* To fasten or grip with or as if with a clamp. ***—phrasal verb:* clamp down** To become more repressive.
clamp·down (klămp′doun′) ▸ *n.* An imposing of restrictions or controls.
clan (klăn) ▸ *n.* **1.** A traditional social unit in the Scottish Highlands, consisting of a number of families claiming a common ancestor. **2.** A division of a tribe tracing descent from a common ancestor. **3.** A large group of relatives or associates. **—clan′nish** *adj.* **—clan′nish·ness** *n.* **—clans′man** *n.* **—clans′wom′an** *n.*
clan·des·tine (klăn-dĕs′tĭn) ▸ *adj.* Kept or done in secret.
clang (klăng) ▸ *n.* A loud, resonant, metallic sound. **—clang** *v.*
clan·gor (klăng′ər, klăng′gər) ▸ *n.* **1.** A repeated clanging. **2.** A din. **—clan′gor** *v.*
clank (klăngk) ▸ *n.* A sharp, hard metallic sound. **—clank** *v.*
clap (klăp) ▸ *v.* **clapped, clap·ping.** **1.** To strike the palms of the hands together with a sudden explosive sound, as in applauding. **2.** To come together suddenly with a sharp sound. **3.** To strike lightly with the open hand, as in greeting. **4.** To put or send promptly or suddenly: *clapped the thief in jail.* ▸ *n.* **1.** The act or sound of clapping the hands. **2.** A loud or explosive sound: *a clap of thunder.* **3.** A slap.
clap·board (klăb′ərd, klăp′bôrd′) ▸ *n.* A long narrow board with one edge thicker than the other, overlapped horizontally to cover the outer walls of frame structures.
clap·per (klăp′ər) ▸ *n.* One that claps, esp. the hammerlike tongue of a bell.
clap·trap (klăp′trăp′) ▸ *n.* Pretentious, insincere, or empty language.
claque (klăk) ▸ *n.* A group of persons hired to applaud at a performance.
clar·et (klăr′ĭt) ▸ *n.* A dry red table wine.
clar·i·fy (klăr′ə-fī′) ▸ *v.* **-fied, -fy·ing.** To make or become clear. **—clar′i·fi·ca′tion** *n.*
clar·i·net (klăr′ə-nĕt′) ▸ *n.* A woodwind instrument having a straight cylindrical tube with a flaring bell and a single-reed mouthpiece. **—clar′i·net′ist, clar′i·net′tist** *n.*
clar·i·on (klăr′ē-ən) ▸ *adj.* Loud and clear.
clar·i·ty (klăr′ĭ-tē) ▸ *n.* The quality or condition of being clear.
Clark (klärk), **William** (1770–1838) ▸ Amer. explorer.
clash (klăsh) ▸ *v.* **1.** To collide or strike together with a loud harsh noise. **2.** To conflict; disagree. ▸ *n.* **1.** A loud

THESAURUS

civilized *adj.* —*See* CULTURED.
civilizing *adj.* —*See* CULTURAL.
clabber *v.* —*See* COAGULATE.
clack *v.* 1. To make a light, sharp noise ▸ click, snap. [*Compare* CRACKLE.] 2. To make or cause to make a succession of short, sharp sounds ▸ brattle, chatter, clank, clatter, rattle. [*Compare* KNOCK, SHAKE.] —*See also* CHATTER (1).
clack *n.* A light, sharp noise ▸ click, crackle, snap. [*Compare* CRACK.] —*See also* CHATTER.
clad *v.* —*See* FACE (2).
claim *v.* To defend, maintain, or insist on the recognition of ▸ assert, challenge, demand, postulate, vindicate. *Idioms:* have dibs on, lay claim to, stake a claim. —*See also* ASSERT, DEMAND (1).
claim *n.* 1. A legitimate or asserted right to demand something as one's due ▸ pretense, pretension, title. *Slang:* dibs. 2. A right or legal share in something ▸ interest, portion, stake, title. [*Compare* CUT, RIGHT.] —*See also* ASSERTION, DEBT (1), DEMAND (1).
claimant *n.* One that makes a formal complaint, especially in court ▸ accuser, complainant, plaintiff.
clamber *v.* —*See* ASCEND.
clammy *adj.* Slightly wet ▸ damp, dank, dewy, moist. [*Compare* STICKY, WET.]
clamor *n.* —*See* NOISE (1), ROAR, VOCIFERATION.
clamor *v.* —*See* SHOUT.
clamorous *adj.* —*See* LOUD, VOCIFEROUS.
clamp *n.* —*See* FASTENER.
clamp *v.* —*See* ATTACH (1), FASTEN.
clampdown *n.* Forceful subjugation, as against an uprising ▸ crackdown, lockdown, repression, suppression. [*Compare* OPPRESSION, RESTRAINT.]
clan *n.* —*See* FAMILY (2).
clandestine *adj.* —*See* SECRET (1).
clandestinely *adv.* —*See* SECRETLY.
clandestinity or **clandestineness** *n.* —*See* SECRECY.
clang *v.* —*See* BANG.
clang *n.* —*See* CLASH.
clangor *n.* —*See* NOISE (1).
clank *v.* To make or cause to make a succession of short, sharp sounds ▸ brattle, chatter, clack, clatter, rattle. [*Compare* KNOCK, SHAKE.]
clap *v.* To express approval audibly, as by clapping ▸ applaud, cheer, root. *Idioms:* give a big hand (*or* welcome), give an ovation, give someone a hand, put one's hands together. —*See also* BANG, CRACK (2), SLAP.
clap *n.* —*See* CRACK (1).
claptrap *n.* —*See* BOMBAST, NONSENSE.
clarification *n.* —*See* EXPLANATION, PURIFICATION (1).
clarifier *n.* —*See* PURIFIER.
clarify *v.* 1. To make clear or clearer ▸ clear (up), define, elucidate, illuminate, illustrate, simplify. *Idiom:* shed (*or* throw) light on (*or* upon). [*Compare* EXPLAIN, SHOW.] 2. To remove impurities from ▸ clean, cleanse, purify, refine. [*Compare* CLEAN.]
clarity *n.* The quality of being clear and easy to perceive or understand ▸ clearness, comprehensibility, distinctness, explicitness, intelligibility, legibility, limpidity, limpidness, lucidity, lucidness, pellucidity, pellucidness, perspicuity, perspicuousness, plainness, preciseness, precision, simplicity. —*See also* PURITY, VISIBILITY.
clash *v.* —*See* BANG, CONFLICT, CONTEND.
clash *n.* A loud, harsh striking noise ▸ clang, crash, slap, smack, smash,

metallic noise. 2. A usu. hostile conflict.
clasp (klăsp) ▸ *n.* 1. A fastening, such as a hook, used to hold two objects or parts together. 2a. An embrace. b. A grip of the hand. ▸ *v.* 1. To fasten with or as if with a clasp. 2. To hold in a tight embrace. 3. To grip firmly in or with the hand.
class (klăs) ▸ *n.* 1. A group whose members have certain attributes in common; category. 2. A division based on quality or grade. 3. A social or economic stratum whose members share similar characteristics. 4. *Informal* Elegance of style or manner. 5a. A group of students or alumni who have the same year of graduation. b. A group of students who meet to study the same subject. 6. *Biol.* A taxonomic category ranking below a phylum and above an order. ▸ *v.* To classify.
class action ▸ *n.* A lawsuit brought by one or more plaintiffs on behalf of a large group of others who have a common interest.
clas·sic (klăs′ĭk) ▸ *adj.* 1a. Of highest rank or class. b. Serving as the established model or standard: *a classic example.* 2. Adhering to established standards and principles. 3. Relating to ancient Greek and Roman literature and art; classical. 4. Having lasting historical or literary associations. ▸ *n.* 1. An artist, author, or work gen. considered to be of the highest rank. 2. **classics** The languages and literature of ancient Greece and Rome. 3. A typical example. 4. *Informal* An outstanding example of its kind: *His excuse was a classic.* 5. A traditional event, as in sports.
clas·si·cal (klăs′ĭ-kəl) ▸ *adj.* 1a. Of or relating to the ancient Greeks and Romans, esp. their art, literature, or culture. b. Conforming to the artistic models of ancient Greece and Rome. 2. *Mus.* a. Of European music during the later 18th and early 19th cent. b. Of concert music, such as symphony and opera, as opposed to popular or folk music. 3. Standard and authoritative rather than new or experimental. **—clas′si·cal·ly** *adv.*
clas·si·cism (klăs′ĭ-sĭz′əm) ▸ *n.* 1. Aesthetic attitudes and principles manifested in the art, architecture, and literature of ancient Greece and Rome and characterized by emphasis on form, simplicity, proportion, and restraint. 2. Adherence to such attitudes and principles. 3. Classical scholarship.
clas·si·cist (klăs′ĭ-sĭst) ▸ *n.* 1. A classical scholar. 2. An adherent of classicism.
clas·si·fied (klăs′ə-fīd′) ▸ *adj.* 1. Arranged in classes or categories. 2. Available to authorized persons only; secret.
clas·si·fy (klăs′ə-fī′) ▸ *v.* **-fied, -fy·ing.** 1. To arrange or organize according to class or category. 2. To designate (e.g., a document) as confidential, secret, or top secret. **—clas′si·fi·ca′tion** *n.* **—clas′si·fi′er** *n.*
class·less (klăs′lĭs) ▸ *adj.* Lacking social or economic distinctions of class.
class·mate (klăs′māt′) ▸ *n.* A member of the same class at school.
class·room (klăs′ro͞om′, -ro͝om′) ▸ *n.* A room in which academic classes meet.
class·y (klăs′ē) ▸ *adj.* **-i·er, -i·est.** *Informal* Highly stylish; elegant. **—class′i·ness** *n.*
clat·ter (klăt′ər) ▸ *v.* To make or cause to make a rattling sound. ▸ *n.* 1. A rattling sound. 2. A din; racket.
Clau·di·us I (klô′dē-əs) (10 B.C.–A.D. 54) ▸ Emperor of Rome (A.D. 41–54).
clause (klôz) ▸ *n.* 1. *Gram.* A group of words containing a subject and a predicate and forming part of a compound or complex sentence. 2. A distinct article, stipulation, or provision in a document. **—claus′al** *adj.*
claus·tro·pho·bi·a (klô′strə-fō′bē-ə) ▸ *n.* An abnormal fear of being in narrow or enclosed spaces. **—claus′tro·phobe′** *n.* **—claus′tro·pho′bic** *adj.*
clav·i·chord (klăv′ĭ-kôrd′) ▸ *n. Mus.* An early keyboard instrument. **—clav′i·chord′ist** *n.*
clav·i·cle (klăv′ĭ-kəl) ▸ *n.* Either of two slender bones that connect the sternum and the scapula; collarbone.
cla·vier (klə-vîr′, klā′vē-ər, klăv′ē-) ▸ *n. Mus.* 1. A keyboard. 2. A stringed keyboard instrument.
claw (klô) ▸ *n.* 1. A sharp curved nail on the toe of a mammal, reptile, or bird. 2. A pincerlike part, as of a lobster. 3. Something resembling a claw. ▸ *v.* To scratch or dig with or as if with claws.
clay (klā) ▸ *n.* 1. A fine-grained, firm earth that is pliable when wet and hardens when heated, used in making bricks, tiles, and pottery. 2. Moist sticky earth. 3. The mortal human body. **—clay′ey** (klā′ē), **clay′ish** *adj.*
clay·more mine (klā′môr′) ▸ *n.* A ground-emplaced antipersonnel mine.
clay pigeon ▸ *n.* A clay disk thrown as a flying target for skeet and trapshooting.
clean (klēn) ▸ *adj.* **-er, -est.** 1. Free from dirt or impurities. 2. Free from foreign matter, pollution, or infection. 3. Even; regular: *a clean, straight line.* 4. Thorough; complete: *a clean getaway.* 5. Morally pure; virtuous. 6. Obeying the rules; honest or fair. ▸ *adv.* **-er, -est.** 1. In a clean manner. 2. *Informal* Entirely; wholly: *clean forgot.* ▸ *v.* To make or become clean. ***—phrasal verbs:*** **clean out** *Informal* 1. To deprive completely, as of money. 2. To drive or force out. **clean up** *Slang* To make a large profit. ***—idiom:*** **clean house** *Slang* To eliminate or discard what is undesirable. **—clean′a·ble** *adj.* **—clean′er** *n.* **—clean′ness** *n.*
clean-cut (klēn′kŭt′) ▸ *adj.* 1. Clearly defined. 2. Neat and trim in appearance.
clean·ly (klĕn′lē) ▸ *adj.* **-li·er, -li·est.** Habitually neat and clean. ▸ *adv.* (klēn′lē) In a clean manner. **—clean′li·ness** (klĕn′lē-nĭs) *n.*

THESAURUS

whack. [*Compare* BLOW[2], CRACK, SLAM.] —*See also* ARGUMENT, BATTLE, CONFLICT.
clasp *n.* —*See* EMBRACE, FASTENER, HOLD (1).
clasp *v.* —*See* EMBRACE (1), GRASP.
class *n.* 1. A subdivision of a larger group ▸ category, classification, department, division, family, genre, group, order, set. [*Compare* KIND.] 2. A division of persons or things by quality, rank, or grade ▸ bracket, caste, grade, hierarchy, league, level, order, range, rank, school, stratum, tier. [*Compare* PLACE.] 3. Degree of excellence ▸ caliber, grade, quality. [*Compare* DEGREE.] —*See also* ELEGANCE.
classic *adj.* —*See* BARE (1), TYPICAL, VINTAGE.
classical *adj.* —*See* TYPICAL, VINTAGE.
classification *n.* —*See* ARRANGEMENT (1), CLASS (1).
classified *adj.* —*See* CONFIDENTIAL (3).
classify *v.* To arrange or organize according to class ▸ assort, catalog, categorize, class, coordinate, distribute, divide, grade, group, pigeonhole, place, range, rank, rate, separate, size, sort (out), stereotype, stratify. [*Compare* ARRANGE, POSITION.]
classy *adj.* —*See* ELEGANT, EXCLUSIVE (3), FASHIONABLE.
clatter *v.* To make or cause to make a succession of short, sharp sounds ▸ brattle, chatter, clack, clank, rattle. [*Compare* KNOCK, SHAKE.]
clay *n.* The substance of the body, especially after decay or cremation ▸ ashes, cremains, dust, remains. —*See also* EARTH (1).
clean *adj.* 1. Free from dirt, stain, or impurities ▸ antiseptic, cleanly, fresh, immaculate, scrubbed, spick-and-span, spotless, stainless, unsmirched, unsoiled, unsullied. *Idioms:* clean as a whistle, squeaky clean. [*Compare* NEAT, STERILE.] 2. Not lewd or obscene ▸ decent, inoffensive, modest, wholesome. *Informal:* G-rated. [*Compare* CORRECT, ETHICAL.] 3. According to the rules ▸ fair, sporting, sportsmanlike, sportsmanly. —*See also* DEXTEROUS, INNOCENT (1), INNOCENT (2), PERFECT.
clean *adv.* —*See* COMPLETELY (1).
clean *v.* 1. To rid of dirt, stains, trash, or other impurities ▸ bathe, cleanse, launder, lave, rinse, wash. [*Compare* SCRAPE, REFINE.] 2. To remove impurities from ▸ clarify, cleanse, purify, refine. —*See also* TIDY (1), TIDY (2).
clean out *v.* —*See* EMPTY, RUIN.
clean up *v. Slang:* To make a large profit ▸ batten, cash in, profit. *Idioms:* make a killing, make out like a bandit.
cleaner *n.* —*See* PURIFIER.
cleaning *n.* —*See* PURIFICATION (1).
cleanliness *n.* —*See* PURITY.
cleanly *adj.* —*See* CLEAN (1).
cleanly *adv.* —*See* FAIR[1].

clean room ▸ *n.* A room kept virtually free of contaminants, used for laboratory work and in the production of precision parts.

cleanse (klĕnz) ▸ *v.* **cleansed, cleans·ing.** To free from dirt, defilement, or guilt. **—cleans′er** *n.*

clean·up (klēn′ŭp′) ▸ *n.* **1.** A thorough cleaning or ordering. **2.** *Slang* A very large profit. **3.** *Baseball* The 4th position in the batting order. **—clean′up′** *adj.*

clear (klîr) ▸ *adj.* **-er, -est. 1.** Free from anything that dims, obscures, or darkens. **2.** Free from impediment; open. **3.** Easily seen through; transparent. **4.** Evident. **5.** Easily perceptible; distinct. **6.** Discerning or perceiving easily: *a clear mind.* **7.** Free from doubt or confusion. **8.** Free from qualification or limitation. **9.** Free from burden, obligation, or guilt. **10.** Freed from contact or connection: *clear of the danger; clear of the reef.* ▸ *adv.* **1.** Distinctly; clearly. **2.** Out of the way. **3.** *Informal* Completely; entirely. ▸ *v.* **1.** To make or become light, clear, or bright. **2.** To rid of impurities or blemishes. **3.** To make plain or intelligible. **4.** To rid of obstructions. **5.** To remove the occupants of: *clear the theater.* **6.** To free from a charge of guilt. **7.** To pass by, under, or over without contact. **8.** To gain as net profit. **9.** To pass through a clearing-house, as a check. **10.** To authorize. **11.** To free (the throat) of phlegm. ***—phrasal verb:*** **clear out** *Informal* To leave a place, usu. quickly. **—clear′ly** *adv.* **—clear′ness** *n.*

clear·ance (klîr′əns) ▸ *n.* **1.** The act or process of clearing. **2.** The amount by which a moving object clears something. **3.** Permission to proceed.

clear-cut (klîr′kŭt′) ▸ *adj.* **1.** Distinctly defined or outlined. **2.** Not ambiguous; obvious. ▸ *v.* To log (an area) by removing all the trees at one time.

clear·ing (klîr′ĭng) ▸ *n.* An open space, esp. a tract of woodland clear of trees.

clear·ing-house (klîr′ĭng-hous′) ▸ *n.* An office where banks exchange checks and drafts and settle accounts.

cleat (klēt) ▸ *n.* A wooden, metallic, or hard rubber projection used to grip, provide support, or prevent slipping.

cleav·age (klē′vĭj) ▸ *n.* **1.** The act of splitting or cleaving. **2.** A fissure or division.

cleave[1] (klēv) ▸ *v.* **cleft** (klĕft) or **cleaved** or **clove** (klōv), **cleft** or **cleaved** or **clo·ven** (klō′vən), **cleav·ing. 1.** To split; divide. **2.** To pierce.

cleave[2] (klēv) ▸ *v.* **cleaved, cleav·ing.** To adhere, cling, or stick fast.

cleav·er (klē′vər) ▸ *n.* A heavy, broad-bladed knife or hatchet used esp. by butchers.

clef (klĕf) ▸ *n. Mus.* A symbol indicating the pitch represented by one line of a staff, from which the others can be determined.

cleft (klĕft) ▸ *v.* P.t. and p.part of **cleave[1]**. ▸ *adj.* Divided; split. ▸ *n.* A crevice.

cleft lip ▸ *n.* A congenital cleft or pair of clefts in the upper lip.

cleft palate ▸ *n.* A congenital fissure of the roof of the mouth.

clem·a·tis (klĕm′ə-tĭs, klĭ-măt′ĭs) ▸ *n.* Any of a genus of vines having showy, variously colored flowers.

clem·en·cy (klĕm′ən-sē) ▸ *n., pl.* **-cies. 1.** Leniency; mercy. **2.** Mildness, as of weather.

Clem·ens (klĕm′ənz), **Samuel Langhorne** Pen name Mark Twain (1835–1910) ▸ Amer. author.

clem·ent (klĕm′ənt) ▸ *adj.* **1.** Lenient or merciful. **2.** Mild; pleasant: *clement weather.* **—clem′ent·ly** *adv.*

clench (klĕnch) ▸ *v.* **1.** To close tightly: *clench one's teeth; clenched my fists in anger.* **2.** To grasp or grip tightly. **3.** To clinch (e.g., a bolt). ▸ *n.* **1.** A tight grip or grasp. **2.** A device that clenches.

Cle·o·pat·ra (klē′ə-păt′rə) (69–30 B.C.) ▸ Egyptian queen (51–49 and 48–30).

clere·sto·ry (klîr′stôr′ē) ▸ *n., pl.* **-ries.** A windowed wall above the roofed section of a building.

cler·gy (klûr′jē) ▸ *n., pl.* **-gies.** The body of people ordained or recognized by a religious community as ritual or spiritual leaders.

cler·gy·man (klûr′jē-mən) ▸ *n.* A man who is a member of the clergy.

cler·gy·wom·an (klûr′jē-wo͝om′ən) ▸ *n.* A woman who is a member of the clergy.

cler·ic (klĕr′ĭk) ▸ *n.* A member of the clergy.

cler·i·cal (klĕr′ĭ-kəl) ▸ *adj.* **1.** Of or relating to clerks or office workers or their work. **2.** Of the clergy.

cler·i·cal·ism (klĕr′ĭ-kə-lĭz′əm) ▸ *n.* A policy of supporting the power and influence of the clergy in political or secular matters.

clerk (klûrk; *British* klärk) ▸ *n.* **1.** One who works in an office performing such tasks as keeping records and filing. **2.** One who performs the business of a court or legislative body. **3.** A salesclerk. ▸ *v.* To work or serve as a clerk. **—clerk′ship′** *n.*

Cleve·land (klēv′lənd) ▸ A city of NE OH on Lake Erie.

Cleveland, (Stephen) Grover (1837–1908) ▸ The 22nd and 24th US President.

clev·er (klĕv′ər) ▸ *adj.* **-er, -est. 1.** Mentally quick and

THESAURUS

cleanness *n.* —*See* PURITY.

cleanse *v.* To remove impurities from ▸ clarify, clean, purify, refine. —*See also* CLEAN (1), PURIFY (1).

cleanser *n.* —*See* PURIFIER.

cleansing *n.* —*See* PURIFICATION (1).

clear *adj.* **1.** Free from what obscures or dims ▸ crystal, crystal clear, crystalline, hyaline, limpid, lucid, pellucid, see-through, translucent, transparent. [*Compare* FILMY, SHEER[2].] **2.** Free from clouds or mist ▸ bright, cloudless, fair, fine, sunny, unclouded. **3.** Free from obstructions ▸ free, open, unbarred, unblocked, unhindered, unimpeded, unobstructed, unplugged. *Idiom:* wide open. [*Compare* PASSABLE.] —*See also* APPARENT (1), DECIDED, DEFINITE (1), EMPTY (1), OBVIOUS, PERFECT, PURE, SHARP (2).

clear *v.* **1.** To become brighter or fairer ▸ brighten, clear up, kindle, illuminate, lighten. **2.** To rid of obstructions ▸ free, open, remove, unblock. [*Compare* RID.] **3.** To free from a charge or imputation of guilt ▸ absolve, acquit, discharge, exculpate, exonerate, justify, purge, vindicate. *Idiom:* get off the hook. [*Compare* FORGIVE.] **4.** To pass by or over safely or successfully ▸ hurdle, negotiate, surmount. —*See also* ANNIHILATE, CLARIFY (1), EMPTY, EXTRICATE, RID, PASS (6), RETURN (3), SETTLE (3), TIDY (1).

clear *adv.* —*See* COMPLETELY (1).

clear out *v.* —*See* RUN (2).

clear up *v.* —*See* SOLVE (1).

clearance *n.* —*See* ELIMINATION.

clear-cut *adj.* —*See* APPARENT (1), DECIDED, DEFINITE (1).

clearing *n.* ▸ field, meadow, pasture. [*Compare* LOT.]

clearness *n.* —*See* CLARITY, VISIBILITY.

clear-sightedness *n.* —*See* DISCERNMENT.

cleavage *n.* —*See* CRACK (2).

cleave[1] *v.* —*See* CRACK (1), CUT (2).

cleave[2] *v.* —*See* BOND.

cleft *n.* —*See* CRACK (2).

clemency *n.* —*See* MERCY.

clement *adj.* Free from extremes in temperature ▸ balmy, mild, moderate, temperate. [*Compare* PLEASANT.] —*See also* TOLERANT.

clench *v.* —*See* GRASP.

clench *n.* —*See* HOLD (1).

clergyman or **clergywoman** *n.* —*See* CLERIC.

cleric *n.* A person ordained for service in a Christian church ▸ abbé, abbot, bishop, chaplain, churchman, churchwoman, clergyman, clergywoman, clerical, clerk, curate, deacon, divine, ecclesiastic, minister, monk, parson, pastor, preacher, prelate, priest, rector, vicar. *Informal:* padre, reverend.

clerical *adj.* Of or relating to the clergy, especially in a Christian church ▸ ecclesiastical, episcopal, ministerial, pastoral, priestly, sacerdotal. [*Compare* SPIRITUAL.]

clerical *n.* —*See* CLERIC.

clerk *n.* —*See* CLERIC, SELLER.

clever *adj.* **1.** Mentally quick and original ▸ acute, alert, bright, ingenious, intelligent, inventive, keen, quick, quick-thinking, quick-witted, resourceful, sharp, sharp-witted, shrewd, smart. *Idioms:* nobody's fool, on the ball (*or* beam), quick on the uptake, sharp as a tack, smart as a whip. [*Compare* ARTFUL,

original. 2. Dexterous. 3. Ingenious. **—clev′er·ly** *adv.* **—clev′er·ness** *n.*
clev·is (klĕv′ĭs) ▸ *n.* A U-shaped metal fastener.
clew (klo͞o) ▸ *n.* 1. A ball of yarn or thread. 2. *Naut.* A metal loop attached to the lower corner of a sail.
cli·ché (klē-shā′) ▸ *n.* A trite expression or idea.
cli·chéd (klē-shād′) ▸ *adj.* Trite; hackneyed.
click (klĭk) ▸ *n.* 1. A brief sharp sound. 2. An act of clicking. ▸ *v.* 1. To make or cause to make a click. 2. *Comp. Sci.* To press down and release a button on a pointing device, as to select an icon. 3. *Slang* **a.** To be a great success. **b.** To function well together.
click·er (klĭk′ər) ▸ *n.* One that clicks, as: **a.** A remote control. **b.** A computer mouse.
cli·ent (klī′ənt) ▸ *n.* 1. One for whom professional services are rendered. 2. A customer. 3. A computer or program that can download files, run applications, or request services from a file server.
cli·en·tele (klī′ən-tĕl′, klē′än-) ▸ *n.* Clients or customers collectively.
cliff (klĭf) ▸ *n.* A high, steep, or overhanging face of rock. **—cliff′y** *adj.*
cliff dweller ▸ *n.* A member of an Anasazi people of the SW US who built dwellings in the sides of cliffs. **—cliff dwelling** *n.*
cliff·hang·er (klĭf′hăng′ər) ▸ *n.* 1. A melodramatic serial in which each episode ends in suspense. 2. A close, suspenseful contest.
cli·mac·ter·ic (klī-măk′tər-ĭk, klī′măk-tĕr′ĭk) ▸ *n.* 1. A period of life marked in women by the end of reproductive capacity and terminating with the completion of menopause. 2. A critical period.
cli·mac·tic (klī-măk′tĭk) ▸ *adj.* Of or constituting a climax. **—cli·mac′ti·cal·ly** *adv.*
cli·mate (klī′mĭt) ▸ *n.* 1. The prevailing weather conditions in a particular region. 2. A region having certain weather conditions: *lives in a cold climate.* 3. A general atmosphere or attitude: *a climate of unrest.* **—cli·mat′ic** (-măt′ĭk) *adj.* **—cli·mat′i·cal·ly** *adv.*
cli·ma·tol·o·gy (klī′mə-tŏl′ə-jē) ▸ *n.* The meteorological study of climate. **—cli′ma·to·log′ic** (-mə-tl-ŏj′ĭk), **cli′ma·to·log′i·cal** *adj.* **—cli′ma·tol′o·gist** *n.*
cli·max (klī′măks′) ▸ *n.* 1. The point of greatest intensity, force, or effect in an ascending series. 2. See **orgasm.** 3. *Ecol.* A stage in which a community of organisms, esp. plants, reaches a stable, self-perpetuating balance. ▸ *v.* To bring to or reach a climax.
climb (klīm) ▸ *v.* 1a. To move up or ascend, esp. by using the hands and feet. **b.** To move in a specified direction: *climbed down the ladder.* 2. To grow upward. 3. To rise: *prices climbed in June.* ▸ *n.* 1. An act of climbing. 2. A place to be climbed. **—climb′er** *n.*
clime (klīm) ▸ *n.* Climate.
clinch (klĭnch) ▸ *v.* 1. To fasten securely, as with a nail or bolt. 2. To settle conclusively. 3. *Sports* To embrace so as to immobilize an opponent's arms. ▸ *n.* An act or instance of clinching.
clinch·er (klĭn′chər) ▸ *n.* One that clinches, esp. a decisive point, fact, or remark.
cling (klĭng) ▸ *v.* **clung** (klŭng), **cling·ing.** 1. To hold fast or adhere to something or someone. 2. To remain emotionally attached. **—cling′y** *adj.*
cling·stone (klĭng′stōn′) ▸ *n.* A fruit, esp. a peach, having flesh that adheres closely to the stone. **—cling′stone′** *adj.*
clin·ic (klĭn′ĭk) ▸ *n.* 1. A facility, often associated with a hospital, that deals mainly with outpatients. 2. A medical establishment run by several specialists working in cooperation. 3. A center that offers special counseling or instruction. 4. A training session in which medical students observe the examination and treatment of patients, as at the bedside.
clin·i·cal (klĭn′ĭ-kəl) ▸ *adj.* 1. Of or connected with a clinic. 2. Of or based on direct observation of patients. 3. Objective; analytical. **—clin′i·cal·ly** *adv.*
cli·ni·cian (klĭ-nĭsh′ən) ▸ *n.* A physician, psychologist, or psychiatrist specializing in clinical studies or practice.
clink[1] (klĭngk) ▸ *v.* To make or cause to make a light sharp ringing sound. **—clink** *n.*
clink[2] (klĭngk) ▸ *n.* *Slang* A prison or jail.
clink·er (klĭng′kər) ▸ *n.* 1. A fused lump of incombustible residue that remains after coal has burned. 2. A mistake.
Clinton (klĭn′tən), **William Jefferson.** "Bill" (b. 1946) ▸ The 42nd US President (1993–2001).
cli·o·met·rics (klī′ə-mĕt′rĭks) ▸ *n.* *(takes sing. v.)* The study of history using advanced mathematical methods of data processing and analysis. **—cli′o·met′ric** *adj.*
clip[1] (klĭp) ▸ *v.* **clipped, clip·ping.** 1. To cut off or out with or as if with shears. 2. To shorten; trim. 3. *Informal* To hit with a sharp blow. 4. *Slang* To cheat; swindle. ▸ *n.* 1. Something clipped off, esp. a short extract from a film or videotape. 2. *Informal* A sharp blow. 3. *Informal* A brisk pace. 4. **clips** A pair of clippers.
clip[2] (klĭp) ▸ *n.* 1. A clasp or fastener. 2. A container for holding cartridges. ▸ *v.* **clipped, clip·ping.** 1. To hold tightly; fasten. 2. *Football* To block (an opponent) illegally.
clip·board (klĭp′bôrd′) ▸ *n.* A small writing board with a spring clip at the top for holding papers or a pad.
clip·per (klĭp′ər) ▸ *n.* 1. often **clippers** A tool for cutting, clipping, or shearing. 2. A sailing vessel built for great speed.
clip·ping (klĭp′ĭng) ▸ *n.* Something cut out, esp. an item from a newspaper.
clique (klēk, klĭk) ▸ *n.* A small, exclusive group of people. **—cliqu′ey, cliqu′y** *adj.*
clit·o·ris (klĭt′ər-ĭs, klĭ-tôr′-, klī′tər-) ▸ *n.* A small erectile organ at the upper part of the vulva, homologous with the penis. **—clit′o·ral** *adj.*
clo·a·ca (klō-ā′kə) ▸ *n., pl.* **-cae** (-sē′). 1. The cavity into which the intestinal, genital, and urinary tracts open in reptiles, birds, amphibians, and most fishes. 2. A similar cavity in certain invertebrates.

THESAURUS

INTELLIGENT, SHREWD.] 2. Exhibiting or employing wit or originality ▸ humorous, scintillating, smart, sparkling, witty. [*Compare* FUNNY, SARCASTIC.] —*See also* DEXTEROUS.
cleverness *n.* —*See* ART, DEXTERITY, INTELLIGENCE.
cliché *n.* A trite expression or idea ▸ banality, bromide, commonplace, platitude, saw, stereotype, truism. *Idiom:* old chestnut.
clichéd *adj.* —*See* TRITE.
click *n.* A light, sharp noise ▸ clack, crackle, snap. [*Compare* CRACK.]
click *v.* To make a light, sharp noise ▸ clack, snap. [*Compare* CRACKLE.] —*See also* RELATE (2), SUCCEED (2).
client *n.* —*See* CONSUMER.
clientele or **clientage** *n.* —*See* PATRONAGE (3).
climacteric *n.* —*See* CRISIS.
climacteric *adj.* —*See* URGENT (1).
climactic *adj.* Of or constituting a climax ▸ crowning, culminating, peak. [*Compare* LAST.] —*See also* DRAMATIC (2).
climate *n.* —*See* ENVIRONMENT (2), TEMPER (3).
climax *n.* The highest point or state ▸ acme, apex, apogee, cap, crest, crown, culmination, fastigium, height, meridian, peak, pinnacle, pitch, roof, summit, top, vertex, zenith. *Informal:* payoff. [*Compare* FACE.] —*See also* CRISIS.
climax *v.* To reach or bring to a climax ▸ cap (off), crescendo, crest, crown, culminate, peak, top (off *or* out).
climb *v.* —*See* ASCEND, RISE (2), RISE (3).
climb *n.* —*See* ASCENT (1).
climbing *v.* —*See* ASCENT (1).
clinch *v.* —*See* DECIDE, EMBRACE (1), GUARANTEE (2).
clinch *n.* —*See* EMBRACE.
clincher *n.* *Informal* A key resource to be used at an opportune moment ▸ ace, trump, trump card. *Idiom:* ace in the hole.
cling *v.* —*See* BOND.
clinging *adj.* Fearful of the loss of position or affection ▸ clutching, green-eyed, jealous, possessive. [*Compare* ENVIOUS.] —*See also* TIGHT (1).
clink *n.* —*See* JAIL.
clinker *n.* —*See* BLUNDER, FAILURE (1).
clip[1] *v.* —*See* CHEAT (1), CUT (3), HIT.
clip *n.* *Informal* Rate of motion or performance ▸ pace, speed, tempo, velocity. —*See also* BLOW[2].
clip[2] *v.* —*See* ATTACH (1), FASTEN.
clip *n.* —*See* FASTENER.
clippers *n.* —*See* SHEARS.
clique *n.* —*See* CIRCLE (3).
cloaca *n.* —*See* PIT[1].

cloak (klōk) ► *n.* **1.** A loose outer garment, such as a cape. **2.** Something that covers or conceals: *a cloak of secrecy.* ► *v.* **1.** To cover with a cloak. **2.** To conceal.

cloak-and-dag·ger (klōk′ən-dăg′ər) ► *adj.* Marked by melodramatic intrigue and spying.

clob·ber (klŏb′ər) ► *v. Slang* **1.** To hit or pound with great force. **2.** To defeat decisively.

cloche (klōsh) ► *n.* A close-fitting woman's hat with a bell-like shape.

clock (klŏk) ► *n.* An instrument for measuring or indicating time. ► *v.* **1.** To time, as with a stopwatch. **2.** To measure the speed of. **—clock′er** *n.*

clock·wise (klŏk′wīz′) ► *adv. & adj.* In the same direction as the rotating hands of a clock.

clock·work (klŏk′wûrk′) ► *n.* A mechanism of geared wheels driven by a wound spring, as in a mechanical clock. ***—idiom:* like clockwork** With machinelike precision.

clod (klŏd) ► *n.* **1.** A lump or chunk, esp. of earth or clay. **2.** A dull, stupid person; dolt. **—clod′dish** *adj.*

clod·hop·per (klŏd′hŏp′ər) ► *n.* **1.** A rube or bumpkin. **2.** A big heavy shoe.

clog (klôg, klŏg) ► *n.* **1.** An obstruction or hindrance. **2.** A heavy, usu. wooden-soled shoe. ► *v.* **clogged, clog·ging. 1.** To make or become obstructed. **2.** To hamper or impede.

cloi·son·né (kloi′zə-nā′, klə-wä′zə-) ► *n.* Enamelware in which the surface decoration is formed by different colors of enamel separated by thin strips of metal. **—cloi·son·né′** *adj.*

clois·ter (kloi′stər) ► *n.* **1.** A covered walk with an open colonnade on one side, running along the walls of buildings that face a quadrangle. **2.** A monastery or convent. ► *v.* To seclude in or as if in a cloister. **—clois′tral** *adj.*

clone (klōn) ► *n.* **1.** One or more organisms descended asexually from and genetically identical to a single common ancestor. **2.** A replica of a DNA sequence, such as a gene, produced by genetic engineering. **3.** One that closely resembles another, as in appearance or function. ► *v.* **cloned, clon·ing. 1.** To make multiple identical copies of (a DNA sequence). **2.** To reproduce asexually. **3.** To propagate (an organism) as a clone. **—clon′al** *adj.*

clop (klŏp) ► *n.* A sharp hollow sound, as of a horse's hoof striking pavement. **—clop** *v.*

close (klōs) ► *adj.* **clos·er, clos·est. 1.** Being near in space, time, or relation. **2.** Bound by mutual interests or affections; intimate. **3.** Compact: *a close weave.* **4.** Being near a surface, as of the skin: *a close haircut.* **5.** Decided by a narrow margin; almost even: *a close election.* **6.** Faithful to the original: *a close copy.* **7.** Rigorous; thorough: *close attention.* **8.** Shut or shut in. **9.** Confined in space; crowded. **10.** Fitting tightly. **11.** Lacking fresh air; stuffy. **12.** Confined to specific persons; restricted. **13.** Hidden; secluded. **14.** Taciturn in manner; reticent. **15.** Stingy; miserly. ► *v.* (klōz) **closed, clos·ing. 1a.** To shut or become shut. **b.** To shut in; enclose. **2.** To fill or stop up. **3.** To bring or come to an end; finish. **4.** To join or unite; bring into contact. **5.** To reach an agreement. **6.** To cease operation: *The shop closes at six.* ***—phrasal verb:* close out** To dispose of (a line of merchandise) at reduced prices. ► *n.* (klōz) A conclusion; finish. ► *adv.* (klōs) **clos·er, clos·est.** In a close manner. **—close′ly** *adv.* **—close′ness** *n.*

closed-cap·tioned (klōzd′kăp′shənd) ► *adj.* Broadcast with captions that can be seen only on a specially equipped receiver.

closed circuit (klōzd) ► *n.* **1.** An electric circuit providing an uninterrupted, endless path for the flow of current. **2.** Television that is transmitted to a limited number of receivers. **—closed′-cir′cuit** *adj.*

closed shop ► *n.* See **union shop.**

close-fist·ed (klōs′fĭs′tĭd) ► *adj.* Stingy.

close-mind·ed (klōs′mīn′dĭd, klōz′-) or **closed-mind·ed** (klōzd′-) ► *adj.* Intolerant of the beliefs and opinions of others. **—close′-mind′ed·ness** *n.*

close-mouthed (klōs′mouthd′, -moutht′) ► *adj.* Giving little information; tightlipped.

close·out (klōz′out′) ► *n.* A sale in which all remaining stock is disposed of, usu. at greatly reduced prices.

clos·et (klŏz′ĭt, klô′zĭt) ► *n.* **1.** A small room for storing supplies or clothing. **2.** A small private room. **3.** A state of secrecy or cautious privacy. ► *v.* To enclose in a private room, as for discussion. ► *adj.* Private; secret: *a closet liberal.*

clos·et·ed (klŏz′ĭ-tĭd, klô′zĭ-) ► *adj.* Being in a state of secrecy or cautious privacy.

close-up (klōs′ŭp′) ► *n.* **1.** A photograph or film shot in which the subject is tightly framed and shown at a relatively large scale. **2.** An intimate view or description. **—close′-up′** *adj.*

clos·ing (klō′zĭng) ► *n.* **1.** A concluding part. **2.** A meeting for concluding esp. a real estate transaction.

clo·sure (klō′zhər) ► *n.* **1.** The act of closing or the state of being closed. **2.** Something that closes or shuts. **3.** See **cloture.**

clot (klŏt) ► *n.* A thick or solid mass or lump formed from liquid. ► *v.* **clot·ted, clot·ting.** To form or cause to form into a clot.

cloth (klôth, klŏth) ► *n., pl.* **cloths** (klôths, klô*th*z, klŏths, klŏ*th*z). **1.** Fabric formed by weaving, knitting, or pressing natural or synthetic fibers. **2.** A piece of fabric used for a specific purpose, as a tablecloth. **3.** The characteristic attire of a profession, esp. that of the clergy.

clothe (klō*th*) ► *v.* **clothed** or **clad** (klăd), **cloth·ing. 1.** To

THESAURUS

cloak *n.* —*See* VEIL, WRAP.

cloak *v.* —*See* CLOTHE, CONCEAL, DISGUISE, WRAP (2).

cloak-and-dagger *adj.* —*See* SECRET (1).

clobber *v.* —*See* BEAT (1), OVERWHELM (1).

clobbering *n.* —*See* DEFEAT.

clock *v.* To record the speed or duration of ► time. [*Compare* MEASURE.]

clod *n.* —*See* DULLARD, LUMP[1].

cloddish *adj.* —*See* AWKWARD (1), STUPID.

cloddishness *n.* —*See* STUPIDITY.

clodhopper *n.* A clumsy, unsophisticated person ► bumpkin, hick, peasant, rustic, yokel. *Informal:* hillbilly. *Slang:* hayseed, rube. [*Compare* BOOR, OAF.]

clog *n.* —*See* BAR (1).

clog *v.* —*See* DELAY (1), FILL (2), OBSTRUCT.

cloister *v.* To put into solitude ► isolate, seclude, sequester, sequestrate. [*Compare* ENCLOSE, IMPRISON, ISOLATE.]

clomp *v.* —*See* THUD.

clone *v.* —*See* COPY, MIMIC.

clone *n.* —*See* DOUBLE.

close *adj.* **1.** Not far from another in space, time, or relation ► adjacent, contiguous, immediate, near, nearby, neighboring, nigh, proximate. *Idioms:* a stone's throw, at hand, next to, under one's nose, within an inch, within hailing (*or* spitting) distance. [*Compare* ADJOINING.] **2.** Consistent with correctness, accuracy, or completeness ► exact, faithful, full, rigorous, strict. [*Compare* CAREFUL, THOROUGH.] **3.** Almost even ► nip and tuck, tight. *Idiom:* neck and neck. —*See also* AIRLESS (1), CONFIDENTIAL (2), INTIMATE[1] (1), STINGY, TACITURN, THICK (2), TIGHT (4).

close *v.* **1.** To move a door, for example, in order to cover an opening ► clench, seal, shut, slam. **2.** To come together from different directions ► converge, join, meet, unite. [*Compare* COMBINE.] —*See also* CONCLUDE, ENCLOSE (1), FILL (2).

close in *v.* —*See* ENCLOSE (2).

close off *v.* —*See* ISOLATE (1).

close out *v.* To get rid of by selling ► dispose of, dump, sell off, unload.

close *n.* —*See* COURT (1), END (1), END (2).

close *adv.* To a point near in time, space, or relation ► closely, hard, near, nearby, nigh.

closed-door *adj.* Belonging or confined to a particular person or group as opposed to the public or the government ► personal, private, privy. [*Compare* CONFIDENTIAL, SECRET.]

closefisted *adj.* —*See* STINGY.

closely *adv.* —*See* CLOSE.

close-minded *adj.* —*See* INTOLERANT (1).

close-mouthed *adj.* —*See* TACITURN.

closeness *n.* —*See* FRIENDSHIP, THICKNESS.

closet *v.* —*See* ENCLOSE (1).

closing *adj.* —*See* LAST[1] (1).

closing *n.* —*See* END (1), END (2).

closure *n.* —*See* END (1).

clot *v.* —*See* COAGULATE.

clot *n.* —*See* LUMP[1].

clothe *v.* To cover as if with clothes ►

put clothes on; dress. 2. To cover as if with clothing.

clothes (klōz, klōthz) ▸ *pl.n.* Articles of dress; wearing apparel; garments.

clothes·horse (klōz′hôrs′, klōthz′-) ▸ *n.* 1. A frame on which clothes are hung to dry. 2. One excessively concerned with dress.

clothes·pin (klōz′pĭn′, klōthz′-) ▸ *n.* A clip for fastening clothes to a line.

cloth·ier (klōth′yər, klō′thē-ər) ▸ *n.* One that makes or sells clothing or cloth.

cloth·ing (klō′thĭng) ▸ *n.* Clothes collectively.

clo·ture (klō′chər) ▸ *n.* A parliamentary procedure by which debate is ended and an immediate vote is taken.

cloud (kloud) ▸ *n.* 1a. A visible body of fine water droplets or ice particles suspended in the earth's atmosphere. **b.** A similar mass, as of dust, suspended in the atmosphere or in outer space. 2. A swarm. 3. Something that darkens or fills with gloom. ▸ *v.* 1. To cover with or as if with clouds. 2. To become overcast. 3. To make or become gloomy or troubled. 4. To cast aspersions on. —**cloud′less** *adj.*

cloud·burst (kloud′bûrst′) ▸ *n.* A sudden heavy rainstorm; downpour.

cloud chamber ▸ *n.* A device in which the path of charged subatomic particles can be detected by the formation of chains of droplets on ions generated by their passage.

cloud nine ▸ *n.* *Informal* A state of elation or great happiness.

cloud·y (klou′dē) ▸ *adj.* **-i·er, -i·est.** 1. Full of or covered with clouds. 2. Of or like clouds. 3. Not transparent. 4. Obscure or vague. —**cloud′i·ly** *adv.* —**cloud′i·ness** *n.*

clout (klout) ▸ *n.* 1. A blow, esp. with the fist. 2. *Informal* a. Influence; pull. b. Power; muscle. ▸ *v.* To hit, esp. with the fist.

clove[1] (klōv) ▸ *n.* An evergreen tree whose aromatic dried flower buds are used as a spice.

clove[2] (klōv) ▸ *n.* A small section of a separable bulb, as that of garlic.

clove[3] (klōv) ▸ *v.* P.t. of **cleave**[1].

clo·ven (klō′vən) ▸ *v.* P.part. of **cleave**[1]. ▸ *adj.* Split; divided: *a cloven hoof.*

clo·ver (klō′vər) ▸ *n.* Any of various plants having compound leaves with three leaflets and small flowers.

clo·ver·leaf (klō′vər-lēf′) ▸ *n.* A highway interchange whose curving entrance and exit ramps resemble a four-leaf clover.

clown (kloun) ▸ *n.* 1. A buffoon who entertains by jokes, antics, and tricks, as in a circus. 2. A coarse, rude person. ▸ *v.* To behave like a clown. —**clown′ish** *adj.* —**clown′ish·ly** *adv.*

cloy (kloi) ▸ *v.* To surfeit, esp. with something too rich or sweet. —**cloy′ing·ly** *adv.* —**cloy′ing·ness** *n.*

club (klŭb) ▸ *n.* 1. A heavy stick, usu. thicker at one end, suitable for use as a weapon. 2. *Sports* A stick used in some games to drive a ball. 3. *Games* Any of a suit of playing cards marked with a black figure shaped like a clover leaf. 4. A group of people organized for a common purpose. 5. The facilities used for the meetings of a club. 6. A nightclub. ▸ *v.* **clubbed, club·bing.** 1. To strike or beat with or as if with a club. 2. To contribute or combine for common purpose.

club·foot (klŭb′fo͝ot′) ▸ *n.* 1. A congenital deformity of the foot, usu. marked by a curled shape of the ankle, heel, and toes. 2. A foot so deformed. —**club′foot′ed** *adj.*

club·house (klŭb′hous′) ▸ *n.* 1. A building occupied by a club. 2. The locker room of an athletic team.

club sandwich ▸ *n.* A sandwich, usu. of three slices of bread with a filling of various meats, tomato, lettuce, and mayonnaise.

club soda ▸ *n.* See **soda water** 1.

club steak ▸ *n.* See **Delmonico steak.**

cluck (klŭk) ▸ *n.* 1. The low, short, throaty sound made by a hen when brooding or calling its chicks. 2. *Informal* A stupid or foolish person. —**cluck** *v.*

clue (klo͞o) ▸ *n.* Something that guides or directs in the solution of a problem or mystery. ▸ *v.* **clued, clue·ing** or **clu·ing.** To give guiding information to.

clue·less (klo͞o′lĭs) ▸ *adj.* Lacking understanding or knowledge.

clump (klŭmp) ▸ *n.* 1. A clustered mass or thick grouping; lump. 2. A heavy dull sound. ▸ *v.* 1. To form clumps (of). 2. To walk with a heavy dull sound.

clum·sy (klŭm′zē) ▸ *adj.* **-si·er, -si·est.** 1. Lacking physical coordination, skill, or grace; awkward. 2. Gauche; inept: *a clumsy excuse.* —**clum′si·ly** *adv.* —**clum′si·ness** *n.*

clung (klŭng) ▸ *v.* P.t. and p.part. of **cling.**

clunk (klŭngk) ▸ *n.* A dull heavy sound. —**clunk** *v.*

clunk·y (klŭng′kē) ▸ *adj.* **-i·er, -i·est.** Clumsy in form or manner; awkward.

clus·ter (klŭs′tər) ▸ *n.* A group of things gathered or occurring closely together; bunch. ▸ *v.* To gather, grow, or form into clusters.

clutch[1] (klŭch) ▸ *v.* 1. To grasp or attempt to grasp and hold tightly. 2. To work a motor vehicle's clutch. ▸ *n.* 1. A hand, claw, talon, or paw in the act of grasping. 2. A tight grasp. 3. often **clutches** Control or power. 4. A device for engaging and disengaging two working parts of a shaft or of a shaft and a driving mechanism. 5. A tense, critical situation.

clutch[2] (klŭch) ▸ *n.* 1. A set of eggs incubated at one time. 2. A brood of chickens. 3. A cluster.

clut·ter (klŭt′ər) ▸ *n.* A confused or disordered state or collection. —**clut′ter** *v.*

Clydes·dale (klīdz′dāl′) ▸ *n.* A large powerful draft horse having white feathered hair on the fetlocks.

cm ▸ *abbr.* centimeter

Cm ▸ The symbol for the element **curium.**

Cn ▸ The symbol for the element **copernicium.**

cni·dar·i·an (nī-dâr′ē-ən) ▸ *n.* Any of a phylum of chiefly marine invertebrates having a radially symmetrical body and saclike internal cavity and including the jellyfishes and corals.

Co ▸ The symbol for the element **cobalt.**

CO ▸ *abbr.* Colorado

co– ▸ *pref.* 1. Together; joint; jointly: *coeducation.* 2a. Partner or associate in an activity: *coauthor.* **b.** Subordinate or assistant: *copilot.* 3. To the same extent or degree: *coextensive.* 4. Complement of an angle: *cotangent.*

coach (kōch) ▸ *n.* 1a. A bus. **b.** A railroad passenger car. 2. A large, closed, four-wheeled carriage with an elevated exterior seat for the driver. 3. An economical passenger

THESAURUS

cloak, coat, drape, jacket, mantle, robe, shawl, vest. *—See also* DRESS (1), WRAP (2).

clothing or **clothes** *n.* *—See* DRESS (1).

cloud *n.* *—See* CROWD.

cloud *v.* *—See* DENIGRATE, DRUG (2), OBSCURE.

cloudburst *n.* *—See* RAIN.

clouded *adj.* *—See* AMBIGUOUS (1), MURKY (1).

cloudiness *n.* *—See* VAGUENESS.

cloudless *adj.* *—See* CLEAR (2).

cloud nine *n.* *—See* HEAVEN.

cloudy *adj.* *—See* AMBIGUOUS (2), MURKY (1), UNCLEAR.

clout *n.* *—See* BLOW[2], INFLUENCE.

clout *v.* *—See* HIT.

clown *n.* *—See* JOKER.

clown *v.* *Informal* To make jokes; behave playfully ▸ jest, joke, quip. *Informal:* clown around, fool around, horse around. ***Idioms:*** crack wise, play the fool. [*Compare* PLAY.]

cloy *v.* *—See* SATIATE.

club *n.* *—See* UNION (1).

club *v.* *—See* BEAT (1).

clue *n.* *—See* HINT (2), TIP[3].

clueless *adj.* *—See* IGNORANT (1), IGNORANT (3).

clump *n.* *—See* GROUP, LUMP[1].

clump *v.* *—See* BLUNDER, THUD.

clumsy *adj.* *—See* AWKWARD (1), AWKWARD (2), TACTLESS, UNSKILLFUL.

clunk *n.* *—See* BEAT (1).

clunk *v.* *—See* THUD.

clunker *n.* *—See* FAILURE (1).

cluster *n.* *—See* GROUP.

cluster *v.* *—See* ASSEMBLE.

clutch[1] *v.* *—See* CATCH (2), GRASP.

clutch *n.* *—See* CATCH (1), CRISIS, HOLD (1), PURSE.

clutch[2] *n.* *—See* GROUP.

clutching *adj.* Fearful of the loss of position or affection ▸ clinging, green-eyed, jealous, possessive. [*Compare* ENVIOUS.]

clutter *n.* *—See* DISORDER (1).

clutter *v.* *—See* DISORDER.

cluttered *adj.* *—See* BUSY (3).

coach *v.* *—See* EDUCATE.

coach *n.* *—See* EDUCATOR.

class on an airplane or train. **4.** One who trains or directs athletes or athletic teams. **5.** One who gives private instruction. ▸ *v.* To train or instruct; teach.
coach·man (kōch′mən) ▸ *n.* A man who drives a coach.
co·ad·ju·tor (kō′ə-jo͞o′tər, kō-ăj′ə-tər) ▸ *n.* **1.** An assistant or coworker. **2.** An assistant to a bishop.
co·ag·u·lant (kō-ăg′yə-lənt) ▸ *n.* An agent that causes coagulation. **—co·ag′u·lant** *adj.*
co·ag·u·late (kō-ăg′yə-lāt′) ▸ *v.* **-lat·ed, -lat·ing.** To form a soft semisolid or solid mass. **—co·ag′u·la′tion** *n.*
coal (kōl) ▸ *n.* **1.** A natural dark brown to black carbon-containing material formed from fossilized plants and used as a fuel. **2.** An ember.
co·a·lesce (kō′ə-lĕs′) ▸ *v.* **-lesced, -lesc·ing.** To grow or come together so as to form one whole; fuse; unite. **—co′a·les′cence** *n.* **—co′a·les′cent** *adj.*
coal gas ▸ *n.* A gaseous mixture distilled from bituminous coal and used as a fuel.
co·a·li·tion (kō′ə-lĭsh′ən) ▸ *n.* An alliance or union, esp. a temporary one.
coal oil ▸ *n.* See **kerosene.**
coal tar ▸ *n.* A viscous black liquid distilled from bituminous coal, used for waterproofing and insulating and in many dyes, drugs, and paints.
coarse (kôrs) ▸ *adj.* **coars·er, coars·est. 1.** Of inferior quality. **2a.** Lacking refinement. **b.** Vulgar or indecent. **3.** Consisting of large particles: *coarse sand.* **4.** Rough, esp. to the touch: *a coarse tweed.* **—coarse′ly** *adv.* **—coarse′ness** *n.*
coars·en (kôr′sən) ▸ *v.* To make or become coarse.
coast (kōst) ▸ *n.* **1.** Land next to the sea. **2.** A hill or slope. **3.** The act of coasting. ▸ *v.* **1.** To slide down an incline through the effect of gravity. **2.** To move without accelerating. **3.** To act or move aimlessly. **4.** To sail along the coast (of). **—coast′al** (kō′stəl) *adj.*
coast·er (kō′stər) ▸ *n.* **1.** One that coasts. **2.** A disk or small mat used to protect a table top or other surface beneath.
coast guard also **Coast Guard** ▸ *n.* The branch of a nation's armed forces that is responsible for coastal defense, protection of life and property at sea, and enforcement of customs, immigration, and navigation laws.
coast·line (kōst′līn′) ▸ *n.* The shape or outline of a coast.
coat (kōt) ▸ *n.* **1.** A sleeved outer garment extending from the shoulders to the waist or below. **2.** A natural or outer covering, such as the fur of an animal. **3.** A layer of material covering something else. ▸ *v.* To provide or cover with a coat or layer. **—coat′ed** *adj.* **—coat′ing** *n.*
co·a·ti (kō-ä′tē) ▸ *n.* An omnivorous mammal of tropical America related to and resembling the raccoon.
co·a·ti·mun·di (kō-ä′tē-mŭn′dē) ▸ *n.* A coati.
coat of arms ▸ *n., pl.* **coats of arms.** A shield blazoned with heraldic bearings indicating ancestry and distinction.
coat of mail ▸ *n., pl.* **coats of mail.** An armored coat made of chain mail.
coat·tail (kōt′tāl′) ▸ *n.* The lower back part of a coat. ***—idiom:* on (someone's) coattails** With the help or on the success of another.
co·au·thor (kō-ô′thər) ▸ *n.* A joint author. **—co·au′thor** *v.*
coax (kōks) ▸ *v.* **1.** To persuade by pleading or flattery. **2.** To obtain by persistent persuasion.
co·ax·i·al (kō-ăk′sē-əl) ▸ *adj.* Having or mounted on a common axis.
coaxial cable ▸ *n.* A cable consisting of a conducting outer metal tube insulated from a central conducting core, used for transmission of electronic signals.
cob (kŏb) ▸ *n.* **1.** A corncob. **2.** A male swan. **3.** A thickset, short-legged horse.
co·balt (kō′bôlt′) ▸ *n. Symbol* **Co** A hard, brittle metallic element used for magnetic alloys, high-temperature alloys, and for blue glass and ceramic pigments. At. no. 27.
cobalt blue ▸ *n.* A vivid blue to greenish blue.
cob·ble (kŏb′əl) ▸ *v.* **-bled, -bling. 1.** To make or mend (boots or shoes). **2.** To put together clumsily.
cob·bler¹ (kŏb′lər) ▸ *n.* One who mends or makes boots and shoes.
cob·bler² (kŏb′lər) ▸ *n.* A deep-dish fruit pie with a thick top crust.
cob·ble·stone (kŏb′əl-stōn′) ▸ *n.* A naturally rounded paving stone.
CO·BOL or **Co·bol** (kō′bôl′) ▸ *n.* A programming language, used esp. for business applications, that is closer to English than many other high-level languages.
co·bra (kō′brə) ▸ *n.* A venomous snake of Asia and Africa capable of expanding the skin of the neck to form a flattened hood.
cob·web (kŏb′wĕb′) ▸ *n.* **1a.** The web spun by a spider to catch its prey. **b.** A single thread of such a web. **2.** Something resembling a cobweb.
co·ca (kō′kə) ▸ *n.* **1.** An Andean evergreen shrub whose leaves contain cocaine. **2.** Dried coca leaves that are chewed for a stimulating effect and are used for extraction of cocaine.
co·caine (kō-kān′, kō′kān′) ▸ *n.* A narcotic alkaloid extracted from coca leaves, sometimes used as a local anesthetic and widely as an illegal drug.
coc·cus (kŏk′əs) ▸ *n., pl.* **coc·ci** (kŏk′sī, kŏk′ī). A bacterium having a spherical or spheroidal shape.
-coccus ▸ *suff.* A microorganism of spheroidal shape: *streptococcus.*
coc·cyx (kŏk′sĭks) ▸ *n., pl.* **coc·cy·ges** (kŏk-sī′jēz, kŏk′sĭ-jēz′). A small bone at the base of the spinal column.
coch·i·neal (kŏch′ə-nēl′, kŏch′ə-nēl′, kō′chə-, kō′chə-) ▸ *n.* A brilliant red dye made of the dried bodies of a tropical American insect.
Co·chise (kō-chēs′, -chēz′) (1812?–74) ▸ Apache leader.
coch·le·a (kŏk′lē-ə, kō′klē-ə) ▸ *n., pl.* **-le·ae** (-lē-ē′, -lē-ī′) also **-le·as.** A spiral tube of the inner ear that contains nerve endings essential for hearing. **—coch′le·ar** *adj.*
cock¹ (kŏk) ▸ *n.* **1a.** An adult male chicken; rooster. **b.** An adult male of various other birds. **2.** A faucet or valve. **3a.** The hammer of a firearm. **b.** Its position when ready for firing. ▸ *v.* **1.** To set the hammer of (a firearm) in position for firing. **2.** To tilt: *cock an eyebrow.* **3.** To raise or draw back in preparation to throw or hit.
cock² (kŏk) ▸ *n.* A cone-shaped pile of straw or hay.

THESAURUS

coaction *n.* —*See* COOPERATION.
coactive *adj.* —*See* COOPERATIVE.
coadjutant or **coadjutor** *n.* —*See* ASSISTANT.
coagulate *v.* To change or be changed from a liquid into a soft, semisolid, or solid mass ▸ clot, congeal, curdle, gelatinize, jell, jelly, set, stiffen. *Chiefly Regional:* clabber. [*Compare* HARDEN.]
coalesce *v.* —*See* COMBINE (1), MIX (1).
coalition *n.* —*See* ALLIANCE, UNIFICATION.
coarse *adj.* **1.** Lacking in delicacy or refinement ▸ barbarian, barbaric, boorish, churlish, common, crass, crude, gross, ill-bred, indelicate, inelegant, philistine, plebeian, rough, rude, tasteless, unbecoming, uncivilized, uncouth, uncultivated, uncultured, unpolished, unrefined, vulgar. *Informal:* tacky. [*Compare* ABRUPT, IMPROPER, RUSTIC.] **2.** Consisting of or covered with large particles ▸ grainy, granular, gravelly, gritty, rough, sabulous, sandy. —*See also* BAD (1), OBSCENE, ROUGH (1).
coarseness *n.* —*See* IRREGULARITY, OBSCENITY (1).
coast *v.* To ride or be pulled on a sled in the snow ▸ sled, sledge, sleigh-ride, slide. ***Idiom:*** go sledding (*or* coasting *or* sleigh-riding). —*See also* BREEZE, GLIDE (1).
coat *n.* **1.** An outer garment that has sleeves ▸ anorak, jacket, mackintosh, overcoat, parka, raincoat, slicker, sport coat, sport jacket, sports coat, sports jacket, suit coat, suit jacket, trench coat, windbreaker. **2.** A layer of material covering something else ▸ blanket, coating, covering, crust, dusting, layer, overlay, sheet. [*Compare* FACE, FINISH, SKIN.]
coat *v.* —*See* CLOTHE, COVER (1), FINISH.
coating *n.* —*See* COAT (2).
coax *v.* To persuade or try to persuade by gentle persistent urging or flattery ▸ blandish, cajole, honey, wheedle. *Informal:* soft-soap, sweet-talk. [*Compare* FLATTER.] —*See also* PERSUADE.
cock *n.* —*See* FAUCET.

cock·ade (kŏ-kād′) ▸ *n.* An ornament, such as a rosette, usu. worn on the hat as a badge.
cock·a·tiel also **cock·a·teel** (kŏk′ə-tēl′) ▸ *n.* A small crested Australian parrot having gray and yellow plumage.
cock·a·too (kŏk′ə-to͞o′) ▸ *n., pl.* **-toos.** A large parrot of Australia and adjacent areas, having a long erectile crest.
cock·a·trice (kŏk′ə-trĭs, -trīs′) ▸ *n. Myth.* A serpent having the power to kill by its glance.
cocked hat (kŏkt) ▸ *n.* A three-cornered hat.
cock·er·el (kŏk′ər-əl) ▸ *n.* A young rooster.
cock·er spaniel (kŏk′ər) ▸ *n.* A dog having long drooping ears and a variously colored silky coat.
cock·eyed (kŏk′īd′) ▸ *adj. Informal* **1.** Foolish; ridiculous: *a cockeyed idea.* **2.** Askew; crooked. **3.** Intoxicated; drunk.
cock·fight (kŏk′fīt′) ▸ *n.* A fight between gamecocks, often fitted with metal spurs, held as a spectacle. **—cock′fight′ing** *n.*
cock·le[1] (kŏk′əl) ▸ *n.* **1.** Any of various bivalve mollusks having rounded or heart-shaped ribbed shells. **2.** *Naut.* A cockleshell.
cock·le[2] (kŏk′əl) ▸ *n.* Any of several weedy plants growing esp. in grain fields.
cock·le·shell (kŏk′əl-shĕl′) ▸ *n.* **1.** The shell of a cockle. **2.** A small light boat.
cock·ney (kŏk′nē) ▸ *n., pl.* **-neys.** **1.** often **Cockney** A native of the East End of London. **2.** The dialect or accent of cockneys.
cock·pit (kŏk′pĭt′) ▸ *n.* **1.** The space set apart in the fuselage of an aircraft for the pilot and crew. **2.** A pit or enclosed area for cockfights. **3.** An area in a small vessel toward the stern, from which it is steered.
cock·roach (kŏk′rōch′) ▸ *n.* Any of various oval, flat-bodied insects common as household pests.
cocks·comb (kŏks′kōm′) ▸ *n.* **1.** The comb of a rooster. **2.** The cap of a jester, decorated to resemble a rooster's comb. **3.** An annual plant having fan-shaped or plume-like clusters of red or yellow flowers.
cock·sure (kŏk′sho͝or′) ▸ *adj.* **1.** Completely sure; certain. **2.** Too sure; overconfident.
cock·tail (kŏk′tāl′) ▸ *n.* **1.** A mixed alcoholic drink. **2.** An appetizer, usu. seafood or fruit. **3.** A combination of drugs used as part of a treatment regimen.
cock·y (kŏk′ē) ▸ *adj.* **-i·er, -i·est.** Overly self-assertive or self-confident. **—cock′i·ly** *adv.* **—cock′i·ness** *n.*
co·coa (kō′kō) ▸ *n.* **1.** A powder made from processed cacao seeds. **2.** A beverage made by mixing this powder with sugar in hot water or milk.
co·co·nut also **co·coa·nut** (kō′kə-nŭt′, -nət) ▸ *n.* **1.** The fruit of the coconut palm, consisting of a fibrous husk surrounding a large seed. **2.** The hard-shelled seed of the coconut, having edible white flesh and a hollow center filled with milky fluid.
coconut palm ▸ *n.* A tropical feather-leaved palm cultivated for food, beverages, oil, thatching, and fiber.
co·coon (kə-ko͞on′) ▸ *n.* **1.** A protective case of silk or fibrous material spun by the larvae of moths and other insects. **2.** A private, comfortable retreat; refuge. **—co·coon′** *v.*
cod (kŏd) ▸ *n., pl.* **cod** or **cods.** An important food fish of N Atlantic waters.
Cod, Cape ▸ A hook-shaped peninsula of SE MA.
co·da (kō′də) ▸ *n. Mus.* The final passage of a movement or work.
cod·dle (kŏd′l) ▸ *v.* **-dled, -dling.** **1.** To cook in water just below the boiling point. **2.** To treat indulgently; baby. **—cod′dler** *n.*
code (kōd) ▸ *n.* **1.** A systematic, comprehensive collection of laws or rules. **2a.** A system of signals used in transmitting messages. **b.** A system of symbols or words given arbitrary meanings, used for transmitting brief or secret messages. **3.** A system of symbols and rules used to represent instructions to a computer. **4.** The genetic code. ▸ *v.* **cod·ed, cod·ing.** **1.** To arrange or convert into a code. **2.** To write or revise a computer program.
co·deine (kō′dēn′, -dē-ĭn) ▸ *n.* An alkaloid narcotic derived from opium or morphine and used esp. for relieving pain.
co·de·pen·dent (kō′dĭ-pĕn′dənt) ▸ *adj.* **1.** Mutually dependent. **2.** Of a relationship in which one person is psychologically dependent on someone addicted to self-destructive behavior. **—co′-de·pen′dence** *n.*
co·dex (kō′dĕks′) ▸ *n., pl.* **co·di·ces** (kō′dĭ-sēz′, kŏd′ĭ-). A manuscript volume, esp. of an ancient text.
cod·fish (kŏd′fĭsh′) ▸ *n.* See **cod.**
codg·er (kŏj′ər) ▸ *n. Informal* A somewhat eccentric man, esp. an old one.
cod·i·cil (kŏd′ə-sĭl) ▸ *n.* A supplement or appendix to a will.
cod·i·fy (kŏd′ĭ-fī′, kō′də-) ▸ *v.* **-fied, -fy·ing.** To arrange or systematize. **—cod′i·fi·ca′tion** *n.*
cod-liv·er oil (kŏd′lĭv′ər) ▸ *n.* Oil obtained from the liver esp. of a cod and used as a source of vitamins A and D.
Co·dy (kō′dē), **William Frederick.** "Buffalo Bill" (1846–1917) ▸ Amer. frontier scout and performer.
co·ed (kō′ĕd′) *Informal* ▸ *n.* A woman who attends a coeducational college or university. ▸ *adj.* Coeducational.
co·ed·u·ca·tion (kō-ĕj′ə-kā′shən) ▸ *n.* The education of both men and women at the same institution. **—co·ed′u·ca′tion·al** *adj.*
co·ef·fi·cient (kō′ə-fĭsh′ənt) ▸ *n.* **1.** A number or symbol multiplied with a variable in an algebraic term, as 4 in the term $4x$. **2.** A numerical measure of a physical or chemical property that is constant for a specified system.
coe·len·ter·ate (sĭ-lĕn′tə-rāt′, -tər-ĭt) ▸ *n.* Any of a phylum of aquatic invertebrates such as the jellyfishes and hydras, having a radially symmetrical, saclike body.
coe·lom (sē′ləm) ▸ *n.* The body cavity of all animals higher than the coelenterates.
co·e·qual (kō-ē′kwəl) ▸ *adj.* Equal with one another, as in rank or size. ▸ *n.* An equal. **—co′e·qual′i·ty** (-kwŏl′ĭ-tē) *n.*
co·erce (kō-ûrs′) ▸ *v.* **-erced, -erc·ing.** **1.** To force to act or think in a certain way; compel. **2.** To dominate, restrain, or control forcibly. **3.** To bring about by force. **—co·erc′er** *n.* **—co·erc′i·ble** *adj.* **—co·er′cion** (kō-ûr′zhən, -shən) *n.* **—co·er′cive** *adj.*
co·e·val (kō-ē′vəl) ▸ *adj.* Of, originating, or existing during the same period or time. **—co·e′val** *n.* **—co·e′val·ly** *adv.*
co·ev·o·lu·tion (kō′ĕv-ə-lo͞o′shən, -ē-və-) ▸ *n.* The evolution of two or more interdependent species, each adapting to changes in the other. **—co′ev·o·lu′tion·ar·y** *adj.* **—co′e·volve′** (-ĭ-vŏlv′) *v.*
co·ex·ist (kō′ĭg-zĭst′) ▸ *v.* **1.** To exist together, at the same time, or in the same place. **2.** To live in peace with another or others despite differences. **—co′ex·is′tence** *n.*
co·ex·ten·sive (kō′ĭk-stĕn′sĭv) ▸ *adj.* Having the same limits, boundaries, or scope.
cof·fee (kô′fē, kŏf′ē) ▸ *n.* **1a.** A stimulating, aromatic beverage prepared from the roasted ground beanlike seeds of a tropical tree. **b.** The whole or ground seeds themselves. **2.** A dark brown.
cof·fee·cake (kô′fē-kāk′, kŏf′ē-) ▸ *n.* A cake or sweetened bread, often containing nuts or raisins.
cof·fee·house also **coffee house** (kô′fē-hous′, kŏf′ē-) ▸ *n.* A restaurant serving coffee and refreshments and some-

THESAURUS

cock-and-bull story *n.* —*See* LIE[2].
cockcrow *n.* —*See* DAWN.
cockeyed *adj.* —*See* DRUNK, FOOLISH.
cocktail lounge *n.* —*See* BAR (2).
cocky *adj.* —*See* BOASTFUL.
coddle *v.* —*See* BABY, COOK.
codify *v.* —*See* ARRANGE (1).
coequal *n.* —*See* PEER[2].
coequal *adj.* —*See* EQUAL.
coequality *n.* —*See* EQUIVALENCE.
coerce *v.* To compel by threats ▸ blackjack, dragoon, force. *Informal:* hijack, strong-arm. [*Compare* INTIMIDATE.] —*See also* FORCE (1).
coercion *n.* —*See* FORCE (1).
coercive *adj.* Accomplished by force ▸ forced, forcible, violent. *Informal:* strong-arm.
coercively *adv.* With force and violence ▸ forcibly, violently. *Idioms:* against one's will, by force, under duress.
coetaneous *adj.* —*See* CONTEMPORARY (1).
coeval *adj.* —*See* CONTEMPORARY (1).
coeval *n.* One of the same time or age as another ▸ contemporary.
coexistent or **coexisting** *adj.* —*See* CONTEMPORARY (1).

times having musical entertainment.
coffee klatch or **coffee klatsch** (klăch, klăch) ▸ *n.* A casual social gathering for coffee and conversation.
cof·fee·mak·er (kô′fē-mā′kər, kŏf′ē-) ▸ *n.* An apparatus used to brew coffee.
cof·fee·pot (kô′fē-pŏt′, kŏf′ē-) ▸ *n.* A pot for brewing or serving coffee.
coffee shop ▸ *n.* A small restaurant in which coffee and light meals are served.
coffee table ▸ *n.* A long low table, often placed before a sofa.
cof·fer (kô′fər, kŏf′ər) ▸ *n.* **1.** A strongbox. **2.** often **coffers** Financial resources; funds.
cof·fer·dam (kô′fər-dăm′, kŏf′ər-) ▸ *n.* A temporary watertight enclosure that is pumped dry to expose the bottom of a body of water so that construction, as of piers, may be undertaken.
cof·fin (kô′fĭn, kŏf′ĭn) ▸ *n.* A box in which a corpse is buried.
cog (kŏg, kôg) ▸ *n.* **1.** One of the teeth on the rim of a wheel or gear. **2.** A subordinate member of an organization.
co·gen·er·a·tion (kō-jĕn′ə-rā′shən) ▸ *n.* A process in which a factory uses its waste energy to produce heat or electricity.
co·gent (kō′jənt) ▸ *adj.* Forcefully convincing: *a cogent argument.* **—co′gen·cy** (-jən-sē) *n.* **—co′gent·ly** *adv.*
cog·i·tate (kŏj′ĭ-tāt′) ▸ *v.* **-tat·ed, -tat·ing.** To think carefully (about); ponder. **—cog′i·ta′tion** *n.*
co·gnac (kōn′yăk′, kŏn′-, kôn′-) ▸ *n.* A fine French brandy.
cog·nate (kŏg′nāt′) ▸ *adj.* **1.** Having a common ancestor or origin, esp. culturally or linguistically akin. **2.** Analogous in nature. **—cog′nate′** *n.*
cog·ni·tion (kŏg-nĭsh′ən) ▸ *n.* **1.** The mental process or faculty of knowing. **2.** That which comes to be known. **—cog′ni·tive** *adj.*
cog·ni·zance (kŏg′nĭ-zəns) ▸ *n.* **1.** Conscious knowledge or recognition; awareness. **2.** Observance; notice. **—cog′ni·zant** *adj.*
cog·no·men (kŏg-nō′mən) ▸ *n., pl.* **-no·mens** or **-nom·i·na** (-nŏm′ə-nə). **1.** A surname. **2.** A nickname.
co·gno·scen·te (kŏn′yə-shĕn′tē, kŏg′nə-) ▸ *n., pl.* **-ti** (-tē). A connoisseur.
cog·wheel (kŏg′hwēl′, -wēl′, kôg′-) ▸ *n.* A toothed gear wheel within a mechanism.
co·hab·it (kō-hăb′ĭt) ▸ *v.* To live together as spouses, esp. when not legally married. **—co·hab′i·ta′tion** *n.*
co·here (kō-hîr′) ▸ *v.* **-hered, -her·ing. 1.** To stick or hold together. **2.** To be logically connected. **—co·her′ence, co·her′en·cy** *n.* **—co·her′ent** *adj.*
co·he·sion (kō-hē′zhən) ▸ *n.* **1.** The process or condition of cohering. **2.** *Phys.* The attraction by which the elements of a body are held together. **—co·he′sive** (-sĭv, -zĭv) *adj.* **—co·he′sive·ly** *adv.* **—co·he′sive·ness** *n.*
co·hort (kō′hôrt′) ▸ *n.* **1.** A group or band of people. **2.** A companion or associate.
co·host or **co-host** (kō′hōst′) ▸ *n.* A joint host, as of a social event. **—co′host′** *v.*
coif (koif) ▸ *n.* **1.** (*also* kwäf) A coiffure. **2.** A tight-fitting cap. ▸ *v.* (*also* kwäf) To style or dress (the hair).
coif·fure (kwä-fyo͝or′) ▸ *n.* A hairstyle.
coil (koil) ▸ *n.* **1.** A series of connected spirals or concentric rings formed by gathering or winding. **2.** A spiral or ring. **3.** *Elect.* A wound spiral of insulated wire. **—coil** *v.*
coin (koin) ▸ *n.* **1.** A piece of metal authorized by a government for use as money. **2.** Metal money collectively. ▸ *v.* **1.** To make coins from metal. **2.** To invent (a new word or phrase). **—coin′er** *n.*
coin·age (koi′nĭj) ▸ *n.* **1.** The process of making coins. **2.** Metal currency.
co·in·cide (kō′ĭn-sīd′) ▸ *v.* **-cid·ed, -cid·ing. 1.** To occupy the same position in space. **2.** To happen at the same time. **3.** To correspond exactly.
co·in·ci·dence (kō-ĭn′sĭ-dəns, -dĕns′) ▸ *n.* **1.** The act or state of coinciding. **2.** A sequence of events that although accidental seems to have been planned or arranged. **—co·in′ci·den′tal, co·in′ci·dent** *adj.* **—co·in′ci·den′tal·ly** *adv.*
co·i·tus (kō′ĭ-təs, kō-ē′-) ▸ *n.* Sexual intercourse. **—co′i·tal** *adj.*
coke[1] (kōk) ▸ *n.* The solid residue of coal after removal of volatile material, used as fuel.
coke[2] (kōk) ▸ *n.* *Slang* Cocaine.
Col. ▸ *abbr.* Colorado
col–[1] ▸ *pref.* Var. of **com–**.
col–[2] ▸ *pref.* Var. of **colo–**.
co·la[1] (kō′lə) ▸ *n.* A carbonated soft drink containing an extract of the cola nut.
co·la[2] (kō′lə) ▸ *n.* Pl. of **colon**[2].
co·la[3] also **ko·la** (kō′lə) ▸ *n.* Either of two African evergreens having nutlike seeds used in carbonated beverages and pharmaceuticals.
col·an·der (kŏl′ən-dər, kŭl′-) ▸ *n.* A perforated, bowl-shaped kitchen utensil for draining off liquids.
cold (kōld) ▸ *adj.* **-er, -est. 1.** Having a low temperature. **2.** Having a subnormal body temperature. **3.** Feeling uncomfortably chilled. **4.** Lacking emotion; objective. **5.** Not friendly; aloof. **6.** No longer fresh: *a cold scent.* **7.** Unconscious: *knocked cold.* ▸ *adv.* Totally; thoroughly. ▸ *n.* **1.** Relative lack of warmth. **2.** The sensation of lacking warmth. **3.** A viral infection of the mucous membranes of the upper respiratory passages. ***—idiom:* out in the cold** Neglected; ignored. **—cold′ly** *adv.* **—cold′ness** *n.*
cold-blood·ed (kōld′blŭd′ĭd) ▸ *adj.* **1.** Lacking feeling or emotion: *a cold-blooded killer.* **2.** Ectothermic. **—cold′-blood′ed·ly** *adv.* **—cold′-blood′ed·ness** *n.*
cold cream ▸ *n.* An emulsion for softening and cleansing the skin.
cold cuts ▸ *pl.n.* Slices of cold cooked meat.
cold drink ▸ *n.* *Regional* See **soft drink**.
cold duck ▸ *n.* A beverage made of sparkling Burgundy and champagne.
cold feet ▸ *pl.n.* *Slang* Failure of nerve.
cold frame ▸ *n.* An unheated outdoor structure consisting of a usu. wooden frame and glass top, used for protecting young plants.
cold-heart·ed (kōld′här′tĭd) ▸ *adj.* Lacking sympathy or feeling. **—cold′-heart′ed·ly** *adv.* **—cold′-heart′ed·ness** *n.*

THESAURUS

cogency *n.* The power of an argument to convince or compel agreement ▸ force, forcefulness, justice, persuasiveness, weight. *Idiom:* sound reason. [*Compare* ELOQUENCE, VERACITY, VERISIMILITUDE.]
cogent *adj.* —*See* CONVINCING, SOUND[2].
cogitate *v.* —*See* PONDER, THINK (1).
cogitation *n.* —*See* THOUGHT.
cogitative *adj.* —*See* THOUGHTFUL.
cognate *adj.* —*See* KINDRED.
cognizable *adj.* —*See* PERCEPTIBLE.
cognizance *n.* —*See* AWARENESS, NOTICE (1).
cognizant *adj.* —*See* AWARE.
cognomen *n.* —*See* NAME (1).
cohere *v.* —*See* BOND.
coherence *n.* —*See* CONSISTENCY.
coherent *adj.* —*See* UNDERSTANDABLE.
cohesion *n.* —*See* BOND (3), CONSISTENCY.
cohort *n.* —*See* ASSOCIATE (1), BAND[2], FOLLOWER.
coil *v.* —*See* WIND[7].
coil *n.* —*See* CURL, LOOP.
coin *v.* —*See* INVENT.
coincide *v.* To occur at the same time ▸ concur, harmonize, synchronize. —*See also* AGREE (2).
coincidence *n.* —*See* CHANCE (2).
coincident *adj.* —*See* CONCURRENT.
cold *adj.* **1.** Marked by a low temperature ▸ arctic, boreal, chill, chilly, cool, freezing, frigid, frosty, gelid, glacial, icy, nippy, polar, shivery, wintry. *Idiom:* bitter (*or* bitterly) cold. **2.** Lacking feeling or emotion ▸ cold-blooded, dispassionate, dry, emotionless, impassible, impassive, indifferent, insensible, insensitive, insusceptible, matter-of-fact, neutral, passionless, phlegmatic, stolid, thick-skinned, unaffected, unemotional, unmoved, unresponsive, unimpressionable, unsusceptible. [*Compare* APATHETIC, CALLOUS.] —*See also* COOL, FRIGID, UNCONSCIOUS.
cold *n.* Lack of warmth ▸ chill, chilliness, coldness, coolness, frigidity, frigidness, frostiness, frozenness, iciness, nip, wintriness.
cold-blooded *adj.* —*See* CALLOUS, COLD (2).
cold feet *n.* —*See* FEAR.
cold-hearted *adj.* —*See* CALLOUS.
coldness *n.* —*See* COLD, INHOSPITALITY.

cold shoulder ► *n. Informal* Deliberate coldness or disregard. **—cold′shoul′der** *v.*
cold sore ► *n.* A small blister occurring on the lips, caused by a herpes virus.
cold turkey ► *n. Slang* Immediate, complete withdrawal esp. from an addictive drug.
cold war ► *n.* A state of political tension and military rivalry between nations that stops short of full-scale war. **—cold warrior** *n.*
Cole·ridge (kōl′rĭj, kō′lə-rĭj), **Samuel Taylor** (1772–1834) ► British poet and critic.
cole·slaw also **cole slaw** (kōl′slô′) ► *n.* A salad of shredded raw cabbage.
co·le·us (kō′lē-əs) ► *n.* A plant of the mint family, cultivated for its showy leaves.
col·ic (kŏl′ĭk) ► *n.* Severe abdominal pain. **—col′ick·y** (kŏl′ĭ-kē) *adj.*
col·i·se·um (kŏl′ĭ-sē′əm) ► *n.* A large public amphitheater.
co·li·tis (kə-lī′tĭs) ► *n.* Inflammation of the colon.
col·lab·o·rate (kə-lăb′ə-rāt′) ► *v.* **-rat·ed, -rat·ing. 1.** To work together, esp. in a joint intellectual effort. **2.** To cooperate treasonably. **—col·lab′o·ra′tion** *n.* **—col·lab′o·ra′tive** *adj.* **—col·lab′o·ra′tor** *n.*
col·lage (kō-läzh′, kə-) ► *n.* An artistic composition of materials and objects pasted over a surface.
col·la·gen (kŏl′ə-jən) ► *n.* The fibrous protein constituent of bone, cartilage, and connective tissue.
col·lapse (kə-lăps′) ► *v.* **-lapsed, -laps·ing. 1.** To fall down or inward suddenly; cave in. **2.** To break down suddenly in strength or health and thereby cease to function. **3.** To fold compactly: *collapse a folding bed for storage.* **—col·lapse′** *n.* **—col·laps′i·ble** *adj.*
col·lar (kŏl′ər) ► *n.* **1.** The part of a garment that encircles the neck. **2.** A restraining or identifying band around the neck of an animal. **3.** *Biol.* An encircling structure or bandlike marking suggestive of a collar. **4.** A ringlike device used to limit, guide, or secure a part. **5.** *Slang* An arrest. ► *v. Slang* To seize or detain. **—col′lared** *adj.*
col·lar·bone (kŏl′ər-bōn′) ► *n.* See **clavicle.**
col·lard (kŏl′ərd) ► *n.* **1.** See **kale. 2. collards** The leaves of kale, used as a vegetable.
col·late (kə-lāt′, kŏl′āt′, kō′lāt′) ► *v.* **-lat·ed, -lat·ing. 1.** To examine and compare (texts) carefully. **2.** To assemble pages in proper sequence.
col·lat·er·al (kə-lăt′ər-əl) ► *adj.* **1.** Situated or running side by side. **2.** Serving to corroborate. **3.** Of a secondary nature; subordinate. **4.** Of or guaranteed by a security pledged against the performance of an obligation. **5.** Having an ancestor in common but descended from a different line. ► *n.* Property acceptable as security for a loan.
col·la·tion (kə-lā′shən, kŏ-, kō-) ► *n.* **1.** The act or process of collating. **2.** A light meal.
col·league (kŏl′ēg′) ► *n.* A fellow member of a profession; associate.
col·lect ► *v.* **1.** To bring or come together in a group; gather. **2.** To accumulate: *collect signatures.* **3.** To obtain payment of: *collect taxes.* **4.** To recover control of: *collect one's emotions.* ► *adv. & adj.* With payment to be made by the receiver: *called collect.* **—col·lect′i·ble, col·lect′a·ble** *adj. & n.* **—col·lec′tion** *n.* **—col·lec′tor** *n.*
col·lect·ed (kə-lĕk′tĭd) ► *adj.* Self-possessed; composed.
col·lec·tive (kə-lĕk′tĭv) ► *adj.* **1.** Assembled into a whole. **2.** Of or made by a number of people acting as a group: *a collective decision.* ► *n.* An undertaking or business controlled by the workers involved. **—col·lec′tive·ly** *adv.* **—col′lec·tiv′i·ty** *n.* **—col·lec′tiv·ize′** *v.* **—col·lec′tiv·i·za′tion** *n.*
collective bargaining ► *n.* Negotiation between the representatives of organized workers and an employer.
collective noun ► *n.* A noun denoting a group of persons or things regarded as a unit.
col·lec·tiv·ism (kə-lĕk′tə-vĭz′əm) ► *n.* The principles or system of ownership and control of the means of production and distribution by the people collectively. **—col·lec′tiv·ist** *n.*
col·leen (kŏ-lēn′, kŏl′ēn′) ► *n.* An Irish girl.
col·lege (kŏl′ĭj) ► *n.* **1.** An institution of higher learning that grants the bachelor's degree. **2.** An undergraduate division or school of a university. **3.** A technical or professional school. **4.** The building or buildings occupied by any such school. **5.** A body of persons having a common purpose or shared duties. **—col·le′giate** (kə-lē′jĭt, -jē-ĭt) *adj.*
col·le·gi·al (kə-lē′jē-əl, -jəl) ► *adj.* Having power and authority vested equally among colleagues.
col·le·gian (kə-lē′jən, -jē-ən) ► *n.* A college student or recent college graduate.
col·le·gi·um (kə-lē′jē-əm, -lĕg′ē-) ► *n., pl.* **-gi·a** (-lē′jē-ə, -lĕg′ē-ə) or **-le·gi·ums.** A governing council in which all members have equal authority.
col·lide (kə-līd′) ► *v.* **-lid·ed, -lid·ing. 1.** To come together with violent, direct impact. **2.** To clash; conflict. **—col·li′sion** (-lĭzh′ən) *n.*
col·lie (kŏl′ē) ► *n.* A large, long-haired dog orig. used to herd sheep.
col·lier (kŏl′yər) ► *n.* **1.** A coal miner. **2.** A coal ship.
col·lier·y (kŏl′yə-rē) ► *n., pl.* **-ies.** A coal mine and its outbuildings.
col·lin·e·ar (kə-lĭn′ē-ər, kŏ-) ► *adj.* **1.** Lying on the same line. **2.** Containing a common line; coaxial.
col·lo·cate (kŏl′ə-kāt′) ► *v.* **-cat·ed, -cat·ing.** To place together, esp. side by side. **—col′lo·ca′tion** *n.*
col·lo·di·on (kə-lō′dē-ən) ► *n.* A highly flammable, syrupy solution used in topical medications and photographic plates.
col·loid (kŏl′oid′) ► *n.* A suspension of finely divided particles in a continuous medium from which the particles do not settle out rapidly and cannot be readily filtered. **—col·loi′dal** (kə-loid′l, kŏ-) *adj.*
col·lo·qui·al (kə-lō′kwē-əl) ► *adj.* Characteristic of or appropriate to informal speech or writing. **—col·lo′qui·al·ism** *n.* **—col·lo′qui·al·ly** *adv.*

THESAURUS

coldshoulder *v.* *—See* SNUB.
cold shoulder *n.* *—See* SNUB.
collaborate *v.* *—See* COOPERATE.
collaboration *n.* *—See* COOPERATION.
collaborative *adj.* *—See* COOPERATIVE.
collapse *v.* **1.** To suddenly lose all health or strength ► break (down), cave in, crack, drop, give out, succumb. *Informal:* crack up. *Slang:* conk out. *Idiom:* give way. [*Compare* FADE, FAINT, TIRE.] **2.** To undergo sudden financial failure ► crash, fail, go under. *Informal:* fold. *Idioms:* go bankrupt, go belly up, go broke, go bust, go down the tubes, go on the rocks, go to the wall. [*Compare* FAIL, RUIN.] **3.** To undergo capture, defeat, or ruin ► fall, go down, go under, topple. [*Compare* SUCCUMB, SURRENDER.] *—See also* BREAK (3), BUCKLE.
collapse *n.* **1.** A sudden sharp decline in mental, emotional, or physical health ► breakdown. *Informal:* crackup. [*Compare* INFIRMITY.] **2.** An abrupt disastrous failure ► breakdown, catastrophe, crash, debacle, disaster, smash, smashup, wreck. [*Compare* FAILURE.] **3.** A disastrous defeat or ruin ► fall, downfall, waterloo. [*Compare* DEFEAT.] *—See also* BREACH (2).
collar *n.* *—See* ARREST, FASTENER.
collar *v.* *—See* ARREST.
collate *v.* *—See* COMPARE.
collateral *adj.* Lying in the same plane and not intersecting ► parallel. *Idiom:* side by side. *—See also* AUXILIARY (1), MINOR (1).
collateral *n.* *—See* PAWN[1].
collateralize *v.* *—See* PAWN[1].
collation *n.* *—See* CONTRAST, REFRESHMENT.
colleague *n.* *—See* ASSOCIATE (1), PEER[2].
collect[1] *v.* *—See* ACCUMULATE, ASSEMBLE, COMPOSE (4).
collect[2] *n.* *—See* PRAYER[1] (2).
collected *adj.* *—See* CALM.
collectedness *n.* *—See* BALANCE (2).
collectible *adj.* *—See* DUE (1).
collection *n.* *—See* ACCUMULATION (1), GROUP.
collective *adj.* *—See* COOPERATIVE.
collide *v.* To come together with force ► bump, crash, knock, hit, impact, run into, slam, strike. [*Compare* CRASH.] *—See also* CONFLICT, CONTEND.
collision *n.* A violent forcible contact ► bump, concussion, crash, foul, hit, impact, jar, jolt, knock, percussion, shock, smash. [*Compare* CRASH, SLAM.]
collocate *v.* *—See* ARRANGE (1).
collocation *n.* *—See* EXPRESSION (3).
colloquial *adj.* *—See* CONVERSATIONAL.

col·lo·qui·um (kə-lō′kwē-əm) ▸ *n., pl.* **-qui·ums** or **-qui·a** (-kwē-ə). 1. An informal conference. 2. An academic seminar.
col·lo·quy (kŏl′ə-kwē) ▸ *n., pl.* **-quies.** A conversation, esp. a formal one.
col·lude (kə-lo͞od′) ▸ *v.* **-lud·ed, -lud·ing.** To act together secretly to achieve a fraudulent, illegal, or deceitful purpose; conspire. **—col·lu′sion** *n.* **—col·lu′sive** *adj.*
Colo. ▸ *abbr.* Colorado
colo– or **col–** ▸ *pref.* Colon: *colostomy.*
co·logne (kə-lōn′) ▸ *n.* A scented liquid made of alcohol and fragrant oils.
Co·lom·bi·a (kə-lŭm′bē-ə) ▸ A country of NW South America with coastlines on the Pacific Ocean and the Caribbean Sea. **—Co·lom′bi·an** *adj. & n.*
co·lon[1] (kō′lən) ▸ *n., pl.* **-lons.** A punctuation mark (:) used to introduce a quotation, explanation, example, or series.
co·lon[2] (kō′lən) ▸ *n., pl.* **-lons** or **-la** (-lə). The section of the large intestine extending from the cecum to the rectum. **—co·lon′ic** (kə-lŏn′ĭk) *adj.*
co·lon[3] (kō-lōn′) ▸ *n., pl.* **co·lons** or **co·lo·nes** (-lō′nās′). See **currency** table in Appendix.
colo·nel (kûr′nəl) ▸ *n.* A rank, as in the US Army, above lieutenant colonel and below brigadier general. **—colo′nel·cy** *n.*
co·lo·ni·al (kə-lō′nē-əl) ▸ *adj.* 1. Of or possessing a colony or colonies. 2. often **Colonial** Of or relating to the 13 original colonies that became the United States of America. ▸ *n.* A native or inhabitant of a colony. **—co·lo′ni·al·ly** *adv.*
co·lo·ni·al·ism (kə-lō′nē-ə-lĭz′əm) ▸ *n.* A policy by which a nation maintains or extends its control over foreign dependencies. **—co·lo′ni·al·ist** *n.*
col·o·nist (kŏl′ə-nĭst) ▸ *n.* An inhabitant or original settler of a colony.
col·o·nize (kŏl′ə-nīz′) ▸ *v.* **-nized, -niz·ing.** To establish a colony (in). **—col′o·ni·za′tion** *n.* **—col′o·niz′er** *n.*
col·on·nade (kŏl′ə-nād′) ▸ *n. Archit.* A series of regularly spaced columns. **—col′on·nad′ed** *adj.*
col·o·ny (kŏl′ə-nē) ▸ *n., pl.* **-nies.** 1. A group of emigrants who settle in a distant territory but remain subject to their parent country. 2. A region controlled by a distant country. 3. A group of people with the same interests concentrated in a particular area. 4. A group of the same kind of organisms living together.
col·o·phon (kŏl′ə-fŏn′, -fən) ▸ *n.* An inscription placed usu. at the end of a book, giving facts about its publication.
col·or (kŭl′ər) ▸ *n.* 1. The visible aspect of things caused by differing qualities of the light reflected or emitted by them. 2. A dye, pigment, or paint that imparts a hue. 3. Skin tone. 4. **colors** A flag or banner, as of a country or military unit. 5. Outward appearance, often deceptive. 6. Vivid, picturesque detail. ▸ *v.* 1. To impart color to. 2. To give a distinctive character to; influence. 3. To misrepresent. 4. To blush. **—col′or·er** *n.*
Col·o·ra·do (kŏl′ə-răd′ō, -rä′dō) ▸ A state of the W-central US. Cap. Denver. **—Col′o·ra′dan** *adj. & n.*
Colorado River ▸ 1. A river of the SW US rising in the Rocky Mts. and flowing about 2,333 km (1,450 mi) to the Gulf of California in NW Mexico. 2. A river rising in NW TX and flowing about 1,438 km (894 mi) to an inlet of the Gulf of Mexico.
col·or·ant (kŭl′ər-ənt) ▸ *n.* Something, esp. a dye, that colors something else.
col·or·a·tion (kŭl′ə-rā′shən) ▸ *n.* Arrangement of colors.
col·or·a·tu·ra (kŭl′ər-ə-to͝or′ə, -tyo͝or′ə) ▸ *n.* Ornamental trills and runs in vocal music.
col·or·blind or **col·or-blind** (kŭl′ər-blīnd′) ▸ *adj.* 1. Partially or totally unable to distinguish certain colors. 2. Not subject to racial prejudices. **—col′or·blind′ness** *n.*
col·or-code (kŭl′ər-kōd′) ▸ *v.* To color, as wires or papers, according to a code for easy identification.
col·ored (kŭl′ərd) ▸ *adj.* 1. Having color. 2. *Often Offensive* Of or belonging to a racial group not categorized as white. 3. Distorted or biased, as by incorrect information.
col·or·ful (kŭl′ər-fəl) ▸ *adj.* 1. Full of color. 2. Vividly distinctive. **—col′or·ful·ly** *adv.*
color guard ▸ *n.* A ceremonial escort for the flag, esp. of a country.
col·or·ing (kŭl′ər-ĭng) ▸ *n.* 1. A substance used to color something. 2. Appearance with regard to color. 3. False or misleading appearance.
col·or·less (kŭl′ər-lĭs) ▸ *adj.* 1. Lacking color. 2. Drab; lifeless. **—col′or·less·ly** *adv.* **—col′or·less·ness** *n.*
color line ▸ *n.* A barrier, created by custom, law, or economic differences, separating nonwhite persons from whites.
co·los·sal (kə-lŏs′əl) ▸ *adj.* Immense in size, extent, or degree. **—co·los′sal·ly** *adv.*
Co·los·sians (kə-lŏsh′ənz) ▸ *pl.n. (takes sing. v.)* See **Bible** table in Appendix.
co·los·sus (kə-lŏs′əs) ▸ *n., pl.* **-los·si** (-lŏs′ī′) or **-sus·es.** 1. A huge statue. 2. Something of enormous size or importance.
co·los·to·my (kə-lŏs′tə-mē) ▸ *n., pl.* **-mies.** Surgical construction of an artificial excretory opening from the colon.
co·los·trum (kə-lŏs′trəm) ▸ *n.* The thin yellowish fluid secreted by the mammary glands at the time of parturition.
col·our (kŭl′ər) ▸ *n. & v. Chiefly Brit.* Var. of **color.**
colt (kōlt) ▸ *n.* A young male horse. **—colt′ish** *adj.* **—colt′ish·ness** *n.*
Co·lum·bi·a (kə-lŭm′bē-ə) ▸ The capital of SC, in the central part.
Columbia River ▸ A river rising in SE British Columbia, Canada, and flowing about 1,947 km (1,210 mi) along the WA-OR border to the Pacific.
col·um·bine (kŏl′əm-bīn′) ▸ *n.* Any of various plants with variously colored flowers that have five spurred petals.
Co·lum·bus (kə-lŭm′bəs) ▸ The capital of OH, in the central part.
Columbus, Christopher (1451–1506) ▸ Italian explorer in the service of Spain and discoverer (1492) of the New World.
Columbus Day ▸ *n.* Oct. 12, observed in the US on the 2nd Monday in Oct. in honor of Christopher Columbus.
col·umn (kŏl′əm) ▸ *n.* 1. A supporting pillar used in building construction. 2. Something resembling a pillar in form or function. 3. *Print.* One of two or more vertical

THESAURUS

colloquium *n.* —*See* CONFERENCE (1).
colloquy *n.* —*See* CONVERSATION.
collude *v.* —*See* PLOT (2).
collusion *n.* —*See* PLOT (1).
colonist or **colonial** *n.* —*See* SETTLER.
colonize *v.* —*See* OCCUPY (2).
colonizer *n.* —*See* SETTLER.
colony *n.* —*See* POSSESSION.
colophon *n.* —*See* MARK (1).
color *n.* 1. That aspect of things that is caused by differing qualities of the light reflected or emitted by them ▸ cast, hue, shade, tinge, tinct, tint, tone, undertone, wash. 2. Something that imparts color ▸ colorant, coloring, dye, dyestuff, paint, pigment, stain, tincture. [*Compare* FINISH.] 3. Skin tone, especially of the face ▸ coloring, complexion. 4. A fresh rosy complexion ▸ bloom, blush, flush, glow. —*See also* VERISIMILITUDE.
color *v.* 1. To impart color to ▸ dye, emblazon, imbue, pigment, stain, tincture, tinge, tint, wash. [*Compare* FINISH.] 2. To give a deceptively attractive appearance to ▸ gild, gloss (over), gloze (over), overlay, sugarcoat, varnish, veneer, whitewash. *Idioms:* paper over, put a good face on. [*Compare* DISGUISE, EXTENUATE.] —*See also* BLUSH, DISTORT.
colorant *n.* —*See* COLOR (2).
colorfast *adj.* Retaining original color ▸ fast, indelible.
colorful *adj.* 1. Full of color ▸ bright, deep, fluorescent, gay, rich, vibrant, vivid. [*Compare* BRIGHT.] 2. Evoking strong mental images through distinctiveness ▸ graphic, picturesque, striking, vivid. —*See also* DESCRIPTIVE, MULTICOLORED.
coloring *n.* Skin tone, especially of the face ▸ color, complexion. [*Compare* BLOOM[1].] —*See also* COLOR (2).
colorless *adj.* Without definite or distinctive characteristics ▸ bland, indistinctive, neutral. [*Compare* BORING.] —*See also* DULL (1), PALE (1).
colorlessness *n.* —*See* DULLNESS.
colors *n.* —*See* FLAG[1].
colossal *adj.* —*See* ENORMOUS.
coltish *adj.* —*See* LIVELY.
column *n.* A sturdy vertical structural support ▸ pier, pilaster, pillar, post,

sections of a page. **4.** A feature article that appears regularly in a publication. **5.** A formation in rows or ranks, as of troops. **—co·lum′nar** (kə-lŭm′nər) *adj.* **—col′umned** *adj.*

col·um·nist (kŏl′əm-nĭst, -ə-mĭst) ► *n.* A writer of a column in a publication.

com– or **col–** or **con–** ► *pref.* Together; jointly: *commingle.*

co·ma (kō′mə) ► *n.* A deep prolonged unconsciousness, usu. the result of injury, disease, or poison.

Co·man·che (kə-măn′chē) ► *n., pl.* **-che** or **-ches. 1.** A member of a Native American people formerly of the S Great Plains, now living in Oklahoma. **2.** The Uto-Aztecan language of the Comanche.

co·ma·tose (kō′mə-tōs′, kŏm′ə-) ► *adj.* **1.** Of or affected with coma; unconscious. **2.** Lethargic; torpid.

comb (kōm) ► *n.* **1.** A thin toothed strip, as of plastic, used to arrange the hair. **2.** Something resembling a comb in shape or use. **3.** The fleshy crest on the crown of the head of domestic fowl and other birds. **4.** A honeycomb. ► *v.* **1.** To arrange with or as if with a comb. **2.** To card (wool or other fiber). **3.** To search thoroughly.

com·bat (kəm-băt′, kŏm′băt′) ► *v.* **-bat·ed, -bat·ing** or **-bat·ted, -bat·ting. 1.** To fight against. **2.** To oppose vigorously. ► *n.* (kŏm′băt′) Fighting, esp. armed battle. **—com·bat′ant** *n.*

combat fatigue ► *n.* A nervous disorder characterized by anxiety, depression, and irritability, caused by the stress of combat.

com·bat·ive (kəm-băt′ĭv) ► *adj.* Eager or disposed to fight; belligerent. **—com·bat′ive·ly** *adv.* **—com·bat′ive·ness** *n.*

comb·er (kō′mər) ► *n.* **1.** One that combs. **2.** A long cresting wave.

com·bi·na·tion (kŏm′bə-nā′shən) ► *n.* **1.** The act of combining or the state of being combined. **2.** A sequence of numbers or letters used to open certain locks.

com·bine (kəm-bīn′) ► *v.* **-bined, -bin·ing. 1.** To make or become united. **2.** To join (two or more substances) to make a single substance. ► *n.* (kŏm′bīn′) **1.** A harvesting machine that cuts, threshes, and cleans grain. **2.** An association of people united for political or commercial interests.

com·bo (kŏm′bō) ► *n., pl.* **-bos.** A small jazz band.

com·bust (kəm-bŭst′) ► *v.* **1a.** To catch fire. **b.** To burn. **2.** To become suddenly angry.

com·bus·ti·ble (kəm-bŭs′tə-bəl) ► *adj.* Capable of igniting and burning. ► *n.* A combustible substance. **—com·bus′ti·bil′i·ty** *n.* **—com·bus′ti·bly** *adv.*

com·bus·tion (kəm-bŭs′chən) ► *n.* **1.** The process of burning. **2.** A chemical change, esp. oxidation, accompanied by heat and light. **—com·bus′tive** (-tĭv) *adj.*

come (kŭm) ► *v.* **came** (kām), **come, com·ing. 1.** To advance; approach. **2.** To make progress. **3.** To arrive. **4.** To move into view. **5.** To occur: *Happiness came to her late in life.* **6.** To arrive at a particular result or condition. **7.** To issue forth; originate. **8.** To become: *The knot came loose.* **9.** To be obtainable. ***—phrasal verbs:*** **come about** To happen. **come across 1.** To meet by chance. **2.** *Slang* To give an impression: *come across as honest.* **come around 1.** To recover. **2.** To change one's opinion. **come by** To acquire. **come into** To inherit. **come off 1.** To happen. **2.** To be successful. **come out 1.** To become known. **2.** To be issued. **come through** To do what is required. **come to** To recover consciousness. ***—idioms:*** **come clean** To confess all. **come to grips with** To confront squarely and resolutely. **come to light** To be clearly revealed or disclosed. **come up with** To produce or discover.

come·back (kŭm′băk′) ► *n.* **1.** A return to former status or prosperity. **2.** A retort.

co·me·di·an (kə-mē′dē-ən) ► *n.* **1.** A professional entertainer who tells jokes or performs various other comic acts. **2.** A writer of comedy.

co·me·di·enne (kə-mē′dē-ĕn′) ► *n.* A female professional entertainer who tells jokes or performs various other comic acts.

come·down (kŭm′doun′) ► *n.* **1.** A decline in status or level. **2.** A cause or feeling of disappointment or depression.

com·e·dy (kŏm′ĭ-dē) ► *n., pl.* **-dies. 1.** A dramatic work that is humorous and usu. has a happy ending. **2.** The genre made up of such works. **3.** A literary work having humorous themes or characters. **4.** Popular entertainment composed of jokes and satire.

come·ly (kŭm′lē) ► *adj.* **-li·er, -li·est.** Pleasing in appearance; attractive. **—come′li·ness** *n.*

come-on (kŭm′ŏn′, -ôn′) ► *n.* Something offered to allure or attract; inducement.

com·er (kŭm′ər) ► *n.* **1.** One that comes. **2.** One showing promise of attaining success.

co·mes·ti·ble (kə-mĕs′tə-bəl) ► *adj.* Edible. **—co·mes′ti·ble** *n.*

com·et (kŏm′ĭt) ► *n.* A celestial body consisting of a dense nucleus of frozen gases and dust, which develops a luminous halo and tail when its orbit approaches the sun.

come·up·pance (kŭm′ŭp′əns) ► *n.* A punishment that one deserves.

THESAURUS

shaft, stud. [*Compare* BEAM, SUPPORT.] —*See also* LINE.

columnist *n.* —*See* PRESS.

comatose *adj.* —*See* UNCONSCIOUS.

comb *v.* —*See* SCOUR[2].

combat *v.* —*See* CONTEND, OPPOSE.

combat *n.* —*See* BATTLE, OPPOSITION (1).

combatant *n.* One who engages in a combat or struggle ► belligerent, fighter, soldier, warrior. [*Compare* AGGRESSOR, SOLDIER.]

combatant *adj.* —*See* BELLIGERENT.

combative *adj.* —*See* AGGRESSIVE, ARGUMENTATIVE.

combativeness *n.* —*See* AGGRESSION, FIGHT (2).

combination *n.* The result of combining ► brew, composite, compound, conjugation, entente, hybrid, incorporation, merger, unification, union, unity. [*Compare* ASSORTMENT, MIXTURE.] —*See also* ALLIANCE, ASSOCIATION (1).

combine *v.* **1.** To bring or come together into a united whole ► articulate, coalesce, compound, concrete, conjoin, conjugate, connect, consolidate, couple, integrate, join, link, marry, meld, unify, unite, wed, yoke. [*Compare* MIX, HARMONIZE.] **2.** To make a part of a united whole ► embody, incorporate, integrate. —*See also* ASSOCIATE (1), BAND[2], COOPERATE.

combine *n.* —*See* ALLIANCE.

combined *adj.* —*See* COOPERATIVE, IMPURE (2).

combust *v.* —*See* BURN (2).

come *v.* To have as one's home or place of origin ► hail, originate. [*Compare* DESCEND, STEM.] —*See also* ADVANCE (2), AMOUNT, ARRIVE (1), BECOME (1), HAPPEN (1), STEM.

come across *v.* —*See* CONTRIBUTE (1), ENCOUNTER (1).

come around or **round** *v.* —*See* RECOVER (2), VISIT.

come back *v.* —*See* RETURN (1).

come between *v.* —*See* ESTRANGE.

come by *v.* —*See* GET (1), VISIT.

come in *v.* To complete a race or competition in a specified position ► finish, place, run. —*See also* ENTER (1).

come into *v.* To receive from one who has died ► inherit. *Idiom:* be (*or* fall) heir to.

come on *v.* —*See* ENCOUNTER (1).

come off *v.* —*See* SUCCEED (2).

come out *v.* **1.** To be made public ► break, get out, out, transpire. *Informal:* leak (out). *Idioms:* come out of the closet, come to light. [*Compare* AIR, ANNOUNCE.] **2.** To make one's formal entry, as into society ► debut. *Idiom:* make one's bow. —*See also* APPEAR (1).

come over *v.* —*See* VISIT.

come through *v.* —*See* SURVIVE (1).

come to *v.* —*See* ACCOMPLISH, STRIKE (2).

come together *v.* —*See* BAND[2].

comeback *n.* A return to former prosperity or status ► recovery, reestablishment, restoration. [*Compare* RENEWAL, REVIVAL.] —*See also* ANSWER (1).

comedian *n.* —*See* JOKER.

comedic *adj.* —*See* FUNNY (1).

comedown *n.* —*See* DESCENT.

comedy *n.* —*See* HUMOR.

come-hither *adj.* —*See* SEDUCTIVE.

comely *adj.* —*See* APPROPRIATE, BEAUTIFUL.

come-on *n.* —*See* LURE (1).

comer *n.* **1.** One that arrives ► arrival, newcomer, visitor. [*Compare* ADDITION, COMPANY.] **2.** One showing much promise ► candidate, hopeful, prospect, rising star, up-and-comer.

comestible *adj.* Fit to be eaten ► eatable, edible, esculent, palatable.

comestibles *n.* —*See* FOOD.

comeuppance *n.* —*See* DUE.

com·fit (kŭm′fĭt, kŏm′-) ▸ *n.* A confection; candy.
com·fort (kŭm′fərt) ▸ *v.* To soothe in time of affliction or distress. ▸ *n.* 1. A condition of pleasurable ease or well-being. 2. Solace. 3. One that brings or provides comfort. 4. The capacity to give physical ease. **—com′fort·ing** *adj.*
com·fort·a·ble (kŭm′fər-tə-bəl, kŭmf′tə-bəl, kŭmf′tər-) ▸ *adj.* 1. Providing comfort. 2. At ease. 3. Sufficient; adequate: *comfortable earnings.* **—com′fort·a·ble·ness** *n.* **—com′fort·a·bly** *adv.*
com·fort·er (kŭm′fər-tər) ▸ *n.* 1. One that comforts. 2. A quilted bedcover.
com·frey (kŭm′frē) ▸ *n.* Any of a genus of Eurasian herbs used in herbal medicine.
com·fy (kŭm′fē) ▸ *adj.* **-fi·er, -fi·est.** *Informal* Comfortable.
com·ic (kŏm′ĭk) ▸ *adj.* 1. Of or relating to comedy. 2. Amusing; humorous. ▸ *n.* 1. A comedian. 2. **comics** Comic strips.
com·i·cal (kŏm′ĭ-kəl) ▸ *adj.* Causing amusement; funny. **—com′i·cal′i·ty** (-kăl′ĭ-tē), **com′i·cal·ness** *n.* **—com′i·cal·ly** *adv.*
comic book ▸ *n.* A book of comic strips.
comic relief ▸ *n.* A humorous incident introduced into a serious literary work to relieve tension or heighten emotional impact.
comic strip ▸ *n.* A narrative series of cartoons.
com·ing (kŭm′ĭng) ▸ *adj.* 1. Approaching; next. 2. Showing promise of success. ▸ *n.* Arrival; advent.
com·i·ty (kŏm′ĭ-tē) ▸ *n., pl.* **-ties.** Civility; courtesy.
com·ma (kŏm′ə) ▸ *n.* A punctuation mark (,) used to indicate a separation of ideas or elements within the structure of a sentence.
com·mand (kə-mănd′) ▸ *v.* 1. To give orders to. 2. To have authority (over). 3. To receive as due; exact: *command respect.* 4. To dominate by position; overlook. ▸ *n.* 1. The act of commanding. 2. An order given with authority. 3. *Comp. Sci.* A signal that initiates an operation defined by an instruction. 4. Ability to control. 5. A military unit or region under the control of one officer.
com·man·dant (kŏm′ən-dănt′, -dänt′) ▸ *n.* The commanding officer of a military organization.
com·man·deer (kŏm′ən-dîr′) ▸ *v.* 1. To seize for military use; confiscate. 2. To take or seize arbitrarily.
com·mand·er (kə-măn′dər) ▸ *n.* 1. One who commands. 2. A rank, as in the US Navy, above lieutenant commander and below captain.
commander in chief ▸ *n., pl.* **commanders in chief.** The supreme commander of all the armed forces of a nation.
com·mand·ing (kə-măn′dĭng) ▸ *adj.* 1. Having command; controlling. 2. Dominating: *a commanding view; a commanding lead.*
com·mand·ment (kə-mănd′mənt) ▸ *n.* 1. A command. 2. One of the Ten Commandments.
command module ▸ *n.* The portion of a spacecraft in which the astronauts live and operate controls during a flight.
com·man·do (kə-măn′dō) ▸ *n., pl.* **-dos** or **-does.** A member of a small military unit specially trained to make quick raids.
com·mem·o·rate (kə-mĕm′ə-rāt′) ▸ *v.* **-rat·ed, -rat·ing.** 1. To honor the memory of. 2. To serve as a memorial to. **—com·mem′o·ra′tion** *n.* **—com·mem′o·ra·tive** (-ər-ə-tĭv, -ə-rā′-) *adj.* & *n.*
com·mence (kə-mĕns′) ▸ *v.* **-menced, -menc·ing.** To make or have a beginning; start.
com·mence·ment (kə-mĕns′mənt) ▸ *n.* 1. A beginning; start. 2. A graduation ceremony.
com·mend (kə-mĕnd′) ▸ *v.* 1. To represent as worthy or qualified; recommend. 2. To praise. 3. To put in the care of another; entrust. **—com·mend′a·ble** *adj.* **—com·mend′a·bly** *adv.*
com·men·da·tion (kŏm′ən-dā′shən) ▸ *n.* 1. The act of commending. 2. An official award or citation.
com·men·da·to·ry (kə-mĕn′də-tôr′ē) ▸ *adj.* Serving to commend.
com·men·sal·ism (kə-mĕn′sə-lĭz′əm) ▸ *n. Biol.* A symbiotic relationship between two organisms of different species in which one derives some benefit while the other is unaffected.
com·men·su·ra·ble (kə-mĕn′sər-ə-bəl, -shər-) ▸ *adj.* Measurable by a common standard. **—com·men′su·ra·bly** *adv.*
com·men·su·rate (kə-mĕn′sər-ĭt, -shər-) ▸ *adj.* 1. Of the same size, extent, or duration. 2. Corresponding in scale; proportionate. **—com·men′su·rate·ly** *adv.* **—com·men′su·ra′tion** *n.*
com·ment (kŏm′ĕnt) ▸ *n.* 1. An explanation, illustration,

THESAURUS

comfort *v.* To give support in time of grief or pain ▸ condole, console, reassure, solace, soothe, succor. [*Compare* ENCOURAGE, FEEL, HELP, RELIEVE.]
comfort *n.* A consoling in time of grief or pain ▸ consolation, reassurance, solace, succor. [*Compare* HELP, PITY.] *—See also* EASE (1), PROSPERITY (2).
comfortable *adj.* Affording pleasurable ease ▸ cozy, easeful, easy, restful, snug, soothing. *Informal:* comfy, cushy, homey, soft. *—See also* PROSPEROUS, SUFFICIENT.
comfortless *adj.* *—See* GLOOMY, UNCOMFORTABLE.
comforts *n.* *—See* AMENITIES (1).
comfy *adj.* *—See* COMFORTABLE.
comic *adj.* *—See* FUNNY (1).
comic *n.* *—See* JOKER.
comical *adj.* *—See* FUNNY (1).
comicalness *n.* *—See* HUMOR.
coming *adj.* 1. In the relatively near future ▸ approaching, due, forthcoming, upcoming. *Idioms:* around the corner, on the horizon. [*Compare* CLOSE, IMMINENT.] 2. Showing great promise ▸ promising, up-and-coming. *Idiom:* on the way up. [*Compare* ENCOURAGING.] *—See also* FOLLOWING (1), FUTURE.
coming *n.* 1. The act of arriving ▸ advent, arrival, appearance. [*Compare* ENTRANCE.] 2. The act or fact of coming near ▸ approach, convergence, imminence, nearness. [*Compare* ADVANCE, APPEARANCE.]
coming-out *n.* The instance or occasion of being presented for the first time to society ▸ debut, presentation.
command *v.* 1. To give orders to ▸ adjure, bid, call, charge, dictate, direct, enjoin, instruct, order, summon, tell. *Idioms:* call the shots, say the word. [*Compare* BOSS, GOVERN.] 2. To have at one's disposal ▸ boast, enjoy, have, hold, own, possess. *Idiom:* have at the ready. *—See also* DOMINATE (1), DOMINATE (2).
command *n.* 1. An order ▸ behest, bidding, charge, commandment, dictate, dictation, direction, directive, fiat, imperative, injunction, instructions, mandate, order, word, writ. [*Compare* LAW, RULING.] 2. The capacity to lead others ▸ lead, leadership. *—See also* ABILITY (1), AUTHORITY, DOMINANCE, DOMINATION, GOVERNMENT (1).
commandeer *v.* *—See* SEIZE (1).
commander *n.* The person in charge of a ship ▸ captain, shipmaster, skipper. *—See also* CHIEF.
commanding *adj.* Exercising authority ▸ authoritative, dominant, lordly, masterful. [*Compare* ADMINISTRATIVE.] *—See also* DOMINANT (1), NOTICEABLE.
commandment *n.* *—See* COMMAND (1).
command post *n.* *—See* BASE[1] (1).
comme il faut *adj.* *—See* APPROPRIATE.
commemorate *v.* 1. To honor or keep alive the memory of ▸ memorialize. [*Compare* IMMORTALIZE.] 2. To mark a day or an event with ceremonies of respect, festivity, or rejoicing ▸ celebrate, keep, observe, solemnize. [*Compare* SANCTIFY.]
commemoration *n.* Something, as a structure or custom, serving to honor or keep alive a memory ▸ memorial, monument, remembrance. [*Compare* TESTIMONIAL.] *—See also* CELEBRATION (2).
commemorative *adj.* Serving to honor or keep alive a memory ▸ memorial, monumental.
commence *v.* *See* BEGIN, START (1).
commencement *n.* *—See* BEGINNING, BIRTH (2).
commend *v.* To pay a compliment to ▸ compliment, congratulate, felicitate, praise. *Idioms:* pay tribute to, raise a glass to, take off one's hat to. [*Compare* HONOR.] *—See also* ENTRUST (1), PRAISE (1).
commendable *adj.* *—See* ADMIRABLE.
commendation *n.* *—See* COMPLIMENT, DISTINCTION (2), PRAISE (1).
commendatory *adj.* *—See* COMPLIMENTARY (1).
commensurate or **commensurable** *adj.* *—See* PROPORTIONAL (1).
comment *n.* An expression of fact or opinion ▸ aside, editorial, note, obiter dictum, observation, reflection, remark, word. [*Compare* EXPRESSION.]

or criticism. **2.** A statement of opinion. **—com′ment** *v.*

com·men·tar·y (kŏm′ən-tĕr′ē) ▸ *n., pl.* **-ies.** A series of explanations or interpretations.

com·men·tate (kŏm′ən-tāt′) ▸ *v.* **-tat·ed, -tat·ing.** To serve as commentator.

com·men·ta·tor (kŏm′ən-tā′tər) ▸ *n.* A broadcaster or writer who reports and analyzes events in the news.

com·merce (kŏm′ərs) ▸ *n.* The buying and selling of goods, esp. on a large scale.

com·mer·cial (kə-mûr′shəl) ▸ *adj.* **1.** Of or engaged in commerce. **2.** Having profit as a chief aim. **3.** Supported by advertising. ▸ *n.* An advertisement on television or radio. **—com·mer′cial·ism** *n.* **—com·mer′cial·ist** *n.* **—com·mer′cial·is′tic** *adj.* **—com·mer′cial·ly** *adv.*

commercial bank ▸ *n.* A bank whose principal functions are to receive demand deposits and to make short-term loans.

com·mer·cial·ize (kə-mûr′shə-līz′) ▸ *v.* **-ized, -iz·ing.** To apply methods of business to for profit. **—com·mer′cial·i·za′tion** *n.*

com·min·gle (kə-mĭng′gəl) ▸ *v.* **-gled, -gling.** To blend together; mix.

com·mis·er·ate (kə-mĭz′ə-rāt′) ▸ *v.* **-at·ed, -at·ing.** To feel or express sympathy (for). **—com·mis′er·a′tion** *n.* **—com·mis′er·a′tive** *adj.* **—com·mis′er·a′tor** *n.*

com·mis·sar (kŏm′ĭ-sär′) ▸ *n.* A Communist Party official in charge of indoctrination and enforcement of party loyalty.

com·mis·sar·i·at (kŏm′ĭ-sâr′ē-ĭt) ▸ *n.* An army department in charge of providing food and supplies.

com·mis·sar·y (kŏm′ĭ-sĕr′ē) ▸ *n., pl.* **-ies. 1.** A store where food and equipment are sold, esp. on a military post. **2.** A cafeteria, esp. in a film studio.

com·mis·sion (kə-mĭsh′ən) ▸ *n.* **1a.** Authorization to carry out a task. **b.** The authority so granted. **c.** The task so authorized. **d.** A document conferring such authorization. **2.** A group authorized to perform certain duties or functions. **3.** A committing; perpetrating: *the commission of a crime.* **4.** An allowance to a sales representative or agent for services rendered. **5.** A document conferring the rank of a military officer. ▸ *v.* **1.** To grant a commission to. **2.** To place an order for. ***—idioms:*** **in commission** In use or in usable condition. **out of commission** Not in use or in working condition.

com·mis·sioned officer (kə-mĭsh′ənd) ▸ *n.* A military officer who holds a commission and ranks above an enlisted person, a noncommissioned officer, or a warrant officer.

com·mis·sion·er (kə-mĭsh′ə-nər) ▸ *n.* **1.** A member of a commission. **2.** A government official in charge of a department. **3.** An administrative head of a professional sport.

com·mit (kə-mĭt′) ▸ *v.* **-mit·ted, -mit·ting. 1.** To do, perform, or perpetrate: *commit murder.* **2.** To consign; entrust. **3.** To place in confinement or custody. **4.** To pledge or obligate (oneself). **—com·mit′ment** *n.* **—com·mit′ta·ble** *adj.* **—com·mit′tal** *n.*

com·mit·tee (kə-mĭt′ē) ▸ *n.* A group of people officially delegated to perform a function, such as investigating, considering, reporting, or acting on a matter. **—com·mit′tee·man** *n.* **—com·mit′tee·wom′an** *n.*

com·mode (kə-mōd′) ▸ *n.* **1.** A low cabinet or chest of drawers. **2.** A movable stand containing a washbowl. **3.** A toilet.

com·mo·di·ous (kə-mō′dē-əs) ▸ *adj.* Spacious; roomy. **—com·mo′di·ous·ly** *adv.* **—com·mo′di·ous·ness** *n.*

com·mod·i·ty (kə-mŏd′ĭ-tē) ▸ *n., pl.* **-ties. 1.** Something useful that can be turned to commercial advantage. **2.** A transportable article of trade or commerce, esp. an agricultural or mining product.

com·mo·dore (kŏm′ə-dôr′) ▸ *n.* **1.** A rank, as in the US Navy, above captain and below rear admiral. **2.** The senior captain of a naval squadron or merchant fleet.

com·mon (kŏm′ən) ▸ *adj.* **-er, -est. 1.** Belonging equally to all; joint. **2.** Of or relating to the whole community; public: *the common good.* **3.** Widespread; prevalent. **4.** Frequent or habitual; usual. **5.** Most widely known; ordinary. **6.** Without noteworthy characteristics; average. **7.** Unrefined; coarse. ▸ *n.* **1.** often **Commons** See **House of Commons. 2.** A tract of land belonging to a whole community. ***—idiom:*** **in common** Equally with or by all. **—com′mon·ly** *adv.* **—com′mon·ness** *n.*

com·mon·al·ty (kŏm′ə-nəl-tē) ▸ *n., pl.* **-ties.** The common people, as distinct from the upper classes.

common denominator ▸ *n.* **1.** A quantity into which all the denominators of a set of fractions may be divided without a remainder. **2.** A commonly shared trait.

com·mon·er (kŏm′ə-nər) ▸ *n.* A person without noble rank.

Common Era ▸ *n.* The period coinciding with the Christian era.

common fraction ▸ *n.* A fraction whose numerator and denominator are both integers.

common ground ▸ *n.* A foundation for mutual understanding.

common law ▸ *n.* An unwritten system of law based on court decisions, customs, and usages. **—com′mon-law′** *adj.*

common logarithm ▸ *n.* A logarithm to the base 10.

Common Market ▸ See **European Economic Community.**

common multiple ▸ *n.* A quantity into which each of two or more quantities may be divided with zero remainder.

com·mon·place (kŏm′ən-plās′) ▸ *adj.* Unremarkable; ordinary. ▸ *n.* Something ordinary or common, esp. a trite or obvious remark.

THESAURUS

—See also COMMENTARY.

comment *v.* To state facts, opinions, or explanations ▸ commentate, editorialize, note, observe, opine, reflect, remark. [*Compare* SAY.]

commentaries *n.* *—See* MEMOIR.

commentary *n.* Critical explanation or analysis ▸ annotation, comment, criticism, critique, exposition, exegesis, interpretation, note, notice, review. [*Compare* EXPLANATION.]

commentate *v.* *—See* COMMENT.

commentator *n.* *—See* CRITIC (1), PRESS.

commerce *n.* *—See* BUSINESS (1).

commingle *v.* *—See* MIX (1).

comminute *v.* *—See* CRUSH (2).

commiserate *v.* To experience or express compassion ▸ ache, condole, feel, sympathize. *Idioms:* be (*or* feel) sorry, have one's heart ache (*or* bleed) for someone, have one's heart go out to someone. [*Compare* COMFORT, PITY.]

commiseration *n.* *—See* PITY (1).

commiserative *adj.* *—See* SYMPATHETIC.

commission *n.* *—See* LICENSE (3), MISSION (1).

commission *v.* *—See* AUTHORIZE.

commit *v.* **1.** To be responsible for or guilty of an error or crime ▸ carry out, do, perpetrate. *Informal:* pull off. [*Compare* PERFORM.] **2.** To be morally bound to do ▸ bind, charge, obligate, oblige, pledge. *Idiom:* be duty bound. [*Compare* FORCE, PLEDGE.] **3.** To place officially in confinement ▸ consign, institutionalize. *Informal:* send up. [*Compare* IMPRISON.] *—See also* ENTRUST (1), PLEDGE (2).

commitment *n.* *—See* DUTY (1), ENGAGEMENT (1), PROMISE (1).

committed *adj.* *—See* FAITHFUL, OBLIGED (2).

commix *v.* *—See* MIX (1).

commixture *n.* *—See* MIXTURE.

commodious *adj.* Having plenty of room ▸ ample, capacious, roomy, spacious. [*Compare* BIG, BROAD.]

commodity *n.* *—See* GOOD (2).

common *adj.* **1.** Occurring or encountered regularly ▸ accustomed, average, commonplace, customary, daily, everyday, familiar, frequent, general, habitual, normal, ordinary, regular, routine, typical, usual, widespread, wonted. [*Compare* INTERMITTENT, ORDINARY, PREVAILING.] **2.** Belonging to, shared by, or applicable to all alike ▸ communal, conjoint, cooperative, general, joint, mutual, public, shared. [*Compare* OPEN.] *—See also* ACCEPTABLE (2), BAD (1), COARSE (1), GENERAL (1), LOWLY (1), NOTORIOUS, ORDINARY.

common *n.* A tract of land set aside for public use ▸ green, lawn, park, plaza, square. [*Compare* RESERVATION.]

commonalty or **commonality** or **commoners** *n.* The common people ▸ commons, crowd, hoi polloi, masses, mob, multitude, plebs, plebeians, populace, proletariat, public, rank and file, ruck, third estate. *Idioms:* the great unwashed, men (*or* women) in the street. [*Compare* RIFFRAFF.]

commonly *adv.* *—See* USUALLY.

commonplace *adj.* *—See* COMMON (1), ORDINARY, TRITE.

commonplace *n.* *—See* CLICHÉ, USUAL.

commons *n.* *—See* COMMONALTY.

common sense ▸ *n.* Native good judgment.

common time ▸ *n. Mus.* A meter with four quarter notes to the measure.

com·mon·weal (kŏm′ən-wēl′) ▸ *n.* 1. The public good. 2. *Archaic* A commonwealth.

com·mon·wealth (kŏm′ən-wĕlth′) ▸ *n.* 1. The people of a nation or state. 2. A nation or state governed by the people; republic. 3. A union of self-governing states.

Commonwealth of Independent States ▸ A federation of self-governing states in E Europe, Asia Minor, and central Asia; formerly republics of the Soviet Union.

Commonwealth of Nations also **British Commonwealth** ▸ An association comprising the United Kingdom, its dependencies, and many former British colonies.

com·mo·tion (kə-mō′shən) ▸ *n.* Violent or turbulent motion; agitation; tumult.

com·mu·nal (kə-myo͞o′nəl, kŏm′yə-) ▸ *adj.* 1. Of or relating to a commune or community. 2. Public. **—com·mu′nal·ly** *adv.*

com·mune[1] (kə-myo͞on′) ▸ *v.* **-muned, -mun·ing.** 1. To experience heightened receptivity: *hikers communing with nature.* 2. To receive the Eucharist.

com·mune[2] (kŏm′yo͞on′, kə-myo͞on′) ▸ *n.* 1a. A small, often rural community whose members share work and income and often own property collectively. b. The members of a commune. 2. The smallest local political division of various European countries.

com·mu·ni·ca·ble (kə-myo͞o′nĭ-kə-bəl) ▸ *adj.* 1. Capable of being transmitted or communicated. 2. Talkative. **—com·mu′ni·ca·bil′i·ty** *n.* **—com·mu′ni·ca·bly** *adv.*

com·mu·ni·cant (kə-myo͞o′nĭ-kənt) ▸ *n.* 1. A person who receives Communion. 2. One who communicates.

com·mu·ni·cate (kə-myo͞o′nĭ-kāt′) ▸ *v.* **-cat·ed, -cat·ing.** 1. To make known; impart. 2. To spread, as a disease. 3. To receive Communion. **—com·mu′ni·ca′tive** (-kā′tĭv, -kə-tĭv) *adj.* **—com·mu′ni·ca′tive·ly** *adv.* **—com·mu′ni·ca′tive·ness** *n.* **—com·mu′ni·ca′tor** *n.*

com·mu·ni·ca·tion (kə-myo͞o′nĭ-kā′shən) ▸ *n.* 1. The act of communicating. 2. The exchange of thoughts, messages, or information. 3. Something communicated; message. 4. **communications** a. A system for communicating. b. The art and technology of communicating. **—com·mu′ni·ca′tion·al** *adj.*

com·mun·ion (kə-myo͞on′yən) ▸ *n.* 1. A sharing of thoughts or feelings. 2. Religious or spiritual fellowship. 3. A Christian denomination. 4. **Communion** a. The Eucharist. b. The consecrated elements of the Eucharist.

com·mu·ni·qué (kə-myo͞o′nĭ-kā′, -myo͞o′nĭ-kā′) ▸ *n.* An official announcement.

com·mu·nism (kŏm′yə-nĭz′əm) ▸ *n.* 1. An economic system characterized by collective ownership of property and by the organization of labor for common advantage. 2. **Communism** a. A system of government in which the state plans and controls the economy and a single, often authoritarian party holds power. b. The Marxist-Leninist version of Communist doctrine. **—com′mu·nist** *n.* **—com′mu·nis′tic** *adj.* **—com′mu·nis′ti·cal·ly** *adv.*

com·mu·ni·ty (kə-myo͞o′nĭ-tē) ▸ *n., pl.* **-ties.** 1a. A group of people living in the same locality and under the same government. b. The locality in which such a group lives. 2. A group of people having common interests. 3. Similarity: *a community of interests.* 4. Society as a whole. 5. *Ecol.* A group of plants and animals living with one another in a specific region.

community college ▸ *n.* A junior college without residential facilities that is often funded by the government.

community property ▸ *n. Law* Property owned jointly by spouses.

com·mu·nize (kŏm′yə-nīz′) ▸ *v.* **-nized, -niz·ing.** 1. To subject to public ownership or control. 2. To convert to Communist principles or control. **—com′mu·ni·za′tion** *n.*

com·mu·ta·tion (kŏm′yə-tā′shən) ▸ *n.* 1. A substitution or exchange. 2. The travel of a commuter. 3. *Law* Reduction of a penalty to a less severe one.

com·mu·ta·tive (kŏm′yə-tā′tĭv, kə-myo͞o′tə-tĭv) ▸ *adj.* 1. Of or involving substitution, interchange, or exchange. 2. Logically or mathematically independent of order. **—com·mu′ta·tiv′i·ty** (kə-myo͞o′tə-tĭv′ĭ-tē) *n.*

com·mu·ta·tor (kŏm′yə-tā′tər) ▸ *n.* A device in a direct current motor or generator that reverses current direction.

com·mute (kə-myo͞ot′) ▸ *v.* **-mut·ed, -mut·ing.** 1. To travel as a commuter. 2. To substitute; interchange. 3. To change (a penalty or payment) to a less severe one. ▸ *n.* A trip made by a commuter.

com·mut·er (kə-myo͞o′tər) ▸ *n.* One who travels regularly from one place to another, esp. between home and work.

Com·o·ros (kŏm′ə-rōz′) ▸ An island country in the **Comoro Islands** of the Indian Ocean between Mozambique and Madagascar.

com·pact[1] (kəm-păkt′, kŏm-, kŏm′păkt′) ▸ *adj.* 1. Closely and firmly packed together. 2. Occupying little space. 3. Concise. ▸ *v.* (kəm-păkt′) To press or join together. ▸ *n.* (kŏm′păkt′) 1. A small cosmetic case. 2. A small automobile. **—com·pact′ly** *adv.* **—com·pact′ness** *n.*

com·pact[2] (kŏm′păkt′) ▸ *n.* An agreement or a covenant.

com·pact disk (kŏm′păkt′) or **compact disc** ▸ *n.* A small optical disk on which data or music is digitally encoded.

com·pac·tor or **com·pact·er** (kəm-păk′tər, kŏm′păk′-) ▸ *n.* An apparatus that compresses refuse for disposal.

com·pan·ion (kəm-păn′yən) ▸ *n.* 1. An associate; comrade. 2. A person employed to live or travel with another. 3. One of a pair or set of things. **—com·pan′ion·ship′** *n.*

com·pan·ion·a·ble (kəm-păn′yə-nə-bəl) ▸ *adj.* Sociable; friendly. **—com·pan′ion·a·bly** *adv.*

com·pan·ion·way (kəm-păn′yən-wā′) ▸ *n.* A staircase leading below deck on a ship.

com·pa·ny (kŭm′pə-nē) ▸ *n., pl.* **-nies.** 1. A group of persons. 2. One's companions or associates. 3. A guest or

THESAURUS

common sense *n.* The ability to make sensible decisions ▸ judgment, mother wit, reason, sense, wisdom. *Informal:* gumption, horse sense. [*Compare* DISCERNMENT, PRUDENCE.]

commonsensical or **commonsensible** *adj.* —*See* SENSIBLE.

commotion *n.* —*See* AGITATION (1), AGITATION (3), DISORDER (2).

communal *adj.* —*See* COMMON (2), POPULAR.

communalize *v.* To place under government or group ownership or control ▸ nationalize, socialize.

communicable *adj.* —*See* CONTAGIOUS, OUTGOING.

communicate *v.* 1. To make known ▸ break, carry, convey, disclose, divulge, get across, impart, pass, report, reveal, tell, transmit. [*Compare* AIR, ANNOUNCE, INFORM.] 2. To spread a disease to others ▸ carry, convey, give, infect, pass, spread, transfer, transmit. —*See also* EXPRESS (1), RELATE (2), SAY.

communication *n.* 1. The exchange of ideas by writing, speech, or signals ▸ communion, conference, conversation, correspondence, discussion, exchange, intercommunication, interaction, intercourse, interface. [*Compare* CONVERSATION, DELIBERATION.] 2. A situation allowing exchange of ideas or messages ▸ contact, correspondence, intercommunication, touch. —*See also* ANNOUNCEMENT, MESSAGE.

communicative *adj.* —*See* CONVERSATIONAL, OUTGOING.

communion *n.* —*See* COMMUNICATION (1).

communiqué *n.* —*See* MESSAGE.

community *n.* —*See* NEIGHBORHOOD (1), PUBLIC (1), VILLAGE.

commutation *n.* —*See* CHANGE (2).

commutative *adj.* —*See* CHANGEABLE (1).

commute *v.* —*See* CHANGE (3).

comp *n. Informal* A free ticket entitling one to transportation or admission ▸ pass. *Slang:* freebie.

compact[1] *adj.* —*See* LITTLE, PITHY, STOCKY, THICK (2).

compact *v.* —*See* CONSTRICT (1), SQUEEZE (1).

compact[2] *n.* —*See* AGREEMENT (1).

compactness *n.* —*See* THICKNESS.

companion *n.* —*See* ASSOCIATE (2), CONCOMITANT, MATE.

companion *v.* —*See* ACCOMPANY.

companionable *adj.* —*See* AMIABLE, SOCIAL.

companionless *adj.* —*See* SOLITARY.

companionship *n.* —*See* COMPANY (3), FRIENDSHIP.

company *n.* 1. A commercial organization ▸ business, concern, conglomerate,

guests. **4.** Companionship; fellowship. **5.** A business enterprise; firm. **6.** A troupe of dramatic or musical performers. **7.** *Military* A subdivision of a regiment or battalion. **8.** A ship's crew and officers.

com·pa·ra·ble (kŏm′pər-ə-bəl) ► *adj.* **1.** Admitting of comparison. **2.** Similar or equivalent. **—com′pa·ra·bil′i·ty** *n.* **—com′pa·ra·bly** *adv.*

com·par·a·tive (kəm-păr′ə-tĭv) ► *adj.* **1.** Of, based on, or involving comparison. **2.** Relative: *a comparative newcomer.* **3.** *Gram.* Of or being the intermediate degree of comparison of adjectives or adverbs. ► *n. Gram.* **1.** The comparative degree. **2.** An adjective, such as *bigger,* or adverb, such as *more distinctly,* expressing the comparative degree. **—com·par′a·tive·ly** *adv.*

com·pare (kəm-pâr′) ► *v.* **-pared, -par·ing. 1.** To describe as similar, equal, or analogous. **2.** To examine in order to note the similarities or differences of. **3.** *Gram.* To form the positive, comparative, or superlative degree of (an adjective or adverb). ► *n.* Comparison: *rich beyond compare.* ***—idiom:* compare notes** To exchange ideas or opinions.

com·par·i·son (kəm-păr′ĭ-sən) ► *n.* **1.** The act of comparing. **2.** Similarity. **3.** *Gram.* The modification or inflection of an adjective or adverb to denote the positive, comparative, or superlative degree.

com·part·ment (kəm-pärt′mənt) ► *n.* One of the parts or spaces into which an area is subdivided. **—com′part·ment′al** (kŏm′pärt-mĕn′tl) *adj.*

com·part·men·tal·ize (kŏm′pärt-mĕn′tl-īz′, kəm-pärt′-) ► *v.* **-ized, -iz·ing.** To separate into distinct areas or categories. **—com′part·men′tal·i·za′tion** (-ĭ-zā′shən) *n.*

com·pass (kŭm′pəs, kŏm′-) ► *n.* **1.** A device used to determine geographic direction, usu. consisting of a magnetic needle that is free to pivot until aligned with the magnetic field of Earth. **2.** A hinged V-shaped device for drawing circles or circular arcs. **3.** An enclosing line or boundary; circumference. **4.** A restricted space or area. **5.** Range or scope. ► *v.* **1.** To make a circuit of; circle. **2.** To surround; encircle. **3.** To accomplish. **4.** To scheme; plot.

com·pas·sion (kəm-păsh′ən) ► *n.* Deep awareness of the suffering of another.

com·pas·sion·ate (kəm-păsh′ə-nĭt) ► *adj.* Feeling or showing compassion. **—com·pas′sion·ate·ly** *adv.*

com·pat·i·ble (kəm-păt′ə-bəl) ► *adj.* **1.** Capable of existing or functioning well with another or others. **2.** *Medic.* Capable of being grafted or transplanted from one individual to another without rejection. **—com·pat′i·bil′i·ty** *n.* **—com·pat′i·bly** *adv.*

com·pa·tri·ot (kəm-pā′trē-ət, -ŏt′) ► *n.* A person from one's own country.

com·peer (kŏm′pîr′, kəm-pîr′) ► *n.* A person of equal status; peer.

com·pel (kəm-pĕl′) ► *v.* **-pelled, -pel·ling.** To force; constrain.

com·pel·ling (kəm-pĕl′ĭng) ► *adj.* **1.** Urgently requiring attention. **2.** Drivingly forceful.

com·pen·di·um (kəm-pĕn′dē-əm) ► *n., pl.* **-di·ums** or **-di·a** (-dē-ə). **1.** A short detailed summary. **2.** A list or collection of items.

com·pen·sate (kŏm′pən-sāt′) ► *v.* **-sat·ed, -sat·ing. 1.** To make up for; offset; counterbalance. **2.** To make payment to; reimburse. **—com′pen·sa′tion** *n.* **—com·pen′sa·to′ry** (kəm-pĕn′sə-tôr′ē) *adj.*

com·pete (kəm-pēt′) ► *v.* **-pet·ed, -pet·ing.** To strive with another or others.

com·pe·tence (kŏm′pĭ-təns) also **com·pe·ten·cy** (-tən-sē) ► *n.* **1.** The state or quality of being competent. **2.** A specific range of skill, knowledge, or ability.

com·pe·tent (kŏm′pĭ-tənt) ► *adj.* **1.** Properly or well qualified. **2.** Adequate for the purpose. **3.** Legally qualified to perform an act. **—com′pe·tent·ly** *adv.*

com·pe·ti·tion (kŏm′pĭ-tĭsh′ən) ► *n.* **1.** The act of competing. **2.** A contest. **3.** A competitor: *The competition has cornered the market.* **—com·pet′i·tive** (kəm-pĕt′ĭ-tĭv) *adj.* **—com·pet′i·tive·ly** *adv.* **—com·pet′i·tive·ness** *n.*

com·pet·i·tor (kəm-pĕt′ĭ-tər) ► *n.* One who competes, as in sports or business; rival.

com·pile (kəm-pīl′) ► *v.* **-piled, -pil·ing. 1.** To gather into a single book. **2.** To compose from materials gathered from several sources. **3.** *Comp. Sci.* To translate (a program) into machine language. **—com′pi·la′tion** (kŏm′pə-lā′shən) *n.* **—com·pil′er** *n.*

com·pla·cence (kəm-plā′səns) also **com·pla·cen·cy** (-sən-sē) ► *n.* **1.** Contented self-satisfaction. **2.** Lack of concern. **—com·pla′cent** *adj.* **—com·pla′cent·ly** *adv.*

com·plain (kəm-plān′) ► *v.* **1.** To express feelings of pain, dissatisfaction, or resentment. **2.** To make a formal

THESAURUS

corporation, enterprise, establishment, firm, house, monopoly, multinational, partnership. *Informal:* outfit. [*Compare* ALLIANCE.] 2. A person or persons visiting one ► caller, guest, visitant, visitor. 3. A pleasant association among people ► brotherhood, camaraderie, companionship, comradeship, fellowship, sisterhood, society. [*Compare* FRIENDSHIP.] *—See also* ASSEMBLY, BAND[2].

company *v.* *—See* ACCOMPANY.

comparable *adj.* Estimated by comparison ► comparative, relative. *—See also* LIKE[2].

comparative *adj.* Estimated by comparison ► comparable, relative.

compare *v.* To examine in order to note the similarities and differences of ► balance, collate, contrast, counterpoint, counterpose, juxtapose, weigh. *—See also* EQUAL (1), LIKEN.

comparison *n.* *—See* CONTRAST, LIKENESS (1).

compass *n.* The ability or power to seize or attain ► capacity, grasp, range, reach, scope. [*Compare* INFLUENCE.] *—See also* CIRCUMFERENCE, RANGE (1).

compass *v.* *—See* KNOW (1), SURROUND, UNDERSTAND (1).

compassion *n.* *—See* PITY (1).

compassionate *adj.* *—See* HUMANITARIAN, SYMPATHETIC.

compassionless *adj.* *—See* CALLOUS.

compatible *adj.* *—See* AGREEABLE.

compatriot *n.* A person who is from one's own country ► countryman, countrywoman, fellow citizen, kinsman, kinswoman. *—See also* ASSOCIATE (1).

compeer *n.* *—See* PEER[2].

compel *v.* *—See* FORCE (1).

compellation *n.* *—See* NAME (1).

compelled *adj.* *—See* OBLIGED (2).

compelling *adj.* *—See* CONVINCING, URGENT (1).

compendious *adj.* *—See* BRIEF.

compensate *v.* To give compensation to ► indemnify, pay, recompense, recoup, redress, reimburse, remit, remunerate, reward, repay, requite. [*Compare* SETTLE.] *—See also* BALANCE (2), CANCEL (2).

compensation *n.* Something to make up for loss or damage ► amends, damages, indemnification, indemnity, offset, payment, quittance, recompense, recoupment, redress, reimbursement, remuneration, reparation, repayment, requital, restitution, reward, satisfaction, settlement, setoff. *—See also* DUE, WAGE.

compensatory or **compensative** *adj.* Affording compensation ► reimbursable, remunerative.

compete *v.* To strive against others for victory ► contend, contest, bid, emulate, play, race, rival, vie. ***Idioms:*** give a run for one's money, take on. [*Compare* CONTEND.]

competence or **competency** *n.* *—See* ABILITY (2).

competent *adj.* *—See* ABLE, SUFFICIENT.

competition *n.* 1. A vying with others for victory or supremacy ► battle, contention, contest, corrivalry, race, rivalry, strife, striving, struggle, tug of war, war, warfare. [*Compare* CONFLICT.] 2. A test of skill or ability ► bout, contest, event, fight, game, match, meet, tournament, tourney, trial. [*Compare* TEST, TILT.] *—See also* COMPETITOR.

competitive *adj.* Given to competition ► cutthroat, dog-eat-dog, emulous, rivalrous. [*Compare* ARGUMENTATIVE.]

competitor *n.* One that competes ► challenger, competition, contender, contestant, corrival, emulator, opponent, rival. [*Compare* OPPONENT.]

complain *v.* To express feelings of pain, dissatisfaction, or resentment ► carp, fuss, grouch, grumble, grump, grunt, moan, mutter, murmur, nag, repine, snivel, whimper, whine. *Informal:* crab, gripe, grouse, holler, kick, squawk, yammer. *Slang:* beef, bellyache, bitch, kvetch. ***Idioms:*** bitch and

accusation or bring a formal charge. **—com·plain′er** *n.*
com·plain·ant (kəm-plā′nənt) ► *n.* A party that files a formal charge, as in a court of law; plaintiff.
com·plaint (kəm-plānt′) ► *n.* **1.** An expression of pain, dissatisfaction, or resentment. **2.** A cause or reason for complaining; grievance. **3.** A bodily disorder or disease. **4.** A formal charge or accusation.
com·plai·sance (kəm-plā′səns, -zəns) ► *n.* Willing compliance; amiability. **—com·plai′sant** *adj.* **—com·plai′sant·ly** *adv.*
com·ple·ment (kŏm′plə-mənt) ► *n.* **1.** Something that completes or makes up a whole. **2.** The quantity or number needed to make up a whole. **3.** An angle related to another so that the sum of their measures is 90°. **4.** *Gram.* A word or group of words that completes a predicate construction. ► *v.* (-mĕnt′) To serve as a complement to.
com·ple·men·ta·ry (kŏm′plə-mĕn′tə-rē, -trē) ► *adj.* **1.** Forming or serving as a complement. **2.** Supplying mutual needs or offsetting mutual lacks. **—com′ple·men′ta·ri·ly** *adv.* **—com′ple·men′ta·ri·ness** *n.*
com·plete (kəm-plēt′) ► *adj.* **-plet·er, -plet·est.** **1.** Having all necessary or normal parts. **2.** Ended; concluded. **3.** Thorough; total: *a complete coward.* ► *v.* **-plet·ed, -plet·ing.** **1.** To end. **2.** To make whole. **—com·plete′ly** *adv.* **—com·plete′ness** *n.* **—com·ple′tion** *n.*
com·plex (kəm-plĕks′, kŏm′plĕks′) ► *adj.* **1.** Consisting of two or more interconnected parts. **2.** Intricate; complicated. **3.** *Gram.* **a.** Containing at least one bound morpheme. Used of a word. **b.** Consisting of an independent clause and at least one other clause. Used of a sentence. ► *n.* (kŏm′plĕks′) **1.** A whole composed of interconnected parts. **2.** *Psychol.* A group of repressed ideas and impulses that compel patterns of feelings and behavior. No longer in scientific use. **—com·plex′i·ty** *n.* **—com·plex′ly** *adv.* **—com·plex′ness** *n.*
complex fraction ► *n.* A fraction in which the numerator or the denominator or both contain fractions.
com·plex·ion (kəm-plĕk′shən) ► *n.* **1.** The natural color, texture, and appearance of the skin. **2.** General character or appearance.
complex number ► *n.* A number of the form $a + bi$, where a and b are real numbers and $i^2 = -1$.
com·pli·ance (kəm-plī′əns) also **com·pli·an·cy** (-ən-sē) ► *n.* **1.** The act of complying with a wish, request, or demand. **2.** A disposition or tendency to yield to others. **—com·pli′ant** *adj.* **—com·pli′ant·ly** *adv.*
com·pli·cate (kŏm′plĭ-kāt′) ► *v.* **-cat·ed, -cat·ing.** To make or become complex, intricate, or perplexing. **—com′pli·ca′tion** *n.*
com·pli·cat·ed (kŏm′plĭ-kā′tĭd) ► *adj.* **1.** Containing intricately combined parts. **2.** Convoluted.
com·plic·i·ty (kəm-plĭs′ĭ-tē) ► *n., pl.* **-ties.** Involvement as an accomplice in a questionable act or a crime.
com·pli·ment (kŏm′plə-mənt) ► *n.* **1.** An expression of praise or admiration. **2. compliments** Good wishes; regards. ► *v.* To pay a compliment to.
com·pli·men·ta·ry (kŏm′plə-mĕn′tə-rē, -trē) ► *adj.* **1.** Expressing a compliment. **2.** Given free as a favor or courtesy. **—com′pli·men′ta·ri·ly** *adv.*
com·ply (kəm-plī′) ► *v.* **-plied, -ply·ing.** To act in accordance with another's command or wish.
com·po·nent (kəm-pō′nənt) ► *n.* An element of a system. ► *adj.* Being or functioning as a constituent. **—com′po·nen′tial** (kŏm′pə-nĕn′shəl) *adj.*

THESAURUS

moan, have a bone to pick, kick up a fuss (*or* row), make a fuss (*or* stink). [*Compare* OBJECT, QUIBBLE.]
complainant *n.* One that makes a formal complaint, especially in court ► accuser, claimant, plaintiff.
complainer *n.* *—See* GROUCH.
complaint *n.* An expression of pain or dissatisfaction ► carp, fuss, grievance, grouch, grumble, grunt, murmur, mutter, squawk, whimper, whine. *Informal:* gripe, grouse, yammer. *Slang:* beef, bellyache, bitch, kick, kvetch, stink. ***Idiom:*** bone to pick. *—See also* DISEASE, OBJECTION, SICKNESS.
complaisance *n.* *—See* OBEDIENCE.
complaisant *adj.* *—See* OBEDIENT, OBLIGING.
complement *n.* *—See* ENHANCEMENT, MATE.
complement *v.* *—See* PERFECT, SUPPLEMENT.
complementary or **complemental** *adj.* Supplying mutual needs or offsetting mutual lacks ► correlative, interdependent, interrelated, mutual, reciprocal, supplemental, symbiotic. [*Compare* AGREEABLE.]
complete *adj.* **1.** Including every constituent or individual ► all, entire, full, gross, intact, integral, perfect, round, total, whole. **2.** Not shortened by omissions ► full-length, unabbreviated, unabridged, uncensored, uncut, unedited, unexpurgated. [*Compare* CONTINUAL.] **3.** Having reached completion ► closed, concluded, consummated, done, ended, executed, finished, over, performed, terminated, through. *—See also* THOROUGH, UTTER[2].
complete *v.* *—See* CONCLUDE, PERFECT, SUPPLEMENT.
completely *adv.* **1.** To the fullest extent ► absolutely, all, altogether, dead, downright, entirely, flat, fully, just, perfectly, purely, quite, thoroughly, totally, utterly, well, wholly. *Informal:* clean, clear. ***Idioms:*** hook, line, and sinker, in toto, root and branch, through and through, to the nth degree. [*Compare* ABSOLUTELY, CONSIDERABLY, REALLY, UNUSUALLY, VERY.] **2.** In a painstakingly complete manner ► comprehensively, exhaustively, intensively, thoroughly. ***Idioms:*** backwards and forwards, down to the ground, from soup to nuts, in and out, up and down.
completeness *n.* The state of being entirely whole ► entirety, fullness, integrity, oneness, totality, wholeness.
completion *n.* *—See* END (1), FULFILLMENT (1).
complex *adj.* **1.** Difficult to understand because of intricacy ► advanced, baffling, baroque, bewildering, byzantine, complicated, confounding, confusing, convoluted, crabbed, daedal, Daedalian, difficult, elaborate, entangled, inextricable, intricate, involute, involved, knotty, labyrinthine, mazy, mystifying, perplexing, puzzling, sophisticated, tangled, tortuous. [*Compare* AMBIGUOUS, INCOMPREHENSIBLE, MYSTERIOUS.] **2.** Consisting of two or more parts ► composite, compound, manifold, multiple, multiplex. [*Compare* VARIOUS.]
complex *n.* **1.** An entity composed of interconnected parts ► conglomerate, group, network, syndrome, system, tissue, web. [*Compare* MIXTURE.] **2.** An exaggerated concern ► anxiety, neurosis, phobia. *Informal:* hang-up. [*Compare* ANXIETY, OBSESSION.] *—See also* BASE[1] (1).
complexion *n.* Skin tone, especially of the face ► color, coloring. [*Compare* BLOOM, COLOR.] *—See also* CHARACTER (1), DISPOSITION.
complexity *n.* Something complex ► bewilderment, complication, elaborateness, entanglement, intricacy, perplexity. [*Compare* TANGLE.]
compliance or **compliancy** *n.* An act of willingly carrying out the wishes of others ► obedience, observance. *—See also* OBEDIENCE.
compliant *adj.* *—See* OBEDIENT.
complicate *v.* To make complex, intricate, or perplexing ► embarrass, embroil, entangle, involve, knot, obfuscate, perplex, ravel, snarl, tangle, vex. [*Compare* CONFUSE.]
complicated *adj.* *—See* COMPLEX (1), DIFFICULT (1), ELABORATE.
complication *n.* *—See* COMPLEXITY, DIFFICULTY.
compliment *n.* An expression of admiration or congratulation ► accolade, commendation, congratulations, felicitations, praise, tribute. *Informal:* congrats. ***Idiom:*** pat on the back. *—See also* PRAISE (1).
compliment *v.* To pay a compliment to ► commend, congratulate, felicitate, praise. ***Idioms:*** pay tribute to, raise a glass to, take off one's hat to. [*Compare* HONOR.] *—See also* DRINK (4), PRAISE (1).
complimentary *adj.* **1.** Serving to compliment ► acclamatory, approbatory, commendatory, congratulatory, encomiastic, eulogistic, laudatory. **2.** Costing nothing ► free, gratis, gratuitous. ***Idioms:*** as a freebie, for free, for nothing, on the house.
comply *v.* *—See* FOLLOW (4).
component *n.* *—See* PART (1).
component *adj.* *—See* BUILT-IN.

com·port (kəm-pôrt′) ▸ *v.* **1.** To conduct (oneself) in a particular manner. **2.** To agree; harmonize. **—com·port′ment** *n.*
com·pose (kəm-pōz′) ▸ *v.* **-posed, -pos·ing.** **1.** To make up; constitute: *the many ethnic groups that compose our nation.* **2.** To make by putting together parts or elements. **3.** To create (a literary or musical piece). **4.** To make calm or tranquil. **5.** To settle; adjust. **6.** *Print.* To arrange or set (type). **—com·pos′er** *n.*
com·posed (kəm-pōzd′) ▸ *adj.* Serenely self-possessed; calm. **—com·pos′ed·ly** (-pō′zĭd-lē) *adv.*
com·pos·ite (kəm-pŏz′ĭt) ▸ *adj.* **1.** Made up of distinct components or elements. **2.** *Math.* Having factors. **3.** Of or belonging to a family of flowering plants, such as the daisy, having flower heads consisting of many small flowers. ▸ *n.* **1.** A composite structure or entity. **2.** A composite plant. **—com·pos′ite·ly** *adv.*
com·po·si·tion (kŏm′pə-zĭsh′ən) ▸ *n.* **1.** The act of composing. **2.** General makeup: *the changing composition of the electorate.* **3.** The arrangement of artistic parts so as to form a unified whole. **4a.** A work of music, literature, or art. **b.** A short essay. **5.** Typesetting. **—com′po·si′tion·al** *adj.*
com·pos·i·tor (kəm-pŏz′ĭ-tər) ▸ *n.* A typesetter.
com·post (kŏm′pōst′) ▸ *n.* A mixture of decaying organic matter used as fertilizer. ▸ *v.* **1.** To fertilize with compost. **2.** To convert (organic matter) to compost.
com·po·sure (kəm-pō′zhər) ▸ *n.* Calmness and self-possession; equanimity.
com·pote (kŏm′pōt) ▸ *n.* **1.** Fruit stewed or cooked in syrup. **2.** A long-stemmed dish used for holding fruit, nuts, or candy.
com·pound[1] (kŏm-pound′, kŏm′pound′) ▸ *v.* **1.** To combine; mix. **2.** To produce by combining. **3.** To compute (interest) on the principal and accrued interest. **4.** To add to; increase. ▸ *adj.* (kŏm′pound′, kŏm-pound′) Consisting of two or more parts. ▸ *n.* (kŏm′pound′) **1.** A combination of two or more elements or parts. **2.** A word, such as *loudspeaker* or *baby-sit,* that consists of two or more elements that are independent words. **3.** A substance consisting of atoms or ions of two or more different elements in definite proportions, usu. having properties unlike those of its constituent elements. **—com·pound′a·ble** *adj.* **—com·pound′er** *n.*
com·pound[2] (kŏm′pound′) ▸ *n.* A building or buildings set off and enclosed by a barrier.
compound eye ▸ *n.* The eye of most insects and some crustaceans, composed of many visual units that each form a portion of an image.
compound fraction ▸ *n.* See **complex fraction.**
compound interest ▸ *n.* Interest computed on accumulated unpaid interest as well as on the original principal.
compound number ▸ *n.* A quantity expressed in two or more different units, such as 3 feet 4 inches.
compound sentence ▸ *n.* A sentence of two or more independent clauses.
com·pre·hend (kŏm′prĭ-hĕnd′) ▸ *v.* **1.** To understand the meaning or importance of. **2.** To take in; include. **—com′pre·hen′si·ble** *adj.* **—com′pre·hen′si·bly** *adv.* **—com′pre·hen′sion** *n.*
com·pre·hen·sive (kŏm′prĭ-hĕn′sĭv) ▸ *adj.* Large in scope; including much. **—com′pre·hen′sive·ly** *adv.* **—com′pre·hen′sive·ness** *n.*
com·press (kəm-prĕs′) ▸ *v.* **1.** To press together; compact. **2.** To make smaller or shorter; condense. ▸ *n.* (kŏm′prĕs′) A soft pad applied to a part of the body to control bleeding or reduce pain. **—com·press′i·bil′i·ty** *n.* **—com·press′i·ble** *adj.* **—com·pres′sion** *n.*
com·pres·sor (kəm-prĕs′ər) ▸ *n.* One that compresses, esp. a machine used to compress gases.
com·prise (kəm-prīz′) ▸ *v.* **-prised, -pris·ing.** **1.** To consist of. **2.** To include. **—com·pris′a·ble** *adj.*
com·pro·mise (kŏm′prə-mīz′) ▸ *n.* **1.** A settlement of differences in which each side makes concessions. **2.** Something that combines qualities of different things. ▸ *v.* **-mised, -mis·ing.** **1a.** To settle by concessions. **b.** To make a compromise. **2.** To expose to danger, suspicion, or disrepute. **—com′pro·mis′er** *n.*
comp·trol·ler (kən-trō′lər, kŏmp-trō′-) ▸ *n.* Var. of **controller** 2.
com·pul·sion (kəm-pŭl′shən) ▸ *n.* **1.** The act of compelling. **2.** The state of being compelled. **3.** An irresistible impulse to act. **—com·pul′sive** *adj.* **—com·pul′sive·ly** *adv.* **—com·pul′sive·ness** *n.*
com·pul·so·ry (kəm-pŭl′sə-rē) ▸ *adj.* **1.** Obligatory; required. **2.** Coercive. **—com·pul′so·ri·ly** *adv.*
com·punc·tion (kəm-pŭngk′shən) ▸ *n.* A strong uneasiness caused by guilt.
com·pute (kəm-pyo͞ot′) ▸ *v.* **-put·ed, -put·ing.** **1.** To determine by mathematics, esp. by numerical methods. **2.** To determine by use of a computer. **—com·put′a·ble** *adj.* **—com′pu·ta′tion** (kŏm′pyo͞o-tā′shən) *n.* **—com′pu·ta′tion·al** *adj.*
com·put·er (kəm-pyo͞o′tər) ▸ *n.* **1.** A device that computes, esp. a programmable electronic machine that performs high-speed mathematical or logical operations or that assembles, stores, correlates, or processes information. **2.** One who computes.
com·put·er·ize (kəm-pyo͞o′tə-rīz′) ▸ *v.* **-ized, -iz·ing.** **1.** To furnish with a computer or computer system. **2.** To enter, process, or store (information) in a computer or computer system. **—com·put′er·i·za′tion** *n.*

THESAURUS

comport *v.* —*See* ACT (1), AGREE (1).
comportment *n.* —*See* BEHAVIOR (1).
compose *v.* 1. To form by artistic effort ▸ create, design, draft, indite, orchestrate, pen, produce, score, write. [*Compare* INVENT.] 2. To devise and set down ▸ draft, draw up, formulate, frame. 3. To be the constituent parts of ▸ form, make up. [*Compare* CONTAIN.] 4. To bring one's emotions under control ▸ calm down, collect (oneself), contain (oneself), control (oneself), cool (down), simmer down. *Slang:* chill (out). *Idiom:* cool it. [*Compare* CALM.] —*See also* MAKE, PUBLISH (2).
composed *adj.* —*See* CALM.
composite *adj.* —*See* COMPLEX (2).
composite *n.* —*See* COMBINATION, MIXTURE.
composition *n.* 1. Something that is the result of creative effort ▸ creation, invention, opus, output, piece, production, work, writing. [*Compare* INVENTION, MASTERPIECE.] 2. A relatively brief discourse written especially as an exercise ▸ essay, paper, theme. —*See also* COMPROMISE.
compos mentis *adj.* Mentally healthy ▸ lucid, normal, rational, sane. *Idioms:* all there, in one's right mind, of sound mind. [*Compare* HEALTHY.]
composure *n.* —*See* BALANCE (2).
compound *v.* —*See* COMBINE (1).
compound *adj.* —*See* COMPLEX (2).
compound *n.* —*See* COMBINATION.
comprehend *v.* —*See* CONTAIN (1), KNOW (1), UNDERSTAND (1).
comprehensibility *n.* —*See* CLARITY.
comprehensible *adj.* —*See* UNDERSTANDABLE.
comprehension *n.* Intellectual hold ▸ apprehension, grasp, grip, hold, understanding. [*Compare* KNOWLEDGE.]
comprehensive *adj.* —*See* DETAILED, GENERAL (2).
comprehensively *adv.* —*See* COMPLETELY (2).
compress *v.* —*See* CONSTRICT (1), SQUEEZE (1).
compressed *adj.* —*See* THICK (2).
compression *n.* —*See* CONSTRICTION.
comprise *v.* —*See* CONTAIN (1).
compromise *n.* A settlement of differences through mutual concession ▸ accommodation, arbitration, arrangement, composition, concession, give-and-take, mediation, settlement, tradeoff. [*Compare* AGREEMENT.]
compromise *v.* To make a concession ▸ accommodate, arrange, concede, settle. *Idioms:* come to an understanding, give and take, go fifty-fifty, make a deal, meet someone halfway, steer a middle course, strike a bargain. [*Compare* AGREE, SETTLE.] —*See also* ENDANGER.
compulsion *n.* —*See* FORCE (1), OBSESSION.
compulsory *adj.* —*See* REQUIRED.
compunction *n.* —*See* PENITENCE, QUALM.
compunctious *adj.* —*See* SORRY.
computation *n.* 1. The act, process, or result of calculating ▸ calculation, cast, figuring, reckoning. 2. Arithmetic calculations ▸ arithmetic, figures, numbers. [*Compare* ADDITION.]
compute *v.* —*See* CALCULATE.

com·rade (kŏm′răd′, -rəd) ▸ *n.* A friend, associate, or companion. **—com′rade·ship′** *n.*

con¹ (kŏn) ▸ *adv.* Against. ▸ *n.* An argument or opinion against something.

con² (kŏn) ▸ *v.* **conned, con·ning. 1.** To study, peruse, or examine carefully. **2.** To memorize.

con³ (kŏn) *Slang* ▸ *v.* **conned, con·ning.** To swindle or dupe. ▸ *n.* A swindle. ▸ *adj.* Of or involving a swindle.

con⁴ (kŏn) ▸ *n. Slang* A convict.

con– ▸ *pref.* Var. of **com–.**

con·cat·e·nate (kŏn-kăt′n-āt′, kən-) ▸ *v.* **-nat·ed, -nat·ing.** To connect or link in a series. **—con·cat′e·nate** (-nĭt, -nāt′) *adj.* **—con·cat′e·na′tion** *n.*

con·cave (kŏn-kāv′, kŏn′kāv′) ▸ *adj.* Curved like the inner surface of a sphere. **—con·cave′ly** *adv.* **—con·cav′i·ty** (-kăv′ĭ-tē) *n.*

con·ceal (kən-sēl′) ▸ *v.* To keep from being seen, found, or discovered; hide. **—con·ceal′a·ble** *adj.* **—con·ceal′er** *n.* **—con·ceal′ment** *n.*

con·cede (kən-sēd′) ▸ *v.* **-ced·ed, -ced·ing. 1.** To acknowledge, often reluctantly, as being true. **2.** To grant (e.g., a privilege). **3.** To make a concession; yield. **—con·ced′er** *n.*

con·ceit (kən-sēt′) ▸ *n.* **1.** An unduly high opinion of oneself. **2.** An elaborate metaphor.

con·ceit·ed (kən-sē′tĭd) ▸ *adj.* Vain. **—con·ceit′ed·ly** *adv.* **—con·ceit′ed·ness** *n.*

con·ceive (kən-sēv′) ▸ *v.* **-ceived, -ceiv·ing. 1.** To become pregnant (with). **2.** To form in the mind; devise. **3.** To think; imagine. **—con·ceiv′a·ble** *adj.* **—con·ceiv′a·bly** *adv.* **—con·ceiv′er** *n.*

con·cen·trate (kŏn′sən-trāt′) ▸ *v.* **-trat·ed, -trat·ing. 1.** To direct or draw toward a common center; focus. **2.** To direct one's thoughts or attention. **3.** To make (a solution) less dilute. ▸ *n.* A product of concentration: *orange juice concentrate.* **—con′cen·tra′tive** *adj.* **—con′cen·tra′tor** *n.*

con·cen·tra·tion (kŏn′sən-trā′shən) ▸ *n.* **1.** The act of concentrating or state of being concentrated. **2.** Something concentrated. **3.** *Chem.* The amount of one substance in a unit amount of another substance.

concentration camp ▸ *n.* A camp where prisoners of war, enemy aliens, and political prisoners are confined.

con·cen·tric (kən-sĕn′trĭk) also **con·cen·tri·cal** (-trĭ-kəl) ▸ *adj.* Having a common center. **—con·cen′tri·cal·ly** *adv.* **—con′cen·tric′i·ty** (kŏn′sĕn-trĭs′ĭ-tē) *n.*

con·cept (kŏn′sĕpt′) ▸ *n.* **1.** A general idea derived from specific instances. **2.** A thought or notion. **3.** A plan. **—con·cep′tu·al** (kən-sĕp′cho͞o-əl) *adj.* **—con·cep′tu·al·ly** *adv.*

con·cep·tion (kən-sĕp′shən) ▸ *n.* **1.** Formation of a viable zygote by the union of the male sperm and the female ovum; fertilization. **2.** The ability to form or understand mental concepts. **3.** A concept, plan, design, or thought. **—con·cep′tion·al** *adj.*

con·cep·tu·al·ize (kən-sĕp′cho͞o-ə-līz′) ▸ *v.* **-ized, -iz·ing.** To form concepts (of). **—con·cep′tu·al·i·za′tion** *n.*

con·cern (kən-sûrn′) ▸ *v.* **1.** To have to do with; relate to. **2.** To engage the attention of; involve. **3.** To cause anxiety or uneasiness in. ▸ *n.* **1.** A matter that relates to or affects one. **2.** Serious interest in. **3.** A troubled state of mind. **4.** A business establishment.

con·cerned (kən-sûrnd′) ▸ *adj.* **1.** Interested. **2.** Anxious; troubled.

con·cern·ing (kən-sûr′nĭng) ▸ *prep.* In reference to.

con·cert (kŏn′sûrt′, -sərt) ▸ *n.* **1.** A public musical performance. **2.** Agreement in purpose, feeling, or action. ▸ *v.* (kən-sûrt′) To plan by mutual agreement. ***—idiom:* in concert** All together; in agreement.

con·cert·ed (kən-sûr′tĭd) ▸ *adj.* Planned or accomplished together: *a concerted effort to solve the problem.* **—con·cert′ed·ly** *adv.*

con·cer·ti·na (kŏn′sər-tē′nə) ▸ *n.* A small hexagonal accordion with buttons for keys.

con·cert·mas·ter (kŏn′sərt-măs′tər) ▸ *n.* The first violinist in a symphony orchestra.

con·cer·to (kən-chĕr′tō) ▸ *n., pl.* **-tos** or **-ti** (-tē). A composition for an orchestra and one or more solo instruments.

con·ces·sion (kən-sĕsh′ən) ▸ *n.* **1.** The act of conceding. **2.** Something conceded. **3.** Land granted by a government to be used for a specific purpose. **4a.** The privilege of maintaining a subsidiary business in a certain place. **b.** The business itself.

con·ces·sion·aire (kən-sĕsh′ə-nâr′) ▸ *n.* The holder or operator of a concession.

conch (kŏngk, kŏnch) ▸ *n., pl.* **conchs** (kŏngks) or **conch·es** (kŏn′chĭz). A tropical marine mollusk having a large spiral shell and edible flesh.

con·cierge (kôɴ-syârzh′) ▸ *n.* A staff member of a hotel or apartment complex, esp. in France, who assists guests or residents.

con·cil·i·ate (kən-sĭl′ē-āt′) ▸ *v.* **-at·ed, -at·ing. 1.** To overcome the distrust of; appease. **2.** To make compatible; reconcile. **—con·cil′i·a′tion** *n.* **—con·cil′i·a′tor** *n.* **—con·cil′i·a·to′ry** (-ə-tôr′ē) *adj.*

THESAURUS

comrade *n.* —*See* ASSOCIATE (2), FRIEND.

comradeship *n.* —*See* COMPANY (3), FRIENDSHIP.

con *v.* To commit to memory ▸ learn, memorize. *Idiom:* learn by heart (*or* rote). [*Compare* LEARN, REMEMBER.] —*See also* CHEAT (1), EXAMINE (1).

con *n.* —*See* CHEAT (1), CRIMINAL.

concatenation *n.* —*See* SERIES.

concave *adj.* —*See* HOLLOW (2).

concavity *n.* —*See* DEPRESSION (1).

conceal *v.* To prevent something from being known ▸ camouflage, cloak, cover (up), enshroud, hide, hush (up), mask, obscure, screen, shroud, veil. *Idioms:* keep in the dark, keep under cover, keep under one's hat, keep under wraps. [*Compare* DISGUISE.] —*See also* BLOCK, HIDE¹.

concealed *adj.* —*See* HIDDEN (1), ULTERIOR (1).

concealment *n.* —*See* SECRECY.

concede *v.* To let have as a favor, prerogative, or privilege ▸ accord, award, give, grant, vouchsafe. [*Compare* YIELD.] —*See also* ACKNOWLEDGE (1), COMPROMISE, SURRENDER (1).

conceit *n.* —*See* EGOTISM, FANCY.

conceited *adj.* —*See* EGOTISTIC (1).

conceivable *adj.* Capable of being anticipated, considered, or imagined ▸ earthly, imaginable, likely, mortal, possible, thinkable. *Idioms:* humanly possible, within the bounds (*or* range *or* realm) of possibility. [*Compare* POSSIBLE.]

conceivably *adv.* —*See* MAYBE.

conceive *v.* —*See* BELIEVE (3), DESIGN (1), IMAGINE, UNDERSTAND (1).

concentrate *v.* To direct toward a common center ▸ center, channel, concenter, converge, focalize, focus, hone in, zero in. [*Compare* ASSEMBLE.] —*See also* APPLY (1).

concentrated *adj.* **1.** Not diffused or dispersed ▸ exclusive, intensive, undivided, unswerving, whole. [*Compare* THICK.] **2.** Having a high concentration of the distinguishing ingredient ▸ potent, stiff, strong. [*Compare* STRAIGHT.] —*See also* [illegible]

concentration *n.* —*See* ATTENTION, INTENSITY, JUNCTION.

concept *n.* —*See* DOCTRINE, IDEA.

conception *n.* —*See* BEGINNING, IDEA.

conceptual *adj.* —*See* IMAGINARY, THEORETICAL (1), THEORETICAL (2).

conceptualization *n.* —*See* THEORY (1), THOUGHT.

conceptualize *v.* —*See* THINK (1).

concern *v.* —*See* APPLY (2), WORRY.

concern *n.* **1.** Something that concerns or involves one personally ▸ affair, business, interest, lookout. **2.** A cause of distress or anxiety ▸ care, stressor, trouble, worry. [*Compare* ANXIETY, BURDEN¹.] —*See also* ANXIETY, COMPANY (1), CONSIDERATION (1), CURIOSITY (1), IMPORTANCE, QUALM.

concerned *adj.* Having concern ▸ affected, connected, engaged, interested, involved. —*See also* ANXIOUS, SYMPATHETIC.

concernment *n.* —*See* CURIOSITY (1), IMPORTANCE.

concert *n.* —*See* AGREEMENT (2), COOPERATION, HARMONY (1).

concert *v.* —*See* COOPERATE.

concerted *adj.* —*See* COOPERATIVE.

concertize *v.* To make music ▸ perform, play, render.

concession *n.* —*See* ACKNOWLEDGMENT (1), COMPROMISE.

conciliate *v.* To reestablish friendship between ▸ make up, reconcile, reunite. —*See also* PACIFY.

conciliation *n.* A reestablishment of friendship or harmony ▸ rapprochement, reconcilement, reconciliation, settlement. [*Compare* AGREEMENT, ATONEMENT, COMPROMISE.]

conciliatory *adj.* —*See* PEACEABLE.

con·cise (kən-sīs′) ▸ *adj.* Expressing much in few words; clear and succinct. **—con·cise′ly** *adv.* **—con·cise′ness** *n.* **—con·ci′sion** (-sĭzh′ən) *n.*

con·clave (kŏn′klāv′, kŏng′-) ▸ *n.* A secret meeting, esp. one in which the cardinals of the Catholic Church meet to elect a pope.

con·clude (kən-klo͞od′) ▸ *v.* **-clud·ed, -clud·ing.** **1.** To bring or come to an end; close. **2.** To come to an agreement or settlement of. **3.** To reach a decision about. **4.** To arrive at (a logical conclusion) by reasoning.

con·clu·sion (kən-klo͞o′zhən) ▸ *n.* **1.** The close or finish. **2.** A result; outcome. **3.** A determination. **4.** A final arrangement.

con·clu·sive (kən-klo͞o′sĭv) ▸ *adj.* Serving to put an end to doubt. **—con·clu′sive·ly** *adv.*

con·coct (kən-kŏkt′) ▸ *v.* **1.** To prepare by mixing ingredients. **2.** To devise: *concoct an excuse.* **—con·coct′er, con·coc′tor** *n.* **—con·coc′tion** *n.*

con·com·i·tant (kən-kŏm′ĭ-tənt) ▸ *adj.* Occurring or existing concurrently. ▸ *n.* One that is concomitant with another. **—con·com′i·tant·ly** *adv.* **—con·com′i·tance** *n.*

con·cord (kŏn′kôrd′, kŏng′-) ▸ *n.* Agreement of interests or feelings; accord.

Con·cord (kŏng′kərd) ▸ **1.** A town of E MA WNW of Boston; site of an early battle of the Revolutionary War. **2.** The capital of NH, in the S-central part.

con·cor·dance (kən-kôr′dns) ▸ *n.* **1.** Agreement; concord. **2.** An index of the words in a text or texts, showing every context in which they occur.

con·cor·dant (kən-kôr′dnt) ▸ *adj.* Harmonious; agreeing. **—con·cor′dant·ly** *adv.*

con·cor·dat (kən-kôr′dăt′) ▸ *n.* A formal agreement.

con·course (kŏn′kôrs′, kŏng′-) ▸ *n.* **1.** A large open space for the gathering or passage of crowds. **2.** A broad thoroughfare. **3.** A crowd; throng.

con·cres·cence (kən-krĕs′əns) ▸ *n.* *Biol.* The growing together of related parts. **—con·cres′cent** *adj.*

con·crete (kŏn-krēt′, kŏng-, kŏn′krēt′, kŏng′-) ▸ *adj.* **1.** Relating to an actual, specific thing or instance; particular. **2.** Existing in reality or in real experience. **3.** Formed by the coalescence of separate particles or parts into one mass; solid. **4.** Made of concrete. ▸ *n.* (kŏn′krēt′, kŏng′-, kŏn-krēt′, kŏng-) **1.** A construction material consisting of sand, conglomerate gravel, broken stone, or slag in a mortar or cement matrix. **2.** A mass formed by the coalescence of particles. ▸ *v.* (kŏn′krēt′, kŏng′-, kŏn-krēt′, kŏng-) **-cret·ed, -cret·ing.** **1.** To build, treat, or cover with concrete. **2.** To form into a mass by coalescence or cohesion of particles. **—con·crete′ly** *adv.* **—con·crete′ness** *n.*

con·cre·tion (kən-krē′shən) ▸ *n.* **1.** The act or process of concreting into a mass; coalescence. **2.** A solid, hard mass.

con·cu·bine (kŏng′kyə-bīn′, kŏn′-) ▸ *n.* *Law* A woman who cohabits with a man without being legally married to him.

con·cu·pis·cence (kŏn-kyo͞o′pĭ-səns) ▸ *n.* Sexual desire; lust. **—con·cu′pis·cent** *adj.*

con·cur (kən-kûr′) ▸ *v.* **-curred, -cur·ring.** **1.** To agree. **2.** To act together. **3.** To occur at the same time. **—con·cur′rence** *n.* **—con·cur′rent** *adj.* **—con·cur′rent·ly** *adv.*

con·cus·sion (kən-kŭsh′ən) ▸ *n.* **1.** A violent jarring. **2.** An injury to an organ, esp. the brain, produced by a violent blow. **—con·cus′sive** (-kŭs′ĭv) *adj.*

con·demn (kən-dĕm′) ▸ *v.* **1.** To express disapproval of. **2.** To pronounce judgment against; sentence. **3.** To declare unfit for use. **4.** *Law* To appropriate (property) for public use. **—con·dem′na·ble** (-dĕm′nə-bəl) *adj.* **—con′dem·na′tion** (kŏn′dĕm-nā′shən) *n.* **—con·dem′na·to′ry** (-nə-tôr′ē) *adj.*

con·dense (kən-dĕns′) ▸ *v.* **-densed, -dens·ing.** **1.** To make or become more compact. **2.** To abridge. **3.** To cause (a gas or vapor) to change to a liquid. **—con·dens′a·bil′i·ty** *n.* **—con·dens′a·ble, con·dens′i·ble** *adj.* **—con′den·sa′tion** (kŏn′dĕn-sā′shən) *n.*

con·dens·er (kən-dĕn′sər) ▸ *n.* **1.** One that condenses, esp. an apparatus that condenses vapor. **2.** See **capacitor.**

con·de·scend (kŏn′dĭ-sĕnd′) ▸ *v.* **1.** To descend to the level of one considered inferior. **2.** To deal with people in a patronizing manner. **—con′de·scend′ing** *adj.* **—con′de·scend′ing·ly** *adv.* **—con′de·scen′sion** *n.*

con·dign (kən-dīn′) ▸ *adj.* Deserved; adequate: *condign censure.*

THESAURUS

concise *adj.* —*See* BRIEF.

conclave *n.* —*See* ASSEMBLY, CONVENTION.

conclude *v.* To bring or come to a natural or proper end ▸ close, complete, consummate, end, finish, play out, see through, terminate, wind up, wrap up. [*Compare* ABOLISH, STOP.] —*See also* DECIDE, INFER, SETTLE (2), SETTLE (1).

concluded *adj.* —*See* COMPLETE (3).

concluding *adj.* —*See* LAST[1] (1).

conclusion *n.* A position arrived at by reasoning from premises ▸ deduction, inference, judgment. [*Compare* BELIEF.] —*See also* DECISION (1), END (1), END (2).

conclusive *adj.* —*See* AUTHORITATIVE (1), CERTAIN (2), DECISIVE, DEFINITIVE.

conclusively *adv.* In conclusion ▸ finally, last, lastly, ultimately. ***Idioms:*** at last, in the end. [*Compare* ULTIMATELY.]

concoct *v.* —*See* DESIGN (1), INVENT.

concoction *n.* —*See* INVENTION (2).

concomitant *n.* One that accompanies another ▸ accompaniment, accompanist, associate, attendant, companion. [*Compare* ASSOCIATE.]

concomitant *adj.* —*See* CONCURRENT.

concord *n.* An identity or coincidence of interests, purposes, or sympathies among the members of a group ▸ oneness, solidarity, union, unity. [*Compare* ALLIANCE, UNION.] —*See also* AGREEMENT (2), HARMONY (1), TREATY.

concordance *n.* —*See* AGREEMENT (2).

concordant *adj.* Having components pleasingly combined ▸ balanced, congruous, harmonious, symmetrical. [*Compare* HARMONIOUS, PLEASANT.] —*See also* AGREEABLE, UNANIMOUS.

concordat *n.* —*See* TREATY.

concourse *n.* —*See* CROWD, JUNCTION.

concrete *adj.* —*See* PHYSICAL, REAL (1).

concrete *v.* —*See* COMBINE (1), HARDEN (2).

concretize *v.* —*See* EMBODY (1).

concupiscence *n.* —*See* DESIRE (2).

concupiscent *adj.* —*See* LASCIVIOUS.

concur *v.* To occur at the same time ▸ coincide, harmonize, synchronize. —*See also* AGREE (2), ASSENT, COOPERATE.

concurrent *adj.* Occurring or existing at the same time ▸ accompanying, attendant, attending, coexisting, coincident, concomitant, contemporary, contemporaneous, parallel, simultaneous, synchronic, synchronous. —*See also* CONTEMPORARY (1).

concurrently *adv.* At the same time ▸ simultaneously, synchronously, together. ***Idioms:*** all at once, all together. [*Compare* TOGETHER.]

concussion *n.* —*See* COLLISION.

condemn *v.* To pronounce judgment against ▸ convict, damn, doom, proscribe, sentence. ***Idioms:*** pass judgment (*or* sentence) on, seal someone's doom (*or* fate). [*Compare* CRITICIZE, PUNISH, SLAM.] —*See also* DEPLORE (1).

condemnable *adj.* —*See* DEPLORABLE.

condemnation *n.* —*See* CRITICISM, DISAPPROVAL, VITUPERATION.

condemned *adj.* Sentenced to terrible, irrevocable punishment ▸ damned, doomed, fallen, fated, foredoomed, hellbound, lost, reprobate, sentenced. ***Idiom:*** gone to blazes.

condensation *n.* Moisture accumulated on a surface through sweating or condensation ▸ lather, perspiration, sweat, transudation. —*See also* SYNOPSIS.

condense *v.* To make thick or thicker, especially through evaporation or condensation ▸ inspissate, reduce, thicken. [*Compare* COAGULATE.] —*See also* SHORTEN.

condescend *v.* **1.** To bring oneself down to a level considered inappropriate to one's dignity ▸ deign, descend, lower, sink, stoop, vouchsafe. ***Idioms:*** come down a peg, slum it. **2.** To treat in a superciliously indulgent manner ▸ patronize. *Informal:* high-hat. ***Idioms:*** lord it over, queen it, speak (*or* talk) down to. [*Compare* INSULT, SNUB.]

condescension or **condescendence** *n.* Superciliously indulgent treatment, especially of those considered inferior ▸ haughtiness, patronization, snobbery. *Informal:* snootiness. [*Compare* ARROGANCE.]

con·di·ment (kŏn′də-mənt) ▸ *n.* A substance, such as a relish, vinegar, or spice, used to complement food.
con·di·tion (kən-dĭsh′ən) ▸ *n.* **1.** A mode or state of being. **2.** A state of health. **3.** A disease or ailment. **4.** A prerequisite. **5.** A qualification. **6. conditions** The existing circumstances. **7.** *Gram.* The dependent clause of a conditional sentence. ▸ *v.* **1.** To make conditional. **2.** To render fit for work or use. **3.** To adapt: *condition oneself to physical labor.* **4.** *Psychol.* To cause to respond in a specific manner to a specific stimulus.
con·di·tion·al (kən-dĭsh′ə-nəl) ▸ *adj.* **1.** Imposing, depending on, or containing a condition. **2.** *Gram.* Stating or implying a condition. ▸ *n. Gram.* A mood, tense, clause, or word expressing a condition. **—con·di′tion·al·ly** *adv.*
con·di·tioned (kən-dĭsh′ənd) ▸ *adj.* **1.** Subject to conditions. **2.** Physically fit. **3.** Prepared for a specific action. **4.** *Psychol.* Exhibiting or trained to exhibit a specific response.
con·do (kŏn′dō′) ▸ *n., pl.* **-dos.** *Informal* A condominium.
con·dole (kən-dōl′) ▸ *v.* **-doled, -dol·ing.** To express sympathy or sorrow. **—con·do′lence** *n.*
con·dom (kŏn′dəm, kŭn′-) ▸ *n.* A usu. latex sheath used to cover the penis during sex to prevent conception or disease.
con·do·min·i·um (kŏn′də-mĭn′ē-əm) ▸ *n., pl.* **-min·i·ums** also **-min·i·a** (-mĭn′ē-ə). **1a.** An apartment complex in which individuals own their apartments and share joint ownership in common elements with other unit owners. **b.** A unit in such a complex. **2.** Joint sovereignty, esp. joint rule over a territory.
con·done (kən-dōn′) ▸ *v.* To overlook, forgive, or disregard (an offense) without protest or censure. **—con·don′a·ble** *adj.*
con·dor (kŏn′dôr′, -dər) ▸ *n.* Either of two large vultures of the Andes or mountains of California.
con·duce (kən-do͞os′, -dyo͞os′) ▸ *v.* **-duced, -duc·ing.** To lead to a specific result. **—con·du′cive** *adj.* **—con·du′cive·ness** *n.*
con·duct (kən-dŭkt′) ▸ *v.* **1.** To direct the course of; control. **2.** To lead or guide. **3.** To serve as a medium for conveying; transmit. **4.** To behave (oneself) in a specified way. ▸ *n.* (kŏn′dŭkt′) **1.** The way one acts; behavior. **2.** Management. **—con·duct′i·ble** *adj.*
con·duc·tance (kən-dŭk′təns) ▸ *n.* A measure of a material's ability to conduct electric charge.
con·duc·tion (kən-dŭk′shən) ▸ *n.* The transmission of something through a medium or passage, esp. the transmission of electric charge or heat. **—con·duc′tive** *adj.* **—con′duc·tiv′i·ty** (kŏn′dŭk-tĭv′ĭ-tē) *n.*
con·duc·tor (kən-dŭk′tər) ▸ *n.* **1.** One who conducts. **2.** One in charge of a train, bus, or streetcar. **3.** One who directs a musical group. **4.** A substance that conducts heat, light, sound, or esp. an electric charge.
con·duit (kŏn′do͞o-ĭt, -dĭt) ▸ *n.* **1.** A pipe or channel for conveying fluids. **2.** A tube or duct for enclosing electric wires or cable. **3.** A means of passing or transmitting.
cone (kōn) ▸ *n.* **1.** *Math.* **a.** The surface generated by a straight line passing through a fixed point or vertex and moving along a fixed curve. **b.** The figure formed by such a surface, bound by its vertex and an intersecting plane. **2.** *Bot.* A scaly, rounded or cylindrical seed-bearing structure, as of a pine. **3.** *Physiol.* A photoreceptor in the retina.
cone·flow·er (kōn′flou′ər) ▸ *n.* Any of various North American plants having disk flowers on a cone-shaped central receptacle surrounded by colorful rays.
Con·es·to·ga wagon (kŏn′ĭ-stō′gə) ▸ *n.* A heavy covered wagon with broad wheels, used by American pioneers.
co·ney also **co·ny** (kō′nē, kŭn′ē) ▸ *n., pl.* **-neys** also **-nies. 1.** A rabbit, esp. of an Old World species. **2.** The fur of a rabbit. **3.** See **pika**. **4.** See **hyrax**.
con·fab·u·late (kən-făb′yə-lāt′) ▸ *v.* **-lat·ed, -lat·ing.** To talk casually; chat. **—con·fab′u·la′tion** *n.*
con·fec·tion (kən-fĕk′shən) ▸ *n.* A sweet preparation, such as candy. **—con·fec′tion·er** *n.*
con·fec·tion·er·y (kən-fĕk′shə-nĕr′ē) ▸ *n., pl.* **-ies. 1.** Candies and other confections collectively. **2.** A confectioner's shop.
con·fed·er·a·cy (kən-fĕd′ər-ə-sē) ▸ *n., pl.* **-cies. 1.** A political union of persons, parties, or states; league. **2. Confederacy** The 11 Southern states that seceded from the US in 1860 and 1861.
con·fed·er·ate (kən-fĕd′ər-ĭt) ▸ *n.* **1.** An associate; ally. **2.** An accomplice. **3. Confederate** A supporter of the American Confederacy. ▸ *v.* (-ə-rāt′) **-at·ed, -at·ing.** To form into or become part of a confederacy. **—con·fed′er·ate** (-ĭt) *adj.*
con·fed·er·a·tion (kən-fĕd′ə-rā′shən) ▸ *n.* **1a.** The act of confederating. **b.** The state of being confederated. **2.** A confederacy.
con·fer (kən-fûr′) ▸ *v.* **-ferred, -fer·ring. 1.** To bestow (e.g., an honor). **2.** To hold a meeting. **—con′fer·ee′** (kŏn′fə-rē′) *n.* **—con·fer′ral** *n.* **—con·fer′rer** *n.*
con·fer·ence (kŏn′fər-əns, -frəns) ▸ *n.* **1.** A meeting for con-

THESAURUS

condiment *n.* —*See* FLAVORING.
condition *n.* **1.** Manner of being or form of existence ▸ case, mode, situation, state, status. **2.** Something indispensable ▸ essential, must, necessary, necessity, need, precondition, prerequisite, requirement, requisite, sine qua non. *Idiom:* be-all and end-all. [*Compare* ELEMENT, STANDARD.] —*See also* CIRCUMSTANCE (2), PLACE (1), PROVISION, SHAPE.
condition *v.* —*See* ACCUSTOM.
conditional *adj.* Depending on or containing a condition or conditions ▸ conditioned, contingent, dependent, provisional, provisory, relative, specified, stipulated, subject, tentative. [*Compare* QUALIFIED.]
conditioned *adj.* —*See* ACCUSTOMED (1), CONDITIONAL, QUALIFIED.
conditioning *n.* —*See* ADAPTATION, PRACTICE.
conditions *n.* Existing surroundings that affect an activity ▸ circumstances, context, environment, estate, setting, surroundings. *Slang:* scene. [*Compare* AIR, ENVIRONMENT.]
condolatory *adj.* —*See* SYMPATHETIC.
condole *v.* To experience or express compassion ▸ ache, commiserate, feel, sympathize. *Idioms:* be (*or* feel) sorry, have one's heart ache (*or* bleed) for someone, have one's heart go out to someone. [*Compare* PITY.] —*See also* COMFORT.
condolence *n.* —*See* PITY (1).
condonable *adj.* —*See* PARDONABLE.
condonation *n.* —*See* FORGIVENESS.
condone *v.* —*See* FORGIVE.
conduce *v.* —*See* CONTRIBUTE (2).
conducive *adj.* Tending to contribute to a result ▸ contributive, contributory, helpful, participatory. [*Compare* AUXILIARY.]
conduct *v.* **1.** To control the course of an activity ▸ carry on, control, direct, engineer, handle, manage, operate, run, steer. *Slang:* quarterback. [*Compare* ADMINISTER, MANEUVER.] **2.** To engage in (a war or campaign, for example) ▸ carry on, carry out, wage. [*Compare* OPPOSE.] **3.** To serve as a conduit ▸ carry, channel, convey, mediate, pass on, transfer, transmit. [*Compare* CARRY, SEND.] —*See also* GUIDE, LEAD.
conduct *n.* —*See* BEHAVIOR (1), MANAGEMENT.
conductor *n.* —*See* GUIDE.
confab *n.* —*See* CONVERSATION.
confab *v.* —*See* CONVERSE[1].
confabulate *v.* —*See* CONVERSE[1].
confabulation *n.* —*See* CONVERSATION.
confabulator *n.* —*See* CONVERSATIONALIST.
confabulatory *adj.* —*See* CONVERSATIONAL.
confederacy *n.* —*See* ALLIANCE.
confederate *n.* —*See* ACCESSORY, ASSOCIATE (1).
confederate *v.* —*See* ALLY.
confederation *n.* —*See* ALLIANCE, UNION (1).
confer *v.* **1.** To meet and exchange views to reach a decision ▸ advise, consult, debate, deliberate, negotiate, parley, talk. *Informal:* huddle, powwow. [*Compare* CONVERSE, DISCUSS.] **2.** To give formally or officially ▸ accord, award, bestow, give (away), grant, hand out, impart, present.
conference *n.* **1.** A meeting for the exchange of views ▸ colloquium, discussion, forum, panel, parley, roundtable, seminar, summit, symposium, workshop. *Informal:* powwow. *Slang:* rap session. **2.** A group of athletic teams that play each other ▸ association, circuit, division, league, loop. [*Compare* UNION.] —*See also* ASSEMBLY, COMMUNICATION (1), CONFERMENT, CONVENTION, DELIBERATION (1).

sultation or discussion. 2. *Sports* An association of teams.

con·fess (kən-fĕs′) ▸ *v.* 1. To disclose (something damaging about oneself); admit. 2. To tell one's sins to a priest for absolution. 3. To recognize the reality or truth of. **—con·fess′ed·ly** (-ĭd-lē) *adv.*

con·fes·sion (kən-fĕsh′ən) ▸ *n.* 1. The act of confessing. 2. Something confessed, esp. disclosure of one's sins to a priest for absolution. 3. A formal statement acknowledging one's guilt. 4. A church or group of worshipers adhering to a specific creed.

con·fes·sion·al (kən-fĕsh′ə-nəl) ▸ *n.* A small booth in which a priest hears confessions.

con·fes·sor (kən-fĕs′ər) ▸ *n.* 1. One who confesses. 2. A priest who hears confessions.

con·fet·ti (kən-fĕt′ē) ▸ *pl.n.* *(takes sing. v.)* Small pieces of colored paper scattered during festive occasions.

con·fi·dant (kŏn′fĭ-dănt′, -dänt′, kŏn′fĭ-dănt′, -dänt′) ▸ *n.* One to whom secrets or private matters are disclosed.

con·fide (kən-fīd′) ▸ *v.* **-fid·ed, -fid·ing.** 1. To tell (something) in confidence. 2. To put into another's keeping.

con·fi·dence (kŏn′fĭ-dəns) ▸ *n.* 1. Trust or faith in a person or thing. 2. A trusting relationship. 3a. Something confided. b. A feeling of assurance that a confidant will keep a secret. 4. Self-assurance. **—con′fi·dent** *adj.* **—con′fi·dent·ly** *adv.*

confidence game ▸ *n.* A swindle in which the victim is defrauded after his or her confidence has been won.

confidence man ▸ *n.* A man who swindles his victims by using a confidence game.

con·fi·den·tial (kŏn′fĭ-dĕn′shəl) ▸ *adj.* 1. Told in confidence; secret. 2. Entrusted with the confidence of another. **—con′fi·den′ti·al′i·ty** (-shē-ăl′ĭ-tē) *n.* **—con′fi·den′tial·ly** *adv.*

con·fig·u·ra·tion (kən-fĭg′yə-rā′shən) ▸ *n.* Arrangement of parts or elements. **—con·fig′u·ra′tive, con·fig′u·ra′tion·al** *adj.*

con·fig·ure (kən-fĭg′yər) ▸ *v.* **-ured, -ur·ing.** To design, arrange, or shape for specific applications or uses.

con·fine (kən-fīn′) ▸ *v.* **-fined, -fin·ing.** 1. To keep within bounds; restrict. 2. To imprison. **—con·fin′a·ble, con·fine′a·ble** *adj.* **—con·fine′ment** *n.* **—con·fin′er** *n.*

con·fines (kŏn′fīnz′) ▸ *pl.n.* 1. The limits of a space or area. 2. Restraining elements: *escape the confines of bureaucracy.*

con·firm (kən-fûrm′) ▸ *v.* 1. To establish the validity of; verify. 2. To make firmer; strengthen. 3. To ratify. 4. To administer the religious rite of confirmation to. **—con·firm′a·ble** *adj.* **—con·firm′a·to′ry** (-fûr′mə-tôr′ē) *adj.*

con·fir·ma·tion (kŏn′fər-mā′shən) ▸ *n.* 1. The act of confirming. 2. A verification. 3a. A Christian rite admitting a baptized person to full membership in a church. b. A ceremony in Judaism that marks the end of a young person's religious training.

con·firmed (kən-fûrmd′) ▸ *adj.* 1. Firmly settled in habit. 2. Ratified; verified. 3. Having received confirmation. **—con·firm′ed·ly** (-fûr′mĭd-lē) *adv.*

con·fis·cate (kŏn′fĭ-skāt′) ▸ *v.* **-cat·ed, -cat·ing.** 1. To seize (private property) for the public treasury. 2. To seize by or as if by authority. **—con′fis·ca′tion** *n.* **—con′fis·ca′tor** *n.* **—con·fis′ca·to′ry** (kən-fĭs′kə-tôr′ē) *adj.*

con·fla·gra·tion (kŏn′flə-grā′shən) ▸ *n.* A large destructive fire.

con·flict (kŏn′flĭkt′) ▸ *n.* 1. Prolonged fighting. 2. Disharmony between incompatible or antithetical persons, ideas, or interests. 3. *Psychol.* A struggle, often unconscious, between mutually exclusive impulses or desires. ▸ *v.* (kən-flĭkt′) To be in opposition; differ. **—con·flic′tive** *adj.*

con·flu·ence (kŏn′flo͞o-əns) ▸ *n.* 1a. A flowing together of two or more streams. b. The point where such streams meet. 2. A gathering together. **—con′flu·ent** *adj.*

con·flux (kŏn′flŭks′) ▸ *n.* A confluence.

con·form (kən-fôrm′) ▸ *v.* 1. To correspond; be similar. 2. To act or be in agreement; comply. 3. To act in accordance with current customs or modes. **—con·form′a·bil′i·ty** *n.* **—con·form′a·ble** *adj.* **—con·form′a·bly** *adv.* **—con·form′er** *n.*

THESAURUS

conferment or **conferral** *n.* The act of conferring, as of an honor ▸ accordance, bestowal, bestowment, conference, grant, presentation.

confess *v.* *—See* ACKNOWLEDGE (1).

confession *n.* *—See* ACKNOWLEDGMENT (1), RELIGION.

confessor *n.* One in whom secrets are confided ▸ confidant, confidante, intimate, repository. [*Compare* FRIEND.]

confidant or **confidante** *n.* One in whom secrets are confided ▸ confessor, intimate, repository. *—See also* FRIEND.

confide *v.* To tell in confidence ▸ breathe, share, unbosom, whisper. [*Compare* COMMUNICATE, REVEAL, SAY.] *—See also* ENTRUST (1).

confide in *v.* *—See* DEPEND ON (1).

confidence *n.* A firm belief in one's own powers ▸ aplomb, assurance, certitude, self-assurance, self-confidence, self-possession. [*Compare* BALANCE, COURAGE.] *—See also* SURENESS, TRUST.

confident *adj.* Having a firm belief in one's own powers ▸ assured, poised, secure, self-assured, self-confident, self-possessed. [*Compare* BRAVE.] *—See also* OPTIMISTIC, SURE (1).

confidential *adj.* 1. Known about by very few ▸ inside, private, privy, secret. *Informal:* hush-hush. [*Compare* SECRET.] 2. Indicating intimacy and mutual trust ▸ close, familiar, innermost, intimate, inward, personal. 3. Of or being information available only to authorized persons ▸ classified, privileged, restricted, sensitive, top secret.

configuration *n.* *—See* FORM (1).

configure *v.* *—See* MAKE.

confine *v.* *—See* ENCLOSE (1), IMPRISON, LIMIT.

confined *adj.* *—See* RESTRICTED.

confinement *n.* *—See* DETENTION, RESTRICTION.

confines *n.* *—See* LIMITS.

confining *adj.* *—See* TIGHT (4).

confirm *v.* 1. To assure the certainty or validity of ▸ affirm, attest, authenticate, avouch, back (up), bear out, corroborate, declare, evidence, justify, substantiate, sustain, testify (to), validate, verify, warrant. [*Compare* ACKNOWLEDGE, CERTIFY, LEGALIZE, PROVE.] 2. To make firmer in a particular conviction or habit ▸ fortify, harden, reinforce, strengthen. [*Compare* BACK, ESTABLISH.] 3. To accept officially ▸ accredit, adopt, affirm, approve, certify, endorse, pass, ratify, sanction. [*Compare* ACCEPT.] *—See also* PROVE.

confirmation *n.* 1. An act of confirming officially ▸ accreditation, adoption, affirmation, approval, certification, endorsement, passage, ratification, sanction, verification. [*Compare* ACCEPTANCE.] 2. That which confirms ▸ attestation, authentication, avouchment, backing, circumstantiation, corroboration, demonstration, documentation, evidence, justification, proof, substantiation, sustainment, testament, testimonial, testimony, validation, verification, warrant. [*Compare* TESTIMONY.]

confirmed *adj.* 1. Firmly established by long standing ▸ deep-rooted, deep-seated, entrenched, established, hard-shell, incorrigible, incurable, indelible, ineradicable, ingrained, inveterate, irradicable, old-line, rooted, set, settled, vested. [*Compare* FIRM[1], FIXED.] 2. Subject to a disease or habit for a long time ▸ chronic, habitual, habituated, inveterate. [*Compare* STUBBORN.]

confiscate *v.* *—See* SEIZE (1).

confiscation *n.* *—See* SEIZURE (2).

conflagrant *adj.* *—See* BURNING.

conflagration *n.* The visible signs of combustion ▸ blaze, fire, flame, flare-up.

conflict *n.* A state of disagreement and disharmony ▸ clash, confrontation, contention, difference, difficulty, disaccord, disagreement, discord, discordance, disharmony, dissension, dissent, dissentience, dissidence, dissonance, faction, friction, inharmony, schism, strife, variance, warfare. [*Compare* ARGUMENT, OPPOSITION.] *—See also* BATTLE.

conflict *v.* To fail to be in accord ▸ clash, collide, contradict, contrast, differ, disaccord, disagree, discord, diverge, jar, mismatch, oppose, vary. *Idiom:* go (*or* run) counter to.

conflicting *adj.* *—See* DISCREPANT, INCONGRUOUS, INHARMONIOUS (1), OPPOSING.

confluence *n.* *—See* JUNCTION.

conflux *n.* *—See* JUNCTION.

conform *v.* *—See* ADAPT, AGREE (1), CONVENTIONALIZE, FOLLOW (4), HARMONIZE (1).

conformable *adj.* *—See* AGREEABLE, OBEDIENT.

con·for·mance (kən-fôr′məns) ▸ *n.* Conformity.

con·for·ma·tion (kŏn′fər-mā′shən) ▸ *n.* **1.** The structure or shape of an item or entity. **2.** A symmetrical arrangement of parts.

con·form·ist (kən-fôr′mĭst) ▸ *n.* A person who uncritically conforms to the customs or styles of a group. **—con·form′ist** *adj.*

con·form·i·ty (kən-fôr′mĭ-tē) ▸ *n., pl.* **-ties. 1.** Similarity; agreement. **2.** Behavior conforming to current customs or styles.

con·found (kən-found′, kŏn-) ▸ *v.* **1.** To confuse or perplex. **2.** To mix up. **—con·found′er** *n.*

con·found·ed (kən-foun′dĭd, kŏn-) ▸ *adj.* **1.** Confused; befuddled. **2.** Used as an intensive: *a confounded fool.* **—con·found′ed·ly** *adv.* **—con·found′ed·ness** *n.*

con·fra·ter·ni·ty (kŏn′frə-tûr′nĭ-tē) ▸ *n., pl.* **-ties.** An association of persons united in a common purpose or profession.

con·frere (kŏn′frâr′) ▸ *n.* A colleague.

con·front (kən-frŭnt′) ▸ *v.* **1.** To bring or come face to face with, esp. with hostility. **2.** To meet; encounter. **—con′fron·ta′tion** (kŏn′frŭn-tā′shən) *n.* **—con′fron·ta′tion·al** *adj.*

Con·fu·cius (kən-fyo͞o′shəs) (c. 551–479 B.C.) ▸ Chinese philosopher. **—Con·fu′cian** *adj. & n.* **—Con·fu′cian·ism** *n.* **—Con·fu′cian·ist** *n.*

con·fuse (kən-fyo͞oz′) ▸ *v.* **-fused, -fus·ing. 1.** To cause to be unclear in mind or purpose. **2.** To mistake (one thing for another). **3.** To make unclear; blur. **—con·fu′sion** *n.*

con·fused (kən-fyo͞ozd′) ▸ *adj.* **1.** Unclear in mind; addled. **2a.** Lacking logical order or sense: *a confused set of instructions.* **b.** Chaotic; jumbled. **—con·fus′ed·ly** (-fyo͞o′zĭd-lē) *adv.* **—con·fus′ed·ness** *n.*

con·fute (kən-fyo͞ot′) ▸ *v.* **-fut·ed, -fut·ing.** To prove to be wrong or false; refute decisively. **—con·fut′a·ble** *adj.* **—con′fu·ta′tion** (kŏn′fyo͞o-tā′shən) *n.*

con·geal (kən-jēl′) ▸ *v.* **1.** To solidify by or as if by freezing. **2.** To coagulate; jell. **—con·geal′a·ble** *adj.* **—con·geal′ment** *n.*

con·gen·ial (kən-jēn′yəl) ▸ *adj.* **1.** Having the same tastes or temperament. **2.** Friendly. **3.** Suited to one's needs or nature; agreeable. **—con·ge′ni·al′i·ty** (-jē′nē-ăl′ĭ-tē), **con·gen′ial·ness** *n.* **—con·gen′ial·ly** *adv.*

con·gen·i·tal (kən-jĕn′ĭ-tl) ▸ *adj.* **1.** Existing at or before birth. **2.** Constitutional; inherent. **—con·gen′i·tal·ly** *adv.*

con·ger (kŏng′gər) ▸ *n.* A large scaleless marine eel.

con·ge·ries (kən-jîr′ēz′, kŏn′jə-rēz′) ▸ *n.* *(takes sing. v.)* A collection; aggregation.

con·gest (kən-jĕst′) ▸ *v.* **1.** To overfill; clog. **2.** To cause the accumulation of excessive blood or fluid in (a vessel or organ). **—con·ges′tion** *n.* **—con·ges′tive** *adj.*

con·glom·er·ate (kən-glŏm′ə-rāt′) ▸ *v.* **-at·ed, -at·ing.** To form or cause to form into an adhering or rounded mass. ▸ *n.* (-ər-ĭt) **1.** A corporation made up of several different companies in diversified fields. **2.** A collected heterogeneous mass; cluster. **3.** *Geol.* A rock consisting of pebbles and gravel embedded in cement. **—con·glom′er·ate** (-ĭt) *adj.* **—con·glom′er·a′tion** *n.*

Con·go (kŏng′gō) ▸ **1.** Officially **Democratic Republic of the Congo** Formerly (1971–97) **Za·ire** (zī′îr, zä-îr′) A country of central Africa astride the equator. **2.** Officially **Republic of the Congo** A country of W-central Africa with a short coastline on the Atlantic Ocean. **—Con′go·lese′** (-lēz′, -lēs′) *adj. & n.*

Congo River also **Zaire River** ▸ A river of central Africa flowing about 4,666 km (2,900 mi) through Dem. Rep. of the Congo to the Atlantic.

con·grat·u·late (kən-grăch′ə-lāt′, -grăj′-, kəng-) ▸ *v.* **-lat·ed, -lat·ing.** To extend congratulations to. **—con·grat′u·la′tor** *n.* **—con·grat′u·la·to′ry** (-lə-tôr′ē) *adj.*

con·grat·u·la·tion (kən-grăch′ə-lā′shən, -grăj′-, kəng-) ▸ *n.* **1.** The act of expressing joy or acknowledgment, as for the achievement or good fortune of another. **2.** often **congratulations** An expression of such joy or acknowledgment.

con·gre·gate (kŏng′grĭ-gāt′) ▸ *v.* **-gat·ed, -gat·ing.** To bring or come together in a group; assemble. **—con′gre·ga′tor** *n.*

con·gre·ga·tion (kŏng′grĭ-gā′shən) ▸ *n.* **1.** The act of assembling. **2.** An assemblage; gathering. **3.** The members of a specific religious group who regularly worship at a church or synagogue.

con·gre·ga·tion·al (kŏng′grĭ-gā′shə-nəl) ▸ *adj.* **1.** Of or relating to a congregation. **2. Congregational** Of or relating to a Protestant denomination in which each member church is self-governing. **—con′gre·ga′tion·al·ism** *n.* **—con′gre·ga′tion·al·ist** *n.*

con·gress (kŏng′grĭs) ▸ *n.* **1.** A formal assembly to discuss problems. **2.** The national legislative body of a nation, esp.

THESAURUS

conformance *n.* —*See* AGREEMENT (2).

conformation *n.* —*See* ADAPTATION, AGREEMENT (2).

conformist *adj.* —*See* CONVENTIONAL.

conformity *n.* —*See* AGREEMENT (2).

confound *v.* To take one thing mistakenly for another ▸ confuse, mistake, mix up. —*See also* BAFFLE, CONFUSE (1), EMBARRASS.

confounded *adj.* —*See* CONFUSED (1), DAMNED.

confront *v.* To meet face-to-face, especially defiantly ▸ encounter, face, front, meet. *Idiom:* stand up to. [*Compare* CONTEST, DEFY.]

confrontation *n.* A face-to-face, usually hostile meeting ▸ duel, encounter, face-off, mano a mano, meeting, showdown. [*Compare* ARGUMENT, FIGHT.] —*See also* BATTLE, CONFLICT.

confuse *v.* **1.** To cause to be unclear in mind or intent ▸ addle, befuddle, bewilder, confound, discombobulate, disorient, dizzy, fuddle, jumble, mix up, muddle, mystify, perplex, puzzle. *Informal:* throw. *Idioms:* make one's head reel, make one's head swim, make one's head whirl. [*Compare* AGITATE, COMPLICATE, DAZE.] **2.** To take one thing mistakenly for another ▸ confound, mistake, mix up. **3.** To put into total disorder ▸ ball up, cross up, disorder, garble, jumble, mess up, muddle, muddy, scramble, snarl. *Slang:* snafu. *Idioms:* make a hash (*or* mess) of, play havoc with. [*Compare* COMPLICATE, DISORDER.] —*See also* EMBARRASS.

confused *adj.* **1.** Mentally uncertain ▸ addled, addlepated, baffled, befuddled, bemused, bewildered, confusional, confounded, discombobulated, disconcerted, disoriented, dizzy, dumbfounded, flustered, haywire, lost, muddle-headed, mystified, nonplused, perplexed, punch-drunk, puzzled, stuck, stumped, turbid. *Informal:* mixed-up. *Idioms:* at a loss, at sea, in a fog (*or* haze *or* state *or* tizzy). [*Compare* AGITATED, IGNORANT.] **2.** Characterized by physical confusion ▸ amiss, chaotic, deranged, disarranged, disarrayed, disordered, disorganized, disrupted, disturbed, garbled, helter-skelter, higgledy-piggledy, jumbled, messy, muddled, pell-mell, scrambled, snarled, topsy-turvy, unsettled, unsystematic, upside-down, willy-nilly. *Informal:* mixed-up. *Slang:* snafu. *Idiom:* at sixes and sevens. [*Compare* COMPLEX, MESSY.]

confusedness *n.* —*See* DISORDER (1).

confusion *n.* —*See* DAZE, DISORDER (1), DISORDER (2), EMBARRASSMENT, MISUNDERSTANDING.

confute *v.* —*See* REFUTE.

con game *n.* —*See* TRICK (1).

congeal *v.* —*See* COAGULATE, HARDEN (2).

congener *n.* —*See* PARALLEL.

congenial *adj.* —*See* AGREEABLE, AMIABLE, PLEASANT.

congeniality or **congenialness** *n.* —*See* AMIABILITY.

congenital *adj.* —*See* CONSTITUTIONAL, INNATE.

congeries *n.* —*See* ACCUMULATION (1).

congest *v.* —*See* FILL (2).

congested *adj.* —*See* OVERCROWDED.

conglomerate *n.* —*See* COMPANY (1), COMPLEX (1).

conglomeration *n.* The act of accumulating ▸ accumulation, agglomeration, buildup. [*Compare* INCREASE.] —*See also* ASSORTMENT.

congrats *n.* —*See* COMPLIMENT.

congratulate *v.* To pay a compliment to ▸ commend, compliment, felicitate, praise. *Idioms:* pay tribute to, raise a glass to. [*Compare* HONOR.]

congratulation *n.* —*See* COMPLIMENT.

congratulatory *adj.* —*See* COMPLIMENTARY (1).

congregate *v.* —*See* ASSEMBLE.

congregation *n.* The steadfast believers in a faith or cause ▸ adherents, faithful, fold. [*Compare* FOLLOWER, ASSEMBLY.] —*See also* ASSEMBLY.

congress *n.* —*See* ASSEMBLY, CONVENTION, UNION (1).

a republic. 3. **Congress** The US legislature, consisting of the Senate and the House of Representatives. **—con·gres′sion·al** (kən-grĕsh′ə-nəl, kəng-) *adj.* **—con·gres′sion·al·ly** *adv.* **—con′gress·man** *n.* **—con′gress·per′son** *n.* **—con′gress·wom′an** *n.*
con·gru·ent (kŏng′gro͞o-ənt, kən-gro͞o′-) ▸ *adj.* 1. Corresponding; congruous. 2. *Math.* Coinciding exactly when superimposed. **—con′gru·ence, con′gru·en·cy** *n.* **—con′gru·ent·ly** *adv.*
con·gru·ous (kŏng′gro͞o-əs) ▸ *adj.* 1. Corresponding in character or kind; harmonious. 2. *Math.* Congruent. **—con·gru′i·ty** (kən-gro͞o′ĭ-tē, kŏn-) *n.* **—con′gru·ous·ly** *adv.* **—con′gru·ous·ness** *n.*
con·ic (kŏn′ĭk) or **con·i·cal** (-ĭ-kəl) ▸ *adj.* Of or shaped like a cone.
conic section ▸ *n.* The intersection of a cone and a plane, which generates a group of curves, including the circle, ellipse, hyperbola, and parabola.
con·i·fer (kŏn′ə-fər, kō′nə-) ▸ *n.* A cone-bearing tree such as a pine or fir. **—co·nif′er·ous** (kō-nĭf′ər-əs, kə-) *adj.*
conj. ▸ *abbr.* conjunction
con·jec·tur·al (kən-jĕk′chər-əl) ▸ *adj.* Based on or involving conjecture. **—con·jec′tur·al·ly** *adv.*
con·jec·ture (kən-jĕk′chər) ▸ *n.* Inference based on incomplete evidence; guesswork. ▸ *v.* **-tured, -tur·ing.** To guess. **—con·jec′tur·a·ble** *adj.* **—con·jec′tur·er** *n.*
con·join (kən-join′) ▸ *v.* To join together; unite. **—con·join′er** *n.* **—con·joint′** *adj.* **—con·joint′ly** *adv.*
con·ju·gal (kŏn′jə-gəl, kən-jo͞o′-) ▸ *adj.* Of or relating to marriage or the marital relationship. **—con′ju·gal′i·ty** *n.* **—con′ju·gal·ly** *adv.*
con·ju·gate (kŏn′jə-gāt′) ▸ *v.* **-gat·ed, -gat·ing.** To inflect (a verb). ▸ *adj.* (-gĭt, -gāt′) Joined together, esp. in pairs. **—con′ju·gate′ly** *adv.* **—con′ju·ga′tive** *adj.*
con·ju·ga·tion (kŏn′jə-gā′shən) ▸ *n.* 1a. The inflection of a verb. b. A presentation of the inflected forms of a verb. 2. *Biol.* A process in which two one-celled organisms unite to transfer nuclear material. **—con′ju·ga′tion·al** *adj.* **—con′ju·ga′tion·al·ly** *adv.*
con·junct (kən-jŭngkt′, kŏn′jŭngkt′) ▸ *adj.* Joined together; united. **—con·junct′ly** *adv.*
con·junc·tion (kən-jŭngk′shən) ▸ *n.* 1. The act of joining or state of being joined. 2. A joint or simultaneous occurrence. 3. A word such as *and, but,* and *because* that connects other words, phrases, clauses, or sentences. **—con·junc′tion·al** *adj.* **—con·junc′tion·al·ly** *adv.*
con·junc·ti·va (kŏn′jŭngk-tī′və) ▸ *n., pl.* **-vas** or **-vae** (-vē). The mucous membrane that lines the inner surface of the eyelid and the exposed surface of the eyeball. **—con′junc·ti′val** *adj.*
con·junc·tive (kən-jŭngk′tĭv) ▸ *adj.* 1. Connective. 2. Joined together; combined. 3. *Gram.* Used as a conjunction. ▸ *n.* A conjunction. **—con·junc′tive·ly** *adv.*
con·junc·ti·vi·tis (kən-jŭngk′tə-vī′tĭs) ▸ *n.* Inflammation of the conjunctiva.
con·junc·ture (kən-jŭngk′chər) ▸ *n.* A critical set of circumstances; crisis.
con·jure (kŏn′jər, kən-jo͝or′) ▸ *v.* **-jured, -jur·ing.** 1. To summon (a spirit) by magical power. 2. To evoke: *a song that conjured up old memories.* 3. To perform magic tricks. **—con′ju·ra′tion** *n.* **—con′jur·er, con′jur·or** *n.*
conk (kŏngk) ▸ *v. Slang* To hit, esp. on the head. ***—phrasal verb:* conk out** 1. To stop functioning; fail. 2. To fall asleep, esp. suddenly or heavily.
con man ▸ *n. Slang* A confidence man.
Conn. ▸ *abbr.* Connecticut
con·nect ▸ *v.* 1. To join or become joined together. 2. To associate or consider as related. 3. To join to or by means of a communications circuit. 4. To make a connection. **—con·nec′tor, con·nect′er** *n.*
Con·nect·i·cut (kə-nĕt′ĭ-kət) ▸ A state of the NE US. Cap. Hartford.
con·nec·tion (kə-nĕk′shən) ▸ *n.* 1. Union; junction. 2. A link. 3. An association or relation. 4. The logical ordering of words or ideas; coherence. 5. Reference to something else; context. 6. A person, esp. one of influence, with whom one is associated. 7. A scheduled run providing service between means of transportation. 8. A line of communication between two points in a telephone system.
con·nec·tive (kə-nĕk′tĭv) ▸ *adj.* Serving or tending to connect. ▸ *n.* A connecting word, such as a conjunction. **—con·nec′tive·ly** *adv.* **—con′nec·tiv′i·ty** *n.*
connective tissue ▸ *n.* Tissue, such as cartilage and bone, that forms the supporting and connecting structures of the body.
con·nip·tion (kə-nĭp′shən) ▸ *n. Informal* A fit of violent emotion.
con·nive (kə-nīv′) ▸ *v.* **-nived, -niv·ing.** 1. To cooperate secretly in an illegal action. 2. To scheme; plot. 3. To feign ignorance of a wrong, thus implying consent. **—con·niv′ance** *n.* **—con·niv′er** *n.* **—con·niv′er·y** *n.*
con·nois·seur (kŏn′ə-sûr′, -so͝or′) ▸ *n.* A person of discriminating taste.
con·note (kə-nōt′) ▸ *v.* **-not·ed, -not·ing.** 1. To suggest or imply in addition to literal meaning: *Spring connotes flowers and new life.* 2. To have as a related condition: *For a political leader, hesitation is apt to connote weakness.* **—con′no·ta′tion** (kŏn′ə-tā′shən) *n.* **—con′no·ta′tive** *adj.*
con·nu·bi·al (kə-no͞o′bē-əl, -nyo͞o′-) ▸ *adj.* Relating to marriage or the married state; conjugal. **—con·nu′bi·al·ly** *adv.*
con·quer ▸ *v.* 1. To defeat or subdue by or as if by force of arms. 2. To overcome; surmount: *conquered my fear of heights.* **—con′quer·a·ble** *adj.* **—con′quer·or, con′quer·er** *n.*

THESAURUS

congruity or **congruence** *n.* —*See* AGREEMENT (2), CONSISTENCY.
congruous *adj.* Having components pleasingly combined ▸ concordant, balanced, harmonious, symmetrical. [*Compare* PLEASANT.] —*See also* AGREEABLE.
conjectural *adj.* —*See* SUPPOSED.
conjecture *n.* —*See* GUESS, THEORY (1).
conjecture *v.* —*See* GUESS.
conjectured *adj.* —*See* UNTRIED.
conjoin *v.* —*See* ASSOCIATE (1), COMBINE (1).
conjoining *adj.* —*See* ADJOINING.
conjoint *adj.* —*See* COMMON (2).
conjugal *adj.* —*See* MARITAL.
conjugality *n.* —*See* MARRIAGE.
conjugate *v.* —*See* COMBINE (1).
conjugation *n.* —*See* COMBINATION.
conjunction *n.* —*See* ASSOCIATION (1).
conjuration *n.* —*See* MAGIC (1), MAGIC (2).
conjure *v.* —*See* EVOKE.
conjure up *v.* —*See* IMAGINE.
conjurer *n.* —*See* WIZARD.
conjuring *n.* —*See* MAGIC (2).
conk *n.* —*See* BLOW[2], HEAD (1).
conk *v.* —*See* HIT.
conk out *v.* —*See* COLLAPSE (1), MALFUNCTION.
connatural or **connate** *adj.* —*See* CONSTITUTIONAL, INNATE, KINDRED.
connect *v.* To come together by arrangement ▸ hook up, get together, meet (up), rendezvous. —*See also* ASSOCIATE (1), ASSOCIATE (3), ATTACH (1), COMBINE (1), RELATE (2).
connected *adj.* —*See* CONCERNED.
connection *n.* 1. Something, such as a feeling or idea, associated with a specific person or thing ▸ association, connotation, impression, suggestion. [*Compare* HINT.] 2. An acquaintance who is in a position to help ▸ contact, source. [*Compare* GO-BETWEEN.] —*See also* ASSOCIATION (1), JOINT (1), PUSHER, RELATION (1).
conniption or **conniption fit** *n.* —*See* TEMPER (2).
connivance *n.* —*See* PLOT (2).
connive *v.* —*See* PLOT (2).
connive at *v.* —*See* BLINK AT.
conniving *adj.* Coldly planning to achieve selfish aims ▸ calculating, designing, manipulative, scheming. [*Compare* ARTFUL.]
connoisseur *n.* —*See* EXPERT.
connotation *n.* Something, such as a feeling or idea, associated with a specific person or thing ▸ association, connection, impression, suggestion. [*Compare* HINT.] —*See also* MEANING.
connotative *adj.* Tending to bring a memory, mood, or image, for example, subtly or indirectly to mind ▸ allusive, evocative, impressionistic, reminiscent, suggestive. [*Compare* DESIGNATIVE, SYMBOLIC.]
connote *v.* —*See* MEAN[1].
connubial *adj.* —*See* MARITAL.
connubiality *n.* —*See* MARRIAGE.
conquer *v.* —*See* DEFEAT, OCCUPY (2).
conquering *adj.* —*See* VICTORIOUS.
conqueror *n.* One that conquers ▸ conquistador, master, subduer, subjugator, surmounter, vanquisher, victor, winner. —*See also* WINNER.

con·quest (kŏn′kwĕst′, kŏng′-) ▸ *n.* **1.** The act or process of conquering. **2.** Something acquired by conquering.

con·quis·ta·dor (kŏn-kwĭs′tə-dôr′, kŏng-kē′stə-) ▸ *n., pl.* **-dors** or **-dor·es** (-dôr′ās, -ēz). One of the 16th-cent. Spanish conquerors of Mexico, Central America, or Peru.

con·san·guin·e·ous (kŏn′săn-gwĭn′ē-əs, -săng-) also **con·san·guine** (kŏn-săng′gwĭn, kən-) ▸ *adj.* Having a common ancestor. **—con′san·guin′e·ous·ly** *adv.* **—con′san·guin′i·ty** *n.*

con·science (kŏn′shəns) ▸ *n.* **1.** The awareness of a moral or ethical aspect to one's conduct. **2.** Conformity to one's own sense of right conduct.

con·sci·en·tious (kŏn′shē-ĕn′shəs) ▸ *adj.* **1.** Guided by one's conscience; principled. **2.** Thorough and careful: *a conscientious worker.* **—con′sci·en′tious·ly** *adv.* **—con′sci·en′tious·ness** *n.*

conscientious objector ▸ *n.* One who refuses to participate in military service on the basis of moral or religious beliefs.

con·scious (kŏn′shəs) ▸ *adj.* **1a.** Having an awareness of one's environment and one's own existence. **b.** Not asleep; awake. **2.** Capable of thought, will, or perception. **3.** Subjectively known: *conscious remorse.* **4.** Deliberate: *a conscious insult.* **5.** Sensible; mindful: *conscious of being stared at.* **—con′scious·ly** *adv.*

con·scious·ness (kŏn′shəs-nĭs) ▸ *n.* **1.** A sense of one's personal or collective identity. **2.** Special awareness of or sensitivity to a particular issue or situation.

con·script (kŏn′skrĭpt′) ▸ *n.* One compulsorily enrolled for service, esp. in the armed forces. **—con·script′** (kən-skrĭpt′) *v.* **—con·scrip′tion** *n.*

con·se·crate (kŏn′sĭ-krāt′) ▸ *v.* **-crat·ed, -crat·ing. 1.** To declare or set apart as sacred. **2.** *Christianity* To change (bread and wine) into the body and blood of Jesus. **3.** To initiate (a priest) into the order of bishops. **4.** To dedicate to a service or goal. **—con′se·cra′tion** *n.* **—con′se·cra′tive** *adj.* **—con′se·cra′tor** *n.*

con·sec·u·tive (kən-sĕk′yə-tĭv) ▸ *adj.* Following one after another without interruption. **—con·sec′u·tive·ly** *adv.* **—con·sec′u·tive·ness** *n.*

con·sen·su·al (kən-sĕn′sho͞o-əl) ▸ *adj.* **1.** *Law* Entered into by mutual consent. **2.** Involving the willing participation of both or all parties. **—con·sen′su·al·ly** *adv.*

con·sen·sus (kən-sĕn′səs) ▸ *n.* **1.** An opinion or position reached by a group as a whole or by majority will. **2.** General agreement.

con·sent (kən-sĕnt′) ▸ *v.* To give assent; agree. ▸ *n.* Acceptance; agreement.

con·se·quence (kŏn′sĭ-kwĕns′, -kwəns) ▸ *n.* **1.** Something that follows from an action or condition. **2.** Significance; importance: *an issue of consequence.*

con·se·quent (kŏn′sĭ-kwĕnt′, -kwənt) ▸ *adj.* Following as an effect, result, or conclusion. **—con′se·quent′ly** *adv.*

con·se·quen·tial (kŏn′sĭ-kwĕn′shəl) ▸ *adj.* **1.** Having important consequences. **2.** Important; influential. **—con′se·quen′ti·al′i·ty** *n.* **—con′se·quen′tial·ly** *adv.*

con·ser·va·tion (kŏn′sûr-vā′shən) ▸ *n.* **1.** The act or process of conserving. **2.** The controlled use and systematic protection of natural resources. **—con′ser·va′tion·al** *adj.* **—con′ser·va′tion·ist** *n.*

con·ser·va·tism (kən-sûr′və-tĭz′əm) ▸ *n.* **1.** The inclination, esp. in politics, to maintain the existing or traditional order. **2.** Caution or moderation, as in behavior or outlook.

con·ser·va·tive (kən-sûr′və-tĭv) ▸ *adj.* **1.** Favoring traditional views and values; tending to oppose change. **2.** Traditional in style. **3.** Moderate; cautious: *a conservative estimate.* **4.** Of or relating to a branch of Judaism that allows certain authorized modifications in the law. ▸ *n.* A conservative person. **—con·ser′va·tive·ly** *adv.* **—con·ser′va·tive·ness** *n.*

con·ser·va·tor (kən-sûr′və-tər, kŏn′sər-vā′tər) ▸ *n.* **1.** A person in charge of maintaining or restoring valuable items. **2.** *Law* A guardian.

con·ser·va·to·ry (kən-sûr′və-tôr′ē) ▸ *n., pl.* **-ries. 1.** A greenhouse, esp. one in which plants are arranged for display. **2.** A school of music or drama.

con·serve (kən-sûrv′) ▸ *v.* **-served, -serv·ing. 1a.** To protect from loss or depletion; preserve. **b.** To use carefully or sparingly: *conserve energy.* **2.** To preserve (fruits). ▸ *n.* (kŏn′sûrv′) A jam that is made of stewed fruits. **—con·serv′a·ble** *adj.*

con·sid·er (kən-sĭd′ər) ▸ *v.* **1.** To think carefully about. **2.** To regard as. **3.** To take into account.

con·sid·er·a·ble (kən-sĭd′ər-ə-bəl) ▸ *adj.* **1.** Large in amount, extent, or degree. **2.** Worthy of consideration; significant. **—con·sid′er·a·bly** *adv.*

THESAURUS

conquest *n.* The act of conquering ▸ knockout, subjugation, triumph, victory, win. [*Compare* ACCOMPLISHMENT, DEFEAT.]

conquistador *n.* —*See* CONQUEROR.

consanguine or **consanguineous** *adj.* —*See* KINDRED.

conscience *n.* —*See* DECENCY (1).

conscienceless *adj.* —*See* UNSCRUPULOUS.

conscientious *adj.* —*See* DILIGENT, ETHICAL.

conscientiousness *n.* —*See* DILIGENCE.

conscious *adj.* —*See* CAREFUL (1), DELIBERATE (1).

consciousness *n.* —*See* AWARENESS, SPIRIT (2).

conscript *v.* To enroll compulsorily in military service ▸ draft, impress, induct, levy.

conscription *n.* —*See* DRAFT (2).

consecrate *v.* To make sacred by a religious rite ▸ bless, hallow, sanctify. [*Compare* EXALT.] —*See also* DEVOTE.

consecrated *adj.* —*See* DIVINE (2), HOLY.

consecution *n.* —*See* SERIES.

consecutive *adj.* Following one after another in an orderly pattern ▸ back-to-back, chronological, numerical, sequent, sequential, serial, seriate, successional, successive. ***Idioms:*** in order, in turn. [*Compare* FOLLOWING, GRADUAL.]

consensual *adj.* —*See* UNANIMOUS.

consensus *n.* —*See* AGREEMENT (2).

consent *v.* —*See* ASSENT, PERMIT (2).

consent *n.* —*See* ACCEPTANCE (1), PERMISSION.

consequence *n.* —*See* EFFECT (1), IMPORTANCE.

consequent *adj.* —*See* FOLLOWING (2), LOGICAL (2).

consequential *adj.* —*See* FOLLOWING (2), IMPORTANT, INFLUENTIAL, PREGNANT (2).

conservancy *n.* —*See* CONSERVATION.

conservation *n.* The careful guarding of an asset ▸ conservancy, husbandry, maintenance, management, preservation, protection. [*Compare* CARE, DEFENSE, ECONOMY.]

conservational *n.* —*See* PRESERVATIVE.

conservative *adj.* **1.** Favoring traditional view and values, especially as a political philosophy ▸ neoconservative, orthodox, right, rightist, right-wing, Tory, traditionalist, traditionalistic. *Informal:* neocon. [*Compare* ULTRACONSERVATIVE.] **2.** Kept within sensible limits ▸ careful, cautious, discreet, guarded, moderate, modest, reasonable, restrained, temperate. —*See also* CONVENTIONAL, PRESERVATIVE.

conservative *n.* A person with politically conservative views ▸ neoconservative, orthodox, rightist, right-winger, Tory, traditionalist. *Informal:* neocon. [*Compare* ULTRACONSERVATIVE.]

conservator *n.* One who is legally responsible for the care and management of the person or property of an incompetent or a minor ▸ caretaker, custodian, guardian, keeper. [*Compare* REPRESENTATIVE.]

conserve *v.* To protect an asset from loss or destruction ▸ husband, preserve, save. [*Compare* DEFEND.] —*See also* PRESERVE (1), SCRIMP.

consider *v.* To receive an idea and think about it in order to form an opinion about it ▸ entertain, hear of, think about, think of. —*See also* BELIEVE (3), DEAL (1), DISCUSS, LOOK (1), PONDER, REGARD, VALUE.

considerable *adj.* —*See* BIG, IMPORTANT.

considerably *adv.* To a considerable extent ▸ abundantly, amply, expansively, extensively, far, largely, much, quite, significantly, sizably, spaciously, substantially, well. ***Idioms:*** by a long shot (*or* way), by a wide margin, by far. [*Compare* ABSOLUTELY, COMPLETELY, REALLY, UNUSUALLY, VERY.]

con·sid·er·ate (kən-sĭd′ər-ĭt) ▸ *adj.* Having regard for the needs or feelings of others; thoughtful. **—con·sid′er·ate·ly** *adv.* **—con·sid′er·ate·ness** *n.*
con·sid·er·a·tion (kən-sĭd′ə-rā′shən) ▸ *n.* **1.** Careful thought. **2.** A factor to be considered in making a decision. **3.** Thoughtful concern for others. **4.** Recompense.
con·sid·ered (kən-sĭd′ərd) ▸ *adj.* Reached after careful thought; deliberate.
con·sid·er·ing (kən-sĭd′ər-ĭng) ▸ *prep.* In view of; taking into consideration. ▸ *adv. Informal* All things considered: *We had a good trip, considering.*
con·sign (kən-sīn′) ▸ *v.* **1.** To give over to the care of another; entrust. **2.** To deliver (merchandise) for sale. **3.** To set apart, as for a special use or purpose. **—con·sign′a·ble** *adj.* **—con·sig′nor, con·sign′er** *n.*
con·sign·ment (kən-sīn′mənt) ▸ *n.* **1.** The act of consigning. **2.** Something consigned. ***—idiom:*** **on consignment** With the provision that payment is expected only on completed sales.
con·sist (kən-sĭst′) ▸ *v.* **1.** To be made up or composed. **2.** To reside: *Its beauty consists in its simplicity.*
con·sis·ten·cy (kən-sĭs′tən-sē) ▸ *n., pl.* **-cies. 1.** Agreement or coherence among things or parts. **2.** Uniformity of successive results or events. **3.** Degree or texture of firmness. **—con·sis′tent** *adj.* **—con·sis′tent·ly** *adv.*
con·sis·to·ry (kən-sĭs′tə-rē) ▸ *n., pl.* **-ries. 1.** *Rom. Cath. Ch.* An assembly of cardinals presided over by the pope. **2.** A council.
con·so·la·tion (kŏn′sə-lā′shən) ▸ *n.* **1a.** The act or an instance of consoling. **b.** The state of being consoled. **2.** One that consoles; a comfort: *Your kindness was a consolation to me in my grief.*
con·sole[1] (kən-sōl′) ▸ *v.* **-soled, -sol·ing.** To allay the sorrow or grief of. **—con·sol′a·ble** *adj.* **—con′so·la′tion** *n.* **—con·so′la·to′ry** (-sō′lə-tôr′ē, -sŏl′ə-) *adj.* **—con·sol′er** *n.*
con·sole[2] (kŏn′sōl′) ▸ *n.* **1.** A freestanding cabinet for a radio, television set, or phonograph. **2.** *Mus.* The part of an organ containing the keyboard, stops, and pedals. **3.** A central control panel for a mechanical or electronic system. **4.** *Archit.* A usu. scroll-shaped bracket.
con·sol·i·date (kən-sŏl′ĭ-dāt′) ▸ *v.* **-dat·ed, -dat·ing. 1.** To unite into one system or whole; combine. **2.** To make strong or secure; strengthen. **—con·sol′i·da′tion** *n.* **—con·sol′i·da′tor** *n.*
con·som·mé (kŏn′sə-mā′, kŏn′sə-mā′) ▸ *n.* A clear soup made of meat or vegetable stock.
con·so·nance (kŏn′sə-nəns) ▸ *n.* **1.** Agreement; harmony. **2.** The repetition of consonants esp. at the ends of words, as in *blank* and *think.*
con·so·nant (kŏn′sə-nənt) ▸ *adj.* **1.** In agreement or accord. **2.** Harmonious in sound. ▸ *n.* **1.** A speech sound produced by partial or complete obstruction of the air stream. **2.** A letter or character representing a consonant. **—con′so·nan′tal** *adj.* **—con′so·nan′tal·ly** *adv.* **—con′so·nant·ly** *adv.*
con·sort (kŏn′sôrt′) ▸ *n.* A husband or wife, esp. of a monarch. ▸ *v.* (kən-sôrt′) **1.** To keep company; associate. **2.** To be in agreement.
con·sor·ti·um (kən-sôr′tē-əm, -shē-əm) ▸ *n., pl.* **-ti·a** (-tē-ə, -shē-ə). **1.** An association of businesses, financial institutions, or investors engaging in a joint venture. **2.** A cooperative arrangement among institutions.
con·spic·u·ous (kən-spĭk′yo͞o-əs) ▸ *adj.* **1.** Obvious. **2.** Attracting attention; noticeable. **—con·spic′u·ous·ly** *adv.* **—con·spic′u·ous·ness** *n.*
con·spir·a·cy (kən-spîr′ə-sē) ▸ *n., pl.* **-cies.** A plot, esp. an illegal one.
con·spire (kən-spīr′) ▸ *v.* **-spired, -spir·ing. 1.** To plan together secretly to commit an illegal act. **2.** To join or act together; combine. **—con·spir′a·tor** (-spîr′ə-tər) *n.* **—con·spir′a·tor′i·al** *adj.* **—con·spir′a·tor′i·al·ly** *adv.*
con·sta·ble (kŏn′stə-bəl, kŭn′-) ▸ *n.* **1.** A peace officer with less authority than a sheriff. **2.** *Chiefly Brit.* A police officer.
con·stab·u·lar·y (kən-stăb′yə-lĕr′ē) ▸ *n., pl.* **-ies. 1.** The body of constables of a district or city. **2.** An armed police force organized like a military unit.
con·stant (kŏn′stənt) ▸ *adj.* **1.** Continually occurring; persistent. **2.** Unchanging; invariable. **3.** Steadfast; faithful. ▸ *n.* **1.** Something unchanging. **2.** A condition, factor, or quantity that is invariant in specified circumstances. **—con′stan·cy** *n.* **—con′stant·ly** *adv.*
Con·stan·tine I (kŏn′stən-tēn′, -tīn′). "Constantine the Great" (A.D. 285?–337) ▸ Emperor of Rome (306–337).
Con·stan·ti·no·ple (kŏn′stăn-tə-nō′pəl) ▸ See **Istanbul.**
con·stel·la·tion (kŏn′stə-lā′shən) ▸ *n.* **1.** A formation of stars perceived as a figure or design. **2.** The configuration of planets at one's birth, regarded by astrologers as determining one's character or fate. **3.** A gathering or assemblage.
con·ster·na·tion (kŏn′stər-nā′shən) ▸ *n.* Great agitation or dismay.
con·sti·pa·tion (kŏn′stə-pā′shən) ▸ *n.* Difficult, incomplete, or infrequent evacuation of the bowels. **—con′sti·pate′** *v.*
con·stit·u·en·cy (kən-stĭch′o͞o-ən-sē) ▸ *n., pl.* **-cies. 1a.** The voters represented by an elected legislator or official. **b.** The district so represented. **2.** A group of supporters.
con·stit·u·ent (kən-stĭch′o͞o-ənt) ▸ *adj.* **1.** Serving as part of a whole; component. **2.** Authorized to make or amend a constitution: *a constituent assembly.* ▸ *n.* **1.** A component. **2.** A resident of a district represented by an elected official. **—con·stit′u·ent·ly** *adv.*
con·sti·tute (kŏn′stĭ-to͞ot′, -tyo͞ot′) ▸ *v.* **-tut·ed, -tut·ing. 1.** To be the parts of; compose. **2.** To set up; establish. **3.** To appoint to an office; designate.
con·sti·tu·tion (kŏn′stĭ-to͞o′shən, -tyo͞o′-) ▸ *n.* **1.** The act or

THESAURUS

considerate *adj.* —*See* ATTENTIVE, OBLIGING.
consideration *n.* **1.** Thoughtful attention to others ▸ attentiveness, concern, helpfulness, hospitality, kindness, loving kindness, regard, solicitousness, solicitude, sweetness, tenderness, thoughtfulness, warm-heartedness. [*Compare* AMIABILITY, BENEVOLENCE, GENEROSITY.] **2.** Careful thought ▸ advisement, deliberation, study. [*Compare* EXAMINATION, SCRUTINY.] —*See also* ATTENTION, DELIBERATION (1), ESTEEM.
considered *adj.* —*See* CALCULATED, DELIBERATE (2).
consign *v.* To place officially in confinement ▸ commit, institutionalize. *Informal:* send up. [*Compare* IMPRISON.] —*See also* ENTRUST (1), SEND (1).
consignment *n.* —*See* DELIVERY.
consist *v.* To have an inherent basis ▸ dwell, exist, inhere, lie, repose, reside, rest. [*Compare* ENDURE, LIVE.] —*See also* AGREE (1).
consistency or **consistence** *n.* Logical agreement among parts ▸ coherence, cohesion, congruence, congruity, uniformity. [*Compare* AGREEMENT, PROPORTION.] —*See also* CHANGELESSNESS.
consistent *adj.* —*See* AGREEABLE, UNCHANGING.
consistently *adv.* —*See* USUALLY.
consolation *n.* ▸ comfort, reassurance, solace, succor. [*Compare* HELP, PITY.]
console *v.* —*See* COMFORT.
consolidate *v.* —*See* COMBINE (1).
consolidated *adj.* —*See* THICK (2).
consolidation *n.* —*See* UNIFICATION.
consonance *n.* —*See* AGREEMENT (2), HARMONY (1).
consonant *adj.* —*See* AGREEABLE, HARMONIOUS (2), UNANIMOUS.
consort *n.* —*See* SPOUSE.
consort *v.* —*See* ASSOCIATE (2).
consortium *n.* —*See* ALLIANCE.
conspicuous *adj.* —*See* APPARENT (1), NOTICEABLE.
conspiracy *n.* —*See* PLOT (2).
conspirator *n.* —*See* ACCESSORY.
conspire *v.* —*See* PLOT (2).
constable *n.* —*See* POLICE OFFICER.
constancy *n.* —*See* CHANGELESSNESS, FIDELITY.
constant *adj.* —*See* CONTINUAL, FAITHFUL, FIRM[1] (3), UNCHANGING.
consternate *v.* —*See* DISMAY.
consternation *n.* —*See* FEAR.
constituency *n.* —*See* PATRONAGE (3).
constituent *adj.* —*See* BUILT-IN.
constituent *n.* —*See* PART (1).
constitute *v.* To be the constituent parts of ▸ compose, form, make up. [*Compare* CONTAIN.] —*See also* EQUAL (1), ESTABLISH (2), FOUND.
constitution *n.* The physical characteristics of a person ▸ body, build, figure, form, frame, habit, habitus, make, makeup, physique, shape.

process of composing or establishing. **2a.** The composition of something. **b.** The physical makeup of a person. **3a.** The system of laws and principles that prescribes the functions and limits of a government. **b.** The written document describing such a system.

con·sti·tu·tion·al (kŏn′stĭ-to͞o′shə-nəl, -tyo͞o′-) ▸ *adj.* **1.** Of or relating to a constitution. **2.** Consistent with, sanctioned by, or operating under a constitution. **3.** Basic; inherent: *a constitutional inability to lie.* ▸ *n.* A walk taken regularly for one's health. **—con′sti·tu′tion·al′i·ty** *n.* **—con′sti·tu′tion·al·ly** *adv.*

con·sti·tu·tive (kŏn′stĭ-to͞o′tĭv, -tyo͞o′-) ▸ *adj.* Inherent; essential.

con·strain (kən-strān′) ▸ *v.* **1.** To compel; oblige. **2.** To confine. **3.** To restrain. **—con·strain′a·ble** *adj.* **—con·strain′er** *n.*

con·straint (kən-strānt′) ▸ *n.* **1.** Force used to compel another; coercion. **2.** Restraint; confinement. **3.** Something that restricts; check. **4.** Reticence; awkwardness.

con·strict (kən-strĭkt′) ▸ *v.* **1.** To make smaller or narrower; compress. **2.** To restrict; cramp: *lives constricted by poverty.* **—con·stric′tion** *n.* **—con·stric′tive** *adj.*

con·stric·tor (kən-strĭk′tər) ▸ *n.* **1.** One that constricts, as a muscle that contracts a part of the body. **2.** A snake, such as the boa, that coils around and asphyxiates its prey.

con·struct (kən-strŭkt′) ▸ *v.* To form by assembling or combining parts; build. ▸ *n.* (kŏn′strŭkt′) **1.** Something formed from parts. **2.** A schematic idea. **—con·struct′i·ble** *adj.* **—con·struc′tor, con·struct′er** *n.*

con·struc·tion (kən-strŭk′shən) ▸ *n.* **1.** The act, process, or business of building. **2.** A structure. **3.** An interpretation: *put a favorable construction on his reply.* **4.** *Gram.* An arrangement of words that forms a phrase, clause, or sentence.

construction paper ▸ *n.* A heavy paper in a variety of colors, used in artwork.

con·struc·tive (kən-strŭk′tĭv) ▸ *adj.* **1.** Serving to improve; helpful. **2.** Structural. **—con·struc′tive·ly** *adv.* **—con·struc′tive·ness** *n.*

con·strue (kən-stro͞o′) ▸ *v.* **-strued, -stru·ing.** **1.** To interpret. **2.** To translate.

con·sul (kŏn′səl) ▸ *n.* **1.** An official appointed by a government to reside in a foreign country and represent its interests there. **2.** Either of the two chief magistrates of the Roman Republic. **—con′su·lar** *adj.* **—con′sul·ship′** *n.*

con·su·late (kŏn′sə-lĭt) ▸ *n.* The residence or official premises of a consul.

con·sult (kən-sŭlt′) ▸ *v.* **1.** To seek advice or information of. **2.** To exchange views. **3.** To work or serve in an advisory capacity. **—con·sul′tant** *n.* **—con′sul·ta′tion** *n.* **—con′sul·ta′tive** *adj.*

con·sul·tan·cy (kən-sŭl′tn-sē) ▸ *n., pl.* **-cies.** A business offering expert advice in a field.

con·sume (kən-so͞om′) ▸ *v.* **-sumed, -sum·ing.** **1.** To eat or drink up. **2.** To expend; use up. **3.** To purchase (goods or services) for use or ownership. **4.** To squander. **5.** To destroy totally; ravage. **6.** To absorb; engross. **—con·sum′a·ble** *adj. & n.*

con·sum·er (kən-so͞o′mər) ▸ *n.* One that consumes, esp. a buyer of goods or services.

consumer goods ▸ *pl.n.* Goods, such as food and clothing, that satisfy human wants through their direct consumption or use.

con·sum·er·ism (kən-so͞o′mə-rĭz′əm) ▸ *n.* **1.** A movement seeking to protect and inform consumers by requiring honest packaging and advertising, product guarantees, and improved standards. **2.** Materialism. **—con·sum′er·ist** *n.*

consumer price index ▸ *n.* An index of prices used to measure the change in the cost of basic goods and services in comparison with a fixed base period.

con·sum·mate (kŏn′sə-māt′) ▸ *v.* **-mat·ed, -mat·ing.** **1.** To bring to completion; conclude. **2.** To complete (a marriage) with the first act of sexual intercourse. ▸ *adj.* (kən-sŭm′ĭt, kŏn′sə-mət) **1.** Complete; lacking nothing. **2.** Supremely accomplished. **—con·sum′mate·ly** *adv.* **—con′sum·ma′tion** *n.* **—con′sum·ma′tor** *n.*

con·sump·tion (kən-sŭmp′shən) ▸ *n.* **1a.** The act or process of consuming. **b.** An amount consumed. **2.** The using up of goods and services esp. by consumer purchasing. **3.** *Pathol.* **a.** A wasting away of body tissue. **b.** Pulmonary tuberculosis.

con·sump·tive (kən-sŭmp′tĭv) ▸ *adj.* **1.** Wasteful. **2.** *Pathol.* Of or afflicted with consumption. ▸ *n.* A person afflicted with consumption. **—con·sump′tive·ly** *adv.*

con·tact (kŏn′tăkt′) ▸ *n.* **1.** A coming together or touching, as of objects or surfaces. **2.** Interaction; communication. **3.** An association; relationship. **4.** A useful person; connection. **5.** A connection between two electric conductors. **6.** A contact lens. ▸ *v.* (kŏn′tăkt′, kən-tăkt′) **1.** To bring or put in contact. **2.** To get in touch with.

THESAURUS

[*Compare* CHARACTER, FORM.] *—See also* FOUNDATION.

constitutional *adj.* Forming an essential element, as arising from the basic structure of an individual ▸ basal, built-in, congenital, connate, connatural, elemental, immanent, inborn, inbred, indigenous, indwelling, ingrained, inherent, innate, intrinsic, native, natural. *Idioms:* in one's blood, runs in the family. [*Compare* CONFIRMED, ELEMENTAL, INNATE.] *—See also* ESSENTIAL (2).

constitutional *n.* *—See* WALK (1).

constitutive *adj.* *—See* ESSENTIAL (2).

constrain *v.* To check the freedom and spontaneity of ▸ constrict, cramp, inhibit. *—See also* FORCE (1), RESTRAIN.

constrained *adj.* *—See* AWKWARD (3), OBLIGED (2), RESERVED.

constraint *n.* *—See* FORCE (1), RESERVE (1), RESTRAINT, RESTRICTION.

constrict *v.* **1.** To make smaller or narrower by binding or squeezing ▸ compact, compress, constringe, contract, narrow, shrink, tighten. [*Compare* DECREASE, SHORTEN.] **2.** To check the freedom and spontaneity of ▸ constrain, cramp, inhibit. [*Compare* RESTRAIN.] *—See also* SQUEEZE (1).

constriction *n.* The act or process of constricting ▸ compression, contraction, narrowing, shrinkage, squeeze. [*Compare* DECREASE.]

constringe *v.* *—See* CONSTRICT (1), SQUEEZE (1).

construct *v.* *—See* BASE[1] (2), BUILD, MAKE.

construable *adj.* *—See* EXPLAINABLE.

construction *n.* Something built, especially for human use ▸ building, edifice, erection, pile, structure.

constructive *adj.* *—See* BENEFICIAL, EFFECTIVE (1).

constructor *n.* *—See* BUILDER.

construe *v.* To understand in a particular way ▸ interpret, read, take. *Idioms:* read between the lines, see in a special light, take to mean. *—See also* EXPLAIN (1), TRANSLATE.

construe *n.* *—See* TRANSLATION.

consuetude *n.* *—See* CUSTOM.

consul *n.* *—See* REPRESENTATIVE.

consult *v.* *—See* CONFER (1).

consultant *n.* *—See* ADVISER.

consultation *n.* *—See* DELIBERATION (1).

consulting *adj.* *—See* ADVISORY.

consume *v.* **1.** To engulf completely ▸ desolate, devastate, devour, dispatch, eat (up), ravage, swallow (up), waste. *Informal:* polish off, put away. *Idioms:* do away with, lay waste. [*Compare* ANNIHILATE, DESTROY.] **2.** To be depleted ▸ exhaust, go, spend. *Idiom:* go down the drain. *—See also* ABSORB (1), EAT (1), ERODE, EXHAUST (1).

consumer *n.* One who buys goods and services ▸ buyer, client, customer, patron, purchaser, shopper, user.

consummate *v.* *—See* CONCLUDE.

consummate *adj.* *—See* DEFINITIVE, PERFECT, UTTER[2].

consummation *n.* *—See* END (1), FULFILLMENT (1).

consumption *n.* The act of consuming ▸ depletion, expenditure, usage, use, utilization. [*Compare* USE.]

contact *n.* **1.** A coming together or touching ▸ contingence, taction, touch. [*Compare* BRUSH[1], TOUCH.] **2.** A situation allowing exchange of ideas or messages ▸ communication, correspondence, intercommunication, touch. [*Compare* COMMUNICATION.] **3.** An acquaintance who is in a position to help ▸ connection, source. *—See also* GO-BETWEEN.

contact *v.* To succeed in communicating with ▸ reach. *Informal:* catch, get. *Idioms:* catch up with, get hold of, get in touch with, get through to, get to.

contact lens ▸ *n.* A thin corrective lens fitted directly over the cornea.

con·ta·gion (kən-tā′jən) ▸ *n.* **1a.** Disease transmission by direct or indirect contact. **b.** A disease so transmitted. **2.** The tendency to spread, as of a doctrine, influence, or emotional state.

con·ta·gious (kən-tā′jəs) ▸ *adj.* **1.** Transmissible by direct or indirect contact; communicable. **2.** Carrying or capable of transmitting disease. **3.** Tending to spread: *a contagious smile.* **—con·ta′gious·ly** *adv.* **—con·ta′gious·ness** *n.*

con·tain (kən-tān′) ▸ *v.* **1.** To have within; hold. **2.** To include; comprise. **3.** To hold back; restrain. **—con·tain′a·ble** *adj.*

con·tain·er (kən-tā′nər) ▸ *n.* A receptacle.

con·tain·er·ize ▸ *v.* **-ized, -iz·ing.** To package (cargo) in large standardized containers for efficient shipping and handling. **—con·tain′er·i·za′tion** *n.*

con·tain·ment (kən-tān′mənt) ▸ *n.* **1.** A policy of checking the expansion of a hostile power or ideology. **2.** A system designed to prevent the accidental release of radioactive materials from a reactor.

con·tam·i·nate (kən-tăm′ə-nāt′) ▸ *v.* **-nated, -nat·ing. 1.** To make impure or unclean by contact or mixture. **2.** To permeate with radioactivity. **—con·tam′i·nant** *n.* **—con·tam′i·na′tion** *n.* **—con·tam′i·na′tive** *adj.* **—con·tam′i·na′tor** *n.*

con·temn (kən-tĕm′) ▸ *v.* To view with contempt.

con·tem·plate (kŏn′təm-plāt′) ▸ *v.* **-plat·ed, -plat·ing. 1.** To consider or ponder thoughtfully. **2.** To intend or anticipate. **—con′tem·pla′tion** *n.* **—con·tem′pla·tive** (kən-tĕm′plə-tĭv) *adj.* **—con·tem′pla·tive·ly** *adv.* **—con′tem·pla′tor** *n.*

con·tem·po·ra·ne·ous (kən-tĕm′pə-rā′nē-əs) ▸ *adj.* Existing or happening during the same period of time. **—con·tem′po·ra·ne′ous·ly** *adv.*

con·tem·po·rar·y (kən-tĕm′pə-rĕr′ē) ▸ *adj.* **1.** Contemporaneous. **2.** Current; modern. ▸ *n., pl.* **-ies. 1.** One of the same time or age. **2.** A person of the present age. **—con·tem′po·rar′i·ly** (-râr′ə-lē) *adv.*

con·tempt (kən-tĕmpt′) ▸ *n.* **1.** Disparaging or haughty disdain; scorn. **2.** The state of being despised; disgrace. **3.** Open disrespect or willful disobedience of the authority of a court of law.

con·tempt·i·ble (kən-tĕmp′tə-bəl) ▸ *adj.* Deserving of contempt; despicable. **—con·tempt′i·bil′i·ty** *n.* **—con·tempt′i·bly** *adv.*

con·temp·tu·ous (kən-tĕmp′cho͞o-əs) ▸ *adj.* Manifesting or feeling contempt; scornful. **—con·temp′tu·ous·ly** *adv.* **—con·temp′tu·ous·ness** *n.*

con·tend (kən-tĕnd′) ▸ *v.* **1.** To strive in opposition; struggle. **2.** To compete. **3.** To maintain or assert. **—con·tend′er** *n.*

con·tent[1] (kŏn′tĕnt′) ▸ *n.* **1.** often **contents** Something contained in a receptacle. **2.** often **contents** The subject matter of a written work. **3.** The meaning or significance of a literary or artistic work. **4.** The proportion of a specified substance.

con·tent[2] (kən-tĕnt′) ▸ *adj.* Satisfied; happy. ▸ *v.* To make satisfied. ▸ *n.* Contentment; satisfaction.

con·tent·ed (kən-tĕn′tĭd) ▸ *adj.* Satisfied; happy. **—con·tent′ed·ly** *adv.*

con·ten·tion (kən-tĕn′shən) ▸ *n.* **1.** Controversy; dispute. **2.** Rivalry: *in contention for first place.*

con·ten·tious (kən-tĕn′shəs) ▸ *adj.* Quarrelsome. **—con·ten′tious·ly** *adv.* **—con·ten′tious·ness** *n.*

con·tent·ment (kən-tĕnt′mənt) ▸ *n.* The state of being contented.

con·ter·mi·nous (kən-tûr′mə-nəs) also **co·ter·mi·nous** (kō-) ▸ *adj.* Having a boundary in common; contiguous. **—con·ter′mi·nous·ly** *adv.*

con·test (kŏn′tĕst′) ▸ *n.* **1.** A struggle between rivals. **2.** A competition. ▸ *v.* (kən-tĕst′, kŏn′tĕst′) **1.** To compete for. **2.** To dispute: *contest a will.* **—con·test′a·ble** *adj.* **—con′tes·ta′tion** *n.* **—con·test′er** *n.*

con·tes·tant (kən-tĕs′tənt, kŏn′tĕs′tənt) ▸ *n.* A competitor, as in a contest or game.

THESAURUS

contagion *n.* —*See* CONTAMINANT, POISON.

contagious *adj.* Capable of transmission by infection ▸ catching, communicable, infectious, pestilent, pestilential, taking, transferable, transmittable, virulent.

contain *v.* **1.** To have as a part ▸ comprehend, comprise, consist of, embody, embrace, encompass, have, include, involve, subsume, take in. **2.** To be filled by ▸ have, hold. [*Compare* CONSTITUTE.] **3.** To have the room or capacity for ▸ accommodate, hold. —*See also* COMPOSE (4), ENCLOSE (1).

container *n.* An object, such as a carton, can, or jar, in which material is held or carried ▸ holder, receptacle, repository, vessel. [*Compare* DEPOSITORY, PACKAGE.]

contaminant *n.* One that contaminates ▸ adulterant, adulterator, contagion, contamination, contaminator, disease, impurity, infection, pestilence, poison, pollutant, pollution, taint. [*Compare* CONTAMINATION, POISON.]

contaminate *v.* To make impure, unclean, or inferior by contact or mixture ▸ adulterate, corrupt, debase, doctor, foul, infect, load, poison, pollute, sophisticate, taint. [*Compare* CORRUPT, DILUTE, DIRTY.] —*See also* CORRUPT.

contaminated *adj.* —*See* IMPURE (2).

contamination *n.* The state of being contaminated ▸ adulteration, corruption, defilement, dirtiness, foulness, impurity, infection, pollution, sophistication, uncleanliness, uncleanness, unwholesomeness. [*Compare* DECAY, DIRTINESS.] —*See also* CONTAMINANT.

contaminative *adj.* —*See* UNWHOLESOME (2).

contaminator *n.* —*See* CONTAMINANT.

contemn *v.* —*See* DESPISE.

contemplate *v.* —*See* INTEND, LOOK (1), PONDER.

contemplative *adj.* —*See* THOUGHTFUL.

contemplation *n.* An act of directing the eyes on an object ▸ look, regard, sight, view. [*Compare* GAZE, WATCH.] —*See also* ATTENTION, THOUGHT.

contemporaneous *adj.* —*See* CONCURRENT, CONTEMPORARY (1).

contemporary *adj.* **1.** Belonging to the same period of time ▸ coetaneous, coeval, coexistent, concurrent, contemporaneous, synchronal, synchronic, synchronous. **2.** Characteristic of recent times or informed of what is current ▸ au courant, current, cutting-edge, latest, latter-day, modern, modernistic, present, recent, state-of-the-art, topical, up-to-date, up-to-the-minute, ultramodern. [*Compare* FASHIONABLE, NEW.] —*See also* CONCURRENT, PRESENT[1].

contemporary *n.* **1.** One of the same time or age as another ▸ coeval. **2.** A person of the present age ▸ modern.

contempt *n.* —*See* DEFIANCE (2), DESPISAL, HATE (1).

contemptible *adj.* —*See* OFFENSIVE (1).

contemptuous *adj.* —*See* DISDAINFUL, DISRESPECTFUL.

contend *v.* To strive in opposition ▸ battle, clash, collide, combat, duel, encounter, engage, fence, fight, grapple, joust, meet, scuffle, spar, strive, struggle, take on, tilt, tussle, war, wrestle. *Idioms:* lock horns with, go to the mat with. [*Compare* CONFRONT, OPPOSE.] —*See also* ARGUE (1), ARGUE (2), ASSERT, COMPETE.

contender *n.* —*See* COMPETITOR.

content *adj.* Having achieved satisfaction, as of one's goal ▸ fulfilled, gratified, happy, satisfied.

content *v.* —*See* SATISFY (2).

contentedness *n.* The condition of being satisfied ▸ contentment, fulfillment, gratification, satisfaction. [*Compare* HAPPINESS, SATIATION.] —*See also* HAPPINESS.

contention *n.* —*See* ARGUMENT, ASSERTION, COMPETITION (1), CONFLICT, THEORY (2).

contentious *adj.* —*See* AGGRESSIVE, ARGUMENTATIVE, DEBATABLE.

contentiousness *n.* —*See* AGGRESSION, FIGHT (2).

contentment *n.* The condition of being satisfied ▸ contentedness, fulfillment, gratification, satisfaction. [*Compare* HAPPINESS, SATIATION.] —*See also* HAPPINESS.

conterminous *adj.* —*See* ADJOINING.

contest *n.* —*See* COMPETITION (1), COMPETITION (2).

contest *v.* To take a stand against ▸ buck, challenge, dispute, oppose, resist, traverse. *Idiom:* go against. [*Compare* CONFRONT, OBJECT, OPPOSE.] —*See also* COMPETE.

contestable *adj.* —*See* DEBATABLE.

contestant *n.* —*See* COMPETITOR.

con·text (kŏn′tĕkst′) ▸ *n.* **1.** The part of a text or statement that surrounds a particular word or passage and determines its meaning. **2.** The circumstances in which an event occurs. **—con·tex′tu·al** (kən-tĕks′cho͞o-əl) *adj.* **—con·tex′tu·al·ly** *adv.*

con·tig·u·ous (kən-tĭg′yo͞o-əs) ▸ *adj.* **1.** Touching. **2.** Neighboring; adjacent. **—con′ti·gu′i·ty** (kŏn′tĭ-gyo͞o′ĭ-tē) **—con·tig′u·ous·ly** *adv.* **—con·tig′u·ous·ness** *n.*

con·ti·nence (kŏn′tə-nəns) ▸ *n.* **1.** Self-restraint; moderation. **2.** Voluntary control over bladder and bowel functions. **3.** Sexual abstinence. **—con′ti·nent** *adj.*

con·ti·nent (kŏn′tə-nənt) ▸ *n.* **1.** One of the principal land masses of the earth. **2. the Continent** The mainland of Europe.

con·ti·nen·tal (kŏn′tə-nĕn′tl) ▸ *adj.* **1.** Of or relating to a continent. **2.** often **Continental** European. **3. Continental** Of the American colonies during the Revolutionary War. ▸ *n.* **1.** often **Continental** A European. **2. Continental** An American Revolutionary War soldier. **—con′ti·nen′tal·ly** *adv.*

continental divide ▸ *n.* A watershed that separates continental river systems flowing in opposite directions.

Continental Divide ▸ A series of mountain ridges extending from AK to Mexico that forms the watershed of North America.

continental shelf ▸ *n.* A submerged, relatively shallow border of a continent.

con·tin·gen·cy (kən-tĭn′jən-sē) ▸ *n., pl.* **-cies.** An event that may occur; possibility. **—con·tin′gen·cy** *adj.*

con·tin·gent (kən-tĭn′jənt) ▸ *adj.* **1.** Liable to occur but not certain; possible. **2.** Conditional. ▸ *n.* **1.** A share or quota, as of troops. **2.** A representative group. **—con·tin′gent·ly** *adv.*

con·tin·u·al (kən-tĭn′yo͞o-əl) ▸ *adj.* **1.** Recurring frequently. **2.** Not interrupted; constant. **—con·tin′u·al·ly** *adv.*

con·tin·u·ance (kən-tĭn′yo͞o-əns) ▸ *n.* **1.** The act or fact of continuing. **2.** Duration. **3.** A continuation or sequel. **4.** *Law* Postponement or adjournment to a future date.

con·tin·u·a·tion (kən-tĭn′yo͞o-ā′shən) ▸ *n.* **1.** The act of continuing. **2.** An extension. **3.** A resumption after an interruption.

con·tin·ue (kən-tĭn′yo͞o) ▸ *v.* **-ued, -u·ing.** **1.** To persist. **2.** To endure; last. **3.** To remain in a state, capacity, or place. **4.** To go on after an interruption; resume. **5.** To extend. **6.** To retain. **7.** To postpone or adjourn. **—con·tin′u·er** *n.*

con·ti·nu·i·ty (kŏn′tə-no͞o′ĭ-tē, -nyo͞o′-) ▸ *n., pl.* **-ties.** **1.** The state of being continuous. **2.** An uninterrupted succession.

con·tin·u·ous (kən-tĭn′yo͞o-əs) ▸ *adj.* Uninterrupted in time, sequence, substance, or extent. **—con·tin′u·ous·ly** *adv.* **—con·tin′u·ous·ness** *n.*

con·tin·u·um (kən-tĭn′yo͞o-əm) ▸ *n., pl.* **-tin·u·a** (-tĭn′yo͞o-ə) or **-tin·u·ums.** A continuous extent or whole, no part of which can be distinguished from neighboring parts except by arbitrary division.

con·tort (kən-tôrt′) ▸ *v.* To twist or wrench out of shape. **—con·tor′tion** *n.* **—con·tor′tive** *adj.*

con·tor·tion·ist (kən-tôr′shə-nĭst) ▸ *n.* One who contorts, esp. an acrobat capable of twisting into extraordinary positions. **—con·tor′tion·is′tic** *adj.*

con·tour (kŏn′to͝or′) ▸ *n.* **1.** The outline of a figure or body. **2.** often **contours** A surface, esp. of a curving form. ▸ *v.* To make or shape the outline of. ▸ *adj.* Following the contour of something.

contour map ▸ *n.* A map showing elevations and surface configuration by means of spaced lines.

contra– ▸ *pref.* Against; opposite; contrasting: *contraindicate.*

con·tra·band (kŏn′trə-bănd′) ▸ *n.* Goods prohibited in trade. **—con′tra·band′ist** *n.*

con·tra·bass (kŏn′trə-bās′) ▸ *n.* See **double bass.**

con·tra·cep·tion (kŏn′trə-sĕp′shən) ▸ *n.* Prevention of conception, as by use of a device, drug, or chemical agent. **—con′tra·cep′tive** *adj. & n.*

con·tract (kŏn′trăkt′) ▸ *n.* An enforceable agreement between parties. ▸ *v.* (kən-trăkt′, kŏn′trăkt′) **1.** To enter into or establish by contract. **2.** To catch (a disease). **3.** To shrink by drawing together. **4.** To shorten (a word or words) by omitting some of the letters or sounds. **—con·tract′i·bil′i·ty** *n.* **—con·tract′i·ble** *adj.* **—con·trac′tion** *n.*

con·trac·tile (kən-trăk′təl, -tīl′) ▸ *adj.* Capable of contracting, as muscle tissue.

con·trac·tor (kŏn′trăk′tər) ▸ *n.* One that agrees to perform services at a specified price, esp. for construction work.

con·trac·tu·al (kən-trăk′cho͞o-əl) ▸ *adj.* Of or like a contract. **—con·trac′tu·al·ly** *adv.*

con·tra·dict (kŏn′trə-dĭkt′) ▸ *v.* **1.** To assert the opposite of. **2.** To deny the statement of. **3.** To be contrary to or inconsistent with. **—con′tra·dict′a·ble** *adj.* **—con′tra·dict′er, con′tra·dic′tor** *n.* **—con′tra·dic′tion** *n.* **—con′tra·dic′to·ry** *adj.*

con·tra·dis·tinc·tion (kŏn′trə-dĭ-stĭngk′shən) ▸ *n.* Distinction by contrasting qualities. **—con′tra·dis·tinc′tive** *adj.* **—con′tra·dis·tinc′tive·ly** *adv.*

THESAURUS

context *n.* —*See* CONDITIONS, ENVIRONMENT (2).

contexture *n.* —*See* TEXTURE.

contiguous *adj.* —*See* ADJOINING, CLOSE (1).

continence *n.* —*See* TEMPERANCE (1).

continent *adj.* —*See* CHASTE, TEMPERATE (2).

contingence *n.* A coming together or touching ▸ contact, taction, touch. [*Compare* BRUSH[1], TOUCH.]

contingency *n.* —*See* CHANCE (2), POSSIBILITY (1).

contingent *adj.* —*See* ACCIDENTAL, CONDITIONAL, PROBABLE.

continual *adj.* Existing or occurring without interruption or end ▸ around-the-clock, ceaseless, constant, continuous, endless, eternal, everlasting, incessant, interminable, never-ending, nonstop, ongoing, perennial, perpetual, persistent, relentless, round-the-clock, timeless, unbroken, unceasing, undying, unending, unfailing, uninterrupted, unremitting. [*Compare* AGELESS, CONTINUING, ENDLESS, UNCHANGING.]

continually *adv.* Without stop or interruption ▸ ceaselessly, constantly, continuously, endlessly, forever, incessantly, interminably, nonstop, perpetually, persistently, relentlessly, steadily, unceasingly, unfailingly, unremittingly. *Slang:* 24-7. *Idioms:* around (*or* round) the clock, all the time, seven days a week. [*Compare* FOREVER, USUALLY.]

continuance *n.* —*See* CONTINUATION (1).

continuation *n.* **1.** Uninterrupted existence or succession ▸ continuance, continuity, continuum, durability, duration, endurance, permanence, persistence, persistency, survival. [*Compare* ENDLESSNESS, STABILITY.] **2.** A continuing after interruption ▸ renewal, resumption, resurgence, revival. [*Compare* REVIVAL.]

continue *v.* To begin or go on after an interruption ▸ pick up, proceed, renew, reopen, restart, resume, take up. —*See also* ENDURE (2), EXTEND (1).

continuing *adj.* Existing or remaining in the same state for an indefinitely long time ▸ abiding, durable, enduring, lasting, long-lasting, long-lived, long-standing, maintaining, old, perdurable, perennial, permanent, persevering, persistent, persisting. [*Compare* CONTINUAL, ENDLESS, UNCHANGING.] —*See also* CHRONIC (2).

continuity *n.* —*See* CONTINUATION (1).

continuous *adj.* —*See* CONTINUAL.

continuum *n.* —*See* CONTINUATION (1).

contort *v.* —*See* DEFORM.

contortion *n.* —*See* DEFORMITY.

contour *n.* —*See* FORM (1).

contrabandist *n.* A person who engages in smuggling ▸ bootlegger, runner, smuggler. *Slang:* mule.

contract *n.* —*See* AGREEMENT (1).

contract *v.* **1.** To enter into a formal agreement ▸ bargain, covenant, stipulate. *Idioms:* shake hands on, sign on the dotted line, strike a bargain. [*Compare* AGREE, PLEDGE, SETTLE.] **2.** To become affected with a disease ▸ catch, develop, get, incur, sicken, take. *Informal:* pick up. *Idiom:* come down with. [*Compare* DEVELOP, GET.] —*See also* CONSTRICT (1), PLEDGE (2).

contraction *n.* —*See* CONSTRICTION.

contractor *n.* —*See* BUILDER.

contradict *v.* —*See* CONFLICT, DENY.

contradiction *n.* —*See* DENIAL (1), OPPOSITE, OPPOSITION (1).

contradictory *adj.* —*See* CONTRARY, DISCREPANT, OPPOSITE.

contradictory *n.* —*See* OPPOSITE.

contradistinction *n.* —*See* OPPOSITION (1).

con·trail (kŏn′trāl′) ▸ *n.* A visible trail of condensed water vapor or ice crystals formed in the wake of an aircraft at high altitudes.
con·tra·in·di·cate (kŏn′trə-ĭn′dĭ-kāt′) ▸ *v.* To indicate the inadvisability of. **—con′tra·in′di·ca′tion** *n.* **—con′tra·in·dic′a·tive** (-ĭn-dĭk′ə-tĭv) *adj.*
con·tral·to (kən-trăl′tō) ▸ *n., pl.* **-tos**. **1.** The lowest female voice or voice part. **2.** A woman having a contralto voice.
con·trap·tion (kən-trăp′shən) ▸ *n.* A mechanical device; gadget.
con·tra·pun·tal (kŏn′trə-pŭn′tl) ▸ *adj. Mus.* Of or using counterpoint. **—con′tra·pun′tal·ly** *adv.*
con·trar·i·an (kən-trâr′ē-ən) ▸ *n.* An investor who makes decisions that contradict prevailing wisdom.
con·trar·i·wise (kŏn′trĕr′ē-wīz′, kən-trâr′-) ▸ *adv.* **1.** From a contrasting point of view. **2.** In the opposite way.
con·trar·y (kŏn′trĕr′ē) ▸ *adj.* **1.** Opposed; counter: *contrary opinions.* **2.** Opposite, as in character or direction. **3.** Adverse; unfavorable. **4.** (*also* kən-trâr′ē) Willful or perverse. ▸ *n., pl.* **-ies**. Something that is opposite or contrary. ▸ *adv.* Contrariwise; counter. **—con′trar′i·ly** (kŏn′trĕr′ə-lē, kən-trâr′-) *adv.* **—con′tra·ri′e·ty** (-trə-rī′ĭ-tē) *n.* **—con′trar′i·ness** *n.*
con·trast (kən-trăst′, kŏn′trăst′) ▸ *v.* **1.** To set in opposition in order to show differences. **2.** To show differences when compared. ▸ *n.* (kŏn′trăst′) **1.** The act of contrasting or the state of being contrasted. **2.** A difference between things compared. **3.** One thing that is strikingly different from another. **—con·trast′a·ble** *adj.* **—con·trast′ing·ly** *adv.*
con·tra·vene (kŏn′trə-vēn′) ▸ *v.* **-vened, -ven·ing**. **1.** To act or be counter to; violate. **2.** To contradict. **—con′tra·ven′tion** (-vĕn′shən) *n.*
con·tre·temps (kŏn′trə-täɴ′, kôɴ′trə-täɴ′) ▸ *n., pl.* **-temps** (-täɴz′, -täɴz′). An inopportune or embarrassing occurrence.
con·trib·ute (kən-trĭb′yo͞ot) ▸ *v.* **-ut·ed, -ut·ing**. **1.** To give or supply a share (to); participate (in). **2.** To help bring about a result. **—con′tri·bu′tion** (kŏn′trĭ-byo͞o′shən) *n.* **—con·trib′u·tive** *adj.* **—con·trib′u·tor** *n.* **—con·trib′u·to′ry** (-tôr′ē) *adj.*
con·trite (kən-trīt′, kŏn′trīt′) ▸ *adj.* Repentant; penitent. **—con·trite′ly** *adv.*
con·tri·tion (kən-trĭsh′ən) ▸ *n.* Remorse for wrongdoing.
con·triv·ance (kən-trī′vəns) ▸ *n.* **1.** A mechanical device. **2.** A clever plan; scheme.
con·trive (kən-trīv′) ▸ *v.* **-trived, -triv·ing**. **1.** To plan with ingenuity; devise. **2.** To invent or fabricate, esp. by improvisation. **3.** To bring about or manage. **—con·triv′er** *n.*
con·trived (kən-trīvd′) ▸ *adj.* Not spontaneous; labored: *a contrived plot.* **—con·triv′ed·ly** (-trī′vĭd-lē, -trīvd′lē) *adv.*
con·trol (kən-trōl′) ▸ *v.* **-trolled, -trol·ling**. **1.** To exercise authority or influence over; direct. **2.** To hold in restraint; check. **3.** To verify or regulate by systematic comparison. ▸ *n.* **1.** Power to manage, direct, or dominate. **2.** often **controls** A set of instruments used to operate a machine. **3.** A restraint; curb. **4.** A standard of comparison for verifying experimental results. **—con·trol′la·bil′i·ty** *n.* **—con·trol′la·ble** *adj.*
con·trolled substance (kən-trōld′) ▸ *n.* A drug or chemical substance whose possession and use are regulated by law.
con·trol·ler (kən-trō′lər) ▸ *n.* **1.** One that controls, esp. a regulating mechanism in a vehicle or machine. **2.** also **comp·trol·ler** (kən-trō′lər, kŏmp-trō′-) An executive or official who supervises financial affairs.
control stick ▸ *n.* A lever used to control the motion of an aircraft by changing the angle of the elevators and ailerons.
control tower ▸ *n.* An observation tower at an airfield from which air traffic is controlled by radio.
con·tro·ver·sy (kŏn′trə-vûr′sē) ▸ *n., pl.* **-sies**. A dispute, esp. a public one, between sides holding opposing views. **—con′tro·ver′sial** (-shəl, -sē-əl) *adj.* **—con′tro·ver′sial·ly** *adv.*
con·tro·vert (kŏn′trə-vûrt′, kŏn′trə-vûrt′) ▸ *v.* To argue against; contradict. **—con′tro·vert′i·ble** *adj.*
con·tu·ma·cious (kŏn′tə-mā′shəs, -tyə-) ▸ *adj.* Obstinately disobedient or rebellious; insubordinate. **—con′tu·ma′cious·ly** *adv.*
con·tu·me·ly (kŏn′to͞o-mə-lē, -tyo͞o-, -təm-lē) ▸ *n., pl.* **-lies**. Insulting treatment; insolence.
con·tuse (kən-to͞oz′, -tyo͞oz′) ▸ *v.* **-tused, -tus·ing**. To injure without breaking the skin; bruise. **—con·tu′sion** *n.*
co·nun·drum (kə-nŭn′drəm) ▸ *n.* **1.** A riddle. **2.** A dilemma.
con·ur·ba·tion (kŏn′ər-bā′shən) ▸ *n.* A predominantly urban region including adjacent towns.
con·va·lesce (kŏn′və-lĕs′) ▸ *v.* **-lesced, -lesc·ing**. To recuperate from an illness or injury. **—con′va·les′cence** *n.* **—con′va·les′cent** *adj. & n.*

THESAURUS

contraindicated *adj.* —*See* UNWISE.
contralto *adj.* —*See* LOW (1).
contraposition *n.* —*See* OPPOSITION (1).
contrapositive *n.* —*See* OPPOSITE.
contraption *n.* —*See* DEVICE (1), GADGET.
contrariness or **contrariety** *n.* —*See* OPPOSITION (1).
contrary *adj.* Marked by a disposition to oppose ▸ antagonistic, balky, contradictory, contrarious, difficult, froward, hostile, impossible, inimical, ornery, perverse, wayward. [*Compare* OPPOSING.] —*See also* DIFFERENT, OPPOSITE.
contrary *n.* —*See* OPPOSITE.
contrast *v.* —*See* COMPARE, CONFLICT, DIFFER.
contrast *n.* The act or state of being contrasted ▸ collation, comparison, counterpoint, juxtaposition. —*See also* DIFFERENCE.
contrasting *adj.* —*See* DIFFERENT, DISCREPANT, OPPOSITE.
contravene *v.* —*See* DENY, VIOLATE (1).
contravention *n.* —*See* BREACH (1).
contretemps *n.* —*See* ACCIDENT.
contribute *v.* **1.** To give in common with others ▸ ante, chip in, donate, give, subscribe. *Informal:* kick in. *Slang:* come across with. *Idiom:* do one's bit. [*Compare* GIVE.] **2.** To help bring about a result ▸ chip in, conduce, partake, participate, share. *Idioms:* have a hand in, take part. [*Compare* ADVANCE, HELP, PARTICIPATE.] —*See also* DONATE.
contribution *n.* —*See* DONATION.
contributive *adj.* Tending to contribute to a result ▸ conducive, contributory, helpful, participatory. [*Compare* AUXILIARY.]
contributor *n.* A person instrumental in the growth of something, especially in its early stages ▸ creator, producer. [*Compare* DEVELOPER.] —*See also* DONOR, PATRON.
contributory *adj.* Tending to contribute to a result ▸ conducive, contributive, helpful, participatory. —*See also* AUXILIARY (1).
contrite *adj.* —*See* SORRY.
contriteness *n.* —*See* PENITENCE.
contrition *n.* —*See* PENITENCE.
contrivance *n.* —*See* DEVICE (1), GADGET, INVENTION (2).
contrive *v.* —*See* DESIGN (1), INVENT.
contrived *adj.* Not natural or spontaneous ▸ effortful, forced, labored, strained. [*Compare* AWKWARD, STIFF.] —*See also* CALCULATED.
control *v.* —*See* ADMINISTER (1), COMPOSE (4), CONDUCT (1), DOMINATE (1), GOVERN.
control *n.* —*See* AUTHORITY, DOMINANCE, DOMINATION, GOVERNMENT (1), RESERVE (1), RESTRAINT.
controllable *adj.* Capable of being governed ▸ administrable, governable, manageable, rulable. [*Compare* LOYAL, OBEDIENT.]
controlled *adj.* —*See* RESERVED, RESTRICTED.
controlling *adj.* —*See* DOMINANT (1), REPRESSIVE.
controversy *n.* —*See* ARGUMENT.
controvert *v.* —*See* DENY.
contumacious *adj.* —*See* DEFIANT.
contumacy *n.* —*See* DEFIANCE (2).
contumelious *adj.* —*See* ABUSIVE, IMPUDENT.
contumely *n.* —*See* INDIGNITY, VITUPERATION.
contuse *v.* To make a bruise or bruises on ▸ bruise. *Idiom:* beat (*or* leave) black-and-blue. [*Compare* HURT.]
contusion *n.* An injury that does not break the skin ▸ black-and-blue mark, bruise. [*Compare* BLACK EYE, HARM, TRAUMA.]
conundrum *n.* —*See* MYSTERY.
convalesce *v.* —*See* RECOVER (2).
convalescence *n.* The process or period of a return to health ▸ rally, recovery, recuperation.

con·vect (kən-vĕkt′) ▸ *v.* To transfer by or undergo convection.

con·vec·tion (kən-vĕk′shən) ▸ *n.* Heat transfer in a gas or liquid by the circulation of currents from one region to another. **—con·vec′tion·al** *adj.* **—con·vec′tive** *adj.*

con·vene (kən-vēn′) ▸ *v.* **-vened, -ven·ing. 1.** To meet or assemble formally. **2.** To convoke. **—con·ven′a·ble** *adj.* **—con·ven′er** *n.*

con·ven·ience (kən-vēn′yəns) ▸ *n.* **1.** Suitability to one's purposes or needs; handiness. **2.** Personal comfort or advantage. **3.** Something that increases comfort or saves work.

con·ven·ient (kən-vēn′yənt) ▸ *adj.* **1.** Suited to one's comfort or needs. **2.** Easy to reach; accessible. **—con·ven′ient·ly** *adv.*

con·vent (kŏn′vənt, -vĕnt′) ▸ *n.* A monastic community or house, esp. of nuns. **—con·ven′tu·al** (kən-vĕn′cho͞o-əl) *adj.*

con·ven·ti·cle (kən-vĕn′tĭ-kəl) ▸ *n.* A religious meeting, esp. a secret one.

con·ven·tion (kən-vĕn′shən) ▸ *n.* **1a.** A formal meeting or assembly, as of a political party. **b.** The delegates attending such an assembly. **2.** An international agreement or compact. **3.** General usage or custom. **4.** An accepted or prescribed practice.

con·ven·tion·al (kən-vĕn′shə-nəl) ▸ *adj.* **1.** Following accepted practice; customary. **2.** Unimaginative or commonplace; ordinary. **3.** Using means other than nuclear weapons or energy. **—con·ven′tion·al′i·ty** *n.* **—con·ven′tion·al·ly** *adv.*

con·ven·tion·al·ize (kən-vĕn′shə-nə-līz′) ▸ *v.* **-ized, -iz·ing.** To make conventional. **—con·ven′tion·al·i·za′tion** *n.*

con·verge (kən-vûrj′) ▸ *v.* **-verged, -verg·ing.** To tend or move toward a common point or result. **—con·ver′gence** *n.* **—con·ver′gent** *adj.*

con·ver·sant (kən-vûr′sənt, kŏn′vər-) ▸ *adj.* Familiar, as by study or experience. **—con·ver′sant·ly** *adv.*

con·ver·sa·tion (kŏn′vər-sā′shən) ▸ *n.* An informal exchange of speech. **—con′ver·sa′tion·al** *adj.* **—con′ver·sa′tion·al·ly** *adv.*

con·ver·sa·tion·al·ist (kŏn′vər-sā′shə-nə-lĭst) ▸ *n.* One given to conversation.

conversation piece ▸ *n.* An unusual object that arouses comment or interest.

con·verse[1] (kən-vûrs′) ▸ *v.* **-versed, -vers·ing.** To engage in conversation. ▸ *n.* (kŏn′vûrs′) Conversation.

con·verse[2] (kən-vûrs′, kŏn′vûrs′) ▸ *adj.* Reversed in position, order, or action. ▸ *n.* (kŏn′vûrs′) The reverse or opposite of something. **—con·verse′ly** *adv.*

con·ver·sion (kən-vûr′zhən, -shən) ▸ *n.* **1.** The act of converting or the state of being converted. **2.** A change in which one adopts a new religion or belief. **3.** The unlawful appropriation of another's property. **4.** *Football* A score made on a try for a point or points after a touchdown.

con·vert (kən-vûrt′) ▸ *v.* **1.** To change into another form, substance, or state. **2.** To adapt to a new or different purpose. **3.** To persuade or be persuaded to adopt a particular religion or belief. **4.** To exchange for something of equal value. **5.** To express in alternative units: *convert feet into meters.* **6.** To misappropriate. **7.** *Football* To make a conversion. ▸ *n.* (kŏn′vûrt′) One who has been converted, esp. from one belief to another. **—con·vert′er, con·ver′tor** *n.*

con·vert·i·ble (kən-vûr′tə-bəl) ▸ *adj.* That can be converted. ▸ *n.* **1.** Something that can be converted. **2.** An automobile with a top that can be folded back or removed.

con·vex (kŏn′vĕks′, kən-vĕks′) ▸ *adj.* Curved outward, as the exterior of a sphere. **—con·vex′i·ty** *n.* **—con′vex′ly** *adv.*

con·vey (kən-vā′) ▸ *v.* **1.** To carry; transport. **2.** To transmit. **3.** To communicate; impart. **4.** *Law* To transfer ownership of or title to. **—con·vey′a·ble** *adj.* **—con·vey′or, con·vey′er** *n.*

con·vey·ance (kən-vā′əns) ▸ *n.* **1.** The act of conveying. **2.** A vehicle. **3.** A document effecting the transfer of title to property.

con·vict (kən-vĭkt′) ▸ *v.* To find or prove guilty of an offense or crime. ▸ *n.* (kŏn′vĭkt′) A person found guilty of a crime, esp. one serving a prison sentence.

con·vic·tion (kən-vĭk′shən) ▸ *n.* **1.** The act of convicting or the state of being convicted. **2.** A strong opinion or belief.

con·vince (kən-vĭns′) ▸ *v.* **-vinced, -vinc·ing.** To bring to

THESAURUS

convene *v.* —*See* ASSEMBLE.

convenience *n.* Unrestricted freedom to choose ▸ discretion, leisure, pleasure, will.

conveniences *n.* —*See* AMENITIES (1).

convenient *adj.* **1.** Suited to one's needs or purpose ▸ appropriate, befitting, expedient, fit, good, handy, meet, proper, suitable, tailor-made, useful. [*Compare* BENEFICIAL, OPPORTUNE.] **2.** Being within easy reach ▸ accessible, handy, nearby, ready. *Idioms:* at one's fingertips, at the ready, close (*or* near) at hand, close by. [*Compare* AVAILABLE, CENTRAL, CLOSE.]

convention *n.* A formal assemblage of the members of a group ▸ assembly, conclave, conference, congress, convocation, council, meeting, session, synod. —*See also* AGREEMENT (1), ASSEMBLY, CULTURE (2), CUSTOM, DOCTRINE, TREATY.

conventional *adj.* Conforming to established practice or standards ▸ button-down, canonical, conformist, conservative, doctrinaire, doctrinal, establishmentarian, normal, orthodox, received, regular, standard, stereotyped, straight, time-honored, traditional, typical, usual. *Slang:* square, uncool. [*Compare* COMMON, ORDINARY, PREVAILING.] —*See also* ACCEPTED, CEREMONIOUS.

conventionalize *v.* To make conventional ▸ conform, homogenize, normalize, regularize, standardize, stereotype, stylize, traditionalize.

converge *v.* To come together from different directions ▸ close, join, meet, unite. [*Compare* COMBINE.] —*See also* CONCENTRATE.

converge on *v.* —*See* APPROACH (1).

convergence *n.* The act or fact of coming near ▸ approach, coming, imminence, nearness. [*Compare* ADVANCE, APPEARANCE.] —*See also* JUNCTION.

conversance *n.* Personal knowledge derived from participation or observation ▸ acquaintance, experience, familiarity. [*Compare* AWARENESS.]

conversant *adj.* Having good knowledge of something ▸ acquainted, familiar, schooled, versant, versed. *Idiom:* up on. [*Compare* ACCUSTOMED, INFORMED.]

conversation *n.* Spoken exchange ▸ chat, colloquy, confabulation, converse, dialogue, discourse, discussion, heart-to-heart, interlocution, interview, pillow talk, speech, talk, tete a tete. *Informal:* bull session, confab, talkfest. *Slang:* gabfest, jaw, rap. [*Compare* CHATTER, GOSSIP.] —*See also* COMMUNICATION (1).

conversational *adj.* In the style of conversation ▸ chatty, chitchatty, colloquial, communicative, confabulatory, cozy, informal. —*See also* TALKATIVE.

conversationalist or **conversationist** *n.* One given to conversation ▸ confabulator, dialogist, discourser, interlocutor, talker. [*Compare* SPEAKER.]

converse[1] *v.* To engage in spoken exchange ▸ buttonhole, chat, confabulate, discourse, speak, talk. *Informal:* confab, visit. [*Compare* CHATTER, CONFER, SAY.] —*See also* DISCUSS.

converse[2] *adj.* —*See* OPPOSITE.

converse *n.* —*See* OPPOSITE.

conversion *n.* **1.** The process or result of changing from one use, function, or appearance to another ▸ change, changeover, metamorphosis, mutation, shift, transfiguration, transformation, translation, transmogrification, transmutation, transubstantiation, turn. [*Compare* CHANGE.] **2.** A fundamental change in one's beliefs ▸ metanoia, rebirth, regeneration. [*Compare* REVIVAL.]

convert *v.* To change into a different form, substance, or state ▸ denature, metamorphose, morph, mutate, reshape, transfigure, transform, translate, transmogrify, transmute, transpose, transubstantiate. [*Compare* CHANGE.] —*See also* CONVINCE.

convertible *adj.* —*See* CHANGEABLE (1).

convey *v.* —*See* BRING (1), CARRY (1), COMMUNICATE (1), COMMUNICATE (2), CONDUCT (1), EXPRESS (1), MEAN[1], SAY, TRANSFER (1).

conveyance *n.* —*See* DELIVERY, GRANT, TRANSPORTATION.

conveyer *n.* —*See* MESSENGER.

convict *v.* —*See* CONDEMN.

convict *n.* —*See* CRIMINAL.

conviction *n.* —*See* BELIEF (1), SURENESS.

convince *v.* To cause another to believe or feel sure about something ▸ assure, bring around (*or* round), convert, persuade, satisfy, sell (on), turn, win over. [*Compare* DISPOSE, PROVE.] —*See also* PERSUADE.

belief by argument or evidence; persuade. **—con·vinc′ing** *adj.* **—con·vinc′ing·ly** *adv.*

con·viv·i·al (kən-vĭv′ē-əl) ▸ *adj.* 1. Fond of social pleasures. 2. Merry; festive. **—con·viv′i·al′i·ty** (-ăl′ĭ-tē) *n.* **—con·viv′i·al·ly** *adv.*

con·vo·ca·tion (kŏn′və-kā′shən) ▸ *n.* 1. The act of convoking. 2. A formal assembly.

con·voke (kən-vōk′) ▸ *v.* **-voked, -vok·ing.** To cause to assemble; convene.

con·vo·lut·ed (kŏn′və-lo͞o′tĭd) ▸ *adj.* 1. Having numerous overlapping coils or folds. 2. Intricate; complex.

con·vo·lu·tion (kŏn′və-lo͞o′shən) ▸ *n.* 1. A form or part that is folded, coiled, or twisted. 2. One of the convex folds of the surface of the brain.

con·voy (kŏn′voi′) ▸ *n.* 1. An accompanying and protecting force, as of ships. 2. A group traveling together for safety. ▸ *v.* (kŏn′voi′, kən-voi′) To accompany, esp. for protection.

con·vulse (kən-vŭls′) ▸ *v.* **-vulsed, -vuls·ing.** 1. To disturb violently. 2. To throw into convulsions. **—con·vul′sive** *adj.* **—con·vul′sive·ly** *adv.*

con·vul·sion (kən-vŭl′shən) ▸ *n.* 1. An intense, paroxysmal, involuntary muscular contraction. 2. An uncontrolled fit, as of laughter; paroxysm. 3. Violent turmoil.

co·ny (kō′nē, kŭn′ē) ▸ *n.* Var. of **coney.**

coo (ko͞o) ▸ *v.* 1. To utter the murmuring sound of a dove or pigeon. 2. To talk in fond or amorous murmurs. **—coo** *n.*

cook (ko͝ok) ▸ *v.* 1. To prepare (food) for eating by applying heat. 2. To prepare or treat by heating. 3. *Slang* To alter or falsify; doctor. ***—phrasal verb:* cook up** *Informal* To concoct: *cook up an excuse.* ▸ *n.* One who prepares food for eating.

Cook, James. "Captain Cook" (1728–79) ▸ British navigator and explorer.

cook·book (ko͝ok′bo͝ok′) ▸ *n.* A book with recipes and advice about food preparation.

cook·er·y (ko͝ok′ə-rē) ▸ *n., pl.* **-ies.** The art or practice of preparing food.

cook·ie also **cook·y** (ko͝ok′ē) ▸ *n., pl.* **-ies.** 1. A small cake, usu. flat and crisp, made from sweetened dough. 2. Information stored on a Web user's computer, used by websites to identify previous visitors to that site.

Cook Islands ▸ An island group of the S Pacific SE of Samoa.

cook·out (ko͝ok′out′) ▸ *n.* A meal cooked and served outdoors.

cool (ko͞ol) ▸ *adj.* **-er, -est.** 1. Moderately cold. 2. Giving or suggesting relief from heat. 3. Marked by calm self-control. 4. Marked by indifference, disdain, or dislike. 5. *Slang* Excellent; first-rate. ▸ *v.* 1. To make or become less warm. 2. To make or become less intense or ardent. ▸ *n.* 1. A cool place, part, or time. 2. *Slang* Composure; poise. ***—idiom:* cool it** *Slang* To calm down; relax. **—cool′ly** *adv.* **—cool′ness** *n.*

cool·ant (ko͞o′lənt) ▸ *n.* Something that cools, esp. a fluid that draws off heat by circulating through or over an engine or part.

cool·er (ko͞o′lər) ▸ *n.* 1. A device or container that cools or that keeps something cool. 2. A tall cold drink. 3. *Slang* A jail.

Coo·lidge (ko͞o′lĭj), **(John) Calvin** (1872–1933) ▸ The 30th US President (1923–29).

coon (ko͞on) ▸ *n. Informal* A raccoon.

coon·skin (ko͞on′skĭn′) ▸ *n.* 1. The pelt of a raccoon. 2. An article made of coonskin.

coop (ko͞op) ▸ *n.* A cage, esp. one for poultry. ▸ *v.* To confine in or as if in a coop.

co-op (kō′ŏp′, kō-ŏp′) ▸ *n.* A cooperative.

coop·er (ko͞o′pər) ▸ *n.* One who makes wooden barrels and tubs. **—coop′er·age** *n.*

Cooper, James Fenimore (1789–1851) ▸ Amer. novelist.

co·op·er·ate (kō-ŏp′ə-rāt′) ▸ *v.* **-at·ed, -at·ing.** To work together for a common end. **—co·op′er·a′tion** *n.* **—co·op′er·a′tor** *n.*

co·op·er·a·tive (kō-ŏp′ər-ə-tĭv, -ə-rā′tĭv, -ŏp′rə-) ▸ *adj.* 1. Willing to cooperate. 2. Engaged in joint economic activity. ▸ *n.* An enterprise owned and operated by those who use its services. **—co·op′er·a·tive·ly** *adv.* **—co·op′er·a·tive·ness** *n.*

co-opt (kō-ŏpt′, kō′ŏpt′) ▸ *v.* 1. To elect or appoint as a fellow member or colleague. 2. To appropriate. 3. To take over through assimilation into an established group or culture. **—co′-op·ta′tion** *n.*

co·or·di·nate (kō-ôr′dn-āt′, -ĭt) ▸ *n.* 1. One that is equal in rank or degree. 2. *Math.* Any of a set of numbers that determines the position of a point in a space of a given dimension. ▸ *adj.* (-ĭt, -āt′) 1. Of equal rank or degree. 2. Of or involving coordination. 3. Of or based on coordinates. ▸ *v.* (-āt′) **-nat·ed, -nat·ing.** 1. To place in the same order, class, or rank. 2. To harmonize in a common action or effort. 3. To be coordinate. **—co·or′di·nate·ly** (-ĭt-lē) *adv.* **—co·or′di·na′tive** *adj.* **—co·or′di·na′tor** *n.*

co·or·di·na·tion (kō-ôr′dn-ā′shən) ▸ *n.* 1. The act of coordinating or the state of being coordinated. 2. Harmonious functioning of muscles in the execution of movements.

coot (ko͞ot) ▸ *n.* 1. A gray water bird with a black head and white bill. 2. *Informal* An eccentric person.

coo·tie (ko͞o′tē) ▸ *n. Slang* A body louse.

cop (kŏp) *Slang* ▸ *n.* A police officer. ▸ *v.* **copped, cop·ping.** 1. To steal. 2. To seize; catch. ***—phrasal verb:* cop out** To avoid fulfilling a commitment or responsibility. ***—idiom:* cop a plea** To plead guilty to a lesser charge to avoid a more serious charge.

co·pa·cet·ic or **co·pa·set·ic** (kō′pə-sĕt′ĭk) ▸ *adj.* Excellent; first-rate.

co·part·ner (kō-pärt′nər, kō′pärt′-) ▸ *n.* A joint partner. **—co·part′ner·ship′** *n.*

THESAURUS

convincing *adj.* Serving to convince ▸ cogent, compelling, effective, efficacious, forceful, forcible, persuasive, satisfactory, telling. [*Compare* BELIEVABLE, DEFINITE, SOUND².] *—See also* AUTHENTIC (2).

convivial *adj.* *—See* CHEERFUL, MERRY, SOCIAL.

conviviality *n.* *—See* MERRIMENT (2).

convocation *n.* *—See* ASSEMBLY, CONVENTION.

convoke *v.* *—See* ASSEMBLE.

convoluted *adj.* *—See* COMPLEX (1), WINDING.

convoy *v.* *—See* ACCOMPANY.

convulse *v.* *—See* AGITATE (1).

convulsion *n.* A condition of anguished struggle and disorder ▸ paroxysm, throes, spasm. *—See also* AGITATION (1), REVOLUTION (2), SEIZURE (1).

cook *v.* To prepare food for eating by the use of heat ▸ bake, barbecue, blanch, boil, braise, broil, brown, charbroil, coddle, deep-fry, fricassee, fry, griddle, grill, pan-broil, pan-fry, parboil, poach, roast, sauté, sear, simmer, steam, stir-fry, stew, toast. *—See also* DISTORT.

cook up *v.* *—See* INVENT.

cook *n.* A person who prepares food for eating ▸ baker, chef, culinary artist.

cooking *n.* *—See* FOOD.

cool *adj.* Not friendly, sociable, or warm in manner ▸ aloof, chill, chilly, detached, distant, formal, frigid, frosty, glacial, icy, impersonal, offish, remote, reserved, reticent, solitary, standoffish, unapproachable, uncommunicative, undemonstrative, withdrawn. [*Compare* COLD.] *—See also* CALM, COLD (1), MARVELOUS.

cool *v.* *—See* COMPOSE (4).

cool *n.* *—See* BALANCE (2).

cooler *n.* *—See* JAIL.

cool-headed *adj.* *—See* CALM.

coolness *n.* *—See* APATHY, BALANCE (2), COLD.

coop *n.* *—See* CAGE, JAIL.

coop up *v.* *—See* ENCLOSE (1).

cooperate *v.* To work together toward a common end ▸ collaborate, combine, concert, concur, join, unite. *Idioms:* act in concert, join forces, pull together, team up. [*Compare* ALLY, COMBINE.]

cooperation *n.* Joint work toward a common end ▸ coaction, collaboration, concert, synergy, teamwork. [*Compare* AGREEMENT, ALLIANCE.] *—See also* ASSOCIATION (1).

cooperative *adj.* Working together toward a common end ▸ coactive, collaborative, collective, combined, concerted, group, joint, synergetic, synergic, synergistic, united. *—See also* COMMON (2).

coordinate *v.* *—See* CLASSIFY, HARMONIZE (1), HARMONIZE (2).

cop *n.* *—See* POLICE OFFICER.

cop *v.* *—See* CAPTURE, STEAL.

cop out *v.* *—See* RENEGE.

copartner *n.* *—See* ASSOCIATE (1).

co·pay·ment (kō′pā′mənt) ▸ *n.* A fixed fee paid by members of a medical plan to a provider of medical services.
cope[1] (kōp) ▸ *v.* **coped, cop·ing.** To contend with difficulties, esp. successfully.
cope[2] (kōp) ▸ *n.* **1.** A long ecclesiastical capelike vestment. **2.** A coping.
Co·pen·ha·gen (kō′pən-hā′gən, -hä′-) ▸ The capital of Denmark, in the E part.
co·per·ni·ci·um (kō′pər-nē′sē-əm, -shē-) ▸ *n. Symbol* **Cn** A synthetic radioactive element. At. no. 112.
Co·per·ni·cus (kō-pûr′nə-kəs, kə-), **Nicolaus** (1473–1543) ▸ Polish astronomer.
cop·i·er (kŏp′ē-ər) ▸ *n.* One that copies, esp. an office machine that makes copies.
co·pi·lot (kō′pī′lət) ▸ *n.* The second or relief pilot of an aircraft.
cop·ing (kō′pĭng) ▸ *n.* The top layer of a wall, usu. slanted to shed water.
co·pi·ous (kō′pē-əs) ▸ *adj.* Ample; abundant. **—co′pi·ous·ly** *adv.* **—co′pi·ous·ness** *n.*
cop-out (kŏp′out′) ▸ *n. Slang* A failure to fulfill a commitment or responsibility.
cop·per (kŏp′ər) ▸ *n.* **1.** *Symbol* **Cu** A ductile, malleable, reddish-brown metallic element that is an excellent conductor of heat and electricity and is used for electrical wiring, water piping, and corrosion-resistant parts. At. no. 29. **2.** A copper object or coin. **3.** A reddish brown. **—cop′per·y** *adj.*
cop·per·head (kŏp′ər-hĕd′) ▸ *n.* A venomous reddish-brown snake of the E US.
co·pra (kō′prə, kŏp′rə) ▸ *n.* Dried coconut meat from which coconut oil is extracted.
co·proc·es·sor (kō′prŏs′ĕs-ər) ▸ *n.* A microprocessor that performs specialized functions not performed by the central processing unit.
copse (kŏps) ▸ *n.* A thicket of small trees.
Copt (kŏpt) ▸ *n.* **1.** A member or descendant of the people of pre-Islamic Egypt. **2.** A member of the Christian church of Egypt. **—Cop′tic** *adj.*
cop·ter (kŏp′tər) ▸ *n. Informal* A helicopter.
cop·u·la (kŏp′yə-lə) ▸ *n.* A verb, such as a form of *be* or *seem,* that identifies the predicate of a sentence with the subject. **—cop′u·lar** *adj.* **—cop′u·la′tive** *adj. & n.*
cop·u·late (kŏp′yə-lāt′) ▸ *v.* **-lat·ed, -lat·ing.** To engage in coitus or sexual intercourse. **—cop′u·la′tion** *n.*
cop·y (kŏp′ē) ▸ *n., pl.* **-ies. 1.** An imitation or reproduction of an original; duplicate. **2.** One specimen of a printed text or picture. **3.** Material, such as a manuscript, that is to be set in type. **4.** Suitable source material for journalism. ▸ *v.* **-ied, -y·ing. 1.** To make a copy or copies (of). **2.** To follow as a model or pattern; imitate. **—cop′y·a·ble** *adj.*
cop·y·book (kŏp′ē-bo͝ok′) ▸ *n.* A book of models of penmanship for imitation.
cop·y·cat (kŏp′ē-kăt′) ▸ *n. Informal* An imitator. **—cop′y·cat′** *adj.*
copy desk ▸ *n.* The desk in a news office where copy is edited and prepared for typesetting.
cop·y·ed·it or **cop·y-ed·it** (kŏp′ē-ĕd′ĭt) ▸ *v.* To correct and prepare (a manuscript) for typesetting. **—cop′y·ed′i·tor** *n.*
cop·y·right (kŏp′ē-rīt′) ▸ *n.* The legal right to exclusive publication, production, sale, or distribution of a literary or artistic work. ▸ *adj.* also **cop·y·right·ed** (-rī′tĭd) Protected by copyright. ▸ *v.* To secure a copyright for.
cop·y·writ·er (kŏp′ē-rī′tər) ▸ *n.* One who writes copy, esp. for advertising.
co·quette (kō-kĕt′) ▸ *n.* A flirtatious woman. **—co·quet′tish** *adj.* **—co·quet′tish·ness** *n.*
cor·a·cle (kôr′ə-kəl, kŏr′-) ▸ *n.* A boat made of waterproof material stretched over a wicker or wooden frame.
cor·al (kôr′əl, kŏr′-) ▸ *n.* **1a.** Any of a class of marine polyps that secrete a rocklike skeleton. **b.** Such skeletons collectively, often forming reefs or islands in warm seas. **c.** The secretions of certain corals used in jewelry. **2.** A strong pink to red or reddish orange. **—cor′al** *adj.*
coral snake ▸ *n.* A venomous snake having red, yellow, and black banded markings.
cor·bel (kôr′bəl, -bĕl′) ▸ *n.* A usu. stone bracket projecting from the face of a wall and used to support a cornice or arch. **—cor′bel** *v.*
cord (kôrd) ▸ *n.* **1.** A string of twisted strands or fibers. **2.** An insulated, flexible electric wire fitted with a plug. **3.** also **chord** *Anat.* A long ropelike structure: *a spinal cord.* **4a.** A raised rib on the surface of cloth. **b.** A fabric with such ribs. **5.** A unit of quantity for cut fuel wood, equal to a stack measuring 4 × 4 × 8 ft or 128 cu ft (3.62 cu m). ▸ *v.* **1.** To fasten or bind with a cord. **2.** To pile (wood) in cords. **—cord′er** *n.*
cord·age (kôr′dĭj) ▸ *n.* Cords or ropes, esp. the ropes in the rigging of a ship.
cor·dial (kôr′jəl) ▸ *adj.* Warm and sincere; friendly. ▸ *n.* **1.** A stimulant; tonic. **2.** A liqueur. **—cor·dial′i·ty** (-jăl′ĭ-tē, -jē-ăl′-) *n.* **—cor′dial·ly** *adv.*
cor·dil·le·ra (kôr′dl-yâr′ə, kôr-dĭl′ər-ə) ▸ *n.* A mountain chain. **—cor′dil·le′ran** (-yâr′ən) *adj.*
Cor·dil·le·ras (kôr′dĭl-yĕr′əz, -dē-yĕ′räs) ▸ The entire complex of mountain ranges in W North America, Mexico, Central America, and South America, extending from AK to Cape Horn.
cord·ite (kôr′dīt′) ▸ *n.* A smokeless explosive powder consisting of nitrocellulose, nitroglycerin, and petrolatum.
cord·less (kôrd′lĭs) ▸ *adj.* Having no cord; battery operated: *a cordless telephone.*
cor·do·ba (kôr′də-bə, -və) ▸ *n.* See **currency** table in Appendix.
cor·don (kôr′dn) ▸ *n.* **1.** A line of people, military posts, or ships stationed around an area to enclose or guard it. **2.** A ribbon worn as an ornament, badge of honor, or decoration. ▸ *v.* To form a cordon around.
cor·do·van (kôr′də-vən) ▸ *n.* A soft fine-grained leather.
cor·du·roy (kôr′də-roi′) ▸ *n.* **1.** A durable ribbed fabric, usu. made of cotton. **2. corduroys** Corduroy trousers.
core (kôr) ▸ *n.* **1.** The hard or fibrous central part of certain fruits, such as the apple, containing the seeds. **2.** The central or innermost part. **3.** The most important part. **4.** An internal computer memory. **5.** The part of a nuclear reactor where fission occurs. ▸ *v.* **cored, cor·ing.** To remove the core of.
co·re·lig·ion·ist (kō′rĭ-lĭj′ə-nĭst) ▸ *n.* One having the same religion as another.
co·re·spon·dent (kō′rĭ-spŏn′dənt) ▸ *n.* A person charged as an adulterer with the defendant in a divorce suit.
co·ri·an·der (kôr′ē-ăn′dər) ▸ *n.* **1.** An aromatic Eurasian herb having seedlike fruit used as a seasoning. **2.** The leafy plantlets of this herb, used in salads and as a flavoring; cilantro.

THESAURUS

cope with *v.* ▸ deal with, handle, treat.
copious *adj.* —*See* GENEROUS (2).
coplanar *adj.* —*See* EVEN (2).
copper *n.* —*See* POLICE OFFICER.
copy *n.* 1. Something closely resembling another ▸ carbon copy, counterpart, ditto, duplicate, facsimile, image, likeness, mirror, photocopy, reduplication, replica, replication, reproduction, simulacrum. [*Compare* DOUBLE, PARALLEL.] 2. An inferior substitute imitating an original ▸ ersatz, imitation, pinchbeck, reprint, simulation. *Informal:* knock-off. [*Compare* COUNTERFEIT.]
copy *v.* To make a copy of ▸ clone, ditto, duplicate, imitate, photocopy, replicate, reprint, reproduce, simulate. *Informal:* knock off. [*Compare* COUNTERFEIT, IMITATE, PLAGIARIZE.] —*See also* FOLLOW (5).
copycat *n.* —*See* MIMIC.
coquet *v.* —*See* FLIRT (2).
coquetry *n.* ▸ dalliance, flirtation.
coquette *n.* A woman who is given to flirting ▸ flirt, tease. *Informal:* vamp. [*Compare* SEDUCTRESS.]
coquettish *adj.* ▸ coy, flirtatious, flirty.
cord *n.* A band or fiber used to bind, tie, connect, or support ▸ bond, cable, chain, cordage, fetter, guy, lace, lacing, line, noose, rope, string, thong. [*Compare* BAND[1], FASTENER, THREAD.]
cordage *n.* —*See* CORD.
cordial *adj.* —*See* AMIABLE.
cordiality or **cordialness** *n.* —*See* AMIABILITY.
cordon *v.* —*See* ENCLOSE (1).
core *n.* —*See* CENTER (3), HEART (1).

Cor·inth (kôr′ĭnth, kŏr′-) ► A city of ancient Greece in the NE Peloponnesus on the Gulf of Corinth.

Co·rin·thi·an (kə-rĭn′thē-ən) ► *adj.* Of or relating to ancient Corinth. ► *n.* **1.** A native or inhabitant of Corinth. **2. Corinthians** *(takes sing. v.)* See **Bible** table in Appendix.

Corinthian order ► *n. Archit.* A classical order marked by slender fluted columns with ornate capitals.

co·ri·um (kôr′ē-əm) ► *n., pl.* **-ri·a** (-ē-ə) *Anat.* See **dermis.**

cork (kôrk) ► *n.* **1.** The lightweight, porous, elastic outer bark of a Mediterranean tree, used for stoppers, insulation, and floats. **2.** Something made of cork, esp. a bottle stopper. **3.** *Bot.* The outermost layer of the bark in woody plants. **—cork** *v.* **—cork′y** *adj.*

cork·er (kôr′kər) ► *n. Slang* One that is remarkable or astounding.

cork·screw (kôrk′skro͞o′) ► *n.* A device for drawing corks from bottles. ► *adj.* Spiral in shape: *a corkscrew turn.*

corm (kôrm) ► *n.* A rounded food-storing underground stem similar to a bulb.

cor·mo·rant (kôr′mər-ənt, -mə-rănt′) ► *n.* A diving bird having dark plumage, webbed feet, and a hooked bill.

corn[1] (kôrn) ► *n.* **1a.** A tall, widely cultivated cereal plant bearing grains or kernels on large ears. **b.** The edible grains or kernels of this plant. **2.** A single grain of various cereal plants. **3.** *Slang* Something trite or overly sentimental. ► *v.* To preserve in brine.

corn[2] (kôrn) ► *n.* A horny thickening of the skin, usu. on or near a toe, resulting from pressure or friction.

corn·ball (kôrn′bôl′) ► *adj. Slang* Mawkish; corny: *cornball humor.*

corn bread or **corn·bread** (kôrn′brĕd′) ► *n.* Bread made from cornmeal.

corn·cob (kôrn′kŏb′) ► *n.* The woody core of an ear of corn.

corn·crib (kôrn′krĭb′) ► *n.* A ventilated structure for storing and drying ears of corn.

cor·ne·a (kôr′nē-ə) ► *n.* The tough transparent membrane of the eyeball, covering the iris and the pupil. **—cor′ne·al** *adj.*

cor·ner (kôr′nər) ► *n.* **1a.** The position at which two lines, surfaces, or edges meet and form an angle. **b.** The area enclosed or bounded by such an angle. **2.** The place where two roads or streets meet. **3.** A position from which escape is difficult. **4.** A remote or secret place. **5.** A speculative monopoly of a stock or commodity created by controlling the available supply so as to raise its price. ► *v.* **1.** To place or drive into a corner. **2.** To form a corner in (a stock or commodity). **3.** To turn, as at a corner.

cor·ner·stone (kôr′nər-stōn′) ► *n.* **1.** A stone at the corner of a building uniting two intersecting walls, esp. one laid with a special ceremony. **2.** A fundamental basis.

cor·net (kôr-nĕt′) ► *n.* A three-valved brass wind instrument resembling a trumpet. **—cor·net′ist** *n.*

corn·flow·er (kôrn′flou′ər) ► *n.* An annual plant having showy blue, purple, pink, or white flowers; bachelor's button.

cor·nice (kôr′nĭs) ► *n.* A horizontal molded projection that crowns or completes a building or wall.

Cor·nish (kôr′nĭsh) ► *adj.* Of or relating to Cornwall or the Cornish language. ► *n.* The extinct Celtic language of Cornwall.

corn·meal (kôrn′mēl′) ► *n.* Coarse meal made from corn.

corn·pone or **corn pone** (kôrn′pōn′) ► *n. Regional* See **johnnycake.**

corn·row (kôrn′rō′) ► *n.* A portion of hair braided close to the scalp to form a row with others. **—corn′row′** *v.*

corn·stalk (kôrn′stôk′) ► *n.* The stalk or stem of a corn plant.

corn·starch (kôrn′stärch′) ► *n.* Starch prepared from corn grains, used industrially and as a thickener in cooking.

corn syrup ► *n.* A syrup that is prepared from cornstarch and is used esp. as a sweetener.

cor·nu·co·pi·a (kôr′nə-kō′pē-ə, -nyə-) ► *n.* **1.** A cone-shaped container overflowing with fruit, flowers, and grain; horn of plenty. **2.** An abundance.

Corn·wall (kôrn′wôl′) ► A region of extreme SW England on a peninsula bounded by the Atlantic Ocean and English Channel.

corn·y (kôr′nē) ► *adj.* **-i·er, -i·est.** Trite, dated, or mawkish. **—corn′i·ness** *n.*

co·rol·la (kə-rŏl′ə, -rō′lə) ► *n.* The petals of a flower considered as a unit.

cor·ol·lar·y (kôr′ə-lĕr′ē, kŏr′-) ► *n., pl.* **-ies.** **1.** A proposition that follows with little or no proof required from one already proven. **2.** A natural consequence or effect; result.

co·ro·na (kə-rō′nə) ► *n., pl.* **-nas** or **-nae** (-nē). **1.** A ring of diffracted light visible esp. around the sun or moon during hazy conditions. **2.** The luminous outer atmosphere of the sun.

Co·ro·na·do (kôr′ə-nä′dō), **Francisco Vásquez de** (1510–54) ► Spanish explorer.

cor·o·nar·y (kôr′ə-nĕr′ē, kŏr′-) ► *adj.* **1.** Of or relating to either of two arteries that originate in the aorta and supply blood directly to the heart tissues. **2.** Relating to the heart. ► *n., pl.* **-ies.** A coronary thrombosis.

coronary thrombosis ► *n.* Obstruction of a coronary artery by a blood clot, often leading to destruction of heart muscle.

cor·o·na·tion (kôr′ə-nā′shən, kŏr′-) ► *n.* The act or ceremony of crowning a sovereign.

cor·o·ner (kôr′ə-nər, kŏr′-) ► *n.* A public officer who investigates any death thought to be of other than natural causes.

cor·o·net (kôr′ə-nĕt′, kŏr′-) ► *n.* **1.** A small crown worn by nobles below the rank of sovereign. **2.** A jeweled headband.

cor·po·ra (kôr′pər-ə) ► *n.* Pl. of **corpus.**

cor·po·ral[1] (kôr′pər-əl, kôr′prəl) ► *adj.* Of the body; bodily. **—cor′po·ral′i·ty** (-pə-răl′ĭ-tē) *n.* **—cor′po·ral·ly** *adv.*

cor·po·ral[2] (kôr′pər-əl, kôr′prəl) ► *n.* The lowest noncommissioned rank, as in the US Army or Marine Corps.

cor·po·rate (kôr′pər-ĭt, kôr′prĭt) ► *adj.* **1.** Formed into a corporation; incorporated. **2.** Of a corporation. **3.** United or combined into one body; collective. **—cor′po·rate·ly** *adv.*

cor·po·ra·tion (kôr′pə-rā′shən) ► *n.* **1.** A body of persons acting under a legal charter as a separate entity having its own rights, privileges, and liabilities. **2.** Such a body created for purposes of government.

cor·po·re·al (kôr-pôr′ē-əl) ► *adj.* **1.** Of the body. **2.** Of a material nature; tangible. **—cor·po′re·al′i·ty** (-ăl′ĭ-tē) *n.* **—cor·po′re·al·ly** *adv.*

corps (kôr) ► *n., pl.* **corps** (kôrz). **1.** A specialized branch or department of the armed forces. **2.** A body of persons under common direction.

corpse (kôrps) ► *n.* A dead body, esp. of a human.

corps·man (kôr′mən, kôrz′mən) ► *n.* An enlisted person in the armed forces trained in first aid.

cor·pu·lence (kôr′pyə-ləns) ► *n.* Excessive fatness; obesity. **—cor′pu·lent** *adj.*

cor·pus (kôr′pəs) ► *n., pl.* **-po·ra** (-pər-ə). **1.** A large collection of specialized writings. **2.** *Anat.* The main part of a bodily structure or organ.

cor·pus·cle (kôr′pə-səl, -pŭs′əl) ► *n.* **1.** An unattached or free-moving body cell, such as a blood or lymph cell. **2.** A minute globular particle. **—cor·pus′cu·lar** (kôr-pŭs′kyə-lər) *adj.*

corpus de·lic·ti (dĭ-lĭk′tī′) ► *n.* **1.** *Law* The material evidence showing that a crime has been committed. **2.** A corpse, esp. of a murder victim.

cor·ral (kə-răl′) ► *n.* An enclosure for confining livestock. ► *v.* **-ralled, -ral·ling.** **1.** To drive into and hold in a corral. **2.** To seize or procure.

cor·rect (kə-rĕkt′) ► *v.* **1a.** To remove errors from. **b.** To

THESAURUS

cork *n.* —*See* PLUG.
cork *v.* —*See* FILL (2).
corkscrew *v.* —*See* WIND².
corner *n.* Exclusive control or possession ► monopoly. [*Compare* DOMINATION.] —*See also* PREDICAMENT.
cornerstone *n.* —*See* BASE¹ (2), BASIS (1).
cornucopia *n.* —*See* PLENTY.
corny *adj.* —*See* SENTIMENTAL, TRITE.
corollary *n.* —*See* EFFECT (1).
corporal *adj.* —*See* BODILY.
corporation *n.* —*See* COMPANY (1).
corporeal *adj.* —*See* BODILY, PHYSICAL.
corporeality *n.* —*See* TANGIBILITY.
corps *n.* —*See* BAND², DETACHMENT (3), FORCE (3).
corpse *n.* —*See* BODY (2).
corpulent *adj.* —*See* FAT (1).
corpus *n.* —*See* QUANTITY (3).
corral *v.* —*See* ENCLOSE (1).
corral *n.* —*See* PEN².
correct *v.* **1.** To make right what is wrong ► amend, emend, fix, mend, rectify, redress, reform, remedy, repair,

mark the errors in. **2.** To punish for the purpose of improving. **3.** To remedy or counteract: *correct a malfunction.* ▸ *adj.* **1.** True; accurate. **2.** Conforming to standards; proper. **—cor·rect′a·ble, cor·rect′i·ble** *adj.* **—cor·rec′tive** *adj. & n.* **—cor·rect′ly** *adv.* **—cor·rect′ness** *n.*

cor·rec·tion (kə-rĕk′shən) ▸ *n.* **1.** The act or process of correcting. **2.** Something offered or substituted for a mistake or fault. **3.** Punishment intended to improve. **4.** A quantity added or subtracted in order to correct. **—cor·rec′tion·al** *adj.*

cor·re·la·tion (kôr′ə-lā′shən, kŏr′-) ▸ *n.* A complementary, parallel, or reciprocal relationship: *a correlation between drug abuse and crime.* **—cor′re·late′** *v. & adj.* **—cor′re·la′tion·al** *adj.*

cor·rel·a·tive (kə-rĕl′ə-tĭv) ▸ *adj.* **1.** Related; corresponding. **2.** *Gram.* Reciprocally related, as the conjunctions *neither* and *nor.* ▸ *n.* **1.** Either of two correlative entities. **2.** *Gram.* A correlative word or expression. **—cor·rel′a·tive·ly** *adv.*

cor·re·spond (kôr′ĭ-spŏnd′, kŏr′-) ▸ *v.* **1.** To be in agreement, harmony, or conformity. **2.** To be similar, parallel, or equivalent, as in nature or function. **3.** To communicate by letter. **—cor′re·spond′ing·ly** *adv.*

cor·re·spon·dence (kôr′ĭ-spŏn′dəns, kŏr′-) ▸ *n.* **1.** The act, fact, or state of agreeing or conforming. **2.** Similarity or analogy. **3a.** Communication by the exchange of letters. **b.** The letters written or received.

cor·re·spon·dent (kôr′ĭ-spŏn′dənt, kŏr′-) ▸ *n.* **1.** One who communicates by letter. **2.** One employed by the media to supply news, esp. from a distant place. **3.** Something that corresponds; correlative. ▸ *adj.* Corresponding.

cor·ri·dor (kôr′ĭ-dər, kŏr′-) ▸ *n.* **1.** A narrow hallway or passageway, often with rooms opening onto it. **2.** A narrow tract of land, esp. through another country. **3.** A thickly populated strip of land connecting urban areas.

cor·ri·gen·dum (kôr′ə-jĕn′dəm, kŏr′-) ▸ *n., pl.* **-da** (-də). **1.** An error to be corrected. **2. corrigenda** A list of errors in a book along with their corrections.

cor·rob·o·rate (kə-rŏb′ə-rāt′) ▸ *v.* **-rat·ed, -rat·ing.** To strengthen or support (other evidence). **—cor·rob′o·ra′tion** *n.* **—cor·rob′o·ra′tive** (-ə-rā′tĭv, -ər-ə-tĭv) *adj.* **—cor·rob′o·ra′tor** *n.*

cor·rode (kə-rōd′) ▸ *v.* **-rod·ed, -rod·ing.** To wear away gradually, esp. by chemical action. **—cor·rod′i·ble, cor·ro′si·ble** (-rō′sə-bəl) *adj.* **—cor·ro′sion** *n.* **—cor·ro′sive** *adj. & n.* **—cor·ro′sive·ness** *n.*

cor·ru·gate (kôr′ə-gāt′, kŏr′-) ▸ *v.* **-gat·ed, -gat·ing.** To make folds or parallel and alternating ridges and grooves (in). **—cor′ru·ga′tion** *n.*

cor·rupt (kə-rŭpt′) ▸ *adj.* **1.** Marked by immorality; depraved. **2.** Open to bribery; dishonest: *a corrupt mayor.* **3.** *Archaic* Tainted; putrid. ▸ *v.* **1.** To make or become corrupt. **2.** To damage (data) in a file or on a disk. **—cor·rupt′er, cor·rup′tor** *n.* **—cor·rupt′i·ble** *adj.* **—cor·rup′tion** *n.* **—cor·rupt′ly** *adv.* **—cor·rupt′ness** *n.*

cor·sage (kôr-säzh′, -säj′) ▸ *n.* A small bouquet worn usu. at the shoulder.

cor·sair (kôr′sâr′) ▸ *n.* **1.** A pirate. **2.** A swift pirate ship.

cor·set (kôr′sĭt) ▸ *n.* A close-fitting undergarment, often reinforced by stays, worn esp. to shape the waist and hips.

Cor·si·ca (kôr′sĭ-kə) ▸ An island of France in the Mediterranean Sea north of Sardinia. **—Cor′si·can** *adj. & n.*

cor·tege (kôr-tĕzh′) ▸ *n.* **1.** A train of attendants. **2.** A ceremonial procession, esp. for a funeral.

Cor·tés (kôr-tĕz′, -tĕs′), **Hernando** (1485–1547) ▸ Spanish explorer and conquistador.

cor·tex (kôr′tĕks′) ▸ *n., pl.* **-ti·ces** (-tĭ-sēz′) or **-tex·es. 1a.** The outer layer of a bodily organ. **b.** The layer of gray matter covering most of the brain. **2.** The region of tissue in a root or stem surrounding the vascular tissue. **—cor′ti·cal** *adj.*

cor·ti·co·ste·roid (kôr′tĭ-kō-stîr′oid′, -stĕr′-) ▸ *n.* Any of the steroid hormones produced by the adrenal cortex or their synthetic equivalents.

cor·ti·sone (kôr′tĭ-sōn′, -zōn′) ▸ *n.* A corticosteroid active in carbohydrate metabolism and used esp. to treat rheumatoid arthritis.

co·run·dum (kə-rŭn′dəm) ▸ *n.* An extremely hard mineral, aluminum oxide, occurring in gem varieties and in a common form used chiefly in abrasives.

cor·us·cate (kôr′ə-skāt′, kŏr′-) ▸ *v.* **-cat·ed, -cat·ing.** To sparkle and glitter. **—cor′us·ca′tion** *n.*

cor·vette (kôr-vĕt′) ▸ *n.* **1.** A fast, lightly armed warship, smaller than a destroyer. **2.** An obsolete sailing warship, smaller than a frigate.

cor·ymb (kôr′ĭmb, -ĭm, kŏr′-) ▸ *n.* A usu. flat-topped flower cluster.

co·ry·za (kə-rī′zə) ▸ *n.* See **cold** 3.

cos ▸ *abbr.* cosine

co·se·cant (kō-sē′kănt′, -kənt) ▸ *n.* The reciprocal of the sine of an angle.

co·sign (kō-sīn′) ▸ *v.* **1.** To sign (a document) jointly. **2.** To

THESAURUS

revise, right, straighten (up *or* out). *Idioms:* put right (*or* to rights), set right (*or* to rights). [*Compare* CURE, FIX.] **2.** To castigate for the purpose of improving ▸ chasten, chide. [*Compare* CHASTISE.] —*See also* PUNISH.

correct *adj.* —*See* ACCURATE, APPROPRIATE.

correction *n.* —*See* PUNISHMENT.

correctional *adj.* —*See* PUNISHING.

corrective *adj.* Tending or intended to correct ▸ amendatory, emendatory, reformative, reformatory, remedial, reparative, reparatory. [*Compare* CURATIVE.]

corrective *n.* —*See* CURE.

correctly *adv.* —*See* FAIR[1].

correctness *n.* —*See* ACCURACY, DECENCY (2), VERACITY.

correlate *v.* —*See* ASSOCIATE (3), HAR[illegible].

correlate *n.* —*See* PARALLEL.

correlation *n.* —*See* RELATION (1).

correlative *n.* —*See* PARALLEL.

correlative *adj.* —*See* COMPLEMENTARY.

correspond *v.* —*See* AGREE (1), EQUAL (1).

correspondence *n.* A situation allowing exchange of ideas or messages ▸ communication, contact, intercommunication, touch. —*See also* AGREEMENT (2), COMMUNICATION (1), LETTER, LIKENESS (1).

correspondent *n.* —*See* PARALLEL, PRESS.

correspondent *adj.* —*See* AGREEABLE.

corresponding *adj.* —*See* AGREEABLE, LIKE[2], PROPORTIONAL (1).

corrival *n.* —*See* COMPETITOR.

corrivalry *n.* —*See* COMPETITION (1).

corroborate *v.* —*See* BACK (2), CONFIRM (1), PROVE.

corroboration *n.* —*See* CONFIRMATION (2).

corrode *v.* —*See* BLAST (2), ERODE.

corrosive *adj.* —*See* BITING, HARMFUL.

corrosiveness *n.* —*See* SARCASM.

corrugate *v.* —*See* [illegible] (1).

corrupt *v.* To ruin morally ▸ animalize, bastardize, bestialize, brutalize, canker, contaminate, debase, debauch, defile, demoralize, deprave, infect, pervert, poison, pollute, soil, stain, suborn, subvert, taint, vitiate, warp. [*Compare* DAMAGE, DEBASE.] —*See also* BLAST (2), BRIBE, CONTAMINATE, DECAY.

corrupt *adj.* **1.** Utterly reprehensible in nature or behavior ▸ debased, degenerate, depraved, miscreant, perverse, perverted, rotten, unhealthy, villainous. [*Compare* DISGRACEFUL, EVIL, OFFENSIVE, SORDID.] **2.** Open to bribery or dishonesty ▸ bribable, dishonest, dishonorable, mercenary, praetorian, profiteering, venal. *Informal:* crooked. *Idioms:* on the pad, on the take. [*Compare* UNDERHAND, UNSCRUPULOUS.] —*See also* ERRONEOUS.

corruption *n.* **1.** Degrading, immoral acts or habits ▸ bestiality, criminality, debauchery, depravity, flagitiousness, immorality, impurity, perversion, rottenness, turpitude, vice, villainousness, villainy, wickedness. [*Compare* CHEAT, CRIME.] **2.** Departure from what is legally, ethically, and morally correct ▸ baseness, corruptness, depravity, dishonesty, improbity, jobbery, malfeasance, venality. *Informal:* crookedness. [*Compare* DISOBEDIENCE, EVIL.] **3.** A misused or incorrect term ▸ barbarism, catachresis, impropriety, malapropism, misusage, solecism. —*See also* CONTAMINATION.

corruptive *adj.* —*See* HARMFUL, UNWHOLESOME (2).

corruptness *n.* —*See* CORRUPTION (2).

corsage *n.* —*See* BOUQUET.

coruscate *v.* —*See* GLITTER.

coruscation *n.* —*See* FLASH (1).

endorse (another's signature), as for a loan. **—co·sign′er** *n.*

co·sig·na·to·ry (kō-sĭg′nə-tôr′ē) ▸ *adj.* Signed jointly. ▸ *n., pl.* **-ries.** A cosigner.

co·sine (kō′sīn′) ▸ *n.* In a right triangle, the ratio of the length of the side adjacent to an acute angle to the length of the hypotenuse.

cos·met·ic (kŏz-mĕt′ĭk) ▸ *adj.* **1.** Serving to beautify the body. **2.** Serving to improve the appearance of a physical feature. **3.** Lacking significance; superficial. ▸ *n.* A cosmetic preparation. **—cos·met′i·cal·ly** *adv.*

cos·me·tol·o·gy (kŏz′mĭ-tŏl′ə-jē) ▸ *n.* The study or art of cosmetics and their use. **—cos′me·tol′o·gist** *n.*

cos·mic (kŏz′mĭk) ▸ *adj.* **1.** Relating to the universe, esp. as distinct from Earth. **2.** Limitless; vast. **—cos′mi·cal·ly** *adv.*

cosmic ray ▸ *n.* A stream of ionizing radiation, consisting chiefly of protons, alpha particles, and other atomic nuclei but including some high-energy electrons, that enters the atmosphere from outer space.

cosmo– or **cosm–** ▸ *pref.* Universe; world: *cosmology.*

cos·mo·chem·is·try (kŏz′mō-kĕm′ĭ-strē) ▸ *n.* The science of the chemical composition of the universe. **—cos′mo·chem′i·cal** *adj.*

cos·mog·o·ny (kŏz-mŏg′ə-nē) ▸ *n.* The study of the origin and evolution of the universe. **—cos·mog′o·nist** *n.*

cos·mog·ra·phy (kŏz-mŏg′rə-fē) ▸ *n., pl.* **-phies. 1.** The study of the visible universe. **2.** A description of the world or universe. **—cos·mog′ra·pher** *n.*

cos·mol·o·gy (kŏz-mŏl′ə-jē) ▸ *n., pl.* **-gies. 1.** The study of the physical universe as a totality of phenomena in time and space. **2.** The astrophysical study of the history, structure, and constituent dynamics of the universe. **—cos′mo·log′ic** (-mə-lŏj′ĭk), **cos′mo·log′i·cal** *adj.* **—cos·mol′o·gist** *n.*

cos·mo·naut (kŏz′mə-nôt′) ▸ *n.* A Soviet astronaut.

cos·mo·pol·i·tan (kŏz′mə-pŏl′ĭ-tn) ▸ *adj.* **1.** Common to the whole world. **2.** Of the entire world or from many different parts of the world. **3.** At home in all parts of the world or in many spheres of interest. ▸ *n.* A cosmopolitan person.

cos·mop·o·lite (kŏz-mŏp′ə-līt′) ▸ *n.* A cosmopolitan person.

cos·mos (kŏz′məs, -mŏs′, -mōs′) ▸ *n.* **1.** The universe regarded as an orderly harmonious whole. **2.** Any system regarded as ordered, harmonious, and whole. **3.** A garden annual with daisylike flowers.

co·spon·sor (kō-spŏn′sər) ▸ *n.* A joint sponsor, as of legislation. **—co·spon′sor** *v.* **—co·spon′sor·ship′** *n.*

Cos·sack (kŏs′ăk) ▸ *n.* A member of a people of S European Russia, noted as cavalrymen esp. during czarist times. **—Cos′sack′** *adj.*

cost (kôst) ▸ *n.* **1.** An amount paid or required in payment for a purchase. **2.** A loss, sacrifice, or penalty. **3. costs** *Law* The charges fixed for litigation. ▸ *v.* **cost, cost·ing.** To require a specified payment, expenditure, effort, or loss.

co·star also **co-star** (kō′stär′) ▸ *n.* A starring actor or actress given equal status with another or others in a play or film. **—co′star′** *v.*

Cos·ta Ri·ca (kŏs′tə rē′kə, kô′stə, kō′-) ▸ A country of Central America between Panama and Nicaragua. **—Cos′ta Ri′can** (-kən) *adj. & n.*

cost·ly (kôst′lē) ▸ *adj.* **-li·er, -li·est. 1.** Of high price or value; expensive. **2.** Entailing great loss or sacrifice. **—cost′li·ness** *n.*

cost of living ▸ *n.* **1.** The average cost of the necessities of life, such as food, shelter, and clothing. **2.** The cost of necessities as defined by an accepted standard.

cost-of-liv·ing adjustment (kôst′əv-lĭv′ĭng) ▸ *n.* An adjustment made in wages that corresponds with a change in the cost of living.

cost-of-living index ▸ *n.* See **consumer price index.**

cost-plus (kôst′plŭs′) ▸ *n.* The cost of production plus a fixed rate of profit.

cos·tume (kŏs′to͞om′, -tyo͞om′) ▸ *n.* **1.** A style of dress characteristic of a particular country or period. **2.** A set of clothes for a particular occasion or season. **3.** An outfit worn by one playing a part. **—cos′tum·er** *n.*

co·sy (kō′zē) ▸ *adj. & v. & n.* Var. of **cozy.**

cot[1] (kŏt) ▸ *n.* A narrow bed, esp. a collapsible one.

cot[2] ▸ *abbr.* cotangent

co·tan·gent (kō-tăn′jənt) ▸ *n.* The reciprocal of the tangent of an angle.

cote (kōt) ▸ *n.* A small shed or shelter for sheep or birds.

Côte d'I·voire (kōt′ dē-vwär′) also **Ivory Coast** ▸ A country of W Africa on the Gulf of Guinea. **—I·vo′ri·an** (ī-vôr′ē-ən) *adj. & n.*

co·ter·ie (kō′tə-rē, kō′tə-rē′) ▸ *n.* A close circle of friends or associates.

co·ter·mi·nous (kō-tûr′mə-nəs) ▸ *adj.* Var. of **conterminous.**

co·til·lion (kō-tĭl′yən, kə-) ▸ *n.* **1.** A formal debutante ball. **2.** A lively group dance.

cot·tage (kŏt′ĭj) ▸ *n.* **1.** A small house, esp. in the country. **2.** A small vacation house. **—cot′tag·er** *n.*

cottage cheese ▸ *n.* A soft mild white cheese made of strained curds of skim milk.

cot·ter (kŏt′ər) ▸ *n.* A bolt or pin inserted through a slot to hold parts together.

cotter pin ▸ *n.* A split cotter inserted through holes in two or more pieces and bent at the ends to fasten the pieces together.

cot·ton (kŏt′n) ▸ *n.* **1a.** Any of various shrubby plants grown for the soft, white, downy fibers surrounding oil-rich seeds. **b.** The fiber of any of these plants, used esp. in making textiles. **2.** Thread or cloth made from cotton fiber. ▸ *v. Informal* To take a liking; become friendly.

cotton candy ▸ *n.* A candy of threaded sugar, often tinted and twirled onto a stick.

cotton gin ▸ *n.* A machine that separates the seeds and seed hulls from cotton fibers.

cot·ton·mouth (kŏt′n-mouth′) ▸ *n.* See **water moccasin.**

cot·ton·seed (kŏt′n-sēd′) ▸ *n.* The seed of the cotton plant, used as a source of oil and meal.

cot·ton·tail (kŏt′n-tāl′) ▸ *n.* A New World rabbit having a tail with a white underside.

cot·ton·wood (kŏt′n-wo͝od′) ▸ *n.* A North American poplar having triangular leaves and seeds with a tuft of cottony hairs.

cot·y·le·don (kŏt′l-ēd′n) ▸ *n.* An embryonic plant leaf, the first to appear from a sprouting seed. **—cot′y·le′do·nous** *adj.*

couch (kouch) ▸ *n.* A sofa. ▸ *v.* To word in a certain manner; phrase.

cou·gar (ko͞o′gər) ▸ *n.* See **mountain lion.**

cough (kôf, kŏf) ▸ *v.* **1.** To expel air from the lungs suddenly and noisily. **2.** To expel by coughing. **—cough** *n.*

could (ko͝od) ▸ *aux.v.* P.t. of **can**[1]. **1.** Used to indicate ability, possibility, or permission in the past. **2.** Used to indicate condition or politeness: *If we could help, we would.*

could·n't (ko͝od′nt) ▸ Could not.

cou·lee (ko͞o′lē) ▸ *n.* A deep ravine, esp. in the W US.

cou·lomb (ko͞o′lŏm′, -lōm′) ▸ *n.* A unit of electric charge

THESAURUS

cosmic *adj.* —*See* HEAVENLY (2), UNIVERSAL (1).

cosmopolitan *adj.* Experienced in the ways of the world; lacking natural simplicity ▸ sophisticated, worldly, worldly-wise. [*Compare* EXPERIENCED, SHREWD, SUAVE.] —*See also* UNIVERSAL (1).

cosmos *n.* —*See* UNIVERSE.

cosset *v.* —*See* BABY.

cost *n.* **1.** An amount paid or to be paid for a purchase ▸ charge, disbursement, expenditure, expense, outlay, payment, price. *Informal:* tab. [*Compare* TOLL[1], WAGE.] **2.** The expenditure at which something is obtained ▸ expense, price, sacrifice, toll. *Informal:* damage.

cost *v.* To require a specified price ▸ go for, sell for. ***Idiom:*** set someone back. [*Compare* BRING, DEMAND.]

costive *adj.* —*See* STINGY.

costly *adj.* Of great value or price ▸ dear, expensive, high, high-priced, inestimable, invaluable, precious, priceless, rich, valuable, worthy. *Informal:* big-ticket, pricey. *Idioms:* beyond price, of great price, worth its weight in gold. [*Compare* STEEP[1].]

costs *n.* —*See* OVERHEAD.

costume *n.* —*See* DISGUISE, DRESS (2).

costume *v.* —*See* DRESS (1).

cote *n.* —*See* CAGE.

coterie *n.* —*See* CIRCLE (3).

cotillion *n.* —*See* DANCE.

cottage *n.* —*See* VILLA.

cotton *v.* —*See* RELATE (2).

couch *v.* —*See* LIE[1] (1), PHRASE.

equal to the quantity of charge in approx. 6×10^{18} electrons.

coun·cil (koun′səl) ▸ *n.* **1.** An assembly of persons called together for deliberation or discussion. **2.** An administrative, legislative, or advisory body. **—coun′cil·man** *n.* **—coun′cil·wom′an** *n.*

coun·cil·or also **coun·cil·lor** (koun′sə-lər, -slər) ▸ *n.* A member of a council.

coun·sel (koun′səl) ▸ *n.* **1.** The act of exchanging opinions and ideas; consultation. **2.** Advice or guidance. **3.** A plan of action. **4.** Private thoughts or opinions: *keep one's own counsel.* **5.** A lawyer or group of lawyers. ▸ *v.* **-seled, -sel·ing** or **-selled, -sel·ling. 1.** To give counsel (to). **2.** To recommend: *counseled caution.*

coun·sel·or also **coun·sel·lor** (koun′sə-lər, -slər) ▸ *n.* **1.** An adviser. **2.** An attorney, esp. a trial lawyer. **3.** One who supervises at a summer camp. **—coun′se·lor·ship′** *n.*

count[1] (kount) ▸ *v.* **1.** To name or list one by one in order to determine a total. **2.** To recite numerals in ascending order. **3.** To include in a reckoning: *ten dogs, counting the puppies.* **4.** To believe or consider to be. **5.** To merit consideration. **6.** To have a specified importance or value: *count for little; counts for two points.* ***—phrasal verb:* count on** To rely on; depend on. ▸ *n.* **1.** The act of counting. **2.** A number reached by counting. **3.** *Law* Any of the charges in an indictment. **—count′a·ble** *adj.*

count[2] (kount) ▸ *n.* A nobleman in some European countries.

count·down (kount′doun′) ▸ *n.* The counting backward to indicate the time remaining before an event or operation, such as the launching of a missile or space vehicle.

coun·te·nance (koun′tə-nəns) ▸ *n.* **1.** Appearance, esp. the expression of the face. **2.** The face. **3.** Support or approval. ▸ *v.* **-nanced, -nanc·ing.** To approve or sanction. **—coun′te·nanc·er** *n.*

coun·ter[1] (koun′tər) ▸ *adj.* Contrary; opposing. ▸ *n.* One that is counter; opposite. ▸ *v.* To move or act in opposition (to). ▸ *adv.* In a contrary manner or direction.

count·er[2] (koun′tər) ▸ *n.* **1.** A flat surface on which money is counted, business is transacted, or food is prepared or served. **2.** A piece, as of wood or ivory, used for keeping a count or a place in games.

count·er[3] (koun′tər) ▸ *n.* One that counts, esp. an electronic or mechanical device that automatically counts occurrences or repetitions of phenomena or events.

counter– ▸ *pref.* **1.** Contrary; opposing: *counteract.* **2.** Reciprocation: *countersign.*

coun·ter·act (koun′tər-ăkt′) ▸ *v.* To oppose and lessen the effects of by contrary action; check. **—coun′ter·ac′tion** *n.*

coun·ter·at·tack (koun′tər-ə-tăk′) ▸ *n.* A return attack. **—coun′ter·at·tack′** *v.*

coun·ter·bal·ance (koun′tər-băl′əns) ▸ *n.* **1.** A force or influence equally counteracting another. **2.** A weight that acts to balance another. **—coun′ter·bal′ance** *v.*

coun·ter·charge (koun′tər-chärj′) ▸ *n.* A charge in opposition to another charge. **—coun′ter·charge′** *v.*

coun·ter·claim (koun′tər-klām′) ▸ *n.* A claim filed in opposition to another claim. **—coun′ter·claim′** *v.* **—coun′ter·claim′ant** *n.*

coun·ter·clock·wise (koun′tər-klŏk′wīz′) ▸ *adv. & adj.* In a direction opposite to the rotating hands of a clock.

coun·ter·cul·ture (koun′tər-kŭl′chər) ▸ *n.* A culture, esp. of young people, with antiestablishment values or lifestyles.

coun·ter·es·pi·o·nage (koun′tər-ĕs′pē-ə-näzh′, -nĭj) ▸ *n.* Espionage undertaken to detect and counteract enemy espionage.

coun·ter·feit (koun′tər-fĭt′) ▸ *v.* **1.** To make a copy of, usu. with intent to defraud; forge. **2.** To pretend; feign. ▸ *adj.* **1.** Made in imitation of what is genuine, usu. with intent to defraud. **2.** Simulated; feigned. ▸ *n.* A fraudulent imitation. **—coun′ter·feit′er** *n.*

coun·ter·in·sur·gen·cy (koun′tər-ĭn-sûr′jən-sē) ▸ *n.* Political and military action undertaken to suppress insurgency. **—coun′ter·in·sur′gent** *n.*

coun·ter·in·tel·li·gence (koun′tər-ĭn-tĕl′ə-jəns) ▸ *n.* The branch of an intelligence service charged with keeping sensitive information from an enemy and preventing subversion and sabotage.

coun·ter·in·tu·i·tive (koun′tər-ĭn-to͞o′ĭ-tĭv, -tyo͞o′-) ▸ *adj.* Contrary to what intuition and common sense would indicate.

coun·ter·mand (koun′tər-mănd′) ▸ *v.* **1.** To reverse (an order). **2.** To recall by a contrary order.

coun·ter·meas·ure (koun′tər-mĕzh′ər) ▸ *n.* A measure or action taken to counter or offset another one.

coun·ter·of·fen·sive (koun′tər-ə-fĕn′sĭv) ▸ *n.* A large-scale counterattack by an armed force, intended to stop an enemy offensive.

coun·ter·pane (koun′tər-pān′) ▸ *n.* A cover for a bed; bedspread.

coun·ter·part (koun′tər-pärt′) ▸ *n.* One that closely resembles another, as in function, characteristics, or relation.

coun·ter·plot (koun′tər-plŏt′) ▸ *n.* **1.** A plot or scheme intended to subvert another plot. **2.** See **subplot.** ▸ *v.* To plot against; thwart with a counterplot.

coun·ter·point (koun′tər-point′) ▸ *n.* **1.** *Mus.* The technique of combining two or more melodic lines so that they establish a harmonic relationship while retaining their linear individuality. **2.** A contrasting but parallel element or theme.

coun·ter·poise (koun′tər-poiz′) ▸ *n.* **1.** A counterbalancing weight. **2.** A force or influence that balances or counteracts

THESAURUS

council *n.* *—See* ASSEMBLY, CONVENTION.

counsel *n.* *—See* ADVICE, DELIBERATION (1), LAWYER.

counsel *v.* *—See* ADVISE.

counseling *adj.* *—See* ADVISORY.

counselor *n.* *—See* ADVISER, LAWYER.

count *v.* **1.** To be of significance or importance ▸ import, matter, signify, weigh. **2.** To note items one by one in order to get a total ▸ enumerate, number, numerate, reckon, score, tally, tell. [*Compare* ADD, CALCULATE, MEASURE.] **3.** To indicate time or rhythm ▸ beat, tap. *Idioms:* keep time, mark time.

count off *v.* *—See* ENUMERATE.

count on *v.* *—See* DEPEND ON (1), EXPECT (1).

count out *v.* *—See* EXCLUDE.

count *n.* **1.** A noting of items one by one ▸ enumeration, numeration, reckoning, score, tally. [*Compare* CALCULATION, TOTAL.] **2.** A gathering of information or opinion from a variety of sources or individuals ▸ canvass, poll, survey.

countenance *n.* *—See* EXPRESSION (4), FACE (1), FACE (3).

countenance *v.* **1.** To lend supportive approval to ▸ encourage, favor, smile on (*or* upon). [*Compare* APPROVE, SUPPORT.] **2.** To be favorably disposed toward ▸ approve, favor, hold with. *Informal:* go for. *Idioms:* be in favor of, take kindly to, think highly (*or* well) of. [*Compare* ASSENT, VALUE.]

counter *adj.* *—See* DISCREPANT, OPPOSITE.

counter *n.* A small often makeshift structure for the display and sale of goods ▸ booth, stand, stall. [*Compare* STORE.] *—See also* OPPOSITE.

counter *v.* *—See* OPPOSE, RETALIATE.

counteract *v.* *—See* BALANCE (2), CANCEL (2).

counterattack *v.* *—See* RETALIATE.

counterattack or **counteraction** *n.* *—See* RETALIATION.

counterbalance *v.* *—See* BALANCE (1), BALANCE (2), CANCEL (2).

counterblow *n.* *—See* RETALIATION.

counterfactual *adj.* *—See* FALSE.

counterfeit *v.* To make a fraudulent copy of ▸ fabricate, fake, falsify, forge. [*Compare* COPY.] *—See also* ACT (2).

counterfeit *adj.* Fraudulently or deceptively imitative ▸ bogus, ersatz, fabricated, factitious, fake, false, forged, fraudulent, phony, sham, spurious, suppositious, supposititious. [*Compare* ARTIFICIAL.]

counterfeit *n.* A fraudulent imitation ▸ fabrication, fake, falsification, forgery, phony, sham. [*Compare* COPY.]

counterfeiter *n.* ▸ fabricator, faker, falsifier, forger.

countermand *v.* *—See* LIFT (3), RETRACT (1).

countermand *n.* *—See* RETRACTION.

countermeasure *n.* *—See* CURE.

counterpart *n.* One that has the same functions and characteristics as another ▸ equivalent, opposite number, vis-à-vis. *—See also* COPY (1), MATE, PARALLEL.

counterpoint *n.* *—See* CONTRAST.

counterpoint *v.* *—See* COMPARE.

counterpoise *n.* *—See* BALANCE (1).

another. 3. The state of being balanced or in equilibrium. **—coun′ter·poise′** *v.*

coun·ter·pro·duc·tive (koun′tər-prə-dŭk′tĭv) ▸ *adj.* Tending to hinder rather than serve one's purpose.

coun·ter·rev·o·lu·tion (koun′tər-rĕv′ə-lo͞o′shən) ▸ *n.* A movement arising in opposition to a previous revolution. **—coun′ter·rev′o·lu′tion·ar′y** *adj. & n.*

coun·ter·sign (koun′tər-sīn′) ▸ *v.* To sign (a previously signed document), as for authentication. ▸ *n.* **1.** A second or confirming signature. **2.** A password.

coun·ter·sig·na·ture (koun′tər-sĭg′nə-chər) ▸ *n.* See **countersign** 1.

coun·ter·sink (koun′tər-sĭngk′) ▸ *n.* **1.** A hole with the top part enlarged so that the head of a screw or bolt will lie flush with or below the surface. **2.** A tool for making such a hole. ▸ *v.* **1.** To make a countersink on or in. **2.** To set into a countersink.

coun·ter·spy (koun′tər-spī′) ▸ *n.* A spy working in opposition to enemy espionage.

coun·ter·ten·or (koun′tər-tĕn′ər) ▸ *n.* A male singer with a range above a tenor's.

coun·ter·weight (koun′tər-wāt′) ▸ *n.* A weight used as a counterbalance.

count·ess (koun′tĭs) ▸ *n.* **1.** A woman holding the title of count or earl. **2.** The wife or widow of a count or earl.

count·ing·house also **count·ing house** (koun′tĭng-hous′) ▸ *n.* An office in which a business firm carries on operations such as accounting and correspondence.

count·less (kount′lĭs) ▸ *adj.* Innumerable.

coun·tri·fied also **coun·try·fied** (kŭn′trĭ-fīd′) ▸ *adj.* **1.** Characteristic of country life; rural. **2.** Lacking sophistication.

coun·try (kŭn′trē) ▸ *n., pl.* **-tries.** **1a.** A nation or state. **b.** The territory or people of a nation or state. **2.** The land of a person's birth or citizenship. **3.** A large tract of land distinguishable by features of topography, biology, or culture. **4.** A rural area. **5.** *Informal* Country music.

country and western ▸ *n.* See **country music.**

country club ▸ *n.* A suburban club for social and sports activities.

coun·try·man (kŭn′trē-mən) ▸ *n.* **1.** A person from one's own country; compatriot. **2.** A rustic.

country mile ▸ *n. Informal* A great distance.

country music ▸ *n.* Popular music based on folk styles of the rural American South and West.

coun·try·side (kŭn′trē-sīd′) ▸ *n.* **1.** A rural region. **2.** The inhabitants of a rural region.

coun·try·wom·an (kŭn′trē-wo͝om′ən) ▸ *n.* **1.** A woman from one's own country; compatriot. **2.** A rustic woman.

coun·ty (koun′tē) ▸ *n., pl.* **-ties.** An administrative subdivision of a state or territory.

coup (ko͞o) ▸ *n., pl.* **coups** (ko͞oz). **1.** A stratagem or plan that is brilliantly executed. **2.** A coup d'état.

coup de grâce (ko͞o′ də gräs′) ▸ *n., pl.* **coups de grâce.** **1.** A deathblow delivered to end the misery of a mortally wounded victim. **2.** A finishing or decisive stroke.

coup d'é·tat (dā-tä′) ▸ *n., pl.* **coups d'état.** The sudden overthrow of a government by a usu. small group of persons in or previously in authority.

coupe (ko͞op) ▸ *n.* A closed two-door automobile.

cou·ple (kŭp′əl) ▸ *n.* **1.** Two items of the same kind; pair. **2.** Something that joins two things; link. **3.** *(takes sing. or pl. v.)* **a.** Two people united, as by marriage. **b.** Two people together. **4.** *Informal* A few; several: *a couple of days.* ▸ *v.* **-pled, -pling.** **1.** To link together. **2.** To form pairs. **—cou′pler** *n.*

cou·plet (kŭp′lĭt) ▸ *n.* Two successive lines of verse, usu. rhyming and having the same meter.

cou·pling (kŭp′lĭng) ▸ *n.* **1.** The act of forming couples. **2.** A device that links or connects.

cou·pon (ko͞o′pŏn′, kyo͞o′-) ▸ *n.* **1.** A negotiable certificate attached to a bond that represents a sum of interest due. **2a.** A redeemable certificate: *a food coupon.* **b.** A certificate that entitles the bearer to certain benefits, such as a cash refund. **3.** A printed form, as in an advertisement, to be used as an order blank.

cour·age (kûr′ĭj, kŭr′-) ▸ *n.* The quality of mind that enables one to face danger with self-possession, confidence, and resolution; bravery. **—cou·ra′geous** (kə-rā′jəs) *adj.* **—cou·ra′geous·ly** *adv.*

cou·ri·er (ko͝or′ē-ər, kûr′-, kŭr′-) ▸ *n.* A messenger, esp. one on urgent or official business.

course (kôrs) ▸ *n.* **1.** Onward movement in a particular direction. **2.** The route or path taken by something, such as a stream, that moves. **3.** Duration: *in the course of a year.* **4.** A mode of action or behavior. **5.** Regular development. **6a.** A body of prescribed studies constituting a curriculum. **b.** A unit of such a curriculum. **7.** A part of a meal served as a unit at one time. ▸ *v.* **coursed, cours·ing.** **1.** To move swiftly (through or over); traverse. **2.** To hunt (game) with hounds. ***—idioms:*** **in due course** At the proper or right time. **of course** Without any doubt; certainly.

cours·er (kôr′sər) ▸ *n.* A swift horse.

court (kôrt) ▸ *n.* **1.** A courtyard. **2.** A short street. **3a.** A royal mansion or palace. **b.** The retinue of a sovereign. **c.** A sovereign's governing body, including ministers and advisers. **4a.** A person or persons whose task is to hear and submit a decision on legal cases. **b.** The place where such cases are heard. **c.** The regular session of a judicial assembly. **5.** An open, level area marked with appropriate lines, upon which a game, such as tennis or basketball, is played. ▸ *v.* **1.** To attempt to gain; seek. **2.** To behave so as to invite: *court disaster.* **3.** To woo. **4.** To attempt to gain the favor of by attention or flattery. ***—idiom:*** **pay court to** **1.** To

THESAURUS

counterpoise *v.* *—See* BALANCE (2), CANCEL (2).

counterpose *v.* *—See* COMPARE.

counterproductive *adj.* *—See* INEFFECTUAL (1).

countervail *v.* *—See* BALANCE (2), CANCEL (2).

countless *adj.* *—See* INCALCULABLE.

country *adj.* Of or relating to the countryside ▸ agrarian, arcadian, bucolic, campestral, georgic, pastoral, provincial, rural, rustic. *Informal:* hick.

country *n.* A remote or rural area ▸ backcountry, backwoods, countryside, God's country, hinterland. *Informal:* sticks. *Slang:* boondocks, boonies, hicksville. [*Compare* DESERT[1], WILDERNESS.] *—See also* STATE (1), TERRITORY.

countryman or **countrywoman** *n.* A person who is from one's own country ▸ compatriot, fellow citizen, kinsman, kinswoman.

countryside *n.* *—See* COUNTRY.

coup *n.* *—See* ACCOMPLISHMENT.

couple *n.* Two items of the same kind together ▸ brace, couplet, doublet, duet, duo, dyad, match, pair, span, two, twosome, yoke. [*Compare* SEVERAL.]

couple *v.* *—See* ASSOCIATE (3), ATTACH (1), COMBINE (1).

couplet *n.* *—See* COUPLE.

coupling *n.* *—See* JOINT (1).

courage *n.* The quality of mind enabling one to face danger or hardship resolutely ▸ backbone, braveness, bravery, courageousness, dauntlessness, doughtiness, fearlessness, fortitude, gallantry, gameness, hardihood, hardiness, heart, heroism, intestinal fortitude, intrepidity, intrepidness, mettle, nerve, pluck, pluckiness, prowess, spine, spirit, stoutheartedness, undauntedness, valiance, valiancy, valiantness, valor. *Informal:* grit, spunk, spunkiness. *Slang:* guts, gutsiness, moxie. [*Compare* DARING, DECISION, TEMERITY.]

courageous *adj.* *—See* BRAVE.

courageousness *n.* *—See* COURAGE.

courier *n.* *—See* MESSENGER.

course *n.* The compass direction in which a ship or aircraft moves ▸ bearing, heading, vector. *—See also* APPROACH (1), DIRECTION, LIFE, SERIES, WAY (2).

course *v.* *—See* FLOW (1).

court *n.* **1.** A roofless area partially or entirely enclosed by walls or buildings ▸ atrium, close, courtyard, enclosure, patio, quad, quadrangle, yard. **2.** A judicial assembly ▸ bar, forum, judicature, judiciary, tribunal.

court *v.* **1.** To behave so as to bring on danger, for example ▸ invite, provoke, solicit, tempt. *Idiom:* ask (*or* go looking) for it. [*Compare* ATTRACT, PROVOKE.] **2.** To attempt to gain the affection of ▸ chase, pursue, run after, spark, woo. *Informal:* romance. *Idiom:* make a play for. [*Compare* APPEAL, FLIRT, SEE.]

flatter in an attempt to obtain something. **2.** To woo.

cour·te·ous (kûr′tē-əs) ▸ *adj.* Graciously considerate of others. **—cour′te·ous·ly** *adv.* **—cour′te·ous·ness** *n.*

cour·te·san (kôr′tĭ-zən) ▸ *n.* A woman prostitute, esp. one whose clients are men of rank or wealth.

cour·te·sy (kûr′tĭ-sē) ▸ *n., pl.* **-sies. 1a.** Polite behavior. **b.** A polite gesture or remark. **2.** Generosity, esp. as a sponsor.

court·house (kôrt′hous′) ▸ *n.* A building housing judicial courts.

court·i·er (kôr′tē-ər, -tyər) ▸ *n.* An attendant at a sovereign's court.

court·ly (kôrt′lē) ▸ *adj.* **-li·er, -li·est.** Elegant in manners. **—court′li·ness** *n.*

court-mar·tial (kôrt′mär′shəl) ▸ *n., pl.* **courts-mar·tial** (kôrts′-). **1.** A military or naval court of officers appointed by a commander to try persons for offenses under military law. **2.** A trial by court-martial. **—court′-mar′tial** *v.*

court order ▸ *n.* An order issued by a court that requires a person to do or refrain from doing something.

court·room (kôrt′ro͞om′, -ro͝om′) ▸ *n.* A room for court proceedings.

court·ship (kôrt′shĭp′) ▸ *n.* The act or period of courting or wooing.

court·yard (kôrt′yärd′) ▸ *n.* An open space surrounded by walls or buildings.

cous·cous (ko͞os′ko͞os′) ▸ *n.* A pasta of North African origin made of crushed and steamed semolina.

cous·in (kŭz′ĭn) ▸ *n.* **1.** A child of one's aunt or uncle. **2.** A relative descended from a common ancestor. **3.** A member of a kindred group.

cou·ture (ko͞o-to͝or′) ▸ *n.* The business of designing, making, and selling highly fashionable clothing for women.

cou·tu·rier (ko͞o-to͝or′ē-ər, -ē-ā′) ▸ *n.* One who designs for or owns an establishment engaged in couture.

co·va·lent bond (kō-vā′lənt) ▸ *n.* A chemical bond formed by the sharing of one or more electrons between atoms.

cove (kōv) ▸ *n.* A small sheltered bay of a sea, river, or lake.

cov·en (kŭv′ən, kō′vən) ▸ *n.* An assembly of 13 witches.

cov·e·nant (kŭv′ə-nənt) ▸ *n.* A formal binding agreement; compact; contract. ▸ *v.* To enter into a covenant (with). **—cov′e·nant·er** *n.*

cov·er (kŭv′ər) ▸ *v.* **1.** To place something upon, over, or in front of so as to protect, shut in, or conceal. **2.** To clothe. **3a.** To spread over the surface of: *Dust covered the table.* **b.** To extend over: *a farm covering 100 acres.* **4.** To hide or conceal: *covered up their mistakes.* **5.** To protect by insurance. **6.** To defray or meet the cost of. **7.** To deal with; treat of. **8.** To travel or pass over. **9.** To report the details of (an event or situation). **10.** To hold within the range and aim of a weapon, such as a firearm. **11.** To act as a substitute during someone's absence. ▸ *n.* **1.** Something that covers. **2.** Something that provides shelter. **3.** Something that screens, conceals, or disguises. **4.** A table setting for one person. **5.** An envelope or wrapper for mail.

cov·er·age (kŭv′ər-ĭj) ▸ *n.* **1.** The extent or degree to which something is observed, analyzed, and reported. **2.** The protection given by an insurance policy.

cov·er·alls (kŭv′ər-ôlz′) ▸ *pl.n.* A loose-fitting one-piece garment worn to protect clothes.

cover charge ▸ *n.* A fixed amount added to the bill at a nightclub, esp. for entertainment.

cover crop ▸ *n.* A crop, such as clover, planted to prevent soil erosion and provide humus or nitrogen when plowed under.

covered wagon (kŭv′ərd) ▸ *n.* A large wagon with an arched canvas top, used esp. by American pioneers for prairie travel.

cov·er·ing (kŭv′ər-ĭng) ▸ *n.* Something that covers, so as to protect or conceal.

cov·er·let (kŭv′ər-lĭt) ▸ *n.* A bedspread.

cov·ert (kŭv′ərt, kō′vərt, kō-vûrt′) ▸ *adj.* **1.** Concealed, hidden, or secret. **2.** Sheltered. ▸ *n.* **1.** A covered shelter or hiding place. **2.** Thick underbrush affording cover for game. **—cov′ert·ly** *adv.*

cov·er-up or **cov·er·up** (kŭv′ər-ŭp′) ▸ *n.* An effort or strategy designed to conceal something, such as a crime or scandal.

cov·et (kŭv′ĭt) ▸ *v.* **1.** To desire (that which is rightfully another's). **2.** To wish for longingly.

cov·et·ous (kŭv′ĭ-təs) ▸ *adj.* Excessively desirous of another's possessions. **—cov′et·ous·ness** *n.*

cov·ey (kŭv′ē) ▸ *n., pl.* **-eys.** A small flock or group, esp. of birds.

cow[1] (kou) ▸ *n.* **1.** The mature female of cattle. **2.** The mature female of other large animals, such as whales or elephants. **3.** A domesticated bovine.

cow[2] (kou) ▸ *v.* To frighten with threats; intimidate.

cow·ard (kou′ərd) ▸ *n.* One who lacks courage in the face of danger, pain, or hardship. **—cow′ard·ly** *adv.*

cow·ard·ice (kou′ər-dĭs) ▸ *n.* Lack of courage or resoluteness.

cow·bird (kou′bûrd′) ▸ *n.* A blackbird that lays its eggs in other birds' nests.

cow·boy (kou′boi′) ▸ *n.* A hired man, esp. in the American

THESAURUS

courteous *adj.* **1.** Characterized by good manners ▸ civil, genteel, gentlemanly, mannerly, polite, well-bred, well-mannered, well-spoken. [*Compare* CEREMONIOUS, CULTURED, SUAVE.] **2.** Characterized by kindness and warm, unaffected courtesy ▸ affable, gracious, hospitable. [*Compare* AMIABLE.] *—See also* ATTENTIVE.

courteousness *n.* *—See* AMENITIES (2), COURTESY.

courter *n.* *—See* BEAU (1).

courtesan *n.* *—See* HARLOT.

courtesy *n.* Well-mannered behavior toward others ▸ civility, courteousness, genteelness, gentility, mannerliness, politeness, politesse. [*Compare* CONSIDERATION, MANNERS.] *—See also* AMENITIES (2), FAVOR (1).

courtier *n.* *—See* SYCOPHANT.

courtliness *n.* *—See* ELEGANCE.

courtly *adj.* *—See* CEREMONIOUS, ELEGANT, GRACIOUS (2).

courtyard *n.* *—See* COURT (1).

cove *n.* *—See* HARBOR.

covenant *n.* *—See* AGREEMENT (1), PROMISE (1).

covenant *v.* *—See* CONTRACT (1), PLEDGE (1).

cover *v.* **1.** To extend over the surface of ▸ blanket, cap, carpet, coat, overlay, overspread, pave, plate, spread. [*Compare* FINISH.] **2.** To journey over ▸ cross, go, make, traverse. *Informal:* do. [*Compare* CROSS, JOURNEY.] *—See also* CONCEAL, DEFEND (1), FACE (2), GO (4).

cover for *v.* *—See* SUBSTITUTE.

cover *n.* **1.** Something that physically protects, especially from danger ▸ ark, asylum, covert, coverture, harbor, haven, port, protection, refuge, retreat, safe house, sanctuary, screen, shelter. [*Compare* DEFENSE, FORT, HIDE-OUT.] **2.** Something that covers, especially to prevent contents from spilling ▸ cap, covering, lid, top. [*Compare* PLUG.] *—See also* FAÇADE (2), SUBSTITUTE, VEIL, WRAPPER.

coverage *n.* *—See* EXTENT.

covering *n.* Something that covers, especially to prevent contents from spilling ▸ cap, cover, lid, top. [*Compare* PLUG.] *—See also* COAT (2), WRAPPER.

covert *adj.* *—See* HIDDEN (1), SECRET (1), ULTERIOR (1).

covert *n.* A hiding place ▸ den, hideaway, hide-out, lair. *—See also* COVER (1).

covertly *adv.* *—See* SECRETLY.

covertness *n.* *—See* SECRECY.

covet *v.* To feel envy toward or for ▸ begrudge, envy, grudge. *—See also* DESIRE.

covetous *adj.* *—See* ENVIOUS, GREEDY.

covetousness *n.* *—See* ENVY, GREED.

cow *v.* *—See* INTIMIDATE.

coward *n.* An ignoble, uncourageous person ▸ caitiff, craven, cur, dastard, funk, milksop, milquetoast, mouse, poltroon, recreant, sissy. *Informal:* nervous Nellie, scaredy-cat. *Slang:* chicken, fraidy cat, yellow-belly. [*Compare* DEFECTOR, SNEAK, WEAKLING.]

cowardice *n.* Ignoble lack of courage ▸ chickenheartedness, cowardliness, cravenness, dastardliness, faintheartedness, funk, poltroonery, pusillanimity, recreance, spinelessness, unmanliness, white feather. *Slang:* gutlessness, yellowness, yellow streak. [*Compare* FEAR.]

cowardliness *n.* *—See* COWARDICE.

cowardly *adj.* Ignobly lacking in courage ▸ caitiff, chickenhearted, chicken-livered, craven, dastardly, faint-hearted, lily-livered, pusillanimous, recreant, sissy, spineless, supine, unmanly, weak-kneed. *Slang:* chicken, gutless, wimpy, yellow, yellow-bellied. [*Compare* AFRAID.]

West, who tends cattle, typically on horseback.
cow·catch·er (kou′kăch′ər, -kĕch′-) ▸ *n.* The metal frame projecting from the front of a locomotive and serving to clear the track of obstructions.
cow·er (kou′ər) ▸ *v.* To cringe in fear.
cow·girl (kou′gûrl′) ▸ *n.* A hired woman, esp. in the American West, who tends cattle, typically on horseback.
cow·hand (kou′hănd′) ▸ *n.* A cowboy or cowgirl.
cow·herd (kou′hûrd′) ▸ *n.* One who herds or tends cattle.
cow·hide (kou′hīd′) ▸ *n.* **1.** The hide of a cow. **2.** The leather made from this hide.
cowl (koul) ▸ *n.* **1.** The hood or hooded robe worn esp. by a monk. **2.** A draped neckline on a woman's garment.
cow·lick (kou′lĭk′) ▸ *n.* A projecting tuft of hair on the head that will not lie flat.
cowl·ing (kou′lĭng) ▸ *n.* A removable metal covering esp. for an aircraft engine.
co·work·er (kō′wûr′kər) ▸ *n.* A colleague.
cow·poke (kou′pōk′) ▸ *n.* A cowhand.
cow·pox (kou′pŏks′) ▸ *n.* A skin disease of cattle caused by a virus that is isolated and used to vaccinate humans against smallpox.
cow·punch·er (kou′pŭn′chər) ▸ *n.* A cowhand.
cow·rie or **cow·ry** (kou′rē) ▸ *n., pl.* **-ries**. Any of various tropical marine gastropods having glossy, often brightly marked shells.
cow·slip (kou′slĭp′) ▸ *n.* **1.** A Eurasian primrose having fragrant yellow flowers. **2.** See **marsh marigold**.
cox·comb (kŏks′kōm′) ▸ *n.* A conceited dandy; fop.
cox·swain (kŏk′sən, -swān′) ▸ *n.* **1.** One who steers a ship's boat. **2.** One who directs the crew of a racing shell.
coy (koi) ▸ *adj.* **-er, -est**. **1.** Shy, esp. flirtatiously so. **2.** Annoyingly unforthcoming. **—coy′ly** *adv.* **—coy′ness** *n.*
coy·o·te (kī-ō′tē, kī′ōt′) ▸ *n.* A small wolflike predator native to W North America, now widely dispersed.
coz·en (kŭz′ən) ▸ *v.* To deceive; cheat.
co·zy also **co·sy** (kō′zē) ▸ *adj.* **-zi·er, -zi·est** also **-si·er, -si·est**. Snug, comfortable, and warm. ▸ *v.* **-zied, -zy·ing** also **-sied, -sy·ing**. *Informal* To ingratiate oneself: *cozy up to the boss.* ▸ *n., pl.* **-zies** also **-sies**. A padded insulating cover for a teapot. **—co′zi·ly** *adv.* **—co′zi·ness** *n.*
CPA ▸ *abbr.* certified public accountant
CPU ▸ *abbr.* central processing unit
Cr ▸ The symbol for the element **chromium**.
crab¹ (krăb) ▸ *n.* **1.** Any of various chiefly marine crustaceans having a broad flattened body with a shell-like covering. **2.** A horseshoe crab. **3.** A crab louse.
crab² (krăb) ▸ *n.* A quarrelsome, ill-tempered person. **—crab** *v.*
crab apple ▸ *n.* **1.** A tree with white, pink, or reddish flowers. **2.** The small tart applelike fruit of such a tree.
crab·bed (krăb′ĭd) ▸ *adj.* **1.** Irritable; ill-tempered. **2.** Difficult to read, as handwriting. **—crab′bed·ly** *adv.* **—crab′bed·ness** *n.*
crab·by (krăb′ē) ▸ *adj.* **-bi·er, -bi·est**. Grouchy; ill-tempered. **—crab′bi·ly** *adv.* **—crab′bi·ness** *n.*
crab·grass (krăb′grăs′) ▸ *n.* A coarse spreading grass usu. considered a weed in lawns.
crab louse ▸ *n.* A body louse that infests the pubic region and causes severe itching.
crack (krăk) ▸ *v.* **1.** To break with a sharp snapping sound. **2.** To break without complete separation of parts. **3.** To change sharply in pitch or timbre, as the voice from emotion. **4.** To strike. **5.** To break open or into. **6.** To discover the solution to, esp. after great effort. **7.** *Informal* To tell (a joke). **8.** To reduce (petroleum) to simpler compounds. ***—phrasal verbs:*** **crack down** *Informal* To become more severe or strict. **crack up** *Informal* **1.** To crash; collide. **2.** To have a mental or physical breakdown. **3.** To laugh or cause to laugh boisterously. ▸ *n.* **1.** A sharp snapping sound. **2a.** A partial split or break; fissure. **b.** A narrow space: *The window was open a crack.* **3.** A sharp resounding blow. **4.** A cracking of the voice. **5.** A try; chance: *gave him a crack at it.* **6.** A witty or sarcastic remark. **7.** *Slang* Chemically purified crystallized cocaine prepared for smoking. ▸ *adj.* Superior; first rate.
crack·down (krăk′doun′) ▸ *n.* An act or instance of cracking down.
cracked (krăkt) ▸ *adj.* **1.** Broken without dividing into parts: *a cracked mirror.* **2.** *Informal* Crazy.
crack·er (krăk′ər) ▸ *n.* **1.** A thin crisp wafer or biscuit. **2.** A firecracker.
crack·er·jack (krăk′ər-jăk′) ▸ *adj.* *Slang* Of excellent quality. **—crack′er·jack′** *n.*
crack·le (krăk′əl) ▸ *v.* **-led, -ling**. **1.** To make or cause to make a succession of slight sharp snapping noises. **2.** To develop a network of fine cracks. **—crack′le** *n.* **—crack′ly** *adj.*
crack·pot (krăk′pŏt′) ▸ *n.* An eccentric or harebrained person.
crack·up (krăk′ŭp′) ▸ *n.* *Informal* **1.** A crash or collision, as of an automobile. **2.** A mental or physical breakdown.
-cracy ▸ *suff.* Government; rule: *technocracy.*
cra·dle (krād′l) ▸ *n.* **1.** A low bed for an infant, often with rockers. **2.** A place of origin. **3.** The part of a telephone on which the handset is supported. **4.** A supporting framework. ▸ *v.* **-dled, -dling**. To place gently in or as if in a cradle.
craft (krăft) ▸ *n.* **1.** Skill in doing or making something, as in the arts. **2.** Skill in evasion or deception; guile. **3a.** A trade, esp. one requiring skilled artistry. **b.** The membership of such a trade; guild. **4.** *pl.* **craft**. A boat, ship, or aircraft. ▸ *v.* To make or devise, esp. with great care. **—crafts′man** *n.*

THESAURUS

cower *v.* —*See* FLINCH.
coxcomb *n.* A man who is vain about his clothes ▸ beau, dandy, fop, peacock, swell.
coy *adj.* Given to flirting ▸ coquettish, flirtatious, flirty. —*See also* SHY¹.
coyness *n.* —*See* SHYNESS.
cozen *v.* —*See* CHEAT (1), DECEIVE.
cozener *n.* —*See* CHEAT (2).
cozy *adj.* —*See* COMFORTABLE, INTIMATE¹ (1).
crab *n.* —*See* GROUCH.
crab *v.* —*See* COMPLAIN.
crabbed *adj.* —*See* COMPLEX (1), ILL-TEMPERED.
crabby *adj.* —*See* ILL-TEMPERED.
crack *v.* **1.** To undergo partial breaking ▸ break, cleave, crackle, craze, fissure, fracture, rift, rupture, split. [*Compare* CUT, TEAR¹.] **2.** To make a sudden, sharp noise ▸ bang, bark, clap, pop, snap. [*Compare* BLAST, CRACKLE, SNAP.] —*See also* BANG, BREAK (1), COLLAPSE (1), DECIPHER, OPEN (1).
crack up *v.* —*See* BREAK (3), COLLAPSE (1), CRASH.
crack *n.* **1.** A sudden sharp, explosive noise ▸ bang, bark, clap, detonation, explosion, pop, rat-a-tat-tat, report, snap. [*Compare* BLAST, CRACKLE, SNAP.] **2.** A partial opening caused by splitting and rupture ▸ breach, break, chink, cleavage, cleft, cranny, crevice, fault, fissure, fracture, niche, rift, rupture, split. [*Compare* CUT, HOLE.] **3.** A flippant or sarcastic remark ▸ barb, dig, jest, quip. *Slang:* wisecrack. [*Compare* JOKE.] —*See also* ATTEMPT, BLOW², FLASH (2).
crack *adj.* —*See* EXPERT.
crackdown *n.* Forceful subjugation, as against an uprising ▸ clampdown, lockdown, repression, suppression. [*Compare* OPPRESSION, RESTRAINT.]
cracked *adj.* —*See* INSANE, OPEN (1).
crackerjack *adj.* —*See* EXPERT.
crackerjack *n.* —*See* EXPERT.
crackle *v.* To make a series of short, sharp noises ▸ crepitate, splutter, sputter. [*Compare* CRACK, HISS, SNAP.] —*See also* BURN (2), CRACK (1).
crackle *n.* A light, sharp noise ▸ clack, click, snap. [*Compare* CRACK.]
crackpot *n.* A person regarded as strange, eccentric, or crazy ▸ crazy, eccentric, lunatic. *Informal:* crank, loon, loony. *Slang:* cuckoo, ding-a-ling, freak, kook, nut, screwball, space cadet, weirdie, weirdo. [*Compare* CHARACTER.]
crackup *n.* *Informal* A sudden sharp decline in mental, emotional, or physical health ▸ breakdown, collapse. [*Compare* INFIRMITY.] —*See also* CRASH (2).
craft *n.* **1.** A conveyance that travels over water ▸ bark, barque, boat, ship, vessel, watercraft. **2.** The technique, style, and quality of working ▸ craftsmanship, work, workmanship. [*Compare* APPROACH.] —*See also* ABILITY (1), ART, BUSINESS (2), DISHONESTY (2).
craftiness *n.* —*See* ART, DISHONESTY (2).
craftsmanship *n.* The technique, style, and quality of working ▸ craft, work, workmanship. [*Compare* APPROACH.]

—crafts′man·ship′ *n.* **—crafts′per′son** *n.* **—crafts′wom′an** *n.*

craft·y (krăf′tē) ► *adj.* **-i·er, -i·est.** Marked by underhandedness, deviousness, or deception. **—craft′i·ly** *adv.* **—craft′i·ness** *n.*

crag (krăg) ► *n.* A steeply projecting mass of rock. **—crag′gy** *adj.*

cram (krăm) ► *v.* **crammed, cram·ming. 1.** To squeeze into an insufficient space; stuff. **2.** To fill too tightly. **3.** To gorge with food. **4.** *Informal* To study intensively just before an examination.

cramp[1] (krămp) ► *n.* **1.** A sudden painful involuntary muscular contraction. **2.** A temporary partial paralysis of habitually or excessively used muscles. **3. cramps** Sharp persistent abdominal pains. ► *v.* To be affected with or as if with a cramp.

cramp[2] (krămp) ► *n.* Something that confines or restricts. ► *v.* **1.** To restrict; hamper. **2.** To jam (a wheel) by a short turn.

cram·pon (krăm′pŏn′, -pən) ► *n.* An iron spike attached to the shoe to prevent slipping on ice.

cran·ber·ry (krăn′bĕr′ē) ► *n.* A mat-forming, evergreen shrub of E North America, bearing tart red edible berries and used in jellies and relishes.

crane (krān) ► *n.* **1.** A large wading bird having a long neck, long legs, and a long bill. **2.** A machine for hoisting heavy objects. ► *v.* **craned, cran·ing.** To stretch (one's neck) for a better view.

cra·ni·um (krā′nē-əm) ► *n., pl.* **-ni·ums** or **-ni·a** (-nē-ə). **1.** The skull of a vertebrate. **2.** The portion of the skull enclosing the brain. **—cra′ni·al** *adj.*

crank (krăngk) ► *n.* **1.** A device for transmitting rotary motion, consisting of a handle attached at right angles to a shaft. **2.** *Informal* **a.** A grouchy person. **b.** An eccentric person. ► *v.* To start or operate by turning a crank. ***—phrasal verb:* crank out** To produce rapidly and mechanically.

crank·case (krăngk′kās′) ► *n.* The metal case enclosing a crankshaft.

crank·shaft (krăngk′shăft′) ► *n.* A shaft that turns or is turned by a crank.

crank·y (krăng′kē) ► *adj.* **-i·er, -i·est. 1.** Ill-tempered; peevish. **2.** Eccentric; odd. **3.** Working or operating unpredictably.

cran·ny (krăn′ē) ► *n., pl.* **-nies.** A small opening, as in a wall; crevice.

crap (krăp) ► *n. Slang* **1.** Nonsense; bunk. **2.** Worthless or shoddy material or work. **3.** Junk; clutter. **4.** Insolent talk or behavior.

crape (krāp) ► *n.* **1.** See **crepe** 1. **2.** A black band worn as a sign of mourning.

crap·pie (krŏp′ē) ► *n., pl.* **-pies.** Either of two edible North American sunfishes.

craps (krăps) ► *pl.n. (takes sing. or pl. v.)* A gambling game played with two dice.

crap·shoot (krăp′sho͞ot′) ► *n. Slang* A risky enterprise.

crap·shoot·er (krăp′sho͞o′tər) ► *n.* One who plays craps.

crash (krăsh) ► *v.* **1.** To fall or collide violently or noisily. **2.** To make a sudden loud noise. **3.** To fail suddenly, as a market or computer. **4.** To cause to collide or fail. **5.** *Informal* To join or enter uninvited: *crash a party.* ► *n.* **1.** A sudden loud noise. **2.** A wreck or collision. **3.** A sudden economic or business failure. **4.** *Comp. Sci.* A sudden failure of a hard drive, program, or operating system. ► *adj. Informal* All-out: *a crash diet.*

crash-land (krăsh′lănd′) ► *v.* To land and usu. damage an aircraft or spacecraft under emergency conditions. **—crash landing** *n.*

crass (krăs) ► *adj.* **-er, -est.** Crude and undiscriminating; coarse. **—crass′ly** *adv.* **—crass′ness** *n.*

—crat ► *suff.* A participant in or supporter of a specified form of government: *technocrat.*

crate (krāt) ► *n.* An often slatted wooden shipping box. ► *v.* **crat·ed, crat·ing.** To pack into a crate.

cra·ter (krā′tər) ► *n.* **1.** A bowl-shaped depression at the mouth of a volcano. **2.** A depression or pit made by an explosion or impact. **—cra′ter** *v.*

cra·ton (krā′tŏn′) ► *n.* A large portion of a continental plate that has been relatively undisturbed since the Precambrian Era.

cra·vat (krə-văt′) ► *n.* A necktie.

crave (krāv) ► *v.* **craved, crav·ing. 1.** To want intensely. **2.** To beg earnestly for; implore.

cra·ven (krā′vən) ► *adj.* Cowardly. **—cra′ven·ly** *adv.* **—cra′ven·ness** *n.*

crav·ing (krā′vĭng) ► *n.* A consuming desire.

craw (krô) ► *n.* The crop of a bird or stomach of an animal.

craw·dad (krô′dăd′) ► *n. Regional* See **crayfish.**

crawl (krôl) ► *v.* **1.** To move slowly by dragging the body along the ground. **2.** To advance slowly or feebly. **3.** To be or feel as if covered with moving things. ► *n.* **1.** A very slow pace. **2.** A rapid swimming style with alternating overarm strokes. **—crawl′er** *n.* **—crawl′y** *adj.*

cray·fish (krā′fĭsh′) also **craw·fish** (krô′-) ► *n., pl.* **-fish** or **-fish·es.** A small freshwater lobsterlike crustacean.

cray·on (krā′ŏn′, -ən) ► *n.* A stick of colored wax, charcoal, or chalk, used for drawing. **—cray′on′** *v.*

craze (krāz) ► *v.* **crazed, craz·ing.** To drive insane. ► *n.* A fad.

cra·zy (krā′zē) ► *adj.* **-zi·er, -zi·est. 1.** Mentally unbalanced;

THESAURUS

crafty *adj.* —*See* ARTFUL.

craggy or **cragged** *adj.* —*See* ROUGH (1).

cram *v. Informal* To study or work hard, especially when pressed for time ► lucubrate, study. *Informal:* bone up, grind. *Idioms:* burn the midnight oil, hit the books. [*Compare* EXAMINE.] —*See also* CROWD, FILL (1).

cramp[1] *n.* —*See* PAIN.

cramp[2] *n.* —*See* RESTRAINT.

cramp *v.* To check the freedom and spontaneity of ► constrain, constrict, inhibit. [*Compare* RESTRAIN.]

cramped *adj.* —*See* TIGHT (4).

cranium *n.* The bony framework of the head ► braincase, brainpan, skull. [*Compare* HEAD.]

crank *n.* —*See* CRACKPOT, GROUCH.

crank up *v.* —*See* ELEVATE (2).

crankiness *n.* —*See* TEMPER (1).

cranky *adj.* —*See* ECCENTRIC, ILL-TEMPERED.

cranny *n.* —*See* CRACK (2).

crap *n.* —*See* FILTH, NONSENSE.

crapehanger *n.* —*See* PESSIMIST (2).

crappy *adj.* —*See* SHODDY.

crapulence *n.* Unpleasant physical and mental effects following overindulgence in alcohol ► hangover, katzenjammer. *Informal:* head. —*See also* DRUNKENNESS.

crapulous or **crapulent** *adj.* —*See* DRUNK.

crash *v.* To wreck a vehicle ► rear-end, sideswipe, smash, total, wreck. *Informal:* crack up, pile up. —*See also* BANG, BLAST (1), COLLAPSE (2), COLLIDE, MALFUNCTION, RETIRE (1).

crash *n.* **1.** A forceful movement causing a loud noise ► bang, slam, smash, wham. **2.** A wrecking of a vehicle ► accident, rear-ender, sideswipe, smash, smashup, wreck. *Informal:* crackup, fender-bender, pileup. —*See also* BLAST (1), CLASH, COLLAPSE (2), COLLISION.

crash *adj. Informal* Designed to meet emergency needs as quickly as possible ► *Informal:* hurry-up, rush.

crashing *adj.* —*See* UTTER[2].

crass *adj.* —*See* COARSE (1).

crate *n.* —*See* CAGE, PACKAGE.

crave *v.* To have a greedy, obsessive desire ► hunger, itch, lust, thirst. [*Compare* DESIRE.] —*See also* APPEAL (1).

craven *adj.* —*See* COWARDLY.

craven *n.* —*See* COWARD.

cravenness *n.* —*See* COWARDICE.

craving *n.* —*See* DESIRE (1).

crawl *v.* **1.** To move along in a crouching or prone position ► creep, sinuate, slide, snake, squiggle, squirm, undulate, waggle, wiggle, worm, wriggle, writhe. **2.** To advance slowly ► creep, drag, inch, poke. [*Compare* TRUDGE.] —*See also* TEEM[1].

crawl *n.* A very slow rate of speed ► creep, footpace, slow motion. *Idiom:* snail's pace.

crawling *adj.* —*See* BUSY (2), SLOW (1).

craze *v.* —*See* CRACK (1), DERANGE.

craze *n.* —*See* ENTHUSIASM (2), FASHION.

craziness *n.* —*See* FOOLISHNESS, INSANITY.

crazy *adj.* —*See* ENTHUSIASTIC, FOOLISH, INSANE.

crazy *n.* —*See* CRACKPOT.

insane. 2. *Informal* Departing from proportion or moderation. **—cra′zi·ly** *adv.* **—cra′zi·ness** *n.*
Crazy Horse (1849?–77) ▸ Sioux leader.
crazy quilt ▸ *n.* A patchwork quilt with irregular pieces of cloth arranged haphazardly.
creak (krēk) ▸ *v.* To make or move with a squeaking sound. ▸ *n.* A grating or squeaking sound. **—creak′i·ly** *adv.* **—creak′i·ness** *n.* **—creak′y** *adj.*
cream (krēm) ▸ *n.* **1.** The yellowish fatty part of milk. **2.** A yellowish white. **3.** The choicest part. ▸ *v.* **1.** To beat into a creamy consistency. **2.** To prepare in a cream sauce. **3.** *Slang* To defeat overwhelmingly. **—cream′i·ness** *n.* **—cream′y** *adj.*
cream cheese ▸ *n.* A soft white cheese made of cream and milk.
cream·er (krē′mər) ▸ *n.* **1.** A small pitcher for cream. **2.** A substitute for cream.
cream·er·y (krē′mə-rē) ▸ *n., pl.* **-ies.** An establishment where dairy products are prepared or sold.
cream puff ▸ *n.* **1.** A light pastry filled with whipped cream or custard. **2.** *Slang* A weakling.
cream sauce ▸ *n.* A white sauce made by mixing flour and butter with milk or cream.
crease (krēs) ▸ *n.* A line made by pressing, folding, or wrinkling. **—crease** *v.* **—crease′less** *adj.* **—crease′proof′** *adj.*
cre·ate (krē-āt′) ▸ *v.* **-at·ed, -at·ing.** **1.** To cause to exist. **2.** To cause; produce.
cre·a·tion (krē-ā′shən) ▸ *n.* **1.** The act of creating. **2.** A product of invention or imagination. **3.** The world and all things in it. **4. Creation** In various religions, the divine act by which the world was created.
cre·a·tion·ism (krē-ā′shə-nĭz′əm) ▸ *n.* Belief in the literal interpretation of the account of the Creation in the Bible. **—cre·a′tion·ist** *n.*
cre·a·tive (krē-ā′tĭv) ▸ *adj.* Characterized by originality; imaginative. **—cre·a′tive·ly** *adv.* **—cre′a·tiv′i·ty, cre·a′tive·ness** *n.*
cre·a·tor (krē-ā′tər) ▸ *n.* One that creates.
crea·ture (krē′chər) ▸ *n.* **1.** A living being, esp. an animal. **2.** A human.
crèche (krĕsh) ▸ *n.* A representation of the Nativity.
cre·dence (krēd′ns) ▸ *n.* Acceptance as true; belief.
cre·den·tial (krĭ-dĕn′shəl) ▸ *n.* **1.** Something that entitles one to confidence or authority. **2. credentials** Evidence concerning one's authority.
cre·den·za (krĭ-dĕn′zə) ▸ *n.* A buffet or sideboard, esp. one without legs.
cred·i·ble (krĕd′ə-bəl) ▸ *adj.* **1.** Believable. **2.** Trustworthy; reliable. **—cred′i·bil′i·ty** *n.* **—cred′i·bly** *adv.*
cred·it (krĕd′ĭt) ▸ *n.* **1.** Confidence in the truth of something. **2.** The quality of being trustworthy. **3.** A source of honor: *a credit to her family.* **4.** Approval; praise. **5.** often **credits** An acknowledgment of work done, as in a motion picture. **6.** Certification of completion of a course of study. **7.** Reputation for solvency and integrity. **8.** An arrangement for deferred payment of a loan or purchase. **9.** *Accounting* Deduction of a payment made by a debtor from an amount due. **10.** The amount remaining in a person's account. ▸ *v.* **1.** To believe in; trust. **2.** To ascribe to; attribute. **3.** To give credit to.
cred·it·a·ble (krĕd′ĭ-tə-bəl) ▸ *adj.* Deserving of commendation. **—cred′it·a·bly** *adv.*
credit card ▸ *n.* A card authorizing the holder to buy goods or services on credit.
cred·i·tor (krĕd′ĭ-tər) ▸ *n.* One to whom money is owed.
credit union ▸ *n.* A cooperative organization that makes low-interest loans to its members.
cre·do (krē′dō, krā′-) ▸ *n., pl.* **-dos.** A creed.
cred·u·lous (krĕj′ə-ləs) ▸ *adj.* Disposed to believe too readily; gullible. **—cre·du′li·ty** (krĭ-do͞o′lĭ-tē, -dyo͞o′-) *n.* **—cred′u·lous·ly** *adv.* **—cred′u·lous·ness** *n.*
Cree (krē) ▸ *n., pl.* **Cree** or **Crees.** **1.** A member of a Native American people formerly of central Canada, now living from E Canada to Alberta. **2.** Their Algonquian language.
creed (krēd) ▸ *n.* A formal statement of religious belief.
creek (krēk, krĭk) ▸ *n.* A small stream, often a tributary to a river. ***—idiom:* up the creek** *Informal* In a difficult position.
Creek (krēk) ▸ *n., pl.* **Creek** or **Creeks.** **1a.** A member of a Native American people formerly of Alabama, Georgia, and NW Florida, now chiefly in Oklahoma. **b.** The Muskogean language of the Creek. **2.** A member of a confederacy of the Creek and various smaller tribes.
creel (krēl) ▸ *n.* A wicker basket used to carry fish.
creep (krēp) ▸ *v.* **crept** (krĕpt), **creep·ing.** **1.** To move with the body close to the ground. **2.** To move stealthily or slowly. **3.** *Bot.* To grow along a surface, as a vine. **4.** To have a tingling sensation. ▸ *n.* **1.** The act of creeping. **2.** *Slang* An annoying or repulsive person. **3. creeps** *Informal* A sensation of fear or repugnance.
creep·er (krē′pər) ▸ *n.* A plant that spreads by means of stems that creep.
creep·y (krē′pē) ▸ *adj.* **-i·er, -i·est.** *Informal* **1.** Inducing a sensation of uneasiness or fear, as of things crawling on one's skin. **2.** Annoyingly unpleasant. **—creep′i·ness** *n.*
cre·mate (krē′māt′, krĭ-māt′) ▸ *v.* **-mat·ed, -mat·ing.** To incinerate (a corpse). **—cre·ma′tion** *n.*
cre·ma·to·ri·um (krē′mə-tôr′ē-əm) ▸ *n., pl.* **-to·ri·ums** or **-to·ri·a** (-tôr′ē-ə). A furnace or establishment for the incineration of corpses.
cre·ma·to·ry (krē′mə-tôr′ē, krĕm′ə-) ▸ *n., pl.* **-ries.** A crematorium.
cren·e·lat·ed also **cren·el·lat·ed** (krĕn′ə-lā′tĭd) ▸ *adj.* Having battlements. **—cren′e·la′tion** *n.*
cren·shaw (krĕn′shô′) ▸ *n.* A winter melon with a greenish rind and pink flesh.
Cre·ole (krē′ōl′) ▸ *n.* **1.** A person of European descent

THESAURUS

cream *n.* —*See* BEST (1), OINTMENT.
cream *v.* —*See* BEAT (6), FOAM, OVERWHELM (1).
creaming *n.* —*See* DEFEAT.
cream puff *n.* —*See* BABY (2), WEAKLING.
crease *n.* —*See* FOLD (1), WRINKLE (1).
crease *v.* —*See* FOLD, WRINKLE.
create *v.* —*See* COMPOSE (1), FOUND, PRODUCE (1).
creation *n.* —*See* COMPOSITION (1), FOUNDATION, MYTH (2), UNIVERSE.
creative *adj.* Relating to or appreciative of the arts ▸ aesthetic, artistic. *Informal:* artsy, arty. —*See also* INVENTIVE.
creativeness *n.* —*See* INVENTION (1).
creativity *n.* —*See* IMAGINATION, INVENTION (1).
creator *n.* —*See* DEVELOPER, ORIGINATOR.
creature *n.* —*See* HUMAN BEING.
credence *n.* Mental acceptance of the actuality of something ▸ belief, credit, faith. [*Compare* TRUST.]
credential *n.* A quality that makes a person suitable for a particular position or task ▸ attainment, endowment, qualification, skill.
credibility or **credibleness** *n.* —*See* VERISIMILITUDE.
credible *adj.* —*See* AUTHENTIC (2), BELIEVABLE.
credit *n.* Mental acceptance of the actuality of something ▸ belief, credence, faith. [*Compare* TRUST.] —*See also* ACCEPTANCE (2).
credit *v.* To have confidence in the truthfulness of ▸ believe, trust. *Idioms:* give credence to, have faith (*or* trust *or* confidence) in, take at one's word. [*Compare* DEPEND ON.] —*See also* ATTRIBUTE.
creditability or **creditableness** *n.* —*See* VERISIMILITUDE.
creditable *adj.* —*See* ADMIRABLE, BELIEVABLE.
credo *n.* —*See* DOCTRINE.
credulous *adj.* —*See* GULLIBLE.
creed *n.* —*See* DOCTRINE, RELIGION.
creek *n.* —*See* BROOK[1].
creel *n.* A container that is made of interwoven material ▸ basket, hamper, pannier, wicker basket. [*Compare* CONTAINER.]
creep *v.* To advance slowly ▸ crawl, drag, inch, poke. *Idiom:* go at a snail's pace. [*Compare* TRUDGE.] —*See also* CRAWL (1), SNEAK.
creep *n.* **1.** A very slow rate of speed ▸ crawl, footpace, slow motion. *Idiom:* snail's pace. **2.** *Slang* A repulsive, despicable, or immoral person ▸ insect, jackal, lowlife, reptile, snake, weasel. *Slang:* louse, maggot, rat, skunk, sleaze, sleazebag, slimeball, toad, troll, worm. [*Compare* BETRAYER, INFORMER, SNEAK.]
creepy *adj.* —*See* WEIRD.
crème de la crème *n.* —*See* BEST (1), SOCIETY (1).

born in the West Indies or Spanish America. **2a.** A person descended from the original French settlers of Louisiana. **b.** The French dialect of these people. **3.** often **creole** A person of mixed Black and European, esp. French or Spanish descent. **4. creole** A pidgin that has developed and become the native language of its users. ▸ *adj.* **creole** Cooked with a spicy sauce containing tomatoes, onions, and peppers.

cre·o·sote (krē′ə-sōt′) ▸ *n.* An oily liquid obtained from coal tar and used as a wood preservative and disinfectant.

crepe also **crêpe** (krāp) ▸ *n.* **1.** A thin crinkled fabric of silk, cotton, wool, or other fiber. **2.** See **crape** 2. **3.** Crepe paper. **4.** (*also* krĕp) A thin small pancake.

crepe paper ▸ *n.* Crinkled tissue paper, used for decorations.

crept (krĕpt) ▸ *v.* P.t. and p.part. of **creep**.

cre·pus·cu·lar (krĭ-pŭs′kyə-lər) ▸ *adj.* **1.** Of or like twilight. **2.** *Zool.* Active at twilight.

cres·cen·do (krə-shĕn′dō) ▸ *n., pl.* **-dos**. **1.** *Mus.* A gradual increase in the volume of sound. **2.** A steady increase in intensity or force. **—cres·cen′do** *adj. & adv.*

cres·cent (krĕs′ənt) ▸ *n.* **1.** The figure of the moon in its first or last quarter, with concave and convex edges terminating in points. **2.** Something shaped like a crescent. ▸ *adj.* Crescent-shaped.

cress (krĕs) ▸ *n.* Any of several related plants with pungent leaves, often used in salads.

crest (krĕst) ▸ *n.* **1.** A tuft or similar projection on the head of a bird or other animal. **2.** *Her.* A device placed above the shield on a coat of arms. **3.** The top, as of a hill or wave. ▸ *v.* **1.** To form into a crest. **2.** To reach the crest (of).

crest·fall·en (krĕst′fô′lən) ▸ *adj.* Dispirited; dejected.

Cre·ta·ceous (krĭ-tā′shəs) *Geol.* ▸ *adj.* Of or being the 3rd and last period of the Mesozoic Era, marked by the development of flowering plants and the disappearance of dinosaurs. ▸ *n.* The Cretaceous Period.

Crete (krēt) ▸ An island of SE Greece in the E Mediterranean Sea. **—Cre′tan** *adj. & n.*

cre·tin (krēt′n) ▸ *n.* A person afflicted with cretinism. **—cre′tin·oid′** *adj.*

cre·tin·ism (krēt′n-ĭz′əm) ▸ *n.* A thyroid deficiency resulting in dwarfed stature and intellectual disability.

cre·tonne (krĭ-tŏn′, krē′tŏn′) ▸ *n.* A heavy unglazed cotton or linen fabric used for draperies and slipcovers.

cre·vasse (krĭ-văs′) ▸ *n.* **1.** A deep fissure, as in a glacier. **2.** A crack in a levee.

crev·ice (krĕv′ĭs) ▸ *n.* A narrow crack.

crew[1] (kro͞o) ▸ *n.* **1.** A group of people working together. **2.** All personnel operating a boat, ship, or aircraft. **3.** A team of rowers.

crew[2] (kro͞o) ▸ *v.* *Chiefly Brit.* P.t. of **crow**[2].

crew·cut or **crew cut** (kro͞o′kŭt′) ▸ *n.* A closely cropped haircut.

crewed (kro͞od) ▸ *adj.* Operated by an onboard crew: *a crewed space flight.*

crew·el (kro͞o′əl) ▸ *n.* Loosely twisted worsted yarn used for embroidery.

crew neck ▸ *n.* A round, close-fitting neckline.

crib (krĭb) ▸ *n.* **1.** A child's bed with high sides. **2.** A small building for storing corn. **3.** A rack or trough for fodder. **4a.** A petty theft. **b.** Plagiarism. **c.** See **pony** 2. ▸ *v.* **cribbed, crib·bing**. **1.** To confine in or as if in a crib. **2.** To plagiarize. **3.** To steal. **—crib′ber** *n.*

crib·bage (krĭb′ĭj) ▸ *n.* A card game scored by inserting pegs into holes on a board.

crib death ▸ *n.* See **sudden infant death syndrome**.

crick[1] (krĭk) ▸ *n.* A painful cramp, as in the neck.

crick[2] (krĭk) ▸ *n.* *Regional* A creek.

crick·et[1] (krĭk′ĭt) ▸ *n.* A leaping insect, the male of which produces a shrill chirping sound.

crick·et[2] (krĭk′ĭt) ▸ *n.* A game played with bats, a ball, and wickets by two teams of 11 players each. **—crick′et·er, crick′et·eer′** (-ĭ-tîr′) *n.*

cri·er (krī′ər) ▸ *n.* One who shouts out public announcements.

crime (krīm) ▸ *n.* **1.** An act committed or omitted in violation of a law. **2.** An unjust or senseless act.

Cri·me·a (krī-mē′ə, krĭ-) ▸ A region and peninsula of S Ukraine on the Black Sea and Sea of Azov. **—Cri·me′an** *adj.*

crim·i·nal (krĭm′ə-nəl) ▸ *adj.* **1.** Of or involving crime. **2.** Guilty of crime. ▸ *n.* One who has committed a crime. **—crim′i·nal′i·ty** (-năl′ĭ-tē) *n.* **—crim′i·nal·ly** *adv.*

crim·i·nal·ize (krĭm′ə-nə-līz′) ▸ *v.* **-ized, -iz·ing**. To make criminal; outlaw. **—crim′i·nal·i·za′tion** *n.*

crim·i·nol·o·gy (krĭm′ə-nŏl′ə-jē) ▸ *n.* The scientific study of crime and criminals. **—crim′i·no·log′i·cal** (-nə-lŏj′ĭ-kəl) *adj.* **—crim′i·no·log′i·cal·ly** *adv.* **—crim′i·nol′o·gist** *n.*

crimp (krĭmp) ▸ *v.* **1.** To press or pinch into small folds or ridges. **2.** To curl (hair). **3.** To have a hampering or obstructive effect on. ▸ *n.* **1.** The act of crimping. **2.** An obstructing agent or force. **—crimp′er** *n.*

crim·son (krĭm′zən) ▸ *n.* A vivid purplish red. **—crim′son** *adj. & v.*

cringe (krĭnj) ▸ *v.* **cringed, cring·ing**. **1.** To shrink back, as in fear; cower. **2.** To fawn. **—cringe** *n.*

crin·kle (krĭng′kəl) ▸ *v.* **-kled, -kling**. To form wrinkles or ripples. **—crin′kle** *n.* **—crin′kly** *adj.*

crin·o·line (krĭn′ə-lĭn) ▸ *n.* **1.** A stiff fabric used to line garments. **2.** A petticoat made of this fabric.

crip·ple (krĭp′əl) ▸ *n.* One that is partially disabled or lame. ▸ *v.* **-pled, -pling**. To disable or damage.

cri·sis (krī′sĭs) ▸ *n., pl.* **-ses** (-sēz). **1.** A crucial point or situation; turning point. **2.** A sudden change in a disease or fever toward improvement or deterioration.

crisp (krĭsp) ▸ *adj.* **-er, -est**. **1.** Firm but easily broken; brittle. **2.** Firm and fresh: *crisp celery.* **3.** Bracing; invigorating. **4.** Clear and concise: *a crisp reply.* **—crisp** *v.* **—crisp′ly**

THESAURUS

crepitate *v.* To make a series of short, sharp noises ▸ crackle, splutter, sputter. [*Compare* CRACK, HISS, SNAP.]

crescendo *v.* —*See* CLIMAX.

crescent *n.* —*See* BEND.

crest *n.* —*See* CLIMAX.

crest *v.* To put a topping on ▸ cap, crown, tip, top (off). [*Compare* COVER.] —*See also* CLIMAX.

crevice *n.* —*See* CRACK (2).

crew *n.* —*See* CIRCLE (3), CROWD, FORCE (3).

crib *v.* —*See* PLAGIARIZE, STEAL.

crib *n.* —*See* TRANSLATION.

cribber *n.* One who reproduces another's work without permission ▸ pirate, plagiarist, plagiarizer. [*Compare* FORGER.]

crime *n.* **1.** An act that violates public law ▸ felony, illegality, malefaction, misdeed, misdemeanor, offense, tort. [*Compare* BREACH.] **2.** A wicked act or wicked behavior ▸ deviltry, diablerie, evil, evildoing, immorality, iniquity, misdeed, offense, peccancy, sin, wickedness, wrong, wrongdoing. [*Compare* CORRUPTION, CRUELTY, OUTRAGE.] **3.** A great disappointment or regrettable fact ▸ pity, shame. *Slang:* bummer. *Idiom:* a crying shame. —*See also* INJUSTICE (1).

criminal *adj.* **1.** Of, involving, or being a crime ▸ felonious, illegal, illegitimate, illicit, lawless, unlawful, wrongful. [*Compare* FORBIDDEN.] **2.** Contrary to accepted, especially moral conventions ▸ illicit, unlawful.

criminal *n.* A person who commits a crime ▸ convict, culprit, delinquent, desperado, felon, gangster, lawbreaker, malefactor, offender, outlaw, perpetrator, scofflaw, transgressor. *Informal:* crook, mobster. *Slang:* con, perp. [*Compare* EVILDOER, FUGITIVE, LARCENIST, THUG.]

criminality *n.* —*See* CORRUPTION (1).

criminate *v.* To cause to appear involved in or guilty of a crime or fault ▸ incriminate, implicate, inculpate. [*Compare* ACCUSE.]

crimination *n.* —*See* ACCUSATION.

crimp *v.* —*See* FOLD, WRINKLE.

crimp *n.* —*See* FOLD (1).

crimson *v.* —*See* BLUSH.

cringe *v.* —*See* FAWN, FLINCH.

cringe *n.* —*See* RECOIL.

crinkle *v.* —*See* FOLD, WRINKLE.

crinkle *n.* —*See* FOLD (1), WRINKLE (1).

cripple *v.* To deprive of a limb or bodily member or its use ▸ amputate, castrate, dismember, maim, mangle, mutilate. [*Compare* BATTER, CUT.] —*See also* DISABLE (1).

crisis *n.* A decisive point ▸ climacteric, climax, clutch, crossroads, crunch, crux, exigence, exigency, head, juncture, pass, turning point, zero hour. *Idiom:* moment of truth. [*Compare* PREDICAMENT.] —*See also* EMERGENCY.

crisp *adj.* —*See* BRIEF.

adv. **—crisp′ness** *n.* **—crisp′·y** *adj.*
criss·cross (krĭs′krôs′, -krŏs′) ▸ *v.* **1.** To mark with crossing lines. **2.** To move back and forth through or over. ▸ *n.* A pattern of crossing lines. **—criss′cross′** *adj. & adv.*
cri·te·ri·on (krī-tîr′ē-ən) ▸ *n., pl.* **-te·ri·a** (-tîr′ē-ə) or **-te·ri·ons.** A standard or test on which a judgment can be based.
crit·ic (krĭt′ĭk) ▸ *n.* **1.** One who analyzes, interprets, or evaluates artistic works. **2.** A faultfinder.
crit·i·cal (krĭt′ĭ-kəl) ▸ *adj.* **1.** Inclined to judge severely. **2.** Marked by careful evaluation. **3.** Of or relating to critics or criticism. **4.** Of or forming a crisis: *a critical food shortage.* **5.** Crucial; decisive. **—crit′i·cal·ly** *adv.*
crit·i·cism (krĭt′ĭ-sĭz′əm) ▸ *n.* **1.** The act of criticizing, esp. adversely. **2.** A critical comment or judgment. **3.** The practice of analyzing, interpreting, or evaluating artistic works. **4.** A critical essay; critique.
crit·i·cize (krĭt′ĭ-sīz′) ▸ *v.* **-cized, -ciz·ing. 1.** To find fault with. **2.** To judge the merits and faults of; evaluate. **—crit′i·ciz′er** *n.*
cri·tique (krĭ-tēk′) ▸ *n.* A critical review or commentary. **—cri·tique′** *v.*
crit·ter (krĭt′ər) ▸ *n. Regional* A creature, esp. a domestic animal.
croak (krōk) ▸ *n.* A low hoarse sound, as that of a frog. ▸ *v.* **1.** To utter a croak. **2.** *Slang* To die.
Cro·at (krō′ăt′, -ät′, krōt) ▸ *n.* **1.** A native or inhabitant of Croatia. **2.** The Croatian language.
Cro·a·tia (krō-ā′shə, -shē-ə) ▸ A country of SE Europe along the NE Adriatic coast.
Cro·a·tian (krō-ā′shən) ▸ *n.* **1.** A Croat. **2.** The Slavic language of Croatia. ▸ *adj.* Of or relating to Croatia or the Croats.
cro·chet (krō-shā′) ▸ *v.* **-cheted** (-shād′), **-chet·ing** (-shā′ĭng). To make (a piece of needlework) by looping thread with a hooked needle. ▸ *n.* Needlework made by crocheting.
crock (krŏk) ▸ *n.* An earthenware vessel.
crocked (krŏkt) ▸ *adj. Slang* Drunk.
crock·er·y (krŏk′ə-rē) ▸ *n.* Earthenware.
Crock·ett (krŏk′ĭt), **David.** "Davy" (1786–1836) ▸ Amer. pioneer and politician.
croc·o·dile (krŏk′ə-dīl′) ▸ *n.* **1.** A large tropical aquatic reptile with armorlike skin and long tapering jaws. **2.** A similar or related reptile, such as a caiman. **—croc′o·dil′i·an** (krŏk′ə-dĭl′ē-ən, -dĭl′yən) *adj. & n.*
cro·cus (krō′kəs) ▸ *n., pl.* **-cus·es** or **-ci** (-sī, -kī). A garden plant with showy, variously colored flowers.
Croe·sus (krē′səs) (d. c. 546 B.C.) ▸ Last king of Lydia (560–546).
Crohn's disease (krōnz) ▸ *n.* A form of ileitis that is marked by abdominal pain, ulceration, and fibrous tissue buildup.
crois·sant (krwä-säɴ′, krə-sänt′) ▸ *n.* A rich, crescent-shaped roll.
Cro-Mag·non (krō-măg′nən, -măn′yən) ▸ *n.* An early form of modern human of Europe in the late Paleolithic Era. **—Cro-Mag′non** *adj.*
Crom·well (krŏm′wĕl′, -wəl, krŭm′-), **Oliver** (1599–1658) ▸ English military, political, and religious leader.
crone (krōn) ▸ *n.* **1.** An old woman. **2.** A hag.
cro·ny (krō′nē) ▸ *n., pl.* **-nies.** A close friend or companion.
cro·ny·ism (krō′nē-ĭz′əm) ▸ *n.* Favoritism shown to old friends without regard for their qualifications.
crook (kro͝ok) ▸ *n.* **1.** A bent or curved implement, such as a staff. **2.** A curve or bend. **3.** *Informal* A thief; swindler. ▸ *v.* To curve or bend.
crook·ed (kro͝ok′ĭd) ▸ *adj.* **1.** Having bends or curves. **2.** *Informal* Dishonest; fraudulent. **—crook′ed·ly** *adv.* **—crook′ed·ness** *n.*
croon (kro͞on) ▸ *v.* To hum or sing softly. **—croon′er** *n.*
crop (krŏp) ▸ *n.* **1a.** Agricultural produce. **b.** The total yield of such produce. **2.** A group. **3.** A short haircut. **4a.** A short riding whip. **b.** The stock of a whip. **5.** *Zool.* A pouchlike enlargement of a bird's gullet in which food is digested or stored. ▸ *v.* **cropped, crop·ping. 1.** To cut or bite off the tops of. **2.** To cut very short. **3.** To trim. ***—phrasal verb:*** **crop up** To appear unexpectedly.
crop-dust·ing (krŏp′dŭs′tĭng) ▸ *n.* The process of spraying crops with insecticides from an airplane. **—crop′-dust′** *v.*
crop·per (krŏp′ər) ▸ *n.* A sharecropper.
cro·quet (krō-kā′) ▸ *n.* An outdoor game in which players drive wooden balls through wickets using mallets.
cro·quette (krō-kĕt′) ▸ *n.* A small cake of minced food usu. fried in deep fat.
cro·sier or **cro·zier** (krō′zhər) ▸ *n.* A crooked staff, esp. of a bishop.
cross (krôs, krŏs) ▸ *n.* **1.** An upright post with a transverse piece near the top. **2a.** often **Cross** A symbolic representation of the structure on which Jesus was crucified. **b.** Any of various modifications of the cross design. **3.** A trial or affliction. **4.** A pattern formed by the intersection of two lines. **5.** *Biol.* **a.** A hybrid plant or animal. **b.** A hybridization. ▸ *v.* **1.** To go or extend across. **2.** To intersect. **3.** To draw a line across. **4.** To place crosswise. **5.** To encounter in passing. **6.** To thwart or obstruct. **7.** *Biol.* To breed by hybridizing. ▸ *adj.* **1.** Lying crosswise. **2.** Contrary or opposing. **3.** Showing ill humor; annoyed. **4.** Hybrid. **—cross′er** *n.* **—cross′ly** *adv.* **—cross′ness** *n.*
cross·bar (krôs′bär′, krŏs′-) ▸ *n.* A horizontal bar or line.
cross·bones (krôs′bōnz′, krŏs′-) ▸ *pl.n.* Two bones placed crosswise, usu. under a skull.

THESAURUS

crisscross *v.* —*See* CROSS (2).
criterion *n.* —*See* STANDARD.
critic *n.* **1.** A person who evaluates and reports on the worth of something ▸ appraiser, assessor, commentator, judge, pundit, reviewer. **2.** A person who finds fault ▸ blamer, carper, caviler, censurer, criticizer, faultfinder, hypercritic, mudslinger, nagger, niggler, nitpicker, pettifogger, quibbler. *Informal:* Monday morning quarterback. [*Compare* SCOLD.]
critical *adj.* **1.** Inclined to judge too severely ▸ captious, carping, censorious, faultfinding, hypercritical, judgmental, nagging, overcritical, reproachful. [*Compare* SEVERE.] **2.** Keenly perceptive or discerning ▸ acute, discerning, discriminating, incisive, keen, penetrating, perceptive, probing, sensitive, sharp, trenchant. [*Compare* CAREFUL, CLEVER, INTELLIGENT, SHREWD.] —*See also* ESSENTIAL (1), URGENT (1).
criticism *n.* The act or an instance of finding fault ▸ blame, censure, condemnation, denunciation, finger-pointing, judgment, reprehension, reprobation. *Informal:* flak, guilt trip, pan. *Slang:* knock. [*Compare* DISAPPROVAL, REBUKE.] —*See also* COMMENTARY.
criticize *v.* **1.** To find fault with ▸ blame, carp at, censure, fault, judge, rap, reprove, scapegoat. *Informal:* guilt-trip, pan, zing. *Slang:* knock, put down. ***Idioms:*** find fault with, lay (*or* put) a guilt trip on, pick apart (*or* to pieces), point the finger at, speak ill of. [*Compare* CHASTISE, MALIGN, SLAM.] **2.** To write a critical report on ▸ critique, review. [*Compare* ESTIMATE.]
criticizer *n.* —*See* CRITIC (2).
critique *n.* —*See* COMMENTARY.
critique *v.* To write a critical report on ▸ criticize, review. [*Compare* ESTIMATE.]
croak *v.* —*See* DIE, GASP.
croaker *n.* —*See* PESSIMIST (2).
croaky or **croaking** *adj.* —*See* HOARSE.
crocked *adj.* —*See* DRUNK.
crone *n.* —*See* WITCH (2).
crony *n.* —*See* ASSOCIATE (2), FRIEND.
crook *n.* —*See* BEND, CHEAT (2), CRIMINAL, STICK (2).
crook *v.* —*See* BEND (1).
crooked *adj.* —*See* BENT, CORRUPT (2), DISHONEST, IRREGULAR.
crookedness *n.* —*See* CORRUPTION (2), DISHONESTY (1), IRREGULARITY.
croon *v.* —*See* SING.
crooner *n.* —*See* VOCALIST.
crop *n.* —*See* HARVEST.
crop *v.* —*See* BROWSE (2), CUT (3), GATHER.
crop up *v.* —*See* BEGIN.
cross *n.* —*See* BURDEN[1] (1).
cross *v.* **1.** To go or extend across ▸ ford, pass, span, track, transit, traverse. **2.** To pass through or over ▸ crisscross, crosscut, cut across, decussate, intersect. [*Compare* CLOSE.] —*See also* CANCEL (1), COVER (2), FRUSTRATE.
cross up *v.* —*See* BETRAY (1), CONFUSE (3), DESTROY (1).
cross *adj.* —*See* ANGRY, ILL-TEMPERED.
crossbeam *n.* —*See* BEAM (2).

cross·bow (krôs′bō′, krŏs′-) ▸ *n.* A weapon consisting of a bow fixed crosswise on a wooden stock.

cross·breed (krôs′brēd′, krŏs′-) ▸ *v.* To hybridize. ▸ *n.* A hybrid.

cross-coun·try (krôs′kŭn′trē, krŏs′-) ▸ *adj.* **1.** Moving across open country rather than roads. **2.** From one side of a country to the opposite side. **—cross′-coun′try** *adv.*

cross-country skiing ▸ *n.* The sport of skiing over the countryside rather than downhill.

cross-cul·tur·al (krôs′kŭl′chər-əl, krŏs′-) ▸ *adj.* Comparing or dealing with different cultures. **—cross′-cul′tur·al·ly** *adv.*

cross·cur·rent (krôs′kûr′ənt, -kŭr′-, krŏs′-) ▸ *n.* **1.** A current flowing across another. **2.** A conflicting tendency.

cross·cut (krôs′kŭt′, krŏs′-) ▸ *v.* To cut or run crosswise. ▸ *adj.* **1.** Used for cutting crosswise. **2.** Cut across the grain.

cross-dress (krôs′drĕs′, krŏs′-) ▸ *v.* To dress in the clothing characteristic of the opposite sex.

cross-ex·am·ine (krôs′ĭg-zăm′ĭn, krŏs′-) ▸ *v.* To question (a person) closely, esp. with regard to answers or information given previously. **—cross′-ex·am′i·na′tion** *n.* **—cross′-ex·am′in·er** *n.*

cross-eye (krôs′ī′, krŏs′ī′) ▸ *n.* A form of strabismus in which one or both eyes deviate toward the nose. **—cross′-eyed′** *adj.*

cross·fire (krôs′fīr′, krŏs′-) ▸ *n.* **1.** Lines of gunfire crossing each other. **2.** Rapid, heated discussion.

cross·hatch (krôs′hăch′, krŏs′-) ▸ *v.* To shade with sets of intersecting parallel lines.

cross·ing (krô′sĭng, krŏs′ĭng) ▸ *n.* **1.** An intersection, as of roads. **2.** A place at which something, as a river, may be crossed.

cross·piece (krôs′pēs′, krŏs′-) ▸ *n.* A transverse or horizontal piece, as of a structure.

cross-pol·li·nate (krôs′pŏl′ə-nāt′, krŏs′-) ▸ *v.* To fertilize (a flower) with pollen from another. **—cross′pol′li·na′tion** *n.*

cross-pur·pose (krôs′pûr′pəs, krŏs′-) ▸ *n.* A conflicting or contrary purpose. ***—idiom:* at cross-purposes** Acting under a misunderstanding of each other's purposes.

cross-ques·tion (krôs′kwĕs′chən, krŏs′-) ▸ *v.* To cross-examine. **—cross′ques′tion** *n.*

cross-ref·er·ence (krôs′rĕf′ər-əns, -rĕf′rəns, krŏs′-) ▸ *n.* A reference from one part of a book or file to another part containing related information. **—cross′re·fer′** *v.*

cross·road (krôs′rōd′, krŏs′-) ▸ *n.* **1.** A road that intersects another. **2. crossroads** *(takes sing. v.)* A place where two or more roads meet. **3.** A crucial point.

cross section ▸ *n.* **1a.** A section formed by a plane cutting through an object, usu. at right angles to an axis. **b.** A piece so cut or a graphic representation of it. **2.** A sample meant to be representative of the whole.

cross-train (krôs′trān′, krŏs′-) ▸ *v.* **1.** To train in different tasks or skills. **2.** To train in different sports, esp. by alternating regimens.

cross·walk (krôs′wôk′, krŏs′-) ▸ *n.* A street crossing marked for pedestrians.

cross·wise (krôs′wīz′, krŏs′-) also **cross·ways** (-wāz′) ▸ *adv.* So as to be in a cross direction; across. **—cross′wise′** *adj.*

cross·word (krôs′wûrd′, krŏs′-) ▸ *n.* A puzzle consisting of numbered squares to be filled with words in answer to clues.

crotch (krŏch) ▸ *n.* The angle formed by the junction of two parts, as branches or legs. **—crotched** (krŏcht) *adj.*

crotch·et (krŏch′ĭt) ▸ *n.* An odd or whimsical notion. **—crotch′et·y** *adj.*

crouch (krouch) ▸ *v.* **1.** To stoop, esp. with the knees bent. **2.** To cower or cringe. **—crouch** *n.*

croup (kro͞op) ▸ *n.* Inflammation of the larynx, esp. in children, marked by labored breathing and a hoarse cough. **—croup′ous, croup′y** *adj.*

crou·pi·er (kro͞o′pē-ər, -pē-ā′) ▸ *n.* An attendant at a gaming table.

crou·ton (kro͞o′tŏn′, kro͞o-tŏn′) ▸ *n.* A small piece of toasted bread.

crow[1] (krō) ▸ *n.* A large, glossy black bird with a raucous call. ***—idiom:* as the crow flies** In a straight line.

crow[2] (krō) ▸ *v.* **1.** To utter the shrill cry of a rooster. **2.** To exult loudly; boast. **3.** To make an inarticulate sound of pleasure or delight. **—crow** *n.*

Crow ▸ *n., pl.* **Crow** or **Crows. 1.** A member of a Native American people of the N Great Plains, now chiefly in SE Montana. **2.** The Siouan language of the Crow.

crow·bar (krō′bär′) ▸ *n.* A metal bar with the working end shaped like a forked chisel, used as a lever.

crowd (kroud) ▸ *n.* **1.** A large number of persons gathered together. **2.** A particular group: *the over-30 crowd.* ▸ *v.* **1.** To gather closely together; throng. **2.** To advance by pressing or shoving. **3.** To press or force tightly together.

crown (kroun) ▸ *n.* **1.** An ornamental circlet worn as a symbol of sovereignty. **2.** often **Crown** The power of a monarch. **3.** A distinction for achievement, esp. a title signifying championship in a sport. **4.** Something resembling a crown in shape. **5.** A former British coin. **6.** The top part of something, as the head. **7.** The part of a tooth above the gum line. ▸ *v.* **1.** To put a crown on. **2.** To invest with regal power. **3.** To confer honor upon. **4.** To be the highest part of.

crown prince ▸ *n.* The male heir apparent to a throne.

crown princess ▸ *n.* **1.** The female heir apparent to a throne. **2.** The wife of a crown prince.

crow's-feet (krōz′fēt′) ▸ *pl.n.* Wrinkles at the outer corner of the eye.

crow's-nest (krōz′nĕst′) ▸ *n.* A small lookout platform near the top of a ship's mast.

cro·zier (krō′zhər) ▸ *n.* Var. of **crosier.**

cru·ces (kro͞o′sēz) ▸ *n.* Pl. of **crux.**

cru·cial (kro͞o′shəl) ▸ *adj.* **1.** Extremely significant or important. **2.** Vital to the resolution of a crisis. **—cru′cial·ly** *adv.*

cru·ci·ble (kro͞o′sə-bəl) ▸ *n.* **1.** A vessel used for melting materials at high temperatures. **2.** A severe test.

cru·ci·fix (kro͞o′sə-fĭks′) ▸ *n.* An image of Jesus on the cross.

cru·ci·fix·ion (kro͞o′sə-fĭk′shən) ▸ *n.* **1.** Execution on a cross. **2. Crucifixion** The crucifying of Jesus. **3.** A crucifix.

cru·ci·form (kro͞o′sə-fôrm′) ▸ *adj.* Shaped like a cross.

cru·ci·fy (kro͞o′sə-fī′) ▸ *v.* **-fied, -fy·ing. 1.** To put to death by nailing or binding to a cross. **2.** To torture; torment.

crude (kro͞od) ▸ *adj.* **crud·er, crud·est. 1.** In an unrefined or natural state; raw. **2.** Lacking tact, refinement, or taste.

THESAURUS

crosscut *v.* —*See* CROSS (2).

cross-examine *v.* —*See* ASK (1).

cross-examiner *n.* —*See* INQUIRER.

cross-eyed *adj.* Marked by or affected with a squint ▸ squint-eyed, squinty, strabismal, strabismic.

crossfire *n.* —*See* BARRAGE.

crossing *adj.* —*See* TRANSVERSE.

crossing *n.* —*See* JOURNEY.

crossroads *n.* —*See* CRISIS, JUNCTION.

crosstie *n.* —*See* BEAM (2).

crosswise or **crossways** *adj.* —*See* TRANSVERSE.

crouch *v.* —*See* STOOP.

crow *v.* —*See* BOAST, EXULT (1).

crow *n.* —*See* WITCH (2).

crowd *n.* An enormous number of persons gathered together ▸ army, cloud, concourse, crew, crush, drove, flock, gaggle, herd, horde, host, legion, mass, mob, multitude, pack, press, rout, ruck, scores, stable, swarm, throng, troop. [*Compare* BAND[2], FLOCK, GROUP.] —*See also* ASSEMBLY, CIRCLE (3), COMMONALTY.

crowd *v.* To move into an area or space in large numbers ▸ cram, crush, flock, flood, jam, pile, pour, press, squeeze, swarm, throng, troop. —*See also* FILL (1), PUSH (1).

crowded *adj.* —*See* BUSY (3), THICK (2), TIGHT (4).

crown *n.* —*See* CIRCLE (1), CLIMAX, HEAD (1).

crown *v.* To put a topping on ▸ cap, crest, tip, top (off). [*Compare* COVER.] —*See also* CLIMAX.

crowning *adj.* ▸ climactic, culminating, peak. [*Compare* LAST.]

crow's-foot *n.* —*See* WRINKLE (1).

crow's nest *n.* —*See* LOOKOUT (2).

crucial *adj.* —*See* DECISIVE, IMPORTANT, PRIMARY (1), URGENT (1).

crucible *n.* —*See* TRIAL (1).

crucify *v.* To subject another to extreme physical cruelty, as in punishing ▸ harrow, rack, torment, torture. *Idioms:* put on the rack (*or* wheel), put the screws to. [*Compare* PUNISH.]

crud *n.* —*See* FILTH.

crude *adj.* Being in a natural state ▸ native, raw, rough, rude, unprocessed, unrefined, virgin. [*Compare* WILD.] —*See also* AMATEURISH,

3. Roughly made. ► *n.* Unrefined petroleum. **—crude′ly** *adv.* **—cru′di·ty, crude′ness** *n.*

cru·el (kro͞o′əl) ► *adj.* **-el·er, -el·est** or **-el·ler, -el·lest.** Causing suffering; painful. **—cru′el·ly** *adv.* **—cru′el·ty** *n.*

cru·et (kro͞o′ĭt) ► *n.* A small glass bottle for vinegar or oil.

cruise (kro͞oz) ► *v.* **cruised, cruis·ing. 1.** To sail or travel about, as for pleasure. **2.** To travel at a steady or efficient speed. **—cruise** *n.*

cruise missile ► *n.* An unpiloted aircraft that serves as a self-contained bomb.

cruis·er (kro͞o′zər) ► *n.* **1.** One of a class of fast warships of medium tonnage. **2.** A cabin cruiser. **3.** See **squad car.**

crul·ler (krŭl′ər) ► *n.* A small cake of deep-fried sweet dough.

crumb (krŭm) ► *n.* **1.** A very small piece broken from bread or pastry. **2.** A fragment or scrap. ► *v.* **1.** To break into crumbs. **2.** To cover with crumbs.

crum·ble (krŭm′bəl) ► *v.* **-bled, -bling. 1.** To break into small pieces. **2.** To disintegrate. **—crum′bly** *adj.*

crum·my also **crumb·y** (krŭm′ē) ► *adj.* **-mi·er, -mi·est** also **-i·er, -i·est.** *Slang* **1.** Miserable. **2.** Shabby; cheap.

crum·pet (krŭm′pĭt) ► *n.* A small flat round of bread, baked on a griddle.

crum·ple (krŭm′pəl) ► *v.* **-pled, -pling. 1.** To crush together into wrinkles; rumple. **2.** To fall apart; collapse. **—crum′ply** *adj.*

crunch (krŭnch) ► *v.* **1.** To chew with a crackling noise. **2.** To crush or grind noisily. **—crunch** *n.* **—crunch′y** *adj.*

cru·sade (kro͞o-sād′) ► *n.* **1.** often **Crusade** Any of the Christian military expeditions undertaken in the 11th, 12th, and 13th cent. to seize the Holy Land from the Muslims. **2.** A vigorous concerted movement for a cause or against an abuse. ► *v.* **-sad·ed, -sad·ing.** To engage in a crusade. **—cru·sad′er** *n.*

crush (krŭsh) ► *v.* **1.** To press or squeeze so as to break or injure. **2.** To break, pound, or grind into small fragments or powder. **3.** To put down; subdue. **4.** To shove or crowd. **5.** To extract by pressing or squeezing. ► *n.* **1.** The act of crushing. **2.** A throng. **3.** *Informal* A temporary infatuation. **—crush′er** *n.*

crust (krŭst) ► *n.* **1.** The usu. hard outer surface of bread. **2.** A stale piece of bread. **3.** A pastry shell, as of a pie. **4.** A hard covering or surface. **5.** *Geol.* The exterior layer of the earth. ► *v.* To cover with or harden into a crust. **—crust′y** *adj.*

crus·ta·cean (krŭ-stā′shən) ► *n.* Any of a class of chiefly aquatic arthropods, including lobsters, crabs, and shrimps, having a segmented body with a hard outer shell.

crutch (krŭch) ► *n.* **1.** A staff or support used as an aid in walking, usu. designed to fit under the armpit. **2.** Something that is depended upon for support.

crux (krŭks, kro͝oks) ► *n., pl.* **crux·es** or **cru·ces** (kro͞o′sēz). **1.** A central or critical point. **2.** A puzzling problem.

cru·zei·ro (kro͞o-zâr′ō, -zā′ro͞o) ► *n., pl.* **cru·zei·ros.** A monetary unit formerly used in Brazil.

cry (krī) ► *v.* **cried** (krīd), **cry·ing. 1.** To sob or shed tears, as out of grief or pain. **2.** To call loudly; shout. **3.** To proclaim or announce in public. **4.** To utter a characteristic sound or call, as does an animal. **5.** To demand or require remedy: *grievances crying out for redress.* ► *n., pl.* **cries** (krīz). **1.** A loud shout, exclamation, or utterance. **2.** A fit of weeping. **3.** An urgent appeal. **4.** The characteristic call of an animal. ***—idioms:*** **cry over spilled milk** To regret in vain what cannot be undone. **cry wolf** To raise a false alarm.

cry·ba·by (krī′bā′bē) ► *n.* One who cries or complains frequently with little cause.

cryo– ► *pref.* Cold; freezing: *cryogenics.*

cry·o·gen (krī′ə-jən) ► *n.* A refrigerant that produces very low temperatures. **—cry′o·gen′ic** *adj.*

cry·o·gen·ics (krī′ə-jĕn′ĭks) ► *n.* *(takes sing. or pl. v.)* The study of low-temperature phenomena.

crypt (krĭpt) ► *n.* An underground vault, esp. one used as a burial place.

cryp·tic (krĭp′tĭk) ► *adj.* Having an ambiguous or hidden meaning. **—cryp′ti·cal·ly** *adv.*

crypto– or **crypt–** ► *pref.* Hidden; secret: *cryptogram.*

cryp·to·gram (krĭp′tə-grăm′) ► *n.* A piece of writing in code or cipher.

cryp·tog·ra·phy (krĭp-tŏg′rə-fē) ► *n.* The process or skill of using or deciphering secret writings. **—cryp·tog′ra·pher** *n.*

crys·tal (krĭs′təl) ► *n.* **1.** A homogenous solid formed by a repeating, three-dimensional pattern of atoms, ions, or molecules and having fixed distances between constituent parts. **2.** A mineral, esp. a transparent form of quartz, having a crystalline structure. **3.** A high-quality clear glass. **4.** A clear protective cover for a watch or clock face. **—crys′tal·line** *adj.*

crys·tal·lize (krĭs′tə-līz′) ► *v.* **-lized, -liz·ing. 1.** To form or cause to form a crystalline structure. **2.** To assume or cause to assume a definite and permanent form. **—crys′tal·li·za′tion** (-lĭ-zā′shən) *n.*

crys·tal·log·ra·phy (krĭs′tə-lŏg′rə-fē) ► *n.* The science of crystal structure and phenomena. **—crys′tal·log′ra·pher** *n.*

Cs ► The symbol for the element **cesium.**

csc ► *abbr.* cosecant

C-sec·tion (sē′sĕk′shən) ► *n.* A cesarean section.

CT ► *abbr.* Connecticut

ct. ► *abbr.* cent

THESAURUS

COARSE (1), ROUGH (4), RUDE (1).

crude *n.* —*See* OIL.

cruel *adj.* Characterized by or inflicting suffering or pain ► barbarous, brutal, ferocious, fierce, grim, inhuman, inhumane, merciless, pitiless, ruthless, sadistic, savage, truculent, vicious. [*Compare* FIENDISH, MALEVOLENT, MURDEROUS.] —*See also* BITTER (2).

cruelty *n.* The quality or condition of being cruel ► barbarity, bestiality, brutality, ferocity, fiendishness, fierceness, grimness, inhumanity, mercilessness, pitilessness, ruthlessness, sadism, savagery, truculence, truculency. [*Compare* CRIME, MALEVOLENCE.]

cruise *n.* —*See* JOURNEY.

crumb *n.* —*See* BIT[1] (1), BIT[1] (2).

crumble *v.* —*See* BREAK (3), DECAY, DISINTEGRATE.

crummy *adj.* —*See* SHODDY.

crump *v.* —*See* CHEW.

crumple *v.* —*See* BREAK (3), BUCKLE, WRINKLE.

crumple *n.* —*See* FOLD (1).

crunch *v.* To rub together noisily ► gnash, grind. —*See also* CHEW.

crunch *n.* —*See* CRISIS.

crusade *n.* A goal served with great or uncompromising dedication ► cause, holy war, jihad. —*See also* DRIVE (1).

crush *v.* **1.** To press forcefully so as to reduce to a pulpy mass ► flatten, mash, mush, pulp, smash, squash. [*Compare* SQUEEZE.] **2.** To break up into tiny particles ► atomize, bray, comminute, granulate, grind, levigate, mill, pestle, pound, powder, pulverize, smash, triturate. [*Compare* BREAK.] **3.** To extract from by applying pressure ► express, press, squeeze. —*See also* BREAK (2), CROWD, DESTROY (1), OVERWHELM (1), OVERWHELM (2), PUSH (1), SUPPRESS.

crush *n.* An extravagant, short-lived romantic attachment ► *Informal:* infatuation, thing. ***Idiom:*** passing fancy. [*Compare* LOVE, OBSESSION.] —*See also* CROWD.

crust *n.* —*See* COAT (2), IMPUDENCE.

crusty *adj.* —*See* ABRUPT (1).

crutch *n.* —*See* SUPPORT.

crux *n.* —*See* CRISIS.

cry *v.* To shed tears ► bawl, blubber, howl, keen, lament, mewl, pule, sniffle, snivel, sob, squall, wail, weep, whimper, whine, yowl. *Idioms:* cry one's eyes out, turn on the waterworks. [*Compare* BAWL, GRIEVE.] —*See also* EXCLAIM, SHOUT.

cry up *v.* —*See* PROMOTE (3).

cry *n.* **1.** A fit of crying ► bawling, blubbering, lament, lamentation, plaint, sobbing, tears, wailing, weeping, whimpering, whining. [*Compare* HOWL.] **2.** A rallying term used by proponents of a cause ► battle cry, call to arms, call to battle, motto, rallying cry, slogan, war cry, watchword. —*See also* DEMAND (1), SHOUT.

crybaby *n.* —*See* BABY (2).

crying *adj.* —*See* URGENT (1).

crypt *n.* —*See* GRAVE[1].

cryptic *adj.* —*See* AMBIGUOUS (1), MYSTERIOUS.

crystal *adj.* —*See* CLEAR (1).

crystal clear *adj.* —*See* APPARENT (1), CLEAR (1).

crystalline *adj.* —*See* CLEAR (1).

Ct. ▸ *abbr.* 1. Connecticut 2. count (title) 3. court
Cu ▸ The symbol for the element **copper** 1.
cu. ▸ *abbr.* cubic
cub (kŭb) ▸ *n.* **1.** The young of certain carnivorous animals, such as the bear. **2.** A youth or novice.
Cu·ba (kyo͞o′bə) ▸ An island country in the Caribbean Sea S of FL. **—Cu′ban** *adj.* *& n.*
Cuban sandwich ▸ *n.* *Regional* See **submarine** 2.
cub·by·hole (kŭb′ē-hōl′) ▸ *n.* A small or cramped space.
cube (kyo͞ob) ▸ *n.* **1.** *Math.* A solid having six congruent square faces. **2a.** Something shaped like a cube. **b.** A cubicle, used for work or study. **3.** *Math.* The third power of a number or quantity. ▸ *v.* **cubed, cub·ing.** **1.** *Math.* To raise (a quantity or number) to the third power. **2.** To form or cut into cubes; dice.
cu·bic (kyo͞o′bĭk) ▸ *adj.* **1.** Having the shape of a cube. **2a.** Having three dimensions. **b.** Having a volume equal to a cube whose edge is of a stated length: *a cubic foot.* **3.** *Math.* Of the third power, order, or degree.
cu·bi·cal (kyo͞o′bĭ-kəl) ▸ *adj.* **1.** Cubic. **2.** Of or relating to volume. **—cu′bi·cal·ly** *adv.*
cu·bi·cle (kyo͞o′bĭ-kəl) ▸ *n.* A small compartment, as for work or sleeping.
cub·ism (kyo͞o′bĭz′əm) ▸ *n.* A 20th-cent. school of painting and sculpture characterized by abstract, often geometric structures. **—cub′ist** *n.* **—cu·bis′tic** *adj.*
cu·bit (kyo͞o′bĭt) ▸ *n.* An ancient unit of linear measure, approx. 17 to 22 in. (43 to 56 cm).
cuck·old (kŭk′əld, ko͝ok′-) ▸ *n.* A man married to an adulterous wife. ▸ *v.* To make a cuckold of.
cuck·oo (ko͞o′ko͞o, ko͝ok′o͞o) ▸ *n., pl.* **-oos.** **1.** A grayish European bird that lays its eggs in the nests of other birds. **2.** Its two-note call. ▸ *adj.* *Slang* Foolish or crazy.
cu·cum·ber (kyo͞o′kŭm′bər) ▸ *n.* **1.** A vine bearing an edible cylindrical fruit with a green rind and crisp white flesh. **2.** The fruit itself.
cud (kŭd) ▸ *n.* Food regurgitated from the first stomach to the mouth of a ruminant and chewed again.
cud·dle (kŭd′l) ▸ *v.* **-dled, -dling.** **1.** To hug tenderly. **2.** To nestle; snuggle. **—cud′dly** *adj.*
cudg·el (kŭj′əl) ▸ *n.* A short heavy club. **—cudg′el** *v.*
cue[1] (kyo͞o) ▸ *n.* A long tapered rod used to strike the cue ball in billiards and pool. **—cue** *v.*
cue[2] (kyo͞o) ▸ *n.* **1.** A word or signal, as in a play, used esp. to prompt another actor's speech or entrance. **2.** A reminder or hint. ▸ *v.* **cued, cu·ing.** To give a cue to.
cue ball ▸ *n.* The white ball propelled with the cue in billiards and pool.
cuff[1] (kŭf) ▸ *n.* **1.** A fold or band at the bottom of a sleeve. **2.** The turned-up fold at the bottom of a trouser leg. ***—idiom:*** **off the cuff** Extemporaneously.
cuff[2] (kŭf) ▸ *v.* To strike with the open hand; slap. **—cuff** *n.*
cuff link ▸ *n.* A paired or jointed fastening for a shirt cuff.
cui·sine (kwĭ-zēn′) ▸ *n.* **1.** A manner or style of preparing food: *Cuban cuisine.* **2.** Food; fare.
cul-de-sac (kŭl′dĭ-săk′, ko͝ol′-) ▸ *n., pl.* **culs-de-sac** (kŭlz′-, ko͝olz′-) or **cul-de-sacs.** **1.** A dead-end street. **2.** An impasse.
cu·li·nar·y (kyo͞o′lə-nĕr′ē, kŭl′ə-) ▸ *adj.* Of or relating to cooking or cookery.
cull (kŭl) ▸ *v.* **1.** To pick out from others; select. **2.** To gather; collect. **—cull′er** *n.*
cul·mi·nate (kŭl′mə-nāt′) ▸ *v.* **-nat·ed, -nat·ing.** **1.** To reach the highest point or degree. **2.** To end. **—cul′mi·na′tion** *n.*
cu·lottes (ko͞o-lŏts′, kyo͞o-, ko͞o′lŏts′, kyo͞o′-) ▸ *pl.n.* A woman's full trousers cut to resemble a skirt.
cul·pa·ble (kŭl′pə-bəl) ▸ *adj.* Deserving of blame. **—cul′pa·bil′i·ty** *n.* **—cul′pa·bly** *adv.*
cul·prit (kŭl′prĭt) ▸ *n.* One charged with or guilty of a crime.
cult (kŭlt) ▸ *n.* **1.** A system of religious worship and ritual. **2.** A religion or sect considered extremist or false. **3a.** Obsessive devotion to a person or principle. **b.** The object of such devotion. **—cult′ish** *adj.* **—cult′ism** *n.* **—cult′ist** *n.*
cul·ti·var (kŭl′tə-vär′, -vâr′) ▸ *n.* A plant variety produced by selective breeding.
cul·ti·vate (kŭl′tə-vāt′) ▸ *v.* **-vat·ed, -vat·ing.** **1.** To improve and prepare (land) for raising crops. **2.** To grow or tend (a plant or crop). **3.** To foster. **4.** To form and refine, as by education. **5.** To seek the acquaintance or good will of. **—cul′ti·va′tion** *n.* **—cul′ti·va′tor** *n.*
cul·ture (kŭl′chər) ▸ *n.* **1.** The behavior patterns, arts, beliefs, institutions, and all other products of human work and thought, esp. as expressed in a particular community or period. **2.** Intellectual and artistic activity and the works produced. **3.** Development of the intellect through training or education. **4.** The breeding of animals or growing of plants, esp. to improve stock. **5.** *Biol.* The growing esp. of microorganisms in a specially prepared nutrient medium. ▸ *v.* **-tured, -tur·ing.** To grow (microorganisms) in a nutrient medium. **—cul′tur·al** *adj.* **—cul′tur·al·ly** *adv.* **—cul′tured** *adj.*
cul·vert (kŭl′vərt) ▸ *n.* A drain crossing under a road or embankment.
cum·ber (kŭm′bər) ▸ *v.* To weigh down. **—cum′brous** *adj.*
cum·ber·some (kŭm′bər-səm) ▸ *adj.* Unwieldy and burdensome.
cum·in (kŭm′ĭn, ko͞o′mĭn, kyo͞o′-) ▸ *n.* A plant having aromatic seedlike fruit used for seasoning.
cum·mer·bund (kŭm′ər-bŭnd′) ▸ *n.* A broad pleated sash worn with a tuxedo.
Cum·mings (kŭm′ĭngz), **Edward Estlin.** e. e. cummings (1894–1962) ▸ Amer. poet.
cu·mu·la·tive (kyo͞om′yə-lā′tĭv, -yə-lə-tĭv) ▸ *adj.* Increasing or enlarging by successive addition.
cu·mu·lo·nim·bus (kyo͞om′yə-lō-nĭm′bəs) ▸ *n., pl.* **-bus·es** or **-bi** (-bī). An extremely dense cumulus extending to great heights, usu. producing heavy rains or thunderstorms.
cu·mu·lus (kyo͞om′yə-ləs) ▸ *n., pl.* **-li** (-lī′). A dense, white, fluffy flat-based cloud with a multiple rounded top and a well-defined outline.

THESAURUS

cuckoo *n.* *—See* CRACKPOT.
cuckoo *adj.* *—See* ENTHUSIASTIC, INSANE.
cuddle *v.* *—See* CARESS, SNUGGLE.
cudgel *n.* *—See* BEAT (1).
cue *n.* *—See* HINT (2).
cue in *v.* *—See* INFORM (1).
cuff *n.* *—See* SLAP.
cuff *n.* *—See* SLAP.
cul-de-sac *n.* A course leading nowhere ▸ blind alley, dead end.
cull *v.* *—See* CHOOSE (1), GLEAN.
culminate *v.* *—See* CLIMAX.
culminating *adj.* ▸ climactic, crowning, peak. [*Compare* LAST[1].]
culmination *n.* *—See* CLIMAX, FULFILLMENT (1).
culpability *n.* *—See* BLAME.
culpable *adj.* *—See* BLAMEWORTHY.
culprit *n.* *—See* CRIMINAL.
cult *n.* *—See* RELIGION.
cultivate *v.* *—See* GROW, NURTURE, PROMOTE (2), TILL.
cultivated *adj.* *—See* CULTURED.
cultivation *n.* *—See* CULTURE (3).
cultrate *adj.* *—See* POINTED.
cultural *adj.* Promoting culture ▸ advancing, aesthetic, civilizing, cultivating, edifying, enlightening, fostering, humanizing, refining. [*Compare* INTELLECTUAL.]
culture *n.* **1.** The total product of human creativity and intellect ▸ civilization, Kultur, society. **2.** Behavior patterns, traits, and products considered as an expression of a certain people or period ▸ civilization, convention, custom, ethos, folkways, lifestyle, mores, society, tradition. **3.** Excellent taste resulting from intellectual development ▸ breeding, civilization, cultivation, enlightenment, refinement, sophistication. [*Compare* COURTESY, EDUCATION, ELEGANCE.]
culture *v.* *—See* TILL.
cultured *adj.* Characterized by discriminating taste and broad knowledge as a result of development or education ▸ civilized, cultivated, educated, highbrow, polished, refined, sophisticated, urbane, well-bred. [*Compare* COURTEOUS, DELICATE, SUAVE.]
cumber *v.* *—See* BURDEN[1].
cumbersome or **cumbrous** *adj.* *—See* BULKY (1).
cumshaw *n.* *—See* GRATUITY.
cumulate *v.* *—See* ACCUMULATE.
cumulation *n.* *—See* ACCUMULATION (1).
cumulative *adj.* Increasing, as in force, by successive additions ▸ accumulative, additive.
cumulus *n.* *—See* HEAP (1).

cu·ne·i·form (kyo͞o′nē-ə-fôrm′, kyo͞o-nē′-) ► *adj.* Wedge-shaped, as the characters used in ancient Mesopotamian writing. ► *n.* Cuneiform writing.

cun·ning (kŭn′ĭng) ► *adj.* **1.** Shrewdly deceptive. **2.** Exhibiting ingenuity. **3.** Delicately pleasing; cute. ► *n.* **1.** Skill in deception; guile. **2.** Dexterity. **—cun′ning·ly** *adv.*

cup (kŭp) ► *n.* **1a.** A small open container used for drinking. **b.** Such a container and its contents. **2.** See **measurement** table in Appendix. **3.** A cuplike object. ► *v.* **cupped, cup·ping.** To shape like a cup: *cup one's hand.*

cup·board (kŭb′ərd) ► *n.* A storage closet or cabinet.

cup·cake (kŭp′kāk′) ► *n.* A small, cup-shaped cake.

Cu·pid (kyo͞o′pĭd) ► *n.* **1.** *Rom. Myth.* The god of love. **2. cupid** A representation of Cupid as a boy having wings and a bow and arrow.

cu·pid·i·ty (kyo͞o-pĭd′ĭ-tē) ► *n.* Excessive desire, esp. for wealth.

cu·po·la (kyo͞o′pə-lə) ► *n.* A small, usu. domed structure surmounting a roof.

cur (kûr) ► *n.* **1.** A mongrel dog. **2.** A base person.

Cu·ra·çao (ko͝or′ə-sou′, kyo͝or′-, ko͝or′ə-sou′, kyo͝or′-) ► An island of the Netherlands Antilles in the S Caribbean Sea off the NW coast of Venezuela.

cu·ra·re also **cu·ra·ri** (ko͞o-rä′rē, kyo͞o-) ► *n.* A South American plant extract used as an arrow poison and medicinally as a muscle relaxant.

cu·rate (kyo͝or′ĭt) ► *n.* **1.** A cleric who has charge of a parish. **2.** A cleric who assists a rector or vicar.

cu·ra·tive (kyo͝or′ə-tĭv) ► *adj.* Serving or tending to cure. **—cur′a·tive** *n.*

cu·ra·tor (kyo͞o-rā′tər, kyo͝or′ə-tər) ► *n.* One in charge of a collection, as at a museum or library. **—cu′ra·to′ri·al** (kyo͝or′ə-tôr′ē-əl) *adj.* **—cu·ra′tor·ship′** *n.*

curb (kûrb) ► *n.* **1.** A concrete or stone edging along a street. **2.** Something that checks or restrains. **3.** A chain or strap used with a bit to restrain a horse. ► *v.* To check, restrain, or control.

curb·stone (kûrb′stōn′) ► *n.* A stone or row of stones that constitutes a curb.

curd (kûrd) ► *n.* The coagulated part of sour milk, used to make cheese.

cur·dle (kûr′dl) ► *v.* **-dled, -dling.** To change into curd.

cure (kyo͝or) ► *n.* **1.** Restoration of health. **2.** A method or course of medical treatment. **3.** An agent, such as a drug, that restores health. ► *v.* **cured, cur·ing. 1.** To restore to health. **2.** To effect a recovery from. **3.** To preserve (e.g., meat), as by salting, smoking, or aging. **—cur′a·ble** *adj.* **—cur′er** *n.* **—cure′less** *adj.*

cure-all (kyo͝or′ôl′) ► *n.* Something that cures all diseases or evils; panacea.

cu·ret·tage (kyo͝or′ĭ-täzh′) ► *n.* Surgical scraping of a body cavity.

cur·few (kûr′fyo͞o) ► *n.* **1.** A regulation requiring certain or all people to leave the streets at a prescribed hour. **2.** The signal, as a bell, announcing the hour of a curfew.

cu·ri·a or **Cu·ri·a** (ko͝or′ē-ə, kyo͝or′-) ► *n., pl.* **-ri·ae** (-ē-ē′). The central administration governing the Catholic Church. **—cu′ri·al** *adj.*

cu·rie (kyo͝or′ē, kyo͞o-rē′) ► *n.* A unit of radioactivity, equal to the amount of a radioactive isotope that decays at the rate of 3.7×10^{10} disintegrations per second.

Cu·rie (kyo͝or′ē, kyo͞o-rē′), **Marie** (1867–1934) ► Polish-born French chemist; shared a 1903 Nobel with her husband, **Pierre Curie** (1859–1906), and won a second Nobel in 1911.

cu·ri·o (kyo͝or′ē-ō′) ► *n., pl.* **-os.** An unusual object.

cu·ri·ous (kyo͝or′ē-əs) ► *adj.* **1.** Eager to learn. **2.** Unduly inquisitive; prying. **3.** Unusual or extraordinary; singular. **—cu′ri·ous·ly** *adv.* **—cu′ri·os′i·ty** (-ŏs′ĭ-tē) *n.*

cu·ri·um (kyo͝or′ē-əm) ► *n.* *Symbol* **Cm** A silvery metallic synthetic radioactive element. At. no. 96.

curl (kûrl) ► *v.* **1.** To form or twist into ringlets or coils. **2.** To assume or form into a coiled or spiral shape. ► *n.* **1.** A ringlet of hair. **2.** Something with a spiral or coiled shape. **—curl′y** *adj.* **—curl′i·ness** *n.* **—curl′er** *n.*

cur·lew (kûrl′yo͞o, kûr′lo͞o) ► *n.* A brownish, long-legged shore bird with a slender, downward-curving bill.

curl·i·cue (kûr′lĭ-kyo͞o′) ► *n.* A fancy twist or curl.

curl·ing (kûr′lĭng) ► *n.* A game in which two four-person teams slide stones toward the center of a circle at either end of a length of ice.

cur·mudg·eon (kər-mŭj′ən) ► *n.* A cantankerous person.

cur·rant (kûr′ənt, kŭr′-) ► *n.* **1.** Any of a genus of shrubs having edible, variously colored berries. **2.** The fruits of any of these plants. **3.** A small seedless raisin.

cur·ren·cy (kûr′ən-sē, kŭr′-) ► *n., pl.* **-cies. 1.** Money in any form when in actual use as a medium of exchange. See **currency** table in Appendix on pages 844-845. **2.** General acceptance or use: *the currency of a slang term.*

cur·rent (kûr′ənt, kŭr′-) ► *adj.* **1.** Belonging to the present time. **2.** Prevalent, esp. at the present time. ► *n.* **1.** A steady onward movement. **2.** The part of a body of liquid or gas that is in flow. **3.** *Symbol* **I a.** A flow of electric charge. **b.** The amount of charge flowing past a specified circuit point per unit time. **—cur′rent·ly** *adv.*

cur·ric·u·lum (kə-rĭk′yə-ləm) ► *n., pl.* **-la** (-lə) or **-lums.** The courses of study offered by an educational institution. **—cur·ric′u·lar** *adj.*

curriculum vi·tae (vī′tē, vē′tī) ► *n., pl.* **curricula vitae.** A summary of one's education, professional history, and job qualifications.

THESAURUS

cunning *adj.* —*See* ARTFUL.
cunning *n.* —*See* ART.

cupidity *n.* —*See* GREED.

cupola *n.* —*See* LOOKOUT (2).

cur *n.* —*See* COWARD.

curate *n.* —*See* CLERIC.

curative *adj.* Serving to cure ► antidotal, healing, medicinal, remedial, restorative, therapeutic. [*Compare* CORRECTIVE, TONIC.]
curative *n.* —*See* CURE.

curatorial *adj.* —*See* PRESERVATIVE.

curb *n.* —*See* BRAKE, RESTRAINT.
curb *v.* —*See* RESTRAIN.

curdle *v.* —*See* COAGULATE, DECAY.

cure *n.* An agent used to restore health ► antidote, corrective, countermeasure, curative, elixir, medicament, medication, medicine, nostrum, physic, remedy, restorative, treatment. [*Compare* DRUG.]
cure *v.* To restore to health ► heal, rehabilitate, remedy, salve. *Informal:* doctor. [*Compare* FIX, REVIVE.] —*See also* PREPARE, PRESERVE (1).

cure-all *n.* Something that is believed to cure all human disorders ► catholicon, elixir, panacea. [*Compare* CURE.]

cureless *adj.* —*See* HOPELESS.

curio *n.* —*See* NOVELTY (3).

curiosity *n.* **1.** Mental acquisitiveness ► concern, concernment, curiousness, inquisitiveness, interest, interestedness, regard. *Idiom:* thirst for knowledge. **2.** Undue interest in the affairs of others ► curiousness, inquisitiveness, intrusiveness, meddlesomeness, prying. *Informal:* nosiness, snoopiness. —*See also* MYSTERY.

curious *adj.* **1.** Unduly interested in the affairs of others ► busy, inquisitive, inquisitorial, interfering, interposing, intrusive, meddlesome, meddling, obtrusive, officious, prying. *Informal:* nosy, snoopy. **2.** Eager to acquire knowledge ► acquisitive, inquiring, inquisitive, interested, intrigued, investigative, questioning, speculative. [*Compare* EAGER, ENTHUSIASTIC.] **3.** Agreeably curious, especially in an old-fashioned or unusual way ► funny, odd, quaint. —*See also* ECCENTRIC, FUNNY (3).

curiously *adv.* —*See* UNUSUALLY.

curiousness *n.* —*See* CURIOSITY (1), CURIOSITY (2).

curl *v.* —*See* WAVE (1), WIND[2].
curl up *v.* To take repose, as by sleeping or lying quietly ► lie (down), recline, repose, rest, stretch (out). [*Compare* NAP, SLEEP.]
curl *n.* Something with a curled or spiral shape ►, coil, curlicue, frizzle, kink, lock, ringlet, spiral, swirl, twist, whorl, winding. [*Compare* BEND.]

curly *adj.* Shaped like or having curls ► coiled, frizzled, helical, kinky, spiral, swirly, twisted, twisty, whorled. [*Compare* BENT.] —*See also* WAVY.

currency *n.* —*See* MONEY (1).

current *adj.* —*See* CONTEMPORARY (2), PRESENT[1], PREVAILING.
current *n.* —*See* FLOW.

currently *adv.* —*See* NOW (1).

cur·ry[1] (kûr′ē, kŭr′ē) ▸ *v.* **-ried, -ry·ing.** 1. To groom (a horse) with a currycomb. 2. To prepare (tanned hides) for use. ***—idiom:* curry favor** To seek favor by flattery.

cur·ry[2] (kûr′ē, kŭr′ē) ▸ *n., pl.* **-ries.** 1. A pungent seasoning made from ground spices, including cumin and coriander. 2. A sauce or dish seasoned with curry. ▸ *v.* **-ried, -ry·ing.** To season (food) with curry.

cur·ry·comb (kûr′ē-kōm′, kŭr′-) ▸ *n.* A comb with metal teeth, used for grooming horses.

curse (kûrs) ▸ *n.* 1a. An appeal for evil or misfortune to befall a person or thing. b. Evil or misfortune resulting from or as if from a curse. 2. A source or cause of evil. 3. A profane word or phrase. ▸ *v.* **cursed** or **curst** (kûrst), **curs·ing.** 1. To invoke evil upon. 2. To swear (at). 3. To bring a curse upon.

curs·ed (kûr′sĭd, kûrst) also **curst** (kûrst) ▸ *adj.* Detestable; damned.

cur·sive (kûr′sĭv) ▸ *adj.* Having the successive letters joined: *cursive writing.*

cur·sor (kûr′sər) ▸ *n. Comp. Sci.* A bright, usu. blinking, movable indicator on a display, marking the position at which a character can be entered or deleted.

cur·so·ry (kûr′sə-rē) ▸ *adj.* Performed with haste and scant attention to detail. **—cur′so·ri·ly** *adv.*

curt (kûrt) ▸ *adj.* **-er, -est.** 1. Rudely brief or abrupt. 2. Concise. **—curt′ly** *adv.* **—curt′ness** *n.*

cur·tail (kər-tāl′) ▸ *v.* To cut short; abbreviate. **—cur·tail′ment** *n.*

cur·tain (kûr′tn) ▸ *n.* 1. Material that hangs in a window or other opening as a decoration, shade, or screen. 2. Something resembling a screen: *a curtain of fire.* 3. The drape in a theater that separates the stage from the auditorium. **—cur′tain** *v.*

curt·sy or **curt·sey** (kûrt′sē) ▸ *n., pl.* **-sies** or **-seys.** A gesture of respect or reverence made chiefly by women by bending the knees with one foot forward. **—curt′sy** *v.*

cur·va·ceous (kûr-vā′shəs) ▸ *adj.* Having a full or voluptuous figure.

cur·va·ture (kûr′və-cho͝or′, -chər) ▸ *n.* The act of curving or the state of being curved.

curve (kûrv) ▸ *n.* 1a. A line that deviates from straightness in a smooth, continuous fashion. b. A surface that deviates from planarity in such a fashion. 2. Something that has the shape of a curve. ▸ *v.* **curved, curv·ing.** To move in, form, or cause to form a curve. **—curv′y** *adj.*

cush·ion (ko͝osh′ən) ▸ *n.* 1. A soft pad or pillow for resting, reclining, or kneeling. 2. Something that absorbs or softens an impact. 3. The rim bordering a billiard table. ▸ *v.* 1. To absorb the shock of. 2. To protect from impacts or disturbing effects.

Cush·it·ic (ko͞o-shĭt′ĭk) ▸ *n.* A branch of the Afro-Asiatic language family spoken in Somalia, Ethiopia, and N Kenya.

cush·y (ko͝osh′ē) ▸ *adj.* **-i·er, -i·est.** *Informal* Making few demands; comfortable.

cusp (kŭsp) ▸ *n.* A point or pointed end, as of a tooth or crescent.

cus·pid (kŭs′pĭd) ▸ *n.* See **canine** 2.

cus·pi·dor (kŭs′pĭ-dôr′) ▸ *n.* A spittoon.

cuss (kŭs) *Informal* ▸ *v.* To curse (at). ▸ *n.* 1. A curse. 2. A stubborn individual.

cus·tard (kŭs′tərd) ▸ *n.* A dish of milk, eggs, flavoring, and sugar, cooked until set.

Cus·ter (kŭs′tər), **George Armstrong** (1839–76) ▸ Amer. soldier.

cus·to·di·al (kŭ-stō′dē-əl) ▸ *adj.* Of or relating to custody or a custodian.

cus·to·di·an (kŭ-stō′dē-ən) ▸ *n.* 1. One that has charge of something; caretaker. 2. A janitor. **—cus·to′di·an·ship′** *n.*

cus·to·dy (kŭs′tə-dē) ▸ *n., pl.* **-dies.** 1. The act or right of guarding, esp. such a right granted by a court. 2. Charge; supervision. 3. The state of being held under guard.

cus·tom (kŭs′təm) ▸ *n.* 1. A practice followed by people of a particular group or region. 2. A person's habitual practice. 3. **customs** a. Duties or taxes on imported goods. b. *(takes sing. v.)* The governmental agency authorized to collect these duties. ▸ *adj.* 1. Made to order. 2. Specializing in made-to-order goods.

cus·tom·ar·y (kŭs′tə-mĕr′ē) ▸ *adj.* 1. Commonly practiced or used; usual. 2. Established by custom. **—cus′tom·ar′i·ly** (-mâr′ə-lē) *adv.*

cus·tom·er (kŭs′tə-mər) ▸ *n.* One that buys goods or services.

cus·tom·house (kŭs′təm-hous′) ▸ *n.* A building or office where customs are collected.

cus·tom·ize (kŭs′tə-mīz′) ▸ *v.* **-ized, -iz·ing.** To make or alter to individual specifications. **—cus′tom·i·za′tion** *n.*

cus·tom-made (kŭs′təm-mād′) ▸ *adj.* Made according to the specifications of the buyer.

customs union ▸ *n.* An international association organized to eliminate customs restrictions between member nations and to set a tariff policy toward nonmembers.

cut (kŭt) ▸ *v.* **cut, cut·ting.** 1. To penetrate with or as if with

THESAURUS

curse *n.* 1. A denunciation invoking a wish or threat of evil or injury ▸ anathema, ban, damnation, execration, hex, imprecation, malediction, oath. *Slang:* whammy. [*Compare* SPELL[2].] 2. Something or someone believed to bring bad luck ▸ evil eye, hex, hoodoo, Jonah. *Informal:* jinx. [*Compare* CHARM, MAGIC.] 3. A cause of suffering or harm ▸ affliction, bane, evil, ill, misery, plague, scourge, sorrow, woe. [*Compare* BURDEN[1], DISASTER.] *—See also* SWEARWORD.

curse *v.* 1. To invoke evil upon ▸ anathematize, damn, hex, imprecate. [*Compare* CHARM.] 2. To bring bad luck or evil to ▸ hex, hoodoo. *Informal:* jinx. 3. To use profane or obscene language ▸ blaspheme, damn, curse. *Informal:* cuss. *See also* AFFLICT.

cursed *adj.* *—See* DAMNED.

cursive *n.* *—See* SCRIPT (1).

cursory *adj.* *—See* PERFUNCTORY, SUPERFICIAL.

curt *adj.* *—See* ABRUPT (1), BRIEF.

curtail *v.* *—See* SHORTEN.

curtailment *n.* *—See* DECREASE.

curtains *n.* *—See* DEATH (1).

curtsy *n.* *—See* BOW[1].

curtsy *v.* *—See* BOW[1] (1).

curvaceous *adj.* *—See* SHAPELY.

curvature *n.* *—See* BEND.

curve *n.* *—See* BEND.

curve *v.* *—See* BEND (1), WAVE (1).

curved or **curvilinear** *adj.* *—See* BENT.

curving *adj.* Having bends, curves, or angles ▸ bending, crooked, curved. [*Compare* BENT.]

curvy *adj.* *—See* SHAPELY, WAVY, WINDING.

cushy *adj.* *—See* COMFORTABLE.

cusp *n.* *—See* POINT (1).

cuspate or **cuspated** *adj.* *—See* POINTED.

cuspidate or **cuspidated** *adj.* *—See* POINTED.

cuss *v.* 1. *Informal* To use profane or obscene language ▸ blaspheme, curse, damn, swear. 2. To hurl strong deprecations, curses, or insults at ▸ *Informal:* cuss at, cuss out, mouth off at, swear at. [*Compare* CURSE, INSULT, REVILE.]

cuss *n.* *—See* SWEARWORD.

custodian *n.* A person who is legally responsible for the care and management of the person or property of an incompetent or a minor ▸ caretaker, conservator, guardian, keeper. [*Compare* REPRESENTATIVE.]

custody *n.* *—See* CARE (2), DETENTION.

custom *n.* A habitual way of behaving ▸ consuetude, convention, form, habit, habitude, manner, observance, practice, praxis, precedent, routine, usage, usance, use, way, wont. [*Compare* ADDICTION, APPROACH, BEHAVIOR, FASHION.] *—See also* CEREMONY (1), CULTURE (2), PATRONAGE (2), PATRONAGE (3).

custom *adj.* Made according to the specifications of the buyer ▸ bespoke, custom-built, customized, custom-made, made-to-order, tailored, tailor-made. *Idiom:* made-to-measure.

customarily *adv.* *—See* USUALLY.

customariness *n.* *—See* USUALNESS.

customary *adj.* *—See* ACCEPTED, COMMON (1).

custom-built *adj.* *—See* CUSTOM.

customer *n.* *—See* CONSUMER.

customized or **custom-made** *adj.* *—See* CUSTOM.

customs *n.* *—See* TAX.

cut *v.* 1. To penetrate with a sharp edge ▸ bayonet, bore, drill, gash, gore, gouge, hack, impale, incise, indent, knife, lacerate, lance, nick,

a sharp edge. **2.** To separate into parts with a sharp-edged instrument; slice. **3.** To trim; shorten. **4.** To mow; harvest. **5.** To have (a new tooth) grow through the gums. **6.** To form or shape by incising. **7.** To sever or detach. **8.** *Comp. Sci.* To remove (e.g., text) from a file for storage in a buffer. **9.** To reduce the size, amount, or duration of. **10.** To dilute. **11.** To hurt keenly. **12.** To fail to attend purposely: *cut a class.* **13.** *Informal* To stop: *cut the noise.* **14.** To stop filming (a movie scene). **15.** To make a recording of. ***—phrasal verbs:*** **cut back** To prune. **cut down 1.** To kill. **2.** To reduce consumption or use. **cut in 1.** To enter a line out of turn. **2.** To interrupt. **cut off 1.** To isolate. **2.** To discontinue. **cut out 1.** To be suited: *not cut out to be a hero.* **2.** To stop. **cut up** *Informal* To behave in a playful way. ▸ *n.* **1.** The act or result of cutting. **2.** A piece cut from an animal: *a cut of beef.* **3.** A passage made by digging or eroding. **4.** A reduction. **5.** The style in which a garment is cut. **6.** *Informal* A share. **7.** An insult. **8a.** An engraved block or plate. **b.** A print made from such a block. ***—idiom:*** **cut corners** To do something in the easiest or cheapest way.

cut-and-dried (kŭt′n-drīd′) ▸ *adj.* In accordance with a standard formula; routine.

cu·ta·ne·ous (kyo͞o-tā′nē-əs) ▸ *adj.* Of or affecting the skin.

cut·back (kŭt′băk′) ▸ *n.* A decrease; curtailment: *cutbacks in federal funding.*

cute (kyo͞ot) ▸ *adj.* **cut·er, cut·est. 1.** Delightfully pretty or dainty. **2.** Clever. **—cute′ly** *adv.* **—cute′ness** *n.*

cute·sy (kyo͞ot′sē) ▸ *adj.* **-si·er, -si·est.** *Informal* Deliberately or affectedly cute.

cu·ti·cle (kyo͞o′tĭ-kəl) ▸ *n.* **1.** The epidermis. **2.** The strip of hardened skin at the base of a fingernail or toenail.

cut·lass (kŭt′ləs) ▸ *n.* A short heavy sword with a curved blade.

cut·ler·y (kŭt′lə-rē) ▸ *n.* Cutting instruments and tools, esp. tableware.

cut·let (kŭt′lĭt) ▸ *n.* A thin slice of meat, usu. veal or lamb, cut from the leg or ribs.

cut·off (kŭt′ôf′, -ŏf′) ▸ *n.* **1.** A designated limit or end. **2.** A shortcut or bypass. **3.** A device that cuts off a flow of fluid.

cut·out (kŭt′out′) ▸ *n.* Something cut out or intended to be cut out from something else.

cut-rate (kŭt′rāt′) ▸ *adj.* Reduced in price.

cut·ter (kŭt′ər) ▸ *n.* **1.** A person or device that cuts. **2.** A ship's boat used for transporting stores or passengers. **3.** A small, lightly armed Coast Guard boat.

cut·throat (kŭt′thrōt′) ▸ *n.* **1.** A murderer. **2.** A ruthless person. ▸ *adj.* **1.** Cruel; murderous. **2.** Merciless: *cutthroat competition.*

cut·ting (kŭt′ĭng) ▸ *n.* A part cut off from a main body, esp. a shoot removed from a plant for rooting or grafting.

cut·tle·bone (kŭt′l-bōn′) ▸ *n.* The chalky internal shell of a cuttlefish, used as a dietary supplement for cage birds.

cut·tle·fish (kŭt′l-fĭsh′) ▸ *n.* A ten-armed, squidlike marine mollusk that has a chalky internal shell.

cut·up (kŭt′ŭp′) ▸ *n.* *Informal* A prankster.

cwt ▸ *abbr.* hundredweight

–cy ▸ *suff.* **1.** Condition; quality: *bankruptcy.* **2.** Rank; office: *baronetcy.* **3.** Action; practice: *conspiracy.*

cy·an (sī′ăn′, -ən) ▸ *n.* A greenish blue, considered a primary color in printing and photography.

cy·a·nide (sī′ə-nīd′) ▸ *n.* Any of various compounds containing a CN group, esp. the poisonous compounds potassium cyanide and sodium cyanide.

cyano– or **cyan–** ▸ *pref.* **1.** Blue: *cyanosis.* **2.** Cyanide: *cyanogen.*

cy·an·o·gen (sī-ăn′ə-jən) ▸ *n.* A colorless, flammable, highly poisonous gas, C_2N_2, used as a rocket propellant.

cy·a·no·sis (sī′ə-nō′sĭs) ▸ *n.* A bluish discoloration of the skin and mucous membranes resulting from inadequate oxygenation of the blood. **—cy′a·not′ic** (-nŏt′ĭk) *adj.*

cyber– ▸ *pref.* **1.** Computer: *cyberpunk.* **2.** Computer network: *cyberspace.*

cy·ber·net·ics (sī′bər-nĕt′ĭks) ▸ *n.* *(takes sing. v.)* The theoretical study of control processes in biological, mechanical, and electronic systems. **—cy′ber·net′ic** *adj.*

cy·ber·punk (sī′bər-pŭnk′) ▸ *n.* Fast-paced science fiction involving futuristic computer-based societies.

cy·ber·space (sī′bər-spās′) ▸ *n.* The electronic medium of computer networks, in which online communication takes place.

cy·cla·mate (sī′klə-māt′, sĭk′lə-) ▸ *n.* A salt of cyclamic acid formerly used as an artificial sweetener.

cy·cla·men (sī′klə-mən, sĭk′lə-) ▸ *n.* A plant with showy, variously colored flowers.

cyc·la·mic acid (sĭk′lə-mĭk′, sī′klə-) ▸ *n.* A crystalline acid used to produce cyclamates.

cy·cle (sī′kəl) ▸ *n.* **1.** An interval of time during which a regularly repeated event occurs. **2a.** A single occurrence of a periodically repeated phenomenon. **b.** A periodically repeated sequence of events. **3.** The orbit of a celestial body. **4.** A group of literary or musical works about a central theme or hero. **5.** A bicycle or motorcycle. ▸ *v.* **-cled, -cling. 1.** To occur in or pass through a cycle. **2.** To ride a bicycle or motorcycle. **—cy′cler** *n.* **—cy′clic** (sī′klĭk, sĭk′lĭk), **cy′cli·cal** *adj.*

cy·clist (sī′klĭst) ▸ *n.* One who rides a vehicle such as a bicycle or motorcycle.

cyclo– or **cycl–** ▸ *pref.* Circle: *cyclometer.*

cy·clom·e·ter (sī-klŏm′ĭ-tər) ▸ *n.* **1.** An instrument that records the revolutions of a wheel to indicate distance traveled. **2.** An instrument that measures circular arcs.

cy·clone (sī′klōn′) ▸ *n.* **1.** An atmospheric system characterized by the rapid inward circulation of air masses about a low-pressure center. **2.** A violent rotating windstorm. **—cy·clon′ic** (-klŏn′ĭk) *adj.*

Cy·clops (sī′klŏps) ▸ *n., pl.* **Cy·clo·pes** (sī-klō′pēz′) *Gk. Myth.* **1.** Any of three one-eyed Titans. **2.** Any of a race

THESAURUS

notch, pierce, prick, punch, puncture, ream, scarify, slash, slit, spear, stab, stick, sting, transfix. [*Compare* BREACH, CRACK, PENETRATE.] **2.** To separate into parts with or as if with a sharp-edged instrument ▸ carve, cleave, dice, dissever, quarter, sever, slice, slit, snip, split. [*Compare* DIVIDE.] **3.** To decrease, as in length or amount, by or as if by severing or excising ▸ chop, clip, crop, cut back, cut down, lop, lower, mow, pare, prune, reap, scythe, shave, shear, sickle, skive, slash, snip, trim, truncate. [*Compare* DECREASE, DROP, SHORTEN.] **4.** To fail to attend on purpose ▸ duck, shirk, truant. *Informal:* skip. *Idioms:* go AWOL, play hooky (*or* truant). [*Compare* AVOID.] *—See also* CENSOR (1), DILUTE, SNUB, SWERVE.

cut across *v.* *—See* CROSS (2).

cut back *v.* *—See* CUT (3).

cut down *v.* *—See* CUT (3), DROP (3), KILL[1].

cut in *v.* *—See* INTERRUPT (2), INTRUDE.

cut off *v.* To block the progress of and force to change direction ▸ head off, intercept. *—See also* ISOLATE (1), KILL[1].

cut out *v.* To take the place of another against the other's will ▸ displace, force out, supplant, usurp. [*Compare* ASSUME, OCCUPY, SEIZE.] *—See also* BREAK (5), GO (1).

cut up *v.* *—See* CRITICIZE (1), MISBEHAVE, SHRED, SLAM (1).

cut *adj.* *—See* DILUTE.

cut *n.* **1.** An opening made by a sharp object ▸ gash, gouge, groove, incision, nick, notch, score, slash, slice, slit, split. [*Compare* IMPRESSION, PRICK, SCRAPE.] **2.** A part severed from a whole ▸ paring, piece, portion, shaving, slab, slice, sliver, snip, snippet, wedge. [*Compare* FLAKE, PART.] **3.** A deliberate slight ▸ rebuff, snub, spurn. *Informal:* cold shoulder, go-by. *—See also* ABSENCE (1), ALLOTMENT, DECREASE, TAUNT.

cut-and-dried *adj.* *—See* ORDINARY.

cutback *n.* *—See* DECREASE.

cute *adj.* *—See* ATTRACTIVE, DELIGHTFUL.

cutoff *n.* *—See* END (1), LIMIT (1), STOP (1).

cutthroat *n.* *—See* MURDERER.

cutthroat *adj.* *—See* COMPETITIVE, MURDEROUS.

cutting *adj.* *—See* BITING.

cutting edge *n.* *—See* FOREFRONT.

cutting-edge *adj.* *—See* CONTEMPORARY (2).

cutup *n.* *—See* RASCAL.

cycle *n.* *—See* CIRCLE (2).

cyclic or **cyclical** *adj.* *—See* PERIODIC.

cyclopean *adj.* *—See* ENORMOUS.

of one-eyed giants reputedly descended from these Titans.

cy·clo·tron (sīʹklə-trŏnʹ) ▸ *n.* A device that accelerates charged subatomic particles in a spiral path by an alternating electric field in a constant magnetic field.

cyg·net (sĭgʹnĭt) ▸ *n.* A young swan.

Cyg·nus (sĭgʹnəs) ▸ *n.* A constellation in the Northern Hemisphere.

cyl·in·der (sĭlʹən-dər) ▸ *n.* **1.** *Math.* **a.** The surface generated by a straight line intersecting and moving along a closed plane curve while remaining parallel to a fixed straight line that is not on or parallel to the plane of the closed curve. **b.** A solid bounded by two parallel planes and such a surface having a closed curve, esp. a circle. **2.** A cylindrical object. **3.** The chamber in which a piston moves. **4.** The rotating chamber of a revolver that holds the cartridges. **—cy·linʹdri·cal** *adj.* **—cy·linʹdri·cal·ly** *adv.*

cym·bal (sĭmʹbəl) ▸ *n. Mus.* A concave brass plate that makes a loud clashing tone when hit with a drumstick or when used in pairs.

cyn·ic (sĭnʹĭk) ▸ *n.* A person who believes all people are motivated by selfishness. **—cynʹi·cal** *adj.* **—cynʹi·cal·ly** *adv.* **—cynʹi·cism** *n.*

cy·no·sure (sīʹnə-sho͝orʹ, sĭnʹə-) ▸ *n.* A focal point of attention and admiration.

cy·press (sīʹprĭs) ▸ *n.* Any of a genus of evergreen trees or shrubs having scalelike leaves and woody cones.

Cy·prus (sīʹprəs) ▸ An island country in the E Mediterranean S of Turkey. **—Cypʹri·an** (sĭpʹre-ən), **Cypʹri·ot** (-ət, -ŏtʹ) *adj. & n.*

Cy·ra·no de Ber·ge·rac (sîrʹə-nō də bûrʹzhə-răkʹ, bĕrʹ-), **Savinien de** (1619–55) ▸ French satirist and duelist.

Cyr·il (sîrʹəl) Saint (827–869) ▸ Christian missionary and theologian.

Cy·ril·lic (sə-rĭlʹĭk) ▸ *adj.* Of or being an alphabet based esp. on that of Byzantine Greek and used for some Slavic languages, such as Russian and Serbian.

cyst (sĭst) ▸ *n. Pathol.* An abnormal membranous sac containing a gaseous, liquid, or semisolid substance.

cys·tic fibrosis (sĭsʹtĭk) ▸ *n.* A hereditary disease of the exocrine glands, marked by production of viscous mucus and resulting in chronic respiratory infections and impaired pancreatic function.

cys·to·scope (sĭsʹtə-skōpʹ) ▸ *n.* A tubular instrument used to examine the urinary bladder.

-cyte ▸ *suff.* Cell: *leukocyte.*

cyto– or **cyt–** ▸ *pref.* Cell: *cytoplasm.*

cy·tol·o·gy (sī-tŏlʹə-jē) ▸ *n.* The branch of biology that deals with the formation, structure, and function of cells. **—cyʹto·logʹic** (-tə-lŏjʹĭk), **cyʹto·logʹi·cal** *adj.* **—cy·tolʹo·gist** *n.*

cy·to·plasm (sīʹtə-plăzʹəm) ▸ *n.* The protoplasm outside the cell nucleus. **—cyʹto·plasʹmic** *adj.*

cy·to·sine (sīʹtə-sēnʹ) ▸ *n.* A pyrimidine base that is an essential constituent of RNA and DNA.

czar (zär, tsär) ▸ *n.* **1.** also **tsar** or **tzar** (zär, tsär) A king or emperor, esp. one of the former emperors of Russia. **2.** An autocrat. **3.** *Informal* An official having special authority: *an energy czar.*

cza·ri·na (zä-rēʹnə, tsä-) ▸ *n.* The wife of a czar.

czar·ism (zärʹĭzʹəm, tsärʹ-) ▸ *n.* The system of government in Russia under the czars. **—czarʹist** *adj. & n.*

Czech (chĕk) ▸ *n.* **1.** A native or inhabitant of the Czech Republic. **2.** The Slavic language of the Czech Republic. **—Czech** *adj.*

Czech·o·slo·va·ki·a (chĕkʹə-slə-väʹkē-ə, -ō-slō-) ▸ A former country of central Europe; divided in Jan. 1993 into the Czech Republic and Slovakia. **—Czechʹo·sloʹvak, Czechʹo·slo·vaʹki·an** *adj. & n.*

Czech Republic ▸ A country of central Europe.

THESAURUS

cynic *n.* A person who habitually expects only the worst from people ▸ misanthrope, misanthropist, pessimist. [*Compare* SKEPTIC.]

cynical *adj.* *—See* DISTRUSTFUL, SARCASTIC.

cynicism *n.* *—See* DISTRUST, SARCASM.

cynosure *n.* *—See* CENTER (3).

D

d or **D** (dē) ▸ *n., pl.* **d's** or **D's** also **ds** or **Ds**. **1.** The 4th letter of the English alphabet. **2.** The 4th in a series. **3.** *Mus.* The 2nd tone of the C major scale. **4. D** The lowest passing grade given to a student.
D[1] also **d** ▸ The symbol for the Roman numeral 500.
D[2] ▸ *abbr.* 1. day 2. Democrat
d. ▸ *abbr.* 1. date 2. daughter 3. died 4. *Chiefly British* penny (of a shilling)
DA ▸ *abbr.* district attorney
dab (dăb) ▸ *v.* **dabbed, dab·bing. 1.** To apply with short poking strokes. **2.** To pat lightly. ▸ *n.* **1.** A small amount. **2.** A quick light pat.
dab·ble (dăb′əl) ▸ *v.* **-bled, -bling. 1.** To splash or spatter with or as if with a liquid. **2.** To undertake something superficially or without serious intent.
dab·bler (dăb′lər) ▸ *n.* One who dabbles in a subject or activity.
da ca·po (dä kä′pō) ▸ *adv. Mus.* From the beginning.
dace (dās) ▸ *n., pl.* **dace** or **dac·es**. A small freshwater fish related to the carps and minnows.
da·cha (dä′chə) ▸ *n.* A Russian country house.
dachs·hund (däks′ho͝ont′, dăk′sənt, -sənd) ▸ *n.* A small dog having a long body, drooping ears, and very short legs.
Da·cron (dā′krŏn′, dăk′rŏn′) ▸ A trademark for a synthetic polyester fabric or fiber.
dac·tyl (dăk′təl) ▸ *n.* A metrical foot consisting of one accented syllable followed by two unaccented ones. **—dac·tyl′ic** (-tĭl′ĭk) *adj. & n.*
dad (dăd) ▸ *n. Informal* A father.
Da·da (dä′dä) ▸ *n.* A European artistic and literary movement (1916–23) that flouted conventional values in works marked by nonsense and incongruity. **—Da′da·ism** *n.* **—Da′da·ist** *adj. & n.*
dad·dy (dăd′ē) ▸ *n., pl.* **-dies.** *Informal* A father.
daddy long·legs (lông′lĕgz′, lŏng′-) ▸ *n., pl.* **daddy longlegs.** A spiderlike arachnid with a small rounded body and long slender legs.
da·do (dā′dō) ▸ *n., pl.* **-does. 1.** The section of a pedestal between the base and cornice or cap. **2.** The lower portion of an interior wall, decorated differently from the upper section.
daf·fo·dil (dăf′ə-dĭl) ▸ *n.* A bulbous plant having showy, usu. yellow flowers with a trumpet-shaped central crown.
daf·fy (dăf′ē) ▸ *adj.* **-fi·er, -fi·est.** *Informal* **1.** Silly; zany. **2.** Crazy. **—daf′fi·ly** *adv.* **—daf′fi·ness** *n.*
daft (dăft) ▸ *adj.* **-er, -est. 1.** Mad; crazy. **2.** Foolish; stupid. **—daft′ly** *adv.* **—daft′ness** *n.*
dag·ger (dăg′ər) ▸ *n.* **1.** A short pointed weapon with sharp edges. **2.** *Print.* See **obelisk** 2. ***—idiom:* look daggers at** To glare at angrily.
da·guerre·o·type (də-gâr′ə-tīp′) ▸ *n.* **1.** An early photographic process with the image developed on a light-sensitive silver-coated metallic plate. **2.** A photograph made by this process.
dahl·ia (dăl′yə, däl′-, dāl′-) ▸ *n.* A New World plant cultivated for its showy, variously colored flowers.
dai·kon (dī′kŏn′, -kən) ▸ *n.* A large white radish of Japan.
dai·ly (dā′lē) ▸ *adj.* Happening or done every day. ▸ *adv.* **1.** Every day. **2.** Once a day. ▸ *n., pl.* **-lies.** A newspaper published every day.
daily double ▸ *n.* A bet won by choosing both winners of two specified races on one day, as in horse racing.
dain·ty (dān′tē) ▸ *adj.* **-ti·er, -ti·est. 1.** Delicately beautiful; exquisite. **2.** Delicious or choice. **3.** Of refined taste. **4.** Fastidious; squeamish. ▸ *n., pl.* **-ties.** A delicacy. **—dain′ti·ly** *adv.* **—dain′ti·ness** *n.*
daiq·ui·ri (dăk′ə-rē, dī′kə-) ▸ *n., pl.* **-ris.** An iced cocktail of rum, lime or lemon juice, and sugar.
dair·y (dâr′ē) ▸ *n., pl.* **-ies. 1.** An establishment for processing or selling milk and milk products. **2.** A dairy farm. **3.** Food containing milk or milk products. **—dair′y** *adj.* **—dair′y·maid′** *n.* **—dair′y·man** *n.* **—dair′y·wom′an** *n.*
dair·y·ing (dâr′ē-ĭng) ▸ *n.* The business of operating a dairy or a dairy farm.
da·is (dā′ĭs, dī′-) ▸ *n.* A raised platform, as in a lecture hall, for honored guests.
dai·sy (dā′zē) ▸ *n., pl.* **-sies.** Any of several plants of the composite family, esp. a widely naturalized species having flower heads with a yellow center and white rays.
Da·ko·ta (də-kō′tə) ▸ *n., pl.* **-ta** or **-tas. 1.** A Sioux, esp. a member of the Santee branch. **2.** The Siouan language of the Dakota. **—Da·ko′tan** *adj. & n.*
Da·lai Lama (dä′lī) ▸ *n.* The traditional ruler of the dominant sect of Buddhism in Tibet and Mongolia.
da·la·si (dä-lä′sē) ▸ *n., pl.* **da·la·si.** See **currency** table in Appendix.
dale (dāl) ▸ *n.* A valley.
Da·li (dä′lē), **Salvador** (1904–89) ▸ Spanish surrealist artist. **—Da′li·esque′** *adj.*
Da·lit (dä′lĭt) ▸ *n.* A member of the lowest class in traditional Indian society. Dalits fall outside the Hindu caste categories.
Dal·las (dăl′əs) ▸ A city of NE TX E of Fort Worth.
dal·ly (dăl′ē) ▸ *v.* **-lied, -ly·ing. 1.** To play amorously. **2.** To waste time; dawdle. **—dal′li·ance** *n.* **—dal′li·er** *n.*
Dal·ma·tian (dăl-mā′shən) ▸ *n.* **1.** A native or inhabitant of Dalmatia. **2.** also **dalmatian** A dog with a short white coat covered with black spots. ▸ *adj.* Relating to Dalmatia.
dam[1] (dăm) ▸ *n.* A barrier built across a waterway to control the flow of water. ▸ *v.* **dammed, dam·ming. 1.** To build a dam across. **2.** To hold back; check.
dam[2] (dăm) ▸ *n.* A female parent of a four-legged animal.
dam·age (dăm′ĭj) ▸ *n.* **1.** Impairment of the usefulness or value of person or property; harm. **2. damages** *Law* Money ordered to be paid as compensation for injury or loss. ▸

THESAURUS

dab *v.* *—See* SMEAR, TAP[1] (1).
dab *n.* *—See* BIT[1] (1).
dabbler *n.* *—See* AMATEUR.
dab hand *n.* *—See* EXPERT.
dacha *n.* *—See* VILLA.
dad or **daddy** *n.* *—See* FATHER.
daedal or **Daedalian** *adj.* *—See* COMPLEX (1).
daffiness *n.* *—See* FOOLISHNESS.
daffy *adj.* *—See* FOOLISH, INSANE.
daft *adj.* *—See* FOOLISH, INSANE.
daftness *n.* *—See* FOOLISHNESS.
daily *adj.* *—See* COMMON (1), EVERYDAY.
dainty *adj.* *—See* DELICATE (1), FUSSY.
dainty *n.* *—See* DELICACY.
dais *n.* *—See* STAGE (1).
dale *n.* *—See* VALLEY.
dalliance *n.* **1.** The practice of flirting ▸ coquetry, flirtation. **2.** A usually brief romance entered into lightly or frivolously ▸ fling, flirtation. [*Compare* LOVE.]
dally *v.* To treat lightly or flippantly ▸ flirt, play, toy, trifle. *—See also* DELAY (2), FLIRT (2), HESITATE.
dam *v.* *—See* OBSTRUCT.
dam *n.* *—See* BAR (1).
damage *n.* Harm done to property or a person ▸ breakage, destruction, deterioration, disfigurement, impairment, injury, wastage, wreckage. [*Compare* DECAY, DESTRUCTION, RUIN.] *—See also* ACCOUNT (2), HARM.
damage *v.* To spoil the soundness or perfection of ▸ blemish, detract from,

v. **-aged, -ag·ing.** To cause damage to. **—dam′age·a·ble** *adj.* **—dam′ag·ing·ly** *adv.*

Da·mas·cus (də-măs′kəs) ▸ The capital of Syria, in the SW part. **—Dam′a·scene′** (dăm′ə-sēn′) *adj. & n.*

dam·ask (dăm′əsk) ▸ *n.* **1.** A rich patterned fabric esp. of silk or wool. **2.** A fine twilled table linen.

damask rose ▸ *n.* A rose with fragrant red or pink flowers used as a source of attar.

dame (dām) ▸ *n.* **1.** A married woman. **2.** *Slang* A woman. **3.** *Chiefly Brit.* **a.** A woman holding a nonhereditary title. **b.** The wife of a knight.

damn (dăm) ▸ *v.* **1.** To criticize adversely. **2.** To bring to ruin. **3.** To condemn to everlasting punishment; doom. **4.** To swear at. ▸ *interj.* Used to express anger, contempt, or disappointment. ▸ *n.* *Informal* The least bit; jot: *not worth a damn.* ▸ *adv. & adj.* Damned. **—dam·na′tion** (-nā′shən) *n.*

dam·na·ble (dăm′nə-bəl) ▸ *adj.* Deserving condemnation; odious. **—dam′na·bly** *adv.*

damned (dămd) ▸ *adj.* **-er, -est.** **1.** Condemned; doomed. **2.** *Informal* Dreadful; awful. **3.** Used as an intensive: *a damned fool.* ▸ *adv.* **-er, -est.** Used as an intensive: *a damned poor excuse.* ▸ *n.* Souls doomed to eternal punishment.

Dam·o·cles (dăm′ə-klēz′) (fl. 4th cent. B.C.) ▸ Greek courtier who according to legend was forced to sit under a sword suspended by a single hair.

damp (dămp) ▸ *adj.* **-er, -est.** Slightly wet; moist. ▸ *n.* **1.** Moisture; humidity. **2.** Foul or poisonous gas in coal mines. ▸ *v.* **1.** To moisten. **2.** To restrain or check. **3.** *Phys.* To decrease the amplitude of (a wave). **—damp′ish** *adj.* **—damp′ly** *adv.* **—damp′ness** *n.*

damp·en (dăm′pən) ▸ *v.* **1.** To make or become damp. **2.** To depress: *dampen one's spirits.* **3.** To soundproof.

damp·er (dăm′pər) ▸ *n.* **1.** One that deadens or depresses: *Rain put a damper on our plans.* **2.** An adjustable plate in a flue for controlling the draft.

dam·sel (dăm′zəl) ▸ *n.* A young woman or girl; maiden.

dam·sel·fly (dăm′zəl-flī′) ▸ *n.* A predatory insect related to the dragonfly but having wings that fold together at rest.

dam·son (dăm′zən, -sən) ▸ *n.* A Eurasian plum tree bearing oval, bluish-black fruit.

dance (dăns) ▸ *v.* **danced, danc·ing.** **1.** To move rhythmically usu. to music. **2.** To leap or skip about. **3.** To bob up and down. ▸ *n.* **1.** A series of motions and steps, usu. performed to music. **2.** The art of dancing. **3.** A party at which people dance. **4.** One round or turn of dancing: *May I have this dance?* **—dance′a·ble** *adj.* **—danc′er** *n.*

dan·de·li·on (dăn′dl-ī′ən) ▸ *n.* A weedy plant having many-rayed yellow flower heads.

dan·der¹ (dăn′dər) ▸ *n.* *Informal* Temper: *got my dander up.*

dan·der² (dăn′dər) ▸ *n.* Scurf from the coat or feathers of various animals, often of an allergenic nature.

dan·dle (dăn′dl) ▸ *v.* **-dled, -dling.** To move (a small child) up and down on one's knees in a playful way.

dan·druff (dăn′drəf) ▸ *n.* Small flakes of dead skin shed from the scalp.

dan·dy (dăn′dē) ▸ *n., pl.* **-dies.** **1.** A man who affects extreme elegance in clothes; fop. **2.** *Informal* Something very good of its kind. ▸ *adj.* **-di·er, -di·est.** **1.** Foppish. **2.** *Informal* Fine; good. **—dan′di·fy′** *v.* **—dan′dy·ism** *n.*

Dane (dān) ▸ *n.* A native or inhabitant of Denmark.

dan·ger (dān′jər) ▸ *n.* **1.** Exposure or vulnerability to harm or risk. **2.** A source of risk or peril.

dan·ger·ous (dān′jər-əs) ▸ *adj.* **1.** Full of danger. **2.** Able or likely to do harm. **—dan′ger·ous·ly** *adv.* **—dan′ger·ous·ness** *n.*

dan·gle (dăng′gəl) ▸ *v.* **-gled, -gling.** To hang or cause to hang loosely and swing to and fro. **—dan′gler** *n.*

dan·gling (dăng′glĭng) ▸ *adj.* Of or being a modifier, especially a participle or participial phrase, that grammatically modifies the subject of its sentence but semantically modifies another element or an unstated referent, as *approaching Dallas* in the sentence *Approaching Dallas, the skyline came into view.*

Dan·iel (dăn′yəl) ▸ *n.* *Bible* **1.** A Hebrew prophet of the 6th cent. B.C. **2.** See **Bible** table in Appendix.

Dan·ish (dā′nĭsh) ▸ *adj.* Of Denmark, the Danes, or the Danish language. ▸ *n.* **1.** The Germanic language of the Danes. **2.** *pl.* **-ish** or **-ish·es.** A Danish pastry.

Danish pastry ▸ *n.* A sweet buttery pastry made with raised dough.

dank (dăngk) ▸ *adj.* **-er, -est.** Disagreeably damp or humid. **—dank′ly** *adv.* **—dank′ness** *n.*

Dan·te A·li·ghie·ri (dän′tā ä′lē-gyĕ′rē, dăn′tē) (1265–1321) ▸ Italian poet. **—Dan′te·an** *adj. & n.* **—Dan·tesque′** (dän-tĕsk′, dăn-) *adj.*

Dan·ube (dăn′yo͞ob) ▸ A river of S-central Europe rising in SW Germany and flowing about 2,848 km (1,770 mi) to the Black Sea.

dap·per (dăp′ər) ▸ *adj.* **1a.** Neatly dressed; trim. **b.** Stylish. **2.** Spry. **—dap′per·ly** *adv.* **—dap′per·ness** *n.*

dap·ple (dăp′əl) ▸ *v.* **-pled, -pling.** To mark or mottle with spots. ▸ *adj.* Dappled.

dap·pled (dăp′əld) ▸ *adj.* Spotted; mottled.

Dar·da·nelles (där′dn-ĕlz′). Formerly **Hellespont** ▸ A strait connecting the Aegean Sea with the Sea of Marmara.

dare (dâr) ▸ *v.* **dared, dar·ing.** **1.** To have the courage required for. **2.** To challenge (someone) to do something requiring boldness. **3.** To confront boldly. ▸ *n.* A challenge. **—dar′er** *n.*

THESAURUS

disserve, flaw, harm, hurt, impair, injure, mar, prejudice, tarnish, vitiate. [*Compare* ABUSE, BATTER, DEFORM.]

damages *n.* *—See* COMPENSATION.

damn *v.* **1.** To invoke evil upon ▸ anathematize, curse, hex, imprecate. [*Compare* CHARM.] **2.** To use profane or obscene language ▸ blaspheme, curse, swear. *Informal:* cuss. *—See also* CONDEMN.

damn *adj.* *—See* DAMNED.

damnation *n.* *—See* CURSE (1).

damned *adj.* *Informal* So annoying or detestable as to deserve condemnation ▸ abominable, accursed, blasted, blessed, bloody, confounded, cursed, damn, darn, execrable, infernal. *Informal:* blamed, dang, danged, doggone, gosh-darn. *Slang:* freaking. *Regional:* dadblame, dadblasted, dadburn, dadgum, durn, gol-durn. [*Compare* VEXATIOUS.] *—See also* CONDEMNED, UTTER².

damp *adj.* Slightly wet ▸ clammy, dank, dewy, moist. [*Compare* STICKY, WET.] *—See also* RAINY.

damp *v.* *—See* EXTINGUISH, MUFFLE.

dampen *v.* To make moist ▸ bathe, moisten, wash, wet. *—See also* DEPRESS, HINDER, MUFFLE.

damsel *n.* *—See* GIRL.

dance *v.* To move rhythmically to music, using patterns of steps or gestures ▸ foot, step. *Slang:* boogie, hoof. ***Idioms:*** cut a rug, foot it, get down, trip the light fantastic. *—See also* GAMBOL.

dance *n.* A party or gathering for dancing ▸ ball, cotillion, formal, hoedown, masquerade, mixer, prom, promenade, rave. *Informal:* hop, sock-hop. [*Compare* PARTY.]

dancer *n.* A person who dances, especially professionally ▸ chorine, chorus boy, chorus girl, terpsichorean. *Slang:* hoofer.

dander¹ *n.* *—See* ANGER, TEMPER (1).

dander² or **dandruff** *n.* Scaly pieces of dry skin that have been shed ▸ furfur, scale, scurf. [*Compare* FLAKE.]

dandy *adj.* *—See* EXCELLENT, GOOD (1), MARVELOUS.

dandy *n.* A man who is very preoccupied with or shows vanity about his clothes ▸ beau, coxcomb, fop, peacock, swell.

danger *n.* Exposure to harm, loss, or injury ▸ endangerment, hazard, imperilment, jeopardy, menace, peril, pitfall, risk, sword of Damocles, threat. [*Compare* TRAP.]

dangerous *adj.* Involving or likely to cause risk, loss, or injury ▸ adventurous, chancy, grave, hazardous, insidious, jeopardous, menacing, parlous, perilous, risky, threatening, treacherous, unsafe, venturesome, venturous. *Slang:* dicey, hairy.

dangle *v.* *—See* HANG (1).

dangling *adj.* *—See* HANGING, LOOSE (1).

dangly *adj.* *—See* HANGING.

dank *adj.* Slightly wet ▸ clammy, damp, dewy, moist. [*Compare* STICKY, WET.]

dapper *adj.* *—See* NEAT.

dapple *v.* *—See* SPECKLE.

dare *v.* To call on another to do

Dare, Virginia (1587–87?) ▸ The first child of English parents born in America.

dare·dev·il (dâr′dĕv′əl) ▸ *n.* One who is recklessly bold. ▸ *adj.* Recklessly bold.

dare·say (dâr′sā′) ▸ *v.* To think very likely. Used in the 1st person sing. present tense: *I daresay you're wrong.*

dar·ing (dâr′ĭng) ▸ *adj.* Bold and venturesome. ▸ *n.* Audacious bravery. **—dar′ing·ly** *adv.* **—dar′ing·ness** *n.*

dark (därk) ▸ *adj.* **-er, -est.** **1.** Lacking light or brightness. **2.** Of a shade of color tending toward black. **3.** Gloomy; dismal. **4.** Sullen or threatening: *a dark scowl.* **5.** Obscure; mysterious. **6.** Lacking enlightenment: *a dark era.* **7.** Evil; sinister. ▸ *n.* **1.** Absence of light. **2.** Night; nightfall. ***—idiom:* in the dark** **1.** In secret. **2.** In ignorance; uninformed. **—dark′ish** *adj.* **—dark′ly** *adv.* **—dark′ness** *n.*

Dark Ages ▸ *pl.n.* The early part of the Middle Ages from about A.D. 476 to A.D. 1000.

dark·en (där′kən) ▸ *v.* **1.** To make or become dark or darker. **2.** To make somber or gloomy. **3.** To tarnish: *darkened their good name.* **—dark′en·er** *n.*

dark horse ▸ *n.* A little-known, unexpectedly successful entrant in a race or contest.

dark matter ▸ *n.* Non-luminous physical objects, such as very dim stars, believed to be part of the universe's missing mass.

dark·room (därk′ro͞om′, -ro͝om′) ▸ *n.* A room in which photographic materials are processed in complete darkness or with a safelight.

dar·ling (där′lĭng) ▸ *n.* **1.** A dearly beloved person. **2.** A favorite. ▸ *adj.* **1.** Much loved. **2.** *Informal* Charming or adorable: *a darling hat.*

darm·stadt·ium (därm′shtät′ē-əm) ▸ *n. Symbol* **Ds** A synthetic radioactive element. At. no. 110.

darn[1] (därn) ▸ *v.* To mend by weaving thread across a hole. ▸ *n.* A hole repaired by darning. **—darn′er** *n.*

darn[2] (därn) ▸ *v. & interj. & n. & adv. & adj.* Damn.

darned (därnd) ▸ *adj. & adv.* Damned.

darn·ing needle (där′nĭng) ▸ *n.* **1.** A long, large-eyed needle used in darning. **2.** A dragonfly.

Dar·row (dăr′ō), **Clarence Seward** (1857–1938) ▸ Amer. lawyer.

dart (därt) ▸ *n.* **1.** A slender pointed missile thrown by hand or shot from a blowgun. **2. darts** *(takes sing. or pl. v.)* A game in which darts are thrown at a target. **3.** A sudden rapid movement. **4.** A tapered tuck sewn in a garment. ▸ *v.* To move suddenly and rapidly.

dart·er (där′tər) ▸ *n.* Any of various small, often brilliantly colored freshwater fishes.

Dar·win (där′wĭn), **Charles Robert** (1809–82) ▸ British naturalist. **—Dar·win′i·an** *adj. & n.*

Dar·win·ism (där′wĭ-nĭz′əm) ▸ *n.* A theory of biological evolution developed by Charles Darwin and others, stating that species of organisms arise and develop through the natural selection of inherited variations that increase the individual's ability to survive and reproduce. **—Dar′win·ist** *n.* **—Dar′win·is′tic** *adj.*

dash (dăsh) ▸ *v.* **1.** To break or smash to pieces. **2.** To hurl or thrust violently. **3.** To splash; spatter. **4.** To move with haste; rush: *dashed inside.* **5.** To perform or complete hastily: *dash off a letter.* **6.** To ruin. ▸ *n.* **1.** A swift blow or stroke. **2a.** A splash. **b.** A small amount of an added ingredient. **3.** A sudden movement; rush. **4.** *Sports* A relatively short footrace run at top speed. **5.** Verve. **6.** A punctuation mark (—) used to indicate a break or omission. **7.** A long sound or symbol used esp. in Morse code. **8.** A dashboard. **—dash′er** *n.*

dash·board (dăsh′bôrd′) ▸ *n.* A panel under the windshield of a vehicle, containing indicator dials and controls.

da·shi·ki (də-shē′kē) ▸ *n., pl.* **-kis.** A loose, brightly colored African tunic.

dash·ing (dăsh′ĭng) ▸ *adj.* **1.** Bold and gallant; spirited. **2.** Stylish; splendid. **—dash′ing·ly** *adv.*

das·tard (dăs′tərd) ▸ *n.* A sneaking, malicious coward. **—das′tard·li·ness** *n.* **—das′tard·ly** *adj.*

da·ta (dā′tə, dăt′ə, dä′tə) ▸ *pl.n. (takes sing. or pl. v.)* **1.** Factual information, esp. information organized for analysis or used to make decisions. **2.** Numerical information suitable for processing by computer. **3.** Pl. of **datum** 1.

da·ta·base (dā′tə-bās′, dăt′ə-) ▸ *n. Comp. Sci.* A collection of data arranged for ease of search and retrieval.

data processing ▸ *n.* **1.** Conversion of data into a form that can be processed by computer. **2.** The storing or processing of such data. **—data processor** *n.*

date[1] (dāt) ▸ *n.* **1a.** Time stated in terms of the day, month, and year. **b.** A statement of calendar time, as on a document. **2.** A specified day of a month. **3.** A particular time at which something happened or is expected to happen. **4.** The period to which something belongs. **5a.** An appointment, esp. to go out socially. **b.** A person's companion on such an outing. **6.** An engagement for a performance. ▸ *v.* **dat·ed, dat·ing.** **1.** To mark or supply with a date: *date a letter.* **2.** To determine the date of. **3.** To betray the age of. **4.** To have origin in a particular time in the past: *This statue dates from 500 B.C.* **5.** To go on a date or dates (with). ***—idiom:* to date** Up to the present time. **—dat′a·ble, date′a·ble** *adj.*

date[2] (dāt) ▸ *n.* The sweet edible oblong fruit of the date palm.

dat·ed (dā′tĭd) ▸ *adj.* **1.** Marked with a date. **2.** Old-fashioned. **—dat′ed·ness** *n.*

date·line (dāt′līn′) ▸ *n.* A phrase in a news story that gives its date and place of origin.

date palm ▸ *n.* A palm tree native to W Asia and N Africa, having featherlike leaves and clusters of dates.

THESAURUS

something bold ▸ challenge, defy. *Idiom:* throw down the gauntlet. —*See also* DEFY (1), VENTURE.

dare *n.* An act of taunting another to do something bold or rash ▸ challenge, gauntlet, provocation. [*Compare* DEFIANCE.]

daredevil *n.* One who seeks adventure ▸ adventurer, quester, venturer.

daredevil *adj.* —*See* ADVENTUROUS.

daredevilry or **daredeviltry** *n.* —*See* DARING.

daring *n.* Willingness to take risks ▸ adventuresomeness, adventurousness, audaciousness, audacity, boldness, daredevilry, daredeviltry, daringness, derring-do, fearlessness, venturesomeness, venturousness. [*Compare* COURAGE, TEMERITY.]

daring *adj.* —*See* ADVENTUROUS.

dark *adj.* **1.** Deficient in brightness ▸ dim, dusky, ill-lit, murky, obscure, shadowy, shady, stygian. [*Compare* SHADY.] **2.** Having a dark color or complexion ▸ black, brown, brunet, dusky, swarthy, tawny. —*See also* BLACK (2), BLEAK (2), EVIL, FATEFUL (1), GLOOMY.

dark *n.* Absence or deficiency of light ▸ darkness, dimness, duskiness, murk, murkiness, obscureness, obscurity. [*Compare* SHADE.] —*See also* NIGHT.

darken *v.* —*See* SHADE (2).

darkness *n.* The condition of not being able to see ▸ blindness, legal blindness, sightlessness, visual impairment. —*See also* DARK, IGNORANCE (1).

darling *n.* **1.** A person who is much loved ▸ beloved, dear, honey, love, precious, sugar, sweet, sweetheart, truelove. *Informal:* babe, baby, honeybun, honeybunch, sweetie, sweetiepie, sweetpea. *Idiom:* light of one's life. **2.** One liked or preferred above all others ▸ favorite, pet. *Idiom:* apple of one's eye.

darling *adj.* Regarded with much love and tenderness ▸ beloved, dear, desired, loved, precious. —*See also* DELIGHTFUL, FAVORITE.

darn *adj.* —*See* DAMNED.

dart *v.* —*See* FLY (2), RUSH, THROW.

dash *v.* —*See* BLAST (2), RUSH, SPLASH (1), THROW.

dash *n.* —*See* BIT[1] (1), ENERGY, POINT (2), RUN (1), SHADE (2), SPIRIT (1).

dashing *adj.* —*See* BRAVE, FASHIONABLE, LIVELY.

dastard *n.* —*See* COWARD.

dastardliness *n.* —*See* COWARDICE.

dastardly *adj.* —*See* COWARDLY.

data *n.* —*See* INFORMATION.

date *n.* A commitment, as for a performance by an entertainer ▸ booking, engagement. *Slang:* gig. —*See also* ENGAGEMENT (1).

date *v.* To be with another person socially on a regular basis ▸ go out (with), go with, see. *Informal:* take out. *Idioms:* go steady, go together.

dated *adj.* —*See* OLD-FASHIONED.

da·tive (dā′tĭv) ▸ *adj.* Of or being the grammatical case that marks the indirect object. ▸ *n.* The dative case.

da·tum (dā′təm, dăt′əm, dä′təm) ▸ *n.* **1.** *pl.* **-ta** (-tə). A fact or proposition used to draw a conclusion or make a decision. 2. *pl.* **-tums**. A point, line, or surface used as a reference, as in surveying.

daub (dôb) ▸ *v.* **1.** To cover or smear with a soft sticky substance. **2.** To paint crudely. **—daub** *n.* **—daub′er** *n.*

daugh·ter (dô′tər) ▸ *n.* 1. One's female child. 2. A female descendant. 3. A woman who is considered as if in a relationship of child to parent: *a daughter of the nation.* **—daugh′ter·ly** *adj.*

daugh·ter-in-law (dô′tər-ĭn-lô′) ▸ *n., pl.* **daugh·ters-in-law** (-tərz-). The wife of one's son.

daunt (dônt, dänt) ▸ *v.* To intimidate or discourage.

daunt·less (dônt′lĭs, dänt′-) ▸ *adj.* Fearless. **—daunt′less·ly** *adv.*

dau·phin (dô′fĭn) ▸ *n.* The eldest son of the king of France from 1349 to 1830.

dau·phine (dô-fēn′) ▸ *n.* The wife of a dauphin.

dav·en·port (dăv′ən-pôrt′) ▸ *n.* A large sofa.

Da·vid (dā′vĭd) (d. c. 962 B.C.) ▸ The 2nd king of Judah and Israel.

Da·vis (dā′vĭs), **Jefferson** (1808–89) ▸ Amer. soldier and president of the Confederacy (1861–65).

dav·it (dăv′ĭt, dā′vĭt) ▸ *n.* A small crane that projects over the side of a ship, used to hoist boats, anchors, and cargo.

daw·dle (dôd′l) ▸ *v.* **-dled, -dling**. 1. To take more time than necessary. 2. To waste time; idle. **—daw′dler** *n.*

dawn (dôn) ▸ *n.* 1. The time each morning at which daylight begins. 2. A first appearance. ▸ *v.* **1.** To begin to become light in the morning. **2.** To begin to exist. 3. To become apparent: *The truth dawned on us.*

day (dā) ▸ *n.* 1. The period of light between dawn and nightfall. 2a. The 24-hour period during which the earth completes one rotation on its axis. **b.** The analogous period of a celestial body. 3. One of the numbered 24-hour periods into which a week, month, or year is divided. 4. The portion of a day that is devoted to work or school: *an eight-hour day.* 5. A period of activity or prominence: *a writer who has had her day.* 6. often **days** A period of time: *in the days of the Roman Empire.* **—*idiom:* day in, day out** All the time; continuously.

day bed ▸ *n.* A couch convertible into a bed.

day·book (dā′bo͝ok′) ▸ *n.* 1. A book in which daily entries are recorded. 2. A diary.

day·break (dā′brāk′) ▸ *n.* Dawn.

day·care or **day care** (dā′kâr′) ▸ *n.* Provision of daytime supervision, training, and recreation, esp. for preschool children.

day·dream (dā′drēm′) ▸ *n.* A dreamlike musing or fantasy while awake. ▸ *v.* To have daydreams. **—day′dream′er** *n.*

Day-Glo (dā′glō′) ▸ A trademark for fluorescent coloring agents and materials.

day labor ▸ *n.* Labor hired and paid by the day. **—day laborer** *n.*

day·light (dā′līt′) ▸ *n.* 1. The light of day. 2a. Dawn. **b.** Daytime. 3. Exposure to public notice. 4. An approaching end, as of a complicated task. 5. **daylights** *Slang* One's wits: *scared the daylights out of me.*

day·light-sav·ing time (dā′lĭt-sā′vĭng) ▸ *n.* Time during which clocks are set one hour or more ahead of standard time to provide more daylight at the end of the working day.

day lily ▸ *n.* A perennial garden plant with yellow, orange, or purplish lilylike flowers.

Day of Atonement ▸ *n.* See **Yom Kippur**.

day school ▸ *n.* A private school for pupils living at home.

day·time (dā′tīm′) ▸ *n.* The time between sunrise and sunset. **—day′time′** *adj.*

day-to-day (dā′tə-dā′) ▸ *adj.* 1. Occurring on a daily basis. 2. Subsisting one day at a time.

day-trip·per (dā′trĭp′ər) ▸ *n.* One who takes a one-day trip without staying overnight.

daze (dāz) ▸ *v.* **dazed, daz·ing**. 1. To stun, as with a blow or shock. 2. To dazzle. ▸ *n.* A stunned or bewildered condition.

daz·zle (dăz′əl) ▸ *v.* **-zled, -zling**. 1. To dim the vision of, esp. to blind with intense light. 2. To amaze or bewilder with spectacular display. **—daz′zle** *n.* **—daz′zling·ly** *adv.*

dB ▸ *abbr.* decibel

Db ▸ The symbol for the element **dubnium**.

DC ▸ *abbr.* 1. direct current 2. District of Columbia

D-day (dē′dā′) ▸ *n.* The unnamed day on which an operation or offensive is to be launched.

DDT (dē′dē-tē′) ▸ *n.* An insecticide banned since 1972 from US agricultural use for its persistent toxicity in the environment.

DE ▸ *abbr.* Delaware

de– ▸ *pref.* 1. Reverse: *deactivate.* 2. Remove: *defog.* 3. Out of: *deplane.* 4. Reduce: *degrade.*

dea·con (dē′kən) ▸ *n.* 1. A cleric ranking just below a priest in the Anglican, Eastern Orthodox, and Roman Catholic churches. 2. A lay assistant to a Protestant minister. **—dea′con·ry** *n.*

dea·con·ess (dē′kə-nĭs) ▸ *n.* A laywoman serving as assistant to a Protestant minister.

de·ac·ti·vate (dē-ăk′tə-vāt′) ▸ *v.* 1. To render inactive or ineffective. 2. To remove from active military status. **—de·ac′ti·va′tion** *n.*

dead (dĕd) ▸ *adj.* **-er, -est**. 1. No longer alive. 2. Lacking feeling; unresponsive. 3. Weary and worn-out. 4a. Inanimate. b. Lifeless; barren: *dead soil.* 5a. No longer in existence or use. b. No longer relevant. c. Dormant: *a dead volcano.* 6. Not circulating; stagnant: *dead air.* 7. Dull;

THESAURUS

daub *v.* —*See* SMEAR.
daub *n.* —*See* SMEAR.
daunt *v.* —*See* DISCOURAGE, DISMAY.
dauntless *adj.* —*See* BRAVE.
dauntlessness *n.* —*See* COURAGE.
dawdle *v.* —*See* DELAY (2), IDLE (2), PUTTER.
dawdler *n.* —*See* LAGGARD.
dawdling *n.* —*See* [illegible]
dawn *n.* The first appearance of daylight in the morning ▸ aurora, cockcrow, dawning, daybreak, first light, morn, morning, sunrise, sunup. *Idioms:* break of day, crack of dawn. —*See also* BIRTH (2).
dawn *v.* —*See* BEGIN.
dawn on or **upon** *v.* To come as a realization ▸ register, sink in, soak in. [*Compare* DISCOVER, STRIKE, UNDERSTAND.]
dawning *n.* —*See* DAWN.
day *n.* —*See* AGE (2), LIFE.
daybreak *n.* —*See* DAWN.
daydream *n.* —*See* DREAM (1).
daydream *v.* —*See* DREAM.
daydreamer *n.* —*See* DREAMER (1).
daydreaming *n.* —*See* TRANCE.
daydreaming *adj.* —*See* DREAMY.
daze *v.* 1. To dull the senses, as with a heavy blow, a shock, or fatigue ▸ bedaze, bemuse, benumb, bewilder, stagger, stun, stupefy. *Chiefly Regional:* maze. *Slang:* zonk. [*Compare* CONFUSE.] 2. To confuse with bright light ▸ bedazzle, blind, dazzle. —*See also* DRUG (2).
daze *n.* A stunned or bewildered condition ▸ bafflement, befuddlement, bewilderedness, bewilderment, confusion, discombobulation, disorientation, distraction, fog, haze, muddle, mystification, perplexity, puzzlement, stupefaction, stupor, trance.
dazed *adj.* —*See* DIZZY (1).
dazzle *v.* To confuse with bright light ▸ bedazzle, blind, daze.
dazzle *n.* An intense blinding light ▸ blaze, flare, glare. [*Compare* BRILLIANCE, GLITTER.]
dazzling *adj.* —*See* BRILLIANT, GLORIOUS.
deacon *n.* —*See* CLERIC.
deactivate *v.* —*See* DISCHARGE.
dead *adj.* 1. No longer alive ▸ asleep, deceased, defunct, departed, expired, extinct, gone, late, lifeless, perished. *Idioms:* at rest, dead and buried, dead as a doornail, pushing up daisies, six feet under. 2. Lacking physical feeling or sensitivity ▸ asleep, benumbed, deadened, dull, inert, insensible, insensitive, lifeless, numb, stuporous, torpid, unfeeling, unresponsive. [*Compare* UNCONSCIOUS.] 3. Completely lacking sensation or consciousness ▸ inanimate, insensate, insentient, lifeless. —*See also* BARREN (2), TIRED (1), UTTER[2].
dead *adv.* —*See* COMPLETELY (1),

quiet: *a dead town; a dead party.* 8. Having grown cold: *dead coals.* 9. Lacking elasticity or bounce. 10. Not running or working: *The motor is dead.* 11a. Sudden; abrupt: *a dead stop.* b. Complete: *dead silence.* c. Exact: *dead center.* 12a. Lacking connection to a source of electric current. b. Discharged: *a dead battery.* ▸ *n.* 1. One who has died. 2. A period of greatest intensity: *the dead of winter.* ▸ *adv.* 1. Absolutely; altogether: *dead sure.* 2. Directly; exactly: *dead ahead.* 3. Suddenly: *stop dead.* **—dead′ness** *n.*

dead·beat (dĕd′bēt′) ▸ *n.* *Slang* 1. One who does not pay one's debts. 2. A lazy person; loafer.

dead bolt ▸ *n.* A bolt on a lock that is moved by turning the key or knob without activation of a spring.

dead·en (dĕd′n) ▸ *v.* 1. To make less intense, sensitive, or strong: *deaden the pain; deaden curiosity.* 2. To make soundproof. 3. To make dull.

dead end ▸ *n.* 1. An end of a passage that affords no exit. 2. An impasse.

dead-end (dĕd′ĕnd′) ▸ *adj.* 1. Having no exit. 2. Permitting no opportunity for advancement: *a dead-end job.* **—dead′-end′** *v.*

dead·eye (dĕd′ī′) ▸ *n.* *Slang* An expert shooter.

dead heat ▸ *n.* A race in which two or more contestants finish at the same time.

dead letter ▸ *n.* An unclaimed or undelivered letter.

dead·line (dĕd′līn′) ▸ *n.* A time limit, as for completion of a task.

dead·lock (dĕd′lŏk′) ▸ *n.* A standstill resulting from the opposition of two unrelenting forces. ▸ *v.* To bring or come to a deadlock.

dead·ly (dĕd′lē) ▸ *adj.* **-li·er, -li·est.** 1. Causing or capable of causing death. 2. Suggestive of death. 3. Mortal; implacable: *deadly enemies.* 4. Destructive in effect. 5. Absolute; utter. 6. Dull: *a deadly lecture.* ▸ *adv.* To an extreme: *deadly serious.* **—dead′li·ness** *n.*

deadly nightshade ▸ *n.* See **belladonna** 1.

deadly sin ▸ *n.* One of the seven sins—anger, covetousness, envy, gluttony, lust, pride, and sloth—supposed to be fatal to one's spiritual development.

dead·pan (dĕd′păn′) ▸ *adj. & adv.* With a blank expressionless face. **—dead′pan′** *v.*

dead reckoning ▸ *n.* Navigation without astronomical observations, as by applying to a previously determined position the course and distance traveled since.

Dead Sea ▸ A salt lake between Israel and Jordan.

dead weight ▸ *n.* 1. The unrelieved weight of a heavy motionless mass. 2. An oppressive burden or difficulty.

dead·wood (dĕd′wo͝od′) ▸ *n.* One that is burdensome or superfluous.

deaf (dĕf) ▸ *adj.* **-er, -est.** 1. Partially or completely unable to hear. 2. Unwilling to listen: *was deaf to our pleas.* ▸ *n.* *(takes pl. v.)* 1. Deaf people collectively. 2. **Deaf** The community of deaf people who use American Sign Language as a primary means of communication. **—deaf′en** *v.* **—deaf′ly** *adv.* **—deaf′ness** *n.*

deaf-mute also **deaf mute** (dĕf′myo͞ot′) ▸ *n.* *Often Offensive* A person who can neither hear nor speak. **—deaf-mute′** *adj.*

deal[1] (dēl) ▸ *v.* **dealt** (dĕlt), **deal·ing.** 1. To distribute or apportion. 2. To sell. 3. To administer; deliver: *deal a blow.* 4. To distribute (playing cards) among players. 5. To have to do; treat: *a book that deals with ecology.* 6. To behave in a specified way toward another or others. 7. To take action: *deal with a complaint.* 8. To do business; trade: *deal in furs.* ▸ *n.* 1. The act of dealing. 2a. The cards dealt in a card game; hand. b. The right or turn of a player to deal. 3. An indefinite quantity or degree: *a great deal of luck.* 4. An often secret arrangement or pact. 5a. A business transaction. b. An agreement. 6. *Informal* A good buy. 7. *Informal* Treatment received: *a fair deal.*

deal[2] (dēl) ▸ *n.* Fir or pine wood, esp. cut to standard size.

deal·er (dē′lər) ▸ *n.* 1. One who buys and sells. 2. *Games* The one who deals the cards.

deal·er·ship (dē′lər-shĭp′) ▸ *n.* A franchise to sell specified items in a certain area.

deal·ing (dē′lĭng) ▸ *n.* 1. **dealings** Transactions or relations with others, usu. in business. 2. Conduct in relation to others.

dean (dēn) ▸ *n.* 1. An administrative officer in a high school, college, or university. 2. The senior member of a body or group.

dear (dîr) ▸ *adj.* **-er, -est.** 1. Loved and cherished. 2. Highly esteemed or regarded. 3. High-priced. ▸ *n.* A greatly loved person; darling. ▸ *interj.* Used as a polite exclamation. **—dear′ly** *adv.* **—dear′ness** *n.*

dearth (dûrth) ▸ *n.* A scarce supply; lack.

death (dĕth) ▸ *n.* 1. The act of dying or state of being dead; termination of life. 2. The cause or manner of dying. 3. Termination; extinction. ***—idiom:* to death** To an extreme degree: *worried to death.*

death·bed (dĕth′bĕd′) ▸ *n.* 1. The bed on which a person dies. 2. The last hours before death.

death·blow (dĕth′blō′) ▸ *n.* A fatal blow or event.

death·less (dĕth′lĭs) ▸ *adj.* Undying; immortal. **—death′less·ness** *n.*

death·ly (dĕth′lē) ▸ *adj.* Of, resembling, or characteristic of death. ▸ *adv.* Extremely; very: *deathly pale.*

THESAURUS

DIRECTLY (1), DIRECTLY (3).

deadbeat *n.* —*See* WASTREL (2).

dead duck *n.* *Slang* One that is ruined or doomed ▸ *Slang:* dead meat, goner, toast.

deaden *v.* To render less sensitive ▸ benumb, blunt, desensitize, dull, numb. *Idioms:* put to sleep, take the edge off. [*Compare* DRUG.] —*See also* MUFFLE.

dead end *n.* A course leading nowhere ▸ blind alley, cul-de-sac.

dead heat *n.* An equality of scores, votes, or performances in a contest ▸ deadlock, draw, stalemate, standoff, tie.

deadliness *n.* The quality or condition of causing death or disaster ▸ fatality, fatefulness, lethality, lethalness.

deadlock *n.* An equality of scores, votes, or performances in a contest ▸ dead heat, draw, stalemate, standoff, tie.

deadly *adj.* Causing or tending to cause death ▸ deathly, fatal, lethal, mortal, pestilent. [*Compare* POISONOUS.] —*See also* BORING, DULL (1), GHASTLY (2).

dead meat *n.* *Slang* One that is ruined or doomed ▸ *Slang:* dead duck, goner, toast.

deadpan *adj.* —*See* EXPRESSIONLESS.

deafening *adj.* —*See* LOUD.

deal *n.* 1. A business agreement involving goods or services ▸ auction, barter, bargain, exchange, sale, trade, transaction. 2. *Informal* Something offered or bought at a low price ▸ bargain, find. *Informal:* buy. *Slang:* steal. —*See also* AGREEMENT (1), QUANTITY (2).

deal *v.* 1. To have for sale ▸ carry, keep, offer, stock. [*Compare* SELL.] 2. To engage in the illicit sale of narcotics ▸ peddle. *Slang:* push. [*Compare* SELL.] 3. To mete out by means of some action ▸ administer, deliver, give. —*See also* DISTRIBUTE, SELL.

deal with *v.* 1. To be concerned with something ▸ address, consider, take up, treat. *Idiom:* have to do with. 2. To behave in a specified way toward someone ▸ cope with, handle, treat.

dealer *n.* A person engaged in buying and selling ▸ businessperson, entrepreneur, merchandiser, merchant, trader, tradesman, trafficker. [*Compare* SELLER.] —*See also* GO-BETWEEN, PUSHER.

dear *adj.* —*See* COSTLY, DARLING.

dear *n.* —*See* DARLING (1).

dearth *n.* The condition of lacking something ▸ absence, lack, want. [*Compare* NEED, SHORTAGE.]

death *n.* 1. The act or fact of dying ▸ decease, demise, dissolution, end, expiration, expiry, extinction, passing, quietus, rest. *Slang:* curtains. 2. A loss of life, or one who has lost life, usually as a result of accident, disaster, or war ▸ casualty, fatality, kill, loss. [*Compare* VICTIM.]

deathless *adj.* ▸ immortal, undying. [*Compare* ENDLESS.]

deathlike *adj.* —*See* GHASTLY (2).

deathly *adj.* —*See* DEADLY, GHASTLY (2).

death rate ▸ *n.* The ratio of deaths to total population in a specified community over a specified period of time.
death rattle ▸ *n.* A gurgling or rattling sound sometimes made in the throat of a dying person.
death row (rō) ▸ *n.* The part of a prison for housing inmates who have received the death penalty.
death's-head (dĕths′hĕd′) ▸ *n.* The human skull as a symbol of mortality or death.
death·trap (dĕth′trăp′) ▸ *n.* An unsafe building or other structure.
Death Valley ▸ An arid desert basin of E CA and W NV.
death·watch (dĕth′wŏch′) ▸ *n.* A vigil kept beside a dying or dead person.
deb (dĕb) ▸ *n. Informal* A debutante.
de·ba·cle (dĭ-bä′kəl, -băk′əl, dĕb′ə-kəl) ▸ *n.* A sudden disastrous collapse, downfall, or defeat.
de·bar (dē-bär′) ▸ *v.* **-barred, -bar·ring. 1.** To exclude or shut out; bar. **2.** To forbid or prevent. **—de·bar′ment** *n.*
de·bark (dĭ-bärk′) ▸ *v.* To unload; disembark. **—de′bar·ka′tion** (dē′bär-kā′shən) *n.*
de·base (dĭ-bās′) ▸ *v.* **-based, -bas·ing.** To lower in character, quality, or value; degrade. **—de·base′ment** *n.* **—de·bas′er** *n.*
de·bate (dĭ-bāt′) ▸ *v.* **-bat·ed, -bat·ing. 1.** To consider; deliberate. **2.** To discuss opposing points. **3.** To discuss or argue formally. ▸ *n.* **1.** An argument. **2.** Deliberation; consideration. **3.** A formal contest of argumentation in which two opposing teams defend and attack a given proposition. **—de·bat′a·ble** *adj.* **—de·bat′er** *n.*
de·bauch (dĭ-bôch′) ▸ *v.* **1.** To corrupt morally. **2.** To reduce the value or quality of; debase. **—de·bauch′er** *n.* **—de·bauch′er·y** *n.*
de·ben·ture (dĭ-bĕn′chər) ▸ *n.* **1.** A voucher acknowledging a debt. **2.** An unsecured bond issued by a civil or governmental agency.
de·bil·i·tate (dĭ-bĭl′ĭ-tāt′) ▸ *v.* **-tat·ed, -tat·ing.** To sap the strength of; enervate. **—de·bil′i·ta′tion** *n.*
de·bil·i·ty (dĭ-bĭl′ĭ-tē) ▸ *n., pl.* **-ties.** Feebleness.
deb·it (dĕb′ĭt) ▸ *n.* **1.** An item of debt as recorded in an account. **2.** The sum of such entries. ▸ *v.* **1.** To enter a debit in an account. **2.** To charge with a debit.
debit card ▸ *n.* A bankcard used in charging electronic transactions against funds on deposit.
deb·o·nair also **deb·o·naire** (dĕb′ə-nâr′) ▸ *adj.* **1.** Suave; urbane. **2.** Carefree; jaunty. **—deb′o·nair′ly** *adv.*
de·brief (dē-brēf′) ▸ *v.* To question to obtain knowledge gathered, esp. on a military mission. **—de·brief′ing** *n.*
de·bris also **dé·bris** (də-brē′, dā-, dā′brē′) ▸ *n.* The scattered remains of something broken or destroyed; rubble or wreckage.
debt (dĕt) ▸ *n.* **1.** Something owed, as money, goods, or services. **2.** The condition of owing; indebtedness. **—debt′or** *n.*
de·bug (dē-bŭg′) ▸ *v.* **-bugged, -bug·ging. 1.** To remove a hidden electronic surveillance device from. **2.** To search for and eliminate malfunctioning elements or errors in (e.g., computer software). **—de·bug′ger** *n.*
de·bunk (dē-bŭngk′) ▸ *v.* To expose or ridicule the falseness or exaggerated claims of. **—de·bunk′er** *n.*
de·but also **dé·but** (dā-byo͞o′, dā′byo͞o′) ▸ *n.* **1.** A first public appearance. **2.** The formal presentation of a young woman to society. **3.** The beginning of something. ▸ *v.* **-buted** (-byo͞od′), **-but·ing** (-byo͞o′ĭng). To make a debut.
deb·u·tante (dĕb′yo͝o-tänt′, dā′byo͞o-) ▸ *n.* A young woman making a formal debut into society.
Dec. ▸ *abbr.* December
deca– or **dec–** also **deka–** or **dek–** ▸ *pref.* Ten: *decagram.*
dec·ade (dĕk′ād′, dĕ-kād′) ▸ *n.* A period of ten years.
dec·a·dence (dĕk′ə-dəns, dĭ-kād′ns) ▸ *n.* A process, condition, or period of deterioration; decay. **—dec′a·dent** *adj. & n.* **—dec′a·dent·ly** *adv.*
de·caf (dē′kăf′) ▸ *n. Informal* Decaffeinated coffee.
de·caf·fein·at·ed (dē-kăf′ə-nā′tĭd, -kăf′ē-ə-) ▸ *adj.* Having the caffeine removed. **—de·caf′fein·ate′** *v.* **—de·caf′fein·a′tion** *n.*
dec·a·gon (dĕk′ə-gŏn′) ▸ *n.* A polygon with ten sides. **—de·cag′o·nal** (dĭ-kăg′ə-nəl) *adj.* **—de·cag′o·nal·ly** *adv.*
dec·a·gram or **dek·a·gram** (dĕk′ə-grăm′) ▸ *n.* See **measurement** table in Appendix.
dec·a·he·dron (dĕk′ə-hē′drən) ▸ *n., pl.* **-drons** or **-dra** (-drə). A polyhedron with ten faces. **—dec′a·he′dral** *adj.*
de·cal (dē′kăl′, dĭ-kăl′) ▸ *n.* **1.** A design transferred by decalcomania. **2.** A decorative sticker.
de·cal·ci·fy (dē-kăl′sə-fī′) ▸ *v.* **-fied, -fy·ing.** To remove calcium or calcium compounds from. **—de·cal′ci·fi·ca′tion** *n.*
de·cal·co·ma·ni·a (dē-kăl′kə-mā′nē-ə, -mān′yə) ▸ *n.* The process of transferring designs printed on specially prepared paper to materials such as glass or metal.
dec·a·li·ter or **dek·a·li·ter** (dĕk′ə-lē′tər) ▸ *n.* See **measurement** table in Appendix.
Dec·a·logue or **Dec·a·log** (dĕk′ə-lôg′, -lŏg′) ▸ *n. Bible* The Ten Commandments.
dec·a·me·ter or **dek·a·me·ter** (dĕk′ə-mē′tər) ▸ *n.* See **measurement** table in Appendix.
de·camp (dĭ-kămp′) ▸ *v.* **1.** To depart secretly or suddenly. **2.** To break camp. **—de·camp′ment** *n.*
de·cant (dĭ-kănt′) ▸ *v.* **1.** To pour off (e.g., wine) without disturbing the sediment. **2.** To pour (a liquid) from one container into another. **—de′can·ta′tion** (dē′kăn-tā′shən) *n.*
de·cant·er (dĭ-kăn′tər) ▸ *n.* A vessel used for decanting, esp. a bottle for serving wine.
de·cap·i·tate (dĭ-kăp′ĭ-tāt′) ▸ *v.* **-tat·ed, -tat·ing.** To cut off the head of. **—de·cap′i·ta′tion** *n.* **—de·cap′i·ta′tor** *n.*
dec·a·syl·la·ble (dĕk′ə-sĭl′ə-bəl) ▸ *n.* A line of verse having ten syllables. **—dec′a·syl·lab′ic** (-sə-lăb′ĭk) *adj.*
de·cath·lon (dĭ-kăth′lən, -lŏn′) ▸ *n.* An athletic contest in which each contestant participates in ten track and field events. **—de·cath′lete** *n.*

THESAURUS

debacle *n.* —*See* COLLAPSE (2), DISASTER.
debar *v.* —*See* EXCLUDE, FORBID.
debark *v.* To come ashore from a seacraft ▸ alight, disembark, land, light.
debase *v.* To lower in character, quality, or value ▸ abase, cheapen, degrade, demean, devalue, downgrade. [*Compare* BELITTLE, HUMBLE.] —*See also* CONTAMINATE, CORRUPT, DISGRACE.
debased *adj.* —*See* CORRUPT (1), IMPURE (1), IMPURE (2), UNSCRUPULOUS.
debasement *n.* —*See* DEGRADATION (1).
debatable *adj.* In doubt or dispute ▸ arguable, contentious, contestable, contested, disputable, doubtful, exceptionable, indefinite, moot, mootable, problematic, problematical, questionable, suspect, uncertain, unconfirmed, unsettled. *Informal:* iffy.
debate *v.* —*See* ARGUE (2), CONFER (1), DISCUSS.
debate *n.* —*See* ARGUMENT, DELIBERATION (1).
debauch *v.* —*See* CORRUPT.
debaucher *n.* A man who seduces women ▸ Don Juan, Lothario, seducer. —*See also* WANTON.
debauchery *n.* —*See* CORRUPTION (1).
debilitate *v.* —*See* ENERVATE.
debilitated *adj.* —*See* WEAK (1).
debilitation *n.* The sapping away of strength or energy ▸ attenuation, depletion, devitalization, enervation, enfeeblement, impairment, impoverishment, incapacitation, weakening.
debit *n.* —*See* DEBT (1).
debonair *adj.* Gracious and tactful in social manner ▸ smooth, suave, urbane. [*Compare* COURTEOUS, CULTURED, SOPHISTICATED.] —*See also* LIGHTHEARTED.
debris *n.* —*See* GARBAGE, RUIN (2).
debt *n.* **1.** Something, such as money, owed by one person to another ▸ arrearage, arrears, claim, debit, due, indebtedness, liability, obligation, score. **2.** A condition of owing something to another ▸ arrearage, arrears, encumbrance, indebtedness, liability, obligation.
debunk *v.* —*See* DISCREDIT.
debut *n.* The instance or occasion of being presented for the first time to society ▸ coming-out, presentation.
debut *v.* To make one's formal entry, as into society ▸ come out.
decadence *n.* —*See* DETERIORATION (1).
decamp *v.* —*See* ESCAPE (1).
decampment *n.* —*See* ESCAPE (1).
decant *v.* —*See* POUR.

de·cay (dĭ-kā′) ► *v.* 1. To decompose; rot. 2. *Phys.* To diminish by radioactive decay. 3. To decline or decrease in quality or quantity. ► *n.* 1. Decomposition. 2. *Phys.* Radioactive decay. 3. A gradual deterioration. 4. A falling into ruin.

de·cease (dĭ-sēs′) ► *v.* **-ceased, -ceas·ing.** To die. ► *n.* Death.

de·ceased (dĭ-sēst′) ► *adj.* No longer living; dead. ► *n., pl.* **deceased.** A dead person.

de·ce·dent (dĭ-sēd′nt) ► *n. Law* A dead person.

de·ceit (dĭ-sēt′) ► *n.* 1. Misrepresentation; deception. 2. A stratagem; trick. **—de·ceit′ful** *adj.* **—de·ceit′ful·ly** *adv.* **—de·ceit′ful·ness** *n.*

de·ceive (dĭ-sēv′) ► *v.* **-ceived, -ceiv·ing.** To cause to believe what is not true; mislead. **—de·ceiv′er** *n.* **—de·ceiv′ing·ly** *adv.*

de·cel·er·ate (dē-sĕl′ə-rāt′) ► *v.* **-at·ed, -at·ing.** To decrease in speed. **—de·cel′er·a′tion** *n.*

De·cem·ber (dĭ-sĕm′bər) ► *n.* The 12th month of the Gregorian calendar. See **calendar** table in Appendix.

de·cen·ni·al (dĭ-sĕn′ē-əl) ► *adj.* 1. Of or lasting for ten years. 2. Occurring every ten years. ► *n.* A tenth anniversary. **—de·cen′ni·al·ly** *adv.*

de·cent (dē′sənt) ► *adj.* 1. Conforming to standards of propriety. 2. Free from indelicacy; modest. 3. Meeting accepted standards; adequate. 4. Kind or obliging. 5. *Informal* Properly or modestly dressed. **—de′cen·cy** *n.* **—de′cent·ly** *adv.* **—de′cent·ness** *n.*

de·cen·tral·ize (dē-sĕn′trə-līz′) ► *v.* **-ized, -iz·ing.** 1. To distribute the functions of (a central authority) among local authorities. 2. To cause to withdraw from an area of concentration. **—de·cen′tral·i·za′tion** *n.*

de·cep·tion (dĭ-sĕp′shən) ► *n.* 1. The use of deceit. 2. The fact or state of being deceived.

de·cep·tive (dĭ-sĕp′tĭv) ► *adj.* Intended or tending to deceive. **—de·cep′tive·ly** *adv.* **—de·cep′tive·ness** *n.*

deci– ► *pref.* One tenth (10^{-1}): *decigram.*

de·ci·bel (dĕs′ə-bəl, -bĕl′) ► *n.* A unit used to express relative difference in power, usu. between acoustic or electric signals, equal to ten times the common logarithm of the ratio of the two levels.

de·cide (dĭ-sīd′) ► *v.* **-cid·ed, -cid·ing.** 1. To settle conclusively all uncertainty about. 2. To influence or determine the outcome of. 3. To make up one's mind. **—de·cid′a·ble** *adj.* **—de·cid′er** *n.*

de·cid·ed (dĭ-sī′dĭd) ► *adj.* 1. Without doubt or question; definite. 2. Resolute. **—de·cid′ed·ly** *adv.* **—de·cid′ed·ness** *n.*

de·cid·u·ous (dĭ-sĭj′o͞o-əs) ► *adj.* 1. Falling off at a specific season or stage of growth. 2. Shedding foliage at the end of the growing season: *deciduous trees.* **—de·cid′u·ous·ly** *adv.* **—de·cid′u·ous·ness** *n.*

dec·i·gram (dĕs′ĭ-grăm′) ► *n.* See **measurement** table in Appendix.

de·cil·lion (dĭ-sĭl′yən) ► *n.* 1. The cardinal number equal to 10^{33}. 2. *Chiefly Brit.* The cardinal number equal to 10^{60}. **—de·cil′lion** *adj.* **—de·cil′lionth** *adj. & n.*

dec·i·mal (dĕs′ə-məl) ► *n.* 1. A linear array of integers that represents a fraction, every decimal place indicating a multiple of a negative power of 10. For example, the decimal 0.1 = $^1/_{10}$, 0.12 = $^{12}/_{100}$, 0.003 = $^3/_{1000}$. 2. A number written using the base 10. ► *adj.* 1. Expressed or expressible as a decimal. 2a. Based on 10. b. Numbered or ordered by groups of 10. **—dec′i·mal·ly** *adv.*

decimal place ► *n.* The position of a digit to the right of a decimal point, usu. identified by successive ascending ordinal numbers with the digit immediately to the right of the decimal point being first.

decimal point ► *n.* A dot written in a decimal number to indicate where the place values change from positive to negative powers of 10.

dec·i·mate (dĕs′ə-māt′) ► *v.* **-mat·ed, -mat·ing.** 1. To destroy or kill a large part of. 2. *Informal* a. To inflict great damage on: *Deer decimated the new garden.* b. To reduce markedly in amount: *hospital bills that decimated our savings.* **—dec′i·ma′tion** *n.*

dec·i·me·ter (dĕs′ə-mē′tər) ► *n.* See **measurement** table in Appendix.

de·ci·pher (dĭ-sī′fər) ► *v.* 1. To read or interpret (obscure or illegible matter). 2. To decode. **—de·ci′pher·a·ble** *adj.*

de·ci·sion (dĭ-sĭzh′ən) ► *n.* 1. The passing of judgment on an issue. 2. A conclusion or judgment; verdict. 3. Firmness of character or action; determination. 4. *Sports* A victory in boxing won on points when no knockout has occurred.

de·ci·sive (dĭ-sī′sĭv) ► *adj.* 1. Conclusive. 2. Determined; resolute. 3. Beyond doubt; unmistakable. **—de·ci′sive·ly** *adv.* **—de·ci′sive·ness** *n.*

deck[1] (dĕk) ► *n.* 1. A platform extending horizontally from one side of a ship to the other. 2. A similar platform or surface, esp. a roofless floored area adjoining a house. 3. A pack of playing cards.

THESAURUS

decay *v.* To become or cause to become rotten or unsound ► blight, break down, corrupt, crumble, curdle, decompose, deteriorate, disintegrate, fester, molder, putrefy, rot, spoil, taint, turn. ***Idioms:*** go bad, go to pot, go to seed.

decay *n.* The condition of being decayed ► blight, breakdown, decomposition, decrepitude, deterioration, disintegration, putrefaction, putrescence, putridness, rot, rottenness, spoilage.

decayed *adj.* —*See* BAD (2), SHABBY.

decaying *adj.* —*See* SHABBY.

decease *v.* —*See* DIE.

decease *n.* —*See* DEATH (1).

deceased *adj.* —*See* DEAD (1).

deceit *n.* The act or practice of deceiving ► cunning, deceitfulness, deception, double-dealing, duplicity, fraud, guile, shiftiness, trickery. —*See also* CHEAT (1).

deceitful *adj.* —*See* DISHONEST.

deceitfulness *n.* —*See* ART, DECEIT, DISHONESTY (1).

deceive *v.* To cause to accept something false by trickery or misrepresentation ► beguile, betray, bluff, cheat, cozen, delude, double-cross, dupe, fool, hoodwink, humbug, mislead, string along, swindle, take in, trick. *Informal:* bamboozle, beat, burn, have, sucker. *Slang:* four-flush, punk, snow. ***Idioms:*** lead astray, play false, pull the wool over someone's eyes, put something over on, slip one over on, take for a ride. [*Compare* FLATTER.]

deceiver *n.* —*See* CHEAT (2), LIAR.

decency *n.* 1. A sense of rightness ► conscience, grace, properness, propriety. 2. Conformity to recognized standards, as of conduct or appearance ► correctness, decentness, decorousness, decorum, properness, propriety, respectability, respectableness, seemliness. —*See also* CHASTITY.

decent *adj. Informal* Proper in appearance ► modest, presentable, respectable, tasteful. —*See also* ACCEPTABLE (2), APPROPRIATE, CHASTE, CLEAN (2), GOOD (1), SUFFICIENT.

deception *n.* —*See* DECEIT, TRICK (1).

deceptive *adj.* —*See* DISHONEST, FALLACIOUS (2).

decide *v.* To make up or cause to make up one's mind ► clinch, conclude, determine, resolve, settle. —*See also* CHOOSE (1), JUDGE.

decided *adj.* Without any doubt ► clear, clear-cut, definite, distinct, pronounced, set, settled, unquestionable. —*See also* DEFINITE (1), FIRM[1] (3), INTENT.

decidedly *adv.* —*See* VERY.

decidedness *n.* —*See* DECISION (2).

deciding *adj.* —*See* DECISIVE.

decimate *v.* —*See* MASSACRE.

decimation *n.* —*See* DESTRUCTION, MASSACRE.

decipher *v.* To find the key to a code or cipher ► break, crack, decrypt, puzzle out, unlock, unscramble. —*See also* EXPLAIN (1), SOLVE (1).

decipherable *adj.* —*See* EXPLAINABLE.

decipherment *n.* —*See* EXPLANATION.

decision *n.* 1. A position that is reached after consideration or deliberation ► conclusion, determination, resolution. [*Compare* DEDUCTION.] 2. Unwavering firmness of character, action, or will ► assuredness, decidedness, decisiveness, determination, firmness, purpose, purposefulness, resoluteness, resolution, resolve, toughness, will, willpower. [*Compare* COURAGE, DRIVE.] —*See also* CHOICE, RULING.

decisive *adj.* Determining or having the power to determine an outcome ► conclusive, crucial, deciding, definitive, determinative. —*See also* CERTAIN (2), DEFINITE (1), DEFINITIVE, FIRM[1] (3).

decisiveness *n.* —*See* DECISION (2).

deck[1] *v.* —*See* DROP (3).

deck² (dĕk) ▸ *v.* **1.** To clothe with finery; adorn. **2.** To decorate.
deck chair ▸ *n.* A folding chair, usu. with arms and a leg rest.
de·claim (dĭ-klām′) ▸ *v.* To speak loudly and with rhetorical effect. **—de·claim′er** *n.* **—dec′la·ma′tion** (dĕk′lə-mā′shən) *n.* **—de·clam′a·to′ry** (dĭ-klăm′ə-tôr′ē) *adj.*
de·clare (dĭ-klâr′) ▸ *v.* **-clared, -clar·ing. 1.** To make known formally, officially, or authoritatively. **2.** To reveal or show. **3.** To make a full statement of (e.g., dutiable goods). **4.** To proclaim one's support or opinion. **—dec′la·ra′tion** (dĕk′lə-rā′shən) *n.* **—de·clar′a·tive** *adj.* **—de·clar′er** *n.*
de·clas·si·fy (dē-klăs′ə-fī′) ▸ *v.* To remove official security classification from (a document). **—de·clas′si·fi·ca′tion** *n.*
de·clen·sion (dĭ-klĕn′shən) ▸ *n.* **1.** *Ling.* **a.** In certain languages, the inflection of nouns, pronouns, and adjectives for case, number, and gender. **b.** A class of words with the same inflections. **2.** A descent. **3.** A decline or deterioration. **—de·clen′sion·al** *adj.*
de·cline (dĭ-klīn′) ▸ *v.* **-clined, -clin·ing. 1.** To express polite refusal. **2.** To slope downward. **3.** To deteriorate gradually; fail. **4.** *Gram.* To inflect (a noun, pronoun, or adjective). ▸ *n.* **1.** The process or result of declining. **2.** A downward slope. **3.** A disease that gradually weakens the body. **—de·clin′a·ble** *adj.* **—dec′li·na′tion** (dĕk′lə-nā′shən) *n.* **—dec′li·na′tion·al** *adj.* **—de·clin′er** *n.*
de·cliv·i·ty (dĭ-klĭv′ĭ-tē) ▸ *n., pl.* **-ties.** A downward slope.
de·code (dē-kōd′) ▸ *v.* To convert from code into plain text. **—de·cod′er** *n.*
dé·colle·tage (dā′kôl-täzh′) ▸ *n.* A low neckline, esp. on a dress.
dé·colle·té (dā′kôl-tā′) ▸ *adj.* Cut low at the neckline.
de·col·o·nize (dē-kŏl′ə-nīz′) ▸ *v.* To free (a colony) from dependent status. **—de·col′o·ni·za′tion** *n.*
de·com·mis·sion (dē′kə-mĭsh′ən) ▸ *v.* To withdraw (e.g., a ship) from active service.
de·com·pose (dē′kəm-pōz′) ▸ *v.* **1.** To separate into components or basic elements. **2.** To rot or cause to rot. **—de′com·pos′a·ble** *adj.* **—de′com·pos′er** *n.* **—de·com′po·si′tion** (dē-kŏm′pə-zĭsh′ən) *n.*
de·com·press (dē′kəm-prĕs′) ▸ *v.* To relieve of pressure. **—de′com·pres′sion** *n.*
decompression sickness ▸ *n.* A disorder, seen esp. in deep-sea divers, caused by nitrogen bubbles in the blood and characterized by severe pain and paralysis.
de·con·gest (dē′kən-jĕst′) ▸ *v.* To relieve the congestion of (e.g., sinuses). **—de′con·ges′tion** *n.* **—de′con·ges′tive** *adj.*
de·con·ges·tant (dē′kən-jĕs′tənt) ▸ *n.* A medication that breaks up congestion, esp. in the sinuses.
de·con·tam·i·nate (dē′kən-tăm′ə-nāt′) ▸ *v.* **1.** To eliminate contamination in. **2.** To make safe by eliminating poisonous or harmful substances, such as radioactive material. **—de′con·tam′i·nant** *n.* **—de′con·tam′i·na′tion** *n.*
de·con·trol (dē′kən-trōl′) ▸ *v.* To stop control of, esp. by the government.
dé·cor or **de·cor** (dā′kôr′, dā-kôr′) ▸ *n.* **1.** Decoration. **2.** A decorative style or scheme, as of a room.
dec·o·rate (dĕk′ə-rāt′) ▸ *v.* **-rat·ed, -rat·ing. 1.** To provide or adorn with something ornamental. **2.** To confer a medal or other honor on. **—dec′o·ra′tion** *n.* **—dec′o·ra·tive** *adj.* **—dec′o·ra·tive·ly** *adv.*
dec·o·ra·tor (dĕk′ə-rā′tər) ▸ *n.* One that decorates, esp. an interior decorator.
dec·o·rous (dĕk′ər-əs, dĭ-kôr′əs) ▸ *adj.* Marked by decorum; proper. **—dec′o·rous·ly** *adv.* **—dec′o·rous·ness** *n.*
de·co·rum (dĭ-kôr′əm) ▸ *n.* **1.** Appropriateness of behavior or conduct; propriety. **2.** Artistic or literary appropriateness.
de·cou·page also **dé·cou·page** (dā′ko͞o-päzh′) ▸ *n.* The technique of decorating a surface with cutouts, as of paper.
de·coy (dē′koi′, dĭ-koi′) ▸ *n.* **1.** A living or artificial animal used to entice game. **2.** A means used to mislead or lead into danger. ▸ *v.* (dĭ-koi′) To lure or entrap by or as if by a decoy. **—de·coy′er** *n.*
de·crease (dĭ-krēs′) ▸ *v.* **-creased, -creas·ing.** To diminish gradually; reduce. ▸ *n.* (dē′krēs′) The act or process of decreasing.
de·cree (dĭ-krē′) ▸ *n.* **1.** An authoritative order; edict. **2.** *Law* The judgment of a court of equity, admiralty, probate, or divorce. ▸ *v.* **-creed, -cree·ing.** To ordain, establish, or decide by decree.
dec·re·ment (dĕk′rə-mənt) ▸ *n.* **1.** A gradual decrease. **2.** The amount lost by gradual diminution or waste. **—dec′re·ment′al** *adj.*
de·crep·it (dĭ-krĕp′ĭt) ▸ *adj.* Weakened, worn out, or broken down by old age, illness, or hard use. **—de·crep′it·ly** *adv.* **—de·crep′i·tude′** *n.*
de·cre·scen·do (dā′krə-shĕn′dō, dē′-) ▸ *n., pl.* **-dos** *Mus.* A gradual decrease in force or loudness. **—de′cre·scen′do** *adv. & adj.*
de·crim·i·nal·ize (dē-krĭm′ə-nə-līz′) ▸ *v.* **-ized, -iz·ing.** To reduce or abolish criminal penalties for. **—de·crim′i·nal·i·za′tion** *n.*
de·cry (dĭ-krī′) ▸ *v.* **-cried, -cry·ing.** To condemn openly. **—de·cri′er** *n.*
ded·i·cate (dĕd′ĭ-kāt′) ▸ *v.* **-cat·ed, -cat·ing. 1.** To set apart for a special use. **2.** To commit (oneself) to a course of action. **3.** To inscribe (e.g., a book) to another. **4.** To open to public use: *dedicate a new library.* **—ded′i·ca′tion** *n.* **—ded′i·ca′tive, ded′i·ca·to′ry** (-kə-tôr′ē) *adj.*
de·duce (dĭ-do͞os′, -dyo͞os′) ▸ *v.* **-duced, -duc·ing.** To infer

THESAURUS

deck² *v.* *—See* ADORN (1), DRESS UP.
declaim *v.* *—See* RANT.
declaimer *n.* *—See* SPEAKER (1).
declamation *n.* *—See* ORATORY, SPEECH (2).
declamatory *adj.* *—See* ORATORICAL.
declaration *n.* *—See* ANNOUNCEMENT, ASSERTION, MESSAGE.
declare *v.* *—See* ANNOUNCE, ASSERT, CONFIRM (1), SAY.
déclassé or **declassed** *adj.* *—See* LOWLY (1).
declension *n.* *—See* DETERIORATION (1).
declination *n.* A marked loss of strength or effectiveness ▸ decline, deterioration, failure. *—See also* DETERIORATION (1).
decline *v.* To be unwilling to accept, consider, or receive ▸ deny, disallow, disapprove, dismiss, pass (on), rebuff, refuse, reject, spurn, turn down, withhold. *Slang:* nix. ***Idiom:*** turn thumbs down on. [*Compare* DEPRIVE, FORBID.] *—See also* DETERIORATE, DROP (2), FADE, FALL (4).
decline *n.* A marked loss of strength or effectiveness ▸ declination, deterioration, failure. *—See also* DETERIORATION (1), DROP (3), FALL (3).
declivity *n.* *—See* DROP (3).
décolleté *adj.* *—See* LOW (2).
decompose *v.* *—See* DECAY, DISINTEGRATE.
decomposition *n.* *—See* DECAY.
decontaminate *v.* To render free of microorganisms ▸ disinfect, irradiate, sanitize, sterilize. [*Compare* CLEAN.]
decorate *v.* *—See* ADORN (1).
decoration *n.* An emblem of honor worn on one's clothing ▸ badge, medal, ribbon. *—See also* ADORNMENT.
decorous *adj.* *—See* APPROPRIATE.
decorousness *n.* *—See* DECENCY (2).
decorticate *v.* *—See* SKIN.
decorum *n.* *—See* DECENCY (2), MANNERS.
decoy *n.* Something that leads one into danger or entrapment ▸ bait, lure. [*Compare* TRAP, TRICK.]
decrease *v.* To become or cause to become gradually less ▸ abate, diminish, drain, dwindle, ebb, lessen, lower, peter out, ratchet down, reduce, shrink, tail away, tail off, taper off, wane. [*Compare* DEPRECIATE, FALL, SHORTEN, SUBSIDE.]
decrease *n.* The act or process of decreasing ▸ abatement, curtailment, cut, cutback, decrement, diminishment, diminution, drain, reduction, shrinkage, slash, slowdown, taper, tapering (off), wane, waning. [*Compare* FALL, WANING.]
decree *n.* *—See* RULING.
decree *v.* *—See* DICTATE, JUDGE.
decrement *n.* *—See* DECREASE.
decrepit *adj.* *—See* SHABBY, WEAK (1).
decrepitude *n.* *—See* DECAY, INFIRMITY.
decriminalize *v.* *—See* LEGALIZE.
decry *v.* *—See* BELITTLE, DEPLORE (1), DISAPPROVE.
decrypt *v.* *—See* DECIPHER.
decumbent *adj.* *—See* FLAT (1).
decussate *v.* *—See* CROSS (2).
dedicate *v.* *—See* APPLY (1), DEVOTE.
dedicated *adj.* *—See* FAITHFUL.
deduce *v.* *—See* INFER.

from a general principle; reason deductively. **—de·duc′i·ble** *adj.*
de·duct (dĭ-dŭkt′) ▸ *v.* To take away or subtract.
de·duct·i·ble (dĭ-dŭk′tə-bəl) ▸ *adj.* That can be deducted, esp. for income taxes. ▸ *n.* **1.** Something, such as an expense, that can be deducted. **2.** A clause in an insurance policy exempting the insurer from paying an initial specified amount after an accident. **—de·duct′i·bil′i·ty** *n.*
de·duc·tion (dĭ-dŭk′shən) ▸ *n.* **1.** The act of deducting; subtraction. **2.** An amount that is or may be deducted. **3.** *Logic* **a.** The process of reasoning in which a conclusion follows necessarily from the stated premises. **b.** A conclusion reached by this process. **—de·duc′tive** *adj.* **—de·duc′tive·ly** *adv.*
deed (dēd) ▸ *n.* **1.** An act; feat; exploit. **2.** Action or performance in general: *Deeds, not words, matter most.* **3.** *Law* A document sealed as an instrument of bond, contract, or conveyance, esp. relating to property. ▸ *v.* To transfer by means of a deed.
deem (dēm) ▸ *v.* To judge; consider; think.
deep (dēp) ▸ *adj.* **-er, -est. 1.** Extending far downward, inward, backward, or from side to side; far down or in. **2.** Difficult to understand. **3.** Of a grave or extreme nature. **4.** Very absorbed or involved. **5.** Profound in quality or feeling. **6.** Of an intense shade of color. **7.** Low in pitch; resonant. ▸ *adv.* To a great depth; deeply. ▸ *n.* **1.** A deep place in land or in a body of water. **2.** The most intense or extreme part. **3.** The ocean. ***—idiom:*** **in deep water** In difficulty. **—deep′ly** *adv.* **—deep′ness** *n.*
deep·en (dē′pən) ▸ *v.* To make or become deep or deeper.
deep-fry (dēp′frī′) ▸ *v.* To fry by immersing in a deep pan of fat or oil. **—deep′-fried′** *adj.*
deep-root·ed (dēp′rōō′tĭd, -rŏŏt′ĭd) ▸ *adj.* Firmly implanted; well-established.
deep-sea (dēp′sē′) ▸ *adj.* Of or occurring in deep parts of the sea.
deep-seat·ed (dēp′sē′tĭd) ▸ *adj.* Deeply rooted; ingrained.
deep-set (dēp′sĕt′) ▸ *adj.* Deeply set or placed: *deep-set eyes.*
deep-six (dēp′sĭks′) ▸ *v.* *Slang* **1.** To toss overboard. **2.** To get rid of.
deep space ▸ *n.* The regions that are located beyond the gravitational influence of Earth, encompassing interplanetary, interstellar, and intergalactic space.
deer (dîr) ▸ *n., pl.* **deer.** Any of various hoofed mammals, including the elk, moose, and caribou, having seasonally shed antlers borne chiefly by the males.
deer fly ▸ *n.* Any of various blood-sucking flies smaller than the related horsefly.
deer·skin (dîr′skĭn′) ▸ *n.* Leather made from the hide of a deer.
de·es·ca·late (dē-ĕs′kə-lāt′) ▸ *v.* To decrease the scope or intensity of. **—de-es′ca·la′tion** *n.*
de·face (dĭ-fās′) ▸ *v.* **-faced, -fac·ing.** To mar or spoil the appearance or surface of. **—de·face′ment** *n.* **—de·fac′er** *n.*
de fac·to (dĭ făk′tō, dā) ▸ *adv.* In reality or fact; actually. ▸ *adj.* **1.** Actual: *de facto segregation.* **2.** Actually exercising power.
de·fal·cate (dĭ-făl′kāt′, -fôl′-, dĕf′əl-) ▸ *v.* **-cat·ed, -cat·ing.** To embezzle. **—de′fal·ca′tion** *n.* **—de·fal′ca′tor** *n.*
de·fame (dĭ-fām′) ▸ *v.* **-famed, -fam·ing.** To damage the reputation or good name of by slander or libel. **—def′a·ma′tion** (dĕf′ə-mā′shən) *n.* **—de·fam′a·to′ry** (dĭ-făm′ə-tôr′ē) *adj.*
de·fault (dĭ-fôlt′) ▸ *n.* **1.** Failure to perform a task or fulfill an obligation. **2.** Failure to participate in a contest. **3.** *Comp. Sci.* A particular value for a variable assigned automatically by an operating system. ▸ *v.* **1a.** To fail to do what is required. **b.** To fail to pay money when it is due. **2.** To lose by not appearing, completing, or participating. **—de·fault′er** *n.*
de·feat (dĭ-fēt′) ▸ *v.* **1.** To win victory over; beat. **2.** To prevent the success of; thwart: *defeat one's own purposes.* ▸ *n.* The act of defeating or state of being defeated.
de·feat·ism (dĭ-fē′tĭz′əm) ▸ *n.* Acceptance of or resignation to the prospect of defeat. **—de·feat′ist** *adj. & n.*
def·e·cate (dĕf′ĭ-kāt′) ▸ *v.* **-cat·ed, -cat·ing.** To void feces from the bowels. **—def′e·ca′tion** *n.*
de·fect (dē′fĕkt′, dĭ-fĕkt′) ▸ *n.* **1.** The lack of something necessary or desirable. **2.** An imperfection; shortcoming. ▸ *v.* (dĭ-fĕkt′) To disown allegiance to a country, position, or group and adopt or join another. **—de·fec′tion** *n.* **—de·fec′tor** *n.*
de·fec·tive (dĭ-fĕk′tĭv) ▸ *adj.* Having a defect. **—de·fec′tive·ly** *adv.* **—de·fec′tive·ness** *n.*
de·fence (dĭ-fĕns′) ▸ *n. & v.* *Chiefly Brit.* Var. of **defense.**
de·fend (dĭ-fĕnd′) ▸ *v.* **1.** To protect from danger or harm.

THESAURUS

deduct *v.* To take away a quantity from another quantity ▸ abate, discount, rebate, remove, subtract, take away, take off, withdraw. *Informal:* knock off, shave off. *—See also* INFER.
deduction *n.* **1.** An amount deducted ▸ abatement, discount, rebate, reduction. **2.** A position arrived at by reasoning from premises ▸ conclusion, inference, judgment. [*Compare* BELIEF.] *—See also* LOGIC.
deed *n.* *—See* ACCOMPLISHMENT, ACT (1), OWNERSHIP.
deed *v.* *—See* TRANSFER (1).
deem *v.* *—See* BELIEVE (3), REGARD.
de-emphasize *v.* *Informal* To make less emphatic or obvious ▸ play down, soft-pedal, tone down. [*Compare* MODERATE.]
deep *adj.* **1.** Extending far downward or inward from a surface ▸ abysmal, bottomless, low, profound. **2.** Beyond the understanding of an average mind ▸ abstract, abstruse, difficult, esoteric, formidable, inscrutable, profound, recondite. *Slang:* heavy. [*Compare* INCOMPREHENSIBLE.] **3.** Resulting from or affecting one's innermost feelings ▸ great, heartfelt, intense, powerful, profound, strong. *—See also* COLORFUL (1), LOW (1).
deep *n.* Something of immeasurable and vast extent ▸ abysm, abyss, chasm, deeps, depth, depths, gulf.
deepen *v.* *—See* INTENSIFY.
deep-fry *v.* *—See* COOK.
deepness *n.* **1.** The extent or measurement downward from a surface ▸ depth, drop, drop-off. **2.** Intellectual penetration or range ▸ depth, profoundness, profundity, weightiness. [*Compare* DISCERNMENT, INTELLIGENCE, WISDOM.]
deep-seated or **deep-rooted** *adj.* *—See* CONFIRMED (1).
deep-six *v.* *—See* DISCARD.
deep water *n.* *—See* PREDICAMENT.
deface *v.* *—See* DEFORM.
defamation *n.* *—See* LIBEL.
defamatory *adj.* *—See* LIBELOUS.
defame *v.* *—See* MALIGN.
default *n.* *—See* FAILURE (2).
defeasance *n.* *—See* ABOLITION.
defeat *v.* To win a victory over, as in battle or a competition ▸ beat, best, checkmate, conquer, master, outgun, outplay, overcome, prevail over, subdue, subjugate, surmount, triumph over, vanquish, worst. *Informal:* trim. *Slang:* ace, KO, lick. ***Idioms:*** carry (*or* win) the day, get (*or* have) the best of, get (*or* have) the better of, go someone one better. [*Compare* ANNIHILATE, OVERWHELM.] *—See also* FRUSTRATE.
defeat *n.* The act of defeating or the condition of being defeated ▸ beating, blowout, checkmate, clobbering, drubbing, overthrow, rout, thrashing, trouncing, vanquishment, waterloo. *Informal:* massacre, trimming, whipping. *Slang:* creaming, dusting, licking, shellacking.
defect *n.* Something that mars the appearance or causes inadequacy or failure ▸ blemish, bug, failing, fault, flaw, glitch, imperfection, shortcoming, wart, weakness. ***Idiom:*** fly in the ointment. [*Compare* ABNORMALITY, DEFORMITY.] *—See also* SHORTAGE.
defect *v.* To abandon one's cause or party usually to join another ▸ apostatize, desert, disavow, forsake, quit, renegade, renounce, secede, tergiversate, turn. *Slang:* rat. ***Idioms:*** change sides, turn one's coat. [*Compare* ABANDON, REPUDIATE.]
defection *n.* An instance of defecting from or abandoning a cause ▸ abandonment, apostasy, disavowal, recreance, recreancy, renouncement, secession, tergiversation. *—See also* EMIGRATION.
defective *adj.* Having a defect or defects ▸ amiss, blemished, faulty, flawed, imperfect. [*Compare* SHABBY, TRICK.] *—See also* DEFICIENT.
defector *n.* A person who has defected ▸ apostate, deserter, recreant, renegade, runagate, tergiversator, traitor, turncoat. *Informal:* rat.
defend *v.* **1.** To keep safe from danger, attack, or harm ▸ cover, guard, hedge,

2. To support or maintain; justify. **3.** *Law* **a.** To represent (a defendant) in a civil or criminal action. **b.** To contest (an action or claim). **—de·fend′a·ble** *adj.* **—de·fend′er** *n.*

de·fen·dant (dĭ-fĕn′dənt) ▸ *n. Law* The party against which an action is brought.

de·fense (dĭ-fĕns′) ▸ *n.* **1.** The act of defending. **2.** A means or method of defending or protecting. **3.** An argument in support or justification. **4.** *Law* **a.** The action of the defendant in opposition to complaints against him or her. **b.** The defendant and his or her legal counsel. **5.** (*often* dē′fĕns′) *Sports* The players on a team attempting to stop the opposition from scoring. **—de·fense′less** *adj.* **—de·fense′less·ly** *adv.* **—de·fense′less·ness** *n.*

defense mechanism ▸ *n.* A physical or psychological reaction of an organism used in self-protection.

de·fen·si·ble (dĭ-fĕn′sə-bəl) ▸ *adj.* Capable of being defended or justified. **—de·fen′si·bil′i·ty** *n.* **—de·fen′si·bly** *adv.*

de·fen·sive (dĭ-fĕn′sĭv) ▸ *adj.* **1.** Of, intended for, or relating to defense. **2.** *Psychol.* Constantly protecting oneself from perceived threats to the ego. ▸ *n.* An attitude or position of defense. ***—idiom:* on the defensive** Prepared to withstand attack. **—de·fen′sive·ly** *adv.* **—de·fen′sive·ness** *n.*

de·fer[1] (dĭ-fûr′) ▸ *v.* **-ferred, -fer·ring.** To put off; postpone. **—de·fer′ra·ble** *adj.*

de·fer[2] (dĭ-fûr′) ▸ *v.* **-ferred, -fer·ring.** To submit to the opinion, wishes, or decision of another. **—de·fer′rer** *n.*

def·er·ence (dĕf′ər-əns, dĕf′rəns) ▸ *n.* **1.** Submission or courteous yielding to the opinion, wishes, or judgment of another. **2.** Courteous respect. **—def′er·en′tial** *adj.* **—def′er·en′tial·ly** *adv.*

de·fer·ment (dĭ-fûr′mənt) ▸ *n.* **1.** The act or an instance of delaying. **2.** Official postponement of compulsory military service.

de·fer·ral (dĭ-fûr′əl) ▸ *n.* Deferment.

de·fi·ant (dĭ-fī′ənt) ▸ *adj.* **1.** Marked by bold resistance to authority or an opposing force. **2.** Deliberately provocative. **—de·fi′ance** *n.* **—de·fi′ant·ly** *adv.*

deficiency disease ▸ *n.* A disease, such as scurvy, caused by a dietary deficiency of specific nutrients.

de·fi·cient (dĭ-fĭsh′ənt) ▸ *adj.* **1.** Lacking an essential quality or element. **2.** Inadequate; insufficient. **—de·fi′cien·cy** *n.* **—de·fi′cient·ly** *adv.*

def·i·cit (dĕf′ĭ-sĭt) ▸ *n.* **1.** Inadequacy or insufficiency. **2.** The amount by which a sum of money falls short of the required amount.

deficit spending ▸ *n.* The spending of public funds obtained by borrowing rather than taxation.

de·fi·er (dĭ-fī′ər) ▸ *n.* One that defies: *a defier of tradition.*

de·file[1] (dĭ-fīl′) ▸ *v.* **-filed, -fil·ing.** **1.** To make filthy or dirty. **2.** To corrupt. **3.** To profane or sully (e.g., a good name). **4.** To desecrate. **5.** To violate the chastity of. **—de·file′ment** *n.* **—de·fil′er** *n.*

de·file[2] (dĭ-fīl′) ▸ *v.* **-filed, -fil·ing.** To march in single file or in columns. ▸ *n.* **1.** A narrow gorge or pass. **2.** A march in a line.

de·fine (dĭ-fīn′) ▸ *v.* **-fined, -fin·ing.** **1.** To state the precise meaning of (e.g., a word). **2.** To describe the basic qualities of. **3.** To delineate. **4.** To specify distinctly; distinguish. **—de·fin′a·ble** *adj.* **—de·fin′a·bly** *adv.* **—de·fin′er** *n.*

def·i·nite (dĕf′ə-nĭt) ▸ *adj.* **1.** Having distinct limits. **2.** Indisputable; certain. **3.** Clearly defined; precise. **—def′i·nite·ly** *adv.* **—def′i·nite·ness** *n.*

definite article ▸ *n.* A determiner that particularizes a noun. In English, *the* is the definite article.

def·i·ni·tion (dĕf′ə-nĭsh′ən) ▸ *n.* **1a.** A statement conveying fundamental character. **b.** A statement of the meaning of a word, phrase, or term, as in a dictionary entry. **2.** The act of making clear and distinct. **3.** A determination of outline, extent, or limits.

de·fin·i·tive (dĭ-fĭn′ĭ-tĭv) ▸ *adj.* **1.** Precisely defined or explicit. **2.** Being a final settlement; conclusive. **3.** Authoritative and complete. **—de·fin′i·tive·ly** *adv.* **—de·fin′i·tive·ness** *n.*

de·flate (dĭ-flāt′) ▸ *v.* **-flat·ed, -flat·ing.** **1a.** To release contained air or gas from. **b.** To collapse by such a release. **2.** To reduce or lessen the size or importance of. **3.** *Econ.* To reduce the amount or availability of (currency or credit), effecting a decline in prices. **—de·fla′tion** *n.* **—de·fla′tion·ar·y** *adj.* **—de·fla′tor** *n.*

de·flect (dĭ-flĕkt′) ▸ *v.* To turn aside or cause to turn aside. **—de·flect′a·ble** *adj.* **—de·flec′tion** *n.* **—de·flec′tive** *adj.* **—de·flec′tor** *n.*

De·foe (dĭ-fō′), **Daniel** (1660–1731) ▸ British writer.

de·fog (dē-fôg′, -fŏg′) ▸ *v.* To remove fog from. **—de·fog′ger** *n.*

THESAURUS

preserve, protect, safeguard, secure, shield, ward. **2.** To support against arguments, attack, or criticism ▸ apologize, bolster, justify, maintain, uphold, vindicate. ***Idioms:*** make a case for, speak up for, stand up for, stick up for.

defendable *adj.* Capable of being defended against armed attack ▸ defensible, tenable. [*Compare* SAFE.]

defendant *n.* A person against whom an action is brought ▸ accused, respondent.

defender *n.* *—See* ADVOCATE.

defense *n.* The act or a means of defending ▸ barricade, guard, hedge, preservation, protection, safeguard, security, shield, ward. *—See also* APOLOGY (1).

defenseless *adj.* *—See* VULNERABLE.

defenselessness *n.* *—See* EXPOSURE.

defensible *adj.* **1.** Capable of being defended against armed attack ▸ defendable, tenable. [*Compare* SAFE.] **2.** Capable of being justified ▸ excusable, justifiable, tenable. [*Compare* LOGICAL, SOUND[2].]

defensive *adj.* *—See* PREVENTIVE (2).

defer[1] *v.* To put off until a later time ▸ adjourn, delay, hold off, hold up, postpone, put off, remit, shelve, stall, stay, suspend, table, waive. ***Informal:*** wait. ***Idioms:*** put on the back burner, put on hold, keep (*or* put) on ice.

defer[2] *v.* To conform to the will or judgment of another, especially out of respect or courtesy ▸ bow, submit, yield. ***Idioms:*** give ground, give way, stand aside, take a back seat. [*Compare* HUMOR.] *—See also* SURRENDER (1).

deference *n.* *—See* HONOR (1), OBEDIENCE.

deferential *adj.* Marked by courteous submission or respect ▸ duteous, dutiful, obeisant, polite, respectful, submissive, yielding.

deferment or **deferral** *n.* *—See* DELAY (1).

defiance *n.* **1.** The act or an instance of defying ▸ challenge, disobedience, insubordination, insurgence, naughtiness, noncompliance, opposition, provocation, rebellion, resistance. **2.** An attitude or behavior that is intentionally provocative or contemptuous ▸ contempt, contumaciousness, contumacy, despite, disregard, recalcitrance, recalcitrancy, rebelliousness.

defiant *adj.* Marked by defiance ▸ contumacious, disobedient, insubordinate, rebellious, recalcitrant.

deficiency *n.* *—See* DEPRIVATION, SHORTAGE.

deficient *adj.* Lacking an essential element ▸ defective, inadequate, incomplete, lacking, sketchy, wanting. *—See also* INSUFFICIENT.

deficit *n.* *—See* SHORTAGE.

defile *v.* *—See* CORRUPT, DENIGRATE, DIRTY, VIOLATE (3).

defilement *n.* *—See* CONTAMINATION.

define *v.* *—See* CLARIFY (1), DETERMINE.

definite *adj.* **1.** Clearly, fully, and emphatically expressed ▸ categorical, clear, clear-cut, decided, decisive, emphatic, explicit, express, positive, precise, ringing, specific, straightforward, strong, strongly worded, unambiguous, unequivocal. [*Compare* APPARENT, ASSERTIVE, CONVINCING, SHARP.] **2.** Having distinct limits ▸ determinate, fixed, limited, precise, specific, unambiguous. ***Idioms:*** cast in stone, fixed in stone, set in cement, set in concrete, set in stone. **3.** Known positively ▸ absolute, certain, positive, sure, unimpeachable. ***Idioms:*** beyond a doubt, beyond the shadow of a doubt, for certain (*or* sure). *—See also* DECIDED.

definitely *adv.* *—See* ABSOLUTELY.

definitive *adj.* Serving the function of deciding or settling with finality ▸ authoritative, conclusive, consummate, decisive, determinative, final, ultimate. [*Compare* AUTHENTIC, COMPLETE, PERFECT.] *—See also* DECISIVE.

definitude *n.* *—See* ACCURACY.

deflate *v.* *—See* DISCREDIT, HUMBLE.

deflect *v.* *—See* BEND (2), REPEL, TURN (2).

deflection *n.* An act of reflection ▸ glance, reflection, scattering. [*Compare* BOUNCE.]

de·fo·li·ant (dē-fō′lē-ənt) ► *n.* A chemical sprayed or dusted on plants to cause the leaves to fall off.
de·fo·li·ate (dē-fō′lē-āt′) ► *v.* **-at·ed, -at·ing.** To deprive of leaves, esp. by the use of chemicals. **—de·fo′li·ate** (-ĭt) *adj.* **—de·fo′li·a′tion** *n.* **—de·fo′li·a′tor** *n.*
de·for·est (dē-fôr′ĭst, -fŏr′-) ► *v.* To clear away trees from. **—de·for′es·ta′tion** *n.*
de·form (dĭ-fôrm′) ► *v.* **1.** To spoil the beauty or appearance of; disfigure. **2.** To become disfigured. **—de·form′a·ble** *adj.* **—de′for·ma′tion** (dē′fôr-mā′shən, dĕf′ər-) *n.*
de·for·mi·ty (dĭ-fôr′mĭ-tē) ► *n., pl.* **-ties. 1.** The state of being deformed. **2.** A bodily malformation or disfigurement. **3.** A deformed person or thing.
de·fraud (dĭ-frôd′) ► *v.* To swindle. **—de′fraud·a′tion** *n.* **—de·fraud′er** *n.*
de·fray (dĭ-frā′) ► *v.* To undertake the payment of; pay. **—de·fray′a·ble** *adj.* **—de·fray′al** *n.*
de·frock (dē-frŏk′) ► *v.* To strip of priestly or other privileges and functions.
de·frost (dē-frôst′, -frŏst′) ► *v.* **1.** To remove ice or frost from. **2.** To cause to thaw. **3.** To become thawed. **—de·frost′er** *n.*
deft (dĕft) ► *adj.* **-er, -est.** Skillful; adroit: *a deft maneuver.* **—deft′ly** *adv.* **—deft′ness** *n.*
de·funct (dĭ-fŭngkt′) ► *adj.* No longer in existence, operation, or use.
de·fuse (dē-fyo͞oz′) ► *v.* **-fused, -fus·ing. 1.** To remove the fuse from (an explosive). **2.** To make less dangerous or hostile.
de·fy (dĭ-fī′) ► *v.* **-fied, -fy·ing. 1.** To oppose or resist with boldness. **2.** To resist or withstand. **3.** To dare (someone) to do something.
deg. ► *abbr.* degree
de·gauss (dē-gous′) ► *v.* **1.** To neutralize the magnetic field of. **2.** To erase information from (e.g., a magnetic disk).
de·gen·er·ate (dĭ-jĕn′ər-ĭt) ► *adj.* Having declined, as in function, from a former state. ► *n.* A depraved or corrupt person. ► *v.* (-ə-rāt′) **-at·ed, -at·ing. 1.** To fall below a normal or desirable state. **2.** To decline in quality. **—de·gen′er·ate·ly** *adv.* **—de·gen′er·ate·ness, de·gen′er·a·cy** *n.* **—de·gen′er·a′tion** *n.* **—de·gen′er·a·tive** *adj.*
de·grad·a·ble (dĭ-grā′də-bəl) ► *adj.* That can be chemically degraded: *degradable plastic.* **—de·grad′a·bil′i·ty** *n.*
de·grade (dĭ-grād′) ► *v.* **-grad·ed, -grad·ing. 1.** To reduce in rank or status. **2.** To dishonor or disgrace. **3.** To reduce in worth or value. **—deg′ra·da′tion** (dĕg′rə-dā′shən) *n.*
de·gree (dĭ-grē′) ► *n.* **1.** One of a series of steps in a process or course; stage. **2.** Relative social or official rank or position. **3.** Relative intensity. **4.** The extent or measure of a state of being or action. **5.** A unit division of a temperature scale. **6.** *Math.* A unit of angular measure equal in magnitude to 1/360 of a complete revolution. **7.** A unit of latitude or longitude, equal to 1/360 of a great circle. **8.** *Math.* The greatest sum of the exponents of the variables in a term of a polynomial or polynomial equation. **9.** An academic title given to someone who has completed a course of study or as an honorary distinction. **10.** *Law* A classification of a crime or injury according to its seriousness. **11.** *Gram.* One of the forms used in the comparison of adjectives and adverbs. **12.** *Mus.* One of the seven notes of a diatonic scale. ***—idiom:* to a degree** In a limited way.
de·gree-day (dĭ-grē′dā′) ► *n.* A unit of measurement equal to a difference of one degree between the mean outdoor temperature on a certain day and a reference temperature, used in estimating the energy needs for heating or cooling a building.
de·hisce (dĭ-hĭs′) ► *v.* **-hisced, -hisc·ing. 1.** *Bot.* To open at definite places, discharging seeds or other contents, as the ripe capsules or pods of some plants. **2.** *Medic.* To rupture or break open. **—de·hisc′ent** *adj.* **—de·hisc′ence** *n.*
de·hu·man·ize (dē-hyo͞o′mə-nīz′) ► *v.* **1.** To deprive of human qualities such as individuality or compassion. **2.** To render mechanical and routine. **—de·hu′man·i·za′tion** *n.*
de·hu·mid·i·fy (dē′hyo͞o-mĭd′ə-fī′) ► *v.* To remove atmospheric moisture from. **—de′hu·mid′i·fi·ca′tion** *n.* **—de′hu·mid′i·fi′er** *n.*
de·hy·drate (dē-hī′drāt′) ► *v.* **1.** To lose water or bodily fluids. **2.** To deplete the bodily fluids of. **—de′hy·dra′tion** *n.* **—de·hy′dra′tor** *n.*
de·hy·dro·gen·ate (dē′hī-drŏj′ə-nāt′, dē-hī′drə-jə-) ► *v.* To remove hydrogen from. **—de·hy′dro·gen·a′tion** *n.*
de·ice (dē-īs′) ► *v.* To make or keep free of ice. **—de·ic′er** *n.*
de·i·fy (dē′ə-fī′, dā′-) ► *v.* **-fied, -fy·ing. 1.** To make a god of. **2.** To worship; exalt. **—de′i·fi·ca′tion** *n.*
deign (dān) ► *v.* To consider appropriate to one's dignity; condescend.
de·in·sti·tu·tion·al·ize (dē-ĭn′stĭ-to͞o′shə-nə-līz′, -tyo͞o′-) ► *v.* **1.** To remove the status of an institution from. **2.** To release (e.g., a mental health patient) from an institution for placement and care in the community. **—de·in′sti·tu′tion·al·i·za′tion** *n.*
de·ism (dē′ĭz′əm) ► *n.* An 18th-cent. system of natural religion affirming the existence of God while denying the validity of revelation. **—de′ist** *n.* **—de·is′tic** *adj.* **—de·is′ti·cal·ly** *adv.*
de·i·ty (dē′ĭ-tē, dā′-) ► *n., pl.* **-ties. 1.** A god or goddess. **2.** Divinity. **3. Deity** God.
dé·jà vu (dā′zhä vü′) ► *n.* An impression of having seen or experienced something before.
de·ject (dĭ-jĕkt′) ► *v.* To lower the spirits of; dishearten. **—de·jec′tion** *n.*
de·ject·ed (dĭ-jĕk′tĭd) ► *adj.* Being in low spirits; depressed. **—de·ject′ed·ly** *adv.* **—de·ject′ed·ness** *n.*
de ju·re (dē jo͝or′ē, dā yo͝or′ā) ► *adv. & adj.* According to law; by right.
dek– or **deka–** ► *pref.* Vars. of **deca–.**
Del. ► *abbr.* Delaware
Del·a·ware[1] (dĕl′ə-wâr′) ► *n., pl.* **-ware** or **-wares. 1.** A member of a group of Native American peoples formerly

THESAURUS

deform *v.* To alter and spoil the natural form or appearance of ► blemish, contort, deface, dent, disfigure, distort, injure, mar, misshape, mutilate, pit, pock, ravage, scar, twist, warp. [*Compare* DAMAGE.]
deformity *n.* A disfiguring abnormality of shape or form ► blemish, contortion, defacement, deformation, dent, disfigurement, distortion, malformation, pit, pock, scar, warping. [*Compare* ABNORMALITY, DEFECT.]
defraud *v.* —*See* CHEAT (1).
defrauder *n.* —*See* CHEAT (2).
deft *adj.* —*See* DEXTEROUS.
deftness *n.* —*See* AGILITY, DEXTERITY.
defunct *adj.* —*See* DEAD (1).
defy *v.* **1.** To confront boldly and courageously ► beard, brave, buck, challenge, dare, face, front, oppose. *Idioms:* beard the lion, fly in the face of, snap one's fingers at, stand up to, thumb one's nose at. [*Compare* CONFRONT, CONTEST.] **2.** To call on another to do something bold ► challenge, dare. *Idiom:* throw down the gauntlet. —*See also* DISOBEY.
degeneracy *n.* —*See* DETERIORATION (1).
degenerate *adj.* —*See* CORRUPT (1).
degenerate *v.* To undergo moral deterioration ► fall, sink, slip. —*See also* DETERIORATE, FADE.
degeneration *n.* —*See* DEGRADATION (1), DETERIORATION (1).
degradation *n.* **1.** A lowering in or deprivation of character or self-esteem ► abasement, debasement, degeneration, disgracing, dishonor, dishonoring, humiliation, mortification. [*Compare* DISGRACE, SHAME.] **2.** The act or an instance of demoting ► demotion, downgrade, reduction.
degrade *v.* —*See* DEBASE, DEMOTE, DISGRACE, HUMBLE.
degraded *adj.* —*See* UNSCRUPULOUS.
degrading *adj.* —*See* DISGRACEFUL.
degree *n.* **1.** One of the units in a course, as on an ascending or descending scale ► grade, interval, level, mark, peg, point, rank, rung, stage, step, unit. *Informal:* notch. **2.** Relative intensity or amount, as of a quality or attribute ► extent, level, magnitude, measure, proportion, range, scope. —*See also* LENGTH.
dehydrate *v.* —*See* DRY, PRESERVE (1).
deific *adj.* —*See* DIVINE (1).
deification *n.* —*See* EXALTATION.
deign *v.* —*See* CONDESCEND (1).
deject *v.* —*See* DEPRESS.
dejected *adj.* —*See* DEPRESSED (1), DESPONDENT.
dejection *n.* —*See* DEPRESSION (2).

of the Delaware and lower Hudson river valleys, now chiefly in Oklahoma. 2. The Algonquian language of the Delaware.

Del·a·ware[2] (dĕl′ə-wâr′) ▸ A state of the E US on the Atlantic Ocean. Cap. Dover.

Delaware River ▸ A river rising in SE NY and flowing about 451 km (280 mi) to the **Delaware Bay** in N DE.

de·lay (dĭ-lā′) ▸ *v.* 1. To postpone; defer. 2. To cause to be later than expected. 3. To procrastinate. ▸ *n.* 1. The act of delaying or condition of being delayed; postponement. 2. The period of time one is delayed. **—de·lay′er** *n.*

de·lec·ta·ble (dĭ-lĕk′tə-bəl) ▸ *adj.* 1. Delightful. 2. Pleasing to the taste. **—de·lec′ta·bil′i·ty** *n.* **—de·lec′ta·bly** *adv.*

de·lec·ta·tion (dē′lĕk-tā′shən) ▸ *n.* Delight; pleasure.

del·e·gate (dĕl′ĭ-gat′, -gĭt) ▸ *n.* 1. A person authorized to act as representative for another. 2. A representative to a convention. ▸ *v.* (-gāt′) **-gat·ed, -gat·ing.** 1. To authorize and send (another person) as one's representative. 2. To commit or entrust to another.

del·e·ga·tion (dĕl′ĭ-gā′shən) ▸ *n.* 1. The act of delegating. 2. A body of delegates.

de·lete (dĭ-lēt′) ▸ *v.* **-let·ed, -let·ing.** To remove by striking out or canceling. **—de·le′tion** *n.*

del·e·te·ri·ous (dĕl′ĭ-tîr′ē-əs) ▸ *adj.* Harmful; injurious. **—del′e·te′ri·ous·ly** *adv.* **—del′e·te′ri·ous·ness** *n.*

delft (dĕlft) ▸ *n.* A style of glazed earthenware, usu. blue and white.

Del·hi (dĕl′ē) ▸ A city of N-central India on the Yamuna R.

del·i (dĕl′ē) ▸ *n., pl.* **-is.** *Informal* A delicatessen.

de·lib·er·ate (dĭ-lĭb′ər-ĭt) ▸ *adj.* 1. Done with full consciousness of the effects; intentional. 2. Marked by careful consideration. 3. Unhurried in action or manner. ▸ *v.* (-ə-rāt′) **-at·ed, -at·ing.** To consider or discuss a matter carefully. **—de·lib′er·ate·ly** *adv.* **—de·lib′er·ate·ness** *n.*

de·lib·er·a·tion (dĭ-lĭb′ə-rā′shən) ▸ *n.* 1. The act or process of deliberating. 2. **deliberations** Careful discussion and consideration. **—de·lib′er·a′tive** *adj.* **—de·lib′er·a′tive·ly** *adv.*

del·i·ca·cy (dĕl′ĭ-kə-sē) ▸ *n., pl.* **-cies.** 1. The quality of being delicate. 2. A choice food. 3. Elegance; refinement; sensitivity; tact.

del·i·cate (dĕl′ĭ-kĭt) ▸ *adj.* 1. Pleasing to the senses, esp. in a subtle way. 2. Exquisitely fine or dainty; easily damaged. 3. Frail in constitution. 4. Sensitive; considerate. 5. Concerned with propriety; fastidious; precise. 6. Tactful; skillful; subtle. **—del′i·cate·ly** *adv.* **—del′i·cate·ness** *n.*

del·i·ca·tes·sen (dĕl′ĭ-kə-tĕs′ən) ▸ *n.* A shop that sells prepared foods ready for serving.

de·li·cious (dĭ-lĭsh′əs) ▸ *adj.* Highly pleasing to the taste. **—de·li′cious·ly** *adv.* **—de·li′cious·ness** *n.*

de·light (dĭ-līt′) ▸ *n.* 1. Great pleasure; joy. 2. Something that gives great pleasure or enjoyment. ▸ *v.* 1. To take great pleasure or joy. 2. To please greatly. **—de·light′ed·ly** *adv.* **—de·light′ed·ness** *n.*

de·light·ful (dĭ-līt′fəl) ▸ *adj.* Greatly pleasing. **—de·light′ful·ly** *adv.*

De·li·lah (də-lī′lə) ▸ In the Bible, Samson's lover who betrayed him by having his hair shorn, thus depriving him of his strength.

de·lim·it (dĭ-lĭm′ĭt) ▸ *v.* To establish the limits of. **—de·lim′i·ta′tion** *n.* **—de·lim′it·er** *n.*

de·lin·e·ate (dĭ-lĭn′ē-āt′) ▸ *v.* **-at·ed, -at·ing.** 1. To draw or trace the outline of. 2. To depict; describe. **—de·lin′e·a′tion** *n.* **—de·lin′e·a′tive** *adj.* **—de·lin′e·a′tor** *n.*

de·lin·quent (dĭ-lĭng′kwənt, -lĭn′-) ▸ *adj.* 1. Failing to do what is required. 2. Overdue in payment: *a delinquent account.* ▸ *n.* 1. A juvenile delinquent. 2. A person who fails to do what is required. **—de·lin′quen·cy** *n.* **—de·lin′quent·ly** *adv.*

del·i·quesce (dĕl′ĭ-kwĕs′) ▸ *v.* **-quesced, -quesc·ing.** To dissolve and become liquid by absorbing moisture from the air. **—del′i·ques′cence** *n.* **—del′i·ques′cent** *adj.*

de·lir·i·um (dĭ-lîr′ē-əm) ▸ *n., pl.* **-i·ums** or **-i·a** (-ē-ə). 1. A temporary state of mental confusion resulting from high fever, intoxication, or shock, marked by anxiety, disorientation,

THESAURUS

delay *v.* 1. To cause to be later or slower than expected or desired ▸ clog, detain, hang up, hinder, hold up, impede, keep (back), retard, set back, slacken, slow (down *or* up), stall. *Idiom:* make late. [*Compare* RESTRAIN, STOP.] 2. To go or move slowly so that progress is hindered ▸ dally, dawdle, dilly-dally, drag, lag, linger, loiter, procrastinate, stall, tarry, trail. *Idioms:* drag one's feet (*or* heels), mark time, take one's time. [*Compare* REMAIN, WAIT.] *—See also* DEFER[1].

delay *n.* 1. The act of putting off or the condition of being put off ▸ adjournment, deferment, deferral, holdup, moratorium, postponement, procrastination, shelving, stay, suspension, tabling, waiver. *Idiom:* putting on ice. 2. The condition or fact of being made late or slow ▸ detainment, holdup, lag, retardation.

delectable *adj.* *—See* DELICIOUS, DELIGHTFUL.

delectation *n.* *—See* DELIGHT.

delegate *n.* *—See* REPRESENTATIVE.

delegate *v.* *—See* ENTRUST (1).

delete *v.* *—See* CANCEL (1).

deleterious *adj.* *—See* HARMFUL.

deletion *n.* *—See* ERASURE.

deliberate *adj.* 1. Done or said on purpose ▸ conscious, intended, intentional, premeditated, purposeful, voluntary, willful, witting. 2. Arising from or marked by careful consideration ▸ advised, calculated, considered, studied, studious, thought out. [*Compare* SANE, WARY.] 3. Careful and slow in acting, moving, or deciding ▸ cautious, circumspect, judicious, leisurely, measured, methodic, methodical, prudent, sober, unhurried. [*Compare* LETHARGIC, SLOW.] *—See also* CALCULATED.

deliberate *v.* *—See* CONFER (1), DISCUSS, PONDER, THINK (1).

deliberation *n.* 1. An exchange of views in an attempt to reach a decision ▸ conference, consideration, consultation, counsel, debate, discussion, parley. 2. Careful thought ▸ advisement, deliberation, study. [*Compare* ATTENTION, EXAMINATION, SCRUTINY.] *—See also* THOUGHT.

deliberative *adj.* *—See* THOUGHTFUL.

delicacy *n.* Something fine and delicious, especially a food ▸ dainty, morsel, sweetmeat, tidbit, treat. *Informal:* goody. [*Compare* LUXURY.] *—See also* INFIRMITY, SUBTLETY, TACT.

delicate *adj.* 1. Appealing to refined taste ▸ choice, dainty, elegant, exquisite, fine, genteel, gentle. [*Compare* CULTURED.] 2. Showing sensitivity and skill in dealing with others ▸ diplomatic, discreet, graceful, politic, sensitive, tactful. 3. Requiring great tact or skill ▸ demanding, difficult, exacting, precarious, sensitive, ticklish, touch-and-go, touchy, tricky. 4. So slight as to be difficult to notice or appreciate ▸ fine, finespun, nice, precise, refined, subtle. *—See also* FINE[1] (2), FRAGILE, GENTLE (2), WEAK (1).

delicateness *n.* *—See* INFIRMITY.

delicious *adj.* Highly pleasing, especially to the sense of taste ▸ ambrosial, appetizing, delectable, flavorful, heavenly, luscious, mouth-watering, palatable, savory, scrumptious, tasteful, tasty, toothsome. *Slang:* yummy. *—See also* DELIGHTFUL.

delight *n.* A feeling of extreme gratification aroused by something good or desired ▸ bliss, delectation, ecstasy, elation, enchantment, enjoyment, glee, joy, pleasure. *—See also* AMUSEMENT, HAPPINESS, LUXURY.

delight *v.* 1. To give great or keen pleasure to ▸ amuse, cheer, elate, enchant, excite, gladden, gratify, overjoy, please, pleasure, thrill, tickle. [*Compare* CHARM.] 2. To feel or take joy or pleasure ▸ exult, pleasure, rejoice. [*Compare* ENJOY, LUXURIATE.] *—See also* ADORE (2).

delighted *adj.* *—See* WILLING.

delightful *adj.* Giving great pleasure or delight ▸ adorable, amusing, blissful, charming, cute, delectable, delicious, enchanting, heavenly, lovable, lovely, luscious, pleasing, pleasurable, sweet. *Informal:* darling. [*Compare* ATTRACTIVE, PLEASANT.]

delimit or **delimitate** *v.* *—See* DETERMINE.

delineate *v.* *—See* DRAFT (1), REPRESENT (2).

delineation *n.* *—See* FORM (1), REPRESENTATION.

delineative *adj.* *—See* DESCRIPTIVE.

delinquency *n.* *—See* BREACH (1), FAILURE (2).

delinquent *n.* *—See* CRIMINAL.

deliquesce *v.* *—See* MELT.

delirious *adj.* *—See* FRANTIC.

hallucinations, delusions, trembling, and incoherence. **2.** Uncontrolled excitement or emotion. **—de·lir′i·ous** *adj.* **—de·lir′i·ous·ly** *adv.* **—de·lir′i·ous·ness** *n.*

delirium tre·mens (trē′mənz) ▸ *n.* An acute delirium caused by withdrawal from alcohol.

de·liv·er (dĭ-lĭv′ər) ▸ *v.* **1.** To take to the proper place or recipient. **2.** To throw or hurl. **3.** To utter. **4a.** To give birth to. **b.** To assist (a woman) in giving birth. **5.** To give forth or produce. **6.** To set free. **7.** To produce what is expected; make good. **—de·liv′er·a·bil′i·ty** *n.* **—de·liv′er·a·ble** *adj.* **—de·liv′er·ance** *n.* **—de·liv′er·er** *n.*

de·liv·er·y (dĭ-lĭv′ə-rē, -lĭv′rē) ▸ *n., pl.* **-ies. 1.** The act of delivering. **2.** Something delivered. **3.** The act or manner of throwing or discharging. **4.** Childbirth. **5.** The act or manner of speaking or singing.

dell (dĕl) ▸ *n.* A small wooded valley.

Del·phi (dĕl′fī′) ▸ An ancient town of central Greece near Mount Parnassus.

del·phin·i·um (dĕl-fĭn′ē-əm) ▸ *n.* A tall cultivated plant having showy, variously colored spurred flowers.

del·ta (dĕl′tə) ▸ *n.* **1.** The 4th letter of the Greek alphabet. **2.** A usu. triangular deposit at the mouth of a river.

del·toid (dĕl′toid′) ▸ *n.* A thick triangular muscle covering the shoulder joint, used to raise the arm from the side.

de·lude (dĭ-lo͞od′) ▸ *v.* **-lud·ed, -lud·ing.** To deceive the mind or judgment of. **—de·lud′er** *n.*

del·uge (dĕl′yo͞oj) ▸ *n.* **1.** A great flood; downpour. **2.** Something that overwhelms. **3. Deluge** The Flood. ▸ *v.* **-uged, -ug·ing.** To overrun with or as if with water; inundate.

de·lu·sion (dĭ-lo͞o′zhən) ▸ *n.* **1.** The act of deluding or state of being deluded. **2.** A false belief or opinion. **—de·lu′sion·al, de·lu′sive** *adj.* **—de·lu′sive·ly** *adv.*

de·luxe also **de luxe** (dĭ-lŭks′, -lo͝oks′) ▸ *adj.* Particularly elegant and luxurious. ▸ *adv.* In an elegant manner.

delve (dĕlv) ▸ *v.* **delved, delv·ing.** To search deeply and laboriously.

Dem. ▸ *abbr.* **1.** Democrat **2.** Democratic

de·mag·net·ize (dē-măg′nĭ-tīz′) ▸ *v.* To remove magnetic properties from. **—de·mag′net·i·za′tion** *n.*

dem·a·gogue or **dem·a·gog** (dĕm′ə-gôg′, -gŏg′) ▸ *n.* A leader who obtains power by appealing to the emotions and prejudices of the populace. **—dem′a·gog′ic** (-gŏj′ĭk, -gŏg′-), **dem′a·gog′i·cal** *adj.* **—dem′a·gogu′er·y** *n.* **—dem′a·gog′y** (-gŏj′ē, -gô′jē, -gŏg′ē) *n.*

de·mand (dĭ-mănd′) ▸ *v.* **1.** To ask for insistently. **2.** To claim as just or due. **3.** To require; call for. ▸ *n.* **1.** The act of demanding. **2.** Something demanded. **3.** An urgent requirement or need. **4.** The state of being sought after. **5.** *Econ.* **a.** The desire to possess something combined with the ability to purchase it. **b.** The amount of something that people are ready to buy for a given price. **—de·mand′a·ble** *adj.* **—de·mand′er** *n.*

de·mand·ing (dĭ-măn′dĭng) ▸ *adj.* Requiring much effort or attention. **—de·mand′ing·ly** *adv.*

de·mar·cate (dĭ-mär′kāt′, dē′mär-kāt′) ▸ *v.* **-cat·ed, -cat·ing.** To set the boundaries of; delimit. **—de·mar′ca′tor** *n.*

de·mar·ca·tion (dē′mär-kā′shən) ▸ *n.* **1.** The setting or marking of boundaries or limits. **2.** A separation.

de·mean[1] (dĭ-mēn′) ▸ *v.* To behave (oneself) in a particular manner.

de·mean[2] (dĭ-mēn′) ▸ *v.* To debase in dignity or social standing.

de·mean·or (dĭ-mē′nər) ▸ *n.* The way a person behaves.

de·ment·ed (dĭ-mĕn′tĭd) ▸ *adj.* Mentally ill; insane.

de·men·tia (dĭ-mĕn′shə) ▸ *n.* Deterioration of intellectual faculties resulting from an organic disease of the brain.

de·mer·it (dĭ-mĕr′ĭt) ▸ *n.* A mark made against one's record for a fault or misconduct.

de·mesne (dĭ-mān′, -mēn′) ▸ *n.* **1.** The grounds of an estate. **2.** An extensive piece of landed property. **3.** A district; territory.

De·me·ter (dĭ-mē′tər) ▸ *n. Gk. Myth.* The goddess of the harvest.

dem·i·god (dĕm′ē-gŏd′) ▸ *n.* **1.** *Myth.* **a.** A male being, the offspring of a deity and a mortal. **b.** A minor god. **2.** A person who is highly revered.

dem·i·john (dĕm′ē-jŏn′) ▸ *n.* A large bottle usu. encased in wickerwork.

de·mil·i·ta·rize (dē-mĭl′ĭ-tə-rīz′) ▸ *v.* To prohibit or eliminate military forces or installations. **—de·mil′i·ta·ri·za′tion** *n.*

dem·i·mon·daine (dĕm′ē-mŏn-dān′, -mŏn′dān′) ▸ *n.* A woman belonging to the demimonde.

dem·i·monde (dĕm′ē-mŏnd′) ▸ *n.* **1a.** A class of women kept by wealthy lovers or protectors. **b.** Women prostitutes collectively. **2.** A group whose respectability is dubious.

de·min·er·al·ize (dē-mĭn′ər-ə-līz′) ▸ *v.* To remove minerals or mineral salts from (a liquid). **—de·min′er·al·i′zer** *n.*

de·mise (dĭ-mīz′) ▸ *n.* **1.** Death. **2.** The end; termination.

dem·i·tasse (dĕm′ē-tăs′, -täs′) ▸ *n.* A small cup of strong coffee.

dem·o (dĕm′ō) ▸ *n., pl.* **-os.** *Informal* **1.** A demonstration, as of a product. **2.** A recording used to illustrate the qualities of a musician. **—dem′o** *v.*

de·mo·bil·ize (dē-mō′bə-līz′) ▸ *v.* To discharge from military service or use. **—de·mo′bil·i·za′tion** *n.*

de·moc·ra·cy (dĭ-mŏk′rə-sē) ▸ *n., pl.* **-cies. 1.** Government by the people, exercised either directly or through elected representatives. **2.** A political unit that has such a government. **3.** Majority rule. **4.** The principles of social equality and respect for the individual within a community.

dem·o·crat (dĕm′ə-krăt′) ▸ *n.* **1.** An advocate of democracy. **2. Democrat** A member of the Democratic Party.

dem·o·crat·ic (dĕm′ə-krăt′ĭk) ▸ *adj.* **1.** Characterized by or advocating democracy. **2.** Of or for the people in general. **3.** Believing in or practicing social equality. **4. Democratic** Of or relating to the Democratic Party. **—dem′o·crat′i·cal·ly** *adv.*

THESAURUS

deliver *v.* **1.** To mete out by means of some action ▸ administer, deal, give. **2.** To yield oneself unrestrainedly, as to an impulse ▸ abandon, relinquish, surrender. *Idiom:* give oneself up (*or* over). *—See also* BEAR (4), GIVE (1), RESCUE, SAY.

deliverance *n.* *—See* RESCUE.

deliverer *n.* *—See* RESCUER.

delivery *n.* The act of delivering or the condition of being delivered ▸ consignment, conveyance, shipment, surrender, transfer, transmission, transmittal. *—See also* BIRTH (1), RESCUE.

dell *n.* *—See* VALLEY.

delude *v.* *—See* DECEIVE.

deluge *n.* *—See* FLOOD, RAIN.

deluge *v.* To affect as if by an outpouring of water ▸ flood, inundate, overwhelm, swamp. *—See also* FLOOD (1).

delusion *n.* *—See* ILLUSION, MYTH (2).

delusive or **delusory** *adj.* *—See* FALLACIOUS (2), ILLUSIVE.

deluxe *adj.* *—See* LUXURIOUS.

delve *v.* *—See* DIG, EXPLORE.

demand *v.* **1.** To ask for urgently or insistently ▸ appeal for, call for, claim, exact, importune, insist on, order, require, requisition. *Idiom:* cry out for. [*Compare* URGE.] **2.** To have as a need or prerequisite ▸ ask, beg, call for, entail, involve, necessitate, need, require, take, want. [*Compare* LACK.] *—See also* CLAIM.

demand *n.* **1.** The act of demanding ▸ appeal, behest, call, claim, cry, exaction, order, requisition. **2.** Something asked for or needed ▸ desire, exigence, exigency, need, requirement, want.

demanding *adj.* *—See* DELICATE (3), DIFFICULT (1), FUSSY, SEVERE (1), TROUBLESOME (2).

demarcate *v.* *—See* DETERMINE.

demarcation *n.* *—See* DISTINCTION (1).

demean[1] *v.* *—See* ACT (1).

demean[2] *v.* *—See* DEBASE, HUMBLE.

demeanor *n.* *—See* BEARING (1).

dement *v.* *—See* DERANGE.

demented *adj.* *—See* INSANE.

dementia *n.* *—See* INSANITY.

demise *n.* *—See* DEATH (1).

demise *v.* *—See* DIE.

demit *v.* To relinquish one's engagement in or occupation with ▸ leave, quit, resign, terminate. *Idioms:* give it up, hang it up, throw in the towel. [*Compare* BREAK.] *—See also* ABANDON (1).

demobilize *v.* *—See* DISCHARGE.

democratic *adj.* *—See* POPULAR.

Democratic Party ▸ *n.* One of the two major US political parties.

de·moc·ra·tize (dĭ-mŏk′rə-tīz′) ▸ *v.* **-tized, -tiz·ing.** To make democratic. **—de·moc′ra·ti·za′tion** *n.*

De·moc·ri·tus (dĭ-mŏk′rĭ-təs) (460?–370? B.C.) ▸ Greek philosopher.

de·mod·u·late (dē-mŏj′ə-lāt′, -mŏd′yə-) ▸ *v.* **-lat·ed, -lat·ing.** To extract (information) from a modulated carrier wave. **—de·mod′u·la′tion** *n.* **—de·mod′u·la′tor** *n.*

dem·o·graph·ics (dĕm′ə-grăf′ĭks, dē′mə-) ▸ *n.* *(takes pl. v.)* The characteristics of human population segments, esp. for identifying consumer markets.

de·mog·ra·phy (dĭ-mŏg′rə-fē) ▸ *n.* The statistical study of human populations. **—de·mog′ra·pher** *n.* **—dem′o·graph′ic** (dĕm′ə-grăf′ĭk, dē′mə-) *adj.* **—dem′o·graph′i·cal·ly** *adv.*

de·mol·ish (dĭ-mŏl′ĭsh) ▸ *v.* To tear down completely; raze.

dem·o·li·tion (dĕm′ə-lĭsh′ən, dē′mə-) ▸ *n.* The act or process of destroying, esp. by explosives. **—dem′o·li′tion·ist** *n.*

de·mon (dē′mən) ▸ *n.* **1.** An evil supernatural being; devil. **2.** A persistently tormenting person, force, or passion. **3.** One who is extremely zealous or diligent. **—de·mon′ic** (dĭ-mŏn′ĭk) *adj.* **—de·mon′i·cal·ly** *adv.*

de·mon·e·tize (dē-mŏn′ĭ-tīz′, -mŭn′-) ▸ *v.* To divest (currency) of monetary value. **—de·mon′e·ti·za′tion** *n.*

de·mo·ni·ac (dĭ-mō′nē-ăk′) also **de·mo·ni·a·cal** (dē′mə-nī′ə-kəl) ▸ *adj.* **1.** Possessed by or as if by a demon. **2.** Devilish; fiendish. **—de′mo·ni′a·cal·ly** *adv.*

de·mon·ize (dē′mə-nīz′) ▸ *v.* **-ized, -iz·ing.** **1.** To turn into or as if into a demon. **2.** To represent as evil. **—de′mon·i·za′tion** *n.*

de·mon·ol·o·gy (dē′mə-nŏl′ə-jē) ▸ *n.* The study of demons. **—de′mon·ol′o·gist** *n.*

de·mon·stra·ble (dĭ-mŏn′strə-bəl) ▸ *adj.* Capable of being shown or proved. **—de·mon′stra·bil′i·ty** *n.* **—de·mon′stra·bly** *adv.*

dem·on·strate (dĕm′ən-strāt′) ▸ *v.* **-strat·ed, -strat·ing.** **1.** To show clearly and deliberately. **2.** To show to be true by reasoning or evidence. **3.** To explain and illustrate. **4.** To show the use of (a product) to a prospective buyer. **5.** To participate in a public display of opinion. **—dem′on·stra′tion** *n.* **—dem′on·stra′tor** *n.*

de·mon·stra·tive (dĭ-mŏn′strə-tĭv) ▸ *adj.* **1.** Serving to manifest or prove. **2.** Given to the open expression of emotion. **3.** *Gram.* Specifying the person or thing referred to: *the demonstrative pronouns these and that.* ▸ *n. Gram.* A demonstrative pronoun or adjective. **—de·mon′stra·tive·ly** *adv.*

de·mor·al·ize (dĭ-môr′ə-līz′, -mŏr′-) ▸ *v.* **-ized, -iz·ing.** **1.** To undermine the confidence or morale of; dishearten. **2.** To corrupt. **—de·mor′al·i·za′tion** *n.* **—de·mor′al·iz′er** *n.*

De·mos·the·nes (dĭ-mŏs′thə-nēz′) (384–322 B.C.) ▸ Greek orator.

de·mote (dĭ-mōt′) ▸ *v.* **-mot·ed, -mot·ing.** To reduce in grade or rank. **—de·mo′tion** *n.*

de·mot·ic (dĭ-mŏt′ĭk) ▸ *adj.* **1.** Of or relating to the common people; popular. **2.** Of or written in a simplified ancient Egyptian hieratic script. **3. Demotic** Relating to a form of modern Greek based on colloquial use.

de·mul·cent (dĭ-mŭl′sənt) ▸ *adj.* Soothing. ▸ *n.* A soothing, usu. jellylike or oily substance, used to relieve pain.

de·mur (dĭ-mûr′) ▸ *v.* **-murred, -mur·ring.** To voice opposition; object.

de·mure (dĭ-myŏŏr′) ▸ *adj.* **-mur·er, -mur·est.** **1.** Modest in manner; reserved. **2.** Affectedly modest or reserved. **—de·mure′ly** *adv.* **—de·mure′ness** *n.*

de·mys·ti·fy (dē-mĭs′tə-fī′) ▸ *v.* To make less mysterious; clarify.

de·my·thol·o·gize (dē′mĭ-thŏl′ə-jīz′) ▸ *v.* To rid of mythological elements. **—de′my·thol′o·gi·za′tion** *n.*

den (dĕn) ▸ *n.* **1.** The shelter or retreat of a wild animal; lair. **2.** A hidden or squalid dwelling place. **3.** A secluded room for study or relaxation. **4.** A unit of about eight to ten Cub Scouts.

De·na·li (də-nä′lē) ▸ See Mount **McKinley**.

den·ar (dĕn′är) ▸ *n., pl.* **den·a·ri** (-är-ē). See **currency** table in Appendix.

de·na·ture (dē-nā′chər) ▸ *v.* **-tured, -tur·ing.** To render unfit to eat or drink, esp. to add methanol to. **—de·na′tur·ant** *n.*

den·drite (dĕn′drīt′) ▸ *n.* A branched protoplasmic extension of a nerve cell that conducts impulses toward the cell body.

dendro– or **dendri–** or **dendr–** ▸ *pref.* Tree; treelike: *dendrite.*

den·gue (dĕng′gē, -gā) ▸ *n.* An acute infectious tropical disease transmitted by mosquitoes.

de·ni·a·ble (dĭ-nī′ə-bəl) ▸ *adj.* **1.** Possible to declare untrue: *deniable charges.* **2.** Being such that plausible disavowal is possible. **—de·ni′a·bil′i·ty** *n.* **—de·ni′a·bly** *adv.*

de·ni·al (dĭ-nī′əl) ▸ *n.* **1.** A refusal to comply with a request. **2.** A refusal to grant the truth of a statement. **3.** A disavowal; repudiation. **4.** Self-denial.

den·ier (dən-yā′, dĕn′yər) ▸ *n.* A unit of fineness for rayon, nylon, and silk fibers.

den·i·grate (dĕn′ĭ-grāt′) ▸ *v.* **-grat·ed, -grat·ing.** To attack the reputation of; defame. **—den′i·gra′tion** *n.* **—den′i·gra′tor** *n.*

den·im (dĕn′ĭm) ▸ *n.* A coarse cotton cloth used for jeans, overalls, and work uniforms.

den·i·zen (dĕn′ĭ-zən) ▸ *n.* An inhabitant; resident.

Den·mark (dĕn′märk′) ▸ A country of N Europe on Jutland and adjacent islands.

de·nom·i·na·tion (dĭ-nŏm′ə-nā′shən) ▸ *n.* **1.** An organized group of religious congregations. **2.** A unit of specified value in a system of currency or weights. **3.** A name or designation, esp. for a class or group. **—de·nom′i·na′tion·al** *adj.* **—de·nom′i·na′tion·al·ly** *adv.*

de·nom·i·na·tor (dĭ-nŏm′ə-nā′tər) ▸ *n.* **1.** *Math.* The expression written below the line in a fraction that indicates the number of parts into which one whole is divided. **2.** A common trait or characteristic.

de·note (dĭ-nōt′) ▸ *v.* **-not·ed, -not·ing.** **1.** To mark; indicate. **2.** To signify directly; refer to specifically. **—de′no·ta′tion** *n.* **—de·no′ta·tive** *adj.* **—de·no′ta·tive·ly** *adv.*

THESAURUS

demolish *v.* —*See* DESTROY (1), DESTROY (2).

demolition *n.* —*See* DESTRUCTION.

demon *n.* An intensely energetic, enthusiastic person ▸ dynamo, hustler. *Informal:* eager beaver, firebreather, go-getter, live wire. —*See also* FIEND.

demonstrate *v.* To demonstrate and clarify with examples ▸ evidence, exemplify, illustrate, instance. [*Compare* EXPLAIN, SHOW.] —*See also* PROVE, SHOW (1).

demonstration *n.* —*See* CONFIRMATION (2), DISPLAY.

demoralize *v.* —*See* CORRUPT, DISCOURAGE.

demoralizing *adj.* —*See* UNWHOLESOME (2).

demote *v.* To lower in rank or grade ▸ break, bump, degrade, downgrade, reduce. *Slang:* bust.

demotion *n.* The act or an instance of demoting ▸ degradation, downgrade, reduction.

demur *v.* —*See* OBJECT.

demur *n.* —*See* OBJECTION.

demure *adj.* —*See* SHY[1].

demureness *n.* —*See* SHYNESS.

demystify *v.* —*See* EXPLAIN (1).

den *n.* **1.** A place used as an animal's dwelling ▸ burrow, hole, lair. [*Compare* CAVE.] **2.** A hiding place ▸ covert, hideaway, hide-out, lair. —*See also* PIT[1].

denature *v.* —*See* CONVERT.

denial *n.* **1.** A refusal to grant the truth of a statement or charge ▸ abnegation, contradiction, disaffirmance, disavowal, disaffirmation, disclaimer, negation, rejection, renunciation, repudiation, traversal. **2.** A turning down of a request ▸ disallowance, nonacceptance, refusal, rejection, turndown. [*Compare* FORBIDDANCE.]

denigrate *v.* To attack the reputation or honor of ▸ befoul, besmear, besmirch, bespatter, blacken, blot, cloud, defile, dirty, smear, smudge, smut, soil, spatter, stain, sully, taint, tarnish, tear down. ***Idioms:*** drag through the mud (*or* dirt), give a black eye to, give someone a bad name, sling (*or* throw) mud on. [*Compare* DISGRACE, LIBEL, MALIGN, SLAM.] —*See also* BELITTLE.

denigration *n.* —*See* BELITTLEMENT, LIBEL.

denizen *n.* —*See* INHABITANT.

denominate *v.* —*See* CALL, NAME (1).

denomination *n.* —*See* KIND[2], NAME (1), RELIGION.

denotation *n.* —*See* MEANING.

denotative or **denotive** *adj.* —*See* DESIGNATIVE.

denote *v.* —*See* DESIGNATE, MEAN[1].

de·noue·ment also **dé·noue·ment** (dā′no͞o-mäN′) ► *n.* **1.** The resolution of a dramatic or narrative plot. **2.** The outcome of a sequence of events.

de·nounce (dĭ-nouns′) ► *v.* **-nounced, -nounc·ing. 1.** To condemn openly as being evil or reprehensible. **2.** To accuse formally. **—de·nounce′ment** *n.* **—de·nounc′er** *n.*

dense (dĕns) ► *adj.* **dens·er, dens·est. 1.** Having relatively high density. **2.** Crowded together. **3.** Thick. **4.** Stupid. **—dense′ly** *adv.* **—dense′ness** *n.*

den·si·ty (dĕn′sĭ-tē) ► *n., pl.* **-ties. 1a.** The quantity of something per unit measure, esp. per unit length, area, or volume. **b.** The mass per unit volume of a substance under specified conditions of pressure and temperature. **2.** Thickness of consistency. **3.** Stupidity.

dent (dĕnt) ► *n.* **1.** A depression in a surface made by pressure or a blow. **2.** *Informal* Meaningful progress; headway. ► *v.* To make a dent in.

den·tal (dĕn′tl) ► *adj.* **1.** Of or relating to the teeth. **2.** *Ling.* Articulated with the tip of the tongue near or against the upper front teeth. ► *n. Ling.* A dental consonant.

dental floss ► *n.* A thread used to clean between the teeth.

dental hygienist ► *n.* One who assists a dentist.

denti– or **dent–** ► *pref.* Tooth: *dentition.*

den·ti·frice (dĕn′tə-frĭs′) ► *n.* A substance, such as a paste, for cleaning the teeth.

den·tin (dĕn′tĭn) or **den·tine** (-tēn′) ► *n.* The calcified part of a tooth, beneath the enamel. **—den′tin·al** (dĕn′tə-nəl, dĕn-tē′-) *adj.*

den·tist (dĕn′tĭst) ► *n.* A person trained and licensed in the diagnosis, prevention, and treatment of diseases of the teeth and gums. **—den′tist·ry** *n.*

den·ti·tion (dĕn-tĭsh′ən) ► *n.* The type, number, and arrangement of a set of teeth.

den·ture (dĕn′chər) ► *n.* A set of artificial teeth.

de·nude (dĭ-no͞od′, -nyo͞od′) ► *v.* **-nud·ed, -nud·ing.** To strip of covering; make bare. **—de′nu·da′tion** (dē′no͞o-dā′shən, -nyo͞o-, dĕn′yo͞o-) *n.*

de·nun·ci·a·tion (dĭ-nŭn′sē-ā′shən, -shē-) ► *n.* The act of denouncing, esp. a public condemnation. **—de·nun′ci·a′tive, de·nun′ci·a·to′ry** (-ə-tôr′ē) *adj.*

Den·ver (dĕn′vər) ► The capital of CO, in the N-central part.

de·ny (dĭ-nī′) ► *v.* **-nied, -ny·ing. 1.** To declare untrue. **2.** To refuse to believe; reject. **3.** To refuse to recognize. **4a.** To decline to grant: *deny a request.* **b.** To restrain (oneself) esp. from indulgence in pleasures.

de·o·dor·ant (dē-ō′dər-ənt) ► *n.* A substance used to counteract undesirable odors.

de·o·dor·ize (dē-ō′də-rīz′) ► *v.* **-ized, -iz·ing.** To mask or neutralize the odor of. **—de·o′dor·i·za′tion** *n.* **—de·o′dor·iz′er** *n.*

de·ox·y·ri·bo·nu·cle·ic acid (dē-ŏk′sē-rī′bō-no͞o-klē′ĭk, -klā′-, -nyo͞o-) ► *n.* DNA.

de·part (dĭ-pärt′) ► *v.* **1.** To go away; leave. **2.** To die. **3.** To vary; deviate: *depart from custom.*

de·part·ment (dĭ-pärt′mənt) ► *n.* **1.** A distinct, usu. specialized division of an organization, business, government, or institution. **2.** *Informal* An area of particular knowledge or responsibility. **—de′part·men′tal** (dē′pärt-mĕn′tl) *adj.* **—de′part·men′tal·ly** *adv.*

de·part·men·tal·ize (dē′pärt-mĕn′tl-īz′) ► *v.* **-ized, -iz·ing.** To organize into departments. **—de′part·men′tal·i·za′tion** *n.*

department store ► *n.* A large retail store offering a variety of merchandise.

de·par·ture (dĭ-pär′chər) ► *n.* **1.** The act of leaving. **2.** A starting out, as on a trip. **3.** A divergence, as from a set procedure.

de·pend (dĭ-pĕnd′) ► *v.* **1.** To rely, esp. for support: *I depend on my parents during college.* **2.** To place trust: *You can depend on her.* **3.** To be determined or contingent. **4.** To have a dependence.

de·pend·a·ble (dĭ-pĕn′də-bəl) ► *adj.* Trustworthy. **—de·pend′a·bil′i·ty** *n.* **—de·pend′a·bly** *adv.*

de·pen·dence also **de·pen·dance** (dĭ-pĕn′dəns) ► *n.* **1.** The state of being dependent, as for support. **2.** Condition; contingency. **3.** Trust; reliance. **4.** A compulsive or chronic need; addiction.

de·pen·den·cy also **de·pen·dan·cy** (dĭ-pĕn′dən-sē) ► *n., pl.* **-cies. 1.** Dependence. **2.** A territory under the jurisdiction of another country of which it is not an integral part.

de·pen·dent (dĭ-pĕn′dənt) ► *adj.* **1.** Contingent on another. **2.** Subordinate. **3.** Relying on the aid of another for support: *dependent children.* ► *n.* also **de·pen·dant** One who relies on another for financial support. **—de·pen′dent·ly** *adv.*

de·pict (dĭ-pĭkt′) ► *v.* **1.** To represent in a picture. **2.** To describe in words. **—de·pic′tion** *n.*

de·pil·a·to·ry (dĭ-pĭl′ə-tôr′ē) ► *n., pl.* **-ries.** A substance used to remove hair. **—de·pil′a·to′ry** *adj.*

de·plane (dē-plān′) ► *v.* **-planed, -plan·ing.** To disembark from an airplane.

de·plete (dĭ-plēt′) ► *v.* **-plet·ed, -plet·ing.** To use up or empty out. **—de·ple′tion** *n.*

THESAURUS

dénouement *n.* —*See* END (1).

denounce *v.* —*See* ACCUSE, DEPLORE (1), DISAPPROVE.

denouncement *n.* —*See* ACCUSATION.

denouncer *n.* One that accuses ► accuser, arraigner, indicter, recriminator.

dense *adj.* —*See* BACKWARD (1), STUPID, THICK (2), THICK (3).

density *n.* —*See* STUPIDITY, THICKNESS.

dent *v.* —*See* DEFORM.

dent *n.* —*See* DEFORMITY, DEPRESSION (1), IMPRESSION (1).

dentate *adj.* —*See* SAW-TOOTHED.

denude *v.* —*See* BARE.

denuded *adj.* —*See* EMPTY (2).

denunciation *n.* —*See* ACCUSATION, CRITICISM, DISAPPROVAL, VITUPERATION.

denunciative or **denunciatory** *adj.* —*See* ACCUSATORIAL.

deny *v.* To refuse to admit the truth, reality, value, or worth of ► abnegate, contradict, contravene, controvert, disaffirm, disavow, dismiss, dispute, gainsay, negate, negative, oppugn, renounce, traverse. [*Compare* CONTEST.] —*See also* DECLINE, DEPRIVE, REPUDIATE.

depart *v.* —*See* DEVIATE, DIE, DIFFER, DISAPPEAR (2), GO (1).

departed *adj.* —*See* DEAD (1).

departing *adj.* —*See* PARTING.

department *n.* —*See* AREA (1), BRANCH (3), CLASS (1).

departure *n.* The act of leaving or bidding farewell ► adieu, departing, egress, embarkation, embarkment, exit, exodus, farewell, going, goodbye, leave-taking, parting, retirement, valediction, withdrawal. —*See also* DEVIATION, DIFFERENCE, DIGRESSION, DISAPPEARANCE.

depend on or **upon** *v.* **1.** To place trust or confidence in ► bank on (*or* upon), believe in, confide in, count on (*or* upon), reckon on (*or* upon), rely on (*or* upon), trust (in). ***Idiom:*** put faith in. **2.** To be determined by or contingent on something unknown, uncertain, or changeable ► hang on (*or* upon), hinge on (*or* upon), rest on (*or* upon), revolve around, turn on (*or* upon). —*See also* EXPECT (1).

dependable *adj.* Capable of being depended on ► honest, reliable, responsible, solid, sound, stable, steadfast, steady, steady-going, trustworthy, trusty.

dependence *n.* The state or relation of being determined or controlled ► dependency, reliance. [*Compare* AUTHORITY, DOMINANCE, NEED, RELATION.] —*See also* ADDICTION, TRUST.

dependency *n.* The state or relation of being determined or controlled ► dependence, reliance. [*Compare* AUTHORITY, DOMINANCE, NEED, RELATION.] —*See also* POSSESSION.

dependent *adj.* Subject to the authority or control of another ► subject, subordinate, subservient. [*Compare* AUXILIARY.] —*See also* CONDITIONAL.

dependent or **dependant** *n.* A person who relies on another for support ► charge, ward.

depict *v.* —*See* INTERPRET (2), REPRESENT (2).

depiction *n.* —*See* INTERPRETATION, REPRESENTATION.

deplete *v.* —*See* DRY UP (2), EXHAUST (1).

depletion *n.* The act of consuming ► consumption, expenditure, usage, use, utilization. [*Compare* USE.]

de·plore (dĭ-plôr′) ▸ *v.* **-plored, -plor·ing.** **1.** To feel or express strong disapproval of. **2.** To regret; bemoan. **—de·plor′a·ble** *adj.* **—de·plor′a·bly** *adv.*

de·ploy (dĭ-ploi′) ▸ *v.* **1.** To distribute (persons or forces) systematically or strategically. **2.** To put into use or action. **—de·ploy′a·bil′i·ty** *n.* **—de·ploy′a·ble** *adj.* **—de·ploy′ment** *n.*

de·po·nent (dĭ-pō′nənt) ▸ *n.* One who testifies under oath, esp. in writing.

de·pop·u·late (dē-pŏp′yə-lāt′) ▸ *v.* To reduce sharply the population of. **—de·pop′u·la′tion** *n.*

de·port (dĭ-pôrt′) ▸ *v.* **1.** To expel from a country. **2.** To conduct (oneself) in a given manner. **—de′por·ta′tion** (dē′pôr-tā′shən) *n.* **—de′por·tee′** *n.*

de·port·ment (dĭ-pôrt′mənt) ▸ *n.* Personal conduct; behavior.

de·pose (dĭ-pōz′) ▸ *v.* **-posed, -pos·ing.** **1.** To remove from office or power. **2.** *Law* **a.** To give a deposition; testify. **b.** To take a deposition from.

de·pos·it (dĭ-pŏz′ĭt) ▸ *v.* **1.** To put or set down. **2.** To lay down by a natural process. **3.** To place for safekeeping, as money in a bank. **4.** To give as partial payment or security. ▸ *n.* **1.** Something entrusted for safekeeping, as money in a bank. **2.** The condition of being deposited: *funds on deposit with a broker.* **3.** A partial or initial payment of a cost or debt. **4.** Something deposited, esp. by a natural process: *rich deposits of natural gas.* **—de·pos′i·tor** *n.*

dep·o·si·tion (dĕp′ə-zĭsh′ən) ▸ *n.* **1.** The act of deposing, as from high office. **2.** The act of depositing. **3.** A deposit. **4.** *Law* Testimony under oath, esp. a written statement admissible in court. **—dep′o·si′tion·al** *adj.*

de·pos·i·to·ry (dĭ-pŏz′ĭ-tôr′ē) ▸ *n., pl.* **-ries.** A place where something is deposited, as for safekeeping.

de·pot (dē′pō, dĕp′ō) ▸ *n.* **1.** A railroad or bus station. **2.** A warehouse or storehouse. **3.** A storage installation for military equipment and supplies.

de·prave (dĭ-prāv′) ▸ *v.* **-praved, -prav·ing.** To debase, esp. morally. **—de·praved′** *adj.* **—de·prav′i·ty** (-prăv′ĭ-tē) *n.*

dep·re·cate (dĕp′rĭ-kāt′) ▸ *v.* **-cat·ed, -cat·ing.** **1.** To express disapproval of. **2.** To belittle; depreciate. **—dep′re·ca′tion** *n.* **—dep′re·ca′tor** *n.* **—dep′re·ca·to′ry** (-kə-tôr′ē) *adj.*

de·pre·ci·ate (dĭ-prē′shē-āt′) ▸ *v.* **-at·ed, -at·ing.** **1.** To diminish in price or value. **2.** To belittle. **—de·pre′ci·a′tion** *n.* **—de·pre′ci·a′tor** *n.* **—de·pre′cia·to′ry** (-shə-tôr′ē), **de·pre′cia·tive** *adj.*

dep·re·da·tion (dĕp′rĭ-dā′shən) ▸ *n.* **1.** An act of plunder or ravage. **2.** Damage or destruction.

de·press (dĭ-prĕs′) ▸ *v.* **1.** To lower in spirits; deject. **2.** To push or press down; lower. **3.** To lessen the activity or force of; weaken. **—de·pres′sive** *adj.* **—de·pres′sive·ly** *adv.* **—de·pres′sor** *n.*

de·pres·sant (dĭ-prĕs′ənt) ▸ *adj.* Tending to slow vital physiological activities. ▸ *n.* A depressant drug.

de·pressed (dĭ-prĕst′) ▸ *adj.* **1.** Low in spirits; dejected. **2.** Suffering from psychological depression. **3.** Lower in amount, degree, or position. **4.** Suffering from socioeconomic hardship.

de·pres·sion (dĭ-prĕsh′ən) ▸ *n.* **1.** The act of depressing or condition of being depressed. **2.** A sunken area; hollow. **3.** The condition of feeling sad or despondent. **4.** *Psychol.* A condition marked by an inability to concentrate, insomnia, and feelings of dejection and hopelessness. **5.** A period of drastic decline in an economy. **6.** A region of low barometric pressure.

de·prive (dĭ-prīv′) ▸ *v.* **-prived, -priv·ing.** **1.** To take something away from. **2.** To keep from possessing or enjoying.

THESAURUS

deplorable *adj.* Worthy of severe disapproval ▸ condemnable, disgraceful, reprehensible, shameful, unfortunate, woeful, wretched. [*Compare* DISGRACEFUL, OFFENSIVE, MISERABLE.] *—See also* SORROWFUL.

deplore *v.* **1.** To express strong disapproval of ▸ bemoan, bewail, censure, condemn, decry, denounce, reprehend, reprobate. [*Compare* DISAPPROVE, CONDEMN, HATE.] **2.** To feel or express sorrow for ▸ regret, repent, rue, sorrow (over). [*Compare* FEEL, GRIEVE.]

deploy *v.* *—See* ARRANGE (1).

deployment *n.* *—See* ARRANGEMENT (1).

depone *v.* *—See* TESTIFY.

deponent *n.* One who testifies, especially in court ▸ attestant, attester, testifier, witness.

deport *v.* *—See* ACT (1), BANISH.

deportation *n.* *—See* EXILE.

deportee *n.* *—See* ÉMIGRÉ.

deportment *n.* *—See* BEHAVIOR (1).

depose *v.* *—See* OVERTHROW, TESTIFY.

deposit *v.* *—See* BANK², PAWN¹, POSITION.

deposit *n.* **1.** A partial or initial payment ▸ down payment, installment, security. **2.** Matter that settles on a bottom or collects on a surface by a natural process ▸ accumulation, alluvium, dregs, lees, precipitate, precipitation, sediment. [*Compare* COAT.]

deposition *n.* A formal declaration of truth or fact given under oath ▸ affidavit, testimony, witness.

depository *n.* A place where something is deposited for safekeeping ▸ archive, bank, cache, depot, lockbox, repository, safe, store, storehouse, strongbox, treasure house, treasury, vault, warehouse. [*Compare* HOARD.]

depot *n.* A stopping place along a route for picking up or dropping off passengers ▸ station, stop, terminal, terminus. *—See also* BASE¹ (1), DEPOSITORY.

deprave *v.* *—See* CORRUPT.

depraved *adj.* *—See* CORRUPT (1).

depravity *n.* *—See* CORRUPTION (1), CORRUPTION (2).

deprecate *v.* *—See* BELITTLE, DISAPPROVE.

deprecation *n.* *—See* BELITTLEMENT, DISAPPROVAL.

deprecatory or **deprecative** *adj.* *—See* DISPARAGING.

depreciate *v.* To make less in price or value ▸ cheapen, depress, devaluate, devalue, downgrade, lessen, lower, mark down, reduce, write down. [*Compare* DECREASE.] *—See also* BELITTLE, DETERIORATE, FALL (4).

depreciation *n.* A lowering of price or value ▸ cheapening, depression, devaluation, lessening, markdown, reduction, shrinkage, write-down. [*Compare* DECREASE.] *—See also* BELITTLEMENT, DETERIORATION (1), FALL (3).

depreciative or **depreciatory** *adj.* *—See* DISPARAGING.

depredate *v.* *—See* SACK².

depress *v.* To make sad or gloomy ▸ dampen, deject, dishearten, dispirit, oppress, sadden, weigh down. *Slang:* bum out. ***Idioms:*** get one down, give one the blues (*or* blahs), make one blue. [*Compare* DISCOURAGE.] *—See also* DEPRECIATE, LOWER², PUSH (1).

depressant *n.* *—See* DRUG (2).

depressed *adj.* **1.** In low spirits ▸ blue, brokenhearted, dejected, desolate, disconsolate, discouraged, dismayed, dispirited, down, downcast, downhearted, dull, dyspeptic, dysphoric, gloomy, heartbroken, heartsick, heavy-hearted, low, melancholic, melancholy, sad, sorrowful, spiritless, tristful, unhappy, wistful. *Informal:* blah. ***Idioms:*** down at (*or* in) the mouth, down in the dumps. [*Compare* ANXIOUS, DESPONDENT, GLUM, LONELY.] **2.** Economically and socially below standard ▸ backward, deprived, disadvantaged, impoverished, poor, underprivileged. [*Compare* POOR.] *—See also* HOLLOW (2).

depressing *adj.* *—See* BLEAK (2), SORROWFUL.

depression *n.* **1.** An area sunk below its surroundings ▸ basin, cavity, concavity, dent, dip, hollow, indentation, pit, recess, sag, sink, sinkhole. [*Compare* HOLE, IMPRESSION.] **2.** A feeling or spell of dismally low spirits ▸ blues, dejection, despondence, despondency, disconsolation, discouragement, disheartenment, doldrums, dolefulness, downheartedness, dumps, dysphoria, funk, gloom, glumness, heartsickness, heavy-heartedness, lowness, melancholy, mopes, mournfulness, sadness, sorrow, sorrowfulness, unhappiness, wistfulness. *Informal:* blahs. **3.** A period of decreased business activity and high unemployment ▸ downturn, recession, slowdown, slump. *—See also* DEPRECIATION.

deprivation or **deprival** *n.* The condition of being deprived of what one once had or ought to have ▸ deficiency, destitution, dispossession, divestiture, hardship, loss, penury, poverty, privation. [*Compare* LACK, NEED, POVERTY, SEIZURE.] *—See also* MISERY.

deprive *v.* To take or keep something away from ▸ deny, dispossess, divest, rob, strip, withhold. [*Compare* DECLINE, SEIZE.]

—**de·priv′a·ble** *adj.* —**dep′ri·va′tion** (dĕp′rə-vā′shən) *n.*

de·pro·gram (dē-prō′grăm′, -grəm) ▸ *v.* To counteract the effect of an indoctrination, esp. a cult indoctrination.

dept. ▸ *abbr.* 1. department 2. deputy

depth (dĕpth) ▸ *n.* **1.** The quality of being deep. **2.** The extent or dimension downward, backward, or inward. **3.** often **depths** A deep part or place. **4.** The most profound or intense part or stage. **5.** The severest or worst part. **6.** Intellectual complexity; profundity. **7.** The range of one's competence: *out of my depth.* **8.** Thoroughness.

depth charge ▸ *n.* A charge designed for detonation under water, used esp. against submarines.

dep·u·ta·tion (dĕp′yə-tā′shən) ▸ *n.* **1.** A person or group appointed to represent others. **2.** The act of deputing.

de·pute (dĭ-pyo͞ot′) ▸ *v.* **-put·ed, -put·ing.** To appoint or authorize as a representative.

dep·u·tize (dĕp′yə-tīz′) ▸ *v.* **-tized, -tiz·ing.** To appoint as a deputy.

dep·u·ty (dĕp′yə-tē) ▸ *n., pl.* **-ties.** **1.** A person empowered to act for another. **2.** An assistant exercising full authority in the absence of a superior. **3.** A legislative representative in certain countries.

de·rail (dē-rāl′) ▸ *v.* **1.** To run or cause to run off the rails. **2.** To come or bring to a sudden halt: *a campaign derailed by lack of funds.* —**de·rail′ment** *n.*

de·rail·leur (dĭ-rā′lər) ▸ *n.* A device for shifting gears on a bicycle by moving the chain between sprocket wheels of different sizes.

de·range (dĭ-rānj′) ▸ *v.* **-ranged, -rang·ing.** **1.** To disarrange. **2.** To make insane. —**de·range′ment** *n.*

der·by (dûr′bē; *British* där′bē) ▸ *n., pl.* **-bies.** **1.** An annual horse race, esp. for three-year-olds. **2.** A race open to all contestants. **3.** A stiff felt hat with a round crown and narrow brim.

der·e·lict (dĕr′ə-lĭkt′) ▸ *adj.* **1.** Deserted by an owner; abandoned. **2.** Neglectful of duty. ▸ *n.* **1.** Abandoned property, esp. a ship abandoned at sea. **2.** A homeless or vagrant person.

der·e·lic·tion (dĕr′ə-lĭk′shən) ▸ *n.* **1.** Willful neglect, as of duty. **2.** Abandonment.

de·ride (dĭ-rīd′) ▸ *v.* **-rid·ed, -rid·ing.** To speak of or treat with contemptuous mirth. —**de·ri′sion** (-rĭzh′ən) *n.* —**de·ri′sive** (-rī′sĭv) *adj.* —**de·ri′sive·ly** *adv.*

de ri·gueur (də rē-gœr′) ▸ *adj.* Socially obligatory.

der·i·va·tion (dĕr′ə-vā′shən) ▸ *n.* **1.** The act or process of deriving. **2.** The origin or source of something. **3.** The historical origin and development of a word; etymology. —**der′i·va′tion·al** *adj.*

de·riv·a·tive (dĭ-rĭv′ə-tĭv) ▸ *adj.* **1.** Resulting from derivation. **2.** Unoriginal: *a derivative prose style.* ▸ *n.* **1.** Something derived. **2.** A word formed from another by derivation. —**de·riv′a·tive·ly** *adv.*

de·rive (dĭ-rīv′) ▸ *v.* **-rived, -riv·ing.** **1a.** To obtain from a source. **b.** To originate. **2.** To deduce or infer. **3.** To trace the origin or development of (a word). **4.** To produce or obtain (a compound) from another substance by chemical reaction. —**de·riv′a·ble** *adj.*

der·ma (dûr′mə) ▸ *n.* See **dermis.**

der·ma·ti·tis (dûr′mə-tī′tĭs) ▸ *n.* Inflammation of the skin.

der·ma·tol·o·gy (dûr′mə-tŏl′ə-jē) ▸ *n.* The medical study of the skin and its diseases. —**der′ma·tol′o·gist** *n.*

der·mis (dûr′mĭs) ▸ *n.* The layer of the skin below the epidermis, containing nerve endings, sweat glands, and blood and lymph vessels. —**der′mal** *adj.*

der·o·gate (dĕr′ə-gāt′) ▸ *v.* **-gat·ed, -gat·ing.** **1.** To take away; detract. **2.** To disparage; belittle. —**der′o·ga′tion** *n.*

de·rog·a·to·ry (dĭ-rŏg′ə-tôr′ē) ▸ *adj.* Disparaging; belittling: *a derogatory comment.* —**de·rog′a·to′ri·ly** *adv.*

der·rick (dĕr′ĭk) ▸ *n.* **1.** A machine for hoisting and moving heavy objects. **2.** A tall framework over a drilled hole, esp. an oil well, used to support equipment.

der·ri·ère also **der·ri·ere** (dĕr′ē-âr′) ▸ *n.* The buttocks.

der·ring-do (dĕr′ĭng-do͞o′) ▸ *n.* Daring or reckless action.

der·rin·ger (dĕr′ĭn-jər) ▸ *n.* A small, short-barreled pistol.

der·vish (dûr′vĭsh) ▸ *n.* A member of any of various Muslim ascetic orders, some of which perform whirling dances in ecstatic devotion.

de·sal·i·nate (dē-săl′ə-nāt′) ▸ *v.* **-nat·ed, -nat·ing.** To desalinize. —**de·sal′i·na′tion** *n.* —**de·sal′i·na′tor** *n.*

de·sal·i·nize (dē-săl′ə-nīz′) ▸ *v.* **-nized, -niz·ing.** To remove salts and other chemicals from (e.g., seawater). —**de·sal′i·ni·za′tion** *n.*

des·cant (dĕs′kănt′) ▸ *n.* **1.** *Mus.* An ornamental melody sung or played above a theme. **2.** A discourse on a theme. —**des′cant′** *v.*

Des·cartes (dā-kärt′), **René** (1596–1650) ▸ French mathematician and philosopher.

de·scend (dĭ-sĕnd′) ▸ *v.* **1.** To move from a higher to a lower place; come or go down. **2.** To slope, extend, or incline downward. **3.** To come from an ancestor. **4.** To pass by inheritance. **5.** To lower oneself; stoop. **6.** To arrive or attack in an overwhelming manner: *tourists descending on the village.*

de·scen·dant (dĭ-sĕn′dənt) ▸ *n.* One descended from specified ancestors. ▸ *adj.* Var. of **descendent.**

de·scen·dent also **de·scen·dant** (dĭ-sĕn′dənt) ▸ *adj.* **1.** Moving downward. **2.** Proceeding from an ancestor.

de·scent (dĭ-sĕnt′) ▸ *n.* **1.** The act or an instance of descending. **2.** A downward incline. **3.** Hereditary deriva-

THESAURUS

deprived *adj.* —*See* DEPRESSED (2), EMPTY (2).

depth *n.* **1.** The extent or measurement downward from a surface ▸ deepness, drop, drop-off. **2.** Intellectual penetration or range ▸ deepness, profoundness, profundity, weightiness. [*Compare* DISCERNMENT, INTELLIGENCE, WISDOM.] —*See also* DEEP, INTENSITY.

depths *n.* —*See* DEEP, INTENSITY.

deputation *n.* A diplomatic office or headquarters in a foreign country ▸ embassy, legation, mission.

deputy *n.* —*See* ASSISTANT, REPRESENTATIVE.

derailed *adj.* —*See* INSANE.

derange *v.* To make insane ▸ craze, dement, madden, unbalance, unhinge. *Idiom:* push off (*or* over) the deep end. —*See also* DISORDER, UPSET.

derangement *n.* —*See* DISORDER (1), INSANITY.

derelict *adj.* —*See* ABANDONED (1), NEGLIGENT.

derelict *n.* —*See* PAUPER.

dereliction *n.* The act of forsaking ▸ abandonment, desertion. [*Compare* DEFECTION.] —*See also* BREACH (1), FAILURE (2).

deride *v.* —*See* RIDICULE.

de rigueur *adj.* —*See* APPROPRIATE.

derision *n.* Words or actions intended to evoke contemptuous laughter ▸ mockery, ridicule. [*Compare* SARCASM, TAUNT.] —*See also* DISGRACE.

derisive *adj.* —*See* DISPARAGING, SARCASTIC.

derivation *n.* —*See* ANCESTRY, DERIVATIVE, ORIGIN.

derivational *adj.* Stemming from an original source ▸ derivative, derived, secondary.

derivative *n.* Something derived from another ▸ byproduct, derivation, descendant, offshoot, outgrowth, spin-off. [*Compare* COPY.]

derivative or **derivate** *adj.* Stemming from an original source ▸ derivational, derived, secondary. —*See also* IMITATIVE (1).

derive *v.* **1.** To obtain from another source ▸ draw, extract, gain, get, receive, take. **2.** To arrive at through reasoning ▸ determine, educe, evolve, excogitate, work out. [*Compare* DECIDE, INFER.] —*See also* DESCEND, STEM.

derived *adj.* Stemming from an original source ▸ derivational, derivative, secondary.

derogate *v.* —*See* BELITTLE.

derogation *n.* —*See* BELITTLEMENT.

derogatory or **derogative** *adj.* —*See* DISPARAGING.

derrière *n.* —*See* BUTTOCKS.

derring-do *n.* —*See* DARING.

descend *v.* To have hereditary derivation ▸ come, derive, issue, spring. *Idiom:* trace one's descent. —*See also* CONDESCEND (1), DETERIORATE, DROP (2), FALL (1).

descendant *n.* —*See* DERIVATIVE, PROGENY.

descending or **descendent** *adj.* Moving or sloping down ▸ downward, drooping, falling, plummeting, plunging, sinking.

descent *n.* A sudden drop to a lower

tion; lineage. **4.** A decline, as in status. **5.** A sudden attack.
de·scribe (dĭ-skrīb′) ▸ *v.* **-scribed, -scrib·ing. 1.** To give a verbal account of. **2.** To depict. **3.** To trace the outline of. **—de·scrib′a·ble** *adj.*
de·scrip·tion (dĭ-skrĭp′shən) ▸ *n.* **1.** The act of describing. **2.** An account describing something. **3.** A kind or sort: *cars of every description.* **—de·scrip′tive** *adj.* **—de·scrip′tive·ly** *adv.* **—de·scrip′tive·ness** *n.*
de·scry (dĭ-skrī′) ▸ *v.* **-scried, -scry·ing. 1.** To catch sight of. **2.** To discover by careful observation.
des·e·crate (dĕs′ĭ-krāt′) ▸ *v.* **-crat·ed, -crat·ing.** To violate the sacredness of; profane. **—des′e·crat′er, des′e·cra′tor** *n.* **—des′e·cra′tion** *n.*
de·seg·re·gate (dē-sĕg′rĭ-gāt′) ▸ *v.* To abolish segregation in. **—de·seg′re·ga′tion** *n.* **—de·seg′re·ga′tion·ist** *n.*
de·sen·si·tize (dē-sĕn′sĭ-tīz′) ▸ *v.* To make less sensitive. **—de·sen′si·ti·za′tion** *n.*
des·ert¹ (dĕz′ərt) ▸ *n.* A dry, often sandy region of little rainfall and sparse vegetation.
de·sert² (dĭ-zûrt′) ▸ *n.* often **deserts** Something deserved, esp. a punishment.
de·sert³ (dĭ-zûrt′) ▸ *v.* **1.** To forsake or leave alone; abandon. **2.** To forsake one's duty or post, esp. in the armed forces. **—de·sert′er** *n.* **—de·ser′tion** *n.*
de·sert·i·fi·ca·tion (dĭ-zûr′tə-fĭ-kā′shən) ▸ *n.* The transformation of arable or habitable land to desert.
de·serve (dĭ-zûrv′) ▸ *v.* **-served, -serv·ing.** To be worthy of; merit.
de·served (dĭ-zûrvd′) ▸ *adj.* Merited or earned. **—de·serv′ed·ly** (-zûr′vĭd-lē) *adv.*
de·serv·ing (dĭ-zûr′vĭng) ▸ *adj.* Worthy, as of reward or praise. **—de·serv′ing·ly** *adv.*
des·ic·cant (dĕs′ĭ-kənt) ▸ *n.* A substance used as a drying agent.
des·ic·cate (dĕs′ĭ-kāt′) ▸ *v.* **-cat·ed, -cat·ing. 1.** To dry out thoroughly. **2.** To preserve (foods) by removing the moisture. **—des′ic·ca′tion** *n.* **—des′ic·ca′tive** *adj.*
de·sid·er·a·tum (dĭ-sĭd′ə-rā′təm, -rä′-) ▸ *n., pl.* **-ta** (-tə). Something necessary or desirable.
de·sign (dĭ-zīn′) ▸ *v.* **1.** To conceive; invent. **2.** To formulate a plan for; devise. **3.** To have as a goal or purpose; intend. ▸ *n.* **1.** A drawing or sketch, esp. a detailed plan for construction or manufacture. **2.** The purposeful arrangement of parts or details. **3.** The art or practice of making designs. **4.** An ornamental pattern. **5.** A plan or project. **6.** A reasoned purpose; intent. **7.** often **designs** A secretive plot or scheme. **—de·sign′er** *n.*
des·ig·nate (dĕz′ĭg-nāt′) ▸ *v.* **-nat·ed, -nat·ing. 1.** To indicate or specify. **2.** To give a name to. **3.** To select and set aside for a duty, office, or purpose. ▸ *adj.* (-nĭt) Appointed but not yet installed in office. **—des′ig·na′tion** *n.* **—des′ig·na′tive** *adj.*
des·ig·nat·ed driver (dĕz′ĭg-nā′tĭd) ▸ *n.* One who agrees to remain sober, as at a party, in order to drive others home safely.
designated hitter ▸ *n. Baseball* A player designated to bat instead of the pitcher.
de·sign·ing (dĭ-zī′nĭng) ▸ *adj.* Conniving.
de·sir·a·ble (dĭ-zīr′ə-bəl) ▸ *adj.* **1.** Worth having or seeking. **2.** Worth doing. **3.** Arousing desire. **—de·sir′a·bil′i·ty, de·sir′a·ble·ness** *n.* **—de·sir′a·bly** *adv.*
de·sire (dĭ-zīr′) ▸ *v.* **-sired, -sir·ing. 1.** To wish or long for; want. **2.** To express a wish for. ▸ *n.* **1.** A wish or longing. **2.** A request. **3.** The object of longing. **4.** Sexual appetite. **—de·sir′er** *n.*
de·sir·ous (dĭ-zīr′əs) ▸ *adj.* Wanting; desiring. **—de·sir′ous·ly** *adv.*
de·sist (dĭ-sĭst′, -zĭst′) ▸ *v.* To cease doing something.
desk (dĕsk) ▸ *n.* **1.** A piece of furniture typically having a flat top for writing. **2.** A counter or booth at which specified services are performed. **3.** A specialized department of a large organization: *a newspaper city desk.*
desk·top (dĕsk′tŏp′) ▸ *adj.* **1.** Designed for use on a desk. **2.** Small enough to fit conveniently in an individual workspace.
desktop publishing ▸ *n.* The design and production of publications using personal computers with graphics capability.
Des Moines (dĭ moin′) ▸ The capital of IA, in the S-central part.

THESAURUS

condition or status ▸ comedown, dip, down, downfall, downgrade, plunge, slide, tumble. *—See also* ANCESTRY, DROP (3), FALL (1), FALL (3).
describe *v.* To communicate the facts, details, or particulars of something ▸ detail, narrate, recite, recount, rehearse, relate, report, tell. [*Compare* CALL, EXPLAIN.] *—See also* REPRESENT (2).
description *n.* *—See* KIND², REPRESENTATION, STORY (1).
descriptive *adj.* Serving to describe ▸ colorful, delineative, graphic, representative, vivid. [*Compare* ELOQUENT, EXPRESSIVE.]
descry *v.* *—See* DISCERN, NOTICE, SEE (1).
desecrate *v.* *—See* VIOLATE (3).
desecration *n.* *—See* SACRILEGE.
desegregate *v.* To open to all people regardless of race ▸ integrate.
desensitize *v.* *—See* DEADEN.
desert¹ *n.* [illegible] region ▸ badlands, barren, barrens, dust bowl, tundra, waste, wasteland. [*Compare* COUNTRY, WILDERNESS.]
desert *adj.* *—See* BARREN (2), DRY (2).
desert² *v.* *—See* ABANDON (1), DEFECT.
deserted *adj.* *—See* ABANDONED (1), LONELY (1).
deserter *n.* *—See* DEFECTOR.
desertion *n.* The act of forsaking ▸ abandonment, dereliction. [*Compare* DEFECTION.]
deserts *n.* *—See* DUE, PUNISHMENT.
deserve *v.* *—See* EARN (1).
deserved *adj.* *—See* JUST.
deserving *adj.* *—See* ADMIRABLE.
desiccate *v.* *—See* DRY, DRY UP (2).
design *v.* **1.** To form a strategy for ▸ blueprint, cast, chart, conceive, concoct, contrive, devise, formulate, frame, lay, originate, plan, predetermine, premeditate, project, scheme, strategize, work out. *Informal:* dope out. ***Idiom:*** lay plans. [*Compare* INVENT, PLOT.] **2.** To work out and arrange the parts and details of ▸ blueprint, draft, lay out, map (out), outline, plan, set out, sketch. [*Compare* DRAFT.] *—See also* COMPOSE (1), INTEND.
design *n.* An element or component in a decorative composition ▸ device, figure, motif, motive. *—See also* APPROACH (1), FORM (1), INTENTION.
designate *v.* To make known or identify, as by signs ▸ denote, earmark, identify, indicate, mark, pinpoint, point out, signal, signify, specify. [*Compare* MARK, REPRESENT, SHOW.] *—See also* APPOINT, APPROPRIATE, CALL, NAME (1).
designation *n.* *—See* APPOINTMENT, NAME (1).
designative or **designatory** *adj.* Serving to designate or indicate ▸ denotative, denotive, exhibitive, exhibitory, indicative, indicatory, significant. [*Compare* SYMBOLIC.]
designed *adj.* *—See* CALCULATED.
designing *adj.* Coldly planning to achieve selfish aims ▸ calculating, conniving, manipulative, scheming. [*Compare* ARTFUL.]
designs *n.* *—See* PLOT (2).
desirable *adj.* Arousing erotic desire ▸ alluring, enticing, sexy. *Slang:* foxy, hot, sizzling. ***Idiom:*** to die for. [*Compare* SEDUCTIVE, SENSUAL.] *—See also* ADVISABLE, ATTRACTIVE.
desire *v.* To have a strong longing for ▸ ache, aspire, covet, dream, hanker, hope, long, pant, pine, want, wish, yearn. *Informal:* die for, hone. ***Idioms:*** be dying (*or* itching) to, give the world for, set one's heart on. [*Compare* LUST.] *—See also* CHOOSE (2).
desire *n.* **1.** A strong wanting of what promises enjoyment or pleasure ▸ appetence, appetency, appetite, craving, hankering, hunger, itch, longing, lust, thirst, wish, yearning. **2.** Sexual hunger ▸ amativeness, appetite, concupiscence, eroticism, erotism, itch, libidinousness, libido, lust, lustfulness, passion, prurience, pruriency, urge. *Slang:* horniness. *—See also* DEMAND (2), DREAM (3).
desired *adj.* *—See* DARLING.
desirous *adj.* Having desire for something ▸ desiring, hankering, hungry. [*Compare* VORACIOUS.]
desist *v.* *—See* ABANDON (2), STOP (1).

des·o·late (dĕs′ə-lĭt, dĕz′-) ▸ *adj.* **1.** Devoid of inhabitants; deserted. **2.** Rendered unfit for habitation or use. **3.** Dreary; dismal. **4.** Lonely; forlorn. ▸ *v.* (-lāt′) **-lat·ed, -lat·ing.** To make desolate. **—des′o·late·ly** *adv.* **—des′o·la′tion** *n.*

de So·to (dĭ sō′tō, dĕ), **Hernando** or **Fernando** (1496?–1542) ▸ Spanish explorer.

de·spair (dĭ-spâr′) ▸ *v.* To lose all hope. ▸ *n.* **1.** Complete loss of hope. **2.** One that causes despair.

des·per·a·do (dĕs′pə-rä′dō, -rā′-) ▸ *n., pl.* **-does** or **-dos.** A bold or desperate outlaw.

des·per·ate (dĕs′pər-ĭt) ▸ *adj.* **1.** Having lost all hope; despairing. **2.** Reckless or violent because of despair. **3.** Undertaken as a last resort. **4.** Nearly hopeless; critical. **5.** Extreme; great: *a desperate urge.* **—des′per·ate·ly** *adv.* **—des′per·a′tion** (dĕs′pə-rā′shən) *n.*

de·spic·a·ble (dĭ-spĭk′ə-bəl, dĕs′pĭ-kə-) ▸ *adj.* Deserving of contempt or scorn; vile. **—de·spic′a·ble·ness** *n.* **—de·spic′a·bly** *adv.*

de·spise (dĭ-spīz′) ▸ *v.* **-spised, -spis·ing.** **1.** To regard with scorn. **2.** To dislike intensely. **—de·spis′er** *n.*

de·spite (dĭ-spīt′) ▸ *prep.* In spite of.

de·spoil (dĭ-spoil′) ▸ *v.* To sack; plunder. **—de·spoil′ment** *n.* **—de·spo′li·a′tion** (-spō′lē-ā′shən) *n.*

de·spond (dĭ-spŏnd′) ▸ *v.* To become discouraged. ▸ *n.* Despondency. **—de·spond′ing·ly** *adv.*

de·spon·den·cy (dĭ-spŏn′dən-sē) ▸ *n.* Loss of hope; dejection. **—de·spon′dent** *adj.* **—de·spon′dent·ly** *adv.*

des·pot (dĕs′pət) ▸ *n.* A ruler with absolute power; tyrant. **—des·pot′ic** (dĭ-spŏt′ĭk) *adj.* **—des·pot′i·cal·ly** *adv.* **—des′pot·ism′** *n.*

des·sert (dĭ-zûrt′) ▸ *n.* A usu. sweet dish served at the end of a meal.

de·sta·bi·lize (dē-stā′bə-līz′) ▸ *v.* **-lized, -liz·ing.** **1.** To upset the stability of. **2.** To undermine the power of (a government). **—de·sta′bi·li·za′tion** *n.*

des·ti·na·tion (dĕs′tə-nā′shən) ▸ *n.* **1.** The place to which one is going or directed. **2.** An ultimate purpose or goal.

des·tine (dĕs′tĭn) ▸ *v.* **-tined, -tin·ing.** **1.** To determine beforehand. **2.** To assign for a specific end, use, or purpose. **3.** To direct toward a given destination.

des·ti·ny (dĕs′tə-nē) ▸ *n., pl.* **-nies.** **1.** One's inevitable fate. **2.** A predetermined course of events. **3.** The power or agency thought to predetermine events.

des·ti·tute (dĕs′tĭ-to͞ot′, -tyo͞ot′) ▸ *adj.* **1.** Utterly lacking; devoid: *destitute of any experience.* **2.** Lacking means of subsistence; impoverished. **—des′ti·tu′tion** *n.*

de·stroy (dĭ-stroi′) ▸ *v.* **1.** To ruin completely. **2.** To tear down; demolish. **3.** To kill.

de·stroy·er (dĭ-stroi′ər) ▸ *n.* **1.** One that destroys. **2.** A small fast warship.

de·struct (dĭ-strŭkt′, dē′strŭkt′) ▸ *n.* The intentional, usu. remote-controlled destruction of a space vehicle, rocket, or missile after launching. **—de·struct′** *v.*

de·struc·ti·ble (dĭ-strŭk′tə-bəl) ▸ *adj.* Easily destroyed. **—de·struc′ti·bil′i·ty** *n.*

de·struc·tion (dĭ-strŭk′shən) ▸ *n.* **1.** The act of destroying or condition of having been destroyed. **2.** The cause or means of destroying. **—de·struc′tive** *adj.* **—de·struc′tive·ly** *adv.* **—de·struc′tive·ness** *n.*

des·ue·tude (dĕs′wĭ-to͞od′, -tyo͞od′) ▸ *n.* A state of disuse.

des·ul·to·ry (dĕs′əl-tôr′ē, dĕz′-) ▸ *adj.* **1.** Without purpose or intent; aimless. **2.** Occurring haphazardly; random. **—des′ul·to′ri·ly** *adv.*

de·tach (dĭ-tăch′) ▸ *v.* To separate; disconnect. **—de·tach′a·bil′i·ty** *n.* **—de·tach′a·ble** *adj.*

de·tached (dĭ-tăcht′) ▸ *adj.* **1.** Separated; disconnected. **2.** Free from emotional involvement; cool; aloof.

de·tach·ment (dĭ-tăch′mənt) ▸ *n.* **1.** The act or process of disconnecting; separation. **2.** Indifference to the concerns of others; aloofness. **3.** Impartiality; disinterest. **4a.** The dispatch of troops or ships from a larger body for special duty. **b.** A small permanent unit organized for special duties.

de·tail (dĭ-tāl′, dē′tāl′) ▸ *n.* **1.** An individual part. **2.** Itemized or minute treatment of particulars: *attention to detail.*

THESAURUS

desolate *adj.* —*See* ABANDONED (1), BARREN (2), GLOOMY, LONELY (1), LONELY (2).

desolate *v.* —*See* CONSUME (1).

despair *v.* To lose all hope ▸ despond, give in, give up. ***Idiom:*** throw in the sponge (*or* towel). [*Compare* ABANDON, SURRENDER.]

despair *n.* Utter lack of hope ▸ desperateness, desperation, despond, despondence, despondency, discouragement, dismay, hopelessness. [*Compare* DEPRESSION.]

despairing *adj.* —*See* DESPONDENT.

desperado *n.* —*See* CRIMINAL.

desperate *adj.* —*See* DESPONDENT, INTENSE, URGENT (1).

desperation or **desperateness** *n.* —*See* DESPAIR.

despicable or **despisable** *adj.* —*See* OFFENSIVE (1).

despisal *n.* The feeling of despising ▸ abhorrence, contempt, despite, disdain, dislike, hatred, loathing, revulsion, scorn. [*Compare* DISRESPECT, ENMITY, HATE.]

despise *v.* To regard with utter contempt ▸ abominate, contemn, disdain, dismiss, scorn, scout, sneer at, sniff at, spit on. ***Idioms:*** have no use for, look down on (*or* upon), look down one's nose at. [*Compare* DISLIKE, REVILE, SNUB.] —*See also* HATE.

despite *n.* —*See* DEFIANCE (2), DESPISAL, INDIGNITY.

despiteful *adj.* —*See* MALEVOLENT.

despitefulness *n.* —*See* MALEVOLENCE.

despoil *v.* —*See* SACK², VIOLATE (3).

despond *v.* To lose all hope ▸ despair, give in, give up. ***Idiom:*** throw in the sponge (*or* towel). [*Compare* ABANDON, SURRENDER.]

despond *n.* —*See* DESPAIR.

despondence or **despondency** *n.* —*See* DEPRESSION (2), DESPAIR.

despondent *adj.* Having lost all hope ▸ dejected, despairing, desperate, discouraged, forlorn, hopeless, wretched. [*Compare* DEPRESSED, GLUM, MISERABLE.]

despot *n.* —*See* AUTHORITARIAN, DICTATOR.

despotic *adj.* —*See* ABSOLUTE, AUTHORITARIAN.

despotism *n.* —*See* ABSOLUTISM (2), ABSOLUTISM (1), TYRANNY.

desquamate *v.* —*See* FLAKE.

destiny *n.* —*See* FATE (1), FATE (2).

destitute *adj.* —*See* EMPTY (2), POOR.

destitution *n.* —*See* DEPRIVATION, POVERTY.

destroy *v.* **1.** To cause the complete ruin or wreckage of ▸ annihilate, bankrupt, break down, cross up, crush, demolish, devastate, finish, ravage, ruin, shatter, sink, smash, spoil, torpedo, undo, wash up, wrack, wreck. *Slang:* total. ***Idioms:*** lay waste to, put the kibosh on. [*Compare* ANNIHILATE, BOTCH, DAMAGE.] **2.** To pull down or break up so that reconstruction is impossible ▸ demolish, dismantle, dynamite, knock down, level, obliterate, pull down, pulverize, raze, tear down, wreck. —*See also* BREAK (2), KILL¹, MURDER.

destroyer *n.* —*See* RUIN (1).

destruction *n.* The act of destroying or state of being destroyed ▸ annihilation, bane, decimation, demolition, devastation, havoc, pulverization, ruin, ruination, undoing, wrack, wreck, wreckage. —*See also* DAMAGE, RUIN (1).

destructive *adj.* —*See* HARMFUL.

desuetude *n.* —*See* OBSOLETENESS.

desultory *adj.* —*See* AIMLESS, RANDOM.

detach *v.* To remove from association with ▸ abstract, disassociate, disconnect, disengage, dissociate, separate, uncouple, withdraw. —*See also* DIVIDE.

detached *adj.* **1.** Lacking interest in one's surroundings or worldly affairs ▸ aloof, disconnected, disinterested, incurious, indifferent, remote, unconcerned, uninterested, uninvolved. **2.** Feeling or showing no strong emotional involvement ▸ disinterested, dispassionate, impersonal, indifferent, neutral. —*See also* APATHETIC, CALM, COOL, FAIR¹ (1), SOLITARY.

detachment *n.* **1.** The act or process of detaching ▸ abstraction, disassociation, disconnection, disengagement, dissociation, separation, uncoupling, withdrawal. **2.** Dissociation from one's surroundings or worldly affairs ▸ aloofness, disinterest, distance, indifference, remoteness, unconcern, uninvolvement. **3.** A unit of troops on special assignment ▸ brigade, corps, detail, patrol, squad. —*See also* APATHY, DIVISION (1), FAIRNESS, FORCE (3).

detail *n.* A small, often specialized element of a whole ▸ fine print, item,

3. An inconsequential item or aspect. **4a.** A group of military personnel selected to do a specified task. **b.** The task assigned. ▸ *v.* (dĭ-tāl′) **1.** To report or relate minutely. **2.** To name or state explicitly. **3.** To provide with decorative detail.

de·tain (dĭ-tān′) ▸ *v.* **1.** To keep from proceeding; delay. **2.** To keep in custody or confinement. **—de·tain′ment** *n.* **—de′tain·ee′** (dē′tā-nē′, dĭ-tā′-) *n.*

de·tect (dĭ-tĕkt′) ▸ *v.* To discover or ascertain the existence, presence, or fact of. **—de·tect′a·ble, de·tect′i·ble** *adj.* **—de·tec′tion** *n.* **—de·tect′er** *n.*

de·tec·tive (dĭ-tĕk′tĭv) ▸ *n.* A person, usu. a member of a police force, who investigates crimes and obtains evidence.

de·tec·tor (dĭ-tĕk′tər) ▸ *n.* One that detects, esp. a mechanical or electrical device that identifies and records a stimulus.

dé·tente (dā-tänt′, -täɴt′) ▸ *n.* A relaxing of tension between nations.

de·ten·tion (dĭ-tĕn′shən) ▸ *n.* **1.** The act of detaining or condition of being detained. **2.** A forced or punitive confinement.

de·ter (dĭ-tûr′) ▸ *v.* **-terred, -ter·ring.** To prevent or discourage from acting, as by means of fear or doubt. **—de·ter′ment** *n.*

de·ter·gent (dĭ-tûr′jənt) ▸ *n.* A cleansing substance made from chemical compounds rather than fats and lye. ▸ *adj.* Having cleansing power.

de·te·ri·o·rate (dĭ-tîr′ē-ə-rāt′) ▸ *v.* **-rat·ed, -rat·ing.** **1.** To diminish in quality or value. **2.** To weaken or disintegrate. **—de·te′ri·o·ra′tion** *n.*

de·ter·mi·nant (dĭ-tûr′mə-nənt) ▸ *adj.* Determinative. ▸ *n.* An influencing or determining factor.

de·ter·mi·nate (dĭ-tûr′mə-nĭt) ▸ *adj.* **1.** Precisely limited or defined; definite. **2.** Conclusively settled; final.

de·ter·mi·na·tion (dĭ-tûr′mə-nā′shən) ▸ *n.* **1a.** The act of arriving at a decision. **b.** The decision reached. **2.** Firmness of purpose; resolve. **3.** The ascertaining or fixing of the quantity, quality, position, or character of something.

de·ter·mi·na·tive (dĭ-tûr′mə-nā′tĭv, -nə-) ▸ *adj.* Tending, able, or serving to determine. ▸ *n.* A determining factor. **—de·ter′mi·na′tive·ly** *adv.*

de·ter·mine (dĭ-tûr′mĭn) ▸ *v.* **-mined, -min·ing.** **1.** To decide, establish, or ascertain definitely. **2.** To cause to come to a conclusion or resolution; influence. **3.** To limit; regulate. **4.** To give direction to. **—de·ter′min·a·ble** *adj.* **—de·ter′min·a·bly** *adv.*

de·ter·mined (dĭ-tûr′mĭnd) ▸ *adj.* Showing determination. **—de·ter′mined·ly** *adv.*

de·ter·min·er (dĭ-tûr′mə-nər) ▸ *n.* A word belonging to a group of noun modifiers that includes articles, demonstratives, and possessive adjectives, and, in English, occupying the first position in a noun phrase.

de·ter·min·ism (dĭ-tûr′mə-nĭz′əm) ▸ *n.* The philosophical doctrine that every state of affairs, including every human event, act, and decision, is the inevitable consequence of antecedent states of affairs. **—de·ter′min·is′tic** *adj.*

de·ter·rent (dĭ-tûr′ənt, -tŭr′-) ▸ *adj.* Tending to deter. ▸ *n.* Something that deters. **—de·ter′rence** *n.*

de·test (dĭ-tĕst′) ▸ *v.* To dislike intensely; abhor. **—de·test′a·ble** *adj.* **—de·test′a·bly** *adv.* **—de′tes·ta′tion** (dē′tĕ-stā′shən) *n.*

de·throne (dē-thrōn′) ▸ *v.* **-throned, -thron·ing.** To remove from the throne; depose. **—de·throne′ment** *n.*

det·o·nate (dĕt′n-āt′) ▸ *v.* **-nat·ed, -nat·ing.** To explode or cause to explode. **—det′o·na′tion** *n.* **—det′o·na′tor** *n.*

de·tour (dē′to͝or′, dĭ-to͝or′) ▸ *n.* A roundabout way, esp. a road used temporarily instead of a main route. ▸ *v.* To go or cause to go by a detour.

de·tox (dē-tŏks′) *Informal* ▸ *v.* To detoxify. ▸ *n.* (dē′tŏks′) A place where patients are detoxified.

de·tox·i·fy (dē-tŏk′sə-fī′) ▸ *v.* **-fied, -fy·ing.** **1.** To remove poison or the effects of poison from. **2.** To treat (an individual) for alcohol or drug dependence, usu. under medical supervision. **—de·tox′i·fi·ca′tion** *n.*

de·tract (dĭ-trăkt′) ▸ *v.* To take away (from); diminish. **—de·trac′tion** *n.* **—de·trac′tor** *n.*

de·train (dē-trān′) ▸ *v.* To leave or cause to leave a railroad train.

det·ri·ment (dĕt′rə-mənt) ▸ *n.* **1.** Damage, harm, or loss. **2.** Something that causes damage, harm, or loss. **—det′ri·men′tal** *adj.* **—det′ri·men′tal·ly** *adv.*

de·tri·tus (dĭ-trī′təs) ▸ *n., pl.* **-tus.** **1.** Loose fragments or grains worn away from rock. **2.** Debris: *the detritus of past civilizations.*

De·troit (dĭ-troit′) ▸ A city of SE MI opposite Windsor, Ontario.

deuce[1] (do͞os, dyo͞os) ▸ *n.* **1.** A playing card or side of a die having two spots. **2.** A tied score in tennis in which each player or side has 40 points.

deuce[2] (do͞os, dyo͞os) ▸ *n.* *Informal* The devil. Used as a mild oath.

deu·te·ri·um (do͞o-tîr′ē-əm, dyo͞o-) ▸ *n.* A hydrogen isotope with an atomic weight of 2.014.

Deu·ter·on·o·my (do͞o′tə-rŏn′ə-mē, dyo͞o′-) ▸ *n.* See **Bible** table in Appendix.

THESAURUS

minutia, nicety, particular, singularity, specialty, technicality, trivia. [*Compare* NITTY-GRITTY.] —*See also* CIRCUMSTANCE (2), DETACHMENT (3), ELEMENT (2).

detail *v.* To state specifically ▸ particularize, provide, specify, stipulate. [*Compare* ASSERT, DESIGNATE, DICTATE.] —*See also* DESCRIBE.

detailed *adj.* Characterized by attention to detail ▸ all-inclusive, blow-by-blow, circumstantial, comprehensive, elaborate, exhaustive, full, in-depth, minute, particular, thorough. —*See also* ELABORATE.

detain *v.* To keep in custody ▸ hold. —*See also* DELAY (1), IMPRISON.

detainment *n.* —*See* DELAY (1), DETENTION.

detect *v.* —*See* DISCERN, DISCOVER, NOTICE, SEE (1).

detectable *adj.* —*See* PERCEPTIBLE.

detective *n.* A person whose work is investigating crimes or obtaining hidden evidence or information ▸ investigator, plainclothesman, private eye, private investigator, sherlock, sleuth. *Informal:* eye. *Slang:* dick, gumshoe.

detention *n.* The state of being detained by legal authority ▸ arrest, charge, confinement, custody, detainment, imprisonment, incarceration, internment, quarantine, ward.

deter *v.* —*See* DISSUADE.

deteriorate *v.* To become lower in quality, character, or condition ▸ atrophy, decline, degenerate, depreciate, descend, ebb, languish, retrograde, sink, wane, weaken, worsen. *Idioms:* go bad, go to pot, go downhill, go to seed, go to the dogs, hit the skids. [*Compare* DECREASE, FALL.] —*See also* DECAY, FADE.

deterioration *n.* **1.** Descent to a lower level or condition ▸ atrophy, decadence, declension, declination, decline, degeneracy, degeneration, depreciation, retrogradation, wane, weakening, worsening. **2.** A marked loss of strength or effectiveness ▸ declination, decline, failure. —*See also* DAMAGE, DECAY.

determinant *n.* That which produces an effect ▸ antecedent, cause, occasion, reason. [*Compare* IMPACT, ORIGIN, STIMULUS.]

determinate *adj.* —*See* DEFINITE (2).

determination *n.* The act or process of ascertaining dimensions, quantity, or capacity ▸ measure, measurement, mensuration, quantification. [*Compare* COMPUTATION, ESTIMATION.] —*See also* ANSWER (2), DECISION (1), DECISION (2), INTENTION, RULING.

determinative *adj.* —*See* DECISIVE, DEFINITIVE.

determine *v.* To fix the limits of ▸ bound, circumscribe, define, delimit, delimitate, demarcate, limit, mark (out *or* off), measure, restrict. —*See also* DECIDE, DERIVE (2), DICTATE, DISCOVER, GOVERN, JUDGE.

determined *adj.* —*See* AMBITIOUS, FIRM[1] (3), INTENT.

deterrence *n.* —*See* PREVENTION.

deterrent *adj.* —*See* PREVENTIVE.

deterrent *n.* —*See* RESTRAINT.

detest *v.* —*See* HATE.

detestable *adj.* —*See* OFFENSIVE (1).

detestation *n.* —*See* HATE.

detonate *v.* —*See* EXPLODE (1).

detonation *n.* —*See* BLAST (2), CRACK (1).

detour *v.* —*See* SKIRT.

detract from *v.* —*See* DAMAGE.

detraction *n.* —*See* BELITTLEMENT, LIBEL.

detractive *adj.* —*See* DISPARAGING, LIBELOUS.

detriment *n.* —*See* DISADVANTAGE, HARM.

detrimental *adj.* —*See* HARMFUL.

deutsche mark (doich′ märk′) ► *n.* The primary unit of currency in Germany before the adoption of the euro.

de·val·ue (dē-văl′yo͞o) also **de·val·u·ate** (-văl′yo͞o-āt′) ► *v.* **-ued, -u·ing** also **-at·ed, -at·ing.** 1. To lessen the value of. 2. To lower the exchange value of (a currency). **—de·val′u·a′tion** *n.*

dev·as·tate (dĕv′ə-stāt′) ► *v.* **-tat·ed, -tat·ing.** 1. To lay waste; destroy. 2. To overwhelm; confound. **—dev′as·ta′tion** *n.* **—dev′as·ta′tor** *n.*

de·vel·op (dĭ-vĕl′əp) ► *v.* 1. To bring, grow, or evolve from latency to or toward fulfillment. 2. To expand or enlarge; elaborate. 3. To appear, disclose, or acquire. 4. To make available and usable. 5. To process (a photosensitive material), esp. with chemicals, to render a recorded image visible. **—de·vel′op·er** *n.* **—de·vel′op·ment** *n.* **—de·vel′op·ment′al** *adj.* **—de·vel′op·men′tal·ly** *adv.*

de·vi·ant (dē′vē-ənt) ► *adj.* Differing or deviating from accepted social or moral standards. **—de′vi·ance** *n.* **—de′vi·ant** *n.*

de·vi·ate (dē′vē-āt′) ► *v.* **-at·ed, -at·ing.** To differ or move away from an established course, way, or prescribed mode of behavior. ► *n.* (-ĭt) A deviant. **—de′vi·a′tion** *n.*

de·vice (dĭ-vīs′) ► *n.* 1. Something designed for a particular purpose, esp. a machine. 2. A plan or scheme; trick. 3. A literary contrivance, such as parallelism or personification, used to achieve a particular effect. 4. A decorative design, figure, or pattern, as one used in embroidery. 5. A graphic symbol or motto, esp. in heraldry.

dev·il (dĕv′əl) ► *n.* 1. often **Devil** In some religions, the major spirit of evil and foe of God. Used with *the.* 2. A subordinate evil spirit; demon. 3. A wicked or malevolent person. 4. A person: *a handsome devil; the poor devil.* 5. A mischievous or daring person. 6. A printer's apprentice. ► *v.* **-iled, -il·ing** or **-illed, -il·ling.** 1. To season (food) heavily. 2. To annoy, torment, or harass.

dev·il·ish (dĕv′ə-lĭsh) ► *adj.* 1. Of or like a devil; fiendish. 2. Mischievous. 3. Excessive; extreme: *devilish heat.* ► *adv.* Extremely; very. **—dev′il·ish·ly** *adv.*

dev·il·try (dĕv′əl-trē) or **dev·il·ry** (-əl-rē) ► *n., pl.* **-tries** or **-ries.** 1. Reckless mischief. 2. Wickedness. 3. Evil magic.

de·vi·ous (dē′vē-əs) ► *adj.* 1. Not straightforward; deceitful. 2. Deviating from the straight or direct course: *a devious route.* **—de′vi·ous·ly** *adv.* **—de′vi·ous·ness** *n.*

de·vise (dĭ-vīz′) ► *v.* **-vised, -vis·ing.** 1. To plan or arrange in the mind; invent. 2. *Law* To transmit (real property) by will. ► *n. Law* 1. The act of transmitting real property by will. 2. A will or clause in a will devising real property. **—de·vis′a·ble** *adj.* **—de·vis′er** *n.*

de·vi·tal·ize (dē-vīt′l-īz′) ► *v.* To diminish or destroy the strength or vitality of.

de·void (dĭ-void′) ► *adj.* Completely lacking; destitute: *a novel devoid of wit.*

de·volve (dĭ-vŏlv′) ► *v.* **-volved, -volv·ing.** To pass on or be passed on to a substitute or successor. **—dev′o·lu′tion** (dĕv′ə-lo͞o′shən) *n.*

De·vo·ni·an (dĭ-vō′nē-ən) *Geol.* ► *adj.* Of or being the 4th period of the Paleozoic Era, marked by the appearance of forests and amphibians. ► *n.* The Devonian Period.

de·vote (dĭ-vōt′) ► *v.* **-vot·ed, -vot·ing.** 1. To give or apply (one's time, attention, or self) entirely: *devoted my time to studying.* 2. To set apart for a specific purpose. 3. To dedicate or consecrate.

de·vot·ed (dĭ-vō′tĭd) ► *adj.* Feeling or displaying strong affection or attachment; ardent. **—de·vot′ed·ly** *adv.*

dev·o·tee (dĕv′ə-tē′, -tā′) ► *n.* An enthusiast.

de·vo·tion (dĭ-vō′shən) ► *n.* 1. Ardent attachment or affection. 2. Religious ardor. 3. often **devotions** Prayers, esp. when private. **—de·vo′tion·al** *adj.*

de·vour (dĭ-vour′) ► *v.* 1. To eat up greedily. 2. To destroy, consume, or waste. 3. To take in eagerly. 4. To prey upon voraciously; engulf: *devoured by jealousy.*

de·vout (dĭ-vout′) ► *adj.* **-er, -est.** 1. Deeply religious; pious. 2. Sincere; earnest. **—de·vout′ly** *adv.* **—de·vout′ness** *n.*

dew (do͞o, dyo͞o) ► *n.* 1. Water droplets condensed from the air, usu. at night, onto cool surfaces. 2. Something moist, fresh, pure, or renewing. **—dew′i·ly** *adv.* **—dew′i·ness** *n.* **—dew′y** *adj.*

dew·ber·ry (do͞o′bĕr′ē, dyo͞o′-) ► *n.* 1. Any of several trailing plants. 2. The edible fruit of the dewberry.

dew·claw (do͞o′klô′, dyo͞o′-) ► *n.* A vestigial digit on the feet of certain mammals.

dew·drop (do͞o′drŏp′, dyo͞o′-) ► *n.* A drop of dew.

dew·lap (do͞o′lăp′, dyo͞o′-) ► *n.* A fold of loose skin hanging from the neck of certain animals.

THESAURUS

devaluate *v.* —*See* DEPRECIATE.

devaluation *n.* —*See* DEPRECIATION.

devalue *v.* —*See* DEBASE, DEPRECIATE.

devastate *v.* —*See* CONSUME (1), DESTROY (1).

devastation *n.* —*See* DESTRUCTION.

develop *v.* 1. To come gradually to have ► acquire, form, grow, incur, manifest, sustain. 2. To be disclosed gradually ► disentangle, evolve, unfold, unfurl, unravel. [*Compare* REVEAL.] —*See also* CHANGE (2), CONTRACT (2), ELABORATE, GAIN (1), HAPPEN (1), INCREASE, MATURE, PRODUCE (1).

developed *adj.* —*See* MATURE.

developer *n.* A person instrumental in the growth of something, especially in its early stages ► builder, contributor, creator, innovator, pioneer, producer. [*Compare* ORIGINATOR.]

development *n.* A progression from a simple form to a more complex one ► advancement, blossoming, evolution, evolvement, growth, maturing, maturation, progress, unfolding. —*See also* BUILDUP (2), CHANGE (1), EVENT (1), IMPROVEMENT (1), PROGRESS, VARIATION.

deviance or **deviancy** *n.* —*See* ABNORMALITY.

deviant *adj.* —*See* ABNORMAL, ERRANT (2).

deviant *n.* One whose sexual behavior differs from the accepted norm ► deviate, pervert. *Slang:* freak.

deviate *v.* To turn away from a prescribed course of action or conduct ► depart, digress, divagate, diverge, drift, stray, swerve, vary, veer. *Idiom:* go off on a tangent. —*See also* DIFFER, DIGRESS, TURN (2).

deviate *n.* One whose sexual behavior differs from the accepted norm ► deviant, pervert. *Slang:* freak.

deviation *n.* A departing from what is prescribed ► aberration, departure, divagation, divergence, divergency, diversion, variation. —*See also* ABNORMALITY, DIGRESSION.

device *n.* 1. Something, as a machine, that is devised for a particular function ► apparatus, appliance, contraption, contrivance, equipment, instrument, machine, mechanism. [*Compare* GADGET, TOOL.] 2. An element or component in a decorative composition ► design, figure, motif, motive. —*See also* INVENTION (2), TRICK (1).

devil *n.* —*See* FIEND, RASCAL.

devilish *adj.* —*See* FIENDISH, MISCHIEVOUS.

devilment *n.* —*See* MISCHIEF.

deviltry or **devilry** *n.* —*See* CRIME (2), MISCHIEF.

devious *adj.* —*See* ERRATIC, INDIRECT (1), UNDERHAND.

deviousness *n.* —*See* ART, DISHONESTY (2).

devise *v.* —*See* DESIGN (1), INVENT, LEAVE[1] (1).

devised *adj.* —*See* CALCULATED.

devitalization *n.* —*See* DEBILITATION.

devitalize *v.* —*See* ENERVATE.

devoid *adj.* —*See* EMPTY (2).

devoir *n.* —*See* DUTY (1).

devote *v.* To give over by or as if by vow to a higher purpose ► bless, consecrate, dedicate, enshrine, hallow, pledge, sacrifice. [*Compare* SANCTIFY.] —*See also* APPLY (1).

devoted *adj.* —*See* AFFECTIONATE, DIVINE (2), FAITHFUL, PIOUS.

devotee *n.* One zealously devoted to a religion ► acolyte, adherent, believer, disciple, enthusiast, fanatic, sectary, votary, zealot. [*Compare* FOLLOWER.] —*See also* FAN[2].

devotion *n.* A state of often extreme religious ardor ► adoration, devoutness, faith, faithfulness, pietism, piety, piousness, religionism, religiosity, religiousness, reverence, spirituality, zeal. [*Compare* ADORATION.] —*See also* LOVE (1), LOVE (2).

devotional *adj.* —*See* PIOUS.

devotions *n.* —*See* PRAYER[1] (2).

devour *v.* To be avidly interested in ► feast on, relish. *Slang:* eat up. —*See also* CONSUME (1), EAT (1).

devout *adj.* —*See* DIVINE (2), PIOUS, REVERENT.

devoutness *n.* —*See* DEVOTION.

dew point ▸ *n.* The temperature at which air becomes saturated and produces dew.
dex·ter·i·ty (dĕk-stĕr′ĭ-tē) ▸ *n.* **1.** Skill in the use of the hands or body; adroitness. **2.** Mental skill or cleverness.
dex·ter·ous (dĕk′stər-əs, -strəs) also **dex·trous** (-strəs) ▸ *adj.* **1.** Skillful in the use of the hands or mind. **2.** Done with dexterity. **—dex′ter·ous·ly** *adv.*
dex·trin (dĕk′strĭn) ▸ *n.* A pale powder obtained from starch, used mainly as an adhesive.
dex·trose (dĕk′strōs′) ▸ *n.* A colorless sugar, $C_6H_{12}O_6 \cdot H_2O$, found in animal and plant tissue and also made synthetically from starch.
dg ▸ *abbr.* decigram
dhar·ma (där′mə, dûr′-) ▸ *n. Hinduism & Buddhism* **1.** The principle or law that orders the universe. **2.** Individual conduct in conformity with this principle.
Dhu′l-Hij·jah (do͞ol-hĭj′ä) ▸ *n.* The 12th month of the Muslim calendar.
Dhu′l-Qa·'dah (do͞ol-kä′dä) ▸ *n.* The 11th month of the Muslim calendar.
di– ▸ *pref.* **1.** Two; twice; double: *digraph.* **2.** Containing two atoms, radicals, or groups: *dioxide.*
di·a·be·tes (dī′ə-bē′tĭs, -tēz) ▸ *n.* Any of several metabolic disorders marked by excessive discharge of urine and persistent thirst, esp. diabetes mellitus. **—di′a·bet′ic** (-bĕt′ĭk) *adj. & n.*
diabetes mel·li·tus (mə-lī′təs, mĕl′ĭ-) ▸ *n.* A chronic disease of pancreatic origin marked by insulin deficiency that results in excess sugar in the blood and urine.
di·a·bol·i·cal (dī′ə-bŏl′ĭ-kəl) also **di·a·bol·ic** (-ĭk) ▸ *adj.* Fiendish; wicked. **—di′a·bol′i·cal·ly** *adv.*
di·a·crit·ic (dī′ə-krĭt′ĭk) ▸ *adj.* **1.** Diacritical. **2.** *Medic.* Diagnostic or distinctive. ▸ *n.* A mark added to a letter to indicate a special phonetic value.
di·a·crit·i·cal (dī′ə-krĭt′ĭ-kəl) ▸ *adj.* **1.** Marking a distinction; distinguishing. **2.** Able to distinguish. **3.** Serving as a diacritic. **—di′a·crit′i·cal·ly** *adv.*
Dí·a de la Ra·za (dē′ä dĕ lä rä′sä) ▸ *n.* Oct. 12, celebrated in many Spanish-speaking areas to commemorate the arrival of Christopher Columbus in the New World.
di·a·dem (dī′ə-dĕm′, -dəm) ▸ *n.* **1.** A crown or headband. **2.** Royal power or dignity.
di·aer·e·sis (dī-ĕr′ĭ-sĭs) ▸ *n.* Var. of **dieresis.**
di·ag·no·sis (dī′əg-nō′sĭs) ▸ *n., pl.* **-ses** (-sēz). Identification, esp. of a disease, by examination and analysis. **—di′ag·nose′** *v.* **—di′ag·nos′tic** (-nŏs′tĭk) *adj.* **—di′ag·nos′ti·cal·ly** *adv.* **—di′ag·nos·ti′cian** (-stĭsh′ən) *n.*
di·ag·o·nal (dī-ăg′ə-nəl) ▸ *adj.* **1.** *Math.* Joining two nonadjacent vertices. **2.** Having a slanted or oblique direction. ▸ *n. Math.* A diagonal line or plane. **—di·ag′o·nal·ly** *adv.*
di·a·gram (dī′ə-grăm′) ▸ *n.* A schematic plan or drawing designed to explain how something works or to clarify the relationship between the parts of a whole. ▸ *v.* **-grammed, -gram·ming** or **-gramed, -gram·ing.** To represent by a diagram. **—di′a·gram·mat′ic** (-grə-măt′ĭk), **di′a·gram·mat′i·cal** *adj.*
di·al (dī′əl) ▸ *n.* **1.** A graduated surface or face on which a measurement, as of time, speed, or temperature, is indicated by a moving pointer. **2.** A sundial. **3.** A rotatable disk, as of a telephone, radio, or television, for making connections or changing frequency channels. ▸ *v.* **-aled, -al·ing** or **-alled, -al·ling.** **1.** To indicate or select by means of a dial. **2.** To call on a telephone.
di·a·lect (dī′ə-lĕkt′) ▸ *n.* **1.** A regional variety of a language. **2.** A language considered as part of a larger family of languages or a linguistic branch. **—di′a·lec′tal** *adj.*
di·a·lec·tic (dī′ə-lĕk′tĭk) ▸ *n.* **1.** The art or practice of arriving at the truth by the exchange of logical arguments. **2. dialectics** *(takes sing. v.)* A method of argument that weighs contradictory facts or ideas with a view to resolving real or apparent contradictions. **—di′a·lec′ti·cal, di′a·lec′tic** *adj.*
di·a·logue or **di·a·log** (dī′ə-lôg′, -lŏg′) ▸ *n.* **1.** A conversation between two or more people. **2.** Conversation between characters in a drama or narrative. **3.** An exchange of ideas or opinions.
dial-up (dī′əl-ŭp′, dīl′-) ▸ *adj.* Relating to a network connection, usu. to the Internet, made by dialing a phone number.
di·al·y·sis (dī-ăl′ĭ-sĭs) ▸ *n., pl.* **-ses** (-sēz′). The separation of smaller molecules from larger molecules or of dissolved substances from colloidal particles in a solution by selective diffusion through a semipermeable membrane.
di·a·mag·net·ic (dī′ə-măg-nĕt′ĭk) ▸ *adj.* Of or relating to a substance that is repelled by a magnet. **—di′a·mag′ne·tism** *n.*
di·am·e·ter (dī-ăm′ĭ-tər) ▸ *n.* **1a.** A straight line segment passing through the center of a figure, esp. of a circle or sphere. **b.** The length of such a segment. **2.** Thickness or width.
di·a·met·ri·cal (dī′ə-mĕt′rĭ-kəl) also **di·a·met·ric** (-rĭk) ▸ *adj.* **1.** Of or along a diameter. **2.** Exactly opposite; contrary. **—di′a·met′ri·cal·ly** *adv.*
di·a·mond (dī′ə-mənd, dī′mənd) ▸ *n.* **1.** An extremely hard, highly refractive crystalline form of carbon, usu. colorless, used as a gemstone when pure and chiefly in abrasives and cutting tools otherwise. **2.** A rhombus or lozenge. **3.** Any of a suit of playing cards marked with a red, diamond-shaped symbol. **4.** *Baseball* **a.** An infield. **b.** The whole playing field.
di·a·mond·back rattlesnake (dī′ə-mənd-băk′, dī′mənd-) ▸ *n.* A large venomous rattlesnake of SW North America.
Diamond Head ▸ A promontory, 232.1 m (761 ft), on the SE coast of Oahu, HI.
Di·an·a (dī-ăn′ə) ▸ *n. Rom. Myth.* The goddess of chastity, hunting, and the moon.
di·a·pa·son (dī′ə-pā′zən, -sən) ▸ *n. Mus.* **1.** The entire range of an instrument or voice. **2.** Either of the two principal stops on a pipe organ that form the tonal basis for the entire scale of the instrument.
di·a·per (dī′ə-pər, dī′pər) ▸ *n.* A piece of absorbent material, such as paper or cloth, that is placed between a baby's legs and fastened at the waist to serve as underpants. ▸ *v.* To put a diaper on.
di·aph·a·nous (dī-ăf′ə-nəs) ▸ *adj.* **1.** Of such fine texture as to be transparent or translucent. **2.** Vague or insubstantial. **—di·aph′a·nous·ly** *adv.*
di·a·pho·re·sis (dī′ə-fə-rē′sĭs, dī-ăf′ə-) ▸ *n.* Copious perspiration, esp. when medically induced.
di·a·phragm (dī′ə-frăm′) ▸ *n.* **1.** A muscular membranous partition separating the abdominal and thoracic cavities and functioning in respiration. **2.** A similar membranous part that divides or separates. **3.** A thin disk, esp. in a microphone or telephone receiver, that vibrates in response to sound waves to produce electric signals, or vice versa. **4.** A contraceptive device consisting of a flexible disk that covers the uterine cervix. **5.** A disk used to restrict the amount of light that passes through a lens or optical system. **—di′a·phrag·mat′ic** (-frăg-măt′ĭk) *adj.*

THESAURUS

dexterity *n.* Skillfulness in the use of the hands or body ▸ adroitness, cleverness, deftness, dexterousness, facility, grace, nimbleness, prowess, quickness, skill, sleight. [*Compare* AGILITY.]
dexterous *adj.* Exhibiting or possessing skill and ease in performance ▸ adroit, agile, artful, clean, clever, deft, facile, handy, neat, nimble, skillful, slick. [*Compare* ABLE, ENERGETIC, EXPERT, FLUENT.]
diablerie *n.* —*See* CRIME (2), MISCHIEF.
diabolic or **diabolical** *adj.* —*See* FIENDISH.
diagnosis *n.* —*See* EXAMINATION (2).
diagonal *adj.* —*See* OBLIQUE.
diagram *n.* —*See* DRAFT (1).
diagram *v.* —*See* DRAFT (1).
dial *n.* The outer surface of an instrument on which a measurement is indicated by a moving pointer ▸ face, gauge, indicator.
dial *v.* —*See* TELEPHONE.
dialect *n.* A variety of a language that differs from the standard form ▸ argot, cant, jargon, lingo, patois, vernacular. —*See also* LANGUAGE (1), LANGUAGE (2).
dialogist *n.* —*See* CONVERSATIONALIST.
dialogue or **dialog** *n.* —*See* CONVERSATION, DISCOURSE, SCRIPT (2).
diametric or **diametrical** *adj.* —*See* OPPOSITE.
diamond *n.* A small sparkling decoration ▸ glitter, rhinestone, sequin, spangle.
diaphanous *adj.* —*See* SHEER[2].

di·ar·rhe·a also **di·ar·rhoe·a** (dī′ə-rē′ə) ▸ *n.* Excessively frequent bowel movements, usu. indicating gastrointestinal disorder.

di·a·ry (dī′ə-rē) ▸ *n., pl.* **-ries**. 1. A daily record, esp. of personal experiences and observations; journal. 2. A book for keeping such a record. **—di′a·rist** *n.*

di·as·to·le (dī-ăs′tə-lē) ▸ *n.* The normal rhythmically occurring relaxation and dilatation of the heart chambers, esp. the ventricles, during which they fill with blood. **—di′as·tol′ic** (dī′ə-stŏl′ĭk) *adj.*

di·a·ther·my (dī′ə-thûr′mē) ▸ *n.* The therapeutic generation of local heat in body tissues by high-frequency electromagnetic currents. **—di′a·ther′mic** *adj.*

di·a·tom (dī′ə-tŏm′) ▸ *n.* Any of a class of microscopic one-celled algae having cell walls of silica consisting of two interlocking valves.

di·a·tom·ic (dī′ə-tŏm′ĭk) ▸ *adj.* Made up of two atoms: *a diatomic molecule.*

di·a·ton·ic (dī′ə-tŏn′ĭk) ▸ *adj. Mus.* Of or using the seven tones of a standard scale. **—di′a·ton′i·cal·ly** *adv.* **—di′a·ton′i·cism** (-ĭ-sĭz′əm) *n.*

di·a·tribe (dī′ə-trīb′) ▸ *n.* A bitter, abusive denunciation.

di·az·e·pam (dī-ăz′ə-păm′) ▸ *n.* An antianxiety drug.

dib·ble (dĭb′əl) ▸ *n.* A pointed implement used to make holes in soil, esp. for planting bulbs. **—dib′ble** *v.*

dibs (dĭbz) ▸ *pl.n. Slang* A claim; rights.

dice (dīs) ▸ *n.* 1. *Games* Pl. of **die**[2] 2. 2. *pl.* **dice** also **dic·es**. A small cube, as of food. ▸ *v.* **diced, dic·ing**. 1. *Games* To play or gamble with dice. 2. To cut into small cubes.

dic·er (dī′sər) ▸ *n.* A device used for dicing food.

dic·ey (dī′sē) ▸ *adj.* **-i·er, -i·est**. Involving or full of danger or risk.

di·chot·o·my (dī-kŏt′ə-mē) ▸ *n., pl.* **-mies**. Division into two usu. contradictory parts, categories, or opinions. **—di·chot′o·mous** *adj.*

dick (dĭk) ▸ *n. Slang* A detective.

dick·ens (dĭk′ənz) ▸ *n. Informal* 1. A severe reprimand. Used with *the.* 2. Used as an intensive: *What in the dickens is that?*

Dickens, Charles John Huffam (1812–70) ▸ British writer. **—Dick·en′si·an** (dĭ-kĕn′zē-ən) *adj.*

dick·er (dĭk′ər) ▸ *v.* To bargain; barter.

dick·ey also **dick·ie** or **dick·y** (dĭk′ē) ▸ *n., pl.* **-eys** also **-ies**. 1a. A woman's blouse front worn under a jacket or low-necked garment. b. A man's detachable shirt front. 2. A small bird.

Dick·in·son (dĭk′ĭn-sən), **Emily Elizabeth** (1830–86) ▸ Amer. poet.

di·cot·y·le·don (dī′kŏt′l-ēd′n) also **di·cot** (dī′kŏt′) ▸ *n.* A plant with two embryonic seed leaves that usu. appear at germination. **—di′cot′y·le′don·ous** *adj.*

dic·tate (dĭk′tāt′, dĭk-tāt′) ▸ *v.* **-tat·ed, -tat·ing**. 1. To say or read aloud for transcription. 2. To prescribe or command with authority. ▸ *n.* (dĭk′tāt′) 1. A directive; command. 2. A guiding principle: *the dictates of conscience.* **—dic·ta′tion** *n.*

dic·ta·tor (dĭk′tā′tər, dĭk-tā′-) ▸ *n.* 1. A ruler having absolute power, esp. a tyrant. 2. One who dictates. **—dic·ta′tor·ship** *n.*

dic·ta·to·ri·al (dĭk′tə-tôr′ē-əl) ▸ *adj.* 1. Domineering. 2. Relating to or characteristic of a dictator or dictatorship; autocratic. **—dic′ta·to′ri·al·ly** *adv.*

dic·tion (dĭk′shən) ▸ *n.* 1. Choice and use of words in speech or writing. 2. Clarity and distinctness of pronunciation.

dic·tion·ar·y (dĭk′shə-nĕr′ē) ▸ *n., pl.* **-ies**. A reference book containing an alphabetical list of words, with information given for each word, usu. including meaning, pronunciation, and etymology, or equivalent translations into another language.

dic·tum (dĭk′təm) ▸ *n., pl.* **-ta** (-tə) or **-tums**. 1. An authoritative, often formal pronouncement. 2. *Law* See **obiter dictum** 1.

did (dĭd) ▸ *v.* P.t. of **do**[1].

di·dac·tic (dī-dăk′tĭk) also **di·dac·ti·cal** (-tĭ-kəl) ▸ *adj.* 1. Intended to instruct. 2. Morally instructive. **—di·dac′ti·cal·ly** *adv.*

did·dle[1] (dĭd′l) ▸ *v.* **-dled, -dling**. *Slang* To cheat or swindle. **—did′dler** *n.*

did·dle[2] (dĭd′l) ▸ *v.* 1. To toy or fiddle: *diddling with the controls.* 2. To waste time: *diddled around all day.*

did·n't (dĭd′nt) ▸ Did not.

didst (dĭdst) ▸ *v. Archaic* 2nd pers. sing. p.t. of **do**[1].

die[1] (dī) ▸ *v.* **died, dy·ing** (dī′ĭng). 1. To cease living; become dead; expire. 2. To cease existing, esp. by degrees. 3. *Informal* To desire greatly. 4. To lose force or vitality; cease operation. ***—phrasal verb:* die out** To become extinct: *customs that died out centuries ago.*

die[2] (dī) ▸ *n.* 1. *pl.* **dies**. A device used for cutting out, forming, punching, or stamping materials. 2. *pl.* **dice** (dīs). A small cube marked on each side with from one to six dots, usu. used in pairs in gambling and in various other games. ***—idiom:* no dice** No. Used as a refusal to a request.

die-hard also **die·hard** (dī′härd′) ▸ *adj.* Stubbornly resisting change or clinging to a cause. **—die′-hard′** *n.*

di·e·lec·tric (dī′ĭ-lĕk′trĭk) ▸ *n.* A nonconductor of electricity. **—di′e·lec′tric** *adj.*

di·er·e·sis or **di·aer·e·sis** (dī-ĕr′ĭ-sĭs) ▸ *n., pl.* **-ses** (-sēz′). A mark (¨) placed over the second of two adjacent vowels to indicate that they are to be pronounced as separate sounds rather than a diphthong.

die·sel (dē′zəl, -səl) ▸ *n.* A vehicle powered by a diesel engine.

diesel engine ▸ *n.* An internal-combustion engine that uses the heat of highly compressed air to ignite a spray of fuel introduced after the start of the compression stroke.

di·et[1] (dī′ĭt) ▸ *n.* 1. One's usual food and drink. 2. A

THESAURUS

diary *n.* —*See* MEMOIR.

diaspora *n.* —*See* EMIGRATION.

diatribe *n.* —*See* TIRADE.

dibs *n.* —*See* CLAIM (1).

dice *v.* —*See* CUT (2).

dicey *adj.* —*See* DANGEROUS.

dick *n.* —*See* DETECTIVE.

dicker *v.* —*See* HAGGLE.

dictate *v.* To set forth expressly and authoritatively ▸ decree, determine, direct, fix, impose, lay down, mandate, ordain, prescribe, rule. ***Idioms:*** call the shots (*or* tune), lay down the law, lay it on the line. [*Compare* STIPULATE.] —*See also* ADMINISTER (1), BOSS, COMMAND (1).

dictate *n.* —*See* COMMAND (1), RULE.

dictated *adj.* —*See* REQUIRED.

dictation *n.* —*See* COMMAND (1).

dictator *n.* An absolute ruler, especially one who is harsh and oppressive ▸ autarchist, authoritarian, autocrat, Big Brother, despot, führer, man on horseback, oligarch, oppressor, strongman, totalitarian, tyrant, usurper. —*See also* AUTHORITARIAN.

dictatorial *adj.* Given to asserting one's will or authority over others ▸ authoritarian, bossy, dogmatic, domineering, imperious, inquisitorial, magisterial, masterful, megalomaniacal, overassertive, overbearing, overweening, peremptory. [*Compare* AGGRESSIVE, DOMINANT, SEVERE.] —*See also* ABSOLUTE, AUTHORITARIAN.

dictatorship *n.* —*See* ABSOLUTISM (1), ABSOLUTISM (2), TYRANNY.

diction *n.* —*See* WORDING.

dictionary *n.* An alphabetical list of words often defined or translated ▸ glossary, lexicon, vocabulary, wordbook.

dictum *n.* —*See* MESSAGE, RULING.

didactic or **didactical** *adj.* Inclined to teach or moralize excessively ▸ academic, expositive, expository, didactical, moralizing, preachy, prescriptive. [*Compare* INSTRUCTIVE, PEDANTIC.] —*See also* MORAL.

diddle[1] *v.* —*See* CHEAT (1).

diddle[2] *v.* —*See* IDLE (1).

diddler *n.* —*See* CHEAT (2).

die *v.* To cease living ▸ decease, demise, depart, drop, expire, go, pass away, pass (on), perish, succumb. *Informal:* pop off. *Slang:* check out, croak, kick in, kick off. ***Idioms:*** bite the dust, breathe one's last, buy the farm, cash in, give up the ghost, go to one's grave, kick the bucket, meet one's end (*or* Maker), pass on to the Great Beyond, turn up one's toes. —*See also* DISAPPEAR (2), FADE AWAY, SUBSIDE.

die for *v.* —*See* DESIRE.

die-hard *adj.* —*See* STUBBORN (1), ULTRACONSERVATIVE.

die-hard *n.* —*See* ULTRACONSERVATIVE.

die-hardism *n.* —*See* STUBBORNNESS.

diet *n.* —*See* FOOD.

regulated selection of foods, esp. as for medical reasons or cosmetic weight loss. ► *v.* To eat and drink according to a regulated or prescribed system. **—di′e·tar′y** *adj.* **—di′et·er** *n.*

di·et² (dī′ĭt) ► *n.* A legislative assembly.

di·e·tet·ic (dī′ĭ-tĕt′ĭk) ► *adj.* Specially prepared or processed for restrictive diets.

di·e·tet·ics (dī′ĭ-tĕt′ĭks) ► *n.* *(takes sing. v.)* The study of diet and nutrition.

di·e·ti·tian or **di·e·ti·cian** (dī′ĭ-tĭsh′ən) ► *n.* A person specializing in dietetics.

dif·fer (dĭf′ər) ► *v.* **1.** To be unlike. **2.** To disagree with something or have a different opinion.

dif·fer·ence (dĭf′ər-əns, dĭf′rəns) ► *n.* **1.** The fact, condition, or degree of being unlike. **2a.** A disagreement, controversy, or quarrel. **b.** A cause of disagreement. **3.** *Math.* **a.** The amount by which one quantity is greater or less than another. **b.** A remainder.

dif·fer·ent (dĭf′ər-ənt, dĭf′rənt) ► *adj.* **1.** Unlike or dissimilar. **2.** Distinct or separate. **3.** Unusual or distinctive. **—dif′fer·ent·ly** *adv.* **—dif′fer·ent·ness** *n.*

dif·fer·en·tial (dĭf′ə-rĕn′shəl) ► *adj.* Of, showing, or constituting a difference. ► *n.* **1.** An amount or degree of difference between similar kinds or individuals: *a wage differential.* **2.** A differential gear.

differential gear ► *n.* An arrangement of gears that permits one turning shaft to drive two others at different speeds.

dif·fer·en·ti·ate (dĭf′ə-rĕn′shē-āt′) ► *v.* **-at·ed, -at·ing. 1.** To constitute or perceive a distinction. **2.** To make or become different, distinct, or specialized. **—dif′fer·en′ti·a′tion** *n.*

dif·fi·cult (dĭf′ĭ-kŭlt′, -kəlt) ► *adj.* **1.** Hard to do, accomplish, or comprehend; arduous. **2.** Hard to please, satisfy, or manage. **—dif′fi·cult′ly** *adv.*

dif·fi·cul·ty (dĭf′ĭ-kŭl′tē, -kəl-) ► *n., pl.* **-ties. 1.** The condition or quality of being difficult. **2.** often **difficulties a.** A troublesome or embarrassing state of affairs: *in financial difficulty.* **b.** Problems or conflicts: *emotional difficulties.* **3.** Great effort; trouble.

dif·fi·dent (dĭf′ĭ-dənt, -dĕnt′) ► *adj.* Lacking self-confidence; timid. **—dif′fi·dence** *n.*

dif·frac·tion (dĭ-frăk′shən) ► *n.* Change in the directions and intensities of light or other radiation after passing by an obstacle or through an aperture.

dif·fuse (dĭ-fyo͞oz′) ► *v.* **-fused, -fus·ing.** To pour or spread out and disperse. ► *adj.* (dĭ-fyo͞os′) **1.** Widely spread or scattered. **2.** Verbose; wordy. **—dif·fuse′ly** (-fyo͞os′lē) *adv.* **—dif·fu′sion** *n.*

dig (dĭg) ► *v.* **dug** (dŭg), **dig·ging. 1.** To break up, turn over, or remove (e.g., earth or sand) with a tool or the hands. **2.** To make (an excavation) by or as if by digging. **3.** To learn or discover: *dug up the evidence.* **4.** To thrust against; poke or prod: *dug me in the ribs.* **5.** *Slang* To understand, take notice of, or enjoy. ***—phrasal verb:* dig in 1.** To begin to work intensively. **2.** To begin to eat heartily. ► *n.* **1.** A poke or thrust. **2.** A sarcastic remark; gibe. **3.** An archaeological excavation. **—dig′ger** *n.*

dig·er·a·ti (dĭj′ə-rä′tē) ► *pl.n.* People knowledgeable about digital technologies.

di·gest (dī-jĕst′, dĭ-) ► *v.* **1.** To convert (food) into a form that can easily be absorbed and assimilated by the body. **2.** To absorb mentally; comprehend. **3.** To organize into a systematic arrangement. ► *n.* (dī′jĕst′) A collection of written material in condensed form. **—di·gest′i·ble** *adj.* **—di·ges′tion** *n.* **—di·ges′tive** *adj.*

digestive system ► *n.* The alimentary canal along with the glands, such as the liver, salivary glands, and pancreas, that produce substances needed in digestion.

dig·it (dĭj′ĭt) ► *n.* **1.** A finger or toe. **2.** One of the ten Arabic number symbols, 0 through 9.

dig·i·tal (dĭj′ĭ-tl) ► *adj.* **1.** Of a digit. **2.** Expressed as or giving a readout in digits: *a digital clock.* **3.** *Comp. Sci.* **a.** Relating to a device that can read, write, or store data in numerical form. **b.** Capable of being read by a computer. **—dig′i·tal·ly** *adv.*

digital computer ► *n.* A computer that performs calculations and logical operations with quantities represented as digits, usu. in the binary number system.

dig·i·tal·is (dĭj′ĭ-tăl′ĭs) ► *n.* A drug prepared from the seeds and dried leaves of the foxglove, used in medicine as a cardiac stimulant.

dig·ni·fy (dĭg′nə-fī′) ► *v.* **-fied, -fy·ing.** To give dignity or honor to.

dig·ni·tar·y (dĭg′nĭ-tĕr′ē) ► *n., pl.* **-ies.** A person of high rank or position.

dig·ni·ty (dĭg′nĭ-tē) ► *n., pl.* **-ties. 1.** The quality or state of being worthy of esteem or respect. **2.** Nobility of character, manner, or language. **3.** A high office or rank.

di·graph (dī′grăf′) ► *n.* A pair of letters representing a single speech sound.

di·gress (dī-grĕs′, dĭ-) ► *v.* To stray, esp. from the main

THESAURUS

differ *v.* To be unlike or dissimilar ► contrast, depart, deviate, disagree, diverge, vary. ***Idiom:*** be at variance. *—See also* CONFLICT.

difference *n.* The condition of being unlike or dissimilar ► contrast, departure, disagreement, discrepancy, disparity, dissimilarity, dissimilitude, distinction, divarication, divergence, divergency, nonconformity, separateness, unlikeness, variance, variation. [*Compare* ABNORMALITY, INEQUALITY.] *—See also* CONFLICT, GAP (3).

different *adj.* Not like another in nature, quality, amount, or form ► contrary, contrasting, disparate, dissimilar, distinct, divergent, diverse, separate, unlike, variant, various. *—See also* NEW.

differentiate *v.* *—See* DISTINGUISH (1), DISTINGUISH (2).

differentiation *n.* *—See* DISTINCTION (1).

difficult *adj.* **1.** Not easy to do, achieve, or master ► arduous, challenging, complicated, demanding, effortful, exacting, exigent, hard, laborious, serious, tall, tough, uphill. [*Compare* BURDENSOME.] **2.** Causing difficulty, trouble, or discomfort ► incommodious, inconvenient, troublesome. [*Compare* DISTURBING.] *—See also* COMPLEX (1), CONTRARY, DEEP (2), DELICATE (3), TROUBLESOME (2).

difficultly *adv.* *—See* HARD (2).

difficulty *n.* Something that obstructs progress and requires great effort to overcome ► asperity, complication, hardship, impediment, obstacle, obstruction, plight, problem, rigor, stumbling block, trial, trouble, vicissitude. ***Idioms:*** a hard (*or* tough) nut to crack, a hard (*or* tough) row to hoe, heavy sledding. [*Compare* BAR, DISTRESS.] *—See also* ARGUMENT, CONFLICT, PREDICAMENT.

diffidence *n.* *—See* SHYNESS.

diffident *adj.* *—See* SHY¹.

diffuse *v.* *—See* SPREAD (1).

diffuse *adj.* *—See* DIGRESSIVE, WORDY (1).

diffuseness *n.* *—See* WORDINESS.

diffusion *n.* *—See* DISTRIBUTION (2), WORDINESS.

dig *v.* To break, turn over, or remove (earth or sand, for example) with or as if with a tool ► bore, burrow, delve, excavate, gouge, grub, scoop, shovel, spade. *—See also* ENJOY, EXPLORE, PLUNGE, PUSH (1), TILL, UNCOVER, UNDERSTAND (1).

dig out or **up** *v.* *—See* DISCOVER.

dig *n.* An act of thrusting into or against, as to attract attention ► jab, jog, nudge, poke, prod, punch, stab. [*Compare* PUSH.] *—See also* CRACK (3), TAUNT.

digest *v.* *—See* ABSORB (2).

digest *n.* *—See* SYNOPSIS.

digestion *n.* *—See* ABSORPTION (1).

dignification *n.* *—See* EXALTATION.

dignified *adj.* *—See* CEREMONIOUS, SERIOUS (1).

dignify *v.* To lend dignity or honor to by an act or favor ► enrich, favor, grace, honor. [*Compare* HONOR.] *—See also* DISTINGUISH (3), EXALT.

dignitary *n.* An important, influential person ► character, eminence, leader, lion, luminary, magnate, nabob, notability, notable, personage, worthy. *Informal:* bigfoot, big name, big-timer, heavyweight, high-up, somebody, someone, VIP. *Slang:* big gun, big shot, big wheel, bigwig, muckamuck.

dignity *n.* *—See* ELEGANCE, HONOR (2), SERIOUSNESS (1).

digress *v.* To turn aside, especially from the main subject in writing or speaking ► deviate, divagate, diverge, drift, maunder, ramble, stray, veer,

subject in writing or speaking. **—di·gres′sion** *n.* **—di·gres′sive** *adj.* **—di·gres′sive·ly** *adv.*

dike (dīk) ► *n.* **1.** A wall or embankment of earth and rock built to hold back water and prevent floods. **2.** A ditch or channel.

di·lap·i·dat·ed (dĭ-lăp′ĭ-dā′tĭd) ► *adj.* In a state of disrepair, deterioration, or ruin. **—di·lap′i·da′tion** *n.*

dil·a·ta·tion (dĭl′ə-tā′shən, dī′lə-) ► *n.* **1.** The process of expanding; dilation. **2.** The condition of being expanded.

di·late (dī-lāt′, dī′lāt′) ► *v.* **-lat·ed, -lat·ing.** To make or become wider or larger; expand. **—di·lat′a·ble** *adj.* **—di·la′tion** *n.* **—di·la′tor** *n.*

dilation and curettage also **dilatation and curettage** ► *n.* A surgical procedure performed for the diagnosis and treatment of various uterine conditions.

dil·a·to·ry (dĭl′ə-tôr′ē) ► *adj.* Tending to delay. **—dil′a·to′ri·ly** *adv.*

di·lem·ma (dĭ-lĕm′ə) ► *n.* A situation that requires a choice between options, usu. equally unfavorable or mutually exclusive.

dil·et·tante (dĭl′ĭ-tänt′, dĭl′ĭ-tänt′, -tän′tē) ► *n., pl.* **-tantes** also **-tan·ti** (-tän′tē, -tăn′-). A dabbler in an art or a field of knowledge. **—dil′et·tan′tism** *n.*

dil·i·gent (dĭl′ə-jənt) ► *adj.* Marked by or done with persevering, painstaking effort and care. **—dil′i·gence** *n.* **—dil′i·gent·ly** *adv.*

dill (dĭl) ► *n.* An herb having aromatic leaves and seeds used as seasoning.

dil·ly (dĭl′ē) ► *n., pl.* **-lies.** *Slang* One that is remarkable, as in size.

dil·ly-dal·ly (dĭl′ē-dăl′ē) ► *v.* **-lied, -lying.** To waste time, esp. in indecision; dawdle or vacillate.

dil·u·ent (dĭl′yo͞o-ənt) ► *n. Chem.* An inert substance used to dilute. **—dil′u·ent** *adj.*

di·lute (dī-lo͞ot′, dĭ-) ► *v.* **-lut·ed, -lut·ing.** To make thinner or weaker, as by adding a liquid such as water. ► *adj.* Weakened; diluted. **—di·lu′tion** *n.*

dim (dĭm) ► *adj.* **dim·mer, dim·mest. 1.** Faintly lighted. **2.** Lacking luster; dull. **3.** Obscure or indistinct; faint. **4.** Lacking sharpness or clarity in sight or understanding. **5.** Negative, unfavorable, or disapproving. ► *v.* **dimmed, dim·ming. 1.** To make or become dim. **2.** To put on low beam: *dimmed the headlights.* ► *n.* Low beam. **—dim′ly** *adv.* **—dim′ness** *n.*

dime (dīm) ► *n.* A US or Canadian coin worth ten cents.

di·men·sion (dĭ-mĕn′shən, dī-) ► *n.* **1.** A measure of spatial extent, esp. width, height, or length. **2.** often **dimensions** Extent or magnitude; scope. **3.** *Math.* One of the least number of independent coordinates required to specify uniquely a point in space. **4.** *Phys.* A physical property, such as mass, length, or time, regarded as a fundamental measure. **—di·men′sion·al** *adj.* **—di·men′sion·al′i·ty** (-shə-năl′ĭ-tē) *n.* **—di·men′sion·al·ly** *adv.*

dime store ► *n.* See **five-and-ten.**

di·min·ish (dĭ-mĭn′ĭsh) ► *v.* **1.** To make or become smaller or less important. **2.** To taper. **—di·min′ish·a·ble** *adj.*

di·min·u·en·do (dĭ-mĭn′yo͞o-ĕn′dō) ► *n. & adv. & adj. Mus.* Decrescendo.

dim·i·nu·tion (dĭm′ə-no͞o′shən, -nyo͞o′-) ► *n.* The act, process, or result of diminishing.

di·min·u·tive (dĭ-mĭn′yə-tĭv) ► *adj.* **1.** Extremely small in size; tiny. **2.** Of or being a suffix that indicates smallness or affection, as *-let* in *booklet.* ► *n.* A diminutive suffix, word, or name.

dim·i·ty (dĭm′ĭ-tē) ► *n., pl.* **-ties.** A sheer crisp cotton fabric with raised woven stripes or checks.

dim·mer (dĭm′ər) ► *n.* A device used to vary the brightness of an electric light.

dim·ple (dĭm′pəl) ► *n.* **1.** A small natural indentation in the flesh on a part of the human body, esp. in the cheek or chin. **2.** A slight depression in a surface. ► *v.* **-pled, -pling.** To form dimples, as by smiling.

dim sum (dĭm′ so͝om′) ► *n.* Small portions of a variety of traditional Chinese foods, including steamed or fried dumplings, served in succession.

dim·wit (dĭm′wĭt′) ► *n. Slang* A stupid person. **—dim′wit′ted** *adj.*

din (dĭn) ► *n.* A jumble of loud, usu. discordant sounds. ► *v.* **dinned, din·ning. 1.** To instill by wearying repetition. **2.** To stun with or make a din.

di·nar (dĭ-när′, dē′när′) ► *n.* See **currency** table in Appendix.

dine (dīn) ► *v.* **dined, din·ing. 1.** To have dinner. **2.** To give dinner to.

din·er (dī′nər) ► *n.* **1.** One that dines. **2.** A railroad dining car. **3.** A restaurant shaped like a dining car.

di·nette (dī-nĕt′) ► *n.* A nook or alcove used for informal meals.

ding[1] (dĭng) ► *v.* To ring or cause to ring; clang. ► *n.* A ringing sound.

ding[2] (dĭng) ► *n. Informal* A small dent or nick, as in the body of a car. **—ding** *v.*

din·ghy (dĭng′ē) ► *n., pl.* **-ghies.** A small open boat, esp. a rowboat.

din·go (dĭng′gō) ► *n., pl.* **-goes.** A wild dog of Australia, having a reddish-brown or yellow coat.

din·gus (dĭng′əs) ► *n. Slang* An article whose name is unknown or forgotten.

din·gy (dĭn′jē) ► *adj.* **-gi·er, -gi·est. 1.** Dirty, soiled, or grimy. **2.** Shabby, drab, or squalid. **—din′gi·ly** *adv.* **—din′gi·ness** *n.*

din·ky (dĭng′kē) ► *adj.* **-ki·er, -ki·est.** *Informal* Of small size or consequence; insignificant.

din·ner (dĭn′ər) ► *n.* **1.** The main meal of the day. **2.** A formal banquet.

dinner jacket ► *n.* See **tuxedo.**

di·no·saur (dī′nə-sôr′) ► *n.* Any of various extinct, often gigantic, carnivorous or herbivorous reptiles of the Mesozoic Era.

dint (dĭnt) ► *n.* **1.** Force or effort: *succeeded by dint of hard work.* **2.** A dent.

THESAURUS

wander. *Idioms:* go off at (*or* on) a tangent, go off the subject. *—See also* DEVIATE.

digression *n.* An instance of digressing ► aside, departure, deviation, divagation, divergence, divergency, diversion, excursion, excursus, irrelevancy, parenthesis, rambling, straying, tangent, wandering.

digressive *adj.* Marked by or given to digression ► diffuse, discursive, excursive, long-winded, meandering, parenthetic, parenthetical, rambling, tangential.

digs *n.* *—See* HOME (1).

dilapidated *adj.* *—See* SHABBY.

dilate *v.* *—See* BROADEN, ELABORATE.

dilatory *adj.* *—See* SLOW (1).

dilemma *n.* *—See* PREDICAMENT.

dilettante *n.* *—See* AMATEUR.

dilettantish *adj.* *—See* AMATEURISH.

diligence *n.* Steady attention and effort, as to one's occupation ► application, assiduity, assiduousness, conscientiousness, industriousness, industry, perseverance, persistence, pertinacity, sedulousness, studiousness. *Informal:* stick-to-itiveness.

diligent *adj.* Characterized by steady attention and effort ► assiduous, conscientious, dogged, industrious, painstaking, persistent, pertinacious, sedulous, studious, unflagging, unremitting.

dilly-dallier *n.* *—See* LAGGARD.

dilly-dally *v.* To shift from one attitude, interest, condition, or emotion to another ► swing, vacillate, waver. *—See also* DELAY (2), HESITATE.

dilute *v.* To lessen the strength of by or as if by admixture ► adulterate, attenuate, cut, thin, water (down), weaken.

dilute *adj.* Lower than normal in strength or concentration due to admixture ► adulterated, cut, thin, washy, watered-down, waterish, watery, weak.

dim *adj.* *—See* BACKWARD (1), BLEAK (2), DARK (1), DULL (2), PALE (2), UNCLEAR.

dim *v.* *—See* DRUG (2), OBSCURE.

dimensions *n.* *—See* SIZE (1).

diminish *v.* *—See* DECREASE, SUBSIDE.

diminishment *n.* *—See* DECREASE, WANING.

diminution *n.* *—See* DECREASE.

diminutive *adj.* *—See* TINY.

dimness *n.* *—See* DARK.

dimwit *n.* *—See* DULLARD.

dimwitted *adj.* *—See* BACKWARD (1), STUPID.

din *n.* *—See* NOISE (1).

ding *v.* *—See* BANG (1), RING[2].

ding-a-ling *n.* *—See* CRACKPOT.

ding-dong *n.* *—See* FOOL.

dingy *adj.* *—See* DIRTY, SHABBY.

dint *n.* *—See* IMPRESSION (1).

di·o·cese (dī′ə-sĭs, -sēs′, -sēz′) ► *n.* The district or churches under the jurisdiction of a bishop; bishopric. **—di·oc′e·san** (dī-ŏs′ə-sən) *adj.*

di·ode (dī′ōd′) ► *n.* A two-terminal semiconductor device, esp. one that restricts current flow chiefly to one direction.

Di·og·e·nes (dī-ŏj′ə-nēz′) (d. c. 320 B.C.) ► Greek philosopher.

Di·o·nys·i·an (dī′ə-nĭsh′ən, -nĭzh′ən, -nĭs′ē-ən) ► *adj.* **1.** *Gk. Myth.* Of or relating to Dionysus. **2.** often **dionysian** Of an orgiastic or irrational nature.

Di·o·ny·sus (dī′ə-nī′səs, -nē′-) ► *n. Gk. & Rom. Myth.* The god of wine, drama, and of an orgiastic religion celebrating the power and fertility of nature.

di·o·ram·a (dī′ə-răm′ə, -rä′mə) ► *n.* A three-dimensional scene with modeled figures against a painted background.

di·ox·ide (dī-ŏk′sīd) ► *n.* A compound with two oxygen atoms per molecule.

di·ox·in (dī-ŏk′sĭn) ► *n.* Any of several carcinogenic or teratogenic hydrocarbons that occur as impurities in petroleum-derived herbicides.

dip (dĭp) ► *v.* **dipped, dip·ping. 1.** To plunge briefly into a liquid. **2.** To immerse (an animal) in a disinfectant solution. **3.** To scoop up (liquid). **4.** To lower and raise (a flag) in salute. **5.** To drop or sink suddenly. **6.** To slope downward; decline. **7.** To dabble: *dip into medieval history.* ► *n.* **1.** A brief plunge or immersion, esp. a quick swim. **2.** A liquid into which something is dipped. **3.** A savory creamy mixture into which crackers or other foods may be dipped. **4.** An amount taken up by dipping. **5.** A downward slope. **6.** A decline: *a dip in prices.* **7.** A hollow or depression. **8.** *Slang* A foolish or stupid person.

diph·the·ri·a (dĭf-thîr′ē-ə, dĭp-) ► *n.* An acute infectious bacterial disease marked by high fever, weakness, and the formation of a false membrane in the throat and other respiratory passages, causing difficulty in breathing. **—diph′the·rit′ic** (-thə-rĭt′ĭk), **diph·ther′ic** (-thĕr′ĭk), **diph·the′ri·al** *adj.*

diph·thong (dĭf′thông′, -thŏng′, dĭp′-) ► *n.* A complex speech sound that begins with one vowel and gradually changes to another vowel within the same syllable, as (oi) in *boil.*

dip·loid (dĭp′loid′) ► *adj.* Having two sets of chromosomes. **—dip′loid′** *n.*

di·plo·ma (dĭ-plō′mə) ► *n.* **1.** A document issued by an educational institution, such as a university, testifying that the recipient has earned a degree or successfully completed a course of study. **2.** A certificate conferring a privilege or honor.

di·plo·ma·cy (dĭ-plō′mə-sē) ► *n.* **1.** The art or practice of conducting international relations. **2.** Tact and skill in dealing with people.

dip·lo·mat (dĭp′lə-măt′) ► *n.* One skilled or working in diplomacy.

dip·lo·mat·ic (dĭp′lə-măt′ĭk) ► *adj.* **1.** Of or involving diplomacy or diplomats. **2.** Tactful. **—dip′lo·mat′i·cal·ly** *adv.*

di·pole (dī′pōl′) ► *n.* **1.** *Phys.* A pair of electric charges or magnetic poles, of equal magnitude but of opposite sign or polarity, separated by a small distance. **2.** *Electron.* An antenna, usu. fed from the center, consisting of two equal rods extending outward in a straight line. **—di·po′lar** *adj.*

dip·per (dĭp′ər) ► *n.* **1.** One that dips, esp. a long-handled cup for taking up water. **2.** A small bird that dives into swift streams and feeds along the bottom.

dip·so·ma·ni·a (dĭp′sə-mā′nē-ə, -mān′yə) ► *n.* An insatiable, often periodic craving for alcoholic beverages. **—dip′so·ma′ni·ac′** *adj. & n.*

dip·stick (dĭp′stĭk′) ► *n.* A graduated rod for measuring the depth of liquid.

dire (dīr) ► *adj.* **dir·er, dir·est. 1.** Warning of disaster. **2.** Urgent; desperate: *in dire poverty.* **—dire′ful** *adj.* **—dire′ful·ly** *adv.* **—dire′ly** *adv.*

di·rect (dĭ-rĕkt′, dī-) ► *v.* **1.** To conduct the affairs of; manage. **2.** To have or take charge of; control. **3.** To aim, guide, or address (something or someone). **4.** To give interpretive dramatic guidance and instruction to the actors in a play or film. **5.** To conduct (musicians) in a performance or rehearsal. ► *adj.* **1.** Proceeding in a straight course or line. **2.** Straightforward. **3.** Having no intervening persons, conditions, or agencies; immediate. **4.** By action of voters, rather than through elected delegates. **5.** Being of unbroken descent; lineal. **6.** Consisting of the exact words of the writer or speaker: *a direct quotation.* **7.** Absolute; total: *direct opposites.* **8.** *Math.* Varying in the same manner as another quantity, esp. increasing if another quantity increases or decreasing if it decreases. ► *adv.* Straight; directly. **—di·rect′ness** *n.*

direct current ► *n.* An electric current flowing in one direction only.

direct deposit ► *n.* The electronic transfer of a payment from the payer's account to that of the payee.

di·rec·tion (dĭ-rĕk′shən, dī-) ► *n.* **1.** The act or function of directing. **2.** often **directions** An instruction or series of instructions for doing or finding something. **3.** An order or command. **4a.** The distance-independent relationship between two points in space that specifies the angular position of either with respect to the other. **b.** A position to which motion or another position is referred. **c.** The line or course along which a person or thing moves. **5.** Tendency toward a particular end or goal. **—di·rec′tion·al** *adj.* **—di·rec′tion·al′i·ty** *n.*

di·rec·tive (dĭ-rĕk′tĭv, dī-) ► *n.* An order or instruction, esp. from a central authority.

di·rect·ly (dĭ-rĕkt′lē, dī-) ► *adv.* **1.** In a direct line or manner. **2.** Without anyone or anything intervening. **3.** Exactly. **4.** Instantly.

direct object ► *n.* The word or phrase in a sentence referring to the receiver of the action of a transitive verb. For example, in *The lawyer telephoned him, him* is the direct object.

di·rec·tor (dĭ-rĕk′tər, dī-) ► *n.* **1.** A manager. **2.** One of a group chosen to govern the affairs of an institution or corporation. **3.** One who supervises or guides the performers

THESAURUS

dip *v.* **1.** To plunge briefly in or into a liquid ► douse, duck, dunk, immerge, immerse, souse, submerge, submerse. [*Compare* STEEP[2], WET.] **2.** To take a substance, as liquid, from a container by plunging the hand or a utensil into it ► bail, dredge, lade, ladle, scoop (up), spoon. *—See also* DROP (2), STEAL.

dip into *v.* *—See* BROWSE (1).

dip *n.* *—See* DEPRESSION (1), DESCENT, DRIP (2), FALL (3), FOOL, PLUNGE.

diplomacy *n.* *—See* TACT.

diplomatic *adj.* *—See* DELICATE (2), GRACIOUS (2).

dippiness *n.* *—See* FOOLISHNESS.

dippy *adj.* *—See* FOOLISH.

dipsomaniac or **dipso** *n.* *—See* DRUNKARD.

dire *adj.* Having or threatening severe negative consequences ► grave, grievous, serious, severe. [*Compare* DISASTROUS.] *—See also* FATEFUL (1), FEARFUL, URGENT (1).

direct *v.* To mark a written communication with its destination ► address, superscribe. [*Compare* TICKET.] *—See also* ADMINISTER (1), ADVISE, AIM (1), APPLY (1), COMMAND (1), CONDUCT (1), DICTATE, GUIDE, STAGE.

direct *adj.* **1.** Proceeding or lying in an uninterrupted line or course ► linear, straight, straightforward, through, undeviating, unswerving. **2.** Marked by the absence of any intervention ► firsthand, immediate, primary. **3.** Of unbroken descent or lineage ► genealogical, hereditary, lineal, ancestral. [*Compare* DIRECT.] *—See also* FRANK.

direct *adv.* *—See* DIRECTLY (1), DIRECTLY (3).

direction *n.* The spatial path along which motion or orientation is referred ► course, heading, route, way. *—See also* ADVICE, COMMAND (1), GOVERNMENT (1), MANAGEMENT.

directionless *adj.* *—See* AIMLESS.

directive *n.* *—See* COMMAND (1).

directly *adv.* **1.** In a direct line ► dead, direct, due, right, straight, straightaway, undeviatingly, unswervingly. **2.** Without intermediary ► firsthand, immediately. **3.** With precision or absolute conformity ► bang, dead, direct, exactly, fair, flush, just, plumb, precisely, right, smack, spot-on, square, squarely, straight. *Slang:* smack-dab. *—See also* FLATLY, IMMEDIATELY (1).

director *n.* *—See* BOSS, CHIEF, EXECUTIVE, GUIDE.

in a play, film, or musical performance. **—di·rec′to′ri·al** (-tôr′ē-əl) *adj.* **—di·rec′tor·ship′** *n.*
di·rec·tor·ate (dĭ-rĕk′tər-ĭt, dī-) ▸ *n.* **1.** The office or position of a director. **2.** A board of directors.
di·rec·to·ry (dĭ-rĕk′tə-rē, dī-) ▸ *n., pl.* **-ries. 1.** An alphabetical or classified listing of names, addresses, and usu. telephone numbers. **2.** *Comp. Sci.* A listing of the files contained in a storage device.
dirge (dûrj) ▸ *n.* **1.** A funeral song. **2.** A slow mournful piece of music.
dir·ham (dîr′həm) ▸ *n.* See **currency** table in Appendix.
dir·i·gi·ble (dîr′ə-jə-bəl, də-rĭj′ə-bəl) ▸ *n.* See **airship.**
dirk (dûrk) ▸ *n.* A dagger.
dirn·dl (dûrn′dl) ▸ *n.* A full skirt with a gathered waistband.
dirt (dûrt) ▸ *n.* **1.** Earth or soil. **2.** A filthy or soiling substance, such as mud. **3.** One that is contemptible or vile. **4a.** Obscene language. **b.** Scandalous gossip.
dirt bike ▸ *n.* A motorbike or bicycle designed for use on rough surfaces.
dirt-cheap (dûrt′chēp′) ▸ *adv. & adj.* Very cheap.
dirt·y (dûr′tē) ▸ *adj.* **-i·er, -i·est. 1.** Soiled or grimy; unclean. **2.** Obscene or indecent. **3.** Dishonorable or unfair: *a dirty fighter.* **4.** Expressing hostility: *a dirty look.* **5.** Dull in color. **6.** Stormy: *dirty weather.* ▸ *v.* **-ied, -y·ing.** To make or become soiled. **—dirt′i·ly** *adv.* **—dirt′i·ness** *n.*
dis (dĭs) ▸ *v.* **dissed, dis·sing.** *Informal* To show disrespect to.
dis– ▸ *pref.* **1.** Not: *dissimilar.* **2a.** Absence of: *disinterest.* **b.** Opposite of: *disfavor.* **3.** Undo: *disarrange.* **4a.** Deprive of: *disfranchise.* **b.** Remove: *disbar.*
dis·a·bil·i·ty (dĭs′ə-bĭl′ĭ-tē) ▸ *n.* **1.** The condition of being disabled; incapacity. **2.** A disadvantage or deficiency, esp. a physical or mental impairment that prevents or restricts normal achievement.
dis·a·ble (dĭs-ā′bəl) ▸ *v.* **-bled, -bling.** To deprive of capability or effectiveness, esp. to impair the physical abilities of.
dis·a·bled (dĭs-ā′bəld) ▸ *adj.* **1.** Inoperative: *a disabled vehicle.* **2.** Impaired, as in physical functioning: *a disabled veteran.* ▸ *n.* Physically impaired people as a group: *the disabled.*
dis·a·buse (dĭs′ə-byo͞oz′) ▸ *v.* **-bused, -bus·ing.** To free from a falsehood or misconception.
di·sac·cha·ride (dī-săk′ə-rīd′) ▸ *n.* Any of a class of carbohydrates, including lactose and sucrose, that yield two monosaccharides upon hydrolysis.
dis·ad·van·tage (dĭs′əd-văn′tĭj) ▸ *n.* **1.** An unfavorable condition or circumstance. **2.** Damage, harm, or loss. **—dis·ad′van·ta′geous** (dĭs-ăd′vən-tā′jəs) *adj.*
dis·ad·van·taged (dĭs′əd-văn′tĭjd) ▸ *adj.* **1.** Socially or economically deprived. **2.** Being at a disadvantage. ▸ *n.* *(takes pl. v.)* Deprived people collectively: *the disadvantaged.*
dis·af·fect (dĭs′ə-fĕkt′) ▸ *v.* To cause to lose affection or loyalty. **—dis′af·fect′ed** *adj.* **—dis′af·fec′tion** *n.*
dis·a·gree (dĭs′ə-grē′) ▸ *v.* **1.** To fail to correspond. **2.** To have a differing opinion. **3.** To dispute; quarrel. **4.** To have bad effects. **—dis′a·gree′ment** *n.*
dis·a·gree·a·ble (dĭs′ə-grē′ə-bəl) ▸ *adj.* **1.** Unpleasant, distasteful, or offensive. **2.** Bad-tempered. **—dis′a·gree′a·ble·ness** *n.* **—dis′a·gree′a·bly** *adv.*
dis·al·low (dĭs′ə-lou′) ▸ *v.* To refuse to allow; reject. **—dis′al·low′ance** *n.*
dis·ap·pear (dĭs′ə-pîr′) ▸ *v.* **1.** To pass out of sight. **2.** To cease to exist. **—dis′ap·pear′ance** *n.*
dis·ap·point (dĭs′ə-point′) ▸ *v.* To fail to satisfy the hope, desire, or expectation of. **—dis′ap·point′ing·ly** *adv.* **—dis′ap·point′ment** *n.*
dis·ap·pro·ba·tion (dĭs-ăp′rə-bā′shən) ▸ *n.* Moral disapproval; condemnation.
dis·ap·prov·al (dĭs′ə-pro͞o′vəl) ▸ *n.* The act of disapproving; condemnation or censure.

THESAURUS

directorial *adj.* —*See* ADMINISTRATIVE.
directorship *n.* —*See* MANAGEMENT.
directory *n.* —*See* LIST[1].
direful *adj.* —*See* FATEFUL (1), FEARFUL.
dirt *n.* —*See* EARTH (1), FILTH, OBSCENITY (2).
dirt-cheap *adj.* —*See* CHEAP.
dirtiness *n.* The condition or state of being dirty ▸ filth, filthiness, foulness, griminess, grubbiness, muckiness, nastiness, smuttiness, squalor, uncleanliness, uncleanness. —*See also* CONTAMINATION, OBSCENITY (1).
dirty *adj.* Covered with or stained by dirt or other impurities ▸ black, dingy, filthy, foul, grimy, grubby, miry, muddy, nasty, smutty, soiled, squalid, unclean, uncleanly, vile. *Slang:* grungy. [*Compare* SLIMY, TURBID.] —*See also* IMPURE (2), OBSCENE, ROUGH (2), UNFAIR.
dirty *v.* To make dirty ▸ bedaub, befoul, begrime, bemire, besmirch, besoil, bespatter, black, blacken, defile, foul, mire, muck up, mud, muddy, slush, smudge, smutch, soil, sully. [*Compare* CONTAMINATE, SMEAR, STAIN.] —*See also* DENIGRATE.
disability *n.* —*See* DISADVANTAGE.
disable *v.* **1.** To render powerless or motionless, as by inflicting severe injury ▸ cripple, handicap, immobilize, impair, incapacitate, invalidate, knock out, paralyze. *Idiom:* put out of action (*or* commission). [*Compare* ENERVATE.] **2.** To make incapable, as of doing a job ▸ disqualify, unfit.
disabuse *v.* To free from false hopes or ideas ▸ disenchant, disillusion, undeceive. *Idioms:* bring down to earth, burst someone's bubble, open someone's eyes. [*Compare* DISAPPOINT, FREE.]
disaccord *n.* —*See* CONFLICT.
disaccord *v.* —*See* CONFLICT.
disacknowledge *v.* —*See* REPUDIATE.
disadvantage *n.* An unfavorable condition, circumstance, or characteristic ▸ detriment, disability, downside, drawback, flaw, handicap, inconvenience, liability, minus, problem, shortcoming. [*Compare* WEAKNESS.]
disadvantaged *adj.* —*See* DEPRESSED (2).
disadvantageous *adj.* —*See* UNFAVORABLE (1).
disaffect *v.* —*See* ESTRANGE.
disaffection *n.* —*See* BREACH (2).
disaffirm *v.* —*See* DENY.
disaffirmation or **disaffirmance** *n.* —*See* DENIAL (1).
disagree *v.* —*See* CONFLICT, DIFFER.
disagreeability *n.* —*See* TEMPER (1).
disagreeable *adj.* —*See* ARGUMENTATIVE, BITTER (3), ILL-TEMPERED, OBJECTIONABLE, UNPLEASANT.
disagreement *n.* —*See* ARGUMENT, CONFLICT, DIFFERENCE, GAP (3), OBJECTION.
disallow *v.* —*See* DECLINE, FORBID.
disallowed *adj.* —*See* FORBIDDEN.
disallowance *n.* A turning down of a request ▸ denial, nonacceptance, refusal, rejection, turndown. —*See also* FORBIDDANCE.
disappear *v.* **1.** To pass out of sight either gradually or suddenly ▸ dissipate, dissolve, ebb, evanesce, evaporate, fade, fade out, melt (away), vanish, wane. [*Compare* LIFT.] **2.** To cease to exist ▸ cease, depart, die (away *or* out), end, expire, perish. [*Compare* DIE.]
disappearance *n.* The act or an example of passing out of sight ▸ departure, dissipation, dissolution, evanescence, evaporation, expiration, fade-out, fading, vanishment, waning.
disappoint *v.* To cause unhappiness by failing to satisfy the hopes, desires, or expectations of ▸ discontent, discourage, disenchant, disgruntle, dishearten, disillusion, dissatisfy, dispirit, embitter, fail, frustrate, let down, sour. *Idioms:* dash someone's hopes, fall short, shatter someone's dream.
disappointing *adj.* Disturbing because of failure to measure up to a standard or produce the desired results ▸ anticlimactic, discouraging, disheartening, inadequate, inferior, insufficient, sorry, underwhelming, unlucky, unsatisfactory, unsatisfying.
disappointment *n.* **1.** Unhappiness caused by the failure of one's hopes, desires, or expectations ▸ discontent, discontentment, discouragement, disenchantment, disgruntlement, disheartenment, disillusion, disillusionment, dissatisfaction, frustration, nonfulfillment, regret, unfulfillment. **2.** Something that disappoints ▸ anticlimax, bust, fiasco, letdown, washout. *Informal:* dud, fizzle, flop, lemon, nonevent. [*Compare* FAILURE.]
disapprobation *n.* —*See* DISAPPROVAL.
disapproval *n.* Unfavorable opinion or judgment ▸ condemnation, denunciation, deprecation, disapprobation, disesteem, disfavor, displeasure, dissatisfaction, rejection, reproach, reproof. [*Compare* DISLIKE, OBJECTION, REBUKE.]

dis·ap·prove (dĭs′ə-pro͞ov′) ▸ *v.* **1.** To have an unfavorable opinion (of). **2.** To refuse to approve. **—dis′ap·prov′ing·ly** *adv.*

dis·arm (dĭs-ärm′) ▸ *v.* **1a.** To divest or deprive of weapons. **b.** To render helpless or harmless. **2.** To overcome the hostility of. **3.** To reduce one's arms or armed forces.

dis·ar·ma·ment (dĭs-är′mə-mənt) ▸ *n.* A reduction of armed forces and armaments.

dis·ar·range (dĭs′ə-rānj′) ▸ *v.* To upset the arrangement of. **—dis′ar·range′ment** *n.*

dis·ar·ray (dĭs′ə-rā′) ▸ *n.* **1.** A state of disorder; confusion. **2.** Disordered dress. ▸ *v.* To throw into confusion; upset.

dis·as·sem·ble (dĭs′ə-sĕm′bəl) ▸ *v.* To take or come apart.

dis·as·so·ci·ate (dĭs′ə-sō′shē-āt′, -sē-) ▸ *v.* To dissociate. **—dis′as·so′ci·a′tion** *n.*

dis·as·ter (dĭ-zăs′tər, -săs′-) ▸ *n.* Great destruction, distress, or misfortune. **—dis·as′trous** *adj.* **—dis·as′trous·ly** *adv.*

dis·a·vow (dĭs′ə-vou′) ▸ *v.* To disclaim knowledge of, responsibility for, or association with. **—dis′a·vow′al** *n.*

dis·band (dĭs-bănd′) ▸ *v.* To dissolve or become dissolved. **—dis·band′ment** *n.*

dis·bar (dĭs-bär′) ▸ *v.* **-barred, -bar·ring.** To expel (an attorney) from the legal profession. **—dis·bar′ment** *n.*

dis·be·lieve (dĭs′bĭ-lēv′) ▸ *v.* To refuse to believe (in). **—dis′be·lief′** *n.*

dis·burse (dĭs-bûrs′) ▸ *v.* **-bursed, -burs·ing.** To pay out, as from a fund; expend. **—dis·burse′ment, dis·bur′sal** *n.*

disc (dĭsk) ▸ *n.* Var. of **disk.**

dis·card (dĭ-skärd′) ▸ *v.* **1.** To throw away; reject. **2.** *Games* To throw out (a playing card) from one's hand. ▸ *n.* (dĭs′kärd′) **1.** The act of discarding. **2.** One that is discarded or rejected.

dis·cern (dĭ-sûrn′, -zûrn′) ▸ *v.* **1.** To detect or perceive with the eyes or intellect. **2.** To perceive the distinctions of; discriminate. **—dis·cern′i·ble** *adj.* **—dis·cern′i·bly** *adv.* **—dis·cern′ment** *n.*

dis·cern·ing (dĭ-sûr′nĭng, -zûr′-) ▸ *adj.* Insightful or perceptive.

dis·charge (dĭs-chärj′) ▸ *v.* **-charged, -charg·ing. 1.** To relieve or be relieved of a burden or of contents. **2.** To unload or empty (contents). **3.** To release or dismiss: *discharge a patient; discharge an employee.* **4.** To send or pour forth; emit. **5.** To shoot (a projectile or weapon). **6.** To perform the obligations or demands of (a duty). **7.** To comply with the terms of (e.g., a debt or promise). **8.** To cause or undergo electrical discharge. ▸ *n.* (dĭs′chärj′, dĭs-chärj′) **1.** The act of removing a load or burden. **2.** The act of shooting a projectile or weapon. **3a.** A pouring forth; emission: *a discharge of pus.* **b.** The amount or rate of emission or ejection. **c.** Something that is discharged: *a watery discharge.* **4.** A relieving from an obligation. **5a.** Dismissal or release from employment, service, care, or confinement. **b.** An official document certifying such release, esp. from military service. **6.** *Elect.* **a.** Release of stored energy in a capacitor by the flow of current between its terminals. **b.** Conversion of chemical energy to electric energy in a storage battery. **c.** A flow of electricity in a dielectric, esp. in a rarefied gas.

dis·ci·ple (dĭ-sī′pəl) ▸ *n.* **1.** One who embraces and assists in spreading the teachings of another. **2.** often **Disciple** One of the 12 original followers of Jesus.

dis·ci·pli·nar·i·an (dĭs′ə-plə-nâr′ē-ən) ▸ *n.* One that enforces or believes in strict discipline.

dis·ci·pli·nar·y (dĭs′ə-plə-nĕr′ē) ▸ *adj.* Of or used for discipline.

dis·ci·pline (dĭs′ə-plĭn) ▸ *n.* **1.** Training expected to produce a specific character or pattern of behavior. **2.** Controlled behavior resulting from such training. **3.** A state of order based on submission to rules and authority. **4.** Punishment intended to correct or train. **5.** A set of rules or methods. **6.** A branch of knowledge or teaching. ▸ *v.* **-plined, -plin·ing. 1.** To train by instruction and practice. **2.** To punish.

dis·ci·plined (dĭs′ə-plĭnd) ▸ *adj.* Possessing or indicative of discipline: *a disciplined mind.*

disc jockey also **disk jockey** ▸ *n.* An announcer who presents popular recorded music, esp. on the radio.

dis·claim (dĭs-klām′) ▸ *v.* **1.** To deny or renounce any claim to or connection with. **2.** To renounce a legal right or claim (to).

dis·claim·er (dĭs-klā′mər) ▸ *n.* A repudiation or denial of responsibility, connection, or claim.

dis·close (dĭ-sklōz′) ▸ *v.* **1.** To expose to view. **2.** To make known (something secret). **—dis·clo′sure** (-sklō′zhər) *n.*

THESAURUS

disapprove *v.* To have or express an unfavorable opinion of ▸ decry, denounce, deprecate, discountenance, disesteem, disfavor, dislike, frown on (*or* upon), object to, reject, reprobate, sniff at. *Idioms:* hold no brief for, look askance at, not go for, take a dim view of, take exception to. [*Compare* CONDEMN, DEPLORE, DISAPPROVE, HATE.] *—See also* DECLINE.

disarrange *v.* *—See* DISORDER, TOUSLE.

disarrangement *n.* *—See* DISORDER (1).

disarray *n.* *—See* DISORDER (1).

disarray *v.* *—See* DISORDER.

disassemble *v.* To divide into component parts ▸ break down, dismantle, dismount, take apart (*or* down).

disassociate *v.* *—See* DETACH.

disassociation *n.* *—See* DETACHMENT (1), DIVISION (1).

disaster *n.* An occurrence inflicting widespread destruction and distress ▸ calamity, cataclysm, catastrophe, debacle, fiasco, holocaust, mishap, tragedy. *—See also* COLLAPSE (2).

disastrous *adj.* Causing ruin or great destruction ▸ calamitous, cataclysmic, catastrophic, fatal, fateful, ruinous. [*Compare* HARMFUL, UNFORTUNATE.]

disavow *v.* *—See* DEFECT, DENY, REPUDIATE.

disavowal *n.* *—See* DEFECTION, DENIAL (1).

disband *v.* *—See* DIVIDE, SCATTER (2).

disbelief *n.* The refusal or reluctance to believe ▸ discredit, distrust, doubt, dubiety, incredulity, incredulousness, mistrust, rejection, skepticism, unbelief. *—See also* ATHEISM.

disbelieve *v.* To give no credence to ▸ discredit, distrust, doubt, mistrust, question, reject. *Idiom:* place (*or* put *or* take) no stock in. [*Compare* REPUDIATE.] *—See also* DISTRUST, DOUBT.

disbelieving *adj.* *—See* ATHEISTIC, INCREDULOUS.

disburden *v.* *—See* RID.

disburse *v.* *—See* DISTRIBUTE, SPEND (1).

disbursement *n.* *—See* COST (1), DISTRIBUTION (1).

disc *n.* *See* DISK.

discard *v.* To let go or get rid of as being useless or defective, for example ▸ dispose of, dump, junk, scrap, shed, slough, throw away, throw out, toss. *Informal:* chuck (out), jettison, shuck (off). *Slang:* deep-six, ditch, eighty-six. [*Compare* ABANDON.]

discarnate *adj.* *—See* IMMATERIAL.

discern *v.* To perceive and fix the identity of, especially with difficulty ▸ ascertain, descry, detect, distinguish, find out, make out, pick out, recognize, spot. *—See also* DISCOVER, DISTINGUISH (1), NOTICE, SEE (1).

discernible *adj.* *—See* PERCEPTIBLE, VISIBLE.

discerning *adj.* *—See* CRITICAL (2), DISCRIMINATING.

discernment *n.* Skill in perceiving, discriminating, or judging ▸ acumen, astuteness, clear-sightedness, discrimination, eye, insight, intelligence, judgment, keenness, nose, penetration, perception, perceptiveness, percipience, percipiency, perspicacity, sagaciousness, sagacity, sageness, sensitivity, sharpness, shrewdness, wit. *—See also* DISTINCTION (1).

discharge *v.* To release from military duty ▸ deactivate, demobilize, muster out, release, separate. *—See also* CLEAR (3), DISMISS (1), EXCUSE (1), FREE (1), FULFILL, OOZE, PERFORM (1), POUR, RID, SETTLE (3).

discharge *n.* *—See* BARRAGE, BLAST (2), DISMISSAL, PERFORMANCE.

disciple *n.* *—See* DEVOTEE, FOLLOWER.

disciplinary *adj.* *—See* PUNISHING.

discipline *n.* An area of academic study that is part of a larger body of learning ▸ branch, field, specialty. [*Compare* AREA.] *—See also* PUNISHMENT.

discipline *v.* *—See* EDUCATE, PUNISH.

disclaim *v.* *—See* REPUDIATE.

disclaimer *n.* *—See* DENIAL (1).

disclose *v.* *—See* AIR (2), COMMUNICATE (1), REVEAL.

disclosure *n.* *—See* REVELATION.

dis·co (dĭs′kō) ▸ *n., pl.* **-cos.** **1.** A discotheque. **2.** Popular dance music, esp. of the late 1970s, marked by strong repetitive bass rhythms. **—dis′co** *adj.*
dis·col·or (dĭs-kŭl′ər) ▸ *v.* To make or become a different color, as by staining or fading. **—dis·col′or·a′tion** *n.*
dis·com·bob·u·late (dĭs′kəm-bŏb′yə-lāt′) ▸ *v.* **-lat·ed, -lat·ing.** To throw into a state of confusion; upset.
dis·com·fit (dĭs-kŭm′fĭt) ▸ *v.* **1.** To make uneasy or perplexed; disconcert. **2.** To thwart the plans of; frustrate. **—dis·com′fi·ture** *n.*
dis·com·fort (dĭs-kŭm′fərt) ▸ *n.* **1.** Mental or bodily distress. **2.** Something that disturbs comfort. ▸ *v.* To make uncomfortable.
dis·com·mode (dĭs′kə-mōd′) ▸ *v.* **-mod·ed, -mod·ing.** To inconvenience; disturb.
dis·com·pose (dĭs′kəm-pōz′) ▸ *v.* **1.** To disturb the composure of; perturb. **2.** To put into disorder. **—dis′com·po′sure** *n.*
dis·con·cert (dĭs′kən-sûrt′) ▸ *v.* **1.** To upset; perturb. **2.** To throw into confusion or disarray. **—dis′con·cert′ing·ly** *adv.*
dis·con·nect (dĭs′kə-nĕkt′) ▸ *v.* **1.** To sever the connection of or between. **2.** To shut off the current to. **—dis′con·nec′tion** *n.*
dis·con·nect·ed (dĭs′kə-nĕk′tĭd) ▸ *adj.* **1.** Not connected. **2.** Marked by unrelated parts; incoherent. **—dis′con·nect′ed·ly** *adv.*
dis·con·so·late (dĭs-kŏn′sə-lĭt) ▸ *adj.* **1.** Hopelessly sad; extremely dejected. **2.** Gloomy; dismal. **—dis·con′so·late·ly** *adv.* **—dis·con′so·late·ness** *n.*
dis·con·tent (dĭs′kən-tĕnt′) ▸ *n.* Absence of contentment; dissatisfaction. ▸ *adj.* Discontented. ▸ *v.* To make discontented. **—dis′con·tent′ment** *n.*
dis·con·tent·ed (dĭs′kən-tĕn′tĭd) ▸ *adj.* Restlessly unhappy; not satisfied; malcontent. **—dis′con·tent′ed·ly** *adv.* **—dis′con·tent′ed·ness** *n.*
dis·con·tin·ue (dĭs′kən-tĭn′yo͞o) ▸ *v.* **1.** To put a stop to. **2.** To give up; abandon. **3.** To come to an end. **—dis′con·tin′u·ance, dis′con·tin′u·a′tion** *n.*
dis·con·tin·u·ous (dĭs′kən-tĭn′yo͞o-əs) ▸ *adj.* Marked by breaks or interruptions. **—dis·con′ti·nu′i·ty** (dĭs-kŏn′tə-no͞o′ĭ-tē, -nyo͞o′-) *n.* **—dis′con·tin′u·ous·ly** *adv.*
dis·cord (dĭs′kôrd′) ▸ *n.* **1.** Lack of agreement; dissension. **2.** A harsh mingling of sounds. **3.** *Mus.* An inharmonious combination of simultaneously sounded tones; dissonance. **—dis·cor′dant** *adj.* **—dis·cor′dant·ly** *adv.*
dis·co·theque (dĭs′kə-tĕk′, dĭs′kə-tĕk′) ▸ *n.* A nightclub, usu. with showy lighting, featuring dancing to recorded or live music.
dis·count (dĭs′kount′, dĭs-kount′) ▸ *v.* **1.** To deduct or subtract from a cost or price. **2a.** To purchase or sell (a promissory note) after deducting the interest. **b.** To lend money after deducting the interest. **3.** To offer for sale at a reduced price. **4.** To disregard as being untrustworthy or exaggerated. **5.** To anticipate and make allowance for. ▸ *n.* (dĭs′kount′) **1.** A reduction from the full amount of a price or debt. **2a.** The interest deducted prior to purchasing or selling a promissory note. **b.** The rate of interest so deducted. **3.** The act or an instance of discounting.
dis·coun·te·nance (dĭs-koun′tə-nəns) ▸ *v.* **1.** To view with disfavor. **2.** To disconcert.
discount store ▸ *n.* A store that sells merchandise below the suggested retail price.
dis·cour·age (dĭ-skûr′ĭj, -skŭr′-) ▸ *v.* **-aged, -ag·ing.** **1.** To deprive of confidence, hope, or spirit. **2.** To hamper. **3.** To try to deter, as by raising objections. **—dis·cour′age·ment** *n.* **—dis·cour′ag·ing·ly** *adv.*
dis·course (dĭs′kôrs′) ▸ *n.* **1.** Verbal exchange; conversation. **2.** A formal discussion of a subject, either written or spoken. ▸ *v.* (dĭ-skôrs′) **-coursed, -cours·ing.** To speak or write formally and at length.
dis·cour·te·ous (dĭs-kûr′tē-əs) ▸ *adj.* Lacking courtesy; not polite. **—dis·cour′te·ous·ly** *adv.* **—dis·cour′te·sy** *n.*
dis·cov·er (dĭ-skŭv′ər) ▸ *v.* **1.** To obtain knowledge of through observation or study. **2.** To be the first to find, learn of, or observe. **—dis·cov′er·a·ble** *adj.* **—dis·cov′er·er** *n.*
dis·cov·er·y (dĭ-skŭv′ə-rē) ▸ *n., pl.* **-ies.** **1.** The act or an instance of discovering. **2.** Something discovered.
dis·cred·it (dĭs-krĕd′ĭt) ▸ *v.* **1.** To disgrace; dishonor. **2.** To cast doubt on. **3.** To refuse to believe. ▸ *n.* **1.** Damage to one's reputation. **2.** Lack or loss of trust or belief. **—dis·cred′it·a·ble** *adj.*
dis·creet (dĭ-skrēt′) ▸ *adj.* Having or showing prudence

THESAURUS

discolor *v.* —*See* STAIN.
discombobulate *v.* —*See* CONFUSE (1).
discombobulation *n.* —*See* DAZE.
discomfit *v.* —*See* EMBARRASS.
discomfiture *n.* —*See* EMBARRASSMENT.
discomfort *n.* **1.** The state or quality of being inconvenient ▸ incommodiousness, incommodity, inconvenience, trouble. [*Compare* BOTHER.] **2.** Something that causes difficulty, trouble, or lack of ease ▸ discommodity, incommodity, inconvenience. [*Compare* ANNOYANCE.] —*See also* EMBARRASSMENT.
discomfort *v.* —*See* EMBARRASS, INCONVENIENCE.
discommode *v.* —*See* INCONVENIENCE.
discommodity *n.* Something that causes difficulty, trouble, or lack of ease ▸ discomfort, incommodity, inconvenience. [*Compare* ANNOYANCE, BOTHER.]
discompose *v.* —*See* AGITATE (2).
discomposure *n.* —*See* EMBARRASSMENT.
disconcert *v.* —*See* DISMAY, EMBARRASS, UPSET.
disconcertment *n.* —*See* AGITATION (2).
disconnect *v.* —*See* DETACH, DIVIDE.
disconnected *adj.* —*See* DETACHED (1).
disconnection *n.* —*See* DETACHMENT (1).
disconsolate *adj.* —*See* DEPRESSED (1).
discontent *n.* —*See* DISAPPOINTMENT (1).
discontent *v.* —*See* DISAPPOINT.
discontentment *n.* —*See* DISAPPOINTMENT (1).
discontinuation or **discontinuance** *n.* —*See* BREAK, STOP (1), STOP (2).
discontinue *v.* To bring an activity or relationship to an end suddenly ▸ break off, cease, interrupt, suspend, terminate. —*See also* ABANDON (2), DROP (4), STOP (1), STOP (2).
discontinuity *n.* —*See* BREAK.
discord *n.* —*See* CONFLICT.
discord *v.* —*See* CONFLICT.
discordance *n.* —*See* CONFLICT.
discordant *adj.* —*See* DISCREPANT, INCONGRUOUS, INHARMONIOUS (1), INHARMONIOUS (2).
discount *v.* —*See* BELITTLE, DEDUCT, LEND.
discount *n.* —*See* DEDUCTION (1).
discountenance *v.* —*See* DISAPPROVE, EMBARRASS.
discourage *v.* To make less hopeful or enthusiastic ▸ daunt, demoralize, dishearten, dismay, dispirit, unnerve. *Idiom:* dampen the spirits of. [*Compare* DISILLUSION.] —*See also* DISAPPOINT, DISSUADE.
discouraged *adj.* —*See* DEPRESSED (1), DESPONDENT.
discouraging *adj.* —*See* BLEAK (2), DISAPPOINTING, SORROWFUL.
discourse *n.* A formal discussion of a subject, either written or spoken ▸ dialogue, disquisition, dissertation, essay, expatiation, lecture, monograph, talk, thesis, tract, treatise. [*Compare* TIRADE.] —*See also* CONVERSATION, SPEECH (1).
discourse *v.* —*See* CONVERSE[1], ELABORATE.
discourser *n.* —*See* CONVERSATIONALIST.
discourteous *adj.* —*See* DISRESPECTFUL, OFFENSIVE (2), RUDE (2).
discourtesy *n.* —*See* IMPUDENCE.
discover *v.* To obtain knowledge or awareness of something not known before ▸ ascertain, detect, determine, dig (up *or* out), discern, ferret out, find (out), hear, learn, observe, realize, turn up, unearth. *Idiom:* get wind of. [*Compare* DISCERN.]
discovery *n.* Something that has been discovered ▸ ascertainment, find, finding, result, strike. [*Compare* DEDUCTION, INVENTION, NOVELTY.]
discredit *v.* To cause to be no longer believed or valued ▸ debunk, deflate, explode, puncture. *Informal:* shoot down. *Idioms:* knock holes in, knock the bottom out of, shoot full of holes. —*See also* DISBELIEVE, DISGRACE.
discredit *n.* —*See* DISBELIEF, DISGRACE.
discreditable *adj.* —*See* DISGRACEFUL.
discreet *adj.* —*See* CONSERVATIVE (2), DELICATE (2).

and self-restraint in speech and behavior. **—dis·creet′ly** *adv.* **—dis·creet′ness** *n.*

dis·crep·an·cy (dĭ-skrĕp′ən-sē) ► *n., pl.* **-cies.** Lack of agreement, as between facts or claims; difference.

dis·crep·ant (dĭ-skrĕp′ənt) ► *adj.* Marked by discrepancy.

dis·crete (dĭ-skrēt′) ► *adj.* **1.** Individually distinct; separate. **2.** Consisting of unconnected distinct parts.

dis·cre·tion (dĭ-skrĕsh′ən) ► *n.* **1.** The quality of being discreet. **2.** Freedom of action or judgment: *The choice was left to our discretion.* **—dis·cre′tion·ar′y** *adj.*

dis·crim·i·nate (dĭ-skrĭm′ə-nāt′) ► *v.* **-nat·ed, -nat·ing. 1.** To make a clear distinction; differentiate. **2.** To make distinctions on the basis of preference or prejudice: *accused of discriminating against women.* **—dis·crim′i·na′tion** *n.* **—dis·crim′i·na′tive, dis·crim′i·na·to′ry** *adj.*

dis·crim·i·nat·ing (dĭ-skrĭm′ə-nā′tĭng) ► *adj.* **1.** Able to recognize or draw fine distinctions; discerning. **2.** Showing careful judgment or fine taste.

dis·cur·sive (dĭ-skûr′sĭv) ► *adj.* Covering a wide field of subjects; digressive. **—dis·cur′sive·ly** *adv.* **—dis·cur′sive·ness** *n.*

dis·cus (dĭs′kəs) ► *n.* A disk, typically wooden or plastic, that is thrown for distance in athletic competitions.

dis·cuss (dĭ-skŭs′) ► *v.* **1.** To speak with others about; talk over. **2.** To examine (a subject) in speech or writing. **—dis·cus′sion** *n.*

dis·cus·sant (dĭ-skŭs′ənt) ► *n.* A participant in a formal discussion.

dis·dain (dĭs-dān′) ► *v.* **1.** To regard or treat with contempt. **2.** To reject aloofly. ► *n.* Haughty contempt. **—dis·dain′ful** *adj.* **—dis·dain′ful·ly** *adv.*

dis·ease (dĭ-zēz′) ► *n.* A condition of an organism that impairs physiological functioning, resulting from causes such as infection, genetic defect, or environmental stress. **—dis·eased′** *adj.*

dis·em·bark (dĭs′ĕm-bärk′) ► *v.* **1.** To put, go, or cause to go ashore from a ship. **2.** To leave an aircraft or vehicle. **—dis·em′bar·ka′tion** *n.*

dis·em·bod·y (dĭs′ĕm-bŏd′ē) ► *v.* **1.** To free (the spirit) from the body. **2.** To divest of material form or existence. **—dis′em·bod′i·ment** *n.*

dis·em·bow·el (dĭs′ĕm-bou′əl) ► *v.* **-eled, -el·ing** or **-elled, -el·ling.** To remove the entrails from. **—dis′em·bow′el·ment** *n.*

dis·en·chant (dĭs′ĕn-chănt′) ► *v.* To free from enchantment or false belief; disillusion. **—dis′en·chant′ment** *n.*

dis·en·cum·ber (dĭs′ĕn-kŭm′bər) ► *v.* To relieve of burdens or hardships.

dis·en·fran·chise (dĭs′ĕn-frăn′chīz′) ► *v.* To disfranchise. **—dis′en·fran′chise′ment** (-chīz′mənt, -chĭz-) *n.*

dis·en·gage (dĭs′ĕn-gāj′) ► *v.* To release from something that holds fast, connects, or obliges. **—dis′en·gage′ment** *n.*

dis·en·tan·gle (dĭs′ĕn-tăng′gəl) ► *v.* To free from entanglement. **—dis′en·tan′gle·ment** *n.*

dis·es·tab·lish (dĭs′ĭ-stăb′lĭsh) ► *v.* To alter the established status of, esp. of a nationally established church. **—dis′es·tab′lish·ment** *n.*

dis·fa·vor (dĭs-fā′vər) ► *n.* **1.** Disapproval. **2.** The condition of being regarded with disapproval. **—dis·fa′vor** *v.*

dis·fig·ure (dĭs-fĭg′yər) ► *v.* **-ured, -ur·ing.** To spoil the appearance or shape of; mar. **—dis·fig′ure·ment** *n.*

dis·fran·chise (dĭs-frăn′chīz′) ► *v.* To deprive of a privilege, an immunity, or a right of citizenship, esp. the right to vote. **—dis·fran′chise′ment** *n.*

dis·gorge (dĭs-gôrj′) ► *v.* **-gorged, -gorg·ing. 1.** To vomit. **2.** To discharge violently; spew. **—dis·gorge′ment** *n.*

dis·grace (dĭs-grās′) ► *n.* **1.** Loss of honor, respect, or reputation; shame. **2.** The condition of being strongly disapproved. **3.** One that brings disgrace. ► *v.* **-graced, -grac·ing.** To bring shame or dishonor on. **—dis·grace′ful** *adj.* **—dis·grace′ful·ly** *adv.*

THESAURUS

discrepancy *n.* —*See* DIFFERENCE, GAP (3).

discrepant *adj.* In sharp opposition ► conflicting, contradictory, contrary, contrasting, counter, discordant, incompatible, incongruent, incongruous, inconsistent, opposite. [*Compare* DIFFERENT, OPPOSITE.] —*See also* INCONGRUOUS.

discrete *adj.* —*See* DISTINCT, INDIVIDUAL (2).

discretely *adv.* —*See* SEPARATELY.

discreteness *n.* —*See* INDIVIDUALITY.

discretion *n.* Unrestricted freedom to choose ► convenience, leisure, pleasure, will. —*See also* CHOICE, DISTINCTION (1), PRUDENCE, TACT.

discretionary *adj.* —*See* ARBITRARY, OPTIONAL.

discriminate *v.* —*See* DISTINGUISH (1), DISTINGUISH (2).

discriminate *adj.* —*See* DISCRIMINATING.

discriminating *adj.* Able to recognize small differences or draw fine distinctions ► astute, discerning, discriminate, discriminative, discriminatory, percipient, perspicacious, select, selective, subtle. [*Compare* CRITICAL.] —*See also* CRITICAL (2).

discrimination *n.* **1.** The ability to distinguish, especially to recognize small differences or draw fine distinctions ► acuteness, astuteness, percipience, percipiency, perspicacity, refinement, selectiveness, selectivity, subtlety, taste. **2.** Lack of equality, as of opportunity, treatment, or status ► inequality, unfairness, unjustness. [*Compare* BIAS.] **3.** Irrational suspicion or hatred of a particular group, race, or religion ► bigotry, intolerance, prejudice. [*Compare* HATE.] —*See also* DISCERNMENT, DISTINCTION (1).

discriminative *adj.* —*See* DISCRIMINATING.

discriminatory *adj.* —*See* BIASED, DISCRIMINATING, UNFAIR.

discursive *adj.* —*See* DIGRESSIVE.

discuss *v.* To speak together and exchange ideas and opinions about ► argue, bandy, consider, converse, debate, deliberate, moot, parley, reason, talk over, thrash out (*or* over), thresh out (*or* over), toss around. *Informal:* hash over, kick around, knock about (*or* around). *Slang:* rap. *Idioms:* go into a huddle, put heads together. [*Compare* CONFER.]

discussion *n.* —*See* COMMUNICATION (1), CONFERENCE (1), CONVERSATION, DELIBERATION (1).

disdain *v.* —*See* DESPISE.

disdain or **disdainfulness** *n.* —*See* ARROGANCE, DESPISAL.

disdainful *adj.* Showing scorn and disrespect toward someone or something ► contemptuous, dismissive, disrespectful, haughty, intolerant, scornful, slighting, sneering, supercilious, superior. *Idiom:* on one's high horse. [*Compare* DISPARAGING, DISRESPECTFUL.] —*See also* ARROGANT.

disease *n.* A pathological condition of mind or body ► ailment, complaint, disorder, ill, illness, infection, infirmity, malady, pathology, sickness. [*Compare* DISTRESS, INFIRMITY.] —*See also* CONTAMINANT.

disembark *v.* To come ashore from a seacraft ► alight, debark, land, light.

disembarrass *v.* —*See* RID.

disembodied *adj.* —*See* IMMATERIAL.

disenchant *v.* —*See* DISABUSE, DISAPPOINT.

disencumber *v.* —*See* RID.

disengage *v.* —*See* DETACH, DIVIDE, EXTRICATE, UNDO.

disengagement *n.* —*See* DETACHMENT (1).

disentangle *v.* —*See* DEVELOP (2), EXTRICATE.

disfavor or **disesteem** *n.* —*See* DISAPPROVAL, DISGRACE.

disfavor or **disesteem** *v.* —*See* DISAPPROVE.

disfavorable *adj.* —*See* DISGRACEFUL.

disfigure *v.* —*See* DEFORM.

disfigurement *n.* —*See* DAMAGE, DEFORMITY.

disgorge *v.* —*See* ERUPT.

disgrace *n.* Loss of honor, respect, or admiration ► bad name, bad odor, derision, discredit, disesteem, disfavor, dishonor, disrepute, humiliation, ignominy, ill repute, obloquy, odium, opprobrium, reproach, scorn, shame. [*Compare* DEGRADATION, INFAMY, REFLECTION, STAIN.]

disgrace *v.* To bring disgrace on ► abase, besmirch, blot, debase, degrade, discredit, dishonor, humiliate, pillory, shame, stigmatize, sully, tarnish. *Idioms:* be a reproach to, cause to lose face, heap dishonor (*or* ignominy) on, put to shame. [*Compare* DENIGRATE, HUMBLE, RIDICULE.]

disgraceful *adj.* Meriting or causing shame or dishonor ► degrading, discreditable, disfavorable, dishonorable, disreputable, humiliating, ignominious, opprobrious, reproachable, shameful. —*See also* DEPLORABLE.

disgracefulness *n.* —*See* INFAMY.

dis·grun·tle (dĭs-grŭn′tl) ► *v.* **-tled, -tling.** To make discontented or ill-humored. **—dis·grun′tle·ment** *n.*

dis·guise (dĭs-gīz′) ► *v.* **-guised, -guis·ing.** 1. To modify the manner or appearance of in order to prevent recognition. 2. To conceal or obscure by false show; misrepresent. ► *n.* 1. Clothes or accessories worn to conceal one's true identity. 2. A pretense or misrepresentation.

dis·gust (dĭs-gŭst′) ► *v.* To make (someone) feel sick, repelled, averse, or offended. ► *n.* A feeling of profound aversion, repugnance, or offensiveness. **—dis·gust′ed** *adj.* **—dis·gust′ed·ly** *adv.*

dis·gust·ing (dĭs-gŭs′tĭng) ► *adj.* Arousing disgust; repugnant. **—dis·gust′ing·ly** *adv.*

dish (dĭsh) ► *n.* 1. A flat or shallow container for holding, cooking, or serving food. 2. A particular variety or preparation of food. 3. Something shaped like a dish. 4. *Electron.* A dish antenna. ► *v.* 1. To serve in or as if in a dish. ***—phrasal verb:* dish out** To dispense freely.

dis·ha·bille (dĭs′ə-bēl′, -bē′) ► *n.* The state of being partially, casually, or sloppily dressed.

dish antenna ► *n.* A transmitter or receiver of electromagnetic energy, esp. microwaves or radiowaves, consisting of a concave parabolic reflector.

dis·har·mo·ny (dĭs-här′mə-nē) ► *n.* Lack of harmony. **—dis′har·mo′ni·ous** (-mō′nē-əs) *adj.*

dish·cloth (dĭsh′klôth′, -klŏth′) ► *n.* A cloth for washing dishes; dishrag.

dis·heart·en (dĭs-här′tn) ► *v.* To shake or destroy the courage, spirit, or resolution of. **—dis·heart′en·ing·ly** *adv.*

di·shev·el (dĭ-shĕv′əl) ► *v.* **-eled, -el·ing** or **-elled, -el·ling.** To put into disarray or disorder, esp. hair or clothing. **—di·shev′el·ment** *n.*

dis·hon·est (dĭs-ŏn′ĭst) ► *adj.* 1. Disposed to lie, cheat, defraud, or deceive; untrustworthy. 2. Resulting from or marked by fraud. **—dis·hon′est·ly** *adv.* **—dis·hon′es·ty** *n.*

dis·hon·or (dĭs-ŏn′ər) ► *n.* 1. Loss of honor, respect, or reputation; disgrace. 2. A cause of loss of honor. 3. Failure to pay a note, bill, or other commercial obligation. ► *v.* 1. To bring shame or disgrace upon. 2. To fail or refuse to pay. **—dis·hon′or·a·ble** *adj.* **—dis·hon′or·a·bly** *adv.*

dishonorable discharge ► *n.* Discharge from the armed forces for a grave offense, such as cowardice, murder, or sabotage.

dish·rag (dĭsh′răg′) ► *n.* See **dishcloth.**

dish·wash·er (dĭsh′wŏsh′ər, -wô′shər) ► *n.* One, esp. a machine, that washes dishes.

dis·il·lu·sion (dĭs′ĭ-lo͞o′zhən) ► *v.* To free or deprive of illusion; disenchant. **—dis′il·lu′sion·ment** *n.*

dis·in·cline (dĭs′ĭn-klīn′) ► *v.* To make or be reluctant. **—dis·in′cli·na′tion** (-klə-nā′shən) *n.*

dis·in·fect (dĭs′ĭn-fĕkt′) ► *v.* To rid of disease-carrying microorganisms. **—dis′in·fec′tant** *adj. & n.* **—dis′in·fec′tion** *n.*

dis·in·gen·u·ous (dĭs′ĭn-jĕn′yo͞o-əs) ► *adj.* Not straightforward or candid; crafty. **—dis′in·gen′u·ous·ly** *adv.* **—dis′in·gen′u·ous·ness** *n.*

dis·in·her·it (dĭs′ĭn-hĕr′ĭt) ► *v.* To exclude from inheriting or the right to inherit.

dis·in·te·grate (dĭs-ĭn′tĭ-grāt′) ► *v.* 1. To separate into pieces; fragment. 2. To decay or undergo a transformation, as an atomic nucleus. **—dis·in′te·gra′tion** *n.* **—dis·in′te·gra′tive** *adj.* **—dis·in′te·gra′tor** *n.*

dis·in·ter (dĭs′ĭn-tûr′) ► *v.* To remove from a grave or tomb. **—dis′in·ter′ment** *n.*

dis·in·ter·est·ed (dĭs-ĭn′trĭ-stĭd, -ĭn′tə-rĕs′tĭd) ► *adj.* 1. Free of bias and self-interest; impartial. 2. *Informal* Not interested; indifferent. **—dis·in′ter·est** *n.* **—dis·in′ter·est·ed·ly** *adv.* **—dis·in′ter·est·ed·ness** *n.*

dis·join (dĭs-join′) ► *v.* To separate.

dis·joint (dĭs-joint′) ► *v.* 1. To take or come apart at the joints. 2. To separate or disconnect; disjoin.

dis·joint·ed (dĭs-join′tĭd) ► *adj.* 1. Separated at the joints. 2. Lacking order or coherence. **—dis·joint′ed·ly** *adv.* **—dis·joint′ed·ness** *n.*

disk also **disc** (dĭsk) ► *n.* 1. A thin, flat, circular object or plate. 2. The central part of a composite flower, such as the daisy. 3. *Anat.* A broad cartilaginous plate lying be-

THESAURUS

disgruntle *v.* —*See* DISAPPOINT.

disgruntlement *n.* —*See* DISAPPOINTMENT (1).

disguise *v.* To change or modify so as to prevent recognition of the true identity or character of ► camouflage, cloak, dissemble, dissimulate, mask, masquerade, veil.

disguise *n.* Clothes or other personal effects, such as makeup, worn to conceal one's identity ► costume, guise, mask, masquerade, veil. *Informal:* getup. —*See also* ACT (2), FAÇADE (2).

disguised *adj.* —*See* HIDDEN (1).

disgust *v.* To offend the senses or feelings of ► appall, nauseate, repel, repulse, revolt, sicken, turn off. *Slang:* gross out. *Idiom:* turn one's stomach. —*See also* OFFEND (2).

disgust *n.* Extreme aversion caused by something offensive ► abhorrence, loathing, nausea, queasiness, repugnance, revulsion. [*Compare* HATE.]

disgusted *adj.* Out of patience ► fed up, sick, tired, weary. *Idiom:* sick and tired. [*Compare* ANGRY.]

disgusting *adj.* —*See* OFFENSIVE (1), UNPALATABLE.

disharmonious *adj.* —*See* INHARMONIOUS (2).

disharmony *n.* —*See* CONFLICT.

dishearten *v.* —*See* DEPRESS, DISAPPOINT, DISCOURAGE, DISMAY.

disheartening *adj.* —*See* DISAPPOINTING, SORROWFUL.

disheartenment *n.* —*See* DEPRESSION (2).

dishevel *v.* —*See* TOUSLE.

disheveled *adj.* —*See* MESSY (1).

dishonest *adj.* Given to or marked by deliberate concealment or misrepresentation of the truth ► ambidextrous, deceitful, deceiving, deceptive, disingenuous, double-dealing, double-faced, duplicitous, false-hearted, insincere, lying, mendacious, perfidious, two-faced, untrustworthy, untruthful. *Informal:* crooked. [*Compare* HYPOCRITICAL, UNDERHAND.] —*See also* CORRUPT (2).

dishonesty *n.* 1. Lack of integrity ► deceitfulness, duplicitousness, duplicity, improbity, inveracity, mendacity, untrustworthiness. *Informal:* crookedness. 2. Lack of straightforwardness and honesty in action ► chicanery, craft, craftiness, deviousness, indirection, shadiness, shiftiness, slyness, sneakiness, trickery, trickiness, underhandedness, wiliness. *Informal:* crookedness. [*Compare* DECEIT, HYPOCRISY, TRICK.] —*See also* CORRUPTION (2).

dishonor *n.* —*See* DEGRADATION (1), DISGRACE, DISRESPECT.

dishonor *v.* —*See* DISGRACE.

dishonorable *adj.* —*See* CORRUPT (2), DISGRACEFUL.

dishonorableness *n.* —*See* INFAMY.

disillusion *v.* —*See* DISABUSE, DISAPPOINT.

disillusion *n.* —*See* DISAPPOINTMENT (1).

disinclination *n.* An attitude or feeling of distaste or mild aversion ► dislike, disrelish, distaste, mislike. [*Compare* DISAPPROVAL, DISGUST, ENMITY, HATE.] —*See also* INDISPOSITION.

disincline *v.* —*See* DISSUADE.

disinclined *adj.* —*See* INDISPOSED.

disinfect *v.* To render free of microorganisms ► decontaminate, irradiate, sanitize, sterilize.

disinfectant *n.* —*See* PURIFIER.

disinfection *n.* —*See* PURITY.

disinformation *n.* —*See* PROPAGANDA.

disingenuous *adj.* —*See* DISHONEST, UNDERHAND.

disingenuousness *n.* —*See* ART, INSINCERITY.

disintegrate *v.* To reduce or become reduced to pieces or fragments ► atomize, break apart (*or* down *or* up), crumble, decompose, dissolve, fragment, fragmentize. *Idioms:* fall apart (*or* to pieces), turn to dust (*or* ashes). [*Compare* BREAK, DESTROY, DIVIDE.] —*See also* DECAY.

disintegration *n.* —*See* DECAY.

disinter *v.* —*See* UNCOVER.

disinterest *n.* —*See* APATHY, DETACHMENT (2), FAIRNESS.

disinterested *adj.* Feeling or showing no strong emotional involvement ► detached, dispassionate, impersonal, indifferent, neutral. —*See also* APATHETIC, DETACHED (1), FAIR[1] (1).

disinterestedness *n.* —*See* FAIRNESS.

disinvolve *v.* —*See* EXTRICATE.

disjoin or **disjoint** *v.* —*See* DIVIDE.

disjunction or **disjuncture** *n.* —*See* DIVISION (1).

disk or **disc** *n.* —*See* CIRCLE (1).

tween adjacent vertebrae. **4.** *Comp. Sci.* **a.** An optical disk, esp. a compact disk. **b.** A magnetic disk, esp. a floppy or hard disk. **5.** often **disc** A phonograph record.

disk drive ▸ *n.* *Comp. Sci.* A device that reads data stored on a disk and writes data onto it for storage.

disk operating system ▸ *n.* DOS.

dis·like (dĭs-līk′) ▸ *v.* To regard with distaste or aversion. ▸ *n.* An attitude or feeling of distaste or aversion.

dis·lo·cate (dĭs′lō-kāt′, dĭs-lō′kāt) ▸ *v.* **1.** To move out of the normal position, esp. to displace (a bone) from a socket or joint. **2.** To disrupt. **—dis′lo·ca′tion** *n.*

dis·lodge (dĭs-lŏj′) ▸ *v.* To force out of a position previously occupied. **—dis·lodge′ment, dis·lodg′ment** *n.*

dis·loy·al (dĭs-loi′əl) ▸ *adj.* Lacking loyalty. **—dis·loy′al·ly** *adv.* **—dis·loy′al·ty** *n.*

dis·mal (dĭz′məl) ▸ *adj.* Causing or showing gloom or depression; dreary. **—dis′mal·ly** *adv.*

dis·man·tle (dĭs-măn′tl) ▸ *v.* **-tled, -tling. 1.** To take apart; tear down; disassemble. **2.** To strip of furnishings or equipment. **—dis·man′tle·ment** *n.*

dis·may (dĭs-mā′) ▸ *v.* To fill with dread or apprehension; daunt. ▸ *n.* Consternation or apprehension.

dis·mem·ber (dĭs-mĕm′bər) ▸ *v.* **1.** To cut, tear, or pull off the limbs of. **2.** To divide into pieces. **—dis·mem′ber·ment** *n.*

dis·miss (dĭs-mĭs′) ▸ *v.* **1.** To discharge, as from employment or service. **2.** To direct or allow to leave: *dismiss students.* **3a.** To rid one's mind of; dispel. **b.** To reject or repudiate. **4.** *Law* To put (a claim or action) out of court without further hearing. **—dis·miss′i·ble** *adj.* **—dis·miss′al** *n.*

dis·mis·sive (dĭs-mĭs′ĭv) ▸ *adj.* **1.** Serving to dismiss. **2.** Showing indifference or disregard. **—dis·mis′ive·ly** *adj.*

dis·mount (dĭs-mount′) ▸ *v.* **1.** To get off or down, as from a horse or vehicle. **2.** To remove (a rider) from a horse. **3.** To remove from a support, setting, or mounting. **4.** To disassemble (e.g., a mechanism). **—dis′mount′** *n.* **—dis·mount′a·ble** *adj.*

Dis·ney (dĭz′nē), **Walter Elias** "Walt" (1901–66) ▸ Amer. animator and film producer.

dis·o·be·di·ence (dĭs′ə-bē′dē-əns) ▸ *n.* Refusal or failure to obey. **—dis′o·be′di·ent** *adj.* **—dis′o·be′di·ent·ly** *adv.*

dis·o·bey (dĭs′ə-bā′) ▸ *v.* To fail to obey.

dis·o·blige (dĭs′ə-blīj′) ▸ *v.* **1.** To refuse or fail to comply with the wishes of. **2.** To inconvenience. **3.** To offend.

dis·or·der (dĭs-ôr′dər) ▸ *n.* **1.** A lack of order; confusion. **2.** A public disturbance. **3.** An ailment. ▸ *v.* To throw into disorder.

dis·or·der·ly (dĭs-ôr′dər-lē) ▸ *adj.* **1.** Not neat or tidy. **2.** Undisciplined; unruly. **3.** *Law* Disturbing the public peace. **—dis·or′der·li·ness** *n.*

dis·or·gan·ize (dĭs-ôr′gə-nīz′) ▸ *v.* To destroy the systematic arrangement of. **—dis·or′gan·i·za′tion** *n.*

dis·o·ri·ent (dĭs-ôr′ē-ĕnt′) ▸ *v.* To cause to lose orientation. **—dis·o′ri·en·ta′tion** *n.*

dis·own (dĭs-ōn′) ▸ *v.* To refuse to acknowledge or accept as one's own; repudiate.

dis·par·age (dĭ-spăr′ĭj) ▸ *v.* **-aged, -ag·ing.** To speak of in a slighting way; belittle. **—dis·par′age·ment** *n.* **—dis·par′ag·ing·ly** *adv.*

dis·pa·rate (dĭs′pər-ĭt, dĭ-spăr′ĭt) ▸ *adj.* Entirely distinct or different. **—dis′pa·rate·ly** *adv.* **—dis·par′i·ty** (dĭ-spăr′ĭ-tē) *n.*

dis·pas·sion·ate (dĭs-păsh′ə-nĭt) ▸ *adj.* Not influenced by emotion or bias. **—dis·pas′sion** *n.* **—dis·pas′sion·ate·ly** *adv.*

THESAURUS

dislike *v.* To regard with distaste or mild aversion ▸ disrelish, mislike. *Idioms:* be averse to, be cool toward, have an aversion to (*or* distaste for), have no use for, not be crazy (*or* nuts *or* wild) about, not care for. [*Compare* DESPISE, HATE.] *—See also* DISAPPROVE.

dislike *n.* An attitude or feeling of distaste or mild aversion ▸ disinclination, disrelish, distaste, mislike. [*Compare* DISAPPROVAL, DISGUST, ENMITY, HATE.] *—See also* DESPISAL.

dislocate *v.* *—See* DISTURB, SLIP (2).

dislocation *n.* *—See* DISPLACEMENT.

disloyal *adj.* *—See* FAITHLESS.

disloyalty *n.* *—See* FAITHLESSNESS.

dismal *adj.* *—See* BLEAK (2), GLOOMY, SORROWFUL.

dismantle *v.* To take something apart ▸ break down, disassemble, dismount, take down. *—See also* DESTROY (2).

dismay *v.* To deprive of courage or the power to act as a result of fear, anxiety, or disgust ▸ alarm, appall, consternate, daunt, disconcert, dishearten, dispirit, shake, shock, unnerve. [*Compare* DISTRESS, FRIGHTEN.] *—See also* DISCOURAGE.

dismay *n.* *—See* DESPAIR, FEAR.

dismayed *adj.* *—See* DEPRESSED (1).

dismaying *adj.* *—See* FEARFUL.

dismember *v.* *—See* CRIPPLE.

dismiss *v.* **1.** To end the employment or service of ▸ cashier, discharge, drop, lay off, let go, release, terminate. *Informal:* ax, fire, pink-slip. *Slang:* boot, bounce, can, sack. *Idioms:* give someone his or her walking papers, give someone the ax (*or* gate *or* pink slip), let go, show someone the door. **2.** To direct or allow to leave ▸ banish, cast out, dispatch, drive out, excuse, expel, release, run out, send away. *Idioms:* send about one's business, send packing, show someone the door. **3.** To rid one's mind of ▸ banish, cast out, dispel, reject, repudiate, shut out. *—See also* DECLINE, DENY, DESPISE, DROP (4), EJECT (1).

dismissal *n.* The act of dismissing or the condition of being dismissed from employment ▸ discharge, expulsion, removal, termination. *Informal:* ax, pink slip. *Slang:* boot, bounce, sack. *—See also* EJECTION.

dismissive *adj.* *—See* DISDAINFUL, DISPARAGING.

dismount *v.* To take something apart ▸ break down, disassemble, dismantle, take down.

disobedience *n.* *—See* DEFIANCE (1).

disobedient *adj.* Refusing or failing to obey ▸ bad, ill-behaved, insubordinate, naughty, noncompliant, ungovernable, unmanageable. *—See also* DEFIANT.

disobey *v.* To refuse or fail to obey ▸ break, defy, disregard, flout, oppose, rebel, resist, transgress, violate. *Idiom:* pay no attention to. [*Compare* DEFY.]

disorder *n.* **1.** A lack of order or regular arrangement ▸ chaos, clutter, confusedness, confusion, derangement, disarrangement, disarray, disorderedness, disorderliness, disorganization, imbroglio, jumble, mess, mix-up, muddle, muss, scramble, shambles, topsyturviness, tumble. *Slang:* snafu. **2.** A lack of civil order or peace ▸ anarchy, brouhaha, chaos, commotion, confusion, disturbance, fracas, lawlessness, melee, misrule, mob rule, riot, ruckus, tumult, turmoil, unrest, uproar. *—See also* AGITATION (1), DISEASE.

disorder *v.* To put out of proper order ▸ clutter, derange, disarrange, disarray, disorganize, disrupt, disturb, jumble, mess up, mix up, muddle, scatter, tumble, unsettle, upset. *—See also* CONFUSE (3), DISTURB, TOUSLE, UPSET.

disordered *adj.* *—See* CONFUSED (2), INSANE.

disorderedness *n.* *—See* DISORDER (1).

disordering *n.* *—See* UPSET.

disorderliness *n.* The state of being messy or unkempt ▸ chaos, disorganization, messiness, sloppiness, slovenliness, topsy-turviness, untidiness. *—See also* DISORDER (1), UNRULINESS.

disorderly *adj.* Upsetting civil order or peace ▸ disruptive, lawless, obstreperous, riotous, rowdy, turbulent. *—See also* CONFUSED (2), UNRULY.

disorganization *n.* *—See* DISORDER (1), DISORDERLINESS, UPSET.

disorganize *v.* *—See* DISORDER, TOUSLE.

disorient *v.* *—See* AGITATE (2), CONFUSE (1).

disorientation *n.* *—See* DAZE.

disoriented *adj.* *—See* CONFUSED (1), LOST (1).

disown *v.* *—See* REPUDIATE.

disparage *v.* *—See* BELITTLE.

disparagement *n.* *—See* BELITTLEMENT.

disparaging *adj.* Tending or intending to belittle ▸ belittling, deprecative, deprecatory, depreciative, depreciatory, derisive, derogative, derogatory, detractive, dismissive, low, mocking, pejorative, slighting, uncomplimentary. [*Compare* DISDAINFUL, SARCASTIC.]

disparate *adj.* *—See* DIFFERENT, VARIOUS.

disparity *n.* *—See* DIFFERENCE, GAP (3), INEQUALITY (1).

dispassion *n.* *—See* FAIRNESS.

dispassionate *adj.* *—See* COLD (2), FAIR[1] (1).

dispassionately *adv.* *—See* FAIRLY (1).

dispassionateness *n.* *—See* FAIRNESS.

dis·patch (dĭ-spăch′) ► *v.* **1.** To send to a specific destination. **2.** To perform promptly. **3.** To kill. ► *n.* **1.** The act of dispatching. **2.** Speed in performance or movement. **3.** An important message. **4.** (*also* dĭs′păch′) A news item sent to a news organization, as by a correspondent. **—dis·patch′er** *n.*

dis·pel (dĭ-spĕl′) ► *v.* **-pelled, -pel·ling.** To rid of by or as if by scattering: *dispel doubts.*

dis·pens·a·ble (dĭ-spĕn′sə-bəl) ► *adj.* Capable of being dispensed with.

dis·pen·sa·ry (dĭ-spĕn′sə-rē) ► *n., pl.* **-ries.** A place where medical supplies, preparations, and treatments are dispensed.

dis·pen·sa·tion (dĭs′pən-sā′shən, -pĕn-) ► *n.* **1a.** The act of dispensing. **b.** Something dispensed. **2.** A system for ordering or administering affairs. **3.** An official exemption or release from an obligation or rule. **4.** A religious system or code of commands considered to have been divinely appointed.

dis·pense (dĭ-spĕns′) ► *v.* **-pensed, -pens·ing. 1.** To deal out in portions; distribute. **2.** To prepare and give out (medicines). **3.** To carry out or administer (e.g., laws). ***—phrasal verb:* dispense with 1.** To manage without; forgo. **2.** To get rid of. **—dis·pens′er** *n.*

dis·perse (dĭ-spûrs′) ► *v.* **-persed, -pers·ing. 1.** To break up and scatter. **2.** To disseminate or distribute. **—dis·pers′i·ble** *adj.* **—dis·per′sion** (-spûr′zhən, -shən), **dis·per′sal** *n.*

dis·pir·it (dĭ-spĭr′ĭt) ► *v.* To lower the spirits of; dishearten.

dis·pir·it·ed (dĭ-spĭr′ĭ-tĭd) ► *adj.* Affected or marked by low spirits; dejected. **—dis·pir′it·ed·ly** *adv.*

dis·place (dĭs-plās′) ► *v.* **1.** To move from the usual place or position. **2.** To take the place of; supplant. **3.** To cause a displacement of.

dis·place·ment (dĭs-plās′mənt) ► *n.* **1.** The act of displacing. **2a.** The weight or volume of a fluid displaced by a floating body. **b.** The distance from an initial position to a subsequent position assumed by a body.

displacement ton ► *n.* A unit for measuring the displacement of a ship afloat, equivalent to one long ton.

dis·play (dĭ-splā′) ► *v.* **1.** To present or hold up to view. **2.** *Comp. Sci.* To provide (information or graphics) on a computer screen. ► *n.* **1a.** The act of displaying. **b.** Something displayed, esp. an elaborate public exhibition. **2.** *Comp. Sci.* A device that accepts video signals from a computer and gives information in a visual form, as on a screen.

dis·please (dĭs-plēz′) ► *v.* To cause annoyance or vexation (to). **—dis·pleas′ing·ly** *adv.* **—dis·pleas′ure** (-plĕzh′ər) *n.*

dis·port (dĭ-spôrt′) ► *v.* To play; frolic.

dis·pos·a·ble (dĭ-spō′zə-bəl) ► *adj.* **1.** Designed to be disposed of after use: *disposable razors.* **2a.** Remaining after taxes have been deducted: *disposable income.* **b.** Free for use; available: *all disposable means.* ► *n.* An article that can be disposed of after one use. **—dis·pos′a·bil′i·ty** *n.*

dis·pos·al (dĭ-spō′zəl) ► *n.* **1.** A particular order, distribution, or placement. **2.** A method of attending to or settling matters. **3.** Transference by gift or sale. **4.** The act of throwing out or away. **5.** A device installed below a sink that grinds and flushes garbage away. **6.** The power to use something.

dis·pose (dĭ-spōz′) ► *v.* **-posed, -pos·ing. 1.** To place in a particular order; arrange. **2.** To put into a certain frame of mind. **3.** To settle a matter. ***—phrasal verb:* dispose of** To get rid of, as by attending to, selling, or throwing out. **—dis·pos′er** *n.*

dis·po·si·tion (dĭs′pə-zĭsh′ən) ► *n.* **1.** Temperament. **2.** A tendency or inclination. **3.** Arrangement, positioning, or distribution. **4.** A final settlement. **5.** An act of disposing of something.

dis·pos·sess (dĭs′pə-zĕs′) ► *v.* To deprive of possession of (e.g., land or property). **—dis′pos·ses′sion** *n.*

dis·praise (dĭs-prāz′) ► *v.* To disparage. ► *n.* Disapproval; reproach.

dis·pro·por·tion (dĭs′prə-pôr′shən) ► *n.* Absence of proper proportion or harmony. **—dis′pro·por′tion·al, dis′pro·por′tion·ate** (-nĭt) *adj.* **—dis′pro·por′tion·al·ly, dis′pro·por′tion·ate·ly** *adv.*

dis·prove (dĭs-pro͞ov′) ► *v.* To prove to be false. **—dis·prov′al** *n.*

dis·pu·ta·tion (dĭs′pyə-tā′shən) ► *n.* **1.** An argument or debate. **2.** An oral defense of a thesis done as an academic exercise.

dis·pu·ta·tious (dĭs′pyə-tā′shəs) ► *adj.* Inclined to dispute. **—dis′pu·ta′tious·ly** *adv.* **—dis′pu·ta′tious·ness** *n.*

dis·pute (dĭ-spyo͞ot′) ► *v.* **-put·ed, -put·ing. 1.** To argue (about); debate. **2.** To question the truth or validity of; doubt. **3.** To strive against; oppose. ► *n.* **1.** An argument; debate. **2.** A quarrel. **—dis·put′a·ble** *adj.* **—dis·put′a·bly** *adv.* **—dis·pu′tant, dis·put′er** *n.*

dis·qual·i·fy (dĭs-kwŏl′ə-fī′) ► *v.* To declare or render unqualified or ineligible. **—dis·qual′i·fi·ca′tion** *n.*

dis·qui·et (dĭs-kwī′ĭt) ► *v.* To trouble; bother. ► *n.* Disquietude.

THESAURUS

dispatch *v.* —*See* CONSUME (1), DISMISS (2), KILL[1], SEND (1).

dispatch *n.* —*See* HASTE (1), ITEM, LETTER.

dispel *v.* To cause to separate and go in various directions ► disperse, dissipate, scatter. [*Compare* DIVIDE, SEPARATE.] —*See also* DISMISS (3).

dispensable *adj.* —*See* UNNECESSARY.

dispensation *n.* —*See* DISTRIBUTION (1).

dispense *v.* —*See* ADMINISTER (2), ADMINISTER (3), DISTRIBUTE, EXCUSE (1).

dispersal *n.* —*See* DISTRIBUTION (2).

disperse *v.* To cause to separate and go in various directions ► dispel, dissipate, scatter. [*Compare* DIVIDE, SEPARATE.] —*See also* LIFT (2), SCATTER (2), SPREAD (2).

dispersion *n.* —*See* DISTRIBUTION (2).

dispirit *v.* —*See* DEPRESS, DISAPPOINT, DISCOURAGE, DISMAY.

dispirited *adj.* —*See* DEPRESSED (1).

dispiriting *adj.* —*See* SORROWFUL.

displace *v.* **1.** To substitute for or fill the place of ► replace, supersede, supplant, surrogate. *Idioms:* fill someone's shoes, take over from, take the reins from. [*Compare* SUBSTITUTE.] **2.** To take the place of another against the other's will ► cut out, force out, supplant, usurp. [*Compare* ASSUME, OCCUPY, SEIZE.] —*See also* DISTURB.

displacement *n.* A change in normal place or position ► dislocation, dislodging, disturbance, move, movement, rearrangement, relocation, shift. [*Compare* REMOVAL, UPSET.]

display *v.* To make a public and an especially ostentatious show of ► brandish, disport, exhibit, expose, flash, flaunt, parade, promenade, show (off), showcase, sport, strut, wear. —*See also* BEAR (3), EXPRESS (1), REVEAL, SHOW (1).

display *n.* An act of showing or displaying ► demonstration, exhibit, exhibition, exposition, manifestation, presentation, show. —*See also* ARRAY.

displease *v.* —*See* OFFEND (1), OFFEND (2).

displeasing *adj.* —*See* OFFENSIVE (2), UNPLEASANT.

displeasure *n.* —*See* DISAPPROVAL, OFFENSE.

disport *v.* —*See* DISPLAY, PLAY (1).

disport *n.* —*See* AMUSEMENT.

disposal *n.* The act of getting rid of something useless or used up ► discarding, dispatching, disposition, dumping, elimination, jettison, junking, removal, riddance, scrapping, unloading. —*See also* ARRANGEMENT (1).

dispose *v.* —*See* ARRANGE (1), INFLUENCE.

dispose of *v.* To get rid of by selling ► close out, dump, sell off, unload. —*See also* DISCARD, SETTLE (1).

disposed *adj.* —*See* INCLINED.

disposition *n.* A person's customary manner of emotional response ► bent, complexion, habit, humor, nature, temper, temperament. [*Compare* MOOD.] —*See also* ARRANGEMENT (1), CHARACTER (1), INCLINATION (1).

dispossess *v.* —*See* DEPRIVE.

dispossession *n.* —*See* DEPRIVATION.

disproportion *n.* —*See* INEQUALITY (1).

disproportionately *adv.* —*See* UNDULY.

disprove *v.* —*See* REFUTE.

disputable *adj.* —*See* DEBATABLE.

disputatious *adj.* —*See* ARGUMENTATIVE.

dispute *v.* —*See* ARGUE (1), ARGUE (2), CONTEST, DENY.

dispute *n.* —*See* ARGUMENT, OBJECTION.

disqualify *v.* To make incapable, as of doing a job ► disable, unfit.

disquiet *v.* —*See* AGITATE (2).

disquiet *n.* —*See* ANXIETY (1), RESTLESSNESS.

disquieting *adj.* —*See* DISTURBING.

dis·qui·e·tude (dĭs-kwī′ĭ-to͞od′, -tyo͞od′) ▸ *n.* A condition of worried unease; anxiety.
dis·qui·si·tion (dĭs′kwĭ-zĭsh′ən) ▸ *n.* A formal discourse or treatise.
dis·re·gard (dĭs′rĭ-gärd′) ▸ *v.* To pay no attention to; ignore. ▸ *n.* Lack of thoughtful attention or due regard.
dis·re·pair (dĭs′rĭ-pâr′) ▸ *n.* The condition of being in need of repair.
dis·rep·u·ta·ble (dĭs-rĕp′yə-tə-bəl) ▸ *adj.* Lacking respectability, as in character or behavior. **—dis·rep′u·ta·bly** *adv.*
dis·re·pute (dĭs′rĭ-pyo͞ot′) ▸ *n.* Damage to or loss of reputation; disgrace.
dis·re·spect (dĭs′rĭ-spĕkt′) ▸ *n.* Lack of respect; rudeness. **—dis′re·spect′** *v.* **—dis′re·spect′ful** *adj.* **—dis′re·spect′ful·ly** *adv.*
dis·robe (dĭs-rōb′) ▸ *v.* To undress.
dis·rupt (dĭs-rŭpt′) ▸ *v.* **1.** To throw into confusion. **2.** To break apart. **—dis·rupt′er, dis·rup′tor** *n.* **—dis·rup′tion** *n.* **—dis·rup′tive** *adj.*
dis·sat·is·fac·tion (dĭs-săt′ĭs-făk′shən) ▸ *n.* **1.** Discontent. **2.** A cause of discontent. **—dis·sat′is·fac′to·ry** (-tə-rē) *adj.*
dis·sat·is·fy (dĭs-săt′ĭs-fī′) ▸ *v.* To fail to satisfy; disappoint.
dis·sect (dĭ-sĕkt′, dī-, dī′sĕkt′) ▸ *v.* **1.** To cut apart or separate (tissue), esp. for anatomical study. **2.** To analyze or criticize in minute detail. **—dis·sec′tion** *n.*
dis·sem·ble (dĭ-sĕm′bəl) ▸ *v.* **-bled, -bling. 1.** To conceal the real nature or motives of. **2.** To simulate; feign. **—dis·sem′bler** *n.*
dis·sem·i·nate (dĭ-sĕm′ə-nāt′) ▸ *v.* **-nat·ed, -nat·ing.** To spread or become spread; diffuse. **—dis·sem′i·na′tion** *n.* **—dis·sem′i·na′tor** *n.*
dis·sen·sion (dĭ-sĕn′shən) ▸ *n.* A difference of opinion, esp. one causing strife within a group.
dis·sent (dĭ-sĕnt′) ▸ *v.* **1.** To disagree; differ. **2.** To withhold assent. ▸ *n.* **1.** Difference of opinion. **2.** The refusal to conform to the authority or doctrine of an established church. **—dis·sent′er** *n.* **—dis·sent′ing** *adj.*
dis·ser·ta·tion (dĭs′ər-tā′shən) ▸ *n.* A treatise, esp. one written as a doctoral thesis.
dis·ser·vice (dĭs-sûr′vĭs) ▸ *n.* A harmful action.
dis·si·dent (dĭs′ĭ-dənt) ▸ *adj.* Disagreeing, as in opinion or belief. ▸ *n.* One who disagrees; dissenter. **—dis′si·dence** *n.*
dis·sim·i·lar (dĭ-sĭm′ə-lər) ▸ *adj.* Different or distinct; unlike. **—dis·sim′i·lar′i·ty** (-lăr′ĭ-tē) *n.* **—dis·sim′i·lar·ly** *adv.*
dis·si·mil·i·tude (dĭs′ə-mĭl′ĭ-to͞od′, -tyo͞od′) ▸ *n.* Lack of resemblance.
dis·sim·u·late (dĭ-sĭm′yə-lāt′) ▸ *v.* **-lat·ed, -lat·ing.** To disguise under a feigned appearance; dissemble. **—dis·sim′u·la′tion** *n.* **—dis·sim′u·la′tor** *n.*
dis·si·pate (dĭs′ə-pāt′) ▸ *v.* **-pat·ed, -pat·ing. 1.** To break up and drive away. **2.** To vanish or disappear. **3.** To spend wastefully; squander. **4.** To indulge in the intemperate pursuit of pleasure. **—dis′si·pat′ed** *adj.* **—dis′si·pa′tion** *n.*
dis·so·ci·ate (dĭ-sō′shē-āt′, -sē-) ▸ *v.* **-at·ed, -at·ing.** To separate or cause to separate. **—dis·so′ci·a′tion** *n.* **—dis·so′ci·a′tive** *adj.*
dis·so·lute (dĭs′ə-lo͞ot′) ▸ *adj.* Lacking in moral restraint; wanton. **—dis′so·lute′ly** *adv.* **—dis′so·lute′ness** *n.*
dis·so·lu·tion (dĭs′ə-lo͞o′shən) ▸ *n.* **1.** Decomposition into fragments; disintegration. **2.** Sensual indulgence; debauchery. **3.** Termination or extinction by dispersion. **4.** Death. **5.** Termination of a legal bond or contract. **6.** Formal dismissal of an assembly. **7.** Reduction to a liquid form.
dis·solve (dĭ-zŏlv′) ▸ *v.* **-solved, -solv·ing. 1.** To enter or cause to pass into solution. **2.** To make or become liquid; melt. **3.** To vanish or cause to vanish. **4.** To break or become broken into component parts. **5.** To terminate or dismiss. **6.** To collapse emotionally. **—dis·solv′a·ble** *adj.* **—dis·solv′er** *n.*
dis·so·nance (dĭs′ə-nəns) ▸ *n.* **1.** A harsh, disagreeable combination of sounds; discord. **2.** *Mus.* A combination of harsh tones considered to suggest unrelieved tension. **—dis′so·nant** *adj.* **—dis′so·nant·ly** *adv.*
dis·suade (dĭ-swād′) ▸ *v.* **-suad·ed, -suad·ing.** To deter from a course of action or purpose. **—dis·sua′sion** *n.* **—dis·sua′sive** *adj.*

THESAURUS

disquietude *n.* —*See* ANXIETY (1), RESTLESSNESS.
disquisition *n.* —*See* DISCOURSE.
disregard *v.* —*See* BLINK AT, DISOBEY, NEGLECT (1), NEGLECT (2), SNUB.
disregard *n.* —*See* DEFIANCE (1), NEGLECT, THOUGHTLESSNESS (2).
disregardful *adj.* —*See* THOUGHTLESS.
disrelish *v.* To regard with distaste ▸ dislike, mislike. *Idioms:* be averse to, be cool toward, have an aversion to (*or* distaste for), have no use for, not be crazy (*or* nuts *or* wild) about, not care for. [*Compare* DESPISE, DISAPPROVE, HATE.]
disrelish *n.* An attitude or feeling of distaste or mild aversion ▸ disinclination, dislike, distaste, mislike. [*Compare* DISAPPROVAL, DISGUST, ENMITY, HATE.]
disremember *v. Informal* To fail to remember ▸ forget. *Idioms:* draw a blank, go blank, have a senior moment, have no recollection (*or* memory).
disreputable *adj.* —*See* DISGRACEFUL.
disreputability or **disreputableness** *n.* —*See* INFAMY.
disrepute *n.* —*See* DISGRACE.
disrespect *n.* Lack of proper respect ▸ affront, dishonor, impoliteness, irreverence, lese majesty, rudeness. [*Compare* DESPISAL, THOUGHTLESSNESS.] —*See also* IMPUDENCE.
disrespectful *adj.* Having or showing a lack of respect ▸ cheeky, contemptuous, discourteous, ill-bred, impertinent, impolite, impudent, insolent, insulting, irreverent, rude, sassy, scornful, unmannered, unmannerly. —*See also* DISDAINFUL, RUDE (2).
disrobe *v.* To remove all the clothing from ▸ strip, unclothe, undress. —*See also* BARE.
disrupt *v.* To break up the order or progress of ▸ disturb, interfere, interrupt, intrude, mess up, muddle, obstruct, upset. —*See also* DISORDER, DISTURB.
disruption *n.* —*See* BREAK, UPSET.
disruptive *adj.* —*See* DISORDERLY, DISTURBING.
dissatisfaction *n.* —*See* DISAPPOINTMENT (1), DISAPPROVAL.
dissatisfactory *adj.* —*See* BAD (1).
dissatisfy *v.* —*See* DISAPPOINT.
dissect *v.* —*See* ANALYZE.
dissection *n.* —*See* ANALYSIS.
dissemblance *n.* —*See* ACT (2).
dissemble *v.* —*See* ACT (2), DISGUISE.
disseminate *v.* —*See* SPREAD (2).
dissemination *n.* —*See* DISTRIBUTION (2).
dissension *n.* —*See* CONFLICT, DIVISION (2).
dissent *v.* —*See* CONFLICT.
dissent *n.* —*See* CONFLICT, DIVISION (2).
dissenter *n.* —*See* OPPONENT, REBEL (2), SEPARATIST.
dissentience *n.* —*See* CONFLICT.
dissertation *n.* A thorough, written presentation of an original point of view ▸ thesis. —*See also* DISCOURSE.
disserve *v.* —*See* DAMAGE.
disservice *n.* —*See* INJUSTICE (1).
dissever *v.* —*See* CUT (2), DIVIDE.
disseverance or **disseverment** *n.* —*See* DIVISION (1).
dissidence *n.* —*See* CONFLICT.
dissident *n.* —*See* SEPARATIST.
dissident *adj.* —*See* INHARMONIOUS (1).
dissimilar *adj.* —*See* DIFFERENT.
dissimilarity or **dissimilitude** *n.* —*See* DIFFERENCE.
dissimulate *v.* —*See* ACT (2), DISGUISE.
dissimulation *n.* —*See* ACT (2).
dissipate *v.* To cause to separate and go in various directions ▸ dispel, disperse, scatter. [*Compare* DIVIDE, SEPARATE.] —*See also* DISAPPEAR (1), LIFT (2), WASTE.
dissipated *adj.* —*See* ABANDONED (2).
dissipation *n.* —*See* DISAPPEARANCE.
dissipative *adj.* —*See* EXTRAVAGANT.
dissociate *v.* —*See* DETACH.
dissociation *n.* —*See* DETACHMENT (1), DIVISION (1).
dissolute *adj.* —*See* ABANDONED (2).
dissoluteness *n.* —*See* LICENSE (2).
dissolution *n.* —*See* DEATH (1), DISAPPEARANCE, LICENSE (2).
dissolve *v.* To make a film image disappear gradually ▸ fade out. —*See also* DISAPPEAR (1), DISINTEGRATE, MELT.
dissonance *n.* —*See* CONFLICT.
dissonant *adj.* —*See* INCONGRUOUS, INHARMONIOUS (1), INHARMONIOUS (2).
dissuade *v.* To persuade a person not to do something ▸ deter, discourage, disincline, divert, put off. *Idiom:* talk out of. [*Compare* DISCOURAGE.]

dis·taff (dĭs′tăf′) ▸ *n.* 1. A staff that holds on its cleft end the flax, wool, or tow in spinning. 2. Women collectively.

distaff side ▸ *n.* The maternal family line.

dis·tal (dĭs′təl) ▸ *adj.* 1. Anatomically located far from the point of attachment, as a bone. 2. Situated farthest from the middle front of the jaw, as a tooth.

dis·tance (dĭs′təns) ▸ *n.* 1. Separation in space or time. 2. The interval separating any two specified instants in time. 3. *Math.* The length of a line segment joining two points. 4a. The degree of deviation or difference that separates two things in a relationship. b. The degree of progress between two points in a trend or course. 5. A point or area that is far away. 6. The whole way: *went the distance.* 7. Chillness of manner; aloofness. ▸ *v.* **-tanced, -tanc·ing.** 1. To place at or as if at a distance. 2. To outrun or outstrip.

dis·tant (dĭs′tənt) ▸ *adj.* 1a. Separate or apart in space or time. b. Far removed; remote. 2. Coming from, located at, or going to a distance. 3. Far apart in relationship: *a distant cousin.* 4. Aloof or chilly. **—dis′tant·ly** *adv.*

dis·taste (dĭs-tāst′) ▸ *n.* Dislike. **—dis·taste′ful** *adj.* **—dis·taste′ful·ly** *adv.*

dis·tem·per (dĭs-tĕm′pər) ▸ *n.* An infectious, often fatal viral disease occurring in dogs, cats, and certain other mammals.

dis·tend (dĭ-stĕnd′) ▸ *v.* To swell or cause to swell. **—dis·ten′si·ble** *adj.* **—dis·ten′tion, dis·ten′sion** *n.*

dis·till also **dis·til** (dĭ-stĭl′) ▸ *v.* **-tilled, -till·ing.** 1. To subject to or derive from distillation. 2. To separate from. 3. To exude in drops. **—dis·till′er** *n.* **—dis·till′er·y** *n.*

dis·til·late (dĭs′tə-lāt′, -lĭt, dĭ-stĭl′ĭt) ▸ *n.* A liquid condensed from vapor in distillation.

dis·til·la·tion (dĭs′tə-lā′shən) ▸ *n.* The evaporation of a liquid and subsequent condensation and collection of the vapors as a means of purification or of extraction of volatile components.

dis·tinct (dĭ-stĭngkt′) ▸ *adj.* 1. Distinguishable from all others. 2. Easily perceived; clear. 3. Clearly defined; unquestionable: *at a distinct disadvantage.* **—dis·tinct′ly** *adv.* **—dis·tinct′ness** *n.*

dis·tinc·tion (dĭ-stĭngk′shən) ▸ *n.* 1. The act of distinguishing; differentiation. 2. A difference. 3. A distinguishing factor or characteristic. 4. Excellence or eminence. 5. Honor: *graduated with distinction.*

dis·tinc·tive (dĭ-stĭngk′tĭv) ▸ *adj.* Serving to distinguish or set apart from others. **—dis·tinc′tive·ly** *adv.* **—dis·tinc′tive·ness** *n.*

dis·tin·guish (dĭ-stĭng′gwĭsh) ▸ *v.* 1. To recognize as being distinct. 2. To perceive distinctly; discern. 3. To discriminate. 4. To set apart. 5. To make eminent. **—dis·tin′guish·a·ble** *adj.* **—dis·tin′guish·a·bly** *adv.*

dis·tin·guished (dĭ-stĭng′gwĭsht) ▸ *adj.* 1. Characterized by excellence or distinction; eminent. 2. Dignified in conduct or appearance.

dis·tort (dĭ-stôrt′) ▸ *v.* 1. To twist out of a proper or natural shape or position. 2. To give a false or misleading account of; misrepresent. **—dis·tor′tion** *n.*

dis·tract (dĭ-străkt′) ▸ *v.* 1. To sidetrack; divert. 2. To upset emotionally; unsettle. **—dis·tract′ing·ly** *adv.* **—dis·trac′tion** *n.*

dis·traught (dĭ-strôt′) ▸ *adj.* 1. Deeply agitated or anxious. 2. Mad; crazed.

dis·tress (dĭ-strĕs′) ▸ *v.* 1. To cause anxiety or suffering to. 2. To mar or treat (e.g., an object or fabric) to give the appearance of an antique. ▸ *n.* 1. Pain or suffering of mind or body. 2. Severe psychological strain. 3. The condition of being in need of immediate assistance. **—dis·tress′ful** *adj.* **—dis·tress′ing·ly** *adv.*

dis·trib·ute (dĭ-strĭb′yo͞ot) ▸ *v.* **-ut·ed, -ut·ing.** 1. To divide and give out in portions. 2. To market, esp. as a wholesaler. 3. To deliver or hand out. 4. To spread or diffuse over an area. 5. To classify. **—dis′tri·bu′tion** *n.* **—dis·trib′u·tive** *adj.*

dis·trib·u·tor (dĭ-strĭb′yə-tər) ▸ *n.* 1. One that distributes, esp. a device that applies electric current to the spark plugs of an engine. 2. One that markets goods, esp. a wholesaler.

dis·trict (dĭs′trĭkt) ▸ *n.* 1. A division of an area, as for ad-

THESAURUS

distance *n.* 1. An extent, measured or unmeasured, of linear space ▸ gap, interval, length, range, reach, space, span, stretch. *Informal:* piece, way. [*Compare* EXTENT, GAP.] 2. The fact or condition of being far removed or apart ▸ farness, remoteness, separateness, separation. *—See also* DETACHMENT (2), EXPANSE (1).

distance *v.* *—See* ESTRANGE.

distant *adj.* Far from others in space, time, or relationship ▸ far, faraway, far-flung, far-off, remote, removed. *Idiom:* at a distance (*or* remove). *—See also* COOL.

distaste *n.* An attitude or feeling of mild aversion ▸ disinclination, dislike, disrelish, mislike. [*Compare* DISAPPROVAL, DISGUST, ENMITY, HATE.]

distasteful *adj.* *—See* BITTER (3), UNPALATABLE.

distend *v.* *—See* BROADEN, SWELL.

distill *v.* *—See* DRIP.

distinct *adj.* Distinguished from others by nature or qualities ▸ discrete, individual, separate, several, various. [*Compare* UNIQUE.] *—See also* APPARENT (1), DECIDED, DIFFERENT, SHARP (2).

distinction *n.* 1. The act or an instance of distinguishing ▸ demarcation, differentiation, discernment, discretion, discrimination, separation. 2. Recognition of achievement or superiority or a sign of this ▸ accolade, award, citation, commendation, honor, kudos, laurels, medal, prize, ribbon, trophy. [*Compare* REWARD.] *—See also* DIFFERENCE, FAME, VIRTUE.

distinctive *adj.* *—See* SPECIAL.

distinctiveness *n.* *—See* IDENTITY (1), INDIVIDUALITY.

distinctness *n.* *—See* CLARITY.

distinguish *v.* 1. To recognize as being different ▸ differentiate, discern, discriminate, know, separate, single out, tell. 2. To make noticeable or different ▸ characterize, differentiate, discriminate, identify, individualize, mark, set apart, signalize, single out, singularize. *—See also* DISCERN, NOTICE. 3. To cause to be eminent or recognized ▸ dignify, elevate, ennoble, exalt, glorify, honor, praise, signalize. [*Compare* CELEBRATE, EXALT, HONOR.]

distinguishable *adj.* *—See* PERCEPTIBLE.

distinguished *adj.* *—See* FAMOUS, NOTICEABLE.

distort *v.* To give an inaccurate view of by representing falsely or misleadingly ▸ alter, belie, bend, color, cook, falsify, fudge, load, misrepresent, misstate, pervert, slant, stretch, twist, warp, wrench, wrest. *Idiom:* give a false coloring to. [*Compare* BIAS, EQUIVOCATE, LIE^{2}.] *—See also* DEFORM.

distortion *n.* *—See* DEFORMITY, EQUIVOCATION, LIE^{2}.

distract *v.* *—See* AGITATE (2).

distracted *v.* *—See* ABSENT-MINDED.

distraction *n.* *—See* AMUSEMENT, DAZE.

distrait *adj.* *—See* ABSENT-MINDED.

distraught *adj.* *—See* ANXIOUS, INSANE.

distress *v.* To cause emotional suffering or painful sorrow to ▸ aggrieve, anguish, grieve, harrow, hurt, injure, pain, traumatize, trouble, vex, wound. [*Compare* AFFLICT, AGITATE, ANNOY, OFFEND.] *—See also* WORRY.

distress *n.* A state of physical or mental suffering ▸ affliction, agony, anguish, grief, hurt, injury, misery, pain, sorrow, torment, torture, vexation, woe, wound, wretchedness. *Slang:* murder. [*Compare* ANNOYANCE, DIFFICULTY.] *—See also* ANXIETY (1), EMERGENCY, HARM.

distressed *adj.* *—See* ANXIOUS.

distressing or **distressful** *adj.* *—See* DISTURBING.

distribute *v.* To give out in portions or shares ▸ admeasure, allocate, allot, allow, apportion, assign, deal (out), disburse, dish (out), dispense, divide, dole out, give (out), hand out, issue, measure out, mete out, parcel out, portion (out), ration (out), share. *Slang:* divvy. [*Compare* APPROPRIATE.] *—See also* CLASSIFY, SPREAD (2).

distribution *n.* 1. The act of distributing or the condition of being distributed ▸ admeasurement, allocation, allotment, apportionment, assignment, disbursement, dispensation, division, dishing out, doling out, meting out, portioning out, rationing out, sharing. 2. The passing out or spreading about of something over a wide area ▸ circulation, diffusion, dispersal, dispersion, dissemination, scattering. *—See also* ALLOTMENT, ARRANGEMENT (1).

district *n.* *—See* AREA (2), NEIGHBOR-

ministrative purposes. **2.** A region having a distinguishing feature. ▸ *v.* To divide into districts.
district attorney ▸ *n.* The prosecuting officer of a judicial district.
District of Columbia ▸ A federal district of the E US on the Potomac R. between VA and MD; coextensive with the city of Washington.
dis·trust (dĭs-trŭst′) ▸ *n.* Lack of trust or confidence; suspicion. ▸ *v.* To have no confidence in. **—dis·trust′ful** *adj.* **—dis·trust′ful·ly** *adv.* **—dis·trust′ful·ness** *n.*
dis·turb (dĭ-stûrb′) ▸ *v.* **1.** To destroy the tranquillity or settled state of. **2.** To trouble emotionally or mentally. **3.** To intrude on or interfere with; interrupt. **4.** To disarrange. **—dis·tur′bance** *n.* **—dis·turb′er** *n.* **—dis·turb′ing·ly** *adv.*
dis·u·nite (dĭs′yo͞o-nīt′) ▸ *v.* **-nit·ed, -nit·ing.** To separate; divide.
dis·u·ni·ty (dĭs-yo͞o′nĭ-tē) ▸ *n., pl.* **-ties.** Lack of unity; dissension.
dis·use (dĭs-yo͞os′) ▸ *n.* The state of not being used or no longer being in use.
ditch (dĭch) ▸ *n.* A trench dug in the ground. ▸ *v.* **1.** To dig or make a ditch. **2.** To drive (a vehicle) into a ditch. **3.** *Slang* To discard. **4.** To crash-land on water.
dith·er (dĭ*th*′ər) ▸ *n.* Indecisive agitation. **—dith′er** *v.*
dit·to (dĭt′ō) ▸ *n., pl.* **-tos. 1.** The same as stated above or before. **2.** A duplicate or copy. **3.** A pair of small marks (") used as a symbol for the word *ditto.*
dit·ty (dĭt′ē) ▸ *n., pl.* **-ties.** A simple song.
di·u·ret·ic (dī′ə-rĕt′ĭk) ▸ *adj.* Tending to increase the discharge of urine. **—di′u·ret′ic** *n.*
di·ur·nal (dī-ûr′nəl) ▸ *adj.* **1.** Of or occurring in a 24-hour period; daily. **2.** Occurring or active during the daytime. **—di·ur′nal·ly** *adv.*
di·va (dē′və) ▸ *n., pl.* **-vas** or **-ve** (-vā). **1.** An operatic prima donna. **2.** A very successful female singer of nonoperatic music.
di·va·gate (dī′və-gāt′, dĭv′ə-) ▸ *v.* **-gat·ed, -gat·ing.** To wander or drift about. **—di′va·ga′tion** *n.*
di·va·lent (dī-vā′lənt) ▸ *adj.* Having a valence of 2.
di·van (dĭ-văn′, dī′văn′) ▸ *n.* A long backless sofa; couch.
dive (dīv) ▸ *v.* **dived** or **dove** (dōv), **dived, div·ing. 1.** To plunge, esp. headfirst, into water. **2.** To submerge: *dive for pearls.* **3.** To fall or drop sharply and rapidly; plummet. **4.** To lunge, leap, or dash. ▸ *n.* **1.** The act or an instance of diving. **2.** A quick pronounced drop. **3.** *Slang* A disreputable or run-down bar or nightclub. **—div′er** *n.*
dive-bomb (dīv′bŏm′) ▸ *v.* To bomb from an airplane at the end of a steep dive toward the target. **—dive′-bomb′er** *n.*
di·verge (dĭ-vûrj′, dī-) ▸ *v.* **-verged, -verg·ing. 1.** To extend in different directions from a common point. **2.** To differ, as in opinion. **3.** To deviate from a norm. **—di·ver′gent** *adj.* **—di·ver′gent·ly** *adv.*
di·ver·gence (dĭ-vûr′jəns, dī-) ▸ *n.* **1.** An act or instance of diverging. **2.** Departure from a norm; deviation. **3.** Difference, as of opinion.
di·vers (dī′vərz) ▸ *adj.* Various; sundry.
di·verse (dĭ-vûrs′, dī-, dī′vûrs′) ▸ *adj.* **1.** Distinct in kind; unlike. **2.** Having variety in form; diversified. **—di·verse′ly** *adv.* **—di·verse′ness** *n.*
di·ver·si·fy (dĭ-vûr′sə-fī′, dī-) ▸ *v.* **-fied, -fy·ing. 1.** To make diverse; vary. **2.** To spread out activities or investments, esp. in business. **—di·ver′si·fi·ca′tion** *n.*
di·ver·sion (dĭ-vûr′zhən, -shən, dī-) ▸ *n.* **1.** The act or an instance of diverting. **2.** That which diverts.
di·ver·si·ty (dĭ-vûr′sĭ-tē, dī-) ▸ *n., pl.* **-ties. 1.** The fact or quality of being diverse; difference. **2.** Variety or multiformity.
di·vert (dĭ-vûrt′, dī-) ▸ *v.* **1.** To turn aside from a course or direction. **2.** To distract. **3.** To amuse or entertain.
di·ver·ti·men·to (dĭ-vĕr′tə-mĕn′tō) ▸ *n., pl.* **-tos** also **-ti** (-tē). A chiefly 18th-cent. form of instrumental chamber music having several short movements.
di·vest (dĭ-vĕst′, dī-) ▸ *v.* **1.** To strip, as of clothes. **2.** To deprive, as of rights; dispossess. **—di·vest′ment** *n.*
di·ves·ti·ture (dĭ-vĕs′tĭ-chər, -cho͝or′, dī-) ▸ *n.* **1.** An act of divesting. **2.** The sale, liquidation, or spinoff of a corporate division or subsidiary.
di·vide (dĭ-vīd′) ▸ *v.* **-vid·ed, -vid·ing. 1.** To separate or become separated into parts, sections, or groups. **2.** To classify. **3.** To set at odds; disunite. **4.** To separate from something else; cut off. **5.** To distribute among a number; apportion. **6.** *Math.* **a.** To subject to the process of division. **b.** To be an exact divisor of. **7.** To branch out, as a river. ▸ *n.* A watershed.
div·i·dend (dĭv′ĭ-dĕnd′) ▸ *n.* **1.** *Math.* A quantity to be divided. **2.** A share of profits received by a stockholder. **3.** A bonus.

THESAURUS

HOOD (1), TERRITORY.
distrust *n.* Lack of trust ▸ cynicism, doubt, leeriness, mistrust, skepticism, suspicion, wariness. *—See also* DISBELIEF, DOUBT.
distrust *v.* To lack trust or confidence in ▸ disbelieve, doubt, misdoubt, mistrust, question, suspect. *—See also* DISBELIEVE, DOUBT.
distrustful *adj.* Lacking trust or confidence ▸ cynical, distrusting, doubting, leery, mistrustful, skeptical, suspicious, untrusting, wary. [*Compare* INCREDULOUS.] *—See also* DOUBTFUL (2).
distrustfully *adv.* *—See* SKEPTICALLY.
distrusting *adj.* *—See* DISTRUSTFUL.
disturb *v.* To alter the settled state or position of ▸ dislocate, disorder, displace, disrupt, move, shake, shift, upset. *—See also* AGITATE (2), ANNOY, DISORDER, DISRUPT.
disturbance *n.* *—See* AGITATION (1), DISORDER (2), DISPLACEMENT, INSANITY.
disturbed *adj.* *—See* ANXIOUS.
disturbing *adj.* Troubling to the mind or emotions ▸ agitating, annoying, bothersome, burdensome, disquieting, disruptive, distressing, distressful, galling, intrusive, irksome, irritating, nettlesome, perturbing, plaguy, provoking, troublesome, troubling, troublous, unsettling, upsetting, vexatious, vexing, worrisome. [*Compare* UNCOMFORTABLE.]
disunion *n.* *—See* DIVISION (1), DIVISION (2).
disunite *v.* *—See* DIVIDE, ESTRANGE.
disunity *n.* *—See* DIVISION (2).
disuse *n.* *—See* OBSOLETENESS.
ditch *n.* *—See* FURROW.
ditch *v.* *—See* DISCARD.
dither *n.* *—See* AGITATION (2).
dither *v.* *—See* HESITATE.
dithyrambic *adj.* *—See* PASSIONATE.
ditsiness *n.* *—See* FOOLISHNESS.
ditsy *adj.* *—See* FOOLISH.
ditto *n.* *—See* COPY (1).
ditto *v.* *—See* COPY.
ditty *n.* *—See* SONG.
ditz *n.* *—See* FOOL.
divagate *v.* *—See* DEVIATE, DIGRESS.
divagation *n.* *—See* DEVIATION, DIGRESSION.
divarication *n.* *—See* DIFFERENCE.
dive *v.* *—See* FALL (1), FALL (4), PLUNGE.
dive into *v.* *—See* ATTACK (2).
dive *n.* *Slang* A disreputable or rundown bar or restaurant ▸ *Slang:* dump, honky-tonk, joint, juke house, juke joint. *Idiom:* hole in the wall. *—See also* FALL (1), FALL (3).
diverge *v.* *—See* BRANCH, CONFLICT, DEVIATE, DIFFER, DIGRESS.
divergence or **divergency** *n.* *—See* ABNORMALITY, DEVIATION, DIFFERENCE, DIGRESSION, DIVISION (2).
divergent *adj.* *—See* ABNORMAL, DIFFERENT.
divers *adj.* *—See* SEVERAL, VARIOUS.
diverse *adj.* *—See* DIFFERENT, VARIOUS.
diversification or **diverseness** *n.* *—See* VARIETY.
diversified *adj.* Not limited to a single class ▸ general, indefinite. *—See also* VARIOUS.
diversiform *adj.* *—See* IRREGULAR.
diversify *v.* *—See* BRANCH.
diversion *n.* *—See* AMUSEMENT, DEVIATION, DIGRESSION.
diversity *n.* *—See* VARIETY.
divert *v.* *—See* AMUSE, DISSUADE, TURN (2).
diverting *adj.* *—See* PLEASANT.
divest *v.* *—See* BARE, DEPRIVE.
divestiture *n.* *—See* DEPRIVATION.
divide *v.* To break up the unity of something; separate into parts, sections, or branches ▸ break, break apart (*or* up), detach, disband, disconnect, disengage, disjoin, disjoint, dissever, disunite, divorce, part, partition, section, segment, separate, split (up), uncouple. [*Compare* BREAK, CUT, DISINTEGRATE, TEAR[1].] *—See also* BRANCH, CLASSIFY, DISTRIBUTE.
divide *n.* *—See* GAP (1).

di·vid·er (dĭ-vī′dər) ▸ *n.* **1.** One that divides, esp. a partition. **2.** A compasslike device used for dividing lines and transferring measurements.

div·i·na·tion (dĭv′ə-nā′shən) ▸ *n.* **1.** The art or act of foretelling future events or revealing occult knowledge by means of augury or alleged supernatural agency. **2.** An inspired guess or presentiment.

di·vine (dĭ-vīn′) ▸ *adj.* **-vin·er, -vin·est. 1a.** Being a deity. **b.** Of or relating to a deity. **2.** Superhuman; godlike. **3.** Supremely good; magnificent. ▸ *n.* **1.** A cleric. **2.** A theologian. ▸ *v.* **-vined, -vin·ing. 1.** To prophesy through or practice divination. **2.** To guess, infer, or conjecture. **—di·vine′ly** *adv.* **—di·vin′er** *n.*

diving board ▸ *n.* A flexible board from which a dive may be executed.

di·vin·ing rod (dĭ-vī′nĭng) ▸ *n.* A forked rod believed to indicate underground water or minerals by bending downward when held over a source.

di·vin·i·ty (dĭ-vĭn′ĭ-tē) ▸ *n., pl.* **-ties. 1.** The state or quality of being divine. **2. the Divinity** God. **3.** Theology.

di·vis·i·ble (dĭ-vĭz′ə-bəl) ▸ *adj.* Capable of being divided. **—di·vis′i·bil′i·ty** *n.*

di·vi·sion (dĭ-vĭzh′ən) ▸ *n.* **1.** The act or process of dividing or the state of being divided. **2.** Something that serves to divide or separate. **3.** One of the parts, sections, or groups into which something is divided. **4.** A self-contained military unit smaller than a corps. **5.** Disagreement; disunion. **6.** *Math.* The operation of determining how many times one quantity is contained in another. **—di·vi′sion·al** *adj.*

di·vi·sive (dĭ-vī′sĭv) ▸ *adj.* Creating dissension or discord. **—di·vi′sive·ly** *adv.* **—di·vi′sive·ness** *n.*

di·vi·sor (dĭ-vī′zər) ▸ *n.* The quantity by which another, the dividend, is divided.

di·vorce (dĭ-vôrs′) ▸ *n.* **1.** The legal dissolution of a marriage. **2.** A complete severance. ▸ *v.* **-vorced, -vorc·ing. 1.** To dissolve the marriage bond between. **2.** To separate or disunite.

di·vor·cé (dĭ-vôr-sā′, -sē′) ▸ *n.* A divorced man.

di·vor·cée (dĭ-vôr-sā′, -sē′) ▸ *n.* A divorced woman.

div·ot (dĭv′ət) ▸ *n.* A piece of turf torn up by a golf club in striking a ball.

di·vulge (dĭ-vŭlj′) ▸ *v.* **-vulged, -vulg·ing.** To make known (something secret). **—di·vul′gence** *n.*

div·vy (dĭv′ē) ▸ *v.* **-vied, -vy·ing.** *Slang* To divide: *divvied up the loot.*

Dix (dĭks), **Dorothea Lynde** (1802–87) ▸ Amer. reformer and educator.

Dix·ie (dĭk′sē) ▸ A region of the S and E US, usu. comprising the states that joined the Confederacy during the Civil War.

Dix·ie·land (dĭk′sē-lănd′) ▸ *n.* An instrumental jazz style associated with New Orleans and marked by a two-beat rhythm and improvisation.

di·zy·got·ic (dī′zī-gŏt′ĭk) ▸ *adj.* Derived from two separately fertilized eggs. Used esp. of fraternal twins.

diz·zy (dĭz′ē) ▸ *adj.* **-zi·er, -zi·est. 1.** Having a whirling sensation. **2.** Bewildered or confused. **3.** *Slang* Scatterbrained or silly. **—diz′zi·ly** *adv.* **—diz′zi·ness** *n.* **—diz′zy** *v.*

DJ ▸ *abbr.* disc jockey

Dja·kar·ta (jə-kär′tə) ▸ See **Jakarta.**

Dji·bou·ti (jĭ-bo͞o′tē) ▸ A country of E Africa on the Gulf of Aden.

DNA (dē′ĕn-ā′) ▸ *n.* A nucleic acid that carries the genetic information which determines individual hereditary characteristics, consists of two long chains of nucleotides twisted into a double helix, and is the major constituent of chromosomes.

Dnie·per (nē′pər) ▸ A river rising in W-central Russia and flowing about 2,285 km (1,420 mi) through Belarus and Ukraine to the Black Sea.

do[1] (do͞o) ▸ *v.* **did** (dĭd), **done** (dŭn), **do·ing, does** (dŭz). **1.** To perform or execute. **2.** To fulfill; complete. **3.** To produce: *do a play on Broadway.* **4.** To bring about; effect: *Crying won't do any good now.* **5.** To render: *do equal justice to both sides.* **6.** To put forth; exert: *Do the best you can.* **7.** To prepare, as by cleaning or washing: *did the dishes.* **8.** To work at: *What do you do?* **9.** To work out: *do homework.* **10.** *Informal* To travel (a specified distance). **11a.** To meet the needs of sufficiently; suit. **b.** To be adequate. **12.** To set or style (the hair). **13.** *Informal* To serve (a prison term). **14.** *Slang* To cheat; swindle: *did her out of an inheritance.* **15.** To behave; act: *Do as I say.* **16.** To get along; fare: *doing well.* **17.** Used as a substitute for an antecedent verb: *worked as hard as everyone else did.* **—aux. 1.** Used in questions, negative statements, and inverted phrases: *Do you understand? I did not sleep well. Little did we know.* **2.** Used for emphasis: *I do want to be sure.* ***—phrasal verbs:* do away with 1.** Make an end of; eliminate. **2.** To destroy; kill. **do in** *Slang* **1.** To tire completely; exhaust. **2.** To kill. **do up** To adorn or dress lavishly. ▸ *n., pl.* **do's** or **dos.** A statement of what should be done: *a list of the do's and don'ts.*

do[2] (dō) ▸ *n. Mus.* The 1st tone of the diatonic scale.

do·a·ble (do͞o′ə-bəl) ▸ *adj.* Possible to do.

Do·ber·man pin·scher (dō′bər-mən pĭn′shər) ▸ *n.* A fairly large dog of a breed originating in Germany, with a smooth short-haired coat.

THESAURUS

divination *n.* —*See* MAGIC (1), PROPHECY.

divine *adj.* **1.** Of, from, like, or being a god or God ▸ celestial, deific, godlike, godly, heavenly, holy, supernal. **2.** In the service or worship of God or a god ▸ anointed, consecrated, devoted, devout, faithful, hallowed, holy, ordained, pious, religious, sacred, sacrosanct, sanctified. [*Compare* HOLY.] —*See also* HEAVENLY (1), MARVELOUS.

divine *n.* —*See* CLERIC.

divine *v.* —*See* FORESEE, PROPHESY, SOLVE (1).

divineness *n.* —*See* HOLINESS.

diviner *n.* —*See* PROPHET.

divine spark *n.* —*See* SPIRIT (2).

divinitory *adj.* —*See* PROPHETIC.

division *n.* **1.** The act or an instance of separating one thing from another ▸ detachment, disassociation, disjunction, disjuncture, disseverance, disseverment, dissociation, disunion, divorce, divorcement, fission, fissure, parting, partition, segmentation, separation, severance, split. **2.** The condition of being divided, as in opinion ▸ dissension, dissent, disunion, disunity, divergence, divergency, schism. [*Compare* BREACH, CONFLICT.] —*See also* ALLOTMENT, BRANCH (1), BRANCH (3), CLASS (1), CONFERENCE (2), DISTRIBUTION (1), FORCE (3), PART (1).

divorce *n.* —*See* DIVISION (1).

divorce *v.* —*See* DIVIDE, SEPARATE (1).

divorcement *n.* —*See* DIVISION (1).

divulge *v.* —*See* AIR (2), BETRAY (2), COMMUNICATE (1).

divulgence *n.* —*See* REVELATION.

divvy *v.* —*See* DISTRIBUTE.

divvy *n.* —*See* ALLOTMENT.

dizziness *n.* A sensation of whirling or falling ▸ giddiness, grogginess, lightheadedness, unsteadiness, vertiginousness, vertigo, wooziness.

dizzy *adj.* **1.** Having a sensation of whirling or falling ▸ dazed, giddy, groggy, lightheaded, reeling, spinning, staggered, unsteady, vertiginous, woozy. **2.** Producing dizziness or vertigo ▸ dizzying, giddy, sickening, vertiginous. [*Compare* STEEP[1].] —*See also* CONFUSED (1), GIDDY (2).

dizzy *v.* —*See* CONFUSE (1).

dizzying *adj.* Producing dizziness or vertigo ▸ dizzy, giddy, sickening, vertiginous. [*Compare* STEEP[1].]

do *v.* **1.** To meet a need or requirement ▸ answer, serve, suffice, suit. **2.** To be responsible for or guilty of an error or crime ▸ carry out, commit, perpetrate. *Informal:* pull off. [*Compare* PERFORM.] **3.** *Informal* To spend or complete time, as a prison term ▸ put in, serve. **4.** To work at, especially as a profession ▸ follow, practice, pursue. ***Idiom:*** hang out one's shingle. [*Compare* LABOR.] —*See also* ACT (1), ACT (3), CHEAT (1), COVER (2), FULFILL, MANAGE, PERFORM (1), SATISFY (1), STAGE.

do for *v.* To work and care for ▸ attend, minister to, serve, wait on (*or* upon). [*Compare* HELP, TEND[2], WORK.]

do in *v.* —*See* MURDER, RUIN, TIRE (1).

do over *v.* To do or perform an act again ▸ duplicate, play over, redo, repeat, replay. [*Compare* COPY.]

do up *v.* To cover and tie something, as with paper and string ▸ package, wrap.

do *n.* —*See* PARTY.

doable *adj.* —*See* POSSIBLE.

do·bra (dō′brə) ► *n.* See **currency** table in Appendix.
doc·ile (dŏs′əl, -īl′) ► *adj.* Easily managed or taught; tractable. **—do·cil′i·ty** (dŏ-sĭl′ĭ-tē, dō-) *n.*
dock[1] (dŏk) ► *n.* **1.** The area of water between two piers or alongside a pier that receives a ship. **2.** A pier or wharf. **3.** often **docks** A group of piers on a commercial waterfront. **4.** A loading platform for trucks or trains. ► *v.* **1.** To maneuver into or next to a dock. **2.** To couple (two or more spacecraft) in space.
dock[2] (dŏk) ► *v.* **1.** To clip short or cut off (e.g., an animal's tail). **2.** To withhold or deduct a part from (one's salary or wages).
dock[3] (dŏk) ► *n.* An enclosed place where the defendant stands or sits in a court of law.
dock[4] (dŏk) ► *n.* See **sorrel**[1].
dock·age (dŏk′ĭj) ► *n.* **1.** A charge for docking privileges. **2.** Facilities for docking vessels.
dock·et (dŏk′ĭt) ► *n.* **1a.** A calendar of the cases awaiting action in a court. **b.** A brief entry of the court proceedings in a legal case. **c.** The book containing such entries. **2.** A list of things to be done; agenda. **3.** A label affixed to a package listing contents or directions. ► *v.* To enter in a court calendar.
dock·hand (dŏk′hănd′) ► *n.* A dockworker.
dock·work·er (dŏk′wûr′kər) ► *n.* A worker who loads and unloads ships; stevedore.
dock·yard (dŏk′yärd′) ► *n.* A shipyard.
doc·tor (dŏk′tər) ► *n.* **1.** A person, esp. a physician, dentist, or veterinarian, trained in the healing arts and licensed to practice. **2.** One holding the highest academic degree awarded by a college or university. ► *v.* **1.** *Informal* To give medical treatment to. **2.** To repair, esp. in a makeshift manner. **3.** To falsify or change. **4.** To add ingredients to. **—doc′tor·al** *adj.*
doc·tor·ate (dŏk′tər-ĭt) ► *n.* The degree or status of an academic doctor.
doc·tri·naire (dŏk′trə-nâr′) ► *adj.* Marked by inflexible attachment to a practice or theory without regard to its practicality. **—doc′tri·nair′ism** *n.*
doc·trine (dŏk′trĭn) ► *n.* **1.** A body of principles presented for acceptance or belief, as by a religious, political, or philosophic group. **2.** A statement of official government policy, esp. in foreign affairs. **—doc′tri·nal** (dŏk′trə-nəl, dŏk-trī′-) *adj.*
doc·u·dra·ma (dŏk′yə-drä′mə, -drăm′ə) ► *n.* A television or movie dramatization based on fact.
doc·u·ment (dŏk′yə-mənt) ► *n.* **1.** A paper that provides evidence or information. **2.** Something, such as a photograph or computer file, that contains information. ► *v.* (-mĕnt′) To support (a claim) with evidence. **—doc′u·men·ta′tion** *n.*
doc·u·men·ta·ry (dŏk′yə-mĕn′tə-rē) ► *adj.* **1.** Of or based on documents. **2.** Of or being a documentary. ► *n., pl.* **-ries.** A work, such as a film or television program, presenting factual information without editorial comment or fictional elements.
dod·der (dŏd′ər) ► *v.* To shake or tremble, as from old age.
do·dec·a·gon (dō-dĕk′ə-gŏn′) ► *n.* A polygon with 12 sides.
do·dec·a·he·dron (dō′dĕk-ə-hē′drən) ► *n., pl.* **-drons** or **-dra** (-drə). A polyhedron with 12 faces.
dodge (dŏj) ► *v.* **dodged, dodg·ing. 1.** To avoid by moving quickly aside. **2.** To evade by cunning or deceit. **3.** To move aside by twisting suddenly. ► *n.* **1.** The act of dodging. **2.** An ingenious expedient intended to evade or trick. **—dodg′er** *n.*
Dodg·son (dŏj′sən), **Charles Lutwidge** Lewis Carroll (1832–98) ► British mathematician and writer.
do·do (dō′dō) ► *n., pl.* **-does** or **-dos. 1.** A large flightless bird extinct since the 17th cent. **2.** *Informal* **a.** One who is hopelessly passé. **b.** A stupid person.
doe (dō) ► *n., pl.* **doe** or **does.** The female of a deer or certain other animals, such as the hare or kangaroo.
do·er (dōō′ər) ► *n.* One who does something, esp. an active, energetic person.
does (dŭz) ► *v.* 3rd pers. sing. pr.t. of **do**[1].
doe·skin (dō′skĭn′) ► *n.* **1.** Soft leather made from the skin of a doe. **2.** A fine, soft, smooth woolen fabric.
does·n't (dŭz′ənt) ► Does not.
doff (dôf, dŏf) ► *v.* **1.** To take off: *doff one's clothes.* **2.** To tip or lift (one's hat) in salutation.
dog (dôg, dŏg) ► *n.* **1.** A domesticated canine mammal that is related to the foxes and wolves. **2.** Any of various other canines, such as the dingo. **3.** A male canine animal. **4.** *Informal* A person: *a lucky dog.* **5.** A person who is contemptible. **6.** An inferior product or creation. **7. dogs** *Slang* The feet. **8.** *Slang* A hot dog. ► *v.* **dogged, dog·ging. 1.** To track or trail persistently. ***—idiom:* go to the dogs** To go to ruin.
dog·cart (dôg′kärt′, dŏg′-) ► *n.* A one-horse vehicle for two persons seated back to back.
dog·catch·er (dôg′kăch′ər, dŏg′-) ► *n.* An official charged with impounding stray dogs.
doge (dōj) ► *n.* The elected chief magistrate of the former republics of Venice and Genoa.
dog-ear (dôg′îr′, dŏg′-) ► *n.* A turned-down corner of a page in a book. **—dog′-ear′** *v.* **—dog′-eared′** *adj.*
dog-eat-dog (dôg′ēt-dôg′, dŏg′ēt-dŏg′) ► *adj.* Ruthlessly acquisitive or competitive.
dog·fight (dôg′fīt′, dŏg′-) ► *n.* An aerial battle between fighter planes.
dog·fish (dôg′fĭsh′, dŏg′-) ► *n.* Any of various small sharks.
dog·ged (dô′gĭd, dŏg′ĭd) ► *adj.* Stubbornly persevering; tenacious. **—dog′ged·ly** *adv.* **—dog′ged·ness** *n.*
dog·ger·el (dô′gər-əl, dŏg′ər-) ► *n.* Clumsy verse, often irregular in form and humorous in effect.
dog·gy or **dog·gie** (dô′gē, dŏg′ē) ► *n., pl.* **-gies.** A dog, esp. a small one.
dog·house (dôg′hous′, dŏg′-) ► *n.* A shelter for a dog. ***—idiom:* in the doghouse** *Slang* In trouble.
do·gie also **do·gy** (dō′gē) ► *n., pl.* **-gies.** *Regional* A stray or motherless calf.
dog·leg (dôg′lĕg′, dŏg′-) ► *n.* A sharp bend or turn. **—dog′-leg′** *v.*
dog·ma (dôg′mə, dŏg′-) ► *n., pl.* **-mas** or **-ma·ta** (-mə-tə). **1.** A corpus of doctrines set forth by a religion. **2.** An authoritative principle or belief, esp. one considered to be absolutely true.
dog·mat·ic (dôg-măt′ĭk, dŏg-) ► *adj.* Marked by an authoritative,

THESAURUS

docent *n.* —*See* GUIDE.
docile *adj.* Capable of being educated ► educable, teachable, trainable. —*See also* GENTLE (1), OBEDIENT.
docket *n.* —*See* PROGRAM (1).
docket *v.* To enter on a schedule ► calendar, program, slate, schedule. —*See also* LIST[1].
doctor *v.* To alter something so as to give it a false character ► fake, falsify. —*See also* ADMINISTER (3), BIAS (2), CONTAMINATE, CURE, FIX (1).
doctored *adj.* —*See* IMPURE (2).
doctrinaire *adj.* —*See* CONVENTIONAL, NARROW (1).
doctrinal *adj.* —*See* CONVENTIONAL.
doctrine *n.* A statement presented for acceptance or belief, as by a religious or political group ► article of faith, belief, canon, concept, convention, credo, creed, dogma, gospel, ideology, line, opinion, orthodoxy, policy, position, precept, principle, proposition, teaching, tenet, theory, thesis. [*Compare* LAW.]
document *v.* —*See* PROVE.
documentation *n.* —*See* CONFIRMATION (2).
dodder *v.* —*See* STAGGER (1).
doddering *adj.* Of or relating to the mental or physical deterioration that often accompanies old age ► doting, senile. [*Compare* OLD, INFIRM.]
dodge *v.* —*See* AVOID, EVADE (1).
dodge *n.* —*See* BUSINESS (2), TRICK (1).
dodger *n.* —*See* CHEAT (2).
doff *v.* —*See* REMOVE (3).
dog *v.* —*See* FOLLOW (8).
dog days *n.* The season occurring between spring and autumn ► summer, summertime.
dog-eat-dog *adj.* —*See* COMPETITIVE.
dogged *adj.* —*See* DILIGENT, STUBBORN (1).
doggedness *n.* —*See* STUBBORNNESS.
doggone *adj.* —*See* DAMNED.
dogma *n.* —*See* DOCTRINE.
dogmatic *adj.* —*See* DICTATORIAL,

arrogant assertion of unproved principles. **—dog·mat′i·cal·ly** *adv.* **—dog′ma·tism′** *n.* **—dog′ma·tist** *n.*

do-good·er (do͞o′go͝od′ər) ► *n.* A naive idealist who supports philanthropic or humanitarian causes.

dog paddle ► *n.* A prone swimming stroke in which the limbs remain submerged.

dog tag ► *n.* **1.** An identification disk attached to a dog's collar. **2.** A metal identification tag worn around the neck by members of the armed forces.

dog·trot (dôg′trŏt′, dŏg′-) ► *n.* A steady trot like that of a dog. **—dog′trot′** *v.*

dog·wood (dôg′wo͝od′, dŏg′-) ► *n.* A tree with small greenish flowers surrounded by large, showy white or pink petallike bracts.

doi·ly (doi′lē) ► *n., pl.* **-lies.** A small ornamental mat, usu. of lace or linen.

do·ings (do͞o′ĭngz) ► *pl.n.* Activities, esp. social activities.

do-it-your·self (do͞o′ĭt-yər-sĕlf′) ► *adj.* Of or designed to be done by an amateur or as a hobby. **—do′-it-your·self′er** *n.*

dol·drums (dōl′drəmz′, dôl′-, dŏl′-) ► *pl.n. (takes sing. or pl. v.)* **1a.** A period of stagnation or slump. **b.** A period of depression or unhappy listlessness. **2.** An ocean region near the equator, marked by calms.

dole (dōl) ► *n.* **1.** Charitable dispensation of goods, esp. money, food, or clothing. **2.** A share of such goods. **3.** *Chiefly Brit.* Government welfare or relief. ► *v.* **doled, dol·ing. 1.** To dispense as charity. **2.** To distribute, esp. sparingly: *doled out the food rations.*

dole·ful (dōl′fəl) ► *adj.* Filled with grief; mournful. **—dole′ful·ly** *adv.* **—dole′ful·ness** *n.*

doll (dŏl) ► *n.* **1.** A child's toy having the likeness of a human. **2.** *Slang* **a.** An attractive person. **b.** A woman. **c.** A sweetheart. ► *v.* To dress smartly: *dolled themselves up for the party.*

dol·lar (dŏl′ər) ► *n.* See **currency** table in Appendix.

dol·lop (dŏl′əp) ► *n.* A lump or portion, as of ice cream.

dol·ly (dŏl′ē) ► *n., pl.* **-lies. 1.** *Informal* A doll. **2.** A low wheeled platform used for transporting heavy loads. **3.** A wheeled apparatus used to transport a movie or television camera about a set.

dol·men (dōl′mən, dŏl′-) ► *n.* See **portal tomb.**

dol·o·mite (dō′lə-mīt′, dŏl′ə-) ► *n.* A magnesia-rich sedimentary rock resembling limestone. **—dol′o·mit′ic** (-mĭt′ĭk) *adj.*

do·lor (dō′lər) ► *n.* Sorrow; grief. **—do′lor·ous** *adj.* **—do′lor·ous·ly** *adv.* **—do′lor·ous·ness** *n.*

dol·phin (dŏl′fĭn, dôl′-) ► *n.* **1.** Any of a family of marine mammals related to the whales but smaller and having a beaklike snout. **2.** Either of two marine game fishes having iridescent coloring.

dolt (dōlt) ► *n.* A stupid person. **—dolt′ish** *adj.*

-dom ► *suff.* **1.** State; condition: *stardom.* **2a.** Domain; position; rank: *dukedom.* **b.** A group having a specified position, office, or character: *officialdom.*

do·main (dō-mān′) ► *n.* **1.** A territory over which control is exercised. **2.** A sphere of activity, concern, or function. **3.** *Comp. Sci.* A group of networked computers having a common communications address.

dome (dōm) ► *n.* **1.** A vaulted roof of gen. hemispherical shape. **2.** A geodesic dome. **3.** Something resembling a dome. **—domed** *adj.*

do·mes·tic (də-mĕs′tĭk) ► *adj.* **1.** Of or relating to the family or household. **2.** Fond of home life and household affairs. **3.** Tame or domesticated. **4.** Of or relating to a country's internal affairs. **5.** Produced in or indigenous to a particular country. ► *n.* A household servant. **—do·mes′ti·cal·ly** *adv.* **—do′mes·tic′i·ty** (dō′mĕ-stĭs′ĭ-tē) *n.*

do·mes·ti·cate (də-mĕs′tĭ-kāt′) ► *v.* **-cat·ed, -cat·ing.** To adapt or make fit for domestic use or life; tame. **—do·mes′ti·ca′tion** *n.*

domestic partner ► *n.* A person, other than a spouse, with whom one cohabits.

dom·i·cile (dŏm′ĭ-sīl′, -səl, dō′mĭ-) ► *n.* A legal residence; home. **—dom′i·cile′** *v.*

dom·i·nant (dŏm′ə-nənt) ► *adj.* **1.** Exercising the most influence or control. **2.** Most prominent, as in position. **3.** *Genet.* Producing the same phenotypic effect whether inherited with an identical or dissimilar gene. **—dom′i·nance** *n.* **—dom′i·nant·ly** *adv.*

dom·i·nate (dŏm′ə-nāt′) ► *v.* **-nat·ed, -nat·ing. 1.** To control, govern, or rule. **2.** To enjoy a commanding position in or over. **3.** To overlook from a height. **4.** To occupy a position more elevated or superior to others. **—dom′i·na′tion** *n.* **—dom′i·na′tor** *n.*

dom·i·neer (dŏm′ə-nîr′) ► *v.* To rule over arrogantly; tyrannize.

Dom·i·ni·ca (dŏm′ə-nē′kə, də-mĭn′ĭ-kə) ► An island country of the E Caribbean between Guadeloupe and Martinique. **—Dom′i·ni′can** *adj. & n.*

Do·min·i·can Republic (də-mĭn′ĭ-kən) ► A country of the West Indies on the E part of the island of Hispaniola. **—Do·min′i·can** *adj. & n.*

do·min·ion (də-mĭn′yən) ► *n.* **1.** Control or exercise of control; sovereignty. **2.** A sphere of influence or control; realm. **3.** often **Dominion** A self-governing nation within the British Commonwealth.

Dominion Day ► *n.* See **Canada Day.**

THESAURUS

INTOLERANT (1), NARROW (1).

doing *n.* —*See* ACT (1).

doldrums *n.* —*See* BOREDOM, DEPRESSION (2).

dole *n.* —*See* ALLOTMENT, RELIEF (2).
  dole out *v.* —*See* DISTRIBUTE.

doleful *adj.* —*See* SORROWFUL.

dolefulness *n.* —*See* DEPRESSION (2).

do-little *n.* —*See* WASTREL (2).

doll *n.* —*See* BEAUTY, GIRL.
  doll up *v.* —*See* ADORN (1), DRESS UP.

dollop *n.* —*See* BIT[1] (2).

dolorous *adj.* —*See* SORROWFUL.

dolt *n.* —*See* DULLARD.

doltish *adj.* —*See* STUPID.

doltishness *n.* —*See* STUPIDITY.

domain *n.* —*See* AREA (1).

dome *n.* —*See* HEAD (1).

domestic *adj.* **1.** Of or relating to the family or household ► familial, family, home, homely, homey, household, residential. **2.** Trained or bred to live with and be of use to people ► broken (in), domesticated, housebroken, housetrained, naturalized, pet, tame. **3.** Of, from, or within a country's own territory ► aboriginal, autochthonous, home, homegrown, indigenous, internal, national, native. [*Compare* INDIGENOUS.]

domesticate *v.* To train to live with and be of use to people ► break in, domesticize, gentle, housebreak, house-train, master, naturalize, tame.

domesticated *adj.* —*See* DOMESTIC (2).

domesticize *v.* —*See* DOMESTICATE.

domicile *n.* —*See* HOME (1).
  domicile *v.* —*See* LIVE[1], LODGE.

dominance *n.* The condition or fact of being dominant ► ascendance, ascendancy, authority, command, control, domination, dominion, hegemony, lead, paramountcy, power, predominance, preeminence, preponderance, preponderancy, prepotency, rule, supremacy, sway. [*Compare* AUTHORITY.] —*See also* DOMINATION.

dominant *adj.* **1.** Exercising controlling power or influence ► ascendant, chief, commanding, controlling, dominating, dominative, governing, key, leading, main, major, paramount, predominant, preeminent, preponderant, prepotent, prevailing, primary, prime, principal, regnant, reigning, ruling, supreme. [*Compare* PRIMARY.] **2.** Exercising authority ► authoritative, commanding, lordly, masterful. [*Compare* ADMINISTRATIVE.]

dominate *v.* **1.** To occupy the preeminent position in ► command, control, lead, predominate, preponderate, prevail, reign, rule. *Idioms:* be cock of the walk, have the ascendancy, lord it over, reign supreme. **2.** To rise above, especially so as to afford a view of ► command, dwarf, overbear, overlook, overshadow, tower above (*or* over). —*See also* ADMINISTER (1), BOSS, ENSLAVE.

dominating *adj.* —*See* DOMINANT (1).

domination *n.* The act of exercising controlling power or the condition of being so controlled ► command, control, dominance, dominion, mastery, reign, repression, rule, subjugation, suppression, sway. —*See also* AUTHORITY, DOMINANCE, OPPRESSION.

dominative *adj.* —*See* DOMINANT (1).

domineer *v.* —*See* BOSS.

domineering *adj.* —*See* DICTATORIAL.

dominion *n.* —*See* AUTHORITY, DOMINANCE, DOMINATION, OWNERSHIP.

dom·i·no[1] (dŏm′ə-nō′) ► *n., pl.* **-noes** or **-nos. 1.** A small rectangular block marked by one to six dots. **2. dominoes** or **dominos** *(takes sing. or pl. v.)* A game played with dominoes.

dom·i·no[2] (dŏm′ə-nō′) ► *n., pl.* **-noes** or **-nos. 1a.** A hooded robe worn with an eye mask at a masquerade. **b.** The mask so worn. **2.** One wearing this costume.

domino effect ► *n.* An effect produced when one event sets off a chain of similar events.

don[1] (dŏn) ► *n.* **1. Don** A Spanish courtesy title for a man. **2.** *Chiefly Brit.* A teacher at a college of Oxford or Cambridge. **3.** The leader of an organized-crime family.

don[2] (dŏn) ► *v.* **donned, don·ning.** To put on (clothing).

Don ► A river of W Russia flowing about 1,963 km (1,220 mi) into the NE Sea of Azov.

Do·ña (dō′nyä) ► *n.* A Spanish courtesy title for a woman.

do·nate (dō′nāt′, dō-nāt′) ► *v.* **-nat·ed, -nat·ing.** To give to a fund or cause; contribute. **—do·na′tion** *n.* **—do′na·tor** *n.*

done (dŭn) ► *v.* P.part. of **do**[1]. ► *adj.* **1.** Completely accomplished or finished. **2.** Cooked adequately. **3.** Socially acceptable.

dong (dông, dŏng) ► *n.* See **currency** table in Appendix.

don·key (dŏng′kē, dŭng′-, dông′-) ► *n., pl.* **-keys. 1.** The domesticated ass. **2.** *Slang* An obstinate or stupid person.

Donne (dŭn), **John** (1572–1631) ► English metaphysical poet.

don·ny·brook (dŏn′ē-bro͝ok′) ► *n.* A free-for-all.

do·nor (dō′nər) ► *n.* One that contributes, gives, or donates.

don't (dōnt) ► Do not.

do·nut (dō′nŭt′, -nət) ► *n.* Var. of **doughnut.**

doo·dad (do͞o′dăd′) ► *n. Informal* An unnamed or nameless gadget or trinket.

doo·dle (do͞od′l) ► *v.* **-dled, -dling.** To scribble aimlessly, esp. when preoccupied. **—doo′dle** *n.*

doo·dle·bug (do͞od′l-bŭg′) ► *n.* See **ant lion** 2.

doom (do͞om) ► *n.* **1.** Condemnation to a severe penalty. **2.** Fate, esp. a tragic or ruinous one. **3.** Inevitable destruction or ruin. ► *v.* To condemn to ruination or death.

doom·say·er (do͞om′sā′ər) ► *n.* One who predicts calamity at every opportunity.

dooms·day (do͞omz′dā′) ► *n.* Judgment Day.

door (dôr) ► *n.* **1.** A movable panel used to close off an entrance. **2.** An entrance to a room, building, or passage. **3.** A means of approach or access.

do-or-die (do͞o′ər-dī′) ► *adj.* Requiring supreme effort to avoid dire consequences: *a do-or-die situation.*

door·jamb (dôr′jăm′) ► *n.* Either of the two vertical pieces framing a doorway.

door·keep·er (dôr′kē′pər) ► *n.* One employed to guard an entrance or gateway.

door·knob (dôr′nŏb′) ► *n.* A knob-shaped handle for opening and closing a door.

door·man (dôr′măn′, -mən) ► *n.* An attendant at the entrance of a building.

door·mat (dôr′măt′) ► *n.* **1.** A mat placed before a doorway for wiping the shoes. **2.** *Slang* One who submits meekly to mistreatment by others.

door prize ► *n.* A prize awarded by lottery to a ticketholder at a function.

door·step (dôr′stĕp′) ► *n.* A step leading to a door.

door·yard (dôr′yärd′) ► *n.* The yard in front of the door of a house.

doo·zy or **doo·zie** (do͞o′zē) ► *n., pl.* **-zies.** *Slang* Something extraordinary or bizarre.

do·pa (dō′pə) ► *n.* An amino acid formed in the liver and converted to dopamine in the brain.

do·pa·mine (dō′pə-mēn′) ► *n.* A monoamine neurotransmitter formed in the brain, essential to the normal functioning of the central nervous system.

dope (dōp) ► *n.* **1.** *Informal* **a.** A narcotic. **b.** An illicit drug, esp. marijuana. **2.** A narcotic preparation used to stimulate a racehorse. **3.** *Informal* A stupid person. **4.** *Informal* Factual information. ► *v.* **doped, dop·ing.** *Informal* **1.** To add or administer a narcotic to. **2.** To figure out (e.g., a puzzle). **—dop′er** *n.*

dope·ster (dōp′stər) ► *n.* One who forecasts future events, as in sports or politics.

dop·ey also **dop·y** (dō′pē) ► *adj.* **-i·er, -i·est.** *Slang* **1.** Dazed or lethargic, as if drugged. **2.** Stupid; foolish.

Dop·pler effect (dŏp′lər) ► *n. Phys.* An apparent change in the frequency of waves when the source and observer are either approaching or moving apart.

Dor·ic (dôr′ĭk, dŏr′-) ► *n.* A dialect of ancient Greek. **—Dor′ic** *adj.*

Doric order ► *n. Archit.* A classical order marked by heavy fluted columns with plain, saucer-shaped capitals and no base.

dork (dôrk) ► *n. Slang* A stupid, inept, or foolish person. **—dork′y** *adj.*

dorm (dôrm) ► *n. Informal* A dormitory.

dor·mant (dôr′mənt) ► *adj.* **1.** In a state resembling sleep. **2.** Latent. **3.** Temporarily inactive: *a dormant volcano.* **4.** *Biol.* In a condition of suspended growth or development. **—dor′man·cy** *n.*

dor·mer (dôr′mər) ► *n.* A window set vertically in a gable projecting from a sloping roof.

dor·mi·to·ry (dôr′mĭ-tôr′ē) ► *n., pl.* **-ries. 1.** A room providing sleeping quarters for several people. **2.** A residence hall, as at a school.

dor·mouse (dôr′mous′) ► *n.* A small squirrellike Old World rodent.

dor·sal (dôr′səl) ► *adj.* Of, toward, on, or near the back. **—dor′sal·ly** *adv.*

do·ry (dôr′ē) ► *n., pl.* **-ries.** A small flat-bottomed boat with high sides.

DOS (dŏs, dôs) ► *n. Comp. Sci.* An operating system that resides on a disk.

dose (dōs) ► *n.* A specified quantity of a therapeutic agent to be taken at one time or at stated intervals. ► *v.* **dosed, dos·ing.** To give a dose to. **—dos′age** *n.*

THESAURUS

don *v.* To put an article of clothing on one's person ► assume, get on, pull on, put on, slip into (*or* on). *—See also* DRESS (1).

donate *v.* To present as a gift to a charity or cause ► award, bequeath, bestow, contribute, endow, give (away), grant, hand out, pledge, present, subscribe. [*Compare* GIFT.] *—See also* CONTRIBUTE (1).

donation *n.* Something given to a charity or cause ► alms, award, benefaction, beneficence, bequest, charity, contribution, endowment, gift, grant, gratuity, handout, largess, offering, pledge, present, subscription. [*Compare* GIFT, GRATUITY, RELIEF.]

donator *n.* *—See* DONOR.

done *adj.* Having no further relationship ► finished, through. *—See also* COMPLETE (3), THROUGH (2).

done for *adj.* *—See* THROUGH (2).

done in *adj.* *—See* TIRED (1).

Don Juan *n.* A man who seduces women ► debaucher, Lothario, seducer. [*Compare* FLIRT, LECHER.] *—See also* GALLANT, PHILANDERER.

donnish *adj.* *—See* PEDANTIC.

donnybrook *n.* *—See* FIGHT (1).

donor *n.* A person who gives to a charity or cause ► benefactor, benefactress, contributor, donator, fairy godmother, giver, grantor, humanitarian, patron, patroness, philanthropist, provider, subscriber, supplier. *Informal:* angel. [*Compare* PATRON, SPONSOR.]

do-nothing *adj.* *—See* LAZY.

do-nothing *n.* *—See* WASTREL (2).

do-nothingism *n.* *—See* LAZINESS.

doodad or **doohickey** *n.* *—See* GADGET.

doodle *v.* *—See* PUTTER.

doom *n.* *—See* FATE (2).

doom *v.* *—See* CONDEMN.

doomed *adj.* *—See* CONDEMNED.

doomsayer *n.* *—See* PESSIMIST (2).

doormat *n.* *—See* WEAKLING.

dope *n.* *—See* DRUG (2), FOOL, INFORMATION.

dope *v.* *—See* DRUG (1).

dope out *v.* *—See* DESIGN (1), SOLVE (1).

doped *adj.* *—See* DRUGGED.

dopey *adj.* *—See* FOOLISH, LETHARGIC, STUPID.

dopeyness *n.* *—See* FOOLISHNESS.

dork *n.* *—See* DRIP (2), FOOL.

dormancy *n.* *—See* ABEYANCE.

dormant *adj.* *—See* LATENT.

dose *v.* *—See* ADMINISTER (3), DRUG (1).

do·sim·e·ter (dō-sĭm′ĭ-tər) ▸ *n.* An instrument that measures amounts of x-rays or radiation.

dos·si·er (dŏs′ē-ā′, dô′sē-ā′) ▸ *n.* A collection of papers giving detailed information about a particular person or subject.

dot (dŏt) ▸ *n.* **1.** A tiny round mark made by or as if by a pointed instrument; spot. **2.** The short sound or signal used in combination with the dash to represent letters or numbers in a code. **3.** *Mus.* A mark after a note indicating an increase in time value by half. **4.** A decimal point. **5.** *Comp. Sci.* A period that separates strings of characters, as in e-mail addresses or URLs. ▸ *v.* **dot·ted, dot·ting.** **1.** To mark with a dot. **2.** To cover with or as if with dots.

dot·age (dō′tĭj) ▸ *n.* A deterioration of the mind; senility.

dot·ard (dō′tərd) ▸ *n.* A senile person.

dot-com (dŏt′kŏm′) ▸ *adj.* Of or relating to business conducted on the Internet: *dot-com advertising.* ▸ *n.* A dot-com company.

dote (dōt) ▸ *v.* **dot·ed, dot·ing.** To show excessive love or fondness.

doth (dŭth) ▸ *v. Archaic* 3rd pers. sing. pr.t. of **do**[1].

dot matrix ▸ *n.* A dense grid of dots used to form characters or designs, as by some computer printers.

dot·ty (dŏt′ē) ▸ *adj.* **-ti·er, -ti·est.** Eccentric; daft; absurd.

dou·ble (dŭb′əl) ▸ *adj.* **1.** Twice as much in size, strength, number, or amount. **2.** Composed of two parts. **3.** Twofold; dual. **4.** Designed for two. **5.** Duplicitous. ▸ *n.* **1.** Something increased twofold. **2.** A duplicate; counterpart. **3.** An actor's understudy or stand-in. **4.** A sharp turn; reversal. **5. doubles** *Sports* A game, such as tennis or handball, having two players on each side. **6.** *Baseball* A hit enabling the batter to reach second base. **7.** *Games* A bid doubling one's opponent's bid in bridge. ▸ *v.* **-bled, -bling.** **1.** To make or become twice as great. **2.** To be twice as much as. **3.** To fold in two. **4.** *Baseball* To make a double. **5.** *Games* To challenge with a double in bridge. **6.** To reverse one's direction. **7.** To serve in an additional capacity. ▸ *adv.* **1.** To twice the amount or extent; doubly. **2.** Two together; in pairs. **3.** In two: *bent double.* ***—phrasal verb:* double up** **1.** To bend suddenly, as in pain or laughter. **2.** To share accommodations meant for one person. **—dou′bly** *adv.*

double agent ▸ *n.* A spy working simultaneously for two opposed governments.

double bass (bās) ▸ *n.* The largest and lowest-pitched member of the violin family.

dou·ble-breast·ed (dŭb′əl-brĕs′tĭd) ▸ *adj.* Fastened by lapping one edge of the front over the other: *a double-breasted jacket.*

dou·ble-click (dŭb′əl-klĭk′) ▸ *v.* To press a button, esp. on a pointing device, twice in rapid succession to activate a command.

dou·ble-cross (dŭb′əl-krôs′, -krŏs′) ▸ *v.* To betray by acting in contradiction to a prior agreement. **—dou′ble-cross′** *n.* **—dou′ble-cross′er** *n.*

dou·ble-deal·ing (dŭb′əl-dē′lĭng) ▸ *n.* Duplicity; treachery. **—dou′ble-deal′er** *n.* **—dou′ble-deal′ing** *adj.*

dou·ble-deck·er (dŭb′əl-dĕk′ər) ▸ *n.* Something, as a vehicle or sandwich, that has two decks or layers. **—dou′ble-deck′er** *adj.*

dou·ble-dig·it (dŭb′əl-dĭj′ĭt) ▸ *adj.* Being between 10 and 99 percent: *double-digit inflation.*

dou·ble-en·ten·dre (dŭb′əl-än-tän′drə, do͞o-blän-täɴ′drə) ▸ *n.* A word or phrase having a double meaning, esp. when one meaning is risqué.

dou·ble-head·er (dŭb′əl-hĕd′ər) ▸ *n.* Two games or events held in succession on the same program, esp. in baseball.

double helix ▸ *n.* The coiled structure of double-stranded DNA in which strands form a spiral configuration.

double jeopardy ▸ *n.* The act of putting a person through a second trial for an offense for which he or she has already been prosecuted or convicted.

dou·ble-joint·ed (dŭb′əl-join′tĭd) ▸ *adj.* Having unusually flexible joints, esp. of the limbs or fingers.

double negative ▸ *n. Gram.* A construction that employs two negatives, esp. to express a single negation.

double play ▸ *n. Baseball* A play in which two players are put out.

dou·ble·speak (dŭb′əl-spēk′) ▸ *n.* See **double talk** 2.

double star ▸ *n.* See **binary star.**

dou·blet (dŭb′lĭt) ▸ *n.* **1.** A close-fitting jacket formerly worn by European men. **2.** One of a pair of similar things.

double take ▸ *n.* A delayed reaction to an unusual remark or circumstance.

double talk ▸ *n.* **1.** Meaningless speech that consists of nonsense syllables mixed with intelligible words; gibberish. **2.** Deliberately ambiguous or evasive language.

dou·bloon (dŭ-blo͞on′) ▸ *n.* An obsolete Spanish gold coin.

doubt (dout) ▸ *v.* **1.** To be uncertain or skeptical about. **2.** To distrust. ▸ *n.* **1.** A lack of certainty or conviction. **2.** A lack of trust. **—doubt′er** *n.*

doubt·ful (dout′fəl) ▸ *adj.* **1.** Subject to or causing doubt. **2.** Experiencing or showing doubt. **3.** Of uncertain outcome. **4.** Questionable in character; suspicious. **—doubt′ful·ly** *adv.* **—doubt′ful·ness** *n.*

doubt·less (dout′lĭs) ▸ *adv.* **1.** Certainly. **2.** Presumably; probably. ▸ *adj.* Certain; assured. **—doubt′less·ly** *adv.*

THESAURUS

dot *n.* *—See* BIT[1] (1), POINT (2).
dot *v.* *—See* SPECKLE.

dotage *n.* The condition of being senile ▸ anecdotage, anility, caducity, senility. [*Compare* AGE.]

dote on *v.* **1.** To like or enjoy enthusiastically, often excessively ▸ adore, delight (in), love. *Slang:* eat up, groove on. **2.** To overindulge with affection or attention ▸ spoil. [*Compare* BABY, RAVE.]

doting *adj.* Relating to the mental deterioration that often accompanies old age ▸ doddering, senile. [*Compare* OLD, INFIRM.] *—See also* AFFECTIONATE.

dotty *adj.* *—See* INSANE.

double *adj.* **1.** Consisting of two identical or similar related things, parts, or elements ▸ dual, matched, paired, twin. [*Compare* EQUAL.] **2.** Composed of two parts or things ▸ biform, binary, dual, duple, duplex, duplicate, geminate, twofold, two-part, two-piece. *—See also* DISHONEST.
double *n.* One exactly resembling another ▸ clone, duplicate, image, picture, portrait, second, spitting image, twin. *Slang:* ringer. [*Compare* COPY.] *—See also* MATE, SUBSTITUTE.
double *v.* **1.** To make or become twice as great ▸ duplicate, geminate, redouble, twin. **2.** To turn sharply around ▸ about-face, double back, reverse. ***Idiom:*** turn on one's heels. *—See also* FOLD.

double-cross *v.* *—See* BETRAY (1), DECEIVE.
double cross or **double-cross** *n.* *—See* BETRAYAL.

double-crosser *n.* *—See* BETRAYER.

double-dealing *adj.* *—See* DISHONEST.
double-dealing *n.* *—See* DECEIT.

double-edged *adj.* *—See* AMBIGUOUS (2).

double-entendre *n.* *—See* AMBIGUITY.

double-faced *adj.* *—See* DISHONEST.

doublespeak *n.* *—See* GIBBERISH.

doublet *n.* *—See* COUPLE.

double talk *n.* *—See* BABBLE, GIBBERISH.

doubt *n.* A lack of conviction or certainty ▸ distrust, doubtfulness, dubiety, dubiousness, incertitude, misgiving, mistrust, qualm, query, question, reservation, skepticism, suspicion, uncertainty, wonder. *—See also* DISBELIEF, DISTRUST.
doubt *v.* To be uncertain, disbelieving, or skeptical about ▸ disbelieve, distrust, misdoubt, mistrust, query, question, waver, wonder. ***Idiom:*** have one's doubts. *—See also* DISBELIEVE, DISTRUST.

doubter *n.* *—See* SKEPTIC.

doubtful *adj.* **1.** Not likely ▸ dubious, improbable, problematic, questionable, unapt, unlikely. **2.** Experiencing doubt ▸ ambivalent, distrustful, doubting, dubious, hesitant, irresolute, skeptical, suspicious, tentative, uncertain, undecided, unsure, vacillating, wavering. ***Idiom:*** in doubt. [*Compare* DISTRUSTFUL, WARY.] *—See also* AMBIGUOUS (1), DEBATABLE, SHADY (1).

doubtfully *adv.* *—See* SKEPTICALLY.

doubtfulness *n.* *—See* DOUBT.

doubting *adj.* *—See* DISTRUSTFUL, DOUBTFUL (2).

doubting Thomas *n.* *—See* SKEPTIC.

doubtless *adv.* *—See* ABSOLUTELY.
doubtless *adj.* *—See* SURE (1).

doubtlessly *adv.* *—See* ABSOLUTELY.

doubtlessness *n.* *—See* SURENESS.

douche (do͞osh) ▸ *n.* **1.** A stream of fluid or air applied to a body part or cavity. **2.** An instrument for applying a douche. **—douche** *v.*

dough (dō) ▸ *n.* **1.** A soft thick mixture of flour and other ingredients that is kneaded, shaped, and baked, esp. as bread or pastry. **2.** *Slang* Money. **—dough′y** *adj.*

dough·boy (dō′boi′) ▸ *n.* An American infantryman in World War I.

dough·nut also **do·nut** (dō′nŭt′, -nət) ▸ *n.* A small ring-shaped cake made of rich light dough that is fried in deep fat.

dough·ty (dou′tē) ▸ *adj.* **-ti·er, -ti·est.** Courageous; brave.

Doug·las (dŭg′ləs), **Stephen Arnold** (1813–1861) ▸ Amer. politician.

Douglas fir ▸ *n.* A tall evergreen timber tree of NW North America.

Doug·lass (dŭg′ləs), **Frederick** (1817–95) ▸ Amer. abolitionist.

dour (do͝or, dour) ▸ *adj.* **-er, -est. 1.** Stern; forbidding. **2.** Silently ill-humored; gloomy. **—dour′ness** *n.*

douse[1] (dous) ▸ *v.* **doused, dous·ing. 1.** To plunge into liquid; immerse. **2.** To wet thoroughly; drench. **3.** To put out; extinguish. **—dous′er** *n.*

douse[2] (douz) ▸ *v.* Var. of **dowse.**

dove[1] (dŭv) ▸ *n.* **1.** A pigeon or related bird, esp. an undomesticated species. **2.** A person who advocates peace and negotiation instead of war. **—dov′ish** *adj.* **—dov′ish·ness** *n.*

dove[2] (dōv) ▸ *v.* P.t. of **dive.**

Do·ver (dō′vər) ▸ The capital of DE, in the central part.

Dover, Strait of ▸ A narrow channel at the E end of the English Channel between SE England and N France.

dove·tail (dŭv′tāl′) ▸ *n.* A fan-shaped tenon that forms a tight interlocking joint when fitted into a corresponding mortise. ▸ *v.* **1.** To join by means of dovetails. **2.** To combine or interlock into a unified whole.

dow·a·ger (dou′ə-jər) ▸ *n.* **1.** A widow with a title derived from her husband. **2.** An elderly woman of high social station.

dow·dy (dou′dē) ▸ *adj.* **-di·er, -di·est.** Lacking stylishness; shabby. **—dow′di·ness** *n.*

dow·el (dou′əl) ▸ *n.* A usu. round pin that fits into a corresponding hole to fasten or align two adjacent pieces. **—dow′el** *v.*

dow·er (dou′ər) ▸ *n.* **1.** The part of a deceased man's real estate allotted by law to his widow for her lifetime. **2.** See **dowry.** ▸ *v.* To give a dower to; endow.

down[1] (doun) ▸ *adv.* **1.** From a higher to a lower place. **2.** In or to a lower position, point, or condition. **3.** Southward: *flew down to Florida.* **4.** To a source: *tracking a rumor down.* **5.** From earlier times or people: *tradition handed down.* **6.** To a concentrated form: *pared the lecture down.* **7.** In writing; on paper: *wrote it all down.* **8.** In partial payment at the time of purchase: *put ten dollars down.* ▸ *adj.* **1a.** Moving or directed downward: *a down elevator.* **b.** Low or lower: *Stock prices are down.* **2.** Sick: *down with a cold.* **3.** Malfunctioning or not operating, esp. temporarily: *The computer is down.* **4.** Low in spirits; depressed: *feeling down today.* **5.** *Sports & Games* Trailing an opponent: *down 20 points.* **6.** Learned or known perfectly: *had algebra down.* ▸ *prep.* In a descending direction along, upon, into, or through. ▸ *n.* **1.** A downward movement; descent. **2.** *Football* Any of a series of four plays during which a team must advance at least ten yards to retain possession of the ball. ▸ *v.* **1.** To bring, put, strike, or throw down. **2.** To swallow hastily. ***—idiom:*** **down on** Hostile toward.

down[2] (doun) ▸ *n.* **1.** Fine, soft, fluffy feathers. **2.** Something similar to down. **—down′y** *adj.*

down[3] (doun) ▸ *n.* often **downs** A rolling, grassy, upland expanse.

down-and-out (doun′ənd-out′, -ən-) ▸ *adj.* **1.** Lacking funds, resources, or prospects; destitute. **2.** Incapacitated; prostrate.

down·beat (doun′bēt′) ▸ *n.* **1.** The downward stroke of a conductor to indicate the first beat of a measure of music. **2.** The first beat of a measure. ▸ *adj.* Cheerless; pessimistic.

down·cast (doun′kăst′) ▸ *adj.* **1.** Directed downward: *a downcast glance.* **2.** Low in spirits; depressed.

down·er (dou′nər) ▸ *n.* *Slang* **1.** A depressant or sedative drug, such as a barbiturate or tranquilizer. **2.** A depressing experience.

down·fall (doun′fôl′) ▸ *n.* **1.** A sudden loss of wealth or reputation; ruin. **2.** A downpour. **—down′fall′en** *adj.*

down·grade (doun′grād′) ▸ *n.* A descending slope, as in a road. ▸ *v.* **1.** To lower the status or salary of. **2.** To minimize the importance or value of.

down·heart·ed (doun′här′tĭd) ▸ *adj.* Low in spirit; depressed.

down·hill (doun′hĭl′) ▸ *adv.* **1.** Down the slope of a hill. **2.** Toward a worse condition. **—down′hill′** *adj.*

down-home (doun′hōm′) ▸ *adj.* Of or reminiscent of a simple life, esp. that associated with the rural S US.

Down·ing Street (dou′nĭng) ▸ *n.* The British government.

down·load (doun′lōd′) ▸ *v.* **1.** To unload. **2.** To transfer (data or programs) from a server or host computer to one's own computer or device.

down payment ▸ *n.* A partial payment made at the time of purchase.

down·play (doun′plā′) ▸ *v.* To minimize the significance of.

down·pour (doun′pôr′) ▸ *n.* A heavy fall of rain.

down·range (doun′rānj′) ▸ *adv. & adj.* In a direction away from the launch site and along the flight line of a missile test range.

down·right (doun′rīt′) ▸ *adj.* **1.** Thoroughgoing; unequivocal: *a downright lie.* **2.** Forthright; candid. ▸ *adv.* Thoroughly.

down·size (doun′sīz′) ▸ *v.* To reduce in size, as a corporation.

down·stage (doun′stāj′) ▸ *adv.* Toward or at the front of a stage. **—down′stage′** *adj.*

down·stairs (doun′stârz′) ▸ *adv.* **1.** Down the stairs. **2.** To or on a lower floor. **—down′stairs′** *adj.* **—down′stairs′** *n.*

down·stream (doun′strēm′) ▸ *adj.* In the direction of a stream's current. **—down′stream′** *adv.*

down·swing (doun′swĭng′) ▸ *n.* **1.** A swing downward, as of a golf club. **2.** A decline, as of a business.

Down syndrome (doun) or **Down's syndrome** (dounz) ▸ *n.* A congenital disorder that is marked by moderate to severe

THESAURUS

dough *n.* —*See* MONEY (1).
doughtiness *n.* —*See* COURAGE.
doughty *adj.* —*See* BRAVE.
doughy *adj.* —*See* PALE (1), SOFT (1).
dour *adj.* —*See* BLEAK (1), FORBIDDING, GLUM.
douse *v.* —*See* DIP (1), EXTINGUISH, WET (1).
doused *adj.* —*See* WET.
dove *n.* —*See* INNOCENT (1).
dovetail *v.* To be the proper size and shape for something ▸ interlock, fit. *Idiom:* fit like a glove. —*See also* AGREE (1).
dovish *adj.* —*See* PEACEABLE.
dowdy *adj.* —*See* OLD-FASHIONED.
dowel *n.* —*See* ANCHOR.
down *adj.* —*See* DEPRESSED (1), SICK (1), SLOW (2).
down *n.* —*See* DESCENT, HILL.
down *v.* —*See* DRINK (1), DROP (3), GULP.
down-and-out *adj.* —*See* POOR.
down-and-outer *n.* —*See* PAUPER.
down-at-heel or **down-at-the-heel** *adj.* —*See* SHABBY.
downbeat *adj.* —*See* BLEAK (2).
downcast *adj.* —*See* DEPRESSED (1).
downer *n.* —*See* KILLJOY.
downfall *n.* A disastrous defeat or ruin ▸ collapse, fall, waterloo. [*Compare* DEFEAT.] —*See also* DESCENT, RAIN, RUIN (1).
downgrade *n.* The act or an instance of demoting ▸ demotion, degradation, reduction. —*See also* DESCENT.
downgrade *v.* —*See* BELITTLE, DEBASE, DEMOTE, DEPRECIATE.
downhearted *adj.* —*See* DEPRESSED (1).
downheartedness *n.* —*See* DEPRESSION (2).
down payment *n.* A partial or intial payment ▸ deposit, installment, security.
downpour *n.* —*See* FLOOD, RAIN.
downright *adj.* —*See* FRANK, UTTER[2].
downright *adv.* —*See* COMPLETELY (1).
downside *n.* —*See* DEPRESSION, DISADVANTAGE.
downswing or **downslide** *n.* —*See* FALL (3).

intellectual disabilities and short stature.
down·time (doun′tīm′) ▸ *n.* The period of time when something is not in operation.
down-to-earth (doun′to͞o-ûrth′, -tə-) ▸ *adj.* Realistic; sensible.
down·town (doun′toun′) ▸ *n.* The business center of a city or town. ▸ *adv.* (doun′toun′) To, toward, or in the business center of a city or town. **—down′town′** *adj.*
down·trod·den (doun′trŏd′n) ▸ *adj.* Oppressed; tyrannized.
down·turn (doun′tûrn′) ▸ *n.* A tendency downward, esp. in economic activity.
down·ward (doun′wərd) ▸ *adv. & adj.* **1.** From a higher to a lower place, point, or level. **2.** From a prior source or earlier time. **—down′ward·ly** *adv.* **—down′wards** *adv.*
down·wind (doun′wĭnd′) ▸ *adv.* In the direction in which the wind blows. **—down′wind′** *adj.*
dow·ry (dou′rē) ▸ *n., pl.* **-ries.** Money or property brought by a bride to her husband at marriage.
dowse also **douse** (douz) ▸ *v.* **dowsed, dows·ing** also **doused, dous·ing.** To use a divining rod to search for underground water or minerals.
dows·er (dou′zər) ▸ *n.* **1.** A person who dowses. **2.** A divining rod.
dox·ol·o·gy (dŏk-sŏl′ə-jē) ▸ *n., pl.* **-gies.** An expression of praise to God, esp. a short hymn sung as part of a Christian liturgy. **—dox′o·log′i·cal** (dŏk′sə-lŏj′ĭ-kəl) *adj.*
doze (dōz) ▸ *v.* **dozed, doz·ing.** To sleep lightly; nap. **—doze** *n.*
doz·en (dŭz′ən) ▸ *n.* **1.** *pl.* **dozen.** A set of twelve. **2. dozens** Many: *dozens of errands to run.* ▸ *adj.* Twelve. **—doz′enth** *adj.*
dr ▸ *abbr.* dram
Dr. ▸ *abbr.* **1.** doctor **2.** drive
drab¹ (drăb) ▸ *adj.* **drab·ber, drab·best. 1.** Of a dull light brown or khaki color. **2.** Dull or commonplace; dreary. **—drab** *n.* **—drab′ly** *adv.* **—drab′ness** *n.*
drab² (drăb) ▸ *n.* A negligible amount.
drach·ma (drăk′mə) ▸ *n., pl.* **drach·mas** or **drach·mae** (-mē). **1.** The primary unit of currency in Greece before the adoption of the euro. **2.** An ancient Greek silver coin.
dra·co·ni·an (drā-kō′nē-ən, drə-) ▸ *adj.* Exceedingly harsh; very severe: *draconian budget cuts.*
draft (drăft) ▸ *n.* **1.** A current of air. **2.** A device that controls air circulation. **3a.** The act of pulling loads; traction. **b.** The load pulled or drawn. **4.** *Naut.* The depth of a vessel's keel below the water line. **5.** A document for transferring money. **6a.** A gulp, swallow, or inhalation. **b.** The amount taken in by such an act. **7.** The drawing, or the amount drawn, of a liquid, as from a keg. **8a.** The selection of individuals from a group, as for military duty. **b.** Compulsory enrollment in the armed forces; conscription. **9.** *Sports* A system in which new players are distributed among professional teams. **10.** A preliminary outline of a plan, document, or picture. ▸ *v.* **1.** To take, as for compulsory military service. **2.** To draw up a preliminary version of. ▸ *adj.* **1.** Suited for drawing heavy loads. **2.** Drawn from a cask or tap.
draft·ee (drăf-tē′) ▸ *n.* One who is drafted, esp. for military service.
draft·ing (drăf′tĭng) ▸ *n.* The drawing of mechanical and architectural structures to scale.
drafts·man (drăfts′mən) ▸ *n.* One who draws plans or designs, as of structures to be built. **—drafts′man·ship′** *n.*
draft·y (drăf′tē) ▸ *adj.* **-i·er, -i·est.** Having or exposed to drafts of air. **—draft′i·ness** *n.*
drag (drăg) ▸ *v.* **dragged, drag·ging. 1.** To pull along with effort, esp. by force; haul. **2.** To pull along the ground. **3.** To search or sweep the bottom of (a body of water), as with a grappling hook. **4.** *Comp. Sci.* **a.** To move (e.g., a mouse) while pressing one of its buttons. **b.** To move (e.g., an icon) on a screen using a pointing device. **5.** To prolong tediously. **6.** To proceed slowly or laboriously. **7.** To draw on a cigarette, pipe, or cigar. ▸ *n.* **1.** The act of dragging. **2.** Something, as a harrow, dragged along the ground. **3.** Something that retards motion or progress. **4.** The degree of resistance involved in dragging or hauling. **5.** *Slang* Something obnoxiously tiresome. **6.** A puff on a cigarette, pipe, or cigar. **7.** *Slang* A street or road: *the main drag.* **8.** The clothing characteristic of one sex when worn by a member of the opposite sex. **—drag′ger** *n.*
drag·net (drăg′nĕt′) ▸ *n.* **1.** A system of procedures for apprehending criminal suspects. **2.** A net for trawling.
drag·o·man (drăg′ə-mən) ▸ *n., pl.* **-mans** or **-men.** An interpreter of Arabic, Turkish, or Persian.
drag·on (drăg′ən) ▸ *n.* A mythical monster usu. represented as a gigantic winged reptile with lion's claws.
drag·on·fly (drăg′ən-flī′) ▸ *n.* Any of an order of large slender insects with two pairs of net-veined wings.
dra·goon (drə-go͞on′, dră-) ▸ *n.* Formerly, a heavily armed trooper. ▸ *v.* To subjugate or compel by violent measures; coerce.
drag race ▸ *n.* An acceleration race between two cars. **—drag racer** *n.* **—drag racing** *n.*
drain (drān) ▸ *v.* **1.** To draw or flow off by a gradual process. **2.** To make or become empty or dry. **3.** To deplete gradually, esp. to the point of exhaustion. ▸ *n.* **1.** A pipe or channel by which liquid is drawn off. **2.** The act or process of draining. **3a.** A gradual loss; consumption or depletion. **b.** Something that causes a gradual loss. **—drain′er** *n.*
drain·age (drā′nĭj) ▸ *n.* **1.** The action or a method of draining. **2.** A system of drains. **3.** Something drained off.
drain·pipe (drān′pīp′) ▸ *n.* A pipe for carrying off water or sewage.
drake (drāk) ▸ *n.* A male duck.
Drake, Sir **Francis** (1540?–96) ▸ English naval hero and explorer.
dram¹ (drăm) ▸ *n.* See **measurement** table in Appendix.
dram² (dräm) ▸ *n.* See **currency** table in Appendix.
dra·ma (drä′mə, drăm′ə) ▸ *n.* **1.** A prose or verse composition, esp. one for performance by actors; a play. **2.** Plays

THESAURUS

downtime *n.* —*See* REST¹ (1).
down-to-earth *adj.* —*See* REALISTIC (1).
downtrend *n.* —*See* FALL (3).
downturn *n.* A period of decreased business activity and high unemployment ▸ depression, recession, slowdown, slump. —*See also* FALL (3).
downward *adj.* —*See* DESCENDING.
doze *v.* —*See* NAP.
doze *n.* —*See* NAP.
dozy *adj.* —*See* SLEEPY.
drab *adj.* —*See* DULL (1), DULL (2).
drabness *n.* —*See* DULLNESS.
draconian *adj.* —*See* SEVERE (1).
draft *n.* **1.** A preliminary plan or version, as of a written work ▸ blueprint, diagram, framework, layout, outline, rough, skeleton, sketch. **2.** Compulsory enrollment in military service ▸ conscription, impressment, induction, levy, selective service. —*See also* BREEZE (1), DRINK (2), PULL (1), PULL (2).
draft *v.* **1.** To draw up a preliminary plan or version of ▸ adumbrate, block in (*or* out), delineate, diagram, lay out, map out, outline, plan, plot, rough in (*or* out), sketch. **2.** To enroll compulsorily in military service ▸ conscript, impress, induct, levy. **3.** To devise and set down ▸ compose, draw up, formulate, frame. —*See also* COMPOSE (1).
drag *v.* **1.** To hang down and be pulled along behind ▸ draggle, trail, train. **2.** To advance slowly ▸ crawl, creep, inch, poke. ***Idiom:*** go at a snail's pace. [*Compare* TRUDGE.] —*See also* DELAY (2), PULL (1).
drag *n.* —*See* BRAKE, BURDEN¹ (1), PULL (1), PULL (2), RESTRAINT.
dragging *adj.* —*See* LONG¹ (2).
draggle *v.* To hang down and be pulled along behind ▸ drag, trail, train. [*Compare* PULL.]
dragoon *v.* —*See* COERCE.
drain *v.* **1.** To remove a liquid by a steady, gradual process ▸ bleed, draw (off), drink up, evaporate, let out, milk, pump, strain, tap. **2.** To lessen or weaken severely, as by removing something essential ▸ deplete, exhaust, impoverish, sap, use up. —*See also* DECREASE, DRY, EXHAUST (1), POUR, TIRE (1).
drain *n.* —*See* BURDEN¹ (1), DECREASE.
drainage basin *n.* The region drained by a river system ▸ basin, watershed.
drained *adj.* —*See* TIRED (1).
draining *adj.* Causing fatigue ▸ exhausting, fatiguing, tiring, wearing, wearying. [*Compare* BURDENSOME.]
dram *n.* —*See* BIT¹ (1), DROP (4).

of a given type or period. **3.** The art of writing or producing dramatic works. **4.** A situation that involves conflicts or suspense and builds to a climax. **—dra·mat′ic** *adj.* **—dra·mat′i·cal·ly** *adv.*

dra·mat·ics (drə-măt′ĭks) ▸ *n.* *(takes sing. or pl. v.)* **1.** The art or practice of acting and stagecraft. **2.** Dramatic or stagy behavior.

dram·a·tist (drăm′ə-tĭst, drä′mə-) ▸ *n.* One who writes plays; playwright.

dram·a·tize (drăm′ə-tīz′, drä′mə-) ▸ *v.* **-tized, -tiz·ing. 1.** To adapt (a literary work) for dramatic presentation, as in a theater. **2.** To present or view in a dramatic or melodramatic way. **—dram′a·ti·za′tion** *n.*

drank (drăngk) ▸ *v.* P.t. of **drink.**

drape (drāp) ▸ *v.* **draped, drap·ing. 1.** To cover, dress, or hang with or as if with cloth in loose folds. **2.** To arrange in loose folds. **3.** To hang or rest limply: *draped my legs over the chair.* ▸ *n.* **1.** A drapery; curtain. **2.** A cloth arranged over a patient's body during a medical procedure. **3.** The way cloth falls or hangs.

drap·er·y (drā′pə-rē) ▸ *n., pl.* **-ies. 1.** Cloth gracefully arranged in loose folds. **2.** Heavy fabric hanging straight in loose folds, used as a curtain. **3.** Cloth; fabric.

dras·tic (drăs′tĭk) ▸ *adj.* Severe or radical in nature; extreme. **—dras′ti·cal·ly** *adv.*

draught (drăft) ▸ *n. & v. & adj. Chiefly Brit.* Var. of **draft.**

draughts (drăfts, dräfts) ▸ *n.* *(takes sing. or pl. v.) Chiefly Brit.* The game of checkers.

Dra·vid·i·an (drə-vĭd′ē-ən) ▸ *n.* **1.** A large family of languages spoken esp. in S India and N Sri Lanka that includes Tamil, Telugu, and Malayalam. **2.** A speaker of a Dravidian language. **—Dra·vid′i·an** *adj.*

draw (drô) ▸ *v.* **drew** (dro͞o), **drawn** (drôn), **draw·ing. 1a.** To cause to move in a given direction by applying continuous force; drag. **b.** To cause to move in a given direction or to a given position, as by leading: *drew us into the room.* **2.** To cause to flow forth: *a blow that drew blood.* **3.** To suck or take in (e.g., air); inhale. **4.** To take or pull out; extract. **5.** To eviscerate; disembowel. **6.** To attract; entice. **7.** To select or take in. **8.** To bring on oneself as a result; provoke. **9.** To elicit: *drew jeers from the audience.* **10.** To earn; gain: *draw interest.* **11.** To withdraw (money). **12.** To receive on a regular basis: *draw a pension.* **13.** To take or receive by chance: *draw lots.* **14.** *Games* To take (cards) from a dealer or stack. **15.** To end or leave (a contest) tied. **16.** To pull back the string of (a bow). **17a.** To inscribe (a line or lines) with a marking implement. **b.** To make a likeness of on a surface; depict with lines. **18.** To formulate or devise from evidence at hand: *draw a comparison.* **19.** To compose in legal format: *draw a deed.* ***—phrasal verbs:*** **draw out** To prolong; protract. **draw up** To compose or write in a set form. ▸ *n.* **1.** An act or result of drawing. **2.** Something drawn, esp. a lot or card. **3.** An inhalation, as on a pipe or cigar. **4.** Something that attracts interest, customers, or spectators. **5.** A contest ending with neither side winning. ***—idioms:*** **draw a blank** To fail to find or remember something. **draw straws** To decide by a lottery with straws of unequal lengths.

draw·back (drô′băk′) ▸ *n.* A disadvantage or inconvenience.

draw·bridge (drô′brĭj′) ▸ *n.* A bridge that can be raised or drawn aside to permit passage beneath it.

draw·er (drô′ər) ▸ *n.* **1.** One that draws, esp. one that draws an order for the payment of money. **2.** (*also* drôr) A sliding boxlike compartment in furniture. **3. drawers** (drôrz) Underpants.

draw·ing (drô′ĭng) ▸ *n.* **1.** The art of representing objects or forms on a surface by means of lines. **2.** A work so produced.

drawing card ▸ *n.* An attraction drawing large audiences.

drawing room ▸ *n.* **1.** A large room in which guests are entertained. **2.** A large private room on a railroad sleeping car.

drawl (drôl) ▸ *v.* To speak with lengthened or drawn-out vowels. **—drawl** *n.*

drawn (drôn) ▸ *v.* P.part. of **draw.** ▸ *adj.* Haggard, as from fatigue or ill health.

draw·string (drô′strĭng′) ▸ *n.* A cord or ribbon run through a hem or casing and pulled to tighten or close an opening.

dray (drā) ▸ *n.* A low heavy cart without sides.

dread (drĕd) ▸ *v.* **1.** To be in terror of. **2.** To anticipate with alarm, distaste, or reluctance. ▸ *n.* **1.** Profound fear; terror. **2.** Fearful or distasteful anticipation. ▸ *adj.* **1.** Causing terror or fear. **2.** Inspiring awe.

dread·ful (drĕd′fəl) ▸ *adj.* **1.** Inspiring dread; terrible. **2.** Extremely unpleasant; distasteful or shocking. **—dread′ful·ly** *adv.* **—dread′ful·ness** *n.*

dread·locks (drĕd′lŏks′) ▸ *pl.n.* **1.** A natural hairstyle in which the hair is twisted into long matted or ropelike locks. **2.** A similar hairstyle consisting of long thin braids.

dread·nought (drĕd′nôt′) ▸ *n.* A heavily armed battleship.

dream (drēm) ▸ *n.* **1.** A series of images, ideas, emotions, and sensations occurring during sleep. **2.** A daydream; reverie. **3.** A wild fancy or hope. **4.** An ambition; aspiration. **5.** One that is exceptionally gratifying, excellent, or beautiful. ▸ *v.* **dreamed** or **dreamt** (drĕmt), **dream·ing. 1.** To experience a dream in sleep. **2.** To daydream. **3.** To aspire. **4.** To conceive of; imagine. **5.** To pass (time) idly or in reverie. ***—phrasal verb:*** **dream up** To invent; concoct. **—dream′er** *n.* **—dream′i·ly** *adv.* **—dream′i·ness** *n.* **—dream′y** *adj.*

THESAURUS

dramatic *adj.* **1.** Of or relating to drama or the theater ▸ dramaturgic, dramaturgical, histrionic, histrionical, theatric, theatrical, thespian. **2.** Suggesting drama or a stage performance, as in emotionality or suspense ▸ climactic, emotional, exaggerated, exciting, flamboyant, histrionic, histrionical, melodramatic, moving, sensational, spectacular, suspenseful, tense, theatric, theatrical, thrilling, vivid. [*Compare* SHOWY.]

dramatics *n.* The art and occupation of an actor ▸ acting, stage, theater, theatrics. *—See also* THEATRICS (2).

dramatize *v.* *—See* ACT (3), STAGE.

dramaturgic or **dramaturgical** *adj.* *—See* DRAMATIC (1).

drape *v.* *—See* CLOTHE, DRESS (1), SPRAWL.

draw *v.* *—See* ATTRACT, DERIVE (1), DRAIN (1), EVOKE, INFER, POUR, PULL (1), REPRESENT (2), RETURN (3).

draw back *v.* *—See* RETREAT.

draw down *v.* *—See* EXHAUST (1).

draw in *v.* **1.** To pull back in ▸ retract, withdraw. **2.** To involve someone in an activity ▸ engage. [*Compare* INVOLVE.] *—See also* DRINK (3).

draw into *v.* *—See* INVOLVE (1).

draw on *v.* *—See* USE.

draw out *v.* *—See* LENGTHEN.

draw up *v.* To devise and set down ▸ compose, draft, formulate, frame. [*Compare* COMPOSE.]

draw *n.* An equality of scores, votes, or performances in a contest ▸ dead heat, deadlock, stalemate, standoff, tie. *—See also* ADVANTAGE (3), ATTRACTION, LURE (1), PULL (1), PULL (7).

drawback *n.* *—See* DISADVANTAGE.

drawing *n.* *—See* REPRESENTATION.

drawn *adj.* *—See* HAGGARD.

drawn-out *adj.* *—See* LONG[1] (2).

dread *v.* To be afraid ▸ fear. *Idioms:* break out in a cold sweat, have butterflies (in one's stomach), have knots (*or* a knot) in one's stomach, have one's heart in one's mouth, sweat blood (*or* bullets).

dread *n.* *—See* FEAR.

dreadful *adj.* *—See* FEARFUL, GHASTLY (1), TERRIBLE.

dreadfully *adv.* *—See* VERY.

dream *n.* **1.** An illusory mental image ▸ daydream, fancy, fantasy, fiction, figment, hallucination, illusion, phantasm, phantasma, phantasmagoria, phantasmagory, reverie, vision. **2.** A fantastic, impracticable plan or desire ▸ bubble, castle in the air, chimera, fantasy, illusion, pipe dream, rainbow. **3.** A fervent hope ▸ ambition, aspiration, desire, goal, hope, ideal, vision, wish. *—See also* TRANCE.

dream *v.* To experience dreams or daydreams ▸ daydream, fancy, fantasize, hallucinate, imagine, muse, stargaze, woolgather. [*Compare* IMAGINE.] *—See also* DESIRE.

dream up *v.* *—See* IMAGINE, INVENT.

dreamer *n.* **1.** A person inclined to be imaginative or idealistic but impractical ▸ daydreamer, fantasist, idealist, romantic, stargazer, theorist, theorizer, utopian, visionary, wishful thinker. **2.** One who aspires ▸ aspirant, aspirer, hopeful, seeker. *Informal:* wannabe.

dream·land (drēm′lănd′) ▸ *n.* 1. An ideal or imaginary land. 2. A state of sleep.
drear (drîr) ▸ *adj.* Dreary.
drea·ry (drîr′ē) ▸ *adj.* **-ri·er, -ri·est.** 1. Dismal; bleak. 2. Boring; dull. **—drea′ri·ly** *adv.* **—drea′ri·ness** *n.*
dredge[1] (drĕj) ▸ *n.* 1. A machine used to deepen harbors and waterways. 2. *Naut.* A boat or barge equipped with a dredge. 3. A net fixed to a frame, used for gathering shellfish. ▸ *v.* **dredge, dredg·ing.** To deepen or bring up with or as if with a dredge. **—dredg′er** *n.*
dredge[2] (drĕj) ▸ *v.* **dredged, dredg·ing.** To coat (food) by sprinkling, as with flour.
dregs (drĕgz) ▸ *pl.n.* 1. The sediment in a liquid; lees. 2. The least desirable portion.
drei·del also **drei·dl** (drād′l) ▸ *n.* A small spinning top used in games played at Hanukkah.
drench (drĕnch) ▸ *v.* To wet thoroughly; soak.
dress (drĕs) ▸ *v.* 1. To put clothes on; clothe. 2. To decorate or adorn. 3. To arrange a display in. 4. To apply medication or bandages. 5. To arrange (the hair). 6. To clean (fish or fowl) for cooking or sale. 7. To wear formal clothes. ***—phrasal verbs:*** **dress down** To scold; reprimand. **dress up** To wear formal or fancy clothes. ▸ *n.* 1. Clothing; apparel. 2. A style of clothing. 3. A one-piece outer garment for women or girls. ▸ *adj.* 1. Suitable for formal occasions. 2. Requiring formal clothes.
dres·sage (drə-säzh′, drĕ-) ▸ *n.* The guiding of a horse through a series of complex maneuvers by slight movements of the hands, legs, and weight.
dress·er[1] (drĕs′ər) ▸ *n.* One that dresses or assists in dressing.
dress·er[2] (drĕs′ər) ▸ *n.* A chest of drawers used for holding clothes and personal items.
dress·ing (drĕs′ĭng) ▸ *n.* 1. Therapeutic material applied to a wound. 2. A sauce, as for salads. 3. A stuffing, as for poultry.
dressing table ▸ *n.* A low table with a mirror at which one sits while applying makeup.
dress·mak·er (drĕs′mā′kər) ▸ *n.* A tailor of women's clothing. **—dress′mak′ing** *n.*
dress·y (drĕs′ē) ▸ *adj.* **-i·er, -i·est.** 1. Showy or elegant in dress. 2. Smart; stylish. **—dress′i·ness** *n.*
drew (dro͞o) ▸ *v.* P.t. of **draw.**
drib·ble (drĭb′əl) ▸ *v.* **-bled, -bling.** 1. To flow or fall in drops or an unsteady stream; trickle. 2. To let saliva drip from the mouth; drool. 3. *Sports* To move (a ball) by repeated light bounces or kicks, as in basketball or soccer. **—drib′ble** *n.* **—drib′bler** *n.*
drib·let (drĭb′lĭt) ▸ *n.* 1. A falling drop of liquid. 2. A small amount or portion.
dried (drīd) ▸ *v.* P.t. and p.part. of **dry.**
dri·er[1] also **dry·er** (drī′ər) ▸ *n.* A substance added to paint, varnish, or ink to speed drying.
dri·er[2] (drī′ər) ▸ *adj.* Comp. of **dry.**
dries (drīz) ▸ *v.* 3rd pers. sing. pr.t. of **dry.**
dri·est (drī′ĭst) ▸ *adj.* Superl. of **dry.**
drift (drĭft) ▸ *v.* 1. To be carried along by currents of air or water. 2. To move unhurriedly and smoothly. 3. To move from place to place, esp. without purpose or regular employment. 4. To wander; stray. 5. To be piled up in banks or heaps by the force of a current. ▸ *n.* 1. The act or condition of drifting. 2. Something that drifts. 3. A bank or pile, as of sand or snow, heaped up by currents of air or water. 4. A general trend, as of opinion. 5. The main idea; gist. **—drift′y** *adj.*
drift·er (drĭf′tər) ▸ *n.* A person who moves aimlessly from place to place or job to job.
drift net ▸ *n.* A large fishing net buoyed up by floats that is carried along with the current or tide.
drift·wood (drĭft′wo͝od′) ▸ *n.* Wood floating in or washed up by the water.
drill[1] (drĭl) ▸ *n.* 1. An implement for boring holes in hard materials. 2. Disciplined, repetitious exercise as a means of teaching a skill or procedure. 3. A task or exercise for teaching a skill or procedure. ▸ *v.* 1. To make a hole with a drill. 2. To instruct thoroughly by repetition. **—drill′er** *n.*
drill[2] (drĭl) ▸ *n.* 1. A shallow trench or furrow in which seeds are planted. 2. A row of planted seeds. 3. An implement for planting seeds. **—drill** *v.*
drill[3] (drĭl) ▸ *n.* Durable cotton or linen twill.
drill instructor ▸ *n.* A noncommissioned officer who instructs recruits in military drill and discipline.
drill·mas·ter (drĭl′măs′tər) ▸ *n.* A military drill instructor.
drill press ▸ *n.* A powered vertical drilling machine in which the drill is pressed to the work automatically or by a hand lever.
drink (drĭngk) ▸ *v.* **drank** (drăngk), **drunk** (drŭngk), **drink·ing.** 1. To swallow (a liquid). 2. To soak up; absorb. 3. To take in eagerly through the senses or intellect: *The students drank in every word.* 4a. To propose (a toast). b. To toast (e.g., a person). 5. To imbibe alcoholic liquors, esp. to excess. ▸ *n.* 1. A liquid for drinking; beverage. 2. An amount of liquid that is swallowed. 3. An alcoholic beverage. 4. Excessive indulgence in alcohol. **—drink′a·bil′i·ty** *n.* **—drink′a·ble** *adj.* **—drink′er** *n.*

THESAURUS

dreamlike *adj.* —*See* ILLUSIVE.
dreamy *adj.* Given to daydreams or reverie ▸ daydreaming, fanciful, fantasizing, moony, musing, stargazing, starry-eyed, visionary, woolgathering. —*See also* MARVELOUS.
dreariness *n.* —*See* DULLNESS.
dreary or **drear** *adj.* —*See* BORING, GLOOMY.
dredge *v.* —*See* DIP (2).
dregs *n.* —*See* DEPOSIT (2), GARBAGE, RIFFRAFF.
drench *v.* —*See* WET (1).
drenched *adj.* —*See* WET.
dress *v.* 1. To put clothes on ▸ apparel, attire, clothe, costume, don, drape, garb, garment, invest, outfit, robe. *Informal:* tog. [*Compare* CLOTHE.] 2. To apply therapeutic materials to a wound ▸ bandage, bind, plaster, swathe, truss. 3. To add fertilizer to soil ▸ fertilize, manure, topdress. —*See also* ADORN (1), LINE.
dress down *v.* —*See* CHASTISE.
dress up *v.* To dress in formal or special clothing ▸ array, attire, bedeck, deck (out), prank, preen, primp. *Informal:* trick out (*or* up). *Slang:* doll up.
dress *n.* 1. Articles worn to cover the body ▸ apparel, attire, clothes, clothing, garb, garments, habiliments, raiment. *Informal:* duds, togs. *Slang:* threads. 2. A set or style of clothing ▸ costume, ensemble, garb, gear, guise, habiliments, outfit, toilette, turnout, wardrobe. *Informal:* getup, rig. 3. A one-piece skirted outer garment for women and children ▸ frock, gown, jumper, muumuu, pinafore, shift, smock.
dressy *adj.* —*See* FORMAL.
dribble *v.* —*See* DRIP, DROOL.
dribble *n.* The process or sound of dripping ▸ drip, drizzle, mizzle, trickle.
driblet *n.* —*See* DROP (1).
drift *v.* To move along with or be carried away by the action of water ▸ float, wash. —*See also* BLOW[1] (2), DEVIATE, DIGRESS, GLIDE (1), HEAP (1), ROVE.
drift *n.* —*See* FLOW, HEAP (1), IMPORT, THRUST.
drifter *n.* —*See* HOBO.
drill *n.* —*See* PRACTICE.
drill *v.* To engage in activities in order to strengthen or condition ▸ exercise, practice, train, work out. —*See also* CUT (1), INDOCTRINATE (1), INSTILL.
drink *v.* 1. To take into the mouth and swallow a liquid ▸ down, drink up, gulp, guzzle, imbibe, lap up, pull on, quaff, sip, slurp, sup, swill. *Informal:* swig, toss back (*or* down). *Slang:* belt. ***Idiom:*** wet one's whistle. 2. To take alcoholic liquor, especially excessively or habitually ▸ guzzle, imbibe, tipple. *Informal:* nip. *Slang:* booze, chug, chugalug, lush, soak, tank up. ***Idioms:*** bend the elbow, hit the bottle. 3. To take in moisture or liquid ▸ absorb, draw in, imbibe, osmose, soak (up), sop up, sponge up, take up. 4. To salute by raising and drinking from a glass ▸ compliment, honor, pledge, salute, toast.
drink in *v.* —*See* ABSORB (2).
drink up *v.* —*See* DRAIN (1).
drink *n.* 1. Any liquid that is fit for drinking ▸ beverage, brew, drinkable, libation, liquor, potable, potation, potion, refreshment. 2. An act of drinking or the amount swallowed ▸ draft, potation, pull, quaff, sip, sup, swallow, swill, taste, tot. *Informal:* swig. *Slang:* belt.
drinkable *n.* —*See* DRINK (1).

drip (drĭp) ▸ *v.* **dripped, drip·ping.** **1.** To fall or let fall in drops. **2.** To shed drops. ▸ *n.* **1.** The process of forming and falling in drops. **2.** Liquid that falls in drops. **3.** The sound made by dripping liquid. **4.** *Slang* A tiresome person.

drip·pings (drĭp′ĭngz) ▸ *pl.n.* The fat and juices exuded from roasting meat.

drive (drīv) ▸ *v.* **drove** (drōv), **driv·en** (drĭv′ən), **driv·ing.** **1.** To push, propel, or urge onward forcibly. **2.** To repulse forcefully; put to flight. **3a.** To guide, control, or direct (a vehicle). **b.** To operate or be transported in a vehicle. **4.** To motivate; cause to function: *Steam drives the engine.* **5.** To compel or force to work, often excessively. **6.** To force into a particular act or state: *drives me crazy.* **7.** To force to go through or penetrate: *drive a nail.* **8.** To carry through vigorously to a conclusion. **9.** To throw or strike (e.g., a ball), hard or rapidly. **10.** To rush or advance violently: *The wind drove into my face.* ***—phrasal verb:*** **drive at** To mean to do or say. ▸ *n.* **1.** A trip or journey in a vehicle. **2.** A road, esp. a driveway, for vehicles. **3.** The apparatus for transmitting motion or power to or in a machine. **4.** *Comp. Sci.* A device that reads data from and writes data onto a storage medium, such as a floppy disk. **5.** A strong organized effort to accomplish a purpose. **6.** Energy; initiative. **7.** *Psychol.* A strong motivating tendency or instinct. **8.** A massive sustained military offensive. **9.** The act of propelling a ball forcefully. **10.** The act of driving cattle. **—driv′a·bil′i·ty** *n.* **—driv′a·ble** *adj.*

drive-by (drīv′bī′) ▸ *adj.* Performed from a moving vehicle: *a drive-by shooting.* **—drive′-by′** *n.*

drive-in (drīv′ĭn′) ▸ *n.* An establishment, esp. an outdoor movie theater, that permits customers to remain in their motor vehicles while being accommodated. **—drive′-in′** *adj.*

driv·el (drĭv′əl) ▸ *v.* **-eled, -el·ing** or **-elled, -el·ling.** **1.** To slobber; drool. **2.** To talk stupidly or childishly. **—driv′el** *n.* **—driv′el·er** *n.*

driv·er (drī′vər) ▸ *n.* **1.** One that drives. **2.** A tool, such as a screwdriver, used to impart forceful pressure on another object. **3.** A golf club used for long shots from the tee.

drive shaft ▸ *n.* A rotating shaft that transmits mechanical power from an engine to a point of application.

drive·way (drīv′wā′) ▸ *n.* A short private road, as to a house or garage.

driz·zle (drĭz′əl) ▸ *v.* **-zled, -zling.** To rain gently in fine mistlike drops. **—driz′zle** *n.* **—driz′zly** *adj.*

drogue (drōg) ▸ *n.* A parachute used to slow a fast-moving object, such as a spacecraft during reentry.

droll (drōl) ▸ *adj.* **-er, -est.** Amusingly odd or whimsically comical. **—droll′er·y, droll′ness** *n.* **—drol′ly** *adv.*

-drome ▸ *suff.* **1.** Racecourse: *hippodrome.* **2.** Field; arena: *airdrome.*

drom·e·dar·y (drŏm′ĭ-dĕr′ē, drŭm′-) ▸ *n., pl.* **-ies.** The one-humped domesticated camel of N Africa and W Asia.

drone¹ (drōn) ▸ *n.* **1.** A male bee, esp. a honeybee. **2.** An idle person who lives off others. **3.** A pilotless, remote-controlled aircraft.

drone² (drōn) ▸ *v.* **droned, dron·ing.** **1.** To make a continuous low dull humming sound. **2.** To speak in a monotonous tone. **—drone** *n.*

drool (dro͞ol) ▸ *v.* **1.** To let saliva run from the mouth; drivel. **2.** *Informal* To make an extravagant show of desire. **—drool** *n.*

droop (dro͞op) ▸ *v.* **1.** To bend or hang downward. **2.** To sag in dejection or exhaustion. **—droop** *n.* **—droop′i·ly, droop′ing·ly** *adv.* **—droop′y** *adj.*

drop (drŏp) ▸ *n.* **1.** A quantity of liquid heavy enough to fall in a spherical mass. **2.** Something resembling a drop. **3.** The act of falling. **4.** A swift decline or decrease, as in quality. **5.** The vertical distance from a higher to a lower level. **6.** A sheer incline, such as a cliff. **7.** Personnel and equipment landed by parachute. **8.** A place where something, such as mail, is brought and distributed. ▸ *v.* **dropped, drop·ping.** **1.** To fall or let fall in drops. **2.** To fall or let fall from a higher to a lower place. **3.** To become less, as in amount or intensity. **4.** To descend. **5.** To sink into a state of exhaustion. **6.** To pass into a specified condition: *dropped into a doze.* **7.** To say or offer casually: *drop a hint.* **8.** To write at leisure: *drop me a note.* **9.** To cease consideration or treatment of: *drop the subject.* **10.** To stop participating in; quit: *drop a course.* **11.** To fire. **12.** To leave out (e.g., a letter) in speaking or writing. ***—phrasal verbs:*** **drop by** To visit briefly. **drop off**

THESAURUS

drip *v.* To fall or let fall in drops of liquid ▸ distill, dribble, drizzle, drop, tear, trickle, weep.

drip *n.* **1.** The process or sound of dripping ▸ dribble, drizzle, mizzle, trickle. **2.** *Slang:* An unpleasant, tiresome person ▸ bore, chump. *Slang:* dip, dork, dweeb, jerk, lamer, nerd, nimrod, pill, poop, schmo, schmuck, turkey, twerp, twit. [*Compare* FOOL.]

dripping *adj.* —*See* WET.

drippy *adj.* —*See* SENTIMENTAL.

drive *v.* **1.** To run and control a motor vehicle ▸ chauffeur, motor, pilot, steer, taxi, wheel. *Slang:* tool. **2.** To force to move or advance with or as if with blows or pressure ▸ butt, jolt, propel, push, ram, shove, slam, thrust. [*Compare* BEAT, HIT.] **3.** To urge to move along ▸ chase, herd, hustle, push, run, wrangle. [*Compare* MANEUVER, PROVOKE.] **4.** To force to work hard ▸ push, task, tax, work. *Idiom:* crack the whip. [*Compare* FORCE.] —*See also* ADVANCE (1), HUNT, INSTILL, LABOR, PLUNGE, URGE.

drive away *v.* —*See* ESTRANGE.

drive out *v.* —*See* DISMISS (2).

drive *n.* **1.** An organized effort to accomplish a purpose ▸ campaign, crusade, movement, push. [*Compare* CAUSE.] **2.** An aggressive readiness along with energy to undertake taxing efforts ▸ enterprise, initiative, hustle, punch. *Informal:* get-up-and-go, gumption, push. [*Compare* ENTHUSIASM.] **3.** A trip in a motor vehicle ▸ jaunt, ride, run. *Informal:* spin, turn, whirl. —*See also* ATTACK, WAY (2).

drivel *v.* —*See* CHATTER (1), DROOL.

drivel *n.* Saliva running from the mouth ▸ drool, salivation, slaver, slobber. —*See also* BABBLE, CHATTER, NONSENSE.

driven *adj.* —*See* AMBITIOUS.

driver *n.* A person who operates a motor vehicle ▸ chauffeur, motorist, operator.

driving *adj.* —*See* ENERGETIC.

drizzle *n.* The process or sound of dripping ▸ dribble, drip, mizzle, trickle. —*See also* RAIN.

drizzle *v.* —*See* DRIP, RAIN (2).

droll *adj.* —*See* FUNNY (1).

drollery or **drollness** *n.* —*See* HUMOR.

drone¹ *n.* —*See* DRUDGE (1), DRUDGE (2), WASTREL (2).

drone² *v.* —*See* HUM.

drone *n.* —*See* HUM.

drool *n.* Saliva running from the mouth ▸ drivel, salivation, slaver, slobber.

drool *v.* To let saliva run from the mouth ▸ dribble, drivel, salivate, slaver, slobber.

drool over *v.* *Informal* To make an excessive show of desire for or interest in ▸ *Informal:* ogle, slobber over. [*Compare* ADORE, DESIRE, LUST, RAVE.]

droop *v.* —*See* DROP (1), SLOUCH (2), TIRE (2), WILT.

drooping *adj.* —*See* LANGUID, LIMP.

droopy *adj.* —*See* LIMP.

drop *n.* **1.** A quantity of liquid falling or resting in a spherical mass ▸ bead, driblet, droplet, glob, globule, tear, teardrop. **2.** The extent or measurement downward from a surface ▸ deepness, depth, drop-off. **3.** A downward slope or distance ▸ decline, declivity, descent, drop-off, fall, pitch. **4.** A small amount of liquor ▸ belt, dram, jigger, shot, sip, splash, taste, tot. *Informal:* nip, slug. *Slang:* snort. —*See also* ADVANTAGE (3), BIT¹ (1), FALL (1), FALL (3).

drop *v.* **1.** To go from a more erect posture to a less erect posture ▸ droop, fall, sag, sink, slump. [*Compare* SLOUCH.] **2.** To slope downward ▸ decline, descend, dip, fall, pitch, sink. **3.** To bring down, as from a shot or blow ▸ chop down, cut down, down, fell, flatten, floor, ground, hew, knock down, level, mow down, prostrate, strike down, throw. *Slang:* deck. *Idiom:* lay low. **4.** To cease completely the consideration or treatment of ▸ abandon, discontinue, dismiss, end, forget, give over (*or* up), quit, relinquish, skip, stop, write off. *Idioms:* have done with, wash one's hands of. [*Compare* ABANDON.] **5.** To take or leave out ▸ eliminate, exclude, let go, omit, prune, remove. [*Compare* DISCARD, REMOVE.] —*See*

To fall asleep. **drop out** 1. To leave school without graduating. 2. To withdraw from society.

drop·let (drŏp′lĭt) ► *n.* A tiny drop.

drop-off (drŏp′ôf′, -ŏf′) ► *n.* 1. An abrupt downward slope. 2. A noticeable decrease.

drop·out (drŏp′out′) ► *n.* One who drops out, as from school.

drop·per (drŏp′ər) ► *n.* A small tube with a suction bulb at one end for drawing in a liquid and releasing it in drops.

drop·sy (drŏp′sē) ► *n.* Edema. No longer in scientific use. **—drop′si·cal** (-sĭ-kəl) *adj.*

dro·soph·i·la (drō-sŏf′ə-lə, drə-) ► *n.* A fruit fly used extensively in genetic research.

dross (drŏs, drôs) ► *n.* 1. A waste product formed on the surface of molten metal. 2. Worthless or trivial matter. **—dross′y** *adj.*

drought (drout) also **drouth** (drouth) ► *n.* 1. A long period of low rainfall. 2. A prolonged dearth or shortage.

drove[1] (drōv) ► *v.* P.t. of **drive.**

drove[2] (drōv) ► *n.* A flock, herd, or large group being driven or moving in a body.

drov·er (drō′vər) ► *n.* One who drives cattle or sheep.

drown (droun) ► *v.* 1. To die or kill by suffocating in water or another liquid. 2. To cover with or as if with a liquid. 3. To mask (a sound) by a louder sound.

drowse (drouz) ► *v.* **drowsed, drows·ing.** To be half-asleep; doze. **—drowse** *n.*

drows·y (drou′zē) ► *adj.* **-i·er, -i·est.** 1. Sleepy. 2. Causing sleepiness; soporific. **—drows′i·ly** *adv.* **—drows′i·ness** *n.*

drub (drŭb) ► *v.* **drubbed, drub·bing.** 1. To thrash with a stick. 2. To instill forcefully. 3. To defeat thoroughly. **—drub′ber** *n.*

drudge (drŭj) ► *n.* A person who does tedious, menial, or unpleasant work. ► *v.* **drudged, drudg·ing.** To do the work of a drudge. **—drudg′er·y** *n.*

drug (drŭg) ► *n.* 1. A medicine used in treating a disease. 2. A narcotic or hallucinogen. ► *v.* **drugged, drug·ging.** 1. To administer a drug to. 2. To mix a drug into (food or drink). 3. To stupefy or dull with or as if with a drug.

drug·gist (drŭg′ĭst) ► *n.* A pharmacist.

drug·store also **drug store** (drŭg′stôr′) ► *n.* A store where prescriptions are filled and drugs and other articles are sold.

dru·id also **Dru·id** (dro͞o′ĭd) ► *n.* A member of an order of priests in ancient Gaul and Britain who appear in legend as prophets and sorcerers. **—dru·id′ic, dru·id′i·cal** *adj.* **—dru′id·ism** *n.*

drum (drŭm) ► *n.* 1. A percussion instrument consisting of a hollow cylinder with a membrane stretched tightly over one or both ends, played by beating with the hands or sticks. 2. Something like a drum in shape or structure. ► *v.* **drummed, drum·ming.** 1. To play or perform on a drum. 2. To thump or tap rhythmically or continually. 3. To summon by or as if by beating a drum. 4. To instill by constant repetition: *drummed the answers into my head.* 5. To expel or dismiss in disgrace: *was drummed out of the army.* ***—phrasal verb:*** **drum up** To bring about by continuous effort: *drum up new business.* **—drum′mer** *n.*

drum·beat (drŭm′bēt′) ► *n.* The sound produced by beating a drum.

drum·lin (drŭm′lĭn) ► *n.* An elongated hill or ridge of glacial drift.

drum major ► *n.* A man who leads a marching band, often twirling a baton.

drum ma·jor·ette (mā′jə-rĕt′) ► *n.* A woman who leads a marching band, often twirling a baton.

drum·stick (drŭm′stĭk′) ► *n.* 1. A stick for beating a drum. 2. The lower part of the leg of a cooked fowl.

drunk (drŭngk) ► *v.* P.part. of **drink.** ► *adj.* 1. Intoxicated with alcohol; inebriated. 2. Overcome by emotion: *drunk with power.* ► *n.* 1. A drunkard. 2. A bout of drinking.

drunk·ard (drŭng′kərd) ► *n.* One who is habitually drunk.

drunk·en (drŭng′kən) ► *adj.* 1. Intoxicated: *a drunken guest.* 2. Habitually drunk. 3. Of or occurring during intoxication: *a drunken brawl.* **—drunk′en·ly** *adv.* **—drunk′en·ness** *n.*

drupe (dro͞op) ► *n.* A fleshy fruit, as a peach or plum, with a single hard stone that encloses a seed.

drupe·let (dro͞op′lĭt) ► *n.* A small drupe, such as one of the many subdivisions of a raspberry or blackberry.

dry (drī) ► *adj.* **dri·er, dri·est** or **dry·er, dry·est.** 1. Free or freed from liquid or moisture. 2. Marked by little or no rain. 3. Not under water. 4. No longer yielding milk: *a dry cow.* 5. Lacking a mucous or watery discharge: *a dry cough.* 6. Thirsty. 7. Of solid rather than liquid commodities: *dry weight.* 8. Not sweet: *a dry wine.* 9. Matter-of-fact; impersonal. 10. Wearisome; dull: *a dry lecture.* 11. Humorous in a subtle way: *dry wit.* 12. Prohibiting the sale of alcoholic beverages. ► *v.* **dried, dry·ing.** 1. To

THESAURUS

also COLLAPSE (1), DIE, DISMISS (1), DRIP, FALL (1), FALL (2), FALL (4), LOWER[2].

drop by or **in** *v.* *—See* VISIT.

drop off *v.* *—See* NAP.

droplet *n.* *—See* DROP (1).

drop-off *n.* The extent or measurement downward from a surface ► deepness, depth, drop. *—See also* FALL (3).

drossy *adj.* *—See* WORTHLESS.

droughty *adj.* *—See* DRY (2).

drove *n.* *—See* CROWD, FLOCK.

drown *v.* *—See* FLOOD (1).

drowsy *adj.* *—See* SLEEPY.

drub *v.* *—See* BEAT (1), OVERWHELM (1), SLAM (1).

drubbing *n.* *—See* DEFEAT.

drudge *n.* 1. A person who does tedious, menial, or unpleasant work ► drone, foot soldier, hack, menial, scullion, slave. *Slang:* grunt. 2. One who works or toils tirelessly ► drone, grind, grub, plodder. *Informal:* workhorse.

drudge *v.* *—See* GRIND (2).

drudgery *n.* *—See* LABOR.

drug *n.* 1. A substance used in the treatment of disease ► medicament, medication, medicine, pharmaceutical, pill, prescription. [*Compare* CURE.] 2. A substance that affects the central nervous system and is often addictive ► depressant, hallucinogen, narcotic, opiate, psychotropic, sedative, stimulant. *Informal:* dope. [*Compare* SOPORIFIC.]

drug *v.* 1. To administer especially a pain-killing drug to someone ► anesthetize, chloroform, dose, etherize, knock out, medicate, narcotize, opiate, physic, put under, sedate, tranquilize. *Informal:* dope (up). [*Compare* DEADEN.] 2. To addle the mind, as with a narcotic or alcohol ► befuddle, besot, blur, cloud, daze, dim, dull, fog, fuddle, impair, stupefy. [*Compare* CONFUSE, DAZE.]

drug abuse *n.* *—See* ADDICTION.

drugged *adj.* Stupefied, intoxicated, or otherwise influenced by the taking of drugs ► *Informal:* doped. *Slang:* baked, buzzed, high, hopped-up, lit (up), potted, ripped, spaced-out, stoned, tripping, turned-on, wasted, wiped-out, wired, zonked. *Idiom:* under the influence.

drum *v.* *—See* BEAT (5).

drunk *adj.* Stupefied, excited, or muddled with alcoholic liquor ► besotted, bibulous, crapulent, crapulous, drunken, inebriate, inebriated, intoxicated, sodden, sottish, tipsy. *Informal:* cockeyed, stewed. *Slang:* blind, blotto, bombed, boozed, boozy, crocked, high, lit (up), loaded, looped, pickled, pie-eyed, pixilated, plastered, polluted, potted, sloshed, smashed, soused, sozzled, stinking, stinko, stoned, tanked, tight, zonked. *Idioms:* drunk as a skunk, half-seas over, high as a kite, in one's cups, three sheets in (*or* to) the wind.

drunk *n.* *—See* BENDER, DRUNKARD.

drunkard *n.* A person who is habitually drunk ► alcoholic, dipsomaniac, drunk, inebriate, sot, tippler, toper. *Slang:* alky, boozehound, boozer, dipso, lush, rummy, soak, souse, sponge, stiff, wino.

drunken *adj.* *—See* DRUNK.

drunkenness *n.* The condition of being intoxicated with alcoholic liquor ► crapulence, inebriation, inebriety, insobriety, intoxication, tipsiness. [*Compare* BENDER, BINGE.]

druthers *n.* *—See* CHOICE.

dry *adj.* 1. Having little or no liquid or moisture ► anhydrous, bone-dry, dried up, moistureless, sere, waterless. 2. Having little or no precipitation ► arid, desert, droughty, parched, rainless, scorched, thirsty. [*Compare* BARREN.] 3. Needing or desiring drink ► parched, thirsty. *—See also* BARE (1), BORING, COLD (2), DULL (1), HARSH, SOUR.

dry *v.* To make or become free of moisture ► dehydrate, desiccate, drain,

make or become dry. 2. To preserve food by extracting the moisture. **—dry′ly, dri′ly** *adv.* **—dry′ness** *n.*

dry·ad (drī′əd, -ăd′) ▸ *n. Gk. Myth.* A wood nymph.

dry cell ▸ *n.* An electric cell having an electrolyte in the form of moist paste.

dry-clean (drī′klēn′) ▸ *v.* To clean (fabrics) with chemical solvents that have little or no water. **—dry cleaner** *n.* **—dry cleaning** *n.*

dry dock ▸ *n.* A large basinlike dock from which the water can be emptied, used for building or repairing a ship below its water line.

dry·er (drī′ər) ▸ *n.* 1. An appliance that removes moisture. 2. Var. of **drier**[1].

dry farming ▸ *n.* Farming practiced in arid areas without irrigation. **—dry′-farm′** *v.*

dry goods ▸ *pl.n.* Textiles, clothing, and related articles of trade.

dry ice ▸ *n.* Solid carbon dioxide used primarily as a coolant.

dry measure ▸ *n.* A system of units for measuring dry commodities such as grains.

dry rot ▸ *n.* A fungous disease of plants in which the tissue remains relatively dry.

dry run ▸ *n.* A trial exercise or rehearsal, as a military exercise without live ammunition.

dry wall or **dry·wall** (drī′wôl′) ▸ *n.* Plasterboard.

Ds ▸ The symbol for the element **darmstadtium**.

DTs or **DT's** (dē′tēz′) ▸ *n. (takes sing. or pl. v.)* Delirium tremens.

du·al (do͞o′əl, dyo͞o′-) ▸ *adj.* 1. Composed of two parts; double. 2. Having a double character or purpose. **—du·al′i·ty** (-ăl′ĭ-tē) *n.* **—du′al·ly** *adv.*

du·al·ism (do͞o′ə-lĭz′əm, dyo͞o′-) ▸ *n.* 1. The condition of being dual. 2. *Philos.* The view that the world consists of two fundamental entities, such as mind and matter. **—du′al·is′tic** *adj.*

dub[1] (dŭb) ▸ *v.* **dubbed, dub·bing.** 1. To confer knighthood on. 2. To give a nickname to.

dub[2] (dŭb) ▸ *v.* **dubbed, dub·bing.** 1a. To transfer (recorded material) onto a new recording medium. **b.** To copy (a record or tape). 2. To insert a new sound track into (a film). 3. To add (sound) into a film or tape. **—dub** *n.* **—dub′ber** *n.*

Du·bai (do͞o-bī′) ▸ A sheikdom and city of E United Arab Emirates on the Persian Gulf.

du·bi·e·ty (do͞o-bī′ĭ tē, dyo͞o-) ▸ *n., pl.* **-ties.** 1. A feeling of uncertainty. 2. A matter of doubt.

du·bi·ous (do͞o′bē-əs, dyo͞o′-) ▸ *adj.* 1. Fraught with uncertainty; undecided. 2. Arousing doubt; questionable. **—du′bi·ous·ly** *adv.* **—du′bi·ous·ness** *n.*

Dub·lin (dŭb′lĭn) ▸ The capital of Ireland, in the E-central part on the Irish Sea. **—Dub′lin·er** *n.*

dub·ni·um (do͞ob′nē-əm) ▸ *n. Symbol* **Db** A short-lived, synthetic radioactive element. At. no. 105.

Du Bois (do͞o bois′), **W(illiam) E(dward) B(urghardt)** (1868–1963) ▸ Amer. writer and civil rights leader.

du·cal (do͞o′kəl, dyo͞o′-) ▸ *adj.* Of a duke or dukedom.

duc·at (dŭk′ət) ▸ *n.* Any of various gold coins formerly used in Europe.

duch·ess (dŭch′ĭs) ▸ *n.* 1. A woman holding title to a duchy. 2. The wife or widow of a duke.

duch·y (dŭch′ē) ▸ *n., pl.* **-ies.** The territory ruled by a duke or duchess; dukedom.

duck[1] (dŭk) ▸ *n.* 1. Any of various water birds having a broad flat bill, short legs, and webbed feet. 2. A female duck.

duck[2] (dŭk) ▸ *v.* 1. To lower quickly, esp. to avoid something. 2. To evade; dodge. 3. To push suddenly under water. **—duck** *n.*

duck[3] (dŭk) ▸ *n.* 1. A durable, closely woven cotton fabric. 2. **ducks** Clothing that is made of duck, esp. white trousers.

duck·bill (dŭk′bĭl′) ▸ *n.* See **platypus.**

duck·board (dŭk′bôrd′) ▸ *n.* A board or boardwalk laid across wet or muddy ground or flooring.

duck·ling (dŭk′lĭng) ▸ *n.* A young duck.

duck·pin (dŭk′pĭn′) ▸ *n.* 1. A bowling pin shorter and squatter than a tenpin. 2. **duckpins** *(takes sing. v.)* A bowling game played with such pins.

duck·weed (dŭk′wēd′) ▸ *n.* Any of various small, free-floating, stemless aquatic flowering plants.

duck·y (dŭk′ē) ▸ *adj.* **-i·er, -i·est.** *Slang* Excellent; fine.

duct (dŭkt) ▸ *n.* 1. A channel for conveying a substance, esp. a liquid or gas. 2. *Anat.* A tubular bodily passage, esp. one for carrying glandular secretions. 3. A tube or pipe for enclosing electrical cables or wires. **—duct′ed** *adj.* **—duct′less** *adj.*

duc·tile (dŭk′təl, -tīl′) ▸ *adj.* 1. Easily drawn into wire or hammered thin. 2. Capable of being readily influenced; tractable. **—duc·til′i·ty** (-tĭl′ĭ-tē), **duc′ti·li·bil′i·ty** *n.*

duct·less gland (dŭkt′lĭs) ▸ *n.* See **endocrine gland.**

dud (dŭd) ▸ *n.* 1. A bomb, shell, or explosive that fails to detonate. 2. *Informal* One that is disappointingly ineffective or unsuccessful. 3. **duds** *Informal* Clothing or personal belongings.

dude (do͞od, dyo͞od) ▸ *n.* 1. *Informal* An Easterner or city person vacationing on a ranch in the West. 2. *Informal* A dandy. 3. *Slang* A fellow; chap. ▸ *v.* **dud·ed, dud·ing.** *Slang* To dress elaborately.

dude ranch ▸ *n.* A resort patterned after a Western ranch, featuring outdoor activities.

dudg·eon (dŭj′ən) ▸ *n.* A sullen, angry, or indignant humor.

due (do͞o, dyo͞o) ▸ *adj.* 1. Payable immediately or on demand. 2. Owed as a debt or right; owing. 3. Meeting special requirements; sufficient. 4. Expected or scheduled. 5. Anticipated; looked for. 6. Capable of being attributed. ▸ *n.* 1. Something owed or deserved. 2. **dues** A membership fee. ▸ *adv.* Straight; directly: *due west.*

du·el (do͞o′əl, dyo͞o′-) ▸ *n.* 1. A prearranged formal combat between two persons that is usu. fought to settle a point of honor. 2. A struggle for domination between two persons or two groups. ▸ *v.* **-eled, -el·ing** or **-elled, -el·ling.** To

THESAURUS

dry out, exsiccate, parch. *—See also* HARDEN (2).

dry up *v.* 1. To make or become no longer fresh or shapely because of loss of moisture ▸ frizzle, mummify, pucker, sear, shrivel, wither, wizen. 2. To make or become no longer active or productive ▸ deplete, desiccate, give out, play out, run out. [*Compare* EXHAUST.]

dryness *n.* *—See* DULLNESS, TEMPERANCE (2).

dry run *n.* *—See* TEST (1).

dual *adj.* Consisting of two identical or similar related things, parts, or elements ▸ double, matched, paired, twin. [*Compare* EQUAL.] *—See also* DOUBLE (2).

dub *v.* *—See* NAME (1).

dub *n.* *—See* BLUNDERER.

dubiety *n.* *—See* DISBELIEF, DOUBT.

dubious *adj.* *—See* AMBIGUOUS (1), DOUBTFUL (1), DOUBTFUL (2), INCREDULOUS, SHADY (1).

dubiously *adv.* *—See* SKEPTICALLY.

dubiousness *n.* *—See* DOUBT.

dubitable *adj.* *—See* AMBIGUOUS (1).

duck *v.* *—See* AVOID, CUT (4), DIP (1), EVADE (1).

duck *n.* *—See* PLUNGE.

duck soup *n.* *—See* BREEZE (2).

duct *n.* *—See* VESSEL (2).

ductile *adj.* *—See* FLEXIBLE (3), MALLEABLE.

ductility *n.* *—See* FLEXIBILITY (1).

dud *n.* *—See* DISAPPOINTMENT (2), FAILURE (1).

dudgeon *n.* *—See* OFFENSE.

duds *n.* *—See* DRESS (1).

due *adj.* 1. Owed as a debt ▸ collectible, mature, outstanding, owed, owing, payable, receivable, unpaid, unsatisfied, unsettled. 2. Known to be about to arrive ▸ anticipated, expected, scheduled, slated. 3. In the relatively near future ▸ approaching, coming, forthcoming, upcoming. *Idioms:* around the corner, on the horizon. [*Compare* CLOSE, IMMINENT.] *—See also* JUST.

due *n.* Something justly deserved ▸ comeuppance, compensation, deserts, guerdon, payment, recompense, reward, satisfaction, wages. *Informal:* lumps. *Idioms:* what is coming to one, what one has coming. *—See also* DEBT (1), RIGHT.

due *adv.* *—See* DIRECTLY (1).

duel *v.* *—See* CONTEND.

fight in a duel. **—du′el·er, du′el·ist** *n.*
due process ▸ *n.* An established course for judicial proceedings designed to safeguard the legal rights of the individual.
du·et (do͞o-ĕt′, dyo͞o-) ▸ *n.* **1.** *Mus.* A composition for two voices or instruments. **2.** The two performers of such a composition.
due to ▸ *prep.* Because of.
duff·er (dŭf′ər) ▸ *n.* *Informal* An incompetent or dull-witted person.
duf·fle bag (dŭf′əl) or **duf·fel bag** ▸ *n.* A large cylindrical cloth bag for carrying personal belongings.
dug¹ (dŭg) ▸ *n.* A breast or teat.
dug² (dŭg) ▸ *v.* P.t. and p.part. of **dig**.
dug·out (dŭg′out′) ▸ *n.* **1.** A boat or canoe made of a hollowed-out log. **2.** A pit dug into the ground or on a hillside and used as a shelter. **3.** *Baseball* A sunken shelter at the side of a field where players stay while not on the field.
duh (dŭ) ▸ *interj.* Used to express disdain, esp. for something deemed obvious.
du jour (də zho͝or′, do͞o) ▸ *adj.* **1.** Offered on a given day: *the soup du jour.* **2.** Current: *the trend du jour.*
duke (do͞ok, dyo͞ok) ▸ *n.* **1.** A nobleman with the highest hereditary rank, esp. in Great Britain. **2.** A sovereign prince who rules an independent duchy. **3.** often **dukes** *Slang* A fist: *Put up your dukes!* ▸ *v.* **duked, duk·ing.** To fight, esp. with fists: *duking it out.* **—duke′dom** *n.*
dul·cet (dŭl′sĭt) ▸ *adj.* **1.** Pleasing to the ear; melodious. **2.** Soothing; agreeable.
dul·ci·mer (dŭl′sə-mər) ▸ *n.* *Mus.* **1.** A zitherlike instrument played by striking with padded hammers. **2.** A long, narrow, usu. four-stringed fretted instrument played by plucking or strumming.
dull (dŭl) ▸ *adj.* **-er, -est. 1.** Intellectually obtuse; stupid. **2.** Lacking alertness; insensitive. **3.** Dispirited; depressed. **4.** Not brisk or rapid; sluggish. **5.** Not having a sharp edge; blunt. **6.** Not keenly felt. **7.** Uninteresting; boring. **8.** Not bright or vivid. **9.** Muffled; indistinct. ▸ *v.* To make or become dull. **—dull′ish** *adj.* **—dull′ness, dul′ness** *n.* **—dul′ly** *adv.*
dull·ard (dŭl′ərd) ▸ *n.* A mentally dull person; dolt.
du·ly (do͞o′lē, dyo͞o′-) ▸ *adv.* **1.** In a proper manner. **2.** At the expected time.
dumb (dŭm) ▸ *adj.* **-er, -est. 1.** Stupid; silly. **2.** Unintentional: *dumb luck.* **3.** Lacking the power or faculty of speech: *a dumb animal.* **4.** Temporarily speechless, as with shock or fear. **—dumb′ly** *adv.* **—dumb′ness** *n.*
dumb·bell (dŭm′bĕl′) ▸ *n.* **1.** A weight consisting of a short bar with a metal ball or disk at each end lifted for muscular exercise. **2.** *Slang* A stupid person.
dumb·found also **dum·found** (dŭm′found′) ▸ *v.* To fill with astonishment and perplexity; confound.
dum-dum (dŭm′dŭm′) ▸ *n.* **1.** A soft-nosed bullet designed to expand on impact. **2.** *Slang* A stupid person.
dum·my (dŭm′ē) ▸ *n., pl.* **-mies. 1.** An imitation of a real object used as a substitute. **2a.** A mannequin used in displaying clothes. **b.** A figure of a person or animal manipulated by a ventriloquist. **3.** A stupid person. **4.** A person secretly in the service of another. **5.** *Print.* A model page with text and illustrations to direct the printer. **6.** *Games* **a.** The partner in bridge who exposes his or her hand to be played by the declarer. **b.** The hand thus exposed. **7.** *Comp. Sci.* A piece of information entered into a computer only to meet prescribed conditions, such as word length. ▸ *adj.* **1.** Simulating or replacing something but lacking its function. **2.** Serving as a front for another: *a dummy corporation.* **3.** *Comp. Sci.* Entered or provided only to meet prescribed conditions: *a dummy variable.*
dump (dŭmp) ▸ *v.* **1.** To release in a large mass. **2.** To empty (material) out of a container or vehicle. **3.** To get rid of; discard. **4.** To place (e.g., goods or stock) on the market in large quantities at a low price. **5.** *Comp. Sci.* To transfer (data) from one place to another, as from a memory to a printout, without processing. ▸ *n.* **1.** A place where refuse is dumped. **2.** A storage place; depot. **3.** *Comp. Sci.* An instance or the result of dumping stored data. **4.** *Slang* A poorly maintained or disreputable place. **—dump′er** *n.*
dump·ling (dŭmp′lĭng) ▸ *n.* **1.** A piece of dough, sometimes filled, cooked in liquid such as soup. **2.** Sweetened dough wrapped around fruit and served as a dessert.
dumps (dŭmps) ▸ *pl.n.* A gloomy, melancholy state of mind; depression.
dump truck ▸ *n.* A truck having a bed that tilts backward to dump loose material.
dump·y¹ (dŭm′pē) ▸ *adj.* **-i·er, -i·est.** Short and stout; squat. **—dump′i·ness** *n.*
dum·py² (dŭm′pē) ▸ *adj.* **-i·er, -i·est.** Resembling a dump; shabby; disreputable.
dun¹ (dŭn) ▸ *v.* **dunned, dun·ning.** To importune (a debtor) for payment. **—dun** *n.*
dun² (dŭn) ▸ *n.* A neutral brownish gray.
dunce (dŭns) ▸ *n.* A stupid person.
dun·der·head (dŭn′dər-hĕd′) ▸ *n.* A dunce.
dune (do͞on, dyo͞on) ▸ *n.* A hill or ridge of wind-blown sand.
dune buggy ▸ *n.* A recreational vehicle having oversize tires designed for use on sand.
dung (dŭng) ▸ *n.* Animal excrement; manure.
dun·ga·ree (dŭng′gə-rē′) ▸ *n.* **1.** A sturdy, often blue denim fabric. **2. dungarees** Trousers or overalls made of denim.
dun·geon (dŭn′jən) ▸ *n.* A dark, often underground prison cell.

THESAURUS

duel *n.* —*See* CONFRONTATION.
due process *n.* The state, action, or principle of treating all persons equally in accordance with the law ▸ equity, justice. [*Compare* FAIRNESS.]
dues *n.* —*See* TOLL¹ (1).
duet *n.* —*See* COUPLE.
due to *preposition* —*See* BECAUSE OF.
dugout *n.* A hollow beneath the earth's surface ▸ cave, cavern, grotto, tunnel. [*Compare* HOLE.]
dulcet *adj.* —*See* MELODIOUS.
dulcify *v.* —*See* PACIFY.
dull *adj.* **1.** Lacking liveliness, charm, or surprise ▸ arid, aseptic, colorless, deadly, drab, dry, earthbound, flat, flavorless, lackluster, leaden, lifeless, lusterless, matter-of-fact, pedestrian, plodding, prosaic, spiritless, sterile, stodgy, unimaginative, uninspired. *Informal:* blah. [*Compare* INSIPID, ORDINARY.] **2.** Lacking vividness or color ▸ dim, drab, flat, gray, lackluster, lusterless, mat, muddy, murky. [*Compare* PALE.] **3.** Not physically sharp or keen ▸ blunt, edgeless, obtuse, unpointed, unsharpened. —*See also* BACKWARD (1), BLIND (3), BORING, DEAD (2), DEPRESSED (1), GLOOMY, SLOW (2).
dull *v.* To make or become less sharp-edged ▸ blunt, hebetate, round, turn. *Idiom:* take the edge off. —*See also* DEADEN, DRUG (2), MUFFLE, OBSCURE.
dullard *n.* A mentally dull person ▸ blockhead, chump, clod, dolt, dummkopf, dummy, dunce, idiot, imbecile, moron, nincompoop, nitwit, numskull, simpleton, softhead, thickhead, woodenhead. *Informal:* bonehead, knucklehead, lamebrain, muttonhead. *Slang:* airhead, boob, cretin, dimwit, dumbbell, dumbo, fathead, half-wit, lunkhead, pinhead, simp. [*Compare* DRIP, FOOL, OAF, SQUARE.]
dullness *n.* A lack of excitement, liveliness, or interest ▸ asepticism, blandness, colorlessness, drabness, dreariness, dryness, familiarity, flatness, flavorlessness, insipidity, insipidness, jejuneness, lifelessness, mediocrity, routinism, sluggishness, staleness, sterileness, sterility, stodginess, tameness, tediousness, tedium, vapidity, vapidness, weariness. [*Compare* MONOTONY.] —*See also* LETHARGY.
dumb *adj.* —*See* MUTE, SPEECHLESS, STUPID, WORTHLESS.
dumbbell *n.* —*See* DULLARD.
dumbfound *v.* —*See* STAGGER (2).
dumbfounded *adj.* —*See* CONFUSED (1).
dumbness *n.* —*See* SILENCE (2), STUPIDITY.
dumbo *n.* —*See* DULLARD.
dumbstruck *adj.* —*See* SPEECHLESS.
dummy or **dummkopf** *n.* —*See* DULLARD.
dump *v.* —*See* DISCARD, DUMP, RID.
dump *n.* *Slang* A disreputable or run-down bar or restaurant ▸ *Slang:* dive, honky-tonk, joint, juke house, juke joint. *Idiom:* hole in the wall.
dumping *n.* —*See* DISPOSAL.
dumps *n.* —*See* DEPRESSION (2).
dumpy *adj.* —*See* STOCKY.
dun *v.* —*See* BILL¹.
dunce *n.* —*See* DULLARD.

dung·hill (dŭng′hĭl′) ▸ *n.* A heap of dung.

dunk (dŭngk) ▸ *v.* **1.** To plunge into liquid; immerse. **2.** To dip (food) into a liquid food, such as sauce, before eating it. **3.** *Basketball* To slam (a ball) through the basket. **4.** To submerge oneself briefly in water. **—dunk** *n.*

du·o (do͞o′ō, dyo͞o′ō) ▸ *n., pl.* **-os. 1.** *Mus.* A duet. **2.** A pair.

du·o·dec·i·mal (do͞o′ə-dĕs′ə-məl, dyo͞o′-) ▸ *adj.* Of or based on the number 12.

du·o·de·num (do͞o′ə-dē′nəm, dyo͞o′-, do͞o-ŏd′n-əm, dyo͞o-) ▸ *n., pl.* **du·o·de·na** (-nə) or **du·o·de·nums.** The beginning portion of the small intestine. **—du′o·de′nal** *adj.*

dupe (do͞op, dyo͞op) ▸ *n.* **1.** An easily deceived person. **2.** A person who functions as the tool of another. ▸ *v.* **duped, dup·ing.** To deceive. **—dup′a·bil′i·ty** *n.* **—dup′er** *n.*

du·ple (do͞o′pəl, dyo͞o′-) ▸ *adj.* **1.** Double. **2.** *Mus.* Consisting of two or a multiple of two beats to the measure.

du·plex (do͞o′plĕks′, dyo͞o′-) ▸ *adj.* Twofold; double. ▸ *n.* A house divided into two living units, usu. with separate entrances.

du·pli·cate (do͞o′plĭ-kĭt, dyo͞o′-) ▸ *adj.* **1.** Identically copied from an original. **2.** Existing in two corresponding parts; double. ▸ *n.* An identical copy; facsimile. ▸ *v.* (-kāt′) **-cat·ed, -cat·ing. 1.** To make an exact copy of. **2.** To make or perform again; repeat. **—du′pli·ca′tion** *n.*

du·pli·ca·tor (do͞o′plĭ-kā′tər, dyo͞o′-) ▸ *n.* A machine that reproduces printed or written material.

du·plic·i·ty (do͞o-plĭs′ĭ-tē, dyo͞o-) ▸ *n., pl.* **-ties.** Deliberate deceptiveness in behavior or speech. **—du·plic′i·tous** *adj.*

du·ra·ble (do͝or′ə-bəl, dyo͝or′-) ▸ *adj.* **1.** Capable of withstanding wear and tear. **2.** *Econ.* Not depleted or consumed by use. **—du′ra·bil′i·ty, du′ra·ble·ness** *n.* **—du′ra·bly** *adv.*

du·ra ma·ter (do͝or′ə mā′tər, mä′-, dyo͝or′ə) ▸ *n.* The tough fibrous membrane covering the brain and spinal cord.

du·rance (do͝or′əns, dyo͝or′-) ▸ *n.* Imprisonment.

du·ra·tion (do͝o-rā′shən, dyo͝o-) ▸ *n.* **1.** Continuance in time. **2.** A period of existence or persistence.

du·ress (do͝o-rĕs′, dyo͝o-) ▸ *n.* **1.** Constraint by threat; coercion. **2.** *Law* Illegal coercion or confinement.

dur·ing (do͝or′ĭng, dyo͝or′-) ▸ *prep.* **1.** Throughout the course of. **2.** At some time in.

du·rum (do͝or′əm, dyo͝or′-, dûr′-, dŭr′-) ▸ *n.* A hardy wheat used chiefly in making pasta.

dusk (dŭsk) ▸ *n.* The darker stage of twilight.

dusk·y (dŭs′kē) ▸ *adj.* **-i·er, -i·est. 1.** Marked by inadequate light; shadowy. **2.** Rather dark in color. **—dusk′i·ness** *n.*

dust (dŭst) ▸ *n.* **1.** Fine dry particles of matter. **2.** The earthy remains of a dead body. **3.** The surface of the ground. **4.** Something of no worth. ▸ *v.* **1.** To remove dust from by wiping or brushing. **2.** To sprinkle with a powdery substance. ***—idiom:* in the dust** Far behind, as in a race. **—dust′y** *adj.*

dust bowl ▸ *n.* A region reduced to aridity by drought and dust storms.

dust devil ▸ *n.* A small whirlwind that swirls dust and debris.

dust·er (dŭs′tər) ▸ *n.* **1.** One that dusts. **2.** A cloth or brush used to remove dust. **3.** A smock worn to protect clothing from dust. **4.** A woman's loose housecoat.

dust·ing (dŭs′tĭng) ▸ *n.* **1.** A light sprinkling. **2.** *Slang* A beating or defeat.

dust·pan (dŭst′păn′) ▸ *n.* A short-handled pan into which dust is swept.

Dutch (dŭch) ▸ *adj.* **1.** Of or relating to the Netherlands or its people or language. **2.** *Archaic* German. ▸ *n.* **1.** The people of the Netherlands. **2.** The Germanic language of the Netherlands. **3.** *Slang* Anger or temper. ***—idioms:* go Dutch** To pay one's own expenses on a date. **in Dutch** In trouble. **—Dutch′man** *n.* **—Dutch′wom′an** *n.*

Dutch door ▸ *n.* A door divided horizontally so that either part can be left open or closed.

Dutch elm disease ▸ *n.* A disease of elm trees caused by a fungus and resulting in death.

Dutch oven ▸ *n.* A large heavy pot, usu. of cast iron, used for slow cooking.

Dutch treat ▸ *n.* An outing, as for dinner or a movie, in which all persons pay their own expenses.

du·te·ous (do͞o′tē-əs, dyo͞o′-) ▸ *adj.* Obedient; dutiful. **—du′te·ous·ly** *adv.*

du·ti·a·ble (do͞o′tē-ə-bəl, dyo͞o′-) ▸ *adj.* Subject to import tax.

du·ti·ful (do͞o′tĭ-fəl, dyo͞o′-) ▸ *adj.* **1.** Careful to fulfill obligations. **2.** Expressing or filled with a sense of duty. **—du′ti·ful·ly** *adv.* **—du′ti·ful·ness** *n.*

du·ty (do͞o′tē, dyo͞o′-) ▸ *n., pl.* **-ties. 1.** An act or course of action required of one. **2.** Moral obligation. **3.** A task assigned to one, esp. in the armed forces. **4.** Function or work; service: *jury duty.* **5.** A tax charged by a government, esp. on imports.

DVD (dē′vē-dē′) ▸ *n.* A high-density compact disk esp. for high-resolution audio-visual data.

dwarf (dwôrf) ▸ *n., pl.* **dwarfs** or **dwarves** (dwôrvz). **1.** An abnormally small, often atypically proportioned person, animal, or plant. **2.** A small creature appearing in fairy tales. ▸ *v.* **1.** To check the growth of; stunt. **2.** To cause to appear small by comparison. **—dwarf′ish** *adj.* **—dwarf′ish·ness** *n.*

dwarf planet ▸ *n.* A celestial body that orbits the sun and is massive enough to assume a nearly spherical shape, but that does not clear other bodies from the neighborhood around its own orbit and is not a satellite of a planet.

dwell (dwĕl) ▸ *v.* **dwelt** (dwĕlt) or **dwelled, dwell·ing. 1.** To live as a resident; reside. **2.** To exist in a given place or state. **3a.** To fasten one's attention: *dwelling on what went wrong.* **b.** To speak or write at length: *dwelt on balancing the budget.* **—dwell′er** *n.*

dwell·ing (dwĕl′ĭng) ▸ *n.* A place to live in; abode.

dwin·dle (dwĭn′dl) ▸ *v.* **-dled, -dling.** To make or become gradually less until little remains.

Dy ▸ The symbol for the element **dysprosium.**

dy·ad (dī′ăd′, -əd) ▸ *n.* Two individuals or units regarded as a pair. ▸ *adj.* Made up of two units.

THESAURUS

dunk *v.* —*See* DIP (1).

dunk *n.* —*See* PLUNGE.

duo *n.* —*See* COUPLE.

dupable *adj.* —*See* GULLIBLE.

dupe *n.* A person who is easily deceived or victimized ▸ butt, cat's-paw, fool, gull, lamb, pushover, tool, victim. *Informal:* sucker. *Slang:* fall guy, gudgeon, mark, monkey, patsy, pigeon, sap. —*See also* PAWN[2].

dupe *v.* —*See* DECEIVE.

duplex or **duple** *adj.* —*See* DOUBLE (2).

duplicate *n.* —*See* COPY (1), DOUBLE, MATE.

duplicate *v.* **1.** To make or become twice as great ▸ double, geminate, redouble, twin. **2.** To do or perform an act or performance again ▸ do over, play over, redo, repeat, replay. —*See also* COPY.

duplicate *adj.* —*See* DOUBLE (2).

duplicitous *adj.* —*See* DISHONEST, UNDERHAND.

duplicity *n.* —*See* DECEIT, DISHONESTY (1).

durability *n.* —*See* CONTINUATION (1), ENDURANCE.

durable *adj.* —*See* CONTINUING.

duration *n.* —*See* CONTINUATION (1), LIFE, PERIOD (1).

duress *n.* —*See* FORCE (1).

dusk *n.* —*See* EVENING.

dusky *adj.* —*See* DARK (1), DARK (2).

dust *n.* The substance of the body, especially after decay or cremation ▸ ashes, clay, cremains, remains.

dust *v.* —*See* SPRINKLE.

dust bowl *n.* —*See* DESERT[1].

dusting *n.* —*See* COAT (2), DEFEAT.

dusty *adj.* —*See* FINE[1] (1).

dutiful or **duteous** *adj.* —*See* DEFERENTIAL, OBEDIENT.

dutifulness *n.* —*See* OBEDIENCE.

duty *n.* **1.** An act or course of action that is demanded of one, as by position, custom, law, or religion ▸ burden, charge, commitment, devoir, imperative, liability, must, need, obligation, onus, requirement, responsibility. **2.** The condition of being put to use ▸ adoption, application, employment, service, use, utilization. [*Compare* EXERCISE.] —*See also* TASK (1), TAX.

dwarf *adj.* —*See* TINY.

dwarf *v.* —*See* DOMINATE (2).

dweeb *n.* —*See* DRIP (2), FOOL.

dwell *v.* —*See* BROOD, CONSIST, LIVE[1].

dwell on *v.* —*See* BELABOR.

dweller *n.* —*See* INHABITANT.

dwelling *n.* —*See* HOME (1).

dwindle *v.* —*See* DECREASE.

dyad *n.* —*See* COUPLE.

dyb·buk (dĭb′o͝ok, dē-bo͝ok′) ▸ *n., pl.* **-buks** or **dyb·buk·im** (dĭ-bo͝ok′ĭm, dē′bo͞o-kēm′). In Jewish folklore, the soul of a dead person that enters and takes control of the body of a living person.

dye (dī) ▸ *n.* **1.** A substance used to color materials. **2.** A color imparted by dyeing. ▸ *v.* **dyed, dye·ing. 1.** To color (a material) with a dye. **2.** To take on or impart color. **—dy′er** *n.*

dye·stuff (dī′stŭf′) ▸ *n.* See **dye** 1.

dy·ing (dī′ĭng) ▸ *adj.* **1.** About to die. **2.** Drawing to an end; declining. **3.** Done or uttered just before death.

dy·nam·ic (dī-năm′ĭk) ▸ *adj.* also **dy·nam·i·cal** (-ĭ-kəl) **1.** Of or relating to energy or to objects in motion. **2.** Marked by continuous change or activity. **3.** Marked by intensity and vigor; forceful. ▸ *n.* **1.** An interactive system, esp. one involving conflicting forces. **2.** A force, esp. political, social, or psychological. **—dy·nam′i·cal·ly** *adv.*

dy·nam·ics (dī-năm′ĭks) ▸ *n.* **1.** *(takes sing. v.)* The branch of mechanics concerned with the effects of forces on the motion of a body or system, esp. of forces not originating in the system. **2.** *(takes pl. v.)* The social, intellectual, or moral forces that produce activity and change in a given sphere.

dy·na·mite (dī′nə-mīt′) ▸ *n.* **1.** A powerful explosive composed of nitroglycerin or ammonium nitrate dispersed in an absorbent medium. **2.** *Slang* Something exceptionally exciting or dangerous. ▸ *v.* **-mit·ed, -mit·ing.** To blow up or destroy with or as if with dynamite. ▸ *adj. Slang* Outstanding; superb. **—dy′na·mit′er** *n.*

dy·na·mo (dī′nə-mō′) ▸ *n., pl.* **-mos. 1.** A generator, esp. one for producing direct current. **2.** An energetic and forceful person.

dy·na·mom·e·ter (dī′nə-mŏm′ĭ-tər) ▸ *n.* An instrument used to measure mechanical power. **—dy′na·mom′e·try** *n.*

dy·nas·ty (dī′nə-stē) ▸ *n., pl.* **-ties. 1.** A succession of rulers from the same family or line. **2.** A group that maintains power for several generations. **—dy·nas′tic** (dī-năs′tĭk) *adj.*

dys– ▸ *pref.* Abnormal; impaired; difficult; bad: *dysplasia.*

dys·en·ter·y (dĭs′ən-tĕr′ē) ▸ *n.* An inflammatory disorder of the lower intestinal tract, resulting in severe diarrhea often with blood and mucus. **—dys′en·ter′ic** *adj.*

dys·func·tion (dĭs-fŭngk′shən) ▸ *n.* Abnormal or impaired functioning, esp. of a bodily system or organ. **—dys·func′tion·al** *adj.*

dys·lex·i·a (dĭs-lĕk′sē-ə) ▸ *n.* A learning disorder marked by impairment of the ability to read. **—dys·lex′ic** *adj. & n.*

dys·pep·sia (dĭs-pĕp′shə, -sē-ə) ▸ *n.* Indigestion. **—dys·pep′tic** *adj. & n.*

dys·pla·sia (dĭs-plā′zhə, -zhē-ə) ▸ *n.* Abnormal development of tissues, organs, or cells. **—dys·plas′tic** (-plăs′tĭk) *adj.*

dys·pro·si·um (dĭs-prō′zē-əm, -zhē-əm) ▸ *n. Symbol* **Dy** A soft, silvery rare-earth element used in nuclear research. At. no. 66.

dys·tro·phy (dĭs′trə-fē) ▸ *n.* **1.** A degenerative disorder caused by inadequate nutrition. **2.** Any of several disorders, esp. muscular dystrophy, in which the muscles weaken and atrophy. **—dys·troph′ic** *adj.*

THESAURUS

dye *n.* —*See* COLOR (2).
dye *v.* —*See* COLOR (1).
dying *adj.* —*See* PARTING.
dynamic or **dynamical** *adj.* —*See* ENERGETIC, FORCEFUL.
dynamism *n.* —*See* ENERGY.
dynamite *v.* —*See* DESTROY (2).
dynamite *adj.* —*See* EXCELLENT.
dynamo *n.* A person who is intensely energetic and enthusiastic ▸ demon, hustler. *Informal:* eager beaver, firebreather, go-getter, live wire.
dyspeptic *adj.* —*See* DEPRESSED (1).
dysphoria *n.* —*See* DEPRESSION (2).
dysphoric *adj.* —*See* DEPRESSED (1).

E

e[1] or **E** (ē) ▸ *n., pl.* **e's** or **E's** also **es** or **Es**. **1.** The 5th letter of the English alphabet. **2.** The 5th in a series. **3.** *Mus.* The 3rd tone of the C major scale. **4.** **E** A failing grade.

e[2] ▸ *abbr.* electron

E ▸ *abbr.* **1.** east **2.** *Baseball* error

e– ▸ *pref.* Computer or computer network: *e-commerce.*

ea. ▸ *abbr.* each

each (ēch) ▸ *adj.* Being one of two or more considered individually; every. ▸ *pron.* Every one of a group considered individually; each one. ▸ *adv.* For or to each one; apiece.

each other ▸ *pron.* Each the other. Used to indicate a reciprocal relationship or action: *The children like each other.*

ea·ger (ē′gər) ▸ *adj.* **-er, -est.** Having or showing keen interest or impatient expectancy. **—ea′ger·ly** *adv.* **—ea′ger·ness** *n.*

ea·gle (ē′gəl) ▸ *n.* **1.** A large bird of prey with a powerful hooked bill and strong soaring flight. **2.** A former US gold coin having a face value of ten dollars. **3.** A golf score of two under par on a hole.

ea·glet (ē′glĭt) ▸ *n.* A young eagle.

ear[1] (îr) ▸ *n.* **1.** *Anat.* **a.** The vertebrate organ of hearing, responsible for maintaining equilibrium and sensing sound. **b.** The visible outer part of this organ. **2.** The sense of hearing. **3.** Aural sensitivity, esp. to differences in musical pitch. **4.** Sympathetic attention. **5.** Something resembling the vertebrate ear. **6.** **ears** *Informal* Headphones. ***—idioms:*** **all ears** *Informal* Acutely attentive. **play it by ear** *Informal* To improvise. **up to (one's) ears** *Informal* Deeply involved. **—eared** *adj.* **—ear′less** *adj.*

ear[2] (îr) ▸ *n.* The seed-bearing spike of a cereal plant, such as corn.

ear·ache (îr′āk′) ▸ *n.* Pain in the ear.

ear·drum (îr′drŭm′) ▸ *n.* The thin membrane that separates the middle ear from the external ear.

ear·flap (îr′flăp′) ▸ *n.* A flap attached to a cap used to cover the ears.

ear·ful (îr′fo͝ol′) ▸ *n.* **1.** An excessive amount of something heard. **2.** Scandalous gossip. **3.** A reprimand.

Ear·hart (âr′härt′), **Amelia** (1897?–1937) ▸ Amer. aviator.

earl (ûrl) ▸ *n.* A British nobleman next in rank above a viscount and below a marquis. **—earl′dom** *n.*

ear·lobe (îr′lōb′) ▸ *n.* The soft pendulous lower part of the external ear.

ear·ly (ûr′lē) ▸ *adj.* **-li·er, -li·est.** **1.** Of or occurring near the beginning of a series, period of time, or course of events. **2.** Belonging to a previous or remote period of time: *early mammals.* **3.** Occurring or developing before the expected time. **4.** Occurring in the near future: *predicted an early end to the negotiations.* ▸ *adv.* **-lier, -liest.** **1.** Near the beginning of a given series, period of time, or course of events. **2.** At or during a remote or initial period. **3.** Before the expected or usual time: *arrived early.* **—ear′li·ness** *n.*

ear·mark (îr′märk′) ▸ *n.* **1.** An identifying feature or characteristic. **2.** A brand on the ear of a domestic animal. ▸ *v.* **1.** To set aside for a particular purpose. **2.** To brand with an earmark.

ear·muff (îr′mŭf′) ▸ *n.* Either of a pair of ear coverings worn to protect against the cold.

earn (ûrn) ▸ *v.* **1.** To gain esp. for the performance of service or labor. **2.** To acquire or deserve as a result of effort or action. **3.** To yield as return or profit. **—earn′er** *n.*

earned run (ûrnd) ▸ *n.* *Baseball* A run scored without the aid of an error.

ear·nest[1] (ûr′nĭst) ▸ *adj.* **1.** Showing deep sincerity or seriousness. **2.** Of an important nature; grave. ***—idiom:*** **in earnest** With a purposeful or sincere intent. **—ear′nest·ly** *adv.* **—ear′nest·ness** *n.*

ear·nest[2] (ûr′nĭst) ▸ *n.* Money paid in advance as part payment to bind a contract or bargain.

earn·ings (ûr′nĭngz) ▸ *pl.n.* **1.** Salary or wages. **2.** Profits from business or investments.

ear·phone (îr′fōn′) ▸ *n.* A device that converts electric signals to audible sound and fits over or in the ear.

ear·piece (îr′pēs′) ▸ *n.* **1.** A part, as of a telephone receiver, that fits in or is held next to the ear. **2.** See **earphone.** **3.** Either of the two parts of an eyeglasses frame that extend over the ear.

ear·plug (îr′plŭg′) ▸ *n.* **1.** A soft plug fitted into the ear canal to keep out water or sound. **2.** An earphone that fits into the ear.

ear·ring (îr′rĭng, îr′ĭng) ▸ *n.* An ornament worn on the ear, esp. the earlobe.

ear·shot (îr′shŏt′) ▸ *n.* The range within which sound can be heard.

ear·split·ting (îr′splĭt′ĭng) ▸ *adj.* Loud and shrill enough to hurt the ears.

earth (ûrth) ▸ *n.* **1a.** The land surface of the world. **b.** Soil, esp. productive soil. **2.** often **Earth** The 3rd planet from the sun, at a mean distance of approx. 149 million km

THESAURUS

eager *adj.* Intensely desirous or interested ▸ agog, ardent, athirst, avid, bursting, hot, impatient, keen, solicitous, thirsting, thirsty. *Informal:* raring. *Idioms:* champing at the bit, hot to trot, ready and willing. *—See also* WILLING.

eager beaver *n.* *Informal* An intensely energetic, enthusiastic person ▸ demon, dynamo, hustler. *Informal:* firebreather, go-getter, live wire.

eagerness *n.* *—See* ENTHUSIASM (1).

ear *n.* The sense by which sound is perceived ▸ audition, hearing.

earlier *adj.* *—See* ADVANCE, PAST.

earlier *adv.* **1.** At or during a time in the past ▸ already, before, beforehand, erenow, erstwhile, formerly, once, previously. *Idioms:* ahead of time, in advance. **2.** Up to this time ▸ before, heretofore, previously, yet.

earliest *adj.* *—See* FIRST.

early *adj.* **1.** Of, existing, or occurring in a distant period ▸ ancient, antediluvian, prehistoric, primal, primeval, primitive, primordial. [*Compare* FIRST.] **2.** Developing, occurring, or appearing before the expected time ▸ precocious, premature, untimely. *—See also* BEGINNING.

early *adv.* Before the expected time ▸ ahead, beforehand, betimes. *Idioms:* ahead of schedule, ahead of time, in advance, with time to spare.

earmark *v.* To attach a ticket to ▸ flag, label, mark, tag, ticket. *—See also* APPROPRIATE, DESIGNATE.

earmark *n.* *—See* TICKET (1).

earn *v.* **1.** To acquire as a result of one's behavior or effort ▸ deserve, gain, get, merit, win. *Informal:* rate. **2.** To receive, as wages, for one's labor ▸ draw, gain, get, make, win. *Informal:* bring in, pull down, pull in, rake in. *Idioms:* bring home the bacon, earn one's keep. *—See also* RETURN (3).

earnest[1] *adj.* *—See* GRAVE[2] (1), SERIOUS (1).

earnest[2] *n.* *—See* PAWN[1].

earnestness *n.* *—See* SERIOUSNESS (1).

earnings *n.* Something earned, won, or otherwise acquired ▸ gain, profit, return. [*Compare* INCREASE.] *—See also* WAGE.

earshot *n.* Range of audibility ▸ hearing, sound. [*Compare* RANGE.]

earsplitting *adj.* *—See* LOUD.

earth *n.* **1.** The soft part of the land surface of the world ▸ clay, dirt, ground, humus, loam, mud, sod, soil,

(92.96 million mi) and with an average radius of 6,374 km (3,959 mi). **3.** The realm of mortal existence. **4.** Worldly pursuits. ***—idioms:*** **down to earth** Sensible; realistic. **on earth** Among all the possiblities: *Why on earth did you go?*

earth·en (ûr′thən, -*th*ən) ► *adj.* Made of earth or clay.

earth·en·ware (ûr′thən-wâr′, -*th*ən-) ► *n.* Pottery made from a porous clay fired at low temperatures.

earth·ling (ûrth′lĭng) ► *n.* One that inhabits the planet Earth.

earth·ly (ûrth′lē) ► *adj.* **1.** Of or characteristic of this earth; terrestrial. **2.** Not heavenly or divine; worldly. **3.** Conceivable; possible: *no earthly reason.* **—earth′li·ness** *n.*

earth·quake (ûrth′kwāk′) ► *n.* A sudden movement of the earth's crust caused by stress accumulated along geologic faults or by volcanic activity.

earth science ► *n.* Any of several geologic sciences concerned with the origin, structure, and physical phenomena of the earth.

earth·shak·ing (ûrth′shā′kĭng) ► *adj.* Of great consequence or importance.

earth·ward (ûrth′wərd) ► *adv. & adj.* To or toward the earth. **—earth′wards** *adv.*

earth·work (ûrth′wûrk′) ► *n.* An earthen embankment, esp. one used as a fortification.

earth·worm (ûrth′wûrm′) ► *n.* Any of a class of annelid worms that burrow into and aerate soil.

earth·y (ûr′thē) ► *adj.* **-i·er, -i·est. 1.** Of, consisting of, or resembling earth. **2.** Crude; indecent. **3.** Hearty or uninhibited. **—earth′i·ly** *adv.* **—earth′i·ness** *n.*

ear·wax (îr′wăks′) ► *n.* The waxlike secretion of certain glands lining the canal of the external ear.

ear·wig (îr′wĭg′) ► *n.* An elongate insect having a pair of pincerlike appendages protruding from the rear of the abdomen.

ease (ēz) ► *n.* **1.** Freedom from pain, worry, or agitation. **2.** Freedom from constraint or embarrassment; naturalness. **3.** Freedom from difficulty, hardship, or effort. **4.** Freedom from financial difficulty; affluence. **5.** Dexterity in performance; facility. ► *v.* **eased, eas·ing. 1.** To free or become free from pain, worry, or agitation. **2.** To lessen the discomfort or pain of. **3.** To give respite from. **4.** To slacken; loosen. **5.** To reduce the difficulty of. **6.** To maneuver slowly and carefully.

ea·sel (ē′zəl) ► *n.* An upright frame for supporting an artist's canvas.

ease·ment (ēz′mənt) ► *n.* **1.** The act of easing or the condition of being eased. **2.** *Law* A right afforded a person to make limited use of another's real property.

east (ēst) ► *n.* **1a.** The direction of the earth's axial rotation; the general direction of sunrise. **b.** The compass point 90° clockwise from north. **2.** often **East** The eastern part of a region or country. **3.** often **East** Asia. ► *adj.* **1.** To, toward, of, or in the east. **2.** Coming from the east: *an east wind.* ► *adv.* In, from, or toward the east. **—east′ward, east′ward·ly** *adj. & adv.* **—east′wards** *adv.*

East Asia ► A region of Asia coextensive with the Far East. **—East Asian** *adj. & n.*

Eas·ter (ē′stər) ► *n.* A Christian feast commemorating the Resurrection of Jesus, observed on a Sunday in March or April.

Easter Island ► An island of Chile in the S Pacific about 3,701 km (2,300 mi) W of the mainland, famous for its colossal heads carved from volcanic rock.

east·er·ly (ē′stər-lē) ► *adj.* **1.** Situated toward the east. **2.** From the east: *easterly winds.* **—east′er·ly** *adv.*

east·ern (ē′stərn) ► *adj.* **1.** Of, in, or toward the east. **2.** From the east: *eastern breezes.* **3.** often **Eastern** Of or characteristic of eastern regions or the East. **4. Eastern a.** Of the Eastern Church. **b.** Of the Eastern Orthodox Church.

Eastern Church ► *n.* Any of the Christian churches formerly within or founded from the Byzantine Empire, esp. the Eastern Orthodox Church.

east·ern·er also **East·ern·er** (ē′stər-nər) ► *n.* A native or inhabitant of the east, esp. the E US.

Eastern Europe ► The countries of E Europe, esp. those allied with the USSR in the Warsaw Pact (1955–91).

Eastern Hemisphere ► The half of the earth comprising Europe, Africa, Asia, and Australia.

Eastern Orthodox Church ► *n.* Any of the Christian churches in communion with the patriarch of Constantinople.

East Germany ► A former country of N Europe on the Baltic Sea (1949–90). **—East German** *adj. & n.*

East Indies ► **1.** The islands comprising Indonesia. **2.** A general term formerly used for India and SE Asia. **—East Indian** *adj.*

East Timor ► A country of the W Pacific Ocean made up of the E part of Timor and an offshore island.

eas·y (ē′zē) ► *adj.* **-i·er, -i·est. 1.** Capable of being accomplished without difficulty. **2.** Free from worry, anxiety, trouble, or pain. **3.** Causing little hardship or distress. **4.** Socially at ease. **5a.** Relaxed in attitude; easygoing. **b.** Not strict or severe; lenient. **6.** Readily exploited, imposed on, or tricked. **7.** Not hurried or forced; moderate. ► *adv.* Without strain or difficulty; in a relaxed manner. **—eas′i·ly** *adv.* **—eas′i·ness** *n.*

easy chair ► *n.* A large comfortable chair.

eas·y·go·ing (ē′zē-gō′ĭng) ► *adj.* Living without worry or concern; relaxed.

eat (ēt) ► *v.* **ate** (āt), **eat·en** (ēt′n), **eat·ing. 1.** To consume (food). **2.** To consume or ravage as if by eating. **3.** To

THESAURUS

terrain, topsoil, turf. **2.** The celestial body where humans live ► globe, orb, planet, world. *—See also* HUMANKIND.

earthbound *adj.* *—See* DULL (1), EARTHLY.

earthen or **earthlike** *adj.* Consisting of or resembling soil ► earthlike, earthy, terrestrial. *—See also* EARTHLY.

earthling *n.* *—See* HUMAN BEING.

earthly *adj.* Relating to or characteristic of the earth or of human life on earth ► earthbound, earthen, earthlike, earthy, mundane, secular, sublunary, tellurian, telluric, temporal, terrene, terrestrial, worldly. [*Compare* PHYSICAL, PROFANE.] *—See also* CONCEIVABLE.

earthquake *n.* A shaking of the earth ► quake, seism, temblor, tremor. *Informal:* shake.

earth-shaking *adj.* *—See* IMPORTANT.

earthwork *n.* *—See* BULWARK.

earthy *adj.* Consisting of or resembling soil ► earthen, earthlike, terrestrial. *—See also* EARTHLY, RACY.

ease *n.* **1.** Freedom from constraint, formality, embarrassment, or awkwardness ► casualness, comfort, easiness, informality, naturalness, poise, spontaneity, unceremoniousness, unrestraint. [*Compare* ABANDON.] **2.** The ability to perform without apparent effort ► easiness, effortlessness, facileness, facility, readiness. [*Compare* ABILITY.] *—See also* PROSPERITY (2), RELIEF (1), REST[1] (2).

ease *v.* **1.** To reduce in tension, pressure, or rigidity ► let up, loose, loosen, relax, slack, slacken, untighten. **2.** To make less difficult ► expedite, facilitate, grease, help along. *Idioms:* clear (*or* prepare *or* smooth the way for, grease the wheels (*or* skids) for, open the door for (*or* to). **3.** To maneuver gently and slowly into place ► glide, slide, slip. **4.** To advance carefully and gradually ► edge, sidle. [*Compare* CRAWL, SNEAK.] *—See also* RELIEVE (1), SUBSIDE.

ease off *v.* *—See* WEAKEN.

easeful *adj.* *—See* COMFORTABLE.

easiness *n.* *—See* EASE (2), EASE (1).

easy *adj.* **1.** Posing no difficulty ► effortless, facile, simple, smooth. *Informal:* snap. *Idioms:* easy as ABC (*or* falling off a log *or* one-two-three *or* pie), like taking candy from a baby, nothing to it. [*Compare* BREEZE.] **2.** Requiring little effort or exertion ► light, moderate, undemanding. *Informal:* cushy, soft. *—See also* COMFORTABLE, EASYGOING, FLUENT, GRADUAL (2), GULLIBLE, PROSPEROUS, TOLERANT, WANTON (1).

easygoing *adj.* Unconstrained by rigid standards or ceremony ► casual, easy, informal, mellow, natural, relaxed, spontaneous, unceremonious, unrestrained. *Informal:* laid-back. [*Compare* LOOSE, TOLERANT.] *—See also* CALM.

easy street *n.* *—See* PROSPERITY (2).

eat *v.* **1.** To take food into the body as nourishment ► consume, devour, ingest, partake. *Informal:* put away,

erode or corrode. **4.** *Slang* To absorb the cost of. **5.** *Informal* To bother or annoy. ***—idioms:*** **eat crow** To be forced to accept a humiliating defeat. **eat (one's) words** To retract an assertion. **eat out of (someone's) hand** To be manipulated by another. **—eat′a·ble** *adj.* & *n.* **—eat′er** *n.*

eat·er·y (ē′tə-rē) ▸ *n., pl.* **-ies.** *Informal* A restaurant.

eat·ing disorder (ē′tĭng) ▸ *n.* A psychological disorder, such as anorexia nervosa, that involves insufficient or excessive food intake.

eaves (ēvz) ▸ *pl.n.* The projecting overhang at the lower edge of a roof.

eaves·drop (ēvz′drŏp′) ▸ *v.* **-dropped, -drop·ping.** To listen secretly to private conversations.

ebb (ĕb) ▸ *n.* **1.** The period of a tide between high tide and a following low tide. **2.** A period of decline or diminution. ▸ *v.* **1.** To recede, as the tide. **2.** To decline or diminish.

eb·on·ite (ĕb′ə-nīt′) ▸ *n.* A hard rubber used as an electrical insulating material.

eb·on·y (ĕb′ə-nē) ▸ *n., pl.* **-ies.** **1.** The hard dark wood of a tropical Asian tree. **2.** The color black. ▸ *adj.* Of or like ebony; black.

e·bul·lient (ĭ-bo͝ol′yənt, ĭ-bŭl′-) ▸ *adj.* **1.** Zestfully enthusiastic. **2.** Boiling or seeming to boil; bubbling. **—e·bul′lience** *n.* **—e·bul′lient·ly** *adv.*

eb·ul·li·tion (ĕb′ə-lĭsh′ən) ▸ *n.* **1.** The state or process of boiling. **2.** A sudden outpouring, as of emotion.

ec·cen·tric (ĭk-sĕn′trĭk, ĕk-) ▸ *adj.* **1.** Departing from a conventional pattern. **2.** Deviating from a circular path, as in an elliptical orbit. **3.** Not situated at or in the geometric center. ▸ *n.* **1.** One that deviates from conventional patterns. **2.** *Phys.* A disk or wheel having its axis of revolution displaced from its center so that it is capable of imparting reciprocating motion. **—ec·cen′tri·cal·ly** *adv.* **—ec′cen·tric′i·ty** *n.*

Ec·cle·si·as·tes (ĭ-klē′zē-ăs′tēz′) ▸ *n.* *(takes sing. v.)* See **Bible** table in Appendix.

ec·cle·si·as·tic (ĭ-klē′zē-ăs′tĭk) ▸ *adj.* Ecclesiastical. ▸ *n.* A minister or priest; cleric.

ec·cle·si·as·ti·cal (ĭ-klē′zē-ăs′tĭ-kəl) ▸ *adj.* Of or relating to a church, esp. as an institution. **—ec·cle′si·as′ti·cal·ly** *adv.*

Ec·cle·si·as·ti·cus (ĭ-klē′zē-ăs′tĭ-kəs) ▸ *n.* See **Bible** table in Appendix.

ec·dy·sis (ĕk′dĭ-sĭs) ▸ *n., pl.* **-ses** (-sēz′). The shedding of an outer integument or layer of skin, as by insects, crustaceans, and snakes; molting.

ech·e·lon (ĕsh′ə-lŏn′) ▸ *n.* **1.** A steplike formation, as of troops or aircraft. **2.** A subdivision of a military force. **3.** A level of authority in a hierarchy; rank.

ech·i·na·ce·a (ĕk′ə-nā′sē-ə, -nā′shə) ▸ *n.* Any of several usu. pinkish-purple coneflower plants used in herbal medicine.

e·chi·no·derm (ĭ-kī′nə-dûrm′) ▸ *n.* Any of various gen. spiny marine invertebrates having an internal calcareous skeleton, including starfishes and sea urchins.

ech·o (ĕk′ō) ▸ *n., pl.* **-oes.** **1a.** Repetition of a sound by reflection of sound waves from a surface. **b.** The sound produced in this manner. **2.** A remnant or vestige. **3.** One who imitates another. **4.** A consequence or repercussion. ▸ *v.* **-oed, -o·ing.** **1.** To repeat or be repeated by or as if by an echo; imitate: *followers echoing the cries of their leader.* **2.** To resound; reverberate. **—ech′o·er** *n.* **—e·cho′ic** *adj.*

Echo ▸ *n.* *Gk. Myth.* A nymph whose unrequited love for Narcissus caused her to pine away until only her voice remained.

ech·o·gram (ĕk′ō-grăm′) ▸ *n.* See **sonogram.**

ech·o·lo·ca·tion (ĕk′ō-lō-kā′shən) ▸ *n.* **1.** *Zool.* A sensory system, as in bats or dolphins, in which usu. high-pitched sounds are emitted and their echoes interpreted to determine the direction and distance of objects. **2.** *Electron.* Ranging by acoustical echo analysis. **—ech′o·lo·cate′** *v.*

é·clair (ā-klâr′, ā′klâr′) ▸ *n.* An elongated pastry filled with custard or whipped cream and usu. iced with chocolate.

é·clat (ā-klä′, ā′klä′) ▸ *n.* **1.** Great brilliance, as of achievement. **2.** Great acclamation.

e·clec·tic (ĭ-klĕk′tĭk) ▸ *adj.* Selecting or employing individual elements from a variety of sources, systems, or styles. **—e·clec′tic** *n.* **—e·clec′ti·cal·ly** *adv.* **—e·clec′ti·cism′** *n.*

e·clipse (ĭ-klĭps′) ▸ *n.* **1a.** The partial or complete obscuring of one celestial body by another. **b.** The period of time during which such an obscuration occurs. **2.** A fall into obscurity or disuse; decline. ▸ *v.* **e·clipsed, e·clips·ing.** **1.** To cause an eclipse of. **2.** To surpass; outshine.

e·clip·tic (ĭ-klĭp′tĭk) ▸ *n.* The apparent path of the sun and the planets among the stars in one year.

ec·logue (ĕk′lôg′, -lŏg′) ▸ *n.* A pastoral poem.

e·col·o·gy (ĭ-kŏl′ə-jē) ▸ *n.* **1.** The science of the relationships between organisms and their environments. **2.** The study of the detrimental effects of human civilization on the environment. **—ec′o·log′i·cal** (ĕk′ə-lŏj′ĭ-kəl, ē′kə-), **ec′o·log′ic** *adj.* **—ec′o·log′i·cal·ly** *adv.* **—e·col′o·gist** *n.*

e-com·merce (ē′kŏm′ərs) ▸ *n.* Commerce transacted electronically, as over the Internet.

e·con·o·met·rics (ĭ-kŏn′ə-mĕt′rĭks) ▸ *n.* *(takes sing. v.)* Application of mathematical and statistical techniques to economics.

ec·o·nom·ic (ĕk′ə-nŏm′ĭk, ē′kə-) ▸ *adj.* **1.** Of or relating to the production, development, and management of material wealth, as of a country. **2.** Of or relating to the necessities of life. **3.** Efficient; economical.

ec·o·nom·i·cal (ĕk′ə-nŏm′ĭ-kəl, ē′kə-) ▸ *adj.* **1.** Prudent and thrifty; not wasteful. **2.** Intended to save money, as by efficient operation. **—ec′o·nom′i·cal·ly** *adv.*

ec·o·nom·ics (ĕk′ə-nŏm′ĭks, ē′kə-) ▸ *n.* **1.** *(takes sing. v.)* The science that deals with the production, distribution, and consumption of goods and services. **2.** *(takes sing. or*

THESAURUS

tuck into. *Slang:* chow down, polish off. [*Compare* CHEW, GULP.] **2.** To have or take a meal ▸ breakfast, dine, lunch, snack, sup. ***Idioms:*** break bread, have (*or* take) a bite. **3.** To include as part of one's diet by nature or preference ▸ exist on, feed on, live on, subsist on. **4.** To do away with completely and destructively ▸ consume, devour, swallow (up), waste. —*See also* ERODE.

eat up *v.* *Slang* To be avidly interested in ▸ devour, feast on, relish. —*See also* CONSUME (1), EXHAUST (1), ADORE (2).

eatable *adj.* Fit to be eaten ▸ comestible, edible, esculent, palatable.

eats *n.* —*See* FOOD.

ebb *v.* —*See* DECREASE, DETERIORATE, DISAPPEAR (1), LANGUISH, RECEDE, SUBSIDE.

ebb *n.* —*See* WANING.

ebony or **ebon** *adj.* —*See* BLACK (1).

ebullient *adj.* —*See* LIVELY.

eccentric *adj.* Deviating from what is conventional or customary ▸ antic, bizarre, cranky, curious, erratic, fantastic, freakish, grotesque, idiosyncratic, odd, outlandish, peculiar, quaint, queer, quirky, singular, strange, unconventional, unnatural, unorthodox, unusual, weird. *Slang:* kooky, screwball. [*Compare* EXOTIC, INSANE.]

eccentric *n.* —*See* CHARACTER (5), CRACKPOT.

eccentricity *n.* Peculiar behavior ▸ idiosyncrasy, peculiarity, quirk, quirkiness, singularity. [*Compare* ABNORMALITY.]

ecclesiastic *n.* —*See* CLERIC.

ecclesiastical *adj.* Of or relating to a church or to an established religion ▸ church, churchly, religious, spiritual. [*Compare* CLERICAL, DIVINE, HOLY, RITUAL.] —*See also* CLERICAL.

echelon *n.* —*See* PLACE (1).

echinate *adj.* —*See* THORNY (1).

echo *n.* **1.** Imitative reproduction, as of the style of another ▸ imitation, reflection, reflex, repetition, reproduction. [*Compare* MIMICRY.] **2.** Repetition of sound by reflection of sound waves from a surface ▸ repercussion, reverberation. —*See also* MIMIC, REPETITION.

echo *v.* To send back the sound of ▸ bounce back, rebound, reecho, reflect, repeat, resound, reverberate. —*See also* MIMIC.

echoic *adj.* Imitating sounds ▸ imitative, mimetic, onomatopoeic, onomatopoetic.

echoism *n.* The formation of words in imitation of sounds ▸ mimesis, onomatopoeia.

eclipse *v.* —*See* OBSCURE.

economical *adj.* Careful in the use of material resources ▸ canny, chary, frugal, provident, prudent, saving, sparing, thrifty. [*Compare* STINGY.]

pl. v.) Economic matters. **—e·con′o·mist** (ĭ-kŏn′ə-mĭst) *n.*

e·con·o·mize (ĭ-kŏn′ə-mīz′) ▸ *v.* **-mized, -miz·ing.** To practice economy, as by avoiding waste. **—e·con′o·miz′er** *n.*

e·con·o·my (ĭ-kŏn′ə-mē) ▸ *n., pl.* **-mies. 1a.** Careful, thrifty management of resources. **b.** An example of such management. **2.** The system of economic activity in a country or region. **3.** Efficient or sparing use.

e·co·sys·tem (ē′kō-sĭs′təm, ĕk′ō-) ▸ *n.* An ecological community together with its environment, functioning as a unit.

ec·ru (ĕk′rōō, ā′krōō) ▸ *n.* A light tan color.

ec·sta·sy (ĕk′stə-sē) ▸ *n., pl.* **-sies.** Intense joy or delight; rapture. **—ec·stat′ic** (ĕk-stăt′ĭk) *adj.* **—ec·stat′i·cal·ly** *adv.*

-ectomy ▸ *suff.* Surgical removal: *tonsillectomy.*

ec·top·ic pregnancy (ĕk-tŏp′ĭk) ▸ *n.* Implantation and subsequent development of a fertilized ovum outside the uterus, as in a fallopian tube.

ec·to·therm (ĕk′tə-thûrm′) ▸ *n.* An organism that regulates its body temperature largely by exchanging heat with its surroundings. **—ec′to·ther′mic, ec′to·ther′mal** *adj.*

Ec·ua·dor (ĕk′wə-dôr′) ▸ A country of NW South America on the Pacific Ocean. **—Ec′ua·dor′i·an** *adj. & n.*

ec·u·men·i·cal (ĕk′yə-mĕn′ĭ-kəl) also **ec·u·men·ic** (-mĕn′ĭk) ▸ *adj.* **1.** Of worldwide scope or applicability; universal. **2.** Of or relating to ecumenism. **—ec′u·men′i·cal·ly** *adv.*

ec·u·me·nism (ĕk′yə-mə-nĭz′əm, ĭ-kyōō′-) ▸ *n.* A movement promoting unity among Christian churches or denominations. **—ec′u·men′ist** *n.*

ec·ze·ma (ĕk′sə-mə, ĕg′zə-, ĭg-zē′-) ▸ *n.* A noncontagious skin inflammation marked by redness, itching, and lesions.

ed. ▸ *abbr.* **1.** edition **2.** editor

-ed[1] ▸ *suff.* Used to form the past tense of regular verbs: *waited.*

-ed[2] ▸ *suff.* Used to form the past participle of regular verbs: *linked.*

-ed[3] ▸ *suff.* Having; characterized by; resembling: *pointed.*

E·dam (ē′dəm, ē′dăm′) ▸ *n.* A mild yellow Dutch cheese, usu. covered with red wax.

ed·dy (ĕd′ē) ▸ *n., pl.* **-dies.** A current, as of water or air, moving contrary to the direction of the main current, esp. in a circular motion. **—ed′dy** *v.*

Eddy, Mary (Morse) Baker (1821–1910) ▸ Amer. religious leader who founded Christian Science (1879).

e·del·weiss (ā′dəl-vīs′, -wīs′) ▸ *n.* An alpine plant having downy leaves and small whitish flowers.

e·de·ma (ĭ-dē′mə) ▸ *n. Pathol.* An excessive accumulation of serous fluid in tissues. **—e·dem′a·tous** (ĭ-dĕm′ə-təs) *adj.*

E·den (ēd′n) ▸ *n.* **1.** *Bible* The garden of God and first home of Adam and Eve. **2.** A state of innocence or bliss. **—E·den′ic** (ē-dĕn′ĭk) *adj.*

edge (ĕj) ▸ *n.* **1.** A thin sharpened side, as of the blade of a cutting instrument. **2.** Keenness; zest. **3.** The line of intersection of two surfaces. **4.** A rim or brink. **5.** A dividing line; border. **6.** An advantage. ▸ *v.* **edged, edg·ing. 1.** To give an edge to. **2.** To advance or push gradually. ***—idiom:*** **on edge** Highly tense or nervous; irritable. **—edg′er** *n.*

edge·wise (ĕj′wīz′) also **edge·ways** (-wāz′) ▸ *adv.* With the edge foremost.

edg·ing (ĕj′ĭng) ▸ *n.* Something that forms an edge or border.

edg·y (ĕj′ē) ▸ *adj.* **-i·er, -i·est. 1.** Nervous or irritable. **2.** Having a sharp or biting edge. **—edg′i·ly** *adv.* **—edg′i·ness** *n.*

ed·i·ble (ĕd′ə-bəl) ▸ *adj.* Fit to be eaten. **—ed′i·bil′i·ty, ed′i·ble·ness** *n.* **—ed′i·ble** *n.*

e·dict (ē′dĭkt′) ▸ *n.* A proclamation issued by an authority.

ed·i·fice (ĕd′ə-fĭs) ▸ *n.* A building, esp. one of imposing size.

ed·i·fy (ĕd′ə-fī′) ▸ *v.* **-fied, -fy·ing.** To instruct, esp. to encourage moral or spiritual improvement. **—ed′i·fi·ca′tion** *n.* **—ed′i·fi′er** *n.*

Ed·in·burgh (ĕd′n-bûr′ə, -bŭr′ə, -brə) ▸ The capital of Scotland, in the E part on the Firth of Forth.

Ed·i·son (ĕd′ĭ-sən), **Thomas Alva** (1847–1931) ▸ Amer. inventor.

ed·it (ĕd′ĭt) ▸ *v.* **1.** To prepare (e.g., a manuscript) for publication, as by correcting or revising. **2.** To supervise the publication of. **3.** To assemble the components of (e.g., a film or soundtrack), as by cutting and splicing. **—ed′it** *n.* **—ed′i·tor** *n.* **—ed′i·tor·ship′** *n.*

e·di·tion (ĭ-dĭsh′ən) ▸ *n.* **1.** The form in which a book is published: *a paperback edition.* **2.** The entire number of copies of a publication issued at one time. **3.** One that resembles an original; version.

ed·i·to·ri·al (ĕd′ĭ-tôr′ē-əl) ▸ *n.* **1.** An article in a publication expressing the opinion of its editors or publishers. **2.** A commentary on television or radio expressing the opinion of the station or network. ▸ *adj.* **1.** Of or relating to editing. **2.** Of or like an editorial. **—ed′i·to′ri·al·ist** *n.* **—ed′i·to′ri·al·ly** *adv.*

ed·i·to·ri·al·ize (ĕd′ĭ-tôr′ē-ə-līz′) ▸ *v.* **-ized, -iz·ing. 1.** To express an opinion in or as if in an editorial. **2.** To present an opinion in the guise of an objective report.

Ed·mon·ton (ĕd′mən-tən) ▸ The capital of Alberta, Canada, in the central part of the province.

ed·u·ca·ble (ĕj′ə-kə-bəl) ▸ *adj.* Capable of being educated. **—ed′u·ca·bil′i·ty** *n.*

ed·u·cate (ĕj′ə-kāt′) ▸ *v.* **-cat·ed, -cat·ing. 1.** To provide esp. with formal knowledge or training. **2.** To provide with information. **3.** To bring to an understanding. **—ed′u·ca′tor** *n.*

ed·u·cat·ed (ĕj′ə-kā′tĭd) ▸ *adj.* **1.** Having an education, esp. one above the average. **2.** Showing evidence of schooling, training, or experience. **3.** Based on experience or knowledge: *an educated guess.*

THESAURUS

economize *v.* —*See* SCRIMP.

economy *n.* Careful use of material resources ▸ frugality, providence, prudence, thrift, thriftiness. [*Compare* CONSERVATION.]

economy *adj.* —*See* CHEAP.

ecosystem or **ecosphere** *n.* —*See* ENVIRONMENT (3).

ecstasy *n.* —*See* DELIGHT, HEAVEN.

ecumenical *adj.* —*See* UNIVERSAL (1).

edacious *adj.* —*See* GLUTTONOUS, VORACIOUS.

edacity *n.* —*See* VORACITY.

eddy *v.* To move or cause to move like a rapidly rotating current of liquid ▸ swirl, whirl. [*Compare* TURN.]

eddy *n.* —*See* BREEZE (1), WHIRLPOOL.

edge *n.* A cutting quality ▸ bite, incisiveness, keenness, sharpness, sting. —*See also* ADVANTAGE (3), BLADE, BORDER (1), OUTSKIRTS, TONE (2).

edge *v.* To advance carefully and gradually ▸ ease, sidle. [*Compare* CRAWL, SNEAK.] —*See also* BORDER, INSINUATE, SHARPEN.

edginess *n.* —*See* RESTLESSNESS.

edging *n.* —*See* BORDER (1).

edgy *adj.* Feeling or exhibiting nervous tension ▸ fidgety, jittery, jumpy, nervous, restive, restless, skittish, taut, tense, twitchy. *Slang:* antsy, hyper, uptight. *Idioms:* a bundle of nerves, all wound up, on edge. [*Compare* ANXIOUS.]

edible *adj.* Fit to be eaten ▸ comestible, eatable, esculent, palatable.

edibles *n.* —*See* FOOD.

edict *n.* —*See* LAW (1), MESSAGE, RULING.

edification *n.* The condition of being informed spiritually ▸ enlightenment, illumination. [*Compare* EDUCATION.]

edifice *n.* Something built, especially for human use ▸ building, construction, erection, pile, structure.

edify *v.* To indulge in moral reflection, usually pompously ▸ moralize, pontificate, preach, sermonize. [*Compare* CHASTISE.] —*See also* ILLUMINATE (2).

edifying *adj.* —*See* CULTURAL, EDUCATIONAL (2), MORAL.

edit *v.* —*See* CENSOR (1), REVISE.

edition *n.* —*See* BOOK, PUBLICATION (2).

editor *n.* —*See* PRESS.

editorial *n.* —*See* COMMENT.

editorialist *n.* —*See* PRESS.

editorialize *v.* —*See* COMMENT.

educable *adj.* Capable of being educated ▸ docile, teachable, trainable. [*Compare* OBEDIENT.]

educate *v.* To impart knowledge and skill to ▸ coach, discipline, form, instruct, school, teach, train, tutor. [*Compare* INDOCTRINATE.] —*See also* INFORM (1).

educated *adj.* Showing evidence of schooling, training, or experience ▸ degreed, enlightened, erudite, informed, knowledgeable, learned, lettered, literate, scholarly, schooled, trained, versed, well-read, well-taught, wise. [*Compare* FAMILIAR, PEDANTIC, STUDIOUS.] —*See also* CULTURED, INFORMED.

ed·u·ca·tion (ĕj′ə-kā′shən) ▸ *n.* **1.** The act or process of educating or being educated. **2.** The knowledge or skill obtained. **3.** The field of study concerned with teaching and learning. **—ed′u·ca′tion·al** *adj.*

e·duce (ĭ-do͞os′, ĭ-dyo͞os′) ▸ *v.* **e·duced, e·duc·ing. 1.** To draw out; elicit. **2.** To deduce.

Ed·ward (ĕd′wərd) Prince of Wales. "the Black Prince." (1330–76) ▸ English soldier during the Hundred Years' War.

-ee[1] ▸ *suff.* **1.** One that receives or benefits from a specified action: *addressee.* **2.** One that performs a specified action: *standee.*

-ee[2] ▸ *suff.* **1.** One resembling: *goatee.* **2.** A particular, esp. a diminutive kind of: *bootee.*

eel (ēl) ▸ *n., pl.* **eel** or **eels.** Any of various long snakelike marine or freshwater fishes.

-eer ▸ *suff.* One concerned with or engaged in: *auctioneer.*

ee·rie or **ee·ry** (îr′ē) ▸ *adj.* **-ri·er, -ri·est. 1.** Inspiring inexplicable fear or uneasiness. **2.** Suggestive of the supernatural; mysterious. **—ee′ri·ly** *adv.* **—ee′ri·ness** *n.*

ef·face (ĭ-fās′) ▸ *v.* **-faced, -fac·ing. 1.** To wipe out; erase. **2.** To make indistinct. **3.** To conduct (oneself) inconspicuously. **—ef·face′ment** *n.*

ef·fect (ĭ-fĕkt′) ▸ *n.* **1.** Something brought about by a cause or agent; result. **2.** The power to achieve a result; influence. **3.** Advantage; avail. **4.** The condition of being in full force. **5.** Something that produces a specific impression. **6.** The basic or general meaning: *words to that effect.* **7. effects** Movable belongings. ▸ *v.* **1.** To bring into existence. **2.** To produce as a result. ***—idiom:* in effect** In essence; to all purposes.

ef·fec·tive (ĭ-fĕk′tĭv) ▸ *adj.* **1.** Having an intended or expected effect. **2.** Producing a strong impression or response; striking. **3.** Operative; in effect. **—ef·fec′tive·ly** *adv.*

ef·fec·tor (ĭ-fĕk′tər) ▸ *n.* A muscle, gland, or organ capable of responding to a stimulus, esp. a nerve impulse.

ef·fec·tu·al (ĭ-fĕk′cho͞o-əl) ▸ *adj.* Producing or sufficient to produce a desired effect; fully adequate. **—ef·fec′tu·al·ly** *adv.*

ef·fec·tu·ate (ĭ-fĕk′cho͞o-āt′) ▸ *v.* **-at·ed, -at·ing.** To bring about; effect. **—ef·fec′tu·a′tion** *n.*

ef·fem·i·nate (ĭ-fĕm′ə-nĭt) ▸ *adj.* Having qualities or characteristics more often associated with women than men. **—ef·fem′i·na·cy** *n.* **—ef·fem′i·nate·ly** *adv.*

ef·fer·ent (ĕf′ər-ənt) ▸ *adj.* **1.** Directed away from a central organ or section. **2.** Carrying impulses from the central nervous system to an effector.

ef·fer·vesce (ĕf′ər-vĕs′) ▸ *v.* **-vesced, -vesc·ing. 1.** To emit small bubbles of gas, as a carbonated liquid. **2.** To show high spirits or excitement. **—ef′fer·ves′cence** *n.* **—ef′fer·ves′cent** *adj.*

ef·fete (ĭ-fēt′) ▸ *adj.* **1.** Depleted of vitality or effectiveness; exhausted. **2.** Marked by self-indulgence or triviality. **—ef·fete′ly** *adv.* **—ef·fete′ness** *n.*

ef·fi·ca·cious (ĕf′ĭ-kā′shəs) ▸ *adj.* Producing a desired effect; effective. **—ef′fi·ca′cious·ly** *adv.* **—ef′fi·ca′cious·ness** *n.* **—ef′fi·ca·cy** (ĕf′ĭ-kə-sē) *n.*

ef·fi·cient (ĭ-fĭsh′ənt) ▸ *adj.* **1.** Acting to produce an effect with a minimum of waste or effort. **2.** Exhibiting a high ratio of output to input. **—ef·fi′cien·cy** *n.* **—ef·fi′cient·ly** *adv.*

ef·fi·gy (ĕf′ə-jē) ▸ *n., pl.* **-gies.** A likeness or image, esp. a crude figure or dummy representing a hated person or group.

ef·flo·resce (ĕf′lə-rĕs′) ▸ *v.* **-resced, -resc·ing.** To blossom; bloom.

ef·flo·res·cence (ĕf′lə-rĕs′əns) ▸ *n.* **1.** *Bot.* A state or time of flowering. **2a.** A gradual process of unfolding or developing. **b.** The highest point; culmination. **—ef′flo·res′cent** *adj.*

ef·flu·ent (ĕf′lo͞o-ənt) ▸ *adj.* Flowing out or forth. ▸ *n.* Something that flows out or forth, esp. outflow from a sewer or a discharge of liquid waste. **—ef′flu·ence** *n.*

ef·flu·vi·um (ĭ-flo͞o′vē-əm) ▸ *n., pl.* **-vi·a** (-vē-ə) or **-vi·ums.** A usu. invisible emanation, often foul or harmful. **—ef·flu′vi·al** *adj.*

ef·fort (ĕf′ərt) ▸ *n.* **1.** The use of physical or mental energy to do something; exertion. **2.** An earnest attempt. **3.** Something done through exertion; achievement. **—ef′fort·less** *adj.*

ef·front·er·y (ĭ-frŭn′tə-rē) ▸ *n., pl.* **-ies.** Brazen boldness; presumptuousness.

THESAURUS

education *n.* **1.** The act, process, or art of imparting knowledge and skill ▸ edification, instruction, pedagogics, pedagogy, schooling, teaching, training, tuition, tutelage, tutoring. **2.** Known facts, ideas, and skills that have been imparted ▸ erudition, instruction, knowledge, learning, scholarship, science. **3.** Training in the proper forms of social and personal conduct ▸ breeding, upbringing. [*Compare* COURTESY, MANNERS.]

educational *adj.* **1.** Of or relating to education ▸ academic, instructional, pedagogic, pedagogical, scholastic, teaching. **2.** Serving to educate or inform ▸ edifying, educative, enlightening, illuminative, informative, instructional, instructive. [*Compare* CULTURAL.]

educative *adj.* *—See* EDUCATIONAL (2).

educator *n.* One who educates ▸ coach, instructor, master, pedagogue, schoolmaster, schoolmistress, schoolteacher, teacher, trainer, tutor. [*Compare* ADVISER.]

educe *v.* *—See* DERIVE (2), EVOKE.

eerie or **eery** *adj.* *—See* WEIRD.

efface *v.* *—See* CANCEL (1).

effacement *n.* *—See* ERASURE.

effect *n.* **1.** Something brought about by a cause ▸ aftermath, consequence, corollary, end product, event, fruit, harvest, issue, outcome, precipitate, ramification, result, resultant, sequel, sequence, sequent, upshot. [*Compare* DERIVATIVE.] **2.** The power or capacity to produce a desired result ▸ effectiveness, effectuality, effectualness, efficaciousness, efficacy, efficiency, influence, potency. [*Compare* ABILITY.] **3.** The condition of being in full force or operation ▸ actualization, being, force, realization. [*Compare* EXERCISE.]

effect *v.* To succeed in doing ▸ accomplish, achieve, bring about, bring off, carry out, carry through, effectuate, execute, put through. *Informal:* swing. [*Compare* ACCOMPLISH, FULFILL, PERFORM, SUCCEED.] *—See also* CAUSE, ENFORCE, PERFORM (1).

effective *adj.* **1.** Producing or able to produce a desired effect ▸ constructive, effectual, efficacious, efficient, instrumental, productive. [*Compare* ABLE, BENEFICIAL.] **2.** In effect ▸ operational, operative. ***Idiom:*** in force (*or* operation). [*Compare* ACTIVE.] *—See also* CONVINCING, FORCEFUL.

effectiveness *n.* *—See* EFFECT (2).

effects *n.* One's portable property ▸ belongings, chattel, goods, lares and penates, movables, personal effects, personal property, possessions, property, things. *Informal:* stuff. [*Compare* HOLDINGS.]

effectual *adj.* *—See* EFFECTIVE (1).

effectuality or **effectualness** *n.* *—See* EFFECT (2).

effectuate *v.* *—See* CAUSE, EFFECT, ENFORCE.

effectuation *n.* *—See* PERFORMANCE.

effeminacy *n.* The quality of being effeminate ▸ effeminateness, effeteness, femininity, unmanliness, womanishness. [*Compare* ANDROGYNY.]

effeminate *adj.* Having qualities traditionally attributed to a woman ▸ epicene, feminine, sissified, sissyish, unmanly, womanish. [*Compare* ANDROGYNOUS.]

effeminateness *n.* *—See* EFFEMINACY.

effervesce *v.* *—See* BOIL, FOAM.

effervescence *n.* *—See* FOAM.

effervescent *adj.* *—See* LIVELY.

effete *adj.* *—See* PALE (2).

effeteness *n.* *—See* EFFEMINACY.

efficacious *adj.* *—See* CONVINCING, EFFECTIVE (1).

efficacy or **efficaciousness** *n.* *—See* EFFECT (2).

efficiency *n.* The quality of being efficient ▸ productiveness, productivity. [*Compare* ABILITY, DILIGENCE.] *—See also* APARTMENT, EFFECT (2).

efficient *adj.* Acting effectively with minimal waste ▸ productive, streamlined, well-oiled. [*Compare* DILIGENT, METHODICAL.] *—See also* EFFECTIVE (1).

effloresce *v.* *—See* BLOOM[1] (1).

efflorescence *n.* *—See* BLOOM[1] (1).

efflux *n.* *—See* FLOW.

effort *n.* The use of energy to do something ▸ endeavor, exertion, pains, strain, striving, struggle, trouble, while. *Informal:* elbow grease. [*Compare* DILIGENCE, LABOR, STRENGTH.] *—See also* ACCOMPLISHMENT, ATTEMPT, TASK (2).

effortful *adj.* Not natural or spontaneous ▸ contrived, forced, labored, strained. [*Compare* AWKWARD, STIFF.] *—See also* DIFFICULT (1).

effortless *adj.* *—See* EASY (1), FLUENT.

effortlessness *n.* *—See* EASE (2).

effrontery *n.* *—See* IMPUDENCE.

ef·ful·gent (ĭ-fo͝ol′jənt, ĭ-fŭl′-) ▸ *adj.* Shining brilliantly; resplendent. **—ef·ful′gence** *n.*

ef·fuse (ĭ-fyo͞os′) ▸ *adj. Bot.* Spreading out loosely. ▸ *v.* (ĭ-fyo͞oz′) **-fused, -fus·ing. 1.** To pour out (a liquid). **2.** To radiate; diffuse.

ef·fu·sion (ĭ-fyo͞o′zhən) ▸ *n.* **1.** Pouring forth; effusing. **2.** An unrestrained outpouring of feeling. **—ef·fu′sive** *adj.* **—ef·fu′sive·ly** *adv.* **—ef·fu′sive·ness** *n.*

eft (ĕft) ▸ *n.* An immature newt.

e.g. ▸ *abbr. Lat.* exempli gratia (for example)

e·gal·i·tar·i·an (ĭ-găl′ĭ-târ′ē-ən-) ▸ *adj.* Affirming political, economic, and social equality for all. **—e·gal′i·tar′i·an** *n.* **—e·gal′i·tar′i·an·ism** *n.*

egg[1] (ĕg) ▸ *n.* **1a.** A female reproductive cell; ovum. **b.** The round or oval reproductive body of various animals, such as birds, reptiles, fishes, and insects, containing the embryo and covered with a shell or membrane. **2.** A hen's egg used as food.

egg[2] (ĕg) ▸ *v.* To encourage or incite to action: *egged them on.*

egg·beat·er (ĕg′bē′tər) ▸ *n.* A kitchen utensil with rotating blades for beating or mixing.

egg·head (ĕg′hĕd′) ▸ *n. Informal* An intellectual; highbrow.

egg·nog (ĕg′nŏg′) ▸ *n.* A drink consisting of milk, sugar, and eggs, often mixed with an alcoholic liquor.

egg·plant (ĕg′plănt′) ▸ *n.* **1.** A plant cultivated for its large, ovoid, purple-skinned fruit. **2.** The fruit of this plant.

egg roll ▸ *n.* A deep-fried cylindrical casing of thin egg dough, filled with minced vegetables and often meat.

egg·shell (ĕg′shĕl′) ▸ *n.* **1.** The thin, brittle, exterior covering of an egg. **2.** A yellowish white. **—egg′shell′** *adj.*

e·gis (ē′jĭs) ▸ *n.* Var. of **aegis.**

eg·lan·tine (ĕg′lən-tīn′, -tēn′) ▸ *n.* See **sweetbrier.**

e·go (ē′gō) ▸ *n., pl.* **e·gos. 1.** The self, esp. as distinct from all others. **2.** In psychoanalysis, the part of the psyche that is conscious, controls thought and behavior, and is most in touch with external reality. **3.** An exaggerated sense of self-importance; conceit.

e·go·cen·tric (ē′gō-sĕn′trĭk) ▸ *adj.* Interested only in one's own needs or affairs; self-centered. **—e′go·cen′tric** *n.* **—e′go·cen·tric′i·ty** (-trĭs′ĭ-tē) *n.* **—e′go·cen′trism** *n.*

e·go·ism (ē′gō-ĭz′əm) ▸ *n.* **1.** The belief that self-interest is the just and proper motive for all human conduct. **2.** Egotism; conceit. **—e′go·ist** *n.* **—e′go·is′tic, e′go·is′ti·cal** *adj.* **—e′go·is′ti·cal·ly** *adv.*

e·go·ma·ni·a (ē′gō-mā′nē-ə, -măn′yə) ▸ *n.* Obsessive preoccupation with the self. **—e′go·ma′ni·ac′** *n.* **—e′·go·ma·ni′a·cal** (-mə-nī′ə-kəl) *adj.* **—e′go·ma·ni′a·cal·ly** *adv.*

e·go·tism (ē′gə-tĭz′əm) ▸ *n.* **1.** The tendency to speak or write of oneself excessively and boastfully. **2.** An inflated sense of one's own importance; conceit. **—e′go·tist** *n.* **—e′go·tis′tic, e′go·tis′ti·cal** *adj.* **—e′go·tis′ti·cal·ly** *adv.*

ego trip ▸ *n. Slang* An act, experience, or course of behavior that gratifies the ego.

e·gre·gious (ĭ-grē′jəs, -jē-əs) ▸ *adj.* Conspicuously bad or offensive. **—e·gre′gious·ly** *adv.* **—e·gre′gious·ness** *n.*

e·gress (ē′grĕs′) ▸ *n.* An act of or opening for going out.

e·gret (ē′grĭt, ĕg′rĭt) ▸ *n.* Any of several usu. white herons having long, showy, drooping plumes.

E·gypt (ē′jĭpt) ▸ A country of NE Africa on the Mediterranean Sea.

E·gyp·tian (ĭ-jĭp′shən) ▸ *n.* **1.** A native or inhabitant of Egypt. **2.** The extinct Afro-Asiatic language of the ancient Egyptians. **—E·gyp′tian** *adj.*

ei·der (ī′dər) ▸ *n.* A large sea duck of northern regions, having soft, commercially valuable down.

ei·der·down also **eider down** (ī′dər-doun′) ▸ *n.* The down of the eider.

eight (āt) ▸ *n.* **1.** The cardinal number equal to 7 + 1. **2.** The 8th in a set or sequence. **—eight** *adj. & pron.*

eight ball ▸ *n. Games* A black pool ball that bears the number 8. ***—idiom:* behind the eight ball** *Slang* In an unfavorable position.

eight·een (ā-tēn′) ▸ *n.* **1.** The cardinal number equal to 17 + 1. **2.** The 18th in a set or sequence. **—eight·een′** *adj. & pron.*

eight·eenth (ā-tēnth′) ▸ *n.* **1.** The ordinal number matching the number 18 in a series. **2.** One of 18 equal parts. **—eight·eenth′** *adv. & adj.*

eighth (ātth, āth) ▸ *n.* **1.** The ordinal number matching the number 8 in a series. **2.** One of eight equal parts. **—eighth** *adv. & adj.*

eight·i·eth (ā′tē-ĭth) ▸ *n.* **1.** The ordinal number matching the number 80 in a series. **2.** One of 80 equal parts. **—eight′i·eth** *adv. & adj.*

eight·y (ā′tē) ▸ *n., pl.* **-ies.** The cardinal number equal to 8 × 10. **—eight′y** *adj. & pron.*

Ein·stein (īn′stīn′), **Albert** (1879–1955) ▸ German-born Amer. theoretical physicist; 1921 Nobel.

ein·stei·ni·um (īn-stī′nē-əm) ▸ *n. Symbol* **Es** A synthetic radioactive element first produced in a thermonuclear explosion. At. no. 99.

Eir·e (âr′ə, ī′rə) ▸ See **Ireland**[2]**.**

Ei·sen·how·er (ī′zən-hou′ər), **Dwight David** (1890–1969) ▸ 34th US President (1953–61).

ei·ther (ē′thər, ī′thər) ▸ *pron.* One or the other of two: *Either wwill be fine.* ▸ *conj.* Used before the first of two or more coordinates or clauses linked by *or*: *Either we go now or we remain here forever.* ▸ *adj.* **1.** Any one of two; one or the other: *Wear either coat.* **2.** One and the other; each: *rings on either hand.* ▸ *adv.* Likewise; also: *If you don't order a dessert, I won't either.*

e·jac·u·late (ĭ-jăk′yə-lāt′) ▸ *v.* **-lat·ed, -lat·ing. 1.** To eject abruptly, esp. to discharge (semen) in orgasm. **2.** To utter suddenly and passionately; exclaim. ▸ *n.* (-lĭt) Semen ejaculated in orgasm. **—e·jac′u·la′tion** *n.* **—e·jac′u·la′tor** *n.* **—e·jac′u·la·to′ry** (-lə-tôr′ē) *adj.*

THESAURUS

effulgence *n.* —*See* BRILLIANCE (1).

effulgent *adj.* —*See* BRIGHT.

effuse *v.* —*See* POUR.

egghead *n.* —*See* MIND (2).

egg on *v.* —*See* PROVOKE.

ego *n.* —*See* EGOTISM, PRIDE.

egocentric *adj.* Holding the philosophical view that the self is the center and norm of existence and experience ▸ egoistic, egoistical, individualistic, solipsistic. —*See also* EGOTISTIC (2).

egocentric *n.* —*See* EGOTIST.

egocentricity or **egocentrism** *n.* —*See* EGOTISM.

egoism *n.* —*See* EGOTISM.

egoist *n.* —*See* EGOTIST.

egoistic or **egoistical** *adj.* Holding the philosophical view that the self is the center and norm of existence and experience ▸ egocentric, individualistic, solipsistic. —*See also* EGOTISTIC (1), EGOTISTIC (2).

egomania *n.* —*See* EGOTISM.

egomaniac *n.* —*See* EGOTIST.

egomaniacal *adj.* —*See* EGOTISTIC (2).

egotism *n.* Exaggerated love for oneself or belief in one's own importance ▸ amour-propre, conceit, ego, egocentricity, egocentrism, egoism, egomania, megalomania, narcissism, pride, self-absorption, self-centeredness, self-importance, self-involvement, selfishness, vainglory, vainness, vanity. *Informal:* big head, bigheadedness, swelled head. *Slang:* ego trip. [*Compare* PRIDE, ARROGANCE, PRETENTIOUSNESS.]

egotist *n.* A conceited, self-centered person ▸ egocentric, egoist, egomaniac, narcissist. [*Compare* BRAGGART.]

egotistic or **egotistical** *adj.* **1.** Thinking too highly of oneself ▸ conceited, egoistic, egoistical, narcissistic, vain, vainglorious. *Informal:* bigheaded, stuck-up, swellheaded. *Idiom:* full of (*or* stuck on) oneself. [*Compare* ARROGANT, BOASTFUL.] **2.** Concerned only with oneself ▸ egocentric, egoistic, egoistical, egomaniacal, self-absorbed, self-centered, self-involved, selfish, self-seeking, self-serving. *Idiom:* wrapped up in oneself.

ego trip *n.* —*See* EGOTISM.

egregious *adj.* Conspicuously bad or offensive ▸ flagrant, glaring, gross, rank. [*Compare* OFFENSIVE, OUTRAGEOUS, SHAMELESS.]

egregiousness *n.* The quality or state of being conspicuously flagrant ▸ flagrancy, glaringness, grossness, rankness. [*Compare* IMPUDENCE, OUTRAGEOUSNESS.]

egress *n.* —*See* DEPARTURE.

eighty-six *v.* —*See* DISCARD.

ejaculate *v.* —*See* EXCLAIM.

ejaculation *n.* —*See* SHOUT.

e·ject (ĭ-jĕkt′) ► *v.* To throw out forcefully; expel. **—e·jec′tion** *n.* **—e·jec′tor** *n.*

ejection seat ► *n.* A seat designed to eject the occupant clear of an aircraft during an in-flight emergency.

eke (ēk) ► *v.* **eked, ek·ing.** To make or supplement with effort: *eked out an income by working two jobs.*

e·lab·o·rate (ĭ-lăb′ər-ĭt) ► *adj.* **1.** Planned or executed with attention to details. **2.** Intricate and rich in detail. ► *v.* (-ə-rāt′) **-rat·ed, -rat·ing. 1.** To work out carefully; develop thoroughly. **2.** To express at greater length or in greater detail. **—e·lab′o·rate·ly** *adv.* **—e·lab′o·rate·ness** *n.* **—e·lab′o·ra′tion** *n.*

é·lan (ā-läɴ′, ā-län′) ► *n.* **1.** Enthusiastic vigor and liveliness. **2.** Distinctive style or flair.

e·land (ē′lənd) ► *n., pl.* **eland** also **e·lands.** Either of two large African antelopes having spirally twisted horns.

el·a·pid (ĕl′ə-pĭd) ► *n.* Any of a family of venomous snakes that includes cobras, mambas, and coral snakes.

e·lapse (ĭ-lăps′) ► *v.* **e·lapsed, e·laps·ing.** To slip by, as time; pass.

e·las·mo·branch (ĭ-lăz′mə-brăngk′) ► *n.* Any of a class of cartilaginous fishes that includes sharks, rays, and skates.

e·las·tic (ĭ-lăs′tĭk) ► *adj.* **1.** Easily resuming original shape after being stretched or expanded; flexible. **2.** Quick to recover, as from disappointment. **3.** Capable of adapting to change or a variety of circumstances. ► *n.* **1.** A flexible, stretchable fabric. **2.** A rubber band. **—e·las′ti·cal·ly** *adv.* **—e·las·tic′i·ty** (ĭ-lă-stĭs′ĭ-tē, ē′lă-) *n.*

e·late (ĭ-lāt′) ► *v.* **e·lat·ed, e·lat·ing.** To make proud or joyful; fill with delight. **—e·la′tion** *n.*

El·ba (ĕl′bə) ► An island of Italy in the Tyrrhenian Sea between Corsica and the mainland.

el·bow (ĕl′bō′) ► *n.* **1a.** The joint or bend of the arm between the forearm and the upper arm. **b.** The bony outer projection of this joint. **2.** Something, esp. a length of pipe, bent like an elbow. ► *v.* **1.** To push or jostle with the elbow. **2.** To make one's way by elbowing.

elbow grease ► *n. Informal* Strenuous effort.

el·bow·room (ĕl′bō-ro͞om′, -ro͝om′) ► *n.* Room to move around or work freely.

El·brus (ĕl-bro͞os′), **Mount** ► A peak, 5,645.6 m (18,510 ft), in the Caucasus Mts. of SW Russia; highest mountain of Europe.

eld·er[1] (ĕl′dər) ► *adj.* **1.** Older. **2.** Superior to another, as in rank. ► *n.* **1.** An older person. **2.** An older, influential member of a family, tribe, or community. **3.** A governing officer of a church.

el·der[2] (ĕl′dər) ► *n.* Any of various shrubs having small white flowers and red or black drupes.

el·der·ber·ry (ĕl′dər-bĕr′ē) ► *n.* **1.** The small edible fruit of an elder. **2.** The elder.

eld·er·ly (ĕl′dər-lē) ► *adj.* **1.** Approaching old age. **2.** Of or characteristic of older persons. ► *n., pl.* **elderly.** *(takes pl. v.)* Older people collectively. Used with *the.*

eld·est (ĕl′dĭst) ► *adj.* Greatest in age or seniority.

El Do·ra·do (ĕl də-rä′dō) ► *n.* A place of fabulous wealth.

e·lect (ĭ-lĕkt′) ► *v.* **1.** To select by vote for an office or for membership. **2.** To pick out; select. ► *adj.* **1.** Chosen deliberately; singled out. **2.** Elected but not yet installed: *the governor-elect.* ► *n.* **1.** One that is chosen or selected. **2.** *(takes pl. v.)* An exclusive group of people. **—e·lec′tion** *n.*

e·lec·tion·eer (ĭ-lĕk′shə-nîr′) ► *v.* To work actively for a candidate or political party.

e·lec·tive (ĭ-lĕk′tĭv) ► *adj.* **1.** Filled or obtained by election. **2.** Having the power to elect. **3.** Optional. ► *n.* An optional academic course or subject.

e·lec·tor (ĭ-lĕk′tər) ► *n.* **1.** A qualified voter. **2.** A member of the Electoral College. **—e·lec′tor·al** *adj.*

Electoral College ► *n.* A body of electors chosen to elect the President and Vice President of the US.

e·lec·tor·ate (ĭ-lĕk′tər-ĭt) ► *n.* A body of qualified voters.

E·lec·tra (ĭ-lĕk′trə) ► *n. Gk. Myth.* Daughter of Agamemnon who with her brother Orestes avenged their father's murder by killing their mother Clytemnestra.

e·lec·tric (ĭ-lĕk′trĭk) ► *adj.* **1.** Of or operated by electricity. **2.** Amplified by an electronic device: *an electric guitar.* **3.** Emotionally exciting; thrilling. **—e·lec′tri·cal·ly** *adv.*

electric chair ► *n.* **1.** A chair used in the electrocution of a prisoner sentenced to death. **2.** The sentence of death by electrocution.

electric eel ► *n.* An eellike freshwater fish of South America that produces a powerful electric discharge.

electric eye ► *n.* See **photoelectric cell.**

e·lec·tri·cian (ĭ-lĕk-trĭsh′ən, ē′lĕk-) ► *n.* One whose occupation is the installation, maintenance, repair, or operation of electric equipment and circuitry.

e·lec·tric·i·ty (ĭ-lĕk-trĭs′ĭ-tē, ē′lĕk-) ► *n.* **1.** The physical phenomena arising from the attraction of particles with opposite charges and the repulsion of particles with the same charge. **2.** Electric current used or regarded as a source of power. **3.** Intense emotional excitement.

e·lec·tri·fy (ĭ-lĕk′trə-fī′) ► *v.* **-fied, -fy·ing. 1.** To produce electric charge on or in. **2.** To wire or equip for the use of electric power. **3.** To thrill, startle greatly, or shock. **—e·lec′tri·fi·ca′tion** *n.*

electro– or **electr–** ► *pref.* **1.** Electric; electricity: *electrochemistry.* **2.** Electron: *electrode.*

THESAURUS

eject *v.* **1.** To put out by force ► bump, cast out, dismiss, evict, expel, oust, throw out. *Informal:* chuck. *Slang:* boot (out), bounce, kick out. *Idioms:* give someone the boot (*or* heave-ho *or* old heave-ho), send packing, show someone the door, throw out on one's ear. [*Compare* DISMISS.] **2.** To catapult oneself from a disabled aircraft ► bail out, jump. *—See also* ERUPT.

ejection *n.* The act of ejecting or the state of being ejected ► dismissal, ejectment, eviction, expulsion, ouster, removal. *Slang:* boot, bounce. [*Compare* DISMISSAL, EXILE.]

elaborate *adj.* Rich in detail ► complicated, detailed, fancy, fussy, intricate, ornate. [*Compare* BUSY, ORNATE.] *—See also* COMPLEX (1), DETAILED.

elaborate *v.* To express at greater length or in greater detail ► amplify (on *or* upon), develop, dilate (on *or* upon), discourse (on *or* upon), enlarge (on *or* upon), expand (on *or* upon), expatiate (on *or* upon), flesh out. *Idioms:* fill in the details, get down to brass tacks, go into detail, go on and on. [*Compare* BELABOR, EXPLAIN.]

élan or **élan vital** *n.* *—See* SPIRIT (1).

elapse *v.* To move past in time ► go by, lapse, pass (away *or* by), slip (away *or* by), tick away.

elastic *adj.* *—See* ADAPTABLE, FLEXIBLE (1), FLEXIBLE (3).

elasticity *n.* The ability to recover quickly from depression or discouragement ► bounce, buoyancy, flexibility, resilience, resiliency. *—See also* FLEXIBILITY (1).

elate *v.* To raise the spirits of ► animate, buoy (up), elevate, exhilarate, flush, inspire, inspirit, lift, uplift. [*Compare* DELIGHT, ENCOURAGE.] *—See also* DELIGHT (1).

elated *adj.* Feeling great delight and joy ► animated, elate, elevated, euphoric, exalted, exhilarated, inspired, overjoyed, uplifted. *Slang:* high, up. *Idioms:* flying (*or* riding) high, on cloud nine, on top of the world. [*Compare* EXULTANT, THRILLED.]

elation *n.* High spirits ► animation, elatedness, euphoria, exaltation, exhilaration, inspiration, lift, uplift. [*Compare* HAPPINESS, HIGH, MERRIMENT.] *—See also* DELIGHT.

elbow *v.* *—See* MUSCLE, PUSH (1).

elbow grease *n.* *—See* EFFORT.

elbowroom *n.* *—See* LICENSE (1).

elder *n.* One who stands above another in rank ► better, senior, superior. *Informal:* higher-up. *—See also* SENIOR (2), CHIEF.

elder *adj.* *—See* OLD (2).

elderliness *n.* *—See* AGE (1).

elderly *adj.* *—See* OLD (2).

elect *v.* To select by vote for an office ► vote (in). *—See also* APPOINT, CHOOSE (1).

elect *adj.* Singled out in preference ► choice, chosen, exclusive, select. [*Compare* EXCELLENT, FAVORITE.]

elect *n.* One that is selected ► choice, chosen, pick, select. [*Compare* BEST.]

election *n.* *—See* APPOINTMENT, CHOICE.

elective *adj.* *—See* OPTIONAL.

elector *n.* One who votes ► balloter, voter. *Idiom:* member of the electorate.

electrify *v.* *—See* ENRAPTURE, STARTLE.

e·lec·tro·car·di·o·gram (ĭ-lĕk′trō-kär′dē-ə-grăm′) ▸ *n.* The curve traced by an electrocardiograph.

e·lec·tro·car·di·o·graph (ĭ-lĕk′trō-kär′dē-ə-grăf′) ▸ *n.* An instrument that measures electrical potentials associated with heart muscle activity. **—e·lec′tro·car′di·o·graph′ic** *adj.* **—e·lec′tro·car′di·og′ra·phy** (-kär′dē-ŏg′rə-fē) *n.*

e·lec·tro·chem·is·try (ĭ-lĕk′trō-kĕm′ĭ-strē) ▸ *n.* The science of the interaction of electric and chemical phenomena. **—e·lec′tro·chem′i·cal·ly** *adv.* **—e·lec′tro·chem′ist** *n.*

e·lec·tro·con·vul·sive therapy (ĭ-lĕk′trō-kən-vŭl′sĭv) ▸ *n.* Administration of electric current to the brain to induce unconsciousness and brief convulsions, used esp. to treat acute depression.

e·lec·tro·cute (ĭ-lĕk′trə-kyo͞ot′) ▸ *v.* **-cut·ed, -cut·ing. 1.** To kill with electricity. **2.** To execute (a prisoner) by electricity. **—e·lec′tro·cu′tion** *n.*

e·lec·trode (ĭ-lĕk′trōd′) ▸ *n.* A solid electric conductor through which an electric current enters or leaves an electrolytic cell or other medium.

e·lec·tro·dy·nam·ics (ĭ-lĕk′trō-dī-năm′ĭks) ▸ *n.* *(takes sing. v.)* The physics of the relationship between electric current and magnetic or mechanical phenomena. **—e·lec′tro·dy·nam′ic** *adj.*

e·lec·tro·en·ceph·a·lo·gram (ĭ-lĕk′trō-ĕn-sĕf′ə-lə-grăm′) ▸ *n.* A graphic record of the electrical activity of the brain as recorded by an electroencephalograph.

e·lec·tro·en·ceph·a·lo·graph (ĭ-lĕk′trō-ĕn-sĕf′ə-lə-grăf′) ▸ *n.* An instrument that measures electrical potentials on the scalp and generates a record of the electrical activity of the brain. **—e·lec′tro·en·ceph′a·lo·graph′ic** *adj.* **—e·lec′tro·en·ceph′a·log′ra·phy** (-lŏg′rə-fē) *n.*

e·lec·trol·o·gist (ĭ-lĕk-trŏl′ə-jĭst, ē′lĕk-) ▸ *n.* One who removes body hair by means of an electric current.

e·lec·trol·y·sis (ĭ-lĕk-trŏl′ĭ-sĭs, ē′lĕk-) ▸ *n.* **1.** Chemical change, esp. decomposition, produced in an electrolyte by an electric current. **2.** Destruction of living tissue, esp. of hair roots, by an electric current.

e·lec·tro·lyte (ĭ-lĕk′trə-līt′) ▸ *n.* **1.** A chemical compound that ionizes when dissolved or molten to produce an electrically conductive medium. **2.** *Physiol.* Any of various ions required by cells to regulate the electric charge and flow of water molecules across the cell membrane.

e·lec·tro·lyt·ic (ĭ-lĕk′trə-lĭt′ĭk) ▸ *adj.* **1.** Of or relating to electrolysis. **2.** Of electrolytes. **—e·lec′tro·lyt′i·cal·ly** *adv.*

e·lec·tro·mag·net (ĭ-lĕk′trō-măg′nĭt) ▸ *n.* A magnet consisting of a coil of insulated wire wrapped around a soft iron core that is magnetized only when current flows through the wire.

electromagnetic spectrum ▸ *n.* The entire range of radiation that includes, in order of decreasing frequency, cosmic-rays, gamma rays, x-rays, ultraviolet radiation, visible light, infrared radiation, microwaves, and radio waves.

e·lec·tro·mag·net·ism (ĭ-lĕk′trō-măg′nĭ-tĭz′əm) ▸ *n.* **1.** Magnetism produced by electric charge in motion. **2.** The physics of electricity and magnetism. **—e·lec′tro·mag·net′ic** *adj.*

e·lec·tro·mo·tive (ĭ-lĕk′trō-mō′tĭv) ▸ *adj.* Of or producing electric current.

electromotive force ▸ *n.* The energy per unit charge that is converted reversibly from chemical, mechanical, or other forms of energy into electrical energy in a battery or dynamo.

e·lec·tron (ĭ-lĕk′trŏn′) ▸ *n.* A stable elementary particle having a unit negative electric charge and a rest mass of approx. 9.1×10^{-28} gram.

e·lec·tron·ic (ĭ-lĕk-trŏn′ĭk, ē′lĕk-) ▸ *adj.* **1.** Of or involving electrons or electronics. **2.** Implemented on or controlled by a computer. **—e·lec′tron′i·cal·ly** *adv.*

e·lec·tron·ics (ĭ-lĕk′trŏn′ĭks, ē′lĕk-) ▸ *n.* **1.** *(takes sing. v.)* The science dealing with the controlled conduction of electrons, esp. in a vacuum, gas, or semiconductor. **2.** *(takes pl. v.)* Electronic devices and systems.

electron microscope ▸ *n.* A microscope that uses electrons rather than visible light to produce images that are magnified.

electron tube ▸ *n.* A sealed enclosure, either highly evacuated or containing a controlled quantity of gas, in which electrons can be made sufficiently mobile to act as the principal carriers of current between at least one pair of electrodes.

electron volt ▸ *n.* A unit of energy equal to the energy acquired by an electron falling through a potential difference of one volt.

e·lec·tro·pho·re·sis (ĭ-lĕk′trō-fə-rē′sĭs) ▸ *n.* The migration of charged colloidal particles or molecules through a solution under the influence of an applied electric field.

e·lec·tro·plate (ĭ-lĕk′trə-plāt′) ▸ *v.* **-plat·ed, -plat·ing.** To coat or cover electrolytically with a thin layer of metal.

e·lec·tro·shock (ĭ-lĕk′trō-shŏk′) ▸ *n.* See **electroconvulsive therapy.** ▸ *v.* To administer electroconvulsive therapy to.

e·lec·tro·stat·ic (ĭ-lĕk′trō-stăt′ĭk) ▸ *adj.* **1.** Of or relating to electric charges at rest. **2.** Of electrostatics. **—e·lec′tro·stat′i·cal·ly** *adv.*

e·lec·tro·stat·ics (ĭ-lĕk′trō-stăt′ĭks) ▸ *n.* *(takes sing. v.)* The physics of electrostatic phenomena.

e·lec·tro·type (ĭ-lĕk′trə-tīp′) ▸ *n.* A metal plate used in letterpress, made by electroplating a mold of the page to be printed. **—e·lec′tro·type′** *v.* **—e·lec′tro·typ′er** *n.* **—e·lec′tro·typ′ic** (-trō-tĭp′ĭk) *adj.*

el·ee·mos·y·nar·y (ĕl′ə-mŏs′ə-nĕr′ē, ĕl′ē-ə-) ▸ *adj.* Of or dependent on charity.

el·e·gance (ĕl′ĭ-gəns) ▸ *n.* **1.** Refinement and grace in movement, appearance, or manners. **2.** Tasteful opulence in form, decoration, or presentation. **3.** Scientific exactness and precision.

el·e·gant (ĕl′ĭ-gənt) ▸ *adj.* Marked by refined, tasteful beauty of manner, form, or style. **—el′e·gant·ly** *adv.*

el·e·gi·ac (ĕl′ə-jī′ək, ĭ-lē′jē-ăk′) ▸ *adj.* **1.** Of or relating to an elegy. **2.** Expressing sorrow; mournful. **—el′·e·gi′ac** *n.* **—el′e·gi′a·cal** *adj.* **—el′e·gi′a·cal·ly** *adv.*

el·e·gy (ĕl′ə-jē) ▸ *n., pl.* **-gies.** A mournful poem or song, esp. one lamenting a dead person. **—el′e·gist** *n.* **—el′e·gize′** *v.*

el·e·ment (ĕl′ə-mənt) ▸ *n.* **1.** A substance composed of atoms having an identical number of protons in each nucleus and not reducible to a simpler substance. **2.** A fundamental or essential part of a whole. **3.** *Math.* **a.** A member of a set. **b.** A point, line, or plane. **c.** A part of a geometric configuration, as an angle in a triangle. **4. elements** The forces that constitute the weather, esp. inclement weather. **5.** An environment naturally suited to or associated with an individual.

el·e·men·tal (ĕl′ə-mĕn′tl) ▸ *adj.* **1.** Of, relating to, or being an element. **2.** Fundamental or essential. **3.** Of or resembling a force of nature in power or effect. **—el′e·men′tal** *n.* **—el′e·men′tal·ly** *adv.*

el·e·men·ta·ry (ĕl′ə-mĕn′tə-rē, -trē) ▸ *adj.* **1.** Of or constituting the essential or fundamental part. **2.** Of or involving the fundamental or simplest aspects of a subject. **3.** Of or relating to an elementary school. **4.** Of, relating to, or being an elementary particle. **—el′e·men·ta′ri·ly** (-tĕr′ə-lē) *adv.* **—el′e·men′ta·ri·ness** *n.*

elementary particle ▸ *n.* A subatomic particle, esp. one regarded as irreducible.

THESAURUS

eleemosynary *adj.* Of or concerned with charity ▸ altruistic, benevolent, charitable, philanthropic.

elegance or **elegancy** *n.* Refinement of manner, form, and style ▸ chic, courtliness, dignity, elegancy, grace, polish, quality, sophistication, style, taste, tastefulness, urbanity. *Informal:* class. [*Compare* ATTRACTION, CULTURE, PROPORTION.]

elegant *adj.* Exhibiting refined, tasteful beauty of manner, form, or style ▸ chic, courtly, exquisite, graceful, refined, tasteful. *Informal:* classy. [*Compare* CULTURED.] *—See also* DELICATE (1), GRACIOUS (2), GRAND.

element *n.* **1.** An irreducible constituent of a whole ▸ basic, essential, fundamental, rudiment. *Idiom:* part and parcel. [*Compare* NITTY-GRITTY.] **2.** An individually considered portion of a whole ▸ article, detail, item, particular, point. *—See also* PART (1).

elemental *adj.* Of or being an irreducible element ▸ basic, elementary, essential, fundamental, primal, primitive, ultimate, underlying. *—See also* CONSTITUTIONAL.

elementary *adj.* **2.** Of or treating the most basic aspects ▸ basal, basic, beginning, rudimental, rudimentary. [*Compare* CONSTITUTIONAL.] *—See also* ELEMENTAL.

elementary school ▸ *n.* A school attended for the first six to eight years of a child's formal education.

el·e·phant (ĕl′ə-fənt) ▸ *n.* A very large herbivorous mammal of Africa and Asia with a long flexible trunk and long tusks.

el·e·phan·ti·a·sis (ĕl′ə-fən-tī′ə-sĭs) ▸ *n.* Enlargement and hardening of tissues, esp. of the lower body, resulting from lymphatic obstruction and usually caused by parasitic worms.

el·e·phan·tine (ĕl′ə-făn′tēn′, -tīn′, ĕl′ə-fən-) ▸ *adj.* **1.** Of or relating to an elephant. **2a.** Enormous in size or strength. **b.** Ponderously clumsy.

el·e·vate (ĕl′ə-vāt′) ▸ *v.* **-vat·ed, -vat·ing. 1.** To raise to a higher position; lift. **2.** To promote to a higher rank. **3.** To raise to a higher moral, cultural, or intellectual level. **4.** To lift the spirits of; elate.

el·e·va·tion (ĕl′ə-vā′shən) ▸ *n.* **1.** The act of elevating or condition of being elevated. **2.** An elevated place or position. **3.** The height to which something is elevated above a point of reference such as the ground.

el·e·va·tor (ĕl′ə-vā′tər) ▸ *n.* **1.** A platform or enclosure raised and lowered in a vertical shaft to transport people or freight. **2.** A movable control surface on an aircraft, used to move the aircraft up or down. **3.** A granary with devices for hoisting and discharging grain.

e·lev·en (ĭ-lĕv′ən) ▸ *n.* **1.** The cardinal number equal to 10 + 1. **2.** The 11th in a set or sequence. **—e·lev′en** *adj. & pron.*

e·lev·enth (ĭ-lĕv′ənth) ▸ *n.* **1.** The ordinal number matching the number 11 in a series. **2.** One of 11 equal parts. **—e·lev′enth** *adv. & adj.*

elf (ĕlf) ▸ *n., pl.* **elves** (ĕlvz). A small, often mischievous fairy. **—elf′in** *adj.* **—elf′ish** *adj.*

El Grec·o (grĕk′ō) ▸ See El **Greco.**

e·lic·it (ĭ-lĭs′ĭt) ▸ *v.* **1.** To bring or draw out. **2.** To call forth; evoke. **—e·lic′i·ta′tion** *n.*

e·lide (ĭ-līd′) ▸ *v.* **e·lid·ed, e·lid·ing. 1.** To omit or slur over (a syllable or word) in pronunciation. **2.** To eliminate or leave out of consideration.

el·i·gi·ble (ĕl′ĭ-jə-bəl) ▸ *adj.* **1.** Qualified to be chosen. **2.** Worthy of choice, esp. for marriage. **—el′i·gi·bil′i·ty** *n.* **—el′i·gi·bly** *adv.*

e·lim·i·nate (ĭ-lĭm′ə-nāt′) ▸ *v.* **-nat·ed, -nat·ing. 1.** To get rid of; remove. **2.** To leave out or omit; reject. **3.** *Physiol.* To excrete (bodily wastes). **—e·lim′i·na′tion** *n.* **—e·lim′i·na′tive, e·lim′i·na·to′ry** (-nə-tôr′ē) *adj.* **—e·lim′i·na′tor** *n.*

El·i·ot (ĕl′ē-ət), **George** Pen name of Mary Ann Evans. (1819–80) ▸ British writer.

Eliot, T(homas) S(tearns) (1888–1965) ▸ Amer.-born British writer; 1948 Nobel.

e·lite or **é·lite** (ĭ-lēt′, ā-lēt′) ▸ *n., pl.* **elite** or **e·lites. 1.** A group or class enjoying superior intellectual, social, or economic status. **2.** A size of type on a typewriter, equal to 12 characters per linear inch. **—e·lite′** *adj.*

e·lit·ism or **é·lit·ism** (ĭ-lē′tĭz′əm, ā-lē′-) ▸ *n.* **1.** The belief that certain persons or members of certain classes or groups deserve favored treatment. **2a.** The sense of entitlement enjoyed by such a group or class. **b.** Control, rule, or domination by such a group or class. **—e·lit′ist** *adj. & n.*

e·lix·ir (ĭ-lĭk′sər) ▸ *n.* **1.** A sweetened aromatic solution of alcohol and water containing medicine. **2.** A substance believed to cure all ills.

E·liz·a·beth II, (ĭ-lĭz′ə-bəth) (b. 1926) ▸ Queen of Great Britain and Northern Ireland (since 1952).

E·liz·a·be·than (ĭ-lĭz′ə-bē′thən, -bĕth′ən) ▸ *adj.* Of or characteristic of Elizabeth I of England or her reign. **—E·liz′a·be′than** *n.*

elk (ĕlk) ▸ *n., pl.* **elk** or **elks. 1.** See **wapiti. 2.** The moose.

ell[1] (ĕl) ▸ *n.* A wing of a building at right angles to the main structure.

ell[2] (ĕl) ▸ *n.* An English linear measure equal to 45 in. (114 cm).

El·ling·ton (ĕl′ĭng-tən), **Edward Kennedy.** "Duke" (1899–1974) ▸ Amer. jazz composer and musician.

el·lipse (ĭ-lĭps′) ▸ *n.* A plane curve that is the locus of points for which the sum of the distances from each point to two fixed points is equal.

el·lip·sis (ĭ-lĭp′sĭs) ▸ *n., pl.* **-ses** (-sēz). **1.** The omission of a word or phrase that is not necessary for understanding. **2.** A mark or series of marks, often three periods (. . .), used to indicate an omission.

el·lip·soid (ĭ-lĭp′soid′) ▸ *n.* A geometric surface whose plane sections are ellipses or circles. **—el·lip′soid′, el′lip·soi′dal** (-soid′l) *adj.*

el·lip·tic (ĭ-lĭp′tĭk) or **el·lip·ti·cal** (-tĭ-kəl) ▸ *adj.* **1.** Of or shaped like an ellipse. **2.** Containing an ellipsis. **3.** Obscure or incomplete. **—el·lip′ti·cal·ly** *adv.*

El·lis Island (ĕl′ĭs) ▸ An island of Upper New York Bay SW of Manhattan; chief immigration station of the US (1892–1943).

elm (ĕlm) ▸ *n.* **1.** Any of various deciduous trees having arching or curving branches and serrate leaves. **2.** The wood of an elm.

El Ni·ño (nēn′yō) ▸ *n.* A periodic warming of the ocean surface off the W coast of South America that affects Pacific and other weather patterns.

el·o·cu·tion (ĕl′ə-kyo͞o′shən) ▸ *n.* The art of public speaking, emphasizing gesture and vocal delivery. **—el′o·cu′tion·ar′y** *adj.* **—el′o·cu′tion·ist** *n.*

e·lon·gate (ĭ-lông′gāt′, ĭ-lŏng′-) ▸ *v.* **-gat·ed, -gat·ing.** To make or grow longer. **—e·lon′ga′tion** *n.*

THESAURUS

elephantine *adj.* —*See* ENORMOUS, PONDEROUS.

elevate *v.* **1.** To move something to a higher position ▸ boost, heave, hike (up), hitch up, hoist, jack (up), lift, pick up, raise, rear, take up, uphold, uplift, upraise, uprear. **2.** To increase markedly in level or intensity, especially of sound ▸ amplify, heighten, raise. *Slang:* crank up, pump up. [*Compare* INCREASE.] —*See also* DISTINGUISH (3), ELATE, EXALT, PROMOTE (1).

elevated *adj.* **1.** Being positioned above a given level ▸ boosted, raised, uplifted, upraised. *Idiom:* on high. [*Compare* HIGHER.] **2.** Abnormally increased, especially in intensity ▸ heightened, high, raised, supernormal. *Idioms:* off the charts, on the high end, over the top. [*Compare* EXCESSIVE.] **3.** Being on a high intellectual or moral level ▸ high-minded, moral, noble, sublime. **4.** Exceedingly dignified in form, tone, or style ▸ eloquent, exalted, grand, high, high-flown, lofty, soaring, vaulting. [*Compare* GRANDIOSE.] **5.** At the upper end of a degree of measure ▸ great, high, large. [*Compare* EXALTED, EXTREME.] —*See also* ELATED, EXALTED, HIGH (1).

elevation *n.* The distance of something from a given level ▸ altitude, height, loftiness, tallness. [*Compare* ASCENT.] —*See also* ADVANCEMENT, EXALTATION.

elf *n.* —*See* FAIRY, URCHIN.

elfish *adj.* —*See* MISCHIEVOUS.

elicit *v.* —*See* EVOKE.

eligibility *n.* —*See* QUALIFICATION.

eligible *adj.* Satisfying certain requirements, as for selection ▸ equal, fit, fitted, qualified, suitable, suited, up to, worthy. [*Compare* APPROPRIATE.] —*See also* SINGLE.

eliminate *n.* To get rid of, especially by banishment or execution ▸ eradicate, liquidate, purge, remove, wipe out. *Idioms:* do away with, put an end to. [*Compare* ANNIHILATE, BANISH, KILL, RID.] —*See also* DROP (5), EXCLUDE.

elimination *n.* The act or process of eliminating ▸ clearance, eradication, exclusion, liquidation, purge, removal, riddance. [*Compare* ABOLITION, EJECTION.] —*See also* DISPOSAL.

eliminative or **eliminatory** *adj.* Of, relating to, or tending to eliminate ▸ cathartic, emetic, evacuant, evacuative, excretory, purgative, urinary.

elite or **élite** *n.* —*See* BEST (1), SOCIETY (1).

elite or **élite** *adj.* —*See* EXCLUSIVE (3), NOBLE.

elitist or **élitist** *n.* One who despises people or things regarded as inferior, especially because of social or intellectual pretension ▸ prig, snob. *Informal:* snoot.

elitist or **élitist** *adj.* —*See* SNOBBISH.

elixir *n.* Something believed to cure all human disorders ▸ catholicon, cure-all, panacea. [*Compare* CURE.] —*See also* CURE.

ellipse *n.* —*See* OVAL.

ellipsoid *n.* —*See* OVAL.

ellipsoid or **ellipsoidal** *adj.* —*See* OVAL.

elliptical *adj.* —*See* OVAL.

elocution *n.* —*See* ORATORY.

elocutionary *adj.* —*See* ORATORICAL.

elongate *v.* —*See* LENGTHEN.

elongated or **elongate** *adj.* —*See* LONG[1] (1).

elongation *n.* —*See* EXTENSION (1).

e·lope (ĭ-lōp′) ▸ *v.* **e·loped, e·lop·ing.** To run away with a lover, esp. to get married. **—e·lope′ment** *n.*
el·o·quent (ĕl′ə-kwənt) ▸ *adj.* **1.** Marked by fluent, persuasive discourse. **2.** Vividly or movingly expressive. **—el′o·quence** *n.* **—el′o·quent·ly** *adv.*
El Sal·va·dor (săl′və-dôr′) ▸ A country of Central America bordering on the Pacific Ocean. **—El Sal′va·dor′i·an** *adj. & n.*
else (ĕls) ▸ *adj.* **1.** Other; different: *Ask somebody else.* **2.** Additional; more: *Would you like anything else?* ▸ *adv.* **1.** In a different time, place, or manner: *Where else would you like to go?* **2.** If not; otherwise: *Be careful, or else you may err.*
else·where (ĕls′hwâr′, -wâr′) ▸ *adv.* In or to another place.
e·lu·ci·date (ĭ-lo͞o′sĭ-dāt′) ▸ *v.* **-dat·ed, -dat·ing.** To make clear or plain; clarify. **—e·lu′ci·da′tion** *n.*
e·lude (ĭ-lo͞od′) ▸ *v.* **e·lud·ed, e·lud·ing.** **1.** To evade or escape from, as by daring or skill. **2.** To escape the understanding or grasp of.
E·lul (ĕl′o͝ol, ĕ-lo͞ol′) ▸ *n.* A month of the Jewish calendar.
e·lu·sive (ĭ-lo͞o′sĭv, -zĭv) ▸ *adj.* **1.** Tending to elude. **2.** Evasive; slippery. **—e·lu′sive·ly** *adv.* **—e·lu′sive·ness** *n.*
e·lute (ĭ-lo͞ot′) ▸ *v.* **e·lut·ed, e·lut·ing.** To extract (one material) from another. **—e·lu′tion** *n.*
el·ver (ĕl′vər) ▸ *n.* A young or immature eel.
elves (ĕlvz) ▸ *n.* Pl. of **elf.**
E·ly·si·um (ĭ-lĭz′ē-əm, ĭ-lĭzh′-) ▸ *n.* A place or condition of ideal happiness. **—E·ly′sian** (-lĭzh′ən) *adj.*
em (ĕm) ▸ *n. Print.* **1.** The width of a square piece of type, used as a unit of measure for matter set in that size of type. **2.** A pica.
em–[1] ▸ *pref.* Var. of **en–**[1].
em–[2] ▸ *pref.* Var. of **en–**[2].
'em (əm) ▸ *pron. Informal* Them.
e·ma·ci·ate (ĭ-mā′shē-āt′) ▸ *v.* **-at·ed, -at·ing.** To make or become extremely thin, esp. from starvation. **—e·ma′ci·a′tion** *n.*
e-mail or **e·mail** (ē′māl′) ▸ *n.* A message or messages sent and received electronically over a computer network. **—e′-mail′** *v.*
em·a·lan·ge·ni (ĕm′ə-läng-gĕn′ē) ▸ *n.* Pl. of **lilangeni.**
em·a·nate (ĕm′ə-nāt′) ▸ *v.* **-nat·ed, -nat·ing.** To come or send forth from a source; issue; stem. **—em′a·na′tion** *n.*
e·man·ci·pate (ĭ-măn′sə-pāt′) ▸ *v.* **-pat·ed, -pat·ing.** To free from bondage, oppression, or restraint; liberate. **—e·man′ci·pa′tion** *n.* **—e·man′ci·pa′tor** *n.*
e·mas·cu·late (ĭ-măs′kyə-lāt′) ▸ *v.* **-lat·ed, -lat·ing.** **1.** To castrate. **2.** To make weak. **—e·mas′cu·la′tion** *n.* **—e·mas′cu·la′tive, e·mas′cu·la·to′ry** (-lə-tôr′ē) *adj.* **—e·mas′cu·la′tor** *n.*
em·balm (ĕm-bäm′) ▸ *v.* To treat (a corpse) with preservatives in order to prevent decay. **—em·balm′er** *n.* **—em·balm′ment** *n.*
em·bank (ĕm-băngk′) ▸ *v.* To confine, support, or protect with a bank, as of earth or stone. **—em·bank′ment** *n.*
em·bar·ca·de·ro (ĕm-bär′kə-dâr′ō) ▸ *n., pl.* **-ros.** *Regional* A pier or wharf, esp. on a river.
em·bar·go (ĕm-bär′gō) ▸ *n., pl.* **-goes.** **1.** A government order prohibiting the movement of merchant ships into or out of its ports. **2.** A prohibition by a government on certain or all trade with a foreign nation. ▸ *v.* To impose an embargo on.
em·bark (ĕm-bärk′) ▸ *v.* **1.** To board or cause to board a vessel or aircraft, esp. at the start of a journey. **2.** To set out; commence. **—em′bar·ka′tion** *n.*
em·bar·rass (ĕm-băr′əs) ▸ *v.* **1.** To cause to feel self-conscious or ill at ease; disconcert. **2.** To hamper with financial difficulties. **—em·bar′rass·ing·ly** *adv.* **—em·bar′rass·ment** *n.*
em·bas·sy (ĕm′bə-sē) ▸ *n., pl.* **-sies.** **1.** A building containing the offices of an ambassador and staff. **2.** The position or function of an ambassador. **3.** A mission headed by an ambassador.
em·bat·tled (ĕm-băt′ld) ▸ *adj.* Beset with attackers, criticism, or controversy.
em·bed (ĕm-bĕd′) also **im·bed** (ĭm-) ▸ *v.* **-bed·ded, -bed·ding.** To fix or become fixed firmly in a surrounding mass.
em·bel·lish (ĕm-bĕl′ĭsh) ▸ *v.* **1.** To make beautiful, as by ornamentation; decorate. **2.** To add fictitious details to. **—em·bel′lish·ment** *n.*
em·ber (ĕm′bər) ▸ *n.* **1.** A piece of live coal or wood from a fire. **2. embers** The smoldering remains of a fire.
em·bez·zle (ĕm-bĕz′əl) ▸ *v.* **-zled, -zling.** To take (e.g., money) for one's own use in violation of a trust. **—em·bez′zle·ment** *n.* **—em·bez′zler** *n.*
em·bit·ter (ĕm-bĭt′ər) ▸ *v.* **1.** To make bitter. **2.** To arouse bitter feelings in. **—em·bit′ter·ment** *n.*
em·bla·zon (ĕm-blā′zən) ▸ *v.* **1.** To ornament richly, esp. with heraldic devices. **2.** To make resplendent with brilliant colors. **3.** To mark or inscribe boldly. **—em·bla′zon·er** *n.* **—em·bla′zon·ment** *n.*
em·blem (ĕm′bləm) ▸ *n.* **1.** An object or representation that functions as a symbol. **2.** A distinctive badge, design, or device. **—em′blem·at′ic** *adj.* **—em′blem·at′i·cal·ly** *adv.*
em·bod·y (ĕm-bŏd′ē) ▸ *v.* **-bod·ied, -bod·y·ing.** **1.** To give a bodily form to. **2.** To personify. **3.** To make part of a system or whole; incorporate. **—em·bod′i·ment** *n.*

THESAURUS

eloquence *n.* Smooth or effective skill in communicating ▸ articulacy, articulateness, eloquentness, expression, expressiveness, expressivity, facility, fluency, fluidity, glibness, rhetoric, silver tongue, volubility. ***Idiom:*** gift of gab.
eloquent *adj.* Fluently persuasive and forceful ▸ articulate, silver-tongued, smooth-spoken, voluble, well-spoken. [*Compare* CONVINCING, FLUENT, GLIB.] *—See also* ELEVATED (4), EXPRESSIVE, ORATORICAL.
eloquentness *n.* *—See* ELOQUENCE.
elsewhere *adj.* *—See* ABSENT.
elucidate *v.* *—See* CLARIFY (1), EXPLAIN (1).
elucidation *n.* *—See* EXPLANATION.
elucidative *adj.* *—See* EXPLANATORY.
elude *v.* To fail to be fixed by the mind, memory, or senses of ▸ escape, evade. ***Idiom:*** slip away from. [*Compare* FORGET.] *—See also* AVOID, LOSE (3).
elusive *adj.* **1.** Inclined or intended to evade ▸ evasive, fugitive, slippery. [*Compare* SLICK, UNDERHAND.] **2.** Deliberately ambiguous or vague ▸ evasive, equivocal, indirect, misleading. [*Compare* AMBIGUOUS.]
emaciated *adj.* *—See* HAGGARD.
emanate *v.* *—See* STEM.
emancipate *v.* *—See* FREE (1).
emancipated *adj.* *—See* FREE (1), LOOSE (2).
emancipation *n.* *—See* LIBERTY, RESCUE.
embark *v.* *—See* START (1).
embarkation *n.* *—See* BIRTH (2), DEPARTURE.
embarkment *n.* *—See* DEPARTURE.
embarrass *v.* To cause a person to be self-consciously distressed ▸ abash, chagrin, confound, confuse, discomfit, discomfort, disconcert, discountenance, faze, mortify. ***Idiom:*** put on the spot. [*Compare* BAFFLE, SHAME.] *—See also* COMPLICATE.
embarrassing *adj.* *—See* AWKWARD (3).
embarrassment *n.* Self-conscious distress ▸ abashment, chagrin, confusion, discomfiture, discomfort, discomposure, mortification. [*Compare* DISGRACE.] *—See also* EXCESS (1).
embassy *n.* A diplomatic office or headquarters in a foreign country ▸ deputation, legation, mission.
embed or **imbed** *v.* *—See* FIX (2).
embellish *v.* To endow with beauty and elegance ▸ beautify, enhance, grace, set off. *—See also* ADORN (1).
embellishment *n.* *—See* ADORNMENT.
embezzle *v.* *—See* STEAL.
embitter *v.* *—See* DISAPPOINT.
embittered *adj.* *—See* RESENTFUL.
embitterment *n.* *—See* RESENTMENT.
emblazon *v.* *—See* ADORN (1), COLOR (1).
emblem *n.* An object or expression associated with and serving to identify something else ▸ attribute, metaphor, signifier, symbol, token. [*Compare* EXPRESSION, SIGN, TERM.] *—See also* SIGN (1).
emblematic or **emblematical** *adj.* *—See* SYMBOLIC.
embodiment *n.* A concrete entity typifying an abstraction ▸ allegory, exemplification, exteriorization, externalization, hypostasis, illustration, image, incarnation, incorporation, instantiation, manifestation, materialization, objectification, personalization, personification, prosopopeia, reification, substantiation, type, typification. [*Compare* REPRESENTATION, SYMBOL.] *—See also* EXAMPLE (1).
embody *v.* **1.** To represent (an abstrac-

em·bold·en (ĕm-bōl′dən) ▸ *v.* To foster boldness or courage in.
em·bo·lism (ĕm′bə-lĭz′əm) ▸ *n.* **1.** Obstruction or occlusion of a blood vessel by an embolus. **2.** An embolus.
em·bo·lus (ĕm′bə-ləs) ▸ *n., pl.* **-li** (-lī′). A mass in the bloodstream that lodges so as to block a blood vessel.
em·boss (ĕm-bôs′, -bŏs′) ▸ *v.* **1.** To mold or carve in relief. **2.** To decorate with a raised design.
em·bou·chure (äm′bo͞o-sho͝or′) ▸ *n.* **1.** The mouthpiece of a wind instrument. **2.** The manner in which the lips and tongue are applied to such a mouthpiece.
em·bow·er (ĕm-bou′ər) ▸ *v.* To enclose in or as if in a bower.
em·brace (ĕm-brās′) ▸ *v.* **-braced, -brac·ing. 1.** To clasp or hold close with the arms. **2.** To surround; enclose: *The warm water embraced us.* **3.** To include as part of something broader. **4.** To take up willingly or eagerly: *embrace a cause.* ▸ *n.* An act of embracing. **—em·brace′a·ble** *adj.* **—em·brace′ment** *n.*
em·bra·sure (ĕm-brā′zhər) ▸ *n.* **1.** An opening in a thick wall for a door or window. **2.** A flared opening for a gun in a wall or parapet.
em·bro·cate (ĕm′brə-kāt′) ▸ *v.* **-cat·ed, -cat·ing.** To moisten and rub (a part of the body) with a liniment or lotion. **—em′bro·ca′tion** *n.*
em·broi·der (ĕm-broi′dər) ▸ *v.* **1.** To ornament with needlework. **2.** To add embellishments or fanciful details to. **—em·broi′der·er** *n.*
em·broi·der·y (ĕm-broi′də-rē) ▸ *n., pl.* **-ies. 1.** The act or art of embroidering. **2.** Something that has been embroidered.
em·broil (ĕm-broil′) ▸ *v.* **1.** To involve in argument, contention, or hostile actions. **2.** To throw into confusion or disorder; entangle. **—em·broil′ment** *n.*
em·bry·o (ĕm′brē-ō′) ▸ *n., pl.* **-os. 1.** An organism in its early stages of development, esp. before it has reached a distinctively recognizable form. **2.** A rudimentary or beginning stage. **—em′bry·on′ic** (-ŏn′ĭk) *adj.* **—em′bry·on′i·cal·ly** *adv.*
em·bry·ol·o·gy (ĕm′brē-ŏl′ə-jē) ▸ *n.* The branch of biology that deals with the formation, early growth, and development of living organisms. **—em′bry·o·log′ic** (-ə-lŏj′ĭk), **em′bry·o·log′i·cal** *adj.* **—em′bry·ol′o·gist** *n.*
em·cee (ĕm′sē′) ▸ *n.* A master of ceremonies. ▸ *v.* **-ceed, -cee·ing.** To act as master of ceremonies (of).
e·mend (ĭ-mĕnd′) ▸ *v.* To improve (a text) by critical editing. **—e·men′da′tion** *n.* **—e·mend′er** *n.*
em·er·ald (ĕm′ər-əld, ĕm′rəld) ▸ *n.* **1.** A brilliant transparent green beryl, used as a gemstone. **2.** A strong yellowish green. **—em′er·ald** *adj.*
e·merge (ĭ-mûrj′) ▸ *v.* **e·merged, e·merg·ing. 1.** To rise up or come forth; issue. **2.** To become evident. **3.** To come into existence. **—e·mer′gence** *n.* **—e·mer′gent** *adj.* **—e·mer′gent·ly** *adv.*
e·mer·gen·cy (ĭ-mûr′jən-sē) ▸ *n., pl.* **-cies.** A serious, unexpected situation or occurrence that demands immediate action.
e·mer·i·tus (ĭ-mĕr′ĭ-təs) ▸ *adj.* Retired but retaining an honorary title: *a professor emeritus.*
Em·er·son (ĕm′ər-sən), **Ralph Waldo** (1803–82) ▸ Amer. writer and philosopher.
em·er·y (ĕm′ə-rē, ĕm′rē) ▸ *n.* A fine-grained impure corundum used for grinding and polishing.
e·met·ic (ĭ-mĕt′ĭk) ▸ *adj.* Causing vomiting. **—e·met′ic** *n.*
–emia or **–hemia** also **–aemia** or **–haemia** ▸ *suff.* Blood: *leukemia.*
em·i·grate (ĕm′ĭ-grāt′) ▸ *v.* **-grat·ed, -grat·ing.** To leave one country or region to settle in another. **—em′i·grant** (-grənt) *n.* **—em′i·gra′tion** *n.*
é·mi·gré (ĕm′ĭ-grā′) ▸ *n.* One who has left a native country, esp. for political reasons.
em·i·nence (ĕm′ə-nəns) ▸ *n.* **1.** A position of great distinction or superiority. **2.** A rise of ground; hill. **3.** A person of high station or great achievements.
em·i·nent (ĕm′ə-nənt) ▸ *adj.* **1.** Rising above others; prominent. **2.** Of high rank or station. **3.** Outstanding; distinguished. **—em′i·nent·ly** *adv.*
eminent domain ▸ *n.* The right of a government to appropriate private property for public use.
e·mir (ĭ-mîr′, ā-mîr′) ▸ *n.* A prince, chieftain, or governor, esp. in the Middle East.
e·mir·ate (ĕm′ə-rĭt, -rāt′) ▸ *n.* **1.** The office of an emir. **2.** The nation or territory ruled by an emir.
em·is·sar·y (ĕm′ĭ-sĕr′ē) ▸ *n., pl.* **-ies.** An agent sent on a mission to represent another.
e·mit (ĭ-mĭt′) ▸ *v.* **e·mit·ted, e·mit·ting. 1.** To release or send out matter or energy. **2.** To utter; express. **3.** To put (currency) into circulation. **—e·mis′sion** (ĭ-mĭsh′ən) *n.* **—e·mit′ter** *n.*
e·mol·lient (ĭ-mŏl′yənt) ▸ *adj.* Softening and soothing, esp. to the skin. **—e·mol′lient** *n.*
e·mol·u·ment (ĭ-mŏl′yə-mənt) ▸ *n.* Payment for an office or employment; compensation.
e·mote (ĭ-mōt′) ▸ *v.* **e·mot·ed, e·mot·ing.** To express emotion, esp. in an excessive or theatrical manner.
e·mo·ti·con (ĭ-mō′tĭ-kŏn′) ▸ *n.* A series of keyed characters used, as in e-mail, to indicate an emotion or attitude, as :-) to indicate intended humor.

THESAURUS

tion, for example) in or as if in bodily form ▸ allegorize, body forth, concretize, exteriorize, externalize, hypostatize, incarnate, instantiate, manifest, materialize, objectify, personalize, personify, reify, substantiate. [*Compare* REALIZE.] 2. To make a part of a united whole ▸ combine, incorporate, integrate. [*Compare* ASSEMBLE, COMBINE.] —*See also* CONTAIN (1).
embolden *v.* —*See* ENCOURAGE (1).
embrace *v.* 1. To put one's arms around affectionately ▸ clasp, enfold, hold, hug, press, squeeze. *Slang:* clinch. *Idioms:* fold to one's bosom, give a bear hug, take in one's arms, wrap one's arms around. [*Compare* GRASP, SNUGGLE.] 2. To receive something given or offered willingly and gladly ▸ accept, take (up), welcome. —*See also* ADOPT, CONTAIN (1), SURROUND.
embrace *n.* The act of embracing ▸ bear hug, clasp, hug, squeeze. *Slang:* clinch. [*Compare* HOLD.]
embracement *n.* —*See* ACCEPTANCE (1).
embrangle *v.* —*See* INVOLVE (1).
embranglement *n.* —*See* ENTANGLEMENT.
embroil *v.* —*See* COMPLICATE, INVOLVE (1).
embroilment *n.* —*See* ENTANGLEMENT.
embryo *n.* —*See* GERM (2).
emend *v.* —*See* CORRECT (1), REVISE.
emendate *v.* —*See* REVISE.
emendation *n.* —*See* REVISION.
emendatory *adj.* —*See* CORRECTIVE.
emerge *v.* —*See* APPEAR (1), BEGIN.
emergence *n.* —*See* APPEARANCE (2).
emergency *n.* A situation requiring immediate assistance or remedial action ▸ crisis, distress, exigence, exigency, extremity, flash point, front burner, hot water, pinch, straits, trauma, trouble, urgency.
emergency *adj.* —*See* AUXILIARY (2).
emergent *adj.* —*See* URGENT (1).
emigrant *n.* One who emigrates ▸ migrant. [*Compare* ÉMIGRÉ, FOREIGNER, SETTLER.]
emigrate *v.* To leave one's native land and settle in another ▸ immigrate (to), migrate, resettle, transmigrate. [*Compare* MOVE, SETTLE.]
emigration *n.* Departure from one's native land to settle in another ▸ defection, diaspora, exodus, expatriation, migration, transmigration. *Idiom:* brain drain. [*Compare* IMMIGRATION, EXILE.]
émigré *n.* One forced to emigrate, usually for political reasons ▸ deportee, displaced person, DP, exile, expatriate, expellee, refugee. —*See also* FOREIGNER.
eminence *n.* —*See* DIGNITARY, FAME, HILL.
eminency *n.* —*See* FAME.
eminent *adj.* —*See* EXALTED, FAMOUS, NOTICEABLE.
eminently *adv.* —*See* VERY.
emir *n.* —*See* CHIEF.
emissary *n.* —*See* REPRESENTATIVE.
emit *v.* To discharge material, as vapor or fumes, usually suddenly and violently ▸ exhale, give, give forth, give off, give out, issue, let off, let out, release, send forth, throw off, vent. [*Compare* ERUPT.] —*See also* SHED[1] (1).
emollient *n.* —*See* OINTMENT.
emolument *n.* —*See* WAGE.

e·mo·tion (ĭ-mō′shən) ▸ *n.* **1.** A strong feeling, as of joy, sorrow, or hate. **2.** A state of mental agitation or disturbance.

e·mo·tion·al (ĭ-mō′shə-nəl) ▸ *adj.* **1.** Of or exhibiting emotion. **2.** Readily affected with emotion. **3.** Arousing the emotions: *an emotional appeal.* **—e·mo′tion·al·ism** *n.* **—e·mo′tion·a·lize′** *v.* **—e·mo′tion·al·ly** *adv.*

e·mo·tive (ĭ-mō′tĭv) ▸ *adj.* **1.** Of or relating to emotion. **2.** Expressing or exciting emotion: *an emotive trial lawyer.* **—e·mo′tive·ly** *adv.* **—e·mo′tive·ness** *n.*

em·pa·na·da (ĕm′pə-nä′də) ▸ *n.* A turnover with a flaky crust and a spicy or sweet filling.

em·pan·el (ĕm-păn′əl) ▸ *v.* Var. of **impanel.**

em·pa·thy (ĕm′pə-thē) ▸ *n.* Identification with and understanding of another's situation, feelings, and motives. **—em′pa·thet′ic, em·path′ic** (-păth′ĭk) *adj.* **—em′pa·thize′** *v.*

em·per·or (ĕm′pər-ər) ▸ *n.* The male ruler of an empire.

em·pha·sis (ĕm′fə-sĭs) ▸ *n., pl.* **-ses** (-sēz′). **1.** Special forcefulness of expression that gives importance to something singled out. **2.** Stress given to a syllable, word, or words. **—em′pha·size′** *v.* **—em·phat′ic** (-făt′ĭk) *adj.* **—em·phat′i·cal·ly** *adv.*

em·phy·se·ma (ĕm′fĭ-sē′mə, -zē′-) ▸ *n.* A disease of the lungs marked by an abnormal increase in the size of the air spaces, resulting in labored breathing and an increased susceptibility to infection. **—em′phy·se′mic** *adj. & n.*

em·pire (ĕm′pīr′) ▸ *n.* **1.** A political unit having an extensive territory or comprising a number of territories or nations and ruled by a single supreme authority. **2.** An extensive enterprise under a central authority: *a publishing empire.* **3.** Imperial sovereignty, domination, or control.

em·pir·i·cal (ĕm-pîr′ĭ-kəl) ▸ *adj.* **1.** Based on observation or experiment. **2.** Guided by practical experience and not theory. **—em·pir′i·cal·ly** *adv.*

em·pir·i·cism (ĕm-pîr′ĭ-sĭz′əm) ▸ *n.* **1.** The view that experience, esp. of the senses, is the only source of knowledge. **2.** Employment of empirical methods, as in science. **—em·pir′i·cist** *n.*

em·place·ment (ĕm-plās′mənt) ▸ *n.* **1.** A prepared position for a military weapon. **2.** Position; location.

em·ploy (ĕm-ploi′) ▸ *v.* **1.** To engage the services of; put to work. **2.** To put to use or service. ▸ *n.* Employment. **—em·ploy′a·bil′i·ty** *n.* **—em·ploy′a·ble** *adj.* **—em·ploy′er** *n.*

em·ploy·ee also **em·ploy·e** (ĕm-ploi′ē, ĭm-, ĕm′ploi-ē′) ▸ *n.* A person who works for another in return for compensation.

em·ploy·ment (ĕm-ploi′mənt) ▸ *n.* **1.** The act of employing. **2.** The state of being employed. **3.** The work in which one is engaged; occupation.

em·po·ri·um (ĕm-pôr′ē-əm) ▸ *n., pl.* **-po·ri·ums** or **-po·ri·a** (-pôr′ē-ə). **1.** A marketplace. **2.** A large retail store carrying a variety of goods.

em·pow·er (ĕm-pou′ər) ▸ *v.* To invest esp. with legal power. **—em·pow′er·ment** *n.*

em·press (ĕm′prĭs) ▸ *n.* **1.** The woman ruler of an empire. **2.** The wife or widow of an emperor.

emp·ty (ĕmp′tē) ▸ *adj.* **-ti·er, -ti·est. 1.** Containing nothing. **2.** Having no occupants or inhabitants; vacant. **3.** Lacking purpose or substance; meaningless. ▸ *v.* **-tied, -ty·ing. 1.** To make or become empty. **2.** To pour or discharge: *The river empties into a bay.* ▸ *n., pl.* **-ties.** *Informal* An empty container. **—emp′ti·ly** *adv.* **—emp′ti·ness** *n.*

emp·ty-hand·ed (ĕmp′tē-hăn′dĭd) ▸ *adj.* **1.** Bearing nothing. **2.** Having received or gained nothing.

em·py·re·an (ĕm′pī-rē′ən, ĕm-pîr′ē-ən) ▸ *n.* **1.** The highest reaches of heaven. **2.** The sky. **—em′py·re′an** *adj.*

e·mu (ē′myo͞o) ▸ *n.* A large flightless Australian bird related to and resembling the ostrich.

em·u·late (ĕm′yə-lāt′) ▸ *v.* **-lat·ed, -lat·ing.** To strive to equal or excel, esp. through imitation. **—em′u·la′tion** *n.* **—em′u·la′tive** *adj.* **—em′u·la′tor** *n.*

e·mul·si·fy (ĭ-mŭl′sə-fī′) ▸ *v.* **-fied, -fy·ing.** To make into an

THESAURUS

emotion *n.* A subjective mental state, such as love or hate ▸ affect, affection, affectivity, feeling, passion, sentiment. [*Compare* PASSION.]

emotional *adj.* **1.** Relating to, arising from, or appealing to the emotions ▸ affectional, affective, emotive. **2.** Readily stirred by emotion ▸ feeling, sensitive. [*Compare* PASSIONATE.] *—See also* DRAMATIC (2).

emotionless *adj.* *—See* COLD (2).

emotive *adj.* Relating to, arising from, or appealing to the emotions ▸ affectional, affective, emotional.

empathetic or **empathic** *adj.* *—See* SYMPATHETIC.

empathize *v.* **1.** To understand or be sensitive to another's feelings or ideas ▸ sympathize, understand. *Idioms:* feel someone's pain, put oneself (*or* walk) in someone else's shoes. **2.** To associate or affiliate oneself closely with a person or group ▸ identify, relate, sympathize. [*Compare* UNDERSTAND.]

empathy *n.* A very close understanding between persons ▸ sympathy, understanding. *—See also* PITY (1).

emperor *n.* *—See* CHIEF.

emphasis *n.* Special attention given to something considered important ▸ accent, accentuation, stress, weight. [*Compare* IMPORTANCE, NOTICE.]

emphasize *v.* To accord emphasis to ▸ accent, accentuate, feature, highlight, italicize, play up, point up, spotlight, stress, underline, underscore. *Idioms:* call attention to, lay stress on. [*Compare* CONCENTRATE.]

emphatic *adj.* *—See* ASSERTIVE, DEFINITE (1).

emphatically *adv.* *—See* FLATLY.

emplace *v.* *—See* POSITION.

emplacement *n.* *—See* POSITION (1).

employ *v.* **1.** To obtain the use or services of ▸ enlist, engage, hire, recruit, retain, sign (on *or* up), take on. *Idioms:* bring aboard, put on the payroll. [*Compare* AUTHORIZE.] **2.** To make busy ▸ busy, engage, occupy. [*Compare* ABSORB, INVOLVE.] *—See also* ABSORB (1), OPERATE, USE.

employ *n.* The state of being employed ▸ employment, hire, service.

employable *adj.* *—See* OPEN (4), USABLE.

employed *adj.* Having a job ▸ hired, jobholding, placed, retained, wage-earning, working. *Idioms:* bringing home the bacon, gainfully employed, off the dole. *—See also* BUSY (1).

employee *n.* One who is employed by another ▸ help, hireling, jobholder, staffer, staff member, wage earner, worker. *Informal:* hire, hired hand, nine-to-fiver. [*Compare* ASSISTANT, LABORER.]

employer *n.* One that employs persons for wages ▸ hirer. [*Compare* BOSS.]

employment *n.* **1.** The act of employing for wages ▸ engagement, hire, hiring, retention. **2.** The state of being employed ▸ employ, hire, service. *—See also* BUSINESS (2), DUTY (2), EXERCISE (1).

emporium *n.* A retail establishment where merchandise is sold ▸ boutique, outlet, shop, store.

empower *v.* To give the means, ability, or opportunity to do ▸ enable, permit. *Idioms:* clear the path (*or* road *or* way for, smooth the way for. [*Compare* EASE, PERMIT.] *—See also* AUTHORIZE.

emprise *n.* *—See* ADVENTURE.

emptiness *n.* **1.** A desolate sense of loss ▸ blankness, desolation, emptiness, hollowness, vacuum, void. **2.** Total lack of ideas, meaning, or substance ▸ bareness, barrenness, blankness, hollowness, inanity, meaninglessness, vacancy, vacuity, vacuousness. [*Compare* FUTILITY, INSIPIDITY.] *—See also* NOTHINGNESS (2).

empty *adj.* **1.** Containing nothing ▸ bare, barren, blank, clear, null, vacant, vacuous, void. *Idiom:* clean as a whistle. **2.** Deprived of a quality or aspect that is desirable ▸ bankrupt, barren, bereft, denuded, deprived, destitute, devoid, innocent, lacking, void, wanting. *Idioms:* crying out for, in want (*or* need) of. *—See also* HOLLOW (1), VACANT, WORTHLESS.

empty *v.* To remove the contents of ▸ clean out, clear, empty out, evacuate, gut, strip, vacate, void. *—See also* POUR, RID.

empty-headed *adj.* *—See* GIDDY (2), VACANT.

empyreal *adj.* *—See* HEAVENLY (2).

emulate *v.* *—See* COMPETE, FOLLOW (5).

emulation *n.* A strong desire to achieve something ▸ ambition, ambitiousness, aspiration. [*Compare* DRIVE, ENTHUSIASM, THIRST.] *—See also* MIMICRY.

emulative *adj.* *—See* IMITATIVE (1).

emulator *n.* *—See* COMPETITOR.

emulous *adj.* *—See* AMBITIOUS, COMPETITIVE.

emulsion. **—e·mul′si·fi·ca′tion** *n.* **—e·mul′si·fi′er** *n.*

e·mul·sion (ĭ-mŭl′shən) ▸ *n.* 1. A suspension of small globules of one liquid in a second liquid with which the first will not mix. 2. A photosensitive coating, usu. of silver halide grains in a thin gelatin layer, on photographic film, paper, or glass. **—e·mul′sive** *adj.*

en (ĕn) ▸ *n. Print.* A space equal to half the width of an em.

en–[1] or **em–** or **in–** ▸ *pref.* 1a. To put into or onto: *encapsulate.* b. To go into or onto: *entrain.* 2. To cover or provide with: *enrobe.* 3. To cause to be: *endear.* 4. Thoroughly. Used often as an intensive: *entangle.*

en–[2] or **em–** ▸ *pref.* In; into; within: *endemic.*

–en[1] ▸ *suff.* 1a. To cause to be: *cheapen.* b. To become: *redden.* 2a. To cause to have: *hearten.* b. To come to have: *lengthen.*

–en[2] ▸ *suff.* Made of; resembling: *earthen.*

en·a·ble (ĕ-nā′bəl) ▸ *v.* **-bled, -bling.** 1. To supply with the means, knowledge, or opportunity; make able. 2. To give legal power, capacity, or sanction to. 3. To make (e.g., a device) operational. **—en·a′bler** *n.*

en·act (ĕn-ăkt′) ▸ *v.* 1. To make (a bill) into law. 2. To act out, as on a stage. **—en·act′ment** *n.* **—en·ac′tor** *n.*

e·nam·el (ĭ-năm′əl) ▸ *n.* 1. A vitreous, usu. opaque protective coating on metal, glass, or ceramic ware. 2. A paint that dries to a hard glossy finish. 3. The hard substance covering the exposed portion of a tooth. ▸ *v.* **-eled, -el·ing** or **-elled, -el·ling.** To coat or decorate with enamel. **—e·nam′el·ware′** *n.*

en·am·or (ĭ-năm′ər) ▸ *v.* To inspire with love; captivate.

en·am·our (ĭ-năm′ər) ▸ *v. Chiefly Brit.* Var. of **enamor.**

enc. ▸ *abbr.* 1. enclosed 2. enclosure

en·camp (ĕn-kămp′) ▸ *v.* To set up or live in a camp. **—en·camp′ment** *n.*

en·cap·su·late (ĕn-kăp′sə-lāt′) ▸ *v.* **-lat·ed, -lat·ing.** 1. To encase in or as if in a capsule. 2. To express in a brief summary. **—en·cap′su·la′tion** *n.*

en·case (ĕn-kās′) also **in·case** (ĭn-) ▸ *v.* **-cased, -cas·ing.** To enclose in or as if in a case. **—en·case′ment** *n.*

–ence ▸ *suff.* 1. State or condition: *dependence.* 2. Action: *emergence.*

en·ceph·a·li·tis (ĕn-sĕf′ə-lī′tĭs) ▸ *n.* Inflammation of the brain. **—en·ceph′a·lit′ic** (-lĭt′ĭk) *adj.*

encephalo– or **encephal–** ▸ *pref.* Brain: *encephalitis.*

en·ceph·a·lo·gram (ĕn-sĕf′ə-lə-grăm′, -ə-lō-) ▸ *n.* An x-ray picture of the brain. **—en·ceph′a·log′ra·phy** (-lŏg′rə-fē) *n.*

en·ceph·a·lon (ĕn-sĕf′ə-lŏn′) ▸ *n., pl.* **-la** (-lə). The brain of a vertebrate. **—en·ceph′a·lous** *adj.*

en·chain (ĕn-chān′) ▸ *v.* To bind with or as if with chains. **—en·chain′ment** *n.*

en·chant (ĕn-chănt′) ▸ *v.* 1. To cast a spell over; bewitch. 2. To attract and delight; entrance. **—en·chant′er** *n.* **—en·chant′ment** *n.* **—en·chant′ress** *n.*

en·chi·la·da (ĕn′chə-lä′də) ▸ *n.* A rolled tortilla with a meat or cheese filling, served with a sauce spiced with chili.

en·ci·pher (ĕn-sī′fər) ▸ *v.* To put (a message) into cipher. **—en·ci′pher·ment** *n.*

en·cir·cle (ĕn-sûr′kəl) ▸ *v.* **-cled, -cling.** 1. To form a circle around. 2. To move or go around; make a circuit of. **—en·cir′cle·ment** *n.*

encl. ▸ *abbr.* 1. enclosed 2. enclosure

en·clave (ĕn′klāv′, ŏn′-) ▸ *n.* A distinctly bounded area enclosed within a larger unit, esp. a country or part of a country lying wholly within the boundaries of another.

en·close (ĕn-klōz′) also **in·close** (ĭn-) ▸ *v.* **-closed, -clos·ing.** 1. To surround on all sides; close in. 2. To include in the same envelope or package: *enclose a check with the order.* **—en·clo′sure** (-klō′zhər) *n.*

en·code (ĕn-kōd′) ▸ *v.* **-cod·ed, -cod·ing.** 1. To put (e.g., a message) into code. 2. *Comp. Sci.* To convert into machine language. **—en·cod′er** *n.*

en·co·mi·um (ĕn-kō′mē-əm) ▸ *n., pl.* **-mi·ums** or **-mi·a** (-mē-ə). Lofty praise; tribute.

en·com·pass (ĕn-kŭm′pəs) ▸ *v.* 1. To enclose. 2. To constitute or include. **—en·com′pass·ment** *n.*

en·core (ŏn′kôr′) ▸ *n.* 1. A demand by an audience for an additional performance. 2. An additional performance in response to such a demand. ▸ *interj.* Used to demand an encore.

en·coun·ter (ĕn-koun′tər) ▸ *n.* 1. A meeting, esp. one that is unexpected or brief. 2. A hostile confrontation; clash. ▸ *v.* 1. To meet, esp. unexpectedly. 2. To confront in battle.

en·cour·age (ĕn-kûr′ĭj, -kŭr′-) ▸ *v.* **-aged, -ag·ing.** 1. To inspire with hope, courage, or confidence. 2. To give support to; foster. **—en·cour′age·ment** *n.* **—en·cour′ag·er** *n.* **—en·cour′ag·ing·ly** *adv.*

en·croach (ĕn-krōch′) ▸ *v.* To take another's possessions or rights gradually or stealthily. **—en·croach′er** *n.* **—en·croach′ment** *n.*

en·crust (ĕn-krŭst′) also **in·crust** (ĭn-) ▸ *v.* To cover with or as if with a crust. **—en′crust·a′tion** *n.*

en·crypt (ĕn-krĭpt′) ▸ *v.* 1. To put into code or cipher. 2. *Comp. Sci.* To alter (e.g., a file) using a secret code so as to be unintelligible to unauthorized parties. **—en·cryp′tion** *n.*

THESAURUS

enable *v.* To give the means, ability, or opportunity to do ▸ empower, permit. *Idioms:* clear the path (*or* road *or* way for, smooth the way for. [*Compare* EASE, PERMIT.] *—See also* AUTHORIZE.

enact *v.* *—See* ACT (3), ESTABLISH (2), STAGE.

enactment *n.* *—See* INTERPRETATION, LAW (2).

enamel *n.* *—See* FINISH.

enamel *v.* *—See* FINISH (2).

enamored *adj.* *—See* INFATUATED.

enceinte *adj.* *—See* PREGNANT (1).

enchant *v.* *—See* CHARM (1), CHARM (2), DELIGHT (1).

enchanter *n.* *—See* WIZARD.

enchanting *adj.* *—See* ATTRACTIVE, DELIGHTFUL.

enchantment *n.* *—See* ATTRACTION, DELIGHT, SPELL[2].

enchantress *n.* A woman who practices magic ▸ hag, lamia, sorceress, witch. [*Compare* WIZARD.] *—See also* SEDUCTRESS.

encircle *v.* To form a circle around ▸ band, begird, belt, cincture, circle, circumnavigate, circumscribe, gird, girdle, girt, loop, orbit, ring, surround. [*Compare* TURN.] *—See also* SURROUND.

enclose *v.* 1. To confine within a limited area ▸ bar, box (in), cage, close (in), closet, confine, contain, coop (in up), cordon (off), corral, fence (in), immure, impound, pen, shut (away in up), wall (in off up). [*Compare* IMPRISON, SURROUND.] 2. To surround and advance upon ▸ besiege, close in, encompass, envelop, hedge, hem, picket. [*Compare* BESIEGE, SURROUND.]

enclosure *n.* *—See* COURT (1).

encomiastic *adj.* *—See* COMPLIMENTARY (1).

encomium *n.* *—See* PRAISE (1).

encompass *v.* *—See* CONTAIN (1), ENCLOSE (2), SURROUND.

encounter *v.* 1. To find or meet by chance ▸ alight on (*or* upon), bump into, chance on (*or* upon), come across, come on (*or* upon), find, happen on (*or* upon), hit (on *or* upon), light on (*or* upon), meet, run across, run into, see, stumble on (*or* upon), tumble on. *Idiom:* meet up with. 2. To meet face-to-face, especially defiantly ▸ confront, face, front, meet. *Idiom:* stand up to. [*Compare* CONTEST, DEFY.] *—See also* CONTEND, EXPERIENCE.

encounter *n.* *—See* BATTLE, CONFRONTATION.

encourage *v.* 1. To impart courage, inspiration, and resolution to ▸ animate, cheer (on), embolden, inspire, inspirit, motivate. [*Compare* PROVOKE, URGE.] 2. To impart emotional, moral, or mental strength to ▸ buck up, cheer (up), fortify, hearten, nerve, perk up. [*Compare* COMFORT, ENERGIZE.] 3. To lend supportive approval to ▸ countenance, favor, smile on (*or* upon). [*Compare* APPROVE, SUPPORT.] *—See also* PROMOTE (2).

encouragement *n.* Something that gives courage or confidence ▸ boost, exhortation, inspiration, lift, motivation, stimulation. *Informal:* pep talk. *Idiom:* shot in the arm. *—See also* PATRONAGE (1), STIMULUS.

encouraging *adj.* Inspiring confidence or hope ▸ cheering, heartening, hopeful, likely, promising. [*Compare* FAVORABLE, OPTIMISTIC.]

encroach *v.* *—See* INTRUDE.

encroachment *n.* *—See* TRESPASS (2).

en·cum·ber (ĕn-kŭm′bər) ▸ *v.* **1.** To weigh down; burden. **2.** To hinder or impede. **3.** To burden with legal or financial obligations. **—en·cum′brance** *n.*
–ency ▸ *suff.* Condition or quality: *complacency.*
en·cyc·li·cal (ĕn-sĭk′lĭ-kəl) ▸ *n. Rom. Cath. Ch.* A papal letter addressed to the bishops.
en·cy·clo·pe·di·a (ĕn-sī′klə-pē′dē-ə) ▸ *n.* A comprehensive reference work containing articles on a wide range of subjects or on numerous aspects of a particular field. **—en·cy′clo·pe′dic** *adj.*
en·cyst (ĕn-sĭst′) ▸ *v.* To enclose or become enclosed in a cyst. **—en·cyst′ment, en′cys·ta′tion** *n.*
end (ĕnd) ▸ *n.* **1.** Either extremity of something that has length. **2.** The point in time when an action, event, or phenomenon ceases or is completed; conclusion. **3.** A result; outcome. **4.** Something toward which one strives; goal. **5.** Death. **6.** The ultimate extent; the very limit. **7.** A remainder; remnant. **8.** A share of a responsibility or obligation. **9.** *Football* Either of the players in the outermost position on the line of scrimmage. ▸ *v.* **1.** To bring or come to a conclusion. **2.** To form the concluding part of. **3.** To destroy. ***—idioms:*** **in the end** Eventually; ultimately. **no end** A great deal.
en·dan·ger (ĕn-dān′jər) ▸ *v.* To expose to harm or danger; imperil. **—en·dan′ger·ment** *n.* **—en·dan′gered** *adj.*
endangered species ▸ *n.* A species present in such small numbers that it is at risk of extinction.
en·dear (ĕn-dîr′) ▸ *v.* To make beloved.
en·dear·ment (ĕn-dîr′mənt) ▸ *n.* An expression of affection.
en·deav·or (ĕn-dĕv′ər) ▸ *n.* A concerted effort toward an end; earnest attempt. ▸ *v.* To attempt through concerted effort: *endeavored to improve my grades.*
en·dem·ic (ĕn-dĕm′ĭk) ▸ *adj.* Prevalent in or peculiar to a particular locality, region, or people. **—en·dem′i·cal·ly** *adv.*
en·dive (ĕn′dīv′, ŏn′dēv′) ▸ *n.* **1.** A plant with crisp succulent leaves used in salads. **2.** A variety of chicory with a narrow pointed cluster of whitish leaves used in salads.
end·less (ĕnd′lĭs) ▸ *adj.* **1.** Being or seeming to be without an end or limit; boundless. **2.** Formed with the ends joined; continuous. **—end′less·ly** *adv.* **—end′less·ness** *n.*
end·most (ĕnd′mōst′) ▸ *adj.* Being at or closest to the end; last.
endo– or **end–** ▸ *pref.* Inside; within: *endogenous.*
en·do·crine (ĕn′də-krĭn, -krēn′, -krīn′) ▸ *adj.* **1.** Secreting internally. **2.** Of or relating to endocrine glands or the hormones secreted by them.
endocrine gland ▸ *n.* A gland, such as the thyroid, adrenal, or pituitary, having hormonal secretions that pass directly into the bloodstream.
en·do·cri·nol·o·gy (ĕn′də-krə-nŏl′ə-jē) ▸ *n.* The study of the glands and hormones of the body and their disorders. **—en′do·cri′no·log′ic** (-krĭn′ə-lŏj′ĭk), **en′do·crin′o·log′i·cal** *adj.* **—en′do·cri·nol′o·gist** *n.*
en·do·don·tics (ĕn′dō-dŏn′tĭks) ▸ *n. (takes sing. v.)* The branch of dentistry that deals with diseases of the tooth root, dental pulp, and surrounding tissue. **—en′do·don′tic** *adj.* **—en′do·don′tist** *n.*
en·dog·e·nous (ĕn-dŏj′ə-nəs) ▸ *adj. Biol.* Originating within an organism or part. **—en·dog′e·nous·ly** *adv.*
en·do·me·tri·o·sis (ĕn′dō-mē′trē-ō′sĭs) ▸ *n.* A usu. painful condition marked by the abnormal occurrence of endometrial tissue outside the uterus.
en·do·me·tri·um (ĕn′dō-mē′trē-əm) ▸ *n., pl.* **-tri·a** (-trē-ə). The glandular mucous membrane that lines the uterus. **—en′do·me′tri·al** *adj.*
en·do·plasm (ĕn′də-plăz′əm) ▸ *n.* A central, less viscous portion of the cytoplasm distinguishable in certain cells. **—en′do·plas′mic** *adj.*
en·dor·phin (ĕn-dôr′fĭn) ▸ *n.* Any of a group of peptide hormones that bind to opiate receptors and are found mainly in the brain.
en·dorse (ĕn-dôrs′) also **in·dorse** (ĭn-) ▸ *v.* **-dorsed, -dors·ing.** **1.** To write one's signature on the back of (e.g., a check), esp. in return for the cash or credit indicated on its face. **2.** To give approval of or support to, esp. by public statement; sanction. **—en·dorse′ment** *n.* **—en·dors′er, en·dor′sor** *n.*
en·do·scope (ĕn′də-skōp′) ▸ *n.* An instrument for viewing the interior of a body canal or a hollow organ such as the colon or stomach. **—en′do·scop′ic** (-skŏp′ĭk) *adj.* **—en·dos′co·py** (ĕn-dŏs′kə-pē) *n.*
en·do·therm (ĕn′də-thûrm′) ▸ *n.* An organism that generates heat to maintain its body temperature, typically above the temperature of its surroundings **—en·do·ther′mic** *adj.*
en·dow (ĕn-dou′) ▸ *v.* **1.** To provide with property, income, or a source of income. **2.** To equip or supply with a talent or quality. **—en·dow′ment** *n.*
en·due (ĕn-do͞o′, -dyo͞o′) ▸ *v.* **-dued, -du·ing.** To provide with a quality or trait.
en·dure (ĕn-do͝or′, -dyo͝or′) ▸ *v.* **-dured, -dur·ing.** **1.** To carry on through, despite hardships; undergo. **2.** To con-

THESAURUS

encumber *v.* —*See* BURDEN[1], HINDER.
encumbrance *n.* An excessive, unwelcome burden ▸ imposition, infliction, intrusion, obtrusion. [*Compare* MEDDLING.] —*See also* BAR (1), BURDEN[1] (2), DEBT (2).
end *n.* **1.** A concluding or terminating ▸ cessation, close, closing, closure, completion, conclusion, consummation, cutoff, dénouement, ending, end of the line, expiration, finis, finish, period, shutdown, stopping point, termination, terminus, wind-up, wrap-up. [*Compare* STOP.] **2.** The last part ▸ close, closing, conclusion, ending, envoy, epilogue, finale, finish, last, termination, wind-up, wrap-up. **3.** Residual matter ▸ butt, fragment, heel, leftovers, odds and ends, ort, scrap, shard, stub. [*Compare* BALANCE.] —*See also* BACK, DEATH (1), FATE (2), INTENTION, LENGTH, LIMITS.
end *v.* —*See* CONCLUDE, DISAPPEAR (2), DROP (4), LAPSE.
endanger *v.* To expose to danger or destruction ▸ compromise, hazard, imperil, jeopardize, menace, peril, risk, threaten. *Idioms:* lay open, put in jeopardy (*or* harm's way).
endangerment *n.* —*See* DANGER, EXPOSURE.
endeavor *n.* Something undertaken, especially something requiring extensive planning and work ▸ enterprise, project, undertaking, venture. [*Compare* TASK.] —*See also* ACCOMPLISHMENT, ATTEMPT, EFFORT.
endeavor *v.* —*See* ATTEMPT.
ended *adj.* —*See* COMPLETE (3).
endemic *adj.* —*See* INDIGENOUS.
ending *n.* —*See* END (1), END (2).
endless *adj.* **1.** Having no ends or limits ▸ boundless, illimitable, immeasurable, infinite, limitless, measureless, unbounded, unlimited. [*Compare* INCALCULABLE.] **2.** Enduring for all time ▸ amaranthine, ceaseless, eternal, eterne, everlasting, immortal, neverending, perpetual, sempiternal, unending. [*Compare* CONTINUING, FOREVER, UNCHANGING.] —*See also* CONTINUAL.
endlessly *adv.* —*See* FOREVER.
endlessness *n.* The quality or state of having no end ▸ ceaselessness, eternality, eternalness, eternity, everlastingness, interminability, perpetuity. [*Compare* INFINITY.]
endmost *adj.* —*See* LAST[1] (2).
end of the line *n.* —*See* END (1).
endorse *v.* —*See* CONFIRM (3), PERMIT (2), SIGN, SUPPORT (1).
endorsement *n.* An indication of commendation or approval ▸ backing, blessing, recommendation, support. *Informal:* plug. [*Compare* PATRONAGE, REFERENCE.] —*See also* CONFIRMATION (1), PERMISSION.
endow *v.* —*See* DONATE, GIFT.
endowed *adj.* —*See* GIFTED.
endowment *n.* A quality, ability, or accomplishment that makes a person suitable for a particular position or task ▸ attainment, credential, qualification, skill. [*Compare* QUALIFICATION.] —*See also* DONATION.
end product *n.* —*See* EFFECT (1).
endurable *adj.* —*See* BEARABLE.
endurance *n.* The quality or power of withstanding hardship or stress ▸ durability, fortitude, hardiness, stamina, staying power, sticking power, toughness. [*Compare* COURAGE, DECISION, STRENGTH.] —*See also* CONTINUATION (1).
endure *v.* **1.** To put up with or continue despite difficulties ▸ abide, accept, bear (with), brook, go on, hang on, keep on, live through, persevere, persist, sit through, soldier on, stand (for), stick

tinue in existence; last. **3.** To suffer patiently without yielding. **—en·dur′a·ble** *adj.* **—en·dur′ance** *n.*

end·wise (ĕnd′wīz′) also **end·ways** (-wāz′) ▸ *adv.* **1.** On end; upright. **2.** With the end foremost.

end zone ▸ *n. Football* The area at either end of the playing field between the goal line and the end line.

ENE ▸ *abbr.* east-northeast

-ene ▸ *suff.* An unsaturated organic compound, esp. one containing a double bond between carbon atoms: *ethylene.*

en·e·ma (ĕn′ə-mə) ▸ *n.* The injection of liquid into the rectum for cleansing or other therapeutic purposes.

en·e·my (ĕn′ə-mē) ▸ *n., pl.* **-mies. 1.** One who feels hatred toward, intends injury to, or opposes the interests of another; foe. **2.** A hostile power or force, such as a nation. **3.** A group of foes or hostile forces. **—en′e·my** *adj.*

en·er·get·ic (ĕn′ər-jĕt′ĭk) ▸ *adj.* **1.** Possessing, exerting, or displaying energy. **2.** Of or relating to energy. **—en′er·get′i·cal·ly** *adv.*

en·er·gize (ĕn′ər-jīz′) ▸ *v.* **-gized, -giz·ing. 1.** To give energy to; invigorate. **2.** To supply with an electric current. **—en′er·giz′er** *n.*

en·er·gy (ĕn′ər-jē) ▸ *n., pl.* **-gies. 1.** The capacity for work or vigorous activity. **2.** Exertion of vigor or power. **3.** Usable heat or power. **4.** *Phys.* The capacity of a physical system to do work.

en·er·vate (ĕn′ər-vāt′) ▸ *v.* **-vat·ed, -vat·ing.** To weaken or destroy the strength or vitality of. **—en′er·va′tion** *n.* **—en′er·va′tive** *adj.*

en·fee·ble (ĕn-fē′bəl) ▸ *v.* **-bled, -bling.** To make feeble. **—en·fee′ble·ment** *n.*

en·fi·lade (ĕn′fə-lād′, -läd′) ▸ *n.* Gunfire directed along the length of a target, as a column of troops.

en·fold (ĕn-fōld′) ▸ *v.* **1.** To cover with or as if with folds; envelop. **2.** To embrace.

en·force (ĕn-fôrs′) ▸ *v.* **-forced, -forc·ing.** To compel observance of or obedience to. **—en·force′a·bil′i·ty** *n.* **—en·force′a·ble** *adj.* **—en·force′ment** *n.* **—en·forc′er** *n.*

en·fran·chise (ĕn-frăn′chīz′) ▸ *v.* **-chised, -chis·ing. 1.** To bestow a franchise on. **2.** To endow with the rights of citizenship, esp. the right to vote. **3.** To free, as from bondage. **—en·fran′chise′ment** *n.*

en·gage (ĕn-gaj′) ▸ *v.* **-gaged, -gag·ing. 1.** To hire; employ. **2.** To reserve. **3.** To pledge, esp. to marry. **4.** To attract and hold: *a project that engaged her interest.* **5.** To participate: *engage in conversation.* **6.** To enter into conflict with: *engage the enemy.* **7.** To interlock or cause to interlock; mesh. **8.** To assume an obligation; agree.

en·gaged (ĕn-gājd′) ▸ *adj.* **1.** Employed, occupied, or busy. **2.** Pledged to marry; betrothed. **3.** Involved in conflict or battle. **4.** Being in gear; meshed.

en·gage·ment (ĕn-gāj′mənt) ▸ *n.* **1.** The act of engaging or the state of being engaged. **2.** Betrothal. **3.** A promise or agreement to be at a particular place at a particular time. **4.** Employment, esp. for a specified time. **5.** A hostile encounter; battle.

en·gag·ing (ĕn-gā′jĭng) ▸ *adj.* Charming; attractive. **—en·gag′ing·ly** *adv.*

en garde (äɴ gärd′) ▸ *interj.* Used to warn a fencer to assume the position preparatory to a match.

Eng·els (ĕng′əlz, -əls), **Friedrich** (1820–95) ▸ German social theorist and writer.

en·gen·der (ĕn-jĕn′dər) ▸ *v.* **1.** To give rise to. **2.** To propagate.

en·gine (ĕn′jĭn) ▸ *n.* **1.** A machine that converts energy into mechanical force or motion. **2.** A mechanical appliance, instrument, or tool. **3.** A locomotive. **4.** *Comp. Sci.* A search engine.

engine block ▸ *n.* The cast metal block containing the cylinders of an internal-combustion engine.

en·gi·neer (ĕn′jə-nîr′) ▸ *n.* **1.** One trained or professionally engaged in a branch of engineering. **2.** One who operates an engine. ▸ *v.* **1.** To plan, construct, or manage as an engineer. **2.** To alter or produce by methods of genetic engineering. **3.** To plan, manage, and put through by contrivance; maneuver.

en·gi·neer·ing (ĕn′jə-nîr′ĭng) ▸ *n.* The application of scientific principles to practical ends, as the design, manufacture, and operation of structures and machines.

Eng·land (ĭng′glənd) ▸ A division of the United Kingdom, in S Great Britain.

Eng·lish (ĭng′glĭsh) ▸ *adj.* **1.** Of or characteristic of England or its people or culture. **2.** Of the English language. ▸ *n.* **1.** The people of England. **2.** The Germanic language of England, the US, and other countries. **3.** A course in the study of English language, literature, or composition. **4.** often **english** *Sports & Games* The spin given to a ball by

THESAURUS

out, stomach, suffer, support, sustain, swallow, take, tolerate, withstand. *Informal:* lump. *Slang:* sweat out, tough out. ***Idioms:*** hang in there, go the distance, keep going, keep it up, learn to live with (*or* accept), make one's peace with, never say die, resign oneself to, put up with. [*Compare* DEAL WITH, SURVIVE.] **2.** To be in existence or in a certain state for an indefinitely long time ▸ abide, bide, continue, go on, hold out, hold steady, keep, last, perdure, perseverate, persist, remain, stand, stay. *—See also* BEAR UP.

enduring *adj.* *—See* CONTINUING, PATIENT, VINTAGE.

enemy *n.* *—See* OPPONENT.

energetic *adj.* Possessing, exerting, or displaying energy ▸ active, brisk, driving, dynamic, dynamical, enterprising, forceful, fresh, kinetic, lively, sprightly, spry, strenuous, vigorous, zippy. *Informal:* peppy, snappy. ***Idiom:*** ready (*or* raring) to go. [*Compare* LUSTY, STRONG.]

energetically *adv.* *—See* HARD (1).

energize *v.* To give or impart vitality and energy to ▸ exhilarate, invigorate, stimulate, vitalize. *Informal:* jazz up, jump-start, pep up. *Slang:* pump up. ***Idioms:*** get the lead out of, light a fire under, put zip into. [*Compare* FIRE, INSPIRE, PROVOKE, REFRESH.]

energizer *n.* *—See* TONIC.

energizing *adj.* *—See* INVIGORATING.

energy *n.* Capacity for work or vigorous activity ▸ animation, dash, dynamism, force, liveliness, might, potency, power, punch, sprightliness, starch, steam, strength, verve, vibrancy, vigor, vigorousness, vim, vitality. *Informal:* get-up-and-go, go, jump, pep, peppiness, snap, zip. ***Idiom:*** vim and vigor. [*Compare* SPIRIT.]

enervate *v.* To lessen or deplete the nerve, power, or vitality of ▸ attenuate, debilitate, devitalize, enfeeble, eviscerate, gut, sap, undermine, undo, unnerve, weaken. [*Compare* DEPLETE, TIRE.]

enervated *adj.* *—See* LETHARGIC, WEAR (1).

enervation *n.* *—See* DEBILITATION, LETHARGY.

enfeeble *v.* *—See* ENERVATE.

enfeeblement *n.* *—See* DEBILITATION.

enfold *v.* *—See* EMBRACE (1), WRAP (1), WRAP (2).

enforce *v.* To compel observance of ▸ carry out, effect, effectuate, execute, implement, invoke, prosecute. ***Idioms:*** put in force, put into action (*or* effect *or* operation).

enforcement *n.* Carrying a law or judgment into effect ▸ execution, implementation. [*Compare* EFFECT, EXERCISE.]

engage *v.* **1.** To involve someone in an activity ▸ draw in. [*Compare* INVOLVE.] **2.** To make busy ▸ busy, employ, occupy. [*Compare* ABSORB, INVOLVE.] **3.** To come or bring together and interlock ▸ mesh. [*Compare* ATTACH, FIT[1].] *—See also* ABSORB (1), BOOK, CONTEND, EMPLOY (1), GRIP, PARTICIPATE, PLEDGE (1), PLEDGE (2).

engaged *adj.* Pledged to marry ▸ affianced, bespoken, betrothed, intended, pledged, plighted, promised. *—See also* BUSY (1), CONCERNED.

engagement *n.* **1.** An arrangement to appear at a certain time and place ▸ appointment, assignation, commitment, date, rendezvous, tryst. **2.** A commitment, as for a performance by an entertainer ▸ booking, date. *Slang:* gig. **3.** The act or condition of being pledged to marry ▸ betrothal, espousal, troth. **4.** The act or fact of participating ▸ involvement, partaking, participation, sharing. **5.** The act of employing for wages ▸ employment, hire, hiring, retention. *—See also* ABSORPTION (2), BATTLE, PROMISE (1).

engaging *adj.* *—See* ATTRACTIVE.

engender *v.* *—See* BREED, PRODUCE (1).

engineer *v.* *—See* CONDUCT (1), MANEUVER (2).

striking it on one side or releasing it with a sharp twist. **—Eng′lish·man** *n.* **—Eng′lish·wom′an** *n.*

English Channel ► An arm of the Atlantic between W France and S England.

English horn ► *n.* A double-reed woodwind instrument similar to but larger than the oboe and pitched lower by a fifth.

English setter ► *n.* Any of a breed of medium-sized dog developed in England having a long silky white coat usu. with black or brownish markings.

en·gorge (ĕn-gôrj′) ► *v.* **-gorged, -gorg·ing. 1.** To devour greedily. **2.** To fill to excess, as with fluid. **—en·gorge′ment** *n.*

en·graft (ĕn-grăft′) ► *v.* To graft (a scion) onto or into another plant.

en·grave (ĕn-grāv′) ► *v.* **-graved, -grav·ing. 1.** To carve, cut, or etch into a material. **2a.** To cut into a block or surface used for printing. **b.** To print from a block or plate made by such a process. **3.** To impress deeply as if by carving or etching. **—en·grav′er** *n.*

en·grav·ing (ĕn-grā′vĭng) ► *n.* **1.** The art or technique of one that engraves. **2.** An engraved surface for printing. **3.** A print made from an engraved plate or block.

en·gross (ĕn-grōs′) ► *v.* To occupy exclusively; absorb.

en·gulf (ĕn-gŭlf′) ► *v.* To swallow up or overwhelm by or as if by overflowing and enclosing.

en·hance (ĕn-hăns′) ► *v.* **-hanced, -hanc·ing.** To make greater, as in value, reputation, or usefulness. **—en·hance′ment** *n.* **—en·hanc′er** *n.*

e·nig·ma (ĭ-nĭg′mə) ► *n.* One that is puzzling, ambiguous, or inexplicable. **—en′ig·mat′ic** (ĕn′ĭg-măt′ĭk), **en′ig·mat′i·cal** *adj.*

en·join (ĕn-join′) ► *v.* **1.** To direct or impose with authority and emphasis. **2.** To forbid. **—en·join′ment** *n.*

en·joy (ĕn-joi′) ► *v.* **1.** To receive pleasure or satisfaction from. **2.** To have the use or benefit of: *enjoys good health.* **—en·joy′a·ble** *adj.* **—en·joy′a·bly** *adv.* **—en·joy′ment** *n.*

en·large (ĕn-lärj′) ► *v.* **-larged, -larg·ing. 1.** To make or become larger. **2.** To give greater scope to; expand. **3.** To speak or write at greater length or in greater detail; elaborate. **—en·large′ment** *n.* **—en·larg′er** *n.*

en·light·en (ĕn-līt′n) ► *v.* **1.** To give spiritual or intellectual insight to. **2.** To inform or instruct. **—en·light′en·ment** *n.*

en·list (ĕn-lĭst′) ► *v.* **1.** To engage (a person) for service in the armed forces. **2.** To engage the support or cooperation of. **3.** To enter the armed forces. **—en·list′ment** *n.*

en·liv·en (ĕn-lī′vən) ► *v.* To make lively or spirited; animate. **—en·liv′en·ment** *n.*

en masse (ŏn măs′) ► *adv.* In one group or body; all together.

en·mesh (ĕn-mĕsh′) also **im·mesh** (ĭm-) ► *v.* To entangle, involve, or catch in or as if in a mesh.

en·mi·ty (ĕn′mĭ-tē) ► *n., pl.* **-ties.** Deep-seated, often mutual hatred.

en·no·ble (ĕn-nō′bəl) ► *v.* **-bled, -bling. 1.** To make noble. **2.** To confer nobility upon. **—en·no′ble·ment** *n.*

en·nui (ŏn-wē′, ŏn′wē) ► *n.* Listlessness and dissatisfaction resulting from lack of interest; boredom.

e·nor·mi·ty (ĭ-nôr′mĭ-tē) ► *n., pl.* **-ties. 1.** Excessive wickedness or outrageousness. **2.** A monstrous offense or evil; outrage. **3.** *Informal* Great size; immensity.

e·nor·mous (ĭ-nôr′məs) ► *adj.* Very great in size, extent, number, or degree. **—e·nor′mous·ly** *adv.* **—e·nor′mous·ness** *n.*

e·nough (ĭ-nŭf′) ► *adj.* Sufficient to meet a need or satisfy a desire; adequate. ► *pron.* An adequate quantity. ► *adv.* **1.** To a satisfactory amount or degree. **2.** Very; quite: *glad enough to leave.* **3.** Tolerably; rather: *She sang well enough.* ► *interj.* Used to express impatience or exasperation.

en·quire (ĕn-kwīr′) ► *v.* Var. of **inquire. —en·quir′er** *n.* **—en·quir′y** *n.*

en·rage (ĕn-rāj′) ► *v.* **-raged, -rag·ing.** To put into a rage; infuriate.

en·rap·ture (ĕn-răp′chər) ► *v.* **-tured, -tur·ing.** To fill with

THESAURUS

englut *v.* —*See* GULP.

engorge *v.* —*See* GULP, SATIATE.

engorgement *n.* —*See* SATIATION.

engrave *v.* **1.** To cut a design or inscription into a hard surface, especially for printing ► carve, chase, chisel, etch, grave, incise, inscribe. **2.** To produce a deep impression of ► etch, fix, grave, impress, imprint, inscribe, stamp. [*Compare* IMPRESS.]

engross *v.* —*See* ABSORB (1), WRITE.

engrossed *adj.* —*See* RAPT.

engrossment *n.* —*See* ABSORPTION (2).

engulf *v.* —*See* FLOOD (1), OVERWHELM (2).

enhance *v.* **1.** To endow with beauty and elegance ► beautify, embellish, grace, set off. [*Compare* ADORN.] **2.** To look good on or with ► become, flatter, suit. ***Idiom:*** put in the best light. —*See also* IMPROVE, INTENSIFY, SUPPLEMENT.

enhancement *n.* Something added to another for embellishment or completion ► accompaniment, add-on, bells and whistles, complement, enrichment, extra, supplement. [*Compare* ADDITION, ATTACHMENT.] —*See also* IMPROVEMENT (1).

enigma *n.* —*See* MYSTERY.

enigmatic *adj.* —*See* AMBIGUOUS (1), MYSTERIOUS.

enjoin *v.* —*See* COMMAND (1), FORBID.

enjoy *v.* To receive pleasure from ► appreciate, care for, like, relish, savor. *Informal:* go for, go in for. *Slang:* be into, dig. ***Idioms:*** be big on, be crazy (*or* wild) about, be fond of, get a charge (*or* bang *or* kick out of, get off on, have a thing about (*or* soft spot for), lap up. [*Compare* LIKE[1].] —*See also* COMMAND (2).

enjoyable *adj.* —*See* GOOD (1), PLEASANT.

enjoyment *n.* —*See* AMUSEMENT, DELIGHT.

enkindle *v.* —*See* FIRE (1), LIGHT[1] (1).

enlace *v.* —*See* WEAVE.

enlarge *v.* —*See* BROADEN, ELABORATE, GAIN (1), INCREASE.

enlargement *n.* —*See* BUILDUP (2), INCREASE (1).

enlighten *v.* —*See* ILLUMINATE (2), INFORM (1).

enlightened *adj.* —*See* EDUCATED, INFORMED.

enlightening *adj.* —*See* CULTURAL, EDUCATIONAL (2).

enlightenment *n.* The condition of being informed spiritually ► edification, illumination. [*Compare* EDUCATION.] —*See also* CULTURE (3).

enlist *v.* —*See* EMPLOY (1), JOIN (1), MOBILIZE.

enliven *v.* **1.** To make lively or animated ► animate, brighten, light (up), perk up. **2.** To make alive ► animate, quicken, vitalize, vivify. [*Compare* ELATE, ENERGIZE, PROVOKE.]

enlivening *adj.* —*See* INVIGORATING.

enmesh *v.* —*See* CATCH (1).

enmeshment *n.* —*See* ENTANGLEMENT.

enmity *n.* Deep-seated hatred, as between longtime opponents or rivals ► animosity, animus, antagonism, antipathy, feud, hostility, ill feeling, ill will, rancor. ***Idioms:*** bad blood, blood feud, hard feelings, no love lost. [*Compare* DESPISAL, HATE, RESENTMENT.]

ennoble *v.* —*See* DISTINGUISH (3), EXALT.

ennobled *adj.* —*See* EXALTED.

ennoblement *n.* —*See* EXALTATION.

ennui *n.* —*See* BOREDOM.

enormity *n.* —*See* OUTRAGE, OUTRAGEOUSNESS.

enormous *adj.* Of extraordinary size and power ► astronomical, behemoth, Brobdingnagian, Bunyanesque, colossal, cyclopean, elephantine, gargantuan, giant, gigantesque, gigantic, herculean, heroic, huge, immense, jumbo, mammoth, massive, massy, mastodonic, mighty, monstrous, monumental, mountainous, prodigious, pythonic, stupendous, super-size, titanic, tremendous, vast. *Informal:* monster, walloping. *Slang:* humongous, whopping. [*Compare* BIG, BULKY, GRAND.]

enormousness *n.* The quality of being enormous ► hugeness, immenseness, immensity, monumentality, prodigiousness, stupendousness, tremendousness, vastness. [*Compare* BULK, SIZE.]

enough *adj.* —*See* SUFFICIENT.

enough *pron.* An adequate quantity ► adequacy, sufficiency.

enounce *v.* —*See* ASSERT, PRONOUNCE.

enquire *v.* *See* INQUIRE.

enquirer *n.* *See* INQUIRER.

enquiring *adj.* *See* INQUIRING.

enquiry *n.* *See* INQUIRY.

enrage *v.* —*See* ANGER (1).

enrapture *v.* To have a powerful emotional effect on someone ► carry away, electrify, excite, ravish, thrill,

rapture or delight. **—en·rap′ture·ment** *n.*
en·rich (ĕn-rĭch′) ▸ *v.* 1. To make rich or richer. 2. To make fuller, more meaningful, or more rewarding. 3. To add nutrients to. 4. To add to the beauty or character of; adorn. **—en·rich′ment** *n.*
en·roll also **en·rol** (ĕn-rōl′) ▸ *v.* **-rolled, -roll·ing.** To enter or register in a roll, list, or record. **—en·roll′ment, en·rol′ment** *n.*
en route (ŏn ro͞ot′, ĕn) ▸ *adv. & adj.* On or along the way.
en·sconce (ĕn-skŏns′) ▸ *v.* **-sconced, -sconc·ing.** 1. To settle securely or comfortably. 2. To place or conceal in a secure place.
en·sem·ble (ŏn-sŏm′bəl) ▸ *n.* 1. A unit or group of complementary parts that contribute to a single effect. 2. A coordinated outfit or costume. 3. A group of musicians, singers, dancers, or actors who perform together. 4. *Mus.* A work for two or more vocalists or instrumentalists.
en·shrine (ĕn-shrīn′) ▸ *v.* **-shrined, -shrin·ing.** 1. To enclose in or as if in a shrine. 2. To cherish as sacred. **—en·shrine′ment** *n.*
en·shroud (ĕn-shroud′) ▸ *v.* To cover with or as if with a shroud.
en·sign (ĕn′sən, -sīn′) ▸ *n.* 1. A standard or banner, as of a military unit. 2. (ĕn′sən) The lowest commissioned rank in the US Navy or Coast Guard. 3. A badge of office or power; emblem.
en·si·lage (ĕn′sə-lĭj) ▸ *n.* The process of storing and fermenting green fodder in a silo. **—en′sil·age** *v.*
en·sile (ĕn-sīl′) ▸ *v.* **-siled, -sil·ing.** To store (fodder) in a silo.
en·slave (ĕn-slāv′) ▸ *v.* **-slaved, -slav·ing.** To make into or as if into a slave. **—en·slave′ment** *n.* **—en·slav′er** *n.*
en·snare (ĕn-snâr′) ▸ *v.* **-snared, -snar·ing.** To catch in or as if in a snare. **—en·snare′ment** *n.* **—en·snar′er** *n.*
en·sue (ĕn-so͞o′) ▸ *v.* **-sued, -su·ing.** 1. To follow as a result. 2. To take place subsequently.
en·sure (ĕn-sho͝or′) ▸ *v.* **-sured, -sur·ing.** To make sure or certain; insure.
-ent ▸ *suff.* 1a. Performing, promoting, or causing a specified action: *absorbent.* b. Being in a specified state or condition: *different.* 2. One that performs, promotes, or causes a specified action: *resident.*
en·tail (ĕn-tāl′, ĭn-) ▸ *v.* 1. To have, impose, or require as a necessary accompaniment or consequence. 2. To limit the inheritance of (property) to a specified succession of heirs. **—en·tail′ment** *n.*
en·tan·gle (ĕn-tăng′gəl) ▸ *v.* **-gled, -gling.** 1. To twist together into a confusing mass; snarl. 2. To complicate; confuse. 3. To involve in or as if in a tangle. **—en·tan′gle·ment** *n.*
en·tente (ŏn-tŏnt′) ▸ *n.* 1. An agreement between two or more governments or powers for cooperative action or policy. 2. The parties to such an agreement.
en·ter (ĕn′tər) ▸ *v.* 1. To come or go into. 2. To penetrate; pierce. 3. To insert. 4. To become or cause to become a participant, member, or part of; join or enroll. 5. To embark on; begin. 6. To write or put in. 7. To place formally on record; submit. 8. To go to or occupy in order to claim possession of (land). ***—phrasal verbs:*** **enter into** 1. To participate in. 2. To become party to (a contract). **enter on (**or **upon)** To set out on; begin.
en·ter·ic (ĕn-tĕr′ĭk) also **en·ter·al** (ĕn′tər-əl) ▸ *adj.* Of or being within the intestine.
en·ter·i·tis (ĕn′tə-rī′tĭs) ▸ *n.* Inflammation of the intestine.
en·ter·prise (ĕn′tər-prīz′) ▸ *n.* 1. An undertaking, esp. one of some scope, complication, and risk. 2. A business organization. 3. Industrious, systematic activity, esp. when directed toward profit. 4. Willingness to undertake new ventures; initiative.
en·ter·pris·ing (ĕn′tər-prī′zĭng) ▸ *adj.* Willing and eager to undertake new projects.
en·ter·tain (ĕn′tər-tān′) ▸ *v.* 1. To hold the attention of with something amusing or diverting. 2. To extend hospitality to. 3. To consider; contemplate. **—en′ter·tain′er** *n.* **—en′ter·tain′ment** *n.*
en·thrall (ĕn-thrôl′) ▸ *v.* 1. To hold spellbound. 2. To enslave. **—en·thrall′ment** *n.*
en·throne (ĕn-thrōn′) ▸ *v.* **-throned, -thron·ing.** 1. To seat on a throne. 2. To raise to a lofty position; exalt. **—en·throne′ment** *n.*
en·thuse (ĕn-tho͞oz′) ▸ *v.* **-thused, -thus·ing.** *Informal* To make or act enthusiastic.
en·thu·si·asm (ĕn-tho͞o′zē-ăz′əm) ▸ *n.* 1. Great excitement for or interest in a subject or cause. 2. A source or cause of great excitement or interest. **—en·thu′si·ast′** *n.* **—en·thu′si·as′tic** *adj.* **—en·thu′si·as′ti·cal·ly** *adv.*

THESAURUS

transport. *Slang:* send. [*Compare* CHARM, DELIGHT.]
enraptured *adj.* —*See* INFATUATED.
enrich *v.* 1. To lend dignity or honor to by an act or favor ▸ favor, grace, dignify, honor. [*Compare* DISTINGUISH, EXALT, HONOR.] 2. To make fertile ▸ fecundate, fertilize, pollinate. [*Compare* IMPREGNATE.] —*See also* IMPROVE, SUPPLEMENT.
enrichment *n.* —*See* ENHANCEMENT.
enroll *v.* —*See* JOIN (1), LIST[1].
ensanguine *v.* To cover with blood ▸ bloodstain, bloody, incarnadine.
ensconce *v.* —*See* ESTABLISH (1), HIDE[1].
ensemble *n.* —*See* DRESS (2).
enshrine *v.* —*See* DEVOTE.
enshroud *v.* —*See* CONCEAL, WRAP (2).
ensign *n.* —*See* FLAG[1].
enslave *v.* To make subservient or subordinate ▸ dominate, enthrall, indenture, make tributary, subject, subjugate, subordinate, take captive. [*Compare* DEFEAT.]
enslavement *n.* —*See* SLAVERY.
ensnare *v.* —*See* CATCH (1).
ensnarement *n.* —*See* ENTANGLEMENT.
ensnarl *v.* —*See* CATCH (1), ENTANGLE.
ensue *v.* To occur as a consequence ▸ attend, follow, result. [*Compare* STEM.] —*See also* FOLLOW (1).
ensuing *adj.* —*See* FOLLOWING.
ensure *v.* —*See* GUARANTEE (2).
entail *v.* To have as a condition or a consequence ▸ carry, involve. —*See also* DEMAND (2), IMPLY.
entangle *v.* To twist together so that separation is or becomes difficult ▸ ensnarl, foul, mat, snarl, tangle. [*Compare* WEAVE.] —*See also* CATCH (1), COMPLICATE.
entanglement *n.* The condition of being entangled or implicated ▸ embranglement, embroilment, enmeshment, ensnarement, implication, involvement. —*See also* TANGLE.
entente *n.* —*See* COMBINATION, TREATY.
enter *v.* 1. To come or go into a place ▸ come in, go in, penetrate. ***Idioms:*** gain admittance (*or* entrance *or* entry), make an entrance, set foot in, walk through the door. 2. To gain entry into a computer network or database ▸ access, log in (*or* on). ***Idioms:*** gain access (*or* admittance *or* entry), get connected. —*See also* JOIN (1), LIST[1], PENETRATE, START (1).
enter into *v.* —*See* PARTICIPATE.
enterprise *n.* Something undertaken, especially something requiring extensive planning and work ▸ endeavor, project, undertaking, venture. [*Compare* TASK.] —*See also* ADVENTURE, BUSINESS (1), COMPANY (1), DRIVE (2).
enterprising *adj.* —*See* ADVENTUROUS, AMBITIOUS, ENERGETIC.
entertain *v.* To receive an idea and think about it in order to form an opinion about it ▸ consider, hear of, think about (of). —*See also* AMUSE, BEAR (2), PONDER.
entertaining *adj.* —*See* PLEASANT.
entertainment *n.* —*See* AMUSEMENT.
enthrall *v.* —*See* CHARM (2), ENSLAVE, GRIP.
enthralling *adj.* —*See* SEDUCTIVE.
enthrallment *n.* —*See* ABSORPTION (2).
enthuse *v.* —*See* RAVE.
enthusiasm *n.* 1. Passionate devotion to or interest in a cause or subject ▸ ardency, ardor, eagerness, excitation, excitement, fanaticism, fervor, fever, fire, passion, verve, vigor, zeal, zealousness. [*Compare* PASSION.] 2. A subject or activity that inspires lively interest ▸ craze, fad, fancy, hobbyhorse, infatuation, mania, passion, rage. [*Compare* FASHION, OBSESSION.] —*See also* OPTIMISM.
enthusiast *n.* —*See* DEVOTEE, FAN[2].
enthusiastic *adj.* Showing or having enthusiasm ▸ ardent, exuberant, fanatic, fanatical, fervent, fervid, keen, mad, obsessive, rabid, warm, zealous. *Informal:* crazy, gaga, wild. *Slang:* cuckoo, gung ho, nuts. [*Compare* EXTREME, PASSIONATE.] —*See also* OPTIMISTIC.

en·tice (ĕn-tīs′) ▸ *v.* **-ticed, -tic·ing.** To attract by arousing hope or desire; lure. **—en·tice′ment** *n.* **—en·tic′er** *n.* **—en·tic′ing·ly** *adv.*

en·tire (ĕn-tīr′) ▸ *adj.* **1.** Having no part excluded or left out. **2.** Complete: *gave us his entire attention.* **—en·tire′ly** *adv.*

en·tire·ty (ĕn-tī′rĭ-tē, -tīr′tē) ▸ *n., pl.* **-ties. 1.** Wholeness. **2.** The entire amount or extent.

en·ti·tle (ĕn-tīt′l) ▸ *v.* **-tled, -tling. 1.** To give a name to. **2.** To furnish with a right or claim to something. **—en·ti′tle·ment** *n.*

en·ti·ty (ĕn′tĭ-tē) ▸ *n., pl.* **-ties. 1.** Something that exists as a particular and discrete unit. **2.** The fact of existence; being.

en·tomb (ĕn-to͞om′) ▸ *v.* **1.** To place in or as if in a tomb or grave. **2.** To serve as a tomb for. **—en·tomb′ment** *n.*

en·to·mol·o·gy (ĕn′tə-mŏl′ə-jē) ▸ *n.* The scientific study of insects. **—en′to·mo·log′ic** (-mə-lŏj′ĭk), **en′to·mo·log′i·cal** *adj.* **—en′to·mol′o·gist** *n.*

en·tou·rage (ŏn′to͞o-räzh′) ▸ *n.* A group of attendants or associates; retinue.

en·tr'acte (ŏn′trăkt′, äɴ-träkt′) ▸ *n.* **1.** The interval between two acts of a theatrical performance. **2.** Another performance, as of music or dance, provided between two acts of a theatrical performance.

en·trails (ĕn′trālz′, -trəlz) ▸ *pl.n.* The internal organs, esp. the intestines.

en·train (ĕn-trān′) ▸ *v.* To go or put aboard a train.

en·trance¹ (ĕn′trəns) ▸ *n.* **1.** The act or an instance of entering. **2.** A means or point by which to enter. **3.** Permission or power to enter; admission.

en·trance² (ĕn-trăns′) ▸ *v.* **-tranced, -tranc·ing. 1.** To put into a trance. **2.** To fill with delight, wonder, or enchantment. **—en·trance′ment** *n.* **—en·tranc′ing·ly** *adv.*

en·trant (ĕn′trənt) ▸ *n.* One that enters a competition.

en·trap (ĕn-trăp′) ▸ *v.* **-trapped, -trap·ping. 1.** To catch in or as if in a trap. **2.** To lure into danger or a compromising situation. **—en·trap′ment** *n.*

en·treat (ĕn-trēt′) ▸ *v.* To make an earnest request of; plead. **—en·treat′ing·ly** *adv.* **—en·treat′ment** *n.*

en·treat·y (ĕn-trē′tē) ▸ *n., pl.* **-ies.** An earnest request; plea.

en·trée or **en·tree** (ŏn′trā, ŏn-trā′) ▸ *n.* **1.** The main dish of a meal. **2.** The power or liberty to enter.

en·trench (ĕn-trĕnch′) ▸ *v.* **1.** To dig or provide with a trench. **2.** To fix (e.g., an idea or custom) firmly. **3.** To encroach or trespass. **—en·trench′ment** *n.*

en·tre·pre·neur (ŏn′trə-prə-nûr′, -no͝or′) ▸ *n.* A person who organizes, operates, and assumes the risk for a business venture. **—en′tre·pre·neur′i·al** *adj.* **—en′tre·pre·neur′ism** *n.* **—en′tre·pre·neur′ship′** *n.*

en·tro·py (ĕn′trə-pē) ▸ *n., pl.* **-pies. 1.** For a closed thermodynamic system, a measure of the amount of thermal energy not available to do work. **2.** A measure of the disorder or randomness of a system. **—en·tro′pic** (ĕn-trō′pĭk, -trŏp′ĭk) *adj.*

en·trust (ĕn-trŭst′) also **in·trust** (ĭn-) ▸ *v.* **1.** To give over (something) to another for care, protection, or performance. **2.** To give as a trust to (someone).

en·try (ĕn′trē) ▸ *n., pl.* **-tries. 1.** The act or an instance of entering. **2.** A means by which to enter. **3a.** The inclusion of an item, as in a record. **b.** An item entered in this way. **4.** An entry word, as in a dictionary; headword. **5.** One entered in a competition.

en·twine (ĕn-twīn′) ▸ *v.* **-twined, -twin·ing.** To twine around or together.

e·nu·mer·ate (ĭ-no͞o′mə-rāt′, ĭ-nyo͞o′-) ▸ *v.* **-at·ed, -at·ing. 1.** To name one by one; list. **2.** To determine the number of; count. **—e·nu′mer·a′tion** *n.* **—e·nu′mer·a′tive** (-mə-rā′tĭv, -mər-ə-) *adj.* **—e·nu′mer·a′tor** *n.*

e·nun·ci·ate (ĭ-nŭn′sē-āt′) ▸ *v.* **-at·ed, -at·ing. 1.** To pronounce, esp. with clarity; articulate. **2.** To announce; proclaim. **—e·nun′ci·a′tion** *n.* **—e·nun′ci·a′tor** *n.*

en·vel·op (ĕn-vĕl′əp) ▸ *v.* **-oped, -op·ing.** To enclose completely with or as if with a covering. **—en·vel′op·er** *n.* **—en·vel′op·ment** *n.*

en·ve·lope (ĕn′və-lōp′, ŏn′-) ▸ *n.* **1.** A flat, folded paper container, esp. for a letter. **2.** Something that envelops or encloses. **3.** The bag containing the gas in a balloon or airship.

en·ven·om (ĕn-vĕn′əm) ▸ *v.* **1.** To make poisonous or noxious. **2.** To embitter.

en·vi·a·ble (ĕn′vē-ə-bəl) ▸ *adj.* So desirable as to arouse envy. **—en′vi·a·bly** *adv.*

en·vi·ous (ĕn′vē-əs) ▸ *adj.* Feeling, expressing, or characterized by envy. **—en′vi·ous·ly** *adv.* **—en′vi·ous·ness** *n.*

en·vi·ron·ment (ĕn-vī′rən-mənt, -vī′ərn-) ▸ *n.* **1.** The circumstances or conditions that surround one; surroundings. **2.** The totality of circumstances surrounding an organism or a group of organisms. **—en·vi′ron·men′tal** *adj.* **—en·vi′ron·men′tal·ly** *adv.*

en·vi·ron·men·tal·ism (ĕn-vī′rən-mĕn′tl-ĭz′əm, -vī′ərn-) ▸ *n.* Advocacy for or work toward protecting the natural environment from destruction or pollution. **—en·vi′ron·men′tal·ist** *n.*

en·vi·rons (ĕn-vī′rənz, -vī′ərnz) ▸ *pl.n.* A surrounding area, esp. of a city.

en·vis·age (ĕn-vĭz′ĭj) ▸ *v.* **-aged, -ag·ing.** To conceive an image or picture of, esp. as a future possibility.

en·vi·sion (ĕn-vĭzh′ən) ▸ *v.* To picture in the mind; imagine.

THESAURUS

entice *v.* —*See* ATTRACT, SEDUCE.

enticement *n.* —*See* ATTRACTION, LURE (1).

enticer *n.* —*See* SEDUCER (1).

enticing *adj.* —*See* ATTRACTIVE, DESIRABLE, SEDUCTIVE.

entire *adj.* —*See* COMPLETE (1), GOOD (2).

entirely *adv.* —*See* COMPLETELY (1).

entirety *n.* —*See* COMPLETENESS, WHOLE.

entitle *v.* —*See* AUTHORIZE, NAME (1).

entitlement *n.* —*See* LICENSE (1), RIGHT.

entity *n.* —*See* EXISTENCE, SYSTEM, THING (1).

entomb *v.* —*See* BURY.

entombment *n.* —*See* BURIAL.

entourage *n.* —*See* RETINUE.

entrails *n.* —*See* VISCERA.

entrance¹ *n.* The act of entering ▸ entry, incoming, ingress, ingression, penetration. —*See also* ADMISSION.

entrance² *v.* —*See* CHARM (1), CHARM (2).

entrancing *adj.* —*See* SEDUCTIVE.

entrap *v.* —*See* CATCH (1).

entreat *v.* —*See* APPEAL (1).

entreaty *n.* —*See* APPEAL.

entrée *n.* —*See* ADMISSION.

entrench *v.* —*See* FIX (2).

entrenched *adj.* —*See* CONFIRMED (1).

entrenchment *n.* —*See* TRESPASS (2).

entrepreneur *n.* —*See* DEALER.

entrust *v.* **1.** To put in the charge of another for care, use, or performance ▸ commend, commit, confide, consign, delegate, give (over), hand over, relegate, remand, remit, trust, turn over. *Idioms:* give in trust (*or* charge), give (*or* put) into custody. **2.** To place a trust upon ▸ charge, trust. [*Compare* AUTHORIZE.]

entry *n.* An item inserted, as in a diary, register, or reference book ▸ heading, headword, insertion, item, lemma, minute, note, posting, record. —*See also* ADMISSION, ENTRANCE¹.

entwine *v.* —*See* WEAVE, WIND².

enumerate *v.* To name or specify one by one ▸ count off, inventory, itemize, list, numerate, tick off. —*See also* COUNT (2).

enumeration *n.* —*See* COUNT (1).

enunciate *v.* —*See* ASSERT, PRONOUNCE.

enunciation *n.* —*See* VOICING.

envelop *v.* —*See* ENCLOSE (2), WRAP (1), WRAP (2).

envelope *n.* —*See* WRAPPER.

envenom *v.* —*See* POISON.

envious *adj.* Resentfully or painfully desirous of another's advantages ▸ begrudging, covetous, grudging, invidious, jaundiced, jealous. *Idiom:* green with envy.

enviousness *n.* —*See* ENVY.

environ *v.* —*See* SURROUND.

environment *n.* **1.** A surrounding area ▸ environs, locale, locality, neighborhood, precincts, purlieu, surroundings, vicinity. [*Compare* LIMITS, OUTSKIRTS.] **2.** The surrounding conditions and circumstances affecting growth or development ▸ ambiance, atmosphere, climate, context, medium, milieu, mise en scène, surroundings, world. **3.** The ecological circumstances in which organisms live ▸ biome, biosphere, ecosphere, ecosystem, habitat, natural world, nature, world. [*Compare* HABITAT, UNIVERSE.] —*See also* CONDITIONS.

environs *n.* —*See* ENVIRONMENT (1), OUTSKIRTS.

envisage *v.* —*See* IMAGINE.

envision *v.* —*See* FORESEE, IMAGINE.

en·voy[1] (ĕn′voi′, ŏn′-) ▸ *n.* **1.** A representative of a government who is sent on a special diplomatic mission. **2.** A messenger; agent.

en·voy[2] also **en·voi** (ĕn′voi′, ŏn′-) ▸ *n.* A short closing stanza in certain verse forms dedicating the poem to a patron or summarizing its main ideas.

en·vy (ĕn′vē) ▸ *n., pl.* **-vies. 1.** Discontent and resentment aroused by desire for the possessions or qualities of another. **2.** The object of such feeling. ▸ *v.* **-vied, -vy·ing.** To feel envy toward. **—en′vi·er** *n.*

en·zyme (ĕn′zīm) ▸ *n.* Any of numerous proteins that are produced by living organisms and function as biochemical catalysts. **—en′zy·mat′ic** (-zə-măt′ĭk) *adj.*

eo– ▸ *pref.* Most primitive; earliest: *Eocene.*

E·o·cene (ē′ə-sēn′) *Geol.* ▸ *adj.* Of or being the 2nd epoch of the Tertiary Period, marked by the rise of mammals. ▸ *n.* The Eocene Epoch.

e·o·li·an (ē-ō′lē-ən, ē-ōl′yən) ▸ *adj.* Relating to, caused by, or carried by the wind.

e·on also **ae·on** (ē′ŏn′, ē′ən) ▸ *n.* **1.** An indefinitely long period of time; age. **2.** The longest division of geologic time, containing two or more eras.

E·os (ē′ŏs′) ▸ *n. Gk. Myth.* The goddess of the dawn.

e·o·sin (ē′ə-sən) ▸ *n.* An acidic dye, used in biology to stain cells.

–eous ▸ *suff.* Characterized by; resembling: *beauteous.*

ep·au·let also **ep·au·lette** (ĕp′ə-lĕt′, ĕp′ə-lĕt′) ▸ *n.* A shoulder ornament, esp. a fringed strap on a uniform.

é·pée also **e·pee** (ā-pā′, ĕp′ā) ▸ *n.* A fencing sword with a bowl-shaped guard and a long narrow blade that has no cutting edge.

e·phed·rine (ĭ-fĕd′rĭn, ĕf′ĭ-drēn′) ▸ *n.* A white odorless alkaloid, $C_{10}H_{15}NO$, used in the treatment of allergies and asthma.

e·phem·er·al (ĭ-fĕm′ər-əl) ▸ *adj.* Lasting for a brief time; fleeting; evanescent. **—e·phem′er·al·ly** *adv.*

E·phe·sian (ĭ-fē′zhən) ▸ *n.* **1.** A native or inhabitant of ancient Ephesus. **2. Ephesians** *(takes sing. v.)* See **Bible** table in Appendix. **—E·phe′sian** *adj.*

epi– or **ep–** ▸ *pref.* **1.** On; upon: *epiphyte.* **2.** Over; above: *epicenter.* **3.** Around; covering: *epithelium.*

ep·ic (ĕp′ĭk) ▸ *n.* **1.** A long narrative poem celebrating the feats of a traditional hero. **2.** A literary or dramatic work that suggests the characteristics of epic poetry. ▸ *adj.* **1.** Of or resembling an epic; heroic; grand. **2.** Of great size or duration.

ep·i·cene (ĕp′ĭ-sēn′) ▸ *adj.* **1.** Having the characteristics of both the male and the female. **2.** Effeminate. **3.** Sexless. ▸ *n.* One that is epicene.

ep·i·cen·ter (ĕp′ĭ-sĕn′tər) ▸ *n.* The point of the earth's surface directly above the focus of an earthquake.

Ep·ic·te·tus (ĕp′ĭk-tē′təs) (A.D. 55?–135?) ▸ Phrygian-born Stoic philosopher.

ep·i·cure (ĕp′ĭ-kyŏŏr′) ▸ *n.* A person with refined taste, esp. in food.

ep·i·cu·re·an (ĕp′ĭ-kyŏŏ-rē′ən, -kyŏŏr′ē-) ▸ *adj.* **1.** Devoted to the pursuit of pleasure. **2.** Suited to the tastes of an epicure. **—ep′i·cu·re′an** *n.*

Ep·i·cu·rus (ĕp′ĭ-kyŏŏr′əs) (341?–270 B.C.) ▸ Greek philosopher.

ep·i·dem·ic (ĕp′ĭ-dĕm′ĭk) ▸ *adj.* Spreading rapidly among many individuals in an area. ▸ *n.* **1.** A contagious disease that spreads rapidly. **2.** A rapid spread or development.

ep·i·der·mis (ĕp′ĭ-dûr′mĭs) ▸ *n.* The outer, protective layer of the skin. **—ep′i·der′mal** *adj.*

ep·i·du·ral (ĕp′ĭ-dŏŏr′əl, -dyŏŏr′-) ▸ *adj.* Located on or over the dura mater. ▸ *n.* An injection, esp. of an anesthetic, into the epidural space of the spine.

ep·i·glot·tis (ĕp′ĭ-glŏt′ĭs) ▸ *n.* The elastic flap of cartilage located at the root of the tongue that prevents food from entering the windpipe during swallowing.

ep·i·gram (ĕp′ĭ-grăm′) ▸ *n.* A short witty poem or remark. **—ep′i·gram·mat′ic** *adj.*

ep·i·graph (ĕp′ĭ-grăf′) ▸ *n.* **1.** An inscription, as on a statue or building. **2.** A motto or quotation, as at the beginning of a book, setting forth a theme. **—ep′i·graph′ic** *adj.*

e·pig·ra·phy (ĭ-pĭg′rə-fē) ▸ *n.* The study esp. of ancient inscriptions. **—e·pig′ra·pher** *n.*

ep·i·lep·sy (ĕp′ə-lĕp′sē) ▸ *n.* Any of various neurological disorders marked by loss of consciousness or convulsive seizures. **—ep′i·lep′tic** *adj. & n.*

ep·i·logue (ĕp′ə-lôg′, -lŏg′) ▸ *n.* **1.** A short poem or speech spoken directly to the audience at the end of a play. **2.** A short section at the end of a literary or dramatic work, often discussing the future of its characters; afterword.

ep·i·neph·rine also **ep·i·neph·rin** (ĕp′ə-nĕf′rĭn) ▸ *n.* **1.** An adrenal hormone that constricts blood vessels and raises blood pressure; adrenaline. **2.** A crystalline compound, $C_9H_{13}NO_3$, used as a heart stimulant, vasoconstrictor, and bronchial relaxant.

e·piph·a·ny (ĭ-pĭf′ə-nē) ▸ *n., pl.* **-nies. 1. Epiphany** A Christian feast observed on Jan. 6 celebrating the visit of the Magi to Jesus. **2.** A revelatory manifestation esp. of a divine being.

ep·i·phyte (ĕp′ə-fīt′) ▸ *n.* A plant, such as Spanish moss or a tropical orchid, that grows on another plant or object that provides support but not nutrients. **—ep′i·phyt′ic** (-fĭt′ĭk) *adj.*

e·pis·co·pa·cy (ĭ-pĭs′kə-pə-sē) ▸ *n., pl.* **-cies. 1.** See **episcopate** 3. **2.** A system of church government that is headed by bishops.

e·pis·co·pal (ĭ-pĭs′kə-pəl) ▸ *adj.* **1.** Of or relating to a bishop. **2.** Governed by bishops. **3. Episcopal** Of the Episcopal Church.

Episcopal Church ▸ *n.* The church in the US that is in communion with the see of Canterbury.

E·pis·co·pa·lian (ĭ-pĭs′kə-pā′lē-ən, -pāl′yən) ▸ *adj.* Of or belonging to the Episcopal Church. **—E·pis′co·pa′lian** *n.*

e·pis·co·pate (ĭ-pĭs′kə-pĭt, -pāt′) ▸ *n.* **1.** The position, term, or office of a bishop. **2.** The jurisdiction of a bishop; diocese. **3.** Bishops collectively.

e·pis·i·ot·o·my (ĭ-pĭz′ē-ŏt′ə-mē, ĭ-pē′zē-) ▸ *n., pl.* **-mies.** Surgical incision of the perineum during childbirth to ease delivery.

ep·i·sode (ĕp′ĭ-sōd′) ▸ *n.* **1.** An incident in the course of an experience. **2.** An incident that forms a unit in a narrative or dramatic work. **—ep′i·sod′ic** (-sŏd′ĭk) *adj.*

e·pis·te·mol·o·gy (ĭ-pĭs′tə-mŏl′ə-jē) ▸ *n.* The branch of philosophy that studies the nature and theory of knowledge. **—e·pis′te·mo·log′i·cal** *adj.* **—e·pis′te·mol′o·gist** *n.*

THESAURUS

envoy[1] *n.* —*See* MESSENGER, REPRESENTATIVE.

envoy[2] *n.* —*See* END (2).

envy *n.* Resentful or painful desire for another's advantages ▸ covetousness, enviousness, green-eyed monster, jaundice, jealousy. [*Compare* RESENTMENT.]

envy *v.* To feel envy toward or for ▸ begrudge, covet, grudge.

enwrap *v.* —*See* WRAP (2).

eon or **aeon** *n.* —*See* AGES.

ephemeral *adj.* —*See* TRANSITORY.

epicene *adj.* —*See* ANDROGYNOUS, EFFEMINATE.

epicenism *n.* The quality of being androgynous ▸ androgyny, gender neutrality, sexlessness. [*Compare* EFFEMINACY, MASCULINITY.]

epicure *n.* —*See* SYBARITE.

epicurean *adj.* **1.** Characterized by or devoted to pleasure and luxury as a lifestyle ▸ hedonic, hedonistic, sybaritic, voluptuary, voluptuous. [*Compare* LUXURIOUS, SENSUAL.] **2.** Relating to, suggestive of, or appealing to sense gratification ▸ sensual, sensuous, sensualistic, voluptuous.

epicurean *n.* —*See* SYBARITE.

epidemic *n.* —*See* ERUPTION.

epidemic *adj.* —*See* PREVAILING.

epidermis *n.* The tissue forming the external covering of the body ▸ integument, skin.

epigrammatic or **epigrammatical** *adj.* —*See* PITHY.

epilogue *n.* —*See* END (2).

episcopal *adj.* —*See* CLERICAL.

episode *n.* —*See* CIRCUMSTANCE (1), EVENT (1).

episodic *adj.* Happening or appearing consistently or repeatedly ▸ recurrent, regular, repeating, repetitive. [*Compare* PERIODIC, PERVASIVE, THEMATIC.] —*See also* INTERMITTENT.

e·pis·tle (ĭ-pĭs′əl) ▸ *n.* **1.** A letter, esp. a formal one. **2.** **Epistle** *Bible* A letter written by an Apostle and included in the New Testament. **—e·pis′to·lar′y** (-tə-lĕr′ē) *adj.*

ep·i·taph (ĕp′ĭ-tăf′) ▸ *n.* An inscription, as on a tombstone, in memory of a deceased person.

ep·i·the·li·um (ĕp′ə-thē′lē-əm) ▸ *n., pl.* **-li·ums** or **-li·a** (-lē-ə). A membranous tissue composed of one or more layers of cells that covers most internal and external surfaces of the body and its organs. **—ep′i·the′li·al** *adj.*

ep·i·thet (ĕp′ə-thĕt′) ▸ *n.* A term, often abusive or contemptuous, used to characterize a person or thing.

e·pit·o·me (ĭ-pĭt′ə-mē) ▸ *n.* **1.** A typical or perfect example of its kind. **2.** A brief summary.

e·pit·o·mize (ĭ-pĭt′ə-mīz′) ▸ *v.* **-mized, -miz·ing.** **1.** To make an epitome of; sum up. **2.** To be a typical example of; embody.

ep·och (ĕp′ək, ē′pŏk′) ▸ *n.* **1.** A particular period of history, esp. one that is noteworthy; era. **2.** A unit of geologic time that is a division of a period. **—ep′och·al** *adj.*

ep·o·nym (ĕp′ə-nĭm′) ▸ *n.* A real or mythical person whose name is the source of the name of something, such as an era or city. **—e·pon′y·mous** (ĭ-pŏn′ə-məs) *adj.*

ep·ox·y (ĭ-pŏk′sē) ▸ *n., pl.* **-ies.** Any of various usu. thermosetting resins used esp. in surface coatings and adhesives. **—ep·ox′y** *v.*

ep·si·lon (ĕp′sə-lŏn′, -lən) ▸ *n.* The 5th letter of the Greek alphabet.

Ep·som salts (ĕp′səm) ▸ *pl.n.* *(takes sing. v.)* Hydrated magnesium sulfate, used as a cathartic and to reduce inflammation.

eq·ua·ble (ĕk′wə-bəl, ē′kwə-) ▸ *adj.* **1.** Unvarying; steady. **2.** Even-tempered. **—eq′ua·bil′i·ty** *n.* **—eq′ua·bly** *adv.*

e·qual (ē′kwəl) ▸ *adj.* **1.** Having the same capability, quantity, effect, measure, or value as another. **2.** *Math.* Being identical to in value. **3.** Having the same privileges, status, or rights. **4.** Having the requisite qualities for a task or situation. ▸ *n.* One that is equal to another. ▸ *v.* **e·qualed, e·qual·ing** or **e·qualled, e·qual·ling.** **1.** To be equal to, esp. in value. **2.** To do, make, or produce something equal to: *equaled the world record.* **—e·qual′i·ty** (ĭ-kwŏl′ĭ-tē) *n.* **—e′qual·ly** *adv.*

e·qual·ize (ē′kwə-līz′) ▸ *v.* **-ized, -iz·ing.** To make equal, uniform, or balanced. **—e′qual·i·za′tion** *n.* **—e′qual·iz′er** *n.*

equal sign ▸ *n.* The symbol (=) used to indicate mathematical equality.

e·qua·nim·i·ty (ē′kwə-nĭm′ĭ-tē, ĕk′wə-) ▸ *n.* Calmness; composure.

e·quate (ĭ-kwāt′) ▸ *v.* **e·quat·ed, e·quat·ing.** To make, treat, or regard as equal or equivalent.

e·qua·tion (ĭ-kwā′zhən, -shən) ▸ *n.* **1.** The act or process of equating or the condition of being equated. **2.** A statement, as in mathematics, that two expressions are equal. **3.** A complex of variable elements or factors.

e·qua·tor (ĭ-kwā′tər) ▸ *n.* **1.** The imaginary great circle around the earth's surface, equidistant from the poles and perpendicular to the earth's axis of rotation, that divides the earth into the Northern Hemisphere and the Southern Hemisphere. **2.** A similar great circle on a celestial body. **—e′qua·to′ri·al** (ē′kwə-tôr′ē-əl, ĕk′wə-) *adj.*

Equatorial Guinea ▸ A country of W-central Africa including islands in the Gulf of Guinea.

eq·uer·ry (ĕk′wə-rē) ▸ *n., pl.* **-ries.** **1.** An attendant to the British royal household. **2.** An officer in charge of the horses in a royal or noble household.

e·ques·tri·an (ĭ-kwĕs′trē-ən) ▸ *adj.* **1.** Of or relating to horseback riding. **2.** Depicted or represented on horseback. ▸ *n.* One who rides a horse or performs on horseback. **—e·ques′tri·an·ism** *n.*

equi– ▸ *pref.* Equal; equally: *equiangular.*

e·qui·an·gu·lar (ē′kwē-ăng′gyə-lər, ĕk′wē-) ▸ *adj.* Having all angles equal.

e·qui·dis·tant (ē′kwĭ-dĭs′tənt, ĕk′wĭ-) ▸ *adj.* Equally distant. **—e′qui·dis′tance** *n.*

e·qui·lat·er·al (ē′kwə-lăt′ər-əl, ĕk′wə-) ▸ *adj.* Having all sides equal. **—e′qui·lat′er·al** *n.*

e·qui·lib·ri·um (ē′kwə-lĭb′rē-əm, ĕk′wə-) ▸ *n.* A condition of balance between opposed forces, influences, or actions.

e·quine (ē′kwīn′, ĕk′wīn′) ▸ *adj.* **1.** Of or like a horse. **2.** Of the taxonomic family which includes the horses, asses, and zebras. **—e′quine′** *n.*

e·qui·noc·tial (ē′kwə-nŏk′shəl, ĕk′wə-) ▸ *adj.* Relating to an equinox.

e·qui·nox (ē′kwə-nŏks′, ĕk′wə-) ▸ *n.* Either of the two times during a year when the sun crosses the celestial equator and when the length of day and night are approx. equal.

e·quip (ĭ-kwĭp′) ▸ *v.* **e·quipped, e·quip·ping.** To supply with the necessary materials for an undertaking.

e·quip·ment (ĭ-kwĭp′mənt) ▸ *n.* **1.** The act of equipping or the state of being equipped. **2.** The things with which one is equipped.

e·qui·poise (ē′kwə-poiz′, ĕk′wə-) ▸ *n.* **1.** Equality in distribution, as of weight. **2.** A counterbalance.

eq·ui·ta·ble (ĕk′wĭ-tə-bəl) ▸ *adj.* Just and fair; impartial. **—eq′ui·ta·ble·ness** *n.* **—eq′ui·ta·bly** *adv.*

eq·ui·ta·tion (ĕk′wĭ-tā′shən) ▸ *n.* The art and practice of riding a horse.

eq·ui·ty (ĕk′wĭ-tē) ▸ *n., pl.* **-ties.** **1.** The state or quality of being just, impartial, and fair. **2.** Something that is equitable. **3.** *Law* A system of rules and principles supplementing civil and common law. **4.** The residual value of a business or property beyond any mortgage or liability. **5.** Corporate stock.

e·quiv·a·lent (ĭ-kwĭv′ə-lənt) ▸ *adj.* **1.** Equal. **2.** Similar or identical in function or effect. **—e·quiv′a·lence, e·quiv′a·len·cy** *n.* **—e·quiv′a·lent** *n.* **—e·quiv′a·lent·ly** *adv.*

e·quiv·o·cal (ĭ-kwĭv′ə-kəl) ▸ *adj.* **1.** Ambiguous. **2.** Ques-

THESAURUS

epistle *n.* —*See* LETTER.

epithet *n.* —*See* NAME (1), SWEARWORD.

epitome *n.* An ideally representative example of a type ▸ archetype, exemplar, mirror, model, paragon, pattern, prototype. [*Compare* MODEL.] —*See also* SYNOPSIS.

epitomize *v.* —*See* REPRESENT (1), REVIEW (1).

epizoic *adj.* —*See* PARASITIC.

epoch *n.* —*See* AGE (2).

equable *adj.* —*See* UNCHANGING.

equal *adj.* Agreeing exactly in value, quantity, or effect ▸ coequal, equipollent, equivalent, even, identical, same, tantamount. ***Idioms:*** on a par, one and the same. [*Compare* LIKE[2].] —*See also* ELIGIBLE, FAIR[1] (1).

equal *n.* —*See* PEER[2].

equal *v.* **1.** To be equal or alike ▸ amount, be equivalent, be tantamount, compare, constitute, correspond, match, measure up, parallel, touch. *Informal:* stack up. ***Idioms:*** be one and the same as, have all the earmarks of, keep pace with. [*Compare* RESEMBLE.] **2.** To do or make something equal to ▸ match, meet, tie.

equality *n.* —*See* EQUIVALENCE.

equalize *v.* To make equal ▸ align, democratize, equate, even, level (off), square, symmetrize. ***Idiom:*** put in line. [*Compare* CONVENTIONALIZE, EVEN[1].] —*See also* BALANCE (1).

equanimity *n.* —*See* BALANCE (2).

equate *v.* —*See* EQUALIZE, LIKEN.

equation *n.* —*See* EQUIVALENCE.

equidistant *adj.* —*See* CENTRAL.

equilibrium *n.* —*See* BALANCE (1).

equip *v.* —*See* FURNISH.

equipment *n.* —*See* DEVICE (1), OUTFIT.

equipoise *n.* —*See* BALANCE (1).

equipollent *adj.* —*See* EQUAL.

equitable *adj.* —*See* FAIR[1] (1).

equitableness *n.* —*See* FAIRNESS.

equitably *adv.* —*See* FAIRLY (1).

equity *n.* The state, action, or principle of treating all persons equally in accordance with the law ▸ due process, justice. [*Compare* FAIRNESS.]

equivalence *n.* The state of being equivalent ▸ coequality, equality, equation, equivalency, par, parity, sameness. [*Compare* LIKENESS, SAMENESS.]

equivalency *n.* —*See* EQUIVALENCE.

equivalent *adj.* —*See* EQUAL, LIKE[2], PROPORTIONAL (1).

equivalent *n.* One that has the same functions and characteristics as another ▸ counterpart, opposite number, vis-à-vis. —*See also* PEER[2].

equivocal *adj.* Deliberately ambiguous or vague ▸ elusive, evasive, indirect, misleading. —*See also* AMBIGUOUS (1), AMBIGUOUS (2), SHADY (1).

tionable or inconclusive. **—e·quiv′o·cal·ly** *adv.*

e·quiv·o·cate (ĭ-kwĭv′ə-kāt′) ▸ *v.* **-cat·ed, -cat·ing.** To use ambiguous language; hedge. **—e·quiv′o·ca′tion** *n.* **—e·quiv′o·ca′tor** *n.*

Er ▸ The symbol for the element **erbium.**

ER ▸ *abbr.* emergency room

–er[1] ▸ *suff.* **1a.** One that performs a specified action: *swimmer.* **b.** One that undergoes a specified action: *broiler.* **c.** One that has: *ten-pounder.* **d.** One associated or involved with: *banker.* **2a.** Native or resident of: *New Yorker.* **b.** One that is: *foreigner.*

–er[2] ▸ *suff.* Used to form the comparative degree of adjectives and adverbs: *darker; faster.*

e·ra (îr′ə, ĕr′ə) ▸ *n.* **1.** A period of time using a specific date in history as a basis. **2.** A period of time characterized by a particular circumstance, event, or person. **3.** The longest division of geologic time, made up of one or more periods.

ERA ▸ *abbr.* **1.** earned run average **2.** Equal Rights Amendment

e·rad·i·cate (ĭ-răd′ĭ-kāt′) ▸ *v.* **-cat·ed, -cat·ing.** To get rid of or remove completely; uproot. **—e·rad′i·ca·ble** *adj.* **—e·rad′i·ca′tion** *n.* **—e·rad′i·ca′tor** *n.*

e·rase (ĭ-rās′) ▸ *v.* **e·rased, e·ras·ing. 1.** To remove (e.g., something written) by or as if by rubbing. **2.** To remove (recorded material) from a magnetic tape or diskette. **3.** To remove all traces of. **—e·ras′a·ble** *adj.* **—e·ras′er** *n.* **—e·ra′sure** *n.*

er·bi·um (ûr′bē-əm) ▸ *n. Symbol* **Er** A soft, malleable, silvery rare-earth element. At. no. 68.

ere (âr) ▸ *prep.* Previous to; before. ▸ *conj.* Rather than; before.

Er·e·bus (ĕr′ə-bəs), **Mount** ▸ A volcanic peak, 3,796.6 m (12,448 ft), on Ross I. in Antarctica.

e·rect (ĭ-rĕkt′) ▸ *adj.* **1.** Being in a vertical, upright position. **2.** *Physiol.* Stiff; rigid. ▸ *v.* **1.** To build or construct. **2.** To raise upright. **3.** To set up; establish. **—e·rect′ly** *adv.* **—e·rect′ness** *n.* **—e·rec′tor** *n.*

e·rec·tile (ĭ-rĕk′təl, -tīl′) ▸ *adj. Physiol.* Of or relating to vascular tissue that is capable of filling with blood and becoming rigid.

e·rec·tion (ĭ-rĕk′shən) ▸ *n.* **1.** The act of erecting or the state of being erected. **2.** *Physiol.* The condition of erectile tissue when filled with blood.

ere·long (âr-lông′, -lŏng′) ▸ *adv.* Before long; soon.

er·e·mite (âr′ə-mīt′) ▸ *n.* A hermit, esp. a religious recluse.

erg (ûrg) ▸ *n.* A unit of energy or work equal to 10^{-7} joule.

er·go (ûr′gō, âr′-) ▸ *conj. & adv.* Consequently; therefore.

er·go·nom·ics (ûr′gə-nŏm′ĭks) ▸ *n.* *(takes sing. v.)* The applied science of equipment design intended to reduce operator fatigue and discomfort. **—er′go·nom′ic, er′go·no·met′ric** *adj.*

er·got (ûr′gət, -gŏt′) ▸ *n.* **1.** A fungus that infects rye and other cereal plants. **2.** The disease caused by such a fungus. **3.** A drug or medicine made from dried ergot.

Er·ic·son (ĕr′ĭk-sən), **Leif** (fl. c. 1000) ▸ Norwegian navigator.

Er·ic the Red (ĕr′ĭk) (fl. 10th cent.) ▸ Norwegian navigator.

E·rie (îr′ē) ▸ *n., pl.* **E·rie** or **E·ries. 1.** A member of a Native American people formerly inhabiting the S shore of Lake Erie. **2.** The Iroquoian language of the Erie.

Erie, Lake ▸ One of the Great Lakes, bounded by S Ontario, W NY, NW PA, N OH, and SE MI.

Erie Canal ▸ An artificial waterway extending about 579 km (360 mi) across central NY from Albany to Buffalo; now part of the New York State Barge Canal.

Er·in (ĕr′ĭn) ▸ A poetic name for Ireland.

Er·i·tre·a (ĕr′ĭ-trē′ə) ▸ A country N of Ethiopia bordering on the Red Sea; it was part of Ethiopia from 1952–93. **—Er′i·tre′an** *adj. & n.*

er·mine (ûr′mĭn) ▸ *n.* **1.** A weasel having dark brown fur that in winter changes to white. **2.** The white fur of this animal.

e·rode (ĭ-rōd′) ▸ *v.* **e·rod·ed, e·rod·ing. 1.** To wear away or destroy gradually by or as if by abrasion. **2.** To eat into or away; corrode. **—e·rod′i·ble** *adj.*

e·rog·e·nous (ĭ-rŏj′ə-nəs) ▸ *adj.* **1.** Responsive to sexual stimulation. **2.** Arousing sexual desire.

Er·os (ĕr′ŏs′, îr′-) ▸ *n. Gk. Myth.* The god of love, son of Aphrodite.

e·ro·sion (ĭ-rō′zhən) ▸ *n.* The process of eroding or the condition of being eroded. **—e·ro′sive** *adj.* **—e·ro′sive·ness** *n.*

e·rot·ic (ĭ-rŏt′ĭk) ▸ *adj.* **1.** Of, concerning, or tending to arouse sexual desire. **2.** Dominated by sexual desire. **—e·rot′i·cal·ly** *adv.* **—e·rot′i·cism** *n.*

e·rot·i·ca (ĭ-rŏt′ĭ-kə) ▸ *pl.n.* *(takes sing. or pl. v.)* Literature or art intended to arouse sexual desire.

err (ûr, ĕr) ▸ *v.* **1.** To make an error or mistake. **2.** To sin.

er·rand (ĕr′ənd) ▸ *n.* **1.** A short trip taken to perform a specified task. **2.** The purpose or object of an errand.

er·rant (ĕr′ənt) ▸ *adj.* **1.** Roving, esp. in search of adventure. **2.** Straying from proper moral standards. **3.** Roving aimlessly. **—er′rant·ly** *adv.* **—er′rant·ry** *n.*

er·rat·ic (ĭ-răt′ĭk) ▸ *adj.* **1.** Lacking consistency or uniformity; irregular. **2.** Unconventional; eccentric. **—er·rat′i·cal·ly** *adv.*

THESAURUS

equivocality or **equivocalness** *n.* —*See* AMBIGUITY, VAGUENESS.

equivocate *v.* **1.** To use evasive or deliberately vague language ▸ euphemize, fence, hedge, shuffle, tergiversate, weasel. *Informal:* pussyfoot, waffle. ***Idioms:*** beat about (*or* around) the bush, give one the runaround, hem and haw, mince words. [*Compare* EVADE.] **2.** To stray from truthfulness or sincerity ▸ palter, prevaricate, shuffle. ***Idiom:*** bend (*or* stretch) the truth. [*Compare* DISTORT, LIE[2].]

equivocation *n.* The use of an instance of equivocal language ▸ ambiguity, distortion, equivoque, euphemism, fence, hedge, misrepresentation, prevarication, shuffle, tergiversation, weasel word. *Informal:* waffle. [*Compare* LIE[2].] —*See also* AMBIGUITY.

era *n.* —*See* AGE (2).

eradicate *v.* —*See* ANNIHILATE, ELIMINATE.

eradication *n.* —*See* ANNIHILATION, ELIMINATION.

erase *v.* —*See* ANNIHILATE, CANCEL (1).

erasure *n.* The act of erasing or the condition of being erased ▸ cancellation, deletion, effacement, expunction, obliteration.

erect *adj.* —*See* RIGID.

erect *v.* To raise upright ▸ pitch, put up, raise, rear, set up, upraise, uprear. —*See also* BUILD.

erector *n.* —*See* BUILDER.

eristic *adj.* —*See* ARGUMENTATIVE.

erode *v.* To reduce gradually, as by chemical reaction, weather, or friction ▸ abrade, bite (into), consume, corrode, eat (away *or* into), gnaw (away *or* down), grind (away *or* down), wear (away *or* down). [*Compare* DECAY, DISINTEGRATE.]

erogenous *adj.* —*See* EROTIC.

erotic *adj.* Concerning or arousing sexual love or desire ▸ amatory, amorous, aphrodisiac, erogenous, libidinal, lascivious, salacious, sensual, sensuous, sexual, sexy, sizzling, spicy, steamy, suggestive. *Slang:* hot. [*Compare* LASCIVIOUS, DESIRABLE, OBSCENE.]

eroticism *n.* The quality of being erotic ▸ amorousness, lasciviousness, salaciousness, sensualism, sensuality, sensuousness, sexuality, sexiness, suggestiveness. *Slang:* sizzle. [*Compare* OBSCENITY, SENSUALITY.] —*See also* DESIRE (2), SENSUALITY (1).

erotism *n.* —*See* DESIRE (2).

err *v.* To make an error or mistake ▸ blunder, lapse, miscue, mistake, slip (up), stumble, trip (up). *Informal:* fluff. *Slang:* goof (up), screw up. ***Idioms:*** get (*or* start) off on the wrong foot, go astray (*or* awry), take a wrong step. [*Compare* BLUNDER, BOTCH.] —*See also* OFFEND (3).

errand *n.* —*See* MISSION (1).

errant *adj.* **1.** Traveling about, especially in search of adventure ▸ itinerant, rambling, roaming, roving, wandering. [*Compare* NOMADIC.] **2.** Straying from a proper course or standard ▸ aberrant, deviant, erring, stray. ***Idioms:*** far afield, off the map, wide of the mark, wide off the mark. [*Compare* ABNORMAL, WRONG.] —*See also* AIMLESS.

erratic *adj.* Without a fixed or regular course ▸ devious, stray, uncontrolled, unfixed, unstable, wandering, wayward. —*See also* CAPRICIOUS, ECCENTRIC, UNEVEN.

er·ra·tum (ĭ-rä′təm, ĭ-rā′-) ▸ *n., pl.* **-ta** (-tə). An error in a printed text.
er·ro·ne·ous (ĭ-rō′nē-əs) ▸ *adj.* Incorrect or mistaken. **—er·ro′ne·ous·ly** *adv.*
er·ror (ĕr′ər) ▸ *n.* **1.** An unintentional deviation from what is correct, right, or true. **2.** The condition of being incorrect or wrong. **3.** *Baseball* A defensive misplay. **—er′ror·less** *adj.*
er·satz (ĕr′zäts′, ĕr-zäts′) ▸ *adj.* Being a substitute; artificial.
Erse (ûrs) ▸ *n.* **1.** See **Irish Gaelic**. **2.** See **Scottish Gaelic**. **—Erse** *adj.*
erst·while (ûrst′hwīl′, -wīl′) ▸ *adv.* In the past. ▸ *adj.* Former.
e·ruct (ĭ-rŭkt′) ▸ *v.* To belch. **—e·ruc·ta′tion** *n.*
er·u·dite (ĕr′yə-dīt′, ĕr′ə-) ▸ *adj.* Marked by erudition; scholarly. **—er′u·dite′ly** *adv.*
er·u·di·tion (ĕr′yə-dĭsh′ən, ĕr′ə-) ▸ *n.* Deep, extensive learning; scholarship.
e·rupt (ĭ-rŭpt′) ▸ *v.* **1.** To break out violently from restraint or limits: *erupt in anger.* **2.** To become violently active, as a volcano. **3.** To appear on the skin. Used of a rash or blemish. **—e·rup′tion** *n.* **—e·rup′tive** *adj.*
–ery or **–ry** ▸ *suff.* **1.** A place for: *bakery.* **2.** A collection or class: *finery.* **3.** A state or condition: *slavery.* **4.** Act; practice: *bribery.* **5.** Characteristics or qualities of: *snobbery.*
er·y·sip·e·las (ĕr′ĭ-sĭp′ə-ləs, ĭr′-) ▸ *n.* An acute disease of the skin caused by a streptococcus and marked by spreading inflammation and fever.
e·ryth·ro·cyte (ĭ-rĭth′rə-sīt′) ▸ *n.* See **red blood cell**. **—e·ryth′ro·cyt′ic** (-sĭt′ĭk) *adj.*
e·ryth·ro·my·cin (ĭ-rĭth′rə-mī′sĭn) ▸ *n.* An antibiotic obtained from a strain of fungus and effective against many bacteria.
Es ▸ The symbol for the element **einsteinium**.
–es[1] ▸ *suff.* Var. of **–s**[1].
–es[2] ▸ *suff.* Var. of **–s**[2].
E·sau (ē′sô) ▸ In the Bible, the eldest son of Isaac and Rebecca.
es·ca·late (ĕs′kə-lāt′) ▸ *v.* **-lat·ed, -lat·ing.** To increase or intensify. **—es′ca·la′tion** *n.*
es·ca·la·tor (ĕs′kə-lā′tər) ▸ *n.* A moving stairway consisting of steps attached to a continuously circulating belt.
es·ca·pade (ĕs′kə-pād′) ▸ *n.* A reckless adventure.
es·cape (ĭ-skāp′) ▸ *v.* **-caped, -cap·ing. 1.** To break out (of). **2.** To avoid capture, danger, or harm. **3.** To succeed in avoiding. **4.** To elude: *Her name escapes me.* **5.** To leak or issue (from). ▸ *n.* **1.** The act or a means of escaping. **2.** A leakage. **3.** *Comp. Sci.* A key used esp. to interrupt a command or exit a program. **—es·cap′er** *n.*
es·cap·ee (ĭ-skā′pē′, ĕs′kā-) ▸ *n.* One that has escaped, esp. an escaped prisoner.
escape velocity ▸ *n.* The minimum velocity that a body must attain to overcome the gravitational attraction of another body, such as the earth.
es·cap·ism (ĭ-skā′pĭz′əm) ▸ *n.* The avoidance of reality through daydreaming, fantasy, or entertainment. **—es·cap′ist** *adj. & n.*
es·ca·role (ĕs′kə-rōl′) ▸ *n.* A salad plant having leaves with frilled edges.
es·carp·ment (ĭ-skärp′mənt) ▸ *n.* **1.** A steep slope or long cliff. **2.** A steep slope in front of a fortification.
–escence ▸ *suff.* State; process: *luminescence.*
–escent ▸ *suff.* **1.** Beginning to be; becoming: *obsolescent.* **2.** Characterized by; resembling: *evanescent.*
es·chew (ĕs-cho͞o′) ▸ *v.* To avoid or shun.
es·cort (ĕs′kôrt′) ▸ *n.* **1.** One that accompanies another to guide, protect, or show honor. **2.** A man who is the companion of a woman, esp. socially. ▸ *v.* (ĭ-skôrt′, ĕs′kôrt′) To accompany as an escort.
es·cri·toire (ĕs′krĭ-twär′) ▸ *n.* A writing table.
es·crow (ĕs′krō′, ĕ-skrō′) ▸ *n.* Money, property, a deed, or a bond put into the custody of a third party until fulfillment of certain conditions.
es·cu·do (ĭ-sko͞o′dō) ▸ *n., pl.* **-dos. 1.** See **currency** table in Appendix. **2.** The primary unit of currency in Portugal before the adoption of the euro.
es·cutch·eon (ĭ-skŭch′ən) ▸ *n.* A shield or shield-shaped emblem bearing a coat of arms.
ESE ▸ *abbr.* east-southeast
–ese ▸ *suff.* **1.** Of, characteristic of, or originating in a specified place: *Vietnamese.* **2.** Native or inhabitant of: *Taiwanese.* **3a.** Language or dialect of: *Chinese.* **b.** Literary style or diction of: *journalese.*
Es·ki·mo (ĕs′kə-mō′) ▸ *n., pl.* **-mo** or **-mos. 1.** A member of a group of peoples inhabiting the Arctic coast of North America and parts of Greenland and NE Siberia. **2.** Any of the languages of the Eskimo. **—Es′ki·mo′, Es′ki·mo′an** *adj.*
ESL ▸ *abbr.* English as a second language
e·soph·a·gus (ĭ-sŏf′ə-gəs) ▸ *n., pl.* **-gi** (-jī′, -gī′). A muscular tube for passing food from the pharynx to the stomach. **—e·soph′a·ge′al** (-jē′əl) *adj.*
es·o·ter·ic (ĕs′ə-tĕr′ĭk) ▸ *adj.* **1.** Intended for or understood by only a few. **2.** Not publicly disclosed; confidential. **—es′o·ter′i·cal·ly** *adv.*
ESP (ē′ĕs-pē′) ▸ *n.* Communication or perception by means other than the physical senses.
esp. ▸ *abbr.* especially
es·pa·drille (ĕs′pə-drĭl′) ▸ *n.* A shoe usu. having a fabric upper and a rope or rubber sole.
es·pal·ier (ĭ-spăl′yər, -yā′) ▸ *n.* A tree or shrub trained to

THESAURUS

erratum *n.* —*See* ERROR.
erring *adj.* —*See* ERRANT (2).
erroneous *adj.* Containing an error or errors ▸ corrupt, fallacious, false, faulty, inaccurate, incorrect, mistaken, off, unsound, untrue, wrong. *Idioms:* all wet, in error, off base, off (*or* wide of) the mark.
error *n.* An unintentional deviation from what is correct, right, or true ▸ erratum, false step, inaccuracy, incorrectness, lapse, miscue, miss, misstep, mistake, omission, oversight, slip, slip-up, trip. [*Compare* BLUNDER, DEFECT, MESS.] —*See also* FALLACY (1).
errorless *adj.* —*See* ACCURATE.
ersatz *n.* —*See* COPY (2).
ersatz *adj.* —*See* ARTIFICIAL (1), COUNTERFEIT.
erstwhile *adv.* —*See* EARLIER (1).
erstwhile *adj.* —*See* LATE (2).
eruct *v.* —*See* ERUPT.
erudite *adj.* —*See* EDUCATED.
erudition *n.* —*See* EDUCATION (2).
erupt *v.* To send forth confined matter violently ▸ belch, disgorge, eject, eruct, expel, spew, vomit. [*Compare* POUR, SPURT.] —*See also* BREAK OUT.
eruption *n.* A sudden emergence or increase ▸ breakout, burst, epidemic, explosion, flare, flare-up, irruption, outbreak, outburst, paroxysm, plague, rash, surge. —*See also* BLAST (2), OUTBURST.
escalate *v.* —*See* INCREASE, INTENSIFY.
escalation *n.* —*See* INCREASE (1).
escapade *n.* —*See* ADVENTURE.
escape *v.* **1.** To break loose and leave suddenly, as from confinement or a difficult situation ▸ abscond, bail out, break out, decamp, flee, fly, get away, run away. *Informal:* make off, skip (out). *Slang:* lam. *Chiefly Regional:* absquatulate. *Idioms:* cut and run, blow (*or* fly) the coop, get clear of, give someone the slip, make a getaway, make good one's escape, make oneself scarce, skip town, take flight, take it on the lam, wriggle off the hook. [*Compare* EVADE.] **2.** To fail to be fixed by the mind, memory, or senses of ▸ elude, evade. *Idiom:* slip away from. [*Compare* FORGET.] —*See also* AVOID.
escape *n.* **1.** The act or an instance of escaping, as from confinement or difficulty ▸ break, breakout, decampment, escapement, flight, getaway. *Slang:* lam. [*Compare* RESCUE.] **2.** The act, an instance, or a means of avoiding ▸ avoidance, bypass, circumvention, evasion. [*Compare* PREVENTION.]
escaped *adj.* Fleeing or having fled, as from confinement or the police ▸ fugitive, fleeing, runaway. *Idiom:* on the lam (*or* loose *or* run).
escapee *n.* One who flees, as from confinement or the police ▸ fugitive, outlaw, refugee, runaway. [*Compare* CRIMINAL.]
escapement *n.* —*See* ESCAPE (1).
eschew *v.* —*See* AVOID.
escort *n.* —*See* GUIDE.
escort *v.* —*See* ACCOMPANY, GUIDE.
esculent *adj.* Fit to be eaten ▸ comestible, eatable, edible, palatable.
esoteric *adj.* —*See* DEEP (2), MYSTERIOUS, OBSCURE (1).

grow in a flat plane against a wall or framework, often in a pattern. **—es·pal′ier** *v.*
es·pe·cial (ĭ-spĕsh′əl) ▸ *adj.* Of special importance or significance; particular; exceptional. **—es·pe′cial·ly** *adv.*
Es·pe·ran·to (ĕs′pə-răn′tō, -rän′-) ▸ *n.* An artificial international language based on many European languages.
es·pi·o·nage (ĕs′pē-ə-näzh′, -nĭj) ▸ *n.* The act or practice of spying.
es·pla·nade (ĕs′plə-näd′, -nād′) ▸ *n.* A flat, open stretch of pavement or grass used as a promenade.
es·pous·al (ĭ-spou′zəl, -səl) ▸ *n.* **1a.** A betrothal. **b.** A wedding ceremony. **2.** Adoption of or support for an idea or cause.
es·pouse (ĭ-spouz′) ▸ *v.* **-poused, -pous·ing. 1.** To marry. **2.** To give one's loyalty or support to; adopt.
es·pres·so (ĭ-sprĕs′ō, ĕ-sprĕs′ō) ▸ *n., pl.* **-sos.** A strong coffee brewed by forcing steam through darkly roasted, powdered beans.
es·prit (ĕ-sprē′) ▸ *n.* **1.** Liveliness of mind and expression; spirit. **2.** Esprit de corps.
esprit de corps (də kôr′) ▸ *n.* A common spirit of enthusiasm and devotion among members of a group.
es·py (ĭ-spī′) ▸ *v.* **-pied, -py·ing.** To catch sight of; glimpse.
–esque ▸ *suff.* In the manner of; resembling: *picturesque.*
es·quire (ĕs′kwīr′, ĭ-skwīr′) ▸ *n.* **1.** A member of the English gentry ranking directly below a knight. **2. Esquire** Used as an honorific, usu. in its abbreviated form *Esq.*, esp. after the name of an attorney or a consular officer. **3.** A candidate for knighthood serving a knight as attendant.
–ess ▸ *suff.* Female: *lioness.*
es·say (ĕs′ā′) ▸ *n.* **1.** A short literary composition on a single subject, usu. presenting the personal view of the author. **2.** (*also* ĕ-sā′) An attempt or endeavor, esp. a tentative one. ▸ *v.* (ĕ-sā′, ĕs′ā′) To make an attempt at; try. **—es·say′er** *n.*
es·say·ist (ĕs′ā′ĭst) ▸ *n.* A writer of essays.
es·sence (ĕs′əns) ▸ *n.* **1.** The intrinsic or indispensable properties that identify something. **2.** A concentrated extract of a substance that retains its fundamental properties. **3.** A perfume or scent.
es·sen·tial (ĭ-sĕn′shəl) ▸ *adj.* **1.** Constituting or being part of the essence of something; inherent. **2.** Basic or indispensable; necessary. ▸ *n.* Something essential. **—es·sen′ti·al′i·ty, es·sen′tial·ness** *n.* **—es·sen′tial·ly** *adv.*
–est¹ ▸ *suff.* Used to form the superlative degree of adjectives and adverbs: *greatest; earliest.*
–est² or **–st** ▸ *suff.* Used to form the archaic 2nd person sing. of English verbs: *comest.*
es·tab·lish (ĭ-stăb′lĭsh) ▸ *v.* **1.** To found or create; set up. **2.** To place or settle in a secure position or condition. **3.** To cause to be recognized and accepted. **4.** To prove the truth of. **—es·tab′lish·er** *n.*
es·tab·lish·ment (ĭ-stăb′lĭsh-mənt) ▸ *n.* **1.** The act of establishing or the condition of being established. **2.** A place of residence or business with its members, staff, and possessions. **3.** often **the Establishment** An exclusive or powerful group who control or strongly influence a government, society, or field of activity.
es·tate (ĭ-stāt′) ▸ *n.* **1.** A landed property, usu. of considerable size. **2.** All of one's possessions, esp. those left at death. **3.** A stage, condition, or status of life.
es·teem (ĭ-stēm′) ▸ *v.* **1.** To regard with respect; prize. **2.** To regard as; consider. ▸ *n.* Favorable regard; respect.
es·ter (ĕs′tər) ▸ *n.* Any of a class of organic compounds usu. resulting from the reaction of an oxygen-containing acid and an alcohol.
Es·ther (ĕs′tər) ▸ *n.* **1.** In the Bible, the Jewish queen of Persia who saved her people from massacre. **2.** See **Bible** table in Appendix.
es·the·sia also **aes·the·sia** (ĕs-thē′zhə) ▸ *n.* The ability to receive sense impressions.
es·thete (ĕs′thēt) ▸ *n.* Var. of **aesthete. —es·thet′ic** (ĕs-thĕt′ĭk) *adj.* **—es·thet′i·cal·ly** *adv.* **—es·thet′i·cism** *n.* **—es·thet′ics** *n.*
es·ti·ma·ble (ĕs′tə-mə-bəl) ▸ *adj.* **1.** Possible to estimate. **2.** Deserving of esteem; admirable. **—es′ti·ma·bly** *adv.*
es·ti·mate (ĕs′tə-māt′) ▸ *v.* **-mat·ed, -mat·ing. 1.** To calculate approximately the amount, extent, magnitude, position, or value of. **2.** To evaluate. ▸ *n.* (-mĭt) **1.** A rough calculation. **2.** A preliminary statement of the cost of work to be done. **3.** An opinion. **—es′ti·ma′tion** *n.* **—es′ti·ma′tor** *n.*
es·ti·vate also **aes·ti·vate** (ĕs′tə-vāt′) ▸ *v.* **-vat·ed, -vat·ing** *Zool.* To pass the summer in a dormant or torpid state. **—es′ti·va′tion** *n.*
Es·to·ni·a (ĕ-stō′nē-ə) ▸ A country of NE Europe.
Es·to·ni·an (ĕ-stō′nē-ən) ▸ *n.* **1.** A native or inhabitant of Estonia. **2.** The Finno-Ugric language of Estonia. **—Es·to′ni·an** *adj.*
es·trange (ĭ-strānj′) ▸ *v.* **-tranged, -trang·ing.** To make hostile,

THESAURUS

especial *adj.* —*See* EXCEPTIONAL, SPECIAL.
espial *n.* —*See* NOTICE (1).
espousal *n.* The act or condition of being pledged to marry ▸ betrothal, engagement, troth. —*See also* ACCEPTANCE (1), WEDDING.
espouse *v.* —*See* ADOPT, MARRY.
esprit or **esprit de corps** *n.* A strong sense of enthusiasm and dedication to a common goal that unites a group ▸ esprit de corps, group spirit, morale, team spirit. [*Compare* CONFIDENCE, MOOD.] —*See also* SPIRIT (1).
espy *v.* —*See* SEE (1).
essay *n.* A relatively brief discourse written especially as an exercise ▸ composition, paper, theme. —*See also* ATTEMPT, DISCOURSE, TEST (1).
essay *v.* —*See* ATTEMPT, TEST (1).
essence *n.* A basic trait or set of traits that define and establish the character of something ▸ being, essentiality, grain, nature, quiddity, quintessence, sine qua non, substance, texture. [*Compare* ELEMENT.] —*See also* FRAGRANCE, HEART (1).
essential *adj.* **1.** Incapable of being dispensed with ▸ critical, indispensable, necessary, needed, needful, prerequisite, required, requisite. [*Compare* REQUIRED.] **2.** Constituting or forming part of the essence of something ▸ basic, constitutional, constitutive, fundamental, integral, quintessential, vital. [*Compare* PRIMARY.] —*See also* ELEMENTAL.
essential *n.* —*See* CONDITION (2), ELEMENT (1).
essentiality *n.* —*See* ESSENCE.
essentially *adv.* In regard to the essence of a matter ▸ basically, fundamentally, underlyingly. ***Idioms:*** at bottom (*or* heart *or* root), at the end of the day, in essence, when all is said and done.
establish *v.* **1.** To place securely in a position or condition ▸ ensconce, fix, install, invest, seat, set (up), settle. **2.** To put in force or cause to be by legal authority ▸ constitute, enact, institute, legislate, legitimate, make, ordain, promulgate. [*Compare* CONFIRM, LEGALIZE.] —*See also* BASE¹, FOUND, GOVERN, PROVE.
established *adj.* —*See* ACCEPTED, CONFIRMED (1).
establishment *n.* —*See* COMPANY (1), FOUNDATION.
establishmentarian *adj.* —*See* CONVENTIONAL.
estate *n.* —*See* CONDITIONS, HOLDINGS, LAND, VILLA.
esteem *n.* A feeling of deference, approval, and liking ▸ account, admiration, appreciation, consideration, estimation, favor, honor, regard, respect. [*Compare* ADORATION, HONOR.] —*See also* ACCEPTANCE (2).
esteem *v.* —*See* REGARD, VALUE.
estimable *adj.* —*See* ADMIRABLE.
estimate *v.* **1.** To make a judgment as to the worth or value of ▸ appraise, assay, assess, calculate, evaluate, gauge, judge, rate, size up, valuate, value, weigh. ***Idiom:*** take the measure of. [*Compare* REGARD, TEST.] **2.** To calculate approximately ▸ approximate, place, put, reckon, set. *Informal:* guesstimate. [*Compare* PREDICT.]
estimate *n.* **1.** The act or result of evaluating or appraising ▸ appraisal, appraisement, assessment, estimation, evaluation, judgment, valuation. **2.** A rough or tentative calculation ▸ approximation, estimation. *Informal:* guesstimate. ***Idioms:*** ballpark figure, educated guess, rough measure. [*Compare* GUESS.] —*See also* BELIEF (1).
estimation *n.* —*See* BELIEF (1), ESTEEM, ESTIMATE (1), ESTIMATE (2).
estrange *v.* To make distant, hostile, or unsympathetic ▸ alienate, antagonize, come between, disaffect, distance,

unsympathetic, or indifferent; alienate. **—es·trange′ment** *n.*

es·tro·gen (ĕs′trə-jən) ▸ *n.* Any of several hormones produced chiefly by the ovaries that act to regulate certain female reproductive functions and maintain female secondary sex characteristics. **—es′tro·gen′ic** (-jĕn′ĭk) *adj.* **—es′tro·gen′i·cal·ly** *adv.*

es·trus (ĕs′trəs) ▸ *n.* The state of sexual excitement in most female mammals that immediately precedes ovulation; heat. **—es′trous** *adj.*

es·tu·ar·y (ĕs′cho͞o-ĕr′ē) ▸ *n., pl.* **-ies.** 1. The wide lower course of a river where its current is met by the tides. 2. An inland arm of the sea that meets the mouth of a river.

–et ▸ *suff.* 1. Small: *eaglet.* 2. Something worn on: *anklet.*

e·ta (ā′tə, ē′tə) ▸ *n.* The 7th letter of the Greek alphabet.

e-tail·er (ē′tā′lər) ▸ *n.* One that sells goods or commodities electronically, as over the Internet.

et al. ▸ *abbr. Lat.* et alii (and others)

etc. ▸ *abbr.* et cetera

et cet·er·a (ĕt sĕt′ər-ə, sĕt′rə) ▸ And other unspecified things of the same class; and so forth.

etch (ĕch) ▸ *v.* 1. To make (a pattern) on a surface with acid. 2. To impress, delineate, or imprint clearly. **—etch′er** *n.*

etch·ing (ĕch′ĭng) ▸ *n.* 1. The art or technique of preparing etched plates, esp. metal plates. 2. A design etched on a plate. 3. An impression made from an etched plate.

e·ter·nal (ĭ-tûr′nəl) ▸ *adj.* 1. Being without beginning or end. 2. Forever true or changeless: *eternal truths.* 3. Seemingly endless; interminable. 4. Of or relating to existence after death. **—e·ter′nal·ly** *adv.* **—e·ter′nal·ness** *n.*

e·ter·ni·ty (ĭ-tûr′nĭ-tē) ▸ *n., pl.* **-ties.** 1. Continuance without beginning or end. 2. The state or quality of being eternal. 3. Immortality. 4. A very long or seemingly endless time.

–eth[1] or **–th** ▸ *suff.* Used to form the archaic 3rd person sing. of English verbs: *leadeth.*

–eth[2] ▸ *suff.* Var. of **–th**[2].

eth·ane (ĕth′ān′) ▸ *n.* A colorless, odorless gas, C_2H_6, that occurs in natural gas and is used as a fuel and refrigerant.

eth·a·nol (ĕth′ə-nôl′, -nōl′, -nŏl′) ▸ *n.* See **alcohol** 1.

e·ther (ē′thər) ▸ *n.* 1. Any of a class of organic compounds in which two hydrocarbon groups are linked by an oxygen atom. 2. A highly flammable liquid, $C_2H_5OC_2H_5$, widely used as a reagent, solvent, and anesthetic. 3. The regions of space beyond the earth's atmosphere; the clear sky. 4. An all-pervading, infinitely elastic, massless medium formerly postulated as the medium of propagation of electromagnetic waves.

e·the·re·al (ĭ-thîr′ē-əl) ▸ *adj.* 1. Highly refined; delicate. 2. Heavenly. **—e·the′re·al·ly** *adv.* **—e·the′re·al·ness** *n.*

eth·ic (ĕth′ĭk) ▸ *n.* 1. A principle of right or good conduct or a body of such principles. 2. A system of moral principles or values. 3. **ethics** *(takes sing. v.)* The study of the general nature of morals and of specific moral choices. 4. **ethics** *(takes sing. or pl. v.)* The rules or standards governing the conduct of the members of a profession.

eth·i·cal (ĕth′ĭ-kəl) ▸ *adj.* 1. Of or dealing with ethics. 2. Being in accordance with the accepted principles that govern the conduct of a group, esp. of a profession. **—eth′i·cal·ly** *adv.*

E·thi·o·pi·a (ē′thē-ō′pē-ə) ▸ A country of NE Africa. **—E′thi·o′pi·an** *adj. & n.*

eth·nic (ĕth′nĭk) ▸ *adj.* Of or relating to sizable groups of people sharing a common and distinctive racial, national, religious, linguistic, or cultural heritage. ▸ *n.* A member of an ethnic group. **—eth′ni·cal·ly** *adv.*

ethnic cleansing ▸ *n.* The systematic elimination of an ethnic group from a region or society, as by expulsion or genocide.

eth·nic·i·ty (ĕth-nĭs′ĭ-tē) ▸ *n.* Ethnic character, background, or affiliation.

ethno– ▸ *pref.* Race; people: *ethnology.*

eth·no·cen·trism (ĕth′nō-sĕn′trĭz′əm) ▸ *n.* Belief in the superiority of one's own ethnic group. **—eth′no·cen′tric** *adj.* **—eth′no·cen′tri·cal·ly** *adv.*

eth·nol·o·gy (ĕth-nŏl′ə-jē) ▸ *n.* 1. The science that analyzes and compares human cultures, as in social structure, language, religion, and technology. 2. The branch of anthropology that deals with the origin, distribution, and characteristics of ethnic groups and the relations among them. **—eth′no·log′ic** (ĕth′nə-lŏj′ĭk), **eth′no·log′i·cal** *adj.* **—eth′no·log′i·cal·ly** *adv.* **—eth·nol′o·gist** *n.*

e·thol·o·gy (ĭ-thŏl′ə-jē, ē-thŏl′-) ▸ *n.* 1. The scientific study of animal behavior. 2. The study of human ethos. **—eth′o·log′i·cal** (ĕth′ə-lŏj′ĭ-kəl) *adj.* **—e·thol′o·gist** *n.*

e·thos (ē′thŏs′) ▸ *n.* The character or values peculiar to a specific person, people, culture, or movement.

eth·yl (ĕth′əl) ▸ *n.* An organic radical, C_2H_5.

ethyl alcohol ▸ *n.* See **alcohol** 1.

eth·yl·ene (ĕth′ə-lēn′) ▸ *n.* A colorless flammable gas, C_2H_4, derived from natural gas and petroleum.

ethylene glycol ▸ *n.* A colorless syrupy alcohol used as an antifreeze.

e·ti·ol·o·gy (ē′tē-ŏl′ə-jē) ▸ *n., pl.* **-gies.** 1. The study of causes, origins, or reasons. 2. The cause or origin of a disease or disorder as determined by medical diagnosis. **—e′ti·o·log′ic** (-ə-lŏj′ĭk), **e′ti·o·log′i·cal** *adj.* **—e′ti·o·log′i·cal·ly** *adv.* **—e′ti·ol′o·gist** *n.*

et·i·quette (ĕt′ĭ-kĕt′, -kĭt) ▸ *n.* The practices and forms prescribed by social convention or by authority.

Et·na (ĕt′nə), **Mount** ▸ An active volcano, 3,325.1 m (10,902 ft), of E Sicily.

E·trus·can (ĭ-trŭs′kən) ▸ *n.* 1. A native or inhabitant of ancient Etruria. 2. The extinct language of the Etruscans, of unknown affiliation. **—E·trus′can** *adj.*

–ette ▸ *suff.* 1. Small; diminutive: *kitchenette.* 2. Female: *suffragette.* 3. An imitation or inferior kind of cloth: *leatherette.*

e·tude (ā′to͞od′, -tyo͞od′) ▸ *n. Mus.* A composition for developing a specific point of technique.

et·y·mol·o·gy (ĕt′ə-mŏl′ə-jē) ▸ *n., pl.* **-gies.** 1. The origin and development of a word. 2. An account of the history of a word. 3. The branch of linguistics that deals with etymolo-

THESAURUS

disunite, drive away. *Slang:* turn off. *Idioms:* set at odds, turn against one. [*Compare* DIVIDE.]

estrangement *n.* —*See* BREACH (2).

estuary *n.* —*See* INLET, RIVER.

etceteras *n.* —*See* ODDS AND ENDS.

etch *v.* —*See* ENGRAVE (1), ENGRAVE (2).

eternal *adj.* Existing unchanged forever ▸ ageless, timeless. [*Compare* ENDLESS.] —*See also* CONTINUAL, ENDLESS (2).

eternality or **eternalness** *n.* —*See* ENDLESSNESS.

eternalize *v.* To cause to last endlessly ▸ eternize, immortalize, perpetuate. *Idiom:* cast (*or* etch *or* fix *or* set in stone. [*Compare* HONOR, MEMORIALIZE.]

eternally *adv.* —*See* FOREVER.

eterne *adj.* —*See* ENDLESS (2).

eternity *n.* 1. The totality of time without beginning or end ▸ infinity, perpetuity, sempiternity. [*Compare* FOREVER.] 2. A place or state beyond death ▸ afterworld, empyrean, far shore, great beyond, happy hunting ground, heaven, hereafter, nirvana, paradise, Valhalla. —*See also* AGES, ENDLESSNESS, IMMORTALITY.

eternize *v.* To cause to last endlessly ▸ eternalize, immortalize, perpetuate. *Idiom:* cast (*or* etch *or* fix *or* set) in stone. [*Compare* HONOR, MEMORIALIZE.]

ether *n.* The gaseous mixture enveloping the earth ▸ air, atmosphere.

ethereal *adj.* —*See* IMMATERIAL, SHEER[2].

ethic *n.* —*See* ETHICS (2).

ethical *adj.* In accordance with principles of right or good conduct ▸ conscientious, humane, moral, principled, proper, right, righteous, rightful, right-minded, scrupulous, virtuous, upright. [*Compare* FRANK, HONEST.]

ethicality or **ethicalness** *n.* —*See* ETHICS (1).

ethics *n.* 1. The quality of being in accord with standards of conduct ▸ ethicality, ethicalness, morality, propriety, rectitude, righteousness, rightness. 2. A set of principles of right conduct ▸ ethic, morality, morals, mores, principles, standards.

ethos *n.* —*See* CULTURE (2), PSYCHOLOGY.

etiolate *v.* —*See* PALE.

etiquette *n.* —*See* CEREMONY (2), MANNERS.

gies. **—et′y·mo·log′i·cal** (-mə-lŏj′ĭ-kəl) *adj.* **—et′y·mol′o·gist** *n.*

Eu ▸ The symbol for the element **europium.**

EU ▸ *abbr.* European Union

eu– ▸ *pref.* Good; well; true: *euphony.*

eu·ca·lyp·tus (yo͞o′kə-lĭp′təs) ▸ *n., pl.* **-tus·es** or **-ti** (-tī′). Any of numerous Australian trees yielding valuable timber and an aromatic medicinal oil.

Eu·cha·rist (yo͞o′kər-ĭst) ▸ *n.* The Christian sacrament instituted at the Last Supper, in which bread and wine are consecrated and consumed in remembrance of Jesus's death; Communion. **—Eu′cha·ris′tic** *adj.*

eu·chre (yo͞o′kər) ▸ *n.* A card game played usu. with the highest 32 cards. ▸ *v.* **-chred, -chring.** To deceive or cheat.

Eu·clid (yo͞o′klĭd) (3rd cent. B.C.) ▸ Greek mathematician.

Eu·clid·e·an (yo͞o-klĭd′ē-ən) ▸ *adj.* Of or relating to Euclid's geometric principles.

eu·gen·ics (yo͞o-jĕn′ĭks) ▸ *n. (takes sing. v.)* The study of hereditary improvement of the human race by controlled selective breeding. **—eu·gen′ic** *adj.*

eu·kar·y·ote (yo͞o-kăr′ē-ōt, -ē-ət) ▸ *n.* An organism whose cells contain a distinct membrane-bound nucleus. **—eu·kar′y·ot′ic** (-ŏt′ĭk) *adj.*

eu·lo·gize (yo͞o′lə-jīz′) ▸ *v.* **-gized, -giz·ing.** To praise highly in speech or writing. **—eu′lo·giz′er** *n.*

eu·lo·gy (yo͞o′lə-jē) ▸ *n., pl.* **-gies.** A spoken or written tribute, esp. one praising someone who has died. **—eu′lo·gist** *n.* **—eu′lo·gis′tic** *adj.*

eu·nuch (yo͞o′nək) ▸ *n.* A castrated man.

eu·phe·mism (yo͞o′fə-mĭz′əm) ▸ *n.* The substitution of an inoffensive term for one considered blunt or offensive. **—eu′phe·mist** *n.* **—eu′phe·mis′tic** *adj.* **—eu′phe·mis′ti·cal·ly** *adv.* **—eu′phe·mize′** *v.*

eu·pho·ny (yo͞o′fə-nē) ▸ *n., pl.* **-nies.** Agreeable sound, esp. of words pleasing to the ear. **—eu·pho′ni·ous** (-fō′nē-əs) *adj.* **—eu·pho′ni·ous·ly** *adv.*

eu·pho·ri·a (yo͞o-fôr′ē-ə) ▸ *n.* A feeling of great happiness or well-being. **—eu·phor′ic** (-fôr′ĭk, -fŏr′-) *adj.*

eu·pho·ri·ant (yo͞o-fôr′ē-ənt) ▸ *n.* A drug that induces euphoria. **—eu·pho′ri·ant** *adj.*

Eu·phra·tes (yo͞o-frā′tēz) ▸ A river of SW Asia flowing about 2,735 km (1,700 mi) from central Turkey to Iraq, where it joins the Tigris R. to form the Shatt al Arab.

Eur·a·sia (yo͞o-rā′zhə) ▸ The land mass comprising the continents of Europe and Asia.

Eur·a·sian (yo͞o-rā′zhən) ▸ *adj.* **1.** Of or relating to Eurasia. **2.** Of mixed European and Asian descent. ▸ *n.* A person of mixed European and Asian descent.

eu·re·ka (yo͞o-rē′kə) ▸ *interj.* Used to express triumph upon finding or discovering something.

Eu·rip·i·des (yo͞o-rĭp′ĭ-dēz′) (480?–406 B.C.) ▸ Greek dramatist.

eu·ro or **Eu·ro** (yo͝or′ō) ▸ *n., pl.* **-ros.** See **currency** table in Appendix.

Eu·ro-A·mer·i·can (yo͝or′ō-ə-mĕr′ĭ-kən) ▸ *n.* A US citizen or resident of European descent. ▸ *adj.* **1.** Relating to Euro-Americans. **2.** Relating to Europe and America.

Eu·ro·cen·tric (yo͝or′ō-sĕn′trĭk) ▸ *adj.* Centered or focused on Europe or European peoples. **—Eu′ro·cen′trism** *n.*

Eu·ro·cur·ren·cy (yo͝or′ō-kûr′ən-sē, -kŭr′-) ▸ *n., pl.* **-cies.** Currency held and traded in a bank outside the currency's country of origin.

Eu·ro·dol·lar (yo͝or′ō-dŏl′ər) ▸ *n.* A US dollar on deposit in a foreign bank.

Eu·ro·pa (yo͞o-rō′pə) ▸ *n. Gk. Myth.* A Phoenician princess abducted to Crete by Zeus, who had assumed the form of a white bull.

Eu·rope (yo͝or′əp) ▸ The sixth-largest continent, consisting of the section of Eurasia that extends W from the Dardanelles, Black Sea, and Ural Mountains.

Eu·ro·pe·an (yo͝or′ə-pē′ən) ▸ *n.* **1.** A native or inhabitant of Europe. **2.** A person of European descent. ▸ *adj.* Of Europe or its peoples, languages, or cultures.

European Community ▸ An economic and political organization formed in 1965 by the members of the European Economic Community.

European Economic Community. Informally the **Common Market** ▸ An economic union among the countries of W Europe.

European plan ▸ *n.* A hotel plan in which the rates include only the charges for a room and not for meals.

European Union ▸ An economic and political union established in 1993 orig. by members of the European Community, with many other European countries joining since then.

eu·ro·pi·um (yo͞o-rō′pē-əm) ▸ *n. Symbol* **Eu** A silvery-white, soft rare-earth element used in lasers and nuclear research. At. no. 63.

Eu·ryd·i·ce (yo͞o-rĭd′ĭ-sē) ▸ *n. Gk. Myth.* The wife of Orpheus.

eu·sta·chian tube or **Eu·sta·chian tube** (yo͞o-stā′shən, -shē-ən, -kē-ən) ▸ *n.* A narrow tube that connects the middle ear with the pharynx and serves to equalize air pressure on either side of the eardrum.

eu·tha·na·sia (yo͞o′thə-nā′zhə, -zhē-ə) ▸ *n.* The act of painlessly ending the life of a person for reasons of mercy. **—eu′than·ize′** *v.*

eu·then·ics (yo͞o-thĕn′ĭks) ▸ *n. (takes sing. v.)* The study of the improvement of human functioning and well-being by improvement of living conditions. **—eu·then′ist** *n.*

e·vac·u·ate (ĭ-văk′yo͞o-āt′) ▸ *v.* **-at·ed, -at·ing.** **1a.** To remove the contents of. **b.** To create a vacuum in. **2.** To excrete waste matter from (the bowel). **3.** To withdraw, esp. from a threatened area. **—e·vac′u·a′tion** *n.*

e·vac·u·ee (ĭ-văk′yo͞o-ē′) ▸ *n.* A person evacuated from a dangerous or threatened area.

e·vade (ĭ-vād′) ▸ *v.* **e·vad·ed, e·vad·ing.** To escape or avoid by cleverness or deceit. **—e·vad′er** *n.*

e·val·u·ate (ĭ-văl′yo͞o-āt′) ▸ *v.* **-at·ed, -at·ing.** To ascertain or fix the value of. **—e·val′u·a′tion** *n.* **—e·val′u·a·tor** *n.*

ev·a·nesce (ĕv′ə-nĕs′) ▸ *v.* **-nesced, -nesc·ing.** To dissipate gradually; fade away like vapor. **—ev′a·nes′cence** *n.* **—ev′a·nes′cent** *adj.* **—ev′a·nes′cent·ly** *adv.*

e·van·gel·i·cal (ē′văn-jĕl′ĭ-kəl, ĕv′ən-) also **e·van·gel·ic** (-jĕl′ĭk) ▸ *adj.* **1.** Of or in accordance with the Christian gospel or Gospels. **2. Evangelical** Of or being a Protestant church that stresses personal spiritual transformation and the inerrancy of the Bible. **—E′van·gel′i·cal** *n.* **—e′van·gel′i·cal·ism** *n.* **—e′van·gel′i·cal·ly** *adv.*

e·van·gel·ism (ĭ-văn′jə-lĭz′əm) ▸ *n.* Zealous preaching of the gospel, as through missionary work. **—e·van′gel·is′tic** *adj.* **—e·van′gel·is′ti·cal·ly** *adv.*

e·van·gel·ist (ĭ-văn′jə-lĭst) ▸ *n.* **1.** often **Evangelist** Any one of the authors of the New Testament Gospels. **2.** One who practices evangelism, esp. a Protestant preacher or missionary.

e·van·gel·ize (ĭ-văn′jə-līz′) ▸ *v.* **-ized, -iz·ing.** **1.** To preach

THESAURUS

eulogistic *adj.* —*See* COMPLIMENTARY (1).

eulogize *v.* —*See* HONOR (1).

eulogy *n.* —*See* PRAISE (1).

euphemism *n.* —*See* EQUIVOCATION.

euphemize *v.* —*See* EQUIVOCATE (1).

euphonious or **euphonic** *adj.* —*See* MELODIOUS.

euphoria *n.* —*See* ELATION.

euphoric *adj.* —*See* ELATED.

evacuant *adj.* —*See* ELIMINATIVE.

evacuate *v.* —*See* EMPTY, RETREAT.

evacuation *n.* —*See* RETREAT.

evacuative *adj.* —*See* ELIMINATIVE.

evade *v.* **1.** To avoid fulfilling or answering completely ▸ dodge, duck, fence, hedge, sidestep, skirt. *Idioms:* weasel out of, wiggle (*or* wriggle *or* worm) one's way out of. [*Compare* MANEUVER, EQUIVOCATE, ESCAPE.] **2.** To fail to be fixed by the mind, memory, or senses of ▸ elude, escape. *Idiom:* slip away from. [*Compare* FORGET.] —*See also* AVOID, LOSE (3).

evaluate *v.* —*See* ESTIMATE (1), TEST (1).

evaluation *n.* —*See* ESTIMATE (1), TEST (1).

evanesce *v.* —*See* DISAPPEAR (1).

evanescence *n.* —*See* DISAPPEARANCE.

evanescent *adj.* —*See* TRANSITORY.

evangelism *n.* —*See* PROPAGANDA.

evangelist *n.* A person doing religious or charitable work in a foreign country ▸ apostle, missionary, missioner. [*Compare* CLERIC, REPRESENTATIVE.] —*See also* PROPAGANDIST.

evangelize *v.* To deliver a sermon, especially as a vocation ▸ preach, sermonize.

the gospel (to). 2. To convert to Christianity.
e·vap·o·rate (ĭ-văp′ə-rāt′) ▸ *v.* **-rat·ed, -rat·ing.** 1. To change into a vapor. 2. To remove or be removed in or as if in a vapor. 3. To vanish. **—e·vap′o·ra′tion** *n.* **—e·vap′o·ra′tive** *adj.* **—e·vap′o·ra′tor** *n.*
e·va·sion (ĭ-vā′zhən) ▸ *n.* 1. The act of evading. 2. A means of evading.
e·va·sive (ĭ-vā′sĭv) ▸ *adj.* 1. Inclined or intended to evade. 2. Intentionally vague or ambiguous. **—e·va′sive·ly** *adv.* **—e·va′sive·ness** *n.*
eve (ēv) ▸ *n.* 1. The evening or day preceding a holiday. 2. The period immediately preceding a certain event: *the eve of war.* 3. Evening.
Eve ▸ In the Bible, the first woman and the wife of Adam.
e·ven[1] (ē′vən) ▸ *adj.* 1a. Flat: *an even floor.* b. Smooth. c. Level; parallel: *The picture is even with the window.* 2a. Uniform, steady, or regular: *an even rhythm of breathing.* b. Placid; calm: *an even temperament.* 3. Equal in degree, extent, or amount; balanced. 4. *Math.* a. Exactly divisible by 2. b. Characterized by a number exactly divisible by 2. 5a. Having an even number in a series. b. Having an even number of members. 6. Exact: *an even pound.* ▸ *adv.* 1. To a greater degree: *an even worse condition.* 2. In fact: *unhappy, even weeping.* 3. At that very time: *Even as we watched, the building collapsed.* 4. In spite of: *Even with his head start, I beat him.* ▸ *v.* To make or become even. **—e′ven·ly** *adv.* **—e′ven·ness** *n.*
e·ven[2] (ē′vən) ▸ *n. Archaic* Evening.
e·ven·hand·ed (ē′vən-hăn′dĭd) ▸ *adj.* Showing no partiality; fair. **—e′ven·hand′ed·ly** *adv.* **—e′ven·hand′ed·ness** *n.*
eve·ning (ēv′nĭng) ▸ *n.* Late afternoon and early night.
evening star ▸ *n.* A planet, esp. Venus or Mercury, that is prominent in the west shortly after sunset.
e·vent (ĭ-vĕnt′) ▸ *n.* 1. An occurrence or incident, esp. one of significance. 2. A social gathering or activity. 3. A contest or an item in a sports program.
e·vent·ful (ĭ-vĕnt′fəl) ▸ *adj.* 1. Full of events. 2. Important; momentous. **—e·vent′ful·ly** *adv.* **—e·vent′ful·ness** *n.*
e·ven·tide (ē′vən-tīd′) ▸ *n.* Evening.
e·ven·tu·al (ĭ-vĕn′cho͞o-əl) ▸ *adj.* Occurring at an unspecified time in the future: *her eventual success.* **—e·ven′tu·al·ly** *adv.*
e·ven·tu·al·i·ty (ĭ-vĕn′cho͞o-ăl′ĭ-tē) ▸ *n., pl.* **-ties.** Something that may occur; possibility.
e·ven·tu·ate (ĭ-vĕn′cho͞o-āt′) ▸ *v.* **-at·ed, -at·ing.** To result ultimately; culminate.
ev·er (ĕv′ər) ▸ *adv.* 1. At all times; always: *ever hoping to strike it rich.* 2. At any time: *Have you ever been to India?* 3. In any way; at all: *How did they ever manage?* 4. To a great extent or degree: *He was ever so sorry. Was she ever mad!*
Ev·er·est (ĕv′ər-ĭst, ĕv′rĭst), **Mount** ▸ A mountain, 8,853.5 m (29,035 ft), of the central Himalayas on the border of Xizang (Tibet) and Nepal.
ev·er·glade (ĕv′ər-glād′) ▸ *n.* A tract of marshland, usu. under water.
Ev·er·glades (ĕv′ər-glādz′) ▸ A subtropical swamp area of S FL including **Everglades National Park.**
ev·er·green (ĕv′ər-grēn′) ▸ *adj.* Having foliage that persists and remains green throughout the year. ▸ *n.* An evergreen tree, shrub, or plant.
ev·er·last·ing (ĕv′ər-lăs′tĭng) ▸ *adj.* Lasting forever; eternal. **—ev′er·last′ing·ly** *adv.*
ev·er·more (ĕv′ər-môr′) ▸ *adv.* Forever; always.
eve·ry (ĕv′rē) ▸ *adj.* 1. Each without exception: *every student in the class.* 2. Being each of a specified series: *every third seat; every two hours.* 3. Being of the highest degree or expression: *showed us every attention.* **—*idioms:* every bit** *Informal* In all ways; equally. **every so often** Occasionally.
eve·ry·bod·y (ĕv′rē-bŏd′ē, -bŭd′ē) ▸ *pron.* Every person; everyone.
eve·ry·day (ĕv′rē-dā′) ▸ *adj.* 1. Appropriate for ordinary occasions. 2. Commonplace; ordinary.
eve·ry·one (ĕv′rē-wŭn′) ▸ *pron.* Every person; everybody.
eve·ry·thing (ĕv′rē-thĭng′) ▸ *pron.* All things or all relevant matters.
eve·ry·where (ĕv′rē-hwâr′, -wâr′) ▸ *adv.* In every place; in all places.
e·vict (ĭ-vĭkt′) ▸ *v.* 1. To expel (a tenant) by legal process. 2. To eject. **—e·vic′tion** *n.* **—e·vic′tor** *n.*
ev·i·dence (ĕv′ĭ-dəns) ▸ *n.* 1. The data on which a conclusion or judgment can be established. 2. Something indicative; an outward sign: *the house showed evidence of neglect.* 3. The statements and material objects admissible as testimony in a court of law. ▸ *v.* **-denced, -denc·ing.** To indicate clearly. **—*idiom:* in evidence** Plainly visible; conspicuous.
ev·i·dent (ĕv′ĭ-dənt) ▸ *adj.* Easily seen or understood; obvious. **—ev′i·dent·ly** *adv.*
ev·i·den·tial (ĕv′ĭ-dĕn′shəl) ▸ *adj.* Of, providing, or constituting legal evidence.
e·vil (ē′vəl) ▸ *adj.* **-er, -est.** 1. Morally bad or wrong; wicked.

THESAURUS

[*Compare* ADDRESS, MORALIZE.]
evaporate *v.* To turn into vapor, especially when heated ▸ boil away, burn off, fume, steam, sublimate, sublime, vaporize, volatilize. *—See also* DISAPPEAR (1), DRAIN (1).
evaporation *n.* *—See* DISAPPEARANCE.
evasion *n.* *—See* ESCAPE (2).
evasive *adj.* 1. Inclined or intended to evade ▸ elusive, fugitive, slippery. [*Compare* SLICK, UNDERHAND.] 2. Deliberately ambiguous or vague ▸ elusive, equivocal, indirect, misleading. [*Compare* AMBIGUOUS.]
eve *n.* *—See* EVENING.
even *adj.* 1. Having no irregularities, roughness, or indentations ▸ flat, flush, level, mirrorlike, planar, plane, smooth, straight, unruffled, unwrinkled. [*Compare* GLOSSY.] 2. On the same plane or line ▸ coplanar, flush, in line, level, square, uniplanar. 3. Owing or being owed nothing ▸ quit, quits, square. *Informal:* even-steven. 4. Neither favorable nor unfavorable ▸ balanced, fifty-fifty, nip and tuck. 5. Being an exact amount or number ▸ exact. ***Idiom:*** on the button (*or* money *or* nose). *—See also* CALM, EQUAL, FAIR[1] (1), GRADUAL (2), UNCHANGING.
even *adv.* 1. To a more extreme degree ▸ ever more so, still, yet. 2. Not just this but also ▸ a fortiori, indeed, moreover, yea. *Idioms:* all the more, not to mention, what is more. *—See also* EXACTLY.
even *v.* To make even, smooth, or level ▸ align, flat, flatten, flush, level, plane, relax, roll (out), smooth, steamroll, steamroller, straighten. *—See also* BALANCE (1), EQUALIZE.
evenhanded *adj.* *—See* FAIR[1] (1).
evenhandedly *adv.* *—See* FAIRLY (1).
evenhandedness *n.* *—See* FAIRNESS.
evening *n.* The period between afternoon and nighttime ▸ dusk, eve, eventide, gloaming, nightfall, sundown, sunset, twilight. *Idiom:* close of day.
event *n.* 1. Something significant that happens ▸ circumstance, development, episode, happening, incident, news, phenomenon, occasion, occurrence, thing. *Idioms:* something to write home about, turn of events. 2. Something demonstrated to exist or known to have existed ▸ actuality, fact, phenomenon, reality. ***Idiom:*** hard (*or* cold *or* plain) fact. [*Compare* INFORMATION.] *—See also* CIRCUMSTANCE (1), COMPETITION (2), EFFECT (1).
even-tempered *adj.* *—See* CALM.
eventide *n.* *—See* EVENING.
eventual *adj.* *—See* FUTURE.
eventuality *n.* *—See* POSSIBILITY (1).
eventually *adv.* *—See* ULTIMATELY (1).
everlasting *adj.* *—See* CONTINUAL, ENDLESS (2).
everlastingly *adv.* *—See* FOREVER.
everlastingness *n.* *—See* ENDLESSNESS, IMMORTALITY.
evermore *adv.* *—See* FOREVER.
everyday *adj.* Of or suitable for ordinary days or routine occasions ▸ casual, daily, quotidian, workaday, workday. [*Compare* ORDINARY.] *—See also* COMMON (1).
everyday *n.* *—See* USUAL.
everything *n.* *—See* WHOLE.
evict *v.* *—See* EJECT (1).
eviction *n.* *—See* EJECTION.
evidence *n.* *—See* CONFIRMATION (2), SIGN (1).
evidence *v.* To demonstrate and clarify with examples ▸ demonstrate, exemplify, illustrate, instance. [*Compare* EXPLAIN.] *—See also* CONFIRM (1), PROVE, SHOW (1).
evident *adj.* *—See* APPARENT (1).
evidently *adv.* *—See* APPARENTLY.
evil *adj.* Morally objectionable ▸ bad,

2. Harmful or injurious. ► *n.* **1.** The quality of being morally bad or wrong; wickedness. **2.** Something that causes harm, misfortune, suffering, or destruction. **—e′vil·ly** *adv.* **—e′vil·ness** *n.*

e·vil·do·er (ē′vəl-do͞o′ər) ► *n.* One that performs evil acts. **—e′vil·do′ing** *n.*

evil eye ► *n.* A look believed to have the power to cause injury to others, esp. by magic or supernatural means.

e·vince (ĭ-vĭns′) ► *v.* **e·vinced, e·vinc·ing.** To show or demonstrate clearly; manifest. **—e·vinc′i·ble** *adj.*

e·vis·cer·ate (ĭ-vĭs′ə-rāt′) ► *v.* **-at·ed, -at·ing. 1.** To remove the entrails of. **2.** To take away a vital or essential part of. **—e·vis′cer·a′tion** *n.*

ev·i·ta·ble (ĕv′ĭ-tə-bəl) ► *adj.* Avoidable.

e·voke (ĭ-vōk′) ► *v.* **e·voked, e·vok·ing.** To summon or call forth; elicit: *evoke memories.* **—ev′o·ca·ble** (ĕv′ə-kə-bəl, ĭ-vō′kə-) *adj.* **—ev′o·ca′tion** *n.* **—e·voc′a·tive** (ĭ-vŏk′ə-tĭv) *adj.* **—e·voc′a·tive·ly** *adv.*

ev·o·lu·tion (ĕv′ə-lo͞o′shən, ē′və-) ► *n.* **1.** A gradual process in which something changes into a different and usu. more complex form. **2.** *Biol.* **a.** The theory that groups of organisms change with the passage of time, mainly as a result of natural selection, so that descendants differ morphologically and physiologically from their ancestors. **b.** The historical development of a related group of organisms; phylogeny. **3.** *Math.* The extraction of a root of a quantity. **—ev′o·lu′tion·ar′y** *adj.* **—ev′o·lu′tion·ism** *n.* **—ev′o·lu′tion·ist** *n.*

e·volve (ĭ-vŏlv′) ► *v.* **e·volved, e·volv·ing. 1.** To develop or work out; achieve gradually: *evolve a plan.* **2.** *Biol.* To develop by evolutionary processes. **—e·volve′ment** *n.*

e·vul·sion (ĭ-vŭl′shən) ► *n.* A forcible extraction.

ewe (yo͞o) ► *n.* A female sheep.

ew·er (yo͞o′ər) ► *n.* A pitcher, esp. one with a flaring spout.

ex[1] (ĕks) ► *prep.* Not including; without: *a stock price ex dividend.*

ex[2] (ĕks) ► *n. Slang* A former spouse or partner.

ex– ► *pref.* **1.** Outside; out of; away from: *exurbia.* **2.** Former: *ex-president.*

ex·ac·er·bate (ĭg-zăs′ər-bāt′) ► *v.* **-bat·ed, -bat·ing.** To increase the severity of; aggravate: *exacerbate tensions; exacerbate pain.* **—ex·ac′er·ba′tion** *n.*

ex·act (ĭg-zăkt′) ► *adj.* Strictly accurate; precise. ► *v.* To obtain by or as if by force or authority. **—ex·act′ly** *adv.* **—ex·act′ness** *n.*

ex·act·ing (ĭg-zăk′tĭng) ► *adj.* **1.** Making rigorous demands. **2.** Requiring great care or effort. **—ex·act′ing·ly** *adv.*

ex·ac·ti·tude (ĭg-zăk′tĭ-to͞od, -tyo͞od′) ► *n.* The state or quality of being exact.

ex·ag·ger·ate (ĭg-zăj′ə-rāt′) ► *v.* **-at·ed, -at·ing.** To enlarge, increase, or represent (something) beyond normal bounds. **—ex·ag′ger·a′tion** *n.* **—ex·ag′ger·a′tive, ex·ag′ger·a·to′ry** (-ə-tôr′ē) *adj.* **—ex·ag′ger·a′tor** *n.*

ex·alt (ĭg-zôlt′) ► *v.* **1.** To raise in rank or status; elevate. **2.** To glorify, praise, or honor. **3.** To inspire; heighten: *art that exalts the imagination.* **—ex′al·ta′tion** (ĕg′zôl-tā′shən) *n.*

ex·am (ĭg-zăm′) ► *n.* An examination; test.

ex·am·i·na·tion (ĭg-zăm′ə-nā′shən) ► *n.* **1.** The act of examining or the state of being examined. **2.** A set of questions or exercises testing knowledge or skill. **—ex·am′i·na′tion·al** *adj.*

ex·am·ine (ĭg-zăm′ĭn) ► *v.* **-ined, -in·ing. 1.** To inspect or analyze (a person, thing, or situation) in detail. **2.** To determine the aptitude or skills of by questioning. **3.** To

THESAURUS

black, dark, immoral, iniquitous, peccant, reprobate, sinful, vicious, wicked, wrong. [*Compare* CORRUPT, SORDID.] —*See also* FATEFUL (1), HARMFUL, MALEVOLENT.

evil *n.* **1.** The quality or state of being morally bad or objectionable ► iniquity, peccancy, sin, vice, wickedness, wrong. [*Compare* CORRUPTION, MALEVOLENCE.] **2.** Whatever is destructive or harmful ► bad, badness, ill, worse. [*Compare* HARM.] —*See also* CRIME (2), CURSE (3).

evildoer *n.* One that performs evil acts ► miscreant, scoundrel, sinner, villain, wrongdoer. *Informal:* baddie, bad guy. *Slang:* black hat. [*Compare* CRIMINAL, FIEND, RASCAL.]

evildoing *n.* —*See* CRIME (2).

evil eye *n.* Something or someone believed to bring bad luck ► curse, hex, hoodoo, Jonah. *Informal:* jinx. [*Compare* CHARM, MAGIC.]

evince *v.* —*See* SHOW (1).

eviscerate *v.* —*See* ENERVATE.

evocative *adj.* Tending to bring a memory, mood, or image, for example, subtly or indirectly to mind ► allusive, connotative, impressionistic, reminiscent, suggestive. [*Compare* DESIGNATIVE, SYMBOLIC.]

evoke *v.* To bring out something latent, hidden, or unexpressed ► call forth (*or* up), conjure (up), draw (out), educe, elicit, invoke, rouse, summon (forth). [*Compare* AROUSE, REVIVE.]

evolution *n.* —*See* CHANGE (1), DEVELOPMENT.

evolve *v.* —*See* CHANGE (2), DERIVE (2), DEVELOP (2).

evolvement *n.* —*See* DEVELOPMENT.

exacerbate *v.* —*See* INTENSIFY.

exact *adj.* **1.** Strictly distinguished from others ► precise, very. **2.** Being an exact amount or number ► even. *Idioms:* on the button (*or* money *or* nose), spot on. —*See also* ACCURATE, CLOSE (2).

exact *v.* To establish and apply as compulsory ► assess, impose, levy, put. —*See also* DEMAND (1), EXTORT.

exacting *adj.* —*See* DELICATE (3), DIFFICULT (1), FUSSY, SEVERE (1).

exaction *n.* —*See* DEMAND (1), TOLL[1] (1).

exactitude *n.* —*See* ACCURACY, VERACITY.

exactly *adv.* In an exact manner ► even, faithfully, just, literally, precisely, strictly, verbatim. *Idioms:* in all respects (*or* every respect), just so, letter for letter, to a T, to the letter, word for word. —*See also* DIRECTLY (3).

exactment *n.* —*See* TOLL[1] (1).

exactness *n.* —*See* ACCURACY, VERACITY.

exaggerate *v.* To make something seem greater than is actually the case ► aggrandize, hyperbolize, inflate, magnify, overcharge, overemphasize, overstate, puff (up). *Idioms:* blow out of proportion, lay it on thick, stretch the truth. [*Compare* BOAST, DISTORT.] —*See also* INCREASE.

exaggerated *adj.* Represented as greater than is actually the case ► farfetched, hyperbolic, inflated, magnified, overblown, overdrawn, overstated. [*Compare* ASTONISHING, DOUBTFUL, IMAGINARY, OUTRAGEOUS.] —*See also* DRAMATIC (2).

exaggeration *n.* The act or an instance of exaggerating ► hyperbole, hyperbolism, overstatement, tall talk. *Informal:* fish story, tall tale. [*Compare* LIE[2].]

exalt *v.* To raise to a high position or status ► aggrandize, apotheosize, dignify, elevate, ennoble, glorify, magnify, uplift. *Idiom:* put (*or* place) on a pedestal. —*See also* DISTINGUISH (3), HONOR (1), PRAISE (3), PROMOTE (1).

exaltation *n.* The act of raising to a high position or status or the condition of being so raised ► aggrandizement, apotheosis, beatification, canonization, deification, dignification, elevation, ennoblement, glorification, lionization. —*See also* ELATION, PRAISE (2).

exalted *adj.* Raised to or occupying a high position or rank ► august, elevated, ennobled, eminent, grand, high-ranking, illustrious, lofty, noble, venerable. [*Compare* FAMOUS.] —*See also* ELEVATED (4).

exam *n.* —*See* EXAMINATION (2), TEST (2).

examination *n.* **1.** The act of examining carefully or critically ► analysis, audit, check, checkup, inquest, inquisition, inquiry, inspection, investigation, perusal, probe, research, review, scrutiny, search, study, survey, view. *Informal:* going-over, once-over. **2.** A medical inquiry into a patient's state of health ► analysis, checkup, diagnosis, exam, probe. *Informal:* workup. —*See also* TEST (2).

examine *v.* **1.** To look at or study carefully or critically ► analyze, audit, check (out), con, go over, inspect, investigate, peruse, pore over, research, review, scrutinize, study, survey, traverse, view. *Informal:* case. *Slang:* scope out. *Idioms:* bone up on, give the once-over (*or* a going-over), go over with a fine-tooth comb, put under a microscope. [*Compare* ESTIMATE, EXPLORE, STUDY, TEST.] **2.** To subject to a test of knowledge or skill ► catechize, quiz, test. —*See also* ASK (1), TEST (1).

question formally to elicit facts; interrogate. **—ex·am′in·ee′** *n.* **—ex·am′in·er** *n.*

ex·am·ple (ĭg-zăm′pəl) ▸ *n.* **1.** One that is representative of a group as a whole. **2.** One serving as a pattern of a specific kind: *set a good example.* **3.** One that serves as a warning or deterrent. **4.** A problem used to illustrate a principle.

ex·as·per·ate (ĭg-zăs′pə-rāt′) ▸ *v.* **-at·ed, -at·ing.** To make very angry or impatient; provoke. **—ex·as′per·at′ing·ly** *adv.* **—ex·as′per·a′tion** *n.*

ex·ca·vate (ĕk′skə-vāt′) ▸ *v.* **-vat·ed, -vat·ing. 1.** To dig or hollow out. **2.** To remove (soil) by digging. **3.** To uncover by digging. **—ex′ca·va′tion** *n.* **—ex′ca·va′tor** *n.*

ex·ceed (ĭk-sēd′) ▸ *v.* **1.** To be greater than; surpass. **2.** To go or be beyond the limits of: *exceeded their authority.*

ex·ceed·ing (ĭk-sē′dĭng) ▸ *adj.* Extreme; extraordinary. **—ex·ceed′ing·ly** *adv.*

ex·cel (ĭk-sĕl′) ▸ *v.* **-celled, -cel·ling.** To be superior to; surpass; outdo.

ex·cel·lence (ĕk′sə-ləns) ▸ *n.* **1.** The quality or condition of excelling; superiority. **2.** Something in which one excels. **3. Excellence** Excellency.

Ex·cel·len·cy (ĕk′sə-lən-sē) ▸ *n., pl.* **-cies.** Used with *His, Her,* or *Your* as a title for certain high officials.

ex·cel·lent (ĕk′sə-lənt) ▸ *adj.* Of the highest or finest quality; exceptionally good; superb. **—ex′cel·lent·ly** *adv.*

ex·cel·si·or (ĭk-sĕl′sē-ər) ▸ *n.* Wood shavings used esp. for packing.

ex·cept (ĭk-sĕpt′) ▸ *prep.* Other than; but. ▸ *conj.* If it were not for the fact that; only. ▸ *v.* To leave out; exclude.

ex·cept·ing (ĭk-sĕp′tĭng) ▸ *prep.* With the exception of; except.

ex·cep·tion (ĭk-sĕp′shən) ▸ *n.* **1.** The act of excepting; exclusion. **2.** One that is excepted. **3.** An objection.

ex·cep·tion·a·ble (ĭk-sĕp′shə-nə-bəl) ▸ *adj.* Open to objection. **—ex·cep′tion·a·bly** *adv.*

ex·cep·tion·al (ĭk-sĕp′shə-nəl) ▸ *adj.* Uncommon; extraordinary. **—ex·cep′tion·al·ly** *adv.*

ex·cerpt (ĕk′sûrpt′) ▸ *n.* A passage or segment taken from a longer work, such as a speech, book, or film. **—ex·cerpt′** *v.*

ex·cess (ĭk-sĕs′, ĕk′sĕs′) ▸ *n.* **1.** An amount or quantity beyond what is required; surplus. **2.** Intemperance; overindulgence: *drank to excess.* ▸ *adj.* Being more than what is required. **—ex·ces′sive** *adj.* **—ex·ces′sive·ly** *adv.* **—ex·ces′sive·ness** *n.*

ex·change (ĭks-chānj′) ▸ *v.* **-changed, -chang·ing. 1.** To give and receive reciprocally; trade; interchange. **2.** To turn in for replacement. ▸ *n.* **1.** The act or an instance of exchanging. **2.** A place where things are exchanged, esp. a center where securities are traded. **3.** A central system that establishes connections between individual telephones. **4.** A bill of exchange. **5.** A rate of exchange. **—ex·change′a·ble** *adj.*

ex·cheq·uer (ĕks′chĕk′ər, ĭks-chĕk′ər) ▸ *n.* A treasury, as of a nation or organization.

ex·cip·i·ent (ĭk-sĭp′ē-ənt) ▸ *n.* An inert substance used as a diluent or vehicle for a drug.

ex·cise[1] (ĕk′sīz′) ▸ *n.* A tax on the production, sale, or consumption of a commodity within a country.

ex·cise[2] (ĭk-sīz′) ▸ *v.* **-cised, -cis·ing.** To remove by or as if by cutting. **—ex·ci′sion** (-sĭzh′ən) *n.*

ex·cit·a·ble (ĭk-sī′tə-bəl) ▸ *adj.* Capable of being easily excited. **—ex·cit′a·bil′i·ty, ex·cit′a·ble·ness** *n.* **—ex·cit′a·bly** *adv.*

ex·ci·tant (ĭk-sīt′nt) ▸ *n.* An agent or stimulus that excites; stimulant. **—ex·ci′tant** *adj.*

ex·cite (ĭk-sīt′) ▸ *v.* **-cit·ed, -cit·ing. 1.** To stir to activity; stimulate. **2.** To call forth; elicit: *excited my curiosity.* **3.** To arouse strong feeling in; provoke. **4.** *Phys.* To raise (e.g., an atom) to a higher energy level. **—ex′ci·ta′tion** (ĕk′sī-tā′shən) *n.* **—ex·cit′ed·ly** *adv.* **—ex·cite′ment** *n.* **—ex·cit′ing·ly** *adv.*

ex·claim (ĭk-sklām′) ▸ *v.* To cry out or speak suddenly or vehemently.

ex·cla·ma·tion (ĕk′sklə-mā′shən) ▸ *n.* **1.** A sudden forceful utterance. **2.** *Gram.* An interjection. **—ex·clam′a·to′ry** (ĭk-sklăm′ə-tôr′ē, -tōr′ē) *adj.*

exclamation point ▸ *n.* A punctuation mark (!) used after an exclamation.

ex·clude (ĭk-sklo͞od′) ▸ *v.* **-clud·ed, -clud·ing. 1.** To prevent from entering; keep out; bar. **2.** To put out; expel. **—ex·**

THESAURUS

example *n.* **1.** One that is representative of a group or class ▸ case, embodiment, exemplar, exemplification, exponent, illustration, instance, instantiation, representative, sample, specimen. **2.** An instance that warns or discourages prospective imitators ▸ caveat, cautionary tale, exemplar, lesson, object lesson, warning. [*Compare* PREVENTIVE, WARNING.] *—See also* MODEL.

exasperate *v. —See* ANGER (1), ANNOY.

exasperation *n. —See* ANNOYANCE (1).

excavate *v. —See* DIG.

exceed *v.* To go beyond the limits of ▸ overleap, overpass, overreach, overrun, overshoot, overstep, surpass, transcend, transgress. *—See also* SURPASS.

exceedingly *adv. —See* VERY.

excel *v. —See* SURPASS.

excellence *n.* The quality of being exceptionally good of its kind ▸ fineness, incomparability, preeminence, superbness, superiority, transcendence, virtuosity. [*Compare* DISTINCTION.]

excellent *adj.* Exceptionally good of its kind ▸ ace, banner, blue-ribbon, brag, capital, champion, dandy, fine, first-class, first-rate, prime, prize, quality, remarkable, splendid, superb, superior, terrific, tiptop, top, world-class. *Informal:* A-OK, A-one, bang-up, bully, great, jim-dandy, smashing, swell, topflight, topnotch. *Slang:* awesome, bad, boss, cool, corking, crackerjack, dynamite, hot, killer, phat, primo, super-duper, tops. *Idioms:* out of this world, to die for. [*Compare* BEST, CHOICE, EXCEPTIONAL, MARVELOUS.]

except *v. —See* EXCLUDE, OBJECT.

exception *n. —See* ABNORMALITY, OBJECTION.

exceptionable *adj. —See* DEBATABLE, OBJECTIONABLE.

exceptional *adj.* Beyond what is usual, normal, or customary ▸ especial, exquisite, extraordinary, magnificent, memorable, notable, noteworthy, outstanding, preeminent, rare, remarkable, singular, special, sublime, towering, uncommon, unprecedented, unusual. *Informal:* standout. *Slang:* awesome, out of sight. [*Compare* BEST, EXCELLENT, NOTICEABLE, UNIQUE.] *—See also* CHOICE (1).

exceptionally *adv. —See* UNUSUALLY, VERY.

excess *n.* **1.** A condition of going or being beyond what is needed, desired, or appropriate ▸ embarrassment, excessiveness, exorbitance, extravagance, extravagancy, extravagantness, inordinacy, inordinateness, overabundance, oversufficiency, plethora, superabundance, superfluity, superfluousness, surfeit. *Idiom:* fifth wheel. **2.** Immoderate indulgence, as in food or drink ▸ immoderacy, immoderateness, immoderation, intemperance, overindulgence, surfeit. *—See also* SURPLUS.

excess *adj. —See* SUPERFLUOUS.

excessive *adj.* Exceeding a normal or reasonable limit ▸ exorbitant, extravagant, extreme, immoderate, intemperate, inordinate, overabundant, overmuch, unbridled, undue, unrestrained. *Idioms:* out of all bounds (*or* proportion), out of control. [*Compare* FLAGRANT, OUTRAGEOUS.] *—See also* WANTON (2).

excessively *adv. —See* UNDULY.

excessiveness *n. —See* EXCESS (1).

exchange *v.* To give and receive mutually, as words ▸ bandy, interchange, swap, trade. *Idiom:* give as good as one gets. [*Compare* RECIPROCATE, RETALIATE.] *—See also* CHANGE (3).

exchange *n. —See* CHANGE (2), COMMUNICATION (1), DEAL (1).

excitation *n. —See* ENTHUSIASM (1).

excite *v. —See* DELIGHT (1), ENRAPTURE, PROVOKE.

excited *adj. —See* THRILLED.

excitement *n. —See* AGITATION (3), ENTHUSIASM (1).

exciting *adj. —See* DRAMATIC (2), INVIGORATING.

exclaim *v.* To speak suddenly or sharply, as from surprise or emotion ▸ blurt (out), burst out, cry (out), ejaculate, rap out. [*Compare* SHOUT.]

exclamation *n. —See* SHOUT.

exclude *v.* To keep from being admit-

clu′sion *n.* **—ex·clu′sion·ar′y** *adv.* (-zhə-nĕr′ē) *adj.*

ex·clu·sive (ĭk-skloo͞′sĭv) ▸ *adj.* **1.** Not divided or shared with others: *exclusive rights.* **2.** Admitting only certain people, as for membership or participation. **3.** Fancy; expensive: *exclusive shops.* ▸ *n.* **1.** A news item initially released to only one publication or broadcaster. **2.** An exclusive right. **—ex·clu′sive·ly** *adv.* **—ex·clu′sive·ness, ex′clu·siv′i·ty** (ĕk′skloo͞-sĭv′ĭ-tē) *n.*

ex·com·mu·ni·cate (ĕks′kə-myoo͞′nĭ-kāt′) ▸ *v.* **-cat·ed, -cat·ing.** To deprive of the right of church membership by ecclesiastical authority. ▸ *n.* (-kĭt) A person who has been excommunicated. **—ex′com·mu′ni·ca′tion** *n.* **—ex′com·mu′ni·ca′tor** *n.*

ex·co·ri·ate (ĭk-skôr′ē-āt′) ▸ *v.* **-at·ed, -at·ing. 1.** To tear or wear off the skin of. **2.** To censure strongly; denounce. **—ex·co′ri·a′tion** *n.*

ex·cre·ment (ĕk′skrə-mənt) ▸ *n.* Bodily waste, esp. fecal matter. **—ex′cre·men′tal** *adj.*

ex·cres·cence (ĭk-skrĕs′əns) ▸ *n.* An outgrowth or enlargement, esp. an abnormal one. **—ex·cres′cent** *adj.*

ex·cre·ta (ĭk-skrē′tə) ▸ *pl.n.* Waste matter, such as sweat, urine, or feces, discharged from the body.

ex·crete (ĭk-skrēt′) ▸ *v.* **-cret·ed, -cret·ing.** To separate and discharge (waste matter) from the blood, tissues, or organs. **—ex·cre′tion** *n.* **—ex′cre·to′ry** (-skrĭ-tôr′ē) *adj.*

ex·cru·ci·at·ing (ĭk-skroo͞′shē-ā′tĭng) ▸ *adj.* Intensely painful or distressing. **—ex·cru′ci·at′ing·ly** *adv.*

ex·cul·pate (ĕk′skəl-pāt′, ĭk-skŭl′-) ▸ *v.* **-pat·ed, -pat·ing.** To clear of guilt or blame. **—ex′cul·pa′tion** *n.* **—ex·cul′pa·to′ry** (ĭk-skŭl′pə-tôr′ē) *adj.*

ex·cur·sion (ĭk-skûr′zhən) ▸ *n.* **1.** A usu. short journey; outing. **2.** A short pleasure trip. **3.** A digression from a main topic. **—ex·cur′sion·ist** *n.*

ex·cur·sive (ĭk-skûr′sĭv) ▸ *adj.* Marked by digression; rambling. **—ex·cur′sive·ly** *adv.* **—ex·cur′sive·ness** *n.*

ex·cuse (ĭk-skyoo͞z′) ▸ *v.* **-cused, -cus·ing. 1.** To offer an apology or explanation for (a fault or offense). **2a.** To pardon; forgive. **b.** To make allowance for; overlook. **3.** To justify: *Brilliance does not excuse bad manners.* **4.** To free, as from an obligation. ▸ *n.* (ĭk-skyoo͞s′) **1.** An explanation offered to obtain forgiveness. **2.** A reason for being excused. **3.** *Informal* An inferior example: *a poor excuse for a car.* **—ex·cus′a·ble** *adj.* **—ex·cus′er** *n.*

ex·e·cra·ble (ĕk′sĭ-krə-bəl) ▸ *adj.* **1.** Detestable or hateful. **2.** Extremely inferior. **—ex′e·cra·bly** *adv.*

ex·e·crate (ĕk′sĭ-krāt′) ▸ *v.* **-crat·ed, -crat·ing. 1.** To protest vehemently against; denounce. **2.** To loathe; abhor. **—ex′e·cra′tion** *n.* **—ex′e·cra′tor** *n.*

ex·e·cute (ĕk′sĭ-kyoo͞t′) ▸ *v.* **-cut·ed, -cut·ing. 1.** To carry out; perform. **2.** To make valid or legal, as by signing. **3.** To carry out what is required by: *execute a will.* **4.** To put to death, esp. by a lawful sentence. **5.** *Comp. Sci.* To run (a program or instruction). **—ex′e·cut′a·ble** *adj.* **—ex′e·cut′er** *n.* **—ex′e·cu′tion** *n.*

ex·e·cu·tion·er (ĕk′sĭ-kyoo͞′shə-nər) ▸ *n.* One who administers capital punishment.

ex·ec·u·tive (ĭg-zĕk′yə-tĭv) ▸ *n.* **1.** A person or group having administrative or managerial authority in an organization. **2.** The branch of government charged with putting a country's laws into effect. ▸ *adj.* **1.** Relating to or capable of carrying out or executing: *executive powers.* **2.** Of or relating to the executive branch of government.

ex·ec·u·tor (ĭg-zĕk′yə-tər, ĕk′sĭ-kyoo͞′tər) ▸ *n.* *Law* A person designated to execute the terms of a will.

ex·e·ge·sis (ĕk′sə-jē′sĭs) ▸ *n., pl.* **-ses** (-sēz). Critical interpretation or explanation of a text. **—ex′e·get′ic** (-jĕt′ĭk), **ex′e·get′i·cal** *adj.*

ex·em·plar (ĭg-zĕm′plär′, -plər) ▸ *n.* **1.** One that is worthy of imitation; model. **2.** One that is typical; example. **—ex·em′pla·ry** *adj.*

ex·em·pli·fy (ĭg-zĕm′plə-fī′) ▸ *v.* **-fied, -fy·ing. 1.** To illustrate by example. **2.** To serve as an example of. **—ex·em′pli·fi·ca′tion** *n.*

ex·empt (ĭg-zĕmpt′) ▸ *v.* To free from an obligation, duty, or liability to which others are subject. **—ex·empt′** *adj.* **—ex·empt′i·ble** *adj.* **—ex·emp′tion** *n.*

ex·er·cise (ĕk′sər-sīz′) ▸ *n.* **1.** An act of using or putting

THESAURUS

ted, included, or considered ▸ ban, bar, blackball, blacklist, boycott, count out, debar, eliminate, except, keep out, ostracize, reject, rule out, shut out, vote down. [*Compare* BANISH, FORBID, DECLINE.] *—See also* DROP (5).

exclusion *n.* *—See* ELIMINATION, PREVENTION.

exclusive *adj.* **1.** Not divided among or shared with others ▸ particular, prerogative, private, single, sole. [*Compare* INDIVIDUAL.] **2.** Singled out in preference ▸ choice, chosen, elect, select. [*Compare* EXCELLENT, FAVORITE.] **3.** Catering to, used by, or admitting only the wealthy or socially superior ▸ chic, chichi, classy, elite, fancy, hoity-toity, posh, selective, smart, sophisticated, swank, swanky, tony. *Informal:* ritzy. [*Compare* SNOBBISH.] *—See also* CONCENTRATED (1), PREVENTIVE (1).

exclusively *adv.* *—See* SOLELY.

excogitate *v.* *—See* DERIVE (2), PONDER.

excogitation *n.* *—See* THOUGHT.

excogitative *adj.* *—See* THOUGHTFUL.

excoriate *v.* *—See* CHAFE, SLAM (1).

excretory *adj.* *—See* ELIMINATIVE.

excruciate *v.* *—See* AFFLICT.

excruciating *adj.* *—See* TORMENTING.

exculpate *v.* *—See* CLEAR (3).

exculpation *n.* A freeing or clearing from accusation or guilt ▸ absolution, acquittal, exoneration, justification, remission, vindication. [*Compare* FORGIVENESS.]

excursion *n.* A usually short journey taken for pleasure ▸ jaunt, junket, outing, trip. [*Compare* EXPEDITION, JOURNEY.] *—See also* DIGRESSION.

excursionist *n.* *—See* TOURIST.

excursive *adj.* *—See* DIGRESSIVE.

excursus *n.* *—See* DIGRESSION.

excusable *adj.* Capable of being justified ▸ defensible, justifiable, tenable. [*Compare* LOGICAL, SOUND[2].] *—See also* PARDONABLE.

excuse *v.* **1.** To free from an obligation or duty ▸ absolve, discharge, dispense, exempt, let off, release, remise, remit, relieve, spare. ***Idioms:*** let off the hook, make excuses for. **2.** To show to be just, right, or valid ▸ justify, rationalize, vindicate. ***Idiom:*** make a case for. *—See also* DISMISS (2), FORGIVE.

excuse *n.* **1.** An explanation offered to justify an action or make it better understood ▸ justification, plea, pretext, rationale, rationalization. *Informal:* alibi. [*Compare* ACCOUNT, PRETENSE.] **2.** A statement of acknowledgment expressing regret or asking pardon ▸ apology, mea culpa, regrets. [*Compare* ACKNOWLEDGMENT.] *—See also* FORGIVENESS.

exec *n.* *—See* EXECUTIVE.

execrable *adj.* *—See* DAMNED.

execrate *v.* *—See* HATE, REVILE.

execration *n.* *—See* CURSE (1), HATE (2).

execute *v.* *—See* ADMINISTER (2), EFFECT, ENFORCE, FULFILL, INTERPRET (2), KILL[1], PERFORM (1).

execution *n.* Carrying a law or judgment into effect ▸ enforcement, implementation. [*Compare* EFFECT, EXERCISE.] *—See also* INTERPRETATION, PERFORMANCE.

executive *n.* A person having administrative or managerial authority in an organization ▸ administrant, administrator, CEO, chair, chairman (of the board), chairwoman, chief executive, director, functionary, manager, middle manager, officer, official, president. *Informal:* exec, higher-up. [*Compare* BOSS.]

executive *adj.* *—See* ADMINISTRATIVE.

exegesis *n.* *—See* COMMENTARY, EXPLANATION.

exegetic *adj.* *—See* EXPLANATORY.

exemplar *n.* *—See* EPITOME, EXAMPLE (1), EXAMPLE (2), MODEL.

exemplary *adj.* Beyond reproach ▸ blameless, faultless, good, lily-white, irreprehensible, irreproachable, unblamable. *—See also* ADMIRABLE, IDEAL.

exemplification *n.* *—See* EMBODIMENT, EXAMPLE (1).

exemplify *v.* To demonstrate and clarify with examples ▸ demonstrate, evidence, illustrate, instance. [*Compare* EXPLAIN, SHOW.] *—See also* REPRESENT (1).

exempt *v.* *—See* EXCUSE (1).

exemption *n.* Temporary immunity from penalties ▸ grace, immunity, reprieve, respite. [*Compare* DELAY, FORGIVENESS.]

exercise *n.* **1.** The act of putting into

into effect. 2. The discharge of a duty, function, or office. 3. Physical activity, esp. to develop or maintain fitness. 4. A task, problem, or other effort designed to develop understanding or skill. 5. **exercises** A public program that includes speeches, awards, and other ceremonial activities. ▸ *v.* **-cised, -cis·ing.** 1. To take exercise. 2. To put into operation; employ. 3. To put through exercises. 4. To worry, upset, or make anxious. **—ex′er·cis′er** *n.*

ex·ert (ĭg-zûrt′) ▸ *v.* 1. To bring to bear: *exert influence.* 2. To put (oneself) to strenuous effort. **—ex·er′tion** *n.*

ex·hale (ĕks-hāl′, ĕk-sāl′) ▸ *v.* **-haled, -hal·ing.** 1. To breathe out. 2. To emit (e.g., smoke). **—ex′ha·la′tion** (ĕks′hə-lā′shən, ĕk′sə-) *n.*

ex·haust (ĭg-zôst′) ▸ *v.* 1. To wear out completely; tire. 2. To use up completely; consume. 3. To treat or cover thoroughly: *exhaust all possibilities.* 4. To let out or draw off (a liquid or gas). ▸ *n.* 1a. The escape or release of waste gases or vapors, as from an engine. b. Vapors or gases so released. 2. A device or system that pumps gases out or allows them to escape. **—ex·haust′i·bil′i·ty** *n.* **—ex·haust′i·ble** *adj.* **—ex·haus′tion** *n.*

ex·haus·tive (ĭg-zô′stĭv) ▸ *adj.* Comprehensive; thorough: *an exhaustive study.* **—ex·haus′tive·ly** *adv.* **—ex·haus′tive·ness** *n.*

ex·hib·it (ĭg-zĭb′ĭt) ▸ *v.* To show or display, esp. to public view. ▸ *n.* 1. The act of exhibiting. 2. Something exhibited. 3. *Law* Something introduced as evidence in court. **—ex·hib′i·tor** *n.* **—ex′hi·bi′tion** (ĕk′sə-bĭsh′ən) *n.*

ex·hi·bi·tion·ism (ĕk′sə-bĭsh′ə-nĭz′əm) ▸ *n.* The practice of behaving so as to attract attention. **—ex′hi·bi′tion·ist** *n.* **—ex′hi·bi′tion·is′tic** *adj.*

ex·hil·a·rate (ĭg-zĭl′ə-rāt′) ▸ *v.* **-rat·ed, -rat·ing.** 1. To make joyous and energetic; elate. 2. To invigorate or stimulate. **—ex·hil′a·ra′tion** *n.* **—ex·hil′a·ra′tive** *adj.*

ex·hort (ĭg-zôrt′) ▸ *v.* To urge by strong argument, admonition, advice, or appeal. **—ex′hor·ta′tion** *n.* **—ex·hor′ta·tive** *adj.* **—ex·hort′er** *n.*

ex·hume (ĭg-zo͞om′, -zyo͞om′, ĕks-hyo͞om′) ▸ *v.* **-humed, -hum·ing.** 1. To remove from a grave. 2. To bring to light, esp. after a period of obscurity. **—ex′hu·ma′tion** *n.*

ex·i·gence (ĕk′sə-jəns) ▸ *n.* Exigency.

ex·i·gen·cy (ĕk′sə-jən-sē, ĭg-zĭj′ən-) ▸ *n., pl.* **-cies.** 1. A pressing or urgent situation. 2. often **exigencies** Urgent requirements. **—ex′i·gent** *adj.*

ex·ig·u·ous (ĭg-zĭg′yo͞o-əs, ĭk-sĭg′-) ▸ *adj.* Scanty; meager. **—ex′i·gu′i·ty** (ĕk′sĭ-gyo͞o′ĭ-tē) *n.* **—ex·ig′u·ous·ly** *adv.*

ex·ile (ĕg′zīl′, ĕk′sīl′) ▸ *n.* 1. Enforced removal or self-imposed absence from one's native country. 2. One who chooses or is sent into exile. ▸ *v.* **-iled, -il·ing.** To send into exile; banish.

ex·ist (ĭg-zĭst′) ▸ *v.* 1. To have actual being; be real. 2. To have life; live. 3. To occur.

ex·is·tence (ĭg-zĭs′təns) ▸ *n.* 1. The fact or state of existing. 2. Presence; occurrence. **—ex·is′tent** *adj.*

ex·is·ten·tial (ĕg′zĭ-stĕn′shəl, ĕk′sĭ-) ▸ *adj.* 1. Of or relating to existence. 2. Based on experience; empirical. 3. Of or relating to existentialism. **—ex′is·ten′tial·ly** *adv.*

ex·is·ten·tial·ism (ĕg′zĭ-stĕn′shə-lĭz′əm, ĕk′sĭ-) ▸ *n.* A philosophy that emphasizes the uniqueness and isolation of the individual in a hostile or indifferent universe and stresses freedom of choice and responsibility for the consequences of one's acts. **—ex′is·ten′tial·ist** *adj. & n.*

ex·it (ĕg′zĭt, ĕk′sĭt) ▸ *n.* 1. The act of going out. 2. A passage or way out. 3. The departure of a performer from the stage. **—ex′it** *v.*

exo– ▸ *pref.* Outside; external: *exoskeleton.*

ex·o·bi·ol·o·gy (ĕk′sō-bī-ŏl′ə-jē) ▸ *n.* The scientific search for extraterrestrial life. **—ex′o·bi·ol′o·gist** *n.*

ex·o·crine (ĕk′sə-krĭn, -krēn, -krīn′) ▸ *adj.* Having or secreting through a duct: *an exocrine gland.*

ex·o·dus (ĕk′sə-dəs) ▸ *n.* 1. A departure or emigration of a large number of people. 2. **Exodus** See **Bible** table in Appendix.

ex of·fi·ci·o (ĕks′ ə-fĭsh′ē-ō′) ▸ *adv. & adj.* By virtue of office or position.

ex·og·e·nous (ĕk-sŏj′ə-nəs) ▸ *adj.* Originating outside an organism or part: *an exogenous disease.* **—ex·og′e·nous·ly** *adv.*

ex·on·er·ate (ĭg-zŏn′ə-rāt′) ▸ *v.* **-at·ed, -at·ing.** To free from blame or responsibility. **—ex·on′er·a′tion** *n.* **—ex·on′er·a′tive** *adj.* **—ex·on′er·a′tor** *n.*

ex·or·bi·tant (ĭg-zôr′bĭ-tənt) ▸ *adj.* Exceeding reasonable

THESAURUS

play ▸ administration, adoption, application, employment, exertion, implementation, operation, play, recourse, resort, usage, use, utilization. 2. Energetic physical action ▸ activity, exertion, workout. —*See also* PRACTICE.

exercise *v.* 1. To bring to bear steadily or forcefully, as influence ▸ exert, ply, wield. *Idiom:* throw one's weight around. 2. To engage in activities in order to strengthen or condition ▸ drill, practice, train, work out. —*See also* FULFILL, PRACTICE (1), USE.

exert *v.* To bring to bear steadily or forcefully, as influence ▸ exercise, ply, wield. *Idiom:* throw one's weight around. —*See also* APPLY (1).

exertion *n.* Energetic physical action ▸ activity, exercise, workout. —*See also* EFFORT, EXERCISE (1).

exfoliate *v.* —*See* FLAKE.

exhalation *n.* —*See* BREATH.

exhale *v.* —*See* BREATHE (1), EMIT.

exhaust *v.* 1. To use all of ▸ consume, deplete, drain, draw down, eat up, expend, finish, play out, run through, sap, spend, use up. *Informal:* polish off. [*Compare* DRY.] 2. To be depleted ▸ consume, go, spend. *Idiom:* go down the drain. —*See also* TIRE (1).

exhausted *adj.* —*See* TIRED (1).

exhausting *adj.* Causing fatigue ▸ draining, fatiguing, tiring, wearing, wearying. [*Compare* BURDENSOME.]

exhaustion *n.* The condition of being extremely tired ▸ burnout, fatigue, prostration, tiredness, weariness. [*Compare* DEBILITATION, LETHARGY.]

exhaustive *adj.* —*See* DETAILED, THOROUGH.

exhaustively *adv.* —*See* COMPLETELY (2).

exhibit *v.* —*See* BEAR (3), DISPLAY, SHOW (1).

exhibit *n.* —*See* DISPLAY, EXHIBITION.

exhibition *n.* A large public display, as of goods or works of art ▸ bazaar, exhibit, expo, exposition, fair, festival, installation, retrospective, salon, show. [*Compare* MARKET, DISPLAY.] —*See also* DISPLAY.

exhibitionism *n.* —*See* THEATRICALISM.

exhibitory or **exhibitive** *adj.* —*See* DESIGNATIVE.

exhilarant *adj.* —*See* INVIGORATING.

exhilarate *v.* —*See* ELATE, ENERGIZE.

exhilarated *adj.* —*See* CHEERFUL.

exhilarating *adj.* —*See* INVIGORATING.

exhilaration *n.* —*See* ELATION.

exhort *v.* —*See* URGE.

exhume *v.* —*See* UNCOVER.

exigency or **exigence** *n.* A condition in which something necessary or desirable is required or wanted ▸ necessity, need. —*See also* CRISIS, DEMAND (2), EMERGENCY.

exigent *adj.* —*See* DIFFICULT (1), URGENT (1).

exiguous *adj.* —*See* MEAGER.

exile *n.* Enforced removal from one's native country by official decree ▸ banishment, deportation, expatriation, extradition, ostracism, proscription, transportation. —*See also* ÉMIGRÉ, OUTCAST.

exile *v.* —*See* BANISH.

exist *v.* To have reality or life ▸ be, breathe, live, subsist. *Idioms:* be around, draw breath, have one's being, walk the earth. [*Compare* ENDURE, SURVIVE.] —*See also* CONSIST.

exist on *v.* To include as part of one's diet by nature or preference ▸ eat, feed on, live on, subsist on.

existence *n.* The fact or state of existing or of being actual ▸ actuality, being, entity, reality, substantiality, substantiveness. [*Compare* CERTAINTY, FACT.] —*See also* LIFE, LIVING, THING (1).

existent *adj.* Occurring or existing in act or fact ▸ actual, extant, real, true. [*Compare* PHYSICAL.] —*See also* ALIVE, PRESENT[1].

existing *adj.* —*See* ALIVE, PRESENT[1].

exit *n.* —*See* DEPARTURE.

exit *v.* —*See* GO (1).

exodus *n.* —*See* DEPARTURE, EMIGRATION.

exonerate *v.* —*See* CLEAR (3).

exoneration *n.* —*See* EXCULPATION.

exorbitance *n.* —*See* EXCESS (1).

exorbitant *adj.* —*See* EXCESSIVE, STEEP[1] (2).

bounds or limits; excessive. **—ex·or′bi·tance** *n.* **—ex·or′bi·tant·ly** *adv.*

ex·or·cise (ĕk′sôr-sīz′, -sər-) ► *v.* **-cised, -cis·ing. 1.** To expel (an evil spirit) by or as if by incantation or prayer. **2.** To free from evil spirits. **—ex′or·cism** *n.* **—ex′or·cist** *n.*

ex·o·skel·e·ton (ĕk′sō-skĕl′ĭ-tn) ► *n.* A hard outer structure, such as the shell of an insect or crustacean, that provides protection or support for an organism. **—ex′o·skel′e·tal** (-ĭ-tl) *adj.*

ex·o·sphere (ĕk′sō-sfîr′) ► *n.* The outermost layer of the earth's atmosphere.

ex·o·ther·mic (ĕk′sō-thûr′mĭk) also **ex·o·ther·mal** (-məl) ► *adj.* Releasing heat: *an exothermic reaction.* **—ex′o·ther′mi·cal·ly** *adv.*

ex·ot·ic (ĭg-zŏt′ĭk) ► *adj.* **1.** From another part of the world. **2.** Intriguingly unusual, different, or beautiful. **—ex·ot′ic** *n.* **—ex·ot′i·cal·ly** *adv.*

exp ► *abbr.* **1.** exponent **2.** exponential

ex·pand (ĭk-spănd′) ► *v.* **1.** To increase or become increased in size, quantity, or scope. **2.** To express in detail; enlarge on: *expanded his remarks.* **3.** To spread out; unfold. **—ex·pand′a·ble** *adj.*

ex·panse (ĭk-spăns′) ► *n.* A wide, open extent, as of land, sea, or sky.

ex·pan·sion (ĭk-spăn′shən) ► *n.* **1.** The act or process of expanding or the state of being expanded. **2.** A product of expanding.

ex·pan·sion·ism (ĭk-spăn′shə-nĭz′əm) ► *n.* A nation's practice or policy of territorial or economic expansion. **—ex·pan′sion·ar′y** *adj.* **—ex·pan′sion·ist** *adj. & n.*

ex·pan·sive (ĭk-spăn′sĭv) ► *adj.* **1.** Capable of expanding or tending to expand. **2.** Broad; comprehensive. **3.** Kind and generous; outgoing. **—ex·pan′sive·ly** *adv.* **—ex·pan′sive·ness** *n.*

ex par·te (ĕks pär′tē) ► *adv. & adj.* *Law* From or on one side only.

ex·pa·ti·ate (ĭk-spā′shē-āt′) ► *v.* **-at·ed, -at·ing.** To speak or write at length; elaborate. **—ex·pa′ti·a′tion** *n.*

ex·pa·tri·ate (ĕk-spā′trē-āt′) ► *v.* **-at·ed, -at·ing. 1.** To exile; banish. **2.** To leave one's country to reside in another. **—ex·pa′tri·ate** (-ĭt, -āt′) *adj. & n.* **—ex·pa′tri·a′tion** *n.*

ex·pect (ĭk-spĕkt′) ► *v.* **1.** To look forward to the occurrence or appearance of. **2.** To consider reasonable or due. **3.** *Informal* To presume or suppose. **4.** To be pregnant. Used in progressive tenses: *My wife is expecting.*

ex·pec·tan·cy (ĭk-spĕk′tən-sē) ► *n., pl.* **-cies. 1.** Expectation. **2.** Something expected, esp. an amount calculated on statistical probability: *life expectancy.*

ex·pec·tant (ĭk-spĕk′tənt) ► *adj.* **1.** Expecting. **2.** Pregnant. **—ex·pec′tant·ly** *adv.*

ex·pec·ta·tion (ĕk′spĕk-tā′shən) ► *n.* **1.** The act or condition of expecting. **2.** Eager anticipation. **3. expectations** Prospects or hopes, esp. of success or gain.

ex·pec·to·rant (ĭk-spĕk′tər-ənt) ► *adj.* Promoting secretion or expulsion of mucus or other matter from the respiratory system. **—ex·pec′to·rant** *n.*

ex·pec·to·rate (ĭk-spĕk′tə-rāt′) ► *v.* **-rat·ed, -rat·ing.** To eject from the mouth; spit. **—ex·pec′to·ra′tion** *n.*

ex·pe·di·ence (ĭk-spē′dē-əns) ► *n.* Expediency.

ex·pe·di·en·cy (ĭk-spē′dē-ən-sē) ► *n., pl.* **-cies. 1.** Appropriateness to a purpose. **2.** Adherence to self-serving means.

ex·pe·di·ent (ĭk-spē′dē-ənt) ► *adj.* **1.** Appropriate to a particular purpose. **2.** Serving narrow or selfish interests. ► *n.* Something expedient. **—ex·pe′di·ent·ly** *adv.*

ex·pe·dite (ĕk′spĭ-dīt′) ► *v.* **-dit·ed, -dit·ing. 1.** To speed the progress of; facilitate. **2.** To perform quickly. **—ex′pe·dit′er, ex′pe·di′tor** *n.*

ex·pe·di·tion (ĕk′spĭ-dĭsh′ən) ► *n.* **1a.** A journey undertaken with a definite objective. **b.** The group making such a journey. **2.** Speed in performance.

ex·pe·di·tion·ar·y (ĕk′spĭ-dĭsh′ə-nĕr′ē) ► *adj.* Of or being an expedition, esp. a military one.

ex·pe·di·tious (ĕk′spĭ-dĭsh′əs) ► *adj.* Acting or done with speed and efficiency. **—ex′pe·di′tious·ly** *adv.*

ex·pel (ĭk-spĕl′) ► *v.* **-pelled, -pel·ling. 1.** To force or drive out; eject forcefully. **2.** To dismiss officially. **—ex·pel′la·ble** *adj.* **—ex·pel′ler** *n.*

ex·pend (ĭk-spĕnd′) ► *v.* **1.** To spend. **2.** To use up; waste.

ex·pend·a·ble (ĭk-spĕn′də-bəl) ► *adj.* **1.** Subject to use or consumption. **2.** Nonessential; dispensable.

ex·pen·di·ture (ĭk-spĕn′dĭ-chər) ► *n.* **1.** The act or process of expending. **2.** Something expended, esp. money.

ex·pense (ĭk-spĕns′) ► *n.* **1a.** Something spent to accomplish a purpose. **b.** Something given up for something gained; sacrifice. **2. expenses a.** Charges incurred by an employee in the performance of work. **b.** *Informal*

THESAURUS

exotic *adj.* Very strange or strikingly unusual ► bizarre, fanciful, fantastic, grotesque, outlandish, outré, strange, unorthodox. *Idioms:* from another planet (*or* outer space), off the wall. [*Compare* ECCENTRIC, UNUSUAL.] *—See also* FOREIGN (1).

expand *v.* *—See* BROADEN, ELABORATE, GAIN (1), INCREASE, SPREAD (1).

expandable *adj.* *—See* EXTENSIBLE.

expanse *n.* **1.** A wide and open area, as of land, sky, or water ► distance, expansion, extent, range, reach, space, spread, stretch, sweep, tract, vista. [*Compare* VIEW.] **2.** The extent of something from side to side ► breadth, broadness, wideness, width. [*Compare* DISTANCE.]

expansible or **expansile** *adj.* *—See* EXTENSIBLE.

expansion *n.* The process of increasing in extent or inclusiveness ► broadening, fanning out, extension, proliferation, spread. [*Compare* DISTRIBUTION.] *—See also* EXPANSE (1), INCREASE (1).

expansive *adj.* *—See* BROAD (1), GENERAL (2), OUTGOING.

expansively *adv.* *—See* CONSIDERABLY.

expatiate *v.* *—See* ELABORATE.

expatiation *n.* *—See* DISCOURSE.

expatriate *v.* *—See* BANISH.

expatriate *n.* *—See* ÉMIGRÉ, FOREIGNER.

expatriation *n.* *—See* EMIGRATION, EXILE.

expect *v.* **1.** To look forward to confidently ► anticipate, await, bargain for (*or* on), bet (on), count on, depend on (*or* upon), look for, wager, wait (for). *Informal:* figure on. [*Compare* FORESEE, INTEND.] **2.** To oblige to do or not do by force of authority, propriety, or custom ► oblige, obligate, require, suppose. [*Compare* MUST.] *—See also* SUPPOSE (1).

expectance or **expectancy** *n.* The condition of looking forward to something, especially with eagerness ► anticipation, expectation, high hopes, hopefulness. [*Compare* DESIRE.]

expectant *adj.* Having or marked by expectation ► anticipant, anticipative, anticipatory, awaiting, hopeful, hoping, looking forward to. *Idioms:* in suspense, on tenterhooks (*or* the edge of one's seat), on the lookout (*or* watch) for, with bated breath. [*Compare* EAGER, OPTIMISTIC.] *—See also* PREGNANT (1).

expectation *n.* **1.** The condition of looking forward to something, especially with eagerness ► anticipation, expectance, expectancy, high hopes, hopefulness. [*Compare* DESIRE.] **2.** Something that is eagerly expected ► anticipation, likelihood, promise, prospect. [*Compare* CHANCE, THEORY.]

expected *adj.* *—See* DUE (2).

expecting *adj.* *—See* PREGNANT (1).

expectorate *n.* *—See* SPIT.

expectorate *v.* To expel a small amount of saliva or mucus from the mouth ► hawk, spit. [*Compare* DROOL.]

expediency *n.* *—See* MAKESHIFT.

expedient *adj.* *—See* ADVISABLE, CONVENIENT (1).

expedient *n.* *—See* MAKESHIFT.

expedite *v.* *—See* EASE (2), SPEED.

expedition *n.* A journey undertaken with a specific objective ► grand tour, mission, odyssey, pilgrimage, quest, safari, sortie, tour, trek, voyage. *—See also* HASTE (1).

expeditious *adj.* *—See* FAST (1), QUICK.

expeditiousness *n.* *—See* HASTE (1).

expel *v.* *—See* BANISH, DISMISS (2), EJECT (1), ERUPT.

expellee *n.* *—See* ÉMIGRÉ.

expend *v.* *—See* EXHAUST (1), SPEND (1).

expenditure *n.* The act of consuming ► consumption, depletion, usage, use, utilization. [*Compare* USE.] *—See also* COST (1).

expense *n.* The expenditure at which something is obtained ► cost, price,

Money allotted for payment of such charges. **3.** Something requiring the expenditure of money.

ex·pen·sive (ĭk-spĕn′sĭv) ▸ *adj.* Having a high price; costly. **—ex·pen′sive·ly** *adv.* **—ex·pen′sive·ness** *n.*

ex·pe·ri·ence (ĭk-spîr′ē-əns) ▸ *n.* **1.** The apprehension of an object, thought, or emotion through the senses or mind. **2a.** Activity or practice through which knowledge or skill is gained. **b.** Knowledge or skill so derived. **3a.** An event or a series of events undergone or lived through. **b.** The totality or effect of such events. ▸ *v.* **-enced, -enc·ing.** To have as an experience; undergo.

ex·pe·ri·enced (ĭk-spîr′ē-ənst) ▸ *adj.* Skilled or knowledgeable through experience.

ex·pe·ri·en·tial (ĭk-spîr′ē-ĕn′shəl) ▸ *adj.* Relating to or derived from experience. **—ex·pe′ri·en′tial·ly** *adv.*

ex·per·i·ment (ĭk-spĕr′ə-mənt) ▸ *n.* A test made to demonstrate a known truth, examine the validity of a hypothesis, or determine the nature of something. ▸ *v.* (-mĕnt′) **1.** To conduct an experiment. **2.** To try something new: *experiment with new methods of teaching.* **—ex·per′i·men′tal** *adj.* **—ex·per′i·men′tal·ly** *adv.* **—ex·per′i·men·ta′tion** *n.*

ex·pert (ĕk′spûrt′) ▸ *n.* A person with a high degree of skill in or knowledge of a certain subject or field. ▸ *adj.* (ĕk′spûrt, ĭk-spûrt′) Highly skilled or knowledgeable. **—ex′pert′ly** *adv.* **—ex′pert′ness** *n.*

ex·per·tise (ĕk′spûr-tēz′) ▸ *n.* Expert skill or knowledge.

ex·pi·ate (ĕk′spē-āt′) ▸ *v.* **-at·ed, -at·ing.** To atone or make amends (for). **—ex′pi·a′tion** *n.* **—ex′pi·a′tor** *n.* **—ex′pi·a·to′ry** (-ə-tôr′ē) *adj.*

ex·pire (ĭk-spīr′) ▸ *v.* **-pired, -pir·ing.** **1.** To come to an end; terminate. **2.** To die. **3.** To exhale. **—ex′pi·ra′tion** (ĕk′spə-rā′shən) *n.*

ex·pi·ry (ĭk-spīr′ē) ▸ *n., pl.* **-ries.** **1.** An expiration, esp. of a contract. **2.** Death.

ex·plain (ĭk-splān′) ▸ *v.* **1.** To make plain or comprehensible. **2.** To define; expound. **3.** To offer reasons for; justify. **—ex·plain′a·ble** *adj.* **—ex′pla·na′tion** (ĕk′splə-nā′shən) *n.* **—ex·plan′a·to′ri·ly** *adv.* **—ex·plan′a·to′ry** (-splăn′ə-tôr′ē) *adj.*

ex·ple·tive (ĕk′splĭ-tĭv) ▸ *n.* An exclamation or oath.

ex·plic·a·ble (ĭk-splĭk′ə-bəl, ĕk′splĭ-kə-) ▸ *adj.* Possible to explain. **—ex′plic·a·bly** *adv.*

ex·pli·cate (ĕk′splĭ-kāt′) ▸ *v.* **-cat·ed, -cat·ing.** To explain, esp. in detail. **—ex′pli·ca′tion** *n.* **—ex′pli·ca′tive** *adj.* **—ex′pli·ca′tor** *n.*

ex·plic·it (ĭk-splĭs′ĭt) ▸ *adj.* Fully and clearly expressed, defined, or formulated. **—ex·plic′it·ly** *adv.* **—ex·plic′it·ness** *n.*

ex·plode (ĭk-splōd′) ▸ *v.* **-plod·ed, -plod·ing.** **1.** To cause or undergo an explosion. **2.** To burst or cause to burst by explosion. **3.** To burst forth or break out suddenly. **4.** To increase suddenly, sharply, and without control. **5.** To show to be false; refute. **—ex·plod′a·ble** *adj.*

ex·ploit (ĕk′sploit′, ĭk-sploit′) ▸ *n.* An act or deed, esp. a heroic one. ▸ *v.* (ĭk-sploit′, ĕk′sploit′) **1.** To utilize fully or advantageously. **2.** To make use of selfishly or unethically. **—ex·ploit′a·ble** *adj.* **—ex′ploi·ta′tion** *n.* **—ex·ploit′a·tive** *adj.* **—ex·ploit′er** *n.*

ex·plore (ĭk-splôr′) ▸ *v.* **-plored, -plor·ing.** **1.** To investigate systematically. **2.** To search or travel into for the purpose of discovery. **3.** *Medic.* To examine for diagnostic purposes. **—ex′plo·ra′tion** (ĕk′splə-rā′shən) *n.* **—ex·plor′a·to′ry** (-tôr′ē) *adj.* **—ex·plor′er** *n.*

ex·plo·sion (ĭk-splō′zhən) ▸ *n.* **1a.** A sudden violent release of mechanical, chemical, or nuclear energy. **b.** The loud sound accompanying such a release. **2.** A sudden, often vehement outburst, esp. of emotion. **3.** A sudden sharp increase: *a population explosion.*

ex·plo·sive (ĭk-splō′sĭv) ▸ *adj.* **1.** Of or causing an explosion. **2.** Tending to explode. **3.** Highly unstable; volatile. ▸ *n.* A substance, esp. a prepared chemical, that explodes or causes explosion. **—ex·plo′sive·ly** *adv.* **—ex·plo′sive·ness** *n.*

ex·po·nent (ĭk-spō′nənt, ĕk′spō′nənt) ▸ *n.* **1.** One that ex-

THESAURUS

sacrifice, toll. *Informal:* damage. *—See also* COST (1).

expenses *n.* *—See* OVERHEAD.

expensive *adj.* *—See* COSTLY.

experience *n.* Personal knowledge derived from participation or observation ▸ acquaintance, conversance, familiarity. [*Compare* AWARENESS.] *—See also* ADVENTURE, CIRCUMSTANCE (1).

experience *v.* To participate in or partake of personally ▸ encounter, feel, go through, have, know, meet (with), pass through, sample, see, suffer, taste (of), undergo. ***Idiom:*** run up against.

experienced *adj.* Skilled or knowledgeable through long practice ▸ old, practiced, seasoned, tried, versed, veteran. ***Idiom:*** knowing the ropes. [*Compare* DEPENDABLE, VETERAN.]

experiment or **experimentation** *n.* *—See* TEST (1).

experimental *adj.* *—See* PILOT.

expert *n.* A person with a high degree of knowledge or skill in a particular field ▸ ace, adept, authority, connoisseur, dab hand, master, maven, past master, professional, proficient, specialist, wizard, world-beater. *Informal:* pro, whiz. *Slang:* crackajack, crackerjack.

expert *adj.* Having or demonstrating a high degree of knowledge or skill ▸ adept, crack, master, masterful, masterly, professional, proficient, skilled, skillful. *Informal:* pro. *Slang:* crackajack, crackerjack. [*Compare* ABLE.]

expertise or **expertness** *n.* *—See* ABILITY (1).

expiable *adj.* *—See* PARDONABLE.

expiate *v.* *—See* PURIFY (1).

expiation *n.* The act of making amends ▸ atonement, penance, reconciliation, reparation. [*Compare* COMPENSATION, PURIFICATION.]

expiatory *adj.* *—See* PURGATIVE.

expiration *n.* *—See* BREATH, DEATH (1), DISAPPEARANCE, END (1).

expire *v.* *—See* BREATHE (1), DIE, DISAPPEAR (2), LAPSE.

explain *v.* **1.** To make understandable ▸ construe, decipher, demystify, elucidate, explicate, expound, gloss, interpret, spell out. ***Idioms:*** make perfectly clear, put into plain English, walk someone through. [*Compare* CLARIFY.] **2.** To offer reasons for or a cause of ▸ account for, justify, rationalize. [*Compare* RESOLVE.] *—See also* SOLVE (1).

explain away *v.* *—See* EXTENUATE.

explainable *adj.* Capable of being explained or accounted for ▸ accountable, construable, decipherable, explicable, illustratable, interpretable. [*Compare* JUSTIFIABLE, UNDERSTANDABLE.]

explanation *n.* Something that serves to explain or clarify ▸ clarification, construction, decipherment, elucidation, exegesis, explication, exposition, gloss, illumination, illustration, interpretation, spin. *—See also* ACCOUNT (1), ANSWER (2).

explanatory or **explanative** *adj.* Serving to explain ▸ elucidative, exegetic, explicative, expositive, expository, hermeneutic, hermeneutical, illustrative, interpretative, interpretive. [*Compare* EDUCATIONAL.]

expletive *n.* *—See* SWEARWORD.

explicable *adj.* *—See* EXPLAINABLE.

explicate *v.* *—See* EXPLAIN (1).

explication *n.* *—See* EXPLANATION.

explicative *adj.* *—See* EXPLANATORY.

explicit *adj.* *—See* DEFINITE (1), GRAPHIC (1).

explicitness *n.* *—See* CLARITY.

explode *v.* **1.** To release or cause to release energy suddenly and violently, especially with a loud noise ▸ backfire, blast, blow (up), burst, detonate, fire, fulminate, go off, touch off. **2.** To come open or fly apart suddenly and violently, as from internal pressure ▸ blow (out), burst, pop. *Slang:* bust. **3.** To increase or expand suddenly, rapidly, or without control ▸ balloon, mushroom, snowball. [*Compare* INCREASE.] *—See also* ANGER (2), BREAK OUT, DISCREDIT.

exploit *v.* *—See* ABUSE (1), ABUSE (2), MANIPULATE (1), USE.

exploit *n.* *—See* ACCOMPLISHMENT.

exploitable *adj.* *—See* GULLIBLE.

exploration *n.* The act or an instance of exploring or investigating ▸ investigation, probe, reconnaissance. [*Compare* EXAMINATION.]

explore *v.* To go into or through for the purpose of making discoveries or acquiring information ▸ delve, dig, fathom, inquire, investigate, look into, plumb, probe, reconnoiter, scout, sound. [*Compare* EXAMINE, SNOOP.]

explosion *n.* *—See* BLAST (2), CRACK (1), ERUPTION, OUTBURST.

exponent *n.* *—See* EXAMPLE (1).

pounds, interprets, or advocates. 2. A number or symbol, as 3 in $(x + y)^3$, placed to the right of and above another number, symbol, or expression, denoting the power to which it is to be raised. **—ex′po·nen′tial** (ĕk′spə-nĕn′shəl) *adj.* **—ex′po·nen′tial·ly** *adv.*

ex·port (ĭk-spôrt′, ĕk′spôrt′) ► *v.* 1. To send or transport abroad, esp. for trade or sale. 2. *Comp. Sci.* To send (data) from one program to another. ► *n.* (ĕk′spôrt′) Exportation. **—ex·port′a·ble** *adj.* **—ex·port′er** *n.*

ex·por·ta·tion (ĕk′spôr-tā′shən) ► *n.* 1. The act of exporting. 2. Something exported; export.

ex·pose (ĭk-spōz′) ► *v.* **-posed, -pos·ing.** 1a. To subject or allow to be subjected to an action or influence. b. To subject (a photographic film or plate) to the action of light. 2. To make visible or known; reveal. 3. To lay bare; uncover. **—ex·pos′er** *n.*

ex·po·sé (ĕk′spō-zā′) ► *n.* A public revelation of something discreditable.

ex·po·si·tion (ĕk′spə-zĭsh′ən) ► *n.* 1. The systematic explanation of a subject. 2. A discourse that conveys information about or explains a subject. 3. A public exhibition of broad scope. **—ex·pos′i·tor** (ĭk-spŏz′ĭ-tər) *n.* **—ex·pos′i·to′ry** (-tôr′ē) *adj.*

ex post fac·to (ĕks′ pōst făk′tō) ► *adj.* Formulated, enacted, or operating retroactively.

ex·pos·tu·late (ĭk-spŏs′chə-lāt′) ► *v.* **-lat·ed, -lat·ing.** To reason earnestly with someone, esp. to dissuade or correct. **—ex·pos′tu·la′tion** *n.* **—ex·pos′tu·la′tor** *n.* **—ex·pos′tu·la·to′ry** (-lə-tôr′ē) *adj.*

ex·po·sure (ĭk-spō′zhər) ► *n.* 1. The act or an instance of exposing or the condition of being exposed. 2. A position in relation to direction of weather conditions. 3a. The act or time of exposing a photographic film or plate. b. A film or plate so exposed.

ex·pound (ĭk-spound′) ► *v.* To give a detailed statement (of); explain. **—ex·pound′er** *n.*

ex·press (ĭk-sprĕs′) ► *v.* 1. To make known or indicate, as by words, facial aspect, or symbols. 2. To press out, as juice from an orange. 3. To send by rapid transport. ► *adj.* 1. Definitely and clearly stated. 2a. Sent by rapid direct transportation. b. Direct, rapid, and usu. nonstop: *an express bus.* ► *adv.* By express transportation. ► *n.* 1. A rapid, efficient system for the delivery of goods and mail. 2. A means of transport, such as a train, that travels rapidly, usu. nonstop. **—ex·press′i·ble** *adj.* **—ex·press′ly** *adv.*

ex·pres·sion (ĭk-sprĕsh′ən) ► *n.* 1. Communication, as of an idea or emotion, esp. by words, art, music, or movement. 2. A symbol, sign, or indication. 3. *Math.* A symbol or combination of symbols representing a quantity or a relationship between quantities. 4. A manner of expressing, esp. in speaking, depicting, or performing. 5. A word or phrase. 6. A facial aspect or tone of voice conveying feeling. **—ex·pres′sion·less** *adj.*

ex·pres·sion·ism (ĭk-sprĕsh′ə-nĭz′əm) ► *n.* A movement in the fine arts that emphasized subjective expression of the artist's inner experiences. **—ex·pres′sion·ist** *n.* **—ex·pres′sion·is′tic** *adj.*

ex·pres·sive (ĭk-sprĕs′ĭv) ► *adj.* 1. Expressing or serving to express or indicate. 2. Full of expression or meaning. **—ex·pres′sive·ly** *adv.* **—ex·pres′sive·ness** *n.*

ex·press·way (ĭk-sprĕs′wā′) ► *n.* A major divided highway designed for high-speed travel.

ex·pro·pri·ate (ĕk-sprō′prē-āt′) ► *v.* **-at·ed, -at·ing.** To acquire or take (land or other property) from another, esp. for public use. **—ex·pro′pri·a′tion** *n.* **—ex·pro′pri·a′tor** *n.*

ex·pul·sion (ĭk-spŭl′shən) ► *n.* The act of expelling or the state of being expelled.

ex·punge (ĭk-spŭnj′) ► *v.* **-punged, -pung·ing.** To erase or strike out.

ex·pur·gate (ĕk′spər-gāt′) ► *v.* **-gat·ed, -gat·ing.** To remove obscene or objectionable material from. **—ex′pur·ga′tion** *n.* **—ex′pur·ga′tor** *n.*

ex·qui·site (ĕk′skwĭ-zĭt, ĭk-skwĭz′ĭt) ► *adj.* 1. Beautifully made or designed. 2. Of or having great delicacy or beauty. 3. Acutely refined or discriminating. 4. Intense; keen. **—ex′qui·site·ly** *adv.* **—ex′qui·site·ness** *n.*

ex·tant (ĕk′stənt, ĕk-stănt′) ► *adj.* Still in existence; not destroyed, lost, or extinct.

ex·tem·po·ra·ne·ous (ĭk-stĕm′pə-rā′nē-əs) ► *adj.* Carried out or performed with little or no preparation; impromptu. **—ex·tem′po·ra′ne·ous·ly** *adv.* **—ex·tem′po·ra′ne·ous·ness** *n.*

ex·tem·po·rar·y (ĭk-stĕm′pə-rĕr′ē) ► *adj.* Extemporaneous.

ex·tem·po·re (ĭk-stĕm′pə-rē) ► *adj.* Extemporaneous. ► *adv.* Extemporaneously.

ex·tem·po·rize (ĭk-stĕm′pə-rīz′) ► *v.* **-rized, -riz·ing.** To do or perform (something) extemporaneously; improvise. **—ex·tem′po·ri·za′tion** *n.*

ex·tend (ĭk-stĕnd′) ► *v.* 1. To stretch, spread, or enlarge to greater length, area, or scope; expand. 2. To exert vigorously

THESAURUS

expose *v.* To lay open, as to something undesirable or injurious ► subject, leave open. [*Compare* ENDANGER.] *—See also* BARE, BETRAY (2), DISPLAY, REVEAL.

exposé *n.* *—See* REVELATION.

exposed *adj.* *—See* BLEAK (1), OPEN (2).

exposition *n.* *—See* COMMENTARY, DISPLAY, EXHIBITION, EXPLANATION.

expository or **expositive** *adj.* *—See* DIDACTIC (2), EXPLANATORY.

expostulate *v.* *—See* OBJECT.

expostulation *n.* *—See* OBJECTION.

exposure *n.* The condition of being laid open to something undesirable or injurious ► assailability, defenselessness, endangerment, liability, openness, pregnability, susceptibility, susceptibleness, unprotectedness, vulnerability, vulnerableness. *—See also* NUDITY, PUBLICITY, REVELATION.

expound *v.* *—See* EXPLAIN (1).

express *v.* 1. To give expression to, as by gestures, facial aspects, or bodily posture ► communicate, convey, display, manifest. ***Idioms:*** give a sign (*or* token), make clear (*or* known *or* plain). [*Compare* SHOW.] 2. To extract from by applying pressure ► crush, press, squeeze. *—See also* AIR (2), PHRASE, REPRESENT (2), SAY, SEND (1).

express *adj.* *—See* DEFINITE (1), FAST (1), SPECIAL.

expression *n.* 1. The act or an instance of expressing in words ► airing, articulation, pronunciation, statement, utterance, ventilation, verbalization, vocalization, voice. [*Compare* EMBODIMENT, MESSAGE, WORDING.] 2. Something that takes the place of words in communicating a thought or feeling ► gesture, indication, mark, sign, token. [*Compare* SIGN.] 3. A word or group of words forming a unit and conveying meaning ► collocation, idiom, locution, phrase. [*Compare* PROVERB.] 4. A disposition of the facial features that conveys meaning, feeling, or mood ► aspect, cast, countenance, face, lineaments, look, visage. [*Compare* APPEARANCE, BEARING.] *—See also* ELOQUENCE, REPRESENTATION, TERM.

expressionless *adj.* Lacking expression ► affectless, blank, deadpan, inexpressive, pokerfaced, zombie-like. [*Compare* DULL, RESERVED, VACANT.]

expressive *adj.* Effectively conveying meaning, feeling, or mood ► eloquent, meaning, meaningful, significant. [*Compare* ELOQUENT, PREGNANT.]

expressiveness or **expressivity** *n.* *—See* ELOQUENCE.

expressway *n.* *—See* WAY (2).

expropriate *v.* *—See* SEIZE (1).

expropriation *n.* *—See* SEIZURE (2).

expulsion *n.* *—See* DISMISSAL, EJECTION.

expunction *n.* *—See* ERASURE.

expunge *v.* *—See* ANNIHILATE, CANCEL (1).

expurgate *v.* *—See* CENSOR (1).

exquisite *adj.* *—See* BEAUTIFUL, DELICATE (1), ELEGANT, EXCEPTIONAL.

exsiccate *v.* *—See* DRY.

extant *adj.* Occurring or existing in act or fact ► actual, existent, real, true. [*Compare* PHYSICAL.] *—See also* ALIVE.

extemporaneous or **extemporary** or **extempore** *adj.* Spoken, performed, or composed with little or no preparation or forethought ► ad-lib, extemporary, extempore, impromptu, improvised, offhand, snap, spur-of-the-moment, unrehearsed. *Informal:* off-the-cuff. [*Compare* SPONTANEOUS.]

extemporization *n.* Something improvised ► ad-lib, impromptu, improvisation. [*Compare* MAKESHIFT.]

extemporize *v.* *—See* IMPROVISE (1).

extend *v.* 1. To proceed on a certain course or for a certain distance ►

or to full capacity. **3.** To offer; tender: *extend credit.* **—ex·tend′i·bil′i·ty, ex·ten′si·bil′i·ty** *n.* **—ex·tend′i·ble, ex·ten′si·ble** *adj.*

ex·ten·sion (ĭk-stĕn′shən) ▸ *n.* **1.** The act of extending or condition of being extended. **2.** An extended or added part.

ex·ten·sive (ĭk-stĕn′sĭv) ▸ *adj.* Large in extent, range, or amount. **—ex·ten′sive·ly** *adv.* **—ex·ten′sive·ness** *n.*

ex·ten·sor (ĭk-stĕn′sər) ▸ *n.* A muscle that extends or straightens a limb or body part.

ex·tent (ĭk-stĕnt′) ▸ *n.* **1.** The area or distance over which a thing extends; size. **2.** The range or degree to which a thing extends; scope.

ex·ten·u·ate (ĭk-stĕn′yo͞o-āt′) ▸ *v.* **-at·ed, -at·ing.** To lessen the seriousness of, esp. by providing partial excuses. **—ex·ten′u·a′tion** *n.* **—ex·ten′u·a′tor** *n.*

ex·te·ri·or (ĭk-stîr′ē-ər) ▸ *adj.* Outer; external. ▸ *n.* An outer or outward part, surface, or aspect.

ex·ter·mi·nate (ĭk-stûr′mə-nāt′) ▸ *v.* **-nat·ed, -nat·ing.** To destroy completely; wipe out. **—ex·ter′mi·na′tion** *n.* **—ex·ter′mi·na′tor** *n.*

ex·ter·nal (ĭk-stûr′nəl) ▸ *adj.* **1.** Of, on, or for the outside or outer part. **2.** Acting or coming from the outside. **3.** For outward show; superficial. **4.** Relating to foreign countries. ▸ *n.* **externals** Outward appearances. **—ex·ter′nal·ly** *adv.*

external ear ▸ *n.* The outer portion of the ear including the auricle and the passage leading to the eardrum.

ex·tinct (ĭk-stĭngkt′) ▸ *adj.* **1.** No longer existing or living. **2.** No longer burning or active. **—ex·tinc′tion** *n.*

ex·tin·guish (ĭk-stĭng′gwĭsh) ▸ *v.* **1.** To put out (e.g., a fire); quench. **2.** To put an end to; destroy. **—ex·tin′guish·a·ble** *adj.* **—ex·tin′guish·er** *n.*

ex·tir·pate (ĕk′stər-pāt′) ▸ *v.* **-pat·ed, -pat·ing. 1.** To uproot or cut out. **2.** To destroy totally; exterminate. **—ex′tir·pa′tion** *n.* **—ex′tir·pa′tive** *adj.* **—ex′tir·pa′tor** *n.*

ex·tol also **ex·toll** (ĭk-stōl′) ▸ *v.* **-tolled, -tol·ling.** To praise highly. **—ex·tol′ler** *n.* **—ex·tol′ment** *n.*

ex·tort (ĭk-stôrt′) ▸ *v.* To obtain from by coercion or intimidation. **—ex·tor′tion** *n.* **—ex·tor′tion·ate** (-ĭt) *adj.* **—ex·tor′tion·ist** *n.* **—ex·tor′tive** *adj.*

ex·tra (ĕk′strə) ▸ *adj.* More than what is usual, expected, or necessary. ▸ *n.* **1.** Something that is extra. **2.** A special edition of a newspaper. **3.** A performer hired to play a minor part, as in a crowd scene in a film. ▸ *adv.* Especially; unusually.

extra– ▸ *pref.* Outside; beyond: *extraterrestrial.*

ex·tract (ĭk-străkt′) ▸ *v.* **1.** To draw or pull out forcibly. **2.** To obtain despite resistance, as by threatening. **3.** To obtain in a concentrated form by chemical or mechanical action. **4.** To remove for separate consideration or publication; excerpt. **5.** *Math.* To determine or calculate (a root). ▸ *n.* (ĕk′străkt′) **1.** A literary excerpt. **2.** A substance prepared by extracting; essence; concentrate. **—ex·tract′a·ble, ex·tract′i·ble** *adj.* **—ex·trac′tor** *n.*

ex·trac·tion (ĭk-străk′shən) ▸ *n.* **1.** The act of extracting or the condition of being extracted. **2.** Something obtained by extracting; extract. **3.** Origin; lineage.

ex·tra·cur·ric·u·lar (ĕk′strə-kə-rĭk′yə-lər) ▸ *adj.* Being outside a regular course of study.

ex·tra·dite (ĕk′strə-dīt′) ▸ *v.* **-dit·ed, -dit·ing.** To give up or deliver (e.g., a fugitive) to the legal jurisdiction of another government or authority. **—ex′tra·dit′a·ble** *adj.* **—ex′tra·di′tion** (ĕk′strə-dĭsh′ən) *n.*

ex·tra·ga·lac·tic (ĕk′strə-gə-lăk′tĭk) ▸ *adj.* Located or originating beyond the Milky Way.

ex·tra·le·gal (ĕk′strə-lē′gəl) ▸ *adj.* Not permitted or governed by law. **—ex′tra·le′gal·ly** *adv.*

ex·tra·mar·i·tal (ĕk′strə-măr′ĭ-tl) ▸ *adj.* Violating marriage vows; adulterous.

ex·tra·mu·ral (ĕk′strə-myo͝or′əl) ▸ *adj.* Occurring or situated outside of the walls or boundaries, as of a community or school.

ex·tra·ne·ous (ĭk-strā′nē-əs) ▸ *adj.* **1.** Not essential. **2.** Coming from the outside. **—ex·tra′ne·ous·ly** *adv.* **—ex·tra′ne·ous·ness** *n.*

ex·traor·di·nar·y (ĭk-strôr′dn-ĕr′ē, ĕk′strə-ôr′-) ▸ *adj.* Beyond what is ordinary or usual; exceptional; remarkable. **—ex·traor′di·nar′i·ly** *adv.*

ex·trap·o·late (ĭk-străp′ə-lāt′) ▸ *v.* **-lat·ed, -lat·ing.** To infer (unknown information) from known information. **—ex·trap′o·la′tion** *n.*

ex·tra·sen·so·ry (ĕk′strə-sĕn′sə-rē) ▸ *adj.* Being outside the normal range of sense perception.

ex·tra·ter·res·tri·al (ĕk′strə-tə-rĕs′trē-əl) ▸ *adj.* From or occurring outside Earth or its atmosphere. **—ex′tra·ter·res′tri·al** *n.*

ex·tra·ter·ri·to·ri·al (ĕk′strə-tĕr′ĭ-tôr′ē-əl) ▸ *adj.* Located outside the territorial boundaries of a nation or state.

ex·tra·ter·ri·to·ri·al·i·ty (ĕk′strə-tĕr′ĭ-tôr′ē-ăl′ĭ-tē) ▸ *n.* Exemption from local legal jurisdiction, such as that granted to foreign diplomats.

THESAURUS

carry, continue, go, reach, run, stretch. **2.** To put forward, especially an appendage ▸ outstretch, reach, stretch (out). *—See also* BROADEN, GO (4), INCREASE, LENGTHEN, OFFER (1), SPREAD (1).

extended *adj.* *—See* BROAD (1), GENERAL (2), LONG[1] (1).

extensible or **extendible** or **extensile** *adj.* Capable of being extended or expanded ▸ expandable, expansible, expansile, protractile, stretch, stretchable, stretchy. [*Compare* MALLEABLE.]

extension *n.* **1.** The act of making something longer or the condition of being made longer ▸ drawing out, elongation, lengthening, prolongation, protraction, spinning out, stretching, stringing out. **2.** A part added to a main structure ▸ addition, add-on, annex, arm, wing. *—See also* BRANCH (1), EXPANSION, EXTENT, INCREASE (1), RANGE (1).

extensive *adj.* *—See* BIG, BROAD (1), GENERAL (2).

extensively *adv.* *—See* CONSIDERABLY.

extent *n.* The measure of how far or long something goes in space, time, or degree ▸ coverage, extension, length, reach, span, stretch. [*Compare* DEPTH, WIDTH.] *—See also* DEGREE (2), EXPANSE (1), RANGE (1), SIZE (1).

extenuate *v.* To conceal or make light of a fault or offense ▸ explain away, gloss over, gloze (over), palliate, sleek over, whitewash. [*Compare* BELITTLE, SOFT-PEDAL.]

exteriorization *n.* *—See* EMBODIMENT.

exteriorize *v.* *—See* EMBODY (1).

exterminate *v.* *—See* ANNIHILATE.

extermination *n.* *—See* ANNIHILATION.

external *adj.* *—See* APPARENT (2).

externalization *n.* *—See* EMBODIMENT.

externalize *v.* *—See* EMBODY (1).

externally *adv.* *—See* APPARENTLY.

extinct *adj.* *—See* DEAD (1).

extinction *n.* *—See* ANNIHILATION, DEATH (1).

extinguish *v.* To cause to stop burning or giving light ▸ damp, douse, put out, quench, smother, snuff out. [*Compare* CHOKE.] *—See also* ABOLISH, ANNIHILATE, SUPPRESS.

extinguishment *n.* *—See* ANNIHILATION.

extirpate *v.* *—See* ANNIHILATE.

extirpation *n.* *—See* ANNIHILATION.

extol *v.* *—See* HONOR (1), PRAISE (1), PRAISE (3).

extolment *n.* *—See* PRAISE (2).

extort *v.* To obtain by coercion or intimidation ▸ blackmail, exact, graft, squeeze, wrench, wrest, wring. *Slang:* shake down.

extortionate *adj.* *—See* STEEP[1] (2).

extra *adj.* Being what remains, especially after a part has been removed ▸ leftover, remaining, stray. ***Idiom:*** left behind. *—See also* ADDITIONAL, SUPERFLUOUS.

extra *adv.* *—See* VERY.

extra *n.* *—See* ENHANCEMENT, SURPLUS.

extract *v.* *—See* DERIVE (1), GLEAN, PULL (2).

extraction *n.* *—See* ANCESTRY.

extradite *v.* *—See* BANISH.

extradition *n.* *—See* EXILE.

extramundane *adj.* *—See* SUPERNATURAL (1).

extraneous *adj.* Not part of the essential nature of a thing or person ▸ alien, foreign, extrinsic. [*Compare* IRRELEVANT.] *—See also* IRRELEVANT.

extraordinarily *adv.* *—See* UNUSUALLY.

extraordinary *adj.* *—See* EXCEPTIONAL.

extrasensory *adj.* *—See* SUPERNATURAL (1).

ex·trav·a·gance (ĭk-străv′ə-gəns) ► *n.* **1.** The quality of being extravagant. **2.** Immoderate expense or display. **3.** Something extravagant.

ex·trav·a·gant (ĭk-străv′ə-gənt) ► *adj.* **1.** Lavish or imprudent in spending money. **2.** Exceeding reasonable bounds; excessive. **—ex·trav′a·gant·ly** *adv.*

ex·trav·a·gan·za (ĭk-străv′ə-găn′zə) ► *n.* An elaborate, spectacular entertainment or display.

ex·treme (ĭk-strēm′) ► *adj.* **1.** Most remote; outermost or farthest. **2.** Very great; intense. **3.** Extending far beyond the norm. **4.** Drastic; severe. ► *n.* **1.** The greatest or utmost degree. **2.** Either of the two things at opposite ends of a scale, series, or range. **3.** An extreme condition. **4.** A drastic expedient. **—ex·treme′ly** *adv.* **—ex·treme′ness** *n.*

ex·trem·ist (ĭk-strē′mĭst) ► *n.* One with extreme views, esp. in politics. **—ex·trem′ism** *n.*

ex·trem·i·ty (ĭk-strĕm′ĭ-tē) ► *n., pl.* **-ties. 1.** The outermost or farthest point or part. **2.** The utmost degree. **3.** Grave danger, necessity, or distress. **4.** An extreme or severe measure. **5a.** A bodily limb or appendage. **b.** A hand or foot.

ex·tri·cate (ĕk′strĭ-kāt′) ► *v.* **-cat·ed, -cat·ing.** To release from an entanglement or difficulty. **—ex′tri·ca·ble** (-kə-bəl) *adj.* **—ex′tri·ca′tion** *n.*

ex·trin·sic (ĭk-strĭn′sĭk, -zĭk) ► *adj.* **1.** Not essential or inherent. **2.** Originating from the outside; external. **—ex·trin′si·cal·ly** *adv.*

ex·tro·vert also **ex·tra·vert** (ĕk′strə-vûrt′) ► *n.* One who is socially outgoing and communicative. **—ex′tro·ver′sion** *n.*

ex·trude (ĭk-strōōd′) ► *v.* **-trud·ed, -trud·ing. 1.** To thrust out. **2.** To shape (e.g., a plastic) by forcing through a die. **—ex·tru′sion** *n.* **—ex·tru′sive** *adj.*

ex·u·ber·ant (ĭg-zōō′bər-ənt) ► *adj.* **1.** High-spirited; lively. **2.** Lavish; effusive. **3.** Growing abundantly. **—ex·u′ber·ance** *n.* **—ex·u′ber·ant·ly** *adv.*

ex·ude (ĭg-zōōd′, ĭk-sōōd′) ► *v.* **-ud·ed, -ud·ing. 1.** To ooze or pour forth gradually. **2.** To give off; radiate: *exude confidence.* **—ex′u·date′** (ĕks′yōō-dāt′) *n.* **—ex′u·da′tion** *n.*

ex·ult (ĭg-zŭlt′) ► *v.* To rejoice greatly, as in triumph. **—ex·ul′tant** *adj.* **—ex′ul·ta′tion** (ĕk′səl-tā′shən, ĕg′zəl-) *n.*

ex·urb (ĕk′sûrb′) ► *n.* A mostly rural, often wealthy residential region lying beyond the suburbs of a city. **—ex·ur′ban** *adj.* **—ex·ur′ban·ite′** *n.*

ex·ur·bi·a (ĕk-sûr′bē-ə, ĕg-zûr′-) ► *n.* A typically exurban area.

-ey ► *suff.* Var. of **-y**[1].

eye (ī) ► *n.* **1.** An organ of vision or of light sensitivity. **2.** The faculty of seeing; vision. **3.** The ability to perceive or discern. **4.** A point of view; opinion. **5.** Attention. **6.** Something suggestive of an eye: *the eye of a needle; the eye of a potato.* ► *v.* **eyed, eye·ing** or **ey·ing.** To look at. ***—idiom:* eye to eye** In agreement.

eye·ball (ī′bôl′) ► *n.* The ball-shaped part of the eye enclosed by the socket and eyelids.

eye·brow (ī′brou′) ► *n.* The hairs covering the bony ridge over the eye.

eye·drop·per (ī′drŏp′ər) ► *n.* A dropper for applying liquid medicines, esp. to the eye.

eye·ful (ī′fōōl′) ► *n.* **1.** A good or thorough look. **2.** A pleasing sight.

eye·glass (ī′glăs′) ► *n.* **1a. eyeglasses** Glasses for the eyes. **b.** A monocle. **2.** See **eyepiece.**

eye·lash (ī′lăsh′) ► *n.* Any of the short hairs fringing the edge of the eyelid.

eye·let (ī′lĭt) ► *n.* **1.** A small hole for a lace, cord, or hook to fit through. **2.** A metal ring designed to reinforce such a hole.

eye·lid (ī′lĭd′) ► *n.* Either of two folds of skin and muscle that can be closed over an eye.

eye opener ► *n.* A startling or shocking revelation.

eye·piece (ī′pēs′) ► *n.* The lens or lens group closest to the eye in an optical instrument.

eye shadow ► *n.* A cosmetic applied esp. to the eyelids to enhance the eyes.

eye·sight (ī′sīt′) ► *n.* The faculty or range of sight; vision.

eye·sore (ī′sôr′) ► *n.* An ugly sight.

eye·strain (ī′strān′) ► *n.* Pain and fatigue in one or more of the eye muscles.

eye·tooth (ī′tōōth′) ► *n.* A canine tooth of the upper jaw.

eye·wit·ness (ī′wĭt′nĭs) ► *n.* One who has personally seen someone or something and can bear witness to the fact.

ey·rie (âr′ē, îr′ē) ► *n.* Var. of **aerie.**

E·ze·ki·el (ĭ-zē′kē-əl) ► *n.* **1.** 6th cent. B.C. Hebrew prophet. **2.** See **Bible** table in Appendix.

Ez·ra (ĕz′rə) ► *n.* **1.** 5th cent. B.C. Hebrew high priest. **2.** See **Bible** table in Appendix.

THESAURUS

extravagance or **extravagancy** *n.* Excessive or imprudent expenditure ► extravagancy, lavishness, overgenerosity, prodigality, profligacy, profusion, profuseness, squander, waste, wastefulness. *—See also* EXCESS (1), LUXURY.

extravagant *adj.* Characterized by excessive or imprudent spending ► dissipative, improvident, lavish, prodigal, profligate, profuse, spendthrift, thriftless, uneconomical, unthrifty, wasteful. ***Idiom:*** penny-wise and pound foolish. [*Compare* CARELESS, NEGLIGENT.] *—See also* EXCESSIVE, PROFUSE.

extravagantly *adv.* *—See* UNDULY.

extravagantness *n.* *—See* EXCESS (1).

extraverted *adj.* *—See* EXTROVERTED.

extreme *adj.* **1.** Most distant or remote, as from a center ► farthermost, farthest, furthermost, furthest, outermost, outmost, ultimate, utmost, uttermost. [*Compare* LAST.] **2.** Holding especially political views that deviate drastically from prevailing beliefs ► extremist, fanatic, fanatical, fire-breathing, fire-eating, fundamentalist, hard-line, lunatic, militant, rabid, radical, raving, revolutionary, ultra, wild-eyed, zealous. *Slang:* far-out. [*Compare* ENTHUSIASTIC, REBELLIOUS, ULTRACONSERVATIVE, ULTRALIBERAL.] *—See also* EXCESSIVE, MAXIMUM.

extreme *n.* Either of the two points at the ends of a spectrum or range ► extremity, limit. [*Compare* CLIMAX, LOW.] *—See also* LENGTH.

extremely *adv.* *—See* UNDULY, VERY.

extremist *n.* One who holds extreme views or advocates extreme measures ► fanatic, fire-breather, fire-eater, fundamentalist, hard-liner, militant, radical, revolutionary, revolutionist, ultra, ultraist, zealot. [*Compare* ULTRACONSERVATIVE, ULTRALIBERAL.]

extremist *adj.* *—See* EXTREME (2).

extremity *n.* Either of the two points at the ends of a spectrum or range ► extreme, limit. [*Compare* CLIMAX, LOW.] *—See also* EMERGENCY, LENGTH.

extricate *v.* To free from an entanglement ► clear, disengage, disentangle, disinvolve, free, release, untangle. [*Compare* UNDO.]

extrinsic *adj.* Not part of the essential nature of a thing ► alien, extraneous, foreign. *—See also* IRRELEVANT.

extroverted or **extraverted** *adj.* *—See* OUTGOING.

exuberant *adj.* *—See* ENTHUSIASTIC, LIVELY, PROFUSE.

exude *v.* *—See* OOZE.

exult *v.* **1.** To feel or express an uplifting joy over a success or victory ► crow, gloat, glory, jubilate, triumph. *Slang:* high-five. [*Compare* BOAST, CELEBRATE, REJOICE.] **2.** To feel or take joy or pleasure ► delight, pleasure, rejoice. [*Compare* ENJOY, LUXURIATE.]

exultant *adj.* Feeling or expressing an uplifting joy over a success or victory ► gloating, jubilant, triumphant. [*Compare* BOASTFUL.]

exultation *n.* The act or condition of feeling an uplifting joy over a success or victory ► crowing, exultance, exultancy, gloating, jubilance, jubilation, triumph.

exuviate *v.* *—See* SHED[1] (2).

eye *n.* **1.** An organ of vision ► eyeball, orb. *Slang:* peeper, saucer. ***Idiom:*** window of the soul. **2.** The most intensely active central part ► midst, thick. [*Compare* CENTER.] *—See also* DETECTIVE, DISCERNMENT, LOOP, VIEWPOINT, VISION (1).

eye *v.* *—See* GAZE, LOOK (1), WATCH (1).

eye-catching *adj.* *—See* NOTICEABLE.

eyeless *adj.* *—See* BLIND (1).

eyelet *n.* *—See* HOLE (2), LOOP.

eye opener *n.* *—See* REVELATION.

eyesight *n.* *—See* VISION (1).

eyes-only *adj.* *—See* UNSPEAKABLE (2).

eyesore *n.* *—See* MESS (2).

eyewitness *n.* Someone who sees something occur ► audience, seer, viewer, witness.

F

f[1] or **F** (ĕf) ► *n., pl.* **f's** or **F's** also **fs** or **Fs**. 1. The 6th letter of the English alphabet. 2. **F** A failing grade. 3. *Mus.* The 4th tone of the C major scale.

f[2] ► *abbr.* 1. feminine 2. function

F[1] ► The symbol for the element **fluorine**.

F[2] ► *abbr.* 1. Fahrenheit 2. female 3. Friday

fa (fä) ► *n. Mus.* The 4th tone of the diatonic scale.

fa·ble (fā′bəl) ► *n.* 1. A fictitious story making a moral point and often using animals as characters. 2. A story about legendary persons and exploits. 3. A falsehood; lie. ► *v.* **-bled, -bling.** To recount as if true. **—fab′u·list** (făb′yə-lĭst) *n.*

fa·bled (fā′bəld) ► *adj.* 1. Legendary. 2. Fictitious.

fab·ric (făb′rĭk) ► *n.* 1. A cloth produced esp. by knitting or weaving fibers. 2. A complex underlying structure; framework: *the fabric of society.*

fab·ri·cate (făb′rĭ-kāt′) ► *v.* **-cat·ed, -cat·ing.** 1. To make; create. 2. To construct or build. 3. To make up in order to deceive: *fabricated an excuse.* **—fab′ri·ca′tion** *n.*

fab·u·lous (făb′yə-ləs) ► *adj.* 1. Barely credible; astonishing. 2. Extremely pleasing or successful: *a fabulous vacation.* 3a. Of the nature of a fable; legendary. b. Told of or celebrated in fables. **—fab′u·lous·ly** *adv.* **—fab′u·lous·ness** *n.*

fa·çade also **fa·cade** (fə-säd′) ► *n.* 1. The face of a building, esp. the principal face. 2. An artificial or deceptive appearance: *put on a façade of sincerity.*

face (fās) ► *n.* 1. The surface of the front of the head. 2. A facial expression; countenance. 3. A grimace. 4. Outward appearance; aspect. 5. Value or standing; prestige: *lose face.* 6. Effrontery; impudence. 7. The front or most significant surface of an object: *the face of a clock.* 8. *Geometry* A planar surface of a geometric solid. ► *v.* **faced, fac·ing.** 1. To turn or be turned in the direction of. 2. To front on: *a window that faces the south.* 3a. To confront. b. To encounter: *face problems later on.* 4. To furnish with a surface or cover of a different material. 5. To trim the edge of (cloth), esp. with contrasting material. ***—phrasal verbs:*** **face down** To overcome by a stare or a resolute manner. **face off** *Sports* To start play with a face-off. **face up to** To confront with resolution. ***—idioms:*** **face the music** To accept unpleasant consequences. **face to face** 1. In each other's presence. 2. Directly confronting: *face to face with death.* **in the face of** 1. Despite the opposition of. 2. In view of. **on the face of it** From appearances alone. **to (one's) face** In one's presence. **—face′less** *adj.*

face card ► *n. Games* A king, queen, or jack of a deck of playing cards.

face·less (fās′lĭs) ► *adj.* 1. Having no face. 2. Without character; anonymous.

face-lift also **face·lift** (fās′lĭft′) ► *n.* 1. Plastic surgery to tighten facial tissues. 2. A renovation, as of a building. **—face′-lift′** *v.*

face-off (fās′ôf′, -ŏf′) ► *n.* 1. A method of starting play, as in ice hockey or lacrosse, by releasing the puck or ball between two opposing players. 2. A confrontation.

fac·et (făs′ĭt) ► *n.* 1. One of the flat surfaces cut on a gemstone. 2. *Anat.* A small, smooth, flat surface, as on a bone or tooth. 3. An aspect; phase. **—fac′et·ed** *adj.*

fa·ce·tious (fə-sē′shəs) ► *adj.* Playfully jocular; humorous. **—fa·ce′tious·ly** *adv.* **—fa·ce′tious·ness** *n.*

face value ► *n.* 1. The value printed on the face, as of a bill or bond. 2. Apparent significance or value.

fa·cial (fā′shəl) ► *adj.* Of the face. ► *n.* A cosmetic treatment for the face.

fac·ile (făs′əl) ► *adj.* 1. Simple; easy. 2. Possessing effortless skill or fluency. 3. Excessively simple; superficial: *a facile solution to a complex problem.* **—fac′ile·ly** *adv.* **—fac′ile·ness** *n.*

fa·cil·i·tate (fə-sĭl′ĭ-tāt′) ► *v.* **-tat·ed, -tat·ing.** To make easy or easier; assist. **—fa·cil′i·ta′tion** *n.* **—fa·cil′i·ta′tor** *n.*

fa·cil·i·ty (fə-sĭl′ĭ-tē) ► *n., pl.* **-ties.** 1. Ease in doing resulting from skill or aptitude. 2. often **facilities** Something that facilitates an action or process. 3. **facilities** *Informal* A restroom.

fac·ing (fā′sĭng) ► *n.* 1. A piece of material sewn to the edge of a garment as lining or decoration. 2. A coating applied to a surface for protection or decoration.

fac·sim·i·le (făk-sĭm′ə-lē) ► *n.* 1. An exact copy or reproduction. 2. See **fax**.

fact (făkt) ► *n.* 1. Information presented as true and accurate. 2. Something having real, demonstrable existence. 3.

THESAURUS

fable *n.* A narrative not based on fact ► fiction, novel, romance, story. *—See also* LIE[2], MYTH (1), YARN.

fabled *adj.* *—See* MYTHICAL.

fabric *n.* *—See* TEXTURE.

fabricate *v.* *—See* ACT (2), COUNTERFEIT, INVENT, MAKE.

fabricated *adj.* *—See* MYTHICAL.

fabrication *n.* *—See* COUNTERFEIT, LIE[2], MYTH (2).

fabricator *n.* One who makes a fraudulent copy of something ► counterfeiter, faker, falsifier, forger. *—See also* LIAR.

fabulist *n.* *—See* LIAR.

fabulous *adj.* *—See* ASTONISHING, MARVELOUS, MYTHICAL.

façade *n.* 1. The forward outer surface of a building ► face, front, frontage, frontispiece, frontal. 2. A deceptive outward appearance ► charade, cover, disguise, face, false colors, front, gloss, guise, make-believe, mask, masquerade, pose, pretense, pretext, semblance, show, veneer, window-dressing. *Slang:* put-on. [*Compare* AFFECTATION, ACT, VEIL.]

face *n.* 1. The front surface of the head ► countenance, features, lineaments, muzzle, physiognomy, visage. *Informal:* mug. *Slang:* kisser, map, pan, puss. 2. A contorted facial expression showing pain, contempt, or disgust ► grimace, moue, pout. *Informal:* mug. [*Compare* FROWN, GLARE, SNEER.] 3. An outward appearance ► aspect, countenance, features, lineaments, look, surface. 4. An outer surface, layer, or part of an object ► facet, side, surface. [*Compare* BACK, BOTTOM, FRONT.] 5. The marked outer surface of an instrument ► dial, gauge, indicator. [*Compare* FRONT.] 6. Credit or respect in the eyes of others ► prestige, standing, status. [*Compare* HONOR, PRIDE, REPUTATION.] *—See also* EXPRESSION (4), FAÇADE (1), FAÇADE (2), IMPUDENCE.

face *v.* 1. To have the face or front turned toward ► front, give onto, look (on *or* upon *or* toward). [*Compare* OVERLOOK.] 2. To cover with a different material ► clad, cover, sheathe, side, surface, veneer. [*Compare* GLOSS[1], FINISH.] 3. To meet face-to-face, especially defiantly ► confront, encounter, front, meet. *Idiom:* stand up to. [*Compare* CONTEST.] *—See also* DEFY (1).

face-lift or **face-lifting** *n.* *—See* RENEWAL (1).

face-off *n.* *—See* CONFRONTATION.

facet *n.* An outer surface, layer, or part of an object ► face, side, surface. [*Compare* BACK, BOTTOM, FRONT.] *—See also* VIEWPOINT.

facetious *adj.* *—See* FUNNY (1).

facile *adj.* *—See* DEXTEROUS, EASY (1), GLIB.

facileness *n.* *—See* EASE (2).

facilitate *v.* *—See* EASE (2), PROMOTE (2).

facilitator *n.* *—See* GO-BETWEEN.

facilities *n.* *—See* AMENITIES (1).

facility *n.* *—See* DEXTERITY, EASE (2), ELOQUENCE.

facsimile *n.* *—See* COPY (1).

fact *n.* Something demonstrated to

Something done, esp. a crime: *an accessory before the fact.*
fact-find·ing (făkt′fīn′dĭng) ▸ *n.* Discovery or determination of facts. **—fact′-find′ing** *adj.*
fac·tion[1] (făk′shən) ▸ *n.* **1.** A cohesive, usu. contentious minority within a larger group. **2.** Internal dissension or discord. **—fac′tion·al** *adj.* **—fac′tion·al·ism** *n.*
fac·tion[2] (făk′shən) ▸ *n.* A genre or work of literature or film that mixes fact and fiction.
–faction ▸ *suff.* Production; making: *petrifaction.*
fac·tious (făk′shəs) ▸ *adj.* **1.** Produced or marked by faction. **2.** Tending to cause conflict or dissension; divisive. **—fac′tious·ly** *adv.*
fac·ti·tious (făk-tĭsh′əs) ▸ *adj.* **1.** Produced artificially. **2.** False; sham.
fact of life ▸ *n.* **1.** Something unavoidable that must be dealt with. **2. facts of life** The basic physiological functions involved in sex and reproduction.
fac·toid (făk′toid) ▸ *n.* **1.** A piece of unverified or inaccurate information accepted as true because of frequent repetition. **2.** A brief, somewhat interesting fact.
fac·tor (făk′tər) ▸ *n.* **1.** One that actively contributes to a result or process. **2.** One who acts for someone else; agent. **3.** *Math.* One of two or more quantities that divides a given quantity without a remainder: *2 and 3 are factors of 6.* ▸ *v. Math.* **1.** To determine the factors of. **2.** To figure: *factor in inflation.*
fac·to·ry (făk′tə-rē) ▸ *n., pl.* **-ries.** A building or group of buildings in which goods are manufactured; plant.
fac·to·tum (făk-tō′təm) ▸ *n.* An employee or assistant with a wide range of duties.
fac·tu·al (făk′cho͞o-əl) ▸ *adj.* Based on or containing facts. **—fac′tu·al′i·ty** (-ăl′ĭ-tē) *n.* **—fac′tu·al·ly** *adv.*
fac·ul·ty (făk′əl-tē) ▸ *n., pl.* **-ties. 1.** An inherent power or ability. **2.** An aptitude or power of the human mind. **3a.** A division of learning at a college or university. **b.** The teachers in a college, university, or school.
fad (făd) ▸ *n.* A briefly popular fashion; craze. **—fad′dist** *n.* **—fad′dish** *adj.*
fade (fād) ▸ *v.* **fad·ed, fad·ing. 1.** To lose or cause to lose brightness or loudness; dim. **2.** To lose strength or freshness; wither. **3.** To disappear gradually; vanish.
fade-in (fād′ĭn′) ▸ *n.* A gradual increase in the visibility of an image or the audibility of a sound, as in cinema, television, or radio.
fade-out (fād′out′) or **fade·out** ▸ *n.* A gradual disappearance of an image or sound, as in cinema, television, or radio.
fa·er·ie (fā′ə-rē, fâr′ē) ▸ *n.* **1.** A fairy. **2.** Fairyland.
Faer·oe Islands or **Far·oe Islands** (fâr′ō) ▸ A group of volcanic islands in the N Atlantic between Iceland and the Shetland Is. **—Faer′o·ese′** *adj. & n.*
fag[1] (făg) ▸ *n.* A drudge. ▸ *v.* **fagged, fag·ging.** To exhaust or work to exhaustion; fatigue.
fag[2] (făg) ▸ *n. Slang* A cigarette.
fag end ▸ *n.* **1.** The frayed end of a length of cloth or rope. **2.** The last and least useful part.
fag·ot also **fag·got** (făg′ət) ▸ *n.* A bundle of twigs or sticks. **—fag′ot** *v.*
Fahr. ▸ *abbr.* Fahrenheit
Fahr·en·heit (făr′ən-hīt′, fä′rən-) ▸ *adj.* Of or according to a temperature scale that registers the freezing point of water as 32°F and the boiling point as 212°F at one atmosphere of pressure. See **measurement** table in Appendix.
fa·ience also **fa·ïence** (fī-äns′, -äɴs′, fā-) ▸ *n.* Earthenware decorated with colorful opaque glazes.
fail (fāl) ▸ *v.* **1.** To be deficient or unsuccessful. **2.** To give or receive an unacceptable academic grade. **3.** To decline, weaken, or cease to function. **4.** To disappoint or forsake. **5.** To omit or neglect: *failed to appear.* **6.** To become bankrupt. ▸ *n.* Failure. ***—idiom:*** **without fail** Absolutely.
fail·ing (fā′lĭng) ▸ *n.* A minor fault; shortcoming. ▸ *prep.* In the absence of.
faille (fīl, fāl) ▸ *n.* A ribbed woven fabric of silk, cotton, or rayon.
fail-safe (fāl′sāf′) ▸ *adj.* **1.** Compensating automatically for a failure, as of a mechanical system. **2.** Containing built-in safeguards, as against military attack.
fail·ure (fāl′yər) ▸ *n.* **1.** The act, condition, or fact of failing. **2.** One that fails. **3.** The act or fact of becoming bankrupt.
fain (fān) ▸ *adv.* Happily; gladly. ▸ *adj. Archaic* **1.** Willing; glad. **2.** Obliged or required.
faint (fānt) ▸ *adj.* **-er, -est. 1.** Lacking strength or vigor; feeble. **2a.** Lacking brightness; dim. **b.** Indistinct. **3.** Suddenly dizzy and weak. ▸ *n.* An abrupt, usu. brief loss of consciousness; blackout. ▸ *v.* To fall into a faint. **—faint′ly** *adv.* **—faint′ness** *n.*
faint-hearted (fānt′här′tĭd) ▸ *adj.* Lacking conviction or courage; timid. **—faint′-heart′ed·ly** *adv.* **—faint′-heart′ed·ness** *n.*
fair[1] (fâr) ▸ *adj.* **-er, -est. 1.** Beautiful; lovely. **2.** Light in color: *fair hair.* **3.** Clear and sunny. **4.** Unblemished; clean. **5.** Promising; favorable. **6.** Just; equitable. **7.** Consistent with rules; permissible. **8.** Moderately good; average. ▸ *adv.* **1.** In a fair manner; properly. **2.** Directly; straight. ***—idiom:***

THESAURUS

exist or known to have existed ▸ actuality, event, phenomenon, reality. *Idiom:* hard (*or* cold *or* plain) fact. [*Compare* INFORMATION.] *—See also* CERTAINTY, CIRCUMSTANCE (2).
faction *n.* *—See* ALLIANCE, CONFLICT.
factitious *adj.* *—See* COUNTERFEIT.
factor *n.* *—See* CIRCUMSTANCE (2), PART (1), REPRESENTATIVE.
factory *n.* A building or complex in which an industry is located ▸ mill, plant, works.
facts *n.* *—See* INFORMATION.
factual *adj.* *—See* ACCURATE, REALISTIC (2).
facultative *adj.* *—See* OPTIONAL.
faculty *n.* *—See* ABILITY (2), TALENT.
fad *n.* *—See* ENTHUSIASM (2), FASHION.
fade *v.* To lose strength or power ▸ decline, degenerate, fail, flag, languish, sink, wane, waste away, weaken. *Informal:* fizzle (out), peter out. [*Compare* DECREASE, DETERIORATE, SUBSIDE, TIRE.] *—See also* DISAPPEAR (1), FADE AWAY, PALE.
fade away *v.* To grow weaker in sound ▸ die (away *or* out *or* down), fade (out), quiet (down). [*Compare* SILENCE.] *—See also* LIFT (2).
fade out *v.* To grow weaker in sound ▸ die (away *or* out *or* down), fade (away), quiet (down). [*Compare* SILENCE.] *—See also* DISAPPEAR (1).
faded *adj.* *—See* PALE (1), SHABBY.
fade-out *n.* *—See* DISAPPEARANCE.
fail *v.* **1.** To go wrong or be unsuccessful ▸ choke, fall through, founder, go amiss, go astray, go awry, go wrong, miscarry, misfire, miss, strike out, wash out. *Informal:* fall down, flop, flunk. *Slang:* bomb. *Idioms:* come a cropper, fall flat, fall short, lay an egg, miss fire, miss the mark. **2.** To prove deficient or insufficient ▸ give out, run out. *Idioms:* fall short, run dry, run short. [*Compare* DECREASE.] *—See also* COLLAPSE (2), DISAPPOINT, FADE, MALFUNCTION, NEGLECT (2).
failing *n.* *—See* DEFECT, WEAKNESS.
fail-safe *adj.* *—See* SURE (2).
failure *n.* **1.** A person or enterprise that is unsuccessful ▸ bust, fiasco, loser, miscarriage, nonperformer, washout. *Informal:* clinker, clunker, dud, flop, lead balloon. *Slang:* bomb, turkey. [*Compare* COLLAPSE.] **2.** Nonperformance of what ought to be done ▸ default, delinquency, dereliction, neglect, nonfeasance, omission, shirking. [*Compare* NEGLIGENCE.] **3.** A cessation of proper functioning ▸ breakdown, collapse, malfunction, outage. **4.** A marked loss of strength or effectiveness ▸ declination, decline, deterioration. *—See also* BANKRUPTCY.
fainéant *adj.* *—See* LAZY.
fainéant *n.* *—See* WASTREL (2).
faint *adj.* So soft as to be barely audible ▸ feeble, weak. [*Compare* SOFT.] *—See also* GENTLE (1), LIGHT[2] (1), PALE (2), REMOTE (2), UNCLEAR, WEAK (1).
faint *n.* A temporary loss of consciousness ▸ blackout, fainting spell, swoon, syncope.
faint *v.* To suffer temporary lack of consciousness ▸ black out, keel over, pass out, swoon. *Idioms:* drop (*or* faint *or* fall) dead away, lose consciousness, see stars. [*Compare* COLLAPSE.]
faint-hearted *adj.* *—See* COWARDLY.
faint-heartedness *n.* *—See* COWARDICE.
fair[1] *adj.* **1.** Free from bias in judgment ▸ balanced, detached, disinterested,

fair and square Just and honest. **—fair′ness** *n.*

fair² (fâr) ▸ *n.* **1.** A gathering for buying and selling goods; market. **2.** An exhibition, as of farm products or handicrafts, usu. judged competitively. **3.** A fund-raising event, as for a charity.

fair·ground (fâr′ground′) ▸ *n.* Open land where fairs are held.

fair·ly (fâr′lē) ▸ *adv.* **1.** In a fair or just manner; equitably. **2.** Actually; fully. **3.** Moderately; rather.

fair-mind·ed (fâr′mīn′dĭd) ▸ *adj.* Just and impartial. **—fair′-mind′ed·ness** *n.*

fair-trade (fâr′trād′) ▸ *adj.* Of or being an agreement under which retailers sell a given item at no less than a minimum price set by the manufacturer.

fair·way (fâr′wā′) ▸ *n.* The mowed part of a golf course from the tee to the green.

fair-weath·er (fâr′wĕth′ər) ▸ *adj.* Dependable only in good times: *fair-weather friends.*

fair·y (fâr′ē) ▸ *n., pl.* **-ies.** A tiny imaginary being depicted as possessing magical powers.

fair·y·land (fâr′ē-lănd′) ▸ *n.* **1.** The imaginary land of the fairies. **2.** A charming place.

fairy tale ▸ *n.* **1.** A fanciful tale of legendary deeds and creatures, usu. intended for children. **2.** A fanciful story or explanation. **—fair′y-tale′** *adj.*

fait ac·com·pli (fā′tä-kôɴ-plē′, fĕt′ä-) ▸ *n., pl.* **faits ac·com·plis** (fā′tä-kôɴ-plē′, -plēz′, fĕt′ä-). An accomplished deed or fact.

faith (fāth) ▸ *n.* **1.** Confident belief or trust in a person, idea, or thing. **2.** Loyalty; allegiance. **3.** often **Faith** *Christianity* Secure belief in God and acceptance of God's will. **4.** A religion. **—faith′less** *adj.* **—faith′less·ness** *n.*

faith·ful (fāth′fəl) ▸ *adj.* **1.** Adhering firmly and devotedly; loyal. **2.** Worthy of trust; reliable. **3.** Accurate; true. ▸ *n., pl.* **-ful** or **-fuls. 1.** The practicing members of a religious faith. **2.** An adherent of a cause: *the party faithful.* **—faith′ful·ly** *adv.* **—faith′ful·ness** *n.*

fa·ji·ta (fə-hē′tə) ▸ *n.* often **fajitas** A dish of grilled strips of marinated meat served in a tortilla, usu. with spicy condiments.

fake (fāk) ▸ *adj.* Not genuine; fraudulent. ▸ *n.* One that is not authentic or genuine; a counterfeit, impostor, or sham. ▸ *v.* **faked, fak·ing. 1.** To contrive and present as genuine; counterfeit. **2.** To pretend; feign. **—fak′er** *n.* **—fak′er·y** *n.*

fa·kir (fə-kîr′, fä-, fă-) ▸ *n.* A Muslim or Hindu religious mendicant, esp. one who performs feats of magic or endurance.

fa·la·fel or **fe·la·fel** (fə-lä′fəl) ▸ *n.* Ground spiced chickpeas shaped into balls and fried.

fal·con (făl′kən, fôl′-, fô′kən) ▸ *n.* Any of various swift hawklike birds of prey with long pointed wings.

fal·con·ry (făl′kən-rē, fôl′-, fô′kən-) ▸ *n.* **1.** Hunting of small game with falcons. **2.** The art of training falcons for hunting. **—fal′con·er** *n.*

Falk·land Islands (fôk′lənd, fôlk′-) ▸ A group of islands in the S Atlantic E of the Strait of Magellan.

fall (fôl) ▸ *v.* **fell** (fĕl), **fall·en** (fô′lən), **fall·ing. 1.** To drop freely under the influence of gravity. **2.** To move oneself to a lower position. **3.** To be killed or severely wounded. **4.** To hang down: *Her hair fell in ringlets.* **5.** To assume an expression of disappointment: *His face fell.* **6.** To be conquered or overthrown. **7.** To slope downward. **8.** To lessen in amount or degree. **9.** To pass into a particular state or condition: *We fell silent.* **10.** To decline in rank, status, or importance. **11.** To err or sin. **12.** To come as if by descending: *A hush fell on the crowd.* **13.** To occur at a specified time or place. **14.** To be allotted: *The task fell to me.* **15.** To be within the range of something. **16.** To come to rest by chance: *My gaze fell on the letter.* ***—phrasal verbs:*** **fall back** To retreat. **fall behind** To fail to keep up with. **fall for 1.** To become infatuated with. **2.** To be deceived or swindled by. **fall in** To take one's place in a military formation. **fall on** To attack suddenly. **fall out** To quarrel. **fall through** To fail or miscarry. **fall to** To begin energetically. **fall back on** To rely on. ▸ *n.* **1.** The act or an instance of falling. **2.** Something that has fallen: *a fall of hail.* **3a.** An amount that has fallen: *a light fall of rain.* **b.** The distance that something falls. **4.** Autumn. **5. falls** *(takes sing. or pl. v.)* A waterfall. **6.** A hanging article of dress, as a veil or hairpiece. **7.** An overthrow or collapse: *the fall of a government.* **8.** A decline or reduction. **9.** A moral lapse. ***—idioms:*** **fall back on** To rely

THESAURUS

dispassionate, equal, equitable, even, evenhanded, fair-minded, impartial, indifferent, just, nondiscriminatory, nonpartisan, objective, square, unbiased, unprejudiced. *Idioms:* fair and square, on the level. [*Compare* BROAD-MINDED, HONEST, NEUTRAL.] **2.** Having light hair ▸ blond, fair-haired, flaxen-haired, golden-haired, light-haired, towheaded. **3.** Having a light color or complexion ▸ alabaster, ivory, light, milky, pale. —*See also* ACCEPTABLE (2), AVERAGE, BEAUTIFUL, CLEAR (2), FAVORABLE (1), SPORTSMANLIKE.

fair *adv.* In a fair, sporting manner ▸ cleanly, correctly, fairly, properly, sportingly. *Idioms:* fair and square, on the up and up. —*See also* DIRECTLY (3).

fair² *n.* —*See* EXHIBITION.

fair-haired *adj.* —*See* FAIR¹ (2), FAVORITE.

fairish *adj.* —*See* ACCEPTABLE (2).

fairly *adv.* **1.** In a just or equitable manner ▸ dispassionately, equitably, evenhandedly, impartially, indifferently, justly, objectively, squarely. **2.** To some extent ▸ pretty, quite, rather. *Idioms:* in part, kind of, more or less, sort of, to a (*or* some) degree. [*Compare* APPROXIMATELY, CONSIDERABLY, USUALLY.] —*See also* FAIR¹, REALLY.

fair-minded *adj.* —*See* FAIR¹ (1).

fairness or **fair-mindedness** *n.* The quality or state of being just and unbiased ▸ detachment, disinterest, disinterestedness, dispassion, dispassionateness, equitableness, evenhandedness, impartiality, impartialness, justice, justness, nonpartisanship, objectiveness, objectivity. [*Compare* HONESTY.]

fair-weather *adj.* —*See* UNDEPENDABLE (1).

fairy *n.* A creature or spirit that has supernatural powers ▸ brownie, dryad, elf, goblin, hobgoblin, jinni, kelpie, leprechaun, naiad, nymph, pixie, pooka, puck, selkie, sprite, sylph.

fairy godmother *n.* —*See* DONOR.

fairy tale *n.* —*See* MYTH (1).

fairy-tale *adj.* —*See* MYTHICAL.

faith *n.* Mental acceptance of the actuality of something ▸ belief, credence, credit. —*See also* DEVOTION, RELIGION, TRUST.

faithful *adj.* Adhering firmly to a person, cause, duty, or faith ▸ allegiant, committed, constant, dedicated, devoted, fast, firm, liege, loyal, staunch, steadfast, true, true-blue. [*Compare* DEPENDABLE, FIRM¹.] —*See also* ACCURATE, AUTHENTIC (2), CLOSE (2), DIVINE (2).

faithful *n.* The steadfast believers in a faith or cause ▸ adherents, congregation, fold. [*Compare* FOLLOWER, ASSEMBLY.]

faithfully *adv.* —*See* EXACTLY.

faithfulness *n.* —*See* FIDELITY, VERACITY.

faithless *adj.* Not true to duty or obligation ▸ disloyal, false, false-hearted, perfidious, recreant, traitorous, treacherous, unfaithful, untrue. [*Compare* UNDEPENDABLE.] —*See also* ATHEISTIC.

faithlessness *n.* Betrayal, especially of a duty or obligation ▸ betrayal, disloyalty, false-heartedness, falseness, falsity, foul play, infidelity, perfidiousness, perfidy, traitorousness, treacherousness, treachery, treason, unfaithfulness. [*Compare* DECEIT.] —*See also* ATHEISM.

fake *n.* A person who practices deceit, especially under an assumed identity ▸ charlatan, faker, fraud, humbug, impostor, mountebank, phony, pretender, quack, sham. [*Compare* CHEAT, HYPOCRITE, LIAR.] —*See also* COUNTERFEIT.

fake *v.* To alter something so as to give it a false character ▸ doctor, falsify. —*See also* ACT (2), COUNTERFEIT, IMPROVISE (1).

fake *adj.* —*See* COUNTERFEIT.

faker *n.* One who makes a fraudulent copy of something ▸ counterfeiter, fabricator, falsifier, forger. —*See also* FAKE.

fall *v.* **1.** To move downward in response to gravity ▸ descend, dive, drop, go down, nose-dive, pitch, plummet, plunge, sink, spill, tumble. *Idioms:* fall flat on one's face, go flying, take a fall (*or* header *or* plunge *or* spill *or* tumble). [*Compare* RECEDE, SETTLE, STUMBLE.] **2.** To come

on. **fall flat** To fail miserably. **fall in with** 1. To agree with. 2. To associate with. **fall short** To fail to reach or attain.

fal·la·cious (fə-lā′shəs) ▸ *adj.* 1. Containing or based on a fallacy. 2. Tending to mislead; deceptive. **—fal·la′cious·ly** *adv.*

fal·la·cy (făl′ə-sē) ▸ *n., pl.* **-cies.** 1. A false idea or notion. 2. Incorrectness of reasoning or belief.

fall guy ▸ *n. Slang* 1. A scapegoat. 2. A dupe.

fal·li·ble (făl′ə-bəl) ▸ *adj.* Capable of making an error. **—fal′li·bil′i·ty** *n.* **—fal′li·bly** *adv.*

fall·ing-out (fô′lĭng-out′) ▸ *n., pl.* **fall·ings-out** or **fall·ing-outs.** A quarrel.

fall·ing star (fô′lĭng) ▸ *n.* See **meteor.**

fal·lo·pi·an tube also **Fal·lo·pi·an tube** (fə-lō′pē-ən) ▸ *n.* Either of a pair of slender ducts through which ova pass from the ovaries to the uterus in the female reproductive system of humans and higher mammals.

fall·out (fôl′out′) ▸ *n.* 1a. The slow descent of minute particles of radioactive debris in the atmosphere after a nuclear explosion. b. These particles. 2. An incidental result or side effect: *political fallout.*

fal·low (făl′ō) ▸ *adj.* 1. Plowed but left unseeded during a growing season. 2. Inactive.

fallow deer ▸ *n.* A small Eurasian deer having broad flat antlers in the male.

false (fôls) ▸ *adj.* **fals·er, fals·est.** 1. Contrary to fact or truth. 2. Unfaithful or disloyal. 3. Not real; artificial. 4. *Mus.* Of incorrect pitch. **—false′ly** *adv.* **—false′ness** *n.*

false alarm ▸ *n.* 1. An emergency alarm set off unnecessarily. 2. A groundless warning.

false arrest ▸ *n.* Unlawful arrest.

false-heart·ed (fôls′här′tĭd) ▸ *adj.* Deceitful.

false·hood (fôls′ho͝od′) ▸ *n.* 1. A lie. 2. The practice of lying. 3. Lack of conformity to truth or fact; inaccuracy.

fal·set·to (fôl-sĕt′ō) ▸ *n., pl.* **-tos.** A male voice in an upper register beyond its normal range. **—fal·set′to** *adv.*

fal·si·fy (fôl′sə-fī′) ▸ *v.* **-fied, -fy·ing.** 1. To state untruthfully. 2. To alter (e.g., a document) so as to deceive. 3. To counterfeit; forge. **—fal′si·fi·ca′tion** *n.* **—fal′si·fi′er** *n.*

fal·si·ty (fôl′sĭ-tē) ▸ *n., pl.* **-ties.** 1. The quality or condition of being false. 2. A lie.

fal·ter (fôl′tər) ▸ *v.* 1. To weaken or be unsteady in purpose or action; waver. 2. To stammer. 3. To stumble. ▸ *n.* 1. Unsteadiness in speech or action. 2. A faltering sound. **—fal′ter·er** *n.* **—fal′ter·ing·ly** *adv.*

fame (fām) ▸ *n.* Great reputation and recognition; renown. **—famed** *adj.*

fa·mil·iar (fə-mĭl′yər) ▸ *adj.* 1. Often encountered; common. 2. Having knowledge of something. 3. Intimate. 4. Unduly forward; bold. ▸ *n.* A close friend or associate. **—fa·mil′iar·ly** *adv.*

fa·mil·iar·i·ty (fə-mĭl′yăr′ĭ-tē, -mĭl′ē-ăr′-) ▸ *n., pl.* **-ties.** 1. Considerable acquaintance with or knowledge of something. 2. Close friendship; intimacy. 3. An excessively familiar act; an impropriety.

fa·mil·iar·ize (fə-mĭl′yə-rīz′) ▸ *v.* **-ized, -iz·ing.** To make (oneself or another) acquainted with. **—fa·mil′iar·i·za′tion** *n.*

fam·i·ly (făm′ə-lē, făm′lē) ▸ *n., pl.* **-lies.** 1. Parents and their children. 2. The members of one household. 3. A group of persons related by blood or marriage. 4. A group of like things; class. 5. *Biol.* The category ranking below an order and above a genus in the hierarchy of taxonomic classification. 6. *Ling.* A group of languages descended from the same parent language. **—fa·mil′ial** (fə-mĭl′yəl) *adj.*

THESAURUS

to the ground from an upright position ▸ fall over (*or* down), keel over, tip over, topple, tumble. [*Compare* BUCKLE.] 3. To undergo capture, defeat, or ruin ▸ collapse, go down, go under, topple. [*Compare* SUCCUMB, SURRENDER.] 4. To become lower in value or price ▸ decline, depreciate, dive, drop (off), fall off, nose-dive, plummet, plunge, sag, sink, skid, slip, slump, tumble. *Idioms:* take a sudden downtrend, take a sudden downturn. [*Compare* COLLAPSE, DECREASE, DETERIORATE, SLIP.] 5. To undergo moral deterioration ▸ degenerate, sink, slip. [*Compare* DETERIORATE.] *—See also* DROP (1), DROP (2), HAPPEN (1), SUBSIDE.

fall apart *v.* *—See* BREAK (3), DISINTEGRATE.

fall back *v.* *—See* BACK (1), RELAPSE, RETREAT.

fall down or **flat** *v.* *—See* FAIL (1).

fall off *v.* *—See* SUBSIDE.

fall on or **upon** *v.* *—See* ATTACK (1).

fall out *v.* *—See* ARGUE (1).

fall short *v.* To prove deficient or insufficient ▸ give out, run out. *Idioms:* run dry, run short. [*Compare* DECREASE.] *—See also* FAIL (1).

fall through *v.* *—See* FAIL (1).

fall *n.* 1. A sudden downward motion toward the ground ▸ descent, dive, drop, nosedive, pitch, plunge, spill, tumble. *Informal:* header. 2. A disastrous defeat or ruin ▸ collapse, downfall, waterloo. [*Compare* DEFEAT.] 3. A usually swift downward trend, as in prices ▸ decline, depreciation, descent, dip, dive, downslide, downswing, downtrend, downturn, drop, drop-off, nosedive, plunge, skid, slide, slump, tumble. [*Compare* DECREASE, DEPRECIATION, DEPRESSION.] *—See also* DROP (3).

fallacious *adj.* 1. Containing errors in reasoning ▸ false, illogical, inconsistent, invalid, irrational, self-contradictory, sophistic, specious, spurious, unsound, untenable. [*Compare* BASELESS, FOOLISH, UNREASONABLE.] 2. Tending to lead one into error ▸ deceptive, delusive, delusory, illusive, illusory, insidious, misleading. [*Compare* DISHONEST, FALSE.] *—See also* ERRONEOUS.

fallacy *n.* 1. An erroneous or false idea ▸ error, falsehood, falsity, misapprehension, misconception, misinterpretation, misunderstanding, untruth. [*Compare* ERROR, ILLUSION.] 2. Plausible but invalid reasoning ▸ casuistry, sophism, sophistry, speciousness, spuriousness.

fallback *n.* *—See* RETREAT.

fallen *adj.* *—See* CONDEMNED.

fall guy *n.* *—See* DUPE, SCAPEGOAT.

false *adj.* Not true ▸ apocryphal, counterfactual, fictitious, specious, spurious, truthless, untrue, untruthful, wrong. [*Compare* BASELESS, DISHONEST.] *—See also* COUNTERFEIT, ERRONEOUS, FAITHLESS, FALLACIOUS (1).

false colors *n.* *—See* FAÇADE (1).

false-hearted *adj.* *—See* DISHONEST, FAITHLESS.

false-heartedness *n.* *—See* FAITHLESSNESS.

falsehood *n.* *—See* FALLACY (1), LIE², MENDACITY.

false impression *n.* *—See* MISUNDERSTANDING.

falseness *n.* *—See* FAITHLESSNESS.

falsification *n.* *—See* COUNTERFEIT, MENDACITY.

falsifier *n.* One who makes a fraudulent copy of something ▸ counterfeiter, fabricator, faker, forger. *—See also* LIAR.

falsify *v.* To alter something so as to give it a false character ▸ fake, doctor. *—See also* COUNTERFEIT, DISTORT, LIE².

falsity *n.* *—See* FAITHLESSNESS, FALLACY (1), INSINCERITY, LIE².

falter *v.* *—See* HESITATE, STAGGER (1), STAMMER.

fame *n.* Wide recognition for one's deeds ▸ celebrity, distinction, eminence, eminency, famousness, glory, illustriousness, luster, mark, notability, note, notoriety, popularity, preeminence, prestige, renown, prominence, prominency, reputation, repute. [*Compare* DISTINCTION, ESTEEM, HONOR, REPUTATION.]

famed *adj.* *—See* FAMOUS.

familial *adj.* *—See* ANCESTRAL, DOMESTIC (1).

familiar *adj.* Having good knowledge of something ▸ acquainted, conversant, schooled, versant, versed. *Idiom:* up on. [*Compare* ACCUSTOMED, INFORMED.] *—See also* COMMON (1), CONFIDENTIAL (2), IMPUDENT, INTIMATE¹ (1).

familiar *n.* *—See* FRIEND.

familiarity *n.* Personal knowledge derived from participation or observation ▸ acquaintance, conversance, experience. [*Compare* AWARENESS.] *—See also* DULLNESS, FRIENDSHIP, IMPUDENCE.

familiarize *v.* To make known socially ▸ acquaint, introduce, present. *—See also* ACCUSTOM.

family *n.* 1. A group of people living together as a unit ▸ house, household, ménage. 2. A group of people sharing common ancestry ▸ clan, house, kindred, lineage, stock, tribe. *Idioms:* kith and kin, flesh and blood. *—See also* ANCESTRY, CLASS (1), KIN.

family leave ▸ *n.* A usu. unpaid absence from work granted for taking care of a family member, such as a baby or sick parent.
family name ▸ *n.* See **surname.**
family planning ▸ *n.* The regulation of the number and spacing of children in a family through birth-control techniques.
family tree ▸ *n.* A genealogical diagram of a family's ancestry.
fam·ine (făm′ĭn) ▸ *n.* **1.** A drastic, wide-reaching food shortage. **2.** A drastic lack; dearth.
fam·ish (făm′ĭsh) ▸ *v.* To starve. **—fam′ished** *adj.*
fa·mous (fā′məs) ▸ *adj.* **1.** Well or widely known. **2.** *Informal* First-rate; excellent. **—fa′mous·ly** *adv.*
fan[1] (făn) ▸ *n.* **1.** A hand-held, usu. wedge-shaped device that is waved to create a cool breeze. **2.** An electrical device that rotates rigid vanes in order to move air, as for cooling. **3.** Something resembling an open hand-held fan. ▸ *v.* **fanned, fan·ning. 1.** To direct a current of air upon, esp. in order to cool. **2.** To stir up: *fanned resentment.* **3.** *Baseball* To strike out. **4.** To spread: *fanned out on their search.*
fan[2] (făn) ▸ *n. Informal* An ardent devotee; enthusiast.
fa·nat·ic (fə-năt′ĭk) ▸ *n.* One who is fanatical. ▸ *adj.* Fanatical.
fa·nat·i·cal (fə-năt′ĭ-kəl) ▸ *adj.* Possessed with extreme zeal or enthusiasm. **—fa·nat′i·cal·ly** *adv.* **—fa·nat′i·cism** *n.*
fan·ci·er (făn′sē-ər) ▸ *n.* One who has a special enthusiasm or interest, as for raising a specific plant or animal.
fan·ci·ful (făn′sĭ-fəl) ▸ *adj.* **1.** Created in the fancy; imaginary: *a fanciful story.* **2.** Tending to indulge in fancy. **3.** Quaint or whimsical in design. **—fan′ci·ful·ly** *adv.*
fan·cy (făn′sē) ▸ *n., pl.* **-cies. 1.** Imagination, esp. of a whimsical or fantastic nature. **2.** A notion or whim. **3.** A capricious liking or inclination. ▸ *adj.* **-ci·er, -ci·est. 1a.** Ingeniously or intricately designed. **b.** Stylish: *a fancy outfit.* **2.** Whimsical. **3.** Done with great technical skill: *fancy footwork.* **4.** Of superior grade: *fancy preserves.* ▸ *v.* **-cied, -cy·ing. 1.** To imagine. **2.** To be fond of. **3.** To suppose; guess. **—fan′ci·ly** *adv.* **—fan′ci·ness** *n.*
fancy dress ▸ *n.* A masquerade costume.
fan·cy-free (făn′sē-frē′) ▸ *adj.* **1.** Having no restrictions; carefree. **2.** Not in love; unattached.
fan·cy·work (făn′sē-wûrk′) ▸ *n.* Decorative needlework, such as embroidery.
fan·dan·go (făn-dăng′gō) ▸ *n., pl.* **-gos.** A lively Spanish or Latin dance.
fan·fare (făn′fâr′) ▸ *n.* **1.** A flourish of trumpets. **2.** A spectacular public display.
fang (făng) ▸ *n.* A long pointed tooth, especially: **a.** A hollow, poison-injecting tooth of a venomous snake. **b.** A canine tooth of a carnivorous animal. **—fanged** *adj.*
fan·jet also **fan-jet** (făn′jĕt′) ▸ *n.* An aircraft powered by a jet engine with a ducted fan that draws in extra air.
fan·light (făn′līt′) ▸ *n.* A half-circle window, often with sash bars arranged like the ribs of a fan.
fan·ny (făn′ē) ▸ *n., pl.* **-nies.** *Slang* The buttocks.
fan·tail (făn′tāl′) ▸ *n.* **1.** A fanlike tail or end. **2.** The stern overhang of a ship. **—fan′tailed′** *adj.*
fan·ta·sia (făn-tā′zhə, -zhē-ə, făn′tə-zē′ə) ▸ *n. Mus.* A freeform composition.
fan·ta·size (făn′tə-sīz′) ▸ *v.* **-sized, -siz·ing. 1.** To indulge in fantasies. **2.** To imagine.
fan·tas·tic (făn-tăs′tĭk) also **fan·tas·ti·cal** (-tĭ-kəl) ▸ *adj.* **1.** Strange in conception or appearance. **2.** Bizarre, as in form or appearance; grotesque. **3.** Unreal or illusory. **4.** Superb. **—fan·tas′ti·cal·ly** *adv.*
fan·ta·sy (făn′tə-sē, -zē) ▸ *n., pl.* **-sies. 1.** The creative imagination. **2.** A product of the fancy; illusion. **3.** A delusion. **4.** Fiction marked by highly fanciful elements. **5.** A daydream. **6.** *Mus.* See **fantasia. —fan′ta·sy** *v.*
fan·zine (făn′zēn) ▸ *n.* An amateur-produced fan magazine.
FAQ (făk) ▸ *n.* A list of frequently asked questions and their answers.
far (fär) ▸ *adv.* **far·ther** (fär′*th*ər), **far·thest** (fär′*th*ĭst) or **fur·ther** (fûr′*th*ər), **fur·thest** (fûr′*th*ĭst). **1.** To, from, or at considerable distance. **2.** To or at a specific distance, degree, or position. **3.** To a considerable degree; much: *felt far better.* ▸ *adj.* **farther, farthest** or **further, furthest. 1.** Being at considerable distance: *a far country.* **2.** More distant or remote: *the far corner.* **3.** Extensive or lengthy: *a far trek.* ***—idioms:*** **as far as** To the extent that. **by far** To the most extreme degree. **far and away** By a great margin. **far and wide** Everywhere. **far cry** A long way. **far from** Not at all: *far from satisfied.* **so far** Up to now.
far·ad (făr′əd, -ăd′) ▸ *n.* The unit of capacitance equal to that of a capacitor that acquires a charge of 1 coulomb when a potential difference of 1 volt is applied.
far·a·way (fär′ə-wā′) ▸ *adj.* **1.** Very distant; remote. **2.** Abstracted; dreamy.
farce (färs) ▸ *n.* **1.** A humorous play having a highly improbable plot and exaggerated characters. **2.** A ludicrous, empty show; mockery. **—far′ci·cal** *adj.* **—far′ci·cal·ly** *adv.*
fare (fâr) ▸ *v.* **fared, far·ing. 1.** To get along. **2.** To travel; go. ▸ *n.* **1.** A transportation charge. **2.** A passenger transported for a fee. **3.** Food and drink. **—far′er** *n.*
Far East ▸ The countries and regions of E and SE Asia, esp. China, Japan, North Korea, South Korea, Taiwan, and Mongolia. **—Far Eastern** *adj.*
fare·well (fâr-wĕl′) ▸ *interj.* Used to express an acknowledgment of parting. ▸ *n.* **1.** A goodbye. **2.** A leave-taking.

THESAURUS

family tree *n.* A written record of ancestry ▸ genealogy, pedigree. *—See also* ANCESTRY.
famished *adj.* *—See* HUNGRY (1).
famous *adj.* Widely known ▸ celebrated, distinguished, eminent, famed, glorious, great, illustrious, important, leading, legendary, notable, noted, notorious, popular, preeminent, prestigious, prominent, recognized, redoubtable, renowned, reputable, storied, well-known. ***Idiom:*** of note. [*Compare* EXALTED.]
famousness *n.* *—See* FAME.
fan[1] *v.* *—See* SPREAD (1).
fan[2] *n.* An ardent devotee ▸ admirer, aficionado, bug, devotee, enthusiast, fanatic, fancier, follower, groupie, hound, junkie, lover, maniac, zealot. *Informal:* buff, fiend. *Slang:* freak, head, nut. [*Compare* FOLLOWER.]
fanatic *n.* *—See* DEVOTEE, EXTREMIST, FAN[2].
fanatic or **fanatical** *adj.* *—See* ENTHUSIASTIC, EXTREME (2).
fanaticism *n.* *—See* ENTHUSIASM (1).
fancier *n.* *—See* FAN[2].
fanciful *adj.* Showing invention or whimsy in design ▸ fantastic, imaginative, whimsical. [*Compare* CAPRICIOUS, ELABORATE, ORNATE.] *—See also* DREAMY, EXOTIC, IMAGINARY.
fancy *n.* An impulsive turn of mind ▸ caprice, conceit, freak, humor, impulse, megrim, notion, vagary, whim, whimsy. ***Idiom:*** bee in one's bonnet. [*Compare* MOOD.] *—See also* DREAM (1), ENTHUSIASM (2), IMAGINATION, LIKING, LOVE (2).
fancy *adj.* *—See* ELABORATE, EXCLUSIVE (3), LUXURIOUS.
fancy *v.* *—See* DREAM, GUESS, IMAGINE, LIKE[1].
fancy-free *adj.* *—See* LIGHTHEARTED, SINGLE.
fanfaronade *n.* *—See* BOAST.
fanny *n.* *—See* BUTTOCKS.
fantasist *n.* *—See* DREAMER (1).
fantasize *v.* *—See* DREAM, IMAGINE.
fantastic *adj.* Showing invention or whimsy in design ▸ fanciful, imaginative, whimsical. [*Compare* ELABORATE, ORNATE.] *—See also* ASTONISHING, CAPRICIOUS, ECCENTRIC, EXOTIC, FICTITIOUS, IMAGINARY, MARVELOUS.
fantastical *adj.* *—See* IMAGINARY, MARVELOUS.
fantasy *n.* *—See* DREAM (1), DREAM (2), IMAGINATION, MYTH (2).
fantasy *adj.* *—See* MYTHICAL.
far *adv.* *—See* CONSIDERABLY.
far *adj.* *—See* DISTANT.
faraway *adj.* *—See* ABSENT-MINDED, DISTANT.
farce *n.* *—See* MOCKERY (2), SATIRE.
farceur *n.* *—See* JOKER.
farcical *adj.* Causing or deserving laughter or derision ▸ laughable, ludicrous, ridiculous, risible. [*Compare* FOOLISH.]
farcicality *n.* *—See* HUMOR.
fare *v.* *—See* JOURNEY, MANAGE.
fare *n.* *—See* FOOD, TOLL[1] (1).
farewell *n.* *—See* DEPARTURE.
farewell *adj.* *—See* PARTING.
farewell *interjection* *—See* GOODBYE.

far·fetched (fär′fĕcht′) ▸ *adj.* Implausible.
far·flung (fär′flŭng′) ▸ *adj.* **1.** Remote; distant. **2.** Widely distributed; wide-ranging.
fa·ri·na (fə-rē′nə) ▸ *n.* Fine meal, as of cereal grain, often used as a cooked cereal or in puddings.
far·i·na·ceous (făr′ə-nā′shəs) ▸ *adj.* **1.** Made from or containing starch. **2.** Mealy or powdery in texture.
farm (färm) ▸ *n.* **1.** A tract of land on which crops or animals are raised. **2.** An area of water used for raising aquatic animals: *a trout farm.* ▸ *v.* **1.** To raise crops or livestock. **2.** To use (land) for this purpose. ***—phrasal verb:* farm out** To send out (work) to be done elsewhere. **—farm′er** *n.* **—farm′ing** *n.*
farm hand ▸ *n.* A hired farm laborer.
farm·house (färm′hous′) ▸ *n.* A dwelling on a farm.
farm·land (färm′lănd′, -lənd) ▸ *n.* An expanse of land suitable or used for farming.
farm·stead (färm′stĕd′) ▸ *n.* A farm, including its land and buildings.
farm·yard (färm′yärd′) ▸ *n.* An area surrounded by or adjacent to farm buildings.
far·o (fâr′ō) ▸ *n.* A card game in which the players bet on the top card of the dealer's pack.
Far·oe Islands (fâr′ō) ▸ See **Faeroe Islands**.
far-off (fär′ôf′, -ŏf′) ▸ *adj.* Remote in space or time; distant.
far-out (fär′out′) ▸ *adj. Slang* Extremely unconventional.
far·ra·go (fə-rä′gō, -rā′-) ▸ *n., pl.* **-goes.** An assortment or medley; conglomeration.
far-reach·ing (fär′rē′chĭng) ▸ *adj.* Having a wide range, influence, or effect.
far·row (făr′ō) ▸ *n.* A litter of pigs. ▸ *v.* To give birth to a farrow.
far·see·ing (fär′sē′ĭng) ▸ *adj.* Foresighted.
far·sight·ed or **far-sight·ed** (fär′sī′tĭd) ▸ *adj.* **1.** Able to see distant objects better than objects at close range. **2.** Prudent; foresighted. **—far′sight′ed·ness** *n.*
far·ther (fär′*th*ər) ▸ *adv.* Comp. of **far**. **1.** To or at a more distant point. **2.** To or at a more advanced point or stage. **3.** To a greater extent or degree. ▸ *adj.* Comp. of **far**. More distant; remoter.
far·ther·most (fär′*th*ər-mōst′) ▸ *adj.* Most distant; farthest.
far·thest (fär′*th*ĭst) ▸ *adj.* Superl. of **far**. Most remote or distant. ▸ *adv.* Superl. of **far**. **1.** To or at the most distant or remote point. **2.** To or at the most advanced point or stage. **3.** By the greatest extent or degree.
far·thing (fär′*th*ĭng) ▸ *n.* **1.** A coin formerly used in Great Britain worth one fourth of a penny. **2.** Something of little value.
far·thin·gale (fär′*th*ĭn-gāl′, -thĭng-) ▸ *n.* A support, such as a hoop, worn beneath a skirt by European women in the 16th and 17th cent.
fas·ci·cle (făs′ĭ-kəl) ▸ *n.* **1.** A small bundle. **2.** One of the parts of a book published in separate sections. **—fas′ci·cled** *adj.*
fas·ci·nate (făs′ə-nāt′) ▸ *v.* **-nat·ed, -nat·ing. 1.** To hold an intense interest or attraction for. **2.** To hold motionless; spellbind. **—fas′ci·na′tion** *n.* **—fas′ci·na′tor** *n.*
fas·cism (făsh′ĭz′əm) ▸ *n.* **1.** often **Fascism a.** Totalitarianism marked by right-wing dictatorship and bellicose nationalism. **b.** A political philosophy or movement based on or advocating such a system of government. **2.** Oppressive, dictatorial control. **—fas′cist** *adj. & n.* **—fas·cis′tic** (fə-shĭs′tĭk) *adj.*
fash·ion (făsh′ən) ▸ *n.* **1.** The prevailing style or custom, as in dress. **2.** Manner; way. **3.** Kind; sort. ▸ *v.* **1.** To give shape or form to; make. **2.** To adapt, as to a purpose or an occasion. ***—idiom:* after a fashion** To a limited extent. **—fash′ion·er** *n.*
fash·ion·a·ble (făsh′ə-nə-bəl) ▸ *adj.* **1.** In the current style; stylish. **2.** Associated with persons of fashion. **—fash′ion·a·ble·ness** *n.* **—fash′ion·a·bly** *adv.*
fast[1] (făst) ▸ *adj.* **-er, -est. 1.** Acting or moving quickly; swift. **2.** Accomplished in little time. **3.** Indicating a time ahead of the actual time: *The clock is fast.* **4.** Adapted to or suitable for speed: *a fast running track.* **5.** Designed for a short exposure time: *fast film.* **6.** Flouting moral standards; wild. **7.** Resistant: *fast colors.* **8.** Firmly fixed or fastened. **9.** Secure. **10.** Firm in loyalty: *fast friends.* **11.** Deep; sound: *in a fast sleep.* ▸ *adv.* **1.** Securely; tightly. **2.** Deeply: *fast asleep.* **3.** Rapidly; quickly. **4.** In quick succession: *New ideas followed fast.* **5.** In a dissipated, immoderate way: *living fast.*
fast[2] (făst) ▸ *v.* To abstain from food, esp. as a religious discipline. ▸ *n.* The act or a period of abstention from food.
fast·back (făst′băk′) ▸ *n.* An automobile designed with a curving downward slope from roof to rear.
fas·ten (făs′ən) ▸ *v.* **1.** To attach or become attached to something else; join; connect. **2.** To make fast or secure; close. **3.** To fix or direct steadily. **—fas′ten·er** *n.* **—fas′ten·ing** *n.*
fast food ▸ *n.* Inexpensive food, such as hamburgers, prepared and served quickly. **—fast′-food′** *adj.*
fast-for·ward (făst-fôr′wərd) ▸ *n.* A function on a tape recorder or player that permits rapid advancement of the tape. **—fast-for′ward** *v.*
fas·tid·i·ous (fă-stĭd′ē-əs, fə-) ▸ *adj.* **1.** Attentive to detail. **2.** Difficult to please; exacting. **3.** Scrupulous, esp. in matters of taste or propriety. **—fas·tid′i·ous·ness** *n.*

THESAURUS

far-fetched *adj.* *—See* EXAGGERATED, INCREDIBLE.
far-flung *adj.* Spread out over a large area ▸ broad, widespread. *—See also* DISTANT.
farm *v.* *—See* GROW.
farness *n.* The fact or condition of being far removed or apart ▸ distance, remoteness, separateness, separation.
far-off *adj.* *—See* DISTANT.
far-out *adj.* *—See* EXTREME (2).
far-ranging or **far-reaching** *adj.* *—See* GENERAL (2).
farsighted *adj.* *—See* VISIONARY.
farsightedness *n.* *—See* VISION (2).
farthest or **farthermost** *adj.* *—See* EXTREME (1).
fascinate *v.* *—See* CHARM (1), GRIP.
fascinating *adj.* *—See* ATTRACTIVE.
fascination *n.* *—See* ATTRACTION, OBSESSION.
fascism *n.* *—See* TYRANNY.
fashion *n.* The current custom ▸ craze, fad, furor, mode, rage, style, trend, vogue. *Informal:* thing. *Idioms:* the in thing, the latest thing. [*Compare* CUSTOM.] *—See also* STYLE, WAY (1).
fashion *v.* *—See* ADAPT, FORM (1), MAKE.
fashionable *adj.* In accordance with current fashion ▸ à la mode, chic, dashing, de rigueur, fashion-forward, mod, modish, smart, stylish, swank, swanky. *Informal:* classy, in, sharp, snappy, swish, trendy, with-it. *Slang:* funky, hip, hot, snazzy. *Idioms:* all the rage, up to the minute, up to the second. [*Compare* CONTEMPORARY, ELEGANT, LUXURIOUS.]
fast *adj.* **1.** Characterized by great speed ▸ blinding, breakneck, brisk, expeditious, express, fleet, hasty, high-speed, hurried, quick, rapid, speedy, swift. *Informal:* hell-for-leather, pedal to the metal. *Idiom:* quick as a bunny (*or* wink). **2.** Retaining original color ▸ colorfast, indelible. *—See also* ABANDONED (2), FAITHFUL, FIRM[1] (2), INTIMATE[1] (1), QUICK, TIGHT (1), WANTON (1).
fast *adv.* In a rapid way ▸ apace, hastily, hurriedly, posthaste, quick, quickly, rapidly, swiftly. *Informal:* flat out, hell-for-leather, lickety-split, pedal to the metal, pronto. *Idioms:* full tilt, in a flash, in nothing flat, like a bat out of hell, like a blue streak, like a flash, like a house on fire, like a shot, like a streak, like greased lightning, like the wind, like wildfire, with dispatch.
fasten *v.* To cause to remain firmly in position or place; make secure ▸ anchor, bind, bolt, buckle, catch, chain, clamp, clip, fix, hitch, knot, lash, lock, moor, nail, pin, rivet, screw, secure, strap, tack, tie (up). *Idiom:* make fast. [*Compare* SUPPORT.] *—See also* ATTACH (1), FIX (2), FIX (3).
fasten on or **upon** *v.* *—See* IMPOSE ON.
fastener or **fastening** *n.* A device for locking or for checking motion ▸ bar, binder, binding, buckle, catch, clamp, clasp, clip, collar, harness, hasp, hook, latch, lock, mortise, pawl, snap, vise. [*Compare* ANCHOR, BOND, CORD, NAIL.]
fastidious *adj.* *—See* CAREFUL (2), FUSSY.
fastidiousness *n.* *—See* THOROUGHNESS.
fastigium *n.* *—See* CLIMAX.

fast·ness (făst′nĭs) ▸ *n.* 1. Rapidity; swiftness. 2. A secure or fortified place.

fast-talk (făst′tôk′) ▸ *v. Informal* To persuade, mislead, or obtain with smooth talk. **—fast′-talk′er** *n.*

fast track ▸ *n. Informal* The quickest and most direct route to achievement of a goal. **—fast′-track′** *adj.* **—fast track′er** *n.*

fat (făt) ▸ *n.* 1a. Any of various soft, solid, or semisolid organic compounds occurring widely in animal and plant tissue. b. Organic tissue containing such substances. c. A solidified animal or vegetable oil. 2. Obesity; corpulence. 3. The best or richest part: *living off the fat of the land.* 4. Unnecessary excess. ▸ *adj.* **fat·ter, fat·test.** 1. Having much flesh. 2. Full of fat or oil; greasy. 3. Abounding in desirable elements. 4. Fertile or productive; rich. 5. Having an abundance; well-stocked: *a fat larder.* 6a. Lucrative or rewarding: *a fat promotion.* b. Prosperous; wealthy: *grew fat on profits.* 7. Thick; large: *a fat book.* **—*idiom:* fat chance** *Slang* Little or no chance. **—fat′ly** *adv.* **—fat′ness** *n.* **—fat′ti·ness** *n.* **—fat′ty** *adj.*

fa·tal (făt′l) ▸ *adj.* 1. Causing or capable of causing death. 2. Causing destruction. 3. Of decisive importance; fateful. **—fa′tal·ly** *adv.*

fa·tal·ism (făt′l-ĭz′əm) ▸ *n.* The doctrine that all events are determined by fate and are therefore unalterable. **—fa′tal·ist** *n.* **—fa′tal·is′tic** *adj.* **—fa′tal·is′ti·cal·ly** *adv.*

fa·tal·i·ty (fā-tăl′ĭ-tē, fə-) ▸ *n., pl.* **-ties.** A death resulting from an accident or disaster.

fat·back (făt′băk′) ▸ *n.* Salt-cured fat from the upper part of a side of pork.

fat cat ▸ *n. Slang* 1. A wealthy and privileged person. 2. A wealthy contributor to a political campaign.

fate (fāt) ▸ *n.* 1. The supposed force or power that determines events. 2. A final result; outcome. 3. Unfavorable destiny; doom. 4. **Fates** *Gk. & Rom. Myth.* The three goddesses, Clotho, Lachesis, and Atropos, who control human destiny.

fat·ed (fā′tĭd) ▸ *adj.* 1. Predetermined. 2. Doomed.

fate·ful (fāt′fəl) ▸ *adj.* 1. Being of great consequence; momentous. 2. Controlled by or as if by fate. 3. Bringing death or disaster; fatal. 4. Ominously prophetic; portentous. **—fate′ful·ly** *adv.* **—fate′ful·ness** *n.*

fat·head (făt′hĕd′) ▸ *n. Slang* A stupid person. **—fat′head′ed** *adj.*

fa·ther (fä′*th*ər) ▸ *n.* 1. A man who begets or raises a child. 2. A male ancestor. 3. **Father** God. 4. A title used for a male priest in some Christian churches. ▸ *v.* To beget; sire. **—fa′ther·hood′** *n.* **—fa′ther·li·ness** *n.* **—fa′ther·ly** *adj.*

father figure ▸ *n.* An older man who elicits the emotions usu. reserved for a father.

fa·ther-in-law (fä′*th*ər-ĭn-lô′) ▸ *n., pl.* **fa·thers-in-law** (-ərz-). The father of one's spouse.

fa·ther·land (fä′*th*ər-lănd′) ▸ *n.* One's native land.

fa·ther·less (fä′*th*ər-lĭs) ▸ *adj.* 1. Having no living father. 2. Having no known father. **—fa′ther·less·ness** *n.*

fath·om (fă*th*′əm) ▸ *n., pl.* **-om** or **-oms.** A unit of length equal to 6 ft (1.83 m), used principally in the measurement of marine depths. ▸ *v.* 1. To determine the depth of; sound. 2. To comprehend. **—fath′om·a·ble** *adj.*

fath·om·less (fă*th*′əm-lĭs) ▸ *adj.* 1. Too deep to be fathomed or measured. 2. Too obscure or complicated to be understood.

fa·tigue (fə-tēg′) ▸ *n.* 1. Physical or mental weariness resulting from exertion. 2. **fatigues** Clothing worn by military personnel for labor or field duty. ▸ *v.* **-tigued, -tigu·ing.** To tire out; weary. **—fat′i·ga·ble** (făt′ĭ-gə-bəl) *adj.*

fat·ten (făt′n) ▸ *v.* To make or become plump or fat. **—fat′ten·er** *n.*

fatty acid ▸ *n.* Any of a large group of organic acids, esp. those found in animal and vegetable fats and oils, having the general formula $C_nH_{2n+1}COOH$.

fa·tu·i·ty (fə-to͞o′ĭ-tē, -tyo͞o′-) ▸ *n.* Smug stupidity; utter foolishness.

fat·u·ous (făch′o͞o-əs) ▸ *adj.* Smugly and unconsciously foolish. **—fat′u·ous·ly** *adv.* **—fat′u·ous·ness** *n.*

fat·wa (făt′wä′) ▸ *n.* A ruling issued by an Islamic scholar.

fau·cet (fô′sĭt) ▸ *n.* A device for regulating the flow of a liquid, as from a pipe.

Faulk·ner (fôk′nər), **William** (1897–1962) ▸ Amer. writer; 1949 Nobel.

fault (fôlt) ▸ *n.* 1. A character weakness, esp. a minor one. 2. A mistake; error. 3. Responsibility for a mistake or offense. 4. *Geol.* A fracture in the continuity of a rock formation caused by a shifting or dislodging of the earth's crust, in which adjacent surfaces are differentially displaced parallel to the plane of fracture. 5. *Sports* A bad service, as in tennis. ▸ *v.* 1. To find error or defect in; criticize or blame. 2. *Geol.* To produce a fault in; fracture.

THESAURUS

fastness *n.* —*See* STABILITY.

fast one *n.* —*See* TRICK (1).

fat *adj.* 1. Having too much flesh or a full figure ▸ chubby, corpulent, fatty, flabby, fleshy, full, gross, heavy, meaty, obese, overblown, overweight, paunchy, plump, plumpish, porcine, portly, potbellied, pudgy, roly-poly, rotund, round, stout, tubby, weighty, zaftig. *Slang:* porky. [*Compare* BULKY, STOCKY.] 2. Relatively great in extent from one surface to the opposite ▸ thick. [*Compare* BULKY.] —*See also* FATTY, PROFITABLE.

fat *n.* Adipose tissue ▸ blubber, lard, suet, tallow. [*Compare* OIL.] —*See also* SURPLUS.

fatal *adj.* So critically decisive as to affect the future ▸ fateful, momentous. [*Compare* DECISIVE.] —*See also* DEADLY, DISASTROUS.

fatality *n.* 1. A loss of life, or one who has lost life, usually as a result of accident, disaster, or war ▸ casualty, death, kill, loss, statistic. [*Compare* VICTIM.] 2. The quality or condition of causing death or disaster ▸ deadliness, fatefulness, lethality, lethalness.

fate *n.* 1. The supposed power that predetermines events ▸ destiny, fortune, kismet, luck, predestination, preordination. [*Compare* CHANCE.] 2. A personal outcome or end ▸ destiny, doom, end, fortune, lot, luck, portion. [*Compare* MISFORTUNE, RUIN.]

fated *adj.* Governed by fate ▸ destined, foreordained, ordained, predestined, predetermined, preordained. [*Compare* CERTAIN.] —*See also* CONDEMNED.

fateful *adj.* 1. Bringing or predicting misfortune ▸ bad, baleful, dark, dire, direful, evil, forbidding, foreboding, grave, ill, ill-boding, ill-omened, inauspicious, looming, lowering, malign, menacing, ominous, portentous, sinister, sullen, threatening, unfavorable, unlucky, unpropitious. [*Compare* UNFORTUNATE.] 2. So critically decisive as to affect the future ▸ fatal, momentous. [*Compare* DECISIVE.] —*See also* DISASTROUS.

fatefulness *adj.* The quality or condition of causing death or disaster ▸ deadliness, fatality, lethalness.

fatheadedness *n.* —*See* STUPIDITY.

father *n.* A male parent ▸ begetter, paterfamilias, patriarch, sire. *Informal:* dad, daddy, pa, papa, pappy, pop. *Slang:* old boy, old man. —*See also* ANCESTOR (1), ORIGINAL, ORIGINATOR.

father *v.* To be the biological father of ▸ beget, get, sire. —*See also* BREED.

fatherly or **fatherlike** *adj.* Like a father, especially in caring ▸ fatherlike, paternal, patriarchal. [*Compare* BENEVOLENT.]

fathom *v.* —*See* EXPLORE, KNOW (1), UNDERSTAND (1).

fathomable *adj.* —*See* UNDERSTANDABLE.

fatidic or **fatidical** *adj.* —*See* PROPHETIC.

fatigue *n.* —*See* EXHAUSTION.

fatigue *v.* —*See* BORE[2], TIRE (1).

fatigued *adj.* —*See* TIRED (1).

fatiguing *adj.* Causing fatigue ▸ draining, exhausting, tiring, wearing, wearying. [*Compare* BURDENSOME.]

fatty *adj.* Having the qualities of fat ▸ adipose, blubbery, fat, greasy, oily, oleaginous, unctuous. —*See also* FAT (1).

fatuity *n.* —*See* FOOLISHNESS.

fatuous *adj.* —*See* FOOLISH.

fatuousness *n.* —*See* FOOLISHNESS.

faucet *n.* A device that regulates the flow of a liquid ▸ cock, fixture, petcock, spigot, stopcock, tap.

fault *n.* —*See* BLAME, CRACK (2), DEFECT, WEAKNESS.

fault *v.* —*See* CRITICIZE (1).

3. To commit a mistake or an error. **—idioms: at fault** Guilty. **find fault** To criticize. **to a fault** To an excessive degree. **—fault′i·ly** *adv.* **—fault′i·ness** *n.* **—fault′y** *adj.*

fault·find·ing (fôlt′fīn′dĭng) ▸ *n.* Petty or nagging criticism; carping. ▸ *adj.* Disposed to find fault; critical. **—fault′find′er** *n.*

fault·less (fôlt′lĭs) ▸ *adj.* Being without fault. **—fault′less·ly** *adv.* **—fault′less·ness** *n.*

faun (fôn) ▸ *n. Rom. Myth.* Any of a group of rural deities represented as part man and part goat.

fau·na (fô′nə) ▸ *n., pl.* **-nas** or **-nae** (-nē′). Animals, esp. of a region or period. **—fau′nal** *adj.* **—fau′nal·ly** *adv.*

Faust (foust) also **Faus·tus** (fou′stəs, fô′-) ▸ *n.* A magician and alchemist in German legend who sells his soul to the devil for power and knowledge. **—Faust′i·an** (fou′stē-ən) *adj.*

fau·vism (fō′vĭz′əm) ▸ *n.* An early 20th-cent. movement in painting marked by the use of bold, often distorted forms and vivid colors. **—fau′vist** *adj.*

faux (fō) ▸ *adj.* Artificial; fake: *faux pearls.*

faux pas (fō pä′) ▸ *n., pl.* **faux pas** (fō päz′). A social blunder.

fa·va bean (fä′və) ▸ *n.* See **broad bean.**

fa·vor (fā′vər) ▸ *n.* 1. A gracious, friendly, or obliging act that is freely granted. 2a. Friendly regard; approval or support. b. A state of being held in such regard. 3. Unfair partiality; favoritism. 4a. A privilege or concession. b. **favors** Sexual privileges, esp. as granted by a woman. 5. A small gift given to each guest at a party. 6. Advantage; benefit. ▸ *v.* 1. To oblige. 2. To treat or regard with approval or support. 3. To be partial to. 4. To make easier; facilitate. 5. To be gentle with. 6. *Regional* To resemble: *She favors her father.* **—idiom: in favor of** 1. In support of. 2. To the advantage of.

fa·vor·a·ble (fā′vər-ə-bəl, fāv′rə-) ▸ *adj.* 1. Advantageous; helpful: *favorable winds.* 2. Encouraging; propitious: *a favorable diagnosis.* 3. Manifesting approval; commendatory: *a favorable report.* 4. Winning approval; pleasing: *a favorable impression.* 5. Granting what has been requested. **—fa′vor·a·ble·ness** *n.* **—fa′vor·a·bly** *adv.*

fa·vor·ite (fā′vər-ĭt, fāv′rĭt) ▸ *n.* 1a. One enjoying special favor or regard. b. One trusted or preferred above others, esp. by a superior. 2. A competitor regarded as most likely to win. **—fa′vor·ite** *adj.*

favorite son ▸ *n.* A man favored for nomination as a presidential candidate by his own state delegates at a national political convention.

fa·vor·it·ism (fā′vər-ĭ-tĭz′əm, fāv′rĭ-) ▸ *n.* A display of partiality toward a favored person or group.

fawn[1] (fôn) ▸ *v.* 1. To exhibit affection or attempt to please, as a dog. 2. To seek favor or attention by obsequiousness. **—fawn′er** *n.* **—fawn′ing·ly** *adv.*

fawn[2] (fôn) ▸ *n.* 1. A young deer. 2. A grayish yellow brown.

fax (făks) ▸ *n.* 1. A fax machine. 2. A printed page or image transmitted or received by a fax machine. ▸ *v.* To transmit (printed matter or an image) by electronic means.

fax machine ▸ *n.* A device that sends and receives printed pages over telephone lines.

fay (fā) ▸ *n.* A fairy or elf.

faze (fāz) ▸ *v.* **fazed, faz·ing.** To disconcert.

FBI ▸ *abbr.* Federal Bureau of Investigation

FCC ▸ *abbr.* Federal Communications Commission

Fe ▸ The symbol for the element **iron** 1.

fe·al·ty (fē′əl-tē) ▸ *n., pl.* **-ties.** 1. The fidelity owed by a vassal to his feudal lord. 2. Faithfulness; allegiance.

fear (fîr) ▸ *n.* 1a. A feeling of agitation and anxiety caused by the presence or imminence of danger. b. A state marked by this feeling. 2. A feeling of disquiet or apprehension. 3. Reverence or awe, as toward a deity. 4. A reason for dread or apprehension. ▸ *v.* 1. To be afraid of. 2. To be apprehensive about. 3. To be in awe of. 4. To expect: *I fear you are wrong.* **—fear′er** *n.* **—fear′less** *adj.* **—fear′less·ly** *adv.* **—fear′less·ness** *n.*

fear·ful (fîr′fəl) ▸ *adj.* 1. Causing or capable of causing fear; frightening. 2. Experiencing fear; frightened. 3. Timid; nervous. 4. Indicating anxiety or terror. 5. Feeling dread or awe. 6. Extreme, as in degree or extent. **—fear′ful·ly** *adv.* **—fear′ful·ness** *n.*

fear·some (fîr′səm) ▸ *adj.* 1. Causing or capable of causing fear. 2. Fearful; timid. **—fear′some·ly** *adv.* **—fear′some·ness** *n.*

fea·si·ble (fē′zə-bəl) ▸ *adj.* 1. Capable of being accomplished or brought about; possible. 2. Used successfully; suitable. **—fea′si·bil′i·ty, fea′si·ble·ness** *n.* **—fea′si·bly** *adv.*

feast (fēst) ▸ *n.* 1. A large elaborate meal; banquet. 2. A religious festival. ▸ *v.* 1. To entertain or feed sumptuously. 2. To eat heartily. 3. To experience something

THESAURUS

faultfinder *n.* —*See* CRITIC (2), GROUCH.

faultfinding *adj.* —*See* CRITICAL (1).

faultless *adj.* —*See* EXEMPLARY, INNOCENT (2), PERFECT.

faulty *adj.* Having a defect or defects ▸ amiss, blemished, defective, flawed, imperfect. [*Compare* SHABBY, TRICK.] —*See also* ERRONEOUS.

faux pas *n.* —*See* BLUNDER.

favor *n.* 1. A kindly act ▸ benefaction, beneficence, benevolence, benignity, courtesy, good deed, good turn, grace, indulgence, kindness, kindliness, kind office, philanthropy, service. [*Compare* HELP.] 2. Preferential treatment or bias ▸ favoritism, partiality, partialness, preference. [*Compare* BIAS, PREJUDICE.] —*See also* ACCEPTANCE (2), ADVANTAGE (2), ESTEEM, REMEMBRANCE (1).

favor *v.* 1. To show partiality toward someone ▸ prefer. *Idioms:* be partial, play favorites. [*Compare* ADVANCE, BABY.] 2. To be favorably disposed toward ▸ approve, countenance, hold with. *Informal:* go for. *Idioms:* be in favor of, take kindly to, think highly (*or* well) of. [*Compare* ASSENT, VALUE.] 3. To lend supportive approval to ▸ countenance, encourage, smile on (*or* upon). [*Compare* SUPPORT.] —*See also* LIKE[1], OBLIGE (1), RESEMBLE.

favorable *adj.* 1. Indicative of future success or full of promise ▸ auspicious, benign, bright, brilliant, fair, fortunate, good, propitious. [*Compare* ENCOURAGING.] 2. Giving assent ▸ affirmative, agreeable, approving, assenting, positive. 3. Disposed to favor one over another ▸ partial, preferential. [*Compare* BIASED.] —*See also* BENEFICIAL, OPPORTUNE, PLEASANT.

favored *adj.* —*See* FAVORITE.

favorite *n.* 1. One liked or preferred above all others ▸ darling, pet. *Idiom:* apple of one's eye. 2. A leading contestant or sure winner ▸ frontrunner, leader, number one, vanguard. *Informal:* shoo-in.

favorite *adj.* Being a favorite ▸ darling, fair-haired, favored, pet, popular, preferred, well-liked. [*Compare* SELECT.]

favoritism *n.* Preferential treatment or bias ▸ favor, partiality, partialness, preference. [*Compare* BIAS, PREJUDICE.]

fawn *v.* To behave obsequiously or submissively ▸ bootlick, cringe, grovel, kowtow, slaver, toady, truckle. *Informal:* apple-polish, brownnose. *Slang:* suck up. *Idioms:* curry favor, dance attendance, kiss someone's feet, lick someone's boots. [*Compare* FLATTER.]

fawner *n.* —*See* SYCOPHANT.

faze *v.* —*See* EMBARRASS.

fealty *n.* —*See* FIDELITY.

fear *n.* A feeling of agitation in the face of danger or trouble ▸ affright, alarm, apprehension, consternation, dismay, dread, fearfulness, fright, funk, horror, panic, terror, trepidation. *Slang:* cold feet. *Idiom:* fear and trembling. [*Compare* ANXIETY, COWARDICE.]

fear *v.* To be afraid ▸ dread. *Idioms:* break out in a cold sweat, have butterflies (in one's stomach), have knots (*or* a knot) in one's stomach, have one's heart in one's mouth, sweat blood (*or* bullets). [*Compare* FLINCH.]

fearful *adj.* Causing or capable of causing fear ▸ alarming, appalling, dire, direful, dismaying, dreadful, fearsome, formidable, frightening, frightful, unnerving, redoubtable, scary, terrible. [*Compare* HORRIBLE, SINISTER, WEIRD.] —*See also* AFRAID, TERRIBLE.

fearfulness *n.* —*See* FEAR.

fearless *adj.* —*See* BRAVE.

fearlessness *n.* —*See* COURAGE, DARING.

fearsome *adj.* —*See* AFRAID, FEARFUL.

feasible *adj.* —*See* POSSIBLE.

feast *n.* A large, elaborately prepared meal ▸ banquet, junket. *Informal:* feed, spread.

feast *v.* To sustain a living organism

with gratification or delight. ***—idiom:*** **feast (one's) eyes on** To be delighted by the sight of. **—feast′er** *n.*

feat (fēt) ▸ *n.* A notable act or deed, esp. of courage.

feath·er (fĕth′ər) ▸ *n.* **1.** One of the light, flat, hollow-shafted growths forming the plumage of birds. **2. feathers** Plumage. **3.** Character, kind, or nature. ▸ *v.* **1.** To cover, dress, or decorate with or as if with feathers. **2.** To fit (an arrow) with a feather. **3.** To turn (an oar blade) almost horizontal as it is carried back after each stroke. **4.** To alter the pitch of (a propeller) so that the chords of the blades are parallel with the line of flight. ***—idioms:*** **feather in (one's cap)** An act or deed to one's credit. **feather (one's) nest** To grow wealthy esp. by abusing a position of trust. **in fine feather** In excellent form, health, or humor. **—feath′er·y** *adj.*

feath·er·bed (fĕth′ər-bĕd′) ▸ *v.* **-bed·ded, -bed·ding.** To employ more workers than are needed for a job.

feather bed ▸ *n.* A mattress stuffed with feathers.

feath·er·brain (fĕth′ər-brān′) ▸ *n.* A flighty or empty-headed person. **—feath′er·brained′** *adj.*

feath·er·edge (fĕth′ər-ĕj′) ▸ *n.* A thin fragile edge.

feath·er·stitch (fĕth′ər-stĭch′) ▸ *n.* An embroidery stitch that produces a decorative zigzag line. **—feath′er·stitch′** *v.*

feath·er·weight (fĕth′ər-wāt′) ▸ *n.* **1.** *Sports* A boxer weighing from 119 to 126 lbs. between a bantamweight and a lightweight. **2.** An insignificant person.

fea·ture (fē′chər) ▸ *n.* **1a.** Any of the distinct parts of the face, as the eyes or mouth. **b.** often **features** The overall appearance of the face. **2.** A prominent or distinctive quality or characteristic. **3a.** The main film presentation at a theater. **b.** A full-length film. **4.** A prominent article or story in a newspaper or periodical. **5.** An item offered as an inducement. ▸ *v.* **-tured, -tur·ing. 1.** To publicize or make prominent. **2.** To include as a prominent part or characteristic. **3.** To draw the features of.

Feb. ▸ *abbr.* February

feb·ri·fuge (fĕb′rə-fyo͞oj′) ▸ *n.* A medication that reduces a fever.

feb·rile (fĕb′rəl, fē′brəl) ▸ *adj.* Relating to or having a fever.

Feb·ru·ar·y (fĕb′ro͞o-ĕr′ē, fĕb′yo͞o-) ▸ *n., pl.* **-ies.** The 2nd month of the Gregorian calendar.

fe·ces (fē′sēz) ▸ *pl.n.* Waste eliminated from the bowels; excrement. **—fe′cal** (fēkəl) *adj.*

feck·less (fĕk′lĭs) ▸ *adj.* **1.** Lacking purpose or vitality; ineffective. **2.** Careless; irresponsible. **—feck′less·ly** *adv.* **—feck′less·ness** *n.*

fe·cund (fē′kənd, fĕk′ənd) ▸ *adj.* Capable of producing offspring or vegetation; fruitful. **—fe·cun′di·ty** (fĭ-kŭn′dĭ-tē) *n.*

fe·cun·date (fē′kən-dāt′, fĕk′ən-) ▸ *v.* **-dat·ed, -dat·ing.** To impregnate; fertilize. **—fe′cun·da′tion** *n.*

fed (fĕd) ▸ *v.* P.t. and p.part. of **feed.**

fed. ▸ *abbr.* **1.** federal **2.** federation

fed·er·al (fĕd′ər-əl, fĕd′rəl) ▸ *adj.* **1.** Relating to or being a form of government in which a union of states recognizes a central authority while retaining certain powers of government. **2. Federal** Of or loyal to the Union cause during the American Civil War. **3.** often **Federal** Of or being the central government of the US. ▸ *n.* **1. Federal** A Union soldier or supporter during the American Civil War. **2.** often **Federal** A federal agent or official. **—fed′er·al·ly** *adv.*

fed·er·al·ism (fĕd′ər-ə-lĭz′əm, fĕd′rə-) ▸ *n.* **1.** A system of federal government. **2.** Advocacy of such a system of government. **3. Federalism** The doctrine of the Federalist Party.

fed·er·al·ist (fĕd′ər-ə-lĭst, fĕd′rə-) ▸ *n.* **1.** An advocate of federalism. **2. Federalist** A member of a US political party of the 1790s advocating a strong federal government. **—fed′er·al·ist** *adj.*

fed·er·al·ize (fĕd′ər-ə-līz′, fĕd′rə-) ▸ *v.* **-ized, -iz·ing. 1.** To unite in a federal union. **2.** To put under federal control. **—fed′er·al·i·za′tion** *n.*

fed·er·ate (fĕd′ə-rāt′) ▸ *v.* **-at·ed, -at·ing.** To join or unite in a league, federal union, or similar association. **—fed′er·a′tion** *n.* **—fed′er·a′tive** *adj.* **—fed′er·a′tive·ly** *adv.*

fe·do·ra (fĭ-dôr′ə) ▸ *n.* A soft felt hat with a fairly low crown creased lengthwise and a flexible brim.

fed up ▸ *adj.* Unable or unwilling to put up with something any longer.

fee (fē) ▸ *n.* **1.** A fixed sum charged for a privilege. **2.** A charge for professional services. **3.** *Law* An inherited or heritable estate in land. **4.** In feudal law, an estate granted by a lord to a vassal on condition of homage and service.

fee·ble (fē′bəl) ▸ *adj.* **-bler, -blest. 1.** Lacking strength; weak. **2.** Lacking vigor, force, or effectiveness. **—fee′ble·ness** *n.* **—fee′bly** *adv.*

fee·ble-mind·ed (fē′bəl-mīn′dĭd) ▸ *adj.* **1.** *Offensive* Deficient in intelligence. **2.** Exhibiting a marked lack of intelligent consideration: *feeble-minded excuses.* **—fee′ble-mind′ed·ly** *adv.* **—fee′ble-mind′ed·ness** *n.*

feed (fēd) ▸ *v.* **fed** (fĕd), **feed·ing. 1a.** To give food to; nourish. **b.** To eat. **2.** To supply with something essential for growth, maintenance, or operation. **3.** To distribute (a local broadcast) to a larger audience by network or satellite. **4.** To support or promote; encourage. ▸ *n.* **1.** Food for animals or birds. **2.** *Informal* A meal, esp. a large one. **3a.** Material supplied, as to a machine. **b.** The act of supplying such material. **4.** Distribution of a locally broadcast program by network or satellite to a larger audience. **—feed′er** *n.*

feed·back (fēd′băk′) ▸ *n.* **1a.** The return of a portion of the output of a process or system to the input. **b.** The portion of the output so returned. **2.** An evaluative response.

feed·lot (fēd′lŏt′) ▸ *n.* A place where livestock are fattened for market.

feed·stuff (fēd′stŭf′) ▸ *n.* Food for livestock; fodder.

feel (fēl) ▸ *v.* **felt** (fĕlt), **feel·ing. 1.** To perceive through the sense of touch. **2a.** To touch. **b.** To examine by touching. **3.** To test or explore with caution. **4a.** To undergo the experience of. **b.** To be aware of; sense. **5.** To believe; think. **6.** To have compassion or sympathy. ▸ *n.* **1.** Perception by or as if by touch; sensation. **2.** The sense of touch. **3.** The quality of something perceived by or as if

THESAURUS

with food ▸ feast, feed, regale. *Idiom:* wine and dine. [*Compare* SUPPORT.] —*See also* CELEBRATE (2).

feast on *v.* To be avidly interested in ▸ devour, relish. *Slang:* eat up.

feat *n.* A clever, dexterous act ▸ stunt, trick. *Idiom:* sleight of hand. —*See also* ACCOMPLISHMENT.

feather *n.* —*See* KIND[2].

featherbrained *adj.* —*See* GIDDY (2).

feature *n.* —*See* ITEM, QUALITY (1).

feature *v.* —*See* EMPHASIZE, IMAGINE.

features *n.* —*See* APPEARANCE (1), FACE (1), FACE (3).

febrile or **febrific** *adj.* —*See* FEVERISH.

feckless *adj.* —*See* CARELESS.

fecund *adj.* Capable of reproducing ▸ fertile, fruitful, productive, prolific. —*See also* FERTILE (1).

fecundate *v.* To make fertile ▸ enrich, fertilize, pollinate. [*Compare* IMPREGNATE.]

fecundity *n.* —*See* FERTILITY, INVENTION (1).

federate *v.* —*See* ALLY, ASSOCIATE (1).

federation *n.* —*See* ALLIANCE, UNION (1).

fed up *adj.* Out of patience ▸ disgusted, sick, tired, weary. *Idioms:* sick and tired, sick to death. [*Compare* ANGRY.]

fee *n.* —*See* TOLL[1] (1), WAGE.

feeble *adj.* So soft or quiet as to be barely audible ▸ faint, weak. [*Compare* SOFT.] —*See also* IMPLAUSIBLE, WEAK (1).

feeble-minded *adj.* —*See* BACKWARD (1).

feebleness *n.* —*See* INFIRMITY.

feed *v.* To sustain a living organism with food ▸ feast, nourish, regale. *Idiom:* wine and dine. [*Compare* SUPPORT.] —*See also* PROMOTE (2).

feed on *v.* To include as part of one's diet by nature or preference ▸ eat, exist on, live on, subsist on. [*Compare* EAT.]

feed *n. Informal* A large, elaborately prepared meal ▸ banquet, feast, junket. *Informal:* spread.

feel *v.* **1.** To experience or express compassion ▸ ache, commiserate, condole, sympathize. *Idioms:* be (*or* feel) sorry, have one's heart ache (*or* bleed) for someone, have one's heart go out to someone. [*Compare* COMFORT, PITY.] **2.** To have a belief or impression about something ▸ believe, hold, sense, think. [*Compare*

by touch. **4.** Overall effect; atmosphere. **5.** Intuitive awareness or natural ability. ***—idiom:* feel like** *Informal* To have an inclination for.

feel·er (fē′lər) ▸ *n.* **1.** Something, such as a hint or question, designed to elicit the attitudes or intentions of others. **2.** *Zool.* A sensory organ, such as an antenna.

feel·ing (fē′lĭng) ▸ *n.* **1a.** The sensation involving perception by touch. **b.** A sensation experienced through touch. **c.** A physical sensation. **2.** An awareness or impression. **3.** An emotional state or disposition; an emotion. **4. feelings** Susceptibility to emotional response; sensibilities. **5.** Opinion based on sentiment. **6.** A general impression. **7.** Intuitive awareness or aptitude. ▸ *adj.* **1.** Sensitive. **2.** Sympathetic. **—feel′ing·ly** *adv.*

feet (fēt) ▸ *n.* Pl. of **foot.**

feign (fān) ▸ *v.* **1.** To give a false appearance (of). **2.** To represent falsely; pretend to.

feint (fānt) ▸ *n.* A feigned attack designed to draw defensive action away from an intended target. **—feint** *v.*

feist·y (fī′stē) ▸ *adj.* **-i·er, -i·est. 1.** Touchy; quarrelsome. **2.** Spirited; frisky. **—feist′i·ness** *n.*

fe·la·fel (fə-lä′fəl) ▸ *n.* Var. of **falafel.**

feld·spar (fĕld′spär′, fĕl′-) ▸ *n.* Any of a group of abundant rock-forming minerals consisting of silicates of aluminum with potassium, sodium, calcium, and, rarely, barium.

fe·lic·i·tate (fĭ-lĭs′ĭ-tāt′) ▸ *v.* **-tat·ed, -tat·ing.** To congratulate. **—fe·lic′i·ta′tion** *n.*

fe·lic·i·tous (fĭ-lĭs′ĭ-təs) ▸ *adj.* **1.** Admirably suited; apt. **2.** Exhibiting an agreeable manner or style. **—fe·lic′i·tous·ness** *n.*

fe·lic·i·ty (fĭ-lĭs′ĭ-tē) ▸ *n., pl.* **-ties. 1.** Great happiness; bliss. **2.** A cause of happiness. **3.** An appropriate and pleasing manner or style.

fe·line (fē′līn′) ▸ *adj.* **1.** Of or belonging to cats or related animals, as lions and tigers. **2.** Suggestive of a cat, as in suppleness or stealthiness. ▸ *n.* A feline animal. **—fe·lin′i·ty** (fĭ-lĭn′ĭ-tē) *n.*

fell[1] (fĕl) ▸ *v.* **1.** To cut or knock down. **2.** To kill. **—fell′a·ble** *adj.*

fell[2] (fĕl) ▸ *adj.* **1.** Cruel; fierce. **2.** Deadly; lethal. **3.** Dire; sinister.

fell[3] (fĕl) ▸ *n.* The hide of an animal; pelt.

fell[4] (fĕl) ▸ *v.* P.t. of **fall.**

fel·lah (fĕl′ə, fə-lä′) ▸ *n., pl.* **fel·la·hin** or **-heen** (fĕl′ə-hēn′, fə-lä-hēn′). A peasant or agricultural laborer in Arab countries.

fel·low (fĕl′ō) ▸ *n.* **1.** A man or boy. **2.** *Informal* A boyfriend. **3.** A comrade or associate. **4.** One of a pair; mate. **5.** A member of a learned society. **6.** A graduate student receiving financial aid for further study. ▸ *adj.* Being of the same kind, group, occupation, or locality: *fellow workers.*

fel·low·ship (fĕl′ō-shĭp′) ▸ *n.* **1.** The sharing of similar interests, ideals, or experiences, as by reason of profession, religion, or nationality. **2.** Friendship; comradeship. **3a.** The financial grant made to a fellow in a college or university. **b.** The status of having been awarded such a grant.

fellow traveler ▸ *n.* One who sympathizes with the tenets and program of an organized group, such as the Communist Party, without being a member.

fel·on (fĕl′ən) ▸ *n.* One who has committed a felony.

fel·o·ny (fĕl′ə-nē) ▸ *n., pl.* **-nies.** *Law* A serious crime, such as murder, rape, or burglary. **—fe·lo′ni·ous** (fə-lō′nē-əs) *adj.*

felt[1] (fĕlt) ▸ *n.* **1.** A fabric of matted, compressed fibers, as of wool. **2.** A material resembling this fabric. **—felt** *adj.*

felt[2] (fĕlt) ▸ *v.* P.t. and p.part. of **feel.**

fem. ▸ *abbr.* **1.** female **2.** feminine

fe·male (fē′māl′) ▸ *adj.* **1a.** Relating to or being the sex that produces ova or bears young. **b.** Consisting of members of this sex. **2.** *Bot.* **a.** Of or being an organ, such as a pistil or ovary, that produces seeds after fertilization. **b.** Bearing pistils but not stamens. **3.** Having a recessed part, such as a slot or receptacle, designed to receive a complementary part, such as a plug. ▸ *n.* A member of the female sex. **—fe′male′ness** *n.*

fem·i·nine (fĕm′ə-nĭn) ▸ *adj.* **1.** Of or relating to women or girls. **2.** Marked by qualities gen. attributed to a woman. **3.** *Gram.* Of or being the gender of words referring to things classified as female. ▸ *n. Gram.* **1.** The feminine gender. **2.** A word belonging to this gender. **—fem′i·nine·ly** *adv.* **—fem′i·nine·ness** *n.* **—fem′i·nin′i·ty** *n.*

fem·i·nism (fĕm′ə-nĭz′əm) ▸ *n.* **1.** Belief in the social, political, and economic equality of the sexes. **2.** The movement organized around this belief. **—fem′i·nist** *n.*

THESAURUS

BELIEVE, PERCEIVE, REGARD.] **3.** To give the impression of being ▸ appear, look, seem, sound. ***Idioms:*** have all the earmarks of being, give the idea (*or* impression) of being, strike one as being. [*Compare* RESEMBLE.] *—See also* EXPERIENCE, GROPE, PERCEIVE, TOUCH.

feel for *v.* *—See* PITY.

feel out *v.* To test the attitude of someone ▸ probe, sound (out). ***Idioms:*** put out feelers, run something up the flagpole, send up a trial balloon.

feel *n.* **1.** A particular sensation conveyed by means of physical contact ▸ feeling, touch. [*Compare* CONTACT, BRUSH.] **2.** The faculty or ability to perceive tactile stimulation ▸ feeling, tactility, touch. ***Idiom:*** sense of touch. [*Compare* SENSATION.] **3.** The proper method for doing, using, or handling something ▸ knack, trick. *Informal:* hang. *—See also* AIR (3), TOUCH (1).

feeler *n.* Something, such as a remark, used to determine another person's attitude ▸ probe. ***Idiom:*** trial balloon. [*Compare* ADVANCES, INTRODUCTION.]

feeling *n.* **1.** An intuitive awareness or sense of something ▸ foreboding, forewarning, gut reaction, hunch, idea, impression, inkling, intuition, notion, premonition, presentiment, suspicion. [*Compare* HINT, INSTINCT, QUALM.] **2.** A particular sensation conveyed by means of physical contact ▸ feel, touch. [*Compare* CONTACT, BRUSH.] **3.** The faculty or ability to perceive tactile stimulation ▸ feel, tactility, touch. ***Idiom:*** sense of touch. [*Compare* SENSATION.] **4.** A general cast of mind with regard to something ▸ attitude, sentiment. [*Compare* IDEA.] **5.** The quality or condition of being emotionally and intuitively sensitive ▸ sensibility, sensitiveness, sensitivity. [*Compare* PITY, SYMPATHY.] *—See also* AIR (3), BELIEF (1), EMOTION, SENSATION (1), TOUCH (1).

feeling *adj.* Readily stirred by emotion ▸ emotional, sensitive. [*Compare* PASSIONATE.] *—See also* SYMPATHETIC.

feign *v.* To claim or allege insincerely or falsely ▸ pretend, pretext, profess, purport. *—See also* ACT (2).

feigned *adj.* *—See* ARTIFICIAL (2).

feint *n.* *—See* TRICK (1).

feisty *adj.* *—See* ARGUMENTATIVE.

felicitate *v.* To pay a compliment to ▸ commend, compliment, congratulate, praise. ***Idioms:*** pay tribute to, raise a glass to, take off one's hat to. [*Compare* HONOR.]

felicitations *n.* *—See* COMPLIMENT.

felicitous *adj.* *—See* APPROPRIATE.

felicity *n.* *—See* HAPPINESS.

feline *adj.* *—See* STEALTHY.

fell *v.* *—See* DROP (3).

fellow *n.* A man referred to familiarly or as a member of one's group ▸ brother. *Informal:* boy, chap, guy, jack, lad. *Slang:* dude, hombre, homeboy. *—See also* ASSOCIATE (1), ASSOCIATE (2), BOYFRIEND, MATE, PEER[2].

fellow citizen *n.* A person who is from one's own country ▸ compatriot, countryman, countrywoman, kinsman, kinswoman.

fellowship *n.* *—See* COMPANY (3), FRIENDSHIP, UNION (1).

felon *n.* *—See* CRIMINAL.

felonious *adj.* *—See* CRIMINAL (1).

felony *n.* *—See* CRIME (1).

female *adj.* Relating to or characteristic of women ▸ feminine, womanish, womanly.

femaleness or **feminineness** *n.* The quality or condition of being feminine ▸ feminineness, femininity, womanliness.

feminine *adj.* Relating to or characteristic of women ▸ female, womanish, womanly. *—See also* EFFEMINATE.

femininity *n.* The quality or condition of being feminine ▸ femaleness, feminineness, womanliness. *—See also* EFFEMINACY.

femme fa·tale (fĕm′ fə-tăl′, -täl′) ▸ *n., pl.* **femmes fa·tales** (fĕm′ fə-tăl′, -tălz′, -täl′, -tälz′). **1.** A seductive woman. **2.** An alluring and mysterious woman.

fe·mur (fē′mər) ▸ *n., pl.* **fe·murs** or **fem·o·ra** (fĕm′ər-ə). A bone of the lower or hind limb in vertebrates, situated between the pelvis and knee in humans. **—fem′or·al** *adj.*

fen (fĕn) ▸ *n.* Low swampy land; bog. **—fen′ny** *adj.*

fence (fĕns) ▸ *n.* **1.** An enclosure, barrier, or boundary, usu. made of posts or stakes joined together by boards, wire, or rails. **2a.** One who receives and sells stolen goods. **b.** A place where stolen goods are received and sold. ▸ *v.* **fenced, fenc·ing. 1.** To enclose with or as if with a fence. **2a.** To act as a conduit for stolen goods. **b.** To sell (stolen goods) to a fence. **3.** To practice the art or sport of fencing. **4.** To avoid giving direct answers; hedge. ***—idiom:*** **on the fence** *Informal* Undecided; neutral. **—fenc′er** *n.*

fenc·ing (fĕn′sĭng) ▸ *n.* **1.** The art or sport of using a foil, épée, or saber. **2.** Skillful repartee, esp. as a defense against having to give direct answers. **3.** Material for fences.

fend (fĕnd) ▸ *v.* **1.** To ward off; repel. **2.** To manage; get by: *You'll have to fend for yourself.*

fend·er (fĕn′dər) ▸ *n.* **1.** A guard over a wheel of a vehicle. **2.** A screen or metal framework placed in front of a fireplace.

fen·es·tra·tion (fĕn′ĭ-strā′shən) ▸ *n.* The design and placement of windows in a building.

feng shui (fŭng′ shwā′) ▸ *n.* The traditional Chinese practice of positioning objects, esp. buildings and graves, so as to harmonize with the flow of chi.

Fe·ni·an (fē′nē-ən) ▸ *n.* **1.** One of a legendary group of heroic Irish warriors of the 2nd and 3rd cent. A.D. **2.** A member of a secret revolutionary organization in the US and Ireland in the mid-19th cent. dedicated to the overthrow of British rule in Ireland. **—Fe′ni·an** *adj.* **—Fe′ni·an·ism** *n.*

fen·nel (fĕn′əl) ▸ *n.* **1.** A plant having aromatic seeds used as flavoring. **2.** The seeds or edible stalks of this plant.

–fer ▸ *suff.* One that bears: *conifer.*

fe·ral (fîr′əl, fĕr′-) ▸ *adj.* **1.** Existing in a wild or untamed state. **2.** Of or suggestive of a wild animal; savage.

fer-de-lance (fĕr′dl-ăns′, -äns′) ▸ *n., pl.* **fer-de-lance.** A venomous tropical American pit viper having brown and grayish markings.

fer·ment (fûr′mĕnt′) ▸ *n.* **1.** Something, such as yeast, that causes fermentation. **2.** A state of agitation or unrest. ▸ *v.* (fər-mĕnt′) **1.** To produce by or as if by fermentation. **2.** To undergo or cause to undergo fermentation. **3.** To be turbulent; seethe. **—fer·ment′a·bil′i·ty** *n.* **—fer·ment′a·ble** *adj.*

fer·men·ta·tion (fûr′mən-tā′shən, -mĕn-) ▸ *n.* **1.** A chemical reaction that splits complex organic compounds into relatively simple substances, esp. the conversion of sugar to carbon dioxide and alcohol by yeast. **2.** Unrest; agitation. **—fer·men′ta·tive** (fər-mĕn′tə-tĭv) *adj.*

Fer·mi (fĕr′mē), **Enrico** (1901–54) ▸ Italian-born Amer. physicist; 1938 Nobel.

fer·mi·um (fûr′mē-əm, fĕr′-) ▸ *n. Symbol* **Fm** A synthetic metallic element. At. no. 100.

fern (fûrn) ▸ *n.* Any of numerous flowerless plants having fronds and reproducing by spores. **—fern′y** *adj.*

fe·ro·cious (fə-rō′shəs) ▸ *adj.* **1.** Extremely savage; fierce. **2.** Intense; extreme: *ferocious heat.* **—fe·ro′cious·ly** *adv.* **—fe·ro′cious·ness, fe·roc′i·ty** (fə-rŏs′ĭ-tē) *n.*

–ferous ▸ *suff.* Bearing; producing; containing: *carboniferous.*

fer·ret (fĕr′ĭt) ▸ *n.* **1.** An Old World, usu. albino weasel related to the polecat and often trained to hunt rats or rabbits. **2.** A North American weasel with black masklike markings. ▸ *v.* **1.** To hunt with ferrets. **2.** To drive out, as from a hiding place; expel. **3.** To uncover and bring to light by searching: *ferret out the solution.*

fer·ric (fĕr′ĭk) ▸ *adj.* Of or containing iron, esp. with a valence of 3.

ferric oxide ▸ *n.* A dark red compound, Fe_2O_3, occurring naturally as rust.

Fer·ris wheel also **fer·ris wheel** (fĕr′ĭs) ▸ *n.* A large upright, rotating wheel having suspended seats that remain in a horizontal position as the wheel revolves.

ferro– or **ferr–** ▸ *pref.* Iron: *ferromagnetic.*

fer·ro·mag·net·ic (fĕr′ō-măg-nĕt′ĭk) ▸ *adj.* Of or characteristic of substances such as iron or nickel and various alloys that exhibit magnetic properties. **—fer′ro·mag′net** (-măg′nĭt) *n.* **—fer′ro·mag′net·ism** *n.*

fer·ro·man·ga·nese (fĕr′ō-măng′gə-nēz′, -nēs′) ▸ *n.* An alloy of iron and manganese used in the production of steel.

fer·ro·type (fĕr′ə-tīp′) ▸ *n.* A positive photograph made directly on an iron plate varnished with a thin sensitized film.

fer·rous (fĕr′əs) ▸ *adj.* Of or containing iron, esp. with a valence of 2.

ferrous oxide ▸ *n.* A black powder, FeO, used in the manufacture of steel and glass.

fer·rule (fĕr′əl) ▸ *n.* A metal ring or cap placed around a pole or shaft for reinforcement.

fer·ry (fĕr′ē) ▸ *v.* **-ried, -ry·ing. 1.** To transport by boat across a body of water. **2.** To cross by a ferry. **3.** To transport from one point to another. ▸ *n., pl.* **-ries. 1.** A ferryboat. **2.** A place where a ferryboat embarks. **3.** A service for delivering an aircraft under its own power to its eventual user.

fer·ry·boat (fĕr′ē-bōt′) ▸ *n.* A boat used to ferry passengers, vehicles, or goods.

fer·tile (fûr′tl) ▸ *adj.* **1.** *Biol.* Capable of initiating, sustaining, or supporting reproduction. **2.** Rich in material needed to sustain plant growth: *fertile soil.* **3.** Highly or continuously productive; prolific: *a fertile imagination.* **—fer′tile·ly** *adv.* **—fer·til′i·ty** (fər-tĭl′ĭ-tē), **fer′tile·ness** *n.*

Fertile Crescent ▸ A region of the Middle East extending from the Nile Valley to the Tigris and Euphrates rivers.

fer·til·ize (fûr′tl-īz′) ▸ *v.* **-ized, -iz·ing. 1.** To initiate biological reproduction, esp. to provide with pollen or sperm. **2.** To make fertile, as by spreading fertilizer. **—fer′til·iz′a·ble** *adj.* **—fer′til·i·za′tion** *n.*

fer·til·iz·er (fûr′tl-ī′zər) ▸ *n.* Any of a large number of natural and synthetic materials, including manure and chemical compounds, added to soil to increase its capacity to support plant growth.

fer·ule (fĕr′əl) ▸ *n.* A cane or flat stick used in punishing children.

fer·vent (fûr′vənt) ▸ *adj.* **1.** Greatly emotional or zealous; ardent. **2.** Extremely hot; glowing. **—fer′ven·cy** *n.* **—fer′vent·ly** *adv.*

fer·vid (fûr′vĭd) ▸ *adj.* **1.** Passionate; zealous. **2.** Extremely hot. **—fer′vid·ly** *adv.* **—fer′vid·ness** *n.*

THESAURUS

femme fatale *n.* *—See* SEDUCTRESS.

fen *n.* *—See* SWAMP.

fence *v.* To separate with or as if with a wall ▸ screen, partition, wall. *—See also* CONTEND, ENCLOSE (1), EQUIVOCATE (1), EVADE (1).

fence *n.* *—See* EQUIVOCATION.

fend *v.* *—See* MANAGE, REPEL.

fender-bender *n.* *—See* CRASH (2).

feral *adj.* *—See* WILD (2).

ferment *v.* *—See* BOIL.

ferment *n.* *—See* AGITATION (1), CATALYST.

ferocious *adj.* So intense as to cause extreme suffering ▸ cruel, fierce, savage, vicious. *—See also* CRUEL.

ferociousness *n.* *—See* INTENSITY.

ferocity *n.* *—See* CRUELTY, INTENSITY.

ferret *v.* *—See* SEEK (1).

ferret out *v.* *—See* DISCOVER.

fertile *adj.* **1.** Characterized by great productivity ▸ fecund, fruitful, productive, prolific, rich. [*Compare* INVENTIVE.] **2.** Capable of reproducing ▸ fecund, fruitful, productive, prolific.

fertility *n.* The quality or state of being fertile ▸ fecundity, fruitfulness, productiveness, productivity, prolificacy, prolificness, richness. [*Compare* INVENTION.]

fertilize *v.* **1.** To add fertilizer to ▸ dress, manure, top-dress. **2.** To make fertile ▸ enrich, fecundate, pollinate. [*Compare* IMPREGNATE.]

fervency *n.* *—See* PASSION.

fervent *adj.* *—See* ENTHUSIASTIC, PASSIONATE.

fervid *adj.* *—See* ENTHUSIASTIC, FRANTIC, PASSIONATE.

fer·vor (fûr′vər) ▸ *n.* 1. Great warmth and intensity of emotion. 2. Intense heat.

fes·cue (fĕs′kyo͞o) ▸ *n.* Any of various grasses often cultivated as pasturage.

fes·tal (fĕs′təl) ▸ *adj.* Of a feast or festival; festive.

fes·ter (fĕs′tər) ▸ *v.* 1. To generate pus. 2. To undergo decay; rot. 3. To be or become a source of irritation; rankle. **—fes′ter** *n.*

fes·ti·val (fĕs′tə-vəl) ▸ *n.* 1. A feast or celebration, esp. a religious one. 2. A programmed series of cultural performances, exhibitions, or competitions: *a film festival.* 3. Revelry; conviviality.

fes·tive (fĕs′tĭv) ▸ *adj.* 1. Relating to or appropriate for a feast or festival. 2. Merry; joyous. **—fes′tive·ly** *adv.* **—fes′tive·ness** *n.*

fes·tiv·i·ty (fĕ-stĭv′ĭ-tē) ▸ *n., pl.* **-ties.** 1. A joyous feast or celebration. 2. The gaiety of a festival or celebration. 3. **festivities** The activities of a festival.

fes·toon (fĕ-sto͞on′) ▸ *n.* 1. A garland, as of leaves or flowers, between two looped points. 2. A representation of such a garland, as in painting. ▸ *v.* 1. To decorate with or as if with festoons. 2. To form festoons.

fet·a (fĕt′ə, fā′tə) ▸ *n.* A white semisoft cheese made usu. from goat's or ewe's milk.

fe·tal also **foe·tal** (fēt′l) ▸ *adj.* Of or relating to a fetus.

fetal alcohol syndrome ▸ *n.* A complex of birth defects in an infant born to an alcoholic mother.

fetal position ▸ *n.* A position of the body at rest in which the spine is curved, the head is bowed, and the limbs are drawn in toward the chest.

fetch (fĕch) ▸ *v.* 1. To go after and bring back; retrieve. 2. To cause to come; bring forth. 3. To bring as a price.

fetch·ing (fĕch′ĭng) ▸ *adj.* Attractive; charming. **—fetch′ing·ly** *adv.*

fete also **fête** (fāt, fĕt) ▸ *n.* 1. A festival or feast. 2. An elaborate outdoor party. ▸ *v.* **fet·ed, fet·ing** also **fêt·ed, fêt·ing.** 1. To celebrate or honor with a feast or elaborate entertainment. 2. To pay honor to.

fet·id (fĕt′ĭd, fē′tĭd) also **foe·tid** (fē′tĭd) ▸ *adj.* Having an offensive odor. **—fet′id·ly** *adv.* **—fet′id·ness** *n.*

fet·ish also **fet·ich** (fĕt′ĭsh, fē′tĭsh) ▸ *n.* 1. An object believed to have spiritual powers. 2. An object of excessive attention or reverence. 3. An obsessive attachment; fixation. **—fet′ish·ism** *n.* **—fet′ish·ist** *n.* **—fet′ish·is′tic** *adj.*

fet·lock (fĕt′lŏk′) ▸ *n.* A projection on the lower part of the leg of a horse or related animal, above and behind the hoof.

fet·ter (fĕt′ər) ▸ *n.* 1. A chain or shackle for the ankles. 2. Something that restricts or restrains. ▸ *v.* 1. To shackle. 2. To restrict the freedom of.

fet·tle (fĕt′l) ▸ *n.* Condition; emotional state: *in fine fettle.*

fet·tuc·ci·ne (fĕt′ə-chē′nē) ▸ *n.* Pasta in narrow flat strips.

fe·tus also **foe·tus** (fē′təs) ▸ *n., pl.* **-tus·es.** The unborn young of a viviparous vertebrate; in humans the unborn young from the end of the eighth week after conception to birth, as distinguished from the earlier embryo.

feud (fyo͞od) ▸ *n.* A bitter, often prolonged quarrel or state of enmity. **—feud** *v.*

feu·dal (fyo͞od′l) ▸ *adj.* Of or characteristic of feudalism. **—feu′dal·ly** *adv.*

feu·dal·ism (fyo͞od′l-ĭz′əm) ▸ *n.* A political and economic system of medieval Europe by which a landowner granted land to a vassal in exchange for homage and military service. **—feu′dal·ist** *n.* **—feu′dal·is′tic** *adj.* **—feu′dal·i·za′tion** *n.* **—feu′dal·ize′** *v.*

feu·da·to·ry (fyo͞o′də-tôr′ē) ▸ *n., pl.* **-ries.** 1. A vassal. 2. A feudal fee. ▸ *adj.* Owing feudal allegiance.

fe·ver (fē′vər) ▸ *n.* 1. Abnormally high body temperature. 2. A disease that is marked by such temperature. 3. Heightened activity or excitement. 4. A usu. short-lived enthusiasm or craze. **—fe′ver·ish** *adj.* **—fe′ver·ish·ly** *adv.* **—fe′ver·ish·ness** *n.*

fever blister ▸ *n.* See **cold sore**.

few (fyo͞o) ▸ *adj.* **-er, -est.** Amounting to or consisting of a small number. ▸ *n.* *(takes pl. v.)* 1. An indefinitely small number: *A few of the cars are new.* 2. An exclusive or limited number: *the fortunate few.* ▸ *pron.* *(takes pl. v.)* A small number: *Few of them are left.* **—few′ness** *n.*

fey (fā) ▸ *adj.* Otherworldly, magical, or fairylike. **—fey′ness** *n.*

fez (fĕz) ▸ *n., pl.* **fez·zes.** A man's felt cap shaped like a flat-topped cone, usu. red with a black tassel hanging from the crown.

fi·an·cé (fē′än-sā′, fē-än′sā′) ▸ *n.* A man engaged to be married.

fi·an·cée (fē′än-sā′, fē-än′sā′) ▸ *n.* A woman engaged to be married.

fi·as·co (fē-ăs′kō, -ä′skō) ▸ *n., pl.* **-coes** or **-cos.** A complete failure.

fi·at (fē′ət, -ăt′, -ät′) ▸ *n.* An arbitrary order or decree.

fib (fĭb) ▸ *n.* An insignificant or childish lie. ▸ *v.* **fibbed, fib·bing.** To tell a fib. **—fib′ber** *n.*

fi·ber (fī′bər) ▸ *n.* 1. A slender threadlike structure. 2. *Bot.* An elongated, thick-walled cell strengthening and supporting plant tissue. 3. *Anat.* Any of various elongated cells, esp. a muscle or nerve fiber. 4. A filament, as of cotton or nylon, capable of being spun into yarn. 5a. Something that provides substance or texture. b. Basic strength or toughness; fortitude. 6. Indigestible plant matter, consisting esp. of cellulose, that stimulates intestinal peristalsis. **—fi′brous** (fī′brəs) *adj.*

fi·ber·board (fī′bər-bôrd′) ▸ *n.* A building material composed of wood chips or plant fibers bonded together and compressed into rigid sheets.

fi·ber·glass (fī′bər-glăs′) ▸ *n.* A material consisting of glass fibers in resin.

fiber optics ▸ *n.* *(takes sing. v.)* 1. The technology of light transmission through very fine, flexible glass or plastic fibers. 2. A bundle of such fibers. **—fi′ber-op′tic** *adj.*

fi·bril (fī′brəl, fĭb′rəl) ▸ *n.* A small slender fiber or filament.

fib·ril·la·tion (fĭb′rə-lā′shən, fī′brə-) ▸ *n.* Rapid uncoordinated twitching movements in the atria or ventricles of the heart. **—fib′ril·late′** *v.*

fi·brin (fī′brĭn) ▸ *n.* An elastic, insoluble, whitish protein that forms in blood clots.

fi·brin·o·gen (fī-brĭn′ə-jən) ▸ *n.* A protein in the blood plasma that is a precursor of fibrin.

fibro– or **fibr–** ▸ *pref.* Fiber, esp. fibrous tissue: *fibroma.*

fi·broid (fī′broid′) ▸ *adj.* Composed of or resembling fibrous tissue. ▸ *n.* A fibroma occurring esp. in the uterine wall.

THESAURUS

fervor *n.* —*See* ENTHUSIASM (1), HEAT (1), PASSION.

fess up *v.* —*See* ACKNOWLEDGE (1).

fester *v.* —*See* DECAY.

festering *n.* —*See* IRRITATION.

festinate *v.* —*See* RUSH.

festival *n.* —*See* CELEBRATION (1), EXHIBITION.

festive *adj.* —*See* MERRY.

festiveness *n.* —*See* MERRIMENT (2).

festivity *n.* —*See* CELEBRATION (1), CELEBRATION (3), MERRIMENT (2), PARTY.

festoon *n.* —*See* ADORN (1).

fetch *v.* —*See* BRING (1), BRING (2).

fetching *adj.* —*See* ATTRACTIVE, BECOMING.

fete *n.* —*See* CELEBRATION (1), PARTY.

fetid *adj.* —*See* SMELLY.

fetish *n.* —*See* CHARM, OBSESSION.

fetor *n.* —*See* STENCH.

fetter *n.* —*See* BOND (1), CORD.

  fetter *v.* —*See* HAMPER[1].

fettle *n.* —*See* SHAPE.

feud *n.* —*See* ARGUMENT, ENMITY.

  feud *v.* —*See* ARGUE (1).

fever *n.* —*See* ENTHUSIASM (1).

fevered *adj.* —*See* FRANTIC.

feverish *adj.* Having an above-normal body temperature ▸ febrific, febrile, hectic, hot, pyretic. [*Compare* SICK.] —*See also* FRANTIC, PASSIONATE.

few *adj.* —*See* SEVERAL.

  few *pronoun* —*See* SEVERAL.

fey *adj.* —*See* MAGIC.

fiancé or **fiancée** *n.* —*See* INTENDED.

fiasco *n.* —*See* DISAPPOINTMENT (2), DISASTER, FAILURE (1), MESS (1).

fiat *n.* —*See* COMMAND (1).

fib *n.* —*See* LIE[2].

  fib *v.* —*See* LIE[2].

fibber *n.* —*See* LIAR.

fiber *n.* A very fine continuous strand ▸ fibril, filament, microfiber, thread. [*Compare* CORD.] —*See also* CHARACTER (2), TEXTURE.

fibril *n.* A very fine continuous strand ▸ fiber, filament, microfiber, thread. [*Compare* CORD.]

fi·bro·ma (fī-brō′mə) ► *n., pl.* **-mas** or **-ma·ta** (-mə-tə). A benign, usu. enclosed neoplasm of primarily fibrous tissue.
fi·bro·sis (fī-brō′sĭs) ► *n.* The formation of excessive fibrous tissue. **—fi·brot′ic** (-brŏt′ĭk) *adj.*
fib·u·la (fĭb′yə-lə) ► *n., pl.* **-lae** (-lē′) or **-las**. The outer and narrower of two bones of the human lower leg or of the hind leg of an animal.
-fic ► *suff.* Causing; making: *honorific.*
-fication ► *suff.* Production; making: *certification.*
fiche (fēsh) ► *n.* A microfiche.
fich·u (fĭsh′o͞o, fē-sho͞o′) ► *n.* A woman's triangular scarf, worn over the shoulders and crossed or tied in a loose knot at the breast.
fick·le (fĭk′əl) ► *adj.* Erratic or changeable, esp. in affections; capricious. **—fick′le·ness** *n.* **—fick′ly** *adv.*
fic·tion (fĭk′shən) ► *n.* **1.** An imaginative creation or pretense. **2.** A lie. **3a.** A literary work, such as a novel, whose content is produced by the imagination and is not necessarily based on fact. **b.** The category of literature comprising works of this kind. **—fic′tion·al** *adj.* **—fic′tion·al·i·za′tion** *n.* **—fic′tion·al·ize′** *v.* **—fic′tion·al·ly** *adv.*
fic·ti·tious (fĭk-tĭsh′əs) ► *adj.* **1.** Nonexistent; imaginary. **2.** Purposely deceptive; false: *a fictitious name.* **—fic·ti′tious·ly** *adv.* **—fic·ti′tious·ness** *n.*
fid·dle (fĭd′l) ► *n.* A violin. ► *v.* **-dled, -dling. 1.** To play a violin. **2.** To play idly; tinker: *fiddled with the knobs.* **3.** To meddle; tamper. ***—phrasal verb:* fiddle away** To waste or squander. **—fid′dler** *n.*
fiddler crab ► *n.* A burrowing crab with one of the front claws much larger in the male.
fid·dle·sticks (fĭd′l-stĭks′) ► *interj.* Used to express mild annoyance or impatience.
fi·del·i·ty (fĭ-dĕl′ĭ-tē, fī-) ► *n., pl.* **-ties. 1.** Faithfulness to obligations or duties. **2.** Exact correspondence with fact; accuracy. **3.** The degree to which an electronic system reproduces the sound or image of its input signal.
fidg·et (fĭj′ĭt) ► *v.* To move nervously or restlessly. ► *n.* often **fidgets** Restlessness manifested by nervous movements. **—fidg′et·i·ness** *n.* **—fidg′et·y** *adj.*
fi·du·ci·ar·y (fĭ-do͞o′shē-ĕr′ē, -shə-rē, -dyo͞o′-) ► *adj.* **1.** Relating to a holding in trust for another. **2.** Held in trust. ► *n., pl.* **-ies.** A trustee.
fie (fī) ► *interj.* Used to express distaste or disapproval.
fief (fēf) ► *n.* **1.** See **fee** 4. **2.** A fiefdom.
fief·dom (fēf′dəm) ► *n.* **1.** The estate of a feudal lord. **2.** Something over which one person or group exercises control.
field (fēld) ► *n.* **1a.** A broad, level, open expanse of land. **b.** A meadow. **c.** A cultivated expanse of land. **d.** A portion of land or a geologic formation containing a specified natural resource. **2.** A battleground. **3.** A background area, as on a flag. **4.** *Sports* **a.** An area in which an athletic event takes place. **b.** All the contestants in an event. **5a.** An area of human activity. **b.** Profession, employment, or business. **c.** A setting of practical activity outside an office, school, or laboratory: *a product tested in the field.* **d.** An area where business activities are conducted. **6.** *Phys.* A region of space characterized by a physical property, such as gravitational force, having a determinable value at every point in the region. **7.** *Comp. Sci.* An interface element in a GUI that accepts the input of text. ► *v.* **1.** *Sports* **a.** To retrieve (a ball) and perform the required maneuver, esp. in baseball. **b.** To place in the field to play. **2.** To give an unrehearsed response to (a question). **—field′er** *n.*
field day ► *n.* **1.** A day set aside for sports or athletic competition. **2.** *Informal* A time of great pleasure, activity, or opportunity.
field event ► *n.* A throwing or jumping event of a track-and-field meet.
field glass ► *n.* A portable binocular telescope.
field goal ► *n.* **1.** *Football* A score worth three points made on an ordinary down by kicking the ball over the crossbar and between the goal posts. **2.** *Basketball* A score made by throwing the ball through the basket in regulation play.
field hockey ► *n.* A game played on turf in which two opposing teams use curved sticks to drive a ball into a goal.
field magnet ► *n.* A magnet used to produce a magnetic field in an electrical device such as a generator or motor.
field marshal ► *n.* An officer in some European armies, usu. ranking just below the commander in chief.
field mouse ► *n.* Any of various small mice inhabiting meadows and fields.
field of force ► *n.* A region of space throughout which the force produced by a single agent, such as an electric current, is operative.
field-test (fēld′tĕst′) ► *v.* To test (e.g., a product) in actual operation or use.
field trial ► *n.* **1.** A test of young, untried hunting dogs for their competence in pointing and retrieving. **2.** A trial of a new product in actual use.
field trip ► *n.* A group excursion for firsthand observation, as to a museum.
field·work (fēld′wûrk′) ► *n.* Work done or observations made in the field as opposed to laboratory work. **—field′work′er** *n.*
fiend (fēnd) ► *n.* **1.** An evil spirit; devil. **2.** An evil or wicked person. **3.** *Informal* One obsessed with a job or pastime: *a puzzle fiend.* **—fiend′ish** *adj.* **—fiend′ish·ly** *adv.* **—fiend′ish·ness** *n.*
fierce (fîrs) ► *adj.* **fierc·er, fierc·est. 1.** Having a violent nature; ferocious: *a fierce beast.* **2.** Severe or violent: *a fierce storm.* **3.** Intense or ardent: *fierce loyalty.* **—fierce′ly** *adv.* **—fierce′ness** *n.*
fier·y (fīr′ē, fī′ə-rē) ► *adj.* **-i·er, -i·est. 1.** Consisting of, containing, or like fire. **2a.** Easily excited: *a fiery temper.* **b.** Charged with emotion: *a fiery speech.* **—fier′i·ly** *adv.* **—fier′i·ness** *n.*
fi·es·ta (fē-ĕs′tə) ► *n.* **1.** A festival or religious holiday, esp. in Spanish-speaking regions. **2.** A party.
fife (fīf) ► *n.* A small, high-pitched flute used to accompany drums in a military or marching band. **—fif′er** *n.*
FIFO ► *abbr.* first-in, first-out
fif·teen (fĭf-tēn′) ► *n.* **1.** The cardinal number equal to 14 + 1. **2.** The 15th in a set or sequence. **—fif·teen′** *adj. & pron.*
fif·teenth (fĭf-tēnth′) ► *n.* **1.** The ordinal number matching the

THESAURUS

fibrous *adj.* Containing or consisting of fibers ► sinewy, stringy, threadlike.
fickle *adj.* *—See* CAPRICIOUS.
fiction *n.* A narrative not based on fact ► fable, novel, romance, story. [*Compare* YARN.] *—See also* DREAM (1), LIE[2], MYTH (2).
fictional *adj.* *—See* FICTITIOUS.
fictitious *adj.* Consisting or suggestive of fiction ► fantastic, fictional, fictive, invented, made-up. [*Compare* IMAGINARY.] *—See also* FALSE.
fictive *adj.* *—See* FICTITIOUS.
fiddle *v.* To touch or handle something out of restlessness ► fidget, fool, play, toy, trifle, twiddle. *Informal:* monkey. [*Compare* HANDLE.] *—See also* BIAS (2), PUTTER, TINKER.
fiddle away *v.* *—See* IDLE (2).
fiddle-faddle *n.* *—See* TRIFLE.
fidelity *n.* Faithfulness or devotion to a person, cause, or obligation ► allegiance, constancy, faithfulness, fealty, loyalty, steadfastness. [*Compare* ATTACHMENT.] *—See also* VERACITY.
fidget *v.* *—See* FIDDLE.
fidgets *n.* *—See* JITTERS.
fidgety *adj.* *—See* EDGY.
field *n.* **1.** An area of open land ► clearing, meadow, pasture. [*Compare* LOT.] **2.** An area of academic study that is part of a larger body of learning ► branch, discipline, specialty. *—See also* AREA (1).
field *v.* *—See* ANSWER.
fiend *n.* A perversely mean, cruel, or wicked person ► archfiend, barbarian, beast, brute, demon, devil, ghoul, hun, monster, ogre, savage, villain. [*Compare* EVILDOER, RASCAL.] *—See also* FAN[2].
fiendish *adj.* Perversely mean, cruel, or wicked ► devilish, diabolic, diabolical, ghoulish, hellish, infernal, ogreish, satanic, villainous. [*Compare* EVIL, FIERCE, MALEVOLENT.]
fierce *adj.* *—See* CRUEL, INTENSE.
fiercely *adv.* *—See* HARD (1).
fierceness *n.* *—See* CRUELTY, INTENSITY.
fiery *adj.* *—See* BURNING, HOT (1), PASSIONATE, SPICY.
fiesta *n.* *—See* CELEBRATION (1).

number 15 in a series. 2. One of 15 equal parts. **—fif·teenth′** *adv. & adj.*

fifth (fĭfth) ▸ *n.* 1. The ordinal number matching the number 5 in a series. 2. One of five equal parts. 3. One fifth of a gallon or four fifths of a quart of liquor. 4. *Mus.* A tone five degrees above or below a given tone in a diatonic scale. **—fifth** *adv. & adj.*

fifth column ▸ *n.* A secret organization working within a country to further an enemy's aims.

fifth wheel ▸ *n.* One that is unnecessary.

fif·ti·eth (fĭf′tē-ĭth) ▸ *n.* 1. The ordinal number matching the number 50 in a series. 2. One of 50 equal parts. **—fif′ti·eth** *adv. & adj.*

fif·ty (fĭf′tē) ▸ *n., pl.* **-ties.** The cardinal number equal to 5 × 10. **—fif′ty** *adj. & pron.*

fif·ty-fif·ty (fĭf′tē-fĭf′tē) ▸ *adj.* 1. Divided in two equal portions. 2. Being equally likely and unlikely. **—fif′ty-fif′ty** *adv.*

fig (fĭg) ▸ *n.* 1a. Any of several Mediterranean trees or shrubs widely cultivated for their edible fruit. b. The sweet, pear-shaped fruit of this plant. 2. A trivial amount: *not worth a fig.*

fight (fīt) ▸ *v.* **fought** (fôt), **fight·ing.** 1. To harm or subdue an adversary by blows or with weapons. 2. To quarrel; argue. 3. To strive vigorously and resolutely: *fight for justice.* 4. To contend with physically or in battle. 5. To wage or carry on (a battle). 6. To struggle against: *fight temptation.* 7. To box or wrestle in a ring. ***—phrasal verb:*** **fight off** To defend against or drive back. ▸ *n.* 1. A confrontation in which each opponent attempts to harm or subdue the other. 2. A quarrel or conflict. 3. A physical conflict between two or more individuals. 4. A struggle for an objective. 5. The inclination to fight; pugnacity.

fight·er (fī′tər) ▸ *n.* 1. One that fights. 2. A fast, maneuverable combat aircraft. 3. A pugnacious or determined person.

fig·ment (fĭg′mənt) ▸ *n.* Something invented or made up.

fig·u·ra·tive (fĭg′yər-ə-tĭv) ▸ *adj.* 1. Based on figures of speech; metaphorical. 2. Represented by a figure or resemblance; symbolic. **—fig′u·ra·tive·ly** *adv.*

fig·ure (fĭg′yər) ▸ *n.* 1. A written or printed symbol, esp. a number. 2. **figures** Mathematical calculations. 3. An amount represented in numbers. 4. The outline, form, or silhouette of a thing, esp. a human body. 5. A person, esp. a well-known one. 6. Impression or appearance made. 7. A diagram, design, or pattern. 8. A distinct group of steps or movements in a dance or in ice skating. ▸ *v.* **-ured, -ur·ing.** 1. To calculate with numbers; compute. 2. To make a likeness of; depict. 3. To adorn with a design or figures. 4. *Informal* To conclude, believe, or predict. 5. To be pertinent or involved. 6. *Informal* To seem reasonable or expected: *It figures.* ***—phrasal verbs:*** **figure on** *Informal* 1. To count on. 2. To expect: *figured on an hour's delay.* **figure out** *Informal* To discover, decide, or solve. **—fig′ur·er** *n.*

fig·ure·head (fĭg′yər-hĕd′) ▸ *n.* 1. A person given a position of nominal leadership but having no actual authority. 2. A carved figure on the prow of a ship.

figure of speech ▸ *n.* An expression that uses words in a nonliteral way or that changes normal word order to heighten rhetorical effect.

figure skating ▸ *n.* Ice skating in which the skater traces prescribed, usu. elaborate figures. **—figure skater** *n.*

fig·u·rine (fĭg′yə-rēn′) ▸ *n.* A small sculptured figure; statuette.

Fi·ji (fē′jē) ▸ A country of the SW Pacific comprising about 320 islands. Pop. 856,000.

fil·a·ment (fĭl′ə-mənt) ▸ *n.* 1. A fine thin thread, fiber, or wire. 2. A fine wire heated electrically to incandescence in an electric lamp. **—fil′a·men′tous** (-mĕn′təs), **fil′a·men′ta·ry** (-mĕn′tə-rē, -mĕn′trē) *adj.*

fi·lar·i·a (fə-lâr′ē-ə) ▸ *n., pl.* **-i·ae** (-ē-ē′). Any of various slender parasitic nematode worms often transmitted as larvae by mosquitos. **—fi·lar′i·al, fi·lar′i·an** *adj.*

fil·bert (fĭl′bərt) ▸ *n.* 1. See **hazel** 1. 2. See **hazelnut.**

filch (fĭlch) ▸ *v.* To steal; snitch. **—filch′er** *n.*

file[1] (fīl) ▸ *n.* 1. A container, such as a cabinet or folder, for keeping papers in order. 2. A collection of papers or published materials kept in convenient order. 3. *Comp. Sci.* A collection of related data or program records stored as a unit. 4. A line of persons, animals, or things positioned one behind the other. ▸ *v.* **filed, fil·ing.** 1. To put or keep in useful order; catalog. 2. To enter (a legal document) on record. 3. To send (copy) to a newspaper. 4. To carry out the first stage of: *filed charges against my associate.* 5. To march or walk in a line. ***—idiom:*** **on file** In or as if in a file for easy reference.

file[2] (fīl) ▸ *n.* A tool with sharp, edged ridges for smoothing or grinding esp. metallic surfaces. ▸ *v.* **filed, fil·ing.** To smooth or grind with or as if with a file.

file clerk ▸ *n.* One employed to maintain office files and records.

file server ▸ *n.* A computer that controls a central repository of data.

fi·let[1] (fĭ-lā′, fĭl′ā′) ▸ *n.* A lace with a simple pattern of squares.

fi·let[2] (fĭ-lā′, fĭl′ā′) ▸ *n.* Var. of **fillet** 2. ▸ *v.* Var. of **fillet** 2.

fi·let mi·gnon (fĭ-lā′ mēn-yôɴ′, fĭl′ā) ▸ *n., pl.* **fi·lets mi·gnons** (fĭ-lā′ mēn-yôɴ′, fĭl′ā). A small, round, choice cut of beef from the loin.

fil·i·al (fĭl′ē-əl) ▸ *adj.* Of or befitting a son or daughter: *filial respect.* **—fil′i·al·ly** *adv.*

fil·i·bus·ter (fĭl′ə-bŭs′tər) ▸ *n.* 1. Obstructionist tactics, esp. prolonged speechmaking, used to delay legislative action. 2. An adventurer engaged in private warfare abroad. **—fil′i·bus′ter** *v.* **—fil′i·bus′ter·er** *n.*

fil·i·gree (fĭl′ĭ-grē′) ▸ *n.* Delicate and intricate ornamental work made from gold, silver, or other fine twisted wire. **—fil′i·gree′** *v.*

fil·ing (fī′lĭng) ▸ *n.* A particle removed by a file.

Fil·i·pi·no (fĭl′ə-pē′nō) ▸ *n., pl.* **-nos.** 1. A native or inhabitant of the Philippines. 2. The official language of the

THESAURUS

fifty-fifty *adj.* Neither favorable nor unfavorable ▸ balanced, even, nip and tuck.

fight *n.* 1. A physical conflict involving two or more people ▸ affray, brawl, donnybrook, fistfight, fisticuffs, fracas, fray, free-for-all, melee, riot, row, ruction, scrap, scuffle, tumult, tussle. *Slang:* rumble, slugfest. [*Compare* ATTACK, BRUSH[1], COMBAT, CONFLICT.] 2. The power or will to fight ▸ bellicoseness, bellicosity, belligerence, belligerency, combativeness, contentiousness, pugnacity, pugnaciousness, truculence, truculency. [*Compare* AGGRESSION.] *—See also* ARGUMENT, COMPETITION (2).

fight *v.* To exchange blows with another person ▸ brawl. *Slang:* rumble. *Idioms:* duke it out, mix it up, slug it out, trade blows. [*Compare* WRESTLE.] *—See also* ARGUE (1), CONTEND, OPPOSE.

fight off *v.* *—See* REPEL.

fighter *n.* 1. One who engages in a combat or struggle ▸ belligerent, combatant, soldier, warrior. [*Compare* AGGRESSOR, SOLDIER.] 2. A contestant in a boxing match ▸ boxer, prizefighter, pugilist. *Slang:* pug.

figment *n.* *—See* DREAM (1), MYTH (2).

figurative *adj.* *—See* SYMBOLIC.

figure *n.* 1. An element or component in a decorative composition ▸ design, device, motif, motive. 2. An amount represented in numerals ▸ number, quantity. [*Compare* TOTAL.] *—See also* CELEBRITY, CHARACTER (7), CONSTITUTION, FORM (1), SCULPTURE.

figure *v.* *—See* BELIEVE (3), CALCULATE.

figure on *v.* *—See* EXPECT (1).

figure out *v.* *Informal* To arrive at an answer to a mathematical problem ▸ solve, work out. [*Compare* CALCULATE, DECIPHER.] *—See also* SOLVE (1).

figured *adj.* *—See* CALCULATED.

figures *n.* Arithmetic calculations ▸ arithmetic, computation, numbers. [*Compare* ADDITION, CALCULATION.]

figurine *n.* *—See* SCULPTURE.

figuring *n.* The act, process, or result of calculating ▸ calculation, cast, computation, reckoning.

filament *n.* A very fine continuous strand ▸ fiber, fibril, microfiber, thread. [*Compare* CORD.]

filch *v.* *—See* STEAL.

file[1] *n.* *—See* LINE.

file *v.* *—See* LINE, LIST[1].

file[2] *v.* *—See* SCRAPE (1), SHARPEN.

Philippines, based on Tagalog. **—Fil′i·pi′no** *adj.*

fill (fĭl) ▸ *v.* **1.** To make or become full. **2.** To build up the level of (low-lying land) with material such as earth or gravel. **3.** To stop or plug up. **4.** To satisfy or meet; fulfill. **5.** To complete (something) by insertion or addition: *fill in the blanks.* **6.** To supply as required: *fill a prescription.* **7.** To place a person in: *fill a job vacancy.* **8.** To occupy completely; pervade. ***—phrasal verb:*** **fill in 1.** To provide with missing information. **2.** To take another's place. ▸ *n.* **1.** An amount needed to make full, complete, or satisfied: *eat one's fill.* **2.** Material for filling. ***—idiom:*** **fill the bill** *Informal* To serve a particular purpose.

fill·er (fĭl′ər) ▸ *n.* **1.** Something added to augment weight or size or to fill space. **2.** A material used to fill in flaws in a surface. **3.** A short item to fill space in a publication or radio or television program.

fil·let (fĭl′ĭt) ▸ *n.* **1.** A narrow strip of ribbon or similar material. **2.** also **fi·let** (fĭ-lā′, fĭl′ā′) A boneless piece of meat or fish, esp. the beef tenderloin. ▸ *v.* **1.** To bind or decorate with or as if with a fillet. **2.** also **fi·let** (fĭ-lā′, fĭl′ā′) To make into fillets.

fill·ing (fĭl′ĭng) ▸ *n.* **1.** Something used to fill a space, cavity, or container: *a gold filling in a tooth.* **2.** An edible mixture used to fill pastries, sandwiches, or cakes: *pie filling.* **3.** The horizontal threads that cross the warp in weaving; weft.

filling station ▸ *n.* See **service station.**

fil·lip (fĭl′əp) ▸ *n.* **1.** A snap of the fingers. **2.** An incentive; stimulus. **—fil′lip** *v.*

Fill·more (fĭl′môr′), **Millard** (1800–74) ▸ The 13th US President (1850–53).

fil·ly (fĭl′ē) ▸ *n., pl.* **-lies.** A young female horse.

film (fĭlm) ▸ *n.* **1.** A thin skin or membrane. **2.** A thin covering or coating. **3.** A thin transparent sheet, as of plastic, used in packaging. **4.** A thin sheet or strip of flexible material, such as a cellulose derivative, coated with a photosensitive emulsion and used to make photographic negatives or transparencies. **5a.** A movie. **b.** Movies collectively. ▸ *v.* **1.** To cover with or as if with a film. **2.** To make a movie (of). **—film′i·ly** *adv.* **—film′i·ness** *n.* **—film′y** *adj.*

film·mak·ing (fĭlm′mā′kĭng) ▸ *n.* The making of movies. **—film′mak′er** *n.*

film noir (nwär) ▸ *n.* A movie marked by low-key lighting, a bleak urban setting, and corrupt, cynical characters.

film·strip (fĭlm′strĭp′) ▸ *n.* A length of film containing graphic matter prepared for still projection one frame at a time.

fil·ter (fĭl′tər) ▸ *n.* **1.** A porous material through which a liquid or gas is passed in order to separate the fluid from suspended particulate matter. **2.** Any of various devices used to reject signals, vibrations, or radiations of certain frequencies while passing others. **3.** *Comp. Sci.* A program that blocks access to data that meet a particular criterion. ▸ *v.* **1.** To pass through a filter. **2.** To remove by passing through a filter. **—fil′ter·a·bil′i·ty** *n.* **—fil′ter·a·ble, fil′tra·ble** *adj.*

filth (fĭlth) ▸ *n.* **1.** Foul or dirty matter. **2.** Corruption; vileness. **3.** Something considered obscene or immoral. **—filth′i·ly** *adv.* **—filth′i·ness** *n.* **—filth′y** *adj.*

fil·trate (fĭl′trāt′) ▸ *v.* **-trat·ed, -trat·ing.** To put or go through a filter. ▸ *n.* Material that has passed through a filter. **—fil·tra′tion** *n.*

fin (fĭn) ▸ *n.* **1.** A membranous appendage extending from the body of a fish or other aquatic animal, used for propelling, steering, or balancing the body in the water. **2.** Something, such as an airfoil, that resembles a fin. **3.** See **flipper 2.** **—fin′ny** *adj.*

fi·na·gle (fə-nā′gəl) ▸ *v.* **-gled, -gling.** *Informal* To obtain or achieve by indirect, usu. deceitful methods. **—fi·na′gler** *n.*

fi·nal (fī′nəl) ▸ *adj.* **1.** Forming or occurring at the end; last. **2.** Of or constituting the end result of a succession or process; ultimate. **3.** Definitive; unalterable. ▸ *n.* **1.** The last of a series of contests. **2.** The last examination of an academic course. **—fi·nal′i·ty** (fī-năl′ĭ-tē, fə-) *n.* **—fi′nal·ly** *adv.*

fi·nal·e (fə-năl′ē, -nä′lē) ▸ *n.* The concluding part, esp. of a musical composition.

fi·nal·ist (fī′nə-lĭst) ▸ *n.* A contestant in the final session of a competition.

fi·nal·ize (fī′nə-līz′) ▸ *v.* **-ized, -iz·ing.** To put into final form. **—fi′nal·i·za′tion** *n.*

fi·nance (fə-năns′, fī-, fī′năns′) ▸ *n.* **1.** The management of money, banking, investments, and credit. **2. finances** Monetary resources; funds. ▸ *v.* **-nanced, -nanc·ing. 1.** To provide or raise the funds or capital for. **2.** To furnish credit to. **—fi·nan′cial** *adj.* **—fi·nan′cial·ly** *adv.*

fin·an·cier (fĭn′ən-sîr′, fə-năn′-, fī′nən-) ▸ *n.* One dealing in large-scale financial affairs.

finch (fĭnch) ▸ *n.* Any of various small birds having a short stout bill.

find (fīnd) ▸ *v.* **found** (found), **find·ing. 1.** To come upon, often by accident. **2.** To come upon after a search. **3.** To discover through observation, experience, or study. **4.** To perceive to be: *found the movie dull.* **5.** To recover; regain. **6.** To arrive at; attain: *found happiness at last.* **7.** To decide on and make a declaration about: *find a verdict of guilty.* ***—phrasal verb:*** **find out 1.** To ascertain, as through examination or inquiry. **2.** To detect the true character of;

THESAURUS

fill *v.* **1.** To make full; put as much into as can be held ▸ charge, cram, crowd, freight, heap, jam, load, mob, pack, pile, stuff, top off. *Informal:* jam-pack. **2.** To plug up or block something, such as a hole or conduit ▸ block, choke, clog, close, congest, cork, plug, seal, stop. *—See also* CHARGE (1), SATISFY (1).

fill in *v.* *—See* INFORM (1), PERFECT, SUBSTITUTE.

fill out *v.* *—See* PERFECT.

fill *n.* *—See* FILLER (1).

filler *n.* **1.** Material used to fill a space or container ▸ caulking, fill, packing, padding, stuffing, wadding. **2.** Written material used to fill space in a publication ▸ boilerplate. [*Compare* ITEM.]

fillet *n.* *—See* BAND¹.

fill-in *n.* *—See* SUBSTITUTE.

fill-in *adj.* *—See* TEMPORARY (1).

filling *n.* *—See* PLUG.

filling *adj.* Not readily digested because of richness ▸ heavy, rich.

fillip *n.* *—See* STIMULUS.

film *n.* A motion picture ▸ motion picture, movie, picture. *Slang:* flick. *—See also* SKIN (2).

filmy *adj.* *—See* SHEER², UNCLEAR.

filth *n.* Foul or dirty matter ▸ dirt, grime, muck, mud. *Slang:* crap, crud, grunge. [*Compare* SLIME.] *—See also* DIRTINESS, OBSCENITY (2).

filthiness *n.* *—See* DIRTINESS, OBSCENITY (1).

filthy *adj.* *—See* DIRTY, OBSCENE, OFFENSIVE (1).

finagle *v.* *—See* MANEUVER (2).

final *adj.* Of or relating to a terminative condition, stage, or point ▸ last, latter, terminal, ultimate. [*Compare* CLIMACTIC.] *—See also* DEFINITIVE, LAST¹ (1).

finale *n.* *—See* END (2).

finalize *v.* *—See* SETTLE (1).

finally *adv.* In conclusion ▸ conclusively, last, lastly, ultimately. *Idioms:* at last, in the end. *—See also* ULTIMATELY (1).

finance *n.* The management of money ▸ banking, investment, money management.

finance *v.* To supply capital to or for ▸ back, capitalize, fund, grubstake, stake, subsidize, subvent, underwrite. *Informal:* bankroll. *Idiom:* put up money for. [*Compare* PATRONIZE, SUPPORT.]

finances *n.* The monetary resources of a government, organization, or individual ▸ capital, funds, money (*or* moneys). [*Compare* CAPITAL, MONEY, RESOURCES.]

financial *adj.* Of or relating to finances ▸ fiscal, monetary, pecuniary.

financier *n.* One who is occupied with or expert in large-scale financial affairs ▸ capitalist. *Informal:* moneyman.

financing *n.* *—See* CAPITAL (1), PATRONAGE (1).

find *v.* To look for and discover ▸ locate, pinpoint, spot. *Informal:* scare up. [*Compare* TRACE, UNCOVER.] *—See also* ENCOUNTER (1), INFER.

find out *v.* *—See* DISCERN, DISCOVER.

find *n.* Something offered or bought at a low price ▸ bargain. *Informal:* buy, deal. *Slang:* steal. *—See also* DISCOVERY, TREASURE.

expose. ▸ *n.* **1.** The act of finding. **2.** An unexpectedly valuable discovery. **—find′a·ble** *adj.* **—find′er** *n.*

fin-de-siè·cle (făɴ′də-sē-ĕk′lə) ▸ *adj.* Of or characteristic of the last part of the 19th cent. esp. its artistic climate of effete sophistication.

find·ing (fīn′dĭng) ▸ *n.* **1.** A conclusion reached after examination or investigation. **2.** A document containing an authoritative conclusion.

fine[1] (fīn) ▸ *adj.* **fin·er, fin·est. 1.** Of superior quality, skill, or appearance. **2.** Very small in size, weight, or thickness. **3.** Very sharp: *a blade with a fine edge.* **4.** Exhibiting superior artistry: *fine china.* **5.** Consisting of very small particles: *fine dust.* **6.** Subtle or precise: *a fine difference.* **7.** Marked by refinement or elegance. **8.** First-rate; splendid. **9.** Being in good condition or health. **10.** Used as an intensive: *a fine mess.* ▸ *adv. Informal* Very well: *doing fine.* **—fine′ly** *adv.* **—fine′ness** *n.*

fine[2] (fīn) ▸ *n.* A sum of money imposed as a penalty for an offense. ▸ *v.* **fined, fin·ing.** To impose a fine on. ***—idiom:* in fine 1.** In conclusion. **2.** In brief.

fi·ne[3] (fē′nā) ▸ *n. Mus.* The end.

fine art (fīn) ▸ *n.* **1.** Art intended primarily for beauty rather than utility. **2.** often **fine arts** Any of the art forms, such as sculpture, painting, and music, used to create this art.

fine print ▸ *n.* The portion of a document that contains qualifications or restrictions in small type or obscure language.

fin·er·y (fī′nə-rē) ▸ *n., pl.* **-ies.** Elaborate adornment, esp. fine clothing.

fi·nesse (fə-nĕs′) ▸ *n.* **1.** Refinement and delicacy of performance, execution, or artisanship. **2.** Subtlety; tact. ▸ *v.* **-nessed, -ness·ing.** To handle with subtle or evasive strategy: *finesse an embarrasing question.*

fine-tune (fīn′to͞on′, -tyo͞on′) ▸ *v.* To make small adjustments in for optimal performance or effectiveness.

fin·ger (fĭng′gər) ▸ *n.* **1.** One of the five digits of the hand, esp. one other than the thumb. **2.** The part of a glove that fits a finger. **3.** Something that resembles a finger. ▸ *v.* **1.** To touch with the fingers; handle. **2.** *Mus.* To play (an instrument) by using the fingers in a particular order or way. **3.** *Slang* **a.** To inform on. **b.** To designate, esp. as an intended victim.

fin·ger·board (fĭng′gər-bôrd′) ▸ *n.* A strip of wood on the neck of a stringed instrument against which the strings are pressed in playing.

finger bowl ▸ *n.* A small bowl that holds water for rinsing the fingers at the table.

fin·ger·ing (fĭng′gər-ĭng) ▸ *n.* The indication on a musical score of which fingers are to be used in playing.

fin·ger·ling (fĭng′gər-lĭng) ▸ *n.* A young or small fish.

fin·ger·nail (fĭng′gər-nāl′) ▸ *n.* The nail on a finger.

fin·ger·print (fĭng′gər-prĭnt′) ▸ *n.* **1.** An impression formed by the curves in the ridges on a fingertip, used esp. as a means of identification. **2.** A distinctive mark or characteristic. **—fin′ger·print′** *v.*

fin·ger·tip (fĭng′gər-tĭp′) ▸ *n.* The extreme end of a finger. ***—idiom:* at (one's) fingertips** Readily available.

fin·i·al (fĭn′ē-əl) ▸ *n.* An ornamental projection or terminating part, as on an arch.

fin·ick·y (fĭn′ĭ-kē) ▸ *adj.* **-i·er, -i·est.** Difficult to please; fussy. **—fin′ick·i·ness** *n.*

fin·is (fĭn′ĭs, fī′nĭs, fē-nē′) ▸ *n.* The end.

fin·ish (fĭn′ĭsh) ▸ *v.* **1.** To reach the end (of). **2.** To bring to an end; terminate. **3.** To consume all of; use up. **4.** To give (a surface) a desired texture. **5.** To destroy; kill. ▸ *n.* **1.** The final part; the conclusion. **2.** Surface texture. **3.** Completeness or refinement of execution; polish. **—fin′ish·er** *n.*

fi·nite (fī′nīt′) ▸ *adj.* **1.** Having bounds; limited. **2.** *Math.* Being neither infinite nor infinitesimal. **3.** *Gram.* Limited by person, number, tense, and mood. Used of a verb. **—fi′nite′ly** *adv.* **—fi′nite′ness** *n.*

fink (fĭngk) *Slang* ▸ *n.* **1.** A contemptible person. **2.** An informer. ▸ *v.* **1.** To inform against another person. **2.** To let another down.

Fin·land (fĭn′lənd) ▸ A country of N Europe on the Gulf of Bothnia and the Gulf of Finland. Pop. 5,180,000.

Finn (fĭn) ▸ *n.* A native or inhabitant of Finland.

fin·nan had·die (fĭn′ən hăd′ē) ▸ *n.* Smoked haddock.

Fin·nic (fĭn′ĭk) ▸ *n.* A branch of Finno-Ugric that includes Finnish, Estonian, and Lapp.

Finn·ish (fĭn′ĭsh) ▸ *adj.* Of or relating to Finland or its people or language. ▸ *n.* The Finno-Ugric language of the Finns.

Fin·no-U·gric (fĭn′ō-o͞o′grĭk, -yo͞o′-) also **Fin·no-U·gri·an** (-o͞o′grē-ən, -yo͞o′-) ▸ *n.* A subfamily of the Uralic language family that includes Finnish, Hungarian, and other languages of E and NE Europe. **—Finno-Ugric** *adj.*

fiord (fyôrd) ▸ *n.* Var. of **fjord.**

fir (fûr) ▸ *n.* **1.** Any of a genus of evergreen trees having flattened needles and erect cones. **2.** The wood of a fir.

fire (fīr) ▸ *n.* **1.** A rapid, persistent chemical change that releases heat and light and is accompanied by flame, esp. the burning of a combustible substance. **2a.** Burning fuel. **b.** A destructive burning: *insured against fire.* **3.** Enthusiasm; ardor. **4.** Brilliance; sparkle. **5.** The discharge of firearms. **6.** Intense, repeated attack or criticism. ▸ *v.* **fired, fir·ing. 1.** To ignite. **2.** To maintain fire in. **3.** To bake in a kiln. **4.** To arouse the emotions of. **5.** To detonate or discharge (a weapon). **6.** To throw with force;

THESAURUS

finding *n.* —*See* DISCOVERY, RULING.

fine[1] *adj.* **1.** Consisting of small particles ▸ dusty, powdery, pulverous, pulverulent. [*Compare* MINUTE[2].] **2.** Able to make or detect effects of great subtlety or precision ▸ delicate, nice, sensitive, subtle. [*Compare* ACCURATE.] —*See also* CHOICE (1), CLEAR (2), DELICATE (1), DELICATE (4), EXCELLENT, GOOD (1), POINTED.

fine[2] *n.* A sum of money levied as punishment for an offense ▸ amercement, mulct, penalty. [*Compare* PUNISHMENT.]

fine *v.* To impose a fine on ▸ amerce, mulct, penalize. [*Compare* PUNISH.]

fineness *n.* —*See* EXCELLENCE, SUBTLETY.

fine print *n.* —*See* DETAIL.

finery *n.* —*See* ATTIRE.

finespun *adj.* —*See* DELICATE (4).

finesse *v.* To outmaneuver an opponent ▸ trump. *Informal:* one-up. *Idioms:* play gotcha, pull (*or* put over) a fast one. [*Compare* DECEIVE, OUTWIT.] —*See also* MANEUVER (1), MANEUVER (2).

finest *n.* —*See* POLICE OFFICER.

fine-tune *v.* —*See* ADJUST.

finger *v.* —*See* ACCUSE, PLACE (1), TOUCH.

finger *n.* —*See* BEAM (1).

finger-pointing *n.* —*See* ACCUSATION, CRITICISM.

finicky or **finical** *adj.* —*See* FUSSY.

finis *n.* —*See* END (1).

finish *v.* **1.** To complete a race or competition in a specified position ▸ come in, place, run. **2.** To apply a coating or surface material to ▸ enamel, glaze, lacquer, paint, plaster, polish, polyurethane, shellac, stain, surface, varnish, wax. [*Compare* COVER, FACE, GLOSS[1], SMEAR.] —*See also* CONCLUDE, DESTROY (1), EXHAUST (1), KILL[1], MURDER.

finish *n.* A final coating or material applied to a surface ▸ enamel, glaze, lacquer, paint, plaster, polish, polyurethane, shellac, stain, surface, varnish, wax. [*Compare* COAT, FACE, GLOSS[1].] —*See also* END (1), END (2).

finished *adj.* **1.** Having no further relationship ▸ done, through. **2.** Proficient as a result of practice and study ▸ accomplished, polished, practiced. [*Compare* ABLE, EXPERT.] —*See also* COMPLETE (3), THROUGH (2).

fink *n.* —*See* INFORMER.

fink *v.* —*See* INFORM (2).

fink out *v.* —*See* RENEGE.

fire *n.* **1.** The visible signs of combustion ▸ blaze, conflagration, flame, flare-up. **2.** Liveliness and vivacity of imagination ▸ brilliance, brilliancy, genius, inspiration. [*Compare* INTELLIGENCE, INVENTION.] —*See also* BARRAGE, BRILLIANCE (1), ENTHUSIASM (1), PASSION.

fire *v.* **1.** To arouse the emotions of; make ardent ▸ animate, arouse, enkindle, impassion, inflame, inspire, kindle, rouse, stir. [*Compare* MOVE.] **2.** To discharge a gun or firearm ▸ blast (away), fire away (off), pop (off), shoot (away *or* off). *Idioms:* go bang-bang, open fire, take a shot (*or*

hurl. 7. To discharge from a position; dismiss. ***—idiom:* on fire** 1. Ignited; ablaze. 2. Ardent; impassioned. **—fir′er** *n.*

fire ant ▸ *n.* Any of a genus of ants of the S US and tropical America that inflict a painful sting.

fire·arm (fīr′ärm′) ▸ *n.* A weapon, esp. a pistol or rifle, capable of firing a projectile.

fire·ball (fīr′bôl′) ▸ *n.* 1. A brilliantly burning sphere. 2. A highly luminous, intensely hot spherical cloud generated by a nuclear explosion. 3. An energetic person.

fire·bomb (fīr′bŏm′) ▸ *n.* A bomb designed to start a fire. **—fire′bomb′** *v.*

fire·brand (fīr′brănd′) ▸ *n.* 1. A piece of burning wood. 2. One who stirs up trouble; agitator.

fire·break (fīr′brāk′) ▸ *n.* A strip of cleared or plowed land used to stop the spread of a fire.

fire·brick (fīr′brĭk′) ▸ *n.* A refractory brick, usu. of fire clay, used for lining furnaces, chimneys, or fireplaces.

fire·bug (fīr′bŭg′) ▸ *n. Informal* An arsonist; pyromaniac.

fire clay (fīr′klā′) ▸ *n.* A type of heat-resistant clay used esp. to make firebricks.

fire·crack·er (fīr′krăk′ər) ▸ *n.* A small explosive charge and a fuse in a heavy paper casing, exploded to entertain.

fire·damp (fīr′dămp′) ▸ *n.* A combustible gas, chiefly methane, that occurs in coal mines and forms an explosive mixture with air.

fire engine ▸ *n.* A large truck that carries firefighters and equipment to a fire.

fire escape ▸ *n.* An outside stairway for emergency exit in the event of fire.

fire extinguisher ▸ *n.* A portable apparatus containing chemicals that can be discharged in a jet to extinguish a small fire.

fire·fight (fīr′fīt′) ▸ *n.* An exchange of gunfire, as between infantry units.

fire·fight·er (fīr′fī′tər) ▸ *n.* One who fights fires, esp. for a living. **—fire′fight′ing** *adj. & n.*

fire·fly (fīr′flī′) ▸ *n.* Any of various nocturnal beetles having luminescent chemicals in the posterior tip of the abdomen that produce a flashing light.

fire·house (fīr′hous′) ▸ *n.* See **fire station**.

fire hydrant ▸ *n.* An upright pipe with a nozzle or spout for drawing water from a water main.

fire irons ▸ *pl.n.* Implements, such as tongs and a poker, used to tend a fireplace.

fire·man (fīr′mən) ▸ *n.* 1. A firefighter. 2. A man who tends fires; stoker.

fire·place (fīr′plās′) ▸ *n.* An open recess for holding a fire at the base of a chimney; hearth.

fire·plug (fīr′plŭg′) ▸ *n.* See **fire hydrant**.

fire·pow·er (fīr′pou′ər) ▸ *n.* The capacity, as of a military unit, for delivering fire.

fire·proof (fīr′pro͞of′) ▸ *adj.* Impervious to damage by fire. ▸ *v.* To make fireproof.

fire·side (fīr′sīd′) ▸ *n.* 1. The area immediately surrounding a fireplace. 2. A home.

fire station ▸ *n.* A building for fire equipment and firefighters.

fire tower ▸ *n.* A tower in which a lookout for fires is posted.

fire·trap (fīr′trăp′) ▸ *n.* A building that can catch fire easily or is difficult to escape from in the event of fire.

fire·wall (fīr′wôl) ▸ *n.* 1. A fireproof wall used as a barrier to prevent the spread of fire. 2. *Comp. Sci.* A security scheme that prevents unauthorized users from accessing a network.

fire·wa·ter (fīr′wô′tər, -wŏt′ər) ▸ *n. Slang* Strong liquor, esp. whiskey.

fire·wood (fīr′wo͝od′) ▸ *n.* Wood used as fuel.

fire·works (fīr′wûrks′) ▸ *pl.n.* 1. Explosives and combustibles set off to generate colored lights, smoke, and noise for amusement. 2a. A spectacular display, as of musical virtuosity. b. A fiery verbal attack.

fir·ing line (fīr′ĭng) ▸ *n.* 1. The line of positions from which fire is directed at a target. 2. The forefront of an activity; vanguard.

firing pin ▸ *n.* The part of the bolt of a firearm that strikes the primer and detonates the charge of a projectile.

firm[1] (fûrm) ▸ *adj.* **-er, -est.** 1. Resistant to externally applied pressure. 2. Marked by the tone and resiliency of healthy tissue: *firm muscles.* 3. Securely fixed in place. 4. Indicating determination or resolution. 5. Constant; steadfast. 6. Fixed and definite: *a firm offer.* 7. Strong and sure: *a firm grasp.* ▸ *v.* To make or become firm. ▸ *adv.* **-er, -est.** Resolutely: *stand firm.* **—firm′ly** *adv.* **—firm′ness** *n.*

firm[2] (fûrm) ▸ *n.* A commercial partnership of two or more persons, esp. when unincorporated.

fir·ma·ment (fûr′mə-mənt) ▸ *n.* The vault or expanse of the heavens; the sky.

first (fûrst) ▸ *n.* 1. The ordinal number matching the number 1 in a series. 2. The one coming, occurring, or ranking first. 3. The beginning; outset: *from the first.* 4. The lowest forward gear in a motor vehicle. 5. The winning position in a contest. ▸ *adj.* 1. Coming before all others in order or location. 2. Prior to all others in time; earliest. 3. Ranking above all others; foremost. ▸ *adv.* 1. Before or above all others in time, order, rank, or importance. 2. For the first time. 3. Rather; preferably: *would die first.* 4. To begin with.

first aid ▸ *n.* Emergency treatment administered to an injured or sick person before professional medical care is available. **—first′-aid′** *adj.*

first base ▸ *n. Baseball* The first base to be reached by a runner. **—first baseman** *n.*

first·born (fûrst′bôrn′) ▸ *adj.* First in order of birth. **—first′born′** *n.*

first class ▸ *n.* 1. The first, highest, or best group in a system of classification. 2. The most expensive class of accommodations. 3. A class of mail sealed against inspection. **—first′-class′** *adj. & adv.*

first cousin ▸ *n.* See **cousin** 1.

first-de·gree burn (fûrst′dĭ-grē′) ▸ *n.* A mild burn that produces redness of the skin but no blistering.

first-gen·er·a·tion (fûrst′jĕn′ə-rā′shən) ▸ *adj.* 1. Of or relating to an immigrant to another country. 2. Of or relating to one whose parents are immigrants.

first·hand (fûrst′hănd′) ▸ *adj.* Received from the original source. **—first′hand′** *adv.*

first lieutenant ▸ *n.* A rank, as in the US Army, that is

THESAURUS

potshot). *—See also* DISMISS (1), EXPLODE (1), LIGHT[1] (1), THROW.

fire and brimstone *n.* *—See* BOMBAST, HELL.

firebrand *n.* *—See* AGITATOR.

fired up *adj.* *—See* THRILLED.

fireplace *n.* An open space for holding a fire at the base of a chimney ▸ grate, hearth, ingle.

fireproof *adj.* Resistant to catching fire ▸ fire-resistant, fire-retardant, flameproof, flame-resistant, flame-retardant, incombustible, noncombustible, nonflammable.

fireworks *n.* *—See* ARGUMENT.

firm[1] *adj.* 1. Unyielding to pressure or force ▸ hard, incompressible, solid. 2. Not easily moved or shaken ▸ fast, secure, solid, sound, stable, steady, strong, sturdy, substantial, sure, unshakable. [*Compare* FIXED, MOTIONLESS.] 3. Indicating or possessing determination or resolution ▸ constant, decided, decisive, determined, resolute, resolved, single-minded, steadfast, steady, stiff, tough, unbending, uncompromising, unflinching, unwavering, unyielding. [*Compare* INSISTENT, INTENT, STUBBORN.] *—See also* FAITHFUL, TIGHT (1), UNCHANGING.

firm up *v.* *—See* HARDEN (2).

firm[2] *n.* *—See* COMPANY (1).

firmament *n.* The celestial regions as seen from the earth ▸ air, heavens, sky. ***Idiom:*** wild blue yonder.

firmness *n.* *—See* CHANGELESSNESS, DECISION (2), STABILITY.

first *adj.* Preceding all others in time ▸ earliest, inaugural, initial, maiden, original, pioneer, premier, primary, prime, primordial. [*Compare* BEGINNING.] *—See also* BEST (1), PRIMARY (1).

first-class *adj.* *—See* CHOICE (1), EXCELLENT.

firsthand *adj.* Marked by the absence of any intervention ▸ direct, immediate, primary.

firsthand *adv.* Without intermediary ▸ directly, immediately.

above second lieutenant and below captain.

first·ly (fûrst′lē) ▸ *adv.* To begin with.

first mate ▸ *n.* An officer on a merchant ship ranking immediately below the captain.

first person ▸ *n.* The form of a verb or pronoun designating the speaker of the sentence in which it appears.

first-rate (fûrst′rāt′) ▸ *adj.* Foremost in quality, rank, or importance. ▸ *adv. Informal* Very well; excellently.

first sergeant ▸ *n.* **1.** A rank in the US Army and Marine Corps below sergeant major. **2.** Any of three senior noncommissioned ranks in the US Air Force.

first-string (fûrst′strĭng′) ▸ *adj.* Of or being a regular member of a team rather than a substitute. **—first′-string′er** *n.*

firth (fûrth) ▸ *n. Scots* A long narrow inlet of the sea.

fis·cal (fĭs′kəl) ▸ *adj.* **1.** Of or relating to government expenditures, revenues, and debt. **2.** Of finance or finances. **—fis′cal·ly** *adv.*

fiscal year ▸ *n.* A 12-month period for which an organization plans the use of its funds.

fish (fĭsh) ▸ *n., pl.* **fish** or **fish·es. 1.** Any of numerous cold-blooded aquatic vertebrates having fins, gills, and a streamlined body. **2.** The edible flesh of a fish. ▸ *v.* **1.** To catch or try to catch fish. **2.** To grope: *fished in both pockets for a coin.* **3.** To seek something indirectly: *fish for compliments.* **—fish′er** *n.* **—fish′ing** *n.*

fish·bowl (fĭsh′bōl′) ▸ *n.* **1.** A transparent bowl in which live fish are kept. **2.** *Informal* A place or situation lacking in privacy.

fish·er·man (fĭsh′ər-mən) ▸ *n.* **1.** One who fishes as an occupation or for sport. **2.** A commercial fishing vessel.

fish·er·y (fĭsh′ə-rē) ▸ *n., pl.* **-ies. 1.** The industry devoted to the catching, processing, or selling of fish. **2.** A fishing ground. **3.** A hatchery for fish.

fish·eye (fĭsh′ī′) ▸ *adj.* Of or being a camera lens that covers an angle of about 180°.

fish hawk ▸ *n.* See **osprey.**

fish·hook (fĭsh′ho͝ok′) ▸ *n.* A barbed metal hook for catching fish.

fishing rod ▸ *n.* A rod used with a line for catching fish.

fish ladder ▸ *n.* A steplike series of pools by which fish can pass around a dam.

fish·meal (fĭsh′mēl′) ▸ *n.* Ground dried fish used as animal feed and fertilizer.

fish·net (fĭsh′nĕt′) ▸ *n.* **1.** Netting used to catch fish. **2.** A large-mesh fabric.

fish story ▸ *n. Informal* An implausible, boastful story.

fish·wife (fĭsh′wīf′) ▸ *n.* **1.** A woman who sells fish. **2.** A woman regarded as coarse and abusive.

fish·y (fĭsh′ē) ▸ *adj.* **-i·er, -i·est. 1.** Resembling or suggestive of fish. **2.** *Informal* Inspiring doubt or suspicion. **—fish′i·ly** *adv.* **—fish′i·ness** *n.*

fis·sile (fĭs′əl, -īl′) ▸ *adj.* **1.** Possible to split. **2.** *Phys.* Fissionable, esp. by neutrons of all energies. **—fis·sil′i·ty** (fĭ-sĭl′ĭ-tē) *n.*

fis·sion (fĭsh′ən) ▸ *n.* **1.** The act or process of splitting into parts. **2.** A nuclear reaction in which an atomic nucleus splits into fragments, generating from 100 million to several hundred million electron volts of energy. **3.** *Biol.* An asexual reproductive process in which a unicellular organism divides into two or more independently maturing cells. **—fis′sion·a·ble** *adj.*

fis·sure (fĭsh′ər) ▸ *n.* A long narrow opening; cleft. **—fis′sure** *v.*

fist (fĭst) ▸ *n.* The hand closed tightly with the fingers bent against the palm.

fist·fight (fĭst′fīt′) ▸ *n.* A fight with the bare fists.

fist·ful (fĭst′fo͝ol′) ▸ *n., pl.* **-fuls.** A handful.

fist·i·cuffs (fĭs′tĭ-kŭfs′) ▸ *pl.n.* A fistfight.

fis·tu·la (fĭs′chə-lə) ▸ *n., pl.* **-las** or **-lae** (-lē′). An abnormal duct or passage that connects a hollow organ to the body surface or to another hollow organ.

fit[1] (fĭt) ▸ *v.* **fit·ted** or **fit, fit·ted, fit·ting. 1.** To be the proper size and shape (for). **2.** To be appropriate to; suit. **3.** To make suitable. **4.** To equip; outfit: *fit out a ship.* **5.** To provide a place or time for: *The doctor can fit you in today.* ▸ *adj.* **fit·ter, fit·test. 1.** Suited, adapted, or acceptable for a given circumstance or purpose. **2.** Appropriate; proper. **3.** Physically sound; healthy. ▸ *n.* The manner in which something fits: *a jacket with a tight fit.* **—fit′ly** *adv.* **—fit′ter** *n.*

fit[2] (fĭt) ▸ *n.* **1.** *Medic.* **a.** A seizure or convulsion, esp. one caused by epilepsy. **b.** The sudden appearance of a symptom such as coughing or sneezing. **2.** A sudden outburst: *a fit of jealousy.* **3.** A sudden period of vigorous activity.

fit·ful (fĭt′fəl) ▸ *adj.* Intermittent; irregular. **—fit′ful·ly** *adv.* **—fit′ful·ness** *n.*

fit·ness (fĭt′nĭs) ▸ *n.* The state of being physically fit, esp. as the result of exercise and proper nutrition.

fit·ting (fĭt′ĭng) ▸ *adj.* Suitable; appropriate. ▸ *n.* **1.** The act of trying on clothes for fit. **2.** A small detachable part for a machine. **—fit′ting·ly** *adv.* **—fit′ting·ness** *n.*

Fitz·ger·ald (fĭts-jĕr′əld), **Ella** (1917–96) ▸ Amer. singer.

Fitzgerald, F(rancis) Scott (Key) (1896–1940) ▸ Amer. writer.

five (fīv) ▸ *n.* **1.** The cardinal number equal to 4 + 1. **2.** The 5th in a set or sequence. **—five** *adj. & pron.*

five-and-ten (fīv′ən-tĕn′) ▸ *n.* A retail store selling a wide variety of inexpensive articles.

fix (fĭks) ▸ *v.* **1a.** To place securely. **b.** To secure to another; attach. **2a.** To put into a stable or unalterable form. **b.** To make (a chemical substance) nonvolatile or solid. **c.** To convert (nitrogen) into stable, biologically assimilable compounds. **d.** To prevent discoloration of (a photographic image) by coating with a chemical preservative. **3.** To direct steadily: *fixed her eyes on the road.* **4.** To establish definitely; specify: *fix a time to meet.* **5.** To assign; attribute: *fix blame.* **6.** To correct or set right; adjust. **7.** To restore to proper condition; repair. **8.** To make ready; prepare. **9.** To spay or castrate (an animal). **10.** *Informal* To get even with. **11.** To influence the outcome of by improper or unlawful means. ▸ *n.* **1.** The act of adjusting, correcting, or repairing. **2.** A solution: *a quick fix.* **3.** The position, as of a ship or aircraft, determined by observation or equipment. **4.** An instance of prearranging an improper or illegal outcome, esp. by means of bribery. **5.** A predicament. **6.**

THESAURUS

first-rate *adj.* —*See* CHOICE (1), EXCELLENT.

fiscal *adj.* Of or relating to finances ▸ financial, monetary, pecuniary.

fish *v.* **1.** To try to catch fish ▸ angle, cast, go fishing, troll, trawl. *Idiom:* cast one's hook (*or* net). **2.** To try to obtain something, usually by subtleness and cunning ▸ angle, hint. [*Compare* COAX.]

fish for *v.* —*See* SEEK (1).

fish story *n.* —*See* EXAGGERATION, LIE[2].

fishwife *n.* —*See* SCOLD.

fishy *adj.* —*See* SHADY (1).

fission *n.* —*See* DIVISION (1).

fissure *n.* —*See* BREACH (2), CRACK (2), DIVISION (1).

fissure *v.* —*See* CRACK (1).

fistfight or **fisticuffs** *n.* —*See* FIGHT (1).

fit[1] *v.* To be the proper size and shape for something ▸ dovetail, interlock. *Idiom:* fit like a glove. —*See also* ADAPT, AGREE (1), FURNISH, PREPARE, SUIT (1).

fit out or **up** *v.* —*See* FURNISH.

fit *adj.* —*See* APPROPRIATE, CONVENIENT (1), ELIGIBLE, HEALTHY, JUST.

fit[2] *n.* —*See* OUTBURST, SEIZURE (1), TEMPER (2).

fitful *adj.* —*See* INTERMITTENT.

fitfully *adv.* —*See* INTERMITTENTLY.

fitness *n.* —*See* QUALIFICATION, SHAPE.

fitted *adj.* —*See* ELIGIBLE.

fitting *adj.* —*See* APPROPRIATE, JUST.

fitting *n.* Something attached as a permanent part of something else ▸ apparatus, fixture, installation. [*Compare* ATTACHMENT.]

fix *v.* **1.** To restore to proper condition or functioning ▸ doctor, fix up, mend, overhaul, patch (up), repair, revamp, right, service. *Idioms:* put right (*or* to rights), set right (*or* to rights). [*Compare* CURE, RESTORE.] **2.** To place or set deeply or securely ▸ embed, entrench, fasten, implant, infix, ingrain, lodge, plant, root. **3.** To ascribe the blame for a misdeed or error ▸ affix, ascribe, assign, attribute, blame, fasten, impute, lay, pin, place. [*Compare* ATTRIBUTE.] **4.** To prearrange the outcome of a contest unlawfully ▸ rig, tamper. *Idiom:* stack the deck. —*See also* ADJUST, ATTACH (1), AVENGE, BRIBE, CATCH (3), CORRECT (1), DICTATE,

Slang A dose of a narcotic. **—fix′a·ble** *adj.* **—fix′er** *n.*

fix·ate (fĭk′sāt′) ▸ *v.* **-at·ed, -at·ing.** 1. To make fixed or stationary. 2. To preoccupy obsessively. 3. *Psychol.* To attach (oneself) to a person or thing in an immature or neurotic fashion. **—fix·a′tion** *n.*

fix·a·tive (fĭk′sə-tĭv) ▸ *n.* A substance that fixes or preserves. **—fix′a·tive** *adj.*

fixed (fĭkst) ▸ *adj.* 1. Firmly in position; stationary. 2. Determined; established: *a fixed price.* 3. Invariable; constant: *a fixed income.* 4. *Chem.* a. Nonvolatile. b. In a stable, combined form. 5. Firmly, often dogmatically held: *fixed notions.* 6. Illegally prearranged: *a fixed election.* **—fix′ed·ly** (fĭk′sĭd-lē) *adv.* **—fix′ed·ness** *n.*

fix·ings (fĭk′sĭngz) ▸ *pl.n. Informal* Accessories; trimmings: *turkey with all the fixings.*

fix·i·ty (fĭk′sĭ-tē) ▸ *n.* The quality or condition of being fixed; stability.

fix·ture (fĭks′chər) ▸ *n.* 1. Something attached as a permanent apparatus or appliance: *plumbing fixtures.* 2. One long associated with a place or setting.

fizz (fĭz) ▸ *n.* 1. A hissing or bubbling sound. 2. Effervescence. **—fizz** *v.* **—fizz′y** *adj.*

fiz·zle (fĭz′əl) ▸ *v.* **-zled, -zling.** 1. To make a hissing or sputtering sound. 2. *Informal* To fail or end weakly, esp. after a hopeful beginning. ▸ *n. Informal* A failure.

fjord or **fiord** (fyôrd) ▸ *n.* A long, narrow, deep inlet of the sea between steep slopes.

FL also **Fla.** ▸ *abbr.* Florida

fl. ▸ *abbr.* 1. *Lat.* floruit (flourished) 2. fluid

flab (flăb) ▸ *n.* Soft, fatty body tissue.

flab·ber·gast (flăb′ər-găst′) ▸ *v.* To overwhelm with astonishment; astound.

flab·by (flăb′ē) ▸ *adj.* **-bi·er, -bi·est.** 1. Lacking firmness; slack. 2. Lacking force; feeble. **—flab′bi·ly** *adv.* **—flab′bi·ness** *n.*

flac·cid (flăs′ĭd, flăk′sĭd) ▸ *adj.* Lacking firmness, resilience, or muscle tone. **—flac·cid′i·ty, flac′cid·ness** *n.* **—flac′cid·ly** *adv.*

flack (flăk) ▸ *n.* Var. of **flak.**

flac·on (flăk′ən, -ŏn′) ▸ *n.* A small stoppered bottle.

flag[1] (flăg) ▸ *n.* 1. A piece of cloth of distinctive color and design, used as a symbol, signal, or emblem. 2. A marker; tag. ▸ *v.* **flagged, flag·ging.** 1. To mark with a flag. 2. To signal with or as if with a flag: *flagged the car to stop.* **—flag′ger** *n.*

flag[2] (flăg) ▸ *n.* A plant, as an iris, that has long bladelike leaves.

flag[3] (flăg) ▸ *v.* **flagged, flag·ging.** 1. To hang limply; droop. 2. To decline in vigor or strength.

flag[4] (flăg) ▸ *n.* A flagstone.

flag·el·late (flăj′ə-lāt′) ▸ *v.* **-lat·ed, -lat·ing.** To whip or flog; scourge. **—flag′el·la′tion** *n.*

fla·gel·lum (flə-jĕl′əm) ▸ *n., pl.* **-gel·la** (-jĕl′ə). 1. *Biol.* A whiplike extension of certain cells or unicellular organisms that serves in locomotion. 2. A whip.

flag·on (flăg′ən) ▸ *n.* A large vessel with a handle and spout, used for holding wine or liquors.

flag·pole (flăg′pōl′) ▸ *n.* A pole on which a flag is raised.

fla·grant (flā′grənt) ▸ *adj.* Conspicuously bad, offensive, or reprehensible. **—fla′gran·cy, fla′grance** *n.* **—fla′grant·ly** *adv.*

flag·ship (flăg′shĭp′) ▸ *n.* 1. A ship bearing the flag of a fleet or squadron commander. 2. The chief one of a group: *the flagship of a newspaper chain.*

flag·staff (flăg′stăf′) ▸ *n.* See **flagpole.**

flag·stone (flăg′stōn′) ▸ *n.* A flat, evenly layered paving stone.

flag-wav·ing (flăg′wā′vĭng) ▸ *n.* Excessive or fanatical patriotism. **—flag′-wav′er** *n.*

flail (flāl) ▸ *n.* A manual threshing device with a long wooden handle and a short, free-swinging stick on the end. ▸ *v.* 1. To beat with or as if with a flail. 2. To move wildly.

flair (flâr) ▸ *n.* 1. A talent or aptitude. 2. Instinctive discernment; keenness. 3. Distinctive elegance or style.

flak also **flack** (flăk) ▸ *n.* 1a. Antiaircraft artillery. b. The bursting shells fired from such artillery. 2. *Informal* a. Excessive criticism. b. Dissension; opposition.

flake (flāk) ▸ *n.* 1. A flat thin piece or layer; chip. 2. A crystal of snow. 3. *Slang* A somewhat eccentric person; oddball. ▸ *v.* **flaked, flak·ing.** To break into or come off in flakes. **—flak′er** *n.* **—flak′i·ly** *adv.* **—flak′i·ness** *n.* **—flak′y, flak′ey** *adj.*

flam·bé (fläm-bā′, fläɴ-) ▸ *adj.* Served flaming in ignited liquor. **—flam·bé′** *v.*

flam·boy·ant (flăm-boi′ənt) ▸ *adj.* 1. Highly elaborate; ornate. 2. Richly colored; resplendent. 3. Marked by striking audacity or verve. 4. Ostentatious. **—flam·boy′ance, flam·boy′an·cy** *n.* **—flam·boy′ant·ly** *adv.*

flame (flām) ▸ *n.* 1. The zone of burning gases and fine suspended matter associated with rapid combustion. 2. A violent or intense passion. 3. *Informal* A sweetheart. 4. An insulting or malicious remark, as on a computer network. ▸ *v.* **flamed, flam·ing.** 1. To burn brightly; blaze. 2. To color or flash suddenly. 3. To insult or criticize provokingly, as on a computer network. **—flam′er** *n.*

fla·men·co (flə-mĕng′kō) ▸ *n., pl.* **-cos.** 1. A dance style of the Andalusian Gypsies, with forceful, often improvised rhythms. 2. The guitar music that usu. accompanies such a dance.

flame·out (flām′out′) ▸ *n.* Failure of a jet aircraft engine, esp. in flight.

flame·throw·er (flām′thrō′ər) ▸ *n.* A weapon that projects a steady stream of ignited fuel.

fla·min·go (flə-mĭng′gō) ▸ *n., pl.* **-gos** or **-goes.** A large

THESAURUS

ENGRAVE (2), ESTABLISH (1), FASTEN, GOVERN, LIMIT, PREPARE, SETTLE (1), SETTLE (2), STERILIZE (2).

fix up *v.* —*See* FIX (1), HARDEN (2), RENEW (1).

fix *n.* —*See* BRIBE, PREDICAMENT.

fixate *v.* To dominate the mind or thoughts of ▸ obsess, possess, preoccupy. [*Compare* ABSORB, GRIP.]

fixation *n.* —*See* OBSESSION.

fixed *adj.* Firmly in position ▸ anchored, embedded, fastened, immobile, immovable, riveted, rooted, secured, stationary, steadfast, steady, unmovable, unmoving. ***Idiom:*** cast (*or* etched *or* set in stone. [*Compare* FIRM[1].] —*See also* DEFINITE (2), INTENT, MOTIONLESS, UNCHANGING.

fixture *n.* Something attached as a permanent part of something else ▸ apparatus, fitting, installation. [*Compare* ATTACHMENT.] —*See also* FAUCET.

fizz *n.* —*See* FOAM, HISS (1).

fizz *v.* —*See* FOAM, HISS (1).

fizzle *v.* —*See* FADE, HISS (1).

fizzle *n.* —*See* DISAPPOINTMENT (2), HISS (1).

fizzy *adj.* —*See* FOAMY.

fjord *n.* —*See* INLET.

flabbergast *v.* —*See* STAGGER (2).

flabby *adj.* —*See* FAT (1), LIMP.

flaccid *adj.* —*See* LIMP.

flag[1] *n.* A piece of fabric used as a symbol or emblem ▸ banderole, banner, banneret, colors, ensign, jack, oriflamme, pennant, pennon, standard, streamer. —*See also* TICKET (1).

flag *v.* To attach a ticket to ▸ earmark, label, mark, tag, ticket. —*See also* GESTURE.

flag[2] *v.* —*See* FADE, TIRE (2), WILT.

flagellate *v.* —*See* BEAT (2).

flagitiousness *n.* —*See* CORRUPTION (1).

flagrancy *n.* The quality or state of being flagrant ▸ egregiousness, glaringness, grossness, rankness. [*Compare* IMPUDENCE, OUTRAGEOUSNESS.]

flagrant *adj.* Conspicuously bad extremely or offensive ▸ egregious, glaring, gross, rank. [*Compare* OFFENSIVE, OUTRAGEOUS, SHAMELESS.]

flail *v.* 1. To swing about or strike at wildly ▸ thrash, thresh, toss. [*Compare* STAGGER, SWAY.] 2. To beat plants to separate the grain from the straw ▸ thrash, thresh. —*See also* BEAT (1).

flair *n.* —*See* TALENT.

flak *n.* —*See* BARRAGE, CRITICISM.

flake *n.* A small, thin piece of something ▸ chip, leaf, paring, scale, slice, sliver, shaving. [*Compare* BIT[1], CUT, END.] —*See also* CHARACTER (5).

flake *v.* To come or fall off in small, thin pieces ▸ chip, desquamate, exfoliate, peel, scale, shed.

flamboyant *adj.* —*See* DRAMATIC (2), ORNATE, SHOWY.

flame *n.* The visible signs of combustion ▸ blaze, conflagration, fire, flare-up. —*See also* LOVER.

flame *v.* —*See* BURN (2).

flameproof or **flame-resistant** or **flame-retardant** *adj.* —*See* FIREPROOF.

flaming *adj.* —*See* BURNING, PASSIONATE.

tropical wading bird with pink plumage, long legs, and a long flexible neck.

flam·ma·ble (flăm′ə-bəl) ▸ *adj.* Easily ignited and capable of burning rapidly. **—flam′ma·bil′i·ty** *n.* **—flam′ma·ble** *n.*

flan (flăn, flän, fläɴ) ▸ *n.* **1.** A tart with a filling of custard, fruit, or cheese. **2.** See **crème caramel.**

Flan·ders (flăn′dərz) ▸ A historical region of NW Europe including parts of N France, W Belgium, and SW Netherlands.

flange (flănj) ▸ *n.* A protruding rim or edge, as on a wheel, used to strengthen an object or hold it in place. **—flange** *v.*

flank (flăngk) ▸ *n.* **1.** The fleshy section of the side between the last rib and the hip. **2.** A cut of meat from the flank of an animal. **3.** A lateral part or side. **4.** The right or left side of a military formation. ▸ *v.* **1.** To protect or guard the flank of. **2.** To menace or attack the flank of. **3.** To be placed or situated at the flank of.

flan·nel (flăn′əl) ▸ *n.* **1.** A soft woven cloth of wool or a wool blend. **2. flannels** Trousers or undergarments made of wool.

flan·nel·ette (flăn′ə-lĕt′) ▸ *n.* A soft napped cotton cloth.

flap (flăp) ▸ *n.* **1.** A flat, usu. thin piece attached at only one side, as on an envelope. **2.** The act or sound of flapping. **3.** A blow given with something flat. **4.** *Informal* A commotion or disturbance. ▸ *v.* **flapped, flap·ping. 1.** To wave (e.g., wings) up and down. **2.** To wave loosely; flutter. **3.** To hit with something broad and flat.

flap·jack (flăp′jăk′) ▸ *n.* See **pancake.**

flap·per (flăp′ər) ▸ *n.* **1.** A broad, flexible part, such as a flipper. **2.** A young woman in the 1920s who showed disdain for conventional dress and behavior.

flare (flâr) ▸ *v.* **flared, flar·ing. 1.** To flame up with a bright, wavering light. **2.** To burst into intense, sudden flame. **3.** To erupt or intensify suddenly. **4.** To expand or open outward in shape, as a skirt. ▸ *n.* **1.** A brief, wavering blaze of light. **2.** A device that produces a bright light for signaling or illumination. **3.** An outbreak, as of emotion. **4.** An expanding outward.

flare-up (flâr′ŭp′) ▸ *n.* A sudden outburst, as of flame or anger.

flash (flăsh) ▸ *v.* **1.** To burst forth into or as if into flame. **2.** To give off light or be lighted in sudden or intermittent bursts. **3.** To appear or cause to appear suddenly. **4.** To move rapidly. **5.** To communicate (information) at great speed. **6.** To display ostentatiously; flaunt. ▸ *n.* **1.** A sudden, brief, intense display of light. **2.** A sudden perception. **3.** A split second; instant. **4.** A brief news dispatch or transmission. **5a.** Instantaneous illumination for photography. **b.** A device used to produce such illumination.

flash·back (flăsh′băk′) ▸ *n.* **1.** A literary or cinematic device in which an earlier event is inserted into the normal chronological order of a narrative. **2.** An unexpected recurrence of the effects of a hallucinogenic drug.

flash·bulb or **flash bulb** (flăsh′bŭlb′) ▸ *n.* A glass bulb filled with finely shredded metal foil that is ignited by electricity to produce a bright flash for taking photographs.

flash flood ▸ *n.* A sudden violent flood.

flash-for·ward (flăsh′fôr′wərd) ▸ *n.* A literary or cinematic device in which the chronological sequence of events is interrupted by the interjection of a future event.

flash·gun (flăsh′gŭn′) ▸ *n.* A dry-cell powered photographic apparatus that holds and electrically triggers a flashbulb.

flash·ing (flăsh′ĭng) ▸ *n.* Sheet metal used to reinforce and weatherproof the joints and angles of a roof.

flash lamp ▸ *n.* An electric lamp for producing a brief bright light for use in photography.

flash·light (flăsh′līt′) ▸ *n.* A small portable lamp usu. powered by batteries.

flash point ▸ *n.* The lowest temperature at which the vapor of a combustible liquid can be made to ignite.

flash·y (flăsh′ē) ▸ *adj.* **-i·er, -i·est. 1.** Cheap and showy. **2.** Giving a momentary or superficial brilliance. **—flash′i·ly** *adv.* **—flash′i·ness** *n.*

flask (flăsk) ▸ *n.* **1.** A flat, relatively thin container for liquor. **2.** A vial or round long-necked vessel for laboratory use.

flat[1] (flăt) ▸ *adj.* **flat·ter, flat·test. 1.** Having a horizontal surface without a slope, tilt, or curvature. **2.** Stretched out or lying at full length along the ground; prone. **3.** Free of qualification; absolute: *a flat refusal.* **4.** Fixed; unvarying: *a flat rate.* **5.** Lacking interest or excitement; dull. **6a.** Lacking in flavor. **b.** Having lost effervescence. **7.** Deflated, as a tire. **8.** *Mus.* **a.** Being below the correct pitch. **b.** Being one half step lower than the corresponding natural key. ▸ *adv.* **1.** Level with the ground; horizontally. **2.** On or up against a flat surface; at full length. **3a.** Directly; completely: *flat broke.* **b.** Exactly; precisely: *arrived in six minutes flat.* **4.** *Mus.* Below the intended pitch. ▸ *n.* **1.** A flat surface or part. **2.** often **flats** A stretch of level ground. **3.** A shallow frame or box for seeds or seedlings. **4.** A deflated tire. **5.** A shoe with a flat heel. **6.** *Mus.* **a.** A sign (♭) used to indicate that a note is to be lowered by a half step. **b.** A note that is lowered a half step. ▸ *v.* **flat·ted, flat·ting. 1.** To make flat; flatten. **2.** *Mus.* **a.** To lower (a note) a semitone. **b.** To sing or play below the proper pitch. **—flat′ly** *adv.* **—flat′ness** *n.*

flat[2] (flăt) ▸ *n.* An apartment on one floor of a building.

flat·bed (flăt′bĕd′) ▸ *n.* An open truck bed or trailer with no sides.

flat·boat (flăt′bōt′) ▸ *n.* A boat with a flat bottom used for transporting freight.

flat·car (flăt′kär′) ▸ *n.* A railroad freight car without sides or roof.

flat·fish (flăt′fĭsh′) ▸ *n.* Any of numerous chiefly marine fishes, including flounders and soles, having a laterally compressed body with both eyes on the upper side.

flat·foot (flăt′fo͝ot′) ▸ *n.* **1.** *pl.* **-feet** (-fēt′). A condition in which the arch of the foot is flattened so that the entire sole makes contact with the ground. **2.** *pl.* **-foots.** *Slang* A police officer. **—flat′-foot′ed** *adj.*

Flat·head (flăt′hĕd′) ▸ *n., pl.* **-head** or **-heads. 1.** A member of a Native American people of W Montana and N Idaho. **2.** The Salishan language of the Flathead.

flat·i·ron (flăt′ī′ərn) ▸ *n.* An iron for pressing clothes.

flat·ten (flăt′n) ▸ *v.* **1.** To make or become flat or flatter.

THESAURUS

flammable *adj.* Easily ignited ▸ combustible, ignitable, inflammable.

flank *n.* One of two or more contrasted parts or places identified by its location with respect to a center ▸ hand, side.

flank *v.* —*See* ADJOIN.

flap *v.* **1.** To move the arms or wings up and down ▸ beat, flitter, flop, flutter, waggle, wave. **2.** To move or cause to move about while being fixed at one edge ▸ flutter, fly, wave. —*See also* BLOW[1] (2), FLY (1).

flap *n.* A flat, thin piece that usually hangs over something ▸ fly, skirt. —*See also* AGITATION (1).

flapping *adj.* —*See* LOOSE (1).

flare *v.* —*See* BREAK OUT, BURN (2), GLARE (2).

flare up *v.* —*See* ANGER (2).

flare *n.* An intense blinding light ▸ blaze, dazzle, glare. —*See also* ERUPTION.

flare-up *n.* The visible signs of combustion ▸ blaze, conflagration, fire, flame. —*See also* BLAST (2), ERUPTION, OUTBURST.

flash *n.* **1.** A sudden burst of light ▸ blink, coruscation, flicker, glance, gleam, glimmer, glint, scintillation, spark, twinkle, wink. **2.** A very brief interval of time ▸ blink, crack, instant, minute, moment, second, trice, twinkle, twinkling, wink. *Informal:* jiff, jiffy, sec. —*See also* ITEM.

flash *v.* —*See* DISPLAY, GLITTER, RUSH.

flash point *n.* —*See* EMERGENCY.

flashy *adj.* —*See* GAUDY.

flat *adj.* **1.** Lying down ▸ decumbent, horizontal, procumbent, prone, prostrate, reclining, recumbent, stretched out, supine. **2.** Lacking an appetizing flavor ▸ bland, flavorless, insipid, stale, tasteless, unsavory. —*See also* DULL (1), DULL (2), EVEN (1), UNCHANGING, UTTER[2].

flat *adv.* —*See* COMPLETELY (1).

flat *v.* —*See* EVEN.

flatfoot *n.* —*See* POLICE OFFICER.

flatly *adv.* In a direct, positive manner ▸ directly, emphatically, point-blank, positively. *Informal:* flat out. *Idiom:* in no uncertain terms.

flatness *n.* —*See* CHANGELESSNESS, DULLNESS.

flat out *adv.* —*See* FAST, FLATLY.

flat-out *adj.* —*See* UTTER[2].

flatten *v.* —*See* DROP (3), EVEN.

2. To knock down. **—flat′ten·er** *n.*
flat·ter (flăt′ər) ▸ *v.* **1.** To compliment excessively and often insincerely, esp. to win favor. **2.** To please or gratify the vanity of. **3.** To portray favorably. **—flat′ter·er** *n.* **—flat′ter·ing·ly** *adv.* **—flat′ter·y** *n.*
flat·top (flăt′tŏp′) ▸ *n. Informal* **1.** An aircraft carrier. **2.** A short, level haircut.
flat·u·lent (flăch′ə-lənt) ▸ *adj.* **1.** Afflicted with or caused by excessive gas in the digestive tract. **2.** Pompous; bloated. **—flat′u·lence** *n.* **—flat′u·lent·ly** *adv.*
flat·ware (flăt′wâr′) ▸ *n.* **1.** Tableware that is fairly flat and fashioned usu. of a single piece, as plates. **2.** Table utensils such as knives, forks, and spoons.
flat·worm (flăt′wûrm′) ▸ *n.* Any of various flat-bodied worms, as the tapeworm.
flaunt (flônt) ▸ *v.* To exhibit ostentatiously or shamelessly; show off. **—flaunt′er** *n.* **—flaunt′ing·ly** *adv.*
flau·tist (flô′tĭst, flou′-) ▸ *n.* A flutist.
fla·vor (flā′vər) ▸ *n.* **1.** Distinctive taste; savor. **2.** A distinctive quality. **3.** A flavoring. ▸ *v.* To give flavor to. **—fla′vor·ful** *adj.* **—fla′vor·less** *adj.*
fla·vor·ing (flā′vər-ĭng) ▸ *n.* A substance, as an extract or spice, that imparts flavor.
flaw (flô) ▸ *n.* An imperfection or blemish; defect. ▸ *v.* To make or become defective.
flaw·less (flô′lĭs) ▸ *adj.* Being entirely without flaw or imperfection. **—flaw′less·ly** *adv.* **—flaw′less·ness** *n.*
flax (flăks) ▸ *n.* **1.** Any of several plants having blue flowers and slender fibrous stems. **2.** The fine yellowish textile fiber obtained from flax.
flax·en (flăk′sən) ▸ *adj.* **1.** Made of or resembling flax. **2.** Having the pale yellowish color of flax fiber.
flay (flā) ▸ *v.* **1.** To strip off the skin of. **2.** To scold or criticize harshly. **—flay′er** *n.*
fl. dr. ▸ *abbr.* fluid dram
flea (flē) ▸ *n.* Any of various small, wingless, bloodsucking insects that are parasitic on warm-blooded animals.
flea collar ▸ *n.* A pet collar containing a substance that repels or kills fleas.
flea market ▸ *n.* A market, usu. held outdoors, where antiques, used household goods, and curios are sold.
fleck (flĕk) ▸ *n.* **1.** A tiny mark or spot. **2.** A small bit or flake. ▸ *v.* To spot or streak.
fledg·ling also **fledge·ling** (flĕj′lĭng) ▸ *n.* **1.** A young bird that has recently acquired its flight feathers. **2.** A young or inexperienced person. **—fledg′ling** *adj.*
flee (flē) ▸ *v.* **fled** (flĕd), **flee·ing. 1.** To run away, as from trouble or danger. **2.** To pass swiftly away; vanish. **—fle′er** *n.*
fleece (flēs) ▸ *n.* **1.** The coat of wool of a sheep or similar animal. **2.** A soft woolly covering or mass. ▸ *v.* **fleeced, fleec·ing. 1.** To defraud of money or property; swindle. **2.** To shear the fleece from. **—fleec′er** *n.* **—fleec′i·ly** *adv.* **—fleec′i·ness** *n.* **—fleec′y** *adj.*
fleet[1] (flēt) ▸ *n.* **1.** A number of warships operating under one command. **2.** A group of vessels or vehicles, such as taxicabs, owned or operated as a unit.
fleet[2] (flēt) ▸ *adj.* **-er, -est. 1.** Moving swiftly; rapid or nimble. **2.** Fleeting; evanescent. ▸ *v.* To move or pass swiftly. **—fleet′ly** *adv.* **—fleet′ness** *n.*
Fleet Admiral ▸ *n.* The highest rank in the US Navy.
fleet·ing (flē′tĭng) ▸ *adj.* Passing quickly; ephemeral. **—fleet′ing·ly** *adv.*
Flem·ing (flĕm′ĭng) ▸ *n.* **1.** A native or inhabitant of Flanders. **2.** A Belgian who speaks Flemish.
Flem·ish (flĕm′ĭsh) ▸ *adj.* Of Flanders or the Flemings. ▸ *n.* **1.** The Germanic language of the Flemings. **2.** The Flemings.
fle·ro·vi·um (flə-rō′vē-əm) ▸ *n. Symbol* **Fl** A synthetic radioactive element. At. no. 114.
flesh (flĕsh) ▸ *n.* **1.** The soft tissue of the body, consisting mainly of skeletal muscle and fat. **2.** Soft tissue of an animal, used as food. **3.** *Bot.* The pulpy, usu. edible part of a fruit or vegetable. **4.** The body as opposed to the mind or soul. **5.** Humankind in general; humanity. ▸ *v.* To give substance or detail to; fill out. ***—idiom:* in the flesh 1.** Alive. **2.** In person; present.
flesh·ly (flĕsh′lē) ▸ *adj.* **-li·er, -li·est. 1.** Relating to the body. **2.** Relating to bodily pleasure; sensual.
flesh·y (flĕsh′ē) ▸ *adj.* **-i·er, -i·est. 1.** Of or resembling flesh. **2.** Having abundant flesh; plump. **3.** Having a juicy or pulpy texture. **4.** Fleshly; carnal. **—flesh′i·ness** *n.*
fleur-de-lis (flûr′də-lē′, flo͝or′-) ▸ *n., pl.* **fleurs-de-lis** (flûr′də-lēz′, flo͝or′-). A decorative motif consisting of a stylized three-petaled iris flower.
flew (flo͞o) ▸ *v.* P.t. of **fly**[1].
flex (flĕks) ▸ *v.* **1.** To bend (something pliant or elastic). **2.** To contract (e.g., a muscle). **3.** To exhibit or show off the strength of.
flex·i·ble (flĕk′sə-bəl) ▸ *adj.* **1.** Capable of being bent or flexed; pliable. **2.** Responsive to change; adaptable.

THESAURUS

flatter *v.* **1.** To compliment excessively and ingratiatingly ▸ adulate, blandish, butter up, honey. *Informal:* soft-soap, sweet-talk. [*Compare* COAX, DECEIVE, FAWN, SEDUCE.] **2.** To look good on or with ▸ become, enhance, suit. ***Idiom:*** put in the best light. [*Compare* SUIT.]
flatterer *n.* —*See* SYCOPHANT.
flattering *adj.* Purposefully contrived to gain favor ▸ blandishing, buttery, cajoling, fawning, honey-tongued, ingratiating, ingratiatory, insinuating, saccharine, smooth-tongued, soft-soaping, sugary, wheedling. *Informal:* brownnosing. —*See also* BECOMING.
flattery *n.* Excessive, ingratiating praise ▸ adulation, blandishment, blarney, oil. *Informal:* apple-polishing, soft soap, sweet talk.
flatulent *adj.* —*See* INFLATED.
flaunt *v.* —*See* DISPLAY.
flavor *n.* **1.** A distinctive property of a substance affecting the sense of taste ▸ relish, savor, smack, tang, taste, zest. **2.** A distinctive yet intangible quality felt to be characteristic of a given thing ▸ aroma, atmosphere, savor, smack. [*Compare* QUALITY.] —*See also* FLAVORING.
flavor *v.* To impart flavor to ▸ season, spice (up), zest.
flavorful *adj.* —*See* DELICIOUS.
flavoring *n.* A substance that imparts taste ▸ condiment, flavor, seasoner, seasoning, spice. [*Compare* ZEST.]
flavorless *adj.* —*See* DULL (1), FLAT (2).
flavorlessness *n.* —*See* DULLNESS.
flaw *n.* —*See* DEFECT, DISADVANTAGE.
flaw *v.* —*See* DAMAGE.
flawed *adj.* Having a defect or defects ▸ amiss, blemished, defective, faulty, imperfect. [*Compare* SHABBY, TRICK.]
flawless *adj.* —*See* GOOD (2), PERFECT.
flaxen-haired *adj.* —*See* FAIR[1] (2).
flay *v.* —*See* BARE, BEAT (2), SLAM (1).
fleck *n.* —*See* POINT (2).
fleck *v.* —*See* SPECKLE.
fledgling *n.* —*See* BEGINNER.
flee *v.* —*See* ESCAPE (1).
fleece *v.* —*See* CHEAT (1).
fleecy *adj.* —*See* HAIRY.
fleer *v.* To smile or laugh scornfully or derisively ▸ sneer, snicker, snigger. *Idiom:* curl one's lip. [*Compare* GRIMACE, LAUGH, RIDICULE.]
fleer *n.* A facial expression or laugh conveying scorn or derision ▸ sneer, snicker, snigger. [*Compare* SMILE.] —*See also* TAUNT.
fleet[1] *n.* A group of warships operating under one command ▸ armada, flotilla.
fleet[2] *adj.* —*See* FAST (1), TRANSITORY.
fleet *v.* —*See* RUSH.
fleeting *adj.* —*See* QUICK, TRANSITORY.
fleetness *n.* —*See* HASTE (1).
flesh *n.* —*See* HUMANKIND.
fleshless *adj.* —*See* THIN (1).
fleshliness *n.* —*See* SENSUALITY (1).
fleshly *adj.* —*See* BODILY, SENSUAL (2).
fleshy *adj.* —*See* BODILY, FAT (1), SENSUAL (2).
flex *v.* —*See* BEND (2).
flexibility *n.* **1.** The quality or state of being flexible ▸ bendability, bounce, ductility, elasticity, flexibleness, give, limberness, lissomeness, litheness, malleability, malleableness, plasticity, pliability, pliableness, pliancy, pliantness, resilience, resiliency, spring, springiness, suppleness, tractableness, tractability. **2.** The ability to recover quickly from depression or discouragement ▸ bounce, buoyancy, elasticity, resilience, resiliency.
flexible *adj.* **1.** Capable of withstand-

—flex′i·bil′i·ty, flex′i·ble·ness *n.* **—flex′i·bly** *adv.*
flex·or (flĕk′sər) ▸ *n.* A muscle that when contracted acts to bend a joint or limb in the body.
flex·time (flĕks′tīm′) ▸ *n.* An arrangement by which employees may set their own work schedules.
flex·ure (flĕk′shər) ▸ *n.* A curve, turn, or fold.
flick[1] (flĭk) ▸ *n.* **1.** A light quick blow or touch. **2.** A light splash, dash, or daub. ▸ *v.* **1.** To touch or hit with a light quick blow. **2.** To cause to move with a light blow: *flick a switch.*
flick[2] (flĭk) ▸ *n. Slang* A movie.
flick·er[1] (flĭk′ər) ▸ *v.* **1.** To move waveringly; flutter. **2.** To burn unsteadily or fitfully. ▸ *n.* **1.** A brief movement; tremor. **2.** An inconstant or wavering light. **3.** A brief sensation.
flick·er[2] (flĭk′ər) ▸ *n.* A large woodpecker with a brown back, spotted breast, and white rump.
flied (flīd) ▸ *v.* P.t. and p.part. of **fly**[1] 6.
fli·er also **fly·er** (flī′ər) ▸ *n.* **1.** One that flies, esp. a pilot. **2.** A passenger in an aircraft. **3.** A circular for mass distribution.
flight[1] (flīt) ▸ *n.* **1.** The act or process of flying. **2.** A swift passage or movement. **3.** A scheduled airline trip. **4.** A group, esp. of birds or aircraft, flying together. **5.** An exuberant or transcendent effort or display: *a flight of the imagination.* **6.** A series of stairs rising from one landing to another.
flight[2] (flīt) ▸ *n.* An act of running away.
flight deck ▸ *n.* **1.** The upper deck of an aircraft carrier, used as a runway. **2.** An elevated compartment in certain aircraft, used by the pilot, copilot, and flight engineer.
flight·less (flīt′lĭs) ▸ *adj.* Incapable of flying, as certain birds.
flight recorder ▸ *n.* A device, as on certain aircraft, that documents preflight checks, in-flight procedures, and the landing.
flight·y (flī′tē) ▸ *adj.* **-i·er, -i·est. 1.** Capricious or impulsive. **2.** Irresponsible or silly. **3.** Easily excited. **—flight′i·ly** *adv.* **—flight′i·ness** *n.*
flim·flam (flĭm′flăm′) ▸ *n. Informal* **1.** Nonsense; humbug. **2.** A deception; swindle. **—flim′flam′** *v.* **—flim′flam′mer** *n.* **—flim′flam′mer·y** *n.*
flim·sy (flĭm′zē) ▸ *adj.* **-si·er, -si·est. 1.** Light, thin, and insubstantial. **2.** Lacking solidity or strength. **3.** Lacking plausibility; unconvincing. **—flim′si·ly** *adv.* **—flim′si·ness** *n.*
flinch (flĭnch) ▸ *v.* **1.** To start or wince involuntarily, as from pain. **2.** To recoil, as from something unpleasant. **—flinch** *n.* **—flinch′er** *n.*
fling (flĭng) ▸ *v.* **flung** (flŭng), **fling·ing. 1.** To throw or move quickly and forcefully. **2.** To throw (oneself) into an activity with abandon and energy. **3.** To cast aside; discard. ▸ *n.* **1.** The act of flinging. **2.** A brief period of indulging one's impulses. **3.** *Informal* A usu. brief attempt or effort.
flint (flĭnt) ▸ *n.* **1.** A very hard, fine-grained quartz that sparks when struck with steel. **2.** A small solid cylinder of a spark-producing alloy, used in lighters to ignite the fuel. **—flint′y** *adj.*
flint·lock (flĭnt′lŏk′) ▸ *n.* **1.** An obsolete gunlock in which a flint ignites the charge. **2.** A firearm having a flintlock.
flip (flĭp) ▸ *v.* **flipped, flip·ping. 1.** To throw or toss with a light brisk motion. **2.** To toss in the air, imparting a spin. **3a.** To turn over, esp. with a quick motion. **b.** To turn through; leaf. **4.** To flick. **5.** To move or operate (e.g., a lever or switch). **6.** To turn a somersault. **7a.** *Slang* To go crazy. **b.** To react strongly and esp. enthusiastically. ▸ *n.* The act of flipping, esp.: **a.** A flick. **b.** A short quick movement. **c.** A somersault. ▸ *adj.* **flip·per, flip·pest.** *Informal* Marked by casual disrespect; impertinent.
flip-flop (flĭp′flŏp′) ▸ *n.* **1.** A backward somersault or handspring. **2.** *Informal* A reversal, as of a stand or position. **3.** A backless, often foam rubber sandal. **—flip′-flop′** *v.*
flip·pant (flĭp′ənt) ▸ *adj.* Casually disrespectful; pert. **—flip′pan·cy** *n.* **—flip′pant·ly** *adv.*
flip·per (flĭp′ər) ▸ *n.* **1.** A wide flat limb, as of a seal, adapted for swimming. **2.** A wide rubber covering for the foot, used in swimming.
flirt (flûrt) ▸ *v.* **1.** To make coyly romantic or sexual overtures. **2.** To deal triflingly with: *flirt with danger.* ▸ *n.* One given to flirting. **—flir·ta′tion** *n.* **—flir·ta′tious** *adj.* **—flir·ta′tious·ly** *adv.* **—flir·ta′tious·ness** *n.*
flit (flĭt) ▸ *v.* **flit·ted, flit·ting.** To move quickly and nimbly. **—flit′ter** *n.*
flit·ter (flĭt′ər) ▸ *v.* To flutter.
float (flōt) ▸ *v.* **1a.** To remain or cause to remain suspended in or on a fluid without sinking. **b.** To be or cause to be suspended in space. **2.** To move from place to place at random. **3.** To move easily or lightly. **4.** To release (a security) for sale. **5.** To offer for consideration; suggest: *floated an idea.* ▸ *n.* **1.** Something that floats. **2.** A buoyant object

THESAURUS

ing stress without injury ▸ elastic, flexile, plastic, resilient, springy, supple. [*Compare* EXTENSIBLE.] **2.** Having or showing bodily flexibility ▸ limber, lissome, lithe, lithesome, supple. [*Compare* LIMP.] **3.** Easily altered or influenced ▸ ductile, elastic, flexile, impressionable, malleable, plastic, pliable, pliant, suggestible, supple. [*Compare* OBEDIENT.] *—See also* ADAPTABLE, MALLEABLE.
flexibleness *n.* *—See* FLEXIBILITY (1).
flexile *adj.* *—See* FLEXIBLE (1), FLEXIBLE (3), MALLEABLE.
flexuous *adj.* *—See* MALLEABLE, WINDING.
flexure *n.* *—See* BEND.
flick *n. Slang* A motion picture ▸ film, motion picture, movie, picture. *—See also* BRUSH[1].
flick *v.* *—See* BRUSH[1], TAP[1] (1).
flicker *v.* To move like a bird in flight ▸ flit, flitter, flutter. [*Compare* FLAP.] *—See also* GLITTER, SMOLDER.
flicker *n.* *—See* FLASH (1).
flier *n.* **1.** A person who flies an airplane ▸ aviator, pilot. *Slang:* flyboy. **2.** An announcement that is distributed on paper to a large number of people ▸ circular, handbill, leaflet, notice.
flight *n.* *—See* ESCAPE (1), FLOCK, JOURNEY.
flighty *adj.* *—See* CAPRICIOUS, GIDDY (2).
flimflam *n.* *—See* CHEAT (1).
flimflammer *n.* *—See* CHEAT (2).
flimsiness *n.* *—See* INFIRMITY.
flimsy *adj.* *—See* IMPLAUSIBLE, PALE (2), WEAK (1).
flinch *v.* To draw away or pull back in fear ▸ blench, cower, cringe, quail, recoil, shrink, shy, start, wince. [*Compare* FEAR.]
flinch *n.* *—See* RECOIL.
fling *v.* *—See* THROW.
fling *n.* **1.** *Informal* A brief trial ▸ crack, go, stab, try. *Informal:* shot, whack, whirl. **2.** A usually brief romance entered into lightly or frivolously ▸ dalliance, flirtation. [*Compare* LOVE.] *—See also* BINGE, THROW.
flinty *adj.* *—See* FORBIDDING.
flip *v.* To throw a coin in order to decide something ▸ toss. *Idiom:* call heads or tails.
flip through *v.* *—See* BROWSE (1).
flip *adj.* *—See* IMPUDENT.
flip-flop *n.* *—See* REVERSAL (1).
flippancy *n.* *—See* IMPUDENCE.
flippant *adj.* *—See* IMPUDENT.
flirt *v.* **1.** To treat something lightly or flippantly ▸ dally, play, toy, trifle. **2.** To make amorous advances without serious intentions ▸ coquet, dally, toy, trifle. *Slang:* mash. *Idioms:* come on to, make advances, make a play for, make eyes at. [*Compare* PHILANDER, SEDUCE.]
flirt *n.* **1.** A woman who is given to flirting ▸ coquette, tease. *Informal:* vamp. [*Compare* SEDUCTRESS.] **2.** A man who is given to flirting ▸ wolf. *Slang:* masher. [*Compare* PHILANDERER, SEDUCER.]
flirtation *n.* **1.** The practice of flirting ▸ coquetry, dalliance. **2.** A usually brief romance entered into lightly or frivolously ▸ dalliance, fling. [*Compare* LOVE.]
flirtatious or **flirty** *adj.* Given to flirting ▸ coquettish, coy.
flit *v.* To move like a bird in flight ▸ flicker, flitter, flutter. [*Compare* FLAP.] *—See also* FLY (1), RUSH.
flitter *v.* To move like a bird in flight ▸ flicker, flit, flutter. *—See also* FLAP (1), FLY (1).
float *v.* **1.** To stay on top of the surface of water or stay in mid-air ▸ bob, be buoyed, be buoyant, have buoyancy, hover, stay afloat. **2.** To move along with or be carried away by the action

that holds a net or fishing line afloat. 3. A decorated exhibit on a mobile platform in a parade. 4. A soft drink with ice cream floating in it.

float·er (flō′tər) ▸ *n.* 1. One that floats. 2. One who wanders; drifter. 3. An employee reassigned from job to job or shift to shift within an operation. 4. An insurance policy that protects movable property in transit.

flock¹ (flŏk) ▸ *n.* 1. A group of animals that live, travel, or feed together. 2. A group of people, esp. under the leadership of one person. 3. A large number; host. ▸ *v.* To congregate or travel in a flock or crowd.

flock² (flŏk) ▸ *n.* 1. A tuft, as of fiber or hair. 2. Pulverized fibers applied to paper or cloth to produce a texture or pattern. **—flock** *v.*

floe (flō) ▸ *n.* A large flat mass of floating ice.

flog (flŏg, flôg) ▸ *v.* **flogged, flog·ging.** To beat severely with a whip or rod. **—flog′ger** *n.*

flood (flŭd) ▸ *n.* 1. An overflowing of water onto normally dry land. 2. An abundant flow or outpouring: *a flood of applications.* 3. A floodlight. 4. **Flood** The universal deluge recorded in the Bible. ▸ *v.* 1. To cover with or as if with a flood; inundate. 2. To fill with an abundance or excess.

flood·gate (flŭd′gāt′) ▸ *n.* 1. A gate that controls the flow of a body of water. 2. Something that restrains a flood or outpouring.

flood·light (flŭd′līt′) ▸ *n.* 1. Artificial light in an intensely bright and broad beam. 2. A unit that produces such a beam. ▸ *v.* To illuminate with a floodlight.

flood·plain (flŭd′plān′) ▸ *n.* A plain bordering a river and subject to flooding.

floor (flôr) ▸ *n.* 1. The surface of a room on which one stands. 2. A story or level of a building. 3a. The part of a legislative chamber where members are seated and from which they speak. b. The right to address an assembly. c. The body of assembly members. 4. The part of a room or building where the principal business or work takes place. 5. The ground or lowermost surface, as of a forest or ocean. 6. A lower limit or base: *a pricing floor.* ▸ *v.* 1. To provide with a floor. 2. To knock down. 3. To stun; overwhelm.

floor leader ▸ *n.* The member of a legislature chosen by fellow party members to be in charge of the party's activities on the floor.

floor plan ▸ *n.* A scale diagram of a room or building.

floor·show (flôr′shō′) ▸ *n.* The entertainment presented in a nightclub.

floor·walk·er (flôr′wô′kər) ▸ *n.* An employee of a department store who supervises sales personnel and assists customers.

floo·zy also **floo·zie** (flo͞o′zē) ▸ *n., pl.* **-zies.** *Slang* A gaudy or tawdry woman.

flop (flŏp) ▸ *v.* **flopped, flop·ping.** 1. To fall or lie down heavily and noisily. 2. To move about loosely or limply. 3. *Informal* To fail utterly. ▸ *n.* 1. The act or sound of flopping. 2. *Informal* An utter failure.

flop·house (flŏp′hous′) ▸ *n.* A cheap hotel.

flop·py (flŏp′ē) ▸ *adj.* **-pi·er, -pi·est.** Tending to flop; loose and flexible. ▸ *n., pl.* **-pies.** *Comp. Sci.* A floppy disk. **—flop′pi·ly** *adv.* **—flop′pi·ness** *n.*

floppy disk ▸ *n.* A flexible plastic disk coated with magnetic material, used to store computer data magnetically; diskette.

flo·ra (flôr′ə) ▸ *n., pl.* **flo·ras** or **flo·rae** (flôr′ē′). Plants collectively, esp. the plants of a particular region or time.

flo·ral (flôr′əl) ▸ *adj.* Of or relating to flowers. **—flo′ral·ly** *adv.*

Flor·ence (flôr′əns, flŏr′-) ▸ A city of central Italy E of Pisa. Pop. 352,000.

flo·res·cence (flô-rĕs′əns, flə-) ▸ *n.* A condition, time, or period of flowering. **—flo·res′cent** *adj.*

flor·id (flôr′ĭd, flŏr′-) ▸ *adj.* 1. Flushed with rosy color; ruddy. 2. Very ornate; flowery. **—flo·rid′i·ty** (flə-rĭd′ĭ-tē, flô-), **flor′id·ness** *n.* **—flor′id·ly** *adv.*

Flor·i·da (flôr′ĭ-də, flŏr′-) ▸ A state of the SE US. Cap. Tallahassee. Pop. 16,000,000. **—Flo·rid′i·an** (flə-rĭd′ē-ən), **Flor′i·dan** (-ĭd-n) *adj. & n.*

Florida Keys ▸ A chain of small islands extending about 241 km (150 mi) from S of Miami to Key West.

flor·in (flôr′ĭn, flŏr′-) ▸ *n.* 1. A guilder. 2. A former British coin worth two shillings.

flo·rist (flôr′ĭst, flŏr′-) ▸ *n.* One who raises or sells flowers and plants.

floss (flôs, flŏs) ▸ *n.* 1. Dental floss. 2. Short or waste silk fibers. 3. A soft, loosely twisted thread. 4. A silky fibrous substance. ▸ *v.* To clean between (teeth) with dental floss.

floss·y (flô′sē, flŏs′ē) ▸ *adj.* **-i·er, -i·est.** 1. Superficially stylish; slick. 2. Made of or resembling floss. **—floss′i·ness** *n.*

flo·ta·tion (flō-tā′shən) ▸ *n.* The act or condition of floating.

flo·til·la (flō-tĭl′ə) ▸ *n.* 1. A small fleet. 2. A fleet of small craft.

flot·sam (flŏt′səm) ▸ *n.* Wreckage or cargo that remains afloat after a ship has sunk.

flounce¹ (flouns) ▸ *n.* A strip of usu. gathered material attached by one edge, as to a skirt or curtain.

flounce² (flouns) ▸ *v.* **flounced, flounc·ing.** To move with exaggerated motions expressive esp. of displeasure or impatience. ▸ *n.* An act of flouncing.

floun·der¹ (floun′dər) ▸ *v.* 1. To move or thrash about clumsily. 2. To act or proceed in confusion.

floun·der² (floun′dər) ▸ *n., pl.* **-der** or **-ders.** Any of various marine flatfishes that are important food fishes.

flour (flou′ər, flour) ▸ *n.* 1. A fine powdery foodstuff obtained by grinding grain, esp. wheat. 2. A soft fine powder. ▸ *v.* To cover or coat with flour. **—flour′y** *adj.*

flour·ish (flûr′ĭsh, flŭr′-) ▸ *v.* 1. To grow well or luxuriantly; thrive. 2. To do or fare well; succeed. 3. To wield or exhibit dramatically. ▸ *n.* 1. A dramatic movement or gesture. 2. An embellishment or ornamentation, esp. in handwriting.

flout (flout) ▸ *v.* To show contempt for; scorn. **—flout′er** *n.*

flow (flō) ▸ *v.* 1. To move or run freely in or as if in a

THESAURUS

of water ▸ drift, wash. *—See also* BLOW¹ (2), FLY (2), GLIDE (1), LEND.

flock *n.* A number of animals considered collectively ▸ bevy, drove, flight, gaggle, gang, herd, kennel, litter, pack, pride, rout, school, stable, swarm, troop. *—See also* CROWD.

flock *v.* *—See* BAND², CROWD.

flog *v.* *—See* BEAT (2).

flogging *n.* *—See* BEATING.

flood *n.* An abundant or overwhelming flow of water ▸ alluvion, cataract, deluge, downpour, freshet, inundation, overflow, spate, torrent. [*Compare* ABUNDANCE, EXCESS, FLOW.] *—See also* FLOW, OUTBURST.

flood *v.* 1. To flow over completely ▸ deluge, drown, engulf, flush, inundate, overflow, overwhelm, submerge, submerse. [*Compare* DIP, FLOW.] 2. To affect as if by an outpouring of water ▸ deluge, inundate, overwhelm, swamp. *—See also* CROWD, ILLUMINATE (1).

floor *v.* *—See* DROP (3), STAGGER (2).

floozy *n.* *—See* SLUT.

flop *v.* To drop or sink heavily and noisily ▸ plop, plump, plunk. [*Compare* FALL.] *—See also* FAIL (1), FLAP (1), RETIRE (1), SLOUCH (2).

flop *n.* *—See* DISAPPOINTMENT (2), FAILURE (1).

floppy *adj.* *—See* LIMP.

flora *n.* The plants of an area or region ▸ plant life, vegetation, verdure.

florescence *n.* *—See* BLOOM¹ (1).

floret *n.* *—See* FLOWER.

florid *adj.* *—See* GAUDY, ORNATE, RUDDY.

flotilla *n.* A group of warships operating under one command ▸ armada, fleet.

flotsam *n.* *—See* GARBAGE.

flounce *v.* *—See* STRUT.

flounder *v.* To move about in an indolent or clumsy manner ▸ roll about, roll around, wallow, welter. *—See also* BLUNDER, MUDDLE.

flourish *v.* 1. To wield boldly and dramatically ▸ brandish, sweep, wave. [*Compare* HANDLE.] 2. To grow rapidly and luxuriantly ▸ bloom, blossom, thrive. [*Compare* INCREASE.] 3. To be in one's prime ▸ flower, shine. *Idioms:* cut a figure, have one's day in the sun, make a splash. *—See also* PROSPER.

flourishing *adj.* Improving, growing, or succeeding steadily ▸ booming, boomy, prospering, prosperous, roaring, successful, thrifty, thriving. [*Compare* PROFUSE.]

flout *v.* *—See* DISOBEY.

flow *n.* Something suggestive of run-

stream. **2.** To circulate, as the blood in the body. **3.** To proceed steadily and easily. **4.** To appear smooth, harmonious, or graceful. **5.** To hang loosely and gracefully. **6.** To rise. Used of the tide. **7.** To arise. **8.** To abound or teem. ► *n.* **1.** The smooth motion characteristic of fluids. **2.** A stream or current. **3a.** A continuous output: *a flow of ideas.* **b.** A continuous movement or circulation: *the flow of traffic.* **4.** The amount that flows in a given period of time. **5.** The rising of the tide.

flow chart ► *n.* A schematic representation of a sequence of operations.

flow·er (flou′ər) ► *n.* **1.** The reproductive structure of a seed-bearing plant, having specialized male and/or female organs and usu. colorful petals. **2.** A plant cultivated for its blossoms. **3.** The period of highest development; peak. **4.** The highest example or best representative: *the flower of our generation.* ► *v.* **1.** To produce flowers; blossom. **2.** To develop fully; reach a peak.

flow·er·ing plant (flou′ər-ĭng) ► *n.* A plant that produces flowers and fruit.

flow·er·pot (flou′ər-pŏt′) ► *n.* A pot in which plants are grown.

flow·er·y (flou′ə-rē) ► *adj.* **-i·er, -i·est.** **1.** Full of or suggestive of flowers: *a flowery perfume.* **2.** Full of ornate or grandiloquent expressions. **—flow′er·i·ness** *n.*

flown (flōn) ► *v.* P.part. of **fly**[1].

fl. oz. ► *abbr.* fluid ounce

flu (flo͞o) ► *n. Informal* Influenza.

flub (flŭb) ► *v.* **flubbed, flub·bing.** *Informal* To botch or bungle. **—flub** *n.*

fluc·tu·ate (flŭk′cho͞o-āt′) ► *v.* **-at·ed, -at·ing.** **1.** To change or vary irregularly. **2.** To rise and fall in or as if in waves. **—fluc′tu·ant** (-ənt) *adj.* **—fluc′tu·a′tion** *n.*

flue (flo͞o) ► *n.* A pipe, tube, or channel for conveying hot air, gas, steam, or smoke, as in a chimney.

flu·ent (flo͞o′ənt) ► *adj.* **1.** Having facility in the use of a language. **2.** Flowing smoothly and naturally; polished. **3.** Flowing or capable of flowing; fluid. **—flu′en·cy** *n.* **—flu′ent·ly** *adv.*

fluff (flŭf) ► *n.* **1.** Light down or fuzz. **2.** Something having a light, soft, or frothy consistency or appearance. **3.** Something of little consequence. **4.** *Informal* An error or lapse of memory, esp. by an actor or announcer. ► *v.* **1.** To make light and puffy by shaking or patting into a soft loose mass: *fluff a pillow.* **2.** *Informal* To misread or forget: *fluff a line of dialogue.* **—fluff′i·ness** *n.* **—fluff′y** *adj.*

flu·id (flo͞o′ĭd) ► *n.* A substance, such as air or water, whose molecules move freely past one another and that tends to assume the shape of its container. ► *adj.* **1.** Capable of flowing. **2.** Smooth and graceful. **3.** Readily changing or tending to change; variable. **4.** Convertible into cash: *fluid assets.* **—flu·id′i·ty, flu′id·ness** *n.* **—flu′id·ly** *adv.*

fluid ounce ► *n.* See **measurement** table in Appendix.

fluke[1] (flo͝ok) ► *n.* **1.** Any of various flatfishes, esp. a flounder. **2.** See **trematode.**

fluke[2] (flo͝ok) ► *n.* **1.** The triangular blade at the end of an arm of an anchor. **2.** A barb or barbed head, as on an arrow or harpoon. **3.** Either of the two flattened divisions of a whale's tail.

fluke[3] (flo͝ok) ► *n.* An accidental stroke of good luck. **—fluk′y** *adj.*

flume (flo͞om) ► *n.* **1.** A narrow gorge, usu. with a stream flowing through it. **2.** An open artificial channel or chute for carrying a stream of water.

flum·mox (flŭm′əks) ► *v. Informal* To confuse; perplex.

flung (flŭng) ► *v.* P.t. and p.part. of **fling.**

flunk (flŭngk) ► *v. Informal* To fail, esp. in a course or examination.

flun·ky also **flun·key** (flŭng′kē) ► *n., pl.* **-kies** also **-keys.** **1.** A person of slavish or fawning obedience; lackey. **2.** One who does menial or trivial work; drudge.

fluo·resce (flo͝o-rĕs′, flô-) ► *v.* **-resced, -resc·ing.** To undergo, produce, or show fluorescence.

fluo·res·cence (flo͝o-rĕs′əns, flô-) ► *n.* **1.** The emission of electromagnetic radiation, esp. of visible light, stimulated in a substance by the absorption of incident radiation and persisting only as long as the stimulating radiation is continued. **2.** The radiation so emitted. **—fluo·res′cent** *adj.*

fluorescent lamp ► *n.* A lamp consisting of a glass tube whose inner wall is coated with a material that fluoresces when an electrical current causes a vapor within the tube to discharge electrons.

fluor·i·date (flo͝or′ĭ-dāt′, flôr′-) ► *v.* **-dat·ed, -dat·ing.** To add a fluorine compound to (e.g., a water supply) for the purpose of reducing tooth decay. **—fluor′i·da′tion** *n.*

fluor·ide (flo͝or′īd′, flôr′-) ► *n.* A binary compound of fluorine with another element.

fluor·ine (flo͝or′ēn′, -ĭn, flôr′-) ► *n. Symbol* **F** A pale-yellow, corrosive, poisonous gaseous element used in a wide variety of industrially important compounds. At. no. 9.

fluoro– or **fluor–** ► *pref.* **1.** Fluorine: *fluorocarbon.* **2.** Fluorescence: *fluoroscope.*

fluor·o·car·bon (flo͝or′ō-kär′bən, flôr′-) ► *n.* Any of various compounds in which fluorine replaces hydrogen, used as aerosol propellants, refrigerants, and solvents and in making plastics and resins.

fluor·o·scope (flo͝or′ə-skōp′, flôr′-) ► *n.* A mounted fluorescent screen on which the internal structures of an optically opaque object may be viewed as shadows formed by the transmission of x-rays through the object. **—fluor′o·scope′** *v.* **—fluor′o·scop′ic** (-skŏp′ĭk) *adj.* **—fluo·ros′co·py** (flo͝o-rŏs′kə-pē) *n.*

flur·ry (flûr′ē, flŭr′ē) ► *n., pl.* **-ries.** **1.** A brief light snowfall. **2.** A sudden gust of wind. **3.** A sudden burst of activity; stir: *a flurry of preparations.* **—flur′ry** *v.*

flush[1] (flŭsh) ► *v.* **1.** To redden or cause to redden; blush. **2.** To glow, esp. with a reddish color. **3.** To flow suddenly and abundantly. **4.** To wash out or clean by a rapid brief flow of water. **5.** To excite or elate. ► *n.* **1.** A brief copious flow or rush, as of water. **2.** A reddish tinge; blush. **3.** A rush of strong feeling: *a flush of pride.* **4.** A state of freshness, vigor, or growth. ► *adj.* **-er, -est.** **1.** Having a healthy reddish color; blushing. **2.** Prosperous; affluent. **3.** Abundant; plentiful: *flush times.* **4a.** Having surfaces in the same

THESAURUS

ning water ► cascade, current, drift, efflux, flood, flux, gush, outflow, outpour, outpouring, rush, spate, stream, surge, tide. [*Compare* BROOK[1], FLOOD, SPURT.]

flow *v.* **1.** To move freely as a liquid ► circulate, course, purl, ripple, run, stream, sweep. [*Compare* SWIRL.] **2.** To come forth or issue in abundance ► cascade, gush, pour, run, rush, stream, surge, well. [*Compare* FLOOD, SPURT.] *—See also* POUR, STEM, TEEM[1].

flower *n.* The showy reproductive structure of a plant ► bloom, blossom, floret, floweret, flower head, pompon, posy, spike, spray. [*Compare* BOUQUET.] *—See also* BEST (1), BLOOM[1] (1), SOCIETY (1).

flower *v.* To be in one's prime ► flourish, shine. *Idioms:* cut a figure, have one's day in the sun, make a splash. *—See also* BLOOM[1] (1).

flowery *adj.* *—See* ORATORICAL, ORNATE.

flowing *adj.* *—See* FLUENT.

flub *v.* *—See* BOTCH.

fluctuant *adj.* *—See* CHANGEABLE (1).

fluctuate *v.* *—See* CHANGE (2), SWAY.

fluctuation *n.* *—See* CHANGE (1).

fluency *n.* *—See* ELOQUENCE.

fluent *adj.* Marked by facility of expression ► easy, effortless, flowing, fluid, graceful, smooth. [*Compare* ELOQUENT, GLIB.]

fluff *n.* *—See* BLUNDER.

fluffy *adj.* Having little weight; not heavy ► airy, light, lightweight, weightless. *Idiom:* light as air (*or* a feather). [*Compare* IMMATERIAL, SHEER[2].] *—See also* TRIVIAL.

fluid *adj.* Changing easily, as in expression ► changeable, mobile, plastic. [*Compare* UNSTABLE.] *—See also* CHANGEABLE (1), FLUENT.

fluidity *n.* *—See* ELOQUENCE.

fluke *n.* *—See* CHANCE (1), LUCK.

fluky *adj.* *—See* ACCIDENTAL.

flummox *v.* *—See* BAFFLE.

fluorescent *adj.* *—See* COLORFUL (1).

flunk *v.* *—See* FAIL (1).

flurry *n.* *—See* AGITATION (3).

flurry *v.* *—See* AGITATE (2).

flush *v.* *—See* BLUSH, ELATE, EVEN, FLOOD (1).

plane; even. **b.** Arranged with adjacent sides, surfaces, or edges close together. **5.** Direct or straightforward. ▸ *adv.* **1.** So as to be even, in one plane, or aligned with a margin. **2.** Squarely or solidly: *a hit flush on the face.* **—flush′ness** *n.*

flush² (flŭsh) ▸ *n.* A hand in certain card games in which all the cards are of the same suit but not in numerical sequence.

flush³ (flŭsh) ▸ *v.* To drive or be driven from cover, as a game bird.

flus·ter (flŭs′tər) ▸ *v.* To make or become nervous or upset. ▸ *n.* A state of agitation or excitement.

flute (flo͞ot) ▸ *n.* **1.** A high-pitched tubular woodwind instrument. **2a.** *Archit.* A long, usu. rounded groove incised on the shaft of a column. **b.** A groove in cloth, such as a pleat. **—flut′ed** *adj.* **—flut′ing** *n.*

flut·ist (flo͞o′tĭst) ▸ *n.* One who plays the flute.

flut·ter (flŭt′ər) ▸ *v.* **1.** To wave or flap lightly, rapidly, and irregularly. **2.** To fly by a quick light flapping of the wings. **3.** To vibrate or beat rapidly or erratically. **4.** To move quickly in a nervous, restless, or excited fashion. ▸ *n.* **1.** The act of fluttering. **2.** A condition of nervous excitement or agitation. **—flut′ter·y** *adj.*

flu·vi·al (flo͞o′vē-əl) ▸ *adj.* Of, inhabiting, or produced by a river or stream.

flux (flŭks) ▸ *n.* **1a.** A flow or flowing. **b.** A rush or flood. **2.** Constant or frequent change; fluctuation. **3.** A substance applied to facilitate flowing, as of solder or plastics, or to prevent formation of oxides. ▸ *v.* **1.** To melt; fuse. **2.** To apply a flux to.

fly¹ (flī) ▸ *v.* **flew** (flo͞o), **flown** (flōn), **fly·ing.** **1.** To engage in flight, esp.: **a.** To move through the air by means of wings or winglike parts. **b.** To travel by air. **c.** To operate an aircraft or spacecraft. **2.** To rise, float, or cause to float in the air. **3a.** To hasten; rush. **b.** To try to escape; flee. **4.** To pass by swiftly. **5.** To disappear rapidly; vanish. **6.** *p.t. and p.part* **flied** (flīd). *Baseball* To hit a baseball in a high arc. ▸ *n., pl.* **flies.** **1.** An overlapping fold of cloth that covers a fastening of a garment. **2.** A flap that covers an entrance, as of a tent. **3.** A baseball batted in a high arc. **4. flies** The area directly over the stage and behind the proscenium of a theater. ***—idioms:*** **fly high** To be elated. **fly off the handle** *Informal* To become suddenly enraged. **on the fly** On the run; in a hurry. **—fly′a·ble** *adj.*

fly² (flī) ▸ *n., pl.* **flies.** **1a.** Any of a large order of two-winged insects such as the housefly, horsefly, and fruit fly. **b.** Any of various other flying insects. **2.** A fishing lure simulating a fly.

fly·blown (flī′blōn′) ▸ *adj.* **1.** Contaminated with fly eggs. **2.** Dirty; squalid.

fly·by also **fly-by** (flī′bī′) ▸ *n., pl.* **-bys.** A flight, as of a spacecraft, passing close to a specified target or position.

fly-by-night (flī′bī-nīt′) ▸ *adj. Informal* **1.** Unreliable, esp. in business. **2.** Temporary.

fly·catch·er (flī′kăch′ər, -kĕch′-) ▸ *n.* Any of various birds that feed on insects, usu. catching them in flight.

fly·er (flī′ər) ▸ *n.* Var. of **flier.**

fly-fish (flī′fĭsh′) ▸ *v.* To angle using artificial flies for bait and usu. a fly rod for casting. **—fly′-fish′er** *n.*

fly·ing buttress (flī′ĭng) ▸ *n.* An arched masonry support serving to bear thrust away from a main structure to an outer pier or buttress.

flying fish ▸ *n.* A marine fish having enlarged winglike fins capable of sustaining it in brief gliding flights over the water.

flying saucer ▸ *n.* Any of various unidentified flying objects of presumed extraterrestrial origin, typically described as luminous moving disks.

flying squirrel ▸ *n.* Any of various nocturnal squirrels having membranes between the forelegs and hind legs that enable them to glide between trees.

fly·leaf (flī′lēf′) ▸ *n.* A blank page at the beginning or end of a book.

fly·pa·per (flī′pā′pər) ▸ *n.* Paper coated with a sticky substance used to catch flies.

fly·speck (flī′spĕk′) ▸ *n.* **1.** A stain made by the excrement of a fly. **2.** A minute spot.

fly·way (flī′wā′) ▸ *n.* A seasonal route followed by birds migrating to and from their breeding areas.

fly·weight (flī′wāt′) ▸ *n.* A boxer weighing 112 lbs. or less, lighter than a bantamweight.

fly·wheel (flī′hwēl′, -wēl′) ▸ *n.* A heavy-rimmed rotating wheel used to keep a shaft of a machine turning at a steady speed.

Fm ▸ The symbol for the element **fermium.**

FM ▸ *abbr.* frequency modulation

f-num·ber (ĕf′nŭm′bər) ▸ *n.* The ratio of the focal length of a lens or lens system to the effective diameter of its aperture.

foal (fōl) ▸ *n.* The young offspring of an equine animal, esp. one under a year old. ▸ *v.* To give birth to a foal.

foam (fōm) ▸ *n.* **1a.** A mass of bubbles in a matrix of liquid film, esp. on the surface of a liquid. **b.** A thick chemical froth, such as shaving cream. **2.** Frothy saliva. **3.** Any of various light, porous, semirigid or spongy materials used for thermal insulation or shock absorption, as in packaging. ▸ *v.* To form or issue as foam. **—foam′i·ness** *n.* **—foam′y** *adj.*

foam rubber ▸ *n.* A light, firm, spongy rubber used in upholstery and for insulation.

fob¹ (fŏb) ▸ *n.* **1.** A short chain on a pocket watch. **2.** An ornament attached to a watch chain.

fob² (fŏb) ▸ *v.* **fobbed, fob·bing.** *Archaic* To cheat or deceive (another). ***—phrasal verb:*** **fob off** To dispose of (something) by fraud or deception: *fobbed off the zircon as a diamond.*

fo·cac·ci·a (fə-kä′chē-ə, -chə, fō-) ▸ *n.* A flat Italian bread flavored with olive oil.

focal length ▸ *n.* The distance of the focus from the surface of a lens or mirror.

focal point ▸ *n.* See **focus** 1a.

fo′c′s′le (fōk′səl) ▸ *n.* Var. of **forecastle.**

fo·cus (fō′kəs) ▸ *n., pl.* **-cus·es** or **-ci** (-sī′, -kī′). **1a.** A point at which rays of light or other radiation converge or from which they appear to diverge, as after refraction or reflection in an optical system. **b.** See **focal length.** **2a.** The distinctness or clarity of an image rendered by an optical system. **b.** Ad-

THESAURUS

flush *n.* **1.** A fresh rosy complexion ▸ bloom, blush, color, glow. [*Compare* COLOR, COMPLEXION.] **2.** A feeling of pervasive emotional warmth ▸ glow, tingle. *—See also* BLOOM¹ (1).

flush *adj.* *—See* EVEN (1), EVEN (2), RICH (1), RUDDY.

flush *adv.* *—See* DIRECTLY (3).

flushed *adj.* *—See* RUDDY.

fluster *v.* *—See* AGITATE (2).

fluster *n.* *—See* AGITATION (2).

flutter *v.* **1.** To move or cause to move about while being fixed at one edge ▸ flap, fly, wave. **2.** To move quickly and irregularly like a bird in flight ▸ flicker, flit, flitter. *—See also* BEAT (5), BLINK, BLOW¹ (2), FLAP (1), FLY (1).

flutter *n.* *—See* AGITATION (2), BLINK.

flux *n.* *—See* FLOW, TRANSITION.

flux *v.* *—See* MELT.

fly *v.* **1.** To move through the air with or as if with wings ▸ flap, flit, flitter, flutter, sail, wing. **2.** To move quickly or smoothly through the air ▸ dart, float, glide, sail, shoot, skim, soar. [*Compare* FLOAT, PLUNGE.] **3.** To move or cause to move about while being fixed at one edge ▸ flap, flutter, wave. *—See also* BLOW¹ (2), ESCAPE (1), RUSH.

flyblown *adj.* *—See* BAD (2).

flying *adj.* *—See* QUICK.

foam *n.* A mass of bubbles in or on the surface of a liquid ▸ barm, effervescence, fizz, froth, head, lather, spume, suds, yeast.

foam *v.* To form or cause to form foam ▸ bubble, cream, effervesce, fizz, froth, lather, spume, suds, yeast. *—See also* ANGER (2).

foamy *adj.* Consisting of or resembling foam ▸ barmy, fizzy, frothy, lathery, spumous, spumy, sudsy, yeasty.

fob off *v.* To offer or put into circulation an inferior or fraudulent item ▸ foist, palm off, pass off, put off. [*Compare* DUMP.]

focal *adj.* *—See* CENTRAL.

focalize *v.* *—See* CONCENTRATE.

focus *n.* *—See* CENTER (1), CENTER (3), OBJECT (2).

focus *v.* *—See* APPLY (1), CONCENTRATE.

justment for distinctness or clarity. 3. A center of interest or activity. ▸ *v.* **-cused, -cus·ing** or **-cussed, -cus·sing.** 1. To converge or cause to converge at a focus. 2a. To produce a clear image (of). b. To adjust (e.g., a lens) to produce a clear image. 3. To concentrate (on). **—fo′cal** *adj.* **—fo′cal·ly** *adv.*

fod·der (fŏd′ər) ▸ *n.* Feed for livestock, esp. coarsely chopped hay or straw.

foe (fō) ▸ *n.* 1. A personal enemy. 2. An enemy in war. 3. An adversary; opponent.

foe·tid (fē′tĭd) ▸ *adj.* Var. of **fetid.**

foe·tus (fē′təs) ▸ *n.* Var. of **fetus.** **—foe′tal** *adj.*

fog (fôg, fŏg) ▸ *n.* 1. Condensed water vapor in cloudlike masses close to the ground. 2. A mist or film clouding a surface. 3. Confusion or bewilderment. 4. A dark blur on a developed photographic negative. ▸ *v.* **fogged, fog·ging.** To cover or be obscured with or as if with fog. **—fog′gi·ly** *adv.* **—fog′gi·ness** *n.* **—fog′gy** *adj.*

fog·horn (fôg′hôrn′, fŏg′-) ▸ *n.* A horn used to warn ships of danger in fog or darkness.

fo·gy also **fo·gey** (fō′gē) ▸ *n., pl.* **-gies** also **-geys.** A person of old-fashioned habits and attitudes. **—fo′gy·ish** *adj.*

foi·ble (foi′bəl) ▸ *n.* A minor weakness or failing of character.

foil[1] (foil) ▸ *v.* To prevent from being successful; thwart.

foil[2] (foil) ▸ *n.* 1. A thin flexible leaf or sheet of metal. 2. One that by contrast enhances the distinctive characteristics of another. 3a. An airfoil. b. A hydrofoil.

foil[3] (foil) ▸ *n.* A light fencing sword having a usu. circular guard and a thin flexible blade with a blunt point.

foist (foist) ▸ *v.* 1. To pass off as genuine, valuable, or worthy. 2. To impose upon another by coercion or trickery.

fold[1] (fōld) ▸ *v.* 1. To bend over or double up so that one part lies on another part. 2. To bring from an extended to a closed position. 3. To place together and intertwine: *fold one's arms.* 4. To envelop or clasp; enfold. 5. To blend in (a cooking ingredient) by slowly and gently turning one part over another. 6. *Informal* To close, esp. for lack of financial success; fail. ▸ *n.* 1. The act or an instance of folding. 2. A line, layer, pleat, or crease formed by folding. 3. *Geol.* A bend in a stratum of rock.

fold[2] (fōld) ▸ *n.* 1. A fenced enclosure for domestic animals, esp. sheep. 2. A flock of sheep. 3. A group of people or institutions bound together by common beliefs and aims.

-fold ▸ *suff.* 1. Divided into a specified number of parts: *fourfold.* 2. Multiplied by a specified number: *twofold.*

fold·er (fōl′dər) ▸ *n.* 1. One that folds. 2. A booklet made of one or more folded sheets of paper. 3. A folded sheet of heavy paper used as a holder for loose paper.

fol·de·rol (fŏl′də-rŏl′) ▸ *n.* 1. Nonsense. 2. A trinket.

fold·out (fōld′out′) ▸ *n.* 1. *Print.* A folded insert or section, as of a cover, whose full size exceeds that of the regular page. 2. A piece or part that folds out. **—fold′out′** *adj.*

fo·li·age (fō′lē ĭj, fō′lĭj) ▸ *n.* Plant leaves, esp. tree leaves, collectively.

fo·lic acid (fō′lĭk, fŏl′ĭk) ▸ *n.* A compound of the vitamin B complex, occurring esp. in dark leafy vegetables and citrus fruits.

fo·li·o (fō′lē-ō′) ▸ *n., pl.* **-os.** 1a. A large sheet of paper folded once in the middle. b. A book of the largest common size, consisting of such folded sheets. 2. A page number in a book.

folk (fōk) ▸ *n., pl.* **folk** or **folks.** 1. The common people of a society or region. 2. **folks** *Informal* People in general. 3. often **folks** People of a specified group or kind: *rich folks.* 4. **folks** *Informal* One's family or relatives. ▸ *adj.* Of or originating among the common people: *a folk hero.*

folk·lore (fōk′lôr′) ▸ *n.* The traditional beliefs, legends, and practices of a people, passed down orally. **—folk′lor′ist** *n.*

folk music ▸ *n.* Music originating among the common people of a nation or region.

folk-rock (fōk′rŏk′) ▸ *n.* Music combining elements of rock 'n' roll and folk music.

folk·sing·er (fōk′sĭng′ər) ▸ *n.* A singer of folksongs.

folk·song (fōk′sông′, -sŏng′) ▸ *n.* A song belonging to the folk music of a people or area, often existing in several versions.

folk·sy (fōk′sē) ▸ *adj.* **-si·er, -si·est.** *Informal* Simple; unpretentious. **—folk′si·ness** *n.*

folk·way (fōk′wā′) ▸ *n.* A practice, custom, or belief shared by the members of a group as part of their common culture.

fol·li·cle (fŏl′ĭ-kəl) ▸ *n.* 1. A small body cavity or sac, such as one in the skin from which hair grows. 2. A cavity in an ovary containing a mature ovum.

fol·low (fŏl′ō) ▸ *v.* 1. To come or go after. 2. To pursue. 3. To move along the course of: *follow a path.* 4. To adhere to. 5. To comply with; obey. 6. To engage in. 7. To come after in order, time, or position: *Night follows day.* 8. To result or ensue. 9. To be attentive to. 10. To grasp the meaning or logic of; understand.

fol·low·er (fŏl′ō-ər) ▸ *n.* 1. One that follows. 2. One who subscribes to the teachings or methods of another; adherent. 3. An attendant or servant; subordinate.

fol·low·ing (fŏl′ō-ĭng) ▸ *adj.* 1. Coming next in time or order. 2. Now to be mentioned or listed. ▸ *n.* A group or

THESAURUS

foe *n.* *—See* OPPONENT.

fog *n.* *—See* DAZE, HAZE.

fog *v.* *—See* DRUG (2), OBSCURE.

foggy *adj.* *—See* UNCLEAR.

fogy *n.* *—See* SQUARE.

foible *n.* *—See* WEAKNESS.

foil *v.* *—See* FRUSTRATE.

foist *v.* To offer or put into circulation an item that is inferior or fraudulent ▸ fob off, palm off, pass off, put off. [*Compare* DUMP.] *—See also* INSINUATE.

foist on or **upon** *v.* *—See* IMPOSE ON.

fold *v.* To bend together or form a crease so that one part lies over another ▸ crease, crimp, crinkle, double, plait, pleat, ply, pucker, rimple, ruck, rumple, wrinkle. *—See also* BEAT (6), COLLAPSE (2), SUCCUMB.

fold down *v.* *—See* BREAK (3).

fold *n.* 1. A line or an arrangement made by the doubling of one part over another ▸ crease, crimp, crinkle, crumple, plait, pleat, plica, plication, pucker, rimple, ruck, rumple, wrinkle. 2. The steadfast believers in a faith or cause ▸ adherents, congregation, faithful. [*Compare* FOLLOWER, ASSEMBLY.] *—See also* BEND, PEN[2].

folklore *n.* *—See* LORE (1).

folks *n.* *—See* KIN.

folk tale *n.* *—See* MYTH (1).

folkways *n.* *—See* CULTURE (2), LORE (1).

follow *v.* 1. To occur after in time ▸ come next, ensue, succeed, supervene. ***Idiom:*** follow on (*or* upon) the heels of. 2. To occur as a consequence ▸ attend, ensue, result. [*Compare* STEM.] 3. To keep another under surveillance by moving along behind ▸ chase, dog, heel, shadow, tag, track, trail. *Informal:* bird-dog, tail. [*Compare* HUNT, PURSUE.] 4. To act in compliance or conformity with ▸ abide by, adhere to, carry out, comply with, conform to, heed, keep, live by, mind, obey, observe. ***Idioms:*** keep to the straight and narrow, toe the line (*or* mark), walk the line. 5. To take as a model ▸ copy, emulate, imitate, model oneself (on *or* upon *or* after), pattern oneself (on *or* upon *or* after). ***Idioms:*** follow in the footsteps of, follow suit, follow the example of, take as a model. [*Compare* IMITATE.] 6. To work at, especially as a profession ▸ do, practice, pursue. ***Idiom:*** hang out one's shingle. [*Compare* LABOR.] 7. To pay regular and close attention to ▸ monitor, observe, stake out, survey, watch. ***Idioms:*** have one's (*or* keep an) eye on, keep tabs on, keep track of, ride herd on. *—See also* UNDERSTAND (1).

follower *n.* One who supports and adheres to another ▸ adherent, believer, cohort, disciple, henchman, partisan, satellite, supporter. [*Compare* PAWN[2], STUDENT, SUBORDINATE, SYCOPHANT.] *—See also* FAN[2].

following *adj.* 1. Occurring after another ▸ coming, ensuing, next, subsequent, succeeding, supervening. ***Idioms:*** coming after, in the wake of. [*Compare* CONSECUTIVE.] 2. Occurring as a result ▸ attending, consequent, consequential, ensuing, resulting. [*Compare* LOGICAL.]

gathering of followers. ► *prep.* Subsequent to; after.

fol·low-up or **fol·low·up** (fŏl′ō-ŭp′) ► *n.* **1.** The act of repeating or adding to previous action. **2.** The means used to do this.

fol·ly (fŏl′ē) ► *n., pl.* **-lies. 1.** A lack of good sense, understanding, or foresight. **2a.** An act or instance of foolishness. **b.** A costly undertaking having an absurd or ruinous outcome. **3. follies** *(takes sing. or pl. v.)* An elaborate theatrical revue consisting of music, dance, and skits.

fo·ment (fō-mĕnt′) ► *v.* **1.** To promote the growth of; incite. **2.** To treat (e.g., the skin) with heat and moisture. **—fo′men·ta′tion** *n.*

fond (fŏnd) ► *adj.* **-er, -est. 1.** Having a strong liking, inclination, or affection: *fond of ballet.* **2.** Affectionate; tender. **3.** Foolishly affectionate; doting. **4.** Deeply felt; dear: *my fondest hopes.* **—fond′ly** *adv.* **—fond′ness** *n.*

fon·dle (fŏn′dl) ► *v.* **-dled, -dling.** To handle or stroke lovingly.

fon·due also **fon·du** (fŏn-dōō′, -dyōō′) ► *n.* A hot dish usu. made of melted cheese and wine.

font[1] (fŏnt) ► *n.* **1.** A basin for holding baptismal or holy water. **2.** An abundant source.

font[2] (fŏnt) ► *n. Print.* A complete set of type of one size and face.

food (fōōd) ► *n.* **1.** Material, usu. of plant or animal origin, that contains essential body nutrients, taken in and assimilated by an organism to maintain life and growth; nourishment. **2.** A specified kind of nourishment: *plant food.* **3.** Nourishment eaten in solid form. **4.** Something that stimulates or encourages: *food for thought.*

food chain ► *n.* A succession of organisms, each kind serving as a source of nourishment as it consumes a lower member and in turn is preyed upon by a higher member.

food poisoning ► *n.* An acute, often severe gastrointestinal disorder caused by eating food contaminated with bacteria or natural toxins.

food stamp ► *n.* A stamp or coupon issued by the government to persons with low incomes and redeemable for food at stores.

food·stuff (fōōd′stŭf′) ► *n.* A substance that can be used or prepared for use as food.

food web ► *n.* A complex of interrelated food chains in an ecological community.

fool (fōōl) ► *n.* **1.** A person who is deficient in judgment, sense, or understanding. **2.** One who can easily be tricked; dupe. **3.** A jester. ► *v.* **1.** To deceive or trick; dupe. **2.** To take unawares; surprise. **3.** *Informal* To speak or act in jest; joke. **4.** To toy, tinker, or meddle: *You shouldn't ever fool with matches.* ***—phrasal verb:*** **fool around** *Informal* **1.** To waste time; idle. **2.** To mess around; play.

fool·er·y (fōō′lə-rē) ► *n., pl.* **-ies. 1.** Foolish behavior or speech. **2.** A jest.

fool·har·dy (fōōl′här′dē) ► *adj.* **-di·er, -di·est.** Unwisely bold, daring, or venturesome; rash. **—fool′har′di·ly** *adv.* **—fool′har′di·ness** *n.*

fool·ish (fōō′lĭsh) ► *adj.* **1.** Lacking good sense or judgment; unwise. **2.** Absurd or ridiculous: *a foolish grin.* **—fool′ish·ly** *adv.* **—fool′ish·ness** *n.*

fool·proof (fōōl′prōōf′) ► *adj.* **1.** Designed to be impervious to incompetence, error, or misuse. **2.** Effective; infallible: *a foolproof scheme.*

fools·cap (fōōlz′kăp′) ► *n. Chiefly Brit.* A sheet of writing paper approx. 13 by 16 in.

fool's gold (fōōlz) ► *n.* See **pyrite.**

foot (fŏŏt) ► *n., pl.* **feet** (fēt). **1.** The lower extremity of the leg that is in direct contact with the ground in standing or walking. **2.** An invertebrate structure used for locomotion. **3.** Something suggestive of a foot in position or function: *the foot of a mountain; the foot of a bed.* **4.** A unit of poetic meter consisting of stressed and unstressed syllables in various set combinations. **5.** See **measurement** table in Appendix. ► *v.* **1.** To walk: *had to foot it home.* **2.** To dance. **3.** To add up; total: *footed up the bill.* **4.** To pay: *footed the travel expenses.* ***—idioms:*** **foot in the door** *Slang* An initial opportunity for entry. **on foot** Walking rather than riding. **on (one's) feet 1.** Standing up. **2.** Fully recovered, as after an illness.

foot·age (fŏŏt′ĭj) ► *n.* **1.** Length, extent, or amount based on measurement in feet. **2.** A portion of film or videotape: *news footage.*

foot·ball (fŏŏt′bôl′) ► *n.* **1a.** A game played by two teams of 11 players each on a 100-yard-long field with goal posts at either end. **b.** The inflated oval ball used in this game. **2.** *Chiefly Brit.* **a.** Rugby or soccer. **b.** The ball used in Rugby or soccer.

foot·board (fŏŏt′bôrd′) ► *n.* **1.** An upright board across the foot of a bedstead. **2.** A board or small raised platform on which to support or rest the feet.

foot·bridge (fŏŏt′brĭj′) ► *n.* A bridge designed for pedestrians.

foot·ed (fŏŏt′ĭd) ► *adj.* Having feet or a specified kind or number of feet: *a footed sofa; web-footed; four-footed.*

foot·fall (fŏŏt′fôl′) ► *n.* See **footstep** 1.

foot·hill (fŏŏt′hĭl′) ► *n.* A low hill near the base of a mountain or mountain range.

foot·hold (fŏŏt′hōld′) ► *n.* **1.** A place providing support for the foot in climbing or standing. **2.** A firm or secure position that provides a base for further advancement.

THESAURUS

following *n.* The body of persons who admire a public personality, especially an entertainer ► audience, public. [*Compare* FAN[2].] *—See also* RETINUE.

folly *n.* *—See* FOOLISHNESS.

foment *v.* *—See* PROVOKE.

fomenter *n.* *—See* AGITATOR.

fond *adj.* *—See* AFFECTIONATE.

fondle *v.* *—See* CARESS.

fondness *n.* *—See* LOVE (1), TASTE (1).

font *n.* *—See* ORIGIN.

food or **foodstuff** *n.* Material that is fit to be eaten ► aliment, bread, comestibles, cooking, diet, eatables, edibles, fare, meat, nourishment, nutriment, nutrition, pabulum, provender, provisions, rations, sustenance, viands, victuals. *Slang:* chow, eats, grub, munchies.

fool *n.* A person who is deficient in judgment and good sense ► ass, buffoon, idiot, imbecile, jackass, mooncalf, moron, nincompoop, ninny, nitwit, simpleton. *Informal:* dope, gander, goose. *Slang:* boob, bozo, cretin, ding-dong, dim bulb, dip, ditz, dork, dweeb, geek, goof, jerk, nerd, nimrod, schmo, schmuck, simp, turkey, twit. [*Compare* DRIP, DULLARD, OAF, SQUARE.] *—See also* DUPE.

fool *v.* *—See* DECEIVE, FIDDLE, PUTTER, TINKER.

fool around *v.* **1.** *Informal* To make jokes; behave playfully ► jest, joke, quip. *Informal:* clown (around), horse around. ***Idioms:*** crack wise, play the fool. [*Compare* PLAY.] **2.** *Informal* To be sexually unfaithful to another ► philander. *Informal:* cheat, mess around, play around. *Slang:* two-time. *—See also* MISBEHAVE, NECK, PUTTER.

fool away *v.* *—See* WASTE.

foolery *n.* *—See* FOOLISHNESS.

foolhardiness *n.* *—See* TEMERITY.

foolhardy *adj.* *—See* RASH[1].

foolish *adj.* Displaying a lack of forethought and good sense ► absurd, asinine, brainless, daft, fatuous, harebrained, idiotic, imbecilic, inane, insane, lunatic, ludicrous, mad, mindless, moronic, nonsensical, preposterous, ridiculous, senseless, silly, witless, zany. *Informal:* cockeyed, crazy, daffy, loony, loopy. *Slang:* balmy, dippy, ditsy, dopey, goofy, jerky, wacky. [*Compare* GIDDY, LAUGHABLE, STUPID.]

foolishness *n.* Foolish behavior ► absurdity, daftness, fatuity, fatuousness, folly, foolery, idiocy, imbecility, inanity, insanity, ludicracy, lunacy, madness, nonsense, preposterousness, ridiculousness, senselessness, silliness, tomfoolery, zaniness. *Informal:* boobishness, craziness, daffiness, looniness, loopiness. *Slang:* balminess, dippiness, ditsiness, dopeyness, goofiness, jerkiness, wackiness. [*Compare* NONSENSE.]

foolproof *adj.* *—See* SURE (2).

foot *n.* *—See* BASE[1] (2).

foot *v.* *—See* ADD, DANCE, WALK.

footfall *n.* *—See* WALK (2).

foothold *n.* A place providing support for the foot in climbing ► footing, perch, purchase, toehold.

foot·ing (fo͝ot′ĭng) ▸ *n.* **1.** Secure placement of the feet in standing or moving. **2.** A basis or foundation. **3a.** Position in relation to others. **b.** Terms of social interaction.
foot·lights (fo͝ot′līts′) ▸ *pl.n.* **1.** Lights placed in a row along the front of a stage floor. **2.** The theater as a profession.
foot·lock·er (fo͝ot′lŏk′ər) ▸ *n.* A small trunk for storing personal belongings.
foot·loose (fo͝ot′lo͞os′) ▸ *adj.* Having no attachments or ties.
foot·man (fo͝ot′mən) ▸ *n.* A man employed as a servant to wait at table, attend the door, and run various errands.
foot·note (fo͝ot′nōt′) ▸ *n.* A note of comment or reference at the bottom of a page of a book. **—foot′note′** *v.*
foot·path (fo͝ot′păth′, -päth′) ▸ *n.* A narrow path for persons on foot.
foot·print (fo͝ot′prĭnt′) ▸ *n.* An outline or indentation left by a foot on a surface.
foot·race (fo͝ot′rās′) ▸ *n.* A race run by contestants on foot.
foot·rest (fo͝ot′rĕst′) ▸ *n.* A support on which to rest the feet.
foot soldier ▸ *n.* A soldier in the infantry.
foot·sore (fo͝ot′sôr′) ▸ *adj.* Having sore or tired feet. **—foot′sore′ness** *n.*
foot·step (fo͝ot′stĕp′) ▸ *n.* **1a.** A step with the foot. **b.** The sound of a foot stepping; footfall. **2.** The distance covered by a step: *a footstep away.* **3.** A footprint.
foot·stool (fo͝ot′sto͞ol′) ▸ *n.* A low stool for supporting the feet.
foot·wear (fo͝ot′wâr′) ▸ *n.* Attire, such as shoes or slippers, for the feet.
foot·work (fo͝ot′wûrk′) ▸ *n.* The manner in which the feet are used or maneuvered, as in boxing, figure skating, or dancing.
fop (fŏp) ▸ *n.* A man preoccupied with clothes and manners; dandy. **—fop′per·y** *n.* **—fop′pish** *adj.* **—fop′pish·ly** *adv.* **—fop′pish·ness** *n.*
for (fôr; fər *when unstressed*) ▸ *prep.* **1a.** Used to indicate the object or purpose of an action or activity: *plans to run for senator.* **b.** Used to indicate a destination: *headed for town.* **2a.** On behalf of: *spoke for us all.* **b.** In favor of: *I'm for the proposal.* **3a.** As equivalent or equal to: *word for word.* **b.** As against: *two steps back for one step forward.* **4.** Used to indicate amount, extent, or duration: *walked for miles.* **5.** As being: *mistook me for the boss.* **6.** As a result of: *jumped for joy.* **7.** Used to indicate appropriateness or suitability: *not for us to decide.* **8.** Notwithstanding; despite: *For all the problems, it was worth it.* **9.** Considering the nature of: *was spry for his age.* **10.** In honor of: *named for her.* ▸ *conj.* Because; since.
fo·ra (fôr′ə) ▸ *n.* Pl. of **forum**.
for·age (fôr′ĭj, fŏr′-) ▸ *n.* **1.** Food for domestic animals; fodder. **2.** A search for food or provisions. ▸ *v.* **-aged, -ag·ing.** To search, as for food. **—for′ag·er** *n.*
for·ay (fôr′ā′, fŏr′ā′) ▸ *n.* **1.** A sudden raid or military advance. **2.** A first venture or attempt. **—for′ay′** *v.*
forb (fôrb) ▸ *n.* A broad-leaved herb other than a grass.
for·bear¹ (fôr-bâr′) ▸ *v.* **-bore** (-bôr′), **-borne** (-bôrn′), **-bear·ing.** **1.** To refrain or desist (from); resist. **2.** To be tolerant or patient. **—for·bear′ance** *n.*
for·bear² (fôr′bâr′) ▸ *n.* Var. of **forebear.**
for·bid (fər-bĭd′, fôr-) ▸ *v.* **-bade** (-băd′, -bād′) or **-bad** (-băd′), **-bid·den** (-bĭd′n) or **-bid**, **-bid·ding.** **1.** To command (someone) not to do something. **2.** To command against doing (something). **3.** To preclude. **—for·bid′dance** *n.*
for·bid·ding (fər-bĭd′ĭng, fôr-) ▸ *adj.* Tending to frighten or menace; threatening.
force (fôrs) ▸ *n.* **1a.** Energy, strength, or active power. **b.** The exertion of such power. **2a.** Physical power or violence. **b.** Intellectual power or vigor. **c.** Moral strength. **3.** A body of persons organized for a certain purpose, esp. for the use of military power. **4.** *Phys.* A vector quantity that tends to produce an acceleration of a body in the direction of its application. ▸ *v.* **forced, forc·ing.** **1.** To compel to perform an action. **2a.** To gain by force or coercion. **b.** To move (something) against resistance. **c.** To inflict or impose. **3.** To produce with effort: *force a laugh.* **4.** To move, break down, open, or clear by force: *forced our way.* **5.** *Bot.* To cause to grow or mature artificially. **—*idiom:* in force** **1.** In full strength. **2.** In effect; operative: *a rule now in force.* **—force′ful** *adj.* **—force′ful·ly** *adv.* **—force′ful·ness** *n.*
force-feed (fôrs′fēd′) ▸ *v.* To compel to ingest food, esp. by mechanical means.
force field ▸ *n.* See **field of force.**
for·ceps (fôr′səps, -sĕps) ▸ *n., pl.* **-ceps.** An instrument used for grasping, manipulating, or extracting, esp. in surgery.
forc·i·ble (fôr′sə-bəl) ▸ *adj.* **1.** Effected through force. **2.** Characterized by force; powerful. **—forc′i·bly** *adv.*
ford (fôrd) ▸ *n.* A shallow place in a body of water where

THESAURUS

footing *n.* A place providing support for the foot in climbing ▸ foothold, perch, purchase, toehold. *—See also* BASE¹ (2), BASIS (1), BASIS (3), PLACE (1).
footloose *adj.* *—See* SINGLE.
footpace *n.* A very slow rate of speed ▸ crawl, creep, slow motion. *Idiom:* snail's pace.
footpath *n.* *—See* WAY (2).
footprints *n.* *—See* TRACK.
footstep *n.* *—See* WALK (2).
footstool or **footrest** *n.* A stool or cushion for resting the feet ▸ hassock, ottoman.
foozle *n.* *—See* BLUNDER.
foozler *n.* *—See* BLUNDERER.
fop *n.* A man who is preoccupied with or vain about his clothes ▸ beau, coxcomb, dandy, peacock, swell.
for *conj.* *—See* BECAUSE.
forage *v.* *—See* BROWSE (2), SCOUR².
foray *n.* An act of invading, especially by military forces ▸ incursion, inroad, invasion, raid. [*Compare* ATTACK.]
foray *v.* *—See* INVADE (1).
forbear *v.* *—See* REFRAIN, STOP (2).
forbearance *n.* *—See* PATIENCE, TOLERANCE.
forbearing *adj.* *—See* PATIENT, TOLERANT.
forbid *v.* To refuse to allow ▸ ban, bar, debar, disallow, enjoin, interdict, outlaw, prohibit, proscribe, taboo. [*Compare* EXCLUDE, HINDER, PREVENT.]
forbiddance *n.* A refusal to allow ▸ ban, disallowance, inhibition, interdiction, prohibition, proscription, taboo. [*Compare* REFUSAL, PREVENTION.]
forbidden *adj.* Not allowed ▸ banned, barred, debarred, disallowed, illicit, impermissible, interdicted, outlawed, prohibited, proscribed, taboo, verboten. [*Compare* CRIMINAL, UNSPEAKABLE.]
forbidding *adj.* So disagreeable as to discourage approach ▸ dour, flinty, grim, inhospitable, stern, unhospitable, uninviting. [*Compare* COOL, HOSTILE, SEVERE.] *—See also* BLEAK (1), FATEFUL (1).
force *n.* **1.** Strength or energy that overcomes resistance ▸ coercion, compulsion, constraint, duress, might, power, pressure, strength, violence. **2.** The condition of being in full effect or operation ▸ actualization, being, effect, realization. [*Compare* EXERCISE.] **3.** A group of people organized for a particular purpose ▸ body, corps, crew, detachment, division, gang, patrol, platoon, side, squad, squadron, team, unit. [*Compare* ALLIANCE, ASSEMBLY, BAND², UNION.] *—See also* COGENCY, ENERGY, IMPACT, INFLUENCE.
force *v.* **1.** To cause a person or thing to act or move in spite of resistance ▸ coerce, compel, constrain, make, obligate, oblige, pressure. [*Compare* DRIVE, URGE.] **2.** To compel another to participate in or submit to a sexual act ▸ assault, molest, rape, ravish, violate. *—See also* COERCE.
force out *v.* To take the place of another against the other's will ▸ cut out, displace, supplant, usurp. [*Compare* ASSUME, OCCUPY.]
forced *adj.* **1.** Accomplished by force ▸ coercive, forcible, violent. *Informal:* strong-arm. **2.** Not natural or spontaneous ▸ contrived, effortful, labored, strained. [*Compare* AWKWARD, STIFF.]
forceful *adj.* Full of or displaying force ▸ dynamic, dynamical, effective, forcible, hard-hitting, mighty, potent, powerful, strong, vigorous. [*Compare* INTENSE, SEVERE.] *—See also* ASSERTIVE, CONVINCING, ENERGETIC.
forcefully *adv.* *—See* HARD (1).
forcefulness *n.* *—See* COGENCY, INTENSITY.
forcible *adj.* Accomplished by force ▸ coercive, forced, violent. *Informal:* strong-arm. *—See also* CONVINCING, FORCEFUL.
forcibly *adv.* With force and violence ▸ coercively, violently. *Idioms:* against one's will, by force, under duress. *—See also* HARD (1).
ford *v.* *—See* CROSS (1).

one can walk, ride, or drive across. **—ford** *v.* **—ford′a·ble** *adj.*

Ford, Gerald Rudolph (1913–2006) ▸ The 38th US President (1974–77).

Ford, Henry (1863–1947) ▸ Amer. automobile manufacturer.

fore (fôr) ▸ *adj. & adv.* At, in, near, or toward the front; forward. ▸ *n.* The front part. ▸ *interj. Sports* Used by a golfer to warn those ahead that a ball is headed in their direction.

fore– ▸ *pref.* **1.** Before; earlier: *forebode.* **2.** In front of; front: *foreground.*

fore-and-aft (fôr′ən-ăft′) ▸ *adj.* Parallel with the length of a structure, as a ship.

fore·arm[1] (fôr-ärm′) ▸ *v.* To arm or prepare in advance of a conflict.

fore·arm[2] (fôr′ärm′) ▸ *n.* The part of the arm between the wrist and elbow.

fore·bear also **for·bear** (fôr′bâr′) ▸ *n.* A person from whom one is descended.

fore·bode (fôr-bōd′) ▸ *v.* **1.** To indicate the likelihood of; portend. **2.** To have a premonition of (a future misfortune). **—fore·bod′ing** *n.*

fore·cast (fôr′kăst′) ▸ *v.* **-cast** or **-cast·ed, -cast·ing. 1.** To estimate, calculate, or indicate in advance: *forecast tomorrow's weather.* **2.** To foreshadow. ▸ *n.* A prediction. **—fore′cast′er** *n.*

fore·cas·tle (fōk′səl, fôr′kăs′əl) also **fo'c's'le** (fōk′səl) ▸ *n.* **1.** The section of the upper deck of a ship located forward of the foremast. **2.** The crew's quarters at the bow of a merchant ship.

fore·close (fôr-klōz′) ▸ *v.* **-closed, -clos·ing. 1.** To deprive (a mortgagor) of mortgaged property, as for payment. **2.** To preclude; bar. **—fore·clo′sure** *n.*

fore·court (fôr′kôrt′) ▸ *n.* **1.** A courtyard in front of a building. **2.** *Sports* The part of a court nearest the net or wall, as in tennis or handball.

fore·fa·ther (fôr′fä′*th*ər) ▸ *n.* **1.** An ancestor. **2.** A founder or originator.

fore·fin·ger (fôr′fĭng′gər) ▸ *n.* See **index finger.**

fore·foot (fôr′fo͝ot′) ▸ *n.* Either of the front feet of an animal.

fore·front (fôr′frŭnt′) ▸ *n.* **1.** The foremost part or area. **2.** The most important position.

fore·go[1] (fôr-gō′) ▸ *v.* To precede, as in time or place. **—fore·go′er** *n.*

fore·go[2] (fôr-gō′) ▸ *v.* Var. of **forgo.**

fore·go·ing (fôr-gō′ĭng, fôr′gō′ĭng) ▸ *adj.* Just before or past; previous.

fore·gone ▸ *adj.* (fôr′gôn′, -gŏn′) So certain as to be known in advance: *a foregone conclusion.*

fore·ground (fôr′ground′) ▸ *n.* **1.** The part of a scene or picture nearest to the viewer. **2.** The forefront; vanguard.

fore·hand (fôr′hănd′) ▸ *adj.* Made or done with the hand moving palm forward: *a forehand tennis stroke.* ▸ *n.* A forehand stroke. **—fore′hand′** *adv.*

fore·head (fôr′hĕd′, -ĭd, fŏr′-) ▸ *n.* The part of the face between the eyebrows and the normal hairline.

for·eign (fôr′ĭn, fŏr′-) ▸ *adj.* **1.** Located away from one's native country. **2.** Characteristic of or from a place or country other than one's own: *a foreign custom.* **3.** Conducted or involved with other nations: *foreign trade.* **4.** Situated in an abnormal or improper place. **5.** Not natural; alien. **6.** Irrelevant. **—for′eign·ness** *n.*

for·eign·er (fôr′ə-nər, fŏr′-) ▸ *n.* One who is from a foreign country or place.

foreign minister ▸ *n.* A cabinet minister in charge of a nation's foreign affairs.

foreign office ▸ *n.* The governmental department in charge of foreign affairs in certain countries.

fore·knowl·edge (fôr-nŏl′ĭj) ▸ *n.* Knowledge of something before its occurrence.

fore·leg (fôr′lĕg′) ▸ *n.* Either of the front legs of an animal.

fore·limb (fôr′lĭm′) ▸ *n.* A front part, such as a leg, wing, or flipper.

fore·lock (fôr′lŏk′) ▸ *n.* A lock of hair that grows from or falls on the forehead.

fore·man (fôr′mən) ▸ *n.* **1.** A man in charge of a group of workers, as at a factory or ranch. **2.** A man who chairs and speaks for a jury.

fore·mast (fôr′məst, -măst′) ▸ *n.* The forward mast on a sailing vessel.

fore·most (fôr′mōst′) ▸ *adj. & adv.* First in position or rank.

fore·noon (fôr′no͞on′) ▸ *n.* The period between sunrise and noon; morning.

fo·ren·sic (fə-rĕn′sĭk, -zĭk) ▸ *adj.* Of or used in legal proceedings or formal debate. **—fo·ren′si·cal·ly** *adv.*

fo·ren·sics (fə-rĕn′sĭks, -zĭks) ▸ *n. (takes sing. v.)* The art or study of formal debate.

fore·or·dain (fôr′ôr-dān′) ▸ *v.* To determine or appoint beforehand; predestine.

fore·part (fôr′pärt′) ▸ *n.* The first or foremost part.

fore·quar·ter (fôr′kwôr′tər) ▸ *n.* **1.** The front section of a side of meat. **2.** The foreleg and shoulder of an animal.

fore·run·ner (fôr′rŭn′ər) ▸ *n.* **1.** A predecessor. **2.** One that comes before and indicates the approach of another.

fore·sail (fôr′səl, -sāl′) ▸ *n.* The principal square sail hung to the foremast of a square-rigged sailing vessel.

fore·see (fôr-sē′) ▸ *v.* To see or know beforehand. **—fore·see′a·ble** *adj.*

fore·shad·ow (fôr-shăd′ō) ▸ *v.* To present an indication or hint of beforehand.

fore·shore (fôr′shôr′) ▸ *n.* The part of a shore that is covered at high tide.

fore·short·en (fôr-shôr′tn) ▸ *v.* To shorten the lines of (a figure or design) in a drawing or painting so as to produce an illusion of depth or distance.

fore·sight (fôr′sīt′) ▸ *n.* **1.** The ability to foresee. **2.** Care or prudence in providing for the future. **3.** The act of looking forward. **—fore′sight′ed** *adj.* **—fore′sight′ed·ly** *adv.* **—fore′sight′ed·ness** *n.*

THESAURUS

fore *n.* —*See* FOREFRONT, FRONT.

forearm *v.* —*See* GIRD.

forebear *n.* —*See* ANCESTOR (1).

forebode *v.* —*See* PROPHESY, THREATEN (1).

foreboding *n.* —*See* FEELING (1), OMEN.

foreboding *adj.* —*See* FATEFUL (1).

forecast *v.* —*See* FORESHADOW, PREDICT.

forecast *n.* —*See* PREDICTION.

foredoomed *adj.* —*See* CONDEMNED.

forefather *n.* —*See* ANCESTOR (1).

forefront *n.* The position of greatest advancement or importance ▸ avant-garde, cutting edge, fore, front, lead, vanguard.

foregoing *adj.* Next before the present one ▸ last, latter, preceding, previous. —*See also* PAST.

forehanded *adj.* —*See* WARY.

forehandedness *n.* —*See* PRUDENCE.

foreign *adj.* **1.** From or characteristic of another place or part of the world ▸ alien, exotic, expatriate, immigrant, nonnative, nonresident, strange. [*Compare* DISTANT.] **2.** Not part of the essential nature of a thing ▸ alien, extraneous, extrinsic. [*Compare* IRRELEVANT.]

foreigner *n.* A person coming from another country or into a new community ▸ alien, émigré, expatriate, immigrant, newcomer, nonresident, outlander, outsider, stranger.

foreknow *v.* —*See* FORESEE.

foreknowledge *n.* —*See* VISION (2).

foreman or **forewoman** *n.* —*See* BOSS.

foremost *adj.* —*See* BEST (1), PRIMARY (1).

foremother *n.* —*See* ANCESTOR (1).

forenoon *n.* The time of day from sunrise to noon ▸ A.M., before lunch, before noon, morning. [*Compare* DAWN.]

forepart *n.* —*See* FRONT.

foreperson *n.* —*See* BOSS.

forerun *v.* —*See* FORESHADOW, PRECEDE, PREVENT.

forerunner *n.* One that foreshadows or prepares for something else ▸ harbinger, herald, pioneer, precursor, presager, trailblazer, vanguard. —*See also* ANCESTOR (2), OMEN, ORIGINAL.

foresee *v.* To know in advance ▸ anticipate, divine, envision, foreknow, see. [*Compare* EXPECT, PREDICT.]

foreshadow *v.* To give an indication of something in advance ▸ adumbrate, augur, bode, betoken, forecast, forerun, foreshow, foretell, foretoken, portend, prefigure, presage, prognosticate. [*Compare* MEAN[1], PROPHESY.]

foresight *n.* —*See* PRUDENCE, VISION (2).

foresighted *adj.* —*See* VISIONARY.

foresightedness *n.* —*See* PRUDENCE.

fore·skin (fôr′skĭn′) ▸ *n.* The loose fold of skin that covers the glans of the penis.
for·est (fôr′ĭst, fŏr′-) ▸ *n.* A dense growth of trees, plants, and underbrush covering a large area. **—for′es·ta′tion** *n.*
fore·stall (fôr-stôl′) ▸ *v.* **1.** To delay, hinder, or prevent by taking measures beforehand. **2.** To anticipate.
for·est·ry (fôr′ĭ-strē, fŏr′-) ▸ *n.* The science and art of cultivating, maintaining, and developing forests.
fore·taste (fôr′tāst′) ▸ *n.* An advance realization, token, or warning. **—fore·taste′** *v.*
fore·tell (fôr-tĕl′) ▸ *v.* To tell of or indicate beforehand; predict. **—fore·tell′er** *n.*
fore·thought (fôr′thôt′) ▸ *n.* Advance deliberation, consideration, or planning.
fore·to·ken (fôr-tō′kən) ▸ *v.* To foreshadow; presage. **—fore′·to′ken** *n.*
for·ev·er (fôr-ĕv′ər, fər-) ▸ *adv.* **1.** For all time; eternally. **2.** Always; incessantly.
for·ev·er·more (fôr-ĕv′ər-môr′, fər-) ▸ *adv.* Forever.
fore·warn (fôr-wôrn′) ▸ *v.* To warn in advance.
fore·wing (fôr′wĭng′) ▸ *n.* Either of a pair of front wings of a four-winged insect.
fore·wom·an (fôr′wo͝om′ən) ▸ *n.* **1.** A woman who serves as the leader of a work crew, as in a factory. **2.** A woman who chairs and speaks for a jury.
fore·word (fôr′wərd) ▸ *n.* A preface or introductory note, esp. in a book.
for·feit (fôr′fĭt) ▸ *n.* **1.** Something surrendered as punishment for a crime, offense, or breach of contract. **2.** Something placed in escrow and then redeemed after payment of a fine. **3.** A forfeiture. ▸ *v.* To surrender or be forced to surrender as a forfeit.
for·fei·ture (fôr′fĭ-cho͝or′, -chər) ▸ *n.* **1.** The act of forfeiting. **2.** Something forfeited.
for·gath·er (fôr-găth′ər) ▸ *v.* To gather together; assemble.
forge[1] (fôrj) ▸ *n.* A furnace or hearth where metals are heated and wrought; smithy. ▸ *v.* **forged, forg·ing. 1.** To form (e.g., metal) by heating in a forge and beating or hammering into shape. **2.** To give form or shape to; devise: *forge a treaty.* **3.** To fashion or reproduce fraudulently; counterfeit: *forge a signature.* **—forg′er** *n.* **—for′ger·y** *n.*
forge[2] (fôrj) ▸ *v.* **forged, forg·ing. 1.** To advance gradually but steadily. **2.** To surge forward.
for·get (fər-gĕt′, fôr-) ▸ *v.* **-got** (-gŏt′), **-got·ten** (-gŏt′n) or **-got, -get·ting. 1.** To be unable to remember or call to mind. **2.** To treat with inattention; neglect. **3.** To fail to become aware at the proper moment: *forget an appointment.* **—*idiom:* forget oneself** To lose one's reserve, temper, or self-restraint. **—for·get′ful** *adj.* **—for·get′ful·ly** *adv.* **—for·get′ful·ness** *n.* **—for·get′ta·ble** *adj.*
for·get-me-not (fər-gĕt′mē-nŏt′, fôr-) ▸ *n.* A low-growing plant with small blue flowers.
for·give (fər-gĭv′, fôr-) ▸ *v.* **-gave** (-gāv′), **-giv·en** (-gĭv′ən), **-giv·ing. 1.** To excuse for a fault or offense; pardon. **2.** To stop feeling anger or resentment against. **3.** To absolve from payment of. **—for·giv′a·ble** *adj.* **—for·give′ness** *n.*
for·go also **fore·go** (fôr-gō′) ▸ *v.* **-went** (-wĕnt′), **-gone** (-gôn′, -gŏn′), **-go·ing.** To give up; relinquish.
fo·rint (fôr′ĭnt′) ▸ *n.* See **currency** table in Appendix.
fork (fôrk) ▸ *n.* **1.** A utensil with two or more prongs, used for eating or serving food. **2.** A pronged implement or part, esp. a farm or garden tool used for digging. **3a.** A separation into two or more branches. **b.** The place of such a separation. **c.** One of the branches: *took the right fork.* ▸ *v.* **1.** To raise, carry, or pierce with a fork. **2.** To shape as a fork. **3.** To divide into branches. **4.** *Informal* To pay: *forked over $50.* **—fork′ful′** *n.*
forked (fôrkt, fôr′kĭd) ▸ *adj.* **1.** Having a fork: *a forked river.* **2.** Shaped like a fork: *forked lightning.*
fork·lift (fôrk′lĭft′) ▸ *n.* An industrial vehicle with a power-operated pronged platform that can be raised and lowered for lifting and carrying loads.
for·lorn (fər-lôrn′, fôr-) ▸ *adj.* **1.** Deserted or abandoned. **2.** Pitiful in appearance. **3.** Nearly hopeless; desperate. **—for·lorn′ly** *adv.* **—for·lorn′ness** *n.*
form (fôrm) ▸ *n.* **1a.** The shape and structure of an object. **b.** The body, esp. of a person; figure. **2a.** The essence of something. **b.** The mode in which a thing exists; kind: *a form of animal life.* **3a.** Procedure as determined by regulation or custom. **b.** A fixed order of words or procedures, as in a ceremony. **4.** A document with blanks for the insertion of requested information. **5.** Manners as governed by etiquette. **6.** Performance according to recognized criteria. **7.** Fitness with regard to health or training. **8a.** Style or manner in literary or musical composition. **b.** The structure of a work of art. **9.** A model for making a mold. **10.** A meaningful unit of language. **11.** A grade level esp. in a British school. ▸ *v.* **1a.** To shape or become shaped. **b.** To develop in the mind: *form an opinion.* **2a.** To shape into a particular form. **b.** To draw up; arrange. **c.** To develop by instruction or precept: *form a child's mind.* **3.** To develop or acquire: *form a habit.* **4.** To constitute a part of.
-form ▸ *suff.* Having the form of: *cruciform.*

THESAURUS

forest *n.* A dense growth of trees and underbrush covering an area ▸ backwoods, timberland, woodland, woods. [*Compare* COUNTRY, WILDERNESS.]
forestall *v.* —*See* HINDER, PREVENT.
forestallment *n.* —*See* PREVENTION.
foretaste *n.* A limited or anticipatory experience ▸ sample, sampling, taste. [*Compare* GLANCE.]
foretell *v.* —*See* FORESHADOW, PREDICT, PROPHESY.
foreteller *n.* —*See* PROPHET.
forethought or **forethoughtfulness** *n.* —*See* PRUDENCE.
foretoken *v.* —*See* FORESHADOW.
foretoken *n.* —*See* OMEN.
forever *adv.* For all time; without end ▸ always, endlessly, eternally, everlastingly, evermore, permanently, perpetually, unendingly. *Idioms:* for ever and a day, for ever and ever, for good, for keeps, in perpetuity, till kingdom come, till Doomsday (*or* Judgment Day), till the cows come home, world without end. —*See also* CONTINUALLY.
forever *n.* —*See* AGES.
forewarn *v.* —*See* THREATEN (1), WARN.
forewarning *n.* —*See* FEELING (1), OMEN.
foreword *n.* —*See* INTRODUCTION.
forfeit *v.* —*See* ABANDON (1).
forfend *v.* —*See* PREVENT.
forgather *v.* —*See* ASSEMBLE.
forge[1] *v.* —*See* BEAT (3), COUNTERFEIT, MAKE.
forge[2] *v.* —*See* TRUDGE.
forger *n.* One who makes a fraudulent copy of something ▸ counterfeiter, fabricator, faker, falsifier.
forgery *n.* —*See* COUNTERFEIT.
forget *v.* To fail to remember ▸ *Informal:* disremember. *Idioms:* draw a blank, go blank, have a senior moment, have no memory, have no recollection. —*See also* DROP (4), NEGLECT (2).
forgetful *adj.* —*See* ABSENT-MINDED, CARELESS.
forgivable *adj.* —*See* PARDONABLE.
forgive *v.* To grant forgiveness to or for ▸ condone, excuse, let pass, overlook, pardon, remit. *Idioms:* forgive and forget, let bygones be bygones. [*Compare* CLEAR, EXCUSE.]
forgiveness *n.* The act or an instance of forgiving ▸ absolution, amnesty, condonation, excuse, pardon, remission. [*Compare* EXCULPATION, GRACE.]
forgo *v.* —*See* ABANDON (1).
fork *n.* —*See* BRANCH (1).
fork *v.* —*See* BRANCH, TILL.
fork out or **over** or **up** *v.* —*See* SPEND (1).
forlorn *adj.* —*See* ABANDONED (1), DESPONDENT, LONELY (1), LONELY (2), PITIFUL.
form *n.* **1.** The characteristic surface arrangement of a thing ▸ cast, configuration, contour, delineation, design, figure, outline, pattern, profile, shape, silhouette, structure. [*Compare* ARRANGEMENT, OUTLINE.] **2.** A document used in applying, as for a job ▸ application, paper, sheet. **3.** A hollow device for shaping a fluid or plastic substance ▸ cast, matrix, mold. —*See also* BEHAVIOR (1), CEREMONY (2), CONSTITUTION, CUSTOM, KIND[2], RITUAL, SHAPE, USUAL, VARIATION.
form *v.* **1.** To give form to by or as if by pressing and kneading ▸ model, mold, sculpt, shape. [*Compare* WORK.] **2.** To be the constituent parts of ▸ compose, make up. [*Compare* CONTAIN.] —*See also* DEVELOP (1), EDUCATE, MAKE.

for·mal (fôr′məl) ▸ *adj.* **1a.** Of or involving outward form or structure. **b.** Being or relating to essential form or constitution: *a formal principle.* **2.** Following accepted forms or conventions: *a formal education.* **3.** Marked by strict observation of forms. **4.** Stiff or reserved: *a formal manner.* **5.** Done for the sake of procedure only: *a formal requirement.* ▸ *n.* Something, such as a gown or social affair, that is formal in nature. **—for′mal·ly** *adv.*

for·mal·de·hyde (fôr-măl′də-hīd′) ▸ *n.* A gaseous compound, HCHO, used in aqueous solution as a preservative and disinfectant.

for·mal·ism (fôr′mə-lĭz′əm) ▸ *n.* Rigorous or excessive adherence to recognized forms, as in religion or art. **—for′mal·ist** *adj. & n.* **—for′mal·is′tic** *adj.*

for·mal·i·ty (fôr-măl′ĭ-tē) ▸ *n., pl.* **-ties. 1.** The quality or condition of being formal. **2.** Rigorous or ceremonious adherence to rules. **3.** An established rule or custom.

for·mal·ize (fôr′mə-līz′) ▸ *v.* **-ized, -iz·ing. 1.** To make formal. **2.** To give formal endorsement to. **—for′mal·i·za′tion** *n.*

for·mat (fôr′măt′) ▸ *n.* **1.** A plan for the organization and arrangement of something. **2.** The layout of a publication. **3.** *Comp. Sci.* The arrangement of data for storage or display. ▸ *v.* **-mat·ted, -mat·ting. 1.** To plan or arrange in a specified form. **2.** *Comp. Sci.* **a.** To determine the arrangement of (data) for storage or display. **b.** To divide (a disk) into sectors so that it may store data.

for·ma·tion (fôr-mā′shən) ▸ *n.* **1.** The act or process of forming. **2.** Something formed: *cloud formations.* **3.** The manner in which something is formed; structure. **4.** A specified arrangement, as of troops. **—for·ma′tion·al** *adj.*

for·ma·tive (fôr′mə-tĭv) ▸ *adj.* **1.** Forming or capable of forming. **2.** Of or relating to formation or growth: *his formative years.*

for·mer (fôr′mər) ▸ *adj.* **1.** Occurring earlier in time. **2.** Coming before in place or order. **3.** Being the first of two mentioned. **4.** Having been in the past: *a former ambassador.*

for·mer·ly (fôr′mər-lē) ▸ *adv.* At an earlier or former time; once.

form·fit·ting (fôrm′fĭt′ĭng) ▸ *adj.* Snugly fitting the body's contours: *formfitting jeans.*

For·mi·ca (fôr-mī′kə) ▸ A trademark for a variety of high-pressure laminated plastic sheets used esp. as heat- and chemical-resistant surfaces.

for·mi·da·ble (fôr′mĭ-də-bəl, fôr-mĭd′ə-) ▸ *adj.* **1.** Arousing fear, dread, or awe. **2.** Difficult to surmount. **—for′mi·da·bil′i·ty** *n.* **—for′mi·da·bly** *adv.*

form·less (fôrm′lĭs) ▸ *adj.* Having no definite form. **—form′less·ly** *adv.* **—form′less·ness** *n.*

form letter ▸ *n.* A letter in a standardized format sent to many recipients.

For·mo·sa (fôr-mō′sə) ▸ See **Taiwan.**

for·mu·la (fôr′myə-lə) ▸ *n., pl.* **-las** or **-lae** (-lē′). **1.** A set of words, symbols, or rules for use in a ceremony or procedure. **2.** *Chem.* A set of symbols that show the composition and structure of a compound. **3.** A recipe. **4.** A liquid food that is prescribed for an infant to substitute for or supplement human milk. **5.** *Math.* A statement, esp. an equation, of a fact, rule, principle, or other logical relation. **—for′mu·la′ic** (-lā′ĭk) *adj.*

for·mu·late (fôr′myə-lāt′) ▸ *v.* **-lat·ed, -lat·ing. 1.** To state as a formula. **2.** To express in systematic terms or concepts. **3.** To prepare according to a specified formula. **—for′mu·la′tion** *n.* **—for′mu·la′tor** *n.*

for·ni·ca·tion (fôr′nĭ-kā′shən) ▸ *n.* Sexual intercourse between partners who are not married. **—for′ni·cate′** *v.* **—for′ni·ca′tor** *n.*

for·sake (fôr-sāk′, fər-) ▸ *v.* **-sook** (-so͝ok′), **-sak·en** (-sā′kən), **-sak·ing. 1.** To give up; renounce. **2.** To leave altogether; abandon; desert.

for·sooth (fôr-so͞oth′, fər-) ▸ *adv.* In truth; indeed.

for·swear (fôr-swâr′) ▸ *v.* **-swore** (fôr-swôr′), **-sworn** (fôr-swôrn′), **-swear·ing. 1.** To renounce seriously or under oath. **2.** To commit perjury.

for·syth·i·a (fôr-sĭth′ē-ə, -sī′thē-ə, fər-) ▸ *n.* A widely cultivated shrub with early-blooming yellow flowers.

fort (fôrt) ▸ *n.* A fortified place, esp. an army post.

for·te¹ (fôr′tā′, fôrt) ▸ *n.* Something in which one excels.

for·te² (fôr′tā′) ▸ *adv. & adj. Mus.* In a loud, forceful manner. **—for′te′** *n.*

forth (fôrth) ▸ *adv.* **1.** Forward or onward. **2.** Out into view.

forth·com·ing (fôrth-kŭm′ĭng) ▸ *adj.* **1.** About to appear or take place. **2.** Available when required or as promised. **3.** Willing to help; cooperative.

forth·right (fôrth′rīt′) ▸ *adj.* Direct and without evasion; straightforward. **—forth′right′ly** *adv.* **—forth′right′ness** *n.*

forth·with (fôrth-wĭth′, -wĭth′) ▸ *adv.* At once; immediately.

for·ti·eth (fôr′tē-ĭth) ▸ *n.* **1.** The ordinal number matching the number 40 in a series. **2.** One of 40 equal parts. **—for′ti·eth** *adv. & adj.*

for·ti·fy (fôr′tə-fī′) ▸ *v.* **-fied, -fy·ing. 1.** To strengthen and secure (a position) militarily. **2.** To strengthen physically; invigorate. **3.** To give moral or mental strength to; encourage. **4.** To enrich (food), as by adding vitamins. **5.** To add alcohol to (wine). **—for′ti·fi·ca′tion** *n.*

for·tis·si·mo (fôr-tĭs′ə-mō′) ▸ *adv. & adj. Mus.* In a very loud manner. **—for·tis′si·mo′** *n.*

for·ti·tude (fôr′tĭ-to͞od′, -tyo͞od′) ▸ *n.* Strength of mind that allows one to endure pain or adversity with courage.

fort·night (fôrt′nīt′) ▸ *n.* A period of 14 days; two weeks.

fort·night·ly (fôrt′nīt′lē) ▸ *adj.* Happening or appearing once in or every two weeks. **—fort′night′ly** *adv.*

FOR·TRAN (fôr′trăn′) ▸ *n.* A programming language for problems that can be expressed algebraically.

for·tress (fôr′trĭs) ▸ *n.* A fortified place, esp. one that includes a town.

for·tu·i·tous (fôr-to͞o′ĭ-təs, -tyo͞o′-) ▸ *adj.* Happening by ac-

THESAURUS

formal *adj.* Requiring elegant clothes and fine manners ▸ black-tie, dressy, full-dress, white-tie. *—See also* AUTHORITATIVE (1), CEREMONIOUS, COOL, RITUAL.

formal *n.* *—See* DANCE.

formalistic *adj.* *—See* PEDANTIC.

formality *n.* *—See* CEREMONY (2), RITUAL.

format *n.* *—See* ARRANGEMENT (1), METHOD.

formation *n.* *—See* ARRANGEMENT (1).

former *adj.* *—See* LATE (2), PAST.

formerly *adv.* *—See* EARLIER (1).

formidable *adj.* *—See* BURDENSOME, DEEP (2), FEARFUL.

formless *adj.* *—See* SHAPELESS.

formula *n.* A means or method of entering into or achieving something that is desirable ▸ key, route, secret. *Informal:* ticket. [*Compare* TRICK.] *—See also* LAW (3), WAY (1).

formulaic *adj.* *—See* ORDINARY.

formulate *v.* To devise and set down ▸ compose, draft, draw up, frame. [*Compare* COMPOSE.] *—See also* DESIGN (1), INVENT, PHRASE.

formulated *adj.* *—See* CALCULATED.

fornicator *n.* *—See* PHILANDERER.

forsake *v.* *—See* ABANDON (1), DEFECT.

forsaken *adj.* *—See* ABANDONED (1).

forswear *v.* *—See* ABANDON (1), BREAK (5), LIE², RETRACT (1).

fort *n.* A position or building that has been fortified to be defended by soldiers ▸ bastion, citadel, fortification, fortress, redoubt, stronghold. [*Compare* BASE¹.]

forte *n.* Something at which a person excels ▸ long suit, métier, specialty, strength, strong point, strong suit. *Slang:* bag, thing.

forth *adv.* *—See* FORWARD.

forthcoming *adj.* In the relatively near future ▸ approaching, coming, due, upcoming. *Idioms:* around the corner, on the horizon. [*Compare* CLOSE, IMMINENT.]

forthright *adj.* *—See* FRANK.

forthwith *adv.* *—See* IMMEDIATELY (1).

fortification *n.* *—See* FORT.

fortify *v.* To make firmer in a particular conviction or habit ▸ confirm, harden, reinforce, strengthen. [*Compare* BACK, ESTABLISH.] *—See also* ENCOURAGE (2), GIRD.

fortitude *n.* *—See* COURAGE, ENDURANCE.

fortitudinous *adj.* *—See* BRAVE.

fortress *n.* *—See* FORT.

fortuitous *adj.* Characterized by luck or good fortune ▸ fortunate, happy, lucky, providential. [*Compare* OPPOR-

cident or chance; unplanned. **—for·tu′i·tous·ly** *adv.* **—for·tu′i·tous·ness** *n.*

for·tu·i·ty (fôr-to͞o′ĭ-tē, -tyo͞o′-) ▸ *n., pl.* **-ties.** 1. A chance occurrence or event. 2. The quality or condition of being fortuitous.

for·tu·nate (fôr′chə-nĭt) ▸ *adj.* Occurring by or having good fortune. **—for′tu·nate·ly** *adv.*

for·tune (fôr′chən) ▸ *n.* 1a. Fate; destiny. b. Good or bad luck. 2. **fortunes** The turns of luck in one's lifetime. 3a. Wealth; riches. b. A large sum of money.

for·tune-tell·er (fôr′chən-tĕl′ər) ▸ *n.* One who, usu. for a fee, professes to predict future events. **—for′tune-tell′ing** *adj. & n.*

Fort Worth ▸ A city of NE TX W of Dallas. Pop. 535,000.

for·ty (fôr′tē) ▸ *n., pl.* **-ties.** The cardinal number equal to 4 × 10. **—for′ty** *adj. & pron.*

for·ty-five (fôr′tē-fīv′) ▸ *n.* 1. A .45-caliber pistol. 2. A phonograph record designed to be played at 45 revolutions per minute.

for·ty-nin·er (fôr′tē-nī′nər) ▸ *n.* One who took part in the 1849 California gold rush.

forty winks ▸ *pl.n. Informal* A short nap.

fo·rum (fôr′əm) ▸ *n., pl.* **fo·rums** also **fo·ra** (fôr′ə). 1. The public square or marketplace of an ancient Roman city. 2. A public place or medium for open discussion. 3. A court of law; tribunal.

for·ward (fôr′wərd) ▸ *adj.* 1. At, near, belonging to, or located in the front. 2. Going, tending, or moving toward the front. 3. Presumptuous or bold. 4. Being ahead of current economic, political, or technological trends; progressive. 5. Mentally, physically, or socially advanced; precocious. ▸ *adv.* 1. Toward or tending to the front; frontward: *step forward.* 2. In or toward the future: *looking forward to seeing you.* 3. Earlier or later: *moved the appointment forward.* ▸ *n. Sports* A player in the front line, as in basketball or hockey. ▸ *v.* 1. To send on to a subsequent destination or address. 2. To help advance; promote. **—for′ward·ly** *adv.* **—for′ward·ness** *n.*

for·wards (fôr′wərdz) ▸ *adv.* To or tending to the front; forward.

for·went (fôr-wĕnt′) ▸ *v.* P.t. of **forgo.**

fos·sil (fŏs′əl) ▸ *n.* 1. A remnant or trace of an organism of a past geologic age, such as a skeleton or leaf imprint, embedded in the earth's crust. 2. One that is outdated.

fossil fuel ▸ *n.* A hydrocarbon deposit, such as natural gas, derived from living matter of a previous geologic time and used for fuel.

fos·sil·ize (fŏs′ə-līz′) ▸ *v.* **-ized, -iz·ing.** 1. To convert into or become a fossil. 2. To make or become outmoded, rigid, or fixed; antiquate. **—fos′sil·i·za′tion** *n.*

fos·ter (fô′stər, fŏs′tər) ▸ *v.* 1. To bring up; rear. 2. To promote the development of; cultivate. ▸ *adj.* Giving or receiving parental care although not related legally or by blood: *foster parents.*

fought (fôt) ▸ *v.* P.t. and p.part. of **fight.**

foul (foul) ▸ *adj.* **-er, -est.** 1. Offensive to the senses; revolting: *a foul flavor.* 2. Having an offensive odor. 3. Rotten or putrid. 4a. Dirty; filthy. b. Full of impurities; polluted: *foul air.* 5. Morally detestable; wicked. 6. Vulgar; obscene. 7. Bad or unfavorable; unpleasant: *foul weather.* 8. Unfair; dishonorable: *win by foul means.* 9a. *Sports* Contrary to the rules of a game or sport. b. Designating lines that limit the playing area. 10. Entangled or twisted, as a rope. ▸ *n.* 1a. *Sports* An infraction of the rules. b. *Baseball* A foul ball, hit, or move. 2. An entanglement or collision. ▸ *adv.* In a foul manner. ▸ *v.* 1. To make or become foul; pollute. 2. To bring into dishonor. 3. To clog or obstruct. 4. To entangle or become entangled, as a rope. 5. To commit a foul (against). ***—phrasal verb:* foul up** To blunder or cause to blunder because of mistakes or poor judgment. **—foul′ly** *adv.* **—foul′ness** *n.*

fou·lard (fo͞o-lärd′) ▸ *n.* A lightweight twill or plain-woven fabric of silk, usu. having a printed design, esp. used for neckties.

foul·mouthed (foul′mouthd′, -moutht′) ▸ *adj.* Using abusive or obscene language.

foul play ▸ *n.* Unfair or treacherous action, esp. when involving violence.

foul shot ▸ *n. Basketball* An unobstructed shot awarded to a fouled player and scored as one point if successful.

foul-up (foul′ŭp′) ▸ *n.* 1. A condition of confusion caused by mistakes or poor judgment. 2. A mechanical failure.

found[1] (found) ▸ *v.* 1. To establish or set up (e.g., a college). 2. To establish the foundation or basis of. **—found′er** *n.*

found[2] (found) ▸ *v.* 1. To melt (metal) and pour into a mold. 2. To make (objects) by founding. **—found′er** *n.*

found[3] (found) ▸ *v.* P.t. and p.part. of **find.**

foun·da·tion (foun-dā′shən) ▸ *n.* 1. The act of founding, esp. the establishment of an institution. 2. The basis on which a thing stands; underlying support; base. 3a. An endowment. b. An endowed institution. 4. A cosmetic used as a base for facial makeup. **—foun·da′tion·al** *adj.*

foun·der (foun′dər) ▸ *v.* 1. To sink or cause to sink below the water. 2. To fail utterly; collapse. 3. To go lame, as a horse.

found·ling (found′lĭng) ▸ *n.* An abandoned child of unknown parentage.

foun·dry (foun′drē) ▸ *n., pl.* **-dries.** A place where metal is melted and molded.

fount[1] (fount) ▸ *n.* 1. A fountain. 2. A source.

fount[2] (fount) ▸ *n. Chiefly Brit.* Var. of **font**[2].

foun·tain (foun′tən) ▸ *n.* 1a. An artificially created stream of water. b. A structure or device from which such a stream issues. 2. A spring of water from the earth, esp. a stream's source. 3. A soda fountain. 4. A point of origin.

foun·tain·head (foun′tən-hĕd′) ▸ *n.* 1. A spring that is the source of a stream. 2. A chief and copious source or origin.

fountain pen ▸ *n.* A pen filled from an external source and containing an ink reservoir that automatically feeds the writing point.

four (fôr) ▸ *n.* 1. The cardinal number that is equal to 3 +

THESAURUS

TUNE.] —*See also* ACCIDENTAL, OPPORTUNE.

fortuitousness *n.* —*See* CHANCE (2).

fortuity *n.* —*See* CHANCE (1), CHANCE (2).

fortunate *adj.* Characterized by luck or good fortune ▸ fortuitous, happy, lucky, providential. —*See also* FAVORABLE (1), OPPORTUNE.

fortunateness *n.* —*See* LUCK.

fortune *n.* A large sum of money ▸ mint. *Informal:* bundle, pile, pretty penny, tidy sum, wad. ***Idiom:*** king's ransom. —*See also* CHANCE (2), FATE (1), FATE (2), LUCK, RESOURCES, WEALTH.

fortuneteller *n.* —*See* PROPHET.

forum *n.* —*See* ASSEMBLY, CONFERENCE (1), COURT (2).

forward *v.* —*See* ADVANCE (1), SEND (1).

forward *adj.* —*See* PROGRESSIVE (1).

forward *adv.* Toward the front or beyond a position ▸ ahead, forth, frontward, out, onward. *Idiom:* in advance.

forward-looking or **forward-thinking** *adj.* —*See* PROGRESSIVE (1).

forwardness *n.* —*See* IMPUDENCE.

fossil *n.* —*See* SQUARE, ULTRACONSERVATIVE.

foster *v.* To take care of and educate a child ▸ bring up, parent, raise, rear. —*See also* ADVANCE (1), NURTURE, PROMOTE (2).

foul *adj.* —*See* BAD (2), BLEAK (1), DIRTY, OBSCENE, OFFENSIVE (1), SMELLY.

foul *v.* —*See* CONTAMINATE, DIRTY, ENTANGLE.

foul up *v.* —*See* BOTCH.

foul *n.* —*See* COLLISION.

foulness *n.* —*See* CONTAMINATION, DIRTINESS, OBSCENITY (1).

foul play *n.* —*See* CONTAMINATION, FAITHLESSNESS.

foul-smelling *adj.* —*See* SMELLY.

foul-tasting *adj.* —*See* UNPALATABLE.

foul-up *n.* —*See* MESS (1).

found *v.* To bring into existence formally ▸ constitute, create, establish, institute, organize, originate, set up, start. [*Compare* START.] —*See also* BASE[1].

foundation *n.* The act of founding or establishing ▸ constitution, creation, establishment, institution, organization, origination, start-up. [*Compare* BEGINNING.] —*See also* BASE[1] (2), BASIS (1), BASIS (2).

foundational *adj.* —*See* RADICAL.

founder[1] *v.* —*See* FAIL (1), SINK (1).

founder[2] *n.* —*See* ORIGINATOR.

foundling *n.* —*See* ORPHAN.

fountain or **fount** or **fountainhead** *n.* —*See* ORIGIN.

1\. 2. The 4th in a set or sequence. **—four** *adj. & pron.*

four-flush (fôr′flŭsh′) ► *v.* **1.** *Games* To bluff in poker with a hand having only four out of five cards of the same suit. **2.** *Slang* To mislead; bluff. **—four′-flush′er** *n.*

4-H Club or **Four-H Club** (fôr′āch′) ► *n.* A youth organization sponsored by the Department of Agriculture and teaching agriculture and home economics.

four-in-hand (fôr′ĭn-hănd′) ► *n.* **1.** A team of four horses controlled by one driver. **2.** A necktie tied in a slipknot with long ends left hanging one in front of the other.

four-leaf clover (fôr′lēf′) ► *n.* A clover leaf having four leaflets instead of three, considered an omen of good luck.

four-o'clock (fôr′ə-klŏk′) ► *n.* A plant cultivated for its tubular, variously colored flowers that open late in the afternoon.

401(k) (fôr′ō-wŭn-kā′) ► *n.* A retirement plan for investing a portion of one's wages in a tax-deferred account.

four-post·er (fôr′pō′stər) ► *n.* A bed having tall corner posts orig. intended to support curtains or a canopy.

four·score (fôr′skôr′) ► *adj.* Four times twenty; eighty.

four·some (fôr′səm) ► *n.* **1.** A group of four persons. **2.** Four players in a game, with two on each side, esp. in golf or bridge.

four·square (fôr′skwâr′) ► *adj.* **1.** Square. **2.** Marked by firm, unwavering conviction or expression; forthright. **—four′square′** *adv.*

four·teen (fôr-tēn′) ► *n.* **1.** The cardinal number that is equal to 13 + 1. **2.** The 14th in a set or sequence. **—four·teen′** *adj. & pron.*

four·teenth (fôr-tēnth′) ► *n.* **1.** The ordinal number matching the number 14 in a series. **2.** One of 14 equal parts. **—four·teenth′** *adv. & adj.*

fourth (fôrth) ► *n.* **1.** The ordinal number matching the number 4 in a series. **2.** One of four equal parts. **3.** *Mus.* A tone four degrees above or below a given tone in a diatonic scale. **—fourth** *adv. & adj.*

fourth dimension ► *n.* Time regarded as a coordinate dimension and required, along with three spatial dimensions, to specify completely the location of any event.

fourth estate ► *n.* Journalists collectively.

Fourth of July ► *n.* See **Independence Day**.

four-wheel drive (fôr′hwēl′, -wēl) ► *n.* An automotive drive system in which mechanical power is transmitted from the drive shaft to all four wheels.

fowl (foul) ► *n., pl.* **fowl** or **fowls**. **1.** A bird used as food, esp. the common domesticated chicken. **2.** A bird used as food or hunted as game. ► *v.* To hunt, trap, or shoot wildfowl.

fox (fŏks) ► *n., pl.* **-es** also **fox**. **1a.** A carnivorous mammal related to the dogs and wolves, having a pointed snout and a long bushy tail. **b.** The fur of a fox. **2.** A crafty or sly person. **3.** *Slang* A sexually attractive person. ► *v.* To trick or fool by ingenuity or cunning; outwit. **—fox′i·ly** *adv.* **—fox′i·ness** *n.* **—fox′y** *adj.*

Fox ► *n., pl.* **Fox** or **-es**. **1.** A member of a Native American people formerly of the upper Midwest, now in central Iowa and Oklahoma. **2.** Their Algonquian language.

fox·fire (fŏks′fīr′) ► *n.* A phosphorescent glow, esp. that of fungi on rotting wood.

fox·glove (fŏks′glŭv′) ► *n.* A plant having a long cluster of large, tubular, pinkish-purple flowers and leaves that are the source of the medicinal drug digitalis.

fox·hole (fŏks′hōl′) ► *n.* A pit dug by a soldier for protection against enemy fire.

fox terrier ► *n.* A small terrier having a white coat with dark markings.

fox trot ► *n.* A ballroom dance in 4/4 time, encompassing a variety of slow and fast steps. **—fox′trot′** (fŏks′trŏt′) *v.*

foy·er (foi′ər, foi′ā′) ► *n.* **1.** A lobby, as of a theater or hotel. **2.** An entrance hall; vestibule.

Fr ► The symbol for the element **francium**.

fra·cas (frā′kəs, frăk′əs) ► *n.* A rowdy fight.

frac·tal (frăk′təl) ► *n.* A geometric pattern that is repeated at ever smaller scales to produce irregular shapes that cannot be represented by classical geometry.

frac·tion (frăk′shən) ► *n.* **1.** *Math.* A quotient of two quantities shown as a numerator over a denominator. **2.** A disconnected piece; fragment. **3.** A small part; bit. **—frac′tion·al** *adj.* **—frac′tion·al·ly** *adv.*

frac·tious (frăk′shəs) ► *adj.* **1.** Inclined to make trouble; unruly. **2.** Having a peevish nature; cranky. **—frac′tious·ly** *adv.* **—frac′tious·ness** *n.*

frac·ture (frăk′chər) ► *n.* **1.** The act or process of breaking or the condition of being broken. **2.** A break, rupture, or crack, esp. in bone or cartilage. ► *v.* **-tured, -tur·ing.** To break or cause to break; crack.

frag·ile (frăj′əl, -īl′) ► *adj.* **1.** Easily broken or damaged; delicate. **2.** Tenuous or flimsy: *a fragile claim to fame.* **—frag′ile·ly** *adv.* **—fra·gil′i·ty** (frə-jĭl′ĭ-tē), **frag′ile·ness** *n.*

frag·ment (frăg′mənt) ► *n.* **1.** A small part broken off. **2.** Something incomplete. ► *v.* (-mĕnt′) To break into fragments. **—frag′men·ta′tion** *n.*

frag·men·tar·y (frăg′mən-tĕr′ē) ► *adj.* Consisting of small, disconnected parts. **—frag′men·tar′i·ly** (-târ′ə-lē) *adv.*

fragmentation bomb ► *n.* An aerial antipersonnel bomb that scatters shrapnel over a wide area upon explosion.

fra·grance (frā′grəns) ► *n.* A sweet or pleasant odor. **—fra′grant** *adj.* **—fra′grant·ly** *adv.*

frail (frāl) ► *adj.* **-er, -est.** **1.** Physically weak. **2.** Not substantial; slight. **3.** Easily broken. **—frail′ly** *adv.*

frail·ty (frāl′tē) ► *n., pl.* **-ties**. **1.** The condition or quality of being frail. **2.** A fault, esp. one arising from human weakness.

frame (frām) ► *v.* **framed, fram·ing.** **1.** To build or construct. **2.** To conceive or design. **3.** To arrange or adjust for a purpose. **4.** To put into words; compose. **5.** To enclose in or as if in a frame. **6.** *Informal* To rig evidence or events so as to incriminate (a person) falsely. ► *n.* **1.** Something composed of parts fitted and joined together. **2.** A skeletal structure: *the frame of a house.* **3.** An open structure or rim: *a window frame.* **4.** The human body; physique. **5.** A general structure or system: *the frame of government.* **6.** A general state or condition: *frame of mind.* **7.** A round of play in some games, such as bowling. **8.** A single picture on a roll of movie film, videotape, or television images. **9.** *Comp. Sci.* A segment within a browser's window that can be scrolled independently of other such segments. **—fram′er** *n.*

frame-up (frām′ŭp′) ► *n.* *Informal* A fraudulent scheme, esp. one that involves falsified charges or evidence to incriminate an innocent person.

frame·work (frām′wûrk′) ► *n.* **1.** A structure for support-

THESAURUS

four-flush *v.* *—See* DECEIVE.

fourth estate *n.* *—See* PRESS.

foxiness *n.* *—See* ART.

foxy *adj.* *—See* ARTFUL, DESIRABLE.

fracas *n.* *—See* ARGUMENT, DISORDER (2), FIGHT (1).

fraction *n.* *—See* PART (1).

fractional *adj.* *—See* PARTIAL (1).

fractious *adj.* *—See* ILL-TEMPERED, UNRULY.

fractiousness *n.* *—See* UNRULINESS.

fracture *v.* *—See* BREAK (1), CRACK (1).

fracture *n.* *—See* CRACK (2).

fragile *adj.* Easily broken or damaged ► breakable, brittle, delicate, frangible, friable. *—See also* WEAK (1).

fragility or **fragileness** *n.* *—See* INFIRMITY.

fragment *n.* *—See* BIT[1] (1), END (3).

fragment *v.* *—See* DISINTEGRATE.

fragmentary *adj.* *—See* PARTIAL (1).

fragmentize *v.* *—See* DISINTEGRATE.

fragrance *n.* A sweet or pleasant odor ► aroma, bouquet, essence, perfume, redolence, scent. [*Compare* SMELL, STENCH.]

fragrant *adj.* Having a pleasant odor ► aromatic, odoriferous, odorous, perfumy, redolent, savory, scent-laden, sweet-smelling. [*Compare* SMELLY.]

fraidy cat *n.* *—See* COWARD.

frail *adj.* *—See* WEAK (1).

frailness *n.* *—See* INFIRMITY.

frailty *n.* *—See* INFIRMITY, WEAKNESS.

frame *n.* A structure that supports or encloses something ► case, casing, framing, framework, shell, skeleton, substructure. [*Compare* FORM, STAGE, SUPPORT.] *—See also* CONSTITUTION.

frame *v.* *—See* BUILD, COMPOSE, DESIGN (1), MAKE, PHRASE.

frame of mind *n.* *—See* MOOD.

frame of reference *n.* *—See* VIEWPOINT.

framework *n.* *—See* DRAFT (1), FRAME.

ing or enclosing something. **2.** A fundamental system or design.

franc (frăngk) ▸ *n.* **1.** See **currency** table in Appendix. **2.** The primary unit of currency in Belgium, France, Luxembourg, and Monaco before the adoption of the euro.

France (frăns) ▸ A country of W Europe on the Atlantic and the English Channel. Pop. 59,800,000.

fran·chise (frăn′chīz′) ▸ *n.* **1.** A privilege granted a person or a group; charter. **2.** A constitutional or statutory right, as the right to vote. **3.** Authorization granted to someone to sell a company's goods or services. **4.** The territory or limits within which a privilege or right may be exercised. ▸ *v.* **-chised, -chis·ing.** To grant a franchise to. **—fran′chis·ee′** *n.* **—fran′chis′er, fran′chi′sor** *n.*

Fran·cis Fer·di·nand (frăn′sĭs fûr′dn-ănd′) (1863–1914) ▸ Austrian archduke whose assassination precipitated World War I.

Francis of As·si·si (ə-sē′zē, -sē, ə-sĭs′ē), Saint (1182?–1226) ▸ Italian friar; founder of the Franciscan order (1209). **—Fran·cis′can** *adj. & n.*

fran·ci·um (frăn′sē əm) ▸ *n. Symbol* **Fr** An extremely unstable synthetic radioactive element. At. no. 87.

Franco– ▸ *pref.* French: *Francophone.*

Fran·co·phone (frăng′kə-fōn′) ▸ *n.* A French-speaking person, esp. in a region of linguistic diversity. ▸ *adj.* French-speaking.

fran·gi·ble (frăn′jə-bəl) ▸ *adj.* Easily broken; breakable. **—fran′gi·bil′i·ty, fran′gi·ble·ness** *n.*

frank[1] (frăngk) ▸ *adj.* **-er, -est.** Open and sincere in expression; straightforward. ▸ *v.* **1.** To put an official mark on (a piece of mail) so that it can be sent free of charge. **2.** To send (mail) free of charge. ▸ *n.* **1.** A mark or signature on a piece of mail to indicate the right to send it free. **2.** The right to send mail free. **—frank′ly** *adv.* **—frank′ness** *n.*

frank[2] (frăngk) ▸ *n. Informal* A frankfurter.

Frank ▸ *n.* A member of a Germanic people who conquered Gaul about A.D. 500. **—Frank′ish** *adj.*

Frank (frăngk, frängk), **Anne** (1929–45) ▸ German Jewish diarist.

Frank·en·stein (frăng′kən-stīn′) ▸ *n.* **1.** A creation that destroys its creator. **2.** A monster having the appearance of a man.

Frank·fort (frăngk′fərt) ▸ The capital of KY, in the N-central part NW of Lexington. Pop. 27,700.

Frank·furt (frănk′fərt, frängk′fo͝ort′) also **Frankfurt am Main** (äm mīn′) ▸ A city of W-central Germany on the Main R. Pop. 648,000.

frank·furt·er (frănk′fər-tər) ▸ *n.* A smoked sausage of beef or beef and pork made in long reddish links.

frank·in·cense (frăng′kĭn-sĕns′) ▸ *n.* An aromatic gum resin used chiefly as incense.

Frank·lin (frăngk′lĭn), **Benjamin** (1706–90) ▸ Amer. public official, writer, scientist, and printer.

fran·tic (frăn′tĭk) ▸ *adj.* Distraught, as from fear or worry. **—fran′ti·cal·ly, fran′tic·ly** *adv.*

frappe (frăp) ▸ *n. Regional* See **milk shake.**

frap·pé (fră-pā′, frăp) ▸ *n.* **1.** A frozen mixture similar to sherbet. **2.** A beverage poured over shaved ice.

fra·ter·nal (frə-tûr′nəl) ▸ *adj.* **1a.** Of brothers. **b.** Brotherly. **2.** Of or constituting a fraternity. **3.** *Biol.* Of or being a twin developed from separately fertilized ova. **—fra·ter′nal·ism** *n.* **—fra·ter′nal·ly** *adv.*

fra·ter·ni·ty (frə-tûr′nĭ-tē) ▸ *n., pl.* **-ties.** **1.** A group of people associated or joined by similar backgrounds, occupations, or interests. **2.** A chiefly social organization of male college students. **3.** Brotherhood.

frat·er·nize (frăt′ər-nīz′) ▸ *v.* **-nized, -niz·ing.** **1.** To associate with others in a brotherly or congenial way. **2.** To associate with an enemy or opposing group. **—frat′er·ni·za′tion** *n.*

frat·ri·cide (frăt′rĭ-sīd′) ▸ *n.* **1.** The killing of one's brother or sister. **2.** One who has killed a sibling. **—frat′ri·cid′al** *adj.*

Frau (frou) ▸ *n., pl.* **Frau·en** (frou′ən). A German courtesy title for a woman.

fraud (frôd) ▸ *n.* **1.** A deliberate deception for unfair or unlawful gain; swindle. **2a.** One that defrauds; cheat. **b.** One who assumes a false pose; impostor.

fraud·u·lent (frô′jə-lənt) ▸ *adj.* Constituting or gained by fraud. **—fraud′u·lence** *n.* **—fraud′u·lent·ly** *adv.*

fraught (frôt) ▸ *adj.* **1.** Filled with a specified element; charged: *work fraught with danger.* **2.** Distressful; upsetting.

Fräu·lein (froi′līn′, frou′-) ▸ *n., pl.* **-lein.** A German courtesy title for a girl or young woman.

fray[1] (frā) ▸ *n.* **1.** A fight or scuffle. **2.** A heated dispute.

fray[2] (frā) ▸ *v.* **1.** To strain; chafe: *fray the nerves.* **2.** To wear away, unravel, or tatter by rubbing.

fraz·zle (frăz′əl) ▸ *v.* **-zled, -zling.** *Informal* **1.** To fray. **2.** To exhaust physically or emotionally. **—fraz′zle** *n.*

freak (frēk) ▸ *n.* **1.** A person, thing, or event that is abnormal or markedly unusual. **2.** A whim; vagary. **3.** *Slang* **a.** A drug addict. **b.** A fan or enthusiast. ▸ *adj.* Highly unusual or irregular: *a freak storm.* ▸ *v. Slang* **1.** To experience or cause to experience hallucinations or feelings of paranoia, esp. as induced by a drug. Often used with *out.* **2.** To make or become agitated or excited: *a find that freaked me out.* **—freak′i·ly** *adv.* **—freak′ish** *adj.* **—freak′ish·ly** *adv.* **—freak′ish·ness** *n.* **—freak′y** *adj.*

freak-out (frēk′out′) ▸ *n. Slang* An act or an instance of freaking out.

freck·le (frĕk′əl) ▸ *n.* A brownish spot on the skin, often darkening with exposure to the sun. ▸ *v.* **-led, -ling.** To dot or become dotted with freckles or spots. **—freck′ly** *adj.*

Fred·er·ick II (frĕd′rĭk, -ər-ĭk) "Frederick the Great" (1712–86) ▸ King of Prussia (1740–86).

Fred·er·ic·ton (frĕd′rĭk-tən, -ər-ĭk-) ▸ The capital of New Brunswick, Canada, in the S-central part. Pop. 47,600.

free (frē) ▸ *adj.* **fre·er, fre·est.** **1.** Not bound or constrained; at liberty. **2.** Not under obligation or necessity. **3a.** Having political independence. **b.** Governed by consent and possessing civil liberties. **4a.** Not affected by a given condition or circumstance. **b.** Exempt: *free of all taxes.* **5.** Not literal or exact: *a free translation.* **6.** Costing nothing;

THESAURUS

framing *n.* —*See* FRAME.

franchise *n.* —*See* RIGHT.

frangible *adj.* —*See* FRAGILE.

frank *adj.* Honest and direct, especially in speech; not lying or dissembling ▸ aboveboard, candid, direct, downright, forthright, free, free-spoken, honest, ingenuous, open, outspoken, plain, plainspoken, straight, straightforward, straight-out, unreserved, upfront, vocal. *Informal:* straight-from-the-shoulder, straight-shooting. [*Compare* ARTLESS, GENUINE, SERIOUS.]

frankness *n.* —*See* HONESTY.

frantic *adj.* Characterized by hurried activity and confusion or agitation ▸ delirious, fervid, fevered, feverish, frenetic, frenzied, hectic, mad, wild. [*Compare* ANXIOUS, BUSY.]

frantically *adv.* —*See* HARD (1).

fraternity *n.* —*See* UNION (1).

fraternize *v.* —*See* ASSOCIATE (2).

fraud *n.* —*See* CHEAT (1), DECEIT, FAKE.

fraudulent *adj.* —*See* COUNTERFEIT.

fraught *adj.* —*See* FULL (1).

fray[1] *n.* —*See* FIGHT (1).

fray[2] or **frazzle** *v.* To wear away along the edges ▸ frazzle, tatter. [*Compare* ERODE, SHRED.]

freak *n.* **1.** *Slang* One whose sexual behavior differs from the accepted norm ▸ deviant, deviate, pervert. **5.** MONSTER. —*See also* CRACKPOT, FAN[2], FANCY.

freakish *adj.* Resembling a freak ▸ freaky, grotesque, monstrous. —*See also* CAPRICIOUS, ECCENTRIC, WEIRD.

freaky *adj.* Resembling a freak ▸ freakish, grotesque, monstrous. [*Compare* ECCENTRIC, WEIRD.]

freckle *v.* —*See* SPECKLE.

free *adj.* **1.** Not imprisoned, enslaved, or controlled by another ▸ autonomous, emancipated, freed, independent, liberated, manumitted, released, self-governing, self-ruling, sovereign. [*Compare* VOLUNTARY.] **2.** Costing nothing ▸ complimentary, gratis, gratuitous. *Idioms:* as a freebie, for free, for nothing, on the house. —*See also* CLEAR (3), FRANK, GENEROUS (1), LOOSE (2), LOOSE (3), OPEN (3), OPEN (4).

free *v.* **1.** To set at liberty ▸ discharge, emancipate, liberate, loose, manumit, release. *Slang:* spring.

gratuitous. **7.** Not occupied or used. **8.** Unobstructed. **9.** Guileless; frank. **10.** Taking undue liberties. **11.** Liberal or lavish. ▸ *adv.* **1.** In a free manner. **2.** Without charge. ▸ *v.* **freed, free·ing.** **1.** To set at liberty. **2.** To rid of; release. **3.** To disengage or untangle. **—free′ly** *adv.*

free·base or **free-base** (frē′bās′) ▸ *v.* **-based, -bas·ing.** To prepare or use purified cocaine by burning it and inhaling the fumes.

free·bie also **free·bee** (frē′bē) ▸ *n. Slang* Something given or received free.

free·board (frē′bôrd′) ▸ *n.* The distance between the water line and the uppermost full deck of a ship.

free·boot·er (frē′bo͞o′tər) ▸ *n.* A pirate or plunderer.

free·born (frē′bôrn′) ▸ *adj.* **1.** Born as a free person. **2.** Of or befitting a person born free.

freed·man (frēd′mən) ▸ *n.* A man who has been freed from slavery.

free·dom (frē′dəm) ▸ *n.* **1.** The condition of being free. **2a.** Political independence. **b.** Possession of civil rights. **3.** Ease of movement. **4.** Frankness or boldness. **5.** Unrestricted use or access.

freed·wom·an (frēd′wo͝om′ən) ▸ *n.* A woman who has been freed from slavery.

free enterprise ▸ *n.* The freedom of private businesses to operate competitively for profit with minimal government regulation.

free fall or **free-fall** (frē′fôl′) ▸ *n.* The fall of a body toward the earth without a drag-producing device such as a parachute.

free flight ▸ *n.* Flight, as of a spacecraft, after termination of powered flight.

free-for-all (frē′fər-ôl′) ▸ *n.* A fight or competition in which everyone present takes part.

free·form (frē′fôrm′) ▸ *adj.* Having a usu. flowing asymmetrical shape or outline: *freeform sculpture.* **—free′form′** *adv.*

free·hand (frē′hănd′) ▸ *adj.* Drawn by hand without mechanical aids. **—free′hand′** *adv.*

free hand ▸ *n.* Freedom to do as one sees fit.

free·hand·ed (frē′hăn′dĭd) ▸ *adj.* Openhanded; generous. **—free′hand′ed·ly** *adv.* **—free′hand′ed·ness** *n.*

free·hold (frē′hōld′) ▸ *n.* **1.** An estate held in fee or for life. **2.** The tenure by which such an estate is held. **—free′hold′er** *n.*

free kick ▸ *n.* An unobstructed kick of a stationary ball, as in soccer.

free·lance (frē′lăns′) ▸ *n.* A person, esp. a writer or artist, who sells his or her services to employers as those services are needed. **—free′lance′** *v. & adj.* **—free′lanc′er** *n.*

free·load (frē′lōd′) ▸ *v.* To take advantage of the generosity or hospitality of others. **—free′load′er** *n.*

free love ▸ *n.* The belief in or practice of living together without marriage.

free·man (frē′mən) ▸ *n.* **1.** A person not in slavery. **2.** One who possesses the rights or privileges of a citizen.

Free·ma·son (frē′mā′sən) ▸ *n.* A member of the Free and Accepted Masons, an international fraternal charitable organization with secret rites and signs. **—Free′ma′son·ry** *n.*

free on board ▸ *adj. & adv.* Without charge to the buyer for delivery on board a carrier at a specified location.

free port ▸ *n.* A port where imported goods can be processed free of customs duties before reexport.

free speech ▸ *n.* The right to state or express any opinion in public without censorship or restraint by the government.

free·stand·ing (frē′stăn′dĭng) ▸ *adj.* Standing without support or attachment.

free·stone (frē′stōn′) ▸ *n.* **1.** A stone, such as limestone, soft enough to be cut easily without shattering. **2.** A fruit, esp. a peach, that has a stone not adhering to the pulp.

free·style (frē′stīl′) ▸ *n.* **1.** A swimming event in which any stroke is permissible. **2.** A competition, as in skiing, in which any maneuver is allowed and competitors are judged on their artistic expression and technical skill. **—free′style′** *adv. & adj.*

free·think·er (frē′thĭng′kər) ▸ *n.* One who rejects authority and dogma, esp. in religious thinking. **—free′think′ing** *adj. & n.*

free throw ▸ *n.* See **foul shot.**

free trade ▸ *n.* Trade between nations without protective customs tariffs.

free verse ▸ *n.* Verse composed of lines having no fixed metrical pattern.

free·ware (frē′wâr′) ▸ *n.* Free software, usu. available over the Internet.

free·way (frē′wā′) ▸ *n.* **1.** See **expressway.** **2.** A highway without tolls.

free·wheel·ing (frē′hwē′lĭng, -wē′-) ▸ *adj.* **1.** Free of restraints or rules, as in organization or procedure. **2.** Heedless; carefree.

free·will (frē′wĭl′) ▸ *adj.* Voluntary.

free will ▸ *n.* **1.** The ability or discretion to choose. **2.** The power to make choices that are unconstrained, as by fate.

freeze (frēz) ▸ *v.* **froze** (frōz), **fro·zen** (frō′zən), **freez·ing.** **1a.** To pass or cause to pass from liquid to solid by loss of heat. **b.** To acquire a surface of ice. **2.** To be at that degree of temperature at which ice forms. **3.** To damage or be damaged by cold or frost. **4.** To be uncomfortably cold. **5.** To make or become inoperative by or as if by frost or ice. **6.** To become unable to act or react, as from fear or shyness. **7.** To become icily silent. **8.** To make or become rigid and inflexible. **9.** To preserve by subjecting to freezing temperatures. **10a.** To fix (prices or wages) at a current level. **b.** To prohibit further manufacture or use of. **c.** To prevent or restrict the exchange, liquidation, or granting of by law **11.** To anesthetize by chilling. ***—phrasal verb:* freeze out** To exclude. ▸ *n.* **1.** The act of freezing or the condition of being frozen. **2.** A cold spell; frost.

freeze-dry (frēz′drī′) ▸ *v.* To preserve by rapid freezing and drying in a high vacuum.

freez·er (frē′zər) ▸ *n.* An insulated compartment, cabinet, or room for the rapid freezing and storing of perishable food.

freez·ing point (frē′zĭng) ▸ *n.* The temperature at which a given liquid solidifies under a specified pressure, esp. a pressure equal to that of the atmosphere.

freight (frāt) ▸ *n.* **1.** Goods carried by a vessel or vehicle; cargo. **2.** A burden; load. **3a.** Commercial transportation of goods. **b.** The charge for transporting goods by cargo carrier. **4.** A railway train carrying goods only. ▸ *v.* **1.** To convey commercially as cargo. **2.** To load with cargo. **3.** To load, as with meaning.

freight·er (frā′tər) ▸ *n.* A vehicle, esp. a ship, used for carrying freight.

THESAURUS

Idiom: let loose. [*Compare* RESCUE.] **2.** To rid of obstructions ▸ clear, open, remove, unblock. [*Compare* RID.] —*See also* EXTRICATE, OPEN (1).

freebie *n.* **1.** *Slang* A free ticket entitling one to transportation or admission ▸ pass. *Informal:* comp. **2.** *Slang* Something bestowed voluntarily ▸ bequest, gift, present, presentation. [*Compare* GRANT.]

freedom *n.* The condition of being politically free ▸ autonomy, independence, liberty, self-determination, self-government, self-rule, sovereignty. —*See also* LIBERTY, RIGHT.

free-for-all *n.* —*See* FIGHT (1).

free hand *n.* —*See* LICENSE (1).

freehanded *adj.* —*See* GENEROUS (1).

freehandedness *n.* —*See* GENEROSITY.

freeload *v. Slang* To take advantage of the generosity or hospitality of others ▸ leech, live off. *Informal:* sponge. [*Compare* BEG.]

freeloader *n.* —*See* PARASITE.

freeloading *adj.* —*See* PARASITIC.

freely *adv.* Of one's own free will ▸ by choice, spontaneously, voluntarily, willfully, willingly. *Idioms:* of one's own accord, on one's own volition.

freeman *n.* —*See* CITIZEN.

free-spoken *adj.* —*See* FRANK.

freethinker *n.* —*See* REBEL (2).

freeway *n.* —*See* WAY (2).

free will *n.* The mental faculty by which one deliberately chooses or decides ▸ volition, will. [*Compare* SPIRIT.] —*See also* CHOICE.

freezing *adj.* —*See* COLD (1).

freight *n.* —*See* BURDEN[1] (2), TRANSPORTATION.

freight *v.* —*See* BURDEN[1], FILL (1).

fre·na (frē′nə) ▸ *n.* Pl. of **frenum.**

French (frĕnch) ▸ *adj.* Of or relating to France or its people or language. ▸ *n.* **1.** The Romance language of France, Quebec, and various other areas. **2.** The people of France. **—French′man** *n.* **—French′wom′an** *n.*

French-Canadian also **French Canadian** ▸ *n.* A Canadian of French descent. **—French′-Ca·na′di·an** *adj.*

French door ▸ *n.* A door with glass panes extending for most of its length.

French fry ▸ *n.* A potato strip fried in deep fat.

French-fry (frĕnch′frī′) ▸ *v.* To fry in deep fat.

French Guiana ▸ A French overseas department of NE South America on the Atlantic. Cap. Cayenne. Pop. 182,000.

French horn ▸ *n.* A valved brass wind instrument with a long narrow coiled tube that ends in a flaring bell.

French leave ▸ *n.* An unauthorized departure.

French Polynesia ▸ A French overseas territory in the S-central Pacific, including the Society, Marquesas, and Austral islands and the Tuamotu archipelago. Cap. Papeete, on Tahiti. Pop. 245,000.

French toast ▸ *n.* Sliced bread soaked in a batter of milk and egg and lightly fried.

fre·net·ic or **phre·net·ic** (frə-nĕt′ĭk) also **fre·net·i·cal** or **phre·net·i·cal** (-ĭ-kəl) ▸ *adj.* Wildly excited or active; frantic; frenzied. **—fre·net′i·cal·ly** *adv.*

fre·num (frē′nəm) ▸ *n., pl.* **-nums** or **-na** (-nə) *Anat.* The band of tissue that connects the tongue to the floor of the mouth.

fren·zy (frĕn′zē) ▸ *n., pl.* **-zies. 1.** Violent mental agitation or wild excitement. **2.** Temporary madness. **3.** A mania; craze. **—fren′zied** *adj.* **—fren′zied·ly** *adv.*

fre·quen·cy (frē′kwən-sē) ▸ *n., pl.* **-cies. 1.** The property of occurring at frequent intervals. **2.** *Math. & Phys.* The number of times a specified phenomenon occurs within a specified interval, as the number of complete cycles of a periodic process occurring per unit time.

frequency modulation ▸ *n.* The encoding of a carrier wave by variation of its frequency in accordance with an input signal.

fre·quent (frē′kwənt) ▸ *adj.* Occurring or appearing often or at close intervals. ▸ *v.* (*also* frē-kwĕnt′) To visit (a place) often. **—fre·quent′er** *n.* **—fre′quent·ly** *adv.* **—fre′quent·ness** *n.*

fres·co (frĕs′kō) ▸ *n., pl.* **-coes** or **-cos. 1.** The art of painting on fresh plaster with pigments dissolved in water. **2.** A painting executed in this way.

fresh (frĕsh) ▸ *adj.* **-er, -est. 1.** New to one's experience; not encountered before. **2.** Novel; different. **3.** Recently made, produced, or harvested; not stale or spoiled. **4.** Not preserved, as by canning or freezing. **5.** Not salty: *fresh water.* **6.** Not yet used or soiled; clean: *a fresh sheet of paper.* **7.** Free from impurity or pollution: *fresh air.* **8.** Additional; new: *fresh evidence.* **9.** Not dull or faded: *a fresh memory.* **10.** Having the unspoiled appearance of youth: *a fresh complexion.* **11.** Untried; inexperienced: *fresh recruits.* **12.** Revived; refreshed. **13.** *Informal* Bold and saucy; impudent. ▸ *adv.* Recently; newly: *fresh out of milk.* **—fresh′ly** *adv.* **—fresh′ness** *n.*

fresh·en (frĕsh′ən) ▸ *v.* **1.** To make or become fresh. **2.** To add to or strengthen (a drink). **—fresh′en·er** *n.*

fresh·et (frĕsh′ĭt) ▸ *n.* A sudden overflow of a stream due to a heavy rain or a thaw.

fresh·man (frĕsh′mən) ▸ *n.* **1.** A first-year student of a US high school or college. **2.** A beginner; novice. **—fresh′man** *adj.*

fresh·wa·ter (frĕsh′wô′tər, -wŏt′ər) ▸ *adj.* Of, living in, or consisting of water that is not salty.

fret[1] (frĕt) ▸ *v.* **fret·ted, fret·ting. 1.** To rub or chafe. **2a.** To gnaw or wear away. **b.** To produce a hole or worn spot in. ▸ *n.* Irritation of mind. **—fret′ful** *adj.* **—fret′ful·ly** *adv.*

fret[2] (frĕt) ▸ *n. Mus.* One of several ridges set across the fingerboard of a stringed instrument.

fret[3] (frĕt) ▸ *n.* A design of repeated symmetrical figures within a band or border.

fret·work (frĕt′wûrk′) ▸ *n.* **1.** Ornamental work consisting of three-dimensional frets. **2.** Fretwork represented two dimensionally.

Freud (froid), **Sigmund** (1856–1939) ▸ Austrian physician and founder of psychoanalysis. **—Freud′i·an** *adj.*

Frey (frā) also **Freyr** (frâr) ▸ *n. Myth.* The Norse god of peace and prosperity.

Frey·a also **Frey·ja** (frā′ə) ▸ *n. Myth.* The Norse goddess of love and beauty.

Fri. ▸ *abbr.* Friday

fri·a·ble (frī′ə-bəl) ▸ *adj.* Readily crumbled; brittle.

fri·ar (frī′ər) ▸ *n.* A man who is a member of a usu. mendicant Roman Catholic order.

fric·as·see (frĭk′ə-sē′, frĭk′ə-sē′) ▸ *n.* Poultry or meat cut up and stewed in gravy. **—fric′as·see′** *v.*

fric·a·tive (frĭk′ə-tĭv) ▸ *n.* A consonant, such as *f* or *s* in English, produced by the forcing of breath through a constricted passage. **—fric′a·tive** *adj.*

fric·tion (frĭk′shən) ▸ *n.* **1.** The rubbing of one object or surface against another. **2.** Conflict, as between persons having dissimilar ideas or interests; clash. **3.** *Phys.* A force that resists the relative motion or tendency to such motion of two bodies in contact. **—fric′tion·al** *adj.* **—fric′tion·al·ly** *adv.*

friction tape ▸ *n.* A sturdy, moisture-resistant adhesive tape used chiefly to insulate electrical conductors.

Fri·day (frī′dē, -dā′) ▸ *n.* The 6th day of the week.

fridge (frĭj) ▸ *n. Informal* A refrigerator.

friend (frĕnd) ▸ *n.* **1.** A person whom one knows, likes, and trusts. **2.** One who supports, sympathizes with, or patronizes a group, cause, or movement. **3. Friend** A member of the Society of Friends; Quaker. **—friend′ship** *n.*

friend·ly (frĕnd′lē) ▸ *adj.* **-li·er, -li·est. 1.** Of or befitting a friend. **2.** Favorably disposed; not antagonistic. **3.** Warm; comforting. **4.** Easy for one to use or understand: *a reader-friendly type design.* **—friend′li·ly** *adv.* **—friend′li·ness** *n.*

fri·er (frī′ər) ▸ *n.* Var. of **fryer.**

frieze (frēz) ▸ *n.* A decorative horizontal band, as along the upper part of a wall in a room.

frig·ate (frĭg′ĭt) ▸ *n.* **1.** A US warship larger than a destroyer and smaller than a cruiser. **2.** A high-speed, medium-sized sailing war vessel of the 17th, 18th, and 19th cent.

fright (frīt) ▸ *n.* **1.** Sudden intense fear. **2.** *Informal* Something extremely unsightly or alarming.

fright·en (frīt′n) ▸ *v.* **1.** To make or become suddenly afraid;

THESAURUS

frenetic *adj.* —*See* FRANTIC.

frenzied *adj.* —*See* FRANTIC.

frenziedly *adv.* —*See* HARD (1).

frequent *adj.* —*See* COMMON (1).

frequent *v.* To visit regularly ▸ hang around, haunt, repair to, resort to. *Slang:* hang out. *Idiom:* go regularly to.

frequently *adv.* —*See* USUALLY.

fresh *adj.* **1.** Not polluted or altered by human intervention ▸ pristine, pure, uncontaminated, undeveloped, unpolluted, unspoiled, untouched. [*Compare* PASTORAL.] **2.** Not sour or salted ▸ fresh, uncured, unsalted. —*See also* ADDITIONAL, CLEAN (1), ENERGETIC, IMPUDENT, INEXPERIENCED, NEW, YOUNG.

freshen *v.* To expose to circulating air ▸ aerate, air, ventilate, wind. —*See also* BLOW[1] (1), REFRESH, TIDY (2).

freshet *n.* —*See* FLOOD.

freshman *n.* —*See* BEGINNER.

freshness *n.* —*See* NOVELTY (1).

fret *v.* —*See* ANNOY, BROOD, CHAFE.

fretful *adj.* —*See* ILL-TEMPERED.

friable *adj.* —*See* FRAGILE.

fricassee *v.* —*See* COOK.

friction *n.* —*See* CONFLICT.

friend *n.* A person whom one knows well, likes, and trusts ▸ alter ego, amigo, brother, chum, comrade, confidant, confidante, crony, familiar, intimate, mate, sister, soul mate. *Informal:* bud, buddy, pal. *Slang:* sidekick. [*Compare* ASSOCIATE.] —*See also* PATRON.

friendliness *n.* —*See* AMIABILITY.

friendly *adj.* —*See* AMIABLE, INTIMATE[1] (1), RECEPTIVE.

friendship *n.* The condition of being friends ▸ amity, camaraderie, chumminess, closeness, companionship, comradeship, familiarity, fellowship, intimacy. [*Compare* COMPANY.]

fright *n.* —*See* FEAR, MESS (2).

frighten *v.* To fill with fear ▸ affright, horrify, intimidate, panic, petrify, scare, scarify, startle, terrify, terrorize, unnerve. *Informal:* spook. *Idioms:* chill one to the bone, frighten

alarm. 2. To drive or force by arousing fear. **—fright′en·ing·ly** *adv.*

fright·ful (frīt′fəl) ▸ *adj.* **1.** Causing disgust or shock; horrifying. **2.** Causing fright; terrifying. **3.** *Informal* **a.** Excessive; extreme: *a frightful liar.* **b.** Disagreeable; distressing. **—fright′ful·ly** *adv.* **—fright′ful·ness** *n.*

frig·id (frĭj′ĭd) ▸ *adj.* **1.** Extremely cold. **2.** Lacking warmth of feeling; cold in manner. **—fri·gid′i·ty** (frĭ-jĭd′ĭ-tē), **frig′id·ness** *n.* **—frig′id·ly** *adv.*

Frigid Zone ▸ Either of the earth's two extreme latitude zones, the **North Frigid Zone** or the **South Frigid Zone**, between the polar circles and the poles.

frill (frĭl) ▸ *n.* **1.** A ruffled, gathered, or pleated border or projection. **2.** *Informal* Something desirable but not essential. **—frill** *v.* **—frill′i·ness** *n.* **—frill′y** *adj.*

fringe (frĭnj) ▸ *n.* **1.** A decorative border or edging of hanging threads, cords, or strips. **2.** Something like a fringe. **3.** A marginal or secondary part. **4.** Those members of a group or political party holding extreme views. **5.** A fringe benefit. **—fringe** *v.* **—fring′y** *adj.*

fringe benefit ▸ *n.* An employment benefit given in addition to wages or salary.

frip·per·y (frĭp′ə-rē) ▸ *n., pl.* **-ies. 1.** Gaudy or showy ornaments or dress. **2.** Something trivial or nonessential.

frisk (frĭsk) ▸ *v.* **1.** To move about briskly and playfully. **2.** To search (a person) for something concealed, esp. a weapon, by passing the hands quickly over clothes or through pockets. **—frisk** *n.* **—frisk′er** *n.*

frisk·y (frĭs′kē) ▸ *adj.* **-i·er, -i·est.** Energetic and playful. **—frisk′i·ness** *n.*

frit·ta·ta (frĭ-tä′tə) ▸ *n.* An open-faced omelet with other ingredients mixed into the eggs before cooking.

frit·ter¹ (frĭt′ər) ▸ *v.* To reduce or squander little by little.

frit·ter² (frĭt′ər) ▸ *n.* A small fried cake made of batter and often fruit, vegetables, or fish.

friv·o·lous (frĭv′ə-ləs) ▸ *adj.* **1.** Unworthy of serious attention; trivial. **2.** Inappropriately silly. **—friv′o·lous·ly** *adv.* **—friv′o·lous·ness, fri·vol′i·ty** (frĭ-vŏl′ĭ-tē) *n.*

frizz (frĭz) ▸ *v.* To form or be formed into small tight curls. ▸ *n.* A small tight curl. **—friz′zly, friz′zy** *adj.*

friz·zle¹ (frĭz′əl) ▸ *v.* **-zled, -zling. 1.** To fry until crisp and curled. **2.** To fry or sear with a sizzling noise.

friz·zle² (frĭz′əl) ▸ *v.* **-zled, -zling.** To form or cause to be formed into small tight curls. ▸ *n.* A small tight curl.

fro (frō) ▸ *adv.* Away; back: *moving to and fro.*

frock (frŏk) ▸ *n.* **1.** A woman's dress. **2.** A long loose outer garment; smock. **3.** A robe worn by monks and other clerics; habit.

frock coat ▸ *n.* A man's dress coat or suit coat with knee-length skirts.

frog (frôg, frŏg) ▸ *n.* **1.** Any of numerous tailless, chiefly aquatic amphibians characteristically having a smooth moist skin, webbed feet, and long hind legs adapted for leaping. **2.** An ornamental looped braid or cord with a button or knot for fastening the front of a garment. **3.** *Informal* Hoarseness or phlegm in the throat.

frog·man (frôg′măn′, -mən, frŏg′-) ▸ *n.* A swimmer equipped to execute underwater maneuvers, esp. military maneuvers.

frol·ic (frŏl′ĭk) ▸ *n.* **1.** Gaiety; merriment. **2.** A gay, carefree time. ▸ *v.* **-icked, -ick·ing. 1.** To behave playfully; romp. **2.** To engage in merrymaking. **—frol′ick·er** *n.* **—frol′ic·some** *adj.*

from (frŭm, frŏm; frəm *when unstressed*) ▸ *prep.* **1.** Used to indicate: **a.** A place or time as a starting point: *from six o'clock on.* **b.** A specified point as the first of two limits: *from a to z.* **c.** A source, cause, agent, or instrument: *a note from me.* **d.** Separation, removal, or exclusion: *freed from bondage.* **e.** Differentiation: *know right from wrong.* **2.** Because of: *faint from hunger.*

frond (frŏnd) ▸ *n.* The leaf esp. of a fern or palm.

front (frŭnt) ▸ *n.* **1.** The forward part or surface. **2.** The area, location, or position directly ahead. **3.** A position of leadership or superiority. **4.** Demeanor or bearing, esp. in the presence of danger or difficulty. **5.** A false appearance or manner: *a good front.* **6.** Land bordering a lake, river, or street. **7.** The most forward line of a combat force. **8.** *Meteorol.* The interface between air masses of different temperatures or densities. **9.** A field of activity: *the economic front.* **10a.** A united movement; coalition. **b.** A nominal leader lacking in real authority; figurehead. **c.** An apparently respectable person or business used as a cover for secret or illegal activities. ▸ *adj.* Of, aimed at, or located in the front. ▸ *v.* **1.** To look out on; face. **2.** To confront. **3.** To provide or serve as a front for.

front·age (frŭn′tĭj) ▸ *n.* **1a.** The front part of a piece of property. **b.** The land between a building and the street. **2.** Land adjacent to something, as a street or body of water.

fron·tal (frŭn′tl) ▸ *adj.* **1.** Of, directed toward, or situated at the front. **2.** *Anat.* Of or in the region of the forehead. **3.** Of a meteorological front. **—fron′tal·ly** *adv.*

fron·tier (frŭn-tîr′, frŏn-) ▸ *n.* **1.** An international border or the area along it. **2.** A region just beyond or beside a settled area. **3.** An undeveloped area for discovery or research. **—fron·tiers′man** *n.* **—fron·tiers′wom·an** *n.*

fron·tis·piece (frŭn′tĭ-spēs′) ▸ *n.* An illustration that faces or immediately precedes the title page of a book.

front·line also **front line** (frŭnt′līn′) ▸ *n.* **1.** A front or boundary, esp. between military or political positions. **2.** *Football* A team's linemen. ▸ *adj.* or **front-line 1.** Located or used at a military front. **2.** Being in the forefront; leading. **3.** *Sports* Of the frontline.

front office ▸ *n.* The executive or policymaking officers of an organization.

front-run·ner (frŭnt′rŭn′ər) ▸ *n.* One in a leading position in a competition.

frost (frôst, frŏst) ▸ *n.* A deposit of minute ice crystals formed when water vapor condenses at a temperature below freezing. ▸ *v.* **1.** To cover or become covered with frost. **2.** To damage or kill by frost. **3.** To cover (glass or metal) with frosting. **4.** To decorate with icing.

THESAURUS

(*or* scare) to death, give one the creeps (*or* heebie-jeebies), make one's blood run cold, make one's flesh crawl (*or* creep), make one's hair stand on end, put the fear of God into one, scare out of one's wits, scare silly (*or* stiff), scare the daylights out of, take one's breath away. [*Compare* AGITATE, DISMAY.]

frightened *adj.* —*See* AFRAID.

frightening *v.* —*See* FEARFUL.

frightful *adj.* —*See* FEARFUL, TERRIBLE.

frigid *adj.* Deficient in or lacking sexual desire ▸ ardorless, cold, inhibited, passionless, undersexed, unresponsive. —*See also* COLD (1), COOL.

frigidity or **frigidness** *n.* —*See* COLD.

frill *n.* —*See* LUXURY.

fringe *n.* —*See* BORDER (1), OUTSKIRTS.

fringe *v.* —*See* BORDER.

frippery *n.* —*See* ATTIRE, TRIFLE.

frisk *v.* To examine a person or someone's personal effects in order to find something lost or concealed ▸ inspect, pat down, search. *Slang:* shake down. *Idiom:* do a body search of. —*See also* GAMBOL.

frisk *n.* A thorough search of a place or persons ▸ search. *Slang:* shakedown.

frisky *adj.* —*See* LIVELY, MISCHIEVOUS.

fritter away *v.* —*See* WASTE.

frivolity *n.* —*See* TRIFLE.

frivolous *adj.* —*See* GIDDY (2), TRIVIAL.

frizzle *v.* —*See* DRY (1).

frock *n.* —*See* DRESS (3).

frolic *n.* —*See* PRANK¹.

frolic *v.* —*See* GAMBOL, PLAY (1), REVEL.

frolicsome *adj.* —*See* MISCHIEVOUS.

front *n.* The forward part of something ▸ bow, fore, forepart, front end, front side, head. —*See also* FAÇADE (1), FAÇADE (2), FOREFRONT.

front *v.* **1.** To have the face or front turned toward ▸ face, give onto, look (on *or* upon *or* toward). [*Compare* OVERLOOK.] **2.** To meet face-to-face, especially defiantly ▸ confront, encounter, face, meet. *Idiom:* stand up to. [*Compare* CONTEST, DEFY.] —*See also* DEFY (1).

frontage or **frontal** *n.* —*See* FAÇADE (1).

frontier *n.* —*See* BORDER (2).

frontispiece *n.* —*See* FAÇADE (1).

front-runner *n.* A leading contestant or sure winner ▸ favorite, leader, number one, vanguard. *Informal:* shoo-in.

frontward *adv.* —*See* FORWARD.

Frost, Robert Lee (1874–1963) ▸ Amer. poet.

frost·bite (frôst′bīt′, frŏst′-) ▸ *n.* Destruction of body tissue resulting from prolonged exposure to freezing or subfreezing temperatures. **—frost′bite′** *v.*

frost·ing (frô′stĭng, frŏs′tĭng) ▸ *n.* **1.** Icing, as on a cake. **2.** A roughened or speckled surface imparted to glass or metal.

frost line ▸ *n.* The depth to which frost penetrates the earth.

frost·y (frô′stē, frŏs′tē) ▸ *adj.* **-i·er, -i·est. 1.** Producing or marked by frost; freezing. **2.** Covered with or as if with frost. **3.** Cold in manner. **—frost′i·ly** *adv.* **—frost′i·ness** *n.*

froth (frôth, frŏth) ▸ *n.* **1.** A mass of bubbles in or on a liquid; foam. **2.** Salivary foam released as a result of disease or exhaustion. **3.** Something unsubstantial or trivial. ▸ *v.* (*also* frôth, frŏth) **1.** To cover with foam. **2.** To exude or expel foam. **—froth′i·ly** *adv.* **—froth′i·ness** *n.* **—froth′y** *adj.*

frou·frou also **frou-frou** (frōō′frōō) ▸ *n.* **1.** Fussy or showy dress or ornamentation. **2.** A rustling sound, as of silk.

fro·ward (frō′wərd, -ərd) ▸ *adj.* Stubbornly contrary and disobedient. **—fro′ward·ly** *adv.* **—fro′ward·ness** *n.*

frown (froun) ▸ *v.* **1.** To wrinkle the brow, as in thought or displeasure. **2.** To regard something with disapproval or distaste. ▸ *n.* A wrinkling of the brow; scowl.

frow·zy also **frow·sy** (frou′zē) ▸ *adj.* **-zi·er, -zi·est** also **-si·er, -si·est.** Unkempt; slovenly. **—frow′zi·ness** *n.*

froze (frōz) ▸ *v.* P.t. of **freeze.**

fro·zen (frō′zən) ▸ *v.* P.part. of **freeze.** ▸ *adj.* **1.** Made into, covered with, or surrounded by ice. **2.** Very cold. **3.** Preserved by freezing. **4.** Rendered immobile. **5.** Expressive of cold unfriendliness or disdain. **6a.** Kept at a fixed level: *frozen rents.* **b.** Impossible to withdraw, sell, or liquidate: *frozen assets.*

fruc·ti·fy (frŭk′tə-fī′, frŏŏk′-) ▸ *v.* **-fied, -fy·ing.** To be or make fruitful or productive. **—fruc′ti·fi·ca′tion** *n.*

fruc·tose (frŭk′tōs′, frŏŏk′-) ▸ *n.* A sweet sugar, $C_6H_{12}O_6$, occurring in many fruits and honey.

fru·gal (frōō′gəl) ▸ *adj.* **1.** Practicing or marked by economy. **2.** Costing little; inexpensive. **—fru·gal′i·ty** (frōō-găl′ĭ-tē), **fru′gal·ness** *n.* **—fru′gal·ly** *adv.*

fruit (frōōt) ▸ *n., pl.* **fruit** or **fruits. 1.** The ripened, seed-bearing part of a plant, esp. when fleshy and edible. **2.** The fertile, often spore-bearing structure of a plant that does not bear seeds. **3.** A plant crop or product. **4.** Result; outcome. ▸ *v.* To produce fruit.

fruit·cake (frōōt′kāk′) ▸ *n.* **1.** A heavy spiced cake containing nuts and candied or dried fruits. **2.** *Slang* An eccentric person.

fruit fly ▸ *n.* Any of various small flies that feed on ripening or fermenting fruits and vegetables.

fruit·ful (frōōt′fəl) ▸ *adj.* **1.** Producing fruit. **2.** Producing in abundance; prolific. **3.** Producing results; profitable. **—fruit′ful·ly** *adv.* **—fruit′ful·ness** *n.*

fru·i·tion (frōō-ĭsh′ən) ▸ *n.* **1.** Realization of something desired or worked for. **2.** The condition of bearing fruit.

fruit·less (frōōt′lĭs) ▸ *adj.* **1.** Producing no fruit. **2.** Unproductive of success. **—fruit′less·ly** *adv.* **—fruit′less·ness** *n.*

fruit·y (frōō′tē) ▸ *adj.* **-i·er, -i·est. 1.** Tasting or smelling of fruit. **2.** Excessively sentimental or sweet. **3.** *Slang* Eccentric. **—fruit′i·ness** *n.*

frump (frŭmp) ▸ *n.* A dull, plain, or unfashionable person. **—frump′i·ly** *adv.* **—frump′i·ness** *n.* **—frump′y** *adj.*

frump·ish (frŭm′pĭsh) ▸ *adj.* **1.** Dull or plain. **2.** Prim and sedate. **—frump′ish·ly** *adv.* **—frump′ish·ness** *n.*

frus·trate (frŭs′trāt′) ▸ *v.* **-trat·ed, -trat·ing. 1.** To prevent from accomplishing a purpose or fulfilling a desire; thwart. **2.** To cause discouragement or bafflement in. **3.** To make ineffectual or invalid. **—frus·tra′tion** *n.*

fry[1] (frī) ▸ *v.* **fried** (frīd), **fry·ing.** To cook over direct heat in hot oil or fat. ▸ *n., pl.* **fries** (frīz). **1.** A French fry. **2.** A social gathering at which fried food is served.

fry[2] (frī) ▸ *pl.n.* **1.** Small fish, esp. hatchlings. **2.** Individuals, esp. young persons.

fry·er also **fri·er** (frī′ər) ▸ *n.* **1.** One that fries, as a deep utensil usu. equipped with a basket and used for frying foods. **2.** A young chicken suitable for frying.

fry·ing pan (frī′ĭng) ▸ *n.* A shallow, long-handled pan used for frying food.

f-stop (ĕf′stŏp′) ▸ *n.* A camera lens aperture setting that corresponds to an f-number.

ft. ▸ *abbr.* **1.** or **ft** foot **2. Ft.** fort

FTP (ĕf′tē-pē′) ▸ *n.* A protocol governing file transfers over a computer network. ▸ *v.* **FTPed, FTPing.** To transfer (a file) using FTP.

fuch·sia (fyōō′shə) ▸ *n.* **1.** A widely cultivated plant with showy, drooping purplish, reddish, or white flowers. **2.** A vivid purplish red. **—fuch′sia** *adj.*

fud·dle (fŭd′l) ▸ *v.* **-dled, -dling. 1.** To put into a state of confusion; befuddle. **2.** To make drunk; intoxicate. **—fud′dle** *n.*

fud·dy-dud·dy (fŭd′ē-dŭd′ē) ▸ *n., pl.* **-dies.** An old-fashioned, fussy person.

fudge (fŭj) ▸ *n.* **1.** A soft rich candy made of sugar, milk, and butter. **2.** Nonsense; humbug. ▸ *v.* **fudged, fudg·ing. 1.** To fake or falsify. **2.** To evade; dodge.

fu·el (fyōō′əl) ▸ *n.* Something consumed to produce energy, esp.: **a.** A material such as wood or oil burned to produce heat or power. **b.** Fissionable material used in a nuclear reactor. **c.** Nutritive material metabolized by a living organism; food. ▸ *v.* **-eled, -el·ing** also **-elled, -el·ling.** To provide with or take in fuel. **—fu′el·er** *n.*

fuel cell ▸ *n.* A device in which a fuel and an oxidant react and the energy released is converted into electricity.

fuel oil ▸ *n.* A liquid petroleum product that is used to generate heat or power.

fuel rod ▸ *n.* A protective metal tube containing pellets of fuel for a nuclear reactor.

fu·gi·tive (fyōō′jĭ-tĭv) ▸ *adj.* **1.** Running away or fleeing, as from the law. **2.** Lasting only a short time; fleeting: *fugitive hours.* ▸ *n.* One who flees.

fugue (fyōōg) ▸ *n.* *Mus.* A polyphonic composition in

THESAURUS

frostiness *n.* —*See* COLD.
frosty *adj.* —*See* COLD (1), COOL.
froth *n.* —*See* FOAM, TRIFLE.
froth *v.* —*See* BOIL, FOAM.
frothy *adj.* —*See* FOAMY, GIDDY (2), TRIVIAL.
froward *adj.* —*See* CONTRARY, UNRULY.
frown *v.* To wrinkle one's brow, as in thought, puzzlement, or displeasure ▸ glower, lower, scowl. *Idioms:* knit one's brow, look black, turn one's mouth down. [*Compare* GLARE, GRIMACE.]
frown on or **upon** *v.* —*See* DISAPPROVE.
frown *n.* The act of wrinkling the brow, as in thought, puzzlement, or displeasure ▸ black look, glower, lower, scowl. [*Compare* FACE, GLARE, SNEER.]
frowzy *adj.* —*See* MESSY (1), MOLDY.
frozen *adj.* —*See* MOTIONLESS.
frozenness *n.* —*See* COLD.
frugal *adj.* —*See* CHEAP, ECONOMICAL.
frugality *n.* —*See* ECONOMY.
fruit *n.* —*See* EFFECT (1), HARVEST, PROGENY.
fruitage *n.* —*See* HARVEST.
fruitful *adj.* Capable of reproducing ▸ fertile, fecund, productive, prolific. —*See also* BENEFICIAL, FERTILE (1).
fruitfulness *n.* —*See* FERTILITY.
fruition *n.* —*See* FULFILLMENT (1).
fruitless *adj.* —*See* FUTILE.
fruitlessness *n.* —*See* FUTILITY, STERILITY (2).
fruity *adj.* —*See* INSANE.
frump *n.* —*See* KILLJOY.
frumpy *adj.* —*See* OLD-FASHIONED.
frustrate *v.* To prevent from accomplishing a purpose ▸ baffle, balk, check, checkmate, defeat, foil, stymie, thwart. *Informal:* cross, stump. *Idiom:* cut the ground from under. [*Compare* DISAPPOINT, DISCOURAGE, HINDER, PREVENT.] —*See also* DISAPPOINT.
frustration *n.* —*See* DISAPPOINTMENT (1), PREVENTION.
fry *v.* —*See* COOK.
fuddle *v.* —*See* CONFUSE (1), DRUG (2).
fuddy-duddy *n.* —*See* SQUARE.
fudge *v.* —*See* DISTORT, MUDDLE.
fugacious *adj.* —*See* TRANSITORY.
fugitive *adj.* **1.** Fleeing or having fled, as from confinement or the police ▸ escaped, fleeing, runaway. *Idiom:* on the lam (*or* loose *or* run). **2.** Inclined or intended to evade ▸ elusive, evasive, slippery. [*Compare* SLICK, UNDERHAND.] —*See also* TRANSITORY.
fugitive *n.* One who flees, as from confinement or the police ▸ escapee, outlaw, refugee, runaway. [*Compare* CRIMINAL.]

which one or more themes stated successively are developed contrapuntally. **—fu′gal** (fyo͞o′gəl) *adj.* **—fu′gal·ly** *adv.*

füh·rer also **fueh·rer** (fyo͝or′ər) ► *n.* **1.** A leader, esp. a dictator. **2. Führer** Adolf Hitler's title as the leader of Nazi Germany.

Fu·ji (fo͞o′jē), **Mount.** Also **Fu·ji·ya·ma** (fo͞o′jē-yä′mə, -mä) ► The highest peak, 3,778.6 m (12,389 ft), in Japan, in central Honshu WSW of Tokyo.

–ful ► *suff.* **1.** Full of: *playful.* **a.** Marked by; resembling: *masterful.* **b.** Tending, given, or able to: *useful.* **2.** A quantity that fills: *armful.*

ful·crum (fo͝ol′krəm, fŭl′-) ► *n., pl.* **-crums** or **-cra** (-krə). The point or support on which a lever pivots.

ful·fill also **ful·fil** (fo͝ol-fĭl′) ► *v.* **-filled, -fill·ing.** **1.** To bring into actuality; effect. **2.** To carry out. **3.** To measure up to; satisfy. **4.** To bring to an end; complete. **—ful·fill′ment, ful·fil′ment** *n.*

full[1] (fo͝ol) ► *adj.* **-er, -est.** **1.** Containing all that is normal or possible. **2.** Complete in every particular. **3.** Of maximum or highest degree. **4.** Having a great deal or many: *full of errors.* **5.** Totally qualified or accepted: *a full member.* **6a.** Rounded in shape. **b.** Of generous dimensions; wide. **7.** Satiated, esp. with food or drink. **8.** Having depth and body. ► *adv.* **1.** To a complete extent; entirely: *knowing full well.* **2.** Exactly; directly: *full in the path of the truck.* ► *n.* The maximum or complete size or amount. **—full′ness, ful′ness** *n.*

full[2] (fo͝ol) ► *v.* To increase the weight and bulk of (cloth) by shrinking and beating or pressing.

full·back (fo͝ol′băk′) ► *n.* **1.** *Football* An offensive backfield player whose position is behind the quarterback and halfbacks. **2.** *Sports* A primarily defensive backfield player in field hockey, soccer, or Rugby.

full-blood·ed (fo͝ol′blŭd′ĭd) ► *adj.* **1.** Of unmixed ancestry; purebred. **2.** Vigorous; vital. **—full′-blood′ed·ness** *n.*

full-blown (fo͝ol′blōn′) ► *adj.* **1.** Having blossomed or opened completely. **2.** Fully developed or matured.

full-bod·ied (fo͝ol′bŏd′ēd) ► *adj.* Having richness of flavor or aroma.

full dress ► *n.* Attire appropriate for formal or ceremonial events.

Ful·ler (fo͝ol′ər), **R(ichard) Buckminster** (1895–1983) ► Amer. architect and inventor.

ful·ler·ene (fo͝ol′ə-rēn′) ► *n.* Any of various nearly spherical carbon molecules.

full-fledged (fo͝ol′flĕjd′) ► *adj.* **1.** Having reached full development; mature. **2.** Having full status or rank: *a full-fledged lawyer.*

full moon ► *n.* The moon when it is visible as a fully illuminated disk.

full-scale (fo͝ol′skāl′) ► *adj.* **1.** Of actual or full size. **2.** Employing all resources.

ful·ly (fo͝ol′ē) ► *adv.* **1.** Totally or completely. **2.** At least.

ful·mi·nate (fo͝ol′mə-nāt′, fŭl′-) ► *v.* **-nat·ed, -nat·ing.** **1.** To issue a severe denunciation. **2.** To explode. **—ful′mi·na′tion** *n.*

ful·some (fo͝ol′səm) ► *adj.* Offensively flattering or insincere. **—ful′some·ly** *adv.* **—ful′some·ness** *n.*

Ful·ton (fo͝ol′tən), **Robert** (1765–1815) ► Amer. engineer and inventor.

fum·ble (fŭm′bəl) ► *v.* **-bled, -bling.** **1.** To touch or handle nervously or idly. **2.** To grope awkwardly to find something. **3.** To proceed awkwardly and uncertainly; blunder. **4.** *Sports* To mishandle or drop a ball that is in play. **5.** To bungle. ► *n.* **1.** The act or an instance of fumbling. **2.** *Sports* A ball that has been fumbled. **—fum′bler** *n.*

fume (fyo͞om) ► *n.* **1.** Vapor, gas, or smoke, esp. if irritating, harmful, or strong. **2.** A strong or acrid odor. ► *v.* **fumed, fum·ing.** **1.** To subject to or treat with fumes. **2.** To give off in or as if in fumes. **3.** To feel or show resentment or anger.

fu·mi·gate (fyo͞o′mĭ-gāt′) ► *v.* **-gat·ed, -gat·ing.** To treat with fumes in order to exterminate pests. **—fu′mi·ga′tion** *n.* **—fu′mi·ga′tor** *n.*

fun (fŭn) ► *n.* **1.** A source of enjoyment, amusement, or pleasure. **2.** Enjoyment; amusement. **3.** Playful, often noisy activity. ***—idiom:*** **for fun** As a joke; playfully.

func·tion (fŭngk′shən) ► *n.* **1.** The action for which one is particularly fitted or employed. **2.** The duty, occupation, or role of a person. **3.** An official ceremony or a formal social occasion. **4.** Something closely related to another thing and dependent on it for its existence or value. **5.** *Math.* A rule of correspondence between two sets such that there is a unique element in the second set assigned to each element in the first set. **6.** *Comp. Sci.* A procedure within an application. ► *v.* To have or perform a function; serve.

func·tion·al (fŭngk′shə-nəl) ► *adj.* **1.** Of or relating to a function. **2.** Designed for or adapted to a particular purpose. **3.** Capable of performing; operative. **4.** *Pathol.* Involving functions rather than a physiological or structural cause. **—func′tion·al·ly** *adv.*

func·tion·al·i·ty (fŭngk′shə-năl′ĭ-tē) ► *n.* **1.** The quality of being functional. **2.** A useful function in a computer program. **3.** The capacity of a computer program to provide a useful function.

func·tion·ar·y (fŭngk′shə-nĕr′ē) ► *n., pl.* **-ies.** One who holds an office or performs a particular function; official.

function word ► *n.* A word, such as a preposition or article, that indicates a grammatical relationship.

fund (fŭnd) ► *n.* **1.** A source of supply; stock. **2.** A sum of money or other resources set aside for a specific purpose.

THESAURUS

führer *n.* —*See* DICTATOR.

fulfill *v.* To carry out the functions, requirements, or terms of ► discharge, do, execute, exercise, implement, keep, perform. *Idiom:* live up to. [*Compare* EFFECT.] —*See also* ACCOMPLISH, PERFORM (1), SATISFY (1), SATISFY (2).

fulfilled *adj.* Having achieved satisfaction, as of one's goal ► content, gratified, happy, satisfied.

fulfillment *n.* **1.** The state or condition of being fulfilled ► accomplishment, attainment, completion, consummation, culmination, fruition, materialization, realization. [*Compare* PERFORMANCE.] **2.** The state or condition of being satisfied ► contentedness, contentment, gratification, satisfaction. [*Compare* HAPPINESS, SATIATION.]

full *adj.* **1.** Completely filled ► awash, brimful, brimming, bursting, charged, chockablock, chock-full, crammed, fraught, jammed, jam-packed, loaded, overflowing, packed, replete, running over, stuffed. **2.** Having the appetite satisfied or overwhelmed ► cloyed, engorged, glutted, gorged, replete, sated, satiated, surfeited. **3.** Of full measure; not narrow or restricted ► ample, baggy, capacious, voluminous, wide. [*Compare* LOOSE.] **4.** No less than; at least ► good, round, whole. —*See also* CLOSE (2), COMPLETE (1), DETAILED, FAT (1), UNCONDITIONAL.

full-blooded *adj.* —*See* RUDDY, THOROUGHBRED.

full-blown *adj.* —*See* MATURE.

full-dress *adj.* —*See* FORMAL, THOROUGH.

full-fledged or **full-grown** *adj.* —*See* MATURE, UTTER[2].

full-length *adj.* —*See* COMPLETE (2).

fullness *n.* —*See* COMPLETENESS, SATIATION.

full-strength *adj.* —*See* STRAIGHT.

fully *adv.* —*See* COMPLETELY (1).

fulminate *v.* —*See* EXPLODE (1).

fulminate against *v.* —*See* REVILE.

fulmination *n.* —*See* BLAST (2), TIRADE.

fulsome *adj.* —*See* UNCTUOUS.

fumble *v.* —*See* BOTCH, GROPE, MUDDLE.

fumble *n.* —*See* BLUNDER.

fume *v.* —*See* ANGER (2), EVAPORATE.

fun *n.* —*See* AMUSEMENT, MERRIMENT (2), PLAY.

fun *adj.* —*See* PLEASANT.

function *n.* **1.** The proper activity of a person or thing ► job, purpose, role, task. [*Compare* DUTY, POSITION, TASK.] **2.** One's duty or responsibility in a common effort ► part, piece, role, share. —*See also* PARTY.

function *v.* To act or operate in a specified way ► act, behave, go, operate, perform, run, take, work. [*Compare* OFFICIATE, SUBSTITUTE.]

functional *adj.* —*See* PRACTICAL.

functionary *n.* —*See* EXECUTIVE.

functioning *n.* —*See* BEHAVIOR (2).

functioning *adj.* —*See* ACTIVE.

fund *v.* —*See* FINANCE.

3. **funds** Available money. ▸ *v.* 1. To make provision for paying off (a debt). 2. To furnish money for.

fun·da·men·tal (fŭn′də-mĕn′tl) ▸ *adj.* 1. Basic; elementary: *fundamental laws of nature.* 2. Of central importance; essential. 3. Involving all aspects; radical: *fundamental change.* **–fun′da·men′tal·ly** *adv.*

fun·da·men·tal·ism (fŭn′də-mĕn′tl-ĭz′əm) ▸ *n.* 1. often **Fundamentalism** A Protestant movement holding the Bible to be the sole authority. 2. A movement marked by rigid adherence to basic principles. **–fun′da·men′tal·ist** *adj. & n.*

fund·rais·er (fŭnd′rā′zər) ▸ *n.* 1. One that raises funds. 2. A social function held for raising funds.

Fun·dy (fŭn′dē), **Bay of** ▸ An inlet of the Atlantic in SE Canada between New Brunswick and Nova Scotia.

fu·ner·al (fyo͞o′nər-əl) ▸ *n.* 1. The ceremonies held in connection with the burial or cremation of the dead. 2. The procession accompanying a body to the grave. **–fu′ner·ar′y** (-nə-rĕr′ē) *adj.*

funeral director ▸ *n.* One whose business is to arrange burials or cremations.

funeral home ▸ *n.* An establishment in which the dead are prepared for burial or cremation.

fu·ne·re·al (fyo͞o-nîr′ē-əl) ▸ *adj.* Appropriate for or suggestive of a funeral; mournful. **–fu·ne′re·al·ly** *adv.*

fun·gi·cide (fŭn′jĭ-sīd′, fŭng′gĭ-) ▸ *n.* A substance that destroys fungi. **–fun′gi·cid′al** *adj.*

fun·gus (fŭng′gəs) ▸ *n., pl.* **fun·gi** (fŭn′jī, fŭng′gī) or **-gus·es.** Any of numerous plant organisms which lack chlorophyll, including the yeasts, molds, smuts, and mushrooms. **–fun′gal, fun′gous** *adj.*

fu·nic·u·lar (fyo͞o-nĭk′yə-lər, fə-) ▸ *n.* A cable railway on a steep incline, esp. one with simultaneously ascending and descending cars counterbalancing one another.

funk[1] (fŭngk) ▸ *n.* 1. A state of cowardly fright. 2. A state of severe depression.

funk[2] (fŭngk) ▸ *n.* A type of popular music combining elements of jazz, blues, and soul.

funk·y (fŭng′kē) ▸ *adj.* **-i·er, -i·est.** 1. Having a strong offensive odor. 2. *Slang* Of or relating to music that has an earthy quality reminiscent of the blues. 3. *Slang* Eccentric in style or manner: *funky clothes.* **–funk′i·ness** *n.*

fun·nel (fŭn′əl) ▸ *n.* 1. A conical utensil with a narrow tube at the bottom, used to channel the flow of a substance into a container. 2. A flue or stack, esp. the smokestack of a ship. ▸ *v.* **-neled, -nel·ing** or **-nelled, -nel·ling.** To move through or as if through a funnel.

fun·ny (fŭn′ē) ▸ *adj.* **-ni·er, -ni·est.** 1. Causing laughter or amusement. 2. Strangely or suspiciously odd. ▸ *n., pl.* **-nies.** *Informal* 1. A joke. 2. **funnies** Comic strips. **–fun′ni·ly** *adv.* **–fun′ni·ness** *n.*

funny bone ▸ *n. Informal* 1. A point on the elbow where pressure against the underlying nerve produces a sharp tingling sensation. 2. A sense of humor.

fur (fûr) ▸ *n.* 1. The thick coat of soft hair covering the skin of various mammals. 2. The dressed pelt of such a mammal that is used esp. for clothing. 3. A furlike coating. **–furred** *adj.*

fur·be·low (fûr′bə-lō′) ▸ *n.* 1. A ruffle on a garment. 2. A piece of showy ornamentation.

fur·bish (fûr′bĭsh) ▸ *v.* 1. To brighten by cleaning or rubbing; polish. 2. To renovate.

fu·ri·ous (fyo͝or′ē-əs) ▸ *adj.* 1. Extremely angry; raging. 2. Violent or intense, as in speed or action. **–fu′ri·ous·ly** *adv.*

furl (fûrl) ▸ *v.* To roll up and secure (a flag or sail) to something else.

fur·long (fûr′lông′, -lŏng′) ▸ *n.* See **measurement** table in Appendix.

fur·lough (fûr′lō) ▸ *n.* A leave of absence or vacation, esp. of a member of the armed forces. **–fur′lough** *v.*

fur·nace (fûr′nĭs) ▸ *n.* An enclosure in which heat is generated by the combustion of a suitable fuel.

fur·nish (fûr′nĭsh) ▸ *v.* 1. To equip, esp. with furniture. 2. To supply; give. **–fur′nish·er** *n.*

fur·nish·ings (fûr′nĭ-shĭngz) ▸ *pl.n.* 1. The furniture and other movable articles in a home or building. 2. Clothes and accessories.

fur·ni·ture (fûr′nĭ-chər) ▸ *n.* The movable articles in a room or an establishment that equip it for living or working.

fu·ror (fyo͝or′ôr′, -ər) ▸ *n.* 1. A public uproar. 2. Violent anger; frenzy. 3. Intense excitement.

fur·ri·er (fûr′ē-ər) ▸ *n.* One who designs, sells, or repairs furs.

fur·ring (fûr′ĭng) ▸ *n.* Strips of wood or metal attached to a wall or other surface to provide a level substratum, as for paneling.

fur·row (fûr′ō, fŭr′ō) ▸ *n.* 1. A long shallow trench made in the ground by a plow or other tool. 2. A deep wrinkle in the skin. **–fur′row** *v.*

fur·ry (fûr′ē, fŭr′ē) ▸ *adj.* **-ri·er, -ri·est.** 1. Consisting of or similar to fur. 2. Covered with fur or a furlike substance. **–fur′ri·ness** *n.*

fur·ther (fûr′*th*ər) ▸ *adj.* Comp. of **far.** 1. More distant in degree, time, or space. 2. Additional. ▸ *adv.* Comp. of **far.** 1. To a greater extent; more. 2. In addition; furthermore. 3. At or to a more distant or advanced point. ▸ *v.* To help the progress of. **–fur′ther·ance** *n.*

fur·ther·more (fûr′*th*ər-môr′) ▸ *adv.* In addition; moreover.

fur·ther·most (fûr′*th*ər-mōst′) ▸ *adj.* Most distant or remote.

THESAURUS

fundament *n.* —*See* BUTTOCKS.

fundamental *adj.* —*See* ELEMENTAL, ESSENTIAL (2), RADICAL.

fundamental *n.* —*See* BASIS (1), ELEMENT (1), LAW (3).

fundamentalist *n.* —*See* EXTREMIST.

fundamentalist *adj.* —*See* EXTREME (2).

fundamentally *adv.* —*See* ESSENTIALLY.

funding *n.* —*See* CAPITAL (1).

funds *n.* The monetary resources of a government, organization, or individual ▸ capital, finances, money (*or* moneys). [*Compare* CAPITAL, MONEY, RESOURCES.]

funeral *n.* A ceremony held in connection with a burial or cremation ▸ funeral service, last rites, memorial service, obsequies, requiem. [*Compare* BURIAL.]

funereal *adj.* —*See* GLOOMY.

funk *n.* —*See* COWARD, COWARDICE, DEPRESSION (2), FEAR.

funky *adj.* —*See* AFRAID, FASHIONABLE, MOLDY, RACY.

funniness *n.* —*See* HUMOR.

funny *adj.* 1. Causing laughter or amusement ▸ amusing, comedic, comic, comical, droll, facetious, hilarious, humorous, jocose, jocular, laughable, priceless, risible, sidesplitting, uproarious, witty, zany. *Informal:* hysterical, killing, rich. *Slang:* ripe. *Idioms:* a laugh and a half, a riot, too funny for words. [*Compare* PLEASANT.] 2. Agreeably curious, especially in an old-fashioned or unusual way ▸ curious, odd, quaint. 3. Causing puzzlement; perplexing ▸ curious, odd, peculiar, queer, strange, weird. [*Compare* SHADY, UNUSUAL.]

funny *n.* —*See* JOKE (1).

funny business *n.* —*See* MISCHIEF.

funnyman *n.* —*See* JOKER.

fur *n.* The skin of an animal, sometimes including fur, hair or feathers ▸ hide, leather, pelt.

furbish *v.* —*See* GLOSS[1], RENEW (1).

furfur *n.* —*See* SCURF.

furious *adj.* —*See* ANGRY, INTENSE.

furiously *adv.* —*See* HARD (1).

furlough *n.* A regularly scheduled period spent away from work or duty, often in recreation ▸ holiday, leave, sabbatical, vacation. *Idiom:* time (*or* day) off. [*Compare* BREAK, TRIP.] —*See also* LICENSE (3).

furnish *v.* To supply what is needed for some activity or purpose ▸ accouter, appoint, equip, fit, fit out (*or* up), gear, outfit, rig, turn out. [*Compare* ADORN.] —*See also* GIVE (1), OFFER (2).

furor *n.* —*See* ANGER, FASHION.

furrow *n.* A long, narrow, and usually shallow depression in the ground ▸ channel, ditch, groove, rut, trench, trough. —*See also* WRINKLE (1).

furry *adj.* —*See* HAIRY.

further *adj.* —*See* ADDITIONAL.

further *adv.* —*See* ADDITIONALLY.

further *v.* —*See* ADVANCE (1).

furtherance *n.* —*See* ADVANCE, PATRONAGE (1).

furthermore *adv.* —*See* ADDITIONALLY.

furthermost *adj.* —*See* EXTREME (1).

fur·thest (fûr′*th*ĭst) ▸ *adj.* Superl. of **far**. Most distant in degree, time, or space. ▸ *adv.* Superl. of **far**. **1.** To the greatest extent or degree. **2.** At or to the most distant point in space or time.

fur·tive (fûr′tĭv) ▸ *adj.* Marked by stealth; surreptitious. **—fur′tive·ly** *adv.* **—fur′tive·ness** *n.*

fu·ry (fyo͝or′ē) ▸ *n., pl.* **-ries**. **1.** Violent anger; rage. **2.** Violent, uncontrolled action. **3. Furies** *Gk. & Rom. Myth.* The three terrible, winged goddesses who pursue and punish doers of unavenged crimes.

furze (fûrz) ▸ *n.* See **gorse**.

fuse[1] also **fuze** (fyo͞oz) ▸ *n.* **1.** A cord of readily combustible material that is lighted at one end to carry a flame along its length to detonate an explosive at the other end. **2.** often **fuze** A mechanical or electrical mechanism used to detonate an explosive device. **—fuse** *v.*

fuse[2] (fyo͞oz) ▸ *v.* **fused, fus·ing**. **1.** To liquefy or reduce to a plastic state by heating; melt. **2.** To mix together by or as if by melting. ▸ *n.* A safety device for an electric circuit that melts when current exceeds a specific amperage, thus opening the circuit. **—fus′i·ble** *adj.*

fu·see also **fu·zee** (fyo͞o-zē′) ▸ *n.* **1.** A large friction match that can burn in a wind. **2.** A colored flare used as a warning signal for trucks and trains.

fu·se·lage (fyo͞o′sə-läzh′, -zə-) ▸ *n.* The central body of an aircraft, to which the wings and tail assembly are attached.

fu·sil·lade (fyo͞o′sə-läd′, -lād′, -zə-) ▸ *n.* **1.** A simultaneous or rapid discharge from many firearms. **2.** A barrage: *a fusillade of insults.*

fu·sion (fyo͞o′zhən) ▸ *n.* **1.** The act or procedure of liquefying or melting by heat. **2.** The liquid or melted state that is induced by heat. **3.** The merging of different elements into a union. **4.** *Phys.* A nuclear reaction in which nuclei release energy when combining to form more massive nuclei.

fuss (fŭs) ▸ *n.* **1.** Useless or nervous activity; commotion. **2.** Needless concern or worry. **3.** An angry or fretful protest. **4.** A display of affectionate excitement and attention: *made a fuss over the baby.* ▸ *v.* **1.** To trouble or worry over trifles. **2.** To be excessively careful or solicitous. **3.** To be in a state of nervous activity: *fussed with his collar.* **4.** To fret or complain.

fuss·budg·et (fŭs′bŭj′ĭt) ▸ *n.* A person who fusses over trifles.

fuss·y (fŭs′ē) ▸ *adj.* **-i·er, -i·est**. **1.** Easily upset; given to bouts of ill temper. **2.** Frequently complaining or making demands. **3.** Meticulous; fastidious. **4.** Requiring attention to small details. **—fuss′i·ly** *adv.* **—fuss′i·ness** *n.*

fus·tian (fŭs′chən) ▸ *n.* **1.** A coarse sturdy cloth. **2.** Pompous language. **—fus′tian** *adj.*

fus·ty (fŭs′tē) ▸ *adj.* **-ti·er, -ti·est**. **1.** Smelling of mildew or decay; musty. **2.** Old-fashioned; antique. **—fus′ti·ly** *adv.* **—fus′ti·ness** *n.*

fu·tile (fyo͞ot′l, fyo͞o′tīl′) ▸ *adj.* Having no useful result. **—fu′tile·ly** *adv.* **—fu·til′i·ty** (fyo͞o-tĭl′ĭ-tē) *n.*

fu·ton (fo͞o′tŏn) ▸ *n.* A pad usu. of tufted cotton batting used on a floor or on a raised frame as a bed.

fu·ture (fyo͞o′chər) ▸ *n.* **1.** The indefinite time yet to come. **2.** Something that will happen in time to come. **3.** Chance of success or advancement: *a position with no future.* **4. futures** *Bus.* Commodities or stocks bought or sold upon agreement of delivery in time to come. **5.** *Gram.* The form of a verb used in speaking of action in the future. ▸ *adj.* That is to be or to come.

fu·tur·is·tic (fyo͞o′chə-rĭs′tĭk) ▸ *adj.* **1.** Of or relating to the future. **2.** Expressing a vision of life and society in the future. **—fu′tur·is′ti·cal·ly** *adj.*

fu·tu·ri·ty (fyo͞o-to͝or′ĭ-tē, -tyo͝or′-, -cho͝or′-) ▸ *n., pl.* **-ties**. **1.** The future. **2.** The quality or condition of being in or of the future. **3.** A future event or possibility.

fu·tur·ol·o·gy (fyo͞o′chə-rŏl′ə-jē) ▸ *n.* The study or forecasting of potential developments, as in science, technology, and society, using current conditions and trends as a point of departure.

fuze (fyo͞oz) ▸ *n.* & *v.* Var. of **fuse**[1].

fu·zee (fyo͞o-zē′) ▸ *n.* Var. of **fusee**.

fuzz[1] (fŭz) ▸ *n.* A mass or coating of fine light fibers, hairs, or particles; down. ▸ *v.* To make blurred or indistinct.

fuzz[2] (fŭz) ▸ *n.* *Slang* The police.

fuzz·y (fŭz′ē) ▸ *adj.* **-i·er, -i·est**. **1.** Covered with fuzz. **2.** Of or resembling fuzz. **3.** Not clear; indistinct. **—fuzz′i·ly** *adv.* **—fuzz′i·ness** *n.*

-fy or **-ify** ▸ *suff.* Cause to become; make: *calcify.*

FYI ▸ *abbr.* for your information

THESAURUS

furthest *adj.* —*See* EXTREME (1).

furtive *adj.* —*See* STEALTHY.

furtiveness *n.* —*See* STEALTH.

fury *n.* —*See* ANGER, INTENSITY, SCOLD.

fuse *v.* —*See* ATTACH (1), MELT, MIX (1).

fusillade *n.* —*See* BARRAGE.

fusion *n.* —*See* MIXTURE.

fuss *n.* —*See* AGITATION (3), ARGUMENT, BOTHER, COMPLAINT, OBJECTION.

fuss *v.* —*See* BROOD, COMPLAIN.

fuss at *v.* —*See* NAG.

fussy *adj.* Very difficult to please ▸ choosy, dainty, demanding, exacting, fastidious, finical, finicky, meticulous, nice, particular, persnickety, squeamish. *Informal:* picky. ***Idiom:*** hard to please. [*Compare* CAREFUL, CONTRARY, DISCRIMINATING.] —*See also* BUSY (3), CAREFUL (2), ELABORATE.

fustian *n.* —*See* BOMBAST.

fustian *adj.* —*See* ORATORICAL.

fusty *adj.* —*See* MOLDY, OLD-FASHIONED.

futile *adj.* Having no useful result ▸ barren, bootless, fruitless, pointless, profitless, unavailing, unprofitable, unsuccessful, useless, vain. ***Idioms:*** in vain, to no avail, to no effect. [*Compare* HOLLOW, INEFFECTUAL.]

futility *n.* The condition or quality of being useless or ineffective ▸ barrenness, bootlessness, fruitlessness, pointlessness, profitlessness, unprofitableness, uselessness, vainness, vanity. [*Compare* FAILURE, INEFFECTUALITY.]

future *n.* **1.** Time that is yet to be ▸ by-and-by, futurity, hereafter, tomorrow. ***Idiom:*** time to come. [*Compare* APPROACH, POSSIBILITY.] **2.** Chance of success or advancement ▸ outlook, prospects. [*Compare* CHANCE.]

future *adj.* Being or occurring in the time ahead ▸ approaching, coming, eventual, forthcoming, later, subsequent. ***Idioms:*** down the road, in the cards, just around the corner, to be, to come. [*Compare* COMING, MOMENTARY, POTENTIAL.]

futuristic *adj.* —*See* PROGRESSIVE (1).

futurity *n.* Time that is yet to be ▸ by-and-by, future, hereafter, tomorrow. ***Idiom:*** time to come. [*Compare* APPROACH, POSSIBILITY.]

fuzz *n.* —*See* POLICE OFFICER.

fuzzy *adj.* —*See* HAIRY, UNCLEAR.

G

g[1] or **G** (jē) ▸ *n., pl.* **g's** or **G's** also **gs** or **Gs**. **1.** The 7th letter of the English alphabet. **2.** *Mus.* The 5th tone in the C major scale. **3.** A unit of acceleration equal to the acceleration caused by gravity at the earth's surface, about 9.8 m (32 ft.) per second per second.

g[2] ▸ *abbr.* gram

G[1] (jē) ▸ A trademark for a movie rating granting admission to persons of all ages.

G[2] ▸ *abbr.* gravitational constant

Ga ▸ The symbol for the element **gallium**.

GA ▸ *abbr.* 1. General Assembly 2. also **Ga.** Georgia (US).

gab (găb) ▸ *v.* **gabbed, gab·bing**. *Slang* To talk idly or incessantly; chatter. **—gab** *n.* **—gab′ber** *n.*

gab·ar·dine (găb′ər-dēn′, găb′ər-dēn′) ▸ *n.* A sturdy fabric of cotton, wool, or rayon twill.

gab·ble (găb′əl) ▸ *v.* **-bled, -bling**. **1.** To speak rapidly or incoherently; jabber. **2.** To make low muttering or quacking sounds, as a goose or duck. **—gab′ble** *n.*

gab·by (găb′ē) ▸ *adj.* **-bi·er, -bi·est.** *Slang* Talkative; garrulous. **—gab′bi·ness** *n.*

ga·ble (gā′bəl) ▸ *n.* A usu. triangular end section of wall between the two slopes of a pitched roof. **—ga′bled** *adj.*

Ga·bon (gă-bōN′) ▸ A country of W-central Africa on the Atlantic Ocean. Pop. 1,230,000.

gad (găd) ▸ *v.* **gad·ded, gad·ding**. To move about restlessly, as in search of social activity. **—gad′der** *n.*

gad·a·bout (găd′ə-bout′) ▸ *n.* One who roams about in search of amusement or social activity.

gad·fly (găd′flī′) ▸ *n.* **1.** A persistent, irritating critic. **2.** One that provokes or goads. **3.** Any of various flies that bite or annoy livestock.

gadg·et (găj′ĭt) ▸ *n.* A small specialized mechanical or electronic device. **—gadg′et·ry** *n.*

gad·o·lin·i·um (găd′l-ĭn′ē-əm) ▸ *n.* *Symbol* **Gd** A silvery-white, malleable rare-earth element used in improving the high-temperature characteristics of alloys. At. no. 64.

Gae·a (jē′ə) also **Gai·a** (gā′ə) ▸ *n.* *Gk. Myth.* The goddess of the earth, who bore and married Uranus and became the mother of the Titans and the Cyclops.

Gael (gāl) ▸ *n.* A Gaelic-speaking Celt of Scotland, Ireland, or the Isle of Man.

Gael·ic (gā′lĭk) ▸ *n.* Any of the Celtic languages of Ireland, Scotland, or the Isle of Man. **—Gael′ic** *adj.*

gaff (găf) ▸ *n.* **1.** A large iron hook attached to a pole and used to land large fish. **2.** A spar used to extend the upper edge of a fore-and-aft sail. **—gaff** *v.*

gaffe also **gaff** (găf) ▸ *n.* **1.** A clumsy social error. **2.** A blatant mistake.

gaf·fer (găf′ər) ▸ *n.* **1.** An electrician in charge of lighting on a movie or television set. **2.** *Chiefly Brit.* An old man.

gag (găg) ▸ *n.* **1.** Something forced into or put over the mouth to prevent speaking or crying out. **2.** An obstacle to free speech. **3.** A surgical device placed in the mouth to keep it open. **4a.** A practical joke. **b.** A comic remark. ▸ *v.* **gagged, gag·ging**. **1.** To prevent from speaking by using a gag. **2.** To restrain from exercising free speech. **3.** To choke or retch. **4.** To make jokes.

ga·ga (gä′gä′) ▸ *adj.* *Informal* **1.** Silly; crazy. **2.** Completely absorbed or infatuated.

Ga·ga·rin (gə-gär′ĭn), **Yuri Alekseyevich** (1934–68) ▸ Soviet cosmonaut.

gage[1] (gāj) ▸ *n.* **1.** Something deposited or given as security; pledge. **2.** Something, such as a glove, that is offered or thrown down as a challenge to fight.

gage[2] (gāj) ▸ *n.* & *v.* Var. of **gauge.**

gag·gle (găg′əl) ▸ *n.* **1.** A flock of geese. **2.** A group.

gag order ▸ *n.* A court order forbidding public reporting or commentary on a case currently before the court.

gag rule ▸ *n.* A rule, as in a legislative body, limiting discussion or debate on an issue.

Gai·a (gā′ə) ▸ *n.* *Gk. Myth.* Var. of **Gaea.**

gai·e·ty (gā′ĭ-tē) ▸ *n., pl.* **-ties**. **1.** Joyful exuberance or merriment; vivacity. **2.** Merry activity; festivity.

gai·ly (gā′lē) ▸ *adv.* **1.** In a joyful, cheerful, or happy manner. **2.** Colorfully; showily.

gain (gān) ▸ *v.* **1.** To come into possession of; acquire. **2.** To win. **3.** To obtain through effort or merit. **4.** To earn. **5.** To increase by: *gained 15 pounds.* **6.** To reach. **7.** To increase; grow: *gained in wisdom.* **8.** To close a gap; get closer. ▸ *n.* Something gained or acquired; profit; advantage; increase.

gain·er (gā′nər) ▸ *n.* **1.** One that gains. **2.** *Sports* A dive in which the diver leaves the board facing forward, does a back somersault, and enters the water feet first.

gain·ful (gān′fəl) ▸ *adj.* Providing a gain or profit. **—gain′ful·ly** *adv.*

gain·say (gān-sā′, gān′sā′) ▸ *v.* **-said** (-sād′, -sĕd′), **-say·ing.** To declare false.

Gains·bor·ough (gānz′bûr′ō, -bər-ə), **Thomas** (1727–88) ▸ British portrait and landscape painter.

gait (gāt) ▸ *n.* **1.** A way of moving on foot. **2.** Any of the ways a horse can move by lifting the feet in different order or rhythm. **3.** A rate or pace.

gai·ter (gā′tər) ▸ *n.* **1.** A cloth or leather covering for the legs extending from the instep to the ankle or knee. **2.** An ankle-high shoe with elastic sides. **3.** An overshoe with a cloth top.

gal (găl) ▸ *n.* *Informal* A girl.

gal. ▸ *abbr.* gallon

ga·la (gā′lə, găl′ə, gä′lə) ▸ *n.* A festive occasion, esp. a lavish social event. **—ga′la** *adj.*

THESAURUS

gab *v.* —*See* CHATTER (1).

gab *n.* —*See* CHATTER.

gabble *v.* —*See* BABBLE.

gabble *n.* —*See* BABBLE.

gabby *adj.* —*See* TALKATIVE.

gabfest *n.* —*See* CONVERSATION.

gad *v.* —*See* ROVE.

gadabout *n.* —*See* HOBO.

gadget *n.* A small specialized mechanical device ▸ apparatus, contraption, contrivance, gimmick, jigger, thing. *Informal:* doodad, doohickey, thingamabob, thingamajig, whatchamacallit, whatsit, widget. *Slang:* gizmo. [*Compare* DEVICE, NOVELTY.]

gaffe *n.* —*See* IMPROPRIETY (2).

gag *n.* —*See* JOKE (1), PRANK[1].

gag *v.* —*See* CHOKE, REPRESS.

gaga *adj.* —*See* ENTHUSIASTIC, GIDDY (2), INSANE.

gage *n.* —*See* PAWN[1].

gaggle *n.* —*See* CROWD, FLOCK.

gaiety *n.* —*See* MERRIMENT (1), MERRIMENT (2).

gain *v.* **1.** To achieve an increase of ▸ augment, build up, develop, enlarge, expand. **2.** To reach a goal or objective ▸ arrive at, attain, come to, get to. *Informal:* hit on (*or* upon). —*See also* ACCOMPLISH, BENEFIT, CAPTURE, DERIVE (1), EARN (1), EARN (2), GET (1), RECOVER (2), RETURN (3).

gain on *v.* —*See* APPROACH (1).

gain *n.* Something earned, won, or otherwise acquired ▸ earnings, profit, return. —*See also* ADVANTAGE (2).

gainful *adj.* —*See* PROFITABLE.

gainsay *v.* —*See* DENY.

gait *n.* —*See* WALK (2).

gal *n.* —*See* GIRL.

gala *n.* —*See* PARTY.

gala *adj.* —*See* MERRY.

ga·lac·tose (gə-lăk′tōs′) ▸ *n.* A simple sugar commonly occurring in lactose.

Gal·a·had (găl′ə-hăd′) ▸ *n.* **1.** In Arthurian legend, the purest Knight of the Round Table. **2.** A model of nobleness and purity.

Ga·lá·pa·gos Islands (gə-lä′pə-gəs, -lăp′ə-) ▸ A group of volcanic islands in the Pacific W of Ecuador, to which they belong.

Ga·la·tians (gə-lā′shənz) ▸ *pl.n.* *(takes sing. v.)* See **Bible** table in Appendix.

gal·ax·y (găl′ək-sē) ▸ *n., pl.* **-ies. 1a.** Any of numerous large-scale aggregates of stars, gas, and dust, containing an average of 100 billion solar masses and ranging in diameter from 1,500 to 300,000 light-years. **b.** often **Galaxy** The Milky Way. **2.** An assembly of brilliant, glamorous, or distinguished persons or things. **—ga·lac′tic** (gə-lăk′tĭk) *adj.*

gale (gāl) ▸ *n.* **1.** A very strong wind. **2.** A forceful outburst, as of laughter.

Ga·len (gā′lən) (A.D. 130?–200?) ▸ Greek anatomist, physician, and writer.

ga·le·na (gə-lē′nə) ▸ *n.* A gray mineral, essentially PbS, the principal ore of lead.

Ga·li·cia (gə-lĭsh′ə, -ē-ə) ▸ **1.** A historical region of central Europe in SE Poland and W Ukraine. **2.** A region and ancient kingdom of NW Spain on the Atlantic S of the Bay of Biscay. **—Ga·li′cian** *adj. & n.*

Gal·i·lee (găl′ə-lē′) ▸ A region of N Israel. **—Gal′i·le′an** *adj. & n.*

Galilee, Sea of Formerly **Lake Tiberias** ▸ A freshwater lake of NE Israel.

Ga·li·le·o Ga·li·lei (găl′ə-lē′ō găl′ə-lā′, -lā′ō) (1564–1642) ▸ Italian astronomer and physicist. **—Gal′i·le′an** *adj.*

gall[1] (gôl) ▸ *n.* **1.** See **bile** 1. **2a.** Bitterness of feeling; rancor. **b.** Something bitter to endure. **3.** Outrageous insolence; effrontery.

gall[2] (gôl) ▸ *n.* **1.** A skin sore caused by rubbing. **2.** Exasperation; vexation. ▸ *v.* **1.** To make or become sore by rubbing. **2.** To exasperate.

gall[3] (gôl) ▸ *n.* An abnormal swelling of plant tissue caused by insects, microorganisms, or external injury.

gal·lant (găl′ənt) ▸ *adj.* **1.** Smartly stylish; dashing. **2.** Courageous; valiant. **3.** Nobly or selflessly resolute. **4.** (gə-lănt′, -länt′) **a.** Courteously attentive; chivalrous. **b.** Flirtatious. ▸ *n.* (gə-lănt′, -länt′, găl′ənt) **1.** A fashionable young man. **2a.** A man courteously attentive to women. **b.** A woman's lover; paramour. **—gal′lant·ly** *adv.* **—gal′lant·ry** *n.*

gall·blad·der also **gall bladder** (gôl′blăd′ər) ▸ *n.* A small muscular sac under the right lobe of the liver, in which bile secreted by the liver is stored.

gal·le·on (găl′ē-ən, găl′yən) ▸ *n.* A large three-masted sailing ship used from the 15th to 17th cent. for trade or warfare.

gal·ler·y (găl′ə-rē) ▸ *n., pl.* **-ies. 1a.** A roofed promenade, esp. one along the wall of a building. **b.** A long interior or exterior balcony. **2a.** A long enclosed passage, esp. a corridor between two parts of a building. **b.** An underground tunnel. **3.** *Regional* See **veranda. 4a.** A rear or side balcony in a theater or auditorium. **b.** The seats in such a section. **c.** The cheapest seats in a theater. **d.** The audience occupying these seats. **5.** A group of spectators, as at a tennis match. **6.** The general public. **7a.** A building, institution, or room for the exhibition of artistic work. **b.** An establishment that displays and sells works of art. **8.** A collection; assortment.

gal·ley (găl′ē) ▸ *n., pl.* **-leys. 1a.** A large medieval ship propelled by sails and oars, used for trade or warfare in the Mediterranean. **b.** An ancient Mediterranean ship propelled by oars. **2.** The kitchen of an airliner or a ship. **3.** *Print.* **a.** A long tray for holding composed type. **b.** A printer's proof taken from such type.

Gal·lic (găl′ĭk) ▸ *adj.* Relating to Gaul or France; French.

Gal·li·cism (găl′ĭ-sĭz′əm) ▸ *n.* A French phrase appearing in another language.

gal·li·um (găl′ē-əm) ▸ *n.* *Symbol* **Ga** A rare metallic element, liquid near room temperature, used in semiconductors. At. no. 31.

gal·li·vant (găl′ə-vănt′) ▸ *v.* **1.** To roam about in search of pleasure or amusement. **2.** To flirt.

gal·lon (găl′ən) ▸ *n.* See table at **measurement.**

gal·lop (găl′əp) ▸ *n.* **1.** A natural three-beat gait of a horse, faster than a canter. **2.** A rapid pace. **—gal′lop** *v.*

gal·lows (găl′ōz) ▸ *n., pl.* **gallows** or **-lows·es.** A framework from which a noose is suspended, used for execution by hanging.

gallows humor ▸ *n.* Humorous treatment of a grave or dire situation.

gall·stone (gôl′stōn′) ▸ *n.* A small hard mass formed in the gallbladder or in a bile duct.

ga·lore (gə-lôr′) ▸ *adj.* In great numbers; in abundance: *opportunities galore.*

ga·losh (gə-lŏsh′) ▸ *n.* A waterproof overshoe.

gal·van·ic (găl-văn′ĭk) ▸ *adj.* **1.** Of or relating to direct-current electricity, esp. when produced chemically. **2.** Having the effect of an electric shock; jolting. **—gal′van·ism** *n.*

gal·va·nize (găl′və-nīz′) ▸ *v.* **-nized, -niz·ing. 1.** To stimulate or shock with an electric current. **2.** To arouse to awareness or action; spur. **3.** To coat (iron or steel) with rust-resistant zinc. **—gal′va·ni·za′tion** *n.*

gal·va·nom·e·ter (găl′və-nŏm′ĭ-tər) ▸ *n.* An instrument used to detect or measure small electric currents by means of mechanical effects produced by a coil in a magnetic field. **—gal′va·no·met′ric** (-nō-mĕt′rĭk), **gal′va·no·met′ri·cal** *adj.*

Ga·ma (găm′ə, gä′mə), **Vasco da** (1460?–1524) ▸ Portuguese explorer and colonial administrator.

Gam·bi·a (găm′bē-ə) ▸ A country of W Africa on the Atlantic. Pop. 1,460,000. **—Gam′bi·an** *adj. & n.*

gam·bit (găm′bĭt) ▸ *n.* **1.** A chess opening in which a minor piece, as a pawn, is offered in exchange for a favorable position. **2.** A maneuver or ploy. **3.** A remark intended to open a conversation.

gam·ble (găm′bəl) ▸ *v.* **-bled, -bling. 1a.** To bet on an uncertain outcome, as of a contest. **b.** To play a game of chance for stakes. **2.** To take a risk in the hope of gaining an advantage. **3.** To expose to hazard: *gamble one's life.* ▸ *n.* **1.** A wager. **2.** A risk. **—gam′bler** *n.*

THESAURUS

galaxy *n.* *—See* ASSEMBLY.

gale *n.* *—See* STORM.

gall[1] *n.* *—See* IMPUDENCE, RESENTMENT.

gall[2] *v.* *—See* ANNOY, CHAFE.

gallant *adj.* Respectfully attentive, especially to women ▸ chivalric, chivalrous, gentlemanly, knightly. *—See also* ATTENTIVE, BRAVE, GRACIOUS (2).

gallant *n.* A man amorously attentive to women ▸ amorist, Casanova, Don Juan, lady's man, Lothario, Romeo. [*Compare* BEAU.]

gallantry *n.* Respectful attention, especially toward women ▸ chivalrousness, chivalry. [*Compare* CONSIDERATION, COURTESY.] *—See also* COURAGE.

gallimaufry *n.* *—See* ASSORTMENT.

galling *adj.* *—See* BITTER (3), DISTURBING.

gallivant *v.* *—See* ROVE.

gallop *v.* *—See* RUN (1).

gallop *n.* *—See* RUN (1).

galumph *v.* *—See* BLUNDER.

galvanize *v.* *—See* PROVOKE.

gamble *v.* **1.** To make a bet ▸ bet, game, lay, play, wager. ***Idiom:*** put one's money on something. **2.** To place something at risk, as in a speculation or a game of chance ▸ bet, chance, lay (down), post, put, risk, stake, venture, wager. *Informal:* go. **3.** To take a risk in the hope of gaining advantage ▸ speculate, venture. ***Idioms:*** go for broke, go out on a limb, play fast and loose, stick one's neck out, take a flier, take a shot (*or* stab) in the dark, tempt fate (*or* fortune), trust to chance (*or* luck).

gamble *n.* An undertaking depending on chance ▸ bet, long shot, plunge, risk, speculation, tossup, venture, wager. *Informal:* flier. *Slang:* crapshoot. ***Idioms:*** leap (*or* shot) in the dark, roll of the dice, toss of a coin. [*Compare* ATTEMPT, TRY.] *—See also* RISK.

gambler *n.* **1.** One who gambles ▸ cardsharp, crapshooter, bettor, gamester, player, sharper. *Slang:* high roller. **2.** One who speculates for

gam·bol (găm′bəl) ► *v.* **-boled, -bol·ing** or **-bolled, -bol·ling.** To leap about playfully; frolic. **—gam′bol** *n.*

gam·brel roof (găm′brəl) ► *n.* A ridged roof with two slopes on each side, the lower slope having the steeper pitch.

game[1] (gām) ► *n.* **1.** An activity providing entertainment or amusement; pastime. **2a.** A competitive activity or sport. **b.** A single instance of such an activity. **3.** The total number of points required to win a game. **4.** A particular style or manner of playing a game. **5.** *Informal* A business or occupation: *the insurance game.* **6.** *Informal* A calculated strategy; scheme: *saw through their game.* **7.** Wild animals, birds, or fish hunted for food or sport. **8.** An object of attack or pursuit: *fair game.* ► *v.* **gamed, gam·ing.** To gamble. ► *adj.* **gam·er, gam·est. 1.** Unyielding in spirit; resolute. **2.** Ready and willing. **—game′ly** *adv.* **—game′ness** *n.*

game[2] (gām) ► *adj.* **gam·er, gam·est.** Lame.

game·cock (gām′kŏk′) ► *n.* A rooster trained for cockfighting.

game·keep·er (gām′kē′pər) ► *n.* One employed to protect and maintain wildlife, esp. on an estate or preserve.

games·man·ship (gāmz′mən-shĭp′) ► *n.* The practice of using dubious maneuvers to further one's aims or better one's position.

game·ster (gām′stər) ► *n.* A habitual gambler.

gam·ete (găm′ēt′, gə-mēt′) ► *n.* A reproductive cell, esp. a mature sperm or egg capable of participating in fertilization. **—ga·met′ic** (-mĕt′ĭk) *adj.*

gam·in (găm′ĭn) ► *n.* A boy who lives on or roams the streets.

ga·mine (gă-mēn′, găm′ēn) ► *n.* **1.** A girl who lives on or roams the streets. **2.** A girl or woman of impish appeal.

gam·ma (găm′ə) ► *n.* The 3rd letter of the Greek alphabet.

gamma globulin ► *n.* A protein fraction of blood serum containing numerous antibodies, used in the prevention and treatment esp. of measles, polio, and hepatitis.

gamma ray ► *n.* Electromagnetic radiation emitted by radioactive decay and having energies from ten thousand to ten million electron volts.

gam·mon (găm′ən) ► *n.* A victory in backgammon reached before the loser has removed a single piece.

–gamous ► *suff.* Having a specified number of marriages: *monogamous.*

gam·ut (găm′ət) ► *n.* A complete range or extent.

gam·y also **gam·ey** (gā′mē) ► *adj.* **-i·er, -i·est. 1.** Having the flavor or odor of game, esp. slightly spoiled game. **2.** Spirited; plucky. **3a.** Corrupt; tainted. **b.** Racy; risqué. **—gam′i·ness** *n.*

–gamy ► *suff.* Marriage: *polygamy.*

gan·der (găn′dər) ► *n.* **1.** A male goose. **2.** *Informal* A look or glance.

Gan·dhi (gän′dē, găn′-), **Indira Nehru** (1917–84) ► Indian prime minister (1966–77 and 1980–84); assassinated.

Gandhi, Mohandas Karamchand. "Mahatma" (1869–1948) ► Indian nationalist and spiritual leader; assassinated.

gang (găng) ► *n.* **1.** A group of criminals or hoodlums. **2.** A group of youths who band together for social and often criminal purposes. **3.** *Informal* A group of people who associate or work together. **4.** A work crew. **5.** A matched set, as of tools. ► *v.* To band together as a group or gang. ***—phrasal verb:*** **gang up** To join together esp. in opposition or attack.

Gan·ges (găn′jēz′) ► A river of N India and Bangladesh rising in the Himalayas and flowing about 2,510 km (1,560 mi) to the Bay of Bengal.

gan·gling (găng′glĭng) ► *adj.* Awkwardly tall or long-limbed.

gan·gli·on (găng′glē-ən) ► *n., pl.* **-gli·a** (-glē-ə) or **-gli·ons.** A group of nerve cells forming a nerve center, esp. one located outside the brain or spinal cord. **—gan′gli·on′ic** (-ŏn′ĭk) *adj.*

gan·gly (găng′glē) ► *adj.* **-gli·er, -gli·est.** Gangling.

gang·plank (găng′plăngk′) ► *n.* A board or ramp used as a removable footway between a ship and a pier.

gan·grene (găng′grēn′, găng-grēn′) ► *n.* Death and decay of body tissue caused by insufficient blood supply, usu. following injury or disease. **—gan′grene** *v.* **—gan′gre·nous** (găng′grə-nəs) *adj.*

gang·ster (găng′stər) ► *n.* A member of an organized group of criminals; racketeer. **—gang′ster·dom** *n.* **—gang′ster·ism** *n.*

gang·way (găng′wā′) ► *n.* **1.** A passage along a ship's upper deck. **2.** See **gangplank.** ► *interj.* Used to clear a passage through a crowded area.

gan·ja (gän′jə) ► *n.* Marijuana.

gan·net (găn′ĭt) ► *n.* A large sea bird of N Atlantic coastal regions, having white plumage with black wingtips.

gant·let (gônt′lĭt, gänt′-) ► *n.* **1.** Var. of **gauntlet[1]**. **2.** Var. of **gauntlet[2]**.

gan·try (găn′trē) ► *n., pl.* **-tries. 1.** A bridgelike mount for a traveling crane. **2.** A massive vertical frame used in assembling or servicing a rocket.

gaol (jāl) ► *n. & v.* *Chiefly Brit.* Var. of **jail.**

gap (găp) ► *n.* **1.** An opening, as in a wall; breach. **2.** A pass through mountains. **3.** A space between objects or points. **4.** An interruption of continuity. **5.** A wide difference; disparity: *the gap between rich and poor.*

gape (gāp, găp) ► *v.* **gaped, gap·ing. 1.** To open the mouth wide; yawn. **2.** To stare wonderingly or stupidly, often with the mouth open. **3.** To open wide. ► *n.* **1.** An act of gaping. **2.** A large opening.

gar (gär) ► *n.* Any of several fishes having long narrow jaws, an elongated body, and a long snout.

ga·rage (gə-räzh′, -räj′) ► *n.* **1.** A structure for housing a motor vehicle. **2.** A commercial establishment where cars are repaired, serviced, or parked. **—ga·rage′** *v.*

garage sale ► *n.* A sale of used household items or clothing held at one's home.

garb (gärb) ► *n.* **1.** A distinctive style of clothing; dress. **2.** An outward appearance; guise. **—garb** *v.*

gar·bage (gär′bĭj) ► *n.* **1a.** Food wastes, as from a kitchen. **b.** Refuse; trash. **2.** Worthless matter.

THESAURUS

quick profits ► adventurer, operator, speculator.

gambol *v.* To leap and skip about playfully ► caper, cavort, dance, frisk, frolic, rollick, romp. [*Compare* BOUND[1].]

game *n.* An object for children to play with ► game, toy. [*Compare* AMUSEMENT.] *—See also* COMPETITION (3), PLAY.

game *v.* To make a bet ► bet, gamble, lay, play, wager. *Idiom:* put one's money on something. *—See also* CHEAT (1).

game *adj.* *—See* BRAVE, WILLING.

gameness *n.* *—See* COURAGE.

game plan *n.* *—See* APPROACH (1).

gamesome *adj.* *—See* MISCHIEVOUS.

gamester *n.* *—See* GAMBLER (1).

gamin or **gamine** *n.* *—See* URCHIN.

gamut *n.* *—See* SERIES.

gamy *adj.* *—See* MOLDY.

gander *n.* *—See* FOOL, GLANCE (1).

gang *n.* An organized group of criminals, hoodlums, or wrongdoers ► band, pack, ring. *Informal:* mob. *—See also* CIRCLE (3), FLOCK, FORCE (3).

gang *v.* *—See* BAND[2].

gang up on *v.* *—See* ATTACK (1).

gangling or **gangly** *adj.* Tall, thin, and awkwardly built ► lanky, rangy, scraggy, spindling, spindly. [*Compare* THIN.]

gangsta *n.* *—See* THUG.

gangster *n.* *—See* CRIMINAL.

gap *n.* **1.** A space between objects or points ► chasm, divide, gulf, interspace, interstice, interval, separation. [*Compare* HOLE.] **2.** An interval during which continuity is suspended ► break, hiatus, interlude, interim, interregnum, lacuna, lull, void. [*Compare* BREAK.] **3.** A marked lack of correspondence or agreement ► difference, disagreement, discrepancy, disparity, imbalance, incompatibility, incongruity, inconsistency. [*Compare* DIFFERENCE.] *—See also* BREACH, DISTANCE (1).

gap *v.* **1.** To make a hole or other opening in ► breach, break (through), hole, perforate, pierce, puncture. **2.** To open wide ► gape, yawn. [*Compare* OPEN, WIDEN.]

gape *v.* **1.** To open the mouth wide with a deep breath, as when tired or bored ► yawn. **2.** To open wide ► gap, yawn. [*Compare* OPEN, WIDEN.] *—See also* GAZE.

gape *n.* An intent fixed look ► gaze, stare. [*Compare* LOOK.]

gaping *adj.* Open wide ► abysmal, abyssal, cavernous, yawning. [*Compare* BROAD, OPEN.]

garb *n.* *—See* DRESS (1), DRESS (2).

garb *v.* *—See* DRESS (1).

garbage *n.* Items or material discarded

gar·ban·zo (gär-bän′zō) ▸ *n., pl.* **-zos.** See **chickpea.**

gar·ble (gär′bəl) ▸ *v.* **-bled, -bling.** To mix up or distort (e.g., a message) to such an extent as to make misleading or unintelligible. **—gar′bler** *n.*

Gar·cí·a Lor·ca (gär-sē′ə lôr′kä, gär-thē′ä), **Federico** (1898–1936) ▸ Spanish writer.

gar·den (gär′dn) ▸ *n.* **1.** A plot of land used for growing flowers, vegetables, herbs, or fruit. **2.** often **gardens** Grounds laid out with ornamental plants and trees and used for public recreation or display. **3.** A yard or lawn. **4.** A fertile, well-cultivated region. ▸ *v.* To plant or tend a garden. **—gar′den·er** *n.*

gar·de·nia (gär-dēn′yə) ▸ *n.* **1.** A shrub having glossy evergreen leaves. **2.** The large fragrant white flower of this plant.

gar·den-va·ri·e·ty (gär′dn-və-rī′ĭ-tē) ▸ *adj.* Common; unremarkable.

Gar·field (gär′fēld′), **James Abram** (1831–81) ▸ The 20th President of the US (1881); assassinated.

gar·gan·tu·an (gär-găn′cho͞o-ən) ▸ *adj.* Of immense size; gigantic.

gar·gle (gär′gəl) ▸ *v.* **-gled, -gling. 1.** To force exhaled air through a liquid held in the back of the mouth in order to cleanse or medicate the mouth or throat. **2.** To produce the sound of gargling when speaking or singing. ▸ *n.* **1.** A medicated solution for gargling. **2.** A gargling sound.

gar·goyle (gär′goil′) ▸ *n.* A roof spout in the form of a grotesque or fantastic creature.

gar·ish (gâr′ĭsh, găr′-) ▸ *adj.* Excessively or stridently decorated. **—gar′ish·ly** *adv.* **—gar′ish·ness** *n.*

gar·land (gär′lənd) ▸ *n.* A wreath or festoon, esp. of plaited flowers or leaves. ▸ *v.* To ornament with a garland.

gar·lic (gär′lĭk) ▸ *n.* **1.** An onionlike plant having a bulb with a strong distinctive odor and flavor. **2.** The bulb of this plant, divisible into separate cloves and used as a seasoning. **—gar′lick·y** *adj.*

gar·ment (gär′mənt) ▸ *n.* An article of clothing.

gar·ner (gär′nər) ▸ *v.* To amass; acquire.

gar·net (gär′nĭt) ▸ *n.* **1.** Any of several common, usu. crystallized silicate minerals, colored red, brown, black, green, yellow, or white and used as gemstones and abrasives. **2.** A dark to very dark red.

gar·nish (gär′nĭsh) ▸ *v.* **1.** To embellish; adorn. **2.** To decorate (food or drink) with small items such as parsley or lemon slices. **3.** *Law* To garnishee. **—gar′nish** *n.*

gar·nish·ee (gär′nĭ-shē′) ▸ *v.* **-eed, -ee·ing.** To attach by garnishment.

gar·nish·ment (gär′nĭsh-mənt) ▸ *n.* A proceeding whereby money or property belonging to a debtor but in the possession of another is turned over to the creditor.

gar·ret (găr′ĭt) ▸ *n.* An attic room or rooms, typically under a pitched roof.

gar·ri·son (găr′ĭ-sən) ▸ *n.* A permanent military post or the troops stationed there. ▸ *v.* To assign (troops) to a military post.

gar·rote or **gar·rotte** (gə-rŏt′, -rōt′) ▸ *n.* **1a.** A method of execution by strangulation with an iron collar. **b.** The collar used for this. **2a.** Strangulation, esp. in order to rob. **b.** A cord or wire used for strangling. **—gar·rote′** *v.* **—gar·rot′er** *n.*

gar·ru·lous (găr′ə-ləs, găr′yə-) ▸ *adj.* Tiresomely talkative; rambling. **—gar′ru·lous·ly** *adv.* **—gar′ru·lous·ness** *n.*

gar·ter (gär′tər) ▸ *n.* An elastic band or suspender worn to hold up hose. **—gar′ter** *v.*

garter snake ▸ *n.* A nonvenomous North American snake with longitudinal stripes.

gas (găs) ▸ *n., pl.* **gas·es** or **gas·ses. 1a.** The state of matter distinguished from the solid and liquid states by relatively low density and viscosity, the ability to diffuse readily, and the spontaneous tendency to become distributed uniformly throughout any container. **b.** A substance in this state. **2.** A gaseous fuel, such as natural gas. **3.** Gasoline. **4.** A gaseous asphyxiant, irritant, or poison. **5.** A gaseous anesthetic. **6.** Flatulence. **7.** *Slang* Idle or boastful talk. **8.** *Slang* One that provides great fun or entertainment. ▸ *v.* **gassed, gas·sing. 1.** To treat chemically with gas. **2.** To overcome or kill with poisonous fumes. ***—phrasal verb:* gas up** To supply a vehicle with gasoline. **—gas′e·ous** (găs′ē-əs, găsh′əs) *adj.*

gas chamber ▸ *n.* A sealed enclosure in which prisoners are executed by poison gas.

gash (găsh) ▸ *v.* To make a long deep cut in. **—gash** *n.*

gas·ket (găs′kĭt) ▸ *n.* Any of a variety of seals or packings used between matched machine parts or around pipe joints to prevent the escape of a gas or fluid.

gas·light (găs′līt′) ▸ *n.* **1.** Light produced by burning illuminating gas. **2.** A gas lamp.

gas mask ▸ *n.* A respirator that contains a chemical air filter and is worn over the face as protection against toxic gases.

gas·o·hol (găs′ə-hôl′) ▸ *n.* A blend of ethyl alcohol and unleaded gasoline used as a fuel.

gas·o·line (găs′ə-lēn′, găs′ə-lēn′) ▸ *n.* A volatile mixture of flammable liquid hydrocarbons derived chiefly from crude petroleum and used as a fuel for internal-combustion engines and as a solvent and thinner.

gasp (găsp) ▸ *v.* **1.** To draw in or catch the breath sharply, as from shock. **2.** To make violent or labored attempts at breathing. **—gasp** *n.*

gas·sy (găs′ē) ▸ *adj.* **-si·er, -si·est.** Containing, full of, or resembling gas. **—gas′si·ness** *n.*

gas·tric (găs′trĭk) ▸ *adj.* Of or associated with the stomach.

gastric juice ▸ *n.* The watery, acidic digestive fluid secreted by glands in the stomach.

gas·tri·tis (gă-strī′tĭs) ▸ *n.* Chronic or acute inflammation of the stomach.

gastro– or **gastr–** ▸ *pref.* Stomach: *gastritis.*

gas·tro·en·ter·i·tis (găs′trō-ĕn′tə-rī′tĭs) ▸ *n.* Inflammation of the mucous membrane of the stomach and intestines.

gas·tro·in·tes·ti·nal (găs′trō-ĭn-tĕs′tə-nəl) ▸ *adj.* Of the stomach and intestines.

gas·trol·o·gy (gă-strŏl′ə-jē) ▸ *n.* The medical study of the stomach and its diseases. **—gas′tro·log′i·cal** (găs′trə-lŏj′ĭ-kəl), **gas′tro·log′ic** *adj.* **—gas′tro·log′i·cal·ly** *adv.* **—gas·trol′o·gist** *n.*

gas·tron·o·my (gă-strŏn′ə-mē) ▸ *n., pl.* **-mies. 1.** The art or science of good eating. **2.** Cooking, as of a particular region. **—gas′tro·nome′** (găs′trə-nōm′) *n.* **—gas′tro·nom′ic** (găs′trə-nŏm′ĭk) *adj.*

gas·tro·pod (găs′trə-pŏd′) ▸ *n.* Any of a class of mollusks, such as the snail or slug, having a single, usu. coiled shell or no shell at all and a muscular foot for locomotion.

gas·works (găs′wûrks′) ▸ *pl.n. (takes sing. v.)* A factory where gas for heating and lighting is produced.

gate (gāt) ▸ *n.* **1a.** A structure that can be swung, drawn, or lowered to block an entrance or passageway. **b.** A gateway. **2.** A passageway, as in an airport terminal, through which passengers arrive or depart. **3.** The total

THESAURUS

or rejected as useless or worthless ▸ debris, dregs, flotsam, jetsam, litter, refuse, rubbish, trash, waste. *Informal:* gunk. *Idiom:* flotsam and jetsam. *—See also* NONSENSE.

garble *v.* *—See* CONFUSE (3).

garden *adj.* *—See* ORDINARY.

garden *v.* *—See* GROW.

garden-variety *adj.* *—See* ORDINARY.

gargantuan *adj.* *—See* ENORMOUS.

garish *adj.* *—See* GAUDY.

garland *n.* *—See* BOUQUET.

garment *v.* *—See* DRESS (1).

garments *n.* *—See* DRESS (1).

garner *v.* *—See* ACCUMULATE, GATHER, GLEAN.

garner *n.* The amount or quantity produced ▸ output, production, yield.

garnish *v.* *—See* ADORN (1).

garniture or **garnishment** *n.* *—See* ADORNMENT.

garrulous *adj.* *—See* TALKATIVE.

gas *n.* *—See* BOAST, CHATTER, SCREAM (2).

gas *v.* *—See* CHATTER (1).

gasconade *v.* *—See* BOAST.

gasconade *n.* *—See* BOAST.

gash *v.* *—See* CUT (1).

gash *n.* *—See* CUT (1).

gasp *v.* To utter in a breathless or hoarse manner ▸ croak, heave, pant, rasp, snort, wheeze. [*Compare* SHOUT.] *—See also* PANT.

gassy *adj.* *—See* INFLATED.

gate *n.* The amount of money collected as admission, especially to a

paid attendance at a public event. **4.** A device for controlling the passage of water or gas through a dam or conduit. **5.** *Electron.* A circuit with one output that is energized only by certain combinations of two or more inputs.

gate·crash·er (gāt′krăsh′ər) ▸ *n. Slang* One who gains admittance, as to a party or concert, without being invited or without paying. **—gate′crash′** *v.*

gat·ed community (gā′tĭd) ▸ *n.* A private neighborhood with entry permitted only to residents and guests.

gate·way (gāt′wā′) ▸ *n.* **1.** An opening, as in a wall or fence, that may be closed by a gate. **2.** A means of access.

gath·er (găth′ər) ▸ *v.* **1.** To bring or come together. **2.** To accumulate gradually. **3.** To harvest or pick. **4.** To grow or increase by degrees: *gather speed.* **5.** To draw (e.g., cloth) into small folds or puckers. **6.** To draw about or bring closer: *gathered the shawl about my shoulders.* **7.** To conclude; infer: *I gather you're ready.* **8.** To summon up: *gathered up my courage.* ▸ *n.* **1.** An act of gathering. **2.** A small fold or pucker in cloth. **—gath′er·er** *n.* **—gath′er·ing** *n.*

ga·tor or **ga·ter** (gā′tər) ▸ *n. Informal* An alligator.

gauche (gōsh) ▸ *adj.* Lacking social polish; tactless. **—gauche′ly** *adv.* **—gauche′ness** *n.*

gau·cho (gou′chō) ▸ *n., pl.* **-chos.** A cowboy of the South American pampas.

gaud·y (gô′dē) ▸ *adj.* **-i·er, -i·est.** Showy in a tasteless or vulgar way. **—gaud′i·ly** *adv.* **—gaud′i·ness** *n.*

gauge also **gage** (gāj) ▸ *n.* **1a.** A standard or scale of measurement. **b.** A standard dimension, quantity, or capacity. **2.** An instrument for measuring or testing. **3.** A means of estimating or evaluating. **4a.** The distance between the two rails of a railroad. **b.** The distance between two wheels on an axle. **5.** The diameter of a shotgun barrel. **6.** Thickness or diameter, as of sheet metal or wire. ▸ *v.* **gauged, gaug·ing** also **gaged, gag·ing. 1.** To measure precisely. **2.** To determine the capacity, volume, or contents of. **3.** To evaluate.

Gau·guin (gō-găɴ′), **(Eugène Henri) Paul** (1848–1903) ▸ French artist.

Gaul^{1} (gôl) ▸ *n.* A Celt of ancient Gaul.

Gaul^{2} (gôl) ▸ An ancient region of W Europe corresponding roughly to modern-day France and Belgium.

Gaul·ish (gô′lĭsh) ▸ *n.* The extinct Celtic language of Gaul.

gaunt (gônt) ▸ *adj.* **-er, -est. 1.** Thin and bony. **2.** Emaciated. **3.** Bleak; desolate. **—gaunt′ly** *adv.* **—gaunt′ness** *n.*

gaunt·let^{1} also **gant·let** (gônt′lĭt, gänt′-) ▸ *n.* **1.** A protective glove. **2.** A challenge to fight or compete.

gaunt·let^{2} also **gant·let** (gônt′lĭt, gänt′-) ▸ *n.* **1.** A form of punishment in which two lines of persons facing each other and armed with sticks or clubs beat the person forced to run between them. **2.** A severe trial; ordeal: *run the gauntlet of public scrutiny.*

gauze (gôz) ▸ *n.* A thin transparent fabric with a loose open weave. **—gauz′i·ly** *adv.* **—gauz′i·ness** *n.* **—gauz′y** *adj.*

gave (gāv) ▸ *v.* P.t. of **give.**

gav·el (găv′əl) ▸ *n.* A small mallet used by a presiding officer or an auctioneer to signal for attention or order or to conclude a transaction. **—gav′el** *v.*

ga·votte (gə-vŏt′) ▸ *n.* A French peasant dance in duple meter.

gawk (gôk) ▸ *n.* An awkward, loutish person; oaf. ▸ *v.* To stare or gape stupidly. **—gawk′er** *n.* **—gawk′y** *adj.*

gay (gā) ▸ *adj.* **-er, -est. 1.** Of or having a sexual orientation to persons of the same sex. **2.** Cheerful and lighthearted; merry. **3.** Bright or lively, esp. in color. ▸ *n.* A person whose sexual orientation is to persons of the same sex. **—gay′ness** *n.*

Ga·za (gä′zə, găz′ə) ▸ A city of SW Asia in the **Gaza Strip,** a narrow coastal area along the Mediterranean Sea adjoining Israel and Egypt. Pop. 118,000.

gaze (gāz) ▸ *v.* **gazed, gaz·ing.** To look steadily, intently, and with fixed attention. **—gaze** *n.* **—gaz′er** *n.*

ga·ze·bo (gə-zā′bō, -zē′-) ▸ *n., pl.* **-bos** or **-boes.** A small, usu. open-sided roofed structure in a garden or park.

ga·zelle (gə-zĕl′) ▸ *n.* Any of various small swift antelopes of Africa and Asia.

ga·zette (gə-zĕt′) ▸ *n.* **1.** A newspaper. **2.** An official journal.

gaz·et·teer (găz′ĭ-tîr′) ▸ *n.* A geographic dictionary or index.

gaz·pa·cho (gə-spä′chō, gəz-pä′-) ▸ *n.* A chilled soup of chopped tomatoes, cucumbers, onions, peppers, and herbs.

GB ▸ *abbr.* **1.** gigabyte **2.** Great Britain

G clef ▸ *n.* See **treble clef.**

Gd ▸ The symbol for the element **gadolinium.**

GDP ▸ *abbr.* gross domestic product

Ge ▸ The symbol for the element **germanium.**

gear (gîr) ▸ *n.* **1a.** A toothed machine part, such as a wheel or cylinder, that meshes with another toothed part to transmit motion or to change speed or direction. **b.** A transmission configuration for a specific ratio of engine to axle torque in a motor vehicle. **2.** Equipment, such as tools or clothing, used for a particular activity. **3.** Personal belongings. ▸ *v.* **1a.** To equip with or connect by gears. **b.** To put into gear. **2.** To adjust or adapt.

gear·box (gîr′bŏks′) ▸ *n.* **1.** See **transmission** 3. **2.** A casing for a system of gears.

gear·shift (gîr′shĭft′) ▸ *n.* A mechanism for changing from one gear to another in a transmission.

geck·o (gĕk′ō) ▸ *n., pl.* **-os** or **-oes.** Any of various usu. small tropical and subtropical lizards having toes with adhesive pads for climbing.

gee (jē) ▸ *interj.* Used as an exclamation, as of surprise.

geek (gēk) ▸ *n. Slang* **1a.** An inept or clumsy person. **b.** One accomplished in scientific or technical pursuits but regarded as socially inept. **2.** A carnival performer featuring bizarre acts. **—geek′y** *adj.*

geese (gēs) ▸ *n.* Pl. of **goose.**

gee·zer (gē′zər) ▸ *n.* An eccentric old man.

Gei·ger counter (gī′gər) ▸ *n.* An instrument that detects and measures the intensity of radiation, such as particles from radioactive material.

gei·sha (gā′shə, gē′-) ▸ *n., pl.* **-sha** or **-shas.** One of a class of professional women in Japan trained to entertain men.

gel (jĕl) ▸ *n.* A jellylike mixture formed when the particles of a colloid become relatively large. **—gel** *v.*

gel·a·tin also **gel·a·tine** (jĕl′ə-tn) ▸ *n.* **1.** A transparent brittle protein formed by boiling the specially prepared skin, bones, and connective tissue of animals and used in foods, drugs, and photographic film. **2.** A jelly made with gelatin. **—ge·lat′i·nous** (jə-lăt′n-əs) *adj.*

geld (gĕld) ▸ *v.* **geld·ed** or **gelt** (gĕlt), **geld·ing.** To castrate (e.g., a horse). **—geld′ing** *n.*

THESAURUS

sporting event ▸ box office, take, receipts.

gatecrash *v.* —*See* INTRUDE.

gather *v.* To collect ripe crops ▸ crop, garner, harvest, pick, pluck, reap. —*See also* ACCUMULATE, ASSEMBLE, GLEAN, INFER.

gathering *n.* —*See* ACCUMULATION (1), ASSEMBLY, JUNCTION, PARTY.

gauche *adj.* —*See* TACTLESS, UNSKILLFUL.

gaudy *adj.* Tastelessly showy ▸ chintzy, flashy, florid, garish, loud, meretricious, tawdry, tinsel, vulgar. *Informal:* glitzy, tacky. [*Compare* ORNATE, SHOWY.]

gauge *n.* The marked outer surface of an instrument ▸ dial, face, indicator. —*See also* STANDARD.

gauge *v.* To ascertain the dimensions, quantity, or capacity of ▸ measure, quantify, quantitate. ***Idiom:*** take the dimensions (*or* measure) of. —*See also* ESTIMATE (1).

gaunt *adj.* —*See* HAGGARD, THIN (1).

gauzy *adj.* —*See* SHEER^{2}.

gawk *n.* —*See* OAF.

gawk *v.* —*See* GAZE.

gawky *adj.* —*See* AWKWARD (1).

gay *adj.* Having a sexual orientation to persons of the same sex ▸ homophile, homosexual, lesbian. —*See also* CHEERFUL, COLORFUL (1).

gaze *v.* To look intently and fixedly ▸ eye, gape, gawk, goggle, ogle, peer, stare. *Slang:* rubberneck. ***Idioms:*** gaze open-mouthed, fix (*or* rivet) the eyes (on). [*Compare* GLARE, LOOK, WATCH, SQUINT.]

gaze *n.* An intent fixed look ▸ gape, stare. [*Compare* LOOK.]

gear *n.* —*See* DRESS (2), OUTFIT.

gear *v.* —*See* FURNISH.

geek *n.* —*See* FOOL.

gelatinize *v.* —*See* COAGULATE.

gelatinous *adj.* —*See* VISCOUS.

geld *v.* —*See* STERILIZE (2).

gel·id (jĕl′ĭd) ▸ *adj.* Very cold. **—ge·lid′i·ty** (jə-lĭd′ĭ-tē), **gel′id·ness** *n.*

gel·ig·nite (jĕl′ĭg-nīt′) ▸ *n.* An explosive mixture composed of nitroglycerine, guncotton, wood pulp, and potassium nitrate.

gem (jĕm) ▸ *n.* **1.** A pearl or mineral that has been cut and polished for use as an ornament. **2.** Something valued highly. **—gem′my** *adj.*

Gem·i·ni (jĕm′ə-nī′, -nē′) ▸ *pl.n.* *(takes sing. v.)* **1.** A constellation in the Northern Hemisphere containing the stars Castor and Pollux. **2.** The 3rd sign of the zodiac.

gem·ol·o·gy or **gem·mol·o·gy** (jĕ-mŏl′ə-jē) ▸ *n.* The study of precious or semiprecious stones. **—gem′o·log′i·cal** (jĕm′ə-lŏj′ĭ-kəl) *adj.* **—gem·ol′o·gist** *n.*

gem·stone (jĕm′stōn′) ▸ *n.* A precious or semiprecious stone that may be used as a jewel when cut and polished.

-gen or **-gene** ▸ *suff.* Producer: *androgen.*

gen·darme (zhän′därm′, zhäN′därm′) ▸ *n.* A member of the French national police.

gen·der (jĕn′dər) ▸ *n.* **1.** *Gram.* A category used in the analysis of nouns, pronouns, adjectives, and, in some languages, verbs that determines agreement with modifiers, referents, or grammatical forms. **2.** Sexual category; males or females as a group. **—gen′der·less** *adj.*

gene (jēn) ▸ *n.* A hereditary unit that occupies a specific location on a chromosome, determines a particular characteristic in an organism, and can undergo mutation.

ge·ne·al·o·gy (jē′nē-ŏl′ə-jē, -ăl′-, jĕn′ē-) ▸ *n., pl.* **-gies. 1.** A record of ancestral descent; family tree. **2.** Direct descent from an ancestor. **3.** The study of ancestry. **—ge′ne·a·log′i·cal** (-ə-lŏj′ĭ-kəl) *adj.* **—ge′ne·al′o·gist** *n.*

gene pool ▸ *n.* The collective genetic information contained within a population of sexually reproducing organisms.

gen·er·a (jĕn′ər-ə) ▸ *n.* Pl. of **genus.**

gen·er·al (jĕn′ər-əl) ▸ *adj.* **1.** Applicable to or affecting the whole or every member of a category. **2.** Widespread; prevalent. **3.** Of or affecting the entire body: *general malaise; general anesthetic.* **4.** Being usually the case. **5.** Not limited in scope or category: *a general rule; general merchandise.* **6.** Broad but not thorough: *a general grasp of the subject.* **7.** Highest or superior in rank: *the general manager.* ▸ *n.* A rank, as in the US Army, above lieutenant general. ***—idiom:* in general** For the most part. **—gen′er·al·ly** *adv.*

general assembly ▸ *n.* **1.** A legislative body. **2. General Assembly** The main deliberative body of the United Nations, in which each member nation has one vote.

gen·er·al·is·si·mo (jĕn′ər-ə-lĭs′ə-mō′) ▸ *n., pl.* **-mos.** The commander in chief of all the armed forces in certain countries.

gen·er·al·i·ty (jĕn′ə-răl′ĭ-tē) ▸ *n., pl.* **-ties. 1.** The state of being general. **2.** An observation or principle having general application; generalization. **3.** A vague statement or idea.

gen·er·al·ize (jĕn′ər-ə-līz′) ▸ *v.* **-ized, -iz·ing. 1.** To render general rather than specific. **2.** To draw inferences or a general conclusion (from). **3.** To deal in generalities; speak or write vaguely. **—gen′er·al·i·za′tion** *n.*

General of the Air Force ▸ *n.* The highest rank in the US Air Force.

General of the Army ▸ *n.* The highest rank in the US Army.

general practitioner ▸ *n.* A physician who does not specialize in a particular area but treats a variety of medical problems.

general relativity ▸ *n.* The geometric theory of gravitation developed by Albert Einstein, extending the theory of special relativity to accelerated frames of reference and introducing the principle that gravitational and inertial forces are equivalent.

gen·er·al·ship (jĕn′ər-əl-shĭp′) ▸ *n.* **1.** The rank, office, or tenure of a general. **2.** Skill in the conduct of war. **3.** Leadership.

gen·er·ate (jĕn′ə-rāt′) ▸ *v.* **-at·ed, -at·ing.** To bring into being; produce. **—gen′er·a·tive** (-ər-ə-tĭv, -ə-rā′-) *adj.*

gen·er·a·tion (jĕn′ə-rā′shən) ▸ *n.* **1.** All of the offspring that are at the same stage of descent from a common ancestor. **2.** The average interval of time between the birth of parents and the birth of their offspring. **3.** A group of contemporaneous individuals. **4.** A period of sequential technological development and innovation. **5.** The act of generating. **—gen·er·a′tion·al** *adj.*

Generation X ▸ *n.* The generation following the post–World War II baby boom, esp. in the US and Canada.

gen·er·a·tor (jĕn′ə-rā′tər) ▸ *n.* One that generates, esp. a machine that converts mechanical energy into electrical energy.

ge·ner·ic (jə-nĕr′ĭk) ▸ *adj.* **1.** Relating to or descriptive of an entire group. **2.** *Biol.* Of or relating to a genus. **3.** Not having a trademark or brand name. ▸ *n.* A product or substance sold under a generic name. **—ge·ner′i·cal·ly** *adv.*

gen·er·ous (jĕn′ər-əs) ▸ *adj.* **1.** Liberal in giving or sharing. **2.** Not petty or mean; magnanimous. **3.** Abundant; ample. **—gen′er·os′i·ty** (-ə-rŏs′-ĭ-tē) *n.* **—gen′er·ous·ly** *adv.* **—gen′er·ous·ness** *n.*

gen·e·sis (jĕn′ĭ-sĭs) ▸ *n., pl.* **-ses** (-sēz′). **1.** The origin of something. **2. Genesis** See **Bible** table in Appendix.

-genesis ▸ *suff.* Origin; production: *morphogenesis.*

gene therapy ▸ *n.* Treatment of esp. genetic disorders by introducing engineered genes into a subject's cells.

ge·net·ic (jə-nĕt′ĭk) also **ge·net·i·cal** (-ĭ-kəl) ▸ *adj.* **1a.** Of or relating to genetics. **b.** Affecting or affected by genes. **2.**

THESAURUS

gelid *adj.* —*See* COLD (1).

gelidity or **gelidness** *n.* —*See* COLD.

gelt *n.* —*See* MONEY (1).

gem *n.* —*See* TREASURE.

geminate *v.* To make or become twice as great ▸ double, duplicate, redouble, twin.

geminate *adj.* —*See* DOUBLE (2).

gendarme *n.* —*See* POLICE OFFICER.

gender-neutral *adj.* —*See* ANDROGYNOUS.

gender-neutrality *n.* The quality of being androgynous ▸ androgyny, epicenism, sexlessness. [*Compare* EFFEMINACY, MASCULINITY.]

genealogical *adj.* Of unbroken descent or lineage ▸ direct, hereditary, lineal, natural. —*See also* ANCESTRAL.

genealogy *n.* A written record of ancestry ▸ family tree, pedigree. —*See also* ANCESTRY.

general *adj.* **1.** Concerned with, applicable to, or affecting the whole ▸ blanket, common, generic, total, universal. **2.** Covering a wide scope ▸ all-around, all-inclusive, all-round, broad, broad-spectrum, comprehensive, expansive, extended, extensive, far-ranging, far-reaching, global, inclusive, large, overall, popular, sweeping, wide-ranging, wide-reaching, widespread. *Idiom:* across-the-board. **3.** Not limited to a single class ▸ diversified, indefinite. —*See also* COMMON (1), COMMON (2), LOOSE (3), POPULAR, PREVAILING.

general *n.* —*See* CHIEF.

generally *adv.* —*See* USUALLY.

generate *v.* —*See* CAUSE, PRODUCE (1).

generation *n.* —*See* LIFE, PROGENY, REPRODUCTION.

generative *adj.* —*See* INVENTIVE.

generic *adj.* —*See* GENERAL (1).

generosity *n.* The quality or state of being generous ▸ big-heartedness, bounteousness, bountifulness, bounty, freehandedness, generousness, great-heartedness, large-heartedness, largess, lavishness, liberality, magnanimity, magnanimousness, munificence, openhandedness, unselfishness, unsparingness. [*Compare* BENEVOLENCE, CONSIDERATION.]

generous *adj.* **1.** Willing to give of oneself and one's possessions ▸ big, big-hearted, bountiful, free, freehanded, great-hearted, handsome, large-hearted, lavish, liberal, magnanimous, munificent, openhanded, princely, prodigal, ungrudging, unselfish, unsparing, unstinting, warmhearted. [*Compare* BENEVOLENT, HUMANITARIAN, SELFLESS.] **2.** Characterized by abundance; as much as one needs or desires ▸ abounding, abundant, ample, bounteous, bountiful, copious, heavy, plenitudinous, plenteous, plentiful, substantial, voluminous. [*Compare* PROFUSE.] —*See also* OBLIGING.

generousness *n.* —*See* GENEROSITY.

genesis *n.* —*See* BIRTH (2).

Of or influenced by the origin or development of something. **—ge·net′i·cal·ly** *adv.*

genetic code ▸ *n.* The nucleotide sequence in DNA or RNA that determines protein synthesis and constitutes the basis of heredity.

genetic engineering ▸ *n.* Scientific alteration of the structure of genetic material in a living organism. **—genetic engineer** *n.*

ge·net·ics (jə-nĕt′ĭks) ▸ *n. (takes sing. v.)* The branch of biology that deals with heredity, esp. the mechanisms of hereditary transmission and the variation of inherited characteristics. **—ge·net′i·cist** *n.*

Ge·ne·va (jə-nē′və) ▸ A city of SW Switzerland, bisected by the Rhone R. Metro. area pop. 175,000.

Gen·ghis Khan (jĕng′gĭs kän′, gĕng′-) also **Jen·ghis Khan** (jĕn′gĭs kän′, jĕng′-) (1162?–1227) ▸ Mongol conqueror.

gen·ial (jēn′yəl) ▸ *adj.* Having a pleasant or friendly disposition or manner. **—ge′ni·al′i·ty** (jē′nē-ăl′ĭ-tē), **gen′ial·ness** *n.* **—gen′ial·ly** *adv.*

-genic ▸ *suff.* 1. Producing; generating: *allergenic.* 2. Produced or generated by: *psychogenic.* 3. Suitable for production or reproduction by a specified medium: *photogenic.*

ge·nie (jē′nē) ▸ *n.* A supernatural creature who does one's bidding when summoned.

gen·i·tal (jĕn′ĭ-tl) ▸ *adj.* 1. Of or relating to biological reproduction. 2. Of the genitalia. 3. Of the third and final stage of psychosexual development in psychoanalytic theory. ▸ *n.* **genitals** The genitalia. **—gen′i·tal·ly** *adv.*

gen·i·ta·li·a (jĕn′ĭ-tā′lē-ə, -tāl′yə) ▸ *pl.n.* The reproductive organs, esp. the external sex organs.

gen·i·tive (jĕn′ĭ-tĭv) ▸ *adj.* Of or designating a grammatical case that expresses possession, measurement, or source. ▸ *n.* The genitive case.

gen·i·to·u·ri·nar·y (jĕn′ĭ-tō-yŏŏr′ə-nĕr′ē) ▸ *adj.* Of or relating to the genital and urinary organs or their functions.

gen·ius (jēn′yəs) ▸ *n., pl.* **-ius·es.** 1a. Extraordinary intellectual and creative power. b. A person of extraordinary intellect and talent. 2. A strong natural talent or aptitude. 3. The distinctive character of a place, person, or era. 4. *pl.* **ge·ni·i** (jē′nē-ī′) *Rom. Myth.* The guardian spirit of a person or place.

Gen·o·a (jĕn′ō-ə) ▸ A city of NW Italy on the Ligurian Sea. Pop. 602,000. **—Gen′o·ese′** (-ēz′, -ēs′), **Gen′o·vese′** (-vēz′, -vēs′) *adj. & n.*

gen·o·cide (jĕn′ə-sīd′) ▸ *n.* The systematic, planned extermination of an entire national, racial, political, or ethnic group. **—gen′o·cid′al** (-sīd′l) *adj.* **—gen′o·cid′al·ly** *adv.*

ge·nome (jē′nōm′) ▸ *n.* 1. The genetic material contained in a haploid set of chromosomes in eukaryotes, in a single chromosome in bacteria, or in the DNA or RNA of viruses. 2. An organism's genetic material. **—ge·nom′ic** (-nŏm′ĭk) *adj.*

gen·o·type (jĕn′ə-tīp′, jē′nə-) ▸ *n.* 1. The genetic constitution of an organism or group of organisms. 2. A group or class of organisms having the same genetic constitution. **—gen′o·typ′ic** (-tĭp′ĭk), **gen′o·typ′i·cal** *adj.*

-genous ▸ *suff.* 1. Producing; generating: *erogenous.* 2. Produced by or in a specified manner: *endogenous.*

gen·re (zhän′rə) ▸ *n.* 1. A type or class. 2. An established class or category of artistic composition, as in literature or film. 3. A realistic style of painting that depicts everyday life.

gent (jĕnt) ▸ *n. Informal* A gentleman.

gen·teel (jĕn-tēl′) ▸ *adj.* 1. Refined in manner; well-bred and polite. 2. Elegantly stylish. 3. Striving to convey an appearance of refinement and respectability. **—gen·teel′ly** *adv.* **—gen·teel′ness** *n.*

gen·tian (jĕn′shən) ▸ *n.* Any of numerous plants having showy, usu. blue flowers.

gen·tile or **Gen·tile** (jĕn′tīl′) ▸ *n.* 1. One who is not a Jew. 2. A Christian. 3. *Archaic* A pagan or heathen.

gen·til·i·ty (jĕn-tĭl′ĭ-tē) ▸ *n.* 1. The quality of being well-mannered. 2. The condition of being born to the gentry.

gen·tle (jĕn′tl) ▸ *adj.* **-tler, -tlest.** 1. Considerate or kindly. 2. Not harsh or severe; soft; mild. 3. Easily managed or handled; docile. 4. Not steep or sudden; gradual. 5. Of good family; wellborn. **—gen′tle** *v.* **—gen′tle·ness** *n.* **—gen′tly** *adv.*

gen·tle·man (jĕn′tl-mən) ▸ *n.* 1. A man of superior social position. 2. A polite or well-mannered man. 3. A man of independent means who does not need to work for a living. 4. A man. **—gen′tle·man·ly** *adj.*

gen·tle·wom·an (jĕn′tl-wŏŏm′ən) ▸ *n.* 1. A woman of superior social position. 2. A polite or well-mannered woman.

gen·tri·fi·ca·tion (jĕn′trə-fĭ-kā′shən) ▸ *n.* The restoration and upgrading of deteriorated urban property by the middle classes, often resulting in displacement of lower-income people. **—gen′tri·fy′** *v.*

gen·try (jĕn′trē) ▸ *n., pl.* **-tries.** 1. People of good family or high social position. 2. The class of English landowners ranking just below the nobility.

gen·u·flect (jĕn′yə-flĕkt′) ▸ *v.* To bend the knee or touch one knee to the floor or ground, as in worship. **—gen′u·flec′tion** *n.*

gen·u·ine (jĕn′yōō-ĭn) ▸ *adj.* 1. Actually possessing the alleged or apparent attribute or character. 2. Not spurious or counterfeit. **—gen′u·ine·ly** *adv.* **—gen′u·ine·ness** *n.*

ge·nus (jē′nəs) ▸ *n., pl.* **gen·er·a** (jĕn′ər-ə). 1. *Biol.* The category ranking below a family and above a species in the hierarchy of taxonomic classification. 2. A class, group, or kind with common attributes.

-geny ▸ *suff.* Production; origin: *ontogeny.*

geo- ▸ *pref.* 1. Earth: *geocentric.* 2. Geography: *geopolitics.*

ge·o·cen·tric (jē′ō-sĕn′trĭk) ▸ *adj.* 1. Of or measured from the center of the earth. 2. Having the earth as a center. **—ge′o·cen′tri·cal·ly** *adv.*

ge·o·chro·nol·o·gy (jē′ō-krə-nŏl′ə-jē) ▸ *n.* The chronology of the earth's history as determined by geologic events. **—ge′o·chron′o·log′ic** (-krŏn′ə-lŏj′ĭk), **ge′o·chron′o·log′i·cal** *adj.* **—ge′o·chro·nol′o·gist** *n.*

ge·ode (jē′ōd′) ▸ *n.* A hollow, usu. spheroidal rock with crystals lining the inside wall.

ge·o·des·ic (jē′ə-dĕs′ĭk, -dē′sĭk) ▸ *n.* The shortest line between two points on any mathematically defined surface, such as a sphere. ▸ *adj.* Of geodeosy or a geodesic.

geodesic dome ▸ *n.* A domed or vaulted structure of lightweight straight elements that form interlocking polygons.

ge·od·e·sy (jē-ŏd′ĭ-sē) ▸ *n.* The geologic science of the size and shape of the earth. **—ge·od′e·sist** *n.*

ge·og·ra·phy (jē-ŏg′rə-fē) ▸ *n., pl.* **-phies.** 1. The science dealing

THESAURUS

genial *adj.* —*See* AMIABLE.

geniality or **genialness** *n.* —*See* AMIABILITY.

genius *n.* Liveliness and vivacity of imagination ▸ brilliance, brilliancy, fire, inspiration. [*Compare* INTELLIGENCE, INVENTION.] *See also* MIND (2), TALENT.

genius *adj.* —*See* INTELLIGENT.

genocide *n.* —*See* MASSACRE.

genre *n.* —*See* CLASS (1).

genteel *adj.* —*See* COURTEOUS (1), DELICATE (1), GRACIOUS (2), PRUDISH.

genteelness *n.* —*See* COURTESY.

gentility *n.* —*See* COURTESY, SOCIETY (1).

gentle *adj.* 1. Of a sympathetic, considerate character ▸ compassionate, kindly, mild, sensitive, soft, softhearted, tender, tenderhearted. [*Compare* ATTENTIVE, SYMPATHETIC.] 2. Free from severity or violence, as in sound or movement ▸ balmy, delicate, faint, mild, moderate, slight, smooth, soothing, soft. 3. Easily managed or handled ▸ docile, domesticated, meek, mild, tame, yielding. [*Compare* COOPERATIVE, OBEDIENT, OBLIGING.] —*See also* DELICATE (1), GRADUAL (2), LIGHT[2] (2).

gentle *v.* To make an animal docile ▸ break, bust, master, tame. —*See also* DOMESTICATE, PACIFY.

gentlemanly *adj.* —*See* COURTEOUS (1), GALLANT.

gentry *n.* —*See* SOCIETY (1).

genuflect *v.* —*See* BOW[1] (1).

genuflection *n.* —*See* BOW[1].

genuine *adj.* Free from hypocrisy or pretense ▸ heartfelt, hearty, honest, natural, plain, real, sincere, true, unaffected, unfeigned. [*Compare* ARTLESS, FRANK, HONEST, SERIOUS.] —*See also* AUTHENTIC (1), PURE.

genuinely *adv.* —*See* REALLY.

genuineness *n.* —*See* VERACITY.

genus *n.* —*See* KIND[2].

with the earth's natural features, climate, resources, and population. 2. The physical characteristics, esp. the surface features, of an area. 3. A book on geography. **—ge·og′ra·pher** *n.* **—ge′o·graph′ic** (jē′ə-grăf′ĭk) *adj.* **—ge′o·graph′i·cal·ly** *adv.*

ge·ol·o·gy (jē-ŏl′ə-jē) ▸ *n., pl.* **-gies.** 1. The science of the origin, history, and structure of the earth. 2. The structure of a specific region of the earth's crust. **—ge′o·log′ic** (jē′ə-lŏj′ĭk), **ge′o·log′i·cal** *adj.* **—ge′o·log′i·cal·ly** *adv.* **—ge·ol′o·gist** *n.*

ge·o·mag·net·ism (jē′ō-măg′nĭ-tĭz′əm) ▸ *n.* The magnetism of the earth. **—ge′o·mag·net′ic** (-nĕt′ĭk) *adj.* **—ge′o·mag·net′i·cal·ly** *adv.*

geometric progression ▸ *n. Math.* A sequence, such as 1, 3, 9, 27, 81, in which each term is multiplied by the same factor to obtain the next term.

ge·om·e·try (jē-ŏm′ĭ-trē) ▸ *n., pl.* **-tries.** 1. The mathematics of the properties, measurement, and relationships of points, lines, angles, surfaces, and solids. 2. Configuration; arrangement. 3. A surface shape. **—ge′o·met′ric** (jē′ə-mĕt′rĭk) *adj.* **—ge′o·met′ri·cal·ly** *adv.* **—ge·om′e·tri′cian** (jē-ŏm′ĭ-trĭsh′ən, jē′ə-mĭ-), **ge·om′e·ter** *n.*

ge·o·phys·ics (jē′ō-fĭz′ĭks) ▸ *n. (takes sing. v.)* The physics of geologic phenomena. **—ge′o·phys′i·cal** *adj.* **—ge′o·phys′i·cal·ly** *adv.* **—ge′o·phys′i·cist** (-ĭ-sĭst) *n.*

ge·o·pol·i·tics (jē′ō-pŏl′ĭ-tĭks) ▸ *n. (takes sing. v.)* The study of the relationship between politics and geography. **—ge′o·po·lit′i·cal** (-pə-lĭt′ĭ-kəl) *adj.* **—ge′o·po·lit′i·cal·ly** *adv.*

George III (jôrj) (1738–1820) ▸ King of Great Britain and Ireland (1760–1820).

Geor·gia (jôr′jə) ▸ 1. A country of Asia Minor in the Caucasus on the Black Sea S of Russia. Pop. 4,960,000. 2. A state of the SE US. Cap. Atlanta. Pop. 8,190,000. **—Geor′gian** *adj. & n.*

Georgia, Strait of ▸ A channel that separates Vancouver I. from mainland British Columbia and N WA State.

ge·o·sta·tion·ar·y (jē′ō-stā′shə-nĕr′ē) ▸ *adj.* Of or being a satellite that travels above the earth's equator at a speed matching that of the earth's rotation, thus remaining stationary in relation to the earth.

ge·o·syn·chro·nous (jē′ō-sĭng′krə-nəs, -sĭn′-) ▸ *adj.* Geostationary. **—ge′o·syn′chro·nous·ly** *adv.*

ge·o·ther·mal (jē′ō-thûr′məl) also **ge·o·ther·mic** (-mĭk) ▸ *adj.* Of or relating to the internal heat of the earth. **—ge′o·ther′mal·ly** *adv.*

ge·ra·ni·um (jə-rā′nē-əm) ▸ *n.* 1. A plant having palmately divided leaves and pink or purplish flowers. 2. A related plant widely cultivated for its rounded, often variegated leaves and showy clusters of red, pink, or white flowers.

ger·bil (jûr′bəl) ▸ *n.* A small mouselike rodent of arid regions of Africa and Asia Minor.

ger·i·at·rics (jĕr′ē-ăt′rĭks) ▸ *n. (takes sing. v.)* The branch of medicine that deals with the diagnosis and treatment of diseases and problems specific to old age. **—ger′i·at′ric** *adj. & n.*

germ (jûrm) ▸ *n.* 1. *Biol.* A small mass of protoplasm or cells from which a new organism or one of its parts may develop. 2. The earliest form of an organism; a seed, bud, or spore. 3. A microorganism, esp. a pathogen. 4. Something that may serve as the basis of further growth or development.

Ger·man (jûr′mən) ▸ *adj.* Of or relating to Germany or its people or language. ▸ *n.* 1. A native or inhabitant of Germany. 2. The Germanic language of Germany, Austria, and part of Switzerland.

ger·mane (jər-mān′) ▸ *adj.* Being both pertinent and fitting. **—ger·mane′ly** *adv.* **—ger·mane′ness** *n.*

Ger·man·ic (jər-măn′ĭk) ▸ *adj.* 1. Of or relating to Germany. 2. Teutonic. 3. Of or relating to the Germanic languages. ▸ *n.* A branch of the Indo-European language family that includes English.

ger·ma·ni·um (jər-mā′nē-əm) ▸ *n. Symbol* **Ge** A brittle, crystalline, gray-white element, widely used as a semiconductor and as an alloying agent and catalyst. At. no. 32.

German measles ▸ *n. (takes sing. or pl. v.)* See **rubella.**

German shepherd ▸ *n.* A large dog having a dense brownish or black coat and often trained to assist police or the blind.

Ger·ma·ny (jûr′mə-nē) ▸ A country of N-central Europe bordered on the N by the Baltic and North seas; formerly divided into **East Germany** and **West Germany** (1949–90). Pop. 83,300,000.

germ cell ▸ *n.* An ovum or a sperm cell or one of its developmental precursors.

ger·mi·cide (jûr′mĭ-sīd′) ▸ *n.* An agent that kills germs; disinfectant. **—ger′mi·cid′al** (-sīd′l) *adj.*

ger·mi·nal (jûr′mə-nəl) ▸ *adj.* 1. Of or relating to a germ cell. 2. Of or relating to the earliest stage of development. **—ger′mi·nal·ly** *adv.*

ger·mi·nate (jûr′mə-nāt′) ▸ *v.* **-nat·ed, -nat·ing.** To begin or cause to sprout or grow. **—ger′mi·na′tion** *n.* **—ger′mi·na′tive** *adj.*

Ge·ron·i·mo (jə-rŏn′ə-mō′) (1829–1909) ▸ Apache leader.

ger·on·toc·ra·cy (jĕr′ən-tŏk′rə-sē) ▸ *n., pl.* **-cies.** Government based on rule by elders. **—ge·ron′to·crat′** (jə-rŏn′tə-krăt′) *n.* **—ge·ron′to·crat′ic** *adj.*

ger·on·tol·o·gy (jĕr′ən-tŏl′ə-jē) ▸ *n.* The study of the biological, psychological, and sociological phenomena associated with old age and aging. **—ge·ron′to·log′i·cal** (jə-rŏn′tə-lŏj′ĭ-kəl), **ge·ron′to·log′ic** *adj.* **—ger′on·tol′o·gist** *n.*

ger·ry·man·der (jĕr′ē-măn′dər, gĕr′-) ▸ *v.* To divide (a geographic area) into voting districts so as to give unfair advantage to one party in elections. **—ger′ry·man′der** *n.*

Gersh·win (gûrsh′wĭn), **George** (1898–1937) ▸ Amer. composer.

ger·und (jĕr′ənd) ▸ *n.* A verbal noun ending in *-ing,* as *singing* in *We admired the choir's singing.* **—ge·run′di·al** (jə-rŭn′dē-əl) *adj.*

ge·run·dive (jə-rŭn′dĭv) ▸ *n.* A Latin verbal adjective that expresses the notion of fitness or obligation or is used as a future passive participle.

ge·stalt or **Ge·stalt** (gə-shtält′, -shtôlt′, -stält′, -stôlt′) ▸ *n.* A configuration or pattern of elements so unified as a whole that its properties cannot be derived from a simple summation of its parts.

Gestalt psychology ▸ *n.* The school in psychology holding that psychological, physiological, and behavioral phenomena are irreducible experiential configurations.

Ge·sta·po (gə-stä′pō, -shtä′-) ▸ *n.* The German internal security police during the Nazi regime.

ges·ta·tion (jĕ-stā′shən) ▸ *n.* The period of development in the uterus from conception until birth; pregnancy. **—ges′tate′** *v.* **—ges′ta·to′ry** (jĕs′tə-tôr′ē), **ges·ta′tion·al** *adj.*

ges·tic·u·late (jĕ-stĭk′yə-lāt′) ▸ *v.* **-lat·ed, -lat·ing.** To make gestures, esp. while speaking. **—ges·tic′u·la′tive** *adj.* **—ges·tic′u·la′tor** *n.*

ges·tic·u·la·tion (jĕ-stĭk′yə-lā′shən) ▸ *n.* 1. The act of gesticulating. 2. An emphatic gesture.

ges·ture (jĕs′chər) ▸ *n.* 1. A motion of the limbs or body made to express thought or to emphasize speech. 2. An act or remark made as a sign of intention or attitude. **—ges′ture** *v.* **—ges′tur·er** *n.*

ge·sund·heit (gə-zo͝ont′hīt′) ▸ *interj.* Used to wish good health to a person who has just sneezed.

get (gĕt) ▸ *v.* **got** (gŏt), **got·ten** (gŏt′n) or **got** or **get·ting.** 1.

THESAURUS

georgic *adj.* —*See* COUNTRY.

germ *n.* 1. A tiny organism usually producing disease ▸ bacterium, bug, microbe, microorganism, parasite, pathogen, virus. 2. A source of further growth and development ▸ bud, embryo, kernel, nucleus, seed, spark. [*Compare* ORIGIN.]

germane *adj.* —*See* RELEVANT.

germaneness *n.* —*See* RELEVANCE.

gestation *n.* The condition of carrying a developing fetus within the uterus ▸ gravidity, gravidness, parturiency, pregnancy.

gesticulate *v.* —*See* GESTURE.

gesticulation *n.* —*See* GESTURE.

gesture *n.* An expressive, meaningful bodily movement ▸ gesticulation, indication, motion, nod, sign, signal, wag, wave. *Informal:* high sign. *Idiom:* thumbs up (*or* down). —*See also* EXPRESSION (2).

gesture *v.* To make bodily motions so as to convey an idea or complement speech ▸ beckon, flag, gesticulate, motion, pantomime, sign, signal, signalize, wave. *Idiom:* give the high sign.

get *v.* 1. To come into possession of ▸ acquire, attain, come by, gain, glean, obtain, procure, reap, receive, secure,

To receive: *got a present from a friend.* **2a.** To go after and bring. **b.** To buy. **3a.** To obtain or acquire: *get knowledge from a book.* **b.** To earn. **4.** To capture. **5.** To reach or catch: *get the bus.* **6.** To contract; catch: *get the flu.* **7.** To understand: *They don't get your point.* **8.** To hear: *Did you get her name?* **9.** To cause to be in a specific condition: *got the shirt clean.* **10a.** To cause to move or go: *Get me out of here!* **b.** To go or come: *We'll get to the hotel at noon.* **11.** To prevail upon: *Get him to come early.* **12.** To take revenge on: *I'll get you for that.* **13.** *Informal* To hit or strike: *The bullet got him in the arm.* **14.** To puzzle or annoy: *His cold manner gets me.* **15.** To begin: *Let's get working on this.* **16.** To become or be: *Get well soon.* **17.** Used in the present perfect: **a.** To have or possess: *I've got lots of friends.* **b.** To have as an obligation: *You've got to see this.* ***—phrasal verbs:*** **get across** To make or be understandable. **get along 1.** To be on friendly terms. **2.** To manage with reasonable success. **get around 1.** To evade or circumvent. **2.** To become known; circulate. **get away** To escape. **get by** To manage; survive. **get into** To be interested or involved in: *got into computers.* **get off 1.** To write and send. **2.** To escape from punishment. **get on 1.** To be on friendly terms. **2.** To make progress; continue. **get out 1.** To leave or escape. **2.** To become public: *The secret got out.* **get over** To recover from. **get through** To finish or complete. **get to 1.** To start to deal with: *finally got to the housework.* **2.** To annoy. **get up 1.** To arise, as from bed. **2.** To create or organize. **3.** To find within oneself: *got up the courage to speak.* ▸ *n.* Progeny; offspring. ***—idioms:*** **get around to** To find the time for. **get away with** To escape the consequences of. **get down to** To give one's attention to. **get even** To obtain revenge. **get somewhere** *Informal* To make progress.

get·a·way (gĕt′ə-wā′) ▸ *n.* **1.** An act of escaping. **2.** The start, as of a race.

get-to·geth·er (gĕt′tə-gĕth′ər) ▸ *n. Informal* A casual social gathering.

Get·tys·burg (gĕt′ēz-bûrg′) ▸ A town of S PA ESE of Chambersburg; site of a Union victory in the Civil War (July 1–3, 1863). Pop. 7,490.

get·up (gĕt′ŭp′) ▸ *n. Informal* An outfit or costume.

gew·gaw (gyo͞o′gô′, go͞o′-) ▸ *n.* A trinket; bauble.

gey·ser (gī′zər) ▸ *n.* A natural hot spring that intermittently ejects a column of water and steam into the air.

Gha·na (gä′nə, găn′ə) ▸ A country of W Africa on the N shore of the Gulf of Guinea. Pop. 20,200,000. **—Gha′na·ian** (gä′nə-yən, gə-nā′ən), **Gha′ni·an** (gä′nē-ən) *adj.* & *n.*

ghast·ly (găst′lē) ▸ *adj.* **-li·er, -li·est. 1.** Inspiring shock or revulsion; terrifying. **2.** Resembling ghosts. **3.** Extremely unpleasant. **—ghast′li·ness** *n.*

gher·kin (gûr′kĭn) ▸ *n.* A small cucumber, esp. one used for pickling.

ghet·to (gĕt′ō) ▸ *n., pl.* **-tos** or **-toes. 1.** A usually poor section of a city inhabited primarily by people of the same race, religion, or social background, often because of discrimination. **2.** An often walled quarter in a European city to which Jews were restricted beginning in the Middle Ages.

ghet·to·ize (gĕt′ō-īz′) ▸ *v.* **-ized, -iz·ing.** To set apart in or as if in a ghetto. **—ghet′to·i·za′tion** *n.*

ghost (gōst) ▸ *n.* **1.** The spirit of a dead person, esp. one believed to haunt living persons. **2.** A faint trace. **3.** A faint false image produced along with the correct television or photographic image. **4.** *Informal* A ghostwriter. ▸ *v. Informal* To ghostwrite. **—ghost′ly** *adj.*

ghost town ▸ *n.* A once thriving town, esp. a boomtown of the American West, that has been abandoned.

ghost·writ·er (gōst′rī′tər) ▸ *n.* One who writes for and gives credit of authorship to another. **—ghost′write′** *v.*

ghoul (go͞ol) ▸ *n.* **1.** One who delights in the revolting, morbid, or loathsome. **2.** A grave robber. **3.** An evil spirit in Muslim folklore believed to plunder graves and feed on corpses. **—ghoul′ish** *adj.* **—ghoul′ish·ly** *adv.* **—ghoul′ish·ness** *n.*

GI (jē′ī′) ▸ *n.* An enlisted person in or a veteran of the US armed forces. **—GI** *adj.*

gi·ant (jī′ənt) ▸ *n.* **1.** A person of great size, power, or importance. **2.** *Myth.* A humanlike being of enormous strength and stature. ▸ *adj.* Of exceptionally great size, magnitude, or power.

gi·ant·ess (jī′ən-tĭs) ▸ *n.* A female giant.

gib·ber·ish (jĭb′ər-ĭsh) ▸ *n.* **1.** Unintelligible or nonsensical talk or writing. **2.** Unnecessarily pretentious or vague language. **—gib′ber** *v.*

gib·bet (jĭb′ĭt) ▸ *n.* A gallows. ▸ *v.* **-bet·ed, -bet·ing** or **-bet·ted, -bet·ting. 1.** To execute by hanging on a gibbet. **2.** To expose to public ridicule.

THESAURUS

take, win. *Informal:* land, pick up. *Slang:* bag. [*Compare* OBTAIN.] **2.** To succeed in communicating with ▸ *Informal:* contact, reach. *Informal:* catch. **3.** To be the biological father of ▸ beget, father, sire. *—See also* ANNOY, AVENGE, BECOME (1), BRING (2), CAPTURE, CONTRACT (2), DERIVE (1), EARN (1), EARN (2), LEARN (1), MOVE (1), UNDERSTAND (1).

get across *v. —See* COMMUNICATE (1).

get ahead *v.* To gain success ▸ arrive, get on, rise, succeed. ***Idioms:*** go far, go places, make good, make it. *—See also* RISE (3).

get along *v.* To grow old ▸ age, get on. *—See also* ADVANCE (2), MANAGE, RELATE (2).

get around *v.* To become known far and wide ▸ circulate, go around, spread, travel. ***Idiom:*** go (*or* make) the rounds. *—See also* AVOID.

get away *v. —See* ESCAPE (1), GO (1).

get behind *v. —See* SUPPORT (1).

get by *v. —See* MANAGE.

get in *v. —See* ARRIVE (1).

get off *v. —See* GO (1), START (1).

get on *v.* **1.** To gain success ▸ arrive, get ahead, rise, succeed. ***Idioms:*** go far, go places, make good, make it. **2.** To grow old ▸ age, get along. *—See also* DON, RELATE (2).

get out *v.* To be made public ▸ break, come out, out, transpire. *Informal:* leak (out). [*Compare* AIR, ANNOUNCE, APPEAR.] *—See also* RUN (2).

get through *v. —See* SURVIVE (1).

get to *v. —See* ACCOMPLISH, ANNOY, PERSUADE.

get together *v.* **2.** To come together by arrangement ▸ connect, hook up, meet (up), rendezvous. *—See also* ASSEMBLE, AGREE (2).

get up *v. —See* RISE (1), STAND (1).

get *n. —See* PROGENY.

getaway *n. —See* ESCAPE (1).

gettable *adj. —See* AVAILABLE.

get-together *n. —See* ASSEMBLY, PARTY, VISIT (1).

getup *n. —See* DISGUISE, DRESS (2).

get-up-and-go *n. —See* DRIVE (2), ENERGY.

gewgaw *n. —See* NOVELTY (3).

ghastly *adj.* **1.** Shockingly repellent ▸ appalling, dreadful, grim, grisly, gruesome, hideous, horrible, horrid, loathsome, lurid, macabre, terrifying. [*Compare* FEARFUL, OFFENSIVE.] **2.** Gruesomely suggestive of ghosts or death ▸ cadaverous, deadly, deathlike, deathly, ghostlike, ghostly, morbid, spectral, wraithlike. [*Compare* PALE, PHANTASMAGORIC, WEIRD.] *—See also* TERRIBLE.

ghettoize *v. —See* ISOLATE (1).

ghost *n.* An immaterial supernatural being, especially the spirit of a dead person ▸ apparition, bogey, bogeyman, bogle, eidolon, phantasm, phantasma, phantom, revenant, shade, shadow, soul, specter, spirit, visitant, wraith. *Informal:* spook. *Chiefly Regional:* haunt. [*Compare* FAIRY.] *—See also* SHADE (2).

ghostly or **ghostlike** *adj. —See* GHASTLY (2).

ghoul *n. —See* FIEND.

ghoulish *adj. —See* FIENDISH.

GI *n. —See* SOLDIER (2).

giant *n.* One that is extraordinarily large and powerful ▸ behemoth, colossus, elephant, gargantua, Goliath, Hercules, hulk, jumbo, leviathan, mammoth, monster, ogre, titan, whale. *Slang:* whopper.

giant *adj. —See* ENORMOUS.

gibber *v. —See* BABBLE.

gibberish *n.* Highly technical, often deliberately deceptive language ▸ abracadabra, doublespeak, double talk, gobbledygook, Greek, hocus-pocus, jabberwocky, mumbo jumbo. [*Compare* NONSENSE.] *—See also* BABBLE.

gibbet *v.* To execute by suspending by the neck ▸ hang. *Informal:* string up. *Slang:* swing.

gib·bon (gĭb′ən) ▸ *n.* Any of several small arboreal apes of SE Asia and the East Indies, having a slender body, long arms, and no tail.

gib·bous (gĭb′əs) ▸ *adj.* More than half but less than fully illuminated: *the gibbous moon.* **–gib′bous·ly** *adv.*

gibe also **jibe** (jīb) ▸ *v.* **gibed, gib·ing** also **jibed, jib·ing.** To make taunting, heckling, or jeering remarks. **–gibe** *n.* **–gib′er** *n.* **–gib′ing·ly** *adv.*

gib·lets (jĭb′lĭts) ▸ *pl.n.* The heart, liver, and gizzard of a fowl.

Gi·bral·tar (jə-brôl′tər) ▸ A British colony at the NW end of the **Rock of Gibraltar,** a peninsula on the S-central coast of Spain in the **Strait of Gibraltar,** connecting the Mediterranean and the Atlantic between Spain and N Africa. Pop. 27,700.

gid·dy (gĭd′ē) ▸ *adj.* **-di·er, -di·est. 1a.** Dizzy. **b.** Causing dizziness: *a giddy climb.* **2.** Frivolous; flighty. ▸ *v.* **-died, -dy·ing.** To become or make giddy. **–gid′di·ly** *adv.* **–gid′di·ness** *n.*

gift (gĭft) ▸ *n.* **1.** Something bestowed voluntarily and without compensation. **2.** The act, right, or power of giving. **3.** A talent or aptitude.

gift·ed (gĭf′tĭd) ▸ *adj.* **1.** Endowed with great natural ability, intelligence, or talent. **2.** Revealing special talent. **–gift′ed·ly** *adv.* **–gift′ed·ness** *n.*

gig¹ (gĭg) ▸ *n.* **1.** A light, two-wheeled horse-drawn carriage. **2.** A long, light ship's boat.

gig² (gĭg) ▸ *n.* A pronged spear for fishing. **–gig** *v.*

gig³ (gĭg) ▸ *n. Slang* A demerit given in the military. **–gig** *v.*

gig⁴ (gĭg) ▸ *n. Slang* A job, esp. a booking for musicians.

giga– ▸ *pref.* One billion (10^9): *gigahertz.*

gig·a·byte (jĭg′ə-bīt′, gĭg′-) ▸ *n.* A unit of computer memory equal to 1,024 megabytes (2^{30} bytes).

gig·a·hertz (jĭg′ə-hûrtz′, gĭg′-) ▸ *n.* One billion cycles per second.

gi·gan·tic (jī-găn′tĭk) ▸ *adj.* Extremely large or extensive; huge. **–gi·gan′ti·cal·ly** *adv.*

gig·gle (gĭg′əl) ▸ *v.* **-gled, -gling.** To laugh in a half-suppressed or nervous way. **–gig′gle** *n.* **–gig′gler** *n.* **–gig′gly** *adj.*

gig·o·lo (jĭg′ə-lō′, zhĭg′-) ▸ *n., pl.* **-los. 1.** A man supported financially by a woman in return for sexual favors. **2.** A professional male escort.

Gi·la monster (hē′lə) ▸ *n.* A venomous lizard of arid regions of the SW US and W Mexico.

Gila River ▸ A river rising in the mountains of W NM and flowing about 1,014 km (630 mi) across S AZ to the Colorado R.

Gilbert Islands ▸ A group of islands of W Kiribati in the central Pacific.

gild (gĭld) ▸ *v.* **gild·ed** or **gilt** (gĭlt), **gild·ing. 1.** To cover with or as if with a thin layer of gold. **2.** To give an often deceptively attractive appearance to.

gill¹ (gĭl) ▸ *n.* The respiratory organ of most aquatic animals that breathe water to obtain oxygen. **–gilled** *adj.*

gill² (jĭl) ▸ *n.* **1.** See **measurement** table in Appendix. **2.** A unit of volume or capacity equal to ¼ of a British Imperial pint (142 ml).

gil·ly·flow·er (jĭl′ē-flou′ər) ▸ *n.* A carnation or other plant with fragrant flowers.

gilt (gĭlt) ▸ *v.* P.t. and p.part. of **gild.** ▸ *adj.* Gilded. ▸ *n.* A thin layer of gold or goldlike material applied in gilding.

gilt-edged (gĭlt′ĕjd′) ▸ *adj.* **1.** Having gilded edges, as book pages. **2.** Of the highest quality or value: *gilt-edged securities.*

gim·bal (gĭm′bəl, jĭm′-) ▸ *n.* often **gimbals** A device consisting of two rings mounted on axes at right angles to each other so that an object, such as a ship's compass, will remain suspended in a horizontal plane between them regardless of any motion of its support.

gim·crack (jĭm′krăk′) ▸ *n.* A cheap showy object of little or no use. **–gim′crack′er·y** *n.*

gim·let (gĭm′lĭt) ▸ *n.* **1.** A small hand tool used for boring holes. **2.** A cocktail made with vodka or gin and sweetened lime juice.

gim·mick (gĭm′ĭk) ▸ *n.* **1.** A device employed to cheat, deceive, or trick. **2.** A stratagem used esp. to promote a project. **3.** A significant feature that is obscured or misrepresented; catch. **–gim′mick·ry** *n.* **–gim′mick·y** *adj.*

gimp (gĭmp) ▸ *n. Slang* A limp or limping gait. **–gimp** *v.* **–gimp′y** *adj.*

gin¹ (jĭn) ▸ *n.* A strong, colorless alcoholic liquor distilled from grain spirits and flavored usu. with juniper berries. **–gin′ny** *adj.*

gin² (jĭn) ▸ *n.* **1.** A snare or trap for game. **2.** A cotton gin. ▸ *v.* **ginned, gin·ning.** To remove the seeds from (cotton) with a cotton gin.

gin³ (jĭn) ▸ *n.* Gin rummy.

gin·ger (jĭn′jər) ▸ *n.* **1.** A plant of SE Asia having a pungent aromatic rhizome. **2.** The rhizome of this plant, used as a spice. **3.** *Informal* Liveliness; vigor. **–gin′ger·y** *adj.*

ginger ale ▸ *n.* A carbonated soft drink flavored with ginger.

gin·ger·bread (jĭn′jər-brĕd′) ▸ *n.* **1.** A dark molasses cake flavored with ginger. **2.** Elaborate ornamentation, esp. in architecture.

gin·ger·ly (jĭn′jər-lē) ▸ *adv.* With great care; cautiously. **–gin′ger·li·ness** *n.* **–gin′ger·ly** *adj.*

gin·ger·snap (jĭn′jər-snăp′) ▸ *n.* A flat brittle cookie spiced with ginger and sweetened with molasses.

ging·ham (gĭng′əm) ▸ *n.* A yarn-dyed cotton fabric woven in stripes, checks, plaids, or solid colors.

gin·gi·va (jĭn′jə-və, jĭn-jī′-) ▸ *n., pl.* **-vae** (-vē′). See **gum².**

gin·gi·vi·tis (jĭn′jə-vī′tĭs) ▸ *n.* Inflammation of the gums.

gink·go also **ging·ko** (gĭng′kō) ▸ *n., pl.* **-goes** also **-koes.** A Chinese tree having fan-shaped leaves and fleshy yellowish seeds with a disagreeable odor.

gin rummy ▸ *n.* A variety of rummy in which a player may win by matching all his or her cards or may end the game by melding.

gin·seng (jĭn′sĕng′) ▸ *n.* A plant of E Asia or North America, having forked roots believed to have medicinal properties.

gip (jĭp) ▸ *v. & n. Slang* Var. of **gyp.**

Gip·sy (jĭp′sē) ▸ *n.* Var. of **Gypsy.**

gi·raffe (jə-răf′) ▸ *n., pl.* **-raffes** or **-raffe.** An African ruminant with a long neck and legs, a tan coat with orange-brown blotches, and short horns.

gird (gûrd) ▸ *v.* **gird·ed** or **girt** (gûrt), **gird·ing. 1.** To encir-

THESAURUS

gibe or **jibe** *v.* —*See* RIDICULE.

gibe *n.* —*See* TAUNT.

giddiness *n.* —*See* DIZZINESS.

giddy *adj.* **1.** Producing dizziness or vertigo ▸ dizzy, dizzying, sickening, vertiginous. [*Compare* STEEP.] **2.** Given to lighthearted silliness ▸ emptyheaded, featherbrained, flighty, frivolous, frothy, harebrained, lighthearted, scatterbrained, silly. *Informal:* gaga. *Slang:* birdbrained, dizzy. [*Compare* FOOLISH, STUPID.] —*See also* DIZZY (1).

gift *n.* Something bestowed voluntarily ▸ bequest, present, presentation. *Slang:* freebie. [*Compare* GRANT.] —*See also* DONATION, TALENT.

gift *v.* To present with a gift ▸ award, endow, endue, give, invest. [*Compare* GRANT.]

gifted *adj.* Possessing great natural ability or talent ▸ born, endowed, natural, precocious, talented. *Informal:* whiz-bang. [*Compare* ABLE, EXPERT.]

gig *n. Slang* A commitment, as for a performance by an entertainer ▸ booking, date, engagement. —*See also* POSITION (3).

gigantic *adj.* —*See* ENORMOUS.

giggle *v.* —*See* LAUGH.

giggle *n.* —*See* LAUGH.

gigolo *n.* —*See* LECHER, WANTON.

gild *v.* —*See* ADORN (1), COLOR (2), SWEETEN.

gilded or **gilt** *adj.* —*See* ORNATE.

gimcrack *n.* —*See* NOVELTY (3).

gimmick *n.* —*See* GADGET, NOVELTY (3), TRICK (1), WRINKLE (2).

ginger *n.* —*See* SPIRIT (1).

gingerliness *n.* —*See* CARE (1), CAUTION.

gingerly *adj.* —*See* WARY.

gird *v.* To prepare oneself for action ▸ arm, brace, forearm, fortify, ready, steel, strengthen. *Idioms:* clear the deck, gird (*or* gird up) one's loins, screw up one's courage. —*See also* ENCIRCLE.

cle or fasten with a belt or band. **2.** To surround. **3.** To prepare (oneself) for action.

gird·er (gûr′dər) ► *n.* A strong horizontal beam used as a main support in building.

gir·dle (gûr′dl) ► *n.* **1.** A belt or sash worn around the waist. **2.** A woman's elasticized flexible undergarment worn over the waist and hips. ► *v.* **-dled, -dling.** To encircle with or as if with a belt. **—gird′ler** *n.*

girl (gûrl) ► *n.* A female child or youth. **—girl′hood′** *n.* **—girl′ish** *adj.* **—girl′ish·ly** *adv.* **—girl′ish·ness** *n.*

girl·friend (gûrl′frĕnd′) ► *n.* **1.** A favored female companion or sweetheart. **2.** A female friend.

Girl Scout ► *n.* A member of an organization of young women and girls founded for character development and citizenship training.

girth (gûrth) ► *n.* **1.** The distance around something; circumference. **2.** A strap encircling an animal's body in order to secure a load or saddle.

gist (jĭst) ► *n.* The central idea; essence.

give (gĭv) ► *v.* **gave** (gāv), **giv·en** (gĭv′ən), **giv·ing. 1.** To make a present of: *We gave her flowers.* **2.** To place in the hands of; pass: *Give me the scissors.* **3.** To deliver in exchange or recompense; pay: *give five dollars for the book.* **4.** To administer: *gave him some medicine.* **5a.** To convey: *Give her my best wishes.* **b.** To inflict, esp. as punishment: *She gave me a bloody nose.* **6.** To grant or bestow: *give permission.* **7.** To furnish or contribute: *gave time to help others.* **8.** To permit one to have or take: *Give me an hour to get ready.* **9.** To emit or utter: *gave a groan.* **10.** To submit for consideration or opinion: *give me your opinion.* **11.** To offer as entertainment: *give a party.* **12.** To cause to catch: *The draft gave me a cold.* **13.** To yield or produce: *Cows give milk.* ***—phrasal verbs:* give away 1.** To make a gift of. **2.** To present (a bride) to the bridegroom at a wedding ceremony. **3.** To expose or betray. **give back** To return. **give in** To surrender; yield. **give off** To send forth; emit: *The radiator gave off heat.* **give out 1.** To distribute. **2.** To break down. **3.** To become used up. **give up 1.** To surrender. **2.** To stop: *gave up smoking.* **3.** To part with; relinquish. ► *n.* Resilience; springiness. ***—idioms:* give it to** *Informal* To punish or reprimand. **give way 1.** To yield the right of way. **2.** To collapse. **—giv′er** *n.*

give-and-take (gĭv′ən-tāk′) ► *n.* **1.** The practice of compromise. **2.** Lively exchange of ideas or conversation.

give·a·way (gĭv′ə-wā′) ► *n.* **1.** Something given away at no charge. **2.** Something that accidentally exposes or betrays.

giv·en (gĭv′ən) ► *v.* P.part. of **give.** ► *adj.* **1.** Specified; fixed: *meet at a given time.* **2.** Granted as a supposition; acknowledged or assumed. **3.** Having a tendency; inclined: *given to lavish spending.* **—giv′en** *n.*

given name ► *n.* A name given at birth or at baptism as distinguished from a surname.

Gi·za (gē′zə) ► A city of N Egypt on the Nile R.; site of the Great Pyramids and the Sphinx. Pop. 2,600,000.

giz·zard (gĭz′ərd) ► *n.* A digestive organ in birds, often containing ingested grit.

gla·cial (glā′shəl) ► *adj.* **1.** Of or derived from a glacier. **2.** Marked or dominated by the existence of glaciers: *a glacial epoch.* **3.** Extremely cold. **—gla′cial·ly** *adv.*

gla·ci·ate (glā′shē-āt′, -sē-) ► *v.* **-at·ed, -at·ing. 1.** To subject to glacial action. **2.** To freeze. **—gla′ci·a′tion** *n.*

gla·cier (glā′shər) ► *n.* A huge mass of ice slowly flowing over a land mass, formed from compacted snow.

glad (glăd) ► *adj.* **glad·der, glad·dest. 1.** Experiencing, showing, or giving joy and pleasure. **2.** Very willing: *glad to help.* **—glad′ly** *adv.* **—glad′ness** *n.*

glad·den (glăd′n) ► *v.* To make glad.

glade (glād) ► *n.* An open space in a forest.

glad hand ► *n. Informal* A hearty but often insincere greeting. **—glad′-hand′** *v.* **—glad′-hand′er** *n.*

glad·i·a·tor (glăd′ē-ā′tər) ► *n.* A man trained to entertain the public by engaging in mortal combat in ancient Roman arenas. **—glad′i·a·to′ri·al** (-ə-tôr′ē-əl) *adj.*

glad·i·o·lus (glăd′ē-ō′ləs) ► *n., pl.* **-li** (-lī, -lē) or **-lus·es.** Any of a genus of plants having sword-shaped leaves and showy, variously colored flowers.

glad·some (glăd′səm) ► *adj.* Causing or showing gladness or joy. **—glad′some·ly** *adv.*

glam·or·ize also **glam·our·ize** (glăm′ə-rīz′) ► *v.* **-ized, -iz·ing.** To make glamorous. **—glam′or·i·za′tion** *n.* **—glam′or·iz′er** *n.*

glam·our also **glam·or** (glăm′ər) ► *n.* An air of compelling charm, romance, and excitement. **—glam′or·ous** *adj.* **—glam′or·ous·ly** *adv.* **—glam′or·ous·ness** *n.*

glance (glăns) ► *v.* **glanced, glanc·ing. 1.** To direct the gaze briefly. **2.** To strike a surface and be deflected. ► *n.* **1.** A brief or cursory look. **2.** A gleam.

THESAURUS

girder *n.* —*See* BEAM (2).

girdle *n.* —*See* BAND[1].

girdle *v.* —*See* ENCIRCLE.

girl *n. Informal:* A woman referred to informally ► lass. *Informal:* chick, damsel, doll, gal, missy, sis, sister. *Slang:* homegirl, momma.

girlfriend *n.* A woman who is a man's romantic partner ► girl, inamorata, lady friend. *Slang:* old lady. [*Compare* DARLING, LOVER.]

girt *v.* —*See* ENCIRCLE.

gist *n.* —*See* HEART (1), THRUST.

give *v.* **1.** To relinquish to the possession or control of another ► deliver, furnish, hand, hand in, hand over, provide, render, supply, transfer, turn over. **2.** To present as a gift to a charity or cause ► bestow, contribute, donate, hand out. **3.** To mete out by means of some action ► administer, deal, deliver. **4.** To let have as a favor, prerogative, or privilege ► accord, award, concede, grant, vouchsafe. [*Compare* YIELD.] —*See also* ADMINISTER (3), ALLOT, APPLY (1), BEND (3), BUCKLE, COMMUNICATE (2), CONFER (2), DISTRIBUTE, ENTRUST (1), GIFT, PERMIT (3), PRODUCE (1), SPEND (1).

give away *v.* —*See* BETRAY (2), DONATE.

give back *v.* —*See* REINSTALL. —*See also* RETURN (2).

give forth *v.* —*See* EMIT, PRODUCE (1).

give in *v.* To lose all hope ► despair, despond, give up. *Idioms:* throw in the sponge (*or* towel). [*Compare* abandon.] —*See also* SURRENDER (1).

give off *v.* —*See* EMIT.

give onto *v.* To have the face or front turned toward ► face, front, look (on *or* upon *or* toward). [*Compare* OVERLOOK.]

give out *v.* To prove deficient or insufficient ► fail, run out. *Idioms:* fall short, run dry, run short. [*Compare* DECREASE.] —*See also* COLLAPSE (1), DRY UP (2), EMIT, MALFUNCTION, TIRE (2).

give over *v.* To yield oneself unrestrainedly, as to an impulse ► deliver, relinquish, surrender. *Idioms:* give oneself up (or over). —*See also* DROP (4)

give up *v.* **1.** To lose all hope ► despair, despond, give in. *Idioms:* throw in the sponge (or towel). [*Compare* ABANDON.] **2.** To yield oneself unrestrainedly, as to an impulse ► deliver, relinquish, surrender. *Idioms:* give oneself up (or over). —*See also* BREAK (5), DROP (4), SURRENDER (1).

give *n.* —*See* FLEXIBILITY (1).

give-and-take *n.* —*See* COMPROMISE.

given *adj.* —*See* INCLINED, PRESUMPTIVE.

given *n.* —*See* ASSUMPTION.

giver *n.* —*See* DONOR.

gizmo *n.* —*See* GADGET.

glacial *adj.* —*See* COLD (1), COOL, SLOW (1).

glad *adj.* —*See* CHEERFUL, MERRY, WILLING.

gladden *v.* —*See* DELIGHT (1).

gladly *adv.* —*See* YES.

gladness *n.* —*See* HAPPINESS, MERRIMENT (1).

gladsome *adj.* —*See* MERRY.

glamorous *adj.* —*See* ATTRACTIVE.

glamour *n.* —*See* ATTRACTION, GLITTER (2).

glance *v.* **1.** To strike a surface at such an angle as to be deflected ► carom, fly off, graze, ricochet, skim, skip. [*Compare* BOUNCE.] **2.** To look briefly and quickly ► glimpse, peek, peep. [*Compare* LOOK.] —*See also* GLITTER.

glance at *or* **over** *or* **through** *v.* —*See* BROWSE (1).

glance *n.* **1.** A quick look ► glimpse, look, peek, peep, scan. *Informal:* gander, look-see. **2.** An act of reflection ► deflection, reflection, scattering. [*Compare* BOUNCE.] —*See also* FLASH (1).

glanc·ing (glăn′sĭng) ▸ *adj.* **1.** Oblique in direction; deflected. **2.** Not straightforward; indirect. **—glanc′ing·ly** *adv.*

gland (glănd) ▸ *n.* An organ that produces a secretion for use elsewhere in the body. **—glan′du·lar** (glăn′jə-lər) *adj.* **—glan′du·lar·ly** *adv.*

glans (glănz) ▸ *n., pl.* **glan·des** (glăn′dēz). The tip of the penis or clitoris.

glare[1] (glâr) ▸ *v.* **glared, glar·ing. 1.** To stare fixedly and angrily. **2.** To shine intensely and blindingly. **3.** To stand out obtrusively. ▸ *n.* **1.** A fierce or angry stare. **2.** An intense, blinding light.

glare[2] (glâr) ▸ *n.* A sheet of glassy and very slippery ice.

glar·ing (glâr′ĭng) ▸ *adj.* **1.** Shining intensely. **2.** Conspicuous; obvious. **3.** Staring with anger or hostility. **—glar′ing·ly** *adv.*

Glas·gow (glăs′kō, -gō, glăz′-) ▸ A city of SW Scotland on the Clyde R. Pop. 630,000.

glas·nost (gläs′nəst, -nôst) ▸ *n.* An official policy of the former Soviet government emphasizing candid discussion of social problems.

glass (glăs) ▸ *n.* **1.** Any of a large class of materials that solidify from the molten state without crystallization, are gen. transparent or translucent, and are considered to be supercooled liquids rather than true solids. **2.** Something usu. made of glass, esp.: **a.** A drinking vessel. **b.** A mirror. **c.** A window or windowpane. **3. glasses** A pair of lenses mounted in a light frame, used to correct faulty vision or protect the eyes. **4.** The quantity contained by a drinking vessel; glassful. **—glass′i·ly** *adv.* **—glass′i·ness** *n.* **—glass′y** *adj.*

glass ceiling ▸ *n.* An unofficial discriminatory barrier that keeps women and minorities from positions of power, as in a corporation.

glau·co·ma (glou-kō′mə, glô-) ▸ *n.* An eye disease characterized by abnormally high intraocular fluid pressure, hardening of the eyeball, and partial to complete loss of vision.

glau·cous (glô′kəs) ▸ *adj.* Of a pale grayish green.

glaze (glāz) ▸ *n.* **1.** A thin, smooth, shiny coating, as on ceramics. **2.** A thin glassy coating of ice. **3.** A coating, as of syrup, applied to food. ▸ *v.* **glazed, glaz·ing. 1.** To furnish with glass: *glaze a window.* **2.** To apply a glaze to: *glaze a cake.* **3.** To become glassy. **—glaz′er** *n.*

gla·zier (glā′zhər) ▸ *n.* One that cuts and fits glass, as for windows. **—gla′zier·y** *n.*

gleam (glēm) ▸ *n.* **1.** A brief flash of light. **2.** A steady but subdued shining; glow. **3.** A brief or dim indication: *a gleam of intelligence.* ▸ *v.* **1.** To flash or glow. **2.** To be manifested briefly or faintly.

glean (glēn) ▸ *v.* **1.** To gather grain left behind by reapers. **2.** To collect bit by bit. **—glean′er** *n.* **—glean′ings** *pl.n.*

glee (glē) ▸ *n.* **1.** Jubilant delight; joy. **2.** An unaccompanied choral song. **—glee′ful** *adj.* **—glee′ful·ly** *adv.*

glee club ▸ *n.* A group of singers who perform usu. short pieces of choral music.

glen (glĕn) ▸ *n.* A valley.

glib (glĭb) ▸ *adj.* **glib·ber, glib·best.** Marked by verbal ease and fluency that often suggests insincerity or superficiality. **—glib′ly** *adv.* **—glib′ness** *n.*

glide (glīd) ▸ *v.* **glid·ed, glid·ing. 1.** To move smoothly and effortlessly. **2.** To fly without propulsion. **—glide** *n.*

glid·er (glī′dər) ▸ *n.* **1.** A light engineless aircraft designed to glide after being towed aloft. **2.** A swinging couch suspended from a vertical frame.

glim·mer (glĭm′ər) ▸ *n.* **1.** A dim or unsteady light. **2.** A faint suggestion or indication. ▸ *v.* **1.** To give off a glimmer. **2.** To appear faintly.

glimpse (glĭmps) ▸ *n.* A brief, incomplete look. ▸ *v.* **glimpsed, glimps·ing.** To get a glimpse of.

glint (glĭnt) ▸ *n.* A brief flash of light; sparkle. **—glint** *v.*

glis·san·do (glĭ-sän′dō) ▸ *n., pl.* **-di** (-dē) or **-dos.** A rapid slide through a series of consecutive musical tones.

glis·ten (glĭs′ən) ▸ *v.* To shine with reflected light. **—glis′ten** *n.*

glitch (glĭch) ▸ *n.* **1.** A minor malfunction. **2.** A false electronic signal caused by a brief power surge.

glit·ter (glĭt′ər) ▸ *n.* **1.** A sparkling or glistening light. **2.** Showy, often superficial attractiveness. **3.** Small pieces of reflective decorative material. ▸ *v.* To sparkle brilliantly; glisten. **—glit′ter·ing·ly** *adv.* **—glit′ter·y** *adj.*

glitz (glĭts) ▸ *n. Informal* Ostentatious showiness; flashiness. **—glitz′i·ness** *n.* **—glitz′y** *adj.*

gloam·ing (glō′mĭng) ▸ *n.* Twilight; dusk.

gloat (glōt) ▸ *v.* To feel or express great, often malicious,

THESAURUS

glare *v.* **1.** To stare fixedly and angrily ▸ glower, lower, scowl. ***Idioms:*** give the evil eye, look daggers. [*Compare* FROWN, GAZE, SNEER.] **2.** To shine intensely and blindingly ▸ beat down, blaze, flare, pulse, throb, vibrate. [*Compare* BEAM.] **3.** To be obtrusively conspicuous or obvious ▸ stand out, stick out. ***Idioms:*** stare someone in the face, stick out like a sore thumb.

glare *n.* **1.** A fixed angry stare ▸ glower, lower, scowl. [*Compare* FACE, SNEER.] **2.** An intense blinding light ▸ blaze, dazzle, flare. **3.** Light that is reflected ▸ highlight, reflection. [*Compare* FLASH.]

glaring *adj.* Conspicuously bad or offensive ▸ egregious, flagrant, gross, rank. [*Compare* OFFENSIVE, OUTRAGEOUS, SHAMELESS.] *—See also* APPARENT (1), BRILLIANT.

glaringness *n.* The quality or state of being flagrant ▸ egregiousness, flagrancy, grossness, rankness. [*Compare* IMPUDENCE, OUTRAGEOUSNESS.]

glary *adj.* *—See* BRILLIANT.

glassy *adj.* Of or resembling glass ▸ glasslike, hyaline, vitrescent, vitreous. [*Compare* TRANSLUCENT.] *—See also* GLOSSY.

glaze *n.* *—See* FINISH, GLOSS[1].

glaze *v.* *—See* FINISH (2), GLOSS[1].

gleam *v.* To shine brightly and steadily but without a flame ▸ glow, incandesce, luminesce. *—See also* BEAM, GLITTER.

gleam *n.* *—See* FLASH (1).

gleaming *adj.* *—See* GLOSSY.

glean *v.* To collect something bit by bit ▸ cherry-pick, cull, extract, garner, gather, harvest, pick up. [*Compare* ACCUMULATE.] *—See also* GET (1).

glee *n.* *—See* DELIGHT, HAPPINESS, MERRIMENT (1).

gleeful *adj.* *—See* CHEERFUL.

gleefulness *n.* *—See* MERRIMENT (1).

glen *n.* *—See* VALLEY.

glib *adj.* Marked by ease and fluency of speech that is often insincere or superficial ▸ facile, offhand, slick, smooth, smooth-talking, smooth-tongued. [*Compare* ELOQUENT, FLUENT, SUAVE, TALKATIVE.]

glibness *n.* *—See* ELOQUENCE.

glide *v.* **1.** To move smoothly, continuously, and effortlessly ▸ coast, drift, float, glissade, skate, skim, slide, slip, slither, waft. **2.** To maneuver gently and slowly into place ▸ ease, slide, slip. [*Compare* EASE.] *—See also* FLY (2), SNEAK.

glimmer *n.* *—See* FLASH (1).

glimmer *v.* *—See* GLITTER.

glimpse *n.* *—See* GLANCE (1).

glimpse *v.* To look briefly and quickly ▸ glance, peek, peep. ***Idiom:*** steal a glance (*or* look). [*Compare* LOOK.]

glint *n.* *—See* FLASH (1), GLITTER (1).

glint *v.* *—See* GLITTER.

glisten *v.* *—See* GLITTER.

glisten *n.* *—See* GLITTER (1).

glistening *adj.* *—See* GLOSSY, SPARKLING.

glister *v.* *—See* GLITTER.

glister *n.* *—See* GLITTER (1).

glitch *n.* *—See* DEFECT.

glitter *n.* **1.** Sparkling, brilliant light ▸ glint, glisten, glister, scintillation, shimmer, sparkle, twinkle. [*Compare* FLASH.] **2.** Brilliant, showy splendor ▸ brilliance, brilliancy, glamorousness, glamour, gorgeousness, magnificence, pageantry, pomp, resplendence, resplendency, showiness, sparkle, sumptuousness. *Informal:* glitz, razzle-dazzle. *Slang:* bling, bling bling. [*Compare* ARRAY, GLORY.] **3.** A small sparkling decoration ▸ diamond, rhinestone, sequin, spangle.

glitter *v.* To emit light in sudden or intermittent bursts ▸ blink, coruscate, flash, flicker, glance, gleam, glimmer, glint, glisten, glister, scintillate, shimmer, spangle, sparkle, twinkle, wink. [*Compare* BEAM.]

glitz *n.* *—See* GLITTER (2).

glitzy *adj.* *—See* GAUDY.

gloaming *n.* *—See* EVENING.

gloat *v.* *—See* EXULT (1), PRIDE.

pleasure or self-satisfaction. **—gloat′er** *n.*

glob (glŏb) ▸ *n.* **1.** A globule. **2.** A soft lump or mass.

glob·al (glō′bəl) ▸ *adj.* **1.** Involving the entire earth; worldwide. **2.** Comprehensive; total. **3.** *Comp. Sci.* Of an entire program or document. **—glob′al·i·za′tion** *n.* **—glob′al·ize′** *v.* **—glob′al·ly** *adv.*

Global Positioning System ▸ *n.* A system for determining one's position on the earth by comparing radio signals received from different satellites.

global warming ▸ *n.* An increase in the average temperature of the earth's atmosphere, esp. one sufficient to cause climatic change.

globe (glōb) ▸ *n.* **1.** A spherical body, esp. a model of the earth as a hollow ball. **2.** The earth. **3.** A spherical or bowllike object.

globe·trot (glōb′trŏt′) ▸ *v.* To travel widely, esp. for sightseeing. **—globe′trot′ter** *n.* **—globe′trot′ting** *n.*

glob·u·lar (glŏb′yə-lər) ▸ *adj.* **1.** Spherical. **2.** Consisting of globules. **—glob′u·lar·ly** *adv.* **—glob′u·lar·ness** *n.*

glob·ule (glŏb′yo͞ol) ▸ *n.* A small spherical mass, as of liquid.

glob·u·lin (glŏb′yə-lĭn) ▸ *n.* Any of a class of proteins found extensively in blood plasma, milk, muscle, and plant seeds.

glock·en·spiel (glŏk′ən-spēl′, -shpēl′) ▸ *n.* A percussion instrument with a series of metal bars played with two light hammers.

gloom (glo͞om) ▸ *n.* **1.** Partial or total darkness. **2.** A state of melancholy or depression.

gloom·y (glo͞o′mē) ▸ *adj.* **-i·er, -i·est. 1.** Partially or totally dark. **2.** Showing or filled with gloom. **3.** Causing gloom; depressing. **—gloom′i·ly** *adv.* **—gloom′i·ness** *n.*

glo·ri·fy (glôr′ə-fī′) ▸ *v.* **-fied, -fy·ing. 1.** To give honor or high praise to; exalt. **2.** To exaggerate the glory or excellence of. **3.** To worship; extol. **—glo′ri·fi·ca′tion** *n.* **—glo′ri·fi′er** *n.*

glo·ri·ous (glôr′ē-əs) ▸ *adj.* **1.** Having or deserving glory; famous. **2.** Splendid; magnificent. **3.** Delightful. **—glo′ri·ous·ly** *adv.* **—glo′ri·ous·ness** *n.*

glo·ry (glôr′ē) ▸ *n., pl.* **-ries. 1.** Great honor or distinction; renown. **2.** A highly praiseworthy asset. **3.** Adoration and praise offered in worship. **4.** Majestic beauty. **5.** A height of achievement, enjoyment, or prosperity. ▸ *v.* **-ried, -ry·ing.** To rejoice triumphantly; exult.

gloss¹ (glôs, glŏs) ▸ *n.* **1.** Surface shine; luster. **2.** A superficially attractive appearance. ▸ *v.* To make attractive or acceptable esp. by superficial treatment: *glossed over the candidate's faults.*

gloss² (glôs, glŏs) ▸ *n.* **1.** A brief explanatory note or translation of a difficult or technical expression. **2.** A translation or commentary accompanying a text. ▸ *v.* To provide (e.g., a text) with a gloss. **—gloss′er** *n.*

glos·sa·ry (glô′sə-rē, glŏs′ə-) ▸ *n., pl.* **-ries.** A list of difficult or specialized words with their definitions.

gloss·y (glô′sē, glŏs′ē) ▸ *adj.* **-i·er, -i·est. 1.** Having a smooth shiny surface. **2.** Superficially attractive; slick. ▸ *n., pl.* **-ies.** A photographic print on smooth shiny paper. **—gloss′i·ly** *adv.* **—gloss′i·ness** *n.*

glot·tal stop (glŏt′l) ▸ *n.* A speech sound produced by closure and release of the glottis.

glot·tis (glŏt′ĭs) ▸ *n., pl.* **-tis·es** or **glot·ti·des** (glŏt′ĭ-dēz′). The opening between the vocal cords at the upper part of the larynx.

glove (glŭv) ▸ *n.* **1.** A fitted covering for the hand with a separate sheath for each finger and the thumb. **2.** *Sports* An oversized padded leather covering for the hand, esp. one used in baseball or boxing. **—glove** *v.*

glow (glō) ▸ *v.* **1.** To shine brightly and steadily, esp. without a flame. **2.** To have a bright ruddy color. **3.** To be exuberant or radiant: *glowing with pride.* ▸ *n.* **1.** A light produced by a heated body. **2.** Brilliance or warmth of color. **3.** A warm feeling. **—glow′ing** *adj.*

glow·er (glou′ər) ▸ *v.* To look or stare angrily or sullenly. **—glow′er** *n.* **—glow′er·ing·ly** *adv.*

glow·worm (glō′wûrm′) ▸ *n.* Any of various luminous female beetles or beetle larvae.

glox·in·i·a (glŏk-sĭn′ē-ə) ▸ *n.* A tropical South American plant grown as a houseplant for its showy, variously colored flowers.

gloze (glōz) ▸ *v.* **glozed, gloz·ing.** To minimize; gloss: *glozed over the errors.*

glu·ca·gon (glo͞o′kə-gŏn′) ▸ *n.* A pancreatic hormone that raises blood sugar levels.

glu·cose (glo͞o′kōs′) ▸ *n.* **1.** A monosaccharide sugar, $C_6H_{12}O_6$, that occurs widely in most plant and animal tissue and is the major energy source of the body. **2.** A syrupy mixture of dextrose and maltose with water, used in confectionery and alcoholic fermentation.

glue (glo͞o) ▸ *n.* **1.** A strong liquid adhesive, esp. one made from animal parts. **2.** An adhesive force or factor. ▸ *v.* **glued, glu·ing.** To stick or fasten with or as if with glue. **—glu′ey** *adj.* **—glu′i·ness** *n.*

glum (glŭm) ▸ *adj.* **glum·mer, glum·mest.** Moody and

THESAURUS

gloating *n.* —*See* EXULTATION.

gloating *adj.* Feeling or expressing an uplifting joy over a success or victory ▸ exultant, jubilant, triumphant. [*Compare* BOASTFUL.]

glob *n.* —*See* DROP (1).

global *adj.* —*See* GENERAL (2), UNIVERSAL (1).

globe *n.* The celestial body where humans live ▸ earth, orb, planet, world. —*See also* BALL.

globetrotter *n.* —*See* TOURIST.

globular or **globoid** *adj.* —*See* ROUND (1).

globule *n.* —*See* DROP (1).

gloom *n.* —*See* DARK, DEPRESSION (2).

gloom *v.* —*See* OBSCURE, SHADE (2).

gloomy *adj.* Dark and depressing ▸ black, bleak, blue, cheerless, comfortless, dark, desolate, dismal, drear, dreary, dull, funereal, glum, joyless, murky, sepulchral, somber, stygian, tenebrific. —*See also* BLEAK (2), DEPRESSED (1), GLUM, SORROWFUL.

glorification *n.* —*See* EXALTATION, PRAISE (2).

glorify *v.* —*See* DISTINGUISH (3), EXALT, HONOR (1), PRAISE (3).

glorious *adj.* Marked by extraordinary beauty and splendor ▸ brilliant, dazzling, gorgeous, magnificent, proud, radiant, resplendent, shining, splendid, splendiferous, splendorous, wonderful, wondrous. [*Compare* BEAUTIFUL, GRAND, SHOWY.] —*See also* FAMOUS, MARVELOUS.

glory *n.* A height of achievement or acclaim ▸ brilliance, grandeur, grandiosity, grandness, greatness, magnificence, majesty, splendor. —*See also* FAME, PRAISE (2).

glory *v.* —*See* EXULT (1).

gloss¹ *n.* A surface shininess ▸ burnish, glaze, luster, polish, sheen, shine, sleekness, varnish. [*Compare* FINISH.] —*See also* FACADE (2).

gloss *v.* To give a bright sheen or luster to ▸ buff, burnish, furbish, glaze, polish, shine, sleek, varnish. —*See also* COLOR (2).

gloss over *v.* —*See* EXTENUATE, NEGLECT (1).

gloss² *n.* —*See* EXPLANATION.

gloss *v.* —*See* EXPLAIN (1).

glossary *n.* An alphabetical list of words often defined or translated ▸ dictionary, lexicon, vocabulary, wordbook.

glossy *adj.* Having a high, radiant sheen ▸ brilliant, burnished, glassy, glazed, gleaming, glistening, lustrous, polished, shining, shiny. [*Compare* SLEEK, SPARKLING.]

glow *v.* To shine brightly and steadily but without a flame ▸ gleam, incandesce, luminesce. —*See also* BEAM, BLUSH.

glow *n.* **1.** A fresh rosy complexion ▸ bloom, blush, color, flush. [*Compare* COLOR, COMPLEXION.] **2.** A feeling of pervasive emotional warmth ▸ flush, tingle. —*See also* LIGHT¹ (1).

glower *v.* **1.** To wrinkle one's brow, as in thought, puzzlement, or displeasure ▸ frown, lower, scowl. *Idioms:* knit one's brow, look black, turn one's mouth down. [*Compare* GRIMACE.] **2.** To stare fixedly and angrily ▸ glare, lower, scowl. *Idioms:* give the evil eye, look daggers. [*Compare* GAZE, SNEER.]

glower *n.* A fixed angry stare ▸ glare, lower, scowl. [*Compare* FACE, SNEER.] —*See also* FROWN.

glowing *adj.* —*See* BRIGHT, PASSIONATE, RUDDY.

gloze *v.* —*See* COLOR (2), EXTENUATE.

gluey *adj.* —*See* STICKY (1).

glum *adj.* Broodingly and sullenly unhappy ▸ dour, gloomy, low, moody,

melancholy; dejected. **—glum′ly** *adv.* **—glum′ness** *n.*
glu·on (glo͞o′ŏn) ► *n. Phys.* A hypothetical particle believed to mediate the strong interaction that binds quarks.
glut (glŭt) ► *v.* **glut·ted, glut·ting. 1.** To fill beyond capacity, esp. with food; satiate. **2.** To flood (a market) so that supply exceeds demand. ► *n.* An oversupply.
glu·ten (glo͞ot′n) ► *n.* A mixture of plant proteins occurring in cereal grains. **—glu′ten·ous** *adj.*
glu·te·us (glo͞o′tē-əs, glo͞o-tē′-) ► *n., pl.* **-te·i** (-tē-ī′, -tē′ī′). Any of three large muscles of the buttocks. **—glu′te·al** *adj.*
glu·ti·nous (glo͞ot′n-əs) ► *adj.* Gluey; sticky. **—glu′ti·nous·ness, glu′ti·nos′i·ty** (-ŏs′ĭ-tē) *n.*
glut·ton (glŭt′n) ► *n.* One who eats or consumes immoderate amounts. **—glut′ton·y** *n.*
glut·ton·ous (glŭt′n-əs) ► *adj.* **1.** Given to gluttony; greedy. **2.** Inordinately fond or eager. **—glut′ton·ous·ly** *adv.*
glyc·er·in also **glyc·er·ine** (glĭs′ər-ĭn) ► *n.* Glycerol.
glyc·er·ol (glĭs′ə-rôl′, -rōl′, -rŏl′) ► *n.* A syrupy liquid obtained from fats and oils and used as a solvent, antifreeze, and sweetener and in making dynamite, soaps, and lubricants.
gly·co·gen (glī′kə-jən) ► *n.* A polysaccharide, $(C_6H_{10}O_5)_n$, that is the main form of carbohydrate storage in animals and occurs primarily in the liver. **—gly′co·gen′ic** (-jĕn′ĭk) *adj.*
glyph (glĭf) ► *n.* **1.** *Archit.* A vertical groove. **2.** A symbol, such as an informative figure or arrow, on a sign.
gnarl (närl) ► *n.* A protruding knot on a tree. **—gnarled** *adj.*
gnash (năsh) ► *v.* To grind (the teeth) together.
gnat (năt) ► *n.* Any of various small biting flies.
gnaw (nô) ► *v.* **1.** To bite or chew on with the teeth. **2.** To erode or diminish gradually as if by gnawing. **3.** To cause persistent worry or pain. **—gnaw′er** *n.*
gneiss (nīs) ► *n.* A banded, granitelike metamorphic rock.
gnoc·chi (nyô′kē) ► *pl.n.* Dumplings made of flour or potatoes.
gnome (nōm) ► *n.* One of a fabled race of dwarflike creatures who live underground and guard treasure hoards. **—gnom′ish** *adj.*
Gnos·tic (nŏs′tĭk) ► *adj.* **1. gnostic** Of or relating to intellectual or spiritual knowledge. **2.** Of Gnosticism. **—Gnos′tic** *n.*
Gnos·ti·cism (nŏs′tĭ-sĭz′əm) ► *n.* The doctrines of certain pre-Christian pagan, Jewish, and early Christian sects.
GNP ► *abbr.* gross national product
gnu (no͞o, nyo͞o) ► *n.* A large bearded African antelope with curved horns.
go[1] (gō) ► *v.* **went** (wĕnt), **gone** (gôn, gŏn), **go·ing, goes** (gōz). **1.** To move or travel. **2.** To move away; depart. **3.** To extend in a certain direction: *The road goes west.* **4.** To function properly: *The car won't go.* **5.** Used to indicate future intent or expectation: *I am going to do it.* **6.** To become: *go mad.* **7.** To continue in a certain condition or continue an activity: *go barefoot all day.* **8.** To belong: *Where do the plates go?* **9.** To be allotted. **10.** To serve: *It goes to show how it is.* **11.** To elapse, as time. **12.** To be used up. **13.** To be discarded or abolished: *The foolish policy has to go.* **14.** To fail: *Her eyes are going.* **15.** To come apart or break up. **16.** To die. **17.** To get along; fare. **18.** To be suitable; harmonize: *The shirt and tie don't go.* **19.** To participate up to: *go halves on a dessert.* **20.** *Informal* To say. ***—phrasal verbs:* go about** To undertake: *went about my chores.* **go along** To cooperate. **go down 1.** To fall or sink. **2.** To be accepted: *His proposal went down well.* **3.** To be remembered. **go for** *Informal* To have a liking for. **go off 1.** To be fired; explode. **2.** To make a noise: *The siren went off at noon.* **go on 1.** To happen. **2.** To continue: *Life goes on.* **3.** To proceed. **go out 1.** To be extinguished. **2.** To socialize outside the home. **go over 1.** To gain acceptance. **2.** To examine. **go through 1.** To examine carefully. **2.** To experience; undergo. **go under** To fail or be ruined. ► *n., pl.* **goes. 1.** An attempt; try: *had a go at it.* **2.** A turn, as in a game. **3.** *Informal* Energy; vitality: *had lots of go.* ***—idioms:* go back on** To fail to honor. **go in for** To have an interest in. **go places** *Informal* To be successful. **go steady** To date someone exclusively. **go to pieces** To lose one's self-control. **on the go** Constantly busy. **to go** To be taken out, as restaurant food.
go[2] (gō) ► *n.* A Japanese board game.
goad (gōd) ► *n.* **1.** A long pointed stick for prodding animals. **2.** A means of prodding; stimulus. **—goad** *v.*
go-a·head (gō′ə-hĕd′) ► *n. Informal* Permission to proceed.
goal (gōl) ► *n.* **1.** A desired purpose; objective. **2.** *Sports* **a.** The finish line of a race. **b.** A structure or zone into or

THESAURUS

morose, sad, saturnine, sour, sulky, sullen, surly. [*Compare* DEPRESSED, DESPONDENT, ILL-TEMPERED.] *—See also* GLOOMY.
glumness *n.* *—See* DEPRESSION (2).
glut *v.* *—See* GULP, SATIATE.
glut *n.* *—See* SURPLUS.
glutinous *adj.* *—See* STICKY (1), VISCOUS.
glutinousness *n.* *—See* VISCOSITY.
glutton *n.* A person who eats or consumes immoderate amounts of food and drink ► hog, overeater, pig. [*Compare* SYBARITE.]
gluttonous *adj.* Wanting to eat or drink more than one can reasonably consume ► edacious, greedy, hoggish, piggish, ravenous, voracious. *—See also* VORACIOUS.
gnash *v.* To rub together noisily ► crunch, grind. *—See also* CHEW.
gnaw *v.* *—See* CHEW, ERODE.
gnawing *adj.* *—See* SHARP (3).
gnomic *adj.* *—See* PITHY.
go *v.* **1.** To move away from a place ► depart, exit, get away, get off, go away, leave, pull out, quit, remove, retire, run (along *or* away), set forth (off *or* out), withdraw. *Informal:* cut out, push off, shove off. *Slang:* blow, bug out (*or* off), split, take off, vamoose. *Idioms:* get going (*or* moving), hit the road, light out for the territory, make oneself scarce, make tracks, pull up stakes, take leave. **2.** To move along a particular course ► pass, proceed, push on, wend. *Idiom:* make (*or* wend) one's way. [*Compare* ADVANCE, JOURNEY, ROVE.] **3.** To act or operate in a specified way ► act, behave, work. **4.** To change or fluctuate within limits ► cover, extend, range, run, vary. **5.** To have a proper or suitable place ► belong, fit. **6.** To be depleted ► dry up, give out, run out. *Idioms:* go down the drain, go up in smoke. [*Compare* DISAPPEAR, EXHAUST, WASTE.] **7.** *Informal* To make an offer of ► bid, offer. *—See also* AGREE (1), BEAR (5), BUCKLE, COVER (2), DIE, EXTEND (1), GAMBLE (2), RESORT.
go along *v.* To agree to cooperate or participate ► *Informal:* play along.
go around *v.* To become known far and wide ► circulate, get around, spread, travel. *—See also* SKIRT, TURN (1).
go at *v.* *—See* ATTACK (1), ATTACK (2).
go away *v.* To come to an end ► pass, pass away. [*Compare* DISAPPEAR.] *—See also* GO (1).
go back *v.* *—See* RETURN (1).
go by *v.* *—See* ELAPSE, VISIT.
go down *v.* To undergo capture, defeat, or ruin ► collapse, fall, go under, topple. [*Compare* SUCCUMB, SURRENDER.] *—See also* FALL (1), SINK (1).
go for *v.* **1.** To require a specified price ► cost, sell for. [*Compare* DEMAND.] **2.** To be favorably disposed toward ► approve, countenance, favor, hold with. *Idioms:* be in favor of, take kindly to, think highly (*or* well) of. [*Compare* ASSENT, VALUE.] *—See also* BRING (2), ENJOY.
go in *v.* *—See* ENTER (1).
go off *v.* *—See* EXPLODE (1).
go on *v.* *—See* CHATTER (1), ENDURE (1), ENDURE (2).
go out *v.* To be with another person socially on a regular basis ► date, go with, see. *Informal:* take out. *Idioms:* go steady, go together.
go over *v.* *—See* EXAMINE (1), PRACTICE (1), REVIEW (1), SUCCEED (2), VISIT.
go through *v.* *—See* EXPERIENCE, PRACTICE (1).
go under *v.* To undergo capture, defeat, or ruin ► collapse, fall, go down, topple. [*Compare* SUCCUMB, SURRENDER.] *—See also* COLLAPSE (2), SINK (1).
go up *v.* *—See* ASCEND.
go with *v.* To be with another person socially on a regular basis ► date, go out (with), see. *Informal:* take out. *Idioms:* go steady, go together. *—See also* CHOOSE (1), SUIT (1).
go *n.* *—See* ATTEMPT, ENERGY, TURN (1).
goad *n.* *—See* PROVOCATION (1), STIMULUS.
goad *v.* *—See* PROVOKE.
go-ahead *adj.* *—See* ASSERTIVE.
go-ahead *n.* *—See* PERMISSION.
goal *n.* *—See* DREAM (3), INTENTION.

over which players try to advance a ball or puck. **c.** The score awarded for this.

goal·ie (gō′lē) ▸ *n.* See **goalkeeper.**

goal·keep·er (gōl′kē′pər) ▸ *n.* A player assigned to protect the goal in various sports.

goal line ▸ *n.* **1.** *Sports* A line crossing either end of a playing area, on which a goal or goal post is positioned. **2.** *Football* A line crossing either end of the playing field over which the ball must be moved to score a touchdown.

goat (gōt) ▸ *n.* **1.** Any of a genus of horned, bearded mammals widely domesticated for wool, milk, and meat. **2.** A lecherous man. **—goat′ish** *adj.*

goat antelope ▸ *n.* Any of various ruminants resembling both goats and antelopes.

goat·ee (gō-tē′) ▸ *n.* A pointed chin beard.

goat·skin (gōt′skĭn′) ▸ *n.* **1.** The skin of a goat, used for leather. **2.** A container, as for wine, made from goatskin.

gob[1] (gŏb) ▸ *n.* **1.** A small mass or lump. **2.** often **gobs** *Informal* A large quantity.

gob[2] (gŏb) ▸ *n. Slang* A sailor.

gob·ble[1] (gŏb′əl) ▸ *v.* **-bled, -bling. 1.** To devour greedily. **2.** To take greedily; grab: *gobble up scarce resources.*

gob·ble[2] (gŏb′əl) ▸ *n.* The guttural chortling sound of a male turkey. **—gob′ble** *v.* **—gob′bler** *n.*

gob·ble·dy·gook also **gob·ble·de·gook** (gŏb′əl-dē-gŏŏk′) ▸ *n.* Unclear, wordy jargon.

go-be·tween (gō′bĭ-twēn′) ▸ *n.* An intermediary between two sides.

Go·bi (gō′bē) ▸ A desert of SE Mongolia and N China.

gob·let (gŏb′lĭt) ▸ *n.* A drinking glass with a stem and base.

gob·lin (gŏb′lĭn) ▸ *n.* A grotesque elfin creature thought to work mischief or evil.

god (gŏd) ▸ *n.* **1. God** A being conceived as the perfect, omnipotent, omniscient originator and ruler of the universe, the principal object of faith and worship in monotheistic religions. **2.** A being of supernatural powers, believed in and worshiped by a people. **3.** One that is worshiped or idealized. **—god′hood′** *n.* **—god′like′** *adj.*

god·child (gŏd′chīld′) ▸ *n.* A child for whom a person serves as sponsor at baptism.

god·daugh·ter (gŏd′dô′tər) ▸ *n.* A female godchild.

god·dess (gŏd′ĭs) ▸ *n.* **1.** A female deity. **2.** A woman of great beauty or grace.

god·fa·ther (gŏd′fä′*th*ər) ▸ *n.* **1.** A man who sponsors a child at baptism. **2.** *Slang* The leader of an organized crime family.

god·for·sak·en (gŏd′fər-sā′kən) ▸ *adj.* Located in a dismal or remote area.

god·head (gŏd′hĕd′) ▸ *n.* Divinity; godhood.

god·less (gŏd′lĭs) ▸ *adj.* **1.** Recognizing or worshiping no god. **2.** Wicked or impious. **—god′less·ly** *adv.* **—god′less·ness** *n.*

god·ly (gŏd′lē) ▸ *adj.* **-li·er, -li·est. 1.** Pious. **2.** Divine. **—god′li·ness** *n.*

god·moth·er (gŏd′mŭ*th*′ər) ▸ *n.* A woman who sponsors a child at baptism.

god·par·ent (gŏd′pâr′ənt, -păr′-) ▸ *n.* A godfather or godmother.

god·send (gŏd′sĕnd′) ▸ *n.* Something wanted or needed that comes unexpectedly.

god·son (gŏd′sŭn′) ▸ *n.* A male godchild.

God·win Aus·ten (gŏd′wĭn ô′stən), **Mount** ▸ See **K2.**

goes (gōz) ▸ *v.* 3rd pers. sing. pr.t. of **go**[1].

Goe·the (gœ′tə), **Johann Wolfgang von** (1749–1832) ▸ German writer and scientist.

go-get·ter (gō′gĕt′ər, -gĕt′-) ▸ *n. Informal* An enterprising person.

gog·gle (gŏg′əl) ▸ *v.* **-gled, -gling.** To stare with wide and bulging eyes. ▸ *n.* **goggles** Tight-fitting, often tinted eyeglasses worn to protect the eyes, as from dust, glare, or flying debris. **—gog′gly** *adj.*

go-go (gō′gō′) ▸ *adj. Informal* Of or relating to discotheques or to the energetic music and dancing performed at discotheques.

go·ing (gō′ĭng) ▸ *n.* **1.** Departure. **2.** The condition underfoot as it affects walking or riding. **3.** *Informal* Progress toward a goal. ▸ *adj.* **1.** Working; running. **2.** Current; prevailing: *The going rates are high.*

goi·ter (goi′tər) ▸ *n.* A noncancerous enlargement of the thyroid gland, visible as a swelling at the front of the neck. **—goi′trous** (-trəs) *adj.*

Go·lan Heights (gō′län′) ▸ An upland region between NE Israel and SW Syria NE of the Sea of Galilee.

gold (gōld) ▸ *n.* **1a.** *Symbol* **Au** A soft, yellow, corrosion-resistant, highly malleable and ductile metallic element used as an international monetary standard, in jewelry, for decoration, and as a plated coating on a wide variety of electrical and mechanical components. At. no. 79. **b.** Coinage made of gold. **2.** Money; riches. **3.** A moderate to vivid yellow. **—gold** *adj.*

gold·brick (gōld′brĭk′) ▸ *n. Slang* One who avoids work; shirker. **—gold′brick′** *v.*

Gold Coast ▸ A section of coastal W Africa along the Gulf of Guinea roughly corresponding to present-day Ghana.

gold·en (gōl′dən) ▸ *adj.* **1.** Made of or containing gold. **2.** Having the color of gold. **3.** Suggestive of gold, as in richness or splendor: *a golden voice.* **4.** Precious: *golden memories.* **5.** Marked by prosperity: *a golden era.* **6.** Excellent: *a golden opportunity.*

golden eagle ▸ *n.* A large eagle with a brownish-yellow head and neck.

Golden Gate ▸ A strait in W CA joining the Pacific and San Francisco Bay.

golden mean ▸ *n.* The course between extremes.

gold·en·rod (gōl′dən-rŏd′) ▸ *n.* Any of a genus of North American plants having feathery clusters of small yellow flowers.

gold·finch (gōld′fĭnch′) ▸ *n.* A small American finch having yellow plumage with a black forehead, wings, and tail.

gold·fish (gōld′fĭsh′) ▸ *n.* A typically reddish freshwater Asian fish bred in many ornamental forms as an aquarium fish.

gold leaf ▸ *n.* Gold beaten into extremely thin sheets, used for gilding.

Gold·man (gōld′mən), **Emma** (1869–1940) ▸ Russian-born Amer. anarchist.

gold rush ▸ *n.* A rush of migrants to an area where gold has been discovered.

gold·smith (gōld′smĭth′) ▸ *n.* An artisan who makes or deals in articles of gold.

gold standard ▸ *n.* A monetary standard under which the basic unit of currency is equal in value to a specified amount of gold.

THESAURUS

goat *n.* —*See* LECHER, SCAPEGOAT.

gob[1] *n.* —*See* HEAP (2), LUMP[1].

gob[2] *n.* —*See* MOUTH (1).

gob[3] *n.* —*See* SAILOR.

gobble *v.* —*See* GULP.

gobbledygook *n.* —*See* BABBLE, GIBBERISH.

go-between *n.* One who acts as an intermediate agent between persons or groups ▸ broker, contact, dealer, facilitator, interceder, intercessor, intermediary, intermediate, intermediator, mediator, middleman, negotiant, negotiator, ombudsman, troubleshooter. [*Compare* AGENT, JUDGE.]

go-by *n.* —*See* SNUB.

goddess *n.* —*See* BEAUTY.

godforsaken *adj.* —*See* LONELY (1).

godless *adj.* —*See* ATHEISTIC.

godlessness *n.* —*See* ATHEISM.

godlike *adj.* —*See* DIVINE (1).

godliness *n.* —*See* HOLINESS.

godly *adj.* —*See* DIVINE (1), PIOUS.

God's country *n.* —*See* COUNTRY.

godsend *n.* —*See* LUCK.

gofer *n.* —*See* ASSISTANT.

go-getter *n. Informal* An intensely energetic, enthusiastic person ▸ demon, dynamo, hustler. *Informal:* eager beaver, firebreather, live wire.

goggle *v.* —*See* GAZE.

going *n.* —*See* DEPARTURE.

going *adj.* —*See* ACTIVE.

going-over *n.* —*See* EXAMINATION (1).

goldbrick *v.* —*See* IDLE (1).

golden ager *n.* —*See* SENIOR (2).

golden-haired *adj.* —*See* FAIR[1] (2).

go·lem (gō′ləm) ► *n.* In Jewish folklore, an artificially created human supernaturally endowed with life.
golf (gŏlf, gôlf) ► *n.* A game played on a 9- or 18-hole course, the object being to hit a small ball with the use of various clubs into each hole with as few strokes as possible. **—golf** *v.* **—golf′er** *n.*
Gol·go·tha (gŏl′gə-thə, gŏl-gŏth′ə) ► See **Calvary**.
Go·li·ath (gə-lī′əth) ► In the Bible, a giant warrior who was slain by David.
Go·mor·rah (gə-môr′ə, -mŏr′ə) ► An ancient city of Palestine near Sodom.
–gon ► *suff.* A figure having a specified kind or number of angles: *polygon.*
go·nad (gō′năd′) ► *n.* An organ in animals that produces gametes, esp. a testis or ovary. **—go·nad′al, go·nad′ic** *adj.*
gon·do·la (gŏn′dl-ə, gŏn-dō′lə) ► *n.* **1.** A lightweight narrow barge used on the canals of Venice. **2.** An open shallow freight car with low sides. **3.** A compartment suspended from a balloon or dirigible. **4.** An enclosed passenger cabin that moves along an overhead cable.
gon·do·lier (gŏn′dl-îr′) ► *n.* The person who propels a Venetian gondola.
gone (gôn, gŏn) ► *v.* P.part. of **go**[1]. ► *adj.* **1.** Past; bygone. **2.** Dying or dead. **3.** Ruined; lost. **4.** Carried away; absorbed. **5.** Used up; exhausted. **6.** *Slang* Infatuated.
gon·er (gô′nər, gŏn′ər) ► *n. Slang* One that is ruined or doomed.
gong (gông, gŏng) ► *n.* A metal disk struck to produce a loud sonorous tone.
gon·or·rhe·a (gŏn′ə-rē′ə) ► *n.* A sexually transmitted disease of the genital and urinary tracts, often marked by a purulent discharge and painful or difficult urination.
goo (go͞o) ► *n. Informal* A sticky, wet, viscous substance. **—goo′ey** *adj.*
goo·ber (go͞o′bər) ► *n.* A peanut.
good (go͝od) ► *adj.* **bet·ter** (bĕt′ər), **best** (bĕst). **1.** Being positive or desirable in nature. **2a.** Having desirable qualities. **b.** Suitable; appropriate. **3a.** Not spoiled. **b.** In excellent condition; sound. **4.** Superior to the average: *a good student.* **5a.** Of high quality: *good books.* **b.** Discriminating: *good taste.* **6.** Beneficial; salutary: *a good night's rest.* **7.** Competent; skilled. **8.** Complete; thorough. **9a.** Reliable; sure. **b.** Valid or true. **c.** Genuine; real. **10.** In effect; operativea. **11a.** Ample; substantial. **b.** Bountiful. **12.** Full: *a good mile away.* **13a.** Pleasant; enjoyable. **b.** Favorable. **14a.** Virtuous; upright. **b.** Benevolent; kind. **15a.** Well-behaved; obedient. **b.** Socially correct; proper. ► *n.* **1.** Something good. **2.** Welfare; benefit. **3.** Goodness; virtue. **4. goods a.** Commodities; wares. **b.** Portable personal property. ***—idioms:*** **as good as** Nearly; almost. **for good** Permanently. **good and** *Informal* Very; thoroughly.
good·bye or **good-bye** also **good-by** (go͝od-bī′) ► *interj.* Used to express farewell. **—good·bye′** *n.*
Good Friday ► *n.* The Friday before Easter, observed by Christians in commemoration of the crucifixion of Jesus.
good·heart·ed (go͝od′här′tĭd) ► *adj.* Kind and generous. **—good′heart′ed·ly** *adv.* **—good′heart′ed·ness** *n.*
Good Hope, Cape of ► A promontory on the SW coast of South Africa S of Cape Town.
good-hu·mored (go͝od′hyo͞o′mərd) ► *adj.* Cheerful; amiable. **—good′-hu′mored·ly** *adv.* **—good′-hu′mored·ness** *n.*
good-look·ing (go͝od′lo͝ok′ĭng) ► *adj.* Of a pleasing appearance; attractive.
good·ly (go͝od′lē) ► *adj.* **-li·er, -li·est. 1.** Of pleasing appearance; comely. **2.** Somewhat large; considerable. **—good′li·ness** *n.*
good-na·tured (go͝od′nā′chərd) ► *adj.* Having an easygoing, cheerful disposition. **—good′-na′tured·ly** *adv.*
good·ness (go͝od′nĭs) ► *n.* **1.** The state or quality of being good. **2.** The beneficial part. ► *interj.* Used to express mild surprise.
Good Samaritan ► *n.* A person who unselfishly helps others.
good·will also **good will** (go͝od′wĭl′) ► *n.* **1.** An attitude of kindness or friendliness; benevolence. **2.** Cheerful willingness. **3.** A good relationship, as between nations.
good·y (go͝od′ē) ► *n., pl.* **-ies.** *Informal* Something attractive or delectable, esp. something sweet to eat. **—good′y** *interj.*
good·y-good·y (go͝od′ē-go͝od′ē) ► *adj.* Affectedly sweet, good, or virtuous. **—good′y-good′y** *n.*
goof (go͞of) ► *n. Slang* **1.** An incompetent, foolish, or stupid person. **2.** A careless mistake; slip. ► *v.* **1.** To blunder. **2.** To waste or kill time: *goofed off all day.* **—goof′i·ly** *adv.* **—goof′i·ness** *n.* **—goof′y** *adj.*
goof·ball (go͞of′bôl′) ► *n. Slang* **1.** A foolish or goofy person. **2.** A barbiturate or tranquilizer in pill form. **—goof′ball** *adj.*
goo·gol (go͞o′gôl′) ► *n.* The number 10 raised to the power 100 (10^{100}).
gook (go͝ok, go͞ok) ► *n.* Var. of **guck.**
goon (go͞on) ► *n. Slang* **1.** A thug hired to intimidate or harm opponents. **2.** A stupid or oafish person.
goose (go͞os) ► *n., pl.* **geese** (gēs). **1.** Any of various water birds related to the ducks and swans. **2.** The female of such a bird. **3.** The flesh of such a bird used as food. **4.** *Informal* A silly person.
goose·ber·ry (go͞os′bĕr′ē, -bə-rē, go͞oz′-) ► *n.* **1.** A spiny shrub having edible greenish berries. **2.** The fruit of this plant.
goose bumps ► *pl.n.* Momentary roughness of the skin in response to cold or fear.
goose flesh ► *n.* See **goose bumps.**
goose·neck (go͞os′nĕk′) ► *n.* A slender curved object or part, such as the flexible shaft of a type of desk lamp. **—goose′necked′** *adj.*
goose step ► *n.* A military parade step executed by swinging the legs from the hips with the knees locked. **—goose′-step′** *v.*

THESAURUS

Goliath *n.* —*See* GIANT.
gone *adj.* —*See* ABSENT, DEAD (1), INFATUATED, LOST (2), PREGNANT (1).
goner *n. Slang* One that is ruined or doomed ► dead duck, dead meat, toast. [*Compare* THROUGH.]
good *adj.* 1. Having pleasant desirable qualities ► bonny, dandy, decent, enjoyable, fine, jolly, nice, worthy. *Informal:* all-right. [*Compare* ACCEPTABLE, CHOICE, EXCELLENT.] 2. In excellent condition ► entire, flawless, intact, perfect, sound, unblemished, unbroken, undamaged, unharmed, unhurt, unimpaired, uninjured, unmarred, whole. 3. No less than; at least ► full, round, whole. —*See also* ABLE, AUTHENTIC (1), BENEFICIAL, BENEVOLENT (1), BIG, CONVENIENT (1), EXEMPLARY, FAVORABLE (1), HONEST, PLEASANT.
good *n.* 1. The quality or state of being morally sound ► goodness, morality, probity, rectitude, righteousness, rightfulness, rightness, uprightness, virtue, virtuousness. [*Compare* ETHIC.] 2. A product or products bought and sold in commerce ► commodity, goods, inventory, line, merchandise, stock, ware, wares. [*Compare* PRODUCT.] —*See also* INTEREST (1).
goodbye *interjection* Used upon taking leave ► farewell, fare-thee-well. *Informal:* adiós, auf Wiedersehen, au revoir, ciao, hasta mañana, later, see you, so long, take care. *Idioms:* catch you later, go in peace (*or* with God), see you later.
goodbye *n.* —*See* DEPARTURE.
goodbye *adj.* —*See* PARTING.
good deed *n.* —*See* FAVOR (1).
good-for-nothing *n.* —*See* RIFFRAFF, WASTREL (2).
good-for-nothing *adj.* —*See* WORTHLESS.
goodhearted *adj.* —*See* BENEVOLENT (1).
goodish *adj.* —*See* ACCEPTABLE (2).
good-looking *adj.* —*See* BEAUTIFUL.
goodly *adj.* —*See* BIG.
good name *n.* —*See* HONOR (2).
good-natured *adj.* —*See* AMIABLE.
goodness *n.* —*See* GOOD (1).
goods *n.* —*See* EFFECTS, GOOD (2).
good-tempered *adj.* —*See* AMIABLE.
good turn *n.* —*See* FAVOR (1).
goodwill *n.* —*See* BENEVOLENCE.
goody *n.* —*See* DELICACY.
gooey *adj.* —*See* SENTIMENTAL, STICKY (1).
goof *n.* —*See* BLUNDER, FOOL.
goof *v.* —*See* IDLE (1).
goof up *v.* —*See* BOTCH, ERR.
goofiness *n.* —*See* FOOLISHNESS.
goofy *adj.* —*See* FOOLISH.
goon *n.* —*See* OAF, THUG.
goose *n.* —*See* FOOL.

GOP ▸ *abbr.* Grand Old Party (Republican Party)

go·pher (gō′fər) ▸ *n.* Any of various burrowing North American rodents having external cheek pouches.

Gor·ba·chev (gôr′bə-chôf′, -chŏf′), **Mikhail Sergeyevich** (b. 1931) ▸ Soviet politician; 1990 Nobel Peace Prize.

gore¹ (gôr) ▸ *v.* **gored, gor·ing.** To pierce or stab with a horn or tusk.

gore² (gôr) ▸ *n.* A triangular or tapering piece of cloth, as in a skirt or sail. **—gore** *v.* **—gored** *adj.*

gore³ (gôr) ▸ *n.* Blood, esp. from a wound.

gorge (gôrj) ▸ *n.* **1.** A deep narrow passage with steep sides. **2.** The throat; gullet. **3.** Something swallowed. ▸ *v.* **gorged, gorg·ing. 1.** To stuff (oneself) with food; glut. **2.** To eat greedily.

gor·geous (gôr′jəs) ▸ *adj.* **1.** Dazzlingly beautiful or magnificent: *a gorgeous gown.* **2.** *Informal* Wonderful; delightful. **—gor′geous·ly** *adv.* **—gor′geous·ness** *n.*

go·ril·la (gə-rĭl′ə) ▸ *n.* An African ape, the largest of the great apes, having a stocky body and coarse dark hair.

gor·mand·ize (gôr′mən-dīz′) ▸ *v.* **-ized, -iz·ing.** To eat gluttonously. **—gor′mand·iz′er** *n.*

gorse (gôrs) ▸ *n.* A spiny European shrub having fragrant yellow flowers.

go·ry (gôr′ē) ▸ *adj.* **-ri·er, -ri·est. 1.** Covered with gore; bloody. **2.** Full of bloodshed and violence. **—gor′i·ly** *adv.* **—gor′i·ness** *n.*

gosh (gŏsh) ▸ *interj.* Used to express mild surprise.

gos·hawk (gŏs′hôk′) ▸ *n.* A large hawk having broad rounded wings and gray or brownish plumage.

gos·ling (gŏz′lĭng) ▸ *n.* A young goose.

gos·pel (gŏs′pəl) ▸ *n.* **1.** often **Gospel** The proclamation of the redemption preached by Jesus and the Apostles. **2.** often **Gospel** *Bible* One of the first four books of the New Testament. **3.** Gospel music. **4.** Something accepted as unquestionably true.

gospel music ▸ *n.* An American religious music associated with Christian evangelism and blending elements of folk music, spirituals, and jazz.

gos·sa·mer (gŏs′ə-mər) ▸ *n.* **1.** A soft, sheer, gauzy fabric. **2.** Something delicate or flimsy. **3.** A fine film of cobwebs often seen floating in the air. **—gos′sa·mer, gos′sa·mer·y** *adj.*

gos·sip (gŏs′əp) ▸ *n.* **1.** Rumor or talk of a personal, sensational, or intimate nature. **2.** A person who habitually indulges in gossip. **—gos′sip** *v.* **—gos′sip·er** *n.* **—gos′sip·y** *adj.*

got (gŏt) ▸ *v.* P.t. and p.part. of **get.**

Goth (gŏth) ▸ *n.* A member of a Germanic people who invaded the Roman Empire in the early centuries of the Christian era.

Goth·ic (gŏth′ĭk) ▸ *adj.* **1a.** Of the Goths or their language. **b.** Germanic. **2.** Medieval. **3.** Of an architectural style prevalent in W Europe from the 12th through the 15th cent. marked esp. by pointed arches and strong vertical elements. **4.** often **gothic** Of a style of fiction that emphasizes the grotesque and mysterious: *a gothic novel.* ▸ *n.* The extinct Germanic language of the Goths.

got·ten (gŏt′n) ▸ *v.* P.part. of **get.**

gouge (gouj) ▸ *n.* **1.** A chisel with a rounded troughlike blade. **2.** A groove or hole scooped with or as if with such a chisel. ▸ *v.* **gouged, goug·ing. 1.** To cut or scoop out with or as if with a gouge. **2.** *Informal* To extort from. **3.** *Slang* To swindle. **—goug′er** *n.*

gou·lash (gōō′läsh′, -lăsh′) ▸ *n.* A meat and vegetable stew seasoned esp. with paprika.

gourd (gôrd, gŏŏrd) ▸ *n.* **1.** A vine related to the pumpkin and cucumber and bearing fruits with a hard rind. **2.** The fruit of such a plant. **3.** The dried and hollowed-out shell of one of these fruits, often used as a drinking utensil.

gourde (gŏŏrd) ▸ *n.* See **currency** table in Appendix.

gour·mand (gŏŏr-mänd′, gŏŏr′mənd) ▸ *n.* **1.** A lover of good food. **2.** A gluttonous eater.

gour·met (gŏŏr-mā′, gŏŏr′mā′) ▸ *n.* A connoisseur of fine food and drink.

gout (gout) ▸ *n.* **1.** A disease of uric-acid metabolism occurring esp. in males, marked by arthritis and painful inflammation of the joints. **2.** A large blob or clot. **—gout′i·ness** *n.* **—gout′y** *adj.*

gov·ern (gŭv′ərn) ▸ *v.* **1.** To make and administer public policy and affairs. **2.** To regulate. **3.** To control; restrain. **4.** To decide or determine. **—gov′ern·a·ble** *adj.* **—gov′er·nance** *n.*

gov·er·ness (gŭv′ər-nĭs) ▸ *n.* A woman employed to educate and train the children of a private household.

gov·ern·ment (gŭv′ərn-mənt) ▸ *n.* **1.** The act or process of governing, esp. the administration of public policy. **2.** The means by which a governing agent or agency uses authority. **3.** A governing body or organization. **4.** Political science. **—gov′ern·men′tal** (-mĕn′tl) *adj.* **—gov′ern·men′tal·ly** *adv.*

gov·er·nor (gŭv′ər-nər) ▸ *n.* **1.** A person who governs, esp. the chief executive of a state in the US. **2.** The manager or administrative head of an organization or institution. **3.** A commandant. **4.** A device on an engine that regulates speed, pressure, or temperature. **—gov′er·nor·ship′** *n.*

govt. ▸ *abbr.* government

gown (goun) ▸ *n.* **1.** A long, loose, flowing garment, as a robe or nightgown. **2.** A woman's formal dress. **3.** A distinctive outer robe worn on ceremonial occasions, as by scholars or clerics. **4.** The faculty and student body of a university: *town and gown.*

GPA ▸ *abbr.* grade point average

GPO ▸ *abbr.* general post office

GPS ▸ *abbr.* Global Positioning System

gr. ▸ *abbr.* **1.** grain (measurement) **2.** gram

grab (grăb) ▸ *v.* **grabbed, grab·bing. 1.** To take or grasp suddenly. **2.** To capture or restrain; arrest. **3.** To obtain

THESAURUS

gore *v.* —*See* CUT (1).

gorge *v.* —*See* GULP, SATIATE.

gorge *n.* —*See* VALLEY.

gorgeous *adj.* —*See* BEAUTIFUL, GLORIOUS.

gorgeousness *n.* —*See* GLITTER (2).

gorilla *n.* —*See* THUG.

gory *adj.* —*See* BLOODY, MURDEROUS.

gospel *n.* —*See* DOCTRINE.

gossamer or **gossamery** *adj.* —*See* SHEER².

gossip *n.* **1.** Idle, often sensational and groundless talk about others ▸ gossipry, hearsay, prattle, report, rumor, scandal, slander, talebearing, talk, tattle, tittle-tattle, word. *Slang:* scuttlebutt. **2.** A person habitually engaged in idle talk about others ▸ bigmouth, blab, chatterbox, gossiper, gossipmonger, newsmonger, rumormonger, scandalmonger, snoop, tabby, talebearer, taleteller, tattle, tattler, tattletale, telltale, whisperer. *Slang:* yenta. [*Compare* BUSYBODY.]

gossip *v.* To engage in or spread gossip ▸ blab, chatter, jabber, noise, prattle, rumor, talk, tattle, tittle-tattle, whisper. *Idioms:* dish the dirt, spread a story, tell tales, tell tales out of school.

gossiper or **gossipmonger** *n.* —*See* GOSSIP (2).

gossipry *n.* —*See* GOSSIP (1).

gossipy *adj.* Inclined to gossip ▸ blabby, talebearing, taletelling.

gouge *v.* —*See* CHEAT (1), CUT (1), DIG.

gouge *n.* —*See* CUT (1).

govern *v.* To control the functioning or outcome of ▸ control, determine, establish, fix, guide, regulate. *Idioms:* call the shots, pull the strings. —*See also* ADMINISTER (1).

governable *adj.* Capable of being governed ▸ administrable, controllable, manageable, rulable. [*Compare* LOYAL, OBEDIENT.]

governance *n.* —*See* GOVERNMENT (1).

governing *adj.* —*See* DOMINANT (1).

government *n.* **1.** The continuous exercise of authority over a political unit ▸ administration, command, control, direction, governance, rule. [*Compare* AUTHORITY.] **2.** A group of people who govern a political unit ▸ administration, authorities, ministry, officials, regime, state. *Idiom:* powers that be. [*Compare* STATE.] —*See also* MANAGEMENT.

governmental *adj.* Of or relating to government ▸ bureaucratic, gubernatorial, legislative, official, political, regulatory. —*See also* ADMINISTRATIVE.

gown *n.* —*See* DRESS (3).

grab *v.* —*See* CATCH (2), GRASP, GRIP, SEIZE (1).

or appropriate unscrupulously or illegally. 4. To take hurriedly. **—grab** *n.* **—grab′ber** *n.* **—grab′by** *adj.*

grab bag ► *n.* 1. A container filled with articles, such as party gifts, to be drawn unseen. 2. *Slang* A miscellaneous collection.

grace (grās) ► *n.* 1. Seemingly effortless beauty of movement, form, or proportion. 2. A pleasing characteristic or quality. 3. A sense of fitness or propriety. 4a. Good will. b. Mercy; clemency. 5. A temporary immunity or exemption; reprieve. 6. **Graces** *Gk. & Rom. Myth.* Three sister goddesses who dispense charm and beauty. 7a. Divine love and protection bestowed freely on people. b. The state of being protected by God. 8. A short prayer said at mealtime. 9. **Grace** Used with *His, Her,* or *Your* as a title for a duke, duchess, or archbishop. ► *v.* **graced, grac·ing.** 1. To honor or favor. 2. To give beauty, elegance, or charm to. ***—idiom:* in the good (**or **bad) graces of** In (or out of) favor with. **—grace′ful** *adj.* **—grace′ful·ly** *adv.* **—grace′ful·ness** *n.* **—grace′less** *adj.* **—grace′less·ly** *adv.* **—grace′less·ness** *n.*

grace period ► *n.* 1. A period in which a debt may be paid without accruing further interest or penalty. 2. A period in which an insurance policy is effective even though the premium is past due.

gra·cious (grā′shəs) ► *adj.* 1. Marked by kindness and warm courtesy. 2. Tactful. 3. Merciful or compassionate. 4. Marked by elegance and good taste. **—gra′cious·ly** *adv.* **—gra′cious·ness** *n.*

grack·le (grăk′əl) ► *n.* Any of several American blackbirds with iridescent blackish plumage.

grad (grăd) ► *n. Informal* A graduate.

gra·da·tion (grā-dā′shən) ► *n.* 1. A series of gradual, successive stages. 2. A degree or stage in such a progression. 3. The act of arranging in grades. **—gra·da′tion·al** *adj.*

grade (grād) ► *n.* 1. A stage or degree in a process. 2. A position in a scale. 3. An accepted standard. 4. A set of persons or things all falling in the same specified limits; class. 5. A class at an elementary school or the pupils in it. 6. A mark indicating a student's level of accomplishment. 7. A military, naval, or civil service rank. 8. The degree of inclination of a slope or other surface. 9. A slope or gradual inclination, esp. of a road or railroad track. ► *v.* **grad·ed, grad·ing.** 1. To arrange in degrees; rank; sort. 2a. To evaluate. b. To give a grade to. 3. To level or smooth (a surface) to a desired gradient. **—grad′er** *n.*

grade school ► *n.* See **elementary school. —grade′-school′er** *n.*

gra·di·ent (grā′dē-ənt) ► *n.* A rate of inclination; slope.

grad·u·al (grăj′o͞o-əl) ► *adj.* Occurring in small stages or advancing by regular or continuous degrees. **—grad′u·al·ism** *n.* **—grad′u·al·ly** *adv.* **—grad′u·al·ness** *n.*

grad·u·ate (grăj′o͞o-āt′) ► *v.* **-at·ed, -at·ing.** 1. To grant or be granted an academic degree or diploma. 2. To arrange into categories, steps, or grades. 3. To divide into marked intervals, esp. for use in measurement. ► *n.* (-ĭt) One who has received an academic degree or diploma. ► *adj.* (-ĭt) 1. Possessing an academic degree or diploma. 2. Of studies beyond a bachelor's degree.

grad·u·a·tion (grăj′o͞o-ā′shən) ► *n.* 1. Conferral or receipt of an academic degree or diploma marking completion of studies. 2. A commencement ceremony. 3. An interval on a graduated scale.

graf·fi·to (grə-fē′tō) ► *n., pl.* **-ti** (-tē). often **graffiti** A drawing or inscription made on a wall or other surface, usu. to be seen by the public.

graft[1] (grăft) ► *v.* 1. To unite (a shoot, bud, or plant) with a growing plant by insertion or placing in close contact. 2. To transplant or implant (tissue) into a bodily part. ► *n.* 1a. A detached shoot or bud grafted onto a growing plant. b. The point of union of such plant parts. 2. Material, esp. tissue or an organ, grafted onto a bodily part. **—graft′er** *n.*

graft[2] (grăft) ► *n.* 1. Illegal use of one's position for profit or advantages. 2. Money or advantage thus gained. **—graft** *v.* **—graft′er** *n.*

graham flour ► *n.* Whole-wheat flour.

grail (grāl) ► *n.* 1. **Grail** A legendary cup or plate used by Jesus at the Last Supper, later the object of chivalrous quests. 2. often **Grail** The object of a prolonged endeavor.

grain (grān) ► *n.* 1a. A small, one-seeded fruit of a cereal grass. b. The fruits of cereal grasses collectively, esp. after harvesting. 2. Cereal grasses collectively. 3. A small amount. 4. See table at **measurement** in Appendix. 5. The arrangement, direction, or pattern of the fibrous tissue in wood. 6. Texture. 7. Basic temperament; disposition. ***—idiom:* with a grain of salt** With reservations; skeptically. **—grain′i·ness** *n.* **—grain′y** *adj.*

grain alcohol ► *n.* See **alcohol** 1.

grain elevator ► *n.* A tall building used for storing grain.

gram (grăm) ► *n.* See **measurement** table in Appendix.

-gram ► *suff.* Something written or drawn; a record: *cardiogram.*

gram·mar (grăm′ər) ► *n.* 1a. The study of how words and their component parts combine to form sentences. b. The study of structural relationships in language or in a language. 2. The system of inflections, syntax, and word formation of a language. 3a. A normative or prescriptive set of rules setting forth the current standard of usage. b. Writing or speech judged with regard to such rules. 4. A book containing the inflectional, syntactic, and semantic rules for a language. **—gram·mar′i·an** (grə-mâr′ē-ən) *n.* **—gram·mat′i·cal** (grə-măt′ĭ-kəl) *adj.* **—gram·mat′i·cal·ly** *adv.*

grammar school ► *n.* See **elementary school.**

gram-mo·lec·u·lar weight (grăm′mə-lĕk′yə-lər) ► *n.* The mass in grams of one mole of a substance.

gram molecule ► *n.* See **mole**[4].

THESAURUS

grab *n.* —*See* CATCH (1), SEIZURE (2).

grab bag *n.* —*See* ASSORTMENT.

grabbiness *n.* —*See* GREED.

grabble *v.* —*See* GROPE.

grabby *adj.* —*See* GREEDY.

grace *n.* 1. Temporary immunity from penalties ► exemption, immunity, reprieve, respite. [*Compare* DELAY.] 2. A short prayer said at meals ► benediction, blessing, thanks, thanksgiving. [*Compare* PRAYER[1].] —*See also* BENEVOLENCE, DECENCY (1), DEXTERITY, ELEGANCE, FAVOR (1), HOLINESS, MERCY.

grace *v.* 1. To lend dignity or honor to by an act or favor ► enrich, favor, dignify, honor. [*Compare* DISTINGUISH, EXALT, HONOR.] 2. To endow with beauty and elegance ► beautify, embellish, enhance, set off. [*Compare* ADORN.]

graceful *adj.* —*See* ATTRACTIVE, DELICATE (2), ELEGANT, FLUENT.

graceless *adj.* —*See* AWKWARD (1).

gracious *adj.* 1. Characterized by kindness and warm, unaffected courtesy ► affable, courteous, hospitable. [*Compare* AMIABLE, ATTENTIVE, COURTEOUS.] 2. Characterized by elaborate, usually formal courtesy ► chivalrous, circumstantial, courtly, diplomatic, elegant, gallant, genteel, stately, tactful. [*Compare* CEREMONIOUS.]

graciousness *n.* —*See* AMENITIES (2).

gradation *n.* —*See* SHADE (1).

gradational *adj.* Proceeding steadily by degrees ► gradual, piecemeal, progressive, step-by-step. ***Idioms:*** one foot after another, one step at a time. [*Compare* CONSECUTIVE, METHODICAL, SLOW.]

grade *n.* Degree of excellence ► caliber, class, quality. —*See also* ASCENT (2), CLASS (2), DEGREE (1), INCLINATION (2).

grade *v.* To evaluate and assign a grade to ► correct, mark, score. —*See also* CLASSIFY.

gradient *n.* —*See* ASCENT (2), INCLINATION (2).

gradual *adj.* 1. Proceeding steadily by degrees ► gradational, piecemeal, progressive, step-by-step. ***Idioms:*** one foot after another, one step at a time. [*Compare* CONSECUTIVE, METHODICAL, SLOW.] 2. Not steep or abrupt ► easy, even, gentle, mild, moderate, steady.

gradually *adv.* In a gradual manner ► by degrees, in stages, piecemeal, progressively. ***Idioms:*** bit by bit, inch by inch, slowly but surely, step by step.

graft *n.* —*See* BRIBE, PLUNDER.

graft *v.* —*See* EXTORT.

grain *n.* A fertilized plant ovule capable of germinating ► kernel, pip, pit, seed. —*See also* BIT[1] (1), ESSENCE, TEXTURE.

grainy *adj.* —*See* COARSE (2).

gram·o·phone (grăm′ə-fōn′) ▸ *n.* A phonograph.
gram·pus (grăm′pəs) ▸ *n.* A marine mammal related to and resembling the dolphins.
gran·a·ry (grăn′ə-rē, grā′nə-) ▸ *n., pl.* **-ries**. A building for storing threshed grain.
grand (grănd) ▸ *adj.* **-er, -est. 1.** Large and impressive in size, scope, or extent. **2a.** Rich and sumptuous. **b.** Of a solemn or stately nature. **3.** Wonderful; very pleasing. **4.** Having higher rank than others of the same category: *a grand admiral.* **5.** Most important; principal: *the grand ballroom.* **6.** Including or covering all units or aspects: *the grand total.* ▸ *n.* **1.** A grand piano. **2.** *Slang* A thousand dollars. **—grand′ly** *adv.* **—grand′ness** *n.*
gran·dam (grăn′dăm′, -dəm) also **gran·dame** (-dām′, -dăm, -dəm) ▸ *n.* **1.** A grandmother. **2.** An old woman.
Grand Canyon ▸ A gorge of the Colorado R. in NW AZ, up to 1.6 km (1 mi) deep, 6.4–29 km (4–18 mi) wide, and more than 321.8 km (200 mi) long.
grand·child (grănd′chīld′, grăn′-) ▸ *n.* A child of one's son or daughter.
grand·daugh·ter (grăn′dô′tər) ▸ *n.* A daughter of one's son or daughter.
gran·deur (grăn′jər, -jo͝or′) ▸ *n.* The quality of being grand; magnificence.
grand·fa·ther (grănd′fä′*th*ər, grăn′-) ▸ *n.* **1.** The father of one's mother or father. **2.** A forefather; ancestor. ▸ *v.* To exempt (one already existing) from new regulations.
gran·dil·o·quence (grăn-dĭl′ə-kwəns) ▸ *n.* Pompous or bombastic speech or expression. **—gran·dil′o·quent** *adj.* **—gran·dil′o·quent·ly** *adv.*
gran·di·ose (grăn′dē-ōs′, grăn′dē-ōs′) ▸ *adj.* **1.** Great in scope or intent; grand. **2.** Affectedly grand; pompous. **—gran′di·os′i·ty** (-ŏs′ĭ-tē), **gran′di·ose′ness** *n.*
grand jury ▸ *n.* A jury convened in private to evaluate criminal accusations against persons and to determine whether the evidence warrants indictment.
grand·ma (grănd′mä′, grăn′-, grăm′mä′, grăm′ə) ▸ *n. Informal* A grandmother.
grand mal (grăn′ mäl′, măl′, grănd′) ▸ *n.* A severe form of epilepsy marked by severe seizures and loss of consciousness.
grand·moth·er (grănd′mŭ*th*′ər, grăn′-) ▸ *n.* **1.** The mother of one's father or mother. **2.** A female ancestor.
grand·pa (grănd′pä′, grăn′-, grăm′pä′, grăm′pə) ▸ *n. Informal* A grandfather.
grand·par·ent (grănd′pâr′ənt, -păr′-, grăn′-) ▸ *n.* A parent of one's mother or father.
grand piano ▸ *n.* A piano having the strings strung in a horizontal harp-shaped frame.
grand slam ▸ *n.* **1.** The winning of all the tricks during a hand in bridge. **2.** *Baseball* A home run hit with three runners on base.
grand·son (grănd′sŭn′, grăn′-) ▸ *n.* A son of one's son or daughter.
grand·stand (grănd′stănd′, grăn′-) ▸ *n.* A roofed stand for spectators at a stadium or racetrack. ▸ *v.* To act ostentatiously to impress an audience. **—grand′stand′er** *n.*
grange (grānj) ▸ *n.* **1. Grange** A US farmers' association founded in 1867. **2.** *Chiefly Brit.* A farm with its outbuildings.
gran·ite (grăn′ĭt) ▸ *n.* A common, coarse-grained, hard igneous rock consisting chiefly of quartz and feldspar, used esp. in monuments and for building. **—gra·nit′ic** (gră-nĭt′ĭk, grə-) *adj.*
gran·ny or **gran·nie** (grăn′ē) ▸ *n., pl.* **-nies**. *Informal* A grandmother.
gra·no·la (grə-nō′lə) ▸ *n.* Rolled oats often mixed with dried fruit, brown sugar, and nuts and used esp. as a breakfast cereal.
grant (grănt) ▸ *v.* **1.** To consent to the fulfillment of. **2.** To accord as a favor. **3a.** To bestow; confer. **b.** To transfer (property) by a deed. **4.** To concede; acknowledge. ▸ *n.* **1.** The act of granting. **2a.** Something granted. **b.** A giving of funds for a specific purpose. **3a.** A transfer of property by deed. **b.** The property so transferred. **c.** The deed of transfer. **—grant′er, gran′tor** *n.*
Grant, Ulysses Simpson (1822–1885) ▸ The 18th US President (1869–77) and a Civil War general.
gran·u·lar (grăn′yə-lər) ▸ *adj.* **1.** Composed of granules or grains. **2.** Having a grainy texture. **—gran′u·lar′i·ty** (-lăr′ĭ-tē) *n.*
gran·u·late (grăn′yə-lāt′) ▸ *v.* **-lat·ed, -lat·ing. 1.** To form into grains or granules. **2.** To make rough and grainy. **—gran′u·la′tion** *n.* **—gran′u·la′tive** *adj.*
gran·ule (grăn′yo͞ol) ▸ *n.* A small grain or particle.
grape (grāp) ▸ *n.* **1.** Any of a genus of woody vines bearing clusters of edible fruit. **2.** The fleshy, smooth-skinned, purple, red, or green fruit of a grape. **3.** Grapeshot.
grape·fruit (grāp′fro͞ot′) ▸ *n.* **1.** A large round citrus fruit having a yellow rind and juicy acid pulp. **2.** The semitropical tree bearing this fruit.
grape·shot (grāp′shŏt′) ▸ *n.* A cluster of small iron balls formerly used as a cannon charge.
grape sugar ▸ *n.* Dextrose from grapes.
grape·vine (grāp′vīn′) ▸ *n.* **1.** A vine on which grapes grow. **2.** The informal transmission of information or rumor from person to person.
graph (grăf) ▸ *n.* **1.** A diagram that exhibits a relationship between two sets of numbers. **2.** Any drawing or diagram used to display quantitative relationships. ▸ *v.* **1.** To represent by a graph. **2.** To plot (a function) on a graph.
-graph ▸ *suff.* **1.** Something written or drawn: *monograph.* **2.** An instrument for writing, drawing, or recording: *seismograph.*
-grapher ▸ *suff.* One who writes about a specified subject or in a specified manner: *stenographer.*
graph·ic (grăf′ĭk) ▸ *adj.* also **graph·i·cal** (-ĭ-kəl) **1.** Relating to written or pictorial representation. **2.** Relating to a graph. **3.** Vividly described or set forth. **4.** Of the graphic arts. ▸ *n.* **1.** A work of graphic art. **2.** A graphic image or display, esp. one generated by a computer. **—graph′i·cal·ly** *adv.*
graphical user interface ▸ *n.* GUI.
graphic arts ▸ *pl.n.* The arts, such as painting, drawing, and engraving, that involve representing, writing, or printing on two-dimensional surfaces.
graph·ics (grăf′ĭks) ▸ *n.* **1.** *(takes sing. v.)* The making of

THESAURUS

grand *adj.* Impressive in size, proportion, or appearance ▸ august, awe-inspiring, awesome, baronial, elegant, grandiose, great, imperial, imposing, lordly, magnific, magnificent, majestic, marvelous, noble, palatial, princely, regal, royal, splendid, stately, sublime, superb. [*Compare* BIG, EXCELLENT, LUXURIOUS.] —*See also* ELEVATED (4), EXALTED, IMPORTANT.
grandiloquence *n.* —*See* BOMBAST.
grandiloquent *adj.* —*See* ORATORICAL.
grandiose *adj.* —*See* GRAND, POMPOUS.
grandioseness *n.* —*See* PRETENTIOUSNESS.
grandiosity *n.* —*See* GLORY, PRETENTIOUSNESS.
grandness *n.* —*See* GLORY.
grant *v.* To let have as a favor, prerogative, or privilege ▸ accord, award, concede, give, vouchsafe. [*Compare* YIELD.] —*See also* ACKNOWLEDGE (1), CONFER (2), DONATE, TRANSFER (1).
grant *n.* **1.** Money or other resources that are granted for a particular purpose or reason ▸ appropriation, budget, subsidy, subvention. **2.** Legal transfer of ownership or title ▸ alienation, assignment, conveyance, transfer, transferal. —*See also* CONFERMENT, DONATION.
grantor *n.* —*See* DONOR.
granular *adj.* —*See* COARSE (2).
granulate *v.* —*See* CRUSH (2).
graph *v.* —*See* PLOT (1).
graphic *adj.* **1.** Depicted in sharp and accurate detail ▸ explicit, lifelike, lucid, photographic, pictorial, picturesque, realistic, uncompromising, vivid. [*Compare* ACCURATE, CLEAR, DETAILED.] **2.** Evoking strong mental images through distinctiveness ▸ colorful, picturesque, striking, vivid. [*Compare* GHASTLY.] **3.** Of or relating to representation by means of writing ▸ calligraphic, scriptural, written. **4.** Of or relating to representation by drawings or pictures ▸ hieroglyphic, illustrative, photographic, pictographic, pictorial, symbolic. —*See also* DESCRIPTIVE.

drawings, as in engineering or architecture. **2.** *(takes sing. or pl. v.)* The pictorial representation and manipulation of data, as used in computer-aided design, typesetting, and the graphic arts.

graph·ite (grăf′īt′) ▸ *n.* A soft, steel-gray to black form of carbon used in lead pencils, lubricants, paints, and coatings. **—gra·phit′ic** (gră-fĭt′ĭk) *adj.*

gra·phol·o·gy (gră-fŏl′ə-jē) ▸ *n.* The study of handwriting. **—graph′o·log′i·cal** (grăf′ə-lŏj′ĭ-kəl) *adj.* **—gra·phol′o·gist** *n.*

-graphy ▸ *suff.* **1.** A writing or representation produced in a specified manner or by a specified process: *photography.* **2.** A writing about a specified subject: *oceanography.*

grap·nel (grăp′nəl) ▸ *n.* **1.** A small anchor with three or more flukes. **2.** See **grapple** 1a.

grap·ple (grăp′əl) ▸ *n.* **1a.** An iron shaft with claws at one end, esp. one formerly used for drawing and holding an enemy ship alongside. **b.** See **grapnel** 1. **2.** The act of grappling. ▸ *v.* **-pled, -pling. 1.** To seize and hold fast. **2.** To grip or grasp firmly, as in wrestling. **3.** To struggle: *grapple with one's conscience.* **—grap′pler** *n.*

grappling iron ▸ *n.* See **grapple** 1a.

grasp (grăsp) ▸ *v.* **1.** To seize or attempt to seize firmly; clutch. **2.** To comprehend. ▸ *n.* **1.** A firm hold or grip. **2.** The ability or power to seize; reach. **3.** Understanding; comprehension.

grasp·ing (grăs′pĭng) ▸ *adj.* Greedy; avaricious. **—grasp′ing·ly** *adv.*

grass (grăs) ▸ *n.* **1a.** Any of various plants with narrow leaves, jointed stems, and spikes or clusters of minute flowers. **b.** Such plants collectively. **2.** Ground, such as a lawn, covered with grass. **3.** *Slang* Marijuana. **—grass′y** *adj.*

grass·hop·per (grăs′hŏp′ər) ▸ *n.* Any of various related insects having long powerful hind legs adapted for jumping.

grass·land (grăs′lănd′) ▸ *n.* An area, such as a prairie, of grass or grasslike vegetation.

grass roots ▸ *pl.n. (takes sing. or pl. v.)* People or society at a local level rather than at the center of a political organization. **—grass′-roots′** *adj.*

grate[1] (grāt) ▸ *v.* **grat·ed, grat·ing. 1.** To shred or pulverize by rubbing against a rough surface. **2.** To make or cause to make a harsh rasping sound. **3.** To irritate persistently. ▸ *n.* A harsh rasping sound. **—grat′er** *n.*

grate[2] (grāt) ▸ *n.* **1.** A framework of parallel or latticed bars over an opening. **2.** A framework of metal bars to hold fuel or food in a stove or fireplace. **—grat′ed** *adj.*

grate·ful (grāt′fəl) ▸ *adj.* **1.** Appreciative; thankful. **2.** Expressing gratitude. **3.** Pleasing; agreeable. **—grate′ful·ly** *adv.* **—grate′ful·ness** *n.*

grat·i·fy (grăt′ə-fī′) ▸ *v.* **-fied, -fy·ing. 1.** To please or satisfy. **2.** To give what is desired to; indulge. **—grat′i·fi·ca′tion** *n.* **—grat′i·fi′er** *n.* **—grat′i·fy′ing** *adj.*

grat·ing (grā′tĭng) ▸ *n.* A grill or network of bars; grate.

grat·is (grăt′ĭs, grä′tĭs, grā′-) ▸ *adv. & adj.* Without charge.

grat·i·tude (grăt′ĭ-to͞od′, -tyo͞od′) ▸ *n.* Thankfulness.

gra·tu·i·tous (grə-to͞o′ĭ-təs, -tyo͞o′-) ▸ *adj.* **1.** Given without return; unearned. **2.** Unnecessary or unwarranted: *gratuitous criticism.* **—gra·tu′i·tous·ly** *adv.* **—gra·tu′i·tous·ness** *n.*

gra·tu·i·ty (grə-to͞o′ĭ-tē, -tyo͞o′-) ▸ *n., pl.* **-ties.** A tip for service.

grave[1] (grāv) ▸ *n.* **1.** An excavation for a burial. **2.** A place of burial.

grave[2] (grāv) ▸ *adj.* **grav·er, grav·est. 1.** Requiring serious thought; momentous. **2.** Fraught with danger or harm. **3.** Dignified in conduct or character. **4.** (*also* gräv) Written with the mark (`), as the è in *Sèvres.* ▸ *n.* (*also* gräv) The grave accent. **—grave′ly** *adv.* **—grave′ness** *n.*

grave[3] (grāv) ▸ *v.* **graved, grav·en** (grā′vən) or **graved, grav·ing.** To engrave. **—grav′er** *n.*

grav·el (grăv′əl) ▸ *n.* A loose mixture of rock fragments or pebbles. **—grav′el·ly** *adj.*

grave·stone (grāv′stōn′) ▸ *n.* A tombstone.

grave·yard (grāv′yärd′) ▸ *n.* A cemetery.

graveyard shift ▸ *n.* A work shift that runs during the early morning hours, as from midnight to 8 A.M.

grav·id (grăv′ĭd) ▸ *adj.* Pregnant. **—gra·vid′i·ty** (grə-vĭd′ĭ-tē) *n.*

grav·i·met·ric (grăv′ə-mĕt′rĭk) also **grav·i·met·ri·cal** (-rĭ-kəl) ▸ *adj.* Of measurement by weight. **—grav′i·met′ri·cal·ly** *adv.*

grav·i·tate (grăv′ĭ-tāt′) ▸ *v.* **-tat·ed, -tat·ing. 1.** To move in response to the force of gravity. **2.** To be attracted. **—grav′i·tat′er** *n.*

grav·i·ta·tion (grăv′ĭ-tā′shən) ▸ *n.* **1a.** The natural phenomenon of attraction between massive bodies. **b.** The act of gravitating. **2.** A movement toward a source of attraction. **—grav′i·ta′tion·al** *adj.* **—grav′i·ta′tion·al·ly** *adv.* **—grav′i·ta′tive** *adj.*

grav·i·ton (grăv′ĭ-tŏn′) ▸ *n.* A massless particle hypothesized to be the quantum of gravitational interaction.

grav·i·ty (grăv′ĭ-tē) ▸ *n.* **1.** *Phys.* **a.** The force of attraction between any two massive bodies, which is directly proportional to the product of their masses and inversely proportional to the square of the distance between them, esp.

THESAURUS

grapnel *n.* —*See* ANCHOR.

grapple *v.* —*See* CONTEND, GRASP.

grapple *n.* —*See* HOLD (1).

grasp *v.* To take firmly with the hand and maintain a hold on ▸ clasp, clench, clutch, fist, grab, grapple, grip, seize. *Idiom:* grab ahold (*or* hold) of. [*Compare* HANDLE.] —*See also* ABSORB (2), KNOW (1), UNDERSTAND (1).

grasp *n.* **1.** Firm control or influence ▸ grip, handle, hold. [*Compare* CONTROL, DOMINANCE.] **2.** The ability or power to seize or attain ▸ capacity, compass, range, reach, scope. [*Compare* INFLUENCE.] **3.** Intellectual hold ▸ apprehension, comprehension, grip, hold, understanding. [*Compare* KNOWLEDGE.] —*See also* HOLD (1).

grasping *adj.* —*See* GREEDY.

graspingness *n.* —*See* GREED.

grate[1] *v.* —*See* SCRAPE (1), SHRED.

grate[2] *n.* An open space for holding a fire at the base of a chimney ▸ fireplace, hearth, ingle.

grateful *adj.* Showing or feeling gratitude ▸ appreciative, thankful. —*See also* OBLIGED (1), PLEASANT.

gratefulness *n.* —*See* APPRECIATION.

gratification *n.* The condition of being satisfied ▸ contentedness, contentment, fulfillment, satisfaction. [*Compare* HAPPINESS, SATIATION.]

gratified *adj.* Having achieved satisfaction, as of one's goal ▸ content, fulfilled, happy, satisfied.

gratify *v.* To comply with the wishes or ideas of another ▸ cater (to), humor, indulge. [*Compare* DEFER[2].] —*See also* DELIGHT (1), SATISFY (2).

gratifying *adj.* —*See* PLEASANT.

grating *adj.* —*See* HARSH.

gratis *adj.* Costing nothing ▸ free, complimentary, gratuitous. *Idioms:* as a freebie, for free, for nothing, on the house.

gratitude *n.* —*See* APPRECIATION.

gratuitous *adj.* Costing nothing ▸ complimentary, free, gratis. *Idioms:* as a freebie, for free, for nothing, on the house. —*See also* WANTON (2).

gratuity *n.* A material favor or gift, usually money, given in return for service ▸ baksheesh, cumshaw, largess, perquisite, tip. *Informal:* perk. [*Compare* BRIBE, REWARD.] —*See also* DONATION.

grave[1] *n.* A burial place or receptacle for human remains ▸ burial chamber, burial plot, catacomb, cinerarium, crypt, gravesite, mausoleum, ossuary, sepulcher, sepulture, tomb, vault.

grave[2] *adj.* **1.** Having great consequence or weight ▸ earnest, heavy, momentous, serious, severe, weighty. [*Compare* IMPORTANT.] **2.** Having or threatening severe negative consequences ▸ dire, grievous, serious, severe. [*Compare* DISASTROUS.] —*See also* DANGEROUS, FATEFUL (1), SERIOUS (1).

grave[3] *v.* —*See* ENGRAVE (1), ENGRAVE (2).

gravelly *adj.* —*See* COARSE (2), HOARSE.

graveness *n.* The condition of being grave and of involving serious consequences ▸ gravity, momentousness, seriousness, weightiness. —*See also* SERIOUSNESS (1).

gravid *adj.* —*See* PREGNANT (1).

gravitas *n.* —*See* SERIOUSNESS (1).

gravitate *v.* —*See* SINK (1).

gravitation *n.* —*See* ATTRACTION.

gravity *n.* The condition of being grave and of involving serious consequences ▸ graveness, gravity, heaviness, momentousness, seriousness, weightiness.

the gravitational force exerted by a celestial body such as the earth. **b.** Gravitation. **2.** Grave consequence; seriousness. **3.** Solemnity or dignity of manner.

gra·vure (grə-vyo͝or′) ▸ *n.* **1.** A method of printing with etched plates or cylinders. **2.** Photogravure.

gra·vy (grā′vē) ▸ *n., pl.* **-vies.** **1.** The juices that drip from cooking meat. **2.** A sauce made from these juices. **3.** *Slang* Money or profit gained easily.

gray also **grey** (grā) ▸ *n.* A neutral color between black and white. ▸ *adj.* **-er, -est.** **1.** Of the color gray. **2.** Dull or dark; gloomy. **3.** Having gray hair. **4.** Intermediate in character or position. **—gray′ish** *adj.* **—gray′ness** *n.*

gray·beard (grā′bîrd′) ▸ *n.* An old man.

gray matter ▸ *n.* **1.** The brownish-gray nerve tissue of the brain and spinal cord. **2.** *Informal* Brains; intellect.

gray whale ▸ *n.* A baleen whale of N Pacific waters having grayish-black coloring with white blotches.

gray wolf ▸ *n.* A large, tawny gray wolf of N North America and Eurasia.

graze[1] (grāz) ▸ *v.* **grazed, graz·ing.** **1.** To feed on growing grasses and herbage. **2.** *Informal* To eat frequent snacks. **—graz′er** *n.*

graze[2] (grāz) ▸ *v.* **grazed, graz·ing.** To touch or scrape lightly in passing. **—graze** *n.*

grease (grēs) ▸ *n.* **1.** Melted animal fat. **2.** A thick oil or viscous lubricant. ▸ *v.* (grēs, grēz) **greased, greas·ing.** **1.** To coat, smear, lubricate, or soil with grease. **2.** To facilitate the progress of, as with money or bribes. **—grease′less** *adj.*

grease·paint (grēs′pānt′) ▸ *n.* Theatrical makeup.

grease·wood (grēs′wo͝od′) ▸ *n.* A spiny shrub of W North America, having white stems and greenish flowers.

greas·y (grē′sē, -zē) ▸ *adj.* **-i·er, -i·est.** **1.** Coated or soiled with grease. **2.** Containing grease, esp. too much grease. **—greas′i·ly** *adv.* **—greas′i·ness** *n.*

great (grāt) ▸ *adj.* **-er, -est.** **1.** Very large in size, quantity, or number. **2.** Remarkable in magnitude or extent: *a great crisis.* **3.** Of outstanding importance: *a great work of art.* **4.** Powerful; influential. **5.** Eminent; distinguished: *a great leader.* **6.** *Informal* Very good: *great at algebra.* **7.** *Informal* First-rate: *had a great time.* **8.** Being one generation removed from the relative specified: *a great-granddaughter.* ▸ *n.* One that is great: *the greats of the opera world.* **—great′ly** *adv.* **—great′ness** *n.*

great ape ▸ *n.* Any of a family of apes including chimpanzees, gorillas, and orangutans.

Great Barrier Reef ▸ The world's largest coral reef, about 2,011 km (1,250 mi), off the NE coast of Australia.

Great Britain ▸ **1.** An island off the W coast of Europe comprising England, Scotland, and Wales. **2.** See **United Kingdom.**

great circle ▸ *n.* A circle described by the intersection of the surface of a sphere with a plane passing through its center.

great·coat (grāt′kōt′) ▸ *n.* A heavy overcoat.

Great Dane ▸ *n.* A large powerful dog having a short smooth coat and narrow head.

great·er (grā′tər) ▸ *adj.* Of or being a city considered together with its suburbs.

Greater Antilles ▸ An island group of the N West Indies including Cuba, Jamaica, Hispaniola, and Puerto Rico.

great horned owl ▸ *n.* A large North American owl having prominent ear tufts and brownish plumage with a white throat.

Great Lakes ▸ A group of five freshwater lakes of central North America between the US and Canada, including Lakes Superior, Huron, Erie, Ontario, and Michigan.

Great Plains ▸ A vast grassland region of central North America extending from the Canadian provinces of Alberta, Saskatchewan, and Manitoba S to TX.

Great Salt Lake ▸ A saline lake of NW UT.

great white shark ▸ *n.* A large shark of temperate and tropical waters that feeds on marine mammals.

grebe (grēb) ▸ *n.* Any of various diving birds having a pointed bill and lobed fleshy membranes along each toe.

Gre·cian (grē′shən) ▸ *adj.* Greek. ▸ *n.* A native or inhabitant of Greece.

Grec·o (grĕk′ō), **El** (1541–1614) ▸ Greek-born Spanish painter of religious works.

Grec·o-Ro·man (grĕk′ō-rō′mən, grē′kō-) ▸ *adj.* Relating to both Greece and Rome.

Greece (grēs) ▸ A country of SE Europe on the S Balkan Peninsula and including numerous islands in the Mediterranean, Aegean, and Ionian seas. Pop. 10,600,000.

greed (grēd) ▸ *n.* An excessive desire for more than one needs or deserves.

greed·y (grē′dē) ▸ *adj.* **-i·er, -i·est.** Wishing to possess more than one needs or deserves. **—greed′i·ly** *adv.* **—greed′i·ness** *n.*

Greek (grēk) ▸ *n.* **1.** The Indo-European language of the Greeks. **2.** A native or inhabitant of Greece. **3.** *Informal* Something unintelligible: *Quantum mechanics is Greek to me.* **—Greek** *adj.*

Greek Orthodox Church ▸ *n.* The state church of Greece, an autonomous part of the Eastern Orthodox Church.

green (grēn) ▸ *n.* **1a.** Any of a group of colors whose hue is that of growing grass. **b.** The hue of the visible spectrum lying between yellow and blue. **2. greens** Leafy plants or plant parts used as food or for decoration. **3.** A grassy lawn or plot: *a putting green.* ▸ *adj.* **-er, -est.** **1.** Of the color green. **2.** Covered with green growth or foliage. **3.** Made with leafy vegetables. **4.** Not mature or ripe. **5.** Inexperienced. ▸ *v.* To make or become green. **—green′ish** *adj.* **—green′ness** *n.*

green·back (grēn′băk′) ▸ *n.* A note of US currency.

green bean ▸ *n.* See **string bean.**

green card ▸ *n.* An official document issued by the US government to aliens, allowing them to work legally in the US.

green·er·y (grē′nə-rē) ▸ *n., pl.* **-ies.** Green foliage; verdure.

green-eyed (grēn′īd′) ▸ *adj.* Jealous.

green·horn (grēn′hôrn′) ▸ *n.* An inexperienced or immature person, esp. one who is easily deceived.

green·house (grēn′hous′) ▸ *n.* A structure, usu. of glass, in which temperature and humidity can be controlled for the cultivation or protection of plants.

greenhouse effect ▸ *n.* The phenomenon whereby the earth's atmosphere traps solar radiation, caused by gases such as carbon dioxide and methane that allow incoming sunlight to pass through but absorb heat radiated back from the earth's surface.

greenhouse gas ▸ *n.* An atmospheric gas that contributes to the greenhouse effect.

THESAURUS

[*Compare* SEVERITY.] —*See also* SERIOUSNESS (1).

gray *adj.* —*See* DULL (2).

gray matter *n.* *Informal:* The seat of the faculty of intelligence and reason ▸ brain, mind. [*Compare* IMAGINATION.] —*See also* INTELLIGENCE.

graze[1] *v.* —*See* BRUSH[1], GLANCE (1).

graze *n.* —*See* BRUSH[1].

graze[2] *v.* —*See* BROWSE (2).

grease *n.* —*See* BRIBE, OIL.

grease *v.* —*See* EASE (2), OIL.

greasy *adj.* —*See* FATTY.

great *adj.* At the upper end of a degree of measure ▸ elevated, high, large. [*Compare* EXALTED, EXTREME.] —*See also* BIG, DEEP (3), EXCELLENT, FAMOUS, GRAND, IMPORTANT, MARVELOUS.

greater *adj.* Being at a rank or level above another ▸ higher, senior, superior, upper. —*See also* BEST (2).

great-hearted *adj.* —*See* GENEROUS (1).

great-heartedness *n.* —*See* GENEROSITY.

greatly *adv.* —*See* VERY.

greatness *n.* —*See* GLORY, SIZE (2).

greed *n.* Excessive desire for more than one needs or deserves ▸ acquisitiveness, avarice, avariciousness, avidity, covetousness, cupidity, graspingness, hoggishness, rapacity. *Informal.* grabbiness. [*Compare* VORACITY.]

greedy *adj.* Having a strong urge to obtain or retain something, especially material wealth ▸ acquisitive, avaricious, avid, covetous, grasping, hungry. *Informal.* grabby. [*Compare* EGOTISTIC, STINGY.] —*See also* GLUTTONOUS, VORACIOUS.

green *n.* —*See* COMMON, MONEY (1).

green *adj.* —*See* INEXPERIENCED, SOUR, YOUNG.

green-eyed *adj.* Fearful of the loss of position or affection ▸ clinging, clutching, jealous, possessive. —*See also* ENVIOUS.

greenhorn *n.* —*See* BEGINNER.

Green·land (grēn′lənd, -lănd′) ▸ An island of Denmark in the N Atlantic off NE Canada. **—Green·land′ic** *adj.*
green light ▸ *n.* **1.** The green-colored light that signals traffic to proceed. **2.** *Informal* Permission to proceed.
green·sward (grēn′swôrd′) ▸ *n.* Ground that is green with grass; turf.
green tea ▸ *n.* Tea made from leaves that are not fermented before being dried.
green thumb ▸ *n.* An unusual ability to make plants grow well.
Green·wich (grĕn′ĭch) ▸ A borough of Greater London in SE England; on the prime meridian. Pop. 215,000.
Greenwich time ▸ *n.* See **universal time.**
greet (grēt) ▸ *v.* **1.** To welcome or salute in a friendly and respectful way. **2.** To receive with a specified reaction. **3.** To be perceived by: *A din greeted our ears.* **—greet′er** *n.*
greet·ing (grē′tĭng) ▸ *n.* A word or gesture of welcome or salutation.
gre·gar·i·ous (grĭ-gâr′ē-əs) ▸ *adj.* **1.** Seeking and enjoying the company of others; sociable. **2.** Tending to move in or form a group. **—gre·gar′i·ous·ly** *adv.* **—gre·gar′i·ous·ness** *n.*
Gre·go·ri·an calendar (grĭ-gôr′ē-ən) ▸ *n.* The calendar in use throughout most of the world, sponsored by Pope Gregory XIII in 1582.
Gregorian chant ▸ *n. Rom. Cath. Ch.* An unaccompanied, monophonic liturgical chant.
grem·lin (grĕm′lĭn) ▸ *n.* An imaginary gnomelike creature to whom mechanical problems are attributed.
Gre·na·da (grə-nā′də) ▸ A country in the Windward Is. of the West Indies comprising the island of **Grenada** and the S Grenadines. Pop. 89,200.
gre·nade (grə-nād′) ▸ *n.* A small bomb detonated by a fuse and thrown by hand or fired from a launcher.
gren·a·dier (grĕn′ə-dîr′) ▸ *n.* Formerly, a foot soldier equipped with grenades.
gren·a·dine (grĕn′ə-dēn′, grĕn′ə-dēn′) ▸ *n.* A thick sweet syrup made from pomegranates.
Gren·a·dines (grĕn′ə-dēnz′) ▸ An archipelago in the Windward Is. of the E Caribbean, divided between Grenada and the country of St. Vincent and the Grenadines.
grew (gro͞o) ▸ *v.* P.t. of **grow.**
grey (grā) ▸ *adj. & n.* Var. of **gray.**
grey·hound (grā′hound′) ▸ *n.* A slender, swift-running dog having a narrow head and long legs.
grid (grĭd) ▸ *n.* **1.** A framework of crisscrossed or parallel bars. **2.** A pattern of regularly spaced horizontal and vertical lines forming squares, as on a map, used as a reference for locating points. **3a.** An interconnected system for the distribution of electricity or electromagnetic signals over a wide area, esp. a network of high-tension cables and power stations. **b.** A conducting plate in a storage battery. **c.** A network or coil of fine wires located between the plate and the filament in an electron tube.
grid·dle (grĭd′l) ▸ *n.* A flat pan or metal surface used for frying.
grid·dle·cake (grĭd′l-kāk′) ▸ *n.* See **pancake.**
grid·i·ron (grĭd′ī′ərn) ▸ *n.* **1.** A football field. **2.** A flat metal grid or grate used for broiling.
grid·lock (grĭd′lŏk′) ▸ *n.* A traffic jam in which no vehicular movement is possible. **—grid′lock′** *v.* **—grid′locked′** *adj.*
grief (grēf) ▸ *n.* **1.** Deep mental anguish, as that arising from bereavement. **2.** A source of sorrow or anguish. **3.** Annoyance or frustration.
Grieg (grĕg, grĭg), **Edvard Hagerup** (1843–1907) ▸ Norwegian composer.
griev·ance (grē′vəns) ▸ *n.* **1.** A circumstance regarded as just cause for protest. **2.** A complaint based on such a circumstance.
grieve (grēv) ▸ *v.* **grieved, griev·ing. 1.** To cause sorrow to; distress. **2.** To feel or express grief.
griev·ous (grē′vəs) ▸ *adj.* **1.** Causing grief, pain, or anguish. **2.** Serious; grave. **—griev′ous·ly** *adv.* **—griev′ous·ness** *n.*
grif·fin also **grif·fon** or **gryph·on** (grĭf′ən) ▸ *n.* A fabulous beast with the head and wings of an eagle and the body of a lion.
grill (grĭl) ▸ *n.* **1.** A cooking surface of parallel metal bars. **2.** Food broiled on a grill. **3.** A restaurant where grilled foods are served. **4.** Var. of **grille.** ▸ *v.* **1.** To broil on a grill. **2.** *Informal* To question relentlessly; cross-examine.
grille also **grill** (grĭl) ▸ *n.* A usu. metal grating used as a screen or barrier, as in a window or on the front of an automobile.
grim (grĭm) ▸ *adj.* **grim·mer, grim·mest. 1.** Unrelenting; stern. **2.** Terrible in aspect; forbidding. **3.** Ghastly; sinister. **4.** Dismal; gloomy. **—grim′ly** *adv.* **—grim′ness** *n.*
grim·ace (grĭm′ĭs, grĭ-mās′) ▸ *n.* A contortion of the face expressive of pain, contempt, or disgust. **—grim′ace** *v.*
grime (grīm) ▸ *n.* Black dirt or soot clinging to or ingrained in a surface. **—grim′i·ness** *n.* **—grim′y** *adj.*
Grimm (grĭm), **Jakob Ludwig Karl** (1785–1863) and **Wilhelm Karl** (1786–1859) ▸ German philologists and folklorists.
grin (grĭn) ▸ *v.* **grinned, grin·ning.** To smile broadly, showing the teeth. **—grin** *n.* **—grin′ner** *n.*
grind (grīnd) ▸ *v.* **ground** (ground), **grind·ing. 1a.** To crush or pulverize by friction. **b.** To shape, sharpen, or refine with friction: *grind a lens.* **2a.** To rub together harshly; gnash: *grind the teeth.* **b.** To move with noisy friction: *grind to a halt.* **3.** To bear down on harshly; crush. **4.** To oppress or weaken gradually. **5.** To operate or produce by turning a crank. **6.** To produce mechanically or without inspiration: *grinding out novels.* **7.** *Informal* To devote oneself to study or work. ▸ *n.* **1.** The act of grinding. **2.** A specific degree

THESAURUS

green light *n.* —*See* PERMISSION.
greenness *n.* —*See* INEXPERIENCE, YOUTH (1).
greet *v.* **1.** To address in a friendly and respectful way ▸ hail, salute, welcome. **2.** To approach for the purpose of speech ▸ accost, hail, salute. [*Compare* ENCOUNTER, INTERRUPT, WELCOME.]
greeting *n.* An expression, in words or gestures, marking a meeting of persons ▸ hail, salutation, salute, welcome. *Informal:* hello.
greetings *interjection* —*See* HELLO.
gregarious *adj.* —*See* OUTGOING, SOCIAL.
griddle *v.* —*See* COOK.
gridlock *n.* —*See* STOP (2).
grief *n.* Mental anguish or pain caused by loss or despair ▸ anguish, heartache, heartbreak, sorrow, torment. —*See also* DISTRESS.
grievance *n.* —*See* COMPLAINT, OBJECTION.
grieve *v.* To feel, show, or express grief ▸ anguish, bemoan, bewail, lament, mourn, sorrow, suffer, ululate. [*Compare* CRY, REGRET.] —*See also* DISTRESS.
grievous *adj.* Having or threatening severe negative consequences ▸ dire, grave, serious, severe. [*Compare* DISASTROUS, FATEFUL.] —*See also* SORROWFUL.
grift *n.* —*See* CHEAT (1).
grifter *n.* —*See* CHEAT (2).
grigri *n.* —*See* CHARM.
grill *v.* —*See* ASK (1), COOK.
grim *adj.* —*See* BLEAK (1), CRUEL, FORBIDDING, GHASTLY (1), STUBBORN (1).
grimace *n.* A contorted facial expression showing pain, contempt, or disgust ▸ face, moue, pout. *Informal:* mug. [*Compare* FROWN, GLARE, SNEER.]
grimace *v.* To contort one's face to indicate pain, contempt, or disgust ▸ mouth, mug. *Idioms:* make a face, make faces. [*Compare* FROWN, GLARE, SNEER.]
grime *n.* —*See* FILTH.
griminess *n.* —*See* DIRTINESS.
grimness *n.* —*See* STUBBORNNESS.
grimy *adj.* —*See* DIRTY.
grin *v.* —*See* SMILE.
grin *n.* A facial expression marked by an upward curving of the lips ▸ simper, smile, smirk. [*Compare* SNEER.]
grind *v.* **1.** To rub together noisily ▸ crunch, gnash. **2.** To do tedious, difficult or menial work ▸ drudge, grub, plod, slave, slog, struggle. [*Compare* LABOR.] **3.** *Informal* To apply one's mind to the acquisition of knowledge, especially when pressed for time ▸ lucubrate, study. *Informal:* bone up, cram. *Idioms:* burn the midnight oil, hit the books. [*Compare* EXAMINE.] **4.** To treat arbitrarily or cruelly ▸ grind down, oppress, trample. [*Compare* ABUSE, ENSLAVE, SUPPRESS.] —*See also* CRUSH (2), ERODE, SHARPEN.
grind *n.* —*See* DRUDGE (2), LABOR, ROUTINE, TASK (2).

of pulverization, as of coffee beans. 3. *Informal* A laborious task, routine, or study. 4. *Informal* A student thought to work or study excessively. **—grind′ing·ly** *adv.*

grind·er (grīn′dər) ▸ *n.* 1. One that grinds, esp.: a. One who sharpens cutting edges. b. A mechanical device that grinds. 2. See **submarine** 2.

grind·stone (grīnd′stōn′) ▸ *n.* 1. A revolving stone disk used for grinding, polishing, or sharpening tools. 2. A millstone. **—*idiom:* put (one's) nose to the grindstone** *Informal* To work in earnest.

grip (grĭp) ▸ *n.* 1. A tight hold; firm grasp. 2. A manner of grasping and holding. 3. Mastery; command: *a good grip on the subject.* 4. A part designed to be grasped; handle. 5. A suitcase. 6. A stagehand or member of a film crew who helps move scenery or adjust lighting and props. ▸ *v.* **gripped, grip·ping.** 1. To secure and maintain a tight hold on. 2. To hold the interest or attention of. **—grip′per** *n.* **—grip′ping·ly** *adv.*

gripe (grīp) ▸ *v.* **griped, grip·ing.** 1. *Informal* To complain naggingly or petulantly; grumble. 2. To cause or have sharp pains in the bowels. 3. *Informal* To irritate; annoy: *Your meddling really gripes me.* ▸ *n.* 1. *Informal* A complaint. 2. **gripes** Sharp pains in the bowels. **—grip′er** *n.*

grippe also **grip** (grĭp) ▸ *n.* See **influenza.** **—grip′py** *adj.*

gris·ly (grĭz′lē) ▸ *adj.* **-li·er, -li·est.** Horrifying; gruesome: *a grisly murder.* **—gris′li·ness** *n.*

grist (grĭst) ▸ *n.* Grain to be ground or already ground. **—*idiom:* grist for (one's) mill** Something that can be used to advantage.

gris·tle (grĭs′əl) ▸ *n.* Cartilage, esp. in meat. **—gris′tly** *adj.*

grit (grĭt) ▸ *n.* 1. Tiny rough granules, as of sand or stone. 2. *Informal* Indomitable spirit. ▸ *v.* **grit·ted, grit·ting.** To clamp (the teeth) together. **—grit′ti·ly** *adv.* **—grit′ti·ness** *n.* **—grit′ty** *adj.*

grits (grĭts) ▸ *pl.n.* *(takes sing. or pl. v.)* 1. A coarse meal made of ground hominy. 2. A mush made from this meal.

griz·zled (grĭz′əld) ▸ *adj.* Grizzly.

griz·zly (grĭz′lē) ▸ *adj.* **-zli·er, -zli·est.** Grayish or flecked with gray. ▸ *n., pl.* **-zlies.** A grizzly bear.

grizzly bear ▸ *n.* The brown bear of NW North America.

groan (grōn) ▸ *v.* To voice a deep inarticulate sound, as of pain, grief, or displeasure. **—groan** *n.*

groats (grōts) ▸ *pl.n.* *(takes sing. or pl. v.)* Hulled, usu. crushed grain, esp. oats.

gro·cer (grō′sər) ▸ *n.* One that sells foodstuffs and household supplies.

gro·cer·y (grō′sə-rē) ▸ *n., pl.* **-ies.** 1. A store selling foodstuffs and household supplies. 2. **groceries** Goods sold by a grocer.

grog (grŏg) ▸ *n.* An alcoholic liquor, esp. rum diluted with water.

grog·gy (grŏg′ē) ▸ *adj.* **-gi·er, -gi·est.** Unsteady and dazed; shaky. **—grog′gi·ly** *adv.* **—grog′gi·ness** *n.*

groin (groin) ▸ *n.* 1. The crease where the thigh meets the trunk, with the area nearby. 2. *Archit.* The curved edge at the junction of two intersecting vaults.

grom·met (grŏm′ĭt) ▸ *n.* A reinforced eyelet, as in cloth or leather, through which a fastener may be passed.

groom (gro͞om, gro͝om) ▸ *n.* 1. A man or boy employed to take care of horses. 2. A bridegroom. ▸ *v.* 1. To make neat and trim. 2. To clean and brush (an animal). 3. To prepare, as for a specific position. **—groom′er** *n.*

groove (gro͞ov) ▸ *n.* 1. A long narrow furrow or channel. 2. *Slang* A settled routine. 3. *Slang* A pleasurable experience. ▸ *v.* **grooved, groov·ing.** 1. To cut a groove or grooves. 2. *Slang* To enjoy oneself.

groov·y (gro͞o′vē) ▸ *adj.* **-i·er, -i·est.** *Slang* Delightful; wonderful. **—groov′i·ness** *n.*

grope (grōp) ▸ *v.* **groped, grop·ing.** 1. To reach about uncertainly; feel one's way. 2. To search blindly or uncertainly: *grope for an answer.* ▸ *n.* The act of groping. **—grop′er** *n.* **—grop′ing·ly** *adv.*

gros·beak (grōs′bēk′) ▸ *n.* Any of various finches having a thick conical bill.

gross (grōs) ▸ *adj.* **-er, -est.** 1. Exclusive of deductions; total: *gross profits.* 2. Utter: *gross incompetence.* 3. Glaringly obvious; flagrant: *gross injustice.* 4a. Coarse; crude. b. Disgusting. 5. Overweight; corpulent. 6. Broad; general. ▸ *n.* 1. *pl.* **gross·es.** The entire body or amount, as of income. 2. *pl.* **gross.** A group of 144 items; 12 dozen. ▸ *v.* To earn as a total before deductions. **—*phrasal verb:* gross out** *Slang* To fill with disgust. **—gross′ly** *adv.* **—gross′ness** *n.*

gross national product ▸ *n.* The total market value of all the goods and services produced by a nation during a specified period.

grosz (grôsh) ▸ *n., pl.* **gro·szy** (grô′shē). See **currency** table in Appendix.

gro·tesque (grō-tĕsk′) ▸ *adj.* 1. Marked by ludicrous or incongruous distortion, as of appearance. 2. Outlandish or bizarre. **—gro·tesque′** *n.* **—gro·tesque′ly** *adv.* **—gro·tesque′ness** *n.* **—gro·tes′que·ry** *n.*

grot·to (grŏt′ō) ▸ *n., pl.* **-toes** or **-tos.** A cave or cavelike excavation.

grouch (grouch) ▸ *n.* 1. A habitually complaining or irritable person. 2. A complaint. ▸ *v.* To grumble or sulk. **—grouch′i·ly** *adv.* **—grouch′i·ness** *n.* **—grouch′y** *adj.*

ground[1] (ground) ▸ *n.* 1. The solid surface of the earth. 2. Soil; earth. 3. often **grounds** An area of land designated for a particular purpose. 4. **grounds** The land surrounding a building. 5. A position contested in or as if in battle. 6. A background. 7. often **grounds** The foundation or basis for an argument or action. 8. often **grounds** The underlying condition prompting an action; cause: *grounds for suspicion.* 9. **grounds** The sediment at the bottom of a liquid. 10. *Elect.* a.

THESAURUS

grip *v.* To compel the attention, interest, or imagination of ▸ arrest, attract, captivate, capture, catch up, engage, enthrall, fascinate, hold, interest, intrigue, mesmerize, rivet, spellbind, transfix. *Informal:* grab. *Slang:* turn on. *Idioms:* catch one's eye, make one's mouth water, tickle one's fancy. [*Compare* ABSORB, AMUSE, CHARM, POSSESS.] *See also* GRASP.

grip *n.* 1. Firm control or influence ▸ grasp, handle, hold. [*Compare* CONTROL, DOMINANCE, INFLUENCE.] 2. Intellectual hold ▸ apprehension, comprehension, grasp, hold, understanding. [*Compare* KNOWLEDGE.] *—See also* HOLD (1), SUITCASE.

gripe *v.* *—See* COMPLAIN.

gripe *n.* *—See* COMPLAINT.

griper *n.* *—See* GROUCH.

grisly *adj.* *—See* GHASTLY (1).

grit *n.* *—See* COURAGE.

gritty *adj.* *—See* BRAVE, COARSE (2).

grizzled *adj.* *—See* OLD (2).

grogginess *adj.* *—See* DIZZINESS.

groggy *adj.* *—See* DIZZY (1).

groom *v.* *—See* TIDY (2).

groove *n.* *—See* CUT (1), FURROW, ROUTINE.

groove on *v.* *Slang* To like or enjoy enthusiastically, often excessively ▸ adore, delight (in), dote on (or upon), love. *Slang:* eat up.

groovy *adj.* *—See* MARVELOUS.

grope *v.* To reach about or search blindly or uncertainly ▸ feel, fumble, grabble, poke, scrabble. [*Compare* SEEK.] *—See also* NECK.

gross *adj.* Conspicuously bad or offensive ▸ egregious, flagrant, glaring, rank. [*Compare* OFFENSIVE, OUTRAGEOUS, SHAMELESS.] *—See also* COARSE (1), COMPLETE (1), FAT (1), OBSCENE, UNPALATABLE.

gross *n.* *—See* WHOLE.

gross *v.* *—See* RETURN (3).

gross out *v.* *—See* DISGUST.

grossness *n.* The quality or state of being flagrant ▸ egregiousness, flagrancy, glaringness, rankness. [*Compare* IMPUDENCE, OUTRAGEOUSNESS.] *—See also* OBSCENITY (1).

grotesque *adj.* Resembling a freak ▸ freakish, freaky, monstrous. [*Compare* WEIRD.] *See also* ECCENTRIC, EXOTIC.

grotesque *n.* MONSTER.

grotto *n.* *—See* CAVE.

grouch *n.* A person who habitually complains or grumbles ▸ complainer, crab, faultfinder, growler, grumbler, grump, murmurer, mutterer, whiner. *Informal:* crank, griper, grouser. *Slang:* bellyacher, sorehead, sourpuss. [*Compare* KILLJOY.] *—See also* COMPLAINT.

grouch *v.* *—See* COMPLAIN.

grouchy *adj.* *—See* ILL-TEMPERED.

ground *n.* *—See* BASE[1] (2), BASIS (1), EARTH (1).

A large conducting body, such as the earth, used as an arbitrary zero of potential. **b.** A conducting object, such as a wire, connected to such a position of zero potential. ▸ *v.* **1.** To place on or cause to touch the ground. **2.** To provide a basis for; justify. **3.** To supply with basic information. **4a.** To prevent (an aircraft or pilot) from flying. **b.** *Informal* To restrict (someone) to a certain place as a punishment. **5.** *Elect.* To connect (an electric circuit) to a ground. **6.** To run (a vessel) aground. **7.** *Baseball* To hit (a ball) on the ground.
ground² (ground) ▸ *v.* P.t. and p.part. of **grind**.
ground·break·ing (ground′brā′kĭng) ▸ *n.* The act or ceremony of breaking ground to begin a construction project. ▸ *adj.* Highly original; new: *a groundbreaking technology.*
ground floor ▸ *n.* **1.** The floor of a building at or nearest ground level. **2.** *Informal* The beginning of a venture.
ground·hog (ground′hôg′, -hŏg′) ▸ *n.* See **woodchuck**.
ground·less (ground′lĭs) ▸ *adj.* Having no ground or foundation; unsubstantiated. **—ground′less·ly** *adv.*
ground rule ▸ *n.* **1.** *Sports* A rule governing the playing of a game on a particular field, course, or court. **2.** A basic rule.
ground squirrel ▸ *n.* Any of several burrowing or terrestrial squirrels resembling the chipmunk.
ground·swell (ground′swĕl′) ▸ *n.* **1.** A broad gathering of force, as of public opinion. **2.** A deep swell of the ocean.
ground water also **ground·wa·ter** (ground′wô′tər, -wŏt′ər) ▸ *n.* Subterranean water that supplies wells and springs.
ground·work (ground′wûrk′) ▸ *n.* A foundation; basis.
ground zero ▸ *n.* The point of detonation of a nuclear weapon.
group (gro͞op) ▸ *n.* A number of persons or objects gathered, located, or classified together. ▸ *v.* To place in or form a group.
grou·per (gro͞o′pər) ▸ *n., pl.* **-er** or **-pers**. Any of various large food and game fishes which inhabit warm seas.
group·ie (gro͞o′pē) ▸ *n. Slang* A fan, esp. a young woman, who follows a rock group around on tours.
grouse¹ (grous) ▸ *n., pl.* **grouse** or **grous·es**. A plump chickenlike game bird having mottled brown or grayish plumage.
grouse² (grous) ▸ *v.* **groused, grous·ing**. *Informal* To complain. **—grouse** *n.* **—grous′er** *n.*
grout (grout) ▸ *n.* A thin mortar used to fill cracks and crevices in masonry. ▸ *v.* To fill or finish with grout. **—grout′er** *n.*
grove (grōv) ▸ *n.* A small stand of trees that lacks undergrowth.
grov·el (grŏv′əl, grŭv′-) ▸ *v.* **-eled, -el·ing** also **-elled, -el·ling**. To behave in a servile manner; cringe. **—grov′el·er** *n.* **—grov′el·ing·ly** *adv.*
grow (grō) ▸ *v.* **grew** (gro͞o), **grown** (grōn), **grow·ing**. **1a.** To increase or cause to increase in size by a natural process. **b.** To cultivate; raise: *grow vegetables.* **2.** To expand or intensify. **3.** To develop and reach maturity. **4.** To originate; stem: *love that grew from friendship.* **5.** To become: *grow angry; grow closer.* ***—phrasal verbs:*** **grow on** To become more pleasurable or acceptable to: *a way of singing that grows on you.* **grow up** To become an adult. **—grow′er** *n.*
growl (groul) ▸ *n.* A low, guttural, menacing sound, as of a dog. **—growl** *v.* **—growl′er** *n.* **—growl′y** *adj.*
grown (grōn) ▸ *v.* P.part. of **grow**. ▸ *adj.* Adult; mature.
grown·up also **grown-up** (grōn′ŭp′) ▸ *n.* An adult.
grown-up (grōn′ŭp′) ▸ *adj.* Of or intended for adults; mature.
growth (grōth) ▸ *n.* **1.** The process of growing or developing. **2.** Evolution. **3.** An increase, as in size or number. **4.** Something that has grown: *a new growth of grass.* **5.** *Pathol.* An abnormal mass of tissue in or on a living organism.
growth ring ▸ *n.* A growth layer in secondary xylem seen in a cross section.
Groz·ny (grôz′nē) ▸ The capital of Chechnya in SW Russia. Pop. 223,000.
grub (grŭb) ▸ *v.* **grubbed, grub·bing**. **1.** To dig up by or as if by the roots. **2.** To clear of roots and stumps. **3a.** To search laboriously; rummage. **b.** To toil arduously; drudge. **4.** *Slang* To obtain by begging: *grub a cigarette.* ▸ *n.* **1.** The thick wormlike larva of certain insects. **2.** *Slang* Food. **—grub′ber** *n.*
grub·by (grŭb′ē) ▸ *adj.* **-bi·er, -bi·est**. Dirty; grimy. **—grub′bi·ly** *adv.* **—grub′bi·ness** *n.*
grub·stake (grŭb′stāk′) ▸ *n.* Supplies or funds advanced to a mining prospector or a person starting a business in return for a share of the profits. **—grub′stake′** *v.*
grudge (grŭj) ▸ *v.* **grudged, grudg·ing**. To be reluctant to give or admit. ▸ *n.* A feeling of resentment. **—grudg′er** *n.* **—grudg′ing·ly** *adv.*
gru·el (gro͞o′əl) ▸ *n.* A thin watery porridge.
gru·el·ing also **gru·el·ling** (gro͞o′ə-lĭng, gro͞o′lĭng) ▸ *adj.* Physically or mentally demanding. **—gru′el·ing·ly** *adv.*
grue·some (gro͞o′səm) ▸ *adj.* Causing horror and repugnance; frightful and shocking. **—grue′some·ly** *adv.* **—grue′some·ness** *n.*
gruff (grŭf) ▸ *adj.* **-er, -est**. **1.** Brief and unfriendly: *a gruff reply.* **2.** Hoarse; harsh. **—gruff′ly** *adv.* **—gruff′ness** *n.*
grum·ble (grŭm′bəl) ▸ *v.* **-bled, -bling**. To mutter discontentedly. **—grum′ble** *n.* **—grum′bler** *n.* **—grum′bly** *adj.*
grump (grŭmp) ▸ *n.* **1.** A cranky, complaining person. **2.** often **grumps** A fit of ill temper. **—grump** *v.* **—grump′i·ly** *adv.* **—grump′i·ness** *n.* **—grump′y** *adj.*
grunge (grŭnj) ▸ *n. Slang* **1.** Filth; dirt. **2.** Rock music incorporating punk rock and heavy metal styles, often having lyrics exhibiting nihilism, dissatisfaction, or apathy.
grun·gy (grŭn′jē) ▸ *adj.* **-gi·er, -gi·est**. *Slang* In a dirty or run-down condition.
grun·ion (grŭn′yən) ▸ *n.* A small fish of California coastal waters that spawns inshore at night.
grunt (grŭnt) ▸ *v.* To utter (with) a deep guttural sound, as

THESAURUS

ground *v.* —*See* BASE¹, DROP (3).
groundless *adj.* —*See* BASELESS.
groundlessly *adv.* Without basis or foundation in fact ▸ baselessly, unfoundedly, unwarrantedly.
grounds *n.* —*See* BASIS (1), CAUSE (2), LAND, REASON (1).
groundwork *n.* —*See* BASE¹ (2), BASIS (1).
group *n.* A number of individuals making up or considered a unit ▸ array, band, batch, bevy, body, bunch, bundle, clump, cluster, clutch, huddle, collection, knot, lot, party, set. [*Compare* ACCUMULATION, CROWD, SYSTEM.] —*See also* ASSEMBLY, CIRCLE (3), CLASS (1), COMPLEX (1).
group *v.* —*See* ASSEMBLE, BAND², CLASSIFY.
group *adj.* —*See* COOPERATIVE.
groupie *n.* —*See* FAN².
grouping *n.* —*See* ARRANGEMENT (1).
grouse *v.* —*See* COMPLAIN.
grouse *n.* —*See* COMPLAINT.
grouser *n.* —*See* GROUCH.
grovel *v.* —*See* FAWN.
groveler *n.* —*See* SYCOPHANT.
grow *v.* To raise crops or animals ▸ breed, cultivate, farm, garden, propagate, raise, tend, ranch. [*Compare* NURTURE, PLANT, TILL.] —*See also* BECOME (1), DEVELOP (1), INCREASE, MATURE.
growl *v.* —*See* RUMBLE (1), SNAP (3).
growler *n.* —*See* GROUCH.
grown or **grown-up** *adj.* —*See* MATURE.
growth *n.* —*See* BUILDUP (2), BUMP (1), DEVELOPMENT, INCREASE (1).
grub *v.* —*See* DIG, GRIND (2).
grub *n.* —*See* DRUDGE (2), FOOD.
grubbiness *n.* —*See* DIRTINESS.
grubby *adj.* —*See* DIRTY.
grubstake *n.* —*See* CAPITAL (1).
grubstake *v.* —*See* FINANCE.
grudge *v.* To feel envy toward or for ▸ begrudge, covet, envy.
grudging *adj.* —*See* ENVIOUS.
grueling *adj.* —*See* BURDENSOME.
gruesome *adj.* —*See* GHASTLY (1).
gruff *adj.* —*See* ABRUPT (1), HOARSE.
grumble *v.* —*See* COMPLAIN, RUMBLE (1).
grumble *n.* —*See* COMPLAINT.
grumbler *n.* —*See* GROUCH.
grump *n. Informal* An expression of ill-tempered dissatisfaction or a circumstance that is regarded as a cause for such expression ▸ complaint, grievance. *Informal:* gripe. *Slang:* beef, kick. *Idiom:* bone to pick. —*See also* GROUCH.
grump *v.* —*See* COMPLAIN.
grumpy *adj.* —*See* ILL-TEMPERED.
grunge *n.* —*See* FILTH.
grungy *adj.* —*See* DIRTY.
grunt *v.* —*See* COMPLAIN.

a hog does. ▸ *n.* **1.** A deep guttural sound. **2.** Any of various tropical fishes that produce grunting sounds. **3.** *Slang* An infantryman in the US military. **4.** *Slang* A menial; drudge. **—grunt′er** *n.*

gryph·on (grĭf′ən) ▸ *n.* Var. of **griffin.**

GU ▸ *abbr.* Guam

gua·ca·mo·le (gwä′kə-mō′lē) ▸ *n.* A thick paste of mashed and seasoned avocado, served as a dip.

Gua·dal·ca·nal (gwŏd′l-kə-năl′) ▸ A volcanic island of the SE Solomon group in the W Pacific.

Gua·de·loupe (gwŏd′l-o͞op′, gwŏd′l-o͞op′) ▸ An overseas department of France in the Leeward Is. of the West Indies. Cap. Basse-Terre. Pop. 436,000.

Guam (gwäm) ▸ An unincorp. territory of the US, the largest of the Mariana Is. in the W Pacific. Cap. Agana. Pop. 161,000. **—Gua·ma′ni·an** (gwä-mā′nē-ən) *adj. & n.*

Guang·zhou (gwäng′jō′) also **Kwang·chow** (kwăng′chō′). Formerly **Canton** ▸ A city of S China on a delta near the South China Sea. Pop. 3,920,000.

gua·nine (gwä′nēn′) ▸ *n.* A purine base, $C_5H_5ON_5$, that is an essential constituent of both RNA and DNA.

gua·no (gwä′nō) ▸ *n., pl.* **-nos.** The dung of sea birds or bats, used as fertilizer.

Guan·tá·na·mo (gwän-tä′nə-mō′) ▸ A city of SE Cuba N of **Guantánamo Bay,** an inlet of the Caribbean Sea. Pop. 274,000.

guar (gwär) ▸ *n.* An annual plant cultivated in semiarid regions as a forage crop and for its seeds.

gua·ra·ni (gwä′rə-nē′) ▸ *n., pl.* **gua·ra·ni** or **gua·ra·nis.** See **currency** table in Appendix.

Guarani ▸ *n., pl.* **-ni** or **-nis. 1.** A member of a South American Indian people of Paraguay, N Argentina, and S Brazil. **2.** The language of the Guarani.

guar·an·tee (găr′ən-tē′) ▸ *n.* **1.** Something assuring a particular outcome or condition. **2.** An assurance, esp. in writing, attesting to the quality or durability of a product or service. **3.** A guaranty. **4.** A guarantor. ▸ *v.* **-teed, -tee·ing. 1.** To assume responsibility for the debt or default of. **2.** To assume responsibility for the quality or performance of. **3.** To undertake to accomplish. **4.** To make certain. **5.** To furnish security for. **6.** To declare with conviction.

guar·an·tor (găr′ən-tôr′, găr′ən-tər) ▸ *n.* One that gives a promise, assurance, or pledge.

guar·an·ty (găr′ən-tē) ▸ *n., pl.* **-ties. 1.** An agreement by which one person assumes the responsibility of assuring payment of another's debts or obligations. **2a.** Something given as security for the execution or completion of something else. **b.** The act of providing such security. **3.** A guarantor.

guard (gärd) ▸ *v.* **1.** To protect from harm; watch over. **2.** To watch over to prevent escape. **3.** *Sports* To keep (an opposing player) from scoring. **4.** To keep watch at. ▸ *n.* **1.** One who protects or keeps watch. **2.** One who supervises prisoners. **3.** A group of people serving as an escort on ceremonial occasions. **4.** *Football* One of the two offensive linemen on either side of the center. **5.** *Basketball* Either of the two players positioned in the backcourt. **6.** A device or attachment that prevents injury, damage, or loss. **—*idiom:* on (or off) (one's) guard** Being (or not being) alert and watchful. **—guard′er** *n.*

guard·ed (gär′dĭd) ▸ *adj.* **1.** Protected; supervised. **2.** Cautious; restrained. **—guard′ed·ly** *adv.* **—guard′ed·ness** *n.*

guard·house (gärd′hous′) ▸ *n.* **1.** A building that accommodates a military guard. **2.** A military jail.

guard·i·an (gär′dē-ən) ▸ *n.* **1.** One that guards or protects. **2.** One legally responsible for the care and management of the person or property of an incompetent or minor. **—guard′i·an·ship′** *n.*

guards·man (gärdz′mən) ▸ *n.* A member of the National Guard.

guar gum ▸ *n.* A paste made from the seeds of the guar, used as an ingredient in foods and pharmaceuticals.

Gua·te·ma·la (gwä′tə-mä′lə) ▸ A country of N Central America. Pop. 13,300,000.

gua·va (gwä′və) ▸ *n.* The yellow-skinned fruit of a tropical American tree, used for jellies and preserves.

gu·ber·na·to·ri·al (go͞o′bər-nə-tôr′ē-əl, gyo͞o′-) ▸ *adj.* Of or relating to a governor.

Guern·sey[1] (gûrn′zē) ▸ An island of S Great Britain, one of the Channel Is.

Guern·sey[2] (gûrn′zē) ▸ *n., pl.* **-seys.** Any of a breed of brown and white dairy cattle orig. developed on the island of Guernsey.

guer·ril·la or **gue·ril·la** (gə-rĭl′ə) ▸ *n.* A member of an irregular military force operating in small bands in occupied territory to harass and undermine the enemy.

guess (gĕs) ▸ *v.* **1.** To predict (a result or event) without sufficient information. **2.** To estimate correctly. **3.** To suppose; think: *I guess he was wrong.* ▸ *n.* **1.** An act of guessing. **2.** A conjecture arrived at by guessing. **—guess′er** *n.*

guess·work (gĕs′wûrk′) ▸ *n.* The process or result of making guesses.

guest (gĕst) ▸ *n.* **1.** One who receives hospitality at the home or table of another. **2.** One who pays for meals or accommodations at a restaurant or hotel. **3.** A visiting performer or contestant, as on a television program.

guest worker ▸ *n.* A foreigner permitted to work in a country on a temporary basis.

Gue·va·ra (gə-vär′ə), **Ernesto.** "Che" (1928–67) ▸ Argentine-born Cuban revolutionary leader.

guff (gŭf) ▸ *n.* *Slang* **1.** Nonsense; baloney. **2.** Back talk.

guf·faw (gə-fô′) ▸ *n.* A boisterous burst of laughter. **—guf·faw′** *v.*

GUI (go͞o′ē) ▸ *n.* *Comp. Sci.* An interface in which a pointing device, such as a mouse, is used to manipulate graphical images on a monitor.

THESAURUS

grunt *n.* —*See* COMPLAINT, DRUDGE (1), SOLDIER (2).

guarantee *n.* An assumption of responsibility, as one given by a manufacturer, for the quality, worth, or durability of a product ▸ certification, guaranty, surety, warrant, warranty. —*See also* PROMISE (1).

guarantee *v.* **1.** To assume responsibility for the quality, worth, or durability of ▸ certify, guaranty, stand behind, warrant. [*Compare* CONFIRM.] **2.** To render certain ▸ assure, ensure, insure, secure, warrant. *Informal:* cinch, clinch.

guarantor *n.* —*See* SPONSOR.

guaranty *n.* An assumption of responsibility, as one given by a manufacturer, for the quality, worth, or durability of a product ▸ certification, guarantee, surety, warrant, warranty. —*See also* PAWN[1], PROMISE (1), SPONSOR.

guaranty *v.* —*See* GUARANTEE (1).

guard *n.* One assigned to provide protection or keep watch over some one or something ▸ guardian, lookout, monitor, picket, protection, protector, sentinel, sentry, ward, watch, watchdog, watchman. [*Compare* WATCHER.] —*See also* DEFENSE.

guard *v.* —*See* DEFEND (1).

guarded *adj.* —*See* CONSERVATIVE (2), RESERVED.

guardian *n.* One who is legally responsible for the care and management of the person or property of an incompetent or a minor ▸ caretaker, conservator, custodian, keeper. [*Compare* REPRESENTATIVE.] —*See also* GUARD.

guardianship *n.* —*See* CARE (2).

gubernatorial *adj.* —*See* GOVERNMENTAL.

gudgeon *n.* —*See* DUPE.

guerdon *n.* —*See* DUE, REWARD.

guerdon *v.* To bestow a reward on ▸ award, honor, reward. [*Compare* CONFER.]

guess *v.* To predict or assume without sufficient information ▸ conjecture, fancy, imagine, infer, speculate, suppose, surmise, suspect, think. [*Compare* BELIEVE, INFER, SUPPOSE.]

guess *n.* A judgment, estimate, or opinion arrived at by guessing ▸ conjecture, guesswork, speculation, supposition, surmise. *Informal:* guesstimate. *Idiom:* shot in the dark. [*Compare* ASSUMPTION, BELIEF, ESTIMATE.]

guesstimate *v.* —*See* ESTIMATE (2).

guesstimate *n.* —*See* ESTIMATE (2).

guesswork *n.* —*See* GUESS.

guest *n.* A person or persons visiting one ▸ caller, guest, visitant, visitor.

guffaw *n.* —*See* LAUGH.

Gui·an·a (gē-ăn′ə, -ä′nə, gī-) ▸ A region of NE South America including SE Venezuela, part of N Brazil, and French Guiana, Suriname, and Guyana.

guid·ance (gīd′ns) ▸ *n.* **1.** The act or process of guiding. **2.** Counseling; advice. **3.** Any of various processes for guiding the path of a vehicle, esp. a missile.

guide (gīd) ▸ *n.* **1.** One who shows the way by leading, directing, or advising, esp. a person employed to conduct others, as on a tour or expedition. **2.** Something, such as a pamphlet, that offers basic information or instruction. **3.** Something that serves to direct. **4.** A device, such as a ruler, that serves as an indicator or regulates motion. ▸ *v.* **guid·ed, guid·ing. 1.** To serve as a guide for; conduct. **2.** To direct the course of; steer. **3.** To exert control or influence over. **—guid′er** *n.*

guide·book (gīd′bo͝ok′) ▸ *n.* A handbook of information, esp. for travelers or tourists.

guid·ed missile (gī′dĭd) ▸ *n.* A self-propelled missile that can be guided while in flight.

guide dog ▸ *n.* A dog trained to guide a visually impaired or sightless person.

guide·line (gīd′līn′) ▸ *n.* A statement or rule of policy or procedure.

guide·post (gīd′pōst′) ▸ *n.* A post with a sign giving directions for travelers.

gui·don (gī′dŏn′, gīd′n) ▸ *n.* A small flag carried by a military unit.

guild (gĭld) ▸ *n.* An association of persons of the same trade, formed to protect common interests and maintain standards.

guil·der (gĭl′dər) ▸ *n.* The primary unit of currency in the Netherlands before the adoption of the euro.

guile (gīl) ▸ *n.* Treacherous cunning; skillful deceit. **—guile′ful** *adj.* **—guile′ful·ly** *adv.* **—guile′less** *adj.* **—guile′less·ly** *adv.* **—guile′less·ness** *n.*

guil·lo·tine (gĭl′ə-tēn′, gē′ə-) ▸ *n.* A device consisting of a heavy blade held aloft between upright guides and dropped to behead the victim below. ▸ *v.* **-tined, -tin·ing.** To behead with a guillotine.

guilt (gĭlt) ▸ *n.* **1.** The fact of being responsible for the commission of an offense. **2.** *Law* Culpability for a crime that carries a legal penalty. **3a.** Remorseful awareness of having done something wrong. **b.** Self-reproach, as for inadequacy. **—guilt′less** *adj.* **—guilt′less·ly** *adv.*

guilt·y (gĭl′tē) ▸ *adj.* **-i·er, -i·est. 1.** Responsible for a crime or wrongdoing. **2.** Suffering from or prompted by a sense of guilt. **—guilt′i·ly** *adv.* **—guilt′i·ness** *n.*

guin·ea (gĭn′ē) ▸ *n.* A former English gold coin worth one pound and one shilling.

Guinea ▸ A country of W Africa on the Atlantic. Pop. 7,780,000. **—Guin′e·an** *adj.* & *n.*

Guinea, Gulf of ▸ A broad inlet of the Atlantic formed by the great bend in the W-central coast of Africa.

Guin·ea-Bis·sau (gĭn′ē-bĭ-sou′) ▸ A country of W Africa on the Atlantic. Pop. 1,350,000.

guinea fowl ▸ *n.* A domesticated pheasantlike African bird having blackish plumage that is flecked with small white spots.

guinea pig ▸ *n.* **1.** A small, short-eared rodent having variously colored hair and no visible tail, often kept as pets or used as experimental animals. **2.** *Informal* A person who is used for experimentation or research, often unknowingly.

Guin·e·vere (gwĭn′ə-vîr′) also **Guen·e·vere** (gwĕn′-) ▸ *n.* The wife of King Arthur and lover of Lancelot in Arthurian legend.

guise (gīz) ▸ *n.* **1.** Outward appearance; aspect. **2.** False appearance. **3.** Mode of dress.

gui·tar (gĭ-tär′) ▸ *n.* A musical instrument having a large flat-backed sound box, a long fretted neck, and usu. six strings. **—gui·tar′ist** *n.*

gu·lag also **Gu·lag** (go͞o′läg) ▸ *n.* A network of forced labor camps in the former Soviet Union, esp. for political dissidents.

gulch (gŭlch) ▸ *n.* A small ravine.

gulf (gŭlf) ▸ *n.* **1.** A large area of a sea or ocean partially enclosed by land. **2.** A deep, wide chasm; abyss. **3.** A wide gap, as in understanding.

Gulf States ▸ **1.** The countries bordering the Persian Gulf in SW Asia. **2.** The states of the S US with coastlines on the Gulf of Mexico.

Gulf Stream ▸ A generally N-flowing warm ocean current of the N Atlantic off E North America.

gulf·weed (gŭlf′wēd′) ▸ *n.* A brownish, tropical Atlantic seaweed often forming dense floating masses.

gull[1] (gŭl) ▸ *n.* Any of various chiefly coastal water birds having long wings, webbed feet, and usu. gray and white plumage.

gull[2] (gŭl) ▸ *n.* A person who is easily tricked; dupe. ▸ *v.* To deceive or cheat.

Gul·lah (gŭl′ə) ▸ *n.* **1.** One of a group of people of African ancestry inhabiting coastal areas of South Carolina, Georgia, and N Florida. **2.** The English-based creole spoken by the Gullahs.

gul·let (gŭl′ĭt) ▸ *n.* **1.** The esophagus. **2.** The throat.

gul·li·ble (gŭl′ə-bəl) ▸ *adj.* Easily deceived or duped. **—gul′li·bil′i·ty** *n.* **—gul′li·bly** *adv.*

gul·ly (gŭl′ē) ▸ *n., pl.* **-lies.** A deep ditch cut in the earth by running water.

gulp (gŭlp) ▸ *v.* **1.** To swallow greedily or rapidly in large amounts. **2.** To swallow air audibly, as in nervousness. ▸ *n.* **1.** The act of gulping. **2.** A large mouthful.

gum[1] (gŭm) ▸ *n.* **1.** Any of various viscous plant substances that dry into water-soluble, noncrystalline, brittle solids. **2.** A sticky or adhesive substance. **3.** Any of various trees yielding gum. **4.** Chewing gum. ▸ *v.* **gummed, gum·ming. 1.** To cover, seal, or fix in place with gum. **2.** To become sticky or clogged. ***—phrasal verb:* gum up** To ruin or bungle. **—gum′mi·ness** *n.* **—gum′my** *adj.*

gum[2] (gŭm) ▸ *n.* The firm connective tissue that surrounds the bases of the teeth. ▸ *v.* **gummed, gum·ming.** To chew (food) with toothless gums.

gum arabic ▸ *n.* A gum that is exuded by various African trees, used as a thickener and in pills, candies, and mucilage.

gum·bo (gŭm′bō) ▸ *n., pl.* **-bos. 1a.** See **okra** 1. **b.** *Regional* See **okra** 2. **2.** A soup or stew thickened with okra pods.

THESAURUS

guffaw *v.* —*See* LAUGH.

guidance *n.* —*See* ADVICE, MANAGEMENT.

guide *n.* Something or someone that shows the way ▸ cicerone, conductor, director, docent, escort, lead, leader, pilot, shepherd, usher. —*See also* ADVISER.

guide *v.* To show the way to ▸ conduct, direct, escort, lead, marshal, pilot, route, shepherd, show, steer, usher. —*See also* ADVISE, GOVERN, MANEUVER (1).

guideline *n.* —*See* RULE.

guild *n.* —*See* UNION (1).

guile *n.* —*See* ART, DECEIT.

guileful *adj.* —*See* ARTFUL, UNDERHAND.

guileless *adj.* —*See* ARTLESS.

guilt *n.* —*See* BLAME, PENITENCE.

guiltless *adj.* —*See* INNOCENT (2).

guilty *adj.* —*See* BLAMEWORTHY.

guise *n.* —*See* APPEARANCE (1), DISGUISE, DRESS (2), FAÇADE (2).

gulf *n.* A body of water partly enclosed by land but having a wide outlet to the sea ▸ bight, gulf, sound. [*Compare* CHANNEL, HARBOR, INLET.] —*See also* DEEP, GAP (1).

gull *n.* —*See* DUPE.

gull *v.* —*See* CHEAT (1).

gullible *adj.* Easily imposed on or tricked ▸ credulous, dupable, easy, exploitable, naive, simple, susceptible, susceptive, trusting. [*Compare* ARTLESS.]

gulp *v.* To swallow food or drink greedily or rapidly in large amounts ▸ bolt, englut, engorge, glut, gobble, gorge, guzzle, ingurgitate, stuff oneself, swill. *Informal:* down, pig out, wolf (down). ***Idioms:*** eat like a pig (*or* hog), feed (*or* stuff) one's face, make a pig (*or* hog) of oneself. [*Compare* EAT, SWALLOW.] —*See also* DRINK (1), PANT.

gulp *n.* An act of swallowing ▸ ingestion, swallow, swig.

gummy *adj.* —*See* STICKY (1).

gum·drop (gŭm′drŏp′) ▸ *n.* A small candy made of sweetened gum arabic or gelatin.

gump·tion (gŭmp′shən) ▸ *n. Informal* Boldness of enterprise; initiative.

gum·shoe (gŭm′sho͞o′) ▸ *n.* **1.** A rubber overshoe. **2.** *Slang* A detective.

gun (gŭn) ▸ *n.* **1.** A weapon consisting of a metal tube from which a projectile is fired. **2.** A portable firearm. **3.** A device that discharges something under pressure or at great speed: *a grease gun.* ▸ *v.* **gunned, gun·ning. 1.** To shoot (a person): *gun down a robber.* **2.** To open the throttle of: *gunned the engine.* **—*phrasal verb:* gun for** To seek to overcome, ruin, or obtain. **—*idiom:* under the gun** Under great pressure or under threat.

gun·boat (gŭn′bōt′) ▸ *n.* A small armed vessel.

gun·cot·ton (gŭn′kŏt′n) ▸ *n.* See **nitrocellulose.**

gun·fight (gŭn′fīt′) ▸ *n.* A duel or battle with firearms. **—gun′fight′er** *n.*

gun·fire (gŭn′fīr′) ▸ *n.* The firing of guns.

gung ho (gŭng′ hō′) ▸ *adj. Slang* Extremely enthusiastic and dedicated.

gun·lock (gŭn′lŏk′) ▸ *n.* A device for igniting the charge of a firearm.

gun·man (gŭn′mən) ▸ *n.* A man, esp. a criminal, armed with a gun.

gun·met·al (gŭn′mĕt′l) ▸ *n.* **1.** An alloy of copper with tin. **2.** Metal used for guns. **3.** A dark gray.

gun·nel (gŭn′əl) ▸ *n.* **Var.** of gunwale.

gun·ner (gŭn′ər) ▸ *n.* A member of the armed forces who operates a gun.

gun·ner·y (gŭn′ə-rē) ▸ *n.* The science of constructing and operating guns.

gunnery sergeant ▸ *n.* A rank in the US Marine Corps above staff sergeant.

gun·ny (gŭn′ē) ▸ *n.* A coarse heavy fabric made of jute or hemp.

gun·ny·sack (gŭn′ē-săk′) ▸ *n.* A sack made of burlap or gunny.

gun·play (gŭn′plā′) ▸ *n.* An exchange of gunfire.

gun·pow·der (gŭn′pou′dər) ▸ *n.* An explosive powder used to propel projectiles from guns.

gun·shot (gŭn′shŏt′) ▸ *n.* **1.** The shooting of a gun. **2.** The range of a gun: *within gunshot.* **3.** Shot that is fired from a gun.

gun-shy (gŭn′shī′) ▸ *adj.* **1.** Afraid of loud noise, esp. gunfire. **2.** Extremely wary.

gun·smith (gŭn′smĭth′) ▸ *n.* One who makes or repairs firearms.

gun·wale also **gun·nel** (gŭn′əl) ▸ *n.* The upper edge of the side of a ship or boat.

gup·py (gŭp′ē) ▸ *n., pl.* **-pies.** A small, brightly colored freshwater fish popular in home aquariums.

gur·gle (gûr′gəl) ▸ *v.* **-gled, -gling. 1.** To flow in a broken, irregular current with a bubbling sound. **2.** To make a sound similar to this. **—gur′gle** *n.* **—gur′gling·ly** *adv.*

gur·ney (gûr′nē) ▸ *n., pl.* **-neys.** A metal stretcher with wheeled legs, used for transporting patients.

gu·ru (go͝or′o͞o, go͞o-ro͞o′) ▸ *n., pl.* **-rus. 1.** *Hinduism* A personal spiritual teacher. **2.** A revered teacher or mentor. **3.** A recognized leader: *the guru of high finance.*

gush (gŭsh) ▸ *v.* **1.** To flow forth suddenly in great volume. **2.** To make an excessive display of sentiment or enthusiasm. ▸ *n.* A copious outflow. **—gush′i·ly** *adv.* **—gush′i·ness** *n.* **—gush′y** *adj.*

gush·er (gŭsh′ər) ▸ *n.* One that gushes, esp. a gas well or oil well.

gus·set (gŭs′ĭt) ▸ *n.* A triangular insert for added strength or expansion in a garment.

gus·sy (gŭs′ē) ▸ *v.* **-sied, -sy·ing.** *Slang* To dress or adorn elaborately.

gust (gŭst) ▸ *n.* **1.** A strong abrupt rush of wind. **2.** An outburst of emotion. ▸ *v.* To blow in gusts. **—gust′i·ly** *adv.* **—gust′i·ness** *n.* **—gust′y** *adj.*

gus·ta·to·ry (gŭs′tə-tôr′ē) ▸ *adj.* Of or relating to the sense of taste. **—gus′ta·to′ri·ly** *adv.*

gus·to (gŭs′tō) ▸ *n.* Vigorous enjoyment.

gut (gŭt) ▸ *n.* **1.** The alimentary canal or a portion thereof, esp. the intestine or stomach. **2. guts** The bowels; entrails. **3.** *Slang* **a.** One's innermost being. **b. guts** The inner working parts. **4. guts** *Slang* **a.** Courage; fortitude. **b.** Nerve; audacity. **5.** A tough cord made from animal intestines. ▸ *v.* **gut·ted, gut·ting. 1.** To disembowel. **2.** To remove the essence or substance of. **3.** To destroy the interior of: *Fire gutted the house.* ▸ *adj. Slang* Deeply felt: *a gut response.*

Gu·ten·berg (go͞ot′n-bûrg′), **Johann** (1400?–68?) ▸ German printer; traditionally considered the inventor of movable type.

gut·less (gŭt′lĭs) ▸ *adj. Slang* Lacking courage or drive. **—gut′less·ness** *n.*

guts·y (gŭt′sē) ▸ *adj.* **-i·er, -i·est.** *Slang* Courageous; plucky. **—guts′i·ly** *adv.* **—guts′i·ness** *n.*

gut·ta-per·cha (gŭt′ə-pûr′chə) ▸ *n.* A rubbery substance obtained from certain tropical trees, used as an electrical insulator and in golf balls.

gut·ter (gŭt′ər) ▸ *n.* **1.** A channel for draining off water along the edge of a street or roof. **2.** A trough on either side of a bowling alley. **3.** A squalid state of human existence. ▸ *v.* **1.** To flow in channels. **2.** To melt away: *The candle guttered and died.*

gut·ter·snipe (gŭt′ər-snīp′) ▸ *n.* A street urchin.

gut·tur·al (gŭt′ər-əl) ▸ *adj.* **1.** Of or produced in the throat. **2.** Harsh; throaty. **3.** *Ling.* Velar. **—gut′tur·al·ly** *adv.*

guy[1] (gī) ▸ *n.* A rope, cord, or cable used to steady, guide, or secure something. **—guy** *v.*

guy[2] (gī) ▸ *n. Informal* **1.** A man; fellow. **2. guys** Persons of either sex.

Guy·a·na (gī-ăn′ə, -ä′nə) ▸ A country of NE South America on the Atlantic. Pop. 698,000. **—Guy′a·nese′** (-nēz′, -nēs′) *adj. & n.*

guz·zle (gŭz′əl) ▸ *v.* **-zled, -zling.** To drink greedily. **—guz′zler** *n.*

gym (jĭm) ▸ *n.* **1.** A gymnasium. **2.** A school course in physical education.

gym·na·si·um (jĭm-nā′zē-əm) ▸ *n., pl.* **-si·ums** or **-si·a** (-zē-ə). **1.** A room or building equipped for indoor sports. **2.** (gĭm-nä′zē-o͝om′) A college-preparatory school in some European countries.

gym·nas·tics (jĭm-năs′tĭks) ▸ *n. (takes pl. v.)* Physical exercises that develop and display strength, balance, and agility, esp. those performed on or with specialized apparatus. **—gym′nast′** *n.* **—gym·nas′tic** *adj.* **—gym·nas′ti·cal·ly** *adv.*

gym·no·sperm (jĭm′nə-spûrm′) ▸ *n.* A plant, such as a conifer, whose seeds are not enclosed within an ovary. **—gym′no·sper′mous** *adj.* **—gym′no·sper′my** *n.*

THESAURUS

gumption *n.* —*See* COMMON SENSE, DRIVE (2).

gumshoe *n.* —*See* DETECTIVE.

gumshoe *v.* —*See* SNEAK.

gum up *v.* —*See* BOTCH.

gun *v.* To wound or kill with a firearm ▸ gun down, pick off, shoot. *Slang:* plug. *Idiom:* fill full of lead (*or* holes). [*Compare* KILL[1], MURDER.]

gun for *v.* —*See* PURSUE (1).

gung ho *adj.* —*See* ENTHUSIASTIC.

gunk *n.* —*See* GARBAGE, SLIME.

gunsel *n.* —*See* THUG.

gurgle *v.* —*See* BURBLE.

gurgle *n.* —*See* BURBLE.

guru *n.* —*See* ADVISER, SAGE.

gush *v.* —*See* FLOW (2), RAVE.

gush *n.* —*See* FLOW, OUTBURST.

gushy *adj.* —*See* SENTIMENTAL.

gust *n.* —*See* OUTBURST, WIND[1].

gust *v.* —*See* BLOW[1] (1).

gusto *n.* Spirited enjoyment ▸ relish, zest. [*Compare* ENTHUSIASM.]

gusty *adj.* —*See* AIRY (3).

gut *adj.* —*See* EMPTY, INNER (2).

gut *v.* —*See* ENERVATE.

gutless *adj.* —*See* COWARDLY.

gutlessness *n.* —*See* COWARDICE.

gut reaction *n.* —*See* FEELING (1).

guts *n.* —*See* COURAGE, VISCERA.

gutsiness *n.* —*See* COURAGE.

gutsy *adj.* —*See* BRAVE, LUSTY.

gutter *n.* —*See* PIT[1].

gutter *v.* —*See* SMOLDER.

gutty *adj.* —*See* BRAVE.

guy[1] *n.* —*See* CORD.

guy[2] *n.* —*See* FELLOW.

guzzle *v.* —*See* DRINK (1), DRINK (2), GULP.

gy·ne·col·o·gy (gī′nĭ-kŏl′ə-jē, jĭn′ĭ-, jī′nĭ-) ▸ *n.* The branch of medicine dealing with the health of women and esp. of the female reproductive system. **–gy′ne·co·log′i·cal** (-kə-lŏj′ĭ-kəl), **gy′ne·co·log′ic** *adj.* **–gy′ne·col′o·gist** *n.*

gyo·za (gyō′zə) ▸ *n.* A pocket of dough that is stuffed with a filling and fried, steamed, or boiled.

gyp also **gip** (jĭp) *Offensive Slang* ▸ *v.* **gypped, gyp·ping** also **gipped, gip·ping**. To cheat or swindle. ▸ *n.* A fraud or swindle. **–gyp′per** *n.*

gyp·sum (jĭp′səm) ▸ *n.* A white mineral, $CaSO_4 \cdot 2H_2O$, used in the manufacture of plaster of Paris, various plaster products, and fertilizers.

Gyp·sy also **Gip·sy** (jĭp′sē) ▸ *n., pl.* **-sies**. **1.** *Often Offensive* A Romani. **2. gypsy** One inclined to a nomadic way of life.

gypsy moth ▸ *n.* A moth having hairy caterpillars that are destructive to trees.

gy·rate (jī′rāt′) ▸ *v.* **-rat·ed, -rat·ing**. **1.** To revolve around a fixed point or axis. **2.** To revolve in a circle or spiral. **–gy·ra′tion** *n.* **–gy′ra′tor** *n.*

gyr·fal·con (jûr′făl′kən, -fôl′-, -fô′-) ▸ *n.* A large Arctic falcon with color phases from black to gray to white.

gy·ro[1] (jī′rō) ▸ *n., pl.* **-ros**. A gyroscope.

gy·ro[2] (jī′rō, jē′-) ▸ *n., pl.* **-ros**. A sandwich made usu. of sliced roasted lamb, onion, and tomato on pita bread.

gy·ro·com·pass (jī′rō-kŭm′pəs, -kŏm′-) ▸ *n.* A compass with a motorized gyroscope that maintains a true north-south orientation.

gy·ro·scope (jī′rə-skōp′) ▸ *n.* A device consisting of a spinning mass, usu. a disk or wheel, that is mounted on a base so that its axis can turn freely in one or more directions and thereby maintain its orientation regardless of any movement of the base. **–gy′ro·scop′ic** (-skŏp′ĭk) *adj.* **–gy′ro·scop′i·cal·ly** *adv.*

THESAURUS

gyrate *v.* —*See* TURN (1).

gyration *n.* —*See* REVOLUTION (1).

gyre *n.* —*See* CIRCLE (1).

H

h[1] or **H** (āch) ► *n., pl.* **h's** or **H's** also **hs** or **Hs**. The 8th letter of the English alphabet.
h[2] ► *abbr.* 1. height 2. hour
H[1] ► The symbol for the element **hydrogen**.
H[2] ► *abbr.* 1. *Baseball* hit 2. humidity
ha also **hah** (hä) ► *interj.* Used to express surprise, laughter, or triumph.
Ha·bak·kuk (hăb′ə-kŭk′, -ko͝ok′, hə-băk′ək) ► *n.* **1.** A Hebrew prophet of the late 7th cent. B.C. **2.** See **Bible** table in Appendix.
ha·be·as corpus (hā′bē-əs) ► *n.* A writ issued to bring a party before a court or judge, used to protect the party from unlawful restraint.
hab·er·dash·er (hăb′ər-dăsh′ər) ► *n.* A dealer in men's attire.
hab·er·dash·er·y (hăb′ər-dăsh′ə-rē) ► *n., pl.* **-ies. 1.** A haberdasher's shop. **2.** Men's furnishings.
ha·bil·i·ment (hə-bĭl′ə-mənt) ► *n.* **1.** often **habiliments** Clothing or dress, esp. that typical of an occasion or office. **2. habiliments** Characteristic furnishings or equipment; trappings.
hab·it (hăb′ĭt) ► *n.* **1.** A pattern of behavior acquired through repetition. **2.** Customary practice. **3.** An addiction. **4.** Characteristic appearance or manner of growth, as of a plant. **5.** A distinctive costume.
hab·it·a·ble (hăb′ĭ-tə-bəl) ► *adj.* Suitable to live in. **—hab′it·a·bil′i·ty** *n.* **—hab′it·a·bly** *adv.*
hab·i·tat (hăb′ĭ-tăt′) ► *n.* **1.** The area or environment in which an organism or ecological community normally lives or occurs. **2.** The place in which a person or thing is likely to be found.
hab·i·ta·tion (hăb′ĭ-tā′shən) ► *n.* **1.** The act of inhabiting or the state of being inhabited. **2a.** A natural environment or locality. **b.** A place of residence.
hab·it-form·ing (hăb′ĭt-fôr′mĭng) ► *adj.* Tending to become a habit, esp. as a result of physiological dependence.
ha·bit·u·al (hə-bĭch′o͞o-əl) ► *adj.* **1a.** Of the nature of a habit: *habitual lying.* **b.** Being such by force of habit: *a habitual liar.* **2.** Customary; usual. **—ha·bit′u·al·ly** *adv.*
ha·bit·u·ate (hə-bĭch′o͞o-āt′) ► *v.* **-at·ed, -at·ing.** To accustom by repetition or long exposure. **—ha·bit′u·a′tion** *n.*
hab·i·tude (hăb′ĭ-to͞od′, -tyo͞od′) ► *n.* A customary behavior.
ha·bit·u·é (hə-bĭch′o͞o-ā′, hə-bĭch′o͞o-ā′) ► *n.* One who frequents a particular place, as a café or bar.
Habs·burg (hăps′bûrg′) ► See **Hapsburg**.
ha·ci·en·da (hä′sē-ĕn′də) ► *n.* **1.** A large estate in Spanish-speaking countries. **2.** The main house of such an estate.
hack[1] (hăk) ► *v.* **1.** To cut or chop with heavy, irregular blows. **2.** To cough roughly or harshly. **3.** *Slang* To cope with successfully; manage. **4.** *Comp. Sci.* **a.** To alter (a program): *hacked her text editor to read HTML.* **b.** To access illegally: *hacked into a government network.* ► *n.* **1.** A cut made by hacking. **2.** A tool used for hacking. **3.** A rough, dry cough.
hack[2] (hăk) ► *n.* **1.** A hackney. **2.** A worn-out horse for hire. **3a.** A hireling. **b.** A writer hired to produce routine writing. **4.** *Informal* **a.** A taxicab. **b.** See **hackie.** ► *v.* To employ or work as a hack. ► *adj.* **1.** By or for a hack. **2.** Hackneyed.
hack·a·more (hăk′ə-môr′) ► *n.* A halter used in breaking horses to a bridle.
hack·er (hăk′ər) ► *n.* **1a.** A computer buff. **b.** One who illegally gains access to another's electronic system. **2.** An enthusiastic amateur at a sport.
hack·ie (hăk′ē) ► *n.* A taxicab driver.
hack·le (hăk′əl) ► *n.* **1.** Any of the long slender feathers on the neck of a bird. **2. hackles** The erectile hairs along the back of the neck of an animal, esp. a dog. **3.** A tuft of feathers trimming a fishing fly. ***—idiom:*** **get (one's) hackles up** To be extremely insulted or irritated.
hack·ney (hăk′nē) ► *n., pl.* **-neys. 1.** A horse suited for routine riding or driving. **2.** A coach or carriage for hire. ► *v.* To make banal and trite.
hack·neyed (hăk′nēd) ► *adj.* Banal; trite.
hack·saw (hăk′sô′) ► *n.* A tough, fine-toothed saw stretched in a frame, used for cutting metal. **—hack′saw′** *v.*
had (hăd) ► *v.* P.t. and p.part. of **have**.
had·dock (hăd′ək) ► *n., pl.* **-dock** or **-docks**. A N Atlantic food fish related to the cod.
Ha·des (hā′dēz) ► *n.* **1.** *Gk. Myth.* The abode of the dead. **2.** also **hades** Hell.
had·n't (hăd′nt) ► Had not.
Ha·dri·an (hā′drē-ən) (A.D. 76–138) ► Emperor of Rome (117–138).
had·ron (hăd′rŏn′) ► *n.* Any of a class of subatomic particles, including protons and neutrons, that take part in the strong interaction.
had·ro·saur (hăd′rə-sôr′) ► *n.* Any of various amphibious dinosaurs that had webbed feet and a ducklike bill.
hadst (hădst) ► *v.* *Archaic* 2nd pers. sing. p.t. of **have**.
-haemia ► *suff.* Var. of **-emia**.
haf·ni·um (hăf′nē-əm) ► *n.* *Symbol* **Hf** A brilliant silvery metallic element used in nuclear reactor control rods and in the manufacture of tungsten filaments. At. no. 72.
haft (hăft) ► *n.* A handle or hilt, esp. of a tool or weapon.
hag (hăg) ► *n.* **1.** An ugly old woman. **2.** A witch; sorceress. **—hag′gish** *adj.*
Hag·ga·i (hăg′ē-ī′, hăg′ī′) ► *n.* **1.** A Hebrew prophet of the 6th cent. B.C. **2.** See **Bible** table in Appendix.
hag·gard (hăg′ərd) ► *adj.* Appearing worn and gaunt. **—hag′-gard·ly** *adv.* **—hag′gard·ness** *n.*

THESAURUS

habiliments *n.* —*See* DRESS (1), DRESS (2).
habit *n.* Clothing worn by members of a religious order ► robe, vestment. [*Compare* DRESS.] —*See also* CONSTITUTION, CUSTOM, DISPOSITION.
habitable *adj.* Fit to live in ► inhabitable, livable.
habitat *n.* The natural environment specific to an animal or plant ► habitation, niche, range, territory. [*Compare* HAUNT.] —*See also* ENVIRONMENT (3).
habitation *n.* —*See* HABITAT, HOME (1).
habitual *adj.* **1.** Subject to a habit or pattern of behavior ► accustomed, chronic, routine. **2.** Subject to a disease or habit for a long time ► chronic, confirmed, habituated, inveterate. [*Compare* STUBBORN.] —*See also* COMMON (1).
habitually *adv.* —*See* USUALLY.
habitualness *n.* —*See* USUALNESS.
habituate *v.* —*See* ACCUSTOM.
habituated *adj.* **1.** In the habit ► accustomed, used, wont. **2.** Subject to a disease or habit for a long time ► chronic, confirmed, habitual, inveterate. [*Compare* STUBBORN.]
habitude *n.* —*See* CUSTOM.
habitus *n.* —*See* CONSTITUTION.
hack[1] *v.* —*See* CUT (1).
hack[2] *n.* —*See* DRUDGE (1).
hackneyed *adj.* —*See* TRITE.
haft *n.* A protrusion or extension designed to be grasped by the hand ► handgrip, handle, hilt. [*Compare* HOLD, KNOB.]
hag *n.* A woman who practices magic ► enchantress, lamia, sorceress, witch. [*Compare* WIZARD.] —*See also* WITCH (2).
haggard *adj.* Appearing worn and exhausted ► careworn, drawn, emaciated, gaunt, pinched, hollow-eyed, shrunken, skeletal, wan, wasted, worn.

hag·gle (hăg′əl) ► *v.* **-gled, -gling.** To argue in an attempt to bargain. **—hag′gle** *n.* **—hag′gler** *n.*

hag·i·og·ra·phy (hăg′ē-ŏg′rə-fē, hā′jē-) ► *n., pl.* **-phies. 1.** Biography of saints. **2.** A worshipful or idealizing biography. **—hag′i·og′raph·er** *n.* **—hag′i·o·graph′ic** (-ə-grăf′ĭk), **hag′i·o·graph′i·cal** *adj.*

Hague (hāg), **The** ► The de facto capital of the Netherlands, in the W part near the North Sea. Pop. 458,000.

hah (hä) ► *interj.* Var. of **ha.**

Hai·da (hī′də) ► *n., pl.* **-da** or **-das. 1.** A member of a Native American people inhabiting the Queen Charlotte Is. of W British Columbia, Canada, and Prince of Wales I. in S Alaska. **2.** The language of the Haida.

hai·ku (hī′ko͞o) ► *n., pl.* **-ku** also **-kus.** An unrhymed Japanese poem having three lines of five, seven, and five syllables.

hail[1] (hāl) ► *n.* **1.** Precipitation in the form of ice pellets. **2.** Something with the force of a shower of hail: *a hail of criticism.* ► *v.* **1.** To precipitate hail. **2.** To pour down or forth.

hail[2] (hāl) ► *v.* **1a.** To salute or greet. **b.** To greet or acclaim enthusiastically. **2.** To signal or call out to: *hail a cabdriver.* ***—phrasal verb:* hail from** To come or originate from. ► *n.* **1.** The act of hailing. **2.** Hailing distance. ► *interj.* Used to express a greeting or tribute. **—hail′er** *n.*

hail·stone (hāl′stōn′) ► *n.* A pellet of hail.

hail·storm (hāl′stôrm′) ► *n.* A storm with hail.

hair (hâr) ► *n.* **1a.** A fine threadlike outgrowth, esp. from the skin of a mammal. **b.** A covering of such outgrowths, as on the human head. **2a.** A minute distance or narrow margin: *won by a hair.* **b.** A precise degree: *calibrated to a hair.* **—hair′less** *adj.*

hair·breadth (hâr′brĕdth′) ► *adj.* Extremely close: *a hairbreadth escape.*

hair·brush (hâr′brŭsh′) ► *n.* A brush for the hair.

hair·cloth (hâr′klôth′, -klŏth′) ► *n.* A wiry fabric woven esp. from horsehair and used for upholstering.

hair·cut (hâr′kŭt′) ► *n.* **1.** The act or an instance of cutting the hair. **2.** A style in which hair is cut. **—hair′cut′ter** *n.* **—hair′cut′ting** *adj.* & *n.*

hair·do (hâr′do͞o′) ► *n., pl.* **-dos.** A hairstyle.

hair·dress·er (hâr′drĕs′ər) ► *n.* One who cuts or arranges hair. **—hair′dress·ing** *n.*

hair·line (hâr′līn′) ► *n.* **1.** The outline of the growth of hair on the head, esp. across the front. **2.** A very slender line.

hair·piece (hâr′pēs′) ► *n.* A covering or bunch of human or artificial hair used to conceal baldness or give shape to a hairstyle.

hair·pin (hâr′pĭn′) ► *n.* **1.** A thin U-shaped pin used to secure a hairdo or headdress. **2.** A sharp U-shaped turn in a road.

hair-rais·ing (hâr′rā′zĭng) ► *adj.* Causing excitement, terror, or thrills.

hair·split·ting (hâr′splĭt′ĭng) ► *n.* The making of unreasonably fine distinctions. **—hair′split′ter** *n.* **—hair′split′ting** *adj.*

hair spray ► *n.* A preparation sprayed on the hair to keep it in place.

hair·spring (hâr′sprĭng′) ► *n.* A fine coiled spring that regulates the movement of the balance wheel in a watch or clock.

hair·style (hâr′stīl′) ► *n.* A style in which hair is arranged. **—hair′styl′ing** *n.* **—hair′styl′ist** *n.*

hair trigger ► *n.* A gun trigger adjusted to respond to a very slight pressure.

hair-trig·ger (hâr′trĭg′ər) ► *adj.* Responding to the slightest provocation or stimulation: *a hair-trigger temper.*

hair·weav·ing (hâr′wē′vĭng) ► *n.* The process of interweaving a hairpiece of human hair with the wearer's own hair.

hair·y (hâr′ē) ► *adj.* **-i·er, -i·est. 1.** Covered with hair. **2.** Of or like hair. **3.** *Slang* Fraught with difficulties; hazardous. **—hair′i·ness** *n.*

Hai·ti (hā′tē) ► **1.** A country of the West Indies comprising the W part of the island of Hispaniola and two offshore islands. Pop. 7,060,000. **2.** See **Hispaniola. —Hai′tian** *adj.* & *n.*

haj (hăj) ► *n., pl.* **-es.** *Islam* A pilgrimage to Mecca.

haj·i (hăj′ē) ► *n., pl.* **-is.** *Islam* One who has made a pilgrimage to Mecca.

hake (hāk) ► *n., pl.* **hake** or **hakes.** A marine food fish related to the cod.

hal– ► *pref.* Var. of **halo–.**

hal·berd (hăl′bərd, hôl′-) ► *n.* A weapon of the 15th and 16th cent. having an axlike blade and a steel spike mounted on the end of a long shaft.

hal·cy·on (hăl′sē-ən) ► *adj.* **1.** Calm and peaceful. **2.** Prosperous; golden: *halcyon years.*

hale[1] (hāl) ► *adj.* **hal·er, hal·est.** Sound in health. **—hale′ness** *n.*

hale[2] (hāl) ► *v.* **haled, hal·ing.** To compel to go.

Hale, Nathan (1755–76) ► Amer. Revolutionary soldier.

half (hăf) ► *n., pl.* **halves** (hăvz). **1a.** One of two equal parts that constitute a whole. **b.** One part approx. equal to the remaining part. **2.** *Sports* **a.** One of two playing periods into which a game is divided. **b.** A halfback. ► *adj.* **1a.** Being one of two equal parts. **b.** Being approx. a half. **2.** Partial or incomplete: *a half smile.* ► *adv.* **1.** To the extent of exactly or nearly a half: *The tank is half empty.* **2.** Not completely; partly: *only half right.* ***—idioms:* by half 1.** By a considerable extent. **2.** By an excessive amount: *too clever by half.* **by halves** In a reluctant manner; unenthusiastically. **not half** Not at all: *not half bad.*

half·back (hăf′băk′) ► *n.* *Sports* **1.** One of the two football players near the flanks behind the line of scrimmage. **2.** One of several players stationed behind the forward line in various sports.

half-baked (hăf′bākt′) ► *adj.* **1.** Only partly baked. **2.** *Informal* Insufficiently thought out: *a half-baked scheme.* **3.** *Informal* Lacking common sense.

half boot ► *n.* A low boot extending just above the ankle.

half-breed (hăf′brēd′) ► *n.* *Offensive* A person of mixed racial descent.

half brother ► *n.* A brother related through one parent only.

half-caste (hăf′kăst′) ► *n.* *Offensive* A person of mixed racial descent. **—half′-caste′** *adj.*

half·cocked (hăf′kŏkt′) ► *adj.* *Informal* Inadequately or poorly prepared. ► *adv.* In a halfcocked manner: *go off halfcocked.*

half-dol·lar (hăf′dŏl′ər) ► *n.* A US silver coin worth 50 cents.

half·heart·ed (hăf′här′tĭd) ► *adj.* Exhibiting or feeling little interest or enthusiasm. **—half′heart′ed·ly** *adv.* **—half′heart′ed·ness** *n.*

half-life (hăf′līf′) ► *n.* **1.** *Phys.* The time required for half the nuclei in a sample of a specific isotopic species to undergo radioactive decay. **2.** *Biol.* The time required for half the quantity of a drug or other substance to be metabolized or eliminated.

half-mast (hăf′măst′) ► *n.* The position about halfway up a mast or pole at which a flag is flown as a symbol of mourning or as a signal of distress.

half-moon (hăf′mo͞on′) ► *n.* **1.** The moon when only half its

THESAURUS

Idiom: skin and bones. [*Compare* EXHAUSTED, THIN.]

haggle *v.* To argue about the terms, as of a sale ► bargain, chaffer, dicker, higgle, huckster, negotiate, palter, wrangle. [*Compare* ARGUE.]

ha-ha *n.* —*See* JOKE (1).

hail[1] *n.* —*See* BARRAGE.

hail[2] *v.* **1.** To approach for the purpose of speech ► accost, greet, salute. [*Compare* ENCOUNTER, INTERRUPT, WELCOME.] **2.** To address in a friendly and respectful way ► greet, salute, welcome. **3.** To have as one's home or place of origin ► come, originate. [*Compare* DESCEND, STEM.] —*See also* HONOR (1).

hail *n.* An expression, in words or gestures, marking a meeting of persons ► greeting, salutation, salute, welcome. *Informal:* hello.

hair *n.* —*See* SHADE (2).

hairless *adj.* —*See* BARE (3).

hairline *n.* Something suggesting the continuousness of a filament ► strand, thread. [*Compare* THREAD.]

hair-raising *adj.* —*See* HORRIBLE.

hairsplitting *n.* —*See* QUIBBLING.

hairy *adj.* Covered with hair ► bristly, downy, fleecy, flocculent, furry, fuzzy, hirsute, pilose, pubescent, shaggy, tufted, woolly. —*See also* DANGEROUS.

halcyon *adj.* —*See* STILL.

hale *adj.* —*See* HEALTHY.

haleness *n.* —*See* HEALTH (1).

halfhearted *adj.* Lacking warmth, interest, enthusiasm, or involvement ► Laodicean, lukewarm, tepid, unenthusiastic. [*Compare* APATHETIC, COLD, COOL.]

disk is illuminated. 2. Something shaped like a crescent.
half nelson ▸ *n.* A wrestling hold in which one arm is passed under the opponent's arm from behind to the back of the neck.
half note ▸ *n. Mus.* A note having half the value of a whole note.
half sister ▸ *n.* A sister related through one parent only.
half-slip (hăf′slĭp') ▸ *n.* A woman's slip that hangs from the waist.
half sole ▸ *n.* A shoe sole that extends from the shank to the toe.
half-staff (hăf′stăf′) ▸ *n.* See **half-mast**.
half step ▸ *n.* See **semitone**.
half·time (hăf′tīm') ▸ *n.* The intermission between halves in a game, such as basketball or football.
half-track (hăf′trăk') ▸ *n.* A lightly armored military motor vehicle, with caterpillar treads in place of wheels.
half-truth (hăf′trōōth') ▸ *n.* A statement, esp. one intended to deceive, that is only partially true.
half·way (hăf′wā′) ▸ *adj.* **1.** Midway between two points or conditions. **2.** Partial: *halfway measures.* **—half′way′** *adv.*
half-wit (hăf′wĭt') ▸ *n.* A foolish or stupid person. **—half′-wit'ted** *adj.* **—half′-wit'ted·ly** *adv.* **—half′-wit'ted·ness** *n.*
hal·i·but (hăl′ə-bət, hŏl′-) ▸ *n., pl.* **-but** or **-buts.** Any of several large edible flatfishes of N Atlantic or Pacific waters.
hal·ide (hăl′īd', hā′līd') ▸ *n.* A chemical compound of a halogen with a more electropositive element or group.
Hal·i·fax (hăl′ə-făks') ▸ The capital of Nova Scotia, Canada, in the S-central part on the Atlantic. Pop. 359,000.
hal·ite (hăl′īt', hā′līt') ▸ *n.* Rock salt.
hal·i·to·sis (hăl'ĭ-tō′sĭs) ▸ *n.* Stale or foul-smelling breath.
hall (hôl) ▸ *n.* **1.** A corridor or passageway in a building. **2.** A large entrance room; lobby. **3a.** A building with a large room for public gatherings or entertainments. **b.** The room itself. **4.** A building used by a social or religious organization. **5a.** A college or university building. **b.** A large room in such a building. **6.** The main house on a landed estate. **7.** The castle or house of a medieval monarch or noble.
hal·le·lu·jah (hăl'ə-lōō′yə) ▸ *interj.* Used to express praise or joy.
Hal·ley (hăl′ē), **Edmund** or **Edmond** (1656–1742) ▸ English astronomer.
hall·mark (hôl′märk') ▸ *n.* **1.** A mark indicating quality or excellence. **2.** A conspicuous feature or characteristic.
hall of fame ▸ *n.* **1.** A group of persons judged outstanding, as in a sport. **2.** A building housing memorials to illustrious persons.
hal·loo (hə-lōō′) ▸ *interj.* Used to catch someone's attention. ▸ *n.* A shout of "halloo." **—hal·loo′** *n.*
hal·low (hăl′ō) ▸ *v.* **1.** To make or set apart as holy. **2.** To respect or honor greatly; revere.
Hal·low·een also **Hal·low·e'en** (hăl'ə-wēn′, hŏl'-) ▸ *n.* Oct. 31, celebrated by children wearing costumes and begging treats.
hal·lu·ci·na·tion (hə-lōō'sə-nā′shən) ▸ *n.* **1a.** False or distorted perception of objects or events with a compelling sense of their reality. **b.** The objects or events so perceived. **2.** A false or mistaken idea; delusion. **—hal·lu′ci·nate** *v.* **—hal·lu'ci·na′tion·al, hal·lu′ci·na'tive** *adj.* **—hal·lu′ci·na·to'ry** (hə-lōō′sə-nə-tôr'ē) *adj.*
hal·lu·ci·no·gen (hə-lōō′sə-nə-jən) ▸ *n.* A substance that induces hallucination. **—hal·lu'ci·no·gen′ic** (-jĕn′ĭk) *adj.*
hall·way (hôl′wā') ▸ *n.* **1.** A corridor in a building. **2.** An entrance hall.
ha·lo (hā′lō) ▸ *n., pl.* **-los** or **-loes.** **1.** A circular band of colored light around a light source, as around the sun or moon. **2.** A luminous ring of light surrounding the heads or bodies of sacred figures in religious paintings. **—ha′lo** *v.*
halo– or **hal–** ▸ *pref.* **1.** Salt: *halite.* **2.** Halogen: *halocarbon.*
hal·o·car·bon (hăl′ə-kär'bən) ▸ *n.* A compound consisting of carbon and a halogen.
hal·o·gen (hăl′ə-jən) ▸ *n.* Any of a group of five chemically related nonmetallic elements including fluorine, chlorine, bromine, iodine, and astatine. **—ha·log′e·nous** (hă-lŏj′ə-nəs) *adj.*
halt[1] (hôlt) ▸ *n.* A suspension of movement or progress; stop. ▸ *v.* **1.** To cause to stop. **2.** To stop; pause.
halt[2] (hôlt) ▸ *v.* **1.** To proceed or act with uncertainty; waver. **2.** To limp or hobble.
hal·ter (hôl′tər) ▸ *n.* **1.** A device made of rope or leather straps that fits around the head or neck of an animal, used to lead or secure it. **2.** A noose used for execution by hanging. **3.** A bodice for women that ties behind the neck and across the back. ▸ *v.* **1.** To put a halter on. **2.** To control with or as if with a halter.
halt·ing (hôl′tĭng) ▸ *adj.* **1.** Hesitant or wavering: *a halting voice.* **2.** Limping; lame. **—halt′ing·ly** *adv.*
hal·vah (häl-vä′, häl′vä) ▸ *n.* A confection of honey and crushed sesame seeds.
halve (hăv) ▸ *v.* **halved, halv·ing.** **1.** To divide into two equal parts. **2.** To lessen or reduce by half: *halved the recipe.* **3.** *Informal* To share equally: *The twins halve everything.*
halves (hăvz) ▸ *n.* Pl. of **half.**
hal·yard (hăl′yərd) ▸ *n.* A rope used to raise or lower a sail, flag, or yard.
ham (hăm) ▸ *n.* **1.** The thigh of the hind leg of an animal, esp. a hog. **2.** A cut of meat from the ham. **3.** The back of the knee or thigh. **4. hams** The buttocks. **5.** A performer who exaggerates. **6.** A licensed amateur radio operator. ▸ *v.* **hammed, ham·ming.** To exaggerate or overact.
ham·a·dry·ad (hăm'ə-drī′əd) ▸ *n., pl.* **-ads** or **-a·des** (-ə-dēz'). *Gk. & Rom. Myth.* A wood nymph.
Ham·burg (hăm′bûrg') ▸ A city of N Germany on the Elbe R. NE of Bremen. Pop. 1,690,000.
ham·burg·er (hăm′bûr'gər) also **ham·burg** (-bûrg') ▸ *n.* **1a.** Ground meat, usu. beef. **b.** A cooked patty of such meat. **2.** A sandwich made with a patty of ground meat usu. in a roll or bun.
Ham·il·ton (hăm′əl-tən), **Alexander** (1755?–1804) ▸ Amer. politician; killed in a duel with Aaron Burr.
Ham·ite (hăm′īt') ▸ *n.* A member of a group of peoples of N and NE Africa, including the Berbers, the Tuaregs, and the ancient Egyptians. **—Ha·mit′ic** (hă-mĭt′ĭk) *adj.*
ham·let (hăm′lĭt) ▸ *n.* A small village.
ham·mer (hăm′ər) ▸ *n.* **1.** A hand tool used for striking, consisting of a handle with a perpendicularly attached head. **2.** A tool or device similar in function or action, as: **a.** The part of a gunlock that hits the primer or firing pin or explodes the percussion cap. **b.** *Mus.* One of the padded wooden pieces of a piano that strikes the strings. **c.** A part of an apparatus that strikes a gong or bell, as in a clock. **3.** See **malleus.** **4.** *Sports* A metal ball having a long handle from which it is thrown for distance. ▸ *v.* **1.** To hit, esp. repeatedly. **2.** To fashion or shape with or as if with repeated blows. **3.** *Informal* To keep at something continuously: *hammered away at the problem.* **—ham′mer·er** *n.*
ham·mer·head (hăm′ər-hĕd') ▸ *n.* **1.** The head of a hammer. **2.** A large predatory shark having eyes set in wide fleshy extensions at the sides of the head.
ham·mer·lock (hăm′ər-lŏk') ▸ *n.* A wrestling hold in which the opponent's arm is pulled behind the back and twisted upward.

THESAURUS

half-pint *n.* —*See* SQUIRT (2).
half-truth *n.* —*See* LIE[2].
half-wit *n.* —*See* DULLARD.
half-witted *adj.* —*See* BACKWARD (1), STUPID.
halloo *n.* —*See* SHOUT.
 halloo *v.* —*See* SHOUT.
hallow *v.* To make sacred by a religious rite ▸ bless, consecrate, sanctify. [*Compare* EXALT.] —*See also* DEVOTE, REVERE.
hallowed *adj.* —*See* DIVINE (2), HOLY.
hallucinate *v.* —*See* DREAM.
hallucination *n.* An experience of things or events that are not real ▸ phantasmagoria, phantasmagory. *Slang:* trip. —*See also* DREAM (1), ILLUSION.
hallucinatory *adj.* —*See* ILLUSIVE.
hallucinogen *n.* —*See* DRUG (2).
halo *n.* —*See* CIRCLE (1).
halt[1] *n.* —*See* STOP (1), STOP (2).
 halt *v.* —*See* STOP (1), STOP (2).
halt[2] *v.* —*See* HESITATE, STAGGER (1).
halting *adj.* —*See* HESITANT.
hamlet *n.* —*See* VILLAGE.
hammer *v.* —*See* BEAT (1), BEAT (3), BEAT (5).

ham·mock (hăm′ək) ▶ *n.* A hanging bed of canvas or heavy netting suspended between two supports.

ham·per¹ (hăm′pər) ▶ *v.* To prevent the free movement, action, or progress of.

ham·per² (hăm′pər) ▶ *n.* A large basket, usu. with a cover.

ham·ster (hăm′stər) ▶ *n.* A small rodent with large cheek pouches and a short tail, often kept as a pet or used in laboratory research.

ham·string (hăm′strĭng′) ▶ *n.* **1.** Any of the tendons at the rear hollow of the human knee. **2.** or **hamstrings** The muscles constituting the back of the upper leg. **3.** The large tendon in the back of the hock of a quadruped. ▶ *v.* **1.** To cripple by cutting the hamstring. **2.** To hinder the efficiency of.

Han (hän) ▶ *n., pl.* **Han** or **Hans.** A member of the principal ethnic group of China.

Han·cock (hăn′kŏk′), **John** (1737–93) ▶ Amer. politician and Revolutionary leader.

hand (hănd) ▶ *n.* **1.** The terminal part of the human arm, consisting of the wrist, palm, four fingers, and thumb. **2.** A unit of length equal to 4 in. (10.2 cm), used esp. to specify the height of a horse. **3.** Something suggesting the shape or function of the human hand, esp.: **a.** A rotating pointer on the face of a clock. **b.** A pointer on a gauge or dial. **4.** See **index** 3. **5.** Lateral direction: *at my right hand.* **6.** Handwriting; penmanship. **7.** A round of applause. **8.** Assistance; help: *lend a hand.* **9a.** The cards held by or dealt to a player in a card game. **b.** A full round of play: *a hand of poker.* **10a.** A manual laborer: *a factory hand.* **b.** A member of a group or crew. **11.** A participant: *an old hand at diplomacy.* **12.** often **hands a.** Possession or keeping. **b.** Control; care: *His fate is in your hands.* **13a.** Involvement or participation. **b.** An influence or effect: *had a hand in all the decisions.* **c.** Craft or skill. **14.** A pledge to wed. ▶ *v.* **1.** To give or pass with or as if with the hands. **2.** To aid, direct, or conduct with the hands. ***—phrasal verbs:*** **hand down 1.** To bequeath as an inheritance. **2.** To deliver (a verdict). **hand in** To turn in; submit. **hand out** To distribute; disseminate. **hand over** To relinquish to another. ***—idioms:*** **at hand 1.** Close by; near. **2.** Soon; imminent. **by hand** Performed manually. **hand in glove** In close association. **hand it to** To give credit to. **hand over fist** At a tremendous rate. **hands down** Easily: *won hands down.* **in hand 1.** Under control. **2.** Accessible at the present time. **off (one's) hands** No longer in one's care or within one's responsibility. **on hand** Available. **on (one's) hands** In one's care or possession, often as an imposition. **out of hand** Out of control. **show (or tip) (one's) hand** To reveal one's intentions. **to hand 1.** Nearby. **2.** In one's possession.

hand·bag (hănd′băg′) ▶ *n.* **1.** A woman's purse. **2.** A piece of small hand luggage.

hand·ball (hănd′bôl′) ▶ *n.* **1.** A game played by two or more players who hit a ball against a wall with their hands. **2.** The small rubber ball used in this game.

hand·bill (hănd′bĭl′) ▶ *n.* A printed sheet or pamphlet distributed by hand.

hand·book (hănd′bo͝ok′) ▶ *n.* A manual or reference book providing information or instruction about a subject or place.

hand·car (hănd′kär′) ▶ *n.* A small open railroad car propelled by a hand pump or a small motor.

hand·cart (hănd′kärt′) ▶ *n.* A small, usu. two-wheeled cart pulled or pushed by hand.

hand·clasp (hănd′klăsp′) ▶ *n.* A handshake.

hand·cuff (hănd′kŭf′) ▶ *n.* often **handcuffs** A restraining device consisting of a pair of strong connected hoops that can be tightened and locked about the wrists. ▶ *v.* **1.** To restrain with or as if with handcuffs. **2.** To render ineffective.

hand·ed (hăn′dĭd) ▶ *adj.* **1.** Of or relating to dexterity or preference with respect to a hand or hands: *one-handed; left-handed.* **2.** Relating to a specified number of people: *a four-handed card game.*

Han·del (hăn′dl), **George Frideric** (1685–1759) ▶ German-born composer.

hand·ful (hănd′fo͝ol′) ▶ *n., pl.* **-fuls. 1.** The amount that a hand can hold. **2.** A small, undefined number or quantity: *a handful of people.* **3.** *Informal* One that is difficult to control or manage: *Our toddler is a handful.*

hand·gun (hănd′gŭn′) ▶ *n.* A firearm that can be used with one hand.

hand·i·cap (hăn′dē-kăp′) ▶ *n.* **1a.** A race or contest in which advantages or compensations are given different contestants to equalize the chances of winning. **b.** Such an advantage or penalty. **2.** A physical or mental disability. **3.** A hindrance. ▶ *v.* **-capped, -cap·ping. 1.** To assign a handicap to (a contestant). **2.** To hinder; impede.

hand·i·capped (hăn′dē-kăpt′) ▶ *adj.* Physically or mentally disabled. ▶ *n.* Physically or mentally disabled people as a group: *the handicapped.*

hand·i·craft (hăn′dē-krăft′) also **hand·craft** (hănd′krăft′) ▶ *n.* **1.** Skill and facility with the hands. **2.** An occupation requiring such skill. **3.** Work that is produced by skilled hands.

hand·i·work (hăn′dē-wûrk′) ▶ *n.* **1.** Work performed by hand. **2.** The product of a person's efforts and actions.

hand·ker·chief (hăng′kər-chĭf, -chēf′) ▶ *n., pl.* **-chiefs** also **-chieves** (-chĭvz, -chēvz′). A small square of cloth used esp. for wiping the nose or mouth.

han·dle (hăn′dl) ▶ *v.* **-dled, -dling. 1.** To touch, lift, or hold with the hands. **2.** To operate with the hands. **3.** To have responsibility for; manage: *handles legal matters.* **4.** To cope with or dispose of. **5.** To act or function in a given way while in operation: *a car that handles well in the snow.* ▶ *n.* **1.** A part held or operated with the hand. **2.** An opportunity. **3.** *Slang* A person's name. ***—idiom:*** **get a handle on** *Informal* To achieve an understanding of.

han·dle·bar (hăn′dl-bär′) ▶ *n.* often **handlebars** A curved metal steering bar, as on a bicycle.

han·dler (hănd′lər) ▶ *n.* **1.** One that handles or directs something or someone: *the candidate's campaign handlers.* **2.** One who trains or exhibits an animal, such as a dog.

hand·made (hănd′mād′) ▶ *adj.* Made or prepared by hand rather than by machine.

hand·maid (hănd′mād′) also **hand·maid·en** (-mād′n) ▶ *n.* A woman attendant or servant.

hand-me-down (hănd′mē-doun′) ▶ *adj.* **1.** Handed down

THESAURUS

hamper¹ *v.* To restrict the activity or free movement of ▶ chain, fetter, hamstring, handcuff, hobble, leash, manacle, shackle, tie, trammel. *Informal:* hogtie. *—See also* HINDER.

hamper² *n.* **1.** A kind of basket normally used to contain clothes or food ▶ laundry basket, food basket, gift basket, pannier. [*Compare* BASKET.] **2.** A container made of interwoven material ▶ basket, creel, pannier. [*Compare* CONTAINER.]

hamstring *v.* *—See* HAMPER¹.

hand *n.* **1.** Approval expressed by clapping ▶ applause, ovation, plaudit. *Idiom:* round of applause. **2.** One of two or more contrasted parts or places identified by its location with respect to a center ▶ flank, side. *—See also* HELP, LABORER, VIEWPOINT.

hand *v.* *—See* GIVE (1).

hand down *v.* To deliver an indictment or verdict, for example ▶ render, return. *—See also* LEAVE¹ (1).

hand in *v.* *—See* GIVE (1).

hand on *v.* *—See* LEAVE¹ (1).

hand out *v.* *—See* CONFER (2), DISTRIBUTE, DONATE.

hand over *v.* *—See* ABANDON (1), ENTRUST (1), GIVE (1).

handbag *n.* *—See* PURSE.

handbill *n.* An announcement distributed on paper to a large number of people ▶ circular, flier, leaflet, notice.

handcuff *v.* *—See* HAMPER¹.

handcuffs *n.* *—See* BOND (1).

handful *pron.* *—See* SEVERAL.

handicap *n.* *—See* ADVANTAGE (1), DISADVANTAGE.

handicap *v.* *—See* DISABLE (1).

handicraft *n.* *—See* BUSINESS (2).

handle *v.* **1.** To manipulate with the hands ▶ manipulate, ply, wield. **2.** To behave in a specified way toward someone ▶ cope with, treat. *—See also* ACT (1), CONDUCT (1), OPERATE, SELL, TOUCH.

handle *n.* **1.** A protrusion or extension designed to be grasped by the hand ▶ haft, handgrip, hilt. [*Compare* HOLD, KNOB.] **2.** Firm control or influence ▶ grasp, grip, hold. [*Compare* CONTROL, DOMINANCE, INFLUENCE.] *—See also* NAME (1).

hand-me-down *adj.* *—See* USED (2).

to one person after being used and discarded by another. 2. Of inferior quality; shabby. ▸ *n.* Something handed down from one person to another.
hand·off (hănd′ôf′, -ŏf′) ▸ *n. Football* A play in which one player hands the ball to another.
hand·out (hănd′out′) ▸ *n.* **1.** Food, clothing, or money given to the needy. **2.** A folder or leaflet circulated free of charge. **3.** A prepared news or publicity release.
hand·pick (hănd′pĭk′) ▸ *v.* **1.** To gather or pick by hand. **2.** To select personally. **—hand′picked′** *adj.*
hand·rail (hănd′rāl′) ▸ *n.* A narrow railing to be grasped with the hand for support.
hand·set (hănd′sĕt′) ▸ *n.* The handle of a telephone, containing the receiver and transmitter and often a dial or push buttons.
hand·shake (hănd′shāk′) ▸ *n.* The grasping of hands by two people, as in greeting.
hands-off (hăndz′ôf′, -ŏf′) ▸ *adj.* Marked by nonintervention.
hand·some (hăn′səm) ▸ *adj.* **-som·er, -som·est. 1.** Pleasing and dignified in form or appearance. **2.** Generous or copious: *a handsome reward.* **3.** Large: *a handsome price.* **—hand′some·ly** *adv.* **—hand′some·ness** *n.*
hands-on (hăndz′ŏn′, -ôn′) ▸ *adj.* Involving active participation.
hand·spring (hănd′sprĭng′) ▸ *n.* A gymnastic feat in which the body is flipped completely forward or backward from an upright position, landing first on the hands and then on the feet.
hand·stand (hănd′stănd′) ▸ *n.* The act of balancing on the hands with one's feet in the air.
hand-to-hand (hănd′tə-hănd′) ▸ *adj.* Being at close quarters: *hand-to-hand combat.* **—hand to hand** *adv.*
hand-to-mouth (hănd′tə-mouth′) ▸ *adj.* Having or providing only the bare essentials.
hand·work (hănd′wûrk′) ▸ *n.* Work done by hand rather than by machine.
hand·writ·ing (hănd′rī′tĭng) ▸ *n.* **1.** Writing done with the hand. **2.** The writing characteristic of a particular person.
hand·y (hăn′dē) ▸ *adj.* **-i·er, -i·est. 1.** Skillful in using one's hands. **2.** Readily accessible. **3.** Easy to use or handle. **—hand′i·ly** *adv.* **—hand′i·ness** *n.*
hand·y·man (hăn′dē-măn′) ▸ *n.* A man who does odd jobs or various small tasks.
hang (hăng) ▸ *v.* **hung** (hŭng), **hang·ing. 1.** To fasten from above with no support from below; suspend. **2.** To suspend or fasten so as to allow free movement at or about the point of suspension: *hang a door.* **3.** *p.t. and p.part* **hanged** (hăngd). To execute by suspending by the neck. **4.** To attach at an appropriate angle. **5.** To furnish by suspending objects about: *hang a room with curtains.* **6.** To hold or incline downward; droop: *hang one's head.* **7.** To attach to a wall, esp. to display: *hang wallpaper; hang a painting.* **8.** To deadlock (a jury) by failing to render a unanimous verdict. **9.** To attach oneself as a dependent; cling. **10.** To depend: *It all hangs on one vote.* ***—phrasal verbs:* hang around** To loiter. **hang back** To hesitate; hold back. **hang on 1.** To cling to something. **2.** To persevere. **hang out** *Slang* **1.** To spend one's free time in a certain place. **2.** To pass time idly; loiter. **hang up 1.** To end a telephone conversation by replacing the receiver. **2.** To delay or impede; hinder. ▸ *n.* **1.** The way in which something hangs. **2.** Particular meaning or significance. **3.** *Informal* The proper method for doing or using something. ***—idioms:* give** (or **care) a hang** To be concerned. **let it all hang out** *Slang* **1.** To be relaxed. **2.** To be completely candid.
han·gar (hăng′ər, hăng′gər) ▸ *n.* A shelter for housing or repairing aircraft.
hang·dog (hăng′dôg′, -dŏg′) ▸ *adj.* **1.** Shamefaced or guilty. **2.** Downcast; intimidated.
hang·er (hăng′ər) ▸ *n.* **1.** One who hangs something. **2.** A contrivance to which something hangs or by which something is hung.
hang·er-on (hăng′ər-ŏn′, -ôn′) ▸ *n., pl.* **hang·ers-on** (hăng′ərz-). A sycophant; parasite.
hang glider ▸ *n.* **1.** A kitelike device from which a harnessed rider hangs while gliding from a height. **2.** The rider of such a device. **—hang′-glide′** *v.*
hang·ing (hăng′ĭng) ▸ *n.* **1.** Execution on a gallows. **2.** Something, such as a tapestry, that is hung.
hang·man (hăng′mən) ▸ *n.* One employed to execute condemned prisoners by hanging.
hang·nail (hăng′nāl′) ▸ *n.* A small, partly detached piece of dead skin at the side or the base of a fingernail.
hang·out (hăng′out′) ▸ *n. Slang* A frequently visited place.
hang·o·ver (hăng′ō′vər) ▸ *n.* **1.** Unpleasant physical effects following the heavy use of alcohol. **2.** A vestige; holdover.
hang-up (hăng′ŭp′) ▸ *n. Informal* **1.** A psychological or emotional difficulty or inhibition. **2.** An obstacle.
hank (hăngk) ▸ *n.* A coil or loop.
han·ker (hăng′kər) ▸ *v.* To have a strong, often restless desire. **—hank′er·er** *n.* **—hank′er·ing** *n.*
han·kie also **han·ky** (hăng′kē) ▸ *n., pl.* **-kies.** *Informal* A handkerchief.
han·ky-pan·ky (hăng′kē-păng′kē) ▸ *n. Slang* Devious or mischievous activity.
Han·ni·bal (hăn′ə-bəl) (247–183? B.C.) ▸ Carthaginian general.
Ha·noi (hă-noi′, hə-) ▸ The capital of Vietnam, in the N part on the Red R. Pop. 1,070,000.
han·som (hăn′səm) ▸ *n.* A two-wheeled covered carriage with the driver's seat at the rear.
Ha·nuk·kah or **Ha·nu·kah** also **Cha·nu·kah** (KHä′nə-kə, hä′-) ▸ *n. Judaism* An eight-day festival commemorating the victory of the Maccabees over Antiochus Epiphanes.
hao·le (hou′lē, -lā) ▸ *n.* A person, esp. a white person, who is not native Hawaiian.
hap (hăp) ▸ *n.* **1.** Fortune; chance. **2.** An occurrence.
hap·haz·ard (hăp-hăz′ərd) ▸ *adj.* Dependent upon or marked by mere chance. **—hap·haz′ard·ly** *adv.* **—hap·haz′ard·ness** *n.*
hap·less (hăp′lĭs) ▸ *adj.* Luckless. **—hap′less·ly** *adv.*
hap·loid (hăp′loid′) ▸ *adj.* **1.** Having the same number of chromosomes as a gamete or half as many as a somatic cell. **2.** Having a single set of chromosomes.
hap·ly (hăp′lē) ▸ *adv.* By chance or accident.
hap·pen (hăp′ən) ▸ *v.* **1a.** To come to pass. **b.** To come into being. **2.** To take place by chance. **3.** To come upon

THESAURUS

handout *n.* —*See* DONATION, RELIEF (2).
handsome *adj.* —*See* BEAUTIFUL, GENEROUS (1).
handwriting *n.* —*See* SCRIPT (1).
handy *adj.* —*See* CONVENIENT (2), CONVENIENT (1), DEXTEROUS, PRACTICAL.
hang *v.* **1.** To fasten or be fastened at one point with no support from below ▸ dangle, depend, sling, suspend, swing. [*Compare* DRAPE.] **2.** To execute by suspending by the neck ▸ gibbet. *Informal:* string up. *Slang:* swing. **3.** To remain stationary over a place or object ▸ hover, poise. [*Compare* FLOAT.]
hang around *v.* —*See* ASSOCIATE (2), FREQUENT, REMAIN.
hang on *v.* —*See* DEPEND ON (2), ENDURE (1).
hang out *v.* —*See* ASSOCIATE (2), FREQUENT.
hang over *v.* —*See* THREATEN (2).
hang up *v.* —*See* DELAY (1).
hang upon *v.* —*See* DEPEND ON (2).
hang *n. Informal* The proper method for doing, using, or handling something ▸ feel, knack, trick.
hanger-on *n.* —*See* PARASITE.
hanging *adj.* Hung or appearing to be hung from a support ▸ dangling, dangly, pendent, pendulous, pensile, suspended. —*See also* LOOSE (1).
hangout *n.* —*See* HAUNT.
hangover *n.* Unpleasant physical and mental effects following overindulgence in alcohol ▸ crapulence, katzenjammer. *Informal:* head.
hang-up *n. Informal* An exaggerated concern ▸ anxiety, complex, neurosis, phobia. [*Compare* ANXIETY, OBSESSION.]
hanker *v.* —*See* DESIRE.
hanky-panky *n.* —*See* MISCHIEF.
hap *n.* —*See* CHANCE (1), CHANCE (2).
hap *v.* To take place by chance ▸ befall, betide, chance, happen. —*See also* HAPPEN (1).
haphazard *adj.* —*See* RANDOM.
hapless *adj.* —*See* UNFORTUNATE (1).
haplessness *n.* —*See* MISFORTUNE.
happen *v.* **1.** To take place ▸ arrive,

something by chance. 4. To appear by chance; turn up.

hap·pen·ing (hăp′ə-nĭng) ▸ *n.* 1. An occurrence. 2. An improvised, often spontaneous spectacle.

hap·pen·stance (hăp′ən-stăns′) ▸ *n.* A chance circumstance.

hap·py (hăp′ē) ▸ *adj.* **-pi·er, -pi·est.** 1. Lucky; fortunate. 2. Enjoying, showing, or marked by pleasure. 3. Well adapted; felicitous: *a happy turn of phrase.* 4. Cheerful; willing. **—hap′pi·ly** *adv.* **—hap′pi·ness** *n.*

hap·py-go-luck·y (hăp′ē-gō-lŭk′ē) ▸ *adj.* Taking things easily; carefree.

happy hour ▸ *n.* A period of time during which a bar features drinks at reduced prices.

Haps·burg also **Habs·burg** (hăps′bûrg′) ▸ German royal family that supplied rulers to several European states from the late Middle Ages until the 20th cent.

ha·ra-ki·ri (hăr′ĭ-kîr′ē, hä′rē-) ▸ *n., pl.* **-ris.** See **seppuku.**

ha·rangue (hə-răng′) ▸ *n.* 1. A long pompous speech. 2. A tirade. **—ha·rangue** *v.* **—ha·rangu′er** *n.*

ha·rass (hə-răs′, hăr′əs,) ▸ *v.* 1. To irritate or torment persistently. 2. To wear out; exhaust. 3. To exhaust (an enemy) by repeated attacks. **—ha·rass′er** *n.* **—ha·rass′ment** *n.*

har·bin·ger (här′bĭn-jər) ▸ *n.* One that indicates or foreshadows what is to come; forerunner.

har·bor (här′bər) ▸ *n.* 1. A sheltered part of a body of water deep enough to provide anchorage for ships. 2. A place of shelter; refuge. ▸ *v.* 1. To give shelter to. 2. To provide a place or habitat for. 3. To hold or nourish: *harbor a grudge.*

hard (härd) ▸ *adj.* **-er, -est.** 1. Resistant to pressure; not readily penetrated. 2. Physically or mentally tough. 3. Difficult to do, understand, or endure. 4. Intense in force or degree: *a hard blow.* 5a. Stern or strict. b. Lacking compassion; callous. 6. Oppressive or unjust. 7a. Harsh or severe. b. Bitter; resentful. 8. Bad; adverse: *hard luck.* 9. Diligent; assiduous: *a hard worker.* 10a. Real and unassailable: *hard evidence.* b. Definite; firm. 11. Backed by bullion rather than by credit. Used of currency. 12a. Having high alcoholic content. b. Fermented: *hard cider.* 13. Containing salts that interfere with the lathering of soap. Used of water. 14. *Ling.* Velar, as the *c* in *cape.* 15. Physically addictive: *a hard drug.* **—idioms: hard and fast** Fixed and invariable. **hard of hearing** Having a partial loss of hearing. **hard put** Undergoing great difficulty. **hard up** *Informal* In need; poor. **—hard** *adv.* **—hard′ness** *n.*

hard·back (härd′băk′) ▸ *adj. & n.* Hardcover.

hard·ball (härd′bôl′) ▸ *n.* 1. Baseball. 2. *Informal* The use of any means, however ruthless, to attain an objective.

hard-bit·ten (härd′bĭt′n) ▸ *adj.* Toughened by experience.

hard-boiled (härd′boild′) ▸ *adj.* 1. Cooked to a solid consistency by boiling. Used of eggs. 2. Callous or unfeeling; tough.

hard coal ▸ *n.* See **anthracite.**

hard copy ▸ *n.* A printed copy of the output of a computer.

hard-core (härd′kôr′) ▸ *adj.* 1. Intensely loyal; die-hard. 2. Stubbornly resistant to change: *hard-core poverty.* 3. Extremely explicit: *hard-core pornography.*

hard·cov·er (härd′kŭv′ər) ▸ *adj.* Bound in cloth, cardboard, or leather rather than paper. Used of books.

hard disk ▸ *n.* A rigid magnetic disk fixed permanently within a drive unit and used for storing computer data.

hard drive ▸ *n.* A disk drive that reads data stored on hard disks.

hard·en (här′dn) ▸ *v.* 1. To make hard or harder. 2. To enable to withstand hardship. 3. To make unsympathetic or callous.

hard·hat or **hard-hat** (härd′hăt′) ▸ *n.* 1a. A protective helmet worn esp. by construction workers. b. *Informal* A construction worker. 2. *Slang* An aggressively patriotic and politically conservative person. **—hard′hat′** *adj.*

hard·head·ed (härd′hĕd′ĭd) ▸ *adj.* 1. Stubborn; willful. 2. Pragmatic. **—hard′head′ed·ly** *adv.* **—hard′head′ed·ness** *n.*

hard·heart·ed (härd′här′tĭd) ▸ *adj.* Lacking in feeling or compassion; cold. **—hard′heart′ed·ly** *adv.* **—hard′heart′ed·ness** *n.*

har·di·hood (här′dē-ho͝od′) ▸ *n.* 1. Boldness and daring. 2. Impudence or insolence.

Har·ding (här′dĭng), **Warren Gamaliel** (1865–1923) ▸ The 29th US President (1921–23); died in office.

hard line ▸ *n.* An uncompromising position or stance. **—hard′-line′** *adj.* **—hard′-lin′er** *n.*

hard·ly (härd′lē) ▸ *adv.* 1. Barely; just. 2. To almost no de-

THESAURUS

befall, betide, come, come about, come off, develop, fall, hap, occur, pass, transpire, turn out. *Idiom:* come to pass. 2. To take place by chance ▸ befall, betide, chance, hap.

happen on or **upon** *v.* —*See* ENCOUNTER (1).

happening *n.* —*See* CIRCUMSTANCE (1), EVENT (1).

happenstance or **happenchance** *n.* —*See* CHANCE (1).

happiness *n.* A condition of supreme well-being and good spirits ▸ beatitude, blessedness, bliss, cheer, cheerfulness, contentedness, contentment, delight, felicity, gladness, glee, joy, joyfulness. [*Compare* DELIGHT, ELATION, SATISFACTION.]

happy *adj.* 1. Having achieved satisfaction, as of one's goal ▸ content, fulfilled, gratified, satisfied. 2. Characterized by luck or good fortune ▸ fortuitous, fortunate, lucky, providential. [*Compare* OPPORTUNE.] —*See also* CHEERFUL, MERRY, WILLING.

happy-go-lucky *adj.* —*See* LIGHTHEARTED.

harangue *n.* —*See* TIRADE.

harangue *v.* —*See* RANT.

harass *v.* To attack or disturb persistently ▸ annoy, badger, bait, bedevil, beleaguer, beset, besiege, harrow, harry, heckle, hector, hound, importune, persecute, pester, plague, taunt, tease, torment, worry. *Informal:* hassle, needle, ride. *Slang:* rag. [*Compare* INSULT, NAG, RIDICULE.]

harassment *n.* —*See* ANNOYANCE (1).

harbinger *n.* —*See* FORERUNNER, OMEN.

harbor *n.* A protected area of water where ships can anchor or dock ▸ anchorage, cove, haven, lagoon, road, roadstead, port. [*Compare* BAY[1], CHANNEL, INLET.] —*See also* COVER (1).

harbor *v.* To give refuge to ▸ haven, house, shelter, take in. [*Compare* DEFEND.] —*See also* BEAR (2), LODGE.

harborage *n.* —*See* REFUGE (1).

hard *adj.* 1. Unyielding to pressure ▸ firm, incompressible, solid. 2. Physically toughened so as to have great endurance ▸ hard-bitten, hard-handed, hardy, rugged, tempered, tough. *Idioms:* hard (*or* tough) as nails, hard (*or* tough) as tacks. [*Compare* MUSCULAR.] 3. Containing alcohol ▸ alcoholic, intoxicating, intoxicative, spiked, spirituous, stiff, strong. 4. Indulging in drink to an excessive degree ▸ heavy. *Informal:* two-fisted. —*See also* BITTER (2), BLEAK (1), CALLOUS, CERTAIN (2), DIFFICULT (1), REALISTIC (1), RESENTFUL, SEVERE (2), SEVERE (1).

hard *adv.* 1. With great force, energy, or intensity ▸ all out, boldly, con brio, energetically, fervently, fiercely, forcefully, forcibly, frantically, frenziedly, furiously, lustily, powerfully, rabidly, severely, stoutly, strenuously, urgently, warmly, vigorously, wholeheartedly, zealously. *Idioms:* hammer and tongs, like all get-out, like blazes, tooth and nail, with might and main, with no holds barred. [*Compare* VERY.] 2. With effort ▸ arduously, assiduously, difficultly, drudgingly, gruelingly, heavily, laboriously, rigorously, wearisomely. —*See also* CLOSE.

hard-bitten *adj.* —*See* HARD (2).

hard-boiled *adj.* —*See* CALLOUS.

harden *v.* 1. To make resistant to hardship, especially through continued exposure ▸ acclimate, acclimatize, caseharden, indurate, season, strengthen, toughen. [*Compare* DEADEN, GIRD.] 2. To make or become physically hard ▸ cake, cement, concrete, congeal, dry, firm up, fix, indurate, ossify, petrify, set, solidify, stiffen, toughen. [*Compare* COAGULATE, THICKEN.] 3. To make firmer in a particular conviction or habit ▸ confirm, fortify, reinforce, strengthen. [*Compare* BACK, ESTABLISH.]

hardened *adj.* —*See* CALLOUS.

hard-fisted *adj.* —*See* STINGY.

hard-handed *adj.* —*See* HARD (2).

hardheaded *adj.* —*See* REALISTIC (1), STUBBORN (1).

hardheadedness *n.* —*See* STUBBORNNESS.

hardhearted *adj.* —*See* CALLOUS.

hard-hitting *adj.* —*See* FORCEFUL.

hardiness *n.* —*See* ENDURANCE.

hardly *adv.* By a very little; almost not ▸ barely, just, scarce, scarcely. *Idioms:* by a hair (*or* whisker), by the

gree; almost not: *I could hardly hear the speaker.* **3.** Probably or almost surely not.

hard-nosed (härd′nōzd′) ► *adj.* Hardheaded.

hard palate ► *n.* The relatively hard, bony anterior portion of the palate.

hard·pan (härd′păn′) ► *n.* A layer of hard subsoil or clay.

hard-pressed (härd′prĕst′) ► *adj.* Experiencing great difficulty.

hard rock ► *n.* A style of rock 'n' roll marked by harsh, amplified sound and loud, distorted electric guitars.

hard sauce ► *n.* A creamy sauce of butter and sugar with liquor or vanilla flavoring.

hard sell ► *n. Informal* Aggressive, high-pressure selling or promotion.

hard·ship (härd′shĭp′) ► *n.* **1.** Extreme privation; suffering. **2.** A cause of privation or suffering.

hard·tack (härd′tăk′) ► *n.* A hard biscuit or bread made with only flour and water.

hard·top (härd′tŏp′) ► *n.* An automobile designed to look like a convertible but having a rigidly fixed, hard top.

hard·ware (härd′wâr′) ► *n.* **1.** Metal goods and utensils. **2a.** A computer and the associated physical equipment directly involved in data processing or communications. **b.** Machines and other physical equipment that are directly involved in performing an industrial, technological, or military function.

hard-wire (härd′wīr′) ► *v. Comp. Sci.* To implement (a capability) through permanently connected logic circuitry not subject to change by programming.

hard·wood (härd′wo͝od′) ► *n.* **1.** The wood of a broad-leaved flowering tree as distinguished from that of a conifer. **2.** Such a tree.

har·dy (här′dē) ► *adj.* **-di·er, -di·est. 1.** Being in robust and sturdy good health. **2.** Courageous; intrepid. **3.** Brazenly daring; audacious. **4.** Capable of surviving unfavorable conditions, such as cold weather. **—har′di·ly** *adv.* **—har′di·ness** *n.*

Hardy, Thomas (1840–1928) ► British writer.

hare (hâr) ► *n.* A mammal similar to a rabbit but having longer ears and legs.

hare·brained (hâr′brānd′) ► *adj.* Foolish; crazy.

hare·lip (hâr′lĭp′) ► *n.* Cleft lip. No longer in scientific use. **—hare′lipped′** *adj.*

har·em (hâr′əm, hăr′-) ► *n.* **1.** A house or rooms reserved for the women of a Muslim household. **2.** The women occupying a harem.

hark (härk) ► *v.* To listen attentively. ***—idiom:* hark back** To return to a previous point, as in a narrative.

Har·lem (här′ləm) ► A section of New York City in N Manhattan.

har·le·quin (här′lĭ-kwĭn, -kĭn) ► *n.* **1. Harlequin** A conventional buffoon of comic theater, traditionally presented in a mask and parti-colored tights. **2.** A clown; buffoon.

har·lot (här′lət) ► *n.* A prostitute. **—har′lot·ry** (-lə-trē) *n.*

harm (härm) ► *n.* **1.** Physical or psychological injury or damage. **2.** Wrong; evil. ► *v.* To do harm to. **—harm′ful** *adj.* **—harm′ful·ly** *adv.* **—harm′ful·ness** *n.* **—harm′less** *adj.* **—harm′less·ly** *adv.* **—harm′less·ness** *n.*

har·mon·ic (här-mŏn′ĭk) ► *adj.* **1.** Of or relating to musical harmony or harmonics. **2.** Pleasing to the ear. ► *n.* **1.** A tone produced on a stringed instrument by lightly touching a vibrating string at a given fraction of its length so that both segments vibrate. **2. harmonics** *(takes sing. v.)* The theory or study of the physical properties of musical sound. **—har·mon′i·cal·ly** *adv.*

har·mon·i·ca (här-mŏn′ĭ-kə) ► *n.* A small rectangular musical instrument played by exhaling or inhaling through a row of reeds.

har·mo·ni·ous (här-mō′nē-əs) ► *adj.* **1.** Exhibiting accord in feeling or action. **2.** Having elements pleasingly combined. **3.** Marked by harmony of sound; melodious. **—har·mo′ni·ous·ly** *adv.* **—har·mo′ni·ous·ness** *n.*

har·mo·ni·um (här-mō′nē-əm) ► *n.* An organlike keyboard instrument with metal reeds.

har·mo·nize (här′mə-nīz′) ► *v.* **-nized, -niz·ing. 1.** To bring or come into harmony. **2a.** To provide harmony for (a melody). **b.** To sing or play in harmony. **—har′mo·ni·za′tion** *n.* **—har′mo·niz′er** *n.*

har·mo·ny (här′mə-nē) ► *n., pl.* **-nies. 1.** Agreement in feeling or opinion; accord. **2.** A pleasing combination of elements in a whole. **3.** Combination and progression of chords in musical structure.

har·ness (här′nĭs) ► *n.* **1.** The gear or tackle with which a draft animal pulls a vehicle or implement. **2.** Something resembling such gear. ► *v.* **1.** To put a harness on. **2.** To control and direct the force of. ***—idiom:* in harness** On duty or at work. **—har′ness·er** *n.*

harp (härp) ► *n.* A musical instrument consisting of a large upright frame with strings of graded length played by plucking. ► *v.* To play a harp. ***—phrasal verb:* harp on** To dwell on tediously. **—harp′ist** *n.*

Har·pers Ferry (här′pərz) ► A locality of NE WV; scene of John Brown's rebellion (1859).

har·poon (här-po͞on′) ► *n.* A spearlike weapon with a barbed head used in hunting whales and large fish. **—har·poon′** *v.*

THESAURUS

skin of one's teeth. [*Compare* APPROXIMATELY, MERELY, ONLY.]

hardness *n.* —*See* SEVERITY, STABILITY.

hard-shell *adj.* —*See* CONFIRMED (1).

hardship *n.* —*See* DEPRIVATION, DIFFICULTY, MISERY.

hardy *adj.* —*See* BRAVE, HARD (2), HEALTHY, STRONG (2).

harebrained *adj.* —*See* FOOLISH, GIDDY (2).

hark *v.* To make an effort to hear something ► attend, hearken, heed, listen. *Idiom:* give (*or* lend) an ear. —*See also* HEAR.

hark back *v.* To cause one to remember or think of ► recall, suggest. *Idioms:* bring to mind, put one in mind of, take one back, remind one of. [*Compare* REFER, REMIND.]

harlot *n.* A woman who engages in sex for payment ► bawd, call girl, courtesan, harlot, scarlet woman, strumpet, tart. *Slang:* hooker, moll, working girl. *Idioms:* lady of easy virtue, lady of the night, lady of pleasure. [*Compare* PROSTITUTE, SLUT.]

harm *n.* The action or result of inflicting loss or pain ► damage, detriment, distress, hurt, impairment, injury, mischief, trauma. [*Compare* DISTRESS, EVIL, OFFENSE.]

harm *v.* —*See* DAMAGE.

harmful *adj.* Causing harm, injury, or destruction ► adverse, bad, baneful, corrosive, corruptive, damaging, deleterious, destructive, detrimental, evil, hurtful, ill, injurious, malefic, maleficent, malevolent, malign, mischievous, naughty, nocuous, noisome, noxious, pernicious, ruinous, toxic, unhealthy, unwholesome. [*Compare* DISASTROUS.]

harmless *adj.* Devoid of hurtful qualities ► benign, hurtless, innocent, innocuous, inoffensive, safe, unoffensive. —*See also* INNOCENT (2).

harmonic *adj.* —*See* HARMONIOUS (2).

harmonious *adj.* **1.** Having components that are pleasingly combined ► balanced, concordant, congruous, symmetrical. [*Compare* PLEASANT.] **2.** Characterized by harmony of sound ► consonant, harmonic, in tune, musical, symphonic, symphonious, well-voiced. —*See also* AGREEABLE, MELODIOUS, UNANIMOUS.

harmonization *n.* —*See* AGREEMENT (2), ARRANGEMENT (1).

harmonize *v.* **1.** To bring into accord ► accommodate, attune, conform, coordinate, integrate, proportion, reconcile, tune. [*Compare* BALANCE, MIX.] **2.** To combine and adapt in order to attain a particular effect ► arrange, blend, coordinate, correlate, integrate, mesh, orchestrate, synthesize, unify. **3.** To occur at the same time ► coincide, concur, synchronize. —*See also* AGREE (1), AGREE (2), RELATE (2).

harmony *n.* **1.** Pleasing agreement, as of musical sounds ► accord, blend, concert, concord, consonance, euphoniousness, euphony, symphony, tune, tunefulness. **2.** A relationship or an affinity between people or things in which many properties are shared ► sympathy, synch, synchronization, synchrony. **3.** Satisfying arrangement marked by even distribution of elements, as in a design ► balance, proportion, symmetry. —*See also* AGREEMENT (2).

harness *n.* —*See* FASTENER.

harness *v.* —*See* RESTRAIN, USE.

harp on *n.* —*See* BELABOR.

harp·si·chord (härpʹsĭ-kôrdʹ) ▸ *n.* A keyboard instrument whose strings are plucked by means of quills or plectrums. **—harpʹsi·chordʹist** *n.*

Har·py (härʹpē) ▸ *n., pl.* **-pies. 1.** *Gk. Myth.* A monster with the head and trunk of a woman and the tail, wings, and talons of a bird. **2. harpy a.** A predatory person. **b.** A shrewish woman.

har·que·bus (härʹkə-bəs, -kwə-) ▸ *n.* A heavy, portable matchlock gun invented during the 15th cent.

har·ri·dan (hărʹĭ-dn) ▸ *n.* A shrewish woman.

har·ri·er¹ (hărʹē-ər) ▸ *n.* **1.** One that harries. **2.** A slender, narrow-winged hawk.

har·ri·er² (hărʹē-ər) ▸ *n.* **1.** Any of a breed of small hound orig. used in hunting hares and rabbits. **2.** A cross-country runner.

Har·ris·burg (hărʹĭs-bûrgʹ) ▸ The capital of PA, in the SE-central part. Pop. 49,000.

Har·ri·son¹ (hărʹĭ-sən), **Benjamin** (1726–91) ▸ Amer. Revolutionary leader.

Har·ri·son² (hărʹĭ-sən), **Benjamin** (1833–1901) ▸ The 23rd US President (1889–93).

Harrison, William Henry (1773–1841) ▸ The 9th US President (1841).

har·row (hărʹō) ▸ *n.* A farm implement consisting of a heavy frame with sharp teeth or upright disks, used to break up and even off plowed ground. ▸ *v.* **1.** To break up and level (soil) with a harrow. **2.** To inflict great distress or torment on.

har·row·ing (hărʹō-ĭng) ▸ *adj.* Extremely distressing; agonizing.

har·ry (hărʹē) ▸ *v.* **-ried, -ry·ing. 1.** To disturb or distress by or as if by repeated attacks. **2.** To raid; pillage.

harsh (härsh) ▸ *adj.* **-er, -est. 1.** Disagreeable to the senses, esp. to the hearing. **2.** Extremely severe or exacting; stern. **—harshʹly** *adv.* **—harshʹness** *n.*

hart (härt) ▸ *n., pl.* **harts** or **hart.** A male deer, esp. a male red deer.

Hart·ford (härtʹfərd) ▸ The capital of CT, in the N-central part on the Connecticut R. Pop. 122,000.

har·um-scar·um (hârʹəm-skârʹəm, hărʹəm-skărʹəm) ▸ *adj.* Reckless. ▸ *adv.* With abandon; recklessly.

har·vest (härʹvĭst) ▸ *n.* **1.** The gathering in of a crop. **2a.** The crop that ripens or is gathered in a season. **b.** The time or season of such gathering. **3.** The result or consequence of an activity. **—harʹvest** *v.* **—harʹvest·er** *n.*

harvest moon ▸ *n.* The full moon that occurs nearest the autumnal equinox.

has (hăz) ▸ *v.* 3rd pers. sing. pr.t. of **have.**

has-been (hăzʹbĭnʹ) ▸ *n. Informal* One that is no longer famous, successful, or useful.

hash¹ (hăsh) ▸ *n.* **1.** A dish of chopped meat and potatoes, usu. browned. **2.** A jumble; hodgepodge. ▸ *v.* **1.** To chop into pieces; mince. **2.** *Informal* To discuss carefully; review: *hash over future plans.*

hash² (hăsh) ▸ *n. Slang* Hashish.

hash·ish (hăshʹēsh', hă-shēshʹ) ▸ *n.* A purified resin prepared from marijuana.

hash mark ▸ *n.* A service stripe on the sleeve of an enlisted person's uniform.

Ha·sid or **Has·sid** also **Chas·sid** (ᴋʜäʹsĭd, häʹ-) ▸ *n., pl.* **-si·dim** (ᴋʜä-sēʹdĭm, ᴋʜô-, hä-). A member of a Jewish mystic movement founded in 18th-cent. E Europe that reacted against Talmudic learning. **—Ha·siʹdic** *adj.* **—Ha·siʹdism** *n.*

has·n't (hăzʹənt) ▸ Has not.

hasp (hăsp) ▸ *n.* A metal fastener that fits over a staple and is secured by a pin, bolt, or padlock. **—hasp** *v.*

has·si·um (häʹsē-əm) ▸ *n. Symbol* **Hs** A synthetic radioactive element. At. no. 108.

has·sle (hăsʹəl) *Informal* ▸ *n.* **1.** An argument or fight. **2.** Trouble; bother. ▸ *v.* **-sled, -sling. 1.** To argue or fight. **2.** To bother or harass.

has·sock (hăsʹək) ▸ *n.* A thick cushion used as a footstool or for kneeling.

hast (hăst) ▸ *v. Archaic* 2nd pers. sing. pr.t. of **have.**

haste (hāst) ▸ *n.* **1.** Rapidity of action or motion. **2.** Overeagerness to act. **3.** Rash or headlong action. ***—idiom:* make haste** To move or act swiftly; hurry.

has·ten (hāʹsən) ▸ *v.* **1.** To move or cause to move swiftly. **2.** To speed up: *a drug to hasten clotting.*

hast·y (hāʹstē) ▸ *adj.* **-i·er, -i·est. 1.** Marked by speed; rapid. **2.** Done or made too quickly to be accurate or wise; rash: *a hasty decision.* **—hastʹi·ly** *adv.* **—hastʹi·ness** *n.*

hat (hăt) ▸ *n.* A covering for the head, esp. one with a shaped crown and brim. ***—idioms:* at the drop of a hat** At the slightest pretext or provocation. **hat in hand** Humbly. **pass the hat** To take up a collection of money. **take (one's) hat off to** To admire or congratulate.

hatch¹ (hăch) ▸ *n.* **1.** An opening, as in the deck of a ship or in an aircraft. **2.** The cover for such an opening. **3.** A hatchway.

hatch² (hăch) ▸ *v.* **1.** To emerge from an egg. **2.** To produce (young) from an egg. **3.** To cause (an egg) to produce young. **4.** To devise or originate, esp. in secret: *hatch a plot.* **—hatchʹer** *n.*

hatch³ (hăch) ▸ *v.* To shade by drawing fine parallel or crossed lines on. **—hatch** *n.*

hatch·back (hăchʹbăkʹ) ▸ *n.* An automobile having a sloping back with a hatch that opens upward.

hatch·er·y (hăchʹə-rē) ▸ *n., pl.* **-ies.** A place where eggs, esp. of fish or poultry, are hatched.

hatch·et (hăchʹĭt) ▸ *n.* **1.** A small, short-handled ax. **2.** A tomahawk.

hatchet man ▸ *n. Slang* **1.** A man hired to commit murder. **2.** One who is assigned to carry out a disagreeable task.

hatch·ling (hăchʹlĭng) ▸ *n.* A newly hatched bird, amphibian, fish, or reptile.

hatch·way (hăchʹwāʹ) ▸ *n.* **1.** A hatch leading to a hold, compartment, or cellar. **2.** A ladder or stairway within a hatchway.

hate (hāt) ▸ *v.* **hat·ed, hat·ing. 1.** To feel hostility or animosity

THESAURUS

harpy *n.* —*See* SCOLD.

harridan *n.* —*See* SCOLD.

harrow *v.* To subject another to extreme physical cruelty, as in punishing ▸ crucify, rack, torment, torture. *Idioms:* put on the rack (*or* wheel), put the screws to. [*Compare* PUNISH.] —*See also* DISTRESS, HARASS.

harrowing *adj.* —*See* HORRIBLE, TORMENTING.

harry *v.* —*See* HARASS, INVADE (1).

harsh *adj.* Disagreeable to the senses, especially the sense of hearing ▸ dry, grating, hoarse, jarring, rasping, raspy, raucous, rough, scratchy, shrill, squawky, strident. [*Compare* VOCIFEROUS, INHARMONIOUS.] —*See also* BITING, BITTER (2), BLEAK (1), ROUGH (1), SEVERE (1).

harshness *n.* —*See* SEVERITY.

harum-scarum *adj.* —*See* RASH¹.

haruspex *n.* —*See* PROPHET.

harvest *n.* The produce harvested from the land ▸ crop, fruit, fruitage, vintage, yield. —*See also* EFFECT (1).

harvest *v.* —*See* GATHER, GLEAN.

hash *n.* —*See* MESS (1).

hash over *v.* —*See* DISCUSS.

hasp *n.* —*See* FASTENER.

hassle *n.* 4. —*See* ANNOYANCE (2), ARGUMENT, BOTHER.

hassle *v.* —*See* ARGUE (1), HARASS.

hassock *n.* A stool or cushion for resting the feet ▸ footrest, footstool, ottoman.

haste *n.* **1.** Rapidness of movement or activity ▸ alacrity, celerity, dispatch, expedition, expeditiousness, fleetness, hurry, hustle, quickness, rapidity, rapidness, rush, speed, speediness, swiftness. **2.** Careless headlong action ▸ hastiness, hurriedness, precipitance, precipitancy, precipitateness, precipitation, rashness, rush.

haste *v.* —*See* RUSH.

hasten *v.* —*See* RUSH, SPEED.

hastily *adv.* —*See* FAST.

hastiness *n.* —*See* HASTE (2).

hasty *adj.* —*See* FAST (1), QUICK, RASH¹.

hatch *v.* —*See* BREED, INVENT, PLOT (2).

hatchet man *n.* —*See* MURDERER.

hate *v.* To feel hostility toward or strong dislike for something ▸ abhor, abominate, detest, execrate, loathe. *Idioms:* bear antipathy (*or* malice *or* ill will) toward, be repelled (*or* repulsed *or* revolted) by, be sick of, can't stand, hold in contempt. [*Compare* DESPISE, DISLIKE, REVILE.]

hate *n.* **1.** A strong feeling of hostil-

toward; detest. 2. To feel dislike or distaste for. ▸ *n.* 1. Hatred. 2. An object of hatred. **—hate′ful** *adj.* **—hate′ful·ly** *adv.* **—hate′ful·ness** *n.* **—hat′er** *n.*

hate crime ▸ *n.* A crime motivated by prejudice against a social group.

hath (hăth) ▸ *v. Archaic* 3rd pers. sing. pr.t. of **have**.

ha·tha yoga (hŭ′tə, hă′thə) ▸ *n.* A system of yoga exercises emphasizing specific postures and controlled breathing.

ha·tred (hā′trĭd) ▸ *n.* Intense animosity or hostility.

hau·berk (hô′bərk) ▸ *n.* A tunic of chain mail.

haugh·ty (hô′tē) ▸ *adj.* **-ti·er, -ti·est.** Scornfully and condescendingly proud. **—haugh′ti·ly** *adv.* **—haugh′ti·ness** *n.*

haul (hôl) ▸ *v.* 1. To pull or drag forcibly. 2. To transport, as with a truck or cart. ▸ *n.* 1. The act of hauling. 2. A distance, esp. over which something is hauled. 3. Something hauled. 4. An amount collected or acquired: *a haul of fish.* **—haul′er** *n.*

haul·age (hô′lĭj) ▸ *n.* 1. The act or process of hauling. 2. A charge made for hauling.

haunch (hônch, hŏnch) ▸ *n.* 1. The hip, buttock, and upper thigh. 2. The loin and leg of an animal, esp. as used for food.

haunt (hônt, hŏnt) ▸ *v.* 1. To inhabit, visit, or appear to in the form of a ghost or spirit. 2. To frequent. 3. To come to the mind of continually. ▸ *n.* A place much frequented. **—haunt′er** *n.* **—haunt′ing·ly** *adv.*

Hau·sa (hou′sə, -zə) ▸ *n., pl.* **-sa** or **-sas.** 1. A member of a people of N Nigeria and S Niger. 2. Their Chadic language.

haute couture (ōt) ▸ *n.* 1. The leading designers of exclusive fashions for women. 2a. The creation of exclusive fashions for women. b. The fashions created.

haute cuisine ▸ *n.* Elaborate or skillfully prepared food.

hau·teur (hō-tûr′, ō-tœr′) ▸ *n.* Haughtiness; arrogance.

Ha·van·a (hə-văn′ə) ▸ The capital of Cuba, in the NW part on the Gulf of Mexico. Pop. 2,340,000. **—Ha·van′an** *adj. & n.*

Ha·var·ti (hə-vär′tē) ▸ *n.* A mild, pale yellow cheese of Danish origin.

have (hăv) ▸ *v.* **had** (hăd), **hav·ing, has** (hăz). 1. To possess; own. 2. To possess as a characteristic or part: *He has a lot of energy. The car has bad brakes.* 3. To stand in relation to. 4. To hold in the mind; know or entertain. 5. To exhibit: *have compassion.* 6. To accept; take: *I'll have some peas.* 7a. To suffer from: *has a bad cold.* b. To experience: *had a great summer.* 8. To cause to: *had him run an errand.* 9. To permit. 10. To beget or give birth to. 11. To partake of. 12. To be obliged to: *I have to go.* ▸ *v. aux.* Used with a past participle to form the present perfect, past perfect, and future perfect tenses: *I have written you. I had given up smoking for a year. I will have left when you get there.* ***—phrasal verbs:*** **have at** To attack. **have on** 1. To wear. 2. To be scheduled: *We have a dinner party on for tomorrow.* ▸ *n.* One who has wealth. ***—idioms:*** **have done with** To stop; cease. **have had it** 1. To be exhausted or disgusted. 2. To be beyond remedy or repair. **have it in for** To intend to harm. **have it out** To settle, esp. by an argument. **have to do with** To be concerned or associated with.

ha·ven (hā′vən) ▸ *n.* 1. A harbor; port. 2. A place of refuge or rest.

have-not (hăv′nŏt′) ▸ *n.* One having little or no material wealth.

have·n't (hăv′ənt) ▸ Have not.

hav·er·sack (hăv′ər-săk′) ▸ *n.* A bag carried over one shoulder to transport supplies.

hav·oc (hăv′ək) ▸ *n.* 1. Widespread destruction; devastation. 2. Disorder or chaos.

haw[1] (hô) ▸ *v.* To fumble in speaking.

haw[2] (hô) ▸ *n.* 1. The fruit of a hawthorn. 2. A hawthorn or similar tree.

Ha·wai·i (hə-wä′ē, -wī′ē) ▸ A state of the US in the central Pacific comprising the Hawaiian Islands. Cap. Honolulu. Pop. 1,210,000.

Ha·wai·ian (hə-wä′yən) ▸ *n.* 1. A native or inhabitant of Hawaii or the Hawaiian Islands. 2a. A member or descendant of the indigenous Polynesian people of the Hawaiian Islands. b. The Polynesian language of Hawaii. **—Ha·wai′ian** *adj.*

Hawaiian Islands ▸ A group of islands in the central Pacific coextensive with HI.

hawk[1] (hôk) ▸ *n.* 1. Any of various birds of prey characteristically having a short hooked bill and strong claws adapted for seizing. 2. One who favors an aggressive or warlike foreign policy. **—hawk′ish** *adj.* **—hawk′ish·ly** *adv.*

hawk[2] (hôk) ▸ *v.* To peddle goods aggressively, esp. by calling out. **—hawk′er** *n.*

hawk[3] (hôk) ▸ *v.* To clear the throat by or as if by coughing up phlegm. **—hawk** *n.*

hawk-eyed (hôk′īd′) ▸ *adj.* Having very keen eyesight.

haw·ser (hô′zər) ▸ *n.* A cable or rope used in mooring or towing a ship.

haw·thorn (hô′thôrn′) ▸ *n.* A usu. thorny tree or shrub having white or pinkish flowers and reddish fruits.

Haw·thorne (hô′thôrn′), **Nathaniel** (1804–64) ▸ Amer. writer.

hay (hā) ▸ *n.* Grass or other plants cut and dried for fodder. ▸ *v.* To mow and cure grass and herbage for hay.

Haydn (hīd′n), **Franz Joseph** (1732–1809) ▸ Austrian composer.

Hayes (hāz), **Rutherford Birchard** (1822–93) ▸ The 19th US President (1877–81).

hay fever ▸ *n.* An allergic condition affecting the mucous membranes of the upper respiratory tract and the eyes, usu. caused by an abnormal sensitivity to airborne pollen.

hay·fork (hā′fôrk′) ▸ *n.* 1. A pitchfork. 2. A machine-operated fork for moving hay.

hay·loft (hā′lôft′, -lŏft′) ▸ *n.* A loft for storing hay.

hay·seed (hā′sēd′) ▸ *n.* 1. Chaff that falls from hay. 2. *Slang* A bumpkin; yokel.

hay·stack (hā′stăk′) ▸ *n.* A large stack of hay, esp. as left in a field to dry.

hay·wire (hā′wīr′) ▸ *adj. Informal* 1. Crazy. 2. Not functioning properly; broken.

haz·ard (hăz′ərd) ▸ *n.* 1. A chance; accident. 2. A possible

THESAURUS

ity or dislike ▸ abhorrence, abomination, antipathy, aversion, contempt, detestation, hatred, horror, loathing, odium, rancor, repellence, repellency, repugnance, repugnancy, repulsion, revulsion. [*Compare* AGGRESSION, DESPISAL, ENMITY, RESENTMENT.] 2. An object of extreme dislike ▸ abhorrence, abomination, anathema, aversion, bête noire, bugbear, detestation, execration. *Informal:* horror. [*Compare* ANNOYANCE.]

hateful *adj.* *—See* MALEVOLENT, OFFENSIVE (1).

hatred *n.* *—See* DESPISAL, HATE (1).

haughtiness *n.* *—See* ARROGANCE, CONDESCENSION.

haughty *adj.* *—See* ARROGANT, DISDAINFUL.

haul *v.* *—See* CARRY (1), PULL (1).

haul *n.* *—See* BURDEN[1] (2), PULL (1).

hauling *n.* *—See* TRANSPORTATION.

haunt *v.* To come to mind continually ▸ obsess, torment, trouble, weigh on (*or* upon). *—See also* FREQUENT.

haunt *n.* A frequently visited place ▸ meeting place, rendezvous, resort. *Slang:* hangout, stamping ground, stomping ground. [*Compare* HABITAT.] *—See also* GHOST.

hauteur *n.* *—See* ARROGANCE.

have *v.* 1. To be filled by ▸ contain, hold. [*Compare* CONSTITUTE.] 2. To admit to one's possession, presence, or awareness ▸ accept, receive, take. [*Compare* ABSORB.] 3. To organize and carry out an activity ▸ give, hold, stage, throw. [*Compare* CONDUCT.] *—See also* BEAR (3), BEAR (4), CARRY (2), COMMAND (2), CONTAIN (1), DECEIVE, EXPERIENCE, PARTICIPATE, PERMIT (1).

have at *v.* *—See* ATTACK (1).

haven *n.* *—See* COVER (1), HARBOR.

haven *v.* To give refuge to ▸ harbor, house, shelter, take in. [*Compare* DEFEND.]

have-not *n.* *—See* PAUPER.

havoc *n.* *—See* DESTRUCTION.

hawk[1] *v.* To travel about selling goods ▸ huckster, peddle, vend. [*Compare* SELL.]

hawk[2] *v.* To expel a small amount of saliva or mucus from the mouth ▸ expectorate, spit. [*Compare* DROOL.]

hawkish *adj.* *—See* AGGRESSIVE, MILITARY (1).

hayseed *n.* *—See* CLODHOPPER.

haywire *adj.* *—See* INSANE.

hazard *n.* *—See* CHANCE, DANGER, RISK.

source of danger: *a fire hazard.* 3. An obstacle on a golf course. ▸ *v.* To venture: *hazard a guess.* **—haz′ard·ous** *adj.* **—haz′ard·ous·ly** *adv.*

haze¹ (hāz) ▸ *n.* 1. Atmospheric moisture, dust, smoke, and vapor that diminishes visibility. 2. A vague or confused state of mind.

haze² (hāz) ▸ *v.* **hazed, haz·ing.** To persecute or harass with meaningless, difficult, or humiliating tasks. **—haz′er** *n.*

ha·zel (hā′zəl) ▸ *n.* 1. A shrub or small tree bearing edible nuts enclosed in a leafy husk. 2. A light or yellowish brown. **—ha′zel** *adj.*

ha·zel·nut (hā′zəl-nŭt′) ▸ *n.* The nut of a hazel.

haz·y (hā′zē) ▸ *adj.* **-i·er, -i·est.** 1. Marked by the presence of haze. 2. Not clearly defined; unclear or vague. **—haz′i·ly** *adv.* **—haz′i·ness** *n.*

H-bomb (āch′bŏm′) ▸ *n.* A hydrogen bomb.

HDL (āch′dē-ĕl′) ▸ *n.* A complex of lipids and proteins that transports cholesterol in the blood, high levels of which may decrease the risk of heart disease.

HDTV ▸ *abbr.* high-definition television

he (hē) ▸ *pron.* 1. Used to refer to the male previously mentioned or implied. 2. Used to refer to a person whose gender is unspecified or unknown. ▸ *n.* A male person or animal: *Is the cat a he?*

He ▸ The symbol for the element **helium.**

head (hĕd) ▸ *n.* 1. The uppermost or forwardmost part of the body, containing the brain and in vertebrates the eyes, ears, nose, mouth, and jaws. 2. The intellect or mind; intelligence. 3a. Mental ability or aptitude. b. Self-control: *Don't lose your head.* 4. *Slang* A drug user. 5. often **heads** *(takes sing. v.)* The side of a coin having the principal design. 6a. An individual: *charged five dollars a head.* b. *pl.* **head.** A single herd animal: *20 head of cattle.* 7. A leader, chief, or director. 8. The foremost or leading position. 9. Pressure: *a head of steam.* 10. A turning point: *bring matters to a head.* 11. A projecting or striking part. 12. A rounded compact mass, as of leaves or buds: *a head of cabbage.* 13. The uppermost part; the top. 14. The end considered the most important: *the head of the table.* 15. A toilet, esp. on a ship. 16. A headline or heading. ▸ *adj.* 1. Foremost in rank or importance. 2. Placed at the top or the front. ▸ *v.* 1. To be in charge of; lead. 2. To be in the first or foremost position of. 3. To aim or proceed in a certain direction: *headed the horses up the hill; head for town.* 4. To provide with a head. ***—phrasal verb:*** **head off** To intercept. ***—idioms:*** **head over heels** 1. Rolling, as in a somersault. 2. Completely; hopelessly: *head over heels in love.* **off** (or **out of**) **(one's) head** Insane; crazy. **—head′less** *adj.*

head·ache (hĕd′āk′) ▸ *n.* 1. A pain in the head. 2. *Informal* An annoying problem. **—head′ach′y** *adj.*

head·band (hĕd′bănd′) ▸ *n.* A band worn around the head.

head·board (hĕd′bôrd′) ▸ *n.* A board or panel that forms the head, as of a bed.

head·dress (hĕd′drĕs′) ▸ *n.* A covering or an ornament for the head.

head·first (hĕd′fûrst′) ▸ *adv.* 1. With the head leading; headlong. 2. Impetuously; brashly. **—head′first′** *adj.*

head·gear (hĕd′gîr′) ▸ *n.* A covering, such as a hat or helmet, for the head.

head·hunt·ing (hĕd′hŭn′tĭng) ▸ *n.* 1. The custom of cutting off and preserving the heads of enemies as trophies. 2. *Informal* The business of recruiting personnel, esp. executive personnel, as for a corporation. **—head′hunt′er** *n.*

head·ing (hĕd′ĭng) ▸ *n.* 1. The title, subtitle, or topic that stands at the top or beginning, as of a text. 2. The direction in which a ship or an aircraft is moving.

head·land (hĕd′lənd, -lănd′) ▸ *n.* A point of land extending out into a body of water.

head·light (hĕd′līt′) ▸ *n.* 1. A light with a reflector mounted on the front of a vehicle. 2. A lamp mounted on a miner's or spelunker's hard hat.

head·line (hĕd′līn′) ▸ *n.* The title or caption of a newspaper article, usu. set in large type. ▸ *v.* **-lined, -lin·ing.** 1. To supply (a page or passage) with a headline. 2. To receive prominent billing at: *headline a variety show.* **—head′lin′er** *n.*

head·lock (hĕd′lŏk′) ▸ *n.* A wrestling hold in which the head of one wrestler is encircled and locked by the arm and body of the other.

head·long (hĕd′lông′, -lŏng′) ▸ *adv.* 1. Headfirst. 2. In an impetuous manner; rashly. 3. At breakneck speed. **—head′long′** *adj.*

head·man (hĕd′mən, -măn′) ▸ *n.* The chief man esp. of a tribal or traditional village.

head·mas·ter (hĕd′măs′tər) ▸ *n.* A man who is a principal, usu. of a private school.

head·mis·tress (hĕd′mĭs′trĭs) ▸ *n.* A woman who is a principal, usu. of a private school.

head-on (hĕd′ŏn′, -ôn′) ▸ *adj.* 1. Facing forward; frontal. 2. With the front end foremost: *a head-on collision.* **—head′-on′** *adv.*

head·phone (hĕd′fōn′) ▸ *n.* A receiver held to the ear by a headband.

head·piece (hĕd′pēs′) ▸ *n.* 1. A protective covering for the head. 2. A headset.

head·pin (hĕd′pĭn′) ▸ *n.* See **kingpin** 1.

head·quar·ters (hĕd′kwôr′tərz) ▸ *pl.n. (takes sing. or pl. v.)* 1. The offices of a commander, as of a military unit. 2. A center of operations or administration.

head·rest (hĕd′rĕst′) ▸ *n.* A support for the head.

head·room (hĕd′ro͞om′, -ro͝om′) ▸ *n.* Space above one's head, as in a vehicle or tunnel; clearance.

head·set (hĕd′sĕt′) ▸ *n.* A pair of headphones, often with microphone attached.

head shop ▸ *n.* *Slang* A shop that sells paraphernalia for use with illegal drugs.

head·stall (hĕd′stôl′) ▸ *n.* The section of a bridle that fits over a horse's head.

head·stand (hĕd′stănd′) ▸ *n.* A position in which one supports oneself vertically on one's head with the hands braced for support on the floor.

head start ▸ *n.* 1. A start before other contestants in a race. 2. An early start that confers an advantage.

head·stone (hĕd′stōn′) ▸ *n.* 1. A memorial stone set at the head of a grave. 2. See **keystone** 1.

head·strong (hĕd′strông′, -strŏng′) ▸ *adj.* Determined to have one's own way; willful.

head·wait·er (hĕd′wā′tər) ▸ *n.* A waiter in charge of the

THESAURUS

hazard *v.* —*See* ENDANGER, GAMBLE (2), VENTURE.

hazardous *adj.* —*See* DANGEROUS.

haze *n.* A suspension in the air of microscopic particles of water, dust, or smoke ▸ brume, fog, mist, pall, smaze, smog, smudge, steam, vapor. —*See also* DAZE.

hazing *n.* —*See* INITIATION.

hazy *adj.* Heavy, dark, or dense, especially with impurities ▸ murky, smoggy, turbid. [*Compare* DIRTY.] —*See also* UNCLEAR.

head *n.* 1. The uppermost part of the body ▸ crown, noddle, pate, poll. *Slang:* bean, block, conk, dome, noggin, noodle, nut. 2. The seat of the faculty of intelligence and reason ▸ brain, mind. *Informal:* gray matter. [*Compare* IMAGINATION.] 3. A term or terms in large type introducing a text ▸ header, heading, headline. —*See also* BOSS, CHIEF, CRISIS, FOAM, FRONT, TALENT.

head *adj.* —*See* PRIMARY (1).

head *v.* —*See* ADMINISTER (1), AIM (1), BEAR (5).

head off *v.* To block the progress of and force to change direction ▸ cut off, intercept. —*See also* PREVENT.

headache *n.* —*See* ANNOYANCE (2), BOTHER, BURDEN¹ (1).

header *n.* —*See* FALL (1).

heading *n.* 1. A term or terms in large type introducing a text ▸ head, header, headline. 2. The compass direction in which a ship or aircraft moves ▸ bearing, course, vector. —*See also* DIRECTION, ENTRY.

headline *n.* A term or terms in large type introducing a text ▸ head, header, heading. —*See also* NEWS.

headliner *n.* —*See* LEAD.

headlong *adj.* —*See* RASH¹.

headman *n.* —*See* CHIEF.

headquarters *n.* —*See* BASE¹ (1), CENTER (1), HOME (1).

head start *n.* —*See* ADVANTAGE (1).

headstrong *adj.* —*See* STUBBORN (1), UNRULY.

other waiters and waitresses in a restaurant.

head·wa·ters (hĕd′wô′tər z, -wŏt′ərz) ▸ *pl.n.* The waters from which a river rises.

head·way (hĕd′wā′) ▸ *n.* **1.** Forward movement, esp. of a ship. **2.** Progress toward a goal. **3.** Overhead clearance; headroom.

head·wind (hĕd′wĭnd′) ▸ *n.* A wind blowing directly against the course of an aircraft or ship.

head·work (hĕd′wûrk′) ▸ *n.* Mental activity or work; thought. **—head′work′er** *n.*

head·y (hĕd′ē) ▸ *adj.* **-i·er, -i·est. 1.** Intoxicating. **2.** Impetuous; rash. **—head′i·ly** *adv.* **—head′i·ness** *n.*

heal (hēl) ▸ *v.* **1.** To restore to or regain health or soundness. **2.** To set right; repair: *healed the rift between us.* **—heal′a·ble** *adj.* **—heal′er** *n.*

health (hĕlth) ▸ *n.* **1.** The overall condition of an organism at a given time. **2.** Soundness, esp. of body or mind. **3.** A condition of well-being. **—health′ful** *adj.* **—health′ful·ly** *adv.* **—health′ful·ness** *n.*

health care ▸ *n.* The prevention and treatment of illness through the delivery of medical services. **—health-care** *adj.*

health food ▸ *n.* A food believed to be beneficial to one's health. **—health′-food′** *adj.*

health maintenance organization ▸ *n.* An HMO.

health·y (hĕl′thē) ▸ *adj.* **-i·er, -i·est. 1.** Possessing good health. **2.** Conducive to good health; healthful. **3.** Indicative of sound thinking or mind: *a healthy attitude.* **4.** Sizable; considerable: *a healthy portion.* **—health′i·ly** *adv.* **—health′i·ness** *n.*

heap (hēp) ▸ *n.* **1.** A group of things placed or thrown, one on top of the other. **2.** often **heaps** *Informal* A great deal; a lot. **3.** *Slang* An old or run-down car. ▸ *v.* **1.** To put or throw in a pile. **2.** To fill to capacity. **3.** To bestow in abundance: *heaped abuse on them.*

hear (hîr) ▸ *v.* **heard** (hûrd), **hear·ing. 1.** To perceive by the ear. **2.** To learn by hearing. **3a.** To listen to attentively. **b.** To listen to in an official capacity. **c.** To attend: *hear Mass.* **—hear′er** *n.*

hear·ing (hîr′ĭng) ▸ *n.* **1.** The sense by which sound is perceived. **2.** Range of audibility; earshot. **3.** An opportunity to be heard. **4.** A preliminary examination of an accused person. **5.** A session at which testimony is taken from witnesses.

hearing aid ▸ *n.* A small electronic amplifying device that is worn to aid poor hearing.

hear·ing-im·paired (hîr′ĭng-ĭm-pârd′) ▸ *adj.* **1.** Hard of hearing. **2.** Completely incapable of hearing; deaf. **—hear′ing-im·paired′** *n.*

hear·ken (här′kən) ▸ *v.* To listen attentively; give heed.

hear·say (hîr′sā′) ▸ *n.* Information heard from another.

hearse (hûrs) ▸ *n.* A vehicle for conveying a coffin to a church or cemetery.

Hearst (hûrst), **William Randolph** (1863–1951) ▸ Amer. newspaper and magazine publisher.

heart (härt) ▸ *n.* **1.** The chambered, muscular organ that pumps blood received from the veins into the arteries, maintaining the flow of blood through the circulatory system. **2.** The vital center and source of one's being, feelings, and emotions. **3a.** Sympathy or generosity; compassion. **b.** Love; affection. **4.** Resolution; fortitude: *lose heart.* **5.** The most important or essential part. **6.** Any of a suit of playing cards marked with a red, heart-shaped figure. **—*idioms:* by heart** By memory. **heart and soul** Completely; entirely. **take to heart** To take seriously and be affected by. **with all (one's) heart 1.** With great willingness or pleasure. **2.** With deepest feeling.

heart·ache (härt′āk′) ▸ *n.* Emotional anguish; sorrow.

heart attack ▸ *n.* Sudden interruption or insufficiency of blood supply to the heart, typically resulting from obstruction of a coronary artery.

heart·beat (härt′bēt′) ▸ *n.* A single complete pulsation of the heart.

heart·break (härt′brāk′) ▸ *n.* Overwhelming grief or disappointment, esp. in love. **—heart′break′er** *n.* **—heart′break′ing** *adj.* **—heart′break′ing·ly** *adv.*

heart·bro·ken (härt′brō′kən) ▸ *adj.* Suffering from heartbreak. **—heart′bro′ken·ly** *adv.*

heart·burn (härt′bûrn′) ▸ *n.* A burning sensation, usu. in the middle of the chest, caused by acidic stomach fluids.

heart disease ▸ *n.* A structural or functional abnormality of the heart or of the blood vessels supplying the heart.

heart·en (här′tn) ▸ *v.* To give strength, courage, or hope to.

heart·felt (härt′fĕlt′) ▸ *adj.* Deeply or sincerely felt; earnest.

hearth (härth) ▸ *n.* **1.** The floor of a fireplace, usu. extending into a room. **2.** Family life; the home. **3.** The lowest part of a blast furnace, from which the molten metal flows.

hearth·stone (härth′stōn′) ▸ *n.* **1.** Stone used in the construction of a hearth. **2.** Family life; the home.

THESAURUS

headway *n.* —*See* ADVANCE, PROGRESS.

headword *n.* —*See* ENTRY.

headwork *n.* —*See* THOUGHT.

heal *v.* —*See* CURE.

health *n.* **1.** The condition of being physically or mentally sound ▸ haleness, healthiness, heartiness, soundness, wellness, wholeness. [*Compare* CONDITION.] **2.** The act of drinking to someone ▸ pledge, toast.

healthful *adj.* Promoting good health ▸ healthsome, healthy, hearty, hygienic, salubrious, salutary, wholesome. [*Compare* BENEFICIAL, NUTRITIOUS.] —*See also* HEALTHY.

healthiness *n.* —*See* HEALTH (1).

healthsome *adj.* —*See* HEALTHFUL.

healthy *adj.* Having good health ▸ able-bodied, all right, fit, flourishing, hale, hardy, healthful, hearty, normal, right, robust, rosy-cheeked, sound, thriving, vigorous, well, whole, wholesome. *Idioms:* fit as a fiddle, hale and hearty, in fine fettle, in fine (*or* good) health, in fine (*or* good) shape, in the pink. [*Compare* LUSTY, MUSCULAR, STRONG.] —*See also* BIG, HEALTHFUL.

heap *n.* **1.** A group of things gathered haphazardly ▸ agglomeration, bank, cumulus, drift, hill, mass, mess, mound, mountain, pile, shock, stack, tumble. [*Compare* ACCUMULATION.] **2.** *Informal* An indeterminately great amount or number ▸ bunch, lot, multiplicity, ream. *Informal:* billion, bushel, gazillion, gob, jillion, load, million, mountain, oodles, passel, peck, pile, scad, slew, ton, trillion, wad, zillion. —*See also* ABUNDANCE.

heap *v.* **1.** To collect or pile up or onto something ▸ bank, drift, hill, load, lump, mound, pile (up *or* together), stack. [*Compare* LOAD.] **2.** To give in great abundance ▸ lavish, rain, shower. [*Compare* CONFER, DONATE, GIVE.] —*See also* FILL (1).

heap up *v.* —*See* ACCUMULATE.

hear *v.* To perceive by ear, usually attentively ▸ attend, auscultate, hark, heed, listen. *Idiom:* give (*or* lend) one's ear. —*See also* DISCOVER, UNDERSTAND (1).

hear of *v.* To receive an idea and think about it in order to form an opinion about it ▸ consider, entertain, think about (of).

hearing *n.* **1.** The sense by which sound is perceived ▸ audition, auditory system, ear. **2.** Range of audibility ▸ earshot, sound. [*Compare* RANGE.] **3.** A chance to be heard ▸ audience, audition, listen. *Idiom:* one's day in court. **4.** The examination of evidence, charges, and claims in court ▸ court case, inquest, inquiry, trial. [*Compare* EXAMINATION.]

hearken or **harken** *v.* To make an effort to hear something ▸ attend, hark, heed, listen. *Idiom:* give (*or* lend) an ear.

hearsay *n.* —*See* GOSSIP (1).

heart *n.* **1.** The most central or essential part ▸ center, core, essence, gist, kernel, marrow, meat, nub, nucleus, pith, quintessence, root, soul, spirit, stuff, substance. [*Compare* SUBJECT.] **2.** The circulatory organ of the body ▸ blood pump. *Slang:* ticker. **3.** The seat of a person's innermost emotions and feelings ▸ bosom, breast, soul. *Idioms:* bottom (*or* cockles) of one's heart, one's heart of hearts. —*See also* CENTER (1), CENTER (3), COURAGE, PITY (1).

heartache or **heartbreak** *n.* —*See* GRIEF.

heartbreaking *adj.* —*See* SORROWFUL.

heartbroken *adj.* —*See* DEPRESSED (1).

hearten *v.* —*See* ENCOURAGE (2).

heartening *adj.* —*See* ENCOURAGING.

heartfelt *adj.* —*See* DEEP (3), GENUINE.

hearth *n.* An open space for holding a fire at the base of a chimney ▸ fireplace, grate, ingle.

heartiness *n.* —*See* HEALTH (1).

heart·land (härtʹlăndʹ) ▸ *n.* A central region, esp. one that is vital to a nation.
heart·less (härtʹlĭs) ▸ *adj.* Devoid of compassion or feeling; pitiless. **—heartʹless·ly** *adv.* **—heartʹless·ness** *n.*
heart-rend·ing (härtʹrĕnʹdĭng) ▸ *adj.* Causing anguish or arousing deep sympathy.
heart·sick (härtʹsĭkʹ) ▸ *adj.* Profoundly depressed.
heart·strings (härtʹstrĭngzʹ) ▸ *pl.n.* The deepest feelings or affections.
heart·throb (härtʹthrŏbʹ) ▸ *n.* **1.** A heartbeat. **2.** Sentimental emotion. **3.** A sweetheart.
heart-to-heart (härtʹtə-härtʹ) ▸ *adj.* Candid; frank. ▸ *n.* An intimate conversation.
heart·wood (härtʹwo͝odʹ) ▸ *n.* The older inactive central wood of a tree or woody plant.
heart·y (härʹtē) ▸ *adj.* **-i·er, -i·est. 1.** Expressed warmly and exuberantly. **2.** Complete or thorough. **3.** Vigorous; robust. **4.** Nourishing; satisfying: *a hearty stew.* ▸ *n., pl.* **-ies.** A good fellow; comrade. **—heartʹi·ly** *adv.* **—heartʹi·ness** *n.*
heat (hēt) ▸ *n.* **1.** A form of energy associated with the motion of atoms or molecules and transferred from a body at a higher temperature to one at a lower temperature. **2.** The sensation or perception of such energy as warmth or hotness. **3.** A degree of warmth or hotness: *low heat.* **4.** The warming of a room or building, as by a furnace. **5.** Intensity, as of emotion. **6.** Estrus. **7.** *Sports* **a.** One round of several in a competition. **b.** A preliminary contest held to determine finalists. **8.** *Informal* Pressure; stress. **9.** *Slang* An intensification of police activity in pursuing criminals. **10.** *Slang* Adverse comments or criticism. ▸ *v.* **1.** To make or become warm or hot. **2.** To excite the feelings of; inflame.
heat·ed (hēʹtĭd) ▸ *adj.* Angry; vehement: *a heated argument.* **—heatʹed·ly** *adv.*
heat·er (hēʹtər) ▸ *n.* **1.** An apparatus that heats or provides heat. **2.** *Slang* A pistol.
heat exhaustion ▸ *n.* A condition caused by exposure to heat, resulting in dehydration and causing weakness, dizziness, nausea, and often collapse.
heath (hēth) ▸ *n.* **1.** Any of various usu. low-growing shrubs having small evergreen leaves and small, colorful flowers. **2.** A tract of uncultivated open land covered with low shrubs; moor.
hea·then (hēʹthən) ▸ *n., pl.* **-thens** or **-then. 1.** *Offensive* An adherent of a religion other than Judaism, Christianity, or Islam. **2.** An adherent of a Neo-Pagan religion that seeks to revive the religious practices of the ancient Germanic peoples. **3.** One regarded as irreligious, uncivilized, or unenlightened. **—heaʹthen·dom, heaʹthen·ry** *n.*
heath·er (hĕthʹər) ▸ *n.* **1.** A low shrub growing in dense masses and having small evergreen leaves and pinkish-purple flowers. **2.** See **heath** 1.
heat lightning ▸ *n.* Intermittent flashes of light near the horizon without thunder.
heat rash ▸ *n.* An inflammatory skin condition caused by obstruction of the sweat gland ducts and marked by itching or prickling.
heat stroke ▸ *n.* A condition caused by prolonged exposure to excessive heat and marked by cessation of sweating, headache, fever, hot dry skin, and in serious cases, collapse and coma.
heave (hēv) ▸ *v.* **heaved, heav·ing. 1.** To raise or lift, esp. with great effort or force. **2.** To throw, esp. with great effort. **3.** To utter with effort or pain: *heaved a sigh.* **4.** To vomit. **5.** *p.t. and p.part* **hove. a.** To raise or haul by means of a rope, line, or cable. **b.** To position or be positioned in a certain way: *the ship hove alongside.* **c.** To push at a capstan bar. **6.** To rise up or swell. ▸ *n.* **1.** The effort of heaving. **2.** A throw. **3.** An upward movement. **4.** An act of gagging or vomiting. **5. heaves** *(takes sing. or pl. v.)* A pulmonary disease of horses marked by coughing, esp. after exercise.
heav·en (hĕvʹən) ▸ *n.* **1.** often **heavens** The sky or universe; firmament. **2.** often **Heaven** The abode of God, the angels, and the souls of those who are granted salvation. **3. Heaven** God. **4.** A state or place of great happiness. **—heavʹen·li·ness** *n.* **—heavʹen·ly** *adj.*
heav·y (hĕvʹē) ▸ *adj.* **-i·er, -i·est. 1.** Having relatively great weight. **2.** Having relatively high density. **3.** Large, as in number, quantity, or yield: *a heavy turnout.* **4.** Of great intensity: *heavy fighting.* **5a.** Having great power or force. **b.** Violent; rough: *heavy seas.* **6a.** Equipped with massive armaments and weapons: *heavy infantry.* **b.** Large enough to fire powerful shells: *heavy guns.* **7.** Indulging or participating to a great degree: *a heavy drinker.* **8.** Of great import or seriousness; grave. **9a.** Dense; thick: *a heavy fog; a heavy coat.* **b.** Too rich to digest easily: *a heavy dessert.* **10a.** Weighed down; burdened. **b.** Marked by weariness: *heavy lids.* **c.** Sad or painful: *heavy news.* **11a.** Hard to do; arduous. **b.** Not easily borne; oppressive: *heavy taxes.* **12.** Lacking vitality. **13.** Sharply inclined; steep. **14.** Of or involving large-scale production: *heavy industry.* **15.** *Phys.* Of an isotope with an atomic mass greater than the average mass of that element. **16.** *Slang* Of great significance or profundity. ▸ *n., pl.* **-ies. 1.** A serious or tragic role in a play. **2.** *Slang* A villain in a story or play. **3.** *Slang* One that is important or influential. **—heavʹi·ness** *n.* **—heavʹy, heavʹi·ly** *adv.*
heav·y-dut·y (hĕvʹē-do͞oʹtē, -dyo͞oʹ-) ▸ *adj.* Made to withstand hard use or wear.
heav·y-hand·ed (hĕvʹē-hănʹdĭd) ▸ *adj.* **1.** Clumsy; awkward. **2.** Tactless; indiscreet. **3.** Oppressive; harsh. **—heavʹy-handʹed·ly** *adv.* **—heavʹy-handʹed·ness** *n.*
heav·y-heart·ed (hĕvʹē-härʹtĭd) ▸ *adj.* Melancholy; depressed; sad. **—heavʹy-heartʹed·ly** *adv.* **—heavʹy-heartʹed·ness** *n.*
heavy metal ▸ *n.* **1.** A metal with a specific gravity greater

THESAURUS

heartless *adj.* —*See* CALLOUS.
heart-rending *adj.* —*See* AFFECTING, SORROWFUL.
heartsick *adj.* —*See* DEPRESSED (1).
heartsickness *n.* —*See* DEPRESSION (2).
heart-to-heart *n.* —*See* CONVERSATION.
hearty *adj.* —*See* GENUINE, HEALTHFUL, HEALTHY.
heat *n.* **1.** Warmth or degree of warmth ▸ fervor, hotness, temperature, torridity, torridness, warmth. **2.** A stage of a competition ▸ round, stage. [*Compare* COMPETITION, TURN.] —*See also* PASSION, POLICE OFFICER, PRESSURE.
heat up *v.* —*See* PROVOKE.
heated *adj.* —*See* HOT (1), PASSIONATE.
heathen *n.* One who does not believe in God ▸ atheist, infidel, nonbeliever, pagan.
heathen *adj.* Without belief in God ▸ pagan. [*Compare* ATHEISTIC.]
heave *v.* To move vigorously from side to side or up and down ▸ pitch, rock, roll, toss. [*Compare* LURCH.] —*See also* ELEVATE (1), GASP, PANT, THROW, VOMIT.
heave *n.* —*See* LIFT, THROW.
heaven *n.* A supremely beautiful, blissful state or experience ▸ bliss, ecstasy, Eden, nirvana, paradise, rapture, transport. *Informal:* cloud nine, seventh heaven. [*Compare* DELIGHT, HAPPINESS.] —*See also* ETERNITY (2).
heavenly *adj.* **1.** Of or relating to heaven ▸ celestial, divine, paradisaic, paradisaical, paradisal, paradisiac, paradisiacal, supernal. **2.** Of or relating to the heavens ▸ astronomical, celestial, cosmic, empyreal, supernal. —*See also* DELICIOUS, DELIGHTFUL, DIVINE (1).
heavens *n.* The celestial regions as seen from the earth ▸ air, firmament, sky. ***Idiom:*** wild blue yonder.
heavily *adv.* —*See* HARD (2).
heaviness *n.* The state or degree of being heavy ▸ heftiness, mass, massiveness, ponderosity, ponderousness, weight, weightiness. *Informal:* avoirdupois. [*Compare* IMPORTANCE.]
heavy *adj.* **1.** Having relatively great weight ▸ heavyweight, hefty, leaden, massive, ponderous, weighty. **2.** Indulging in drink to an excessive degree ▸ hard. *Informal:* two-fisted. **3.** Not readily digested because of richness ▸ filling, rich. **4.** Bearing a heavy load ▸ heavy-laden, laden, loaded, weighed down. —*See also* BULKY (1), BULKY (2), BURDENSOME, DEEP (2), FAT (1), GENEROUS (2), GRAVE[2] (1), INTENSE, PONDEROUS, ROUGH (2), SEVERE (2), THICK (3), VISCOUS.
heavy *n. Slang* A mean, worthless character in a story or play ▸ bad guy, villain.
heavy-footed *adj.* —*See* PONDEROUS.
heavy-handed *adj.* —*See* PONDEROUS, UNSKILLFUL.
heavy-hearted *adj.* —*See* DEPRESSED (1).
heavy-heartedness *n.* —*See* DEPRESSION (2).
heavy-laden *adj.* Burdened by a weighty load ▸ heavy, laden, loaded, weighed down.

than about 5.0. 2. Very loud, brash rock music.
heav·y·set (hĕv′ē-sĕt′) ▸ *adj.* Having a stout or compact build.
heavy water ▸ *n.* An isotopic variety of water, esp. with deuterium replacing hydrogen.
heav·y·weight (hĕv′ē-wāt′) ▸ *n.* 1. One of above average weight. 2. A contestant in the heaviest weight class of a sport, esp. a boxer weighing more than 175 pounds. 3. *Informal* A person of great importance.
He·bra·ic (hĭ-brā′ĭk) ▸ *adj.* Of or relating to the Hebrews or their language or culture.
He·bra·ism (hē′brā-ĭz′əm) ▸ *n.* 1. A manner or custom of the Hebrews. 2. Judaism.
He·bra·ist (hē′brā′ĭst) ▸ *n.* A Hebrew scholar.
He·brew (hē′bro͞o) ▸ *n.* 1. A member of a Semitic people claiming descent from Abraham, Isaac, and Jacob; Israelite. 2a. The Semitic language of the ancient Hebrews. b. Any of the various later forms of this language, esp. the language of the Israelis. 3. **Hebrews** *(takes sing. v.)* See **Bible** table in Appendix. **—He′brew** *adj.*
Hebrew Scriptures ▸ *pl.n.* The Torah, the Prophets, and the Writings.
Heb·ri·des (hĕb′rĭ-dēz′) ▸ An island group of W and NW Scotland in the Atlantic, divided into the **Inner Hebrides,** closer to the Scottish mainland, and the **Outer Hebrides,** to the NW. **—Heb′ri·de′an** *adj. & n.*
heck (hĕk) ▸ *interj.* Used as a mild oath.
heck·le (hĕk′əl) ▸ *v.* **-led, -ling.** To try to embarrass and annoy, as with gibes. **—heck′ler** *n.*
hec·tare (hĕk′târ′) ▸ *n.* See **measurement** table in Appendix.
hec·tic (hĕk′tĭk) ▸ *adj.* 1. Marked by intense activity, confusion, or haste. 2. Consumptive; feverish. 3. Flushed. **—hec′ti·cal·ly** *adv.*
hecto– or **hect–** ▸ *pref.* One hundred (10^2): *hectare.*
hec·to·gram (hĕk′tə-grăm′) ▸ *n.* See **measurement** table in Appendix.
hec·to·li·ter (hĕk′tə-lē′tər) ▸ *n.* See **measurement** table in Appendix.
hec·to·me·ter (hĕk′tə-mē′tər, hĕk-tŏm′ĭ-tər) ▸ *n.* See **measurement** table in Appendix.
hec·tor (hĕk′tər) ▸ *v.* To intimidate in a blustering way.
Hector ▸ *n. Gk. Myth.* A Trojan prince killed by Achilles in Homer's *Iliad.*
he'd (hēd) ▸ 1. He had. 2. He would.
hedge (hĕj) ▸ *n.* 1. A row of closely planted shrubs forming a boundary. 2. Protection, esp. against financial loss. 3. An intentionally ambiguous statement. ▸ *v.* **hedged, hedg·ing.** 1. To enclose or bound with or as if with hedges. 2. To limit the financial risk of (e.g., a bet) by a counterbalancing transaction. 3. To avoid making a clear, direct response. **—hedg′er** *n.*
hedge·hog (hĕj′hôg′, -hŏg′) ▸ *n.* A small insectivorous Old World mammal having the back covered with dense, erectile spines.
he·don·ism (hēd′n-ĭz′əm) ▸ *n.* 1. Pursuit of or devotion to pleasure. 2. The ethical doctrine that only what is pleasant is intrinsically good. **—he′don·ist** *n.* **—he′don·is′tic** *adj.* **—he′don·is′ti·cal·ly** *adv.*
–hedral ▸ *suff.* Having a specified kind or number of surfaces: *tetrahedral.*
–hedron ▸ *suff.* A crystal or geometric figure having a specified kind or number of surfaces: *polyhedron.*
hee·bie-jee·bies (hē′bē-jē′bēz) ▸ *pl.n. Slang* A feeling of uneasiness; jitters.
heed (hēd) ▸ *v.* To pay attention (to). ▸ *n.* Close attention; notice. **—heed′less** *adj.* **—heed′less·ly** *adv.* **—heed′less·ness** *n.*
heed·ful (hēd′fəl) ▸ *adj.* Attentive; mindful. **—heed′ful·ly** *adv.* **—heed′ful·ness** *n.*
heel[1] (hēl) ▸ *n.* 1a. The rounded posterior portion of the human foot under and behind the ankle. b. The corresponding part of the hind foot of other vertebrates. 2. The part, as of a sock or shoe, that covers or supports the heel. 3. One of the crusty ends of a loaf of bread. 4. A lower, rearward surface. 5. *Informal* A cad. ▸ *v.* 1. To furnish with a heel. 2. *Slang* To furnish, esp. with money. 3. To follow at one's heels. *—idioms:* **down at the heels** Shabby; poor. **on (or upon) the heels of** 1. Directly behind. 2. Immediately following. **take to (one's) heels** To flee.
heel[2] (hēl) ▸ *v.* To tilt or cause to tilt (e.g., a boat) to one side. **—heel** *n.*
heft (hĕft) ▸ *n.* Weight; heaviness. ▸ *v.* 1. To judge the weight of by lifting. 2. To hoist; heave.
heft·y (hĕf′tē) ▸ *adj.* **-i·er, -i·est.** 1. Heavy. 2. Rugged and powerful. 3. *Informal* Large; substantial. **—heft′i·ness** *n.*
He·gel (hā′gəl), **Georg Wilhelm Friedrich** (1770–1831) ▸ German philosopher.
he·gem·o·ny (hĭ-jĕm′ə-nē, hĕj′ə-mō′nē) ▸ *n., pl.* **-nies.** The dominance of one state over others. **—heg′e·mon′ic** (hĕj′ə-mŏn′ĭk) *adj.* **—he·gem′o·nism** *n.* **—he·gem′o·nist** *adj. & n.*
he·gi·ra (hĭ-jī′rə, hĕj′ər-ə) ▸ *n.* 1. A flight to escape danger. 2. also **Hegira** The flight of Muhammad from Mecca to Medina in 622.
heif·er (hĕf′ər) ▸ *n.* A young cow, esp. one that has not calved.
height (hīt) ▸ *n.* 1a. The distance from the base of something to the top. b. Elevation above a given level; altitude. 2a. The condition of being high or tall. b. Stature, esp. of the human body. 3. The highest or uppermost point. 4a. The most advanced degree; zenith. b. The point of highest intensity; climax. 5. An eminence, such as a hill.
height·en (hīt′n) ▸ *v.* 1. To rise or increase in quantity or degree; intensify. 2. To make or become high or higher.
Heim·lich maneuver (hīm′lĭk′, -lĭKH′) ▸ *n.* A firm embrace with clasped hands just below the rib cage, applied from behind to force an object from the trachea of a choking person.
hei·nous (hā′nəs) ▸ *adj.* Grossly wicked or abominable. **—hei′nous·ly** *adv.* **—hei′nous·ness** *n.*
heir (âr) ▸ *n.* A person who inherits or is entitled to inherit the estate, rank, title, or office of another.
heir apparent ▸ *n., pl.* **heirs apparent.** An heir whose right

THESAURUS

heavyset *adj.* —*See* STOCKY.
heavyweight *n.* —*See* DIGNITARY.
heavyweight *adj.* —*See* BIG-LEAGUE, HEAVY (1).
hebetude *n.* —*See* LETHARGY.
hebetudinous *adj.* —*See* LETHARGIC, STUPID.
hecatomb *n.* —*See* OFFERING.
heckle *v.* —*See* HARASS.
hectic *adj.* —*See* BUSY (2), FEVERISH, FRANTIC.
hector *n.* —*See* BULLY.
hector *v.* —*See* HARASS, INTIMIDATE.
hedge *v.* —*See* DEFEND (1), DEFENSE, ENCLOSE (2), EQUIVOCATE (1), EVADE (1), SURROUND.
hedge *n.* —*See* EQUIVOCATION.
hedonist *n.* —*See* SYBARITE.
hedonistic or **hedonic** *adj.* Characterized by or devoted to pleasure and luxury as a lifestyle ▸ epicurean, sybaritic, voluptuary, voluptuous. [*Compare* LUXURIOUS, SENSUAL.]
heebie-jeebies *n.* —*See* JITTERS.
heed *v.* To make an effort to hear something ▸ attend, hark, hearken, listen. *Idiom:* give (*or* lend) an ear. —*See also* FOLLOW (4), HEAR.
heed *n.* —*See* CARE (1), NOTICE (1).
heedful *adj.* —*See* ALERT, CAREFUL (1).
heedfulness *n.* —*See* ATTENTION, CARE (1).
heedless *adj.* —*See* CARELESS.
heedlessness *n.* A careless, often reckless disregard for consequences ▸ abandon, blitheness, carelessness, thoughtlessness. [*Compare* TEMERITY.]
heehaw *n.* —*See* LAUGH.
heehaw *v.* —*See* LAUGH.
heel[1] *v.* —*See* FOLLOW (3).
heel[2] *v.* —*See* INCLINE.
heel *n.* —*See* INCLINATION (2).
heel[3] *n.* —*See* END (3).
heftiness *n.* —*See* HEAVINESS.
hefty *adj.* —*See* BULKY (1), BULKY (2), HEAVY (1), SEVERE (2).
hegemony *n.* —*See* DOMINANCE.
height *n.* The distance of something from a given level ▸ altitude, elevation, loftiness, tallness. [*Compare* ASCENT.] —*See also* CLIMAX, INTENSITY.
heighten *v.* —*See* ELEVATE (2), INTENSIFY.
heightened *adj.* —*See* ELEVATED (2), INTENSE.
heinous *adj.* —*See* OUTRAGEOUS.
heinousness *n.* —*See* OUTRAGEOUSNESS.

to inheritance is indisputable provided he or she survives an ancestor.

heir·ess (âr′ĭs) ▸ *n.* A woman who is an heir.

heir·loom (âr′lo͞om′) ▸ *n.* **1.** A valued possession passed down in a family through succeeding generations. **2.** *Law* An article of personal property included in an inherited estate.

heir presumptive ▸ *n., pl.* **heirs presumptive.** An heir whose claim can be defeated by the birth of a closer relative before the death of the ancestor.

heist (hīst) *Slang* ▸ *v.* To steal; rob. ▸ *n.* A robbery; burglary.

held (hĕld) ▸ *v.* P.t. and p.part. of **hold**[1].

Hel·en (hĕl′ən) ▸ *n.* *Gk. Myth.* The wife of Menelaus whose abduction by Paris caused the Trojan War.

Hel·e·na (hĕl′ə-nə) ▸ The capital of Montana, in the W-central part NNE of Butte. Pop. 25,800.

hel·i·cal (hĕl′ĭ-kəl, hē′lĭ-) ▸ *adj.* Shaped like a helix; spiral. **—hel′i·cal·ly** *adv.*

hel·i·cop·ter (hĕl′ĭ-kŏp′tər) ▸ *n.* An aircraft that derives its lift from blades that rotate about an approx. vertical central axis. **—hel′i·cop′ter** *v.*

helio– or **heli–** ▸ *pref.* Sun: *heliocentric.*

he·li·o·cen·tric (hē′lē-ō-sĕn′trĭk) also **he·li·o·cen·tri·cal** (-trĭ-kəl) ▸ *adj.* Having the sun as a center. **—he′li·o·cen·tric′i·ty** (-sĕn-trĭs′ĭ-tē) *n.*

he·li·o·trope (hē′lē-ə-trōp′) ▸ *n.* **1.** Any of several plants having small, highly fragrant purplish flowers. **2.** Any of various plants that turn toward the sun.

hel·i·port (hĕl′ə-pôrt′) ▸ *n.* A place for helicopters to land and take off.

he·li·um (hē′lē-əm) ▸ *n.* *Symbol* **He** A colorless, odorless inert gaseous element used in lasers and as a refrigerant and a lifting gas for balloons. At. no. 2.

he·lix (hē′lĭks) ▸ *n., pl.* **-lix·es** or **hel·i·ces** (hĕl′ĭ-sēz′, hē′lĭ-). **1.** A three-dimensional curve that lies on a cylinder or cone, so that its angle to a plane perpendicular to the axis is constant. **2.** A spiral form.

hell (hĕl) ▸ *n.* **1.** often **Hell** The abode of condemned souls and devils. **2.** The abode of the dead; underworld. **3a.** A situation or place of evil, misery, or destruction. **b.** Torment; anguish. **4.** *Informal* One that causes trouble, agony, or annoyance. **5.** A sharp scolding: *gave me hell.* ▸ *interj.* Used to express anger, disgust, or impatience. *—idiom:* **for the hell of it** For no particular reason.

he'll (hēl) ▸ **1.** He will. **2.** He shall.

hell-bent (hĕl′bĕnt′) ▸ *adj.* Recklessly determined to do something.

hel·le·bore (hĕl′ə-bôr′) ▸ *n.* Any of various chiefly poisonous plants, esp. a North American species yielding a toxic alkaloid used medicinally.

Hel·lene (hĕl′ēn′) ▸ *n.* A Greek.

Hel·len·ic (hĕ-lĕn′ĭk) ▸ *adj.* Of or relating to the ancient Hellenes or their language; Greek. ▸ *n.* The branch of Indo-European that consists only of Greek.

Hel·le·nism (hĕl′ə-nĭz′əm) ▸ *n.* **1.** A manner or custom of the Greeks. **2.** The civilization of ancient Greece. **3.** Admiration for Greek culture. **—Hel′le·ni·za′tion** *n.* **—Hel′le·nize′** *v.* **—Hel′le·niz′er** *n.*

Hel·le·nist (hĕl′ə-nĭst) ▸ *n.* **1.** A student of Greek literature, language, or civilization. **2.** In ancient times, a non-Greek who adopted Greek language and culture.

Hel·le·nis·tic (hĕl′ə-nĭs′tĭk) ▸ *adj.* **1.** Relating to the Hellenists. **2.** Relating to Greek civilization from the death of Alexander the Great (323 B.C.) to the battle of Actium (31 B.C.); Alexandrian.

Hel·les·pont (hĕl′ĭ-spŏnt′) ▸ See **Dardanelles.**

hell·gram·mite (hĕl′grə-mīt′) ▸ *n.* A large brownish aquatic insect larva, often used as fishing bait.

hell·hole (hĕl′hōl′) ▸ *n.* A place of extreme wretchedness or squalor.

hel·lion (hĕl′yən) ▸ *n.* *Informal* A mischievous, troublesome person.

hell·ish (hĕl′ĭsh) ▸ *adj.* **1.** Of, resembling, or worthy of hell; fiendish. **2.** Highly unpleasant. **—hell′ish·ly** *adv.* **—hell′ish·ness** *n.*

hel·lo (hĕ-lō′, hə-) ▸ *interj.* Used to greet someone, answer the telephone, or express surprise. ▸ *n., pl.* **-los.** A calling or greeting of "hello."

helm (hĕlm) ▸ *n.* **1.** The steering gear of a ship, esp. the tiller or wheel. **2.** A position of leadership or control.

hel·met (hĕl′mĭt) ▸ *n.* A protective head covering, as of metal or plastic.

hel·minth (hĕl′mĭnth′) ▸ *n.* A worm, esp. a parasitic roundworm or tapeworm.

helms·man (hĕlmz′mən) ▸ *n.* A person who steers a ship.

Hé·lo·ise (ĕl′ə-wēz′, ā-lô-ēz′) (1098?–1164) ▸ French philosopher and religious figure; secretly married Peter Abelard (c. 1118).

help (hĕlp) ▸ *v.* **1.** To give assistance (to); aid. **2.** To contribute; promote. **3.** To give relief to: *help the needy.* **4.** To ease; relieve: *medication to help your cold.* **5.** To change for the better; improve. **6.** To refrain from: *couldn't help laughing.* **7.** To wait on, as in a store. ▸ *n.* **1.** Aid or assistance. **2.** Relief; remedy. **3.** One that helps. **4a.** A person employed to help. **b.** Such employees in general. *—idiom:* **help (oneself) to** To serve or provide oneself with.

help·er (hĕl′pər) ▸ *n.* One that helps.

help·ful (hĕlp′fəl) ▸ *adj.* Providing help; useful. **—help′ful·ly** *adv.* **—help′ful·ness** *n.*

help·ing (hĕl′pĭng) ▸ *n.* A single portion of food.

help·less (hĕlp′lĭs) ▸ *adj.* **1.** Unable to manage by oneself; incompetent. **2.** Lacking power or strength; impotent. **3.** Involuntary: *helpless laughter.* **—help′less·ly** *adv.* **—help′less·ness** *n.*

help·mate (hĕlp′māt′) ▸ *n.* A helper and companion, esp. a spouse.

help·meet (hĕlp′mēt′) ▸ *n.* A helpmate.

Hel·sin·ki (hĕl′sĭng′kē, hĕl-sĭng′-) ▸ The capital of Finland, in the S part on the Gulf of Finland. Pop. 560,000.

hel·ter-skel·ter (hĕl′tər-skĕl′tər) ▸ *adv.* **1.** In disorderly haste; confused. **2.** Haphazardly. ▸ *adj.* **1.** Hurried and confused. **2.** Haphazard. ▸ *n.* Turmoil; confusion.

THESAURUS

heist *v.* —*See* ROB, STEAL.

heist *n.* —*See* LARCENY.

hell *n.* A place or experience of excruciating pain or punishment ▸ fire and brimstone, hellfire, inferno, living hell, perdition, persecution, torment, torture. *Idiom:* tortures of the damned. [*Compare* DISTRESS, MISERY.]

hell *v.* —*See* REVEL.

hellbound *adj.* —*See* CONDEMNED.

hellfire *n.* —*See* HELL.

hell-for-leather *adv.* —*See* FAST.

hell-for-leather *adj.* —*See* FAST (1).

hellhole *n.* —*See* PIT[1].

hellish *adj.* —*See* FIENDISH.

hello *interjection* Used as a greeting ▸ good day, greetings, salutations. *Informal:* aloha, hey, hey ho, hey there, hi, hi there, howdy, howdy do. *Slang:* yo, 'sup. *Idioms:* how do you do, what's up.

hello *n.* *Informal* An expression, in words or gestures, marking a meeting of persons ▸ hail, greeting, salutation, salute, welcome.

helot *n.* —*See* SLAVE.

helotry *n.* —*See* SLAVERY.

help *v.* To give support or assistance to ▸ abet, aid, assist, boost, help out, relieve, succor. *Idioms:* come to the aid of, do a service, give (*or* lend) a hand, give a leg up, see someone through. [*Compare* COMFORT, SERVE, SUPPORT.] —*See also* IMPROVE, OBLIGE (1), PROFIT (2).

help along *v.* —*See* EASE (2).

help *n.* The act or an instance of helping ▸ abetment, aid, assist, assistance, hand, relief, succor, support. —*See also* ASSISTANT, EMPLOYEE.

helper *n.* —*See* ASSISTANT.

helpful *adj.* Tending to contribute to a result ▸ conducive, contributive, contributory, participatory. [*Compare* AUXILIARY.] —*See also* BENEFICIAL, BENEVOLENT (1), OBLIGING.

helping *n.* —*See* SERVING.

helping *adj.* —*See* AUXILIARY (1).

helpless *adj.* Lacking power or strength ▸ impotent, powerless, unable. —*See also* INEFFECTUAL (2), VULNERABLE.

helplessness *n.* —*See* INEFFECTUALITY.

helplessly *adv.* Without regard to desire or inclination ▸ inextricably, involuntarily, perforce, willy-nilly.

helpmate or **helpmeet** *n.* —*See* SPOUSE.

helter-skelter *adj.* —*See* CONFUSED (2).

helter-skelter *n.* —*See* AGITATION (1).

hem[1] (hĕm) ▸ *n.* **1.** A smooth, even edge on a piece of cloth made by folding the selvage edge under and stitching it down. **2.** A hemline. ▸ *v.* **hemmed, hem·ming.** **1.** To fold back and stitch down the edge of. **2.** To surround and shut in. **—hem′mer** *n.*

hem[2] (hĕm) ▸ *n.* A short cough or clearing of the throat, as to gain attention, warn another, or hide embarrassment. ▸ *v.* **hemmed, hem·ming.** To utter a hem. ***—idiom:*** **hem and haw** To be hesitant and indecisive.

he-man (hē′măn′) ▸ *n. Informal* A strong, virile man.

he·ma·tite (hē′mə-tīt′) ▸ *n.* A blackish-red to brick-red mineral, essentially Fe_2O_3, the chief ore of iron.

hemato– or **hemat–** ▸ *pref.* Blood: *hematology.*

he·ma·tol·o·gy (hē′mə-tŏl′ə-jē) ▸ *n.* The science encompassing the medical study of the blood and blood-producing organs. **—he′ma·to·log′ic** (-tə-lŏj′ĭk), **he′ma·to·log′i·cal** *adj.* **—he′ma·tol′o·gist** *n.*

he·ma·to·ma (hē′mə-tō′mə) ▸ *n.* A localized swelling filled with blood.

heme (hēm) ▸ *n.* The deep red, nonprotein, ferrous component of hemoglobin.

–hemia ▸ *suff.* Var. of **–emia.**

Hem·ing·way (hĕm′ĭng-wā′), **Ernest Miller** (1899–1961) ▸ Amer. writer; 1954 Nobel.

hem·i·sphere (hĕm′ĭ-sfîr′) ▸ *n.* **1a.** A half of a sphere bounded by a great circle. **b.** A half of a symmetrical, approx. spherical object as divided by a plane of symmetry. **2.** Either the northern or southern half of the earth as divided by the equator or the eastern or western half as divided by a meridian. **3.** *Anat.* Either of the lateral halves of the cerebrum. **—hem′i·spher′ic** (-sfîr′ĭk, -sfĕr′-), **hem′i·spher′i·cal** *adj.*

hem·line (hĕm′līn′) ▸ *n.* **1.** The bottom edge of a skirt, dress, or coat. **2.** The height of a hemline from the floor.

hem·lock (hĕm′lŏk′) ▸ *n.* **1a.** Any of a genus of coniferous evergreen trees having small cones and short flat leaves. **b.** The wood of a hemlock. **2a.** The poison hemlock. **b.** A poison obtained from the poison hemlock.

hemo– ▸ *pref.* Blood: *hemodialysis.*

he·mo·di·al·y·sis (hē′mō-dī-ăl′ĭ-sĭs) ▸ *n., pl.* **-ses** (-sēz′). The removal esp. of metabolic waste products from the bloodstream by dialysis.

he·mo·glo·bin (hē′mə-glō′bĭn) ▸ *n.* The iron-containing respiratory pigment in red blood cells.

he·mo·phil·i·a (hē′mə-fĭl′ē-ə, -fēl′yə) ▸ *n.* Any of several hereditary blood-coagulation disorders occurring only in males, in which the blood fails to clot normally because of a defective clotting factor. **—he′mo·phil′i·ac′** *n.*

hem·or·rhage (hĕm′ər-ĭj) ▸ *n.* Copious or excessive bleeding. **—hem′or·rhage** *v.* **—hem′or·rhag′ic** (hĕm′ə-răj′ĭk) *adj.*

hem·or·rhoid (hĕm′ə-roid′) ▸ *n.* **1.** An itching or painful mass of dilated veins in swollen anal tissue. **2. hemorroids** The pathological condition in which hemorrhoids occur. **—hem′or·rhoi′dal** *adj.*

he·mo·stat (hē′mə-stăt′) ▸ *n.* **1.** An agent used to stop bleeding. **2.** A surgical clamp used to constrict a blood vessel. **—he′mo·stat′ic** *adj.*

hemp (hĕmp) ▸ *n.* **1.** Cannabis. **2.** The tough coarse fiber of the cannabis plant, used to make cordage.

hem·stitch (hĕm′stĭch′) ▸ *n.* A decorative stitch used esp. on hems. **—hem′stitch′** *v.*

hen (hĕn) ▸ *n.* A female bird, esp. the adult female of the domestic fowl.

hence (hĕns) ▸ *adv.* **1.** For this reason; therefore. **2.** From this time; from now. **3.** Away from here.

hence·forth (hĕns′fôrth′) ▸ *adv.* From this time forth; from now on.

hence·for·ward (hĕns-fôr′wərd) ▸ *adv.* Henceforth.

hench·man (hĕnch′mən) ▸ *n.* **1.** A loyal follower or subordinate. **2.** A person who supports a political figure for selfish interests.

hen·na (hĕn′ə) ▸ *n.* **1a.** A tree or shrub having fragrant white or reddish flowers. **b.** A reddish-orange cosmetic dye prepared from the dried and ground leaves of this plant. **2.** A reddish brown. ▸ *v.* To dye with henna. **—hen′na** *adj.*

hen·peck (hĕn′pĕk′) ▸ *v. Informal* To dominate (one's husband) with nagging.

hen·ry (hĕn′rē) ▸ *n., pl.* **hen·ries** or **hen·rys.** The unit of inductance in which an induced electromotive force of one volt is produced when the current is varied at the rate of one ampere per second.

Henry VIII (1491–1547) ▸ King of England (1509–47).

Henry, Patrick (1736–99) ▸ Amer. Revolutionary leader and orator.

hep (hĕp) ▸ *adj. Slang* Var. of **hip**[2]**.**

hep·a·rin (hĕp′ər-ĭn) ▸ *n.* An organic acid, found esp. in lung and liver tissue, that slows blood clotting.

he·pat·ic (hĭ-păt′ĭk) ▸ *adj.* **1.** Of or relating to the liver. **2.** Acting on or occurring in the liver.

he·pat·i·ca (hĭ-păt′ĭ-kə) ▸ *n.* A woodland plant having three-lobed leaves and white or lavender flowers.

hep·a·ti·tis (hĕp′ə-tī′tĭs) ▸ *n.* Inflammation of the liver, caused by infectious or toxic agents and characterized by jaundice, fever, liver enlargement, and abdominal pain.

He·phaes·tus (hĭ-fĕs′təs) ▸ *n. Gk. Myth.* The god of fire and metalworking.

hepta– or **hept–** ▸ *pref.* Seven: *heptagon.*

hep·ta·gon (hĕp′tə-gŏn′) ▸ *n.* A seven-sided polygon. **—hep·tag′o·nal** (-tăg′ə-nəl) *adj.*

her (hər, ər; hûr *when stressed*) ▸ *adj.* The possessive form of **she.** Used as a modifier before a noun: *her mother; her goals.* ▸ *pron.* The objective case of **she. 1.** Used as a direct or indirect object: *I know her; They gave her a ride.* **2.** Used as the object of a preposition: *The call is for her.*

He·ra (hîr′ə) ▸ *n. Gk. Myth.* The sister and wife of Zeus.

Her·a·cli·tus (hĕr′ə-klī′təs) (fl. 500 B.C.) ▸ Greek philosopher. **—Her′a·cli′te·an** (-tē-ən) *adj.*

her·ald (hĕr′əld) ▸ *n.* **1.** One who proclaims important news; messenger. **2.** One that gives a sign or indication of something to come. **3.** An official formerly charged with making royal proclamations. ▸ *v.* To proclaim; announce.

he·ral·dic (hə-răl′dĭk) ▸ *adj.* Of heralds or heraldry. **—he·ral′di·cal·ly** *adv.*

her·ald·ry (hĕr′əl-drē) ▸ *n., pl.* **-ries. 1.** The study or art of devising, granting, and blazoning arms, tracing genealogies, and ruling on questions of rank or protocol. **2.** Armorial ensigns or devices. **3.** Pomp and ceremony; pageantry. **—her′ald·ist** *n.*

herb (ûrb, hûrb) ▸ *n.* **1.** A plant that does not have a woody stem and usu. dies back at the end of each growing season. **2.** Any of various often aromatic plants used in medicine or as seasoning.

her·ba·ceous (hûr-bā′shəs, ûr-) ▸ *adj.* **1.** Relating to an herb as distinguished from a woody plant. **2.** Green and leaflike in appearance or texture.

herb·age (ûr′bĭj, hûr′-) ▸ *n.* **1.** Herbaceous plant growth, esp. as used for pasturage. **2.** The fleshy, often edible parts of plants.

herb·al (ûr′bəl, hûr′-) ▸ *adj.* Relating to or containing herbs. ▸ *n.* A book about plants and herbs, esp. those useful to humans.

herb·al·ism (ûr′bə-lĭz′əm, hûr′-) ▸ *n.* The study or use of medicinal herbs; herbal medicine. **—herb′al·ist** *n.*

herbal medicine ▸ *n.* **1.** The study or use of medicinal herbs to prevent or treat disease. **2.** A medicinal preparation made from plants.

her·bar·i·um (hûr-bâr′ē-əm, ûr-) ▸ *n., pl.* **-i·ums** or **-i·a** (-ē-ə). **1.** A collection of dried plants mounted and labeled for scientific study. **2.** A place where such a collection is kept.

her·bi·cide (hûr′bĭ-sīd′, ûr′-) ▸ *n.* A chemical substance used to destroy plants, esp. weeds. **—her′bi·cid′al** (-sīd′l) *adj.*

her·bi·vore (hûr′bə-vôr′, ûr′-) ▸ *n.* An animal that feeds chiefly on plants.

her·biv·o·rous (hûr-bĭv′ər-əs, ûr-) ▸ *adj.* Feeding on plants; plant-eating. **—her·biv′o·rous·ly** *adv.*

THESAURUS

hem *v.* —*See* ENCLOSE (2), SURROUND.
hem *n.* —*See* BORDER (1).
henchman *n.* —*See* FOLLOWER.
henpeck *v.* —*See* NAG.
herald *n.* —*See* FORERUNNER, MESSENGER.
herald *v.* —*See* ANNOUNCE, PROCLAIM.

Her·cu·les (hûr′kyə-lēz′) ▸ *n. Gk. & Rom. Myth.* A hero of extraordinary strength. **—Her′cu·le′an** (hûr′kyə-lē′ən, hûr-kyo͞o′lē-) *adj.*

herd (hûrd) ▸ *n.* **1.** A group of animals, as domestic cattle kept or living together. **2.** A large number of people; crowd. ▸ *v.* **1.** To come together in a herd. **2.** To gather, keep, or drive in or as if in a herd. **—herd′er** *n.* **—herds′man** *n.*

here (hîr) ▸ *adv.* **1.** At or in this place: *Stop here for a rest.* **2.** At this time; now: *We'll adjourn the meeting here.* **3.** At or on this point or item: *Here I must disagree.* **4.** To this place: *Come here.* ▸ *interj.* Used esp. to respond to a roll call, attract attention, command an animal, or concur. ***—idiom:* neither here nor there** Irrelevant.

here·a·bout (hîr′ə-bout′) also **here·a·bouts** (-bouts′) ▸ *adv.* In this vicinity.

here·af·ter (hîr-ăf′tər) ▸ *adv.* **1.** After this; from here or now on. **2.** In a future time or state. ▸ *n.* The afterlife.

here·by (hîr-bī′) ▸ *adv.* By this means.

he·red·i·tar·y (hə-rĕd′ĭ-tĕr′ē) ▸ *adj.* **1.** *Law* **a.** Passing down by inheritance. **b.** Having title or possession through inheritance. **2.** Genetically transmitted or transmissible. **3.** Derived from or fostered by one's ancestors. **—he·red′i·tar′i·ly** (-târ′ə-lē) *adv.*

he·red·i·ty (hə-rĕd′ĭ-tē) ▸ *n., pl.* **-ties. 1.** The genetic transmission of characteristics from parent to offspring. **2.** The set of characteristics transmitted genetically to an individual organism.

here·in (hîr-ĭn′) ▸ *adv.* In or into this.

here·of (hîr-ŭv′, -ŏv′) ▸ *adv.* Of this.

here·on (hîr-ŏn′, -ôn′) ▸ *adv.* On this.

her·e·sy (hĕr′ĭ-sē) ▸ *n., pl.* **-sies. 1.** An opinion or doctrine at variance with religious orthodoxy. **2a.** A controversial or unorthodox opinion or doctrine, as in politics, philosophy, or science. **b.** Adherence to such opinion.

her·e·tic (hĕr′ĭ-tĭk) ▸ *n.* A person who holds unorthodox opinions. **—he·ret′i·cal** (hə-rĕt′ĭ-kəl) *adj.*

here·to (hîr-to͞o′) ▸ *adv.* To this document or matter.

here·to·fore (hîr′tə-fôr′) ▸ *adv.* Before this; previously.

here·un·to (hîr-ŭn′to͞o) ▸ *adv.* Hereto.

here·up·on (hîr′ə-pŏn′, -pôn′) ▸ *adv.* **1.** Immediately after this. **2.** At or on this.

here·with (hîr-wĭth′, -wĭth′) ▸ *adv.* **1.** Along with this. **2.** By this means; hereby.

her·i·ta·ble (hĕr′ĭ-tə-bəl) ▸ *adj.* Capable of being inherited; hereditary. **—her′i·ta·bil′i·ty** *n.* **—her′i·ta·bly** *adv.*

her·i·tage (hĕr′ĭ-tĭj) ▸ *n.* **1.** Property that is or can be inherited. **2.** Something passed down from preceding generations; tradition.

her·maph·ro·dite (hər-măf′rə-dīt′) ▸ *n.* One having the reproductive organs and many of the secondary sex characteristics of both sexes. **—her·maph′ro·dit′ic** (-dĭt′ĭk) *adj.*

Her·mes (hûr′mēz) ▸ *n. Gk. Myth.* The god of commerce, invention, cunning, and theft.

her·met·ic (hər-mĕt′ĭk) also **her·met·i·cal** (-ĭ-kəl) ▸ *adj.* **1.** Completely sealed, esp. against the escape or entry of air. **2.** Impervious to outside interference or influence. **—her·met′i·cal·ly** *adv.*

her·mit (hûr′mĭt) ▸ *n.* One who lives a solitary existence; recluse. **—her·mit′ic** *adj.*

her·mit·age (hûr′mĭ-tĭj) ▸ *n.* **1.** The habitation of a hermit. **2.** A hideaway or retreat.

hermit crab ▸ *n.* Any of various soft-bodied crabs that occupy and carry the empty shell of a snail or other mollusk.

her·ni·a (hûr′nē-ə) ▸ *n., pl.* **-ni·as** or **-ni·ae** (-nē-ē′). The protrusion of an organ or other bodily structure through the wall that normally contains it; rupture. **—her′ni·al** *adj.*

he·ro (hîr′ō) ▸ *n., pl.* **-roes. 1.** In mythology and legend, a man celebrated for his bold exploits. **2.** A person noted for feats of courage or nobility of purpose. **3.** A person noted for special achievement in a particular field. **4.** The principal male character in a literary work. **5.** See **submarine** 2.

He·rod·o·tus (hĭ-rŏd′ə-təs) (5th cent. B.C.) ▸ Greek historian.

he·ro·ic (hĭ-rō′ĭk) also **he·ro·i·cal** (-ĭ-kəl) ▸ *adj.* **1.** Of or like the heroes of literature, legend, or myth. **2.** Nobly or selflessly brave. **3.** Impressive in size or scope; grand: *heroic undertakings.* ▸ *n.* **heroics 1.** Heroic acts; heroism. **2.** Melodramatic behavior or language. **—he·ro′i·cal·ly** *adv.*

heroic couplet ▸ *n.* A verse unit of two rhymed lines in iambic pentameter.

her·o·in (hĕr′ō-ĭn) ▸ *n.* A white, odorless, highly addictive narcotic derived from morphine.

her·o·ine (hĕr′ō-ĭn) ▸ *n.* **1.** A woman noted for courage and daring action. **2.** A woman noted for special achievement in a particular field. **3.** The principal female character in a literary work.

her·o·ism (hĕr′ō-ĭz′əm) ▸ *n.* **1.** Heroic conduct or behavior. **2.** Selfless courage.

her·on (hĕr′ən) ▸ *n.* Any of various wading birds having a long neck, long legs, and a long pointed bill.

her·pes (hûr′pēz) ▸ *n.* Any of several viral diseases causing the eruption of small blisterlike vesicles on the skin or mucous membranes. **—her·pet′ic** (hər-pĕt′ĭk) *adj.*

herpes sim·plex (sĭm′plĕks′) ▸ *n.* Either of two recurrent viral diseases marked by the eruption of blisters on the mouth and face or on the genitals.

her·pe·tol·o·gy (hûr′pĭ-tŏl′ə-jē) ▸ *n.* The branch of zoology that deals with reptiles and amphibians. **—her′pe·to·log′ic** (-tə-lŏj′ĭk), **her′pe·to·log′i·cal** *adj.* **—her′pe·tol′o·gist** *n.*

Herr (hĕr) ▸ *n., pl.* **Her·ren** (hĕr′ən). A German courtesy title for a man.

her·ring (hĕr′ĭng) ▸ *n., pl.* **-ring** or **-rings**. A commercially important food fish of Atlantic and Pacific waters.

her·ring·bone (hĕr′ĭng-bōn′) ▸ *n.* **1.** A pattern consisting of rows of short, slanted parallel lines with the direction of the slant alternating row by row. **2.** A twilled fabric woven in this pattern.

hers (hûrz) ▸ *pron. (takes sing. or pl. v.)* Used to indicate the one or ones belonging to her: *I found my keys, but not hers.*

her·self (hûr-sĕlf′) ▸ *pron.* **1.** That one identical with her: **a.** Used reflexively as the direct or indirect object of a verb or as the object of a preposition: *She hurt herself.* **b.** Used for emphasis: *She herself saw it.* **2.** Her normal or healthy condition: *She's feeling herself again.*

hertz (hûrts) ▸ *n., pl.* **hertz**. A unit of frequency equal to one cycle per second.

Her·ze·go·vi·na (hĕrt′sə-gō′vē-nə, -gō-vē′-, hûrt′-) ▸ The S region of Bosnia and Herzegovina.

he's (hēz) ▸ **1.** He is. **2.** He has.

Hesh·van also **Hesh·wan** (ᴋʜĕsh′vən, -vän) ▸ *n.* A month of the Jewish calendar.

He·si·od (hē′sē-əd, hĕs′ē-) (fl. 8th cent. B.C.) ▸ Greek poet.

hes·i·tant (hĕz′ĭ-tənt) ▸ *adj.* Inclined or tending to hesi-

THESAURUS

herculean *adj.* —*See* ENORMOUS.

herd *v.* —*See* DRIVE (3).

herd *n.* —*See* CROWD, FLOCK.

hereafter *n.* Time that is yet to be ▸ by-and-by, future, futurity, tomorrow. *Idiom:* time to come. [*Compare* APPROACH, POSSIBILITY.] —*See also* ETERNITY (2).

hereditary *adj.* Of unbroken descent or lineage ▸ direct, genealogical, lineal, natural. —*See also* ANCESTRAL, INNATE.

heretic *n.* —*See* SEPARATIST.

heretofore *adv.* —*See* EARLIER (2).

heritage *n.* **1.** Something immaterial, as a style or philosophy, that is passed from one generation to another ▸ inheritance, legacy, tradition. [*Compare* CULTURE.] **2.** Any special privilege accorded a firstborn ▸ birthright, inheritance, legacy, patrimony. [*Compare* RIGHT.]

hermeneutic *adj.* —*See* EXPLANATORY.

hero *n.* A person revered especially for noble courage ▸ champion, heroine, paladin. *Idiom:* knight in shining armor. [*Compare* WINNER.] —*See also* CELEBRITY.

heroic *adj.* —*See* BRAVE, ENORMOUS.

heroine *n.* A woman revered especially for noble courage ▸ champion, hero, paladin. *Idiom:* knight in shining armor. [*Compare* WINNER.] —*See also* CELEBRITY.

heroism *n.* —*See* COURAGE.

hesitancy *n.* —*See* HESITATION.

hesitant *adj.* Given to or exhibiting hesitation ▸ halting, hesitating, indecisive, irresolute, pendulous, shilly-shally, tentative, timid, unsure, vacillant, vacillatory, wavering. *Idiom:* hemming and hawing. [*Compare* IN-

tate. **—hes′i·tan·cy** *n.* **—hes′i·tant·ly** *adv.*

hes·i·tate (hĕz′ĭ-tāt′) ▸ *v.* **-tat·ed, -tat·ing.** 1. To be slow to act, speak, or decide; waver. 2. To be reluctant. 3. To speak haltingly; falter. **—hes′i·tat′ing·ly** *adv.* **—hes′i·ta′tion** *n.*

Hes·ti·a (hĕs′tē-ə) ▸ *n. Gk. Myth.* The goddess of the hearth.

hetero– or **heter–** ▸ *pref.* Other; different: *heterosexual.*

het·er·o·dox (hĕt′ər-ə-dŏks′) ▸ *adj.* 1. Not in agreement with accepted beliefs, esp. in theology. 2. Holding unorthodox opinions. **—het′er·o·dox′y** *n.*

het·er·o·ge·ne·ous (hĕt′ər-ə-jē′nē-əs, -jēn′yəs) ▸ *adj.* 1. also **het·er·og·e·nous** (hĕt′ə-rŏj′ə-nəs) Consisting of dissimilar elements or parts; not homogeneous. 2. Completely different; incongruous. **—het′er·o′ge·ne′i·ty** *n.* **—het′er·o·ge′ne·ous·ly** *adv.* **—het′er·o·ge′ne·ous·ness** *n.*

het·er·o·sex·u·al (hĕt′ə-rō-sĕk′shōō-əl) ▸ *adj.* 1. Sexually oriented to persons of the opposite sex. 2. Of or relating to different sexes. ▸ *n.* A heterosexual person. **—het′er·o·sex′u·al′i·ty** *n.* **—het′er·o·sex′u·al·ly** *adv.*

het·er·o·troph (hĕt′ər-ə-trŏf′, -trōf′) ▸ *n.* An organism that cannot synthesize its own food and depends on complex organic substances for nutrition. **—het′er·o·troph′ic** (-trŏf′ĭk, -trō′fĭk) *adj.* **—het′er·o·troph′i·cal·ly** *adv.* **—het′er·ot′ro·phy** (-ə-rŏt′rə-fē) *n.*

heu·ris·tic (hyōō-rĭs′tĭk) ▸ *adj.* 1. Of an educational method in which students learn through investigation and discovery. 2. *Comp. Sci.* Of a problem-solving technique in which the best solution is selected at successive stages of a program. **—heu·ris′tic** *n.* **—heu·ris′ti·cal·ly** *adv.* **—heu·ris′tics** *n.*

hew (hyōō) ▸ *v.* **hewed, hewn** (hyōōn) or **hewed, hew·ing.** 1. To make or shape with or as if with an ax. 2. To cut down with an ax. 3. To adhere or conform strictly: *hew to the line.* **—hew′er** *n.*

hex[1] (hĕks) ▸ *n.* 1. An evil spell; curse. 2. One that brings bad luck. ▸ *v.* 1. To put a hex on. 2. To bring or wish bad luck to. **—hex′er** *n.*

hex[2] (hĕks) ▸ *adj.* Hexagonal. Used of hardware; *a hex wrench.*

hexa– or **hex–** ▸ *pref.* Six: *hexagon.*

hex·a·dec·i·mal (hĕk′sə-dĕs′ə-məl) ▸ *adj.* Of or based on the number 16.

hex·a·gon (hĕk′sə-gŏn′) ▸ *n.* A polygon having six sides. **—hex·ag′o·nal** (hĕk-săg′ə-nəl) *adj.* **—hex·ag′o·nal·ly** *adv.*

hex·am·e·ter (hĕk-săm′ĭ-tər) ▸ *n.* A line of verse consisting of six metrical feet. **—hex′a·met′ric** (hĕk-sə-mĕt′rĭk), **hex′a·met′ri·cal** (-rĭ-kəl) *adj.*

hey (hā) ▸ *interj.* Used to attract attention or to express surprise, appreciation, wonder, or pleasure.

hey·day (hā′dā′) ▸ *n.* The period of greatest popularity, success, or power; prime.

Hf ▸ The symbol for the element **hafnium.**

Hg ▸ The symbol for the element **mercury.**

hi (hī) ▸ *interj.* Used to express greeting.

HI ▸ *abbr.* Hawaii

hi·a·tus (hī-ā′təs) ▸ *n., pl.* **-tus·es** or **-tus.** A gap or an interruption in space, time, or continuity; break. **—hi·a′tal** *adj.*

Hi·a·wa·tha (hī′ə-wŏth′ə, -wô′thə, hē′ə-) (fl. 1570) ▸ Onondagan leader.

hi·ba·chi (hĭ-bä′chē) ▸ *n., pl.* **-chis.** A portable charcoal-burning brazier.

hi·ber·nate (hī′bər-nāt′) ▸ *v.* **-nat·ed, -nat·ing.** To pass the winter in a dormant or torpid state. **—hi′ber·na′tion** *n.* **—hi′ber·na′tor** *n.*

Hi·ber·ni·a (hī-bûr′nē-ə) ▸ The Latin and poetic name for Ireland. **—Hi·ber′ni·an** *adj. & n.*

hi·bis·cus (hī-bĭs′kəs) ▸ *n.* Any of a genus of chiefly tropical shrubs or trees having large, showy, variously colored flowers.

hic·cup also **hic·cough** (hĭk′əp) ▸ *n.* 1. A spasm of the diaphragm resulting in a rapid involuntary inhalation that is stopped by the sudden closure of the glottis. 2. **hiccups** also **hiccoughs** An attack of these spasms. ▸ *v.* **-cupped, -cup·ping** also **-coughed, -cough·ing.** To have the hiccups.

hick (hĭk) *Informal* ▸ *n.* A gullible, provincial person; yokel. ▸ *adj.* Provincial; unsophisticated.

Hick·ok (hĭk′ŏk′), **James Butler.** "Wild Bill" (1837–76) ▸ Amer. frontier scout and marshal.

hick·o·ry (hĭk′ə-rē) ▸ *n., pl.* **-ries.** 1. Any of a genus of North American trees having smooth or shaggy bark, compound leaves, and hard nuts with an edible kernel. 2. The wood of a hickory.

hi·dal·go (hĭ-dăl′gō) ▸ *n., pl.* **-gos.** A member of the minor nobility in Spain.

hide[1] (hīd) ▸ *v.* **hid** (hĭd), **hid·den** (hĭd′n) or **hid, hid·ing.** 1. To put or keep out of sight. 2. To prevent the disclosure of. 3. To cut off from sight; cover up. 4. To seek refuge.

hide[2] (hīd) ▸ *n.* The skin of an animal, esp. of a large animal.

hide-and-seek (hīd′n-sēk′) ▸ *n.* A children's game in which one player tries to find and catch others who are hiding.

hide·a·way (hīd′ə-wā′) ▸ *n.* 1. A place of concealment; hide-out. 2. A secluded or isolated place.

hide·bound (hīd′bound′) ▸ *adj.* Stubbornly narrow-minded or inflexible.

hid·e·ous (hĭd′ē-əs) ▸ *adj.* Repulsive, esp. to the sight. **—hid′e·ous·ly** *adv.* **—hid′e·ous·ness** *n.*

hide·out (hīd′out′) ▸ *n.* A place of shelter or concealment.

hie (hī) ▸ *v.* **hied, hie·ing** or **hy·ing** (hī′ĭng). To go quickly; hasten.

hi·er·ar·chy (hī′ə-rär′kē, hī′rär′-) ▸ *n., pl.* **-chies.** 1. A body of persons having authority. 2. An arrangement of persons or things in a graded series, as by rank or ability. **—hi′er·ar′chal, hi′er·ar′chic, hi′er·ar′chi·cal** *adj.* **—hi′er·ar′chi·cal·ly** *adv.*

THESAURUS

DISPOSED.] *—See also* DOUBTFUL (2).

hesitate *v.* To be irresolute in acting or doing ▸ dally, dilly-dally, dither, falter, halt, pause, shilly-shally, stagger, vacillate, waver, wobble. *Idiom:* hem and haw. [*Compare* DELAY.]

hesitation *n.* The act of hesitating or state of being hesitant ▸ dawdling, hesitancy, indecision, indecisiveness, irresoluteness, irresolution, pause, shilly-shally, tentativeness, timidity, timidness, to-and-fro, vacillation, wavering. *Idiom:* hemming and hawing. [*Compare* DELAY.]

heterogeneity or **heterogeneousness** *n.* *—See* VARIETY.

heterogeneous *adj.* *—See* VARIOUS.

hew *v.* *—See* DROP (3).

hex *n.* Something or someone believed to bring bad luck ▸ curse, evil eye, hoodoo, Jonah. *Informal:* jinx. [*Compare* CHARM, MAGIC.] *—See also* CURSE (1).

hex *v.* 1. To bring or wish bad luck or evil to ▸ curse, hoodoo. *Informal:* jinx. [*Compare* AFFLICT.] 2. To invoke an evil spell upon ▸ anathematize, curse, damn, imprecate. [*Compare* CHARM.]

hey *interjection* *—See* HELLO.

heyday *n.* *—See* BLOOM[1] (1).

hi *interjection* *—See* HELLO.

hiatus *n.* *—See* GAP (2), REST[1] (1).

hick *adj.* *—See* COUNTRY.

hick *n.* *—See* CLODHOPPER.

hidden *adj.* 1. Difficult or impossible to see or distinguish ▸ buried, camouflaged, cloaked, concealed, covert, disguised, imperceptible, indiscernible, indistinguishable, invisible, masked, obscured, secret, shrouded, unapparent, unnoticeable, unseen, veiled. [*Compare* IMPERCEPTIBLE, SECRET.] 2. Concealed from view ▸ blind, secluded, screened, secret. *Idioms:* out of sight, out of view. [*Compare* HIDDEN.] *—See also* ULTERIOR (1).

hide[1] *v.* To put or keep out of sight ▸ bury, cache, conceal, ensconce, occult, secrete, squirrel away. *Slang:* plant, stash. [*Compare* SAVE.] *—See also* BLOCK, CONCEAL.

hide out *v.* To shut oneself up in secrecy ▸ *Informal:* hole up. *Idioms:* go underground, lay (*or* lie) low.

hide[2] *n.* The skin of an animal, sometimes including fur, hair or feathers ▸ fur, leather, pelt.

hide *v.* *—See* BEAT (2).

hideaway *n.* A hiding place ▸ covert, den, hide-out, lair.

hidebound *adj.* *—See* INTOLERANT (1).

hideous *adj.* *—See* GHASTLY (1), UGLY.

hideousness *n.* *—See* UGLINESS.

hide-out *n.* A hiding place ▸ covert, den, hideaway, lair.

hiding *n.* *—See* BEATING.

hierarch *n.* *—See* CHIEF.

hierarchy *n.* *—See* CLASS (2).

hi·er·at·ic (hī′ə-răt′ĭk, hī-răt′-) ▸ *adj.* **1.** Of or relating to sacred persons or offices; sacerdotal. **2.** Of or relating to a simplified style of Egyptian hieroglyphic script. **—hi′er·at′i·cal·ly** *adv.*

hi·er·o·glyph (hī′ər-ə-glĭf′, hī′rə-) ▸ *n.* **1.** A symbol used in hieroglyphic writing. **2.** Something that suggests a hieroglyph.

hi·er·o·glyph·ic (hī′ər-ə-glĭf′ĭk, hī′rə-) ▸ *adj.* Of or being a system of writing, such as that of ancient Egypt, in which pictorial symbols represent meaning or sound or both. ▸ *n.* **1a.** A character in hieroglyphic writing. **b.** often **hieroglyphics** *(takes sing. or pl. v.)* Hieroglyphic writing, esp. that of the ancient Egyptians. **2.** Something illegible or undecipherable. **—hi′er·o·glyph′i·cal·ly** *adv.*

hi-fi (hī′fī′) ▸ *n., pl.* **-fis.** *Informal* **1.** High fidelity. **2.** An electronic system, esp. a phonograph, for reproducing high-fidelity sound. **—hi′-fi′** *adj.*

hig·gle·dy-pig·gle·dy (hĭg′əl-dē-pĭg′əl-dē) ▸ *adv.* In utter disorder or confusion.

high (hī) ▸ *adj.* **-er, -est.** **1a.** Relatively great in elevation. **b.** Extending a specified distance. **2a.** At or near a peak or culminating stage. **b.** Advanced in development or complexity. **3.** Piercing in tone or pitch. **4a.** Of great importance: *a high priority on housing.* **b.** Eminent in rank or status: *a high official.* **c.** Serious; grave: *high crimes.* **d.** Constituting a climax: *the high point of a film.* **5.** Lofty or exalted in quality. **6a.** Relatively great, as in quantity or degree. **b.** Favorable: *has a high opinion of him.* **7a.** Indicating excitement or euphoria. **b.** *Slang* Intoxicated by or as if by alcohol or a drug. ▸ *adv.* **-er, -est.** At, in, or to a lofty position, level, or degree. ▸ *n.* **1.** A high level, degree, or point. **2.** The gear configuration of a transmission that produces the highest range of output speeds. **3.** A center of high atmospheric pressure. **4.** *Slang* An intoxicated or euphoric condition. ***—idioms:*** **high and dry** Helpless; stranded. **high and low** Everywhere: *searched high and low.* **—high′ly** *adv.*

high·ball (hī′bôl′) ▸ *n.* A mixed alcoholic beverage served in a tall glass.

high beam ▸ *n.* The beam of a vehicle's headlight that provides long-range illumination.

high·born (hī′bôrn′) ▸ *adj.* Of noble birth.

high·boy (hī′boi′) ▸ *n.* A tall chest of drawers supported on four legs.

high·bred (hī′brĕd′) ▸ *adj.* Of superior breed or stock.

high·brow (hī′brou′) ▸ *adj.* Highly cultured or intellectual. ▸ *n.* One who has or affects a high degree of culture or learning. **—high′brow′, high′browed′** (-broud′) *adj.*

high·chair (hī′châr′) ▸ *n.* A very young child's feeding chair that has long legs.

high-class (hī′klăs′) ▸ *adj.* Of superior quality; first-class.

high·er-up (hī′ər-ŭp′) ▸ *n.* *Informal* One who has a superior rank, position, or status.

high·fa·lu·tin or **hi·fa·lu·tin** (hī′fə-lo͞ot′n) ▸ *adj.* *Informal* Pompous; pretentious.

high fashion ▸ *n.* **1.** See **high style.** **2.** See **haute couture.**

high fidelity ▸ *n.* The electronic reproduction of sound with minimal distortion. **—high′-fi·del′i·ty** *adj.*

high-flown (hī′flōn′) ▸ *adj.* Highly pretentious or inflated.

high frequency ▸ *n.* A radio frequency in the range between 3 and 30 megahertz.

High German ▸ *n.* **1.** German as used in central and S Germany. **2.** See **German** 2.

high·hand·ed (hī′hăn′dĭd) ▸ *adj.* Arrogant; overbearing. **—high′hand′ed·ly** *adv.* **—high′hand′ed·ness** *n.*

high-hat (hī′hăt′) *Informal* ▸ *v.* **-hat·ted, -hat·ting.** To treat condescendingly or superciliously. ▸ *adj.* Snobbish; haughty.

high jinks or **hi·jinks** (hī′jĭnks′) ▸ *pl.n.* Playful, often noisy and rowdy activity.

high jump ▸ *n.* A jump for height made over a horizontal bar in a track-and-field contest. **—high jumper** *n.*

high·land (hī′lənd) ▸ *n.* **1.** Elevated land. **2. highlands** A mountainous section of a country. **—high′land** *adj.* **—high′land·er** *n.*

High·lands (hī′ləndz) ▸ A mountainous region of central and N Scotland. **—High′land** *adj.* **—High′land·er** *n.*

high·light (hī′līt′) ▸ *n.* An especially notable detail or event. ▸ *v.* **1.** To make prominent; emphasize. **2.** To be a highlight of.

high-mind·ed (hī′mīn′dĭd) ▸ *adj.* Elevated in ideals or conduct; noble. **—high′-mind′ed·ly** *adv.* **—high′-mind′ed·ness** *n.*

high·ness (hī′nĭs) ▸ *n.* **1.** The quality or condition of being high. **2. Highness** Used with *His, Her,* or *Your* as a title for a prince or princess.

high-pres·sure (hī′prĕsh′ər) ▸ *adj.* **1.** Relating to pressures higher than normal. **2.** *Informal* Aggressive and persistent. **3.** Full of or imposing great stress or tension.

high profile ▸ *n.* An intentionally conspicuous, well-publicized presence or stance. **—high′-pro′file** *adj.*

high relief ▸ *n.* Sculptural relief in which the modeled forms project from the background by at least half their depth.

high-rise also **high rise** (hī′rīz′) ▸ *n.* A multistoried building equipped with elevators. **—high′-rise′** *adj.*

high·road or **high road** (hī′rōd′) ▸ *n.* **1.** A direct or sure path. **2.** *Chiefly Brit.* A main road; highway.

high school ▸ *n.* A secondary school that usu. includes grades 9 or 10 through 12. **—high′-school′** *adj.* **—high school′er** *n.*

high seas ▸ *pl.n.* The open ocean waters beyond the territorial limits of a country.

high-sound·ing (hī′soun′dĭng) ▸ *adj.* Pretentious; pompous.

high-spir·it·ed (hī′spĭr′ĭ-tĭd) ▸ *adj.* **1.** Having a proud or unbroken spirit. **2.** Vivacious; lively. **—high′-spir′it·ed·ness** *n.*

high-strung (hī′strŭng′) ▸ *adj.* Tending to be very nervous and easily excited.

high style ▸ *n.* The latest in fashion, usu. for an exclusive clientele. **—high′-style′** *adj.*

high·tail (hī′tāl′) ▸ *v.* *Slang* To go as fast as possible, esp. in retreat.

high-tech (hī′tĕk′) ▸ *adj.* *Informal* Of or resembling high technology.

THESAURUS

hieroglyphic *adj.* —*See* GRAPHIC (4).

higgle *v.* —*See* HAGGLE.

higgledy-piggledy *adj.* —*See* CONFUSED (2).

high *adj.* **1.** Being of or at a relatively great height or altitude ▸ aerial, airy, elevated, lofty, sky-high, soaring, tall, towering. *Idiom:* on high. **2.** At the upper end of a degree of measure ▸ elevated, great, large. [*Compare* EXALTED, EXTREME.] **3.** Elevated in pitch ▸ acute, high-pitched, piercing, piping, shrieky, shrill, shrilly, treble. —*See also* COSTLY, DRUGGED, DRUNK, ELATED, ELEVATED (4), ELEVATED (2), INTENSE.

high *n.* —*See* THRILL.

high-and-mighty *adj.* —*See* ARROGANT.

highball *v.* —*See* RUSH.

highborn *adj.* —*See* NOBLE.

highbred *adj.* —*See* NOBLE, THOROUGHBRED.

highbrow *adj.* —*See* CULTURED, INTELLECTUAL.

highbrow *n.* —*See* MIND (2).

higher *adj.* Being at a rank or level above another ▸ greater, senior, superior, upper.

higher-up *n.* *Informal* One who stands above another in rank ▸ better, elder, senior, superior. [*Compare* CHIEF.]

highest *adj.* Of, being, located at, or forming the top ▸ loftiest, top, topmost, upmost, uppermost. [*Compare* CLIMACTIC.] —*See also* BEST (1).

highfalutin or **hifalutin** *adj.* —*See* POMPOUS.

high-flown *adj.* —*See* ELEVATED (4), ORATORICAL.

highflying *adj.* —*See* AMBITIOUS.

high-grade *adj.* —*See* CHOICE (1).

high-hat *v.* To treat in a superciliously indulgent manner ▸ condescend, patronize. *Idioms:* lord it over, queen it, speak (*or* talk) down to. [*Compare* INSULT, SNUB.]

high-hat *adj.* —*See* ARROGANT, SNOBBISH.

high jinks or **hijinks** *n.* —*See* MISCHIEF.

highlight *v.* —*See* EMPHASIZE.

highlight *n.* Light that is reflected ▸ glare, reflection. [*Compare* FLASH.]

highly *adv.* —*See* VERY.

high-minded *adj.* —*See* ELEVATED (3).

high-pitched *adj.* —*See* HIGH (3).

high-priced *adj.* —*See* COSTLY.

high-ranking *adj.* —*See* EXALTED.

high sign *n.* —*See* ALARM, GESTURE.

high-sounding *adj.* —*See* ORATORICAL.

high-speed *adj.* —*See* FAST (1).

high-spirited *adj.* —*See* LIVELY.

hightail *v.* —*See* RUN (2).

high technology ▸ *n.* Technology involving highly advanced systems or devices. **—high′-tech·nol′o·gy** *adj.*
high-ten·sion (hī′tĕn′shən) ▸ *adj.* Having a high voltage.
high-test (hī′tĕst') ▸ *adj.* **1.** Of or being highly volatile high-octane gasoline. **2.** Meeting exacting standards. **—high′test′** *n.*
high tide ▸ *n.* **1a.** The tide at its highest level. **b.** The time at which this tide occurs. **2.** A point of culmination; climax.
high-toned (hī′tōnd') ▸ *adj.* **1.** Intellectually, morally, or socially superior. **2.** *Informal* Pretentiously elegant or fashionable.
high·way (hī′wā') ▸ *n.* A main public road.
high·way·man (hī′wā'mən) ▸ *n.* A robber who holds up travelers on a road.
high wire ▸ *n.* A tightrope for aerialists that is stretched high above the ground. **—high′-wire′** *adj.*
hi·jack also **high·jack** (hī′jăk') ▸ *v. Informal* **1.** To steal (goods) from a vehicle in transit. **2.** To seize control of (a moving vehicle) by force, esp. to reach an alternate destination. **—hi′jack′er** *n.*
hike (hīk) ▸ *v.* **hiked, hik·ing. 1.** To go on a long walk for pleasure or exercise. **2.** To increase in amount. **3.** To pull or raise abruptly: *hiked up her socks.* **4.** *Football* To snap (the ball). ▸ *n.* **1.** A long walk. **2.** An often abrupt increase or rise: *a price hike.* **3.** *Football* See **snap** 9. **—hik′er** *n.*
hi·lar·i·ous (hĭ-lâr′ē-əs, -lăr′-, hī-) ▸ *adj.* Boisterously funny. **—hi·lar′i·ous·ly** *adv.* **—hi·lar′i·ty** *n.*
hill (hĭl) ▸ *n.* **1.** A well-defined natural elevation smaller than a mountain. **2.** A small heap, pile, or mound. **3. Hill** The US Congress. ***—idiom:* over the hill** *Informal* Past one's prime. **—hill′i·ness** *n.* **—hill′y** *adj.*
hill·bil·ly (hĭl′bĭl'ē) ▸ *n., pl.* **-lies.** *Informal* A person from the backwoods or a remote mountain area.
hill·ock (hĭl′ək) ▸ *n.* A small hill.
hill·side (hĭl′sīd') ▸ *n.* The slope of a hill.
hill·top (hĭl′tŏp') ▸ *n.* The crest of a hill.
hilt (hĭlt) ▸ *n.* The handle of a weapon or tool. ***—idiom:* to the hilt** To the limit; completely.
him (hĭm) ▸ *pron.* The objective case of **he. 1.** Used as a direct or indirect object: *They chose him; I gave him a raise.* **2.** Used as the object of a preposition: *This call is for him.*
Him·a·la·ya Mountains (hĭm′ə-lā′ə, hĭ-mäl′yə) ▸ A mountain system of S-central Asia extending about 2,414 km (1,500 mi) through Kashmir, N India, S Xizang (Tibet), Nepal, and Bhutan.
him·self (hĭm-sĕlf′) ▸ *pron.* **1.** That one identical with him: **a.** Used reflexively as the direct or indirect object of a verb or the object of a preposition: *He cut himself.* **b.** Used for emphasis: *He himself did it.* **2.** His normal or healthy condition: *He's feeling himself again.*
hind[1] (hīnd) ▸ *adj.* Located at or forming the back or rear; posterior: *hind legs.*
hind[2] (hīnd) ▸ *n.* A female red deer.
hin·der (hĭn′dər) ▸ *v.* **1.** To be or get in the way of. **2.** To obstruct or delay the progress of. **—hin′der·er** *n.*
Hin·di (hĭn′dē) ▸ *n.* **1.** A group of Indic dialects that are spoken in N India. **2.** The literary and official language that is based on these dialects. **—Hin′di** *adj.*
hind·most (hīnd′mōst') also **hind·er·most** (hīn′dər-) ▸ *adj.* Farthest to the rear; last.
hind·quar·ter (hīnd′kwôr'tər) ▸ *n.* **1.** The back portion of a side of meat. **2. hindquarters** The rump of a four-footed animal.
hin·drance (hĭn′drəns) ▸ *n.* **1.** The act of hindering or condition of being hindered. **2.** One that hinders.
hind·sight (hīnd′sīt') ▸ *n.* Understanding of events after their occurrence.
Hin·du (hĭn′do͞o) ▸ *adj.* Of Hinduism or the Hindus. ▸ *n.* **1.** An adherent of Hinduism. **2.** A native of India, esp. N India.
Hin·du·ism (hĭn′do͞o-ĭz'əm) ▸ *n.* A diverse body of religion, philosophy, and culture native to India.
Hindu Kush (ko͝osh, kŭsh) ▸ A mountain range of SW Asia extending W from N Pakistan to NE Afghanistan.
Hin·du·stan (hĭn'do͞o-stăn′, -stän′) ▸ **1.** A historical region of India considered at various times to include only the upper Ganges R. plateau or all of N India. **2.** The entire Indian subcontinent.
Hin·du·sta·ni (hĭn'do͞o-stä′nē, -stăn′ē) ▸ *n.* A group of Indic dialects that includes Urdu and Hindi. ▸ *adj.* Of or relating to Hindustan or the Hindustani language.
hinge (hĭnj) ▸ *n.* **1.** A jointed device that allows the turning of a part, such as a door, on a frame. **2.** A similar structure or part. ▸ *v.* **hinged, hing·ing. 1.** To attach by or equip with or as if with a hinge. **2.** To be contingent; depend.
hint (hĭnt) ▸ *n.* **1.** A slight indication or intimation. **2.** A barely perceptible amount: *just a hint of color.* ▸ *v.* **1.** To make known in an indirect manner. **2.** To give a hint. **—hint′er** *n.*
hin·ter·land (hĭn′tər-lănd') ▸ *n.* **1.** The land adjacent to and inland from a coast. **2.** A region remote from urban areas.
hip[1] (hĭp) ▸ *n.* **1.** The part of the human body that projects outward over the hipbone between the waist and the thigh. **2.** The hip joint.
hip[2] (hĭp) also **hep** (hĕp) ▸ *adj.* **hip·per, hip·pest** also **hep·per, hep·pest.** *Slang* **1.** Keenly aware of the latest trends or developments. **2.** Cognizant; wise. **3.** Very fashionable or stylish. **—hip′ness** *n.*
hip[3] (hĭp) ▸ *n.* The fleshy, usu. red fruit of the rose, used for tea.
hip·bone (hĭp′bōn') ▸ *n.* Either of two large flat bones each forming one of the halves of the pelvis.
hip-hop (hĭp′hŏp') ▸ *n.* **1.** A popular urban youth culture, closely associated with rap music and the style of inner-city African Americans. **2.** Rap music.
hip joint ▸ *n.* The ball-and-socket joint between the femur and the hipbone.
hip·pie also **hip·py** (hĭp′ē) ▸ *n., pl.* **-pies.** *Slang* A member of a social and political movement advocating such practices as pacifism, nonconformity in dress and behavior, and often the use of psychedelic drugs. **—hip′pie·dom** *n.*
hip·po (hĭp′ō) ▸ *n., pl.* **-pos.** A hippopotamus.
Hip·poc·ra·tes (hĭ-pŏk′rə-tēz') (460?–377? B.C.) ▸ Greek physician. **—Hip'po·crat′ic** (hĭp'ə-krăt′ĭk) *adj.*

THESAURUS

high-up *n.* *—See* DIGNITARY.
highway *n.* *—See* WAY (2).
highwayman *n.* *—See* THIEF.
hijack *v.* *—See* COERCE, SEIZE (1).
hike *v.* **1.** To travel about or journey on foot ▸ backpack, march, tramp, trek. [*Compare* JOURNEY, ROVE, WALK.] **2.** To increase in amount ▸ boost, jack (up), jump, raise, up. *—See also* ELEVATE (1).
hike *n.* *—See* INCREASE (1), INCREASE (2), WALK (1).
hilarious *adj.* *—See* FUNNY (1).
hilarity *n.* *—See* MERRIMENT (1).
hill *n.* A natural land elevation ▸ bump, butte, down, eminence, hummock, knoll, prominence, rise. [*Compare* PLATEAU.] *—See also* HEAP (1).
hill *v.* *—See* HEAP (1).
hillbilly *n.* *—See* CLODHOPPER.
hilt *n.* A protrusion or extension designed to be grasped by the hand ▸ haft, handgrip, handle. [*Compare* HOLD, KNOB.]
hind *adj.* *—See* BACK.
hind end *n.* *—See* BACK.
hinder *v.* To interfere with the progress of ▸ bog (down), dampen, encumber, forestall, hamper, hold back, impede, interfere with, obstruct, retard, stem. *Idioms:* be (*or* stand *or* get) in the way of, put a damper on. [*Compare* FRUSTRATE, RESTRAIN, STOP.] *—See also* DELAY (1).
hindmost or **hindermost** *adj.* *—See* BACK, LAST[1] (2).
hindquarters *n.* *—See* BUTTOCKS.
hindrance *n.* *—See* BAR (1).
hinge on or **upon** *v.* *—See* DEPEND ON (2).
hint *n.* **1.** A subtle quality underlying or felt to underlie a situation, action, or person ▸ glimmering, implication, inkling, suspicion, undercurrent, undertone. **2.** A brief or indirect suggestion ▸ allusion, clue, cue, innuendo, insinuation, intimation, suggestion, wink. *—See also* SHADE (2), TIP[3].
hint *v.* To convey an idea by indirect, subtle means ▸ allude to, hint at, imply, insinuate, intimate, suggest. *Idiom:* drop a hint.
hinterland *n.* *—See* COUNTRY.
hip *adj.* *—See* AWARE, FASHIONABLE.

Hippocratic oath ▸ *n.* An oath of ethical professional behavior sworn by new physicians.

hip·po·drome (hĭp′ə-drōm′) ▸ *n.* An arena used esp. for horse shows.

hip·po·pot·a·mus (hĭp′ə-pŏt′ə-məs) ▸ *n., pl.* **-mus·es** or **-mi** (-mī′). A large African river mammal having thick, dark, almost hairless skin, short legs, and a broad, wide-mouthed muzzle.

hip roof or **hipped roof** (hĭpt) ▸ *n.* A four-sided roof having sloping ends and sides.

hip·ster (hĭp′stər) ▸ *n. Slang* One who is hip.

hi·ra·ga·na (hîr′ə-gä′nə) ▸ *n.* A cursive kana used for polite, informal, or casual writing.

hire (hīr) ▸ *v.* **hired, hir·ing.** To engage the services or use of for a fee: *hired a new clerk; hire a car for the day.* ▸ *n.* **1.** The act of hiring or the condition of being hired. **2.** Payment for services or the use of something. **—hir′er** *n.*

hire·ling (hīr′lĭng) ▸ *n.* One who works solely for compensation, esp. at performing tasks considered offensive.

Hi·ro·hi·to (hîr′ō-hē′tō) (1901–89) ▸ Emperor of Japan (1926–89).

Hi·ro·shi·ma (hîr′ə-shē′mə, hĭ-rō′shə-mə) ▸ A city of SW Honshu, Japan; destroyed by US forces with the first atomic bomb used in warfare (August 6, 1945). Pop. 1,130,000.

hir·sute (hûr′so͞ot′, hîr′-, hər-so͞ot′) ▸ *adj.* Hairy. **—hir′sute′·ness** *n.*

his (hĭz) ▸ *adj.* The possessive form of **he.** Used as a modifier before a noun: *his brother; his ideas.* ▸ *pron. (takes sing. or pl. v.)* Used to indicate the one or ones belonging to him: *If you can't find your hat, take his.*

His·pan·ic (hĭ-spăn′ĭk) ▸ *adj.* **1.** Relating to Spain or Spanish-speaking Latin America. **2.** Relating to Hispanic Americans. ▸ *n.* **1.** A Spanish-speaking person. **2.** A Hispanic American.

Hispanic American ▸ *n.* **1.** A US citizen or resident of Latin-American or Spanish descent. **2.** A Spanish American. **—His·pan′ic-A·mer′i·can** *adj.*

His·pan·io·la (hĭs′pən-yō′lə). Formerly **Haiti** ▸ An island of the West Indies E of Cuba, divided between Haiti and the Dominican Republic.

hiss (hĭs) ▸ *n.* **1.** A sharp sibilant sound similar to a sustained *s.* **2.** An expression of disapproval or contempt conveyed by a hiss. ▸ *v.* **1.** To make a hiss. **2.** To express disapproval by hissing.

his·ta·mine (hĭs′tə-mēn′, -mĭn) ▸ *n.* A white crystalline compound, $C_5H_9N_3$, found in plant and animal tissue, that dilates blood vessels, stimulates gastric secretions, and is released by the body in allergic reactions. **—his′ta·min′ic** (-mĭn′ĭk) *adj.*

his·to·com·pat·i·bil·i·ty (hĭs′tō-kəm-păt′ə-bĭl′ĭ-tē) ▸ *n., pl.* **-ties.** A state or condition in which the absence of immunological interference permits the grafting of tissue or the transfusion of blood without rejection. **—his′to·com·pat′i·ble** *adj.*

his·to·gram (hĭs′tə-grăm′) ▸ *n.* A bar graph of a frequency distribution in which the areas of the bars are proportional to the classes into which the variable has been divided and their frequencies.

his·tol·o·gy (hĭ-stŏl′ə-jē) ▸ *n., pl.* **-gies. 1.** The anatomical study of the microscopic structure of animal and plant tissues. **2.** The microscopic structure of tissue. **—his′to·log′i·cal** (hĭs′tə-lŏj′ĭ-kəl), **his′to·log′ic** *adj.* **—his′to·log′i·cal·ly** *adv.* **—his·tol′o·gist** *n.*

his·to·ri·an (hĭ-stôr′ē-ən, -stŏr′-) ▸ *n.* A writer, student, or scholar of history.

his·tor·ic (hĭ-stôr′ĭk, -stŏr′-) ▸ *adj.* Having importance in or influence on history.

his·tor·i·cal (hĭ-stôr′ĭ-kəl, -stŏr′-) ▸ *adj.* **1.** Of or relating to history. **2.** Based on or concerned with events in history. **3.** Important or famous in history. **—his·tor′i·cal·ly** *adv.*

his·to·ri·og·ra·phy (hĭ-stôr′ē-ŏg′rə-fē) ▸ *n.* **1.** The principles or methodology of historical research. **2.** The writing of history. **3.** Historical literature. **—his·to′ri·og′ra·pher** *n.* **—his·to′ri·o·graph′ic** (-ē-ə-grăf′ĭk), **his·to′ri·o·graph′i·cal** *adj.*

his·to·ry (hĭs′tə-rē) ▸ *n., pl.* **-ries. 1.** A narrative of events; story. **2.** A chronological record of events. **3.** The branch of knowledge that records and analyzes past events. **4.** The events of the past. **5.** An interesting past: *a house with a history.*

his·tri·on·ic (hĭs′trē-ŏn′ĭk) also **his·tri·on·i·cal** (-ĭ-kəl) ▸ *adj.* **1.** Of or relating to actors or acting. **2.** Excessively dramatic or emotional; affected. **—his′tri·on′i·cal·ly** *adv.*

his·tri·on·ics (hĭs′trē-ŏn′ĭks) ▸ *n. (takes sing. or pl. v.)* Exaggerated emotional behavior calculated for effect.

hit (hĭt) ▸ *v.* **hit, hit·ting. 1.** To come or cause to come into contact with forcefully; strike. **2.** To deal a blow to. **3.** To press or push (a key or button). **4.** To propel (e.g., a ball) with a blow. **5.** *Baseball* To execute (a base hit) successfully. **6.** To affect adversely. **7.** *Informal* To discover, esp. by chance. **8.** *Informal* To attain or reach: *Sales hit a new high.* ▸ *n.* **1.** A collision or impact. **2.** A successfully executed shot, blow, or throw. **3.** A successful or popular venture. **4.** *Baseball* A base hit. **5.** *Comp. Sci.* **a.** A match of data in a search string against data that one is searching. **b.** A connection made to a website. **6.** *Slang* A dose of a narcotic drug. **7.** *Slang* A murder, esp. for hire. ***—idioms:*** **hit it off** *Informal* To get along well together. **hit the hay** *Slang* To go to bed. **hit the road** *Slang* To set out; leave. **hit the roof** *Slang* To express vehement anger. **hit the spot** To satisfy a specific desire. **—hit′ter** *n.*

hit-and-run (hĭt′n-rŭn′) ▸ *adj.* Of or being a vehicular accident in which the driver at fault leaves the scene.

hitch (hĭch) ▸ *v.* **1.** To fasten or catch temporarily with or as if with a loop, hook, or noose. **2.** To connect or attach:

THESAURUS

hire *v.* To engage the temporary use of something for a fee ▸ charter, lease, rent (out). *—See also* EMPLOY (1), LEASE (1).

hire *n.* **1.** The act of employing for wages ▸ employment, engagement, hiring, retention. **2.** The state of being employed ▸ employ, employment, service. *—See also* EMPLOYEE, WAGE.

hired *adj.* *—See* EMPLOYED.

hired hand or **hireling** *n.* *—See* EMPLOYEE.

hirer *n.* One that employs persons for wages ▸ employer.

hirsute *adj.* *—See* HAIRY.

hiss *n.* **1.** A sibilant sound ▸ fizz, fizzing, fizzle, fizzling, rustle, rustling, sibilant, sizzle, sizzling, swish, swishing, whiz, whizzing, whoosh, whooshing. **2.** One of various derisive sounds of disapproval ▸ boo, catcall, hoot. *Slang:* bird, Bronx cheer, raspberry, razz.

hiss *v.* **1.** To make a sibilant sound ▸ fizz, fizzle, rustle, sibilate, sizzle, swish, whiz, whoosh. **2.** To make a derisive sound of disapproval ▸ boo, catcall, hoot. *Slang:* bird, Bronx cheer, raspberry, razz. *Idioms:* give (*or* blow) a Bronx cheer, give (*or* blow) a raspberry. *—See also* BURN (2).

hissy fit *n.* *—See* TEMPER (2).

historic *adj.* *—See* IMPORTANT, VINTAGE.

history *n.* **1.** A chronological record of past events ▸ annals, archive, chronicle, historical record. [*Compare* ANTIQUITY.] **2.** One's previous experiences ▸ background, career, credentials, curriculum vitae, life history, past, record, resumé, vita. [*Compare* ACCOMPLISHMENT, QUALIFICATION.] *—See also* STORY (1).

histrionic or **histrionical** *adj.* *—See* DRAMATIC (1), DRAMATIC (2).

histrionics *n.* *—See* THEATRICS (2).

hit *v.* To deliver a sudden, sharp blow to ▸ bash, box, bust, catch, clout, jab, knock, pop, punch, slam, slog, slug, smash, smite, sock, strike, swat, swing at, thwack, whack, wham, whop. *Informal:* biff, bop, clip, wallop. *Slang:* belt, conk, nail, paste. *Idioms:* let fly at, let someone have it, sock it to someone, take a swing (*or* swipe) at. *—See also* COLLIDE, ENCOUNTER (1), KILL[1], STRIKE (2).

hit back *v.* *—See* RETALIATE.

hit on *v.* *—See* ACCOMPLISH.

hit *n.* A dazzling, often sudden instance of success ▸ sleeper. *Informal:* knockout, smash, smash hit, tenstrike, winner, wow. *Slang:* boff, boffo, boffola. [*Compare* ACCOMPLISHMENT.] *—See also* BLOW[2], COLLISION, MURDER, PULL (2).

hitch *v.* *—See* FASTEN, STAGGER (1).

hitch up *v.* *—See* ELEVATE (1).

hitch *n.* **1.** A prison term ▸ stretch, time. **2.** *Informal* A tricky or unsuspected condition ▸ catch, rub, snag.

hitch an ox to the plow. **3.** To move or raise by pulling or jerking. **4.** *Informal* **a.** To obtain (a free ride). **b.** To hitchhike. **5.** To get married. ▸ *n.* **1.** A knot used as a temporary fastening. **2.** A short jerk or tug. **3.** A hobble or limp. **4.** An impediment or delay. **5.** A term of military service. **—hitch′er** *n.*

hitch·hike (hĭch′hīk′) ▸ *v.* **-hiked, -hik·ing.** To travel by soliciting free rides along a road. **—hitch′hik′er** *n.*

hith·er (hĭth′ər) ▸ *adv.* To or toward this place: *Come hither.* ▸ *adj.* Located on the near side.

hith·er·to (hĭth′ər-to͞o′, hĭth′ər-to͞o′) ▸ *adv.* Until this time.

Hit·ler (hĭt′lər), **Adolf** (1889–1945) ▸ Austrian-born German Nazi dictator.

hit man ▸ *n. Slang* A hired killer.

hit-or-miss (hĭt′ər-mĭs′) ▸ *adj.* Haphazard; random. **—hit or miss** *adv.*

hit squad ▸ *n. Slang* A squad or team of hired executioners.

Hit·tite (hĭt′īt′) ▸ *n.* **1.** A member of an ancient people living in Anatolia and N Syria about 2000–1200 B.C. **2.** The Indo-European language of the Hittites.

HIV (āch′ī-vē′) ▸ *n.* A retrovirus that causes AIDS.

hive (hīv) ▸ *n.* **1.** A structure for housing bees, esp. honeybees. **2.** A colony of bees living in a hive. **3.** A place swarming with activity. **—hive** *v.*

hives (hīvz) ▸ *pl.n. (takes sing. or pl. v.)* A skin condition marked by itching welts and caused by an allergic reaction, as to a food, infection, or nervous state.

HMO (āch′ĕm-ō′) ▸ *n.* A corporation providing curative and preventive medicine within certain limits to enrolled members.

Hmong (hmông) ▸ *n., pl.* **Hmong** or **Hmongs.** **1.** A member of a people inhabiting parts of S China, Vietnam, Laos, and Thailand. **2.** The language of the Hmong.

Ho ▸ The symbol for the element **holmium.**

hoa·gie also **hoa·gy** (hō′gē) ▸ *n., pl.* **-gies.** *Regional* See **submarine** 2.

hoard (hôrd) ▸ *n.* A supply hidden or stored for future use. ▸ *v.* To accumulate a hoard (of). **—hoard′er** *n.*

hoar·frost (hôr′frôst′, -frŏst′) ▸ *n.* Frozen dew that forms a white coating on a surface.

hoarse (hôrs) ▸ *adj.* **hoars·er, hoars·est.** Rough or grating in sound. **—hoarse′ly** *adv.* **—hoarse′ness** *n.*

hoar·y (hôr′ē) ▸ *adj.* **-i·er, -i·est.** **1.** Gray or white with or as if with age. **2.** Very old; ancient. **—hoar′i·ness** *n.*

hoax (hōks) ▸ *n.* An act intended to deceive or trick. ▸ *v.* To deceive or cheat by using a hoax. **—hoax′er** *n.*

hob (hŏb) ▸ *n. Chiefly Brit.* A hobgoblin, sprite, or elf.

Hobbes (hŏbz), **Thomas** (1588–1679) ▸ English philosopher and political theorist. **—Hobbes′i·an** *adj.*

hob·ble (hŏb′əl) ▸ *v.* **-bled, -bling.** **1.** To walk with difficulty; limp. **2.** To impede the movement or progress of. ▸ *n.* **1.** A hobbling walk or gait. **2.** A device used to join the legs esp. of a horse so as to hamper but not prevent its movement. **—hob′bler** *n.*

hob·by (hŏb′ē) ▸ *n., pl.* **-bies.** An activity or interest pursued at one's leisure for enjoyment. **—hob′by·ist** *n.*

hob·by·horse (hŏb′ē-hôrs′) ▸ *n.* **1.** A riding toy made of a long stick with an imitation horse's head on one end. **2.** See **rocking horse.** **3.** A favorite or obsessive topic.

hob·gob·lin (hŏb′gŏb′lĭn) ▸ *n.* **1.** An ugly, mischievous elf or goblin. **2.** An object or source of fear or dread; bugaboo.

hob·nail (hŏb′nāl′) ▸ *n.* A short nail with a thick head used to protect the soles of shoes or boots. **—hob′nailed′** *adj.*

hob·nob (hŏb′nŏb′) ▸ *v.* **-nobbed, -nob·bing.** To associate familiarly: *hobnobs with the executives.*

ho·bo (hō′bō) ▸ *n., pl.* **-boes** or **-bos.** A homeless person, esp. a vagrant.

Ho Chi Minh City (hō′ chē′ mĭn′). Formerly **Saigon** ▸ A city of S Vietnam near the South China Sea. Pop. 3,020,000.

hock[1] (hŏk) ▸ *n.* The joint of the hind leg of a quadruped, such as a horse, corresponding to the human ankle.

hock[2] (hŏk) *Slang* ▸ *v.* To pawn. ▸ *n.* **1.** The state of being in pawn. **2.** Debt: *in hock for 500 dollars.*

hock·ey (hŏk′ē) ▸ *n.* **1.** Ice hockey. **2.** Field hockey.

ho·cus-po·cus (hō′kəs-pō′kəs) ▸ *n.* **1.** Nonsense words or phrases used when performing magic tricks. **2.** Deception; trickery.

hod (hŏd) ▸ *n.* **1.** A trough carried over the shoulder for transporting loads, as of bricks or mortar. **2.** A coal scuttle.

hodge·podge (hŏj′pŏj′) ▸ *n.* A haphazard mixture; jumble.

Hodg·kin (hŏj′kĭn), **Dorothy Mary Crowfoot** (1910–94) ▸ Egyptian-born British chemist; 1964 Nobel.

Hodg·kin's disease (hŏj′kĭnz) ▸ *n.* A malignant, progressive, sometimes fatal disease marked by enlargement of the lymph nodes, spleen, and liver.

hoe (hō) ▸ *n.* A tool with a flat blade attached to a long handle, used for weeding, cultivating, and gardening. **—hoe** *v.* **—ho′er** *n.*

hoe·down (hō′doun′) ▸ *n.* A square dance.

hog (hôg, hŏg) ▸ *n.* **1a.** An animal of the pig family, such as the boar or wart hog. **b.** A domesticated pig, esp. one full-grown. **2.** A gluttonous person. ▸ *v.* **hogged, hog·ging.** *Informal* To take more than one's share of. ***—idiom:* high on the hog** In high or lavish style.

ho·gan (hō′gän′, -gən) ▸ *n.* A usu. earth-covered Navajo dwelling, traditionally facing east.

hogs·head (hôgz′hĕd′, hŏgz′-) ▸ *n.* **1.** A large barrel or cask. **2.** A unit of capacity used in the US, equal to 63 gal. (238 l).

hog·tie also **hog-tie** (hôg′tī′, hŏg′-) ▸ *v.* **1.** To tie together the feet or legs of. **2.** *Informal* To impede in movement or action.

hog·wash (hôg′wôsh′, -wŏsh′, hŏg′-) ▸ *n.* **1.** Worthless, false, or ridiculous language; nonsense. **2.** Garbage fed to hogs; swill.

hog-wild (hôg′wīld′, hŏg′-) ▸ *adj. Informal* So excited as to be devoid of good judgment. **—hog′-wild′** *adv.*

hoi pol·loi (hoi′ pə-loi′) ▸ *n.* The common people.

hoist (hoist) ▸ *v.* To raise or haul up. ▸ *n.* **1.** An apparatus for lifting heavy or cumbersome objects. **2.** The act of hoisting; lift. **—hoist′er** *n.*

Ho·kan (hō′kən) ▸ *n.* A proposed grouping of a number of Native American language families of W North America.

Hok·kai·do (hŏ-kī′dō, hô′kī-dō′) ▸ An island of Japan N of Honshu.

hol– ▸ *pref.* Var. of **holo–.**

hold[1] (hōld) ▸ *v.* **held** (hĕld), **hold·ing.** **1.** To have in one's grasp. **2.** To support; keep up. **3.** To retain the attention

THESAURUS

[*Compare* BAR, DISADVANTAGE, TRICK.] *—See also* BOND (2), TURN (1).

hit man *n. —See* MURDERER.

hit-or-miss *adj. —See* RANDOM.

hive *v. —See* ACCUMULATE.

hoard *n.* A supply stored or hidden for possible future use ▸ backlog, cache, inventory, nest egg, provision, reserve, reservoir, stash, stock, stockpile, store, supply, treasure. [*Compare* ACCUMULATION.]

hoard *v. —See* SAVE (1).

hoarse *adj.* Rough, raw, or grating in sound ▸ croaking, croaky, gravelly, gruff, husky, ragged, raw. *—See also* HARSH.

hoary *adj. —See* OLD (2).

hoax *v. —See* CHEAT (1).

hoax *n. —See* CHEAT (1).

hobble *v. —See* HAMPER[1], STAGGER (1).

hobble *n. —See* BOND (1).

hobby *n. —See* AMUSEMENT.

hobbyhorse *n. —See* ENTHUSIASM (2).

hobnob *v. —See* ASSOCIATE (2).

hobo *n.* One who wanders without a permanent home or livelihood ▸ drifter, gadabout, gypsy, itinerant, migrant, nomad, peregrinator, peripatetic, roamer, rover, swagman, tramp, transient, vagabond, vagrant, wanderer. [*Compare* PAUPER.]

hock *v. —See* PAWN[1].

hocus-pocus *n. —See* GIBBERISH.

hodgepodge *n. —See* ASSORTMENT.

hoggish *adj. —See* GLUTTONOUS.

hogtie *v. —See* HAMPER[1].

hogwash *n. —See* NONSENSE.

hoi polloi *n. —See* COMMONALTY.

hoist *v. —See* ELEVATE (1).

hoist *n. —See* LIFT.

hoity-toity *adj. —See* EXCLUSIVE (3), POMPOUS.

hokey *adj. —See* SENTIMENTAL.

hold *v.* **1.** To have and maintain in one's possession ▸ hold back, keep (back), reserve, retain, stick with, withhold. **2.** To be filled by ▸ contain, have. [*Compare* CONSTITUTE.]

of. 4. To contain. 5. To have in one's possession. 6. To maintain control over. 7. To maintain occupation of by force. 8. To maintain in a given condition or situation. 9. To restrain; curb. 10. To stop or delay. 11. To keep from use: *Hold the tickets for us.* 12. To obligate: *held me to my promise.* 13a. To regard or consider. b. To assert; affirm. 14. To cause to take place: *hold a yard sale.* 15. To withstand pressure or stress. 16. To continue in a direction or condition. 17. To be valid or true. ***—phrasal verbs:*** **hold forth** To talk at great length. **hold out** 1. To continue in supply; last. 2. To continue to resist. **hold over** 1. To postpone. 2. To keep in an earlier state. **hold up** 1. To obstruct or delay. 2. To rob. 3. To endure. ▸ *n.* 1. The act or means of grasping. 2. Something that may be grasped, as for support. 3. Control or power. 4. A prison cell. ***—idioms:*** **hold the line** To maintain the current position or state. **hold water** To be valid or acceptable. **on hold** Into a state of delay. **—hold′er** *n.*

hold² (hōld) ▸ *n.* The interior of a ship or airplane in which cargo is stored.

hold·ing (hōl′dĭng) ▸ *n.* 1. Land rented or leased from another. 2. often **holdings** Legally owned property, as land or stocks.

holding company ▸ *n.* A company with partial or complete control over other companies.

hold·out (hōld′out′) ▸ *n.* One that withholds agreement or consent.

hold·o·ver (hōld′ō′vər) ▸ *n.* One that remains from an earlier time.

hold·up (hōld′ŭp′) ▸ *n.* 1. An interruption; delay. 2. An armed robbery.

hole (hōl) ▸ *n.* 1. A cavity in a solid. 2. An opening or perforation; gap. 3. An animal's burrow. 4. An ugly, squalid, or depressing place. 5. A bad situation; predicament. 6. *Sports* a. The small pit lined with a cup into which a golf ball must be hit. b. One of the divisions of a golf course, from tee to cup.

hol·i·day (hŏl′ĭ-dā′) ▸ *n.* 1. A day free from work, esp. one on which custom or the law dictates a halt to ordinary business to commemorate or celebrate a particular event. 2. A holy day. 3. *Chiefly Brit.* A vacation.

Holiday, Eleanora. "Billie" (1915–59) ▸ Amer. singer.

ho·li·ness (hō′lē-nĭs) ▸ *n.* 1. The quality of being holy; sanctity. 2. **Holiness** *Rom. Cath. Ch.* Used with *His* or *Your* as a title for the pope.

ho·lism (hō′lĭz′əm) ▸ *n.* A theory or belief emphasizing the importance of the whole and the interdependence of its parts. **—ho′list** *n.* **—ho·lis′tic** *adj.* **—ho·lis′ti·cal·ly** *adv.*

holistic medicine ▸ *n.* Medical care emphasizing treatment of a person's complete physical and mental state.

Hol·land (hŏl′ənd) ▸ See **Netherlands.**

hol·lan·daise sauce (hŏl′ən-dāz′) ▸ *n.* A sauce of butter, egg yolks, and lemon juice or vinegar.

hol·ler (hŏl′ər) ▸ *v.* To yell. **—hol′ler** *n.*

hol·low (hŏl′ō) ▸ *adj.* **-er, -est.** 1. Having a cavity or space within. 2a. Deeply concave. b. Sunken; indented: *hollow cheeks.* 3. Without substance or character. 4. Devoid of truth; specious. 5. Having a deep reverberating sound. ▸ *n.* 1. A cavity or interior space. 2. An indented or concave surface or area. 3. A void. 4. also **hol·ler** (hŏl′ər) *Regional* A mountain valley. ▸ *v.* To make hollow. **—hol′low·ly** *adv.* **—hol′low·ness** *n.*

hol·ly (hŏl′ē) ▸ *n., pl.* **-lies.** A tree or shrub usu. having bright red berries and glossy evergreen leaves with spiny margins.

hol·ly·hock (hŏl′ē-hŏk′) ▸ *n.* A tall garden plant with showy, variously colored flowers.

Hol·ly·wood (hŏl′ē-wŏŏd′) ▸ A district of Los Angeles, CA; a film and entertainment center.

Holmes (hōmz, hōlmz), **Oliver Wendell, Jr.** (1841–1935) ▸ Amer. jurist; associate justice of the US Supreme Court (1902–32).

hol·mi·um (hōl′mē-əm) ▸ *n. Symbol* **Ho** A relatively soft, malleable, rare-earth element. At. no. 67.

holo– or **hol–** ▸ *pref.* Whole; entire; entirely: *holograph.*

hol·o·caust (hŏl′ə-kôst′, hō′lə-) ▸ *n.* 1. Great or total destruction, esp. by fire. 2. **Holocaust** The genocide of European Jews and others by the Nazis during World War II.

Hol·o·cene (hŏl′ə-sēn′, hō′lə-) *Geol.* ▸ *adj.* Of or being the more recent epoch of the Quaternary Period, extending to the present. ▸ *n.* The Holocene Epoch.

hol·o·gram (hŏl′ə-grăm′, hō′lə-) ▸ *n.* The pattern produced on a photosensitive medium that has been exposed by holography and then photographically developed.

hol·o·graph (hŏl′ə-grăf′, hō′lə-) ▸ *n.* 1. A document that is written wholly in the handwriting of its signer. 2. See **hologram.** **—hol′o·graph′ic, hol′o·graph′i·cal** *adj.* **—hol′o·graph′i·cal·ly** *adv.*

ho·log·raph·y (hō-lŏg′rə-fē) ▸ *n.* A method of producing a three-dimensional image of an object by recording the pattern of interference formed by a split laser beam and then illuminating the pattern.

THESAURUS

3. To have the room or capacity for ▸ accommodate, contain. 4. To view in a certain way ▸ believe, feel, sense, think. [*Compare* PERCEIVE, REGARD.] 5. To prove valid under scrutiny ▸ hold up, prove out, stand up. *Informal:* wash. —*See also* ASSERT, BEAR (1), BELIEVE (3), COMMAND (2), EMBRACE (1), GRIP, HAVE (3), IMPRISON, RESTRAIN, OCCUPY (2), SUPPORT (2).

hold back *v.* —*See* HINDER, REPRESS, RESTRAIN.

hold down *v.* —*See* REPRESS, RESTRAIN.

hold in *v.* —*See* RESTRAIN.

hold off *v.* —*See* DEFER[1], REFRAIN.

hold out *v.* —*See* ENDURE (2), OFFER (1).

hold up *v.* To prove valid under scrutiny ▸ prove out, stand up. *Informal:* wash. —*See also* BEAR, DEFER[1], DELAY (1), ROB.

hold with *v.* To be favorably disposed toward ▸ approve, countenance, favor. *Informal:* go for. *Idioms:* be in favor of, take kindly to, think highly (*or* well) of. [*Compare* ASSENT, VALUE.]

hold *n.* 1. An act or means of holding something ▸ clasp, clench, clutch, grapple, grasp, grip. 2. Intellectual hold ▸ apprehension, comprehension, grasp, grip, understanding. [*Compare* KNOWLEDGE.]

holder *n.* An object, such as a carton, can, or jar, in which material is held or carried ▸ container, receptacle, repository, vessel. [*Compare* DEPOSITORY, PACKAGE.] —*See also* OWNER.

holdings *n.* A thing or set of things, such as land and assets, legally possessed ▸ belongings, estate, possessions, property. [*Compare* EFFECTS.]

holdup *n.* —*See* DELAY (1), DELAY (2), LARCENY.

hole *n.* 1. A space in an otherwise solid mass ▸ cavity, hollow, pocket, space, vacuity, void. [*Compare* CRACK, CUT.] 2. An open space allowing passage ▸ aperture, eyelet, mouth, opening, orifice, outlet, slot, tunnel, vent. [*Compare* GAP, PRICK.] 3. A place used as an animal's dwelling ▸ burrow, den, lair. [*Compare* CAVE.] —*See also* HUT, PREDICAMENT.

hole *v.* —*See* BREACH.

hole up *v. Informal* To shut oneself up in secrecy ▸ hide out. *Idioms:* go underground, lay (*or* lie) low.

holiday *n.* A regularly scheduled period spent away from work or duty, often in recreation ▸ furlough, leave, sabbatical, vacation. *Idiom:* time (*or* day) off. [*Compare* BREAK, TRIP.] —*See also* CELEBRATION (1).

holier-than-thou *adj.* Piously or overly sure of one's own righteousness ▸ moralistic, self-righteous. [*Compare* ARROGANT, HYPOCRITICAL, MORAL.]

holiness *n.* The quality of being or acting in accordance with what is holy or sacred ▸ beatitude, blessedness, divineness, godliness, grace, hallowedness, inviolability, sacredness, sacrosanctity, saintliness, sanctity, venerability, venerableness. [*Compare* DEVOTION.]

holler *v.* —*See* BAWL, COMPLAIN, SHOUT.

holler *n.* SHOUT.

hollow *adj.* 1. Lacking value, use, or substance ▸ empty, idle, otiose, vacant, vain. [*Compare* FUTILE.] 2. Curving inward ▸ carved out, cavernous, concave, depressed, indented, sunken.

hollow *n.* —*See* DEPRESSION (1), HOLE (1), VALLEY.

hollow-eyed *adj.* —*See* HAGGARD.

hollowness *n.* A desolate sense of loss ▸ blankness, desolation, emptiness, vacuum, void. —*See also* EMPTINESS (2).

holocaust *n.* —*See* DISASTER, MASSACRE.

Hol·stein (hōl′stīn′, -stēn′) ► *n.* Any of a breed of large black and white dairy cattle.

hol·ster (hōl′stər) ► *n.* **1.** A leather case shaped to hold a pistol. **2.** A belt designed to carry small tools. **—hol′stered** *adj.*

ho·ly (hō′lē) ► *adj.* **-li·er, -li·est. 1.** Of or associated with a divine power; sacred. **2.** Worthy of veneration or awe; revered. **3.** Spiritually pure; saintly. **—ho′li·ly** *adv.* **—ho′li·ness** *n.*

Holy Ark ► *n. Judaism* The cabinet in a synagogue in which the Torah scrolls are kept.

Holy Communion ► *n.* The Eucharist.

holy day ► *n.* A day for religious observance.

Holy Ghost ► *n.* The Holy Spirit.

Holy Land ► The biblical region of Palestine.

Holy Roman Empire ► A loosely federated political entity of central and W Europe (962–1806).

Holy Spirit ► *n.* The third person of the Christian Trinity.

holy war ► *n.* A war declared for a religious or high moral purpose.

hom·age (hŏm′ĭj, ŏm′-) ► *n.* Special honor or respect shown or expressed publicly.

hom·bre (ŏm′brā′, -brē) ► *n. Slang* A man; fellow.

Hom·burg also **hom·burg** (hŏm′bûrg′) ► *n.* A man's felt hat having a high dented crown and a stiff, slightly rolled brim.

home (hōm) ► *n.* **1.** A place where one lives; residence. **2.** A structure or unit for domestic living. **3.** A household. **4.** A place of origin. **5.** The native habitat, as of a plant or animal. **6a.** *Baseball* Home plate. **b.** *Games* Home base. **7.** An institution where people are cared for. ► *adv.* **1.** At or to the direction of home. **2.** On target: *The arrow struck home.* **3.** To the very center: *Your comment struck home.* ► *v.* **homed, hom·ing. 1.** To go or return home. **2.** To be guided to a target automatically, as by radio waves. **3.** To move toward a goal: *home in on the truth.* ***—idiom:* at home** Comfortable and relaxed.

home base ► *n.* **1a.** *Games* An objective toward which players progress. **b.** *Baseball* Home plate. **2.** A base of operations.

home·bod·y (hōm′bŏd′ē) ► *n., pl.* **-ies.** One whose interests center on the home.

home·boy (hōm′boi′) ► *n. Slang* **1.** A male friend from one's neighborhood or hometown. **2.** A fellow male gang member.

home·com·ing (hōm′kŭm′ĭng) ► *n.* **1.** A return home. **2.** An annual event at schools and colleges for visiting graduates.

home economics ► *n. (takes sing. or pl. v.)* The science and art of home management. **—home economist** *n.*

home front ► *n.* The civilian population or the civilian activities of a country at war.

home·girl (hōm′gûrl′) ► *n. Slang* **1.** A female friend from one's neighborhood or hometown. **2.** A fellow female gang member.

home·land (hōm′lănd′) ► *n.* **1.** One's native land. **2.** A state or region closely identified with a particular people.

home·less (hōm′lĭs) ► *adj.* Having no home or haven. ► *n. (takes pl. v.)* People without homes considered as a group.

home·ly (hōm′lē) ► *adj.* **-li·er, -li·est. 1.** Not attractive or good-looking. **2.** Simple or unpretentious; plain: *homely truths.* **3.** Characteristic of the home. **—home′li·ness** *n.*

home·made (hōm′mād′) ► *adj.* **1.** Made or prepared in the home. **2.** Crudely or simply made.

home·mak·er (hōm′mā′kər) ► *n.* One who manages a household. **—home′mak′ing** *n.*

homeo– ► *pref.* Similar; constant: *homeostasis.*

ho·me·op·a·thy (hō′mē-ŏp′ə-thē) ► *n., pl.* **-thies.** A system for treating disease based on the administration of minute doses of a drug that in massive amounts produces symptoms similar to those of the disease itself. **—ho′me·o·path′** (-ə-păth′), **ho′me·op′a·thist** *n.* **—ho′me·o·path′ic** *adj.*

ho·me·o·sta·sis (hō′mē-ō-stā′sĭs) ► *n.* The ability of an organism or cell to maintain internal equilibrium by adjusting its physiological processes. **—ho′me·o·stat′ic** (-stăt′ĭk) *adj.*

ho·me·o·therm (hō′mē-ə-thûrm′) ► *n.* An organism, such as a mammal or bird, having a constant body temperature independent of the temperature of its surroundings.

home·page or **home page** (hōm′pāj′) ► *n.* The main page of a website, usu. providing information about the site.

home plate ► *n. Baseball* The base at which a batter stands when hitting and which a runner must cross safely in order to score.

hom·er (hō′mər) ► *n. Baseball* A home run. ► *v.* To hit a home run.

Homer (fl. 850 B.C.) ► Greek epic poet.

home rule ► *n.* Self-government in the internal affairs of a dependent country or region.

home run ► *n. Baseball* A hit that allows the batter to make a complete circuit of the diamond and score a run.

home·school (hōm′sko͞ol′) ► *v.* To educate at home rather than in an established school.

home·sick (hōm′sĭk′) ► *adj.* Longing for one's home. **—home′sick′ness** *n.*

home·spun (hōm′spŭn′) ► *adj.* **1.** Spun or woven in the home. **2.** Made of a homespun fabric. **3.** Simple; unpretentious. ► *n.* A plain, coarse cloth made of homespun yarn.

home·stead (hōm′stĕd′) ► *n.* A house, esp. a farmhouse, with adjoining buildings and land. ► *v.* To settle and farm land. **—home′stead′er** *n.*

home·stretch (hōm′strĕch′) ► *n.* **1.** The part of a racetrack from the last turn to the finish line. **2.** The final stage of a task.

home·ward (hōm′wərd) ► *adv. & adj.* Toward home. **—home′wards** (-wərdz) *adv.*

home·work (hōm′wûrk′) ► *n.* **1.** Work, such as schoolwork, done at home. **2.** Preparatory or preliminary work.

hom·ey also **hom·y** (hō′mē) ► *adj.* **-i·er, -i·est.** *Informal* Having a feeling of home; comfortable. **—hom′ey·ness** *n.*

hom·i·cide (hŏm′ĭ-sīd′, hō′mĭ-) ► *n.* **1.** The killing of one person by another. **2.** A person who kills another. **—hom′i·cid′al** *adj.*

hom·i·let·ic (hŏm′ə-lĕt′ĭk) ► *adj.* **1.** Of or like a homily. **2.** Relating to preaching. **—hom′i·let′i·cal·ly** *adv.* **—hom′i·let′ics** *n.*

hom·i·ly (hŏm′ə-lē) ► *n., pl.* **-lies. 1.** A sermon. **2.** A tedious moralizing lecture. **—hom′i·list** *n.*

hom·ing pigeon (hō′mĭng) ► *n.* A pigeon trained to return to its home roost.

hom·i·nid (hŏm′ə-nĭd) ► *n.* A primate of the family

THESAURUS

holy *adj.* Regarded with particular reverence or respect, especially by a religion ► blessed, consecrated, hallowed, inviolable, sacred, sacrosanct, sanctified, venerable, venerated, virtuous. *—See also* DIVINE (1), DIVINE (2), PIOUS.

holy war *n.* A goal served with great or uncompromising dedication ► cause, crusade, jihad. [*Compare* DRIVE.]

homage *n.* *—See* HONOR (1).

home *n.* **1.** A building or shelter where one lives ► abode, domicile, dwelling, habitation, house, lodging, place, residence. *Informal:* address, headquarters, nest, pad. *Slang:* digs. **2.** The natural environment specific to an animal or plant ► habitat, habitation, niche, range, territory. **3.** An institution that provides care and shelter ► asylum, hospice, hospital, sanatorium, shelter. *—See also* BASE¹ (1).

home *adj.* *—See* DOMESTIC.

home base *n.* *—See* BASE¹ (1).

homegrown *adj.* *—See* DOMESTIC (3), INDIGENOUS.

homeliness *n.* *—See* UGLINESS.

homely *adj.* *—See* DOMESTIC (1), ORDINARY, RUSTIC, UGLY.

homemade *adj.* *—See* RUDE (1).

home office *n.* *—See* BASE¹ (1).

homespun *adj.* *—See* RUSTIC.

homey *adj.* *—See* COMFORTABLE, DOMESTIC (1).

homicidal *adj.* *—See* MURDEROUS.

homicide *n.* *—See* MURDER, MURDERER.

homily *n.* *—See* SPEECH (2).

hominoid *adj.* *—See* HUMANLIKE. [*Compare* HUMAN.]

homogenize *v.* *—See* CONVENTIONALIZE, MIX (1).

homophile *adj.* Having a sexual orientation to members of one's own sex ► gay, homosexual, lesbian.

Homo sapiens *n.* *—See* HUMAN BEING, HUMANKIND.

homosexual *adj.* Having a sexual orientation to members of one's own sex ► gay, homophile, lesbian.

homesteader *n.* *—See* SETTLER.

Hominidae, of which *Homo sapiens* is the only extant species. **—hom′i·nid** *adj.*

hom·i·ny (hŏm′ə-nē) ▸ *n.* Hulled and dried kernels of corn, prepared as food by boiling.

homo– or **hom–** ▸ *pref.* Same; like: *homophone.*

ho·mo·ge·ne·ous (hō′mə-jē′nē-əs, -jēn′yəs) ▸ *adj.* **1.** Of the same or similar nature or kind. **2.** Uniform in composition throughout. **—ho′mo·ge·ne′i·ty** (-jə-nē′ĭ-tē, -nā′-) *n.*

ho·mog·e·nize (hə-mŏj′ə-nīz′, hō-) ▸ *v.* **-nized, -niz·ing. 1.** To make homogeneous. **2a.** To reduce to particles and disperse throughout a fluid. **b.** To make uniform in consistency, esp. to render (milk) uniform in consistency by emulsifying the fat content. **—ho·mog′e·ni·za′tion** *n.* **—ho·mog′e·niz′er** *n.*

ho·mog·e·ny (hə-mŏj′ə-nē, hō-) ▸ *n.* Similarity of structure between organs related by common descent. **—ho·mog′e·nous** *adj.*

hom·o·graph (hŏm′ə-grăf′, hō′mə-) ▸ *n.* One of two or more words that have the same spelling but differ in origin and meaning, as *light,* "not dark," and *light,* "not heavy." **—hom′o·graph′ic** *adj.*

ho·mol·o·gous (hə-mŏl′ə-gəs, hō-) ▸ *adj.* **1.** Corresponding or similar esp. in structure or function. **2.** *Biol.* Similar in structure and evolutionary origin but not necessarily in function. **—hom′o·logue′, hom′o·log′** (hŏm′ə-lôg′, -lŏg′, hō′mē-ə-) *n.* **—ho·mol′o·gy** (-ə-jē) *n.*

hom·o·nym (hŏm′ə-nĭm′, hō′mə-) ▸ *n.* One of two or more words that have the same sound and often the same spelling but differ in meaning, as *bear,* "carry"; *bear,* (the animal); and *bare,* "naked." **—hom′o·nym′ic, ho·mon′y·mous** (hō-mŏn′ə-məs, hə-) *adj.*

ho·mo·pho·bi·a (hō′mə-fō′bē-ə) ▸ *n.* Fear of or contempt for lesbians and gay men. **—ho′mo·phobe′** *n.* **—ho′mo·pho′bic** *adj.*

hom·o·phone (hŏm′ə-fōn′, hō′mə-) ▸ *n.* One of two or more words, such as *night* and *knight,* that are pronounced the same but differ in meaning, origin, and sometimes spelling. **—ho·moph′o·nous** (hō-mŏf′ə-nəs) *adj.*

Ho·mo sa·pi·ens (hō′mō sā′pē-ənz, -ĕnz′) ▸ *n.* The modern species of humans.

ho·mo·sex·u·al (hō′mə-sĕk′shōō-əl, -mō-) ▸ *adj.* Of or having a sexual orientation to persons of the same sex. ▸ *n.* A homosexual person; a gay man or lesbian. **—ho′mo·sex′u·al′i·ty** *n.*

hom·y (hō′mē) ▸ *adj.* Var. of **homey.**

hon·cho (hŏn′chō) ▸ *n., pl.* **-chos.** *Slang* One who is in charge; leader.

Hon·du·ras (hŏn-dŏŏr′əs, -dyŏŏr′-) ▸ A country of N Central America. Pop. 6,560,000. **—Hon·du′ran** *adj. & n.*

hone (hōn) ▸ *n.* A fine-grained whetstone for sharpening a tool. ▸ *v.* **honed, hon·ing.** To sharpen on or as if on a hone.

hon·est (ŏn′ĭst) ▸ *adj.* **1.** Marked by or displaying integrity; upright. **2.** Not deceptive or fraudulent; genuine. **3a.** True; not false: *honest reporting.* **b.** Sincere; frank: *an honest critique.* **4.** Without affectation; plain: *honest folk.* **—hon′est·ly** *adv.* **—hon′es·ty** *n.*

hon·ey (hŭn′ē) ▸ *n., pl.* **-eys. 1.** A sweet, thick fluid produced by bees from the nectar of flowers. **2.** Sweetness. **3.** Flattery. **4.** *Informal* Sweetheart.

hon·ey·bee (hŭn′ē-bē′) ▸ *n.* Any of several social bees that produce honey.

hon·ey·comb (hŭn′ē-kōm′) ▸ *n.* **1.** A structure of hexagonal, thin-walled cells constructed from beeswax by honeybees to hold honey and larvae. **2.** Something resembling this structure. ▸ *v.* To fill with or as if with holes; riddle.

hon·ey·dew melon (hŭn′ē-dōō′, -dyōō′) ▸ *n.* A melon having a smooth whitish rind and green flesh.

hon·eyed also **hon·ied** (hŭn′ēd) ▸ *adj.* Sweet; sugary: *honeyed words.*

hon·ey·moon (hŭn′ē-mōōn′) ▸ *n.* **1.** A trip taken by a newly married couple. **2.** An early harmonious period in a relationship. **—hon′ey·moon′** *v.* **—hon′ey·moon′er** *n.*

hon·ey·suck·le (hŭn′ē-sŭk′əl) ▸ *n.* A shrub or vine having fragrant, usu. paired tubular flowers.

Hong Kong (hŏng′kŏng′, hông′kông′) ▸ An administrative region of SE China, on the coast SE of Guangzhou, including **Hong Kong Island** and adjacent areas. Cap. Victoria. Pop. 7,300,000.

honk (hôngk, hŏngk) ▸ *n.* **1.** The raucous, resonant sound of a goose. **2.** A similar sound, esp. the blaring sound of an automobile horn. **—honk** *v.* **—honk′er** *n.*

hon·ky-tonk (hông′kē-tôngk′, hŏng′kē-tŏngk′) ▸ *n. Slang* **1.** A cheap, noisy bar or dance hall. **2.** A type of ragtime music typically played on a tinny piano. **—hon′ky-tonk′** *adj. & v.*

Hon·o·lu·lu (hŏn′ə-lōō′lōō) ▸ The capital of HI, on the SE coast of Oahu. Pop. 372,000.

hon·or (ŏn′ər) ▸ *n.* **1.** High respect; esteem. **2a.** Recognition; distinction. **b.** A token or gesture of respect or distinction: *the place of honor.* **3.** Great privilege. **4. Honor** Used with *His, Her,* or *Your* as a form of address for certain officials, such as judges and mayors. **5. honors a.** Special recognition for unusual academic achievement. **b.** A program of individual advanced study for exceptional students. ▸ *v.* **1a.** To esteem. **b.** To show respect for. **2.** To confer distinction on. **3.** To accept or pay as valid: *honor a check.* **—hon′or·ee′** *n.*

hon·or·a·ble (ŏn′ər-ə-bəl) ▸ *adj.* **1.** Deserving or winning honor and respect. **2.** Bringing distinction or recognition. **3.** Possessing integrity. **4.** Illustrious. **5. Honorable** Used as a title of respect for certain high government officials. **—hon′or·a·bly** *adv.*

honorable discharge ▸ *n.* Discharge from the armed forces with a commendable record.

hon·o·rar·i·um (ŏn′ə-râr′ē-əm) ▸ *n., pl.* **-i·ums** or **-i·a** (-ē-ə). A payment given to a professional person for services for which fees are not legally or traditionally required.

hon·or·ar·y (ŏn′ə-rĕr′ē) ▸ *adj.* Held or given as an honor, without fulfillment of the usual requirements.

hon·or·if·ic (ŏn′ə-rĭf′ĭk) ▸ *adj.* Conferring or showing respect or honor. ▸ *n.* A title or grammatical form conveying respect. **—hon′or·if′i·cal·ly** *adv.*

hon·our (ŏn′ər) ▸ *n. & v. Chiefly Brit.* Var. of **honor.**

Hon·shu (hŏn′shōō) ▸ The largest island of Japan, in the central part between the Sea of Japan and the Pacific.

hood[1] (hŏŏd) ▸ *n.* **1.** A loose pliable covering for the head

THESAURUS

honcho *n.* —*See* CHIEF.

hone[1] *v.* —*See* PERFECT, SHARPEN.

hone in *v.* —*See* CONCENTRATE.

hone[2] *v.* —*See* DESIRE.

honest *adj.* Marked by uprightness in principle and action ▸ aboveboard, good, honorable, incorruptible, respectable, righteous, straight, true, truthful, upright, upstanding, veracious. *Informal:* straight-shooting. *Idiom:* on the up-and-up. [*Compare* ETHICAL, INNOCENT, MORAL.] —*See also* DEPENDABLE, FRANK, GENUINE.

honesty *n.* The quality of being honest ▸ candidness, frankness, honor, honorableness, incorruptibility, integrity, openness, plainspokenness, reliability, righteousness, sincerity, truth, trustworthiness, upstandingness. —*See also* CHARACTER (2).

honey *n.* —*See* DARLING (1).

honey *v.* —*See* COAX, FLATTER (1), SWEETEN.

honeyed *adj.* Having or suggesting the taste of sugar ▸ saccharine, sugary, sweet.

honky-tonk *n. Slang* A disreputable or run-down bar or restaurant ▸ *Slang:* dive, dump, joint, juke house, juke joint. *Idiom:* hole in the wall.

honor *n.* **1.** Great respect or high public esteem accorded as a right or as due ▸ deference, homage, obeisance, reverence, veneration. [*Compare* TESTIMONIAL.] **2.** A person's high standing among others ▸ dignity, good name, good report, prestige, reputation, repute, respect, status. [*Compare* EXALTATION.] —*See also* CHARACTER (2), DISTINCTION (2), ESTEEM, HONESTY.

honor *v.* **1.** To pay tribute or homage to ▸ acclaim, celebrate, eulogize, exalt, extol, glorify, hail, laud, lionize, magnify, panegyrize, praise. *Idiom:* sing someone's praises. [*Compare* REVERE.] **2.** To lend dignity or honor to by an act or favor ▸ enrich, favor, grace, dignify. [*Compare* EXALT.] **3.** To bestow a reward on ▸ award, guerdon, reward. [*Compare* CONFER.] —*See also* DISTINGUISH (5), DRINK (4), VALUE.

honorable *adj.* —*See* ADMIRABLE, HONEST.

honorableness *n.* —*See* HONESTY.

honorarium *n.* —*See* REWARD.

and neck. **2.** Something resembling a hood. **3.** The hinged metal lid over the engine of a motor vehicle. ► *v.* To supply or cover with a hood. **—hood′ed** *adj.*

hood^{2} (hŏŏd) ► *n. Slang* A hoodlum.

Hood, Mount ► A volcanic peak, 3,426.7 m (11,235 ft), in the Cascade Range of NW OR.

-hood ► *suff.* **1a.** Condition; state; quality: *manhood.* **b.** An instance of a specified state or quality: *falsehood.* **2.** A group sharing a specified state or quality: *sisterhood.*

hood·lum (hŏŏd′ləm, hōōd′-) ► *n.* **1.** A gangster; thug. **2.** A tough, often aggressive young man. **—hood′lum·ism** *n.*

hoo·doo (hōō′dōō) ► *n., pl.* **-doos.** **1.** Magic healing and control, esp. in African-based folk medicine. **2.** Voodoo. **3a.** Bad luck. **b.** One that brings bad luck. **—hoo′doo** *v.*

hood·wink (hŏŏd′wĭngk′) ► *v.* To deceive; cheat. **—hood′-wink′er** *n.*

hoo·ey (hōō′ē) ► *n. Slang* Nonsense.

hoof (hŏŏf, hōōf) ► *n., pl.* **hooves** (hŏŏvz, hōōvz) or **hoofs.** **1.** The horny sheath covering the foot of some mammals. **2.** A hoofed foot, esp. of a horse. ► *v. Slang* **1.** To walk. **2.** To dance. **—hoofed** *adj.*

hook (hŏŏk) ► *n.* **1.** A curved or sharply bent device, usu. of metal, used to catch, drag, suspend, or fasten something. **2.** Something shaped like a hook. **3.** *Slang* A means of attracting interest; enticement. **4.** *Sports* **a.** A short swinging blow in boxing delivered with a crooked arm. **b.** A thrown or struck ball that curves. ► *v.* **1.** To catch, suspend, fasten, or connect with or as if with a hook. **2.** *Slang* To steal; snatch. **3.** *Slang* To cause to become addicted. ***—phrasal verb:*** **hook up** **1.** To assemble or wire (a mechanism). **2.** *Slang* To connect. ***—idioms:*** **by hook or (by) crook** By whatever means possible. **off the hook** Freed, as from blame or obligation. **—hooked** *adj.*

hook·ah (hŏŏk′ə) ► *n.* A pipe in which the smoke is cooled by passing through a long tube submerged in an urn of water.

hook and eye ► *n.* A fastener consisting of a small hook that is inserted in a loop.

hook·er (hŏŏk′ər) ► *n. Slang* A prostitute.

hook·up (hŏŏk′ŭp′) ► *n. Elect.* **1.** A system of circuits and equipment designed to operate together. **2.** A configuration of parts or devices providing a link between a supply source and a user.

hook·worm (hŏŏk′wûrm′) ► *n.* A parasitic worm having hooked mouthparts that fasten to the intestinal walls of a host.

hook·y (hŏŏk′ē) ► *n. Informal* Truancy: *play hooky.*

hoo·li·gan (hōō′lĭ-gən) ► *n. Informal* A rowdy or aggressive person; ruffian. **—hoo′li·gan·ism** *n.*

hoop (hōōp, hŏŏp) ► *n.* **1.** A circular band put around a cask or barrel to bind the staves together. **2.** Something resembling a hoop. **3.** A circular support for a hoop skirt. **4.** A circular earring. **5.** *Basketball* The basket. **—hoop** *v.*

hoop·la (hōōp′lä′, hŏŏp′-) ► *n. Slang* **1.** Great commotion or fuss. **2.** Extravagant publicity.

hoop skirt ► *n.* A long full skirt belled out with a series of connected hoops.

hoo·ray (hōō-rā′, hə-) ► *interj. & n. & v.* Var. of **hurrah.**

hoose·gow (hōōs′gou′) ► *n. Slang* A jail.

hoot (hōōt) ► *v.* **1.** To utter the characteristic cry of an owl. **2.** To make a loud, derisive cry. **3.** To drive off with jeering cries. **—hoot** *n.* **—hoot′er** *n.*

hoot·en·an·ny (hōōt′n-ăn′ē) ► *n., pl.* **-nies.** An informal performance by folk singers.

Hoo·ver (hōō′vər), **Herbert Clark** (1874–1964) ► The 31st US President (1929–33).

Hoover, J(ohn) Edgar (1895–1972) ► Amer. director of the FBI (1924–72).

hooves (hŏŏvz, hōōvz) ► *n.* Pl. of **hoof.**

hop^{1} (hŏp) ► *v.* **hopped, hop·ping.** **1.** To move with light bounding skips or leaps. **2.** To jump on one foot. **3.** To make a quick trip, esp. in an airplane. **4.** To jump aboard. ► *n.* **1.** A light springy jump or leap. **2a.** A short distance. **b.** A short trip, esp. by air. **3.** *Informal* A dance or dance party. ***—idiom:*** **hop to it** To begin a task energetically.

hop^{2} (hŏp) ► *n.* **1.** A twining vine having lobed leaves and spikes of green flowers. **2. hops** The dried flowers of this plant, used as a flavoring in brewing beer. ► *v.* **hopped, hop·ping.** To flavor with hops. ***—phrasal verb:*** **hop up** *Slang* **1.** To increase the power of. **2.** To stimulate with or as if with a narcotic.

hope (hōp) ► *v.* **hoped, hop·ing.** To wish for something with expectation. ► *n.* **1.** A desire accompanied by confident expectation. **2.** Something hoped for. **3.** One that is a source of or reason for hope. **—hope′ful** *adj.* **—hope′ful·ness** *n.*

hope·ful·ly (hōp′fə-lē) ► *adv.* **1.** In a hopeful manner. **2.** *Informal* It is to be hoped.

hope·less (hōp′lĭs) ► *adj.* **1.** Having no hope. **2.** Dismal; bleak. **—hope′less·ly** *adv.*

Ho·pi (hō′pē) ► *n., pl.* **-pi** or **-pis.** **1.** A member of a Pueblo people of NE Arizona. **2.** The Uto-Aztecan language of the Hopi.

hop·per (hŏp′ər) ► *n.* **1.** One that hops. **2.** A funnel-shaped container in which materials are held ready for dispensing.

hop·scotch (hŏp′skŏch′) ► *n.* A children's game in which players hop or jump through a pattern of numbered spaces to retrieve a thrown object.

Hor·ace (hôr′əs, hŏr′-) (65–8 B.C.) ► Roman lyric poet.

horde (hôrd) ► *n.* A throng or swarm.

hore·hound (hôr′hound′) ► *n.* An aromatic plant having downy leaves that yield a bitter extract used in flavoring and as a cough remedy.

ho·ri·zon (hə-rī′zən) ► *n.* **1.** The apparent intersection of the earth and sky as seen by an observer. **2.** The range of one's knowledge, experience, or interest.

hor·i·zon·tal (hôr′ĭ-zŏn′tl, hŏr′-) ► *adj.* **1.** Of or near the horizon. **2.** At right angles to a vertical line. ► *n.* Something horizontal. **—hor′i·zon′tal·ly** *adv.*

hor·mone (hôr′mōn′) ► *n.* A substance produced by one

THESAURUS

hoodlum or **hood** *n.* —*See* THUG.

hoodoo *n.* Something or someone believed to bring bad luck ► curse, evil eye, hex, Jonah. *Informal:* jinx. [*Compare* CHARM, MAGIC.]

hoodoo *v.* To bring bad luck or evil to ► curse, hex. *Informal:* jinx. [*Compare* AFFLICT.]

hoodwink *v.* —*See* DECEIVE.

hooey *n.* —*See* NONSENSE.

hoof *v.* —*See* DANCE, WALK.

hoofer *n. Slang* A person who dances, especially professionally ► chorine, chorus boy, chorus girl, dancer, terpsichorean.

hoo-hah *n.* —*See* AGITATION (1), SENSATION (2).

hook *n.* —*See* BEND, FASTENER.

hook *v.* —*See* BEND (1), CATCH (1), CATCH (3), STEAL.

hook up *v.* To come together by arrangement ► connect, get together, meet (up), rendezvous.

hooker *n.* —*See* HARLOT.

hookup *n.* —*See* RELATION (1).

hooky *n.* —*See* ABSENCE (1).

hooligan *n.* —*See* THUG.

hoop *n.* —*See* BASKET (3), CIRCLE (1).

hoopla *n.* —*See* PUBLICITY.

hoosegow *n.* —*See* JAIL.

hoot *n.* —*See* HISS (2), SCREAM (2).

hoot *v.* —*See* HISS (2).

hop *v. Informal* To go aboard a means of transport ► board, catch, take. —*See also* BOUND^{1}.

hop *n.* A bouncing movement ► bounce, bound, rebound. —*See also* BOUND^{1} (2), DANCE.

hope *v.* —*See* DESIRE.

hope *n.* —*See* DREAM (3).

hopeful *adj.* —*See* ENCOURAGING, EXPECTANT.

hopeful *n.* One who aspires ► aspirant, aspirer. *Informal:* wannabe. —*See also* APPLICANT, COMER (2).

hopefulness *n.* The condition of looking forward to something, especially with eagerness ► anticipation, expectance, expectancy, expectation, high hopes. [*Compare* DESIRE.] —*See also* OPTIMISM.

hopeless *adj.* Offering or having no hope or expectation of improvement ► cureless, incurable, irremediable, irreparable, lost, remediless. [*Compare* FUTILE.] —*See also* DESPONDENT.

hopelessness *n.* —*See* DESPAIR.

hopped-up *adj.* —*See* DRUGGED.

hopping *adj.* —*See* BUSY (2).

horde *n.* —*See* CROWD.

horizon *n.* —*See* KEN.

horizontal *adj.* —*See* FLAT (1).

tissue and conveyed by the bloodstream to another to effect physiological activity, such as growth or metabolism. **—hor·mon′al** (-mō′nəl) *adj.* **—hor·mon′al·ly** *adv.*

Hor·muz (hôr′mŭz′, hôr-mo͞oz′), **Strait of.** Also **Strait of Ormuz** ► A waterway linking the Persian Gulf with the Gulf of Oman.

horn (hôrn) ► *n.* **1a.** One of the hard, usu. permanent structures projecting from the head of certain mammals, such as cattle or sheep. **b.** The hard, smooth material forming the outer covering of a horn. **2.** A growth or protuberance similar to a horn. **3.** A container made from a horn: *a powder horn.* **4.** *Mus.* **a.** A brass wind instrument, esp. a French horn. **b.** A trumpet. **c.** A saxophone. **5.** A signaling device that produces a loud, resonant sound: *an automobile horn.* **—horned** *adj.* **—horn′less** *adj.* **—horn′y** *adj.*

Horn, Cape ► A headland of extreme S Chile in the Tierra del Fuego archipelago.

horned toad ► *n.* A lizard having hornlike projections on the head and a spiny body.

hor·net (hôr′nĭt) ► *n.* Any of various stinging wasps that typically build large papery nests.

horn of plenty ► *n., pl.* **horns of plenty.** See **cornucopia** 1.

horn·pipe (hôrn′pīp′) ► *n.* A spirited British folk dance.

ho·rol·o·gy (hô-rŏl′ə-jē) ► *n.* **1.** The science of measuring time. **2.** The art of making timepieces. **—ho·rol′o·gist** *n.*

hor·o·scope (hôr′ə-skōp′, hŏr′-) ► *n.* A diagram of the positions of the planets and stars at a given moment, such as the moment of a person's birth, used by astrologers.

hor·ren·dous (hô-rĕn′dəs, hə-) ► *adj.* Hideous. **—hor·ren′dous·ly** *adv.*

hor·ri·ble (hôr′ə-bəl, hŏr′-) ► *adj.* **1.** Arousing horror; dreadful. **2.** Very unpleasant. **—hor′ri·ble·ness** *n.* **—hor′ri·bly** *adv.*

hor·rid (hôr′ĭd, hŏr′-) ► *adj.* **1.** Causing horror; dreadful. **2.** Extremely disagreeable; offensive. **—hor′rid·ly** *adv.*

hor·rif·ic (hô-rĭf′ĭk, hŏ-) ► *adj.* Terrifying. **—hor·rif′i·cal·ly** *adv.*

hor·ri·fy (hôr′ə-fī′, hŏr′-) ► *v.* **-fied, -fy·ing. 1.** To cause to feel horror. **2.** To cause unpleasant surprise to; shock. **—hor′ri·fi·ca′tion** *n.* **—hor′ri·fy′ing·ly** *adv.*

hor·ror (hôr′ər, hŏr′-) ► *n.* **1.** An intense feeling of repugnance and fear. **2.** Intense dislike; abhorrence. **3.** A cause of horror.

hors de com·bat (ôr′ də kôN-bä′) ► *adv.* & *adj.* Out of action; disabled.

hors d'oeuvre (ôr dûrv′) ► *n., pl.* **hors d'oeuvres** (ôr dûrvz′) or **hors d'oeuvre.** An appetizer served before a meal.

horse (hôrs) ► *n.* **1.** A large hoofed mammal having a long mane and tail, domesticated for riding and for drawing or carrying loads. **2.** A supporting frame, usu. with four legs. **3.** *Sports* A vaulting horse. **4.** often **horses** Horsepower. ► *v.* **horsed, hors·ing.** To provide with a horse. ***—phrasal verb:*** **horse around** *Informal* To indulge in horseplay or frivolous activity. ***—idioms:*** **hold (one's) horses** To restrain oneself. **the horse's mouth** The original source.

horse·back (hôrs′băk′) ► *adv.* & *adj.* On the back of a horse.

horse chestnut ► *n.* **1.** A tree having erect clusters of white flowers and shiny brown seeds. **2.** The seed of this tree.

horse·flesh (hôrs′flĕsh′) ► *n.* **1.** The flesh of a horse. **2.** Horses collectively, esp. for riding or racing.

horse·fly (hôrs′flī′) ► *n.* Any of numerous large flies, the females of which suck the blood of various mammals.

horse·hair (hôrs′hâr′) ► *n.* **1.** The hair of a horse, esp. from the mane or tail. **2.** Cloth made of horsehair.

horse·hide (hôrs′hīd′) ► *n.* **1.** The hide of a horse. **2.** Leather made from this hide.

horse·man (hôrs′mən) ► *n.* A man who rides a horse or breeds and raises horses.

horse·man·ship (hôrs′mən-shĭp′) ► *n.* The skill of riding horses.

horse·play (hôrs′plā′) ► *n.* Rowdy play.

horse·pow·er (hôrs′pou′ər) ► *n.* A unit of power equal to 745.7 watts or 33,000 foot-pounds per minute.

horse·rad·ish (hôrs′răd′ĭsh) ► *n.* **1.** A coarse plant having a thick, whitish, pungent root. **2.** A condiment made of its grated roots.

horse sense ► *n.* *Informal* Common sense.

horse·shoe (hôrs′sho͞o′, hôrsh′-) ► *n.* **1.** A flat U-shaped metal plate fitted and nailed to a horse's hoof. **2. horseshoes** *(takes sing. v.)* A game in which players toss horseshoes at a stake to encircle it.

horseshoe crab ► *n.* A marine arthropod having a large rounded body and a stiff pointed tail.

horse·tail (hôrs′tāl′) ► *n.* A nonflowering plant having a jointed hollow stem and narrow leaves.

horse·whip (hôrs′hwĭp′, -wĭp′) ► *n.* A whip used to control a horse. **—horse′whip′** *v.*

horse·wom·an (hôrs′wo͝om′ən) ► *n.* A woman who rides a horse or breeds and raises horses.

hors·y also **hors·ey** (hôr′sē) ► *adj.* **-i·er, -i·est. 1.** Of or resembling a horse. **2.** Devoted to horses or riding. **3.** Large and clumsy. **—hors′i·ly** *adv.* **—hors′i·ness** *n.*

hor·ta·to·ry (hôr′tə-tôr′ē) ► *adj.* Marked by exhortation.

hor·ti·cul·ture (hôr′tĭ-kŭl′chər) ► *n.* The science or art of cultivating fruits, vegetables, flowers, or ornamental plants. **—hor′ti·cul′tur·al** *adj.* **—hor′ti·cul′tur·al·ly** *adv.* **—hor′ti·cul′tur·ist** *n.*

ho·san·na also **ho·san·nah** (hō-zăn′ə) ► *interj.* Used to express praise or adoration to God.

hose (hōz) ► *n.* **1.** *pl.* **hose.** Stockings; socks. **2.** *pl.* **hos·es.** A flexible tube for conveying liquids or gases. ► *v.* **hosed, hos·ing.** To water or wash with a hose.

Ho·se·a (hō-zē′ə, -zā′ə) ► *n.* **1.** 8th cent. B.C. Hebrew prophet. **2.** See **Bible** table in Appendix.

ho·sier·y (hō′zhə-rē) ► *n.* Socks and stockings.

hos·pice (hŏs′pĭs) ► *n.* **1.** A shelter or lodging for travelers or the needy. **2.** A program that provides medical and other care for terminally ill patients.

hos·pi·ta·ble (hŏs′pĭ-tə-bəl, hŏ-spĭt′ə-bəl) ► *adj.* **1.** Cordial and generous to guests. **2.** Favorable to growth and development. **—hos′pi·ta·bly** *adv.*

hos·pi·tal (hŏs′pĭ-tl, -pĭt′l) ► *n.* An institution that provides medical, surgical, or psychiatric care and treatment for the sick or the injured.

hos·pi·tal·i·ty (hŏs′pĭ-tăl′ĭ-tē) ► *n., pl.* **-ties.** Cordial and generous reception of guests.

hos·pi·tal·ize (hŏs′pĭt-l-īz′) ► *v.* **-ized, -iz·ing.** To place in a hospital for treatment or observation. **—hos′pi·tal·i·za′tion** *n.*

host[1] (hōst) ► *n.* **1.** One who receives or entertains guests. **2.** One that furnishes facilities and resources for an event. **3.** The emcee or interviewer on a radio or television program. **4.** *Biol.* The organism on or in which a parasite lives. ► *v.* *Informal* To serve as host to or for.

host[2] (hōst) ► *n.* **1.** An army. **2.** A great number; multitude.

host[3] also **Host** (hōst) ► *n.* *Eccles.* The consecrated bread or wafer of the Eucharist.

hos·tage (hŏs′tĭj) ► *n.* A person held by force as security that specified terms will be met.

THESAURUS

hornets' nest *n.* *—See* PROBLEM.

horn in *v.* *—See* INTRUDE, MEDDLE.

horniness *n.* *—See* DESIRE (2).

horrendous *adj.* *—See* TERRIBLE.

horrible *adj.* Causing great horror ► bloodcurdling, hair-raising, harrowing, horrid, horrific, horrifying, nightmarish, petrifying, terrific, terrifying. *—See also* GHASTLY (1), TERRIBLE.

horrid *adj.* *—See* GHASTLY (1), HORRIBLE, OFFENSIVE (1).

horrific *adj.* *—See* HORRIBLE.

horrified *adj.* *—See* AFRAID.

horrify *v.* *—See* FRIGHTEN.

horror *n.* *—See* FEAR, HATE (1), HATE (2), OUTRAGE.

hors d'oeuvre *n.* *—See* APPETIZER.

horse around *v.* *Informal* To make jokes; behave playfully ► jest, joke, quip. *Informal:* clown (around), fool around. *Idioms:* crack wise, play the fool. *—See also* MISBEHAVE, PLAY (1).

horseplay *n.* *—See* MISBEHAVIOR.

horse sense *n.* *—See* COMMON SENSE.

hospice *n.* *—See* HOME (3).

hospitable *adj.* Characterized by kindness and warm, unaffected courtesy ► affable, courteous, gracious. [*Compare* AMIABLE, ATTENTIVE, COURTEOUS.]

hospital *n.* *—See* HOME (3).

hospitality *n.* *—See* CONSIDERATION (1).

host *n.* *—See* CROWD.

hostage *n.* *—See* PAWN[1].

hos·tel (hŏs′təl) ▸ *n.* **1.** A supervised inexpensive lodging for young travelers. **2.** An inn. **—hos′tel·er** *n.*

hos·tel·ry (hŏs′təl-rē) ▸ *n., pl.* **-ries.** An inn.

host·ess (hō′stĭs) ▸ *n.* **1.** A woman who receives or entertains guests. **2.** A woman employed to greet and assist patrons, as in a restaurant.

hos·tile (hŏs′təl, -tīl′) ▸ *adj.* **1.** Of or characteristic of an enemy. **2.** Feeling or showing enmity: *a hostile remark.* **—hos′tile** *n.* **—hos′tile·ly** *adv.*

hos·til·i·ty (hŏ-stĭl′ĭ-tē) ▸ *n., pl.* **-ties. 1.** Antagonism or enmity. **2a.** A hostile act. **b. hostilities** Overt warfare.

hos·tler (hŏs′lər, ŏs′-) ▸ *n.* One who tends horses, esp. at an inn.

hot (hŏt) ▸ *adj.* **hot·ter, hot·test. 1a.** Having or giving off great heat. **b.** Being at a high temperature. **2.** Warmer than normal or desirable. **3a.** Causing a burning sensation. **b.** Spicy: *hot peppers.* **4a.** Charged or as if charged with electricity. **b.** Radioactive. **5.** Marked by intensity of emotion. **6.** *Informal* Arousing intense interest or controversy: *a hot topic.* **7.** *Slang* Recently stolen: *a hot car.* **8.** *Informal* **a.** Most recent; new: *a hot news item.* **b.** Currently popular: *the hottest young talents.* **9.** *Slang* **a.** Performing with great skill. **b.** Unusually lucky. ***—idioms:* hot under the collar** *Informal* Angry. **hot water** Trouble; difficulty. **—hot′ly** *adv.* **—hot′ness** *n.*

hot air ▸ *n. Slang* Empty, exaggerated talk.

hot·bed (hŏt′bĕd′) ▸ *n.* An environment conducive to growth or development, esp. of something undesirable: *a hotbed of intrigue.*

hot-blood·ed (hŏt′blŭd′ĭd) ▸ *adj.* Easily excited or aroused. **—hot′-blood′ed·ness** *n.*

hot·box (hŏt′bŏks′) ▸ *n.* An axle or journal box, as on a railway car, overheated by friction.

hot button ▸ *n. Slang* Something that elicits a strong emotional response. **—hot′-but′ton** *adj.*

hot·cake (hŏt′kāk′) ▸ *n.* See **pancake.** ***—idiom:* go** (or **sell**) **like hotcakes** To be in great demand.

hot dog or **hot·dog** (hŏt′dôg′, -dŏg′) ▸ *n.* **1.** A frankfurter. **2.** *Slang* One who performs showy, often dangerous stunts. **—hot′-dog′** *v.* **—hot′-dog′ger** *n.*

ho·tel (hō-tĕl′) ▸ *n.* An establishment that provides lodging and often meals esp. for travelers.

hot flash ▸ *n.* A sudden brief sensation of heat sometimes experienced during menopause.

hot·foot (hŏt′fo͝ot′) ▸ *v. Informal* To go in haste: *hotfoot it out of town.*

hot·head·ed (hŏt′hĕd′ĭd) ▸ *adj.* **1.** Easily angered; quick-tempered. **2.** Impetuous; rash. **—hot′head′** *n.* **—hot′head′ed·ly** *adv.* **—hot′head′ed·ness** *n.*

hot·house (hŏt′hous′) ▸ *n.* A heated greenhouse. ▸ *adj.* Delicate; sensitive.

hot line or **hot·line** (hŏt′līn′) ▸ *n.* A communications line for use in a crisis.

hot plate ▸ *n.* An electrically heated plate for cooking food.

hot rod also **hot-rod** (hŏt′rŏd′) ▸ *n. Slang* An automobile modified for speed and acceleration. **—hot′-rod′** *v.* **—hot rodder, hot′-rod′der** *n.*

hot seat ▸ *n.* **1.** *Slang* The electric chair. **2.** *Informal* A position of stress or discomfort.

hot·shot (hŏt′shŏt′) ▸ *n. Slang* A person of impressive, often aggressive skill. **—hot′shot′** *adj.*

hot tub ▸ *n.* A large tub filled with hot water for bathing or soaking.

hot-wire (hŏt′wīr′) ▸ *v. Informal* To start the engine of (e.g., an automobile) without a key, as by short-circuiting the ignition system.

Hou·di·ni (ho͞o-dē′nē), **Harry.** Ehrich Weiss (1874–1926) ▸ Amer. escape artist.

hound (hound) ▸ *n.* **1a.** Any of various hunting dogs usu. having drooping ears and a deep resonant voice. **b.** A dog. **2.** A scoundrel. **3.** An avid enthusiast. ▸ *v.* **1.** To pursue relentlessly. **2.** To nag.

hour (our) ▸ *n.* **1.** One of the 24 equal parts of a day. **2.** The time of day. **3a.** A customary time: *the dinner hour.* **b. hours** A specified time: *banking hours.*

hour·glass (our′glăs′) ▸ *n.* An instrument that measures time by trickling sand from an upper glass chamber to a lower one.

hou·ri (ho͝or′ē, ho͞o′rē) ▸ *n., pl.* **-ris.** One of the beautiful virgins of the Koranic paradise.

hour·ly (our′lē) ▸ *adj.* **1.** Occurring every hour. **2.** Frequent; continual. **3.** By the hour as a unit: *hourly pay.* ▸ *adv.* **1.** At or during every hour. **2.** Frequently; continually.

house (hous) ▸ *n., pl.* **hous·es** (hou′zĭz, -sĭz). **1a.** A structure serving as a dwelling for one or more persons. **b.** A household. **2a.** A building used for a particular purpose: *a movie house.* **b.** The audience or patrons of such a place: *a full house.* **3a.** A commercial firm: *a brokerage house.* **b.** A publishing company. **4.** often **House** A legislative assembly. ▸ *v.* (houz) **housed, hous·ing. 1.** To provide living quarters for; lodge. **2.** To shelter, keep, or store. **3.** To contain; harbor. ***—idiom:* on the house** At the expense of the establishment; free.

house·boat (hous′bōt′) ▸ *n.* A barge equipped for use as a dwelling.

house·break·ing (hous′brā′kĭng) ▸ *n.* The unlawful breaking into and entering another's house. **—house′break′er** *n.*

house·bro·ken (hous′brō′kən) ▸ *adj.* **1.** Trained to have excretory habits appropriate for indoor living. **2.** Compliant.

house·fly (hous′flī′) ▸ *n.* A common fly that frequents human dwellings and transmits a wide variety of diseases.

house·hold (hous′hōld′) ▸ *n.* A domestic unit consisting of the people who live together in a single dwelling. ▸ *adj.* Commonly known; familiar: *a household name.* **—house′hold′er** *n.*

THESAURUS

hostile *adj.* **1.** Feeling or showing unfriendliness ▸ inimical, unfriendly. [*Compare* MEAN[2].] **2.** Not encouraging life or growth ▸ adverse, inhospitable, unfavorable. [*Compare* SEVERE.] *—See also* AGGRESSIVE, BELLIGERENT, CONTRARY.

hostilities *n.* *—See* BATTLE.

hostility *n.* *—See* AGGRESSION, ENMITY.

hot *adj.* **1.** Marked by much heat ▸ ardent, baking, blistering, boiling, broiling, burning, fiery, heated, red-hot, roasting, scalding, scorching, searing, sizzling, sultry, sweltering, torrid, tropical, white-hot. *Idioms:* hot enough to fry an egg on, piping hot. **2.** *Informal* Of great current interest ▸ live, red-hot. [*Compare* FASHIONABLE, IMPORTANT.] *—See also* DESIRABLE, EAGER, EROTIC, FASHIONABLE, FEVERISH, MARVELOUS, SPICY.

hotbed *n.* *—See* CENTER (1), ORIGIN.

hot-blooded *adj.* *—See* PASSIONATE.

hotdog *n. Slang* A person who behaves ostentatiously or performs dangerous stunts ▸ showoff, showboat. [*Compare* BRAGGART.]

hot-dog *v. Slang* To behave in an ostentatious manner or perform dangerous stunts ▸ show off, showboat. [*Compare* BOAST, SWAGGER.]

hotfoot *v.* *—See* RUN (2), RUSH.

hotheaded *adj.* *—See* ARGUMENTATIVE, RASH[1].

hotheadedness *n.* *—See* TEMPER (1).

hotness *n.* *—See* HEAT (1).

hot pursuit *n.* The following of another in an attempt to overtake and capture ▸ chase, hunt, pursuit.

hot spot *n.* *—See* PREDICAMENT.

hot water *n.* *—See* EMERGENCY, PREDICAMENT.

hound *v.* *—See* HARASS.

hound *n.* *—See* FAN[2].

house *n.* A group of people living together as a unit ▸ family, household, ménage. *—See also* COMPANY (1), FAMILY (2), HOME (1).

house *v.* To give refuge to ▸ harbor, haven, shelter, take in. [*Compare* DEFEND.] *—See also* LIVE[1], LODGE.

housebreak *v.* *—See* DOMESTICATE.

housebreaker *n.* *—See* THIEF.

housebroken *adj.* *—See* DOMESTIC (2).

housecleaning *n. Informal* A thorough or drastic reorganization ▸ overhaul, reengineering, reshuffling, shakeup. [*Compare* RENEWAL, REVOLUTION.]

household *n.* A group of people living together as a unit ▸ family, house, ménage.

household *adj.* *—See* DOMESTIC (1).

house·keep·er (hous′kē′pər) ▸ *n.* One hired to perform or direct the domestic tasks in a household.
house·keep·ing (hous′kē′pĭng) ▸ *n.* 1. Performance or management of household tasks. 2. Routine maintenance; upkeep.
house·moth·er (hous′mŭth′ər) ▸ *n.* A woman employed as supervisor of a residence for young people.
House of Commons ▸ *n.* The lower house of Parliament in the United Kingdom and Canada.
House of Lords ▸ *n.* The upper house of Parliament in the United Kingdom.
house organ ▸ *n.* A periodical published by an organization for its employees or clients.
house·plant (hous′plănt′) ▸ *n.* A usu. decorative plant suitable for growing indoors.
house·wares (hous′wârz′) ▸ *pl.n.* Articles used in a home, esp. in the kitchen.
house·warm·ing (hous′wôr′mĭng) ▸ *n.* A celebration of the occupancy of a new home.
house·wife (hous′wīf′) ▸ *n.* A woman, esp. a married woman, who manages her household as her main occupation. **—house′wife′ly** *adj.* **—house′wif′er·y** *n.*
house·work (hous′wûrk′) ▸ *n.* The tasks, such as cleaning and cooking, performed in housekeeping.
hous·ing (hou′zĭng) ▸ *n.* 1a. Buildings in which people live. b. A dwelling. 2. Provision of lodging or shelter. 3. Something that covers, protects, or supports, esp. something that protects a mechanical part.
Hous·ton (hyōō′stən) ▸ A city of SE TX NW of Galveston. Pop. 1,950,000. **—Hous·to′ni·an** (-stō′nē-ən) *n.*
HOV ▸ *abbr.* high-occupancy vehicle
hove (hōv) ▸ *v.* P.t. and p.part. of **heave** 5.
hov·el (hŭv′əl, hŏv′-) ▸ *n.* A small miserable dwelling.
hov·er (hŭv′ər, hŏv′-) ▸ *v.* 1. To remain floating or suspended in the air. 2. To linger in a place. 3. To remain in an uncertain state; waver.
hov·er·craft (hŭv′ər-krăft′, hŏv′-) ▸ *n.* See **air-cushion vehicle.**
HOV lane (āch′ō-vē′) ▸ *n.* An expressway lane restricted to vehicles with a set minimum of occupants, usu. two.
how (hou) ▸ *adv.* 1. In what manner or way; by what means. 2. In what state or condition. 3. To what extent, amount, or degree. 4. For what reason or purpose; why. 5. With what meaning: *How should I take that remark?* ▸ *conj.* 1. The manner or way in which: *forgot how it was done.* 2. In whatever way or manner: *Cook it how you please.* ***—idioms:*** **how about** What is your thought or feeling regarding: *How about a cup of tea?* **how come** *Informal* How is that; why.
how·be·it (hou-bē′ĭt) ▸ *adv.* Nevertheless.
how·dah (hou′də) ▸ *n.* A covered seat on the back of an elephant or camel.
Howe (hou), **Elias** (1819–67) ▸ Amer. inventor.
Howe, Julia Ward (1819–1910) ▸ Amer. writer and feminist.
how·ev·er (hou-ĕv′ər) ▸ *adv.* 1. In whatever manner or way. 2. To whatever degree or extent. 3. In spite of that; nevertheless. 4. On the other hand; by contrast. ▸ *conj.* In whatever manner or way.
how·it·zer (hou′ĭt-sər) ▸ *n.* A short cannon that delivers shells at a high trajectory.
howl (houl) ▸ *v.* 1. To utter a long mournful sound. 2. To cry or wail loudly. 3. *Slang* To laugh heartily. **—howl** *n.*
howl·er (hou′lər) ▸ *n.* 1. A person or thing that howls. 2. *Slang* A blunder that is laughably stupid.
how·so·ev·er (hou′sō-ev′ər) ▸ *adv.* 1. To whatever extent. 2. By whatever means.
hoy·den (hoid′n) ▸ *n.* A high-spirited, boisterous, or saucy woman. **—hoy′den·ish** *adj.*
hp ▸ *abbr.* horsepower
HQ ▸ *abbr.* headquarters
HR ▸ *abbr.* 1. House of Representatives 2. home run
hr. ▸ *abbr.* hour
hryv·nia (hrĭv′nyä) ▸ *n.* See **currency** table in Appendix.
Hs ▸ The symbol for the element **hassium.**
HTLV–I (āch′tē-ĕl′vē-wŭn′) ▸ *n.* A retrovirus that causes diseases similar to multiple sclerosis.
HTLV–III (āch′tē-ĕl′vē-thrē′) ▸ *n.* HIV.
HTML (āch′tē-ĕm-ĕl′) ▸ *n.* A markup language used to structure and set up hypertext links between documents, esp. on the World Wide Web.
HTTP or **http** (āch′tē-tē-pē′) ▸ *n.* A protocol used to request and transmit files, esp. over the Internet.
Huang He (hwäng′ hə′) also **Hwang Ho** (hwäng′ hō′) or **Yellow River** ▸ A river of N China rising in the Kunlun Mts. and flowing about 4,827 km (3,000 mi) to the Gulf of Bo Hai.
hub (hŭb) ▸ *n.* 1. The center part of a wheel, fan, or propeller. 2. A center of activity or interest.
hub·bub (hŭb′ŭb′) ▸ *n.* 1. Loud noise; din. 2. Confusion; tumult.
hub·cap (hŭb′kăp′) ▸ *n.* A round covering over the hub of an automobile wheel.
hu·bris (hyōō′brĭs) ▸ *n.* Overbearing pride; arrogance.
huck·le·ber·ry (hŭk′əl-bĕr′ē) ▸ *n.* 1. A shrub related to the blueberry. 2. The glossy blackish edible fruit of this plant.
huck·ster (hŭk′stər) ▸ *n.* 1. A peddler or hawker. 2. An aggressive salesperson or promoter. **—huck′ster·ism** *n.*
hud·dle (hŭd′l) ▸ *n.* 1. A densely packed group. 2. *Football* A brief gathering of a team's players behind the line of scrimmage to receive instructions for the next play. 3. A small private conference. ▸ *v.* **-dled, -dling.** 1. To crowd together. 2. To curl up or crouch. 3. *Football* To gather in a huddle. 4. *Informal* To gather together for consultation. **—hud′dler** *n.*
Hud·son (hŭd′sən), **Henry** (d. 1611) ▸ English navigator and explorer.
Hudson Bay ▸ An inland sea of E-central Canada connected to the Atlantic by **Hudson Strait.**
Hudson River ▸ A river rising in NE NY and flowing about 507 km (315 mi) to Upper New York Bay at New York City.
hue (hyōō) ▸ *n.* 1. The property of colors by which they can be perceived as ranging from red through yellow, green, and blue. 2. A particular gradation of color; shade or tint. 3. Color.
hue and cry ▸ *n.* A public clamor, as of protest or demand.
huff (hŭf) ▸ *n.* A fit of anger or annoyance; pique. ▸ *v.* 1. To puff; blow. 2. To bluster. **—huff′i·ly** *adv.* **—huff′i·ness** *n.* **—huff′y** *adj.*
hug (hŭg) ▸ *v.* **hugged, hug·ging.** 1. To clasp or hold closely; embrace. 2. To cherish. 3. To stay close to. ▸ *n.* A close embrace. **—hug′ger** *n.*
huge (hyōōj) ▸ *adj.* **hug·er, hug·est.** Exceedingly large; tremendous. **—huge′ly** *adv.* **—huge′ness** *n.*
Hu·gue·not (hyōō′gə-nŏt′) ▸ *n.* A French Protestant of the 16th and 17th cent.

THESAURUS

house of correction *n.* —*See* JAIL.
house-train *v.* —*See* DOMESTICATE.
house-trained *adj.* —*See* DOMESTIC (2).
housing *n.* Dwellings in general ▸ lodging, shelter. ***Idiom:*** a roof over one's head. [*Compare* HOME, HUT.]
hovel *n.* —*See* HUT.
hover *v.* To remain stationary over a place or object ▸ hang, poise. —*See also* FLOAT (1), THREATEN (2).
however *adv.* —*See* STILL (1).
howl *v.* To utter or emit a long, mournful, plaintive sound ▸ bay, moan, ululate, wail, yowl. —*See also* BAWL, CRY, LAUGH, SHOUT.
howl *n.* A long, mournful cry ▸ bay, moan, ululation, wail, yowl. —*See also* LAUGH, SCREAM (2), SHOUT.
howler *n.* —*See* BLUNDER.
hub *n.* —*See* CENTER (1), CENTER (3).
hubbub *n.* —*See* NOISE (1).
hubris *n.* —*See* ARROGANCE.
huckster *v.* To travel about selling goods ▸ hawk, peddle, vend. —*See also* HAGGLE.
huddle *v.* —*See* CONFER (1), STOOP.
huddle *n.* —*See* GROUP.
hue *n.* —*See* COLOR (1), SHADE (1).
huff *n.* —*See* OFFENSE, TEMPER (2).
huff *v.* —*See* INSULT, PANT.
huffy *adj.* —*See* ANGRY.
hug *v.* —*See* EMBRACE (1).
hug *n.* —*See* EMBRACE.
huge *adj.* —*See* ENORMOUS.
hugely *adv.* —*See* VERY.
hugeness *n.* —*See* ENORMOUSNESS.
huggermugger *n.* —*See* SECRECY.
huggermugger *adj.* —*See* SECRET (1).
huggermugger *adv.* —*See* SECRETLY.
huggermuggery *n.* —*See* SECRECY.

huh (hŭ) ▸ *interj.* Used to express interrogation, surprise, contempt, or indifference.

hu·la (ho͞o′lə) ▸ *n.* A Polynesian dance marked by undulating hips and rhythmic miming movements of the arms and hands.

hulk (hŭlk) ▸ *n.* **1.** An unwieldy or unseaworthy ship. **2.** A wrecked hull. **3.** One that is bulky, clumsy, or unwieldy. ▸ *v.* To loom as a massive form.

hulk·ing (hŭl′kĭng) also **hulk·y** (hŭl′kē) ▸ *adj.* Unwieldy or bulky; massive.

hull (hŭl) ▸ *n.* **1.** The dry outer covering of a fruit, seed, or nut; husk. **2.** The frame or body of a ship. **3.** The outer casing of a rocket, guided missile, or spaceship. ▸ *v.* To remove the hulls of (fruit or seeds).

hul·la·ba·loo also **hul·la·bal·loo** (hŭl′ə-bə-lo͞o′) ▸ *n., pl.* **-loos.** Great noise or excitement; uproar.

hum (hŭm) ▸ *v.* **hummed, hum·ming. 1.** To emit a continuous low droning sound. **2.** To be in a state of busy activity. **3.** To sing without opening the lips. **—hum** *n.* **—hum′ma·ble** *adj.* **—hum′mer** *n.*

hu·man (hyo͞o′mən) ▸ *n.* **1.** A member of the genus *Homo* and esp. of the species *H. sapiens.* **2.** A person: *remarkable humans who explored Antarctica.* ▸ *adj.* **1.** Of or characteristic of humans. **2.** Made up of humans: *formed a human bridge across the ice.* **—hu′man·hood′** *n.* **—hu′man·ly** *adv.* **—hu′man·ness** *n.*

human being ▸ *n.* A human.

hu·mane (hyo͞o-mān′) ▸ *adj.* **1.** Kind or compassionate. **2.** Emphasizing humanistic values and concerns. **—hu·mane′ly** *adv.* **—hu·mane′ness** *n.*

hu·man·ism (hyo͞o′mə-nĭz′əm) ▸ *n.* **1.** A system of thought that centers on humans and their values, capacities, and worth. **2. Humanism** A Renaissance movement that emphasized secular concerns as a result of the rediscovery of classical literature, art, and civilization. **—hu′man·ist** *n.* **—hu′man·is′tic** *adj.*

hu·man·i·tar·i·an (hyo͞o-măn′ĭ-târ′ē-ən) ▸ *n.* One devoted to the promotion of human welfare. ▸ *adj.* Compassionate. **—hu·man′i·tar′i·an·ism** *n.*

hu·man·i·ty (hyo͞o-măn′ĭ-tē) ▸ *n., pl.* **-ties. 1.** Humans considered as a group; the human race. **2.** The condition or quality of being human. **3.** The quality of being humane. **4. humanities** Those disciplines, such as philosophy and art, concerned with human thought and culture; the liberal arts.

hu·man·ize (hyo͞o′mə-nīz′) ▸ *v.* **-ized, -iz·ing. 1.** To make human or humanlike. **2.** To make humane; civilize. **—hu′man·i·za′tion** *n.* **—hu′man·iz′er** *n.*

hu·man·kind (hyo͞o′mən-kīnd′) ▸ *n.* The human race.

hu·man·oid (hyo͞o′mə-noid′) ▸ *adj.* Having human characteristics or form. ▸ *n.* **1.** A being having human form. **2.** See **android.**

hum·ble (hŭm′bəl) ▸ *adj.* **-bler, -blest. 1.** Meek or modest. **2.** Deferentially respectful. **3.** Low in rank or station. ▸ *v.* **-bled, -bling. 1.** To humiliate. **2.** To cause to be meek. **3.** To make lower or lesser; abase. **—hum′ble·ness** *n.* **—hum′bler** *n.* **—hum′bly** *adv.*

Hum·boldt Current (hŭm′bōlt′) ▸ *n.* A cold ocean current of the South Pacific, flowing N along the W coast of South America.

hum·bug (hŭm′bŭg′) ▸ *n.* **1.** A hoax or fraud. **2.** An impostor. **3.** Nonsense; rubbish. ▸ *v.* **-bugged, -bug·ging.** To deceive or trick. **—hum′bug′** *interj.* **—hum′bug′ger·y** *n.*

hum·ding·er (hŭm′dĭng′ər) ▸ *n. Slang* One that is extraordinary.

hum·drum (hŭm′drŭm′) ▸ *adj.* Monotonous; boring.

hu·mer·us (hyo͞o′mər-əs) ▸ *n., pl.* **-mer·i** (-mə-rī′). The long bone of the arm, extending from the shoulder to the elbow.

hu·mid (hyo͞o′mĭd) ▸ *adj.* Containing a high amount of water vapor. **—hu·mid′i·ty** *n.*

hu·mid·i·fy (hyo͞o-mĭd′ə-fī′) ▸ *v.* **-fied, -fy·ing.** To make humid. **—hu·mid′i·fi·ca′tion** *n.* **—hu·mid′i·fi′er** *n.*

hu·mi·dor (hyo͞o′mĭ-dôr′) ▸ *n.* A container designed for storing cigars at a constant humidity.

hu·mil·i·ate (hyo͞o-mĭl′ē-āt′) ▸ *v.* **-at·ed, -at·ing.** To lower the pride, dignity, or self-respect of; degrade. **—hu·mil′i·a′tion** *n.*

hu·mil·i·ty (hyo͞o-mĭl′ĭ-tē) ▸ *n.* The quality or condition of being humble.

hum·ming·bird (hŭm′ĭng-bûrd′) ▸ *n.* Any of a family of very small birds having brilliant iridescent plumage, a long slender bill, and hovering flight.

hum·mock (hŭm′ək) ▸ *n.* A low mound or ridge of earth. **—hum′mock·y** *adj.*

hum·mus (ho͝om′əs, hŭm′-) ▸ *n.* A thick dip or spread made of mashed chickpeas, tahini, oil, lemon juice, and garlic.

hu·mor (hyo͞o′mər) ▸ *n.* **1.** The quality that makes something laughable or amusing. **2.** The ability to perceive, enjoy, or express what is amusing or comical. **3.** *Physiol.* A body fluid, such as blood, lymph, or bile. **4.** A state of mind; mood: *a bad humor.* **5.** A sudden whim. ▸ *v.* To comply with the wishes or ideas of; indulge. **—hu′mor·ist** *n.* **—hu′mor·**

THESAURUS

hulk *n.* —*See* GIANT, OAF.

hulk *v.* —*See* BLUNDER.

hulking or **hulky** *adj.* —*See* BULKY (2).

hull *n.* —*See* SKIN (3).

hull *v.* —*See* SKIN.

hullabaloo *n.* —*See* NOISE (1), VOCIFERATION.

hum *v.* To make a continuous low-pitched droning sound ▸ bombinate, bumble, burr, buzz, drone, purr, whir, whiz.

hum *n.* A continuous low-pitched droning sound ▸ bumble, burr, buzz, buzzing, drone, humming, purr, purring, whir, whirring, whiz, whizzing.

human *adj.* Of or characteristic of human beings or humankind ▸ anthropic, anthropical, anthropoid, mortal. —*See also* HUMANITARIAN.

human *n.* —*See* HUMAN BEING.

human being *n.* A member of the human race ▸ being, body, creature, earthling, Homo sapiens, human, individual, life, man, mortal, party, person, personage, self, soul, spirit.

humane *adj.* —*See* ETHICAL, HUMANITARIAN.

humanistic *adj.* —*See* BROAD-MINDED.

humanitarian *adj.* Concerned with human welfare and the remedying of social ills ▸ charitable, compassionate, human, humane, humanistic, merciful, philanthropic, public-spirited, social-minded. [*Compare* BENEVOLENT, GENEROUS, LIBERAL, SELFLESS.]

humanitarian *n.* —*See* DONOR.

humanity *n.* —*See* BENEVOLENCE, HUMANKIND.

humanize *v.* To fit for companionship with others, especially in attitude or manners ▸ acculturate, civilize, socialize.

humanizing *adj.* —*See* CULTURAL.

humankind *n.* Humans as a group ▸ earth, flesh, Homo sapiens, human beings, humanity, **human race**, man, mankind, men and women, mortals, universe, world. [*Compare* PUBLIC.]

humanlike or **humanoid** *adj.* Resembling a human being ▸ anthropoid, anthropomorphic, anthropomorphous, hominoid, manlike. [*Compare* HUMAN.]

human race *n.* —*See* HUMANKIND.

humble *adj.* **1.** Having or expressing feelings of humility ▸ lowly, meek, modest, unambitious. [*Compare* DEFERENTIAL.] **2.** Of little distinction ▸ lowly, mean, simple. [*Compare* MODEST.] —*See also* LOWLY (1).

humble *v.* To lower the pride or dignity of ▸ abase, debase, deflate, degrade, demean, humiliate, lower, mortify, puncture. *Slang:* put down. *Idioms:* bring low, put in one's place, take (*or* bring) down a notch, take (*or* bring) down a peg. [*Compare* BELITTLE, DISGRACE, SHAME.] —*See also* DEBASE.

humbleness *n.* —*See* MODESTY (1).

humbug *n.* —*See* CHEAT (1), FAKE.

humbug *v.* —*See* DECEIVE.

humdrum *adj.* —*See* BORING, DULL (1), ORDINARY.

humid *adj.* —*See* STICKY (2).

humiliate *v.* —*See* DISGRACE, HUMBLE.

humiliating *adj.* —*See* DISGRACEFUL.

humiliation *n.* —*See* DEGRADATION (1), DISGRACE.

humility *n.* —*See* MODESTY (1).

humming *adj.* —*See* ACTIVE, BUSY (2).

hummock *n.* —*See* HILL.

humor *n.* The quality of being laughable or comical ▸ comedy, comicality, comicalness, drollery, drollness, farcicality, funniness, humorousness, jocoseness, jocosity, jocularity, ludicrousness, ridiculousness, wit, wittiness, zaniness. —*See also* DISPOSITION, FANCY, MOOD.

less *adj.* **—hu′mor·less·ly** *adv.* **—hu′mor·less·ness** *n.* **—hu′mor·ous** *adj.* **—hu′mor·ous·ly** *adv.* **—hu′mor·ous·ness** *n.*

hump (hŭmp) ► *n.* **1.** A rounded mass, as on the back of a camel. **2.** A low mound. ► *v.* **1.** To bend into a hump; arch. **2.** *Slang* To exert (oneself). **3.** *Slang* To hurry. ***—idiom:* over the hump** Past the worst stage.

hump·back (hŭmp′băk′) ► *n.* **1.** See **hunchback** 1. **2.** A humped upper back. **3.** A humpback whale. **—hump′backed′** *adj.*

humpback whale ► *n.* A large baleen whale noted for its communicative songs.

hu·mus (hyo͞o′məs) ► *n.* A brown or black organic substance consisting of decayed vegetable or animal matter.

Hun (hŭn) ► *n.* **1.** A member of a nomadic Mongolian people who invaded Europe in the 4th and 5th cent. A.D. **2.** often **hun** A barbarous person.

hunch (hŭnch) ► *n.* An intuitive feeling. ► *v.* **1.** To bend or draw up into a hump. **2.** To assume a crouched or cramped posture.

hunch·back (hŭnch′băk′) ► *n.* **1.** One whose back is hunched due to abnormal curvature of the upper spine. **2.** An abnormally humped back. **—hunch′backed′** *adj.*

hun·dred (hŭn′drĭd) ► *n., pl.* **-dred** or **-dreds. 1.** The cardinal number equal to 10 × 10 or 10^2. **2. hundreds** The numbers between 100 and 999: *a crowd numbering in the hundreds.* **—hun′dred** *adj. & pron.*

hun·dredth (hŭn′drĭdth) ► *n.* **1.** The ordinal number matching the number 100 in a series. **2.** One of 100 equal parts. **—hun′dredth** *adj.*

hun·dred·weight (hŭn′drĭd-wāt′) ► *n., pl.* **-weight** or **-weights. 1.** A unit of weight equal to 100 lbs. (45.36 kg). **2.** *Chiefly Brit.* A unit equal to 112 lbs. (50.80 kg).

hung (hŭng) ► *v.* P.t. and p.part of **hang.**

Hun·gar·i·an (hŭng-gâr′ē-ən) ► *n.* **1.** A native or inhabitant of Hungary. **2.** The Finno-Ugric language of the Hungarians. **—Hun·gar′i·an** *adj.*

Hun·ga·ry (hŭng′gə-rē) ► A country of central Europe E of Austria.

hun·ger (hŭng′gər) ► *n.* **1a.** A strong desire for food. **b.** The discomfort, weakness, or pain caused by a lack of food. **2.** A strong desire or craving. ► *v.* **1.** To have a need or desire for food. **2.** To have a strong desire or craving; yearn. **—hun′gri·ly** *adv.* **—hun′gri·ness** *n.* **—hun′gry** *adj.*

hung jury ► *n.* A jury unable to agree on a verdict.

hunk (hŭngk) ► *n.* **1.** *Informal* A large piece. **2.** *Slang* An attractive man.

hun·ker (hŭng′kər) ► *v.* **1.** To squat; crouch. **2.** To assume a defensive position: *hunkered down against the unfavorable criticism.*

hun·ky-do·ry (hŭng′kē-dôr′ē) ► *adj. Slang* Perfectly satisfactory; fine.

hunt (hŭnt) ► *v.* **1.** To pursue (game) for food or sport. **2.** To search for prey: *hunted the backwoods.* **3.** To pursue so as to capture. **4.** To search (for). ► *n.* **1.** The act or sport of hunting. **2.** A hunting expedition. **3.** A diligent search. **—hunt′er** *n.* **—hunt′ress** *n.*

hunts·man (hŭnts′mən) ► *n.* A man who hunts, esp. one who manages a pack of hounds in the field.

hur·dle (hûr′dl) ► *n.* **1.** *Sports* **a.** A framelike barrier to be jumped over in certain races. **b. hurdles** A race in which such barriers must be jumped. **2.** An obstacle to be overcome. ► *v.* **-dled, -dling. 1.** To leap over (a barrier). **2.** To overcome; surmount. **—hur′dler** *n.*

hur·dy-gur·dy (hûr′dē-gûr′dē, hûr′dē-gûr′dē) ► *n., pl.* **-dies.** A musical instrument, such as a barrel organ, played by turning a crank.

hurl (hûrl) ► *v.* **1.** To throw forcefully; fling. **2.** To utter vehemently: *hurl insults.* **3.** To pitch a baseball. **—hurl** *n.*

hur·ly-bur·ly (hûr′lē-bûr′lē) ► *n., pl.* **-lies.** Noisy confusion; tumult.

Hu·ron (hyo͝or′ən, -ŏn′) ► *n., pl.* **-ron** or **-rons. 1.** A member of a Native American confederacy formerly of SE Ontario, now in Quebec and Oklahoma. **2.** The Iroquoian language of the Huron.

Huron, Lake ► The second largest of the Great Lakes, between SE Ontario, Canada, and E MI.

hur·rah (ho͝o-rä′, -rô′, hə-) also **hoo·ray** or **hur·ray** (-rā′) ► *interj.* Used as an exclamation of pleasure, approval, elation, or victory. **—hur·rah′** *n. & v.*

hur·ri·cane (hûr′ĭ-kān′, hŭr′-) ► *n.* A tropical cyclone usu. involving heavy rains and winds exceeding 74 mph (119 kph).

hur·ry (hûr′ē, hŭr′-) ► *v.* **-ried, -ry·ing. 1.** To move or cause to move with speed or haste. **2.** To act or cause to act with undue haste; rush. **3.** To speed the completion of; expedite. ► *n., pl.* **-ries. 1.** The act of hurrying. **2.** Haste. **—hur′ried** *adj.* **—hur′ried·ly** *adv.*

hurt (hûrt) ► *v.* **hurt, hurt·ing. 1.** To feel or cause to feel pain. **2.** To aggrieve; distress. **3.** To damage or impair. ► *n.* **1.** Something that hurts. **2.** Mental suffering; anguish. **3.** A wrong; harm. **—hurt′ful** *adj.* **—hurt′ful·ly** *adv.*

hur·tle (hûr′tl) ► *v.* **-tled, -tling. 1.** To move with or as if with great speed. **2.** To throw forcefully; hurl.

hus·band (hŭz′bənd) ► *n.* A male spouse. ► *v.* To use economically: *husband one's energy.*

hus·band·ry (hŭz′bən-drē) ► *n.* **1.** Farming; agriculture. **2.** Careful management of resources; economy.

hush (hŭsh) ► *v.* **1.** To make or become silent. **2.** To calm; soothe. **3.** To suppress mention of: *hush up the evidence.* ► *n.* A silence or stillness.

THESAURUS

humor *v.* To comply with the wishes or ideas of another ► cater (to), gratify, indulge. [*Compare* DEFER².] *—See also* BABY.

humorist *n.* *—See* JOKER.

humorous *adj.* *—See* CLEVER (2), FUNNY (1).

humorousness *n.* *—See* HUMOR.

hump *n.* *—See* BUMP (1).

hump *v.* *—See* STOOP.

humus *n.* *—See* EARTH (1).

hunch *n.* *—See* FEELING (1), LUMP¹.

hunch *v.* *—See* STOOP.

hunger *n.* *—See* APPETITE, DESIRE (1).

hunger *v.* To have a greedy, obsessive desire ► crave, itch, lust, thirst. [*Compare* DESIRE.]

hungry *adj.* **1.** Desiring or craving food ► famished, ravenous, starving, voracious. *Informal:* starved. *Idiom:* hungry as a wolf. **2.** Having desire for something ► desiring, desirous, hankering. [*Compare* VORACIOUS.] *—See also* GREEDY.

hunk *n.* *—See* BEAUTY, LUMP¹.

hunker down *v.* To sit on one's heels ► squat. *—See also* STOOP.

hunt *v.* To look for and pursue game in order to capture or kill it ► chase (down), drive, run (down), stalk. [*Compare* TRACK.] *—See also* PURSUE (1).

hunt down *v.* *—See* TRACE (1).

hunt for *v.* *—See* SEEK (1).

hunt *n.* The following of another in an attempt to overtake and capture ► chase, hot pursuit, pursuit. *—See also* PURSUIT (2).

hurdle *n.* *—See* BAR (1).

hurdle *v.* To pass by or over successfully ► clear, negotiate, surmount. *—See also* JUMP (1).

hurl *v.* *—See* THROW, VOMIT.

hurl *n.* *—See* THROW.

hurried *adj.* *—See* ABRUPT (2), FAST (1), QUICK.

hurriedly *adv.* *—See* FAST.

hurriedness *n.* *—See* HASTE (2).

hurry *v.* *—See* RUSH, SPEED.

hurry *n.* *—See* HASTE (1).

hurry-scurry *n.* *—See* AGITATION (2).

hurry-up *adj.* Designed to meet emergency needs as quickly as possible ► *Informal:* crash, rush.

hurt *v.* **1.** To cause bodily damage to a living thing ► injure, traumatize, wing, wound. [*Compare* CUT, BREAK.] **2.** To cause pain, soreness, or discomfort; be painful ► ache, bite, burn, smart, sting, twinge. **3.** To cause pain, soreness, or discomfort to ► bother, inflame, irritate, pain, pang, twinge. [*Compare* AFFLICT.] *—See also* DAMAGE, DISTRESS, OFFEND (1).

hurt *n.* *—See* DISTRESS, HARM.

hurtful *adj.* *—See* HARMFUL, OFFENSIVE (2), PAINFUL.

hurtle *v.* *—See* SHOOT (3), THROW.

hurtless *adj.* *—See* HARMLESS.

husband *n.* *—See* SPOUSE.

husband *v.* To protect an asset from loss or destruction ► conserve, preserve, save. [*Compare* DEFEND.]

husbandry *n.* *—See* CONSERVATION.

hush *v.* *—See* CENSOR (2), CONCEAL, REPRESS, SILENCE.

hush *n.* *—See* SILENCE (1), STILLNESS.

hushed *adj.* *—See* SILENT (1), SOFT (2).

hush-hush (hŭsh′hŭsh′) ► *adj. Informal* Secret; confidential.

hush puppy ► *n.* A small round cornmeal fritter fried in deep fat.

husk (hŭsk) ► *n.* **1.** The outer covering of some fruits or seeds, as that of an ear of corn. **2.** A shell or outer covering, esp. when considered worthless. ► *v.* To remove the husk from. **—husk′er** *n.*

husk·y[1] (hŭs′kē) ► *adj.* **-i·er, -i·est.** Hoarse or throaty. **—husk′i·ly** *adv.*

husk·y[2] (hŭs′kē) ► *adj.* **-i·er, -i·est.** Strongly built; burly.

hus·ky[3] (hŭs′kē) ► *n., pl.* **-kies.** An Arctic sled dog having a dense, variously colored coat.

hus·sar (hə-zär′, -sär′) ► *n.* A member of any of various European units of light cavalry.

hus·sy (hŭz′ē, hŭs′ē) ► *n., pl.* **-sies. 1.** A brazen or immoral woman. **2.** A saucy or impudent girl.

hus·tle (hŭs′əl) ► *v.* **-tled, -tling. 1.** To jostle or shove roughly. **2.** To hurry along. **3.** To work busily. **4.** *Slang* To sell or get by questionable or aggressive means. ► *n.* Energetic activity; drive. **—hus′tler** *n.*

hut (hŭt) ► *n.* A crude or makeshift dwelling; shack.

hutch (hŭch) ► *n.* **1.** A coop for small animals, esp. rabbits. **2.** A cupboard with drawers and usu. open shelves on top. **3.** A hut.

Hu·tu (ho͞o′to͞o′) ► *n., pl.* **-tu, -tus.** A member of a Bantu people inhabiting Rwanda and Burundi.

Hux·ley (hŭks′lē), **Aldous Leonard** (1894–1963) ► British writer.

huz·zah also **huz·za** (hə-zä′) ► *interj.* Used to express joy, encouragement, or triumph. **—huz·zah′** *n.*

Hwang Ho (hwäng′ hō′) ► See **Huang He.**

hy·a·cinth (hī′ə-sĭnth) ► *n.* A bulbous plant having narrow leaves and variously colored, usu. fragrant flowers.

hy·brid (hī′brĭd) ► *n.* **1.** The offspring of genetically dissimilar parents, esp. of different varieties or species. **2.** Something of mixed origin or composition. **—hy′brid** *adj.* **—hy′brid·ism** *n.*

hy·brid·ize (hī′brĭ-dīz′) ► *v.* **-ized, -iz·ing.** To produce or cause to produce hybrids; crossbreed. **—hy′brid·i·za′tion** *n.*

hy·dra (hī′drə) ► *n.* A small freshwater polyp having a cylindrical body and a mouth surrounded by tentacles.

hy·dran·gea (hī-drān′jə, -drăn′-) ► *n.* A shrub having large rounded clusters of white, pink, or blue flowers.

hy·drant (hī′drənt) ► *n.* A fire hydrant.

hy·drate (hī′drāt′) ► *n.* A solid compound containing water molecules combined in a definite ratio as an integral part of the crystal. ► *v.* **-drat·ed, -drat·ing. 1.** To rehydrate. **2.** To become a hydrate. **—hy·dra′tion** *n.* **—hy′dra′tor** *n.*

hy·drau·lic (hī-drô′lĭk) ► *adj.* **1.** Of, involving, or operated by a fluid, esp. water, under pressure. **2.** Able to set and harden under water, as Portland cement. **3.** Of or relating to hydraulics. **—hy·drau′li·cal·ly** *adv.*

hy·drau·lics (hī-drô′lĭks) ► *n. (takes sing. v.)* The physical science and technology of the static and dynamic behavior of fluids.

hydro– or **hydr–** ► *pref.* **1a.** Water: *hydroelectric.* **b.** Fluid: *hydrodynamics.* **2.** Hydrogen: *hydrocarbon.*

hy·dro·car·bon (hī′drə-kär′bən) ► *n.* An organic compound, such as benzene or methane, that contains only carbon and hydrogen.

hy·dro·ceph·a·lus (hī′drō-sĕf′ə-ləs) also **hy·dro·ceph·a·ly** (-lē) ► *n.* A congenital defect in which accumulation of fluid in the cerebral ventricles causes enlargement of the skull and compression of the brain. **—hy′dro·ce·phal′ic** (-sə-făl′ĭk), **hy′dro·ceph′a·loid′, hy′dro·ceph′a·lous** *adj.*

hy·dro·chlo·ric acid (hī′drə-klôr′ĭk) ► *n.* A clear, fuming, poisonous aqueous solution of hydrogen chloride, HCl, used in petroleum production, food processing, pickling, and metal cleaning.

hy·dro·cor·ti·sone (hī′drə-kôr′tĭ-sōn′, -zōn′) ► *n.* **1.** A steroid hormone, $C_{21}H_{30}O_5$, produced by the adrenal cortex, that regulates carbohydrate metabolism and maintains blood pressure. **2.** A preparation of this hormone used to treat inflammations and adrenal failure.

hy·dro·dy·nam·ics (hī′drō-dī-năm′ĭks) ► *n. (takes sing. v.)* The branch of science that deals with the dynamics of fluids, esp. incompressible fluids, in motion.

hy·dro·e·lec·tric (hī′drō-ĭ-lĕk′trĭk) ► *adj.* Of or relating to electricity generated by conversion of the energy of running water. **—hy′dro·e·lec·tric′i·ty** (-ĭ-lĕk-trĭs′ĭ-tē) *n.*

hy·dro·foil (hī′drə-foil′) ► *n.* **1.** A winglike structure on the hull of a boat that raises the hull out of the water for efficient high-speed operation. **2.** A boat with hydrofoils.

hy·dro·gen (hī′drə-jən) ► *n. Symbol* **H** A colorless, highly flammable gaseous element, the most abundant element in the universe and present in most organic compounds. At. no. 1. **—hy·drog′e·nous** (-drŏj′ə-nəs) *adj.*

hy·dro·gen·ate (hī′drə-jə-nāt′, hī-drŏj′ə-) ► *v.* **-at·ed, -at·ing.** To combine with or subject to the action of hydrogen.

hydrogen bomb ► *n.* A bomb whose explosive power is caused by the fusion of hydrogen nuclei into helium nuclei.

hydrogen peroxide ► *n.* A colorless, strongly oxidizing liquid, H_2O_2, used esp. as an antiseptic, bleaching agent, oxidizing agent, and laboratory reagent.

hy·drol·y·sis (hī-drŏl′ĭ-sĭs) ► *n.* Decomposition of a chemical compound by reaction with water. **—hy′dro·lyte′** (-līt′) *n.* **—hy′dro·lyt′ic** (-drə-lĭt′ĭk) *adj.* **—hy′dro·ly·za′tion** (hī′drə-lĭ-zā′shən) *n.* **—hy′dro·lyze′** *v.*

hy·drom·e·ter (hī-drŏm′ĭ-tər) ► *n.* An instrument used to determine the specific gravity of a fluid.

hy·dro·pho·bi·a (hī′drə-fō′bē-ə) ► *n.* **1.** Fear of water. **2.** Rabies. **—hy′dro·pho′bic** *adj.*

hy·dro·plane (hī′drə-plān′) ► *n.* **1.** See **seaplane. 2.** A motorboat designed to skim the water's surface at high speeds. **3.** See **hydrofoil** 2. ► *v.* **-planed, -plan·ing. 1.** To drive or ride in a hydroplane. **2a.** To skim along on the surface of the water. **b.** To lose control by skimming along the surface of a wet road. Used of a motor vehicle.

hy·dro·pon·ics (hī′drə-pŏn′ĭks) ► *n. (takes sing. v.)* Cultivation of plants in nutrient solution rather than in soil. **—hy′dro·pon′ic** *adj.* **—hy′dro·pon′i·cal·ly** *adv.*

hy·dro·stat·ics (hī′drə-stăt′ĭks) ► *n. (takes sing. v.)* The physics of fluids at rest and under pressure. **—hy′dro·stat′ic, hy′dro·stat′i·cal** *adj.* **—hy′dro·stat′i·cal·ly** *adv.*

hy·dro·ther·a·py (hī′drə-thĕr′ə-pē) ► *n., pl.* **-pies.** External use of water in the treatment of diseases.

hy·drous (hī′drəs) ► *adj.* Containing water, esp. water of crystallization or hydration.

hy·drox·ide (hī-drŏk′sīd′) ► *n.* A chemical compound containing the univalent group OH.

hy·e·na (hī-ē′nə) ► *n.* Any of several carnivorous mammals of Africa and Asia feeding chiefly on carrion.

hy·giene (hī′jēn′) ► *n.* **1.** The science of the promotion and preservation of health. **2.** Conditions and practices that promote or preserve health. **—hy′gien′ic** (-jĕn′ĭk) *adj.* **—hy′gien′i·cal·ly** *adv.* **—hy·gien′ist** (hī-jē′nĭst, -jĕn′ĭst) *n.*

hy·grom·e·ter (hī-grŏm′ĭ-tər) ► *n.* Any of several instruments that measure atmospheric humidity. **—hy′gro·met′ric** (hī′grə-mĕt′rĭk) *adj.* **—hy·grom′e·try** *n.*

hy·ing (hī′ĭng) ► *v.* Pr.part. of **hie.**

hy·men (hī′mən) ► *n.* A membranous fold of tissue closing the external vaginal orifice. **—hy′men·al** *adj.*

hy·me·ne·al (hī′mə-nē′əl) ► *adj.* Of a wedding or marriage.

THESAURUS

hush-hush *adj.* *—See* CONFIDENTIAL (1), SECRET (1).

husk *n.* *—See* SKIN (3).

husk *v.* *—See* SKIN.

husky[1] *adj.* *—See* HOARSE.

husky[2] *adj.* *—See* BULKY (2), MUSCULAR.

hussy *n.* *—See* SLUT.

hustle *v.* *—See* DRIVE (3), RUSH, SPEED.

hustle *n.* *—See* DRIVE (2), HASTE (1), TRICK (1).

hustler *n.* An intensely energetic, enthusiastic person ► demon, dynamo. *Informal:* eager beaver, firebreather, go-getter, live wire. *—See also* PROSTITUTE.

hut *n.* A small, usually roughly built shelter ► cabin, hole, hovel, lean-to, shack, shanty, shed.

hutch *n.* *—See* CAGE.

hutzpah *n.* *See* CHUTZPAH.

hyaline *adj.* Of or resembling glass ► glasslike, glassy, vitreous, vitrescent. [*Compare* TRANSLUCENT.] *—See also* CLEAR (1).

hybrid *n.* *—See* COMBINATION.

hygienic *adj.* *—See* HEALTHFUL, STERILE (1).

hymn (hĭm) ▸ *n.* A song of praise or thanks, esp. to God.
hym·nal (hĭm′nəl) ▸ *n.* A book or collection of church hymns.
hype[1] (hīp) ▸ *n. Slang* **1.** Excessive publicity. **2.** Extravagant claims made esp. in advertising. **—hype** *v.*
hype[2] (hīp) *Slang* ▸ *n.* A hypodermic injection or syringe.
hy·per (hī′pər) ▸ *adj. Slang* **1.** Excitable; high-strung. **2.** Manic; frenzied.
hyper– ▸ *pref.* **1.** Over; above; beyond: *hypersonic.* **2.** Excessive; excessively: *hypercritical.*
hy·per·ac·tive (hī′pər-ăk′tĭv) ▸ *adj.* Highly or excessively active. **—hy′per·ac′tive·ly** *adv.* **—hy′per·ac·tiv′i·ty** *n.*
hy·per·bo·la (hī-pûr′bə-lə) ▸ *n., pl.* **-las** or **-lae** (-lē) *Math.* A plane curve having two branches, formed by the intersection of a plane with both halves of a right circular cone at an angle parallel to the axis of the cone.
hy·per·bo·le (hī-pûr′bə-lē) ▸ *n.* A figure of speech in which exaggeration is used for emphasis or effect, as in *I could sleep for a year.*
hy·per·bol·ic (hī′pər-bŏl′ĭk) also **hy·per·bol·i·cal** (-ĭ-kəl) ▸ *adj.* **1.** Of or employing hyperbole. **2.** *Math.* Of or shaped like a hyperbola. **—hy′per·bol′i·cal·ly** *adv.*
hy·per·crit·i·cal (hī′pər-krĭt′ĭ-kəl) ▸ *adj.* Excessively critical; captious. **—hy′per·crit′i·cal·ly** *adv.*
hy·per·gly·ce·mi·a (hī′pər-glī-sē′mē-ə) ▸ *n.* An excess of glucose in the blood. **—hy′per·gly·ce′mic** *adj.*
hy·per·link (hī′pər-lĭngk′) *Comp. Sci.* ▸ *n.* See **link** 3. ▸ *v.* To follow a hypertext link to an electronic document.
hy·per·sen·si·tive (hī′pər-sĕn′sĭ-tĭv) ▸ *adj.* Abnormally sensitive. **—hy′per·sen′si·tive·ness, hy′per·sen′si·tiv′i·ty** *n.*
hy·per·son·ic (hī′pər-sŏn′ĭk) ▸ *adj.* Of or relating to speed equal to or exceeding five times the speed of sound.
hy·per·ten·sion (hī′pər-tĕn′shən) ▸ *n.* **1.** Abnormally high arterial blood pressure. **2.** High emotional tension. **—hy′per·ten′sive** *adj. & n.*
hy·per·text (hī′pər-tĕkst′) ▸ *n.* A computer-based text retrieval system that provides access to particular locations in webpages or other electronic documents by clicking on embedded links.
hy·per·thy·roid·ism (hī′pər-thī′roi-dĭz′əm) ▸ *n.* **1.** Pathologically excessive production of thyroid hormones. **2.** The condition resulting from such production.
hy·per·tro·phy (hī-pûr′trə-fē) ▸ *n., pl.* **-phies.** A nontumorous enlargement of an organ or a tissue.
hy·per·ven·ti·late (hī′pər-vĕn′tl-āt′) ▸ *v.* **-lat·ed, -lat·ing.** **1.** To breathe so as to effect hyperventilation. **2.** To breathe fast or deeply, as from excitement or anxiety.
hy·per·ven·ti·la·tion (hī′pər-vĕn′tl-ā′shən) ▸ *n.* Fast or deep respiration resulting in abnormally low levels of carbon dioxide in the blood.
hy·phen (hī′fən) ▸ *n.* A punctuation mark (-) used between the parts of a compound word or between the syllables of a word, esp. when divided at the end of a line of text.
hy·phen·ate (hī′fə-nāt′) ▸ *v.* **-at·ed, -at·ing.** To divide or connect with a hyphen. **—hy′phen·a′tion** *n.*
hyp·no·sis (hĭp-nō′sĭs) ▸ *n., pl.* **-ses** (-sēz). An induced sleeplike state in which the subject may experience forgotten or suppressed memories, hallucinations, and heightened suggestibility.
hyp·not·ic (hĭp-nŏt′ĭk) ▸ *adj.* **1.** Of or relating to hypnosis. **2.** Inducing or tending to induce sleep. ▸ *n.* An agent or substance that causes sleep. **—hyp·not′i·cal·ly** *adv.*
hyp·no·tism (hĭp′nə-tĭz′əm) ▸ *n.* **1.** The theory, practice, or act of inducing hypnosis. **2.** Hypnosis. **—hyp′no·tist** *n.*
hyp·no·tize (hĭp′nə-tīz′) ▸ *v.* **-tized, -tiz·ing.** **1.** To put into a state of hypnosis. **2.** To fascinate; mesmerize. **—hyp′no·ti·za′tion** *n.* **—hyp′no·tiz′er** *n.*
hy·po (hī′pō) ▸ *n., pl.* **-pos.** *Informal* A hypodermic syringe or injection.
hypo– or **hyp–** ▸ *pref.* **1.** Below; beneath; under: *hypodermic.* **2.** Lower than normal: *hypothermia.*
hy·po·al·ler·gen·ic (hī′pō-ăl′ər-jĕn′ĭk) ▸ *adj.* Having a decreased tendency to provoke an allergic reaction.
hy·po·chon·dri·a (hī′pə-kŏn′drē-ə) ▸ *n.* The neurosis that one is or is becoming ill. **—hy′po·chon′dri·ac′** *adj. & n.*
hy·poc·ri·sy (hĭ-pŏk′rĭ-sē) ▸ *n., pl.* **-sies.** The professing of beliefs or virtues one does not possess.
hyp·o·crite (hĭp′ə-krĭt′) ▸ *n.* A person given to hypocrisy. **—hyp′o·crit′i·cal** *adj.* **—hyp′o·crit′i·cal·ly** *adv.*
hy·po·der·mic (hī′pə-dûr′mĭk) ▸ *adj.* Injected beneath the skin. ▸ *n.* **1.** A hypodermic injection. **2.** A hypodermic needle or syringe. **—hy′po·der′mi·cal·ly** *adv.*
hypodermic needle ▸ *n.* **1.** A hollow needle used with a hypodermic syringe. **2.** A hypodermic syringe with its needle.
hypodermic syringe ▸ *n.* A syringe fitted with a hypodermic needle for giving injections.
hy·po·gly·ce·mi·a (hī′pō-glī-sē′mē-ə) ▸ *n.* An abnormally low level of glucose in the blood. **—hy′po·gly·ce′mic** *adj.*
hy·pot·e·nuse (hī-pŏt′n-o͞os′, -yo͞os′) ▸ *n. Math.* The side of a right triangle opposite the right angle.
hy·po·thal·a·mus (hī′pō-thăl′ə-məs) ▸ *n.* The part of the brain that lies below the thalamus and regulates bodily temperature, certain metabolic processes, and other autonomic activities. **—hy′po·tha·lam′ic** (-thə-lăm′ĭk) *adj.*
hy·po·ther·mi·a (hī′pə-thûr′mē-ə) ▸ *n.* Abnormally low body temperature. **—hy′po·ther′mic** *adj.*
hy·poth·e·sis (hī-pŏth′ĭ-sĭs) ▸ *n., pl.* **-ses** (-sēz′). A tentative explanation that accounts for a set of facts and can be tested by further investigation. **—hy·poth′e·size** *v.*
hy·po·thet·i·cal (hī′pə-thĕt′ĭ-kəl) also **hy·po·thet·ic** (-thĕt′ĭk) ▸ *adj.* **1.** Of or based on a hypothesis. **2.** Suppositional; uncertain. **—hy′po·thet′i·cal** *n.* **—hy′po·thet′i·cal·ly** *adv.*
hy·po·thy·roid·ism (hī′pō-thī′roi-dĭz′əm) ▸ *n.* **1.** Insufficient production of thyroid hormones, marked by lack of energy and a slowed metabolism. **2.** A pathological condition resulting from such an insufficiency.
hys·sop (hĭs′əp) ▸ *n.* A woody plant having spikes of small blue flowers and aromatic leaves.
hys·ter·ec·to·my (hĭs′tə-rĕk′tə-mē) ▸ *n., pl.* **-mies.** Surgical removal of the uterus.
hys·ter·i·a (hĭ-stĕr′ē-ə, -stîr′-) ▸ *n.* **1.** A neurosis marked by a physical ailment with no organic cause, such as sleepwalking or amnesia. **2.** Excessive or uncontrollable emotion, such as fear or panic.
hys·ter·ic (hĭ-stĕr′ĭk) ▸ *n.* **1.** A person suffering from hysteria. **2. hysterics** *(takes sing. or pl. v.)* **a.** A fit of laughing or crying. **b.** An attack of hysteria. ▸ *adj.* Hysterical.
hys·ter·i·cal (hĭ-stĕr′ĭ-kəl) ▸ *adj.* **1.** Marked by or due to hysteria. **2.** Having or prone to having hysterics. **3.** *Informal* Extremely funny. **—hys·ter′i·cal·ly** *adv.*
Hz ▸ *abbr.* hertz

THESAURUS

hymn *n.* —*See* SONG.
hymn *v.* —*See* PRAISE (3).
hype *n.* —*See* PUBLICITY.
hype *v.* —*See* PROMOTE (3).
hyper *adj.* —*See* EDGY.
hyperbole or **hyperbolism** *n.* —*See* EXAGGERATION.
hyperbolic *adj.* —*See* EXAGGERATED.
hyperbolize *v.* —*See* EXAGGERATE.
hypercritic *n.* —*See* CRITIC (2).
hypercritical *adj.* —*See* CRITICAL (1).
hypersensitive *adj.* —*See* OVERSENSITIVE.
hypersensitivity *adj.* —*See* OVERSENSITIVITY.
hypnotic *adj.* —*See* SOPORIFIC.
hypnotic *n.* —*See* SOPORIFIC.
hypnotic state *n.* —*See* TRANCE.
hypnotize *v.* —*See* CHARM (2).
hypocrisy *n.* A show or expression of feelings or beliefs one does not actually hold or possess ▸ lip service, pharisaism, phoniness, piety, sanctimoniousness, sanctimony, tartuffery, two-facedness. [*Compare* ARROGANCE, DECEIT, DISHONESTY, FAITHLESSNESS.]
hypocrite *n.* A person who practices hypocrisy ▸ dissembler, pharisee, phony, poser, tartuffe. [*Compare* LIAR.]
hypocritical *adj.* Of or practicing hypocrisy ▸ Janus-faced, Pecksniffian, pharisaic, phony, pious, sanctimonious, two-faced. [*Compare* ARROGANT, DISHONEST, FAITHLESS, UNDERHAND.]
hypogeal or **hypogean** or **hypogeous** *adj.* —*See* UNDERGROUND.
hypostasis *n.* —*See* EMBODIMENT.
hypostatize *v.* —*See* EMBODY (1).
hypothecate *v.* —*See* PAWN[1].
hypothesis *n.* —*See* THEORY (2).
hypothesize *v.* To formulate as a tentative explanation ▸ speculate, theorize. [*Compare* SUPPOSE.]
hypothesized or **hypothetical** *adj.* —*See* SUPPOSED, THEORETICAL (2), UNTRIED.
hysterical *adj.* —*See* FUNNY (1).

I

i[1] or **I** (ī) ► *n., pl.* **i's** or **I's** also **is** or **Is.** The 9th letter of the English alphabet.
i[2] ► The symbol for **imaginary unit**.
I[1] (ī) ► *pron.* Used to refer to oneself as speaker or writer. ► *n.* The self; the ego.
I[2] ► **1.** The symbol for the element **iodine** 1. **2.** The symbol for **current** 3.
IA or **Ia.** ► *abbr.* Iowa
–ia[1] ► *suff.* **1.** Disease; disorder: *dyslexia.* **2.** Territory; country: *suburbia.*
–ia[2] ► *suff.* Things derived from or relating to: *marginalia.*
–ial ► *suff.* Of, relating to, or characterized by: *axial.*
i·amb (ī′ămb′, ī′ăm′) ► *n., pl.* **i·ambs.** A metrical foot in which a stressed syllable follows an unstressed syllable. **—i·am′bic** *adj. & n.*
–ian ► *suff.* **1.** Of, relating to, or resembling: *Devonian.* **2.** One relating to, belonging to, or resembling: *tragedian.*
–iana ► *suff.* Var. of **–ana.**
–iatric ► *suff.* Of or relating to a specified kind of medical practice: *pediatric.*
–iatrics ► *suff.* Medical treatment: *pediatrics.*
–iatry ► *suff.* Medical treatment: *psychiatry.*
ib. ► *abbr.* ibidem
I·be·ri·a (ī-bîr′ē-ə) ► **1.** An ancient country of Transcaucasia roughly equivalent to E Georgia. **2.** See **Iberian Peninsula.** **—I·be′ri·an** *adj. & n.*
Iberian Peninsula also **Iberia** ► A peninsula of SW Europe occupied by Spain and Portugal.
i·bex (ī′bĕks′) ► *n., pl.* **ibex** or **i·bex·es.** A wild goat native to Eurasia and N Africa and having long curving horns.
ibid. ► *abbr.* ibidem
i·bi·dem (ĭb′ĭ-dĕm′, ĭ-bī′dəm) ► *adv.* In the same place, as in a book cited before.
i·bis (ī′bĭs) ► *n., pl.* **ibis** or **i·bis·es.** Any of a family of storklike wading birds having a long, downward-curving bill.
–ible ► *suff.* Var. of **–able.**
I·bo (ē′bō) ► *n., pl.* **Ibo** or **I·bos.** **1.** A member of a people of SE Nigeria. **2.** The language of the Ibo.
Ib·sen (ĭb′sən, ĭp′-), **Henrik** (1828–1906) ► Norwegian playwright.
i·bu·pro·fen (ī′byo͞o-prō′fən) ► *n.* An anti-inflammatory medication used esp. to treat arthritis and for its analgesic and antipyretic properties.
–ic ► *suff.* **1.** Of, relating to, or characterized by: *seismic.* **2.** Having a valence higher than corresponding *–ous* compounds: *ferric.*
ice (īs) ► *n.* **1.** Water frozen solid. **2.** A dessert consisting of sweetened and flavored crushed ice. **3.** *Slang* Diamonds. **4.** Extreme unfriendliness or reserve. ***—idiom:* on ice** In reserve or readiness. ► *v.* **iced, ic·ing.** **1a.** To form ice; freeze. **b.** To coat with ice. **2.** To chill or freeze. **3.** To cover or decorate with icing. **4.** *Slang* To ensure of victory; clinch.
ice age ► *n.* **1.** A cold period marked by episodes of extensive glaciation. **2. Ice Age** The most recent glacial period.
ice bag ► *n.* See **ice pack** 2.
ice·berg (īs′bûrg′) ► *n.* A massive floating body of ice broken away from a glacier.
ice·boat (īs′bōt′) ► *n.* **1.** A boatlike vehicle with sharp runners, used for sailing on ice. **2.** See **icebreaker** 1. **—ice′boat′er** *n.* **—ice′boat′ing** *n.*
ice·bound (īs′bound′) ► *adj.* Locked in or covered over by ice.
ice·box (īs′bŏks′) ► *n.* A refrigerator.
ice·break·er (īs′brā′kər) ► *n.* **1.** A ship built for breaking a passage through icebound waters. **2a.** Something done or said to relax an unduly formal situation. **b.** A start. **—ice′break′ing** *n.*
ice·cap or **ice cap** (īs′kăp′) ► *n.* An extensive perennial cover of ice and snow.
ice cream ► *n.* A sweet frozen food prepared from milk products and flavorings.
ice hockey ► *n.* A game played on ice in which two teams of skaters use curved sticks to drive a puck into the opponent's goal.
ice·house (īs′hous′) ► *n.* A place where ice is made, stored, or sold.
Ice·land (īs′lənd) ► An island country in the North Atlantic near the Arctic Circle. **—Ice′land·er** *n.*
Ice·land·ic (īs-lăn′dĭk) ► *adj.* Of or relating to Iceland or its people or language. ► *n.* The Germanic language of Iceland.
ice pack ► *n.* **1.** A floating mass of compacted ice fragments. **2.** A sac filled with crushed ice and applied to sore or swollen parts of the body.
ice pick ► *n.* An awl for chipping or breaking ice.
ice skate ► *n.* A boot with a metal blade fitted to the sole, used for skating on ice. **—ice′-skate′** *v.* **—ice skater** *n.*
ice storm ► *n.* A storm in which snow or rain freezes on contact.
ichthyo– or **ichthy–** ► *pref.* Fish: *ichthyology.*
ich·thy·ol·o·gy (ĭk′thē-ŏl′ə-jē) ► *n.* The branch of zoology that studies fishes. **—ich′thy·o·log′ic** (-ə-lŏj′ĭk), **ich′thy·o·log′i·cal** *adj.* **—ich′thy·ol′o·gist** *n.*
ich·thy·o·saur (ĭk′thē-ə-sôr′) also **ich·thy·o·sau·rus** (ĭk′thē-ə-sôr′əs) ► *n.* An extinct fishlike marine reptile of the Mesozoic Era having an elongated, toothed snout.
–ician ► *suff.* One who practices; a specialist: *beautician.*
i·ci·cle (ī′sĭ-kəl) ► *n.* **1.** A tapering spike of ice formed by the freezing of dripping water. **2.** *Informal* An aloof person.
ic·ing (ī′sĭng) ► *n.* A sweet glaze used on cakes and cookies.
i·con (ī′kŏn′) ► *n.* **1.** An image or representation. **2.** A religious painting, usu. on wood, venerated in some Christian churches. **3.** *Comp. Sci.* A picture on a screen that represents a specific file, directory, window, or program.
i·con·o·clast (ī-kŏn′ə-klăst′) ► *n.* **1.** One who attacks traditional ideas or institutions. **2.** One who destroys sacred images. **—i·con′o·clasm′** *n.* **—i·con′o·clas′tic** *adj.* **—i·con′o·clas′ti·cal·ly** *adv.*
–ics ► *suff.* **1.** Study; knowledge; skill: *graphics.* **2.** Actions, activities, or practices of: *athletics.* **3.** Qualities or operations of: *mechanics.*
ic·tus (ĭk′təs) ► *n., pl.* **-tus** or **-tus·es.** *Medic.* A sudden seizure.
ICU ► *abbr.* intensive care unit
ic·y (ī′sē) ► *adj.* **-i·er, -i·est.** **1.** Containing or covered with ice. **2.** Bitterly cold; freezing. **3.** Chilling in manner: *an icy smile.* **—ic′i·ly** *adv.* **—ic′i·ness** *n.*
id (ĭd) ► *n.* In psychoanalysis, the part of the psyche that is the source of instinctual impulses and demands for satisfaction of primitive needs
ID[1] (ī′dē′) *Informal* ► *n.* A form of identification, such as a card or passport. ► *v.* **ID'ed, ID'·ing.** To check the identification of; card.
ID[2] ► *abbr.* **1.** also **Id.** Idaho **2.** identification
id. ► *abbr.* idem
I'd (īd) ► **1.** I had. **2.** I would. **3.** I should.
I·da·ho (ī′də-hō′) ► A state of the northwest US. Cap.

THESAURUS

I-beam *n.* —*See* BEAM (2).
ice *v.* —*See* KILL[1].
iciness *n.* —*See* COLD.
icky *adj.* —*See* UNPALATABLE, UNPLEASANT.
iconoclast *n.* —*See* REBEL (2).
icy *adj.* —*See* COLD (1), COOL.

Boise. —**I′da·ho′an** *adj.* & *n.*

-ide ▸ *suff.* **1.** Chemical compound: *chloride.* **2.** Chemical element with properties similar to another: *lanthanide.*

i·de·a (ī-dē′ə) ▸ *n.* **1.** Something, such as a thought, that exists in the mind as a product of mental activity. **2.** An opinion, conviction, or principle. **3.** A plan, scheme, or method. **4.** A general meaning or purport.

i·de·al (ī-dē′əl, ī-dēl′) ▸ *n.* **1.** A concept of something as perfect. **2.** A standard of perfection or excellence. **3.** An ultimate objective; goal. **4.** An honorable or worthy principle. ▸ *adj.* **1.** Of or embodying an ideal. **2.** Considered the best of its kind. **3.** Completely satisfactory. **4.** Existing only in the mind; imaginary. —**i·de′al·ly** *adv.*

i·de·al·ism (ī-dē′ə-lĭz′əm) ▸ *n.* **1.** The practice of envisioning things in an ideal form. **2.** Pursuit of one's ideals. **3.** *Philos.* The theory that things, in themselves or as perceived, consist of ideas. —**i·de′al·ist** *n.* —**i·de′al·is′tic** *adj.* —**i·de′al·is′ti·cal·ly** *adv.*

i·de·al·ize (ī-dē′ə-līz′) ▸ *v.* **-ized, -iz·ing.** To regard, envision, or represent as ideal. —**i·de′al·i·za′tion** *n.* —**i·de′al·iz′er** *n.*

i·de·ate (ī′dē-āt′) ▸ *v.* **-at·ed, -at·ing.** To form an idea (of). —**i′de·a′tion** *n.* —**i′de·a′tion·al** *adj.*

i·dem (ī′dĕm′) ▸ *pron.* Something mentioned previously.

i·den·ti·cal (ī-dĕn′tĭ-kəl) ▸ *adj.* **1.** Being the same. **2.** Exactly equal and alike. **3.** *Biol.* Of or relating to a twin or twins developed from the same ovum. —**i·den′ti·cal·ly** *adv.* —**i·den′ti·cal·ness** *n.*

i·den·ti·fi·ca·tion (ī-dĕn′tə-fĭ-kā′shən) ▸ *n.* **1.** The act of identifying. **2.** The state of being identified. **3.** Proof of identity. **4.** *Psychol.* A person's association with the characteristics or views of another person.

i·den·ti·fy (ī-dĕn′tə-fī′) ▸ *v.* **-fied, -fy·ing.** **1.** To establish the identity of. **2.** To ascertain the origin, nature, or characteristics of. **3.** To equate. **4.** To associate (oneself) closely with a person or group. —**i·den′ti·fi′a·ble** *adj.* —**i·den′ti·fi′a·bly** *adv.*

i·den·ti·ty (ī-dĕn′tĭ-tē) ▸ *n., pl.* **-ties.** **1.** The collective aspect of the set of characteristics by which a thing is definitively recognizable or known. **2.** The set of characteristics by which an individual is recognizable. **3.** The quality or condition of being the same as something else. **4.** *Math.* An equation satisfied by any number that replaces the letter for which the equation is defined.

identity element ▸ *n. Math.* The element of a set of numbers that when combined with another number in an operation leaves that number unchanged: *Zero is the identity element under addition for the real numbers.*

ideo– ▸ *pref.* Idea: *ideogram.*

id·e·o·gram (ĭd′ē-ə-grăm′, ī′dē-) ▸ *n.* **1.** A character or symbol representing an idea or a thing without expressing the pronunciation of a particular word or words for it. **2.** A graphic symbol, such as &, $, or @. —**id′e·o·gram·mat′ic** (-grə-măt′ĭk) *adj.* —**id′e·o·gram·mat′i·cal·ly** *adv.*

i·de·o·logue (ī′dē-ə-lôg′, -lŏg′, ĭd′ē-) ▸ *n.* An advocate of a particular ideology.

i·de·ol·o·gy (ī′dē-ŏl′ə-jē, ĭd′ē-) ▸ *n., pl.* **-gies.** **1.** The body of ideas reflecting the social needs and aspirations of an individual, group, class, or culture. **2.** A systematic set of doctrines or beliefs. —**i′de·o·log′i·cal** (ī′dē-ə-lŏj′ĭ-kəl, ĭd′ē-) *adj.* —**i′de·o·log′i·cal·ly** *adv.* —**i′de·ol′o·gist** *n.*

ides (īdz) ▸ *pl.n. (takes sing. or pl. v.)* The 15th day of March, May, July, or October or the 13th day of the other months in the ancient Roman calendar.

id·i·o·cy (ĭd′ē-ə-sē) ▸ *n., pl.* **-cies.** **1.** Extreme folly or stupidity. **2.** The condition of profound mental retardation.

id·i·om (ĭd′ē-əm) ▸ *n.* **1.** An expression having a meaning that cannot be understood from the individual meanings of its elements, as in *hand over fist.* **2.** The specific grammatical, syntactic, and structural character of a given language. **3.** Regional speech or dialect. —**id′i·o·mat′ic** (-ə-măt′ĭk) *adj.* —**id′i·o·mat′i·cal·ly** *adv.*

id·i·op·a·thy (ĭd′ē-ŏp′ə-thē) ▸ *n.* A disease of unknown cause. —**id′i·o·path′ic** (-ə-păth′ĭk) *adj.*

id·i·o·syn·cra·sy (ĭd′ē-ō-sĭng′krə-sē) ▸ *n., pl.* **-sies.** A structural or behavioral peculiarity; eccentricity. —**id′i·o·syn·crat′ic** (-sĭn-krăt′ĭk) *adj.* —**id′i·o·syn·crat′i·cal·ly** *adv.*

id·i·ot (ĭd′ē-ət) ▸ *n.* **1.** A foolish or stupid person. **2.** A person of profound mental retardation, gen. unable to learn connected speech or guard against common dangers. No longer in use. —**id′i·ot′ic** (-ŏt′ĭk) *adj.* —**id′i·ot′i·cal·ly** *adv.*

i·dle (īd′l) ▸ *adj.* **i·dler, i·dlest.** **1a.** Not employed or busy. **b.** Avoiding work or employment; lazy. **c.** Not in use or operation. **2.** Lacking substance or basis. ▸ *v.* **i·dled, i·dling.** **1.** To pass time without working. **2.** To move lazily. **3.** To run or cause to run at a slow speed or out of gear. —**i′dle·ness** *n.* —**i′dler** *n.* —**i′dly** *adv.*

i·dol (īd′l) ▸ *n.* **1.** An image used as an object of worship. **2.** One that is adored.

i·dol·a·try (ī-dŏl′ə-trē) ▸ *n., pl.* **-tries.** **1.** Worship of idols. **2.** Excessive devotion. —**i·dol′a·ter** *n.* —**i·dol′a·trous** *adj.* —**i·dol′a·trous·ly** *adv.*

i·dol·ize (īd′l-īz′) ▸ *v.* **-ized, -iz·ing.** **1.** To regard with excessive admiration or devotion. **2.** To worship as an idol.

THESAURUS

idea *n.* That which exists in the mind as the product of careful mental activity ▸ concept, conception, image, notion, perception, thought. [*Compare* DECISION, THOUGHT, UNDERSTANDING.] —*See also* APPROACH (1), BELIEF (1), FEELING (1), IMPORT.

ideal *adj.* Conforming to an ultimate form of perfection or excellence ▸ archetypal, archetypical, exemplary, idealized, model, perfect, quintessential, supreme. [*Compare* EXCELLENT, PERFECT.] —*See also* THEORETICAL (2).

ideal *n.* —*See* DREAM (3), MODEL.

idealist *n.* —*See* DREAMER (1).

idealistic *adj.* Characterized by ideals that often conflict with practical considerations ▸ blue-sky, impractical, quixotic, romantic, starry-eyed, unrealistic, utopian, visionary. ***Idiom:*** having one's head in the clouds. [*Compare* IMPOSSIBLE, OPTIMISTIC.]

ideate *v.* —*See* THINK (1).

ideation *n.* —*See* THOUGHT.

identical *adj.* —*See* EQUAL, SAME.

identicalness *n.* The quality or condition of being exactly the same as something else ▸ identity, oneness, sameness, selfsameness. [*Compare* LIKENESS.]

identify *v.* To associate or affiliate oneself closely with a person or group ▸ empathize, relate, sympathize. [*Compare* UNDERSTAND.] —*See also* ASSOCIATE (3), DESIGNATE, DISTINGUISH (2), LIKEN, MARK (1), PLACE (1).

identity *n.* **1.** The set of behavioral or personal characteristics by which an individual is recognizable ▸ distinctiveness, individualism, individuality, peculiarity, selfhood, singularity, uniqueness. [*Compare* CHARACTER.] **2.** The quality or condition of being exactly the same as something else ▸ identicalness, oneness, sameness, selfsameness. [*Compare* LIKENESS.]

ideological *adj.* —*See* THEORETICAL (1).

ideology *n.* —*See* DOCTRINE.

idiocy *n.* —*See* FOOLISHNESS, NONSENSE, STUPIDITY.

idiom *n.* —*See* EXPRESSION (3), LANGUAGE (2).

idiosyncrasy *n.* —*See* ECCENTRICITY.

idiosyncratic *adj.* —*See* ECCENTRIC.

idiot *n.* —*See* DULLARD, FOOL.

idiotic *adj.* —*See* FOOLISH, STUPID.

idle *adj.* **1.** Marked by a lack of activity or use ▸ inactive, inert, inoperative, unemployed, unoccupied, unused, vacant. [*Compare* EMPTY, MOTIONLESS, STILL.] **2.** Having no job ▸ jobless, unemployed, unoccupied, workless. ***Idiom:*** out of a job (*or* employ *or* work). —*See also* BASELESS, HOLLOW (1), LAZY.

idle *v.* **1.** To pass time without working or in avoiding work ▸ bum (around), laze (around), loaf (around), loiter, lounge (around), piddle (around), shirk, slack off. *Informal:* vegetate. *Slang:* diddle (around), goldbrick, goof (off). ***Idioms:*** kill (*or* waste) time, twiddle one's thumbs. [*Compare* DELAY.] **2.** To spend (time) idly or pleasantly ▸ dawdle (away), fiddle away, idle away, kill, trifle away, waste, while (away), wile (away). [*Compare* SPEND.] —*See also* STOP (2).

idleness *n.* —*See* INACTION, LAZINESS, STOP (2).

idler *n.* —*See* WASTREL (2).

idol *n.* —*See* CELEBRITY.

idolization *n.* The act of adoring, especially reverently ▸ adoration, reverence, veneration, worship. [*Compare* DEVOTION, HONOR, PRAISE.]

idolize *v.* —*See* DROOL, REVERE.

—i′dol·i·za′tion (-zā′shən) *n.* **—i′dol·iz′er** *n.*

i·dyll also **i·dyl** (īd′l) ▸ *n.* **1.** A short poem idealizing rural life. **2.** A scene or event of a simple and tranquil nature. **3.** A romantic interlude. **—i·dyl′lic** (ī-dĭl′ĭk) *adj.* **—i·dyl′li·cal·ly** *adv.*

i.e. ▸ *abbr. Lat.* id est (that is)

–ie ▸ *suff.* Var. of **–y**[3].

if (ĭf) ▸ *conj.* **1a.** In the event that: *If I were to go, I would be late.* **b.** Granting that: *If that is true, what can we do?* **c.** On the condition that: *She will sing only if she is paid.* **2.** Even though: *a handsome if useless trinket.* **3.** Whether: *Ask if he plans to come.* **4.** Used to introduce an exclamatory clause, indicating a wish: *If only he were here!* ▸ *n.* A possibility, condition, or stipulation: *no ifs, ands, or buts.*

if·fy (ĭf′ē) ▸ *adj.* **-fi·er, -fi·est.** *Informal* Doubtful; uncertain: *an iffy proposition.* **—if′fi·ness** *n.*

–ify ▸ *suff.* Var. of **–fy.**

ig·loo (ĭg′lo͞o) ▸ *n., pl.* **-loos.** An Inuit or Eskimo dwelling, esp. one built of blocks of packed snow.

ig·ne·ous (ĭg′nē-əs) ▸ *adj.* **1.** Of or relating to fire. **2.** *Geol.* Formed by solidification from a molten state.

ig·nis fat·u·us (ĭg′nĭs făch′o͞o-əs) ▸ *n., pl.* **ig·nes fat·u·i** (ĭg′nēz făch′o͞o-ī′). **1.** A phosphorescent light that hovers over swampy ground at night. **2.** An illusion.

ig·nite (ĭg-nīt′) ▸ *v.* **-nit·ed, -nit·ing. 1.** To set fire to or catch fire. **2.** To excite; kindle.

ig·ni·tion (ĭg-nĭsh′ən) ▸ *n.* **1.** An act or instance of igniting. **2.** An electrical system that provides the spark to ignite the fuel mixture in an internal-combustion engine.

ig·no·ble (ĭg-nō′bəl) ▸ *adj.* **1.** Not noble in quality or purpose; base or mean. **2.** Not of the nobility; common. **—ig′no·bil′i·ty** *n.* **—ig·no′bly** *adv.*

ig·no·min·y (ĭg′nə-mĭn′ē, -mə-nē) ▸ *n., pl.* **-ies. 1.** Personal dishonor or humiliation. **2.** Shameful or disgraceful conduct. **—ig′no·min′i·ous** *adj.* **—ig′no·min′i·ous·ly** *adv.*

ig·no·ra·mus (ĭg′nə-rā′məs) ▸ *n., pl.* **-mus·es.** An ignorant person.

ig·no·rant (ĭg′nər-ənt) ▸ *adj.* **1.** Lacking education or knowledge. **2.** Showing a lack of education or knowledge. **3.** Unaware or uninformed. **—ig′nor·ance** *n.* **—ig′no·rant·ly** *adv.*

ig·nore (ĭg-nôr′) ▸ *v.* **-nored, -nor·ing.** To refuse to pay attention to; disregard. **—ig·nor′a·ble** *adj.* **—ig·nor′er** *n.*

i·gua·na (ĭ-gwä′nə) ▸ *n.* A large tropical American lizard.

IL ▸ *abbr.* Illinois

il– ▸ *pref.* Var. of **in–**[1].

–ile ▸ *suff.* Of, relating to, or capable of: *infantile.*

il·e·i·tis (ĭl′ē-ī′tĭs) ▸ *n.* Inflammation of the ileum.

il·e·um (ĭl′ē-əm) ▸ *n., pl.* **-e·a** (-ē-ə). The portion of the small intestine extending from the jejunum to the cecum. **—il′e·al** *adj.*

il·i·um (ĭl′ē-əm) ▸ *n., pl.* **-i·a** (-ē-ə). The uppermost of the three fused bones constituting either half of the pelvis. **—il′i·ac′** (-ăk′) *adj.*

ilk (ĭlk) ▸ *n.* Type or kind: *a remark of that ilk.*

ill (ĭl) ▸ *adj.* **worse** (wûrs), **worst** (wûrst). **1a.** Not healthy; sick. **b.** Unsound; bad: *ill health.* **2.** Resulting in suffering; distressing. **3.** Hostile or unfriendly. **4.** Not favorable; unpropitious: *ill omen.* **5.** Not up to standard: *ill treatment.* ▸ *adv.* **worse, worst. 1.** In a sickly manner; not well. **2.** Scarcely or with difficulty. ▸ *n.* **1.** Evil. **2.** Disaster or harm. **3.** Something that causes suffering.

Ill. ▸ *abbr.* Illinois

I'll (īl) ▸ **1.** I will. **2.** I shall.

ill-ad·vised (ĭl′əd-vīzd′) ▸ *adj.* Done without wise counsel or careful deliberation. **—ill′-ad·vis′ed·ly** (-vī′zĭd-lē) *adv.*

ill-bred (ĭl′brĕd′) ▸ *adj.* Badly brought up; impolite and crude.

il·le·gal (ĭ-lē′gəl) ▸ *adj.* **1.** Prohibited by law. **2.** *Sports & Games* Prohibited by official rules. **3.** *Comp. Sci.* Not performable by a computer. **—il′le·gal′i·ty** (ĭl′ē-găl′ĭtē) *n.* **—il·le′gal·ly** *adv.*

il·leg·i·ble (ĭ-lĕj′ə-bəl) ▸ *adj.* Not legible. **—il·leg′i·bil′i·ty** *n.* **—il·leg′i·bly** *adv.*

il·le·git·i·mate (ĭl′ĭ-jĭt′ə-mĭt) ▸ *adj.* **1.** Illegal. **2.** Born out of wedlock. **3.** Incorrectly deduced; illogical. **—il′le·git′i·ma·cy** *n.* **—il′le·git′i·mate·ly** *adv.*

ill-fat·ed (ĭl′fā′tĭd) ▸ *adj.* **1.** Destined for misfortune; doomed. **2.** Disastrous; unlucky.

ill-fa·vored (ĭl′fā′vərd) ▸ *adj.* **1.** Ugly or unattractive. **2.** Objectionable; offensive.

ill-found·ed (ĭl′foun′dĭd) ▸ *adj.* Having no factual basis.

ill-got·ten (ĭl′gŏt′n) ▸ *adj.* Obtained by dishonest or immoral means: *ill-gotten gains.*

ill-hu·mored (ĭl′hyo͞o′mərd) ▸ *adj.* Irritable; surly. **—ill′-hu′mored·ly** *adv.*

il·lib·er·al (ĭ-lĭb′ər-əl) ▸ *adj.* Narrow-minded; bigoted. **—il·lib′er·al′i·ty** (-ə-răl′ĭ-tē), **il·lib′er·al·ness** *n.*

il·lic·it (ĭ-lĭs′ĭt) ▸ *adj.* Not permitted by custom or law; unlawful. **—il·lic′it·ly** *adv.*

il·lim·it·a·ble (ĭ-lĭm′ĭ-tə-bəl) ▸ *adj.* Limitless. **—il·lim′it·a·bly** *adv.*

THESAURUS

idyllic *adj.* Charmingly simple and carefree ▸ arcadian, pastoral. [*Compare* COUNTRY, FRESH, STILL.]

i.e. *adv.* *—See* NAMELY.

iffy *adj.* *—See* AMBIGUOUS (1), DEBATABLE.

ignis fatuus *n.* *—See* ILLUSION.

ignite *v.* *—See* LIGHT[1] (1).

ignoble *adj.* *—See* LOWLY (1), SORDID.

ignominious *adj.* *—See* DISGRACEFUL.

ignominiousness *n.* *—See* INFAMY.

ignominy *n.* *—See* DISGRACE.

ignorance *n.* **1.** The condition of being ignorant; lack of knowledge or learning ▸ backwardness, benightedness, darkness, illiteracy, illiterateness, nescience, unintelligence. [*Compare* INEXPERIENCE, STUPIDITY.] **2.** The condition of being uninformed or unaware ▸ innocence, nescience, obliviousness, unawareness, unconsciousness, unfamiliarity. [*Compare* ARTLESSNESS, MISUNDERSTANDING.]

ignorant *adj.* **1.** Without education or knowledge ▸ clueless, illiterate, lowbrow, nescient, uncultivated, uneducated, uninstructed, unlearned, unlettered, unread, unscholarly, unschooled, unstudious, untaught, untutored. *Idiom:* in the dark. [*Compare* ARTLESS, BACKWARD, INEXPERIENCED.] **2.** Exhibiting lack of education or knowledge ▸ backward, benighted, primitive, unenlightened, uninformed. [*Compare* DUMB, STUPID.] **3.** Not aware or informed ▸ clueless, ill-informed, innocent, misguided, misinformed, oblivious, unacquainted, unaware, unconscious, unenlightened, unfamiliar, unilluminated, uninformed, unknowing, unwitting. *Idioms:* in the dark, without a clue. [*Compare* BLIND, CONFUSED.]

ignore *v.* *—See* BLINK AT, NEGLECT (1), NEGLECT (2), SNUB.

ilk *n.* *—See* KIND[2].

ill *adj.* *—See* FATEFUL (1), HARMFUL, SICK (1).

ill *n.* Whatever is destructive or harmful ▸ bad, badness, evil, worse. [*Compare* HARM.] *—See also* CURSE (3), DISEASE.

ill-advised *adj.* *—See* UNWISE.

ill-behaved *adj.* *—See* UNRULY.

ill-boding *adj.* *—See* FATEFUL (1).

ill-bred *adj.* *—See* COARSE (1), DISRESPECTFUL, RUDE (2).

ill-chosen *adj.* *—See* UNFORTUNATE (2).

ill-considered *adj.* *—See* RASH[1], UNWISE.

illegal *adj.* Prohibited by law ▸ illegitimate, illicit, lawless, outlawed, unlawful, wrongful. *Idiom:* against the law. [*Compare* FORBIDDEN.] *—See also* CRIMINAL (1).

illegality *n.* The state or quality of being illegal ▸ illegitimacy, illicitness, lawlessness, unlawfulness. *—See also* CRIME (1).

illegitimacy *n.* The state or quality of being illegal ▸ illegality, illicitness, lawlessness, unlawfulness.

illegitimate *adj.* Born to parents who are not married to each other ▸ baseborn, bastard, misbegotten, natural, spurious, unlawful. *Idiom:* born out of wedlock. *—See also* CRIMINAL (1), ILLEGAL.

ill-fated *adj.* *—See* UNFORTUNATE (1).

ill-favored *adj.* *—See* OBJECTIONABLE, UGLY.

illiberal *adj.* *—See* INTOLERANT (1).

illicit *adj.* Contrary to accepted, especially moral conventions ▸ criminal, unlawful. *—See also* CRIMINAL (1), FORBIDDEN, ILLEGAL.

illicitness *n.* The state or quality of being illegal ▸ illegality, illegitimacy, lawlessness, unlawfulness.

illimitable *adj.* *—See* ENDLESS (1).

Il·li·nois[1] (ĭl′ə-noi′) ▸ *n., pl.* **-nois.** **1.** A member of a Native American confederacy formerly inhabiting parts of Wisconsin, Illinois, Iowa, and Missouri. **2.** The Algonquian language of the Illinois.

Il·li·nois[2] (ĭl′ə-noi′) ▸ A state of the N-central US. Cap. Springfield. **—Il′li·nois′an** (-noi′ən) *adj. & n.*

il·lit·er·ate (ĭ-lĭt′ər-ĭt) ▸ *adj.* **1.** Having little or no formal education, esp. unable to read and write. **2.** Unfamiliar with language and literature. **3.** Ignorant of the fundamentals of a given art or branch of knowledge. **—il·lit′er·a·cy** *n.* **—il·lit′er·ate** *n.*

ill-man·nered (ĭl′măn′ərd) ▸ *adj.* Lacking good manners; rude.

ill-na·tured (ĭl′nā′chərd) ▸ *adj.* Surly; disagreeable. **—ill′-na′tured·ly** *adv.*

ill·ness (ĭl′nĭs) ▸ *n.* Sickness.

il·log·i·cal (ĭ-lŏj′ĭ-kəl) ▸ *adj.* Contradicting or disregarding the principles of logic. **—il·log′i·cal′i·ty** (-kăl′ĭ-tē) *n.* **—il·log′i·cal·ly** *adv.*

ill-starred (ĭl′stärd′) ▸ *adj.* Ill-fated; unlucky.

ill-tem·pered (ĭl′tĕm′pərd) ▸ *adj.* Having a bad temper; irritable. **—ill′-tem′pered·ly** *adv.*

ill-treat (ĭl′trēt′) ▸ *v.* To treat unkindly or harshly; maltreat. **—ill′-treat′ment** *n.*

il·lu·mi·nate (ĭ-lo͞o′mə-nāt′) ▸ *v.* **-nat·ed, -nat·ing.** **1.** To provide or brighten with light. **2.** To make understandable; clarify. **3.** To enable to understand; enlighten. **4.** To adorn (a page of a book) with designs in brilliant colors. **—il′lu·mi·na′tion** *n.* **—il·lu′mi·na′tor** *n.*

il·lu·mine (ĭ-lo͞o′mĭn) ▸ *v.* **-mined, -min·ing.** To give light to; illuminate.

ill·us·age (ĭl′yo͞o′sĭj, -zĭj) ▸ *n.* Bad treatment; ill-use.

ill-use (ĭl′yo͞oz′) ▸ *v.* To treat badly or unjustly; maltreat. **—ill′-use′** (ĭl′yo͞os′) *n.*

il·lu·sion (ĭ-lo͞o′zhən) ▸ *n.* **1a.** An erroneous perception of reality. **b.** An erroneous concept or belief. **2.** Illusionism. **3.** A misleading visual image. **—il·lu′sion·al, il·lu′sion·ar′y** (-zhə-nĕr′ē) *adj.*

il·lu·sion·ism (ĭ-lo͞o′zhə-nĭz′əm) ▸ *n.* The use of techniques such as foreshortening to produce the illusion of reality, esp. in visual art. **—il·lu′sion·ist** *n.* **—il·lu′sion·is′tic** *adj.*

il·lu·sive (ĭ-lo͞o′sĭv) ▸ *adj.* Illusory. **—il·lu′sive·ly** *adv.* **—il·lu′sive·ness** *n.*

il·lu·so·ry (ĭ-lo͞o′sə-rē, -zə-rē) ▸ *adj.* Produced by or based on an illusion; deceptive.

il·lus·trate (ĭl′ə-strāt′, ĭ-lŭs′trāt′) ▸ *v.* **-trat·ed, -trat·ing.** **1a.** To clarify, as by use of examples. **b.** To serve as an instructive example of. **2.** To provide (a publication) with explanatory or decorative graphic features. **—il′lus·tra′tor** *n.*

il·lus·tra·tion (ĭl′ə-strā′shən) ▸ *n.* **1a.** The act of illustrating. **b.** The state of being illustrated. **2.** Material used to clarify; example. **3.** Visual matter used to explain or decorate a text.

il·lus·tra·tive (ĭ-lŭs′trə-tĭv, ĭl′ə-strā′tĭv) ▸ *adj.* Acting or serving as an illustration.

il·lus·tri·ous (ĭ-lŭs′trē-əs) ▸ *adj.* Highly distinguished; eminent. **—il·lus′tri·ous·ly** *adv.* **—il·lus′tri·ous·ness** *n.*

ill will ▸ *n.* Unfriendly feeling; enmity.

Il·lyr·i·a (ĭ-lîr′ē-ə) ▸ An ancient region of the Balkan Peninsula on the Adriatic coast. **—Il·lyr′i·an** *adj. & n.*

im–[1] ▸ *pref.* Var. of **in–**[1].

im–[2] ▸ *pref.* Var. of **in–**[2].

I'm (īm) ▸ I am.

im·age (ĭm′ĭj) ▸ *n.* **1.** A reproduction of the form of a person or object, esp. a sculptured likeness. **2.** *Phys.* An optically formed duplicate of an object, especially one formed by a lens or mirror. **3.** One that closely resembles another. **4.** An outward impression of character, esp. one projected to the public. **5.** A personification: *the image of good health.* **6.** A mental picture of something not real or present. **7a.** A vivid description or representation. **b.** A figure of speech. **c.** A concrete representation evocative of something else: *night as an image of death.* ▸ *v.* **-aged, -ag·ing.** **1.** To make a likeness of. **2.** To mirror or reflect. **3.** To picture mentally; imagine. **4.** To describe, especially vividly.

im·age·ry (ĭm′ĭj-rē) ▸ *n., pl.* **-ries.** **1.** Mental images. **2.** The use of vivid or figurative language to represent objects, actions, or ideas.

i·mag·i·na·ble (ĭ-măj′ə-nə-bəl) ▸ *adj.* Capable of being imagined. **—i·mag′i·na·bly** *adv.*

i·mag·i·nar·y (ĭ-măj′ə-nĕr′ē) ▸ *adj.* **1.** Having existence

THESAURUS

illiteracy *n.* —*See* IGNORANCE (1).

illiterate *adj.* —*See* IGNORANT (1).

illiterateness *n.* —*See* IGNORANCE (1).

ill-mannered *adj.* —*See* RUDE (2).

illness *n.* —*See* DISEASE, SICKNESS.

illogical *adj.* Not governed by or predicated on reason ▸ irrational, unreasonable, unreasoned. *Idioms:* out of bounds, without rhyme or reason. [*Compare* FOOLISH.] —*See also* FALLACIOUS (1).

illogicality or **illogicalness** *n.* The absence of reason ▸ irrationality, unreason, unreasonableness. [*Compare* FALLACY, FOOLISHNESS.]

ill-omened *adj.* —*See* FATEFUL (1).

ill repute *n.* —*See* DISGRACE.

ill-starred *adj.* —*See* UNFORTUNATE (1).

ill-suited *adj.* —*See* IMPROPER (2).

ill-tempered *adj.* Having or showing a bad temper ▸ bad-tempered, cantankerous, churlish, crabbed, cranky, cross, curmudgeonly, disagreeable, fractious, fretful, grouchy, grumpy, ill-humored, ill-natured, irascible, irritable, nasty, peevish, petulant, querulous, short-tempered, snappish, snappy, splenetic, surly, testy, ugly, waspish. *Informal:* crabby, mean. *Slang:* snarky. *Idiom:* out of sorts. [*Compare* ABRUPT, ARGUMENTATIVE, TESTY.]

ill-timed *adj.* Not occurring at a favorable time ▸ inconvenient, inopportune, untimely. [*Compare* FATEFUL.] —*See also* UNSEASONABLE.

ill-treat *v.* —*See* ABUSE (1).

ill-treatment *n.* —*See* ABUSE (2).

illume *v.* —*See* ILLUMINATE (1), ILLUMINATE (2).

illuminate *v.* **1.** To cover or fill with light ▸ flood, illume, illumine, light (up), lighten. [*Compare* BEAM.] **2.** To enable one to understand, especially in a spiritual or intellectual sense ▸ edify, enlighten, illume, illumine. *Idioms:* make plain, remove the scales from someone's eyes, shed (*or* throw) light upon. [*Compare* EXPLAIN.] —*See also* CLARIFY (1), CLEAR (1).

illumination *n.* **1.** The act of physically illuminating or the condition of being filled with light ▸ light, lighting. [*Compare* BRILLIANCE.] **2.** The condition of being informed spiritually ▸ edification, enlightenment. [*Compare* EDUCATION.] —*See also* EXPLANATION, LIGHT[1] (1).

illuminative *adj.* —*See* EDUCATIONAL (2).

illumine *v.* —*See* ILLUMINATE (1), ILLUMINATE (2).

ill-usage *n.* —*See* ABUSE (1).

ill-use *v.* —*See* ABUSE (1).

illusion *n.* A phenomenon that causes a misperception ▸ delusion, hallucination, ignis fatuus, mirage, phantasm, phantasma, phantasmagoria, phantasmagory, will-o'-the-wisp. —*See also* DREAM (1), DREAM (2), MAGIC (2).

illusive or **illusory** *adj.* Of, relating to, or in the nature of an illusion; lacking reality ▸ chimeric, chimerical, delusive, delusory, dreamlike, hallucinatory, phantasmagoric, phantasmal, phantasmic, unreal, visionary. [*Compare* IMAGINARY.] —*See also* FALLACIOUS (2).

illustratable *adj.* —*See* EXPLAINABLE.

illustrate *v.* To demonstrate and clarify with examples ▸ demonstrate, evidence, exemplify, instance. [*Compare* EXPLAIN, SHOW.] —*See also* CLARIFY (1), REPRESENT (1).

illustration *n.* —*See* EMBODIMENT, EXAMPLE (1), EXPLANATION, REPRESENTATION.

illustrative *adj.* —*See* EXPLANATORY, GRAPHIC (4).

illustrious *adj.* —*See* EXALTED, FAMOUS.

illustriousness *n.* —*See* FAME.

ill will *n.* —*See* ENMITY, MALEVOLENCE.

image *n.* **1.** An image caused by reflection ▸ likeness, reflection. **2.** The character projected or given by someone to the public ▸ appearance, impression. [*Compare* FAÇADE.] —*See also* COPY (1), DOUBLE, EMBODIMENT, IDEA.

image *v.* To send back or form an image of ▸ mirror, reflect. —*See also* IMAGINE, MIMIC, REPRESENT (2).

imaginable *adj.* —*See* CONCEIVABLE.

imaginary *adj.* Existing only in the

only in the imagination. 2. *Math.* Of or being an imaginary number.

imaginary number ▸ *n. Math.* A complex number in which the real part is zero and the coefficient of the imaginary unit is not zero.

imaginary unit ▸ *n. Symbol* **i** The square root of –1.

i·mag·i·na·tion (ĭ-măj′ə-nā′shən) ▸ *n.* **1.** The formation of a mental image of something not real or present. **2.** Creative power. **3.** Resourcefulness. **—i·mag′i·na·tive** (ĭ-măj′ə-nə-tĭv, -nā′tĭv) *adj.* **—i·mag′i·na·tive·ly** *adv.* **—i·mag′i·na·tive·ness** *n.*

i·mag·ine (ĭ-măj′ĭn) ▸ *v.* **-ined, -in·ing. 1.** To form a mental image of. **2.** To think; conjecture. **3.** To fancy.

i·ma·go (ĭ-mā′gō, ĭ-mä′-) ▸ *n., pl.* **-goes** or **-gi·nes** (-gə-nēz′). An insect in its sexually mature adult stage.

i·mam also **I·mam** (ĭ-mäm′) ▸ *n. Islam* The caliph who is successor to Muhammad as the leader of the Islamic community.

im·bal·ance (ĭm-băl′əns) ▸ *n.* A lack of balance, as in distribution. **—im·bal′anced** *adj.*

im·be·cile (ĭm′bə-sĭl, -səl) ▸ *n.* **1.** A stupid or silly person. **2.** *Psychol.* A person of moderate to severe mental retardation. No longer in use. **—im′be·cil′ic** *adj.* **—im′be·cil′i·ty** *n.*

im·bed (ĭm-bĕd′) ▸ *v.* Var. of **embed.**

im·bibe (ĭm-bīb′) ▸ *v.* **-bibed, -bib·ing. 1.** To drink. **2.** To absorb or take in as if by drinking. **—im·bib′er** *n.*

im·bro·glio (ĭm-brōl′yō) ▸ *n., pl.* **-glios. 1a.** A difficult or intricate situation. **b.** A confused or complicated disagreement. **2.** A confused heap; tangle.

im·bue (ĭm-byo͞o′) ▸ *v.* **-bued, -bu·ing. 1.** To permeate or invade. **2.** To stain or dye deeply.

im·i·tate (ĭm′ĭ-tāt′) ▸ *v.* **-tat·ed, -tat·ing. 1a.** To copy the actions, appearance, mannerisms, or speech of. **b.** To copy or use the style of. **2.** To copy exactly; reproduce. **3.** To appear like; resemble. **—im′i·ta·ble** *adj.* **—im′i·ta′tor** *n.*

im·i·ta·tion (ĭm′ĭ-tā′shən) ▸ *n.* **1.** The act of imitating. **2.** Something derived or copied from an original. **—im′i·ta′tion** *adj.*

im·i·ta·tive (ĭm′ĭ-tā′tĭv) ▸ *adj.* **1.** Of or involving imitation. **2.** Not original; derivative. **3.** Tending to imitate. **4.** Onomatopoeic. **—im′i·ta′tive·ly** *adv.*

im·mac·u·late (ĭ-măk′yə-lĭt) ▸ *adj.* **1.** Impeccably clean. **2.** Free from stain or blemish; pure. **3.** Free from fault or error. **—im·mac′u·late·ly** *adv.* **—im·mac′u·late·ness** *n.*

im·ma·nent (ĭm′ə-nənt) ▸ *adj.* **1.** Existing or remaining within; inherent. **2.** Restricted entirely to the mind; subjective. **—im′ma·nence, im′ma·nen·cy** *n.* **—im′ma·nent·ly** *adv.*

im·ma·te·ri·al (ĭm′ə-tîr′ē-əl) ▸ *adj.* **1.** Of no importance; inconsequential. **2.** Having no material body or form. **—im′ma·te′ri·al·ly** *adv.*

im·ma·ture (ĭm′ə-tyo͝or′, -to͝or′, -cho͝or′) ▸ *adj.* **1.** Not fully grown or developed. **2.** Marked by or suggesting a lack of normal maturity. **—im′ma·ture′ly** *adv.* **—im′ma·tur′i·ty** *n.*

im·meas·ur·a·ble (ĭ-mĕzh′ər-ə-bəl) ▸ *adj.* **1.** Impossible to measure. **2.** Vast; limitless. **—im·meas′ur·a·bil′i·ty, im·meas′ur·a·ble·ness** *n.* **—im·meas′ur·a·bly** *adv.*

im·me·di·a·cy (ĭ-mē′dē-ə-sē) ▸ *n., pl.* **-cies. 1.** Directness. **2.** Urgency.

im·me·di·ate (ĭ-mē′dē-ĭt) ▸ *adj.* **1.** Occurring at once; instant. **2.** Of or near the present time: *in the immediate future.* **3.** Close at hand; near: *in the immediate vicinity.* **4.** Next in line: *an immediate successor.* **5.** Occurring without interposition; direct. **—im·me′di·ate·ly** *adv.*

im·me·mo·ri·al (ĭm′ə-môr′ē-əl) ▸ *adj.* Reaching beyond the limits of memory, tradition, or history. **—im′me·mo′ri·al·ly** *adv.*

im·mense (ĭ-mĕns′) ▸ *adj.* **1.** Extremely large; huge. **2.** Of immeasurable size or extent. **3.** *Informal* Excellent. **—im·mense′ly** *adv.* **—im·men′si·ty** *n.*

im·merse (ĭ-mûrs′) ▸ *v.* **-mersed, -mers·ing. 1.** To cover completely in a liquid. **2.** To baptize by submerging in water. **3.** To engage deeply; absorb. **—im·mer′sion** *n.*

im·mesh (ĭm-mĕsh′) ▸ *v.* Var. of **enmesh.**

im·mi·grant (ĭm′ĭ-grənt) ▸ *n.* **1.** One who immigrates. **2.** A plant or animal that establishes itself in a new area or habitat.

im·mi·grate (ĭm′ĭ-grāt′) ▸ *v.* **-grat·ed, -grat·ing.** To enter

THESAURUS

imagination ▸ chimeric, chimerical, conceptual, fanciful, fantastic, fantastical, invented, make-believe, notional, unreal, visionary. *Idiom:* pie in the sky. [*Compare* FICTITIOUS, ILLUSIVE, MYTHICAL.]

imagination *n.* The power of the mind to form images ▸ creativity, inventiveness, fancy, fantasy, imaginativeness, mind's eye. [*Compare* INVENTION.] *—See also* VISION (2).

imaginative *adj.* Showing invention or whimsy in design ▸ fanciful, fantastic, whimsical. [*Compare* CAPRICIOUS, ELABORATE, ORNATE.] *—See also* VISIONARY.

imaginativeness *n.* *—See* IMAGINATION.

imagine *v.* To form mental images of ▸ call up, conceive, conjure up, dream up, envisage, envision, fancy, fantasize, image, make up, picture, see, think, vision, visualize. *Informal:* feature. [*Compare* INVENT.] *—See also* DREAM, GUESS, SUPPOSE (1).

imbalance *n.* *—See* GAP (3), INEQUALITY (1).

imbecile *n.* *—See* DULLARD, FOOL.

imbecilic *adj.* *—See* FOOLISH, STUPID.

imbecility *n.* *—See* FOOLISHNESS, STUPIDITY.

imbed *v.* *See* EMBED.

imbibe *v.* *—See* ABSORB (2), DRINK (1), DRINK (2), DRINK (3).

imbibing *adj.* *—See* ABSORBENT.

imbroglio *n.* *—See* DISORDER (1), TANGLE.

imbue *v.* *—See* CHARGE (1), COLOR (1).

imitate *v.* To copy the manner or expression of another, especially in an exaggerated or mocking way ▸ ape, burlesque, caricature, impersonate, mimic, mock, parody, simulate, travesty. *Idioms:* do a takeoff on, do (*or* make) like. [*Compare* ACT, IMPERSONATE.] *—See also* COPY, FOLLOW (5), MIMIC.

imitation *n.* *—See* COPY (2), ECHO (1), MIMICRY, SATIRE.

imitation *adj.* *—See* ARTIFICIAL (1).

imitative *adj.* **1.** Of or involving imitation ▸ apish, derivative, emulative, mimetic, slavish. [*Compare* COUNTERFEIT.] **2.** Imitating sounds ▸ echoic, mimetic, onomatopoeic, onomatopoetic.

imitator *n.* *—See* MIMIC.

immaculacy *n.* *—See* PURITY.

immaculate *adj.* *—See* CLEAN (1).

immanent *adj.* *—See* CONSTITUTIONAL.

immaterial *adj.* Having no body, form, or substance ▸ bodiless, discarnate, disembodied, ethereal, impalpable, incorporeal, insubstantial, intangible, metaphysical, nonphysical, spiritual, unbodied, uncorporal, unsubstantial. [*Compare* SUPERNATURAL.] *—See also* IRRELEVANT.

immature *adj.* *—See* CHILDISH, INEXPERIENCED, YOUNG.

immaturity *n.* *—See* INEXPERIENCE.

immeasurable *adj.* *—See* ENDLESS (1), INCALCULABLE.

immeasurability or **immeasurableness** *n.* *—See* INFINITY (1).

immediate *adj.* **1.** Occurring at once ▸ instant, instantaneous. [*Compare* FAST, QUICK.] **2.** Marked by the absence of any intervention ▸ direct, firsthand, primary. *—See also* CLOSE (1), PRESENT[1].

immediately *adv.* **1.** Without delay ▸ ASAP, directly, forthwith, instant, instantly, now, promptly, right away, right off, straightaway, straight off. *Informal:* lickety-split, PDQ, yesterday. *Slang:* pronto. *Idioms:* at once, before you can say Jack Sprat (*or* Jack Robinson), first off, in the blink of an eye, like a shot, on the double, this instant (*or* minute *or* second). [*Compare* FAST.] **2.** Without intermediary ▸ directly, firsthand.

immemorial *adj.* *—See* OLD (1).

immense *adj.* *—See* ENORMOUS.

immensity or **immenseness** *n.* *—See* ENORMOUSNESS.

immerge *v.* *—See* DIP (1).

immerse *v.* *—See* ABSORB (1), DIP (1).

immersed *adj.* *—See* RAPT.

immersion *n.* *—See* ABSORPTION (2).

immigrant *n.* One who immigrates ▸ migrant. [*Compare* ÉMIGRÉ, SETTLER.] *—See also* FOREIGNER.

immigrant *adj.* *—See* FOREIGN (1).

immigrate *v.* To leave one's native land and settle in another ▸ emigrate (from), migrate, resettle, transmigrate. [*Compare* MOVE, SETTLE.]

and settle in a foreign country. **—im′mi·gra′tion** *n.*

im·mi·nent (ĭm′ə-nənt) ▸ *adj.* About to occur. **—im′mi·nence** *n.* **—im′mi·nent·ly** *adv.*

im·mo·bile (ĭ-mō′bəl, -bēl′, -bīl′) ▸ *adj.* **1.** Immovable; fixed. **2.** Not moving; motionless. **—im′mo·bil′i·ty** (-bĭl′-ĭ-tē) *n.*

im·mo·bi·lize (ĭ-mō′bə-līz′) ▸ *v.* **-lized, -liz·ing.** To render immobile. **—im·mo′bi·li·za′tion** *n.*

im·mod·er·ate (ĭ-mŏd′ər-ĭt) ▸ *adj.* Extreme; excessive. **—im·mod′er·ate·ly** *adv.* **—im·mod′er·ate·ness, im·mod′er·a′tion** *n.*

im·mod·est (ĭ-mŏd′ĭst) ▸ *adj.* **1.** Lacking modesty. **2.** Indecent or offensive. **—im·mod′est·ly** *adv.* **—im·mod′es·ty** *n.*

im·mo·late (ĭm′ə-lāt′) ▸ *v.* **-lat·ed, -lat·ing. 1.** To kill as a sacrifice. **2.** To kill (oneself) by fire. **3.** To destroy. **—im′mo·la′tion** *n.* **—im′mo·la′tor** *n.*

im·mor·al (ĭ-môr′əl, -mŏr′-) ▸ *adj.* Contrary to established moral principles. **—im′mor·al′i·ty** *n.* **—im·mor′al·ly** *adv.*

im·mor·tal (ĭ-môr′tl) ▸ *adj.* **1.** Not subject to death. **2.** Having enduring fame; undying. **—im·mor′tal** *n.* **—im′mor·tal′i·ty** *n.* **—im·mor′tal·ize′** *v.* **—im·mor′tal·ly** *adv.*

im·mov·a·ble (ĭ-mo͞o′və-bəl) ▸ *adj.* **1a.** Impossible to move. **b.** Incapable of movement. **2.** Unyielding; steadfast. **3.** Impassive; insensitive. **—im·mov′a·bil′i·ty** *n.* **—im·mov′a·bly** *adv.*

im·mune (ĭ-myo͞on′) ▸ *adj.* **1.** Exempt. **2.** Resistant to infection by a specific pathogen. **—im·mun′i·ty** *n.*

immune response ▸ *n.* An integrated bodily response to an antigen, esp. one mediated by lymphocytes and involving recognition of antigens by specific antibodies or previously sensitized lymphocytes.

immune system ▸ *n.* The integrated body system of organs, tissues, cells, and cell products such as antibodies that differentiates self from nonself and neutralizes potentially pathogenic organisms or substances.

im·mu·nize (ĭm′yə-nīz′) ▸ *v.* **-nized, -niz·ing.** To render immune. **—im′mu·ni·za′tion** *n.*

immuno– ▸ *pref.* Immune; immunity: *immunology.*

im·mu·no·de·fi·cien·cy (ĭm′yə-nō-dĭ-fĭsh′ən-sē, ĭ-myo͞o′-) ▸ *n., pl.* **-cies.** An inability to develop a normal immune response. **—im′mu·no·de·fi′cient** *adj.*

im·mu·no·glob·u·lin (ĭm′yə-nō-glŏb′yə-lĭn, ĭ-myo͞o′-) ▸ *n.* Any of a group of proteins that function as antibodies in the body's immune response.

im·mu·nol·o·gy (ĭm′yə-nŏl′ə-jē) ▸ *n.* The branch of medicine dealing with the immune system. **—im′mu·no·log′ic** (-nə-lŏj′ĭk), **im′mu·no·log′i·cal** *adj.* **—im′mu·no·log′i·cal·ly** *adv.* **—im′mu·nol′o·gist** *n.*

im·mu·no·sup·pres·sion (ĭm′yə-nō-sə-prĕsh′ən, ĭ-myo͞o′-) ▸ *n.* Suppression of the immune response, as by drugs or radiation. **—im′mu·no·sup·pres′sant** (-prĕs′ənt) *n.* **—im′mu·no·sup·pres′sive** *adj.*

im·mure (ĭ-myo͝or′) ▸ *v.* **-mured, -mur·ing. 1.** To confine within or as if within walls; imprison. **2.** To build into or entomb within a wall. **—im·mure′ment** *n.*

im·mu·ta·ble (ĭ-myo͞o′tə-bəl) ▸ *adj.* Not susceptible to change. **—im·mu′ta·bil′i·ty** *n.* **—im·mu′ta·bly** *adv.*

imp (ĭmp) ▸ *n.* **1.** A mischievous child. **2.** A small demon. **—imp′ish** *adj.* **—imp′ish·ly** *adv.* **—imp′ish·ness** *n.*

im·pact (ĭm′păkt′) ▸ *n.* **1.** A collision. **2.** The force transmitted by a collision. **3.** The effect or impression of one thing on another. ▸ *v.* (ĭm-păkt′) **1.** To pack firmly together. **2.** To strike forcefully. **3.** To affect or change. **—im·pac′tion** *n.*

im·pact·ed (ĭm-păk′tĭd) ▸ *adj.* Wedged inside the gum in a manner prohibiting eruption into a normal position: *an impacted tooth.*

im·pair (ĭm-pâr′) ▸ *v.* To diminish in strength, value, or quality; damage. **—im·pair′ment** *n.*

im·paired (ĭm-pârd′) ▸ *adj.* **1.** Diminished; weakened: *structurally impaired.* **2.** Functioning poorly or incompetently: *an impaired driver.* **3.** Having a physical or mental disability: *learning-impaired.* ▸ *n.* People who have a physical or mental disability considered as a group: *the visually impaired.*

im·pa·la (ĭm-pä′lə) ▸ *n.* An African antelope noted for its leaping ability.

im·pale (ĭm-pāl′) ▸ *v.* **-paled, -pal·ing. 1.** To pierce with or as if with a sharp point. **2.** To torture or kill by impaling. **—im·pale′ment** *n.* **—im·pal′er** *n.*

im·pal·pa·ble (ĭm-păl′pə-bəl) ▸ *adj.* **1.** Not perceptible to the touch; intangible. **2.** Difficult for the mind to grasp. **—im·pal′pa·bil′i·ty** *n.* **—im·pal′pa·bly** *adv.*

im·pan·el (ĭm-păn′əl) also **em·pan·el** (ĕm-) ▸ *v.* **-eled, -el·ing** or **-elled, -el·ling.** To enroll (a jury) upon a panel or list. **—im·pan′el·ment** *n.*

im·part (ĭm-pärt′) ▸ *v.* **1.** To grant a share of; bestow. **2.** To make known; disclose.

im·par·tial (ĭm-pär′shəl) ▸ *adj.* Not partial or biased; unprejudiced. **—im′par·ti·al′i·ty** (-shē-ăl′ĭ-tē) *n.* **—im·par′tial·ly** *adv.*

im·pass·a·ble (ĭm-păs′ə-bəl) ▸ *adj.* Impossible to pass or cross. **—im·pass′a·bil′i·ty** *n.* **—im·pass′a·bly** *adv.*

im·passe (ĭm′păs′) ▸ *n.* **1.** A road or passage having no exit. **2.** A situation allowing for no further progress; stalemate: *reached an impasse in the negotiations.*

THESAURUS

immigration *n.* Settling in a country to which one is not native ▸ migration, transmigration. [*Compare* EMIGRATION.]

imminence *n.* The act or fact of coming near ▸ approach, coming, convergence, nearness. [*Compare* ADVANCE, APPEARANCE.]

imminent *adj.* About to occur at any moment ▸ at hand, approaching, brewing, impending, in store, looming, proximate. *Idioms:* around the corner, in no time at all, in the offing, in the wind, on the horizon. [*Compare* CLOSE, COMING.]

immobile *adj.* —*See* FIXED, MOTIONLESS.

immobilization *n.* —*See* STOP (2).

immobilize *v.* —*See* DISABLE (1), STOP (2).

immoderate *adj.* —*See* EXCESSIVE.

immoderation or **immoderacy** *n.* —*See* EXCESS (2).

immodest *adj.* —*See* IMPROPER (1).

immolate *v.* To offer as a sacrifice ▸ offer up, sacrifice, victimize.

immolation *n.* —*See* OFFERING.

immoral *adj.* —*See* EVIL, IMPURE (1).

immorality *n.* —*See* CORRUPTION (1), CRIME (2).

immortal *adj.* Not being subject to death ▸ deathless, undying. —*See also* ENDLESS (2).

immortality *n.* Endless life after death ▸ afterlife, deathlessness, eternal life, eternity, everlasting life, everlastingness, life eternal, life everlasting. [*Compare* ENDLESSNESS, ETERNITY.]

immortalize *v.* To cause to last endlessly ▸ eternalize, eternize, perpetuate. *Idiom:* cast (*or* etch *or* fix *or* set) in stone. [*Compare* HONOR, MEMORIALIZE.]

immovable *adj.* —*See* FIXED.

immune *adj.* —*See* RESISTANT, SAFE (2).

immunity *n.* **1.** The capacity to withstand ▸ imperviousness, insusceptibility, resistance, unsusceptibility. [*Compare* ENDURANCE, STABILITY.] **2.** Temporary immunity from penalties ▸ exemption, grace, reprieve, respite. [*Compare* DELAY.] —*See also* SAFETY.

immure *v.* —*See* ENCLOSE (1), IMPRISON.

immutability *n.* —*See* CHANGELESSNESS.

immutable *adj.* Incapable of changing or being modified ▸ inalterable, inconvertible, inflexible, invariable, ironclad, rigid, unalterable, unchangeable, unmodifiable. [*Compare* CONTINUING, FIRM[1], FIXED.] —*See also* UNCHANGING.

imp *n.* —*See* RASCAL, URCHIN.

impact *n.* The strong effect exerted by one person or thing on another ▸ bearing, force, impression, influence, repercussion, reverberation. [*Compare* CAUSE, EFFECT, STIMULUS.] —*See also* COLLISION.

impact *v.* —*See* COLLIDE, INFLUENCE.

impair *v.* —*See* DAMAGE, DISABLE (1), DRUG (2).

impairment *n.* —*See* DAMAGE, DEBILITATION, HARM.

impale *v.* —*See* CUT (1).

impalpable *adj.* —*See* IMMATERIAL, IMPERCEPTIBLE (1).

impart *v.* —*See* COMMUNICATE (1), CONFER (2).

impartial *adj.* —*See* FAIR[1] (1), NEUTRAL (1).

impartially *adv.* —*See* FAIRLY (1).

impartiality or **impartialness** *n.* —*See* FAIRNESS.

impassable *adj.* Incapable of being negotiated or overcome ▸ insuperable, insurmountable, unconquerable. [*Compare* IMPOSSIBLE, INVINCIBLE.]

impasse *n.* —*See* PREDICAMENT.

im·pas·si·ble (ĭm-păs′ə-bəl) ▸ *adj.* **1.** Not subject to suffering or pain. **2.** Unfeeling.

im·pas·sioned (ĭm-păsh′ənd) ▸ *adj.* Filled with passion; fervent.

im·pas·sive (ĭm-păs′ĭv) ▸ *adj.* **1.** Revealing no emotion; expressionless. **2.** Not susceptible to emotion. **—im·pas′sive·ly** *adv.* **—im·pas′sive·ness, im′pas·siv′i·ty** *n.*

im·pa·tiens (ĭm-pā′shənz, -shəns) ▸ *n.* Any of various plants of a genus which includes the jewelweed.

im·pa·tient (ĭm-pā′shənt) ▸ *adj.* **1.** Unable to wait patiently or tolerate delay; restless. **2.** Unable to endure opposition; intolerant. **3.** Restively eager or desirous; anxious. **—im·pa′tience** *n.* **—im·pa′tient·ly** *adv.*

im·peach (ĭm-pēch′) ▸ *v.* **1.** To charge (a public official) with improper conduct in office before a proper tribunal. **2.** To try to discredit; challenge: *impeach a witness's credibility.* **—im·peach′a·ble** *adj.* **—im·peach′er** *n.* **—im·peach′ment** *n.*

im·pec·ca·ble (ĭm-pĕk′ə-bəl) ▸ *adj.* **1.** Having no flaws. **2.** Incapable of sin. **—im·pec′ca·bil′i·ty** *n.* **—im·pec′ca·bly** *adv.*

im·pe·cu·ni·ous (ĭm′pĭ-kyo͞o′nē-əs) ▸ *adj.* Lacking money; penniless. **—im′pe·cu′ni·ous·ly** *adv.* **—im′pe·cu′ni·ous·ness** *n.*

im·ped·ance (ĭm-pēd′ns) ▸ *n.* *Symbol* **Z** A measure of the total opposition to current flow in an alternating current circuit.

im·pede (ĭm-pēd′) ▸ *v.* **-ped·ed, -ped·ing.** To retard or obstruct the progress of. **—im·ped′er** *n.*

im·ped·i·ment (ĭm-pĕd′ə-mənt) ▸ *n.* **1.** Something that impedes; hindrance or obstruction. **2.** A speech defect preventing clear articulation.

im·ped·i·men·ta (ĭm-pĕd′ə-mĕn′tə) ▸ *pl.n.* Objects, such as baggage, that impede or encumber.

im·pel (ĭm-pĕl′) ▸ *v.* **-pelled, -pel·ling.** **1.** To urge to action. **2.** To drive forward; propel.

im·pel·ler (ĭm-pĕl′ər) ▸ *n.* A rotor or rotor blade.

im·pend (ĭm-pĕnd′) ▸ *v.* **1.** To be about to take place. **2.** To threaten to happen; menace.

im·pen·e·tra·ble (ĭm-pĕn′ĭ-trə-bəl) ▸ *adj.* **1.** Impossible to penetrate or enter. **2.** Impossible to understand. **—im·pen′e·tra·bil′i·ty** *n.* **—im·pen′e·tra·bly** *adv.*

im·pen·i·tent (ĭm-pĕn′ĭ-tənt) ▸ *adj.* Not repentant. **—im·pen′i·tence** *n.* **—im·pen′i·tent** *n.* **—im·pen′i·tent·ly** *adv.*

im·per·a·tive (ĭm-pĕr′ə-tĭv) ▸ *adj.* **1.** Expressing a command or plea. **2.** Having the authority to command or control. **3.** *Gram.* Of or relating to the mood that expresses a command. **4.** Pressing; urgent. **—im·per′a·tive** *n.* **—im·per′a·tive·ly** *adv.*

im·per·cep·ti·ble (ĭm′pər-sĕp′tə-bəl) ▸ *adj.* **1.** Impossible or difficult to perceive. **2.** Insignificantly small or slight. **—im′per·cep′ti·bil′i·ty** *n.* **—im′per·cep′ti·bly** *adv.*

im·per·fect (ĭm-pûr′fĭkt) ▸ *adj.* **1.** Not perfect. **2.** *Gram.* Of or being a verb tense expressing a past action or condition as incomplete or continuous. ▸ *n.* *Gram.* **1.** The imperfect tense. **2.** A verb in the imperfect tense. **—im·per′fect·ly** *adv.*

im·per·fec·tion (ĭm′pər-fĕk′shən) ▸ *n.* **1.** The quality or condition of being imperfect. **2.** A defect; flaw.

im·pe·ri·al (ĭm-pîr′ē-əl) ▸ *adj.* **1.** Of or relating to an empire, emperor, or empress. **2.** Ruling over extensive territories or over colonies or dependencies. **3.** Regal; majestic. **—im·pe′ri·al·ly** *adv.*

im·pe·ri·al·ism (ĭm-pîr′ē-ə-lĭz′əm) ▸ *n.* The policy of extending a nation's authority by economic and political means over other nations. **—im·pe′ri·al·ist** *adj. & n.* **—im·pe′ri·al·is′tic** *adj.* **—im·pe′ri·al·is′ti·cal·ly** *adv.*

im·per·il (ĭm-pĕr′əl) ▸ *v.* **-iled, -il·ing** or **-illed, -il·ling.** To put into peril. **—im·per′il·ment** *n.*

im·pe·ri·ous (ĭm-pîr′ē-əs) ▸ *adj.* **1.** Arrogantly domineering or overbearing. **2.** Urgent; pressing. **—im·pe′ri·ous·ly** *adv.* **—im·pe′ri·ous·ness** *n.*

im·per·ish·a·ble (ĭm-pĕr′ĭ-shə-bəl) ▸ *adj.* Not perishable. **—im·per′ish·a·bil′i·ty** *n.* **—im·per′ish·a·bly** *adv.*

im·per·ma·nent (ĭm-pûr′mə-nənt) ▸ *adj.* Not lasting; transient. **—im·per′ma·nence** *n.* **—im·per′ma·nent·ly** *adv.*

im·per·me·a·ble (ĭm-pûr′mē-ə-bəl) ▸ *adj.* Impossible to permeate. **—im·per′me·a·bil′i·ty** *n.* **—im·per′me·a·bly** *adv.*

im·per·mis·si·ble (ĭm′pər-mĭs′ə-bəl) ▸ *adj.* Forbidden. **—im′per·mis′si·bil′i·ty** *n.*

im·per·son·al (ĭm-pûr′sə-nəl) ▸ *adj.* **1.** Not being a person: *an impersonal force.* **2.** Showing no emotion: *an impersonal manner.* **3.** Having no personal reference or connection. **—im·per′son·al′i·ty** (-sə-năl′ĭ-tē) *n.* **—im·per′son·al·ly** *adv.*

im·per·son·ate (ĭm-pûr′sə-nāt′) ▸ *v.* **-at·ed, -at·ing.** To assume the character or appearance of. **—im·per′son·a′tion** *n.* **—im·per′son·a′tor** *n.*

im·per·ti·nent (ĭm-pûr′tn-ənt) ▸ *adj.* **1.** Impudent; insolent. **2.** Not pertinent. **—im·per′ti·nence** *n.* **—im·per′ti·nent·ly** *adv.*

im·per·turb·a·ble (ĭm′pər-tûr′bə-bəl) ▸ *adj.* Unshakably calm and collected. **—im′per·turb′a·bil′i·ty** *n.* **—im′per·turb′a·bly** *adv.*

im·per·vi·ous (ĭm-pûr′vē-əs) ▸ *adj.* **1.** Incapable of being penetrated, as by water. **2.** Incapable of being affected: *impervious to fear.* **—im·per′vi·ous·ly** *adv.* **—im·per′vi·ous·ness** *n.*

im·pe·ti·go (ĭm′pĭ-tī′gō) ▸ *n.* A contagious bacterial skin infection marked by pustules.

im·pet·u·ous (ĭm-pĕch′o͞o-əs) ▸ *adj.* Marked by sudden and forceful energy or emotion; impulsive. **—im·pet′u·os′i·ty** (ĭm-pĕch′o͞o-ŏs′ĭ-tē) *n.* **—im·pet′u·ous·ly** *adv.* **—im·pet′u·ous·ness** *n.*

THESAURUS

impassible *adj.* —*See* COLD (2).

impassion *v.* —*See* FIRE (1).

impassioned *adj.* —*See* PASSIONATE.

impassive *adj.* —*See* APATHETIC, COLD (2), VACANT.

impassivity or **impassiveness** *n.* —*See* APATHY.

impatient *adj.* Being unable or unwilling to endure irritation or opposition, for example ▸ intolerant, unforbearing, unindulgent. [*Compare* ILL-TEMPERED, INTOLERANT.] —*See also* ANXIOUS, EAGER.

impeach *v.* —*See* ACCUSE.

impeachment *n.* —*See* ACCUSATION.

impeccable *adj.* —*See* PERFECT.

impecuniosity or **impecuniousness** *n.* —*See* POVERTY.

impecunious *adj.* —*See* POOR.

impede *v.* —*See* DELAY (1), HINDER.

impediment *n.* —*See* BAR (1), DIFFICULTY.

impel *v.* —*See* PROVOKE.

impelled *adj.* —*See* OBLIGED (2).

impend *v.* —*See* THREATEN (2).

impending *adj.* —*See* IMMINENT.

impenetrability *n.* —*See* SAFETY.

impenetrable *adj.* —*See* INCOMPREHENSIBLE, MYSTERIOUS, SAFE (2).

impenitent *adj.* Devoid of remorse ▸ remorseless, unrepentant.

imperative *adj.* —*See* REQUIRED, URGENT (1).

imperative *n.* —*See* COMMAND (1), DUTY (1).

imperceptible *adj.* **1.** Incapable of being apprehended by the mind or the senses ▸ impalpable, imponderable, inappreciable, indiscernible, indistinguishable, insensible, intangible, invisible, subtle, unnoticeable, unobservable. [*Compare* AMBIGUOUS, REMOTE, UNCLEAR.] **2.** So small as not to be discernible ▸ infinitesimal, microscopic. [*Compare* TINY.] *See also* HIDDEN (1).

imperfect *adj.* Having a defect or defects ▸ amiss, blemished, defective, faulty, flawed. [*Compare* SHABBY, TRICK.] —*See also* ROUGH (4).

imperfection *n.* —*See* DEFECT.

imperial *adj.* —*See* AUTHORITATIVE (1), GRAND.

imperil *v.* —*See* ENDANGER.

imperilment *n.* —*See* DANGER.

imperious *adj.* —*See* DICTATORIAL.

impermanent *adj.* —*See* TEMPORARY (2).

impermissible *adj.* —*See* FORBIDDEN.

impersonal *adj.* Feeling or showing no strong emotional involvement ▸ detached, disinterested, dispassionate, indifferent, neutral. —*See also* COOL.

impersonate *v.* To assume the character or appearance of ▸ attitudinize, masquerade, pass for, pose as, posture. *Idiom:* pass oneself off as. —*See also* ACT (3), IMITATE.

impersonation *n.* —*See* MIMICRY, SATIRE.

impersonator *n.* —*See* MIMIC.

impertinence *n.* —*See* IMPUDENCE.

impertinent *adj.* —*See* DISRESPECTFUL, IMPUDENT, IRRELEVANT, OFFENSIVE (2).

imperturbability or **imperturbableness** *n.* —*See* BALANCE (2).

imperturbable *adj.* —*See* CALM.

impervious *adj.* —*See* RESISTANT.

imperviousness *n.* The capacity to withstand ▸ immunity, insusceptibility, resistance, unsusceptibility. [*Compare* ENDURANCE, STABILITY.]

impetuous *adj.* —*See* RASH[1].

im·pe·tus (ĭm′pĭ-təs) ▸ *n., pl.* **-tus·es.** 1. An impelling force; impulse. 2. The force or energy associated with a moving body. 3. Something that incites; stimulus.
im·pi·e·ty (ĭm-pī′ĭ-tē) ▸ *n., pl.* **-ties.** 1. The quality or state of being impious. 2. An impious act.
im·pinge (ĭm-pĭnj′) ▸ *v.* **-pinged, -ping·ing.** 1. To collide or strike. 2. To encroach; trespass. **—im·pinge′ment** *n.* **—im·ping′er** *n.*
im·pi·ous (ĭm′pē-əs, ĭm-pī′-) ▸ *adj.* Lacking reverence; not pious. **—im′pi·ous·ly** *adv.* **—im′pi·ous·ness** *n.*
im·plac·a·ble (ĭm-plăk′ə-bəl, -plā′kə-) ▸ *adj.* Impossible to reconcile or appease: *implacable foes.* **—im·plac′a·bil′i·ty** *n.* **—im·plac′a·bly** *adv.*
im·plant (ĭm-plănt′) ▸ *v.* 1. To set or fix firmly. 2. To establish securely, as in the mind; instill. 3. *Medic.* To insert or embed (a tissue or device) surgically. 4. To become attached to the uterine lining. Used of a fertilized egg. **—im′plant′** *n.* **—im′plan·ta′tion** *n.*
im·plau·si·ble (ĭm-plô′zə-bəl) ▸ *adj.* Difficult to believe; not plausible. **—im·plau′si·bil′i·ty** *n.* **—im·plau′si·bly** *adv.*
im·ple·ment (ĭm′plə-mənt) ▸ *n.* A tool or utensil. ▸ *v.* (-mĕnt′) To put into effect. **—im′ple·men·ta′tion** *n.*
im·pli·cate (ĭm′plĭ-kāt′) ▸ *v.* **-cat·ed, -cat·ing.** 1. To involve, esp. incriminatingly. 2. To imply. **—im′pli·ca′tion** *n.*
im·plic·it (ĭm-plĭs′ĭt) ▸ *adj.* 1. Implied or understood though not directly expressed. 2. Contained in the nature of something though not readily apparent. 3. Having no reservations; unquestioning: *implicit trust.* **—im·plic′it·ly** *adv.* **—im·plic′it·ness** *n.*
im·plode (ĭm-plōd′) ▸ *v.* **-plod·ed, -plod·ing.** To burst inward. **—im·plo′sion** (-plō′zhən) *n.*
im·plore (ĭm-plôr′) ▸ *v.* **-plored, -plor·ing.** To appeal to; beseech. **—im·plor′ing·ly** *adv.*
im·ply (ĭm-plī′) ▸ *v.* **-plied, -ply·ing.** 1. To involve by logical necessity; entail. 2. To express or indicate indirectly.
im·po·lite (ĭm′pə-līt′) ▸ *adj.* Not polite; discourteous. **—im′po·lite′ly** *adv.* **—im′po·lite′ness** *n.*
im·pol·i·tic (ĭm-pŏl′ĭ-tĭk) ▸ *adj.* Not wise or expedient. **—im·pol′i·tic·ly** *adv.*
im·pon·der·a·ble (ĭm-pŏn′dər-ə-bəl) ▸ *adj.* That cannot undergo precise evaluation. **—im·pon′der·a·ble** *n.* **—im·pon′der·a·bil′i·ty** *n.* **—im·pon′der·a·bly** *adv.*
im·port (ĭm-pôrt′, ĭm′pôrt′) ▸ *v.* 1. To bring in from an outside source, esp. from a foreign country, for sale. 2. *Comp. Sci.* To receive (data) from one program into another. 3. To signify. 4. To be significant. ▸ *n.* (ĭm′pôrt′) 1. Something imported. 2. The occupation of importing goods or materials. 3. Signification. 4. Importance; significance. **—im·port′er** *n.*
im·por·tant (ĭm-pôr′tnt) ▸ *adj.* 1. Strongly affecting the course of events. 2. Having or suggesting an air of authority; authoritative. **—im·por′tance** *n.* **—im·por′tant·ly** *adv.*
im·por·ta·tion (ĭm′pôr-tā′shən) ▸ *n.* 1. The act or business of importing. 2. Something imported.
im·por·tu·nate (ĭm-pôr′chə-nĭt) ▸ *adj.* Troublesomely urgent or persistent. **—im·por′tu·nate·ly** *adv.* **—im·por′tu·nate·ness** *n.*
im·por·tune (ĭm′pôr-to͞on′, -tyo͞on′, ĭm-pôr′chən) ▸ *v.* **-tuned, -tun·ing.** To beset with insistent requests. **—im′por·tune′ly** *adv.* **—im′por·tun′er** *n.* **—im′por·tu′ni·ty** *n.*
im·pose (ĭm-pōz′) ▸ *v.* **-posed, -pos·ing.** 1. To establish as compulsory; levy: *impose a tax.* 2. To apply by or as if by authority: *impose a settlement.* 3. To force (oneself) on others. 4. To pass off on others. 5. To take unfair advantage: *imposing on their generosity.* **—im·pos′er** *n.* **—im′po·si′tion** (ĭm′pə-zĭsh′ən) *n.*
im·pos·ing (ĭm-pō′zĭng) ▸ *adj.* Impressive. **—im·pos′ing·ly** *adv.*
im·pos·si·ble (ĭm-pŏs′ə-bəl) ▸ *adj.* 1. Incapable of existing or occurring. 2. Not capable of being accomplished. 3. Unac-

THESAURUS

impetus *n.* —*See* STIMULUS.
impiety *n.* —*See* ATHEISM, SACRILEGE.
impinge *v.* —*See* ADJOIN.
impingement *n.* —*See* TRESPASS (2).
impious *adj.* Showing irreverence and contempt for something sacred ▸ blasphemous, profane, sacrilegious. —*See also* ATHEISTIC.
impish *adj.* —*See* MISCHIEVOUS.
impishness *n.* —*See* MISCHIEF.
implacability *n.* —*See* STUBBORNNESS.
implacable *adj.* —*See* STUBBORN (1), VINDICTIVE.
implant *v.* —*See* FIX (2), INSTILL, INTRODUCE (2).
implausible *adj.* Not plausible or believable ▸ feeble, flimsy, improbable, inconceivable, incredible, insubstantial, lame, shaky, tenuous, thin, unbelievable, unconceivable, unconvincing, unlikely, unsubstantial, weak. *Idiom:* beyond belief. [*Compare* DOUBTFUL, FALLACIOUS, IMPOSSIBLE.]
implement *v.* —*See* ENFORCE, FULFILL, USE.
implement *n.* A device used to do work or perform a task ▸ instrument, tool, utensil. [*Compare* AGENT, DEVICE, GADGET.]
implementation *n.* Carrying a law or judgment into effect ▸ enforcement, execution. [*Compare* EFFECT.] —*See also* EXERCISE (1).
implicate *v.* To cause to appear involved in or guilty of a crime or fault ▸ criminate, incriminate, inculpate. [*Compare* ACCUSE.] —*See also* IMPLY, INVOLVE (1).
implicating *adj.* —*See* INSINUATING.
implication *n.* —*See* ENTANGLEMENT, HINT (1).
implicit *adj.* 1. Conveyed indirectly without words or speech ▸ hinted, implied, inferred, insinuated, suggested, tacit, unarticulated, understood, unexpressed, unsaid, unspoken, unstated, unuttered, unvocalized, wordless. *Idiom:* taken for granted. [*Compare* CONSTITUTIONAL, SILENT.] 2. Having no reservations ▸ absolute, unconditional, undoubting, unfaltering, unhesitating, unquestioning, unreserved, wholehearted. *Idiom:* without reservations. [*Compare* DEFINITE, SURE.]
implied *adj.* —*See* IMPLICIT (1).
imploration *n.* —*See* APPEAL.
implore *v.* —*See* APPEAL (1).
imply *v.* To involve by logical necessity ▸ entail, implicate, involve, lead to, point to, suggest. [*Compare* DEMAND, MEAN[1], SUPPOSE.] —*See also* HINT.
impolite *adj.* —*See* DISRESPECTFUL, OFFENSIVE (2), RUDE (2).
impoliteness *n.* —*See* DISRESPECT.
impolitic *adj.* —*See* TACTLESS, UNWISE.
imponderable *adj.* —*See* IMPERCEPTIBLE (1).
import *v.* —*See* COUNT (1), MEAN[1].
import *n.* The general sense or significance, as of an action or statement ▸ amount, burden, drift, gist, idea, purport, substance, tenor. *Idioms:* sum and substance, sum total. [*Compare* HEART, THRUST.] —*See also* IMPORTANCE, MEANING.
importance *n.* The quality or state of being important ▸ concern, concernment, consequence, import, magnitude, moment, significance, significancy, weight, weightiness. [*Compare* IMPORT, MEANING.]
important *adj.* Having great significance ▸ big, consequential, considerable, crucial, earth-shaking, grand, great, historic, key, large, material, meaningful, momentous, monumental, significant, substantial, world-shaking. *Informal:* bigtime. [*Compare* BIG-LEAGUE, CRITICAL, ESSENTIAL, PRIMARY.] —*See also* FAMOUS, INFLUENTIAL.
importunate *adj.* Firm or obstinate, as in making a demand or maintaining a stand ▸ importune, insistent, persistent, urgent. [*Compare* FIRM[1], STUBBORN.]
importune *v.* —*See* DEMAND (1), HARASS.
importune *adj.* Firm or obstinate, as in making a demand or maintaining a stand ▸ importunate, insistent, persistent, urgent. [*Compare* FIRM[1], STUBBORN.]
impose *v.* To establish and apply as compulsory ▸ assess, exact, levy, put. [*Compare* BILL[1], DEMAND.] —*See also* DICTATE, INFLICT.
impose on or **upon** *v.* To force another to accept a burden ▸ charge with, fasten on (*or* upon), foist on (*or* upon), inflict on (*or* upon), lay on (*or* upon), put on (*or* upon), saddle with, tax with, yoke with. *Informal:* stick with. *Idioms:* weigh down with, weight down with. —*See also* ABUSE (1), INCONVENIENCE.
imposing *adj.* —*See* GRAND.
imposition *n.* An excessive, unwelcome burden ▸ encumbrance, infliction, intrusion, obtrusion. [*Compare* BURDEN[1], MEDDLING.]
impossible *adj.* Not capable of happening or being done ▸ blue-sky, im-

ceptable. **4.** Extremely difficult to deal with or tolerate: *an impossible situation.* **—im·pos′si·bil′i·ty** *n.* **—im·pos′si·bly** *adv.*
im·post (ĭm′pōst′) ▸ *n.* A tax or duty.
im·pos·tor (ĭm-pŏs′tər) ▸ *n.* One who deceives under an assumed identity.
im·pos·ture (ĭm-pŏs′chər) ▸ *n.* The act or instance of engaging in deception under an assumed identity.
im·po·tent (ĭm′pə-tənt) ▸ *adj.* **1.** Lacking physical strength or vigor. **2.** Lacking in power; helpless. **3.** *Physiol.* Incapable of penile erection. **—im′po·tence** *n.* **—im′po·tent·ly** *adv.*
im·pound (ĭm-pound′) ▸ *v.* **1.** To confine in or as if in a pound: *impound stray dogs.* **2.** To seize and retain in legal custody. **3.** To set aside in a fund rather than spend as prescribed. **4.** To accumulate and store (water) in a reservoir. **—im·pound′age, im·pound′ment** *n.*
im·pov·er·ish (ĭm-pŏv′ər-ĭsh) ▸ *v.* **1.** To reduce to poverty. **2.** To deprive of natural richness or strength. **—im·pov′er·ish·ment** *n.*
im·prac·ti·ca·ble (ĭm-prăk′tĭ-kə-bəl) ▸ *adj.* Impossible to do or carry out. **—im·prac′ti·ca·bil′i·ty** *n.* **—im·prac′ti·ca·bly** *adv.*
im·prac·ti·cal (ĭm-prăk′tĭ-kəl) ▸ *adj.* **1.** Unwise to implement or maintain in practice. **2.** Unable to deal efficiently with practical matters. **3.** Impracticable. **—im·prac′ti·cal′i·ty** (-kăl′ĭ-tē), **im·prac′ti·cal·ness** *n.*
im·pre·ca·tion (ĭm′prĭ-kā′shən) ▸ *n.* A curse.
im·pre·cise (ĭm′prĭ-sīs′) ▸ *adj.* Not precise. **—im′pre·cise′ly** *adv.* **—im′pre·ci′sion** (-sĭzh′ən) *n.*
im·preg·na·ble (ĭm-prĕg′nə-bəl) ▸ *adj.* **1.** Impossible to capture or enter by force. **2.** Beyond challenge or refutation.
im·preg·nate (ĭm-prĕg′nāt) ▸ *v.* **-nat·ed, -nat·ing.** **1.** To make pregnant; inseminate. **2.** To fertilize (an ovum). **3.** To fill throughout; saturate. **4.** To permeate or imbue. **—im′preg·na′tion** *n.* **—im·preg′na′tor** *n.*
im·pre·sa·ri·o (ĭm′prĭ-sär′ē-ō′, -sâr′-) ▸ *n., pl.* **-os.** One who sponsors or produces entertainment, esp. the director of an opera company.
im·press[1] (ĭm-prĕs′) ▸ *v.* **1.** To affect strongly, often favorably. **2.** To produce vivid impression of. **3.** To mark or stamp with or as if with pressure. **4.** To apply with pressure. ▸ *n.* (ĭm′prĕs′) **1.** The act of impressing. **2.** A mark or pattern produced by or as if by impressing. **3.** A stamp or seal to be impressed. **—im·press′i·bil′i·ty** *n.* **—im·press′i·ble** *adj.*
im·press[2] (ĭm-prĕs′) ▸ *v.* **1.** To compel (a person) to serve in a military force. **2.** To confiscate (property). **—im·press′ment** *n.*
im·pres·sion (ĭm-prĕsh′ən) ▸ *n.* **1.** An effect, feeling, or image retained after an experience. **2.** A vague notion, remembrance, or belief. **3.** A mark produced on a surface by pressure. **4.** *Print.* **a.** All the copies of a publication printed at one time from the same set of type. **b.** A single copy of such a printing. **5.** A humorous imitation esp. of a famous person.
im·pres·sion·a·ble (ĭm-prĕsh′ə-nə-bəl) ▸ *adj.* Readily or easily influenced; suggestible. **—im·pres′sion·a·bil′i·ty, im·pres′sion·a·ble·ness** *n.*
im·pres·sion·ism (ĭm-prĕsh′ə-nĭz′əm) ▸ *n.* A style of painting marked by concentration on the immediate visual impression produced by a scene and by the use of unmixed primary colors and small strokes to simulate actual reflected light. **—im·pres′sion·ist** *n.* **—im·pres′sion·is′tic** *adj.*
im·pres·sive (ĭm-prĕs′ĭv) ▸ *adj.* Making a strong or vivid impression; remarkable: *an impressive achievement.* **—im·pres′sive·ly** *adv.* **—im·pres′sive·ness** *n.*
im·pri·ma·tur (ĭm′prə-mä′to͝or, -mā′tər) ▸ *n.* **1.** Official approval or license to print or publish. **2.** Official approval; sanction.
im·print (ĭm-prĭnt′) ▸ *v.* **1.** To produce (a mark or pattern) on a surface. **2.** To impart a strong impression of. **3.** To fix firmly, as in the mind. ▸ *n.* (ĭm′prĭnt′) **1.** A mark or pattern produced by imprinting. **2.** A distinguishing influence or effect: *the imprint of Islamic rule.* **3.** A publisher's name, often with the date, address, and edition, printed at the bottom of a title page.
im·pris·on (ĭm-prĭz′ən) ▸ *v.* To put in or as if in prison. **—im·pris′on·a·ble** *adj.* **—im·pris′on·ment** *n.*
im·prob·a·ble (ĭm-prŏb′ə-bəl) ▸ *adj.* Unlikely to happen or be true. **—im·prob′a·bil′i·ty** *n.* **—im·prob′a·bly** *adv.*
im·promp·tu (ĭm-prŏmp′to͞o, -tyo͞o) ▸ *adj.* **1.** Prompted by the occasion rather than being planned in advance. **2.** Extemporaneous. **—im·promp′tu** *adv.* *&* *n.*
im·prop·er (ĭm-prŏp′ər) ▸ *adj.* **1.** Not suited to circumstances or needs; unsuitable. **2.** Not in keeping with conventional mores; indecorous. **3.** Not consistent with

THESAURUS

practicable, impractical, infeasible, unachievable, unattainable, unimaginable, unobtainable, unrealizable, unthinkable, unworkable. *Idioms:* beyond the bounds of possiblity (*or* reason), hardly possible, out of the question. [*Compare* IMPLAUSIBLE, INCREDIBLE, INSUPERABLE, FOOLISH.] *—See also* CONTRARY, UNBEARABLE.
impost *n.* *—See* TAX.
impostor *n.* *—See* FAKE.
imposture *n.* *—See* TRICK (1).
impotence *n.* *—See* INEFFECTUALITY, STERILITY (2).
impotent *adj.* Lacking power or strength ▸ helpless, powerless, unable. *—See also* BARREN (1), INEFFECTUAL (2).
impound *v.* *—See* ENCLOSE (1), SEIZE [illegible]
impoundment *n.* *—See* SEIZURE (2).
impoverish *v.* *—See* RUIN.
impoverished *adj.* *—See* DEPRESSED (2), POOR.
impoverishment *n.* *—See* DEBILITATION, POVERTY.
impracticable *adj.* *—See* IMPOSSIBLE, UNWORKABLE.
impractical *adj.* *—See* IDEALISTIC, IMPOSSIBLE, INEFFICIENT, THEORETICAL (1), THEORETICAL (2), UNWISE.
imprecate *v.* To invoke evil upon ▸ anathematize, curse, damn, hex. [*Compare* CHARM.]
imprecation *n.* *—See* CURSE (1).
imprecise *adj.* *—See* INDEFINITE (1), LOOSE (3).
imprecision *n.* *—See* VAGUENESS.
impregnability *n.* *—See* SAFETY.
impregnable *adj.* *—See* SAFE (2).
impregnate *v.* To make pregnant ▸ inseminate. *Slang:* knock up. *Idioms:* get (*or* put) in a family way, get with child. [*Compare* FERTILIZE.] *—See also* CHARGE (1).
impress[1] *v.* *—See* ENGRAVE (2), INSTILL, MOVE (1), STRIKE (2).
impress *n.* *—See* IMPRESSION (1).
impress[2] *v.* To enroll compulsorily in military service ▸ conscript, draft, induct, levy.
impressible *adj.* *—See* SENSITIVE (1).
impression *n.* **1.** The visible effect made on a surface by pressure ▸ dent, dint, impress, imprint, indent, indentation, mark, print, stamp. [*Compare* DEPRESSION.] **2.** The character projected or given by someone to the public ▸ appearance, image. [*Compare* FAÇADE.] **3.** Something, such as a feeling or idea, associated with a specific person or thing ▸ association, connection, connotation, suggestion. *—See also* FEELING (1), IMPACT, MIMICRY, SENSATION (1).
impressionable *adj.* *—See* FLEXIBLE (3), SENSITIVE (1).
impressionistic *adj.* Tending to bring a memory, mood, or image, for example, subtly or indirectly to mind ▸ allusive, connotative, evocative, reminiscent, suggestive. [*Compare* DESIGNATIVE, SYMBOLIC.]
impressive *adj.* *—See* AFFECTING, NOTICEABLE.
impressment *n.* *—See* DRAFT (2).
imprimatur *n.* *—See* PERMISSION.
imprint *v.* *—See* ENGRAVE (2).
imprint *n.* *—See* IMPRESSION (1), MARK (1).
imprison *v.* To put in or as if in prison ▸ confine, detain, hold, immure, incarcerate, intern, jail, lock (away *or* in *or* up), shut (away *or* in *or* up). *Informal:* put away. *Idioms:* clap in jail (*or* prison *or* irons), put behind bars, throw in the cooler (*or* slammer). [*Compare* ENCLOSE, RESTRAIN.]
imprisonment *n.* *—See* DETENTION.
improbable *adj.* *—See* DOUBTFUL (1), IMPLAUSIBLE.
improbity *n.* *—See* CORRUPTION (2), DISHONESTY (1).
impromptu *adj.* *—See* EXTEMPORANEOUS.
impromptu *n.* Something improvised ▸ ad-lib, extemporization, improvisation. [*Compare* MAKESHIFT.]
improper *adj.* **1.** Not in keeping with conventional mores ▸ immodest, indecent, indecorous, indelicate, indiscreet, naughty, risqué, unbecoming, unbefitting, unjudicious, ungentlemanly, unladylike, unseemly, untoward. *Idiom:*

fact; incorrect. **—im·prop'er·ly** *adv.*

improper fraction ▸ *n.* A fraction in which the numerator is larger than or equal to the denominator.

im·pro·pri·e·ty (ĭm'prə-prī'ĭ-tē) ▸ *n., pl.* **-ties.** 1. The quality of being improper. 2. An improper act or expression.

im·prove (ĭm-pro͞ov') ▸ *v.* **-proved, -prov·ing.** 1. To make or become better. 2. To increase the productivity or value of (property).

im·prove·ment (ĭm-pro͞ov'mənt) ▸ *n.* 1a. The act or process of improving. b. The state of being improved. 2. A change or addition that improves.

im·prov·i·dent (ĭm-prŏv'ĭ-dənt) ▸ *adj.* Not providing for the future; thriftless. **—im·prov'i·dence** *n.* **—im·prov'i·dent·ly** *adv.*

im·pro·vise (ĭm'prə-vīz') ▸ *v.* **-vised, -vis·ing.** 1. To invent, compose, or recite without preparation. 2. To make or provide from available materials: *improvised a hasty dinner.* **—im·prov'i·sa'tion** (ĭm-prŏv'ĭ-zā'shən) *n.* **—im'pro·vis'er** *n.*

im·pru·dent (ĭm-pro͞od'nt) ▸ *adj.* Unwise or indiscreet; not prudent. **—im·pru'dence** *n.* **—im·pru'dent·ly** *adv.*

im·pu·dent (ĭm'pyə-dənt) ▸ *adj.* Brashly bold; insolent; impertinent. **—im'pu·dence** *n.* **—im'pu·dent·ly** *adv.*

im·pugn (ĭm-pyo͞on') ▸ *v.* To attack as false or questionable; challenge. **—im·pugn'a·ble** *adj.* **—im·pugn'er** *n.*

im·pulse (ĭm'pŭls') ▸ *n.* 1a. An impelling force. b. The motion produced by such a force. 2. A sudden wish or urge that prompts an unpremeditated act. 3. A motivating force. 4. *Physiol.* The electrochemical transmission of a signal along a nerve fiber that produces a response at a target tissue.

im·pul·sive (ĭm-pŭl'sĭv) ▸ *adj.* 1. Inclined to act on impulse rather than thought. 2. Resulting from impulse; spontaneous. 3. Having power to impel. **—im·pul'sive·ly** *adv.* **—im·pul'sive·ness** *n.*

im·pu·ni·ty (ĭm-pyo͞o'nĭ-tē) ▸ *n.* Exemption from punishment or penalty.

im·pure (ĭm-pyo͝or') ▸ *adj.* 1. Not clean or pure; contaminated. 2. Immoral or sinful. 3. Mixed with another substance; adulterated. **—im·pure'ly** *adv.* **—im·pure'ness** *n.* **—im·pu'ri·ty** *n.*

im·pute (ĭm-pyo͞ot') ▸ *v.* **-put·ed, -put·ing.** 1. To charge with the fault or responsibility for. 2. To attribute; credit. **—im·put'a·ble** *adj.* **—im'pu·ta'tion** *n.*

in[1] (ĭn) ▸ *prep.* 1. Within the limits, bounds, or area of. 2. From the outside to the inside of; into: *threw it in the wastebasket.* 3. To or at a situation or condition of: *in love.* 4. Having the activity, occupation, or function of: *a life in politics.* 5. By means of: *paid in cash.* 6. With reference to: *six inches in depth.* ▸ *adv.* 1. To or toward the inside. 2. To or toward a place. 3. Within a place, as of business or residence. ▸ *adj.* 1. Located inside; inner. 2. Incoming. 3. Holding office; having power. 4. *Informal* Currently fashionable. ▸ *n.* 1. One with position, influence, or power. 2. *Informal* Influence.

in[2] or **in.** ▸ *abbr.* inch

In ▸ The symbol for the element **indium.**

IN ▸ *abbr.* Indiana

in–[1] or **il–** or **im–** or **ir–** ▸ *pref.* Not: *inarticulate.*

in–[2] or **im–** or **ir–** ▸ *pref.* 1. In; into; within: *irradiate.* 2. Var. of **en–**[1].

–in ▸ *suff.* 1. Neutral chemical compound: *globulin.* 2. Enzyme: *pepsin.* 3. A pharmaceutical: *niacin.* 4. An antibiotic: *penicillin.* 5. Var. of **–ine**[2] 1.

in·a·bil·i·ty (ĭn'ə-bĭl'ĭ-tē) ▸ *n.* Lack of ability or means.

in ab·sen·tia (ĭn ăb-sĕn'shə, -shē-ə) ▸ *adv.* While or although not present.

in·ac·ces·si·ble (ĭn'ăk-sĕs'ə-bəl) ▸ *adj.* Not accessible; un-

THESAURUS

out of line. [*Compare* ABANDONED, FOOLISH, RUDE, WRONG.] 2. Not suited to circumstances ▸ ill-fitted, ill-suited, inappropriate, inapt, incongruous, incorrect, inept, infelicitous, malapropos, mismatched, unapt, unbecoming, unbefitting, unfit, unfitting, unseemly, unsuitable, unsuited. ***Idiom:*** out of line (*or* place). [*Compare* DEFICIENT, INADEQUATE.] *—See also* OBJECTIONABLE.

improperness *n.* *—See* IMPROPRIETY (1).

impropriety *n.* 1. The condition of being improper ▸ improperness, inappropriateness, incongruity, incorrectness, indecency, indecorousness, indiscretion, unbecomingness, unfitness, unseemliness, unsuitability, unsuitableness. [*Compare* IMPUDENCE.] 2. An improper act or statement ▸ gaffe, gaucherie, indecency, indecorum, indelicacy, indiscretion, solecism. [*Compare* BLUNDER, BREACH.] *—See also* CORRUPTION (3).

improve *v.* To advance to a more desirable state ▸ ameliorate, amend, better, enhance, enrich, help, meliorate, upgrade. [*Compare* CORRECT, RENEW.] *—See also* RECOVER (2).

improvement *n.* 1. The act of making better or the condition of being made better ▸ advancement, amelioration, amendment, betterment, development, enhancement, melioration, refinement, rehabilitation, upgrade. [*Compare* CHANGE, REVISION.] 2. Steady improvement, as of an individual or a society ▸ amelioration, betterment, development, melioration, progress.

improvident *adj.* *—See* EXTRAVAGANT, RASH[1].

improvisation *n.* Something improvised ▸ ad-lib, extemporization, impromptu. [*Compare* MAKESHIFT.]

improvise *v.* 1. To compose or recite without preparation ▸ ad-lib, extemporize, fake, make up. ***Idioms:*** make it up as one goes along, play by ear, speak off the cuff, think on one's feet, wing it. [*Compare* INVENT.] 2. To make or provide from available materials ▸ cobble together, jerry-rig, jury-rig, rig up, slap together, throw together. ***Idiom:*** make do with. [*Compare* INVENT.]

improvised *adj.* *—See* EXTEMPORANEOUS.

imprudent *adj.* *—See* UNWISE.

impudence *n.* The state or quality of being impudent or arrogantly self-confident ▸ assumption, audaciousness, audacity, blatancy, boldness, brashness, brazenness, cheek, cheekiness, chutzpah, discourtesy, disrespect, effrontery, face, familiarity, flippancy, forwardness, gall, impertinence, impudency, incivility, insolence, nerve, nerviness, overconfidence, pertness, presumptuousness, pushiness, rudeness, sassiness, sauciness, shamelessness. *Informal:* brass, brassiness, crust, sauce, uppishness, uppityness. [*Compare* BACK TALK, FLAGRANCY.]

impudent *adj.* Rude and disrespectful; without shame ▸ assuming, assumptive, audacious, bald-faced, barefaced, blatant, bold, boldfaced, brash, brazen, brazenfaced, cheeky, contumelious, familiar, flippant, forward, impertinent, insolent, malapert, nervy, overconfident, pert, presuming, presumptuous, pushy, sassy, saucy, shameless, smart, snippy, unabashed, unblushing. *Informal:* brassy, flip, fresh, smart-alecky, snippety, uppish, uppity. *Slang:* snotty, wise. [*Compare* DISRESPECTFUL, FLAGRANT, OFFENSIVE, RUDE.]

impulse *n.* *—See* FANCY, STIMULUS.

impulsive *adj.* *—See* CAPRICIOUS, RASH[1], SPONTANEOUS.

impulsivity *n.* *—See* SPONTANEITY.

impure *adj.* 1. Not chaste or moral ▸ corrupted, debased, debauched, defiled, immoral, unchaste, unclean, uncleanly, unvirtuous. [*Compare* EVIL, IMPROPER, OBSCENE.] 2. Mixed with other substances ▸ adulterated, alloyed, blended, combined, contaminated, corrupted, cut, debased, diluted, dirty, doctored, infected, loaded, mixed, polluted, sophisticated, sullied, tainted, tampered with, vitiated. [*Compare* DIRTY.]

impurity *n.* *—See* CONTAMINANT, CONTAMINATION, CORRUPTION (1).

imputation *n.* An implied criticism ▸ reflection, slur. [*Compare* CRACK, LIBEL.] *—See also* ACCUSATION.

impute *v.* *—See* FIX (3).

in *adj.* *—See* FASHIONABLE.

inability *n.* Lack of ability or capacity ▸ incapability, incapacity, incompetence, incompetency, inefficiency, ineptitude, ineptness, powerlessness. [*Compare* DISADVANTAGE, FUTILITY, INEFFECTUALITY.]

inaccessible *adj.* 1. Unable to be reached ▸ inapproachable, unapproachable, unattainable, unavailable, unobtainable, unreachable. ***Idioms:*** beyond reach, out of reach, out of the way. [*Compare* DISTANT, REMOTE.] 2. Not accessible or handy ▸ inconvenient, unhandy. ***Idioms:*** beyond reach,

approachable. **—in′ac·ces′si·bil′i·ty** *n.* **—in′ac·ces′si·bly** *adv.*
in·ac·cu·rate (ĭn-ăk′yər-ĭt) ▸ *adj.* Mistaken or incorrect; not accurate. **—in·ac′cu·ra·cy** *n.* **—in·ac′cu·rate·ly** *adv.*
in·ac·tion (ĭn-ăk′shən) ▸ *n.* Lack or absence of action.
in·ac·ti·vate (ĭn-ăk′tə-vāt′) ▸ *v.* **-vat·ed, -vat·ing.** To render inactive. **—in·ac′ti·va′tion** *n.*
in·ac·tive (ĭn-ăk′tĭv) ▸ *adj.* 1. Not active or functioning; idle. 2. Retired from duty or service. **—in·ac′tive·ly** *adv.* **—in′ac·tiv′i·ty, in·ac′tive·ness** *n.*
in·ad·e·quate (ĭn-ăd′ĭ-kwĭt) ▸ *adj.* Not adequate; insufficient. **—in·ad′e·qua·cy** *n.* **—in·ad′e·quate·ly** *adv.*
in·ad·mis·si·ble (ĭn′əd-mĭs′ə-bəl) ▸ *adj.* Not admissible. **—in′ad·mis′si·bil′i·ty** *n.* **—in′ad·mis′si·bly** *adv.*
in·ad·ver·tent (ĭn′əd-vûr′tnt) ▸ *adj.* 1. Not duly attentive. 2. Unintentional. **—in′ad·ver′tence** *n.* **—in′ad·ver′tent·ly** *adv.*
in·ad·vis·a·ble (ĭn′əd-vī′zə-bəl) ▸ *adj.* Not recommended; unwise. **—in′ad·vis′a·bil′i·ty** *n.*
in·al·ien·a·ble (ĭn-āl′yə-nə-bəl, -ā′lē-ə-) ▸ *adj.* That cannot be transferred to another. **—in·al′ien·a·bil′i·ty** *n.* **—in·al′ien·a·bly** *adv.*
in·ane (ĭn-ān′) ▸ *adj.* **-an·er, -an·est.** Lacking sense or substance. **—in·ane′ly** *adv.* **—in·an′i·ty** (ĭ-năn′ĭ-tē) *n.*
in·an·i·mate (ĭn-ăn′ə-mĭt) ▸ *adj.* Lacking the qualities of active, living organisms; not animate. **—in·an′i·mate·ly** *adv.* **—in·an′i·mate·ness** *n.*
in·a·ni·tion (ĭn′ə-nĭsh′ən) ▸ *n.* Exhaustion, as from lack of nourishment or vitality.
in·ap·pli·ca·ble (ĭn-ăp′lĭ-kə-bəl, ĭn′ə-plĭk′ə-) ▸ *adj.* Not applicable. **—in·ap′pli·ca·bil′i·ty** *n.*
in·ap·pre·cia·ble (ĭn′ə-prē′shə-bəl) ▸ *adj.* Too small to be noticed; negligible. **—in′ap·pre′cia·bly** *adv.*
in·ap·pro·pri·ate (ĭn′ə-prō′prē-ĭt) ▸ *adj.* Unsuitable or improper; not appropriate. **—in′ap·pro′pri·ate·ly** *adv.* **—in′ap·pro′pri·ate·ness** *n.*
in·apt (ĭn-ăpt′) ▸ *adj.* Inappropriate. **—in·apt′ly** *adv.* **—in·apt′ness** *n.*
in·ar·tic·u·late (ĭn′är-tĭk′yə-lĭt) ▸ *adj.* 1. Uttered without the use of normal words or syllables. 2. Unable to speak; speechless. 3. Unable to speak with clarity or eloquence. 4. Going unexpressed: *inarticulate sorrow.* **—in′ar·tic′u·late·ly** *adv.* **—in′ar·tic′u·late·ness** *n.*
in·as·much as (ĭn′əz-mŭch′) ▸ *conj.* Because of the fact that; since.
in·at·ten·tion (ĭn′ə-tĕn′shən) ▸ *n.* Lack of attention, notice, or regard. **—in′at·ten′tive** *adj.* **—in′at·ten′tive·ly** *adv.* **—in′at·ten′tive·ness** *n.*
in·au·di·ble (ĭn-ô′də-bəl) ▸ *adj.* Impossible to hear. **—in·au′di·bil′i·ty** *n.* **—in·au′di·bly** *adv.*
in·au·gu·ral (ĭn-ô′gyər-əl) ▸ *adj.* 1. Of or relating to an inauguration. 2. Initial; first. ▸ *n.* An inaugural speech.
in·au·gu·rate (ĭn-ô′gyə-rāt′) ▸ *v.* **-rat·ed, -rat·ing.** 1. To induct into office by a formal ceremony. 2. To begin, esp. formally. 3. To open with a ceremony; dedicate. **—in·au′gu·ra′tor** *n.*
in·au·gu·ra·tion (ĭn-ô′gyə-rā′shən) ▸ *n.* 1. Formal induction into office. 2. A formal beginning or introduction.
in·aus·pi·cious (ĭn′ô-spĭsh′əs) ▸ *adj.* Not favorable; not auspicious. **—in′aus·pi′cious·ly** *adv.* **—in′aus·pi′cious·ness** *n.*
in·board (ĭn′bôrd′) ▸ *adj.* 1. Within the hull of a vessel. 2. Close to the fuselage of an aircraft: *the inboard engines.* **—in′board′** *adv.*
in·born (ĭn′bôrn′) ▸ *adj.* Hereditary; innate.
in·bound (ĭn′bound′) ▸ *adj.* Incoming: *inbound traffic.*
in·bred (ĭn′brĕd′) ▸ *adj.* 1. Produced by inbreeding. 2. Innate; deep-seated.
in·breed (ĭn′brēd′) ▸ *v.* To breed by the continued mating of closely related individuals. **—in′breed′er** *n.*
Inc. ▸ *abbr.* incorporated
In·ca (ĭng′kə) ▸ *n., pl.* **-ca** or **-cas.** 1. A member of a Quechuan people who established an empire centered in highland Peru before the Spanish conquest. 2. A ruler of the Inca empire. **—In′can** *adj.*
in·cal·cu·la·ble (ĭn-kăl′kyə-lə-bəl) ▸ *adj.* 1. Impossible to calculate, esp. too great to be conceived. 2. Unforeseeable; unpredictable. **—in·cal′cu·la·bly** *adv.*
in·can·des·cent (ĭn′kən-dĕs′ənt) ▸ *adj.* 1. Emitting visible light as a result of being heated. 2. Shining brilliantly; very bright. **—in′can·des′cence** *n.* **—in′can·des′cent·ly** *adv.*
incandescent lamp ▸ *n.* An electric lamp in which a filament is heated to incandescence by an electric current.
in·can·ta·tion (ĭn′kăn-tā′shən) ▸ *n.* 1. Ritual recitation of verbal charms or spells to produce a magic effect. 2. A charm or spell used in ritual recitation. **—in′can·ta′tion·al** *adj.* **—in·can′ta·to′ry** (-tə-tôr′ē) *adj.*
in·ca·pa·ble (ĭn-kā′pə-bəl) ▸ *adj.* Lacking the necessary ability, capacity, or power to perform adequately. **—in·ca′pa·bil′i·ty, in·ca′pa·ble·ness** *n.* **—in·ca′pa·bly** *adv.*
in·ca·pac·i·tate (ĭn′kə-păs′ĭ-tāt′) ▸ *v.* **-tat·ed, -tat·ing.** To deprive of strength or ability; disable. **—in′ca·pac′i·ta′tion** *n.*
in·ca·pac·i·ty (ĭn′kə-păs′ĭ-tē) ▸ *n., pl.* **-ties.** Inadequate capacity, strength, or ability.
in·car·cer·ate (ĭn-kär′sə-rāt′) ▸ *v.* **-at·ed, -at·ing.** 1. To imprison. 2. To confine. **—in·car′cer·a′tion** *n.*
in·car·nate (ĭn-kär′nĭt) ▸ *adj.* 1. Invested with bodily nature and form. 2. Personified: *evil incarnate.* ▸ *v.* (-nāt′) **-nat·ed, -nat·ing.** 1. To give bodily, esp. human, form to. 2. To personify; embody.
in·car·na·tion (ĭn′kär-nā′shən) ▸ *n.* 1. The act of incarnating

THESAURUS

out of reach, out of the way. [*Compare* AWKWARD.] *—See also* COOL.
inaccuracy *n.* *—See* ERROR.
inaccurate *adj.* *—See* ERRONEOUS.
inaction *n.* A lack of action or activity ▸ idleness, inactivity, inertness, inoperativeness, lifelessness, sedentariness, stagnation, vegetation. [*Compare* ABEYANCE, LAZINESS, STILLNESS.]
inactive *adj.* *—See* IDLE (1), LATENT.
inadequacy *n.* *—See* INEFFECTUALITY, SHORTAGE.
inadequate *adj.* *—See* BAD (1), DEFICIENT, DISAPPOINTING, INEFFECTUAL (2), INEFFICIENT, INSUFFICIENT.
inadmissible *adj.* *—See* OBJECTIONABLE.
inadvertent *adj.* *—See* ACCIDENTAL, CARELESS, UNINTENTIONAL.
inadvisable *adj.* *—See* UNWISE.
inalterable *adj.* *—See* IMMUTABLE.
inane *adj.* *—See* FOOLISH, VACANT.
inanimate *adj.* Completely lacking sensation or consciousness ▸ dead, insensate, insentient, lifeless. [*Compare* DEAD.]
inanity *n.* *—See* EMPTINESS (2), FOOLISHNESS.
inapplicable *adj.* *—See* IRRELEVANT.
inapposite *adj.* *—See* IRRELEVANT.
inappreciable *adj.* *—See* IMPERCEPTIBLE (1).
inapproachable *adj.* *—See* INACCESSIBLE (1).
inappropriate *adj.* *—See* IMPROPER (2), UNFORTUNATE (2).
inappropriateness *n.* *—See* IMPROPRIETY (1).
inapt *adj.* *—See* IMPROPER (2), INEFFICIENT.
inarguable *adj.* *—See* CERTAIN (2).
inarticulate *adj.* *—See* MUTE, SPEECHLESS.
inasmuch as *conj.* *—See* BECAUSE.
inattentive *adj.* *—See* ABSENT-MINDED, CARELESS.
inaudible *adj.* *—See* SILENT (1).
inaugural *n.* *—See* INITIATION.
inaugural *adj.* *—See* BEGINNING, FIRST.
inaugurate *v.* *—See* INITIATE, START (1).
inauguration *n.* *—See* BEGINNING, INITIATION.
inauspicious *adj.* *—See* BLEAK (2), FATEFUL (1).
in-between *adj.* *—See* MIDDLE.
inborn *adj.* *—See* CONSTITUTIONAL, INNATE, INSTINCTIVE.
inbred *adj.* *—See* CONSTITUTIONAL.
incalculable *adj.* Too great to be calculated ▸ boundless, countless, immeasurable, incomputable, inestimable, infinite, innumerable, measureless, uncountable, unfathomable, unlimited. [*Compare* ENDLESS.]
incandesce *v.* To shine brightly and steadily but without a flame ▸ gleam, glow, luminesce. *—See also* BEAM.
incandescent *adj.* *—See* BRIGHT.
incantation *n.* *—See* SPELL².
incapability *n.* *—See* INABILITY, INEFFECTUALITY.
incapable *adj.* *—See* INEFFECTUAL (2), INEFFICIENT.
incapacitate *v.* *—See* DISABLE (1).
incapacitation *n.* *—See* DEBILITATION.
incapacity *n.* *—See* INABILITY.
incarcerate *v.* *—See* IMPRISON.
incarceration *n.* *—See* DETENTION.
incarnate *v.* *—See* EMBODY (1).
incarnate *adj.* *—See* BODILY.
incarnation *n.* *—See* EMBODIMENT.

or condition of being incarnated. 2. **Incarnation** The Christian doctrine that God the Son became man. 3. One who personifies something.

in·case (ĭn-kās′) ► *v.* Var. of **encase.**

in·cau·tious (ĭn-kô′shəs) ► *adj.* Not cautious; rash. **—in·cau′tious·ly** *adv.* **—in·cau′tious·ness** *n.*

in·cen·di·ar·y (ĭn-sĕn′dē-ĕr′ē) ► *adj.* 1. Producing intensely hot fire, as a military weapon. 2. Of or involving arson. 3. Tending to inflame; inflammatory. **—in·cen′di·ar′y** *n.*

in·cense[1] (ĭn-sĕns′) ► *v.* **-censed, -cens·ing.** To cause to be extremely angry; infuriate.

in·cense[2] (ĭn′sĕns′) ► *n.* 1. An aromatic substance burned to produce a pleasant odor. 2. The smoke or odor produced by the burning of incense.

in·cen·tive (ĭn-sĕn′tĭv) ► *n.* Something, such as a punishment or reward, that induces action.

in·cep·tion (ĭn-sĕp′shən) ► *n.* The beginning of something. **—in·cep′tive** *adj.*

in·cer·ti·tude (ĭn-sûr′tĭ-to͞od′, -tyo͞od′) ► *n.* 1. Uncertainty. 2. Insecurity or instability.

in·ces·sant (ĭn-sĕs′ənt) ► *adj.* Continuing without interruption. **—in·ces′san·cy** *n.* **—in·ces′sant·ly** *adv.*

in·cest (ĭn′sĕst′) ► *n.* Sexual relations between persons so closely related that their marriage is illegal or forbidden by custom. **—in·ces′tu·ous** (ĭn-sĕs′cho͞o-əs) *adj.* **—in·ces′tu·ous·ly** *adv.* **—in·ces′tu·ous·ness** *n.*

inch (ĭnch) ► *n.* 1. See **measurement** table in Appendix. 2. A very small degree or amount: *won't budge an inch.* ► *v.* To move or cause to move slowly or by small degrees. ***—idiom:* every inch** In every respect; entirely.

in·cho·ate (ĭn-kō′ĭt) ► *adj.* In an initial or early stage; incipient. **—in·cho′ate·ly** *adv.* **—in·cho′ate·ness** *n.*

inch·worm (ĭnch′wûrm′) ► *n.* See **measuring worm.**

in·ci·dence (ĭn′sĭ-dəns) ► *n.* Extent or frequency of occurrence.

in·ci·dent (ĭn′sĭ-dənt) ► *n.* 1. An occurrence; event. 2. An event that causes a crisis. ► *adj.* 1. Tending to arise or occur as a result. 2. *Phys.* Striking a surface: *incident radiation.*

in·ci·den·tal (ĭn′sĭ-dĕn′tl) ► *adj.* 1. Occurring or likely to occur as a minor consequence. 2. Of a minor or casual nature: *incidental expenses.* ► *n.* A minor accompanying item or expense. **—in′ci·den′tal·ly** *adv.*

in·cin·er·ate (ĭn-sĭn′ə-rāt′) ► *v.* **-at·ed, -at·ing.** To consume by fire; burn to ashes. **—in·cin′er·a′tion** *n.*

in·cin·er·a·tor (ĭn-sĭn′ə-rā′tər) ► *n.* An apparatus for burning waste.

in·cip·i·ent (ĭn-sĭp′ē-ənt) ► *adj.* Beginning to exist or appear. **—in·cip′i·en·cy, in·cip′i·ence** *n.* **—in·cip′i·ent·ly** *adv.*

in·cise (ĭn-sīz′) ► *v.* **-cised, -cis·ing.** 1. To cut into or mark with a sharp instrument. 2. To engrave (e.g., designs) into a surface; carve.

in·ci·sion (ĭn-sĭzh′ən) ► *n.* 1. The act of incising. 2. A cut, esp. a surgical cut into soft tissue.

in·ci·sive (ĭn-sī′sĭv) ► *adj.* Penetrating, clear, and sharp: *incisive comments.* **—in·ci′sive·ly** *adv.* **—in·ci′sive·ness** *n.*

in·ci·sor (ĭn-sī′zər) ► *n.* A tooth adapted for cutting or gnawing, located at the apex of the dental arch.

in·cite (ĭn-sīt′) ► *v.* **-cit·ed, -cit·ing.** To provoke to action; stir up: *incite a mob.* **—in·cite′ment** *n.* **—in·cit′er** *n.*

in·ci·vil·i·ty (ĭn′sĭ-vĭl′ĭ-tē) ► *n., pl.* **-ties.** Rudeness.

incl. ► *abbr.* 1. including 2. inclusive

in·clem·ent (ĭn-klĕm′ənt) ► *adj.* 1. Stormy: *inclement weather.* 2. Unmerciful. **—in·clem′en·cy** *n.* **—in·clem′ent·ly** *adv.*

in·cli·na·tion (ĭn′klə-nā′shən) ► *n.* 1. A bend or tilt. 2a. A slant: *the inclination of the roof.* b. An incline; slope. 3. A tendency or disposition toward something.

in·cline (ĭn-klīn′) ► *v.* **-clined, -clin·ing.** 1. To deviate or cause to deviate from the horizontal or vertical. 2. To dispose or be disposed; tend. 3. To lower or bend (the head or body), as in a nod or bow. ► *n.* (ĭn′klīn′) An inclined surface; slope. **—in·clin′er** *n.*

in·clined plane (ĭn-klīnd′) ► *n.* A plane set at an angle to the horizontal, esp. a simple machine used in raising or lowering loads.

in·close (ĭn-klōz′) ► *v.* Var. of **enclose.**

in·clude (ĭn-klo͞od′) ► *v.* **-clud·ed, -clud·ing.** 1. To have as a part, element, or member; contain. 2. To place into a group, class, or total. **—in·clu′sion** *n.* **—in·clu′sive** *adj.* **—in·clu′sive·ly** *adv.* **—in·clu′sive·ness** *n.*

in·cog·ni·to (ĭn′kŏg-nē′tō, ĭn-kŏg′nĭ-tō′) ► *adv. & adj.* With one's identity disguised or concealed.

in·co·her·ent (ĭn′kō-hîr′ənt) ► *adj.* 1. Lacking cohesion; not coherent. 2. Unable to express one's thoughts in an orderly manner. **—in′co·her′ence** *n.* **—in′co·her′ent·ly** *adv.*

in·com·bus·ti·ble (ĭn′kəm-bŭs′tə-bəl) ► *adj.* Incapable of burning. **—in′com·bus′ti·bil′i·ty** *n.* **—in′com·bus′ti·ble** *n.* **—in′com·bus′ti·bly** *adv.*

in·come (ĭn′kŭm′) ► *n.* The amount of money or its equivalent received in exchange for labor or services, from the sale of goods or property, or as profit from investments.

income tax ► *n.* A tax levied on net income.

in·com·ing (ĭn′kŭm′ĭng) ► *adj.* Coming in or about to come in.

in·com·men·su·rate (ĭn′kə-mĕn′sər-ĭt, -shər-) ► *adj.* 1. Not commensurate; disproportionate. 2. Inadequate. **—in′com·men′su·rate·ly** *adv.*

in·com·mode (ĭn′kə-mōd′) ► *v.* **-mod·ed, -mod·ing.** To inconvenience; disturb.

THESAURUS

incautious *adj.* —*See* RASH[1].

incautiousness *n.* —*See* TEMERITY.

incendiary *n.* —*See* AGITATOR.

incense *v.* —*See* ANGER (1).

incentive *n.* —*See* STIMULUS.

inception *n.* —*See* BEGINNING, BIRTH (2).

inceptive *adj.* —*See* BEGINNING.

incertitude *n.* —*See* DOUBT.

incessant *adj.* —*See* CONTINUAL.

inch *v.* To advance slowly ► crawl, creep, drag, poke. ***Idiom:*** go at a snail's pace. [*Compare* TRUDGE.]

inchoate *adj.* —*See* SHAPELESS.

incident *n.* —*See* CIRCUMSTANCE (1), EVENT (1).

incidental *adj.* Not part of the real or essential nature of a thing ► adscititious, adventitious, inessential, supervenient. [*Compare* IRRELEVANT, UNNECESSARY.] —*See also* ACCIDENTAL.

incidentals *n.* —*See* ODDS AND ENDS.

incinerate *v.* —*See* BURN (1).

incipience or **incipiency** *n.* —*See* BEGINNING.

incipient *adj.* —*See* BEGINNING.

incise *v.* —*See* CUT (1), ENGRAVE (1).

incision *n.* —*See* CUT (1).

incisive *adj.* —*See* CRITICAL (2).

incisiveness *n.* —*See* EDGE.

incite *v.* —*See* PROVOKE.

incitement or **incitation** *n.* —*See* PROVOCATION (1).

inciter *n.* —*See* AGITATOR.

incivility *n.* —*See* IMPUDENCE, INDIGNITY.

inclement *adj.* —*See* BLEAK (1).

inclination *n.* 1. A natural or habitual preference for something ► affinity, bent, bias, cast, disposition, leaning, partiality, penchant, predilection, predisposition, prejudice, proclivity, proneness, propensity, tendency, trend, urge, turn. [*Compare* FANCY, LIKING, LOVE.] 2. Deviation from a particular direction ► cant, grade, gradient, heel, incline, lean, list, rake, slant, slope, tilt, tip. [*Compare* BEND, HILL.]

incline *v.* To depart or cause to depart from true vertical or horizontal ► cant, heel, lean, list, rake, slant, slope, tilt, tip. [*Compare* BEND, TURN.] —*See also* INFLUENCE, TEND[1].

incline *n.* —*See* INCLINATION (2).

inclined *adj.* Having or showing a tendency or likelihood ► apt, disposed, given, liable, likely, predisposed, prone, tending, wont. —*See also* OBLIQUE.

inclined plane *n.* —*See* ASCENT (2).

include *v.* To construct as an integral part ► build in, incorporate, integrate. —*See also* CONTAIN (1).

inclusive *adj.* —*See* GENERAL (2).

incombustible *adj.* —*See* FIREPROOF.

income *n.* —*See* LIVING.

incoming *n.* —*See* ENTRANCE[1].

incommode *v.* —*See* INCONVENIENCE.

incommodious *adj.* Causing difficulty, trouble, or discomfort ► difficult, inconvenient, troublesome. [*Compare* AWKWARD, DISTURBING.]

incommodiousness *n.* The state or quality of being inconvenient ► discomfort, incommodity, inconvenience, trouble. [*Compare* BOTHER.]

incommodity *n.* 1. The state or quality of being inconvenient ► discomfort, incommodiousness, inconvenience, trouble. [*Compare* BOTHER.] 2. Something that causes difficulty, trouble, or lack of ease ► discomfort, discommodity, inconvenience. [*Compare* ANNOYANCE.]

in·com·mu·ni·ca·do (ĭn′kə-myo͞o′nĭ-kä′dō) ► *adv.* & *adj.* Without the means or right of communicating with others.

in·com·pa·ra·ble (ĭn-kŏm′pər-ə-bəl) ► *adj.* **1.** Being such that comparison is impossible. **2.** Beyond comparison; unsurpassed. **—in·com′pa·ra·bil′i·ty, in·com′pa·ra·ble·ness** *n.* **—in·com′pa·ra·bly** *adv.*

in·com·pat·i·ble (ĭn′kəm-păt′ə-bəl) ► *adj.* **1.** Not compatible; not in harmony or agreement. **2.** Inconsistent. **—in′com·pat′i·bil′i·ty** *n.* **—in′com·pat′i·bly** *adv.*

in·com·pe·tent (ĭn-kŏm′pĭ-tənt) ► *adj.* Not competent. **—in·com′pe·tence, in·com′pe·ten·cy** *n.* **—in·com′pe·tent** *n.* **—in·com′pe·tent·ly** *adv.*

in·com·plete (ĭn′kəm-plēt′) ► *adj.* Not complete. **—in′com·plete′ly** *adv.* **—in′com·plete′ness, in′com·ple′tion** *n.*

in·com·pre·hen·si·ble (ĭn′kŏm-prĭ-hĕn′sə-bəl, ĭn-kŏm′-) ► *adj.* Impossible to understand; unintelligible. **—in′com·pre·hen′si·bil′i·ty** *n.* **—in′com·pre·hen′si·bly** *adv.* **—in′com·pre·hen′sion** *n.*

in·com·press·i·ble (ĭn′kəm-prĕs′ə-bəl) ► *adj.* Impossible to compress. **—in′com·press′i·bil′i·ty** *n.*

in·con·ceiv·a·ble (ĭn′kən-sē′və-bəl) ► *adj.* **1.** Impossible to comprehend or grasp fully. **2.** Implausible; incredible. **—in′con·ceiv′a·bil′i·ty** *n.* **—in′con·ceiv′a·bly** *adv.*

in·con·clu·sive (ĭn′kən-klo͞o′sĭv) ► *adj.* Not conclusive. **—in′con·clu′sive·ly** *adv.* **—in′con·clu′sive·ness** *n.*

in·con·gru·ent (ĭn-kŏng′gro͞o-ənt, ĭn′kŏn-gro͞o′ənt) ► *adj.* Not congruent. **—in·con′gru·ence** *n.* **—in·con′gru·ent·ly** *adv.*

in·con·gru·ous (ĭn-kŏng′gro͞o-əs) ► *adj.* **1.** Lacking in harmony; incompatible. **2.** Not in keeping with what is correct, proper, or logical; inappropriate. **—in′con·gru′i·ty** (ĭn′kŏn-gro͞o′ĭ-tē) *n.* **—in·con′gru·ous·ly** *adv.* **—in·con′gru·ous·ness** *n.*

in·con·se·quen·tial (ĭn-kŏn′sĭ-kwĕn′shəl, ĭn′kŏn-) ► *adj.* Lacking importance. **—in·con′se·quence** (-kwəns) *n.* **—in·con′se·quen′ti·al′i·ty** (-kwĕn′shē-ăl′ĭ-tē) *n.* **—in·con′se·quen′tial·ly** *adv.*

in·con·sid·er·a·ble (ĭn′kən-sĭd′ər-ə-bəl) ► *adj.* Trivial. **—in′con·sid′er·a·bly** *adv.*

in·con·sid·er·ate (ĭn′kən-sĭd′ər-ĭt) ► *adj.* **1.** Thoughtless of others. **2.** Ill-considered. **—in′con·sid′er·ate·ly** *adv.* **—in′con·sid′er·ate·ness** *n.*

in·con·sis·tent (ĭn′kən-sĭs′tənt) ► *adj.* Displaying a lack of consistency, esp. erratic, contradictory, or incompatible. **—in′con·sis′ten·cy** *n.* **—in′con·sis′tent·ly** *adv.*

in·con·sol·a·ble (ĭn′kən-sō′lə-bəl) ► *adj.* Impossible to console; forlorn. **—in′con·sol′a·bil′i·ty** *n.* **—in′con·sol′a·bly** *adv.*

in·con·spic·u·ous (ĭn′kən-spĭk′yo͞o-əs) ► *adj.* Not readily noticeable. **—in′con·spic′u·ous·ly** *adv.* **—in′con·spic′u·ous·ness** *n.*

in·con·stant (ĭn-kŏn′stənt) ► *adj.* **1.** Changing, esp. often and erratically. **2.** Fickle. **—in·con′stan·cy** *n.* **—in·con′stant·ly** *adv.*

in·con·test·a·ble (ĭn′kən-tĕs′tə-bəl) ► *adj.* Beyond dispute; unquestionable. **—in′con·test′a·bil′i·ty** *n.* **—in′con·test′a·bly** *adv.*

in·con·ti·nent (ĭn-kŏn′tə-nənt) ► *adj.* **1.** Not restrained. **2.** Lacking normal voluntary control of excretory functions. **—in·con′ti·nence** *n.* **—in·con′ti·nent·ly** *adv.*

in·con·tro·vert·i·ble (ĭn-kŏn′trə-vûr′tə-bəl, ĭn′kŏn-) ► *adj.* Impossible to dispute; unquestionable. **—in·con′tro·vert′i·bil′i·ty** *n.* **—in·con′tro·vert′i·bly** *adv.*

in·con·ven·ience (ĭn′kən-vēn′yəns) ► *n.* **1.** The state or quality of being inconvenient. **2.** Something inconvenient. ► *v.* **-ienced, -ienc·ing.** To cause inconvenience to.

in·con·ven·ient (ĭn′kən-vēn′yənt) ► *adj.* Not convenient, esp.: **a.** Not accessible. **b.** Not suited to one's purpose or needs. **c.** Inopportune. **—in′con·ven′ient·ly** *adv.*

in·cor·po·rate (ĭn-kôr′pə-rāt′) ► *v.* **-rat·ed, -rat·ing. 1.** To unite or combine (one thing) with something else. **2.** To form or cause to form into a legal corporation. **3.** To give material form to; embody. **—in·cor′po·ra′tion** *n.* **—in·cor′po·ra′tive** *adj.* **—in·cor′po·ra′tor** *n.*

in·cor·po·re·al (ĭn′kôr-pôr′ē-əl) ► *adj.* Lacking material form or substance. **—in′cor·po′re·al′i·ty** (-ăl′ĭ-tē) *n.*

in·cor·rect (ĭn′kə-rĕkt′) ► *adj.* **1.** Not correct; erroneous. **2.** Improper; inappropriate. **—in′cor·rect′ly** *adv.* **—in′cor·rect′ness** *n.*

in·cor·ri·gi·ble (ĭn-kôr′ĭ-jə-bəl, -kŏr′-) ► *adj.* Incapable of being corrected or reformed. **—in·cor′ri·gi·bil′i·ty, in·cor′ri·gi·ble·ness** *n.* **—in·cor′ri·gi·bly** *adv.*

in·cor·rupt·i·ble (ĭn′kə-rŭp′tə-bəl) ► *adj.* **1.** Incapable of being morally corrupted. **2.** Not subject to decay. **—in′cor·rupt′i·bil′i·ty** *n.* **—in′cor·rupt′i·bly** *adv.*

THESAURUS

incommunicative *adj.* —*See* TACITURN.
incomparability *n.* —*See* EXCELLENCE.
incomparable *adj.* —*See* UNIQUE.
incompatibility *n.* —*See* GAP (3).
incompatible *adj.* —*See* DISCREPANT, INCONGRUOUS, OPPOSITE.
incompetence or **incompetency** *n.* —*See* INABILITY.
incompetent *adj.* —*See* INEFFICIENT.
incomplete *adj.* —*See* DEFICIENT, PARTIAL (1), ROUGH (4).
incompliance or **incompliancy** *n.* —*See* STUBBORNNESS.
incompliant *adj.* —*See* STUBBORN (1).
incomprehensible *adj.* Incapable of being grasped by the intellect or understanding ► impenetrable, inscrutable, uncomprehensible, unfathomable, unintelligible. [*Compare* COMPLEX, DEEP, MYSTERIOUS.]
incompressible *adj.* Unyielding to pressure ► firm, hard, solid.
incomputable *adj.* —*See* INCALCULABLE.
inconceivable *adj.* —*See* IMPLAUSIBLE, INCREDIBLE.
inconclusive *adj.* —*See* AMBIGUOUS (1).
incongruent *adj.* —*See* DISCREPANT, INCONGRUOUS.
incongruity *n.* —*See* GAP (3), IMPROPRIETY (1), INEQUALITY (1).
incongruous *adj.* Made up of parts or qualities that are disparate or otherwise markedly lacking in consistency ► conflicting, discordant, discrepant, dissonant, incompatible, incongruent, inconsistent, inconsonant, irregular, jarring, mismatched. [*Compare* INHARMONIOUS, OPPOSITE.] —*See also* DISCREPANT, IMPROPER (2).
inconsequence *n.* —*See* TRIFLE.
inconsequent or **inconsequential** *adj.* —*See* TRIVIAL.
inconsiderable *adj.* —*See* TRIVIAL.
inconsiderableness *n.* —*See* TRIFLE.
inconsiderate *adj.* —*See* THOUGHTLESS.
inconsideration or **inconsiderateness** *n.* —*See* THOUGHTLESSNESS (2).
inconsistency *n.* —*See* GAP (3), INSTABILITY.
inconsistent *adj.* —*See* CAPRICIOUS, DISCREPANT, FALLACIOUS (1), INCONGRUOUS, UNEVEN.
inconsonant *adj.* —*See* INCONGRUOUS, INHARMONIOUS (1).
inconspicuous *adj.* Not readily noticed or seen ► obscure, unassuming, unconspicuous, undistinguished, unnoticeable, unobtrusive. *Idiom:* having (*or* keeping) a low profile. [*Compare* HIDDEN, MODEST, SECLUDED.]
inconstant *adj.* —*See* CAPRICIOUS, CHANGEABLE (1).
incontestable *adj.* —*See* CERTAIN (2).
incontinence *n.* —*See* ABANDON (1).
incontrovertible *adj.* —*See* CERTAIN (2).
inconvenience *n.* **1.** The state or quality of being inconvenient ► discomfort, incommodiousness, incommodity, trouble. [*Compare* BOTHER.] **2.** Something that causes difficulty, trouble, or lack of ease ► discomfort, discommodity, incommodity. [*Compare* ANNOYANCE.] —*See also* DISADVANTAGE.
inconvenience *v.* To cause inconvenience for ► discomfort, discommode, impose on (*or* upon), incommode, put out, trouble. [*Compare* ANNOY.]
inconvenient *adj.* **1.** Not accessible or handy ► inaccessible, unhandy. *Idioms:* beyond reach, out of reach, out of the way. [*Compare* AWKWARD, REMOTE.] **2.** Causing difficulty, trouble, or discomfort ► difficult, incommodious, troublesome. [*Compare* DISTURBING.] **3.** Not occurring at a favorable time ► ill-timed, inopportune, mistimed, untimely. [*Compare* FATEFUL.]
incorporate *v.* **1.** To construct as an integral part ► build, include, integrate. **2.** To make a part of a united whole ► combine, embody, integrate. —*See also* ABSORB (2), ASSOCIATE (1).
incorporated *adj.* —*See* BUILT-IN.
incorporation *n.* —*See* ABSORPTION (1), COMBINATION, EMBODIMENT.
incorporeal *adj.* —*See* IMMATERIAL.
incorrect *adj.* —*See* ERRONEOUS, IMPROPER (2).
incorrectness *n.* —*See* ERROR, IMPROPRIETY (1).
incorrigible *adj.* —*See* CONFIRMED (1).
incorruptibility *n.* —*See* HONESTY.
incorruptible *adj.* —*See* HONEST.

in·crease (ĭn-krēs′) ► *v.* **-creased, -creas·ing.** 1. To make or become greater or larger. 2. To multiply; reproduce. ► *n.* (ĭn′krēs′) 1. The act of increasing. 2. The amount or rate by which something is increased. **—in·creas′ing·ly** *adv.*

in·cred·i·ble (ĭn-krĕd′ə-bəl) ► *adj.* 1. So implausible as to elicit disbelief. 2. Astonishing. **—in·cred′i·bil′i·ty, in·cred′i·ble·ness** *n.* **—in·cred′i·bly** *adv.*

in·cred·u·lous (ĭn-krĕj′ə-ləs) ► *adj.* 1. Skeptical; disbelieving. 2. Expressive of disbelief. **—in′cre·du′li·ty** (ĭn′krĭ-dōō′lĭ-tē, -dyōō′-) *n.* **—in·cred′u·lous·ly** *adv.* **—in·cred′u·lous·ness** *n.*

in·cre·ment (ĭn′krə-mənt, ĭng′-) ► *n.* 1. The process of increasing. 2. Something added or gained, esp. one of a series of regular, usu. small additions. **—in′cre·men′tal** (-mĕn′tl) *adj.* **—in′cre·men′tal·ly** *adv.*

in·crim·i·nate (ĭn-krĭm′ə-nāt′) ► *v.* **-nat·ed, -nat·ing.** To accuse of or implicate in a crime or other wrongful act. **—in·crim′i·na′tion** *n.* **—in·crim′i·na·to′ry** (-nə-tôr′ē) *adj.*

in·crust (ĭn-krŭst′) ► *v.* Var. of **encrust.**

in·cu·bate (ĭn′kyə-bāt′, ĭng′-) ► *v.* **-bat·ed, -bat·ing.** 1. To warm (eggs) esp. with the body to promote hatching. 2. To maintain at optimal environmental conditions for development. **—in′cu·ba′tion** *n.*

in·cu·ba·tor (ĭn′kyə-bā′tər, ĭng′-) ► *n.* 1. An apparatus in which environmental conditions, such as temperature and humidity, can be controlled, used for incubating or culturing. 2. An apparatus for maintaining a young or premature infant in an environment of controlled temperature, humidity, and oxygen.

in·cu·bus (ĭn′kyə-bəs, ĭng′-) ► *n., pl.* **-bus·es** or **-bi** (-bī′). 1. An evil spirit believed to violate sleeping women. 2. An oppressive nightmare.

in·cul·cate (ĭn-kŭl′kāt′, ĭn′kŭl-) ► *v.* **-cat·ed, -cat·ing.** To teach or impress by frequent instruction or repetition; instill. **—in′cul·ca′tion** *n.* **—in·cul′ca′tor** *n.*

in·cul·pa·ble (ĭn-kŭl′pə-bəl) ► *adj.* Free of guilt; blameless.

in·cul·pate (ĭn-kŭl′pāt′, ĭn′kŭl-) ► *v.* **-pat·ed, -pat·ing.** To incriminate. **—in′cul·pa′tion** *n.*

in·cum·bent (ĭn-kŭm′bənt) ► *adj.* 1. Imposed as an obligation or duty; obligatory. 2. Lying, leaning, or resting on something else. 3. Currently holding a specified office. ► *n.* A person who holds an office. **—in·cum′ben·cy** *n.*

in·cu·nab·u·lum (ĭn′kyə-năb′yə-ləm, ĭng′-) ► *n., pl.* **-la** (-lə). A book printed before 1501.

in·cur (ĭn-kûr′) ► *v.* **-curred, -cur·ring.** 1. To acquire or come into; sustain: *incurred substantial losses.* 2. To become liable or subject to as a result of one's actions; bring upon oneself.

in·cur·a·ble (ĭn-kyŏŏr′ə-bəl) ► *adj.* 1. Impossible to cure. 2. Inveterate: *an incurable optimist.* **—in·cur′a·bil′i·ty** *n.* **—in·cur′a·ble** *n.* **—in·cur′a·bly** *adv.*

in·cu·ri·ous (ĭn-kyŏŏr′ē-əs) ► *adj.* Lacking curiosity. **—in·cu′ri·ous·ly** *adv.*

in·cur·sion (ĭn-kûr′zhən, -shən) ► *n.* A raid or invasion.

in·cus (ĭng′kəs) ► *n., pl.* **in·cu·des** (ĭng-kyōō′dēz). An anvil-shaped bone in the middle ear.

Ind. ► *abbr.* Indiana

in·debt·ed (ĭn-dĕt′ĭd) ► *adj.* Obligated to another; beholden. **—in·debt′ed·ness** *n.*

in·de·cent (ĭn-dē′sənt) ► *adj.* 1. Offensive to good taste. 2. Morally offensive. **—in·de′cen·cy** *n.* **—in·de′cent·ly** *adv.*

in·de·ci·pher·a·ble (ĭn′dĭ-sī′fər-ə-bəl) ► *adj.* Impossible to decipher. **—in′de·ci′pher·a·bil′i·ty** *n.* **—in′de·ci′pher·a·bly** *adv.*

in·de·ci·sion (ĭn′dĭ-sĭzh′ən) ► *n.* Inability to make up one's mind; irresolution.

in·de·ci·sive (ĭn′dĭ-sī′sĭv) ► *adj.* 1. Characterized by indecision. 2. Inconclusive. **—in′de·ci′sive·ly** *adv.* **—in′de·ci′sive·ness** *n.*

in·dec·o·rous (ĭn-dĕk′ər-əs) ► *adj.* Lacking propriety or good taste. **—in·dec′o·rous·ly** *adv.* **—in·dec′o·rous·ness** *n.*

in·deed (ĭn-dēd′) ► *adv.* 1. Without a doubt; certainly. 2. In fact; in reality. ► *interj.* Used to express surprise, skepticism, or irony.

indef. ► *abbr.* indefinite

in·de·fat·i·ga·ble (ĭn′dĭ-făt′ĭ-gə-bəl) ► *adj.* Untiring. **—in′de·fat′i·ga·bil′i·ty** *n.* **—in′de·fat′i·ga·bly** *adv.*

in·de·fen·si·ble (ĭn′dĭ-fĕn′sə-bəl) ► *adj.* 1. Inexcusable; unpardonable. 2. Invalid; untenable. 3. Not capable of being defended. **—in′de·fen′si·bly** *adv.*

in·de·fin·a·ble (ĭn′dĭ-fī′nə-bəl) ► *adj.* Impossible to define, describe, or analyze. **—in′de·fin′a·bil′i·ty** *n.* **—in′de·fin′a·bly** *adv.*

in·def·i·nite (ĭn-dĕf′ə-nĭt) ► *adj.* 1. Unclear; vague. 2. Lack-

THESAURUS

increase *v.* To make or become greater or larger ► aggrandize, amplify, augment, blow up, boost, build, build up, burgeon, develop, enlarge, escalate, exaggerate, expand, extend, grow, magnify, mount, multiply, proliferate, ratchet up, rise, rocket, run up, skyrocket, snowball, soar, step up, surge, swell, upsurge, wax. *Informal:* beef up. [*Compare* ADVANCE, BROADEN, ELEVATE, RAISE.] —*See also* BREED.

increase *n.* 1. The act of increasing or rising ► aggrandizement, amplification, augment, augmentation, boost, buildup, burgeoning, enlargement, escalation, expansion, extension, growth, hike, jump, magnification, multiplication, proliferation, raise, rise, snowballing, soaring, swell, upsurge, upswing, upturn. [*Compare* ADVANCEMENT, PROGRESS.] 2. The amount by which something is increased ► advance, boost, hike, increment, jump, raise, rise.

incredible *adj.* Not to be believed ► far-fetched, inconceivable, unbelievable, unimaginable, unthinkable. *Idioms:* beyond belief, contrary to all reason. [*Compare* DOUBTFUL, OUTRAGEOUS.] —*See also* ASTONISHING, IMPLAUSIBLE.

incredibly *adv.* —*See* UNUSUALLY.

incredulity *n.* —*See* DISBELIEF.

incredulous *adj.* Refusing or reluctant to believe ► disbelieving, dubious, questioning, skeptical, unbelieving, unconvinced. [*Compare* DISTRUSTFUL, DOUBTFUL.]

incredulousness *n.* —*See* DISBELIEF.

increment *n.* —*See* INCREASE (2).

incriminate *v.* To cause to appear involved in or guilty of a crime or fault ► criminate, implicate, inculpate. [*Compare* ACCUSE.] —*See also* ACCUSE.

incriminating *adj.* —*See* ACCUSATORIAL, INSINUATING.

incrimination *n.* —*See* ACCUSATION.

incriminatory *adj.* —*See* ACCUSATORIAL.

inculcate *v.* —*See* INDOCTRINATE (1), INSTILL.

inculpable *adj.* —*See* INNOCENT (2).

inculpate *v.* To cause to appear involved in or guilty of a crime or fault ► criminate, implicate, incriminate. [*Compare* ACCUSE.] —*See also* ACCUSE.

inculpation *n.* —*See* ACCUSATION.

inculpatory *adj.* —*See* ACCUSATORIAL.

incumbency *n.* The holding of a position ► occupancy, occupation, tenure. [*Compare* PERIOD.]

incur *v.* —*See* ASSUME, CONTRACT (2), DEVELOP (1).

incurable *adj.* —*See* CONFIRMED (1), HOPELESS.

incuriosity *n.* —*See* APATHY.

incurious *adj.* —*See* APATHETIC, DETACHED (1).

incuriousness *n.* —*See* APATHY.

incursion *n.* An act of invading, especially by military forces ► foray, inroad, invasion, raid. [*Compare* ATTACK.]

indebted *adj.* —*See* OBLIGED (1).

indebtedness *n.* —*See* DEBT (1), DEBT (2).

indecency *n.* —*See* IMPROPRIETY (1), IMPROPRIETY (2).

indecent *adj.* —*See* IMPROPER (1), OBSCENE.

indecision *n.* —*See* HESITATION.

indecisive *adj.* —*See* AMBIGUOUS (1), HESITANT.

indecisiveness *n.* —*See* HESITATION.

indecorous *adj.* —*See* IMPROPER (1).

indecorum *n.* An improper act or statement ► impropriety, indecency, indelicacy. —*See also* IMPROPRIETY (2).

indeed *adv.* In point of fact ► actually, really. —*See also* EVEN (2), REALLY, YES.

indefatigable *adj.* —*See* TIRELESS.

indefectible *adj.* —*See* PERFECT.

indefensible *adj.* —*See* INEXCUSABLE.

indefinable *adj.* —*See* UNSPEAKABLE (1).

indefinite *adj.* 1. Lacking precise limits ► imprecise, indeterminate, inexact, undefined, undetermined. [*Compare* ENDLESS, INCALCULABLE.] 2. Marked by lack of firm decision or commitment; of questionable outcome ► open, uncertain, undecided, undetermined, unresolved, unsettled, unspecified, unsure, vague. *Idiom:* up in the air. [*Compare* AMBIGUOUS.] 3. Not limited

ing precise limits. 3. Uncertain; undecided. **—in·def′i·nite·ly** *adv.* **—in·def′i·nite·ness** *n.*

indefinite article ► *n.* An article, such as English *a* or *an,* that does not fix the identity of the noun modified.

in·del·i·ble (ĭn-dĕl′ə-bəl) ► *adj.* 1. Impossible to remove, erase, or wash away. 2. Making a mark not easily erased or washed away. **—in·del′i·bil′i·ty** *n.* **—in·del′i·bly** *adv.*

in·del·i·cate (ĭn-dĕl′ĭ-kĭt) ► *adj.* 1. Offensive to propriety; improper. 2. Tasteless. 3. Tactless. **—in·del′i·ca·cy** *n.* **—in·del′i·cate·ly** *adv.*

in·dem·ni·fy (ĭn-dĕm′nə-fī′) ► *v.* **-fied, -fy·ing.** 1. To protect against damage or loss; insure. 2. To compensate for damage suffered. **—in·dem′ni·fi·ca′tion** *n.* **—in·dem′ni·fi′er** *n.*

in·dem·ni·ty (ĭn-dĕm′nĭ-tē) ► *n., pl.* **-ties.** 1. Security against damage or injury. 2. A legal exemption from liability for damages. 3. Compensation for damage, loss, or injury suffered.

in·dent[1] (ĭn-dĕnt′) ► *v.* 1. To set (the first line of a paragraph) in from the margin. 2. To notch or serrate the edge of; make jagged. ► *n.* (ĭn-dĕnt′, ĭn′dĕnt′) An indentation.

in·dent[2] (ĭn-dĕnt′) ► *v.* 1. To make a dent in. 2. To impress; stamp.

in·den·ta·tion (ĭn′dĕn-tā′shən) ► *n.* 1. The act of indenting or condition of being indented. 2. The blank space between a margin and the beginning of an indented line. 3. A notch or jagged cut in an edge. 4. A recess, as in a border or coastline.

in·den·ture (ĭn-dĕn′chər) ► *n.* 1. often **indentures** A contract binding one party into the service of another for a specified term. 2. A deed or legal contract. ► *v.* **-tured, -tur·ing.** To bind by indenture.

Independence Day ► *n.* July 4, celebrated in the US to commemorate the adoption in 1776 of the Declaration of Independence.

in·de·pen·dent (ĭn′dĭ-pĕn′dənt) ► *adj.* 1. Not governed by a foreign power. 2. Free from the influence, guidance, or control of others; self-reliant. 3. Not contingent. 4. Not committed to any one political party. 5a. Financially self-sufficient. b. Providing or being sufficient income to enable one to live without working. ► *n.* One that is independent, esp. a voter not committed to any one party. **—in′de·pen′dence** *n.* **—in′de·pen′dent·ly** *adv.*

in-depth (ĭn′dĕpth′) ► *adj.* Detailed; thorough.

in·de·scrib·a·ble (ĭn′dĭ-skrī′bə-bəl) ► *adj.* 1. Impossible to describe. 2. Beyond description. **—in′de·scrib′a·bly** *adv.*

in·de·struc·ti·ble (ĭn′dĭ-strŭk′tə-bəl) ► *adj.* Impossible to destroy. **—in′de·struc′ti·bil′i·ty** *n.* **—in′de·struc′ti·bly** *adv.*

in·de·ter·mi·nate (ĭn′dĭ-tûr′mə-nĭt) ► *adj.* 1a. Not precisely determined. b. Not precisely fixed. 2. Lacking clarity or precision. **—in′de·ter′mi·na·cy** *n.* **—in′de·ter′mi·nate·ly** *adv.*

in·dex (ĭn′dĕks′) ► *n., pl.* **-dex·es** or **-di·ces** (-dĭ-sēz′). 1. An alphabetized list of names, places, and subjects treated in a printed work. 2. Something that reveals or indicates; sign. 3. *Print.* A character (☞) used in printing to call attention to a particular paragraph. 4. *Math.* A number or symbol, often a subscript or superscript to a mathematical expression, that indicates a specific element of a set or sequence. 5. A number derived from a formula, used to characterize a set of data: *adjusted the cost-of-living index.* ► *v.* 1. To furnish with or enter in an index. 2. To indicate or signal. **—in′dex′er** *n.*

index finger ► *n.* The finger next to the thumb.

index of refraction ► *n.* The ratio of the speed of light in a vacuum to the speed of light in a medium under consideration.

In·di·a (ĭn′dē-ə) ► 1. A peninsula and subcontinent of S Asia S of the Himalayas, comprising India, Nepal, Bhutan, Sikkim, Pakistan, and Bangladesh. 2. A country of S Asia.

In·di·an (ĭn′dē-ən) ► *n.* 1. A native or inhabitant of India or of the East Indies. 2. See **Native American**. 3. Any of the languages of the Native Americans. **—In′di·an** *adj.*

In·di·an·a (ĭn′dē-ăn′ə) ► A state of the N-central US. Cap. Indianapolis. **—In′di·an′an, In′di·an′i·an** *adj. & n.*

In·di·an·ap·o·lis (ĭn′dē-ə-năp′ə-lĭs) ► The capital of IN, in the central part SSW of Fort Wayne.

Indian corn ► *n.* See **corn[1]** 1.

Indian Ocean ► A body of water extending from S Asia to Antarctica and from E Africa to SE Australia.

Indian pipe ► *n.* A waxy white woodland plant with scale-like leaves and a nodding flower.

Indian summer ► *n.* A period of mild weather occurring in late autumn.

In·dic (ĭn′dĭk) ► *n.* A branch of Indo-European that comprises the languages of the Indian subcontinent and Sri Lanka. **—In′dic** *adj.*

in·di·cate (ĭn′dĭ-kāt′) ► *v.* **-cat·ed, -cat·ing.** 1. To show the way to or point out. 2. To serve as a sign, symptom, or token of; signify. 3. To suggest the necessity or advisability of. 4. To state or express briefly. **—in′di·ca′tion** *n.* **—in′di·ca′tor** *n.*

in·dic·a·tive (ĭn-dĭk′ə-tĭv) ► *adj.* 1. Serving to indicate. 2. *Gram.* Of or being the mood of the verb used in ordinary objective statements. ► *n. Gram.* 1. The indicative mood. 2. A verb in the indicative mood. **—in·dic′a·tive·ly** *adv.*

in·di·ces (ĭn′dĭ-sēz′) ► *n.* Pl. of **index**.

in·dict (ĭn-dīt′) ► *v.* 1. To accuse of wrongdoing. 2. *Law* To make a formal accusation against (a party) by the findings of a grand jury. **—in·dict′a·ble** *adj.* **—in′dict·ee′** (ĭn′dī-tē′) *n.* **—in·dict′er, in·dict′or** *n.* **—in·dict′ment** *n.*

In·dies (ĭn′dēz) ► 1. See **East Indies**. 2. See **West Indies**.

in·dif·fer·ent (ĭn-dĭf′ər-ənt, -dĭf′rənt) ► *adj.* 1. Not partial; unbiased. 2. Not mattering one way or the other. 3. Having no marked feeling for or against. 4. Having no particular interest in or concern for; apathetic. 5. Neither good nor bad; mediocre. **—in·dif′fer·ence** *n.* **—in·dif′fer·ent·ly** *adv.*

THESAURUS

to a single class ► diversified, general. —*See also* DEBATABLE, UNCLEAR.

indefiniteness *n.* —*See* VAGUENESS.

indelible *adj.* Retaining original color ► colorfast, fast. —*See also* CONFIRMED (1).

indelicacy *n.* —*See* IMPROPRIETY (2).

indelicate *adj.* —*See* COARSE (1), IMPROPER (1), TACTLESS.

indemnification *n.* —*See* COMPENSATION.

indemnify *v.* —*See* COMPENSATE.

indemnity *n.* —*See* COMPENSATION.

indent *n.* —*See* IMPRESSION (1).

indent *v.* —*See* CUT (1).

indentation *n.* —*See* DEPRESSION (1), IMPRESSION (1).

indented *adj.* —*See* HOLLOW (2).

indenture *v.* —*See* ENSLAVE.

independence *n.* The capacity to manage one's own affairs, make one's own judgments, and provide for oneself ► autonomy, self-containment, self-control, self-determination, self-reliance, self-sufficiency. —*See also* FREEDOM.

independent *adj.* 1. Free from the influence, guidance, or control of others ► autonomous, individualistic, self-contained, self-determined, self-directed, self-reliant, self-sufficient. 2. Able to support oneself financially ► self-sufficient, self-supporting. —*See also* FREE (1).

independent *n.* —*See* REBEL (2).

independently *adv.* —*See* SEPARATELY.

in-depth *adj.* —*See* DETAILED.

indiscreet *adj.* —*See* IMPROPER (1), UNWISE.

indescribable *adj.* —*See* UNSPEAKABLE (1).

indeterminate *adj.* —*See* AMBIGUOUS (1), INDEFINITE (1).

index *n.* —*See* LIST[1], SIGN (1).

indicate *v.* 1. To give grounds for believing in the existence or presence of ► argue, attest, bespeak, betoken, mark, point to, testify, witness. 2. To lead to by logical inference ► imply, point to, suggest. —*See also* DESIGNATE, MEAN[1], SHOW (2).

indication *n.* —*See* EXPRESSION (2), GESTURE, SIGN (1).

indicative *adj.* —*See* DESIGNATIVE.

indicator *n.* The marked outer surface of an instrument ► dial, face, gauge. —*See also* SIGN (1).

indicatory *adj.* —*See* DESIGNATIVE.

indict *v.* —*See* ACCUSE.

indicter or **indictor** *n.* One that accuses ► accuser, arraigner, denouncer, recriminator.

indictment *n.* —*See* ACCUSATION.

indifference *n.* —*See* APATHY, DETACHMENT (2), TRIFLE.

indifferent *adj.* —*See* APATHETIC, AVERAGE, COLD (2), DETACHED (1), FAIR[1] (1), ORDINARY.

indifferently *adv.* —*See* FAIRLY (1).

in·dig·e·nous (ĭn-dĭj′ə-nəs) ▸ *adj.* Originating and living or occurring naturally in an area or environment; native. **—in·dig′e·nous·ly** *adv.*

in·di·gent (ĭn′dĭ-jənt) ▸ *adj.* Lacking the means of subsistence; impoverished. **—in′di·gence** *n.* **—in′di·gent** *n.* **—in′di·gent·ly** *adv.*

in·di·gest·i·ble (ĭn′dĭ-jĕs′tə-bəl, -dī-) ▸ *adj.* Difficult or impossible to digest. **—in′di·gest′i·bil′i·ty** *n.* **—in′di·gest′i·bly** *adv.*

in·di·ges·tion (ĭn′dĭ-jĕs′chən, -dī-) ▸ *n.* **1.** Inability to properly digest food. **2.** Discomfort or illness resulting from indigestion.

in·dig·nant (ĭn-dĭg′nənt) ▸ *adj.* Feeling or expressing indignation. **—in·dig′nant·ly** *adv.*

in·dig·na·tion (ĭn′dĭg-nā′shən) ▸ *n.* Anger aroused by something unjust or mean.

in·dig·ni·ty (ĭn-dĭg′nĭ-tē) ▸ *n., pl.* **-ties. 1.** Humiliating or degrading treatment. **2.** A source of offense, as to a person's pride or sense of dignity; affront.

in·di·go (ĭn′dĭ-gō′) ▸ *n., pl.* **-gos** or **-goes. 1.** A plant that yields a blue dyestuff. **2.** A blue dye obtained from this plant or produced synthetically. **3a.** A dark to purplish blue. **b.** The hue of the visible spectrum lying between blue and violet.

indigo bunting ▸ *n.* A small New World finch, the male of which has deep blue plumage.

in·di·rect (ĭn′dĭ-rĕkt′, -dī-) ▸ *adj.* **1.** Diverging from a direct course; roundabout. **2a.** Not proceeding straight to the point. **b.** Not forthright and candid; devious. **3.** Not directly planned for; secondary: *indirect benefits.* **—in′di·rec′tion** *n.* **—in′di·rect′ly** *adv.* **—in′di·rect′ness** *n.*

indirect object ▸ *n.* An object indirectly affected by the action of a verb, as *me* in *Sing me a song.*

in·dis·cern·i·ble (ĭn′dĭ-sûr′nə-bəl, -zûr′-) ▸ *adj.* Impossible to perceive; imperceptible. **—in′dis·cern′i·bly** *adv.*

in·dis·creet (ĭn′dĭ-skrēt′) ▸ *adj.* Lacking discretion; injudicious. **—in′dis·creet′ly** *adv.* **—in′dis·creet′ness** *n.* **—in′dis·cre′tion** (ĭn′dĭ-skrĕsh′ən) *n.*

in·dis·crim·i·nate (ĭn′dĭ-skrĭm′ə-nĭt) ▸ *adj.* **1.** Not making or based on careful distinctions; unselective. **2.** Widespread; wholesale: *indiscriminate violence.* **3.** Random; haphazard. **4.** Confused; chaotic. **—in′dis·crim′i·nate·ly** *adv.*

in·dis·pens·a·ble (ĭn′dĭ-spĕn′sə-bəl) ▸ *adj.* Not to be dispensed with; essential. **—in′dis·pens′a·bil′i·ty, in′dis·pens′a·ble·ness** *n.* **—in′dis·pens′a·bly** *adv.*

in·dis·posed (ĭn′dĭ-spōzd′) ▸ *adj.* **1.** Mildly ill. **2.** Averse; disinclined. **—in·dis′po·si′tion** (ĭn-dĭs′pə-zĭsh′ən) *n.*

in·dis·put·a·ble (ĭn′dĭ-spyōō′tə-bəl) ▸ *adj.* Beyond doubt; undeniable. **—in′dis·put′a·ble·ness** *n.* **—in′dis·put′a·bly** *adv.*

in·dis·sol·u·ble (ĭn′dĭ-sŏl′yə-bəl) ▸ *adj.* Impossible to dissolve, disintegrate, or undo. **—in′dis·sol′u·bil′i·ty** *n.* **—in′dis·sol′u·bly** *adv.*

in·dis·tinct (ĭn′dĭ-stĭngkt′) ▸ *adj.* **1.** Not clearly or sharply delineated. **2.** Hazy, vague. **—in′dis·tinct′ly** *adv.* **—in′dis·tinct′ness** *n.*

in·dis·tin·guish·a·ble (ĭn′dĭ-stĭng′gwĭ-shə-bəl) ▸ *adj.* **1.** Impossible to differentiate or tell apart. **2.** Impossible to discern; imperceptible. **—in′dis·tin′guish·a·bly** *adv.*

in·dite (ĭn-dīt′) ▸ *v.* **-dit·ed, -dit·ing.** To write; compose.

in·di·um (ĭn′dē-əm) ▸ *n. Symbol* **In** A soft, malleable, silvery-white metallic element used as a plating over silver in making mirrors and in compounds for making transistors. At. no. 49.

in·di·vid·u·al (ĭn′də-vĭj′ōō-əl) ▸ *adj.* **1a.** Of or relating to a single human. **b.** By or for one person: *an individual portion.* **2.** Existing singly; separate: *individual words.* **3.** Distinguished by particular attributes; distinctive: *an individual way of dressing.* ▸ *n.* **1.** A human or organism considered by itself. **2.** A particular person. **—in′di·vid′u·al·ly** *adv.*

in·di·vid·u·al·ism (ĭn′də-vĭj′ōō-ə-lĭz′əm) ▸ *n.* **1.** Belief in the primary importance of the individual and personal independence. **2.** The doctrine that the interests of the individual should take precedence over those of the state. **3.** Individuality.

in·di·vid·u·al·ist (ĭn′də-vĭj′ōō-ə-lĭst) ▸ *n.* **1.** A person of independent thought and action. **2.** An advocate of individualism. **—in′di·vid′u·al·is′tic** *adj.*

in·di·vid·u·al·i·ty (ĭn′də-vĭj′ōō-ăl′ĭ-tē) ▸ *n.* **1.** The aggregate of qualities that distinguish one individual from another. **2.** The quality of being individual.

in·di·vid·u·al·ize (ĭn′də-vĭj′ōō-ə-līz′) ▸ *v.* **-ized, -iz·ing. 1.** To give individuality to. **2.** To consider or treat individually. **3.** To modify to suit a particular individual. **—in′di·vid′u·al·i·za′tion** *n.*

individual retirement account ▸ *n.* A personal investment account in which contributions and interest are tax-deferred until retirement.

in·di·vis·i·ble (ĭn′də-vĭz′ə-bəl) ▸ *adj.* Incapable of division. **—in′di·vis′i·bly** *adv.*

In·do·chi·na (ĭn′dō-chī′nə) ▸ **1.** A peninsula of SE Asia comprising Vietnam, Laos, Cambodia, Thailand, Myanmar, and the mainland territory of Malaysia. **2.** The former French colonial empire in SE Asia, including much of the E part of the Indochinese peninsula. **—In′do·chi′nese′** (-nēz′, -nēs′) *adj.* & *n.*

in·doc·tri·nate (ĭn-dŏk′trə-nāt′) ▸ *v.* **-nat·ed, -nat·ing. 1.** To

THESAURUS

indigence *n.* —*See* POVERTY.

indigenous *adj.* Existing, born, or produced in a land or region ▸ aboriginal, autochthonal, autochthonic, autochthonous, endemic, homegrown, local, native, regional. *Idiom:* native to the soil. —*See also* CONSTITUTIONAL, DOMESTIC (3).

indigent *adj.* —*See* POOR.

indigestible *adj.* —*See* BITTER (3).

indignant *adj.* —*See* ANGRY.

indignation *n.* —*See* ANGER.

indignity *n.* An act that offends a person's sense of pride or dignity ▸ affront, aspersion, contumely, despite, incivility, insult, offense, outrage, putdown, slight. *Idioms:* backhanded (*or* lefthanded) compliment, kick in the teeth, slap in the face. [*Compare* INJUSTICE, OUTRAGE, SNUB, VITUPERATION.]

indirect *adj.* **1.** Not proceeding straight to the point or object ▸ anfractuous, backhanded, circuitous, circular, circumlocutory, curving, devious, meandering, oblique, out-of-the-way, rambling, roundabout, tortuous, twisting, wandering, winding, zigzag. [*Compare* DIGRESSIVE.] **2.** Deliberately ambiguous or vague ▸ elusive, equivocal, evasive, misleading. [*Compare* AMBIGUOUS.] —*See also* UNDERHAND.

indirection *n.* —*See* DISHONESTY (2).

indiscernible *adj.* —*See* HIDDEN (1), IMPERCEPTIBLE (1).

indiscreet *adj.* —*See* UNWISE.

indiscretion *n.* —*See* IMPROPRIETY (1), IMPROPRIETY (2).

indiscriminate *adj.* —*See* RANDOM.

indispensable *adj.* —*See* ESSENTIAL (1).

indisposed *adj.* Not inclined or willing to do or undertake ▸ against, averse, disinclined, loath, opposed, reluctant, resistant, unwilling. *Idioms:* not feeling like, not in the mood. [*Compare* HESITANT, WARY.] —*See also* SICK (1).

indisposition *n.* The state of not being disposed or inclined ▸ averseness, aversion, disinclination, opposition, reluctance, resistance, unwillingness. [*Compare* OBJECTION.] —*See also* SICKNESS.

indisputable *adj.* —*See* CERTAIN (2).

indistinct *adj.* —*See* UNCLEAR.

indistinctive *adj.* Without definite or distinctive characteristics ▸ bland, colorless, neutral. [*Compare* BORING.]

indistinguishable *adj.* —*See* HIDDEN (1), IMPERCEPTIBLE (1).

indite *v.* —*See* COMPOSE (1), WRITE.

individual *adj.* **1.** Belonging to, relating to, or affecting a particular person ▸ intimate, personal, private. **2.** Being or related to a distinct entity ▸ discrete, lone, particular, separate, single, singular, sole. —*See also* DISTINCT, SPECIAL.

individual *n.* —*See* HUMAN BEING, THING (1).

individualism *n.* —*See* IDENTITY (1).

individualistic *adj.* Holding the philosophical view that the self is the center and norm of existence ▸ egocentric, egoistic, egoistical, solipsistic. [*Compare* EGOTISTIC.] —*See also* INDEPENDENT (1).

individuality *n.* The quality of being individual ▸ discreteness, distinctiveness, particularity, separateness, singularity. [*Compare* NOVELTY, UNIQUENESS.] —*See also* IDENTITY (1).

individualize *v.* —*See* DISTINGUISH (2).

individually *adv.* —*See* SEPARATELY.

indocile *adj.* —*See* UNRULY.

indocility *n.* —*See* UNRULINESS.

indoctrinate *v.* **1.** To instruct by rote

instruct in a body of doctrine. **2.** To imbue with a partisan point of view. **—in·doc′tri·na′tion** *n.*

In·do-Eu·ro·pe·an (ĭn′dō-yo͝or′ə-pē′ən) ▸ *n.* **1a.** A family of languages consisting of most of the languages of Europe as well as those of Iran, the Indian subcontinent, and other parts of Asia. **b.** Proto-Indo-European. **2.** A member of any of the peoples speaking an Indo-European language. **—In′do-Eu′ro·pe′an** *adj.*

In·do-I·ra·ni·an (ĭn′dō-ĭ-rā′nē-ən) ▸ *n.* **1.** A subfamily of the Indo-European language family that comprises the Indic and Iranian branches. **2.** A member of any of the peoples speaking an Indo-Iranian language. **—In′do-I·ra′ni·an** *adj.*

in·do·lent (ĭn′də-lənt) ▸ *adj.* Disinclined to work; habitually lazy. **—in′do·lence** *n.* **—in′do·lent·ly** *adv.*

in·dom·i·ta·ble (ĭn-dŏm′ĭ-tə-bəl) ▸ *adj.* Impossible to overcome; unconquerable. **—in·dom′i·ta·bly** *adv.*

In·do·ne·sia (ĭn′də-nē′zhə, -shə, -dō-) ▸ A country of SE Asia in the Malay Archipelago comprising Sumatra, Java, Sulawesi, the Moluccas, parts of Borneo, New Guinea, and Timor, and many smaller islands.

In·do·ne·sian (ĭn′də-nē′zhən, -shən) ▸ *n.* **1.** A native or inhabitant of Indonesia. **2.** A subfamily of Austronesian that includes Malay, Tagalog, and the languages of Indonesia. **—In′do·ne′sian** *adj.*

in·door (ĭn′dôr′) ▸ *adj.* Of, situated in, or intended for use in the interior of a building.

in·doors (ĭn-dôrz′) ▸ *adv.* In or into a building.

in·dorse (ĭn-dôrs′) ▸ *v.* Var. of **endorse.**

in·du·bi·ta·ble (ĭn-do͞o′bĭ-tə-bəl, -dyo͞o′-) ▸ *adj.* Too apparent to be doubted; unquestionable. **—in·du′bi·ta·bly** *adv.*

in·duce (ĭn-do͞os′, -dyo͞os′) ▸ *v.* **-duced, -duc·ing. 1.** To persuade or move to action; influence. **2.** To bring about the occurrence of; cause: *a drug used to induce labor.* **—in·duc′i·ble** *adj.* **—in·duce′ment** *n.*

in·duct (ĭn-dŭkt′) ▸ *v.* **1.** To place formally in office; install. **2.** To admit as a member; initiate. **3.** To take into military service. **—in′duc·tee′** *n.*

in·duc·tance (ĭn-dŭk′təns) ▸ *n.* A circuit element in which electromotive force is generated by electromagnetic induction.

in·duc·tion (ĭn-dŭk′shən) ▸ *n.* **1.** The act of inducting or the process of being inducted. **2.** *Elect.* **a.** The generation of electromotive force in a closed circuit by a varying magnetic flux through the circuit. **b.** The charging of an isolated conducting object by momentarily grounding it while a charged body is nearby. **3.** *Logic* The process of deriving general principles from particular facts or instances.

in·duc·tive (ĭn-dŭk′tĭv) ▸ *adj.* **1.** Of or using logical induction. **2.** *Elect.* Of or arising from inductance. **—in·duc′tive·ly** *adv.* **—in·duc′tive·ness** *n.*

in·dulge (ĭn-dŭlj′) ▸ *v.* **-dulged, -dulg·ing. 1.** To yield to the desires and whims of; humor. **2a.** To yield to; gratify: *indulge a craving for chocolate.* **b.** To allow (oneself) a special pleasure. **—in·dulg′er** *n.*

in·dul·gence (ĭn-dŭl′jəns) ▸ *n.* **1.** The act of indulging or state of being indulgent. **2.** Something indulged in. **3.** Liberal or lenient treatment; tolerance. **4.** Something that is granted as a favor or privilege. **5.** *Rom. Cath. Ch.* The remission of temporal punishment due for a sin that has been absolved.

in·dul·gent (ĭn-dŭl′jənt) ▸ *adj.* Showing, characterized by, or given to indulgence; lenient. **—in·dul′gent·ly** *adv.*

in·du·rate (ĭn′də-rāt′, -dyə-) ▸ *v.* **-rat·ed, -rat·ing. 1.** To make or become hard; harden. **2.** To inure, as to hardship or ridicule. **—in′dur·a′tion** *n.*

in·du·ra·tion (ĭn′də-rā′shən, -dyə-) ▸ *n.* **1.** The quality or condition of being hardened. **2.** The act or process of becoming hardened. **3.** *Pathol.* The hardening of a normally soft tissue or organ, especially the skin, because of inflammation, infiltration of a neoplasm, or an accumulation of blood.

In·dus (ĭn′dəs) ▸ A river of S-central Asia rising in SW Xizang (Tibet) and flowing about 3,057 km (1,900 mi) through N India and Pakistan to the Arabian Sea.

in·dus·tri·al (ĭn-dŭs′trē-əl) ▸ *adj.* **1.** Of or relating to industry. **2.** Having highly developed industries. **3.** Used in industry: *industrial diamonds.* **—in·dus′tri·al·ly** *adv.*

in·dus·tri·al·ist (ĭ-dŭs′trē-ə-lĭst) ▸ *n.* One who owns or has a financial interest in an industrial enterprise.

in·dus·tri·al·ize (ĭn-dŭs′trē-ə-līz′) ▸ *v.* **-ized, -iz·ing.** To make or become industrial. **—in·dus′tri·al·i·za′tion** *n.*

in·dus·tri·ous (ĭn-dŭs′trē-əs) ▸ *adj.* Hard-working; diligent. **—in·dus′tri·ous·ly** *adv.* **—in·dus′tri·ous·ness** *n.*

in·dus·try (ĭn′də-strē) ▸ *n., pl.* **-tries. 1.** Commercial production and sale of goods. **2.** A specific branch of manufacture and trade. **3.** The sector of an economy made up of manufacturing enterprises. **4.** Hard work; diligence.

–ine¹ ▸ *suff.* **1.** Of or relating to: *Benedictine.* **2.** Made of; resembling: *opaline.*

–ine² ▸ *suff.* **1.** also **-in** A chemical substance, esp.: **a.** Halogen: *bromine.* **b.** Basic compound: *amine.* **c.** Alkaloid: *quinine.* **2.** Amino acid: *glycine.* **3.** A mixture of compounds: *gasoline.* **4.** Commercial material: *glassine.*

in·e·bri·ate (ĭn-ē′brē-āt′) ▸ *v.* **-at·ed, -at·ing.** To make drunk; intoxicate. ▸ *n.* (-ĭt) An intoxicated person. **—in·e′bri·a′tion** *n.*

in·ed·i·ble (ĭn-ĕd′ə-bəl) ▸ *adj.* Not edible. **—in·ed′i·bil′i·ty** *n.* **—in·ed′i·bly** *adv.*

in·ef·fa·ble (ĭn-ĕf′ə-bəl) ▸ *adj.* **1.** Incapable of being expressed; indescribable. **2.** Not to be uttered; taboo. **—in·ef′fa·bly** *adv.*

in·ef·face·a·ble (ĭn′ĭ-fā′sə-bəl) ▸ *adj.* Impossible to efface; indelible.

in·ef·fec·tive (ĭn′ĭ-fĕk′tĭv) ▸ *adj.* **1.** Not effective; ineffectual. **2.** Incompetent. **—in′ef·fec′tive·ly** *adv.* **—in′ef·fec′tive·ness** *n.*

in·ef·fec·tu·al (ĭn′ĭ-fĕk′cho͞o-əl) ▸ *adj.* **1.** Not having a desired

THESAURUS

or discipline, as in a body of doctrine or belief ▸ catechize, drill, inculcate. *Idioms:* beat (*or* drum *or* pound) something into someone's head, put someone through his or her paces. [*Compare* EDUCATE, PRACTICE.] **2.** To teach to accept a system of thought or beliefs uncritically ▸ brainwash, program, propagandize. [*Compare* BIAS, INFLUENCE.]

indoctrination *n.* *—See* PROPAGANDA.

indolence *n.* *—See* LAZINESS.

indolent *adj.* *—See* LAZY.

indomitable *adj.* Incapable of being conquered or subjugated ▸ invincible, unbeatable, unconquerable, undefeatable. [*Compare* INSUPERABLE, SAFE.]

indubitability *n.* *—See* SURENESS.

indubitable *adj.* *—See* AUTHENTIC (1), CERTAIN (2).

indubitably *adv.* *—See* ABSOLUTELY, YES.

induce *v.* *—See* CAUSE, PERSUADE, URGE.

inducement *n.* *—See* LURE (1), STIMULUS.

induct *v.* To enroll compulsorily in military service ▸ conscript, draft, impress, levy. *—See also* INITIATE.

induction *n.* *—See* DRAFT (2), INITIATION, INTRODUCTION, LOGIC.

inductive *adj.* *—See* INTRODUCTORY.

indulge *v.* To comply with the wishes or ideas of another ▸ cater (to), gratify, humor. [*Compare* DEFER².] *—See also* BABY, LUXURIATE, OBLIGE (1), PARTICIPATE, SATISFY (2).

indulgence *n.* *—See* FAVOR (1), LICENSE (2), LUXURY, TOLERANCE.

indulgent *adj.* *—See* OBLIGING, TOLERANT.

indurate *v.* *—See* HARDEN (1), HARDEN (2).

industrious *adj.* *—See* DILIGENT.

industriousness *n.* *—See* DILIGENCE.

industry *n.* *—See* BUSINESS (1), DILIGENCE.

inebriate *adj.* *—See* DRUNK.

inebriate *n.* *—See* DRUNKARD.

inebriated *adj.* *—See* DRUNK.

inebriation or **inebriety** *n.* *—See* DRUNKENNESS.

inedible *adj.* *—See* UNPALATABLE.

ineffable *adj.* *—See* UNSPEAKABLE (1).

ineffective *adj.* *—See* INEFFECTUAL (1), INEFFECTUAL (2).

ineffectiveness *n.* *—See* INEFFECTUALITY.

ineffectual *adj.* **1.** Not having the desired effect ▸ counterproductive, inefficacious, inefficient, useless. *Idioms:* all wind, to no avail. **2.** Not capable of accomplishing anything ▸ helpless, impotent, inadequate, incapable, ineffective, inefficient, insufficient, lame, powerless, unable, useless, weak. *Idiom:* all gas and no motor.

effect; vain. 2. Lacking forcefulness; weak. **—in′ef·fec′tu·al·ly** *adv.*

in·ef·fi·cient (ĭn′ĭ-fĭsh′ənt) ▸ *adj.* Not efficient; wasteful of time, energy, or materials. **—in′ef·fi′cien·cy** *n.* **—in′ef·fi′cient·ly** *adv.*

in·el·e·gant (ĭn-ĕl′ĭ-gənt) ▸ *adj.* Lacking refinement; not elegant. **—in·el′e·gance** *n.* **—in·el′e·gant·ly** *adv.*

in·el·i·gi·ble (ĭn-ĕl′ĭ-jə-bəl) ▸ *adj.* Disqualified by law or rule. **—in·el′i·gi·bil′i·ty** *n.* **—in·el′i·gi·bly** *adv.*

in·e·luc·ta·ble (ĭn′ĭ-lŭk′tə-bəl) ▸ *adj.* Not to be avoided or escaped; inevitable. **—in′e·luc′ta·bly** *adv.*

in·ept (ĭn-ĕpt′) ▸ *adj.* 1. Not apt or fitting; inappropriate. 2. Lacking judgment or sense; foolish. 3. Bungling or clumsy; incompetent. **—in·ept′ly** *adv.* **—in·ept′ness, in·ep′ti·tude′** (-ĕp′tĭ-to͞od′, -tyo͞od′) *n.*

in·e·qual·i·ty (ĭn′ĭ-kwŏl′ĭ-tē) ▸ *n., pl.* **-ties.** 1. The condition of being unequal. 2. Social or economic disparity. 3. Lack of regularity; unevenness. 4. A mathematical statement that two quantities are not equal.

in·eq·ui·ta·ble (ĭn-ĕk′wĭ-tə-bəl) ▸ *adj.* Not equitable; unfair. **—in·eq′ui·ta·bly** *adv.*

in·eq·ui·ty (ĭn-ĕk′wĭ-tē) ▸ *n., pl.* **-ties.** 1. Injustice; unfairness. 2. An instance of unfairness.

in·er·ran·cy (ĭn-ĕr′ən-sē) ▸ *n.* Freedom from error or untruths; infallibility.

in·ert (ĭn-ûrt′) ▸ *adj.* 1. Unable to move or act. 2. Sluggish in action or motion; lethargic. 3. *Chem.* Not readily reactive with other elements; forming few or no chemical compounds. **—in·ert′ly** *adv.* **—in·ert′ness** *n.*

in·er·tia (ĭ-nûr′shə) ▸ *n.* 1. *Phys.* The tendency of a body to remain at rest or stay in motion unless acted on by an outside force. 2. Resistance to motion, action, or change. **—in·er′tial** *adj.*

in·es·cap·a·ble (ĭn′ĭ-skā′pə-bəl) ▸ *adj.* Impossible to escape; inevitable. **—in′es·cap′a·bly** *adv.*

in·es·ti·ma·ble (ĭn-ĕs′tə-mə-bəl) ▸ *adj.* 1. Impossible to estimate or compute. 2. Of immeasurable worth; invaluable. **—in·es′ti·ma·bly** *adv.*

in·ev·i·ta·ble (ĭn-ĕv′ĭ-tə-bəl) ▸ *adj.* 1. Impossible to avoid or prevent. 2. Predictable. **—in·ev′i·ta·bil′i·ty** *n.* **—in·ev′i·ta·bly** *adv.*

in·ex·act (ĭn′ĭg-zăkt′) ▸ *adj.* Not accurate or precise; not exact. **—in′ex·act′ly** *adv.* **—in′ex·act′ness** *n.*

in·ex·cus·a·ble (ĭn′ĭk-skyo͞o′zə-bəl) ▸ *adj.* Impossible to excuse; unpardonable. **—in′ex·cus′a·bly** *adv.*

in·ex·haust·i·ble (ĭn′ĭg-zô′stə-bəl) ▸ *adj.* 1. That cannot be used up. 2. Never wearying; tireless. **—in′ex·haust′i·bil′i·ty, in′ex·haust′i·ble·ness** *n.* **—in′ex·haust′i·bly** *adv.*

in·ex·o·ra·ble (ĭn-ĕk′sər-ə-bəl) ▸ *adj.* Not capable of being persuaded by entreaty; relentless. **—in·ex′o·ra·bil′i·ty** *n.* **—in·ex′o·ra·bly** *adv.*

in·ex·pen·sive (ĭn′ĭk-spĕn′sĭv) ▸ *adj.* Not costly; cheap. **—in′ex·pen′sive·ly** *adv.*

in·ex·pe·ri·ence (ĭn′ĭk-spîr′ē-əns) ▸ *n.* Lack of experience. **—in′ex·pe′ri·enced** *adj.*

in·ex·pert (ĭn-ĕk′spûrt′) ▸ *adj.* Not expert; unskilled. **—in·ex′pert′ly** *adv.*

in·ex·pli·ca·ble (ĭn-ĕk′splĭ-kə-bəl, ĭn′ĭk-splĭk′ə-bəl) ▸ *adj.* Impossible to explain or account for. **—in·ex′pli·ca·bly** *adv.*

in·ex·press·i·ble (ĭn′ĭk-sprĕs′ə-bəl) ▸ *adj.* Impossible to express; indescribable. **—in′ex·press′i·bly** *adv.*

in·ex·tin·guish·a·ble (ĭn′ĭk-stĭng′gwĭ-shə-bəl) ▸ *adj.* Difficult or impossible to extinguish.

in ex·tre·mis (ĭn ĕk-strē′mĭs) ▸ *adv.* At the point of death.

in·ex·tri·ca·ble (ĭn-ĕk′strĭ-kə-bəl, ĭn′ĭk-strĭk′ə-bəl) ▸ *adj.* 1. Difficult or impossible to disentangle or untie. 2. Too involved or complicated to solve. **—in·ex′tri·ca·bil′i·ty** *n.* **—in·ex′tri·ca·bly** *adv.*

inf. ▸ *abbr.* infinitive

in·fal·li·ble (ĭn-făl′ə-bəl) ▸ *adj.* 1. Incapable of erring. 2. Incapable of failing; certain: *an infallible antidote.* **—in·fal′li·bil′i·ty** *n.* **—in·fal′li·bly** *adv.*

in·fa·mous (ĭn′fə-məs) ▸ *adj.* 1. Having an exceedingly bad reputation; notorious. 2. Causing or deserving infamy. **—in′fa·mous·ly** *adv.* **—in′fa·mous·ness** *n.*

in·fa·my (ĭn′fə-mē) ▸ *n., pl.* **-mies.** 1. Evil fame or reputation. 2. The condition of being infamous. 3. An infamous act.

in·fan·cy (ĭn′fən-sē) ▸ *n., pl.* **-cies.** 1. The state or period of being an infant. 2. An early stage of existence.

in·fant (ĭn′fənt) ▸ *n.* 1. A child in the earliest period of life; baby. 2. *Law* A minor. **—in′fant** *adj.*

THESAURUS

[*Compare* INEFFICIENT, FUTILE.]

ineffectuality *n.* The condition or state of being incapable of accomplishing anything ▸ helplessness, impotence, inadequacy, incapability, ineffectiveness, ineffectualness, inefficacy, insufficiency, powerlessness, uselessness. [*Compare* FUTILITY, INABILITY.]

inefficacious *adj.* —*See* INEFFECTUAL (1).

inefficacy *n.* —*See* INEFFECTUALITY.

inefficiency *n.* —*See* INABILITY.

inefficient *adj.* Lacking the qualities, as efficiency or skill, required to produce desired results ▸ bungling, impractical, inadequate, inapt, incapable, incompetent, inept, inexpert, unable, unequal, unfit, unqualified, unskilled, unskillful, unworkmanlike. [*Compare* AMATEURISH, IMPROPER.] —*See also* INEFFECTUAL (1).

inelastic *adj.* —*See* RIGID.

inelegant *adj.* —*See* COARSE (1).

ineluctable *adj.* —*See* CERTAIN (1).

inept *adj.* —*See* AWKWARD (1), IMPROPER (2), INEFFICIENT, UNFORTUNATE (2), UNSKILLFUL.

ineptitude *n.* —*See* INABILITY.

inequality *n.* 1. The condition or fact of being unequal, as in age, rank, or degree ▸ disparity, disproportion, disproportionateness, imbalance, incongruity. [*Compare* DIFFERENCE.] 2. Lack of equality, as of opportunity, treatment, or status ▸ discrimination, unfairness, unjustness. [*Compare* BIAS.] —*See also* IRREGULARITY.

inequitable *adj.* —*See* UNFAIR.

inequity *n.* —*See* INJUSTICE (1), INJUSTICE (2).

ineradicable *adj.* —*See* CONFIRMED (1).

inert *adj.* —*See* DEAD (2), IDLE (1), LETHARGIC.

inertness *n.* —*See* INACTION, LETHARGY.

inescapable *adj.* —*See* CERTAIN (1).

inessential *adj.* Not part of the real or essential nature of a thing ▸ adscititious, adventitious, incidental, supervenient. [*Compare* IRRELEVANT.] —*See also* UNNECESSARY.

inestimable *adj.* —*See* COSTLY, INCALCULABLE.

inevitable *adj.* —*See* CERTAIN (1).

inexact *adj.* —*See* INDEFINITE (1), LOOSE (3).

inexcusable *adj.* Impossible to excuse, pardon, or justify ▸ indefensible, inexpiable, irremissible, unforgivable, unjustifiable, unpardonable, unwarrantable. [*Compare* EVIL, DEPLORABLE.]

inexhaustibility or **inexhaustibleness** *n.* —*See* INFINITY (1).

inexhaustible *adj.* —*See* TIRELESS.

inexorability or **inexorableness** *n.* —*See* STUBBORNNESS.

inexorable *adj.* —*See* STUBBORN (1).

inexpedient *adj.* —*See* UNWISE.

inexpensive *adj.* —*See* CHEAP.

inexperience *n.* Lack of experience and the knowledge gained from it ▸ greenness, immaturity, inexpertness, newness, rawness. [*Compare* ARTLESSNESS, IGNORANCE.]

inexperienced *adj.* Lacking experience and the knowledge gained from it ▸ fresh, green, immature, inexpert, new, raw, unconversant, uninitiate, uninitiated, unpracticed, unseasoned, untried, unversed. ***Idiom:*** wet behind the ears. [*Compare* ARTLESS, IGNORANT.]

inexpert *adj.* —*See* INEFFICIENT, INEXPERIENCED.

inexpertness *n.* —*See* INEXPERIENCE.

inexpiable *adj.* —*See* INEXCUSABLE.

inexplicable *adj.* That cannot be explained ▸ unaccountable, unexplainable. [*Compare* MYSTERIOUS.]

inexplicit *adj.* —*See* AMBIGUOUS (2).

inexpressible *adj.* —*See* UNSPEAKABLE (1).

inexpressive *adj.* —*See* EXPRESSIONLESS.

inextricable *adj.* —*See* COMPLEX (1).

infallible *adj.* —*See* SURE (2).

infamous *adj.* —*See* NOTORIOUS, OFFENSIVE (1).

infamy or **infamousness** *n.* The condition of being infamous ▸ disgracefulness, dishonorableness, disreputability, disreputableness, ignominiousness, shamefulness. [*Compare* DISGRACE.] —*See also* NOTORIETY.

infant *n.* —*See* BABY (1).

infant *adj.* —*See* YOUNG.

in·fan·ti·cide (ĭn-făn′tĭ-sīd′) ▸ *n.* **1.** The killing of an infant. **2.** One who kills an infant.

in·fan·tile (ĭn′fən-tīl′, -tĭl) ▸ *adj.* **1.** Of or relating to infants or infancy. **2.** Immature; childish.

infantile paralysis ▸ *n.* See **poliomyelitis.**

in·fan·try (ĭn′fən-trē) ▸ *n., pl.* **-tries.** The combat arm made up of units trained to fight on foot. **—in′fan·try·man** *n.*

in·farct (ĭn′färkt′, ĭn-färkt′) ▸ *n.* A necrotic area of tissue due to the obstruction of local blood supply. **—in·farct′ed** *adj.* **—in·farc′tion** *n.*

in·fat·u·ate (ĭn-făch′o͞o-āt′) ▸ *v.* **-at·ed, -at·ing.** To inspire with unreasoning love or attachment. **—in·fat′u·at′ed** *adj.* **—in·fat′u·a′tion** *n.*

in·fea·si·ble (ĭn-fē′zə-bəl) ▸ *adj.* Not feasible; impracticable.

in·fect (ĭn-fĕkt′) ▸ *v.* **1.** To contaminate with a pathogenic microorganism. **2.** To communicate a disease to. **3.** To contaminate or corrupt: *a land infected by hate.* **—in·fec′tion** *n.*

in·fec·tious (ĭn-fĕk′shəs) ▸ *adj.* **1.** Capable of causing infection. **2.** Caused or transmitted by infection. **3.** Easily or readily communicated, as laughter. **—in·fec′tious·ly** *adv.*

infectious mononucleosis ▸ *n.* An acute infectious disease caused by Epstein-Barr virus and marked by fever, swollen lymph nodes, sore throat, and lymphocyte abnormalities.

in·fe·lic·i·tous (ĭn′fĭ-lĭs′ĭ-təs) ▸ *adj.* Inappropriate or ill-chosen, as a remark. **—in′fe·lic′i·tous·ly** *adv.* **—in′fe·lic′i·ty** *n.*

in·fer (ĭn-fûr′) ▸ *v.* **-ferred, -fer·ring.** **1.** To conclude from evidence or premises. **2.** To lead to as a result or conclusion.

in·fer·ence (ĭn′fər-əns) ▸ *n.* **1.** The act or process of inferring. **2.** Something inferred.

in·fe·ri·or (ĭn-fîr′ē-ər) ▸ *adj.* **1.** Low or lower in order, degree, rank, quality, or estimation. **2.** Situated under or beneath. **—in·fe′ri·or** *n.* **—in·fe′ri·or′i·ty** (-ôr′ĭ-tē, -ŏr′-) *n.*

in·fer·nal (ĭn-fûr′nəl) ▸ *adj.* **1.** Of or relating to hell. **2.** Fiendish; diabolical. **3.** Abominable; awful. **—in·fer′nal·ly** *adv.*

in·fer·no (ĭn-fûr′nō) ▸ *n., pl.* **-nos.** **1.** Hell. **2.** A place of fiery heat or destruction.

in·fer·tile (ĭn-fûr′tl) ▸ *adj.* Not fertile; unproductive or barren. **—in′fer·til′i·ty** (-fər-tĭl′ĭ-tē) *n.*

in·fest (ĭn-fĕst′) ▸ *v.* To inhabit or overrun in numbers large enough to be harmful or obnoxious. **—in′fes·ta′tion** *n.*

in·fi·del (ĭn′fĭ-dəl, -dĕl′) ▸ *n.* **1.** An unbeliever with respect to a particular religion, esp. Christianity or Islam. **2.** One with no religious beliefs.

in·fi·del·i·ty (ĭn′fĭ-dĕl′ĭ-tē) ▸ *n., pl.* **-ties.** **1.** Lack of fidelity or loyalty, esp. to a spouse. **2.** Lack of religious belief.

in·field (ĭn′fēld′) ▸ *n. Baseball* **1.** The area of the field within the baselines. **2.** The defensive positions of first base, second base, third base, and shortstop. **—in′field′er** *n.*

in·fight·ing (ĭn′fī′tĭng) ▸ *n.* **1.** Contentious rivalry within an organization. **2.** *Sports* Fighting at close range. **—in′fight′er** *n.*

in·fil·trate (ĭn-fĭl′trāt′, ĭn′fĭl-) ▸ *v.* **-trat·ed, -trat·ing.** **1.** To pass, enter, or join gradually or surreptitiously. **2.** To pass or cause (a liquid or gas) to pass into. **—in′fil·tra′tion** *n.* **—in·fil′tra·tor** *n.*

in·fi·nite (ĭn′fə-nĭt) ▸ *adj.* **1.** Having no boundaries or limits. **2.** Immeasurably great or large. **3.** *Math.* **a.** Being beyond or greater than any arbitrarily large value. **b.** Spatially unlimited. **—in′fin·ite** *n.* **—in′fi·nite·ly** *adv.*

in·fin·i·tes·i·mal (ĭn′fĭn-ĭ-tĕs′ə-məl) ▸ *adj.* **1.** Immeasurably or incalculably small. **2.** *Math.* Capable of having values approaching zero as a limit. **—in′fin·i·tes′i·mal·ly** *adv.*

in·fin·i·tive (ĭn-fĭn′ĭ-tĭv) ▸ *n.* A verb form that in English is often preceded by *to* and may be followed by an object or complement, as *be* in *I want to be president.*

in·fin·i·tude (ĭn-fĭn′ĭ-to͞od′, -tyo͞od′) ▸ *n.* **1.** The state or quality of being infinite. **2.** An immeasurably large quantity, number, or extent.

in·fin·i·ty (ĭn-fĭn′ĭ-tē) ▸ *n., pl.* **-ties.** **1.** The quality or condition of being infinite. **2.** Unbounded space, time, or quantity. **3.** An indefinitely large number or amount.

in·firm (ĭn-fûrm′) ▸ *adj.* **1.** Weak in body, esp. from old age or disease; feeble. **2.** Not strong or stable; shaky. **—in·firm′ly** *adv.*

in·fir·ma·ry (ĭn-fûr′mə-rē) ▸ *n., pl.* **-ries.** A place for the care of the sick or injured.

in·fir·mi·ty (ĭn-fûr′mĭ-tē) ▸ *n., pl.* **-ties.** **1.** A bodily ailment or weakness. **2.** Frailty; feebleness. **3.** A defect in a person's character.

in·flame (ĭn-flām′) ▸ *v.* **-flamed, -flam·ing.** **1.** To arouse to strong feeling or action. **2.** To intensify. **3.** To produce or be affected by an inflammation. **4.** To set on fire; kindle.

in·flam·ma·ble (ĭn-flăm′ə-bəl) ▸ *adj.* **1.** Easily ignited and capable of burning rapidly; flammable. **2.** Quickly aroused to strong emotion. **—in·flam′ma·bil′i·ty** *n.* **—in·flam′ma·ble** *n.*

in·flam·ma·tion (ĭn′flə-mā′shən) ▸ *n.* A localized reaction of tissue to irritation, injury, or infection, characterized by pain, redness, heat, and swelling.

in·flam·ma·to·ry (ĭn-flăm′ə-tôr′ē) ▸ *adj.* **1.** Arousing strong emotion, esp. anger. **2.** Marked or caused by inflammation.

in·flate (ĭn-flāt′) ▸ *v.* **-flat·ed, -flat·ing.** **1.** To fill and swell with air or gas. **2.** To raise or expand abnormally or improperly. **3.** To cause (e.g., wages) to undergo inflation. **—in·fla′tor, in·flat′er** *n.*

in·fla·tion (ĭn-flā′shən) ▸ *n.* **1.** The act of inflating or the state of being inflated. **2.** A persistent increase in prices

THESAURUS

infantile *adj.* —*See* BABYISH, CHILDISH.

infantine *adj.* —*See* BABYISH.

infatuated or **infatuate** *adj.* Affected with intense romantic attraction ▸ beguiled, besotted, captivated, charmed, enamored, enraptured, obsessed, smitten, spellbound, taken. *Slang:* gone. ***Idioms:*** crazy (*or* mad *or* nuts *or* wild) about, cuckoo over, hung up on.

infatuation *n.* An extravagant, short-lived romantic attachment ▸ *Informal:* crush, thing. ***Idiom:*** passing fancy. [*Compare* LOVE.] —*See also* ENTHUSIASM (2), OBSESSION.

infeasible *adj.* —*See* IMPOSSIBLE.

infect *v.* —*See* COMMUNICATE (2), CONTAMINATE, CORRUPT, POISON.

infection *n.* —*See* CONTAMINANT, CONTAMINATION, DISEASE.

infectious *adj.* —*See* CONTAGIOUS.

infelicitous *adj.* —*See* IMPROPER (2), UNFORTUNATE (2).

infer *v.* To arrive at a conclusion from evidence or reasoning ▸ conclude, deduce, deduct, draw, find, gather, judge, reason, understand. [*Compare* BELIEVE, DERIVE, SUPPOSE.] —*See also* GUESS.

inference *n.* A position arrived at by reasoning from premises ▸ conclusion, deduction, judgment. [*Compare* BELIEF.]

inferential *adj.* —*See* SUPPOSED.

inferior *adj.* —*See* BAD (1), DISAPPOINTING, MINOR (1).

inferior *n.* —*See* SUBORDINATE.

infernal *adj.* —*See* DAMNED, FIENDISH.

inferred *adj.* —*See* IMPLICIT (1).

infertile *adj.* —*See* BARREN (1), BARREN (2).

infertility *n.* —*See* STERILITY (2).

infidel *n.* One who does not believe in God ▸ atheist, heathen, nonbeliever, pagan.

infidelity *n.* —*See* FAITHLESSNESS.

infiltrate *v.* —*See* INSINUATE.

infinite *adj.* —*See* ENDLESS (1), INCALCULABLE.

infiniteness *n.* —*See* INFINITY (1).

infinitesimal *adj.* So small as not to be discernible ▸ imperceptible, microscopic. [*Compare* TINY.]

infinity *n.* **1.** The state or quality of being infinite ▸ boundlessness, immeasurability, immeasurableness, inexhaustibility, inexhaustibleness, infiniteness, infinitude, limitlessness, measurelessness, unboundedness, unlimitedness. [*Compare* ENDLESSNESS.] **2.** The totality of time without beginning or end ▸ eternity, perpetuity, sempiternity. [*Compare* FOREVER.]

infirm *adj.* —*See* INSECURE (2), WEAK (1).

infirmity *n.* The condition of being infirm or physically weak ▸ debility, decrepitude, delicacy, delicateness, feebleness, flimsiness, fragileness, fragility, frailness, frailty, insubstantiality, puniness, unsoundness, unsubstantiality, weakliness, weakness. [*Compare* BREAKDOWN.] —*See also* DISEASE, SICKNESS, WEAKNESS.

infix *v.* —*See* FIX (2).

inflame *v.* —*See* FIRE (1), HURT (3), PROVOKE.

inflamed *adj.* —*See* PAINFUL.

inflammation *n.* —*See* IRRITATION.

inflate *v.* —*See* EXAGGERATE, SWELL.

inflated *adj.* Filled up with or as if with something insubstantial ▸ flatulent, gassy, overblown, tumescent, tumid, turgid, windy. —*See also* EXAGGERATED, ORATORICAL, SWOLLEN.

or a persistent decline in the purchasing power of money. **—in·fla′tion·ar′y** (-shə-nĕr′ē) *adj.*

in·flect (ĭn-flĕkt′) ▸ *v.* 1. To alter (the voice) in tone or pitch; modulate. 2. *Gram.* To alter (a word) by inflection. 3. To turn from a course; bend. **—in·flec′tive** *adj.*

in·flec·tion (ĭn-flĕk′shən) ▸ *n.* 1. Alteration in pitch or tone of the voice. 2a. A change in the form of a word in accordance with grammar, syntax, or meaning, as in *near, nearer* or *man, men's.* b. The paradigm of a word. c. A pattern of forming paradigms, as of nouns or verbs. **—in·flec′tion·al** *adj.* **—in·flec′tion·al·ly** *adv.*

in·flex·i·ble (ĭn-flĕk′sə-bəl) ▸ *adj.* 1. Not easily bent; rigid. 2. Incapable of being changed; unalterable. 3. Unyielding. **—in·flex′i·bil′i·ty** *n.* **—in·flex′i·bly** *adv.*

in·flict (ĭn-flĭkt′) ▸ *v.* 1. To mete out (e.g., punishment); impose. 2. To afflict. **—in·flict′er, in·flic′tor** *n.* **—in·flic′tion** *n.*

in·flo·res·cence (ĭn′flə-rĕs′əns) ▸ *n.* A characteristic arrangement of flowers on a stem or in a cluster. **—in′flo·res′cent** *adj.*

in·flow (ĭn′flō′) ▸ *n.* A flowing in or into.

in·flu·ence (ĭn′flo͞o-əns) ▸ *n.* 1. A power indirectly or intangibly affecting a person or course of events. 2a. Power to sway or affect based on prestige, wealth, ability, or position. b. One exercising such power. ▸ *v.* **-enced, -enc·ing.** 1. To affect or sway. 2. To modify. ***—idiom:* under the influence** Intoxicated, esp. with alcohol. **—in′flu·en′tial** (-ĕn′shəl) *adj.* **—in′flu·en′tial·ly** *adv.*

in·flu·en·za (ĭn′flo͞o-ĕn′zə) ▸ *n.* An acute viral infection marked by inflammation of the respiratory tract and by fever, chills, and pain.

in·flux (ĭn′flŭks′) ▸ *n.* A flowing in.

in·fo (ĭn′fō) ▸ *n.* *Informal* Information.

in·fold (ĭn-fōld′) ▸ *v.* 1. To fold inward. 2. To enfold.

in·form (ĭn-fôrm′) ▸ *v.* 1. To impart information to. 2. To imbue with a quality. 3. To give or disclose information.

in·for·mal (ĭn-fôr′məl) ▸ *adj.* 1. Not formal or ceremonious; casual. 2. Not in accord with prescribed regulations. 3. Suited for everyday use: *informal clothes.* **—in′for·mal′i·ty** (-măl′ĭ-tē) *n.* **—in·for′mal·ly** *adv.*

in·for·mant (ĭn-fôr′mənt) ▸ *n.* 1. One that gives information. 2. An informer.

in·for·ma·tion (ĭn′fər-mā′shən) ▸ *n.* 1. Knowledge derived from study or experience. 2. Knowledge of an event or situation; intelligence. 3. A collection of facts or data. 4. Informing or being informed; communication of knowledge. 5. *Comp. Sci.* Processed, stored, or transmitted data. **—in′for·ma′tion·al** *adj.*

in·for·ma·tive (ĭn-fôr′mə-tĭv) ▸ *adj.* Providing or disclosing information; instructive. **—in·for′ma·tive·ly** *adv.*

in·formed (ĭn-fôrmd′) ▸ *adj.* 1. Possessing or based on reliable information. 2. Knowledgeable; educated: *the informed consumer.*

in·form·er (ĭn-fôr′mər) ▸ *n.* An informant, esp. one who informs against others.

infra– ▸ *pref.* Inferior to, below, or beneath: *infrasonic.*

in·frac·tion (ĭn-frăk′shən) ▸ *n.* The act or an instance of infringing; violation.

in·fra·red (ĭn′frə-rĕd′) ▸ *adj.* Of or relating to the range of invisible radiation wavelengths longer than red in the visible spectrum and on the border of the microwave region.

in·fra·son·ic (ĭn′frə-sŏn′ĭk) ▸ *adj.* Generating or using waves or vibrations with frequencies below that of audible sound.

in·fra·struc·ture (ĭn′frə-strŭk′chər) ▸ *n.* 1. An underlying base esp. for an organization or system. 2. The basic facilities, services, and installations needed for a community or society.

in·fre·quent (ĭn-frē′kwənt) ▸ *adj.* 1. Not occurring regularly; rare. 2. Situated at wide intervals in time or space. **—in·fre′quence, in·fre′quen·cy** *n.* **—in·fre′quent·ly** *adv.*

in·fringe (ĭn-frĭnj′) ▸ *v.* **-fringed, -fring·ing.** 1. To transgress; violate. 2. To encroach; trespass. **—in·fringe′ment** *n.*

in·fu·ri·ate (ĭn-fyo͝or′ē-āt′) ▸ *v.* **-at·ed, -at·ing.** To make furious; enrage. **—in·fu′ri·at′ing·ly** *adv.*

in·fuse (ĭn-fyo͞oz′) ▸ *v.* **-fused, -fus·ing.** 1. To put into as if by pouring. 2. To fill; imbue. 3. To steep or soak without boiling. **—in·fus′er** *n.* **—in·fus′i·ble** *adj.* **—in·fu′sion** *n.*

–ing[1] ▸ *suff.* 1. Used to form the present participle of verbs: *seeing.* 2. Used to form adjectives resembling present participles but not derived from verbs: *swashbuckling.*

–ing[2] ▸ *suff.* 1. Action, process, or art: *dancing.* 2. Something necessary to perform an action or process: *mooring.* 3. The result of an action or process: *drawing.* 4. Something connected with a specified thing or concept: *siding.*

in·gen·ious (ĭn-jēn′yəs) ▸ *adj.* 1. Marked by inventive skill; creative. 2. Imaginative and resourceful; clever. **—in·gen′ious·ly** *adv.* **—in·gen′ious·ness** *n.*

in·gé·nue (ăN′zhə-no͞o′) ▸ *n.* 1. An artless, innocent girl or

THESAURUS

inflection *n.* —*See* TONE (2).

inflexibility or **inflexibleness** *n.* —*See* STUBBORNNESS.

inflexible *adj.* —*See* IMMUTABLE, NARROW (1), RIGID, STUBBORN (1).

inflict *v.* To cause to undergo or bear (something unwelcome or damaging, for example) ▸ bring, impose, play, visit, wreak.

inflict on or **upon** *v.* —*See* IMPOSE ON.

infliction *n.* An excessive, unwelcome burden ▸ encumbrance, imposition, intrusion, obtrusion. [*Compare* BURDEN[1], MEDDLING.] —*See also* PUNISHMENT.

influence *n.* Power to sway or affect based on prestige, wealth, ability, or position ▸ force, leverage, power, sway, weight. *Informal:* clout, muscle. *Slang:* pull. —*See also* EFFECT (2), IMPACT.

influence *v.* To have an impact on in a certain way ▸ act on, affect, dispose, impact, incline, lead (into), predispose, sway, work on. [*Compare* BIAS, CHANGE, PERSUADE.] —*See also* MOVE (1).

influential *adj.* Having or exercising influence ▸ consequential, guiding, important, powerful, seminal, weighty. [*Compare* DOMINANT, FAMOUS, IMPORTANT, PRIMARY.]

infold *v.* —*See* WRAP (2).

inform *v.* 1. To impart information to ▸ acquaint, advise, apprise, cue in, educate, enlighten, fill in, notify, tell. *Idiom:* break the news. [*Compare* COMMUNICATE, DESCRIBE, REVEAL, SAY.] 2. To give incriminating information about others, especially to the authorities ▸ report, talk, tattle, tell, tip (off). *Slang:* finger, fink, rat (out), sing, snitch, squeal, stool. *Idioms:* blow the whistle, drop a dime on, name names, put the finger on. [*Compare* ACCUSE, BETRAY.]

informal *adj.* —*See* CONVERSATIONAL, EASYGOING.

informality *n.* —*See* EASE (1).

informant *n.* —*See* INFORMER.

information *n.* That which is known about a specific subject or situation ▸ data, facts, intelligence, knowledge, lore. info, low-down. *Slang:* dope, poop. [*Compare* EDUCATION, KNOWLEDGE.] —*See also* NEWS.

informative *adj.* —*See* EDUCATIONAL (2).

informed *adj.* Provided with information; made aware ▸ acquainted, advised, educated, enlightened, instructed, knowing, knowledgeable, up on. *Idioms:* in the know, up to date. [*Compare* AWARE, FAMILIAR.] —*See also* EDUCATED.

informer *n.* One who gives incriminating information about others ▸ informant, mole, source, talebearer, tattler, tattletale, telltale, whistleblower. *Informal:* rat, tipster. *Slang:* canary, finger, fink, nark, snitch, snitcher, squealer, stoolie, stool pigeon. [*Compare* BETRAYER, GOSSIP.]

infraction *n.* —*See* BREACH (1).

infrequent *adj.* Rarely occurring or appearing ▸ occasional, rare, scarce, sporadic, uncommon, unusual. *Idioms:* few and far between, like a snowball in summer, once in a lifetime. [*Compare* INTERMITTENT, UNIQUE.]

infrequently *adv.* At rare intervals ▸ inhabitually, little, occasionally, rarely, seldom, sporadically, uncommonly. *Idioms:* every now and then hardly (*or* scarcely) ever, once in a blue moon, once in a great while, when the spirit moves.

infringe *v.* —*See* VIOLATE (1).

infringement *n.* —*See* BREACH (1), TRESPASS (2).

infuriate *v.* —*See* ANGER (1).

infuriated *adj.* —*See* ANGRY.

infuse *v.* —*See* INTRODUCE (2), STEEP[2].

ingenerate *v.* —*See* CAUSE.

ingenious *adj.* —*See* CLEVER (1), INVENTIVE.

ingénue *n.* —*See* INNOCENT (2).

young woman. 2. An actress playing an ingenue.
in·ge·nu·i·ty (ĭn′jə-no͞o′ĭ-tē, -nyo͞o′-) ▸ *n., pl.* **-ties.** Inventive skill or imagination; cleverness.
in·gen·u·ous (ĭn-jĕn′yo͞o-əs) ▸ *adj.* 1. Unsophisticated; artless. 2. Straightforward; candid. **—in·gen′u·ous·ly** *adv.* **—in·gen′u·ous·ness** *n.*
in·gest (ĭn-jĕst′) ▸ *v.* To take into the body by or as if by swallowing. **—in·ges′tion** *n.*
in·glo·ri·ous (ĭn-glôr′ē-əs) ▸ *adj.* 1. Ignominious; disgraceful. 2. Not famous or renowned. **—in·glo′ri·ous·ly** *adv.*
in·got (ĭng′gət) ▸ *n.* A mass of metal cast in a shape for convenient storage or shipment.
in·grain (ĭn-grān′) ▸ *v.* To fix deeply or indelibly, as in the mind. ▸ *n.* (ĭn′grān′) Yarn or fiber dyed before manufacture.
in·grained (ĭn-grānd′) ▸ *adj.* 1. Firmly established; deep-seated: *ingrained prejudice.* 2. Worked deeply into the fiber: *ingrained dirt.*
in·grate (ĭn′grāt′) ▸ *n.* An ungrateful person.
in·gra·ti·ate (ĭn grā′shē-āt′) ▸ *v.* **-at·ed, -at·ing.** To bring (oneself) into the favor of another.
in·grat·i·tude (ĭn-grăt′ĭ-to͞od′, -tyo͞od′) ▸ *n.* Lack of gratitude; ungratefulness.
in·gre·di·ent (ĭn-grē′dē-ənt) ▸ *n.* An element in a mixture or compound; constituent.
in·gress (ĭn′grĕs′) ▸ *n.* 1. A going in or entering. 2. A means of entering.
in-group (ĭn′gro͞op′) ▸ *n.* A clique.
in·grown (ĭn′grōn′) ▸ *adj.* 1. Grown abnormally into the flesh. 2. Inbred; innate: *ingrown habits.*
in·gui·nal (ĭng′gwə-nəl) ▸ *adj.* Relating to or located in the groin.
in·hab·it (ĭn-hăb′ĭt) ▸ *v.* To live or reside in. **—in·hab′it·a·bil′i·ty** *n.* **—in·hab′it·a·ble** *adj.*
in·hab·i·tant (ĭn-hăb′ĭ-tənt) ▸ *n.* A permanent resident.
in·ha·lant (ĭn-hā′lənt) ▸ *n.* A medication to be inhaled.
in·hale (ĭn-hāl′) ▸ *v.* **-haled, -hal·ing.** To draw into the lungs by breathing. **—in′ha·la′tion** (-hə-lā′shən) *n.*
in·hal·er (ĭn-hā′lər) ▸ *n.* 1. One that inhales. 2. A device that produces a vapor to ease breathing.
in·here (ĭn-hîr′) ▸ *v.* **-hered, -her·ing.** To be inherent or innate. **—in·her′ence** (-hîr′əns, -hĕr′-), **in·her′en·cy** *n.*
in·her·ent (ĭn-hîr′ənt, -hĕr′-) ▸ *adj.* Existing as an essential constituent or characteristic; intrinsic. **—in·her′ent·ly** *adv.*
in·her·it (ĭn-hĕr′ĭt) ▸ *v.* 1. To receive by legal succession or will. 2. *Biol.* To receive from one's parents by genetic transmission. **—in·her′it·a·bil′i·ty** *n.* **—in·her′it·a·ble** *adj.* **—in·her′i·tor** *n.*
in·her·i·tance (ĭn-hĕr′ĭ-təns) ▸ *n.* 1. Something inherited or to be inherited. 2. Something regarded as a heritage.
in·hib·it (ĭn-hĭb′ĭt) ▸ *v.* 1. To hold back; restrain. 2. To prohibit; forbid. **—in·hib′i·tive, in·hib′i·to′ry** (-tôr′ē) *adj.*
in·hi·bi·tion (ĭn′hə-bĭsh′ən, ĭn′ə-) ▸ *n.* 1. The act of inhibiting or the state of being inhibited. 2. *Psychol.* Restraint of a behavioral process, desire, or impulse.
in·hib·i·tor also **in·hib·it·er** (ĭn-hĭb′ĭ-tər) ▸ *n.* One that inhibits, as a substance that retards or stops a chemical reaction.
in·hos·pi·ta·ble (ĭn-hŏs′pĭ-tə-bəl, ĭn′hŏ-spĭt′ə-bəl) ▸ *adj.* 1. Displaying no hospitality; unfriendly. 2. Unfavorable to life or growth; hostile. **—in·hos′pi·ta·ble·ness** *n.* **—in·hos′pi·ta·bly** *adv.*
in-house (ĭn′hous′) ▸ *adj.* Conducted or being within an organization or firm.
in·hu·man (ĭn-hyo͞o′mən) ▸ *adj.* 1a. Lacking kindness or pity; cruel. b. Deficient in emotional warmth; cold. 2. Not suited for human needs. 3. Not of ordinary human form; monstrous. **—in·hu′man·ly** *adv.*
in·hu·mane (ĭn′hyo͞o-mān′) ▸ *adj.* Lacking pity or compassion. **—in′hu·mane′ly** *adv.*
in·hu·man·i·ty (ĭn′hyo͞o-măn′ĭ-tē) ▸ *n., pl.* **-ties.** 1. Lack of pity or compassion; cruelty. 2. An inhuman or cruel act.
in·im·i·cal (ĭ-nĭm′ĭ-kəl) ▸ *adj.* 1. Injurious or harmful. 2. Unfriendly; hostile. **—in·im′i·cal·ly** *adv.*
in·im·i·ta·ble (ĭ-nĭm′ĭ-tə-bəl) ▸ *adj.* Defying imitation; matchless. **—in·im′i·ta·bly** *adv.*
in·iq·ui·ty (ĭ-nĭk′wĭ-tē) ▸ *n., pl.* **-ties.** 1. Wickedness; sinfulness. 2. A wicked sin. **—in·iq′ui·tous** *adj.*
in·i·tial (ĭ-nĭsh′əl) ▸ *adj.* Of or occurring at the beginning; first. ▸ *n.* The first letter of a name or word. ▸ *v.* **-tialed, -tial·ing** also **-tialled, -tial·ling.** To mark or sign with initials, esp. as authorization or approval. **—in·i′tial·ly** *adv.*
in·i·ti·ate (ĭ-nĭsh′ē-āt′) ▸ *v.* **-at·ed, -at·ing.** 1. To begin or originate. 2. To introduce to a new field, interest, skill, or activity. 3. To admit into membership, as with ceremonies or

THESAURUS

ingenuity or **ingeniousness** *n.* *—See* INVENTION (1).
ingenuous *adj.* *—See* ARTLESS, FRANK.
ingest *v.* To cause to pass from the mouth into the stomach ▸ swallow, take. [*Compare* DRINK, GULP.] *—See also* EAT (1).
ingestion *n.* An act of swallowing ▸ gulp, swallow, swig.
ingle *n.* An open space for holding a fire at the base of a chimney ▸ fireplace, grate, hearth.
ingrain *v.* *—See* FIX (2), INSTILL.
ingrained *adj.* *—See* CONFIRMED (1), CONSTITUTIONAL.
ingratiating *adj.* *—See* FLATTERING.
ingredient *n.* *—See* PART (1).
ingress *n.* *—See* ADMISSION, ENTRANCE[1].
ingression *n.* *—See* ADMISSION, ENTRANCE[1].
in-group *n.* *—See* CIRCLE (3).
ingurgitate *v.* *—See* GULP.
inhabit *v.* To live in a place, as does a people ▸ occupy, people, populate. [*Compare* LIVE[1], SETTLE.]
inhabitable *adj.* Fit to live in ▸ habitable, livable.
inhabitant *n.* One who resides in a place, especially on a permanent basis ▸ denizen, dweller, native, occupant, resident, tenant, townsman, townswoman, villager. *Informal:* local. [*Compare* CITIZEN.]
inhalation *n.* *—See* BREATH.
inhale *v.* *—See* BREATHE (1).
inharmonic or **inharmonical** *adj.* *—See* INHARMONIOUS (2).
inharmonious *adj.* 1. Devoid of harmony and accord ▸ conflicting, differing, disagreeing, discordant, dissident, dissonant, inconsonant, uncongenial, unharmonious. ***Idioms:*** at odds, at opposite poles, at sixes and sevens, at war, out of accord. [*Compare* DISCREPANT, INCONGRUOUS.] 2. Characterized by unpleasant discordance of sound ▸ cacophonous, discordant, disharmonious, dissonant, inharmonic, tuneless, unharmonious, unmelodious, unmusical, untuneful. [*Compare* HARSH.]
inharmony *n.* *—See* CONFLICT.
inhere *v.* *—See* CONSIST.
inherent *adj.* *—See* CONSTITUTIONAL, INSTINCTIVE.
inherit *v.* To receive from one who has died ▸ come into. *Idiom:* be (or fall) heir to.
inheritance *n.* 1. Any special privilege accorded a firstborn ▸ birthright, heritage, legacy, patrimony. [*Compare* RIGHT.] 2. Something immaterial, as a style or philosophy, that is passed from one generation to another ▸ heritage, legacy, tradition.
inherited *adj.* *—See* ANCESTRAL, INNATE.
inhibit *v.* To check the freedom and spontaneity of ▸ constrain, constrict, cramp. *—See also* RESTRAIN.
inhibited *adj.* *—See* FRIGID, RESERVED.
inhibition *n.* *—See* FORBIDDANCE, RESTRAINT.
inhibitive or **inhibitory** *adj.* *—See* REPRESSIVE.
inhospitable *adj.* Not encouraging life or growth ▸ adverse, hostile, unfavorable. [*Compare* SEVERE.] *—See also* FORBIDDING.
inhospitality *n.* Lack of cordiality and hospitableness ▸ aloofness, coldness, inhospitableness, uncivility, uncongeniality, unfriendliness, ungraciousness, unreceptiveness, unwelcome, unwelcomeness.
inhuman *adj.* *—See* CRUEL, OUTRAGEOUS.
inhumane *adj.* *—See* CRUEL.
inhumanity *n.* *—See* CRUELTY, OUTRAGE.
inhumation *n.* *—See* BURIAL.
inhume *v.* *—See* BURY.
inimical *adj.* Feeling or showing unfriendliness ▸ hostile, unfriendly. [*Compare* MEAN[2].] *—See also* CONTRARY.
iniquitous *adj.* *—See* EVIL.
iniquity *n.* *—See* CRIME (2), EVIL (1), INJUSTICE (2).
initial *adj.* *—See* BEGINNING, FIRST.
initiate *v.* To admit formally into membership or office, as with ritual ▸

ritual. ▸ *n.* (-ĭt) One who has been initiated. **—in·i′ti·a′tion** *n.* **—in·i′ti·a′tor** *n.* **—in·i′ti·a·to′ry** (-ə-tôr′ē) *adj.*

in·i·tia·tive (ĭ-nĭsh′ə-tĭv) ▸ *n.* **1.** The ability to begin or follow through with a plan or task; enterprise. **2.** A first step: *took the initiative in breaking the deadlock.* **3.** The right and procedure by which citizens can propose a law by petition and ensure its submission to the electorate.

in·ject (ĭn-jĕkt′) ▸ *v.* **1.** To force or drive (a fluid) into. **2.** To introduce into conversation or consideration: *injected a note of humor.* **3.** To place into an orbit, trajectory, or stream. **—in·jec′tion** *n.* **—in·jec′tor** *n.*

in·ju·di·cious (ĭn′jo͞o-dĭsh′əs) ▸ *adj.* Showing a lack of judgment or discretion; unwise. **—in′ju·di′cious·ly** *adv.*

in·junc·tion (ĭn-jŭngk′shən) ▸ *n.* **1.** A command, directive, or order. **2.** A court order prohibiting or requiring a specific action. **—in·junc′tive** *adj.*

in·jure (ĭn′jər) ▸ *v.* **-jured, -jur·ing. 1.** To cause harm or damage to. **2.** To commit an injustice or offense against.

in·ju·ri·ous (ĭn-jo͝or′ē-əs) ▸ *adj.* Causing injury; harmful. **—in·ju′ri·ous·ly** *adv.*

in·ju·ry (ĭn′jə-rē) ▸ *n., pl.* **-ries. 1.** An act that harms or damages. **2.** A wound or other particular form of hurt, damage, or loss. **3.** Injustice.

in·jus·tice (ĭn-jŭs′tĭs) ▸ *n.* **1.** Violation of another's rights or of what is right; lack of justice. **2.** An unjust act; wrong.

ink (ĭngk) ▸ *n.* **1.** A pigmented liquid or paste used esp. for writing or printing. **2.** A dark liquid ejected for protection, as by the squid and octopus. ▸ *v.* To cover or stain with ink. **—ink′y** *adj.*

ink·blot (ĭngk′blŏt′) ▸ *n.* **1.** A blotted pattern of spilled ink. **2.** A pattern resembling an inkblot that is used in inkblot tests.

inkblot test ▸ *n.* A psychological test in which a subject's interpretation of inkblots is analyzed.

ink-jet printer (ĭngk′jĕt′) ▸ *n.* A printer that directs electrically charged ink streams onto a page.

in·kling (ĭng′klĭng) ▸ *n.* **1.** A slight hint or indication. **2.** A vague idea or notion.

ink·well (ĭngk′wĕl′) ▸ *n.* A small reservoir for ink.

in·laid (ĭn′lād′) ▸ *v.* P.t. and p.part. of **inlay.** ▸ *adj.* Decorated with a pattern set into a surface.

in·land (ĭn′lənd) ▸ *adj.* **1.** Of or located in the interior part of a country. **2.** *Chiefly Brit.* Operating or applying within a country; domestic. **—in′land** *adv. & n.*

in-law (ĭn′lô′) ▸ *n.* A relative by marriage.

in·lay (ĭn′lā′, ĭn-lā′) ▸ *v.* **-laid** (-lād′), **-lay·ing.** To set into a surface to form a design. ▸ *n.* **1.** An inlaid object, design, or decoration. **2.** A solid filling, as of gold, fitted and cemented to a tooth.

in·let (ĭn′lĕt′, -lĭt) ▸ *n.* **1.** A stream or bay leading inland, as from the ocean; estuary. **2.** A narrow passage of water, as between two islands.

in·mate (ĭn′māt′) ▸ *n.* An occupant of a communal dwelling, esp. a person confined to an institution such as a prison or hospital.

in me·di·as res (ĭn mē′dē-əs rās′) ▸ *adv.* In or into the middle of a sequence of events.

in me·mo·ri·am (ĭn′ mə-môr′ē-əm) ▸ *prep.* In memory of.

inn (ĭn) ▸ *n.* **1.** A hotel. **2.** A tavern.

in·nards (ĭn′ərdz) ▸ *pl.n. Informal* **1.** Internal bodily organs; viscera. **2.** The inner parts, as of a machine.

in·nate (ĭ-nāt′, ĭn′āt′) ▸ *adj.* **1.** Possessed at birth; inborn. **2.** Possessed as an essential characteristic; inherent. **—in·nate′ly** *adv.*

in·ner (ĭn′ər) ▸ *adj.* **1.** Located farther inside: *an inner room.* **2.** Of or relating to the mind or spirit. **3.** More exclusive, influential, or important: *the inner circles of government.* **—in′ner·ness** *n.*

inner city ▸ *n.* The usu. older central part of a city, esp. when crowded, neglected, and decaying. **—in′ner-cit′y** *adj.*

in·ner-di·rect·ed (ĭn′ər-dĭ-rĕk′tĭd, -dī-) ▸ *adj.* Guided, as in behavior, by one's own set of values rather than external standards.

inner ear ▸ *n.* The part of the vertebrate ear that includes the semicircular canals, vestibule, and cochlea.

Inner Hebrides ▸ See **Hebrides.**

Inner Mongolia ▸ See **Nei Monggol.**

in·ner·most (ĭn′ər-mōst′) ▸ *adj.* **1.** Situated farthest within. **2.** Most intimate.

inner planet ▸ *n.* Any of the four planets, Mercury, Venus, Earth, and Mars, whose orbits are closest to the sun.

inner tube ▸ *n.* A flexible, airtight hollow ring, usu. made of rubber, inserted into the casing of a pneumatic tire for holding compressed air.

in·ning (ĭn′ĭng) ▸ *n.* A division of a baseball game in which each team has a turn at bat.

inn·keep·er (ĭn′kē′pər) ▸ *n.* One who owns or manages an inn or hotel.

in·no·cent (ĭn′ə-sənt) ▸ *adj.* **1.** Uncorrupted by evil, malice, or wrongdoing; sinless. **2.** Not guilty of a specific crime or offense; legally blameless. **3.** Not dangerous or harmful; innocuous. **4a.** Not experienced or worldly;

THESAURUS

inaugurate, induct, install, instate, invest. [*Compare* ADMIT, INDOCTRINATE.] —*See also* START (1).

initiate *n.* —*See* BEGINNER.

initiation *n.* The act or process of formally admitting a person to membership or office ▸ hazing, inaugural, inauguration, induction, installation, instatement, investiture. [*Compare* ADMISSION.] —*See also* BEGINNING.

initiative *n.* —*See* DRIVE (2).

initiatory *adj.* —*See* BEGINNING.

inject *v.* —*See* INTRODUCE (2).

injudicious *adj.* —*See* UNWISE.

injunction *n.* —*See* COMMAND (1).

injure *v.* To cause bodily damage to a living thing ▸ hurt, traumatize, wing, wound. [*Compare* CUT, BREAK.] —*See also* DAMAGE, DEFORM, DISTRESS, OFFEND (1).

injurious *adj.* —*See* HARMFUL, LIBELOUS.

injury *n.* —*See* DAMAGE, HARM, INJUSTICE (1).

injustice *n.* **1.** An unjust act ▸ crime, disservice, inequity, injury, malpractice, offense, outrage, raw deal, wrong. [*Compare* BREACH, CRIME, INDIGNITY.] **2.** Lack of justice ▸ inequity, iniquity, unfairness, unjustness, wrong. [*Compare* FAVORITISM, INEQUALITY, PREJUDICE.] —*See also* OPPRESSION.

inkling *n.* —*See* FEELING (1), HINT (1).

inky *adj.* —*See* BLACK (2).

inlet *n.* A usually narrow stretch of water leading inland ▸ estuary, fjord, mouth. [*Compare* BAY[1], CHANNEL, HARBOR.]

inlying *adj.* Located inside or farther in ▸ inner, inside, interior, internal. [*Compare* CENTRAL, SECLUDED.]

inmost *adj.* —*See* CENTRAL.

inn *n.* —*See* BAR (2).

innate *adj.* Possessed at birth ▸ congenital, connate, connatural, hereditary, inborn, inherited, native. [*Compare* ESSENTIAL.] —*See also* CONSTITUTIONAL, INSTINCTIVE.

inner *adj.* **1.** Located inside or farther in ▸ inlying, inside, interior, internal. [*Compare* CENTRAL, SECLUDED.] **2.** Arising from one's mental or spiritual being ▸ interior, internal, intimate, inward, visceral. *Slang:* gut. [*Compare* CONSTITUTIONAL, ESSENTIAL, PERSONAL.]

innermost *adj.* —*See* CENTRAL, CONFIDENTIAL (2).

innerving *adj.* —*See* INVIGORATING.

inning *n.* —*See* TURN (1).

innocence *n.* The stage of life between birth and puberty ▸ childhood, early years, preadolescence, prepubescence. [*Compare* YOUTH.] —*See also* ARTLESSNESS, CHASTITY, IGNORANCE (2).

innocent *adj.* **1.** Free from evil and corruption ▸ angelic, angelical, clean, lily-white, pure, sinless, unblemished, uncorrupted, undefiled, unstained, unsullied, untainted, virginal. ***Idiom:*** pure as the driven snow. [*Compare* CLEAN, ETHICAL, INEXPERIENCED, MORAL.] **2.** Free from guilt or blame ▸ blameless, faultless, guiltless, harmless, inculpable, irreproachable, lily-white, unblamable, unoffending. *Slang:* clean. ***Idioms:*** above suspicion, in the clear. [*Compare* HONEST.] —*See also* ARTLESS, EMPTY (2), HARMLESS, IGNORANT (3).

innocent *n.* **1.** A pure, uncorrupted person ▸ angel, cherub, dove, lamb, virgin. **2.** A guileless, unsophisticated person ▸ babe, child, ingénue, naive. ***Idioms:*** babe in the woods, pure heart, simple soul. [*Compare* FOOL.] —*See also* CHILD (1).

naive. **b.** Without deception or guile; artless. **—in′no·cence** *n.* **—in′no·cent** *n.* **—in′no·cent·ly** *adv.*

in·noc·u·ous (ĭ-nŏk′yo͞o-əs) ▸ *adj.* **1.** Having no adverse effect; harmless. **2.** Not likely to provoke strong emotion; insipid. **—in·noc′u·ous·ly** *adv.* **—in·noc′u·ous·ness** *n.*

in·nom·i·nate (ĭ-nŏm′ə-nĭt) ▸ *adj.* **1.** Having no name. **2.** Anonymous.

in·no·vate (ĭn′ə-vāt′) ▸ *v.* **-vat·ed, -vat·ing. 1.** To begin or introduce (something new). **2.** To be creative. **—in′no·va′tive** *adj.* **—in′no·va′tor** *n.*

in·no·va·tion (ĭn′ə-vā′shən) ▸ *n.* **1.** The act of innovating. **2.** Something, such as a method or product, newly introduced. **—in′no·va′tion·al** *adj.*

in·nu·en·do (ĭn′yo͞o-ĕn′dō) ▸ *n., pl.* **-does.** An indirect or subtle, usu. derogatory insinuation.

in·nu·mer·a·ble (ĭ-no͞o′mər-ə-bəl, ĭ-nyo͞o′-) ▸ *adj.* Too numerous to be counted.

in·oc·u·late (ĭ-nŏk′yə-lāt′) ▸ *v.* **-lat·ed, -lat·ing.** To introduce a serum, vaccine, or antigenic substance into, esp. to produce or boost immunity to a specific disease. **—in·oc′u·la′tion** *n.*

in·oc·u·lum (ĭ-nŏk′yə-ləm) ▸ *n., pl.* **-la** (-lə) or **-lums.** The material used in an inoculation.

in·of·fen·sive (ĭn′ə-fĕn′sĭv) ▸ *adj.* Giving no offense; unobjectionable.

in·op·er·a·ble (ĭn-ŏp′ər-ə-bəl, -ŏp′rə-) ▸ *adj.* **1.** Not working; inoperative. **2.** Not able to be treated surgically.

in·op·er·a·tive (ĭn-ŏp′ər-ə-tĭv, -ŏp′rə-) ▸ *adj.* Not working or functioning.

in·op·por·tune (ĭn-ŏp′ər-to͞on′, -tyo͞on′) ▸ *adj.* Inappropriate or ill-timed. **—in·op′por·tune′ly** *adv.* **—in·op′por·tune′ness** *n.*

in·or·di·nate (ĭn-ôr′dn-ĭt) ▸ *adj.* **1.** Exceeding reasonable limits; immoderate. **2.** Not regulated; disorderly. **—in·or′di·nate·ly** *adv.*

in·or·gan·ic (ĭn′ôr-găn′ĭk) ▸ *adj.* **1a.** Involving neither organic life nor the products of organic life. **b.** Not composed of organic matter. **2.** *Chem.* Of or relating to compounds not usu. classified as organic. **—in′or·gan′i·cal·ly** *adv.*

in·pa·tient (ĭn′pā′shənt) ▸ *n.* A patient who is admitted to a hospital for treatment.

in·put (ĭn′po͝ot′) ▸ *n.* **1.** Something put in. **2.** Energy, work, or power put into a system or machine. **3.** Information put into a computer system for processing. **4.** *Informal* **a.** Contribution of information, comments, or viewpoint to a common effort. **b.** Information in general. **—in′put′** *v.*

in·quest (ĭn′kwĕst′) ▸ *n.* **1.** A judicial inquiry, usu. held before a jury. **2.** An investigation.

in·quire (ĭn-kwīr′) also **en·quire** (ĕn-) ▸ *v.* **-quired, -quir·ing. 1.** To ask or ask about. **2.** To make an inquiry or investigation. **—in·quir′er** *n.* **—in·quir′ing·ly** *adv.*

in·quir·y (ĭn-kwīr′ē, ĭn′kwə-rē) also **en·quir·y** (ĕn-kwīr′ē, ĕn′kwə-rē) ▸ *n., pl.* **-ies. 1.** The act or process of inquiring. **2.** A question; query. **3.** A close examination of a matter in a search for information or truth.

in·qui·si·tion (ĭn′kwĭ-zĭsh′ən, ĭng′-) ▸ *n.* **1.** An investigation, such as an inquest. **2. Inquisition** A former Roman Catholic tribunal established to suppress heresy. **3.** A rigorous interrogation or scrutiny. **—in·quis′i·tor** (-kwĭz′ĭ-tər) *n.* **—in·quis′i·to′ri·al** (-kwĭz′ĭ-tôr′ē-əl) *adj.*

in·quis·i·tive (ĭn-kwĭz′ĭ-tĭv) ▸ *adj.* **1.** Unduly curious. **2.** Eager for knowledge. **—in·quis′i·tive·ly** *adv.* **—in·quis′i·tive·ness** *n.*

in re (ĭn rā′, rē′) ▸ *prep.* *Law* In the matter or case of; in regard to.

in·road (ĭn′rōd′) ▸ *n.* **1.** A hostile invasion; raid. **2.** An advance, esp. at another's expense; encroachment.

in·rush (ĭn′rŭsh′) ▸ *n.* A sudden influx.

ins. ▸ *abbr.* inches

in·sa·lu·bri·ous (ĭn′sə-lo͞o′brē-əs) ▸ *adj.* Not promoting health; unwholesome.

in·sane (ĭn-sān′) ▸ *adj.* **1a.** Of, exhibiting, or afflicted with mental disorder. **b.** Characteristic of or associated with persons who are insane. **2.** Very foolish; absurd. **—in·sane′ly** *adv.* **—in·san′i·ty** (-săn′ĭ-tē) *n.*

in·sa·tia·ble (ĭn-sā′shə-bəl, -shē-ə-) ▸ *adj.* Impossible to satiate or satisfy. **—in·sa′tia·bil′i·ty, in·sa′tia·ble·ness** *n.* **—in·sa′tia·bly** *adv.*

in·scribe (ĭn-skrīb′) ▸ *v.* **-scribed, -scrib·ing. 1.** To write, print, carve, or engrave (words or letters) on or in a surface. **2.** To mark or engrave with words or letters. **3.** To enter (a name) on a list. **4.** To dedicate to someone. **5.** *Math.* To draw (one figure) within another figure so that every vertex of the enclosed figure touches the outer figure. **—in·scrib′er** *n.* **—in·scrip′tion** (-skrĭp′shən) *n.*

THESAURUS

innocuous *adj.* —*See* HARMLESS, INSIPID.

innocuousness *n.* —*See* INSIPIDITY.

innovate *v.* —*See* INTRODUCE (1).

innovation *n.* A new and unusual thing ▸ novelty. ***Idioms:*** the latest craze (*or* fashion *or* thing), the in thing, whole new ball of wax. —*See also* INVENTION (2), VISION (2).

innovative *adj.* —*See* INVENTIVE, NEW.

innovativeness *n.* —*See* NOVELTY (1).

innovator *n.* —*See* DEVELOPER.

innuendo *n.* —*See* HINT (2).

innumerable *adj.* —*See* INCALCULABLE.

inobservant *adj.* —*See* CARELESS.

inobtrusive *adj.* —*See* MODEST (1).

inoffensive *adj.* —*See* CLEAN (2), HARMLESS, INSIPID.

inoperative *adj.* —*See* IDLE (1).

inoperativeness *n.* —*See* INACTION.

inopportune *adj.* Not occurring at a favorable time ▸ ill-timed, inconvenient, untimely. [*Compare* FATEFUL.] —*See also* UNSEASONABLE.

inordinacy *n.* —*See* EXCESS (1).

inordinate *adj.* —*See* EXCESSIVE.

inordinately *adv.* —*See* UNDULY.

inordinateness *n.* —*See* EXCESS (1).

input *n.* The right or chance to express an opinion or participate in a decision ▸ say, suffrage, voice, vote. *Informal:* say-so.

inquest *n.* The examination of evidence, charges, and claims in court ▸ court case, hearing, inquiry, trial. —*See also* EXAMINATION (1).

inquietude *n.* —*See* RESTLESSNESS.

inquire or **enquire** *v.* —*See* ASK (1), EXPLORE.

inquirer or **enquirer** *n.* One who inquires ▸ cross-examiner, inquisitor, interrogator, interviewer, investigator, prober, querier, quester, questioner, researcher. [*Compare* BUSYBODY.]

inquiring or **enquiring** *adj.* —*See* CURIOUS (2).

inquiry or **enquiry** *n.* **1.** A request for data ▸ interrogation, query, question, questioning. [*Compare* DEMAND, PROBLEM.] **2.** The examination of evidence, charges, and claims in court ▸ court case, hearing, inquest, trial. —*See also* EXAMINATION (1).

inquisition *n.* —*See* EXAMINATION (1).

inquisitive *adj.* —*See* CURIOUS (1), CURIOUS (2).

inquisitiveness *n.* —*See* CURIOSITY (2), CURIOSITY (1).

inquisitor *n.* —*See* INQUIRER.

inquisitorial *adj.* —*See* CURIOUS (1), DICTATORIAL.

inroad *n.* An act of invading, especially by military forces ▸ foray, incursion, invasion, raid. [*Compare* ATTACK.]

insalubrious *adj.* —*See* MORBID, UNWHOLESOME (1).

insane *adj.* Afflicted with or exhibiting irrationality and mental unsoundness ▸ brainsick, certifiable, crazed, crazy, daft, demented, derailed, disordered, distraught, dotty, lunatic, mad, maniac, maniacal, mentally ill, moonstruck, non compos mentis, off, sick, touched, unsound, wrong. *Informal:* bonkers, cracked, daffy, gaga, haywire, loony, unhinged. *Slang:* bananas, bats, batty, buggy, cuckoo, fruity, loco, nuts, nutty, psycho, screwy, unbalanced, wacko, wacky, whack. ***Idioms:*** around the bend, bereft of reason, crazy as a loon, having a screw loose, mad as a hatter (*or* March hare), not all there, not playing with a full deck, nutty as a fruitcake, off one's nut (*or* rocker), off (*or* out of) one's head, off the wall, out of one's mind (*or* gourd *or* skull *or* tree *or* wits), sick (*or* soft) in the head, stark raving mad, of unsound mind. —*See also* FOOLISH.

insaneness *n.* —*See* INSANITY.

insanity *n.* Serious mental illness impairing a person's capacity to function normally ▸ brainsickness, craziness, dementia, derangement, disturbance, insaneness, lunacy, madness, mania, mental illness, psychopathy, unbalance. —*See also* FOOLISHNESS.

insatiable *adj.* —*See* VORACIOUS.

insatiability *n.* —*See* VORACITY.

inscribe *v.* —*See* ENGRAVE (1), ENGRAVE (2), LIST[1], SIGN, WRITE.

in·scru·ta·ble (ĭn-skro͞o′tə-bəl) ▸ *adj.* Difficult to fathom or understand. **—in·scru′ta·bil′i·ty, in·scru′ta·ble·ness** *n.* **—in·scru′ta·bly** *adv.*

in·seam (ĭn′sēm′) ▸ *n.* The inside seam of a pant leg.

in·sect (ĭn′sĕkt′) ▸ *n.* Any of a class of small, usu. winged invertebrate animals, such as flies, beetles, and moths, having three pairs of legs and a three-segmented body.

in·sec·ti·cide (ĭn-sĕk′tĭ-sīd′) ▸ *n.* A substance used to kill insects. **—in·sec′ti·cid′al** *adj.*

in·sec·ti·vore (ĭn-sĕk′tə-vôr′) ▸ *n.* An insect-eating organism. **—in′sec·tiv′o·rous** (-tĭv′ər-əs) *adj.*

in·se·cure (ĭn′sĭ-kyo͝or′) ▸ *adj.* 1. Inadequately guarded or protected; unsafe. 2. Not firm or fixed; shaky. 3. Lacking self-confidence. **—in′se·cure′ly** *adv.* **—in′se·cu′ri·ty** *n.*

in·sem·i·nate (ĭn-sĕm′ə-nāt′) ▸ *v.* **-nat·ed, -nat·ing.** To introduce or inject semen into the reproductive tract of (a female). **—in·sem′i·na′tion** *n.* **—in·sem′i·na′tor** *n.*

in·sen·sate (ĭn-sĕn′sāt′, -sĭt) ▸ *adj.* 1a. Inanimate. b. Unconscious. 2. Lacking sensibility; unfeeling. 3. Lacking sense; foolish.

in·sen·si·ble (ĭn-sĕn′sə-bəl) ▸ *adj.* 1. Imperceptible; inappreciable. 2a. Unconscious. b. Inanimate. c. Insensitive; numb. 3a. Unaware. b. Callous; indifferent. **—in·sen′si·bil′i·ty** *n.* **—in·sen′si·bly** *adv.*

in·sen·si·tive (ĭn-sĕn′sĭ-tĭv) ▸ *adj.* 1. Not physically sensitive; numb. 2. Unresponsive to or unaffected by the feelings of others; unfeeling. **—in·sen′si·tive·ly** *adv.* **—in·sen′si·tiv′i·ty** *n.*

in·sen·tient (ĭn-sĕn′shənt) ▸ *adj.* Devoid of sensation or consciousness. **—in·sen′tience** *n.*

in·sep·a·ra·ble (ĭn-sĕp′ər-ə-bəl, -sĕp′rə-) ▸ *adj.* 1. Impossible to separate. 2. Very closely associated. **—in·sep′a·ra·bil′i·ty** *n.* **—in·sep′a·ra·bly** *adv.*

in·sert (ĭn-sûrt′) ▸ *v.* 1. To put, place, or set into: *inserted a key in a lock.* 2. To interpolate. ▸ *n.* (ĭn′sûrt′) Something inserted or intended for insertion, as a chart into a text. **—in·ser′tion** *n.*

in·set (ĭn′sĕt′, ĭn-sĕt′) ▸ *v.* To set in; insert. **—in′set′** *n.*

in·shore (ĭn′shôr′) ▸ *adv. & adj.* Close to or coming toward a shore.

in·side (ĭn-sīd′, ĭn′sīd′) ▸ *n.* 1. An inner or interior part. 2. An inner side or surface. 3. **insides** *Informal* a. The inner organs; entrails. b. The inner parts or workings: *the insides of a TV set.* ▸ *adv.* Into or in the interior; within. ▸ *prep.* 1. Within: *inside an hour.* 2. Into the interior of: *going inside the house.* **—*idioms:* inside of** Within: *inside of an hour.* **inside out** 1. With the inner surface turned out. 2. *Informal* Thoroughly: *knew the city inside out.* **on the inside** In a position of confidence or influence. **—in·side′** *adj.*

in·sid·er (ĭn-sī′dər) ▸ *n.* 1. An accepted member of a group. 2. One who has special knowledge or access to confidential information.

inside track ▸ *n. Informal* An advantageous position, as in a competition.

in·sid·i·ous (ĭn-sĭd′ē-əs) ▸ *adj.* 1. Working or spreading harmfully in a subtle or stealthy manner. 2. Intended to entrap; treacherous. 3. Beguiling but harmful. **—in·sid′i·ous·ly** *adv.* **—in·sid′i·ous·ness** *n.*

in·sight (ĭn′sīt′) ▸ *n.* The capacity to discern the true nature of a situation; penetration. **—in′sight′ful** *adj.* **—in·sight′ful·ness** *n.*

in·sig·ni·a (ĭn-sĭg′nē-ə) ▸ *n., pl.* **-ni·a** or **-ni·as.** A distinguishing badge of office, rank, membership, or nationality; emblem.

in·sig·nif·i·cant (ĭn′sĭg-nĭf′ĭ-kənt) ▸ *adj.* 1. Lacking in importance; trivial. 2. Small in size, power, value, or amount. 3. Having little or no meaning. **—in′sig·nif′i·cance** *n.* **—in′sig·nif′i·cant·ly** *adv.*

in·sin·cere (ĭn′sĭn-sîr′) ▸ *adj.* Not sincere; hypocritical. **—in′sin·cere′ly** *adv.* **—in′sin·cer′i·ty** (-sĕr′ĭ-tē) *n.*

in·sin·u·ate (ĭn-sĭn′yo͞o-āt′) ▸ *v.* **-at·ed, -at·ing.** 1. To introduce (e.g., a thought) gradually and insidiously. 2. To introduce or insert (oneself) by subtle and artful means. 3. To hint. **—in·sin′u·a′tion** *n.*

in·sip·id (ĭn-sĭp′ĭd) ▸ *adj.* 1. Lacking flavor or zest; not tasty. 2. Lacking excitement or interest; dull. **—in·sip′id·ly** *adv.*

in·sist (ĭn-sĭst′) ▸ *v.* 1. To be firm in one's demand or course. 2. To assert or demand (something) vehemently and persistently. **—in·sis′tence, in·sis′ten·cy** *n.* **—in·sis′tent** *adj.* **—in·sis′tent·ly** *adv.*

in si·tu (ĭn sī′to͞o, sē′-) ▸ *adv. & adj.* In the original position.

in·so·far as (ĭn′sō-fär′) ▸ *conj.* To the extent that.

THESAURUS

inscrutable *adj.* —*See* DEEP (2), INCOMPREHENSIBLE, MYSTERIOUS.

insecure *adj.* 1. Inadequately protected ▸ ill-protected, unattended, undefended, unfortified, unguarded, unprotected, unsafe, unshielded. [*Compare* OPEN, VULNERABLE.] 2. Lacking stability ▸ infirm, precarious, rickety, shaky, teetering, tottering, tottery, unstable, unsteady, unsure, wavering, weak, wiggly, wobbly. [*Compare* WEAK.]

insecurity or **insecureness** *n.* —*See* INSTABILITY.

inseminate *v.* To make pregnant ▸ impregnate. *Slang:* knock up. *Idioms:* get (*or* put) in a family way, get with child. [*Compare* FERTILIZE.]

insensate *adj.* Completely lacking sensation or consciousness ▸ dead, inanimate, insentient, lifeless. [*Compare* DEAD.] —*See also* CALLOUS, FOOLISH.

insensibility or **insensibleness** *n.* —*See* APATHY.

insensible *adj.* —*See* BLIND (3), CALLOUS, COLD (2), DEAD (2), IMPERCEPTIBLE (1), UNCONSCIOUS.

insensitive *adj.* —*See* CALLOUS, COLD (2), DEAD (2), TACTLESS, THOUGHTLESS.

insensitivity *n.* —*See* THOUGHTLESSNESS (2).

insentient *adj.* Completely lacking sensation or consciousness ▸ dead, inanimate, insensate, lifeless. [*Compare* DEAD.]

insert *v.* —*See* INTRODUCE (2), LIST[1].

insertion *n.* —*See* ENTRY.

inside *adj.* Located inside or farther in ▸ inlying, inner, interior, internal. [*Compare* CENTRAL, SECLUDED.] —*See also* CONFIDENTIAL (1).

insides *n.* —*See* VISCERA.

inside track *n.* —*See* ADVANTAGE (3).

insidious *adj.* —*See* DANGEROUS, FALLACIOUS (2).

insight *n.* —*See* DISCERNMENT, INSTINCT, WISDOM (1).

insightful *adj.* —*See* VISIONARY.

insignificance *n.* —*See* OBSCURITY, TRIFLE.

insignificant *adj.* —*See* OBSCURE (2), TRIVIAL.

insincere *adj.* —*See* ARTIFICIAL (2), DISHONEST.

insincerity *n.* Lack of sincerity ▸ ambidexterity, artificiality, disingenuousness, falsity, phoniness, pretense. [*Compare* DISHONESTY, HYPOCRISY.]

insinuate *v.* To introduce or insert by subtle and artful means ▸ edge, foist, infiltrate, wind, work, worm. [*Compare* MANEUVER.] —*See also* HINT.

insinuating *adj.* Provoking a change of outlook and especially gradual doubt and suspicion ▸ implicating, incriminating, insinuative, insinuatory, suggestive. —*See also* FLATTERING.

insinuation *n.* —*See* HINT (2).

insinuative or **insinuatory** *adj.* —*See* INSINUATING.

insipid *adj.* Lacking vigor, intensity, or bite ▸ bland, innocuous, inoffensive, jejune, milk-and-water, namby-pamby, vapid, washy, watered down, waterish, watery, white-bread. *Informal:* wishy-washy. [*Compare* DULL, HARMLESS, TRITE.] —*See also* FLAT (2).

insipidity or **insipidness** *n.* The state or quality of being insipid ▸ banality, blandness, innocuousness, jejuneness, vapidity, vapidness, washiness, wateriness. *Informal:* wishy-washiness. [*Compare* EMPTINESS.] —*See also* DULLNESS.

insist *v.* To take and maintain a stand obstinately ▸ be resolute, carry on, persevere, persist. *Idioms:* make (*or* take) a stand, not take no for an answer, stand firm (*or* tall), stick to one's guns, hold (*or* stand) one's ground. [*Compare* CARRY ON, CONTINUE, ENDURE.] —*See also* ASSERT.

insist on or **upon** *v.* —*See* DEMAND (1).

insistence or **insistency** *n.* 1. The state or quality of being insistent ▸ perseverance, persistence, persistency. [*Compare* DECISION.] 2. Urgent solicitation ▸ persuasion, pressing, urging. [*Compare* DEMAND.]

insistent *adj.* Firm or obstinate, as in making a demand or maintaining a stand ▸ importunate, importune, persistent, urgent. [*Compare* FIRM[1], STUBBORN.] —*See also* ASSERTIVE.

insobriety *n.* —*See* DRUNKENNESS.

in·sole (ĭn′sōl′) ▸ *n.* **1.** The inner sole of a shoe or boot. **2.** An extra strip of material put inside a shoe for comfort or protection.
in·so·lent (ĭn′sə-lənt) ▸ *adj.* Disrespectfully arrogant; impertinent; rude. **—in′so·lence** *n.* **—in′so·lent·ly** *adv.*
in·sol·u·ble (ĭn-sŏl′yə-bəl) ▸ *adj.* **1.** Incapable of being dissolved. **2.** Difficult or impossible to solve or explain. **—in·sol′u·bil′i·ty** *n.* **—in·sol′u·bly** *adv.*
in·sol·vent (ĭn-sŏl′vənt) ▸ *adj.* Unable to pay one's debts. **—in·sol′ven·cy** *n.*
in·som·ni·a (ĭn-sŏm′nē-ə) ▸ *n.* Chronic inability to sleep. **—in·som′ni·ac′** (-ăk′) *adj. & n.*
in·so·much as (ĭn′sō-mŭch′) ▸ *conj.* Inasmuch as; since.
in·sou·ci·ant (ĭn-so͞o′sē-ənt) ▸ *adj.* Blithely unconcerned. **—in·sou′ci·ance** *n.*
in·spect (ĭn-spĕkt′) ▸ *v.* **1.** To examine carefully and critically, esp. for flaws. **2.** To review or examine officially. **—in·spec′tion** *n.* **—in·spec′tor** *n.*
inspector general ▸ *n., pl.* **inspectors general.** An officer with general investigative powers within a civil, military, or other organization.
in·spi·ra·tion (ĭn′spə-rā′shən) ▸ *n.* **1a.** Stimulation of the mind or emotions to a high level of feeling or activity. **b.** The condition of being so stimulated. **2.** One that inspires. **3.** Something that is inspired. **4.** Inhalation. **—in′spi·ra′tion·al** *adj.* **—in′spi·ra′tion·al·ly** *adv.*
in·spire (ĭn-spīr′) ▸ *v.* **-spired, -spir·ing. 1.** To fill with noble or reverent emotion; exalt. **2.** To stimulate creativity or action. **3.** To elicit or create in another. **4.** To inhale. **—in·spir′er** *n.*
in·spir·it (ĭn-spĭr′ĭt) ▸ *v.* To instill courage or life into; animate.
inst. ▸ *abbr.* **1.** institute **2.** institution
in·sta·bil·i·ty (ĭn′stə-bĭl′ĭ-tē) ▸ *n., pl.* **-ties.** Lack of stability.
in·stall also **in·stal** (ĭn-stôl′) ▸ *v.* **-stalled, -stall·ing. 1.** To set in position and connect or adjust for use. **2.** To induct into an office, rank, or position. **3.** To put or place. **—in′stal·la′tion** (-stə-lā′shən) *n.* **—in·stall′er** *n.*
in·stall·ment also **in·stal·ment** (ĭn-stôl′mənt) ▸ *n.* **1.** One of a number of successive payments of a debt. **2.** A portion of something, such as a publication, issued at intervals.
in·stance (ĭn′stəns) ▸ *n.* **1.** A case or example. **2.** An occurrence or occasion. **3.** A suggestion or request: *called at the instance of his attorney.* ▸ *v.* **-stanced, -stanc·ing.** To offer as an example; cite.
in·stant (ĭn′stənt) ▸ *n.* **1.** A very brief space of time; moment. **2.** A particular point in time. ▸ *adj.* **1.** Immediate. **2.** Imperative; urgent: *an instant need.* **3.** Designed, prepared, or processed for quick preparation: *instant coffee.*
in·stan·ta·ne·ous (ĭn′stən-tā′nē-əs) ▸ *adj.* **1.** Occurring or completed without perceptible delay: *Relief was instantaneous.* **2.** Present or occurring at a specific instant. **—in′stan·ta′ne·ous·ly** *adv.* **—in′stan·ta′ne·ous·ness** *n.*
in·stant·ly (ĭn′stənt-lē) ▸ *adv.* At once.
in·stead (ĭn-stĕd′) ▸ *adv.* In the place of that previously mentioned. ***—Idiom:*** **instead of** In place of; rather than.
in·step (ĭn′stĕp′) ▸ *n.* The arched middle part of the human foot between the toes and ankle.
in·sti·gate (ĭn′stĭ-gāt′) ▸ *v.* **-gat·ed, -gat·ing. 1.** To urge on. **2.** To incite. **—in′sti·ga′tion** *n.* **—in′sti·ga′tor** *n.*
in·still also **in·stil** (ĭn-stĭl′) ▸ *v.* **-stilled, -still·ing. 1.** To introduce gradually; implant. **2.** To pour in (e.g., medicine) drop by drop. **—in′stil·la′tion** (-stə-lā′shən) *n.* **—in·still′er** *n.*
in·stinct (ĭn′stĭngkt′) ▸ *n.* **1.** An inner pattern of behavior that is not learned and results in complex animal responses such as building of nests and nursing of young. **2.** A powerful motivation or impulse. **3.** A natural capability or aptitude. **—in·stinc′tive** *adj.* **—in·stinc′tive·ly** *adv.* **—in·stinc′tu·al** (-stĭngk′cho͞o-əl) *adj.*
in·sti·tute (ĭn′stĭ-to͞ot′, -tyo͞ot′) ▸ *v.* **-tut·ed, -tut·ing. 1.** To establish, organize, and set in operation. **2.** To initiate; begin. ▸ *n.* **1.** Something instituted, esp. an authoritative rule. **2.** An organization founded to promote a cause. **3.** An educational institution. **4.** A seminar or workshop.
in·sti·tu·tion (ĭn′stĭ-to͞o′shən, -tyo͞o′-) ▸ *n.* **1.** The act of instituting. **2.** An established custom, practice, or relationship in a society. **3a.** An organization or foundation, esp. one dedicated to education, public service, or culture. **b.** The building housing such an organization. **c.** A place for care of the disabled or mentally ill. **—in′sti·tu′tion·al** *adj.* **—in′sti·tu′tion·al·ly** *adv.*
in·sti·tu·tion·al·ize (ĭn′stĭ-to͞o′shə-nə-līz′, -tyo͞o′-) ▸ *v.* **-ized,**

THESAURUS

insolence *n.* —*See* ARROGANCE, IMPUDENCE.
insolent *adj.* —*See* ARROGANT, DISRESPECTFUL, IMPUDENT.
insolvency *n.* —*See* BANKRUPTCY.
insolvent *n.* —*See* PAUPER.
insolvent *adj.* —*See* POOR.
insouciant *adj.* —*See* CARELESS.
inspect *v.* To examine a person or someone's personal effects in order to find something lost or concealed ▸ frisk, pat down, search. *Slang:* shake down. *Idiom:* do a body search of. —*See also* EXAMINE (1).
inspection *n.* —*See* EXAMINATION (1).
inspiration *n.* **1.** Liveliness and vivacity of imagination ▸ brilliance, brilliancy, fire, genius. [*Compare* INTELLIGENCE, INVENTION.] **2.** A sudden exciting thought ▸ brainstorm, bright idea. *Informal:* brain wave. [*Compare* IDEA.] —*See also* BREATH, ELATION, ENCOURAGEMENT, VISION (2).
inspire *v.* —*See* BREATHE (1), CAUSE, ELATE, ENCOURAGE (1), FIRE (1), PROVOKE.
inspired *adj.* —*See* VISIONARY.
inspirit *v.* —*See* ELATE, ENCOURAGE (1).
inspissate *v.* To make thick or thicker, especially through evaporation or condensation ▸ condense, reduce, thicken. [*Compare* COAGULATE.]
instability *n.* The quality or condition of being erratic and undependable ▸ flightiness, inconsistency, inconstancy, insecureness, insecurity, irregularity, precariousness, shakiness, unpredictability, unreliability, unstableness, unsteadiness, unsureness. [*Compare* CHANGE.]
install *v.* —*See* ESTABLISH (1), INITIATE, POSITION.
installation *n.* Something attached as a permanent part of something else ▸ apparatus, fitting, fixture. [*Compare* ATTACHMENT.] —*See also* BASE[1] (1), EXHIBITION, INITIATION.
installment *n.* A partial or intial payment ▸ deposit, down payment, security.
instance *n.* —*See* EXAMPLE (1), LAWSUIT.
instance *v.* To demonstrate and clarify with examples ▸ demonstrate, evidence, exemplify, illustrate. [*Compare* EXPLAIN, SHOW.] —*See also* NAME (2).
instant *n.* —*See* FLASH (2), OCCASION (1).
instant *adj.* Occurring at once ▸ immediate, instantaneous. *Idioms:* on-the-spot, split-second. [*Compare* FAST, QUICK.] —*See also* URGENT (1).
instant *adv.* —*See* IMMEDIATELY (1).
instantaneous *adj.* Occurring at once ▸ immediate, instant. *Idioms:* on-the-spot, split-second. [*Compare* FAST, QUICK.]
instantiate *v.* —*See* EMBODY (1).
instantiation *n.* —*See* EMBODIMENT, EXAMPLE (1).
instantly *adv.* —*See* IMMEDIATELY (1).
instate *v.* —*See* INITIATE.
instatement *n.* —*See* INITIATION.
instigate *v.* —*See* PROVOKE.
instigation *n.* —*See* PROVOCATION (1).
instigator *n.* —*See* AGITATOR.
instill *v.* To fix (an idea, for example) in someone's mind by reemphasis and repetition ▸ beat into, drill, drive, implant, impress, inculcate, ingrain, pound. *Idiom:* drum (*or* hammer *or* knock) into someone's head. [*Compare* INDOCTRINATE, TEACH.]
instinct *n.* The power to discern the true nature of a person or situation ▸ clairvoyance, insight, intuitiveness, intuition, penetration, sense, sixth sense. [*Compare* DISCERNMENT, FEELING, INCLINATION.] —*See also* TALENT.
instinctive *adj.* Derived from or prompted by a natural tendency or impulse ▸ inborn, inherent, innate, instinctual, intuitive, unlearned, untaught, visceral. [*Compare* CONSTITUTIONAL.] —*See also* SPONTANEOUS.
instinctual *adj.* —*See* INSTINCTIVE.
institute *v.* —*See* ESTABLISH (2), FOUND, START (1).
institute *n.* —*See* LAW (1).
institution *n.* —*See* FOUNDATION.
institutionalize *v.* To place officially in confinement ▸ commit, consign.

-iz·ing. 1. To make into an institution. 2. To (confine) in an institution. **—in′sti·tu′tion·al·i·za′tion** *n.*

in·struct (ĭn-strŭkt′) ▸ *v.* 1. To teach; educate. 2. To give orders to; direct. **—in·struc′tive** *adj.* **—in·struc′tive·ly** *adv.*

in·struc·tion (ĭn-strŭk′shən) ▸ *n.* 1. The act, practice, or profession of instructing. 2a. Something learned. b. A lesson. 3. *Comp. Sci.* A sequence of bits that tells a central processing unit to perform a particular operation. 4a. An authoritative direction; order. b. **instructions** Detailed directions on procedure. **—in·struc′tion·al** *adj.*

in·struc·tor (ĭn-strŭk′tər) ▸ *n.* One who instructs, esp. a college teacher ranking below assistant professor. **—in·struc′tor·ship′** *n.*

in·stru·ment (ĭn′strə-mənt) ▸ *n.* 1. A means by which something is done; agency. 2. An implement used to facilitate work. 3. A device for recording or measuring, esp. one functioning as part of a control system. 4. A device for playing or producing music. 5. A legal document. ▸ *v.* (-mĕnt′) To provide with instruments.

in·stru·men·tal (ĭn′strə-mĕn′tl) ▸ *adj.* 1. Serving as a means or agency. 2. *Mus.* Performed on or written for an instrument as opposed to a voice or voices. **—in′stru·men′tal·ly** *adv.*

in·stru·men·tal·ist (ĭn′strə-mĕn′tl-ĭst) ▸ *n.* One who plays a musical instrument.

in·stru·men·tal·i·ty (ĭn′strə-mĕn-tăl′ĭ-tē) ▸ *n., pl.* **-ties.** A means; agency.

in·stru·men·ta·tion (ĭn′strə-mĕn-tā′shən) ▸ *n.* 1. The application or use of instruments. 2. The arrangement of music for instruments.

in·sub·or·di·nate (ĭn′sə-bôr′dn-ĭt) ▸ *adj.* Not submissive to authority. **—in′sub·or′di·nate·ly** *adv.* **—in′sub·or′di·na′tion** *n.*

in·sub·stan·tial (ĭn′səb-stăn′shəl) ▸ *adj.* 1. Lacking substance or reality. 2. Not firm or solid; flimsy. **—in′sub·stan′ti·al′i·ty** (-shē-ăl′ĭ-tē) *n.*

in·suf·fer·a·ble (ĭn-sŭf′ər-ə-bəl, -sŭf′rə-) ▸ *adj.* Impossible to endure; intolerable. **—in·suf′fer·a·bly** *adv.*

in·suf·fi·cient (ĭn′sə-fĭsh′ənt) ▸ *adj.* Not sufficient; inadequate. **—in′suf·fi′cien·cy** *n.* **—in′suf·fi′cient·ly** *adv.*

in·su·lar (ĭn′sə-lər, ĭns′yə-) ▸ *adj.* 1. Of or constituting an island. 2a. Isolated. b. Narrow-minded. **—in′su·lar′i·ty** *n.*

in·su·late (ĭn′sə-lāt′, ĭns′yə-) ▸ *v.* **-lat·ed, -lat·ing.** 1. To detach. 2. To prevent the passage of heat, electricity, or sound into or out of, esp. by surrounding with a nonconducting material. **—in′su·la′tion** *n.* **—in′su·la′tor** *n.*

in·su·lin (ĭn′sə-lĭn) ▸ *n.* 1. A pancreatic hormone that regulates the metabolism of carbohydrates and fats by controlling blood glucose levels. 2. A pharmaceutical preparation containing this hormone.

insulin shock ▸ *n.* Acute hypoglycemia usu. resulting from excessive insulin in the blood.

in·sult (ĭn-sŭlt′) ▸ *v.* To speak to or treat with disrespect or contempt. ▸ *n.* (ĭn′sŭlt′) An offensive or disrespectful action or remark.

in·su·per·a·ble (ĭn-so͞o′pər-ə-bəl) ▸ *adj.* Impossible to overcome; insurmountable. **—in·su′per·a·bil′i·ty** *n.* **—in·su′per·a·bly** *adv.*

in·sup·port·a·ble (ĭn′sə-pôr′tə-bəl) ▸ *adj.* 1. Not endurable; intolerable. 2. Unjustifiable. **—in′sup·port′a·bly** *adv.*

in·sur·ance (ĭn-sho͝or′əns) ▸ *n.* 1. The act of insuring or state of being insured. 2. The business of insuring persons or property. 3a. A contract binding a company to indemnify an insured party against specified loss. b. The sum for which something is insured. 4. A protective measure or device.

in·sure (ĭn-sho͝or′) ▸ *v.* **-sured, -sur·ing.** 1. To cover with insurance. 2. To make sure, certain, or secure. **—in·sur′a·ble** *adj.* **—in·sur′er** *n.*

in·sured (ĭn-sho͝ord′) ▸ *n.* One that is covered by insurance.

in·sur·gent (ĭn-sûr′jənt) ▸ *adj.* Rising in revolt; rebellious. ▸ *n.* 1. One who revolts against civil authority. 2. A member of a political party who rebels against its leadership. **—in·sur′gence, in·sur′gen·cy** *n.*

in·sur·mount·a·ble (ĭn′sər-moun′tə-bəl) ▸ *adj.* Impossible to surmount; insuperable. **—in′sur·mount′a·bil′i·ty** *n.* **—in′sur·mount′a·bly** *adv.*

in·sur·rec·tion (ĭn′sə-rĕk′shən) ▸ *n.* The act or an instance of open revolt against civil authority or a constituted government. **—in′sur·rec′tion·ist** *n.*

int. ▸ *abbr.* 1. interest 2. international 3. intransitive

in·tact (ĭn-tăkt′) ▸ *adj.* Not impaired in any way. **—in·tact′ness** *n.*

in·ta·glio (ĭn-tăl′yō, -täl′-) ▸ *n., pl.* **-glios.** A figure or design carved deeply into the surface of hard metal or stone.

in·take (ĭn′tāk′) ▸ *n.* 1. An opening by which a fluid enters a container or pipe. 2a. The act of taking in. b. The quantity taken in.

in·tan·gi·ble (ĭn-tăn′jə-bəl) ▸ *adj.* 1. Incapable of being perceived by the senses; lacking physical substance. 2. Incapable of being realized or defined. ▸ *n.* Something intangible. **—in·tan′gi·bil′i·ty, in·tan′gi·ble·ness** *n.* **—in·tan′gi·bly** *adv.*

in·te·ger (ĭn′tĭ-jər) ▸ *n.* A member of the set of positive whole numbers (1, 2, 3, . . .), negative whole numbers (–1, –2, –3, . . .), and zero (0).

in·te·gral (ĭn′tĭ-grəl, ĭn-tĕg′rəl) ▸ *adj.* 1. Essential or necessary for completeness; constituent. 2. Whole; entire. 3.

THESAURUS

Informal: send up. [*Compare* IMPRISON.]

instruct *v.* —*See* COMMAND (1), EDUCATE.

instructed *adj.* —*See* INFORMED.

instruction *n.* —*See* COMMAND (1), EDUCATION (1), EDUCATION (2).

instructional *adj.* —*See* EDUCATIONAL (1), EDUCATIONAL (2).

instructive *adj.* —*See* EDUCATIONAL (2).

instructor *n.* —*See* EDUCATOR.

instrument *n.* A device used to do work or perform a task ▸ implement, tool, utensil. [*Compare* GADGET.] —*See also* AGENT, DEVICE (1), PAWN[2].

instrumental *adj.* —*See* EFFECTIVE (1).

instrumentalist *n.* —*See* PLAYER (2).

instrumentality *n.* —*See* AGENT.

insubordinate *adj.* —*See* DEFIANT, UNRULY.

insubordination *n.* —*See* DEFIANCE (1).

insubstantial *adj.* —*See* IMMATERIAL, IMPLAUSIBLE, MEAGER, WEAK (1).

insubstantiality *n.* —*See* INFIRMITY.

insufferable *adj.* —*See* UNBEARABLE.

insufficiency *n.* —*See* INEFFECTUALITY, SHORTAGE.

insufficient *adj.* Not enough to meet a demand or requirement ▸ deficient, inadequate, scarce, short, shy, under, wanting. ***Idioms:*** in short supply, on the short end. [*Compare* DEFICIENT, INEFFICIENT, MEAGER.] —*See also* DISAPPOINTING, INEFFECTUAL (2).

insular *adj.* —*See* NARROW (1), REMOTE (1).

insulate *v.* —*See* ISOLATE (1).

insulation *n.* —*See* ISOLATION.

insult *v.* To cause resentment or hurt by callous, rude behavior ▸ affront, huff, miff, offend, outrage, pique. *Informal:* badmouth, slam. *Slang:* dis, put down. ***Idioms:*** add insult to injury, call names, give offense, hurt someone's feelings, step on someone's toes. [*Compare* REVILE, RIDICULE, SNUB.] —*See also* OFFEND (1).

insult *n.* —*See* INDIGNITY, TAUNT.

insulting *adj.* —*See* DISRESPECTFUL, OFFENSIVE (2).

insuperable *adj.* Incapable of being negotiated or overcome ▸ impassable, insurmountable, unconquerable. [*Compare* IMPOSSIBLE, INVINCIBLE.]

insupportable *adj.* —*See* UNBEARABLE.

insure *v.* —*See* GUARANTEE (2).

insurgence *n.* —*See* DEFIANCE (1), REBELLION.

insurgency *n.* —*See* REBELLION.

insurgent *adj.* —*See* REBELLIOUS.

insurgent *n.* —*See* REBEL (1).

insurmountable *adj.* Incapable of being negotiated or overcome ▸ impassable, insuperable, unconquerable. [*Compare* IMPOSSIBLE, INVINCIBLE.]

insurrection *n.* —*See* REBELLION.

insurrectionary or **insurrectionist** *n.* —*See* REBEL (1).

insusceptibility *n.* The capacity to withstand ▸ immunity, imperviousness, resistance, unsusceptibility. [*Compare* ENDURANCE, STABILITY.]

insusceptible *adj.* —*See* COLD (2), RESISTANT.

intact *adj.* —*See* COMPLETE (1), GOOD (2).

intake *n.* —*See* ABSORPTION (1).

intangible *adj.* —*See* IMMATERIAL, IMPERCEPTIBLE (1).

integral *adj.* —*See* BUILT-IN, COMPLETE (1), ESSENTIAL (2).

(ĭn′tĭ-grəl) *Math.* Expressed or expressible as or in terms of integers. ▸ *n.* A complete unit; whole.

integral calculus ▸ *n. Math.* The study of integration and its use in finding volumes, areas, and solutions of differential equations.

in·te·grate (ĭn′tĭ-grāt′) ▸ *v.* **-grat·ed, -grat·ing. 1.** To make into a whole; unify. **2.** To join with something else; unite. **3.** To open to people of all races or ethnic groups without restriction; desegregate. **—in′te·gra′tion** *n.* **—in′te·gra′tion·ist** *adj. & n.* **—in′te·gra′tive** *adj.*

in·te·grat·ed circuit (ĭn′tĭ-grā′tĭd) ▸ *n.* A complex set of electronic components and their interconnections that are etched or imprinted on a chip.

in·teg·ri·ty (ĭn-tĕg′rĭ-tē) ▸ *n.* **1.** Steadfast adherence to a strict moral or ethical code. **2.** Soundness. **3.** Completeness; unity.

in·teg·u·ment (ĭn-tĕg′yo͞o-mənt) ▸ *n.* A natural outer covering, such as the skin or a seed coat.

in·tel·lect (ĭn′tl-ĕkt′) ▸ *n.* **1a.** The ability to learn, reason, and understand. **b.** The ability to think abstractly or profoundly. **2.** A person of great intellectual ability.

in·tel·lec·tu·al (ĭn′tl-ĕk′cho͞o-əl) ▸ *adj.* **1a.** Of, engaging, or requiring use of the intellect. **b.** Rational. **2a.** Having a superior intellect. **b.** Given to abstract or philosophical thought. ▸ *n.* An intellectual person. **—in′tel·lec′tu·al·ly** *adv.*

in·tel·lec·tu·al·ize (ĭn′tl-ĕk′cho͞o-ə-līz′) ▸ *v.* **-ized, -iz·ing. 1.** To make rational. **2.** *Psychol.* To analyze (an emotional problem) intellectually, esp. so as to avoid a more direct confrontation. **—in′tel·lec′tu·al·i·za′tion** *n.*

in·tel·li·gence (ĭn-tĕl′ə-jəns) ▸ *n.* **1a.** The capacity to acquire and apply knowledge. **b.** The faculty of thought and reason. **c.** Superior powers of mind. **2.** Information; news. **3a.** Secret information, esp. about an enemy. **b.** The work of gathering such information; espionage.

intelligence quotient ▸ *n.* The ratio of tested mental age to chronological age, usu. expressed as a quotient multiplied by 100.

in·tel·li·gent (ĭn-tĕl′ə-jənt) ▸ *adj.* **1.** Having intelligence: *intelligent life.* **2.** Having a high degree of intelligence. **3.** Showing intelligence: *an intelligent act.* **—in·tel′li·gent·ly** *adv.*

in·tel·li·gent·si·a (ĭn-tĕl′ə-jĕnt′sē-ə, -gĕnt′-) ▸ *n.* The intellectual elite of a society.

in·tel·li·gi·ble (ĭn-tĕl′ĭ-jə-bəl) ▸ *adj.* Capable of being understood; comprehensible. **—in·tel′li·gi·bil′i·ty** *n.* **—in·tel′li·gi·bly** *adv.*

in·tem·per·ance (ĭn-tĕm′pər-əns, -prəns) ▸ *n.* Lack of temperance, esp. in the drinking of alcoholic beverages. **—in·tem′per·ate** *adj.* **—in·tem′per·ate·ly** *adv.*

in·tend (ĭn-tĕnd′) ▸ *v.* **1.** To have in mind; plan. **2.** To design for a specific purpose. **3.** To signify or mean.

in·tend·ed (ĭn-tĕn′dĭd) ▸ *adj.* **1.** Deliberate; intentional. **2.** Prospective; future. ▸ *n. Informal* One engaged to be married.

in·tense (ĭn-tĕns′) ▸ *adj.* **-tens·er, -tens·est. 1.** Displaying a distinctive feature to an extreme degree. **2.** Extreme in degree, strength, or size. **3.** Involving or showing great concentration or strain. **4.** Deeply felt; profound. **—in·tense′ly** *adv.* **—in·tense′ness** *n.*

in·ten·si·fy (ĭn-tĕn′sə-fī′) ▸ *v.* **-fied, -fy·ing.** To make or become intense or more intense. **—in·ten′si·fi·ca′tion** *n.*

in·ten·si·ty (ĭn-tĕn′sĭ-tē) ▸ *n., pl.* **-ties. 1.** Exceptionally great concentration, power, or force. **2.** Degree; strength. **3.** *Phys.* The amount or degree of strength of electricity, light, heat, or sound per unit area or volume.

in·ten·sive (ĭn-tĕn′sĭv) ▸ *adj.* **1.** Relating to or marked by intensity: *intensive training.* **2.** *Gram.* Adding emphasis. ▸ *n. Gram.* A word or word element, such as the adverb *awfully,* that adds emphasis but no new meaning. **—in·ten′sive·ly** *adv.*

in·tent (ĭn-tĕnt′) ▸ *n.* **1.** An aim or purpose. **2.** *Law* The state of one's mind at the time one carries out an action. **3.** Meaning or significance. ▸ *adj.* **1.** Firmly fixed; concentrated. **2.** Engrossed. **3.** Determined on a specific purpose. **—in·tent′ly** *adv.* **—in·tent′ness** *n.*

in·ten·tion (ĭn-tĕn′shən) ▸ *n.* **1.** A plan of action; design. **2.** An aim that guides action; objective.

in·ten·tion·al (ĭn-tĕn′shə-nəl) ▸ *adj.* Done deliberately; intended. **—in·ten′tion·al′i·ty** (-năl′ĭ-tē) *n.* **—in·ten′tion·al·ly** *adv.*

THESAURUS

integral *n.* —*See* SYSTEM.

integrate *v.* **1.** To construct as an integral part ▸ build in, include, incorporate. **2.** To make a part of a united whole ▸ combine, embody, incorporate. **3.** To open to all people regardless of race ▸ desegregate. —*See also* COMBINE (1), HARMONIZE (2), HARMONIZE (1).

integrity *n.* —*See* CHARACTER (2), COMPLETENESS, HONESTY, SOUNDNESS.

integument *n.* The tissue forming the external covering of the body ▸ epidermis, skin.

intellect *n.* —*See* INTELLIGENCE, MIND (2).

intellection *n.* —*See* THOUGHT.

intellective *adj.* —*See* MENTAL.

intellectual *adj.* Appealing to or engaging the intellect ▸ cerebral, mental, sophisticated, thoughtful. *Informal:* eggheaded, highbrow. *Slang:* pointy-headed. [*Compare* COMPLEX, EDUCATED.] —*See also* INTELLIGENT, MENTAL.

intellectual *n.* —*See* MIND (2).

intelligence *n.* The faculty of thinking, reasoning, and applying knowledge ▸ aptitude, brainpower, brains, brightness, cleverness, intellect, mentality, mind, quick-wittedness, sense, smartness, understanding, wit. *Informal:* eggheadedness, gray matter. *Slang:* smarts. ***Idioms:*** intellectual (*or* mental) grasp, mental aptitude (*or* capacity), power of the mind (*or* thought). [*Compare* COMMON SENSE.] —*See also* DISCERNMENT, INFORMATION, NEWS, WISDOM (1).

intelligent *adj.* Having or showing intelligence, often of a high order ▸ bright, brilliant, genius, intellectual, knowing, knowledgeable, smart. *Informal:* brainy. [*Compare* CRITICAL, SHREWD, WISE[1].] —*See also* CLEVER (1), LOGICAL (2).

intelligibility *n.* —*See* CLARITY.

intelligible *adj.* —*See* UNDERSTANDABLE.

intend *v.* To have in mind as a goal or purpose ▸ aim, contemplate, design, mean, plan, project, propose, purpose, target. *Chiefly Regional:* mind. ***Idioms:*** be fixing to, have one's heart set on, set one's sights on. [*Compare* AIM, DECIDE, EXPECT.] —*See also* MEAN[1].

intended *adj.* —*See* DELIBERATE (1), ENGAGED.

intended *n. Informal* A person to whom one is engaged to be married ▸ betrothed, bride-to-be, fiancé, fiancée, future husband, future wife, husband-to-be, prospective spouse, wife-to-be.

intense *adj.* Extreme in activity, strength, or effect ▸ all-out, concentrated, desperate, fierce, furious, heavy, heightened, high, intensive, overpowering, overwhelming, strong, terrible, vehement, violent. [*Compare* FORCEFUL, SEVERE, SHARP.] —*See also* DEEP (3).

intensely *adv.* —*See* VERY.

intensify *v.* To make greater in intensity or severity ▸ aggravate, deepen, enhance, escalate, exacerbate, heighten, redouble, sharpen, step up. *Slang:* hop up. ***Idiom:*** add fuel to the fire (*or* flame). [*Compare* EMPHASIZE, INCREASE, SUPPORT.]

intensity *n.* Concentrated power or force, as of effort, opinion, or emotion ▸ concentration, depth, depths, ferociousness, ferocity, fever pitch, fierceness, forcefulness, fury, height, pitch, severity, strain, vehemence, vehemency, violence. [*Compare* FORCE, PASSION, STRENGTH.]

intensive *adj.* —*See* CONCENTRATED (1), INTENSE.

intensively *adv.* —*See* COMPLETELY (2).

intent *n.* —*See* INTENTION, MEANING, THRUST.

intent *adj.* Committed to or unwavering in a course of action ▸ bent, decided, determined, fixed, resolute, resolved, set, single-minded, unhesitating. [*Compare* FIRM[1], INSISTENT, STUBBORN.] —*See also* ALERT, RAPT.

intention *n.* What one intends to do or achieve ▸ aim, ambition, design, determination, end, goal, intent, mark, meaning, object, objective, point, projection, purpose, target, view, why. ***Idioms:*** end in view, why and wherefore. [*Compare* APPROACH, DREAM, MISSION.]

intentional *adj.* —*See* CALCULATED, DELIBERATE (1).

in·ter (ĭn-tûr′) ▸ *v.* **-terred, -ter·ring.** To place in a grave; bury.
inter– ▸ *pref.* **1.** Between; among: *international.* **2.** Mutual; reciprocal: *interdependent.*
in·ter·act (ĭn′tər-ăkt′) ▸ *v.* To act on each other.
in·ter·ac·tion (ĭn′tər-ăk′shən) ▸ *n.* **1.** The act or process of interacting. **2.** *Phys.* Any of four ways that elementary particles and bodies can influence each other, classified as strong, weak, electromagnetic, and gravitational.
in·ter·ac·tive (ĭn′tər-ăk′tĭv) ▸ *adj.* **1.** Acting on each other. **2.** *Comp. Sci.* Of or relating to a program that responds to user activity. **3.** Of a form of television entertainment in which the viewer can affect events on the screen. **—in′ter·ac′tive·ly** *adv.*
in·ter a·li·a (ĭn′tər ā′lē-ə, ä′lē-ə) ▸ *adv.* Among other things.
in·ter·breed (ĭn′tər-brēd′) ▸ *v.* **1.** To crossbreed. **2.** To breed or cause to breed within a narrow range; inbreed.
in·ter·ca·lar·y (ĭn-tûr′kə-lĕr′ē, ĭn′tər-kăl′ə-rē) ▸ *adj.* **1.** Inserted in the calendar, as an extra day or month. **2.** Inserted between other elements or parts; interpolated.
in·ter·cede (ĭn′tər-sēd′) ▸ *v.* **-ced·ed, -ced·ing. 1.** To plead on another's behalf. **2.** To mediate.
in·ter·cel·lu·lar (ĭn′tər-sĕl′yə-lər) ▸ *adj. Biol.* Located among or between cells.
in·ter·cept (ĭn′tər-sĕpt′) ▸ *v.* **1.** To stop or interrupt the progress of. **2.** *Math.* To include or bound (a part of a space or curve) between two points or lines. **—in′ter·cept′** *n.* **—in′ter·cep′tion** *n.* **—in′ter·cep′tor** *n.*
in·ter·ces·sion (ĭn′tər-sĕsh′ən) ▸ *n.* **1.** A prayer or petition to God in behalf of another. **2.** Mediation. **—in′ter·ces′sion·al** *adj.* **—in′ter·ces′sor** *n.* **—in′ter·ces′so·ry** *adj.*
in·ter·change (ĭn′tər-chānj′) ▸ *v.* **1.** To switch each into the place of the other. **2.** To exchange. **3.** To alternate. ▸ *n.* (ĭn′tər-chānj′) **1.** An exchange. **2.** A highway intersection allowing traffic to move freely from one road to another without crossing another line of traffic. **—in′ter·change′a·ble** *adj.* **—in′ter·change′a·bly** *adv.*
in·ter·col·le·giate (ĭn′tər-kə-lē′jĭt, -jē-ĭt) ▸ *adj.* Involving two or more colleges.
in·ter·com (ĭn′tər-kŏm′) ▸ *n.* An electronic two-way communication system, as between two rooms.
in·ter·com·mu·ni·cate (ĭn′tər-kə-myōō′nĭ-kāt′) ▸ *v.* **1.** To communicate with each other. **2.** To be connected or adjoined, as rooms or passages. **—in′ter·com·mu′ni·ca′tion** *n.*
in·ter·con·nect (ĭn′tər-kə-nĕkt′) ▸ *v.* To connect or be connected with each other. **—in′ter·con·nec′tion** *n.*
in·ter·con·ti·nen·tal (ĭn′tər-kŏn′tə-nĕn′tl) ▸ *adj.* **1.** Taking place between continents. **2.** Traveling from one continent to another.
in·ter·cos·tal (ĭn′tər-kŏs′təl) ▸ *adj.* Located or occurring between the ribs.
in·ter·course (ĭn′tər-kôrs′) ▸ *n.* **1.** Social interchange; communication. **2.** Sexual intercourse.
in·ter·de·pen·dent (ĭn′tər-dĭ-pĕn′dənt) ▸ *adj.* Mutually dependent. **—in′ter·de·pen′dence** *n.*
in·ter·dict (ĭn′tər-dĭkt′) ▸ *v.* **1.** To prohibit or forbid, esp. authoritatively. **2.** To confront and halt the activities or entry of. **—in′ter·dict′** *n.* **—in′ter·dic′tion** *n.*
in·ter·dis·ci·pli·nar·y (ĭn′tər-dĭs′ə-plə-nĕr′ē) ▸ *adj.* Of or involving two or more usu. distinct academic disciplines.
in·ter·est (ĭn′trĭst, -tər-ĭst, -trĕst′) ▸ *n.* **1a.** A state of curiosity or concern about or attention to something. **b.** Something that evokes this mental state. **2.** often **interests** Advantage or benefit. **3.** A right, claim, or legal share in something: *an interest in the will.* **4.** A charge for a loan, usu. a percentage of the amount loaned. ▸ *v.* **1.** To arouse interest in. **2.** To cause to become involved or concerned.
in·ter·est·ed (ĭn′trĭ-stĭd, -tər-ĭ-stĭd, -tə-rĕs′tĭd) ▸ *adj.* **1.** Having or showing interest. **2.** Possessing a right, claim, or share.
in·ter·est·ing (ĭn′trĭ-stĭng, -tər-ĭ-stĭng, -tə-rĕs′tĭng) ▸ *adj.* Arousing or holding the attention; absorbing. **—in′ter·est·ing·ly** *adv.*
in·ter·face (ĭn′tər-fās′) ▸ *n.* **1.** A surface forming a common boundary between adjacent regions. **2.** A point at which independent systems or diverse groups interact. **3.** *Comp. Sci.* The point of interaction or communication between a computer and another entity, such as a printer or human operator. **—in′ter·face′** *v.* **—in′ter·fa′cial** (-fā′shəl) *adj.*
in·ter·fere (ĭn′tər-fîr′) ▸ *v.* **-fered, -fer·ing. 1.** To hinder or impede. **2.** *Sports* To impede illegally the catching of a pass or the playing of a ball or puck. **3.** To intervene or intrude in the affairs of others; meddle. **4.** To inhibit or prevent clear reception of broadcast signals. **—in′ter·fer′ence** *n.* **—in′ter·fer′er** *n.*
in·ter·fe·rom·e·ter (ĭn′tər-fə-rŏm′ĭ-tər) ▸ *n.* An instrument that uses interference phenomena between waves to make measurements, as of wavelengths or very small distances. **—in′ter·fe·rom′e·try** *n.*
in·ter·fer·on (ĭn′tər-fîr′ŏn′) ▸ *n.* A cellular protein produced in response to and acting to prevent replication of an infectious viral form within an infected cell.
in·ter·ga·lac·tic (ĭn′tər-gə-lăk′tĭk) ▸ *adj.* Between galaxies.
in·ter·im (ĭn′tər-ĭm) ▸ *n.* A period between two events. ▸ *adj.* Serving or taking place during an interim.
in·te·ri·or (ĭn-tîr′ē-ər) ▸ *adj.* **1.** Of or located on the inside; inner. **2.** Inland. ▸ *n.* **1.** The internal portion or area; inside. **2.** One's mental or spiritual life. **3.** The inland part of a geographic area. **4.** A representation of the inside of a building or room.
interior decoration ▸ *n.* The arrangement, furnishing, and decoration of an architectural interior. **—interior decorator** *n.*
interj. ▸ *abbr.* interjection
in·ter·ject (ĭn′tər-jĕkt′) ▸ *v.* To insert between elements; interpose. **—in′ter·jec′to·ry** *adj.*
in·ter·jec·tion (ĭn′tər-jĕk′shən) ▸ *n.* **1.** An exclamation. **2.** A part of speech usu. expressing emotion and capable of standing alone grammatically, such as *Ugh!* or *Wow!*
in·ter·lard (ĭn′tər-lärd′) ▸ *v.* To insert something foreign or different into.

THESAURUS

inter *v.* —*See* BURY.
interaction *n.* —*See* COMMUNICATION (1).
interceder or **intercessor** *n.* —*See* GO-BETWEEN.
intercept *v.* To block the progress of and force to change direction ▸ cut off, head off.
interchange *v.* To take turns ▸ alternate, rotate, shift. —*See also* CHANGE (3), EXCHANGE.
interchange *n.* Occurrence in successive turns ▸ alternation, rotation, shift. —*See also* CHANGE (2).
intercommunication *n.* A situation allowing exchange of ideas or messages ▸ communication, correspondence, contact, touch. [*Compare* COMMUNICATION.] —*See also* COMMUNICATION (1).
interconnection *n.* —*See* RELATION (1).
intercourse *n.* —*See* COMMUNICATION (1).
interdependence *n.* —*See* RELATION (1).
interdependent *adj.* —*See* COMPLEMENTARY.
interdict *v.* —*See* FORBID.
interdict *n.* A coercive measure intended to ensure compliance or conformity ▸ interdiction, penalty, sanction. [*Compare* RESTRICTION, PUNISHMENT.]
interdiction *n.* A coercive measure intended to ensure compliance or conformity ▸ interdict, penalty, sanction. [*Compare* RESTRICTION, PUNISHMENT.] —*See also* FORBIDDANCE.
interdictive *adj.* —*See* PREVENTIVE (1).
interest *n.* **1.** Something that contributes to or increases one's well-being ▸ advantage, benefit, good, interests, profit, use. [*Compare* ADVANTAGE.] **2.** A right or legal share in something ▸ claim, portion, stake, title. [*Compare* CUT, RIGHT.] **3.** Something that concerns or involves one personally ▸ affair, business, concern, lookout. —*See also* CURIOSITY (1).
interest *v.* —*See* GRIP.
interested *adj.* —*See* CONCERNED, CURIOUS (2).
interestedness *n.* —*See* CURIOSITY (1).
interface *n.* —*See* COMMUNICATION (1).
interfere *v.* —*See* DISRUPT, MEDDLE.
interfere with *v.* —*See* HINDER.
interference *n.* —*See* MEDDLING.
interfering *adj.* —*See* CURIOUS (1).
interim *n.* —*See* GAP (2).
interim *adj.* —*See* TEMPORARY (2), TEMPORARY (1).
interior *adj.* Located inside or farther in ▸ inlying, inner, inside, internal. [*Compare* CENTRAL, SECLUDED.] —*See also* INNER (2).
interject *v.* —*See* INTRODUCE (2).
interlace *v.* —*See* WEAVE.
interlard *v.* —*See* INTRODUCE (2).

in·ter·leu·kin (ĭn′tər-lo͞o′kĭn) ▸ *n.* Any of a group of proteins produced by the immune system that regulate the body's immune response.
in·ter·lin·ing (ĭn′tər-lī′nĭng) ▸ *n.* An extra lining between the outer fabric and regular lining of a garment.
in·ter·lock (ĭn′tər-lŏk′) ▸ *v.* **1.** To unite or join closely. **2.** To connect together (e.g., parts of a mechanism) so that the operating parts affect one another.
in·ter·loc·u·tor (ĭn′tər-lŏk′yə-tər) ▸ *n.* One who takes part in a conversation or dialogue, often officially.
in·ter·loc·u·to·ry (ĭn′tər-lŏk′yə-tôr′ē) ▸ *adj.* Of or relating to a temporary decree that is made during the course of a trial or suit.
in·ter·lop·er (ĭn′tər-lō′pər) ▸ *n.* One who interferes; meddler. **—in′ter·lope′** *v.*
in·ter·lude (ĭn′tər-lo͞od′) ▸ *n.* **1.** An intervening episode, feature, or period of time. **2.** An entertainment between the acts of a play. **3.** *Mus.* A short piece inserted between the parts of a longer composition.
in·ter·mar·ry (ĭn′tər-măr′ē) ▸ *v.* **1.** To marry a member of another religion, nationality, race, or group. **2.** To be bound together by the marriages of members. **3.** To marry within one's own group. **—in′ter·mar′riage** *n.*
in·ter·me·di·ar·y (ĭn′tər-mē′dē-ĕr′ē) ▸ *adj.* **1.** In between; intermediate. **2.** Acting as a mediator. ▸ *n., pl.* **-ies. 1.** A mediator; go-between. **2.** An intermediate state or stage.
in·ter·me·di·ate (ĭn′tər-mē′dē-ĭt) ▸ *adj.* Lying or occurring between two extremes; in between. ▸ *n.* **1.** One that is intermediate. **2.** An intermediary. **—in′ter·me′di·ate·ly** *adv.*
in·ter·ment (ĭn-tûr′mənt) ▸ *n.* The act or ritual of interring or burying.
in·ter·mez·zo (ĭn′tər-mĕt′sō, -mĕd′zō) ▸ *n., pl.* **-zos** or **-zi** (-sē, -zē) *Mus.* **1.** A short movement separating the major sections of a lengthy composition or work. **2.** A short independent instrumental composition.
in·ter·mi·na·ble (ĭn-tûr′mə-nə-bəl) ▸ *adj.* Tiresomely long. **—in·ter′mi·na·bly** *adv.*
in·ter·min·gle (ĭn′tər-mĭng′gəl) ▸ *v.* To mix or become mixed together.
in·ter·mis·sion (ĭn′tər-mĭsh′ən) ▸ *n.* A temporary suspension of activity, esp. the period between the acts of a theatrical or musical performance.
in·ter·mit·tent (ĭn′tər-mĭt′nt) ▸ *adj.* Stopping and starting at intervals. **—in′ter·mit′tent·ly** *adv.*
in·tern also **in·terne** (ĭn′tûrn′) ▸ *n.* An advanced student or a recent graduate, as of a medical school, undergoing supervised practical training. ▸ *v.* **1.** To train or serve as an intern. **2.** (*also* ĭn-tûrn′) To detain or confine, esp. in wartime. **—in·tern′ment** *n.* **—in′tern·ship′** *n.*
in·ter·nal (ĭn-tûr′nəl) ▸ *adj.* **1.** Inner; interior. **2.** Intrinsic; inherent. **3.** Located, acting, or effective within the body. **4.** Of or relating to the domestic affairs of a nation, group, or business. **—in·ter′nal·ly** *adv.*
in·ter·nal-com·bus·tion engine (ĭn-tûr′nəl-kəm-bŭs′chən) ▸ *n.* An engine in which fuel is burned within the engine.
in·ter·nal·ize (ĭn-tûr′nə-līz′) ▸ *v.* **-ized, -iz·ing.** To make internal, personal, or subjective. **—in·ter′nal·i·za′tion** *n.*
internal medicine ▸ *n.* The branch of medicine dealing with diseases affecting the internal organs, esp. in adults.
in·ter·na·tion·al (ĭn′tər-năsh′ə-nəl) ▸ *adj.* Of or involving two or more nations or nationalities. **—in′ter·na′tion·al·ly** *adv.*
International Date Line ▸ *n.* An imaginary line through the Pacific Ocean roughly corresponding to 180° longitude, to the east of which, by international agreement, the calendar date is one day earlier than to the west.
in·ter·na·tion·al·ism (ĭn′tər-năsh′ə-nə-lĭz′əm) ▸ *n.* A policy of cooperation among nations, esp. in politics and economics. **—in′ter·na′tion·al·ist** *n.*
in·ter·na·tion·al·ize (ĭn′tər-năsh′ə-nə-līz′) ▸ *v.* **-ized, -iz·ing.** To put under international control. **—in′ter·na′tion·al·i·za′tion** *n.*
international law ▸ *n.* A set of rules gen. accepted as binding between nations.
in·ter·nec·ine (ĭn′tər-nĕs′ēn′, -ĭn, -nē′sīn′) ▸ *adj.* **1.** Relating to struggle within a nation, organization, or group. **2.** Mutually destructive.
in·tern·ee (ĭn′tûr-nē′) ▸ *n.* One who is interned, esp. in wartime.
In·ter·net (ĭn′tər-nĕt′) ▸ *n.* An interconnected system of networks that connects computers around the world.
in·ter·nist (ĭn-tûr′nĭst) ▸ *n.* A physician specializing in internal medicine.
in·ter·of·fice (ĭn′tər-ô′fĭs, -ŏf′ĭs) ▸ *adj.* Transmitted or taking place between offices, esp. of an organization.
in·ter·per·son·al (ĭn′tər-pûr′sə-nəl) ▸ *adj.* Relating to or occurring among several people. **—in′ter·per′son·al·ly** *adv.*
in·ter·plan·e·tar·y (ĭn′tər-plăn′ĭ-tĕr′ē) ▸ *adj.* Existing or occurring between planets.
in·ter·play (ĭn′tər-plā′) ▸ *n.* Reciprocal action and reaction; interaction. **—in′ter·play′** *v.*
in·ter·po·late (ĭn-tûr′pə-lāt′) ▸ *v.* **-lat·ed, -lat·ing. 1.** To insert or introduce between other elements or parts. **2.** To change (a text) by introducing new or false material. **—in·ter′po·la′tion** *n.* **—in·ter′po·la′tor** *n.*
in·ter·pose (ĭn′tər-pōz′) ▸ *v.* **-posed, -pos·ing. 1a.** To insert or introduce between parts. **b.** To place (oneself) between. **2.** To introduce or interject into a discourse or conversation. **3.** To intervene. **—in′ter·pos′er** *n.* **—in′ter·po·si′tion** (-pə-zĭsh′ən) *n.*
in·ter·pret (ĭn-tûr′prĭt) ▸ *v.* **1.** To explain or clarify the meaning of. **2.** To conceive the significance of; construe. **3.** To perform or present according to one's artistic understanding. **4.** To serve as translator for speakers of different languages. **—in·ter′pret·a·ble** *adj.* **—in·ter′pret·er** *n.*
in·ter·pre·ta·tion (ĭn-tûr′prĭ-tā′shən) ▸ *n.* **1.** An explanation. **2.** A concept of a work of art as expressed by its representation or performance. **—in·ter′pre·ta′tion·al** *adj.*
in·ter·pre·tive (ĭn-tûr′prĭ-tĭv) also **in·ter·pre·ta·tive** (-tā′tĭv) ▸ *adj.* Marked by interpretation; explanatory. **—in·ter′pre·tive·ly** *adv.*

THESAURUS

interlock *v.* To be the proper size and shape for something ▸ dovetail, fit. *Idiom:* fit like a glove.
interlocution *n.* —*See* CONVERSATION.
interlocutor *n.* —*See* CONVERSATIONALIST.
interlope *v.* —*See* INTRUDE, MEDDLE.
interloper *n.* —*See* BUSYBODY.
interlude *n.* —*See* GAP (2).
intermeddle *v.* —*See* MEDDLE.
intermediary *n.* —*See* AGENT, GO-BETWEEN.
intermediary *adj.* —*See* MIDDLE.
intermediate *n.* —*See* GO-BETWEEN.
intermediate *adj.* —*See* MIDDLE.
intermediator *n.* —*See* GO-BETWEEN.
interment *n.* —*See* BURIAL.
interminability *n.* —*See* ENDLESSNESS.
interminable *adj.* —*See* CONTINUAL, LONG[1] (2).
intermingle *v.* —*See* MIX (1).
intermission *n.* —*See* ABEYANCE, REST[1] (1).
intermittent *adj.* Happening or appearing now and then ▸ episodic, fitful, irregular, occasional, periodic, periodical, sporadic. *Informal:* on-again, off-again. *Idioms:* here and there, on and off. [*Compare* INFREQUENT, RANDOM.]
intermittently *adv.* Once in a while; at times ▸ betimes, fitfully, occasionally, periodically, sometimes, sporadically. *Idioms:* ever and again (*or* anon), now and again (*or* then).
intermix *v.* —*See* MIX (1).
intern *v.* —*See* IMPRISON.
internal *adj.* Located inside or farther in ▸ inlying, inner, inside, interior. [*Compare* CENTRAL, SECLUDED.] —*See also* DOMESTIC (3), INNER (2).
internment *n.* —*See* DETENTION.
interpolate *v.* —*See* INTRODUCE (2).
interpose *v.* —*See* INTRODUCE (2).
interpret *v.* **1.** To understand in a particular way ▸ construe, read, take. *Idioms:* read between the lines, see in a special light, take to mean. [*Compare* UNDERSTAND.] **2.** To perform according to one's artistic conception ▸ depict, execute, play, present, render, represent. [*Compare* ACT.] —*See also* EXPLAIN (1), TRANSLATE.
interpretable *adj.* —*See* EXPLAINABLE.
interpretation *n.* A performer's distinctive personal version of a song, dance, piece of music, or role ▸ depiction, enactment, execution, performance, portrayal, presentation, reading, realization, rendering, rendition, representation. —*See also* COMMENTARY, EXPLANATION, TRANSLATION.
interpretive or **interpretative** *adj.* —*See* EXPLANATORY.

in·ter·ra·cial (ĭn′tər-rā′shəl) ▸ *adj.* Of or between different races.

in·ter·reg·num (ĭn′tər-rĕg′nəm) ▸ *n., pl.* **-nums** or **-na** (-nə). 1. The interval of time between two successive reigns or governments. 2. A gap in continuity. **—in′ter·reg′nal** *adj.*

in·ter·re·late (ĭn′tər-rĭ-lāt′) ▸ *v.* To place in or come into mutual relationship. **—in′ter·re·la′tion** *n.* **—in′ter·re·la′tion·ship′** *n.*

in·ter·ro·gate (ĭn-tĕr′ə-gāt′) ▸ *v.* **-gat·ed, -gat·ing.** To question formally. **—in·ter′ro·ga′tion** *n.* **—in·ter′ro·ga′tion·al** *adj.* **—in·ter′ro·ga′tor** *n.*

in·ter·rog·a·tive (ĭn′tə-rŏg′ə-tĭv) ▸ *adj.* 1. Of the nature of a question. 2. *Gram.* Used to ask a question: *an interrogative pronoun.* **—in′ter·rog′a·tive** *n.* **—in′ter·rog′a·tive·ly** *adv.*

in·ter·rog·a·to·ry (ĭn′tə-rŏg′ə-tôr′ē) ▸ *adj.* Interrogative. ▸ *n., pl.* **-ries.** *Law.* A formal question, as to a witness, usu. answered under oath. **—in′ter·rog′a·to′ri·ly** *adv.*

in·ter·rupt (ĭn′tə-rŭpt′) ▸ *v.* 1. To break the continuity or uniformity of. 2. To stop (someone) by breaking in on. 3. To break in on another's speech or action. **—in′ter·rupt′er** *n.* **—in′ter·rup′tion** *n.* **—in′ter·rup′tive** *adj.*

in·ter·sect (ĭn′tər-sĕkt′) ▸ *v.* 1. To cut across or through. 2. To form an intersection (with); cross.

in·ter·sec·tion (ĭn′tər-sĕk′shən) ▸ *n.* 1. The act or result of intersecting. 2. A place where things intersect, esp. where roads cross. 3. *Math.* The point or locus of points common to two or more geometric figures.

in·ter·sperse (ĭn′tər-spûrs′) ▸ *v.* **-spersed, -spers·ing.** 1. To distribute randomly among other things. 2. To supply or diversify with things distributed randomly. **—in′ter·sper′sion** (-spûr′zhən, -shən) *n.*

in·ter·state (ĭn′tər-stāt′) ▸ *adj.* Involving, between, or connecting two or more states. ▸ *n.* One of a system of highways connecting the major cities of the 48 contiguous US states.

in·ter·stel·lar (ĭn′tər-stĕl′ər) ▸ *adj.* Between the stars.

in·ter·stice (ĭn-tûr′stĭs) ▸ *n., pl.* **-stic·es** (-stĭ-sēz′, -sĭz). A small or narrow space between things or parts. **—in′ter·sti′tial** (ĭn′tər-stĭsh′əl) *adj.*

in·ter·twine (ĭn′tər-twīn′) ▸ *v.* To join or become joined by twining together.

in·ter·ur·ban (ĭn′tər-ûr′bən) ▸ *adj.* Relating to, between, or connecting urban areas.

in·ter·val (ĭn′tər-vəl) ▸ *n.* 1. A space between two objects or points. 2. A period of time between two events. 3. *Math.* The set of all numbers that lie between two given numbers, sometimes including either or both of the given numbers. 4. *Mus.* The difference, usu. expressed in the number of steps, between two pitches.

in·ter·vene (ĭn′tər-vēn′) ▸ *v.* **-vened, -ven·ing.** 1. To come or occur between two things, events, or points of time. 2a. To come in or between so as to hinder or alter an action: *intervened to prevent a fight.* b. To interfere, usu. through force, in the affairs of another nation. **—in′ter·ven′tion** (-vĕn′shən) *n.*

in·ter·view (ĭn′tər-vyo͞o′) ▸ *n.* 1. A formal face-to-face meeting, esp. one conducted for the assessment of an applicant. 2. A conversation between a reporter and one from whom facts or statements are elicited. **—in′ter·view′** *v.* **—in′ter·view·ee′** *n.* **—in′ter·view′er** *n.*

in·ter·weave (ĭn′tər-wēv′) ▸ *v.* 1. To weave together. 2. To intertwine.

in·tes·tate (ĭn-tĕs′tāt′, -tĭt) ▸ *adj.* 1. Having made no legal will. 2. Not disposed of by a legal will.

in·tes·tine (ĭn-tĕs′tĭn) ▸ *n.* often **intestines** The portion of the alimentary canal extending from the outlet of the stomach to the anus. **—in·tes′ti·nal** *adj.* **—in·tes′ti·nal·ly** *adv.*

in·ti·mate[1] (ĭn′tə-mĭt) ▸ *adj.* 1. Marked by close acquaintance, association, or familiarity. 2. Essential; innermost. 3. Comfortably private: *an intimate café.* 4. Very personal. 5. Of or involving a sexual relationship. ▸ *n.* A close friend or confidant. **—in′ti·ma·cy** *n.* **—in′ti·mate·ly** *adv.*

in·ti·mate[2] (ĭn′tə-māt′) ▸ *v.* **-mat·ed, -mat·ing.** To imply subtly. **—in′ti·ma′tion** *n.*

in·tim·i·date (ĭn-tĭm′ĭ-dāt′) ▸ *v.* **-dat·ed, -dat·ing.** 1. To make timid; fill with fear. 2. To coerce, inhibit, or discourage by or as if by threats. **—in·tim′i·dat′ing·ly** *adv.* **—in·tim′i·da′tion** *n.* **—in·tim′i·da′tor** *n.*

intl. ▸ *abbr.* international

in·to (ĭn′to͞o) ▸ *prep.* 1. To the inside of. 2. To the activity or occupation of: *go into banking.* 3. To the condition or form of. 4. So as to be in or within. 5. *Informal* Interested in or involved with: *into vegetarianism.* 6. To a time or place in the course of: *well into the week.* 7. Toward: *pointed into the sky.* 8. Against: *crashed into a tree.*

in·tol·er·a·ble (ĭn-tŏl′ər-ə-bəl) ▸ *adj.* Unbearable: *intolerable agony.* **—in·tol′er·a·bly** *adv.*

in·tol·er·ant (ĭn-tŏl′ər-ənt) ▸ *adj.* 1. Not tolerant of differences in beliefs of others; bigoted. 2. Unable to endure: *intolerant of certain drugs.* **—in·tol′er·ance** *n.* **—in·tol′er·ant·ly** *adv.*

in·to·na·tion (ĭn′tə-nā′shən, -tō-) ▸ *n.* 1. The act of intoning or chanting. 2. A manner of producing musical tones, esp. with regard to pitch. 3. The way in which the voice rises and falls in pitch to convey meaning: *a questioning intonation.* 4. A use of pitch characteristic of a speaker or dialect.

in·tone (ĭn-tōn′) ▸ *v.* **-toned, -ton·ing.** To recite in a singing or chanting voice.

THESAURUS

interregnum *n.* —*See* GAP (2).

interrelated *adj.* —*See* COMPLEMENTARY.

interrelationship *n.* —*See* RELATION (1).

interrogate *v.* —*See* ASK (1).

interrogation *n.* A request for data ▸ inquiry, query, question, questioning. [*Compare* DEMAND, PROBLEM.]

interrogator or **interrogater** *n.* —*See* INQUIRER.

interrupt *v.* 1. To stop suddenly, as a conversation, activity, or relationship ▸ break off, cease, discontinue, suspend, terminate. 2. To interject remarks or questions into another's discourse ▸ barge in, break in, chime in, chip in, cut in. *Idioms:* break one's train of thought, talk out of turn. [*Compare* INTRUDE, MEDDLE.] 3. To stop for an indefinite period ▸ pause, suspend. *Idiom:* put on hold (*or* on ice). [*Compare* REST[1].] —*See also* DISRUPT.

interruption *n.* —*See* BREAK.

intersect *v.* —*See* CROSS (2).

interstice or **interspace** *n.* —*See* GAP (1).

intertwine *v.* —*See* WEAVE.

interval *n.* —*See* BIT[1] (3), DEGREE (1), DISTANCE (1), GAP (1).

intervention *n.* —*See* MEDDLING.

interview *n.* —*See* CONVERSATION.

intestinal fortitude *n.* —*See* COURAGE.

intestines *n.* —*See* VISCERA.

intimacy *n.* —*See* FRIENDSHIP.

intimate[1] *adj.* 1. Very closely associated ▸ bosom, chummy, close, cozy, familiar, fast, friendly, inseparable, near. *Informal:* solid, thick. *Slang:* tight. *Idioms:* buddy-buddy with, hand in glove with. [*Compare* FAITHFUL.] 2. Belonging to, relating to, or affecting a particular person ▸ individual, personal, private. —*See also* CONFIDENTIAL (2), INNER (2).

intimate *n.* One in whom secrets are confided ▸ confessor, confidant, confidante, repository. —*See also* FRIEND.

intimate[2] *v.* —*See* HINT.

intimation *n.* —*See* HINT (2), SHADE (2).

intimidate *v.* To frighten into submission, compliance, or acquiescence ▸ bludgeon, browbeat, bulldoze, bully, bullyrag, cow, hector, lean on, menace, push around, threaten. *Informal:* strong-arm. *Idioms:* flex one's muscles, put the screws (*or* squeeze) on, threaten with bodily harm, turn the heat on, twist someone's arm. [*Compare* COERCE, HARASS.] —*See also* FRIGHTEN.

intimidation *n.* An expression of the intent to hurt or punish another ▸ menace, threat.

intimidator *n.* —*See* BULLY.

intolerable *adj.* —*See* OUTRAGEOUS, UNBEARABLE.

intolerance *n.* Irrational suspicion or hatred of a particular group, race, or religion ▸ bigotry, discrimination, prejudice. [*Compare* HATE.]

intolerant *adj.* 1. Not tolerant of the beliefs or opinions of others ▸ bigoted, close-minded, dogmatic, hidebound, illiberal, judgmental, narrow-minded, opinionated, puritanical. [*Compare* BIASED, NARROW, STUBBORN.] 2. Being unable or unwilling to endure irritation or opposition, for example ▸ impatient, unforbearing, unindulgent. [*Compare* ILL-TEMPERED, INTOLERANT.] —*See also* DISDAINFUL.

intonation *n.* —*See* TONE (2).

intone *v.* —*See* SING.

in to·to (ĭn tō′tō) ▸ *adv.* Totally; altogether.

in·tox·i·cate (ĭn-tŏk′sĭ-kāt′) ▸ *v.* **-cat·ed, -cat·ing. 1.** To make drunk. 2. To stimulate or excite. **—in·tox′i·cant** (-kənt) *adj. & n.* **—in·tox′i·ca′tion** *n.*

intr. ▸ *abbr.* intransitive

intra– ▸ *pref.* Within: *intracellular.*

in·tra·cel·lu·lar (ĭn′trə-sĕl′yə-lər) ▸ *adj.* Occurring or situated within a cell or cells.

in·trac·ta·ble (ĭn-trăk′tə-bəl) ▸ *adj.* Difficult to manage or govern; stubborn. **—in·trac′ta·bil′i·ty** *n.* **—in·trac′ta·bly** *adv.*

in·tra·mu·ral (ĭn′trə-myo͝or′əl) ▸ *adj.* Existing or carried on within an institution, esp. a school.

in·tra·net (ĭn′trə-nĕt′) ▸ *n.* A restricted-access computer network, as within an organization.

in·tran·si·gent (ĭn-trăn′sə-jənt, -zə-) ▸ *adj.* Refusing to moderate a position, esp. an extreme one; uncompromising. **—in·tran′si·gence, in·tran′si·gen·cy** *n.* **—in·tran′si·gent** *n.* **—in·tran′si·gent·ly** *adv.*

in·tran·si·tive (ĭn-trăn′sĭ-tĭv, -zĭ-) ▸ *adj.* Designating a verb that does not require a direct object to complete its meaning. ▸ *n.* An intransitive verb. **—in·tran′si·tive·ly** *adv.* **—in·tran′si·tive·ness, in·tran′si·tiv′i·ty** *n.*

in·tra·oc·u·lar (ĭn′trə-ŏk′yə-lər) ▸ *adj.* Within the eyeball.

in·tra·state (ĭn′trə-stāt′) ▸ *adj.* Existing within the boundaries of a state.

in·tra·u·ter·ine (ĭn′trə-yo͞o′tər-ĭn, -tə-rīn′) ▸ *adj.* Within the uterus.

intrauterine device ▸ *n.* A birth control device inserted into the uterus to prevent implantation.

in·tra·ve·nous (ĭn′trə-vē′nəs) ▸ *adj.* Within or administered into a vein. **—in′tra·ve′nous·ly** *adv.*

in·trep·id (ĭn-trĕp′ĭd) ▸ *adj.* Resolutely courageous; fearless. **—in·trep′id·ness —in·trep′id·ly** *adv.*

in·tri·cate (ĭn′trĭ-kĭt) ▸ *adj.* **1.** Having many complexly arranged elements. 2. Comprehensible only with painstaking effort. **—in′tri·ca·cy** (-kə-sē) *n.* **—in′tri·cate·ly** *adv.*

in·trigue (ĭn′trēg′, ĭn-trēg′) ▸ *n.* **1.** A secret or underhand scheme; plot. 2. A secret love affair. ▸ *v.* (ĭn-trēg′) **-trigued, -trigu·ing. 1.** To engage in or effect by secret scheming or plotting. 2. To arouse the interest or curiosity of. **—in·trigu′er** *n.*

in·trin·sic (ĭn-trĭn′zĭk, -sĭk) ▸ *adj.* Relating to the essential nature of a thing; inherent. **—in·trin′si·cal·ly** *adv.*

in·tro (ĭn′trō′) ▸ *n., pl.* **-tros.** *Informal* An introduction.

intro– ▸ *pref.* Inward: *introvert.*

in·tro·duce (ĭn′trə-do͞os′, -dyo͞os′) ▸ *v.* **-duced, -duc·ing. 1.** To identify and present, esp. to make (strangers) acquainted. **2.** To bring forward (e.g., a plan) for consideration. **3.** To inform (someone) of something for the first time. **4.** To originate. **5.** To put into; insert or inject. **6.** To preface. **—in′tro·duc′tion** (-dŭk′shən) *n.*

in·tro·duc·to·ry (ĭn′trə-dŭk′tə-rē) ▸ *adj.* Serving to introduce.

in·tro·spec·tion (ĭn′trə-spĕk′shən) ▸ *n.* Contemplation of one's own thoughts and feelings; self-examination. **—in′tro·spect′** *v.* **—in′tro·spec′tive** *adj.* **—in′tro·spec′tive·ly** *adv.*

in·tro·vert (ĭn′trə-vûrt′) ▸ *n.* One whose thoughts and feelings are directed inward. **—in′tro·ver′sion** *n.*

in·trude (ĭn-tro͞od′) ▸ *v.* **-trud·ed, -trud·ing.** To put or force in without being wanted or asked; barge in. **—in·trud′er** *n.* **—in·tru′sion** *n.* **—in·tru′sive** *adj.* **—in·tru′sive·ly** *adv.*

in·trust (ĭn-trŭst′) ▸ *v.* Var. of **entrust.**

in·tu·it (ĭn-to͞o′ĭt, -tyo͞o′-) ▸ *v.* To know intuitively.

in·tu·i·tion (ĭn′to͞o-ĭsh′ən, -tyo͞o-) ▸ *n.* **1a.** The faculty of knowing as if by instinct without conscious reasoning. **b.** A perception based on this faculty. **2.** Sharp insight; impression. **—in′tu·i′tion·al** *adj.* **—in·tu′i·tive** (ĭn-to͞o′ĭ-tĭv, -tyo͞o′-) *adj.* **—in·tu′i·tive·ly** *adv.* **—in·tu′i·tive·ness** *n.*

In·u·it (ĭn′yo͞o-ĭt) ▸ *n., pl.* **-it** or **-its. 1.** A member of a group of Eskimoan peoples inhabiting the Arctic from N Alaska eastward to E Greenland. **2.** Any of the Eskimoan languages of the Inuit.

in·un·date (ĭn′ŭn-dāt′) ▸ *v.* **-dat·ed, -dat·ing.** To cover or overwhelm with or as if with a flood. **—in′un·da′tion** *n.*

in·ure (ĭn-yo͝or′) ▸ *v.* **-ured, -ur·ing.** To make used to something undesirable; harden. **—in·ure′ment** *n.*

in u·ter·o (ĭn yo͞o′tə-rō) ▸ *adv. & adj.* In the uterus.

in·vade (ĭn-vād′) ▸ *v.* **-vad·ed, -vad·ing. 1.** To enter by force in order to conquer. **2.** To trespass or intrude on; violate. **3.** To overrun or infest. **4.** To enter and permeate, esp. harmfully. **—in·vad′er** *n.*

in·va·lid¹ (ĭn′və-lĭd) ▸ *n.* One incapacitated by a chronic illness or injury. ▸ *adj.* Incapacitated by illness or injury.

in·val·id² (ĭn-văl′ĭd) ▸ *adj.* **1.** Not legally valid; null. **2.** Falsely based or reasoned; unjustified. **—in′va·lid′i·ty** (-və-lĭd′ĭ-tē) *n.* **—in·val′id·ly** *adv.*

in·val·i·date (ĭn-văl′ĭ-dāt′) ▸ *v.* **-dat·ed, -dat·ing.** To make invalid; nullify. **—in·val′i·da′tion** *n.* **—in·val′i·da′tor** *n.*

in·val·u·a·ble (ĭn-văl′yo͞o-ə-bəl) ▸ *adj.* Of inestimable value; priceless. **—in·val′u·a·bly** *adv.*

in·var·i·a·ble (ĭn-vâr′ē-ə-bəl) ▸ *adj.* Not changing or subject

THESAURUS

intoxicate *v.* *—See* POISON.

intoxicated *adj.* *—See* DRUNK.

intoxicating *adj.* *—See* HARD (3), INVIGORATING.

intoxication *n.* *—See* DRUNKENNESS.

intoxicative *adj.* *—See* HARD (3).

intractability or **intractableness** *n.* *—See* UNRULINESS.

intractable *adj.* *—See* UNRULY.

intransigence or **intransigency** *n.* *—See* STUBBORNNESS.

intransigent *adj.* *—See* STUBBORN (1).

intrepid *adj.* *—See* BRAVE.

intrepidity or **intrepidness** *n.* *—See* COURAGE.

intricacy *n.* *—See* COMPLEXITY.

intricate *adj.* *—See* COMPLEX (1), ELABORATE.

intrigue *n.* *—See* PLOT (2).

intrigue *v.* *—See* GRIP, PLOT (2).

intrigued *adj.* *—See* CURIOUS (2).

intrinsic *adj.* *—See* CONSTITUTIONAL.

introduce *v.* **1.** To bring into currency, use, fashion, or practice ▸ innovate, launch, originate, pioneer, popularize, put forward, usher in. ***Idiom:*** start the ball rolling. [*Compare* FOUND, START.] **2.** To put or set into, between, or among another or other things ▸ implant, infuse, inject, insert, interject, interlard, interpolate, interpose, put in, stick in, throw in. [*Compare* ATTACH, FIX.] **3.** To begin something with preliminary or prefatory material ▸ lead, precede, preface, ring in, usher in. ***Idiom:*** pave the way. [*Compare* START.] **4.** To make known socially ▸ acquaint, familiarize, present. *—See also* BROACH, PROCLAIM.

introduction *n.* A short section of preliminary remarks ▸ foreword, induction, lead-in, overture, preamble, preface, prelude, prolegomenon, prologue. *—See also* ADMISSION, BEGINNING.

introductory *adj.* Serving to introduce or prepare for something ▸ inductive, prefatory, preliminary, preparatory. *—See also* BEGINNING.

intromission *n.* *—See* ADMISSION.

intromit *v.* *—See* ACCEPT (3).

introversion *n.* *—See* RESERVE (1).

introverted *adj.* *—See* RESERVED, SHY¹.

intrude *v.* To force or come in as an improper or unwanted element ▸ barge in, charge in, cut in, encroach, gatecrash, horn in, interlope, obtrude, trespass. [*Compare* INTERRUPT, MEDDLE.] *—See also* DISRUPT.

intrusion *n.* An excessive, unwelcome burden ▸ encumbrance, imposition, infliction, obtrusion. [*Compare* BURDEN¹.] *—See also* MEDDLING, TRESPASS (2).

intrusive *adj.* *—See* CURIOUS (1), DISTURBING.

intuit *v.* *—See* PERCEIVE.

intuition *n.* *—See* FEELING (1), INSTINCT.

intuitive *adj.* *—See* INSTINCTIVE, VISIONARY.

intuitiveness *n.* *—See* INSTINCT.

inundate *v.* To affect as if by an outpouring of water ▸ deluge, flood, overwhelm, swamp. *—See also* FLOOD (1).

inundation *n.* *—See* FLOOD.

inure *v.* *—See* ACCUSTOM.

inured *adj.* *—See* ACCUSTOMED (1).

invade *v.* **1.** To enter so as to attack, plunder, destroy, or conquer ▸ foray, harry, maraud, overrun, raid. ***Idioms:*** enter by force, take by storm. [*Compare* ATTACK, SACK².] **2.** To enter forcibly or illegally ▸ break in, burglarize, trespass. [*Compare* ROB, STEAL.] *—See also* OCCUPY (2).

invalid *adj.* *—See* FALLACIOUS (1).

invalidate *v.* *—See* ABOLISH, DISABLE (1).

invaluable *adj.* *—See* COSTLY.

invariable *adj.* *—See* IMMUTABLE, UNCHANGING.

to change; constant. **—in·var′i·a·bil′i·ty, in·var′i·a·ble·ness** *n.* **—in·var′i·a·bly** *adv.*

in·va·sion (ĭn-vā′zhən) ▸ *n.* **1.** The act of invading, esp. entrance by force. **2.** A large-scale onset of something harmful, such as a disease. **3.** An intrusion or encroachment: *invasion of privacy.*

in·va·sive (ĭn-vā′sĭv) ▸ *adj.* **1.** Of or engaging in armed aggression. **2.** Tending to spread, esp. into healthy tissue.

in·vec·tive (ĭn-vĕk′tĭv) ▸ *n.* Harsh and insulting language used to attack or denounce.

in·veigh (ĭn-vā′) ▸ *v.* To protest or disapprove vehemently.

in·vei·gle (ĭn-vā′gəl, -vē′-) ▸ *v.* **-gled, -gling. 1.** To win over or lead astray by guile or deception. **2.** To obtain by deception or flattery. **—in·vei′gle·ment** *n.* **—in·vei′gler** *n.*

in·vent (ĭn-vĕnt′) ▸ *v.* **1.** To conceive of or produce first; originate. **2.** To make up; fabricate: *invent a likely excuse.* **—in·ven′tor** *n.*

in·ven·tion (ĭn-vĕn′shən) ▸ *n.* **1.** The act or process of inventing. **2.** A new device, method, or process developed from study and experimentation. **3.** A mental fabrication, esp. a falsehood. **4.** Skill in inventing.

in·ven·tive (ĭn-vĕn′tĭv) ▸ *adj.* **1.** Of or characterized by invention. **2.** Skillful at inventing. **—in·ven′tive·ly** *adv.* **—in·ven′tive·ness** *n.*

in·ven·to·ry (ĭn′vən-tôr′ē) ▸ *n., pl.* **-ries. 1a.** A detailed list of things, esp. a periodic survey of all goods and materials in stock. **b.** The process of making such a list. **c.** The items so listed. **2.** The supply of goods on hand; stock. **—in′ven·to′ry** *v.*

in·verse (ĭn-vûrs′, ĭn′vûrs′) ▸ *adj.* Reversed in order, nature, or effect. ▸ *n.* (ĭn′vûrs′, ĭn-vûrs′) Something opposite, as in sequence, effect, or character; reverse. **—in·verse′ly** *adv.*

in·ver·sion (ĭn-vûr′zhən, -shən) ▸ *n.* **1.** The act of inverting or the state of being inverted. **2.** A reversal of position or order in a sequence. **3.** *Meteorol.* An atmospheric condition in which the air temperature rises with increasing altitude, holding surface air down along with its pollutants.

in·vert (ĭn-vûrt′) ▸ *v.* **1.** To turn inside out or upside down. **2.** To reverse the position, order, or condition of. **—in·vert′er** *n.* **—in·vert′i·ble** *adj.*

in·ver·te·brate (ĭn-vûr′tə-brĭt, -brāt′) ▸ *adj.* Lacking a backbone or spinal column; not vertebrate. **—in·ver′te·brate** *n.*

in·vest (ĭn-vĕst′) ▸ *v.* **1.** To commit (money or capital) in order to gain a financial return. **2.** To spend or devote (time or effort) for future benefit. **3.** To endow with authority or power. **4.** To install in office; inaugurate. **5.** To surround or envelop. **—in·ves′tor** *n.*

in·ves·ti·gate (ĭn-vĕs′tĭ-gāt′) ▸ *v.* **-gat·ed, -gat·ing.** To observe or inquire into in detail; examine systematically. **—in·ves′ti·ga′tive** *adj.* **—in·ves′ti·ga′tor** *n.*

in·ves·ti·ga·tion (ĭn-vĕs′tĭ-gā′shən) ▸ *n.* **1.** The act or process of investigating. **2.** A detailed inquiry or systematic examination.

in·ves·ti·ture (ĭn-vĕs′tĭ-cho͝or′, -chər) ▸ *n.* The act or ceremony of conferring the authority and symbols of a high office.

in·vest·ment (ĭn-vĕst′mənt) ▸ *n.* **1.** The act of investing or the conditon of being invested. **2.** An amount invested. **3.** Property acquired for future income. **4.** Investiture.

in·vet·er·ate (ĭn-vĕt′ər-ĭt) ▸ *adj.* **1.** Firmly and long established. **2.** Persisting in an ingrained habit: *an inveterate liar.* **—in·vet′er·a·cy** (-ər-ə-sē), **—in·vet′er·ate·ly** *adv.*

in·vid·i·ous (ĭn-vĭd′ē-əs) ▸ *adj.* **1.** Tending to rouse ill will or envy. **2.** Containing or implying a slight. **—in·vid′i·ous·ly** *adv.* **—in·vid′i·ous·ness** *n.*

in·vig·or·ate (ĭn-vĭg′ə-rāt′) ▸ *v.* **-at·ed, -at·ing.** To impart vigor or vitality to; animate. **—in·vig′or·at′ing·ly** *adv.* **—in·vig′or·a′tion** *n.* **—in·vig′or·a′tive** *adj.*

in·vin·ci·ble (ĭn-vĭn′sə-bəl) ▸ *adj.* Unconquerable. **—in·vin′ci·bil′i·ty** *n.* **—in·vin′ci·bly** *adv.*

in·vi·o·la·ble (ĭn-vī′ə-lə-bəl) ▸ *adj.* **1.** Secure from violation or profanation. **2.** Impregnable. **—in·vi′o·la·bil′i·ty** *n.* **—in·vi′o·la·bly** *adv.*

in·vi·o·late (ĭn-vī′ə-lĭt) ▸ *adj.* Not violated or profaned; intact. **—in·vi′o·late·ly** *adv.* **—in·vi′o·late·ness** *n.*

in·vis·i·ble (ĭn-vĭz′ə-bəl) ▸ *adj.* **1.** Incapable of being seen. **2.** Hidden from view. **3.** Inconspicuous. **—in·vis′i·bil′i·ty** *n.* **—in·vis′i·bly** *adv.*

in·vi·ta·tion (ĭn′vĭ-tā′shən) ▸ *n.* **1.** The act of inviting. **2.** A request for someone's presence or participation. **3.** An allurement or enticement. **—in′vi·ta′tion·al** *adj. & n.*

in·vite (ĭn-vīt′) ▸ *v.* **-vit·ed, -vit·ing. 1.** To request the presence or participation of. **2.** To request formally. **3.** To welcome: *invite questions.* **4.** To tend to bring on; provoke. **5.** To entice; lure. ▸ *n.* (ĭn′vīt′) *Informal* An invitation.

THESAURUS

invariant *adj.* —*See* UNCHANGING.

invasion *n.* An act of invading, especially by military forces ▸ foray, incursion, inroad, raid. [*Compare* ATTACK.]

invective *n.* —*See* VITUPERATION.

invective *adj.* —*See* ABUSIVE.

inveigh *v.* —*See* OBJECT.

inveigle *v.* —*See* SEDUCE.

inveiglement *n.* —*See* LURE (1).

inveigler *n.* —*See* SEDUCER (1).

invent *v.* To use ingenuity in making, developing, or achieving ▸ coin, concoct, contrive, devise, dream up, fabricate, formulate, hatch, make up, mint, think up. *Informal:* cook up. *Idiom:* come up with. [*Compare* DESIGN, INTRODUCE, PRODUCE, MAKE.] —*See also* LIE².

invented *adj.* —*See* FICTITIOUS.

invention *n.* **1.** The power or ability to invent ▸ creativeness, creativity, fecundity, ingeniousness, ingenuity, inventiveness, originality, resourcefulness. [*Compare* ABILITY, BRILLIANCE, IMAGINATION.] **2.** A new thing, method or process that is invented ▸ brainchild, concoction, contrivance, device, innovation, origination. [*Compare* DEVICE, DISCOVERY, NOVELTY.] —*See also* BEGINNING, COMPOSITION (1), LIE², MYTH (2).

inventive *adj.* Characterized by or productive of new things or new ideas ▸ artistic, creative, generative, ingenious, innovative, original, resourceful, seminal. [*Compare* FERTILE, VISIONARY.] —*See also* CLEVER (1), NEW.

inventiveness *n.* —*See* INVENTION (1).

inventor *n.* —*See* ORIGINATOR.

inventory *n.* —*See* GOOD (2), HOARD, LIST¹.

inventory *v.* —*See* ENUMERATE.

inveracity *n.* —*See* LIE², MENDACITY.

inverse *n.* —*See* OPPOSITE.

inverse *adj.* —*See* OPPOSITE.

inversion *n.* —*See* REVERSAL (1).

invert *v.* —*See* OVERTURN, REVERSE (1).

inverted *adj.* —*See* UPSIDE-DOWN.

invest *v.* —*See* BANK², BESIEGE, DRESS (1), ESTABLISH (1), GIFT, INITIATE, WRAP (2).

investigate *v.* —*See* EXAMINE (1), EXPLORE.

investigation *n.* The act or an instance of exploring or investigating ▸ exploration, probe, reconnaissance. —*See also* EXAMINATION (1).

investigative *adj.* —*See* CURIOUS (2).

investigator *n.* —*See* DETECTIVE, INQUIRER.

investiture *n.* —*See* INITIATION.

investment *n.* **1.** The management of money ▸ banking, finance, money management. **2.** A prolonged encirclement of an objective by hostile troops ▸ beleaguerment, besiegement, blockade, siege. [*Compare* ATTACK.]

inveterate *adj.* Subject to a disease or habit for a long time ▸ chronic, confirmed, habitual, habituated. [*Compare* STUBBORN.] —*See also* CONFIRMED (1).

invidious *adj.* —*See* ENVIOUS, LIBELOUS.

invigorate *v.* —*See* ENERGIZE.

invigorating *adj.* Producing or stimulating physical, mental, or emotional vigor ▸ animating, bracing, energizing, enlivening, exciting, exhilarant, exhilarating, innerving, intoxicating, quickening, refreshing, reinvigorating, renewing, restorative, roborant, rousing, stimulating, tonic, vitalizing, vivifying. [*Compare* CURATIVE, PLEASANT.]

invincible *adj.* Incapable of being conquered or subjugated ▸ indomitable, unbeatable, unconquerable, undefeatable. [*Compare* SAFE.]

inviolability *n.* The quality or condition of being safe from assault, trespass, or violation ▸ sacredness, sacrosanctity, sanctity. —*See also* HOLINESS.

inviolable *adj.* —*See* HOLY, SAFE (2).

invisible *adj.* —*See* HIDDEN (1), IMPERCEPTIBLE (1).

invitation *n.* A spoken or written request for someone to take part or be present ▸ call, bid, summons. *Informal:* invite. [*Compare* REQUEST.] —*See also* LURE (1), OFFER.

invite *v.* To request that someone take

in·vit·ing (ĭn-vī′tĭng) ▸ *adj.* Attractive; tempting. **—in·vit′ing·ly** *adv.*

in vi·tro (ĭn vē′trō) ▸ *adv. & adj.* In an artificial environment outside the living organism.

in vi·vo (vē′vō) ▸ *adv. & adj.* Within a living organism.

in·vo·ca·tion (ĭn′və-kā′shən) ▸ *n.* **1.** The act of invoking, esp. an appeal to a higher power. **2.** A prayer or other formula used in invoking.

in·voice (ĭn′vois′) ▸ *n.* **1.** A list of goods shipped or services rendered, detailing all costs. **2.** The goods or services so itemized. **—in′voice′** *v.*

in·voke (ĭn-vōk′) ▸ *v.* **-voked, -vok·ing. 1.** To call on (a higher power) for help or inspiration. **2.** To appeal to; petition. **3.** To call for earnestly. **4.** To conjure. **5.** To use or apply: *invoked the veto power.* **—in·vok′er** *n.*

in·vol·un·tar·y (ĭn-vŏl′ən-tĕr′ē) ▸ *adj.* **1.** Performed against one's will. **2.** Not subject to control: *an involuntary twitch.* **—in·vol′un·tar′i·ly** (-târ′ə-lē) *adv.* **—in·vol′un·tar′i·ness** *n.*

in·vo·lu·tion (ĭn′və-lo͞o′shən) ▸ *n.* **1.** The act of involving or the state of being involved. **2.** Something, such as a long grammatical construction, that is intricate or complex. **3.** *Math.* The multiplying of a quantity by itself a specified number of times; raising to a power.

in·volve (ĭn-vŏlv′) ▸ *v.* **-volved, -volv·ing. 1.** To contain as a part; include. **2.** To have as a necessary feature or consequence. **3.** To engage or draw in; embroil. **4.** To engross. **5.** To make complex; complicate. **—in·volve′ment** *n.*

in·vul·ner·a·ble (ĭn-vŭl′nər-ə-bəl) ▸ *adj.* **1.** Immune to attack; impregnable. **2.** Impossible to damage or injure. **—in·vul′ner·a·bil′i·ty** *n.* **—in·vul′ner·a·bly** *adv.*

in·ward (ĭn′wərd) ▸ *adj.* **1.** Located inside; inner. **2.** Directed or moving toward the interior. **3.** Existing in the mind. ▸ *adv.* **1.** Toward the inside or center. **2.** Toward the mind or the self. **—in′wards** *adv.*

in·ward·ly (ĭn′wərd-lē) ▸ *adv.* **1.** On or in the inside; within. **2.** To oneself; privately.

i·o·dide (ī′ə-dīd′) ▸ *n.* A binary compound of iodine with a more electropositive atom or group.

i·o·dine (ī′ə-dīn′, -dĭn, -dēn′) ▸ *n.* **1.** *Symbol* **I** A grayish-black, corrosive, poisonous element having radioactive isotopes used as tracers and in thyroid disease diagnosis and therapy, and compounds used as germicides, antiseptics, and dyes. At. no. 53. **2.** A liquid containing iodine dissolved in ethyl alcohol, used as an antiseptic for wounds.

i·o·dize (ī′ə-dīz′) ▸ *v.* **-dized, -diz·ing.** To treat or combine with iodine or an iodide.

iodo– or **iod–** ▸ *pref.* Iodine: *iodize.*

i·on (ī′ən, ī′ŏn′) ▸ *n.* An atom or molecule having a net electric charge acquired by gaining or losing one or more electrons from an initially neutral configuration. **—i·on′ic** (-ŏn′ĭk) *adj.*

–ion ▸ *suff.* **1a.** Action or process: *completion.* **b.** Result of an action or process: *invention.* **2.** State or condition: *dehydration.*

ionic bond ▸ *n.* A chemical bond formed by the complex transfer of one or more electrons from one kind of atom to another.

Ionic order ▸ *n. Archit.* A classical order marked by two opposed volutes in the column capital.

i·on·ize (ī′ə-nīz′) ▸ *v.* **-ized, -iz·ing.** To convert or be converted totally or partially into ions. **—i′on·i·za′tion** *n.*

i·on·o·sphere (ī-ŏn′ə-sfîr′) ▸ *n.* An electrically conducting set of layers of the earth's atmosphere, extending from altitudes of 70 km (43 mi) to 400 km (250 mi).

i·o·ta (ī-ō′tə) ▸ *n.* **1.** The 9th letter of the Greek alphabet. **2.** A very small amount; bit.

IOU (ī′ō-yo͞o′) ▸ *n.* A usu. written promise to pay a debt.

–ious ▸ *suff.* Characterized by or full of: *bilious.*

I·o·wa[1] (ī′ə-wə) ▸ *n., pl.* **-wa** or **-was. 1.** A member of a Native American people formerly of Iowa and SW Minnesota, later in Nebraska, Kansas, and Oklahoma. **2.** The Siouan language of the Iowa.

I·o·wa[2] (ī′ə-wə) ▸ A state of the N-central US. Cap. Des Moines. **—I′o·wan** *adj. & n.*

ip·e·cac (ĭp′ĭ-kăk′) ▸ *n.* A preparation made from the roots of a tropical American shrub, used to induce vomiting.

ip·so fac·to (ĭp′sō făk′tō) ▸ *adv.* By the fact itself; by that very fact.

IQ ▸ *abbr.* intelligence quotient

I·qal·u·it (ĭ-kăl′o͞o-ĭt, ē-kä′lo͞o-ēt) ▸ The capital of Nunavut, Canada, on Baffin Island.

Ir ▸ The symbol for the element **iridium.**

ir–[1] ▸ *pref.* Var. of **in–**[1].

ir–[2] ▸ *pref.* Var. of **in–**[2].

IRA ▸ *abbr.* individual retirement account

I·ran (ĭ-răn′, ĭ-rän′) ▸ A country of SW Asia.

I·ra·ni·an (ĭ-rā′nē-ən, ĭ-rä′-) ▸ *n.* **1.** A native or inhabitant of Iran. **2.** A branch of the Indo-European language family that includes Persian, Kurdish, and Pashto. **—I·ra′ni·an** *adj.*

I·raq (ĭ-răk′, ĭ-räk′) ▸ A country of SW Asia. **—I·ra′qi** (-răk′ē, -rä′kē) *adj. & n.*

i·ras·ci·ble (ĭ-răs′ə-bəl, ī-răs′-) ▸ *adj.* Prone to outbursts of temper; easily angered; ill-tempered. **—i·ras′ci·bil′i·ty** *n.* **—i·ras′ci·bly** *adv.*

i·rate (ī-rāt′, ī′rāt′) ▸ *adj.* Extremely angry; enraged. **—i·rate′ly** *adv.*

ire (īr) ▸ *n.* Anger; wrath.

ire·ful (īr′fəl) ▸ *adj.* Full of ire. **—ire′ful·ly** *adv.*

Ire·land[1] (īr′lənd) ▸ An island in the N Atlantic W of Great Britain.

Ire·land[2] (īr′lənd) also **Eire** ▸ A country occupying most of the island of Ireland.

Ireland, Northern ▸ See **Northern Ireland.**

ir·i·des·cent (ĭr′ĭ-dĕs′ənt) ▸ *adj.* Producing a display of lustrous, rainbowlike colors: *an iridescent oil slick.* **—ir′i·des′cence** *n.*

i·rid·i·um (ĭ-rĭd′ē-əm) ▸ *n. Symbol* **Ir** A hard, brittle, exceptionally corrosion-resistant whitish-yellow metallic element used as an alloy with platinum. At. no. 77.

i·ris (ī′rĭs) ▸ *n., pl.* **i·ris·es** or **i·ri·des** (ī′rĭ-dēz′, ĭr′ĭ-). **1.** The pigmented, round, contractile membrane of the eye, situated between the cornea and lens and perforated by the pupil. **2.** A plant having narrow sword-shaped leaves and showy, variously colored flowers.

THESAURUS

part in or be present at a particular occasion ▸ ask, bid, summon. *Idioms:* extend an invitation to, request the presence of. [*Compare* APPEAL, REQUEST.] —*See also* COURT (1).

invite *n. Informal* A spoken or written request for someone to take part or be present ▸ call, bid, invitation, summons. [*Compare* REQUEST.]

inviting *adj.* —*See* SEDUCTIVE.

invocation *n.* The act of praying ▸ benediction, prayer, supplication. [*Compare* APPEAL.]

invoice *n.* —*See* ACCOUNT (2), LIST[1].

invoice *v.* —*See* BILL[1].

invoke *v.* To offer a reverent petition to God or a god ▸ pray, supplicate. [*Compare* APPEAL.] —*See also* CITE, ENFORCE, EVOKE.

involuntarily *adv.* —*See* HELPLESSLY, SPONTANEOUSLY (1).

involuntary *adj.* —*See* SPONTANEOUS, UNINTENTIONAL.

involute *adj.* —*See* COMPLEX (1).

involve *v.* **1.** To draw in so that extrication is difficult ▸ catch up, draw into, embrangle, embroil, implicate, mix up, suck, wrap up. [*Compare* CATCH.] **2.** To have as a condition or a consequence ▸ carry, entail. —*See also* ABSORB (1), COMPLICATE, CONTAIN (1), DEMAND (2), IMPLY.

involved *adj.* —*See* COMPLEX (1), CONCERNED.

involvement *n.* The act or fact of participating ▸ engagement, partaking, participation, sharing. —*See also* ABSORPTION (2), ENTANGLEMENT.

invulnerability *n.* —*See* SAFETY.

invulnerable *adj.* —*See* SAFE (2).

inward *adj.* —*See* CONFIDENTIAL (2), INNER (2).

in-your-face *adj.* —*See* ASSERTIVE.

iota *n.* —*See* BIT[1] (1).

irascibility or **irascibleness** *n.* —*See* TEMPER (1).

irascible *adj.* —*See* ILL-TEMPERED, TESTY.

irate *adj.* —*See* ANGRY.

irateness *n.* —*See* ANGER.

ire *n.* —*See* ANGER.

ireful *adj.* —*See* ANGRY.

irenic *adj.* —*See* PEACEABLE.

I·rish (īʹrĭsh) ▸ *adj.* Of or relating to Ireland or its people or language. ▸ *n.* **1.** The people of Ireland. **2a.** See **Irish Gaelic**. **b.** English as spoken by the Irish. **3.** *Informal* Fieriness of temper or passion. **—Iʹrish·man** *n.* **—Iʹrish·womʹan** *n.*

Irish bull ▸ *n.* A statement containing an incongruity or a logical absurdity, usu. unbeknown to the speaker.

Irish Gaelic ▸ *n.* The Celtic language of Ireland.

Irish moss ▸ *n.* An edible North Atlantic seaweed that yields carrageenan.

Irish Sea ▸ An arm of the N Atlantic between Ireland and Great Britain.

Irish setter ▸ *n.* A setter having a silky reddish-brown coat.

irk (ûrk) ▸ *v.* To annoy; irritate.

irk·some (ûrkʹsəm) ▸ *adj.* Annoying; bothersome; tedious. **—irkʹsome·ly** *adv.* **—irkʹsome·ness** *n.*

i·ron (īʹərn) ▸ *n.* **1.** *Symbol* **Fe** A silvery-white, malleable, magnetic or magnetizable metallic element used alloyed in many important structural materials. At. no. 26. **2.** An implement made of iron alloy or similar metal, esp. a bar heated for use in branding or curling hair. **3.** Great hardness or strength: *a will of iron.* **4.** A golf club with a metal head. **5.** An appliance with a weighted flat bottom, used when heated to press fabric. **6. irons** Fetters; shackles. ▸ *adj.* Of or like iron. ▸ *v.* To press and smooth with a heated iron. ***—phrasal verb:* iron out** To discuss and settle; work out. **—iʹron·er** *n.* **—iʹron·ing** *n.*

Iron Age ▸ *n.* The period of human culture succeeding the Bronze Age, marked by the introduction of iron metallurgy and in Europe beginning around the 8th cent. B.C.

i·ron·clad (īʹərn-klădʹ) ▸ *adj.* **1.** Covered with iron plates for protection. **2.** Rigid; fixed: *an ironclad rule.*

iron curtain or **Iron Curtain** ▸ *n.* The military, political, and ideological barrier existing between the Soviet bloc and western Europe from 1945 until 1990.

i·ron·ic (ī-rŏnʹĭk) also **i·ron·i·cal** (-ĭ-kəl) ▸ *adj.* **1.** Marked by or constituting irony. **2.** Given to the use of irony. **—i·ronʹi·cal·ly** *adv.* **—i·ronʹi·cal·ness** *n.*

iron lung ▸ *n.* A tank that encloses all of the body except the head and forces the lungs to inhale and exhale through regulated changes in air pressure.

i·ron·stone (īʹərn-stōnʹ) ▸ *n.* **1.** A hard white pottery. **2.** An iron ore.

i·ron·ware (īʹərn-wârʹ) ▸ *n.* Iron utensils and other products made of iron.

i·ron·work (īʹərn-wûrkʹ) ▸ *n.* Work in iron, such as gratings and rails.

i·ron·work·er (īʹərn-wûrʹkər) ▸ *n.* **1.** A construction worker who builds steel structures. **2.** One who makes iron articles.

i·ron·works (īʹərn-wûrksʹ) ▸ *pl.n. (takes sing. or pl. v.)* A building or establishment where iron is smelted or iron products are made.

i·ro·ny (īʹrə-nē, īʹər-) ▸ *n., pl.* **-nies. 1.** The use of words to convey the opposite of their literal meaning. **2.** Incongruity between what might be expected and what actually occurs. **—iʹro·nist** *n.*

Ir·o·quoi·an (îrʹə-kwoiʹən) ▸ *n.* **1.** A family of Native American languages of E North America. **2.** A member of an Iroquoian-speaking people. **—Irʹo·quoiʹan** *adj.*

Ir·o·quois (îrʹə-kwoiʹ) ▸ *n., pl.* **-quois** (-kwoiʹ, -kwoizʹ). **1.** A member of a Native American confederacy of New York State composed of the Mohawk, Oneida, Onondaga, Cayuga, Seneca, and later the Tuscarora peoples. **2.** Any of the languages of the Iroquois.

ir·ra·di·ate (ĭ-rāʹdē-ātʹ) ▸ *v.* **-at·ed, -at·ing. 1.** To expose to or treat with radiation. **2.** To shed light on; illuminate. **3.** To emit in or as if in rays; radiate. **—ir·raʹdi·aʹtion** *n.* **—ir·raʹdi·aʹtive** *adj.* **—ir·raʹdi·aʹtor** *n.*

ir·ra·tion·al (ĭ-răshʹə-nəl) ▸ *adj.* **1a.** Not endowed with reason. **b.** Incoherent, as from shock. **c.** Illogical: *an irrational dislike.* **2.** *Math.* Relating to an irrational number. **—ir·raʹtion·alʹi·ty** (-ə-nălʹĭ-tē) *n.* **—ir·raʹtion·al·ly** *adv.*

irrational number ▸ *n.* Any real number that cannot be expressed as a ratio between two integers.

ir·rec·on·cil·a·ble (ĭ-rĕkʹən-sīʹlə-bəl, ĭ-rĕkʹən-sīʹ-) ▸ *adj.* Impossible to reconcile. **—ir·recʹon·cilʹa·bilʹi·ty** *n.* **—ir·recʹon·cilʹa·bly** *adv.*

ir·re·cov·er·a·ble (ĭrʹĭ-kŭvʹər-ə-bəl) ▸ *adj.* Impossible to recover; irreparable: *irrecoverable losses.* **—irʹre·covʹer·a·ble·ness** *n.* **—irʹre·covʹer·a·bly** *adv.*

ir·re·deem·a·ble (ĭrʹĭ-dēʹmə-bəl) ▸ *adj.* **1.** That cannot be bought back or paid off. **2.** Not convertible into coin. **3.** Impossible to redeem or reform. **—irʹre·deemʹa·bly** *adv.*

ir·re·den·tist (ĭrʹĭ-dĕnʹtĭst) ▸ *n.* One who advocates the recovery of territory culturally or historically related to one's nation but now subject to a foreign government. **—irʹre·denʹtism** *n.*

ir·re·duc·i·ble (ĭrʹĭ-dōōʹsə-bəl, -dyōōʹ-) ▸ *adj.* Impossible to reduce to a simpler or smaller form or amount. **—irʹre·ducʹi·bilʹi·ty** *n.* **—irʹre·ducʹi·bly** *adv.*

ir·ref·u·ta·ble (ĭ-rĕfʹyə-tə-bəl, ĭrʹĭ-fyōōʹ-) ▸ *adj.* Impossible to refute or disprove. **—ir·refʹu·ta·bilʹi·ty** *n.* **—ir·refʹu·ta·bly** *adv.*

ir·re·gard·less (ĭrʹĭ-gärdʹlĭs) ▸ *adv. Nonstandard* Regardless.

ir·reg·u·lar (ĭ-rĕgʹyə-lər) ▸ *adj.* **1.** Contrary to rule, accepted order, or general practice. **2.** Not straight, uniform, or symmetrical. **3.** Of uneven rate, occurrence, or duration. **4.** Deviating from a type; atypical. **5.** Not up to standard or specification; imperfect. **6.** *Gram.* Departing from the usual pattern of inflection. **7.** Not belonging to a permanent, organized military force. ▸ *n.* **1.** One that is irregular. **2.** A guerrilla. **—ir·regʹu·larʹi·ty** (-yə-lărʹĭ-tē) *n.* **—ir·regʹu·lar·ly** *adv.*

ir·rel·e·vant (ĭ-rĕlʹə-vənt) ▸ *adj.* Unrelated to the matter at hand. **—ir·relʹe·vance, ir·relʹe·van·cy** *n.* **—ir·relʹe·vant·ly** *adv.*

ir·re·li·gious (ĭrʹĭ-lĭjʹəs) ▸ *adj.* Hostile or indifferent to religion. **—irʹre·liʹgious·ly** *adv.* **—irʹre·liʹgious·ness** *n.*

ir·re·me·di·a·ble (ĭrʹĭ-mēʹdē-ə-bəl) ▸ *adj.* Impossible to remedy, correct, or repair. **—irʹre·meʹdi·a·bly** *adv.*

ir·rep·a·ra·ble (ĭ-rĕpʹər-ə-bəl) ▸ *adj.* Impossible to repair, rectify, or amend. **—ir·repʹa·ra·bilʹi·ty, ir·repʹa·ra·ble·ness** *n.* **—ir·repʹa·ra·bly** *adv.*

ir·re·place·a·ble (ĭrʹĭ-plāʹsə-bəl) ▸ *adj.* Impossible to replace.

ir·re·press·i·ble (ĭrʹĭ-prĕsʹə-bəl) ▸ *adj.* Impossible to control or hold back. **—irʹre·pressʹi·bilʹi·ty** *n.* **—irʹre·pressʹi·bly** *adv.*

ir·re·proach·a·ble (ĭrʹĭ-prōʹchə-bəl) ▸ *adj.* Being beyond re-

THESAURUS

irk *v.* —*See* ANNOY.

irksome *adj.* —*See* BORING, DISTURBING.

iron *adj.* —*See* LUSTY, STUBBORN (1).

iron *v.* —*See* PRESS (2).

ironbound *adj.* —*See* ROUGH (1).

ironclad *adj.* —*See* IMMUTABLE.

ironic or **ironical** *adj.* —*See* SARCASTIC.

irons *n.* —*See* BOND (1).

irony *n.* —*See* SARCASM.

irradiant *adj.* —*See* BRIGHT.

irradiate *v.* To render free of microorganisms ▸ decontaminate, disinfect, sanitize, sterilize. —*See also* SHED[1] (1).

irradicable *adj.* —*See* CONFIRMED (1).

irrational *adj.* Not governed by or predicated on reason ▸ illogical, unreasonable, unreasoned. *Idioms:* out of bounds, without rhyme or reason. [*Compare* FOOLISH.] —*See also* FALLACIOUS (1).

irrationality *n.* The absence of reason ▸ illogicality, illogicalness, unreason, unreasonableness. [*Compare* FALLACY, FOOLISHNESS.]

irrefutable *adj.* —*See* CERTAIN (2).

irregular *adj.* Not straight, uniform, or symmetrical ▸ asymmetric, asymmetrical, crooked, diversiform, nonuniform, variform. [*Compare* UNEVEN, ROUGH.] —*See also* ABNORMAL, INCONGRUOUS, INTERMITTENT.

irregularity *n.* Lack of smoothness or regularity ▸ abrasiveness, asymmetry, bumpiness, choppiness, coarseness, crookedness, inequality, jaggedness, pockedness, raggedness, roughness, unevenness, ununiformity. —*See also* ABNORMALITY.

irrelevancy *n.* —*See* DIGRESSION.

irrelevant *adj.* Not relevant or pertinent to the subject; not applicable ▸ extraneous, extrinsic, immaterial, impertinent, inapplicable, inapposite, unconnected, ungermane, unrelated. *Idioms:* beside the point, neither here nor there, off the subject (*or* topic), out of place. [*Compare* DIGRESSIVE, TRIVIAL.]

irreligious *adj.* —*See* ATHEISTIC.

irremediable *adj.* —*See* HOPELESS.

irremissible *adj.* —*See* INEXCUSABLE.

irreparable *adj.* —*See* HOPELESS.

irreprehensible *adj.* —*See* EXEMPLARY.

irreproachable *adj.* —*See* EXEMPLARY, INNOCENT (2).

proach: *irreproachable conduct.* **—ir′re·proach′a·bly** *adv.*

ir·re·sis·ti·ble (ĭr′ĭ-zĭs′tə-bəl) ▸ *adj.* **1.** Impossible to resist. **2.** Overwhelming. **—ir′re·sis′ti·bil′i·ty, ir′re·sis′ti·ble·ness** *n.* **—ir′re·sis′ti·bly** *adv.*

ir·res·o·lute (ĭ-rĕz′ə-lo͞ot′) ▸ *adj.* **1.** Unsure of how to act or proceed; undecided. **2.** Lacking in resolution; indecisive. **—ir·res′o·lute′ly** *adv.* **—ir·res′o·lute′ness, ir·res′o·lu′tion** *n.*

ir·re·spec·tive of (ĭr′ĭ-spĕk′tĭv) ▸ *prep.* Without consideration of; regardless of.

ir·re·spon·si·ble (ĭr′ĭ-spŏn′sə-bəl) ▸ *adj.* **1.** Marked by a lack of responsibility: *irresponsible accusations.* **2.** Unreliable. **—ir′re·spon′si·bil′i·ty, ir′re·spon′si·ble·ness** *n.* **—ir′re·spon′si·bly** *adv.*

ir·re·triev·a·ble (ĭr′ĭ-trē′və-bəl) ▸ *adj.* Impossible to retrieve or recover. **—ir′re·triev′a·ble·ness, ir′re·triev′a·bil′i·ty** *n.* **—ir′re·triev′a·bly** *adv.*

ir·rev·er·ence (ĭ-rĕv′ər-əns) ▸ *n.* **1.** Lack of reverence or due respect. **2.** A disrespectful act or remark. **—ir·rev′er·ent** *adj.* **—ir·rev′er·ent·ly** *adv.*

ir·re·vers·i·ble (ĭr′ĭ-vûr′sə-bəl) ▸ *adj.* Impossible to reverse. **—ir′re·vers′i·bil′i·ty** *n.* **—ir′re·vers′i·bly** *adv.*

ir·rev·o·ca·ble (ĭ-rĕv′ə-kə-bəl) ▸ *adj.* Impossible to retract or revoke. **—ir·rev′o·ca·bil′i·ty, ir·rev′o·ca·ble·ness** *n.* **—ir·rev′o·ca·bly** *adv.*

ir·ri·gate (ĭr′ĭ-gāt′) ▸ *v.* **-gat·ed, -gat·ing. 1.** To supply land or crops with water by means of ditches, pipes, or streams. **2.** *Medic.* To wash out with water or a medicated fluid. **—ir′ri·ga·ble** (ĭr′ĭ-gə-bəl) *adj.* **—ir′ri·ga′tion** *n.* **—ir′ri·ga′tion·al** *adj.* **—ir′ri·ga′tor** *n.*

ir·ri·ta·ble (ĭr′ĭ-tə-bəl) ▸ *adj.* **1.** Easily irritated or annoyed. **2.** *Pathol.* Abnormally sensitive. **3.** *Physiol.* Responsive to stimuli. **—ir′ri·ta·bil′i·ty, ir′ri·ta·ble·ness** *n.* **—ir′ri·ta·bly** *adv.*

ir·ri·tant (ĭr′ĭ-tənt) ▸ *adj.* Causing irritation, esp. physical irritation. ▸ *n.* A source of irritation.

ir·ri·tate (ĭr′ĭ-tāt′) ▸ *v.* **-tat·ed, -tat·ing. 1.** To make impatient or angry; annoy. **2.** To chafe or inflame. **—ir′ri·ta′tion** *n.* **—ir′ri·ta′tor** *n.*

ir·rupt (ĭ-rŭpt′) ▸ *v.* To break or burst in; invade. **—ir·rup′tion** *n.* **—ir·rup′tive** *adj.*

IRS ▸ *abbr.* Internal Revenue Service

is (ĭz) ▸ *v.* 3rd pers. sing. pr. indic. of **be.**

Is. ▸ *abbr.* island

I·saac (ī′zək) ▸ In the Bible, the son of Abraham.

I·sa·iah (ī-zā′ə, ī-zī′ə) ▸ *n.* **1.** A Hebrew prophet of the 8th cent. B.C. **2.** See **Bible** table in Appendix.

is·che·mi·a (ĭ-skē′mē-ə) ▸ *n.* A decrease in the blood supply to a bodily organ or part caused by constriction or obstruction of the blood vessels. **—i·sche′mic** *adj.*

-ish ▸ *suff.* **1.** Of, relating to, or being: *Swedish.* **2a.** Characteristic of: *girlish.* **b.** Having the qualities of: *childish.* **3.** Approximately; somewhat: *greenish.* **4.** Tending toward; preoccupied with: *selfish.*

i·sin·glass (ī′zən-glăs′, ī′zĭng-) ▸ *n.* **1.** A transparent gelatin prepared from the air bladder esp. of the sturgeon. **2.** Mica in thin, transparent sheets.

I·sis (ī′sĭs) ▸ *n.* *Myth.* An ancient Egyptian goddess of fertility, the sister and wife of Osiris.

Isl. ▸ *abbr.* island

Is·lam (ĭs-läm′, ĭs′läm′, ĭz′-) ▸ *n.* **1.** A monotheistic religion marked by the profession of submission to God and to Muhammad as the chief and last prophet of God. **2.** The people or nations that practice Islam; the Muslim world. **—Is·lam′ic** *adj.*

Is·lam·a·bad (ĭs-lä′mə-bäd′) ▸ The capital of Pakistan, in the NE.

Islamic calendar ▸ *n.* The lunar calendar used by Muslims, reckoned from the year of the Hegira in A.D. 622.

is·land (ī′lənd) ▸ *n.* **1.** A land mass, esp. one smaller than a continent, surrounded by water. **2.** Something that is completely isolated or surrounded. **—is′land·er** *n.*

isle (īl) ▸ *n.* An island, esp. a small one.

is·let (ī′lĭt) ▸ *n.* A very small island.

ism (ĭz′əm) ▸ *n.* *Informal* A distinctive doctrine, system, or theory.

-ism ▸ *suff.* **1.** Action, process; practice: *terrorism.* **2.** Characteristic behavior or quality: *heroism.* **3a.** State; condition; quality: *pauperism.* **b.** State or condition resulting from an excess of something specified: *strychninism.* **4.** Distinctive or characteristic trait: *Latinism.* **5a.** Doctrine; theory; system of principles: *pacifism.* **b.** An attitude of prejudice against a given group: *racism.*

is·n't (ĭz′ənt) ▸ Is not.

iso– or **is–** ▸ *pref.* **1.** Equal; uniform: *isobar.* **2.** Isomeric: *isopropyl.*

i·so·bar (ī′sə-bär′) ▸ *n.* A line on a weather map connecting points of equal barometric pressure. **—i′so·bar′ic** (-bär′ĭk, -băr′-) *adj.*

i·so·gon (ī′sə-gŏn′) ▸ *n.* A polygon whose angles are equal. **—i′so·gon′ic** *adj.*

i·so·late (ī′sə-lāt′) ▸ *v.* **-lat·ed, -lat·ing. 1.** To set apart or cut off from a group or whole. **2.** To place in quarantine. **—i′so·la′tion** *n.* **—i′so·la′tor** *n.*

i·so·la·tion·ism (ī′sə-lā′shə-nĭz′əm) ▸ *n.* A national policy of abstaining from political or economic entanglements with other countries. **—i′so·la′tion·ist** *n.*

i·so·mer (ī′sə-mər) ▸ *n.* **1.** *Chem.* A compound having the same elements in the same proportions as another but differing in chemical or physical properties. **2.** *Phys.* An atom whose nucleus can exist in any of several bound excited states for a measurable period. **—i′so·mer′ic** (-mĕr′ĭk) *adj.*

i·so·met·ric (ī′sə-mĕt′rĭk) also **i·so·met·ri·cal** (-rĭ-kəl) ▸ *adj.* **1.** Exhibiting equality in dimensions or measurements. **2.** *Physiol.* Involving muscular contraction against resistance in which the length of the muscle remains the same. ▸ *n.* A line connecting isometric points.

i·so·met·rics (ī′sə-mĕt′rĭks) ▸ *n.* *(takes sing. or pl. v.)* Exercise in which isometric contraction is used to strengthen and tone muscles.

i·so·morph (ī′sə-môrf′) ▸ *n.* An organism or substance exhibiting isomorphism.

i·so·mor·phism (ī′sə-môr′fĭz′əm) ▸ *n.* Similarity of form, as in organisms of different ancestry, or of structure, as in chemical substances. **—i′so·mor′phic** *adj.*

i·so·pro·pyl alcohol (ī′sə-prō′pəl) ▸ *n.* A clear, colorless, flammable mobile liquid used in antifreeze compounds, lotions, cosmetics, and as a solvent.

i·sos·ce·les (ī-sŏs′ə-lēz′) ▸ *adj.* Having two equal sides: *an isosceles triangle.*

i·so·therm (ī′sə-thûrm′) ▸ *n.* A line on a weather map linking all points of equal or constant temperature. **—i′so·ther′mal** *adj.*

THESAURUS

irresistible *adj.* —*See* CERTAIN (1).

irresolute *adj.* —*See* DOUBTFUL (2), HESITANT.

irresolution or **irresoluteness** *n.* —*See* HESITATION.

irresponsible *adj.* —*See* CARELESS, UNDEPENDABLE (1).

irreverence *n.* —*See* DISRESPECT.

irreverent *adj.* —*See* DISRESPECTFUL.

irrevocable *adj.* That cannot be revoked or undone ▸ irretrievable, irreversible, unalterable. *Idioms:* beyond recall, past the point of no return. [*Compare* IMMUTABLE, UNCHANGEABLE.]

irritability *n.* —*See* TEMPER (1).

irritable *adj.* —*See* ILL-TEMPERED.

irritant *n.* —*See* ANNOYANCE (2).

irritate *v.* —*See* ANGER (1), ANNOY, CHAFE, HURT (3).

irritated *adj.* —*See* ANGRY.

irritating *adj.* —*See* DISTURBING, PAINFUL.

irritation *n.* An instance of being irritated, as in a part of the body ▸ festering, inflammation, rankling, redness, sensitiveness, soreness, tenderness. [*Compare* BUMP, DISEASE, PAIN.] —*See also* ANNOYANCE (1), ANNOYANCE (2).

isochronal or **isochronous** *adj.* —*See* PERIODIC.

isolate *v.* **1.** To set apart or cut off from others ▸ alienate, close off, cut off, ghettoize, insulate, seclude, segregate, separate, sequester, sequestrate, set apart. [*Compare* EXCLUDE.] **2.** To put into solitude ▸ cloister, seclude, sequester, sequestrate. [*Compare* ENCLOSE, IMPRISON.]

isolate *adj.* —*See* SOLITARY.

isolated *adj.* —*See* REMOTE (1), SOLITARY.

isolation *n.* The act or process of isolating ▸ alienation, insulation, segregation, separation, sequestration. [*Compare* BREACH.] —*See also* SECLUSION, SOLITUDE.

i·so·tope (ī′sə-tōp′) ▸ *n.* One of two or more atoms whose nuclei have the same number of protons but different numbers of neutrons. **—i′so·top′ic** (-tŏp′ĭk) *adj.* **—i′so·top′i·cal·ly** *adv.*

i·so·tro·pic (ī′sə-trō′pĭk, -trŏp′ĭk) ▸ *adj.* Invariant with respect to direction; identical in all directions. **—i·sot′ro·py** (ī-sŏt′rə-pē), **i·sot′ro·pism** (-pĭz′əm) *n.*

Is·ra·el[1] (ĭz′rē-əl) ▸ *n.* **1a.** In the Bible, Jacob. **b.** The descendants of Jacob. **2.** *Judaism* The Hebrew people, past, present, and future.

Is·ra·el[2] (ĭz′rē-əl) ▸ **1.** An ancient kingdom of the Hebrews founded by Saul c. 1025 B.C. **2.** A country of SW Asia on the E Mediterranean.

Is·rae·li (ĭz-rā′lē) ▸ *adj.* Of or relating to modern-day Israel or its people. ▸ *n., pl.* **-lis.** A citizen of modern-day Israel.

Is·ra·el·ite (ĭz′rē-ə-līt′) ▸ *n.* **1.** A native or inhabitant of ancient Israel. **2.** A Jew.

is·sue (ĭsh′o͞o) ▸ *n.* **1.** The act or an instance of flowing, passing, or giving out. **2a.** Something produced, published, or offered, as stamps or coins. **b.** A single copy of a periodical. **3.** The final result of an action. **4.** Proceeds from estates or fines. **5.** Something proceeding from a specified source. **6.** Offspring; progeny. **7.** A point of discussion. **8.** An outlet. **9.** *Pathol.* A discharge, as of blood. ▸ *v.* **-sued, -su·ing. 1.** To go or come out. **2.** To be born or be descended. **3.** To publish or be published. **4.** To circulate, as coins. **5.** To come forth or cause to come forth. **6.** To end or result. ***—idioms:*** **at issue** In dispute. **take issue** To disagree. **—is′su·ance** *n.* **—is′su·er** *n.*

-ist ▸ *suff.* **1a.** One that performs a specified action: *lobbyist.* **b.** One that produces, operates, or is connected with a specified thing: *novelist.* **2.** A specialist in a specified field: *biologist.* **3.** An adherent or advocate of a specified doctrine, theory, or school of thought: *anarchist.* **4.** One that is characterized by a specified trait or quality: *romanticist.*

Is·tan·bul (ĭs′tăn-bo͞ol′, -tän-, ĭ-stän′bo͞ol). Formerly **Con·stan·ti·no·ple** (kŏn′stăn-tə-nō′pəl) ▸ The largest city of Turkey, in the NW part on the Bosporus at its entrance into the Sea of Marmara.

isth·mus (ĭs′məs) ▸ *n.* **1.** A narrow strip of land connecting two larger masses of land. **2.** *Anat.* **a.** A narrow strip of tissue joining two larger organs or parts of an organ. **b.** A narrow passage connecting two larger cavities. **—isth′mi·an** *adj.*

it (ĭt) ▸ *pron.* **1.** Used to refer to a nonhuman entity, an animal or human whose sex is unknown or irrelevant, a group of persons, or an abstraction. **2.** Used as the subject of an impersonal verb: *It is snowing.* **3.** Used to refer to a general condition or state of affairs: *She couldn't stand it.* ▸ *n. Games* A player, as in tag, who attempts to find or catch the other players.

ital. ▸ *abbr.* **1.** italic **2.** italics

I·tal·ian (ĭ-tăl′yən) ▸ *adj.* Of or relating to Italy or its people or language. ▸ *n.* **1a.** A native or inhabitant of Italy. **b.** A person of Italian descent. **2.** The Romance language of the Italians and parts of Switzerland.

I·tal·ic (ĭ-tăl′ĭk, ī-tăl′-) ▸ *adj.* **1.** Of or relating to ancient Italy. **2.** Of or relating to Italic. **3. italic** Of or being a style of printing type with the letters slanting to the right: *This sentence is in italic type.* ▸ *n.* **1.** A branch of Indo-European that includes Latin. **2.** often **italics** Italic print or typeface.

i·tal·i·cize (ĭ-tăl′ĭ-sīz′, ī-tăl′-) ▸ *v.* **-cized, -ciz·ing.** To print in italic type. **—i·tal′i·ci·za′tion** *n.*

It·a·ly (ĭt′l-ē) ▸ A country of S Europe comprising the peninsula of Italy, Sardinia, Sicily, and several smaller islands.

itch (ĭch) ▸ *n.* **1.** A skin sensation causing a desire to scratch. **2.** A skin disorder marked by intense irritation and itching. **3.** A restless desire or craving. **—itch** *v.* **—itch′i·ness** *n.* **—itch′y** *adj.*

-ite[1] ▸ *suff.* **1.** Native or resident of: *urbanite.* **2.** Adherent or follower of: *Trotskyite.* **3.** A part of an organ or body: *dendrite.* **4a.** Rock; mineral: *graphite.* **b.** Fossil: *trilobite.* **5a.** Product: *metabolite.* **b.** A commercial product: *ebonite.*

-ite[2] ▸ *suff.* A salt or ester of an acid named with an adjective ending in *-ous: sulfite.*

i·tem (ī′təm) ▸ *n.* **1.** A single article or unit in a group, series, or list. **2a.** A bit of information. **b.** A short piece in a newspaper or magazine.

i·tem·ize (ī′tə-mīz′) ▸ *v.* **-ized, -iz·ing.** To set down by item; list. **—i′tem·i·za′tion** *n.* **—i′tem·iz′er** *n.*

it·er·ate (ĭt′ə-rāt′) ▸ *v.* **-at·ed, -at·ing.** To say or perform again. **—it′er·a′tion** *n.*

i·tin·er·ant (ī-tĭn′ər-ənt, ĭ-tĭn′-) ▸ *adj.* Traveling from place to place, esp. to perform work. ▸ *n.* An itinerant person. **—i·tin′er·an·cy, i·tin′er·a·cy** *n.*

i·tin·er·ar·y (ī-tĭn′ə-rĕr′ē, ĭ-tĭn′-) ▸ *n., pl.* **-ies. 1.** A route or proposed route of a journey. **2.** An account or record of a journey. **3.** A traveler's guidebook.

-itis ▸ *suff.* Inflammation or disease of: *laryngitis.*

it'll (ĭt′l) ▸ **1.** It will. **2.** It shall.

its (ĭts) ▸ *adj.* The possessive form of **it.** Used as a modifier before a noun: *The airline canceled its early flight to Atlanta.*

it's (ĭts) ▸ **1.** It is. **2.** It has.

it·self (ĭt-sĕlf′) ▸ *pron.* **1.** That one identical with it. Used: **a.** Reflexively as the direct or indirect object of a verb or the object of a preposition: *The cat scratched itself.* **b.** For emphasis: *The trouble is in the machine itself.* **2.** Its normal condition or state: *The car is acting itself again since the oil change.*

-ity ▸ *suff.* State; quality: *abnormality.*

-ium ▸ *suff.* Chemical element or group: *iridium.*

IV ▸ *abbr.* intravenous

I·van III Va·sil·ie·vich (ī′vən, ē-vän′; və-sĭl′yə-vĭch′). "the Great" (1440–1505) ▸ Grand duke of Muscovy (1462–1505).

Ivan IV Vasilievich. "the Terrible" (1530–84) ▸ The first czar of Russia (1547–84).

-ive ▸ *suff.* Performing or tending toward a specified action: *demonstrative.*

I've (īv) ▸ I have.

i·vo·ry (ī′və-rē, īv′rē) ▸ *n., pl.* **-ries. 1.** A hard, smooth, yellowish-white substance that forms the tusks of certain animals, esp. the elephant. **2.** An article made of ivory. **3.** A substance resembling ivory. **4.** A yellowish white. **5.** often **ivories a.** Piano keys. **b.** Dice. **c.** *Slang* The teeth. **—i′vo·ry** *adj.*

Ivory Coast ▸ See **Côte d'Ivoire.**

ivory tower ▸ *n.* A place or attitude of retreat, esp. preoccupation with intellectual considerations rather than practical life.

i·vy (ī′vē) ▸ *n., pl.* **i·vies.** Any of a genus of climbing or trailing plants having lobed evergreen leaves.

I·wo Ji·ma (ē′wə jē′mə, ē′wō) ▸ The largest of the Volcano Is. of Japan, in the NW Pacific E of Taiwan.

I·yar also **Iy·yar** (ē-yär′, ē′yär′) ▸ *n.* A month in the Jewish calendar.

-ization ▸ *suff.* Action, process, or result of doing or making: *colonization.*

-ize ▸ *suff.* **1a.** To cause to be or become: *dramatize.* **b.** To cause to conform to or resemble: *Hellenize.* **c.** To treat as: *idolize.* **2a.** To treat or affect with: *anesthetize.* **b.** To subject to: *tyrannize.* **3.** To treat according to or practice the method of: *pasteurize.* **4.** To become; become like: *materialize.* **5.** To perform, engage in, or produce: *botanize.*

THESAURUS

issue *n.* *—See* EFFECT (1), PROBLEM, PROGENY, PUBLICATION (1).

issue *v.* *—See* APPEAR (1), DESCEND, DISTRIBUTE, EMIT, POUR, PUBLISH (1), STEM.

italicize *v.* *—See* EMPHASIZE.

itch *n.* *—See* DESIRE (1), DESIRE (2).

itch *v.* To have a greedy, obsessive desire ▸ crave, hunger, lust, thirst. [*Compare* DESIRE.]

item *n.* A detail of news or information ▸ article, bit, bulletin, dispatch, feature, flash, news flash, notice, paragraph, piece, squib, story, write-up. [*Compare* MESSAGE, NEWS, STORY.] *—See also* DETAIL, ELEMENT (2), ENTRY, OBJECT (1).

item *adv.* *—See* ADDITIONALLY.

itemize *v.* *—See* ENUMERATE.

iterate *v.* To happen again or repeatedly ▸ reappear, recur, reoccur, repeat. *—See also* REPEAT (1).

iteration *n.* *—See* REPETITION.

iterative *adj.* Characterized by repetition ▸ reiterative, repetitious, repetitive. [*Compare* BORING, SUPERFLUOUS, WORDY.]

itinerant *adj.* Moving from one area to another in search of work ▸ migrant, migratory. *—See also* ERRANT (1), NOMADIC.

iterant *n.* *—See* HOBO.

ivory *adj.* *—See* FAIR[1] (3).

ivory-tower *adj.* *—See* THEORETICAL (1).

J

j or **J** (jā) ▸ *n., pl.* **j's** or **J's** also **js** or **Js**. The 10th letter of the English alphabet.
jab (jăb) ▸ *v.* **jabbed, jab·bing**. 1. To poke abruptly, esp. with something sharp. 2. To punch with short blows. ▸ *n.* A quick stab or blow.
jab·ber (jăb′ər) ▸ *v.* To talk rapidly, unintelligibly, or idly. **—jab′ber** *n.*
ja·bot (zhă-bō′, jăb′ō) ▸ *n.* A cascade of ruffles down the front of a shirt.
jac·a·ran·da (jăk′ə-răn′də) ▸ *n.* 1. A tropical American tree having purple flowers. 2. The wood of this tree.
jack (jăk) ▸ *n.* 1. often **Jack** *Informal* A man; fellow. 2. *Games* A playing card showing the figure of a knave and ranking below a queen. 3. *Games* a. **jacks** *(takes sing. or pl. v.)* A game played with a set of small six-pointed metal pieces and a rubber ball, the object being to pick up the pieces in various combinations. b. One of the metal pieces so used. 4. A usu. portable device for raising heavy objects. 5. A small flag flown at the bow of a ship, usu. to indicate nationality. 6. The male of certain animals, esp. the ass. 7. A socket that accepts a plug at one end and attaches to electric circuitry at the other. ▸ *v.* 1. To hoist with a jack. 2. To raise: *jack up prices.*
jack·al (jăk′əl, -ôl′) ▸ *n.* A doglike mammal of Africa and S Asia.
jack·ass (jăk′ăs′) ▸ *n.* 1. A male ass or donkey. 2. A foolish or stupid person.
jack·boot (jăk′bo͞ot′) ▸ *n.* A stout military boot extending above the knee.
jack·daw (jăk′dô′) ▸ *n.* A Eurasian crow.
jack·et (jăk′ĭt) ▸ *n.* 1. A short coat usu. extending to the hips. 2. An outer covering or casing. **—jack′et·ed** *adj.*
jack·ham·mer (jăk′hăm′ər) ▸ *n.* A hand-held pneumatic machine for drilling rock and breaking up pavement. **—jack′ham′mer** *v.*
jack-in-the-box (jăk′ĭn-*thə*-bŏks′) ▸ *n., pl.* **-box·es** or **jacks-in-the-box** (jăks′-). A clownlike puppet that springs out of a box when the lid is raised.
jack-in-the-pul·pit (jăk′ĭn-*thə*-po͝ol′pĭt, -pŭl′-) ▸ *n., pl.* **-pits**. A plant having a leaflike spathe enclosing a clublike spadix.
jack·knife (jăk′nīf′) ▸ *n.* 1. A large clasp knife. 2. A dive in which one bends at the waist, touches the toes, and then straightens out. ▸ *v.* To fold or double like a jackknife.
jack-of-all-trades (jăk′əv-ôl′trādz′) ▸ *n., pl.* **jacks-of-all-trades** (jăks′-). One who can do many kinds of work.
jack-o'-lan·tern (jăk′ə-lăn′tərn) ▸ *n.* A lantern made from a hollowed pumpkin with a carved face.
jack·pot (jăk′pŏt′) ▸ *n.* A cumulative pool or top prize in various games.
jack·rab·bit (jăk′răb′ĭt) ▸ *n.* A large, long-eared hare.
Jack·son (jăk′sən) ▸ The capital of MS, in the W-central part.
Jackson, Andrew. "Old Hickory" (1767–1845) ▸ The 7th US President (1829–37).
Jackson, Thomas Jonathan. "Stonewall" (1824–63) ▸ Amer. Confederate general.
Jack·son·ville (jăk′sən-vĭl′) ▸ A city of NE FL near the Atlantic and the GA border.
Ja·cob (jā′kəb) ▸ In the Bible, the son of Isaac and grandson of Abraham.
Jac·o·be·an (jăk′ə-bē′ən) ▸ *adj.* Relating to the reign of James I of England or his times. **—Jac′o·be′an** *n.*
Jac·o·bin (jăk′ə-bĭn) ▸ *n.* 1. A radical leftist. 2. A radical republican during the French Revolution.
Ja·cob's ladder (jā′kəbz) ▸ *n.* 1. *Naut.* A rope or chain ladder with rigid rungs. 2. A plant having blue flowers and compound leaves with numerous leaflets.
Ja·cuz·zi (jə-ko͞o′zē, jă-) ▸ A trademark for a whirlpool bath.
jade[1] (jād) ▸ *n.* Either of two distinct minerals, nephrite and jadeite, that are gen. pale green and used mainly as gemstones.
jade[2] (jād) ▸ *v.* **jad·ed, jad·ing**. 1. To wear out, as by overuse. 2. To become weary or spiritless. ▸ *n.* 1. A broken-down horse; nag. 2. A disreputable woman.
jad·ed (jā′dĭd) ▸ *adj.* 1. Worn out; wearied. 2. Dulled by surfeit; sated. 3. Cynically callous. **—jad′ed·ly** *adv.* **—jad′ed·ness** *n.*
jade·ite (jā′dīt′) ▸ *n.* A rare, usu. emerald to light green but sometimes white, auburn, buff, or violet jade, $NaAlSi_2O_6$.
Jaf·fa (jăf′ə, yä′fə) ▸ See **Yafo**.
jag[1] (jăg) ▸ *n.* A sharp point; barb.
jag[2] (jăg) ▸ *n.* *Slang* A period of overindulgence; spree.
jag·ged (jăg′ĭd) ▸ *adj.* Having sharp or ragged projections. **—jag′ged·ly** *adv.* **—jag′ged·ness** *n.*
jag·uar (jăg′wär′, jăg′yo͞o-är′) ▸ *n.* A large leopardlike mammal of Central and South America.
jai a·lai (hī′ lī′, hī′ ə-lī′, hī′ ə-lī′) ▸ *n.* A fast court game in which players use a long hand-shaped basket to propel the ball against a wall.
jail (jāl) ▸ *n.* A place for the confinement of persons in lawful detention; prison. ▸ *v.* To put in jail; imprison.
jail·bird (jāl′bûrd′) ▸ *n.* *Informal* A prisoner or ex-convict.
jail·break (jāl′brāk′) ▸ *n.* An escape from jail.
jail·er also **jail·or** (jā′lər) ▸ *n.* The keeper of a jail.
Ja·kar·ta or **Dja·kar·ta** (jə-kär′tə) ▸ The capital of Indonesia, on the NE coast of Java.
ja·la·pe·ño (hä′lə-pān′yō) ▸ *n., pl.* **-ños**. A cultivated variety of capsicum pepper having a pungent green or red fruit used in cooking.

THESAURUS

jab *v.* —*See* HIT, PENETRATE, PUSH (1).
jab *n.* —*See* BLOW[2], DIG.
jabber *v.* —*See* BABBLE, CHATTER (1), GOSSIP, MUTTER.
jabber *n.* —*See* BABBLE, CHATTER.
jabberwocky *n.* —*See* BABBLE, GIBBERISH.
jack *n.* —*See* FELLOW, FLAG[1], MONEY (1).
jack *v.* To increase in amount ▸ boost, hike, jack up, jump, raise, up. —*See also* ELEVATE (1).
Jack *n.* —*See* SAILOR.
jackass *n.* —*See* FOOL.
jacket *n.* —*See* COAT (1), WRAPPER.
jacket *v.* —*See* CLOTHE.
Jack-tar *n.* —*See* SAILOR.
jade *n.* —*See* SLUT.
jade *v.* —*See* TIRE (1).
jaded *adj.* —*See* TIRED (1).
jag[1] *n.* —*See* BENDER, BINGE.
jag[2] *n.* —*See* SPIKE.
jagged *adj.* —*See* ROUGH (1).
jaggedness *n.* —*See* IRREGULARITY.
jail *n.* A place for the confinement of persons in lawful detention ▸ brig, house of correction, keep, penitentiary, prison. *Informal:* lockup, pen. *Slang:* big house, calaboose, can, clink, cooler, coop, hoosegow, joint, jug, pokey, slammer, stir.
jail *v.* —*See* IMPRISON.
jailer *n.* A guard or keeper of a prison ▸ turnkey, warden. *Slang:* screw. [*Compare* GUARD, POLICE OFFICER.]

ja·lop·y (jə-lŏp′ē) ► *n., pl.* **-ies.** *Informal* An old dilapidated automobile.
jal·ou·sie (jăl′ə-sē) ► *n.* A blind or shutter having adjustable horizontal slats.
jam[1] (jăm) ► *v.* **jammed, jam·ming. 1.** To drive or squeeze into a tight position. **2.** To activate or apply suddenly. **3.** To lock or cause to lock into an unworkable position. **4.** To fill to excess; cram. **5.** To block or clog. **6.** To interfere electronically with the reception of (broadcast signals). **7.** *Mus.* To play improvisations. ► *n.* **1.** The act of jamming or the condition of being jammed. **2.** A crush or congestion. **3.** A predicament. **—jam′mer** *n.*
jam[2] (jăm) ► *n.* A preserve made from fruit boiled with sugar.
Ja·mai·ca (jə-mā′kə) ► An island country in the Caribbean Sea S of Cuba. **—Ja·mai′can** *adj. & n.*
jamb (jăm) ► *n.* One of the vertical posts of a door or window frame.
jam·ba·lay·a (jŭm′bə-lī′ə) ► *n.* A spicy Creole dish of rice and meat or seafood.
jam·bo·ree (jăm′bə-rē′) ► *n.* **1.** A noisy celebration. **2.** A large assembly, as of Boy Scouts or Girl Scouts.
James (jāmz) ► *n.* See **Bible** table in Appendix.
James, Henry (1843–1916) ► Amer. writer and critic.
jam session ► *n.* An informal gathering of musicians to play improvised or unrehearsed music.
Jan. ► *abbr.* January
jan·gle (jăng′gəl) ► *v.* **-gled, -gling. 1.** To make or cause to make a harsh metallic sound. **2.** To grate on or jar (the nerves). **—jan′gle** *n.* **—jan′gler** *n.*
jan·i·tor (jăn′ĭ-tər) ► *n.* One employed to maintain and clean a building. **—jan′i·to′ri·al** (-tôr′ē-əl) *adj.*
Jan·u·ar·y (jăn′yo͞o-ĕr′ē) ► *n., pl.* **-ies.** The 1st month of the Gregorian calendar.
Ja·nus (jā′nəs) ► *n. Rom. Myth.* The god of gates and doorways, depicted with two faces looking in opposite directions.
ja·pan (jə-păn′) ► *n.* A black enamel used to produce a durable glossy finish. **—ja·pan′** *v.*
Japan ► A country of Asia on an archipelago off the NE coast of the mainland.
Japan, Sea of ► An enclosed arm of the W Pacific between Japan and the Asian mainland.
Japan Current ► *n.* A warm ocean current flowing NE from the Philippine Sea past SE Japan to the North Pacific.
Jap·a·nese (jăp′ə-nēz′, -nēs′) ► *adj.* Of or relating to Japan or its people or language. ► *n., pl.* **-nese. 1a.** A native or inhabitant of Japan. **b.** A person of Japanese ancestry. **2.** The language of the Japanese.
Japanese beetle ► *n.* A metallic-green beetle that is a plant pest in North America.
jape (jāp) ► *v.* **japed, jap·ing.** To joke or quip. ► *n.* A joke or quip. **—jap′er** *n.* **—jap′er·y** *n.*
jar[1] (jär) ► *n.* A cylindrical glass or earthenware vessel with a wide mouth. **—jar′ful′** *n.*
jar[2] (jär) ► *v.* **jarred, jar·ring. 1.** To make or utter a harsh sound. **2.** To disturb or irritate; grate. **3.** To shake from impact. **4.** To clash or conflict. **5.** To bump or cause to move from impact. ► *n.* **1.** A jolt. **2.** A harsh sound. **—jar′ring·ly** *adv.*
jar·di·nière (jär′dn-îr′, zhär′dn-yâr′) ► *n.* A large decorative stand or pot for plants.
jar·gon (jär′gən) ► *n.* **1.** Nonsensical or incoherent talk. **2.** The specialized or technical language of a trade or profession.
Jarls·berg (yärlz′bûrg′) ► A trademark for a mild, pale-yellow, hard Norwegian cheese with large holes.
jas·mine (jăz′mĭn) also **jes·sa·mine** (jĕs′ə-mĭn) ► *n.* Any of a genus of vines or shrubs having fragrant white or yellow flowers.
jas·per (jăs′pər) ► *n.* An opaque red, yellow, or brown quartz.
ja·to (jā′tō) ► *n., pl.* **-tos.** An aircraft takeoff aided by an auxiliary rocket.
jaun·dice (jôn′dĭs, jän′-) ► *n.* Yellowish discoloration of the eyes and tissues caused by deposition of bile salts. ► *v.* **-diced, -dic·ing. 1.** To affect with jaundice. **2.** To affect with envy, prejudice, or hostility.
jaunt (jônt, jänt) ► *n.* A short trip or excursion. **—jaunt** *v.*
jaun·ty (jôn′tē, jän′-) ► *adj.* **-ti·er, -ti·est. 1.** Having a buoyant or self-confident air. **2.** Dapper in appearance. **—jaun′ti·ly** *adv.* **—jaun′ti·ness** *n.*
ja·va (jä′və, jăv′ə) ► *n. Informal* Brewed coffee.
Java ► An island of Indonesia separated from Borneo by the **Java Sea,** an arm of the Pacific. **—Jav′a·nese′** *adj. & n.*
jave·lin (jăv′lĭn, jăv′ə-) ► *n.* **1.** A light spear, thrown as a weapon. **2.** A metal or metal-tipped spear, used in contests of distance throwing.
jaw (jô) ► *n.* **1.** Either of two bony or cartilaginous structures that in most vertebrates form the framework of the mouth and hold the teeth. **2.** Either of two opposed hinged parts in a mechanical device. **3. jaws** A dangerous situation. **4.** *Slang* **a.** Back talk. **b.** A chat. ► *v. Slang* To talk; converse. **—jaw′less** *adj.*
jaw·bone (jô′bōn′) ► *n.* A bone of the jaw, esp. of the lower jaw. ► *v.* **-boned, -bon·ing.** *Slang* To try to influence or pressure through strong persuasion.
jaw·break·er (jô′brā′kər) ► *n.* **1.** A very hard candy. **2.** *Slang* A word difficult to pronounce.
jay (jā) ► *n.* Any of various often crested birds gen. having a loud harsh call.
jay·walk (jā′wôk′) ► *v.* To cross a street in violation of traffic regulations. **—jay′walk′er** *n.*
jazz (jăz) ► *n.* **1.** A style of American music marked by a strong but flexible rhythmic understructure with solo and ensemble improvisations and a highly sophisticated harmonic idiom. **2.** *Slang* **a.** Animation; enthusiasm. **b.** Nonsense. **c.** Miscellaneous, unspecified things. ► *v. Slang* To exaggerate or lie (to): *Don't jazz me.* ***—phrasal verb:*** **jazz up** *Slang* To make more interesting; enliven.
jazz·y (jăz′ē) ► *adj.* **-i·er, -i·est. 1.** Of or resembling jazz. **2.** *Slang* Showy; flashy. **—jazz′i·ly** *adv.* **—jazz′i·ness** *n.*
jct. ► *abbr.* junction
JD ► *abbr.* **1.** *Lat.* Juris Doctor (Doctor of Law) **2.** Justice Department **3.** juvenile delinquent
jeal·ous (jĕl′əs) ► *adj.* **1.** Fearful of losing affection or position. **2.** Resentful or bitter in rivalry; envious. **3.** Arising from feelings of envy, apprehension, or bitterness. **4.** Vigilant in guarding something. **—jeal′ous·ly** *adv.* **—jeal′ous·y, jeal′ous·ness** *n.*
jean (jēn) ► *n.* **1.** A heavy cotton. **2. jeans** Pants made of jean or denim.
jeep (jēp) ► *n.* A small durable US Army motor vehicle with four-wheel drive.
jeer (jîr) ► *v.* To speak or shout derisively. **—jeer** *n.* **—jeer′er** *n.*
Jef·fer·son (jĕf′ər-sən), **Thomas** (1743–1826) ► The 3rd US President (1801–09). **—Jef′fer·so′ni·an** *adj. & n.*
Jefferson City ► The capital of MO, in the central part on the Missouri R.
Je·ho·vah (jĭ-hō′və) ► *n.* In the Old Testament, God.

THESAURUS

jam *v.* —*See* CROWD, FILL (1), PUSH (1).
jam *n.* —*See* PREDICAMENT, PUSH, STOP (2).
jam-pack *v.* —*See* FILL (1).
Janus-faced *adj.* —*See* HYPOCRITICAL.
jape *n.* —*See* JOKE (1).
jar *v.* To bump or cause to move to and fro with short, jerky movements ► jiggle, joggle, shake. [*Compare* JERK.] —*See also* AGITATE (2), BUMP, CONFLICT.
jar *n.* —*See* COLLISION.
jargon *n.* —*See* BABBLE, DIALECT, LANGUAGE (2).
jarring *adj.* —*See* HARSH, INCONGRUOUS.
jaundice *v.* —*See* BIAS (1).
jaundice *n.* —*See* ENVY.
jaundiced *adj.* —*See* ENVIOUS.
jaunt *n.* A usually short journey taken for pleasure ► excursion, junket, outing, trip. [*Compare* EXCURSION, JOURNEY.] —*See also* DRIVE (3).
jaunt *v.* —*See* JOURNEY.
jaunty *adj.* —*See* LIVELY.
jaw *v.* —*See* CHATTER (1).
jazz up *v.* —*See* ENERGIZE.
jealous *adj.* Fearful of the loss of position or affection ► clinging, clutching, green-eyed, possessive. [*Compare* ENVIOUS.] —*See also* ENVIOUS.
jealousy *n.* —*See* ENVY.
jeer *v.* —*See* RIDICULE.
jeer *n.* —*See* TAUNT.
jeering *adj.* —*See* SARCASTIC.

je·june (jə-jo͞on′) ▸ *adj.* 1. Not interesting. 2. Lacking maturity; childish. 3. Lacking in nutrition. **—je·june′ly** *adv.* **—je·june′ness** *n.*

je·ju·num (jə-jo͞o′nəm) ▸ *n., pl.* **-na** (-nə). The section of the small intestine between the duodenum and the ileum.

jell (jĕl) ▸ *v.* 1. To make or become firm or gelatinous. 2. To take shape; crystallize.

jel·ly (jĕl′ē) ▸ *n., pl.* **-lies.** 1. A soft semisolid food typically made by the boiling and setting of fruit juice, sugar, and pectin or gelatin. 2. Something having the consistency of jelly. ▸ *v.* **-lied, -ly·ing.** To make into or become jelly.

jel·ly·bean (jĕl′ē-bēn′) ▸ *n.* A small chewy candy.

jel·ly·fish (jĕl′ē-fĭsh′) ▸ *n.* 1. A gelatinous, free-swimming marine animal often having a bell-shaped stage as the dominant phase of its life cycle. 2. *Informal* A weakling.

jel·ly·roll (jĕl′ē-rōl′) ▸ *n.* A thin sheet of sponge cake layered with jelly and then rolled up.

Jen·ghis Khan (jĕn′gĭz kän′, -gĭs, jĕng′-) ▸ See **Genghis Khan.**

jen·ny (jĕn′ē) ▸ *n., pl.* **-nies.** 1. The female of certain animals, esp. the donkey and wren. 2. A spinning jenny.

jeop·ard·ize (jĕp′ər-dīz′) ▸ *v.* **-ized, -iz·ing.** To expose to loss or injury.

jeop·ard·y (jĕp′ər-dē) ▸ *n., pl.* **-ies.** Risk of loss or injury; danger.

jer·bo·a (jər-bō′ə) ▸ *n.* A small nocturnal leaping rodent of Asia and Africa.

jer·e·mi·ad (jĕr′ə-mī′əd) ▸ *n.* A bitter lament or righteous prophecy of doom.

Jer·e·mi·ah (jĕr′ə-mī′ə) ▸ *n.* 1. A Hebrew prophet of the 7th and 6th cent. B.C. 2. See **Bible** table in Appendix.

Jer·i·cho (jĕr′ĭ-kō′) ▸ An ancient city of Palestine near the NW shore of the Dead Sea.

jerk[1] (jûrk) ▸ *v.* 1. To give a sudden quick thrust, pull, or twist to. 2. To move in sudden abrupt motions. ▸ *n.* 1. A sudden yank, twist, or jolt. 2. A muscle spasm. 3. *Slang* A stupid or foolish person. **—jerk′i·ly** *adv.* **—jerk′i·ness** *n.* **—jerk′y** *adj.*

jerk[2] (jûrk) ▸ *v.* To cut (meat) into long strips and sun-dry or cure by smoking.

jer·kin (jûr′kĭn) ▸ *n.* A close-fitting sleeveless jacket.

jerk·wa·ter (jûrk′wô′tər, -wŏt′ər) ▸ *adj. Informal* Remote and insignificant.

jerk·y (jûr′kē) ▸ *n.* Meat cured by jerking.

jer·o·bo·am (jĕr′ə-bō′əm) ▸ *n.* A wine bottle holding 4/5 gal. (3.03 l).

jer·ry-build (jĕr′ē-bĭld′) ▸ *v.* **-built, -build·ing.** To build shoddily and cheaply.

jer·sey (jûr′zē) ▸ *n., pl.* **-seys.** 1a. A soft, plain-knitted fabric. b. A garment made of jersey. 2. often **Jersey** A breed of fawn-colored dairy cattle.

Jersey ▸ The largest of the Channel Is. in the English Channel.

Je·ru·sa·lem (jə-ro͞o′sə-ləm, -zə-) ▸ The capital of Israel, in the E-central part.

jes·sa·mine (jĕs′ə-mĭn) ▸ *n.* Var. of **jasmine.**

jest (jĕst) ▸ *n.* 1. A playful remark or act. 2. A frivolous mood. 3. An object of ridicule. ▸ *v.* 1. To act or speak playfully. 2. To ridicule. **—jest′ing·ly** *adv.*

jest·er (jĕs′tər) ▸ *n.* One who jests, esp. a paid fool at medieval courts.

Jes·u·it (jĕzh′o͞o-ĭt, jĕz′o͞o-, -yo͞o-) ▸ *n. Rom. Cath. Ch.* A member of the Society of Jesus, an order founded by Saint Ignatius of Loyola in 1534.

Je·sus (jē′zəs) ▸ *n.* The founder of Christianity, regarded by Christians as the Son of God and the Christ.

jet[1] (jĕt) ▸ *n.* 1. A dense black coal that takes a high polish and is used for jewelry. 2. A deep black. **—jet** *adj.*

jet[2] (jĕt) ▸ *n.* 1a. A high-velocity fluid stream forced under pressure out of a small-diameter opening. b. An outlet for emitting such a stream. c. Something emitted in or as if in such a stream. 2. A jet-propelled vehicle, esp. an aircraft. ▸ *v.* **jet·ted, jet·ting.** 1. To travel by jet aircraft. 2. To squirt.

jet engine ▸ *n.* 1. An engine that develops thrust by ejecting a jet of gaseous combustion products. 2. An engine that obtains the oxygen needed from the atmosphere, used esp. to propel aircraft.

jet lag ▸ *n.* A disruption of bodily rhythms caused by high-speed air travel across time zones. **—jet′-lagged′** *adj.*

jet-pro·pelled (jĕt′prə-pĕld′) ▸ *adj.* Driven by one or more jet engines. **—jet propulsion** *n.*

jet·sam (jĕt′səm) ▸ *n.* 1. Cargo or equipment thrown overboard to lighten a ship in distress. 2. Discarded odds and ends.

jet set ▸ *n.* An international social set made up of wealthy people who travel from one fashionable place to another. **—jet′-set′** *adj.* **—jet setter** *n.*

jet stream ▸ *n.* A high-speed, meandering wind current that gen. flows westerly at altitudes of 15 to 25 km (10 to 15 mi).

jet·ti·son (jĕt′ĭ-sən, -zən) ▸ *v.* 1. To cast overboard or off. 2. *Informal* To discard.

jet·ty (jĕt′ē) ▸ *n., pl.* **-ties.** 1. A structure that projects into a body of water to influence the current or to protect a harbor. 2. A wharf.

Jew (jo͞o) ▸ *n.* 1. An adherent of Judaism. 2. A member of the people descended from the ancient Hebrews and sharing an ethnic heritage based on Judaism.

jew·el (jo͞o′əl) ▸ *n.* 1a. A precious stone; gem. b. A small natural or artificial gem used as a bearing in a watch. 2. A costly ornament of precious metal or gems. 3. One that is treasured or esteemed. ▸ *v.* **-eled, -el·ing** or **-elled, -el·ling.** To adorn or fit with jewels. **—jew′el·ry** *n.*

jewel box ▸ *n.* 1. A usu. lined box for holding jewelry. 2. A hinged plastic case for holding a compact disk and usu. a printed insert.

jew·el·er also **jew·el·ler** (jo͞o′ə-lər) ▸ *n.* One who makes, repairs, or deals in jewelry.

jew·el·weed (jo͞o′əl-wēd′) ▸ *n.* Any of several plants having yellowish spurred flowers and dehiscent seed pods.

Jew·ish (jo͞o′ĭsh) ▸ *adj.* Of or relating to the Jews or their culture or religion. **—Jew′ish·ness** *n.*

Jew·ry (jo͞o′rē) ▸ *n.* The Jewish people.

Jew's-harp or **jew's-harp** (jo͞oz′härp′) ▸ *n.* A small musical instrument consisting of a lyre-shaped metal frame held between the teeth and a steel tongue that is plucked to produce a soft twanging sound.

jez·e·bel (jĕz′ə-bĕl′, -bəl) ▸ *n.* A wicked, scheming woman.

jib (jĭb) ▸ *n.* A triangular sail set forward of the mast of a sailing vessel.

THESAURUS

jejune *adj.* —*See* INSIPID.

jejuneness *n.* —*See* DULLNESS, INSIPIDITY.

jell or **jelly** *v.* —*See* COAGULATE.

jellyfish *n.* —*See* WEAKLING.

jeopardize *v.* —*See* ENDANGER.

jeopardous *adj.* —*See* DANGEROUS.

jeopardy *n.* —*See* DANGER.

jeremiad *n.* —*See* TIRADE.

jerk *v.* To move or cause to move with a motion that is sudden and abrupt ▸ lurch, snap, twitch, wrench, yank. [*Compare* MOVE.] —*See also* BUMP, RECOIL.

jerk *n.* A sudden motion, such as a pull ▸ lurch, snap, tug, twitch, wrench, yank. [*Compare* PULL.] —*See also* DRIP (2), FOOL, TREMOR (2).

jerkiness *n.* —*See* FOOLISHNESS.

jerky *adj.* —*See* FOOLISH, TREMULOUS.

jerry-rig *v.* —*See* IMPROVISE (2).

jest *n.* An object of amusement or laughter ▸ butt, joke, laughingstock, mockery. ***Idiom:*** figure of fun. [*Compare* FOOL.] —*See also* CRACK (3), JOKE (1), PLAY.

jest *v.* To make jokes; behave playfully ▸ joke (around), quip. *Informal:* clown (around), fool around, horse around. ***Idioms:*** crack wise, play the fool. [*Compare* PLAY.] —*See also* RIDICULE.

jester *n.* —*See* JOKER.

jet[1] *adj.* —*See* BLACK (1).

jet[2] *n.* A sudden swift stream of ejected liquid ▸ spout, spray, spurt, squirt. [*Compare* FLOW.]

jet *v.* To eject or be ejected in a sudden thin, swift stream ▸ spout, spray, spurt, squirt. [*Compare* ERUPT, FLOW.]

jetsam *n.* —*See* GARBAGE.

jet-setter *n.* —*See* TOURIST.

jettison *v.* —*See* DISCARD.

jetty *adj.* —*See* BLACK (1).

jibe[1] (jīb) ▸ *v.* **jibed, jib·ing.** To shift a fore-and-aft sail from one side of a vessel to the other while sailing before the wind.
jibe[2] (jīb) ▸ *v.* **jibed, jib·ing.** *Informal* To be in accord; agree.
jibe[3] (jīb) ▸ *v. & n.* Var. of **gibe.**
Jid·da (jĭd′ə) ▸ A city of W-central Saudi Arabia on the Red Sea.
jif·fy (jĭf′ē) ▸ *n., pl.* **jif·fies.** *Informal* A moment.
jig (jĭg) ▸ *n.* **1.** Any of various lively dances in triple time. **2.** A fishing lure with one or more hooks. **3.** A device for guiding a tool or for holding work in place. ▸ *v.* **jigged, jig·ging. 1.** To dance a jig. **2.** To bob or jerk rapidly. **3.** To operate a jig.
jig·ger (jĭg′ər) ▸ *n.* A small measure for liquor, usu. holding 1 ½ oz.
jig·gle (jĭg′əl) ▸ *v.* **-gled, -gling.** To move or cause to move jerkily up and down or to and fro. **—jig′gle** *n.* **—jig′gly** *adj.*
jig·saw (jĭg′sô′) ▸ *n.* A saw with a narrow vertical blade, used to cut sharp curves.
jigsaw puzzle ▸ *n.* A puzzle consisting of irregularly shaped pieces that form a picture when fitted together.
ji·had (jĭ-häd′) ▸ *n.* A Muslim holy war against infidels.
jilt (jĭlt) ▸ *v.* To drop (a lover) suddenly or callously.
Jim Crow (jĭm) ▸ *n. Slang* The practice of discriminating against and segregating Black people. **—Jim′-Crow′** *adj.*
jim·my (jĭm′ē) ▸ *n., pl.* **-mies.** A short crowbar with curved ends. ▸ *v.* **-mied, -my·ing.** To pry (something) open with or as if with a jimmy.
jim·son·weed (jĭm′sən-wēd′) ▸ *n.* A coarse poisonous plant having large, trumpet-shaped white or purplish flowers.
jin·gle (jĭng′gəl) ▸ *v.* **-gled, -gling.** To make or cause to make a tinkling or ringing metallic sound. ▸ *n.* **1.** A jingling sound. **2.** A catchy, often musical advertising slogan. **—jin′gly** *adj.*
jin·go·ism (jĭng′gō-ĭz′əm) ▸ *n.* Extreme nationalism marked esp. by a belligerent foreign policy. **—jin′go·ist** *n.* **—jin′go·is′tic** *adj.*
jin·ni (jĭn′ē, jĭ-nē′) ▸ *n., pl.* **jinn** (jĭn). In Muslim legend, a supernatural spirit.
jin·rik·sha (jĭn-rĭk′shô′) ▸ *n.* A small, two-wheeled carriage drawn by one or two persons; ricksha.
jinx (jĭngks) *Informal* ▸ *n.* **1.** A person or thing believed to bring bad luck. **2.** A period of bad luck. ▸ *v.* **jinxed, jinx·ing.** To bring bad luck to.
jit·ney (jĭt′nē) ▸ *n., pl.* **-neys.** A small motor vehicle that transports passengers on a route for a low fare.
jit·ter (jĭt′ər) ▸ *v.* To be nervous or uneasy; fidget. ▸ *n.* **jitters** A fit of nervousness. **—jit′ter·i·ness** *n.* **—jit′ter·y** *adj.*
jit·ter·bug (jĭt′ər-bŭg′) ▸ *n.* A lively dance consisting of various two-step patterns embellished with twirls and acrobatic maneuvers. **—jit′ter·bug′** *v.*
jive (jīv) ▸ *n.* **1a.** Jazz or swing music. **b.** The jargon of jazz musicians. **2.** *Slang* Deceptive, nonsensical, or glib talk. **—jive** *v. & adj.* **—jiv′er** *n.* **—jiv′ey, jiv′y** *adj.*
jnr. ▸ *abbr.* junior
Joan of Arc (jōn), Saint (1412?–31) ▸ French military leader and heroine.
job (jŏb) ▸ *n.* **1.** A regular activity performed for payment. **2.** A position in which one is employed. **3a.** A task that must be done. **b.** A specified duty or responsibility. **4.** A specific piece of work to be done for a set fee. **5.** *Informal* A criminal act, esp. a robbery. ▸ *v.* **jobbed, job·bing. 1.** To work by the piece or at odd jobs. **2.** To act as a jobber. **3.** To subcontract. **—job′less** *adj.* **—job′less·ness** *n.*
Job (jōb) ▸ *n.* **1.** In the Bible, an upright man tested by God. **2.** See **Bible** table in Appendix.
job action (jŏb) ▸ *n.* A temporary action, such as a strike or slowdown, by workers to protest or make demands.
job·ber (jŏb′ər) ▸ *n.* **1.** One who buys merchandise from manufacturers and sells it to retailers. **2.** One who works by the piece.
job·hold·er (jŏb′hōl′dər) ▸ *n.* A person who has a regular job.
job lot ▸ *n.* Miscellaneous merchandise sold in one lot.
job-share (jŏb′shâr′) ▸ *v.* To share one job in alternation with one or more part-time workers.
jock[1] (jŏk) ▸ *n.* **1.** A jockey. **2.** A disc jockey.
jock[2] (jŏk) ▸ *n.* **1.** An athletic supporter. **2.** An athlete.
jock·ey (jŏk′ē) ▸ *n., pl.* **-eys.** One who rides horses in races, esp. as a profession. ▸ *v.* **1.** To ride (a horse) as jockey. **2.** To direct or maneuver by cleverness or skill. **3.** To maneuver for a certain position or advantage.
jock·strap (jŏk′străp′) ▸ *n.* An athletic supporter.
jo·cose (jō-kōs′) ▸ *adj.* Given to joking; merry. **—jo·cose′ly** *adv.* **—jo·cose′ness, jo·cos′i·ty** (-kŏs′ĭ-tē) *n.*
joc·u·lar (jŏk′yə-lər) ▸ *adj.* Given to or marked by joking. **—joc′u·lar′i·ty** (-lăr′ĭ-tē) *n.* **—joc′u·lar·ly** *adv.*
joc·und (jŏk′ənd, jō′kənd) ▸ *adj.* Lighthearted; merry. **—jo·cun′di·ty** (jō-kŭn′dĭ-tē) *n.* **—joc′und·ly** *adv.*
jodh·purs (jŏd′pərz) ▸ *pl.n.* Wide-hipped riding pants of heavy cloth, fitting tightly from knee to ankle.
Jo·el (jō′əl) ▸ *n.* See **Bible** table in Appendix.
jo·ey (jō′ē) ▸ *n., pl.* **-eys.** *Australian* A young animal, esp. a baby kangaroo.
jog[1] (jŏg) ▸ *v.* **jogged, jog·ging. 1.** To jar or move by shoving, bumping, or jerking. **2.** To nudge. **3.** To run or ride at a steady slow trot, esp. for exercise or sport. **4.** To proceed in a leisurely manner. ▸ *n.* **1.** A slight nudge. **2.** A slow steady trot. **—jog′ger** *n.*
jog[2] (jŏg) ▸ *n.* **1.** A protruding or receding part in a surface or line. **2.** An abrupt change in direction. **—jog** *v.*
jog·gle (jŏg′əl) ▸ *v.* **-gled, -gling.** To jar slightly. **—jog′gle** *n.*
Jo·han·nes·burg (jō-hăn′ĭs-bûrg′, -hä′nĭs-) ▸ A city of NE South Africa NW of Durban.
John (jŏn) ▸ *n.* See **Bible** table in Appendix.
John Doe ▸ *n.* **1.** Used as a name in legal proceedings to designate a fictitious or unidentified man. **2.** An average man.
john·ny·cake (jŏn′ē-kāk′) ▸ *n. Regional* A flat cornmeal bread usu. fried on a griddle.
John Paul II (1920–2005) ▸ Pope (1978–2005).
John·son (jŏn′sən), **Andrew** (1808–75) ▸ The 17th US President (1865–69).
Johnson, Lyndon Baines (1908–73) ▸ The 36th US President (1963–69).

THESAURUS

jibber-jabber *v.* —*See* BABBLE.
jibber-jabber *n.* —*See* BABBLE.
jibe[1] *v.* —*See* AGREE (1).
jibe[2] *v. See* GIBE.
jiffy or **jiff** *n.* —*See* FLASH (2).
jig *n.* —*See* TRICK (1).
jigger *n.* —*See* DROP (4), GADGET.
jiggle *v.* To cause to move to and fro with short, jerky movements ▸ jar, joggle, shake. [*Compare* JERK.] —*See also* BUMP.
jihad *n.* A goal served with great or uncompromising dedication ▸ cause, crusade, jihad. [*Compare* DRIVE.]
jillion *n.* —*See* HEAP (2).
jilted *adj.* —*See* ABANDONED (1).
jim-jams *n.* —*See* JITTERS.
jingle *n.* —*See* SONG.
jinx *n. Informal* Something or someone believed to bring bad luck ▸ curse, evil eye, hex, hoodoo, Jonah. [*Compare* CHARM, MAGIC.]
jinx *v. Informal* To bring bad luck or evil to ▸ curse, hex, hoodoo.
jitters *n.* A state of nervous restlessness or agitation ▸ fidgets, jumps, shivers, trembles. *Informal:* all-overs, shakes. *Slang:* heebie-jeebies, jim-jams, whim-whams, willies.
jittery *adj.* —*See* EDGY.
jive *v.* —*See* JOKE (2).
job *n.* —*See* BUSINESS (2), FUNCTION (1), POSITION (3), TASK (1), TASK (2).
jobbery *n.* —*See* CORRUPTION (2).
jobholder *n.* —*See* EMPLOYEE.
jobholding *adj.* —*See* EMPLOYED.
jobless *adj.* Having no job ▸ idle, unemployed, unoccupied, workless. *Idiom:* out of a job (*or* employ *or* work).
jockey *v.* —*See* MANEUVER (1), MANEUVER (2).
jocose *adj.* —*See* FUNNY (1).
jocosity or **jocoseness** *n.* —*See* HUMOR, MERRIMENT (1).
jocular *adj.* —*See* FUNNY (1).
jocularity *n.* —*See* HUMOR, MERRIMENT (1).
jocund *adj.* —*See* CHEERFUL.
jocundity *n.* —*See* MERRIMENT (1).
jog *v.* —*See* PUSH (1), RUN (1).
jog *n.* —*See* DIG, RUN (1).
joggle *v.* To cause to move to and fro with short, jerky movements ▸ jar, jiggle, shake. [*Compare* JERK.]

Johnson, Samuel (1709–84) ▸ British writer and lexicographer.
John the Baptist, Saint (1st cent. B.C.) ▸ Jewish prophet who in the Bible baptized Jesus.
joie de vi·vre (zhwä′ də vē′vrə) ▸ *n.* Carefree enjoyment of life.
join (join) ▸ *v.* **1.** To put or bring together. **2.** To put or bring into close association or relationship. **3.** To connect, as with a straight line. **4.** To meet and merge with. **5.** To become a part or member of. **6.** To come or act together. **7.** To take part; participate.
join·er (joi′nər) ▸ *n.* **1.** A carpenter, esp. a cabinetmaker. **2.** *Informal* A person given to joining groups.
joint (joint) ▸ *n.* **1.** A place or part at which two or more things are joined. **2.** *Anat.* A point of articulation between two or more bones, esp. one that allows motion. **3.** A cut of meat for roasting. **4.** *Slang* A cheap or disreputable gathering place. **5.** *Slang* A marijuana cigarette. ▸ *adj.* **1.** Shared by or common to two or more. **2.** Formed or marked by cooperation or united action. ▸ *v.* **1.** To provide with joints. **2.** To separate (meat) at the joints. **—*idiom:* out of joint 1.** Dislocated, as a bone. **2.** *Informal* **a.** Not harmonious. **b.** Out of order; unsatisfactory. **c.** In bad humor. **—joint′ly** *adv.*
joist (joist) ▸ *n.* Any of the parallel horizontal beams set from wall to wall or across girders to support a floor or ceiling.
jo·jo·ba (hə-hō′bə, hō-) ▸ *n.* A shrub of the SW US and N Mexico having leathery leaves and edible seeds that contain a valuable oil.
joke (jōk) ▸ *n.* **1.** Something said or done to evoke laughter, esp. an amusing story with a punch line. **2.** A mischievous trick. **3.** A ludicrous incident or situation. **4.** *Informal* A laughingstock. ▸ *v.* **joked, jok·ing. 1.** To tell or play jokes. **2.** To speak in fun; be facetious. **—jok′ing·ly** *adv.*
jok·er (jō′kər) ▸ *n.* **1a.** One who tells or plays jokes. **b.** *Informal* A person, esp. an annoying one. **2.** A playing card used in certain games as the highest-ranking card or as a wild card. **3.** A minor clause in a document that voids or changes its original or intended purpose.
Jol·li·et also **Jo·li·et** (jō′lē-ĕt′, jō′lē-ĕt′, zhô-lyā′), **Louis** (1645–1700) ▸ French-Canadian explorer.
jol·li·fi·ca·tion (jŏl′ə-fĭ-kā′shən) ▸ *n.* Festivity; revelry.
jol·li·ty (jŏl′ĭ-tē) ▸ *n.* Merriment; mirth.
jol·ly (jŏl′ē) ▸ *adj.* **-li·er, -li·est. 1.** Full of good humor. **2.** Merry: *a jolly tune.* ▸ *adv. Chiefly Brit.* Very: *a jolly good cook.* **—jol′li·ly** *adv.* **—jol′li·ness** *n.*
jolt (jōlt) ▸ *v.* **1.** To shake or jar with or as if with a sudden hard blow. **2.** To move or cause to move jerkily. ▸ *n.* **1.** A hard jarring or jerking. **2.** A sudden shock, as of surprise. **—jolt′y** *adj.*
Jo·nah (jō′nə) ▸ *n.* **1.** In the Bible, a prophet swallowed by a great fish and disgorged unharmed. **2.** See **Bible** table in Appendix. **3.** One thought to bring bad luck.
Jones (jōnz), **John Paul** (1747–92) ▸ Scottish-born Amer. naval officer.
jon·quil (jŏng′kwəl, jŏn′-) ▸ *n.* An ornamental plant with short-tubed, fragrant yellow flowers.
Jon·son (jŏn′sən), **Benjamin.** "Ben" (1572–1637) ▸ English actor and writer.
Jop·lin (jŏp′lĭn), **Scott** (1868–1917) ▸ Amer. composer.
Jor·dan (jôr′dn) ▸ A country of SW Asia in NW Arabia. **—Jor·da′ni·an** (jôr-dā′nē-ən) *adj. & n.*
Jo·seph[1] (jō′zəf, -səf) ▸ In the Bible, the older son of Jacob and Rachel.
Jo·seph[2] (jō′zəf, -səf). "Chief Joseph" (1840?–1904) ▸ Nez Percé leader.
Joseph, Saint (fl. first century A.D.) ▸ In the Bible, the husband of Mary, mother of Jesus.
josh (jŏsh) ▸ *v.* To tease good-humoredly. **—josh′er** *n.*
Josh·u·a (jŏsh′o͞o-ə) ▸ *n.* **1.** In the Bible, a Hebrew leader. **2.** See **Bible** table in Appendix.
jos·tle (jŏs′əl) ▸ *v.* **-tled, -tling. 1.** To come in rough contact (with); push and shove. **2.** To make one's way by pushing or elbowing. **3.** To vie (with) for advantage or position. **—jos′tle** *n.* **—jos′tler** *n.*
jot (jŏt) ▸ *n.* The smallest bit; iota. ▸ *v.* **jot·ted, jot·ting.** To write down briefly or hastily. **—jot′ting** *n.*
joule (jo͞ol, joul) ▸ *n.* A unit of electrical energy equal to the work done when a current of 1 ampere is passed through a resistance of 1 ohm for 1 second.
jounce (jouns) ▸ *v.* **jounced, jounc·ing.** To move with bumps and jolts; bounce. **—jounce** *n.* **—jounc′y** *adj.*
jour·nal (jûr′nəl) ▸ *n.* **1a.** A personal record of experiences and reflections; diary. **b.** An official record of daily proceedings, as of a legislative body. **2.** A newspaper. **3.** A specialized periodical. **4.** The part of a shaft or axle supported by a bearing.
jour·nal·ese (jûr′nə-lēz′, -lēs′) ▸ *n.* A slick, superficial style of writing often deemed typical of newspapers and magazines.
jour·nal·ism (jûr′nə-lĭz′əm) ▸ *n.* **1.** The collecting, writing, editing, and presentation of news in print or electronic media. **2.** Written material of current or popular interest. **—jour′nal·ist** *n.* **—jour′nal·is′tic** *adj.* **—jour′nal·is′ti·cal·ly** *adv.*
jour·ney (jûr′nē) ▸ *n., pl.* **-neys.** Travel from one place to another; trip. ▸ *v.* To travel. **—jour′ney·er** *n.*
jour·ney·man (jûr′nē-mən) ▸ *n.* **1.** One who has served an apprenticeship in a trade and works in another's employ. **2.** A competent worker.
joust (joust, jŭst, jo͞ost) ▸ *n.* A combat between two mounted

THESAURUS

join *v.* **1.** To become a member of ▸ enlist, enroll, enter, muster in, sign up. *Informal:* sign on. **2.** To come together from different directions ▸ close, converge, meet, unite. *—See also* ADJOIN, ASSOCIATE (1), BAND[2], COMBINE (1), COOPERATE, PARTICIPATE.
join *n.* *—See* JOINT (1).
joint *n.* **1.** A point or position at which two or more things are joined ▸ connection, coupling, join, junction, juncture, seam, union. **2.** *Slang* A disreputable or run-down bar or restaurant ▸ *Slang:* dive, dump, honky-tonk, juke house, juke joint. *Idiom:* hole in the wall. *—See also* JAIL.
joint *adj.* *—See* COMMON (2), COOPERATIVE.
jointly *adv.* In, into, or as a single body ▸ together. *Idioms:* as one, in one breath, in the same breath, in unison, with one accord, with one voice.
joist *n.* *—See* BEAM (2).
joke *n.* **1.** Words intended to excite laughter or amusement ▸ gag, jape, jest, one-liner, quip, sally, witticism. *Informal:* funny, knee-slapper, rib tickler, zinger. *Slang:* ha-ha. [*Compare* CRACK, TAUNT.] **2.** An object of amusement or laughter ▸ butt, jest, laughingstock, mockery. *Idiom:* figure of fun. [*Compare* FOOL.] *—See also* PRANK[1], SCREAM (2).
joke *v.* **1.** To make jokes; behave playfully ▸ jest, joke around, quip. *Informal:* clown (around), fool around, horse around. *Idioms:* crack wise, play the fool. [*Compare* PLAY.] **2.** To tease or mock good-humoredly ▸ banter, chaff, josh. *Informal:* fun, kid, rib, ride. *Slang:* jive, rag, razz. *Idiom:* pull (someone's) leg.
joker *n.* A person whose words or actions provoke or are intended to provoke amusement or laughter ▸ clown, comedian, comic, farceur, funnyman, humorist, jester, jokester, quipster, wag, wit, zany. *Informal:* card. [*Compare* SMART ALECK.]
jollification *n.* *—See* CELEBRATION (3).
jollies *n.* *—See* AMUSEMENT, THRILL.
jolliness *n.* *—See* MERRIMENT (1).
jollity *n.* *—See* MERRIMENT (1), MERRIMENT (2).
jolly *adj.* *—See* CHEERFUL, GOOD (1).
jolt *v.* *—See* BUMP, DRIVE (2), STARTLE.
jolt *n.* *—See* COLLISION, SHOCK[1].
jongleur *n.* *—See* POET.
josh *v.* *—See* JOKE (2).
jostle *v.* *—See* PUSH (1).
jostle *n.* *—See* PUSH.
jot *n.* *—See* BIT[1] (1).
jounce *n.* *—See* BUMP.
journal *n.* *—See* MEMOIR.
journalist *n.* *—See* PRESS.
journey *n.* The act of traveling from one place to another ▸ [illegible] cruising, cruise, flight, odyssey, passage, peregrination, progress, transit, travel, traversal, trip, voyage, wayfaring. [*Compare* EXPEDITION, TRIP.]
journey *v.* To make or go on a journey ▸ fare, jaunt, pass, peregrinate, sightsee, tour, travel, trek, trip, voyage. *Idioms:* hit the road, see the country, see the sights, see the world. [*Compare* HIKE, MIGRATE, ROVE.]
joust *n.* Any competition or test of opposing wills likened to the sport in which knights fought with lances ▸ tilt, tournament, tourney. [*Compare*

knights using lances. ▸ *v.* To engage in a joust. **—joust′er** *n.*

Jove (jōv) ▸ *n. Rom. Myth.* See **Jupiter** 1.

jo·vi·al (jō′vē-əl) ▸ *adj.* Mirthful; jolly. **—jo′vi·al′i·ty** (-ăl′ĭ-tē) *n.* **—jo′vi·al·ly** *adv.*

jowl[1] (joul) ▸ *n.* **1.** The jaw, esp. the lower jaw. **2.** The cheek.

jowl[2] (joul) ▸ *n.* The flesh under the lower jaw, esp. when plump or flabby.

joy (joi) ▸ *n.* **1.** Intense or elated happiness. **2.** A source of great pleasure. ▸ *v.* To rejoice. **—joy′less** *adj.* **—joy′less·ly** *adv.* **—joy′less·ness** *n.*

Joyce (jois), **James** (1882–1941) ▸ Irish writer. **—Joyc′e·an** *adj.*

joy·ful (joi′fəl) ▸ *adj.* Feeling, causing, or showing joy. **—joy′ful·ly** *adv.* **—joy′ful·ness** *n.*

joy·ous (joi′əs) ▸ *adj.* Joyful. **—joy′ous·ly** *adv.* **—joy′ous·ness** *n.*

joy ride ▸ *n. Slang* An often reckless automobile ride taken for fun and thrills.

joy·stick (joi′stĭk′) ▸ *n. Slang* **1.** A control stick. **2.** A manual control lever, as for a video game.

JP ▸ *abbr.* justice of the peace

jr. or **Jr.** ▸ *abbr.* junior

Ju·ba (jo͞o′bə) ▸ The capital of South Sudan, in the southern part.

ju·bi·lant (jo͞o′bə-lənt) ▸ *adj.* Exultingly joyful. **—ju′bi·lance** *n.* **—ju′bi·lant·ly** *adv.*

ju·bi·la·tion (jo͞o′bə-lā′shən) ▸ *n.* **1.** The act of rejoicing. **2.** A joyful celebration.

ju·bi·lee (jo͞o′bə-lē′, jo͞o′bə-lē′) ▸ *n.* **1.** A special anniversary, esp. a 50th anniversary. **2.** A season or occasion of joyful celebration. **3.** Jubilation; rejoicing.

Ju·dah[1] (jo͞o′də) ▸ In the Bible, a son of Jacob and Leah.

Ju·dah[2] (jo͞o′də) ▸ An ancient kingdom of S Palestine between the Mediterranean and the Dead Sea.

Ju·da·ic (jo͞o-dā′ĭk) also **Ju·da·i·cal** (-ĭ-kəl) ▸ *adj.* Of or relating to Jews or Judaism.

Ju·da·ism (jo͞o′dē-ĭz′əm) ▸ *n.* The monotheistic religion of the Jews, having its spiritual and ethical principles embodied chiefly in the Hebrew Scriptures and the Talmud.

Ju·das (jo͞o′dəs) ▸ *n.* One who betrays another under the guise of friendship.

Judas Is·car·i·ot (ĭ-skăr′ē-ət) (d. c. A.D. 30) ▸ In the Bible, one of the 12 Apostles and the betrayer of Jesus.

Jude (jo͞od) ▸ *n.* See **Bible** table in Appendix.

Ju·de·a also **Ju·dae·a** (jo͞o-dē′ə, -dā′ə) ▸ An ancient region of S Palestine comprising present-day S Israel and SW Jordan. **—Ju·de′an** *adj. & n.*

judge (jŭj) ▸ *v.* **judged, judg·ing. 1.** To form an opinion (of). **2.** To hear and decide on in a court of law; try. **3.** To determine or declare after deliberation. **4.** *Informal* To think; suppose. ▸ *n.* **1.** One who makes estimates as to worth, quality, or fitness. **2.** A public official who hears and decides cases brought before a court of law. **3.** One appointed to decide the winners of a contest or competition. **4. Judges** *(takes sing. v.).* See **Bible** table in Appendix. **—judge′ship′** *n.*

judg·ment also **judge·ment** (jŭj′mənt) ▸ *n.* **1.** The act or process of judging. **2.** The mental ability to form an opinion, distinguish relationships, or draw sound conclusions. **3.** An opinion or estimate formed after due consideration: *awaited the judgment of the umpire.* **4.** A judicial decision.

judg·men·tal (jŭj-mĕn′tl) ▸ *adj.* **1.** Of or relating to judgment. **2.** Inclined to make judgments, esp. moral or personal ones. **—judg·men′tal·ly** *adv.*

Judgment Day ▸ *n.* In Judeo-Christian and Muslim traditions, the day when God judges all humans.

ju·di·ca·ture (jo͞o′dĭ-kə-cho͝or′) ▸ *n.* **1.** Administration of justice. **2.** A system of courts of law.

ju·di·cial (jo͞o-dĭsh′əl) ▸ *adj.* **1a.** Of or proper to courts of law or the administration of justice. **b.** Decreed by or proceeding from a court of justice. **2.** Marked by or expressing judgment. **—ju·di′cial·ly** *adv.*

ju·di·ci·ar·y (jo͞o-dĭsh′ē-ĕr′ē, -dĭsh′ə-rē) ▸ *n., pl.* **-ies. 1.** The judicial branch of government. **2a.** A system of courts of law. **b.** The judges of these courts.

ju·di·cious (jo͞o-dĭsh′əs) ▸ *adj.* Having or exhibiting sound judgment. **—ju·di′cious·ly** *adv.* **—ju·di′cious·ness** *n.*

Ju·dith (jo͞o′dĭth) ▸ *n.* See **Bible** table in Appendix.

ju·do (jo͞o′dō) ▸ *n.* A sport using principles of balance and leverage adapted from jujitsu.

jug (jŭg) ▸ *n.* **1.** An often earthenware or glass vessel with a small mouth, a handle, and usu. a stopper or cap. **2.** *Slang* A jail.

jug·ger·naut (jŭg′ər-nôt′) ▸ *n.* An overwhelming advancing force that crushes everything in its path.

jug·gle (jŭg′əl) ▸ *v.* **-gled, -gling. 1.** To keep (two or more objects) in the air at one time by alternately tossing and catching them. **2.** To keep (more than two activities) in progress at one time. **3.** To manipulate (e.g., figures) in order to deceive. **—jug′gler** *n.*

jug·u·lar (jŭg′yə-lər) ▸ *adj.* Of or located in the neck or throat. ▸ *n.* A jugular vein.

juice (jo͞os) ▸ *n.* **1a.** A fluid naturally contained in plant or animal tissue. **b.** A bodily secretion. **2.** *Slang* **a.** Electric current. **b.** Fuel for an engine. ▸ *v.* **juiced, juic·ing.** To extract the juice from.

juic·er (jo͞o′sər) ▸ *n.* An appliance used to extract juice from fruits and vegetables.

juic·y (jo͞o′sē) ▸ *adj.* **-i·er, -i·est. 1.** Full of juice. **2.** Interesting, racy, or titillating. **3.** Rewarding or gratifying: *a juicy raise.* **—juic′i·ly** *adv.* **—juic′i·ness** *n.*

ju·jit·su also **ju·jut·su** (jo͞o-jĭt′so͞o) ▸ *n.* An art of weaponless self-defense developed in China and Japan that uses throws, holds, and blows and derives added power from the attacker's own weight and strength.

ju·jube (jo͞o′jo͞ob′) ▸ *n.* A fruit-flavored, chewy candy.

juke (jo͞ok) *Regional* ▸ *n.* A roadside tavern offering music for dancing. ▸ *v.* **juked, juk·ing.** To dance.

juke·box (jo͞ok′bŏks′) ▸ *n.* A coin-operated phonograph.

ju·li·enne (jo͞o′lē-ĕn′, zhü-lyĕn′) ▸ *adj.* Cut into long thin strips: *julienne potatoes.*

Ju·ly (jo͞o-lī′) ▸ *n.* The 7th month of the Gregorian calendar.

Ju·ma·da (jo͞o-mä′dä) ▸ *n.* Either the 5th or the 6th month of the Muslim calendar.

jum·ble (jŭm′bəl) ▸ *v.* **-bled, -bling. 1.** To mix in a confused way. **2.** To confuse. **—jum′ble** *n.*

THESAURUS

BATTLE, COMPETITION.]

joust *v.* —*See* CONTEND.

jovial *adj.* —*See* CHEERFUL.

joviality *n.* —*See* MERRIMENT (1).

joy *n.* —*See* DELIGHT, HAPPINESS.

joyful *adj.* —*See* CHEERFUL, MERRY.

joyfulness *n.* —*See* HAPPINESS.

joyless *adj.* —*See* GLOOMY, SORROWFUL.

joyous *adj.* —*See* MERRY.

jubilance *n.* —*See* EXULTATION.

jubilant *adj.* Feeling or expressing an uplifting joy over a success or victory ▸ exultant, gloating, triumphant. [*Compare* BOASTFUL.]

jubilate *v.* —*See* EXULT (1).

jubilation *n.* —*See* CELEBRATION (3), EXULTATION.

jubilee *n.* —*See* CELEBRATION (1).

Judas *n.* —*See* BETRAYER.

judge *v.* To make a decision about (a controversy or dispute, for example) after deliberation, as in a court of law ▸ adjudge, adjudicate, arbitrate, decide, decree, determine, referee, rule, umpire. ***Idiom:*** sit in judgment. [*Compare* HEAR.] —*See also* BELIEVE (3), CRITICIZE (1), ESTIMATE (1), INFER.

judge *n.* **1.** A public official who decides cases brought before a court of law in order to administer justice ▸ jurist, jurisprudent, justice, justice of the peace, magistrate. [*Compare* GO-BETWEEN.] **2.** A person, usually appointed, who decides the issues of, decides the results of, or supervises the conduct of a competition or conflict ▸ arbiter, arbitrator, referee, umpire. *Informal:* ref, ump. —*See also* CRITIC (1).

judgment *n.* A position arrived at by reasoning from premises ▸ conclusion, deduction, inference. —*See also* BELIEF (1), COMMON SENSE, CRITICISM, DISCERNMENT, ESTIMATE (1), RULING.

judgmental *adj.* —*See* ARBITRARY, CRITICAL (1), INTOLERANT (1).

judiciary or **judicature** *n.* —*See* COURT (2).

judicious *adj.* —*See* DELIBERATE (3), SENSIBLE.

jug *n.* —*See* JAIL.

juju *n.* —*See* CHARM.

jumble *v.* —*See* CONFUSE (1), CONFUSE (3), DISORDER, SHUFFLE.

jum·bo (jŭm′bō) ▸ *n., pl.* **-bos**. An unusually large person, animal, or thing. **—jum′bo** *adj.*

jump (jŭmp) ▸ *v.* **1.** To spring off the ground or from some other base by a muscular effort of the legs and feet. **2.** To move involuntarily, as in surprise. **3.** To react quickly: *jump at a bargain.* **4.** To enter eagerly into an activity. **5.** To form an opinion hastily. **6.** To spring upon in sudden attack. **7.** To rise suddenly and markedly. **8.** To move discontinuously; skip: *jumps from one subject to another.* **9.** To be displaced suddenly from (e.g., a track). **10.** To move over (an opponent's playing piece) in a board game. **11.** *Slang* To be lively; bustle. ▸ *n.* **1.** The act of jumping; leap. **2.** *Informal* An initial advantage; head start. **3.** A sudden rise, as in price. **4.** A sudden transition. **5a.** An involuntary nervous movement. **b. jumps** A condition of nervousness. ***—idiom:*** **jump the gun** To start something too soon.

jump·er[1] (jŭm′pər) ▸ *n.* **1.** One that jumps. **2.** *Elect.* A short length of wire used temporarily to complete or bypass a circuit.

jump·er[2] (jŭm′pər) ▸ *n.* **1.** A sleeveless dress worn over a blouse or sweater. **2.** A loose protective smock or coat. **3. jumpers** A child's overalls.

jump shot ▸ *n. Basketball* A shot made by a player at the highest point of a jump.

jump suit ▸ *n.* **1.** A parachutist's uniform. **2.** A one-piece garment consisting of a blouse or shirt with attached slacks or shorts.

jump·y (jŭm′pē) ▸ *adj.* **-i·er, -i·est.** On edge; nervous. **—jump′i·ness** *n.*

jun. ▸ *abbr.* junior

jun·co (jŭng′kō) ▸ *n., pl.* **-cos** or **-coes**. A small North American bird having predominantly gray plumage.

junc·tion (jŭngk′shən) ▸ *n.* **1.** The act of joining or the condition of being joined. **2.** A place where two things join or meet.

junc·ture (jŭngk′chər) ▸ *n.* **1.** The act of joining or the condition of being joined. **2.** A place where two things are joined; joint. **3.** A point in time, esp. a critical point.

June (jo͞on) ▸ *n.* The 6th month of the Gregorian calendar.

Ju·neau (jo͞o′nō′) ▸ The capital of AK, in the southeast part.

June beetle or **June bug** ▸ *n.* A North American beetle appearing in late spring and having larvae that often destroy crops.

Jung (yo͝ong), **Carl Gustav** (1875–1961) ▸ Swiss psychiatrist. **—Jung′i·an** *adj. & n.*

jun·gle (jŭng′gəl) ▸ *n.* **1.** Land densely overgrown with tropical vegetation. **2.** A dense thicket or growth. **3.** A bewildering complex or maze. **4.** A place of ruthless competition or struggle for survival. **—jun′gly** (-glē) *adj.*

jungle gym ▸ *n.* A structure of poles and bars for children to climb and play on.

jun·ior (jo͞on′yər) ▸ *adj.* **1.** Younger. Used to distinguish a son from his father when they have the same given name. **2.** Intended for youthful persons: *junior fashions.* **3.** Lower in rank or shorter in length of tenure. **4.** Of the third year of a US high school or college. **5.** Lesser in scale than the usual. ▸ *n.* **1.** A person who is younger than another. **2.** A person lesser in rank or time of service. **3.** A third-year student in a US high school or college.

junior college ▸ *n.* A school offering a two-year course that is the equivalent of the first two years of a four-year college.

junior high school ▸ *n.* A school including the 7th, 8th, and sometimes 9th grades.

ju·ni·per (jo͞o′nə-pər) ▸ *n.* An evergreen tree or shrub with scalelike leaves and aromatic, bluish-gray, berrylike cones.

junk[1] (jŭngk) ▸ *n.* **1.** Discarded material that may be reused in some form. **2.** *Informal* **a.** Cheap or shoddy material. **b.** Something worthless or meaningless. **3.** *Slang* Heroin. ▸ *v.* To throw away or discard as useless. **—junk′y** *adj.*

junk[2] (jŭngk) ▸ *n.* A Chinese flat-bottomed sailing ship.

junk bond ▸ *n.* A corporate bond having a high yield and high risk.

jun·ket (jŭng′kĭt) ▸ *n.* **1.** A dessert made from flavored milk and rennet. **2.** A party or outing. **3.** A trip taken by a public official or businessperson at public or corporate expense. **—jun′ket** *v.* **—jun′ket·er** *n.*

junk food ▸ *n.* A high-calorie food that is low in nutritional value.

junk·ie also **junk·y** (jŭng′kē) ▸ *n., pl.* **-ies.** *Slang* **1.** A narcotics addict, esp. one using heroin. **2.** One who has an insatiable devotion or interest: *a sports junkie.*

junk mail ▸ *n.* Third-class mail, such as advertisements, mailed indiscriminately in large quantities.

junk·yard (jŭngk′yärd′) ▸ *n.* A yard or lot used to store junk.

Ju·no (jo͞o′nō) ▸ *n. Rom. Myth.* The principal goddess of the pantheon, wife and sister of Jupiter.

jun·ta (ho͝on′tə, jŭn′-) ▸ *n.* A group of military officers ruling a country after seizing power.

Ju·pi·ter (jo͞o′pĭ-tər) ▸ *n.* **1.** *Rom. Myth.* The supreme god, brother and husband of Juno. **2.** *Astron.* The largest of the planets and the 5th from the sun, at a mean distance of 777 million km (483 million mi), having a diameter of approx. 138,000 km (86,000 mi).

Ju·ras·sic (jo͝o-răs′ĭk) *Geol.* ▸ *adj.* Of or being the 2nd period of the Mesozoic Era, marked by the appearance of the earliest birds. ▸ *n.* The Jurassic Period. **—Ju·ras′sic** *n.*

ju·rid·i·cal (jo͝o-rĭd′ĭ-kəl) also **ju·rid·ic** (-ĭk) ▸ *adj.* Of or relating to the law and its administration. **—ju·rid′i·cal·ly** *adv.*

ju·ris·dic·tion (jo͝or′ĭs-dĭk′shən) ▸ *n.* **1.** The right and power to interpret and apply the law. **2a.** Authority or control. **b.** The extent of authority or control: *a matter beyond the school's jurisdiction.* **3.** The territorial range of authority or control. **—ju′ris·dic′tion·al** *adj.*

ju·ris·pru·dence (jo͝or′ĭs-pro͞od′ns) ▸ *n.* **1.** The philosophy or science of law. **2.** A division or department of law. **—ju′ris·pru·den′tial** (-pro͞o-dĕn′shəl) *adj.*

ju·rist (jo͝or′ĭst) ▸ *n.* One skilled in the law, esp. a judge or legal scholar.

THESAURUS

jumble *n.* —*See* ASSORTMENT, DISORDER (1).

jumbled *adj.* —*See* CONFUSED (2).

jumbo *n.* —*See* GIANT.

jumbo *adj.* —*See* ENORMOUS.

jump *v.* **1.** To move off the ground by a muscular effort of the legs and feet ▸ hurdle, leap, pounce, spring, vault. [*Compare* PLUNGE.] **2.** To move suddenly and involuntarily ▸ bolt, start. [*Compare* BUMP, JERK.] **3.** To catapult oneself from a disabled aircraft ▸ bail out, eject. **4.** To increase in amount ▸ boost, hike, jack (up), raise, up. —*See also* BOUND[1], PROMOTE (1).

jump on *v.* —*See* CHASTISE.

jump up *v.* —*See* STAND (1).

jump *n.* **1.** The act of jumping ▸ leap, pounce, spring, vault. [*Compare* FALL.] **2.** A sudden and involuntary movement ▸ bolt, start, startle. [*Compare* JERK, RECOIL.] —*See also* ADVANCEMENT, ADVANTAGE (3), BOUND[1] (2), ENERGY, INCREASE (1), INCREASE (2).

jumper *n.* —*See* DRESS (3).

jumpiness *n.* —*See* RESTLESSNESS.

jumps *n.* —*See* JITTERS.

jump-start *v.* —*See* ENERGIZE.

jumpy *adj.* —*See* EDGY.

junction *n.* The act or fact of coming together ▸ concentration, concourse, confluence, conflux, convergence, crossroads, gathering, meeting, terminal. [*Compare* UNIFICATION.] —*See also* JOINT (1).

juncture *n.* A point or position at which two or more things are joined ▸ connection, coupling, joint, junction, seam, union. —*See also* CRISIS, OCCASION (1).

jungle *n.* —*See* TANGLE, WILDERNESS.

junior *adj.* —*See* MINOR (1).

junior *n.* —*See* SUBORDINATE.

junk *v.* —*See* DISCARD.

junk *n.* —*See* ODDS AND ENDS.

junk *adj.* —*See* UNWHOLESOME (1).

junket *n.* **1.** A large, elaborately prepared meal ▸ banquet, feast, junket. *Informal:* feed, spread. **2.** A usually short journey taken for pleasure ▸ excursion, jaunt, outing, trip. [*Compare* EXCURSION, JOURNEY.]

junkie *n.* —*See* FAN[2].

junky *n.* —*See* SHODDY.

jurisdiction *n.* —*See* AUTHORITY.

jurist or **jurisprudent** *n.* A public official who decides cases that are brought before a court of law in order to administer justice ▸ judge, justice, justice of the peace, magistrate. [*Compare* GO-

ju·ris·tic (jo͞o-rĭs′tĭk) also **ju·ris·ti·cal** (-tĭ-kəl) ▸ *adj.* 1. Of or relating to a jurist or to jurisprudence. 2. Of law or legality.
ju·ror (jo͝or′ər, -ôr′) ▸ *n.* A member of a jury.
ju·ry (jo͝or′ē) ▸ *n., pl.* **-ries**. 1. A body of persons summoned by law and sworn to hear and hand down a verdict upon a case presented in court. 2. A committee to select winners or award prizes.
just (jŭst) ▸ *adj.* 1. Honorable and fair in one's dealings and actions. 2. Consistent with what is morally right: *a just cause.* 3. Properly due or merited: *just deserts.* 4. Lawful; legitimate. 5. Suitable; fitting. 6. Based on sound reason; well-founded. ▸ *adv.* (jəst, jĭst; jŭst *when stressed*) 1. Exactly: *just enough salt.* 2. Only a moment ago. 3. By a narrow margin. 4. At a little distance. 5. Merely; only. 6. Simply: *It's just beautiful!* *—idiom:* **just the same** Nevertheless. **—just′ly** *adv.* **—just′ness** *n.*
jus·tice (jŭs′tĭs) ▸ *n.* 1. The quality of being just; fairness. 2. The principle of moral rightness; equity. 3. The upholding of what is just, esp. fair treatment and due reward in accordance with honor, standards, or law. 4. The administration and procedure of law. 5. Conformity to fact or sound reason. 6. A judge. *—idiom:* **do justice to** To treat adequately, fairly, or with full appreciation.
justice of the peace ▸ *n.* A local magistrate who is authorized to act on minor offenses, perform marriages, and administer oaths.
jus·ti·fi·ca·tion (jŭs′tə-fĭ-kā′shən) ▸ *n.* 1. The act of justifying or the condition of being justified. 2. Something, such as a fact or circumstance, that justifies.
jus·ti·fy (jŭs′tə-fī′) ▸ *v.* **-fied, -fy·ing**. 1. To demonstrate to be just, right, or valid. 2. To declare free of blame; absolve. 3. To demonstrate sufficient legal reason for (an action taken). 4. *Print.* To adjust the spacing within (a line or lines) so as to end evenly at a straight margin. **—jus′ti·fi′a·ble** *adj.* **—jus′ti·fi′a·bly** *adv.*
jut (jŭt) ▸ *v.* **jut·ted, jut·ting**. To extend outward or upward; project. **—jut** *n.*
jute (jo͞ot) ▸ *n.* 1. Either of two Asian plants yielding a fiber used for sacking and cordage. 2. The fiber obtained from these plants.
Jute ▸ *n.* A member of a Germanic people who migrated to Britain in the 5th and 6th cent. A.D.
Ju·ve·nal (jo͞o′və-nəl) (A.D. 60?–140?) ▸ Roman satirist.
ju·ve·nile (jo͞o′və-nīl′, -nəl) ▸ *adj.* 1. Not fully grown; young. 2. Intended for or appropriate to children or young people. 3. Immature; childish. ▸ *n.* 1a. A young person; child. b. A young animal that has not reached sexual maturity. 2. An actor who plays children. **—ju′ve·nile′ly** *adv.* **—ju′ve·nile′ness** *n.*
juvenile delinquent ▸ *n.* A juvenile guilty of antisocial or criminal behavior. **—juvenile delinquency** *n.*
jux·ta·pose (jŭk′stə-pōz′) ▸ *v.* **-posed, -pos·ing**. To place side by side. **—jux′ta·po·si′tion** (-pə-zĭsh′ən) *n.*
JV ▸ *abbr.* junior varsity

THESAURUS

BETWEEN, JUDGE.] *—See also* LAWYER.
jury-rig *v.* *—See* IMPROVISE (2).
just *adj.* Consistent with prevailing or accepted standards or circumstances ▸ appropriate, deserved, due, fit, fitting, merited, proper, right, rightful, suitable. [*Compare* RELEVANT.] *—See also* FAIR[1] (1), LAWFUL, SOUND[2].
just *adv.* 1. By a very little; almost not ▸ barely, hardly, scarce, scarcely. *Idioms:* by a hair (*or* whisker), by the skin of one's teeth. [*Compare* APPROXIMATELY, MERELY, ONLY.] 2. Nothing more than ▸ but, merely, only, simply. [*Compare* BARELY, SOLELY.] *—See also* COMPLETELY (1), DIRECTLY (3), EXACTLY, LATELY, SOLELY.
justice *n.* 1. The state, action, or principle of treating all persons equally in accordance with the law ▸ due process, equitableness, equity. [*Compare* LEGALITY.] 2. A public official who decides cases brought before a court of law in order to administer justice ▸ judge, jurisprudent, jurist, justice of the peace, magistrate. [*Compare* GO-BETWEEN, JUDGE.] *—See also* COGENCY, FAIRNESS.
justifiable *adj.* Capable of being justified ▸ defensible, excusable, tenable. [*Compare* LOGICAL, SOUND[2].]
justification *n.* *—See* ACCOUNT (1), APOLOGY (1), BASIS (2), CAUSE (2), CONFIRMATION (2), EXCULPATION, EXCUSE (1).
justify *v.* 1. To show to be just, right, or valid ▸ excuse, rationalize, vindicate. *Idiom:* make a case for. 2. To be an appropriate occasion for ▸ call for, befit, occasion, warrant. [*Compare* SUIT.] 3. To offer reasons for or a cause of ▸ account for, explain, rationalize. [*Compare* CLARIFY, RESOLVE.] *—See also* CLEAR (3), CONFIRM (1), DEFEND (2), PROVE.
justly *adv.* *—See* FAIRLY (1).
justness *n.* *—See* FAIRNESS.
jut *v.* *—See* BULGE.
jut *n.* *—See* PROJECTION.
juvenescence *n.* *—See* YOUTH (1).
juvenile *adj.* Not yet a legal adult ▸ minor, underage. *—See also* CHILDISH, YOUNG.
juvenile *n.* One who is not yet legally of age ▸ child, minor, underage person. [*Compare* CHILD, YOUTH.] *—See also* CHILD (1).
juvenile delinquent *n.* *—See* URCHIN.
juvenility *n.* *—See* YOUTH (1).
juxtapose *v.* *—See* COMPARE.
juxtaposition *n.* *—See* CONTRAST.

K

k[1] or **K** (kā) ▸ *n., pl.* **k's** or **K's** also **ks** or **Ks**. The 11th letter of the English alphabet.

k[2] ▸ *abbr.* karat

K[1] ▸ The symbol for the element **potassium**.

K[2] ▸ *abbr.* 1. kelvin 2. kilobyte 3. kindergarten

K2 (kā′to͞o′). Also **Mount Godwin Austen** ▸ A peak, 8,616.3 m (28,250 ft), in the Karakoram Range of N Kashmir.

kab·ba·lah or **ca·ba·la** (kăb′ə-lə, kə-bä′lə) ▸ *n.* 1. often **Kabbalah** A body of mystical teachings of rabbinical origin, often based on an esoteric interpretation of the Hebrew Scriptures. 2. A secret or esoteric doctrine. **—kab′ba·lism** *n.* **—kab′ba·list** *n.* **—kab′ba·list′ic** *adj.*

ka·bob (kə-bŏb′) ▸ *n.* Var. of **kebab**.

ka·bu·ki (kə-bo͞o′kē) ▸ *n.* A type of popular Japanese drama in which elaborately costumed performers use stylized movements, dances, and songs.

Ka·bul (kä′bo͝ol, kə-bo͝ol′) ▸ The capital of Afghanistan, in the E part.

Kad·dish (kä′dĭsh) ▸ *n. Judaism* A prayer recited in the daily synagogue services and by mourners after the death of a close relative.

Kaf·ka (käf′kə, -kä), **Franz** (1883–1924) ▸ Austrian writer. **—Kaf′ka·esque′** *adj.*

kaf·tan (kăf′tăn′, -tən, kăf-tăn′) ▸ *n.* Var. of **caftan**.

Kai·ser (kī′zər) ▸ *n.* Any of the emperors of the Holy Roman Empire (962–1806), of Austria (1806–1918), or of Germany (1871–1918).

kale (kāl) ▸ *n.* A variety of cabbage having spreading crinkled leaves that do not form a compact head.

ka·lei·do·scope (kə-lī′də-skōp′) ▸ *n.* 1. A tube-shaped optical instrument that is rotated to produce a succession of symmetrical designs by means of mirrors reflecting the constantly changing patterns made by bits of colored objects at one end of the tube. 2. A constantly changing set of colors. 3. A series of changing phases or events. **—ka·lei′do·scop′ic** (-skŏp′ĭk) *adj.* **—ka·lei′do·scop′i·cal·ly** *adv.*

Kam·chat·ka (kăm-chăt′kə) ▸ A peninsula of E Russia between the Sea of Okhotsk and the Bering Sea.

Ka·me·ha·me·ha I (kə-mā′ə-mā′ə) (1758–1819) ▸ King of the Hawaiian Is. (1795–1819).

ka·mi·ka·ze (kä′mĭ-kä′zē) ▸ *n.* 1. A Japanese pilot trained in World War II to make a suicidal crash attack. 2. An airplane loaded with explosives for such an attack.

ka·na (kä′nə) ▸ *n., pl.* **kana** or **-nas**. Japanese syllabic writing.

kan·ga·roo (kăng′gə-ro͞o′) ▸ *n., pl.* **-roo** or **-roos**. Any of various large Australian marsupials having short forelimbs, large hind limbs adapted for leaping, and a long tapered tail.

kangaroo court ▸ *n.* A court set up in violation of established legal procedure, typically marked by dishonesty or incompetence.

Kan·sas (kăn′zəs) ▸ A state of the central US. Cap. Topeka. **—Kan′san** *adj. & n.*

Kansas City ▸ 1. A city of NE KS on the Missouri R. adjacent to Kansas City, MO. 2. A city of W MO on the Missouri R. WNW of St. Louis.

Kant (kănt, känt), **Immanuel** (1724–1804) ▸ German philosopher. **—Kant′i·an** *adj. & n.*

ka·o·lin also **ka·o·line** (kā′ə-lĭn) ▸ *n.* A fine clay used esp. in ceramics and refractories.

ka·pok (kā′pŏk′) ▸ *n.* A silky fiber obtained from the fruit of the silk-cotton tree and used esp. for padding.

kap·pa (kăp′ə) ▸ *n.* The 10th letter of the Greek alphabet.

ka·put also **ka·putt** (kä-po͝ot′, -po͞ot′, kə-) ▸ *adj. Informal* 1. Destroyed; wrecked. 2. Incapacitated.

Ka·ra·chi (kə-rä′chē) ▸ A city of S Pakistan on the Arabian Sea.

Ka·ra·ko·ram Range (kăr′ə-kôr′əm) ▸ A mountain system of N Pakistan and India and SW China.

kar·a·kul (kăr′ə-kəl) ▸ *n.* 1. Any of a breed of Central Asian sheep having a wide tail and wool that is curled and glossy in the young but wiry and coarse in the adult. 2. Fur made from the pelt of a karakul lamb.

kar·a·o·ke (kâr′ē-ō′kē) ▸ *n.* A music entertainment system providing prerecorded accompaniment to songs that a performer sings live.

kar·at also **car·at** (kăr′ət) ▸ *n.* A unit of measure for the fineness of gold, equal to 1/24 part; for example, gold that is 50 percent pure is 12 karat.

ka·ra·te (kə-rä′tē) ▸ *n.* A Japanese art of self-defense in which sharp blows and kicks are administered to an opponent.

kar·ma (kär′mə) ▸ *n.* 1. *Hinduism & Buddhism* The effect of a person's actions during the successive phases of the person's existence, regarded as determining the person's destiny. 2. Fate; destiny. 3. *Informal* A distinctive aura or feeling. **—kar′mic** (-mĭk) *adj.*

karst (kärst) ▸ *n.* A limestone region marked by fissures, sinkholes, underground streams, and caverns.

kar·y·o·type (kăr′ē-ə-tīp′) ▸ *n.* The characterization of the chromosomal complement of an individual or a species according to the number, form, and size of the chromosomes.

Kash·mir (kăsh′mîr′, kăsh-mîr′) ▸ A historical region of NW India and NE Pakistan. **—Kash·mir′i** *adj. & n.*

ka·ta·ka·na (kä′tä-kä′nä) ▸ *n.* An angular kana used for writing foreign words or official documents.

Kath·man·du also **Kat·man·du** (kăt′măn-do͞o′) ▸ The capital of Nepal, in the central part of the country in the E Himalayas.

ka·ty·did (kā′tē-dĭd′) ▸ *n.* A green insect related to the grasshopper, the male of which produces a shrill sound.

Kau·ai (kou′ī′) ▸ An island of HI NW of Oahu.

ka·va (kä′və) ▸ *n.* 1. A shrub native to the Pacific islands. 2. A narcotic beverage made from the roots of this plant.

kay·ak (kī′ăk′) ▸ *n.* 1. A watertight Inuit or Eskimo canoe covered with skins except for a single or double opening in the center. 2. A similar lightweight canoe. **—kay′ak′** *v.* **—kay′ak′er** *n.*

kay·o (kā-ō′, kā′ō′) ▸ *n., pl.* **-os**. A knockout in boxing. **—kay′o** *v.*

Ka·zakh (kä′zäk′, kə-zäk′) ▸ *n., pl.* **-zakh** or **-zakhs**. 1. A member of a Turkic people living in Kazakhstan and NW China. 2. The language of this people.

Ka·zakh·stan (kä′zäk-stän′, kə-zäk′-) ▸ A country S of Russia and NE of the Caspian Sea.

ka·zoo (kə-zo͞o′) ▸ *n., pl.* **-zoos**. A toy musical instrument in which a paper membrane is vibrated by the performer's voice.

kcal ▸ *abbr.* kilocalorie

Keats (kēts), **John** (1795–1821) ▸ British poet. **—Keats′i·an** *adj.*

ke·bab or **ke·bob** also **ka·bob** (kə-bŏb′) ▸ *n.* Shish kebab.

kedge (kĕj) ▸ *n.* A light anchor used for warping a vessel. ▸ *v.* **kedged, kedg·ing.** To move (a vessel) with a kedge.

keel (kēl) ▸ *n.* 1a. The principal structural member of a

THESAURUS

kaleidoscopic *adj.* —*See* CHANGEABLE (1).

kaput *adj.* —*See* THROUGH (2).

katzenjammer *n.* Unpleasant physical and mental effects following overindulgence in alcohol ▸ crapulence, hangover. *Informal:* head. —*See also* VOCIFERATION.

keel *v.* —*See* LURCH (1).

ship, running lengthwise along the center line from bow to stern, to which the frames are attached. **b.** A corresponding structure on an aircraft. **2.** The breastbone of a bird. **3.** A pair of united petals in certain flowers, as those of the pea. ▸ *v.* To capsize. ***—phrasal verb:* keel over** To collapse or fall, as from death or fainting.

keel·boat (kēl′bōt′) ▸ *n.* A riverboat with a keel, used for carrying freight.

keel·haul (kēl′hôl′) ▸ *v.* To punish by dragging under the keel of a ship.

keen[1] (kēn) ▸ *adj.* **-er, -est. 1.** Having a fine sharp edge or point. **2.** Intellectually acute. **3.** Acutely sensitive: *a keen ear.* **4.** Sharp; vivid. **5.** Intense; piercing: *a keen wind.* **6.** Pungent; acrid. **7a.** Ardent; enthusiastic. **b.** Eagerly desirous: *keen on going.* **8.** *Slang* Great; splendid. **—keen′ly** *adv.* **—keen′ness** *n.*

keen[2] (kēn) ▸ *n.* A loud wailing lament for the dead. **—keen** *v.* **—keen′er** *n.*

keep (kēp) ▸ *v.* **kept** (kĕpt), **keep·ing. 1.** To retain possession of. **2.** To provide (e.g., a family) with maintenance and support. **3.** To put customarily; store. **4.** To raise: *keep chickens.* **5.** To maintain: *keep a diary.* **6.** To manage or have charge of. **7.** To remain fresh or unspoiled. **8.** To continue or cause to continue in a state or condition. **9a.** To detain: *was kept after school.* **b.** To prevent: *kept them from entering.* **10.** To refrain from divulging: *keep a secret.* **11.** To save; reserve. **12.** To adhere to: *keep one's word.* **13.** To celebrate; observe. **14.** To continue: *keep talking.* ***—phrasal verbs:* keep down** To prevent from accomplishing or succeeding. **keep up 1.** To maintain in good condition. **2.** To persevere in. **3.** To continue at the same level or pace. ▸ *n.* **1.** Care; charge. **2.** A means of support: *earn one's keep.* **3a.** The stronghold of a castle. **b.** A jail. ***—idiom:* for keeps 1.** For an indefinitely long period. **2.** Permanently: *We're separating for keeps.* **—keep′er** *n.*

keep·sake (kēp′sāk′) ▸ *n.* Something given or kept as a reminder; memento.

keg (kĕg) ▸ *n.* A small barrel.

Kel·ler (kĕl′ər), **Helen Adams** (1880–1968) ▸ Amer. memoirist and lecturer.

kelp (kĕlp) ▸ *n.* Any of various brown, often large seaweeds.

kel·vin (kĕl′vĭn) ▸ *n.* A unit of the absolute temperature scale, the zero point of which equals – 273.16°C.

Kelvin, 1st Baron (1824–1907) ▸ British physicist.

ken (kĕn) ▸ *n.* **1.** Perception; understanding. **2.** Range of vision; view. ▸ *v.* **kenned** or **kent** (kĕnt), **ken·ning** *Scots.* To know.

Ken·ne·dy (kĕn′ĭ-dē), **Cape** ▸ See **Canaveral.**

Kennedy, John Fitzgerald (1917–63) ▸ The 35th US President (1961–63); assassinated.

ken·nel (kĕn′əl) ▸ *n.* **1.** A shelter for a dog. **2.** An establishment where dogs are bred, trained, or boarded. **—ken′nel** *v.*

ken·te (kĕn′tā) ▸ *n.* **1.** A brightly patterned, hand-woven ceremonial cloth of the Ashanti. **2.** A fabric resembling this cloth.

Ken·tuck·y (kən-tŭk′ē) ▸ A state of the E-central US. Cap. Frankfort. **—Ken·tuck′i·an** *adj. & n.*

Ken·ya (kĕn′yə, kēn′-) ▸ A country of E-central Africa bordering on the Indian Ocean. **—Ken′yan** *adj. & n.*

Kenya, Mount ▸ An extinct volcano, 5,202.7 m (17,058 ft), in central Kenya.

ke·pi (kā′pē, kĕp′ē) ▸ *n., pl.* **-pis.** A French military cap with a flat circular top and a visor.

Kep·ler (kĕp′lər), **Johannes** (1571–1630) ▸ German astronomer and mathematician.

kept (kĕpt) ▸ *v.* P.t. and p.part. of **keep.**

ker·a·tin (kĕr′ə-tĭn) ▸ *n.* A tough insoluble protein that is the chief constituent of hair, nails, horns, and hoofs. **—ke·rat′i·nous** (kə-răt′n-əs) *adj.*

kerb (kûrb) ▸ *n. Chiefly Brit.* Var. of **curb 1.**

ker·chief (kûr′chĭf, -chēf′) ▸ *n., pl.* **-chiefs** also **-chieves** (-chĭvz, -chēvz). **1.** A woman's square scarf, often worn as a head covering. **2.** A handkerchief.

kerf (kûrf) ▸ *n.* A groove or notch made by a cutting tool, such as a saw.

ker·nel (kûr′nəl) ▸ *n.* **1.** A grain or seed, as of a cereal grass. **2.** The inner, usu. edible seed of a nut or fruit stone. **3.** The central part; core.

ker·o·sene (kĕr′ə-sēn′, kĕr′ə-sēn′) ▸ *n.* A thin oil distilled from petroleum or shale oil, used as a fuel and as a denaturant for alcohol.

Ker·ou·ac (kĕr′o͞o-ăk′), **Jack** (1922–69) ▸ Amer. writer.

kes·trel (kĕs′trəl) ▸ *n.* Any of various small falcons noted for their habit of hovering.

ketch (kĕch) ▸ *n.* A two-masted fore-and-aft-rigged sailing vessel with a smaller mast aft of the mainmast but forward of the rudder.

ketch·up (kĕch′əp, kăch′-) also **catch·up** (kăch′əp, kĕch′-) or **cat·sup** (kăt′səp, kăch′əp, kĕch′-) ▸ *n.* A thick, smooth, spicy sauce usu. made from tomatoes.

ke·tone (kē′tōn′) ▸ *n.* Any of a class of organic compounds having the group –OH– linked to two hydrocarbon radicals.

ket·tle (kĕt′l) ▸ *n.* A metal pot or container for boiling or stewing.

ket·tle·drum (kĕt′l-drŭm′) ▸ *n.* A large copper or brass drum with a parchment head that can be tuned by adjusting the tension.

key[1] (kē) ▸ *n., pl.* **keys. 1a.** A notched, usu. metal implement that is turned to open or close a lock. **b.** A similar device used for opening or winding. **2.** A means of access, control, or possession. **3a.** A crucial element. **b.** A set of answers to a test. **c.** A table, gloss, or cipher for decoding or explaining. **4.** A device, such as a pin, inserted to lock together mechanical or structural parts. **5a.** A button or lever that is pressed to operate a machine. **b.** A button that is depressed to cause a character or function to be typed or executed by a typewriter or to be accepted as input by a computer. **c.** *Mus.* A button or lever that is pressed to produce or modulate the sound of an instru-

THESAURUS

keel over *v.* To suffer temporary lack of consciousness ▸ black out, faint, pass out, swoon. *Idioms:* drop (*or* faint *or* fall) dead away, see stars. [*Compare* COLLAPSE.] *—See also* FALL (2).

keen[1] *adj.* *—See* CLEVER (1), CRITICAL (2), EAGER, ENTHUSIASTIC, MARVELOUS, POINTED, SHARP (1).

keen[2] *v.* *—See* CRY.

keenness *n.* *—See* DISCERNMENT, EDGE.

keep *v.* **1.** To have for sale ▸ carry, deal (in), offer, stock. [*Compare* SELL.] **2.** To supply with the necessities of life ▸ maintain, provide for, support. *Idioms:* put a roof over someone's head, put food on the table, take care of. [*Compare* NOURISH.] **3.** To have or put in a customary place ▸ cache, put, store. **4.** To remain fresh and unspoiled ▸ last. **5.** To persevere in some condition, action, or belief ▸ keep to, maintain, retain, stay with, stick to, stick with, sustain. **6.** To mark a day or an event with ceremonies of respect, festivity, or rejoicing ▸ celebrate, commemorate, observe, solemnize. [*Compare* SANCTIFY.] *—See also* DELAY (1), ENDURE (2), FOLLOW (4), FULFILL, HOLD (1), REFRAIN, RESTRAIN, SAVE (1).

keep back *v.* *—See* HOLD (1), REPRESS, RESTRAIN.

keep off *v.* *—See* REPEL.

keep on *v.* *—See* ENDURE (1).

keep out *v.* *—See* EXCLUDE.

keep up *v.* To keep in a condition of good repair, efficiency, or use ▸ maintain, preserve, sustain.

keep *n.* *—See* JAIL, LIVING.

keeper *n.* One who is legally responsible for the care and management of the person or property of an incompetent or a minor ▸ caretaker, conservator, custodian, guardian. [*Compare* REPRESENTATIVE.]

keeping *n.* *—See* AGREEMENT (2), CARE (2), CELEBRATION (2).

keepsake *n.* *—See* REMEMBRANCE (1).

keg *n.* *—See* VAT.

ken *n.* The extent of one's perception, understanding, knowledge, or vision ▸ horizon, purview, range, reach, scope. [*Compare* AWARENESS, AREA.]

kennel *n.* *—See* CAGE, FLOCK.

kernel *n.* A fertilized plant ovule capable of germinating ▸ grain, pip, pit, seed. *—See also* GERM (2), HEART (1).

key *n.* A means or method of entering into or achieving something desirable

ment. **6.** *Mus.* A tonal system consisting of seven tones in fixed relationship to a tonic; tonality. **7.** The pitch of a voice or other sound. **8.** A characteristic tone or level of intensity. ▸ *adj.* Of crucial importance; significant. ▸ *v.* **1.** *Mus.* To regulate the pitch of. **2.** To bring into harmony; adjust or adapt. **3.** To supply an explanatory key for. **4a.** To operate (a device) by means of a keyboard. **b.** To enter (data) into a computer by means of a keyboard. ***—phrasal verb:* key up** To make intense, excited, or nervous.

key[2] (kē) ▸ *n., pl.* **keys.** A low offshore island or reef; cay.

Key, Francis Scott (1779–1843) ▸ Amer. lawyer and poet.

key·board (kē′bôrd′) ▸ *n.* **1.** A set of keys, as on a computer terminal or piano. **2.** *Mus.* Any of various, often electronic instruments played by means of a set of piano-like keys. ▸ *v. Comp. Sci.* To enter (text or data) by means of a keyboard. **—key′board′er** *n.*

key·card (kē′kärd′) ▸ *n.* A plastic card with a magnetically coded strip that is scanned to operate a mechanism such as an automated teller machine.

key·hole (kē′hōl′) ▸ *n.* The hole in a lock into which a key fits.

Key Largo ▸ A narrow island off S FL, the largest of the Florida Keys.

key·note (kē′nōt′) ▸ *n.* **1.** The tonic of a musical key. **2.** A prime element or theme.

keynote address ▸ *n.* An opening address, as at a political convention.

key·pad (kē′păd′) ▸ *n.* A computer input device consisting of a set of number and function keys.

key·punch (kē′pŭnch′) ▸ *n.* A keyboard machine used to punch holes in cards or tapes for data-processing systems. ▸ *v.* To process on a keypunch. **—key′punch′er** *n.*

key signature ▸ *n. Mus.* The group of sharps or flats placed to the right of the clef on a staff to identify the key.

key·stone (kē′stōn′) ▸ *n.* **1.** The central wedge-shaped stone of an arch that locks its parts together. **2.** A basic or fundamental element.

key·stroke (kē′strōk′) ▸ *n.* A stroke of a key, as on a computer keyboard.

Key West ▸ A city of extreme S FL on the island of **Key West,** westernmost of the Florida Keys in the Gulf of Mexico.

kg ▸ *abbr.* kilogram

KGB (kā′jē-bē′) ▸ *n.* The intelligence and internal security agency of the former Soviet Union.

khak·i (kăk′ē, kä′kē) ▸ *n.* **1.** A light yellow brown. **2a.** A sturdy cloth of this color. **b. khakis** A uniform or garment of this cloth. **—khak′i** *adj.*

khan (kän, kăn) ▸ *n.* **1.** A ruler, official, or important person in India and some central Asian countries. **2.** A medieval ruler of a Mongol, Tartar, or Turkish tribe.

Khar·kiv (kär′kôf′) ▸ A city of northeast Ukraine east of Kiev.

Khar·toum (kär-to͞om′) ▸ The capital of Sudan, in the E-central part at the confluence of the Blue Nile and the White Nile.

Khmer (kmâr) ▸ *n., pl.* **Khmer** or **Khmers. 1.** A member of a people of Cambodia. **2.** The official language of Cambodia.

Khoi·san (koi′sän′) ▸ *n.* A family of languages of S Africa.

Kho·mei·ni (kō-mā′nē, KHō-), Ayatollah **Ruholla** (1900–89) ▸ Iranian Shiite leader and head of state (1979–89).

Khru·shchev (kro͞osh′chĕf, -chôf), **Nikita Sergeyevich** (1894–1971) ▸ Soviet politician

Khy·ber Pass (kī′bər) ▸ A narrow pass, about 53 km (33 mi), through mountains on the border between W Afghanistan and N Pakistan.

kib·butz (kĭ-bo͝ots′, -bo͞ots′) ▸ *n., pl.* **kib·but·zim** (kĭb′o͝ot-sēm′, -o͞ot-). A collective farm or settlement in modern Israel.

kib·itz (kĭb′ĭts) ▸ *v. Informal* **1.** To look on and offer unwanted advice. **2.** To chat. **—kib′itz·er** *n.*

ki·bosh (kī′bŏsh′, kĭ-bŏsh′) ▸ *n. Informal* A checking or restraining element: *put the kibosh on a plan.*

kick (kĭk) ▸ *v.* **1.** To strike or strike out with the foot. **2.** *Sports* To score or gain ground by kicking a ball. **3.** To recoil, as a gun when fired. **4.** *Informal* To object vigorously; complain or protest. ***—phrasal verbs:* kick around 1.** *Informal* To treat badly; abuse. **2.** To move from place to place. **kick in** *Informal* To contribute (one's share). **kick off 1.** To begin or resume play with a kickoff. **2.** *Informal* To begin; start. **kick out** *Slang* To throw out; eject or expel. ▸ *n.* **1.** A vigorous blow or motion with the foot or feet. **2.** A jolting recoil, as of a gun. **3.** *Slang* A complaint; protest. **4.** *Slang* Power; force. **5.** *Slang* **a.** A feeling of pleasurable stimulation: *got a kick out of the show.* **b. kicks** Fun: *just for kicks.* **6.** *Slang* Temporary, often obsessive interest. **7a.** The act or an instance of kicking a ball. **b.** A kicked ball. **c.** The distance spanned by a kicked ball. ***—idioms:* kick the bucket** *Slang* To die. **kick the habit** *Slang* To free oneself of an addiction.

Kick·a·poo (kĭk′ə-po͞o′) ▸ *n., pl.* **-poo** or **-poos. 1.** A member of a Native American people formerly of S Wisconsin and N Illinois, now chiefly in Kansas and Oklahoma. **2.** Their Algonquian language.

kick·back (kĭk′băk′) ▸ *n.* **1.** A sharp reaction; repercussion. **2.** *Slang* A secret payment to one who has influenced or facilitated a profitable deal.

kick·er (kĭk′ər) ▸ *n.* **1.** One that kicks. **2.** *Informal* A sudden surprising turn of events.

kick·off (kĭk′ôf′, -ŏf′) ▸ *n.* **1.** A place kick in football or soccer with which play is begun. **2.** *Informal* A beginning.

kid (kĭd) ▸ *n.* **1.** A young goat. **2.** Kidskin. **3.** *Informal* A child. ▸ *adj.* **1.** Made of kidskin. **2.** *Informal* Younger than oneself: *my kid brother.* ▸ *v.* **kid·ded, kid·ding. 1.** To mock playfully. **2.** To deceive in fun; fool. **—kid′der** *n.* **—kid′ding·ly** *adv.*

Kidd (kĭd), **William.** "Captain Kidd" (1645?–1701) ▸ British pirate.

kid·nap (kĭd′năp′) ▸ *v.* **-napped, -nap·ping** or **-naped, -nap·ing.** To seize and detain unlawfully and usu. for ransom. **—kid′nap′per, kid′nap′er** *n.*

kid·ney (kĭd′nē) ▸ *n., pl.* **-neys. 1.** Either of a pair of organs in the vertebrate abdominal cavity functioning to maintain proper water balance and to filter the blood of metabolic wastes for excretion. **2.** Kind; sort.

kidney bean ▸ *n.* A bean cultivated in many forms for its edible pods and seeds.

kid·skin (kĭd′skĭn′) ▸ *n.* Soft leather made from the skin of a young goat.

kiel·ba·sa (kĭl-bä′sə, kēl-) ▸ *n.* A spicy smoked Polish sausage.

Ki·ev (kē′ĕf, -ĕv) ▸ The capital of Ukraine, in the N-central part on the Dnieper R.

Ki·ku·yu (kĭ-ko͞o′yo͞o) ▸ *n., pl.* **-yu** or **-yus. 1.** A member of a people of central and S Kenya. **2.** The Bantu language of the Kikuyu.

Kil·i·man·ja·ro (kĭl′ə-mən-jär′ō), **Mount** ▸ The highest mountain in Africa, in NE Tanzania near the Kenya border, rising to 5,895 m (19,340 ft).

THESAURUS

▸ formula, route, secret. *Informal.* ticket. [*Compare* TRICK.] *—See also* ANSWER (2).

key *adj.* *—See* DOMINANT (1), IMPORTANT, PRIMARY (1).

keystone *n.* *—See* BASIS (1).

kibitz *v.* *—See* MEDDLE.

kibitzer *n.* *—See* BUSYBODY.

kick *v.* *—See* BREAK (5), COMPLAIN, OBJECT.

kick around *v.* *—See* DISCUSS.

kick back *v.* *—See* REST[1] (1).

kick in *v.* *—See* CONTRIBUTE (1), DIE.

kick off *v.* *—See* DIE, START (1).

kick out *v.* *—See* EJECT (1).

kick *n.* **1.** *Slang* A stimulating or intoxicating effect ▸ charge, potency. *Informal:* punch, sting, wallop. **2.** *Slang* A temporary concentration of interest ▸ *Slang:* trip. *—See also* COMPLAINT, OBJECTION, THRILL, WRINKLE (2).

kickback *n.* *—See* BRIBE.

kicker *n.* *—See* WRINKLE (2).

kickoff *n.* *—See* BEGINNING.

kicks *n.* *—See* AMUSEMENT.

kid *n.* *—See* CHILD (1), TEENAGER.

kid *v.* *—See* JOKE (2).

kidlike *n.* *—See* BABYISH.

kidnap *v.* To seize and detain a person unlawfully ▸ abduct, snatch, spirit away, take hostage. [*Compare* SEIZE, STEAL.]

kids *n.* *Informal* Young people collectively ▸ young, youth.

kill[1] (kĭl) ▸ *v.* **1a.** To put to death. **b.** To deprive of life. **2a.** To put an end to; extinguish. **b.** To veto: *kill a congressional bill.* **3.** To cause to cease operating: *killed the motor.* **4.** To use up: *kill time.* **5.** To cause extreme discomfort to: *My shoes are killing me.* **6.** To delete. **7.** *Informal* To overwhelm, esp. with hilarity. ***—phrasal verb:*** **kill off** To destroy in such large numbers as to render extinct. ▸ *n.* **1.** The act of killing. **2.** One that is killed, as an animal in hunting. **3.** An enemy aircraft, vessel, or missile that has been destroyed. **—kill′er** *n.*

kill[2] (kĭl) ▸ *n. Regional* A creek.

kill·deer (kĭl′dîr′) ▸ *n., pl.* **-deer** or **-deers.** A New World plover having a distinctive noisy cry.

killer whale ▸ *n.* A black and white predatory whale feeding esp. on large fish and squid.

kill·ing (kĭl′ĭng) ▸ *n.* **1.** Murder; homicide. **2.** A large profit. ▸ *adj.* **1.** Fatal. **2.** Thoroughly exhausting. **3.** *Informal* Hilarious.

kill·joy (kĭl′joi′) ▸ *n.* One who spoils the enthusiasm or fun of others.

kiln (kĭln, kĭl) ▸ *n.* An oven for hardening, firing, or drying.

ki·lo (kē′lō) ▸ *n., pl.* **-los.** A kilogram.

kilo– ▸ *pref.* One thousand (10^3): *kilowatt.*

kil·o·byte (kĭl′ə-bīt′) ▸ *n.* A unit of computer memory equal to 1,024 (2^{10}) bytes.

kil·o·cal·o·rie (kĭl′ə-kăl′ə-rē) ▸ *n.* See **calorie** 2a.

kil·o·cy·cle (kĭl′ə-sī′kəl) ▸ *n.* Kilohertz.

kil·o·gram (kĭl′ə-grăm′) ▸ *n.* See **measurement** table in Appendix.

kil·o·hertz (kĭl′ə-hûrts′) ▸ *n.* A unit of frequency equal to 1,000 hertz.

kil·o·li·ter (kĭl′ə-lē′tər) ▸ *n.* See **measurement** table in Appendix.

kil·o·me·ter (kĭ-lŏm′ĭ-tər, kĭl′ə-mē′tər) ▸ *n.* See **measurement** table in Appendix. **—kil′o·met′ric** (kĭl′ə-mĕt′rĭk) *adj.*

kil·o·ton (kĭl′ə-tŭn′) ▸ *n.* **1.** A unit of weight equal to 1,000 tons. **2.** An explosive force equivalent to that of 1,000 metric tons of TNT.

kil·o·watt (kĭl′ə-wŏt′) ▸ *n.* A unit of power equal to 1,000 watts.

kil·o·watt-hour (kĭl′ə-wŏt-our′) ▸ *n.* A unit of electric power equal to the work done by one kilowatt acting for one hour.

kilt (kĭlt) ▸ *n.* A knee-length pleated skirt, usu. of a tartan wool, traditionally worn by men in the Scottish Highlands.

kil·ter (kĭl′tər) ▸ *n.* Good condition; proper form: *out of kilter.*

ki·mo·no (kə-mō′nō) ▸ *n., pl.* **-nos.** **1.** A long, wide-sleeved Japanese robe worn with an obi. **2.** A loose robe worn chiefly by women.

kin (kĭn) ▸ *n.* **1.** *(takes pl. v.)* One's relatives. **2.** A family member. ▸ *adj.* Related; akin.

-kin ▸ *suff.* Little one: *napkin.*

ki·na (kē′nə) ▸ *n., pl.* **-na** or **-nas.** See **currency** table in Appendix.

kind[1] (kīnd) ▸ *adj.* **-er, -est. 1.** Of a generous or warm-hearted nature. **2.** Showing sympathy or understanding. **3.** Humane: *kind to animals.* **—kind′ness** *n.*

kind[2] (kīnd) ▸ *n.* **1.** A group of individuals linked by traits held in common. **2.** A particular variety; a sort. ***—idioms:*** **in kind 1.** With produce or commodities rather than with money. **2.** In the same manner. **kind of** *Informal* Rather; somewhat.

kin·der·gar·ten (kĭn′dər-gär′tn, -dn) ▸ *n.* A class for four- to six-year-old children. **—kin′der·gart′ner, kin′der·gar′ten·er** *n.*

kind·heart·ed (kīnd′här′tĭd) ▸ *adj.* Having or proceeding from a kind heart. **—kind′heart′ed·ly** *adv.* **—kind′heart′ed·ness** *n.*

kin·dle (kĭn′dl) ▸ *v.* **-dled, -dling. 1.** To start (a fire); ignite. **2.** To glow or cause to glow. **3.** To arouse; stir up.

kin·dling (kĭnd′lĭng) ▸ *n.* Easily ignited material, used to start a fire.

kind·ly (kīnd′lē) ▸ *adj.* **-li·er, -li·est.** Of a sympathetic, helpful, or benevolent nature. ▸ *adv.* **1.** In a kind manner. **2.** In an accommodating manner: *Would you kindly close the door?* **—kind′li·ness** *n.*

kin·dred (kĭn′drĭd) ▸ *n.* **1.** A group of related persons. **2.** *(takes pl. v.)* Kinfolk. ▸ *adj.* Being similar or related.

kine (kīn) ▸ *n. Archaic* Pl. of **cow[1]**.

kin·e·mat·ics (kĭn′ə-măt′ĭks) ▸ *n. (takes sing. v.) Phys.* The study of motion without regard to the influence of mass or force. **—kin′e·mat′ic** *adj.* **—kin′e·mat′i·cal·ly** *adv.*

kin·e·scope (kĭn′ĭ-skōp′, kī′nĭ-) ▸ *n.* **1.** See **picture tube**. **2.** A film of a transmitted television program.

ki·net·ic (kə-nĕt′ĭk, kī-) ▸ *adj.* Of or produced by motion. **—ki·net′i·cal·ly** *adv.*

kinetic energy ▸ *n.* The energy possessed by a body because of its motion.

ki·net·ics (kə-nĕt′ĭks, kī-) ▸ *n. (takes sing. v.)* **1.** See **dynamics** 1. **2.** The branch of chemistry concerned with the rates of change of reactants in a chemical reaction.

kin·folk (kĭn′fōk′) also **kins·folk** (kĭnz′-) or **kin·folks** (kĭn′fōks′) ▸ *pl.n.* One's relatives; kindred.

king (kĭng) ▸ *n.* **1.** A male sovereign. **2.** One that is preeminent in a group, category, or sphere. **3a.** A playing card bearing the figure of a king. **b.** The principal chess piece. **c.** A piece in checkers that has been crowned. **4. Kings** *(takes sing. v.)* See **Bible** table in Appendix. **—king′li·ness** *n.* **—king′ly** *adj. & adv.* **—king′ship′** *n.*

King, Martin Luther, Jr. (1929–68) ▸ Amer. cleric and civil rights leader; assassinated. Won 1964 Nobel Peace Prize.

king·bolt (kĭng′bōlt′) ▸ *n.* A vertical bolt that joins the body of a wagon or other vehicle to its front axle and usu. acts as a pivot.

king crab ▸ *n.* A large edible crab of coastal waters of Alaska, Japan, and Siberia.

king·dom (kĭng′dəm) ▸ *n.* **1.** A land ruled by a king or queen. **2.** An area in which one thing is dominant. **3.** One of the three main divisions (animal, vegetable, and mineral) of the natural world. **4.** *Biol.* The highest taxonomic classification into which organisms are grouped,

THESAURUS

kill[1] *v.* To cause the death of ▸ carry off, cut down, cut off, destroy, dispatch, execute, finish (off), slay. *Slang:* hit, ice, rub out, waste, wipe out, zap. *Idioms:* put an end to, put to death, put to sleep, take the life of. [*Compare* MASSACRE.] *—See also* AFFLICT, ANNIHILATE, CENSOR (2), IDLE (2), MURDER.

kill *n.* A loss of life, or one who has lost life, usually as a result of accident, disaster, or war ▸ casualty, death, fatality, loss. [*Compare* VICTIM.]

kill[2] *n. —See* BROOK[1].

killer *n. —See* MURDERER.

killing *n. —See* MURDER.

killing *adj. —See* FUNNY (1).

killjoy *n.* One who spoils the enthusiasm or fun of others ▸ frump, spoilsport. *Informal:* stick-in-the-mud, wet blanket. *Slang:* bummer, downer, party pooper, pill. *Idiom:* dog in the manger. [*Compare* GROUCH, SQUARE.]

kilter *n. —See* SHAPE.

kin *n.* One's relatives collectively ▸ family, folks, kindred, kinfolk, kith and kin, people. [*Compare* RELATIVE.]

kin *adj. —See* KINDRED, LIKE[2].

kind[1] *adj. —See* BENEVOLENT (1).

kind[2] *n.* A class that is defined by the common attribute or attributes possessed by all its members ▸ brand, breed, cast, denomination, description, feather, form, genus, ilk, lot, manner, mold, nature, order, persuasion, sort, species, stamp, stripe, type, variety. [*Compare* CLASS.]

kindhearted *adj. —See* BENEVOLENT (1).

kindheartedness *n. —See* BENEVOLENCE.

kindle *v. —See* AROUSE, CLEAR (1), FIRE (1), LIGHT[1] (1).

kindliness *n. —See* BENEVOLENCE, FAVOR (1).

kindly *adj. —See* BENEVOLENT (1), GENTLE (1).

kindness *n. —See* AMIABILITY, BENEVOLENCE, CONSIDERATION (1), FAVOR (1).

kind office *n. —See* FAVOR (1).

kindred *n. —See* FAMILY (2), KIN.

kindred *adj.* Connected by or as if by kinship or common origin ▸ agnate, akin, allied, cognate, connate, connatural, consanguine, consanguineous, kin, related. [*Compare* ANCESTRAL.]

kinetic *adj. —See* ENERGETIC.

kinfolk or **kinfolks** *n. —See* KIN.

king *n. —See* CHIEF.

based on fundamental similarities and common ancestry.

king·fish·er (kĭng′fĭsh′ər) ▸ *n.* Any of a family of crested, large-billed birds that feed on fish.

King James Bible ▸ *n.* An English translation of the Bible published in 1611.

king·pin (kĭng′pĭn′) ▸ *n.* **1.** The foremost or central pin in bowling. **2.** The most important person or element. **3.** See **kingbolt.**

King's English (kĭngz) ▸ *n.* English speech or usage that is deemed standard or accepted.

king-size (kĭng′sīz′) or **king-sized** (-sīzd′) ▸ *adj.* **1.** Larger or longer than the usual size. **2.** Very large.

kink (kĭngk) ▸ *n.* **1.** A tight curl or twist in a length of thin material. **2.** A muscle cramp. **3.** A difficulty that is likely to impede operation. **4.** A mental peculiarity; quirk. ▸ *v.* To form a kink (in).

kink·a·jou (kĭng′kə-jo͞o′) ▸ *n.* A furry long-tailed arboreal mammal of tropical America.

kink·y (kĭng′kē) ▸ *adj.* **-i·er, -i·est. 1.** Tightly twisted or curled. **2.** *Slang* Of or relating to eccentric sexual practices. **—kink′i·ness** *n.*

kins·folk (kĭnz′fōk′) ▸ *pl.n.* Var. of **kinfolk.**

kin·ship (kĭn′shĭp′) ▸ *n.* **1.** Connection by blood, marriage, or adoption; family relationship. **2.** Likeness; affinity.

kins·man (kĭnz′mən) ▸ *n.* A male relative.

kins·wom·an (kĭnz′wo͝om′ən) ▸ *n.* A female relative.

ki·osk (kē′ŏsk′, kē-ŏsk′) ▸ *n.* A small, usu. freestanding structure used as a newsstand or booth.

Ki·o·wa (kī′ə-wô′, -wä′, -wā′) ▸ *n., pl.* **-wa** or **-was. 1.** A member of a Native American people formerly inhabiting the S Great Plains, now chiefly in SW Oklahoma. **2.** The Tanoan language of the Kiowa.

Kiowa Apache ▸ *n.* A member of an Athabaskan-speaking Native American people closely associated with the Kiowa.

kip (kĭp) ▸ *n., pl.* **kip.** See **currency** table in Appendix.

kip·per (kĭp′ər) ▸ *n.* A split, salted, and smoked herring or salmon. **—kip′per** *v.*

Kir·ghiz (kîr-gēz′) ▸ *n.* Var. of **Kyrgyz.**

Ki·ri·ba·ti (kēr′ə-bä′tē, kîr′ə-băs′) ▸ An island country of the W-central Pacific near the equator.

kir·i·ga·mi (kĭr′ĭ-gä′mē) ▸ *n.* The Japanese art of cutting and folding paper into ornamental objects or designs.

kirk (kûrk) ▸ *n. Scots* A church.

kirsch (kîrsh) ▸ *n.* A cherry brandy.

Kis·lev (kĭs′ləv, kēs-lĕv′) ▸ *n.* A month of the Jewish calendar.

kis·met (kĭz′mĕt′, -mĭt) ▸ *n.* Fate; fortune.

kiss (kĭs) ▸ *v.* **1.** To touch or caress with the lips, as in affection or greeting. **2.** To touch lightly or gently. ▸ *n.* **1.** A caress or touch with the lips. **2.** A slight touch. **3.** A small piece of candy, esp. of chocolate.

kiss·er (kĭs′ər) ▸ *n.* **1.** One that kisses. **2.** *Slang* The mouth. **3.** *Slang* The face.

kit (kĭt) ▸ *n.* **1a.** A set of articles or implements: *a shaving kit.* **b.** A container for such a set. **2.** A set of parts to be assembled: *a model airplane kit.* **3.** A packaged set of related materials: *a sales kit.* ***—idiom:*** **the (whole) kit and caboodle** The entire collection or lot.

kitch·en (kĭch′ən) ▸ *n.* **1.** A room or area for preparing and cooking food. **2.** A staff that prepares, cooks, and serves food.

kitch·en·ette (kĭch′ə-nĕt′) ▸ *n.* A small kitchen.

kitchen police ▸ *n.* **1.** Enlisted military personnel assigned to work in a kitchen. **2.** Military duty assisting cooks.

kitch·en·ware (kĭch′ən-wâr′) ▸ *n.* Utensils for use in a kitchen.

kite (kīt) ▸ *n.* **1.** A light framework covered with cloth, plastic, or paper, designed to be flown in the wind at the end of a long string. **2.** Any of various predatory birds having a long, often forked tail and long pointed wings.

kith and kin (kĭth) ▸ *pl.n.* One's acquaintances and relatives.

kitsch (kĭch) ▸ *n.* Art or artwork marked by sentimental, often pretentious bad taste. **—kitsch′y** *adj.*

kit·ten (kĭt′n) ▸ *n.* A young cat.

kit·ten·ish (kĭt′n-ĭsh) ▸ *adj.* Playfully coy and frisky. **—kit′ten·ish·ly** *adv.*

kit·ty[1] (kĭt′ē) ▸ *n., pl.* **-ties.** A pool of money, esp. one to which a number of people have contributed.

kit·ty[2] (kĭt′ē) ▸ *n., pl.* **-ties.** A cat or kitten.

Kitty Hawk ▸ A village of NE NC, site of the Wright brothers' first two successful flights (December 17, 1903).

ki·va (kē′və) ▸ *n.* A usu. underground ceremonial chamber in a Pueblo village.

ki·wi (kē′wē) ▸ *n., pl.* **-wis. 1.** A flightless New Zealand bird having vestigial wings and a long slender bill. **2a.** A woody Chinese vine having fuzzy fruit with an edible pulp. **b.** The fruit of this plant.

Klam·ath (klăm′əth) ▸ *n., pl.* **-ath** or **-aths. 1.** A member of a Native American people of S-central Oregon and N California. **2.** The Penutian language of the Klamath.

Kleen·ex (klē′nĕks′) ▸ A trademark for a soft facial tissue.

klep·to·ma·ni·a (klĕp′tə-mā′nē-ə, -mān′yə) ▸ *n.* An obsessive impulse to steal regardless of economic need. **—klep′to·ma′ni·ac′** *n.*

klieg light (klēg) ▸ *n.* A powerful lamp used esp. in making movies.

klutz (klŭts) ▸ *n. Slang* A clumsy or inept person. **—klutz′i·ness** *n.* **—klutz′y** *adj.*

km ▸ *abbr.* kilometer

kmph ▸ *abbr.* kilometers per hour

knack (năk) ▸ *n.* **1.** A clever, expedient way of doing something. **2.** A specific talent for something.

knack·wurst or **knock·wurst** (nŏk′wûrst′, -wo͝orst′) ▸ *n.* A short, thick, highly seasoned sausage.

knap·sack (năp′săk′) ▸ *n.* A sturdy bag with shoulder straps for carrying articles on the back.

knave (nāv) ▸ *n.* **1.** An unprincipled, crafty fellow. **2.** See **jack 2. —knav′er·y** *n.* **—knav′ish** *adj.* **—knav′ish·ly** *adv.* **—knav′ish·ness** *n.*

knead (nēd) ▸ *v.* **1.** To mix and work into a uniform mass, esp. with the hands: *kneading dough.* **2.** To massage.

knee (nē) ▸ *n.* The joint between the thigh and the lower leg. ▸ *v.* **kneed, knee·ing.** To strike with the knee.

knee·cap (nē′kăp′) ▸ *n.* See **patella.**

kneel (nēl) ▸ *v.* **knelt** (nĕlt) or **kneeled, kneel·ing.** To go down or rest on one or both knees.

knell (nĕl) ▸ *v.* **1.** To ring slowly and solemnly, esp. for a funeral; toll. **2.** To signal or proclaim by or as if by tolling. ▸ *n.* **1.** A solemn or mournful toll. **2.** A signal of disaster or destruction.

knew (no͞o, nyo͞o) ▸ *v.* P.t. of **know.**

knick·ers (nĭk′ərz) ▸ *pl.n.* **1.** Full breeches gathered and banded just below the knee. **2.** *Chiefly Brit.* Panties.

knick·knack (nĭk′năk′) ▸ *n.* A small ornamental article; trinket.

THESAURUS

kink *n.* —*See* CURL.

kink *v.* —*See* BEND (3).

kinsman or **kinswoman** *n.* **1.** A person connected to another person by blood or marriage ▸ relation, relative. [*Compare* ANCESTRY, FAMILY, KIN.] **2.** A person who is from one's own country ▸ compatriot, countryman, countrywoman, fellow citizen, kinswoman.

kismet *n.* —*See* FATE (1).

kiss *v.* To touch or caress with the lips, especially as a sign of passion or affection ▸ buss, osculate, smack. *Informal:* peck. *Slang:* lock lips, make out, smooch, suck face, swap spit. [*Compare* NECK.] —*See also* BRUSH[1].

kiss *n.* The act or an instance of kissing ▸ buss, osculation, smack, smacker. *Informal:* peck. *Slang:* smooch. —*See also* BRUSH[1].

kisser *n.* —*See* FACE (1), MOUTH (1).

kit *n.* —*See* PACK (1), SUITCASE.

kith and kin *n.* —*See* KIN.

kitty *n.* —*See* BET.

klutz *n.* —*See* BLUNDERER, OAF.

klutzy *adj.* —*See* AWKWARD (1).

knack *n.* The proper method for doing, using, or handling something ▸ feel, trick. *Informal:* hang. —*See also* ABILITY (1), TALENT.

knapsack *n.* —*See* PACK (1).

knave *n.* —*See* CHEAT (2).

knead *v.* To handle in a way so as to mix, form, and shape ▸ manipulate, squeeze, work. —*See also* RUB.

kneel *v.* —*See* BOW[1] (1).

knee-slapper *n.* —*See* JOKE (1).

knell *v.* —*See* RING[2].

knickknack *n.* —*See* NOVELTY (3).

knife (nīf) ▸ *n., pl.* **knives** (nīvz). **1.** A cutting instrument consisting of a sharp blade attached to a handle. **2.** A cutting edge; blade. ▸ *v.* **knifed, knif·ing. 1.** To use a knife on, esp. to stab. **2.** *Informal* To betray. ***—idiom:*** **under the knife** *Informal* Undergoing surgery.

knight (nīt) ▸ *n.* **1a.** A medieval gentleman-soldier. **b.** A man holding a nonhereditary title conferred by a sovereign. **2.** A member of certain fraternal orders. **3.** A noble defender or champion. **4.** A chess piece, usu. in the shape of a horse's head. ▸ *v.* To raise (a person) to knighthood. **—knight′ly** *adj.*

knight-errant (nīt′ĕr′ənt) ▸ *n., pl.* **knights-errant** (nīts′-). A knight who wanders in search of adventures to prove his chivalry.

knight·hood (nīt′ho͝od′) ▸ *n.* **1.** The rank or vocation of a knight. **2.** Knights collectively.

knish (kə-nĭsh′) ▸ *n.* A piece of dough stuffed with potato, meat, or cheese and baked or fried.

knit (nĭt) ▸ *v.* **knit** or **knit·ted, knit·ting. 1.** To make (a fabric or garment) by intertwining yarn or thread in a series of connected loops. **2.** To join closely. **3.** To draw (the brows) together in wrinkles; furrow. ▸ *n.* A fabric or garment made by knitting. **—knit′ter** *n.*

knob (nŏb) ▸ *n.* **1.** A rounded protuberance. **2a.** A rounded handle. **b.** A rounded control switch or dial. **—knobbed** *adj.* **—knob′by** *adj.*

knock (nŏk) ▸ *v.* **1.** To strike with a hard or sharp blow. **2.** To collide or cause to collide. **3.** To produce by hitting: *knocked a hole in the wall.* **4.** *Slang* To disparage; criticize. **5.** To make the rattling noise of a misfiring engine. ***—phrasal verbs:*** **knock around** (or **about**) **1.** To be rough or brutal with. **2.** To wander from place to place. **knock down 1.** To fell; topple. **2.** To disassemble into parts. **3.** To declare sold at an auction. **4.** *Informal* To reduce in price. **knock off 1.** *Informal* To stop an activity; quit. **2.** *Informal* To produce in routine fashion. **3.** *Slang* To kill. **4.** *Slang* To hold up or rob. **knock out 1.** To render unconscious. **2.** To defeat (a boxing opponent) by a knockout. **3.** To render useless. **4.** *Slang* To overwhelm or amaze. ***—idiom:*** **knock dead** *Slang* To affect strongly and positively. **—knock** *n.*

knock·down (nŏk′doun′) ▸ *adj.* **1.** Strong enough to knock down or overwhelm: *a knockdown blow.* **2.** Easily assembled or disassembled: *knockdown furniture.*

knock·er (nŏk′ər) ▸ *n.* A hinged fixture used for knocking on a door.

knock-knee (nŏk′nē′) ▸ *n.* A deformity of the legs in which the knees are abnormally close together. **—knock′-kneed′** *adj.*

knock·out (nŏk′out′) ▸ *n.* **1.** A victory in boxing in which one's opponent is unable to rise from the canvas within a specified time. **2.** *Slang* A strikingly attractive or impressive person or thing.

knock·wurst (nŏk′wûrst′, -wo͝orst′) ▸ *n.* Var. of **knackwurst**.

knoll (nōl) ▸ *n.* A small rounded hill; hillock.

knot (nŏt) ▸ *n.* **1a.** A compact intersection of interlaced material, such as rope. **b.** A fastening made by tying together lengths of material. **2.** A decorative bow. **3.** A unifying bond, esp. a marriage bond. **4.** A tight cluster of persons or things. **5.** A feeling of tightness: *a knot in my stomach.* **6.** A complex problem. **7a.** A hard node on a tree trunk at a point from which a branch grows. **b.** The round, often darker cross section of such a node in cut lumber. **8.** A protuberant growth or swelling in a tissue. **9.** A unit of speed, one nautical mile per hour. ▸ *v.* **knot·ted, knot·ting. 1.** To tie in or fasten with a knot. **2.** To make or become snarled or entangled. **—knot′ti·ness** *n.* **—knot′ty** *adj.*

knot·hole (nŏt′hōl′) ▸ *n.* A hole in a piece of lumber where a knot once was.

know (nō) ▸ *v.* **knew** (no͞o, nyo͞o), **known** (nōn), **know·ing. 1.** To perceive directly with the mind or senses. **2.** To regard as true beyond doubt. **3.** To be capable of or skilled in: *knows how to cook.* **4.** To have learned: *knows her Latin verbs.* **5.** To have experience of. **6a.** To recognize: *I know that face.* **b.** To be acquainted with. **7.** To be able to distinguish: *knows right from wrong.* ***—idiom:*** **in the know** Possessing special or secret information. **—know′a·ble** *adj.* **—know′er** *n.*

know-how (nō′hou′) ▸ *n.* Practical knowledge or skill.

know·ing (nō′ĭng) ▸ *adj.* **1.** Possessing knowledge, information, or understanding. **2.** Clever; shrewd. **3.** Suggestive of private knowledge: *a knowing glance.* **4.** Deliberate; conscious. **—know′ing·ly** *adv.*

knowl·edge (nŏl′ĭj) ▸ *n.* **1.** The state or fact of knowing. **2.** Familiarity, awareness, or understanding gained through experience or study. **3.** The sum or range of what has been perceived, discovered, or learned. **4.** Learning; erudition. **—knowl′edge·a·ble** *adj.* **—knowl′edge·a·bly** *adv.*

knuck·le (nŭk′əl) ▸ *n.* The rounded prominence of a joint, esp. of one of the joints connecting the fingers to the hand. ▸ *v.* **-led, -ling.** To press, rub, or hit with the knuckles. ***—phrasal verbs:*** **knuckle down** To apply oneself earnestly. **knuckle under** To yield to pressure; give in.

knuck·le·bone (nŭk′əl-bōn′) ▸ *n.* A knobbed bone, as of a knuckle or joint.

knurl (nûrl) ▸ *n.* **1.** A knob or knot. **2.** One of a set of small ridges, as on a thumbscrew, to aid in gripping. **—knurled** *adj.* **—knurl′y** *adj.*

KO (kā′ō′) *Slang* ▸ *v.* **KO'd, KO'ing.** To knock out in boxing. ▸ *n.* (kā-ō′, kā′ō′) A knockout in boxing.

ko·a·la (kō-ä′lə) ▸ *n.* A furry, bearlike arboreal Australian marsupial.

Ko·be (kō′bē′, -bā′) ▸ A city of S Honshu, Japan, SSW of Kyoto.

kohl (kōl) ▸ *n.* A cosmetic preparation used to darken the rims of the eyelids.

kohl·ra·bi (kōl-rä′bē, -răb′ē) ▸ *n., pl.* **-bies.** A plant whose thick basal stem is eaten as a vegetable.

THESAURUS

knife *v.* —*See* BETRAY (1), CUT (1).

knifelike *adj.* —*See* SHARP (3).

knightly *adj.* —*See* GALLANT.

knob *n.* —*See* BUMP (1), PROJECTION.

knock *v.* —*See* BANG (1), COLLIDE, CRITICIZE (1), HIT.

knock about or **around** *v.* —*See* BATTER, DISCUSS, MANHANDLE.

knock down *v.* —*See* DESTROY (2), DROP (3).

knock off *v.* To interrupt regular activity for a short period ▸ break, recess. *Idioms:* take a break, take a breather, take five (*or* ten). [*Compare* REST[1].] —*See also* ABANDON (2), COPY, DEDUCT, MURDER, ROB.

knock out *v.* —*See* DISABLE (1), DRUG (1), STAGGER (2), TIRE (1).

knock over *v.* —*See* OVERTURN, STAGGER (2).

knock together *v.* —*See* BUILD.

knock *n.* The sound made by a light blow ▸ rap, rapping, tap, tapping. —*See also* BEAT (1), COLLISION, CRITICISM.

knockabout *adj.* —*See* ROUGH (3).

knocked-out *adj.* —*See* TIRED (1).

knocked-up *adj.* —*See* PREGNANT (1).

knockoff *n.* —*See* COPY (2).

knockout *n.* —*See* BEAUTY, CONQUEST, HIT.

knoll *n.* —*See* HILL.

knot *n.* —*See* BOND (2), BUMP (1), BUMP (2), GROUP, PROJECTION, TANGLE.

knot *v.* To make fast or firmly fixed, as by means of a cord or rope ▸ bind, fasten, secure, tie, tie up. —*See also* COMPLICATE, FASTEN.

knotty *adj.* —*See* COMPLEX (1).

know *v.* **1.** To perceive directly with the intellect ▸ apprehend, compass, comprehend, fathom, grasp. *Idioms:* be sure, be certain. [*Compare* UNDERSTAND.] **2.** To be acquainted with ▸ know of, know about. *Idioms:* be acquainted with, be aware of. **3.** To undergo an emotional reaction ▸ experience, feel, have, savor, taste. **4.** To perceive to be identical with something held in the memory ▸ recognize. —*See also* DISTINGUISH (1), EXPERIENCE, PLACE (1).

knowable *adj.* —*See* UNDERSTANDABLE.

know-how *n.* —*See* ABILITY (1).

knowing *adj.* Possessing deep knowledge and understanding ▸ sagacious, sage, sapient, wise. —*See also* INTELLIGENT, SHREWD.

know-it-all *n.* —*See* SMART ALECK.

knowledge *n.* The sum of what has been perceived, discovered, or inferred ▸ lore, understanding, wisdom. [*Compare* ACTUALITY.] —*See also* EDUCATION (2), INFORMATION.

knowledgeable *adj.* —*See* EDUCATED, INFORMED, INTELLIGENT.

knuckleheaded *adj.* —*See* STUPID.

KO *v.* —*See* DEFEAT.

ko·la (kō′lə) ▸ *n.* Var. of **cola**[3].

Kol·ka·ta (kŭl-kŭt′ə). Formerly **Cal·cut·ta** (kăl-kŭt′ə) ▸ A city of E India on the Hugli R. in the Ganges delta.

kook (ko͝ok) ▸ *n. Slang* An eccentric or crazy person. **—kook′i·ness** *n.* **—kook′y** *adj.*

kook·a·bur·ra (ko͝ok′ə-bûr′ə, -bŭr′ə) ▸ *n.* A large kingfisher of S and E Australia, having a call like raucous laughter.

ko·pek or **ko·peck** (kō′pĕk) ▸ *n.* A coin equal to 1/100 of the Russian ruble.

Ko·ran or **Qur·'an** (kə-răn′, -rän′, kô-, kō-) ▸ *n.* The sacred text of Islam, considered by Muslims to contain the revelations of God to Muhammad. **—Ko·ran′ic** *adj.*

Ko·re·a (kə-rē′ə, kô-, kō-) ▸ A peninsula and former country of E Asia between the Yellow Sea and the Sea of Japan.

Korea Bay ▸ An inlet of the Yellow Sea between NE China and W North Korea.

Ko·re·an (kə-rē′ən, kô-, kō-) ▸ *n.* **1.** A native or inhabitant of Korea. **2.** The language of the Koreans. **—Ko·re′an** *adj.*

ko·ru·na (kôr′ə-nä′) ▸ *n.* See **currency** table in Appendix.

Kos·ci·us·ko (kŏs′ē-ŭs′kō, kŏs′kē-), **Mount** ▸ A peak, 2,231.4 m (7,316 ft), of SW Australia in the Australian Alps; highest point in continent.

ko·sher (kō′shər) ▸ *adj.* **1.** Conforming to or prepared in accordance with Jewish dietary laws. **2.** *Slang* Legitimate; permissible.

Ko·so·vo (kô′sə-vō′, kō′-) ▸ A republic of SE Europe. **—Ko′so·var′** (-vär′) *adj. & n.*

Kow·loon (kou′lo͞on′) ▸ A city of SE China on **Kowloon Peninsula** opposite Hong Kong I.

kow·tow (kou-tou′, kou′tou′) ▸ *v.* **1.** To kneel and touch the forehead to the ground in expression of deep respect, worship, or submission. **2.** To show servile deference. **—kow′tow′** *n.*

Kr ▸ The symbol for the element **krypton**.

kraal (krôl, kräl) ▸ *n. South African* **1.** A rural village. **2.** An enclosure for livestock.

Kra·ka·tau (krăk′ə-tou′, krä′kə-) or **Kra·ka·to·a** (-tō′ə) ▸ A volcanic island of Indonesia between Sumatra and Java.

Kra·ków (krăk′ou, krä′kou, -ko͝of) ▸ A city of S Poland on the Vistula R. SSE of Warsaw.

Krem·lin (krĕm′lĭn) ▸ *n.* **1.** The citadel of Moscow, housing the offices of the Russian and formerly the Soviet government. **2.** The government of Russia and formerly that of the Soviet Union.

Krem·lin·ol·o·gy (krĕm′lə-nŏl′ə-jē) ▸ *n.* The study of the policies of the Soviet or Russian government. **—Krem′lin·ol′o·gist** *n.*

krill (krĭl) ▸ *n., pl.* **krill**. Small marine crustaceans that are the principal food of baleen whales.

Krish·na (krĭsh′nə) ▸ *n. Hinduism* The 8th and principal avatar of Vishnu.

kro·na[1] (krō′nə) ▸ *n., pl.* **kro·nur** (-nər). See **currency** table in Appendix.

kro·na[2] (krō′nə) ▸ *n., pl.* **kro·nor** (-nôr′, -nər). See **currency** table in Appendix.

kro·ne[1] (krō′nə) ▸ *n., pl.* **kro·ner** (-nər). See **currency** table in Appendix.

kro·ne[2] (krō′nə) ▸ *n., pl.* **kro·ner** (-nər). See **currency** table in Appendix.

kroon (krōn) ▸ *n., pl.* **kroon·i** (krō′nē). See **currency** table in Appendix.

kryp·ton (krĭp′tŏn′) ▸ *n. Symbol* **Kr** A whitish, largely inert gaseous element used chiefly in fluorescent lamps. At. no. 36.

Kry·vyy Rih (krĭ-vĭ′ rĭKH′) ▸ A city of S-central Ukraine NE of Odessa.

KS ▸ *abbr.* Kansas

kt. ▸ *abbr.* **1.** karat **2.** *Naut.* knot

Kt. ▸ *abbr.* knight (title)

Kua·la Lum·pur (kwä′lə lo͝om-po͝or′) ▸ The capital of Malaysia, on the SW Malay Peninsula northwest of Singapore.

Ku·blai Khan (ko͞o′blī kän′) also **Ku·bla Khan** (-blə) (1215–94) ▸ Mongol emperor (1260–94) and founder of the Mongol dynasty in China.

ku·dos (ko͞o′dōz′, -dōs′, -dŏs′, kyo͞o′-) ▸ *n.* Acclaim or praise for exceptional achievement.

ku·du (ko͞o′do͞o) ▸ *n., pl.* **-du** or **-dus**. A large striped African antelope with spirally curved horns in the male.

kud·zu (ko͝od′zo͞o) ▸ *n.* A fast-growing vine native to E Asia and grown for fodder, forage, and erosion control.

ku·lak (ko͞o-lăk′, ko͞o′lăk′, -läk′) ▸ *n.* A prosperous landed peasant in czarist Russia.

kum·quat (kŭm′kwŏt′) ▸ *n.* **1.** A tree or shrub bearing small edible orangelike fruit. **2.** The fruit itself.

ku·na (ko͞o′nə) ▸ *n.* See **currency** table in Appendix.

kung fu (kŭng′ fo͞o′, ko͝ong′) ▸ *n.* The Chinese martial arts, esp. those forms similar to karate.

Kurd (kûrd, ko͝ord) ▸ *n.* A member of a people inhabiting the transnational region of Kurdistan.

Kurd·ish (kûr′dĭsh, ko͝or′-) ▸ *n.* The Iranian language of the Kurds. **—Kurd′ish** *adj.*

Kurd·i·stan (kûr′dĭ-stăn′, ko͝or′dĭ-stän′) ▸ An extensive plateau region of SW Asia.

Ku·ril Islands also **Ku·rile Islands** (ko͝or′ĭl, ko͞o-rēl′) ▸ An island chain of extreme E Russia extending about 1,207 km (750 mi) in the Pacific between Kamchatka Peninsula and N Hokkaido, Japan. **—Ku·ril′i·an** *adj.*

Ku·wait (ko͞o-wāt′) ▸ A country of NE Arabia at the head of the Persian Gulf. **—Ku·wait′i** (-wā′tē) *adj. & n.*

kW ▸ *abbr.* kilowatt

kwa·cha (kwä′chə) ▸ *n.* See **currency** table in Appendix.

Kwa·ki·u·tl (kwä′kē-o͞ot′l) ▸ *n., pl.* **-tl** or **-tls**. **1.** A member of a Native American people of coastal British Columbia and Vancouver Island. **2.** Their language.

kwan·za (kwän′zə) ▸ *n., pl.* **kwan·za** or **kwan·zas**. See **currency** table in Appendix.

Kwan·zaa also **Kwan·za** (kwän′zə) ▸ *n.* An African-American cultural festival celebrated from Dec. 26 to Jan. 1.

kwa·shi·or·kor (kwä′shē-ôr′kôr′) ▸ *n.* Severe protein malnutrition, esp. in children, marked by anemia, potbelly, reduced pigmentation, and growth retardation.

kWh ▸ *abbr.* kilowatt-hour

KY or **Ky.** ▸ *abbr.* Kentucky

kyat (chät) ▸ *n.* See **currency** table in Appendix.

Kyo·to (kē-ō′tō, kyō′-) ▸ A city of W-central Honshu, Japan, NNE of Osaka.

Kyr·gyz or **Kir·ghiz** (kîr-gēz′) ▸ *n., pl.* **-gyz** or **-gyz·es** or **-ghiz** or **-ghiz·es**. **1.** A member of a traditionally nomadic people living principally in Kyrgyzstan. **2.** The language of this people.

Kyr·gyz·stan (kîr′gē-stän′) ▸ A country of W-central Asia bordering on NW China.

Kyu·shu (kē-o͞o′sho͞o, kyo͞o′-) ▸ An island of SW Japan on the East China Sea and the Pacific.

Ky·zyl Kum (kĭ-zĭl′ ko͝om′) ▸ A desert of N-central Uzbekistan and S-central Kazakhstan SE of the Aral Sea.

THESAURUS

kook *n.* —*See* CRACKPOT.

kooky *adj.* —*See* ECCENTRIC.

kosher *adj.* —*See* ACCEPTABLE (1), AUTHENTIC (1).

kowtow *v.* —*See* BOW[1] (1), FAWN.
kowtow *n.* —*See* BOW[1].

kudos *n.* —*See* DISTINCTION (2), PRAISE (1).

Kultur *n.* The total product of human creativity and intellect ▸ civilization, culture, society.

kvetch *v.* —*See* COMPLAIN.
kvetch *n.* —*See* COMPLAINT.

L

l[1] or **L** (ĕl) ► *n., pl.* **l's** or **L's** also **ls** or **Ls**. The 12th letter of the English alphabet.
l[2] ► *abbr.* 1. length 2. liter
L[1] also **l** ► The symbol for the Roman numeral 50.
L[2] ► *abbr.* 1. large 2. left
l. ► *abbr.* line
la (lä) ► *n. Mus.* The 6th tone of the diatonic scale.
La ► The symbol for the element **lanthanum**.
LA ► *abbr.* 1. Los Angeles 2. also **La.** Louisiana
lab (lăb) ► *n.* A laboratory.
la·bel (lā′bəl) ► *n.* 1. Something, such as a small piece of paper or cloth, attached to an article to identify its owner, contents, or destination. 2. A descriptive term; epithet. ► *v.* **-beled, -bel·ing** or **-belled, -bel·ling**. 1. To attach a label to. 2. To identify or classify. **—la′bel·er, la′bel·ler** *n.*
la·bi·al (lā′bē-əl) ► *adj.* 1. Of the lips or labia. 2. *Ling.* Articulated mainly with the lips, as (b), (m), or (w). ► *n. Ling.* A labial consonant. **—la′bi·al·ly** *adv.*
la·bi·um (lā′bē-əm) ► *n., pl.* **-bi·a** (-bē-ə) *Anat.* Any of four folds of tissue of the female external genitalia.
la·bor (lā′bər) ► *n.* 1. Physical or mental exertion. 2. A specific task. 3. Work for wages. 4a. Workers collectively. b. The trade union movement. 5. The physical efforts of childbirth. ► *v.* 1. To work; toil. 2. To strive painstakingly. 3. To proceed with effort; plod. 4. To suffer from distress or a disadvantage: *labored under a misconception.* **—la′bor·er** *n.*
lab·o·ra·to·ry (lăb′rə-tôr′ē) ► *n., pl.* **-ries**. 1. A place equipped for scientific experimentation, research, or testing. 2. A place where drugs and chemicals are manufactured.
Labor Day ► *n.* The 1st Monday in Sep. observed as a holiday in honor of working people.
la·bored (lā′bərd) ► *adj.* 1. Produced or done with effort. 2. Lacking natural ease; strained.
la·bo·ri·ous (lə-bôr′ē-əs) ► *adj.* Marked by or requiring hard or tedious work. **—la·bo′ri·ous·ly** *adv.* **—la·bo′ri·ous·ness** *n.*
labor union ► *n.* An organization of workers formed to promote the members' interests with respect to wages and working conditions.
Lab·ra·dor (lăb′rə-dôr′) ► The mainland territory of Newfoundland and Labrador, Canada, on NE Labrador Peninsula. **—Lab′ra·dor′e·an, Lab′ra·dor′i·an** *adj. & n.*
Labrador Current ► *n.* A cold ocean current flowing S from Baffin Bay along the coast of Labrador.
Labrador Peninsula ► A peninsula of E Canada between Hudson Bay and the Atlantic.
la·bur·num (lə-bûr′nəm) ► *n.* A tree or shrub cultivated for its drooping clusters of yellow flowers.
lab·y·rinth (lăb′ə-rĭnth′) ► *n.* 1. An intricate structure of interconnecting passages through which it is difficult to find one's way; maze. 2. **Labyrinth** *Gk. Myth.* The maze in which the Minotaur was confined. **—lab′y·rin′thine** (-rĭn′thĭn, -thēn′) *adj.*
lac (lăk) ► *n.* A resinous secretion of an Asian insect, used in making shellac.
lace (lās) ► *n.* 1. A cord used to draw and tie together two opposite edges, as of a shoe. 2. A delicate fabric woven in an open weblike pattern. ► *v.* **laced, lac·ing**. 1. To draw together and tie the laces of. 2. To intertwine: *lace garlands through a trellis.* 3. To add a touch of liquor to. **—lac′er** *n.* **—lac′y** *adj.*
lac·er·ate (lăs′ə-rāt′) ► *v.* **-at·ed, -at·ing**. 1. To rip or tear (e.g., the skin). 2. To wound. **—lac′er·a′tion** *n.*
lach·ry·mal also **lac·ri·mal** (lăk′rə-məl) ► *adj.* Of tears or the tear-producing glands.
lach·ry·mose (lăk′rə-mōs′) ► *adj.* Tearful. **—lach′ry·mose′ly** *adv.*
lack (lăk) ► *n.* A deficiency or absence. ► *v.* 1. To be without any or much of. 2. To be wanting or deficient.
lack·a·dai·si·cal (lăk′ə-dā′zĭ-kəl) ► *adj.* Lacking spirit, liveliness, or interest. **—lack′a·dai′si·cal·ly** *adv.* **—lack′a·dai′si·cal·ness** *n.*
lack·ey (lăk′ē) ► *n., pl.* **-eys**. 1. A footman. 2. A servile follower; toady.
lack·lus·ter (lăk′lŭs′tər) ► *adj.* Lacking brightness, luster, or vitality.
la·con·ic (lə-kŏn′ĭk) ► *adj.* Using few words; terse. **—la·con′i·cal·ly** *adv.*
lac·quer (lăk′ər) ► *n.* Any of various clear or colored synthetic or resinous coatings used to impart a high gloss to surfaces. **—lac′quer** *v.*
la·crosse (lə-krôs′, -krŏs′) ► *n.* A game of Native American origin played on a field by two teams using long-handled sticks with webbed pouches to maneuver a ball into the opposing team's goal.
lac·tate (lăk′tāt′) ► *v.* **-tat·ed, -tat·ing**. To secrete or produce milk. **—lac·ta′tion** *n.*
lac·tic (lăk′tĭk) ► *adj.* Of or derived from milk.
lactic acid ► *n.* A syrupy liquid, $C_3H_6O_3$, present in sour milk, molasses, various fruits, and wines.
lacto– or **lact–** ► *pref.* Milk: *lactate.*
lac·tose (lăk′tōs′) ► *n.* A white crystalline sugar, $C_{12}H_{22}O_{11}$, obtained from whey and used in infant foods, bakery prod-

THESAURUS

label *n.* —*See* MARK (1), TICKET (1).
label *v.* To attach a ticket to ► earmark, flag, mark, tag, ticket. —*See also* CALL, MARK (1).
labile *adj.* —*See* CHANGEABLE (1).
labor *n.* Physical exertion that is usually difficult and exhausting ► drudgery, moil, toil, travail, work. *Informal:* grind, sweat. ***Idiom:*** sweat of one's brow. —*See also* BIRTH (1).
labor *v.* To exert oneself steadily, often to the point of exhaustion ► drive, moil, slave, strain, strive, sweat, toil, travail, tug, work. ***Idioms:*** bend over backward, break one's back (*or* neck), break (*or* bust) one's butt, bust a gut, knock oneself out, work one's butt off, work oneself ragged, work one's fingers to the bone. [*Compare* GRIND.] —*See also* BELABOR.
labored *adj.* Not natural or spontaneous ► contrived, effortful, forced, strained. [*Compare* AWKWARD, STIFF.] —*See also* PONDEROUS.
laborer *n.* One who labors ► day laborer, hand, menial, operative, roustabout, toiler, wage slave, worker, working girl, workingman, workingwoman, workman, workwoman. [*Compare* EMPLOYEE.]
laborious *adj.* —*See* BURDENSOME, DIFFICULT (1).
laboriously *adv.* —*See* HARD (2).
labyrinth *n.* —*See* TANGLE.
labyrinthine *adj.* —*See* COMPLEX (1).
lace *n.* —*See* CORD, WEB.
lacerate *v.* —*See* CUT (1), SLAM (1).
laceration *n.* Marked tissue damage, especially when produced by physical injury ► lesion, trauma, traumatism, wound. [*Compare* HARM.]
lachrymose *adj.* —*See* TEARFUL.
lacing *n.* —*See* CORD, WEB.
lack *v.* To be without what is needed, required, or essential ► need, require, want. [*Compare* DEMAND.]
lack *n.* The condition of lacking something ► absence, dearth, want. [*Compare* NEED.] —*See also* SHORTAGE.
lackadaisical *adj.* —*See* LANGUID.
lackey *n.* —*See* SYCOPHANT.
lacking *adj.* —*See* DEFICIENT, EMPTY (2).
lackluster *adj.* —*See* DULL (1), DULL (2).
laconic *adj.* —*See* BRIEF, TACITURN.
lacquer *n.* —*See* FINISH.
lacquer *v.* —*See* FINISH (2).

ucts, confections, and pharmaceuticals.

la·cu·na (lə-kyo͞o′nə) ▸ *n., pl.* **-nae** (-nē) or **-nas**. **1.** An empty space; gap. **2.** *Anat.* A cavity or depression. **—la·cu′nal** *adj.*

lad (lăd) ▸ *n.* A boy or young man.

lad·der (lăd′ər) ▸ *n.* **1.** A structure consisting of two long sides crossed by parallel rungs, used to climb up and down. **2.** A series of ranked stages or levels.

lade (lād) ▸ *v.* **lad·ed, lad·en** (lād′n) or **lad·ed, lad·ing**. **1.** To load or be loaded with or as if with cargo. **2.** To burden; weigh down. **—lad′en** *adj.*

lad·ing (lā′dĭng) ▸ *n.* Cargo; freight.

La·di·no (lə-dē′nō) ▸ *n.* A Romance language with Hebrew elements, spoken by Sephardic Jews esp. in the Balkans.

la·dle (lād′l) ▸ *n.* A long-handled spoon with a deep bowl for serving liquids. **—la′dle** *v.* **—la′dler** *n.*

la·dy (lā′dē) ▸ *n., pl.* **-dies**. **1.** A woman of superior social position. **2.** A well-mannered woman. **3.** A woman who is the head of a household. **4.** A woman. **5.** **Lady** *Chiefly Brit.* A general feminine title of nobility and other rank. **—la′dy·like′** *adj.*

la·dy·bird (lā′dē-bûrd′) ▸ *n.* See **ladybug**.

la·dy·bug (lā′dē-bŭg′) ▸ *n.* A small, rounded, usu. brightly colored beetle, often reddish with black spots.

la·dy·fin·ger (lā′dē-fĭng′gər) ▸ *n.* A small finger-shaped sponge cake.

lady in waiting ▸ *n., pl.* **ladies in waiting**. A lady appointed to attend a queen or princess.

la·dy·ship also **La·dy·ship** (lā′dē-shĭp′) ▸ *n.* Used with *Your* or *Her* as a title for a woman holding the rank of lady.

la·dy's slipper (lā′dēz) ▸ *n.* An orchid having flowers with an inflated pouchlike lip.

lag (lăg) ▸ *v.* **lagged, lag·ging**. **1.** To fail to keep up a pace; straggle. **2.** To weaken or slacken gradually. ▸ *n.* **1.** The act of lagging. **2.** The extent or duration of lagging. **—lag′ger** *n.*

la·ger (lä′gər) ▸ *n.* A beer aged from six weeks to six months to allow sedimentation.

lag·gard (lăg′ərd) ▸ *n.* One that lags; straggler. **—lag′gard·ly** *adv.* **—lag′gard·ness** *n.*

la·gniappe (lăn′yəp, lăn-yăp′) ▸ *n.* *Regional* An extra item or amount; bonus.

la·goon (lə-go͞on′) ▸ *n.* A shallow body of water, esp. one separated from a sea by sandbars or coral reefs.

La·gos (lā′gŏs′, lä′gōs) ▸ The largest city of Nigeria, in the SW part on the Gulf of Guinea.

La·hore (lə-hôr′) ▸ A city of NE Pakistan SE of Rawalpindi.

laid (lād) ▸ *v.* P.t. and p.part. of **lay**[1].

laid-back (lād′băk′) ▸ *adj.* *Informal* Relaxed and casual; easygoing.

lain (lān) ▸ *v.* P.part. of **lie**[1].

lair (lâr) ▸ *n.* The den or dwelling of a wild animal.

lais·sez faire also **lais·ser faire** (lĕs′ā fâr′) ▸ *n.* Noninterference, esp. an economic doctrine that opposes governmental involvement in commerce. **—lais′sez-faire′** *adj.*

la·i·ty (lā′ĭ-tē) ▸ *n.* **1.** Laypeople collectively. **2.** Nonprofessionals.

lake (lāk) ▸ *n.* **1.** A large inland body of water. **2.** A large pool of liquid.

La·ko·ta (lə-kō′tə) ▸ *n., pl.* **-ta** or **-tas**. See **Teton**.

lam (lăm) *Slang* ▸ *v.* **lammed, lam·ming**. To escape, as from prison. ▸ *n.* Flight, esp. from the law: *on the lam.*

la·ma (lä′mə) ▸ *n.* A Buddhist monk of Tibet or Mongolia.

lamb (lăm) ▸ *n.* **1a.** A young sheep. **b.** The flesh of a young sheep used as meat. **2.** A sweet, mild-mannered person.

lam·baste (lăm-bāst′) ▸ *v.* **-bast·ed, -bast·ing**. *Informal* **1.** To give a thrashing to. **2.** To scold sharply; berate.

lamb·da (lăm′də) ▸ *n.* The 11th letter of the Greek alphabet.

lam·bent (lăm′bənt) ▸ *adj.* **1.** Flickering or glowing gently. **2.** Effortlessly light or brilliant: *lambent wit.* **—lam′ben·cy** *n.* **—lam′bent·ly** *adv.*

lamb·skin (lăm′skĭn′) ▸ *n.* The hide of a lamb or a fine leather made from it.

lame (lām) ▸ *adj.* **lam·er, lam·est**. **1.** Disabled so that movement, esp. walking, is difficult. **2.** Weak and ineffectual: *a lame excuse.* ▸ *v.* **lamed, lam·ing**. To make lame. **—lame′ly** *adv.* **—lame′ness** *n.*

la·mé (lă-mā′) ▸ *n.* A fabric woven with metallic threads.

lame duck ▸ *n.* **1.** An elected officeholder continuing in office during the period between the election and inauguration of a successor. **2.** An ineffective person. **—lame′-duck′** *adj.*

la·mel·la (lə-mĕl′ə) ▸ *n., pl.* **-mel·lae** (-mĕl′ē′) or **-mel·las**. A thin scale, plate, or layer. **—la·mel′lar, la·mel′late′** (lə-mĕl′āt′, lăm′ə-lāt′) *adj.*

la·ment (lə-mĕnt′) ▸ *v.* **1.** To express grief for or about; mourn. **2.** To regret deeply; deplore. ▸ *n.* **1.** An expression of grief; lamentation. **2.** A dirge or elegy. **—la·men′ta·ble** *adj.* **—la·men′ta·bly** *adv.* **—la·ment′er** *n.*

lam·en·ta·tion (lăm′ən-tā′shən) ▸ *n.* **1.** The act of lamenting. **2.** A lament. **3.** **Lamentations** *(takes sing. v.)* See **Bible** table in Appendix.

lam·i·na (lăm′ə-nə) ▸ *n., pl.* **-nae** (-nē′) or **-nas**. A thin plate, sheet, or layer. **—lam′i·nar, lam′i·nal** *adj.*

lam·i·nate (lăm′ə-nāt′) ▸ *v.* **-nat·ed, -nat·ing**. **1.** To form into a thin sheet. **2.** To divide into thin layers. **3.** To bond together in layers. ▸ *adj.* (-nĭt, -nāt′) also **lam·i·nat·ed** (-nā′tĭd) Consisting of thin layers. **—lam′i·na′tion** *n.* **—lam′i·na′tor** *n.*

lamp (lămp) ▸ *n.* **1.** A device that generates light, heat, or therapeutic radiation. **2.** A vessel containing oil or alcohol burned through a wick for illumination.

lamp·black (lămp′blăk′) ▸ *n.* Fine soot used as a pigment and in matches, explosives, and fertilizers.

lam·poon (lăm-po͞on′) ▸ *n.* A written attack ridiculing a person, group, or institution. **—lam·poon′** *v.* **—lam·poon′er, lam·poon′ist** *n.* **—lam·poon′er·y** *n.*

lam·prey (lăm′prē) ▸ *n., pl.* **-preys**. A primitive elongated fish having a jawless sucking mouth.

LAN (lăn) ▸ *n.* A system that links computers and related equipment to form a network, as within an office.

la·nai (lə-nī′) ▸ *n., pl.* **-nais**. A veranda or patio.

Lanai ▸ An island of central HI W of Maui.

lance (lăns) ▸ *n.* **1.** A thrusting weapon with a long shaft and a sharp metal head. **2.** A similar implement for spearing fish. **3.** *Medic.* See **lancet**. ▸ *v.* **lanced, lanc·ing**. **1.** To pierce with a lance. **2.** *Medic.* To cut into: *lance a boil.*

lance corporal ▸ *n.* A rank in the US Marine Corps below corporal.

lanc·er (lăn′sər) ▸ *n.* A cavalryman armed with a lance.

lan·cet (lăn′sĭt) ▸ *n.* A surgical knife with a short, wide, pointed double-edged blade.

THESAURUS

lacuna *n.* —*See* GAP (2).

lad *n.* —*See* FELLOW.

laden *adj.* Burdened by a weighty load ▸ heavy, heavy-laden, loaded, weighed down.

ladle *v.* —*See* DIP (2).

lady-killer *n.* —*See* PHILANDERER.

lady's man *n.* —*See* GALLANT, PHILANDERER.

lag *v.* —*See* DELAY (2).

lag *n.* —*See* DELAY (2), LAGGARD.

laggard *adj.* —*See* SLOW (1).

laggard or **lagger** *n.* One that lags ▸ dawdler, dilly-dallier, lag, lingerer, loiterer, poke, procrastinator, snail, straggler, tarrier. *Informal:* slowpoke.

lagging *adj.* —*See* BACKWARD (2).

laid-back *adj.* —*See* EASYGOING.

laid up *adj.* —*See* SICK (1).

lair *n.* **1.** A place used as an animal's dwelling ▸ burrow, den, hole. [*Compare* CAVE.] **2.** A hiding place ▸ covert, den, hideaway, hide-out.

lam *v.* —*See* ESCAPE (1).

lam *n.* —*See* ESCAPE (1).

lamb *n.* —*See* DUPE, INNOCENT (1).

lambaste *v.* —*See* BEAT (1), CHASTISE, SLAM (1).

lambency *n.* —*See* LIGHT[1] (1).

lambent *adj.* —*See* BRIGHT.

lame *adj.* —*See* IMPLAUSIBLE, INEFFECTUAL (2).

lamebrained *adj.* —*See* STUPID.

lament *v.* —*See* CRY, GRIEVE.

lament *n.* —*See* CRY (1).

lamentable *adj.* —*See* PITIFUL, SORROWFUL.

lamentation *n.* —*See* CRY (1).

lamia *n.* A woman who practices magic ▸ enchantress, hag, sorceress, witch. [*Compare* WIZARD.]

lamina *n.* —*See* SKIN (2).

lampoon *n.* —*See* SATIRE.

lampoon *v.* —*See* RIDICULE.

lance *v.* —*See* CUT (1).

land (lănd) ▸ *n.* 1. The solid ground of the earth. 2. A distinct area or region: *desert land.* 3. A nation, country, or realm. 4. Public or private landed property; real estate. ▸ *v.* 1. To put or arrive on land after traveling by water or air. 2. *Informal* To arrive or cause to arrive in a place or condition: *land in jail.* 3. To catch by or as if by fishing. 4. To come to rest; alight.

land·ed (lăn′dĭd) ▸ *adj.* 1. Owning land. 2. Consisting of land.

land·fall (lănd′fôl′) ▸ *n.* 1. The act or an instance of sighting or reaching land. 2. The land sighted or reached.

land·fill (lănd′fĭl′) ▸ *n.* A method of solid waste disposal in which refuse is buried between layers of dirt in low-lying ground. **—land′fill′** *v.*

land grant ▸ *n.* A government grant of public land for a railroad, highway, or state college.

land·hold·er (lănd′hōl′dər) ▸ *n.* One who owns land. **—land′hold′ing** *n.*

land·ing (lăn′dĭng) ▸ *n.* 1. The act or site of coming to land or rest. 2. A platform at the top, bottom, or between flights of stairs.

landing gear ▸ *n.* The structure supporting an aircraft on the ground.

landing strip ▸ *n.* An aircraft runway without airport facilities.

land·la·dy (lănd′lā′dē) ▸ *n.* A woman who owns and rents land, buildings, or dwelling units.

land·locked (lănd′lŏkt′) ▸ *adj.* 1. Surrounded or almost surrounded by land. 2. Confined to inland waters, as certain salmon.

land·lord (lănd′lôrd′) ▸ *n.* One who owns and rents land, buildings, or dwelling units.

land·lub·ber (lănd′lŭb′ər) ▸ *n.* A person unfamiliar with the sea or seamanship. **—land′lub′ber·ly** *adj.*

land·mark (lănd′märk′) ▸ *n.* 1. A prominent identifying feature of a landscape. 2. A fixed marker indicating a boundary line. 3. A historically significant event or site.

land·mass (lănd′măs′) ▸ *n.* A large area of land.

land mine ▸ *n.* An explosive mine laid usu. just below the surface of the ground.

land-of·fice business (lănd′ô′fĭs, -ŏf′ĭs) ▸ *n.* A thriving or rapidly moving volume of trade.

land-poor (lănd′po͝or′) ▸ *adj.* Owning much land but lacking the capital to improve it.

land·scape (lănd′skāp′) ▸ *n.* 1. A view or vista of scenery on land. 2. A picture depicting such a view. ▸ *v.* **-scaped, -scap·ing.** To improve (a section of ground) by contouring and decorative planting. **—land′scap′er** *n.*

land·slide (lănd′slīd′) ▸ *n.* 1. The downward sliding of a mass of earth and rock. 2. An overwhelming victory, esp. in an election.

land·ward (lănd′wərd) ▸ *adv.* & *adj.* To or toward land. **—land′wards** *adv.*

lane (lān) ▸ *n.* 1. A narrow way or road. 2. A set passage or course, as for vehicles or ships.

lan·guage (lăng′gwĭj) ▸ *n.* 1a. Communication of thoughts and feelings through a system of arbitrary signals, such as voice sounds, gestures, or written symbols. b. Such a system, including rules for combining components, such as words. c. Such a system used by a particular group or community. 2. *Comp. Sci.* A system of symbols and rules used for communication with or between computers. 3. The special vocabulary of a scientific, professional, or other group. 4. A particular style of speech or writing: *poetic language.* 5. Communication between nonhumans.

Lan·gue·doc (läng-dôk′, läɴg-) ▸ A former province of S-central France on an arm of the Mediterranean Sea W of the Rhone R.

lan·guid (lăng′gwĭd) ▸ *adj.* 1. Lacking energy or vitality; weak. 2. Apathetic; listless. 3. Lacking force; slow. **—lan′guid·ly** *adv.* **—lan′guid·ness** *n.*

lan·guish (lăng′gwĭsh) ▸ *v.* 1. To lose strength or vigor. 2. To exist in miserable conditions; be neglected. 3. To become downcast; pine. 4. To affect a wistful or languid air.

lan·guor (lăng′gər, lăng′ər) ▸ *n.* 1. Lack of physical or mental energy; lethargy. 2. A dreamy, lazy mood or quality. **—lan′guor·ous** *adj.* **—lan′guor·ous·ly** *adv.*

La Ni·ña (lä nēn′yä) ▸ *n.* A periodic cooling of the ocean surface off the W coast of South America that affects Pacific and other weather patterns.

lank (lăngk) ▸ *adj.* **-er, -est.** 1. Long and lean. 2. Long, straight, and limp: *lank hair.* **—lank′ly** *adv.* **—lank′ness** *n.*

lank·y (lăng′kē) ▸ *adj.* **-i·er, -i·est.** Tall, thin, and ungainly. **—lank′i·ly** *adv.* **—lank′i·ness** *n.*

lan·o·lin (lăn′ə-lĭn) ▸ *n.* A fatty substance obtained from wool and used in soaps, cosmetics, and ointments.

Lan·sing (lăn′sĭng) ▸ The capital of MI, in the S-central part NW of Detroit.

lan·tern (lăn′tərn) ▸ *n.* An often portable case with transparent or translucent sides for holding and protecting a light.

lan·tha·nide (lăn′thə-nīd′) ▸ *n.* See **rare-earth element.**

lan·tha·num (lăn′thə-nəm) ▸ *n.* *Symbol* **La** A soft, silvery-white rare-earth element used esp. in glass manufacture. At. no. 57.

lan·yard also **lan·iard** (lăn′yərd) ▸ *n.* 1. *Naut.* A short rope used for securing rigging. 2. A cord worn around the neck for carrying something, such as a whistle.

Lao (lou) ▸ *n., pl.* **Lao** or **Laos** (louz). 1. A member of a Buddhist people of Laos and Thailand. 2. The Tai language of the Lao.

La·os (lous, lä′ōs′) ▸ A country of SE Asia. **—La·o′tian** (lā-ō′shən, lou′shən) *adj.* & *n.*

Lao Tzu also **Lao-tse** (lou′dzŭ′) (fl. 6th cent. B.C.) ▸ Chinese philosopher.

lap¹ (lăp) ▸ *n.* 1. The front area from the waist to the knees of a seated person. 2. The portion of a garment that covers the lap. **—lap′ful′** *n.*

lap² (lăp) ▸ *v.* **lapped, lap·ping.** 1. To place or lay (something) so as to overlap another. 2. To fold or wrap or wind around (something); encircle. 3. To get ahead of (an opponent) in a race by one or more laps. ▸ *n.* 1. A part that overlaps. 2. One complete round or circuit, esp. of a racetrack. 3. A segment or stage, as of a trip.

lap³ (lăp) ▸ *v.* **lapped, lap·ping.** 1. To take in (a liquid or food) with the tongue. 2. To wash against with soft liquid sounds: *waves lapping the shore.* ***—phrasal verb:*** **lap up** To receive eagerly. **—lap** *n.*

lap·board (lăp′bôrd′) ▸ *n.* A flat board held on the lap and used as a table or desk.

lap dog ▸ *n.* A small, easily held pet dog.

la·pel (lə-pĕl′) ▸ *n.* The part of a garment that is an extension of the collar and folds back against the breast.

THESAURUS

land *n.* Usually extensive real estate ▸ acreage, acres, estate, grounds, lands, manor, property. *—See also* STATE (1).

land *v.* 1. To come ashore from a seacraft ▸ alight, debark, disembark, light. 2. To come to rest on the ground ▸ alight, light, set down, settle, touch down. *—See also* GET (1).

landscape *n.* *—See* VIEW (2).

lane *n.* *—See* WAY (2).

language *n.* 1. A system of terms used by a people sharing a history and culture ▸ dialect, mother tongue, speech, tongue, vernacular. 2. Specialized expressions indigenous to a particular field, subject, trade, or subculture ▸ argot, cant, dialect, idiom, jargon, lexicon, lingo, parlance, patois, terminology, vernacular, vocabulary.

languid *adj.* Lacking energy and vitality ▸ drooping, flagging, lackadaisical, languorous, leaden, limp, listless, lymphatic, sleepy, spiritless, unspirited. [*Compare* APATHETIC, LAZY, SLOW, WEAK.]

languidness *n.* *—See* LETHARGY.

languish *v.* To become downcast from longing or grief ▸ ebb, pine (away), shrivel, waste (away), wither. *—See also* DETERIORATE, FADE.

languor *n.* *—See* LETHARGY.

languorous *adj.* *—See* LANGUID.

lank *adj.* *—See* THIN (1).

lanky *adj.* *—See* GANGLING, THIN (1).

lap *v.* 1. To flow against or along ▸ bathe, lave, lip, wash. [*Compare* FLOW.] 2. To make the sound of moving or disturbed water ▸ splash, swash, wash. [*Compare* SWISH.] *—See also* BURBLE.

lap up *v.* *—See* DRINK (1).

lap *n.* *—See* BURBLE.

lap·i·dar·y (lăp′ĭ-dĕr′ē) ▸ *n., pl.* **-ies.** One who cuts and polishes gems. ▸ *adj.* **1.** Of or relating to precious stones or the art of working with them. **2.** Concise and polished: *lapidary prose.*

lap·in (lăp′ĭn, lä-păɴ′) ▸ *n.* Rabbit fur.

lap·is laz·u·li (lăp′ĭs lăz′ə-lē, -yə-, lăzh′ə-) ▸ *n.* An opaque blue semiprecious gemstone.

Lap·land (lăp′lănd′, -lənd) ▸ A region of extreme N Europe including N Norway, Sweden, and Finland and the Kola Peninsula of NW Russia. **—Lap′land·er** *n.*

Lapp (lăp) ▸ *n.* **1.** A member of a nomadic herding people inhabiting Lapland. **2.** Any of the Finnic languages of the Lapps. **—Lap′pish** *adj.*

lapse (lăps) ▸ *v.* **lapsed, laps·ing. 1.** To fall from a previous standard, as of quality. **2.** To pass or come to an end, esp. gradually. **3.** To be no longer valid or active; expire. ▸ *n.* **1.** A minor or temporary failure; slip. **2.** A deterioration or decline. **3.** A period of time; interval. **4.** *Law* The termination of a right or privilege through disuse, neglect, or death. **—laps′er** *n.*

lap·top (lăp′tŏp′) ▸ *n.* A portable computer small enough to use on one's lap.

lap·wing (lăp′wĭng′) ▸ *n.* Any of several crested Old World birds related to the plovers.

La Ra·za (lä rä′sä) ▸ *n.* Mexicans or Mexican Americans considered as a group.

lar·board (lär′bərd) ▸ *n. Naut.* See **port**[2]. **—lar′board** *adj.*

lar·ce·ny (lär′sə-nē) ▸ *n., pl.* **-nies.** The stealing of another's personal property; theft. **—lar′ce·nous** (-nəs) *adj.*

larch (lärch) ▸ *n.* A deciduous, cone-bearing tree having needlelike leaves and heavy durable wood.

lard (lärd) ▸ *n.* The white rendered fat of a hog. ▸ *v.* **1.** To insert strips of fat in (meat) before cooking. **2.** To embellish throughout: *larded the report with quotations.* **—lard′y** *adj.*

lar·der (lär′dər) ▸ *n.* A place, such as a pantry, where food is stored.

large (lärj) ▸ *adj.* **larg·er, larg·est. 1.** Of greater than average size or amount; big. **2.** Broad; comprehensive. **3.** Tolerant; liberal. ***—idiom:*** **at large 1.** Not in captivity; at liberty. **2.** As a whole; in general. **3.** Not representing a particular country, state, or district. **—large′ness** *n.*

large calorie ▸ *n.* See **calorie** 1.

large intestine ▸ *n.* The portion of the intestine from the ileum to the anus.

large·ly (lärj′lē) ▸ *adv.* **1.** For the most part; mainly. **2.** On a large scale; amply.

large-scale (lärj′skāl′) ▸ *adj.* **1.** Large in scope or extent. **2.** Drawn or made large to show detail.

lar·gess also **lar·gesse** (lär-zhĕs′, -jĕs′, lär′jĕs′) ▸ *n.* **1.** Liberality in giving. **2.** Money or gifts bestowed.

lar·go (lär′gō) ▸ *adv. & adj. Mus.* In a slow, solemn tempo. **—lar′go** *n.*

la·ri (lä′rē) ▸ *n.* See **currency** table in Appendix.

lar·i·at (lăr′ē-ət) ▸ *n.* See **lasso.**

lark[1] (lärk) ▸ *n.* **1.** Any of various chiefly Old World birds with a sustained, melodious song. **2.** Any of several similar birds.

lark[2] (lärk) ▸ *n.* A carefree adventure or prank. ▸ *v.* To engage in fun or pranks. **—lark′er** *n.* **—lark′ish** *adj.*

lark·spur (lärk′spûr′) ▸ *n.* See **delphinium.**

lar·va (lär′və) ▸ *n., pl.* **-vae** (-vē) or **-vas. 1.** The newly hatched, wingless, often wormlike form of many insects. **2.** The newly hatched stage of any of various animals that differ markedly in form and appearance from the adult. **—lar′val** *adj.*

lar·yn·gi·tis (lăr′ĭn-jī′tĭs) ▸ *n.* Inflammation of the larynx. **—lar′yn·git′ic** (-jĭt′ĭk) *adj.*

lar·ynx (lăr′ĭngks) ▸ *n., pl.* **la·ryn·ges** (lə-rĭn′jēz) or **lar·ynx·es.** The part of the respiratory tract between the pharynx and the trachea, containing the vocal cords. **—la·ryn′ge·al** (lə-rĭn′jē-əl) *adj.*

la·sa·gna also **la·sa·gne** (lə-zän′yə) ▸ *n.* Flat wide noodles, usu. baked in layers with sauce and cheese.

las·civ·i·ous (lə-sĭv′ē-əs) ▸ *adj.* **1.** Lustful; lecherous. **2.** Lewd; salacious. **—las·civ′i·ous·ly** *adv.* **—las·civ′i·ous·ness** *n.*

la·ser (lā′zər) ▸ *n.* Any of several devices that convert incident electromagnetic radiation of mixed frequencies to one or more discrete frequencies of highly amplified and coherent radiation.

laser disk ▸ *n.* See **optical disk.**

laser printer ▸ *n.* A printer that uses a laser to produce an image on a rotating drum before electrostatically transferring the image to paper.

lash[1] (lăsh) ▸ *n.* **1.** A stroke or blow with or as if with a whip. **2.** A whip or its thong. **3.** An eyelash. ▸ *v.* **1.** To strike with or as if with a whip. **2.** To strike against with force or violence: *sleet lashing the roof.* **3.** To beat or swing rapidly; thrash. **4.** To attack verbally: *lashed out at her critics.* **5.** To goad; sting. **—lash′er** *n.*

lash[2] (lăsh) ▸ *v.* To secure or bind, as with a rope.

lass (lăs) ▸ *n.* **1.** A girl or young woman. **2.** A sweetheart.

las·sie (lăs′ē) ▸ *n.* A lass.

las·si·tude (lăs′ĭ-to͞od′, -tyo͞od′) ▸ *n.* A state of weariness, lethargy, or listlessness.

las·so (lăs′ō, lă-so͞o′) ▸ *n., pl.* **-sos** or **-soes.** A long rope with a noose at one end, used esp. to catch horses and cattle. **—las′so** *v.* **—las′so·er** *n.*

last[1] (lăst) ▸ *adj.* **1.** Being, coming, or placed after all others; final. **2.** Most recent; latest. **3.** Most authoritative or conclusive. **4.** Least likely or expected: *the last person we would have suspected.* ▸ *adv.* **1.** After all others. **2.** Most recently. **3.** At the end; finally. ▸ *n.* **1.** One that is last. **2.** The end. ***—idiom:*** **at last** Finally. **—last′ly** *adv.*

last[2] (lăst) ▸ *v.* **1.** To continue in existence; go on. **2.** To remain adequate or sufficient.

last[3] (lăst) ▸ *n.* A foot-shaped block or form used in making or repairing shoes.

last-ditch (lăst′dĭch′) ▸ *adj.* Done as a final recourse; desperate.

THESAURUS

lapse *v.* To become void, especially through passage of time or an omission ▸ cease, end, expire, run out, terminate. *—See also* ELAPSE, ERR, RELAPSE, SUBSIDE.

lapse *n.* *—See* ERROR, RELAPSE.

lapsed *adj.* *—See* PAST.

larcenist or **larcener** *n.* *—See* THIEF.

larcenous *adj.* *—See* THIEVISH.

larceny *n.* The crime of taking someone else's property without consent ▸ banditry, brigandage, burglary, holdup, looting, mugging, pilferage, purloining, robbery, steal, stealing, theft, thievery. *Slang:* heist, rip-off, stickup.

lard *n.* Adipose tissue ▸ blubber, fat, suet, tallow. [*Compare* OIL.]

lares and penates *n.* *—See* EFFECTS.

large *adj.* At the upper end of a degree of measure ▸ elevated, great, high. [*Compare* EXALTED, EXTREME.] *—See also* BIG, GENERAL (2), IMPORTANT.

large-hearted *adj.* *—See* GENEROUS (1).

large-heartedness *n.* *—See* GENEROSITY.

largely *adv.* *—See* CONSIDERABLY.

largeness *n.* *—See* SIZE (2).

larger *adj.* *—See* BEST (1).

large-scale *adj.* *—See* BIG.

largess *n.* *—See* DONATION, GENEROSITY, GRATUITY.

largest *adj.* *—See* BEST (2).

largish *adj.* *—See* BIG.

lark *n.* *—See* PRANK[1].

larkish *adj.* *—See* MISCHIEVOUS.

lascivious *adj.* Feeling or preoccupied with sexual love or desire ▸ amorous, concupiscent, lecherous, lewd, libidinous, lubricious, lustful, lusty, passionate, prurient, sexy. [*Compare* OBSCENE, WANTON.] *—See also* EROTIC.

lash *v.* *—See* BEAT (2), FASTEN, SLAM (1).

lashing *n.* *—See* BEATING.

lass *n.* *—See* GIRL.

lassitude *n.* *—See* APATHY, LETHARGY.

last[1] *adj.* **1.** Coming after all others ▸ closing, concluding, final, terminal, ultimate. **2.** Bringing up the rear ▸ aftermost, endmost, hindermost, hindmost, lattermost, rearmost, tail. [*Compare* EXTREME.] **3.** Next before the present one ▸ foregoing, latter, preceding, previous. [*Compare* PAST.] **4.** Of or relating to a terminative condition, stage, or point ▸ final, latter, terminal, ultimate. [*Compare* CLIMACTIC.]

last *adv.* In conclusion ▸ conclusively, finally, lastly, ultimately. *Idioms:* at last, in the end. [*Compare* ULTIMATELY.]

last *n.* *—See* END (2).

last[2] *v.* To remain fresh and unspoiled ▸ keep. *—See also* ENDURE (2), SURVIVE (1).

last·ing (lăs′tĭng) ▸ *adj.* Continuing or remaining for a long time; enduring. **—last′ing·ly** *adv.* **—last′ing·ness** *n.*

Last Judgment ▸ *n. Theol.* The final judgment by God of all humankind.

last rites ▸ *pl.n.* Rites performed for one in danger of dying or for a burial.

last straw ▸ *n.* The last of a series of annoyances or setbacks that leads to a final loss of patience or hope.

Last Supper ▸ *n.* Jesus's supper with his disciples on the night before his crucifixion.

Las Ve·gas (läs vā′gəs) ▸ A city of SE NV near the CA and AZ borders.

latch (lăch) ▸ *n.* **1.** A fastening or lock, as for a door or gate, typically consisting of a movable bar that fits into a notch. **2.** A spring lock opened by a key. ▸ *v.* To close with a latch. **—*idiom:* latch on to** (or **onto**) **1.** To get hold of; obtain. **2.** To cling to.

late (lāt) ▸ *adj.* **lat·er, lat·est. 1.** Coming, occurring, or remaining after the proper or expected time. **2.** Occurring at an advanced hour. **3.** Of or toward the end. **4.** Recent. **5.** Recently deceased: *in memory of the late explorer.* ▸ *adv.* **later, latest. 1.** After the expected or usual time. **2.** At or into an advanced period or stage. **3.** Recently. **—*idiom:* of late** Recently. **—late′ness** *n.*

late·com·er (lāt′kŭm′ər) ▸ *n.* **1.** One that arrives late. **2.** A recent arrival or participant.

Late Greek ▸ *n.* Greek in late antiquity and the early Byzantine period.

Late Latin ▸ *n.* Latin from the 3rd to the 7th cent. A.D.

late·ly (lāt′lē) ▸ *adv.* Not long ago; recently.

la·tent (lāt′nt) ▸ *adj.* Present or potential but not evident or active. **—la′ten·cy** *n.* **—la′tent·ly** *adv.*

lat·er·al (lăt′ər-əl) ▸ *adj.* Of or situated at or on the side. ▸ *n. Football* A pass thrown sideways or backward. **—lat′er·al** *v.* **—lat′er·al·ly** *adv.*

la·tex (lā′tĕks′) ▸ *n.* **1.** The milky sap of certain plants that coagulates on exposure to air. **2.** An emulsion of rubber or plastic globules in water, used in paints, adhesives, and various synthetic rubber products. **—la′tex′** *adj.*

lath (lăth) ▸ *n., pl.* **laths** (lă*th*z, lăths). **1.** A thin strip of wood or metal, usu. nailed in rows as a substructure for plaster, shingles, or tiles. **2.** A similarly used building material.

lathe (lā*th*) ▸ *n.* A machine on which a piece of material, such as wood or metal, is spun and shaped against a fixed cutting tool. **—lathe** *v.*

lath·er (lă*th*′ər) ▸ *n.* **1.** A foam formed esp. by soap agitated in water. **2.** Frothy sweat. **3.** *Informal* An agitated state; dither. ▸ *v.* To produce or coat with lather. **—lath′er·er** *n.* **—lath′er·y** *adj.*

Lat·in (lăt′n) ▸ *n.* **1.** The Indo-European language of the ancient Romans. **2.** A member of a Latin people, esp. a native or inhabitant of Latin America. ▸ *adj.* **1.** Relating to ancient Rome or its language or culture. **2.** Relating to the Romance languages or to the peoples that speak them. **3.** Relating to Latinos or their culture. **4.** Relating to the Roman Catholic Church.

La·ti·na (lə-tē′nə, lă-) ▸ *n.* A Latino woman or girl.

Latin America ▸ The countries of the Western Hemisphere S of the US, esp. those speaking Spanish, Portuguese, or French. **—Latin American** *n.* **—Lat′in-A·mer′i·can** *adj.*

La·ti·no (lə-tē′nō, lă-) ▸ *n., pl.* **-nos. 1.** A Latin American. **2.** A person of Latin-American descent, esp. one living in the US. **—La·ti′no** *adj.*

lat·i·tude (lăt′ĭ-to͞od′, -tyo͞od′) ▸ *n.* **1a.** The angular distance north or south of the equator, measured in degrees along a meridian. **b.** A region considered in relation to this distance. **2.** Freedom from limitations. **3.** Extent; breadth. **—lat′i·tu′din·al** *adj.* **—lat′i·tu′di·nal·ly** *adv.*

lat·i·tu·di·nar·i·an (lăt′ĭ-to͞od′n-âr′ē-ən, -tyo͞od′-) ▸ *adj.* Holding or expressing tolerant views, esp. in religious matters. **—lat′i·tu′di·nar′i·an** *n.* **—lat′i·tu′di·nar′i·an·ism** *n.*

lat·ke (lät′kə) ▸ *n.* A pancake, esp. one made of grated potato.

la·trine (lə-trēn′) ▸ *n.* A communal toilet.

lats (läts) ▸ *n., pl.* **la·ti** (lä′tē′). See **currency** table in Appendix.

lat·ter (lăt′ər) ▸ *adj.* **1.** Being the second of two persons or things mentioned. **2.** Near the end. **—lat′ter·ly** *adv.*

lat·ter-day (lăt′ər-dā′) ▸ *adj.* Belonging to present or recent times; modern.

Latter-day Saint ▸ *n.* See **Mormon.**

lat·tice (lăt′ĭs) ▸ *n.* **1a.** An open framework made of interwoven strips, as of metal or wood. **b.** A structure, such as a window, made of or containing a lattice. **2.** *Phys.* A regular, periodic configuration of points throughout an area or space. **—lat′ticed** *adj.* **—lat′tice·work′** *n.*

Lat·vi·a (lăt′vē-ə) ▸ A country of N Europe on the Baltic Sea.

Lat·vi·an (lăt′vē-ən) ▸ *n.* **1.** A native or inhabitant of Latvia. **2.** The Baltic language of the Latvians. **—Lat′vi·an** *adj.*

laud (lôd) ▸ *v.* To praise highly. ▸ *n.* Praise. **—laud·a′tion** *n.* **—laud′er** *n.*

laud·a·ble (lô′də-bəl) ▸ *adj.* Praiseworthy; commendable. **—laud′a·bil′i·ty, laud′a·ble·ness** *n.* **—laud′a·bly** *adv.*

lau·da·num (lôd′n-əm) ▸ *n.* A tincture of opium, formerly used as a drug.

laud·a·to·ry (lô′də-tôr′ē) ▸ *adj.* Expressing or conferring praise.

laugh (lăf) ▸ *v.* **1.** To express mirth, delight, or derision by a series of unarticulated sounds. **2.** To affect by laughter:

THESAURUS

lasting *adj.* —*See* CONTINUING.

lastly *adv.* In conclusion ▸ conclusively, finally, last, ultimately. ***Idioms:*** at last, in the end. [*Compare* ULTIMATELY.]

last rites *n.* —*See* FUNERAL.

latch *n.* —*See* FASTENER.

late *adj.* **1.** Coming or occurring after the correct, usual, or expected time; not on time ▸ behindhand, belated, delayed, overdue, slow, tardy. **2.** Having been such previously ▸ erstwhile, former, old, once, onetime, past, previous, quondam, sometime, whilom. —*See also* DEAD (1).

late *adv.* Not on time ▸ behind, behindhand, belatedly, slow, tardily. *Idiom:* behind time.

lately *adv.* Not long ago ▸ freshly, just (now), lately, latterly, newly, recently. *Idioms:* of late, only a moment (*or* while) ago.

latency *n.* —*See* ABEYANCE.

lateness *n.* The quality or condition of not being on time ▸ belatedness, slowness, tardiness, unpunctuality.

latent *adj.* Present but not evident or active ▸ abeyant, dormant, hibernating, inactive, lurking, possible, potential, quiescent, sleeping, smoldering, torpid. [*Compare* HIDDEN, IMPLICIT.]

later *adj.* Following something else in time ▸ after, posterior, subsequent, ulterior. [*Compare* FOLLOWING.] —*See also* FUTURE.

later *adv.* At a subsequent time ▸ after, afterward, afterwards, latterly, next, subsequently, ulteriorly. *Idioms:* after a while, by and by, later on.

later *interjection* —*See* GOODBYE.

latest *adj.* —*See* CONTEMPORARY (2).

lather *n.* Moisture accumulated on a surface through sweating or condensation ▸ condensation, perspiration, sweat, transudation. —*See also* AGITATION (2), FOAM.

lather *v.* To excrete moisture through a porous skin or layer ▸ perspire, sweat, transude. —*See also* BEAT (1), FOAM.

lathery *adj.* —*See* FOAMY.

latitude *n.* —*See* LICENSE (1).

latter *adj.* **1.** Of or relating to a terminative condition, stage, or point ▸ final, last, terminal, ultimate. [*Compare* CLIMACTIC.] **2.** Next before the present one ▸ foregoing, last, preceding, previous. [*Compare* PAST.]

latter-day *adj.* —*See* CONTEMPORARY (2).

latterly *adv.* —*See* LATELY, LATER.

lattermost *adj.* —*See* LAST[1] (2).

lattice *n.* —*See* WEB.

laud *v.* —*See* HONOR (1), PRAISE (1), PRAISE (3).

laud *n.* —*See* PRAISE (1).

laudable *adj.* —*See* ADMIRABLE.

laudation *n.* —*See* PRAISE (1), PRAISE (2).

laudatory *adj.* —*See* COMPLIMENTARY (1).

laugh *v.* To express amusement or mirth by smiling and emitting inarticulate sounds ▸ bray, cachinnate, cackle, chortle, chuckle, giggle, guffaw, roar, snicker, snigger, tee-hee, titter. *Informal:* break up, heehaw, yuk. *Slang:* howl. *Idioms:* be in stitches, die laughing, laugh one's head off,

laughed them off the stage. ▸ *n.* **1.** The sound or act of laughing. **2.** *Informal* Something amusing or absurd. **3.** often **laughs** *Informal* Fun; amusement. **—laugh′er** *n.* **—laugh′ing·ly** *adv.*

laugh·a·ble (lăf′ə-bəl) ▸ *adj.* Causing or deserving laughter or derision. **—laugh′a·ble·ness** *n.* **—laugh′a·bly** *adv.*

laugh·ing·stock (lăf′ĭng-stŏk′) ▸ *n.* An object of jokes or ridicule; a butt.

laugh·ter (lăf′tər) ▸ *n.* The act or sound of laughing.

launch[1] (lônch, lănch) ▸ *v.* **1a.** To propel with force; hurl. **b.** To set or thrust in motion: *launch a rocket.* **2.** To put (a boat) into the water. **3.** To set going; initiate. **—launch** *n.* **—launch′er** *n.*

launch[2] (lônch, lănch) ▸ *n.* An open motorboat.

launch pad or **launch·ing pad** (lôn′chĭng, lăn′-) ▸ *n.* The base or platform from which a rocket or space vehicle is launched.

laun·der (lôn′dər, lăn′-) ▸ *v.* **1.** To wash or wash and iron (clothes or linens). **2.** To disguise the source or nature of (money) by channeling through an intermediate agent. **—laun′der·er** *n.* **—laun′dress** (-drĭs) *n.*

Laun·dro·mat (lôn′drə-măt′, lăn′-) ▸ A service mark for a commercial establishment with washing machines and dryers.

laun·dry (lôn′drē, lăn′-) ▸ *n., pl.* **-dries.** **1.** Soiled or laundered clothes. **2.** A place where laundering is done.

lau·re·ate (lôr′ē-ĭt, lŏr′-) ▸ *n.* One awarded a prize for great achievements esp. in the arts or sciences. **—lau′re·ate** *adj.* **—lau′re·ate·ship′** *n.*

lau·rel (lôr′əl, lŏr′-) ▸ *n.* **1.** A Mediterranean evergreen tree having aromatic leaves. **2.** Any of several similar shrubs or trees, such as the mountain laurel. **3.** often **laurels** **a.** A wreath of laurel conferred as a mark of honor. **b.** Honor and glory.

la·va (lä′və, lăv′ə) ▸ *n.* **1.** Molten rock that reaches the earth's surface through a volcano or fissure. **2.** Rock formed by the cooling and solidifying of lava.

lav·age (lăv′ĭj, lä-väzh′) ▸ *n.* A washing, esp. of a hollow bodily organ.

lav·a·liere (lăv′ə-lîr′) ▸ *n.* A pendant worn on a chain around the neck.

lav·a·to·ry (lăv′ə-tôr′ē) ▸ *n., pl.* **-ries.** **1.** A room equipped with washing and toilet facilities; bathroom. **2.** A flush toilet.

lave (lāv) ▸ *v.* **laved, lav·ing.** To wash; bathe.

lav·en·der (lăv′ən-dər) ▸ *n.* **1.** Any of a genus of aromatic plants having small purplish flowers. **2.** A pale to light purple. **—lav′en·der** *adj.*

lav·ish (lăv′ĭsh) ▸ *adj.* **1.** Extravagant; profuse. **2.** Immoderate in giving. ▸ *v.* To give or bestow in abundance; shower. **—lav′ish·er** *n.* **—lav′ish·ly** *adv.* **—lav′ish·ness** *n.*

La·voi·sier (lə-vwä′zē-ā′, lä-vwä-zyā′), **Antoine Laurent** (1743–94) ▸ French chemist.

law (lô) ▸ *n.* **1a.** A rule of conduct established by custom, agreement, or authority. **b.** A body of such rules. **2.** A piece of enacted legislation. **3.** A judicial system or its workings. **4.** The science and study of law; jurisprudence. **5.** **Law** *Judaism* The Pentateuch. **6.** A code of ethics or behavior. **7.** A formulation or generalization based on observed phenomena or consistent experience.

law·a·bid·ing (lô′ə-bī′dĭng) ▸ *adj.* Adhering to the law.

law·break·er (lô′brā′kər) ▸ *n.* One that breaks the law.

law·ful (lô′fəl) ▸ *adj.* Allowed or recognized by law. **—law′ful·ly** *adv.* **—law′ful·ness** *n.*

law·less (lô′lĭs) ▸ *adj.* **1.** Unrestrained by or contrary to the law. **2.** Not governed by law. **—law′less·ly** *adv.* **—law′less·ness** *n.*

law·mak·er (lô′mā′kər) ▸ *n.* One who drafts laws; a legislator. **—law′mak′ing** *n.*

lawn[1] (lôn) ▸ *n.* A plot of grass, usu. tended or mowed.

lawn[2] (lôn) ▸ *n.* A fine light cotton or linen.

Law·rence (lôr′əns, lŏr-), **D(avid) H(erbert)** (1885–1930) ▸ British writer.

Lawrence, T(homas) E(dward). "Lawrence of Arabia" (1888–1935) ▸ Welsh-born British soldier, adventurer, and writer.

law·ren·ci·um (lô-rĕn′sē-əm, lō-) ▸ *n.* *Symbol* **Lr** A short-lived, synthetic radioactive element. At. no. 103.

law·suit (lô′so͞ot′) ▸ *n.* A case brought before a court for settlement.

law·yer (loi′yər) ▸ *n.* One who gives legal advice to clients and represents them in court. **—law′yer·ly** *adv.*

lax (lăks) ▸ *adj.* **-er, -est.** **1.** Lacking due care or concern. **2.** Not strict; lenient. **3.** Not taut; slack. **—lax·a′tion** *n.* **—lax′i·ty, lax′ness** *n.* **—lax′ly** *adv.*

lax·a·tive (lăk′sə-tĭv) ▸ *n.* A food or drug that stimulates evacuation of the bowels. **—lax′a·tive** *adj.*

lay[1] (lā) ▸ *v.* **laid** (lād), **lay·ing.** **1.** To cause to lie down. **2.** To place in or bring to a specified condition. **3.** To bury. **4.** To put or set down: *lay railroad track.* **5.** To produce and deposit (eggs). **6.** To put against: *laid an ear to the door.* **7.** To put forward or impose: *lay the blame on us.* **8.** To devise; contrive. **9.** To spread: *lay paint on a canvas.* **10.** To prepare: *lay the table for lunch.* **11.** To present; submit: *laid the case before us.* ***—phrasal verbs:*** **lay aside** **1.** To give up; abandon. **2.** To save for the future. **lay away** To reserve for the future; save. **lay by** To save. **lay down** **1.** To give up; surrender. **2.** To specify: *laid down the rules.* **lay in** To store for future use. **lay off** **1.** To dismiss or suspend from a job.

THESAURUS

roll in the aisles, split one's sides.

laugh at *v.* *—See* RIDICULE.

laugh *n.* An act of laughing ▸ bray, cachinnation, cackle, chortle, chuckle, giggle, guffaw, laughter, roar, snicker, snigger, tee-hee, titter. *Informal:* heehaw, yuk. *Slang:* howl. *—See also* SCREAM (2).

laughable *adj.* Causing or deserving laughter or derision ▸ farcical, ludicrous, ridiculous, risible. [*Compare* FOOLISH.] *—See also* FUNNY (1).

laughingstock *n.* An object of amusement or laughter ▸ butt, jest, joke, mockery. *Idiom:* figure of fun.

laughter *n.* *—See* LAUGH.

launch *v.* *—See* INTRODUCE (1), START (1), THROW.

launch *n.* *—See* BEGINNING, THROW.

launder *v.* *—See* CLEAN (1).

laurels *n.* *—See* DISTINCTION (2).

lavation *n.* *—See* PURIFICATION (1).

lave *v.* To flow against or along ▸ bathe, lap, lip, wash. [*Compare* FLOW.] *—See also* CLEAN (1).

lavish *adj.* *—See* EXTRAVAGANT, GENEROUS (1), LUXURIOUS, PROFUSE.

lavish *v.* To give in great abundance ▸ heap, rain, shower. [*Compare* CONFER, DONATE, GIVE.]

lavishness *n.* *—See* EXTRAVAGANCE, GENEROSITY.

law *n.* **1.** A principle governing affairs within or among political units ▸ bylaw, canon, charter, edict, institute, ordinance, precept, prescription, regulation, rule, tenet. [*Compare* DOCTRINE.] **2.** The formal product of a legislative or judicial body ▸ act, assize, bill, enactment, legislation, lex, measure, statute. [*Compare* COMMAND, RULING.] **3.** A broad and basic rule or truth ▸ axiom, formula, fundamental, maxim, principle, theorem, truism, universal. *—See also* POLICE OFFICER, RULE.

law *v.* To institute or subject to legal proceedings ▸ litigate, prosecute, sue. *Idioms:* bring suit, haul (*or* drag) into court.

lawbreaker *n.* *—See* CRIMINAL.

lawful *adj.* Within, allowed by, or sanctioned by the law ▸ authorized, just, legal, legitimate, licit, permitted, rightful, valid, warranted. *Slang:* legit. [*Compare* ACCEPTABLE.]

lawfulness *n.* *—See* LEGALITY.

lawless *adj.* *—See* CRIMINAL (1), DISORDERLY, ILLEGAL, UNRULY.

lawlessness *n.* The state or quality of being illegal ▸ illegality, illegitimacy, illicitness, unlawfulness. *—See also* DISORDER (2), UNRULINESS.

lawn *n.* *—See* COMMON.

lawsuit *n.* A legal proceeding to demand justice or enforce a right ▸ action, case, cause, instance, litigation, suit.

lawyer *n.* A person who practices law ▸ attorney, counsel, counselor, jurist, pettifogger. *Slang:* ambulance chaser, legal eagle.

lax *adj.* *—See* LOOSE (1), NEGLIGENT, TOLERANT.

laxity or **laxness** *n.* *—See* LICENSE (2), NEGLIGENCE.

lay[1] *v.* **1.** To arrange tableware upon a table in preparation for a meal ▸ set, spread. **2.** To make a bet ▸ bet,

2. *Slang* To cease; quit. **lay out** 1. To make a plan for. 2. To knock to the ground. 3. To spend (money). **lay over** To make a stopover. **lay up** 1. To store for future needs. 2. *Informal* To confine with an illness or injury. ***—idioms:*** **lay of the land** The nature, arrangement, or disposition of something. **lay waste** To destroy.

lay² (lā) ► *adj.* 1. Of or relating to the laity. 2. Nonprofessional.

lay³ (lā) ► *n.* 1. A narrative poem, such as one sung by medieval minstrels; ballad. 2. A song; tune.

lay⁴ (lā) ► *v.* P.t. of **lie¹**.

lay·a·way (lā′ə-wā′) ► *n.* A payment plan in which merchandise is reserved with a down payment until the balance is paid in full.

lay·er (lā′ər) ► *n.* 1. One that lays, esp. a hen. 2. A single thickness, coating, or level of material. ► *v.* To divide or form into layers.

lay·ette (lā-ĕt′) ► *n.* Clothing and other supplies for a newborn child.

lay·man (lā′mən) ► *n.* 1. A man who is not a cleric. 2. A man who is a nonprofessional.

lay·off (lā′ôf′, -ŏf′) ► *n.* 1. Dismissal of employees, esp. for lack of work. 2. A period of temporary inactivity or rest.

lay·out (lā′out′) ► *n.* 1. An arrangement or plan. 2. *Print.* The overall design of a page, spread, or book.

lay·o·ver (lā′ō′vər) ► *n.* A short stop in a journey.

lay·per·son (lā′pûr′sən) ► *n.* A layman or laywoman. **—lay′peo′ple** *n.*

lay·wom·an (lā′wo͝om′ən) ► *n.* 1. A woman who is not a cleric. 2. A woman who is a nonprofessional.

Laz·a·rus (lăz′ər-əs) ► In the Bible, the brother of Mary and Martha.

Lazarus, Emma (1849–87) ► Amer. writer.

laze (lāz) ► *v.* **lazed, laz·ing.** To be lazy; loaf.

la·zy (lā′zē) ► *adj.* **-zi·er, -zi·est.** 1. Resistant to work or exertion; slothful. 2. Slow-moving; sluggish. **—la′zi·ly** *adv.* **—la′zi·ness** *n.*

lazy Su·san (so͞o′zən) ► *n.* A revolving tray for condiments or food.

lb. ► *abbr.* 1. libra (ancient Roman weight) 2. pound (modern weight)

LCD ► *abbr.* liquid-crystal display

LDL (ĕl′dē-ĕl′) ► *n.* A complex of lipids and proteins that transports cholesterol in the blood, high levels of which may increase the risk of heart disease.

L-do·pa (ĕl-dō′pə) ► *n.* A drug used to treat Parkinson's disease.

lea (lē, lā) ► *n.* A meadow.

leach (lēch) ► *v.* To remove or be removed from by the action of a percolating liquid. **—leach′er** *n.*

lead¹ (lēd) ► *v.* **led** (lĕd), **lead·ing.** 1. To guide, conduct, escort, or direct. 2. To influence; induce. 3. To be ahead or be at the head of: *My name led the list.* 4. To pursue; live: *lead an independent life.* 5. To begin or open with, as in games: *led an ace.* 6. To tend toward a certain goal or result: *policies that led to disaster.* ***—phrasal verbs:*** **lead off** To begin; start. **lead on** To lure; entice. **lead up to** To proceed toward (a main topic) with preliminary remarks. ► *n.* 1. The first or foremost position. 2. The margin by which one is ahead. 3. A clue. 4. Command; leadership. 5. An example; precedent. 6. The principal role in a play. 7. *Games* a. The prerogative or turn to make the first play. b. A card played first in a round. 8. A leash. **—lead′er** *n.* **—lead′er·ship′** *n.*

lead² (lĕd) ► *n.* 1. *Symbol* **Pb** A malleable, bluish-white, dense metallic element used in solder, radiation shields, and alloys. At. no. 82. 2. A weight used to make soundings. 3. Bullets; shot. 4. *Print.* A thin strip of metal used to separate lines of type. 5. A thin stick of graphitic composition, used in pencils. ► *v.* 1. To cover, line, weight, or fill with lead. 2. To secure (window glass) with lead. 3. To treat (e.g., gasoline or paint) with lead. **—lead** *adj.*

lead·en (lĕd′n) ► *adj.* 1. Made of lead. 2. Heavy and inert. 3. Downcast; depressed: *leaden spirits.* 4. Dark gray: *a leaden sky.* **—lead′en·ly** *adv.* **—lead′en·ness** *n.*

lead·ing¹ (lē′dĭng) ► *adj.* 1. In the first or front position. 2. Chief; principal. 3. Performing a lead in a theatrical production. 4. Encouraging a desired response: *a leading question.*

lead·ing² (lĕd′ĭng) ► *n.* 1. A border of lead, as around a windowpane. 2. *Print.* The spacing between lines.

lead-time (lēd′tīm′) ► *n.* The time between the initial stage of a project and the appearance of results.

leaf (lēf) ► *n., pl.* **leaves** (lēvz). 1. A usu. green, flattened plant structure attached to a stem and functioning as a principal organ of photosynthesis. 2. A leaflike part. 3. Leaves collectively; foliage. 4. Any of the sheets of paper bound in a book. 5. A very thin sheet of metal. 6. A hinged or removable section for a table top. 7. A movable section of a folding door, shutter, or gate. ► *v.* 1. To produce leaves. 2. To turn pages: *leafed through the catalog.* **—leaf′i·ness** *n.* **—leaf′less** *adj.* **—leaf′y** *adj.*

leaf·age (lē′fĭj) ► *n.* Foliage.

leaf·let (lē′flĭt) ► *n.* 1. A small leaf or leaflike part. 2. A printed handbill or flier. ► *v.* To hand out leaflets (to).

leaf spring ► *n.* A spring consisting of several layers of flexible metallic strips.

leaf·stalk or **leaf stalk** (lēf′stôk′) ► *n.* See **petiole.**

league¹ (lēg) ► *n.* 1. An association or alliance for common action. 2. An association of sports teams. 3. A level of competition. **—league** *v.*

league² (lēg) ► *n.* A unit of distance equal to 3.0 mi (4.8 km).

THESAURUS

gamble, game, play, wager. *Idiom:* put one's money on something. *—See also* AIM (1), BURY, CITE, DESIGN (1), FIX (3), GAMBLE (2), POSITION.

lay away *v.* *—See* BANK², SAVE (1).

lay down *v.* *—See* ABANDON (1), DICTATE.

lay for *v.* *—See* LURK.

lay into *v.* *—See* ATTACK (1), BEAT (2).

lay off *v.* *—See* ABANDON (2), DISMISS (1).

lay on or **upon** *v.* *—See* IMPOSE ON.

lay out *v.* To plan the details or arrangements of ► arrange, prepare, schedule, work out. *—See also* DESIGN (2), DRAFT (1), PLOT (1), SPEND (1).

lay² *adj.* *—See* PROFANE (2).

layabout *n.* *—See* WASTREL (2).

layer *n.* *—See* COAT (2).

layout *n.* *—See* APPROACH (1), ARRANGEMENT (1), DRAFT (1).

layperson *n.* *—See* AMATEUR.

laze *v.* *—See* IDLE (1).

laziness *n.* The quality or state of being lazy ► fainéance, fainéancy, idleness, indolence, otioseness, otiosity, shiftlessness, sloth, slothfulness, sluggardness, sluggishness. *Informal:* do-nothingism.

lazy *adj.* Resistant to exertion and activity ► fainéant, idle, indolent, otiose, shiftless, slothful, sluggard, sluggish. *Informal:* do-nothing. *Idiom:* bone lazy.

lazybones *n.* *—See* WASTREL (2).

leach *v.* *—See* OOZE.

lead *v.* To go through life in a certain way ► conduct, live, pass, pursue, spend. *—See also* ADMINISTER (1), DOMINATE (1), GUIDE, INFLUENCE, INTRODUCE (3).

lead off *v.* *—See* START (1).

lead to *v.* *—See* CAUSE, IMPLY.

lead *n.* The main performer in a theatrical production ► headliner, leading lady, leading man, prima donna, principal, protagonist, star, starlet. *—See also* DOMINANCE, FOREFRONT, GUIDE, MANAGEMENT, TIP³.

lead balloon *n.* *—See* FAILURE (1).

leaden *adj.* *—See* DULL (1), HEAVY (1), LANGUID, PONDEROUS.

leadenness *n.* *—See* LETHARGY.

leader *n.* A leading contestant or sure winner ► favorite, front-runner, number one, vanguard. *Informal:* shoo-in. *—See also* CHIEF, DIGNITARY, GUIDE.

leadership *n.* The capacity to lead others ► command, lead. *—See also* MANAGEMENT.

lead-in *n.* *—See* INTRODUCTION.

leading *adj.* *—See* BEST (1), BIG-LEAGUE, DOMINANT (1), FAMOUS, PRIMARY (1).

leadoff *n.* *—See* BEGINNING.

leadoff *adj.* *—See* BEGINNING.

leaf *n.* *—See* FLAKE.

leaf *v.* *—See* BROWSE (1).

leafless *adj.* *—See* BARE (3).

leaflet *n.* An announcement distributed on paper to a large number of people ► circular, flier, handbill, notice.

league *n.* *—See* ALLIANCE, CLASS (2), CONFERENCE (2), UNION (1).

league *v.* *—See* ALLY, BAND².

League of Nations ▸ A world organization (1920–46) to promote international cooperation and peace.

leak (lēk) ▸ *v.* **1.** To escape or permit the escape of something through a breach or flaw. **2.** *Informal* To disclose or become known through a breach of secrecy. ▸ *n.* **1.** A crack or flaw that permits something to escape from or enter a container or conduit. **2a.** The act or instance of leaking. **b.** An amount leaked. **3.** *Informal* A disclosure of confidential information. **—leak′er** *n.* **—leak′i·ness** *n.* **—leak′y** *adj.*

leak·age (lē′kĭj) ▸ *n.* **1.** The process of leaking. **2.** An amount that escapes by leaking.

lean^1 (lēn) ▸ *v.* **1.** To bend or cause to bend away from the vertical. **2.** To incline one's weight so as to be supported. **3.** To rely for assistance or support. **4.** To have a tendency or preference. **5.** *Informal* To exert pressure.

lean^2 (lēn) ▸ *adj.* **-er, -est. 1.** Not fleshy or fat; thin. **2.** Containing little or no fat: *a lean steak.* **3.** Not productive or prosperous. ▸ *n.* Meat with little or no fat. **—lean′ly** *adv.* **—lean′ness** *n.*

lean·ing (lē′nĭng) ▸ *n.* A tendency; preference.

lean-to (lēn′to͞o′) ▸ *n., pl.* **-tos. 1.** A structure with a single-pitch roof attached to the side of a building. **2.** A shelter resembling this.

leap (lēp) ▸ *v.* **leaped** or **leapt** (lĕpt, lēpt), **leap·ing. 1a.** To spring upward, as from the ground; jump. **b.** To jump over. **2.** To act quickly, abruptly, or impulsively. ▸ *n.* **1.** The act of leaping; jump. **2.** An abrupt transition. **—leap′er** *n.*

leap·frog (lēp′frôg′, -frŏg′) ▸ *n.* A game in which a player bends over while the next in line leaps over him or her. **—leap′frog′** *v.*

leap year ▸ *n.* A year having 366 days, with Feb. 29 being the extra day.

learn (lûrn) ▸ *v.* **learned** also **learnt** (lûrnt), **learn·ing. 1.** To gain knowledge, comprehension, or mastery of through experience or study. **2.** To memorize. **3.** To become informed. **—learn′er** *n.*

learn·ed (lûr′nĭd) ▸ *adj.* Possessing systematic knowledge. **—learn′ed·ly** *adv.* **—learn′ed·ness** *n.*

learn·ing (lûr′nĭng) ▸ *n.* Acquired knowledge or skill.

learning disability ▸ *n.* Any of various cognitive disorders that impede the ability to learn.

lease (lēs) ▸ *n.* A contract granting use or occupation of property during a specified period for a specified rent. ▸ *v.* **leased, leas·ing. 1.** To grant use of by lease. **2.** To hold under lease.

lease·hold (lēs′hōld′) ▸ *n.* **1.** Possession by lease. **2.** Property held by lease. **—lease′hold′er** *n.*

leash (lēsh) ▸ *n.* A restraining chain, rope, or strap attached to the collar or harness of an animal. **—leash** *v.*

least (lēst) ▸ *adj.* Superl. of **little. 1.** Lowest in importance or rank. **2.** Smallest. ▸ *adv.* Superl. of **little.** To or in the lowest or smallest degree. ▸ *n.* The lowest or smallest. ***—idioms:*** **at least 1.** Not less than. **2.** In any event. **in the least** At all.

least common denominator ▸ *n.* The least common multiple of the denominators of a set of fractions.

least common multiple ▸ *n.* The smallest quantity exactly divisible by two or more given quantities.

leath·er (lĕth′ər) ▸ *n.* The dressed or tanned hide of an animal, usu. with the hair removed. **—leath′er** *adj.* **—leath′er·y** *adj.*

leath·er·neck (lĕth′ər-nĕk′) ▸ *n. Slang* A US Marine.

leave^1 (lēv) ▸ *v.* **left** (lĕft), **leav·ing. 1.** To go out of or away (from). **2a.** To go without taking: *left my book on the bus.* **b.** To omit: *left out the best part.* **3.** To have as a remainder or result. **4.** To allow to remain in a specified state. **5.** To bequeath. **6.** To abandon; forsake. ***—phrasal verb:*** **leave off** To stop; cease.

leave^2 (lēv) ▸ *n.* **1.** Permission. **2.** Official permission to be absent from work or duty. **3.** Departure; farewell.

leav·en (lĕv′ən) ▸ *n.* **1.** An agent, such as yeast, that causes batter or dough to rise, esp. by fermentation. **2.** An element that lightens or enlivens. ▸ *v.* **1.** To add a rising agent to. **2.** To lighten or enliven. **—leav′ened** *adj.*

leav·en·ing (lĕv′ə-nĭng) ▸ *n.* A rising agent; leaven.

leaves (lēvz) ▸ *n.* Pl. of **leaf.**

leave-tak·ing (lēv′tā′kĭng) ▸ *n.* A departure or farewell.

leav·ings (lē′vĭngz) ▸ *pl.n.* Scraps or remains; residue.

Leb·a·non (lĕb′ə-nən, -nŏn′) ▸ A country of southwest Asia on the Mediterranean Sea. **—Leb′a·nese′** (-nēz′, -nēs′) *adj. & n.*

lech·er (lĕch′ər) ▸ *n.* A man given to lewd or lascivious behavior. **—lech′er·ous** *adj.* **—lech′er·ous·ly** *adv.* **—lech′er·y** *n.*

lec·i·thin (lĕs′ə-thĭn) ▸ *n.* Any of a group of fatty compounds found in plant and animal tissues and used in the processing of foods, cosmetics, and plastics.

lec·tern (lĕk′tərn) ▸ *n.* A reading stand for a public speaker.

lec·ture (lĕk′chər) ▸ *n.* **1.** A speech on a given subject delivered before an audience or class, as for the purpose of instruction. **2.** A solemn scolding or admonition. **—lec′ture** *v.*

led (lĕd) ▸ *v.* P.t. and p.part. of **lead**^{1}.

LED (ĕl′ē-dē′, lĕd) ▸ *n.* A semiconductor diode that converts electrical energy to light and is used in digital displays, as of a calculator.

ledge (lĕj) ▸ *n.* **1.** A shelflike projection on a wall or cliff. **2.** A reef.

ledg·er (lĕj′ər) ▸ *n.* A book in which the monetary transactions of a business are posted.

lee (lē) ▸ *n.* **1.** *Naut.* The side away from the wind; the sheltered side. **2.** Cover; shelter.

Lee, Henry. "Lighthorse Harry" (1756–1818) ▸ Amer. Revolutionary politician and soldier.

Lee, Robert Edward (1807–70) ▸ Amer. Confederate general.

leech (lēch) ▸ *n.* **1.** Any of various aquatic bloodsucking worms, of which one species was formerly used by

THESAURUS

leak *v. Informal* To be made public ▸ break, come out, get out, out, transpire. *Informal:* leak out. [*Compare* AIR, ANNOUNCE, APPEAR.] *—See also* BETRAY (2), OOZE.

lean^1 *v.* *—See* INCLINE, TEND^1.

lean^2 *adj.* *—See* BRIEF, THIN (1), TIGHT (3).

leaning *n.* *—See* INCLINATION (1).

leaning *adj.* *—See* OBLIQUE.

lean-to *n.* *—See* HUT.

leap *v.* *—See* BOUND^1, JUMP (1).

leap *n.* The act of jumping ▸ jump, pounce, spring, vault. [*Compare* FALL.] *—See also* BOUND^1 (2).

learn *v.* **1.** To gain knowledge or mastery of by study ▸ acquire, get, master. *Informal:* pick up. **2.** To commit to memory ▸ con, memorize. ***Idiom:*** learn by heart (*or* rote). [*Compare* REMEMBER.] *—See also* ABSORB (2), DISCOVER.

learned *adj.* *—See* EDUCATED.

learner *n.* *—See* BEGINNER, STUDENT.

learning *n.* *—See* EDUCATION (2).

lease *v.* **1.** To give temporary use of in return for payment ▸ hire (out), let (out), rent (out), sublet. **2.** To engage the temporary use of something for a fee ▸ charter, hire, rent.

leash *v.* *—See* HAMPER^1.

leash *n.* *—See* BRAKE.

least *adj.* *—See* MINIMAL.

leather *n.* The skin of an animal, sometimes including fur, hair, or feathers ▸ fur, hide, pelt.

leave^1 *v.* **1.** To give property to another after one's death ▸ bequeath, devise, hand down, hand on, pass (along *or* on), transmit, will. [*Compare* DONATE, GIVE.] **2.** To relinquish one's engagement in or occupation with ▸ demit, quit, resign, terminate. ***Idioms:*** hang it up, throw in the sponge (*or* towel). [*Compare* BREAK.] *—See also* ABANDON (1), GO (1).

leave off *v.* *—See* ABANDON (2), BREAK (5), STOP (1).

leave^2 *n.* A regularly scheduled period spent away from work or duty, often in recreation ▸ furlough, holiday, sabbatical, vacation. ***Idiom:*** time (*or* day) off. [*Compare* BREAK, TRIP.] *—See also* PERMISSION.

leaven *n.* *—See* CATALYST.

leavening *n.* *—See* CATALYST.

leave-taking *n.* *—See* DEPARTURE.

leavings *n.* *—See* BALANCE (4).

lecher *n.* An immoral or licentious man ▸ gigolo, goat, roué, satyr. *Informal:* dirty old man. *Slang:* lech. [*Compare* PHILANDERER, WANTON.]

lecherous *adj.* *—See* LASCIVIOUS.

lecture *n.* *—See* DISCOURSE, REBUKE, SPEECH (2).

lecture *v.* To talk to an audience formally ▸ address, prelect, sermonize, speak. [*Compare* CONVERSE.] *—See also* CHASTISE.

lecturer *n.* *—See* SPEAKER (1).

leech *n.* *—See* PARASITE.

physicians to bleed patients. **2.** One that preys on others; parasite. **3.** *Archaic* A physician. **—leech** *v.*

leek (lēk) ▸ *n.* An edible plant related to the onion, having a white slender bulb and dark-green leaves.

leer (lîr) ▸ *v.* To give a lewd or malicious look. **—leer** *n.* **—leer′ing·ly** *adv.*

leer·y (lîr′ē) ▸ *adj.* **-i·er, -i·est.** Suspicious; wary. **—leer′i·ly** *adv.* **—leer′i·ness** *n.*

lees (lēz) ▸ *pl.n.* Dregs.

Leeu·wen·hoek (lā′vən-ho͝ok′), **Anton van** (1632–1723) ▸ Dutch microscopy pioneer.

lee·ward (lo͞o′ərd, lē′wərd) ▸ *adv. & adj. Naut.* Away from the wind. **—lee′ward** *n.*

Lee·ward Islands (lē′wərd) ▸ **1.** The N group of the Lesser Antilles in the West Indies, from the Virgin Is. SE to Guadeloupe. **2.** A chain of small islets of HI in the central Pacific WNW of the main islands.

lee·way (lē′wā′) ▸ *n.* **1.** The drift of a ship or aircraft to leeward of the course being steered. **2.** A margin of freedom or variation; latitude.

left[1] (lĕft) ▸ *adj.* **1.** Of, located on, or corresponding to the side of the body to the north when one is facing east. **2.** often **Left** Of or belonging to the political left. ▸ *n.* **1a.** The direction or position on the left side. **b.** The left side or hand. **c.** A turn in this direction: *make a left.* **2.** often **Left** The people and groups who pursue liberal or egalitarian political goals. ▸ *adv.* Toward or on the left.

left[2] (lĕft) ▸ *v.* P.t. and p.part. of **leave**[1].

left field ▸ *n.* **1.** *Baseball* The third of the outfield to the left, looking from home plate. **2.** *Informal* A position far from the mainstream, as of opinion. **—left fielder** *n.*

left-hand (lĕft′hănd′) ▸ *adj.* **1.** Of or on the left. **2.** Designed for or done with the left hand.

left-hand·ed (lĕft′hăn′dĭd) ▸ *adj.* **1.** Using the left hand more skillfully or easily than the right. **2.** Done with or made for the left hand. **3.** Awkward; clumsy. **4.** Counterclockwise. ▸ *adv.* With the left hand. **—left′-hand′ed·ly** *adv.* **—left′-hand′ed·ness** *n.*

left-hand·er (lĕft′hăn′dər) ▸ *n.* One who is left-handed.

left·ism also **Left·ism** (lĕf′tĭz′əm) ▸ *n.* The ideology of the political left. **—left′ist** *adj. & n.*

left·o·ver (lĕft′ō′vər) ▸ *adj.* Remaining as an unused portion. ▸ *n.* **1.** A remnant or unused portion. **2. leftovers** Food remaining from a previous meal.

left wing ▸ *n.* **1.** The leftist faction of a group. **2.** See **left**[1] 2. **—left′-wing′** *adj.* **—left′-wing′er** *n.*

left·y (lĕf′tē) ▸ *n., pl.* **-ies.** *Informal* A left-handed person.

leg (lĕg) ▸ *n.* **1.** A limb or appendage used for locomotion or support. **2.** A part resembling a leg in shape or function. **3.** The part of a pair of trousers that covers the leg. **4.** A stage of a journey or course. ▸ *v.* **legged, leg·ging.** *Informal* To go on foot; walk or run: *legged it home.*

leg·a·cy (lĕg′ə-sē) ▸ *n., pl.* **-cies.** **1.** Money or property bequeathed to another by will. **2.** Something handed down from an ancestor or predecessor.

le·gal (lē′gəl) ▸ *adj.* **1.** Of or relating to law or lawyers. **2a.** Authorized by or based on law. **b.** Established by law; statutory. **3.** In conformity with or permitted by law. **—le·gal′i·ty** (lē-găl′ĭ-tē) *n.* **—le′gal·i·za′tion** *n.* **—le′gal·ize′** *v.* **—le′gal·ly** *adv.*

le·gal·ism (lē′gə-lĭz′əm) ▸ *n.* Strict, literal adherence to law. **—le′gal·ist** *n.* **—le′gal·is′tic** *adj.* **—le′gal·is′ti·cal·ly** *adv.*

leg·ate (lĕg′ĭt) ▸ *n.* An official emissary, esp. of the pope.

leg·a·tee (lĕg′ə-tē′) ▸ *n.* The inheritor of a legacy.

le·ga·tion (lĭ-gā′shən) ▸ *n.* A diplomatic mission in a foreign country ranking below an embassy. **—le·ga′tion·ar·y** *adj.*

le·ga·to (lĭ-gä′tō) ▸ *adv. & adj. Mus.* In a smooth, even style.

leg·end (lĕj′ənd) ▸ *n.* **1.** An unverified popular story, esp. one believed to be historical. **2.** One of great fame or popular renown. **3.** An inscription on an object. **4.** An explanatory caption. **—leg′en·dar′y** *adj.*

leg·er·de·main (lĕj′ər-də-mān′) ▸ *n.* Sleight of hand.

leg·ged (lĕg′ĭd, lĕgd) ▸ *adj.* Having a specified kind or number of legs.

leg·ging (lĕg′ĭng) ▸ *n.* **1.** A leg covering usu. extending from the ankle to the knee. **2. leggings** Close-fitting knit trousers.

leg·gy (lĕg′ē) ▸ *adj.* **-gi·er, -gi·est.** Having long slender legs. **—leg′gi·ness** *n.*

leg·horn or **Leg·horn** (lĕg′hôrn′, -ərn) ▸ *n.* Any of a breed of hardy domestic fowl noted for prolific production of eggs.

leg·i·ble (lĕj′ə-bəl) ▸ *adj.* Possible to read or decipher. **—leg′i·bil′i·ty, leg′i·ble·ness** *n.* **—leg′i·bly** *adv.*

le·gion (lē′jən) ▸ *n.* **1.** A unit of the Roman army consisting of 3,000 to 6,000 infantry and 100 to 200 cavalry. **2.** A large number; multitude. **—le′gion·ar′y** *adj. & n.* **—le′gion·naire′** *n.*

leg·is·late (lĕj′ĭ-slāt′) ▸ *v.* **-lat·ed, -lat·ing.** **1.** To create or pass laws. **2.** To bring about by legislation. **—leg′is·la′tor** *n.* **—leg′is·la·to′ri·al** (-lə-tôr′ē-əl) *adj.*

leg·is·la·tion (lĕj′ĭ-slā′shən) ▸ *n.* **1.** The act or process of legislating; lawmaking. **2.** A proposed or enacted law or group of laws.

leg·is·la·tive (lĕj′ĭ-slā′tĭv) ▸ *adj.* **1.** Of or relating to the enactment of laws. **2.** Having the power to create laws.

leg·is·la·ture (lĕj′ĭ-slā′chər) ▸ *n.* A body of people empowered to make laws.

le·git·i·mate (lə-jĭt′ə-mĭt) ▸ *adj.* **1.** Lawful. **2.** Being in accordance with accepted standards. **3.** Reasonable: *a legitimate doubt.* **4.** Authentic; genuine. **5.** Born of legally married parents. ▸ *v.* (-māt′) **-mat·ed, -mat·ing.** To make legitimate. **—le·git′i·ma·cy** (-mə-sē) *n.* **—le·git′i·mate·ly** *adv.*

le·git·i·mize (lə-jĭt′ə-mīz′) ▸ *v.* **-mized, -miz·ing.** To legitimate. **—le·git′i·mi·za′tion** *n.*

leg·ume (lĕg′yo͞om′, lə-gyo͞om′) ▸ *n.* **1.** A pod, such as that

THESAURUS

leech *v.* To take advantage of the generosity of others ▸ live off. *Informal:* sponge. *Slang:* freeload. [*Compare* BEG.]

leeriness *n.* —*See* DISTRUST.

leery *adj.* —*See* DISTRUSTFUL.

lees *n.* —*See* DEPOSIT (2).

leeway *n.* —*See* LICENSE (1).

left *adj.* —*See* LIBERAL.

left-handed *adj.* —*See* UNDERHAND.

leftist *n.* —*See* LIBERAL.

leftist *adj.* —*See* LIBERAL.

leftover *adj.* Being what remains, especially after a part has been removed ▸ extra, remaining, residual, stray. ***Idiom:*** left behind. [*Compare* SUPERFLUOUS.]

leftover *n.* —*See* BALANCE (4), SURPLUS.

leftovers *n.* —*See* BALANCE (4).

left-wing *adj.* —*See* LIBERAL.

left-winger *n.* —*See* LIBERAL.

legacy *n.* **1.** Something immaterial, as a style or philosophy, that is passed from one generation to another ▸ heritage, inheritance, tradition. **2.** Any special privilege accorded a firstborn ▸ birthright, heritage, inheritance, patrimony. [*Compare* RIGHT.]

legal *adj.* —*See* LAWFUL.

legality *n.* The state or quality of being within the law ▸ lawfulness, legitimacy, legitimateness, licitness, permissibility, rightfulness, soundness, validity. [*Compare* JUSTICE.]

legalize *v.* To make lawful ▸ decriminalize, legitimate, legitimatize, legitimize, warrant. [*Compare* AUTHORIZE, CONFIRM, PERMIT.]

legation *n.* A diplomatic office or headquarters in a foreign country ▸ deputation, embassy, mission.

legend *n.* —*See* CELEBRITY, LORE (1), MYTH (1).

legendary *adj.* —*See* FAMOUS, MYTHICAL.

legerdemain *n.* —*See* MAGIC (2).

legibility *n.* —*See* CLARITY.

legion *n.* —*See* CROWD.

legion *adj.* —*See* MANY.

legionnaire or **legionary** *n.* —*See* SOLDIER (2).

legislate *v.* —*See* ESTABLISH (2).

legislation *n.* —*See* LAW (2).

legislative *adj.* —*See* GOVERNMENTAL.

legit *adj.* —*See* AUTHENTIC (1), LAWFUL.

legitimacy or **legitimateness** *n.* —*See* LEGALITY.

legitimate *adj.* **3.** Being so legitimately ▸ rightful, true. —*See also* AUTHENTIC (1), LAWFUL.

legitimate *v.* —*See* ESTABLISH (2), LEGALIZE.

legitimize or **legitimatize** *v.* —*See* LEGALIZE.

legman *n.* —*See* PRESS.

of a pea or bean, that splits in two when mature. **2.** A plant of or related to the pea family. **—le·gu′mi·nous** *adj.*
leg·work (lĕg′wûrk′) ▸ *n. Informal* Work, such as collecting information, that involves walking or traveling about.
lei[1] (lā, lā′ē) ▸ *n., pl.* **leis.** A garland of flowers, esp. one worn around the neck.
lei[2] (lā) ▸ *n.* Pl. of **leu.**
Leib·niz or **Leib·nitz** (līb′nĭts, līp′-), Baron **Gottfried Wilhelm von** (1646–1716) ▸ German philosopher and mathematician.
Leip·zig (līp′sĭg, -sĭk) ▸ A city of E-central Germany SSW of Berlin.
lei·sure (lē′zhər, lĕzh′ər) ▸ *n.* Freedom from time-consuming duties or activities. ***—idiom:* at (one's) leisure** At one's convenience. **—lei′sured** *adj.*
lei·sure·ly (lē′zhər-lē, lĕzh′ər-) ▸ *adj.* Done without haste; unhurried. ▸ *adv.* In an unhurried manner. **—lei′sure·li·ness** *n.*
leit·mo·tif also **leit·mo·tiv** (līt′mō-tēf′) ▸ *n.* **1.** *Mus.* A melodic passage or phrase associated with a specific character or element. **2.** A dominant and recurring theme, as in a novel.
lek (lĕk) ▸ *n.* See **currency** table in Appendix.
lem·ming (lĕm′ĭng) ▸ *n.* A small rodent inhabiting northern regions and known for periodic mass migrations.
lem·on (lĕm′ən) ▸ *n.* **1a.** A spiny evergreen citrus tree cultivated for its yellow, egg-shaped fruit. **b.** The tart juicy fruit of this tree. **2.** *Informal* One that is unsatisfactory or defective. **—lem′on·y** *adj.*
lem·on·ade (lĕm′ə-nād′) ▸ *n.* A drink made of lemon juice, water, and sugar.
lem·pi·ra (lĕm-pîr′ə) ▸ *n.* See **currency** table in Appendix.
le·mur (lē′mər) ▸ *n.* A small arboreal African primate having large eyes and a long tail.
lend (lĕnd) ▸ *v.* **lent** (lĕnt), **lend·ing. 1.** To give or allow the use of temporarily. **2.** To provide (money) temporarily, usu. at interest. **3.** To contribute; impart. **4.** To be suitable for. **—lend′er** *n.*
length (lĕngkth, lĕngth, lĕnth) ▸ *n.* **1.** The measurement of something along its greatest dimension. **2.** Measured distance or dimension. **3.** Extent or duration: *the length of a journey.* **4.** often **lengths** The degree to which an action or policy is carried. ***—idiom:* at length 1.** Eventually. **2.** Fully. **—length′y** *adj.*
length·en (lĕngk′thən, lĕng′-, lĕn′-) ▸ *v.* To make or become long or longer.
length·ways (lĕngkth′wāz′, lĕngth′-, lĕnth′-) ▸ *adv.* Lengthwise.
length·wise (lĕngkth′wīz′, lĕngth′-, lĕnth′-) ▸ *adv. & adj.* Along the direction of the length.
le·ni·ent (lē′nē-ənt, lēn′yənt) ▸ *adj.* Not harsh or strict; merciful or indulgent. **—le′ni·en·cy, le′ni·ence** *n.* **—le′ni·ent·ly** *adv.*
Le·nin (lĕn′ĭn), **Vladimir Ilich** (1870–1924) ▸ Russian revolutionary leader and first head of the USSR (1917–24).
Len·in·grad (lĕn′ĭn-grăd′) ▸ See **Saint Petersburg.**
Len·in·ism (lĕn′ə-nĭz′əm) ▸ *n.* The theory and practice of proletarian revolution as developed by Lenin. **—Len′in·ist** *adj. & n.*
lens (lĕnz) ▸ *n., pl.* **lens·es. 1.** A piece of glass or other transparent material with opposite surfaces either or both of which are curved, by means of which light rays converge or diverge to form an image. **2.** A combination of two or more such pieces used to form an image for viewing or photographing. **3.** A transparent part of the eye that focuses light rays to form an image on the retina.

lent (lĕnt) ▸ *v.* P.t. and p.part. of **lend.**
Lent ▸ *n.* The 40 weekdays from Ash Wednesday until Easter, observed by Christians as a season of penitence.
len·til (lĕn′təl) ▸ *n.* The round, flattened, edible seed of a pealike Old World plant.
len·to (lĕn′tō) ▸ *adv. & adj. Mus.* In a slow tempo.
Le·o (lē′ō) ▸ *n.* **1.** A constellation in the Northern Hemisphere. **2.** The 5th sign of the zodiac.
Le·o·nar·do da Vin·ci (lē′ə-när′dō də vĭn′chē, dä, lā′-) (1452–1519) ▸ Italian painter, engineer, musician, and scientist.
le·one (lē-ōn′) ▸ *n.* See **currency** table in Appendix.
le·o·nine (lē′ə-nīn′) ▸ *adj.* Of or characteristic of a lion.
leop·ard (lĕp′ərd) ▸ *n.* **1.** A large wild cat of Africa and S Asia, having either tawny and black-spotted or all-black fur. **2.** The pelt of this animal.
le·o·tard (lē′ə-tärd′) ▸ *n.* **1.** A snug one-piece garment that covers the torso, worn esp. by dancers. **2. leotards** Tights. **—le′o·tard′ed** *adj.*
lep·er (lĕp′ər) ▸ *n.* **1.** A person affected by leprosy. **2.** A pariah; outcast.
lep·i·dop·ter·ist (lĕp′ĭ-dŏp′tər-ĭst) ▸ *n.* An entomologist specializing in the study of butterflies and moths.
lep·re·chaun (lĕp′rĭ-kŏn′, -kôn′) ▸ *n.* An elf in Irish folklore.
lep·ro·sy (lĕp′rə-sē) ▸ *n.* A chronic, mildly contagious disease marked by ulcers of the skin, bone, and viscera and leading to paralysis, gangrene, and deformation. **—lep′rous** *adj.*
lep·ton (lĕp′tŏn′) ▸ *n.* Any of a family of elementary particles, including the electrons and neutrinos, that take part in the weak interaction.
les·bi·an (lĕz′bē-ən) ▸ *n.* A woman whose sexual orientation is to women. **—les′bi·an** *adj.* **—les′bi·an·ism** *n.*
le·sion (lē′zhən) ▸ *n.* **1.** A wound or injury. **2.** A diseased patch of skin.
Le·so·tho (lə-sō′tō, -so͞o′to͞o) ▸ A country of S Africa forming an enclave within E-central South Africa.
less (lĕs) ▸ *adj.* Comp. of **little. 1.** Not as great in amount or quantity. **2.** Lower in importance, esteem, or rank. **3.** Consisting of a smaller number. ▸ *adv.* Comp. of **little.** To a smaller extent, degree, or frequency. ▸ *n.* A smaller amount.
-less ▸ *suff.* **1.** Without; lacking: *blameless.* **2.** Unable to act or be acted on in a specified way: *dauntless.*
les·see (lĕ-sē′) ▸ *n.* One that holds a lease.
less·en (lĕs′ən) ▸ *v.* To make or become less.
less·er (lĕs′ər) ▸ *adj.* Comp. of **little.** Smaller in size or importance.
Lesser Antilles ▸ An island group of the E West Indies extending in an arc from Curaçao to the Virgin Is.
les·son (lĕs′ən) ▸ *n.* **1.** Something to be learned. **2a.** A period of instruction. **b.** An instructional exercise. **3.** An edifying experience or example. **4.** A rebuke or reprimand. **5.** A reading from a sacred text as part of a religious service.
les·sor (lĕs′ôr′, lĕ-sôr′) ▸ *n.* One that lets property under a lease.
lest (lĕst) ▸ *conj.* For fear that: *tiptoed lest they should hear.*
let[1] (lĕt) ▸ *v.* **let, let·ting. 1.** To give permission or opportunity to; allow: *I let them borrow the car.* **2.** To cause to; make: *Let the news be known.* **3.** Used as an auxiliary in the imperative to express: **a.** A command, request, or proposal: *Let's finish the job!* **b.** A warning or threat: *Just let her try!* **4.** To release or give forth: *let out a yelp.* **5.**

THESAURUS

leisure *n.* Unrestricted freedom to choose ▸ convenience, discretion, pleasure, will. *—See also* REST[1] (2).
leisurely *adj. —See* DELIBERATE (3).
lemma *n. —See* ASSUMPTION, ENTRY.
lend *v.* To supply money, especially on credit ▸ advance, discount, float, loan. *Idiom:* extend credit to.
length *n.* The ultimate point to which an action, thought, discussion, or policy is carried ▸ degree, end, extreme, extremity, limit. *—See also* DISTANCE (1), EXTENT.
lengthen *v.* To make or become longer ▸ draw out, elongate, extend, prolong, prolongate, protract, spin (out), stretch (out), string out. [*Compare* BROADEN, INCREASE.]
lengthening *n. —See* EXTENSION (1).
lengthy *adj. —See* LONG[1] (1), LONG[1] (2).
lenience or **leniency** *n. —See* MERCY, TOLERANCE.
lenient *adj. —See* TOLERANT.
lese majesty *n.* Willful violation of allegiance to one's country ▸ sedition, seditiousness, traitorousness, treason. [*Compare* FAITHLESSNESS.] *—See also* DISRESPECT.
lesion *n.* Marked tissue damage, especially when produced by physical injury ▸ laceration, trauma, traumatism, wound. [*Compare* HARM.]
lessen *v. —See* DECREASE, DEPRECIATE, RELIEVE (1).
lesser *adj. —See* MINOR (1).
lesson *n. —See* EXAMPLE (2), MORAL.
let *v. —See* LEASE (1), PERMIT (1), PERMIT (2), PERMIT (3).
let down *v. —See* DISAPPOINT, LOWER[2].

To rent or lease. *—phrasal verbs:* **let down** 1. To lower. 2. To disappoint. **let on** To allow to be known; admit. **let out** 1. To come to a close. 2. To reveal: *Who let the story out?* **let up** To diminish: *The rain let up.*

let² (lĕt) ▸ *n.* 1. Something that hinders; obstacle. 2. *Sports* An invalid stroke in tennis and other net games that must be repeated.

-let ▸ *suff.* 1. Small: *booklet.* 2. Something worn on: *armlet.*

let·down (lĕt′doun′) ▸ *n.* 1. A decrease, decline, or relaxation, as of effort or energy. 2. A disappointment.

le·thal (lē′thəl) ▸ *adj.* Causing or capable of causing death. **—le·thal′i·ty** (lē-thăl′ĭ-tē) *n.* **—le′thal·ly** *adv.*

leth·ar·gy (lĕth′ər-jē) ▸ *n., pl.* **-gies.** A state of sluggishness, inactivity, and apathy. **—le·thar′gic** (lə-thär′jĭk) *adj.* **—le·thar′gi·cal·ly** *adv.*

le·the (lē′thē) ▸ *n.* 1. **Lethe** *Gk. Myth.* The river of forgetfulness in Hades. 2. Forgetfulness; oblivion.

let's (lĕts) ▸ Let us.

Lett (lĕt) ▸ *n.* A member of a Baltic people constituting the main population of Latvia.

let·ter (lĕt′ər) ▸ *n.* 1. A written character representing a speech sound and being a unit of an alphabet. 2. A written or printed communication. 3. Literal meaning. 4. **letters** *(takes sing. v.)* Learning or knowledge, esp. of literature. ▸ *v.* To write letters on. **—let′ter·er** *n.*

let·tered (lĕt′ərd) ▸ *adj.* 1. Literate. 2. Learned. 3. Inscribed with letters.

let·ter·head (lĕt′ər-hĕd′) ▸ *n.* 1. Stationery with a printed or engraved heading. 2. The heading itself.

let·ter·ing (lĕt′ər-ĭng) ▸ *n.* 1. The act of forming letters. 2. Letters inscribed, as on a sign.

let·ter-per·fect (lĕt′ər-pûr′fĭkt) ▸ *adj.* Correct to the last detail.

let·ter·press (lĕt′ər-prĕs′) ▸ *n.* The process of printing from a raised inked surface.

let·ter-qual·i·ty (lĕt′ər-kwŏl′ĭ-tē) ▸ *adj.* Of or producing printed characters similar in clarity to those produced by a typewriter.

Let·tish (lĕt′ĭsh) ▸ *n.* See **Latvian** 2.

let·tuce (lĕt′əs) ▸ *n.* A plant cultivated for its edible leaves, eaten esp. as salad.

let·up (lĕt′ŭp′) ▸ *n.* 1. A reduction; slowdown. 2. A pause.

le·u (lĕ′o͞o) ▸ *n., pl.* **lei** (lā). See **currency** table in Appendix.

leu·ke·mi·a (lo͞o-kē′mē-ə) ▸ *n.* Any of various acute or chronic diseases in which unrestrained proliferation of white blood cells occurs. **—leu·ke′mic** *adj. & n.*

leuko- or **leuk-** also **leuco-** or **leuc-** ▸ *pref.* 1. White; colorless: *leukocyte.* 2. Leukocyte: *leukemia.*

leu·ko·cyte also **leu·co·cyte** (lo͞o′kə-sīt′) ▸ *n.* A white blood cell. **—leu′ko·cyt′ic** (-sĭt′ĭk) *adj.*

lev (lĕf) ▸ *n., pl.* **lev·a** (lĕv′ə). See **currency** table in Appendix.

Le·vant (lə-vănt′) ▸ The countries bordering on the E Mediterranean Sea. **—Le′van·tine′** (lĕv′ən-tīn′, -tēn′, lə-văn′-) *adj. & n.*

lev·ee (lĕv′ē) ▸ *n.* 1. An embankment raised to prevent a river from overflowing. 2. A landing place on a river.

lev·el (lĕv′əl) ▸ *n.* 1. Relative position or rank on a scale. 2. A natural or proper position, place, or stage. 3. Position along a vertical axis; height or depth. 4a. A horizontal line or plane at right angles to the plumb. b. The position or height of such a line or plane. 5. A flat horizontal surface. 6. A land area of uniform elevation. 7. An instrument for ascertaining whether a surface is horizontal. ▸ *adj.* 1. Having a flat smooth surface. 2. Horizontal. 3. At the same height or position as another; even. 4. Consistent: steady. 5. Rational; sensible. 6. Filled evenly to the top. ▸ *v.* **-eled, -el·ing** or **-elled, -el·ling.** 1. To make horizontal, flat, or even. 2. To tear down; raze. 3. To equalize. 4. To aim or direct. 5. To direct emphatically toward someone: *leveled charges of dishonesty.* 6. *Informal* To be frank and open. *—phrasal verb:* **level off** To move toward stability or consistency. **—lev′el·er** *n.* **—lev′el·ly** *adv.* **—lev′el·ness** *n.*

lev·el·head·ed (lĕv′əl-hĕd′ĭd) ▸ *adj.* Characteristically self-composed and sensible. **—lev′el·head′ed·ness** *n.*

lev·er (lĕv′ər, lē′vər) ▸ *n.* 1. A simple machine consisting of a rigid bar pivoted on a fixed point and used to transmit force. 2. A projecting handle used to adjust or operate a mechanism. 3. A means of accomplishing; tool. ▸ *v.* To move or lift with or as if with a lever.

lev·er·age (lĕv′ər-ĭj, lē′vər-) ▸ *n.* 1. The action or mechanical advantage of a lever. 2. Positional advantage. 3. The use of credit or borrowed funds to improve one's speculative capacity. **—lev′er·age** *v.*

le·vi·a·than (lə-vī′ə-thən) ▸ *n.* 1. Something unusually large of its kind. 2. *Bible* A monstrous sea creature mentioned in the Bible.

Le·vi's (lē′vīz′) ▸ A trademark for denim trousers.

lev·i·tate (lĕv′ĭ-tāt′) ▸ *v.* **-tat·ed, -tat·ing.** To rise or raise into the air and float in apparent defiance of gravity. **—lev′i·ta′tion** *n.*

Le·vit·i·cus (lə-vĭt′ĭ-kəs) ▸ *n.* See **Bible** table in Appendix.

lev·i·ty (lĕv′ĭ-tē) ▸ *n., pl.* **-ties.** Lightness of manner or speech; frivolity.

lev·y (lĕv′ē) ▸ *v.* **-ied, -y·ing.** 1. To impose or collect (a tax). 2. To draft into military service. 3. To wage (a war). 4. To confiscate property. ▸ *n., pl.* **-ies.** 1. The act or process of levying. 2. Money, property, or troops levied. **—lev′i·er** *n.*

lewd (lo͞od) ▸ *adj.* **-er, -est.** 1. Lustful. 2. Obscene; indecent. **—lewd′ly** *adv.* **—lewd′ness** *n.*

Lewis, C(live) S(taples) (1898–1963) ▸ British writer and critic.

Lewis, (Harry) Sinclair (1885–1951) ▸ Amer. novelist; 1930 Nobel.

Lewis, Meriwether (1774–1809) ▸ Amer. soldier and explorer.

lex·i·cog·ra·phy (lĕk′sĭ-kŏg′rə-fē) ▸ *n.* The work of writing or compiling a dictionary. **—lex′i·cog′ra·pher** *n.* **—lex′i·co·graph′ic** (-kə-grăf′ĭk), **lex′i·co·graph′i·cal** *adj.*

lex·i·con (lĕk′sĭ-kŏn′) ▸ *n.* 1. A dictionary. 2. A specialized vocabulary. **—lex′i·cal** *adj.*

THESAURUS

let go *v.* *—See* DISMISS (1), DROP (5).
let in *v.* *—See* ACCEPT (3).
let off *v.* *—See* EMIT, EXCUSE (1).
let out *v.* *—See* BETRAY (2), DRAIN (1), EMIT, LEASE (1).
let up *v.* *—See* EASE (1), SUBSIDE.

letdown *n.* *—See* DISAPPOINTMENT (2).

lethal *adj.* *—See* DEADLY.

lethality or **lethalness** *n.* The quality or condition of causing death or disaster ▸ deadliness, fatality, fatefulness.

lethargic *adj.* Lacking mental and physical alertness and activity ▸ enervated, hebetudinous, inert, slothful, sluggish, stupid, stuporous, torpid. *Slang:* dopey. [*Compare* DULL, LANGUID.] *—See also* APATHETIC.

lethargy *n.* A deficiency in mental and physical alertness and activity ▸ dullness, enervation, hebetude, inertness, languidness, languor, lassitude, leadenness, listlessness, slothfulness, sluggishness, stupor, torpidity, torpor. [*Compare* STUPIDITY.] *—See also* APATHY.

letter *n.* A written communication that is directed to another ▸ correspondence, dispatch, epistle, line, memo, memorandum, message, missive, note. *—See also* CHARACTER (7).

lettered *adj.* *—See* EDUCATED.

lettuce *n.* *—See* MONEY (1).

letup *n.* *—See* WANING.

level *n.* *—See* CLASS (2), DEGREE (1), DEGREE (2), PLACE (1).
level *adj.* *—See* EVEN (1), EVEN (2).
level *v.* *—See* AIM (1), BALANCE (1), DESTROY (2), DROP (3), EQUALIZE, EVEN.

levelheaded *adj.* *—See* SENSIBLE.

levelheadedness *adj.* *—See* BALANCE (2).

leverage *n.* *—See* ADVANTAGE (3), INFLUENCE.

leviathan *n.* *—See* GIANT.

levity *n.* *—See* TRIFLE.

levy *v.* 1. To establish and apply as compulsory ▸ assess, exact, impose, put. 2. To enroll compulsorily in military service ▸ conscript, draft, impress, induct.
levy *n.* *—See* DRAFT (2), TAX.

lewd *adj.* *—See* LASCIVIOUS, OBSCENE.

lewdness *n.* *—See* OBSCENITY (1).

lex *n.* *—See* LAW (2).

lexeme *n.* *—See* TERM.

lexical *adj.* Relating to, consisting of, or having the nature of words ▸ linguistic, verbal, wordy.

lexicon *n.* 1. An alphabetical list of words often defined or translated ▸ dictionary, glossary, vocabulary, word-

Lex·ing·ton (lĕk′sĭng-tən) ► **1.** A city of northeast-central KY east-southeast of Louisville. **2.** A town of NE MA; site of first battle of the American Revolution (April 19, 1775).

Lha·sa (lä′sə, lăs′ə) ► A city of SW China, the capital of Xizang (Tibet).

Li ► The symbol for the element **lithium**.

li·a·bil·i·ty (lī′ə-bĭl′ĭ-tē) ► *n., pl.* **-ties.** **1.** Something for which one is liable; an obligation, responsibility, or debt. **2.** Something that holds one back; handicap.

li·a·ble (lī′ə-bəl) ► *adj.* **1.** Legally obligated; responsible. **2.** Subject; susceptible. **3.** Likely; apt.

li·ai·son (lē′ā-zŏn′, lē-ā′-) ► *n.* **1a.** Communication between groups or units. **b.** One that maintains communication. **2.** A love affair.

li·an·a (lē-ä′nə, -ăn′ə) ► *n.* Any climbing, woody, usu. tropical vine.

li·ar (lī′ər) ► *n.* One that tells lies.

li·ba·tion (lī-bā′shən) ► *n.* **1.** The ritual pouring of a liquid offering or the liquid so poured. **2.** *Informal* An alcoholic drink.

li·bel (lī′bəl) ► *n.* **1.** A written, printed, or pictorial statement that maliciously damages a person's reputation. **2.** The act or offense of publishing a libel. ► *v.* **-beled, -bel·ing** or **-belled, -bel·ling.** To make or publish a libel about. **—li′bel·er, li′bel·ist** *n.* **—li′bel·ous** *adj.* **—li′bel·ous·ly** *adv.*

lib·er·al (lĭb′ər-əl, lĭb′rəl) ► *adj.* **1a.** Open-minded; tolerant. **b.** Favoring civil and political liberties, democratic reforms, and protection from arbitrary authority. **2a.** Tending to give freely; generous. **b.** Abundant; ample. **3.** Not strict or literal; approximate. **4.** Of or based on the traditional arts and sciences of a college or university curriculum: *a liberal education.* ► *n.* A person with liberal ideas or opinions. **—lib′er·al·ism** *n.* **—lib′er·al′i·ty** (lĭb′ə-răl′ĭ-tē) *n.* **—lib′er·al·i·za′tion** *n.* **—lib′er·al·ize′** *v.* **—lib′er·al·ly** *adv.*

lib·er·ate (lĭb′ə-rāt′) ► *v.* **-at·ed, -at·ing.** To set free, as from oppression, confinement, or foreign control. **—lib′er·a′tion** *n.* **—lib′er·a′tion·ist** *n.* **—lib′er·a′tor** *n.*

Li·be·ri·a (lī-bîr′ē-ə) ► A country of W Africa on the Atlantic. **—Li·be′ri·an** *adj. & n.*

lib·er·tar·i·an (lĭb′ər-târ′ē-ən) ► *n.* One who advocates maximizing individual rights and minimizing the role of the state. **—lib′er·tar′i·an·ism** *n.*

lib·er·tine (lĭb′ər-tēn′) ► *n.* A dissolute or licentious person. **—lib′er·tine′** *adj.* **—lib′er·tin·ism′** *n.*

lib·er·ty (lĭb′ər-tē) ► *n., pl.* **-ties.** **1a.** The condition of being free from restriction or control; freedom. **b.** The right to act or believe as one chooses. **2.** Permission; authorization. **3.** often **liberties a.** Undue familiarity. **b.** Latitude; license: *took liberties with the truth.* **4.** Authorized leave from naval duty.

li·bi·do (lĭ-bē′dō, -bī′-) ► *n., pl.* **-dos.** **1.** The psychic and emotional energy associated with biological drives. **2.** Sexual desire. **—li·bid′i·nal** (-bĭd′n-əl) *adj.* **—li·bid′i·nous** *adj.*

Li·bra (lē′brə, lī′-) ► *n.* **1.** A constellation in the Southern Hemisphere near Scorpius and Virgo. **2.** The 7th sign of the zodiac.

li·brar·i·an (lī-brâr′ē-ən) ► *n.* A specialist in library work. **—li·brar′i·an·ship′** *n.*

li·brar·y (lī′brĕr′ē) ► *n., pl.* **-ies.** **1.** A place where written or recorded materials, such as books, periodicals, tapes, or films, are kept for reading, reference, or lending. **2.** A collection of such materials.

li·bret·to (lĭ-brĕt′ō) ► *n., pl.* **-bret·tos** or **-bret·ti** (-brĕt′ē). The text of a dramatic musical work, such as an opera. **—li·bret′tist** *n.*

Lib·y·a (lĭb′ē-ə) ► A country of N Africa on the Mediterranean Sea. **—Lib′y·an** *adj. & n.*

lice (līs) ► *n.* Pl. of **louse** 1.

li·cense (lī′səns) ► *n.* **1a.** Official or legal permission to do or own a specified thing. **b.** Proof of permission granted, usu. in the form of a document, card, plate, or tag. **2.** Deviation from normal rules, practices, or methods. **3.** Latitude of action, esp. in behavior or speech. **4.** Excessive freedom. ► *v.* **-censed, -cens·ing.** **1.** To give permission to or for. **2.** To grant a license to or for. **—li′cens·a·ble** *adj.* **—li′cens·ee′** *n.* **—li′cens·er** *n.*

li·censed practical nurse (lī′sənst) ► *n.* A nurse who has completed a practical nursing program and is licensed by a state to provide routine patient care under the direction of a registered nurse or a physician.

li·cen·tious (lī-sĕn′shəs) ► *adj.* Lacking moral, esp. sexual restraint. **—li·cen′tious·ly** *adv.* **—li·cen′tious·ness** *n.*

li·chee (lē′chē) ► *n.* Var. of **litchi.**

li·chen (lī′kən) ► *n.* A fungus that grows symbiotically with algae, resulting in a composite organism that forms a crustlike or branching growth on rocks or tree trunks. **—li′chen·ous** *adj.*

lic·it (lĭs′ĭt) ► *adj.* Legal. **—lic′it·ly** *adv.* **—lic′it·ness** *n.*

lick (lĭk) ► *v.* **1.** To pass the tongue over or along. **2.** To lap up. **3.** To touch lightly: *waves licked the shore.* **4.** *Slang* To thrash; defeat. ► *n.* **1.** The act of licking. **2.** A small quantity. **3.** A deposit of exposed natural salt licked by passing animals. **4.** A blow. **—lick′er** *n.*

THESAURUS

book. **2.** All the words of a language ► vocabulary, word-hoard. *—See also* LANGUAGE (2).

liability *n.* *—See* DEBT (1), DEBT (2), DISADVANTAGE, DUTY (1), EXPOSURE, RESPONSIBILITY.

liable *adj.* **1.** Legally or officially obligated ► accountable, amenable, answerable, responsible. [*Compare* OBLIGATED.] **2.** Tending to incur ► open, prone, subject, susceptible, susceptive, vulnerable. [*Compare* HELPLESS.] *—See also* INCLINED.

liaison *n.* *—See* LOVE (3).

liar *n.* One who tells lies ► deceiver, dissimulator, fabricator, fabulist, false witness, falsifier, fibber, perjurer, prevaricator. *Informal:* storyteller. [*Compare* HYPOCRITE.]

libation *n.* *—See* DRINK (1).

libel *n.* The expression of injurious, malicious statements about someone ► aspersion, badmouthing, calumniation, calumny, character assassination, defamation, denigration, detraction, mudslinging, obloquy, scandal, slander, smear, smear campaign, traducement, vilification. [*Compare* BELITTLEMENT, VITUPERATION.]

libel *v.* *—See* MALIGN.

libelous *adj.* Damaging to the reputation ► calumnious, defamatory, detractive, injurious, invidious, scandalous, slanderous. [*Compare* DEROGATORY.]

liberal *adj.* Favoring civil liberties and social reform, especially as a political philosophy ► left, leftist, left-wing, liberalistic, neoliberal, progressive, reformist, reform-minded, Whiggish. [*Compare* ULTRALIBERAL.] *—See also* BROAD-MINDED, GENEROUS (1).

liberal *n.* One with politically liberal views ► leftist, left-winger, liberalist, neoliberal, progressive, Whig. [*Compare* ULTRALIBERAL.]

liberality *n.* *—See* GENEROSITY.

liberate *v.* *—See* FREE (1).

liberated *adj.* *—See* LOOSE (2).

liberation *n.* *—See* LIBERTY, RESCUE.

liberator *n.* *—See* RESCUER.

libertine *n.* *—See* WANTON.

libertine *adj.* *—See* WANTON (1).

libertinism *n.* *—See* LICENSE (2).

liberty *n.* The state of not being in confinement or servitude ► emancipation, freedom, liberation, manumission. *—See also* FREEDOM, LICENSE (1).

libidinous or **libidinal** *adj.* *—See* LASCIVIOUS.

libido or **libidinousness** *n.* *—See* DESIRE (2).

libretto *n.* *—See* SCRIPT (2).

license *n.* **1.** Freedom from normal restraints, limitations, or regulations ► elbowroom, entitlement, free hand, latitude, leeway, liberty, margin, play, privilege, room, scope. [*Compare* RIGHT.] **2.** Excessive freedom; lack of restraint ► anarchy, dissoluteness, dissolution, indulgence, laxity, laxness, libertinism, licentiousness, profligacy, slackness. [*Compare* [illegible]CESS.] **3.** A document that gives permission to do something ► commission, furlough, passport, permit, ticket, visa, warrant. *—See also* PERMISSION.

license *v.* *—See* AUTHORIZE, PERMIT (2).

licentious *adj.* *—See* ABANDONED (2).

licentiousness *n.* *—See* LICENSE (2).

licit *adj.* *—See* LAWFUL.

licitness *n.* *—See* LEGALITY.

lick *v.* *—See* BEAT (2), DEFEAT.

lick *n.* *—See* BLOW[2].

lick·e·ty-split (lĭk′ĭ-tē-splĭt′) ► *adv. Informal* With great speed.

lick·ing (lĭk′ĭng) ► *n. Slang* 1. A beating or spanking. 2. A severe loss or defeat.

lic·o·rice (lĭk′ər-ĭs, -ĭsh) ► *n.* 1. A plant having a sweet, distinctively flavored root. 2. A candy made from or flavored with this root.

lid (lĭd) ► *n.* 1. A removable cover for a hollow receptacle. 2. An eyelid.

li·do·caine (lī′də-kān′) ► *n.* A synthetic drug used chiefly as a local anesthetic.

lie[1] (lī) ► *v.* **lay** (lā), **lain** (lān), **ly·ing** (lī′ĭng). 1. To be or place oneself at rest in a flat, horizontal, or recumbent position; recline. 2. To be or remain in a specified condition. 3. To occupy a position or place. 4. To extend. ► *n.* The position in which something lies. ***—idiom:*** **lie** (or **lay**) **low** To keep oneself or one's plans hidden.

lie[2] (lī) ► *n.* A false statement deliberately presented as true. ► *v.* **lied, ly·ing** (lī′ĭng). 1. To tell a lie. 2. To convey a false image or impression: *Appearances often lie.*

Liech·ten·stein (lĭk′tən-stīn′, lĭkн′tən-shtīn′) ► A small Alpine principality in central Europe between Austria and Switzerland. Cap. Vaduz.

lied (lēt) ► *n., pl.* **lie·der** (lē′dər). A German lyric song.

lie detector ► *n.* A machine used to detect possible deception during an interrogation.

lief (lēf) ► *adv.* **-er, -est.** Readily; willingly.

liege (lēj) ► *n.* 1. A feudal lord. 2. A vassal. ► *adj.* Loyal; faithful.

lien (lēn, lē′ən) ► *n.* The right to take and hold or sell the property of a debtor as security or payment for a debt.

lieu (lo͞o) ► *n. Archaic* Place; stead. ***—idiom:*** **in lieu of** In place of; instead of.

lieu·ten·ant (lo͞o-tĕn′ənt) ► *n.* 1a. A rank, as in the US Navy, above lieutenant junior grade and below lieutenant commander. b. A first lieutenant. c. A second lieutenant. 2. An officer in a police or fire department ranking below a captain. 3. One who acts in place of a superior. **—lieu·ten′an·cy** *n.*

lieutenant colonel ► *n.* A rank, as in the US Army, above major and below colonel.

lieutenant commander ► *n.* A rank, as in the US Navy, above lieutenant and below commander.

lieutenant general ► *n.* A rank, as in the US Army, above major general and below general.

lieutenant governor ► *n.* An elected official ranking just below the governor of a state in the US.

lieutenant junior grade ► *n., pl.* **lieutenants junior grade.** A rank, as in the US Navy, above ensign and below lieutenant.

life (līf) ► *n., pl.* **lives** (līvz). 1. *Biol.* The quality that distinguishes living organisms from dead organisms and inanimate matter, manifested in functions such as metabolism, growth, reproduction, and response to stimuli. 2. Living organisms collectively: *marine life.* 3. A living being. 4. The interval between birth and death. 5. A biography. 6. Human existence, relationships, or activities: *everyday life.* 7. A manner of living: *led a hard life.* 8. Liveliness; animation. **—life′less** *adj.* **—life′less·ly** *adv.* **—life′less·ness** *n.*

life·blood (līf′blŭd′) ► *n.* An indispensable or vital part.

life·boat (līf′bōt′) ► *n.* A boat used for abandoning ship or for rescue services.

life buoy ► *n.* A usu. ringlike cork or polystyrene life preserver.

life·guard (līf′gärd′) ► *n.* An expert swimmer employed to safeguard other swimmers.

life insurance ► *n.* Insurance that guarantees a specific sum of money to a designated beneficiary upon the death of the insured.

life·like (līf′līk′) ► *adj.* Accurately representing real life.

life·line (līf′līn′) ► *n.* 1. A line thrown to someone falling or drowning. 2. A means or route by which necessary supplies are transported.

life·long (līf′lông′, -lŏng′) ► *adj.* Continuing for a lifetime.

life preserver ► *n.* A buoyant device designed to keep a person afloat in the water.

life-size (līf′sīz′) also **life-sized** (-sīzd′) ► *adj.* Being of the same size as an original.

life·style also **life-style** or **life style** (līf′stīl′) ► *n.* A way of life that reflects the attitudes and values of a person or group.

life·time (līf′tīm′) ► *n.* The period of time during which an individual is alive.

life·work (līf′wûrk′) ► *n.* The chief or entire work of a person's lifetime.

LIFO (lī′fō) ► *abbr.* last-in, first-out

lift (lĭft) ► *v.* 1a. To elevate; raise. b. To ascend; rise. 2a. To revoke; rescind. b. To bring an end to. 3. To elate. 4. *Informal* To steal. 5. To pay off (a debt). ***—phrasal verb:*** **lift off** To begin flight. ► *n.* 1. The act or process of rising or raising. 2. Power or force available for raising. 3. A load. 4. The extent or height to which something is raised or rises. 5. An elevation of the spirits. 6. A machine or device designed to raise or carry something. 7. *Chiefly Brit.* An elevator. 8. A ride in a vehicle given to help someone. 9. The component of the total aerodynamic force acting on an aircraft, perpendicular to the relative wind and normally exerted in an upward direction. **—lift′a·ble** *adj.* **—lift′er** *n.*

lift·off (lĭft′ôf′, -ŏf′) ► *n.* The moment in which a rocket or other craft leaves the ground.

lig·a·ment (lĭg′ə-mənt) ► *n.* A sheet or band of tough, fibrous tissue connecting bones or cartilages at a joint or supporting an organ.

THESAURUS

lickety-split *adv.* *—See* FAST, IMMEDIATELY (1).

licking *n.* *—See* BEATING, DEFEAT.

lid *n.* Something that covers, especially to prevent contents from spilling ► cap, cover, covering, top. [*Compare* PLUG.] *—See also* LIMIT (1).

lie[1] *v.* 1. To be or place oneself in a prostrate or recumbent position ► couch, lie down, recline, repose, stretch (out). 2. To take repose, as by sleeping or lying quietly ► curl up, recline, repose, rest, stretch (out). [*Compare* NAP, SLEEP.] *—See also* CONSIST.

lie[2] *n.* An untrue declaration ► baldfaced lie, barefaced lie, canard, cock-and-bull story, distortion, fable, fabrication, falsehood, falsity, fib, fiction, half-truth, invention, inveracity, mendacity, misrepresentation, misstatement, prevarication, story, tale, untruth, white lie. *Informal:* fish story, tall tale. *Slang:* whopper.

lie *v.* To present false information with the intention of deceiving ► falsify, fib, forswear, invent, make up, perjure, prevaricate. *Idioms:* lie like a trooper, like through one's teeth, speak with a forked tongue. [*Compare* ACT, DISTORT.]

liege *adj.* *—See* FAITHFUL.

lieu *n.* The function or position customarily occupied by another ► place, stead.

lieutenant *n.* *—See* ASSISTANT, REPRESENTATIVE.

life *n.* The period during which someone or something exists ► course, day, days, duration, existence, generation, lifetime, span, term, time. [*Compare* AGE.] *—See also* HUMAN BEING, SPIRIT (1).

life force *n.* *—See* SPIRIT (2).

lifeless *adj.* Completely lacking sensation or consciousness ► dead, inanimate, insensate, insentient. *—See also* DEAD (1), BARREN (2), DEAD (2), DULL (1), VACANT.

lifelessness *n.* *—See* DULLNESS, INACTION.

lifelike *adj.* *—See* GRAPHIC (1), REALISTIC (2).

lifesaver *n.* *—See* RESCUER.

lifestyle *n.* *—See* CULTURE (2).

lifetime *n.* *—See* LIFE.

lift *v.* 1. To rise up in flight ► lift off, take off. 2. To disappear by or as if by rising ► disperse, dissipate, fade away, scatter, thin out, withdraw. [*Compare* DISAPPEAR.] 3. To take back or remove ► countermand, overturn, pull, quash, recall, repeal, rescind, reverse, revoke. [*Compare* ABOLISH, RETRACT.] *—See also* ELATE, ELEVATE (1), PLAGIARIZE, RISE (2), STEAL.

lift *n.* An instance of lifting or being lifted ► boost, heave, hoist, uplift, upthrust. *—See also* ASCENT (1), ELATION, ENCOURAGEMENT, THRILL.

liftoff *n.* The act of rising in flight ► takeoff.

ligament *n.* *—See* BOND (2).

lig·a·ture (lĭgʹə-cho͝or′, -chər) ▸ *n.* **1.** The act of tying or binding. **2.** A cord, wire, or bandage used for binding. **3.** A character, such as *æ*, combining two or more letters. **4.** *Mus.* A slur.

light[1] (līt) ▸ *n.* **1.** Electromagnetic radiation that may be perceived by the human eye. **2.** The sensation of perceiving light; brightness. **3a.** A source of light, esp. a lamp or electric fixture. **b.** The illumination derived from such a source. **4a.** Daylight. **b.** Dawn; daybreak. **5.** A source of fire, such as a match or cigarette lighter. **6.** A state of awareness or understanding. **7.** Public attention. **8.** A way of looking at or considering a matter; aspect. **9.** A prominent person. ▸ *v.* **light·ed** or **lit** (lĭt), **light·ing**. **1.** To set or be set on fire; ignite. **2.** To cause to give out light: *lit a lamp.* **3.** To illuminate. ▸ *adj.* **-er, -est. 1.** Not dark; bright. **2.** Not dark in color: *light hair.* ***—idiom:*** **in (the) light of** In consideration of. **—lightʹness** *n.*

light[2] (līt) ▸ *adj.* **-er, -est. 1a.** Not heavy. **b.** Of relatively low density. **2.** Having less force, quantity, intensity, or volume than normal. **3a.** Consuming moderate amounts. **b.** Not severe: *a light punishment.* **4.** Not serious or profound. **5.** Free from worries or troubles; blithe. **6.** Liable to change; fickle. **7.** Mildly dizzy. **8.** Moving easily and quickly; nimble. **9.** Easily disturbed: *a light sleeper.* **10.** Low in a potentially harmful ingredient, such as alcohol, fat, or sodium. ▸ *adv.* **-er, -est. 1.** Lightly. **2.** With little weight and few burdens: *traveling light.* ▸ *v.* **light·ed** or **lit** (lĭt), **light·ing. 1.** To get down; alight. **2.** To land. ***—phrasal verbs:*** **light into** *Informal* To assail. **light out** *Informal* To leave hastily. **—lightʹly** *adv.* **—lightʹness** *n.*

light bulb ▸ *n.* An incandescent lamp or its glass housing.

light-e·mit·ting diode (lītʹĭ-mĭt′ĭng) ▸ *n.* LED.

light·en[1] (lītʹn) ▸ *v.* To make or become light or lighter; illuminate or brighten.

light·en[2] (lītʹn) ▸ *v.* **1.** To make or become less heavy. **2.** To make or become less oppressive, troublesome, or severe. **3.** To relieve cares or worries.

light·er[1] (līʹtər) ▸ *n.* **1.** One that ignites. **2.** A device for lighting a cigarette, cigar, or pipe.

light·er[2] (līʹtər) ▸ *n.* A barge used to deliver goods to or from a cargo ship. **—lightʹer** *v.*

light·face (lītʹfās′) ▸ *n.* A typeface with relatively thin, light lines. **—lightʹfaced′** *adj.*

light·head·ed (lītʹhĕdʹĭd) ▸ *adj.* **1.** Faint, giddy, or delirious. **2.** Frivolous; silly. **—lightʹheadʹed·ly** *adv.* **—lightʹheadʹed·ness** *n.*

light·heart·ed (lītʹhärʹtĭd) ▸ *adj.* Happy and carefree. **—lightʹheartʹed·ly** *adv.* **—lightʹheartʹed·ness** *n.*

light heavyweight ▸ *n.* A boxer weighing from 161 to 175 lbs. between a middleweight and a heavyweight.

light·house (lītʹhous′) ▸ *n.* A tall structure topped by a powerful light that guides ships.

light·ing (līʹtĭng) ▸ *n.* **1.** The state of being lighted; illumination. **2.** The method or equipment used to provide artificial illumination. **3.** The act or process of igniting.

light·ning (lītʹnĭng) ▸ *n.* An abrupt, powerful natural electric discharge in the atmosphere, accompanied by a flash of light. ▸ *adj.* Very fast or sudden. **—lightʹning** *v.*

lightning bug ▸ *n.* See **firefly**.

lightning rod ▸ *n.* A metal rod placed high on a structure to prevent damage by conducting lightning to the ground.

light·weight (lītʹwāt′) ▸ *n.* **1.** One that weighs relatively little or less than average. **2.** A boxer weighing from 127 to 135 lbs. between a featherweight and a welterweight. **3.** A person of little intelligence, influence, or importance. **—lightʹweight′** *adj.*

light-year also **light year** (lītʹyîr′) ▸ *n.* **1.** The distance that light travels in a vacuum in one year, approx. 9.46 trillion km or 5.88 trillion mi. **2.** often **light-years** *Informal* A long way.

lig·nin (lĭgʹnĭn) ▸ *n.* A complex polymer that hardens and strengthens the cell walls of plants.

lig·nite (lĭgʹnīt′) ▸ *n.* A soft, brownish-black coal. **—lig·nitʹic** (-nĭtʹĭk) *adj.*

lig·num vi·tae (lĭgʹnəm vīʹtē) ▸ *n., pl.* **-taes. 1.** A tropical American tree having very heavy, durable wood. **2.** The wood of this tree.

lig·ro·in (lĭgʹrō-ĭn) ▸ *n.* A volatile, flammable fraction of petroleum, obtained by distillation and used as a solvent.

lik·a·ble also **like·a·ble** (līʹkə-bəl) ▸ *adj.* Pleasing; attractive. **—likʹa·ble·ness** *n.*

like[1] (līk) ▸ *v.* **liked, lik·ing. 1.** To find pleasant; enjoy. **2.** To want, wish, or prefer. **3.** To feel about; regard. ▸ *n.* Something that is liked; preference.

like[2] (līk) ▸ *prep.* **1.** Resembling closely; similar to. **2.** In the typical manner of: *It's not like you.* **3.** Inclined to: *felt like running away.* **4.** Indicative of: *looks like rain.* **5.** Such as: *saved things like old newspapers.* ▸ *adj.* **1.** Similar. **2.** Alike. ▸ *adv.* As if: *ran like crazy.* ▸ *n.* One similar to or like another: *bolts, screws, and the like.* ▸ *conj. Informal* **1.** In the same way that; as: *To dance like she does takes practice.* **2.** As if: *It looks like we'll finish on time.* ***—idiom:*** **be like** *Informal* To say: *And he's like, "Leave me alone!"*

-like ▸ *suff.* Resembling or characteristic of: *ladylike.*

like·li·hood (līkʹlē-ho͝od′) ▸ *n.* **1.** The state of being probable; probability. **2.** Something probable.

THESAURUS

ligature *n.* —*See* BOND (2).

light[1] *n.* **1.** Electromagnetic radiation that makes vision possible ▸ glow, illumination, lambency, lucency, luminescence. [*Compare* FLASH.] **2.** The act of physically illuminating or the condition of being filled with light ▸ illumination, lighting. [*Compare* BRILLIANCE.] —*See also* VIEWPOINT.

light *v.* **1.** To begin or cause to begin burning ▸ enkindle, fire, ignite, kindle, touch off. *Slang:* torch. *Idioms:* burst into flame, catch fire (*or* on fire), set fire to, set afire (*or* on fire). [*Compare* BURN.] **2.** To make lively or animated ▸ animate, brighten, enliven, light up, perk up. —*See also* ILLUMINATE (1).

light *adj.* —*See* FAIR[1] (3).

light[2] *adj.* **1.** Having little weight; not heavy ▸ airy, fluffy, lightweight, weightless. *Idiom:* light as air (*or* a feather). [*Compare* IMMATERIAL, SHEER[2].] **2.** Of small intensity ▸ faint, gentle, moderate, modest, slight, soft. [*Compare* IMPERCEPTIBLE.] **3.** Requiring little effort or exertion ▸ easy, moderate, undemanding. *Informal:* cushy, soft. —*See also* LIGHTHEARTED, TRIVIAL, WANTON (1).

light *v.* To come ashore from a seacraft ▸ alight, debark, disembark, land. —*See also* LAND (2).

light into *v.* —*See* ATTACK (1), SLAM (1).

light on or **upon** *v.* —*See* ENCOUNTER (1).

light out *v.* —*See* BEAR (5).

lighten[1] *v.* —*See* CLEAR (1), ILLUMINATE (1).

lighten[2] *v.* —*See* RELIEVE (1).

light-fingered *adj.* —*See* THIEVISH.

light-haired *adj.* —*See* FAIR[1] (2).

lightheaded *adj.* —*See* DIZZY (1).

lightheadedness *n.* —*See* DIZZINESS.

lighthearted *adj.* Happy and free from worry or care ▸ airy, blithe, buoyant, carefree, debonair, fancy-free, happy-go-lucky, light, untroubled. *Idioms:* free and easy, free as a bird, without a care in the world. [*Compare* CARELESS, LIVELY, MERRY.] —*See also* CHEERFUL, GIDDY (2).

lightheartedness *n.* —*See* MERRIMENT (1).

lighting *n.* The act of physically illuminating or the condition of being filled with light ▸ illumination, light. [*Compare* BRILLIANCE.]

lightness *n.* —*See* TRIFLE.

lights out *n.* —*See* NIGHT.

lightweight *adj.* Having little weight; not heavy ▸ airy, fluffy, light, weightless. *Idiom:* light as air (*or* a feather). [*Compare* IMMATERIAL, SHEER[2].] —*See also* TRIVIAL.

lightweight *n.* —*See* NONENTITY.

like[1] *v.* To find agreeable ▸ adore, fancy, favor, love, take to. *Idiom:* take a fancy (*or* liking *or* shine) to. [*Compare* VALUE.] —*See also* CHOOSE (2), ENJOY (1).

like[2] *adj.* Possessing the same or almost the same characteristics ▸ akin, alike, analogous, comparable, corresponding, equivalent, kin, matching, parallel, resembling, similar, uniform. [*Compare* EQUAL.]

likeable *adj.* —*See* AMIABLE.

likelihood *n.* Something expected ▸ anticipation, expectation, promise, prospect. [*Compare* THEORY.] —*See also* CHANCE (3).

like·ly (līk′lē) ▸ *adj.* **-li·er, -li·est.** 1. Having a tendency or likelihood: *They are likely to win.* 2. Credible; plausible: *a likely excuse.* 3. Apparently suitable: *a likely candidate for the job.* 4. Promising: *a likely topic for investigation.* ▸ *adv. Informal* Probably.

like-mind·ed (līk′mīn′dĭd) ▸ *adj.* Of the same turn of mind.

lik·en (lī′kən) ▸ *v.* To see, mention, or show as similar; compare.

like·ness (līk′nĭs) ▸ *n.* 1. Similarity; resemblance. 2. An imitative appearance; semblance. 3. A copy or picture of something; image.

like·wise (līk′wīz′) ▸ *adv.* 1. In the same way; similarly. 2. As well; also.

lik·ing (lī′kĭng) ▸ *n.* 1. A feeling of attraction; fondness. 2. Preference or taste.

li·lac (lī′lək, -lŏk, -lăk) ▸ *n.* 1. A shrub widely cultivated for its clusters of fragrant purplish or white flowers. 2. A pale purple. **—li′lac** *adj.*

li·lan·ge·ni (lĭ-läng′gĕ-nē) ▸ *n., pl.* **em·a·lan·ge·ni** (ĕm′ə-läng-gĕn′ē). See **currency** table in Appendix.

Li·li·u·o·ka·la·ni (lē-lē′o͞o-ō-kä-lä′nē), **Lydia Kamekeha Paki** (1838–1917) ▸ Queen of the Hawaiian Islands (1891–93).

lilt (lĭlt) ▸ *n.* 1. A cheerful or lively manner of speaking. 2. A light, happy tune or song.

lil·y (lĭl′ē) ▸ *n., pl.* **-ies.** 1. Any of a genus of plants having variously colored, often trumpet-shaped flowers. 2. A similar plant, such as the day lily.

lil·y-liv·ered (lĭl′ē-lĭv′ərd) ▸ *adj.* Cowardly.

lily of the valley ▸ *n., pl.* **lilies of the valley.** A plant having a cluster of small, fragrant, bell-shaped white flowers.

lily pad ▸ *n.* One of the floating leaves of a water lily.

Li·ma (lē′mə) ▸ The capital of Peru, in the west-central part.

li·ma bean (lī′mə) ▸ *n.* 1. A plant having flat pods containing large, light green, edible seeds. 2. The seed of this plant.

limb (lĭm) ▸ *n.* 1. A large tree branch. 2. One of the jointed appendages of an animal, such as an arm, leg, wing, or flipper.

lim·ber (lĭm′bər) ▸ *adj.* 1. Bending or flexing readily; pliable. 2. Capable of moving, bending, or contorting easily; supple. ▸ *v.* To make or become limber: *limbered up before the game.* **—lim′ber·ness** *n.*

lim·bic system (lĭm′bĭk) ▸ *n.* A group of deep brain structures in mammals associated with primitive brain functions. **—lim′bic** *adj.*

lim·bo¹ (lĭm′bō) ▸ *n., pl.* **-bos.** 1. often **Limbo** In the Roman Catholic Church, the abode of souls excluded from heaven but not condemned to further punishment. 2. A region or condition of oblivion, neglect, or prolonged uncertainty.

lim·bo² (lĭm′bō) ▸ *n., pl.* **-bos.** A West Indian dance in which the dancers bend over backward and pass under a pole lowered slightly each time.

Lim·burg·er (lĭm′bûr′gər) ▸ *n.* A soft white cheese that has a very strong odor and flavor.

lime¹ (līm) ▸ *n.* 1. A spiny evergreen citrus tree cultivated for its green, egg-shaped fruit. 2. The fruit of this tree.

lime² (līm) ▸ *n.* See **linden.**

lime³ (līm) ▸ *n.* 1. Calcium oxide. 2. Birdlime. ▸ *v.* **limed, lim·ing.** To treat with lime. **—lim′y** *adj.*

lime·light (līm′līt′) ▸ *n.* 1. A focus of public attention. 2. An early type of stage light in which lime was heated to incandescence producing brilliant illumination.

lim·er·ick (lĭm′ər-ĭk) ▸ *n.* A humorous or nonsensical verse of five anapestic lines usu. with the rhyme scheme *aabba.*

lime·stone (līm′stōn′) ▸ *n.* A common sedimentary rock consisting mostly of calcium carbonate.

lim·it (lĭm′ĭt) ▸ *n.* 1. The point, edge, or line beyond which something cannot or may not proceed. 2. **limits** A boundary; bounds: *within city limits.* 3. The greatest or least amount or number allowed. ▸ *v.* To confine or restrict within a boundary. **—lim′it·a·ble** *adj.* **—lim′i·ta′tion** *n.* **—lim′it·er** *n.* **—lim′it·less** *adj.*

lim·it·ed (lĭm′ĭ-tĭd) ▸ *adj.* 1. Confined within certain limits. 2. Mediocre or qualified: *a limited success.* 3. Designating trains or buses that make few stops. **—lim′i·ted·ly** *adv.*

limn (lĭm) ▸ *v.* **limned, limn·ing.** 1. To describe. 2. To depict by painting or drawing. **—limn′er** (lĭm′nər) *n.*

lim·o (lĭm′ō) ▸ *n., pl.* **lim·os.** *Informal* A limousine.

lim·ou·sine (lĭm′ə-zēn′, lĭm′ə-zēn′) ▸ *n.* 1. A large, luxurious passenger vehicle, esp. one driven by a chauffeur. 2. A small bus used to carry passengers esp. to airports and hotels.

limp (lĭmp) ▸ *v.* 1. To walk lamely, favoring one leg. 2. To proceed haltingly. ▸ *n.* An irregular, jerky, or awkward gait. ▸ *adj.* **-er, -est.** 1. Lacking rigidity. 2. Weak or spiritless. **—limp′ly** *adv.* **—limp′ness** *n.*

lim·pet (lĭm′pĭt) ▸ *n.* A marine gastropod mollusk having a conical shell and adhering to rocks of tidal areas.

lim·pid (lĭm′pĭd) ▸ *adj.* Crystal clear; transparent. **—lim·pid′i·ty, lim′pid·ness** *n.* **—lim′pid·ly** *adv.*

Lim·po·po (lĭm-pō′pō) ▸ A river of SE Africa rising near Johannesburg in NE South Africa and flowing about 1,770 km (1,100 mi) to the Indian Ocean in S Mozambique.

lin·age also **line·age** (lī′nĭj) ▸ *n.* The number of lines of printed or written material.

linch·pin (lĭnch′pĭn′) ▸ *n.* 1. A locking pin inserted in the end of a shaft, as in an axle, to prevent a wheel from slipping off. 2. A central cohesive element.

Lin·coln (lĭng′kən) ▸ The capital of NE, in the SE part SW of Omaha.

Lincoln, Abraham (1809–65) ▸ The 16th US President (1861–65); assassinated.

Lind·bergh (lĭnd′bûrg′, lĭn′-), **Charles Augustus** (1902–74) ▸ Amer. pioneer aviator.

lin·den (lĭn′dən) ▸ *n.* A shade tree having heart-shaped leaves and drooping clusters of yellowish, often fragrant flowers.

THESAURUS

likely *adj.* —*See* CONCEIVABLE, ENCOURAGING, INCLINED, PRESUMPTIVE, PROBABLE.

likely *adv.* —*See* PROBABLY.

like-minded *adj.* —*See* UNANIMOUS.

liken *v.* To represent as similar ▸ analogize, assimilate, compare, equate, identify, match, parallel, relate. [*Compare* ASSOCIATE.]

likeness *n.* 1. The quality or state of being alike ▸ affinity, alikeness, analogy, comparison, correspondence, parallelism, resemblance, similarity, similitude, uniformity, uniformness. [*Compare* AGREEMENT, SAMENESS.] 2. An image caused by reflection ▸ image, reflection. [*Compare* COPY.] —*See also* COPY (1).

likewise *adv.* —*See* ADDITIONALLY.

likewise *adj.* In a similar manner ▸ similarly, so. ***Idioms:*** by the same token, in like fashion, in like manner, in the same way, like so.

liking *n.* A desire for a particular thing or activity ▸ fancy, mind, pleasure, soft spot, will. [*Compare* INCLINATION, TASTE.] —*See also* LOVE (1).

Lilliputian *adj.* —*See* TINY.

lilt *n.* —*See* TONE (2).

lily-livered *adj.* —*See* COWARDLY.

lily-white *adj.* —*See* EXEMPLARY, INNOCENT (1), INNOCENT (2).

limber *adj.* —*See* FLEXIBLE (2).

limberness *n.* —*See* FLEXIBILITY (1).

limit *n.* 1. The greatest amount or number allowed ▸ brim, cap, ceiling, cutoff, lid, limitation, maximum. [*Compare* ALLOTMENT, MAXIMUM.] 2. Either of the two points at the ends of a spectrum or range ▸ extreme, extremity. [*Compare* CLIMAX, LOW.] —*See also* BORDER (1), LENGTH, LIMITS, RESTRAINT.

limit *v.* To place a limit on ▸ bound, circumscribe, confine, fix, restrict, set. [*Compare* RESTRAIN.] —*See also* DETERMINE.

limitation *n.* —*See* LIMIT (1), PROVISION, RESTRAINT, RESTRICTION.

limited *adj.* —*See* DEFINITE (2), LOCAL, NARROW (1), QUALIFIED, RESTRICTED.

limitless *adj.* —*See* ENDLESS (1).

limitlessness *n.* —*See* INFINITY (1).

limits *n.* The boundary surrounding a certain area ▸ bound, bounds, confines, end, limit, perimeter, periphery, precincts. [*Compare* BORDER, CIRCUMFERENCE, OUTSKIRTS.]

limn *v.* —*See* REPRESENT (2).

limp *v.* —*See* MUDDLE, STAGGER (1).

limp *adj.* Not firm or stiff ▸ drooping, droopy, flabby, flaccid, floppy, soft. [*Compare* FLEXIBLE, LOOSE, MALLEABLE.] —*See also* LANGUID.

limpid *adj.* —*See* CLEAR (1).

limpidity or **limpidness** *n.* —*See* CLARITY.

line[1] (līn) ▸ *n.* **1.** A geometric figure formed by a point moving along a fixed direction and the reverse direction. **2.** A thin continuous mark, as that made by a pen, pencil, or brush. **3.** A crease in the skin; wrinkle. **4.** A border or boundary. **5.** A contour or outline. **6.** A cable, rope, string, cord, or wire. **7.** An electric-power transmission cable. **8.** A telephone connection. **9.** A system of transportation, esp. a company owning such a system. **10.** A course of progress or movement: *a line of flight.* **11.** A general manner or course of procedure: *different lines of thought.* **12.** An official policy: *the party line.* **13.** Alignment: *brought the front wheels into line.* **14a.** One's trade or occupation. **b.** Range of competence: *not in my line.* **15.** Merchandise of a similar nature: *a line of small tools.* **16.** A group of persons or things arranged in a row: *long lines at the box office.* **17.** A horizontal row of printed or written words or symbols. **18.** A brief letter; note. **19a.** A unit of verse ending in a textual or typographic break. **b.** often **lines** The dialogue of a theatrical presentation, such as a play. **20.** *Informal* Glib or insincere talk. **21.** *Football* **a.** A line of scrimmage. **b.** The linemen. ▸ *v.* **lined, lin·ing. 1.** To mark with lines. **2.** To place in a series or row. **3.** To form a bordering line along. ***—phrasal verb:* line up 1.** To form a line. **2.** *Football* To take one's position in a formation before a snap or kickoff. **3.** To organize: *line up support.* ***—idioms:* down the line 1.** Throughout. **2.** In the future. **in line for** Next in order for. **on the line 1.** Ready for immediate payment. **2.** In jeopardy. **out of line 1.** Uncalled for; improper. **2.** Out of control.

line[2] (līn) ▸ *v.* **lined, lin·ing. 1.** To fit or sew a covering to the inside surface of. **2.** To cover the inner surface of.

lin·e·age[1] (lĭn′ē-ĭj) ▸ *n.* Direct descent from a particular ancestor; ancestry.

line·age[2] (lī′nĭj) ▸ *n.* Var. of **linage.**

lin·e·al (lĭn′ē-əl) ▸ *adj.* **1.** In the direct line of descent from an ancestor. **2.** Linear. **—lin′e·al·ly** *adv.*

lin·e·a·ment (lĭn′ē-ə-mənt) ▸ *n.* A distinctive shape, contour, or line, esp. of the face.

lin·e·ar (lĭn′ē-ər) ▸ *adj.* **1.** Of or resembling a line; straight. **2.** Having only one dimension. **—lin′e·ar·ly** *adv.*

linear equation ▸ *n.* An algebraic equation involving only terms of the first degree.

line·back·er (līn′băk′ər) ▸ *n.* *Football* A defensive player positioned behind the ends and tackles.

line drive ▸ *n.* *Baseball* A batted ball hit sharply in a roughly straight line.

line-i·tem veto (līn′ī′təm) ▸ *n.* Authority, as of a government executive, to reject individual provisions of a bill.

line·man (līn′mən) ▸ *n.* **1.** One who installs or repairs telephone, telegraph, or electric power lines. **2.** *Football* A player positioned on the forward line.

lin·en (lĭn′ən) ▸ *n.* **1.** Thread or cloth made from flax. **2.** also **linens** Household articles made from linen or other cloth; bed sheets and tablecloths. **—lin′en** *adj.*

line of scrimmage ▸ *n.* *Football* Either of two imaginary lines parallel to the goal line at the ends of the ball as it rests prior to being snapped and at which each team lines up for a new play.

lin·er[1] (lī′nər) ▸ *n.* **1.** One that makes lines. **2.** A large commercial ship or airplane, esp. one carrying passengers on a regular route.

lin·er[2] (lī′nər) ▸ *n.* **1.** One who puts in linings. **2.** Material used as a lining.

lines·man (līnz′mən) ▸ *n.* **1a.** *Football* An official who marks the downs and the position of the ball. **b.** *Sports* An official in various court games who calls shots that fall out of bounds. **2.** See **lineman 1.**

line·up also **line-up** (līn′ŭp′) ▸ *n.* **1.** A line of people formed for inspection or identification. **2.** *Sports* **a.** The members of a team chosen to start a game. **b.** A list of such players.

–ling ▸ *suff.* **1.** One connected with: *hireling.* **2.** One having a specified quality: *underling.* **3.** One that is young, small, or inferior: *duckling.*

lin·ger (lĭng′gər) ▸ *v.* **1.** To be slow in leaving, esp. out of reluctance; tarry. **2.** To persist: *an aftertaste that lingers.* **3.** To procrastinate. **—lin′ger·er** *n.* **—lin′ger·ing·ly** *adv.*

lin·ge·rie (län′zhə-rā′, län′zhə-rē) ▸ *n.* Women's underwear.

lin·go (lĭng′gō) ▸ *n., pl.* **-goes. 1.** Unintelligible or unfamiliar language. **2.** Specialized language; jargon.

lin·gua fran·ca (lĭng′gwə frăng′kə) ▸ *n., pl.* **lingua fran·cas** (-kəz). A medium of communication between peoples of different languages.

lin·gual (lĭng′gwəl) ▸ *adj.* Of or pronounced with the tongue. **—lin′gual** *n.* **—lin′gual·ly** *adv.*

lin·gui·ne also **lin·gui·ni** (lĭng-gwē′nē) ▸ *n.* Pasta in long, flat, thin strands.

lin·guist (lĭng′gwĭst) ▸ *n.* **1.** A specialist in linguistics. **2.** A polyglot.

lin·guis·tics (lĭng-gwĭs′tĭks) ▸ *n.* *(takes sing. v.)* The study of the nature and structure of human speech. **—lin·guis′tic** *adj.* **—lin·guis′ti·cal·ly** *adv.*

lin·i·ment (lĭn′ə-mənt) ▸ *n.* A medicinal fluid rubbed into the skin.

lin·ing (lī′nĭng) ▸ *n.* A covering or coating for an inside surface.

link (lĭngk) ▸ *n.* **1.** One of the rings or loops forming a chain. **2a.** One of a connected series of units: *links of sausage.* **b.** A unit in a transportation or communications system. **c.** A tie or bond. **3.** *Comp. Sci.* A text segment or graphical item that serves as a cross-reference, as between or within hypertext documents. ▸ *v.* To connect or become connected with or as if with a link.

link·age (lĭng′kĭj) ▸ *n.* **1.** The act or process of linking or the condition of being linked. **2.** A system of connected elements.

link·ing verb (lĭng′kĭng) ▸ *n.* See **copula.**

links (lĭngks) ▸ *pl.n.* A golf course.

Lin·nae·us (lĭ-nē′əs, -nā′-), **Carolus** (1707–78) ▸ Swedish botanist.

lin·net (lĭn′ĭt) ▸ *n.* A small brownish Old World finch.

li·no·le·um (lĭ-nō′lē-əm) ▸ *n.* A durable, washable material made in sheets, used as a covering esp. for floors.

lin·seed (lĭn′sēd′) ▸ *n.* The seed of flax, esp. when used as the source of linseed oil.

lint (lĭnt) ▸ *n.* Clinging bits of fiber and fluff; fuzz. **—lint′y** *adj.*

lin·tel (lĭn′tl) ▸ *n.* The horizontal beam over the top of a window or door.

li·on (lī′ən) ▸ *n.* **1.** A large wild cat of Africa and NW India, having a short tawny coat and, in the male, a long heavy mane. **2.** A celebrity. ***—idiom:* lion's share** The greatest or best part.

li·on·ess (lī′ə-nĭs) ▸ *n.* A female lion.

li·on·heart·ed (lī′ən-här′tĭd) ▸ *adj.* Extraordinarily courageous.

li·on·ize (lī′ə-nīz′) ▸ *v.* **-ized, -iz·ing.** To treat (a person) as a celebrity. **—li′on·i·za′tion** *n.*

THESAURUS

line *n.* A group of people or things arranged in a row ▸ column, file, queue, rank, row, string, tier. [*Compare* SERIES.] —*See also* ANCESTRY, APPROACH (1), BUSINESS (2), CORD, DOCTRINE, GOOD (2), LETTER, STRIPE, WRINKLE (1).

line *v.* To place in or form a line or lines ▸ align, dress, file, line up, queue (up), range. [*Compare* ARRANGE.] —*See also* STREAK.

lineage *n.* —*See* ANCESTRY, FAMILY (2).

lineal *adj.* Of unbroken descent or lineage ▸ direct, genealogical, hereditary, natural. [*Compare* ANCESTRAL.]

lineaments *n.* —*See* EXPRESSION (4), FACE (1), FACE (3).

linear *adj.* —*See* DIRECT (1).

lineup *n.* A list of candidates proposed or endorsed by a political party ▸ ballot, slate, ticket. —*See also* ARRANGEMENT (1), PROGRAM (1).

linger *v.* —*See* DELAY (2), REMAIN.

lingerer *n.* —*See* LAGGARD.

lingering *adj.* —*See* CHRONIC (2).

lingo *n.* —*See* DIALECT, LANGUAGE (2).

linguistic *adj.* Relating to, consisting of, or having the nature of words ▸ lexical, verbal, wordy.

liniment *n.* —*See* OINTMENT.

link *n.* —*See* BOND (2), RELATION (1).

link *v.* —*See* ASSOCIATE (1), ASSOCIATE (3), COMBINE (1).

linkage *n.* —*See* RELATION (1).

lintel *n.* —*See* BEAM (2).

lion *n.* —*See* CELEBRITY, DIGNITARY.

lionization *n.* —*See* EXALTATION.

lip (lĭp) ▸ *n.* **1.** Either of two fleshy folds that surround the opening of the mouth. **2a.** A structure or part that encircles an orifice. **b.** A protruding part of certain flowers. **3a.** The tip of a pouring spout. **b.** A rim. **4.** *Slang* Insolent talk.

lip·id (lĭp′ĭd) ▸ *n.* Any of a group of organic compounds that includes fats, oils, waxes, sterols, and triglycerides. **—lip·id′ic** *adj.*

lipo– or **lip–** ▸ *pref.* **1.** Fat: *liposuction.* **2.** Lipid: *lipoprotein.*

lip·o·pro·tein (lĭp′ō-prō′tēn′, -tē-ĭn, lī′pō-) ▸ *n.* A lipid-protein complex by which lipids are transported in the bloodstream.

lip·o·suc·tion (lĭp′ō-sŭk′shən, lī′pō-) ▸ *n.* A surgical procedure that uses suction to remove excess fat from the body.

lip reading ▸ *n.* A technique for understanding unheard speech by interpreting the lip and facial movements of the speaker. **—lip′-read′** *v.* **—lip reader** *n.*

lip service ▸ *n.* Insincere agreement or allegiance; hypocritical respect.

lip·stick (lĭp′stĭk′) ▸ *n.* A small stick of waxy lip coloring enclosed in a cylindrical case.

lip-synch also **lip-sync** (lĭp′sĭngk′) ▸ *v.* **-synched, -synch·ing** also **-synced, -sync·ing.** To move the lips in synchronization with recorded speech or song.

liq·ue·fy also **liq·ui·fy** (lĭk′wə-fī′) ▸ *v.* To make or become liquid. **—liq′ue·fac′tion** (-făk′shən) *n.*

li·queur (lĭ-kûr′, -kyŏŏr′) ▸ *n.* A strongly flavored alcoholic beverage, usu. served after dinner.

liq·uid (lĭk′wĭd) ▸ *n.* A substance capable of flowing or of being poured. ▸ *adj.* **1.** Of or being a liquid. **2.** Liquefied, esp.: **a.** Melted by heating: *liquid wax.* **b.** Condensed by cooling: *liquid oxygen.* **3.** Readily convertible into cash: *liquid assets.* **—liq′uid·ness** *n.*

liq·ui·date (lĭk′wĭ-dāt′) ▸ *v.* **-dat·ed, -dat·ing. 1a.** To pay off (e.g., a debt); settle. **b.** To settle the affairs of (e.g., a business). **2.** To convert (assets) into cash. **3.** To put an end to; abolish or kill. **—liq′ui·da′tion** *n.* **—liq′ui·da′tor** *n.*

li·quid·i·ty (lĭ-kwĭd′ĭ-tē) ▸ *n.* **1.** The state of being liquid. **2.** The quality of being readily convertible into cash.

liq·uor (lĭk′ər) ▸ *n.* **1.** An alcoholic beverage made by distillation rather than by fermentation. **2.** A liquid substance or solution.

li·ra (lîr′ə, lē′rä) ▸ *n., pl.* **li·re** (lîr′ā, lē′rĕ) or **li·ras. 1.** See **currency** table in Appendix. **2.** The primary unit of currency in Italy and San Marino before the adoption of the euro.

Lis·bon (lĭz′bən) ▸ The capital of Portugal, in the W part on the Tagus R. estuary.

lisle (līl) ▸ *n.* A fine, smooth, tightly twisted thread spun from long-stapled cotton.

lisp (lĭsp) ▸ *n.* A speech defect or mannerism in which the sounds (s) and (z) are pronounced as (th) and (*th*). **—lisp** *v.* **—lisp′er** *n.*

lis·some also **lis·som** (lĭs′əm) ▸ *adj.* Limber; supple; lithe. **—lis′some·ly** *adv.* **—lis′some·ness** *n.*

list[1] (lĭst) ▸ *n.* A series of names, words, or other items written, printed, or imagined one after the other. ▸ *v.* **1.** To make a list of; itemize. **2.** To enter in a list. **3.** To have a stated list price.

list[2] (lĭst) ▸ *n.* An inclination to one side, as of a ship; tilt. **—list** *v.*

lis·ten (lĭs′ən) ▸ *v.* **1.** To make an effort to hear something. **2.** To pay attention. **—lis′ten·er** *n.*

list·ing (lĭs′tĭng) ▸ *n.* **1.** An entry in a list. **2.** A list. **3.** *Comp. Sci.* A printout of a program or data set.

list·less (lĭst′lĭs) ▸ *adj.* Lacking energy or enthusiasm; lethargic. **—list′less·ly** *adv.* **—list′less·ness** *n.*

list price ▸ *n.* A basic published price, often subject to discount.

list·serv·er (lĭst′sûr′vər) ▸ *n.* A file server used in the management of e-mail for members of a discussion group.

Liszt (lĭst), **Franz** (1811–86) ▸ Hungarian composer and pianist.

lit[1] (lĭt) ▸ *v.* P.t. and p.part. of **light**[1].

lit[2] (lĭt) ▸ *v.* P.t. and p.part. of **light**[2].

lit·a·ny (lĭt′n-ē) ▸ *n., pl.* **-nies. 1.** A prayer consisting of petitions recited by a leader alternating with responses by the congregation. **2.** A repetitive recital.

lit·as (lĭt′äs) ▸ *n.* See **currency** table in Appendix.

li·tchi also **li·chee** (lē′chē) ▸ *n.* **1.** A Chinese tree that bears edible fruit. **2.** The nutlike fruit of this tree.

li·ter (lē′tər) ▸ *n.* See **measurement** table in Appendix.

lit·er·a·cy (lĭt′ər-ə-sē) ▸ *n.* The ability to read and write.

lit·er·al (lĭt′ər-əl) ▸ *adj.* **1.** Conforming or limited to the simplest, nonfigurative, or most obvious meaning of a word or words. **2.** Word for word; verbatim: *a literal translation.* **3.** Avoiding exaggeration or embellishment; prosaic. **4.** Consisting of or expressed by letters: *literal notation.* **—lit′er·al·ly** *adv.* **—lit′er·al·ness** *n.*

lit·er·ar·y (lĭt′ə-rĕr′ē) ▸ *adj.* **1.** Of or relating to literature. **2a.** Found in or appropriate to literature: *a literary style.* **b.** Bookish; pedantic: *literary language.* **—lit′er·ar′i·ly** (-râr′ə-lē) *adv.* **—lit′er·ar′i·ness** *n.*

lit·er·ate (lĭt′ər-ĭt) ▸ *adj.* **1.** Able to read and write. **2.** Knowledgeable; well-read. **3.** Well-written. **—lit′er·ate** *n.* **—lit′er·ate·ly** *adv.*

lit·er·a·ti (lĭt′ə-rä′tē) ▸ *pl.n.* The literary intelligentsia.

lit·er·a·ture (lĭt′ər-ə-chŏŏr′, -chər) ▸ *n.* **1.** Imaginative or creative writing. **2.** The body of written works of a particular language, period, or culture. **3.** Printed material of any kind, as for a political campaign.

–lith ▸ *suff.* Rock; stone: *megalith.*

lithe (līth) ▸ *adj.* **lith·er, lith·est. 1.** Readily bent; supple. **2.** Graceful. **—lithe′ly** *adv.* **—lithe′ness** *n.*

lithe·some (līth′səm) ▸ *adj.* Lithe; lissome.

–lithic ▸ *suff.* Stone Age: *Paleolithic.*

lith·i·um (lĭth′ē-əm) ▸ *n.* *Symbol* **Li** A light, silvery, highly reactive metallic element used in ceramics, alloys, and thermonuclear weapons. At. no. 3.

litho– or **lith–** ▸ *pref.* Stone: *lithography.*

lith·o·graph (lĭth′ə-grăf′) ▸ *n.* A print produced by lithography. **—lith′o·graph′** *v.* **—li·thog′raph·er** (lĭ-thŏg′rə-fər) *n.* **—lith′o·graph′ic, lith′o·graph′i·cal** *adj.*

li·thog·ra·phy (lĭ-thŏg′rə-fē) ▸ *n.* A printing process in which the image is rendered on a flat surface and treated to retain ink while the nonimage areas are treated to repel ink.

THESAURUS

lip *n.* *Informal* Insolent talk ▸ back talk, mouth. *Informal:* sass. [*Compare* IMPUDENCE.] —*See also* BORDER (1), PROJECTION.

lip *v.* To flow against or along ▸ bathe, lap, lave, wash. [*Compare* FLOW.]

lip service *n.* —*See* HYPOCRISY.

liquefy *v.* —*See* MELT.

liquidate *v.* —*See* ANNIHILATE, ELIMINATE, MURDER, SETTLE (3).

liquidation *n.* —*See* ANNIHILATION, ELIMINATION, MASSACRE, MURDER.

liquor *n.* —*See* DRINK (1).

lissome *adj.* —*See* FLEXIBLE (2).

lissomeness *n.* —*See* FLEXIBILITY (1).

list[1] *n.* A series, as of names or words, printed or written down ▸ agenda, catalog, checklist, directory, index, inventory, invoice, listing, manifest, register, roll, roster, schedule, table.

list *v.* To place on a list or in a record or book ▸ book, catalog, chronicle, docket, enroll, enter, file, inscribe, insert, log, minute, post, record, register, set down, tabulate, write down. [*Compare* SCHEDULE.] —*See also* ENUMERATE.

list[2] *n.* —*See* INCLINATION (2).

list *v.* —*See* INCLINE.

listen *v.* To make an effort to hear something ▸ attend, hark, hearken, heed. *Idiom:* give (*or* lend) an ear. —*See also* HEAR.

listen *n.* A chance to be heard ▸ audience, audition, hearing.

listing *n.* —*See* LIST[1].

listless *adj.* —*See* APATHETIC, LANGUID.

listlessness *n.* —*See* APATHY, BOREDOM, LETHARGY.

lit *adj.* —*See* DRUGGED, DRUNK.

litany *n.* —*See* PRAYER[1] (2).

literal *adj.* Employing the very same words as another ▸ undeviating, unvarnished, verbal, verbatim, word-for-word. *Idiom:* to the letter. [*Compare* ACCURATE, CLOSE.] —*See also* PEDANTIC.

literally *adv.* —*See* EXACTLY.

literary *adj.* —*See* PEDANTIC.

literate *adj.* —*See* EDUCATED.

lithe or **lithesome** *adj.* —*See* FLEXIBLE (2).

litheness *n.* —*See* FLEXIBILITY (1).

lith·o·sphere (lĭth′ə-sfîr′) ▸ *n.* The outer part of the earth; the earth's crust and upper mantle.

Lith·u·a·ni·a (lĭth′o͞o-ā′nē-ə) ▸ A country of N Europe on the Baltic Sea.

Lith·u·a·ni·an (lĭth′o͞o-ā′nē-ən) ▸ *n.* **1.** A native or inhabitant of Lithuania. **2.** The Baltic language of the Lithuanians. **—Lith′u·a′ni·an** *adj.*

lit·i·gant (lĭt′ĭ-gənt) ▸ *n.* A party in a lawsuit.

lit·i·gate (lĭt′ĭ-gāt′) ▸ *v.* **-gat·ed, -gat·ing.** To engage in or subject to legal proceedings. **—lit′i·ga′tion** *n.* **—lit′i·ga′tor** *n.*

li·ti·gious (lĭ-tĭj′əs) ▸ *adj.* **1.** Of or marked by litigation. **2.** Tending to engage in lawsuits. **—li·ti′gious·ly** *adv.* **—li·ti′gious·ness** *n.*

lit·mus (lĭt′məs) ▸ *n.* A water-soluble blue powder derived from lichens that changes to red with increasing acidity and to blue with increasing basicity.

litmus paper ▸ *n.* White paper impregnated with litmus and used as a pH or acid-base indicator.

litmus test ▸ *n.* **1.** A test for chemical acidity or basicity using litmus paper. **2.** A test that uses a single indicator to prompt a decision.

li·tre (lē′tər) ▸ *n.* *Chiefly Brit.* Var. of **liter.**

lit·ter (lĭt′ər) ▸ *n.* **1a.** A disorderly accumulation; pile. **b.** Carelessly discarded refuse, such as wastepaper. **2.** The offspring produced at one birth by a mammal. **3a.** Straw or other material used as bedding for animals. **b.** A material used to absorb an animal's excretions. **4.** A couch mounted on shafts, used to carry a passenger. **5.** A stretcher for carrying a disabled or dead person. ▸ *v.* **1.** To make untidy by discarding rubbish carelessly. **2.** To scatter about; strew. **—lit′ter·er** *n.*

lit·ter·bug (lĭt′ər-bŭg′) ▸ *n.* *Informal* One who litters public areas.

lit·tle (lĭt′l) ▸ *adj.* **-tler** or **less** (lĕs) also **less·er** (lĕs′ər), **-tlest** or **least** (lēst). **1.** Small in size, quantity, or degree. **2.** Short in extent or duration; brief: *little time.* **3.** Unimportant; trivial. **4.** Narrow; petty. **5.** Without much power or influence. **6.** Young. ▸ *adv.* **less, least.** Not much: *slept little.* ▸ *n.* A small quantity: *Give me a little.* ***—idiom:*** **little by little** Gradually. **—lit′tle·ness** *n.*

Little Dipper ▸ *n.* Ursa Minor.

Little Rock ▸ The capital of Arkansas, in the central part on the Arkansas R.

lit·to·ral (lĭt′ər-əl) ▸ *adj.* Of or on a shore, esp. a seashore. ▸ *n.* A coastal region; shore.

lit·ur·gy (lĭt′ər-jē) ▸ *n., pl.* **-gies. 1.** A prescribed form for public worship. **2.** often **Liturgy** The Christian Eucharist. **—li·tur′gi·cal** (lĭ-tûr′jĭ-kəl) *adj.*

liv·a·ble also **live·a·ble** (lĭv′ə-bəl) ▸ *adj.* **1.** Suitable to live in; habitable. **2.** Endurable. **—liv′a·ble·ness** *n.*

live[1] (lĭv) ▸ *v.* **lived, liv·ing. 1.** To be alive; exist. **2.** To continue to be alive. **3.** To subsist. **4.** To reside. **5.** To conduct one's life in a particular manner: *lived frugally.* **6.** To remain in memory or usage: *an event that lives on in our minds.* ***—phrasal verbs:*** **live down** To overcome the shame or effect of over time. **live with** To resign oneself to.

live[2] (līv) ▸ *adj.* **1.** Having life; alive. **2.** Of current interest. **3.** Glowing; burning. **4.** Not yet exploded: *live ammunition.* **5.** Carrying an electric current. **6.** Broadcast while being performed.

live-in (lĭv′ĭn′) ▸ *adj.* **1.** Residing in the place where one is employed. **2.** Residing together with another, esp. in sexual intimacy. **—live′-in′** *n.*

live·li·hood (līv′lē-ho͝od′) ▸ *n.* Means of support; subsistence.

live·long (lĭv′lông′, -lŏng′) ▸ *adj.* Complete; whole: *the livelong day.*

live·ly (līv′lē) ▸ *adj.* **-li·er, -li·est. 1.** Full of life and energy; vigorous. **2.** Full of spirit; animated: *a lively tune.* **3.** Marked by animated intelligence: *a lively discussion.* **4.** Effervescent; sparkling. ▸ *adv.* With energy or vigor; briskly: *Step lively!* **—live′li·ly** *adv.* **—live′li·ness** *n.*

li·ven (lī′vən) ▸ *v.* To make or become more lively.

liv·er (lĭv′ər) ▸ *n.* A large, reddish-brown, glandular vertebrate organ that secretes bile and is active in the formation of certain blood proteins and in the metabolism of carbohydrates, fats, and proteins.

liv·er·mor·i·um (lĭv′ər-môr′ē-əm) ▸ *n.* *Symbol* **Lv** A synthetic radioactive element. At. no. 116.

liver spot ▸ *n.* A benign brownish patch on the skin, often occurring in old age in fair-skinned people.

liv·er·wort (lĭv′ər-wûrt′, -wôrt′) ▸ *n.* Any of a class of small, green, nonvascular plants related to the mosses.

liv·er·wurst (lĭv′ər-wûrst′, -wo͝orst′) ▸ *n.* A sausage made of or containing ground liver.

liv·er·y (lĭv′ə-rē, lĭv′rē) ▸ *n., pl.* **-ies. 1.** A distinctive uniform worn by the male servants of a household. **2a.** The boarding and care of horses for a fee. **b.** The hiring out of horses and carriages. **—liv′er·ied** *adj.* **—liv′er·y·man** *n.*

lives (līvz) ▸ *n.* Pl. of **life.**

live·stock (līv′stŏk′) ▸ *n.* Domestic animals, such as cattle or horses, raised for home use or for profit.

live wire (līv) ▸ *n.* **1.** A wire carrying electric current. **2.** *Informal* A vivacious, alert, or energetic person.

liv·id (lĭv′ĭd) ▸ *adj.* **1.** Discolored, as from a bruise; black-and-blue. **2.** Ashen or pallid. **3.** Extremely angry. **—li·vid′i·ty, liv′id·ness** *n.* **—liv′id·ly** *adv.*

liv·ing (lĭv′ĭng) ▸ *adj.* **1.** Possessing life; alive. **2.** In active function or use: *a living language.* **3.** True to life; realistic. ▸ *n.* **1.** The condition or action of maintaining life. **2.** A manner or style of life. **3.** A livelihood.

living room ▸ *n.* A room in a private residence intended for social and leisure activities.

living will ▸ *n.* A will in which the signer requests not to be kept alive by medical life-support systems in the event of a terminal illness.

THESAURUS

litigate *v.* To institute or subject to legal proceedings ▸ law, prosecute, sue. *Idioms:* bring suit, haul (*or* drag) into court.

litigation *n.* *—See* LAWSUIT.

litigious *adj.* *—See* ARGUMENTATIVE.

litter *n.* The offspring, as of an animal or bird, for example, that are the result of one breeding season ▸ brood, young. [*Compare* PROGENY.] *—See also* FLOCK, GARBAGE.

little *adj.* Below average in amount, length, size, or scope ▸ bantam, compact, petite, runty, short, small, smallish, undersized. [*Compare* STOCKY, TINY.] *—See also* NARROW (1), TRIVIAL.

little *adv.* *—See* INFREQUENTLY.

little *n.* *—See* BIT[1] (1).

little-known *adj.* *—See* OBSCURE (2).

littlest *adj.* *—See* MINIMAL.

liturgical *adj.* *—See* RITUAL.

liturgy *n.* *—See* CEREMONY (1).

livable *adj.* Fit to live in ▸ habitable, inhabitable.

live[1] *v.* To have as one's domicile, usually for an extended period ▸ abide, domicile, dwell, house, occupy, reside, stay. [*Compare* INHABIT.] *—See also* EXIST, LEAD.

live by *v.* *—See* FOLLOW (4).

live off *v.* To take advantage of the generosity of others ▸ leech. *Informal:* sponge. *Slang:* freeload. [*Compare* [illegible]]

live on *v.* To include as part of one's diet by nature or preference ▸ eat, exist on, feed on, subsist on.

live through *v.* *—See* ENDURE (1).

live[2] *adj.* *Informal* Of great current interest ▸ hot, red-hot. [*Compare* FASHIONABLE, IMPORTANT.] *—See also* ALIVE.

livelihood *n.* *—See* LIVING.

liveliness *n.* *—See* ENERGY, SPIRIT (1).

lively *adj.* Very brisk, alert, and full of high spirits ▸ animated, bouncy, breezy, bubbly, chipper, coltish, dashing, ebullient, effervescent, exuberant, frisky, high-spirited, jaunty, perky, pert, sassy, sparkling, sparkly, spirited, vibrant, vivacious. *Informal:* corky, peppy, snappy. ***Idioms:*** bright-eyed and bushy tailed, full of life. [*Compare* ENTHUSIASTIC, PASSIONATE.] *—See also* ENERGETIC.

live wire *n.* *Informal* An intensely energetic, enthusiastic person ▸ demon, dynamo, hustler. *Informal:* eager beaver, firebreather, go-getter.

livid *adj.* *—See* ANGRY, PALE (1).

living *adj.* *—See* ALIVE.

living *n.* The means needed to support life ▸ alimentation, alimony, bread, bread and butter, existence, income, keep, livelihood, maintenance, subsistence, support, sustenance, upkeep.

living hell *n.* *—See* HELL.

Li·vo·ni·a (lĭ-vō′nē-ə, -vōn′yə) ▸ A region comprising N Latvia and Estonia. **—Li·vo′ni·an** *adj. & n.*

liz·ard (lĭz′ərd) ▸ *n.* **1.** Any of numerous reptiles having a scaly elongated body, movable eyelids, four legs, and a tapering tail. **2.** Leather that is made from the skin of a lizard.

lla·ma (lä′mə) ▸ *n.* A South American mammal related to the camel, raised for its soft fleecy wool and used as a beast of burden.

lo (lō) ▸ *interj.* Used to attract attention or to show surprise.

load (lōd) ▸ *n.* **1a.** A supported weight or mass. **b.** The force to which a structure is subjected. **2.** Something carried, as by a vehicle, person, or animal. **3.** The share of work allocated to or required of a person, machine, group, or organization. **4.** A heavy responsibility; burden. **5.** often **loads** *Informal* A great number or amount. ▸ *v.* **1.** To put (something) into or onto a structure or conveyance. **2.** To fill nearly to overflowing. **3.** To weigh down; burden. **4.** To charge (a firearm) with ammunition. **5.** To insert material into: *loaded the camera with film.* **6.** *Games* To make (dice) heavier on one side. **7.** To charge with meanings or implications. **8.** To dilute. **9.** *Comp. Sci.* To transfer (data) from storage into a computer's memory. **—load′er** *n.*

load·ed (lō′dĭd) ▸ *adj.* **1.** Carrying a load. **2.** Heavy with meaning or emotional import. **3.** *Slang* Intoxicated; drunk. **4.** *Slang* Rich.

loaf[1] (lōf) ▸ *n., pl.* **loaves** (lōvz). A shaped mass of bread or other food baked in one piece.

loaf[2] (lōf) ▸ *v.* To pass time idly. **—loaf′er** *n.*

loam (lōm) ▸ *n.* Soil composed of sand, clay, silt, and organic matter. **—loam′y** *adj.*

loan (lōn) ▸ *n.* **1.** Something lent for temporary use. **2.** A sum of money lent at interest. ▸ *v.* To lend (money or goods). **—loan′er** *n.*

loan·word (lōn′wûrd′) ▸ *n.* A word, such as *honcho*, adopted from another language and at least partly naturalized.

loath (lōth, lō*th*) ▸ *adj.* Unwilling or reluctant.

loathe (lō*th*) ▸ *v.* **loathed, loath·ing.** To dislike greatly; abhor.

loath·ing (lō′*th*ĭng) ▸ *n.* Great dislike; abhorrence. **—loath′ing·ly** *adv.*

loath·some (lō*th*′səm, lōth′-) ▸ *adj.* Arousing loathing; abhorrent. **—loath′some·ness** *n.*

lob (lŏb) ▸ *v.* **lobbed, lob·bing.** To hit, throw, or propel in a high arc. **—lob** *n.*

lob·by (lŏb′ē) ▸ *n., pl.* **-bies.** **1.** A hall, foyer, or waiting room at or near the entrance to a building, such as a hotel. **2.** A group of persons engaged in trying to influence legislators. ▸ *v.* **-bied, -by·ing.** To try to influence public officials for or against a specific cause. **—lob′by·er, lob′by·ist** *n.*

lobe (lōb) ▸ *n.* A rounded part or projection, esp. of an organic structure: *the lobe of an ear.* **—lobed** *adj.*

lo·bot·o·my (lə-bŏt′ə-mē, lō-) ▸ *n., pl.* **-mies.** Surgery on the frontal lobe of the brain to sever one or more nerve tracts.

lob·ster (lŏb′stər) ▸ *n.* **1.** A large edible marine crustacean having five pairs of legs, the first pair of which is modified into large pincers. **2.** Any of several related crustaceans.

lo·cal (lō′kəl) ▸ *adj.* **1.** Of or relating to a particular place: *a local custom.* **2.** Not widespread: *local outbreaks of flu.* **3.** Of or affecting a specific part of the body: *a local infection; local anesthetic.* **4.** Making many stops on a route: *a local train.* ▸ *n.* **1.** A public conveyance that stops at all stations. **2.** A local chapter or branch of an organization, esp. of a labor union. **3.** *Informal* A person from a particular locality. **—lo′cal·ly** *adv.*

lo·cale (lō-kăl′) ▸ *n.* A place, esp. with reference to an event.

lo·cal·i·ty (lō-kăl′ĭ-tē) ▸ *n., pl.* **-ties.** A particular neighborhood, place, or district.

lo·cal·ize (lō′kə-līz′) ▸ *v.* **-ized, -iz·ing.** **1.** To make local. **2.** To confine or restrict to a locality. **—lo′cal·i·za′tion** *n.*

lo·cate (lō′kāt′, lō-kāt′) ▸ *v.* **-cat·ed, -cat·ing.** **1.** To determine the position of. **2.** To find by searching. **3.** To place; situate. **4.** To become established; settle. **—lo′cat′er, lo′cat′or** *n.*

lo·ca·tion (lō-kā′shən) ▸ *n.* **1.** The act or process of locating. **2.** A place where something is located. **3.** A site away from a studio at which part or all of a movie is shot. **—lo·ca′tion·al** *adj.*

loc. cit. ▸ *abbr. Lat.* loco citato (in the place cited)

loch (lŏкн, lŏk) ▸ *n. Scots* **1.** A lake. **2.** An arm of the sea similar to a fjord.

lo·ci (lō′sī′, -kē, -kī′) ▸ *n.* Pl. of **locus.**

lock[1] (lŏk) ▸ *n.* **1.** A device operated by a key, combination, or keycard and used, as on a door, for holding, closing, or securing. **2.** A section of a canal closed off with gates for raising or lowering the water level. **3.** A mechanism in a firearm for exploding the charge. ▸ *v.* **1.** To fasten or become fastened with a lock. **2.** To confine or exclude by or as if by means of a lock. **3.** To clasp or link firmly: *lock arms.* **4.** To bind in close struggle or battle. **5.** To become entangled; interlock. **6.** To become rigid or immobile. **—lock′a·ble** *adj.*

lock[2] (lŏk) ▸ *n.* A length or curl of hair; tress.

Locke (lŏk), **John** (1632–1704) ▸ English philosopher.

lock·er (lŏk′ər) ▸ *n.* **1.** A small, usu. metal compartment that can be locked, esp. one at a public place for the safekeeping of clothing and valuables. **2.** A flat trunk for storage. **3.** A refrigerated cabinet or room for storing frozen foods.

locker room ▸ *n.* A room with lockers and usu. showers, as in a gymnasium, in which to change clothes and store equipment.

lock·et (lŏk′ĭt) ▸ *n.* A small ornamental case for a keepsake, usu. worn as a pendant.

lock·jaw (lŏk′jô′) ▸ *n.* **1.** See **tetanus.** **2.** A symptom of tetanus, in which the jaw is held tightly closed by a spasm of muscles.

lock·out (lŏk′out′) ▸ *n.* The closing down of a workplace by an employer during a labor dispute.

lock·smith (lŏk′smĭth′) ▸ *n.* One who makes or repairs locks.

lock·step (lŏk′stĕp′) ▸ *n.* A way of marching in which the marchers follow each other closely.

lo·co (lō′kō) ▸ *adj. Slang* Mad; insane.

lo·co·mo·tion (lō′kə-mō′shən) ▸ *n.* The act of moving or ability to move from place to place.

lo·co·mo·tive (lō′kə-mō′tĭv) ▸ *n.* A self-propelled vehicle,

THESAURUS

load *n.* —*See* BURDEN[1] (2), HEAP (2).
load *v.* To put explosive material into a weapon ▸ charge, prime, ready. —*See also* BURDEN[1], CONTAMINATE, DISTORT, FILL (1), HEAP (1).

loaded *adj.* Burdened by a weighty load ▸ heavy, heavy-laden, laden, weighed down. —*See also* DRUNK, IMPURE (2), RICH (1).

loaf *v.* —*See* IDLE (1).

loafer *n.* —*See* WASTREL (2).

loam *n.* —*See* EARTH (1).

loan *v.* —*See* LEND.

loath *adj.* —*See* INDISPOSED.

loathe *v.* —*See* HATE.

loathing *n.* —*See* DESPISAL, DISGUST, HATE (1).

loathsome *adj.* —*See* GHASTLY (1), OFFENSIVE (1).

loathsomeness *n.* —*See* UGLINESS.

lob *v.* —*See* THROW.
lob *n.* —*See* THROW.

local *adj.* Confined to a particular location or site ▸ bounded, limited, localized, on-site, regional. —*See also* CITY, INDIGENOUS, NARROW (1).
local *n.* —*See* INHABITANT.

locale *n.* —*See* ENVIRONMENT (1), LOCALITY, SCENE (1).

locality *n.* A particular geographic area ▸ area, locale, location, neighborhood, place, vicinity. [*Compare* POSITION, SCENE.] —*See also* AREA (2), ENVIRONMENT (1).

localized *adj.* —*See* LOCAL.

locate *v.* **1.** To look for and discover ▸ find, pinpoint, spot. *Informal:* scare up. [*Compare* TRACE, UNCOVER.] **2.** To move to a place and reside there ▸ relocate, settle. ***Idioms:*** fix one's residence, make one's home, put down roots, take up residence. [*Compare* EMIGRATE, LIVE[1], MOVE.] —*See also* POSITION.

location *n.* —*See* BEARING (3), LOCALITY, POSITION (1).

lock[1] *n.* —*See* FASTENER.
lock *v.* —*See* FASTEN.
lock away or **in** or **up** *v.* —*See* IMPRISON.

lock[2] *n.* —*See* CURL.

lockup *n.* —*See* JAIL.

loco *adj.* —*See* INSANE.

usu. electric or diesel-powered, that moves railroad cars. ► *adj.* Of or involved in locomotion.
lo·co·mo·tor (lō′kə-mō′tər) ► *adj.* Locomotive.
lo·co·weed (lō′kō-wēd′) ► *n.* Any of several plants of the western and central US that are poisonous to livestock.
lo·cus (lō′kəs) ► *n., pl.* **-ci** (-sī′, -kē, -kī′). **1.** A place. **2.** *Math.* The set of all points that satisfy specified conditions.
lo·cust (lō′kəst) ► *n.* **1.** A grasshopper that travels in destructive swarms that devour vegetation. **2.** The periodical cicada. **3.** A North American tree having compound leaves, clusters of fragrant white flowers, and durable hard wood.
lo·cu·tion (lō-kyo͞o′shən) ► *n.* **1.** A particular word, phrase, or expression. **2.** Style of speaking; phraseology.
lode (lōd) ► *n.* A vein of mineral ore deposited between layers of rock.
lode·star (lōd′stär′) ► *n.* **1.** A star, esp. Polaris, used as a point of reference. **2.** A guiding principle or ambition.
lode·stone (lōd′stōn′) ► *n.* A magnetized piece of magnetite.
lodge (lŏj) ► *n.* **1a.** A cottage or cabin, often rustic, used as a temporary abode or shelter: *a ski lodge.* **b.** An inn. **2.** Any of various Native American dwellings, such as a hogan, wigwam, or longhouse. **3a.** A local chapter of certain fraternal organizations. **b.** The meeting hall of such a chapter. **4.** The den of certain animals, such as the dome-shaped one built by beavers. ► *v.* **lodged, lodg·ing. 1.** To provide with or rent quarters temporarily, esp. for sleeping. **2.** To live in a rented room or rooms. **3.** To register (e.g., a complaint) before an authority. **4.** To vest (authority). **5.** To be or become embedded.
lodg·er (lŏj′ər) ► *n.* One that lodges, esp. one who rents and lives in a furnished room.
lodg·ing (lŏj′ĭng) ► *n.* **1.** Sleeping accommodations. **2.** Rented rooms.
Łódź (lŏdz, wo͞och) ► A city of central Poland WSW of Warsaw.
lo·ess (lō′əs, lĕs, lŭs) ► *n.* A windblown deposit of fine-grained silt or clay.
loft (lôft, lŏft) ► *n.* **1a.** A large, usu. unpartitioned floor in a commercial building. **b.** A loft converted into an apartment or studio. **2.** An open space under a roof; attic. **3.** A gallery or balcony, as in a church. **4.** A high arc given to a struck or thrown object, such as a golf ball or baseball. ► *v.* **1.** To put, store, or keep in a loft. **2.** To propel in a high arc.
loft·y (lôf′tē, lŏf′-) ► *adj.* **-i·er, -i·est. 1.** Of imposing height. **2.** Exalted; noble. **3.** Arrogant; haughty. **—loft′i·ly** *adv.* **—loft′i·ness** *n.*
log[1] (lôg, lŏg) ► *n.* **1.** A section of a trunk or limb of a fallen or felled tree. **2.** A device trailed from a ship to determine its speed through water. **3.** A record of a ship's or aircraft's speed, progress, and navigation. **4.** A regularly kept record; journal. ► *v.* **logged, log·ging. 1a.** To cut down timber (on). **b.** To cut (trees) into logs. **2.** To enter in a ship's or aircraft's log. **3.** To travel (a specified distance, time, or speed). ***—phrasal verbs:*** **log in** (or **on**) To enter into a computer the information required to begin a session. **log out** (or **off**) To enter into a computer the command to end a session. **—log′ger** *n.*
log[2] (lôg, lŏg) ► *n. Math.* A logarithm.
lo·gan·ber·ry (lō′gən-bĕr′ē) ► *n.* An edible blackberrylike red fruit.
log·a·rithm (lô′gə-rĭth′əm, lŏg′ə-) ► *n.* The power to which a fixed number, the base, must be raised to produce a given number. **—log′a·rith′mic, log′a·rith′mi·cal** *adj.* **—log′a·rith′mi·cal·ly** *adv.*
loge (lōzh) ► *n.* **1.** A small compartment, esp. a box in a theater. **2.** The front rows of the mezzanine in a theater.
log·ger·head (lô′gər-hĕd′, lŏg′ər-) ► *n.* A marine turtle having a large beaked head. ***—idiom:*** **at loggerheads** Engaged in a head-on dispute.
log·ic (lŏj′ĭk) ► *n.* **1.** The study of the principles of reasoning. **2.** Valid reasoning, esp. as distinguished from invalid or irrational argumentation. **3.** The mathematical operations performed by a computer, such as sorting and comparing, that involve yes-no decisions. **—lo·gi′cian** (lō-jĭsh′ən) *n.*
log·i·cal (lŏj′ĭ-kəl) ► *adj.* **1.** Of, using, or in accordance with logic. **2.** Reasonable. **3.** Showing consistency of reasoning. **—log′i·cal·ly** *adv.* **—log′i·cal·ness** *n.*
log·in (lôg′ĭn′, lŏg′-) also **log·on** (-ŏn′, -ôn′) ► *n.* The process of identifying oneself to a computer, as by entering one's username and password.
lo·gis·tics (lō-jĭs′tĭks, lə-) ► *n.* *(takes sing. or pl. v.)* The procurement, distribution, maintenance, and replacement of materiel and personnel. **—lo·gis′tic, lo·gis′ti·cal** *adj.* **—lo·gis′ti·cal·ly** *adv.*
log·jam (lôg′jăm′, lŏg′-) ► *n.* **1.** An immovable mass of floating logs crowded together. **2.** A deadlock; impasse.
lo·go (lō′gō′) ► *n., pl.* **-gos.** A distinctive name, symbol, or trademark of a company that is designed for easy recognition.
lo·go·type (lô′gə-tīp′, lŏg′ə-) ► *n.* **1.** A piece of type bearing two or more usu. separate elements. **2.** A logo.
log·roll·ing (lôg′rō′lĭng, lŏg′-) ► *n.* The trading of influence or votes among legislators to achieve passage of projects of interest to one another. **—log′roll′er** *n.*
-logue or **-log** ► *suff.* Speech; discourse: *travelogue.*
lo·gy (lō′gē) ► *adj.* **-gi·er, -gi·est.** Lethargic; sluggish.
-logy ► *suff.* **1.** Discourse; expression: *phraseology.* **2.** Science; theory; study: *geology.*
loin (loin) ► *n.* **1a.** *Anat.* The part of the side and back between the ribs and pelvis. **b.** A cut of meat from this part of an animal. **2. loins a.** The region of the thighs and groin. **b.** The genitals.
loin·cloth (loin′klôth′, -klŏth′) ► *n.* A strip of cloth worn around the loins.
Loire (lwär) ► A river, about 1,014 km (630 mi), rising in SE France and flowing to the Bay of Biscay.
loi·ter (loi′tər) ► *v.* **1.** To stand idly about; linger aimlessly. **2.** To proceed slowly or with many stops. **3.** To delay or dawdle. **—loi′ter·er** *n.*
loll (lŏl) ► *v.* **1.** To recline in an indolent or relaxed way. **2.** To hang or droop laxly. **—loll′er** *n.*
lol·li·pop also **lol·ly·pop** (lŏl′ē-pŏp′) ► *n.* A piece of hard candy on the end of a small stick.
Lom·bar·dy (lŏm′bər-dē, lŭm′-) ► A region of N Italy bordering on Switzerland. **—Lom′bard** *adj. & n.*

THESAURUS

locus *n.* —*See* CENTER (1), POSITION (1).
locution *n.* —*See* EXPRESSION (3), TERM, WORDING.
lodge *v.* To stay in or provide with lodging, especially temporarily ► accommodate, bed (down), berth, bestow, billet, board, bunk, domicile, harbor, house, put up, quarter, room, sojourn, stay, visit. [*Compare* LIVE[1].] —*See also* CATCH (3), FIX (2).
lodging *n.* Dwellings in general ► housing, shelter. *Idiom:* a roof over one's head. [*Compare* HUT.] —*See also* HOME (1).
lodgings *n.* Usually temporary living accommodations ► barracks, quarters, rooms. *Slang:* crash-pad. [*Compare* APARTMENT, HOME.]
loftiest *adj.* Of, being, located at, or forming the top ► highest, top, topmost, upmost, uppermost. [*Compare* CLIMACTIC.]
loftiness *n.* The distance of something from a given level ► altitude, height, loftiness, tallness. [*Compare* ASCENT.] —*See also* ARROGANCE, PRETENTIOUSNESS.
lofty *adj.* —*See* ARROGANT, ELEVATED (4), EXALTED, HIGH (1).
log *v.* —*See* LIST[1].
log in or **on** *v.* To gain entry into a computer network or database ► access, enter. *Idioms:* gain access (*or* admittance *or* entry), get connected.
logic *n.* Exact, valid, and rational reasoning ► analysis, argument, deduction, induction, ratiocination, rationality, reason. —*See also* SENSE.
logical *adj.* **1.** Able to reason validly ► analytic, analytical, ratiocinative, rational. [*Compare* SENSIBLE.] **2.** Consistent with reason and intellect ► consequent, deducible, intelligent, rational, reasonable. [*Compare* SOUND[2].]
loiter *v.* —*See* DELAY (2), IDLE (1).
loiterer *n.* —*See* LAGGARD.
loll *v.* To take on or move with an awkward, slovenly posture ► slouch, slump. [*Compare* BOW[1], STOOP.] —*See also* SLOUCH (2), SPRAWL.

lo mein (lō′ mān′) ▸ *n.* A Chinese dish of wheat noodles boiled then seasoned and stir-fried.

Lon·don (lŭn′dən) ▸ The capital of the United Kingdom, on the Thames R. in SE England.

lone (lōn) ▸ *adj.* 1. Solitary: *a lone tree.* 2. Isolated; unfrequented: *the lone prairie.* 3. Sole: *the lone school in town.*

lone·ly (lōn′lē) ▸ *adj.* **-li·er, -li·est.** 1. Without companions; solitary. 2. Unfrequented by people; desolate. 3a. Sad at being alone. b. Producing such sadness. **—lone′li·ness** *n.*

lon·er (lō′nər) ▸ *n.* One who avoids the company of other people.

lone·some (lōn′səm) ▸ *adj.* 1. Sad at feeling alone. 2. Offering solitude; secluded. **—lone′some·ly** *adv.* **—lone′some·ness** *n.*

long[1] (lông, lŏng) ▸ *adj.* **-er, -est.** 1. Having great length. 2. Of relatively great duration: *a long time.* 3. Of a specified length or duration: *a mile long; an hour long.* 4. Concerned with distant issues; far-reaching: *a long view of the plan.* 5. Risky; chancy: *long odds.* 6. Having an abundance or excess: *long on hope.* 7. Of or being a vowel sound of comparatively great duration, such as those in *made* or *feed.* ▸ *adv.* 1. For an extended period of time. 2. For or throughout a specified period: *all night long.* 3. At a distant point of time: *long before we were born.* ▸ *n.* A long time. **—*idioms:* any longer** For more time: *can't wait any longer.* **as** (or **so**) **long as** Inasmuch as; since. **no longer** Not now as formerly: *We no longer smoke.*

long[2] (lông, lŏng) ▸ *v.* To have an earnest desire; yearn.

long·bow (lông′bō′, lŏng′-) ▸ *n.* A wooden, hand-drawn bow, often 6 ft. or longer.

long distance ▸ *n.* Telephone service between distant points. **—long′-dis′tance** *adj. & adv.*

lon·gev·i·ty (lŏn-jĕv′ĭ-tē, lôn-) ▸ *n.* 1. Long life. 2. Long duration.

Long·fel·low (lông′fĕl′ō, lŏng′-), **Henry Wadsworth** (1807–82) ▸ Amer. writer.

long·hand (lông′hănd′, lŏng′-) ▸ *n.* Cursive writing.

long·horn (lông′hôrn′, lŏng′-) ▸ *n.* Any of a breed of cattle with long horns, formerly bred in the SW US.

long·house (lông′hous′) ▸ *n.* A long communal dwelling, esp. of certain Native American, Polynesian, and Indonesian peoples.

long·ing (lông′ĭng, lŏng′-) ▸ *n.* A persistent yearning or desire. **—long′ing** *adj.* **—long′ing·ly** *adv.*

Long Island ▸ An island of SE NY separated from CT by **Long Island Sound,** an arm of the Atlantic.

lon·gi·tude (lŏn′jĭ-to͞od′, -tyo͞od′, lôn′-) ▸ *n.* Angular distance east or west, measured with respect to the prime meridian at Greenwich, England. **—lon′gi·tu′di·nal** *adj.* **—lon′gi·tu′di·nal·ly** *adv.*

long jump ▸ *n.* A jump in track and field made for distance, usu. from a moving start.

long-lived (lông′lĭvd′, -lĭvd′, lŏng′-) ▸ *adj.* Having a long life. **—long′-lived′ness** *n.*

long-play·ing (lông′plā′ĭng, lŏng′-) ▸ *adj.* Of or being a phonograph record that turns at 33 ⅓ revolutions per minute.

long-range (lông′rānj′, lŏng′-) ▸ *adj.* 1. Of or designed for great distances: *long-range missiles.* 2. Involving an extended span of time: *long-range planning.*

long·shore·man (lông′shôr′mən, lŏng′-) ▸ *n.* A dock worker who loads and unloads ships.

long shot ▸ *n.* An entry, as in a horserace, with only a slight chance of winning.

long-stand·ing (lông′stăn′dĭng, lŏng′-) ▸ *adj.* Of long duration or existence.

long-suf·fer·ing (lông′sŭf′ər-ĭng, lŏng′-) ▸ *adj.* Patiently enduring pain or difficulties.

long-term (lông′tûrm′, lŏng′-) ▸ *adj.* Involving or being in effect for a long time.

long ton ▸ *n.* See **measurement** table in Appendix.

long-wind·ed (lông′wĭn′dĭd, lŏng′-) ▸ *adj.* Wearisomely talkative. **—long′-wind′ed·ly** *adv.* **—long′-wind′ed·ness** *n.*

loo·fa (lo͞o′fə) ▸ *n.* 1. A tropical vine having cylindrical fruit with a fibrous interior. 2. The interior of this fruit, used esp. as a sponge.

look (lo͝ok) ▸ *v.* 1. To use the eyes to see. 2. To search. 3. To focus one's gaze or attention: *look toward the river.* 4. To seem or appear to be: *look ripe.* 5. To face in a specified direction. 6. To have an appearance of conformity with: *look one's age.* **—*phrasal verbs:* look after** To take care of. **look into** To investigate. **look on** 1. To be a spectator. 2. To consider; regard. **look out** To be on guard. **look over** To inspect, esp. in a casual way. **look up** 1. To search for and find, as in a reference book. 2. To visit: *look up an old friend.* 3. To improve. ▸ *n.* 1. The act or instance of looking: *gaze or glance.* 2. Appearance or aspect. 3. **looks** Physical appearance, esp. when pleasing. **—*idioms:* look down on** To regard with contempt or condescension. **look up to** To admire. **—look′er** *n.*

look·ing glass (lo͝ok′ĭng) ▸ *n.* See **mirror** 1.

look·out (lo͝ok′out′) ▸ *n.* 1. The act of observing or keeping watch. 2. A high place commanding a wide view for

THESAURUS

lone *adj.* Alone in a given category ▸ one, only, particular, separate, single, singular, sole, solitary, unique. *Idioms:* all by one's lonesome, all by one's self, first and last, one and only. *—See also* INDIVIDUAL (2), SINGLE, SOLITARY.

loneliness *n.* *—See* SOLITUDE.

lonely or **lonesome** *adj.* 1. Empty of people ▸ deserted, desolate, forlorn, godforsaken, uninhabited, unfrequented, unpeopled, unpopulated, vacant. 2. Dejected due to the awareness of being alone ▸ desolate, forlorn, lorn. [*Compare* DEPRESSED, MISERABLE.] *—See also* REMOTE (1), SOLITARY.

long[1] *adj.* 1. Having great physical length ▸ elongate, elongated, extended, lengthy, outstretched, prolonged, stretching. 2. Extending tediously beyond a standard duration ▸ dragging, drawn-out, interminable, lengthy, long-drawn-out, overlong, prolonged, protracted, sustained, unending.

long *n.* *—See* AGES.

long[2] *v.* *—See* DESIRE.

longanimity *n.* *—See* PATIENCE.

long-drawn-out *adj.* *—See* LONG[1] (2).

long green *n.* *—See* MONEY (1).

longhand *n.* *—See* SCRIPT (1).

longing *n.* *—See* DESIRE (1).

long-lasting or **long-lived** or **long-standing** *adj.* *—See* CONTINUING.

long-suffering *adj.* *—See* PATIENT.

long-suffering *n.* *—See* PATIENCE.

long suit *n.* *—See* FORTE.

long-winded *adj.* *—See* DIGRESSIVE, WORDY (1).

long-windedness *n.* *—See* WORDINESS.

look *v.* 1. To direct the eyes on an object ▸ consider, contemplate, eye, view. *Idiom:* clap (*or* lay *or* set) one's eyes on. [*Compare* GAZE, GLIMPSE, SURVEY, WATCH.] 2. To give the impression of being ▸ appear, feel, seem, sound. *Idioms:* have all the earmarks of being, give the idea (*or* impression) of being, strike one as being. [*Compare* RESEMBLE.]

look after *v.* *—See* TEND[2].

look for *v.* *—See* EXPECT (1), SEEK (1).

look in *v.* *—See* VISIT.

look into *v.* *—See* EXPLORE.

look on or **toward** *v.* To have the face or front turned toward ▸ face, front, give onto. [*Compare* OVERLOOK.]

look out *v.* To be careful ▸ beware, mind, watch out. *Idioms:* be on guard, be on the lookout, keep an eye peeled, take care (*or* heed).

look over *v.* To view broadly or from a height ▸ overlook, scan, survey. *—See also* BROWSE (1).

look through *v.* *—See* BROWSE (1).

look up *v.* *—See* VISIT.

look upon *v.* To have the face or front turned toward ▸ face, front, give onto. [*Compare* OVERLOOK.] *—See also* REGARD.

look *n.* An act of directing the eyes on an object ▸ contemplation, regard, sight, view. [*Compare* GAZE, WATCH.] *—See also* APPEARANCE (1), EXPRESSION (4), FACE (3), GLANCE (1).

looker *n.* *—See* BEAUTY.

looker-on *n.* *—See* WATCHER (1).

look-in *n.* *—See* VISIT (1).

lookout *n.* 1. The act of carefully watching ▸ monitoring, stakeout, surveillance, vigil, vigilance, watch. *Idiom:* watch and ward. [*Compare* WATCH.] 2. A high structure or place commanding a wide view ▸ crow's nest, cupola, observation post, observatory, outlook, overlook, post, vista, watchtower. 3. Something that concerns or involves one personally ▸ af-

observation. 3. A person who keeps watch.

loom[1] (lo͞om) ▸ *v.* 1. To come into view as a massive, distorted, or indistinct image. 2. To appear imminent and usu. theatening.

loom[2] (lo͞om) ▸ *n.* An apparatus for making thread or yarn into cloth by weaving strands together at right angles.

loon[1] (lo͞on) ▸ *n.* A diving bird having mottled plumage and an eerie, laughlike cry.

loon[2] (lo͞on) ▸ *n. Informal* One who is crazy or simpleminded.

loon·y or **loon·ey** (lo͞o′nē) ▸ *adj.* **-i·er, -i·est.** *Informal* 1. Extremely foolish or silly. 2. Crazy; insane. **—loon′i·ness** *n.* **—loon′y** *n.*

loop (lo͞op) ▸ *n.* 1. A length of line, ribbon, or other thin material doubled over and joined at the ends. 2. Something having a shape, order, or path of motion that is circular or curved over on itself. 3. *Comp. Sci.* A sequence of instructions that repeats either a specified number of times or until a particular condition is met. ▸ *v.* 1. To form, or form into, a loop. 2. To fasten, join, or encircle with a loop or loops.

loop·hole (lo͞op′hōl′) ▸ *n.* 1. A means of evasion. 2. A small hole or slit in a wall, esp. one through which small arms may be fired.

loop·y (lo͞o′pē) ▸ *adj.* **-i·er, -i·est.** Offbeat; crazy.

loose (lo͞os) ▸ *adj.* **loos·er, loos·est.** 1. Not tightly fastened or secured. 2. Not tightly stretched, taut, or fixed. 3. Free from confinement. 4. Not tight-fitting. 5. Not bound, bundled, or gathered together. 6. Lacking restraint or responsibility: *loose talk.* 7. Licentious; immoral. 8. Not literal or exact: *a loose translation.* ▸ *adv.* In a loose manner. ▸ *v.* **loosed, loos·ing.** 1. To set free; release. 2. To undo, untie, or unwrap. 3. To make less tight, firm, or compact; loosen. 4. To let fly; discharge: *loosed an arrow.* 5. To relax. **—loose′ly** *adv.* **—loose′ness** *n.*

loos·en (lo͞o′sən) ▸ *v.* 1. To make or become loose or looser. 2. To free from restraint, pressure, or strictness.

loot (lo͞ot) ▸ *n.* 1. Valuables pillaged in war; spoils. 2. Goods stolen or illicitly obtained. ▸ *v.* To pillage; plunder. **—loot′er** *n.*

lop (lŏp) ▸ *v.* **lopped, lop·ping.** 1. To cut off (a part) from, esp. with a single swift blow. 2. To cut off branches or twigs from; trim.

lope (lōp) ▸ *v.* **loped, lop·ing.** To run or ride with a steady, easy gait. ▸ *n.* A steady, easy gait. **—lop′er** *n.*

lop·sid·ed (lŏp′sī′dĭd) ▸ *adj.* Heavier, larger, or higher on one side than on the other. **—lop′sid′ed·ly** *adv.* **—lop′sid′ed·ness** *n.*

lo·qua·cious (lō-kwā′shəs) ▸ *adj.* Very talkative. **—lo·qua′cious·ly** *adv.* **—lo·qua′cious·ness, lo·quac′i·ty** (-kwăs′ĭ tē) *n.*

lord (lôrd) ▸ *n.* 1. The owner of a feudal estate. 2. **Lord** *Chiefly Brit.* The general masculine title of nobility and other rank. 3. **Lord** a. God. b. Jesus. 4. A man of renowned power, authority, or mastery in a given field or activity. ▸ *v.* To domineer: *lorded it over their subordinates.*

lord·ly (lôrd′lē) ▸ *adj.* **-li·er, -li·est.** 1. Of or characteristic of a lord. 2. Dignified and noble. 3. Arrogant and overbearing. **—lord′li·ness** *n.*

lord·ship (lôrd′shĭp′) ▸ *n.* 1. often **Lordship** Used with *Your, His,* or *Their* as a title for a man holding the rank of lord. 2. The position or domain of a lord.

Lord's Prayer (lôrdz prâr) ▸ *n.* The prayer taught by Jesus to his disciples.

lore (lôr) ▸ *n.* Accumulated facts, traditions, or beliefs about a specific subject.

lor·gnette (lôrn-yĕt′) ▸ *n.* Eyeglasses or opera glasses with a short handle.

lorn (lôrn) ▸ *adj.* Bereft; forlorn.

Lor·raine (lō-rān′, lô-, lô-rĕn′) ▸ A region and former province of NE France.

lor·ry (lôr′ē, lŏr′ē) ▸ *n., pl.* **-ries.** *Chiefly Brit.* A motor truck.

Los An·ge·les (lôs ăn′jə-ləs, -lēz′, ăng′gə-ləs) ▸ A city of S CA on the Pacific.

lose (lo͞oz) ▸ *v.* **lost** (lôst, lŏst), **los·ing.** 1. To be unable to find; mislay. 2. To be deprived of: *lost a friend.* 3. To be unable to maintain or keep. 4. To fail to win; be defeated. 5. To fail to take advantage of. 6. To let (oneself) become engrossed. 7. To rid oneself of: *lost five pounds.* 8. To cause the loss of: *Politics lost her the job.* 9. To suffer loss. ***—phrasal verb:* lose out** To fail or be defeated. **—los′er** *n.*

loss (lôs, lŏs) ▸ *n.* 1. The act or an instance of losing or having lost. 2. One that is lost. 3. **losses** People killed, wounded, or captured in wartime; casualties. ***—idiom:* at a loss** Perplexed; puzzled.

loss leader ▸ *n.* A commodity offered at or below cost to attract customers.

lost (lôst, lŏst) ▸ *v.* P.t. and p.part. of **lose.** ▸ *adj.* 1. Unable to find one's way: strayed or missing. 2a. No longer in

THESAURUS

fair, business, concern, interest. *—See also* GUARD, VIEW (2).

looks *n.* *—See* APPEARANCE (1).

loom *v.* *—See* APPEAR (1), THREATEN (2).

looming *adj.* *—See* FATEFUL (1), IMMINENT.

loon *n.* *—See* CRACKPOT.

looniness *n.* *—See* FOOLISHNESS.

loony *adj.* *—See* FOOLISH, INSANE.

loony *n.* *—See* CRACKPOT.

loop *n.* A length of line folded over and joined at the ends so as to form a curve or circle ▸ circuit, coil, eye, eyelet, noose, ring, ringlet. [*Compare* CIRCLE.] *—See also* CONFERENCE (2).

loop *v.* *—See* BEND (1), ENCIRCLE.

looped *adj.* *—See* DRUNK.

loopiness *n.* *—See* FOOLISHNESS.

loopy *adj.* *—See* FOOLISH.

loose *adj.* 1. Not tautly bound, held, or fastened ▸ dangling, flapping, hanging, lax, relaxed, slack, unbound, unfastened. [*Compare* LIMP.] 2. Able to move about at will without bounds or restraint ▸ emancipated, free, liberated, unbridled, unchained, unchecked, unconfined, unfettered, unhindered, unrestrained, untrammeled. ***Idioms:*** at large, at liberty, free as a bird, on the loose. [*Compare* CLEAR.] 3. Lacking literal exactness ▸ approximate, broad, free, general, imprecise, inexact, rough. *—See also* WANTON (1).

loose *v.* *—See* EASE (1), FREE (1), SHOOT (3), UNDO.

loosen *v.* *—See* EASE (1), UNDO.

loot *n.* *—See* PLUNDER.

loot *v.* *—See* SACK[2].

looter *n.* *—See* THIEF.

looting *n.* *—See* LARCENY.

lop[1] *v.* *—See* CUT (3).

lop[2] *v.* *—See* SLOUCH (2).

lope *v.* *—See* RUN (1).

lope *n.* *—See* RUN (1).

loquacious *adj.* *—See* TALKATIVE.

lord *n.* *—See* CHIEF.

lordliness *n.* *—See* ARROGANCE.

lordly *adj.* Exercising authority ▸ authoritative, commanding, dominant, masterful. [*Compare* ADMINISTRATIVE.] *—See also* ARROGANT, GRAND.

lore *n.* 1. A body of traditional beliefs and notions accumulated about a particular subject ▸ folklore, folkways, legend, myth, mythology, mythos, old wives' tale, tradition, superstition. [*Compare* PROVERB.] 2. The sum of what has been perceived, discovered, or inferred ▸ knowledge, understanding, wisdom. [*Compare* ACTUALITY.] *—See also* INFORMATION.

lorn *adj.* *—See* ABANDONED (1), LONELY (2).

lose *v.* 1. To be unable to find ▸ mislay, misplace, miss. ***Idiom:*** have something go missing. 2. To fail to take advantage of ▸ miss, pass up, relinquish, squander, waste. ***Idioms:*** let slip, let slip through one's fingers, lose out on. [*Compare* NEGLECT.] 3. To get away from a pursuer ▸ elude, evade, outrun, shake off, slip, throw off. *Slang:* shake. ***Idiom:*** give someone the shake (*or* slip).

loser *n.* *—See* FAILURE (1), UNFORTUNATE.

loss *n.* 1. The act or an instance of losing something ▸ losing, mislaying, misplacement, missing. 2. A loss of life, or one who has lost life, usually as a result of accident, disaster, or war ▸ casualty, death, fatality, kill. [*Compare* VICTIM.] 3. A sad or tragic deprivation ▸ waste. *—See also* DEPRIVATION.

lost *adj.* 1. Unable to find the correct way or place to go ▸ adrift, astray, disoriented, stray. ***Idiom:*** wandering in the wilderness. 2. No longer in one's possession ▸ gone, mislaid, misplaced, missing, vanished. ***Idiom:*** gone missing. [*Compare* ABSENT.] *—See also*

one's possession or control. **b.** No longer known or practiced: *a lost art.* **3.** Unable to function; helpless; bewildered. **4.** Absorbed or rapt.

lot (lŏt) ▸ *n.* **1.** An object used in making a determination at random. **2.** The use of lots for selection. **3.** One's fate in life. **4.** A number of associated people or things. **5.** *Informal* A large amount or number. **6.** A piece of land having fixed boundaries.

lo·ti (lō′tē) ▸ *n., pl.* **ma·lo·ti** (mä-). See **currency** table in Appendix.

lo·tion (lō′shən) ▸ *n.* A liquid medicine or cosmetic applied to the skin.

lot·ter·y (lŏt′ə-rē) ▸ *n., pl.* **-ies.** A contest in which winners are selected in a drawing of lots.

lo·tus (lō′təs) ▸ *n.* **1a.** An Asian water lily having large leaves and pinkish flowers. **b.** Any of several similar or related plants. **2.** *Gk. Myth.* A fruit said to produce a drugged, indolent state in those who ate it.

lotus position ▸ *n.* A cross-legged sitting position used in yoga.

loud (loud) ▸ *adj.* **-er, -est. 1.** Marked by high volume and intensity of sound. **2.** Producing or capable of producing sound of high volume and intensity. **3.** Offensively bright; flashy. **—loud, loud′ly** *adv.* **—loud′ness** *n.*

loud·mouth (loud′mouth′) ▸ *n. Informal* One given to loud, irritating, or indiscreet talk. **—loud′mouthed′** (-mouthd′, -moutht′) *adj.*

loud·speak·er (loud′spē′kər) ▸ *n.* A device that converts electric signals to sound and projects it.

Lou·is XIV (lo͞o′ē, lo͞o-ē′). "the Sun King" (1638–1715) ▸ King of France (1643–1715).

Louis XV (1710–74) ▸ King of France (1715–74).

Louis XVI (1754–93) ▸ King of France (1774–92); executed.

Lou·i·si·an·a (lo͞o-ē′zē-ăn′ə, lo͞o′zē-) ▸ A state of the S US on the Gulf of Mexico. Cap. Baton Rouge.

Louisiana French ▸ *n.* French as spoken by the descendants of the original French settlers of Louisiana.

Louisiana Purchase ▸ A territory of the W US from the Mississippi R. to the Rocky Mts. between the Gulf of Mexico and the Canadian border; purchased from France in 1803.

lounge (lounj) ▸ *v.* **lounged, loung·ing.** To stand, sit, or lie in a lazy, relaxed way. ▸ *n.* **1.** A comfortably furnished waiting room, as in a hotel or theater. **2.** A bar serving cocktails. **3.** A long couch. **—loung′er** *n.*

lour (lour) ▸ *v. & n.* Var. of **lower**[1].

louse (lous) ▸ *n.* **1.** *pl.* **lice** (līs). Any of numerous small wingless insects parasitic on various animals, including humans. **2.** *pl.* **lous·es.** *Slang* A mean or despicable person. ▸ *v.* **loused, lous·ing.** *Slang* To bungle: *louse up a deal.*

lous·y (lou′zē) ▸ *adj.* **-i·er, -i·est. 1.** Infested with lice. **2.** Mean; nasty. **3.** Inferior or worthless. **4.** Very bad or painful: *a lousy headache.* **—lous′i·ly** *adv.* **—lous′i·ness** *n.*

lout (lout) ▸ *n.* An awkward, stupid person; oaf. **—lout′ish** *adj.* **—lout′ish·ly** *adv.*

lou·ver also **lou·vre** (lo͞o′vər) ▸ *n.* **1.** An opening fitted with fixed or movable horizontal slats for admitting air and light and shedding rain. **2.** One of the slats of a louver. **—lou′vered** *adj.*

love (lŭv) ▸ *n.* **1.** Deep affection and warm feeling for another. **2.** The emotion of sex and romance; strong sexual desire for another person. **3.** A beloved person. **4.** A strong fondness or enthusiasm. **5.** *Sports* A zero score in tennis. ▸ *v.* **loved, lov·ing. 1.** To feel love (for). **2.** To like or desire enthusiastically. ***—idiom:* in love** Feeling love; enamored. **—lov′a·ble, love′a·ble** *adj.* **—love′less** *adj.*

love·bird (lŭv′bûrd′) ▸ *n.* A small parrot often kept as a cage bird.

love·lorn (lŭv′lôrn′) ▸ *adj.* Deprived of love or one's lover.

love·ly (lŭv′lē) ▸ *adj.* **-li·er, -li·est. 1.** Having pleasing or attractive qualities; beautiful. **2.** Enjoyable; delightful. **—love′li·ness** *n.*

love·mak·ing (lŭv′mā′kĭng) ▸ *n.* **1.** Sexual activity between lovers. **2.** Courtship.

lov·er (lŭv′ər) ▸ *n.* **1.** One who loves another, esp. one who feels sexual love. **2. lovers** A couple in love with each other. **3.** A sexual partner. **4.** One who is fond of or devoted to something. **—lov′er·ly** *adv. & adj.*

love seat ▸ *n.* A small sofa that seats two.

love·sick (lŭv′sĭk′) ▸ *adj.* **1.** Pining with love. **2.** Exhibiting or expressing a lover's yearning. **—love′sick′ness** *n.*

lov·ing (lŭv′ĭng) ▸ *adj.* Feeling or showing love; affectionate. **—lov′ing·ly** *adv.*

loving cup ▸ *n.* A large ornamental vessel, usu. with two or more handles, often given as an award in sporting contests.

low[1] (lō) ▸ *adj.* **-er, -est. 1.** Having little height. **2.** Of less than the usual height or depth. **3.** Humble or inferior in status. **4.** Morally base. **5.** Emotionally or mentally depressed; sad. **6.** Below average or standard in degree, intensity, or amount. **7.** Of small value or quality. **8.** Having a pitch corresponding to a relatively small number of sound-wave cycles per second. **9.** Not loud; soft or hushed. **10.** Depreciatory; disparaging: *a low opinion.* ▸ *adv.* **1.** At, in, or to a low position, level, or space. **2.** Softly; quietly: *speak low.* **3.** With or at a low pitch. ▸ *n.* **1.** A low level, position, or degree. **2.** *Meteorol.* A region of atmospheric air that exerts less pressure than the air around it. **3.** The gear configuration that produces the lowest range of output speeds, as in an automotive transmission. **—low′ness** *n.*

low[2] (lō) ▸ *n.* A moo. **—low** *v.*

THESAURUS

ABSENT-MINDED, CONDEMNED, CONFUSED (1), HOPELESS.

lot *n.* **1.** A piece of land ▸ acreage, parcel, patch, plat, plot, tract. [*Compare* FIELD.] **2.** *Informal* An indefinite amount or extent ▸ deal, quantity. *—See also* ABUNDANCE, ALLOTMENT, FATE (2), GROUP, HEAP (2), KIND[2].

Lothario *n.* A man who seduces women ▸ debaucher, Don Juan, seducer. [*Compare* FLIRT, LECHER, PHILANDERER.] *—See also* GALLANT.

lotion *n.* *—See* OINTMENT.

lottery *n.* *—See* CHANCE (2).

loud *adj.* Marked by extremely high volume and intensity of sound ▸ blaring, booming, clamorous, deafening, earsplitting, noisy, piercing, roaring, shrill, stentorian, strident, thunderous. *—See also* GAUDY.

loudmouthed *adj.* *—See* VOCIFEROUS.

lounge *v.* *—See* IDLE (1), REST[1] (1), SPRAWL.

lounge *n.* *—See* BAR (2).

lounger *n.* *—See* WASTREL (2).

louse *n.* *—See* CREEP (2).

louse up *v.* *—See* BOTCH.

lousy *adj.* *—See* OFFENSIVE (1), SHODDY, TERRIBLE.

lout *n.* *—See* OAF.

lovable *adj.* *—See* DELIGHTFUL.

love *n.* **1.** An intense attachment to a person or thing ▸ adoration, affection, attachment, devotion, fondness, heart, liking, love affair, loyalties, passion, romance, tenderness, worship. [*Compare* INCLINATION.] **2.** The passionate affection and desire felt by lovers for each other ▸ amativeness, amorousness, ardor, devotion, fancy, passion, romance. [*Compare* DESIRE.] **3.** An intimate sexual relationship between two people ▸ affair, amour, liaison, love affair, romance. *—See also* DARLING (1).

love *v.* To feel deep devoted love for ▸ adore, worship. *Idioms:* be soft (*or* stuck *or* sweet) on, place (*or* put) on a pedestal, worship the ground someone walks on. *—See also* ADORE (2), LIKE[1].

love affair *n.* *—See* LOVE (3), LOVE (1).

loved *adj.* *—See* DARLING.

lovely *adj.* *—See* ATTRACTIVE, BEAUTIFUL, PLEASANT.

lover *n.* A romantic interest, especially a regular sexual partner ▸ heartthrob, paramour, partner, steady. *Informal:* flame, significant other. *Slang:* main squeeze, squeeze. [*Compare* BOYFRIEND, DARLING, GIRLFRIEND.] *—See also* FAN[2].

loving *adj.* *—See* AFFECTIONATE, SYMPATHETIC.

low *adj.* **1.** Being a sound produced by a relatively small frequency of vibrations ▸ alto, bass, contralto, deep, low-pitched. **2.** Cut to reveal the wearer's neck, chest, and back ▸ décolleté, low-cut, low-neck, low-necked, plunging. *—See also* CHEAP, DEEP (1), DEPRESSED (1), DISPARAGING, MINOR (1), OFFENSIVE (1), SICK (1), SOFT (2), SORDID.

low *n.* A very low or lowest level, position, or degree ▸ bottom, minimum, nadir, rock bottom.

low beam ▸ *n.* The beam of a vehicle's headlight that provides short-range illumination.
low·born (lō′bôrn′) ▸ *adj.* Of humble birth.
low·boy (lō′boi′) ▸ *n.* A low tablelike chest of drawers.
low·bred (lō′brĕd′) ▸ *adj.* Coarse; vulgar.
low·brow (lō′brou′) ▸ *n.* One having uncultivated tastes. **—low′brow′** *adj.*
low-cal (lō′kăl′) ▸ *adj.* Having fewer calories than what is typical: *low-cal foods.*
Low Countries ▸ Belgium, the Netherlands, and Luxembourg.
low·down (lō′doun′) ▸ *n. Slang* All the facts; the whole truth.
low-down (lō′doun′) ▸ *adj.* Despicable; mean.
low·er[1] (lou′ər, lour) also **lour** (lour) ▸ *v.* **1.** To look angry; scowl. **2.** To appear dark or threatening, as the sky. **—low′er** *n.*
low·er[2] (lō′ər) ▸ *adj.* Comp. of **low**[1]. **1.** Below another in rank, position, or authority. **2. Lower** *Geol. & Archaeol.* Being an earlier division of the period named. **3.** Denoting the larger and usu. more representative house of a bicameral legislature. ▸ *v.* **1.** To let, bring, or move something down to a lower level. **2.** To make or become less; reduce or diminish.
low·er·case or **low·er-case** (lō′ər-kās′) ▸ *adj.* Of or relating to small letters as distinguished from capital letters. **—low′er·case′** *n. & v.*
low·er class (lō′ər) ▸ *n.* The socioeconomic class or classes of lower than middle rank in a society. **—low′er-class′** *adj.*
low·est common denominator (lō′ĭst) ▸ *n.* See **least common denominator.**
low frequency ▸ *n.* A radio-wave frequency in the range from 30 to 300 kilohertz.
Low German ▸ *n.* **1.** The German dialects of northern Germany. **2.** The continental Scandinavian and Germanic languages except High German.
low-grade (lō′grād′) ▸ *adj.* **1.** Of inferior quality. **2.** Reduced in degree or intensity: *a low-grade fever.*
low-key (lō′kē′) also **low-keyed** (-kēd′) ▸ *adj.* Restrained, as in style or quality.
low·land (lō′lənd) ▸ *n.* An area of relatively low land. **—low′land** *adj.* **—low′land·er** *n.*
low·ly (lō′lē) ▸ *adj.* **-li·er, -li·est. 1.** Having a low rank or position. **2.** Humble or meek in manner. **—low′li·ness** *n.* **—low′ly** *adv.*
low-mind·ed (lō′mīn′dĭd) ▸ *adj.* Exhibiting a coarse, vulgar character. **—low′-mind′ed·ly** *adv.* **—low′-mind′ed·ness** *n.*
low profile ▸ *n.* Unobtrusive, restrained behavior or activity.
low relief ▸ *n.* Sculptural relief that projects very little from the background; bas-relief.
low road ▸ *n.* Deceitful, immoral behavior or practice.
low-tech (lō′tĕk′) ▸ *adj.* Relating to technology that does not involve highly advanced systems or devices.
low tide ▸ *n.* **1.** The lowest level of the tide. **2.** The time of this level.
lox[1] (lŏks) ▸ *n., pl.* **lox** or **-es.** Smoked salmon.
lox[2] (lŏks) ▸ *n.* Liquid oxygen, esp. when used in rocket fuel.
loy·al (loi′əl) ▸ *adj.* **1.** Steadfast in allegiance, as to one's homeland. **2.** Faithful, as to a person, ideal, cause, or duty. **—loy′al·ly** *adv.* **—loy′al·ty** *n.*
loy·al·ist (loi′ə-lĭst) ▸ *n.* One who maintains loyalty to the lawful government during a revolt.
loz·enge (lŏz′ĭnj) ▸ *n.* **1.** A small medicated candy dissolved slowly in the mouth to soothe irritated throat tissues. **2.** A flat diamond-shaped figure.
LP (ĕl′pē′) ▸ *n.* A long-playing record.
Lr ▸ The symbol for the element **lawrencium.**
LSD (ĕl′ĕs-dē′) ▸ *n.* A powerful drug, lysergic acid diethylamide, $C_{20}H_{25}N_3O$, that induces hallucinations.
ltd. or **Ltd.** ▸ *abbr.* limited
Lu ▸ The symbol for the element **lutetium.**
lu·au (lo͞o-ou′, lo͞o′ou′) ▸ *n.* A traditional Hawaiian feast.
lube (lo͞ob) *Informal* ▸ *v.* **lubed, lub·ing.** To lubricate (e.g., a car's joints). ▸ *n.* A lubricant, esp. one applied to machinery.
lu·bri·cant (lo͞o′brĭ-kənt) ▸ *n.* A substance, such as grease or oil, that reduces friction when applied as a surface coating to moving parts. **—lu′bri·cant** *adj.*
lu·bri·cate (lo͞o′brĭ-kāt′) ▸ *v.* **-cat·ed, -cat·ing.** To apply a lubricant to. **—lu′bri·ca′tion** *n.*
lu·bri·cious (lo͞o-brish′əs) also **lu·bri·cous** (lo͞o′brĭ-kəs) ▸ *adj.* **1.** Slippery. **2.** Shifty or tricky. **3a.** Lewd; wanton. **b.** Salacious. **—lu·bri′cious·ness** *n.* **—lu·bric′i·ty** (-brĭs′ĭ-tē) *n.*
lu·cid (lo͞o′sĭd) ▸ *adj.* **1.** Easily understood: *a lucid explanation.* **2.** Clear-minded; rational. **3.** Translucent. **—lu·cid′i·ty, lu′cid·ness** *n.* **—lu′cid·ly** *adv.*
Lu·ci·fer (lo͞o′sə-fər) ▸ *n.* In Christian tradition, the archangel cast from heaven for leading the revolt of the angels; Satan.
Lu·cite (lo͞o′sīt′) ▸ A trademark for a transparent thermoplastic acrylic resin.
luck (lŭk) ▸ *n.* **1.** The chance happening of good or bad events; fortune. **2.** Good fortune; success. ▸ *v.* To gain success or something desirable by chance: *lucked into a good apartment.*
luck·less (lŭk′lĭs) ▸ *adj.* Unlucky.
luck·y (lŭk′ē) ▸ *adj.* **-i·er, -i·est.** Having, bringing, or attended by good luck. **—luck′i·ly** *adv.* **—luck′i·ness** *n.*

THESAURUS

lowborn *adj.* *—See* LOWLY (1).
lowbrow *adj.* *—See* IGNORANT (1).
low-cost *adj.* *—See* CHEAP.
low-cut *adj.* *—See* LOW (2).
low-down *adj.* *—See* SORDID.
low-down *n.* *—See* INFORMATION.
lower[1] *v.* **1.** To wrinkle one's brow, as though one were in thought, puzzlement, or displeasure ▸ frown, glower, scowl. *Idioms:* knit one's brow, look black, turn one's mouth down. [*Compare* GRIMACE.] **2.** To stare fixedly and angrily ▸ glare, glower, scowl. *Idioms:* give the evil eye, look daggers. [*Compare* GAZE, SNEER.] *—See also* THREATEN (2).
lower *n.* A fixed angry stare ▸ glare, glower, scowl. [*Compare* FACE, SNEER.] *—See also* FROWN.
lower[2] *v.* To cause to descend ▸ cast down, depress, drop, let down, sink, take down. *See also* CONDESCEND (1), CUT (3), DECREASE, DEPRECIATE, HUMBLE.
lower *adj.* *—See* MINOR (1).
lowering *adj.* *—See* FATEFUL (1).
lowest or **lowermost** *adj.* Opposite to or farthest from the top ▸ bottom, nethermost, undermost.
low-grade *adj.* *—See* BAD (1).
low-key or **low-keyed** *adj.* *—See* SOFT (2).
lowland *n.* *—See* VALLEY.
lowlife *n.* *—See* CREEP (2).
lowliness *n.* *—See* MODESTY (1).
lowly *adj.* **1.** Lacking high station or birth ▸ baseborn, common, déclassé, declassed, humble, ignoble, lowborn, low-ranking, mean, plebeian, unwashed, vulgar. [*Compare* POOR.] **2.** Having or expressing feelings of humility ▸ humble, meek, modest, unambitious. [*Compare* DEFERENTIAL.] **3.** Of little distinction ▸ humble, mean, simple. [*Compare* MODEST.]
low-necked or **low-neck** *adj.* *—See* LOW (2).
lowness *n.* *—See* DEPRESSION (2).
low-pitched *adj.* *—See* LOW (1).
low-priced *adj.* *—See* CHEAP.
low-quality *adj.* *—See* BAD (1).
loyal *adj.* *—See* FAITHFUL.
loyalties *n.* *—See* LOVE (1).
loyalty *n.* *—See* FIDELITY.
lube *n.* *—See* OIL.
lube *v.* *—See* OIL.
lubricant *n.* *—See* OIL.
lubricate *v.* *—See* OIL.
lubricious *adj.* *—See* LASCIVIOUS, SLICK, UNDERHAND.
lucency *n.* *—See* LIGHT[1] (1).
lucent *adj.* *—See* BRIGHT.
lucid *adj.* Mentally healthy ▸ compos mentis, normal, rational, sane. *Idioms:* all there, in one's right mind, of sound mind. [*Compare* HEALTHY.] *—See also* CLEAR (1), GRAPHIC (1), UNDERSTANDABLE.
lucidity or **lucidness** *n.* *—See* CLARITY, SANITY.
luck *n.* Success attained as a result of chance ▸ dumb luck, fluke, fortunateness, fortune, godsend, good fortune (*or* luck), luckiness. *Idioms:* gift from above (*or* heaven *or* on high), stroke of luck. *—See also* CHANCE (2), FATE (1), FATE (2).
luckless *adj.* *—See* UNFORTUNATE (1).
lucky *adj.* Characterized by luck or good fortune ▸ fortuitous, fortunate, happy, providential. [*Compare* OPPORTUNE.]

lu·cra·tive (lo͞o′krə-tĭv) ▸ *adj.* Producing wealth; profitable. **—lu′cra·tive·ly** *adv.*

lu·cre (lo͞o′kər) ▸ *n.* Money or profits.

lu·cu·brate (lo͞o′kyo͞o-brāt′) ▸ *v.* **-brat·ed, -brat·ing.** To write or study laboriously.

lu·di·crous (lo͞o′dĭ-krəs) ▸ *adj.* Laughable because of obvious absurdity or incongruity. **—lu′di·crous·ly** *adv.* **—lu′di·crous·ness** *n.*

lug[1] (lŭg) ▸ *n.* 1. A stubby handle or projection, used as a hold or support or to provide traction. 2. A lug nut. 3. *Slang* A clumsy fool.

lug[2] (lŭg) ▸ *v.* **lugged, lug·ging.** To drag or haul with difficulty.

luge (lo͞ozh) ▸ *n. Sports* A racing sled for one or two people lying supine.

lug·gage (lŭg′ĭj) ▸ *n.* Baggage, esp. suitcases.

lug nut ▸ *n.* A heavy rounded nut that fits over a bolt.

lu·gu·bri·ous (lo͝o-go͞o′brē-əs, -gyo͞o′-) ▸ *adj.* Mournful or gloomy, esp. to a ludicrous degree. **—lu·gu′bri·ous·ly** *adv.* **—lu·gu′bri·ous·ness** *n.*

Luke (lo͝ok) ▸ *n.* See **Bible** table in Appendix.

Luke, Saint (1st cent. A.D.) ▸ Companion of Saint Paul and author of the third Gospel of the Bible.

luke·warm (lo͝ok′wôrm′) ▸ *adj.* 1. Mildly warm; tepid. 2. Half-hearted: *lukewarm support for the candidate.* **—luke′warm′ly** *adv.* **—luke′warm′ness** *n.*

lull (lŭl) ▸ *v.* 1. To cause to sleep or rest; soothe. 2. To deceive into trustfulness. ▸ *n.* A relatively calm or inactive interval or period.

lull·a·by (lŭl′ə-bī′) ▸ *n., pl.* **-bies.** A soothing song with which to lull a child to sleep.

lum·ba·go (lŭm-bā′gō) ▸ *n.* A painful condition of the lower back, as one resulting from muscle strain or a slipped disk.

lum·bar (lŭm′bər, -bär′) ▸ *adj.* Of, near, or situated in the part of the back and sides between the lowest ribs and the hips.

lum·ber[1] (lŭm′bər) ▸ *n.* 1. Timber sawed into boards and planks. 2. Something useless or cumbersome. ▸ *v.* To cut down (trees) and prepare as marketable timber. **—lum′ber·er** *n.*

lum·ber[2] (lŭm′bər) ▸ *v.* To walk or move with heavy clumsiness.

lum·ber·jack (lŭm′bər-jăk′) ▸ *n.* One who fells trees and transports the timber to a mill.

lum·ber·yard (lŭm′bər-yärd′) ▸ *n.* An establishment that sells lumber and other building materials from a yard.

lu·men (lo͞o′mən) ▸ *n., pl.* **-mens** or **-mi·na** (-mə-nə). *Anat.* The inner open space or cavity of a tubular organ. **—lu′men·al, lu′min·al** *adj.*

lu·mi·nar·y (lo͞o′mə-nĕr′ē) ▸ *n., pl.* **-ies.** 1. An object, such as a celestial body, that gives light. 2. A notable person in a specific field. **—lu′mi·nar′y** *adj.*

lu·mi·nes·cence (lo͞o′mə-nĕs′əns) ▸ *n.* 1. The production of light without heat, as in fluorescence. 2. The light so produced. **—lu′mi·nes′cent** *adj.*

lu·mi·nous (lo͞o′mə-nəs) ▸ *adj.* 1. Emitting light, esp. self-generated light. 2. Full of light; illuminated. 3. Easily comprehended; clear. **—lu′mi·nos′i·ty** (-nŏs′ĭ-tē), **lu′mi·nous·ness** *n.* **—lu′mi·nous·ly** *adv.*

luminous flux ▸ *n.* The rate of flow of light per unit of time.

lum·mox (lŭm′əks) ▸ *n. Informal* An oaf; lout.

lump[1] (lŭmp) ▸ *n.* 1. An irregularly shaped mass or piece. 2. *Pathol.* A swelling or small palpable mass in a part of the body. 3. **lumps** *Informal* Punishment or criticism: *take one's lumps.* ▸ *adj.* 1. Formed into lumps: *lump sugar.* 2. Not divided into parts: *a lump payment.* ▸ *v.* To put together in a single group or pile. **—lump′i·ness** *n.* **—lump′y** *adj.*

lump[2] (lŭmp) ▸ *v.* To tolerate: *like it or lump it.*

lump·ec·to·my (lŭm-pĕk′tə-mē) ▸ *n., pl.* **-mies.** Surgical excision of a tumor from the breast.

lu·na·cy (lo͞o′nə-sē) ▸ *n., pl.* **-cies.** 1. Insanity. 2. Foolish conduct.

lu·nar (lo͞o′nər) ▸ *adj.* 1. Of, involving, caused by, or affecting the moon. 2. Measured in reference to the revolution of the moon: *a lunar month.*

lu·na·tic (lo͞o′nə-tĭk) ▸ *adj.* 1. Insane. 2. Of or for the insane. 3. Wildly or giddily foolish. **—lu′na·tic** *n.*

lunch (lŭnch) ▸ *n.* A meal eaten at midday. **—lunch** *v.*

lunch·eon (lŭn′chən) ▸ *n.* A lunch, esp. a party at which lunch is served.

lunch·eon·ette (lŭn′chə-nĕt′) ▸ *n.* A small restaurant that serves simple meals.

lung (lŭng) ▸ *n.* Either of two spongy, saclike thoracic organs in most vertebrates, functioning to remove carbon dioxide from the blood and provide it with oxygen.

lunge (lŭnj) ▸ *n.* 1. A sudden thrust or pass, as with a sword. 2. A sudden forward movement. ▸ *v.* **lunged, lung·ing.** To move with a lunge. **—lung′er** *n.*

lung·fish (lŭng′fĭsh′) ▸ *n.* Any of several tropical freshwater fishes that have lunglike organs as well as gills.

lu·pine also **lu·pin** (lo͞o′pən) ▸ *n.* A plant having tall spikes of variously colored flowers.

lu·pus (lo͞o′pəs) ▸ *n.* An autoimmune disease of the connective tissue, usu. involving multiple organ systems.

lurch[1] (lûrch) ▸ *v.* 1. To stagger. 2. To roll or pitch suddenly, as a ship. **—lurch** *n.* **—lurch′ing·ly** *adv.*

lurch[2] (lûrch) ▸ *n.* A difficult position.

lure (lo͝or) ▸ *n.* 1. Something that tempts or attracts with the promise of pleasure or reward. 2. An artificial bait used in catching fish. **—lure** *n.*

THESAURUS

lucrative *adj.* —*See* PROFITABLE.

lucre *n.* —*See* MONEY (1).

lucubrate *v.* To apply one's mind to the acquisition of knowledge, especially when pressed for time ▸ study. *Informal:* bone up, cram, grind. *Idioms:* burn the midnight oil, hit the books. [*Compare* EXAMINE.]

ludicracy *n.* —*See* FOOLISHNESS.

ludicrous *adj.* Causing or deserving laughter or derision ▸ farcical, laughable, ridiculous, risible. —*See also* FOOLISH.

ludicrousness *n.* —*See* HUMOR.

lug[1] *n.* —*See* OAF.

lug[2] *v.* —*See* CARRY (1), PULL (1).

lugubrious *adj.* —*See* SORROWFUL.

lukewarm *adj.* Lacking warmth, interest, enthusiasm, or involvement ▸ half-hearted, Laodicean, tepid, unenthusiastic. [*Compare* APATHETIC, COLD, COOL.]

lull *v.* —*See* PACIFY.

lull *n.* —*See* GAP (2), STILLNESS.

lumber *v.* —*See* BLUNDER.

luminary *n.* —*See* CELEBRITY, DIGNITARY.

luminesce *v.* To shine brightly and steadily but without a flame ▸ gleam, glow, incandesce. [*Compare* BEAM.]

luminescence *n.* —*See* LIGHT[1] (1).

luminosity *n.* —*See* BRILLIANCE (1).

luminous or **luminescent** *adj.* —*See* BRIGHT.

lummox *n.* —*See* OAF.

lump[1] *n.* An irregularly shaped mass of indefinite size ▸ cake, chunk, clod, clot, clump, gob, hunch, nugget, slab, wad. *Informal:* hunk. —*See also* BUMP (1), BUMP (2), OAF.

lump *v.* —*See* BLUNDER, HEAP (1).

lump[2] *v.* —*See* ENDURE (1).

lumpish *adj.* —*See* AWKWARD (1), BULKY (1).

lumps *n.* —*See* DUE.

lumpy *adj.* —*See* BULKY (1).

lunacy *n.* —*See* FOOLISHNESS, INSANITY.

lunatic *adj.* —*See* EXTREME (2), FOOLISH, INSANE.

lunatic *n.* —*See* CRACKPOT.

lunge *v.* —*See* PLUNGE.

lunkheaded *adj.* —*See* STUPID.

lurch *v.* 1. To lean suddenly, unsteadily, and erratically from the vertical axis ▸ keel, pitch, roll, seesaw, yaw. [*Compare* INCLINE, SWAY, TOSS.] 2. To move or cause to move with a sudden abrupt motion ▸ jerk, snap, twitch, wrench, yank. [*Compare* MOVE.] —*See also* BLUNDER, BUMP, STAGGER (1).

lurch *n.* —*See* JERK.

lure *n.* 1. Something that attracts, especially with the promise of pleasure or reward ▸ allurement, attraction, bait, carrot, come-on, draw, enticement, inducement, inveiglement, invitation, magnet, seduction, temptation. 2. Something that leads a person into danger or entrapment ▸ bait, decoy. [*Compare* TRAP, TRICK.] —*See also* ATTRACTION.

lure *v.* —*See* ATTRACT, SEDUCE.

lurer *n.* —*See* SEDUCER (1).

lu·rid (lo͝or′ĭd) ▸ *adj.* 1. Horrible; gruesome. 2. Marked by sensationalism or violence. **—lu′rid·ly** *adv.* **—lu′rid·ness** *n.*

lurk (lûrk) ▸ *v.* 1. To lie in wait, as in ambush. 2. To move furtively; sneak. 3. To read but not contribute to the discussion in a newsgroup or chatroom.

lus·cious (lŭsh′əs) ▸ *adj.* 1. Sweet and pleasant to taste or smell. 2. Sensually appealing. **—lus′cious·ly** *adv.*

lush[1] (lŭsh) ▸ *adj.* **-er, -est.** 1a. Marked by luxuriant growth or vegetation. b. Abundant; plentiful. 2. Luxurious; opulent. **—lush′ly** *adv.* **—lush′ness** *n.*

lush[2] (lŭsh) ▸ *n. Slang* A drunkard.

lust (lŭst) ▸ *n.* 1. Intense, excessive, or unrestrained sexual desire. 2. An overwhelming craving. 3. Intense eagerness or enthusiasm. ▸ *v.* To have an intense desire, esp. sexual desire. **—lust′ful** *adj.* **—lust′ful·ly** *adv.* **—lust′ful·ness** *n.*

lus·ter (lŭs′tər) ▸ *n.* 1. Soft reflected light; sheen. 2. Brilliance or radiance. 3. Glory, distinction, or splendor. **—lus′trous** (-trəs) *adj.* **—lus′trous·ly** *adv.* **—lus′trous·ness** *n.*

lus·tre (lŭs′tər) ▸ *n. Chiefly Brit.* Var. of **luster**.

lust·y (lŭs′tē) ▸ *adj.* **-i·er, -i·est.** Full of vigor; robust. **—lust′i·ly** *adv.* **—lust′i·ness** *n.*

lute (lo͞ot) ▸ *n.* A stringed instrument having a fretted fingerboard and a body shaped like half a pear. **—lu′te·nist, lu′ta·nist** (lo͞ot′n-ĭst), **lut′ist** *n.*

lu·te·ti·um also **lu·te·ci·um** (lo͞o-tē′shē-əm) ▸ *n. Symbol* **Lu** A silvery-white rare-earth element. At. no. 71.

Lu·ther (lo͞o′thər), **Martin** (1483–1546) ▸ German theologian and Reformation leader.

Lu·ther·an (lo͞o′thər-ən) ▸ *adj.* Of or relating to the branch of the Protestant Church adhering to the views of Martin Luther. **—Lu′ther·an** *n.* **—Lu′ther·an·ism** *n.*

Lux·em·bourg also **Lux·em·burg** (lŭk′səm-bûrg′) ▸ A country of NW Europe.

lux·u·ri·ant (lŭg-zho͝or′ē-ənt, lŭk-sho͝or′-) ▸ *adj.* 1a. Marked by rich or profuse growth. b. Producing or yielding in abundance. 2. Excessively florid or elaborate; ornate. **—lux·u′ri·ance** *n.* **—lux·u′ri·ant·ly** *adv.*

lux·u·ri·ate (lŭg-zho͝or′ē-āt′, lŭk-sho͝or′-) ▸ *v.* **-at·ed, -at·ing.** To take luxurious pleasure; indulge oneself.

lux·u·ry (lŭg′zhə-rē, lŭk′shə-) ▸ *n., pl.* **-ries.** 1. Something inessential, usu. expensive, that provides pleasure and comfort. 2. Sumptuous living or surroundings. **—lux·u′ri·ous** (-zho͝or′ēəs, -sho͝or′-) *adj.* **—lux·u′ri·ous·ly** *adv.*

L'viv (lə-vĭv′, -vĭf′) or **L'vov** (lə-vôv′, -vôf′) ▸ A city of W-central Ukraine near the Polish border.

–ly[1] ▸ *suff.* 1. Like; having the characteristics of: *sisterly.* 2. Recurring at a specified interval of time: *hourly.*

–ly[2] ▸ *suff.* 1. In a specified manner; in the manner of: *gradually.* 2. At a specified interval of time: *weekly.* 3. With respect to: *partly.*

ly·ce·um (lī-sē′əm) ▸ *n.* 1. A hall in which public lectures, concerts, and similar programs are presented. 2. An organization sponsoring such programs.

lye (lī) ▸ *n.* 1. The liquid that is obtained by leaching wood ashes. 2. See **potassium hydroxide**. 3. See **sodium hydroxide**.

Lyme disease (līm) ▸ *n.* An inflammatory disease that is caused by a spirochete transmitted by ticks.

lymph (lĭmf) ▸ *n.* A clear watery fluid that contains white blood cells and acts to remove bacteria and certain proteins from the tissues, transport fat from the small intestine, and supply mature lymphocytes to the blood.

lym·phat·ic (lĭm-făt′ĭk) ▸ *adj.* Of or relating to lymph or the lymphatic system. ▸ *n.* A vessel that conveys lymph.

lymphatic system ▸ *n.* The system of spaces and vessels between tissues and organs by which lymph is circulated.

lymph node ▸ *n.* Any of numerous oval or round bodies that supply lymphocytes to the bloodstream and remove bacteria and foreign particles from the lymph.

lym·pho·cyte (lĭm′fə-sīt′) ▸ *n.* A white blood cell formed in lymphoid tissue.

lym·phoid (lĭm′foid′) ▸ *adj.* Of lymph, lymphatic tissue, or the lymphatic system.

lynch (lĭnch) ▸ *v.* To execute without due process of law, esp. to hang by a mob. **—lynch′ing** *n.*

lynx (lĭngks) ▸ *n., pl.* **lynx** or **-es.** A wildcat with soft thick fur, a short tail, and tufted ears.

lynx-eyed (lĭngks′īd′) ▸ *adj.* Keen of vision.

lyre (līr) ▸ *n.* A stringed instrument of the harp family used esp. in ancient Greece.

lyr·ic (lĭr′ĭk) ▸ *adj.* 1. Of or relating to poetry that expresses subjective thoughts and feelings, often in a songlike style or form. 2. Lyrical. ▸ *n.* 1. A lyric poem. 2. often **lyrics** The words of a song. **—lyr′i·cism** (-sĭz′əm) *n.*

lyr·i·cal (lĭr′ĭ-kəl) ▸ *adj.* 1. Expressing deep personal emotion or observations. 2. Highly enthusiastic; rhapsodic. 3. Lyric. **—lyr′i·cal·ly** *adv.*

lyr·i·cist (lĭr′ĭ-sĭst) ▸ *n.* A writer of song lyrics.

ly·ser·gic acid (lĭ-sûr′jĭk, lī-) ▸ *n.* A crystalline alkaloid, $C_{16}H_{16}N_2O_2$, derived from ergot and used in medical research.

lysergic acid di·eth·yl·am·ide (dī′ĕth-əl-ăm′īd′) ▸ *n.* See **LSD**.

ly·sin (lī′sĭn) ▸ *n.* An antibody that acts to destroy red blood cells, bacteria, or other cellular elements.

ly·sis (lī′sĭs) ▸ *n., pl.* **-ses** (-sēz). 1. The dissolution or destruction of cells. 2. The gradual subsiding of the symptoms of an acute disease.

–lysis ▸ *suff.* Decomposition; dissolving: *hydrolysis.*

–lyte ▸ *suff.* A substance that can be decomposed by a specified process: *electrolyte.*

THESAURUS

lurid *adj.* —*See* GHASTLY (1), PALE (1).

luring *adj.* —*See* SEDUCTIVE.

lurk *v.* To wait furtively in order to attack someone ▸ ambush, await, prowl, skulk. *Informal:* lay for. *Idioms:* lay wait for, lie in wait for. [*Compare* AMBUSH.] —*See also* SNEAK.

luscious *adj.* —*See* DELICIOUS, DELIGHTFUL.

lush[1] *adj.* —*See* LUXURIOUS, PROFUSE, THICK (3).

lush[2] *n.* —*See* DRUNKARD.

lush *v.* —*See* DRINK (2).

lust *n.* —*See* DESIRE (1), DESIRE (2).

lust *v.* To have a greedy, obsessive desire ▸ crave, hunger, itch, thirst.

luster *n.* —*See* FAME, GLOSS[1].

lusterless *adj.* —*See* DULL (1), DULL (2).

lustful *adj.* —*See* LASCIVIOUS.

lustfulness *n.* —*See* DESIRE (2).

lustral *adj.* —*See* PURGATIVE.

lustrate *v.* —*See* PURIFY (1).

lustration *n.* —*See* PURIFICATION (2).

lustrative *adj.* —*See* PURGATIVE.

lustrous *adj.* —*See* BRIGHT, GLOSSY.

lusty *adj.* Full of vigor ▸ able-bodied, gutsy, iron, red-blooded, robust, strapping, sturdy, vigorous, vital. [*Compare* ENERGETIC, HEALTHY.] —*See also* LASCIVIOUS.

luxuriance *n.* —*See* PROSPERITY (2).

luxuriant *adj.* —*See* LUXURIOUS, PROFUSE, THICK (3).

luxuriate *v.* To take extravagant pleasure ▸ bask, indulge, revel, roll, rollick, splurge, wallow. [*Compare* ENJOY.]

luxurious *adj.* Characterized by extravagant, ostentatious magnificence ▸ deluxe, fancy, lavish, lush, luxuriant, opulent, palatial, plush, plushy, rich, ritzy, sumptuous. [*Compare* EXCLUSIVE, GLORIOUS, SYBARITIC.]

luxury *n.* Something costly and unnecessary ▸ delight, extravagance, extravagancy, frill, indulgence, rarity, treat. —*See also* PROSPERITY (2).

lying *adj.* —*See* DISHONEST.

lying *n.* —*See* MENDACITY.

lying-in *n.* —*See* BIRTH (1).

lymphatic *adj.* —*See* LANGUID.

lyric or **lyrical** *adj.* Relating to the characteristics of poetry ▸ poetic, poetical. [*Compare* MELODIOUS, RHYTHMICAL.]

lyricism *n.* A creation or experience having beauty suggestive of poetry ▸ poem, poetry.

lyrics *n.* —*See* SONG.

M

m¹ or **M** (ĕm) ▸ *n., pl.* **m's** or **M's** also **ms** or **Ms.** The 13th letter of the English alphabet.
m² ▸ *abbr.* **1.** *Gram.* masculine **2.** *Phys.* mass **3.** meter (measurement)
M¹ also **m** ▸ The symbol for the Roman numeral 1,000.
M² ▸ *abbr.* **1.** male **2.** medium **3.** Monday **4.** month
m. ▸ *abbr.* mile
M. ▸ *abbr.* **1.** master **2.** Monsieur
MA ▸ *abbr.* **1.** *Lat.* Magister Artium (Master of Arts) **2.** Massachusetts
ma'am (măm) ▸ *n.* Used as a form of polite address for a woman: *Is that all, ma'am?*
ma·ca·bre (mə-kä′brə, mə-käb′, -kä′bər) ▸ *adj.* Suggesting the horror of death and decay; gruesome; ghastly.
mac·ad·am (mə-kăd′əm) ▸ *n.* Pavement made of layers of compacted broken stone, now usu. bound with tar or asphalt. **—mac·ad′am·ize** *v.*
Ma·cao also **Ma·cau** (mə-kou′) ▸ An administrative region of SE China. Cap. the city of **Macao.**
ma·caque (mə-kăk′, -käk′) ▸ *n.* A short-tailed monkey of Asia, Japan, Gibraltar, and N Africa.
mac·a·ro·ni (măk′ə-rō′nē) ▸ *n., pl.* **-ni.** Pasta in any of various hollow shapes, especially short curved tubes.
mac·a·roon (măk′ə-ro͞on′) ▸ *n.* A chewy cookie made with sugar, egg whites, and almond paste or coconut.
Mac·Ar·thur (mĭk-är′thər), **Douglas** (1880–1964) ▸ Amer. general.
ma·caw (mə-kô′) ▸ *n.* A large, usu. brilliantly colored tropical American parrot.
Mac·ca·bees (măk′ə-bēz′) ▸ *pl.n. Bible* **1.** A family of Jewish patriots of the 2nd and 1st cent. B.C. **2.** See **Bible** table in Appendix. **—Mac′ca·be′an** *adj.*
mace¹ (mās) ▸ *n.* **1.** A ceremonial staff used as a symbol of authority. **2.** A heavy medieval war club with a spiked head.
mace² (mās) ▸ *n.* An aromatic spice made from the dried seed covering of the nutmeg.
Mace ▸ A trademark for a temporarily disabling liquid sprayed into the face of an attacker.
Mac·e·do·ni·a (măs′ĭ-dō′nē-ə, -dōn′yə) ▸ **1.** Also **Mac·e·don** (-dən, -dŏn′) An ancient kingdom of N Greece. **2.** A historical region of SE Europe on the Balkan Peninsula. **3.** A country of the S-central Balkan Peninsula.
Mac·e·do·ni·an (măs′ĭ-dō′nē-ən) ▸ *adj.* Of or relating to ancient or modern Macedonia. ▸ *n.* **1.** A native or inhabitant of ancient or modern Macedonia. **2.** The language of ancient Macedonia, of uncertain affiliation within Indo-European. **3.** The Slavic language of modern Macedonia, closely related to Bulgarian.
mac·er·ate (măs′ə-rāt′) ▸ *v.* **-at·ed, -at·ing. 1.** To soften or separate by soaking or steeping. **2.** To emaciate, usu. by starvation. **—mac′er·a′tion** *n.*
Mach also **mach** (mäk) ▸ *n.* Mach number.
ma·chet·e (mə-shĕt′ē, -chĕt′ē) ▸ *n.* A large, broad-bladed knife used for cutting and as a weapon.
Ma·chi·a·vel·li (măk′ē-ə-vĕl′ē, mä′kyä-), **Niccolò** (1469–1527) ▸ Italian political theorist.
Ma·chi·a·vel·li·an (măk′ē-ə-vĕl′ē-ən) ▸ *adj.* Of or relating to the political doctrine of Machiavelli, which holds that craft and deceit are justified in pursuing and maintaining political power. **—Ma′chi·a·vel′li·an** *n.* **—Ma′chi·a·vel′li·an·ism** *n.*
mach·i·na·tion (măk′ə-nā′shən, măsh′-) ▸ *n.* A scheme or secret plot usu. meant to achieve an evil end. **—mach′i·nate′** *v.*
ma·chine (mə-shēn′) ▸ *n.* **1a.** A device or system consisting of fixed and moving parts that alters, directs, or modifies mechanical energy and transmits it to accomplish a specific objective. **b.** A simple device, such as a lever, pulley, or screw, that alters an applied force. **2.** A system or device, such as a computer, that performs or assists with a human task. **3.** An automaton. **4.** An organized political group under the control of a strong leader or faction. ▸ *v.* **-chined, -chin·ing.** To shape or finish by machine.
machine gun ▸ *n.* A gun, often mounted, that fires rapidly and repeatedly. **—ma·chine′-gun** *v.* **—machine gunner** *n.*
machine language ▸ *n.* A set of coded instructions that a computer can use directly without further translation.
ma·chin·er·y (mə-shē′nə-rē, -shēn′rē) ▸ *n., pl.* **-ies. 1.** Machines or machine parts collectively. **2.** The working parts of a particular machine. **3.** A system of related elements that operate together: *diplomatic and political machinery.*
ma·chin·ist (mə-shē′nĭst) ▸ *n.* One who makes, operates, or repairs machines.
ma·chis·mo (mä-chēz′mō) ▸ *n.* A strong or exaggerated sense of masculinity.
Mach number also **mach number** (mäk) ▸ *n.* The ratio of the speed of an object to the speed of sound in the surrounding medium.
ma·cho (mä′chō) ▸ *adj.* Marked by machismo. ▸ *n., pl.* **-chos. 1.** Machismo. **2.** A macho person.
Ma·chu Pic·chu (mä′cho͞o pēk′cho͞o, pē′-) ▸ An ancient Inca fortress city in the Andes NW of Cuzco, Peru.
mack·er·el (măk′ər-əl, măk′rəl) ▸ *n., pl.* **-el** or **-els.** Any of several widely distributed marine food fishes.
mack·i·naw (măk′ə-nô′) ▸ *n.* A short double-breasted coat of heavy, usu. plaid, woolen material.
mack·in·tosh also **mac·in·tosh** (măk′ĭn-tŏsh′) ▸ *n. Chiefly Brit.* A raincoat.
mac·ra·mé (măk′rə-mā′) ▸ *n.* Coarse lace work made by weaving and knotting cords.
mac·ro (măk′rō′) ▸ *n., pl.* **-ros.** *Comp. Sci.* A single, user-defined command that is part of an application and executes a series of commands.
macro– or **macr–** ▸ *pref.* **1.** Large: *macroscopic.* **2.** Long: *macrobiotics.* **3.** Inclusive: *macroeconomics.*
mac·ro·bi·ot·ics (măk′rō-bī-ŏt′ĭks) ▸ *n.* *(takes sing. v.)* The theory or practice of promoting well-being and longevity esp. by means of a diet chiefly of whole grains and beans. **—mac′ro·bi·ot′ic** *adj.*
mac·ro·cosm (măk′rə-kŏz′əm) ▸ *n.* **1.** The entire world; universe. **2.** A system that contains subsystems. **—mac′ro·cos′mic** *adj.*
mac·ro·ec·o·nom·ics (măk′rō-ĕk′ə-nŏm′ĭks, -ē′kə-) ▸ *n.* *(takes sing. v.)* The study of the overall workings of a national economy. **—mac′ro·e·con′o·mist** *n.*
mac·ro·in·struc·tion (măk′rō-ĭn-strŭk′shən) ▸ *n.* A macro.
ma·cron (mā′krŏn′, -krən, măk′rŏn′) ▸ *n.* A mark (—) placed above a vowel to indicate a long sound, as the (ā) in *make.*
mac·ro·phage (măk′rə-fāj′) ▸ *n.* A large phagocytic cell.
mac·ro·scop·ic (măk′rə-skŏp′ĭk) also **mac·ro·scop·i·cal** (-ĭ-kəl) ▸ *adj.* Large enough to be seen or examined by the unaided eye.

THESAURUS

macabre *adj.* —*See* GHASTLY (1), MORBID.
macerate *v.* —*See* STEEP².
machinate *v.* —*See* PLOT (2).
machination *n.* —*See* PLOT (2).
machine *n.* —*See* DEVICE (1), SYSTEM.
machismo *n.* —*See* MASCULINITY.
macho *adj.* —*See* MANLY.
mackintosh *n.* —*See* COAT (1).
macrocosm *n.* —*See* UNIVERSE.

mad (măd) ► *adj.* **mad·der, mad·dest. 1.** Feeling anger or resentment. **2.** Suffering from a disorder of the mind; insane. **3.** Lacking restraint, reason, or judgment. **4.** Feeling or showing strong liking or enthusiasm: *mad about sports.* **5.** Marked by extreme excitement, confusion, or agitation; frantic: *a mad scramble for the bus.* **6.** Affected by rabies; rabid. **—mad′ly** *adv.* **—mad′man** *n.* **—mad′ness** *n.* **—mad′wom′an** *n.*

Mad·a·gas·car (măd′ə-găs′kər) ► An island country in the Indian Ocean off southeast Africa. **—Mad′a·gas′can** *adj. & n.*

Mad·am (măd′əm) ► *n.* **1.** *pl.* **Mes·dames** (mā-dăm′, -däm′). Used formerly as a courtesy title before a woman's given name. **2.** Used as a salutation in a letter. **3. madam** Used as a form of polite address for a woman. **4. madam** A woman who manages a house of prostitution.

Ma·dame (mə-dăm′, măd′əm) ► *n., pl.* **Mes·dames** (mā-dăm′, -däm′). A French courtesy title for a woman.

mad·cap (măd′kăp′) ► *adj.* Behaving or acting impulsively or rashly. **—mad′cap′** *n.*

mad·den (măd′n) ► *v.* **1.** To make or become angry. **2.** To make frantic or insane.

mad·der (măd′ər) ► *n.* **1.** A SW Asian plant having small yellow flowers and a fleshy red root. **2.** A red dye obtained from the roots of the madder.

made (mād) ► *v.* P.t. and p.part. of **make.**

Ma·dei·ra (mə-dîr′ə) ► *n.* A fortified dessert wine, esp. from the Madeira Is.

Madeira Islands ► An archipelago of Portugal in the NE Atlantic W of Morocco. **—Ma·dei′ran** *adj. & n.*

Mad·e·moi·selle (măd′ə-mə-zĕl′, măd-mwä-zĕl′) ► *n., pl.* **Mad·e·moi·selles** (-zĕlz) or **Mes·de·moi·selles** (mād′mwä-zĕl′). A French courtesy title for a girl or young woman.

made-to-or·der (mād′to͞o-ôr′dər) ► *adj.* **1.** Made according to particular instructions. **2.** Very suitable.

made-up (mād′ŭp′) ► *adj.* **1.** Fictitious: *a made-up story.* **2.** Wearing makeup.

mad·house (măd′hous′) ► *n.* **1.** Formerly, an insane asylum. **2.** *Informal* A place of disorder and confusion.

Mad·i·son (măd′ĭ-sən) ► The capital of WI, in the S-central part.

Madison, Dolley Payne Todd (1768–1849) ► First Lady of the US (1809–17) as the wife of President James Madison.

Madison, James (1751–1836) ► The 4th US President (1809–17).

Ma·don·na (mə-dŏn′ə) ► *n.* The Virgin Mary.

mad·ras (măd′rəs, mə-drăs′, -dräs′) ► *n.* A fine cotton cloth, usu. with a plaid, striped, or checked pattern.

Ma·dras (mə-drăs′, -dräs′) ► See **Chennai.**

Ma·drid (mə-drĭd′) ► The capital of Spain, in the central part.

mad·ri·gal (măd′rĭ-gəl) ► *n.* **1.** An unaccompanied vocal composition for two or three voices in simple harmony. **2.** A polyphonic song written for four to six voices and usu. unaccompanied.

ma·dro·ña (mə-drō′nyə) also **ma·dro·ño** (-drō′nyō) or **ma·dro·ne** (-drō′nə) ► *n., pl.* **-ñas** also **-ños** or **-nes.** An evergreen tree of W North America, having scaly bark and orange or red edible berries.

mael·strom (māl′strəm) ► *n.* **1.** A violent or turbulent situation. **2.** A large and violent whirlpool.

maes·tro (mīs′trō) ► *n., pl.* **-tros** or **-tri** (-trē). A master in an art, esp. a composer, conductor, or music teacher.

Ma·fi·a (mä′fē-ə) ► *n.* **1.** A secret terrorist organization in Sicily. **2.** A criminal organization believed active, esp. in Italy and the US.

Ma·fi·o·so (mä′fē-ō′sō) ► *n., pl.* **-si** (-sē) or **-sos.** A member of the Mafia.

mag·a·zine (măg′ə-zēn′, măg′ə-zēn′) ► *n.* **1.** A periodical containing articles, stories, pictures, or other features. **2.** A place where goods are stored, esp. ammunition. **3.** A usu. detachable compartment in some types of firearms, in which cartridges are held. **4.** A compartment in a camera for holding film.

Ma·gel·lan (mə-jĕl′ən), **Ferdinand** (1480?–1521) ► Portuguese navigator.

Magellan, Strait of ► A channel separating South America from Tierra del Fuego and connecting the Atlantic and Pacific.

ma·gen·ta (mə-jĕn′tə) ► *n.* A vivid purplish red. **—ma·gen′ta** *adj.*

mag·got (măg′ət) ► *n.* The legless, soft-bodied larva of any of various flies, often found in decaying matter. **—mag′got·y** *adj.*

ma·gi (mā′jī′) ► *n.* Pl. of **magus.**

mag·ic (măj′ĭk) ► *n.* **1.** The art that purports to control or forecast natural events, effects, or forces by invoking the supernatural through the use of charms, spells, or rituals. **2.** The exercise of sleight of hand or conjuring for entertainment. **3.** A mysterious quality of enchantment. **—mag′ic, mag′i·cal** *adj.* **—mag′i·cal·ly** *adv.* **—ma·gi′cian** (mə-jish′ən) *n.*

mag·is·te·ri·al (măj′ĭ-stîr′ē-əl) ► *adj.* **1a.** Authoritative; commanding. **b.** Dogmatic; overbearing. **2.** Of a magistrate or a magistrate's official functions. **—mag′is·te′ri·al·ly** *adv.*

mag·is·trate (măj′ĭ-strāt′, -strĭt) ► *n.* A civil officer with power to administer the law.

mag·ma (măg′mə) ► *n., pl.* **-ma·ta** (-mä′tə) or **-mas.** The molten rock material under the earth's crust that cools and hardens to form igneous rock. **—mag·mat′ic** (-măt′ĭk) *adj.*

Mag·na Car·ta or **Mag·na Char·ta** (măg′nə kär′tə) ► *n.* The charter of English political and civil liberties granted by King John in 1215.

mag·nan·i·mous (măg-năn′ə-məs) ► *adj.* Generous and noble, esp. in forgiving. **—mag′na·nim′i·ty** (-nə-nĭm′ĭ-tē) *n.* **—mag·nan′i·mous·ly** *adv.*

mag·nate (măg′nāt′, -nĭt) ► *n.* A powerful or influential person, esp. in business or industry.

mag·ne·sia (măg-nē′zhə, -shə) ► *n.* A white powdery compound, MgO, used in refractories, electric insulation, and as a laxative and antacid.

mag·ne·si·um (măg-nē′zē-əm, -zhəm) ► *n. Symbol* **Mg** A light, silvery, moderately hard metallic element that burns with a brilliant white flame, used in lightweight structural alloys. At. no. 12.

mag·net (măg′nĭt) ► *n.* **1.** An object that is surrounded by a magnetic field and attracts iron or steel. **2.** An electromagnet. **3.** A person, place, or object that attracts.

mag·net·ic (măg-nĕt′ĭk) ► *adj.* **1a.** Of or relating to magnetism or magnets. **b.** Having the properties of a magnet.

THESAURUS

mad *adj.* —*See* ANGRY, ENTHUSIASTIC, FOOLISH, FRANTIC, INSANE.

madcap *adj.* —*See* RASH[1].

madden *v.* —*See* ANGER (1), DERANGE.

made-to-order *adj.* —*See* CUSTOM.

made up *adj.* Being fictitious and not real, as a name ► assumed, pretended, pseudonymous. [*Compare* FALSE.] —*See also* FICTITIOUS.

madness *n.* —*See* FOOLISHNESS, INSANITY.

maelstrom *n.* —*See* WHIRLPOOL.

magic *n.* **1.** The use of supernatural powers to influence or predict events ► augury, black art, black magic, conjuration, divination, hoodoo, incantation, necromancy, obeah, occultism, sorcery, sortilege, thaumaturgy, theurgy, voodoo, witchcraft, witchery, witching, wizardry. [*Compare* CHARM, PREDICTION.] **2.** The use of skillful tricks and deceptions to produce entertainingly baffling effects ► conjuration, conjuring, illusion, legerdemain, prestidigitation, sleight of hand, trickery. —*See also* SPELL[2].

magic or **magical** *adj.* Having, brought about by, or relating to supernatural powers or magic ► bewitching, enchanted, fey, spellbinding, talismanic, thaumaturgic, thaumaturgical, theurgic, theurgical, witching, wizardly. [*Compare* MYSTERIOUS, SUPERNATURAL.] —*See also* ATTRACTIVE.

magician *n.* —*See* WIZARD.

magisterial *adj.* —*See* DICTATORIAL.

magistrate *n.* A public official who decides cases brought before a court of law in order to administer justice ► judge, jurist, jurisprudent, justice, justice of the peace. [*Compare* GO-BETWEEN, JUDGE.]

magnanimity *n.* —*See* GENEROSITY.

magnanimous *adj.* —*See* GENEROUS (1).

magnanimousness *n.* —*See* GENEROSITY.

magnate *n.* —*See* DIGNITARY.

magnet *n.* —*See* LURE (1).

magnetic *adj.* —*See* ATTRACTIVE.

c. Capable of being magnetized or attracted by a magnet. 2. Relating to the magnetic poles of the earth. 3. Exerting attraction: *a magnetic personality.* **—mag·net′i·cal·ly** *adv.*

magnetic disk ▸ *n. Comp. Sci.* A memory device, such as a hard disk, covered with a magnetic coating on which digital information is stored by magnetization of microscopically small needles.

magnetic field ▸ *n.* A detectable force that exists at every point in the region around a magnet or electric current.

magnetic needle ▸ *n.* A slender bar of magnetized steel, usu. suspended in a magnetic compass to indicate the direction of the earth's magnetic poles.

magnetic north ▸ *n.* The direction of the earth's magnetic pole, to which the north-seeking pole of a magnetic needle points.

magnetic pole ▸ *n.* 1. Either of two limited regions in a magnet at which the magnet's field is strongest. 2. Either of two variable points on the earth, close to but not coinciding with the geographic poles, where the earth's magnetic field is most intense.

magnetic resonance imaging ▸ *n.* The use of nuclear magnetic resonance to produce images of atoms and molecules in solids, esp. human tissues and organs.

magnetic tape ▸ *n.* A plastic tape coated with iron oxide for use in magnetic recording.

mag·net·ism (măg′nĭ-tĭz′əm) ▸ *n.* 1. The properties and effects associated with a magnetic field. 2. The study of magnets and their effects. 3. The force exerted by a magnetic field. 4. Unusual power to attract or influence: *the magnetism of money.*

mag·net·ite (măg′nĭ-tīt′) ▸ *n.* A magnetic black iron ore, Fe_3O_4.

mag·net·ize (măg′nĭ-tīz′) ▸ *v.* **-ized, -iz·ing.** 1. To make magnetic. 2. To attract. **—mag′net·i·za′tion** *n.* **—mag′net·iz′er** *n.*

mag·ne·to (măg-nē′tō) ▸ *n., pl.* **-tos.** A small generator of alternating current that works by means of permanent magnets, used in the ignition systems of some internal-combustion engines.

mag·ne·tom·e·ter (măg′nĭ-tŏm′ĭ-tər) ▸ *n.* A device that measures the strength and direction esp. of the earth's magnetic field.

magnet school ▸ *n.* A public school for students of high ability that attracts its student body from all parts of a city.

mag·nif·i·cent (măg-nĭf′ĭ-sənt) ▸ *adj.* 1. Splendid in appearance; grand: *a magnificent palace.* 2. Grand or noble in thought or deed; exalted. 3. Outstanding or exceptional. **—mag·nif′i·cence** *n.* **—mag·nif′i·cent·ly** *adv.*

mag·ni·fy (măg′nə-fī′) ▸ *v.* **-fied, -fy·ing.** 1. To make greater in size, extent, or effect; enlarge. 2. To cause to appear greater or more important. 3. To increase the apparent size of, esp. by means of a lens. 4. To glorify or praise. **—mag′ni·fi·ca′tion** *n.* **—mag′ni·fi′er** *n.*

mag·ni·fy·ing glass (măg′nə-fī′ĭng) ▸ *n.* A lens or system of lenses that enlarges the image of an object.

mag·ni·tude (măg′nĭ-to͞od′, -tyo͞od′) ▸ *n.* 1. Greatness, esp. in size or extent. 2. Greatness in significance or influence. 3. *Astron.* The relative brightness of a celestial body designated on a numerical scale.

mag·no·lia (măg-nōl′yə) ▸ *n.* A tree having large, usu. white, pink, or purple flowers.

mag·num (măg′nəm) ▸ *n.* A bottle for wine or liquor holding approx. ⅖ gal.

magnum opus ▸ *n.* The greatest single work of an artist, writer, or composer.

mag·pie (măg′pī′) ▸ *n.* 1. A long-tailed, loud-voiced, chiefly black and white bird related to the crows and jays. 2. A person who chatters constantly.

Ma·gritte (mä-grēt′), **René** (1898–1967) ▸ Belgian painter.

ma·guey (mə-gā′, măg′wā) ▸ *n., pl.* **-gueys.** 1. Any of various agaves or related plants. 2. The fiber obtained from a maguey.

ma·gus (mā′gəs) ▸ *n., pl.* **ma·gi** (mā′jī′). 1. **Magus** In the New Testament, one of the three wise men from the East who paid homage to the infant Jesus. 2. A sorcerer; magician.

Mag·yar (măg′yär′, mäg′-) ▸ *n.* 1. An ethnic Hungarian. 2. See **Hungarian** 2. **—Mag′yar** *adj.*

ma·ha·ra·jah or **ma·ha·ra·ja** (mä′hə-rä′jə, -zhə) ▸ *n.* A king or prince in India ranking above a rajah.

ma·ha·ra·ni or **ma·ha·ra·nee** (mä′hə-rä′nē) ▸ *n., pl.* **-nis** or **-nees.** 1. The wife of a maharajah. 2. A princess in India ranking above a rani.

ma·ha·ri·shi (mä′hə-rē′shē, mə-här′ə-shē) ▸ *n., pl.* **-shis.** *Hinduism* A teacher of spiritual knowledge.

Ma·hat·ma (mə-hät′mə, -hăt′-) ▸ *n. Hinduism* Used as a title of respect for a person renowned for spirituality and high-mindedness.

Mah·di (mä′dē) ▸ *n., pl.* **-dis.** *Islam* The messiah expected to appear at the world's end and establish a reign of peace. **—Mah′dism** *n.* **—Mah′dist** *n.*

Ma·hi·can (mə-hē′kən) also **Mo·hi·can** (mō-, mə-) ▸ *n., pl.* **-can** or **-cans.** 1. A member of a Native American confederacy formerly inhabiting the upper Hudson R. valley, now in Oklahoma and Wisconsin. 2. The Algonquian language of the Mahican.

mah·jong also **mah·jongg** (mä′zhŏng′, -zhông′) ▸ *n.* A Chinese game usu. played by four persons with rectangular tiles bearing various designs.

ma·hog·a·ny (mə-hŏg′ə-nē) ▸ *n., pl.* **-nies.** 1a. Any of a genus of tropical American trees valued for their hard, reddish-brown wood. b. The wood of such a tree. 2. Any of several similar trees or their wood.

maid (mād) ▸ *n.* 1. An unmarried girl or woman. 2. A woman servant.

maid·en (mād′n) ▸ *n.* An unmarried girl or woman. ▸ *adj.* 1. Of or befitting a maiden. 2. First or earliest: *a maiden voyage.* **—maid′en·hood′** *n.*

maid·en·hair fern (mād′n-hâr′) ▸ *n.* A fern having feathery fronds with fan-shaped leaflets.

maiden name ▸ *n.* A woman's family name if different from her married name.

maid of honor ▸ *n., pl.* **maids of honor.** The chief unmarried woman attendant of a bride.

Mai·du (mī′do͞o) ▸ *n., pl.* **-du** or **-dus.** 1. A member of a Native American people inhabiting NE California. 2. The Penutian language of the Maidu.

mail[1] (māl) ▸ *n.* 1a. Materials, such as letters and packages, handled in a postal system. b. Postal material for a specific person or organization. 2. often **mails** A postal system. 3. *Comp. Sci.* Messages sent electronically; e-mail. ▸ *v.* To send by mail. **—mail′er** *n.*

mail[2] (māl) ▸ *n.* Flexible armor composed of small overlapping metal rings, loops of chain, or scales. **—mailed** *adj.*

mail·box (māl′bŏks′) ▸ *n.* 1. A public container for deposit of outgoing mail. 2. A private box for the delivery of mail. 3. A computer file for collecting and storing e-mail.

mail·man (māl′măn′, -mən) ▸ *n.* A man who carries and delivers mail.

mail order ▸ *n.* An order for goods to be shipped through the mail.

mail-or·der house (māl′ôr′dər) ▸ *n.* A business that promotes, receives, and fills requests for merchandise through the mail.

maim (mām) ▸ *v.* 1. To disable, mutilate, or cripple. 2. To impair. **—maim′er** *n.*

THESAURUS

magnetism *n.* —*See* ATTRACTION.

magnetize *v.* —*See* ATTRACT.

magnification *n.* —*See* INCREASE (1), PRAISE (2).

magnificence *n.* —*See* GLITTER (2), GLORY.

magnificent *adj.* —*See* EXCEPTIONAL, GLORIOUS, GRAND.

magnified *adj.* —*See* EXAGGERATED.

magnify *v.* —*See* EXAGGERATE, EXALT, HONOR (1), INCREASE, PRAISE (3).

magniloquence *n.* —*See* BOMBAST.

magniloquent *adj.* —*See* ORATORICAL.

magnitude *n.* —*See* BULK (1), DEGREE (2), IMPORTANCE, SIZE (1), SIZE (2).

magnum opus *n.* An outstanding and ingenious work ▸ chef-d'oeuvre, masterpiece, masterwork. [*Compare* ACCOMPLISHMENT, COMPOSITION, TREASURE.]

maiden *adj.* —*See* FIRST.

mail *v.* —*See* SEND (1).

maim *v.* —*See* BATTER, CRIPPLE.

Mai·mon·i·des (mī-mŏn′ĭ-dēz′). Moses Ben Maimon (1135–1204) ▸ Spanish-born Jewish philosopher and physician.

main (mān) ▸ *adj.* **1.** Most important; principal; chief. **2.** Exerted to the utmost; sheer: *by main strength.* **3.** Relating to or being the principal clause or verb of a complex sentence. ▸ *n.* **1.** The chief or largest part: *ideas that are in the main, impractical.* **2.** The principal pipe or conduit in a system for conveying water, gas, oil, or other utility. **3.** Physical strength: *fought with might and main.* **—main′ly** *adv.*

Main (mān, mīn) ▸ A river rising in E Germany and flowing about 499 km (310 mi) to the Rhine R. at Mainz.

Maine (mān) ▸ A state of the NE US. Cap. Augusta.

main·frame (mān′frām′) ▸ *n.* A large, powerful computer, often serving many connected terminals.

main·land (mān′lănd′, -lənd) ▸ *n.* The principal landmass of a country or continent.

main·line (mān′līn′) ▸ *v.* **-lined, -lin·ing.** *Slang* To inject narcotics into a vein.

main·mast (mān′məst, -măst′) ▸ *n.* The principal mast of a sailing ship.

main·sail (mān′səl, -sāl′) ▸ *n.* The principal sail of a sailing ship.

main·spring (mān′sprĭng′) ▸ *n.* **1.** The principal spring mechanism in a device, esp. a timepiece. **2.** The chief motivating force.

main·stay (mān′stā′) ▸ *n.* **1.** A chief support. **2.** A rope that steadies and supports the mainmast of a sailing ship.

main·stream (mān′strēm′) ▸ *n.* The prevailing current or direction of a movement, influence, or activity. ▸ *v.* **1.** To integrate (a disadvantaged student) into regular classes. **2.** To incorporate into the mainstream. **—main′stream′** *adj.*

main·tain (mān-tān′) ▸ *v.* **1.** To carry on; continue. **2.** To preserve or retain. **3.** To keep in good repair. **4.** To provide for; support. **5.** To defend against criticism. **6.** To declare to be true. **—main·tain′a·ble** *adj.* **—main′te·nance** (-tə-nəns) *n.*

mai·tre d′ (mā′trə dē′, mā′tər) ▸ *n., pl.* **mai·tre d′s** (dēz′). *Informal* A maitre d'hôtel.

maî·tre d'hô·tel (mā′trə dō-tĕl′) ▸ *n., pl.* **maî·tres d'hôtel** (-trə). **1.** A headwaiter. **2.** A major-domo.

maize (māz) ▸ *n.* See **corn**[1] 1.

maj·es·ty (măj′ĭ-stē) ▸ *n., pl.* **-ties.** **1.** The greatness and dignity of a sovereign. **2.** Supreme authority or power. **3.** **Majesty** Used with *His, Her,* or *Your* as a title for a sovereign. **4.** Regal splendor, magnificence, or grandeur. **—ma·jes′tic** (mə-jĕs′tĭk) *adj.* **—ma·jes′ti·cal·ly** *adv.*

ma·jor (mā′jər) ▸ *adj.* **1.** Greater in importance, rank, or extent. **2.** Of great concern; very serious: *a major illness.* **3.** *Mus.* Of or based on a major scale. ▸ *n.* **1.** A rank, as in the US Army, above captain and below lieutenant colonel. **2a.** A field of study that is chosen as an academic specialty. **b.** A student who is specializing in such studies. ▸ *v.* To pursue studies in a major field.

Ma·jor·ca (mə-jôr′kə, -yôr′-) ▸ An island of Spain in the W Mediterranean off the E-central coast of the mainland. **—Ma·jor′can** *adj. & n.*

ma·jor-do·mo (mā′jər-dō′mō) ▸ *n., pl.* **-mos.** A head steward or butler.

major general ▸ *n.* A rank, as in the US Army, above brigadier general and below lieutenant general.

ma·jor·i·ty (mə-jôr′ĭ-tē, -jŏr′-) ▸ *n., pl.* **-ties.** **1.** A number more than half of the total number of a given group. **2.** The amount by which the greater number of votes cast, as in an election, exceeds the total number of remaining votes. **3.** The status of legal age.

major league ▸ *n.* A league of principal importance in professional sports, esp. baseball. **—ma′jor-league′** *adj.*

major medical ▸ *n.* Insurance that covers all or most medical bills for major illnesses.

major scale ▸ *n.* *Mus.* A diatonic scale having half steps between the 3rd and 4th and the 7th and 8th degrees.

make (māk) ▸ *v.* **made** (mād), **mak·ing.** **1.** To bring about; create. **2.** To form or construct: *made a dress.* **3.** To cause to be or become: *made him happy.* **4a.** To cause to act in a specified manner. **b.** To compel: *made him leave.* **5.** To prepare; fix. **6.** To carry out; perform. **7.** To achieve or attain: *make peace.* **8.** To arrive at. **9.** To gain or earn. **10.** To develop into: *made a great teacher.* **11.** To constitute. **12.** To act or behave in a specified manner. **13.** To proceed. ***—phrasal verbs:*** **make out** **1.** To see, esp. with difficulty. **2.** To understand. **3.** To write out or draw up. **4.** To fare: *made out well on the deal.* **5.** *Informal* To neck; pet. **make up** **1.** To put together; construct or compose. **2.** To constitute. **3.** To apply cosmetics. **4.** To invent: *made up an excuse.* **5.** To compensate, as for an omission. **6.** To resolve a quarrel. ▸ *n.* **1.** The style or manner in which a thing is made. **2.** A specific line of manufactured goods. ***—idioms:*** **make believe** To pretend. **make do** To get along with the means available. **make good** **1.** To carry out successfully. **2.** To pay back. **make it** To be successful. **make light of** To treat as unimportant. **make love** **1.** To court; woo. **2.** To engage in sexual intercourse. **make no bones about** To be completely frank about. **make the most of** To use to the greatest advantage. **make time** To move or travel fast. **make way** To give room for passage. **—mak′er** *n.*

make-be·lieve (māk′bĭ-lēv′) ▸ *n.* Playful or fanciful pretense. **—make′-be·lieve′** *adj.*

make·shift (māk′shĭft′) ▸ *n.* A temporary expedient or substitute. **—make′shift′** *adj.*

make·up or **make-up** (māk′ŭp′) ▸ *n.* **1.** The way in which something is composed, constructed, or arranged. **2.** The qualities or temperament that constitute a personality. **3.** Cosmetics applied esp. to the face.

mak·ings (mā′kĭngz) ▸ *pl.n.* The material or ingredients needed for making something.

THESAURUS

main *adj.* —*See* DOMINANT (1), PRIMARY (1).

main *n.* —*See* OCEAN.

mainly *adv.* —*See* USUALLY.

mainspring *n.* —*See* CAUSE (2).

maintain *v.* **1.** To keep in a condition of good repair, efficiency, or use ▸ keep up, preserve, sustain. **2.** To supply with the necessities of life ▸ keep, provide for, support. *Idioms:* put a roof over someone's head, put food on the table, take care of. [*Compare* NOURISH.] —*See also* ASSERT, DEFEND (2), KEEP (5).

maintenance *n.* The work of keeping something in proper condition ▸ preservation, repairs, reparation, sustenance, upkeep. [*Compare* CARE.] —*See also* CONSERVATION, LIVING.

majestic *adj.* —*See* GRAND.

majesty *n.* —*See* CHIEF, GLORY.

major *adj.* —*See* BIG-LEAGUE, DOMINANT (1), PRIMARY (1).

major-league *adj.* —*See* BIG-LEAGUE.

make *v.* To create by forming, combining, or altering materials ▸ assemble, build, compose, configure, construct, fabricate, fashion, forge, form, frame, manufacture, mold, pattern, produce, put together, shape, structure. [*Compare* [illegible], DESIGN, INVENT.] —*See also* APPOINT, BEAR (5), CAUSE, COVER (2), EARN (2), ESTABLISH (2), FORCE (1), PREPARE, PRODUCE (1).

make off *v.* —*See* ESCAPE (1).

make out *v.* —*See* DISCERN, MANAGE, NECK, UNDERSTAND (1).

make over *v.* —*See* REVOLUTIONIZE. —*See also* TRANSFER (1).

make up *v.* **1.** To reestablish friendship between ▸ conciliate, reconcile, reunite. [*Compare* PACIFY.] **2.** To be the constituent parts of ▸ compose, form. [*Compare* CONTAIN.] —*See also* BALANCE (2), IMAGINE, IMPROVISE (1), INVENT, LIE[2], RECOVER (1).

make *n.* —*See* CONSTITUTION.

make-believe *n.* —*See* FAÇADE (2).

make-believe *adj.* —*See* IMAGINARY, MYTHICAL.

make-do *n.* —*See* MAKESHIFT.

make-do *adj.* —*See* TEMPORARY (2).

maker *n.* One that assembles or makes something ▸ artificer, artisan, assembler, craftsman, craftsperson, craftswoman, fabricator, manufacturer, modeler, producer. [*Compare* BUILDER.] —*See also* ORIGINATOR.

makeshift *n.* **1.** Something used temporarily or reluctantly when other means are not available ▸ expediency, expedient, make-do, resort, shift, stopgap. [*Compare* SUBSTITUTE.]

makeshift *adj.* —*See* TEMPORARY (2).

makeup or **make-up** *n.* —*See* CHARACTER (1), CONSTITUTION.

makings *n.* Indication of future success

ma·ko (mä′kō) ▸ *n., pl.* **-kos.** A shark having a large heavy body and a nearly symmetrical tail.

mal– ▸ *pref.* Bad; badly: *malformation.*

Mal·a·chi (măl′ə-kī′) ▸ *n.* **1.** A Hebrew prophet of the 6th cent. B.C. **2.** See **Bible** table in Appendix.

mal·a·chite (măl′ə-kīt′) ▸ *n.* A green carbonate mineral used as a source of copper and for ornamental stoneware.

mal·ad·just·ment (măl′ə-jŭst′mənt) ▸ *n.* Faulty or poor adjustment. **—mal′ad·just′ed** *adj.*

mal·a·droit (măl′ə-droit′) ▸ *adj.* Marked by a lack of dexterity; clumsy; inept. **—mal′a·droit′ly** *adv.* **—mal′a·droit′ness** *n.*

mal·a·dy (măl′ə-dē) ▸ *n., pl.* **-dies.** A disease, disorder, or ailment.

Mal·a·gas·y (măl′ə-găs′ē) ▸ *n., pl.* **-gas·y** or **-gas·ies.** **1.** A native or inhabitant of Madagascar. **2.** The Austronesian language of the Malagasy. **—Mal′a·gas′y** *adj.*

mal·aise (mă-lāz′, -lĕz′) ▸ *n.* A vague feeling of illness or depression.

mal·a·mute (măl′ə-myo͞ot′) ▸ *n.* A powerful dog that was developed in Alaska as a sled dog and that has a thick coat and a bushy tail.

mal·a·prop·ism (măl′ə-prŏp-ĭz′əm) ▸ *n.* A ludicrous or humorous misuse of a word.

mal·a·pro·pos (măl′ăp-rə-pō′) ▸ *adj.* Out of place; inappropriate; inopportune. **—mal′a·pro·pos′** *adv.*

ma·lar·i·a (mə-lâr′ē-ə) ▸ *n.* An infectious disease marked by cycles of chills, fever, and sweating, transmitted by the bite of an infected mosquito. **—ma·lar′i·al** *adj.*

ma·lar·key also **ma·lar·ky** (mə-lär′kē) ▸ *n. Slang* Exaggerated or foolish talk, usu. intended to deceive.

Mal·a·thi·on (măl′ə-thī′ŏn′) ▸ A trademark for the organic compound $C_{10}H_{19}O_6PS_2$, used as an insecticide.

Ma·la·wi (mə-lä′wē) ▸ A country of SE Africa. **—Ma·la′wi·an** *adj. & n.*

Ma·lay (mə-lā′, mā′lā′) ▸ *n.* **1.** A member of a people inhabiting Malaysia, the N Malay Peninsula, and parts of the W Malay Archipelago. **2.** The Austronesian language of the Malays. **—Ma·lay′an, Ma·lay′** *adj. & n.*

Mal·a·ya·lam (măl′ə-yä′ləm) ▸ *n.* A Dravidian language spoken in SW India.

Malay Archipelago ▸ An island group of SE Asia between Australia and the Asian mainland.

Malay Peninsula also **Ma·la·ya** (mə-lā′ə, mā-) ▸ A peninsula of SE Asia comprising SW Thailand, W Malaysia, and the island of Singapore.

Ma·lay·sia (mə-lā′zhə, -shə) ▸ A country of SE Asia consisting of the S Malay Peninsula and the N part of Borneo. **—Ma·lay′sian** *adj. & n.*

Mal·colm X (măl′kəm ĕks′) (1925–65) ▸ Amer. activist; assassinated.

mal·con·tent (măl′kən-tĕnt′) ▸ *adj.* Discontented. ▸ *n.* A discontented person.

Mal·dives (môl′dīvz, -dēvz, măl′-) ▸ An island country in the Indian Ocean SW of Sri Lanka. **—Mal·div′i·an** (-dĭv′ē-ən), **Mal·di′van** *adj. & n.*

male (māl) ▸ *adj.* **1a.** Of or being the sex that has organs to produce spermatozoa for fertilizing ova. **b.** Consisting of members of this sex. **2.** *Bot.* **a.** Of or being an organ, as an anther, that produces gametes capable of fertilizing those produced by female organs. **b.** Bearing stamens but not pistils. **3.** Made for insertion into a fitted bore or socket. ▸ *n.* A member of the male sex. **—male′ness** *n.*

Mal·e·cite (măl′ə-sīt′) or **Mal·i·seet** (-sēt′) ▸ *n., pl.* **-cite** or **-cites** or **-seet** or **-seets.** **1.** A member of a Native American people inhabiting New Brunswick and NE Maine. **2.** The Algonquian language of the Malecite.

mal·e·dic·tion (măl′ĭ-dĭk′shən) ▸ *n.* A curse.

mal·e·fac·tor (măl′ə-făk′tər) ▸ *n.* **1.** A criminal. **2.** An evildoer. **—mal′e·fac′tion** *n.*

ma·lef·ic (mə-lĕf′ĭk) ▸ *adj.* **1.** Exerting a malignant influence. **2.** Malicious.

ma·lef·i·cence (mə-lĕf′ĭ-səns) ▸ *n.* **1.** The doing of evil or harm. **2.** Harmful or evil nature or quality. **—ma·lef′i·cent** *adj.*

ma·lev·o·lence (mə-lĕv′ə-ləns) ▸ *n.* **1.** The quality or state of being malevolent. **2.** Malicious behavior.

ma·lev·o·lent (mə-lĕv′ə-lənt) ▸ *adj.* Having or exhibiting ill will; malicious. **—ma·lev′o·lence** *n.* **—ma·lev′o·lent·ly** *adv.*

mal·fea·sance (măl-fē′zəns) ▸ *n. Law* Misconduct or wrongdoing, esp. by a public official.

mal·for·ma·tion (măl′fôr-mā′shən) ▸ *n.* An abnormal or irregular formation or structure; deformity. **—mal·formed′** *adj.*

mal·func·tion (măl-fŭngk′shən) ▸ *v.* To fail to function normally. **—mal·func′tion** *n.*

Ma·li (mä′lē) ▸ A country of western Africa. **—Ma′li·an** *adj. & n.*

mal·ice (măl′ĭs) ▸ *n.* A desire to harm others or to see others suffer; spite. **—ma·li′cious** (mə-lĭsh′əs) *adj.* **—ma·li′cious·ly** *adv.* **—ma·li′cious·ness** *n.*

ma·lign (mə-līn′) ▸ *v.* To speak evil of; defame. ▸ *adj.* **1.** Evil or harmful in influence or effect; injurious. **2.** Malevolent. **—ma·lign′er** *n.*

ma·lig·nant (mə-lĭg′nənt) ▸ *adj.* **1.** Showing great malevolence. **2.** Highly injurious; pernicious. **3.** *Pathol.* Relating to an abnormal growth that tends to spread. **—ma·lig′nan·cy** *n.* **—ma·lig′nant·ly** *adv.*

ma·lig·ni·ty (mə-lĭg′nĭ-tē) ▸ *n., pl.* **-ties.** **1a.** Intense ill will or hatred; great malice. **b.** An act or feeling of great malice. **2.** The condition of being evil or injurious.

ma·lin·ger (mə-lĭng′gər) ▸ *v.* To feign illness or other incapacity to avoid work. **—ma·lin′ger·er** *n.*

mall (môl, măl) ▸ *n.* **1.** A large, often enclosed shopping complex with stores, businesses, and restaurants. **2.** A street lined with shops and closed to vehicles. **3.** A shady public walk or promenade. **4.** *Regional* See **median strip.**

mal·lard (măl′ərd) ▸ *n., pl.* **-lard** or **-lards.** A wild duck with a green head and neck in the male.

THESAURUS

or development ▸ possibility, potential, promise, prospects. [*Compare* MATERIAL.]

maladroit *adj.* —*See* AWKWARD (1), TACTLESS, UNSKILLFUL.

malady *n.* —*See* DISEASE, SICKNESS.

malaise *n.* —*See* SICKNESS.

malapert *adj.* —*See* IMPUDENT.

malapropism *n.* —*See* CORRUPTION (3).

malapropos *adj.* —*See* IMPROPER (2).

malarkey *n.* —*See* NONSENSE.

malcontent *n.* —*See* AGITATOR.

male *adj.* —*See* MANLY.

malediction *n.* —*See* CURSE (1).

malefaction *n.* —*See* CRIME (1).

malefactor *n.* —*See* CRIMINAL.

maleficent or **malefic** *adj.* —*See* HARMFUL.

maleness *n.* —*See* MASCULINITY.

malevolence *n.* A desire to harm others or to see others suffer ▸ despitefulness, ill will, malice, maliciousness, malignancy, malignity, meanness, nastiness, poisonousness, spite, spitefulness, venomousness, viciousness, vindictiveness. [*Compare* CRUELTY, EVIL, HATE.]

malevolent *adj.* Characterized by intense ill will or spite ▸ black, despiteful, evil, evil-minded, hateful, ill-natured, malicious, malign, malignant, mean, nasty, poisonous, rancorous, spiteful, venomous, vicious, vindictive, wicked. *Slang:* bitchy. [*Compare* CRUEL, FIENDISH, ILL-TEMPERED.] —*See also* HARMFUL.

malfeasance *n.* —*See* BREACH (1), CORRUPTION (2).

malformation *n.* —*See* DEFORMITY.

malfunction *v.* To become unusable or stop working properly ▸ act up, break (down), crash, fail, give out. *Slang:* bust, conk out, crap out, poop out. *Idioms:* get out of whack (*or* kilter), go haywire, go on the blink (*or* fritz). [*Compare* COLLAPSE, FAIL.]

malfunction *n.* A cessation of proper functioning ▸ breakdown, collapse, failure, outage.

malice or **maliciousness** *n.* —*See* MALEVOLENCE.

malicious *adj.* —*See* MALEVOLENT.

malign *v.* To make harmful and often untrue statements about ▸ asperse, backbite, calumniate, defame, libel, slander, slur, tear down, traduce, vilify. *Informal:* badmouth. *Idioms:* cast aspersions on, give someone a bad name, speak evil of. [*Compare* BELITTLE, DENIGRATE, SLAM.]

malign *adj.* —*See* FATEFUL (1), HARMFUL, MALEVOLENT.

malignancy *n.* —*See* MALEVOLENCE.

malignant *adj.* —*See* MALEVOLENT, POISONOUS.

malignity *n.* —*See* MALEVOLENCE.

mal·le·a·ble (măl′ē-ə-bəl) ▸ *adj.* **1.** Capable of being shaped or formed; pliable. **2.** Easily controlled; tractable. **—mal′le·a·bil′i·ty, mal′le·a·ble·ness** *n.* **—mal′le·a·bly** *adv.*

mal·let (măl′ĭt) ▸ *n.* **1.** A short-handled hammer, usu. with a cylindrical head of wood. **2.** *Sports* A similar long-handled implement used to strike a ball, as in croquet and polo.

mal·le·us (măl′ē-əs) ▸ *n., pl.* **-le·i** (-ē-ī′). A hammer-shaped bone that is the largest bone in the middle ear.

mal·low (măl′ō) ▸ *n.* A plant having showy pink or white flowers.

mal·nour·ished (măl-nûr′ĭsht, -nŭr′-) ▸ *adj.* Affected by improper or poor nutrition.

mal·nu·tri·tion (măl′no͞o-trĭsh′ən, -nyo͞o-) ▸ *n.* Insufficient or unhealthy nutrition.

mal·oc·clu·sion (măl′ə-klo͞o′zhən) ▸ *n.* Faulty closure between the upper and lower teeth.

mal·o·dor (măl-ō′dər) ▸ *n.* A bad odor. **—mal·o′dor·ous** *adj.* **—mal·o′dor·ous·ly** *adv.* **—mal·o′dor·ous·ness** *n.*

ma·lo·ti (mä-lō′tē) ▸ *n.* Pl. of **loti**.

mal·prac·tice (măl-prăk′tĭs) ▸ *n.* Improper, negligent, or unethical conduct or treatment, esp. by a physician or lawyer. **—mal′prac·ti′tion·er** *n.*

malt (môlt) ▸ *n.* **1.** Grain, usu. barley, that has been allowed to sprout, used chiefly in brewing and distilling. **2.** An alcoholic beverage, such as beer, brewed from malt. **3.** See **malted milk** 2. **—malt** *v.* **—malt′y** *adj.*

Mal·ta (môl′tə) ▸ An island country in the Mediterranean S of Sicily. **—Mal·tese′** *adj. & n.*

malt·ed milk (môl′tĭd) ▸ *n.* **1.** A soluble powder made of dried milk, malted barley, and wheat flour. **2.** A beverage made by mixing milk with this powder and often ice cream and flavoring; malt.

mal·tose (môl′tōs′, -tōz′) ▸ *n.* A crystalline sugar formed in the digestion of starch.

mal·treat (măl-trēt′) ▸ *v.* To treat in a rough or cruel way; abuse. **—mal·treat′ment** *n.*

ma·ma or **mam·ma** (mä′mə, mə-mä′) ▸ *n. Informal* Mother.

mam·ba (mäm′bə) ▸ *n.* A venomous snake of tropical Africa.

mam·bo (mäm′bō) ▸ *n., pl.* **-bos.** A dance of Latin-American origin, resembling the rumba. **—mam′bo** *v.*

mam·mal (măm′əl) ▸ *n.* Any of various warm-blooded vertebrate animals, including humans, marked by a covering of hair on the skin and, in the female, milk-producing glands. **—mam·ma′li·an** (mă-mā′lē ən) *adj. & n.*

mam·mal·o·gy (mă-măl′ə-jē, -mŏl′-) ▸ *n.* The branch of zoology that deals with mammals. **—mam·mal′o·gist** *n.*

mam·ma·ry (măm′ə-rē) ▸ *adj.* Of or relating to a breast or milk-producing organ.

mam·mo·gram (măm′ə-grăm′) ▸ *n.* An x-ray image produced by mammography.

mam·mog·ra·phy (mă-mŏg′rə-fē) ▸ *n., pl.* **-phies.** X-ray examination of the breasts for detection of tumors.

Mam·mon or **mam·mon** (măm′ən) ▸ *n.* Material wealth regarded as having an evil influence.

mam·moth (măm′əth) ▸ *n.* An extinct elephant once widespread in the Northern Hemisphere. ▸ *adj.* Of enormous size; huge.

man (măn) ▸ *n., pl.* **men** (mĕn). **1.** An adult male human. **2.** A human regardless of sex or age; person. **3.** The human race: *man's quest for peace.* **4.** A male human having qualities considered characteristic of manhood. **5.** *Informal* A husband, lover, or sweetheart. **6.** *Games* A piece used in a board game, such as chess or checkers. ▸ *v.* **manned, man·ning. 1.** To supply with men or persons: *man a ship.* **2.** To take one's station at; attend or operate. ***—idiom:* to a man** Without exception.

Man, Isle of ▸ An island of Great Britain in the Irish Sea off NW England.

Man. ▸ *abbr.* Manitoba

man about town ▸ *n., pl.* **men about town.** A sophisticated, socially active man who frequents fashionable places.

man·a·cle (măn′ə-kəl) ▸ *n.* **1.** A device for shackling the hands; handcuff. **2.** Something that confines or restrains. ▸ *v.* **-cled, -cling.** To restrain with or as if with manacles.

man·age (măn′ĭj) ▸ *v.* **-aged, -ag·ing. 1.** To direct, control, or handle. **2.** To make submissive. **3.** To direct business affairs (of). **4.** To contrive or arrange. **5.** To get along; get by. **—man′age·a·bil′i·ty, man′age·a·ble·ness** *n.* **—man′age·a·bly** *adv.*

man·aged care (măn′ĭjd) ▸ *n.* A health care arrangement in which an organization, such as an HMO, acts as an intermediate between patient and physician.

man·age·ment (măn′ĭj-mənt) ▸ *n.* **1.** The act, manner, or practice of managing. **2.** The person or persons who manage an organization. **3.** Executive ability.

man·ag·er (măn′ĭ-jər) ▸ *n.* **1.** One who manages. **2.** One in charge of the training and performance of an athlete or team. **—man′a·ge′ri·al** (-ĭ-jîr′ē-əl) *adj.* **—man′a·ge′ri·al·ly** *adv.* **—man′ag·er·ship′** *n.*

ma·ña·na (mä-nyä′nə) ▸ *adv.* **1.** Tomorrow. **2.** At some future time. **—ma·ña′na** *n.*

ma·nat (mä-nät′) ▸ *n.* See **currency** table in Appendix.

man·a·tee (măn′ə-tē′) ▸ *n.* An aquatic, primarily tropical mammal.

Man·ches·ter (măn′chĕs′tər, -chĭ-stər) ▸ A borough of NW England ENE of Liverpool.

Man·chu (măn′cho͞o, măn-cho͞o′) ▸ *n., pl.* **-chu** or **-chus. 1.** A member of a people native to Manchuria who ruled China during the Qing dynasty (1644–1912). **2.** The Tungusic language of the Manchu. **—Man′chu** *adj.*

Man·chu·ri·a (măn-cho͝or′ē-ə) ▸ A region of NE China. **—Man·chu′ri·an** *adj. & n.*

man·da·la (mŭn′də-lə) ▸ *n.* Any of various ritualistic geometric designs used in Hinduism and Buddhism as an aid to meditation.

man·da·mus (măn-dā′məs) ▸ *n.* A writ issued by a superior court ordering a public official or body or a lower court to perform a duty.

Man·dan (măn′dăn′) ▸ *n., pl.* **-dan** or **-dans. 1.** A member of a Native American people formerly living along the Missouri R. in S-central North Dakota, now in W-central North Dakota. **2.** Their Siouan language.

man·da·rin (măn′də-rĭn) ▸ *n.* **1.** A high-ranking public official in the Chinese Empire. **2. Mandarin** The official standard language of China, based on the dialect of Beijing. **3.** A mandarin orange. **—man′da·rin** *adj.*

mandarin orange ▸ *n.* A small, loose-skinned, orange citrus fruit.

man·date (măn′dāt′) ▸ *n.* **1.** An authoritative command or instruction. **2a.** A commission from the League of Nations authorizing a member nation to administer a territory. **b.** A

THESAURUS

malleability or **malleableness** *n.* —*See* FLEXIBILITY (1).

malleable *adj.* Capable of being shaped, bent, or drawn out, as by hammering or pressure ▸ bendable, ductile, flexible, flexile, flexuous, moldable, plastic, pliable, pliant, supple, tractable, workable. [*Compare* CHANGEABLE, EXTENSIBLE.] —*See also* ADAPTABLE, FLEXIBLE (3).

malodor *n.* —*See* STENCH.

malodorous *adj.* —*See* SMELLY.

malpractice *n.* —*See* INJUSTICE (1).

maltreat *v.* —*See* ABUSE (1).

maltreatment *n.* —*See* ABUSE (2).

mammoth *n.* —*See* GIANT.

mammoth *adj.* —*See* ENORMOUS.

man *n.* —*See* HUMAN BEING, HUMANKIND, POLICE OFFICER.

manacle *n.* —*See* BOND (1).

manacle *v.* —*See* HAMPER[1].

manage *v.* To progress or perform adequately, especially in difficult circumstances ▸ do, fare, fend, get along, get by, muddle through, scrape by, shift, squeak by. *Informal:* make out. *Idioms:* make do, make shift, make the best of it. [*Compare* ENDURE.] —*See also* ADMINISTER (1), CONDUCT (1), OPERATE.

manageable *adj.* Capable of being governed ▸ administrable, controllable, governable, rulable. [*Compare* LOYAL, OBEDIENT.]

management *n.* The act or practice of directing or controlling ▸ administration, charge, conduct, direction, directorship, guidance, government, lead, leadership, oversight, stewardship, superintendence, supervision. [*Compare* DOMINATION, DUTY.] —*See also* CONSERVATION.

manager *n.* —*See* BOSS, EXECUTIVE.

managerial *adj.* —*See* ADMINISTRATIVE.

mandate *n.* —*See* AUTHORITY,

region under administration. **—man′date′** *v.*

man·da·to·ry (măn′də-tôr′ē) ▸ *adj.* **1.** Required or obligatory. **2.** Of or containing a mandate.

Man·de·la (măn-dĕl′ə), **Nelson Rolihlahla** (1918–2013) ▸ South African political leader and president (1994–99); 1993 Nobel Peace Prize.

man·di·ble (măn′də-bəl) ▸ *n.* **1.** The lower jaw of a vertebrate animal. **2.** Either part of a bird's beak. **3.** A jawlike part of an insect. **—man·dib′u·lar** (-dĭb′yə-lər) *adj.*

Man·din·go (măn-dĭng′gō) ▸ *n., pl.* **-gos** or **-goes. 1.** A member of any of various peoples inhabiting a large area of the upper Niger R. valley of W Africa. **2.** A group of related languages in W Africa.

man·do·lin (măn′də-lĭn′, măn′dl-ĭn) ▸ *n.* A stringed musical instrument with a usu. pear-shaped body and a fretted neck.

man·drake (măn′drāk′) ▸ *n.* **1.** A S European plant having a branched root thought to resemble the human body, once widely believed to have magical powers. **2.** See **May apple.**

man·drel or **man·dril** (măn′drəl) ▸ *n.* **1.** A spindle or axle used to secure or support material being machined. **2.** A metal rod or bar around which material, such as metal or glass, may be shaped.

man·drill (măn′drəl) ▸ *n.* A large African baboon having brilliant facial markings in the adult male.

mane (mān) ▸ *n.* **1.** The long hair growing from the neck of certain animals, such as the horse and male lion. **2.** A long thick growth of human hair.

ma·nège also **ma·nege** (mă-nĕzh′) ▸ *n.* The art of training or riding horses.

ma·nes or **Ma·nes** (mā′nēz′, mä′nās′) ▸ *pl.n.* In ancient Roman religion, the spirits of the dead.

ma·neu·ver (mə-no͞o′vər, -nyo͞o′-) ▸ *n.* **1a.** A strategic or tactical military or naval movement. **b.** often **maneuvers** A large-scale tactical exercise that simulates combat. **2.** A physical movement involving skill and dexterity. **3.** An adroit, clever, and artful move or action; stratagem. ▸ *v.* **1.** To carry out a military maneuver. **2.** To use stratagems in gaining an end. **3.** To manipulate or guide adroitly to a desired position or goal. **—ma·neu′ver·a·bil′i·ty** *n.* **—ma·neu′ver·a·ble** *adj.*

man·ful (măn′fəl) ▸ *adj.* Courageous; resolute. **—man′ful·ly** *adv.* **—man′ful·ness** *n.*

man·ga·nese (măng′gə-nēz′, -nēs′) ▸ *n. Symbol* **Mn** A brittle metallic element used chiefly in making alloys of steel. At. no. 25.

mange (mānj) ▸ *n.* A chronic skin disease esp. of domestic animals, marked by itching and loss of hair. **—mang′y** *adj.*

man·ger (mān′jər) ▸ *n.* A trough or an open box in which feed for livestock is placed.

man·gle[1] (măng′gəl) ▸ *v.* **-gled, -gling. 1.** To mutilate or disfigure by battering or hacking. **2.** To ruin or botch. **—man′gler** *n.*

man·gle[2] (măng′gəl) ▸ *n.* A laundry machine for pressing fabrics.

man·go (măng′gō) ▸ *n., pl.* **-goes** or **-gos. 1.** A tropical Asian evergreen tree cultivated for its edible fruit. **2.** The sweet juicy fruit of the mango.

man·grove (măn′grōv′, măng′-) ▸ *n.* A tropical evergreen tree or shrub having stiltlike roots and stems and forming dense thickets in tidal regions.

man·han·dle (măn′hăn′dəl) ▸ *v.* **1.** To handle roughly. **2.** To effect by physical effort.

Man·hat·tan[1] (măn-hăt′n) ▸ A borough of New York City in SE NY, mainly on **Manhattan Island. —Man·hat′tan·ite′** (-īt′) *n.*

Man·hat·tan[2] (măn-hăt′n, mən-) ▸ *n.* A cocktail made of sweet vermouth and whiskey.

man·hole (măn′hōl′) ▸ *n.* A hole, usu. with a cover, through which an underground structure, such as a sewer, can be entered.

man·hood (măn′ho͝od′) ▸ *n.* **1.** The state of being an adult male. **2.** The qualities, such as courage and vigor, often thought to be appropriate to a man. **3.** Men collectively.

man-hour (măn′our′) ▸ *n.* An industrial unit of production equal to the work one person can produce in one hour.

man·hunt (măn′hŭnt′) ▸ *n.* An organized search esp. for a fugitive criminal.

ma·ni·a (mā′nē-ə, mān′yə) ▸ *n.* **1.** An intense enthusiasm; craze. **2.** A mental disorder characterized by excessive physical activity and emotional excitement.

-mania ▸ *suff.* An exaggerated desire or enthusiasm for: *pyromania.*

ma·ni·ac (mā′nē-ăk′) ▸ *n.* **1.** An insane person. **2.** One with an excessive enthusiasm for something. **—ma′ni·ac′, ma·ni′a·cal** (mə-nī′ə-kəl) *adj.*

man·ic (măn′ĭk) ▸ *adj.* Of, affected by, or marked by mania.

man·ic-de·pres·sive (măn′ĭk-dĭ-prĕs′ĭv) *Psychiat.* ▸ *adj.* Bipolar. ▸ *n.* A person with bipolar disorder.

man·i·cot·ti (măn′ĭ-kŏt′ē) ▸ *n.* A dish of large pasta tubes with a filling, as of meat or cheese.

man·i·cure (măn′ĭ-kyo͝or′) ▸ *n.* A cosmetic treatment of the fingernails. ▸ *v.* **-cured, -cur·ing. 1.** To give a manicure to. **2.** To trim evenly. **—man′i·cur′ist** *n.*

man·i·fest (măn′ə-fĕst′) ▸ *adj.* Clearly apparent to the sight or understanding; obvious. ▸ *v.* To show plainly; reveal. ▸ *n.* A list of cargo or passengers. **—man′i·fest′ly** *adv.*

man·i·fes·ta·tion (măn′ə-fĕ-stā′shən) ▸ *n.* An indication of the existence or presence of something.

man·i·fes·to (măn′ə-fĕs′tō) ▸ *n., pl.* **-toes** or **-tos.** A public declaration of principles or intentions, esp. political ones.

man·i·fold (măn′ə-fōld′) ▸ *adj.* **1.** Of many and diverse kinds. **2.** Having many features or forms. ▸ *n.* A pipe having several openings for making multiple connections.

man·i·kin or **man·ni·kin** (măn′ĭ-kĭn) ▸ *n.* **1.** A man short in stature. **2.** A mannequin.

Ma·nil·a (mə-nĭl′ə) ▸ The capital of the Philippines, on **Manila Bay,** an inlet of the South China Sea.

Manila hemp ▸ *n.* The fiber of the abaca, a Philippine plant related to the banana, used to make rope, cordage, and paper.

Manila paper ▸ *n.* A strong paper or thin cardboard, usu. buff in color.

man·i·oc (măn′ē-ŏk′) ▸ *n.* See **cassava.**

ma·nip·u·late (mə-nĭp′yə-lāt′) ▸ *v.* **-lat·ed, -lat·ing. 1.** To operate or control by skilled use of the hands; handle. **2.** To influence or manage shrewdly or deviously. **3.** To tamper with or falsify for personal gain. **—ma·nip′u·la′tion** *n.* **—ma·nip′u·la′tive** *adj.* **—ma·nip′u·la′tor** *n.* **—ma·nip′u·la·to′ry** (-lə-tôr′ē) *adj.*

THESAURUS

COMMAND (1), POSSESSION.

mandate *v.* —*See* DICTATE.

mandatory *adj.* —*See* REQUIRED.

maneuver *n.* **1.** A method of deploying troops and equipment in combat ▸ battle plan, plan of attack, stratagem, strategy, tactic. **2.** An action calculated to achieve an end ▸ measure, move, procedure, step, tactic. —*See also* TRICK (1).

maneuver *v.* **1.** To direct the course of carefully ▸ finesse, guide, jockey, navigate, pilot, steer. *Idiom:* back and fill. [*Compare* DRIVE, OPERATE.] **2.** To use stratagems in gaining an end ▸ angle for, engineer, finesse, jockey, worm. *Informal:* finagle, wangle. *Idiom:* pull strings (*or* wires). [*Compare* PLOT.] —*See also* MANIPULATE (1), MOVE (2).

manful *adj.* —*See* MANLY.

mangle[1] *v.* —*See* BATTER, BOTCH, CRIPPLE.

mangle[2] *v.* —*See* PRESS (2).

mangy *adj.* —*See* SHABBY.

manhandle *v.* To be rough or brutal with ▸ knock about (*or* around), rough up, slap around. *Slang:* mess up. [*Compare* ABUSE, BEAT, HIT.] —*See also* BATTER.

manhood *n.* —*See* MASCULINITY.

mania *n.* —*See* ENTHUSIASM (2), INSANITY, OBSESSION.

maniac *n.* —*See* FAN[2].

maniacal or **maniac** *adj.* —*See* INSANE.

manifest *v.* —*See* DEVELOP (1), EMBODY (1), EXPRESS (1), SHOW (1).

manifest *n.* —*See* LIST[1].

manifest *adj.* —*See* APPARENT (1).

manifestation *n.* —*See* APPEARANCE (2), ARRAY, DISPLAY, EMBODIMENT, SIGN (1).

manifesto *n.* —*See* MESSAGE.

manifold *adj.* —*See* COMPLEX (2).

manipulate *v.* **1.** To influence or manage shrewdly or deviously ▸ exploit, maneuver, play, use. *Idioms:* pull strings, wheel and deal. [*Compare* PLOT, WANGLE.] **2.** To use with or as if with the hands ▸ handle, ply, wield.

Man·i·to·ba (măn′ĭ-tō′bə) ▸ A province of S-central Canada. Cap. Winnipeg. **—Man′i·to′ban** *adj. & n.*
man·i·tou (măn′ĭ-tōō′) ▸ *n., pl.* **-tous.** In Algonquian religious belief, a supernatural power that permeates the world.
man·kind (măn′kīnd′) ▸ *n.* **1.** The human race. **2.** Men as opposed to women.
man·ly (măn′lē) ▸ *adj.* **-li·er, -li·est. 1.** Having qualities traditionally attributed to a man. **2.** Of a man; masculine. ▸ *adv.* In a manly manner. **—man′li·ness** *n.*
man-made or **man·made** (măn′mād′) ▸ *adj.* Made by humans; synthetic.
man·na (măn′ə) ▸ *n.* **1.** In the Bible, the food miraculously provided for the Israelites in the wilderness during their flight from Egypt. **2.** Something of value that comes unexpectedly.
manned (mănd) ▸ *adj.* Transporting or operated by a human: *a manned spacecraft.*
man·ne·quin (măn′ĭ-kĭn) ▸ *n.* **1.** A life-size representation of the human body, used to fit or display clothes; dummy. **2.** One who models clothes.
man·ner (măn′ər) ▸ *n.* **1.** A way of doing something or the way in which a thing is done or happens. **2.** A way of acting; bearing or behavior. **3. manners a.** Socially proper behavior. **b.** The prevailing customs of a society or period, esp. as the subject of a literary work. **4.** Practice, style, or method in the arts. **5.** Kind; sort. ***—idiom:* in a manner of speaking** In a way; so to speak.
man·nered (măn′ərd) ▸ *adj.* **1.** Having manners of a specific kind: *ill-mannered.* **2.** Artificial or affected. **3.** Of or exhibiting mannerisms.
man·ner·ism (măn′ə-rĭz′əm) ▸ *n.* **1.** A distinctive behavioral trait. **2.** Exaggerated or affected style or habit.
man·ner·ly (măn′ər-lē) ▸ *adj.* Having good manners. **—man′ner·li·ness** *n.*
man·ni·kin (măn′ĭ-kĭn) ▸ *n.* Var. of **manikin.**
man·nish (măn′ĭsh) ▸ *adj.* Resembling or suggestive of a man rather than a woman. **—man′nish·ly** *adv.* **—man′nish·ness** *n.*
man-of-war (măn′ə-wôr′) ▸ *n., pl.* **men-of-war** (mĕn′-). **1.** See **warship. 2.** A Portuguese man-of-war.
ma·nom·e·ter (mă-nŏm′ĭ-tər) ▸ *n.* An instrument for measuring the pressure of liquids and gases. **—man′o·met′ric** (măn′ə-mĕt′rĭk), **man′o·met′ri·cal** *adj.* **—ma·nom′e·try** *n.*
man·or (măn′ər) ▸ *n.* **1a.** A landed estate. **b.** The main house on an estate. **2.** The district over which a feudal lord had domain. **—ma·no′ri·al** (mə-nôr′ē-əl) *adj.*
man·pow·er (măn′pou′ər) ▸ *n.* **1.** The power of human physical strength. **2.** Power in terms of the workers available, as for a particular task.
man·qué (mäN-kā′) ▸ *adj.* Unfulfilled; frustrated: *an artist manqué.*
man·sard (măn′särd′) ▸ *n.* A four-sided roof having a double slope on all sides, with the lower slope much steeper than the upper.
manse (măns) ▸ *n.* A cleric's house and land, esp. the residence of a Presbyterian minister.
man·sion (măn′shən) ▸ *n.* A large stately house.
man-sized (măn′sīzd′) also **man-size** (-sīz′) ▸ *adj. Informal* Very large.
man·slaugh·ter (măn′slô′tər) ▸ *n.* The unlawful killing of one human by another without express or implied intent to do injury.
man·ta (măn′tə) ▸ *n.* A large ray of tropical and subtropical seas having winglike pectoral fins and two hornlike fins on the head.
man·tel also **man·tle** (măn′tl) ▸ *n.* **1.** An ornamental facing around a fireplace. **2.** The protruding shelf over a fireplace.
man·tel·piece (măn′tl-pēs′) ▸ *n. Regional* See **mantel.**
man·til·la (măn-tē′yə, -tĭl′ə) ▸ *n.* A lace or silk scarf worn over the head and shoulders by women in Spain and Latin America.
man·tis (măn′tĭs) ▸ *n., pl.* **-es** or **-tes** (-tēz). A predatory insect having two pairs of walking legs and powerful grasping forelimbs.
man·tis·sa (măn-tĭs′ə) ▸ *n.* The decimal part of a logarithm.
man·tle (măn′tl) ▸ *n.* **1.** A loose sleeveless outer garment; cloak. **2.** Something that covers, envelops, or conceals. **3.** Var. of **mantel. 4.** A device in gas lamps consisting of a sheath of threads that glows brightly when heated by the flame. **5.** The layer of the earth between the crust and the core. ▸ *v.* **-tled, -tling.** To cover with or as if with a mantle.
man·tra (măn′trə, mŭn′-) ▸ *n.* **1.** *Hinduism* A sacred verbal formula repeated in prayer, meditation, or incantation. **2.** A commonly repeated word or phrase. **—man′tric** *adj.*
man·u·al (măn′yōō-əl) ▸ *adj.* **1.** Of or relating to the hands. **2.** Done by or operated with the hands. **3.** Employing human rather than mechanical energy: *manual labor.* ▸ *n.* **1.** A small reference book, esp. one giving instructions. **2.** An organ keyboard. **3.** Prescribed movements in the handling of a weapon. **—man′u·al·ly** *adv.*
manual alphabet ▸ *n.* An alphabet used by hearing-impaired people in which finger positions represent the letters.
man·u·fac·to·ry (măn′yə-făk′tə-rē) ▸ *n., pl.* **-ries.** A factory.
man·u·fac·ture (măn′yə-făk′chər) ▸ *v.* **-tured, -tur·ing. 1.** To make or process from raw materials, esp. by means of a large-scale industrial operation. **2.** To make up; fabricate. ▸ *n.* **1.** The act or process of manufacturing. **2.** A manufactured product. **—man′u·fac′tur·er** *n.*
man·u·mit (măn′yə-mĭt′) ▸ *v.* **-mit·ted, -mit·ting.** To free from slavery or bondage. **—man′u·mis′sion** (-mĭsh′ən) *n.*
ma·nure (mə-nŏŏr′, -nyŏŏr′) ▸ *n.* Material, esp. dung, used to fertilize soil. ▸ *v.* **-nured, -nur·ing.** To fertilize (soil) by applying manure.
man·u·script (măn′yə-skrĭpt′) ▸ *n.* **1.** A book or other composition written by hand. **2.** A typewritten or handwritten version of a text prepared and submitted for publication. **3.** Handwriting.
Manx (măngks) ▸ *n., pl.* **Manx. 1.** The people of the Isle of Man. **2.** The extinct Celtic language of the Manx. **—Manx** *adj.* **—Manx′man** *n.* **—Manx′wom′an** *n.*
man·y (mĕn′ē) ▸ *adj.* **more** (môr), **most** (mōst). Amounting to or being one of a large indefinite number: *many friends; many a day.* ▸ *n. (takes pl. v.)* A large indefinite number. ▸ *pron. (takes pl. v.)* A large number of persons or things.

THESAURUS

3. To handle in a way so as to mix, form, and shape ▸ knead, squeeze, work. *—See also* RUB, TOUCH.
manipulation *n.* *—See* TOUCH (1).
manipulative *adj.* Coldly planning to achieve selfish aims ▸ calculating, conniving, designing, scheming. [*Compare* ARTFUL.]
mankind *n.* *—See* HUMANKIND.
manlike *adj.* *—See* HUMANLIKE, MANLY.
manliness *n.* *—See* MASCULINITY.
manly *adj.* Having qualities traditionally attributed to a man ▸ macho, male, manful, manlike, mannish, masculine, virile.
manmade *adj.* *—See* ARTIFICIAL (1).
manner *n.* *—See* BEARING (1), BEHAVIOR (1), CUSTOM, KIND[2], STYLE, WAY (1).
mannered *adj.* Artificially genteel ▸ affected, artificial, precious. *Informal:* la-di-da. *—See also* PRUDISH.
mannerism *n.* *—See* AFFECTATION.
mannerliness *n.* *—See* COURTESY.
mannerly *adj.* *—See* COURTEOUS (1).
manners *n.* Socially correct behavior ▸ decorum, etiquette, good behavior, good form, mores, proprieties, propriety, p's and q's, refinement. [*Compare* COURTESY.]
mannish *adj.* *—See* MANLY.
mannishness *n.* *—See* MASCULINITY.
man on horseback *n.* *—See* DICTATOR.
manor *n.* *—See* LAND, VILLA.
manslaughter *n.* *—See* MURDER.
manslayer *n.* *—See* MURDERER.
mantic *adj.* *—See* PROPHETIC.
mantle *v.* *—See* BLUSH, CLOTHE.
mantle *n.* *—See* VEIL.
manufacture *v.* *—See* MAKE.
manufacture *n.* Something produced by human effort ▸ produce, product, production, work. [*Compare* COMPOSITION, GOOD.]
manufactured *adj.* *—See* ARTIFICIAL (1).
manufacturer *n.* *—See* MAKER.
manumission *n.* *—See* LIBERTY.
manumit *v.* *—See* FREE (1).
manumitted *adj.* *—See* FREE (1).
manuscript *n.* *—See* SCRIPT (2).
many *adj.* Amounting to or consisting of a large, indefinite number ▸ legion, multitudinous, myriad, numerous. *Informal:* umpteen. ***Idioms:*** quite a few, quite a lot. [*Compare* ABUNDANCE,

man·y-sid·ed (mĕn′ē-sī′dĕd) ▸ *adj.* 1. Having many sides. 2. Having many aspects or talents.

man·za·ni·ta (măn′zə-nē′tə) ▸ *n.* A small evergreen tree of the Pacific coast of North America.

Mao·ism (mou′ĭz′əm) ▸ *n.* Marxism-Leninism developed in China chiefly by Mao Zedong. **—Mao′ist** *adj. & n.*

Mao·ri (mou′rē) ▸ *n., pl.* **-ri** or **-ris.** 1. A member of a people of New Zealand, of Polynesian-Melanesian descent. 2. Their Austronesian language. **—Mao′ri** *adj.*

Mao Ze·dong (mou′ dzə′dŏng′) also **Mao Tse-tung** (tsə′-to͝ong′) (1893–1976) ▸ Chinese Communist leader and theorist.

map (măp) ▸ *n.* 1. A representation, usu. on a plane surface, of a region. 2. Something resembling a map, as in schematic representation. ▸ *v.* **mapped, map·ping.** 1. To make a map of. 2. To plan in detail: *map out the future.* **—map′mak′er** *n.* **—map′pa·ble** *adj.* **—map′per** *n.*

ma·ple (mā′pəl) ▸ *n.* 1. Any of a genus of deciduous trees or shrubs having palmate leaves and long-winged fruits borne in pairs. 2. The wood of a maple. 3. The flavor of maple sugar or syrup.

maple sugar ▸ *n.* A sugar that is made by boiling down maple syrup.

maple syrup ▸ *n.* A sweet syrup made from the sap of the sugar maple.

mar (mär) ▸ *v.* **marred, mar·ring.** To damage, disfigure, or spoil.

Mar. ▸ *abbr.* March

mar·a·bou (măr′ə-bo͞o′) ▸ *n.* 1. A large African stork that scavenges for carrion. 2. The soft white down of the marabou, used esp. in trimming garments.

ma·ra·ca (mə-rä′kə) ▸ *n.* A percussion instrument consisting of a hollow gourd containing pebbles or beans.

Ma·ra·cai·bo (mä′rä-kī′bō) ▸ A city of northwest Venezuela on **Lake Maracaibo,** the largest lake of South America.

mar·a·schi·no (măr′ə-skē′nō, -shē′-) ▸ *n., pl.* **-nos.** A cordial made from the fermented juice and crushed pits of a bitter cherry.

maraschino cherry ▸ *n.* A cherry preserved in a syrup flavored with maraschino.

Ma·ra·thi (mə-rä′tē, -răt′ē) ▸ *n.* The principal Indic language of the state of Maharashtra, India.

mar·a·thon (măr′ə-thŏn′) ▸ *n.* 1. A cross-country footrace of 26 mi, 385 yd (42.195 km). 2. A test or contest of endurance. **—mar′a·thon′er** *n.*

ma·raud (mə-rôd′) ▸ *v.* To rove in search of plunder. **—ma·raud′er** *n.*

mar·ble (mär′bəl) ▸ *n.* 1. A metamorphic, often streaked rock formed by alteration of limestone or dolomite, used esp. in architecture and sculpture. 2. Something resembling marble, as in being very hard, smooth, or cold. 3a. A small hard ball, usu. of glass, used in children's games. b. **marbles** *(takes sing. v.)* A game played with marbles. 4. **marbles** *Slang* Common sense; sanity: *lost his marbles.* **—mar′ble** *adj.* **—mar′bly** *adj.*

mar·bled (mär′bəld) ▸ *adj.* 1. Made of or covered with marble. 2. Mottled or streaked: *meat marbled with fat.* **—mar′bling** *n.*

mar·ca·site (mär′kə-sīt′, -zīt′) ▸ *n.* 1. A mineral with the same composition as pyrite, FeS_2, but differing in crystal structure. 2. An ornament of pyrite, polished steel, or white metal.

march[1] (märch) ▸ *v.* 1. To walk or cause to walk steadily and rhythmically forward, usu. in step with others. 2a. To proceed directly and purposefully. b. To advance steadily: *Time marches on.* 3. To participate in an organized walk. ▸ *n.* 1. The act of marching. 2. Steady forward movement or progression. 3. A measured, even step. 4. The distance covered by marching: *a week's march.* 5. *Mus.* A composition in usu. duple meter that is appropriate for marching. 6. An organized walk, as for a public cause. ***—idiom:* on the march** Advancing steadily. **—march′er** *n.*

march[2] (märch) ▸ *n.* A border region; frontier.

March (märch) ▸ *n.* The 3rd month of the Gregorian calendar.

mar·chio·ness (mär′shə-nĭs, mär′shə-nĕs′) ▸ *n.* 1. The wife or widow of a marquis. 2. A noblewoman ranking above a countess and below a duchess.

Mar·co·ni (mär-kō′nē), **Guglielmo** (1874–1937) ▸ Italian engineer and inventor; 1909 Nobel.

Mar·cus Au·re·li·us An·to·ni·nus (mär′kəs ô-rē′lē-əs ăn′tə-nī′nəs) (A.D. 121–180) ▸ Roman philosopher and emperor (161–180).

Mar·di Gras (mär′dē grä′) ▸ *n.* The day before Ash Wednesday, celebrated in many places with carnivals and parades of costumed merrymakers.

mare[1] (mâr) ▸ *n.* A female horse or related animal.

ma·re[2] (mä′rā) ▸ *n., pl.* **-ri·a** (-rē-ə). Any of the large dark areas on the moon or planets, esp. Mars.

mar·ga·rine (mär′jər-ĭn) ▸ *n.* A fatty solid butter substitute consisting of hydrogenated vegetable oils mixed with emulsifiers, vitamins, and coloring matter.

mar·ga·ri·ta (mär′gə-rē′tə) ▸ *n.* A cocktail made with tequila, an orange-flavored liqueur, and lemon or lime juice.

mar·gin (mär′jĭn) ▸ *n.* 1. An edge and the area immediately adjacent to it; border. 2. The blank space bordering the written or printed area on a page. 3. An allowance beyond what is needed: *a margin of safety.* 4. A measure or degree of difference: *a margin of 500 votes.* 5. The difference between cost and selling price, as of securities.

mar·gin·al (mär′jə-nəl) ▸ *adj.* 1. Of, at, or constituting a margin. 2. Barely within a lower standard or limit: *marginal writing ability.* **—mar′gin·al·ly** *adv.*

mar·gi·na·li·a (mär′jə-nā′lē-ə) ▸ *pl.n.* Notes in the margin or margins of a book.

ma·ri·a·chi (mä′rē-ä′chē) ▸ *n., pl.* **-chis.** A street band in Mexico.

Mar·i·an·a Islands (măr′ē-ăn′ə, mâr′-) ▸ A US-administered island group in the W Pacific E of the Philippines, comprising Guam, an independent commonwealth, and the **Northern Mariana Islands.**

Ma·rie An·toi·nette (mə-rē′ ăn′twə-nĕt′) (1755–93) ▸ Queen of France (1774–93) as the wife of Louis XVI; executed.

mar·i·gold (măr′ĭ-gōld′, mâr′-) ▸ *n.* Any of various American plants cultivated for their showy yellow or orange flowers.

mar·i·jua·na also **mar·i·hua·na** (măr′ə-wä′nə) ▸ *n.* 1. The cannabis plant. 2. A preparation made from the dried flower clusters and leaves of the cannabis plant, smoked or eaten to induce euphoria.

ma·rim·ba (mə-rĭm′bə) ▸ *n.* A large wooden percussion instrument with resonators, resembling a xylophone.

ma·ri·na (mə-rē′nə) ▸ *n.* A boat basin that has docks, moorings, and supplies for small boats.

mar·i·nade (măr′ə-nād′) ▸ *n.* A spiced liquid in which food is soaked before cooking.

mar·i·nate (măr′ə-nāt′) ▸ *v.* **-nat·ed, -nat·ing.** To soak (e.g., meat) in a marinade.

ma·rine (mə-rēn′) ▸ *adj.* 1. Of or relating to the sea: *marine exploration.* 2. Of shipping or maritime affairs. 3. Of sea navigation. ▸ *n.* 1a. A soldier serving on a ship. b. **Marine** A member of the US Marine Corps. 2. A picture of the sea.

Marine Corps ▸ *n.* A branch of the US armed forces composed chiefly of amphibious troops.

THESAURUS

GENEROUS, HEAP, INCALCULABLE.]

many-colored or **many-hued** *adj.* —*See* MULTICOLORED.

many-sided *adj.* —*See* VERSATILE.

map *v.* —*See* ARRANGE (2), DESIGN (2), PLOT (1).

map out *v.* —*See* DRAFT (1).

map *n.* —*See* FACE (1).

mar *v.* —*See* DAMAGE, DEFORM.

maraud *v.* —*See* INVADE (1).

marbles *n.* —*See* SANITY.

march[1] *v.* To travel about or journey on foot ▸ backpack, hike, tramp, trek. [*Compare* JOURNEY, WALK, ROVE.] —*See also* ADVANCE (2).

march *n.* —*See* ADVANCE, WALK (1).

march[2] or **marchland** *n.* —*See* BORDER (2).

margin *n.* —*See* BORDER (1), LICENSE (1).

margin *v.* —*See* BORDER.

marinate *v.* —*See* STEEP[2].

marine *adj.* 1. Of or relating to the seas or oceans ▸ briny, maritime, oceangoing, oceanic, pelagic, saltwater, salty, sea, seafaring, seagoing, seawater, thalassic. 2. Of or relating to sea navigation ▸ maritime, nautical, naval, navigational.

mar·i·ner (măr′ə-nər) ▸ *n.* A sailor.

mar·i·o·nette (măr′ē-ə-nĕt′) ▸ *n.* A jointed puppet manipulated by strings.

mar·i·tal (măr′ĭ-tl) ▸ *adj.* Of or relating to marriage. **—mar′i·tal·ly** *adv.*

mar·i·time (măr′ĭ-tīm′) ▸ *adj.* **1.** Of or adjacent to the sea. **2.** Of marine shipping or navigation.

Maritime Provinces ▸ The Canadian provinces of Nova Scotia, New Brunswick, and Prince Edward Island. **—Mar′i·tim′er** *n.*

mar·jo·ram (mär′jər-əm) ▸ *n.* Any of several aromatic plants having opposite leaves used as seasoning.

mark[1] (märk) ▸ *n.* **1.** A visible trace or impression, such as a line or spot. **2.** A written or printed symbol: *a punctuation mark.* **3a.** An academic grade. **b.** often **marks** An appraisal; rating: *earned high marks.* **4.** A name, stamp, or seal placed on merchandise to signify ownership or origin. **5a.** A distinctive trait or property: *a mark of good breeding.* **b.** A lasting effect: *The experience had left its mark.* **6.** A recognized standard of quality. **7.** Importance; note. **8.** A target. **9.** An aim or goal. **10.** An object or a point that serves as a guide. **11.** *Slang* An intended victim. ▸ *v.* **1a.** To make a mark (on). **b.** To form, make, or depict by making a mark. **2a.** To single out or identify by or as if by a mark. **b.** To distinguish or characterize. **3.** To set off or separate, as with a line: *marked off the property.* **4.** To grade (academic work). ***—phrasal verbs:* mark down** To reduce in price. **mark up 1.** To deface by covering with marks. **2.** To increase the price of. ***—idiom:* mark time 1.** To move the feet in a marching rhythm without advancing. **2.** To suspend progress temporarily. **—mark′er** *n.*

mark[2] (märk) ▸ *n.* The deutsche mark.

Mark (märk) ▸ *n.* See **Bible** table in Appendix.

Mark, Saint ▸ Author of the second Gospel in the Bible and disciple of Saint Peter.

mar·ka (mär′kä) ▸ *n.* See **currency** table in Appendix.

Mark An·to·ny (ăn′tə-nē) or **Mark An·tho·ny** (ăn′thə-nē) (83?–30 B.C.) ▸ Roman orator, politician, and soldier.

mark·down (märk′doun′) ▸ *n.* A reduction in price.

marked (märkt) ▸ *adj.* **1.** Having a distinguishing mark. **2.** Clearly defined; noticeable. **3.** Singled out, esp. for a dire fate: *a marked man.* **—mark′ed·ly** (mär′kĭd-lē) *adv.*

mar·ket (mär′kĭt) ▸ *n.* **1.** A public gathering held for buying and selling merchandise. **2.** A place where goods are sold. **3.** A shop that sells a particular type of merchandise: *a meat market.* **4a.** The business of buying and selling a specified commodity: *the soybean market.* **b.** A geographic region considered as a place for sales. **c.** A specific group of buyers: *the student market.* **5.** The extent of demand for merchandise: *a big market for gourmet foods.* ▸ *v.* **1.** To offer for sale. **2.** To sell. **—mar′ket·a·bil′i·ty** *n.* **—mar′ket·a·ble** *adj.* **—mar′ket·er** *n.*

mar·ket·place (mär′kĭt-plās′) ▸ *n.* **1.** An open area in which a public market is set up. **2.** The world of business and commerce.

market price ▸ *n.* The prevailing price at which a commodity is sold.

market value ▸ *n.* The amount a seller may expect to obtain in the open market.

mark·ing (mär′kĭng) ▸ *n.* **1.** An act or result of marking. **2.** The characteristic pattern of coloration of a plant or animal.

mark·ka (mär′kä′) ▸ *n., pl.* **mark·kaa.** The primary unit of currency in Finland before the adoption of the euro.

marks·man (märks′mən) ▸ *n.* A man skilled in shooting. **—marks′man·ship′** *n.*

marks·wom·an (märks′wo͝om′ən) ▸ *n.* A woman skilled in shooting.

mark·up (märk′ŭp′) ▸ *n.* **1.** A raise in price. **2.** An amount added to a cost price in calculating a selling price. **3a.** The set of typesetting instructions written on a manuscript. **b.** *Comp. Sci.* The set of tags describing an electronic document's formatting specifications.

markup language ▸ *n.* A coding system, such as HTML, used to structure and link text files.

marl (märl) ▸ *n.* Clay containing calcium carbonate, used as fertilizer. **—marl′y** *adj.*

mar·lin (mär′lĭn) ▸ *n.* A large saltwater game fish, having an elongated spearlike upper jaw.

mar·line·spike also **mar·lin·spike** (mär′lĭn-spīk′) ▸ *n.* A pointed metal spike, used to separate strands of rope in splicing.

Mar·lowe (mär′lō), **Christopher** (1564–93) ▸ English playwright and poet.

mar·ma·lade (mär′mə-lād′) ▸ *n.* A preserve made from the pulp and rind esp. of citrus fruits.

Mar·ma·ra (mär′mər-ə), **Sea of** ▸ A sea of NW Turkey between Europe and Asia.

mar·mo·re·al (mär-môr′ē-əl) ▸ *adj.* Resembling marble, as in smoothness or hardness.

mar·mo·set (mär′mə-sĕt′, -zĕt′) ▸ *n.* Any of various small tropical American monkeys having soft fur, tufted ears, and long tails.

mar·mot (mär′mət) ▸ *n.* Any of various stocky, short-legged burrowing rodents of the Northern Hemisphere.

ma·roon[1] (mə-ro͞on′) ▸ *v.* **1.** To abandon on a deserted island or coast. **2.** To leave helpless.

ma·roon[2] (mə-ro͞on′) ▸ *n.* A dark purplish red. **—ma·roon′** *adj.*

mar·quee (mär-kē′) ▸ *n.* **1.** A large, often open-sided tent used chiefly for outdoor entertainment. **2.** A rooflike structure, often bearing a signboard, projecting over an entrance, as to a theater.

Mar·que·sas Islands (mär-kā′zəz, -zəz, -səs) ▸ A volcanic archipelago in the S Pacific, part of French Polynesia. **—Mar·que′san** *adj. & n.*

mar·que·try (mär′kĭ-trē) ▸ *n., pl.* **-tries.** Material, such as wood, inlaid into a veneer in an intricate design.

Mar·quette (mär-kĕt′), Père **Jacques** (1637–75) ▸ French missionary and explorer.

mar·quis (mär′kwĭs, mär-kē′) or **mar·quess** (mär′kwĭs) ▸ *n., pl.* **-quis·es** (-kwĭ-sĭz) or **-quis** (-kēz′) or **-quess·es** (-kwĭ-sĭz). A nobleman ranking below a duke and above an earl or count.

mar·quise (mär-kēz′) ▸ *n.* See **marchioness** 2.

mar·qui·sette (mär′kĭ-zĕt′, -kwĭ-) ▸ *n.* A sheer fabric used for clothing, curtains, and mosquito nets.

Mar·ra·kesh or **Mar·ra·kech** (măr′ə-kĕsh′, mə-rä′kĕsh) ▸ A city of W-central Morocco.

mar·riage (măr′ĭj) ▸ *n.* **1a.** The legal union of a man and woman as husband and wife, and in some jurisdictions, between two persons of the same sex. **b.** Wedlock. **2.** A wedding. **3.** A close union. **—mar′riage·a·ble** *adj.*

THESAURUS

mariner *n.* —*See* SAILOR.

marital *adj.* Of, relating to, or typical of marriage ▸ conjugal, connubial, hymeneal, married, matrimonial, nuptial, spousal, wedded.

maritime *adj.* Of or relating to sea navigation ▸ marine, nautical, naval, navigational. —*See also* MARINE (1).

mark *n.* **1.** A name or other device placed on an article to signify its ownership, manufacture, or origin ▸ brand, colophon, imprint, label, monogram, trademark. [*Compare* SYMBOL.] **2.** One that is fired at, attacked, or abused ▸ butt, target. —*See also* CHARACTER (7), DEGREE (1), DUPE, EXPRESSION (2), FAME, IMPRESSION (1), INTENTION, NOTICE (1), QUALITY (1), SIGN (1), STANDARD.

mark *v.* **1.** To set off by or as if by a mark indicating ownership or manufacture ▸ brand, identify, label, tag, trademark. **2.** To attach a ticket to ▸ earmark, flag, label, tag, ticket. **3.** To evaluate and assign a grade to ▸ correct, grade, score. **4.** To make a target of ▸ target. *Idioms:* draw (*or* get) a bead on, get in one's sights. —*See also* DESIGNATE, DETERMINE, DISTINGUISH (2), INDICATE (1), NOTICE, SHOW (2).

mark down *v.* —*See* DEPRECIATE.

markdown *n.* —*See* DEPRECIATION.

marked *adj.* —*See* NOTICEABLE.

market *v.* —*See* PROMOTE (3), SELL.

marketability or **marketableness** *n.* Market appeal ▸ salability, salableness, sell.

marks *n.* —*See* TRACK.

maroon *v.* —*See* ABANDON (1).

marooned *adj.* —*See* ABANDONED (1).

marriage *n.* The state of being married ▸ conjugality, coupling, connubiality, holy matrimony, matrimony, union, wedded bliss, wedlock. [*Compare* UNION.] —*See also* WEDDING.

marriageable *adj.* —*See* SINGLE.

married *adj.* —*See* MARITAL.

mar·row (măr′ō) ▸ *n.* **1.** The soft fatty tissue that fills most bone cavities and is the source of red and many white blood cells. **2.** The inmost, choicest, or most important part.

mar·ry (măr′ē) ▸ *v.* **-ried, -ry·ing.** **1a.** To join as spouses by exchanging vows. **b.** To take as a spouse. **c.** To give in marriage. **2.** To obtain by marriage: *marry money.* **3.** To unite in a close, usu. permanent way. **—mar′ried** *adj.*

Mars (märz) ▸ *n.* **1.** *Rom. Myth.* The god of war. **2.** The 4th planet from the sun, at a mean distance of 227.8 million km (141.6 million mi) and a mean diameter of approx. 6,726 km (4,180 mi).

Mar·seille (mär-sā′) or **Mar·seilles** ▸ A city of SE France on the Mediterranean Sea.

marsh (märsh) ▸ *n.* A grassy or reedy wetland. **—marsh′y** *adj.*

mar·shal (mär′shəl) ▸ *n.* **1.** A military officer of the highest rank in some countries. **2a.** A US federal or city officer who carries out court orders. **b.** The head esp. of a fire department. **3.** A person in charge of a parade or ceremony. **4.** A high official in a royal court. ▸ *v.* **-shaled, -shal·ing** also **-shalled, -shal·ling.** **1.** To place or set in position or order. **2.** To enlist and organize: *marshal public support.* **3.** To guide ceremoniously; usher.

Mar·shall (mär′shəl), **John** (1755–1835) ▸ Amer. jurist and politician; the chief justice of the US Supreme Court (1801–35).

Marshall, Thurgood (1908–93) ▸ Amer. jurist; US Supreme Court justice (1967–91).

Marshall Islands ▸ A self-governing island group in the central Pacific.

marsh·mal·low (märsh′mĕl′ō, -măl′ō) ▸ *n.* **1.** A light spongy confection made of corn syrup, gelatin, sugar, and starch. **2.** often **marsh mallow** A perennial wetland plant having showy pink flowers and a root sometimes used in confectionery.

marsh marigold ▸ *n.* A wetland plant having bright yellow flowers; cowslip.

mar·su·pi·al (mär-so͞o′pē-əl) ▸ *n.* Any of an order of mammals, including kangaroos, opossums, and wombats, found esp. in Australia and the Americas and marked by an abdominal pouch in the female in which the newly born young are sheltered and fed.

mart (märt) ▸ *n.* A market.

mar·ten (mär′tn) ▸ *n., pl.* **-ten** or **-tens.** **1.** A weasellike, chiefly arboreal mammal of northern forests. **2.** The fur of the marten.

mar·tial (mär′shəl) ▸ *adj.* **1.** Of or suggestive of war. **2.** Of or connected with military life. **—mar′tial·ly** *adv.*

martial art ▸ *n.* Any of several arts of combat and self-defense, such as karate or judo.

martial law ▸ *n.* Rule by military authorities, imposed on a civilian population esp. in time of war or when civil authority has broken down.

Mar·tian (mär′shən) ▸ *adj.* Of or relating to the planet Mars. ▸ *n.* A hypothetical inhabitant of the planet Mars.

mar·tin (mär′tn) ▸ *n.* Any of several birds of the swallow family.

mar·ti·net (mär′tn-ĕt′) ▸ *n.* A rigid disciplinarian.

mar·ti·ni (mär-tē′nē) ▸ *n., pl.* **-nis.** A cocktail of gin or vodka and dry vermouth.

Mar·ti·nique (mär′tĭ-nēk′, -tn-ēk′) ▸ An island and overseas department of France in the Windward Is. of the West Indies. Cap. Fort-de-France.

Martin Luther King Day ▸ *n.* The 3rd Monday in Jan. observed in the US in commemoration of the birthday of Martin Luther King, Jr.

mar·tyr (mär′tər) ▸ *n.* **1.** One who chooses to suffer death rather than renounce religious principles. **2.** One who makes great sacrifices for a cause. **3.** One who endures great suffering. **—mar′tyr** *v.* **—mar′tyr·dom** *n.*

mar·vel (mär′vəl) ▸ *n.* One that evokes surprise, admiration, or wonder. ▸ *v.* **-veled, -vel·ing** also **-velled, -vel·ling.** To become filled with wonder.

mar·vel·ous also **mar·vel·lous** (mär′və-ləs) ▸ *adj.* **1.** Causing wonder or astonishment. **2.** Miraculous. **3.** Excellent; superb. **—mar′vel·ous·ly** *adv.* **—mar′vel·ous·ness** *n.*

Marx (märks), **Karl** (1818–83) ▸ German philosopher, economist, and revolutionary. **—Marx′i·an** *adj. & n.*

Marx·ism (märk′sĭz′əm) ▸ *n.* The political and economic ideas of Karl Marx and Friedrich Engels that society inevitably develops through class struggle from oppression under capitalism to eventual classlessness. **—Marx′ist** *n. & adj.*

Marx·ism-Len·in·ism (märk′sĭz′əm-lĕn′ĭ-nĭz′əm) ▸ *n.* The expansion of Marxism to include the concepts of Leninism. **—Marx′ist-Len′in·ist** *adj. & n.*

Mar·y (mâr′ē) ▸ *n.* In the Bible, the mother of Jesus.

Mar·y·land (mĕr′ə-lənd) ▸ A state of the E-central US. Cap. Annapolis. **—Mar′y·land·er** *n.*

Mary Mag·da·lene (măg′də-lən, -lēn′) ▸ In the Bible, a woman whom Jesus cured of evil spirits; also identified with the repentent prostitute who washed Jesus' feet.

mar·zi·pan (mär′zə-păn′, märt′sə-pän′) ▸ *n.* A confection made of ground almonds, egg whites, and sugar.

Ma·sai (mä-sī′, mä′sī) ▸ *n., pl.* **-sai** or **-sais.** **1.** A member of a people of Kenya and parts of Tanzania. **2.** The Nilotic language of this people. **—Ma·sai′** *adj.*

masc. ▸ *abbr.* masculine

mas·car·a (mă-skăr′ə) ▸ *n.* A cosmetic applied to darken the eyelashes.

mas·cot (măs′kŏt′, -kət) ▸ *n.* A person, animal, or object believed to bring good luck.

mas·cu·line (măs′kyə-lĭn) ▸ *adj.* **1.** Of or relating to men or boys. **2.** Marked by qualities gen. attributed to a man. **3.** *Gram.* Of or being the gender of words referring to things classified as male. ▸ *n. Gram.* **1.** The masculine gender. **2.** A word belonging to this gender. **—mas′cu·line·ly** *adv.* **—mas′cu·line·ness** *n.* **—mas′cu·lin′i·ty** *n.*

ma·ser (mā′zər) ▸ *n.* Any of several devices that amplify or generate electromagnetic waves, esp. microwaves.

mash (măsh) ▸ *n.* **1.** A fermentable starchy mixture from which alcohol can be distilled. **2.** A mixture of ground grain and nutrients fed to livestock and fowl. **3.** A soft pulpy mixture or mass. ▸ *v.* **1.** To convert (malt or grain) into mash. **2.** To convert into a soft pulpy mixture: *mash potatoes.* **3.** To crush or grind. **—mash′er** *n.*

mask (măsk) ▸ *n.* **1.** A covering worn on the face to conceal one's identity. **2.** A figure of a head worn by actors in Greek and Roman drama. **3a.** A protective covering for the face or head. **b.** A covering for the nose and mouth that is used

THESAURUS

marrow *n.* —*See* HEART (1).

marrowy *adj.* —*See* PITHY.

marry *v.* To join or be joined in marriage ▸ espouse, mate, unite, wed. *Slang:* get hitched, get hooked. *Idioms:* join in matrimony, join together, lead to the altar, take the plunge, tie the knot. —*See also* COMBINE (1).

marsh *n.* —*See* SWAMP.

marshal *v.* —*See* ARRANGE (1), GUIDE, MOBILIZE.

marshal *n.* —*See* POLICE OFFICER.

marshland *n.* —*See* SWAMP.

martial *adj.* —*See* MILITARY (1), MILITARY (2).

martinet *n.* —*See* AUTHORITARIAN.

martyr *n.* —*See* VICTIM.

marvel *n.* One that evokes great surprise and admiration ▸ astonishment, miracle, phenomenon, prodigy, sensation, stunner, surprise, wonder, wonderment. *Idioms:* one for the books, eighth wonder of the world. [*Compare* DISPLAY.] —*See also* WONDER (1).

marvel *v.* To have a feeling of great awe and rapt admiration ▸ admire, wonder. *Idiom:* be agog (*or* agape *or* awestruck). [*Compare* GAZE, STAGGER.]

marvelous *adj.* Particularly excellent ▸ dandy, divine, fabulous, fantastic, fantastical, glorious, sensational, spectacular, splendid, superb, terrific, wonderful. *Informal:* dreamy, great, ripping, super, swell, tremendous. *Slang:* cool, groovy, hot, keen, neat, nifty, phat. *Idiom:* out of this world. [*Compare* EXCELLENT, EXCEPTIONAL.] —*See also* ASTONISHING, GRAND.

mascot *n.* —*See* CHARM.

masculine *adj.* —*See* MANLY.

masculinity *adj.* The quality of being masculine ▸ machismo, maleness, manhood, manliness, mannishness, virility.

mash *v.* —*See* CRUSH (1), FLIRT (2).

masher *n.* *Slang* A man who is given to flirting ▸ flirt, wolf. [*Compare* PHILANDERER, SEDUCER.]

mask *n.* —*See* DISGUISE, FAÇADE (2).

for inhaling oxygen or an anesthetic. **4.** A mold of a person's face. **5.** The facial markings of certain animals. **6.** Something that disguises or conceals. **7.** Var. of **masque.** ▸ *v.* **1.** To cover with a mask. **2.** To make indistinct or blurred to the senses. **3.** To conceal, protect, or disguise.

mas·och·ism (măs′ə-kĭz′əm) ▸ *n.* **1.** A psychological disorder in which sexual gratification is derived from abuse or physical pain. **2.** The deriving of pleasure from being dominated or mistreated. **—mas′och·ist** *n.* **—mas′och·is′tic** *adj.* **—mas′och·is′ti·cal·ly** *adv.*

ma·son (mā′sən) ▸ *n.* **1.** One who builds or works with stone or brick. **2. Mason** A Freemason.

Ma·son-Dix·on Line (mā′sən-dĭk′sən) ▸ The boundary between PA and MD, regarded as the division between free and slave states before the Civil War.

Ma·son·ic (mə-sŏn′ĭk) ▸ *adj.* Of or relating to Freemasonry.

Mason jar ▸ *n.* A wide-mouthed glass jar with a screw top, used for preserving food.

ma·son·ry (mā′sən-rē) ▸ *n., pl.* **-ries. 1.** The trade or work of a mason. **2.** Stonework or brickwork. **3. Masonry** Freemasonry.

masque also **mask** (măsk) ▸ *n.* **1.** An allegorical dramatic entertainment, popular in the 16th and early 17th cent. **2.** See **masquerade** 1.

mas·quer·ade (măs′kə-rād′) ▸ *n.* **1.** A costume party or ball at which masks are worn. **2.** A disguise or false outward show; pretense. ▸ *v.* **-ad·ed, -ad·ing. 1.** To wear a mask or disguise. **2.** To have a deceptive appearance. **—mas′quer·ad′er** *n.*

mass (măs) ▸ *n.* **1.** A unified body of matter with no specific shape. **2.** A large but nonspecific amount or number. **3.** The principal part; majority. **4.** The physical volume or bulk of a solid body. **5.** *Phys.* The quantity of matter that a body contains, not dependent on gravity and therefore different from but proportional to its weight. **6. masses** The body of common people. ▸ *v.* To gather or form into a mass.

Mass also **mass** ▸ *n.* In certain Christian churches, the celebration of the Eucharist.

Mass. ▸ *abbr.* Massachusetts

Mas·sa·chu·sett also **Mas·sa·chu·set** (măs′ə-cho͞o′sĭt, -zĭt) ▸ *n., pl.* **-sett** or **-setts** also **-set** or **-sets. 1.** A member of a Native American people formerly located along Massachusetts Bay from Plymouth N to Salem. **2.** Their Algonquian language.

Mas·sa·chu·setts (măs′ə-cho͞o′sĭts) ▸ A state of the NE US. Cap. Boston.

mas·sa·cre (măs′ə-kər) ▸ *n.* **1.** The act of killing many humans indiscriminately and cruelly. **2.** *Informal* A severe defeat, as in sports. **—mas′sa·cre** *v.*

mas·sage (mə-säzh′, -säj′) ▸ *n.* The rubbing or kneading of parts of the body to aid circulation or relax the muscles. **—mas·sage′** *v.*

Mas·sa·soit (măs′ə-soit′) (1580?–1661) ▸ Wampanoag leader.

mas·seur (mă-sûr′, mə-) ▸ *n.* A man who gives massages professionally.

mas·seuse (mă-sœz′) ▸ *n.* A woman who gives massages professionally.

mas·sive (măs′ĭv) ▸ *adj.* **1.** Consisting of or making up a large mass. **2.** Imposing, as in quantity or scale. **—mas′sive·ly** *adv.*

mass-mar·ket (măs′mär′kĭt) ▸ *adj.* Of or produced for consumption by large numbers of people.

mass medium ▸ *n., pl.* **mass media.** A means of public communication reaching a large audience.

mass number ▸ *n.* The sum of the number of neutrons and protons in an atomic nucleus.

mass-pro·duce (măs′prə-do͞os′, -dyo͞os′) ▸ *v.* To manufacture in large quantities, often by or as if by assembly-line techniques. **—mass production** *n.*

mast (măst) ▸ *n.* **1.** A tall vertical spar that rises from the keel of a sailing vessel to support the sails and rigging. **2.** A vertical pole.

mas·tec·to·my (mă-stĕk′tə-mē) ▸ *n., pl.* **-mies.** Surgical removal of all or part of a breast.

mas·ter (măs′tər) ▸ *n.* **1.** One having control or authority over another or others. **2.** The captain of a merchant ship. **3.** A male teacher or tutor. **4.** One who holds a master's degree. **5.** An artist or performer of great skill. **6.** An expert. **7. Master** Used as a courtesy title for a boy not considered old enough to be addressed as Mister. **8.** An original audio recording from which copies can be made. ▸ *v.* **1.** To make oneself a master of: *master a language.* **2.** To overcome or defeat.

master chief petty officer ▸ *n.* The highest noncommissioned rank in the US Navy or Coast Guard.

mas·ter·ful (măs′tər-fəl) ▸ *adj.* **1.** Domineering; imperious. **2.** Skillful; expert. **—mas′ter·ful·ly** *adv.* **—mas′ter·ful·ness** *n.*

master gunnery sergeant ▸ *n.* A rank in the US Marine Corps equivalent to sergeant major.

master key ▸ *n.* A key that opens every one of a set of locks.

mas·ter·ly (măs′tər-lē) ▸ *adj.* Showing the knowledge or skill of a master. ▸ *adv.* With the skill of a master. **—mas′ter·li·ness** *n.*

mas·ter·mind (măs′tər-mīnd′) ▸ *n.* One who plans and directs a difficult project. **—mas′ter·mind′** *v.*

master of ceremonies ▸ *n., pl.* **masters of ceremonies.** One who acts as host at a formal event or program of varied entertainment.

mas·ter·piece (măs′tər-pēs′) ▸ *n.* **1.** An outstanding work of art or craft. **2.** Something superlative of its kind.

mas·ter's degree (măs′tərz) ▸ *n.* An academic degree conferred upon those who complete at least one year of study beyond the bachelor's degree.

master sergeant ▸ *n.* **1.** A rank in the US Army and Marine Corps below sergeant major. **2.** A rank in the US Air Force below senior master sergeant.

mas·ter·stroke (măs′tər-strōk′) ▸ *n.* A masterly achievement or action.

mas·ter·work (măs′tər-wûrk′) ▸ *n.* A masterpiece.

mas·ter·y (măs′tə-rē) ▸ *n., pl.* **-ies. 1.** Possession of consummate skill. **2.** The status of master. **3.** Full command of a subject.

mast·head (măst′hĕd′) ▸ *n.* **1.** The top of a ship's mast. **2.** The listing in a newspaper or periodical of information about its staff, operation, and circulation.

mas·tic (măs′tĭk) ▸ *n.* A pastelike cement, esp. one made with powdered lime or brick and tar.

mas·ti·cate (măs′tĭ-kāt′) ▸ *v.* **-cat·ed, -cat·ing.** To chew. **—mas′ti·ca′tion** *n.*

mas·tiff (măs′tĭf) ▸ *n.* A large dog with a short brownish coat.

THESAURUS

mask *v.* —*See* CONCEAL, DISGUISE.

masquerade *n.* —*See* ACT (2), CHEAT (1), DANCE, DISGUISE, FAÇADE (2).

masquerade *v.* —*See* DISGUISE, IMPERSONATE.

masquerader *n.* —*See* CHEAT (2).

mass *n.* The greatest part or portion ▸ bulk, preponderance, preponderancy, weight. [*Compare* CENTER.] —*See also* ABUNDANCE, ACCUMULATION (1), BULK (1), CROWD, HEAP (1), HEAVINESS, OBJECT (1).

mass *v.* —*See* ACCUMULATE.

massacre *n.* The savage killing of many victims ▸ bloodbath, bloodletting, bloodshed, butchering, butchery, carnage, decimation, genocide, holocaust, liquidation, mass murder, slaughter. [*Compare* MURDER.]

massacre *v.* To kill savagely and in discriminately ▸ annihilate, butcher, decimate, kill off, slaughter, wipe out. [*Compare* KILL.] —*See also* OVERWHELM (1).

massage *v.* —*See* BIAS (2), RUB.

masses *n.* —*See* COMMONALTY.

massive *adj.* —*See* BULKY (1), ENORMOUS, HEAVY (1).

massiveness *n.* —*See* HEAVINESS.

massy *adj.* —*See* ENORMOUS.

master *n.* —*See* CHIEF, CONQUEROR, EDUCATOR, EXPERT, ORIGINAL, OWNER.

master *adj.* —*See* EXPERT.

master *v.* —*See* DEFEAT, DOMESTICATE, GENTLE, LEARN (1).

masterful *adj.* Exercising authority ▸ authoritative, commanding, dominant, lordly. [*Compare* ADMINISTRATIVE.] —*See also* DICTATORIAL, EXPERT.

masterly *adj.* —*See* EXPERT.

mastermind *n.* —*See* MIND (2).

masterpiece or **masterwork** *n.* An outstanding and ingenious work ▸ chef-d'oeuvre, magnum opus. [*Compare* ACCOMPLISHMENT, COMPOSITION, TREASURE.]

masterstroke *n.* —*See* ACCOMPLISHMENT.

mastery *n.* —*See* ABILITY (1), AUTHORITY, DOMINATION.

masticate *v.* —*See* CHEW.

mas·ti·tis (mă-stī′tĭs) ▸ *n.* Inflammation of the breast or udder.

mas·to·don (măs′tə-dŏn′) ▸ *n.* An extinct elephantlike mammal.

mas·toid (măs′toid′) ▸ *n.* The mastoid process.

mastoid process ▸ *n.* The rear portion of the temporal bone behind the ear.

mas·tur·bate (măs′tər-bāt′) ▸ *v.* **-bat·ed, -bat·ing.** To excite one's own or another's genitals by means other than intercourse. **—mas′tur·ba′tion** *n.* **—mas′tur·ba′tor** *n.* **—mas′tur·ba·to′ry** *adj.*

mat[1] (măt) ▸ *n.* **1.** A flat piece of material used as a floor covering. **2.** A floor pad to protect athletes, as in wrestling. **3.** A thickly tangled mass. ▸ *v.* **mat·ted, mat·ting.** **1.** To cover or protect with a mat. **2.** To form into a tangled mass.

mat[2] (măt) ▸ *n.* **1.** A border placed around a picture to serve as a frame or provide contrast between the picture and the frame. **2.** also **matte** A dull, often rough finish, as of paint, glass, or paper. ▸ *adj.* also **matte** Having a dull finish. **—mat** *v.*

mat·a·dor (măt′ə-dôr′) ▸ *n.* A bullfighter who performs the final passes and kills the bull.

match[1] (măch) ▸ *n.* **1.** One equal or similar to another. **2.** A pair, each one of which harmonizes with the other. **3.** *Sports* A game or contest. **4.** A marriage or arrangement of marriage. ▸ *v.* **1.** To be or make similar or equal to. **2.** To harmonize with. **3.** To join in marriage. **4.** To place in competition with. **—match′er** *n.*

match[2] (măch) ▸ *n.* A narrow strip of flammable material coated on one end with a compound that ignites easily.

match·book (măch′bo͝ok′) ▸ *n.* A small cardboard folder containing safety matches.

match·less (măch′lĭs) ▸ *adj.* Having no equal.

match·lock (măch′lŏk′) ▸ *n.* A gunlock in which powder is ignited by a match.

match·mak·er (măch′mā′kər) ▸ *n.* **1.** One who arranges marriages. **2.** *Sports* One who arranges athletic competitions. **—match′mak′ing** *n.*

match·up (măch′ŭp′) ▸ *n.* The pairing of two people or things, as for athletic competition or for comparison.

mate[1] (māt) ▸ *n.* **1.** One of a matched pair: *the mate to this glove.* **2.** A spouse. **3.** Either of a pair of breeding animals. **4.** A close associate. **5.** A deck officer on a merchant ship ranking below the master. ▸ *v.* **mat·ed, mat·ing.** **1.** To join closely; pair. **2.** To unite in marriage. **3.** To pair for breeding.

mate[2] (māt) ▸ *n.* A checkmate. ▸ *v.* **mat·ed, mat·ing.** To checkmate.

ma·té (mä′tā, mä-tē′) ▸ *n.* A tealike beverage made from the leaves of a South American tree.

ma·te·ri·al (mə-tîr′ē-əl) ▸ *n.* **1.** The substance out of which a thing is or can be made. **2. materials** Tools or apparatus for the performance of a given task. **3.** Cloth; fabric. ▸ *adj.* **1.** Of or composed of matter. **2.** Of or affecting physical well-being. **3.** Of or concerned with the physical rather than the intellectual or spiritual. **4.** Relevant: *testimony material to the inquiry.* **—ma·te′ri·al·ly** *adv.*

ma·te·ri·al·ism (mə-tîr′ē-ə-lĭz′əm) ▸ *n.* **1.** *Philos.* The theory that physical matter is the only reality and that everything can be explained in terms of matter and physical phenomena. **2.** Excessive regard for worldly concerns. **—ma·te′ri·al·ist** *n.* **—ma·te′ri·al·is′tic** *adj.*

ma·te·ri·al·ize (mə-tîr′ē-ə-līz′) ▸ *v.* **-ized, -iz·ing.** **1.** To cause to become real or actual. **2.** To take physical form or shape. **3.** To appear, esp. suddenly. **—ma·te′ri·al·i·za′tion** *n.*

ma·te·ri·el or **ma·té·ri·el** (mə-tîr′ē-ĕl′) ▸ *n.* The equipment and supplies of a military force or other organization.

ma·ter·nal (mə-tûr′nəl) ▸ *adj.* **1.** Relating to or characteristic of a mother or motherhood; motherly. **2.** Inherited from or related through one's mother. **—ma·ter′nal·ism** *n.* **—ma·ter′nal·ly** *adv.*

ma·ter·ni·ty (mə-tûr′nĭ-tē) ▸ *n.* The state of being a mother; motherhood.

math (măth) ▸ *n.* Mathematics.

math·e·mat·ics (măth′ə-măt′ĭks) ▸ *n.* *(takes sing. v.)* The study of the measurement, properties, and relationships of quantities and sets, using numbers and symbols. **—math′e·mat′i·cal** *adj.* **—math′e·mat′i·cal·ly** *adv.* **—math′e·ma·ti′cian** (-mə-tĭsh′ən) *n.*

Math·er (mă*th*′ər). **Increase** (1639–1723) and **Cotton** (1663–1728) ▸ Amer. clerics and writers.

mat·i·nee or **mat·i·née** (măt′n-ā′) ▸ *n.* An entertainment, such as a dramatic performance or movie, given in the afternoon.

mat·ins (măt′nz) ▸ *n.* *(takes sing. or pl. v.)* *Eccles.* The office that formerly constituted the first of the seven canonical hours.

matri– ▸ *pref.* Mother; maternal: *matrilineal.*

ma·tri·arch (mā′trē-ärk′) ▸ *n.* **1.** A woman who rules a family, clan, or tribe. **2.** A leading or venerable woman. **—ma′tri·ar′chal, ma′tri·ar′chic** *adj.*

ma·tri·ar·chy (mā′trē-är′kē) ▸ *n., pl.* **-chies.** A social system in which the mother is head of the family.

mat·ri·cide (măt′rĭ-sīd′) ▸ *n.* **1.** The act of killing one's mother. **2.** One who kills one's mother. **—mat′ri·cid′al** *adj.*

ma·tric·u·late (mə-trĭk′yə-lāt′) ▸ *v.* **-lat·ed, -lat·ing.** To admit or be admitted into a group, esp. a college or university. **—ma·tric′u·la′tion** *n.*

mat·ri·lin·e·al (măt′rə-lĭn′ē-əl) ▸ *adj.* Based on or tracing ancestral descent through the maternal line. **—mat′ri·lin′e·al·ly** *adv.*

mat·ri·mo·ny (măt′rə-mō′nē) ▸ *n., pl.* **-nies.** The act or state of being married. **—mat′ri·mo′ni·al** *adj.*

ma·trix (mā′trĭks) ▸ *n., pl.* **ma·tri·ces** (mā′trĭ-sēz′, măt′rĭ-) or **ma·trix·es.** **1.** A situation or surrounding substance within which something else originates, develops, or is contained. **2.** A mold or die.

ma·tron (mā′trən) ▸ *n.* **1.** A married woman or widow, esp. a woman in middle age or older. **2.** A woman who acts as a supervisor in a public institution, such as a school or prison. **—ma′tron·li·ness** *n.* **—ma′tron·ly** *adv. & adj.*

THESAURUS

mastodonic *adj.* —*See* ENORMOUS.

mat[1] *v.* —*See* ENTANGLE.

mat[2] or **matte** *adj.* —*See* DULL (2).

match *n.* —*See* COMPETITION (2), COUPLE, MATE, PARALLEL, PEER[2].

match *v.* To do or make something equal to ▸ equal, meet, tie. —*See also* AGREE (1), EQUAL (1), LIKEN, OPPOSE, RESEMBLE, SUIT (1).

matched *adj.* Consisting of two identical or similar related things, parts, or elements ▸ double, dual, paired, twin. [*Compare* DOUBLE, EQUAL.]

matchless *adj.* —*See* UNIQUE.

matchlessness *n.* —*See* UNIQUENESS.

mate *n.* One of a matched pair of things ▸ companion, complement, counterpart, double, duplicate, fellow, match, twin. —*See also* ASSOCIATE (2), FRIEND, SPOUSE.

mate *v.* —*See* MARRY.

materfamilias *n.* —*See* MOTHER.

material *n.* **1.** That from which things are or can be made ▸ matter, medium, stuff, substance. ***Idiom:*** grist for one's mill. **2.** A person considered to have qualities suitable for a particular activity ▸ stuff, timber. [*Compare* COMER, POTENTIAL.] —*See also* OUTFIT.

material *adj.* Of or preoccupied with that which is material rather than spiritual or intellectual ▸ materialistic, sensual. [*Compare* EARTHLY, GREEDY, SUPERFICIAL.] —*See also* IMPORTANT, PHYSICAL, RELEVANT.

materialistic *adj.* Of or preoccupied with that which is material rather than spiritual or intellectual ▸ material, sensual. [*Compare* EARTHLY, GREEDY, SUPERFICIAL.]

materiality *n.* That which occupies space and can be perceived by the senses ▸ matter, substance. [*Compare* ELEMENT, OBJECT, THING.] —*See also* RELEVANCE.

materialization *n.* —*See* APPEARANCE (2), EMBODIMENT, FULFILLMENT (1).

materialize *v.* To make real or actual ▸ actualize, bring about, make happen, realize. ***Idioms:*** bring to pass, carry (*or* put) into effect. [*Compare* EFFECT, PRODUCE.] —*See also* APPEAR (1), EMBODY (1).

materiel or **matériel** *n.* —*See* OUTFIT.

matriarch *n.* —*See* MOTHER.

matrimonial *adj.* —*See* MARITAL.

matrimony *n.* —*See* MARRIAGE.

matrix *n.* A hollow device for shaping a fluid or plastic substance ▸ cast, form, mold.

matron of honor ► *n., pl.* **matrons of honor**. A married woman serving as chief attendant of the bride at a wedding.

matte (măt) ► *n.* Var. of **mat**[2] 2. ► *adj.* Var. of **mat**[2].

mat·ter (măt′ər) ► *n.* **1a.** Something that occupies space and can be perceived by the senses; a physical substance or the physical universe as a whole. **b.** *Phys.* Something that has mass and exists as a solid, liquid, or gas. **2.** A specific type of substance: *inorganic matter.* **3.** The substance of thought or expression. **4.** A subject of concern or action. **5.** Trouble or difficulty: *What's the matter?* **6.** An approximated quantity: *a matter of years.* **7.** Something that is printed or written. ► *v.* To be of importance. —*idioms:* **as a matter of fact** In fact; actually. **no matter** Regardless of.

Mat·ter·horn (măt′ər-hôrn′) ► A mountain, 4,481.1 m (14,692 ft), in the Pennine Alps on the Italian-Swiss border.

mat·ter-of-fact (măt′ər-əv-făkt′) ► *adj.* Relating or adhering to facts; literal. —**mat′ter-of-fact′ly** *adv.* —**mat′ter-of-fact′ness** *n.*

Mat·thew (măth′yo͞o) ► *n.* See **Bible** table in Appendix.

Matthew, Saint (1st cent. A.D.) ► One of the 12 Apostles and the traditionally accepted author of the first Gospel.

mat·ting (măt′ĭng) ► *n.* A coarse fabric used esp. for covering floors.

mat·tock (măt′ək) ► *n.* A digging tool with a flat blade set at right angles to the handle.

mat·tress (măt′rĭs) ► *n.* A pad of heavy cloth filled with soft material used as or on a bed.

ma·ture (mə-tyo͝or′, -to͝or′, -cho͝or′) ► *adj.* **-tur·er, -tur·est. 1.** Fully grown or developed. **2.** In a desired or final condition; ripe. **3.** Worked out fully by the mind; considered. **4.** Payable; due: *a mature bond.* ► *v.* **-tured, -tur·ing. 1.** To bring or come to full development; ripen. **2.** To become due. —**mat′u·ra′tion** (măch′ə-rā′shən) *n.* —**ma·ture′ly** *adv.* —**ma·tur′i·ty, ma·ture′ness** *n.*

mat·zo also **mat·zoh** (mät′sə, -sō) ► *n., pl.* **-zos** also **-zohs** (-səz, -səs, -sōs′). A brittle, flat piece of unleavened bread, eaten esp. during Passover.

maud·lin (môd′lĭn) ► *adj.* Effusively or tearfully sentimental.

Mau·i (mou′ē) ► An island of HI NW of Hawaii I.

maul (môl) ► *n.* A heavy, long-handled hammer used to drive stakes, piles, or wedges. ► *v.* **1.** To injure by or as if by beating. **2.** To handle roughly. —**maul′er** *n.*

Mau·na Ke·a (mou′nə kā′ə) ► An active volcano, about 4,208 m (13,796 ft), of N-central Hawaii I.

Mauna Lo·a (lō′ə) ► An active volcano, 4,172.4 m (13,680 ft), of S-central Hawaii I.

maun·der (môn′dər, män′-) ► *v.* **1.** To talk incoherently or aimlessly. **2.** To move or act aimlessly or vaguely.

Mau·ri·ta·ni·a (môr′ĭ-tā′nē-ə) ► A country of NW Africa bordering on the Atlantic. —**Mau′ri·ta′ni·an** *adj.* & *n.*

Mau·ri·tius (mô-rĭsh′əs, -ē-əs) ► An island country in the SW Indian Ocean. —**Mau·ri′tian** *adj.* & *n.*

mau·so·le·um (mô′sə-lē′əm, -zə-) ► *n., pl.* **-le·ums** or **-le·a** (-lē′ə). A large stately tomb or a building housing such a tomb or tombs.

mauve (mōv) ► *n.* A grayish to reddish purple. —**mauve** *adj.*

ma·ven (mā′vən) ► *n.* An expert.

mav·er·ick (măv′ər-ĭk, măv′rĭk) ► *n.* **1.** An unbranded range calf or colt. **2.** One that resists adherence to a group. —**mav′er·ick** *adj.*

maw (mô) ► *n.* **1.** The mouth or gullet of a voracious animal. **2.** The opening into something deemed insatiable.

mawk·ish (mô′kĭsh) ► *adj.* Excessively and objectionably sentimental. —**mawk′ish·ly** *adv.* —**mawk′ish·ness** *n.*

max. ► *abbr.* maximum

max·il·la (măk-sĭl′ə) ► *n., pl.* **-lae** (-ē) or **-las.** *Anat.* Either of two bones forming the upper jaw. —**max′il·lar′y** (-sə-lĕr′ē) *adj.* & *n.*

max·im (măk′sĭm) ► *n.* A succinct formulation of a fundamental principle or rule of conduct.

max·i·mal (măk′sə-məl) ► *adj.* Of or being a maximum. —**max′i·mal·ly** *adv.*

max·i·mize (măk′sə-mīz′) ► *v.* **-mized, -miz·ing.** To make as great as possible. —**max′i·mi·za′tion** *n.* —**max′i·miz′er** *n.*

max·i·mum (măk′sə-məm) ► *n., pl.* **-mums** or **-ma** (-mə). **1.** The greatest possible quantity, degree, or number. **2.** An upper limit permitted by law or other authority. ► *adj.* The greatest or highest possible or permitted.

Max·well (măks′wĕl′, -wəl), **James Clerk** (1831–79) ► British physicist.

may (mā) ► *aux.v., P.t.* **might** (mīt). **1.** To be allowed to: *May I go? Yes, you may.* **2.** Used to indicate possibility: *It may rain.* **3.** Used to express a fervent wish: *Long may he live!* **4.** Used to express contingency, purpose, or result in clauses introduced by *that* or *so that*: *displayed so that all may see.*

May ► *n.* The 5th month in the Gregorian calendar.

Ma·ya (mä′yə) ► *n., pl.* **-ya** or **-yas. 1.** A member of an American Indian people of SE Mexico, Guatemala, and Belize, whose civilization reached its height around A.D. 300–900. **2.** Any of the Mayan languages.

Ma·yan (mä′yən) ► *adj.* **1.** Of or relating to the Maya. **2.** Of the Mayan linguistic stock. ► *n.* **1.** A Maya. **2.** A linguistic stock of Central America that includes Maya.

May apple ► *n.* A North American plant having a single white flower, oval yellow fruit, and poisonous roots, leaves, and seeds.

may·be (mā′bē) ► *adv.* Perhaps; possibly.

may·day (mā′dā′) ► *n.* An international radiotelephone signal word used by aircraft and ships in distress.

May Day ► *n.* **1.** May 1, a traditional holiday in celebration of spring. **2.** May 1, a holiday in some countries in honor of labor.

may·flow·er (mā′flou′ər) ► *n.* Any of various plants that bloom in May, esp. the trailing arbutus.

may·fly (mā′flī′) ► *n.* A winged insect that lives in the adult stage for only a few days.

may·hem (mā′hĕm′, mā′əm) ► *n.* **1.** *Law* The crime of willfully maiming or crippling a person. **2.** Infliction of wanton

THESAURUS

matter *n.* **1.** Something that occupies space and that can be perceived by the senses ► materiality, substance. [*Compare* ELEMENT, OBJECT, THING.] **2.** Something that is to be done, considered, or dealt with ► affair, business, thing. [*Compare* BUSINESS, TASK.] —*See also* MATERIAL (1), PROBLEM, SUBJECT.

matter *v.* —*See* COUNT (1).

matter-of-fact *adj.* —*See* COLD (2), DULL (1), REALISTIC (1).

maturate *v.* —*See* MATURE.

maturation *n.* —*See* DEVELOPMENT.

mature *adj.* Having reached full growth and development ► adult, advanced, big, developed, evolved, full-blown, full-fledged, full-grown, full-size, grown, grown-up, matured, older, ripe. *Idioms:* in full bloom, in one's prime, of age. [*Compare* AGED.] —*See also* DUE (1), OLD (2).

mature *v.* To bring or come to full development ► age, develop, grow (up), maturate, mellow, ripen. *Idioms:* come of age, reach adulthood. [*Compare* AGE.]

maturity *n.* —*See* AGE (1).

maudlin *adj.* —*See* SENTIMENTAL.

maudlinism *n.* *See* SENTIMENTALITY.

maul *v.* —*See* BATTER, BEAT (1).

maunder *n.* —*See* DIGRESS.

maunder *v.* —*See* MUTTER.

mausoleum *n.* —*See* GRAVE[1].

maven *n.* —*See* EXPERT.

maverick *n.* —*See* REBEL (2).

maw *n.* —*See* MOUTH (1).

mawkish *adj.* —*See* SENTIMENTAL.

mawkishness *n.* —*See* SENTIMENTALITY.

maxim *n.* —*See* LAW (3), MORAL, PROVERB.

maximal *adj.* —*See* MAXIMUM.

maximum *n.* The greatest quantity or highest degree attainable ► outside, top, ultimate, utmost, uttermost. *Slang:* max. *Idioms:* the last word, ne plus ultra. [*Compare* CLIMAX.] —*See also* LIMIT (1).

maximum *adj.* Greatest in quantity or highest in degree that can be attained ► extreme, greatest, highest, maximal, peak, top, topmost, transcendent, ultimate, unsurpassable, utmost, uttermost. *Slang:* max, tops. [*Compare* BEST.]

maybe or **mayhap** *adv.* Possibly but not certainly ► conceivably, feasibly, perchance, perhaps, possibly. [*Compare* PROBABLY.]

destruction. 3. A state of violent disorder or riotous confusion; havoc.

may·n't (mā′ənt, mānt) ▸ May not.

may·on·naise (mā′ə-nāz′, mā′ə-nāz′) ▸ *n.* A dressing made of egg yolk, oil, lemon juice or vinegar, and seasonings.

may·or (mā′ər, mâr) ▸ *n.* The head of government of a city, town, or borough. **—may′or·al** *adj.* **—may′or·al·ty** *n.* **—may′or·ship′** *n.*

May·pole also **may·pole** (mā′pōl′) ▸ *n.* A pole decorated with streamers that May Day celebrants hold while dancing.

maze (māz) ▸ *n.* 1. An intricate, usu. confusing network of interconnecting pathways, as in a garden; labyrinth. 2. Something made up of many confused or conflicting elements; tangle.

ma·zur·ka (mə-zûr′kə, -zŏŏr′-) ▸ *n.* 1. A lively Polish dance. 2. Music for a mazurka.

MB ▸ *abbr.* 1. Manitoba 2. megabyte

MBA ▸ *abbr.* Master of Business Administration

MC (ĕm′sē′) ▸ *n.* A master of ceremonies.

Mc·Clel·lan (mə-klĕl′ən), **George Brinton** (1826–85) ▸ Amer. Union general.

Mc·Cor·mick (mə-kôr′mĭk), **Cyrus Hall** (1809–84) ▸ Amer. inventor.

Mc·Kin·ley (mə-kĭn′lē), **Mount.** Also **De·na·li** (də-nä′lē) ▸ The highest mountain in North America, rising to 6,197.6 m (20,320 ft) in the Alaska Range of S-central AK.

McKinley, William (1843–1901) ▸ The 25th US President (1897–1901); assassinated.

Md ▸ The symbol for the element **mendelevium.**

MD ▸ *abbr.* 1. also **Md.** Maryland 2. *Lat.* Medicinae Doctor (Doctor of Medicine) 3. muscular distrophy

Mdm. ▸ *abbr.* Madam

me (mē) ▸ *pron. The objective case of* **I.** Used as: **a.** The direct object of a verb: *He saw me.* **b.** The indirect object of a verb: *They gave me a ride.* **c.** The object of a preposition: *It's for me.*

ME ▸ *abbr.* 1. also **Me.** Maine 2. Middle English

mead (mēd) ▸ *n.* An alcoholic beverage made from fermented honey.

Mead, Margaret (1901–78) ▸ Amer. anthropologist.

mead·ow (mĕd′ō) ▸ *n.* A tract of grassland used as pasture or for growing hay. **—mead′ow·y** *adj.*

mead·ow·lark (mĕd′ō-lärk′) ▸ *n.* A North American songbird having brownish plumage and a yellow breast.

mea·ger also **mea·gre** (mē′gər) ▸ *adj.* 1. Deficient in quantity, fullness, or extent. 2. Thin; lean. **—mea′ger·ly** *adv.* **—mea′ger·ness** *n.*

meal¹ (mēl) ▸ *n.* 1. Coarsely ground edible grain. 2. Any granular substance. **—meal′i·ness** *n.* **—meal′y** *adj.*

meal² (mēl) ▸ *n.* The food served and eaten in one sitting.

meal·time (mēl′tīm′) ▸ *n.* The usual time for eating a meal.

meal·y-mouthed (mē′lē-mouthd′, -moutht′) ▸ *adj.* Unwilling to speak simply and directly.

mean¹ (mēn) ▸ *v.* **meant** (mĕnt), **mean·ing.** 1a. To be defined as; denote. **b.** To act as a symbol of; represent. 2. To intend to convey or indicate. 3. To have as a consequence: *Friction means heat.* 4. To be of a specified importance: *She meant so much to me.*

mean² (mēn) ▸ *adj.* **-er, -est.** 1. Spiteful and petty; unkind. 2. Ignoble; base. 3. Miserly. 4a. Low in quality or grade. **b.** Low in value or amount. 5. Low in social status. 6. *Informal* Ill-tempered. 7. *Slang* Hard to cope with. **—mean′ly** *adv.* **—mean′ness** *n.*

mean³ (mēn) ▸ *n.* 1. Something midway between extremes; a medium. 2. *Math.* The average value of a set of numbers. 3. **means** *(takes sing. or pl. v.)* A course of action or instrument by which an end can be achieved. 4. **means** *(takes pl. v.)* Money, property, or other wealth. ▸ *adj.* Occupying a middle position between two extremes. ***—idioms:* by all means** Without fail; certainly. **by no means** In no sense; certainly not.

me·an·der (mē-ăn′dər) ▸ *v.* 1. To follow a winding and turning course. 2. To move aimlessly and idly. ▸ *n.* **meanders** Circuitous windings, as of a stream or path.

mean·ing (mē′nĭng) ▸ *n.* 1. Something signified; sense. 2. Something one wishes to convey, esp. by language. 3. Intent; end. **—mean′ing·ful** *adj.* **—mean′ing·ful·ly** *adv.* **—mean′ing·less** *adj.*

mean·time (mēn′tīm′) ▸ *n.* The time between two occurrences. ▸ *adv.* Meanwhile.

mean·while (mēn′hwīl′, -wīl′) ▸ *n.* The intervening time. ▸ *adv.* In the intervening time.

mea·sles (mē′zəlz) ▸ *n. (takes sing. or pl. v.)* 1. An acute, contagious viral disease, marked by red spots on the skin, fever, and coughing. 2. Any of several milder diseases similar to measles.

mea·sly (mēz′lē) ▸ *adj.* **-sli·er, -sli·est.** *Slang* Contemptibly small: *a measly tip.*

meas·ure (mĕzh′ər) ▸ *n.* 1. Dimensions, quantity, or capacity ascertained by a standard. 2. A reference used for the quantitative comparison of properties. 3. A unit specified by a scale, such as an inch, or by variable conditions, such as a day's march. 4. A device used for measuring. 5. The act of measuring. 6. A basis of comparison. 7. Extent or degree. 8. A limited amount or degree. 9. often **measures** An action taken as a means to an end. 10. A legislative bill or enactment. 11. Poetic meter. 12. *Mus.* The metric unit between two bars on the staff; bar. ▸ *v.* **-ured, -ur·ing.** 1. To ascertain the dimensions, quantity, or capacity of. 2. To lay out dimensions by measuring: *measure off an area.* 3. To compare: *measured our strength against theirs.* 4. To consider or choose with care; weigh: *He measures his words.* ***—phrasal verb:* measure up** 1. To be the equal of. 2. To have the necessary qualifications. ***—idiom:* for good measure** In addition to

THESAURUS

maze *n.* —*See* TANGLE.

maze *v.* —*See* DAZE (1).

mea culpa *n.* A statement of acknowledgment expressing regret or asking pardon ▸ apology, excuse, regrets. [*Compare* ACKNOWLEDGMENT.]

meadow *n.* ▸ clearing, field, pasture. [*Compare* LOT.]

meager *adj.* Conspicuously deficient in quantity, fullness, or extent ▸ exiguous, insubstantial, poor, puny, scant, scanty, scrimpy, skimpy, spare, sparse, spartan, stingy, thin. *Slang:* measly. *Idioms:* in short supply, scraping the bottom of the barrel. [*Compare* INSUFFICIENT, LITTLE, TRIVIAL.] —*See also* THIN (1).

mean¹ *v.* To have or convey a particular idea ▸ connote, convey, denote, import, intend, indicate, signify, spell. *Idioms:* add up to, come down to. [*Compare* COMMUNICATE, IMPLY, REPRESENT.] —*See also* INTEND.

mean² *adj.* Of little distinction ▸ humble, lowly, simple. [*Compare* MODEST.] —*See also* BAD (1), ILL-TEMPERED, LOWLY (1), MALEVOLENT, OFFENSIVE (1), SORDID, STINGY, TROUBLESOME (2).

mean³ *n.* —*See* AVERAGE.

mean *adj.* —*See* MIDDLE.

meander *v.* —*See* ROVE, WIND².

meandering *adj.* —*See* DIGRESSIVE, INDIRECT (1), WINDING.

meaning *n.* Something that is conveyed or signified ▸ acceptation, connotation, denotation, import, intent, message, point, purport, sense, significance, significancy, signification, value. [*Compare* FEELING, IDEA, IMPORT, THRUST.] —*See also* INTENTION.

meaning *adj.* —*See* EXPRESSIVE.

meaningful *adj.* —*See* EXPRESSIVE, IMPORTANT, PREGNANT (2).

meaningless *adj.* —*See* MINDLESS.

meaninglessness *n.* —*See* EMPTINESS (2).

meanness *n.* —*See* MALEVOLENCE, TEMPER (1).

means *n.* —*See* AGENT, APPROACH (1), RESOURCES.

measly *adj.* —*See* MEAGER, TRIVIAL.

measure *v.* To ascertain the dimensions, quantity, or capacity of ▸ gauge, quantify, quantitate. *Idiom:* take the dimensions (*or* measure) of. [*Compare* ESTIMATE.] —*See also* DETERMINE.

measure out *v.* —*See* DISTRIBUTE.

measure up *v.* —*See* EQUAL (1).

measure *n.* 1. The act or process of ascertaining dimensions, quantity, or capacity ▸ determination, measurement, mensuration, quantification. [*Compare* COMPUTATION, ESTIMATION.] 2. An action calculated to achieve an end ▸ maneuver, move, procedure, step, tactic. —*See also* ALLOTMENT, DEGREE (2),

the required amount. **—meas′ur·a·ble** *adj.* **—meas′ur·a·bly** *adv.* **—meas′ure·ment** *n.* **—meas′ur·er** *n.*

meas·ure·ment (mĕzh′ər-mənt) ▸ *n.* **1.** The act of measuring or the process of being measured. **2.** A system of measuring: *measurement in miles.* See **measurement** table in Appendix on pages 848–849. **3.** The dimension, quantity, or capacity determined by measuring.

meat (mēt) ▸ *n.* **1.** The edible flesh of animals, esp. mammals. **2.** The edible part, as of a piece of fruit. **3.** The essence, substance, or gist: *the meat of the editorial.* **4.** Food. **—meat′i·ness** *n.* **—meat′y** *adj.*

meat·ball (mēt′bôl′) ▸ *n.* **1.** A ball of cooked ground meat. **2.** *Slang* A stupid person.

mec·ca (mĕk′ə) ▸ *n.* A center of interest or attraction: *a mecca for tourists.*

Mecca ▸ A city of W Saudi Arabia near the coast of the Red Sea; birthplace of Muhammad.

me·chan·ic (mĭ-kăn′ĭk) ▸ *n.* A worker skilled in making, using, or repairing machines.

me·chan·i·cal (mĭ-kăn′ĭ-kəl) ▸ *adj.* **1.** Of or relating to machines or tools. **2.** Operated or produced by a machine. **3.** Of or relating to mechanics. **4.** Performed in a machinelike manner; automatic: *a mechanical task.* **—me·chan′i·cal·ly** *adv.*

mechanical drawing ▸ *n.* **1.** Drafting. **2.** A drawing that enables measurements to be interpreted.

me·chan·ics (mĭ-kăn′ĭks) ▸ *n.* **1.** *(takes sing. v.)* The branch of physics concerned with the analysis of the action of forces on matter or material systems. **2.** *(takes sing. or pl. v.)* Design, construction, and use of machinery or mechanical structures. **3.** *(takes pl. v.)* The functional and technical aspects of an activity: *the mechanics of football.*

mech·a·nism (mĕk′ə-nĭz′əm) ▸ *n.* **1a.** A machine or mechanical appliance. **b.** The arrangement of connected parts in a machine. **2.** A system of parts that operate or interact like those of a machine. **3.** A means or process by which something is done or comes into being. **4.** *Philos.* The doctrine that all natural phenomena are explicable by material causes and mechanical principles.

mech·a·nis·tic (mĕk′ə-nĭs′tĭk) ▸ *adj.* **1.** *Philos.* Of or relating to the philosophy of mechanism. **2.** Automatic and impersonal. **—mech′a·nis′ti·cal·ly** *adv.*

mech·a·nize (mĕk′ə-nīz′) ▸ *v.* **-nized, -niz·ing.** **1.** To equip with machinery. **2.** To make automatic or routine. **—mech′a·ni·za′tion** *n.*

med·al (mĕd′l) ▸ *n.* **1.** A flat piece of metal stamped with a design commemorating an event or person, often given as an award. **2.** A piece of metal stamped with a religious device.

med·al·ist (mĕd′l-ĭst) ▸ *n.* **1.** A recipient of a medal. **2.** One who designs medals.

me·dal·lion (mĭ-dăl′yən) ▸ *n.* **1.** A large medal. **2.** An emblem of registration for a taxicab. **3.** Something resembling a large medal.

med·dle (mĕd′l) ▸ *v.* **-dled, -dling.** To intrude into other people's affairs. **—med′dler** *n.* **—med′dle·some** *adj.*

Mede (mēd) ▸ *n.* A member of an Iranian people inhabiting ancient Media.

med·e·vac (mĕd′ĭ-văk′) ▸ *n.* Air transport of persons to a place where they can receive medical care.

me·di·a (mē′dē-ə) ▸ *n.* Pl. of **medium.**

me·di·ae·val (mē′dē-ē′vəl, mĕd′ē-) ▸ *adj.* Var. of **medieval.**

me·di·al (mē′dē-əl) ▸ *adj.* Of or situated in the middle; median. **—me′di·al·ly** *adv.*

me·di·an (mē′dē-ən) ▸ *adj.* **1.** Of or located in the middle. **2.** *Statistics* Of or being the middle value in a distribution. ▸ *n.* **1a.** A median point, plane, line, or part. **b.** See **median strip.** **2.** *Statistics* The middle value in a distribution, above and below which lie an equal number of values. **3.** *Math.* A line that joins a vertex of a triangle to the midpoint of the opposite side.

median strip ▸ *n.* A paved or landscaped strip that divides opposing traffic lanes of a highway.

me·di·ate (mē′dē-āt′) ▸ *v.* **-at·ed, -at·ing.** **1.** To resolve or seek to resolve (differences) by working with all conflicting parties. **2.** To act as intermediary. **—me′di·a′tion** *n.* **—me′di·a′tor** *n.*

med·ic (mĕd′ĭk) ▸ *n.* **1.** A member of a military medical corps. **2.** A physician or surgeon.

Med·i·caid also **med·i·caid** (mĕd′ĭ-kād′) ▸ *n.* A US government program that pays for medical care for people who cannot finance their own medical expenses.

med·i·cal (mĕd′ĭ-kəl) ▸ *adj.* Of or relating to the study or practice of medicine. **—med′i·cal·ly** *adv.*

me·dic·a·ment (mĭ-dĭk′ə-mənt, mĕd′ĭ-kə-) ▸ *n.* A medicine.

Med·i·care also **med·i·care** (mĕd′ĭ-kâr′) ▸ *n.* A US government program that pays for medical care for people over 65.

med·i·cate (mĕd′ĭ-kāt′) ▸ *v.* **-cat·ed, -cat·ing.** **1.** To treat with medicine. **2.** To add a medicinal substance to.

med·i·ca·tion (mĕd′ĭ-kā′shən) ▸ *n.* **1.** A medicine. **2.** The act of medicating.

med·i·cine (mĕd′ĭ-sĭn) ▸ *n.* **1a.** The science of diagnosing, treating, or preventing disease or bodily injury. **b.** The branch of this science encompassing treatment by means other than surgery. **2.** An agent used to treat disease. **3.** Something serving as a remedy or corrective. **4.** Shamanistic practices or beliefs. **—me·di′ci·nal** (mĭ-dĭs′ə-nəl) *adj.* **—me·di′ci·nal·ly** *adv.*

medicine man ▸ *n.* A male shaman, esp. among Native American peoples.

medicine woman ▸ *n.* A female shaman, esp. among Native American peoples.

med·i·co (mĕd′ĭ-kō′) ▸ *n., pl.* **-cos.** *Informal* A doctor or medical student.

me·di·e·val also **me·di·ae·val** (mē′dē-ē′vəl, mĕd′ē-, mĭ-dē′vəl) ▸ *adj.* **1.** Of or belonging to the Middle Ages. **2.** *Informal* Old-fashioned. **—me′di·e′val·ist** *n.* **—me′di·e′val·ly** *adv.*

Medieval Greek ▸ *n.* The Greek language from about 800 to about 1500.

Medieval Latin ▸ *n.* The Latin language from about 700 to about 1500.

me·di·o·cre (mē′dē-ō′kər) ▸ *adj.* Moderate to inferior in quality; ordinary. **—me′di·oc′ri·ty** (-ŏk′rĭ-tē) *n.*

med·i·tate (mĕd′ĭ-tāt′) ▸ *v.* **-tat·ed, -tat·ing.** **1.** To reflect on; contemplate. **2a.** *Buddhism & Hinduism* To train or empty the mind, as by focusing on one object. **b.** To engage in

THESAURUS

LAW (2), MODERATION, QUANTITY (2), RHYTHM, SIZE (1), STANDARD.

measured *adj.* *—See* DELIBERATE (3), RHYTHMICAL.

measureless *adj.* *—See* ENDLESS (1), INFINITE.

measurelessness *n.* *—See* INFINITY (1).

measurement *n.* The act or process of ascertaining dimensions, quantity, or capacity ▸ determination, measure, mensuration, quantification. [*Compare* CALCULATION, ESTIMATION.]

measurements *n.* *—See* SIZE (1).

meat *n.* *—See* FOOD, HEART (1).

meatball or **meathead** *n.* *—See* OAF.

mechanical *adj.* *—See* PERFUNCTORY.

mechanism *n.* *—See* AGENT, DEVICE (1).

medal *n.* *—See* DECORATION, DISTINCTION (2).

medalist *n.* *—See* WINNER.

meddle *v.* To intervene officiously or indiscreetly in the affairs of others ▸ butt in, horn in, interfere, interlope, intermeddle, obtrude. *Informal* kibitz. *Idioms:* poke one's nose in, stick one's nose in, stick one's oar in. [*Compare* INTERRUPT, SNOOP.] *—See also* TINKER.

meddler *n.* *—See* BUSYBODY.

meddling *n.* The act or an instance of interfering or intruding ▸ interference, interfering, interrupting, intervention, intruding, intrusion, obtrusion, prying, snooping.

meddling or **meddlesome** *adj.* *—See* CURIOUS (1).

media *n.* *—See* PRESS.

median *n.* *—See* AVERAGE, CENTER (2).

median or **medial** *adj.* *—See* CENTRAL, MIDDLE.

mediate *v.* To intervene between disputants in order to bring about an agreement ▸ arbitrate, moderate. [*Compare* CONFER, JUDGE.] *—See also* CONDUCT (3).

mediation *n.* *—See* COMPROMISE.

mediator *n.* *—See* GO-BETWEEN.

medicament *n.* *—See* CURE, DRUG (1).

medicate *v.* *—See* ADMINISTER (3), DRUG (1).

medication *n.* *—See* CURE, DRUG (1).

medicinal *adj.* *—See* CURATIVE.

medicine *n.* *—See* CURE, DRUG (1).

mediocre *adj.* *—See* AVERAGE, BAD (1), ORDINARY.

mediocrity *n.* *—See* DULLNESS.

meditate *v.* *—See* PONDER.

prayer. **—med′i·ta′tion** *n.* **—med′i·ta′tion·al** *adj.* **—med′i·ta′tive** *adj.* **—med′i·ta′tive·ly** *adv.* **—med′i·ta′tor** *n.*

Med·i·ter·ra·ne·an (mĕd′ĭ-tə-rā′nē-ən) ▸ The region surrounding the Mediterranean Sea. **—Med′i·ter·ra′ne·an** *adj. & n.*

Mediterranean fruit fly ▸ *n.* A black and white two-winged fly, the larvae of which destroy fruit crops.

Mediterranean Sea ▸ An inland sea surrounded by Europe, Asia, Asia Minor, the Near East, and Africa.

me·di·um (mē′dē-əm) ▸ *n., pl.* **-di·a** (-dē-ə) or **-di·ums. 1.** A position, condition, or course of action midway between extremes. **2.** An intervening substance through which something else is transmitted or carried on. **3.** An agency by which something is accomplished, conveyed, or transferred. **4.** *pl.* **media.** A means of mass communication. **5.** *pl.* **mediums.** A person thought to have the power to communicate with the spirits of the dead. **6.** *pl.* **media.** An environment in which something functions and thrives. **7.** A means of expression as determined by the materials or the creative methods involved. ▸ *adj.* Midway between extremes; intermediate: *broil a medium steak.*

med·ley (mĕd′lē) ▸ *n., pl.* **-leys. 1.** A jumbled assortment. **2.** A musical arrangement of several melodies.

me·dul·la (mĭ-dŭl′ə) ▸ *n., pl.* **-las** or **-dul·lae** (-dŭl′ē). **1.** The inner core of certain organs or body structures, such as the marrow of bone. **2.** The medulla oblongata. **—me·dul′lar, med′ul·lar′y** (mĕd′l-ĕr′ē, mə-dŭl′ə-rē) *adj.*

medulla ob·lon·ga·ta (ŏb′lông-gä′tə) ▸ *n., pl.* **-tas** or **medullae ob·lon·ga·tae** (-tē). The lowermost portion of the vertebrate brain that controls respiration, circulation, and certain other bodily functions.

meek (mēk) ▸ *adj.* **-er, -est. 1.** Showing patience and humility. **2.** Submissive; passive. **—meek′ly** *adv.* **—meek′ness** *n.*

meer·kat (mîr′kăt′) ▸ *n.* An African burrowing mammal that is related to the mongoose, and has grayish fur and a long tail.

meer·schaum (mîr′shəm, -shôm′) ▸ *n.* **1.** A claylike mineral used esp. to make tobacco pipes. **2.** A pipe made of meerschaum.

meet[1] (mēt) ▸ *v.* **met** (mĕt), **meet·ing. 1.** To come upon. **2.** To be present at the arrival of: *met the train.* **3.** To be introduced to. **4.** To come into conjunction with. **5.** To come into the company of, as for a conference. **6.** To come to the notice of: *more than meets the eye.* **7.** To cope effectively with. **8.** To fulfill. **9.** To come together: *Let's meet tonight.* ▸ *n.* A meeting or contest.

meet[2] (mēt) ▸ *adj.* Fitting; proper. **—meet′ly** *adv.*

meet·ing (mē′tĭng) ▸ *n.* **1.** A coming together. **2.** An assembly or gathering.

mega– ▸ *pref.* **1.** Large: *megalith.* **2.** One million (10^6): *megaton.*

meg·a·byte (mĕg′ə-bīt′) ▸ *n.* A unit of computer memory equal to 1,048,576 (2^{20}) bytes.

meg·a·cy·cle (mĕg′ə-sī′kəl) ▸ *n.* See **megahertz.**

meg·a·fau·na (mĕg′ə-fô′nə) ▸ *n. (takes sing. or pl. v.)* Large animals, as of a particular period, considered as a group.

meg·a·hertz (mĕg′ə-hûrts′) ▸ *n.* One million cycles per second.

meg·a·lith (mĕg′ə-lĭth′) ▸ *n.* A very large stone used in various prehistoric structures or monuments. **—meg′a·lith′ic** *adj.*

megalo– ▸ *pref.* Exaggeratedly large: *megalomania.*

meg·a·lo·ma·ni·a (mĕg′ə-lō-mā′nē-ə, -mān′yə) ▸ *n.* A mental disorder characterized by delusions of wealth, power, or omnipotence. **—meg′a·lo·ma′ni·ac′** *n.*

meg·a·lop·o·lis (mĕg′ə-lŏp′ə-lĭs) ▸ *n.* **1.** A very large city. **2.** An urban complex made up of several large cities and their surrounding areas.

meg·a·phone (mĕg′ə-fōn′) ▸ *n.* A funnel-shaped device used to amplify the voice.

meg·a·ton (mĕg′ə-tŭn′) ▸ *n.* A unit of explosive force equal to that of one million metric tons of TNT. **—meg′a·ton′nage** (-tŭn′ĭj) *n.*

meg·a·vi·ta·min (mĕg′ə-vī′tə-mĭn) ▸ *n.* A dose of a vitamin greatly exceeding the amount required to maintain health.

meg·a·watt (mĕg′ə-wŏt′) ▸ *n.* One million watts. **—meg′a·watt′age** *n.*

mei·o·sis (mī-ō′sĭs) ▸ *n., pl.* **-ses** (-sēz′). Cell division in sexually reproducing organisms that reduces the number of chromosomes in reproductive cells. **—mei·ot′ic** (-ŏt′ĭk) *adj.* **—mei·ot′i·cal·ly** *adv.*

meit·ner·i·um (mīt-nûr′ē-əm) ▸ *n. Symbol* **Mt** A short-lived synthetic radioactive element. At. no. 109.

Me·kong (mā′kông′, -kŏng′) ▸ A river of SE Asia flowing about 4,183 km (2,600 mi) from SE China to the South China Sea through S Vietnam.

mel·an·cho·li·a (mĕl′ən-kō′lē-ə) ▸ *n.* A mental disorder marked by severe depression and apathy.

mel·an·chol·ic (mĕl′ən-kŏl′ĭk) ▸ *adj.* **1.** Affected with melancholy. **2.** Of or relating to melancholia. **—mel′an·chol′ic** *n.* **—mel′an·chol′i·cal·ly** *adv.*

mel·an·chol·y (mĕl′ən-kŏl′ē) ▸ *n.* **1.** Sadness; depression. **2.** Pensive reflection. ▸ *adj.* **1.** Gloomy; sad. **2.** Pensive; thoughtful.

Mel·a·ne·sia (mĕl′ə-nē′zhə, -shə) ▸ A division of Oceania in the SW Pacific comprising the islands NE of Australia and S of the equator.

Mel·a·ne·sian (mĕl′ə-nē′zhən, -shən) ▸ *adj.* Of Melanesia or its peoples, languages, or cultures. ▸ *n.* **1.** A native or inhabitant of Melanesia. **2.** A subfamily of the Austronesian languages spoken in Melanesia.

mé·lange also **me·lange** (mā-läNzh′) ▸ *n.* A mixture.

mel·a·nin (mĕl′ə-nĭn) ▸ *n.* A dark pigment found esp. in skin, hair, fur, and feathers.

mel·a·nism (mĕl′ə-nĭz′əm) ▸ *n.* **1.** See **melanosis. 2.** Dark coloration due to a high concentration of melanin. **—mel′a·nis′tic** *adj.*

melano– or **melan–** ▸ *pref.* Black; dark: *melanism.*

mel·a·no·ma (mĕl′ə-nō′mə) ▸ *n., pl.* **-mas** or **-ma·ta** (-mə-tə). A dark-pigmented malignant tumor usu. occurring in the skin.

mel·a·no·sis (mĕl′ə-nō′sĭs) ▸ *n.* Abnormally dark pigmentation resulting from a disorder of pigment metabolism. **—mel′a·not′ic** (-nŏt′ĭk) *adj.*

Mel·ba toast (mĕl′bə) ▸ *n.* Very thinly sliced crisp toast.

Mel·bourne (mĕl′bərn) ▸ A city of SE Australia SW of Canberra.

meld[1] (mĕld) ▸ *v.* To declare or display (a card or combination of cards) for inclusion in one's score in various card games. **—meld** *n.*

meld[2] (mĕld) ▸ *v.* To merge or become merged; blend.

me·lee (mā′lā′, mā-lā′) also **mê·lée** (mĕ-lā′) ▸ *n.* **1.** Confused, hand-to-hand fighting. **2.** A tumultuous mingling.

THESAURUS

meditation *n.* —*See* THOUGHT.

meditative *adj.* —*See* THOUGHTFUL.

medium *n.* —*See* AGENT, AVERAGE, ENVIRONMENT (2), MATERIAL (1).

medium *adj.* —*See* AVERAGE.

medley *n.* —*See* ASSORTMENT.

meek *adj.* Having or expressing feelings of humility ▸ humble, lowly, modest, unambitious. [*Compare* DEFERENTIAL.] —*See also* GENTLE (3).

meekness *n.* —*See* MODESTY (1).

meet[1] *v.* **1.** To come together face-to-face, especially defiantly ▸ confront, encounter, face, front. *Idiom:* stand up to. [*Compare* CONTEST, DEFY.] **2.** To come together by arrangement ▸ connect, hook up, meet up, get together, rendezvous. [*Compare* ASSEMBLE.] **3.** To come together from different directions ▸ close, converge, join, unite. [*Compare* COMBINE.] **4.** To do or make something equal to ▸ equal, match, tie. —*See also* ADJOIN, CONTEND, ENCOUNTER (1), EXPERIENCE, SATISFY (1).

meet *n.* —*See* COMPETITION (2).

meet[2] *adj.* —*See* CONVENIENT (1).

meeting *n.* —*See* ASSEMBLY, CONFRONTATION, CONVENTION, JUNCTION.

megalomania *n.* ▸ egoism, self-importance. *Informal:* big head. [*Compare* EGOTISM.]

megalomaniacal *adj.* —*See* DICTATORIAL.

megalopolis *n.* —*See* CITY.

megrim *n.* —*See* FANCY.

melancholic *adj.* —*See* DEPRESSED (1).

melancholy *n.* —*See* DEPRESSION (2).

melancholy *adj.* —*See* DEPRESSED (1), SORROWFUL.

mélange *n.* —*See* ASSORTMENT.

meld *v.* —*See* COMBINE (1).

melee *n.* —*See* DISORDER (2), FIGHT (1).

mel·io·rate (mēl′yə-rāt′, mē′lē-ə-) ▸ *v.* **-rat·ed, -rat·ing.** To make or become better; improve. **—mel′io·ra·ble** (-rə-bəl) *adj.* **—mel′io·ra′tion** *n.*

mel·lif·lu·ous (mə-lĭf′lo͞o-əs) ▸ *adj.* Flowing in a smooth or sweet manner. **—mel·lif′lu·ous·ly** *adv.*

mel·low (mĕl′ō) ▸ *adj.* **-er, -est. 1.** Soft, sweet, and full-flavored because of ripeness. **2.** Rich and soft in quality: *a mellow wine.* **3.** Having the gentleness often associated with maturity. **4.** Relaxed; easygoing. **5.** *Slang* Slightly and pleasantly intoxicated. ▸ *v.* To make or become mellow. **—mel′low·ly** *adv.* **—mel′low·ness** *n.*

me·lo·de·on (mə-lō′dē-ən) ▸ *n.* A small harmonium.

me·lo·di·ous (mə-lō′dē-əs) ▸ *adj.* **1.** Tuneful. **2.** Agreeable to hear. **—me·lo′di·ous·ly** *adv.* **—me·lo′di·ous·ness** *n.*

mel·o·dra·ma (mĕl′ə-drä′mə, -drăm′ə) ▸ *n.* **1.** A dramatic work marked by exaggerated emotions, stereotypical characters, and interpersonal conflicts. **2.** Behavior or events having melodramatic characteristics.

mel·o·dra·mat·ic (mĕl′ə-drə-măt′ĭk) ▸ *adj.* **1.** Having the emotional appeal of melodrama. **2.** Exaggeratedly emotional or sentimental. **—mel′o·dra·mat′i·cal·ly** *adv.*

mel·o·dy (mĕl′ə-dē) ▸ *n., pl.* **-dies. 1.** A pleasing succession or arrangement of sounds. **2.** A rhythmic sequence of single tones organized so as to make up a musical phrase. **—me·lod′ic** (mə-lŏd′ĭk) *adj.* **—me·lod′i·cal·ly** *adv.*

mel·on (mĕl′ən) ▸ *n.* Any of several fruits, as cantaloupe or watermelon, having a hard rind and juicy flesh.

melt (mĕlt) ▸ *v.* **1.** To change or be changed from a solid to a liquid state by application of heat or pressure or both. **2.** To dissolve: *Sugar melts in water.* **3.** To disappear or cause to disappear gradually. **4.** To pass imperceptibly into something else. **5.** To become softened in feeling. **—melt′a·ble** *adj.* **—melt′ing·ly** *adv.*

melt·down (mĕlt′doun′) ▸ *n.* **1.** Severe overheating of a nuclear reactor core, resulting in escape of radiation. **2.** *Informal* An emotional breakdown.

melt·ing point (mĕl′tĭng) ▸ *n.* The temperature at which a solid becomes a liquid at standard atmospheric pressure.

melting pot ▸ *n.* A place where immigrants of different cultures or races form an integrated society.

Mel·ville (mĕl′vĭl), **Herman** (1819–91) ▸ Amer. writer.

mem·ber (mĕm′bər) ▸ *n.* **1.** A distinct part of a whole. **2.** A part or an organ of a human or animal body. **3.** One that belongs to a group or organization.

mem·ber·ship (mĕm′bər-shĭp′) ▸ *n.* **1.** The state of being a member. **2.** All the members in a group.

mem·brane (mĕm′brān′) ▸ *n.* **1.** A thin pliable layer of plant or animal tissue covering or separating structures or organs. **2.** A thin sheet of natural or synthetic material that is permeable to substances in solution, as in osmosis. **—mem′bra·nal** (-brə-nəl), **mem′bra·nous** *adj.*

me·men·to (mə-mĕn′tō) ▸ *n., pl.* **-tos** or **-toes.** A reminder of the past; keepsake.

mem·o (mĕm′ō) ▸ *n., pl.* **-os.** *Informal* A memorandum.

mem·oir (mĕm′wär′, -wôr′) ▸ *n.* **1.** often **memoirs** An autobiography or biography. **2. memoirs** The report of the proceedings of a learned society. **—mem′oir·ist** *n.*

mem·o·ra·bil·i·a (mĕm′ər-ə-bĭl′ē-ə, -bĭl′yə) ▸ *pl.n.* **1.** Objects valued for their historical significance. **2.** Events or experiences worthy of remembrance.

mem·o·ra·ble (mĕm′ər-ə-bəl) ▸ *adj.* Worth being remembered or noted. **—mem′o·ra·bil′i·ty, mem′o·ra·ble·ness** *n.* **—mem′o·ra·bly** *adv.*

mem·o·ran·dum (mĕm′ə-răn′dəm) ▸ *n., pl.* **-dums** or **-da** (-də). **1.** A short note written as a reminder. **2.** A written record or communication, as in a business office.

me·mo·ri·al (mə-môr′ē-əl) ▸ *n.* **1.** Something, such as a monument or holiday, intended to honor the memory of a person or event. **2.** A written statement of facts or a formal petition. ▸ *adj.* Commemorative. **—me·mo′ri·al·ize′** *v.* **—me·mo′ri·al·ly** *adv.*

Memorial Day ▸ *n.* May 30, a US holiday commemorating members of the armed forces killed in war, officially observed on the last Monday in May.

mem·o·rize (mĕm′ə-rīz′) ▸ *v.* **-rized, -riz·ing.** To commit to memory; learn by heart. **—mem′o·ri·za′tion** *n.*

mem·o·ry (mĕm′ə-rē) ▸ *n., pl.* **-ries. 1.** The mental faculty of retaining and recalling past experience. **2.** The act of remembering; recollection. **3.** All that a person can remember. **4.** Something remembered: *childhood memories.* **5.** The period of time covered by remembrance or recollection. **6.** *Comp. Sci.* **a.** A unit of a computer that preserves data for retrieval. **b.** Capacity for storing information.

Mem·phis (mĕm′fĭs) ▸ **1.** An ancient city of Egypt S of Cairo. **2.** A city of southwest TN on the Mississippi River.

mem·sa·hib (mĕm′sä′ĭb) ▸ *n.* Used formerly as a respectful address for a European woman in colonial India.

men (mĕn) ▸ *n.* Pl. of **man.**

men·ace (mĕn′ĭs) ▸ *n.* **1.** A threat. **2.** A troublesome or annoying person. ▸ *v.* **-aced, -ac·ing.** To threaten. **—men′ac·er** *n.* **—men′ac·ing·ly** *adv.*

mé·nage (mā-näzh′) ▸ *n.* A household.

me·nag·er·ie (mə-năj′ə-rē, -năzh′-) ▸ *n.* A collection of wild animals on exhibition.

me·nar·che (mə-när′kē) ▸ *n.* The first menstrual period, usu. occurring during puberty. **—me·nar′che·al** *adj.*

mend (mĕnd) ▸ *v.* **1.** To make repairs or restoration to; fix. **2.** To reform or correct. **3.** To improve in health; heal. ▸ *n.* A mended place. ***—idiom:* on the mend** Improving, esp. in health. **—mend′a·ble** *adj.* **—mend′er** *n.*

men·da·cious (mĕn-dā′shəs) ▸ *adj.* **1.** Lying; untruthful. **2.**

THESAURUS

meliorate *v.* *—See* IMPROVE.

melioration *n.* *—See* IMPROVEMENT (1), PROGRESS.

mellifluous *adj.* *—See* MELODIOUS.

mellow *adj.* Brought to full flavor and richness by aging ▸ aged, ripe. [*Compare* MATURE.] *—See also* CALM, EASYGOING, RESONANT.

mellow *v.* *—See* MATURE.

mellow out *v.* *—See* REST[1] (1).

melodious or **melodic** *adj.* Having or producing a pleasing melody or sound ▸ dulcet, euphonic, euphonious, harmonious, mellifluous, melodic, musical, silvery, sweet-sounding, tuneful. [*Compare* HARMONIOUS, PLEASANT.]

melodrama or **melodramatics** *n.* *—See* THEATRICS (2).

melodramatic *adj.* *—See* DRAMATIC (2)

melody *n.* A pleasing succession or arrangement of sound ▸ air, aria, strain, theme, tune. [*Compare* SONG.]

melt *v.* To change from a solid to a liquid ▸ deliquesce, dissolve, flux, fuse, liquefy, run, thaw. *—See also* DISAPPEAR (1).

member *n.* *—See* PART (1).

membrane *n.* *—See* SKIN (2).

memento *n.* *—See* REMEMBRANCE (1).

memo *n.* *—See* LETTER, NOTE.

memoir *n.* A personal narrative or record of experiences ▸ autobiography, commentaries, diary, journal, reminiscences. [*Compare* MEMORY, STORY.]

memorable *adj.* *—See* EXCEPTIONAL.

memorandum *n.* *—See* LETTER, NOTE.

memorial *n.* Something, as a structure or custom, serving to honor or keep alive a memory ▸ commemoration, monument, remembrance. [*Compare* TESTIMONIAL.]

memorial *adj.* Serving to honor or keep alive a memory ▸ commemorative, monumental.

memorialize *v.* To honor or keep alive the memory of ▸ commemorate. [*Compare* IMMORTALIZE.]

memorize *v.* To commit to memory ▸ con, learn. ***Idiom:*** learn by heart (*or* rote). [*Compare* LEARN, REMEMBER.]

memory *n.* **1.** The power of retaining and recalling past experience ▸ recall, recollection, remembrance, reminiscence, retention. ***Idiom:*** power of recall. **2.** An act or instance of remembering ▸ mental image, recollection, remembrance, reminiscence. [*Compare* IDEA.]

menace *n.* An expression of the intent to hurt or punish another ▸ intimidation, threat. *—See also* DANGER.

menace *v.* *—See* ENDANGER, INTIMIDATE, THREATEN (2).

menacing *adj.* *—See* DANGEROUS, FATEFUL (1).

ménage *n.* A group of people living together as a unit ▸ family, house, household.

mend *v.* *—See* CORRECT (1), FIX (1), RECOVER (2).

mendacious *adj.* *—See* DISHONEST.

False; untrue. **—men·da′cious·ly** *adv.* **—men·dac′i·ty** (-dăs′ĭ-tē) *n.*

Men·del (mĕn′dl), **Gregor Johann** (1822–84) ▸ Austrian botanist.

Men·de·le·ev (mĕn′də-lā′əf), **Dmitri Ivanovich** (1834–1907) ▸ Russian chemist.

men·de·le·vi·um (mĕn′də-lē′vē-əm) ▸ *n. Symbol* **Md** A synthetic radioactive element. At. no. 101.

men·di·cant (mĕn′dĭ-kənt) ▸ *adj.* Depending on alms for a living. ▸ *n.* **1.** A beggar. **2.** A friar.

Men·e·la·us (mĕn′ə-lā′əs) ▸ *n. Gk. Myth.* The king of Sparta at the time of the Trojan War.

men·ha·den (mĕn-hād′n) ▸ *n., pl.* **-den** or **-dens.** A fish of American Atlantic and Gulf waters, used as fertilizer and bait.

men·hir (mĕn′hîr′) ▸ *n.* See **standing stone.**

me·ni·al (mē′nē-əl, mēn′yəl) ▸ *adj.* **1.** Of or relating to work regarded as servile. **2.** Of or appropriate for a servant. ▸ *n.* A domestic servant. **—me′ni·al·ly** *adv.*

men·in·gi·tis (mĕn′ĭn-jī′tĭs) ▸ *n.* Inflammation of the meninges of the brain and the spinal cord.

me·ninx (mē′nĭngks) ▸ *n., pl.* **me·nin·ges** (mə-nĭn′jēz). Any of the three membranes enclosing the brain and spinal cord in vertebrates. **—me·nin′ge·al** (mə-nĭn′jē-əl) .

me·nis·cus (mə-nĭs′kəs) ▸ *n., pl.* **-nis·ci** (-nĭs′ī, -kī, -kē) or **-es. 1.** A crescent-shaped body. **2.** The curved upper surface of a liquid in a container.

men·o·pause (mĕn′ə-pôz′) ▸ *n.* The cessation of menstruation, occurring usu. between the ages of 45 and 55. **—men′o·paus′al** *adj.*

me·no·rah (mə-nôr′ə) ▸ *n. Judaism* A nine-branched candelabrum used in celebration of Hanukkah.

men·ses (mĕn′sēz) ▸ *pl.n. (takes sing. or pl. v.)* The monthly flow of blood and cellular debris from the uterus that begins at puberty in women and the females of other primates.

men·stru·ate (mĕn′strōō-āt′) ▸ *v.* **-at·ed, -at·ing.** To undergo menstruation.

men·stru·a·tion (mĕn′strōō-ā′shən) ▸ *n.* The process of discharging the menses. **—men′stru·al** *adj.*

men·su·ra·ble (mĕn′sər-ə-bəl, -shər-) ▸ *adj.* That can be measured. **—men′su·ra·bil′i·ty** *n.*

men·su·ra·tion (mĕn′sə-rā′shən, -shə-) ▸ *n.* The act, process, or art of measuring.

–ment ▸ *suff.* Product, means, action, or state: *curtailment.*

men·tal (mĕn′tl) ▸ *adj.* **1.** Of the mind. **2.** Executed or performed by the mind. **—men′tal·ly** *adv.*

mental age ▸ *n.* A measure of mental development as determined by intelligence tests, gen. restricted to children and expressed as the age of which that level is typical.

men·tal·i·ty (mĕn-tăl′ĭ-tē) ▸ *n., pl.* **-ties. 1.** Cast or turn of mind. **2.** Intellectual capabilities or endowment.

mental retardation ▸ *n.* Subnormal intellectual development or functioning resulting from congenital causes, brain injury, or disease and marked by impaired learning ability.

men·thol (mĕn′thôl′) ▸ *n.* A white crystalline organic compound used in perfumes, flavorings, and inhalants. **—men′tho·lat′ed** *adj.*

men·tion (mĕn′shən) ▸ *v.* To refer to, esp. incidentally. **—men′tion** *n.* **—men′tion·a·ble** *adj.*

men·tor (mĕn′tôr′, -tər) ▸ *n.* A wise and trusted counselor or teacher.

men·u (mĕn′yōō) ▸ *n.* **1.** A list of dishes to be served or available for a meal. **2.** A list or display of options, esp. as displayed on a computer screen.

me·ow (mē-ou′) ▸ *n. Informal* The cry of a cat. **—me·ow′** *v.*

me·phi·tis (mə-fī′tĭs) ▸ *n.* **1.** An offensive smell; stench. **2.** A foul-smelling gas emitted from the earth. **—me·phit′ic** (-fĭt′ĭk) *adj.*

–mer ▸ *suff.* Part; segment: *monomer.*

mer·can·tile (mûr′kən-tēl′, -tīl′, -tĭl) ▸ *adj.* Of or relating to merchants or trade.

Mer·ca·tor (mər-kā′tər), **Gerhardus** (1512–94) ▸ Flemish cartographer.

mer·ce·nar·y (mûr′sə-nĕr′ē) ▸ *adj.* **1.** Motivated by a desire for monetary or material gain. **2.** Hired for service in a foreign army. **—mer′ce·nar′y** *n.*

mer·cer (mûr′sər) ▸ *n. Chiefly Brit.* A dealer in textiles.

mer·cer·ize (mûr′sə-rīz′) ▸ *v.* **-ized, -iz·ing.** To treat (cotton thread) with sodium hydroxide so as to shrink the fiber and increase its luster and affinity for dye.

mer·chan·dise (mûr′chən-dīz′, -dīs′) ▸ *n.* Goods bought and sold in business; commercial wares. ▸ *v.* (-dīz′) **-dised, -dis·ing. 1.** To buy and sell (goods). **2.** To promote merchandise sales. **—mer′chan·dis′er** *n.*

mer·chant (mûr′chənt) ▸ *n.* **1.** One whose occupation is buying and selling goods for profit. **2.** A shopkeeper.

mer·chant·man (mûr′chənt-mən) ▸ *n.* A ship used in commerce.

merchant marine ▸ *n.* **1.** A nation's commercial ships. **2.** The personnel of the merchant marine.

mer·ci·ful (mûr′sĭ-fəl) ▸ *adj.* Full of mercy; compassionate. **—mer′ci·ful·ly** *adv.* **—mer′ci·ful·ness** *n.*

mer·cu·ri·al (mər-kyŏŏr′ē-əl) ▸ *adj.* **1.** Containing or caused by the action of the element mercury. **2.** Quick and changeable in temperament; volatile. **—mer·cu′ri·al·ly** *adv.*

mer·cu·ric (mər-kyŏŏr′ĭk) ▸ *adj.* Relating to or containing bivalent mercury.

mer·cu·rous (mər-kyŏŏr′əs, mûr′kyər-əs) ▸ *adj.* Of or containing monovalent mercury.

mer·cu·ry (mûr′kyə-rē) ▸ *n.* **1.** *Symbol* **Hg** A silvery-white poisonous metallic element, liquid at room temperature, used in thermometers and batteries. At. no. 80. **2.** Temperature: *The mercury fell overnight.*

Mercury ▸ *n.* **1.** *Rom. Myth.* A god that served as messenger to the other gods and was himself the god of commerce, travel, and thievery. **2.** The smallest of the planets and the one that is nearest the sun, at a mean distance of 58.3 million km (36.2 million mi) and a mean radius of approx. 2,414 km (1,500 mi).

mer·cy (mûr′sē) ▸ *n., pl.* **-cies. 1.** Compassionate treatment, esp. of those under one's power. **2.** A disposition to be kind and forgiving. **3.** A blessing. **—mer′ci·less** *adj.* **—mer′ci·less·ly** *adv.* **—mer′ci·less·ness** *n.*

THESAURUS

mendacity *n.* The practice of lying ▸ falsehood, falsification, inveracity, lying, perjury, prevarication, truthlessness, untruthfulness. [*Compare* DECEIT.] —*See also* DISHONESTY (1), LIE[2].

mendicancy or **mendicity** *n.* The condition of being a beggar ▸ beggary, mendicity. [*Compare* POVERTY.]

mendicant *n.* —*See* BEGGAR (1).

mendicant *adj.* —*See* POOR.

menial *adj.* —*See* SERVILE.

menial *n.* —*See* DRUDGE (1), LABORER.

mensuration *n.* The act or process of ascertaining dimensions, quantity, or capacity ▸ determination, measure, measurement, quantification. [*Compare* COMPUTATION, ESTIMATION.]

mental *adj.* Relating to or performed by the mind ▸ cerebral, intellective, intellectual, psychic, psychical, psychological, reasoning, thinking. [*Compare* ARBITRARY.] —*See also* INTELLECTUAL.

mental illness *n.* —*See* INSANITY.

mental image *n.* An act or instance of remembering ▸ memory, recollection, remembrance, reminiscence. [*Compare* IDEA.]

mentality *n.* —*See* INTELLIGENCE, PSYCHOLOGY.

mentally ill *adj.* —*See* INSANE.

mention *v.* —*See* NAME (2), REFER (1).

mentor *n.* —*See* ADVISER.

mentor *v.* —*See* ADVISE.

mephitic or **mephitical** *adj.* —*See* POISONOUS, SMELLY.

mercenary *n.* A freelance fighter ▸ adventurer, soldier of fortune. [*Compare* FIGHTER, SOLDIER.]

mercenary *adj.* —*See* CORRUPT (2).

merchandise *n.* —*See* GOOD (2).

merchandise *v.* —*See* SELL.

merchandiser *n.* —*See* DEALER.

merchant *n.* —*See* DEALER.

merchant *v.* —*See* SELL.

merciful *adj.* —*See* HUMANITARIAN, TOLERANT.

mercifulness *n.* —*See* MERCY.

merciless *adj.* —*See* CALLOUS, CRUEL.

mercurial *adj.* Given to changeable emotional states, especially of anger or gloom ▸ moody, temperamental. [*Compare* TESTY.] —*See also* CAPRICIOUS.

mercy *n.* Kind, forgiving, or compassionate treatment of or disposition toward others ▸ charity, clemency, grace, lenience, leniency, lenity, mercifulness. [*Compare* PITY.]

mere (mîr) ▸ *adj. Superl.* **mer·est. 1.** Being no more than what is specified: *a mere 50 cents.* **2.** Considered apart from anything else: *shocked by the mere idea.* **—mere′ly** *adv.*
me·ren·gue (mə-rĕng′gā) ▸ *n.* A ballroom dance of Dominican and Haitian origin, marked by a sliding step.
mer·e·tri·cious (mĕr′ĭ-trĭsh′əs) ▸ *adj.* Attracting attention in a vulgar manner. **—mer′e·tri′cious·ly** *adv.* **—mer′e·tri′cious·ness** *n.*
mer·gan·ser (mər-găn′sər) ▸ *n.* A fish-eating diving duck having a slim hooked bill.
merge (mûrj) ▸ *v.* **merged, merg·ing.** To blend together or cause to be absorbed, esp. in gradual stages.
merg·er (mûr′jər) ▸ *n.* The act or an instance of merging, esp. the union of two or more commercial interests or corporations.
me·rid·i·an (mə-rĭd′ē-ən) ▸ *n.* **1a.** A great circle on the earth's surface passing through the North and South geographic poles. **b.** Either half of such a circle from pole to pole. **2.** *Astron.* A great circle passing through the two poles of the celestial sphere and the point directly overhead. **3.** The highest point or stage; zenith. **4.** *Regional* See **median strip.**
me·ringue (mə-răng′) ▸ *n.* A dessert topping or pastry shell made from stiffly beaten egg whites and sugar.
me·ri·no (mə-rē′nō) ▸ *n., pl.* **-nos. 1.** A breed of sheep having long fine wool. **2.** A soft lightweight fabric made of fine wool.
mer·it (mĕr′ĭt) ▸ *n.* **1.** Superior quality or worth; excellence. **2.** often **merits** An aspect of character or behavior deserving approval or disapproval. **3. merits a.** *Law* A party's strict legal rights. **b.** The factual content of a matter. ▸ *v.* To earn; deserve. **—mer′it·less** *adj.*
mer·i·to·ri·ous (mĕr′ĭ-tôr′ē-əs) ▸ *adj.* Deserving reward or praise; having merit. **—mer′i·to′ri·ous·ly** *adv.*
mer·maid (mûr′mād′) ▸ *n.* A legendary sea creature having the head and upper body of a woman and the tail of a fish.
mer·man (mûr′măn′, -mən) ▸ *n.* A legendary sea creature having the head and upper body of a man and the tail of a fish.
mer·ry (mĕr′ē) ▸ *adj.* **-ri·er, -ri·est. 1.** Full of high-spirited gaiety. **2.** Marked by fun and festivity. **—mer′ri·ly** *adv.* **—mer′ri·ment** *n.* **—mer′ri·ness** *n.*
mer·ry-go-round (mĕr′ē-gō-round′) ▸ *n.* **1.** A revolving circular platform fitted with seats, often in the form of animals, ridden for amusement. **2.** A busy round; whirl.
mer·ry·mak·ing (mĕr′ē-mā′kĭng) ▸ *n.* **1.** Participation in festive activities. **2.** A festivity; revelry. **—mer′ry·mak′er** *n.*
me·sa (mā′sə) ▸ *n.* A flat-topped elevation with steep sides.
mes·cal (mĕs-kăl′) ▸ *n.* **1.** See **peyote** 1. **2.** A Mexican liquor distilled from fermented agave juice. **3.** See **maguey** 1.
mes·ca·line (mĕs′kə-lēn′, -lĭn) ▸ *n.* A hallucinogenic alkaloid drug, obtained from peyote buttons.
mes·clun (mĕs′klən) ▸ *n.* A mixture of young leafy greens used as salad.
Mes·dames (mā-däm′, -dăm′) ▸ *n.* **1.** Pl. of **Madam** 1. **2.** Pl. of **Madame.**
Mes·de·moi·selles (măd′mwä-zĕl′) ▸ *n.* Pl. of **Mademoiselle.**
mesh (mĕsh) ▸ *n.* **1.** Any of the open spaces in a net or network. **2.** A net or network: *a screen made of wire mesh.* **3.** The engagement of gear teeth. ▸ *v.* **1.** To ensnare. **2.** To engage or cause (gear teeth) to become engaged. **3.** To fit together harmoniously.
mes·mer·ize (mĕz′mə-rīz′, mĕs′-) ▸ *v.* **-ized, -iz·ing.** To hypnotize. **—mes′mer·ism′** *n.* **—mes′mer·ist** *n.* **—mes′mer·iz′er** *n.*
meso– or **mes–** ▸ *pref.* Middle: *mesosphere.*
Mes·o·a·mer·i·ca (mĕz′ō-ə-mĕr′ĭ-kə, mĕs′-) ▸ A region extending S and E from central Mexico to include parts of Guatemala, Belize, Honduras, and Nicaragua. **—Mes′o·a·mer′i·can** *adj. & n.*
Mes·o·lith·ic (mĕz′ə-lĭth′ĭk, mĕs′-) ▸ *adj.* Of or being the Stone Age period between the Paleolithic and Neolithic, marked by the appearance of microlithic tools and weapons. ▸ *n.* The Mesolithic Period.
mes·on (mĕz′ŏn′, mĕs′-) ▸ *n.* Any of a family of subatomic particles that participate in strong interactions and are composed of a quark and an antiquark.
Mes·o·po·ta·mi·a (mĕs′ə-pə-tā′mē-ə) ▸ An ancient region of SW Asia between the Tigris and Euphrates rivers in modern-day Iraq. **—Mes′o·po·ta′mi·an** *adj. & n.*
mes·o·sphere (mĕz′ə-sfîr′, mĕs′-) ▸ *n.* The portion of the atmosphere from about 30 to 80 km (20 to 50 mi) above the earth's surface. **—mes′o·spher′ic** (-sfîr′ĭk, -sfĕr′-) *adj.*
Mes·o·zo·ic (mĕz′ə-zō′ĭk, mĕs′-) ▸ *adj.* Of or being the 3rd geologic era, including the Cretaceous, Jurassic, and Triassic periods and marked esp. by the appearance and extinction of dinosaurs. ▸ *n.* The Mesozoic Era.
mes·quite (mĕ-skēt′, mə-) ▸ *n.* A small spiny shrub native to hot dry regions of North America.
mess (mĕs) ▸ *n.* **1.** A disorderly or dirty accumulation, heap, or jumble. **2.** A confused or troubling condition. **3.** An unspecified amount of food, as for a meal: *a mess of fish.* **4a.** A group, as of soldiers, that regularly eats meals together. **b.** Food served to such a group. ▸ *v.* **1.** To make disorderly or soiled. **2.** To botch; bungle. **3.** To interfere: *messing in our affairs.*
mes·sage (mĕs′ĭj) ▸ *n.* **1.** A usu. short communication transmitted from one person or group to another. **2.** A lesson or moral.
mes·sen·ger (mĕs′ən-jər) ▸ *n.* **1.** One that carries messages

THESAURUS

mere *adj.* Just sufficient ▸ bare, scant, scanty. [*Compare* INSUFFICIENT, MEAGER.]
merely *adv.* Nothing more than ▸ but, just, only, simply. [*Compare* BARELY, SOLELY.]
meretricious *adj.* —*See* GAUDY.
merge *v.* —*See* MIX (1).
merger *n.* —*See* COMBINATION, MIXTURE.
meridian *n.* —*See* CLIMAX.
merit *n.* A level of superiority that is usually high ▸ caliber, quality, stature, value, virtue, worth. [*Compare* ADVANTAGE.] —*See also* USE (2), VIRTUE.
merit *v.* —*See* EARN (1).
merited *adj.* —*See* JUST.
meritless *adj.* —*See* BASELESS.
meritorious *adj.* —*See* ADMIRABLE.
merriment *n.* **1.** A state of joyful exuberance ▸ blitheness, gaiety, gladness, glee, gleefulness, hilarity, jocoseness, jocosity, jocularity, jocundity, jolliness, jollity, joviality, lightheartedness, merriness, mirth, mirthfulness. [*Compare* ELATION.] **2.** Joyful, exuberant activity ▸ celebration, conviviality, festiveness, festivity, fun, gaiety, jollity, merrymaking, revelry, revels. [*Compare* BLAST, CELEBRATION, PARTY.]
merriness *n.* —*See* MERRIMENT (1).
merry *adj.* Providing joy and pleasure, especially in celebration ▸ celebratory, cheerful, cheery, convivial, festive, gala, glad, gladsome, happy, joyful, joyous, mirthful. [*Compare* LIGHTHEARTED.] —*See also* CHEERFUL.
merrymaking *n.* —*See* CELEBRATION (3), MERRIMENT (2).
mesa *n.* A natural, flat land elevation ▸ plateau, table. [*Compare* HILL.]
mesh *n.* —*See* TANGLE, WEB.
mesh *v.* To come or bring together and interlock ▸ engage. [*Compare* ATTACH, FIT[1].] —*See also* HARMONIZE (2).
mesmerize *v.* —*See* CHARM (2), GRIP.
mess *n.* **1.** A confused or ruinous state ▸ botch, fiasco, foul-up, mix-up, muddle, shambles. *Informal:* hash. *Slang:* screwup, snafu. [*Compare* BLUNDER.] **2.** An unsightly object ▸ disaster, eyesore, monstrosity, ugliness. *Informal:* fright, sight, ugly. *Idiom:* something the cat dragged in. —*See also* ABUNDANCE, DISORDER (1), HEAP (1), PREDICAMENT, SERVING.
mess *v.* —*See* TINKER, TOUSLE.
mess around *v. Informal* To be sexually unfaithful to another ▸ philander. *Informal:* cheat, fool around, play around. *Slang:* two-time. —*See also* PUTTER, TINKER.
mess up *v.* —*See* BOTCH, CONFUSE (3), DISORDER, DISRUPT, MANHANDLE.
message *n.* Something announced or communicated ▸ announcement, annunciation, brief, bulletin, communication, communiqué, declaration, dictum, edict, manifesto, notice, notification, proclamation, pronouncement, statement, word. —*See also* LETTER, MEANING.
messenger *n.* A person who carries messages or is sent on errands ▸ bearer, carrier, conveyer, courier, envoy, errand boy, errand girl, herald, runner. *Slang:* gofer. [*Compare* AGENT,

or performs errands. 2. A bearer of news.
Mes·si·ah (mĭ-sī′ə) ▸ *n.* 1. also **Mes·si·as** (mĭ-sī′əs) The anticipated deliverer and king of the Jews. 2. also **Messias** *Christianity* Jesus. 3. **messiah** An expected savior or liberator. **—Mes′si·an′ic** (mĕs′ē-ăn′ĭk) *adj.*
Mes·sieurs (mā-syœ′) ▸ *n.* Pl. of **Monsieur.**
Messrs.[1] (mĕs′ərz) ▸ *n.* Pl. of **Mr.**
Messrs.[2] ▸ *abbr.* Messieurs
mess·y (mĕs′ē) ▸ *adj.* **-i·er, -i·est.** 1. Disorderly and dirty. 2. Unpleasantly difficult to settle or resolve: *a messy court case.* **—mess′i·ly** *adv.* **—mess′i·ness** *n.*
mes·ti·zo (mĕs-tē′zō) ▸ *n., pl.* **-zos** or **-zoes.** A person of mixed racial ancestry, esp. of European and Native American ancestry.
met (mĕt) ▸ *v.* P.t. and p.part. of **meet**[1].
meta– or **met–** ▸ *pref.* 1. Change; transformation: *metastasis.* 2. Situated behind: *metacarpus.*
me·tab·o·lism (mĭ-tăb′ə-lĭz′əm) ▸ *n.* 1. The physical and chemical processes occurring within a living cell or organism that are necessary for life. 2. The functioning of a specific substance within the body: *iodine metabolism.* **—met′a·bol′ic** (mĕt′ə-bŏl′ĭk) *adj.* **—met′a·bol′i·cal·ly** *adv.* **—me·tab′o·lize′** *v.*
me·tab·o·lite (mĭ-tăb′ə-līt′) ▸ *n.* A substance produced by metabolism.
met·a·car·pus (mĕt′ə-kär′pəs) ▸ *n., pl.* **-pi** (-pī). 1. The part of the human hand that includes the five bones between the fingers and the wrist. 2. The corresponding part of the forefoot of a quadruped.
Met·a·com (mĕt′ə-kŏm′) (d. 1676) ▸ Wampanoag leader.
met·al (mĕt′l) ▸ *n.* 1. Any of a category of elements that usu. have a shiny surface, are gen. good conductors of heat and electricity, and can be melted or fused, hammered into thin sheets, or drawn into wires. 2. An alloy of two or more metals. 3. Basic character; mettle. 4. *Mus.* Heavy metal. **—me·tal′lic** (mə-tăl′ĭk) *adj.* **—me·tal′li·cal·ly** *adv.*
metallic bond ▸ *n.* The chemical bond characteristic of metals, in which mobile valence electrons are shared among atoms in a usu. stable crystalline structure.
met·al·lur·gy (mĕt′l-ûr′jē) ▸ *n.* The science that deals with extracting metals from their ores and creating useful objects from them. **—met′al·lur′gic, met′al·lur′gi·cal** *adj.* **—met′al·lur′gist** *n.*
met·al·work (mĕt′l-wûrk′) ▸ *n.* Work done in metal. **—met′al·work′er** *n.*
met·a·mor·phic (mĕt′ə-môr′fĭk) ▸ *adj.* 1. also **met·a·mor·phous** (-fəs) Of metamorphosis. 2. *Geol.* Changed in structure or composition as a result of metamorphism.
met·a·mor·phism (mĕt′ə-môr′fĭz′əm) ▸ *n. Geol.* The process by which rocks are altered in composition, texture, or structure by heat, pressure, and chemical action.
met·a·mor·phose (mĕt′ə-môr′fōz′, -fōs′) ▸ *v.* **-phosed, -phos·ing.** To change by metamorphosis.
met·a·mor·pho·sis (mĕt′ə-môr′fə-sĭs) ▸ *n., pl.* **-ses** (-sēz′). 1. A transformation, as by magic or sorcery. 2. A marked change in appearance, character, condition, or function. 3. *Biol.* A change in form and often habits during development after the embryonic stage, as in insects.
met·a·phor (mĕt′ə-fôr′, -fər) ▸ *n.* A figure of speech in which a word or phrase that ordinarily designates one thing is used to designate another, thus making an implicit comparison, as in *the evening of life.* **—met′a·phor′ic** (-fôr′ĭk, -fŏr′-), **met′a·phor′i·cal** *adj.* **—met′a·phor′i·cal·ly** *adv.*
met·a·phys·i·cal (mĕt′ə-fĭz′ĭ-kəl) ▸ *adj.* 1. Of or relating to metaphysics. 2. Based on speculative or abstract reasoning. 3. Abstruse. **—met′a·phys′i·cal·ly** *adv.*
met·a·phys·ics (mĕt′ə-fĭz′ĭks) ▸ *n. (takes sing. v.)* The branch of philosophy that examines the nature of reality and the relationship between mind and matter. **—met′a·phy·si′cian** (-fĭ-zĭsh′ən) *n.*
me·tas·ta·sis (mə-tăs′tə-sĭs) ▸ *n., pl.* **-ses** (-sēz′). The spreading of a disease from an original site to one or more sites elsewhere in the body. **—me·tas′ta·size′** *v.* **—met′a·stat′ic** (mĕt′ə-stăt′ĭk) *adj.* **—met′a·stat′i·cal·ly** *adv.*
met·a·tar·sus (mĕt′ə-tär′səs) ▸ *n., pl.* **-si** (-sī, -sē). The middle part of the foot, composed of the five bones between the toes and tarsus, that forms the instep. **—met′a·tar′sal** *adj.*
mete (mēt) ▸ *v.* **met·ed, met·ing.** To dole; allot: *mete out punishment.*
me·tem·psy·cho·sis (mə-tĕm′sĭ-kō′sĭs, mĕt′əm-sī-) ▸ *n., pl.* **-ses** (-sēz). Reincarnation.
me·te·or (mē′tē-ər, -ôr′) ▸ *n.* A bright trail or streak that appears in the sky when a meteoroid is heated to incandescence by friction with the earth's atmosphere.
me·te·or·ic (mē′tē-ôr′ĭk, -ŏr′-) ▸ *adj.* 1. Of or formed by a meteoroid. 2. Similar to a meteor in speed or brilliance: *a meteoric rise to fame.* **—me′te·or′i·cal·ly** *adv.*
me·te·or·ite (mē′tē-ə-rīt′) ▸ *n.* A stony or metallic mass of matter that has fallen to the earth's surface from outer space. **—me′te·or·it′ic** (-ə-rĭt′ĭk), **me′te·or·it′i·cal** *adj.*
me·te·or·oid (mē′tē-ə-roid′) ▸ *n.* A solid body, moving in space, that is smaller than an asteroid and at least as large as a speck of dust.
me·te·or·ol·o·gy (mē′tē-ə-rŏl′ə-jē) ▸ *n.* The science that deals with the phenomena of the atmosphere, esp. weather. **—me′te·or·o·log′i·cal** (-ər-ə-lŏj′ĭ-kəl), **me′te·or·o·log′ic** *adj.* **—me′te·or·o·log′i·cal·ly** *adv.* **—me′te·or·ol′o·gist** *n.*
me·ter[1] (mē′tər) ▸ *n.* 1a. The measured arrangement of words in poetry, as by accentual rhythm. b. A particular arrangement of words in a poem, such as iambic pentameter. 2. *Mus.* a. Division into measures or bars. b. A specific rhythm in a measure.
me·ter[2] (mē′tər) ▸ *n.* See **measurement** table in Appendix.
me·ter[3] (mē′tər) ▸ *n.* Any of various devices that measure or indicate and record or regulate. ▸ *v.* 1. To measure or regulate with a meter. 2. To imprint with postage by means of a postage meter or similar device.
–meter ▸ *suff.* Measuring device: *thermometer.*
me·ter-kil·o·gram-sec·ond (mē′tər-kĭl′ə-grăm-sĕk′ənd) ▸ *adj.* Of or relating to a system of units for mechanics, using the meter, the kilogram, and the second as basic units of length, mass, and time.
meth·a·done (mĕth′ə-dōn′) ▸ *n.* A potent synthetic narcotic drug, $C_{21}H_{27}NO$, used in addiction treatment programs.
meth·am·phet·a·mine (mĕth′ăm-fĕt′ə-mēn′, -mĭn) ▸ *n.* An amine derivative of amphetamine used in the form of its crystalline hydrochloride as a stimulant.
meth·ane (mĕth′ān′) ▸ *n.* An odorless, colorless, flammable gas, CH_4, the major constituent of natural gas, used as a fuel and an important source of organic compounds.
meth·a·nol (mĕth′ə-nôl′, -nōl′, -nŏl′) ▸ *n.* A colorless, toxic, flammable liquid, CH_3OH, used as an antifreeze, solvent, fuel, and denaturant for ethyl alcohol.
meth·od (mĕth′əd) ▸ *n.* 1. A systematic means or manner of procedure. 2. Orderly arrangement of parts or steps to ac-

THESAURUS

GO-BETWEEN, REPRESENTATIVE.]
messiness *n.* —*See* DISORDERLINESS.
messy *adj.* 1. Marked by a lack of cleanliness or neatness ▸ careless, disheveled, frowzy, mussy, slapdash, slipshod, sloppy, slovenly, unkempt, untidy. 2. Lacking regular or logical order ▸ disorderly, unsystematic.
metamorphose *v.* —*See* CONVERT, REVOLUTIONIZE.
metamorphosis *n.* —*See* CONVERSION (1), REVOLUTION (2).
metanoia *n.* A fundamental change in one's beliefs ▸ conversion, rebirth, regeneration. [*Compare* REVIVAL.]
metaphor *n.* An object or expression associated with and serving to identify something else ▸ attribute, emblem, signifier, symbol, token. [*Compare* EXPRESSION, SIGN, TERM.]
metaphorical or **metaphoric** *adj.* —*See* SYMBOLIC.
metaphrase *n.* —*See* TRANSLATION.
metaphrase *v.* —*See* TRANSLATE.
metaphysical *adj.* —*See* IMMATERIAL, SUPERNATURAL (1).
mete *v.* —*See* DISTRIBUTE.
meter *n.* —*See* RHYTHM.
method *n.* Systematic arrangement and design ▸ format, order, orderliness, organization, pattern, plan, process, scheme, system, systematization, systemization. [*Compare* ARRANGEMENT, FORM.] —*See also* ROUTINE, WAY (1).
methodical or **methodic** *adj.* Arranged or proceeding in a set, systematized pattern ▸ arranged, neat, ordered, orderly, organized, regular, regulated, structured, systematic, systematical. [*Compare* NEAT,

complish an end. **—me·thod′i·cal** (mə-thŏd′ĭ-kəl), **me·thod′ic** *adj.* **—me·thod′i·cal·ly** *adv.*

Meth·od·ist (mĕth′ə-dĭst) ▸ *n.* A member of an evangelical Protestant church founded on the principles of John and Charles Wesley. **—Meth′od·ism** *n.* **—Meth′od·is′tic** *adj.*

meth·od·ol·o·gy (mĕth′ə-dŏl′ə-jē) ▸ *n., pl.* **-gies. 1.** A body of practices, procedures, and rules used in a discipline. **2.** The branch of logic that deals with the general principles of the formation of knowledge. **—meth′od·o·log′i·cal** (-ə-də-lŏj′ĭ-kəl) *adj.* **—meth′od·o·log′i·cal·ly** *adv.*

meth·yl (mĕth′əl) ▸ *n.* The univalent hydrocarbon radical, CH_3^-. **—me·thyl′ic** (mə-thĭl′ĭk) *adj.*

methyl alcohol ▸ *n.* See **methanol.**

met·i·cal (mĕt′ĭ-kăl′, mĕt′ĭ-käl′) ▸ *n.* See **currency** table in Appendix.

me·tic·u·lous (mĭ-tĭk′yə-ləs) ▸ *adj.* Extremely or excessively careful and precise. **—me·tic′u·los′i·ty** (-lŏs′ĭ-tē), **me·tic′u·lous·ness** *n.* **—me·tic′u·lous·ly** *adv.*

mé·tier (mĕ-tyā′, mā-) ▸ *n.* **1.** A trade or profession. **2.** One's specialty.

me·ton·y·my (mə-tŏn′ə-mē) ▸ *n., pl.* **-mies.** A figure of speech in which one word or phrase is substituted for another with which it is closely associated, as in the use of *Washington* for *the US government.* **—met′o·nym′** (mĕt′ə-nĭm′) *n.* **—met′o·nym′ic, met′o·nym′i·cal** *adj.*

me·tre (mē′tər) ▸ *n. Chiefly Brit.* **1.** Var. of **meter**[1]. **2.** Var. of **meter**[2].

met·ric (mĕt′rĭk) ▸ *adj.* Of or relating to the metric system.

met·ri·cal (mĕt′rĭ-kəl) ▸ *adj.* **1.** Of or composed in poetic meter: *metrical verse.* **2.** Of or relating to measurement. **—met′ri·cal·ly** *adv.*

met·ri·ca·tion (mĕt′rĭ-kā′shən) ▸ *n.* Conversion to the metric system of weights and measures.

met·rics (mĕt′rĭks) ▸ *n. (takes sing. v.)* The study of poetic meter; prosody.

metric system ▸ *n.* A decimal system of units based on the meter as a unit length, the kilogram as a unit mass, and the second as a unit time. See **measurement** table in Appendix.

metric ton ▸ *n.* See **measurement** table in Appendix.

met·ro·nome (mĕt′rə-nōm′) ▸ *n. Mus.* An adjustable device used to mark time at precise intervals. **—met′ro·nom′ic** (mĕt′rə-nŏm′ĭk) *adj.*

me·trop·o·lis (mĭ-trŏp′ə-lĭs) ▸ *n.* **1.** A major city, esp. the chief city of a country or region. **2.** A city or an urban area regarded as the center of a specific activity. **—met′ro·pol′i·tan** (mĕt′rə-pŏl′ĭ-tən) *adj. & n.*

-metry ▸ *suff.* Process or science of measuring: *photometry.*

met·tle (mĕt′l) ▸ *n.* **1.** Courage and fortitude; spirit. **2.** Quality of character and temperament. **—met′tle·some** *adj.*

mew (myo͞o) ▸ *v.* To make the cry of a cat; meow. **—mew** *n.*

mews (myo͞oz) ▸ *pl.n. (takes sing. or pl. v.)* A small street or alley orig. with private stables, often converted into residential apartments.

Mexican American ▸ *n.* A US citizen or resident of Mexican descent. **—Mex′i·can-A·mer′i·can** *adj.*

Mex·i·co (mĕk′sĭ-kō′) ▸ A country of S-central North America. **—Mex′i·can** (-kən) *adj. & n.*

Mexico, Gulf of ▸ An arm of the Atlantic in SE North America bordering on E Mexico, the SE US, and Cuba.

Mexico City ▸ The capital of Mexico, at the S end of the central plateau.

mez·za·nine (mĕz′ə-nēn′, mĕz′ə-nēn′) ▸ *n.* **1.** A partial story between two main stories of a building. **2.** The lowest balcony in a theater or its first few rows.

mez·zo-so·pran·o (mĕt′sō-sə-prăn′ō, -prä′nō, mĕd′zō-) ▸ *n., pl.* **-os. 1.** A woman's singing voice having a range between soprano and contralto. **2.** A woman having a mezzo-soprano voice.

mg ▸ *abbr.* milligram

Mg ▸ Symbol for the element **magnesium.**

mgt. ▸ *abbr.* management

MHz ▸ *abbr.* megahertz

mi (mē) ▸ *n. Mus.* The 3rd tone of the diatonic scale.

MI ▸ *abbr.* Michigan

mi. or **mi** ▸ *abbr.* mile

MIA (ĕm′ī-ā′) ▸ *n.* A member of the armed services reported missing in action.

Mi·am·i (mī-ăm′ē, -ăm′ə) ▸ A city of SE FL on Biscayne Bay S of Fort Lauderdale.

mi·as·ma (mī-ăz′mə, mē-) ▸ *n., pl.* **-mas** or **-ma·ta** (-mə-tə). **1.** A noxious atmosphere or influence. **2.** A poisonous vapor formerly thought to rise from swamps and putrid matter and cause disease. **—mi·as′mal, mi·as′mic** *adj.*

mi·ca (mī′kə) ▸ *n.* Any of a group of chemically and physically related silicate minerals, common in igneous and metamorphic rocks.

Mi·cah (mī′kə) also **Mi·che·as** (mī-kē′əs) ▸ *n.* **1.** A Hebrew prophet of the 8th cent. B.C. **2.** See **Bible** table in Appendix.

mice (mīs) ▸ *n.* Pl. of **mouse.**

Mich. ▸ *abbr.* Michigan

Mi·chel·an·ge·lo Buo·nar·ro·ti (mī′kəl-ăn′jə-lō′ bwôn′ə-rô′tē, mĭk′-, mē′kĕl-än′jĕ-lō bwō′är-rō′tē) (1475–1564) ▸ Italian sculptor, painter, architect, and poet.

Mich·i·gan (mĭsh′ĭ-gən) ▸ A state of the N-central US. Cap. Lansing.

Michigan, Lake ▸ The third largest of the Great Lakes, between WI and MI.

Mic·mac (mĭk′măk′) ▸ *n., pl.* **-mac** or **-macs. 1.** A member of a Native American people of E Canada. **2.** The Algonquian language of the Micmac.

mi·cra (mī′krə) ▸ *n.* Pl. of **micron.**

mi·cro (mī′krō) ▸ *adj.* Basic or small-scale: *the economy's performance at the micro level.*

micro– or **micr–** ▸ *pref.* **1a.** Small: *microcircuit.* **b.** Abnormally small: *microcephaly.* **c.** Requiring or involving microscopy: *microsurgery.* **2.** One-millionth (10^{-6}): *microsecond.*

mi·crobe (mī′krōb′) ▸ *n.* A microorganism. **—mi·cro′bi·al** (-krō′bē-əl) *adj.*

mi·cro·bi·ol·o·gy (mī′krō-bī-ŏl′ə-jē) ▸ *n.* The branch of biology that deals with microorganisms. **—mi′cro·bi′o·log′i·cal** (-bī′ə-lŏj′ĭ-kəl) *adj.* **—mi′cro·bi′o·log′i·cal·ly** *adv.* **—mi′cro·bi·ol′o·gist** *n.*

mi·cro·bus (mī′krō-bŭs′) ▸ *n.* A station wagon in the shape of a small bus.

mi·cro·ceph·a·ly (mī′krō-sĕf′ə-lē) ▸ *n.* Abnormal smallness of the head. **—mi′cro·ce·phal′ic** (-sə-făl′ĭk) *adj. & n.* **—mi′cro·ceph′a·lous** *adj.*

mi·cro·chip (mī′krə-chĭp′) ▸ *n. Comp. Sci.* See **chip** 4a.

mi·cro·cir·cuit (mī′krō-sûr′kĭt) ▸ *n.* An electric circuit consisting of miniaturized components. **—mi′cro·cir′cuit·ry** *n.*

mi·cro·com·put·er (mī′krō-kəm-pyo͞o′tər) ▸ *n.* A personal computer.

mi·cro·cosm (mī′krə-kŏz′əm) ▸ *n.* A small, representative system having analogies to a larger system in constitution, configuration, or development. **—mi′cro·cos′mic** (-kŏz′mĭk), **mi′cro·cos′mi·cal** *adj.*

mi·cro·dot (mī′krə-dŏt′) ▸ *n.* A copy or photograph reduced to an extremely small size.

mi·cro·ec·o·nom·ics (mī′krō-ĕk′ə-nŏm′ĭks, -ēk′ə-) ▸ *n. (takes sing. v.)* The study of specific components of a national economy, such as individual firms, households, and consumers. **—mi′cro·ec′o·nom′ic** *adj.*

mi·cro·e·lec·tron·ics (mī′krō-ĭ-lĕk-trŏn′ĭks) ▸ *n. (takes sing. v.)* The branch of electronics that deals with miniature components. **—mi′cro·e·lec·tron′ic** *adj.*

mi·cro·fiche (mī′krō-fēsh′) ▸ *n., pl.* **-fiche** or **-fich·es.** A sheet of microfilm containing rows of pages in reduced form.

mi·cro·film (mī′krə-fĭlm′) ▸ *n.* A film on which printed materials are photographed greatly reduced in size. **—mi′cro·film′** *v.*

THESAURUS

SYMMETRICAL.] *—See also* DELIBERATE (3).
methodize *v.* *—See* ARRANGE (1).
meticulous *adj.* *—See* CAREFUL (2), FUSSY.
meticulousness *n.* *—See* ACCURACY, THOROUGHNESS.
métier *n.* *—See* BUSINESS (2), FORTE.
metrical *adj.* *—See* RHYTHMICAL.
metropolis *n.* *—See* CITY.
metropolitan *adj.* *—See* CITY.
mettle *n.* *—See* COURAGE.
mettlesome *adj.* *—See* BRAVE.
mewl *v.* *—See* CRY.
miasmic *adj.* *—See* POISONOUS.
microbe or **microorganism** *n.* *—See* GERM (1).

mi·cro·lith (mī′krō-lĭth′) ► *n. Archaeol.* A very small blade made of flaked stone. **—mi′cro·lith′ic** (-lĭth′ĭk) *adj.*

mi·cro·man·age (mī′krō-măn′ĭj) ► *v.* To direct or control in a detailed, often meddlesome manner.

mi·crom·e·ter (mī-krŏm′ĭ-tər) ► *n.* A device for measuring very small distances.

mi·cron (mī′krŏn′) ► *n., pl.* **-crons** or **-cra** (-krə). A unit of length equal to one millionth (10^{-6}) of a meter. No longer in technical use.

Mi·cro·ne·si·a (mī′krō-nē′zhə, -shə) ► The islands of the W Pacific, E of the Philippines and N of the equator.

Mi·cro·ne·sian (mī′krə-nē′zhən, -shən) ► *n.* **1.** A member of any of the peoples inhabiting Micronesia. **2.** A subfamily of the Austronesian language family. **—Mi′cro·ne′sian** *adj.*

mi·cro·or·gan·ism (mī′krō-ôr′gə-nĭz′əm) ► *n.* An organism of microscopic size, esp. a bacterium or protozoan.

mi·cro·phone (mī′krə-fōn′) ► *n.* An instrument that converts sound waves into an electric current, usu. fed into an amplifier, recorder, or broadcast transmitter.

mi·cro·proc·es·sor (mī′krō-prŏs′ĕs-ər) ► *n.* An integrated circuit that contains the entire central processing unit of a computer on a single chip.

mi·cro·scope (mī′krə-skōp′) ► *n.* An optical instrument that uses a combination of lenses to produce magnified images of small objects, esp. of objects too small to be seen by the unaided eye.

mi·cro·scop·ic (mī′krə-skŏp′ĭk) also **mi·cro·scop·i·cal** (-ĭ-kəl) ► *adj.* **1.** Relating to microscopes. **2a.** So small as to require a microscope for viewing. **b.** Tiny; minute. **—mi′cro·scop′i·cal·ly** *adv.*

mi·cros·co·py (mī-krŏs′kə-pē) ► *n.* **1.** The study or use of microscopes. **2.** Investigation employing a microscope.

mi·cro·sec·ond (mī′krō-sĕk′ənd) ► *n.* One millionth (10^{-6}) of a second.

mi·cro·sur·ger·y (mī′krō-sûr′jə-rē) ► *n.* Surgery on minute body structures or cells performed with the aid of microscopes. **—mi′cro·sur′gi·cal** *adj.*

mi·cro·wave (mī′krə-wāv′, -krō-) ► *n.* **1.** An electromagnetic wave intermediate between infrared and short-wave radio wavelengths. **2.** *Informal* A microwave oven. **—mi′cro·wav′a·ble, mi′cro·wave′a·ble** *adj.* **—mi′cro·wave′** *v.*

microwave oven ► *n.* An oven in which microwaves cook the food.

mid (mĭd) ► *adj.* Middle; central.

mid– ► *pref.* Middle: *midsummer.*

mid·air (mĭd′âr′) ► *n.* A point or region in the air. **—mid′air′** *adj.*

Mi·das (mī′dəs) ► *n.* A fabled king who turned all that he touched to gold.

mid·day (mĭd′dā′) ► *n.* Noon. **—mid′day′** *adj.*

mid·den (mĭd′n) ► *n.* A refuse heap.

mid·dle (mĭd′l) ► *adj.* **1.** Equally distant from extremes or limits. **2.** Intermediate; in-between. **3.** Intervening between an earlier and a later period of time. ► *n.* **1.** An area or a point equidistant between extremes. **2.** The waist.

middle age ► *n.* The time of human life gen. between 40 and 60. **—mid′dle-aged′** *adj.*

Middle Ages ► *pl.n.* The period in European history between antiquity and the Renaissance, often dated from A.D. 476 to 1453.

Middle America ► *n.* **1.** That part of the US middle class thought of as being conservative in values and attitudes. **2.** The American heartland thought of as being made up of small towns, small cities, and suburbs.

middle class ► *n.* The members of society occupying a socioeconomic position between the lower working classes and the wealthy.

Middle Dutch ► *n.* Dutch from the middle of the 12th through the 15th cent.

middle ear ► *n.* The space between the eardrum and the inner ear that contains the malleus, incus, and stapes.

Middle East also **Mid·east** (mĭd-ēst′) ► An area comprising the countries of SW Asia and NE Africa. **—Middle Eastern** *adj.* **—Middle Easterner** *n.*

Middle English ► *n.* English from about 1100 to 1500.

Middle High German ► *n.* High German from the 11th through the 15th cent.

Middle Low German ► *n.* Low German from the mid-13th through the 15th cent.

mid·dle·man (mĭd′l-măn′) ► *n.* **1.** A trader who buys from producers and sells to retailers or consumers. **2.** A go-between.

middle management ► *n.* A group of persons occupying intermediate managerial positions. **—middle manager** *n.*

mid·dle-of-the-road (mĭd′l-əv-thə-rōd′) ► *adj.* Pursuing a course of action midway between extremes, esp. in politics.

middle school ► *n.* A school typically including grades five or six through eight.

mid·dle·weight (mĭd′l-wāt′) ► *n.* A boxer weighing from 148 to 160 lbs. between a welterweight and a light heavyweight.

Middle West ► See **Midwest.** **—Middle Western** *adj.* **—Middle Westerner** *n.*

mid·dling (mĭd′lĭng, -lĭn) ► *adj.* **1.** Of medium size, position, or quality. **2.** Mediocre. ► *adv. Informal* Fairly; moderately. **—mid′dling·ly** *adv.*

mid·dy (mĭd′ē) ► *n., pl.* **-dies.** **1.** A midshipman. **2.** A loose blouse with a sailor collar.

Mid·east (mĭd-ēst′) ► See **Middle East.** **—Mid·east′ern** *adj.* **—Mid·east′ern·er** *n.*

midge (mĭj) ► *n.* A gnatlike fly.

midg·et (mĭj′ĭt) ► *n.* **1.** *Offensive* An unusually small or short person of otherwise normal proportions. **2.** A miniature version of something. **—midg′et** *adj.*

mid·land (mĭd′lənd) ► *n.* The middle part of a country or region. **—mid′land** *adj.*

mid·line (mĭd′līn′) ► *n.* A medial line, esp. the medial line of the body.

mid·night (mĭd′nīt′) ► *n.* The middle of the night; 12 o'clock at night.

midnight sun ► *n.* The sun as seen at midnight during the summer within the Arctic and Antarctic regions.

mid·point (mĭd′point′) ► *n.* A point or position at or near the middle.

mid·riff (mĭd′rĭf) ► *n.* **1.** See **diaphragm** 1. **2.** The outer part of the human body from below the breast to the waist.

mid·ship·man (mĭd′shĭp′mən, mĭd-shĭp′mən) ► *n.* A student at a naval academy training to be a commissioned officer.

midst (mĭdst, mĭtst) ► *n.* **1.** The middle position or part; center. **2.** The condition of being surrounded by something: *the midst of chaos.* ► *prep.* Among.

mid·sum·mer (mĭd′sŭm′ər) ► *n.* **1.** The middle of the summer. **2.** The summer solstice, about Jun. 21. **—mid′sum′mer** *adj.*

mid·term (mĭd′tûrm′) ► *n.* **1.** The middle esp. of an academic or political term. **2.** An examination given at the middle of a school term. **—mid′term′** *adj.*

mid·town (mĭd′toun′) ► *n.* A central portion of a city. **—mid′town′** *adj.*

mid·way (mĭd′wā′) ► *n.* The area of a fair, carnival, or circus where sideshows and other amusements are located. ► *adv.* In the middle; halfway. **—mid′way′** *adj.*

Midway Islands ► Two small islands and a surrounding coral atoll in the central Pacific NW of Honolulu.

mid·week (mĭd′wēk′) ► *n.* The middle of the week. **—mid′week′** *adj.* **—mid′week′ly** *adj. & adv.*

THESAURUS

microscopic *adj.* So small as not to be discernible ► imperceptible, infinitesimal. *—See also* TINY.

mid *adj.* *—See* CENTRAL, MIDDLE.

middle *adj.* Being at neither one extreme nor the other ► between, central, in-between, intermediary, intermediate, mean, medial, median, mid, middle-of-the-road, midway. [*Compare* NEUTRAL.] *—See also* CENTRAL.

middle *n.* *—See* CENTER (2).

middleman *n.* *—See* GO-BETWEEN.

middlemost *adj.* *—See* CENTRAL.

middle-of-the-road *adj.* *—See* MIDDLE.

middling *adj.* *—See* AVERAGE, ORDINARY.

midget *adj.* *—See* TINY.

midmost *adj.* *—See* CENTRAL.

midpoint *n.* *—See* AVERAGE, CENTER (2).

midst *n.* The most intensely active central part ► eye, thick. [*Compare* CENTER.] *—See also* CENTER (2).

midway *adj.* *—See* MIDDLE.

Mid·west (mĭd-wĕst′) or **Middle West** ▸ A region of the N-central US around the Great Lakes and the upper Mississippi Valley. **—Mid·west′ern** *adj.* **—Mid·west′ern·er** *n.*
mid·wife (mĭd′wīf′) ▸ *n., pl.* **-wives** (-wīvz′). A person, usu. a woman, trained to assist women in childbirth. **—mid·wife′ry** (-wĭf′ə-rē, mĭd′wīf′rē) *n.*
mid·win·ter (mĭd′wĭn′tər) ▸ *n.* 1. The middle of the winter. 2. The winter solstice, about Dec. 22. **—mid′win′ter** *adj.*
mid·year (mĭd′yîr′) ▸ *n.* 1. The middle of the calendar or academic year. 2. An examination given in the middle of a school year. **—mid′year′** *adj.*
mien (mēn) ▸ *n.* Bearing or manner; appearance.
miff (mĭf) ▸ *v.* To offend; annoy.
might[1] (mīt) ▸ *n.* 1. The power or force held by a person or group. 2. Physical strength.
might[2] (mīt) ▸ *aux.v.* P.t. of **may**. Used to indicate a condition contrary to fact, a possibility weaker than *may,* or to express a higher degree of politeness than *may.*
might·y (mī′tē) ▸ *adj.* **-i·er, -i·est.** 1. Having great power. 2. Imposing or awesome. ▸ *adv. Regional* Very. **—might′i·ly** *adv.* **—might′i·ness** *n.*
mi·graine (mī′grān′) ▸ *n.* A severe, recurring headache, usu. affecting only one side of the head.
mi·grant (mī′grənt) ▸ *n.* 1. One that migrates. 2. A worker who travels from one area to another in search of work. **—mi′grant** *adj.*
mi·grate (mī′grāt′) ▸ *v.* **-grat·ed, -grat·ing.** 1. To move from one country or region and settle in another. 2. To move periodically from one region or climate to another. **—mi·gra′tion** *n.* **—mi′gra·to′ry** (-grə-tôr′ē) *adj.*
mi·ka·do (mĭ-kä′dō) ▸ *n., pl.* **-dos.** An emperor of Japan.
mike (mīk) *Informal* ▸ *n.* A microphone. ▸ *v.* **miked, mik·ing.** To supply with or transmit through a microphone.
mil (mĭl) ▸ *n.* A unit of length equal to one thousandth (10^{-3}) of an inch.
Mi·lan (mĭ-lăn′, -län′) ▸ A city of N Italy NE of Genoa. **—Mil′a·nese′** (mĭl′ə-nēz′, -nēs′) *adj. & n.*
mild (mīld) ▸ *adj.* **-er, -est.** 1. Gentle or kind in disposition or behavior. 2. Not harsh, severe, or strong; moderate. **—mild′ly** *adv.* **—mild′ness** *n.*
mil·dew (mĭl′do͞o′, -dyo͞o′) ▸ *n.* Any of various fungi that form a usu. whitish growth on plants and materials such as cloth and paper. **—mil′dew′** *v.*
mile (mīl) ▸ *n.* 1. See **measurement** table in Appendix. 2. A nautical mile. 3. An air mile.
mile·age (mī′lĭj) ▸ *n.* 1. Distance measured or expressed in miles. 2. Service or wear estimated by miles used or traveled. 3. An allowance for travel expenses established at a specified rate per mile.
mile·post (mīl′pōst′) ▸ *n.* A post indicating distance in miles, as along a highway.
mil·er (mī′lər) ▸ *n.* One who competes in one-mile races.
mile·stone (mīl′stōn′) ▸ *n.* 1. A stone milepost. 2. A turning point.
mi·lieu (mĭl-yo͞o′, mē-lyœ′) ▸ *n., pl.* **-lieus** or **-lieux** (-lyœ′). An environment; setting.
mil·i·tant (mĭl′ĭ-tənt) ▸ *adj.* 1. Fighting or warring. 2. Combative or aggressive esp. for a cause. ▸ *n.* A militant person or party. **—mil′i·tance, mil′i·tan·cy** *n.* **—mil′i·tant·ly** *adv.*
mil·i·ta·rism (mĭl′ĭ-tə-rĭz′əm) ▸ *n.* 1. Glorification of the ideals of a professional military class. 2. Predominance of the armed forces in state policies. **—mil′i·ta·rist** *n.* **—mil′i·ta·ris′tic** *adj.*
mil·i·ta·rize (mĭl′ĭ-tə-rīz′) ▸ *v.* **-rized, -riz·ing.** 1. To equip, train, or prepare for war. 2. To imbue with militarism. **—mil′i·ta·ri·za′tion** *n.*
mil·i·tar·y (mĭl′ĭ-tĕr′ē) ▸ *adj.* Of or relating to the armed forces or war. ▸ *n., pl.* **-y** also **-ies.** Armed forces. **—mil′i·tar′i·ly** (-târ′ə-lē) *adv.*
mil·i·tate (mĭl′ĭ-tāt′) ▸ *v.* **-tat·ed, -tat·ing.** To bring about an effect or change.
mi·li·tia (mə-lĭsh′ə) ▸ *n.* An army composed of ordinary citizens rather than professional soldiers, on call for service in an emergency. **—mi·li′tia·man** *n.*
milk (mĭlk) ▸ *n.* 1. A nourishing whitish liquid produced by the mammary glands of female mammals after they have given birth and used to feed their young. 2. The milk of cows or other animals, used as food by humans. 3. A liquid that resembles milk: *coconut milk.* ▸ *v.* 1. To draw milk from (a female mammal). 2. To draw or extract a liquid from as if by milking. **—milk′er** *n.* **—milk′i·ness** *n.* **—milk′y** *adj.*
milk·maid (mĭlk′mād′) ▸ *n.* A girl or woman who milks cows.
milk·man (mĭlk′măn′) ▸ *n.* A man who sells or delivers milk to customers.
milk of magnesia ▸ *n.* A milky white liquid suspension of magnesium hydroxide, $Mg(OH)_2$, used as an antacid and laxative.
milk shake ▸ *n.* A whipped beverage made of milk, flavoring, and usu. ice cream.
milk tooth ▸ *n.* Any of the temporary first teeth of a young mammal.
milk·weed (mĭlk′wēd′) ▸ *n.* A plant having milky juice and pods that split open to release downy seeds.
Milky Way ▸ *n.* The galaxy containing the solar system, visible as a broad band of faint light in the night sky.
mill[1] (mĭl) ▸ *n.* 1. A building equipped with machinery for grinding grain. 2. A device for crushing or grinding. 3. A building equipped with machinery for processing materials; factory. 4. A place that turns out something routinely in the manner of a factory: *a diploma mill.* ▸ *v.* 1. To grind or crush in or as if in a mill. 2. To move around in churning confusion. **—mill′er** *n.*
mill[2] (mĭl) ▸ *n.* A monetary unit equal to ¹/₁₀₀₀ of a US dollar.
Mil·lay (mĭ-lā′), **Edna Saint Vincent** (1892–1950) ▸ Amer. poet.
mill·dam (mĭl′dăm′) ▸ *n.* A dam to make a millpond.
mil·len·ni·um (mə-lĕn′ē-əm) ▸ *n., pl.* **-ni·ums** or **-ni·a** (ē-ə). 1. A span of 1,000 years. 2. In the New Testament, a thousand-year period in which Jesus is to rule on earth. 3. A hoped-for

THESAURUS

mien *n.* —*See* APPEARANCE (1), BEARING (1).
miff *v.* —*See* INSULT, OFFEND (1).
miff *n.* —*See* OFFENSE.
might *n.* —*See* ABILITY (2), AUTHORITY, ENERGY, FORCE (1), STRENGTH.
mighty *adj.* Having great physical strength ▸ potent, powerful, strong. [*Compare* ENERGETIC, MUSCULAR.] —*See also* STRENUOUS, FORCEFUL.
mighty *adv.* —*See* VERY.
migrant *n.* One who migrates ▸ emigrant, immigrant, transmigrant. [*Compare* ÉMIGRÉ, FOREIGNER, SETTLER.] —*See also* HOBO.
migrant *adj.* Moving from one area to another in search of work ▸ itinerant, migratory. —*See also* MIGRATORY (1).
migrate *v.* 1. To leave one's native land and settle in another ▸ emigrate (from), immigrate (to), resettle, transmigrate. [*Compare* MOVE, SETTLE.] 2. To change habitat seasonally ▸ transmigrate.
migration *n.* Settling in a country to which one is not native ▸ immigration, transmigration. —*See also* EMIGRATION.
migrational *adj.* —*See* MIGRATORY (1).
migratory *adj.* 1. Moving from one habitat to another on a seasonal basis ▸ migrant, migrational, seasonal, transient, transmigratory. [*Compare* MOBILE, NOMADIC.] 2. Moving from one area to another in search of work ▸ itinerant, migrant.
mild *adj.* Free from extremes in temperature ▸ balmy, clement, moderate, temperate. [*Compare* PLEASANT.] —*See also* GENTLE (1), GENTLE (2), GENTLE (3), GRADUAL (2).
mildewed *adj.* —*See* MOLDY.
milieu *n.* —*See* ENVIRONMENT (2).
militance *n.* —*See* AGGRESSION.
militant *adj.* —*See* AGGRESSIVE, BELLIGERENT, EXTREME (2).
militant *n.* —*See* EXTREMIST.
militaristic *adj.* —*See* MILITARY (1).
militarize *v.* —*See* MOBILIZE.
military *adj.* 1. Of or inclined toward war ▸ bellicose, chauvinistic, hawkish, jingoistic, martial, militaristic, warlike, warmongering. [*Compare* AGGRESSIVE.] 2. Relating to armed service ▸ barracks, enlisted, martial, regimental, soldierly. *Idiom:* in uniform.
militiaman *n.* —*See* SOLDIER (2).
milk *v.* —*See* DRAIN (1).
milksop *n.* —*See* BABY (2), COWARD.
milky *adj.* —*See* FAIR[1] (3).
mill *n.* A building or complex in which an industry is located ▸ factory, plant, works.
mill *v.* —*See* CRUSH (2).

period of joy, serenity, and justice. **—mil·len′ni·al** (-əl) *adj.* **—mil·len′ni·al·ism** *n.* **—mil·len′ni·al·ist** *n.* **—mil·len′ni·al·ly** *adv.*

mil·le·pede (mĭl′ə-pēd′) ► *n.* Var. of **millipede.**

mil·let (mĭl′ĭt) ► *n.* **1.** A grass grown for its edible white grain and for hay. **2.** The grain itself.

milli– ► *pref.* One thousandth (10^{-3}): *millisecond.*

mil·liard (mĭl′yərd, -yärd′, mĭl′ē-ärd′) ► *n. Chiefly Brit.* A billion.

mil·li·bar (mĭl′ə-bär′) ► *n.* A unit of atmospheric pressure equal to 100 newtons per square meter.

mil·li·gram (mĭl′ĭ-grăm′) ► *n.* See **measurement** table in Appendix.

mil·li·li·ter (mĭl′ə-lē′tər) ► *n.* See **measurement** table in Appendix.

mil·li·me·ter (mĭl′ə-mē′tər) ► *n.* See **measurement** table in Appendix.

mil·li·ner (mĭl′ə-nər) ► *n.* One who makes or sells esp. women's hats. **—mil′li·ner′y** (-nĕr′ē) *n.*

mil·lion (mĭl′yən) ► *n., pl.* **-lion** or **-lions.** The cardinal number equal to 10^6. **—mil′lion** *adj. & pron.*

mil·lion·aire (mĭl′yə-nâr′) ► *n.* A person whose wealth amounts to at least a million dollars, pounds, or the equivalent in other currency.

mil·lionth (mĭl′yənth) ► *n.* **1.** The ordinal number matching the number million in a series. **2.** One of a million equal parts. **—mil′lionth** *adv. & adj.*

mil·li·pede or **mil·le·pede** (mĭl′ə-pēd′) ► *n.* A crawling, plant-eating myriapod having a long segmented body with two pairs of legs attached to most of its body segments.

mil·li·sec·ond (mĭl′ĭ-sĕk′ənd) ► *n.* One thousandth (10^{-3}) of a second.

mill·pond (mĭl′pŏnd′) ► *n.* A pond formed by a dam to provide power for turning a mill wheel.

mill·race (mĭl′rās′) ► *n.* **1.** The fast stream of water that drives a mill wheel. **2.** The channel in which this stream flows.

mill·stone (mĭl′stōn′) ► *n.* **1.** One of a pair of large circular stones used for grinding grain. **2.** A heavy burden.

mill·stream (mĭl′strēm′) ► *n.* The rapid stream of water in a millrace.

mill wheel ► *n.* A wheel, typically driven by water, that powers a mill.

milque·toast (mĭlk′tōst′) ► *n.* One who has a timid, unassertive nature.

milt (mĭlt) ► *n.* Fish sperm.

Mil·ton (mĭl′tən), **John** (1608–74) ► English poet and scholar.

Mil·wau·kee (mĭl-wô′kē) ► A city of SE WI on Lake Michigan.

mime (mīm) ► *n.* **1.** Pantomime. **2.** A modern performer who specializes in silent comic mimicry. ► *v.* **mimed, mim·ing.** **1.** To mimic. **2.** To pantomime. **—mim′er** *n.*

mim·e·o·graph (mĭm′ē-ə-grăf′) ► *n.* A duplicator that makes copies of written, drawn, or typed material from a stencil fitted around an inked drum. **—mim′e·o·graph′** *v.*

mi·me·sis (mĭ-mē′sĭs, mī-) ► *n.* The representation of aspects of the sensible world, esp. human actions, in literature and art.

mi·met·ic (mĭ-mĕt′ĭk, mī-) ► *adj.* Of, relating to, or exhibiting mimicry. **—mi·met′i·cal·ly** *adv.*

mim·ic (mĭm′ĭk) ► *v.* **-icked, -ick·ing.** **1.** To imitate closely, as in speech or gesture; ape. **2.** To ridicule by imitating; mock. **3.** To resemble closely; simulate. ► *n.* One who mimics. ► *adj.* Of mimicry. **—mim′ick·er** *n.*

mim·ic·ry (mĭm′ĭ-krē) ► *n., pl.* **-ries.** The act or practice of mimicking; imitation.

mi·mo·sa (mĭ-mō′sə, -zə) ► *n.* Any of various shrubs or trees having ball-like clusters of small flowers.

min. ► *abbr.* **1.** minimum **2. Min.** minister **3.** minor **4.** minute

min·a·ret (mĭn′ə-rĕt′) ► *n.* A tall slender tower attached to a mosque, from which a muezzin calls the faithful to prayer.

min·a·to·ry (mĭn′ə-tôr′ē) also **min·a·to·ri·al** (-tôr′ē-əl) ► *adj.* Menacing or threatening.

mince (mĭns) ► *v.* **minced, minc·ing.** **1.** To cut into very small pieces. **2.** To pronounce in an affected way. **3.** To moderate (words) for the sake of decorum; euphemize. **4.** To walk with exaggerated primness. **—minc′er** *n.* **—minc′ing** *adj.*

mince·meat (mĭns′mēt′) ► *n.* A mixture, as of finely chopped apples, raisins, spices, and rum or brandy, used esp. as a pie filling. ***—idiom:*** **make mincemeat of** *Slang* To destroy utterly.

mind (mīnd) ► *n.* **1.** The human consciousness that originates in the brain and is manifested esp. in thought, perception, emotion, will, memory, and imagination. **2.** Intelligence; intellect. **3.** A person of great mental ability. **4.** Memory; recollection. **5.** Opinion or sentiment. **6.** Sanity. ► *v.* **1.** To obey. **2.** To attend to; heed. **3.** To be careful about. **4.** To care or be concerned about. **5.** To object (to); dislike.

mind-blow·ing (mīnd′blō′ĭng) ► *adj. Informal* **1.** Producing hallucinatory effects. **2.** Mind-boggling. **—mind′blow′er** *n.*

mind-bog·gling (mīnd′bŏg′lĭng) ► *adj. Informal* Intellectually or emotionally overwhelming. **—mind′-bog′gler** *n.*

mind-ex·pand·ing (mīnd′ĭk-spăn′dĭng) ► *adj.* Psychedelic.

mind·ful (mīnd′fəl) ► *adj.* Attentive; heedful. **—mind′ful·ness** *n.*

mind·less (mīnd′lĭs) ► *adj.* **1.** Lacking intelligence or sense. **2.** Careless; heedless. **—mind′less·ly** *adv.* **—mind′less·ness** *n.*

mind·set or **mind-set** (mīnd′sĕt′) ► *n.* A fixed mental attitude that determines one's responses to and interpretations of situations.

mine[1] (mīn) ► *n.* **1.** An excavation from which ore or minerals are extracted. **2.** A deposit of ore or minerals. **3.** An abundant source. **4a.** A tunnel dug under an enemy position. **b.** An explosive device, often buried or submerged and designed to be detonated by contact or a time fuse. ► *v.* **mined, min·ing.** **1.** To extract (ore or minerals) from the earth. **2.** To dig a mine in. **3.** To lay explosive mines in or under. **4.** To undermine; subvert. **—min′a·ble, mine′a·ble** *adj.* **—min′er** *n.*

mine[2] (mīn) ► *pron. (takes sing. or pl. v.)* Used to indicate the one or ones belonging to me: *The green gloves are mine.*

mine·field (mīn′fēld′) ► *n.* An area in which explosive mines have been placed.

min·er·al (mĭn′ər-əl) ► *n.* **1.** A natural inorganic substance having a definite chemical composition and characteristic crystalline structure. **2a.** An element, such as gold or silver.

THESAURUS

million *n.* —*See* HEAP (2).

millstone *n.* —*See* BURDEN[1] (1).

milquetoast *n.* —*See* BABY (2), COWARD.

mime *n.* —*See* MIMIC, MIMICRY.

mimesis *n.* The formation of words in imitation of sounds ► echoism, onomatopoeia.

mimetic *adj.* Imitating sounds ► echoic, imitative, onomatopoeic, onomatopoetic. —*See also* IMITATIVE (1).

mimic *v.* To copy another slavishly ► clone, echo, image, imitate, mirror, parrot, reflect, repeat. [*Compare* COPY.] —*See also* IMITATE, RESEMBLE.

mimic *n.* One who imitates ► ape, echo, imitator, impersonator, mime, parrot. *Informal:* copycat.

mimicry *n.* The act, practice, or art of copying the manner or expression of another ► aping, copying, echoing, emulation, imitation, impersonation, impression, mime, mirroring, parroting. [*Compare* MOCKERY.]

mincing *adj.* —*See* PRUDISH.

mind *n.* **1.** The seat of the faculty of intelligence and reason ► brain, head. *Informal:* gray matter. [*Compare* IMAGINATION.] **2.** A person of great mental ability ► brain, genius, highbrow, intellect, intellectual, mastermind, thinker. *Informal:* egghead, whiz. *Slang:* brainiac, pointy-head. [*Compare* EXPERT, SAGE.] —*See also* BELIEF (1), INTELLIGENCE, LIKING, PSYCHOLOGY, SANITY.

mind *v.* To be careful ► beware, look out, watch out. ***Idioms:*** be on guard, be on the lookout, keep an eye peeled, take care (*or* heed). —*See also* CARE, FOLLOW (4), NOTICE, REMEMBER (1), TEND[2].

mind-boggling or **mind-blowing** *adj.* —*See* ASTONISHING.

minded *adj.* —*See* WILLING.

mindful *adj.* —*See* CAREFUL (1).

mindfulness *n.* —*See* CARE (1).

mindless *adj.* Lacking rational direction or purpose ► brainless, meaningless, pointless, purposeless, senseless. ***Idiom:*** without rhyme or reason. [*Compare* BORING, PERFUNCTORY, VACANT.] —*See also* CARELESS, FOOLISH, STUPID.

mindlessness *n.* —*See* STUPIDITY.

mindset or **mind-set** *n.* —*See* MOOD, POSTURE (2), PSYCHOLOGY.

mind's eye *n.* —*See* IMAGINATION.

b. An organic derivative, such as coal or petroleum. 3. A substance that is neither animal nor vegetable; inorganic matter. 4. A nutritionally important inorganic element, such as calcium or zinc. 5. An ore. **—min′er·al** *adj.* **—min′er·al·ize′** *v.*

min·er·al·o·gy (mĭn′ə-rŏl′ə-jē, -răl′-) ▸ *n.* The study of minerals. **—min′er·a·log′i·cal** (-ər-ə-lŏj′ĭ-kəl) *adj.* **—min′er·a·log′i·cal·ly** *adv.* **—min′er·al′o·gist** *n.*

mineral oil ▸ *n.* Any of various oils, esp. a distillate of petroleum used as a laxative.

mineral water ▸ *n.* Water that contains dissolved mineral salts or gases.

mineral wool ▸ *n.* A fibrous insulating material made by steam blasting and cooling molten glass or rock.

Mi·ner·va (mĭ-nûr′və) ▸ *n. Rom. Myth.* The goddess of wisdom, the arts, and warfare.

min·e·stro·ne (mĭn′ĭ-strō′nē, -strōn′) ▸ *n.* A thick soup containing vegetables, beans, and pasta.

mine·sweep·er (mīn′swē′pər) ▸ *n.* A ship equipped for detecting, removing, or neutralizing marine mines.

min·gle (mĭng′gəl) ▸ *v.* **-gled, -gling.** To mix together in close association. **—min′gler** *n.*

min·i (mĭn′ē) ▸ *n., pl.* **min·is.** 1. Something distinctively smaller than others of its class. 2. A miniskirt. **—min′i** *adj.*

mini– ▸ *pref.* Small; miniature: *minibike.*

min·i·a·ture (mĭn′ē-ə-cho͝or′, -chər, mĭn′ə-) ▸ *n.* 1. A very small copy or model. 2. A very small, detailed painting. ▸ *adj.* Very small. **—min′i·a·tur′ist** *n.* **—min′i·a·tur·i·za′tion** *n.* **—min′i·a·tur·ize′** *v.*

min·i·bike (mĭn′ē-bīk′) ▸ *n.* A small motorbike.

min·i·bus (mĭn′ē-bŭs′) ▸ *n.* A small bus.

min·i·com·put·er (mĭn′ē-kəm-pyo͞o′tər) ▸ *n.* A mid-sized computer, usu. fitting within a single cabinet about the size of a refrigerator, that has less memory than a mainframe.

min·im (mĭn′əm) ▸ *n.* 1. A unit of fluid measure equal to 1/60 of a fluid dram. 2. A small portion.

min·i·mal (mĭn′ə-məl) ▸ *adj.* Smallest in amount or degree. **—min′i·mal·ly** *adv.*

min·i·mal·ism (mĭn′ə-mə-lĭz′əm) ▸ *n.* Use of the fewest and barest essentials or elements, as in the arts, literature, or design.

min·i·mal·ist (mĭn′ə-mə-lĭst) ▸ *n.* 1. One who advocates a moderate or conservative policy. 2. A practitioner of minimalism. **—min′i·mal·ist** *adj.*

min·i·mize (mĭn′ə-mīz′) ▸ *v.* **-mized, -miz·ing.** To reduce to or represent as having minimal importance or value. **—min′i·mi·za′tion** *n.* **—min′i·miz′er** *n.*

min·i·mum (mĭn′ə-məm) ▸ *n., pl.* **-mums** or **-ma** (-mə). 1. The least possible quantity or degree. 2. The lowest quantity reached or permitted. **—min′i·mum** *adj.*

minimum wage ▸ *n.* The lowest wage, determined by law or contract, that can be paid for a specified job.

min·ion (mĭn′yən) ▸ *n.* An obsequious follower or dependent.

min·i·se·ries (mĭn′ē-sîr′ēz) ▸ *n.* 1. A televised drama shown in a number of episodes. 2. A short series of athletic contests.

min·i·skirt (mĭn′ē-skûrt′) ▸ *n.* A very short skirt. **—min′i·skirt′ed** *adj.*

min·is·ter (mĭn′ĭ-stər) ▸ *n.* 1. One authorized to perform religious functions in a Christian church. 2. The head of a governmental department. 3. A diplomat ranking below an ambassador. 4. A person serving as an agent for another. ▸ *v.* To attend to the wants and needs of others. **—min′is·te′ri·al** (-stîr′ē-əl) *adj.* **—min′is·te′ri·al·ly** *adv.* **—min′is·trant** *n.* **—min′is·tra′tion** *n.* **—min′is·tra′tive** *adj.*

min·is·try (mĭn′ĭ-strē) ▸ *n., pl.* **-tries.** 1. The act of serving; ministration. 2a. The profession and services of a minister. b. The clergy. c. The period of service of a minister. 3a. A governmental department presided over by a minister. b. The building in which it is housed. c. The duties, functions, or term of a governmental minister.

min·i·van (mĭn′ē-văn′) ▸ *n.* A small passenger van, typically with removable rear seats.

mink (mĭngk) ▸ *n., pl.* **mink** or **minks.** 1. A semiaquatic weasellike mammal having soft, thick, lustrous brown fur. 2. The fur of the mink.

Minn. ▸ *abbr.* Minnesota

Min·ne·ap·o·lis (mĭn′ē-ăp′ə-lĭs) ▸ A city of SE MN on the Mississippi R. adjacent to St. Paul.

Min·ne·so·ta (mĭn′ĭ-sō′tə) ▸ A state of the N US bordering on Lake Superior and Canada. Cap. St. Paul. **—Min′ne·so′tan** *adj. & n.*

min·now (mĭn′ō) ▸ *n., pl.* **-now** or **-nows.** Any of various small freshwater fishes widely used as bait.

Mi·no·an (mĭ-nō′ən) ▸ *adj.* Of or relating to the Bronze Age culture in Crete from about 3000 to 1100 B.C. **—Mi·no′an** *n.*

mi·nor (mī′nər) ▸ *adj.* 1. Lesser or smaller in amount, size, or importance. 2. Lesser in seriousness or danger. 3. *Law* Being under legal age. 4. *Mus.* Of or being a minor scale. ▸ *n.* 1. *Law* One who is under legal age. 2a. A secondary area of academic study. b. One studying a minor: *She is a chemistry minor.* 3. *Mus.* A minor key, scale, or interval. 4. **minors** *Sports* The minor leagues. ▸ *v.* To pursue academic studies in a minor field.

Mi·nor·ca (mĭ-nôr′kə) ▸ A Spanish island in the Balearics of the W Mediterranean Sea. **—Mi·nor′can** *adj. & n.*

mi·nor·i·ty (mə-nôr′ĭ-tē, -nŏr′-, mī-) ▸ *n., pl.* **-ties.** 1. The smaller of two groups forming a whole. 2a. A racial, religious, or other group different from the larger group of which it is part. b. A member of such a group. 3. The state or period of being under legal age.

minor league ▸ *n.* A league of professional sports clubs not belonging to the major leagues. **—mi′nor-league′** *adj.*

minor scale ▸ *n. Mus.* A diatonic scale having a half step between the 2nd and 3rd degrees.

Min·o·taur (mĭn′ə-tôr′, mī′nə-) ▸ *n. Gk. Myth.* A monster who was half man and half bull.

min·ster (mĭn′stər) ▸ *n. Chiefly Brit.* A monastery church.

min·strel (mĭn′strəl) ▸ *n.* 1. A medieval traveling entertainer. 2. A performer in a minstrel show.

minstrel show ▸ *n.* A comic variety show presenting jokes, songs, dances, and skits, usually by white actors in blackface.

mint[1] (mĭnt) ▸ *n.* 1. A place where money is manufactured by a government. 2. An abundant amount, esp. of money. ▸ *v.* 1. To produce (money) by stamping metal. 2. To invent or fabricate (e.g., a phrase). ▸ *adj.* New or as if new: *mint condition.* **—mint′er** *n.*

mint[2] (mĭnt) ▸ *n.* 1. Any of various related plants, many of which yield an aromatic oil used for flavoring. 2. A candy flavored with mint. **—mint′y** *adj.*

mint julep ▸ *n.* A drink made of bourbon, sugar, crushed mint leaves, and shaved ice.

min·u·end (mĭn′yo͞o-ĕnd′) ▸ *n.* The quantity from which

THESAURUS

mingle *v.* To take part in social activities ▸ mix, socialize. —*See also* MIX (1).

miniature or **mini** *adj.* —*See* TINY.

minim *n.* —*See* BIT[1] (1).

minimal *adj.* Comprising the least possible ▸ least, littlest, minimum, minutest, slightest, smallest, tiniest. [*Compare* TRIVIAL.]

minimization *n.* —*See* BELITTLEMENT.

minimize *v.* —*See* BELITTLE.

minimum *adj.* —*See* MINIMAL.

minimum *n.* A very low or lowest level, position, or degree ▸ bottom, low, nadir, rock bottom.

minion *n.* —*See* SUBORDINATE.

minister *n.* —*See* CLERIC, REPRESENTATIVE.

minister to *v.* To work and care for ▸ attend, do for, serve, wait on (*or* upon). [*Compare* HELP, WORK.] —*See also* TEND[2].

ministerial *adj.* —*See* ADMINISTRATIVE, CLERICAL.

ministry *n.* —*See* GOVERNMENT (2).

minor *adj.* 1. Below another in standing, importance, or status ▸ collateral, inferior, junior, lesser, little known, low, lower, minor-league, petty, secondary, second-class, slight, small, subaltern, subordinate, under. *Informal:* smalltime. *Slang:* bush-league. [*Compare* AUXILIARY, TRIVIAL.] 2. Not yet a legal adult ▸ juvenile, underage.

minor *n.* One who is not yet legally of age ▸ child, juvenile, underage person. [*Compare* CHILD, YOUTH.]

minor-league *adj.* —*See* MINOR (1).

minstrel *n.* —*See* POET.

mint *n.* —*See* FORTUNE.

mint *v.* —*See* INVENT.

another quantity is to be subtracted.

min·u·et (mĭn′yo͞o-ĕt′) ▸ *n.* **1.** A stately dance in 3/4 time originating in 17th-cent. France. **2.** Music for a minuet.

mi·nus (mī′nəs) ▸ *prep.* **1.** *Math.* Reduced by; less: *Nine minus three is six.* **2.** *Informal* Without: *I went to work minus my briefcase.* ▸ *adj.* **1.** *Math.* Negative or on the negative part of a scale: *a minus value.* **2.** Ranking on the lower end of a designated scale: *a grade of A minus.* ▸ *n.* **1.** *Math.* **a.** The minus sign (–). **b.** A negative quantity. **2.** A deficiency or defect.

min·us·cule (mĭn′ə-skyo͞ol′, mĭ-nŭs′kyo͞ol′) ▸ *adj.* Very small; tiny.

minus sign ▸ *n.* *Math.* The symbol –, as in 4 – 2 = 2, used to indicate subtraction or a negative quantity.

min·ute[1] (mĭn′ĭt) ▸ *n.* **1.** A unit of time equal to $^1/_{60}$ of an hour or 60 seconds. **2.** A unit of angular measurement equal to $^1/_{60}$ of a degree or 60 seconds. **3.** A moment. **4.** A specific point in time. **5. minutes** An official record of the proceedings at a meeting.

mi·nute[2] (mī-no͞ot′, -nyo͞ot′, mĭ-) ▸ *adj.* **1.** Exceptionally small; tiny. **2.** Beneath notice; insignificant. **3.** Marked by careful examination; detailed. **—mi·nute′ly** *adv.* **—mi·nute′ness** *n.*

min·ute·man (mĭn′ĭt-măn′) ▸ *n.* An armed man ready to fight on a minute's notice during the American Revolutionary War.

mi·nu·ti·a (mĭ-no͞o′shē-ə, -shə, -nyo͞o′-) ▸ *n., pl.* **-ti·ae** (-shē-ē′). A small or trivial detail.

minx (mĭngks) ▸ *n.* An impudent young woman. **—minx′ish** *adj.*

Mi·o·cene (mī′ə-sēn′) *Geol.* ▸ *adj.* Of or being the 4th epoch of the Tertiary Period, marked by the development of grasses and grazing mammals. ▸ *n.* The Miocene Epoch.

mir·a·cle (mĭr′ə-kəl) ▸ *n.* **1.** An event inexplicable by the laws of nature and so held to be supernatural in origin or an act of God. **2.** A marvel. **—mi·rac′u·lous** (mĭ-răk′yə-ləs) *adj.* **—mi·rac′u·lous·ly** *adv.*

mi·rage (mĭ-räzh′) ▸ *n.* **1.** An optical phenomenon that creates the illusion of water, often with inverted reflections of distant objects. **2.** Something illusory or insubstantial.

mire (mīr) ▸ *n.* **1.** A bog. **2.** Deep slimy soil or mud. ▸ *v.* **mired, mir·ing.** **1.** To sink or stick in or as if in mire. **2.** To soil with mud. **—mir′y** *adj.*

mir·in (mĭr′ĭn) ▸ *n.* A sweet Japanese rice wine, used esp. in cooking.

mir·ror (mĭr′ər) ▸ *n.* **1.** A surface capable of reflecting sufficient undiffused light to form a virtual image of an object in front of it. **2.** Something that gives a true picture of something else. ▸ *v.* To reflect in or as in a mirror.

mirth (mûrth) ▸ *n.* Gladness and gaiety. **—mirth′ful** *adj.* **—mirth′ful·ly** *adv.* **—mirth′ful·ness** *n.*

mis– ▸ *pref.* **1.** Bad; badly; wrong; wrongly: *misconduct.* **2.** Failure; lack: *misfire.*

mis·ad·ven·ture (mĭs′əd-vĕn′chər) ▸ *n.* A misfortune; mishap.

mis·al·li·ance (mĭs′ə-lī′əns) ▸ *n.* An unsuitable marriage.

mis·an·thrope (mĭs′ən-thrōp′, mĭz′-) also **mis·an·thro·pist** (mĭs-ăn′thrə-pĭst, mĭz′-) ▸ *n.* One who hates humankind. **—mis′an·throp′ic** (-thrŏp′ĭk) *adj.* **—mis′an·throp′i·cal·ly** *adv.* **—mis·an′thro·py** *n.*

mis·ap·pre·hend (mĭs-ăp′rĭ-hĕnd′) ▸ *v.* To misunderstand. **—mis·ap′pre·hen′sion** *n.*

mis·be·got·ten (mĭs′bĭ-gŏt′n) ▸ *adj.* **1.** Of illegitimate birth. **2.** Of dubious origin.

misc. ▸ *abbr.* miscellaneous

mis·car·riage (mĭs′kăr′ĭj, mĭs-kăr′-) ▸ *n.* **1.** Premature expulsion of a nonviable fetus from the uterus. **2.** Mismanagement.

mis·car·ry (mĭs′kăr′ē, mĭs-kăr′ē) ▸ *v.* **1.** To have a miscarriage. **2.** To go wrong.

mis·ceg·e·na·tion (mĭ-sĕj′ə-nā′shən, mĭs′ĭ-jə-) ▸ *n.* Cohabitation, sexual relations, or marriage between persons of different races.

mis·cel·la·ne·ous (mĭs′ə-lā′nē-əs) ▸ *adj.* Made up of a variety of parts or ingredients. **—mis′cel·la′ne·ous·ly** *adv.*

mis·cel·la·ny (mĭs′ə-lā′nē) ▸ *n., pl.* **-nies.** **1.** A collection of various items or ingredients. **2.** A collection of diverse literary works.

mis·chance (mĭs-chăns′) ▸ *n.* **1.** A mishap. **2.** Bad luck.

mis·chief (mĭs′chĭf) ▸ *n.* **1.** A cause of discomfiture or annoyance. **2.** An inclination to play pranks. **3.** Damage caused by a specific person.

mis·chie·vous (mĭs′chə-vəs) ▸ *adj.* **1.** Causing mischief. **2.** Playful in a naughty or teasing way. **—mis′chie·vous·ly** *adv.* **—mis′chie·vous·ness** *n.*

mis·ci·ble (mĭs′ə-bəl) ▸ *adj.* *Chem.* That can be mixed in all proportions. **—mis′ci·bil′i·ty** *n.*

mis·con·ceive (mĭs′kən-sēv′) ▸ *v.* To misunderstand. **—mis′con·cep′tion** *n.*

mis·con·duct (mĭs-kŏn′dŭkt) ▸ *n.* **1.** Improper or immoral behavior. **2.** Dishonest or bad management. ▸ *v.* (mĭs′kən-dŭct′) **1.** To mismanage. **2.** To behave (oneself) badly.

mis·con·strue (mĭs′kən-stro͞o′) ▸ *v.* To misinterpret. **—mis′con·struc′tion** *n.*

THESAURUS

minus *n.* —*See* DISADVANTAGE.

minuscule *adj.* —*See* TINY.

minute[1] *n.* —*See* ENTRY, FLASH (2).
  minute *v.* —*See* LIST[1].

minute[2] *adj.* —*See* DETAILED, TINY.

minutia *n.* —*See* DETAIL, TRIFLE.

minx *n.* —*See* URCHIN.

miracle *n.* An event inexplicable by the laws of nature ▸ wonder. *Idiom:* act of God. —*See also* MARVEL.

miraculous *adj.* —*See* ASTONISHING, SUPERNATURAL (1).

mirage *n.* —*See* ILLUSION.

mire *n.* —*See* SLIME, SWAMP.
  mire *v.* —*See* DIRTY.

mirror *n.* —*See* EPITOME, MODEL.
  mirror *v.* To send back or form an image of ▸ image, reflect. —*See also* MIMIC.

mirth *n.* —*See* MERRIMENT (1).

mirthful *adj.* —*See* CHEERFUL, MERRY.

mirthfulness *n.* —*See* MERRIMENT (1).

miry *adj.* —*See* DIRTY, SLIMY.

misadventure *n.* —*See* ACCIDENT.

misanthrope or **misanthropist** *n.* A person who expects only the worst from people ▸ cynic, pessimist. [*Compare* SKEPTIC.]

misapplication *n.* —*See* ABUSE (1).

misapply *v.* —*See* ABUSE (2).

misapprehend *v.* —*See* MISUNDERSTAND.

misapprehension *n.* —*See* FALLACY (1), MISUNDERSTANDING.

misappropriate *v.* —*See* ABUSE (2).

misappropriation *n.* —*See* ABUSE (1).

misbegotten *adj.* —*See* ILLEGITIMATE.

misbehave *v.* To behave in a rowdy, improper, or unruly fashion ▸ act out, act up, be naughty, carry on. *Informal:* cut up, fool around, horse around. [*Compare* OFFEND.]

misbehavior *n.* Improper, often rude behavior ▸ bad manners, horseplay, misconduct, misdoing, naughtiness, wrongdoing. [*Compare* CRIME, IMPROPRIETY.]

miscalculate *v.* To count or calculate wrongly ▸ miscount, misestimate, misjudge, misreckon, overestimate, underestimate. [*Compare* ERR, MISUNDERSTAND.]

miscalculation *n.* A wrong calculation ▸ misestimate, misestimation, misjudgment, misreckoning, overestimation, underestimation. [*Compare* ERROR, MISUNDERSTANDING.]

miscarriage *n.* —*See* FAILURE (1).

miscarry *v.* —*See* FAIL (1).

miscellanea *n.* —*See* ODDS AND ENDS.

miscellaneous *adj.* —*See* VARIOUS.

miscellaneousness *n.* —*See* VARIETY.

miscellany *n.* —*See* ASSORTMENT.

mischance *n.* —*See* ACCIDENT.

mischief *n.* Annoying yet harmless, usually playful acts ▸ devilment, devilry, deviltry, diablerie, high jinks, impishness, mischief-making, mischievousness, playfulness, prankishness, pranks, rascality, roguery, roguishness, tomfoolery, tricks. *Informal:* shenanigans. *Slang:* funny business, hanky-panky, monkey business, monkeyshines. [*Compare* PRANK[1].] —*See also* HARM, RASCAL.

mischievous *adj.* Full of mischief or high-spirited fun ▸ arch, devilish, elfish, frisky, frolicsome, gamesome, impish, larkish, playful, prankish, puckish, rascally, roguish, sportful, sportive, trickish, waggish. [*Compare* LIVELY.] —*See also* HARMFUL.

mischievousness *n.* —*See* MISCHIEF.

misconceive *v.* —*See* MISUNDERSTAND.

misconception *n.* —*See* FALLACY (1), MISUNDERSTANDING.

misconduct *n.* —*See* MISBEHAVIOR.

misconstrue *v.* —*See* MISUNDERSTAND.

miscount *v.* —*See* MISCALCULATE.

mis·cre·ant (mĭs′krē-ənt) ▸ *n.* A wrongdoer or offender; villain. **—mis′cre·ant** *adj.*

mis·cue (mĭs-kyo͞o′) ▸ *n.* A mistake. **—mis·cue′** *v.*

mis·deed (mĭs-dēd′) ▸ *n.* A wrongdoing.

mis·de·mean·or (mĭs′dĭ-mē′nər) ▸ *n.* **1.** A misdeed. **2.** *Law* An offense less serious than a felony.

mise en scène (mēz′ äɴ sĕn′) ▸ *n., pl.* **mise en scènes** (sĕn′). The arrangement and setting for a play or film.

mi·ser (mī′zər) ▸ *n.* A stingy person, esp. one who hoards money. **—mi′ser·li·ness** *n.* **—mi′ser·ly** *adj.*

mis·er·a·ble (mĭz′ər-ə-bəl, mĭz′rə-) ▸ *adj.* **1.** Very unhappy; wretched. **2.** Causing discomfort or distress. **3.** Wretchedly poor; squalid. **4.** Of poor quality; inferior. **—mis′er·a·bly** *adv.*

mis·er·y (mĭz′ə-rē) ▸ *n., pl.* **-ies. 1.** Great physical or emotional suffering. **2.** An affliction or trial.

mis·fire (mĭs-fīr′) ▸ *v.* **1.** To fail to ignite, fire, or discharge when expected. **2.** To fail to achieve an anticipated result. **—mis′fire′** *n.*

mis·fit (mĭs′fĭt′, mĭs-fĭt′) ▸ *n.* **1.** A poor fit. **2.** A maladjusted person.

mis·for·tune (mĭs-fôr′chən) ▸ *n.* **1.** Bad fortune. **2.** A mishap.

mis·giv·ing (mĭs-gĭv′ĭng) ▸ *n.* A feeling of doubt or distrust.

mis·guide (mĭs-gīd′) ▸ *v.* To lead in the wrong direction; lead astray. **—mis·guid′ance** *n.* **—mis·guid′ed** *adj.* **—mis·guid′ed·ly** *adv.*

mis·han·dle (mĭs-hăn′dl) ▸ *v.* To deal with clumsily or inefficiently.

mis·hap (mĭs′hăp′, mĭs-hăp′) ▸ *n.* An unfortunate accident.

mish·mash (mĭsh′măsh′) ▸ *n.* A hodgepodge.

mis·in·ter·pret (mĭs′ĭn-tûr′prĭt) ▸ *v.* To interpret or explain inaccurately. **—mis′in·ter′pre·ta′tion** *n.* **—mis′in·ter′pret·er** *n.*

Mis·ki·to (mĭ-skē′tō) ▸ *n., pl.* **-to** or **-tos. 1.** A member of an American Indian people of the Caribbean coast of NE Nicaragua and SE Honduras. **2.** Their language.

mis·lay (mĭs-lā′) ▸ *v.* To put in a place that is afterward forgotten; lose.

mis·lead (mĭs-lēd′) ▸ *v.* **1.** To lead in the wrong direction. **2.** To lead into error.

mis·like (mĭs-līk′) ▸ *v.* To dislike. ▸ *n.* Dislike.

mis·no·mer (mĭs-nō′mər) ▸ *n.* A wrong or inappropriate name.

mi·so (mē′sō) ▸ *n., pl.* **-sos.** A thick fermented paste made of cooked soybeans, salt, and often rice or barley.

mi·sog·a·my (mĭ-sŏg′ə-mē) ▸ *n.* Hatred of marriage. **—mi·sog′a·mist** *n.*

mi·sog·y·ny (mĭ-sŏj′ə-nē) ▸ *n.* Hatred of women. **—mi·sog′y·nist** *n.* **—mi·sog′y·nis′tic, mi·sog′y·nous** *adj.*

mis·place (mĭs-plās′) ▸ *v.* **1a.** To put in a wrong place. **b.** To mislay. **2.** To bestow (e.g., confidence) on an unsuitable or unworthy person. **—mis·place′ment** *n.*

mis·play (mĭs-plā′, mĭs′plā′) ▸ *n.* *Sports & Games* A mistaken play. **—mis·play′** *v.*

mis·read (mĭs-rēd′) ▸ *v.* **1.** To read inaccurately. **2.** To misinterpret.

mis·rep·re·sent (mĭs-rĕp′rĭ-zĕnt′) ▸ *v.* To give a false or misleading representation of. **—mis·rep′re·sen·ta′tion** *n.*

miss[1] (mĭs) ▸ *v.* **1.** To fail to hit, reach, catch, meet, or make contact with. **2.** To fail to perceive or understand. **3.** To fail to achieve or attain. **4.** To fail to attend or perform. **5.** To omit. **6.** To avoid. **7.** To discover or feel the absence of. **8.** To misfire. ▸ *n.* **1.** A failure to hit or succeed. **2.** A misfire.

miss[2] (mĭs) ▸ *n.* **1. Miss** Used as a courtesy title for a young woman or girl. **2.** Used as a polite address for a girl or young woman.

Miss. ▸ *abbr.* Mississippi

mis·sal (mĭs′əl) ▸ *n.* *Rom. Cath. Ch.* A book containing all the prayers and responses necessary for celebrating the Mass.

mis·sile (mĭs′əl, -īl′) ▸ *n.* **1.** An object or weapon fired or projected at a target. **2.** A guided missile. **3.** A ballistic missile. **—mis′sile·ry** *n.*

miss·ing (mĭs′ĭng) ▸ *adj.* Absent; lost; lacking.

mis·sion (mĭsh′ən) ▸ *n.* **1a.** A body of envoys to a foreign country. **b.** A permanent diplomatic office abroad. **2.** A body of missionaries, or the building housing them. **3.** A special assignment given to a person or group. **4.** A vocation.

mis·sion·ar·y (mĭsh′ə-nĕr′ē) ▸ *n., pl.* **-ies. 1.** A propagandist for a belief or cause. **2.** One who attempts to convert others

THESAURUS

miscreant *adj.* —*See* CORRUPT (1).
miscreant *n.* —*See* EVILDOER.
miscue *n.* —*See* ERROR.
miscue *v.* —*See* ERR.
misdeed *n.* —*See* CRIME (1), CRIME (2).
misdemeanor *n.* —*See* CRIME (1).
misdoing *n.* —*See* MISBEHAVIOR.
misdoubt *v.* —*See* DISTRUST, DOUBT.
mise en scène *n.* —*See* ENVIRONMENT (2), SCENE (2).
miser *n.* A stingy person ▸ churl, niggard, pinchpenny, Scrooge, skinflint. *Informal:* penny pincher. *Slang:* cheapskate, piker, stiff, tightwad.
miserable *adj.* Very uncomfortable or unhappy ▸ afflicted, agonized, anguished, suffering, woebegone, woeful, wretched. [*Compare* DEPRESSED, DESPONDENT, GLUM.] —*See also* SHODDY.
miserable *n.* —*See* UNFORTUNATE.
miserly *adj.* —*See* STINGY.
misery *n.* A state of prolonged anguish and privation ▸ deprival, deprivation, hardship, misfortune, suffering, woe, wretchedness. [*Compare* HELL, POVERTY.] —*See also* CURSE (3), DISTRESS, PAIN.
misestimate *v.* To make a mistake in judging ▸ misjudge, mistake, prejudge. [*Compare* MISUNDERSTAND, SUPPOSE.] —*See also* MISCALCULATE.
misestimate or **misestimation** *n.* —*See* MISCALCULATION.
misfire *v.* —*See* FAIL (1).
misfortune *n.* Bad fortune ▸ adversity, bad luck, haplessness, hard luck, ill luck, unfortunateness, unluckiness, untowardness. [*Compare* PREDICAMENT.] —*See also* ACCIDENT, MISERY.
misgiving *n.* —*See* DOUBT, QUALM.
misguided *adj.* —*See* IGNORANT (3).
mishandle *v.* —*See* ABUSE (1), ABUSE (2), BOTCH.
mishandling *n.* —*See* ABUSE (1), ABUSE (2).
mishap *n.* —*See* ACCIDENT, DISASTER.
mishear *v.* —*See* MISUNDERSTAND.
mishmash *n.* —*See* ASSORTMENT.
misinformed *adj.* —*See* IGNORANT (3).
misinterpret *v.* —*See* MISUNDERSTAND.
misinterpretation *n.* —*See* FALLACY (1), MISUNDERSTANDING.
misjudge *v.* To make a mistake in judging ▸ misestimate, mistake, prejudge. [*Compare* MISUNDERSTAND, SUPPOSE.] —*See also* MISCALCULATE.
misjudgment *n.* —*See* MISCALCULATION.
mislaid *adj.* —*See* LOST (2).
mislay *v.* To be unable to find ▸ lose, misplace, miss. *Idiom:* have something go missing.
mislead *v.* —*See* DECEIVE.
misleading *adj.* Deliberately ambiguous or vague ▸ elusive, equivocal, evasive, indirect. [*Compare* AMBIGUOUS.] —*See also* FALLACIOUS (2).
mislike *v.* To regard with distaste ▸ dislike, disrelish. *Idioms:* be averse to, be cool toward, have an aversion to (*or* distaste for), have no use for, not be crazy (*or* nuts *or* wild) about, not care for. [*Compare* DESPISE, DISAPPROVE, HATE.]
mislike *n.* An attitude or feeling of distaste or mild aversion ▸ disinclination, dislike, disrelish, distaste. [*Compare* DISAPPROVAL, DISGUST, ENMITY, HATE.]
mismanage *v.* —*See* BOTCH.
mismatch *v.* —*See* CONFLICT.
mismatched *adj.* —*See* IMPROPER (2), INCONGRUOUS.
misplace *v.* To be unable to find ▸ lose, mislay, miss. *Idiom:* have something go missing.
misplaced *adj.* —*See* LOST (2).
misplacement *n.* —*See* LOSS (1).
misread *v.* —*See* MISUNDERSTAND.
misreckon *v.* —*See* MISCALCULATE.
misreckoning *n.* —*See* MISCALCULATION.
misrepresent *v.* —*See* DISTORT.
misrepresentation *n.* —*See* EQUIVOCATION, LIE[2].
misrule *n.* —*See* DISORDER (2).
miss *v.* To be unable to find ▸ lose, mislay, misplace. *Idiom:* have something go missing. —*See also* FAIL (1), LOSE (2).
miss *n.* —*See* ERROR.
misshape *v.* —*See* DEFORM.
missing *adj.* —*See* ABSENT, LOST (2).
mission *n.* **1.** An assignment one is sent to carry out ▸ charge, commission, errand, operation, undertaking. [*Compare* ADVENTURE, INTENTION, TASK.] **2.** A diplomatic office or headquarters in a foreign country ▸ deputation, embassy, legation. **3.** An inner urge to pursue an activity or perform a service ▸ calling, vocation. [*Compare* DREAM, DUTY, FATE.] —*See also* EXPEDITION.
missionary or **missioner** *n.* A person doing religious or charitable work in

to a particular doctrine or set of principles. **—mis′sion·ar′y** *adj.*

Mis·sis·sip·pi (mĭs′ĭ-sĭp′ē) ▸ A state of the SE US. Cap. Jackson. **—Mis′sis·sip′pi·an** *adj. & n.*

Mis·sis·sip·pi·an (mĭs′ĭ-sĭp′ē-ən) *Geol.* ▸ *adj.* Of or being the 5th period of the Paleozoic Era, marked by widespread shallow seas. ▸ *n.* The Mississippian Period.

Mississippi River ▸ The chief river of the US, rising in N MN and flowing about 3,781 km (2,350 mi) to the Gulf of Mexico.

mis·sive (mĭs′ĭv) ▸ *n.* A written message.

Mis·sou·ri[1] (mĭ-zo͝or′ē) ▸ *n., pl.* **-ri** or **-ris.** **1.** A member of a Native American people formerly of N-central Missouri, now in Oklahoma. **2.** Their Siouan language.

Mis·sou·ri[2] (mĭ-zo͝or′ē, -zo͝or′ə) ▸ A state of the central US. Cap. Jefferson City. **—Mis·sou′ri·an** *adj. & n.*

Missouri River ▸ A river of the US rising in the Rocky Mts. and flowing about 4,127 km (2,565 mi) to the Mississippi R. N of St. Louis, MO.

mis·speak (mĭs-spēk′) ▸ *v.* To speak mistakenly, inappropriately, or rashly.

mis·step (mĭs-stĕp′) ▸ *n.* **1.** A misplaced step. **2.** A social or procedural blunder.

mist (mĭst) ▸ *n.* **1.** A mass of fine droplets of water in the atmosphere. **2.** Water vapor condensed on and clouding a surface. **3.** Fine drops of a liquid sprayed into the air. **4.** Something that dims or conceals. ▸ *v.* To become obscured or misty.

mis·take (mĭ-stāk′) ▸ *n.* **1.** An error or fault. **2.** A misconception or misunderstanding. **—mis·tak′a·ble** *adj.* **—mis·take′** *v.*

mis·tak·en (mĭ-stā′kən) ▸ *adj.* **1.** Wrong in opinion, understanding, or perception. **2.** Based on error. **—mis·tak′en·ly** *adv.*

Mis·ter (mĭs′tər) ▸ *n.* **1.** Used as a courtesy title for a man, usu. written in its abbreviated form *Mr.* **2. mister** *Informal* Used in addressing a man.

mis·tle·toe (mĭs′əl-tō′) ▸ *n.* A plant growing as a parasite on trees and having leathery evergreen leaves and waxy white berries.

mis·treat (mĭs-trēt′) ▸ *v.* To treat roughly or wrongly; abuse. **—mis·treat′ment** *n.*

mis·tress (mĭs′trĭs) ▸ *n.* **1.** A woman in a position of authority, control, or ownership. **2.** Something personified as female that has supremacy or control: *a country that is mistress of the seas.* **3.** A woman who has a continuing sexual relationship with a man who is not her husband. **4. Mistress** Used formerly as a courtesy title for a woman.

mis·tri·al (mĭs′trī′əl, -trīl′, mĭs-trī′əl, -trīl′) ▸ *n.* **1.** A trial declared invalid because of a procedural error. **2.** An inconclusive trial.

mis·trust (mĭs-trŭst′) ▸ *n.* Lack of trust; suspicion. ▸ *v.* To regard with suspicion or doubt. **—mis·trust′ful** *adj.*

mist·y (mĭs′tē) ▸ *adj.* **-i·er, -i·est.** **1.** Consisting of or resembling mist. **2.** Obscured or clouded by or as if by mist. **3.** Vague or hazy. **—mist′i·ly** *adv.* **—mist′i·ness** *n.*

mis·un·der·stand (mĭs′ŭn-dər-stănd′) ▸ *v.* To understand incorrectly; misinterpret.

mis·un·der·stand·ing (mĭs′ŭn-dər-stăn′dĭng) ▸ *n.* **1.** A failure to understand correctly. **2.** A disagreement or quarrel.

mis·use (mĭs-yo͞os′) ▸ *n.* Improper, unlawful, or incorrect use. ▸ *v.* (-yo͞oz′) **1.** To use incorrectly. **2.** To mistreat or abuse.

mite[1] (mīt) ▸ *n.* Any of various small, often parasitic arachnids.

mite[2] (mīt) ▸ *n.* **1.** A very small contribution or amount of money. **2.** A tiny object or amount.

mi·ter (mī′tər) ▸ *n.* **1.** *Eccles.* A tall pointed hat with peaks in front and back, worn esp. by bishops. **2.** A miter joint. ▸ *v.* To fit together with or meet in a miter joint.

miter joint ▸ *n.* A joint made by fitting together two beveled edges to form a 90° corner.

mit·i·gate (mĭt′ĭ-gāt′) ▸ *v.* **-gat·ed, -gat·ing.** To make or become less in force or intensity; moderate. **—mit′i·ga·ble** (-gə-bəl) *adj.* **—mit′i·ga′tion** *n.* **—mit′i·ga′tive, mit′i·ga·to′ry** (-gə-tôr′ē) *adj.*

mi·to·chon·dri·on (mī′tə-kŏn′drē-ən) ▸ *n., pl.* **-dri·a** (-drē-ə). A microscopic structure in nearly all living cells, containing genetic material and enzymes important for cell metabolism. **—mi′to·chon′dri·al** *adj.*

mi·to·sis (mī-tō′sĭs) ▸ *n. Biol.* **1.** The process in cell division by which the nucleus divides, normally resulting in two new nuclei, each of which contains a complete copy of the parental chromosomes. **2.** The entire process of cell division including division of the nucleus and the cytoplasm. **—mi·tot′ic** (-tŏt′ĭk) *adj.* **—mi·tot′i·cal·ly** *adv.*

mi·tre (mī′tər) ▸ *n. & v. Chiefly Brit.* Var. of **miter.**

mitt (mĭt) ▸ *n.* **1.** A woman's glove that extends over the hand and only partially covers the fingers. **2.** A mitten. **3.** A baseball glove, esp. one used by catchers and first basemen. **4.** *Slang* A hand.

mit·ten (mĭt′n) ▸ *n.* A covering for the hand that encases the thumb separately and the four fingers together.

mitz·vah (mĭts′və) ▸ *n., pl.* **-voth** (-vōt′, -vōs′) or **-vahs.** **1.** A commandment of the Jewish law. **2.** A worthy deed.

mix (mĭks) ▸ *v.* **1a.** To combine or blend so that the constituent parts are indistinguishable. **b.** To create or form by blending. **2.** To combine or join: *mix joy with sorrow.* **3.** To associate socially. **4.** To crossbreed. **5a.** To combine (audio tracks or channels) to make an audio recording. **b.** To make in this manner. ***—phrasal verb:* mix up** **1.** To confuse. **2.** To involve: *got mixed up in the scandal.* **3.** To throw into disorder; jumble. ▸ *n.* A mixture, esp. of ingredients packaged and sold commercially. **—mix′a·ble** *adj.*

mixed bag (mĭkst) ▸ *n.* A varied assortment.

mixed drink ▸ *n.* A drink made of one or more kinds of liquor combined with other ingredients, usu. shaken or stirred.

mixed number ▸ *n.* A number, such as $7^1/_4$, consisting of an integer and a fraction or decimal.

mix·er (mĭk′sər) ▸ *n.* **1.** One that mixes, esp. a device that mixes substances or ingredients. **2.** A sociable person. **3.**

THESAURUS

a foreign country ▸ apostle, evangelist. [*Compare* CLERIC, REPRESENTATIVE.] *—See also* PROPAGANDIST.

missive *n.* *—See* LETTER.

misstate *v.* *—See* DISTORT.

misstatement *n.* *—See* LIE[2].

misstep *n.* *—See* ERROR.

missy *n.* *—See* GIRL.

mist *n.* *—See* HAZE, RAIN.

mist *v.* *—See* OBSCURE, RAIN (2).

mistake *n.* *—See* ERROR, MISUNDERSTANDING.

mistake *v.* **1.** To take one thing mistakenly for another ▸ confound, confuse, mix up. **2.** To make a mistake in judgment ▸ misestimate, misjudge, prejudge. [*Compare* MISCALCULATE, SUPPOSE.] *—See also* ERR, MISUNDERSTAND.

mistaken *adj.* *—See* ERRONEOUS.

mistimed *adj.* *—See* UNSEASONABLE.

mistreat *v.* *—See* ABUSE (1), ABUSE (2).

mistreatment *n.* *—See* ABUSE (2).

mistrust *n.* *—See* DISBELIEF, DISTRUST, DOUBT.

mistrust *v.* *—See* DISBELIEVE, DISTRUST, DOUBT.

mistrustful *adj.* *—See* DISTRUSTFUL.

mistrustfully *adv.* *—See* SKEPTICALLY.

misty *adj.* *—See* RAINY, SENTIMENTAL, UNCLEAR.

misunderstand *v.* To understand incorrectly ▸ misapprehend, misconceive, misconstrue, mishear, misinterpret, misread, mistake. ***Idioms:*** get something wrong, get the wrong idea, miss the point. [*Compare* CONFUSE, MISCALCULATE.]

misunderstanding *n.* A failure to understand correctly ▸ confusion, false impression, misapprehension, misconception, misinterpretation, mistake. [*Compare* MISCALCULATION.] *—See also* ARGUMENT, FALLACY (1).

misusage *n.* *—See* ABUSE (2), CORRUPTION (3).

misuse *n.* *—See* ABUSE (1).

misuse *v.* *—See* ABUSE (1), ABUSE (2).

mitigate *v.* *—See* RELIEVE (1).

mitigation *n.* *—See* RELIEF (1).

mix *v.* **1.** To combine into one mass or mixture ▸ admix, alloy, amalgamate, blend, coalesce, commingle, commix, fuse, homogenize, intermingle, intermix, merge, mingle, stir. [*Compare* COMBINE.] **2.** To take part in social activities ▸ mingle, socialize. *—See also* BEAT (6).

mix up *v.* To take one thing mistakenly for another ▸ confound, confuse, mistake. *—See also* CONFUSE (1), DISORDER, INVOLVE (1).

mix *n.* *—See* MIXTURE.

mixed *adj.* *—See* IMPURE (2), VARIOUS.

mixed bag *n.* *—See* ASSORTMENT.

mixed-up *adj.* *—See* CONFUSED (2), CONFUSED (1).

A party affording people an opportunity to get acquainted. **4.** A nonalcoholic beverage, such as soda water, used in mixed drinks.
Mix·tec (mēs′tĕk) ► *n., pl.* **-tec** or **-tecs**. **1.** A member of a Mesoamerican Indian people of S Mexico whose civilization was overthrown by the Aztecs in the 16th cent. **2.** The language of this people.
mix·ture (mĭks′chər) ► *n.* **1.** The act of mixing or the state of being mixed. **2.** Something made by mixing. **3.** One that consists of diverse elements. **4.** *Chem.* A blend of substances not chemically bound to each other.
mix-up also **mix·up** (mĭks′ŭp′) ► *n.* A state or instance of confusion; muddle.
miz·zen or **miz·en** (mĭz′ən) ► *n.* **1.** A fore-and-aft sail set on the mizzenmast. **2.** A mizzenmast. **—miz′zen** *adj.*
miz·zen·mast or **miz·en·mast** (mĭz′ən-məst, -măst′) ► *n.* The third mast aft on sailing ships carrying three or more masts.
mks ► *abbr.* meter-kilogram-second
mL also **ml** ► *abbr.* milliliter
Mlle. ► *abbr.* Mademoiselle
Mlles. ► *abbr.* Mesdemoiselles
mm ► *abbr.* millimeter
Mme. ► *abbr.* Madame
Mmes. ► *abbr.* Mesdames
Mn ► The symbol for the element **manganese**.
MN ► *abbr.* Minnesota
mne·mon·ic (nĭ-mŏn′ĭk) ► *adj.* Assisting or intended to assist the memory. ► *n.* A device, such as a formula or rhyme, used as a mnemonic aid. **—mne·mon′i·cal·ly** *adv.*
Mo ► The symbol for the element **molybdenum**.
MO ► *abbr.* **1.** mail order **2.** also **Mo.** Missouri **3.** modus operandi **4.** money order
mo. ► *abbr.* month
Mo·ab (mō′ăb) ► An ancient kingdom E of the Dead Sea in SW Jordan. **—Mo′ab·ite′** *adj. & n.*
moan (mōn) ► *n.* **1.** A low, sustained, mournful cry, as of sorrow or pain. **2.** A whining complaint. **—moan** *v.* **—moan′er** *n.*
moat (mōt) ► *n.* A deep wide ditch, usu. filled with water, esp. one surrounding a medieval town, fortress, or castle as a defense.
mob (mŏb) ► *n.* **1.** A large disorderly throng. **2.** The mass of common people. **3.** *Informal* An organized gang of criminals. ► *v.* **mobbed, mob·bing**. **1.** To crowd around and jostle, annoy, or attack. **2.** To crowd into (a place).
mo·bile (mō′bəl, -bēl′, -bīl′) ► *adj.* **1.** Capable of moving or of being moved readily. **2.** Changing quickly from one condition to another. ► *n.* (mō′bēl′) A sculpture consisting of parts that move, esp. in response to air currents. **—mo·bil′i·ty** (-bĭl′ĭ-tē) *n.*
mobile home ► *n.* A house trailer installed on a site and used as a home.
mo·bi·lize (mō′bə-līz′) ► *v.* **-lized, -liz·ing**. **1.** To make mobile or capable of movement. **2.** To assemble and prepare for or as if for war. **—mo′bi·li·za′tion** *n.*
mob·ster (mŏb′stər) ► *n. Informal* A member of a criminal gang.
moc·ca·sin (mŏk′ə-sĭn) ► *n.* **1.** A soft leather slipper or shoe. **2.** A water moccasin.
mo·cha (mō′kə) ► *n.* **1.** A rich, pungent Arabian coffee. **2.** A flavoring of coffee mixed with chocolate. **3.** A dark olive brown.
mock (mŏk) ► *v.* **1.** To treat with ridicule or contempt; deride. **2.** To mimic, as in sport or derision. ► *adj.* Simulated; sham. **—mock′er** *n.* **—mock′er·y** *n.* **—mock′ing·ly** *adv.*
mock-he·ro·ic (mŏk′hĭ-rō′ĭk) ► *n.* A satirical imitation or burlesque of the heroic manner or style. **—mock′-he·ro′ic** *adj.*
mock·ing·bird (mŏk′ĭng-bûrd′) ► *n.* A gray and white songbird of the E US that mimics the sounds of other birds.
mock orange ► *n.* Any of numerous deciduous shrubs having white, usu. fragrant flowers.
mock·up also **mock-up** (mŏk′ŭp′) ► *n.* A usu. full-sized scale model of a machine or structure, used for demonstration or testing.
mod (mŏd) ► *n.* Fashionable style of dress. ► *adj.* Fashionably up-to-date.
mode (mōd) ► *n.* **1a.** A manner, way, or method of doing or acting. **b.** A particular form, variety, or manner. **c.** A given condition of functioning; status. **2.** The current fashion or style. **3.** *Mus.* Any of certain arrangements of the diatonic tones of an octave. **4.** *Statistics* The number in a distribution that occurs the most frequently. **—mod′al** *adj.*
mod·el (mŏd′l) ► *n.* **1.** A small representation of an existing object, usu. built to scale. **2.** A preliminary pattern. **3.** A schematic description of a system or theory that accounts for its known properties. **4.** A style or design. **5.** An example to be emulated. **6.** One who poses for an artist. **7.** One who models clothes. ► *v.* **-eled, -el·ing** also **-elled, -el·ling**. **1.** To plan or construct a model (of). **2.** To display (clothes) by wearing or posing. **3.** To serve or work as a model. ► *adj.* **1.** Being or used as a model. **2.** Worthy of imitation; exemplary. **—mod′el·er** *n.*
mo·dem (mō′dəm) ► *n.* A device for transmitting data over telephone wires by modulating the data into an audio signal to send it and demodulating an audio signal into data to receive it.
mod·er·ate (mŏd′ər-ĭt) ► *adj.* **1.** Not excessive or extreme. **2.** Temperate. **3.** Average or mediocre. **4.** Opposed to radical views or measures. ► *n.* One who holds moderate views

THESAURUS

mixture *n.* Something produced by mixing ► admixture, alloy, amalgam, amalgamation, blend, commixture, composite, fusion, merger, mix. [*Compare* COMBINATION, UNIFICATION.] *—See also* ASSORTMENT.
mix-up *n.* *—See* DISORDER (1), MESS (1).
mizzle *n.* The process or sound of dripping ► dribble, drip, drizzle, trickle. *—See also* RAIN.
mizzle *v.* *—See* RAIN (2).
moan *n.* *—See* HOWL.
moan *v.* *—See* COMPLAIN, HOWL.
mob *n.* *Informal* An organized group of criminals, hoodlums, or wrongdoers ► band, gang, pack, ring. *—See also* COMMONALTY, CROWD.
mob *v.* *—See* FILL (1).
mobile *adj.* **1.** Capable of moving or being moved from place to place ► movable, moving, portable, transportable, traveling, unstationary. [*Compare* LOOSE, MIGRANT.] **2.** Changing easily, as in expression ► changeable, fluid, plastic. [*Compare* CHANGEABLE, UNSTABLE.]
mobilization *n.* *—See* PREPARATION.
mobilize *v.* To assemble, prepare, or put into operation, as for war or a similar emergency ► activate, call up, enlist, marshal, militarize, muster, organize, rally, ready. *Idioms:* call to action, call out the troops. [*Compare* ASSEMBLE, ENERGIZE, PROVOKE.]
mobster *n.* *—See* CRIMINAL.
mock *v.* *—See* IMITATE, RIDICULE.
mock *adj.* *—See* ARTIFICIAL (1).
mockery *n.* **1.** Words or actions intended to evoke contemptuous laughter ► derision, ridicule. [*Compare* SARCASM, TAUNT.] **2.** A false, derisive, or impudent imitation of something ► caricature, farce, parody, sham, travesty. [*Compare* COUNTERFEIT, SATIRE.] **3.** An object of amusement or laughter ► butt, jest, joke, laughingstock. *Idiom:* figure of fun. [*Compare* FOOL.]
mocking *adj.* *—See* DISPARAGING, SARCASTIC.
mod *adj.* *—See* FASHIONABLE.
mode *n.* *—See* CONDITION (1), FASHION, STYLE, WAY (1).
model *n.* One that is worthy of imitation or duplication ► beau ideal, example, exemplar, ideal, mirror, nonpareil, paradigm, paragon, pattern, precedent, role model, standard. *Idioms:* man among men, woman among women. [*Compare* CELEBRITY.] *—See also* EPITOME, ORIGINAL.
model *v.* *—See* BASE[1], FOLLOW (5), FORM (1), POSE (1).
model *adj.* *—See* IDEAL, TYPICAL.
moderate *v.* **1.** To make or become less severe or extreme ► mute, play down, qualify, soften, subdue, tame, temper, tone down. [*Compare* DECREASE, RELIEVE.] **2.** To intervene between disputants in order to bring about an agreement ► arbitrate, mediate. [*Compare* CONFER, JUDGE.] *—See also* SUBSIDE.
moderate *adj.* **1.** Free from extremes in temperature ► balmy, clement, mild, temperate. [*Compare* PLEASANT.] **2.** Requiring little effort or exertion ► easy, light, undemanding. *Informal:* cushy,

or opinions. ▸ *v.* (mŏd′ə-rāt′) **-at·ed, -at·ing.** 1. To make or become less violent, severe, or extreme. 2. To preside over as a moderator. **—mod′er·ate·ly** *adv.* **—mod′er·a′tion** *n.*

mod·er·a·tor (mŏd′ə-rā′tər) ▸ *n.* 1. One that moderates. 2. A presiding officer.

mod·ern (mŏd′ərn) ▸ *adj.* 1. Of or relating to recent times or the present. 2. Characteristic of the present; up-to-date. **—mod′ern** *n.* **—mod·ern′i·ty** (mŏ-dûr′nĭ-tē, mō-) *n.* **—mod′ern·i·za′tion** *n.* **—mod′ern·ize′** *v.*

Modern English ▸ *n.* English since about 1500.

Modern Greek ▸ *n.* Greek since the early 16th cent.

Modern Hebrew ▸ *n.* The Hebrew language as used in Israel from 1948 on.

mod·ern·ism (mŏd′ər-nĭz′əm) ▸ *n.* 1. A theory, practice, or belief that is peculiar to modern times. 2. often **Modernism** The use of innovative forms of expression that distinguish many styles in the arts and literature of the 20th cent. **—mod′ern·ist** *n.* **—mod′ern·is′tic** *adj.*

mod·est (mŏd′ĭst) ▸ *adj.* 1. Having or showing a moderate estimation of oneself. 2. Retiring; shy. 3. Observing conventional proprieties; decent. 4. Free from ostentation. 5. Not extreme; moderate: *a modest price.* **—mod′est·ly** *adv.* **—mod′es·ty** *n.*

mod·i·cum (mŏd′ĭ-kəm) ▸ *n.* A small or token amount.

mod·i·fy (mŏd′ə-fī′) ▸ *v.* **-fied, -fy·ing.** 1. To change or become changed; alter. 2. To make or become less extreme, severe, or strong. 3. *Gram.* To qualify or limit the meaning of. **—mod′i·fi·ca′tion** *n.* **—mod′i·fi′er** *n.*

mod·ish (mō′dĭsh) ▸ *adj.* Conforming to the current fashion. **—mod′ish·ly** *adv.* **—mod′ish·ness** *n.*

mo·diste (mō-dēst′) ▸ *n.* One who produces, designs, or deals in women's fashions.

mod·u·late (mŏj′ə-lāt′) ▸ *v.* **-lat·ed, -lat·ing.** 1. To regulate or temper. 2. To change or vary the pitch, intensity, or tone of. 3. *Mus.* To pass from one tonality to another by harmonic progression. 4. *Electron.* To vary the frequency, amplitude, phase, or other characteristic of (electromagnetic waves). **—mod′u·la′tion** *n.* **—mod′u·la′tor** *n.*

mod·ule (mŏj′o͞ol) ▸ *n.* 1. A standard or unit of measurement. 2. A standardized unit or component of a system designed for easy assembly or flexible use. 3. *Electron.* A self-contained assembly of electronic components and circuitry. 4. A self-contained unit of a spacecraft that performs a specific task. **—mod′u·lar** *adj.*

mo·dus op·er·an·di (mō′dəs ŏp′ə-răn′dē, -dī′) ▸ *n., pl.* **mo·di operandi** (mō′dē, -dī). A method of operating or functioning.

mo·gul (mō′gəl) ▸ *n.* A hard mound or bump on a ski slope.

Mo·gul (mō′gəl, mō-gŭl′) ▸ *n.* 1. also **Mo·ghul** (mo͞o-gŭl′) **a.** A member of the force that under Baber conquered India in 1526. **b.** A member of the Muslim dynasty founded by Baber that ruled India until 1857. 2. A Mongol or Mongolian. 3. **mogul** A rich or powerful person.

mo·hair (mō′hâr′) ▸ *n.* 1. The long silky hair of the Angora goat. 2. Fabric made with yarn from this hair.

Mo·ham·med (mō-hăm′ĭd, -hä′mĭd, mo͞o-) ▸ See **Muhammad.**

Mo·ham·med·an (mō-hăm′ĭ-dən) ▸ *n.* Var. of **Muhammadan.** **—Mo·ham′med·an·ism′** *n.*

Mo·hawk (mō′hôk′) ▸ *n., pl.* **-hawk** or **-hawks.** 1. A member of a Native American people formerly of NE New York, now in S Ontario and extreme N New York. 2. The Iroquoian language of the Mohawk.

Mo·he·gan (mō-hē′gən) ▸ *n., pl.* **-gan** or **-gans.** 1. A member of a Native American people formerly of E Connecticut, now in SE Connecticut and Wisconsin. 2. The Algonquian language of the Mohegan.

Mo·hi·can (mō-hē′kən, mə-) ▸ *n.* Var. of **Mahican.**

Mohs scale (mōz) ▸ *n.* A scale for determining the hardness of a mineral ranging from 1 for the softest to 10 for the hardest.

moi·e·ty (moi′ĭ-tē) ▸ *n., pl.* **-ties.** 1. A half. 2. A portion or share.

moil (moil) ▸ *v.* To work hard; toil. **—moil** *n.* **—moil′er** *n.*

moi·ré (mwä-rā′, mô-) ▸ *n.* 1. Fabric, esp. silk, with a wavy or rippled pattern. 2. A similar pattern pressed on cloth by engraved rollers. **—moi·ré′** *adj.*

moist (moist) ▸ *adj.* **-er, -est.** Slightly wet; damp. **—mois′ten** (moi′sən) *v.* **—moist′ly** *adv.* **—moist′ness** *n.*

mois·ture (mois′chər) ▸ *n.* Diffused or condensed liquid; dampness. **—mois′tur·ize′** *v.* **—mois′tur·iz′er** *n.*

Mo·ja·ve Desert also **Mo·ha·ve Desert** (mō-hä′vē) ▸ An arid region of S CA SE of the Sierra Nevada.

mol (mōl) ▸ *n.* Var. of **mole^{4}.**

mol. ▸ *abbr.* 1. molecular 2. molecule

mo·lal (mō′ləl) ▸ *adj.* Being a solution having one mole of solute in 1,000 grams of solvent. **—mo·lal′i·ty** (mō-lăl′ĭ-tē) *n.*

mo·lar (mō′lər) ▸ *n.* A tooth with a broad crown for grinding food, located behind the bicuspids. **—mo′lar** *adj.*

mo·las·ses (mə-lăs′ĭz) ▸ *n.* A thick brownish syrup produced in refining raw sugar.

mold^{1} (mōld) ▸ *n.* 1. A hollow form or matrix for shaping a fluid or plastic substance. 2. A frame or model for forming or shaping something. 3. Something made in or shaped on a mold. 4. General shape or form. 5. Distinctive shape, character, or type. ▸ *v.* To shape in or on a mold. **—mold′a·ble** *adj.* **—mold′er** *n.*

mold^{2} (mōld) ▸ *n.* 1. Any of various fungi that cause disintegration of organic matter. 2. The growth of such fungi. ▸ *v.* To become moldy.

mold^{3} (mōld) ▸ *n.* Loose soil rich in humus and fit for planting.

Mol·da·vi·a (mŏl-dā′vē-ə, -dāv′yə) ▸ 1. A historical region of E Romania E of Transylvania. 2. See **Moldova.** **—Mol·da′vi·an** *adj. & n.*

mold·er (mōl′dər) ▸ *v.* To decay or crumble into dust.

mold·ing (mōl′dĭng) ▸ *n.* 1. The act or process of molding. 2. Something molded. 3. An ornamental strip, as of wood, used to decorate or finish a surface, such as a wall or door.

THESAURUS

soft. *—See also* ACCEPTABLE (2), CONSERVATIVE (2), GENTLE (2), GRADUAL (2), LIGHT^{2} (2).

moderateness *n.* *—See* MODERATION.

moderation *n.* Avoidance of extremes of opinion, feeling, or personal conduct ▸ abstemiousness, measure, moderateness, sobriety, temperance. [*Compare* PRUDENCE, RESTRAINT.] *—See also* WANING.

modern *adj.* *—See* CONTEMPORARY (2).

modern *n.* A person of the present age ▸ contemporary.

modernize *v.* To make modern in appearance or style ▸ streamline, update. *Idioms:* bring into the 21st century, bring up to date. [*Compare* IMPROVE, RENEW.]

modest *adj.* 1. Not showy or obtrusive, as in appearance, style, or behavior ▸ inobtrusive, plain, quiet, restrained, simple, subdued, tasteful, unassuming, unobtrusive, unostentatious, unpretentious. [*Compare* APPROPRIATE, INCONSPICUOUS, RESERVED.] 2. Having or expressing feelings of humility ▸ humble, lowly, meek, unambitious. [*Compare* DEFERENTIAL.] *—See also* ACCEPTABLE (2), CHASTE, CLEAN (2), CONSERVATIVE (2), DECENT (7), LIGHT^{2} (2), SHY^{1}.

modesty *n.* 1. Lack of vanity or self-importance ▸ humbleness, humility, lowliness, meekness, unassumingness, unpretentiousness. 2. Lack of ostentation or pretension ▸ inobtrusiveness, plainness, quietness, restraint, simpleness, simplicity, tastefulness, unassumingness, unobtrusiveness, unostentatiousness, unpretentiousness. *—See also* CHASTITY, SHYNESS.

modicum *n.* *—See* BIT^{1} (1).

modifiable *adj.* *—See* CHANGEABLE (1).

modification *n.* *—See* CHANGE (1), VARIATION.

modified *adj.* *—See* QUALIFIED.

modify *v.* *—See* CHANGE (1), CHANGE (2).

modish *adj.* *—See* FASHIONABLE.

modulate *v.* *—See* ADJUST.

modus operandi *n.* *—See* APPROACH (1), WAY (1).

moil *v.* *—See* LABOR.

moil *n.* *—See* LABOR.

moist *adj.* Slightly wet ▸ clammy, damp, dank, dewy. [*Compare* STICKY, WET.]

moisten *v.* To make moist ▸ bathe, dampen, wash, wet.

moistureless *adj.* *—See* DRY (1).

mold *n.* A hollow device for shaping a fluid or plastic substance ▸ cast, form, matrix. *—See also* KIND^{2}.

mold *v.* *—See* FORM (1), MAKE.

moldable *adj.* *—See* MALLEABLE.

molder *v.* *—See* DECAY.

Mol·do·va (mŏl-dō′və, môl-). Formerly **Mol·da·vi·a** (-dā′vē-ə, -dāv′yə) ▸ A country of E Europe bordering on Romania. **—Mol·do′van** *adj. & n.*

mold·y (mōl′dē) ▸ *adj.* **-i·er, -i·est.** 1. Covered with or containing mold. 2. Musty or stale, as from decay. **—mold′i·ness** *n.*

mole[1] (mōl) ▸ *n.* A small congenital growth on the human skin, usu. dark and slightly raised.

mole[2] (mōl) ▸ *n.* A small burrowing mammal having silky fur, rudimentary eyes, a narrow snout, and strong forefeet for digging.

mole[3] (mōl) ▸ *n.* A massive jetty or breakwater built to protect a harbor.

mole[4] or **mol** (mōl) ▸ *n.* The amount of a substance that contains Avogadro's number of atoms, molecules, or other elementary units.

molecular biology ▸ *n.* The branch of biology dealing with the structure and function of essential molecules, such as nucleic acids, and esp. their role in heredity.

molecular weight ▸ *n.* The sum of the atomic weights of the atoms in a molecule.

mol·e·cule (mŏl′ĭ-kyo͞ol′) ▸ *n.* 1. The smallest particle into which an element or compound can be divided without changing its chemical and physical properties. 2. A small particle; tiny bit. **—mo·lec′u·lar** *adj.*

mole·hill (mōl′hĭl′) ▸ *n.* A small mound of loose earth raised by a burrowing mole.

mole·skin (mōl′skĭn′) ▸ *n.* 1. The fur of a mole. 2. A heavy-napped cotton fabric.

mo·lest (mə-lĕst′) ▸ *v.* 1. To disturb or annoy. 2. To subject to unwanted or improper sexual activity. **—mo′les·ta′tion** (mō′lĕ-stā′shən) *n.* **—mo·lest′er** *n.*

Mo·lière (mōl-yâr′), **Jean Baptiste Poquelin** (1622–73) ▸ French playwright.

moll (mŏl) ▸ *n. Slang* A woman companion of a gangster.

mol·li·fy (mŏl′ə-fī′) ▸ *v.* **-fied, -fy·ing.** 1. To placate; soothe. 2. To soften or ease. **—mol′li·fi·ca′tion** *n.*

mol·lusk also **mol·lusc** (mŏl′əsk) ▸ *n.* Any of a phylum of chiefly marine invertebrates typically having a soft body and a protective shell and including the edible shellfish and the snails.

mol·ly·cod·dle (mŏl′ē-kŏd′l) ▸ *v.* **-dled, -dling.** To spoil by pampering. ▸ *n.* A pampered person.

Mo·lo·kai (mŏl′ə-kī′, mō′lə-) ▸ An island of central HI between Oahu and Maui.

Mo·lo·tov cocktail (mŏl′ə-tôf′, môl′-, mō′lə-) ▸ *n.* A makeshift incendiary bomb made of a bottle filled with flammable liquid and a usu. rag wick.

molt (mōlt) ▸ *v.* To periodically shed an outer covering, such as feathers or skin, for replacement by a new growth. ▸ *n.* The act of molting.

mol·ten (mōl′tən) ▸ *adj.* Made liquid and glowing by heat; melted.

mol. wt. ▸ *abbr.* molecular weight

mo·lyb·de·num (mə-lĭb′də-nəm) ▸ *n. Symbol* **Mo** A hard, silvery-white metallic element used to toughen alloy steels and soften steel alloys. At. no. 42.

mom (mŏm) ▸ *n. Informal* Mother.

mo·ment (mō′mənt) ▸ *n.* 1. A brief interval of time. 2. A specific point in time: *not here at the moment.* 3. A particular period of importance or excellence. 4. Importance.

mo·men·tar·i·ly (mō′mən-târ′ə-lē) ▸ *adv.* 1. For a moment. 2. In a moment; shortly.

mo·men·tar·y (mō′mən-tĕr′ē) ▸ *adj.* 1. Lasting for only a moment. 2. Occurring or present at every moment. **—mo′men·tar′i·ness** *n.*

mo·ment·ly (mō′mənt-lē) ▸ *adv.* From moment to moment.

mo·men·tous (mō-mĕn′təs) ▸ *adj.* Of utmost importance or significance. **—mo·men′tous·ly** *adv.* **—mo·men′tous·ness** *n.*

mo·men·tum (mō-mĕn′təm) ▸ *n., pl.* **-ta** (-tə) or **-tums.** 1. The product of a body's mass and velocity. 2. Impetus.

mom·my ▸ *n., pl.* **-mies.** *Informal* A mother.

Mon. ▸ *abbr.* Monday

mon– ▸ *pref.* Var. of **mono–.**

Mon·a·co (mŏn′ə-kō′, mə-nä′kō) ▸ A principality on the Mediterranean Sea consisting of an enclave in SE France. Cap. **Monaco** or **Monaco-Ville.** **—Mon′a·can** *adj. & n.*

mon·arch (mŏn′ərk, -ärk′) ▸ *n.* 1. A hereditary sovereign, such as a king or queen. 2. One that presides over or rules. 3. A large orange and black butterfly. **—mo·nar′chal** (mə-när′kəl), **mo·nar′chic** *adj.*

mon·ar·chism (mŏn′ər-kĭz′əm, -är′-) ▸ *n.* 1. The system or principles of monarchy. 2. Belief in or advocacy of monarchy. **—mon′ar·chist** *n.* **—mon′ar·chis′tic** *adj.*

mon·ar·chy (mŏn′ər-kē, -är′-) ▸ *n., pl.* **-chies.** 1. Government by a monarch. 2. A state ruled or headed by a monarch.

mon·as·ter·y (mŏn′ə-stĕr′ē) ▸ *n., pl.* **-ries.** The dwelling place of a community of monks. **—mon′as·te′ri·al** (-stîr′ē-əl, -stĕr′-) *adj.*

mo·nas·tic (mə-năs′tĭk) also **mo·nas·ti·cal** (-tĭ-kəl) ▸ *adj.* 1. Of a monastery. 2. Characteristic of life in a monastery or convent, esp.: a. Secluded and contemplative. b. Strictly disciplined. c. Self-abnegating; austere. **—mo·nas′ti·cal·ly** *adv.* **—mo·nas′ti·cism** *n.*

mon·au·ral (mŏn-ôr′əl) ▸ *adj.* 1. Of or designating sound reception by one ear. 2. Using a single channel to record or reproduce sound; monophonic. **—mon·au′ral·ly** *adv.*

Mon·day (mŭn′dē, -dā′) ▸ *n.* The 2nd day of the week.

Mo·net (mō-nā′, mô-), **Claude** (1840–1926) ▸ French painter.

mon·e·ta·rism (mŏn′ĭ-tə-rĭz′əm, mŭn′-) ▸ *n.* A policy of regulating an economy by altering the money supply, esp. by increasing it moderately but steadily. **—mon′e·ta·rist** *adj. & n.*

mon·e·tar·y (mŏn′ĭ-tĕr′ē, mŭn′-) ▸ *adj.* 1. Of or relating to money. 2. Of or relating to a nation's currency or coinage. **—mon′e·tar′i·ly** *adv.*

mon·e·tize (mŏn′ĭ-tīz′, mŭn′-) ▸ *v.* **-tized, -tiz·ing.** 1. To establish as legal tender. 2. To coin (money). **—mon′e·ti·za′tion** *n.*

mon·ey (mŭn′ē) ▸ *n., pl.* **-eys** or **-ies.** 1. A commodity that is legally established as an exchangeable equivalent of all other commodities and used as a measure of their comparative market value. 2. The official currency issued by a government. 3. Assets and property considered in terms of monetary value; wealth. 4. Profit or loss: *made money on the sale.* 5. often **moneys** or **monies** Sums of money; funds: *state tax monies.*

mon·eyed also **mon·ied** (mŭn′ēd) ▸ *adj.* 1. Wealthy. 2. Representing or arising from money or wealth.

mon·ey·lend·er (mŭn′ē-lĕn′dər) ▸ *n.* One that lends money at an interest rate.

THESAURUS

moldy or **moldering** *adj.* Smelling of mildew or decay ▸ frowzy, funky, fusty, gamy, mildewed, musty, rancid, rank, rotten, stale. [*Compare* AIRLESS, BAD, SMELLY.]

mole *n.* —*See* INFORMER.

molecule *n.* —*See* BIT[1] (1).

molest *v.* To compel another to participate in or submit to a sexual act ▸ assault, force, rape, ravish, violate. —*See also* ANNOY.

moll *n.* —*See* HARLOT.

mollify *v.* —*See* PACIFY.

mollycoddle *n.* —*See* BABY (2).

mollycoddle *v.* —*See* BABY.

molt *v.* —*See* SHED[1] (2).

mom *n.* —*See* MOTHER.

moment *n.* —*See* [illegible], IMPORTANCE, OCCASION (1), OPPORTUNITY.

momentary *adj.* —*See* TRANSITORY.

momentous *adj.* So critically decisive as to affect the future ▸ fatal, fateful. [*Compare* DECISIVE.] —*See also* GRAVE[2] (1), IMPORTANT.

momentousness *n.* The condition of being grave and of involving serious consequences ▸ graveness, gravity, heaviness, seriousness, weightiness. [*Compare* SEVERITY.]

momma *n.* —*See* GIRL, MOTHER.

mommy *n.* —*See* MOTHER.

monarch *n.* —*See* CHIEF.

monetary *adj.* Of or relating to finances ▸ financial, fiscal, pecuniary.

money *n.* 1. Something, such as coins or printed bills, used as a medium of exchange ▸ bills, cash, coin, currency, greenbacks, lucre, notes. *Informal:* bucks, wampum. *Slang:* bread, cabbage, dough, gelt, green, jack, juice, lettuce, long green, mazuma, moola, roll, scratch, shekels. [*Compare* WAGE.] 2. The monetary resources of a government, an organization, or an individual ▸ capital, finances, funds. [*Compare* CAPITAL, RESOURCES.] —*See also* WEALTH.

moneyed *adj.* —*See* RICH (1).

mon·ey·mak·ing (mŭn′ē-mā′kĭng) ▸ *n.* Acquisition of money. ▸ *adj.* **1.** Engaged in acquiring wealth. **2.** Profitable. **—mon′ey·mak′er** *n.*

money market ▸ *n.* **1.** The trade in short-term, low-risk securities, such as certificates of deposit and US Treasury notes. **2.** A mutual fund that sells its shares in order to purchase short-term securities.

money order ▸ *n.* An order for the payment of a specified amount of money, usu. issued and payable at a bank or post office.

mon·ger (mŭng′gər, mŏng′-) ▸ *n.* A dealer.

Mon·gol (mŏng′gəl, -gōl′, mŏn′-) ▸ *n.* **1.** A member of any of the traditionally nomadic peoples of Mongolia. **2.** See **Mongolian** 4. **3.** *Anthro.* A member of the Mongoloid racial division. **—Mon′gol** *adj.*

Mon·go·li·a (mŏng-gō′lē-ə, -gōl′yə, mŏn-) ▸ **1.** An ancient region of E-central Asia comprising modern-day Nei Monggol (Inner Mongolia) and the country of Mongolia. **2.** A country of N-central Asia between Russia and China.

Mon·go·li·an (mŏng-gō′lē-ən, -gōl′yən, mŏn-) ▸ *n.* **1.** A native or inhabitant of Mongolia. **2.** A Mongol. **3.** *Anthro.* A member of the Mongoloid racial division. **4a.** A subfamily of the Altaic language family including Mongolian. **b.** Any of the languages of the Mongols.

Mon·gol·ic (mŏng-gŏl′ĭk, mŏn-) ▸ *adj. Anthro.* Of the Mongoloid racial division.

mon·gol·ism also **Mon·gol·ism** (mŏng′gə-lĭz′əm, mŏn′-) ▸ *n. Offensive* Down syndrome.

Mon·gol·oid (mŏng′gə-loid′, mŏn′-) ▸ *adj.* **1.** *Anthro.* Of or being a human racial classification distinguished by yellowish-brown skin color and straight black hair and including peoples indigenous to central and E Asia. **2.** Of or like a Mongol. **3.** also **mongoloid** *Offensive* Relating to Down syndrome. **—Mon′gol·oid′** *n.*

mon·goose (mŏng′go͞os′, mŏn′-) ▸ *n., pl.* **-goos·es.** Any of various weasellike, chiefly African or Asian mammals noted for their ability to kill venomous snakes.

mon·grel (mŭng′grəl, mŏng′-) ▸ *n.* A plant or animal, esp. a dog, of mixed breed. ▸ *adj.* Of mixed origin or character.

mon·ied (mŭn′ēd) ▸ *adj.* Var. of **moneyed.**

mon·ies (mŭn′ēz) ▸ *n.* Pl. of **money.**

mon·i·ker or **mon·ick·er** (mŏn′ĭ-kər) ▸ *n. Slang* A nickname.

mo·nism (mō′nĭz′əm, mŏn′ĭz′əm) ▸ *n.* The view in metaphysics that all reality is composed of and reducible to one substance. **—mo′nist** *n.* **—mo·nis′tic** (mō-nĭs′tĭk, mŏ-) *adj.*

mo·ni·tion (mō-nĭsh′ən, mə-) ▸ *n.* A warning or admonition.

mon·i·tor (mŏn′ĭ-tər) ▸ *n.* **1.** A pupil who assists a teacher. **2a.** A usu. electronic device used to record or control a process or system. **b.** A screen used to check the picture being broadcast or picked up by a camera. **c.** *Comp. Sci.* A device that accepts video signals from a computer and displays information on a screen. ▸ *v.* To check, watch, or keep track of, often by means of an electronic device.

mon·i·to·ry (mŏn′ĭ-tôr′ē) ▸ *adj.* Conveying an admonition or warning.

monk (mŭngk) ▸ *n.* A man who is a member of a religious community living in a monastery. **—monk′ish** *adj.* **—monk′ish·ly** *adv.*

mon·key (mŭng′kē) ▸ *n., pl.* **-keys.** Any of various long-tailed, medium-sized primates including the macaques, baboons, capuchins, and marmosets and excluding apes and prosimians. ▸ *v. Informal* To play or tamper with something.

mon·key·shine (mŭng′kē-shīn′) ▸ *n. Slang* A prank. Often used in the plural.

monkey wrench ▸ *n.* **1.** A hand tool with adjustable jaws for turning nuts. **2.** *Informal* Something that hinders or disrupts.

monks·hood (mŭngks′ho͝od′) ▸ *n.* **1.** See **aconite. 2.** A poisonous perennial plant whose dried leaves and roots yield aconite.

mon·o[1] (mŏn′ō) ▸ *n. Informal* Infectious mononucleosis.

mon·o[2] (mŏn′ō) ▸ *adj. Informal* Monaural.

mono– or **mon–** ▸ *pref.* One; single; alone: *monofilament.*

mon·o·chro·mat·ic (mŏn′ə-krō-măt′ĭk) ▸ *adj.* **1.** Of only one color. **2.** Of or composed of radiation of only one wavelength. **—mon′o·chro·mat′i·cal·ly** *adv.*

mon·o·chrome (mŏn′ə-krōm′) ▸ *n.* **1.** A painting or drawing done in different shades of a single color. **2.** The technique of executing a monochrome. **—mon′o·chro′mic** *adj.*

mon·o·cle (mŏn′ə-kəl) ▸ *n.* An eyeglass for one eye.

mon·o·cline (mŏn′ə-klīn′) ▸ *n.* A geologic structure in which all layers are inclined in the same direction. **—mon′o·cli′nal** *adj.*

mon·o·clo·nal (mŏn′ə-klō′nəl) ▸ *adj.* Of, forming, or derived from a single clone: *a monoclonal antibody.*

mon·o·cot·y·le·don (mŏn′ə-kŏt′l-ēd′n) also **mon·o·cot** (mŏn′ə-kŏt′) ▸ *n.* A plant having a single embryonic seed leaf that appears at germination. **—mon′o·cot′y·le′don·ous** *adj.*

mo·noc·u·lar (mŏ-nŏk′yə-lər, mə-) ▸ *adj.* **1.** Having one eye. **2.** Of or intended for use by only one eye.

mon·o·cul·ture (mŏn′ə-kŭl′chər) ▸ *n.* **1.** The cultivation of a single crop in an area or region. **2.** A single homogeneous society or culture. **—mon′o·cul′tur·al** *adj.*

mon·o·dy (mŏn′ə-dē) ▸ *n., pl.* **-dies.** An ode or elegy. **—mo·nod′ic** (mə-nŏd′ĭk) *adj.* **—mon′o·dist** *n.*

mon·o·fil·a·ment (mŏn′ə-fĭl′ə-mənt) ▸ *n.* A single strand of untwisted synthetic fiber used esp. for fishing line.

mo·nog·a·my (mə-nŏg′ə-mē) ▸ *n.* **1.** The condition or practice of being sexually faithful to one partner during a relationship. **2.** Marriage to only one person at a time. **—mo·nog′a·mist** *n.* **—mo·nog′a·mous** *adj.* **—mo·nog′a·mous·ly** *adv.*

mon·o·gram (mŏn′ə-grăm′) ▸ *n.* A design composed of one or more initials of a name. ▸ *v.* **-grammed, -gram·ming** also **-gramed, -gram·ing.** To mark with a monogram. **—mon′o·gram·mat′ic** (-grə-măt′ĭk) *adj.*

mon·o·graph (mŏn′ə-grăf′) ▸ *n.* A scholarly book or article on a specific, often limited subject. **—mon′o·graph′ic** *adj.*

mon·o·lin·gual (mŏn′ə-lĭng′gwəl) ▸ *adj.* Using or knowing only one language. **—mon′o·lin′gual** *n.* **—mon′o·lin′gual·ism** *n.*

mon·o·lith (mŏn′ə-lĭth′) ▸ *n.* **1.** A large block of stone, esp. one used in architecture or sculpture. **2.** A large organization that acts as a powerful unit. **—mon′o·lith′ic** *adj.*

mon·o·logue also **mon·o·log** (mŏn′ə-lôg′, -lŏg′) ▸ *n.* **1.** A soliloquy. **2.** A series of jokes delivered by a comedian. **3.** A long speech by one person, often monopolizing a conversation. **—mon′o·logu′ist, mo·nol′o·gist** (mə-nŏl′ə-jĭst, mŏn′ə-lôg′ĭst, -lŏg′-) *n.*

mon·o·ma·ni·a (mŏn′ə-mā′nē-ə, -mān′yə) ▸ *n.* **1.** Obsession with one idea. **2.** Intent concentration on one subject. **—mon′o·ma′ni·ac′** *n.* **—mon′o·ma·ni′a·cal** (-mə-nī′ə-kəl) *adj.*

mon·o·mer (mŏn′ə-mər) ▸ *n.* A molecule that can be chemically bound to form a polymer. **—mon′o·mer′ic** (-mĕr′ĭk) *adj.*

mo·no·mi·al (mŏ-nō′mē-əl, mə-) ▸ *n.* **1.** An algebraic expression consisting of only one term. **2.** *Biol.* A taxonomic name consisting of a single word. **—mo·no′mi·al** *adj.*

mon·o·nu·cle·o·sis (mŏn′ō-no͞o′klē-ō′sĭs, -nyo͞o-) ▸ *n.* Infectious mononucleosis.

mon·o·phon·ic (mŏn′ə-fŏn′ĭk) ▸ *adj.* Monaural. **—mon′o·phon′i·cal·ly** *adv.*

mon·o·plane (mŏn′ə-plān′) ▸ *n.* An airplane with only one pair of wings.

mo·nop·o·lize (mə-nŏp′ə-līz′) ▸ *v.* **-lized, -liz·ing. 1.** To acquire

THESAURUS

moneymaking *adj.* —*See* PROFITABLE.

moneyman *n.* One who is occupied with or expert in large-scale financial affairs ▸ capitalist, financier.

money management *n.* The management of money ▸ banking, finance, investment.

moniker or **monicker** *n.* —*See* NAME (1).

monition *n.* —*See* WARNING.

monitor *v.* To pay regular and close attention to ▸ follow, observe, stake out, survey, watch. *Idioms:* have one's (*or* keep an) eye on, keep tabs on, keep track of, ride herd on. —*See also* POLICE, SUPERVISE.

monitor *n.* —*See* GUARD.

monitory *adj.* Giving warning ▸ admonishing, admonitory, cautionary, warning.

monk *n.* —*See* CLERIC.

monkey *n.* —*See* DUPE.

monkey *v.* —*See* FIDDLE, TINKER.

monkey business *n.* —*See* MISCHIEF.

monkeyshine *n.* —*See* PRANK[1].

monocracy *n.* —*See* ABSOLUTISM (2).

monocratic *adj.* —*See* ABSOLUTE.

monogram *n.* —*See* MARK (1).

monograph *n.* —*See* DISCOURSE.

monopolize *v.* —*See* ABSORB (1).

or maintain a monopoly of. **2.** To dominate by excluding others: *monopolized the conversation.* **—mo·nop′o·li·za′tion** *n.* **—mo·nop′o·liz′er** *n.*

mo·nop·o·ly (mə-nŏp′ə-lē) ▸ *n., pl.* **-lies. 1.** Exclusive control or ownership, as of a commodity or service. **2a.** A company or group having such control. **b.** A commodity or service so controlled. **—mo·nop′o·list** *n.* **—mo·nop′o·lis′tic** *adj.*

mon·o·rail (mŏn′ə-rāl′) ▸ *n.* A railway system using a single rail.

mon·o·sac·cha·ride (mŏn′ə-săk′ə-rīd′, -rĭd) ▸ *n.* A carbohydrate that cannot be decomposed by hydrolysis; simple sugar.

mon·o·so·di·um glu·ta·mate (mŏn′ə-sō′dē-əm glōō′tə-māt′) ▸ *n.* A white crystalline compound used as a flavor enhancer.

mon·o·syl·la·ble (mŏn′ə-sĭl′ə-bəl) ▸ *n.* A word of one syllable. **—mon′o·syl·lab′ic** (-sĭ-lăb′ĭk) *adj.*

mon·o·the·ism (mŏn′ə-thē-ĭz′əm) ▸ *n.* The belief that there is only one God. **—mon′o·the′ist** *n.* **—mon′o·the·is′tic** *adj.*

mon·o·tone (mŏn′ə-tōn′) ▸ *n.* A succession of sounds or words uttered in a single tone of voice or sung at a single pitch.

mo·not·o·nous (mə-nŏt′n-əs) ▸ *adj.* **1.** Unvarying in tone or pitch. **2.** Repetitiously dull. **—mo·not′o·nous·ly** *adv.* **—mo·not′o·nous·ness** *n.* **—mo·not′o·ny** *n.*

mon·o·type (mŏn′ə-tīp′) ▸ *n. Biol.* The sole member of its group, such as a single species that constitutes a genus. **—mon′o·typ′ic** (-tĭp′ĭk) *adj.*

mon·o·un·sat·u·rat·ed (mŏn′ō-ŭn-săch′ə-rā′tĭd) ▸ *adj.* Being an unsaturated fat composed esp. of fatty acids having only one double bond in the carbon chain.

mon·o·va·lent (mŏn′ə-vā′lənt) ▸ *adj.* Univalent. **—mon′o·va′lence, mon′o·va′len·cy** *n.*

mon·ox·ide (mə-nŏk′sīd′) ▸ *n.* An oxide with each molecule containing one oxygen atom.

mon·o·zy·got·ic (mŏn′ō-zī-gŏt′ĭk) ▸ *adj.* Derived from a single fertilized ovum. Used esp. of identical twins.

Mon·roe (mən-rō′), **James** (1758–1831) ▸ The 5th US President (1817–25).

Mon·sieur (mə-syœ′) ▸ *n., pl.* **Mes·sieurs** (mā-syœ′, mĕs′ərz). A French courtesy title for a man.

Mon·si·gnor also **mon·si·gnor** (mŏn-sēn′yər) ▸ *n. Rom. Cath. Ch.* A title and office conferred on a cleric by the Pope.

mon·soon (mŏn-sōōn′) ▸ *n.* A wind system that influences large climatic regions and reverses direction seasonally, esp. the Asiatic system producing dry and wet seasons in India and S Asia.

mon·ster (mŏn′stər) ▸ *n.* **1.** A creature having a strange or frightening appearance. **2.** An animal or plant having gross defects or deformities. **3.** Something unusually large. **4.** One who inspires horror or disgust. **—mon·stros′i·ty** (-strŏs′ĭ-te) *n.* **—mon′strous** *adj.* **—mon′strous·ly** *adv.* **—mon′strous·ness** *n.*

mon·strance (mŏn′strəns) ▸ *n. Rom. Cath. Ch.* A receptacle in which the host is held.

Mont. ▸ *abbr.* Montana

mon·tage (mŏn-täzh′, môN-) ▸ *n.* **1.** A single pictorial composition made by juxtaposing several pictures or designs. **2.** A rapid succession of scenes or images, as in a movie, that exhibits different aspects of the same idea or situation.

Mon·tag·nais (mŏn′tən-yā′) ▸ *n., pl.* **-nais. 1.** A member of a Native American people inhabiting Quebec and Labrador. **2.** The Algonquian language of the Montagnais.

Mon·tan·a (mŏn-tăn′ə) ▸ A state of the northwest US bordering on Canada. Cap. Helena. **—Mon·tan′an** *adj. & n.*

mon·tane (mŏn-tān′, mŏn′tān′) ▸ *adj.* Of, growing in, or inhabiting mountain areas.

Mon·te Car·lo (mŏn′tē kär′lō) ▸ A resort town of Monaco on the Mediterranean Sea and the French Riviera.

Mon·te·neg·ro (mŏn′tə-nĕg′rō, -nē′grō) ▸ A country of southeast Europe on the Adriatic Sea. **—Mon′te·neg′rin** *adj. & n.*

Mon·ter·rey (mŏn′tə-rā′, môn′tĕ-) ▸ A city of NE Mexico E of Matamoros.

Mon·tes·so·ri (mŏn′tĭ-sôr′ē), **Maria** (1870–1952) ▸ Italian physician and educator.

Montessori method ▸ *n.* A method of educating children that stresses development of a child's own initiative.

Mon·te·zu·ma II (mŏn′tĭ-zōō′mə) (1466?–1520) ▸ Aztec emperor in Mexico (1502–20).

Mont·gom·er·y (mŏnt-gŭm′ə-rē, -gŭm′rē) ▸ The capital of AL, in the SE-central part SSE of Birmingham.

month (mŭnth) ▸ *n.* **1.** The period during which the moon passes once through its phases, equal to about 30 days or 4 weeks. **2.** One of the usu. 12 divisions of a calendar year. **3.** A period extending from a date in one calendar month to the corresponding date in the next month.

month·ly (mŭnth′lē) ▸ *adj.* **1.** Occurring, appearing, or payable every month. **2.** Continuing or lasting for a month. ▸ *adv.* Once a month; every month. ▸ *n., pl.* **-lies.** A publication appearing once each month.

Mont·pel·ier (mŏnt-pēl′yər) ▸ The capital of VT, in the N-central part.

Mon·tre·al (mŏn′trē-ôl′) ▸ A city of S Quebec, Canada, on **Montreal Island** in the St. Lawrence R.

Mont·ser·rat (mŏnt′sə-răt′) ▸ An island in the Leeward Is. of the British West Indies NW of Guadaloupe.

mon·u·ment (mŏn′yə-mənt) ▸ *n.* **1.** A structure erected as a memorial. **2.** A tombstone. **3.** Something preserved for its historic or aesthetic significance. **4a.** An outstanding or enduring achievement. **b.** An exceptional example.

mon·u·men·tal (mŏn′yə-mĕn′tl) ▸ *adj.* **1.** Of or serving as a monument. **2.** Impressively large and sturdy. **3.** Of outstanding significance. **4.** Astounding: *monumental cowardice.* **—mon′u·men′tal·ly** *adv.*

moo (mōō) ▸ *v.* To emit the deep bellowing sound made by a cow. **—moo** *n.*

mooch (mōōch) ▸ *v. Slang* **1.** To obtain free; beg. **2.** To steal; filch. **—mooch′er** *n.*

mood¹ (mōōd) ▸ *n.* **1.** A state of mind or emotion. **2.** Inclination; disposition.

mood² (mōōd) ▸ *n.* A set of verb forms or inflections used to indicate the factuality or likelihood of the action or condition expressed.

mood·y (mōō′dē) ▸ *adj.* **-i·er, -i·est. 1.** Given to changeable moods; temperamental. **2.** Subject to periods of depression; gloomy. **—mood′i·ly** *adv.* **—mood′i·ness** *n.*

THESAURUS

monopoly *n.* Exclusive control or possession ▸ corner. [*Compare* DOMINATION.] —*See also* ALLIANCE, COMPANY (1).

monotonous *adj.* —*See* BORING.

monotony or **monotonousness** or **monotone** *n.* A tiresome lack of variety ▸ humdrum, invariability, repetition, repititiousness, repetitiveness, sameness, tedium, tediousness. [*Compare* BOREDOM, DULLNESS, ROUTINE.]

monster *n.* A person or animal that is abnormally formed ▸ freak, grotesque, monstrosity, mooncalf, mutant. *Idiom:* freak of nature. [*Compare* DEFORMITY.] —*See also* FIEND, GIANT.

monster *adj.* —*See* ENORMOUS.

monstrosity *n.* —*See* MESS (2), MONSTER, OUTRAGE, UGLINESS.

monstrous *adj.* Resembling a freak ▸ freakish, freaky, grotesque. [*Compare* ECCENTRIC, WEIRD.] —*See also* ENORMOUS, OUTRAGEOUS, UGLY.

monstrousness *n.* —*See* OUTRAGEOUSNESS, UGLINESS.

monument *n.* Something, as a structure or custom, serving to honor or keep alive a memory ▸ commemoration, memorial, remembrance. [*Compare* TESTIMONIAL.]

monumental *adj.* Serving to honor or to keep alive a memory ▸ commemorative, memorial. —*See also* ENORMOUS, IMPORTANT.

monumentality *n.* —*See* ENORMOUSNESS.

mooch *v.* —*See* BEG, STEAL.

moocher *n.* —*See* BEGGAR (1).

mood *n.* A temporary state of mind or feeling ▸ frame of mind, humor, mindset, spirits, state of mind, temper, vein. [*Compare* DISPOSITION, POSTURE.] —*See also* AIR (3), TEMPER (3).

moody *adj.* Given to changeable emotional states, especially of anger or gloom ▸ mercurial, temperamental. [*Compare* CAPRICIOUS, TESTY.] —*See also* GLUM.

moola or **moolah** *n.* —*See* MONEY (1).

moon (mo͞on) ▸ *n.* **1.** often **Moon** The natural satellite of Earth, approx. 356,000 km (221,600 mi) distant at perigee and 406,997 km (252,950 mi) at apogee, and having a mean diameter of 3,475 km (2,160 mi), mass approx. one eightieth that of Earth, and an average period of revolution around Earth of 29 days 12 hours 44 minutes. **2.** A natural satellite revolving around a planet. **3.** The moon as it appears at a particular phase: *the full moon.* **4.** A month. **5.** A disk, globe, or crescent resembling the moon. ▸ *v.* To wander about or pass time in a dreamy or aimless way. **—moon′y** *adj.*
moon·beam (mo͞on′bēm′) ▸ *n.* A ray of moonlight.
moon·light (mo͞on′līt′) ▸ *n.* The light of the moon. ▸ *v. Informal* To work at a second job, often at night. **—moon′light′er** *n.*
moon·lit (mo͞on′lĭt′) ▸ *adj.* Lighted by moonlight.
moon·shine (mo͞on′shīn′) ▸ *n.* **1.** Moonlight. **2.** *Informal* Foolish talk; nonsense. **3.** Illegally distilled whiskey. **—moon′shin′er** *n.*
moon·stone (mo͞on′stōn′) ▸ *n.* A form of feldspar valued for its pearly translucence.
moon·struck (mo͞on′strŭk′) ▸ *adj.* **1.** Dazed or distracted with romantic sentiment. **2.** Mentally unbalanced; crazed.
moor[1] (mo͝or) ▸ *v.* To secure in place with or as if with lines, cables, or anchors. **—moor′age** *n.*
moor[2] (mo͝or) ▸ *n.* A broad area of open, often boggy land, usu. covered with low shrubs.
Moor ▸ *n.* **1.** A member of a Muslim people of mixed Berber and Arab descent, now living chiefly in NW Africa. **2.** One of the Muslims who invaded Spain in the 8th cent. **—Moor′ish** *adj.*
moor·ing (mo͝or′ĭng) ▸ *n.* **1.** A place at which a vessel or aircraft can be moored. **2.** often **moorings** Elements providing stability or security.
moose (mo͞os) ▸ *n., pl.* **moose.** A large deer of N North America, having broad flattened antlers in the male.
moot (mo͞ot) ▸ *v.* To bring up as a subject for discussion or debate. ▸ *adj.* **1.** Subject to debate; arguable. **2.** *Law* Without legal significance. **3.** Irrelevant.
moot court ▸ *n.* A mock court where hypothetical cases are tried by law students as an exercise.
mop (mŏp) ▸ *n.* **1.** A household implement made of absorbent material attached to a handle and used for cleaning floors. **2.** A tangled mass, esp. of hair. ▸ *v.* **mopped, mop·ping.** To wash or wipe with or as if with a mop. ***—phrasal verb:* mop up** **1.** To clear (an area) of remaining enemy troops after a victory. **2.** To conclude a project or activity. **—mop′per** *n.*
mope (mōp) ▸ *v.* **moped, mop·ing.** To be gloomy or dejected. **—mop′er** *n.* **—mop′ish·ly** *adv.*
mo·ped (mō′pĕd′) ▸ *n.* A motorbike that can be pedaled as well as driven by a low-powered gasoline engine.
mop·pet (mŏp′ĭt) ▸ *n.* A young child.
mop-up (mŏp′ŭp′) ▸ *n.* The act of disposing of final or remaining details.
mo·raine (mə-rān′) ▸ *n.* An accumulation of boulders, stones, or other debris carried and deposited by a glacier.
mor·al (môr′əl, mŏr′-) ▸ *adj.* **1.** Of or concerned with the judgment or instruction of goodness or badness of character and behavior. **2.** Conforming to established standards of good behavior. **3.** Arising from conscience. **4.** Having psychological rather than tangible effects. **5.** Based on likelihood rather than evidence. ▸ *n.* **1.** The principle taught by a story or event. **2. morals** Rules or habits of conduct, esp. of sexual conduct. **—mor′al·ly** *adv.*
mo·rale (mə-răl′) ▸ *n.* The state of mind of a person or group as exhibited by confidence, cheerfulness, and discipline.
mor·al·ist (môr′ə-lĭst, mŏr′-) ▸ *n.* **1.** A teacher or student of ethics. **2.** One who follows a system of moral principles. **—mor′a·lis′tic** *adj.* **—mor′a·lis′ti·cal·ly** *adv.*
mo·ral·i·ty (mə-răl′ĭ-tē, mô-) ▸ *n., pl.* **-ties. 1.** The quality of being moral. **2.** A system of ideas of right and wrong conduct. **3.** Virtuous conduct.
mor·al·ize (môr′ə-līz′, mŏr′-) ▸ *v.* **-ized, -iz·ing.** To think about or discuss moral issues. **—mor′al·i·za′tion** *n.* **—mor′al·iz′er** *n.*
mo·rass (mə-răs′, mô-) ▸ *n.* **1.** An area of low-lying, soggy ground. **2.** A difficult, perplexing, or overwhelming situation.
mor·a·to·ri·um (môr′ə-tôr′ē-əm, mŏr′-) ▸ *n., pl.* **-to·ri·ums** or **-to·ri·a** (-tôr′ē-ə). **1.** *Law* An authorization to a debtor permitting temporary suspension of payments. **2.** A suspension or delay of any action or activity.
mo·ray (môr′ā, mə-rā′) ▸ *n.* Any of numerous chiefly tropical marine eels that are ferocious fighters.
mor·bid (môr′bĭd) ▸ *adj.* **1.** Of or caused by disease. **2.** Marked by preoccupation with unwholesome matters. **3.** Gruesome; grisly. **—mor′bid·ly** *adv.* **—mor′bid·ness** *n.*
mor·bid·i·ty (môr-bĭd′ĭ-tē) ▸ *n., pl.* **-ties. 1.** The condition or quality of being morbid. **2.** The rate of incidence of a disease.
mor·da·cious (môr-dā′shəs) ▸ *adj.* **1.** Given to biting. **2.** Caustic; sarcastic. **—mor·da′cious·ly** *adv.* **—mor·dac′i·ty** (-dăs′ĭ-tē) *n.*
mor·dant (môr′dnt) ▸ *adj.* **1.** Bitingly sarcastic. **2.** Incisive and trenchant. **—mor′dan·cy** *n.* **—mor′dant·ly** *adv.*
more (môr) ▸ *adj.* Comp. of **many, much. 1a.** Greater in number. **b.** Greater in size, amount, extent, or degree. **2.** Additional; extra: *She needs some more time.* ▸ *n.* A greater or additional quantity, number, degree, or amount. ▸ *pron. (takes pl. v.)* A greater or additional number of persons or things. ▸ *adv.* Comp. of **much. 1a.** To or in a greater extent or degree: *loved him even more.* **b.** Used to form the comparative of many adjectives and adverbs: *more difficult; more softly.* **2.** In addition: *phoned twice more.* ***—idiom:* more or less** **1.** About; approximately. **2.** To an undetermined degree.
More, Sir **Thomas** (1478–1535) ▸ English politician, scholar, and writer.
mo·rel (mə-rĕl′, mô-) ▸ *n.* An edible mushroom having a brownish spongelike cap.
more·o·ver (môr-ō′vər, môr′ō′vər) ▸ *adv.* Furthermore; besides.
mo·res (môr′āz′, -ēz) ▸ *pl.n.* The accepted customs and rules of a particular social group.

THESAURUS

mooncalf *n.* —*See* FOOL, MONSTER.
moonstruck *adj.* —*See* INSANE.
moony *adj.* —*See* DREAMY.
moor[1] *v.* —*See* ATTACH (1), FASTEN.
moor[2] *n.* —*See* SWAMP.
mooring *n.* —*See* ANCHOR.
moot *v.* —*See* ARGUE (2), BROACH, DISCUSS.
moot *adj.* —*See* DEBATABLE, THEORETICAL (1).
mope *v.* To be sullenly aloof or withdrawn, as in silent resentment or protest ▸ pet, pout, sulk. [*Compare* BROOD.] —*See also* BROOD.
mopes *n.* —*See* DEPRESSION (2).
moppet *n.* —*See* CHILD (1).
moral *adj.* Teaching morality ▸ didactic, didactical, edifying, moralistic, moralizing, preachy. —*See also* CHASTE, ELEVATED (3), ETHICAL.
moral *n.* The principle that is taught by a fable or parable ▸ axiom, lesson, maxim, principle. [*Compare* IDEA, LAW, MEANING.]
morale *n.* A strong sense of enthusiasm and dedication to a common goal that unites a group ▸ esprit, esprit de corps, group spirit, team spirit. [*Compare* CONFIDENCE, MOOD, SPIRIT.]
moralistic *adj.* Piously or overly sure of one's own righteousness ▸ holier-than-thou, self-righteous. [*Compare* ARROGANT, HYPOCRITICAL, MORAL.] —*See also* MORAL.
morality *n.* —*See* CHASTITY, ETHICS (1), ETHICS (2), GOOD (1).
moralize *v.* To indulge in moral reflection, usually pompously ▸ edify, pontificate, preach, sermonize. [*Compare* CHASTISE.]
moralizing *adj.* —*See* DIDACTIC (2), MORAL.
morals *n.* —*See* ETHICS (2).
morass *n.* —*See* SWAMP, TANGLE.
moratorium *n.* —*See* DELAY (1).
morbid *adj.* Characterized by preoccupation with unwholesome thoughts or feelings ▸ insalubrious, macabre, sick, unhealthy, unwholesome. [*Compare* ABNORMAL.] —*See also* GHASTLY (2).
mordacity or **mordancy** *n.* —*See* SARCASM.
mordant or **mordacious** *adj.* —*See* BITING.
more *adj.* —*See* ADDITIONAL.
more *adv.* To a greater extent ▸ better. *Idioms:* more fully, to a greater degree. —*See also* ADDITIONALLY.
moreover *adv.* —*See* ADDITIONALLY, EVEN (2).
mores *n.* —*See* CULTURE (2), ETHICS (2), MANNERS.

morgue (môrg) ► *n.* **1.** A place in which the bodies of persons found dead are temporarily kept. **2.** A reference file in a newspaper or magazine office.

mor·i·bund (môr′ə-bŭnd′, mŏr′-) ► *adj.* At the point of death. **–mor′i·bun′di·ty** *n.* **–mor′i·bund′ly** *adv.*

Mor·mon (môr′mən) ► *n.* A member of the Mormon Church. **–Mor′mon** *adj.* **–Mor′mon·ism** *n.*

Mormon Church ► *n.* A church founded by Joseph Smith in 1830 and having its headquarters in Salt Lake City, Utah.

morn (môrn) ► *n.* Morning.

morn·ing (môr′nĭng) ► *n.* The first or early part of the day, esp. from sunrise to noon.

morning glory ► *n.* Any of various twining vines having funnel-shaped flowers that close late in the day.

mo·roc·co (mə-rŏk′ō) ► *n., pl.* **-cos.** A soft fine leather of goatskin.

Morocco ► A country of NW Africa on the Mediterranean and the Atlantic. **–Mo·roc′can** *adj. & n.*

mo·ron (môr′ŏn′) ► *n.* **1.** A stupid person. **2.** *Psychol.* A person of mild mental retardation having a mental age of from 7 to 12 years. Not in scientific use. **–mo·ron′ic** (mə-rŏn′ĭk, mô-) *adj.*

mo·rose (mə-rōs′, mô-) ► *adj.* Sullenly melancholy; gloomy. **–mo·rose′ly** *adv.* **–mo·rose′ness** *n.*

morph (môrf) ► *v.* **1.** To transform (an image) by computer: *morphed the villain into a snake.* **2.** To be transformed.

–morph ► *suff.* **1.** Form; shape; structure: *isomorph.* **2.** Morpheme: *allomorph.*

mor·pheme (môr′fēm′) ► *n.* A linguistic unit, such as *man,* or *-ed* in *walked,* that has meaning and cannot be divided into smaller meaningful parts. **–mor·phem′ic** *adj.* **–mor·phem′i·cal·ly** *adv.*

mor·phine (môr′fēn′) ► *n.* A powerfully addictive narcotic drug extracted from opium, used in medicine as an anesthetic or sedative.

morpho– or **morph–** ► *pref.* **1.** Form; shape; structure: *morphogenesis.* **2.** Morpheme: *morphology.*

mor·pho·gen·e·sis (môr′fō-jĕn′ĭ-sĭs) ► *n.* Evolutionary or embryological development of the structure of an organism or part. **–mor′pho·ge·net′ic** (-jə-nĕt′ĭk), **mor′pho·gen′ic** *adj.*

mor·phol·o·gy (môr-fŏl′ə-jē) ► *n., pl.* **-gies. 1.** The biological study of the form and structure of organisms. **2.** *Ling.* The study of word formation, including inflection, derivation, and compounds. **–mor′pho·log′i·cal** (-fə-lŏj′ĭ-kəl), **mor′pho·log′ic** *adj.* **–mor′pho·log′i·cal·ly** *adv.* **–mor·phol′o·gist** *n.*

mor·ris (môr′ĭs, mŏr′-) ► *n.* An English folk dance in which a story is enacted by costumed dancers.

Morris chair ► *n.* A large easy chair with an adjustable back and removable cushions.

mor·row (môr′ō, mŏr′ō) ► *n.* The following day.

Morse (môrs), **Samuel Finley Breese** (1791–1872) ► Amer. painter and inventor.

Morse code ► *n.* A code, used esp. in telegraphy, in which letters of the alphabet and numbers are represented by various sequences of dots and dashes or short and long signals.

mor·sel (môr′səl) ► *n.* **1.** A small piece of food. **2.** A tasty tidbit. **3.** A bit or item: *a morsel of wisdom.*

mor·tal (môr′tl) ► *adj.* **1.** Liable or subject to death. **2.** Of or accompanying death. **3.** Causing death; fatal. **4a.** Fought to the death: *mortal combat.* **b.** Unrelentingly antagonistic: *mortal foes.* **5.** Of great intensity or severity; dire: *mortal terror.* ► *n.* A human. **–mor′tal·ly** *adv.*

mor·tal·i·ty (môr-tăl′ĭ-tē) ► *n.* **1.** The condition of being mortal. **2.** Death rate.

mor·tar (môr′tər) ► *n.* **1.** A vessel in which substances are crushed or ground with a pestle. **2.** A muzzleloading cannon used to fire shells in high trajectories. **3.** A bonding material used in building, esp. a mixture of cement or lime with sand and water.

mor·tar·board (môr′tər-bôrd′) ► *n.* **1.** A square board with a handle used for holding and carrying mortar. **2.** An academic cap topped by a flat square and a tassel.

mort·gage (môr′gĭj) ► *n.* **1.** A legal pledge of property to a creditor as security for the payment of a loan or other debt. **2.** A contract or deed specifying the terms of a mortgage. ► *v.* **-gaged, -gag·ing.** To pledge (property) by means of a mortgage. **–mort′ga·gee′** (-gĭ-jē′) *n.* **–mort′ga·gor′** (-jôr′, -jər) *n.*

mor·ti·cian (môr-tĭsh′ən) ► *n.* See **funeral director.**

mor·ti·fy (môr′tə-fī′) ► *v.* **-fied, -fy·ing. 1.** To shame; humiliate. **2.** To discipline (one's body and appetites) by self-denial. **–mor′ti·fi·ca′tion** *n.*

mor·tise (môr′tĭs) ► *n.* A usu. rectangular cavity in a piece of wood, stone, or other material, prepared to receive a tenon and thus form a joint.

mort·main (môrt′mān′) ► *n.* **1.** *Law* Perpetual ownership of real estate by institutions such as churches that cannot transfer or sell it. **2.** The often oppressive influence of the past on the present.

mor·tu·ar·y (môr′chōō-ĕr′ē) ► *n., pl.* **-ies.** A place where dead bodies are kept before burial or cremation.

mos. ► *abbr.* months

mo·sa·ic (mō-zā′ĭk) ► *n.* A picture or decorative design made by setting small colored pieces, as of stone, glass, or tile, into a surface.

Mos·cow (mŏs′kou, -kō) ► The capital of Russia, in the W-central part.

Mos·es (mō′zĭz, -zĭs) ► In the Bible, the Hebrew prophet and lawgiver who led the Israelites out of Egypt. **–Mo·sa′ic** (mō-zā′ĭk) *adj.*

Moses, Anna Mary Robertson. "Grandma Moses" (1860–1961) ► Amer. painter.

mo·sey (mō′zē) ► *v. Informal* To move in a leisurely manner; saunter.

mosh (mŏsh) ► *v.* To knock against others intentionally while dancing at a rock concert; slam-dance.

mosh pit ► *n.* An area in front of a concert stage in which audience members mosh.

Mos·lem (mŏz′ləm, mŏs′-) ► *n. & adj.* Var. of **Muslim.**

mosque (mŏsk) ► *n.* A Muslim house of worship.

mos·qui·to (mə-skē′tō) ► *n., pl.* **-toes** or **-tos.** Any of various two-winged insects of which the females suck blood and in some species transmit diseases.

Mosquito ► *n., pl.* **-to** or **-tos.** See **Miskito.**

moss (môs, mŏs) ► *n.* Any of various small, green, nonflowering plants often forming a dense matlike growth. **–moss′i·ness** *n.* **–moss′y** *adj.*

most (mōst) ► *adj.* Superl. of **many, much. 1a.** Greatest in number. **b.** Greatest in amount, extent, or degree. **2.** In the greatest number of instances: *Most fish have fins.* ► *n.* The greatest amount or degree: *She has the most to gain.* ► *pron. (takes sing. or pl. v.)* The greatest part or number: *Most of the town was destroyed.* ► *adv.* Superl. of **much. 1.** In or to the highest degree, quantity, or extent. Used with many adjectives and adverbs to form the superlative: *most honest; most impatiently.* **2.** Very: *a most impressive book.* **3.** *Informal* Almost: *Most everyone agrees.* **–*idiom:* at (the) most** At the maximum: *two miles at most.*

–most ► *suff.* **1.** Most: *innermost.* **2.** Nearest to: *endmost.*

most·ly (mōst′lē) ► *adv.* **1.** For the greatest part; mainly. **2.** Generally; usually.

THESAURUS

morn *n.* —*See* DAWN.

morning *n.* The time of day from sunrise to noon ► A.M., before lunch, before noon, forenoon. —*See also* DAWN.

moron *n.* —*See* DULLARD, FOOL.

moronic *adj.* —*See* FOOLISH, STUPID.

morose *adj.* —*See* GLUM.

morph *v.* —*See* CONVERT.

morsel *n.* —*See* BIT[1] (1), BIT[1] (2), DELICACY.

mortal *adj.* —*See* BODILY, CONCEIVABLE, DEADLY, HUMAN.

mortal *n.* —*See* HUMAN BEING.

mortgage *v.* —*See* PAWN[1].

mortification *n.* *See* DEGRADATION (1), EMBARRASSMENT.

mortify *v.* To cause to feel embarrassment, dishonor, and often guilt ► brand, reproach, shame, stigmatize. [*Compare* BELITTLE, DENIGRATE.] —*See also* EMBARRASS, HUMBLE.

mortise *n.* —*See* FASTENER.

mosey *v.* —*See* STROLL.

mossback *n.* —*See* SQUARE, ULTRACONSERVATIVE.

mossbacked *adj.* —*See* ULTRACONSERVATIVE.

most *adj.* —*See* BEST (2).

most *adv.* —*See* VERY.

mostly *adv.* —*See* USUALLY.

Mo·sul (mō-so͞ol′, mō′səl) ▸ A city of N Iraq on the Tigris R.
mot (mō) ▸ *n.* A short witty saying or remark.
mote (mōt) ▸ *n.* A speck, esp. of dust.
mo·tel (mō-tĕl′) ▸ *n.* A hotel for motorists providing rooms usu. having direct access to an open parking area.
mo·tet (mō-tĕt′) ▸ *n. Mus.* A polyphonic composition based on a religious text.
moth (môth, mŏth) ▸ *n., pl.* **moths** (mô*th*z, mŏ*th*z, môths, mŏths). Any of numerous insects related to and resembling butterflies but gen. night-flying and having hairlike or feathery antennae.
moth·ball (môth′bôl′, mŏth′-) ▸ *n.* **1.** A marble-sized ball, orig. of camphor but now of naphthalene, stored with clothes to repel moths. **2. mothballs** Protective storage: *put the battleship into mothballs.*
moth·er (mŭ*th*′ər) ▸ *n.* **1.** A female parent. **2.** A woman having some of the authority or responsibility of a mother: *a den mother.* **3.** A creative source; origin: *Philosophy is the mother of the sciences.* ▸ *adj.* **1.** Being a mother: *a mother hen.* **2.** Characteristic of a mother: *mother love.* **3.** Native: *one's mother language.* ▸ *v.* **1.** To give birth to; create and produce. **2.** To watch over, nourish, and protect; care for. **—moth′er·hood′** *n.* **—moth′er·less** *adj.* **—moth′er·li·ness** *n.* **—moth′er·ly** *adj.*
moth·er·board (mŭ*th*′ər-bôrd′) ▸ *n.* The main board of a computer, usu. containing the circuitry for the central processing unit, keyboard, and monitor.
moth·er-in-law (mŭ*th*′ər-ĭn-lô′) ▸ *n., pl.* **moth·ers-in-law** (-ərz-). The mother of one's spouse.
moth·er·land (mŭ*th*′ər-lănd′) ▸ *n.* **1.** One's native land. **2.** The land of one's ancestors.
moth·er-of-pearl (mŭ*th*′ər-əv-pûrl′) ▸ *n.* The pearly internal layer of certain mollusk shells, used to make decorative objects.
mother superior ▸ *n., pl.* **mothers superior** or **mother superiors.** A woman in charge of a religious community of women.
moth·proof (môth′pro͞of′, mŏth′-) ▸ *adj.* Resistant to damage by moth larvae. **—moth′proof′** *v.*
mo·tif (mō-tēf′) ▸ *n.* A recurrent thematic element in a musical, artistic, or literary work.
mo·tile (mōt′l, mō′tīl′) ▸ *adj. Biol.* Moving or having the power to move spontaneously. **—mo·til′i·ty** (mō-tĭl′ĭ-tē) *n.*
mo·tion (mō′shən) ▸ *n.* **1.** The act or process of changing position or place. **2.** A meaningful or expressive change in the position of a part of the body; gesture. **3.** A formal proposal put to the vote under parliamentary procedures. ▸ *v.* **1.** To signal to or direct by making a gesture. **2.** To gesture meaningfully: *motioned to her to enter.* **—mo′tion·less** *adj.* **—mo′tion·less·ly** *adv.* **—mo′tion·less·ness** *n.*
motion picture ▸ *n.* **1.** A movie. **2. motion pictures** The movie industry. **—mo′tion-pic′ture** *adj.*
motion sickness ▸ *n.* Nausea and dizziness caused by motion, as in travel by aircraft, car, or ship.
mo·ti·vate (mō′tə-vāt′) ▸ *v.* **-vat·ed, -vat·ing.** To provide with an incentive; move to action; impel. **—mo′ti·va′tion** *n.* **—mo′ti·va′tion·al** *adj.* **—mo′ti·va′tor** *n.*
mo·tive (mō′tĭv) ▸ *n.* An emotion, desire, need, or similar impulse that causes a person to act in a particular way. ▸ *adj.* Causing or able to cause motion.
mot·ley (mŏt′lē) ▸ *adj.* **1.** Having elements of great variety; heterogenous; varied. **2.** Multicolored.
mo·to·cross (mō′tō-krôs′, -krŏs′) ▸ *n.* A cross-country motorcycle race.
mo·tor (mō′tər) ▸ *n.* **1.** Something that produces or imparts motion. **2.** A device that converts any other energy into mechanical energy, esp. an internal-combustion engine or a device that converts electric current into mechanical power. ▸ *adj.* **1.** Causing or producing motion. **2.** Driven by or having a motor. **3.** Of or for motors or motor vehicles: *motor oil.* **4.** *Physiol.* Relating to movements of the muscles. ▸ *v.* To travel in a motor vehicle. **—mo′tor·i·za′tion** *n.* **—mo′tor·ize′** *v.*
mo·tor·bike (mō′tər-bīk′) ▸ *n.* **1.** A lightweight motorcycle. **2.** A bicycle powered by an attached motor.
mo·tor·boat (mō′tər-bōt′) ▸ *n.* A boat propelled by an internal-combustion engine.
mo·tor·cade (mō′tər-kād′) ▸ *n.* A procession of motor vehicles.
mo·tor·car (mō′tər-kär′) ▸ *n.* See **automobile.**
motor court ▸ *n.* See **motel.**
mo·tor·cy·cle (mō′tər-sī′kəl) ▸ *n.* A two-wheeled vehicle resembling a heavy bicycle, propelled by a gasoline engine. **—mo′tor·cy′cle** *v.* **—mo′tor·cy′clist** *n.*
motor home ▸ *n.* A large motor vehicle having self-contained living quarters, used for recreational travel.
motor inn ▸ *n.* An urban motel usu. having several stories and a guest parking lot.
mo·tor·ist (mō′tər-ĭst) ▸ *n.* One who drives or rides in an automobile.
motor lodge ▸ *n.* See **motel.**
mo·tor·man (mō′tər-mən) ▸ *n.* One who drives a streetcar or subway train.
motor scooter ▸ *n.* A small two-wheeled vehicle with a low-powered gasoline engine.
motor vehicle ▸ *n.* A self-propelled wheeled vehicle that does not run on rails.
mot·tle (mŏt′l) ▸ *v.* **-tled, -tling.** To mark with spots or blotches of different shades or colors.
mot·to (mŏt′ō) ▸ *n., pl.* **-toes** or **-tos.** A brief statement used to express a principle, goal, or ideal.
moue (mo͞o) ▸ *n.* A grimace; pout.
mould[1] (mōld) ▸ *n. & v. Chiefly Brit.* Var. of **mold**[1].
mould[2] (mōld) ▸ *n. & v. Chiefly Brit.* Var. of **mold**[2].
mound (mound) ▸ *n.* **1.** A raised mass, as of earth, sand, or rocks. **2.** A natural elevation, such as a small hill. **3.** A pile; heap. **4.** *Baseball* The slightly elevated pitcher's area in the center of the diamond. **—mound** *v.*
Mound Builder ▸ *n.* A Native American culture flourishing from the 5th cent. B.C. to the 16th cent. A.D. esp. in the Ohio and Mississippi valleys, known for its large burial and effigy mounds.
mount[1] (mount) ▸ *v.* **1.** To climb or ascend. **2.** To get up on: *mount a horse.* **3.** To increase in amount, extent, or intensity. **4a.** To fix securely to a support: *mount an engine in a car.* **b.** To place or fix in an appropriate setting for display, study, or use. **5.** To prepare and set in motion. **6.** To set (guns) in position. ▸ *n.* **1.** A horse or other ani-

THESAURUS

mother *n.* A female parent ▸ materfamilias, matriarch. *Informal:* ma, mama, mammy, mom, momma, mommy, mum, mummy. *Slang:* old lady. —*See also* ANCESTOR (1), ORIGIN.
motif *n.* An element or component in a decorative composition ▸ design, device, figure, motive.
motion *n.* The act or process of moving ▸ action, activity, move, movement, moving, stir, stirring. [*Compare* CHANGE.] —*See also* GESTURE, PROPOSAL (1).
motion *v.* —*See* GESTURE.
motionless *adj.* Not moving ▸ at rest, fixed, frozen, halted, immobile, paralyzed, resting, rigid, static, stationary, still, stock-still, transfixed, unmoving. *Idioms:* at a dead calm, at a quiet stop, at a standstill, at a deadlock. [*Compare* DORMANT, FIXED, INACTIVE.]
motivate *v.* —*See* ENCOURAGE (1), PROVOKE.
motivation *n.* Something that encourages ▸ encouragement, inspiration, stimulation. —*See also* CAUSE (2), STIMULUS.
motive *n.* An element or component in a decorative composition ▸ design, device, figure, motif. —*See also* CAUSE (2).
motivic *adj.* Of, constituting, or relating to a theme or themes ▸ thematic, topical.
motley *adj.* —*See* MULTICOLORED, VARIOUS.
motor *v.* —*See* DRIVE (1).
motorist *n.* A person who operates a motor vehicle ▸ chauffeur, driver, operator.
mottle *v.* —*See* SPECKLE.
mottled *adj.* —*See* MULTICOLORED.
motto *n.* —*See* CRY (2), PROVERB.
moue *n.* A contorted facial expression showing pain, contempt, or disgust ▸ face, pout. *Informal:* mug. [*Compare* FROWN, GLARE, SNEER.]
mound *n.* —*See* HEAP (1).
mound *v.* —*See* HEAP (1).
mount *v.* —*See* ASCEND, INCREASE,

mal on which to ride. **2.** An object to which another is affixed for accessibility, display, or use. **—mount′a·ble** *adj.*

mount² (mount) ▸ *n.* A mountain or hill: *Mount Rainier.*

moun·tain (moun′tən) ▸ *n.* A natural elevation of the earth's surface greater in height than a hill.

mountain ash ▸ *n.* Any of various deciduous trees having clusters of small white flowers and bright orange-red berries.

moun·tain·eer (moun′tə-nîr′) ▸ *n.* **1.** An inhabitant of a mountainous area. **2.** One who climbs mountains for sport. ▸ *v.* To climb mountains for sport.

mountain goat ▸ *n.* A hoofed mammal of the NW North American mountains, having short curved black horns and shaggy yellowish-white hair and beard.

mountain laurel ▸ *n.* An evergreen shrub of E North America, having leathery poisonous leaves and pink or white flowers.

mountain lion ▸ *n.* A large wild cat of mountainous regions of the Western Hemisphere, having an unmarked tawny body.

moun·tain·ous (moun′tə-nəs) ▸ *adj.* **1.** Having many mountains. **2.** Massive; huge.

mountain range ▸ *n.* A series of mountain ridges alike in form, direction, and origin.

moun·tain·side (moun′tən-sīd′) ▸ *n.* The sloping side of a mountain.

moun·tain·top (moun′tən-tŏp′) ▸ *n.* The summit of a mountain.

moun·te·bank (moun′tə-băngk′) ▸ *n.* **1.** A peddler of quack medicines. **2.** An impostor or swindler.

Mount·ie also **Mount·y** (moun′tē) ▸ *n., pl.* **-ies.** *Informal* A member of the Royal Canadian Mounted Police.

mount·ing (moun′tĭng) ▸ *n.* A supporting structure or frame: *a mounting for a gem.*

Mount Ver·non (vûr′nən) ▸ An estate of NE VA on the Potomac R.; home of George Washington (1752–99).

mourn (môrn) ▸ *v.* To feel or express grief or sorrow (for). **—mourn′er** *n.*

mourn·ful (môrn′fəl) ▸ *adj.* **1.** Feeling or expressing grief. **2.** Causing or suggesting sadness. **—mourn′ful·ly** *adv.* **—mourn′ful·ness** *n.*

mourn·ing (môr′nĭng) ▸ *n.* **1.** Expression of grief. **2.** Outward signs of grief for the dead, such as wearing black clothes. **3.** The period during which a death is mourned.

mourning dove ▸ *n.* A wild dove of North America, noted for its mournful call.

mouse (mous) ▸ *n., pl.* **mice** (mīs). **1.** Any of numerous small, usu. long-tailed rodents, some living in or near human dwellings. **2.** A hand-held, button-activated input device that controls the movement of an indicator on a computer screen, allowing the user to select operations or manipulate text or graphics. ▸ *v.* (mouz) **moused, mous·ing.** To hunt or catch mice. **—mous′er** (mou′zər, -sər) *n.*

mouse·pad (mous′păd′) ▸ *n. Comp. Sci.* A flat pad that provides a surface on which to use a mouse.

mouse·trap (mous′trăp′) ▸ *n.* A trap for catching mice.

mous·sa·ka (mo͞o-sä′kə, mo͞o′sä-kä′) ▸ *n.* A Greek baked dish of ground meat, sliced eggplant, and cheese.

mousse (mo͞os) ▸ *n.* **1.** A chilled dessert made with whipped cream, gelatin, eggs, and flavoring. **2.** A foam for styling the hair.

mous·tache (mŭs′tăsh′, mə-stăsh′) ▸ *n.* Var. of **mustache.**

mous·y (mou′sē, -zē) ▸ *adj.* **-i·er, -i·est.** **1.** Of a drab, mouselike color. **2.** Timid or shy. **—mous′i·ness** *n.*

mouth (mouth) ▸ *n., pl.* **mouths** (mou*th*z). **1.** The body opening and related organs through which food is taken in, chewed, and swallowed and sounds and speech are articulated. **2.** A natural opening, as the part of a river that empties into a larger body of water or the entrance to a harbor, valley, or cave. **3.** The opening by which a container is filled or emptied. ▸ *v.* (mou*th*) **1.** To declare in a pompous manner; declaim. **2.** To put, take, or move around in the mouth. ***—phrasal verb:*** **mouth off** *Slang* To criticize, brag, or talk back loudly. **—mouth′ful′** *n.*

mouth organ ▸ *n.* See **harmonica.**

mouth·part (mouth′pärt′) ▸ *n.* Any of the parts of the mouth of an insect or other arthropod.

mouth·piece (mouth′pēs′) ▸ *n.* **1.** A part, as of a musical instrument, used in or near the mouth. **2.** A protective device worn over the teeth by athletes. **3.** A spokesperson.

mouth-to-mouth resuscitation (mouth′tə-mouth′) ▸ *n.* A technique of artificial resuscitation in which the rescuer's mouth is placed over the victim's and air is forced into the victim's lungs.

mouth·wash (mouth′wŏsh′, -wôsh′) ▸ *n.* A flavored, usu. antiseptic solution used for cleaning the mouth and freshening the breath.

mouth·wa·ter·ing or **mouth-wa·ter·ing** (mouth′wô′tər-ĭng) ▸ *adj.* Appealing to the sense of taste; appetizing.

mouth·y (mou′*th*ē, -thē) ▸ *adj.* **-i·er, -i·est.** Annoyingly talkative; bombastic. **—mouth′i·ness** *n.*

move (mo͞ov) ▸ *v.* **moved, mov·ing.** **1.** To change in position from one point to another. **2.** To settle in a new place. **3.** To change hands commercially: *Woolens move slowly in the summer.* **4.** To take action; act. **5.** To stir the emotions (of). **6.** To make a formal motion in parliamentary procedure. **7.** To evacuate (the bowels). **8.** To transfer (a piece) in a board game. ▸ *n.* **1.** The act of moving. **2.** A change of residence or place of business. **3a.** The act of transferring a piece in board games. **b.** A player's turn to move a piece. **4.** A calculated action taken to achieve an end. ***—idioms:*** **get a move on** *Informal* To get going. **move in on** To attempt to seize control of. **on the move** Busily moving about or making progress. **—mov′a·bil′i·ty, mov′a·ble·ness** *n.* **—mov′a·ble, move′a·ble** *adj.*

move·ment (mo͞ov′mənt) ▸ *n.* **1.** The act of moving or a change in position. **2.** A change in the location of troops, ships, or aircraft for strategic purposes. **3.** A large-scale organized effort: *the labor movement.* **4.** Activity, esp. in business or commerce. **5.** An evacuation of the bowels. **6.** *Mus.* A self-contained section of an extended composition. **7.** A mechanism, such as the works of a watch, that produces or transmits motion.

mov·er (mo͞o′vər) ▸ *n.* **1.** One that moves. **2.** One that

THESAURUS

RISE (2), RISE (3), STAGE.

mountain *n.* —*See* ABUNDANCE, HEAP (1), HEAP (2).

mountainous *adj.* —*See* ENORMOUS.

mountebank *n.* —*See* FAKE.

mounting *n.* —*See* ASCENT (1).

mourn *v.* —*See* GRIEVE.

mournful *adj.* —*See* SORROWFUL.

mournfulness *n.* —*See* DEPRESSION (2).

mouse *n. Slang* A bruise surrounding the eye ▸ black eye. *Slang:* shiner. [*Compare* BRUISE.] —*See also* COWARD.

mouse *v.* —*See* SNEAK.

mouth *n.* **1.** The opening in the body through which food is ingested ▸ chops, maw. *Slang:* gob, hole, jaws, kisser, pie hole, puss, smacker, trap, yap. **2.** Insolent talk ▸ back talk. *Informal:* lip, sass. [*Compare* IMPUDENCE.] —*See also* HOLE (2), INLET, SPEAKER (2).

mouth *v.* To contort one's face to indicate pain, contempt, or disgust ▸ grimace, mug. *Idioms:* make a face, make faces. [*Compare* FROWN, GLARE, SNEER.] —*See also* RANT.

mouthful *n.* —*See* BIT¹ (1).

mouthpiece *n.* —*See* SPEAKER (2).

mouth-watering *adj.* —*See* DELICIOUS.

movable *adj.* —*See* MOBILE (1).

movables *n.* —*See* EFFECTS.

move *v.* **1.** To stir the emotions of ▸ affect, get (to), impress, influence, strike, touch. *Idioms:* hit (*or* touch) a soft spot, touch a chord, tug at one's heartstrings. [*Compare* DISTURB, ENCOURAGE.] **2.** To go or cause to go from one place to another ▸ maneuver, remove, shift, transfer, travel. [*Compare* GO, JOURNEY.] **3.** To change one's residence or place of business, for example ▸ relocate, remove, transfer. *Idiom:* pull up stakes. [*Compare* EMIGRATE, SETTLE.] **4.** To move or cause to move slightly ▸ budge, shift, stir. —*See also* ADVANCE (2), DISTURB, PERSUADE, PROPOSE, PROVOKE.

move apart *v.* —*See* SCATTER (2).

move *n.* **1.** The act of moving from one place to another ▸ relocation, remotion, removal. *Idiom:* change of address (*or* residence). [*Compare* DEPARTURE.] **2.** An action calculated to achieve an end ▸ maneuver, measure, procedure, step, tactic. —*See also* MOTION, DISPLACEMENT, TRANSITION.

movement *n.* —*See* DISPLACEMENT, DRIVE (1), MOTION, PLOT (1).

transports furnishings as an occupation.

mov·ie (mo͞o′vē) ▸ *n.* **1a.** A sequence of filmed images projected onto a screen in rapid succession to create the illusion of motion and continuity; motion picture. **b.** A cinematic narrative represented in this form; film. **2. movies** The movie industry.

mov·ing (mo͞o′vĭng) ▸ *adj.* **1.** Of or causing motion or transfer. **2.** Arousing deep emotion. **—mov′ing·ly** *adv.*

moving picture ▸ *n.* A movie.

mow¹ (mou) ▸ *n.* A place, usu. a barn, where hay or grain is stored.

mow² (mō) ▸ *v.* **mowed, mowed** or **mown** (mōn), **mow·ing. 1.** To cut down (grass or grain) with a scythe or machine. **2.** To cut (grass or grain) from. ***—phrasal verb:* mow down** To destroy in great numbers, as in battle. **—mow′er** *n.*

mox·ie (mŏk′sē) ▸ *n. Slang* Courage in adversity.

Mo·zam·bique (mō′zəm-bēk′, -zăm-) ▸ A country of SE Africa. **—Mo′zam·bi′can** (-bē′kən) *adj. & n.*

Mo·zart (mōt′särt), **Wolfgang Amadeus** (1756–91) ▸ Austrian composer.

moz·za·rel·la (mŏt′sə-rĕl′ə, mōt′-) ▸ *n.* A mild white Italian cheese, often melted, as on pizza.

MP ▸ *abbr.* **1.** member of Parliament **2.** military police **3.** nounted police

mpg ▸ *abbr.* miles per gallon

mph ▸ *abbr.* miles per hour

Mr. (mĭs′tər) ▸ *n., pl.* **Messrs.** (mĕs′ərz). Used as a courtesy title before the surname or full name of a man.

MRI ▸ *abbr.* magnetic resonance imaging

Mrs. (mĭs′ĭz) ▸ *n., pl.* **Mmes.** (mā-däm′, -dăm′). Used as a courtesy title for a married or widowed woman.

ms ▸ *abbr.* **1.** or **ms.** manuscript **2.** millisecond

MS ▸ *abbr.* **1.** *Lat.* Magister Scientiae (Master of Science) **2.** Mississippi **3.** multiple sclerosis

Ms. also **Ms** (mĭz) ▸ *n., pl.* **Mses.** also **Mss.** (mĭz′ĭz). Used as a courtesy title for a woman or girl.

MSG ▸ *abbr.* monosodium glutamate

Mt ▸ The symbol for the element **meitnerium.**

MT ▸ *abbr.* Montana

Mt. ▸ *abbr.* **1.** mount **2.** mountain

Mts. ▸ *abbr.* mountains

mu (myo͞o, mo͞o) ▸ *n.* The 12th letter of the Greek alphabet.

much (mŭch) ▸ *adj.* **more** (môr), **most** (mōst). Great in quantity, degree, or extent: *not much rain.* ▸ *n.* **1.** A large quantity or amount. **2.** Something great or remarkable: *I've never been much to look at.* ▸ *adv.* **more, most. 1.** To a great degree or extent: *much smarter.* **2.** Just about; almost: *much the same.*

mu·ci·lage (myo͞o′sə-lĭj) ▸ *n.* A sticky substance used as an adhesive. **—mu′ci·lag′i·nous** (-lăj′ə-nəs) *adj.*

muck (mŭk) ▸ *n.* **1.** A moist sticky mixture, esp. of mud and filth. **2.** Moist farmyard dung. **3.** Dark fertile soil that is rich in humus. ▸ *v.* To soil or make dirty with or as if with muck. ***—phrasal verb:* muck up** *Informal* To botch. **—muck′y** *adj.*

muck·rake (mŭk′rāk′) ▸ *v.* **-raked, -rak·ing.** To search for and expose misconduct in public life. **—muck′rak′er** *n.*

mu·co·sa (myo͞o-kō′sə) ▸ *n., pl.* **-sae** (-sē) or **-sas.** See **mucous membrane.**

mu·cous (myo͞o′kəs) ▸ *adj.* Containing or secreting mucus.

mucous membrane ▸ *n.* A membrane lining all body passages that communicate with the air, the glands of which secrete mucus.

mu·cus (myo͞o′kəs) ▸ *n.* The viscous substance secreted as a protective lubricant coating by glands of the mucous membranes.

mud (mŭd) ▸ *n.* **1.** Wet, sticky, soft earth. **2.** Slanderous or defamatory charges. **—mud′di·ly** *adv.* **—mud′di·ness** *n.* **—mud′dy** *adj. & v.*

mud·dle (mŭd′l) ▸ *v.* **-dled, -dling. 1.** To make turbid or muddy. **2.** To mix confusedly; jumble. **3.** To befuddle (the mind), as with alcohol. **4.** To botch; bungle. ***—phrasal verb:* muddle through** To persist successfully in a disorganized, blundering way. ▸ *n.* A mess or jumble. **—mud′dler** *n.*

mud·guard (mŭd′gärd′) ▸ *n.* A shield over or behind a vehicle's wheel.

mud·sling·er (mŭd′slĭng′ər) ▸ *n.* One who makes malicious charges to discredit an opponent. **—mud′sling′ing** *n.*

mues·li (myo͞oz′lē) ▸ *n.* A mixture of rolled oats, nuts, and dried fruit, often used as a breakfast cereal.

mu·ez·zin (myo͞o-ĕz′ĭn, mo͞o-) ▸ *n. Islam* The crier who calls the faithful to prayer five times a day.

muff¹ (mŭf) ▸ *v.* To perform clumsily; bungle. **—muff** *n.*

muff² (mŭf) ▸ *n.* A small, cylindrical, usu. fur cover, open at both ends, used to keep the hands warm.

muf·fin (mŭf′ĭn) ▸ *n.* A small, cup-shaped bread, often sweetened.

muf·fle (mŭf′əl) ▸ *v.* **-fled, -fling. 1.** To wrap up snugly for warmth, protection, or secrecy. **2.** To wrap or pad in order to deaden a sound. **3.** To deaden (a sound). **4.** To suppress; stifle: *muffle political opposition.*

muf·fler (mŭf′lər) ▸ *n.* **1.** A heavy scarf worn around the neck for warmth. **2.** A device that absorbs noise, esp. one used with an internal-combustion engine.

muf·ti (mŭf′tē) ▸ *n.* Civilian dress, esp. when worn by one usu. in uniform.

mug¹ (mŭg) ▸ *n.* A heavy cylindrical drinking cup usu. having a handle.

mug² (mŭg) ▸ *n.* **1.** *Informal* **a.** The human face. **b.** A grimace. **2.** A hoodlum. ▸ *v.* **mugged, mug·ging. 1.** *Informal* To take a photograph of for police files. **2.** To waylay and assault with intent to rob. **3.** To grimace, esp. for humorous effect. **—mug′ger** *n.*

mug·gy (mŭg′ē) ▸ *adj.* **-gi·er, -gi·est.** Warm and extremely humid. **—mug′gi·ness** *n.*

mug shot ▸ *n. Informal* A photograph of a person's face, esp. for police files.

Mu·ham·mad (mo͞o-hăm′ĭd, -hä′mĭd) also **Mo·ham·med** (mō-, mo͞o-) (570?–632) ▸ Arab prophet of Islam.

Mu·ham·mad·an (mo͞o-hăm′ĭ-dən) or **Mo·ham·med·an** (mō-) ▸ *adj.* Of or relating to Muhammad or Islam; Muslim. ▸ *n. Offensive* A Muslim.

Mu·har·ram (mo͞o-hăr′əm) ▸ *n.* The 1st month of the Muslim calendar.

THESAURUS

moves *n.* —*See* ADVANCES.

movie *n.* A motion picture ▸ film, motion picture, picture. *Slang:* flick.

moving *adj.* —*See* AFFECTING, DRAMATIC (2), MOBILE (1).

mow *v.* —*See* CUT (3).

moxie *n.* —*See* COURAGE.

Mrs. Grundy *n.* —*See* PRUDE.

much *n.* —*See* ABUNDANCE.

much *adv.* —*See* CONSIDERABLY.

muchness *n.* —*See* PLENTY.

mucilaginous *adj.* —*See* STICKY (1), VISCOUS.

muck *n.* —*See* FILTH, SLIME.

muck up *v.* —*See* BOTCH, DIRTY.

muckamuck *n.* —*See* DIGNITARY.

muckiness *n.* —*See* DIRTINESS.

mucky *adj.* —*See* SLIMY.

mud *v.* —*See* DIRTY.

mud *n.* —*See* FILTH.

muddle *v.* To proceed or perform in an unsteady, faltering manner ▸ blunder, bumble, bungle, flounder, fudge, fumble, limp, shuffle, stagger, stumble. —*See also* BOTCH, CONFUSE (1), CONFUSE (3), DISORDER, DISRUPT.

muddle through *v.* —*See* MANAGE.

muddle *n.* —*See* DAZE, DISORDER (1), MESS (1).

muddled *adj.* —*See* CONFUSED (2).

muddle-headed *adj.* —*See* CONFUSED (1).

muddy *adj.* —*See* DIRTY, DULL (2), MURKY (1).

muddy *v.* —*See* CONFUSE (3), DIRTY.

mudslinger *n.* —*See* CRITIC (2).

mudslinging *n.* —*See* LIBEL.

muff *v.* —*See* BOTCH.

muff *n.* —*See* BLUNDER.

muffle *v.* To decrease or dull the sound of ▸ damp (down), dampen, deaden, dull, mute, stifle. [*Compare* DECREASE, SILENCE, SOFTEN.] —*See also* REPRESS.

muffler *n.* WRAP.

mug *n. Informal* A contorted facial expression showing pain, contempt, or disgust ▸ face, grimace, moue, pout. [*Compare* FROWN, GLARE, SNEER.] —*See also* FACE (1), THUG.

mug *v.* To contort one's face to indicate pain, contempt, or disgust ▸ grimace, mouth. *Idioms:* make a face, make faces. [*Compare* FROWN, GLARE, SNEER.] —*See also* ROB.

muggy *adj.* —*See* STICKY (2).

mu·ja·hi·deen also **mu·ja·he·deen** or **mu·ja·hi·din** (mo͞o-jä′hĕ-dēn′) ▸ *pl.n.* Muslim guerrilla warriors engaged in a jihad.
muk·luk (mŭk′lŭk′) ▸ *n.* **1.** A soft Eskimo boot made of reindeer skin or sealskin. **2.** A slipper similar to a mukluk.
mu·lat·to (mo͞o-lăt′ō, -lä′tō, myo͞o-) ▸ *n., pl.* **-tos** or **-toes. 1.** A person having one white and one Black parent. **2.** A person of mixed white and Black ancestry.
mul·ber·ry (mŭl′bĕr′ē, -bə-rē) ▸ *n.* **1.** A tree bearing sweet reddish or purplish berrylike fruit. **2.** The fruit itself.
mulch (mŭlch) ▸ *n.* A protective covering, as of leaves or hay, placed around plants to prevent evaporation of moisture, freezing of roots, and growth of weeds. ▸ *v.* To cover with mulch.
mulct (mŭlkt) ▸ *n.* A penalty such as a fine. ▸ *v.* **1.** To penalize by fining. **2.** To defraud or swindle.
mule[1] (myo͞ol) ▸ *n.* **1.** The sterile hybrid offspring of a male donkey and female horse. **2.** *Informal* A stubborn person. **—mul′ish** *adj.* **—mul′ish·ly** *adv.* **—mul′ish·ness** *n.*
mule[2] (myo͞ol) ▸ *n.* An open slipper or shoe that leaves the heel bare.
mule deer ▸ *n.* A long-eared deer of W North America, having a black-tipped tail.
mule·skin·ner (myo͞ol′skĭn′ər) ▸ *n.* *Informal* A driver of mules.
mu·le·teer (myo͞o′lə-tîr′) ▸ *n.* A driver of mules.
mull[1] (mŭl) ▸ *v.* To heat and spice (e.g., wine).
mull[2] (mŭl) ▸ *v.* To ponder or ruminate: *mull over a plan.*
mul·lah also **mul·la** (mŭl′ə, mo͝ol′ə) ▸ *n.* *Islam* A religious teacher or leader, esp. one trained in law.
mul·lein (mŭl′ən) ▸ *n.* Any of various tall plants having closely clustered yellow flowers and downy leaves.
mul·let (mŭl′ĭt) ▸ *n., pl.* **-let** or **-lets**. Any of various saltwater and freshwater edible fishes of tropical and temperate waters.
mul·li·ga·taw·ny (mŭl′ĭ-gə-tô′nē) ▸ *n., pl.* **-nies**. An East Indian soup made with meat or chicken and curry.
mul·lion (mŭl′yən) ▸ *n.* A vertical strip, as of wood or stone, dividing the panes of a window. **—mul′lioned** *adj.*
multi– ▸ *pref.* **1.** Many; much; multiple: *multicolored.* **2a.** More than one: *multiparous.* **b.** More than two: *multilateral.*
mul·ti·cel·lu·lar (mŭl′tē-sĕl′yə-lər, -tī-) ▸ *adj.* Having many cells. **—mul′ti·cel′lu·lar′i·ty** (-lăr′ĭ-tē) *n.*
mul·ti·col·ored (mŭl′tĭ-kŭl′ərd) also **mul·ti·col·or** (-kŭl′ər) ▸ *adj.* Having many colors.
mul·ti·cul·tur·al (mŭl′tē-kŭl′chər-əl, -tī-) ▸ *adj.* Of or including several cultures or ethnic groups.
mul·ti·di·men·sion·al (mŭl′tĭ-dĭ-mĕn′shə-nəl) ▸ *adj.* Having several dimensions. **—mul′ti·di·men′sion·al′i·ty** (-shə-năl′ĭ-tē) *n.*
mul·ti·di·rec·tion·al (mŭl′tē-dĭ-rĕk′shə-nəl, -dī-, -tī-) ▸ *adj.* Reaching out or operating in several directions.
mul·ti·dis·ci·pli·nar·y (mŭl′tē-dĭs′ə-plə-nĕr′ē, -tī-) ▸ *adj.* Involving or making use of several academic disciplines at once.
mul·ti·eth·nic (mŭl′tē-ĕth′nĭk, -tī-) ▸ *adj.* Of or including a variety of ethnic groups.
mul·ti·fac·et·ed (mŭl′tē-făs′ĭ-tĭd, -tī-) ▸ *adj.* Having many facets or aspects.
mul·ti·fam·i·ly (mŭl′tē-făm′ə-lē, -tī-) ▸ *adj.* Of or intended for use by several families.
mul·ti·far·i·ous (mŭl′tə-fâr′ē-əs) ▸ *adj.* Having great variety. **—mul′ti·far′i·ous·ly** *adv.* **—mul′ti·far′i·ous·ness** *n.*
mul·ti·form (mŭl′tə-fôrm′) ▸ *adj.* Occurring in or having many forms or shapes. **—mul′ti·for′mi·ty** *n.*
mul·ti·lane (mŭl′tē-lān′, -tī-) ▸ *adj.* Having several lanes: *a multilane highway.*
mul·ti·lat·er·al (mŭl′tĭ-lăt′ər-əl) ▸ *adj.* **1.** Having many sides. **2.** Involving more than two nations or parties. **—mul′ti·lat′er·al·ly** *adv.*
mul·ti·lay·ered (mŭl′tē-lā′ərd, -tī-) ▸ *adj.* Consisting of several layers or levels.
mul·ti·lev·el (mŭl′tə-lĕv′əl) ▸ *adj.* Having several levels: *a multilevel parking garage.*
mul·ti·lin·gual (mŭl′tē-lĭng′gwəl, -tī-) ▸ *adj.* **1.** Of, including, or expressed in several languages. **2.** Fluent in several languages.
mul·ti·me·di·a (mŭl′tē-mē′dē-ə, -tī-) ▸ *pl.n.* *(takes sing. v.)* **1.** The combined use of several media, such as slides and music. **2.** The use of several mass media, such as television and print, as for advertising. ▸ *adj.* **1.** Relating to the combined use of media. **2.** *Comp. Sci.* Relating to an application that can integrate text, graphics, video, and sound.
mul·ti·mil·lion·aire (mŭl′tē-mĭl′yə-nâr′, -tī-) ▸ *n.* A person whose wealth amounts to two or more million dollars, pounds, or the equivalent in other currency.
mul·ti·na·tion·al (mŭl′tē-năsh′ə-nəl, -năsh′nəl, -tī-) ▸ *adj.* Of or involving more than two countries.
mul·tip·a·rous (mŭl-tĭp′ər-əs) ▸ *adj.* **1.** Having given birth two or more times. **2.** Giving birth to more than one offspring at a time.
mul·ti·ple (mŭl′tə-pəl) ▸ *adj.* Of, having, or consisting of more than one individual, element, or part. ▸ *n.* *Math.* A number into which another number may be divided with no remainder.
mul·ti·ple-choice (mŭl′tə-pəl-chois′) ▸ *adj.* Offering several answers from which the correct one is to be chosen.
multiple fruit ▸ *n.* A fruit, such as a fig or pineapple, derived from several flowers that are combined into one structure.
multiple sclerosis ▸ *n.* A degenerative disease of the central nervous system causing muscular weakness, loss of coordination, and speech and visual disturbances.
multiple star ▸ *n.* Three or more stars that appear as one to the naked eye.
mul·ti·plex (mŭl′tə-plĕks′) ▸ *adj.* **1.** Multiple; manifold. **2.** Of or being a system of simultaneous communication of two or more messages on the same wire or radio channel. ▸ *n.* A movie theater or dwelling with multiple separate units. **—mul′ti·plex′** *v.*
mul·ti·pli·cand (mŭl′tə-plĭ-kănd′) ▸ *n.* A number to be multiplied by another.
mul·ti·pli·ca·tion (mŭl′tə-plĭ-kā′shən) ▸ *n.* **1.** The act of multiplying or the condition of being multiplied. **2.** The reproduction of plants and animals. **3.** *Math.* The operation of adding a number to itself a certain number of times. **—mul′ti·pli′ca·tive** *adj.*
mul·ti·plic·i·ty (mŭl′tə-plĭs′ĭ-tē) ▸ *n., pl.* **-ties**. **1.** The state of being various or multiple. **2.** A large number.
mul·ti·pli·er (mŭl′tə-plī′ər) ▸ *n.* The number by which another number is multiplied.
mul·ti·ply (mŭl′tə-plī′) ▸ *v.* **-plied, -ply·ing**. **1.** To increase in amount, number, or degree. **2.** *Math.* To perform multiplication (on). **3.** To breed; reproduce.
mul·ti·pur·pose (mŭl′tē-pûr′pəs, -tī-) ▸ *adj.* Designed or used for several purposes.
mul·ti·ra·cial (mŭl′tē-rā′shəl, -tī-) ▸ *adj.* **1.** Made up of, involving, or acting on behalf of various races: *a multiracial society.* **2.** Having ancestors of several or various races.

THESAURUS

mulct *n.* A sum of money levied as punishment for an offense ▸ amercement, fine, penalty. [*Compare* PUNISHMENT.]
mulct *v.* To impose a fine on ▸ amerce, fine, penalize. [*Compare* PUNISH.] —*See also* CHEAT (1).
mule *n.* *Slang* A person who engages in smuggling ▸ bootlegger, contrabandist, runner, smuggler.
mulish *adj.* —*See* STUBBORN (1).
mulishness *n.* —*See* STUBBORNNESS.
mull *v.* —*See* PONDER.
multicolored *adj.* Having many different colors ▸ colorful, many-colored, many-hued, motley, mottled, pied, polychromatic, polychrome, polychromic, polychromous, varicolored, variegated, versicolor, versicolored. ***Idiom:*** of all the colors in the rainbow. [*Compare* BRIGHT, COLORFUL.]
multifaceted *adj.* —*See* VERSATILE.
multifarious *adj.* —*See* VARIOUS.
multifariousness *n.* —*See* VARIETY.
multiform *adj.* —*See* VARIOUS.
multiformity *n.* —*See* VARIETY.
multinational *n.* —*See* COMPANY (1).
multiple or **multiplex** *adj.* —*See* COMPLEX (2).
multiplication *n.* —*See* BUILDUP (2), INCREASE (1), REPRODUCTION.
multiplicity *n.* —*See* HEAP (2), VARIETY.
multiply *v.* —*See* BREED, INCREASE.
multipurpose or **multitalented** *adj.* —*See* VERSATILE.

mul·ti·stage (mŭl′tĭ-stāj′) ▸ *adj.* Functioning by stages: *a multistage rocket.*
mul·ti·sto·ry (mŭl′tĭ-stôr′ē) ▸ *adj.* Having several stories: *a multistory hotel.*
mul·ti·task·ing (mŭl′tē-tăsk′kĭng, -tī-) ▸ *n.* The concurrent operation by one central processing unit of two or more processes.
mul·ti·tude (mŭl′tĭ-to͞od′, -tyo͞od′) ▸ *n.* A very great number. **—mul′ti·tu′di·nous** *adj.* **—mul′ti·tu′di·nous·ly** *adv.*
mul·ti·va·lent (mŭl′tĭ-vā′lənt, mŭl-tĭv′ə-lənt) ▸ *adj.* Polyvalent. **—mul′ti·va′lence** *n.*
mul·ti·vi·ta·min (mŭl′tə-vī′tə-mĭn) ▸ *adj.* Containing many vitamins. ▸ *n.* A preparation containing many vitamins.
mum[1] (mŭm) ▸ *adj.* Not talking.
mum[2] (mŭm) ▸ *n.* A chrysanthemum.
Mum·bai (mŭm′bī′). Formerly **Bom·bay** (bŏm-bā′) ▸ A city of W-central India.
mum·ble (mŭm′bəl) ▸ *v.* **-bled, -bling.** To speak or utter indistinctly by lowering the voice or partially closing the mouth. **—mum′ble** *n.* **—mum′bler** *n.* **—mum′bly** *adj.*
mum·bo jum·bo (mŭm′bō jŭm′bō) ▸ *n.* **1.** Confusing or incomprehensible language or activity. **2.** An obscure ritual or incantation.
mum·mer (mŭm′ər) ▸ *n.* One who acts or plays in a mask or costume. **—mum′mer·y** *n.*
mum·my (mŭm′ē) ▸ *n., pl.* **-mies.** A body embalmed after death, as by the ancient Egyptians. **—mum′mi·fi·ca′tion** *n.* **—mum′mi·fy** *v.*
mumps (mŭmps) ▸ *pl.n. (takes sing. or pl. v.)* A contagious viral disease marked by painful swelling esp. of the salivary glands and sometimes of the ovaries or testes.
munch (mŭnch) ▸ *v.* To chew (food) noisily or with pleasure.
mun·dane (mŭn-dān′, mŭn′dān′) ▸ *adj.* **1.** Of this world; worldly. **2.** Of or concerned with the ordinary. **—mun·dane′ly** *adv.*
mung bean (mŭng) ▸ *n.* An Asian plant cultivated for its edible seeds and pods and the chief source of bean sprouts.
Mu·nich (myo͞o′nĭk) ▸ A city of SE Germany.
mu·nic·i·pal (myo͞o-nĭs′ə-pəl) ▸ *adj.* **1.** Of or typical of a municipality. **2.** Having local self-government. **—mu·nic′i·pal·ly** *adv.*
municipal bond ▸ *n.* An often tax-exempt bond, such as one that is issued by a city or county, for financing public projects.
mu·nic·i·pal·i·ty (myo͞o-nĭs′ə-păl′ĭ-tē) ▸ *n., pl.* **-ties.** A political unit, such as a city or town, that is incorporated for local self-government.
mu·nif·i·cent (myo͞o-nĭf′ĭ-sənt) ▸ *adj.* Extremely liberal in giving; very generous. **—mu·nif′i·cence** *n.* **—mu·nif′i·cent·ly** *adv.*
mu·ni·tions (myo͞o-nĭsh′ənz) ▸ *pl.n.* War materiel.
mu·on (myo͞o′ŏn′) ▸ *n.* An elementary particle in the lepton family having a mass 209 times that of the electron.
mu·ral (myo͝or′əl) ▸ *n.* A painting or photograph applied directly to a wall or ceiling. **—mu′ral·ist** *n.*
mur·der (mûr′dər) ▸ *n.* The unlawful killing of one human by another, esp. with premeditated malice. ▸ *v.* **1.** To kill (a human) unlawfully. **2.** To mar or spoil by ineptness: *murder the English language.* **3.** *Slang* To defeat decisively. **—mur′der·er** *n.* **—mur′der·ess** *n.*
mur·der·ous (mûr′dər-əs) ▸ *adj.* **1.** Capable of, guilty of, or intending murder. **2.** Characteristic of murder; brutal. **3.** *Informal* Very difficult or dangerous: *a murderous exam.* **—mur′der·ous·ly** *adv.* **—mur′der·ous·ness** *n.*
mu·rex (myo͝or′ĕks) ▸ *n., pl.* **mu·ri·ces** (myo͝or′ĭ-sēz′) or **mu·rex·es.** Any of various tropical marine gastropods having rough spiny shells.
murk (mûrk) ▸ *n.* Partial or total darkness; gloom. **—murk′i·ly** *adv.* **—murk′i·ness** *n.* **—murk′y** *adj.*
mur·mur (mûr′mər) ▸ *n.* **1.** A low, indistinct, continuous sound. **2.** A grumbled complaint. **3.** *Medic.* An abnormal sound, usu. in the heart. **—mur′mur** *v.*
mus·cat (mŭs′kăt′, -kət) ▸ *n.* A sweet white grape used for making wine or raisins.
mus·ca·tel (mŭs′kə-tĕl′) ▸ *n.* A rich sweet wine made from muscat grapes.
mus·cle (mŭs′əl) ▸ *n.* **1.** A tissue composed of fibers capable of contracting and relaxing to effect bodily movement. **2.** A contractile organ consisting of muscle tissue. **3.** Muscular strength. **4.** *Informal* Power or authority. ▸ *v.* **-cled, -cling.** *Informal* To force one's way.
mus·cle·bound also **mus·cle-bound** (mŭs′əl-bound′) ▸ *adj.* Having stiff, overdeveloped muscles, usu. from excessive exercise.
Mus·co·vite (mŭs′kə-vīt′) ▸ *adj.* A native or resident of Moscow or Muscovy. **—Mus′co·vite′** *adj.*
mus·cu·lar (mŭs′kyə-lər) ▸ *adj.* **1.** Of or consisting of muscle. **2.** Having well-developed muscles. **—mus′cu·lar′i·ty** (-lăr′ĭ-tē) *n.* **—mus′cu·lar·ly** *adv.*
muscular dystrophy ▸ *n.* A chronic noncontagious genetic disease in which gradual irreversible muscle deterioration results in complete incapacitation.
mus·cu·la·ture (mŭs′kyə-lə-cho͝or′) ▸ *n.* The system of muscles in a body or a body part.
muse (myo͞oz) ▸ *v.* **mused, mus·ing.** To ponder, consider, or deliberate at length. **—mus′er** *n.*
Muse ▸ *n.* **1.** *Gk. Myth.* Any of the nine daughters of Zeus, each of whom presided over a different art or science. **2. muse** A source of inspiration, esp. of a poet.

THESAURUS

multitude *n.* —*See* COMMONALTY, CROWD.
multitudinous *adj.* —*See* MANY.
mum *adj.* —*See* SPEECHLESS.
mumble *v.* —*See* MUTTER.
mumble *n.* —*See* MURMUR.
mumbo jumbo *n.* —*See* GIBBERISH.
mummify *v.* —*See* DRY (1).
mummy *n.* —*See* BODY (2).
munch *v.* —*See* CHEW.
mundane *adj.* —*See* EARTHLY, ORDINARY.
municipal *adj.* —*See* CITY.
municipality *n.* —*See* CITY.
munificence *n.* —*See* GENEROSITY.
munificent *adj.* —*See* GENEROUS (1).
murder *n.* The crime of murdering someone ▸ assassination, blood, homicide, killing, liquidation, manslaughter, slaying. *Slang:* hit, rubout, wipeout.
murder *v.* To take the life of a person or persons unlawfully ▸ assassinate, destroy, finish (off), kill, liquidate, slay. *Informal:* put away. *Slang:* bump off, do in, ice, snuff, knock off, off, pop off, rub out, snuff out, take out, waste, wipe out, zap. ***Idiom:*** do away with. [*Compare* MASSACRE.] —*See also* OVERWHELM (1).
murderer *n.* One who murders another ▸ assassin, butcher, cutthroat, exterminator, homicide, killer, liquidator, manslayer, massacrer, murderess, slaughterer, slayer, triggerman. *Slang:* axman, hatchet man, hired gun, hit man.
murderous *adj.* Marked by or giving rise to murder or bloodshed ▸ bloodthirsty, bloody, bloody-minded, cutthroat, death-dealing, homicidal, gory, killing, man-killing, sanguinary, sanguineous, slaughterous. [*Compare* DEADLY, FIERCE.]
murk or **murkiness** *n.* —*See* DARK.
murky *adj.* **1.** Darkened or clouded with sediment ▸ clouded, cloudy, muddy, roiled, roily, sedimentary, turbid, unsettled. **2.** Heavy, dark, or dense, especially with impurities ▸ hazy, smoggy, turbid. [*Compare* DIRTY.] —*See also* DARK (1), DULL (2), UNCLEAR.
murmur *n.* A low, indistinct, and often continuous sound ▸ mumble, rustle, sigh, sough, susurration, susurrus, whisper. [*Compare* HUM.] —*See also* BURBLE, COMPLAINT.
murmur *v.* To make a low, continuous, and indistinct sound ▸ rustle, sigh, sough, whisper. [*Compare* HUM.] —*See also* BURBLE, COMPLAIN, MUTTER.
murmurer *n.* —*See* GROUCH.
muscle *n.* —*See* AUTHORITY, BRAWN, INFLUENCE, STRENGTH.
muscle *v.* *Informal* To force one's way into a place or situation ▸ bulldoze, elbow, push, shoulder, shove. [*Compare* PUSH.]
muscular *adj.* Characterized by marked muscular development ▸ athletic, beefy, brawny, burly, husky, rugged, robust, sinewy, strapping, studly, sturdy. *Slang:* buff, built. [*Compare* HEALTHY, RUGGED, STRONG.]
muscularity *n.* —*See* BRAWN.
muse[1] *v.* —*See* DREAM, PONDER.
muse *n.* —*See* TRANCE.
muse[2] *n.* —*See* POET.

mu·se·um (myoo-zē′əm) ▸ *n.* A place devoted to the acquisition, study, and exhibition of objects of scientific, historical, or artistic value.

mush[1] (mŭsh) ▸ *n.* **1.** Cornmeal boiled in water or milk. **2.** Something thick, soft, and pulpy. **3.** *Informal* Mawkish sentimentality.

mush[2] (mŭsh) ▸ *v.* To drive (a team of dogs) over snow.

mush·room (mŭsh′ro͞om′, -ro͝om′) ▸ *n.* Any of various fleshy fungi having an umbrella-shaped cap borne on a stalk. ▸ *v.* To grow or spread rapidly.

mush·y (mŭsh′ē, mo͝osh′ē) ▸ *adj.* **-i·er, -i·est.** **1.** Thick, soft, and pulpy. **2.** *Informal* Marked by maudlin sentimentality. **—mush′i·ness** *n.*

mu·sic (myo͞o′zĭk) ▸ *n.* **1.** The art of arranging sounds in time to produce a composition that elicits an aesthetic response in a listener. **2.** Vocal or instrumental sounds having some degree of melody, harmony, or rhythm. **3.** A musical composition. **4.** Aesthetically pleasing or harmonious sound or combination of sounds.

mu·si·cal (myo͞o′zĭ-kəl) ▸ *adj.* **1.** Of or producing music. **2.** Melodious. **3.** Set to or accompanied by music. **4.** Devoted to or skilled in music. ▸ *n.* **1.** A play or movie having musical numbers. **2.** A musical comedy. **—mu′si·cal·ly** *adv.*

musical comedy ▸ *n.* A comedic play in which dialogue is interspersed with songs and dances.

mu·si·cale (myo͞o′zĭ-kăl′) ▸ *n.* A program of music performed at a social gathering.

music box ▸ *n.* A box containing a mechanical device that produces music.

mu·si·cian (myo͞o-zĭsh′ən) ▸ *n.* One who composes, conducts, or performs music. **—mu·si′cian·ship′** *n.*

mu·si·col·o·gy (myo͞o′zĭ-kŏl′ə-jē) ▸ *n.* The historical and scientific study of music. **—mu′si·col′o·gist** *n.*

musk (mŭsk) ▸ *n.* An odorous substance secreted by an Asian deer or produced synthetically, used in perfumes. **—musk′i·ness** *n.* **—musk′y** *adj.*

mus·keg (mŭs′kĕg′) ▸ *n.* A peaty bog of N North America.

mus·kel·lunge (mŭs′kə-lŭnj′) ▸ *n., pl.* **-lunge** or **-lung·es.** A large pike of the N US and S Canada.

mus·ket (mŭs′kĭt) ▸ *n.* A smoothbore shoulder gun used from the late 16th through the 18th cent. **—mus′ket·eer** *n.*

mus·ket·ry (mŭs′kĭ-trē) ▸ *n.* **1.** Muskets collectively. **2.** Musketeers collectively.

musk·mel·on (mŭsk′mĕl′ən) ▸ *n.* Any of several edible melons, such as the cantaloupe, having a rough rind and juicy flesh.

Mus·ko·ge·an (mŭs-kō′gē-ən) ▸ *n.* A family of Native American languages of the SE US that includes Choctaw, Chickasaw, and Creek.

Mus·ko·gee (mŭs-kō′gē) ▸ *n.* See **Creek.**

musk·ox or **musk ox** (mŭsk′ŏks′) ▸ *n.* A large ox of N Canada and Greenland, having broad, flat, downward-curving horns and a shaggy coat.

musk·rat (mŭs′krăt′) ▸ *n., pl.* **-rat** or **-rats.** A large aquatic rodent of North America.

Mus·lim (mŭz′ləm, mo͝oz′-, mŭs′-, mo͝os′-) or **Mos·lem** (mŏz′ləm, mŏs′-) ▸ *n.* A believer or adherent of Islam. **—Mus′lim** *adj.*

mus·lin (mŭz′lĭn) ▸ *n.* Any of various sturdy cotton fabrics of plain weave, used esp. for sheets.

muss (mŭs) ▸ *v.* To make messy or untidy; rumple: *The wind has mussed up my hair.* ▸ *n.* A state of disorder; a mess. **—muss′i·ly** *adv.* **—muss′i·ness** *n.* **—muss′y** *adj.*

mus·sel (mŭs′əl) ▸ *n.* Any of various narrow-shelled bivalve mollusks, esp. an edible marine species.

Mus·so·li·ni (mo͞o′sə-lē′nē), **Benito.** "Il Duce" (1883–1945) ▸ Italian Fascist dictator and prime minister (1922–43).

must[1] (mŭst) ▸ *aux.v.* Used to indicate: **a.** Necessity or obligation: *Citizens must register in order to vote.* **b.** Insistence: *You must not go there alone.* **c.** Inevitability or certainty: *We all must die.* **d.** Probability: *It must be almost midnight.* ▸ *n.* An absolute requirement.

must[2] (mŭst) ▸ *n.* Staleness.

must[3] (mŭst) ▸ *n.* Unfermented or fermenting fruit juice, usu. grape.

mus·tache also **mous·tache** (mŭs′tăsh′, mə-stăsh′) ▸ *n.* The hair growing on the human upper lip.

mus·ta·chio (mə-stăsh′ō, -stăsh′ē-ō′) ▸ *n., pl.* **-chios.** A mustache, esp. a luxuriant one.

mus·tang (mŭs′tăng′) ▸ *n.* A small, hardy wild horse of the W North American plains.

mus·tard (mŭs′tərd) ▸ *n.* **1.** Any of various plants having yellow flowers and often pungent seeds. **2.** A condiment made from mustard seeds. **—mus′tard·y** *adj.*

mustard gas ▸ *n.* An oily volatile liquid used in warfare as a blistering agent.

mus·ter (mŭs′tər) ▸ *v.* **1.** To summon or assemble (troops). **2.** To gather or summon up: *mustering up her strength for the ordeal.* ***—phrasal verbs:*** **muster in** To enlist (someone) in military service. **muster out** To discharge (someone) from military service. ▸ *n.* A gathering, esp. of troops, for service, inspection, or roll call.

must·n't (mŭs′ənt) ▸ Must not.

must·y (mŭs′tē) ▸ *adj.* **-i·er, -i·est.** Stale or moldy in odor or taste. **—must′i·ness** *n.*

mu·ta·ble (myo͞o′tə-bəl) ▸ *adj.* **1.** Subject to change. **2.** Fickle. **—mu′ta·bil′i·ty, mu′ta·ble·ness** *n.* **—mu′ta·bly** *adv.*

mu·ta·gen (myo͞o′tə-jən, -jĕn′) ▸ *n.* An agent, such as ultraviolet light or a radioactive element, that can induce mutation in an organism. **—mu′ta·gen′ic** *adj.*

mu·tant (myo͞ot′nt) ▸ *n.* An organism or a new genetic character differing from the parental strain as a result of mutation. **—mu′tant** *adj.*

mu·tate (myo͞o′tāt, myo͞o-tāt′) ▸ *v.* **-tat·ed, -tat·ing.** To undergo or cause to undergo mutation. **—mu′ta′tive** (-tā′tĭv, -tə-tĭv) *adj.*

mu·ta·tion (myo͞o-tā′shən) ▸ *n.* **1.** A change, as in nature, form, or quality. **2.** Any heritable alteration of an organism.

mute (myo͞ot) ▸ *adj.* **mut·er, mut·est.** **1.** Incapable of producing speech or vocal sound. **2.** Unable to speak. **3.** Expressed without speech; unspoken. ▸ *n.* **1.** *Often Offensive* One who is incapable of speech. **2.** *Mus.* A device used to muffle or soften the tone of an instrument. ▸ *v.* **mut·ed, mut·ing.** To soften the sound, color, or shade of. **—mute′ly** *adv.* **—mute′ness** *n.*

mu·ti·late (myo͞ot′l-āt′) ▸ *v.* **-lat·ed, -lat·ing.** **1.** To deprive of a limb or an essential part. **2.** To disfigure by damaging irreparably. **—mu′ti·la′tion** *n.* **—mu′ti·la′tive** *adj.* **—mu′ti·la′tor** *n.*

mu·ti·ny (myo͞ot′n-ē) ▸ *n., pl.* **-nies.** Open rebellion against constituted authority, esp. by military personnel against superior officers. **—mu′ti·neer′** *n.* **—mu′ti·nous** *adj.* **—mu′ti·nous·ly** *adv.* **—mu′ti·ny** *v.*

mutt (mŭt) ▸ *n.* *Informal* A mongrel dog.

THESAURUS

mush *v.* —*See* CRUSH (1).
mush or **mushiness** *n.* —*See* SENTIMENTALITY.
mushroom *v.* To increase or expand suddenly, rapidly, or without control ▸ balloon, explode, snowball. [*Compare* INCREASE.]
mushy *adj.* —*See* SENTIMENTAL, SOFT (1).
musical *adj.* —*See* HARMONIOUS (2), MELODIOUS.
musician *n.* —*See* PLAYER (2).
muskeg *n.* —*See* SWAMP.
muss *v.* —*See* TOUSLE.
muss *n.* —*See* DISORDER (1).
mussy *adj.* —*See* MESSY (1).
must *v.* To be required to do ▸ be compelled, be obliged, need, ought, should. *Idioms:* have got to, have to.
must *n.* —*See* CONDITION (2), DUTY (1).
muster *v.* —*See* ASSEMBLE, MOBILIZE.
muster in *v.* —*See* JOIN (1).
muster out *v.* —*See* DISCHARGE.
muster *n.* —*See* ASSEMBLY.
musty *adj.* —*See* MOLDY, TRITE.
mutable *adj.* —*See* CHANGEABLE (1).
mutant *n.* MONSTER.
mutate *v.* —*See* CHANGE (1), CHANGE (2), CONVERT.
mutation *n.* —*See* CHANGE (1), CONVERSION (1).
mute *adj.* Lacking the power or faculty of speech ▸ aphonic, dumb, inarticulate, silent, speechless, tongueless, tongue-tied, voiceless, wordless. —*See also* SPEECHLESS.
mute *v.* —*See* MODERATE (1), MUFFLE.
muteness *n.* —*See* SILENCE (2).
mutilate *v.* —*See* BATTER, CRIPPLE, DEFORM.
mutineer *n.* —*See* REBEL (1).
mutinous *adj.* —*See* REBELLIOUS.
mutiny *n.* —*See* REBELLION.
mutiny *v.* To vehemently defy and

mut·ter (mŭt′ər) ▸ *v.* **1.** To speak or utter indistinctly in low tones. **2.** To complain or grumble. ▸ *n.* A low, indistinct utterance. **—mut′ter·er** *n.*
mut·ton (mŭt′n) ▸ *n.* The flesh of a fully grown sheep.
mut·ton·chops (mŭt′n-chŏps′) ▸ *pl.n.* Side whiskers narrow at the temple and broad along the lower jawline.
mu·tu·al (myo͞o′cho͞o-əl) ▸ *adj.* **1.** Having the same relationship each to the other: *mutual predators.* **2.** Given and received in equal amount: *mutual respect.* **3.** Possessed in common: *mutual interests.* **—mu′tu·al′i·ty** (-ăl′ĭ-tē) *n.* **—mu′tu·al·ly** *adv.*
mutual fund ▸ *n.* An investment company that by the sale of its shares acquires funds to invest in diversified securities.
muu·muu (mo͞o′mo͞o′) ▸ *n.* A long loose dress.
Mu·zak (myo͞o′zăk′) ▸ A trademark for recorded background music transmitted by wire on a subscription basis.
muz·zle (mŭz′əl) ▸ *n.* **1.** The usu. projecting nose and jaws of certain animals; snout. **2.** A device fitted over an animal's snout to prevent biting or eating. **3.** The front end of the barrel of a firearm. ▸ *v.* **-zled, -zling. 1.** To put a muzzle on (an animal). **2.** To restrain from expressing opinions.
muz·zle·load·er (mŭz′əl-lō′dər) ▸ *n.* A firearm loaded at the muzzle. **—muz′zle·load′ing** *adj.*
my (mī) ▸ *adj.* The possessive form of **I**[1]. Used as a modifier before a noun: *my boots; my brother.* ▸ *interj.* Used as an exclamation of surprise, pleasure, or dismay: *Oh, my! What a day!*
my·al·gi·a (mī-ăl′jē-ə, -jə) ▸ *n.* Muscular pain or tenderness, esp. when diffuse and nonspecific. **—my·al′gic** (-jĭk) *adj.*
Myan·mar (myän-mär′). Formerly **Bur·ma** (bûr′mə) ▸ A country of SE Asia on the Bay of Bengal and the Andaman Sea.
my·as·the·ni·a grav·is (mī′əs-thē′nē-ə grăv′ĭs) ▸ *n.* A disease marked by progressive muscular weakness and fatigue caused by impaired transmission of nerve impulses.
my·ce·li·um (mī-sē′lē-əm) ▸ *n., pl.* **-li·a** (-lē-ə). The vegetative part of a fungus, consisting of a mass of branching, threadlike filaments that forms its main growing structure. **—my·ce′li·al** *adj.*
–mycin ▸ *suff.* A substance derived from a bacterium in the order Actinomycetales: *streptomycin.*
myco– or **myc–** ▸ *pref.* Fungus: *mycology.*
my·col·o·gy (mī-kŏl′ə-jē) ▸ *n.* The branch of botany that deals with fungi. **—my′co·log′i·cal** (-kə-lŏj′ĭ-kəl) *adj.*
my·co·tox·in (mī′kō-tŏk′sĭn) ▸ *n.* A toxin produced by a fungus.
my·e·lin (mī′ə-lĭn) also **my·e·line** (-lĭn, -lēn′) ▸ *n.* A white fatty material that encloses certain axons and nerve fibers.
my·e·li·tis (mī′ə-lī′tĭs) ▸ *n.* Inflammation of the spinal column or bone marrow.
myelo– or **myel–** ▸ *pref.* **1.** Spinal cord: *myelitis.* **2.** Bone marrow: *myeloma.*
my·e·lo·ma (mī′ə-lō′mə) ▸ *n., pl.* **-mas** or **-ma·ta** (-mə-tə). A malignant tumor formed by the cells of the bone marrow.
my·na or **my·nah** (mī′nə) ▸ *n.* An Asian starling, certain species of which can mimic human speech.
my·o·car·di·um (mī′ō-kär′dē-əm) ▸ *n., pl.* **-di·a** (-dē-ə). The muscular tissue of the heart. **—my′o·car′di·al** *adj.*
my·o·pi·a (mī-ō′pē-ə) ▸ *n.* **1.** A visual defect in which distant objects appear blurred because their images are focused in front of the retina rather than on it; nearsightedness. **2.** Shortsightedness in thinking or planning. **—my·op′ic** (-ŏp′ĭk, -ō′pĭk) *adj.* **—my·op′i·cal·ly** *adv.*
my·o·sin (mī′ə-sĭn) ▸ *n.* The commonest protein in muscle cells.
myr·i·ad (mĭr′ē-əd) ▸ *adj.* Constituting a very large, indefinite number. ▸ *n.* A vast number.
myr·i·a·pod (mĭr′ē-ə-pŏd′) ▸ *n.* Any of several arthropods, such as the centipede, having at least nine pairs of legs.
myrrh (mûr) ▸ *n.* An aromatic gum resin obtained from several Asian or African trees and shrubs and used in perfume and incense.
myr·tle (mûr′tl) ▸ *n.* **1.** An Old World shrub having pink or white flowers and blackish berries. **2.** See **periwinkle**[2].
my·self (mī-sĕlf′) ▸ *pron.* **1.** That one identical with me. Used: **a.** Reflexively: *I hurt myself.* **b.** For emphasis: *I myself was certain of the facts.* **2.** My normal or healthy state: *I'm feeling myself again.*
mys·ter·y (mĭs′tə-rē) ▸ *n., pl.* **-ies. 1.** Something that cannot be explained or fully understood. **2.** The quality associated with the unexplained, secret, or unknown. **3.** A work of fiction or drama dealing with a puzzling crime. **4.** A religious truth that is knowable only through divine revelation. **—mys·te′ri·ous** (mĭ-stîr′ē-əs) *adj.* **—mys·te′ri·ous·ly** *adv.* **—mys·te′ri·ous·ness** *n.*
mys·tic (mĭs′tĭk) ▸ *adj.* **1.** Of or relating to religious mysteries or occult rites and practices. **2.** Of or relating to mysticism or mystics. **3.** Mysterious or enigmatic. **4.** Mystical. ▸ *n.* One who practices or believes in mysticism.
mys·ti·cal (mĭs′tĭ-kəl) ▸ *adj.* **1.** Spiritually significant. **2.** Of or relating to mystics, mysticism, or mystic rites or practices. **—mys′ti·cal·ly** *adv.* **—mys′ti·cal·ness** *n.*
mys·ti·cism (mĭs′tĭ-sĭz′əm) ▸ *n.* Consciousness of transcendent reality or of God through deep meditation or contemplation.
mys·ti·fy (mĭs′tə-fī′) ▸ *v.* **-fied, -fy·ing. 1.** To perplex or bewilder. **2.** To make obscure or mysterious. **—mys′ti·fi·ca′tion** *n.* **—mys′ti·fi′er** *n.* **—mys′ti·fy′ing·ly** *adv.*
mys·tique (mĭ-stēk′) ▸ *n.* An aura of mystery or reverence surrounding a particular person, thing, or idea.
myth (mĭth) ▸ *n.* **1.** A traditional story dealing with supernatural beings, ancestors, or heroes that serves as a primordial type in the world view of a people. **2.** A fiction or half-truth. **3.** A fictitious story, person, or thing. **—myth′i·cal, myth′ic** *adj.* **—myth′i·cal·ly** *adv.*
myth·mak·er (mĭth′mā′kər) ▸ *n.* One that creates myths or mythical situations. **—myth′mak·ing** *n.*
my·thol·o·gy (mĭ-thŏl′ə-jē) ▸ *n., pl.* **-gies. 1.** A body of myths about the origin, history, deities, ancestors, and heroes of a people. **2.** The study of myths. **—myth′o·log′i·cal** (mĭth′ə-lŏj′ĭ-kəl) *adj.* **—myth′o·log′i·cal·ly** *adv.* **—my·thol′o·gist** *n.* **—my·thol′o·gize′** *v.*

THESAURUS

break allegiance with ▸ rebel, revolt, rise (up). [*Compare* DEFECT, DEFY.]
mutter *v.* To speak or utter indistinctly, as by lowering the voice or partially closing the mouth ▸ jabber, maunder, mumble, murmur, whisper. ***Idioms:*** speak under one's breath, talk to one's self. *—See also* COMPLAIN.
mutter *n.* *—See* COMPLAINT.
muttonheaded *adj.* *—See* STUPID.
mutual *adj.* Directed and received by each toward the other ▸ exchanged, give-and-take, reciprocal, reciprocative, requited, shared, two-sided. [*Compare* COOPERATIVE.] *—See also* COMMON (2), COMPLEMENTARY.
muumuu *n.* *—See* DRESS (3).
muzzle *v.* *—See* REPRESS.
muzzle *n.* *—See* FACE (1).
myriad *adj.* *—See* MANY.
mysterious *adj.* Difficult to explain or understand ▸ arcane, baffling, cabalistic, confounding, cryptic, enigmatic, esoteric, impenetrable, inexplicable, inscrutable, mystic, mystical, mystifying, occult, perplexing, puzzling, unaccountable. [*Compare* FUNNY, OBSCURE, SECRET, WEIRD.]
mystery *n.* Anything that arouses curiosity or perplexes because it is unexplained, inexplicable, or secret ▸ brainteaser, conundrum, curiousity, enigma, perplexity, puzzle, puzzler, question mark, riddle, stickler, weirdness.
mystical or **mystic** *adj.* *—See* MYSTERIOUS, SUPERNATURAL (1).
mystification *n.* *—See* DAZE.
mystify *v.* *—See* BAFFLE, CONFUSE (1).
mystifying *adj.* *—See* MYSTERIOUS.
myth *n.* **1.** A traditional story or tale that has no proven factual basis ▸ fable, fairy tale, folk tale, just-so story, legend, parable. [*Compare* FICTION, STORY, YARN.] **2.** A fiction or half-truth, especially one that forms part of an ideology ▸ creation, delusion, fabrication, fantasy, fiction, figment, invention. [*Compare* LIE[2].] *—See also* LORE (1).
mythical or **mythic** *adj.* Having the nature of a fable; not real ▸ apocryphal, fabled, fabricated, fabulous, fairy-tale, fantasy, legendary, make-believe, mythologic, mythological. [*Compare* FANCIFUL, FICTITIOUS, IMAGINARY.]
mythological or **mythologic** *adj.* *—See* MYTHICAL.
mythology or **mythos** *n.* *—See* LORE (1).

N

n[1] or **N** (ĕn) ► *n., pl.* **n's** or **N's** also **ns** or **Ns**. The 14th letter of the English alphabet.
n[2] ► *abbr.* **1.** *Gram.* neuter **2.** neutron
N[1] ► The symbol for the element **nitrogen.**
N[2] ► *abbr.* **1.** north **2.** northern
n. ► *abbr.* noun
Na ► The symbol for the element **sodium.**
NA ► *abbr.* **1.** North America **2.** also **n/a** not applicable
nab (năb) ► *v.* **nabbed, nab·bing.** *Informal* **1.** To seize; arrest. **2.** To grab; snatch.
na·bob (nā′bŏb′) ► *n.* A person of wealth and prominence.
na·celle (nə-sĕl′) ► *n.* A streamlined enclosure on an aircraft for housing the crew or an engine.
na·cho (nä′chō′) ► *n., pl.* **-chos.** A piece of tortilla topped with cheese or chili-pepper sauce and broiled.
na·cre (nā′kər) ► *n.* See **mother-of-pearl.**
Na-De·ne also **Na-Dé·né** (nä-dā′nē, -dā-nā′) ► *n.* A North American Indian language family including Athabaskan and Tlingit.
na·dir (nā′dər, -dîr′) ► *n.* **1.** A point on the celestial sphere diametrically opposite the zenith. **2.** The lowest point.
NAFTA ► *abbr.* North American Free Trade Agreement
nag[1] (năg) ► *v.* **nagged, nag·ging. 1.** To annoy by constant scolding, complaining, or urging. **2.** To torment persistently, as with anxiety or pain. **3.** To scold, complain, or find fault constantly: *nagging at the children.* ► *n.* One who nags. **—nag′ger** *n.* **—nag′ging·ly** *adv.*
nag[2] (năg) ► *n.* A horse, esp. an old or worn-out horse.
Na·ga·sa·ki (nä′gə-sä′kē) ► A city of W Kyushu, Japan, on **Nagasaki Bay,** an inlet of the East China Sea.
Na·hua·tl (nä′wät′l) ► *n., pl.* **-tl** or **-tls. 1.** A member of any of various Indian peoples of central Mexico, esp. the Aztecs. **2.** The Uto-Aztecan language of the Nahuatl.
Na·hum (nā′həm, nā′əm) ► *n.* **1.** A Hebrew prophet of the 7th cent. B.C. who predicted the fall of Nineveh. **2.** See **Bible** table in Appendix.
nai·ad (nā′əd, -ăd′, nī′-) ► *n., pl.* **-a·des** (-ə-dēz′) or **-ads.** *Gk. Myth.* One of the nymphs living in brooks, springs, and fountains.
nail (nāl) ► *n.* **1.** A slim, pointed piece of metal hammered into material as a fastener. **2a.** A thin, horny, transparent plate covering the upper surface of the tip of each finger and toe. **b.** A claw or talon. ► *v.* **1.** To fasten with or as if with a nail. **2.** To cover, enclose, or shut by fastening with nails: *nail up a window.* **3.** *Slang* To seize; catch: *nail a suspect.* **4.** *Slang* To strike or hit. ***—phrasal verb:*** **nail down** To settle conclusively.
nai·ra (nī′rə) ► *n.* See **currency** table in Appendix.
Nai·ro·bi (nī-rō′bē) ► The capital of Kenya, in the S-central part.
na·ive or **na·ïve** (nī-ēv′, nä-) also **na·if** or **na·ïf** (-ēf′) ► *adj.* **1.** Lacking worldliness and sophistication. **2.** Simple and credulous; ingenuous. **—na·ive′ly** *adv.* **—na·ive′ness** *n.*
na·ive·té or **na·ïve·té** (nī′ēv-tā′, nä′-, nī-ē′vĭ-tā′, nä-) ► *n.* **1.** The state of being naive. **2.** A naive statement or act.
na·ked (nā′kĭd) ► *adj.* **1.** Without clothing; nude. **2.** Having no covering; bare. **3.** Being without addition, disguise, or embellishment: *naked ambition.* **—na′ked·ly** *adv.* **—na′ked·ness** *n.*
naked eye ► *n.* The eye unassisted by an optical instrument.
nak·fa (näk′fä′) ► *n.* See **currency** table in Appendix.
nam·by-pam·by (năm′bē-păm′bē) ► *adj.* **1.** Insipid and sentimental. **2.** Indecisive; spineless. **—nam′by-pam′by** *n.*
name (nām) ► *n.* **1.** A word or words by which an entity is designated. **2.** A disparaging designation: *called me names.* **3.** Appearance rather than reality: *a democracy in name only.* **4a.** General reputation: *a bad name.* **b.** Renown. **5.** An illustrious person. ► *v.* **named, nam·ing. 1.** To give a name to. **2.** To mention, specify, or cite by name. **3.** To nominate or appoint. **4.** To specify or fix: *name the time and date.* ► *adj. Informal* Well-known by a name: *a name performer.* ***—idioms:*** **in the name of** By the authority of. **to (one's) name** Belonging to one. **—nam′a·ble, name′a·ble** *adj.* **—nam′er** *n.*
name-drop (nām′drŏp′) ► *v.* To mention casually the names of illustrious or famous people as a means of self-promotion. **—name′-drop′per** *n.* **—name′-drop′ping** *n.*
name·less (nām′lĭs) ► *adj.* **1.** Having no name. **2.** Unknown by name; obscure. **3.** Anonymous: *a nameless benefactor.* **4.** Defying description; inexpressible: *nameless horror.* **—name′less·ly** *adv.* **—name′less·ness** *n.*
name·ly (nām′lē) ► *adv.* That is to say; specifically.
name·sake (nām′sāk′) ► *n.* One who is named after another.
Na·mib·i·a (nə-mĭb′ē-ə) ► A country of SW Africa on the Atlantic. **—Na·mib′i·an** *adj. & n.*
Nan·jing (nän′jĭng′) also **Nan·king** (năn′kĭng′, nän′-) ► A city of E-central China on the Chang Jiang (Yangtze R.) NW of Shanghai.
nan·keen (năn-kēn′) also **nan·kin** (-kēn′, -kĭn′) ► *n.* A sturdy yellow or buff cotton cloth.

THESAURUS

nab *v.* —*See* ARREST, CATCH (2).
nabob *n.* —*See* DIGNITARY.
nadir *n.* A very low or lowest level, position, or degree ► bottom, low, minimum, rock bottom.
nag *v.* To scold or find fault with constantly ► carp at, fuss at, niggle, peck at, pick at. *Informal:* henpeck. [*Compare* ANNOY, HARASS, QUIBBLE.] —*See also* COMPLAIN.
nag *n.* —*See* SCOLD.
nagging *adj.* —*See* CRITICAL (1), PAINFUL.
nail *v.* —*See* CAPTURE, FASTEN, HIT.
nail *n.* A bolt or a shaft that is hammered or drilled in place and is used to support or hold together ► bolt, peg, pin, rivet, screw, spike, stud, tack. [*Compare* ANCHOR, CORD, FASTENER.]
naive *adj.* —*See* ARTLESS, GULLIBLE, SUPERFICIAL.
naive *n.* —*See* INNOCENT (2).
naiveté *n.* —*See* ARTLESSNESS.
naked *adj.* —*See* BARE (3), NUDE.
nakedness *n.* —*See* NUDITY.
namby-pamby *adj.* —*See* INSIPID, SENTIMENTAL.
name *n.* **1.** The word or words by which one is called and identified ► appellation, appellative, cognomen, compellation, denomination, designation, epithet, namesake, nickname, pet name, sobriquet, style, tag, title. *Slang:* handle, moniker. **2.** Public estimation of someone ► character, report, reputation, repute. *Informal:* rep. [*Compare* IMAGE, PLACE.] —*See also* CELEBRITY.
name *v.* **1.** To give a name or title to ► baptize, call, christen, denominate, designate, dub, entitle, nickname, style, term, title. *Idiom:* give a handle to. [*Compare* CALL.] **2.** To refer to by name ► cite, instance, mention, point to, refer to, single out, specify. —*See also* APPOINT, CALL.
nameless *adj.* Not known or not widely known by name ► obscure, unheard-of, unknown. —*See also* ANONYMOUS.
namelessness *n.* —*See* OBSCURITY.
namely *adv.* That is to say ► i.e. particularly, scilicet, specifically, videlicet, viz. *Idioms:* by way of explanation, in other words, strictly speaking, that is, to wit.
namesake *n.* —*See* NAME (1).

nan·ny (năn′ē) ▸ *n., pl.* **-nies.** A children's nurse.
nanny goat ▸ *n.* A female goat.
nano– ▸ *pref.* **1.** One-billionth (10^{-9}): *nanosecond.* **2.** Extremely small: *nanotube.*
nan·o·sec·ond (năn′ə-sĕk′ənd) ▸ *n.* One billionth (10^{-9}) of a second.
nan·o·tech·nol·o·gy (năn′ə-tĕk-nŏl′ə-jē) ▸ *n.* The science of building electronic circuits and devices from single atoms and molecules.
nan·o·tube (năn′ə-to͞ob′, -tyo͞ob′) ▸ *n.* An elongated fullerene having a cylindrical configuration.
Nan·tuck·et (năn-tŭk′ĭt) ▸ An island of SE MA S of Cape Cod. **—Nan·tuck′et·er** *n.*
nap[1] (năp) ▸ *n.* A brief sleep, often during the day. ▸ *v.* **napped, nap·ping. 1.** To take a nap. **2.** To be unaware of imminent danger or trouble.
nap[2] (năp) ▸ *n.* A soft or fuzzy surface on fabric or leather.
na·palm (nā′päm′) ▸ *n.* A highly incendiary jelly used in bombs and flamethrowers. **—na′palm′** *v.*
nape (nāp, năp) ▸ *n.* The back of the neck.
na·per·y (nā′pə-rē) ▸ *n.* Household linen, esp. table linen.
naph·tha (năf′thə, năp′-) ▸ *n.* A highly volatile, flammable liquid distilled esp. from petroleum and used as a fuel or solvent and in making chemicals.
naph·tha·lene (năf′thə-lēn′, năp′-) ▸ *n.* A white crystalline compound, $C_{10}H_8$, used in making dyes, moth repellents, and explosives and as a solvent.
nap·kin (năp′kĭn) ▸ *n.* **1.** A piece of cloth or absorbent paper used at table to protect the clothes or wipe the lips and fingers. **2.** A cloth or towel.
Na·ples (nā′pəlz) ▸ A city of S-central Italy on the **Bay of Naples,** an arm of the Tyrrhenian Sea.
Na·po·le·on I (nə-pō′lē-ən, -pōl′yən). Napoleon Bonaparte (1769–1821) ▸ Emperor of the French (1804–14). **—Na·po′le·on′ic** (-ŏn′ĭk) *adj.*
narc (närk) ▸ *n. Slang* A narcotics agent.
nar·cis·sism (när′sĭ-sĭz′əm) ▸ *n.* Excessive love or admiration of oneself. **—nar′cis·sist** *n.* **—nar′cis·sis′tic** *adj.*
nar·cis·sus (när-sĭs′əs) ▸ *n., pl.* **-es** or **-cis·si** (-sĭs′ī′, -sĭs′ē). Any of a genus of plants that includes the daffodil and jonquil.
Narcissus ▸ *n. Gk. Myth.* A youth who fell in love with his own image in a pool of water and was transformed into a flower.
nar·co·lep·sy (när′kə-lĕp′sē) ▸ *n.* A disorder marked by sudden and uncontrollable, often brief, attacks of deep sleep. **—nar′co·lep′tic** (-lĕp′tĭk) *adj. & n.*
nar·co·sis (när-kō′sĭs) ▸ *n., pl.* **-ses** (-sēz). Deep stupor or unconsciousness produced by a drug.
nar·cot·ic (när-kŏt′ĭk) ▸ *n.* An addictive drug that reduces pain, alters mood and behavior, and usu. induces sleep or stupor. **—nar·cot′ic** *adj.*
nar·co·tism (när′kə-tĭz′əm) ▸ *n.* **1.** Addiction to narcotics. **2.** Narcosis.
nar·co·tize (när′kə-tīz′) ▸ *v.* **-tized, -tiz·ing. 1.** To place under the influence of a narcotic. **2.** To put to sleep. **3.** To dull; deaden.
nar·is (nâr′ĭs) ▸ *n., pl.* **-es** (-ēz). A nostril.
Nar·ra·gan·sett (năr′ə-găn′sĭt) ▸ *n., pl.* **-sett** or **-setts. 1.** A member of a Native American people inhabiting parts of Rhode Island. **2.** Their Algonquian language.
nar·rate (năr′āt′, nă-rāt′) ▸ *v.* **-rat·ed, -rat·ing. 1.** To give an account of; tell. **2.** To supply a descriptive commentary for a movie or performance. **—nar·ra′tion** *n.* **—nar′ra′tor** *n.*
nar·ra·tive (năr′ə-tĭv) ▸ *n.* **1.** A narrated account; story. **2.** The act or process of narrating. **—nar′ra·tive** *adj.*
nar·row (năr′ō) ▸ *adj.* **-er, -est. 1.** Of small or limited width. **2.** Limited in area or scope; cramped. **3.** Lacking flexibility; rigid: *narrow opinions.* **4.** Barely sufficient; close: *a narrow margin of victory.* **5.** Painstakingly thorough; meticulous: *narrow scrutiny.* ▸ *v.* To reduce in width or extent; make narrower. ▸ *n.* **narrows** *(takes sing. or pl. v.)* A narrow body of water that connects two larger ones. **—nar′row·ly** *adv.* **—nar′row·ness** *n.*
nar·row-mind·ed (năr′ō-mīn′dĭd) ▸ *adj.* Lacking tolerance or breadth of view; petty. **—nar′row-mind′ed·ly** *adv.* **—nar′row-mind′ed·ness** *n.*
nar·thex (när′thĕks′) ▸ *n.* A portico or lobby to the nave of a church.
nar·whal (när′wəl) ▸ *n.* An Arctic whale marked in the male by a long spirally twisted ivory tusk.
nar·y (nâr′ē) ▸ *adj.* Not one.
NASA (năs′ə) ▸ *abbr.* National Aeronautics and Space Administration
na·sal (nā′zəl) ▸ *adj.* **1.** Of or relating to the nose. **2.** Marked by or resembling a resonant sound produced through the nose: *a nasal whine.* **—na·sal′i·ty** (nā-zăl′ĭ-tē) *n.* **—na′sal·ly** *adv.*
nas·cent (năs′ənt, nā′sənt) ▸ *adj.* Coming into existence; emergent. **—nas′cence** *n.*
Nash·ville (năsh′vĭl′) ▸ The capital of TN, in the N-central part NE of Memphis.
nas·tur·tium (nə-stûr′shəm, nă-) ▸ *n.* A plant having pungent juice, edible round leaves, and usu. yellow, orange, or red irregular flowers.
nas·ty (năs′tē) ▸ *adj.* **-ti·er, -ti·est. 1.** Disgustingly dirty; foul. **2.** Offensive; indecent. **3.** Malicious. **4.** Very unpleasant: *nasty weather.* **5.** Painful or dangerous: *a nasty accident.* **—nas′ti·ly** *adv.* **—nas′ti·ness** *n.*
na·tal (nāt′l) ▸ *adj.* **1.** Of or accompanying birth. **2.** Of the time or place of one's birth.
na·tal·i·ty (nā-tăl′ĭ-tē, nə-) ▸ *n.* See **birthrate.**
Natch·ez (năch′ĭz) ▸ *n., pl.* **Natchez. 1.** A member of an extinct Native American people formerly living along the lower Mississippi R. **2.** The language of the Natchez.
Na·tick (nā′tĭk) ▸ *n.* A dialect of Massachusett.
na·tion (nā′shən) ▸ *n.* **1.** A relatively large group of people organized under a single government. **2.** A people; nationality. **3.** A federation or tribe. **—na′tion·hood′** *n.*
Nation, Carry Amelia Moore (1846–1911) ▸ Amer. temperance crusader.
na·tion·al (năsh′ə-nəl, năsh′nəl) ▸ *adj.* **1.** Of or belonging to a nation. **2.** Characteristic of the people of a nation: *a national trait.* ▸ *n.* A citizen of a particular nation. **—na′tion·al·ly** *adv.*
National Guard ▸ *n.* The military reserve units controlled by each US state and subject to the call of either the federal or the state government.
na·tion·al·ism (năsh′ə-nə-lĭz′əm, năsh′nə-) ▸ *n.* **1.** Devotion to the interests or culture of a particular nation. **2.**

THESAURUS

nap *n.* A brief sleep ▸ catnap, doze, power nap, siesta, snooze. *Informal:* forty winks. [*Compare* REST, SLEEP.]
nap *v.* To sleep for a brief period ▸ catnap, doze (off), drop off, nod (off), snooze. ***Idioms:*** catch (*or* grab *or* take) forty winks, get some shut-eye. [*Compare* REST, SLEEP.]
narc *n.* *—See* POLICE OFFICER.
narcissism or **narcism** *n.* *—See* EGOTISM.
narcissist *n.* *—See* EGOTIST.
narcissistic *adj.* *—See* EGOTISTIC (1).
narcotic *n.* *—See* DRUG (2), SOPORIFIC.
narcotic *adj.* *—See* SOPORIFIC.
narcotize *v.* *—See* DRUG (1).
nark *n.* *—See* INFORMER.
narrate *v.* *—See* DESCRIBE.
narrative or **narration** *n.* *—See* STORY (1).
narrow *adj.* **1.** Restricted in scope, outlook, or understanding ▸ doctrinaire, dogmatic, inflexible, insular, limited, little, local, narrow-minded, parochial, petty, provincial, small, small-minded, small-town. **2.** Having the restricted outlook often characteristic of geographic isolation ▸ insular, limited, local, narrow-minded, parochial, provincial, small-town. *—See also* REMOTE (2), TIGHT (4).
narrow *v.* *—See* CONSTRICT (1).
narrow-minded *adj.* *—See* INTOLERANT (1), NARROW (1).
nascence or **nascency** *n.* *—See* BIRTH (2).
nastiness *n.* *—See* DIRTINESS, MALEVOLENCE, OBSCENITY (1).
nasty *adj.* So objectionable as to elicit despisal or deserve condemnation ▸ abhorrent, abominable, antipathetic, contemptible, despicable, despisable, detestable, disgusting, filthy, foul, infamous, loathsome, lousy, low, mean, nefarious, obnoxious, odious, repugnant, rotten, shabby, vile, wretched. *—See also* BLEAK (1), DIRTY, ILL-TEMPERED, MALEVOLENT, OBSCENE, OFFENSIVE (1).
nation *n.* *—See* STATE (1).
national *adj.* *—See* DOMESTIC (3), POPULAR.
national *n.* *—See* CITIZEN.

Aspirations for national independence. **—na′tion·al·ist** *n.* **—na′tion·al·is′tic** *adj.* **—na′tion·al·is′ti·cal·ly** *adv.*

na·tion·al·i·ty (năsh′ə-năl′ĭ-tē, năsh-năl′-) ▸ *n., pl.* **-ties.** **1.** The status of belonging to a particular nation by origin, birth, or naturalization. **2.** A people having common origins or traditions and often constituting a nation.

na·tion·al·ize (năsh′ə-nə-līz′, năsh′nə-) ▸ *v.* **-ized, -iz·ing.** **1.** To convert from private to governmental ownership and control. **2.** To make national in character or scope. **—na′tion·al·i·za′tion** *n.*

national monument ▸ *n.* A landmark or site of historic interest set aside by a national government for public enjoyment.

national park ▸ *n.* A tract of public land maintained by a national government for recreational and cultural use.

na·tion·wide (nā′shən-wīd′) ▸ *adv. & adj.* Throughout a whole nation.

na·tive (nā′tĭv) ▸ *adj.* **1.** Inborn; innate: *native ability.* **2.** Being such by birth or origin: *a native Scot.* **3.** Being one's own by birth: *our native land.* **4.** Originating or produced in a certain place; indigenous. ▸ *n.* **1a.** One born in a specified place. **b.** An original or lifelong inhabitant of a place. **2.** An animal or plant that originated in a particular place.

Native Alaskan ▸ *n.* See **Alaska Native.**

Native American ▸ *n.* A member of any of the peoples indigenous to the Western Hemisphere before European contact. **—Native American** *adj.*

Native Hawaiian ▸ *n.* A member or descendant of the indigenous Polynesian people of the Hawaiian Islands.

na·tiv·i·ty (nə-tĭv′ĭ-tē, nā-) ▸ *n., pl.* **-ties.** **1.** Birth, esp. the conditions or circumstances of being born. **2. Nativity a.** The birth of Jesus. **b.** Christmas.

natl. ▸ *abbr.* national

NATO (nā′tō) ▸ *abbr.* North Atlantic Treaty Organization

nat·ty (năt′ē) ▸ *adj.* **-ti·er, -ti·est.** Neat, trim, and smart; dapper. **—nat′ti·ly** *adv.* **—nat′ti·ness** *n.*

nat·u·ral (năch′ər-əl, năch′rəl) ▸ *adj.* **1.** Present in or produced by nature. **2.** Of or relating to nature. **3.** Conforming to the usual course of nature: *a natural death.* **4a.** Not acquired; inherent. **b.** Having a particular character by nature: *a natural leader.* **5.** Free from affectation or inhibitions. **6.** Not altered or treated: *natural coloring.* **7.** Expected and accepted. **8.** *Math.* Of or relating to positive integers. **9.** *Mus.* Not sharped or flatted. ▸ *n.* **1.** One especially suited by nature or qualifications: *a natural for the job.* **2.** *Mus.* The sign (♮) placed before a note to cancel a preceding sharp or flat. **—nat′u·ral·ness** *n.*

natural gas ▸ *n.* A mixture of hydrocarbon gases, chiefly methane, occurring with petroleum deposits and used esp. as a fuel.

natural history ▸ *n.* The study of organisms and natural objects, esp. their origins, evolution, and relationships.

nat·u·ral·ism (năch′ər-ə-lĭz′əm, năch′rə-) ▸ *n.* **1.** Factual or realistic representation in art or literature. **2.** The view that all phenomena can be explained in terms of natural causes and laws.

nat·u·ral·ist (năch′ər-ə-lĭst, năch′rə-) ▸ *n.* **1.** One versed in natural history, esp. in zoology or botany. **2.** An adherent of naturalism.

nat·u·ral·is·tic (năch′ər-ə-lĭs′tĭk, năch′rə-) ▸ *adj.* Lifelike; realistic. **—nat′u·ral·is′ti·cal·ly** *adv.*

nat·u·ral·ize (năch′ər-ə-līz′, năch′rə-) ▸ *v.* **-ized, -iz·ing.** **1.** To grant full citizenship to. **2.** To adopt into general use. **3.** To adapt or acclimate (a plant or animal) to a new environment. **—nat′u·ral·i·za′tion** *n.*

nat·u·ral·ly (năch′ər-ə-lē, năch′rə-) ▸ *adv.* **1.** In a natural manner. **2.** By nature; inherently. **3.** Without a doubt; surely.

natural resource ▸ *n.* A material source of wealth, such as timber or a mineral deposit, that occurs in a natural state.

natural science ▸ *n.* A science, such as biology, chemistry, or physics, that deals with the objects, phenomena, or laws of nature and the physical world.

natural selection ▸ *n.* The process in nature by which only the organisms best adapted to their environment tend to survive and transmit their genetic characters to succeeding generations.

na·ture (nā′chər) ▸ *n.* **1.** The material world and its phenomena. **2.** The forces that produce and control such phenomena: *the laws of nature.* **3.** The world of living things and the outdoors. **4.** A primitive state of existence. **5.** A kind or sort. **6.** The essential character of a person or thing. **7.** Disposition; temperament: *a sweet nature.* **—na′tured** *adj.*

na·tur·op·a·thy (nā′chə-rŏp′ə-thē) ▸ *n., pl.* **-thies.** A system of therapy that relies on natural remedies, such as sunlight, diet, and massage, to treat illness. **—na′tur·o·path′** (nā′chər-ə-păth′, nə-choor′-) *n.* **—na′tur·o·path′ic** *adj.*

naught also **nought** (nôt) ▸ *n.* **1.** Nonexistence; nothingness. **2.** The figure 0; zero.

naugh·ty (nô′tē) ▸ *adj.* **-ti·er, -ti·est.** **1.** Disobedient; mischievous. **2.** Indecent; improper. **—naugh′ti·ly** *adv.* **—naugh′ti·ness** *n.*

Na·u·ru (nä-oo′roo) ▸ An island country of the central Pacific S of the equator and W of Kiribati. **—Na·u′ru·an** *adj. & n.*

nau·se·a (nô′zē-ə, -zhə, -sē-ə, -shə) ▸ *n.* **1.** A feeling of sickness in the stomach marked by an urge to vomit. **2.** Strong aversion; disgust.

nau·se·ate (nô′zē-āt′, -zhē-, -sē-, -shē-) ▸ *v.* **-at·ed, -at·ing.** To feel or cause to feel nausea. **—nau′se·at′ing·ly** *adv.*

nau·seous (nô′shəs, -zē-əs) ▸ *adj.* **1.** Causing nausea; sickening. **2.** Affected with nausea.

nau·ti·cal (nô′tĭ-kəl) ▸ *adj.* Of or characteristic of ships, shipping, sailors, or navigation. **—nau′ti·cal·ly** *adv.*

nautical mile ▸ *n.* A unit of length used in sea and air navigation, usu. equal to 1,852 m (about 6,076 ft).

nau·ti·lus (nôt′l-əs) ▸ *n., pl.* **-es** or **-li** (-lī′). A cephalopod mollusk having a partitioned spiral shell.

Nav·a·jo also **Nav·a·ho** (năv′ə-hō′, nä′və-) ▸ *n., pl.* **-jo** or **-jos** also **-ho** or **-hos.** **1.** A member of a Native American people inhabiting reservation lands in Arizona, New Mexico, and SE Utah. **2.** The Athabaskan language of the Navajo. **—Nav′a·jo′** *adj.*

na·val (nā′vəl) ▸ *adj.* **1.** Of or relating to ships or shipping. **2.** Of or relating to a navy.

nave (nāv) ▸ *n.* The central part of a church, extending from the narthex to the chancel and flanked by the aisles.

na·vel (nā′vəl) ▸ *n.* The mark on the abdomen of mammals where the umbilical cord was attached during gestation.

navel orange ▸ *n.* A usu. seedless orange having at its apex a navellike formation enclosing an underdeveloped fruit.

nav·i·ga·ble (năv′ĭ-gə-bəl) ▸ *adj.* **1.** Sufficiently deep or

THESAURUS

nationalize *v.* To place under government or group ownership or control ▸ communalize, socialize.

native *adj.* —*See* CONSTITUTIONAL, CRUDE, DOMESTIC (3), INDIGENOUS, INNATE, WILD (1).

native *n.* —*See* INHABITANT.

nativity *n.* —*See* BIRTH (1).

natter *v.* —*See* CHATTER (1).

natty *adj.* —*See* NEAT.

natural *adj.* **1.** Produced by nature; not artificial or manmade ▸ additive-free, chemical-free, organic, unadulterated, unprocessed, unsynthetic. *Idiom:* pure as the driven snow. [*Compare* AUTHENTIC, PURE.] **2.** Of unbroken descent or lineage ▸ direct, genealogical, hereditary, lineal. [*Compare* ANCESTRAL.] —*See also* ARTLESS, CONSTITUTIONAL, EASYGOING, GENUINE, GIFTED, ILLEGITIMATE, REALISTIC (2), RUSTIC, SPONTANEOUS, WILD (1).

naturalistic *adj.* —*See* REALISTIC (2).

naturalize *v.* —*See* DOMESTICATE.

naturalized *adj.* —*See* DOMESTIC (2).

naturally *adv.* —*See* USUALLY, YES.

naturalness *n.* —*See* ARTLESSNESS, EASE (1).

nature *n.* —*See* CHARACTER (1), DISPOSITION, ENVIRONMENT (3), ESSENCE, KIND[2], UNIVERSE.

naughtiness *n.* —*See* DEFIANCE (1), MISBEHAVIOR.

naughty *adj.* —*See* HARMFUL, IMPROPER (1), UNRULY.

nausea *n.* —*See* DISGUST.

nauseate *v.* —*See* DISGUST.

nauseating *adj.* —*See* OFFENSIVE (1), UNPALATABLE.

nautical or **naval** *adj.* ▸ marine, maritime, navigational. [*Compare* MARINE.]

nave *n.* —*See* CENTER (3).

navigable *adj.* —*See* PASSABLE.

wide to provide passage for vessels. 2. That can be steered. **—nav'i·ga·bil'i·ty, nav'i·ga·ble·ness** *n.*

nav·i·gate (năv'ĭ-gāt') ▸ *v.* **-gat·ed, -gat·ing.** 1. To control the course of a ship or aircraft. 2. To voyage over water in a boat or ship; sail. 3. To make one's way (through). **—nav'i·ga'tion** *n.* **—nav'i·ga'tion·al** *adj.* **—nav'i·ga'tor** *n.*

na·vy (nā'vē) ▸ *n., pl.* **-vies.** 1. All of a nation's warships. 2. A nation's entire military organization for sea warfare and defense. 3. Navy blue.

navy bean ▸ *n.* A variety of the kidney bean cultivated for its edible white seeds.

navy blue ▸ *n.* A dark grayish blue.

nay (nā) ▸ *adv.* 1. No: *voted nay.* 2. And moreover: *He was ill-favored, nay, hideous.* ▸ *n.* 1. A denial or refusal. 2. A negative vote or voter.

Naz·a·reth (năz'ər-əth) ▸ A town of N Israel southeast of Haifa.

Na·zi (nät'sē, năt'-) ▸ *n., pl.* **-zis.** A member of the fascist political party that held power (1933–45) in Germany under Adolf Hitler. **—Na'zi** *adj.* **—Na'zism, Na'zi·ism** *n.*

Nb ▸ The symbol for the element **niobium.**

NB ▸ *abbr.* 1. also **N.B.** New Brunswick 2. nota bene

NC or **N.C.** ▸ *abbr.* North Carolina

Nd ▸ The symbol for the element **neodymium.**

ND or **N.D.** ▸ *abbr.* North Dakota

Ne ▸ The symbol for the element **neon.**

NE ▸ *abbr.* 1. Nebraska 2. New England 3a. northeast b. northeastern

Ne·an·der·thal (nē-ăn'dər-thôl', -tôl', nā-än'dər-täl') ▸ *adj.* 1. Of or being an extinct species or subspecies of humans of the late Pleistocene Epoch, esp. in Europe. 2. *Slang* Crude, boorish, or slow-witted. **—Ne·an'der·thal'** *n.*

neap tide (nēp) ▸ *n.* A tide occuring during the first and third quarters of the moon, when the difference between high and low tides is least.

near (nîr) ▸ *adv.* **-er, -est.** 1. To, at, or within a short distance or interval in space or time. 2. Almost; nearly: *was near exhausted from the work.* 3. With or in a close relationship. ▸ *adj.* **-er, -est.** 1. Close in time, space, position, or degree: *near equals.* 2. Closely related. 3. Nearly so: *a near victory.* 4. Closely resembling an original. 5. Closer of two or more. ▸ *prep.* Close to: *an inn near Tokyo.* ▸ *v.* To come close or closer to; draw near. **—near'ness** *n.*

near·by (nîr'bī') ▸ *adj.* Located a short distance away. ▸ *adv.* Not far away.

Near East ▸ A region of SW Asia generally thought to include the countries of the E Mediterranean, the Arabian Peninsula, and, sometimes, NE Africa. **—Near Eastern** *adj.*

near·ly (nîr'lē) ▸ *adv.* Almost but not quite.

near·sight·ed (nîr'sī'tĭd) ▸ *adj.* Unable to see distant objects clearly; myopic. **—near'sight'ed·ly** *adv.* **—near'sight'ed·ness** *n.*

neat (nēt) ▸ *adj.* **-er, -est.** 1. Clean and tidy. 2. Orderly and precise; systematic. 3. Marked by ingenuity and skill; adroit: *a neat turn of phrase.* 4. Not diluted: *neat whiskey.* 5. *Slang* Wonderful; terrific: *a neat party.* **—neat'ly** *adv.* **—neat'ness** *n.*

neat·en (nēt'n) ▸ *v.* To make neat or tidy.

neath or **'neath** (nēth) ▸ *prep.* Beneath.

neat's-foot oil (nēts'fo͝ot') ▸ *n.* A light yellow oil obtained from the feet and shinbones of cattle, used chiefly to dress leather.

neb (nĕb) ▸ *n.* 1a. A beak of a bird. b. A nose. 2. A projecting part, esp. a nib.

neb·bish (nĕb'ĭsh) ▸ *n.* A weak-willed or timid person. **—neb'bish·y** *adj.*

Ne·bras·ka (nə-brăs'kə) ▸ A state of the central US in the Great Plains. Cap. Lincoln. **—Ne·bras'kan** *adj. & n.*

neb·u·la (nĕb'yə-lə) ▸ *n., pl.* **-lae** (-lē') or **-las.** 1. A diffuse mass of interstellar dust or gas. 2. See **galaxy** 1. **—neb'u·lar** *adj.*

neb·u·lize (nĕb'yə-līz') ▸ *v.* **-lized, -liz·ing.** To convert (a liquid) to a fine spray; atomize. **—neb'u·li·za'tion** *n.* **—neb'u·liz'er** *n.*

neb·u·los·i·ty (nĕb'yə-lŏs'ĭ-tē) ▸ *n., pl.* **-ties.** 1. The quality or condition of being nebulous. 2. A nebula.

neb·u·lous (nĕb'yə-ləs) ▸ *adj.* 1. Cloudy, misty, or hazy. 2. Lacking definite form or limits; vague. 3. Of or characteristic of a nebula. **—neb'u·lous·ly** *adv.* **—neb'u·lous·ness** *n.*

nec·es·sar·i·ly (nĕs'ĭ-sâr'ə-lē, -sĕr'-) ▸ *adv.* Of necessity; inevitably.

nec·es·sar·y (nĕs'ĭ-sĕr'ē) ▸ *adj.* 1. Absolutely essential; indispensable. 2. Unavoidably determined; inevitable. 3. Required, as by obligation, compulsion, or convention. ▸ *n., pl.* **-ies.** Something indispensable.

ne·ces·si·tate (nə-sĕs'ĭ-tāt') ▸ *v.* **-tat·ed, -tat·ing.** To make necessary or unavoidable. **—ne·ces'si·ta'tion** *n.*

ne·ces·si·tous (nə-sĕs'ĭ-təs) ▸ *adj.* 1. Needy; indigent. 2. Urgent.

ne·ces·si·ty (nə-sĕs'ĭ-tē) ▸ *n., pl.* **-ties.** 1a. The condition or quality of being necessary. b. Something necessary. 2. The force exerted by circumstance. 3. Pressing or urgent need.

neck (nĕk) ▸ *n.* 1. The part of the body joining the head to the trunk. 2. The part of a garment around or near the neck. 3. A narrow elongation, projection, or connecting part: *a neck of land; the neck of a flask.* 4. A narrow margin: *won by a neck.* ▸ *v. Informal* To kiss and caress amorously. ***—idiom:* neck and neck** Very close together, as in a race. **—necked** *adj.*

neck·er·chief (nĕk'ər-chĭf, -chēf') ▸ *n.* A kerchief worn around the neck.

neck·lace (nĕk'lĭs) ▸ *n.* An ornament worn around the neck.

neck·line (nĕk'līn') ▸ *n.* The line formed by the edge of a garment at the neck.

neck·tie (nĕk'tī') ▸ *n.* A narrow fabric band worn around the neck and tied in a knot or bow close to the throat.

necro– or **necr–** ▸ *pref.* Death; the dead: *necrosis.*

ne·crol·o·gy (nə-krŏl'ə-jē, nĕ-) ▸ *n., pl.* **-gies.** 1. A list of people who have died, esp. in the recent past. 2. An obituary. **—nec'ro·log'ic** (nĕk'rə-lŏj'ĭk), **nec'ro·log'i·cal** *adj.* **—ne·crol'o·gist** *n.*

nec·ro·man·cy (nĕk'rə-măn'sē) ▸ *n.* 1. The art that professes to communicate with the spirits of the dead so as to predict the future. 2. Black magic; sorcery. **—nec'ro·man'cer** *n.* **—nec'ro·man'tic** *adj.*

ne·crop·o·lis (nə-krŏp'ə-lĭs, nĕ-) ▸ *n., pl.* **-lis·es** or **-leis** (-lās'). A cemetery, esp. a large and elaborate one in an ancient city.

ne·cro·sis (nə-krō'sĭs, nĕ-) ▸ *n., pl.* **-ses** (-sēz'). Death of cells or tissues through injury or disease. **—ne·crot'ic** (-krŏt'ĭk) *adj.*

nec·tar (nĕk'tər) ▸ *n.* 1. A sweet liquid secreted by flowers.

THESAURUS

navigate *v.* *—See* MANEUVER (1).

navigator *n.* *—See* SAILOR.

nay *adv.* *—See* NO.

nay *n.* A negative vote or voter ▸ no. *—See also* NO (1).

near *adv.* *—See* CLOSE.

near *adj.* *—See* CLOSE (1), INTIMATE[1] (1).

near *v.* *—See* APPROACH (1).

nearby *adj.* *—See* CLOSE (1), CONVENIENT (2).

nearby *adv.* *—See* CLOSE.

nearly *adv.* *—See* APPROXIMATELY.

nearness *n.* The act or fact of coming near ▸ approach, coming, convergence, imminence. [*Compare* ADVANCE, APPEARANCE.]

neat *adj.* In good order or clean condition ▸ dapper, natty, orderly, prim, shipshape, snug, spick-and-span, spruce, taut, tidy, trig, trim, well-groomed, well-kept, well-ordered. *Idioms:* in apple pie order, in good order, neat as a pin. [*Compare* CLEAN, METHODICAL.] *—See also* DEXTEROUS, MARVELOUS, METHODICAL, STRAIGHT.

neaten *v.* *—See* TIDY (1), TIDY (2).

neb *n.* *—See* POINT (1).

nebbish *n.* *—See* NONENTITY.

nebulous *adj.* *—See* AMBIGUOUS (2).

nebulousness *n.* *—See* VAGUENESS.

necessary *adj.* *—See* CERTAIN (1), ESSENTIAL (1), REQUIRED.

necessary *n.* *—See* CONDITION (2).

necessitate *v.* *—See* DEMAND (2).

necessitous *adj.* *—See* POOR.

necessity *n.* A condition in which something that is necessary or desirable is required or wanted ▸ exigence, exigency, need. *—See also* CAUSE (2), CONDITION (2).

neck *v.* *Informal* To engage in kissing, caressing, and other amorous behavior ▸ *Informal:* fool around, pet, spoon. *Slang:* grope, make out. *Idioms:* bill and coo, play kissy-face (*or* sucky-face), play post office. [*Compare* CARESS, KISS, SNUGGLE.]

neck *n.* *—See* CHANNEL.

neck of the woods *n.* *—See* AREA (2).

necromancer *n.* *—See* WIZARD.

2. *Gk. & Rom. Myth.* The drink of the gods. 3. A delicious or invigorating drink.
nec·tar·ine (nĕk′tə-rēn′) ▸ *n.* A variety of peach having a smooth waxy skin.
née also **nee** (nā) ▸ *adj.* Born.
need (nēd) ▸ *n.* 1. A lack of something required or desirable. 2. Something required or wanted; requisite. 3. Necessity; obligation. 4. Poverty or misfortune: *in dire need.* ▸ *v.* 1. To have need of; require: *The family needs money.* 2. To be in need or want. *—aux.* To be under the necessity of or the obligation to: *They need not come.*
need·ful (nēd′fəl) ▸ *adj.* Necessary; required. **—need′ful·ly** *adv.* **—need′ful·ness** *n.*
nee·dle (nēd′l) ▸ *n.* 1a. A small slender implement used for sewing, made usu. of steel and having an eye at one end through which a thread is passed. b. A similarly shaped implement, such as one used in knitting. 2. A stylus used to transmit vibrations from the grooves of a phonograph record. 3. A slender pointer or indicator, as on a dial. 4. A hypodermic needle. 5. A narrow stiff leaf, as those of conifers. 6. A fine sharp projection, as a spine of a sea urchin. ▸ *v.* **-dled, -dling.** *Informal* To goad, provoke, or tease.
nee·dle·point (nēd′l-point′) ▸ *n.* Decorative needlework on canvas.
need·less (nēd′lĭs) ▸ *adj.* Not needed or wished for; unnecessary. **—need′less·ly** *adv.* **—need′less·ness** *n.*
nee·dle·work (nēd′l-wûrk′) ▸ *n.* Work, such as embroidery, that is done with a needle.
need·n't (nēd′nt) ▸ Need not.
needs (nēdz) ▸ *adv.* Of necessity; necessarily: *We must needs go.*
need·y (nē′dē) ▸ *adj.* **-i·er, -i·est.** Being in need; impoverished. **—need′i·ness** *n.*
ne'er (nâr) ▸ *adv.* Never.
ne'er-do-well (nâr′dōō-wĕl′) ▸ *n.* An idle, irresponsible person. **—ne'er′-do-well′** *adj.*
ne·far·i·ous (nə-fâr′ē-əs) ▸ *adj.* Extremely wicked. **—ne·far′i·ous·ly** *adv.* **—ne·far′i·ous·ness** *n.*
ne·gate (nĭ-gāt′) ▸ *v.* **-gat·ed, -gat·ing.** 1. To make ineffective or invalid; nullify. 2. To rule out; deny. **—ne·ga′tion** *n.*
neg·a·tive (nĕg′ə-tĭv) ▸ *adj.* 1a. Expressing negation, refusal, or denial. b. Indicating opposition or resistance: *a negative reaction.* 2. Not positive or constructive: *negative criticism.* 3. *Medic.* Not indicating the presence of a disease or specific condition. 4. *Math.* a. Of or being a quantity less than zero. b. Of or being a quantity, number, angle, velocity, or direction in a sense opposite to another understood to be positive. 5. *Phys.* Of or being an electric charge of the same sign as that of an electron, indicated by the symbol (–). ▸ *n.* 1. A negative word, statement, or act. 2. A feature or aspect that is not positive or affirmative. 3. The side in a debate that opposes the question being debated. 4a. An image in which the light areas of the object rendered appear dark and the dark areas appear light. b. A film, plate, or other photographic material containing such an image. ▸ *v.* **-tived, -tiv·ing.** 1. To veto. 2. To deny. **—neg′a·tive·ly** *adv.* **—neg′a·tive·ness, neg′a·tiv′i·ty** (-tĭv′ĭ-tē) *n.*
neg·a·tiv·ism (nĕg′ə-tĭ-vĭz′əm) ▸ *n.* A habitual attitude of skepticism or resistance to the suggestions or instructions of others. **—neg′a·tiv·ist** *n.* **—neg′a·tiv·is′tic** *adj.*
ne·glect (nĭ-glĕkt′) ▸ *v.* 1. To ignore; disregard. 2. To fail to care for or attend to properly: *neglects her appearance.* 3. To fail to do through carelessness or oversight. ▸ *n.* 1. The act or an instance of neglecting something. 2. The state of being neglected. **—ne·glect′er** *n.*
ne·glect·ful (nĭ-glĕkt′fəl) ▸ *adj.* Marked by neglect. **—ne·glect′ful·ly** *adv.* **—ne·glect′ful·ness** *n.*
neg·li·gee also **neg·li·gée** (nĕg′lĭ-zhā′, nĕg′lĭ-zhā′) ▸ *n.* A woman's loose dressing gown.
neg·li·gence (nĕg′lĭ-jəns) ▸ *n.* 1. The state or quality of being negligent. 2. *Law* Failure to exercise the degree of care considered reasonable under the circumstances.
neg·li·gent (nĕg′lĭ-jənt) ▸ *adj.* 1. Marked by or inclined to neglect. 2. Careless or casual. 3. *Law* Guilty of negligence. **—neg′li·gent·ly** *adv.*
neg·li·gi·ble (nĕg′lĭ-jə-bəl) ▸ *adj.* Not worth considering; trifling. **—neg′li·gi·bil′i·ty** *n.* **—neg′li·gi·bly** *adv.*
ne·go·tia·ble (nĭ-gō′shə-bəl, -shē-ə-) ▸ *adj.* 1. Capable of being negotiated. 2. Transferable from one person to another by delivery or endorsement: *negotiable securities.* **—ne·go′tia·bil′i·ty** *n.*
ne·go·ti·ate (nĭ-gō′shē-āt′) ▸ *v.* **-at·ed, -at·ing.** 1. To confer with another in order to come to terms. 2. To arrange or settle by agreement: *negotiate a two-year contract.* 3. To transfer title to or ownership of (e.g., a promissory note) to another party in return for value received. 4. To succeed in coping with: *negotiate a sharp curve.* **—ne·go′ti·a′tion** *n.* **—ne·go′ti·a′tor** *n.*
ne·gri·tude or **Ne·gri·tude** (nē′grĭ-tōōd′, -tyōōd′, nĕg′rĭ-) ▸ *n.* Awareness of and pride in Black culture.
Ne·gro (nē′grō) ▸ *n., pl.* **-groes.** *Often Offensive* A Black person. **—Ne′gro** *adj.*
Ne·groid (nē′groid′) ▸ *adj. Anthro.* Of or being a human racial classification distinguished by brown to black pigmentation and often tightly curled hair and including peoples indigenous to sub-Saharan Africa. **—Ne′groid′** *n.*
Ne·he·mi·ah (nē′hə-mī′ə, nē′ə-) ▸ *n.* 1. A Hebrew leader of the 5th cent. B.C. 2. See **Bible** table in Appendix.
neigh (nā) ▸ *n.* The long, high-pitched sound made by a horse. **—neigh** *v.*
neigh·bor (nā′bər) ▸ *n.* 1. One that lives or is located near another. 2. A fellow human. ▸ *v.* 1. To lie close to or border on. 2. To live or be situated close by.
neigh·bor·hood (nā′bər-hŏŏd′) ▸ *n.* 1. A district or area with distinctive characteristics. 2. The people who live in

THESAURUS

need *n.* A condition in which something necessary or desirable is required or wanted ▸ exigence, exigency, necessity. *—See also* CONDITION (2), DEMAND (2), DUTY (1), POVERTY.
need *v.* To be without what is needed, required, or essential ▸ lack, require, want. [*Compare* DEMAND.] *—See also* DEMAND (1), MUST.
needful *adj.* *—See* ESSENTIAL (1).
neediness *n.* *—See* POVERTY.
needle *n.* *—See* SPIKE.
needle *v.* *—See* HARASS.
needless *adj.* *—See* UNNECESSARY.
needy *adj.* *—See* POOR.
ne'er-do-well *n.* *—See* WASTREL (2).
nefarious *adj.* *—See* OFFENSIVE (1).
negate *v.* *—See* ABOLISH, CANCEL (2), DENY.
negation *n.* *—See* ABOLITION, DENIAL (1).
negative *adj.* *—See* UNFAVORABLE (1).
negative *v.* *—See* DENY, VETO.
neglect *v.* 1. To fail to care for or give proper attention to ▸ be lax about, disregard, gloss over, ignore, let slide, let slip, pass over, slight. *Idioms:* lose sight (*or* track) of, lie down on the job, turn a blind eye to. 2. To fail to do or carry out ▸ disregard, fail (to do something), forget, ignore, omit, overlook, shirk. *Idioms:* leave undone, let slide, let slip, pass over. *—See also* SNUB.
neglect *n.* An act or instance of neglecting ▸ disregard, negligence, omission, oversight, slight. [*Compare* ERROR, NEGLIGENCE.] *—See also* FAILURE (2).
neglectful *adj.* *—See* NEGLIGENT.
negligence *n.* The state or quality of being negligent ▸ carelessness, forgetfulness, heedlessness, inattentiveness, laxity, laxness, remissness, slackness, sloppiness, thoughtlessness. [*Compare* ABANDON, APATHY, FAILURE.] *—See also* BREACH (1), NEGLECT.
negligent *adj.* Guilty of neglect; lacking due care or concern ▸ derelict, lax, neglectful, remiss, slack, slipshod, sloppy, unconcerned. [*Compare* CARELESS.]
negligibility *n.* *—See* TRIFLE.
negligible *adj.* *—See* REMOTE (2), TRIVIAL.
negotiable *adj.* *—See* PASSABLE.
negotiant *n.* *—See* GO-BETWEEN.
negotiate *v.* To pass by or over successfully ▸ clear, hurdle, surmount. *—See also* CONFER (1), HAGGLE, SETTLE (2).
negotiation *n.* The act or process of dealing with another to reach an agreement ▸ parley, talk. [*Compare* CONVERSATION.]
negotiator *n.* *—See* GO-BETWEEN.
neighbor *v.* *—See* ADJOIN.
neighborhood *n.* 1. An area in a city or town with distinctive characteristics ▸ area, community, district, quarter,

a particular district. 3. The surrounding area; vicinity. 4. *Informal* Approximate amount or range: *in the neighborhood of a million dollars.*

neigh·bor·ly (nā′bər-lē) ▸ *adj.* Having or exhibiting the qualities of a friendly neighbor. **—neigh′bor·li·ness** *n.*

Nei Mong·gol (nā′ mŏn′gōl′, mŏng′-) also **Inner Mongolia** ▸ An autonomous region of NE China.

nei·ther (nē′*th*ər, nī′-) ▸ *adj.* Not one or the other; not either: *Neither shoe feels comfortable.* ▸ *pron.* Not either one: *Neither of them fits.* ▸ *conj.* 1. Not either. Used with *nor*: *I got neither the gift nor the card.* 2. Also not: *If he won't go, neither will she.*

nel·son (nĕl′sən) ▸ *n.* A wrestling hold in which the user places an arm under the opponent's arm and presses the wrist or the palm of the hand against the opponent's neck.

Nelson, Horatio. Viscount Nelson (1758–1805) ▸ British admiral.

nem·a·tode (nĕm′ə-tōd′) ▸ *n.* Any of several often parasitic worms having unsegmented cylindrical bodies.

nem·e·sis (nĕm′ĭ-sĭs) ▸ *n., pl.* **-ses** (-sēz′). 1. A source of downfall or ruin. 2. An implacable or unbeatable foe. 3. One that inflicts just retribution; avenger. 4. **Nemesis** *Gk. Myth.* The goddess of retributive justice or vengeance.

neo– ▸ *pref.* New; recent: *Neolithic.*

ne·o·clas·si·cism also **Ne·o·clas·si·cism** (nē′ō-klăs′ĭ-sĭz′əm) ▸ *n.* A revival of classical aesthetics and forms, esp. in art, architecture, or music. **—ne′o·clas′sic, ne′o·clas′si·cal** *adj.* **—ne′o·clas′si·cist** *n.*

ne·o·dym·i·um (nē′ō-dĭm′ē-əm) ▸ *n. Symbol* **Nd** A bright, silvery rare-earth element used esp. for coloring glass. At. no. 60.

Ne·o·lith·ic (nē′ə-lĭth′ĭk) ▸ *adj.* Of or being the Stone Age period beginning in the Middle East around 10,000 B.C. marked by the development of agriculture and the making of polished stone implements. ▸ *n.* The Neolithic Period.

ne·ol·o·gism (nē-ŏl′ə-jĭz′əm) ▸ *n.* A new word, expression, or usage.

ne·on (nē′ŏn′) ▸ *n. Symbol* **Ne** A rare, inert gaseous element that glows red in an electric discharge and is used in display and television tubes. At. no. 10.

ne·o·nate (nē′ə-nāt′) ▸ *n.* A newborn infant. **—ne′o·na′tal** *adj.*

Ne·o-Pa·gan (nē′ō-pā′gən) ▸ *adj.* Of or relating to a religious movement combining worship of pagan nature deities, particularly of the earth, with benign witchcraft. ▸ *n.* An adherent of such a religion. **—Ne·o-Pa·gan·ism** *n.*

ne·o·phyte (nē′ə-fīt′) ▸ *n.* 1. A recent convert. 2. A beginner or novice.

ne·o·plasm (nē′ə-plăz′əm) ▸ *n.* An abnormal new growth of tissue; tumor. **—ne′o·plas′tic** *adj.*

ne·o·prene (nē′ə-prēn′) ▸ *n.* A tough synthetic rubber used esp. in weather-resistant products, adhesives, shoe soles, paints, and rocket fuels.

Ne·pal (nə-pôl′, -päl′, nā-) ▸ A country of central Asia in the Himalayas between India and SW China. **—Nep′al·ese′** (nĕp′ə-lēz′, -lēs′), **Ne·pal′i** *adj. & n.*

ne·pen·the (nĭ-pĕn′thē) ▸ *n.* 1. A legendary drug of ancient times, used as a remedy for grief. 2. Something that eases sorrow or pain.

neph·ew (nĕf′yo͞o) ▸ *n.* A son of one's brother or sister or of the brother or sister of one's spouse.

neph·rite (nĕf′rīt′) ▸ *n.* A white to dark green variety of jade.

ne·phrit·ic (nə-frĭt′ĭk) ▸ *adj.* 1. Of the kidneys. 2. Of or affected with nephritis.

ne·phri·tis (nə-frī′tĭs) ▸ *n.* Inflammation of the kidneys.

nephro– or **nephr–** ▸ *pref.* Kidney: *nephritis.*

nep·o·tism (nĕp′ə-tĭz′əm) ▸ *n.* Favoritism shown or patronage granted to relatives. **—nep′o·tist** *n.*

Nep·tune (nĕp′to͞on′, -tyo͞on′) ▸ *n.* 1. *Rom. Myth.* The god of the sea. 2. The 8th planet from the sun, at a mean distance of 4.5 billion km (2.8 billion mi) and with a mean radius of 24,000 km (15,000 mi). **—Nep·tu′ni·an** *adj.*

nep·tu·ni·um (nĕp-to͞o′nē-əm, -tyo͞o′-) ▸ *n. Symbol* **Np** A naturally radioactive metallic element found in trace quantities in uranium ores. At. no. 93.

nerd (nûrd) ▸ *n. Slang* An unpopular or socially inept person, esp. one regarded as excessively studious. **—nerd′y** *adj.*

Ne·ro (nîr′ō, nē′rō) (A.D. 37–68) ▸ Emperor of Rome (54–68).

nerve (nûrv) ▸ *n.* 1. Any of the cordlike bundles of fibers made up of neurons through which sensory stimuli and motor impulses pass between the central nervous system and other parts of the body. 2. The sensitive tissue in the pulp of a tooth. 3. A sore point: *The criticism touched a nerve.* 4a. Courage: *lost my nerve.* b. Fortitude; stamina. c. Brazen boldness; cheek. 5. **nerves** Nervous agitation caused by fear, anxiety, or stress. ▸ *v.* **nerved, nerv·ing.** To give strength or courage to.

nerve cell ▸ *n.* See **neuron.**

nerve center ▸ *n.* A source of power or control.

nerve gas ▸ *n.* A poisonous gas used in war that attacks the nervous system.

nerve·less (nûrv′lĭs) ▸ *adj.* 1. Lacking strength or energy. 2. Lacking courage. 3. Calm and controlled. **—nerve′less·ly** *adv.* **—nerve′less·ness** *n.*

nerve-rack·ing or **nerve-wrack·ing** (nûrv′răk′ĭng) ▸ *adj.* Intensely distressing.

nerv·ous (nûr′vəs) ▸ *adj.* 1. Of or affecting the nerves or nervous system. 2. High-strung; jumpy. 3. Uneasy; apprehensive. 4. Restless; lively: *nervous energy.* **—nerv′ous·ly** *adv.* **—nerv′ous·ness** *n.*

nervous breakdown ▸ *n.* An episode of severe or incapacitating emotional disorder.

nervous system ▸ *n.* The system of cells, tissues, and organs that regulates the body's responses to internal and external stimuli.

nerv·y (nûr′vē) ▸ *adj.* **-i·er, -i·est.** 1. Arrogantly impudent; brazen. 2. Bold; daring. 3. *Chiefly Brit.* Jumpy; nervous.

Ness (nĕs), **Loch** ▸ A lake of N-central Scotland.

–ness ▸ *suff.* State; quality; condition; degree: *brightness.*

nest (nĕst) ▸ *n.* 1a. A shelter made by a bird to hold its eggs and young. b. A similar structure built by fish, insects, or other animals. 2. A snug, cozy place. 3. A hotbed: *a nest of criminal activity.* 4. A set of objects that can be stacked together: *a nest of tables.* ▸ *v.* 1. To build or occupy a nest. 2. To fit or stack snugly together.

nest egg ▸ *n.* A reserve sum of money.

nes·tle (nĕs′əl) ▸ *v.* **-tled, -tling.** 1. To settle snugly and comfortably. 2. To lie in a sheltered location. 3. To snuggle. **—nes′tler** *n.*

nest·ling (nĕst′lĭng, nĕs′-) ▸ *n.* A bird too young to leave its nest.

net¹ (nĕt) ▸ *n.* 1. An openwork meshed fabric. 2. Something made of net, as a device used to capture animals or act as a barrier: *a fishing net; a mosquito net.* 3. A barrier strung between two posts to divide a court in half, as in tennis. 4. Something that entraps. ▸ *v.* **net·ted, net·ting.** To catch or ensnare in or as if in a net. **—net′ting** *n.*

net² (nĕt) ▸ *adj.* 1. Remaining after all deductions or adjustments have been made: *net profit.* 2. Ultimate; final:

THESAURUS

quarters, ward. *Slang:* 'hood. 2. *Informal* Approximate size or amount ▸ range, vicinity. *Slang:* ballpark. *—See also* AREA (2), ENVIRONMENT (1), LOCALITY.

neighboring *adj.* *—See* ADJOINING, CLOSE (1).

neighborly *adj.* *—See* AMIABLE, ATTENTIVE.

nemesis *n.* *—See* OPPONENT.

neonate *n.* *—See* BABY (1).

neophyte *n.* An entrant who has not yet taken the final vows of a religious order ▸ novice, novitiate, postulant. *—See also* BEGINNER.

nerd *n.* *—See* DRIP (2), FOOL.

nerve *n.* *—See* COURAGE, IMPUDENCE.

nerve *v.* *—See* ENCOURAGE (2).

nerviness *n.* *—See* IMPUDENCE.

nervous *adj.* *—See* ANXIOUS, EDGY.

nervousness *n.* *—See* ANXIETY (1), RESTLESSNESS.

nervy *adj.* *—See* BRAVE (1), IMPUDENT (1).

nescience *n.* *—See* IGNORANCE (1), IGNORANCE (2).

nescient *adj.* *—See* IGNORANT (1).

nest *n.* *—See* HOME (1).

nest egg *n.* *—See* HOARD.

nestle *v.* *—See* SNUGGLE.

net¹ *n.* *—See* BASKET (3), WEB.

net *v.* *—See* CAPTURE, CATCH (1).

net² *v.* *—See* RETURN (3).

the net result. ► *n.* A net amount. ► *v.* **net·ted, net·ting.** To bring in as profit.

Net ► *n.* The Internet.

neth·er (nĕ*th*′ər) ► *adj.* Located beneath or below.

Neth·er·lands (nĕ*th*′ər ləndz). Often called **Holland** ► A country of NW Europe on the North Sea. Caps. Amsterdam and The Hague.

Netherlands Antilles ► An autonomous territory of the Netherlands consisting of several islands in the Caribbean Sea. Cap. Willemstad.

net·i·quette (nĕt′ĭ-kĕt′, -kĭt) ► *n.* Etiquette advocated in communication over a computer network.

net·tle (nĕt′l) ► *n.* A plant with toothed leaves and stinging hairs. ► *v.* **-tled, -tling.** To irritate; vex. **—net′tle·some** *adj.*

net·work (nĕt′wûrk′) ► *n.* **1.** An openwork fabric or structure in which cords, threads, or wires cross at regular intervals. **2.** A complex, interconnected group or system: *a spy network.* **3.** A chain of radio or television broadcasting stations with shared or coordinated programming. **4.** A system of computers interconnected so as to share information. ► *v.* **1.** To interact with others for mutual assistance or support. **2.** *Comp. Sci.* To connect (computers) into a network.

neu·ral (no͝or′əl, nyo͝or′-) ► *adj.* Of or relating to a nerve or the nervous system.

neu·ral·gia (no͞o-răl′jə, nyo͞o-) ► *n.* Intense pain extending along a nerve. **—neu·ral′gic** *adj.*

neu·ras·the·ni·a (no͝or′əs-thē′nē-ə, nyo͝or′-) ► *n.* A neurotic disorder marked by chronic fatigue and weakness, loss of memory, and generalized aches and pains. **—neu′ras·then′ic** (-thĕn′ĭk) *adj. & n.*

neu·ri·tis (no͞o-rī′tĭs, nyo͞o-) ► *n.* Inflammation of a nerve. **—neu·rit′ic** (-rĭt′ĭk) *adj.*

neuro– or **neur–** ► *pref.* Nerve; nervous system: *neuritis.*

neu·rol·o·gy (no͞o-rŏl′ə-jē, nyo͞o-) ► *n.* The medical science that deals with the nervous system and disorders affecting it. **—neu′ro·log′ic** (no͝or′ə-lŏj′ĭk, nyo͝or′-), **neu′ro·log′i·cal** (-ĭ-kəl) *adj.* **—neu′ro·log′i·cal·ly** *adv.* **—neu·rol′o·gist** *n.*

neu·ron (no͝or′ŏn′, nyo͝or′-) also **neu·rone** (-ōn′) ► *n.* Any of the cells that make up the nervous system, consisting of a nucleated cell body with dendrites and a single axon. **—neu·ron′ic** *adj.*

neu·ro·sis (no͞o-rō′sĭs, nyo͞o-) ► *n., pl.* **-ses** (-sēz). Any of various mental or emotional disorders, such as hypochondria, not due to any organic cause.

neu·ro·sur·ger·y (no͝or′ō-sûr′jə-rē, nyo͝or′-) ► *n.* Surgery on a part of the nervous system. **—neu′ro·sur′geon** *n.*

neu·rot·ic (no͞o-rŏt′ĭk, nyo͞o-) ► *adj.* Of or affected with a neurosis. ► *n.* A neurotic person. **—neu·rot′i·cal·ly** *adv.*

neu·ro·trans·mit·ter (no͝or′ō-trăns′mĭt-ər, -trănz′-, nyo͝or′-) ► *n.* A chemical substance, such as dopamine, that transmits nerve impulses across a synapse.

neut. ► *abbr.* **1.** neuter **2.** neutral

neu·ter (no͞o′tər, nyo͞o′-) ► *adj.* **1.** *Gram.* Neither masculine nor feminine in gender. **2.** Having undeveloped sexual organs or parts. ► *n.* **1.** *Gram.* **a.** The neuter gender. **b.** A neuter word. **2.** A castrated or spayed animal. **3.** A sexually undeveloped insect, such as a worker bee. **4.** A plant without stamens or pistils. ► *v.* To castrate or spay.

neu·tral (no͞o′trəl, nyo͞o′-) ► *adj.* **1.** Not aligned with or supporting a side in a war, dispute, or contest. **2.** Belonging to neither kind or side. **3.** *Chem.* Neither acidic nor alkaline. **4.** *Phys.* Having a net electric charge of zero. **5.** Of or indicating a color that lacks hue; achromatic. ► *n.* **1.** A neutral nation or person. **2.** A neutral color. **3.** A position in which a set of gears is disengaged. **—neu′tral·ly** *adv.*

neutral ground ► *n.* See **median strip.**

neu·tral·ism (no͞o′trə-lĭz′əm, nyo͞o′-) ► *n.* Neutrality. **—neu′tral·ist** *adj. & n.*

neu·tral·i·ty (no͞o-trăl′ĭ-tē, nyo͞o-) ► *n.* The state or policy of being neutral, esp. in war.

neu·tral·ize (no͞o′trə-līz′, nyo͞o′-) ► *v.* **-ized, -iz·ing. 1.** To make neutral. **2.** To render ineffective. **—neu′tral·i·za′tion** *n.* **—neu′tral·iz′er** *n.*

neu·tri·no (no͞o-trē′nō, nyo͞o-) ► *n., pl.* **-nos.** Any of three electrically neutral elementary particles in the lepton family.

neu·tron (no͞o′trŏn′, nyo͞o′-) ► *n.* An electrically neutral subatomic particle, stable when bound in an atomic nucleus and having a mean lifetime of about 12 minutes as a free particle.

neutron bomb ► *n.* A nuclear bomb that would produce many neutrons but little blast and thus destroy life but spare property.

Nev. ► *abbr.* Nevada

Ne·vad·a (nə-văd′ə, -vä′də) ► A state of the W US. Cap. Carson City. **—Ne·vad′an, Ne·vad′i·an** *adj. & n.*

nev·er (nĕv′ər) ► *adv.* **1.** Not ever; at no time. **2.** Not at all; in no way.

nev·er·more (nĕv′ər-môr′) ► *adv.* Never again.

nev·er·the·less (nĕv′ər-*th*ə-lĕs′) ► *adv.* In spite of that; however.

ne·vus (nē′vəs) ► *n., pl.* **-vi** (-vī′). A congenital growth or mark on the skin, such as a mole.

new (no͞o, nyo͞o) ► *adj.* **-er, -est. 1.** Not old; recent. **2.** Never used or worn before: *a new car.* **3.** Just found or learned: *new information.* **4.** Unfamiliar. **5.** Different from the former or the old. **6.** Recently arrived or established: *a new president.* **7.** Rejuvenated. **8.** Currently fashionable. **9. New** In the most recent form, period, or development. ► *adv.* Freshly; recently. **—new′ness** *n.*

New Age ► *adj.* **1.** Relating to a complex of spiritual and consciousness-raising movements originating in the 1980s. **2.** Of or being a style of modern music marked esp. by quiet harmonies and drones.

New Amsterdam ► A settlement estab. by the Dutch on S Manhattan I. in 1624 and renamed New York after its capture by the English in 1664.

new·bie (no͞o′bē, nyo͞o′-) ► *n.* One that is new to something, esp. a novice at using computer technology or the Internet.

new·born (no͞o′bôrn′, nyo͞o′-) ► *adj.* **1.** Very recently born. **2.** Born anew. ► *n.* A neonate.

New Brunswick ► A province of E Canada on the Gulf of St. Lawrence. Cap. Fredericton.

new·com·er (no͞o′kŭm′ər, nyo͞o′-) ► *n.* One who has only recently arrived.

New Deal ► *n.* The programs and policies to promote economic recovery and social reform introduced in the 1930s by President Franklin Roosevelt. **—New Dealer** *n.*

New Delhi ► The capital of India, in the N-central part S of Delhi.

new·el (no͞o′əl, nyo͞o′-) ► *n.* **1.** A vertical support at the center of a circular staircase. **2.** A post for a handrail at the bottom or landing of a staircase.

New England ► A region of the NE US comprising ME,

THESAURUS

nethermost *adj.* —*See* BOTTOM.

netting *n.* —*See* WEB.

nettle *v.* —*See* ANNOY.

nettlesome *adj.* Full of irritating difficulties or controversies ► prickly, spiny, thorny. [*Compare* COMPLEX, DELICATE, DISTURBING, TROUBLESOME.] —*See also* DISTURBING.

network *n.* —*See* COMPLEX (1), WEB.

neurosis *n.* An exaggerated concern ► anxiety, complex, phobia. *Informal:* hang-up. [*Compare* ANXIETY, OBSESSION.]

neuter *adj.* —*See* NEUTRAL (1).

neuter *v.* —*See* STERILIZE (2).

neutral *adj.* **1.** Not inclining toward or actively taking either side in a matter under dispute ► impartial, neuter, nonaligned, nonpartisan, unbiased, uncommitted, uninvolved, unprejudiced. *Idiom:* on the fence. [*Compare* FAIR, RECEPTIVE.] **2.** Without definite or distinctive characteristics ► bland, colorless, indistinctive. [*Compare* BORING.] —*See also* COLD (2).

neutralize *v.* —*See* CANCEL (2).

never-ending *adj.* —*See* CONTINUAL, ENDLESS (2).

nevertheless *adv.* —*See* STILL (1).

new *adj.* Not the same as what was previously known or done ► brand new, different, fresh, innovative, inventive, newfangled, novel, original, unfamiliar, unprecedented. [*Compare* CONTEMPORARY, PROGRESSIVE.] —*See also* ADDITIONAL, INEXPERIENCED, PRESENT[1].

newborn *n.* —*See* BABY (1).

newcomer *n.* One that arrives ► arrival, comer, visitor. [*Compare* ADDITION, COMPANY.] —*See also* BEGINNER, FOREIGNER.

NH, VT, MA, CT, and RI. **—New Eng′land·er** *n.*
Newf. ▸ *abbr.* Newfoundland
new·fan·gled (no͞o′făng′gəld, nyo͞o′-) ▸ *adj.* New and often needlessly novel.
new·found (no͞o′found′, nyo͞o′-) ▸ *adj.* Recently discovered.
New·found·land and Labrador (no͞o′fən-lənd, -lănd′, -fənd-, nyo͞o′-) ▸ A province of E Canada including the island of **Newfoundland** and nearby islands and Labrador. Cap. St. John's. **—New′found·land·er** *n.*
New France ▸ The possessions of France in North America from the 16th cent. until the Treaty of Paris (1763), including much of SE Canada, the Great Lakes region, and the Mississippi Valley.
New Guinea ▸ An island in the SW Pacific N of Australia; divided politically between Indonesia and Papua New Guinea. **—New Guinean** *adj. & n.*
New Hamp·shire (hămp′shər, -shîr′, hăm′-) ▸ A state of the NE US between VT and ME. Cap. Concord. **—New Hamp′shir·ite′** *n.*
New Hebrides ▸ See **Vanuatu.**
New Jersey ▸ A state of the E-central US on the Atlantic. Cap. Trenton. **—New Jer′sey·ite′** *n.*
New Latin ▸ *n.* Latin as used since about 1500.
new·ly (no͞o′lē, nyo͞o′-) ▸ *adv.* **1.** Not long ago; recently. **2.** Once more; anew. **3.** In a new or different way; freshly.
new·ly·wed (no͞o′lē-wĕd′, nyo͞o′-) ▸ *n.* A person recently married.
new math ▸ *n.* Mathematics taught in elementary and secondary schools that is based on set theory.
New Mexico ▸ A state of the SW US on the Mexican border. Cap. Santa Fe. **—New Mexican** *adj. & n.*
new moon ▸ *n.* The phase of the moon occurring when it passes between the earth and the sun and is invisible or visible only as a thin crescent at sunset.
New Neth·er·land (nĕ*th*′ər-lənd) ▸ A Dutch colony in North America along the Hudson and lower Delaware rivers; renamed New York in 1664.
New Or·leans (no͞o ôr′lē-ənz, ôr′lənz, ôr-lēnz′, ô′lənz, nyo͞o, nô′lənz) ▸ A city of southeast LA on the Mississippi River.
news (no͞oz, nyo͞oz) ▸ *pl.n. (takes sing. v.)* **1a.** Information about recent events. **b.** A presentation of such information, as in a newspaper. **2.** New information of any kind.
news·cast (no͞oz′kăst′, nyo͞oz′-) ▸ *n.* A radio or television broadcast of the news. **—news′cast′er** *n.*
news·group (no͞oz′gro͞op′, nyo͞oz′-) ▸ *n.* An area on a computer network, esp. the Internet, devoted to discussion of a specified topic.
news·let·ter (no͞oz′lĕt′ər, nyo͞oz′-) ▸ *n.* A printed report giving news or information of interest to a special group.
New Spain ▸ The former Spanish possessions in the New World, including South America (except Brazil), Central America, Mexico, the West Indies, Florida, and much of the land W of the Mississippi R.
news·pa·per (no͞oz′pā′pər, nyo͞oz′-) ▸ *n.* **1.** A publication, usu. issued daily or weekly, containing current news, editorials, feature articles, and advertising. **2.** See **newsprint.** **—news′pa′per·man** *n.* **—news′pa′per·wom′an** *n.*
news·print (no͞oz′prĭnt′, nyo͞oz′-) ▸ *n.* Inexpensive paper used esp. for newspapers.
news·reel (no͞oz′rēl′, nyo͞oz′-) ▸ *n.* A short film dealing with recent events.
news·stand (no͞oz′stănd′, nyo͞oz′-) ▸ *n.* A stand at which newspapers and periodicals are sold.
news·wor·thy (no͞oz′wûr′*th*ē, nyo͞oz′-) ▸ *adj.* Interesting or important enough to warrant news coverage. **—news′wor′thi·ness** *n.*
news·y (no͞o′zē, nyo͞o′-) ▸ *adj.* **-i·er, -i·est.** *Informal* Full of news; informative.
newt (no͞ot, nyo͞ot) ▸ *n.* Any of several small semiaquatic salamanders.
New Testament ▸ *n.* The Gospels, Acts, Epistles, and the Book of Revelation. See **Bible** table in Appendix.
new·ton (no͞ot′n, nyo͞ot′n) ▸ *n.* A unit of force equal to the force needed to accelerate a mass of 1 kilogram 1 meter per second per second.
Newton, Sir **Isaac** (1642–1727) ▸ English mathematician and scientist. **—New·to′ni·an** *adj.*
New World ▸ The Western Hemisphere.
New Year's Day ▸ *n.* Jan. 1, the first day of the year in the Gregorian calendar, celebrated as a holiday in many countries.
New Year's Eve ▸ *n.* The eve of New Year's Day, celebrated with merrymaking.
New York ▸ **1.** A state of the NE US. Cap. Albany. **2.** or **New York City** A city of S NY at the mouth of the Hudson R. **—New York′er** *n.*
New Zea·land (zē′lənd) ▸ An island country in the S Pacific SE of Australia. **—New Zea′land·er** *n.*
next (nĕkst) ▸ *adj.* **1.** Nearest in space or position; adjacent. **2.** Immediately following, as in time or sequence. ▸ *adv.* **1.** In the time, order, or place nearest or immediately following. **2.** On the first subsequent occasion: *when next I write.* ▸ *n.* The next person or thing. ***—idiom:* next to 1.** Adjacent to. **2.** Almost; practically.
nex·us (nĕk′səs) ▸ *n., pl.* **-us** or **-us·es. 1.** A means of connection; link or tie. **2.** A connected series or group. **3.** The core or center.
Nez Perce (nĕz′ pûrs′, nĕs′) ▸ *n., pl.* **Nez Perce** or **-ces** (pûr′sĭz). **1.** A member of a Native American people inhabiting W Idaho and NE Washington. **2.** The language of the Nez Perce.
Nfld. ▸ *abbr.* Newfoundland
NGO ▸ *abbr.* nongovernmental organization
ngul·trum (əng-gŭl′trəm) ▸ *n.* See **currency** table in Appendix.
NH or **N.H.** ▸ *abbr.* New Hampshire
Ni ▸ The symbol for the element **nickel.**
ni·a·cin (nī′ə-sĭn) ▸ *n.* A white crystalline acid that is a component of the vitamin B complex.
Ni·ag·a·ra Falls (nī-ăg′rə, -ər-ə) ▸ Falls in the Niagara R. between W NY and Ontario, Canada.
nib (nĭb) ▸ *n.* The point of a pen.
nib·ble (nĭb′əl) ▸ *v.* **-bled, -bling. 1.** To bite at gently and repeatedly. **2.** To take small or hesitant bites. ▸ *n.* A morsel.
Nic·a·ra·gua (nĭk′ə-rä′gwə) ▸ A country of Central America on the Caribbean Sea and the Pacific. **—Ni′ca·ra′guan** *adj. & n.*
nice (nīs) ▸ *adj.* **nic·er, nic·est. 1.** Pleasing; agreeable. **2.** Pleasant; attractive. **3.** Courteous; polite. **4.** Of good character; respectable. **5.** Fastidious; fussy. **6.** Showing or requiring sensitive discernment; subtle. **7.** Done with skill. **—nice′ly** *adv.* **—nice′ness** *n.*
ni·ce·ty (nī′sĭ-tē) ▸ *n., pl.* **-ties. 1.** Precision or accuracy. **2.** Delicacy of character; scrupulousness. **3.** A fine point or subtle distinction. **4.** An elegant or refined feature.
niche (nĭch, nēsh) ▸ *n.* **1.** A recess in a wall, as for holding a statue. **2.** A situation or activity specially suited to one's interests or abilities.
Nich·o·las (nĭk′ə-ləs), Saint (4th cent. A.D.) ▸ Bishop of Myra in Asia Minor; often associated with Santa Claus.

THESAURUS

newfangled *adj.* —*See* NEW.
newly *adv.* —*See* LATELY.
newness *n.* —*See* INEXPERIENCE, NOVELTY (1).
news *n.* New information, especially about recent events and happenings ▸ advice, headline, information, intelligence, report, tidings, word. *Informal:* scoop. [*Compare* NOTICE.] —*See also* EVENT (1).
newscaster *n.* —*See* PRESS.
news flash *n.* —*See* ITEM.
newshound *n.* —*See* PRESS.
newsmonger *n.* —*See* GOSSIP (2).
newspaperman *n.* —*See* PRESS.
newspaperwoman *n.* —*See* PRESS.
newsperson *n.* —*See* PRESS.
next *adj.* —*See* ADJOINING, FOLLOWING (1).
next *adv.* —*See* LATER.
nexus *n.* —*See* BOND (2).
nib *n.* —*See* POINT (1).
nibble *v.* —*See* BROWSE (2), CHEW.
nice *adj.* —*See* APPROPRIATE, DELICATE (4), FINE[1] (2), FUSSY, GOOD (1), PLEASANT.
nicety *n.* —*See* DETAIL, RITUAL, SHADE (1).
niche *n.* The proper or designated location ▸ place. —*See also* CRACK (2), ENVIRONMENT (3), HABITAT.

Nicholas II (1868–1918) ▸ The last czar of Russia (1894–1917); executed.

nick (nĭk) ▸ *n.* A shallow notch, cut, or chip on an edge or surface. ▸ *v.* **1.** To cut a nick or notch in. **2.** To cut short; check. ***—idiom:*** **in the nick of time** Just at the critical moment.

nick·el (nĭk′əl) ▸ *n.* **1.** *Symbol* **Ni** A silvery, hard, ductile, ferromagnetic metallic element used in alloys, in corrosion-resistant surfaces and batteries, and for electroplating. At. no. 28. **2.** A US coin worth five cents.

nick·el·o·de·on (nĭk′ə-lō′dē-ən) ▸ *n.* **1.** An early movie theater charging an admission of five cents. **2.** A player piano. **3.** A jukebox.

nick·er (nĭk′ər) ▸ *v.* To neigh softly.

nick·name (nĭk′nām′) ▸ *n.* **1.** A descriptive name added to or replacing the actual name of a person, place, or thing. **2.** A familiar or shortened form of a proper name. ▸ *v.* To give a nickname to.

nic·o·tine (nĭk′ə-tēn′) ▸ *n.* A colorless, poisonous alkaloid, $C_{10}H_{14}N_2$, derived from the tobacco plant and used as an insecticide.

nic·o·tin·ic acid (nĭk′ə-tĭn′ĭk, -tē′nĭk) ▸ *n.* See **niacin.**

nic·ti·tate (nĭk′tĭ-tāt′) ▸ *v.* **-tat·ed, -tat·ing.** To wink. **—nic′ti·ta′tion** *n.*

niece (nēs) ▸ *n.* The daughter of one's brother or sister or of the brother or sister of one's spouse.

Nie·tzsche (nē′chə, -chē), **Friedrich Wilhelm** (1844–1900) ▸ German philosopher.

nif·ty (nĭf′tē) ▸ *adj.* **-ti·er, -ti·est.** *Slang* First-rate; great.

Ni·ger (nī′jər, nē-zhâr′) ▸ A country of W-central Africa.

Ni·ger-Con·go (nī′jər-kŏng′gō) ▸ *n.* A large language family of sub-Saharan Africa.

Ni·ge·ri·a (nī-jîr′ē-ə) ▸ A country of W Africa on the Gulf of Guinea. **—Ni·ge′ri·an** *adj. & n.*

Niger River ▸ A river of W Africa rising in Guinea and flowing about 4,183 km (2,600 mi) through Mali, Niger, and Nigeria to the Gulf of Guinea.

nig·gard (nĭg′ərd) ▸ *n.* A stingy person; miser. ▸ *adj.* Stingy; miserly.

nig·gard·ly (nĭg′ərd-lē) ▸ *adj.* **1.** Grudging and petty; stingy. **2.** Scanty; meager. **—nig′gard·li·ness** *n.* **—nig′gard·ly** *adv.*

nig·gling (nĭg′lĭng) ▸ *adj.* **1.** Petty; trifling: *niggling details.* **2.** Overly concerned with details; fussy. **—nig′gling·ly** *adv.*

nigh (nī) ▸ *adv.* **-er, -est. 1.** Near in time, place, or relationship. **2.** Nearly; almost: *talked for nigh onto two hours.* ▸ *adj.* **-er, -est.** Close; near. ▸ *prep.* Near.

night (nīt) ▸ *n.* **1.** The period between sunset and sunrise, esp. the hours of darkness. **2.** Nightfall. **3.** Darkness. **4.** A time or condition of gloom, obscurity, ignorance, or despair.

night blindness ▸ *n.* Abnormally weak vision at night or in dim light. **—night′blind′** *adj.*

night·cap (nīt′kăp′) ▸ *n.* **1.** A usu. alcoholic drink taken just before bedtime. **2.** A cloth cap worn esp. in bed.

night·clothes (nīt′klōz′, -klōthz′) ▸ *pl.n.* Clothes, such as pajamas, worn in bed.

night·club (nīt′klŭb′) ▸ *n.* An establishment that stays open late at night and provides food, drink, and entertainment.

night crawler ▸ *n.* An earthworm that crawls out from the ground at night.

night·dress (nīt′drĕs′) ▸ *n.* See **nightgown.**

night·fall (nīt′fôl′) ▸ *n.* The approach of night.

night·gown (nīt′goun′) ▸ *n.* A loose garment worn in bed by women and girls.

night·hawk (nīt′hôk′) ▸ *n.* **1.** An insectivorous, chiefly nocturnal bird having mottled grayish-brown feathers. **2.** *Informal* A night owl.

night·ie or **night·y** (nī′tē) ▸ *n., pl.* **-ies.** *Informal* A nightgown.

night·in·gale (nīt′n-gāl′, nī′tĭng-) ▸ *n.* A brownish European songbird noted for the melodious song of the male at night.

Nightingale, Florence (1820–1910) ▸ British nursing pioneer.

night·life (nīt′līf′) ▸ *n.* Social activities or entertainment available in the evening.

night·ly (nīt′lē) ▸ *adj.* Of or occurring during the night or every night. **—night′ly** *adv.*

night·mare (nīt′mâr′) ▸ *n.* **1.** An extremely frightening dream. **2.** An event or experience that is intensely distressing. **—night′mar′ish** *adj.*

night owl ▸ *n. Informal* A person who habitually stays up late at night.

night school ▸ *n.* A school that holds classes in the evening.

night·shade (nīt′shād′) ▸ *n.* Any of several related, sometimes poisonous plants, such as belladonna.

night·shirt (nīt′shûrt′) ▸ *n.* A long loose shirt worn in bed.

night·stick (nīt′stĭk′) ▸ *n.* A club carried by a police officer.

night·time (nīt′tīm′) ▸ *n.* The time between sunset and sunrise.

ni·hil·ism (nī′ə-lĭz′əm, nē′-) ▸ *n.* **1.** A doctrine holding that all values are baseless and that nothing can be known or communicated. **2.** The belief that destruction of existing political or social institutions is necessary for future improvement. **—ni′hil·ist** *n.* **—ni′hil·is′tic** *adj.*

-nik ▸ *suff.* One associated with or characterized by: *beatnik.*

Ni·ke (nī′kē) ▸ *n. Gk. Myth.* The goddess of victory.

nil (nĭl) ▸ *n.* Nothing; zero. **—nil** *adj.*

Nile (nīl) ▸ The longest river in the world, flowing about 6,677 km (4,150 mi) through E Africa from its sources in Burundi to a delta on the Mediterranean Sea in NE Egypt.

Ni·lo-Sa·har·an (nī′lō-sə-hăr′ən, -hä′rən) ▸ *n.* A language family of sub-Saharan Africa.

Ni·lot·ic (nī-lŏt′ĭk) ▸ *n.* A subfamily within the Nilo-Saharan languages.

nim·ble (nĭm′bəl) ▸ *adj.* **-bler, -blest. 1.** Quick and light in movement or action; deft. **2.** Quick and clever in devising or understanding. **—nim′ble·ness** *n.* **—nim′bly** *adv.*

nim·bus (nĭm′bəs) ▸ *n., pl.* **-bi** (-bī′) or **-es. 1.** A radiant light usu. in the form of a halo about or over the head in a representation, as of a deity or saint. **2.** A uniformly gray rain cloud.

NIMBY ▸ *abbr.* not in my backyard

nin·com·poop (nĭn′kəm-po͞op′, nĭng′-) ▸ *n.* A silly or foolish person.

nine (nīn) ▸ *n.* **1.** The cardinal number equal to 8 + 1. **2.** The 9th in a set or sequence. **—nine** *adj. & pron.*

nine·teen (nīn-tēn′) ▸ *n.* **1.** The cardinal number equal to 18 + 1. **2.** The 19th in a set or sequence. **—nine·teen′** *adj. & pron.*

nine·teenth (nīn-tēnth′) ▸ *n.* **1.** The ordinal number matching the number 19 in a series. **2.** One of 19 equal parts. **—nine·teenth′** *adv. & adj.*

nine·ti·eth (nīn′tē-ĭth) ▸ *n.* **1.** The ordinal number matching the number 90 in a series. **2.** One of 90 equal parts. **—nine′ti·eth** *adv. & adj.*

nine·ty (nīn′tē) ▸ *n., pl.* **-ties.** The cardinal number equal to 9 × 10. **—nine′ty** *adj. & pron.*

Nin·e·veh (nĭn′ə-və) ▸ An ancient city of Assyria on the Tigris R. opposite the site of present-day Mosul, Iraq

THESAURUS

nick *v.* —*See* CHEAT (1), CUT (1)
nick *n.* —*See* CUT (1), PRICK.
nickname *n.* —*See* NAME (1).
nickname *v.* —*See* NAME (1).
nictitate *v.* —*See* BLINK.
nictitation *n.* —*See* BLINK.
nifty *adj.* —*See* MARVELOUS.
niggard *n.* —*See* MISER.
niggard *adj.* —*See* STINGY.
niggardly *adj.* —*See* STINGY.
niggle *v.* —*See* NAG, QUIBBLE.
niggler *n.* —*See* CRITIC (2).
niggling *adj.* —*See* TRIVIAL.
niggling *n.* —*See* QUIBBLING.
nigh *adv.* —*See* CLOSE.
nigh *adj.* —*See* CLOSE (1).
night *n.* The period of time between sunset and sunrise ▸ after dark, after dinner, bedtime, dark, lights out, nighttime, P.M. *Idioms:* dark of night, hours of darkness, wee hours (of the night), witching hours. [*Compare* EVENING.]
night *adj.* Of or occurring during the night ▸ nightly, nocturnal.
nightclub *n.* *See* BAR (2).
nightfall *n.* —*See* EVENING.
nightly *adj.* Of or occurring during the night ▸ night, nocturnal.
nightmarish *adj.* —*See* HORRIBLE.
nighttime *n.* —*See* NIGHT.
nihility *n.* —*See* NOTHINGNESS (1).
nil *n.* —*See* NOTHING.
nimble *adj.* —*See* DEXTEROUS.
nimbleness *n.* —*See* AGILITY, DEXTERITY.
nimrod *n.* —*See* DRIP (2).
nincompoop *n.* —*See* DULLARD, FOOL.

nin·ja (nĭn′jə) ► *n., pl.* **-ja** or **-jas.** A 14th-cent. Japanese mercenary trained in the martial arts.

nin·ny (nĭn′ē) ► *n., pl.* **-nies.** A fool; simpleton.

ninth (nīnth) ► *n.* **1.** The ordinal number matching the number 9 in a series. **2.** One of nine equal parts. **—ninth** *adv. & adj.*

ni·o·bi·um (nī-ō′bē-əm) ► *n. Symbol* **Nb** A silvery, soft, ductile metallic element used in steel alloys, arc welding, and superconductivity research. At. no. 41.

nip[1] (nĭp) ► *v.* **nipped, nip·ping. 1.** To seize and pinch or bite. **2.** To sever by pinching or snipping. **3.** To sting with the cold. **4.** To check the growth or development of. **5.** *Slang* **a.** To snatch up hastily. **b.** To steal. ► *n.* **1.** A small pinch or bite. **2.** A small amount. **3.** Sharp stinging cold.

nip[2] (nĭp) ► *n.* A small amount of liquor. ► *v.* **nipped, nip·ping.** To sip (liquor) in small amounts.

nip·per (nĭp′ər) ► *n.* **1.** often **nippers** A tool, such as pliers, used for grasping or nipping. **2.** A pincerlike claw.

nip·ple (nĭp′əl) ► *n.* **1.** The small projection of a mammary gland containing the outlets of the milk ducts. **2.** Something resembling a nipple, esp. the rubber cap on a baby's bottle.

nip·py (nĭp′ē) ► *adj.* **-pi·er, -pi·est. 1.** Sharp or biting. **2.** Bitingly cold.

nir·va·na (nîr-vä′nə, nər-) ► *n.* **1.** often **Nirvana** *Buddhism* The ineffable ultimate in which one has attained disinterested wisdom and compassion. **2.** An ideal condition of harmony, stability, or joy.

Ni·san (nĭs′ən, nē-sän′) ► *n.* A month of the Jewish calendar.

Ni·sei (nē-sā′, nē′sā′) ► *n., pl.* **-sei** or **-seis.** A person born in America of parents who emigrated from Japan.

nit (nĭt) ► *n.* The egg or young of a parasitic insect, such as a louse. **—nit′ty** *adj.*

ni·ter (nī′tər) ► *n.* A white or gray mineral of potassium nitrate, used in making gunpowder.

nit·pick (nĭt′pĭk′) ► *v.* To be concerned with insignificant details. **—nit′pick′er** *n.*

ni·trate (nī′trāt′, -trĭt) ► *n.* **1.** The univalent radical NO_3 or a compound containing it, as a salt of nitric acid. **2.** Fertilizer consisting of sodium nitrate or potassium nitrate. ► *v.* **-trat·ed, -trat·ing.** To treat with nitric acid or a nitrate, usu. to change (an organic compound) into a nitrate. **—ni·tra′tion** *n.*

ni·tre (nī′tər) ► *n. Chiefly Brit.* Var. of **niter.**

ni·tric acid (nī′trĭk) ► *n.* A transparent, corrosive liquid, HNO_3, used in the production of fertilizers, explosives, and rocket fuels.

ni·tride (nī′trīd′) ► *n.* A compound containing nitrogen with another more electropositive element.

ni·tri·fy (nī′trə-fī′) ► *v.* **-fied, -fy·ing. 1.** To oxidize (an ammonia compound) into nitric or nitrous acids or salts, esp. by the action of nitrobacteria. **2.** To treat or combine with nitrogen or compounds containing nitrogen. **—ni′tri·fi·ca′tion** *n.*

ni·trite (nī′trīt′) ► *n.* The univalent radical NO_2 or a compound containing it.

nitro– or **nitr–** ► *pref.* **1.** Nitrate; niter: *nitric acid.* **2a.** Nitrogen: *nitrify.* **b.** Containing the univalent group NO_2: *nitrite.*

ni·tro·bac·te·ri·um (nī′trō-băk-tîr′ē-əm) ► *n., pl.* **-te·ri·a** (-tîr′ē-ə). Any of various soil bacteria that oxidize ammonium compounds into nitrites or nitrites into nitrates.

ni·tro·cel·lu·lose (nī′trō-sĕl′yə-lōs′, -lōz′) ► *n.* A cottonlike substance that is derived from cellulose treated with sulfuric and nitric acids and is used in explosives and plastics.

ni·tro·gen (nī′trə-jən) ► *n. Symbol* **N** A colorless, odorless, almost inert gaseous element that constitutes nearly four fifths of the air by volume. At. no. 7. **—ni·tric** (nī′trĭk) *adj.* **—ni·trog′e·nous** (nī-trŏj′ə-nəs) *adj.* **—ni·trous** (nī′trəs) *adj.*

ni·tro·glyc·er·in also **ni·tro·glyc·er·ine** (nī′trō-glĭs′ər-ĭn, -trə-) ► *n.* A thick, pale yellow, explosive liquid, used in dynamite and as a vasodilator in medicine.

ni·trous oxide (nī′trəs) ► *n.* A colorless, sweet-tasting gas, N_2O, used as a mild anesthetic.

nit·ty-grit·ty (nĭt′ē-grĭt′ē) ► *n. Informal* The specific or practical details.

nit·wit (nĭt′wĭt′) ► *n.* A stupid, silly person.

nix (nĭks) *Slang* ► *n.* Nothing. ► *adv.* No. ► *v.* To forbid; veto.

Nix·on (nĭk′sən), **Richard Milhous** (1913–94) ► The 37th US President (1969–74); resigned.

NJ or **N.J.** ► *abbr.* New Jersey

NM or **N.M.** ► *abbr.* New Mexico

NNE ► *abbr.* north-northeast

NNW ► *abbr.* north-northwest

no[1] (nō) ► *adv.* **1.** Used to express refusal, denial, disbelief, or disagreement. **2.** Not at all. Used with the comparative: *no better.* **3.** Not: *whether or no.* ► *n., pl.* **noes** (nōz). A negative response or vote.

no[2] (nō) ► *adj.* **1.** Not any; not one. **2.** Not at all: *He is no child.*

No[1] also **Noh** (nō) ► *n.* The classical drama of Japan, with elaborate costumes and highly stylized music and dance.

No[2] ► The symbol for the element **nobelium.**

no. ► *abbr.* number

No·ah (nō′ə) ► In the Bible, the patriarch who was chosen by God to build an ark to save human and animal life from a flood.

No·bel (nō-bĕl′), **Alfred Bernhard** (1833–96) ► Swedish chemist and philanthropist.

no·bel·i·um (nō-bĕl′ē-əm) ► *n. Symbol* **No** A radioactive element artificially produced in trace amounts. At. no. 102.

Nobel Prize ► *n.* Any of the international prizes awarded annually by the Nobel Foundation for outstanding achievements in physics, chemistry, physiology or medicine, literature, economics, and for the promotion of world peace. **—No·bel′ist** *n.*

no·bil·i·ty (nō-bĭl′ĭ-tē) ► *n., pl.* **-ties. 1.** A class of persons distinguished by high birth or rank. **2.** Noble rank or status. **3.** High moral character.

no·ble (nō′bəl) ► *adj.* **-bler, -blest. 1.** Of or belonging to the nobility. **2a.** Having or showing high moral character. **b.** Lofty; exalted: *a noble ideal.* **3.** Majestic; grand. **4.** *Chem.* Inert. ► *n.* A member of the nobility. **—no′ble·ness** *n.* **—no′bly** *adv.*

no·ble·man (nō′bəl-mən) ► *n.* A man of noble rank.

no·blesse o·blige (nō-blĕs′ ō-blēzh′) ► *n.* Benevolent, honorable behavior considered to be the duty of persons of high birth or rank.

no·ble·wom·an (nō′bəl-wo͝om′ən) ► *n.* A woman of noble rank.

no·bod·y (nō′bŏd′ē, -bŭd′ē, -bə-dē) ► *pron.* No person; not

THESAURUS

ninny *n.* —*See* FOOL.

nip[1] *v.* To try to bite something quickly or eagerly ► snap, snatch, strike. —*See also* BLAST (2), STEAL.

nip *n.* —*See* COLD.

nip[2] *n.* —*See* DROP (4).

nip *v.* —*See* BIT[1] (1), DRINK (2).

nip and tuck *adj.* **1.** Almost even ► tight. *Idiom:* neck and neck. **2.** Neither favorable nor unfavorable ► balanced, even, fifty-fifty.

nippy *adj.* —*See* COLD (1).

nitpick *v.* —*See* QUIBBLE.

nitpicker *n.* —*See* CRITIC (2).

nitpicking *n.* —*See* QUIBBLING.

nitty-gritty *n. Informal* Practical or basic details ► brass tacks, details, nuts and bolts, practicalities, specifics. [*Compare* DETAIL, HEART, ELEMENT.]

nitwit *n.* —*See* DULLARD, FOOL.

nix *n.* —*See* NOTHING.

nix *adv.* —*See* NO.

nix *v.* —*See* DECLINE, VETO.

no *adv.* Not so ► nay, not. *Informal:* nope, noway. *Slang:* negative, nix. *Idioms:* by no means, absolutely not, not at all, not on your life, nothing doing.

no *n.* **1.** A negative response ► nay, naysay, refusal, rejection, thumbs-down. *Slang:* no go. [*Compare* REFUSAL.] **2.** A negative vote or voter ► nay.

nobility *n.* Noble rank or status by birth ► birth, blood, blue blood, high blood, noble blood, noblesse, royalty. [*Compare* ANCESTRY, STATUS.] —*See also* SOCIETY (1).

noble *adj.* Of high birth or social position ► aristocratic, blue-blooded, elite, gentle, highborn, highbred, imperial, patrician, regal, royal, thoroughbred, titled, upper-class, wellborn. *Informal:* upper-crust. —*See also* ELEVATED (3), EXALTED, GRAND.

noblesse *n.* —*See* NOBILITY.

nobody *pron.* No person ► none, not anybody, not one, no one. *Idioms:* no one at all, not a soul.

anyone. ▸ *n., pl.* **-ies**. A person of no importance or influence.

no-brain·er (nō′brā′nər) ▸ *n. Informal* Something so simple as to require no thought.

noc·tur·nal (nŏk-tûr′nəl) ▸ *adj.* **1.** Of or occurring in the night. **2.** Most active at night: *nocturnal animals.* **—noc·tur′nal·ly** *adv.*

noc·turne (nŏk′tûrn′) ▸ *n.* **1.** A painting of a night scene. **2.** A musical composition of a pensive, dreamy mood, esp. one for the piano.

nod (nŏd) ▸ *v.* **nod·ded, nod·ding**. **1.** To lower and raise the head quickly, as in agreement or acknowledgment. **2.** To express with a nod: *nodded agreement.* **3.** To let the head fall forward when sleepy. **4.** To be momentarily inattentive. **5.** To sway or bend, as flowers in the wind. ▸ *n.* A nodding movement. **—nod′der** *n.*

node (nōd) ▸ *n.* **1.** A protuberance or swelling. **2a.** *Bot.* The point on a stem where a leaf is attached. **b.** See **knot** 7. **3.** *Phys.* A point or region of virtually zero amplitude in a periodic system. **—nod′al** *adj.*

nod·ule (nŏj′o͞ol) ▸ *n.* A small knotlike lump or growth. **—nod′u·lar** (nŏj′ə-lər) *adj.*

No·ël also **No·el** (nō-ĕl′) ▸ *n.* **1.** Christmas. **2. noël** also **noel** A Christmas carol.

no-fault (nō′fôlt′) ▸ *adj.* **1.** Of or indicating a system of motor vehicle insurance in which accident victims are compensated by their insurance companies without assignment of blame. **2.** Of or indicating a type of divorce in which blame is assigned to neither party.

no-fly zone (nō′flī′) ▸ *n.* Airspace in which certain, esp. military, aircraft are forbidden to fly.

nog·gin (nŏg′ĭn) ▸ *n.* **1.** A small mug or cup. **2.** A unit of liquid measure equal to ¼ pint. **3.** *Slang* The human head.

Noh (nō) ▸ *n.* Var. of **No**[1].

noise (noiz) ▸ *n.* **1a.** Sound or a sound that is loud, unpleasant, or unexpected. **b.** Sound of any kind. **2.** A loud outcry or commotion. **3.** *Phys.* A usu. persistent disturbance that obscures or reduces the clarity of a signal. ▸ *v.* **noised, nois·ing**. To spread the rumor or report of. **—noise′less** *adj.* **—noise′less·ly** *adv.* **—nois′i·ly** *adv.* **—nois′i·ness** *n.* **—nois′y** *adj.*

noise·mak·er (noiz′mā′kər) ▸ *n.* One that makes noise, esp. a device such as a horn used to make noise at a party.

noi·some (noi′səm) ▸ *adj.* **1.** Offensive; foul. **2.** Harmful or dangerous. **—noi′some·ly** *adv.* **—noi′some·ness** *n.*

no·lo con·ten·de·re (nō′lō kən-tĕn′də-rē) ▸ *n.* A plea made by the defendant in a criminal action that is equivalent to an admission of guilt but permits denial of the alleged facts in other proceedings.

no·mad (nō′măd′) ▸ *n.* **1.** A member of a group of people who have no fixed home and move or migrate from place to place. **2.** A wanderer. **—no·mad′ic** *adj.*

no man's land ▸ *n.* **1.** Land under dispute by two opposing entrenched armies. **2.** An area of uncertainty or ambiguity. **3.** An unclaimed or unowned piece of land.

nom de guerre (nŏm′ də gâr′) ▸ *n., pl.* **noms de guerre** (nŏm′). A fictitious name; pseudonym.

nom de plume (plo͞om′) ▸ *n., pl.* **noms de plume**. See **pen name.**

no·men·cla·ture (nō′mən-klā′chər, nō-mĕn′klə-) ▸ *n.* A system of names used in an art or science.

nom·i·nal (nŏm′ə-nəl) ▸ *adj.* **1.** Of or like a name or names. **2.** Existing in name only. **3.** *Gram.* Of or relating to a noun. **4.** Trifling: *a nominal sum.* **—nom′i·nal·ly** *adv.*

nom·i·nate (nŏm′ə-nāt′) ▸ *v.* **-nat·ed, -nat·ing**. **1.** To propose as a candidate, esp. for election. **2.** To name or appoint, as to an office. **—nom′i·na′tion** *n.* **—nom′i·na′tor** *n.*

nom·i·na·tive (nŏm′ə-nə-tĭv) ▸ *adj.* Of or belonging to a grammatical case that usu. indicates the subject of a verb. ▸ *n.* The nominative case.

nom·i·nee (nŏm′ə-nē′) ▸ *n.* One who has been nominated.

–nomy ▸ *suff.* A system of laws governing or a body of knowledge about a specified field: *astronomy.*

non– ▸ *pref.* Not: *nonfat.*

non·age (nŏn′ĭj, nō′nĭj) ▸ *n.* **1.** Legal minority. **2.** A period of immaturity.

non·a·ge·nar·i·an (nŏn′ə-jə-nâr′ē-ən, nō′nə-) ▸ *n.* A person between 90 and 100 years of age. **—non′a·ge·nar′i·an** *adj.*

non·a·gon (nŏn′ə-gŏn′, nō′nə-) ▸ *n.* A polygon with 9 sides.

non·a·ligned (nŏn′ə-līnd′) ▸ *adj.* Not allied with any other nation or bloc; neutral. **—non′a·lign′ment** *n.*

nonce (nŏns) ▸ *n.* The present or particular occasion: *for the nonce.*

non·cha·lant (nŏn′shə-länt′) ▸ *adj.* Seeming to be coolly unconcerned or indifferent. **—non′cha·lance′** *n.* **—non′cha·lant′ly** *adv.*

non·com (nŏn′kŏm′) ▸ *n. Informal* A noncommissioned officer.

non·com·bat·ant (nŏn′kəm-băt′nt, -kŏm′bə-tnt) ▸ *n.* **1.** A member of the armed forces whose duties lie outside combat. **2.** A civilian in wartime.

non·com·mis·sioned officer (nŏn′kə-mĭsh′ənd) ▸ *n.* An enlisted member of the armed forces, such as a corporal or sergeant, appointed to a rank over other enlisted personnel.

non·com·mit·tal (nŏn′kə-mĭt′l) ▸ *adj.* Refusing commitment to a particular opinion or course of action.

non com·pos men·tis (nŏn kŏm′pəs mĕn′tĭs) ▸ *adj. Law* Not of sound mind and hence not legally responsible.

non·con·duc·tor (nŏn′kən-dŭk′tər) ▸ *n.* A material that conducts little or no electricity, heat, or sound.

non·con·form·ist (nŏn′kən-fôr′mĭst) ▸ *n.* One who does not conform to accepted beliefs, customs, or practices. **—non′con·form′i·ty** *n.*

non·de·script (nŏn′dĭ-skrĭpt′) ▸ *adj.* Lacking distinctive qualities. **—non′de·script′** *n.*

none (nŭn) ▸ *pron.* **1.** No one; nobody. **2.** Not any. **3.** No part: *none of your business.* ▸ *adv.* Not at all; in no way.

non·en·ti·ty (nŏn-ĕn′tĭ-tē) ▸ *n., pl.* **-ties**. **1.** A person of no importance or significance. **2.** Something that does not

THESAURUS

nobody *n.* —*See* NONENTITY.

nocturnal *adj.* Of or occurring during the night ▸ night, nightly.

nod *v.* —*See* ASSENT, BOW[1] (1), NAP.

nod *n.* —*See* ACCEPTANCE (1), BOW[1], GESTURE, PERMISSION.

nodding *adj.* —*See* SLEEPY.

noddle *n.* —*See* HEAD (1).

node or **nodule** *n.* —*See* BUMP (1).

noggin *n.* —*See* HEAD (1).

no-good *adj.* —*See* WORTHLESS.

no-good *n.* —*See* WASTREL (2).

noise *n.* **1.** Sounds or a sound, especially when loud, confused, or disagreeable ▸ babel, cacophony, caterwaul, clamor, clangor, din, hubbub, hullabaloo, pandemonium, racket, row, rumpus, tumult, uproar. *Idiom:* hue and cry. [*Compare* DISORDER, SENSATION.] **2.** Vibrations detected by the ear ▸ sonance, sound. [*Compare* TONE.]

noise *v.* —*See* ANNOUNCE, GOSSIP.

noiseless *adj.* —*See* SILENT (1).

noiselessness *n.* —*See* SILENCE (1).

noisome *adj.* —*See* HARMFUL, SMELLY.

noisy *adj.* —*See* LOUD.

nomad *n.* —*See* HOBO.

nomadic *adj.* Leading the life of a person who does not have a fixed domicile; moving from place to place ▸ drifting, itinerant, peripatetic, roaming, roving, traveling, vagabond, vagrant, wayfaring, wandering. [*Compare* MIGRATORY, MOBILE.]

nominate *v.* —*See* APPOINT.

nomination *n.* —*See* APPOINTMENT, PROPOSAL (1).

nonaligned *adj.* —*See* NEUTRAL (1).

nonappearance *n.* —*See* ABSENCE (1).

nonassertive *adj.* —*See* SHY[1].

nonattendance *n.* —*See* ABSENCE (1).

nonattendant *adj.* —*See* ABSENT.

nonbeing *n.* —*See* NOTHINGNESS (1).

nonbeliever *n.* —*See* SKEPTIC.

nonchalance *n.* —*See* APATHY, BALANCE (2).

nonchalant *adj.* —*See* CALM, CARELESS.

noncombustible *adj.* —*See* FIREPROOF.

noncommittal *adj.* —*See* RESERVED.

noncompliance *n.* —*See* DEFIANCE (1).

noncompliant *adj.* —*See* UNRULY.

non compos mentis *adj.* —*See* INSANE.

nonconformist *n.* —*See* REBEL (2), SEPARATIST.

nonconformity *n.* —*See* DIFFERENCE.

nondescript *adj.* —*See* ORDINARY.

nondiscriminatory *adj.* —*See* FAIR[1] (1).

none *pron.* —*See* NOBODY.

nonentity *n.* A totally insignificant person ▸ cipher, lightweight, menial, nebbish, no-account, nobody, nonperson, nothing, obscurity, scrub, small fry, whippersnapper. *Informal:*

exist or that exists only in the imagination.

nones (nōnz) ▸ *pl.n.* In the ancient Roman calendar, the 7th day of March, May, July, or October and the 5th day of the other months.

none·such (nŭn′sŭch′) ▸ *n.* A person or thing without equal. **—none′such′** *adj.*

none·the·less (nŭn′*thə*-lĕs′) ▸ *adv.* Nevertheless; however.

non·e·vent (nŏn′ĭ-vĕnt′) ▸ *n. Informal* An anticipated event that does not occur or proves anticlimactic.

non·fat (nŏn′făt′) ▸ *adj.* Lacking fat solids or having the fat content removed.

non·fea·sance (nŏn-fē′zəns) ▸ *n. Law* Failure to perform an official duty or legal requirement.

no·nil·lion (nō-nĭl′yən) ▸ *n.* **1.** The cardinal number equal to 10^{30}. **2.** *Chiefly Brit.* The cardinal number equal to 10^{54}. **—no·nil′lion** *adj.* **—no·nil′lionth** *n. & adj.*

non·in·ter·ven·tion (nŏn′ĭn-tər-vĕn′shən) ▸ *n.* Failure or refusal to intervene, esp. in the affairs of another nation. **—non′in·ter·ven′tion·ist** *n.*

non·met·al (nŏn-mĕt′l) ▸ *n.* Any of a number of elements, such as oxygen or sulfur, that lack the properties of metals. **—non′me·tal′lic** (-mə-tăl′ĭk) *adj.*

no-no (nō′nō′) ▸ *n., pl.* **-noes.** *Informal* Something unacceptable or impermissible.

non·pa·reil (nŏn′pə-rĕl′) ▸ *adj.* Having no equal; peerless. ▸ *n.* **1.** One that has no equal. **2.** A small flat chocolate drop covered with white pellets of sugar.

non·per·son (nŏn-pûr′sən) ▸ *n.* A person whose obliteration from the memory of the public is sought, esp. for political reasons.

non·plus (nŏn-plŭs′) ▸ *v.* **-plussed, -plus·sing** also **-plused, -plus·ing.** To put at a loss; bewilder.

non·pro·lif·er·a·tion (nŏn′prə-lĭf′ə-rā′shən) ▸ *adj.* Of or calling for an end to the proliferation of nuclear weapons.

non·rep·re·sen·ta·tion·al (nŏn-rĕp′rĭ-zĕn-tā′shə-nəl) ▸ *adj.* Not representing natural objects realistically.

non·re·stric·tive (nŏn′rĭ-strĭk′tĭv) ▸ *adj. Gram.* Of or being a subordinate clause or phrase that describes but does not identify or restrict the meaning of the modified term.

non·self (nŏn-sĕlf′) ▸ *n.* That which the immune system identifies as foreign to the body.

non·sense (nŏn′sĕns′, -səns) ▸ *n.* **1.** Foolish or absurd language or behavior. **2.** Matter of little or no importance or use. **—non·sen′si·cal** *adj.* **—non·sen′si·cal·ly** *adv.*

non se·qui·tur (nŏn sĕk′wĭ-tər, -to͝or′) ▸ *n.* A statement that does not follow logically from what preceded it.

non·stan·dard also **non·stan·dard** (nŏn-stăn′dərd) ▸ *adj.* **1.** Varying from or not adhering to the standard. **2.** *Ling.* Associated with a language variety used by uneducated speakers or socially disfavored groups.

non·stop (nŏn′stŏp′) ▸ *adj.* Made or done without a stop. **—non′stop′** *adv.*

non·suit (nŏn-so͞ot′) ▸ *n.* A judgment against a plaintiff for failure to prosecute the case or to introduce sufficient evidence.

non·sup·port (nŏn′sə-pôrt′) ▸ *n.* Failure to provide for the maintenance of one's dependents.

non trop·po (nŏn trô′pō, nōn) ▸ *adv. & adj. Mus.* In moderation.

non·un·ion (nŏn-yo͞on′yən) ▸ *adj.* **1.** Not belonging to a labor union. **2.** Not recognizing a labor union or employing union members.

non·vi·o·lence (nŏn-vī′ə-ləns) ▸ *n.* The doctrine or practice of rejecting violence in favor of peaceful tactics as a means of gaining political objectives. **—non·vi′o·lent** *adj.* **—non·vi′o·lent·ly** *adv.*

non·white (nŏn′hwīt′, -wīt′) ▸ *n.* A person who is not white. **—non′white′** *adj.*

noo·dle[1] (no͞od′l) ▸ *n.* A narrow ribbonlike strip of dried dough, usu. made of flour, eggs, and water.

noo·dle[2] (no͞od′l) ▸ *n. Slang* The human head.

nook (no͝ok) ▸ *n.* **1.** A small corner or recess in a room. **2.** A hidden or secluded spot.

noon (no͞on) ▸ *n.* Twelve o'clock in the daytime; midday.

noon·day (no͞on′dā′) ▸ *n.* Midday; noon.

no one ▸ *pron.* No person; nobody.

noon·time (no͞on′tīm′) ▸ *n.* Noon.

noose (no͞os) ▸ *n.* A loop formed in a rope by a slipknot so that it binds tighter as the rope is pulled.

Noot·ka (no͞ot′kə, no͝ot′-) ▸ *n., pl.* **-ka** or **-kas. 1.** A member of a Native American people inhabiting Vancouver Island in British Columbia and an adjacent area in NW Washington. **2.** Their language.

no-par (nō′pär′) ▸ *adj.* Being without face or par value: *a no-par stock certificate.*

nope (nōp) ▸ *adv. Informal* No.

nor (nôr; nər *when unstressed*) ▸ *conj.* And not; or not; not either: *has neither phoned nor written us.*

Nor·dic (nôr′dĭk) ▸ *adj.* **1.** Scandinavian. **2.** Of a human physical type exemplified by the light-skinned, blond-haired peoples of Scandinavia. **3.** Of a ski competition featuring ski jumping and cross-country racing. **—Nor′dic** *n.*

Nor·gay (nôr′gā), **Tenzing** (1914–86) ▸ Sherpa guide; with Sir Edmund Hillary made the first ascent of Mount Everest (1953).

norm (nôrm) ▸ *n.* A standard, model, or pattern regarded as typical.

nor·mal (nôr′məl) ▸ *adj.* **1.** Conforming to a norm or standard; typical: *normal room temperature.* **2a.** Of average intelligence or development. **b.** Free from physical or emotional disorder. ▸ *n.* **1.** A norm. **2.** The usual state, amount, or degree. **—nor′mal·cy** *n.* **—nor·mal′i·ty** (-măl′ĭ-tē) *n.* **—nor′mal·ly** *adv.*

THESAURUS

pip-squeak, squirt, zero. *Slang:* punk, shrimp, small fish, twerp, zilch. *Idioms:* small potatoes, small fish in a big pond. [*Compare* DRIP, FOOL, SQUIRT.] *—See also* NOTHINGNESS (1).

nonessential *adj.* *—See* UNNECESSARY.

nonesuch *n.* A person or thing so excellent as to have no equal or match ▸ nonpareil, paragon, phoenix. [*Compare* BEST, CELEBRITY, MODEL.]

nonetheless *adv.* *—See* STILL (1).

nonevent *n.* *—See* DISAPPOINTMENT (2).

nonexistence *n.* *—See* NOTHINGNESS (1).

nonexistent *adj.* *—See* ABSENT.

nonfeasance *n.* *—See* BREACH (1), FAILURE (2).

nonflammable *adj.* *—See* FIREPROOF.

nonnative *adj.* *—See* FOREIGN (1).

no-nonsense *adj.* *—See* PRACTICAL, SERIOUS (1).

nonpareil *adj.* *—See* UNIQUE.

nonpareil *n.* A person or thing so excellent as to have no equal or match ▸ nonesuch, paragon, phoenix. [*Compare* BEST, CELEBRITY, MODEL.] *—See also* MODEL.

nonpartisan *adj.* *—See* FAIR[1] (1), NEUTRAL (1).

nonpartisanship *n.* *—See* FAIRNESS.

nonperformer *n.* *—See* FAILURE (1).

nonphysical *adj.* *—See* IMMATERIAL.

nonplus *v.* *—See* BAFFLE.

nonprofessional *n.* *—See* AMATEUR.

nonprofessional *adj.* *—See* AMATEURISH.

nonresident *n.* *—See* FOREIGNER.

nonresident *adj.* *—See* FOREIGN (1).

nonresistant *adj.* *—See* PASSIVE.

nonsense *n.* Something that does not have or make sense ▸ balderdash, blather, bunkum, claptrap, drivel, foolishness, garbage, hogwash, idiocy, piffle, poppycock, rigmarole, rot, rubbish, senselessness, silliness, tomfoolery, trash, twaddle. *Informal:* tommyrot. *Slang:* applesauce, baloney, bilge, bull, bunk, crap, hooey, malarkey. [*Compare* EMPTINESS, GIBBERISH.] *—See also* BABBLE, FOOLISHNESS, TRIFLE.

nonsensical *adj.* *—See* FOOLISH.

nonstop *adj.* *—See* CONTINUAL.

nonstop *adv.* *—See* CONTINUALLY.

nonuniform *adj.* *—See* IRREGULAR.

nonviolent *adj.* *—See* PEACEABLE.

noodle *n.* *—See* HEAD (1).

no one *pron.* *—See* NOBODY.

noose *n.* *—See* CORD, LOOP, TRAP (1).

nope *adv.* *—See* NO.

norm *n.* *—See* AVERAGE, STANDARD, USUAL.

normal *adj.* Mentally healthy ▸ compos mentis, lucid, rational, sane. *Idioms:* all there, in one's right mind, of sound mind. [*Compare* HEALTHY.] *—See also* COMMON (1), CONVENTIONAL, HEALTHY.

normalcy or **normality** *n.* *—See* USUALNESS.

nor·mal·ize (nôr′mə-līz′) ▸ *v.* **-ized, -iz·ing.** To make normal or regular. **—nor′mal·i·za′tion** *n.* **—nor′mal·iz′er** *n.*

normal school ▸ *n.* A school that trains teachers, chiefly for the elementary grades.

Nor·man (nôr′mən) ▸ *n.* **1a.** A member of a Scandinavian people who settled in N France in the 10th cent. **b.** A member of a people of Norman and French blood who invaded England in 1066. **2.** A native or inhabitant of Normandy. **—Nor′man** *adj.*

Nor·man·dy (nôr′mən-dē) ▸ A historical region and former province of NW France on the English Channel.

Norman French ▸ *n.* The dialect of Old French used in medieval Normandy.

nor·ma·tive (nôr′mə-tĭv) ▸ *adj.* Of or prescribing a norm or standard. **—nor′ma·tive·ly** *adv.* **—nor′ma·tive·ness** *n.*

Norse (nôrs) ▸ *adj.* **1.** Of or relating to medieval Scandinavia. **2.** Norwegian. **3.** Of or relating to the branch of the Germanic languages that includes Norwegian, Icelandic, and Faeroese. **—Norse** *n.*

Norse·man (nôrs′mən) ▸ *n.* A member of any of the peoples of medieval Scandinavia.

north (nôrth) ▸ *n.* **1a.** The direction along a meridian 90° counterclockwise from east. **b.** The compass point located at 0°. **2.** often **North a.** The northern part of the earth. **b.** The northern part of a region or country. ▸ *adj.* **1.** To, toward, of, or in the north. **2.** Coming from the north: *a north wind.* ▸ *adv.* In, from, or toward the north. **—north′ward** *adj. & adv.* **—north′ward·ly** *adj. & adv.* **—north′wards** *adv.*

North Africa ▸ A region of N Africa usu. considered to include Morocco, Algeria, Tunisia, and Libya. **—North African** *adj. & n.*

North America ▸ The N continent of the Western Hemisphere, extending northward from the Colombia-Panama border and including Central America, Mexico, the islands of the Caribbean Sea, the US, Canada, the Arctic Archipelago, and Greenland. **—North American** *adj. & n.*

North Car·o·li·na (kăr′ə-lī′nə) ▸ A state of the SE US bordering on the Atlantic. Cap. Raleigh. **—North Car·o·lin′i·an** (-lĭn′ē-ən) *adj. & n.*

North Dakota ▸ A state of the N-central US bordering on Canada. Cap. Bismarck. **—North Dakotan** *adj. & n.*

north·east (nôrth-ēst′, nôr-ēst′) ▸ *n.* **1.** The direction halfway between due north and due east. **2.** An area or region lying in the northeast. **—north·east′** *adj. & adv.* **—north·east′er·ly** *adj. & adv.* **—north·east′ern** *adj.* **—north·east′ward** *adj. & adv.* **—north·east′ward·ly** *adj. & adv.* **—north·east′wards** *adv.*

north·east·er (nôrth-ē′stər, nôr-ē′-) ▸ *n.* A storm or gale blowing from the northeast.

north·er·ly (nôr′*th*ər-lē) ▸ *adj.* **1.** In or toward the north. **2.** Coming from the north: *northerly winds.* **—north′er·ly** *adv.*

north·ern (nôr′*th*ərn) ▸ *adj.* **1.** Of, in, or toward the north. **2.** From the north: *northern breezes.*

north·ern·er also **North·ern·er** (nôr′*th*ər-nər) ▸ *n.* A native or inhabitant of a northern region.

Northern Hemisphere ▸ *n.* The half of the earth north of the equator.

Northern Ireland ▸ A division of the United Kingdom in the NE section of the island of Ireland. Cap. Belfast.

northern lights ▸ *pl.n.* See **aurora borealis.**

Northern Mariana Islands ▸ See **Mariana Islands.**

North Korea ▸ A country of NE Asia on the Korean Peninsula. **—North Korean** *adj. & n.*

North Pole ▸ *n.* **1.** The northern end of the earth's axis of rotation. **2.** The celestial zenith of the heavens as viewed from the south terrestrial pole.

North Sea ▸ An arm of the Atlantic between Great Britain and NW Europe.

North Star ▸ *n.* See **Polaris.**

North Vietnam ▸ A former country (1954–75) of SE Asia; now part of Vietnam. **—North Vietnamese** *adj. & n.*

north·west (nôrth-wĕst′, nôr-wĕst′) ▸ *n.* **1.** The direction halfway between due north and due west. **2.** An area or region lying in the northwest. **—north·west′** *adj. & adv.* **—north·west′er·ly** *adj. & adv.* **—north·west′ern** *adj.* **—north·west′ward** *adj. & adv.* **—north·west′ward·ly** *adj. & adv.* **—north·west′wards** *adv.*

Northwest Passage ▸ A water route from the Atlantic to the Pacific through the Arctic Archipelago of N Canada and along the N coast of AK.

Northwest Territories ▸ A territory of N Canada between Yukon Territory and Nunavut including islands of the W Arctic Archipelago. Cap. Yellowknife.

Northwest Territory ▸ A historical region of the N-central US from the Ohio and Mississippi rivers to the Great Lakes.

Nor·way (nôr′wā′) ▸ A country of N Europe in the W part of the Scandinavian Peninsula.

Nor·we·gian (nôr-wē′jən) ▸ *n.* **1.** A native or inhabitant of Norway. **2.** Either of the Germanic languages of the Norwegians. **—Nor·we′gian** *adj.*

nos. or **Nos.** ▸ *abbr.* numbers

nose (nōz) ▸ *n.* **1.** The part of the face that contains the nostrils and organs of smell and forms the beginning of the respiratory tract. **2.** The sense of smell. **3.** The ability to detect, as if by smell: *has a nose for gossip.* **4.** Something, such as the forward end of an aircraft, that resembles a nose. ▸ *v.* **nosed, nos·ing.** **1.** To find out by or as if by smell. **2.** To touch with the nose; nuzzle. **3.** To move or advance carefully. **4.** *Informal* To snoop or pry. ***—idioms:*** **on the nose** Exactly; precisely. **under (someone's) nose** In plain view.

nose·bleed (nōz′blēd′) ▸ *n.* Bleeding from the nose.

nose cone ▸ *n.* The forwardmost, usu. separable section of a rocket or guided missile.

nose·dive (nōz′dīv′) ▸ *n.* **1.** A very steep dive of an aircraft. **2.** A sudden plunge. **—nose′-dive′** *v.*

nose·gay (nōz′gā′) ▸ *n.* A small bouquet of flowers.

nosh (nŏsh) ▸ *v.* *Informal* To eat a snack or light meal. **—nosh** *n.* **—nosh′er** *n.*

nos·tal·gi·a (nŏ-stăl′jə, nə-) ▸ *n.* **1.** A bittersweet longing for the past. **2.** Homesickness. **—nos·tal′gic** *adj.* **—nos·tal′gi·cal·ly** *adv.*

nos·tril (nŏs′trəl) ▸ *n.* Either of the external openings of the nose.

nos·trum (nŏs′trəm) ▸ *n.* A quack medicine or remedy.

nos·y or **nos·ey** (nō′zē) ▸ *adj.* **-i·er, -i·est.** *Informal* Prying; inquisitive. **—nos′i·ly** *adv.* **—nos′i·ness** *n.*

not (nŏt) ▸ *adv.* In no way; to no degree. Used to express negation, denial, refusal, or prohibition: *I will not go. You may not have any.*

no·ta be·ne (nō′tə bĕn′ē, bē′nē) ▸ Used to direct attention to something particularly important.

no·ta·ble (no′tə-bəl) ▸ *adj.* **1.** Worthy of note or notice; remarkable. **2.** Distinguished; eminent. ▸ *n.* A person of distinction. **—no′ta·bil′i·ty** *n.* **—no′ta·bly** *adv.*

no·ta·rize (nō′tə-rīz′) ▸ *v.* **-rized, -riz·ing.** To certify or attest to as a notary public. **—no′ta·ri·za′tion** *n.*

no·ta·ry (nō′tə-rē) ▸ *n., pl.* **-ries.** A notary public.

notary public ▸ *n., pl.* **notaries public.** A person legally em-

THESAURUS

normalize *v.* —*See* CONVENTIONALIZE.

normally *adv.* —*See* USUALLY.

nose *n.* **1.** The human organ of smell ▸ proboscis. *Informal:* beak, snoot. *Slang:* honker, nozzle, schnoz, schnozzle, smeller, sniffer, snout. **2.** The sense by which odors are perceived ▸ olfaction, scent, smell. —*See also* DISCERNMENT.

nose *v. Informal* To look into or inquire about curiously, inquisitively, or in a meddlesome fashion ▸ poke, pry, snoop. *Informal:* sniff about (*or* around). *Idiom:* stick one's nose into. [*Compare* MEDDLE.] —*See also* SMELL (1).

nose out *v.* —*See* TRACE (1).

nosedive *n.* —*See* FALL (1), FALL (3).

nose-dive *v.* —*See* FALL (1), FALL (4).

nosegay *n.* —*See* BOUQUET.

nosey *adj. See* NOSY.

nosh *n.* —*See* REFRESHMENT.

nosiness *n.* —*See* CURIOSITY (2).

nostrum *n.* —*See* CURE.

nosy or **nosey** *adj.* —*See* CURIOUS (1).

not *adv.* —*See* NO.

notability *n.* —*See* DIGNITARY, FAME.

notable *adj.* —*See* EXCEPTIONAL, FAMOUS.

notable *n.* —*See* CELEBRITY, DIGNITARY.

notably *adv.* —*See* VERY.

powered to witness and certify the validity of documents and to take affidavits and depositions.

no·ta·tion (nō-tā′shən) ▸ *n.* **1a.** A system of figures or symbols used to represent numbers, quantities, tones, or values. **b.** The act or process of using such a system. **2.** A brief note; annotation.

notch (nŏch) ▸ *n.* **1.** A V-shaped cut. **2.** A narrow pass between mountains. **3.** *Informal* A level or degree. ▸ *v.* **1.** To cut a notch in. **2.** To record by or as if by making notches.

note (nōt) ▸ *n.* **1.** A brief written record. **2.** A brief informal letter. **3.** A formal written diplomatic or official communication. **4.** A comment or explanation, as on a passage in a text. **5a.** A piece of paper currency. **b.** A promissory note. **6.** *Mus.* **a.** A tone of definite pitch. **b.** A symbol for such a tone. **7.** The vocal sound made by a songbird or other animal. **8.** The sign of a particular quality or emotion: *a note of despair.* **9.** Importance; consequence. **10.** Notice; observation: *took note of the scene.* ▸ *v.* **not·ed, not·ing. 1.** To observe carefully; notice. **2.** To make a note of; write down. **3.** To make mention of; remark.

note·book (nōt′bo͝ok′) ▸ *n.* **1.** A book of blank pages for notes. **2.** A portable computer, gen. thinner than a laptop.

not·ed (nō′tĭd) ▸ *adj.* Well-known; famous.

note·wor·thy (nōt′wûr′thē) ▸ *adj.* Deserving notice or attention; notable. **—note′wor′thi·ness** *n.*

noth·ing (nŭth′ĭng) ▸ *pron.* **1.** No thing; not anything. **2.** No part; no portion: *Nothing remains of the old house.* **3.** One of no consequence or interest. ▸ *n.* **1.** Absence of anything perceptible; nonexistence. **2.** Zero. **3.** A nonentity. ▸ *adv.* Not at all: *She looks nothing like me.*

noth·ing·ness (nŭth′ĭng-nĭs) ▸ *n.* **1.** The condition or quality of being nothing; nonexistence. **2.** Empty space; void.

no·tice (nō′tĭs) ▸ *n.* **1.** Observation; attention. **2.** Respectful attention or consideration. **3.** A written or printed announcement. **4.** A formal announcement or warning. **5.** A critical review. ▸ *v.* **-ticed, -tic·ing. 1.** To observe. **2.** To comment on.

no·tice·a·ble (nō′tĭ-sə-bəl) ▸ *adj.* **1.** Evident; observable. **2.** Worthy of notice; significant. **—no′tice·a·bly** *adv.*

no·ti·fy (nō′tə-fī′) ▸ *v.* **-fied, -fy·ing. 1.** To give notice to; inform. **2.** *Chiefly Brit.* To make known; proclaim. **—no′ti·fi·ca′tion** *n.* **—no′ti·fi′er** *n.*

no·tion (nō′shən) ▸ *n.* **1.** A belief or opinion. **2.** An idea or conception. **3.** A fanciful impulse; whim. **4. notions** Small lightweight items for household use, such as needles, buttons, and thread. **—no′tion·al** *adj.*

no·to·ri·ous (nō-tôr′ē-əs) ▸ *adj.* Known widely and usu. unfavorably; infamous. **—no′to·ri′e·ty** (-tə-rī′ĭ-tē) *n.* **—no·to′ri·ous·ly** *adv.*

not·with·stand·ing (nŏt′wĭth-stănd′ĭng, -wĭth-) ▸ *prep.* In spite of. ▸ *adv.* All the same; nevertheless. ▸ *conj.* Although.

nou·gat (no͞o′gət) ▸ *n.* A candy made from a sugar or honey paste and nuts.

nought (nôt) ▸ *n.* Var. of **naught.**

noun (noun) ▸ *n.* A word used to name a person, place, thing, quality, or action.

nour·ish (nûr′ĭsh, nŭr′-) ▸ *v.* **1.** To provide with food or other substances necessary for life and growth. **2.** To foster the development of; promote. **—nour′ish·ing** *adj.* **—nour′ish·ment** *n.*

nou·veau riche (no͞o′vō rēsh′) ▸ *n., pl.* **nou·veaux riches** (no͞o′vō rēsh′). One who has recently become rich.

Nov. ▸ *abbr.* November

no·va (nō′və) ▸ *n., pl.* **-vae** (-vē) or **-vas.** A star that suddenly becomes much brighter and then returns to its original brightness over a period of weeks to years.

Nova Sco·tia (skō′shə) ▸ A province of E Canada comprising a mainland peninsula and the adjacent Cape Breton I. Cap. Halifax. **—No′va Sco′tian** *adj. & n.*

nov·el[1] (nŏv′əl) ▸ *n.* A fictional prose narrative of considerable length, typically having a plot that is unfolded by the actions, speech, and thoughts of the characters. **—nov′el·is′tic** *adj.*

nov·el[2] (nŏv′əl) ▸ *adj.* Strikingly new, unusual, or different. **—nov′el·ly** *adv.*

nov·el·ette (nŏv′ə-lĕt′) ▸ *n.* A short novel.

nov·el·ist (nŏv′ə-lĭst) ▸ *n.* A writer of novels.

nov·el·ize (nŏv′ə-līz′) ▸ *v.* **-ized, -iz·ing.** To convert into a novelistic format. **—nov′el·i·za′tion** *n.*

no·vel·la (nō-vĕl′ə) ▸ *n.* A short novel.

nov·el·ty (nŏv′əl-tē) ▸ *n., pl.* **-ties. 1.** The quality of being novel; newness. **2.** Something new and unusual. **3.** A small mass-produced article, such as a trinket.

No·vem·ber (nō-vĕm′bər) ▸ *n.* The 11th month of the Gregorian calendar.

THESAURUS

notation *n.* —*See* NOTE.

notch *n.* *Informal* One of the units in a course, as on an ascending or descending scale ▸ degree, grade, level, peg, point, rung, stage, step. —*See also* CUT (1), DEGREE (1), PRICK.

notch *v.* *Informal* To gain a point or points in a game or contest ▸ post, score, tally. ***Idiom:*** make a goal (*or* point). —*See also* CUT (1).

notched *adj.* —*See* SAW-TOOTHED.

note *n.* A brief record written as an aid to the memory ▸ jotting, memorandum, notation, reminder. *Informal:* memo. —*See also* COMMENT, COMMENTARY, ENTRY, FAME, LETTER, NOTICE (1), SIGN (1).

note *v.* —*See* COMMENT, NOTICE, REFER (1).

noted *adj.* —*See* FAMOUS.

noteworthy *adj.* —*See* EXCEPTIONAL.

nothing *n.* No thing; not anything ▸ naught, nil, null. *Informal:* zero. *Slang:* diddly-squat, goose egg, nix, squat, zilch. —*See also* NONENTITY, NOTHINGNESS (1).

nothing *adj.* —*See* WORTHLESS.

nothingness *n.* **1.** The condition or quality of not existing ▸ nihility, nonbeing, nonentity, nonexistence, nonsubsistence, nothing, nullity. **2.** Empty, unfilled space ▸ barrenness, blankness, emptiness, vacancy, vacuity, vacuum, void. [*Compare* DEEP.]

notice *n.* **1.** The act of noting, observing, or taking into account ▸ attention, cognizance, espial, heed, looking, mark, note, observance, observation, regard, remark, seeing, viewing, watching, witnessing. **2.** An announcement distributed on paper to a large number of people ▸ circular, flier, handbill, leaflet. **3.** A report giving information ▸ advisory, bulletin. [*Compare* REPORT, WARNING.] —*See also* COMMENTARY, ITEM, MESSAGE, SIGN (2).

notice *v.* To perceive with a special effort of the senses or the mind ▸ descry, detect, discern, distinguish, mark, mind, note, observe, recognize, remark, see. [*Compare* DISCOVER, SEE.]

noticeable *adj.* Readily attracting notice ▸ arresting, bold, commanding, conspicuous, distinguished, eminent, eye-catching, impressive, marked, observable, outstanding, pointed, prominent, pronounced, remarkable, salient, signal, striking, undisguised. ***Idiom:*** sticking out like a sore thumb. [*Compare* EXCEPTIONAL, OBVIOUS.] —*See also* APPARENT (1), PERCEPTIBLE.

notification *n.* —*See* ANNOUNCEMENT, MESSAGE.

notify *v.* —*See* INFORM (1).

notion *n.* —*See* BELIEF (1), FANCY, FEELING (1), IDEA.

notoriety *n.* Unfavorable, usually unsavory renown ▸ disrepute, ill fame, ill repute, infamousness, infamy, notoriousness. —*See also* FAME.

notorious *adj.* Known widely and unfavorably ▸ common, disreputable, ill-famed, ill-reputed, infamous. [*Compare* EVIL, SHADY.] —*See also* FAMOUS.

nourish *v.* To sustain a living organism with food ▸ feast, feed, regale. ***Idiom:*** wine and dine. [*Compare* SUPPORT.] —*See also* BEAR (2), NURTURE, PROMOTE (2).

nourishing *adj.* —*See* NUTRITIOUS.

nourishment *n.* —*See* FOOD.

novel *adj.* —*See* NEW, UNUSUAL.

novel *n.* A narrative not based on fact ▸ fiction, fable, romance, story. [*Compare* YARN.]

novelty *n.* **1.** The quality of being novel ▸ freshness, imaginativeness, innovativeness, newfangledness, newness, originality, rareness, rarity, recentness, strangeness, uncommonness, uniqueness, unusualness. **2.** A new and unusual thing ▸ innovation. ***Idioms:*** the latest craze (*or* fashion *or* thing), the in thing, whole new ball of wax. **3.** A small showy article ▸ bauble, bibelot, bric-a-brac, curio, gewgaw, gimcrack, gimmick, knickknack, toy, trifle, trinket, whatnot. *Slang:* chachka. [*Compare* GADGET, REMEMBRANCE.]

no·ve·na (nō-vē′nə) ▸ *n. Rom. Cath. Ch.* A recitation of devotions for nine consecutive days.
nov·ice (nŏv′ĭs) ▸ *n.* **1.** A beginner. **2.** One who has entered a religious order but has not yet taken vows.
no·vi·ti·ate (nō-vĭsh′ē-ĭt, -āt′) ▸ *n.* **1.** The period of being a religious novice. **2.** A place where novices live. **3.** See **novice** 2.
No·vo·cain (nō′və-kān′) ▸ A trademark for an anesthetic preparation of procaine.
now (nou) ▸ *adv.* **1.** At the present time. **2.** At once: *Stop now.* **3.** Very recently: *left the room just now.* **4.** At this point in the series of events; then. **5.** In these circumstances; as things are. **6.** Used to introduce a command, reproof, or request: *Now pay attention.* ▸ *conj.* Seeing that; since. ▸ *n.* The present time or moment. ▸ *adj.* **1.** Current. **2.** *Slang* Fashionable; trendy.
now·a·days (nou′ə-dāz′) ▸ *adv.* During the present time; now.
no·way (nō′wā′) also **no·ways** (-wāz′) ▸ *adv. Informal* Nowise.
no·where (nō′hwâr′, -wâr′) ▸ *adv.* **1.** Not anywhere. **2.** To no place or result. ▸ *n.* A remote or unknown place.
no·wise (nō′wīz′) ▸ *adv.* In no way, manner, or degree; not at all.
nox·ious (nŏk′shəs) ▸ *adj.* Injurious to health or morals. **—nox′ious·ly** *adv.*
noz·zle (nŏz′əl) ▸ *n.* A projecting part with an opening for regulating a flow of fluid.
Np ▸ The symbol for the element **neptunium**.
NS also **N.S.** ▸ *abbr.* Nova Scotia
NT ▸ *abbr.* **1.** New Testament **2.** Northwest Territories
nth (ĕnth) ▸ *adj.* **1.** Relating to an unspecified ordinal number. **2.** Highest; utmost: *to the nth degree.*
nt. wt. ▸ *abbr.* net weight
nu (no͞o, nyo͞o) ▸ *n.* The 13th letter of the Greek alphabet.
nu·ance (no͞o′äns′, nyo͞o′-) ▸ *n.* A subtle or slight degree of difference, as in meaning or feeling; gradation. **—nu·anced′** *adj.*
nub (nŭb) ▸ *n.* **1.** A lump or knob. **2.** The essence; core. **—nub′by** *adj.*
Nu·bi·a (no͞o′bē-ə, nyo͞o′-) ▸ A desert region and ancient kingdom in the Nile valley of S Egypt and N Sudan. **—Nu′bi·an** *adj. & n.*
nu·bile (noo′bĭl, -bīl′, nyo͞o′-) ▸ *adj.* Of marriageable age or condition.
nu·cle·ar (no͞o′klē-ər, nyo͞o′-) ▸ *adj.* **1.** *Biol.* Of or forming a nucleus. **2.** *Phys.* Of or relating to atomic nuclei. **3.** Of, using, or derived from nuclear energy.
nuclear energy ▸ *n.* The energy released by a nuclear reaction, esp. by fission or fusion.
nuclear family ▸ *n.* A family unit consisting of a mother and father and their children.
nuclear magnetic resonance ▸ *n.* The absorption of electromagnetic radiation of a specific frequency by an atomic nucleus placed in a strong magnetic field.
nuclear reaction ▸ *n.* A reaction, as in fission, that alters the energy, composition, or structure of an atomic nucleus.
nuclear reactor ▸ *n.* A device in which a nuclear chain reaction is initiated and controlled.
nu·cle·ate (no͞o′klē-ĭt, nyo͞o′-) ▸ *adj.* Having a nucleus or nuclei. ▸ *v.* (-āt′) **-at·ed, -at·ing. 1.** To bring together into or form a nucleus. **2.** To act as a nucleus for. **—nu′cle·a′tion** *n.*
nu·cle·ic acid (no͞o-klē′ĭk, -klā′-, nyo͞o-) ▸ *n.* Any of a group of complex compounds that are found in all living cells and viruses and that control cellular function and heredity.
nucleo– or **nucle–** ▸ *pref.* **1.** Nucleus: *nucleon.* **2.** Nucleic acid: *nucleotide.*
nu·cle·o·lus (no͞o-klē′ə-ləs, nyo͞o-) ▸ *n., pl.* **-li** (-lī′). A small granular body composed of protein and RNA in the nucleus of a cell. **—nu·cle′o·lar** (-lər) *adj.*
nu·cle·on (no͞o′klē-ŏn′, nyo͞o′-) ▸ *n.* A proton or a neutron. **—nu′cle·on′ic** *adj.*
nu·cle·on·ics (no͞o′klē-ŏn′ĭks, nyo͞o′-) ▸ *n. (takes sing. v.)* The study of the behavior of nucleons or atomic nuclei.
nu·cle·o·tide (no͞o′klē-ə-tīd′, nyo͞o′-) ▸ *n.* Any of various compounds that form the basic constituents of DNA and RNA.
nu·cle·us (no͞o′klē-əs, nyo͞o′-) ▸ *n., pl.* **-cle·i** (-klē-ī′) or **-es. 1.** A central or essential part around which other parts are gathered or grouped; core. **2.** *Biol.* A membrane-bound structure within a living cell that contains the cell's hereditary material and controls its metabolism, growth, and reproduction. **3.** *Phys.* The positively charged central region of an atom, composed of protons and neutrons and containing almost all of the mass of the atom.
nu·clide (no͞o′klīd′, nyo͞o′-) ▸ *n.* A type of atom specified by its atomic number, atomic mass, and energy state. **—nu·clid′ic** (no͞o-klĭd′ĭk, nyo͞o-) *adj.*
nude (no͞od, nyo͞od) ▸ *adj.* **nud·er, nud·est.** Being without clothing; naked. ▸ *n.* **1.** An unclothed human figure, esp. in artistic representation. **2.** The condition of being unclothed. **—nu′di·ty** *n.*
nudge (nŭj) ▸ *v.* **nudged, nudg·ing.** To push against gently, esp. in order to gain attention. **—nudge** *n.*
nud·ism (no͞o′dĭz′əm, nyo͞o′-) ▸ *n.* The belief in or practice of going nude, esp. for reasons of health. **—nud′ist** *adj. & n.*
nu·ga·to·ry (no͞o′gə-tôr′ē, nyo͞o′-) ▸ *adj.* **1.** Insignificant; trifling. **2.** Hollow.
nug·get (nŭg′ĭt) ▸ *n.* A small solid lump, esp. of gold.
nui·sance (no͞o′səns, nyo͞o′-) ▸ *n.* One that is inconvenient, annoying, or vexatious; bother.
nuke (no͞ok, nyo͞ok) *Slang* ▸ *n.* **1.** A nuclear device or weapon. **2.** A nuclear power plant. ▸ *v.* **nuked, nuk·ing.** To attack with nuclear weapons.
null (nŭl) ▸ *adj.* **1.** Having no legal force; invalid. **2.** Of no consequence; insignificant. **3.** Amounting to nothing. ▸ *n.* Zero; nothing. **—nul′li·ty** *n.*
null character ▸ *n. Comp. Sci.* A data control character used as a filler between blocks of data.
nul·li·fy (nŭl′ə-fī′) ▸ *v.* **-fied, -fy·ing. 1.** To make null; invalidate. **2.** To counteract the force or effectiveness of. **—nul′li·fi·ca′tion** *n.*
numb (nŭm) ▸ *adj.* **-er, -est. 1.** Unable to feel or move normally. **2.** Stunned, as from shock. **—numb** *v.* **—numb′ly** *adv.* **—numb′ness** *n.*
num·ber (nŭm′bər) ▸ *n.* **1.** *Math.* **a.** A member of the set

THESAURUS

novice or **novitiate** *n.* An entrant who has not yet taken the final vows of a religious order ▸ neophyte, postulant. *—See also* BEGINNER.
now *adv.* **1.** At this moment ▸ actually, at present, currently. *Idioms:* even (*or* just *or* right) now, at this instant (*or* moment *or* time), here and now. [*Compare* SOON.] **2.** At the present; these days ▸ nowadays, today. *Idioms:* in our time, in this day and age. *—See also* IMMEDIATELY (1).
now *n.* The current time ▸ nowadays, present, today. *Idioms:* modern times, the here and now, the present age (*or* day *or* time).
now *adj.* *—See* PRESENT[1].
nowadays *adv.* At the present; these days ▸ now, today. *Idioms:* in our time, in this day and age.
nowadays *n.* *—See* NOW.
noway *adv.* *—See* NO.
noxious *adj.* *—See* HARMFUL, POISONOUS.
nozzle *n.* *—See* NOSE (1).
nuance *n.* *—See* SHADE (1).
nub *n.* *—See* BUMP (1), HEART (1).
nuclear *adj.* *—See* CENTRAL.
nucleus *n.* *—See* CENTER (3), GERM (2), HEART (1).
nude *adj.* Not wearing any clothes ▸ au naturel, bare, disrobed, exposed, naked, stripped, unclad, unclothed, undraped, undressed. *Idioms:* buck naked, in one's birthday suit, in the altogether (*or* buff *or* raw), naked as a jaybird, stark naked, without a stitch. *—See also* BARE (3).
nudeness *n.* *—See* NUDITY.
nudge *v.* *—See* PUSH (1).
nudge *n.* *—See* DIG.
nudity *n.* The state of being without clothes ▸ bareness, exposure, nakedness, nudeness, undress.
nugatory *adj.* *—See* TRIVIAL.
nugget *n.* *—See* LUMP[1].
nuisance *n.* *—See* ANNOYANCE (2).
null *n.* *—See* NOTHING.
null *adj.* *—See* EMPTY (1).
nullification *n.* *—See* ABOLITION.
nullify *v.* *—See* ABOLISH, CANCEL (2).
numb *adj.* *—See* DEAD (2).
numb *v.* *—See* DEADEN, PARALYZE.
number *n.* An amount represented in numerals ▸ figure, quantity. [*Compare* TOTAL.] *—See also* BIT[1] (4), QUANTITY (2), SONG.

of positive integers. **b.** A member of any of the further sets of objects that can be derived from the positive integers. **2. numbers** Arithmetic. **3.** A numeral or series of numerals used for reference or identification: *a telephone number.* **4.** One item in a sequence or series. **5.** A total; sum. **6.** An indefinite quantity: *a number of people.* **7. numbers** A multitude. **8.** *Gram.* The indication of the singularity or plurality of a linguistic form. **9. Numbers** *(takes sing. v.)* See **Bible** table in Appendix. **10.** An item in a program of entertainment. ▸ *v.* **1.** To assign a number to. **2.** To count or enumerate. **3.** To add up to. **4.** To include in a group or category. **5.** To limit in number.

num·ber·less (nŭm′bər-lĭs) ▸ *adj.* Innumerable; countless.

nu·mer·a·ble (no͞o′mər-ə-bəl, nyo͞o′-) ▸ *adj.* That can be counted; countable.

nu·mer·al (no͞o′mər-əl, nyo͞o′-) ▸ *n.* A symbol or mark used to represent a number. **—nu′mer·al** *adj.*

nu·mer·ate (no͞o′mə-rāt′, nyo͞o′-) ▸ *v.* **-at·ed, -at·ing.** To enumerate. **—nu′mer·a′tion** *n.*

nu·mer·a·tor (no͞o′mə-rā′tər, nyo͞o′-) ▸ *n.* The expression written above the line in a common fraction to indicate the number of parts.

nu·mer·i·cal (no͞o-mĕr′ĭ-kəl, nyo͞o-) also **nu·mer·ic** (-mĕr′ĭk) ▸ *adj.* Of, represented by, or being a number or numbers. **—nu·mer′i·cal·ly** *adv.*

nu·mer·ol·o·gy (no͞o′mə-rŏl′ə-jē, nyo͞o′-) ▸ *n.* The study of occult meanings of numbers. **—nu′mer·ol′o·gist** *n.*

nu·mer·ous (no͞o′mər-əs, nyo͞o′-) ▸ *adj.* Amounting to a large number; many. **—nu′mer·ous·ly** *adv.* **—nu′mer·ous·ness** *n.*

nu·mi·nous (no͞o′mə-nəs, nyo͞o′-) ▸ *adj.* **1.** Filled with a sense of a supernatural presence. **2.** Spiritually elevated; sublime.

nu·mis·mat·ics (no͞o′mĭz-măt′ĭks, -mĭs-, nyo͞o′-) ▸ *n. (takes sing. v.)* The study or collection of money, coins, and medals. **—nu′mis·mat′ic** *adj.* **—nu·mis′ma·tist** (-mĭz′mə-tĭst, -mĭs′-) *n.*

num·skull also **numb·skull** (nŭm′skŭl′) ▸ *n.* A stupid person.

nun (nŭn) ▸ *n.* A woman who belongs to a religious order.

Nu·na·vut (no͞o′nə-vo͞ot′) ▸ A territory of N Canada including part of the mainland W of Hudson Bay and N of latitude 60° N, islands in the Hudson Bay, and most of the Arctic Archipelago. Cap. Iqaluit.

nun·ci·o (nŭn′sē-ō′, no͝on′-) ▸ *n., pl.* **-os.** A papal ambassador or representative.

nun·ner·y (nŭn′ə-rē) ▸ *n., pl.* **-ies.** A convent of nuns.

nup·tial (nŭp′shəl, -chəl) ▸ *adj.* Of marriage or the wedding ceremony. ▸ *n.* often **nuptials** A wedding ceremony.

Nu·rem·berg (no͝or′əm-bûrg′, nyo͝or′-) ▸ A city of SE Germany NNW of Munich.

nurse (nûrs) ▸ *n.* **1.** A person trained to care for the sick or disabled. **2a.** A wet nurse. **b.** A nursemaid. ▸ *v.* **nursed, nurs·ing. 1.** To serve as a nurse for. **2.** To suckle. **3.** To treat: *nurse a cough.* **4.** To take special care of. **5.** To assist; attend. **6.** To bear privately in the mind: *nursing a grudge.* **7.** To consume slowly: *nurse a drink.*

nurse·maid (nûrs′mād′) ▸ *n.* A woman employed to take care of children.

nurse practitioner ▸ *n.* A registered nurse with special training for providing primary health care.

nurs·er·y (nûr′sə-rē, nûrs′rē) ▸ *n., pl.* **-ies. 1.** A room set apart for children. **2a.** A place for the temporary care of children. **b.** A nursery school. **3.** A place where plants are grown, esp. for sale.

nursery school ▸ *n.* A school for children, usu. between the ages of three and five.

nurs·ing (nûr′sĭng) ▸ *n.* The profession or tasks of a nurse.

nursing home ▸ *n.* A residential establishment that provides care for the elderly or the chronically ill.

nurs·ling (nûrs′lĭng) ▸ *n.* A nursing infant or young animal.

nur·ture (nûr′chər) ▸ *n.* **1.** Something that nourishes. **2.** Upbringing; rearing. ▸ *v.* **-tured, -tur·ing. 1.** To nourish; feed. **2.** To educate; train. **3.** To foster; cultivate. **—nur′tur·er** *n.*

nut (nŭt) ▸ *n.* **1a.** A fruit or seed with a hard shell and an inner kernel. **b.** The kernel itself. **2.** *Slang* **a.** A crazy or eccentric person. **b.** An enthusiast: *a movie nut.* **3.** *Mus.* A ridge of wood at the top of the fingerboard or neck of a stringed instrument, over which the strings pass. **4.** A small block of metal or wood with a central threaded hole that is designed to fit around and secure a bolt or screw.

nut·crack·er (nŭt′krăk′ər) ▸ *n.* An implement used to crack nuts.

nut·meat (nŭt′mēt′) ▸ *n.* The edible kernel of a nut.

nut·meg (nŭt′mĕg′) ▸ *n.* The hard aromatic seed of an East Indian tree, grated or ground as a spice.

nu·tri·a (no͞o′trē-ə, nyo͞o′-) ▸ *n.* **1.** A beaverlike South American rodent. **2.** Its thick brownish fur.

nu·tri·ent (no͞o′trē-ənt, nyo͞o′-) ▸ *n.* A source of nourishment. ▸ *adj.* Providing nourishment.

nu·tri·ment (no͞o′trə-mənt, nyo͞o′-) ▸ *n.* A source of nourishment, esp. food.

nu·tri·tion (no͞o-trĭsh′ən, nyo͞o-) ▸ *n.* **1.** The process of nourishing or being nourished, esp. the process by which a living organism assimilates and uses food. **2.** The study of food and nourishment. **—nu·tri′tion·al** *adj.* **—nu·tri′tion·al·ly** *adv.* **—nu·tri′tion·ist** *n.* **—nu′tri·tive** (-trĭ-tĭv) *adj.*

nu·tri·tious (no͞o-trĭsh′əs, nyo͞o-) ▸ *adj.* Providing nourishment or nutrition. **—nu·tri′tious·ly** *adv.* **—nu·tri′tious·ness** *n.*

nuts (nŭts) *Slang* ▸ *adj.* **1.** Crazy; insane. **2.** Extremely enthusiastic. ▸ *interj.* Used to express contempt, disappointment, or refusal.

nut·shell (nŭt′shĕl′) ▸ *n.* The shell of a nut. ***—idiom:* in a nutshell** In a few words.

nut·ty (nŭt′ē) ▸ *adj.* **-ti·er, -ti·est. 1.** Full of or tasting like nuts. **2.** *Slang* Crazy: *a nutty idea.* **—nut′ti·ly** *adv.* **—nut′ti·ness** *n.*

nuz·zle (nŭz′əl) ▸ *v.* **-zled, -zling. 1.** To rub or push against gently with the nose or snout. **2.** To nestle together.

NV ▸ *abbr.* Nevada

NW ▸ *abbr.* **1.** northwest **2.** northwestern

NWT or **N.W.T.** ▸ *abbr.* Northwest Territories

n. wt. ▸ *abbr.* net weight

NY or **N.Y.** ▸ *abbr.* New York

NYC ▸ *abbr.* New York City

ny·lon (nī′lŏn′) ▸ *n.* **1a.** Any of a family of high-strength, resilient synthetic resins. **b.** Cloth or yarn made from nylon. **2. nylons** Stockings made of nylon.

nymph (nĭmf) ▸ *n.* **1.** *Gk. & Rom. Myth.* Any of numerous female spirits dwelling in woodlands and waters. **2.** The larval form of certain insects, usu. resembling the adult form but smaller and lacking fully developed wings.

nym·pho·ma·ni·a (nĭm′fə-mā′nē-ə, -mān′yə) ▸ *n.* Abnormal or excessive sexual desire in a female. **—nym′pho·ma′ni·ac** (-nē-ăk) *n.*

NZ ▸ *abbr.* New Zealand

THESAURUS

number *v.* —*See* AMOUNT, COUNT (2).

number one *n.* A leading contestant or sure winner ▸ favorite, front-runner, leader, vanguard. *Informal:* shoo-in.

number one *adj.* —*See* PRIMARY (1).

numbers *n.* Arithmetic calculations ▸ arithmetic, computation, figures. [*Compare* ADDITION, CALCULATION.]

numerate *v.* —*See* COUNT (2), ENUMERATE.

numeration *n.* —*See* COUNT (1).

numerical *adj.* —*See* CONSECUTIVE.

numerous *adj.* —*See* MANY.

numinous *adj.* —*See* SUPERNATURAL (1).

numskull *n.* —*See* DULLARD.

nuptial *adj.* —*See* MARITAL.

nuptials *n.* —*See* WEDDING.

nurse *v.* —*See* BEAR (2), NURTURE.

nursling *n.* —*See* BABY (1).

nurture *v.* To help grow or develop ▸ cultivate, foster, nourish, nurse, provide for, sustain, tend. [*Compare* GROW, REAR², TEND².] —*See also* PROMOTE (2).

nut *n.* —*See* CRACKPOT, FAN², HEAD (1).

nutrient *adj.* —*See* NUTRITIOUS.

nutriment *n.* —*See* FOOD.

nutrition *n.* —*See* FOOD.

nutritious or **nutritional** or **nutritive** *adj.* Providing nourishment ▸ alimentary, nourishing, nutrient. [*Compare* HEALTHFUL.]

nuts *adj.* —*See* ENTHUSIASTIC, INSANE.

nutty *adj.* —*See* INSANE.

nuzzle *v.* —*See* SNUGGLE.

O

o or **O** (ō) ▸ *n., pl.* **o's** or **O's** also **os** or **Os**. **1.** The 15th letter of the English alphabet. **2.** A zero. **3. O** A type of blood in the ABO system.

O[1] (ō) ▸ *interj.* **1.** Used before the name of a person or thing being formally addressed. **2.** Used to express surprise or strong emotion.

O[2] ▸ The symbol for the element **oxygen**.

O[3] ▸ *abbr.* **1.** *Baseball* out **2.** outstanding

O. ▸ *abbr.* **1.** ocean **2.** Ohio

oaf (ōf) ▸ *n.* A stupid, clumsy person. **—oaf′ish** *adj.*

O·a·hu (ō-ä′ho͞o) ▸ An island of central HI between Molokai and Kauai.

oak (ōk) ▸ *n.* **1.** Any of numerous trees bearing acorns as fruit. **2.** The durable wood of these trees. **—oak′en** *adj.*

oa·kum (ō′kəm) ▸ *n.* Loose hemp or jute fiber, sometimes treated with tar, used chiefly for caulking ships.

oar (ôr) ▸ *n.* **1.** A long pole with a blade at one end, used to row or steer a boat. **2.** One who rows a boat.

oars·man (ôrz′mən) ▸ *n.* A rower, esp. in a racing crew.

o·a·sis (o-a′sĭs) ▸ *n., pl.* **-ses** (-sēz). A fertile or green spot in a desert.

oat (ōt) ▸ *n.* often **oats** *(takes sing. or pl. v.)* **1.** A cereal grass widely cultivated for its edible grains. **2.** The grain of this plant. **—oat′en** *adj.*

oath (ōth) ▸ *n., pl.* **oaths** (ōthz, ōths). **1.** A formal promise to fulfill a pledge, often calling on God or a god as witness. **2.** A blasphemous use of a sacred name.

oat·meal (ōt′mēl′) ▸ *n.* **1.** Meal made from oats; rolled or ground oats. **2.** A porridge made from rolled or ground oats.

O·ba·di·ah (ō′bə-dī′ə) ▸ *n.* **1.** A Hebrew prophet of the 6th cent. B.C. **2.** See **Bible** table in Appendix.

O·ba·ma (ō-bä′mə), **Barack Hussein, Jr.** The 44th US President (took office 2009).

ob·bli·ga·to (ŏb′lĭ-gä′tō) ▸ *n., pl.* **-tos** or **-ti** (-tē). *Mus.* An accompaniment that is an indispensable part of a piece.

ob·du·rate (ŏb′do͝o-rĭt, -dyo͝o-) ▸ *adj.* Hardened against influence or feeling; intractable. **—ob′du·ra·cy** *n.* **—ob′du·rate·ly** *adv.*

o·be·di·ent (ō-bē′dē-ənt) ▸ *adj.* Dutifully complying with the orders or instructions of one in authority. **—o·be′di·ence** *n.* **—o·be′di·ent·ly** *adv.*

o·bei·sance (ō-bā′səns, ō-bē′-) ▸ *n.* **1.** A gesture or body movement expressing deference. **2.** An attitude of deference. **—o·bei′sant** *adj.*

ob·e·lisk (ŏb′ə-lĭsk) ▸ *n.* **1.** A tall, four-sided shaft of stone, usu. tapered, that rises to a pointed pyramidal top. **2.** *Print.* The dagger sign (†), used esp. as a reference mark.

o·bese (ō-bēs′) ▸ *adj.* Extremely fat; grossly overweight. **—o·bese′ly** *adv.* **—o·be′si·ty, o·bese′ness** *n.*

o·bey (ō-bā′) ▸ *v.* **1.** To carry out the command of. **2.** To comply with (a command). **—o·bey′er** *n.*

ob·fus·cate (ŏb′fə-skāt′, ŏb-fŭs′kāt′) ▸ *v.* **-cat·ed, -cat·ing.** **1.** To make so confused as to be difficult to understand. **2.** To render indistinct or dim. **—ob′fus·ca′tion** *n.* **—ob·fus′ca·to′ry** (ŏb-fŭs′kə-tôr′ē, əb-) *adj.*

o·bi (ō′bē) ▸ *n.* A wide sash worn by Japanese women as part of the traditional dress.

o·bit (ō′bĭt, ō-bĭt′) ▸ *n.* *Informal* An obituary.

o·bi·ter dic·tum (ō′bĭ-tər dĭk′təm) ▸ *n., pl.* **obiter dic·ta** (dĭk′tə). **1.** *Law* An incidental, nonbinding opinion voiced by a judge. **2.** An incidental remark or observation.

o·bit·u·ar·y (ō-bĭch′o͞o-ĕr′ē) ▸ *n., pl.* **-ies.** A published notice of a death, usu. with a brief biography of the deceased.

ob·ject (ŏb′jĭkt, -jĕkt′) ▸ *n.* **1.** Something perceptible by the senses; a material thing. **2.** A focus of attention or action. **3.** The purpose of a specific action. **4.** *Gram.* A noun that receives or is affected by the action of a verb or that follows and is governed by a preposition. **5.** *Comp. Sci.* A discrete item that can be selected and maneuvered, such as an onscreen graphic. ▸ *v.* (əb-jĕkt′) **1.** To present a dissenting or opposing argument. **2.** To feel or express disapproval. **—ob·jec′tion** *n.* **—ob·jec′tor** *n.*

ob·jec·tion·a·ble (əb-jĕk′shə-nə-bəl) ▸ *adj.* Arousing disapproval; offensive. **—ob·jec′tion·a·bil′i·ty** *n.* **—ob·jec′tion·a·bly** *adv.*

ob·jec·tive (əb-jĕk′tĭv) ▸ *adj.* **1.** Of or having to do with a material object. **2.** Having actual existence. **3a.** Uninfluenced by emotions or personal prejudices. **b.** Based on observable phenomena. **4.** *Gram.* Of or being the case of a noun or pronoun that serves as the object of a verb. ▸ *n.* **1.** Something worked toward or striven for; goal. **2.** *Gram.* The objective

THESAURUS

oaf *n.* A large, ungainly, and dull-witted person ▸ ape, bear, gawk, hulk, lout, lump, ox. *Informal:* lummox. *Slang:* goon, klutz, lug, meatball, meathead, palooka, schlep, schlub. [*Compare* BLUNDERER, DULLARD, FOOL.]

oath *n.* —*See* CURSE (1), PROMISE (1), SWEARWORD.

obduracy or **obdurateness** *n.* —*See* STUBBORNNESS.

obdurate *adj.* —*See* CALLOUS, STUBBORN (1).

obeah *n.* —*See* CHARM, MAGIC (1).

obedience *n.* The quality, state, or act of willingly carrying out the wishes of others ▸ acquiescence, amenability, amenableness, complaisance, compliance, compliancy, deference, dutifulness, observance, submission, submissiveness, tractability, tractableness. [*Compare* LOYALTY.]

obedient *adj.* Willing to carry out the wishes of others ▸ acquiescent, amenable, biddable, complaisant, compliant, conformable, docile, duteous, dutiful, pliant, submissive, supple, tractable. [*Compare* DEFERENTIAL, LOYAL, PASSIVE.]

obeisance *n.* —*See* BOW[1], HONOR (1).

obeisant *adj.* —*See* DEFERENTIAL.

obese *adj.* —*See* FAT (1).

obey *v.* —*See* FOLLOW (4).

obfuscate *v.* —*See* COMPLICATE, OBSCURE.

obiter dictum *n.* —*See* COMMENT.

object *n.* **1.** Something having material existence ▸ article, body, item, mass, something, thing. *Informal:* thingamabob, thingamajig, thingy. [*Compare* GADGET.] **2.** A focus of attention, thought, or action ▸ butt, focus, receiver, recipient, subject, target. —*See also* INTENTION, THING (1).

object *v.* To express opposition, often by argument ▸ challenge, demur, except, expostulate, inveigh, oppose, protest, remonstrate, speak up. *Informal:* kick, squawk. [*Compare* ARGUE, COMPLAIN, CONTEST, QUIBBLE.] —*See also* CARE.

object to *v.* —*See* DISAPPROVE.

objectification *n.* —*See* EMBODIMENT.

objectify *v.* —*See* EMBODY (1).

objection *n.* An expression of opposition ▸ argument, challenge, complaint, demur, demurral, disagreement, dispute, exception, expostulation, fuss, grievance, problem, protest, protestation, remonstrance, remonstration. *Slang:* beef.

objectionable *adj.* Arousing disapproval ▸ disagreeable, exceptionable, ill-favored, improper, inadmissible, unacceptable, undesirable, unsuitable, unwanted, unwelcome. [*Compare* DEPLORABLE, OFFENSIVE.]

objective *adj.* —*See* FAIR[1] (1), PHYSICAL, REAL (1), REALISTIC (1).

objective *n.* —*See* INTENTION.

objectively *adv.* —*See* FAIRLY (1).

objectivity or **objectiveness** *n.* —*See* FAIRNESS.

case or a noun or pronoun in the objective case. **3.** The lens in an optical instrument that first receives light rays from the object. **—ob·jec′tive·ly** *adv.* **—ob·jec′tive·ness** *n.* **—ob′jec·tiv′i·ty** (ŏb′jĕk-tĭv′ĭ-tē) *n.*

object lesson ► *n.* A concrete illustration of a moral or principle.

ob·jet d'art (ôb′zhĕ där′) ► *n., pl.* **ob·jets d'art** (ôb′zhĕ där′). An object of artistic merit.

ob·jur·gate (ŏb′jər-gāt′, ŏb-jûr′gāt′) ► *v.* **-gat·ed, -gat·ing.** To rebuke sharply; berate. **—ob′jur·ga′tion** *n.*

ob·late (ŏb′lāt′, ŏ-blāt′) ► *adj.* Flattened at the poles: *an oblate spheroid.* **—ob′late′ly** *adv.* **—ob′late′ness** *n.*

ob·la·tion (ə-blā′shən, ō-blā′-) ► *n.* The act of offering something to a deity. **—ob·la′tion·al, ob′la·to′ry** (ŏb′lə-tôr′ē) *adj.*

ob·li·gate (ŏb′lĭ-gāt′) ► *v.* **-gat·ed, -gat·ing.** To bind, compel, or constrain by a social, legal, or moral tie.

ob·li·ga·tion (ŏb′lĭ-gā′shən) ► *n.* **1.** The act of binding oneself by a social, legal, or moral tie. **2.** A requirement, such as a contract or promise, that compels one to a particular course of action. **3.** The constraining power of a promise, contract, law, or sense of duty. **4.** The fact or condition of being indebted to another for a favor received.

o·blig·a·to·ry (ə-blĭg′ə-tôr′ē, ŏb′lĭ-gə-) ► *adj.* **1.** Morally or legally binding. **2.** Compulsory. **—o·blig′a·to′ri·ly** *adv.*

o·blige (ə-blīj′) ► *v.* **o·bliged, o·blig·ing. 1.** To constrain. **2.** To make indebted or grateful. **3.** To do a service or favor (for). **—o·blig′ing** *adj.* **—o·blig′ing·ly** *adv.* **—o·blig′ing·ness** *n.*

o·blique (ō-blēk′, ə-blēk′) ► *adj.* **1a.** Slanting or sloping. **b.** *Math.* Neither parallel nor perpendicular. **2.** Indirect or evasive. **3.** *Gram.* Designating any noun case except the nominative or vocative. ► *n.* Something oblique. ► *adv.* (ō-blīk′, ə-blīk′) At an angle of 45°. **—o·blique′ly** *adv.* **—o·blique′ness, o·bliq′ui·ty** (ō-blĭk′wĭ-tē, ə-blĭk′-) *n.*

o·blit·er·ate (ə-blĭt′ə-rāt′, ō-blĭt′-) ► *v.* **-at·ed, -at·ing. 1.** To do away with completely. **2.** To wipe out or erase. **—o·blit′er·a′tion** *n.* **—o·blit′er·a′tive** (-ə-rā′tĭv, -ər-ə-tĭv) *adj.*

o·bliv·i·on (ə-blĭv′ē-ən) ► *n.* **1.** The condition of being completely forgotten. **2.** Forgetfulness.

o·bliv·i·ous (ə-blĭv′ē-əs) ► *adj.* **1.** Lacking all memory; forgetful. **2.** Unaware. **—o·bliv′i·ous·ly** *adv.* **—o·bliv′i·ous·ness** *n.*

ob·long (ŏb′lông′, -lŏng′) ► *adj.* **1a.** Deviating from a square, circular, or spherical form by being elongated in one direction. **b.** Rectangular or elliptical. **2.** *Bot.* Elongated. **—ob′long′** *n.*

ob·lo·quy (ŏb′lə-kwē) ► *n., pl.* **-quies. 1.** Abusively detractive language. **2.** Disgrace; ill repute.

ob·nox·ious (ŏb-nŏk′shəs, əb-) ► *adj.* Very objectionable; odious. **—ob·nox′ious·ly** *adv.* **—ob·nox′ious·ness** *n.*

o·boe (ō′bō) ► *n.* A woodwind instrument with a conical bore and a double reed mouthpiece. **—o′bo·ist** *n.*

ob·scene (ŏb-sēn′, əb-) ► *adj.* **1.** Offensive to accepted standards of decency. **2.** Inciting lust; lewd. **3.** Offensive to the senses. **—ob·scene′ly** *adv.* **—ob·scen′i·ty** (-sĕn′ĭ-tē) *n.*

ob·scur·ant·ism (ŏb-skyo͝or′ən-tĭz′əm, əb-, ŏb′skyo͝o-răn′-) ► *n.* **1.** The practice of deliberate abstruseness. **2.** A policy of withholding information from the public. **—ob·scur′ant·ist** *n.*

ob·scure (ŏb-skyo͝or′, əb-) ► *adj.* **-scur·er, -scur·est. 1.** Dim; dark. **2.** Indistinctly heard or perceived. **3.** Out of sight; hidden. **4.** Of undistinguished station or reputation. **5.** Ambiguous or vague; unclear. ► *v.* **-scured, -scur·ing. 1.** To make dim or unclear. **2.** To conceal or cover. **—ob·scure′ly** *adv.* **—ob·scure′ness, ob·scu′ri·ty** *n.*

ob·se·qui·ous (ŏb-sē′kwē-əs, əb-) ► *adj.* Full of or exhibiting servile compliance. **—ob·se′qui·ous·ly** *adv.* **—ob·se′qui·ous·ness** *n.*

ob·se·quy (ŏb′sĭ-kwē) ► *n., pl.* **-quies.** A funeral rite or ceremony.

ob·ser·vance (əb-zûr′vəns) ► *n.* **1.** The act or practice of complying with a law, custom, command, or rule. **2.** The custom of celebrating a holiday or other ritual occasion. **3.** A customary rite or ceremony.

ob·ser·vant (əb-zûr′vənt) ► *adj.* **1.** Quick to perceive or apprehend; alert. **2.** Diligent in observing a law, custom, or principle. **—ob·ser′vant·ly** *adv.*

ob·ser·va·tion (ŏb′zər-vā′shən) ► *n.* **1.** The act of observ-

THESAURUS

object lesson *n.* —*See* EXAMPLE (2).

objurgate *v.* —*See* CHASTISE.

oblation *n.* —*See* OFFERING.

obligate *v.* To oblige to do or not do by force of authority, propriety, or custom ► expect, oblige, require, suppose. [*Compare* MUST.] —*See also* COMMIT (2), FORCE (1).

obligated *adj.* —*See* OBLIGED (1), OBLIGED (2).

obligation *n.* —*See* DEBT (1), DEBT (2), DUTY (1).

obligatory *adj.* —*See* REQUIRED.

oblige *v.* **1.** To perform a service or a courteous act for ► accommodate, aid, assist, favor, help, indulge, serve. **2.** To cause to do or not do by force of authority, propriety, or custom ► expect, obligate, require, suppose. [*Compare* MUST.] —*See also* COMMIT (2), FORCE (1).

obliged *adj.* **1.** Owing something, such as gratitude, to another ► beholden, grateful, indebted, obligated, thankful. *Idiom:* in someone's debt. **2.** Being legally or morally required to do something ► bound, committed, compelled, constrained, impelled, obligated, pledged, required, sworn. *Idioms:* duty (*or* honor) bound, under obligation (*or* contract *or* oath). [*Compare* LIABLE.]

obliging *adj.* Ready to do favors for another ► accommodating, agreeable, complaisant, considerate, generous, helpful, indulgent. [*Compare* AMIABLE, OBEDIENT, WILLING.]

oblique *adj.* At an angle ► angled, askew, aslant, beveled, bias, biased, canted, diagonal, inclined, leaning, listing, pitched, raked, skewed, slanted, slanting, sloped, sloping, tilted. [*Compare* TRANSVERSE.] —*See also* INDIRECT (1).

obliterate *v.* —*See* ANNIHILATE, CANCEL (1), DESTROY (2).

obliteration *n.* —*See* ANNIHILATION, ERASURE.

oblivion *n.* —*See* OBSCURITY.

oblivious *adj.* —*See* ABSENT-MINDED, IGNORANT (3).

obliviousness *n.* —*See* IGNORANCE (2).

oblong *adj.* —*See* OVAL.

obloquy *n.* —*See* DISGRACE, LIBEL, VITUPERATION.

obnoxious *adj.* —*See* OFFENSIVE (1).

obscene *adj.* Offensive to accepted standards of decency ► barnyard, bawdy, broad, coarse, dirty, filthy, foul, gross, indecent, lewd, nasty, profane, ribald, scatologic, scatological, scurrilous, smutty, vulgar. *Slang:* raunchy. [*Compare* EROTIC, RACY.] —*See also* OUTRAGEOUS.

obscenity *n.* **1.** The quality or state of being obscene ► bawdiness, coarseness, dirtiness, filthiness, foulness, grossness, indecentness, lewdness, nastiness, profaneness, profanity, scurrility, scurrilousness, smuttiness, vulgarity, vulgarness. *Slang:* raunch, raunchiness. **2.** Something that is offensive to accepted standards of decency ► bawdry, dirt, filth, pornography, profanity, ribaldry, scatology, sleaze, smut, vulgarity. *Slang:* porn, raunch. [*Compare* IMPROPRIETY.] —*See also* SWEARWORD.

obscure *adj.* **1.** Not widely understood ► abstruse, arcane, cabalistic, esoteric, occult, recondite. [*Compare* MYSTERIOUS.] **2.** Not widely known ► insignificant, little-known, undistinguished, unheard-of, unknown. [*Compare* ANONYMOUS, REMOTE.] —*See also* AMBIGUOUS (1), AMBIGUOUS (2), DARK (1), INCONSPICUOUS, UNCLEAR.

obscure *v.* To make dim or unclear ► adumbrate, becloud, bedim, befog, blear, blur, cloud, dim, dull, eclipse, fog, gloom, mist, obfuscate, overcast, overshadow, shadow. [*Compare* SHADE.] —*See also* BLOCK, CONCEAL.

obscured *adj.* —*See* HIDDEN (1), ULTERIOR (1).

obscurity *n.* The quality or state of being little known ► anonymity, insignificance, namelessness, oblivion, obscureness, unimportance. —*See also* DARK, VAGUENESS.

obsequious *adj.* —*See* SERVILE.

observable *adj.* —*See* APPARENT (1), NOTICEABLE, PERCEPTIBLE, VISIBLE.

observance *n.* The act of observing, often for an extended time ► observation, scrutiny, watch, watching. —*See also* CELEBRATION (2), CEREMONY (1), CUSTOM, NOTICE (1), OBEDIENCE.

observant *adj.* —*See* ALERT, CAREFUL (1).

observation *n.* The act of observing,

ing or the fact of being observed. **2.** The act of noting and recording something with instruments. **3.** A comment or remark. **—ob′ser·va′tion·al** *adj.* **—ob′ser·va′tion·al·ly** *adv.*

ob·ser·va·to·ry (əb-zûr′və-tôr′ē) ▸ *n., pl.* **-ries.** A place designed for making observations of astronomical, meteorological, or other natural phenomena.

ob·serve (əb-zûrv′) ▸ *v.* **-served, -serv·ing. 1.** To be or become aware of, esp. through careful attention; notice. **2.** To watch attentively. **3.** To make a systematic or scientific observation of. **4.** To say casually; remark. **5.** To adhere to or abide by. **6.** To keep or celebrate (e.g., a holiday). **—ob·serv′a·ble** *adj.* **—ob·serv′a·bly** *adv.* **—ob·serv′er** *n.*

ob·sess (əb-sĕs′, ŏb-) ▸ *v.* To preoccupy the mind of excessively.

ob·ses·sion (əb-sĕsh′ən, ŏb-) ▸ *n.* **1.** Compulsive preoccupation with a fixed idea or unwanted emotion. **2.** A compulsive, often unreasonable idea or emotion. **—ob·ses′sion·al** *adj.* **—ob·ses′sive** *adj.* **—ob·ses′sive·ly** *adv.* **—ob·ses′sive·ness** *n.*

ob·sid·i·an (ŏb-sĭd′ē-ən) ▸ *n.* A hard, usu. black or banded volcanic glass.

ob·so·les·cent (ŏb′sə-lĕs′ənt) ▸ *adj.* Becoming obsolete. **—ob′so·les′cence** *n.* **—ob′so·les′cent·ly** *adv.*

ob·so·lete (ŏb′sə-lēt′, ŏb′sə-lēt′) ▸ *adj.* **1.** No longer in use or in effect. **2.** Outmoded in style or construction. **—ob′so·lete′ly** *adv.* **—ob′so·lete′ness** *n.* **—ob′so·let′ism** *n.*

ob·sta·cle (ŏb′stə-kəl) ▸ *n.* One that opposes, stands in the way of, or holds up progress.

ob·ste·tri·cian (ŏb′stĭ-trĭsh′ən) ▸ *n.* A physician who specializes in obstetrics.

ob·stet·rics (ŏb-stĕt′rĭks, əb-) ▸ *n.* *(takes sing. or pl. v.)* The branch of medicine that deals with the care of women during and after pregnancy and childbirth. **—ob·stet′ric, ob·stet′ri·cal** *adj.*

ob·sti·nate (ŏb′stə-nĭt) ▸ *adj.* **1.** Stubbornly adhering to an attitude or course of action. **2.** Difficult to manage, control, or subdue. **—ob′sti·na·cy** (-nə-sē) *n.* **—ob′sti·nate·ly** *adv.*

ob·strep·er·ous (ŏb-strĕp′ər-əs, əb-) ▸ *adj.* Noisily and stubbornly defiant. **—ob·strep′er·ous·ly** *adv.* **—ob·strep′er·ous·ness** *n.*

ob·struct (əb-strŭkt′, ŏb-) ▸ *v.* **1.** To block (a passage) with obstacles. **2.** To impede; retard. **3.** To get in the way of; hide from sight. **—ob·struct′er, ob·struc′tor** *n.* **—ob·struc′tive** *adj.* **—ob·struc′tive·ly** *adv.* **—ob·struc′tive·ness** *n.*

ob·struc·tion (əb-strŭk′shən, ŏb-) ▸ *n.* **1.** An obstacle. **2.** The act or an instance of obstructing. **3.** The causing of a delay.

ob·struc·tion·ist (əb-strŭk′shə-nĭst, ŏb-) ▸ *n.* One who systematically blocks or delays a process. **—ob·struc′tion·ism** *n.* **—ob·struc′tion·is′tic** *adj.*

ob·tain (əb-tān′, ŏb-) ▸ *v.* **1.** To succeed in gaining possession of; acquire. **2.** To be accepted or customary. **—ob·tain′a·ble** *adj.* **—ob·tain′er** *n.*

ob·trude (ŏb-tro͞od′, əb-) ▸ *v.* **-trud·ed, -trud·ing. 1.** To impose (oneself or one's ideas) on others. **2.** To thrust out; push forward. **—ob·trud′er** *n.* **—ob·tru′sion** (-tro͞o′zhən) *n.* **—ob·tru′sive** (-tro͞o′sĭv, -zĭv) *adj.* **—ob·tru′sive·ly** *adv.*

ob·tuse (ŏb-to͞os′, -tyo͞os′, əb-) ▸ *adj.* **-tus·er, -tus·est. 1.** Lacking quickness of perception or intellect. **2.** Not sharp, pointed, or acute in form; blunt. **—ob·tuse′ly** *adv.* **—ob·tuse′ness** *n.*

obtuse angle ▸ *n.* An angle greater than 90° and less than 180°.

ob·verse (ŏb-vûrs′, əb-, ŏb′vûrs′) ▸ *adj.* **1.** Facing the observer. **2.** Serving as a counterpart or complement. ▸ *n.* (ŏb′vûrs′, ŏb-vûrs′, əb-) **1.** The side of a coin or medal that bears the principal stamp or design. **2.** A counterpart or complement. **—ob·verse′ly** *adv.*

ob·vi·ate (ŏb′vē-āt′) ▸ *v.* **-at·ed, -at·ing.** To prevent or render unnecessary by anticipatory measures. **—ob′vi·a′tion** *n.* **—ob′vi·a′tor** *n.*

ob·vi·ous (ŏb′vē-əs) ▸ *adj.* Easily perceived or understood; apparent. **—ob′vi·ous·ly** *adv.* **—ob′vi·ous·ness** *n.*

oc·a·ri·na (ŏk′ə-rē′nə) ▸ *n.* A small bulb-shaped wind instrument with finger holes and a mouthpiece.

oc·ca·sion (ə-kā′zhən) ▸ *n.* **1.** An event or happening, esp. a significant event. **2.** The time at which an event occurs. **3.** A favorable time; opportunity. **4.** Something that brings on an action. **5.** A reason; ground. **6.** An important social gathering. ▸ *v.* To provide occasion for. ***—idiom:* on occasion** From time to time.

oc·ca·sion·al (ə-kā′zhə-nəl) ▸ *adj.* **1.** Occurring from time to time. **2.** Created for a special occasion. **—oc·ca′sion·al·ly** *adv.*

oc·ci·dent (ŏk′sĭ-dənt, -dĕnt′) ▸ *n.* **1.** The west. **2. Occident** Europe and the Western Hemisphere. **—oc′ci·den′tal, Oc′ci·den′tal** *adj. & n.*

oc·cip·i·tal (ŏk-sĭp′ĭ-tl) ▸ *adj.* Of the occiput or the occipital bone. ▸ *n.* The occipital bone.

occipital bone ▸ *n.* A cranial bone that forms the lower posterior part of the skull.

THESAURUS

often for an extended time ▸ observance, scrutiny, watch, watching. *—See also* COMMENT, NOTICE (1).

observatory *n.* *—See* LOOKOUT (2).

observe *v.* **1.** To mark a day or an event with ceremonies of respect, festivity, or rejoicing ▸ celebrate, commemorate, keep, solemnize. [*Compare* SANCTIFY.] **2.** To pay regular and close attention to ▸ follow, monitor, stake out, survey, watch. *Idioms:* have one's (*or* keep an) eye on, keep tabs on, keep track of, ride herd on. *—See also* COMMENT, DISCOVER, FOLLOW (4), NOTICE, WATCH (1).

observer *n.* *—See* WATCHER (1).

obsess *v.* **1.** To come to mind continually ▸ haunt, torment, trouble, weigh on, weigh upon. **2.** To dominate the mind or thoughts of ▸ fixate, possess, preoccupy. [*Compare* ABSORB, GRIP.]

obsessed *adj.* *—See* INFATUATED.

obsession *n.* An irrational preoccupation ▸ compulsion, fascination, fetish, fixation, infatuation, mania. *Informal:* thing. *Idiom:* bee in one's bonnet. [*Compare* COMPLEX, ENTHUSIASM.]

obsessive *adj.* *—See* ENTHUSIASTIC, VORACIOUS.

obsessiveness *n.* *—See* VORACITY.

obsolescent *adj.* *—See* OBSOLETE.

obsolete *adj.* No longer in use ▸ obsolescent, outdated, outmoded, out-of-date, superannuated, superseded. *Idioms:* in mothballs, on the shelf. [*Compare* OLD-FASHIONED.]

obsoleteness *n.* The quality or state of being obsolete ▸ desuetude, disuse, obsoletism, outdatedness, outmodedness.

obstacle *n.* *—See* BAR (1), DIFFICULTY.

obstinacy *n.* *—See* STUBBORNNESS, UNRULINESS.

obstinate *adj.* Difficult to alleviate or cure ▸ persistent, pertinacious, stubborn. *—See also* STUBBORN (1), UNRULY (1).

obstinateness *n.* *—See* STUBBORNNESS, UNRULINESS.

obstreperous *adj.* *—See* DISORDERLY, UNRULY, VOCIFEROUS.

obstreperousness *n.* *—See* UNRULINESS.

obstruct *v.* To block or fill with obstacles ▸ bar, barricade, block, blockade, choke, clog, dam. *Idioms:* close (*or* cut) off, put obstacles in the way (*or* path) of, stand in the way (*or* path) of. *—See also* BLOCK, DISRUPT, HINDER.

obstruction *n.* *—See* BAR (1), DIFFICULTY.

obtain *v.* *—See* GET (1).

obtainable *adj.* *—See* AVAILABLE.

obtrude *v.* *—See* INTRUDE, MEDDLE.

obtrusion *n.* An excessive, unwelcome burden ▸ encumbrance, imposition, infliction, intrusion. [*Compare* BURDEN.] *—See also* MEDDLING, TRESPASS (2).

obtrusive *adj.* *—See* CURIOUS (1).

obtuse *adj.* *—See* BLIND (3), DULL (3), STUPID.

obtuseness *n.* *—See* STUPIDITY.

obviate *v.* *—See* PREVENT.

obviation *n.* *—See* PREVENTION.

obvious *adj.* Easily seen through due to a lack of subtlety ▸ blatant, broad, clear, overt, patent, plain, transparent, undisguised, unmistakable, unsubtle. *Idiom:* sticking out like a sore thumb. *—See also* APPARENT (1).

occasion *n.* **1.** The general point at which an event occurs ▸ instant, juncture, moment, point, stage, time. *Idiom:* point in time. [*Compare* PERIOD.] **2.** That which produces an effect ▸ antecedent, cause, determinant, reason. [*Compare* IMPACT, ORIGIN, STIMULUS.] *—See also* CAUSE (2), CIRCUMSTANCE (1), EVENT (1), OPPORTUNITY, PARTY.

occasion *v.* *—See* CAUSE, JUSTIFY (2).

occasional *adj.* *—See* INFREQUENT, INTERMITTENT.

occasionally *adv.* *—See* INFREQUENTLY, INTERMITTENTLY.

oc·ci·put (ŏk′sə-pŭt′, -pət) ▸ *n., pl.* **oc·cip·i·ta** (ŏk-sĭp′ĭ-tə) or **-puts.** The back part of the head or skull.

oc·clude (ə-klo͞od′) ▸ *v.* **-clud·ed, -clud·ing. 1.** To close or shut off; obstruct. **2.** *Chem.* To absorb or adsorb and retain (a substance). **3.** To close so that the opposing tooth surfaces fit together. **—oc·clu′sion** *n.*

oc·cult (ə-kŭlt′, ŏk′ŭlt′) ▸ *adj.* **1.** Of or relating to supernatural influences, agencies, or phenomena. **2.** Beyond human comprehension. **3.** Available only to the initiate; secret. **—oc·cult′** *n.* **—oc·cult′ly** *adv.* **—oc·cult′ness** *n.*

oc·cult·ism (ə-kŭl′tĭz′əm, ŏk′ŭl-) ▸ *n.* **1.** The study of the supernatural. **2.** A belief in supernatural powers. **—oc·cult′ist** *n.*

oc·cu·pan·cy (ŏk′yə-pən-sē) ▸ *n., pl.* **-cies. 1.** The act of occupying or the condition of being occupied. **2.** The period during which one occupies a place or position. **—oc′cu·pant** *n.*

oc·cu·pa·tion (ŏk′yə-pā′shən) ▸ *n.* **1.** An activity that serves as one's regular source of livelihood. **2.** The act or process of holding a place. **3.** Invasion, conquest, and control of a nation or territory by foreign armed forces. **—oc′cu·pa′tion·al** *adj.*

occupational therapy ▸ *n.* The use of productive or creative activity in the treatment of disabled people. **—occupational therapist** *n.*

oc·cu·py (ŏk′yə-pī′) ▸ *v.* **-pied, -py·ing. 1.** To fill up (time or space). **2.** To dwell or reside in. **3.** To hold or fill (an office or position). **4.** To seize possession of and maintain control over by or as if by conquest. **5.** To engage or busy (oneself). **—oc′cu·pi′er** *n.*

oc·cur (ə-kûr′) ▸ *v.* **-curred, -cur·ring. 1.** To take place. **2.** To be found to exist or appear. **3.** To come to mind. **—oc·cur′rence** *n.*

o·cean (ō′shən) ▸ *n.* **1.** The entire body of salt water that covers more than 70 percent of the earth's surface. **2.** often **Ocean** Any of the principal divisions of the ocean: *the Indian Ocean.* **3.** A great expanse or amount. **—o′ce·an′ic** (ō′shē-ăn′ĭk) *adj.*

o·cean·ar·i·um (ō′shə-nâr′ē-əm) ▸ *n., pl.* **-i·ums** or **-i·a** (-ē-ə). A large aquarium for the study or display of marine life.

O·ce·an·i·a (ō′shē-ăn′ē-ə, -ä′nē-ə, -ä′nē-ə) ▸ The islands of the S, W, and central Pacific, including Melanesia, Micronesia, Polynesia, and sometimes Australia, New Zealand, and the Malay Archipelago. **—O′ce·an′i·an** *adj. & n.*

o·cean·og·ra·phy (ō′shə-nŏg′rə-fē) ▸ *n.* The exploration and scientific study of the ocean. **—o′cean·og′ra·pher** *n.* **—o′cean·o·graph′ic** (-nə-grăf′ĭk) *adj.*

oc·e·lot (ŏs′ə-lŏt′, ō′sə-) ▸ *n.* A spotted wildcat of the SW US and Central and South America.

o·cher or **o·chre** (ō′kər) ▸ *n.* **1.** Any of several earthy mineral oxides of iron occurring in yellow, brown, or red and used as pigments. **2.** A moderate orange yellow.

o'clock (ə-klŏk′) ▸ *adv.* Of or according to the clock: *three o'clock.*

O'Con·nor (ō-kŏn′ər), **Sandra Day** (b. 1930) ▸ Amer. jurist; first woman associate justice of the US Supreme Court (1981–2006).

Oct. ▸ *abbr.* October

oc·ta·gon (ŏk′tə-gŏn′) ▸ *n.* A polygon with 8 sides. **—oc·tag′o·nal** (ŏk-tăg′ə-nəl) *adj.*

oc·ta·he·dron (ŏk′tə-hē′drən) ▸ *n., pl.* **-drons** or **-dra** (-drə). A polyhedron with 8 surfaces.

oc·tal (ŏk′təl) ▸ *adj.* Of or based on the number 8.

oc·tane (ŏk′tān′) ▸ *n.* **1.** Any of various hydrocarbons with the formula C_8H_{18}. **2.** An octane number.

octane number ▸ *n.* A numerical representation of the antiknock properties of motor fuel compared with a standard reference fuel with a rating of 100.

oc·tant (ŏk′tənt) ▸ *n.* One eighth of a circle. **—oc·tan′tal** (ŏk-tăn′təl) *adj.*

oc·tave (ŏk′tĭv, -tāv′) ▸ *n.* **1.** *Mus.* The interval of eight diatonic degrees between two tones of the same name. **2.** A group or series of eight.

oc·ta·vo (ŏk-tā′vō, -tä′-) ▸ *n., pl.* **-vos.** *Print.* **1.** The page size, from 5 by 8 inches to 6 by 9 1/2 inches, of a book composed of printer's sheets folded into eight leaves. **2.** A book composed of octavo pages.

oc·tet (ŏk-tĕt′) ▸ *n.* **1.** *Mus.* A composition written for eight voices or eight instruments. **2.** A group of eight.

oc·til·lion (ŏk-tĭl′yən) ▸ *n.* **1.** The cardinal number equal to 10^{27}. **2.** *Chiefly Brit.* The cardinal number equal to 10^{48}. **—oc·til′lion** *adj.* **—oc·til′lionth** *n. & adj.*

octo– or **octa–** or **oct–** ▸ *pref.* Eight: *octagon.*

Oc·to·ber (ŏk-tō′bər) ▸ *n.* The 10th month of the Gregorian calendar.

oc·to·ge·nar·i·an (ŏk′tə-jə-nâr′ē-ən) ▸ *n.* A person between 80 and 90 years of age.

oc·to·pus (ŏk′tə-pəs) ▸ *n., pl.* **-pus·es** or **-pi** (-pī′). A marine mollusk with a soft rounded body and eight sucker-bearing tentacles.

oc·tu·plet (ŏk-tŭp′lĭt, -to͞o′plĭt, -tyo͞o′-) ▸ *n.* One of eight offspring born in a single birth.

oc·u·lar (ŏk′yə-lər) ▸ *adj.* **1.** Of or relating to the eye. **2.** Visual. ▸ *n.* The eyepiece of an optical instrument.

oc·u·list (ŏk′yə-lĭst) ▸ *n.* **1.** An ophthalmologist. **2.** An optometrist.

OD (ō′dē′) *Slang* ▸ *n.* **1.** An overdose of a drug. **2.** A person who has taken an overdose. ▸ *v.* **OD'ed, OD'·ing.** To overdose.

odd (ŏd) ▸ *adj.* **-er, -est. 1.** Strange or peculiar. **2.** In excess of a given number: *invited 30-odd guests.* **3.** Being one of an incomplete pair or set. **4.** *Math.* Designating an integer not divisible by 2. **—odd′ly** *adv.* **—odd′ness** *n.*

odd·ball (ŏd′bôl′) ▸ *n.* *Informal* An eccentric person.

odd·i·ty (ŏd′ĭ-tē) ▸ *n., pl.* **-ties. 1.** One that is odd. **2.** The state of being odd.

odd·ment (ŏd′mənt) ▸ *n.* Something left over.

odds (ŏdz) ▸ *pl.n.* **1.** An advantage given to a weaker side in a contest to equalize the chances of all participants. **2.** A ratio expressing the probability of an outcome. **3.** Chances: *The odds are that it will rain.* **—*idiom:* at odds** In disagreement.

odds and ends ▸ *pl.n.* Miscellaneous items.

odds-on (ŏdz′ŏn′, -ôn′) ▸ *adj.* *Informal* More likely than others to win.

ode (ōd) ▸ *n.* A lyric poem, often in the form of an address and having an elevated style and formal structure.

-ode ▸ *suff.* **1.** Way; path: *electrode.* **2.** Electrode: *diode.*

O·des·sa (ō-dĕs′ə) ▸ A city of S Ukraine on **Odessa Bay,** an arm of the Black Sea.

THESAURUS

occult *adj.* —*See* MYSTERIOUS, OBSCURE (1).

occult *v.* —*See* HIDE[1].

occupancy *n.* The holding of something, such as a position ▸ incumbency, occupation, tenure. [*Compare* PERIOD.]

occupant *n.* —*See* INHABITANT.

occupation *n.* The holding of something, such as a position ▸ incumbency, occupancy, tenure. [*Compare* PERIOD.] —*See also* BUSINESS (2).

occupied *adj.* —*See* BUSY (1).

occupy *v.* **1.** To live in a place, as does a people ▸ inhabit, people, populate. [*Compare* LIVE[1], SETTLE.] **2.** To seize or maintain control over by conquest ▸ capture, colonize, conquer, hold, invade, overrun, seize, subjugate, take over. ***Idiom:*** take possession of. [*Compare* CONTROL.] **3.** To make busy ▸ busy, employ, engage. —*See also* ABSORB (1), LIVE[1].

occur *v.* —*See* HAPPEN (1).

occur to *v.* —*See* STRIKE (2).

occurrence *n.* The condition or fact of being present ▸ attendance, presence. [*Compare* EXISTENCE.] —*See also* CIRCUMSTANCE (1), EVENT (1).

ocean *n.* A body of salt water covering a large part of the surface of the earth ▸ brine, briny, deep, high seas, main, sea.

oceanic *adj.* —*See* MARINE (1).

ocular *adj.* Serving, resulting from, or relating to the sense of sight ▸ optic, optical, seeing, visual.

odd *adj.* Agreeably curious, especially in an old-fashioned or unusual way ▸ curious, funny, quaint. —*See also* ACCIDENTAL, ECCENTRIC, FUNNY (3).

oddball *n.* —*See* CHARACTER (5).

oddity *n.* —*See* ABNORMALITY, CHARACTER (5).

oddly *adv.* —*See* UNUSUALLY.

odds *n.* —*See* ADVANTAGE (1), CHANCE (3).

odds and ends *n.* Articles too small or numerous to be specified ▸ bits and pieces, etceteras, incidentals, junk, miscellanea, oddments, sundries, things. [*Compare* ASSORTMENT.] —*See also* END (3).

O·din (ō′dĭn) ▸ *n. Myth.* The Norse god of wisdom, war, and art.

o·di·ous (ō′dē-əs) ▸ *adj.* Arousing strong dislike or intense displeasure. **—o′di·ous·ly** *adv.* **—o′di·ous·ness** *n.*

o·di·um (ō′dē-əm) ▸ *n.* **1.** The state or quality of being odious. **2.** Disgrace resulting from hateful conduct.

o·dom·e·ter (ō-dŏm′ĭ-tər) ▸ *n.* An instrument that indicates distance traveled by a vehicle.

o·don·tol·o·gy (ō′dŏn-tŏl′ə-jē) ▸ *n.* The study of the structure and abnormalities of the teeth. **—o·don′to·log′i·cal** (-tə-lŏj′ĭ-kəl) *adj.* **—o′don·tol′o·gist** *n.*

o·dor (ō′dər) ▸ *n.* **1.** The property or quality of a thing perceived by the sense of smell. **2.** Esteem; repute. **—o′dor·less** *adj.* **—o′dor·less·ly** *adv.* **—o′dor·ous** *adj.* **—o′dor·ous·ly** *adv.* **—o′dor·ous·ness** *n.*

o·dor·if·er·ous (ō′də-rĭf′ər-əs) ▸ *adj.* Having or giving off an odor. **—o′dor·if′er·ous·ly** *adv.* **—o′dor·if′er·ous·ness** *n.*

O·dys·seus (ō-dĭs′yo͞os′, ō-dĭs′ē-əs) ▸ *n. Gk. Myth.* The hero of Homer's *Odyssey.*

od·ys·sey (ŏd′ĭ-sē) ▸ *n., pl.* **-seys.** A long adventurous voyage.

Oed·i·pus (ĕd′ə-pəs, ē′də-) ▸ *n. Gk. Myth.* A Theban prince who unwittingly killed his father and then married his mother.

Oedipus complex ▸ *n. Psychiat.* A subconscious sexual desire in a child, esp. a male child, for the parent of the opposite sex. **—oed′i·pal** *adj.*

o'er (ôr) ▸ *prep. & adv.* Over.

oeu·vre (œ′vrə) ▸ *n., pl.* **oeu·vres** (œ′vrə). **1.** A work of art. **2.** The lifework of an artist.

of (ŭv, ŏv; əv *when unstressed*) ▸ *prep.* **1.** Derived or coming from. **2.** Owing to: *died of cholera.* **3.** Away from. **4.** So as to be separated from: *robbed of one's dignity.* **5.** From the total or group comprising. **6.** Composed or made from. **7.** Associated with. **8.** Belonging or connected to. **9.** Possessing: *a person of honor.* **10.** Containing or carrying. **11.** Specified as: *a depth of ten feet; the Garden of Eden.* **12.** Centering on; directed toward. **13.** Produced by. **14.** Characterized or identified by. **15.** With reference to; about. **16.** Set aside for: *a day of rest.* **17.** Before: *five minutes of two.* **18.** During or on: *of recent years.*

off (ôf, ŏf) ▸ *adv.* **1.** From a place or position. **2.** At a certain distance in space or time. **3.** So as to be no longer operating or functioning. **4.** So as to be smaller, fewer, or less. **5.** So as to be away from work or duty. ▸ *adj.* **1.** Remote. **2.** Not on, attached, or connected. **3.** Not operating or operational. **4.** No longer taking place; canceled. **5.** Inferior. **6.** Incorrect. **7.** Going. **8.** Absent or away from work or duty: *He's off every Tuesday.* ▸ *prep.* **1.** So as to be removed or distant from. **2.** Away or relieved from: *off duty.* **3a.** By consuming: *living off honey.* **b.** With the means provided by: *living off my pension.* **4.** Extending or branching out from. **5.** Not up to the usual standard of: *off her game.* **6.** So as to abstain from. **7.** To seaward of: *a mile off Sandy Hook.* ▸ *v. Slang* To murder. ***—idiom:* off and on** Intermittently.

of·fal (ô′fəl, ŏf′əl) ▸ *n.* **1.** Waste parts, esp. of a butchered animal. **2.** Rubbish.

off·beat (ôf′bēt′, ŏf′-) ▸ *n. Mus.* An unaccented beat in a measure. ▸ *adj.* (ôf′bēt′, ŏf′-) *Slang* Unconventional.

off-col·or (ôf′kŭl′ər, ŏf′-) ▸ *adj.* **1.** Risqué: *an off-color joke.* **2.** Varying from the expected or required color.

of·fend (ə-fĕnd′) ▸ *v.* **1.** To cause anger, resentment, or wounded feelings in. **2.** To be displeasing or disagreeable to. **3.** To violate; transgress. **—of·fend′er** *n.*

of·fense (ə-fĕns′) ▸ *n.* **1.** The act of offending. **2.** A violation of a moral or social code. **3.** A crime. **4.** (ŏf′ĕns′) The act of attacking or assaulting. **5.** (ŏf′ĕns′) *Sports* A team in possession of the ball or puck.

of·fen·sive (ə-fĕn′sĭv) ▸ *adj.* **1.** Disagreeable to the senses. **2.** Causing anger, resentment, or affront. **3.** Making an attack. **4.** (ŏf′ĕn-) *Sports* Relating to the offense. **—of·fen′sive·ly** *adv.* **—of·fen′sive·ness** *n.*

of·fer (ô′fər, ŏf′ər) ▸ *v.* **1.** To present for acceptance or rejection. **2.** To present for sale. **3.** To present as payment; bid. **4.** To present as an act of worship. **5.** To put up; mount. **6.** To produce or introduce on the stage. **—of′fer** *n.* **—of′fer·er, of′fer·or** *n.*

of·fer·ing (ô′fər-ĭng, ŏf′ər-) ▸ *n.* **1.** The act of making an offer. **2.** Something offered. **3.** A presentation made to a deity as an act of worship.

of·fer·to·ry (ô′fər-tôr′ē, ŏf′ər-) ▸ *n., pl.* **-ries. 1.** often **Offertory** The part of the Eucharist at which bread and wine are offered to God. **2.** A collection of offerings at a religious service.

off-guard (ôf′gärd′, ŏf′-) ▸ *adj.* Off one's guard; unprepared.

off·hand (ôf′hănd′, ŏf′-) ▸ *adv. & adj.* Without preparation or forethought. **—off′hand′ed·ly** *adv.* **—off′hand′ed·ness** *n.*

of·fice (ô′fĭs, ŏf′ĭs) ▸ *n.* **1a.** A place in which business, clerical, or professional activities are conducted. **b.** The staff working in such a place. **2.** A duty or function assigned to or assumed by someone. **3.** A position of authority

THESAURUS

odious *adj.* —*See* OFFENSIVE (1).

odiousness *n.* —*See* UGLINESS.

odium *n.* —*See* DISGRACE, HATE (1).

odor *n.* The quality of something that may be perceived by smelling ▸ aroma, scent, smell. [*Compare* FRAGRANCE, STENCH.] —*See also* TRACK.

odorous or **odoriferous** *adj.* —*See* FRAGRANT, SMELLY.

odyssey *n.* —*See* ADVENTURE, EXPEDITION, JOURNEY.

off *adj.* —*See* ABSENT, ERRONEOUS, INSANE, SLOW (2).

off *v.* —*See* MURDER.

offbeat *adj.* —*See* UNUSUAL.

off-color *adj.* —*See* RACY, SICK (1).

offend *v.* **1.** To cause anger, resentment, or hurt feelings in ▸ affront, anger, annoy, chagrin, displease, hurt, injure, insult, miff, outrage, pique, provoke, put out, scandalize, upset, wound, wrong. [*Compare* ANGER, ANNOY, STAGGER.] **2.** To be very disagreeable or displeasing to ▸ disgust, displease, put off, repel, repulse, upset. *Slang:* turn off. *Idioms:* give offense to, not sit right (*or* well) with. **3.** To violate a rule or law ▸ err, sin, transgress, trespass. *Idioms:* break the law (*or* rules), go astray. —*See also* INSULT.

offender *n.* —*See* CRIMINAL.

offense *n.* Extreme displeasure caused by an insult or slight ▸ bad feelings, displeasure, dudgeon, huff, hurt, miff, pique, resentment, ruffled feathers, umbrage. [*Compare* ANGER.] —*See also* ATTACK, CRIME (1), CRIME (2), INDIGNITY, INJUSTICE (1).

offensive *adj.* **1.** So unpleasant or objectionable as to cause scorn or disgust ▸ abhorrent, abominable, antipathetic, atrocious, contemptible, despicable, despisable, detestable, disgusting, filthy, foul, hateful, horrid, infamous, loathsome, lousy, low, mean, nasty, nauseating, nefarious, obnoxious, odious, repellent, repugnant, repulsive, revolting, rotten, shabby, sickening, stomach-churning, ugly, unwholesome, vile, wretched. [*Compare* BAD, DEPLORABLE, DISGRACEFUL, OBSCENE.] **2.** Causing displeasure, anger, or hurt feelings ▸ discourteous, displeasing, hurtful, impertinent, impolite, insulting, rude, uncivil. [*Compare* IMPUDENT, OBJECTIONABLE.] —*See also* UNPLEASANT.

offensive *n.* —*See* ATTACK.

offer *v.* **1.** To put before another for acceptance ▸ advance, extend, hold out, present, proffer, put forward, put up, render, submit, tender, turn in, volunteer. *Idioms:* come forward with, hand to on a silver plate (*or* platter), lay before, lay at someone's feet. [*Compare* DONATE.] **2.** To make something readily available ▸ afford, furnish, make available, present, provide, render, supply. *Idiom:* place (*or* put) at one's disposal. [*Compare* ALLOW.] **3.** To have for sale ▸ carry, deal (in), keep, stock. [*Compare* SELL.] **4.** To make an offer of ▸ bid. *Informal:* go. **5.** To offer as a sacrifice ▸ immolate, sacrifice, victimize. —*See also* PROPOSE.

offer *n.* An act of offering or the thing offered ▸ bid, invitation, presentation, proffer, tender. [*Compare* PROPOSAL.] —*See also* ATTEMPT.

offering *n.* Something, especially a slain animal or group of animals, presented to a deity as an act of worship ▸ hecatomb, immolation, oblation, sacrifice, victim. —*See also* DONATION.

offhand *adj.* —*See* EXTEMPORANEOUS, GLIB.

office *n.* —*See* BRANCH (3), CEREMONY (1), POSITION (3), TASK (1).

given to a person, as in a government or corporation. 4. A subdivision of a governmental department. 5. A public position: *seek office*. 6. often **offices** A favor. 7. *Eccles.* A service, esp. liturgical prayer.

of·fice·hold·er (ô′fĭs-hōl′dər, ŏf′ĭs-) ▸ *n.* One who holds public office.

of·fi·cer (ô′fĭ-sər, ŏf′ĭ-) ▸ *n.* 1. One who holds an office of authority or trust in an organization. 2. One who holds a commission in the armed forces. 3. A person licensed in the merchant marine as master, mate, chief engineer, or assistant engineer. 4. A police officer.

of·fi·cial (ə-fĭsh′əl) ▸ *adj.* 1. Of or relating to an office of authority. 2. Authorized by a proper authority. 3. Holding office in a public capacity. 4. Formal: *an official banquet.* ▸ *n.* 1. One who holds an office or a position. 2. *Sports* A referee or umpire. **—of·fi′cial·dom** *n.* **—of·fi′cial·ly** *adv.*

of·fi·cial·ism (ə-fĭsh′ə-lĭz′əm) ▸ *n.* Rigid adherence to official forms and procedures.

of·fi·ci·ate (ə-fĭsh′ē-āt′) ▸ *v.* **-at·ed, -at·ing.** 1. To perform the functions of an office or position of authority, esp. at a religious service. 2. *Sports* To serve as a referee or umpire. **—of·fi′ci·a′tor** *n.*

of·fi·cious (ə-fĭsh′əs) ▸ *adj.* Overly eager in offering unwanted services or advice. **—of·fi′cious·ly** *adv.* **—of·fi′cious·ness** *n.*

off·ing (ô′fĭng, ŏf′ĭng) ▸ *n.* The near future: *new developments in the offing.*

off·ish (ô′fĭsh, ŏf′ĭsh) ▸ *adj.* Distant; aloof. **—off′ish·ly** *adv.* **—off′ish·ness** *n.*

off-key (ôf′-kē′, ŏf′-) ▸ *adj.* 1. *Mus.* Out of tune; sharp or flat. 2. Inappropriate; improper. **—off′key′** *adv.*

off-lim·its (ôf-lĭm′ĭts, ŏf-) ▸ *adj.* Forbidden to a designated group.

off·line or **off-line** (ôf′līn′, ŏf′-) ▸ *adj.* Not connected to or controlled by a computer.

off·load or **off-load** (ôf′lōd′, ŏf′-) ▸ *v.* 1. To unload (e.g., a vehicle). 2. *Comp. Sci.* To transfer (data) to a peripheral device.

off·print (ôf′prĭnt′, ŏf′-) ▸ *n.* A reproduction of an article from a publication. **—off′print′** *v.*

off-road (ôf′rōd′, ŏf′-) ▸ *adj.* Taking place or designed for use off public roads. **—off′-road′** *adv.*

off-sea·son (ôf′-sē′zən, ŏf′-) ▸ *n.* A part of the year marked by a cessation or lessening of activity. **—off′-sea′son** *adv.* & *adj.*

off·set (ôf′sĕt′, ŏf′-) ▸ *n.* 1. One that balances, counteracts, or compensates. 2. *Archit.* A ledge or recess in a wall. 3. A bend made in a pipe or bar to allow it to pass around an obstruction. 4. Printing by indirect image transfer. ▸ *v.* (ôf′sĕt′, ŏf′-, ôf-sĕt′, ŏf-) **-set, -set·ting.** 1. To counterbalance or compensate for. 2. To produce by offset printing. 3. To make or form an offset in (a wall, bar, or pipe). **—off′set′** *adv.* & *adj.*

off·shoot (ôf′sho͞ot′, ŏf′-) ▸ *n.* Something that branches out or derives its origin from a particular source, as a shoot from a plant stem.

off·shore (ôf′shôr′, ŏf′-) ▸ *adj.* 1. Away from the shore. 2. At a distance from the shore. **—off′shore′** *adv.*

off·side (ôf′sīd′, ŏf′-) also **off·sides** (-sīdz′) ▸ *adv.* & *adj.* *Sports* Illegally ahead of the ball or puck.

off·spring (ôf′sprĭng′, ŏf′-) ▸ *n., pl.* **-spring.** 1. Progeny; young. 2. A result; product.

off·stage (ôf′stāj′, ŏf′-) ▸ *adj.* & *adv.* Away from the area of a stage visible to the audience.

off-the-cuff (ôf′*thə*-kŭf′, ŏf′-) ▸ *adv.* & *adj.* Without preparation; impromptu.

off-the-rec·ord (ôf′*thə*-rĕk′ərd, ŏf′-) ▸ *adv.* & *adj.* Not for publication or attribution.

off-the-wall (ôf′*thə*-wôl′, ŏf′-) ▸ *adj.* *Informal* Very unconventional or unusual.

off-track betting (ôf′trăk′, ŏf′-) ▸ *n.* A system of placing bets away from a racetrack.

off-white (ôf′hwīt′, -wīt′, ŏf′-) ▸ *n.* A grayish or yellowish white. **—off′-white′** *adj.*

off year ▸ *n.* 1. A year in which no major political elections occur. 2. A year of reduced activity or production.

oft (ôft, ŏft) ▸ *adv.* Often.

of·ten (ô′fən, ŏf′ən, ôf′tən, ŏf′-) ▸ *adv.* Many times; frequently.

of·ten·times (ô′fən-tīmz′, ôf′tən-, ŏf′ən-, ŏf′tən-) also **oft·times** (ôf′tīmz′, ŏf′-) ▸ *adv.* Often.

O·gla·la (ō-glä′lə) ▸ *n., pl.* **-la** or **-las.** A member of a Teton Sioux people inhabiting SW South Dakota.

o·gle (ō′gəl, ô′gəl) ▸ *v.* **o·gled, o·gling.** To stare at, esp. impertinently or flirtatiously. **—o′gler** *n.*

o·gre (ō′gər) ▸ *n.* 1. A fabled giant that eats humans. 2. A brutish or cruel person. **—o′gre·ish** (ō′gər-ĭsh, ō′grĭsh) *adj.*

oh (ō) ▸ *interj.* 1. Used to express strong emotion, such as surprise, fear, anger, or pain. 2. Used to indicate understanding.

OH ▸ *abbr.* Ohio

O·hi·o (ō-hī′ō) ▸ A state of the N-central US. Cap. Columbus. **—O·hi′o·an** *adj.* & *n.*

Ohio River ▸ A river formed by the confluence of the Allegheny and Monongahela rivers in W Pennsylvania and flowing about 1,578 km (981 mi) to the Mississippi R. in S IL.

ohm (ōm) ▸ *n.* A unit of electrical resistance equal to that of a conductor in which a current of one ampere is produced by a potential of one volt across its terminals. **—ohm′ic** *adj.*

ohm·me·ter (ōm′mē′tər) ▸ *n.* An instrument for measurement in ohms of the resistance of a conductor.

-oid ▸ *suff.* Resembling; having the appearance of: *humanoid.*

oil (oil) ▸ *n.* 1. Any of numerous mineral, vegetable, and synthetic substances and animal and vegetable fats that are gen. slippery, combustible, viscous, liquid or liquefiable at room temperatures, soluble in various organic solvents such as ether but not in water, and used in a great variety of products, esp. lubricants and fuels. 2. Petroleum. 3. A substance with an oily consistency. 4. Oil paint. 5. An oil painting. ▸ *v.* To lubricate, supply, or cover with oil. **—oil′er** *n.*

oil·cloth (oil′klôth′, -klŏth′) ▸ *n.* Fabric treated with clay and oil to make it waterproof.

oil color ▸ *n.* See **oil paint.**

oil field ▸ *n.* An area with reserves of recoverable petroleum.

oil paint ▸ *n.* A paint in which the vehicle is a drying oil.

oil painting ▸ *n.* 1. A painting done in oil paints. 2. The art of painting with oils.

oil shale ▸ *n.* A black or dark brown shale containing hydrocarbons that yield petroleum by distillation.

oil·skin (oil′skĭn′) ▸ *n.* 1. Cloth treated with oil to make it waterproof. 2. A garment made of oilskin.

oil slick ▸ *n.* A layer of oil on water.

oil well ▸ *n.* A hole drilled or dug in the earth from which petroleum flows or is pumped.

oil·y (oi′lē) ▸ *adj.* **-i·er, -i·est.** 1. Of or relating to oil. 2. Impregnated with oil; greasy. 3. Unctuous. **—oil′i·ly** *adv.* **—oil′i·ness** *n.*

oink (oingk) ▸ *n.* The characteristic grunting noise of a hog. **—oink** *v.*

THESAURUS

officer *n.* —*See* EXECUTIVE, POLICE OFFICER.

official *adj.* —*See* AUTHORITATIVE (1), CEREMONIOUS, GOVERNMENTAL.

official *n.* —*See* EXECUTIVE.

officiate *v.* To peform assigned or official duties ▸ act as, function as, serve as.

officious *adj.* —*See* CURIOUS (1).

offish *adj.* —*See* COOL.

offset *n.* —*See* COMPENSATION.

offset *v.* —*See* BALANCE (2), CANCEL (2).

offshoot *n.* —*See* BRANCH (1), DERIVATIVE, SHOOT.

offspring *n.* —*See* PROGENY.

off-the-cuff *adj.* —*See* EXTEMPORANEOUS.

often *adv.* —*See* USUALLY.

ogle *v.* *Informal* To make an excessive show of desire for or interest in ▸ *Informal:* drool over, slobber over. [*Compare* ADORE, DESIRE, FLIRT, LUST, RAVE.] —*See also* GAZE.

ogre *n.* —*See* FIEND.

ogreish *adj.* —*See* FIENDISH.

oil *n.* A substance that is generally slippery, combustible, and not water-soluble ▸ crude, grease, lube, lubricant, petroleum, unction. [*Compare* FAT, OINTMENT, SLIME.] —*See also* FLATTERY.

oil *v.* To apply oil to something ▸ anoint, grease, lube, lubricate. [*Compare* SMEAR.]

oily *adj.* —*See* FATTY, SLICK, UNCTUOUS.

oint·ment (oint′mənt) ▸ *n.* A highly viscous or semisolid substance used on the skin as a cosmetic or salve.

O·jib·wa (ō-jĭb′wä′, -wə) also **O·jib·way** (-wā′) ▸ *n., pl.* **-wa** or **-was** also **-way** or **-ways. 1.** A member of a Native American people inhabiting a region of the US and Canada around Lake Superior. **2.** The Algonquian language of the Ojibwa.

OK[1] or **o·kay** (ō-kā′) *Informal* ▸ *n.* Approval; agreement. ▸ *v.* **OK'ed** or **OK'd** or **o·kayed, OK'·ing** or **o·kay·ing.** To approve of or agree to; authorize. ▸ *interj.* Used to express approval or agreement. **—OK** *adv. & adj.*

OK[2] ▸ *abbr.* Oklahoma

O·kee·cho·bee (ō′kĭ-chō′bē), **Lake** ▸ A lake of SE FL N of the Everglades.

O'Keeffe (ō-kēf′), **Georgia** (1887–1986) ▸ Amer. painter.

O·khotsk (ō-kŏtsk′), **Sea of** ▸ An arm of the NW Pacific W of the Kamchatka Peninsula and Kuril Is.

O·ki·na·wa (ō′kĭ-nä′wə, -nou′-) ▸ An island and island group of the central Ryukyu Is. in the W Pacific SW of Japan.

O·kla·ho·ma (ō′klə-hō′mə) ▸ A state of the S-central US. Cap. Oklahoma City. **—O′kla·ho′man** *adj. & n.*

Oklahoma City ▸ The capital of OK, in the central part.

o·kra (ō′krə) ▸ *n.* **1.** A tall tropical Asian plant cultivated for its edible green pods. **2.** The pods of this plant, used esp. in soups. **3.** See **gumbo** 2.

–ol ▸ *suff.* An alcohol or phenol: *glycerol.*

old (ōld) ▸ *adj.* **-er, -est. 1.** Having lived or existed for a long time; far advanced in years or life. **2.** Made or acquired long ago; not new. **3.** Wise; mature. **4.** Having a specified age. **5.** Belonging to or being of an earlier time: *her old classmates.* **6.** Known through long acquaintance: *an old friend.* **7.** Used as an intensive or to express affection: *any old time; good old Fido.* ▸ *n.* **1.** An individual of a specified age: *a class of five-year-olds.* **2.** Old people collectively. **3.** Former times; yore: *days of old.* **—old′ness** *n.*

old·en (ōl′dən) ▸ *adj.* Old.

Old English ▸ *n.* English from the middle of the 5th to the beginning of the 12th cent.

old-fash·ioned (ōld′făsh′ənd) ▸ *adj.* Outdated. ▸ *n.* A cocktail made of whiskey, bitters, and fruit.

Old French ▸ *n.* French from the 9th to the early 16th cent.

old guard ▸ *n.* A conservative, often reactionary element of a class or group.

Old High German ▸ *n.* High German from the middle of the 9th to the late 11th cent.

old·ie (ōl′dē) ▸ *n.* Something old, esp. a song that was once popular.

Old Irish ▸ *n.* Irish from 725 to about 950.

Old Italian ▸ *n.* Italian until the middle of the 16th cent.

old-line (ōld′līn′) ▸ *adj.* **1.** Conservative; reactionary. **2.** Long established.

old master ▸ *n.* **1.** A distinguished European artist from about 1500 to the early 1700s. **2.** A work by such an artist.

Old Norse ▸ *n.* The Germanic language of the Scandinavians until the middle of the 14th cent.

Old North French ▸ *n.* The northern dialects of Old French.

Old Persian ▸ *n.* An ancient Iranian language attested in inscriptions dating from the 6th to the 5th cent. B.C.

Old Provençal ▸ *n.* Provençal before the middle of the 16th cent.

old school ▸ *n.* A group committed to traditional ideas or practices.

Old Spanish ▸ *n.* Spanish before the middle of the 16th cent.

old·ster (ōld′stər) ▸ *n. Informal* An elderly person.

Old Testament ▸ *n. Bible* The first of the two main divisions of the Christian Bible, corresponding to the Hebrew Scriptures. See **Bible** table in Appendix.

old-tim·er (ōld′tī′mər) ▸ *n. Informal* **1a.** An oldster. **b.** One with long tenure or experience. **2.** Something very old.

Ol·du·vai Gorge (ōl′də-vī′, ôl′do͝o-) ▸ A ravine in N Tanzania W of Mt. Kilimanjaro.

old wives' tale ▸ *n.* A superstitious belief.

Old World ▸ The Eastern Hemisphere; often used to refer to Europe.

o·le·ag·i·nous (ō′lē-ăj′ə-nəs) ▸ *adj.* **1.** Of or relating to oil. **2.** Unctuous.

o·le·an·der (ō′lē-ăn′dər, ō′lē-ăn′dər) ▸ *n.* A poisonous Eurasian shrub having fragrant white, rose, or purple flowers.

o·le·ic acid (ō-lē′ĭk) ▸ *n.* An oily liquid occurring in animal and vegetable oils.

o·le·o (ō′lē-ō′) ▸ *n., pl.* **-os.** Margarine.

oleo– or **ole–** ▸ *pref.* Oil: *oleomargarine.*

o·le·o·mar·ga·rine (ō′lē-ō-mär′jə-rĭn, -rēn′) ▸ *n.* Margarine.

ol·fac·tion (ŏl-făk′shən, ōl-) ▸ *n.* **1.** The sense of smell. **2.** The act of smelling.

ol·fac·to·ry (ŏl-făk′tə-rē, -trē, ōl-) ▸ *adj.* Of or relating to the sense of smell.

ol·i·gar·chy (ŏl′ĭ-gär′kē, ō′lĭ-) ▸ *n., pl.* **-chies. 1a.** Government by a few. **b.** Those making up such a government. **2.** A state governed by oligarchy. **—ol′i·garch′** *n.* **—ol′i·gar′chic, ol′i·gar′chi·cal** *adj.*

oligo– or **olig–** ▸ *pref.* Few: *oligarchy.*

Ol·i·go·cene (ŏl′ĭ-gō-sēn′, ō′lĭ-) *Geol.* ▸ *adj.* Of or being the 3rd epoch of the Tertiary Period, marked by the rise of true carnivores. ▸ *n.* The Oligocene Epoch.

ol·ive (ŏl′ĭv) ▸ *n.* **1.** A Mediterranean evergreen tree having fragrant white flowers, leathery leaves, and edible fruit. **2.** The small ovoid fruit of the olive, an important food and source of oil. **3.** A dull yellowish green. **—ol′ive** *adj.*

olive branch ▸ *n.* A branch of an olive tree regarded as an emblem of peace.

ol·la (ŏl′ə, ō′yä) ▸ *n. Regional* A rounded earthenware pot, used esp. for cooking or to hold water.

Ol·mec (ŏl′mĕk, ōl′-) ▸ *n., pl.* **-mec** or **-mecs. 1.** An early Mesoamerican Indian civilization of SE Mexico that flourished around 1300–400 B.C. **2.** A member of a people sharing the Olmec culture.

O·lym·pi·a[1] (ō-lĭm′pē-ə, ə-lĭm′-) ▸ A plain of S Greece in the NW Peleponnesus.

THESAURUS

ointment *n.* A substance used on the skin to soothe or heal ▸ balm, cream, emollient, liniment, lotion, salve, unction, unguent.

OK or **okay** *n.* —*See* ACCEPTANCE (1), PERMISSION.

OK or **okay** *v.* —*See* PERMIT (2).

OK or **okay** *adv.* —*See* YES.

OK or **okay** *adj.* —*See* ACCEPTABLE (2).

old *adj.* **1.** Belonging to, existing, or occurring in times long past ▸ age-old, ancient, antediluvian, antiquated, antique, archaic, bygone, of yore, olden, old-time, timeworn, venerable. *Idiom:* old as Methuselah (*or* the hills *or* time). [*Compare* EARLY, SHABBY.] **2.** Far along in life or time ▸ advanced, aged, aging, elder, elderly, grizzled, hoary, mature, older, senescent, senior. *Idioms:* getting along (*or* on) in years, long in the tooth, no spring chicken, over the hill. [*Compare* SENILE.] —*See also* CONTINUING, EXPERIENCED, LATE (2), OLD-FASHIONED.

old *n.* —*See* PAST.

old age *n.* —*See* AGE (1).

old boy *n.* —*See* FATHER.

olden *adj.* —*See* OLD (1).

older *adj.* —*See* OLD (2).

old-fashioned *adj.* Of a style or method formerly in vogue ▸ antiquated, antique, archaic, dated, dowdy, frumpish, frumpy, fusty, old, old-time, out, outdated, outmoded, out-of-date, passé, unfashionable. *Idioms:* old hat, old school. [*Compare* OBSOLETE, TRITE, VINTAGE.]

old hand *n.* One who has had long experience in a given activity or capacity ▸ past master, vet, veteran. *Informal:* old-timer. [*Compare* EXPERT.]

old lady *n.* —*See* GIRLFRIEND, MOTHER.

old-line *adj.* —*See* CONFIRMED (1), ULTRACONSERVATIVE.

old maid *n.* —*See* PRUDE.

old man *n.* —*See* BOYFRIEND, FATHER.

oldster *n.* —*See* SENIOR (2).

old-time *adj.* —*See* OLD-FASHIONED, OLD (1).

old-timer *n. Informal* One who has had long experience in a given activity or capacity ▸ old hand, past master, vet, veteran. [*Compare* EXPERT.] —*See also* SENIOR (2).

oleaginous *adj.* —*See* FATTY, UNCTUOUS.

olfaction *n.* The sense by which odors are perceived ▸ nose, scent, smell.

oligarch *n.* —*See* DICTATOR.

olio *n.* —*See* ASSORTMENT.

O·lym·pi·a² (ō-lĭm′pē-ə, ə-lĭm′-) ▸ The capital of WA, in the W part on the S end of Puget Sound.

O·lym·pi·an (ō-lĭm′pē-ən) ▸ *adj.* **1.** *Gk. Myth.* Of or relating to the gods and goddesses of Mount Olympus. **2.** Surpassing all others in scope. ▸ *n.* **1.** *Gk. Myth.* One of the gods or goddesses of Mount Olympus. **2.** A contestant in the ancient or modern Olympic Games.

O·lym·pic Games (ō-lĭm′pĭk) ▸ *pl.n.* **1.** A group of modern international athletic contests held every four years. **2.** An ancient Greek festival of athletic games and contests of choral poetry and dance. **—O·lym′pic** *adj.*

O·lym·pics (ō-lĭm′pĭks) ▸ *pl.n.* See **Olympic Games** 1.

O·lym·pus (ə-lĭm′pəs, ō-lĭm′-) ▸ A range of N Greece near the Aegean coast; rises to 2,918.9 m (9,570 ft) at **Mount Olympus,** home of the mythical Greek gods.

Om (ōm) ▸ *n. Hinduism & Buddhism* A sacred Sanskrit syllable uttered as a mantra.

–oma ▸ *suff.* Tumor: *melanoma.*

O·ma·ha¹ (ō′mə-hô′, -hä′) ▸ *n., pl.* **-ha** or **-has. 1.** A member of a Native American people inhabiting NE Nebraska. **2.** The Siouan language of the Omaha.

O·ma·ha² (ō′mə-hô′, -hä′) ▸ A city of E NE on the Missouri R.

O·man (ō-män′) ▸ A sultanate of the SE Arabian Peninsula on the **Gulf of Oman,** an arm of the Arabian Sea. Cap. Muscat. **—O·man′i** *adj. & n.*

O·mar Khay·yám (ō′mär kī-yäm′, -ăm′) (1050?–1123) ▸ Persian poet, mathematician, and astronomer.

om·buds·man (ŏm′bŭdz′mən, -bədz-, -bo͝odz′-) ▸ *n.* One who investigates complaints, as from consumers, and mediates grievances and disputes. **—om′buds′man·ship′** *n.*

o·me·ga (ō-mĕg′ə, ō-mē′gə, ō-mā′-) ▸ *n.* The 24th letter of the Greek alphabet.

om·e·let also **om·e·lette** (ŏm′ə-lĭt, ŏm′lĭt) ▸ *n.* A dish of beaten eggs cooked and folded, often around a filling.

o·men (ō′mən) ▸ *n.* Something believed to be a sign of future good or evil.

om·i·cron (ŏm′ĭ-krŏn′, ō′mĭ-) ▸ *n.* The 15th letter of the Greek alphabet.

om·i·nous (ŏm′ə-nəs) ▸ *adj.* **1.** Menacing; threatening. **2.** Of or being an evil omen. **—om′i·nous·ly** *adv.* **—om′i·nous·ness** *n.*

o·mit (ō-mĭt′) ▸ *v.* **o·mit·ted, o·mit·ting. 1.** To fail to include or mention; leave out. **2a.** To pass over; neglect. **b.** To desist or fail in doing. **—o·mis′si·ble** *adj.* **—o·mis′sion** (ō-mĭsh′ən) *n.*

omni– ▸ *pref.* All: *omnidirectional.*

om·ni·bus (ŏm′nĭ-bŭs′, -bəs) ▸ *n.* A bus. ▸ *adj.* Covering many things or classes: *an omnibus trade bill.*

om·ni·di·rec·tion·al (ŏm′nē-dĭ-rĕk′shə-nəl, -dī-) ▸ *adj.* Capable of transmitting or receiving signals in all directions.

om·nip·o·tent (ŏm-nĭp′ə-tənt) ▸ *adj.* Having unlimited power, authority, or force. ▸ *n.* **Omnipotent** God. **—om·nip′o·tence** *n.*

om·ni·pres·ent (ŏm′nĭ-prĕz′ənt) ▸ *adj.* Present everywhere. **—om′ni·pres′ence** *n.*

om·nis·cient (ŏm-nĭsh′ənt) ▸ *adj.* Having total knowledge; knowing everything. **—om·nis′cience** *n.* **—om·nis′cient·ly** *adv.*

om·ni·um-gath·er·um (ŏm′nē-əm-găth′ər-əm) ▸ *n.* A miscellaneous collection; hodgepodge.

om·niv·o·rous (ŏm-nĭv′ər-əs) ▸ *adj.* **1.** Eating both animal and vegetable foods. **2.** Taking in everything available: *an omnivorous mind.* **—om′ni·vore′** (ŏm′nə-vôr′) *n.* **—om·niv′o·rous·ly** *adv.*

on (ŏn, ôn) ▸ *prep.* **1.** Used to indicate: **a.** Position above. **b.** Contact with. **c.** Location at or along. **d.** Proximity. **e.** Attachment to or suspension from. **2.** Used to indicate motion toward or against. **3.** Used to indicate: **a.** Occurrence during: *on July 3rd.* **b.** The particular occasion or circumstance: *On entering the room, she saw him.* **4.** Used to indicate: **a.** The object affected by an action: *The spotlight fell on the actress.* **b.** The agent or agency of a specified action: *cut my foot on the broken glass.* **5.** Used to indicate a source or basis: *live on bread and water.* **6.** Used to indicate: **a.** The state or process of: *on leave; on fire.* **b.** The purpose of: *travel on business.* **c.** A means of conveyance: *ride on a train.* **d.** Availability by means of: *beer on tap.* **7.** Used to indicate belonging: *a nurse on the hospital staff.* **8.** Used to indicate addition or repetition: *heaped error on error.* **9.** Concerning: *a book on dogs.* **10.** *Informal* With: *I haven't a cent on me.* **11.** At the expense of: *drinks on the house.* ▸ *adv.* **1.** In or into a position of being in contact with something: *Put the coffee on.* **2.** In or into a position of covering something: *Put your clothes on.* **3.** In the direction of something: *He looked on while the ship docked.* **4.** Toward a point lying ahead in space or time: *The play moved on to the next city.* **5.** In a continuous course. **6.** In or into performance or operation.

ON ▸ *abbr.* Ontario

–on¹ ▸ *suff.* **1.** Subatomic particle: *baryon.* **2.** Unit; quantum: *photon.*

–on² ▸ *suff.* Inert gas: *radon.*

once (wŭns) ▸ *adv.* **1.** One time only: *once a day.* **2.** At one time in the past; formerly. **3.** At any time; ever. ▸ *n.* A single occurrence; one time: *You can go this once.* ▸ *conj.* As soon as; when. ***—idiom:* at once 1.** All at one time; simultaneously. **2.** Immediately.

once-o·ver (wŭns′ō′vər) ▸ *n.* A quick but comprehensive survey or performance.

on·co·gene (ŏn′kə-jēn, ŏng′-) ▸ *n.* A gene that causes the transformation of normal cells into cancerous tumor cells, esp. a viral gene. **—on′co·gen′ic** (-jĕn′ĭk) *adj.* **—on′co·ge·nic′i·ty** (-jə-nĭs′ĭ-tē) *n.*

on·co·gen·e·sis (ŏn′kō-jĕn′ĭ-sĭs, ŏng′-) ▸ *n.* The formation and development of tumors.

on·col·o·gy (ŏn-kŏl′ə-jē, ŏng-) ▸ *n.* The scientific study of tumors. **—on′co·log′i·cal** (-kə-lŏj′ĭ-kəl), **on′co·log′ic** *adj.* **—on·col′o·gist** *n.*

on·com·ing (ŏn′kŭm′ĭng, ôn′-) ▸ *adj.* Approaching.

one (wŭn) ▸ *adj.* **1.** Being a single entity, unit, object, or living being; not two or more. **2.** United: *They spoke with one voice.* **3.** Being a single member of a group, category, or kind: *I'm just one player on the team.* ▸ *n.* **1.** The cardinal number, represented by the symbol 1, designating the first such unit in a series. **2.** A single person or thing: *This is the one I like best.* ▸ *pron.* **1.** An indefinitely specified individual: *met one of the crew.* **2.** An unspecified individual; anyone. **—one′ness** *n.*

O·nei·da (ō-nī′də) ▸ *n., pl.* **-da** or **-das. 1.** A member of Native American people formerly inhabiting central New York, now in Wisconsin, New York, and Ontario. **2.** The Iroquoian language of the Oneida.

O'Neill (ō-nēl′), **Eugene Gladstone** (1888–1953) ▸ Amer. playwright; 1936 Nobel.

on·er·ous (ŏn′ər-əs, ō′nər-) ▸ *adj.* Troublesome or oppressive; burdensome. **—on′er·ous·ly** *adv.*

THESAURUS

omen *n.* A phenomenon that serves as a sign or warning of some future good or evil ▸ augury, foreboding, forerunner, foreshadowing, foretoken, forewarning, harbinger, portent, prefigurement, presage, prognostic, prognostication, sign, thundercloud, warning. ***Idiom:*** writing (*or* handwriting) on the wall. [*Compare* PREDICTION, SIGN, THREAT.]

ominous *adj.* —*See* FATEFUL (1).

omission *n.* —*See* ERROR, FAILURE (2), NEGLECT.

omit *v.* —*See* DROP (5), NEGLECT (2).

omnipotence *n.* —*See* AUTHORITY.

omnipresent *adj.* Ever present in all places ▸ ubiquitous, universal. [*Compare* RAMPANT.]

omnivorous *adj.* —*See* VORACIOUS.

omnivorousness *n.* —*See* VORACITY.

omphalos *n.* —*See* CENTER (2).

once *adv.* —*See* EARLIER (1).

once *adj.* —*See* LATE (2).

once again *adv.* —*See* ANEW.

once-over *n.* —*See* EXAMINATION (1).

one *adj.* —*See* LONE.

one-dimensional *adj.* —*See* SUPERFICIAL.

one-liner *n.* —*See* JOKE (1).

oneness *n.* **1.** The condition of being one ▸ singleness, singularity, unity. **2.** An identity or coincidence of interests, purposes, or sympathies among the members of a group ▸ concord, solidarity, union, unity. [*Compare* ALLIANCE, UNION.] **3.** The quality or condition of being exactly the same as something else ▸ identicalness, identity, sameness, selfsameness. [*Compare* LIKENESS.] —*See also* COMPLETENESS, UNIQUENESS.

onerous *adj.* —*See* BURDENSOME.

one·self (wŭn-sĕlf′) also **one's self** (wŭn sĕlf′, wŭnz sĕlf′) ▸ *pron.* **1.** One's own self. Used: **a.** Reflexively: *One can congratulate oneself on one's victories.* **b.** In an absolute construction: *When in charge oneself, one may do as one pleases.* **2.** One's normal or healthy condition or state.

one-shot (wŭn′shŏt′) ▸ *adj. Informal* **1.** Effective after only one attempt. **2.** Being the only one and unlikely to be repeated.

one-sid·ed (wŭn′-sī′dĭd) ▸ *adj.* **1.** Biased: *a one-sided view.* **2.** Unequal: *a one-sided contest.* **—one′-sid′ed·ness** *n.*

one·time (wŭn′tīm′) ▸ *adj.* Former: *a onetime boxing champion.*

one-time (wŭn′tīm′) ▸ *adj.* Only once: *a one-time winner in 1970.*

one-to-one (wŭn′tə-wŭn′) ▸ *adj.* Allowing the pairing of each member of a class uniquely with a member of another class.

one-track (wŭn′trăk′) ▸ *adj.* Obsessed with a single idea or purpose.

one-up (wŭn′ŭp′) ▸ *v.* **-upped, -up·ping.** *Informal* To practice one upmanship on.

one-up·man·ship (wŭn-ŭp′mən-shĭp′) ▸ *n.* The art of outdoing or showing up a rival.

one-way (wŭn′wā′) ▸ *adj.* Moving or permitting movement in one direction only: *a one-way street; a one-way ticket.*

on·go·ing (ŏn′gō′ĭng, ôn′-) ▸ *adj.* Currently taking place.

on·ion (ŭn′yən) ▸ *n.* **1.** A bulbous plant widely cultivated as a vegetable. **2.** The pungent bulb of this plant.

on·ion·skin (ŭn′yən-skĭn′) ▸ *n.* A thin, strong, translucent paper.

on·line (ŏn′līn′, ôn′-) ▸ *adj.* **1.** *Comp. Sci.* **a.** Controlled by a central computer. **b.** Connected to a computer network. **c.** Accessible via a computer. **2.** Ongoing: *online editorial projects.*

on·look·er (ŏn′lo͝ok′ər, ôn′-) ▸ *n.* A spectator.

on·ly (ōn′lē) ▸ *adj.* Alone in kind or class; sole. ▸ *adv.* **1.** Without anyone or anything else; alone. **2a.** At the very least. **b.** And nothing else or more. **3.** Exclusively; solely. ▸ *conj.* But; except.

on·o·mat·o·poe·ia (ŏn′ə-măt′ə-pē′ə, -mä′tə-) ▸ *n.* The formation or use of words such as *buzz* or *murmur* that imitate the sounds associated with the objects or actions they refer to. **—on′o·mat′o·poe′ic, on′o·mat′o·po·et′ic** (-pō-ĕt′ĭk) *adj.* **—on′o·mat′o·poe′i·cal·ly, on′o·mat′o·po·et′i·cal·ly** *adv.*

On·on·da·ga (ŏn′ən-dô′gə, -dä′-, -dā′-) ▸ *n., pl.* **-ga** or **-gas.** **1.** A member of a Native American people inhabiting W-central New York, now also in SE Ontario. **2.** Their Iroquoian language. **—On′on·da′gan** *adj.*

on·rush (ŏn′rŭsh′, ôn′-) ▸ *n.* **1.** A forward rush. **2.** An assault. **—on′rush′ing** *adj.*

on·set (ŏn′sĕt′, ôn′-) ▸ *n.* **1.** An onslaught. **2.** A beginning.

on·shore (ŏn′shôr′, ôn′-) ▸ *adj.* **1.** Moving or directed toward the shore. **2.** Located on the shore. **—on′shore′** *adv.*

on·slaught (ŏn′slôt′, ôn′-) ▸ *n.* A violent attack.

Ont. ▸ *abbr.* Ontario

On·tar·i·o (ŏn-târ′ē-ō′) ▸ **1.** A province of E-central Canada. Cap. Toronto. **2.** A city of S CA E of Los Angeles.

Ontario, Lake ▸ The smallest of the Great Lakes, between SE Ontario, Canada, and NW NY.

on·to (ŏn′to͞o′, -tə, ôn′-) ▸ *prep.* **1.** On top of; upon. **2.** *Informal* Aware of: *I'm onto your plans.*

onto– or **ont–** ▸ *pref.* **1.** Existence; being: *ontology.* **2.** Organism: *ontogeny.*

on·tog·e·ny (ŏn-tŏj′ə-nē) ▸ *n., pl.* **-nies.** The origin and development of an individual organism. **—on′to·ge·net′ic** (ŏn′tō-jə-nĕt′ĭk) *adj.* **—on′to·ge·net′i·cal·ly** *adv.*

on·tol·o·gy (ŏn-tŏl′ə-jē) ▸ *n.* The branch of metaphysics that deals with the nature of being. **—on′to·log′i·cal** (ŏn′tə-lŏj′ĭ-kəl) *adj.* **—on′to·log′i·cal·ly** *adv.* **—on·tol′o·gist** *n.*

o·nus (ō′nəs) ▸ *n.* **1.** A burden. **2.** Blame.

on·ward (ŏn′wərd, ôn′-) ▸ *adv.* also **on·wards** (-wərdz) In a direction or toward a position that is ahead. **—on′ward** *adj.*

–onym ▸ *suff.* Word; name: *acronym.*

on·yx (ŏn′ĭks) ▸ *n.* A chalcedony that occurs in bands of different colors.

oo– ▸ *pref.* Egg; ovum: *oogenesis.*

o·o·cyte (ō′ə-sīt′) ▸ *n.* A cell from which an egg or ovum develops by meiosis; a female germ cell.

oo·dles (o͞od′lz) ▸ *pl.n. Informal* A great amount.

o·o·gen·e·sis (ō′ə-jĕn′ĭ-sĭs) ▸ *n.* The formation, development, and maturation of an ovum. **—o′o·ge·net′ic** (-jə-nĕt′ĭk) *adj.*

o·o·go·ni·um (ō′ə-gō′nē-əm) ▸ *n., pl.* **-ni·a** (-nē-ə) or **-ni·ums.** **1.** A cell that differentiates into an oocyte in the ovary. **2.** A female reproductive structure in certain fungi.

o·o·lite (ō′ə-līt′) ▸ *n.* **1.** A small round calcareous grain found esp. in limestones. **2.** Rock, usu. limestone, composed of oolites. **—o′o·lit′ic** (-lĭt′ĭk) *adj.*

o·ol·o·gy (ō-ŏl′ə-jē) ▸ *n.* The branch of ornithology that deals with the study of eggs. **—o′o·log′ic** (ō′ə-lŏj′ĭk), **o′o·log′i·cal** *adj.* **—o′o·log′i·cal·ly** *adv.* **—o·ol′o·gist** *n.*

oomph (o͝omf) ▸ *n. Slang* **1.** Spirited vigor. **2.** Sex appeal.

oops (o͝ops) ▸ *interj.* Used to acknowledge a minor accident or mistake.

ooze[1] (o͞oz) ▸ *v.* **oozed, ooz·ing.** **1.** To flow or leak out slowly. **2.** To disappear or ebb slowly. **—ooze** *n.* **—ooz′i·ness** *n.* **—ooz′y** *adj.*

ooze[2] (o͞oz) ▸ *n.* Soft mud or slime, as on the floor of oceans and lakes. **—ooz′i·ness** *n.* **—ooz′y** *adj.*

o·pal (ō′pəl) ▸ *n.* A translucent mineral of hydrated silica, often used as a gem. **—o′pal·ine′** (ō′pə-līn′, -lēn′) *adj.*

o·pal·es·cent (ō′pə-lĕs′ənt) ▸ *adj.* Exhibiting a milky iridescence like that of an opal. **—o′pal·esce′** *v.* **—o′pal·es′cence** *n.*

o·paque (ō-pāk′) ▸ *adj.* **1a.** Impenetrable by light. **b.** Not reflecting light; dull. **2.** Unintelligible. **3.** Obtuse; dense. **—o·pac′i·ty** (ō-păs′ĭ-tē), **o·paque′ness** *n.* **—o·paque′ly** *adv.*

op art also **Op Art** (ŏp) ▸ *n.* Abstract art marked by the use of geometric shapes and brilliant colors to create optical illusions.

op. cit. ▸ *abbr. Lat.* opere citato (in the work cited)

OPEC (ō′pĕk′) ▸ *abbr.* Organization of Petroleum Exporting Countries

op-ed page (ŏp′ĕd′) ▸ *n.* A newspaper page, usu. opposite the editorial page, with articles expressing personal viewpoints.

o·pen (ō′pən) ▸ *adj.* **1.** Affording unobstructed entrance and exit; not shut or closed. **2.** Having no protecting cover. **3.** Not sealed, tied, or folded. **4.** Having gaps, spaces, or intervals. **5.** Accessible to all; unrestricted. **6.** Susceptible; vulnerable. **7.** Available; obtainable. **8.** Ready to transact business. **9.** Not filled, engaged, or in use. **10.** Frank; candid. ▸ *v.* **1.** To release from a closed or fastened position. **2.** To remove obstructions from; clear.

THESAURUS

one-sided *adj.* —*See* BIASED.

one-sidedness *n.* —*See* BIAS.

onetime *adj.* —*See* LATE (2).

one-up *v. Informal* To outmaneuver an opponent ▸ finesse, trump. *Idioms:* play gotcha, pull (*or* put over) a fast one. [*Compare* DECEIVE, MANEUVER, OUTWIT.] — *See also* SURPASS.

ongoing *adj.* —*See* CONTINUAL.

onlooker *n.* —*See* WATCHER (1).

only *adj.* —*See* LONE, UNIQUE.

only *adv.* Nothing more than ▸ but, just, merely, simply. [*Compare* BARELY.] —*See also* SOLELY.

onomatopoeia *n.* The formation of words in imitation of sounds ▸ echoism, mimesis.

onomatopoetic or **onomatopoeic** *adj.* Imitating sounds ▸ echoic, imitative, mimetic.

onrush *n.* —*See* ATTACK.

onset *n.* —*See* ATTACK, BIRTH (2).

onslaught *n.* —*See* ATTACK, CHARGE (1), TIRADE.

onus *n.* —*See* BLAME, BURDEN[1] (1), DUTY (1), STAIN.

onward *adv.* —*See* FORWARD.

onyx *adj.* —*See* BLACK (1).

oodles *n.* —*See* HEAP (2).

oomph *n.* —*See* SPIRIT (1).

ooze *v.* To flow or leak out or emit something slowly ▸ bleed, discharge, exude, leach, leak, percolate, seep, sweat, transpire, transude, weep. [*Compare* DRIP, FLOW.]

ooze *n.* —*See* SLIME.

oozy *adj.* —*See* SLIMY.

open *adj.* **1.** Not closed, sealed, or fastened ▸ agape, ajar, cracked, unbuttoned, unbuckled, unclosed, undone, unlaced, unlocked, untied, unzipped, wide. [*Compare* LOOSE, YAWNING.] **2.**

3. To make or force an opening in. **4.** To remove the cover or wrapping from; undo. **5.** To spread out or apart. **6.** To get (something) going; initiate; commence. **7.** To make available. **8.** To make or become more responsive or understanding. **9.** To reveal the secrets of. **10.** To come into view; become revealed. **—*phrasal verb:* open up** *Informal* To speak freely and candidly. ▸ *n.* **1.** The outdoors. **2.** A tournament or contest for both professional and amateur players. **—o′pen·er** *n.* **—o′pen·ly** *adv.* **—o′pen·ness** *n.*

o·pen-air (ō′pən-âr′) ▸ *adj.* Outdoor: *an open-air concert.*

o·pen-and-shut (ō′pən-ən-shŭt′) ▸ *adj.* Easily settled or determined.

o·pen-end (ō′pən-ĕnd′) ▸ *adj.* Unlimited.

o·pen-end·ed (ō′pən-ĕn′dĭd) ▸ *adj.* **1.** Not limited; open-end. **2.** Allowing for change. **3.** Inconclusive or indefinite.

o·pen-eyed (ō′pən-īd′) ▸ *adj.* **1.** Having the eyes wide open. **2.** Watchful and alert.

o·pen·hand·ed (ō′pən-hăn′dĭd) ▸ *adj.* Giving freely; generous. **—o′pen·hand′ed·ly** *adv.* **—o′pen·hand′ed·ness** *n.*

o·pen-hearth (ō′pən-härth′) ▸ *adj.* Of a process for producing high-quality steel in a furnace with a heat-reflecting roof.

open house ▸ *n.* **1.** A social event with a general invitation to all. **2.** An occasion when an institution is open for visiting by the public.

o·pen·ing (ō′pə-nĭng) ▸ *n.* **1.** The act of becoming open or being made to open. **2.** An open space. **3.** A breach; aperture. **4.** The first part or stage. **5.** The first performance. **6.** *Games* A series of beginning moves, esp. in chess. **7.** An opportunity. **8.** An unfilled job or position.

o·pen-mind·ed (ō′pən-mīn′dĭd) ▸ *adj.* Receptive to new ideas or to reason. **—o′pen-mind′ed·ly** *adv.* **—o′pen-mind′ed·ness** *n.*

open shop ▸ *n.* A business employing both union and nonunion workers.

o·pen·work (ō′pən-wûrk′) ▸ *n.* Ornamental or structural work containing numerous openings, usu. in set patterns.

op·er·a[1] (ŏp′ər-ə, ŏp′rə) ▸ *n.* **1.** A theatrical presentation in which a dramatic performance is set to music. **2.** A theater designed primarily for operas. **—op′er·at′ic** (ŏp′ə-răt′ĭk) *adj.* **—op′er·at′i·cal·ly** *adv.*

o·pe·ra[2] (ō′pər-ə, ŏp′ər-ə) ▸ *n.* Pl. of **opus.**

op·er·a·ble (ŏp′ər-ə-bəl, ŏp′rə-) ▸ *adj.* **1.** Capable of or suitable for use. **2.** Treatable by surgery. **—op′er·a·bil′i·ty** *n.* **—op′er·a·bly** *adv.*

op·er·a glasses (ŏp′ər-ə, ŏp′rə) ▸ *pl.n.* Small binoculars for use esp. at the theater.

op·er·and (ŏp′ər-ənd) ▸ *n. Math.* A quantity on which an operation is performed.

op·er·ate (ŏp′ə-rāt′) ▸ *v.* **-at·ed, -at·ing. 1.** To perform a function; work. **2.** To perform surgery. **3.** To exert an influence. **4.** To control the functioning of.

op·er·at·ing system (ŏp′ə-rā′tĭng) ▸ *n.* Software designed to control the hardware of a specific computer system in order to allow users and application programs to make use of it.

op·er·a·tion (ŏp′ə-rā′shən) ▸ *n.* **1.** The act or process of operating. **2.** The state of being operative. **3.** *Medic.* A surgical procedure for remedying an injury or ailment. **4.** *Math.* A process, such as addition, performed in accordance with specific rules. **5.** *Comp. Sci.* An action resulting from a single instruction. **6.** A military action or campaign. **—op′er·a′tion·al** *adj.* **—op′er·a′tion·al·ly** *adv.*

op·er·a·tive (ŏp′ər-ə-tĭv, -ə-rā′tĭv, ŏp′rə-) ▸ *adj.* **1.** Being in effect; having force. **2.** Functioning effectively. **3.** Of or relating to a surgical operation. ▸ *n.* **1.** A skilled worker, esp. in industry. **2a.** A spy. **b.** A private detective. **—op′er·a·tive·ly** *adv.*

op·er·a·tor (ŏp′ə-rā′tər) ▸ *n.* **1.** One who operates a machine or system. **2.** The owner or manager of a business. **3.** *Informal* A person adept at accomplishing goals shrewdly or unscrupulously. **4.** *Math.* A symbol that represents an operation.

op·e·ret·ta (ŏp′ə-rĕt′ə) ▸ *n.* A theatrical production that has elements of opera but is lighter and more popular in subject and style.

oph·thal·mic (ŏf-thăl′mĭk, ŏp-) ▸ *adj.* Of or relating to the eye.

ophthalmo– or **ophthalm–** ▸ *pref.* Eye: *opthalmology.*

oph·thal·mol·o·gy (ŏf′thəl-mŏl′ə-jē, -thăl-, ŏp′-) ▸ *n.* The branch of medicine that deals with the anatomy, functions, pathology, and treatment of the eye. **—oph·thal′mo·log′ic** (-thăl′mə-lŏj′ĭk), **oph·thal′mo·log′i·cal** *adj.* **—oph′thal·mol′o·gist** *n.*

o·pi·ate (ō′pē-ĭt, -āt′) ▸ *n.* **1.** A narcotic containing opium or one of its derivatives. **2.** A narcotic. **3.** Something that dulls the senses and induces relaxation. ▸ *adj.* **1.** Containing opium or an opium derivative. **2.** Inducing sleep or sedation.

o·pine (ō-pīn′) ▸ *v.* **o·pined, o·pin·ing.** To hold or state as an opinion.

o·pin·ion (ə-pĭn′yən) ▸ *n.* **1.** A belief or conclusion held with confidence but not substantiated by proof. **2.** A judgment based on special knowledge. **3.** A judgment or estimation.

o·pin·ion·at·ed (ə-pĭn′yə-nā′tĭd) ▸ *adj.* Holding stubbornly to one's opinions.

o·pi·um (ō′pē-əm) ▸ *n.* A bitter, yellowish-brown, addictive narcotic drug prepared from the pods of an Old World poppy.

o·pos·sum (ə-pŏs′əm, pŏs′əm) ▸ *n., pl.* **-sum** or **-sums.** Any of various nocturnal, usu. arboreal marsupials of the Western Hemisphere.

Op·pen·hei·mer (ŏp′ən-hī′mər), **J(ulius) Robert** (1902–67) ▸ Amer. physicist.

op·po·nent (ə-pō′nənt) ▸ *n.* One that opposes another or

THESAURUS

Not covered ▸ exposed, revealed, spread, unconcealed, uncovered, unfurled, unprotected, unrolled, unsheltered. [*Compare* APPARENT, PERCEPTIBLE.] 3. Not restricted or confined to few ▸ free, nonexclusive, open-door, public, unrestricted. [*Compare* COMMON.] 4. Available for use or occupation ▸ accessible, employable, free, operable, operative, practicable, unfilled, uninhabited, unoccupied, unreserved, usable, utilizable, vacant, vacated. [*Compare* AVAILABLE, EMPTY.] *—See also* CLEAR (3), FRANK, INDEFINITE (2), LIABLE (2), RECEPTIVE.

open *v.* 1. To become or cause to become open ▸ crack, free, release, throw wide, unbutton, unbuckle, unclose, undo, unfasten, unlace, unlock, untie, unzip. [*Compare* REVEAL, UNDO.] 2. To rid of obstructions ▸ clear, free, remove, unblock. [*Compare* RID.] *—See also* SPREAD (1), START (1).

open-door *adj.* *—See* OPEN (3).

open-eyed *adj.* *—See* ALERT.

openhanded *adj.* *—See* GENEROUS (1).

openhandedness *n.* *—See* GENEROSITY.

opening *n.* *—See* BEGINNING, BIRTH (2), HOLE (2), OPPORTUNITY.

opening *adj.* *—See* BEGINNING.

open-minded *adj.* *—See* BROAD-MINDED, RECEPTIVE.

open-mindedness *n.* *—See* OPENNESS.

openness *n.* Ready acceptance of new suggestions, ideas, or opinions ▸ amenability, amenableness, open-mindedness, receptiveness, receptivity, responsiveness. [*Compare* ACCEPTANCE.] *—See also* EXPOSURE, HONESTY.

operable *adj.* *—See* OPEN (4).

operate *v.* To control or direct the functioning of ▸ employ, handle, manage, run, use, utilize, wield, work. [*Compare* ADMINISTER, DRIVE, GOVERN, MANEUVER.] *—See also* CONDUCT (1), FUNCTION.

operating *adj.* *—See* ACTIVE.

operation *n.* *—See* BEHAVIOR (2), EXERCISE (1), MISSION (1).

operational *adj.* In effect ▸ effective, operative. *Idiom:* in force (*or* operation). *—See also* USABLE.

operative *adj.* In effect ▸ effective, operational. *Idiom:* in force (*or* operation). *—See also* ACTIVE, OPEN (4).

operative *n.* *—See* LABORER, SPY.

operator *n.* 1. A person who operates a motor vehicle ▸ chauffeur, driver, motorist. 2. One who speculates for quick profits ▸ adventurer, gambler, speculator.

opiate *n.* *—See* DRUG (2), SOPORIFIC.

opiate *adj.* *—See* SOPORIFIC.

opine *v.* *—See* BELIEVE (3), COMMENT.

opinion *n.* *—See* BELIEF (1), DOCTRINE, RULING.

opinionated *adj.* *—See* BIASED, INTOLERANT (1).

opponent *n.* One that opposes the purposes or interests of another ▸ adversary, antagonist, archenemy, dissenter,

others. **—op·po′nent** *adj.* **—op·po′nen·cy** *n.*

op·por·tune (ŏp′ər-to͞on′, -tyo͞on′) ▸ *adj.* Occurring at a fitting or advantageous time. **—op′por·tune′ly** *adv.* **—op′por·tune′ness** *n.*

op·por·tun·ist (ŏp′ər-to͞o′nĭst, -tyo͞o′-) ▸ *n.* One who takes advantage of any opportunity to achieve an end, often with no regard for principles or consequences. **—op′por·tun′ism** *n.* **—op′por·tun·is′tic** *adj.*

op·por·tu·ni·ty (ŏp′ər-to͞o′nĭ-tē, -tyo͞o′-) ▸ *n., pl.* **-ties.** A favorable or advantageous circumstance or combination of circumstances.

op·pose (ə-pōz′) ▸ *v.* **-posed, -pos·ing. 1.** To be in contention or conflict with. **2.** To be resistant to. **3.** To place opposite, esp. in contrast or counterbalance. **—op·pos′a·bil′i·ty** *n.* **—op·pos′a·ble** *adj.* **—op′po·si′tion** (ŏp′ə-zĭsh′ən) *n.* **—op′po·si′tion·al** *adj.* **—op·pos′er** *n.*

op·po·site (ŏp′ə-zĭt) ▸ *adj.* **1.** Placed or located directly across from. **2.** Facing or moving away from each other. **3.** Sharply contrasting: *opposite views.* ▸ *n.* One that is opposite or contrary to another. ▸ *adv.* In an opposite position. ▸ *prep.* Across from or facing. **—op′po·site·ly** *adv.* **—op′po·site·ness** *n.*

op·press (ə-prĕs′) ▸ *v.* **1.** To keep down by unjust use of force or authority. **2.** To weigh heavily on the mind or spirit of. **—op·pres′sion** *n.* **—op·pres′sor** *n.*

op·pres·sive (ə-prĕs′ĭv) ▸ *adj.* **1.** Difficult to bear; burdensome. **2.** Tyrannical. **3.** Weighing heavily on the mind or spirit. **—op·pres′sive·ly** *adv.* **—op·pres′sive·ness** *n.*

op·pro·bri·ous (ə-prō′brē-əs) ▸ *adj.* **1.** Expressing contemptuous reproach. **2.** Shameful or infamous. **—op·pro′bri·ous·ly** *adv.*

op·pro·bri·um (ə-prō′brē-əm) ▸ *n.* **1.** Disgrace arising from shameful conduct. **2.** Scorn; contempt. **3.** A cause of shame.

-opsy ▸ *suff.* Examination: *biopsy.*

opt (ŏpt) ▸ *v.* To choose.

op·tic (ŏp′tĭk) ▸ *adj.* Of or relating to the eye or vision.

op·ti·cal (ŏp′tĭ-kəl) ▸ *adj.* **1.** Of or relating to sight. **2.** Designed to assist sight. **3.** Of or relating to optics. **—op′ti·cal·ly** *adv.*

optical art ▸ *n.* Op art.

optical disk ▸ *n. Comp. Sci.* A plastic-coated disk that stores digital data as tiny pits etched into the surface and is read with a laser scanning the surface; laser disk.

optical illusion ▸ *n.* A deceptive visual image.

op·ti·cian (ŏp-tĭsh′ən) ▸ *n.* One that makes or sells lenses, eyeglasses, and other optical instruments.

op·tics (ŏp′tĭks) ▸ *n.* *(takes sing. v.)* The scientific study of light and vision.

op·ti·mal (ŏp′tə-məl) ▸ *adj.* Most favorable or desirable. **—op′ti·mal·ly** *adv.*

op·ti·mism (ŏp′tə-mĭz′əm) ▸ *n.* **1.** A tendency to expect the best possible outcome or dwell on the most hopeful aspects of a situation. **2.** *Philos.* The doctrine that this world is the best of all possible worlds. **—op′ti·mist** *n.* **—op′ti·mis′tic** *adj.* **—op′ti·mis′ti·cal·ly** *adv.*

op·ti·mize (ŏp′tə-mīz′) ▸ *v.* **-mized, -miz·ing. 1.** To make as perfect or effective as possible. **2.** To make the most of. **—op′ti·mi·za′tion** *n.*

op·ti·mum (ŏp′tə-məm) ▸ *n., pl.* **-ma** (-mə) or **-mums.** The point at which the condition, degree, or amount of something is the most favorable. **—op′ti·mum** *adj.*

op·tion (ŏp′shən) ▸ *n.* **1.** The act of choosing; choice. **2.** The power or freedom to choose. **3.** The right to buy or sell something within a specified time at a set price. **4.** Something available as a choice. **—op′tion·al** *adj.* **—op′tion·al·ly** *adv.*

op·tom·e·try (ŏp-tŏm′ĭ-trē) ▸ *n.* The profession of examining eyes and prescribing corrective lenses or other treatments for visual defects. **—op′to·met′ric** (ŏp′tə-mĕt′rĭk) *adj.* **—op·tom′e·trist** *n.*

op·u·lent (ŏp′yə-lənt) ▸ *adj.* **1.** Possessing great wealth. **2.** Lavish. **—op′u·lence** *n.* **—op′u·lent·ly** *adv.*

o·pus (ō′pəs) ▸ *n., pl.* **o·pe·ra** (ō′pər-ə, ŏp′ər-ə) or **o·pus·es.**

THESAURUS

enemy, foe, nemesis, opposer, opposition, oppositionist, resister. *—See also* COMPETITOR.

opportune *adj.* Suited for a particular purpose or occurring at a suitable time ▸ auspicious, favorable, fortuitous, fortunate, propitious, prosperous, seasonable, timely, well-timed. [*Compare* APPROPRIATE, CONVENIENT.]

opportunity *n.* A favorable or advantageous combination of circumstances ▸ break, chance, main chance, moment, occasion, opening, option. *Informal:* shot. ***Idioms:*** big moment, chance of a lifetime, day in the sun. [*Compare* TURN.]

oppose *v.* To place in opposition or be in opposition to ▸ combat, counter, fight, match, pit, play off, resist, stand against, withstand. ***Idioms:*** bump heads with, meet head-on, mount (*or* offer) resistance, put up a fight, set (*or* be) at odds, set (*or* be) at someone's throat, stand in the way of, stand up to. [*Compare* CONTEND, HINDER.] *—See also* BALANCE (2), CONFLICT, CONTEST, DEFY (1), DISOBEY, OBJECT.

opposed *adj.* *—See* INDISPOSED, OPPOSING.

opposer *n.* *—See* OPPONENT.

opposing *adj.* Acting against or in opposition ▸ adversarial, adverse, antagonistic, antipathetic, conflicting, countervailing, opposed, oppositional, resistant, unfavorable. ***Idioms:*** at odds, in opposition to. [*Compare* CONTRARY, HOSTILE.] *—See also* OPPOSITE.

opposite *adj.* Diametrically opposed ▸ antipodal, antipodean, antithetical, antonymic, antonymous, contradictory, contrary, contrasting, converse, counter, diametric, diametrical, incompatible, inverse, irreconcilable, opposing, polar, reverse. *—See also* DISCREPANT.

opposite *n.* That which is diametrically opposed to another ▸ antipode, antipodes, antithesis, antonym, contradiction, contradictory, contrapositive, contrary, converse, counter, inverse, reverse.

opposite number *n.* One that has the same functions and characteristics as another ▸ counterpart, equivalent, vis-à-vis.

opposition *n.* **1.** The act or condition of conflict ▸ antagonism, antithesis, aversion, combat, contradiction, contradistinction, contraposition, contrariety, contrariness, polarity. [*Compare* CONFLICT, ENMITY.] **2.** The act of resisting ▸ renitence, renitency, resistance. **3.** A clandestine organization of freedom fighters in an oppressed land ▸ resistance, underground. *—See also* INDISPOSITION, OPPONENT.

oppositional *adj.* *—See* OPPOSING.

oppositionist *n.* *—See* OPPONENT.

oppress *v.* To treat arbitrarily or cruelly ▸ grind (down), trample. [*Compare* ENSLAVE, SUPPRESS.] *—See also* ABUSE (1), BURDEN[1], DEPRESS.

oppression *n.* Cruel exercise of power ▸ domination, injustice, persecution, repression, subjugation. [*Compare* CRUELTY, SLAVERY.] *—See also* TYRANNY.

oppressive *adj.* *—See* BURDENSOME.

oppressor *n.* *—See* DICTATOR.

opprobrious *adj.* *—See* ABUSIVE, DISGRACEFUL.

opprobrium *n.* *—See* DISGRACE, REBUKE.

oppugn *v.* *—See* DENY.

opt *v.* *—See* CHOOSE (1).

optic or **optical** *adj.* Serving, resulting from, or relating to the sense of sight ▸ ocular, seeing, visual.

optics *n.* *—See* VISION (1).

optimal *adj.* *—See* BEST (1).

optimism *n.* A tendency to expect a favorable outcome or to dwell on hopeful aspects ▸ assurance, cheerfulness, enthusiasm, hopefulness, sanguineness, sanguinity. [*Compare* SURENESS.]

optimist *n.* One who expects a favorable outcome or dwells on hopeful aspects ▸ Pangloss, Pollyanna, positivist. [*Compare* DREAMER.]

optimistic *adj.* Expecting or suggesting a favorable outcome ▸ assured, cheerful, confident, enthusiastic, Panglossian, positive, roseate, rose-colored, rosy, sanguine, upbeat. ***Idioms:*** looking on the bright side, looking through rose-colored glasses. [*Compare* ENCOURAGING, IDEALISTIC.]

optimum *adj.* *—See* BEST (1).

option *n.* *—See* CHOICE, OPPORTUNITY.

optional *adj.* Not compulsory or automatic ▸ discretionary, elective, facultative, noncompulsory, nonobligatory, permissible, possible. [*Compare* VOLUNTARY.]

opulence *n.* *—See* WEALTH.

opulent *adj.* *—See* LUXURIOUS, PROFUSE.

opus *n.* *—See* COMPOSITION (1), PUBLICATION (2).

A creative work, esp. a musical composition.

or (ôr; ər *when unstressed*) ▸ *conj.* Used to indicate: **a.** An alternative. **b.** The second of two alternatives: *either right or wrong.* **c.** A synonymous or equivalent expression: *acrophobia, or fear of heights.* **d.** Indefiniteness: *two or three.*

OR ▸ *abbr.* **1.** operating room **2.** Oregon

–or[1] ▸ *suff.* One that performs a specified action: *detector.*

–or[2] ▸ *suff.* State; activity: *behavior.*

or·a·cle (ôr′ə-kəl, ŏr′-) ▸ *n.* **1a.** A shrine consecrated to a prophetic deity. **b.** A priest or priestess at such a shrine. **c.** A prophecy made known at such a shrine. **2.** A wise person. **—o·rac′u·lar** (ô-răk′yə-lər, ō-) *adj.*

o·ral (ôr′əl) ▸ *adj.* **1.** Spoken rather than written. **2.** Of the mouth: *oral surgery.* **3.** Used in or taken through the mouth. **4.** Relating to the first stage of psychosexual development in psychoanalytic theory. **—o′ral·ly** *adv.*

or·ange (ôr′ĭnj, ŏr′-) ▸ *n.* **1a.** Any of several citrus trees having white flowers and round, reddish-yellow fruit. **b.** The sectioned pulpy fruit of an orange, having a sweetish acidic juice. **2.** The hue of the visible spectrum lying between red and yellow. **—or′ange** *adj.*

or·ange·ade (ôr′ĭn-jād′, ŏr′-) ▸ *n.* A beverage of orange juice, sugar, and water.

o·rang·u·tan (ô-răng′ə-tăn′, ə-răng′-) also **o·rang·ou·tang** (-ə-tăng′) ▸ *n.* An arboreal anthropoid ape having a shaggy reddish-brown coat and very long arms.

o·rate (ô-rāt′, ôr′āt′) ▸ *v.* **o·rat·ed, o·rat·ing.** To speak in a formal, often pompous manner.

o·ra·tion (ô-rā′shən) ▸ *n.* A formal speech.

or·a·tor (ôr′ə-tər, ŏr′-) ▸ *n.* **1.** One who delivers an oration. **2.** An eloquent and skilled public speaker. **—or′a·tor′i·cal** (-tôr′ĭ-kəl) **—or′a·tor′i·cal·ly** *adv.*

or·a·to·ri·o (ôr′ə-tôr′ē-ō′, ŏr′-) ▸ *n., pl.* **-os.** *Mus.* A composition for voices and orchestra, usu. on a religious theme, without costumes, scenery, or dramatic action.

or·a·to·ry[1] (ôr′ə-tôr′ē, ŏr′-) ▸ *n.* **1.** The art of public speaking. **2.** Eloquence or skill in making public speeches.

or·a·to·ry[2] (ôr′ə-tôr′ē, ŏr′-) ▸ *n., pl.* **-ries.** A small private chapel.

orb (ôrb) ▸ *n.* **1.** A sphere. **2.** A celestial body. **3.** An eye or eyeball. **—or·bic′u·lar** (ôr-bĭk′yə-lər) *adj.*

or·bit (ôr′bĭt) ▸ *n.* **1.** The path of a celestial body or artificial satellite as it revolves around another body. **2.** The path of a body in a field of force surrounding another body. **3.** A range of activity or influence. **4.** An eye socket. ▸ *v.* **1.** To put into an orbit. **2.** To revolve around (a body or center of attraction). **—or′bi·tal** *adj.* **—or′bit·er** *n.*

or·ca (ôr′kə) ▸ *n.* See **killer whale.**

or·chard (ôr′chərd) ▸ *n.* **1.** An area of land devoted to the cultivation of fruit or nut trees. **2.** The trees cultivated in an orchard.

or·ches·tra (ôr′kĭ-strə, -kĕs′trə) ▸ *n.* **1.** A group of musicians who play together on various instruments. **2a.** The front section of seats nearest the stage in a theater. **b.** The entire main floor of a theater. **—or·ches′tral** (-kĕs′trəl) *adj.* **—or·ches′tral·ly** *adv.*

or·ches·trate (ôr′kĭ-strāt′) ▸ *v.* **-trat·ed, -trat·ing. 1.** To compose or arrange (music) for an orchestra. **2.** To arrange or organize; direct. **—or′ches·tra′tion** *n.* **—or′ches·tra′tor** *n.*

or·chid (ôr′kĭd) ▸ *n.* **1a.** Any of a large family of chiefly tropical plants with lipped, three-petaled flowers. **b.** The flower itself. **2.** A light reddish purple. **—or′chid** *adj.*

or·dain (ôr-dān′) ▸ *v.* **1.** To install as a minister, priest, or rabbi. **2.** To order by or as if by decree. **3.** To predestine. **—or·dain′er** *n.* **—or·dain′ment** *n.*

or·deal (ôr-dēl′) ▸ *n.* A difficult or painful experience.

or·der (ôr′dər) ▸ *n.* **1.** A condition of logical or comprehensible arrangement among the separate elements of a group. **2.** The condition or state of something: *a machine in good working order.* **3a.** The established system of social organization. **b.** A condition in which freedom from disorder is maintained through established authority. **4.** A sequence or arrangement of successive things. **5.** The prescribed form or customary procedure. **6.** A command or direction. **7.** A commission or instruction to buy, sell, or supply something. **8.** A request made by a customer at a restaurant for food. **9.** *Eccles.* **a.** Any of several grades of the Christian ministry. **b.** often **orders** Ordination. **10.** A group of persons living under a religious rule. **11.** A group of people upon whom a government or sovereign has formally conferred honor: *the Order of the Garter.* **12.** Degree of quality or importance; rank. **13.** *Archit.* Any of several classical styles marked by the type of column employed. **14.** *Biol.* The category ranking below a class and above a family in the hierarchy of taxonomic classification. ▸ *v.* **1.** To issue a command or instruction. **2.** To request to be supplied with. **3.** To put into a systematic arrangement. **—*idioms:* in order to** For the purpose of. **on the order of** Similar to; like. **to order** According to the buyer's specifications. **—or′der·er** *n.*

or·der·ly (ôr′dər-lē) ▸ *adj.* **1.** Having a systematic arrangement; neat. **2.** Devoid of disruption; peaceful. ▸ *n., pl.* **-lies. 1.** An attendant in a hospital. **2.** A soldier assigned to attend a superior officer. **—or′der·li·ness** *n.*

or·di·nal (ôr′dn-əl) ▸ *adj.* Being of a specified position in a numbered series.

ordinal number ▸ *n.* A number, such as *second* or *tenth,* indicating position in a series.

or·di·nance (ôr′dn-əns) ▸ *n.* **1.** An authoritative command or order. **2.** A municipal statute or regulation.

or·di·nar·i·ly (ôr′dn-âr′ə-lē, ôr′dn-ĕr′-) ▸ *adv.* As a general rule; usually.

or·di·nar·y (ôr′dn-ĕr′ē) ▸ *adj.* **1.** Commonly encountered; usual. **2.** Of no exceptional ability, degree, or quality; average. **—or′di·nar′i·ness** *n.*

or·di·nate (ôr′dn-ĭt, -āt′) ▸ *n.* *Symbol* **y** *Math.* The plane Cartesian coordinate representing the distance from a specified point to the *x*-axis, measured parallel to the *y*-axis.

THESAURUS

oracle *n.* —*See* PROPHECY, PROPHET.

oral *adj.* Expressed or produced in speech or by the voice ▸ articulate, phonetic, phonic, pronounced, spoken, unwritten, uttered, verbal, vocal, voiced, word-of-mouth.

orate *v.* —*See* RANT.

oration *n.* —*See* SPEECH (2).

orator *n.* —*See* SPEAKER (1).

oratorical *adj.* Characterized by elevated language, such as that used in public speaking ▸ aureate, bombastic, declamatory, elocutionary, eloquent, flowery, fustian, grandiloquent, high-flown, high-sounding, inflated, magniloquent, orotund, overblown, rhetorical, sonorous.

oratory *n.* The art of public speaking ▸ declamation, elocution, rhetoric, speech. [*Compare* BOMBAST, ELOQUENCE.]

orb *n.* **1.** The celestial body where humans live ▸ earth, globe, planet, world. **2.** An organ of vision ▸ eye, eyeball. *Slang:* peeper, saucer. *Idiom:* window of the soul. —*See also* BALL.

orbicular *adj.* —*See* ROUND (1).

orbit *n.* —*See* AREA (1), CIRCLE (2), RANGE (1), REVOLUTION (1).

orbit *v.* —*See* ENCIRCLE, TURN (1).

orchestrate *v.* —*See* COMPOSE (1), HARMONIZE (2).

ordain *v.* —*See* DICTATE, ESTABLISH (2).

ordained *adj.* —*See* DIVINE (2).

ordeal *n.* —*See* TRIAL (1).

order *n.* —*See* ARRANGEMENT (1), CLASS (1), CLASS (2), COMMAND (1), DEMAND (1), KIND[2], METHOD, SERIES, SHAPE, UNION (1).

order *v.* —*See* ARRANGE (1), BOSS, COMMAND (1), DEMAND (1).

orderliness *n.* —*See* METHOD.

orderly *adj.* —*See* METHODICAL, NEAT.

orders of the day *n.* —*See* PROGRAM (1).

ordinance *n.* —*See* CEREMONY (1), LAW (1).

ordinarily *adv.* —*See* USUALLY.

ordinariness *n.* —*See* USUALNESS.

ordinary *adj.* Being of no special quality or type ▸ average, bland, boring, common, commonplace, cut-and-dried, formulaic, garden, garden-variety, homely, humdrum, indifferent, mediocre, middling, mundane, nondescript, plain, routine, run-of-the-mill, so-so, standard, stock, undistinguished, unexceptional, unremarkable, white-bread. *Informal:* ho-hum. *Idioms:* fair-to-middling, no great shakes. [*Compare* ACCEPTABLE, HUMBLE, MODEST.] —*See also* COMMON (1).

ordinary *n.* —*See* USUAL.

or·di·na·tion (ôr′dn-ā′shən) ► *n.* The act or ceremony of ordaining, as to the ministry.

ord·nance (ôrd′nəns) ► *n.* **1.** Military materiel, such as weapons and ammunition. **2.** Cannon; artillery.

Or·do·vi·cian (ôr′də-vĭsh′ən) *Geol.* ► *adj.* Of or being the 2nd period of the Paleozoic Era, marked by the appearance of primitive fishes. ► *n.* The Ordovician Period.

or·dure (ôr′jər) ► *n.* Excrement; dung.

ore (ôr) ► *n.* A mineral or rock from which a valuable constituent, esp. a metal, can be mined or extracted.

Ore. ► *abbr.* Oregon

o·re·ad (ôr′ē-ăd′) ► *n.* *Gk. Myth.* A mountain nymph.

o·reg·a·no (ə-rĕg′ə-nō′, ô-rĕg′-) ► *n.* An herb having aromatic leaves used as a seasoning.

Or·e·gon (ôr′ĭ-gən, -gŏn′, ŏr′-) ► A state of the NW US in the Pacific Northwest. Cap. Salem. **—Or′e·go′ni·an** (-gō′nē-ən) *adj. & n.*

or·gan (ôr′gən) ► *n.* **1.** A musical instrument consisting of a number of pipes that sound tones when supplied with air and a keyboard that operates a mechanism controlling the flow of air to the pipes; pipe organ. **2.** An instrument resembling or suggestive of a pipe organ. **3.** *Biol.* A differentiated part of an organism that performs a specific function. **4.** An instrument or agency performing specified functions: *a government organ.* **5.** A periodical.

or·gan·dy (ôr′gən-dē) ► *n., pl.* **-dies.** A stiff transparent fabric of cotton or silk, used for curtains and light apparel.

or·gan·elle (ôr′gə-nĕl′) ► *n.* A differentiated structure within a cell, such as a vacuole, that performs a specific function.

or·gan·ic (ôr-găn′ĭk) ► *adj.* **1.** Of or affecting an organ of the body. **2.** Of or derived from living organisms. **3.** Cultivated or raised without the use of synthetic chemicals, such as pesticides, or drugs, such as hormones. **4.** Resembling a living organism in organization or development: *an organic whole.* **5.** Constituting an integral part of a whole; fundamental. **6.** *Chem.* Of or designating carbon compounds. **—or·gan′i·cal·ly** *adv.* **—or′gan·ic′i·ty** (ôr′gə-nĭs′ĭ-tē) *n.*

or·gan·ism (ôr′gə-nĭz′əm) ► *n.* **1.** A living being. **2.** A system similar to a living body: *the social organism.*

or·gan·ist (ôr′gə-nĭst) ► *n.* One who plays the organ.

or·gan·i·za·tion (ôr′gə-nĭ-zā′shən) ► *n.* **1.** The act of organizing or process of being organized. **2.** Something organized into an ordered whole. **3.** A group of persons organized for a particular purpose; association. **—or′gan·i·za′tion·al** *adj.*

or·gan·ize (ôr′gə-nīz′) ► *v.* **-ized, -iz·ing.** **1.** To put together into an orderly, functional, structured whole. **2.** To arrange in a coherent form; systematize. **3.** To arrange systematically for united action. **4.** To establish as an organization. **5.** To persuade to form or join a labor union. **—or′gan·iz′er** *n.*

or·gan·za (ôr-găn′zə) ► *n.* A sheer stiff fabric of silk or synthetic material.

or·gasm (ôr′găz′əm) ► *n.* The highest point of sexual excitement; climax. **—or·gas′mic, or·gas′tic** *adj.*

or·gy (ôr′jē) ► *n., pl.* **-gies.** **1.** A revel involving unrestrained indulgence, esp. sexual activity. **2.** Uncontrolled indulgence in an activity. **—or′gi·ast** *n.* **—or′gi·as′tic** *adj.*

o·ri·el (ôr′ē-əl) ► *n.* A projecting bay window supported by a bracket.

o·ri·ent (ôr′ē-ənt, -ĕnt′) ► *n.* **Orient** The countries of Asia, esp. of E Asia. ► *v.* (ôr′ē-ĕnt′) **1.** To locate or place in a particular relation to the points of the compass. **2.** To make familiar with or adjusted to a situation. **—o′ri·en·tate′** *v.* **—o′ri·en·ta′tion** *n.*

O·ri·en·tal also **o·ri·en·tal** (ôr′ē-ĕn′tl) ► *adj.* Of or designating the Orient. ► *n.* *Often Offensive* An Asian person.

or·i·fice (ôr′ə-fĭs, ŏr′-) ► *n.* An opening, esp. to a cavity or passage of the body. **—or′i·fi′cial** (-fĭsh′əl) *adj.*

o·ri·ga·mi (ôr′ĭ-gä′mē) ► *n.* The Japanese art of folding paper.

or·i·gin (ôr′ə-jĭn, ŏr′-) ► *n.* **1.** The point at which something comes into existence. **2.** Ancestry. **3.** The fact of originating. **4.** *Math.* The point of intersection of coordinate axes.

o·rig·i·nal (ə-rĭj′ə-nəl) ► *adj.* **1.** Preceding all others; first. **2.** Fresh and unusual; new. **3.** Inventive. ► *n.* **1.** A first form from which other forms are made or developed. **2.** An authentic work of art. **—o·rig′i·nal′i·ty** (-năl′ĭ-tē) *n.* **—o·rig′i·nal·ly** *adv.*

o·rig·i·nate (ə-rĭj′ə-nāt′) ► *v.* **-nat·ed, -nat·ing.** To come or bring into being. **—o·rig′i·na′tion** *n.* **—o·rig′i·na′tor** *n.*

O·ri·no·co (ôr′ə-nō′kō) ► A river rising in SE Venezuela and flowing more than 2,414 km (1,500 mi) to the Atlantic.

o·ri·ole (ôr′ē-ōl′) ► *n.* A songbird with black and bright yellow or orange plumage.

O·ri·on (ō-rī′ən, ə-rī′-) ► *n.* A constellation in the celestial equator near Gemini and Taurus.

or·i·son (ôr′ĭ-sən, -zən, ŏr′-) ► *n.* A prayer.

Ork·ney Islands (ôrk′nē) ► An archipelago in the Atlantic Ocean and the North Sea off the NE coast of Scotland.

Or·lon (ôr′lŏn′) ► A trademark for an acrylic fiber.

Or·mazd (ôr′məzd) ► *n.* The chief deity of Zoroastrianism.

or·mo·lu (ôr′mə-lo͞o′) ► *n.* An alloy resembling gold, used to ornament furniture.

Or·muz (ôr′mŭz′, ôr-mo͞oz′), **Strait of** ► See **Hormuz**.

or·na·ment (ôr′nə-mənt) ► *n.* Something that decorates or adorns; embellishment. ► *v.* (-mĕnt′) To decorate. **—or′na·men′tal** *adj.* **—or′na·men′tal·ly** *adv.* **—or′na·men·ta′tion** *n.*

or·nate (ôr-nāt′) ► *adj.* Elaborately, often excessively ornamented. **—or·nate′ly** *adv.* **—or·nate′ness** *n.*

or·ner·y (ôr′nə-rē) ► *adj.* **-i·er, -i·est.** Mean and stubborn; cantankerous. **—or′ner·i·ness′** *n.*

or·ni·thol·o·gy (ôr′nə-thŏl′ə-jē) ► *n.* The branch of zoology that deals with the study of birds. **—or′ni·tho·log′ic** (-thə-lŏj′ĭk), **or′ni·tho·log′i·cal** *adj.* **—or′ni·thol′o·gist** *n.*

o·ro·tund (ôr′ə-tŭnd′) ► *adj.* **1.** Pompous and bombastic. **2.** Sonorous.

or·phan (ôr′fən) ► *n.* A child whose parents are dead. **—or′phan** *v.* **—or′phan·hood′** *n.*

THESAURUS

organ *n.* *—See* AGENT, BRANCH (3), PUBLICATION (2).

organic *adj.* *—See* NATURAL (1).

organization *n.* *—See* ALLIANCE, ARRANGEMENT (1), FOUNDATION, METHOD, SYSTEM, UNION (1).

organizational *adj.* *—See* ADMINISTRATIVE.

organize *v.* *—See* ARRANGE (1), ARRANGE (2), FOUND, MOBILIZE.

organized *adj.* *—See* METHODICAL.

orgy *n.* *—See* BINGE.

orientation *n.* *—See* BEARING (3).

orifice *n.* *—See* HOLE (2).

oriflamme *n.* *—See* FLAG[1].

origin *n.* A point of origination ► beginning, birthplace, cradle, derivation, font, fount, fountain, fountainhead, hotbed, mother, parent, provenance, provenience, rise, root, rootstock, source, spring, well, wellspring. [*Compare* GERM.] *—See also* ANCESTRY, BIRTH (2).

original *adj.* Not derived from something else ► archetypal, archetypical, primary, prime, primitive, pristine, prototypic, prototypical, seminal. [*Compare* ELEMENTAL.] *—See also* AUTHENTIC (1), FIRST, INVENTIVE, NEW, RADICAL.

original *n.* A first form from which varieties arise or imitations are made ► archetype, father, forerunner, master, model, paradigm, pattern, protoplast, prototype, standard. *—See also* CHARACTER (5), REBEL (2).

originality *n.* *—See* INVENTION (1), NOVELTY (1).

originate *v.* To have as one's home or place of origin ► hail, come. [*Compare* DESCEND.] *—See also* BEGIN, DESIGN (1), FOUND, INTRODUCE (1), PRODUCE (1), STEM.

origination *n.* *—See* BEGINNING, FOUNDATION, INVENTION (2).

originator *n.* One that creates, founds, or originates ► architect, author, begetter, creator, father, framer, founder, initiator, inventor, maker, parent, patriarch, prime mover. [*Compare* DEVELOPER.]

orison *n.* *—See* PRAYER[1] (2).

ornament *n.* *—See* ADORNMENT.

ornament *v.* *—See* ADORN (1).

ornamentation *n.* *—See* ADORNMENT.

ornate *adj.* Elaborately and heavily ornamented ► baroque, decorated, flamboyant, florid, flowery, gilded, gilt, jeweled, ornamented, ostentatious, resplendent, rococo. [*Compare* GAUDY, SHOWY.] *—See also* ELABORATE.

orneriness *n.* *—See* TEMPER (1).

ornery *adj.* *—See* CONTRARY.

orotund *adj.* *—See* ORATORICAL, RESONANT.

orotundity *n.* *—See* BOMBAST.

orphan *n.* A child or young animal

or·phan·age (ôr′fə-nĭj) ► *n.* An institution for the care of orphans.

Or·phe·us (ôr′fē-əs, -fyo͞os′) ► *n. Gk. Myth.* A poet and musician who almost succeeded in rescuing his wife Eurydice from Hades. **—Or′phic** *adj.*

ortho– or **orth–** ► *pref.* 1. Straight; correct: *orthodontics.* 2. Perpendicular: *orthogonal.*

or·tho·don·tia (ôr′thə-dŏn′shə) or **or·tho·don·ture** (-dŏn′chər) ► *n.* Orthodontics.

or·tho·don·tics (ôr′thə-dŏn′tĭks) ► *n. (takes sing. v.)* The dental specialty and practice of correcting irregularities of the teeth. **—or′tho·don′tic** *adj.* **—or′tho·don′tist** *n.*

or·tho·dox (ôr′thə-dŏks′) ► *adj.* 1. Adhering to an accepted or established doctrine. 2. often **Orthodox** Of or relating to the most conservative or traditional form of a religion, philosophy, or ideology. 3. **Orthodox** Of or relating to the Eastern Orthodox Church. 4. Commonly accepted; customary. **—or′tho·dox′ly** *adv.* **—or′tho·dox′y** *n.*

or·thog·o·nal (ôr-thŏg′ə-nəl) ► *adj. Math.* Relating to or composed of right angles. **—or·thog′o·nal·ly** *adv.*

or·thog·ra·phy (ôr-thŏg′rə-fē) ► *n., pl.* **-phies.** 1. Correct spelling. 2. A method of representing the sounds of a language by letters and diacritics. **—or′tho·graph′ic** (ôr′thə-grăf′ĭk) *adj.* **—or′tho·graph′i·cal·ly** *adv.*

or·tho·pe·dics (ôr′thə-pē′dĭks) ► *n. (takes sing. v.)* The branch of medicine that deals with injuries or disorders of the skeletal system. **—or′tho·pe′dic** *adj.* **—or′tho·pe′di·cal·ly** *adv.* **—or′tho·pe′dist** *n.*

or·thot·ics (ôr-thŏt′ĭks) ► *n. (takes sing. v.)* The science that deals with the use of specialized mechanical devices to support or supplement impaired joints or limbs. **—or·thot′ic** *adj. & n.* **—or·thot′ist** (ôr-thŏt′ĭst, ôr′thə-tĭst) *n.*

Or·well (ôr′wĕl′, -wəl), **George.** Eric Arthur Blair (1903–50) ► British writer.

–ory ► *suff.* 1. Of, relating to, or characterized by: *advisory.* 2. A place or thing used for or connected with: *crematory.*

o·ryx (ôr′ĭks, ŏr′-) ► *n., pl.* **oryx** or **-es.** An African antelope having slightly curved horns.

Os ► The symbol for the element **osmium.**

O·sage (ō′sāj′, ō-sāj′) ► *n., pl.* **O·sage** or **O·sag·es.** 1. A member of a Native American people formerly inhabiting W Missouri, now in N-central Oklahoma. 2. Their Siouan language. **—O′sage′** *adj.*

O·sa·ka (ō-sä′kə) ► A city of S Honshu, Japan, on **Osaka Bay,** an inlet of the Pacific.

Os·ce·o·la (ŏs′ē-ō′lə, ō′sē-) (1804?–38) ► Seminole leader.

os·cil·late (ŏs′ə-lāt′) ► *v.* **-lat·ed, -lat·ing.** 1. To swing back and forth steadily. 2. To waver; vacillate. 3. *Phys.* To vary between alternate extremes, usu. within a definable period of time. **—os′cil·la′tion** *n.* **—os′cil·la′tor** *n.*

os·cil·lo·scope (ə-sĭl′ə-skōp′) ► *n.* An electronic instrument that produces an instantaneous trace on the screen of a cathode-ray tube corresponding to oscillations of voltage and current. **—os·cil′lo·scop′ic** (-skŏp′ĭk) *adj.*

os·cu·late (ŏs′kyə-lāt′) ► *v.* **-lat·ed, -lat·ing.** 1. To kiss. 2. To come together; contact. **—os′cu·la′tion** *n.*

–ose[1] ► *suff.* Possessing; having the characteristics of: *comatose.*

–ose[2] ► *suff.* Carbohydrate: *fructose.*

o·sier (ō′zhər) ► *n.* 1. A willow having long rodlike twigs used in basketry. 2. A twig of such a willow.

O·si·ris (ō-sī′rĭs) ► *n. Myth.* The ancient Egyptian god of the underworld, the brother and husband of Isis.

–osis ► *suff.* 1. Condition; process; action: *osmosis.* 2. Diseased or abnormal condition: *cyanosis.*

Os·lo (ŏz′lō, ŏs′-) ► The capital of Norway, in the southeast part.

os·mi·um (ŏz′mē-əm) ► *n. Symbol* **Os** A bluish-white, hard, dense metallic element used as a platinum hardener and in phonograph needles. At. no. 76.

os·mo·sis (ŏz-mō′sĭs, ŏs-) ► *n.* 1. Diffusion of fluid through a semipermeable membrane until there is an equal concentration of fluid on both sides of the membrane. 2. A gradual process of assimilation or absorption. **—os·mot′ic** (-mŏt′ĭk) *adj.* **—os·mot′i·cal·ly** *adv.*

os·prey (ŏs′prē, -prā) ► *n., pl.* **-preys.** A large fish-eating hawk having dark plumage on the back and white below.

os·si·fy (ŏs′ə-fī′) ► *v.* **-fied, -fy·ing.** 1. To change into bone. 2. To become set in a rigidly conventional pattern. **—os·sif′ic** (ŏ-sĭf′ĭk) *adj.* **—os′si·fi·ca′tion** *n.*

os·te·i·tis (ŏs′tē-ī′tĭs) ► *n.* Inflammation of bone or bony tissue.

os·ten·si·ble (ŏ-stĕn′sə-bəl) ► *adj.* Represented or appearing as such; apparent. **—os·ten′si·bly** *adv.*

os·ten·ta·tion (ŏs′tĕn-tā′shən, -tən-) ► *n.* Pretentious display.

os·ten·ta·tious (ŏs′tĕn-tā′shəs, -tən-) ► *adj.* Pretentious. **—os′ten·ta′tious·ly** *adv.*

osteo– or **oste–** ► *pref.* Bone: *osteopathy.*

os·te·op·a·thy (ŏs′tē-ŏp′ə-thē) ► *n.* A system that emphasizes manipulation esp. of the bones for treating disease. **—os′te·o·path′** (ŏs′tē-ə-păth′) *n.* **—os′te·o·path′ic** *adj.* **—os′te·o·path′i·cal·ly** *adv.*

os·te·o·po·ro·sis (ŏs′tē-ō-pə-rō′sĭs) ► *n.* A disease in which the bones become extremely porous, occurring esp. in women following menopause. **—os′te·o·po·rot′ic** (-rŏt′ĭk) *adj.*

os·tra·cize (ŏs′trə-sīz′) ► *v.* **-cized, -ciz·ing.** To banish or exclude from a group. **—os′tra·cism** *n.*

os·trich (ŏs′trĭch, ôs′-) ► *n., pl.* **-trich** or **-trich·es.** A large, swift-running flightless bird of Africa, having a long bare neck and two-toed feet.

Os·tro·goth (ŏs′trə-gŏth′) ► *n.* One of a tribe of eastern Goths that conquered and ruled Italy from A.D. 493 to 555.

OT ► *abbr.* 1. Old Testament 2. overtime

oth·er (ŭth′ər) ► *adj.* 1a. Being the remaining one of two or more. b. Being the remaining ones of several. 2. Different from that or those implied or specified. 3. Additional; extra. 4. Opposite; reverse. 5. Alternate; second: *every other day.* 6. Of the recent past: *the other day.* ► *n.* 1a. The remaining one of two or more. b. **others** The remaining ones of several. 2a. A different one: *one storm after the other.* b. An additional one: *How many others will come later?* ► *pron.* A different person or thing. ► *adv.* In another way.

oth·er·wise (ŭth′ər-wīz′) ► *adv.* 1. In another way; differently. 2. Under other circumstances. 3. In other respects: *an otherwise logical mind.* ► *adj.* Other than supposed; different: *The facts are otherwise.*

oth·er·world·ly (ŭth′ər-wûrld′lē) ► *adj.* 1. Of or characteristic of another world, esp. a mystical world. 2. Concerned with intellectual or imaginative things. **—oth′er·world′li·ness** *n.*

–otic ► *suff.* 1. Of or characterized by a specified condition or process: *mitotic.* 2. Having a specified disease or abnormality: *sclerotic.*

o·ti·ose (ō′shē-ōs′, ō′tē-) ► *adj.* 1. Lazy. 2. Of no use. 3. Futile.

o·ti·tis (ō-tī′tĭs) ► *n.* Inflammation of the ear.

Ot·ta·wa[1] (ŏt′ə-wə, -wä′, -wô′) ► *n., pl.* **-wa** or **-was.** 1. A member of a Native American people of S Ontario and N Michigan. 2. The Ojibwa dialect spoken by the Ottawa.

Ot·ta·wa[2] (ŏt′ə-wə) ► The capital of Canada, in SE Ontario on the Ottawa R.

THESAURUS

without parents ► foundling, ragamuffin, stray, waif.

ort *n.* —*See* BIT[1] (1), END (3).

orthodox *adj.* —*See* ACCEPTED, CONSERVATIVE (1), CONVENTIONAL.

orthodox *n.* —*See* CONSERVATIVE.

orthodoxy *n.* —*See* DOCTRINE.

oscillate *v.* —*See* SWAY.

osculate *v.* —*See* KISS.

osculation *n.* —*See* KISS.

osmose *v.* —*See* DRINK (3).

osmosis *n.* —*See* ABSORPTION (1).

ossify *v.* —*See* HARDEN (2).

ossuary *n.* —*See* GRAVE[1].

ostensible or **ostensive** *adj.* —*See* APPARENT (2).

ostensibly or **ostensively** *adv.* —*See* APPARENTLY.

ostentation *n.* —*See* PRETENTIOUSNESS.

ostentatious *adj.* —*See* ORNATE, SHOWY.

ostracism *n.* —*See* EXILE.

ostracize *v.* —*See* BANISH, EXCLUDE.

other *adj.* —*See* ADDITIONAL.

otherworldly *adj.* —*See* SUPERNATURAL (1), WEIRD.

otiose *adj.* —*See* HOLLOW (1), LAZY.

otiosity or **otioseness** *n.* —*See* LAZINESS.

ot·ter (ŏt′ər) ▸ *n., pl.* **-ter** or **-ters.** 1. Any of several aquatic carnivorous mammals having webbed feet and thick brown fur. 2. The fur of an otter.

ot·to·man (ŏt′ə-mən) ▸ *n., pl.* **-mans.** 1. A backless upholstered sofa. 2. An upholstered footstool.

Ottoman ▸ *n., pl.* **-mans.** A Turk, esp. of the Ottoman Empire. ▸ *adj.* 1. Of the Ottoman Empire. 2. Turkish.

Ottoman Empire ▸ A Turkish sultanate (1299?–1919) of SW Asia, NE Africa, and SE Europe.

ouch (ouch) ▸ *interj.* Used to express sudden pain.

ought[1] (ôt) ▸ *aux.v.* Used to indicate: **a.** Obligation or duty: *You ought to work harder than that.* **b.** Advisability or prudence: *You ought to wear a raincoat.* **c.** Desirability: *You ought to have been there.* **d.** Probability or likelihood: *She ought to finish by next week.*

ought[2] (ôt) ▸ *pron. & adv.* Var. of **aught**[1].

ought[3] (ôt) ▸ *n.* Var. of **aught**[2].

ou·gui·ya (o͞o-gē′yə) ▸ *n.* See **currency** table in Appendix.

ounce (ouns) ▸ *n.* 1a. See **measurement** table in Appendix. **b.** A unit of apothecary weight, equal to 480 grains (31.104 grams). 2. A fluid ounce. 3. A tiny bit.

our (our) ▸ *adj.* The possessive form of **we.** Used as a modifier before a noun: *our deeds; our hometown.*

ours (ourz) ▸ *pron. (takes sing. or pl. v.)* Used to indicate the one or ones belonging to us: *The victory is ours. If your car doesn't start, take ours.*

our·self (our-sĕlf′, är-) ▸ *pron.* Myself. Used as a reflexive, as in a royal proclamation.

our·selves (our-sĕlvz′, är-) ▸ *pron.* 1. Those ones identical with us. Used: **a.** Reflexively as a direct or indirect object or the object of a preposition: *We bought ourselves a new camera.* **b.** For emphasis. 2. Our normal or healthy condition: *We're feeling ourselves again.*

–ous ▸ *suff.* 1. Possessing; full of: *joyous.* 2. Having a valence lower than in compounds or ions named with adjectives ending in *-ic*: *ferrous.*

oust (oust) ▸ *v.* To eject; force out.

oust·er (ous′tər) ▸ *n.* Eviction; expulsion.

out (out) ▸ *adv.* 1. Away from the inside. 2. Away from the center or middle. 3. Away from a usual place. 4. Outside: *went out to play.* 5a. To exhaustion or depletion: *The supplies have run out.* **b.** Into extinction: *The fire has gone out.* **c.** To a finish or conclusion: *Play the game out.* 6. In or into a state of unconsciousness: *The drug put him out for hours.* 7. Into view: *The moon came out.* 8. Into distribution: *giving out free passes.* 9. Into disuse. 10. *Baseball* So as to be retired. 11. On strike. ▸ *adj.* 1. Exterior; external. 2. Outgoing: *the out doorway.* 3. Not operating or operational: *The power was out.* 4. Not to be considered or permitted: *A taxi is out, because I don't have any money.* 5. No longer fashionable. 6. No longer existing in one's possession or supplies: *We're out of coffee.* 7. *Baseball* Retired. 8. *Informal* Openly gay, lesbian, or bisexual. ▸ *prep.* 1. Forth from; through. 2. Within the area of: *a house with a garden out back.* ▸ *n.* 1. One that is out, esp. one who is out of power. 2. A means of escape. 3. *Baseball* A play in which a batter or base runner is retired. ▸ *v.* 1. To be disclosed or revealed: *Truth will out.* 2. To expose (someone) as being gay, lesbian, or bisexual. ***—idiom:* on the outs** *Informal* Not on friendly terms.

out– ▸ *pref.* In a way that surpasses or exceeds: *outdistance.*

out·age (ou′tĭj) ▸ *n.* A temporary suspension of operation, esp. of electric power.

out-and-out (out′n-out′) ▸ *adj.* Complete; thoroughgoing.

out·back (out′băk′) ▸ *n.* The wild, remote part esp. of Australia or New Zealand.

out·bid (out-bĭd′) ▸ *v.* To bid higher than.

out·board (out′bôrd′) ▸ *adj.* 1. Situated outside the hull of a vessel. 2. Situated toward or nearer the end of an aircraft wing. **—out′board′** *adv.*

out·bound (out′bound′) ▸ *adj.* Outward bound.

out·break (out′brāk′) ▸ *n.* A sudden eruption.

out·build·ing (out′bĭl′dĭng) ▸ *n.* A building separate from but associated with a main building.

out·burst (out′bûrst′) ▸ *n.* A sudden violent display, as of activity or emotion.

out·cast (out′kăst′) ▸ *n.* One that has been excluded from a society. **—out′cast′** *adj.*

out·class (out-klăs′) ▸ *v.* To surpass decisively, so as to appear of a higher class.

out·come (out′kŭm′) ▸ *n.* A result; consequence.

out·crop (out′krŏp′) ▸ *n.* A portion of bedrock protruding through the soil level. **—out·crop′** *v.*

out·cry (out′krī′) ▸ *n.* 1. A loud cry or clamor. 2. A strong protest.

out·dat·ed (out-dā′tĭd) ▸ *adj.* Out-of-date; old-fashioned.

out·dis·tance (out-dĭs′təns) ▸ *v.* To surpass by a wide margin.

out·do (out-do͞o′) ▸ *v.* To do better than.

out·door (out′dôr′) also **out-of-door** (out′əv-dôr′) ▸ *adj.* Located in, done in, or suited to the open air.

out·doors (out-dôrz′) also **out-of-doors** (out′əv-dôrz′) ▸ *n.* The open air; the area away from buildings. ▸ *adv.* In or into the outdoors.

out·er (ou′tər) ▸ *adj.* 1. Located on the outside. 2. Farther from the center or middle.

outer ear ▸ *n.* See **external ear.**

out·er·most (ou′tər-mōst′) ▸ *adj.* Farthest out.

outer space ▸ *n.* Space beyond the limits of a celestial body or system.

out·face (out-fās′) ▸ *v.* 1. To overcome with a bold or self-assured look. 2. To defy.

out·fall (out′fôl′) ▸ *n.* The place where a sewer, drain, or stream discharges.

out·field (out′fēld′) ▸ *n.* *Baseball* The playing area extending outward from the diamond. **—out′field′er** *n.*

out·fit (out′fĭt′) ▸ *n.* 1. Clothing or equipment for a specialized purpose. 2. *Informal* An association of persons who work together. ▸ *v.* To provide with an outfit. **—out′fit′ter** *n.*

out·flank (out-flăngk′) ▸ *v.* 1. To maneuver around the flank of (an opposing force). 2. To gain a tactical advantage over.

out·flow (out′flō′) ▸ *n.* 1. The act of flowing out. 2. Something that flows out.

out·fox (out-fŏks′) ▸ *v.* To outsmart.

out·go (out′gō′) ▸ *n., pl.* **-goes.** Something that goes out, esp. money.

out·go·ing (out′gō′ĭng) ▸ *adj.* 1. Going out; departing. 2.

THESAURUS

ottoman *n.* A stool or cushion for resting the feet ▸ footrest, footstool, hassock.

ought *v.* —*See* MUST.

ounce *n.* —*See* BIT[1] (1).

oust *v.* —*See* EJECT (1).

ouster *n.* —*See* EJECTION.

out *v.* To be made public ▸ break, come out, get out, transpire. *Informal:* leak (out). [*Compare* AIR, ANNOUNCE, APPEAR.]

out *adj.* —*See* ABSENT, OLD-FASHIONED, UNCONSCIOUS.

out *adv.* —*See* FORWARD.

outage *n.* A cessation of proper functioning ▸ breakdown, collapse, failure, malfunction.

out-and-out *adj.* —*See* UTTER[2].

outback *n.* —*See* WILDERNESS.

outbreak *n.* —*See* ERUPTION, OUTBURST.

outburst *n.* A sudden violent expression, as of activity or emotion ▸ access, blowup, burst, dambreak, damburst, eruption, explosion, fit, flare-up, flood, gush, gust, outbreak, outpouring, paroxysm, torrent. —*See also* ERUPTION.

outcast *n.* Someone excluded from society ▸ exile, outsider, pariah, persona non grata, reject, untouchable. [*Compare* FUGITIVE.]

outcast *adj.* —*See* ABANDONED (1).

outcome *n.* —*See* EFFECT (1).

outcry *n.* —*See* SHOUT, VOCIFERATION.

outdated *adj.* —*See* OBSOLETE, OLD-FASHIONED.

outdo *v.* —*See* SURPASS.

outdoors *n.* —*See* WILDERNESS.

outermost *adj.* —*See* EXTREME (1).

outfit *n.* Things needed for a task, journey, or other purpose ▸ accouterments, apparatus, equipment, gear, material, materiel, paraphernalia, rig, tackle, turnout. —*See also* COMPANY (1), DRESS (2).

outflow *n.* —*See* FLOW.

outfox *v.* —*See* OUTWIT.

outgoing *adj.* Disposed to be open, sociable, and talkative ▸ communicable, communicative, expansive, extroverted, gregarious, unreserved.

Addressed for sending: *outgoing mail.* 3. Sociable; friendly.

out·grow (out-grō′) ▸ *v.* 1. To grow too large for. 2. To grow too mature for: *outgrow childish games.* 3. To surpass in growth.

out·growth (out′grōth′) ▸ *n.* 1. A product of growing out; offshoot. 2. A consequence.

out·guess (out-gĕs′) ▸ *v.* To anticipate correctly the actions of.

out·house (out′hous′) ▸ *n.* 1. A toilet housed in a small outdoor structure. 2. An outbuilding.

out·ing (ou′tĭng) ▸ *n.* 1. An excursion. 2. A walk outdoors. 3. The exposing of someone as being gay, lesbian, or bisexual.

out·land (out′lănd′, -lənd) ▸ *n.* 1. A foreign land. 2. **outlands** The outlying areas of a country. **—out′land′** *adj.* **—out′land′er** *n.*

out·land·ish (out-lăn′dĭsh) ▸ *adj.* 1. Conspicuously unconventional; bizarre. 2. Strikingly unfamiliar. **—out·land′ish·ly** *adv.* **—out·land′ish·ness** *n.*

out·last (out-lăst′) ▸ *v.* To last longer than.

out·law (out′lô′) ▸ *n.* 1. A fugitive from the law. 2. A person excluded from normal legal protection and rights. ▸ *v.* 1. To declare illegal. 2. To deprive of the protection of the law. **—out′law′** *adj.* **—out′law′ry** *n.*

out·lay (out′lā′) ▸ *n.* 1. The spending or disbursement of money. 2. An amount spent.

out·let (out′lĕt′, -lĭt) ▸ *n.* 1a. A passage for escape or exit; vent. b. A means of release or gratification, as for energies or desires. 2. A commercial market for goods or services. 3. A receptacle connected to a power supply and having a socket for a plug.

out·line (out′līn′) ▸ *n.* 1a. A line marking the outer boundaries of an object or figure. b. Shape; contour. 2. A style of drawing in which objects are delineated in contours without shading. 3. A short description, account, or summary. ▸ *v.* **-lined, -lin·ing.** 1. To draw an outline of. 2. To give the main features of; summarize.

out·live (out-lĭv′) ▸ *v.* To live longer than.

out·look (out′lo͝ok′) ▸ *n.* 1. A point of view; attitude. 2. Expectation for the future; prospect. 3a. A place where something can be viewed. b. The view seen.

out·ly·ing (out′lī′ĭng) ▸ *adj.* Relatively distant or remote from a center.

out·ma·neu·ver (out′mə-no͞o′vər, -nyo͞o′-) ▸ *v.* 1. To overcome by more artful maneuvering. 2. To excel in maneuverability.

out·mod·ed (out-mō′dĭd) ▸ *adj.* 1. Not in fashion. 2. Obsolete.

out·num·ber (out-nŭm′bər) ▸ *v.* To be more numerous than.

out of ▸ *prep.* 1a. From within to the outside of: *got out of the car.* b. From a given condition: *came out of her trance.* c. From a source or cause: *made out of wood.* 2a. In a position or situation beyond the range, boundaries, or sphere of: *flew out of sight.* b. In a state away from the expected or usual: *out of practice.* 3. From among: *five out of six votes.* 4. Because of: *did it out of spite.* 5. In a condition of no longer having: *We're out of coffee.*

out-of-bounds (out′əv-boundz′) ▸ *adv. & adj.* Beyond the designated boundaries or limits.

out-of-date (out′əv-dāt′) ▸ *adj.* Out of style.

out-of-door (out′əv-dôr′) ▸ *adj.* Var. of **outdoor.**

out-of-doors (out′əv-dôrz′) ▸ *adv. & n.* Var. of **outdoors.**

out-of-pock·et (out′əv-pŏk′ĭt) ▸ *adj.* 1. Calling for the spending of cash: *out-of-pocket expenses.* 2. Lacking funds.

out-of-the-way (out′əv-*th*ə-wā′) ▸ *adj.* 1. Remote; secluded. 2. Unusual.

out·pace (out-pās′) ▸ *v.* To surpass; outstrip.

out·pa·tient (out′pā′shənt) ▸ *n.* A patient who receives treatment at a hospital but does not require an overnight stay.

out·place·ment (out′plās′mənt) ▸ *n.* The process by which an employer helps a terminated employee find a new job.

out·play (out-plā′) ▸ *v.* To play better than.

out·post (out′pōst′) ▸ *n.* 1a. A detachment of troops stationed at a distance from a main force. b. The station occupied by such troops. 2. An outlying settlement.

out·pour·ing (out′pôr′ĭng) ▸ *n.* Something that pours out or is poured out.

out·put (out′po͝ot′) ▸ *n.* 1. An amount produced or manufactured during a certain time. 2a. The energy, power, or work produced by a system. b. *Comp. Sci.* The information produced by a program or process from a specific input. **—out′put′** *v.*

output device ▸ *n.* A device, such as a printer or speaker, that presents computer data.

out·rage (out′rāj′) ▸ *n.* 1. An act of extreme violence or viciousness. 2. An act grossly offensive to decency or good taste. 3. Resentful anger. ▸ *v.* **-raged, -rag·ing.** 1. To commit an outrage on. 2. To produce anger or indignity in.

out·ra·geous (out-rā′jəs) ▸ *adj.* 1a. Grossly offensive. b. Beyond the bounds of good taste. 2. Extravagant; immoderate. **—out·ra′geous·ly** *adv.* **—out·ra′geous·ness** *n.*

out·rank (out-răngk′) ▸ *v.* To rank higher than.

ou·tré (o͞o-trā′) ▸ *adj.* Eccentric; bizarre.

out·reach (out-rēch′) ▸ *v.* 1. To surpass in reach. 2. To exceed. ▸ *n.* (out′rēch′) 1. Extent of reach. 2. A systematic attempt to provide services to a community.

out·rid·er (out′rī′dər) ▸ *n.* A mounted attendant.

out·rig·ger (out′rĭg′ər) ▸ *n.* 1. A long thin float attached

THESAURUS

[*Compare* AMIABLE, FRIENDLY, SOCIAL, TALKATIVE.]

outgrowth *n.* —*See* BUMP (1), DERIVATIVE.

outgun *v.* —*See* DEFEAT.

outing *n.* A usually short journey taken for pleasure ▸ excursion, jaunt, junket, trip. [*Compare* EXCURSION, JOURNEY.]

outlander *n.* —*See* FOREIGNER.

outlandish *adj.* —*See* ECCENTRIC, EXOTIC.

outlast *v.* To live, exist, or remain longer than ▸ outlive, outwear, survive. [*Compare* SURVIVE.]

outlaw *v.* —*See* FORBID.

outlaw *n.* One who flees, as from confinement or the police ▸ escapee, fugitive, refugee, runaway. [*Compare* CRIMINAL.] —*See also* CRIMINAL.

outlawed *adj.* —*See* ILLEGAL.

outlay *n.* —*See* COST (1), OVERHEAD.

outlay *v.* —*See* SPEND (1).

outlet *n.* 1. A socket connected to a power supply ▸ plug, electric socket, socket, terminal, wall socket. 2. A retail establishment where merchandise is sold ▸ boutique, emporium, shop, store. —*See also* HOLE (2).

outline *n.* —*See* DRAFT (1), FORM (1), SYNOPSIS.

outline *v.* —*See* DESIGN (2), DRAFT (1).

outlive *v.* To live, exist, or remain longer than ▸ outlast, outwear, survive. [*Compare* SURVIVE.]

outlook *n.* Chance of success or advancement ▸ future, prospects. [*Compare* CHANCE.] —*See also* LOOKOUT (2), POSTURE (2), PREDICTION, VIEW (2), VIEWPOINT.

outlying *adj.* —*See* REMOTE (1).

outmaneuver *v.* —*See* OUTWIT.

outmatch *v.* —*See* SURPASS.

outmoded *adj.* —*See* OBSOLETE, OLD-FASHIONED.

outmost *adj.* —*See* EXTREME (1).

out-of-date *adj.* —*See* OBSOLETE, OLD-FASHIONED.

out of sight *adj.* —*See* EXCEPTIONAL.

out-of-the-way *adj.* —*See* INDIRECT (1), REMOTE (1).

outpace *v.* —*See* PASS (2).

outplay *v.* —*See* DEFEAT.

outpour *n.* —*See* FLOW.

outpouring *n.* —*See* FLOW, OUTBURST.

output *n.* The amount or quantity produced ▸ garner, production, yield. —*See also* COMPOSITION (1).

outrage *n.* A monstrous offense or evil ▸ atrocity, barbarity, enormity, horror, inhumanity, monstrosity. [*Compare* CRIME.] —*See also* ANGER, INDIGNITY, INJUSTICE (1).

outrage *v.* —*See* INSULT, OFFEND (1).

outrageous *adj.* Exceeding the bounds of morality, decency, or reason ▸ appalling, atrocious, heinous, inhuman, intolerable, monstrous, obscene, preposterous, reprehensible, ridiculous, scandalous, shocking, unconscionable, ungodly, unreasonable, unspeakable, wanton. ***Idioms:*** beyond the pale, out of bounds, out of sight. [*Compare* ECCENTRIC, EXCESSIVE, FLAGRANT, OFFENSIVE, SHAMEFUL.]

outrageousness *n.* The quality or state of being outrageous ▸ atrociousness, atrocity, enormity, heinousness, monstrousness, scandalousness. [*Compare* FLAGRANCY.]

outré *adj.* —*See* EXOTIC.

parallel to a seagoing canoe to prevent it from capsizing. 2. A vessel fitted with an outrigger.
out·right (out′rīt′, -rīt′) ▸ *adv.* 1. Without reservation or qualification. 2. Completely; wholly. 3. At once; straightway. ▸ *adj.* (out′rīt′) 1. Unqualified: *an outright gift.* 2. Thoroughgoing; out-and-out.
out·run (out-rŭn′) ▸ *v.* 1. To run faster than. 2. To exceed.
out·sell (out-sĕl′) ▸ *v.* To surpass in sales or selling.
out·set (out′sĕt′) ▸ *n.* Beginning; start.
out·shine (out-shīn′) ▸ *v.* 1. To shine brighter than. 2. To outdo.
out·side (out-sīd′, out′sīd′) ▸ *n.* 1. The outer surface or side; exterior. 2. The space beyond a boundary or limit. 3. The utmost limit; maximum: *We'll be leaving in ten days at the outside.* ▸ *adj.* 1. Of, restricted to, or situated on the outer side; external: *an outside door lock.* 2. Acting, occurring, originating, or being at a place beyond certain limits: *outside assistance.* 3. Extreme; uttermost: *exceeded even our outside estimates.* 4. Unlikely; remote: *an outside chance.* ▸ *adv.* 1. On or to the outer side. 2. Outdoors. ▸ *prep.* 1. On or to the outer side of. 2. Beyond the limits of: *outside the city.* 3. Except: *no information outside the figures given.*
outside of ▸ *prep.* Outside.
out·sid·er (out-sī′dər) ▸ *n.* One who is not part of a group or community.
out·size (out′sīz′) ▸ *n.* An unusual size, esp. a very large size. **—out′size′, out′sized′** *adj.*
out·skirts (out′skûrts′) ▸ *pl.n.* The peripheral parts, as of a city.
out·smart (out-smärt′) ▸ *v.* To outwit.
out·spend (out-spĕnd′) ▸ *v.* 1. To spend beyond the limits of. 2. To outdo in spending.
out·spo·ken (out-spō′kən) ▸ *adj.* 1. Spoken without reserve; candid. 2. Frank in speech. **—out·spo′ken·ly** *adv.* **—out·spo′ken·ness** *n.*
out·spread (out-sprĕd′) ▸ *v.* To spread out; extend. **—out′-spread′** *adj.*
out·stand·ing (out-stăn′dĭng, out′stăn′-) ▸ *adj.* 1. Prominent. 2. Superior; distinguished. 3. Projecting upward or outward. 4. Not settled or resolved. **—out·stand′ing·ly** *adv.*
out·stretch (out-strĕch′) ▸ *v.* To extend.
out·strip (out-strĭp′) ▸ *v.* 1. To leave behind; outrun. 2. To exceed; surpass.
out·take (out′tāk′) ▸ *n.* A shot or scene, as of a movie, that is filmed but not used in the final version.
out·ward (out′wərd) ▸ *adj.* 1. Of or moving toward the outside or exterior. 2. Purely external; superficial. ▸ *adv.* also **out·wards** (-wərdz) Toward the outside. **—out′ward·ly** *adv.*
out·wear (out-wâr′) ▸ *v.* To outlast.
out·weigh (out-wā′) ▸ *v.* 1. To weigh more than. 2. To be more significant than.
out·wit (out-wĭt′) ▸ *v.* **-wit·ted, -wit·ting.** To best or defeat by cleverness or cunning.
out·work (out-wûrk′) ▸ *v.* To work better or faster than.
ou·zo (o͞o′zō) ▸ *n.* A Greek liqueur flavored with anise.
o·va (ō′və) ▸ *n.* Pl. of **ovum**.
o·val (ō′vəl) ▸ *adj.* 1. Egg-shaped. 2. Shaped like an ellipse; elliptical. **—o′val** *n.*
o·va·ry (ō′və-rē) ▸ *n., pl.* **-ries.** 1. The usu. paired female reproductive organ that produces ova. 2. *Bot.* The ovule-bearing part of a pistil. **—o·var′i·an** (ō-vâr′ē-ən) *adj.*
o·vate (ō′vāt′) ▸ *adj.* Oval. **—o′vate′ly** *adv.*
o·va·tion (ō-vā′shən) ▸ *n.* Enthusiastic, prolonged applause.
ov·en (ŭv′ən) ▸ *n.* A compartment for heating or baking food, as in a stove.
o·ver (ō′vər) ▸ *prep.* 1. Above. 2. Above and across. 3. On the other side of. 4. Upon. 5. All through. 6. So as to cover. 7. Higher than. 8. Through the duration of. 9. More than. 10. With reference to: *an argument over methods.* ▸ *adv.* 1. Above. 2a. Across to another or opposite side. b. Across the edge or brim. 3. Across an intervening distance. 4. To a different opinion or allegiance. 5. To a different person, condition, or title: *sign the property over.* 6. So as to be completely enclosed or covered: *The river froze over.* 7. Completely through; thoroughly: *Think the problem over.* 8a. From an upright position. b. From an upward position to an inverted or reversed position. 9. Again. 10. In repetition: *ten times over.* 11. In addition or excess. 12. At an end: *The war is over.* ▸ *adj.* 1. External; outer. 2. Excessive; extreme. 3a. Not yet used up. b. Extra; surplus. ***—idioms:*** **over against** Contrasted with. **over and above** In addition to; besides.
over– ▸ *pref.* 1. Above; upon: *overpass.* 2. Superior: *overlord.* 3. More in amount than proper: *overpay.* 4. Into a reverse position: *overturn.*
o·ver·act (ō′vər-ăkt′) ▸ *v.* To act with unnecessary exaggeration.
o·ver·age¹ (ō′vər-ĭj) ▸ *n.* A surplus; excess.
o·ver·age² (ō′vər-āj′) ▸ *adj.* Beyond the proper or required age.
o·ver·all (ō′vər-ôl′) ▸ *adj.* 1. From one end to the other. 2. Including everything; comprehensive. ▸ *adv.* (ō′vər-ôl′) Generally. ▸ *n.* **overalls** Loose-fitting trousers with a bib front and shoulder straps.
o·ver·arm (ō′vər-ärm′) ▸ *adj. Sports* Executed with the arm raised above the shoulder.
o·ver·awe (ō′vər-ô′) ▸ *v.* To control or subdue by inspiring awe.
o·ver·bal·ance (ō′vər-băl′əns) ▸ *v.* 1. To outweigh. 2. To throw off balance.
o·ver·bear (ō′vər-bâr′) ▸ *v.* 1. To crush or press down on with physical force. 2. To prevail over; dominate.
o·ver·bear·ing (ō′vər-bâr′ĭng) ▸ *adj.* Domineering and arrogant.
o·ver·bite (ō′vər-bīt′) ▸ *n.* A condition of the teeth in which the front upper incisors and canines project over the lower.
o·ver·blown (ō′vər-blōn′) ▸ *adj.* 1. Excessive; overdone. 2. Inflated; exaggerated.
o·ver·board (ō′vər-bôrd′) ▸ *adv.* Over the side of a boat or ship. ***—idiom:*** **go overboard** To go to extremes.
o·ver·build (ō′vər-bĭld′) ▸ *v.* To build beyond the demand or need of (an area).

THESAURUS

outright *adj.* —*See* UTTER².
outrun *v.* —*See* LOSE (3), PASS (2), SURPASS.
outset *n.* —*See* BIRTH (2).
outshine *v.* —*See* SURPASS.
outside *n.* —*See* MAXIMUM.
outside *adj.* —*See* REMOTE (2).
outsider *n.* —*See* FOREIGNER, OUTCAST.
outsize *adj.* —*See* BIG.
outskirts *n.* The periphery of a city or town ▸ city limits, edge, environs, exurbs, fringe, skirts, suburbs, town line. [*Compare* BORDER, LIMITS.]
outsmart *v.* —*See* OUTWIT.
outspoken *adj.* —*See* FRANK.
outstanding *adj.* —*See* DUE (1), EXCEPTIONAL, NOTICEABLE.
outstretch *v.* To put forward, especially an appendage ▸ extend, reach, stretch (out). —*See also* SPREAD (1).
outstretched *adj.* —*See* LONG¹ (1).
outstrip *v.* —*See* PASS (2), SURPASS.
outthink *v.* —*See* OUTWIT.
outward *adj.* —*See* APPARENT (2).
outwardly *adv.* —*See* APPARENTLY.
outwear *v.* To live, exist, or remain longer than ▸ outlast, outlive, survive. [*Compare* SURVIVE.]
outweigh *v.* —*See* CANCEL (2).
outwit *v.* To get the better of by cleverness or cunning ▸ outfox, outguess, outmaneuver, outsmart, outthink, overreach, second-guess, take in. *Idioms:* get the better of, put one over on. [*Compare* BAFFLE, CONFUSE, DECEIVE.]
oval *adj.* Resembling an egg in shape ▸ egg-shaped, ellipsoidal, elliptical, oblong, ovate, oviform, ovoid, ovoidal.
oval *n.* An egg-shaped form or figure ▸ egg-shape, ellipse, ellipsoid, ovoid.
ovate *adj.* —*See* OVAL.
ovation *n.* Approval expressed by clapping ▸ applause, hand, plaudit. *Idiom:* round of applause. —*See also* TESTIMONIAL (2).
over *n.* —*See* COMPLETE (3).
overabundance *n.* —*See* EXCESS (1).
overabundant *adj.* —*See* EXCESSIVE.
over again *adv.* —*See* ANEW.
overage *n.* —*See* SURPLUS.
overall *adj.* —*See* GENERAL (2).
overambitious *adj.* —*See* AMBITIOUS.
overbear *v.* —*See* DOMINATE (2).
overbearing *adj.* —*See* ARROGANT, DICTATORIAL.
overbearingness *n.* —*See* ARROGANCE.
overblown *adj.* —*See* EXAGGERATED, FAT (1), INFLATED, ORATORICAL.

o·ver·cast (ō′vər-kăst′, ō′vər-kăst′) ▸ *adj.* **1.** Clouded over. **2.** Gloomy; melancholy. **3.** Sewn with long overlying stiches.
o·ver·charge (ō′vər-chärj′) ▸ *v.* **1.** To charge too much. **2.** To fill too full. **—o′ver·charge′** *n.*
o·ver·cloud (ō′vər-kloud′) ▸ *v.* To make or become cloudy.
o·ver·coat (ō′vər-kōt′) ▸ *n.* A heavy coat worn over ordinary clothing.
o·ver·come (ō′vər-kŭm′) ▸ *v.* **1.** To defeat; conquer. **2.** To prevail over; surmount. **3.** To overpower, as with emotion.
o·ver·do (ō′vər-do͞o′) ▸ *v.* **1.** To do or use to excess; exaggerate. **2.** To cook too long.
o·ver·dose (ō′vər-dōs′) ▸ *v.* To take or cause to take too large a dose. **—o′ver·dose′** *n.*
o·ver·draft (ō′vər-drăft′) ▸ *n.* **1.** The act of overdrawing a bank account. **2.** The amount overdrawn.
o·ver·draw (ō′vər-drô′) ▸ *v.* **1.** To draw against (a bank account) in excess of credit. **2.** To exaggerate or overstate.
o·ver·drive (ō′vər-drīv′) ▸ *n.* An automotive transmission gear that transmits to the drive shaft a speed greater than engine speed.
o·ver·due (ō′vər-do͞o′, -dyo͞o′) ▸ *adj.* **1.** Being unpaid when due. **2.** Past due; late.
o·ver·ex·pose (ō′vər-ĭk-spōz′) ▸ *v.* **-posed, -pos·ing.** To expose too long or too much. **—o′ver·ex·po′sure** *n.*
o·ver·flow (ō′vər-flō′) ▸ *v.* **1.** To flow over the top, brim, or banks (of). **2.** To spread or cover over. **3.** To teem; abound. ▸ *n.* (ō′vər-flō′) **1.** A flood. **2.** An excess; surplus. **3.** An outlet through which excess liquid may escape.
o·ver·grow (ō′vər-grō′, ō′vər-grō′) ▸ *v.* **1.** To grow over with foliage. **2.** To grow too large for. **3.** To grow beyond normal size. **—o′ver·grown′** *adj.* **—o′ver·growth′** *n.*
o·ver·hand (ō′vər-hănd′) also **o·ver·hand·ed** (ō′vər-hăn′dĭd) ▸ *adj.* Executed with the hand above the level of the shoulder. **—o′ver·hand′** *adv. & n.*
o·ver·hang (ō′vər-hăng′) ▸ *v.* **1.** To project or extend beyond. **2.** To loom over. **—o′ver·hang′** *n.*
o·ver·haul (ō′vər-hôl′, ō′vər-hôl′) ▸ *v.* **1a.** To examine carefully. **b.** To repair thoroughly. **2.** To overtake. **—o′ver·haul′** *n.*
o·ver·head (ō′vər-hĕd′) ▸ *adj.* **1.** Located or functioning from above. **2.** Of or relating to the operating expenses of a business. ▸ *n.* The operating expenses of a business, including rent, utilities, and taxes. **—o′ver·head′** *adv.*
o·ver·hear (ō′vər-hîr′) ▸ *v.* To hear without the speaker's awareness or intent.
o·ver·joy (ō′vər-joi′) ▸ *v.* To fill with joy; delight. **—o′ver·joyed′** (-joid′) *adj.*
o·ver·kill (ō′vər-kĭl′) ▸ *n.* **1.** Destructive nuclear capacity exceeding the amount needed to destroy an enemy. **2.** An excess action or response.
o·ver·land (ō′vər-lănd′, -lənd) ▸ *adj.* Over or across land. **—o′ver·land′** *adv.*
o·ver·lap (ō′vər-lăp′) ▸ *v.* **1.** To extend over and cover part of. **2.** To have something in common with. **—o′ver·lap′** *n.*
o·ver·lay (ō′vər-lā′) ▸ *v.* To lay or spread over or on. **—o′ver·lay′** *n.*
o·ver·look (ō′vər-lo͝ok′) ▸ *v.* **1.** To look over from above. **2.** To afford a view over. **3.** To fail to notice or consider. **4.** To ignore deliberately or indulgently; disregard. **5.** To look over; examine. **6.** To oversee. ▸ *n.* (ō′vər-lo͝ok′) An elevated spot that affords a broad view.
o·ver·lord (ō′vər-lôrd′) ▸ *n.* A lord having supremacy over other lords.
o·ver·ly (ō′vər-lē) ▸ *adv.* Excessively.
o·ver·mas·ter (ō′vər-măs′tər) ▸ *v.* To overcome.
o·ver·match (ō′vər-măch′) ▸ *v.* **1.** To be more than a match for. **2.** To match with a superior opponent.
o·ver·much (ō′vər-mŭch′) ▸ *adj.* Too much. ▸ *adv.* In excess.
o·ver·night (ō′vər-nīt′) ▸ *adj.* **1.** Lasting for or remaining during a night. **2.** Sudden: *an overnight success.* ▸ *adv.* (ō′vər-nīt′) **1.** During or for the length of the night. **2.** Suddenly. **—o′ver·night′** *n.*
o·ver·pass (ō′vər-păs′) ▸ *n.* A roadway or bridge that crosses above another.
o·ver·play (ō′vər-plā′) ▸ *v.* **1.** To overact. **2.** To overestimate the strength of (one's position).
o·ver·pow·er (ō′vər-pou′ər) ▸ *v.* **1.** To overcome by superior force. **2.** To overwhelm.
o·ver·qual·i·fied (ō′vər-kwŏl′ə-fīd′) ▸ *adj.* Educated or skilled beyond what is necessary or desired for a particular job.
o·ver·rate (ō′vər-rāt′) ▸ *v.* To overestimate the merits of.
o·ver·reach (ō′vər-rēch′) ▸ *v.* **1.** To reach or extend over or beyond. **2.** To miss by reaching too far or attempting too much. **3.** To defeat (oneself) by going too far. **—o′ver·reach′** *n.* **—o′ver·reach′er** *n.*
o·ver·ride (ō′vər-rīd′) ▸ *v.* **1.** To ride across. **2.** To trample on. **3.** To prevail over; conquer. **4.** To declare null and void; set aside.
o·ver·rid·ing (ō′vər-rī′dĭng) ▸ *adj.* More important than all others: *an overriding concern.* **—o′ver·rid′ing·ly** *adv.*
o·ver·rule (ō′vər-ro͞ol′) ▸ *v.* **1.** To rule against. **2.** To nullify or reverse.

THESAURUS

overcast *v.* —*See* OBSCURE, SHADE (2).
overcharge *v.* —*See* CHEAT (1), EXAGGERATE.
overcoat *n.* —*See* COAT (1).
overcome *v.* —*See* DEFEAT, OVERWHELM (1), OVERWHELM (2).
overcome *adj.* —*See* ANXIOUS.
overconfidence *n.* —*See* IMPUDENCE.
overconfident *adj.* —*See* IMPUDENT.
overcritical *adj.* —*See* CRITICAL (1).
overcrowded *adj.* Filled beyond capacity ▸ choked, congested, overflowing, overpopulated, swarming, teeming. [*Compare* FULL, TIGHT.]
overdo *v.* To do, use, or stress something to excess ▸ overindulge, overreach, overwork, stretch, strain. ***Idioms:*** bite off more than one can chew, carry too far (*or* to extremes, do to death, go overboard, go too far, go to extremes, go whole hog, kill oneself, knock oneself out. [*Compare* EXAGGERATE, EXCEED.]
overdrawn *adj.* —*See* EXAGGERATED.
overdue *adj.* —*See* LATE (1).
overeater *n.* A person who eats or consumes immoderate amounts of food and drink ▸ glutton, hog, pig. [*Compare* SYBARITE.]
overemphasize *v.* —*See* BELABOR, EXAGGERATE.
overestimate *v.* —*See* MISCALCULATE.
overflow *v.* —*See* FLOOD (1), TEEM[1].
overflow *n.* —*See* FLOOD, SURPLUS.
overflowing *adj.* —*See* FULL (1), OVERCROWDED.
overgenerosity *n.* —*See* EXTRAVAGANCE.
overgrown *adj.* —*See* THICK (3).
overhang *v.* —*See* BULGE, THREATEN (2).
overhang *n.* —*See* PROJECTION.
overhaul *v.* To reorganize thoroughly or drastically ▸ reconfigure, reengineer, reshuffle, shake up. ***Idioms:*** clean house, make a clean sweep. [*Compare* RENEW, RESTORE.] —*See also* FIX (1), PASS (2).
overhaul *n.* A thorough or drastic reorganization ▸ reengineering, reshuffling, shakeup. *Informal:* housecleaning. ***Idiom:*** clean sweep. [*Compare* RENEWAL, REVOLUTION.]
overhead *n.* The expenses associated with running an enterprise ▸ budget, costs, expenses, operating costs, operating expenses, outlay.
overindulge *v.* —*See* BABY, OVERDO.
overindulgence *n.* —*See* EXCESS (2).
overjoy *v.* —*See* DELIGHT (1).
overjoyed *adj.* —*See* ELATED.
overlay *v.* —*See* COLOR (2), COVER (1).
overlay *n.* —*See* COAT (2).
overleap *v.* —*See* EXCEED.
overlong *adj.* —*See* LONG[1] (2).
overlook *v.* To view broadly or from a height ▸ look over, scan, survey. [*Compare* LOOK.] —*See also* BLINK AT, DOMINATE (2), FORGIVE, NEGLECT (2), SUPERVISE.
overlook *n.* —*See* LOOKOUT (2).
overlord *n.* —*See* CHIEF.
overly *adv.* —*See* UNDULY.
overmuch *adj.* —*See* EXCESSIVE.
overmuch *adv.* —*See* UNDULY.
overmuch *n.* —*See* SURPLUS.
overpass *v.* —*See* EXCEED.
overpopulated *adj.* —*See* OVERCROWDED.
overpower *v.* —*See* OVERWHELM (1), OVERWHELM (2).
overpowering *adj.* —*See* INTENSE, SMELLY.
overpriced *adj.* —*See* STEEP[1] (2).
overreach *v.* —*See* EXCEED, OUTWIT, OVERDO.
overrefined *adj.* —*See* PRUDISH.
overripe *adj.* —*See* BAD (2).

o·ver·run (ō′vər-rŭn′) ▸ *v.* **1.** To spread or swarm over destructively. **2.** To spread swiftly throughout. **3.** To overflow. **4.** To run or extend beyond; exceed. ▸ *n.* (ō′vər-rŭn′) **1.** An act of overrunning. **2.** The amount by which something overruns.

o·ver·scale (ō′vər-skāl′) or **o·ver·scaled** (-skāld′) ▸ *adj.* Unusually large or extensive.

o·ver·seas (ō′vər-sēz′, ō′vər-sēz′) ▸ *adv.* Beyond the sea; abroad. **—o′ver·seas′** *adj.*

o·ver·see (ō′vər-sē′) ▸ *v.* **1.** To watch over and direct. **2.** To examine or inspect. **—o′ver·se′er** *n.*

o·ver·sexed (ō′vər-sĕkst′) ▸ *adj.* Having an excessive sexual appetite.

o·ver·shad·ow (ō′vər-shăd′ō) ▸ *v.* **1.** To cast a shadow over. **2.** To surpass; dominate.

o·ver·shoe (ō′vər-sho͞o′) ▸ *n.* An outer shoe worn as protection from water or snow.

o·ver·shoot (ō′vər-sho͞ot′) ▸ *v.* **1.** To shoot or go over or beyond. **2.** To miss by or as if by shooting or going too far.

o·ver·sight (ō′vər-sīt′) ▸ *n.* **1.** An unintentional omission or mistake. **2.** Supervision.

o·ver·size (ō′vər-sīz′) also **o·ver·sized** (-sīzd′) ▸ *adj.* Larger in size than usual.

o·ver·skirt (ō′vər-skûrt′) ▸ *n.* A skirt worn over another.

o·ver·sleep (ō′vər-slēp′) ▸ *v.* To sleep beyond one's intended time for waking.

o·ver·state (ō′vər-stāt′) ▸ *v.* To exaggerate. **—o′ver·state′ment** *n.*

o·ver·stay (ō′vər-stā′) ▸ *v.* To stay beyond the limits or duration of.

o·ver·step (ō′vər-stĕp′) ▸ *v.* To go beyond.

o·ver·stuff (ō′vər-stŭf′) ▸ *v.* **1.** To stuff too much into. **2.** To upholster thickly.

o·ver·sub·scribe (ō′vər-səb-skrīb′) ▸ *v.* To subscribe for in excess of available supply. **—o′ver·sub·scrip′tion** (-skrĭp′shən) *n.*

o·vert (ō-vûrt′, ō′vûrt′) ▸ *adj.* Open and observable; not concealed. **—o·vert′ly** *adv.* **—o·vert′ness** *n.*

o·ver·take (ō′vər-tāk′) ▸ *v.* To catch up with.

o·ver-the-count·er (ō′vər-*thə*-koun′tər) ▸ *adj.* **1.** Not listed or available on an officially recognized stock exchange. **2.** Sold legally without a doctor's prescription.

o·ver·throw (ō′vər-thrō′) ▸ *v.* **1.** To overturn. **2.** To bring about the downfall of; topple. **3.** To throw over and beyond. **—o′ver·throw′** *n.*

o·ver·time (ō′vər-tīm′) ▸ *n.* **1.** Working hours in addition to those of a regular schedule. **2.** Payment for such work. **3.** *Sports* A period of playing time added after the expiration of the set time limit.

o·ver·tone (ō′vər-tōn′) ▸ *n.* **1.** often **overtones** An implication; hint: *overtones of jealousy.* **2.** See **harmonic** 1.

o·ver·top (ō′vər-tŏp′) ▸ *v.* **1.** To tower above. **2.** To take precedence over.

o·ver·ture (ō′vər-cho͝or′) ▸ *n.* **1.** *Mus.* **a.** An instrumental introduction to an extended work. **b.** An independent instrumental composition of similar form. **2.** A first offer or proposal.

o·ver·turn (ō′vər-tûrn′) ▸ *v.* **1.** To turn over; upset. **2.** To overthrow.

o·ver·view (ō′vər-vyo͞o′) ▸ *n.* A comprehensive view; survey.

o·ver·ween·ing (ō′vər-wē′nĭng) ▸ *adj.* **1.** Arrogant; overbearing. **2.** Immoderate.

o·ver·weigh (ō′vər-wā′) ▸ *v.* **1.** To outweigh. **2.** To overburden.

o·ver·whelm (ō′vər-hwĕlm′, -wĕlm′) ▸ *v.* **1.** To submerge; engulf. **2.** To defeat completely. **3.** To turn over; upset.

o·ver·wrought (ō′vər-rôt′) ▸ *adj.* **1.** Nervous or excited. **2.** Extremely elaborate.

ovi– or **ovo–** or **ov–** ▸ *pref.* Egg; ovum: *oviduct.*

Ov·id (ŏv′ĭd) (43 B.C.– A.D. 17) ▸ Roman poet.

o·vi·duct (ō′vĭ-dŭkt′) ▸ *n.* A tube through which ova pass from an ovary.

o·vip·a·rous (ō-vĭp′ər-əs) ▸ *adj.* Producing eggs that hatch outside the body.

o·void (ō′void′) also **o·voi·dal** (ō-void′l) ▸ *adj.* Egg-shaped. **—o′void** *n.*

o·vo·vi·vip·a·rous (ō′vō-vī-vĭp′ər-əs) ▸ *adj.* Producing eggs that hatch within the female's body.

o·vu·late (ō′vyə-lāt′, ŏv′yə-) ▸ *v.* **-lat·ed, -lat·ing.** To produce or discharge ova. **—o′vu·la′tion** *n.*

o·vule (ō′vyo͞ol, ŏv′yo͞ol) ▸ *n.* A minute structure in seed plants that develops into a seed after fertilization. **—o′vu·lar** (ō′vyə-lər, ŏv′yə-) *adj.*

o·vum (ō′vəm) ▸ *n., pl.* **o·va** (ō′və). The female reproductive cell of animals.

owe (ō) ▸ *v.* **owed, ow·ing. 1.** To have to pay or repay: *He owes me five dollars.* **2.** To be in debt to. **3.** To have a moral obligation to: *I owe them an apology.* **4.** To be indebted for.

Ow·ens (ō′ĭnz), **James Cleveland.** "Jesse" (1913–80) ▸ Amer. athlete.

ow·ing (ō′ĭng) ▸ *adj.* Still to be paid; due.

owl (oul) ▸ *n.* Any of various usu. nocturnal birds of prey having large heads, short hooked beaks, and large eyes set forward. **—owl′ish** *adj.*

THESAURUS

overrun *v.* *—See* EXCEED, INVADE (1), OCCUPY (2).
overrun *n.* *—See* SURPLUS.

oversee *v.* *—See* SUPERVISE.

overseer *n.* *—See* BOSS.

oversensitive *adj.* Quick to take offense or become angry or upset ▸ hypersensitive, sensitive, thin-skinned, ticklish, touchy. [*Compare* ILL-TEMPERED.]

oversensitivity *adj.* Quickness to take offense ▸ hypersensitivity, sensitivity, ticklishness, touchiness. *Idiom:* thin skin. [*Compare* TEMPER.]

overshadow *v.* *—See* DOMINATE (2), OBSCURE, SHADE (2).

overshoot *v.* *—See* EXCEED.

oversight *n.* *—See* ERROR, MANAGEMENT, NEGLECT.

oversize or **oversized** *adj.* *—See* BULKY (1).

overspread *v.* *—See* COVER (1).

overstate *v.* *—See* EXAGGERATE.

overstated *adj.* *—See* EXAGGERATED.

overstatement *n.* *—See* EXAGGERATION.

overstep *v.* *—See* EXCEED, VIOLATE (1).

overstock *n.* *—See* SURPLUS.

oversufficiency *n.* *—See* EXCESS (1).

oversupply *n.* *—See* SURPLUS.

overt *adj.* *—See* OBVIOUS.

overtake *v.* To come up even with another ▸ catch (up), pull alongside, pull even. [*Compare* APPROACH, EQUALIZE.] *—See also* PASS (2).

overthrow *v.* To bring about the downfall of ▸ bring down, depose, overturn, subvert, topple, tumble, unhorse, upset. [*Compare* DEFEAT.] *—See also* OVERTURN.
overthrow *n.* *—See* DEFEAT, UPSET.

overture *n.* *—See* ADVANCES, INTRODUCTION.

overturn *v.* To turn or cause to turn from a vertical or horizontal position ▸ capsize, invert, knock over, overthrow, tip over, topple, turn over, upend, upset, upturn. *—See also* LIFT (3), OVERTHROW.
overturn *n.* *—See* UPSET.

overturned *adj.* *—See* UPSIDE-DOWN.

overused *adj.* *—See* TRITE.

overview *n.* A general or comprehensive view or treatment ▸ survey. [*Compare* SYNOPSIS.]

overweening *adj.* *—See* ARROGANT, DICTATORIAL.

overweight *adj.* *—See* FAT (1).

overwhelm *v.* **1.** To render totally ineffective by decisive defeat ▸ crush, drub, overcome, overpower, rout, smash, steamroller, thrash, trounce. *Informal:* clobber, massacre, wallop, whip. *Slang:* cream, murder, shellac, skunk, smear. *Idioms:* clean someone's clock, eat someone alive, eat someone's lunch, kick someone's butt, take to the cleaners. [*Compare* ANNIHILATE, DEFEAT.] **2.** To affect deeply or completely, as with emotion ▸ crush, engulf, overcome, overpower, pierce, prostrate. [*Compare* DAZE, STAGGER.] **3.** To affect as if by an outpouring of water ▸ deluge, flood, inundate, swamp. *See also* BREAK (2), FLOOD (1).

overwhelming *adj.* *—See* ASTONISHING, INTENSE.

overwork *v.* *—See* OVERDO.

overworked *adj.* *—See* TRITE.

overwrought *adj.* *—See* ANXIOUS.

oviform *adj.* *—See* OVAL.

ovoid *n.* *—See* OVAL.
ovoid *adj.* *—See* OVAL.
ovoidal *adj.* *—See* OVAL.

owed or **owing** *adj.* *—See* DUE (1).

owing to *prep.* *—See* BECAUSE OF.

owl·et (ou′lĭt) ▸ *n.* A young owl.
own (ōn) ▸ *adj.* Of or belonging to oneself. ▸ *n.* That which belongs to one. ▸ *v.* **1.** To have or possess. **2.** To admit or acknowledge. ***—idiom:*** **on (one's) own** Completely independent. **—own′er** *n.* **—own′er·ship′** *n.*
ox (ŏks) ▸ *n., pl.* **ox·en** (ŏk′sən). **1.** An adult castrated bull. **2.** A bovine mammal.
ox·al·ic acid (ŏk-săl′ĭk) ▸ *n.* A poisonous, crystalline organic acid used as a bleach and rust remover.
ox·blood red (ŏks′blŭd′) ▸ *n.* A deep reddish brown.
ox·bow (ŏks′bō′) ▸ *n.* **1.** A U-shaped collar for an ox. **2.** A U-shaped bend in a river.
ox·ford (ŏks′fərd) ▸ *n.* **1.** A low shoe that laces over the instep. **2.** A cotton cloth used primarily for shirts.
ox·i·dant (ŏk′sĭ-dənt) ▸ *n.* An oxidizing agent.
ox·i·da·tion (ŏk′sĭ-dā′shən) ▸ *n.* **1.** The combination of a substance with oxygen. **2.** A reaction in which the atoms in an element lose electrons and the element's valence is correspondingly increased. **—ox′i·da′tive** *adj.* **—ox′i·da′tive·ly** *adv.*
ox·ide (ŏk′sīd′) ▸ *n.* A binary compound of an element or radical with oxygen. **—ox·id′ic** (ŏk-sĭd′ĭk) *adj.*
ox·i·dize (ŏk′sĭ-dīz′) ▸ *v.* **-dized, -diz·ing. 1.** To combine with oxygen. **2.** To increase the positive charge or valence of (an element) by removing electrons. **3.** To coat with oxide. **—ox′i·di·za′tion** *n.* **—ox′i·diz′er** *n.*
oxy– ▸ *pref.* Oxygen, esp. additional oxygen: *oxyacetylene.*
ox·y·a·cet·y·lene (ŏk′sē-ə-sĕt′l-ĭn, -ēn′) ▸ *adj.* Of or using a mixture of acetylene and oxygen: *an oxyacetylene torch.*
ox·y·gen (ŏk′sĭ-jən) ▸ *n. Symbol* **O** A gaseous element that constitutes 21 percent of the atmosphere by volume, is essential for plant and animal respiration, and is required for nearly all combustion. At. no. 8. **—ox′y·gen′ic** (-jĕn′ĭk) *adj.* **—ox·yg′e·nous** (ŏk-sĭj′ə-nəs) *adj.*
ox·y·gen·ate (ŏk′sĭ-jə-nāt′) ▸ *v.* **-at·ed, -at·ing.** To treat, combine, or infuse with oxygen. **—ox′y·gen·a′tion** *n.*
oxygen tent ▸ *n.* A canopy placed usu. over the head and shoulders of a patient to provide oxygen at a higher level than normal.
ox·y·mo·ron (ŏk′sē-môr′ŏn′) ▸ *n., pl.* **-mo·ra** (-môr′ə) or **-rons.** A rhetorical figure in which incongruous or contradictory terms are combined, as in *a deafening silence.* **—ox′y·mo·ron′ic** (-mə-rŏn′ĭk) *adj.*
oys·ter (oi′stər) ▸ *n.* Any of several edible bivalve mollusks that have a rough, irregularly shaped shell.
oz also **oz.** ▸ *abbr.* ounce
O·zark Plateau or **O·zark Mountains** (ō′zärk′) ▸ An upland region of the S-central US in SW MO, NW AR, and E OK.
o·zone (ō′zōn′) ▸ *n.* **1.** A blue gaseous allotrope of oxygen, O_3, formed naturally from diatomic oxygen by electric discharge or exposure to ultraviolet radiation, used to purify water and as a bleach. **2.** *Informal* Fresh, pure air.
ozone hole ▸ *n.* An area of the ozone layer that is periodically depleted of ozone, gen. occurring over the Polar Regions.
ozone layer ▸ *n.* A region of the upper atmosphere, between about 15 and 30 km (10 and 20 mi) in altitude, containing a relatively high concentration of ozone that absorbs solar ultraviolet radiation.
o·zo·no·sphere (ō-zō′nə-sfîr′) ▸ *n.* See **ozone layer.**

THESAURUS

own *v.* —*See* ACKNOWLEDGE (1), COMMAND (2).
owner *n.* A person who has legal title to property ▸ holder, landlady, landlord, master, possessor, proprietor, titleholder.
ownership *n.* The fact of possessing or the legal right to possess something ▸ deed, dominion, possession, proprietorship, title.
ox *n.* —*See* OAF.

P

p[1] or **P** (pē) ▸ *n., pl.* **p's** or **P's** also **ps** or **Ps**. The 16th letter of the English alphabet.

p[2] ▸ *abbr.* proton

P ▸ The symbol for the element **phosphorus**.

p. ▸ *abbr.* **1.** page **2.** participle **3.** past **4.** penny **5.** pint

Pa ▸ The symbol for the element **protactinium**.

PA ▸ *abbr.* **1.** or **Pa.** Pennsylvania **2.** power of attorney **3.** prosecuting attorney **4.** public-address system

pa'an·ga (päng′gə, pä-äng′-) ▸ *n.* See **currency** table in Appendix.

pab·u·lum (păb′yə-ləm) ▸ *n.* A substance that gives nourishment, esp. a soft food.

pace (pās) ▸ *n.* **1.** A step made in walking. **2.** The distance spanned by such a step. **3.** Rate of movement or progress. **4.** A manner of walking or running: *a jaunty pace.* **5.** A gait of a horse in which both feet on one side leave and return to the ground together. ▸ *v.* **paced, pac·ing. 1.** To walk or stride back and forth. **2.** To measure by counting the number of steps needed to cover a distance. **3.** To set or regulate the rate of speed for. **4.** To train (a horse) in a particular gait, esp. the pace. **—pac′er** *n.*

pace·mak·er (pās′mā′kər) ▸ *n.* **1.** One who sets the pace in a race. **2.** A leader in a field. **3a.** A part of the body, esp. of the heart, that sets the pace or rhythm of physiological activity. **b.** A surgically implanted electronic device used to regulate the heartbeat. **—pace′mak′ing** *adj. & n.*

pach·y·derm (păk′ĭ-dûrm′) ▸ *n.* A large, thick-skinned, hoofed mammal such as the elephant or rhinoceros.

pach·y·san·dra (păk′ĭ-săn′drə) ▸ *n.* A low-growing plant with evergreen leaves, cultivated as a ground cover.

pa·cif·ic (pə-sĭf′ĭk) ▸ *adj.* **1.** Tending to diminish conflict. **2.** Of a peaceful nature; tranquil. **—pa·cif′i·cal·ly** *adv.*

Pacific Islander ▸ *n.* A native or inhabitant of any of the islands of Oceania.

Pacific Islands, Trust Territory of the ▸ A group of islands and islets of the NW Pacific administered by the US from 1947 to 1978.

Pacific Northwest ▸ A region of the NW US including WA and OR and sometimes SW British Columbia, Canada.

Pacific Ocean ▸ The largest of the world's oceans, divided into the **North Pacific** and the **South Pacific** and extending from the W Americas to E Asia and Australia.

pac·i·fi·er (păs′ə-fī′ər) ▸ *n.* A rubber or plastic nipple for a baby to suck or chew on.

pac·i·fism (păs′ə-fĭz′əm) ▸ *n.* Opposition to war or violence as a means of resolving disputes. **—pac′i·fist** *n.* **—pac′i·fis′tic** *adj.*

pac·i·fy (păs′ə-fī′) ▸ *v.* **-fied, -fy·ing. 1.** To ease the anger or agitation of. **2.** To end fighting or violence in. **—pac′i·fi·ca′tion** *n.*

pack (păk) ▸ *n.* **1a.** A collection of items tied up or wrapped; bundle. **b.** A container made to be carried on the back. **2.** A small package containing a standard number of identical or similar items: *a pack of matches.* **3.** A complete set of related items: *a pack of cards.* **4a.** A group of animals, such as wolves. **b.** A gang or group of people. **5.** A material, such as gauze, that is applied to the body for therapeutic purposes. ▸ *v.* **1.** To fold, roll, or combine into a bundle. **2a.** To put into a receptacle for transporting or storing. **b.** To fill up with items: *pack one's trunk.* **3a.** To crowd together tightly. **b.** To fill up tight; cram. **4.** To wrap tightly, as for protection. **5.** To press together; compact firmly. **6.** *Informal* To carry: *pack a pistol.* **7.** To send unceremoniously: *packed the children off to bed.* **8.** To rig (a voting panel) to be favorable to one's purposes.

pack·age (păk′ĭj) ▸ *n.* **1.** A wrapped or boxed object; parcel. **2.** A proposition or an offer composed of several items: *a benefits package.* ▸ *v.* **-aged, -ag·ing.** To place or make into a package.

package store ▸ *n.* A store that sells sealed bottles of alcoholic beverages for consumption off the premises.

pack·ag·ing (păk′ə-jĭng) ▸ *n.* **1.** Material used for making packages. **2.** The manner in which something is presented to the public.

pack animal ▸ *n.* An animal, such as a mule, used to carry loads.

pack·er (păk′ər) ▸ *n.* **1.** One that packs. **2.** One who processes and packs goods, usu. meat products.

pack·et (păk′ĭt) ▸ *n.* **1.** A small package or bundle. **2.** A regularly scheduled passenger and cargo boat.

pack·ing (păk′ĭng) ▸ *n.* **1.** The processing and packaging of manufactured products, esp. food products. **2.** Material used to prevent breakage or seepage.

pack rat ▸ *n.* **1.** Any of various small North American rodents that collect a great variety of small objects. **2.** *Slang* A collector of miscellaneous objects.

pack·sad·dle (păk′săd′l) ▸ *n.* A saddle on which loads can be secured.

pact (păkt) ▸ *n.* A formal agreement; treaty.

pad[1] (păd) ▸ *n.* **1.** Soft material used esp. to fill, give shape, or protect against injury. **2.** A number of sheets of paper glued together at one end; tablet. **3.** The broad, floating leaf of an aquatic plant such as the water lily. **4.** The cushionlike flesh on the underpart of the feet of many animals. **5.** A launch pad. **6.** *Slang* One's apartment or room. ▸ *v.* **pad·ded, pad·ding. 1.** To line or stuff with soft material. **2.** To lengthen or fill out with extraneous material.

pad[2] (păd) ▸ *v.* **pad·ded, pad·ding.** To go about quietly on foot.

pad·ding (păd′ĭng) ▸ *n.* Material that is used to pad.

pad·dle[1] (păd′l) ▸ *n.* **1.** A wooden implement having a blade at one end or at both ends, used to propel a canoe

THESAURUS

pa *n.* —*See* FATHER.

pabulum *n.* —*See* FOOD.

pace *n.* Rate of motion or performance ▸ speed, tempo, velocity. *Informal:* clip. —*See also* WALK (2).

pace *v.* —*See* WALK.

pacific or **pacifical** *adj.* —*See* PEACEABLE, STILL.

pacifist or **pacifistic** *adj.* —*See* PEACEABLE.

pacify *v.* To ease the anger or agitation of ▸ allay, appease, assuage, becalm, calm (down), conciliate, dulcify, gentle, lull, mollify, placate, propitiate, quiet, settle, soften, soothe, still, sweeten, tranquilize. *Idiom:* pour oil on troubled water. [*Compare* MODERATE, SATIATE.]

pack *n.* **1.** A container carried on the back or around the waist ▸ backpack, belly pack, daypack, fanny pack, haversack, kit, knapsack, rucksack, waist pack. **2.** An organized group of criminals, hoodlums, or wrongdoers ▸ band, gang, ring. *Informal:* mob. —*See also* ABUNDANCE, CROWD, FLOCK.

pack *v.* —*See* CARRY (1), CARRY (2), FILL (1).

package *v.* To cover and tie something, as with paper and string ▸ do up, wrap.

package *n.* Something wrapped or enclosed, as for transporting ▸ box, bundle, carton, crate, mailer, packet, parcel, tin. [*Compare* CONTAINER.]

packaging *n.* —*See* WRAPPER.

packed *adj.* —*See* FULL (1), THICK (2).

packet *n.* —*See* PACKAGE.

packing *n.* —*See* FILLER (1).

pact *n.* —*See* AGREEMENT (1), TREATY.

pad *n.* —*See* HOME (1).

padding *n.* —*See* FILLER (1).

or small boat. **2.** Any of various implements resembling a paddle, used esp. for stirring, mixing, or beating. **3.** A light wooden racket used in playing table tennis. **4.** A board on a paddle wheel. ▸ *v.* **-dled, -dling. 1.** To move or propel through water with or as if with a paddle. **2.** To stir or beat with a paddle. **—pad′dler** *n.*

pad·dle² (păd′l) ▸ *v.* **-dled, -dling.** To dabble about in shallow water; splash gently with the hands or feet.

pad·dle·board (păd′l-bôrd′) ▸ *n.* A long, narrow, floatable board used esp. in surfing.

paddle wheel ▸ *n.* A wheel with boards or paddles around its rim, used to propel a ship.

pad·dock (păd′ək) ▸ *n.* **1.** A fenced area, usu. near a stable, used chiefly for grazing horses. **2.** An enclosure at a racetrack where horses are saddled and paraded before a race.

pad·dy (păd′ē) ▸ *n., pl.* **-dies.** An irrigated or flooded field where rice is grown.

paddy wagon ▸ *n. Slang* A van used by police for taking suspects into custody.

pad·lock (păd′lŏk′) ▸ *n.* A lock with a U-shaped bar that is passed through the staple of a hasp or a link in a chain and then snapped shut. **—pad′lock′** *v.*

pad thai (păd′ tī′, päd′) ▸ *n.* A Thai dish of stir-fried rice noodles, egg, peanuts, and other ingredients.

pae·an (pē′ən) ▸ *n.* A song of joyful praise or exultation.

pa·el·la (pä-ĕl′ə, pä-ā′yä) ▸ *n.* A Spanish dish made with rice, vegetables, meat, and seafood.

pa·gan (pā′gən) ▸ *n.* One who is not a Christian, Muslim, or Jew. **—pa′gan** *adj.* **—pa′gan·ism** *n.*

page¹ (pāj) ▸ *n.* **1.** A sheet of paper or one side of a sheet, as of a book, letter, or manuscript. **2.** *Comp. Sci.* A webpage. ▸ *v.* **paged, pag·ing. 1.** To number the pages of. **2.** To turn the pages of.

page² (pāj) ▸ *n.* **1.** A youth in attendance at court. **2.** One who is employed to run errands, carry messages, or act as a guide, as in a hotel. ▸ *v.* **paged, pag·ing.** To summon or call (a person) by name.

pag·eant (păj′ənt) ▸ *n.* **1.** An elaborate public spectacle depicting a historical event. **2.** A spectacular procession or celebration. **3.** Colorful, showy display. **—pag′eant·ry** *n.*

page·boy (pāj′boi′) ▸ *n.* A hairstyle, usu. shoulder-length, with the ends of the hair curled under smoothly.

pag·i·na·tion (păj′ə-nā′shən) ▸ *n.* **1.** The system by which pages are numbered. **2.** The arrangement and number of pages in a book. **—pag′i·nate** *v.*

pa·go·da (pə-gō′də) ▸ *n.* A many-storied Buddhist tower, erected as a memorial or shrine.

paid (pād) ▸ *v.* P.t. and p.part. of **pay.**

pail (pāl) ▸ *n.* A watertight cylindrical vessel with a handle; bucket.

pain (pān) ▸ *n.* **1.** An unpleasant sensation occurring as a consequence of injury, disease, or emotional disorder. **2.** Suffering or distress. **3. pains** Great care or effort: *take pains with one's work.* **4.** *Informal* A source of annoyance; nuisance. ▸ *v.* To cause or suffer pain. ***—idiom:* on (or under) pain of** Subject to the penalty of a specified punishment, such as death. **—pain′ful** *adj.* **—pain′ful·ly** *adv.* **—pain′less** *adj.* **—pain′less·ly** *adv.*

Paine (pān), **Thomas** (1737–1809) ▸ British-born Amer. Revolutionary leader.

pain·kill·er (pān′kĭl′ər) ▸ *n.* An agent, such as an analgesic drug, that relieves pain. **—pain′kill′ing** *adj.*

pains·tak·ing (pānz′tā′kĭng) ▸ *adj.* Taking pains; very careful and diligent. **—pains′tak′ing·ly** *adv.*

paint (pānt) ▸ *n.* **1a.** A liquid mixture, usu. of a solid pigment in a liquid vehicle, used as a decorative or protective coating. **b.** The dry film formed by such a mixture when applied to a surface. **2.** Makeup. **3.** See **pinto.** ▸ *v.* **1a.** To represent with paints. **b.** To depict vividly in words. **2.** To coat or decorate with paint. **3.** To apply cosmetics to. **4.** To practice the art of painting. **—paint′er** *n.*

paint·brush (pānt′brŭsh′) ▸ *n.* A brush for applying paint.

paint·ing (pān′tĭng) ▸ *n.* **1.** The process, art, or occupation of working with paint. **2.** A picture or design in paint.

pair (pâr) ▸ *n., pl.* **pair** or **pairs. 1.** Two corresponding persons or items similar in form or function: *a pair of shoes.* **2.** One object composed of two joined, similar parts: *a pair of pliers.* **3.** Two persons or animals considered together. ▸ *v.* **1.** To arrange in sets of two; couple. **2.** To form pairs or a pair.

pais·ley (pāz′lē) ▸ *adj.* **1.** Made of a soft wool fabric with a colorful swirled pattern of curved shapes. **2.** Marked with this pattern.

Pai·ute (pī′yo͞ot′) ▸ *n., pl.* **-ute** or **-utes.** A member of either of two distinct Native American peoples, the Northern Paiute and the Southern Paiute, of the Great Basin.

pa·ja·mas (pə-jä′məz, -jăn′əz) ▸ *pl.n.* A loose-fitting garment consisting of trousers and a jacket, worn for sleeping or lounging.

Pak·i·stan (păk′ĭ-stăn′, pä′kĭ-stän′) ▸ A country of S Asia on the Arabian Sea. Pop. 148,000,000. **—Pak′i·stan′i** (-stăn′ē, -stä′nē) *adj. & n.*

pal (păl) *Informal* ▸ *n.* A friend; chum. ▸ *v.* **palled, pal·ling.** To spend time with a friend.

pal·ace (păl′ĭs) ▸ *n.* **1.** The official residence of a royal personage. **2.** A large or splendid residence.

pal·a·din (păl′ə-dĭn) ▸ *n.* A paragon of chivalry.

pal·an·quin (păl′ən-kēn′) ▸ *n.* A covered litter carried on poles on the shoulders of four or more bearers.

pal·at·a·ble (păl′ə-tə-bəl) ▸ *adj.* **1.** Agreeable to the taste. **2.** Acceptable to the mind or sensibilities: *a palatable solution.*

pal·ate (păl′ĭt) ▸ *n.* **1.** The roof of the mouth, consisting of the hard palate and the soft palate. **2.** The sense of taste. **—pal′a·tal** *adj.*

pa·la·tial (pə-lā′shəl) ▸ *adj.* **1.** Of or suitable for a palace. **2.** Of the nature of a palace, as in spaciousness or ornateness.

pa·lat·i·nate (pə-lăt′n-āt′, -ĭt) ▸ *n.* The office or territory of a palatine.

pal·a·tine (păl′ə-tīn′) ▸ *n.* **1.** A title for various officials of the late Roman and Byzantine empires. **2.** A feudal lord exercising sovereign power over his lands. ▸ *adj.* **1.** Belonging to or fit for a palace. **2.** Of a palatine or palatinate.

Pa·lau (pä-lou′, pə-) ▸ A group of volcanic islands in the Caroline Is. of the W Pacific.

pa·lav·er (pə-lăv′ər, -lä′vər) ▸ *n.* Long and idle chatter. **—pa·lav′er** *v.*

THESAURUS

paddock *n.* —*See* PEN².

padre *n.* —*See* CLERIC.

paean *n.* —*See* PRAISE (1).

pagan *n.* One who does not believe in God ▸ atheist, heathen, infidel, nonbeliever. —*See also* SYBARITE.

pagan *adj.* Without belief in God ▸ heathen. [*Compare* ATHEISTIC.]

pageant *n.* —*See* ARRAY.

pageantry *n.* —*See* CELEBRATION (3), GLITTER (2).

pain *n.* A sensation of physical discomfort occurring as the result of disease or injury ▸ ache, burn, cramp, crick, gripes, pang, prick, prickle, shoot, smart, soreness, spasm, stab, sting, stitch, throe, twinge. *Informal:* misery. [*Compare* HARM.] —*See also* ANNOYANCE (2), BURDEN¹ (1), DISTRESS.

pain *v.* —*See* AFFLICT, DISTRESS, HURT (3).

painful *adj.* Marked by, causing, or experiencing physical pain ▸ aching, achy, afflictive, hurtful, inflamed, irritating, nagging, raw, smarting, sore, stabbing, stinging, tender. [*Compare* GRIEVOUS, TORMENTING, UNCOMFORTABLE.] —*See also* BITTER (3).

pains *n.* —*See* EFFORT, THOROUGHNESS.

painstaking *adj.* —*See* CAREFUL (2), DILIGENT.

paint *n.* —*See* COLOR (2), FINISH.

paint *v.* —*See* FINISH (2).

pair *n.* —*See* COUPLE.

paired *adj.* Consisting of two identical or similar related things, parts, or elements ▸ double, dual, matched, twin. [*Compare* EQUAL.]

pal *n.* —*See* ASSOCIATE (2), FRIEND.

pal *v.* —*See* ASSOCIATE (2).

paladin *n.* A person revered especially for noble courage ▸ champion, hero, heroine. *Idiom:* knight in shining armor. [*Compare* WINNER.]

palatable *adj.* Fit to be eaten ▸ comestible, eatable, edible, esculent. —*See also* ACCEPTABLE (2), DELICIOUS.

palatial *adj.* —*See* GRAND, LUXURIOUS.

palaver *n.* —*See* CHATTER.

palaver *v.* —*See* CHATTER (1).

pale[1] (pāl) ▸ *n.* **1.** A stake or pointed stick; picket. **2.** A fence enclosing an area. **3.** The area enclosed by a fence or boundary. ***—idiom:* beyond the pale** Beyond safe or acceptable limits.

pale[2] (pāl) ▸ *adj.* **pal·er, pal·est. 1.** Whitish in complexion; pallid. **2.** Of a low intensity of color; light. **3.** Of a low intensity of light; dim or faint. **—pale** *v.* **—pale′ness** *n.*

paleo– or **pale–** ▸ *pref.* Ancient or prehistoric: *paleography.*

Pa·le·o·cene (pā′lē-ə-sēn′) *Geol.* ▸ *adj.* Of or being the 1st epoch of the Tertiary Period, marked by the appearance of placental mammals. ▸ *n.* The Paleocene Epoch.

pa·le·og·ra·phy (pā′lē-ŏg′rə-fē) ▸ *n.* The study of ancient written documents. **—pa′le·og′ra·pher** *n.* **—pa′le·o·graph′ic** (-ə-grăf′ĭk), **pa′le·o·graph′i·cal** *adj.*

Pa·le·o·lith·ic (pā′lē-ə-lĭth′ĭk) ▸ *adj.* Of or being the Stone Age period beginning with the earliest chipped stone tools, about 750,000 years ago, until the beginning of the Mesolithic, about 15,000 years ago. ▸ *n.* The Paleolithic Period.

pa·le·on·tol·o·gy (pā′lē-ŏn-tŏl′ə-jē) ▸ *n.* The study of the forms of life existing in prehistoric or geologic times. **—pa′le·on′to·log′ic** (-ŏn′tə-lŏj′ĭk), **pa′le·on′to·log′i·cal** *adj.* **—pa′le·on·tol′o·gist** *n.*

Pa·le·o·zo·ic (pā′lē-ə-zō′ĭk) ▸ *adj.* Of or being the 2nd geologic era, including the Cambrian, Ordovician, Silurian, Devonian, Mississippian, Pennsylvanian, and Permian periods. ▸ *n.* The Paleozoic Era.

Pa·ler·mo (pə-lâr′mō, pä-lĕr′-) ▸ A city of NW Sicily, Italy, on the Tyrrhenian Sea.

Pal·es·tine (păl′ĭ-stīn′) ▸ A region of SW Asia on the E Mediterranean shore, roughly coextensive with modern Israel and the West Bank. **—Pal′es·tin′i·an** (-stĭn′ē-ən) *adj. & n.*

pal·ette (păl′ĭt) ▸ *n.* **1.** A board, usu. with a hole for the thumb, on which the artist mixes colors. **2.** The range of colors on a palette.

pal·i·mo·ny (păl′ə-mō′nē) ▸ *n. Informal* An allowance for support made under court order and given by one partner to the other after they have separated.

pal·imp·sest (păl′ĭmp-sĕst′) ▸ *n.* A manuscript, usu. of papyrus or parchment, that has been written on more than once, with the earlier writing incompletely erased.

pal·in·drome (păl′ĭn-drōm′) ▸ *n.* A word, phrase, verse, or sentence that reads the same backward or forward, as *A man, a plan, a canal, Panama!*

pal·ing (pā′lĭng) ▸ *n.* **1.** A pale; picket. **2.** A fence made of pales or pickets.

pal·i·sade (păl′ĭ-sād′) ▸ *n.* A fence of pales forming a defense barrier or fortification.

pall[1] (pôl) ▸ *n.* **1.** A cover for a coffin, bier, or tomb, often made of velvet. **2.** A coffin. **3.** A covering that darkens or obscures: *a pall of smoke.*

pall[2] (pôl) ▸ *v.* **1.** To become insipid, boring, or wearisome. **2.** To cloy; satiate.

pal·la·di·um (pə-lā′dē-əm) ▸ *n. Symbol* **Pd** A steel-white, tarnish-resistant, metallic element alloyed for use in electric contacts, jewelry, watch parts, and surgical instruments. At. no. 46.

pall·bear·er (pôl′bâr′ər) ▸ *n.* One carrying or attending a coffin at a funeral.

pal·let[1] (păl′ĭt) ▸ *n.* A portable platform used for storing or moving cargo or freight.

pal·let[2] (păl′ĭt) ▸ *n.* A narrow, hard bed or straw-filled mattress.

pal·li·ate (păl′ē-āt′) ▸ *v.* **-at·ed, -at·ing. 1.** To make (e.g., a crime) seem less serious; extenuate. **2.** To mitigate. **3.** To soothe without curing. **—pal′li·a′tion** *n.* **—pal′li·a′tive** *adj. & n.*

pal·lid (păl′ĭd) ▸ *adj.* **1.** Pale or wan in color or complexion. **2.** Lacking in vitality; dull.

pal·lor (păl′ər) ▸ *n.* Extreme or unnatural paleness.

palm[1] (päm) ▸ *n.* The inner surface of the hand, extending from the wrist to the base of the fingers. ▸ *v.* To conceal (something) in the palm of the hand. ***—phrasal verb:* palm off** To dispose of or pass off by deception.

palm[2] (päm) ▸ *n.* **1.** Any of various chiefly tropical evergreen trees, shrubs, or woody vines usu. having unbranched trunks with a crown of large pinnate or palmate leaves. **2.** An emblem of victory, success, or joy. **3.** Triumph; victory.

pal·mate (păl′māt′, päl′-, pä′māt′) also **pal·mat·ed** (-mā′tĭd) ▸ *adj.* **1.** Shaped like a hand with the fingers extended. **2.** *Zool.* Webbed. **—pal′mate′ly** *adv.*

pal·met·to (păl-mĕt′ō) ▸ *n., pl.* **-tos** or **-toes.** Any of several small, mostly tropical palms having fan-shaped leaves.

palm·is·try (pä′mĭ-strē) ▸ *n.* The practice or art of telling fortunes from the patterns on the palms of the hands. **—palm′ist** *n.*

Palm Sunday ▸ *n.* The Sunday before Easter, observed by Christians in commemoration of the entry of Jesus into Jerusalem.

palm·y (pä′mē) ▸ *adj.* **-i·er, -i·est. 1.** Of, relating to, or covered with palm trees. **2.** Prosperous; flourishing.

pal·o·mi·no (păl′ə-mē′nō) ▸ *n., pl.* **-nos.** A horse with a golden or tan coat and a white or cream-colored mane and tail.

pal·pa·ble (păl′pə-bəl) ▸ *adj.* **1.** Capable of being touched or felt; tangible. **2.** Easily perceived; obvious. **—pal′pa·bly** *adv.*

pal·pate (păl′pāt′) ▸ *v.* **-pat·ed, -pat·ing.** To examine by touching (an area of the body). **—pal·pa′tion** *n.*

pal·pi·tate (păl′pĭ-tāt′) ▸ *v.* **-tat·ed, -tat·ing. 1.** To tremble, shake, or quiver. **2.** To beat with excessive rapidity; throb. **—pal′pi·ta′tion** *n.*

pal·sy (pôl′zē) ▸ *n., pl.* **-sies.** Complete or partial muscle paralysis. **—pal′sied** *adj.*

pal·try (pôl′trē) ▸ *adj.* **-tri·er, -tri·est. 1.** Lacking in importance or worth; trivial. **2.** Wretched or contemptible. **—pal′tri·ness** *n.*

pam·pa (păm′pə) ▸ *n., pl.* **-pas** (-pəz, -pəs). In South America, a treeless grassland area.

pam·per (păm′pər) ▸ *v.* To treat with excessive indulgence.

pam·phlet (păm′flĭt) ▸ *n.* An unbound printed work, usu. with a paper cover. **—pam′phlet·eer′** (-flĭ-tîr′) *n.*

pan[1] (păn) ▸ *n.* **1.** A shallow, wide, open container, usu. of metal and used for holding liquids, cooking, and other domestic purposes. **2.** A vessel similar in form to a pan. **3a.** A basin or depression in the earth. **b.** Hardpan. ▸ *v.* **panned, pan·ning. 1.** To wash (e.g., gravel) in a pan for gold or other precious metal. **2.** *Informal* To criticize or review harshly. ***—phrasal verb:* pan out** To turn out well; be successful.

pan[2] (păn) ▸ *v.* **panned, pan·ning.** To move (a movie or television camera) to follow an object or create a panoramic effect.

Pan ▸ *n. Gk. Myth.* The god of woods, fields, and flocks.

pan– ▸ *pref.* All: *panchromatic.*

pan·a·ce·a (păn′ə-sē′ə) ▸ *n.* A remedy for all diseases, evils, or difficulties; cure-all.

THESAURUS

pale *adj.* **1.** Lacking color ▸ ashen, ashy, bloodless, cadaverous, colorless, doughy, etiolated, faded, livid, lurid, pallid, pastel, pasty, sallow, wan, washed out, waxen, waxy, whey-faced. *Idioms:* green about the gills, white as a sheet. [*Compare* DULL, HAGGARD, SICK.] **2.** Being weak in quality or substance ▸ anemic, bloodless, dim, effete, faint, flimsy, pallid, sickly, thin, waterish, watery, weak. [*Compare* INSIPID, WEAK.] *—See also* FAIR[1] (3).

pale *v.* To lose normal coloration; turn pale ▸ blanch, bleach, etiolate, fade, peak, sallow, wan, wash out, whiten.

palinode *n.* *—See* RETRACTION.

palliate *v.* *—See* EXTENUATE, RELIEVE (1).

palliation *n.* *—See* RELIEF (1).

pallid *adj.* *—See* PALE (1), PALE (2).

palmist *n.* *—See* PROPHET.

palm off *v.* To offer or put into circulation an inferior or fraudulent item ▸ foist, fob off, pass off, put off. [*Compare* DUMP.]

palpability *n.* *—See* TANGIBILITY.

palpable *adj.* Discernible by touch ▸ tactile, tangible, touchable. *—See also* PERCEPTIBLE, PHYSICAL.

palpableness *n.* *—See* TANGIBILITY.

palpate *v.* *—See* TOUCH.

palpation *n.* *—See* TOUCH (1).

palpitate *v.* *—See* BEAT (5).

palpitation *n.* *—See* BEAT (3).

palter *v.* *—See* EQUIVOCATE (2), HAGGLE.

paltriness *n.* *—See* TRIFLE.

paltry *adj.* *—See* SHODDY, TRIVIAL.

pamper *v.* *—See* BABY.

pamphleteer *n.* *—See* PROPAGANDIST.

pan *n.* *—See* CRITICISM, FACE (1).

pan *v.* *—See* CRITICIZE (1).

pan out *v.* *—See* SUCCEED (2).

panacea *n.* Something believed to cure all human disorders ▸ catholicon, cure-all, elixir. [*Compare* CURE.]

pa·nache (pə-năsh′, -näsh′) ▸ *n.* **1.** Dash; verve. **2.** A bunch of feathers or a plume, esp. on a helmet.

Pan·a·ma (păn′ə-mä′) ▸ A country of SE Central America. **—Pan′a·ma′ni·an** (-mā′nē-ən) *adj. & n.*

Panama, Isthmus of ▸ An isthmus of Central America connecting North and South America and separating the Pacific from the Caribbean Sea.

Panama Canal ▸ A ship canal, about 82 km (51 mi), crossing the Isthmus of Panama between the Caribbean Sea and the Pacific.

Panama hat ▸ *n.* A natural-colored hat made from leaves of a palmlike tropical plant of South and Central America.

Pan-A·mer·i·can (păn′ə-mĕr′ĭ-kən) ▸ *adj.* Of North, South, and Central America.

pan·a·tel·a (păn′ə-tĕl′ə) ▸ *n.* A long, slender cigar.

pan-broil (păn′broil′) ▸ *v.* To cook over direct heat in an uncovered, usu. ungreased skillet.

pan·cake (păn′kāk′) ▸ *n.* A thin cake made of batter that is cooked on both sides.

pan·chro·mat·ic (păn′krō-măt′ĭk) ▸ *adj.* Sensitive to all colors, as film.

pan·cre·as (păng′krē-əs, păn′-) ▸ *n.* A long, irregularly shaped gland that produces insulin and secretes pancreatic juice into the intestine. **—pan′cre·at′ic** (păng′krē-ăt′ĭk, păn′-) *adj.*

pan·cre·a·ti·tis (păng′krē-ə-tī′tĭs, păn′-) ▸ *n.* Inflammation of the pancreas.

pan·da (păn′də) ▸ *n.* **1.** A bearlike black and white mammal of the mountains of China and Tibet. **2.** A small, raccoonlike mammal of NE Asia.

pan·dem·ic (păn-dĕm′ĭk) ▸ *adj.* **1.** Widespread; general. **2.** Epidemic over a wide geographic area. ▸ *n.* A pandemic disease.

pan·de·mo·ni·um (păn′də-mō′nē-əm) ▸ *n.* Wild uproar or noise.

pan·der (păn′dər) ▸ *v.* **1.** To act as a go-between or liaison in sexual intrigues. **2.** To cater to the lower tastes and desires of others or exploit their weaknesses. **—pan′der, pan′der·er** *n.*

Pan·do·ra (păn-dôr′ə) ▸ *n. Gk. Myth.* The first woman, who opened a box containing all the evils of human life.

pan·dow·dy (păn-dou′dē) ▸ *n., pl.* **-dies.** Sliced fruit baked with sugar and spices in a deep dish, with a thick top crust.

pane (pān) ▸ *n.* **1.** A framed, glass-filled division of a window or door. **2.** The glass itself.

pan·e·gyr·ic (păn′ə-jĭr′ĭk, -jī′rĭk) ▸ *n.* **1.** A speech or written composition of commendation or praise. **2.** Elaborate praise; encomium. **—pan′e·gyr′i·cal** *adj.* **—pan′e·gyr′ist** *n.*

pan·el (păn′əl) ▸ *n.* **1.** A flat, usu. rectangular piece forming a raised, recessed, or framed part of the surface in which it is set. **2.** A vertical section of fabric. **3.** A thin wooden board, used as a painting surface. **4.** A board with switches or buttons to control an electric device. **5.** A list or group of persons for jury duty. **6.** A group of people gathered to discuss a topic, judge a contest, or act as a team on a quiz program. ▸ *v.* **-eled, -el·ing** or **-elled, -el·ling. 1.** To cover, decorate, or furnish with panels. **2.** To separate into panels.

pan·el·ing (păn′ə-lĭng) ▸ *n.* A section of panels or paneled wall.

pan·el·ist (păn′ə-lĭst) ▸ *n.* A member of a panel.

panel truck ▸ *n.* A small delivery truck with a fully enclosed body.

pang (păng) ▸ *n.* **1.** A sudden sharp spasm of pain. **2.** A sudden, sharp feeling of emotional distress.

Pan·gae·a (păn-jē′ə) ▸ *n.* A hypothetical landmass comprising all the earth's continents in the late Paleozoic Era.

pan·han·dle[1] (păn′hăn′dl) ▸ *v.* **-dled, -dling.** *Informal* To beg for money or food. **—pan′han′dler** *n.*

pan·han·dle[2] (păn′hăn′dl) ▸ *n.* A narrow strip of territory projecting from a larger, broader area.

pan·ic (păn′ĭk) ▸ *n.* A sudden, overpowering terror, often affecting many people at once. **—pan′ic** *v.* **—pan′ick·y** *adj.*

pan·i·cle (păn′ĭ-kəl) ▸ *n.* A branched cluster of flowers in which the branches are racemes. **—pan′i·cled** *adj.*

Pan·ja·bi (pŭn-jä′bē, -jăb′ē) ▸ *n. & adj.* Var. of **Punjabi.**

pan·nier (păn′yər, păn′ē-ər) ▸ *n.* **1.** A large wicker basket, esp. one carried on the back. **2.** One of a pair of baskets or packs carried on either side of an animal or vehicle, such as a bicycle.

pan·o·ply (păn′ə-plē) ▸ *n., pl.* **-plies. 1.** A splendid or striking array. **2.** Something that covers and protects. **3.** The complete arms and armor of a warrior.

pan·o·ram·a (păn′ə-răm′ə, -rä′mə) ▸ *n.* **1.** An unbroken view of a wide area. **2.** A picture or series of pictures representing a continuous scene. **—pan′o·ram′ic** *adj.*

pan·pipe (păn′pīp′) ▸ *n.* A wind instrument consisting of a series of pipes or reeds of graduated length bound together.

pan·sy (păn′zē) ▸ *n., pl.* **-sies.** Any of various plants having flowers with velvety petals of various colors.

pant (pănt) ▸ *v.* **1.** To breathe rapidly in short gasps, as after exertion. **2.** To utter hurriedly or breathlessly. **3.** To long demonstratively; yearn. ▸ *n.* A short, labored breath; gasp. **—pant′ing·ly** *adv.*

pan·ta·loon (păn′tə-lo͞on′) ▸ *n.* often **pantaloons** Trousers, esp. tight trousers extending from waist to ankle.

pan·the·ism (păn′thē-ĭz′əm) ▸ *n.* A doctrine identifying the deity with the universe. **—pan′the·ist** *n.* **—pan′the·is′tic** *adj.*

pan·the·on (păn′thē-ŏn′, -ən) ▸ *n.* **1.** A temple dedicated to all gods. **2.** All the gods of a people. **3.** A public building commemorating and dedicated to the heroes and heroines of a nation.

pan·ther (păn′thər) ▸ *n.* **1.** The leopard, esp. in its black, unspotted form. **2.** See **mountain lion.**

pant·ies (păn′tēz) ▸ *pl.n.* Short underpants for women or children.

pan·to·mime (păn′tə-mīm′) ▸ *n.* **1.** Communication by means of gesture and facial expression. **2.** A play, dance, or other theatrical performance presented in pantomime. **—pan′to·mime** *v.* **—pan′to·mim′ic** (-mĭm′ĭk) *adj.* **—pan′to·mim′ist** (-mī′mĭst) *n.*

pan·try (păn′trē) ▸ *n., pl.* **-tries.** A small room or closet where food, tableware, linens, and similar items are stored.

pants (pănts) ▸ *pl.n.* **1.** Trousers. **2.** Underpants.

pant·suit also **pants suit** (pănt′so͞ot′) ▸ *n.* A woman's suit having trousers instead of a skirt.

pant·y·hose or **pant·y hose** (păn′tē-hōz′) ▸ *pl.n.* A woman's one-piece undergarment consisting of underpants and stockings.

pant·y·waist (păn′tē-wāst′) ▸ *n. Slang* A sissy.

pap (păp) ▸ *n.* **1.** Soft or semiliquid food, as for infants. **2.** Material lacking real value or substance.

pa·pa (pä′pə, pə-pä′) ▸ *n. Informal* Father.

pa·pa·cy (pā′pə-sē) ▸ *n., pl.* **-cies. 1.** The office and jurisdiction of a pope. **2.** The period of time during which a pope is in office. **3. Papacy** The system of church government headed by the pope.

Pa·pa·go (păp′ə-gō′, pä′pə-) ▸ *n., pl.* **-go** or **-gos. 1.** A member of a Native American people inhabiting S Arizona and NW Mexico. **2.** Their Uto-Aztecan language.

pa·pal (pā′pəl) ▸ *adj.* Of or issued by a pope.

Papal States ▸ A group of territories in central Italy ruled by the popes (754–1870).

THESAURUS

pan-broil *v.* —*See* COOK.

pandemic *adj.* —*See* PREVAILING, UNIVERSAL (1).

pandemonium *n.* —*See* NOISE (1).

panegyric *n.* —*See* PRAISE (1).

panegyrize *v.* —*See* HONOR (1).

panel *n.* —*See* CONFERENCE (1).

pan-fry *v.* —*See* COOK.

pang *n.* —*See* PAIN.

pang *v.* —*See* HURT (3).

Panglossian *adj.* —*See* OPTIMISTIC.

panhandle *v.* —*See* BEG.

panhandler *n.* —*See* BEGGAR (1).

panic *n.* —*See* FEAR, SCREAM (2).

panic *v.* —*See* FRIGHTEN.

panicky or **panic-stricken** *adj.* —*See* AFRAID.

panicmonger *n.* One who needlessly alarms others ▸ alarmist, Chicken Little, scaremonger. ***Idiom:*** one who cries wolf. [*Compare* PESSIMIST.]

panoply *n.* —*See* ARRAY.

panorama *n.* —*See* VIEW (2).

pant *v.* To breathe hard ▸ blow, gasp, gulp, heave, huff, puff, wheeze. *Idiom:* suck air (*or* wind). [*Compare* BREATHE.] —*See also* DESIRE, GASP.

pantomime *v.* —*See* GESTURE.

pantywaist *n.* —*See* WEAKLING.

papa *n.* —*See* FATHER.

pa·paw also **paw·paw** (pô′pô′) ► *n.* **1.** A deciduous North American tree having fleshy edible fruit. **2.** The fruit of this tree. **3.** See **papaya.**

pa·pa·ya (pə-pä′yə) ► *n.* **1.** An evergreen tropical American tree having large, yellow, edible fruit. **2.** The fruit of this tree.

pa·per (pā′pər) ► *n.* **1.** A material made of cellulose pulp, derived mainly from wood, rags, and certain grasses, processed into flexible sheets or rolls, and used for writing, printing, drawing, wrapping, and covering walls. **2.** A sheet of this material. **3.** A written work such as an essay or a treatise. **4.** often **papers** An official document, esp. one establishing the identity of the bearer. **5.** A newspaper. **6.** Wallpaper. ► *v.* To cover, wrap, or line with paper. **—pa′per·er** *n.* **—pa′per·y** *adj.*

pa·per·back (pā′pər-băk′) ► *n.* A book having a flexible paper binding.

pa·per·board (pā′pər-bôrd′) ► *n.* Cardboard; pasteboard.

pa·per·bound (pā′pər-bound′) ► *adj.* Bound in paper; paperback.

pa·per·hang·er (pā′pər-hăng′ər) ► *n.* One whose occupation is hanging wallpaper.

pa·per·less (pā′pər-lĭs) ► *adj.* Not requiring paper to record, convey, and store information.

pa·per·weight (pā′pər-wāt′) ► *n.* A small, heavy object for holding down papers.

pa·per·work (pā′pər-wûrk′) ► *n.* Work involving the handling of reports, letters, and forms.

pa·pier-mâ·ché (pā′pər-mə-shā′, pă-pyā′-) ► *n.* A material, made from paper pulp or shreds of paper mixed with glue or paste, that can be molded into various shapes when wet. **—pa′pier-mâ·ché′** *adj.*

pa·pil·la (pə-pĭl′ə) ► *n., pl.* **-pil·lae** (-pĭl′ē). A small nipplelike projection, such as a protuberance on the tongue. **—pap′il·lar′y** (păp′ə-lĕr′ē, pə-pĭl′ə-rē) *adj.*

pa·pist (pā′pĭst) ► *n. Offensive* A Roman Catholic.

pa·poose (pă-po͞os′, pə-) ► *n.* A Native American infant or very young child.

pa·pri·ka (pă-prē′kə, pə-, păp′rĭ-kə) ► *n.* A mild, powdered seasoning made from sweet red peppers.

Pap smear ► *n.* A test for cancer, esp. of the female genital tract.

Pap·u·a New Guinea (păp′yo͞o-ə, pä′poo-ä′) ► An island country of the SW Pacific comprising the E half of New Guinea and adjacent islands. **—Pap′u·an** *adj. & n.* **—Pap′u·a New Guin′e·an** *adj. & n.*

pa·py·rus (pə-pī′rəs) ► *n., pl.* **-rus·es** or **-ri** (-rī′). **1.** A tall, aquatic, grasslike plant of Northern Africa. **2.** A material on which to write made from the pith or the stems of this plant.

par (pär) ► *n.* **1.** An amount or a level considered to be average; standard. **2.** An equality of status, level, or value; equal footing. **3.** The established value of a monetary unit of a country. **4.** The face value of a stock or bond. **5.** The number of golf strokes considered necessary to complete a hole or course.

para– or **par–** ► *pref.* **1.** Beside; near: *parathyroid gland.* **2.** Beyond: *paranormal.* **3.** Subsidiary; assistant: *paralegal.*

par·a·ble (păr′ə-bəl) ► *n.* A simple story illustrating a moral or religious lesson.

pa·rab·o·la (pə-răb′ə-lə) ► *n.* A plane curve formed by the intersection of a right circular cone and a plane parallel to an element of the cone. **—par′a·bol′ic** (păr′ə-bŏl′ĭk) *adj.*

par·a·chute (păr′ə-sho͞ot′) ► *n.* A light, usu. hemispherical apparatus used to retard free fall from an aircraft. ► *v.* **-chut·ed, -chut·ing.** To drop by means of a parachute. **—par′a·chut′ist** *n.*

pa·rade (pə-rād′) ► *n.* **1.** An organized public procession on a festive or ceremonial occasion. **2.** A ceremonial review of troops. **3.** An extended, usu. showy succession. **4.** An ostentatious show; exhibition: *a parade of wealth.* ► *v.* **-rad·ed, -rad·ing.** **1.** To take part or cause to take part in a parade. **2.** To assemble for a ceremonial military review. **3.** To stroll in public; promenade. **4.** To exhibit ostentatiously; flaunt.

par·a·digm (păr′ə-dīm′, -dĭm′) ► *n.* **1.** An example that serves as a pattern or a model. **2.** A list of all the inflectional forms of a word taken as an illustrative example. **—par′a·dig·mat′ic** (-dĭg-măt′ĭk) *adj.*

par·a·dise (păr′ə-dīs′, -dīz′) ► *n.* **1.** often **Paradise** Heaven. **2.** A place of ideal beauty or loveliness. **—par′a·di·si′a·cal** (-dĭ-sī′ə-kəl, -zī′-) *adj.*

par·a·dox (păr′ə-dŏks′) ► *n.* **1.** A seemingly contradictory statement that may nonetheless be true. **2.** One exhibiting inexplicable or contradictory aspects. **—par′a·dox′i·cal** *adj.* **—par′a·dox′i·cal·ly** *adv.*

par·af·fin (păr′ə-fĭn) ► *n.* **1.** A waxy, white or colorless, solid hydrocarbon mixture used to make candles, wax paper, lubricants, and sealing materials. **2.** *Chiefly Brit.* Kerosene. **—par′af·fin′ic** *adj.*

par·a·foil (păr′ə-foil′) ► *n.* A nonrigid, parachutelike airfoil of ribbed or cellular construction.

par·a·glid·er (păr′ə-glī′dər) ► *n.* A recreational aircraft consisting of a large parafoil from which a harnessed rider hangs.

par·a·gon (păr′ə-gŏn′, -gən) ► *n.* A model of excellence or perfection.

par·a·graph (păr′ə-grăf′) ► *n.* **1.** A distinct division of written or printed matter that consists of one or more sentences and typically deals with a single thought or topic. **2.** A mark (¶) used to indicate where a new paragraph should begin. **3.** A brief article, notice, or announcement, as in a newspaper. ► *v.* To divide or arrange into paragraphs.

Par·a·guay (păr′ə-gwī′, -gwā′) ► A country of S-central South America. **—Par′a·guay′an** *adj. & n.*

par·a·keet (păr′ə-kēt′) ► *n.* Any of various small slender parrots, usu. having long tapering tails.

par·a·le·gal (păr′ə-lē′gəl) ► *adj.* Relating to or being a person with specialized training who assists an attorney. **—par′a·le′gal** *n.*

par·al·lax (păr′ə-lăks′) ► *n.* An apparent change in the direction of an object, caused by a change in the viewer's position.

par·al·lel (păr′ə-lĕl′) ► *adj.* **1.** Being an equal distance apart everywhere and never intersecting. **2a.** Having comparable parts or analogous aspects. **b.** Having the same tendency or direction. ► *adv.* In a parallel relationship or manner. ► *n.* **1.** *Math.* One of a set of parallel geometric figures, such as lines or planes. **2a.** One that closely resembles or is analogous to another. **b.** A comparison indicating likeness; analogy. **3.** Any of the imaginary lines representing degrees of latitude that encircle the earth parallel to the plane of the equator. **4.** *Electron.* An arrangement of components in a circuit that splits the current into two or more paths. ► *v.* **-leled, -lel·ing** also **-lelled, -lel·ling.** **1.** To make parallel. **2.** To be or extend parallel to. **3.** To be similar or analogous to. **—par′al·lel·ism** *n.*

parallel bars ► *pl.n.* An apparatus for gymnastic exercises consisting of two bars set parallel to each other in adjustable upright supports.

paper *n.* **1.** Something that is the result of creative effort ► composition, essay, theme. **2.** A document used in applying, as for a job ► application, form, sheet. —*See also* PUBLICATION (2).

papoose *n.* —*See* BABY (1).

pappy[1] *adj.* —*See* SOFT (1).

pappy[2] *n.* —*See* FATHER.

par *n.* —*See* AVERAGE, EQUIVALENCE.

parable *n.* —*See* MYTH (1).

parade *n.* A formal military inspection ► review. —*See also* ARRAY.

parade *v.* —*See* DISPLAY.

paradigm *n.* —*See* MODEL, ORIGINAL.

paradigmatic *adj.* —*See* TYPICAL.

paradise *n.* —*See* ETERNITY (2), HEAVEN.

paradisiac *adj.* —*See* HEAVENLY (1).

paragon *n.* A person or thing so excellent as to have no equal or match ► nonesuch, nonpareil, phoenix. [*Compare* BEST, CELEBRITY.] —*See also* EPITOME, MODEL.

paragraph *n.* —*See* ITEM.

parallel *adj.* Lying in the same plane and not intersecting ► collateral. *Idiom:* side by side. —*See also* CONCURRENT, LIKE[2].

parallel *n.* Something closely analogous to something else ► analogue, analogy, congener, correlate, correlative, correspondent, counterpart, match. [*Compare* COPY, LIKENESS.]

parallel *v.* —*See* EQUAL (1), LIKEN.

parallelism *n.* —*See* LIKENESS (1).

par·al·lel·e·pi·ped (păr′ə-lĕl′ə-pī′pĭd, -pĭp′ĭd) ▸ *n.* A solid with 6 faces, each a parallelogram and each being parallel to the opposite face.

par·al·lel·o·gram (păr′ə-lĕl′ə-grăm′) ▸ *n.* A four-sided plane figure with opposite sides parallel.

pa·ral·y·sis (pə-răl′ĭ-sĭs) ▸ *n., pl.* **-ses** (-sēz′). **1a.** Loss or impairment of the ability to move a body part. **b.** Loss of sensation over a region of the body. **2.** Total stoppage or severe impairment of activity. **—par′a·lyt′ic** (păr′ə-lĭt′ĭk) *adj. & n.*

par·a·lyze (păr′ə-līz′) ▸ *v.* **-lyzed, -lyz·ing. 1.** To affect with paralysis. **2.** To make inoperative or powerless.

par·a·me·ci·um (păr′ə-mē′sē-əm, -shē-əm) ▸ *n., pl.* **-ci·a** (-sē-ə, -shē-ə) or **-ci·ums.** Any of various freshwater, usu. oval protozoans that move by means of cilia.

par·a·med·ic (păr′ə-mĕd′ĭk) ▸ *n.* A person who is trained to give emergency medical treatment or assist medical professionals. **—par′a·med′i·cal** *adj.*

pa·ram·e·ter (pə-răm′ĭ-tər) ▸ *n.* **1.** *Math.* A constant in an equation that can be varied to represent a family of curves or surfaces, such as the radius in a family of concentric circles. **2.** One of a set of measurable factors, such as temperature, that helps define a system and its behavior. **3.** *Informal* A limiting or restrictive factor. **—par′a·met′ric** (păr′ə-mĕt′rĭk) *adj.*

par·a·mil·i·tar·y (păr′ə-mĭl′ĭ-tĕr′ē) ▸ *adj.* Of or being a group of civilians organized in a military fashion.

par·a·mount (păr′ə-mount′) ▸ *adj.* **1.** Of chief concern or importance. **2.** Supreme in rank or power.

par·a·mour (păr′ə-mo͝or′) ▸ *n.* A lover, esp. one in an adulterous relationship.

par·a·noi·a (păr′ə-noi′ə) ▸ *n.* A psychotic disorder characterized by delusions of persecution or grandeur. **—par′a·noi′ac′** (-ăk′, -ĭk) *n.* **—par′a·noid′** *adj. & n.*

par·a·nor·mal (păr′ə-nôr′məl) ▸ *adj.* Beyond the range of normal experience or scientific explanation.

par·a·pet (păr′ə-pĭt, -pĕt′) ▸ *n.* **1.** A low protective wall or railing along the edge of a raised structure such as a roof or balcony. **2.** An embankment protecting soldiers from enemy fire.

par·a·pher·na·lia (păr′ə-fər-nāl′yə, -fə-nāl′yə) ▸ *pl.n. (takes sing. or pl. v.)* **1.** Personal belongings. **2.** The articles used in a particular activity.

par·a·phrase (păr′ə-frāz′) ▸ *n.* A restatement of a text or passage in another form or other words, often to clarify meaning. **—par′a·phrase′** *v.*

par·a·ple·gi·a (păr′ə-plē′jē-ə, -jə) ▸ *n.* Paralysis of the lower half of the body including both legs. **—par′a·ple′gic** (-jĭk) *adj. & n.*

par·a·pro·fes·sion·al (păr′ə-prə-fĕsh′ə-nəl) ▸ *n.* One trained to assist a professional.

par·a·psy·chol·o·gy (păr′ə-sī-kŏl′ə-jē) ▸ *n.* The study of paranormal phenomena, such as telepathy and clairvoyance.

par·a·quat (păr′ə-kwŏt′) ▸ *n.* A colorless compound, $C_{12}H_{14}Cl_2N_2$, or a related yellow compound, $C_{12}H_{14}N_2(CH_3SO_4)_2$, used as a herbicide.

par·a·site (păr′ə-sīt′) ▸ *n.* **1.** An organism that grows and feeds on or in a different organism while contributing nothing to the survival of its host. **2.** One who habitually takes advantage of the generosity of others. **—par′a·sit·ism** (-sĭ-tĭz′əm, -sī-) *n.* **—par′a·sit·ize′** (-sĭ-tīz′, -sī-) *v.*

par·a·sit·ic (păr′ə-sĭt′ĭk) also **par·a·sit·i·cal** (-ĭ-kəl) ▸ *adj.* **1.** Of or characteristic of a parasite. **2.** Caused by a parasite.

par·a·si·tol·o·gy (păr′ə-sĭ-tŏl′ə-jē, -sī-) ▸ *n.* The scientific study of parasites or parasitic populations. **—par′a·si·tol′o·gist** *n.*

par·a·sol (păr′ə-sôl′, -sŏl′) ▸ *n.* A light, usu. small umbrella carried as protection from the sun.

par·a·sym·pa·thet·ic nervous system (păr′ə-sĭm′pə-thĕt′ĭk) ▸ *n.* The part of the autonomic nervous system that inhibits or opposes the physiological effects of the sympathetic nervous system.

par·a·thy·roid gland (păr′ə-thī′roid) ▸ *n.* Any of four small kidney-shaped glands that lie in pairs near or within the thyroid gland and secrete a hormone necessary for the metabolism of calcium and phosphorus.

par·a·troops (păr′ə-tro͞ops′) ▸ *pl.n.* Infantry trained and equipped to parachute. **—par′a·troop′er** *n.*

par·a·ty·phoid fever (păr′ə-tī′foid′) ▸ *n.* An acute food poisoning, similar to typhoid fever but less severe.

par·boil (pär′boil′) ▸ *v.* To cook partially by boiling for a brief period.

par·cel (pär′səl) ▸ *n.* **1.** Something wrapped up or packaged; package. **2.** A plot of land, usu. a division of a larger area. **3.** A quantity of merchandise offered for sale. **4.** A group or company; pack. ▸ *v.* **-celed, -cel·ing** also **-celled, -cel·ling. 1.** To divide into parts and distribute. **2.** To make into a parcel; package.

parcel post ▸ *n.* A postal service or department that handles and delivers packages.

parch (pärch) ▸ *v.* **1.** To make or become extremely dry, esp. by exposure to heat. **2.** To make or become thirsty.

parch·ment (pärch′mənt) ▸ *n.* **1.** The skin of a sheep or goat prepared as a material on which to write or paint. **2.** A written text or drawing on a sheet of this material.

par·don (pär′dn) ▸ *v.* **1.** To release (a person) from punishment. **2.** To let (an offense) pass without punishment. **3.** To forgive; excuse. ▸ *n.* **1.** Exemption of a convicted person from the penalties of an offense or a crime. **2.** Allowance or forgiveness for an offense or a discourtesy. **—par′don·a·ble** *adj.* **—par′don·er** *n.*

pare (pâr) ▸ *v.* **pared, par·ing. 1.** To remove the outer covering or skin of: *pare apples.* **2.** To reduce by or as if by cutting off outer parts; trim: *pare expenses.* **—par′er** *n.*

par·e·gor·ic (păr′ə-gôr′ĭk, -gŏr′-) ▸ *n.* A camphorated tincture of opium, taken internally for the relief of diarrhea and intestinal pain.

par·ent (pâr′ənt, păr′-) ▸ *n.* **1.** A father or mother. **2.** An ancestor; progenitor. **3.** An organism that produces or generates offspring. **4.** A source or cause; origin. ▸ *v.* To act as a parent (to). **—par′ent·age** *n.* **—pa·ren′tal** (pə-rĕn′tl) *adj.* **—par′ent·hood′** *n.*

THESAURUS

paralyze *v.* To render helpless, as by emotion ▸ benumb, numb, petrify, stun, stupefy, wither. ***Idiom:*** strike dumb (*or* speechless). [*Compare* DAZE, STAGGER.] —*See also* DISABLE (1).

paralyzed *adj.* —*See* MOTIONLESS.

paramount *adj.* —*See* DOMINANT (1), PRIMARY (1).

paramountcy *n.* —*See* DOMINANCE.

paramour *n.* —*See* LOVER, PHILANDERER.

paranormal *adj.* —*See* SUPERNATURAL (1).

parapet *n.* —*See* BULWARK.

paraphernalia *n.* —*See* OUTFIT.

paraphrase *n.* A restating of something in other, especially simpler, words ▸ rendering, rendition, restatement, translation, version. [*Compare* SUMMARY, SYNOPSIS.]

paraphrase *v.* To express the meaning of in other, especially simpler, words ▸ rehash, render, rephrase, restate, reword, translate. [*Compare* REVIEW.]

parasite *n.* One who depends on another for support without reciprocating ▸ bloodsucker, hanger-on, leech, sponge, sponger. *Slang:* freeloader. [*Compare* BEGGAR, SYCOPHANT.] —*See also* GERM (1).

parasitic or **parasitical** *adj.* Of, relating to, or characteristic of a parasite ▸ bloodsucking, epizoic. *Slang:* freeloading.

parboil *v.* —*See* COOK.

parcel *n.* —*See* LOT (1), PACKAGE.

parcel out *v.* —*See* DISTRIBUTE.

parch *v.* —*See* DRY.

parched *adj.* Needing or desiring drink ▸ dry, thirsty. —*See also* DRY (2).

pardon *v.* —*See* FORGIVE, PURIFY (1).

pardon *n.* —*See* FORGIVENESS.

pardonable *adj.* Admitting of forgiveness or pardon ▸ condonable, excusable, expiable, forgivable, remissible, understandable, venial. [*Compare* ACCEPTABLE, JUSTIFIABLE.]

pardoning *n.* —*See* PURIFICATION (2).

pare *v.* To reduce in complexity or scope ▸ boil down, simplify, streamline. ***Idiom:*** reduce to the basics (*or* essentials *or* bare bones). [*Compare* EXPLAIN.] —*See also* CUT (3), SKIN.

parent *n.* —*See* ANCESTOR (1), ORIGIN, ORIGINATOR.

parent *v.* To take care of and educate a child ▸ bring up, foster, raise, rear. [*Compare* NURTURE.] —*See also* BREED.

parentage *n.* —*See* ANCESTRY.

pa·ren·the·sis (pə-rĕn′thĭ-sĭs) ▸ *n., pl.* **-ses** (-sēz′). **1.** Either or both of the upright curved lines, ( ), used to mark off explanatory or qualifying remarks or enclose a mathematical expression. **2.** A qualifying or amplifying word, phrase, or sentence inserted within a passage. **—par′en·thet′i·cal** (păr′ən-thĕt′ĭ-kəl) , **par′en·thet′ic** (-ĭk) *adj.*

pa·re·sis (pə-rē′sĭs, păr′ĭ-sĭs) ▸ *n.* Slight or partial paralysis. **—pa·ret′ic** (pə-rĕt′ĭk) *adj. & n.*

pa·re·ve (pä′rə-və) also **par·ve** (pär′və) ▸ *adj.* Prepared without meat or milk and thus permissible to be eaten with both meat and dairy dishes according to Jewish dietary laws.

par ex·cel·lence (pär ĕk-sə-läns′) ▸ *adj.* Being of the highest degree; quintessential.

par·fait (pär-fā′) ▸ *n.* **1.** A dessert made of cream, eggs, sugar, and flavoring. **2.** A dessert made of several layers of different flavors of ice cream or ices, variously garnished.

par·he·li·on (pär-hē′lē-ən, -hēl′yən) ▸ *n., pl.* **-he·li·a** (-hē′lē-ə, -hēl′yə). A bright spot appearing on either side of the sun, often on a luminous ring or halo.

pa·ri·ah (pə-rī′ə) ▸ *n.* **1.** A social outcast. **2.** An Untouchable.

pa·ri·e·tal (pə-rī′ĭ-təl) ▸ *adj.* **1.** *Anat.* **a.** Of or forming the wall of a body part, organ, or cavity. **b.** Of or in the region of the sides of the skull. **2.** Dwelling or having authority within the walls or buildings of a college.

par·i·mu·tu·el (păr′ĭ-myōō′chōō-əl) ▸ *n.* A system of betting on races whereby the winners divide the total amount bet, after deducting management expenses, in proportion to the sums they have wagered individually.

par·ing (pâr′ĭng) ▸ *n.* Something, such as a peel, that has been pared off.

pa·ri pas·su (păr′ē păs′ōō) ▸ *adv.* At an equal pace; side by side.

Par·is[1] (păr′ĭs) ▸ *n. Gk. Myth.* The prince of Troy whose abduction of Helen provoked the Trojan war.

Par·is[2] (păr′ĭs) ▸ The capital of France, in the N-central part on the Seine R.

par·ish (păr′ĭsh) ▸ *n.* **1a.** An administrative part of a diocese that has its own church. **b.** The members of such a parish. **2.** An administrative subdivision in Louisiana that corresponds to a county in other US states.

pa·rish·ion·er (pə-rĭsh′ə-nər) ▸ *n.* A member of a parish.

par·i·ty (păr′ĭ-tē) ▸ *n., pl.* **-ties. 1.** Equality, as in amount, status, or value. **2.** The equivalent in value of a sum of money in a different currency at a fixed rate of exchange. **3.** A level for farm-product prices maintained by governmental support.

park (pärk) ▸ *n.* **1.** An area of land set aside for public use, as for recreation. **2.** *Sports* A stadium or an enclosed playing field: *a baseball park.* **3.** An area in or near a town designed and usu. zoned for a certain purpose: *a commercial park.* **4.** A place for parking vehicles; parking lot. ▸ *v.* **1.** To put or leave (a vehicle) for a time in a certain location. **2.** *Informal* To place or leave temporarily.

par·ka (pär′kə) ▸ *n.* **1.** A hooded fur pullover outer garment worn in the Arctic. **2.** A coat or jacket with a hood and usu. a warm lining.

Par·kin·son's disease (pär′kĭn-sənz) ▸ *n.* A progressive nervous disease chiefly of later life, marked by muscular tremor and slowing of movement.

park·way (pärk′wā′) ▸ *n.* A broad landscaped highway.

par·lance (pär′ləns) ▸ *n.* A particular manner of speaking; idiom: *legal parlance.*

par·lay (pär′lā′, -lē) ▸ *n.* A bet comprising the sum of a prior wager plus its winnings or a series of bets made in such a manner. **—par′lay′** *v.*

par·ley (pär′lē) ▸ *n., pl.* **-leys.** A discussion or conference, esp. between opponents. ▸ *v.* To have a discussion, esp. with an opponent.

par·lia·ment (pär′lə-mənt) ▸ *n.* **1.** A national legislative body. **2. Parliament** The national legislature of various countries, esp. the United Kingdom. **—par′lia·men′ta·ry** (-mən′tə-rē, -men′trē) *adj.*

par·lia·men·tar·i·an (pär′lə-mĕn-târ′ē-ən) ▸ *n.* **1.** One who is expert in parliamentary procedures, rules, or debate. **2.** A member of a parliament.

par·lor (pär′lər) ▸ *n.* **1.** A room in a private home set apart for the entertainment of visitors. **2.** A business establishment: *a funeral parlor.*

par·lous (pär′ləs) ▸ *adj.* Perilous; dangerous.

Par·me·san (pär′mə-zän′, -zăn′, -zən) ▸ *n.* A hard, sharp, dry Italian cheese usu. served grated as a garnish.

par·mi·gia·na (pär′mĭ-zhä′nə, -jä′-) ▸ *adj.* Made or covered with Parmesan cheese: *eggplant parmigiana.*

Par·nas·sus (pär-năs′əs) ▸ A mountain, about 2,458 m (8,060 ft), of central Greece N of the Gulf of Corinth.

pa·ro·chi·al (pə-rō′kē-əl) ▸ *adj.* **1.** Of, supported by, or located in a parish. **2.** Narrowly restricted in scope or outlook; provincial: *parochial attitudes.* **—pa·ro′chi·al·ism** *n.* **—pa·ro′chi·al·ly** *adv.*

parochial school ▸ *n.* A school supported by a church parish.

par·o·dy (păr′ə-dē) ▸ *n., pl.* **-dies. 1.** A satirical imitation, as of a literary work. **2.** Travesty: *a parody of justice.* **—par′o·dist** *n.* **—par′o·dy** *v.*

pa·role (pə-rōl′) ▸ *n.* **1.** The release of a prisoner whose term has not yet expired on condition of good behavior. **2.** Word of honor. ▸ *v.* **-roled, -rol·ing.** To release on parole. **—pa·rol′ee′** *n.*

pa·rot·id gland (pə-rŏt′ĭd) ▸ *n.* Either of the pair of salivary glands situated below and in front of each ear.

-parous ▸ *suff.* Giving birth to; bearing: *multiparous.*

par·ox·ysm (păr′ək-sĭz′əm) ▸ *n.* **1.** A sudden outburst, as of emotion. **2a.** A sudden attack or intensification of a disease. **b.** A spasm or fit; convulsion. **—par′ox·ys′mal** (-ək-sĭz′məl) *adj.*

par·quet (pär-kā′) ▸ *n.* **1.** A floor made of parquetry. **2.** The art or process of making parquetry. **3a.** The part of the main floor of a theater in front of the balcony. **b.** The entire main floor of a theater.

par·quet·ry (pär′kĭ-trē) ▸ *n., pl.* **-ries.** Inlay of wood, often of different colors, that is used esp. for floors.

par·ri·cide (păr′ĭ-sīd′) ▸ *n.* **1.** The murdering of one's father, mother, or other near relative. **2.** One who commits such a murder. **—par′ri·cid′al** (-sīd′l) *adj.*

par·rot (păr′ət) ▸ *n.* **1.** Any of numerous tropical and semitropical birds, marked by a short hooked bill, brightly colored plumage, and, in some species, the ability to mimic human speech. **2.** One who imitates the words or actions of another, esp. without understanding them. ▸ *v.* To repeat or imitate, esp. without understanding.

parrot fever ▸ *n.* See **psittacosis.**

par·ry (păr′ē) ▸ *v.* **-ried, -ry·ing. 1.** To deflect or ward off. **2.** To evade skillfully; avoid. **—par′ry** *n.*

parse (pärs) ▸ *v.* **parsed, pars·ing. 1.** To provide a grammatical description of a word, group of words, or sentence. **2.** *Comp. Sci.* To analyze or separate (e.g., input) into more easily processed components. **3.** To examine or analyze closely. **—pars′er** *n.*

par·sec (pär′sĕk′) ▸ *n.* A unit of astronomical length equal to 3.258 light-years.

par·si·mo·ny (pär′sə-mō′nē) ▸ *n.* Unusual or excessive frugality;

THESAURUS

parenthesis *n.* *—See* DIGRESSION.

parenthetic or **parenthetical** *adj.* *—See* DIGRESSIVE.

pariah *n.* *—See* OUTCAST.

parity *n.* *—See* EQUIVALENCE.

park *n.* Public land kept for a special purpose ▸ preserve, reserve, reservation, sanctuary. *—See also* COMMON.

parka *n.* *—See* COAT (1).

parlance *n.* *—See* LANGUAGE (2), WORDING.

parley *n.* The act or process of dealing with another to reach an agreement ▸ negotiation, talk. [*Compare* CONVERSATION.] *—See also* CONFERENCE (1), DELIBERATION (1).

parley *v.* *—See* CONFER (1), DISCUSS.

parlous *adj.* *—See* DANGEROUS.

parochial *adj.* *—See* NARROW (1).

parody *n.* *—See* MOCKERY (2), SATIRE.

parody *v.* *—See* IMITATE.

paroxysm *n.* A condition of anguished struggle and disorder ▸ convulsion, throes. *—See also* ERUPTION, OUTBURST, SEIZURE (1), TREMOR (2).

parrot *n.* *—See* MIMIC.

parrot *v.* *—See* MIMIC.

parry *v.* *—See* REPEL.

parsimonious *adj.* *—See* STINGY.

stingingness. **—par'si·mo'ni·ous** *adj.* **—par'si·mo'ni·ous·ly** *adv.*

pars·ley (pär'slē) ▸ *n.* An herb having flat or curled leaves that are used for seasoning or as a garnish.

pars·nip (pär'snĭp) ▸ *n.* **1.** A strong-scented plant cultivated for its long, white, edible root. **2.** Its root.

par·son (pär'sən) ▸ *n.* **1.** An Anglican cleric in charge of a parish. **2.** A Protestant minister.

par·son·age (pär'sə-nĭj) ▸ *n.* The official residence provided by a church for its parson.

part (pärt) ▸ *n.* **1.** A portion, division, or segment of a whole. **2.** A component of a system; detachable piece: *spare parts for cars.* **3.** A role, as in a play. **4.** One's responsibility, duty, or obligation; share. **5.** often **parts** A region, area, land, or territory. **6.** A side in a dispute or controversy. **7.** The line where the hair on the head is parted. **8.** *Mus.* **a.** The music or score for a particular instrument. **b.** One of the melodic divisions or voices of a composition. ▸ *v.* **1.** To divide or break into separate parts. **2.** To break up (a relationship) by separating the elements involved: *parted company.* **3.** To put or keep apart. **4.** To comb (e.g., hair) into a part. **5.** To go apart from one another; separate: *parted as friends.* **6.** To go away; depart. **—*phrasal verb:* part with** To give up or let go of; relinquish. ▸ *adv.* Partially; in part. ▸ *adj.* Not full or complete; partial. **—*idioms:* in part** To some extent; partly. **take part** To join in.

part. ▸ *abbr.* participle

par·take (pär-tāk') ▸ *v.* **-took** (-tŏŏk'), **-tak·en** (-tā'kən), **-tak·ing.** **1.** To take or have a part or share; participate. **2.** To take or be given part or portion. **—par·tak'er** *n.*

par·terre (pär-târ') ▸ *n.* A flower garden whose beds form a pattern.

par·the·no·gen·e·sis (pär'thə-nō-jĕn'ĭ-sĭs) ▸ *n.* Reproduction in which an unfertilized egg develops into a new individual. **—par'the·no·ge·net'ic** (-jə-nĕt'ĭk) *adj.*

par·tial (pär'shəl) ▸ *adj.* **1.** Not total; incomplete. **2.** Favoring one person or side over another or others. **3.** Particularly fond: *partial to detective novels.* **—par'tial·ly** *adv.*

par·ti·al·i·ty (pär'shē-ăl'ĭ-tē, pär-shăl'-) ▸ *n., pl.* **-ties.** **1.** The state of being partial. **2.** Favorable prejudice or bias. **3.** A special fondness.

par·tic·i·pate (pär-tĭs'ə-pāt') ▸ *v.* **-pat·ed, -pat·ing.** To take part or share in something. **—par·tic'i·pant** (-pənt), **par·tic'i·pa'tor** *n.* **—par·tic'i·pa'tion** *n.* **—par·tic'i·pa·to'ry** (-pə-tôr'ē) *adj.*

par·ti·ci·ple (pär'tĭ-sĭp'əl) ▸ *n.* A form of a verb that can function independently as an adjective and can be used with an auxiliary verb to indicate tense, aspect, or voice. **—par'ti·cip'i·al** (-ē-əl) *adj.*

par·ti·cle (pär'tĭ-kəl) ▸ *n.* **1.** A very small piece or part; speck. **2.** A very small or the smallest possible amount. **3.** A subatomic particle. **4.** *Ling.* A word (e.g., a preposition) that has little meaning but specifies, connects, or limits the meanings of other words.

par·ti-col·ored (pär'tē-kŭl'ərd) ▸ *adj.* Having parts or sections colored differently from each other.

par·tic·u·lar (pər-tĭk'yə-lər, pə-tĭk'-) ▸ *adj.* **1.** Belonging to or associated with a specific person, group, thing, or category. **2.** Separate and distinct from others; specific. **3.** Worthy of note; exceptional. **4.** Attentive to or concerned with details, often excessively so; fussy. ▸ *n.* An individual item, fact, or detail. **—par·tic'u·lar'i·ty** (lăr'ĭ-tē) *n.* **—par·tic'u·lar·ly** *adv.*

par·tic·u·lar·ize (pər-tĭk'yə-lə-rīz', pə-tĭk-) ▸ *v.* **-ized, -iz·ing.** **1.** To mention, describe, or treat individually; itemize or specify. **2.** To go into or give details or particulars.

par·tic·u·late (pər-tĭk'yə-lĭt, -lāt', pär-) ▸ *adj.* Of or formed of separate particles. **—par·tic'u·late** *n.*

part·ing (pär'tĭng) ▸ *n.* **1.** The act or process of separating or dividing. **2.** A departure or leave-taking. ▸ *adj.* Given, received, or done on departing or separating.

par·ti·san (pär'tĭ-zən) ▸ *n.* **1.** A strong supporter of a party, cause, faction, person, or idea. **2.** A guerrilla. **—par'ti·san** *adj.* **—par'ti·san·ship'** *n.*

par·tite (pär'tīt') ▸ *adj.* Divided into parts.

par·ti·tion (pär-tĭsh'ən) ▸ *n.* **1a.** The act or process of dividing something into parts. **b.** The state of being so divided. **2.** Something that divides or separates, as a wall dividing one room or cubicle from another. **3.** A part or section into which something has been divided. ▸ *v.* **1.** To divide into parts, pieces, or sections. **2.** To divide or separate by means of a partition.

part·ly (pärt'lē) ▸ *adv.* In part or in some degree; not completely.

part·ner (pärt'nər) ▸ *n.* **1.** One associated with another in an activity or a sphere of common interest. **2.** A member of a business partnership. **3a.** A spouse. **b.** A domestic partner. **4.** Either of two persons who are dancing together. **5.** One of a pair or team in a sport or game. **—part'ner·ship'** *n.*

part of speech ▸ *n., pl.* **parts of speech.** Any of the traditional grammatical classes of words according to their functions in context, including the noun, verb, and adjective.

par·took (pär-tŏŏk') ▸ *v.* P.t. of **partake.**

par·tridge (pär'trĭj) ▸ *n., pl.* **-tridge** or **-tridg·es.** Any of several plump-bodied game birds.

part-time (pärt'tīm') ▸ *adj.* For or during less than the cus-

THESAURUS

parson *n.* —*See* CLERIC.

part *n.* **1.** A separate unit that belongs or contributes to a whole ▸ building block, component, constituent, division, element, factor, fraction, ingredient, member, percentage, piece, portion, section, sector, segment, subdivision. [*Compare* BIT[1], CUT, ELEMENT.] **2.** One's duty or responsibility in a common effort ▸ function, piece, role, share. [*Compare* FUNCTION.] **3.** A particular subdivision of a written work ▸ chapter, passage, section, segment. **4.** A person portrayed in fiction or drama ▸ character, persona, personage, role. —*See also* ALLOTMENT, VIEWPOINT.

part *v.* —*See* BRANCH, DIVIDE, SEPARATE (1).

part *adj.* —*See* PARTIAL (1).

partake *v.* —*See* CONTRIBUTE (2), EAT (1), PARTICIPATE.

partial *adj.* **1.** Not total ▸ fractional, fragmentary, incomplete, part, unfinished. [*Compare* ROUGH.] **2.** Disposed to favor one over another ▸ favorable, preferential. —*See also* BIASED.

partiality *n.* Preferential treatment or bias ▸ favor, favoritism, partialness, preference. [*Compare* PREJUDICE.] —*See also* BIAS, INCLINATION (1), TASTE (1).

partialness *n.* Preferential treatment or bias ▸ favor, favoritism, partiality, preference. [*Compare* BIAS, PREJUDICE.]

participant *n.* One who participates ▸ actor, partaker, participator, party, player, sharer. [*Compare* ASSOCIATE.]

participate *v.* To involve oneself in an activity ▸ carry on, engage, enter into, have, indulge, join (in), partake. *Idioms:* have a hand in, take part. [*Compare* CONTRIBUTE.] —*See also* CONTRIBUTE (2).

participation *n.* The act or fact of participating ▸ engagement, involvement, partaking, sharing.

participatory *adj.* Tending to contribute to a result ▸ conducive, contributive, contributory, helpful. [*Compare* AUXILIARY.]

particle *n.* —*See* BIT[1] (1).

particular *adj.* —*See* DETAILED, EXCLUSIVE (1), FUSSY, INDIVIDUAL (2), LONE, SPECIAL.

particular *n.* —*See* CIRCUMSTANCE (2), DETAIL, ELEMENT (2).

particularity *n.* —*See* INDIVIDUALITY.

particularize *v.* To state specifically ▸ detail, provide, specify, stipulate. [*Compare* ASSERT, DESCRIBE, DESIGNATE, DICTATE.]

particularly *adv.* —*See* NAMELY, VERY.

parting *n.* —*See* DEPARTURE, DIVISION (1).

parting *adj.* Of, done, given, or said on departing ▸ departing, dying, farewell, goodbye, leaving, valedictory. [*Compare* LAST[1].]

partisan *n.* —*See* FOLLOWER.

partisan *adj.* —*See* BIASED.

partisanship *n.* —*See* BIAS.

partition *n.* A solid structure that separates one area from another ▸ barrier, screen, wall. [*Compare* BORDER.] —*See also* DIVISION (1).

partition *v.* To separate with or as if with a wall ▸ fence, screen, wall. —*See also* DIVIDE.

partner *n.* —*See* ASSOCIATE (1), LOVER, SPOUSE.

partnership *n.* —*See* ASSOCIATION (1), COMPANY (1).

tomary or standard time: *a part-time job.* **—part′-time′** *adv.*
par·tu·ri·tion (pär′tyo͞o-rĭsh′ən, -to͞o-, pär′chə-) ▸ *n.* The act of giving birth; childbirth.
part·way (pärt′wā′) ▸ *adv. Informal* To a certain degree or distance; in part.
par·ty (pär′tē) ▸ *n., pl.* **-ties. 1a.** A social gathering. **b.** A group of people who have gathered to participate in a specific task or activity. **2.** A political group organized to promote and support its principles and candidates. **3a.** A participant or accessory: *I refuse to be a party to your scheme.* **b.** A person or group involved in a legal proceeding. ▸ *adj.* **1.** Of or relating to a political organization. **2.** Of or for use at a social gathering. ▸ *v.* **-tied, -ty·ing.** *Informal* To celebrate or carouse at or as if at a party.
party line ▸ *n.* **1.** A telephone circuit connecting two or more subscribers with the same exchange. **2.** One or more of the policies of a political party to which loyal members are expected to adhere.
par·ve·nu (pär′və-no͞o′, -nyo͞o′) ▸ *n.* A person who has suddenly risen to a higher social and economic class and has not yet gained acceptance by others in that class.
pas (pä) ▸ *n., pl.* **pas** (pä). A step or dance.
Pas·cal (pă-skăl′, pä-skäl′), **Blaise** (1623–62) ▸ French philosopher and mathematician.
pas de deux (də dœ) ▸ *n., pl.* **pas de deux.** A dance for two, esp. in ballet.
pa·sha (pä′shə, păsh′ə, pə-shä′) ▸ *n.* Used formerly as a title for military and civil officers, esp. in Turkey and N Africa.
Pash·to (pŭsh′tō) also **Push·tu** (pŭsh′to͞o) ▸ *n.* An Iranian language of Afghanistan and W Pakistan.
pass (păs) ▸ *v.* **1.** To move on or ahead; proceed. **2.** To extend; run: *The river passes through town.* **3.** To move by or past. **4.** To elapse or allow to elapse. **5.** To cause to move: *passed her hand over the curtain.* **6a.** To hand over to someone else: *pass the bread.* **b.** To transfer or be transferred from one to another. **c.** To transfer (a ball or puck) to a teammate. **7.** To be communicated or exchanged. **8.** To come to an end. **9.** To happen; take place. **10.** To be allowed to happen without challenge: *let the remark pass.* **11.** *Games* To decline one's turn to play or bid. **12.** To undergo or cause to undergo a course or test with favorable results. **13.** To serve as a barely acceptable substitute. **14.** To approve or be approved, as by a legislature. **15.** *Law* To pronounce an opinion or judgment. **16.** To discharge (bodily wastes); excrete. ***—phrasal verbs:*** **pass away** To end or die. **pass out** To lose consciousness. **pass up** To reject; turn down. ▸ *n.* **1.** The act of passing. **2.** A narrow passage between mountains; way. **3.** A permit, ticket, or authorization to come or go at will or without charge. **4.** A sweep or run by a military aircraft over a target area. **5.** A complete cycle of operations, as by a computer program. **6.** A critical situation; predicament. **7.** A sexual invitation or overture. ***—idiom:*** **pass the buck** *Slang* To shift blame to another. **—pass′er** *n.*
pass·a·ble (păs′ə-bəl) ▸ *adj.* **1.** That can be passed, traversed, or crossed; navigable. **2.** Satisfactory but not outstanding; adequate. **—pass′a·bly** *adv.*
pas·sage (păs′ĭj) ▸ *n.* **1.** The act or process of passing. **2.** A journey, esp. by air or water. **3.** The right to travel as a passenger, esp. on a ship. **4a.** A path, channel, or duct through, over, or along which something may pass. **b.** A corridor. **5.** Enactment into law of a legislative measure. **6.** A segment of a written work or musical composition.
pas·sage·way (păs′ĭj-wā′) ▸ *n.* A corridor.
Pas·sa·ma·quod·dy (păs′ə-mə-kwŏd′ē) ▸ *n., pl.* **-dy** or **-dies. 1.** A member of a Native American people inhabiting parts of coastal Maine and New Brunswick. **2.** The Algonquian language of the Passamaquoddy.
pass·book (păs′bo͝ok′) ▸ *n.* See **bankbook.**
pas·sé (pă-sā′) ▸ *adj.* **1.** No longer current or in fashion; out-of-date. **2.** Past the prime; faded or aged.
pas·sen·ger (păs′ən-jər) ▸ *n.* A person who travels in a conveyance, such as a car or train.
passe-par·tout (păs-pär-to͞o′) ▸ *n.* Something, such as a master key, that permits one to pass or go at will.
pas·ser·by (păs′ər-bī′, -bī′) ▸ *n., pl.* **pas·sers·by** (păs′ərz-). A person who passes by, esp. casually or by chance.
pas·ser·ine (păs′ə-rīn′) ▸ *adj.* Of the order of birds that includes perching birds and songbirds.
pass-fail (păs′fāl′) ▸ *adj.* Of or being a system of grading in which a student simply passes or fails instead of receiving a letter grade.
pas·sim (păs′ĭm) ▸ *adv.* Throughout or frequently; used to indicate that a word, a passage, or an idea occurs frequently in the work cited.
pass·ing (păs′ĭng) ▸ *adj.* **1.** Moving by; going past. **2.** Of brief duration; transitory: *a passing fancy.* **3.** Cursory or superficial; casual: *a passing glance.* **4.** Satisfactory: *a passing grade.* ▸ *n.* **1.** The act of one that passes. **2.** Death. **—pass′ing·ly** *adv.*
pas·sion (păsh′ən) ▸ *n.* **1.** A powerful emotion, such as love or anger. **2a.** Ardent love. **b.** Strong sexual desire; lust. **c.** The object of such love or desire. **3a.** Boundless enthusiasm: *a passion for sports.* **b.** The object of such enthusiasm. **4. Passion** The sufferings of Jesus after the Last Supper, including the Crucifixion. **—pas′sion·ate** (ə-nĭt) *adj.* **—pas′sion·ate·ly** *adv.* **—pas′sion·less** *adj.*

THESAURUS

parturiency *n.* The condition of carrying a developing fetus within the uterus ▸ gestation, gravidity, gravidness, pregnancy.
parturient *adj.* —*See* PREGNANT (1).
parturition *n.* —*See* BIRTH (1).
party *n.* A social gathering, especially for pleasure ▸ affair, celebration, festivity, fete, function, gala, gathering, get-together, occasion, social, soiree, tea. *Informal:* do. *Slang:* bash. [*Compare* BLAST, CELEBRATION, DANCE.] —*See also* ALLIANCE, BAND[2], GROUP, HUMAN BEING, PARTICIPANT.
party *v.* —*See* CELEBRATE (2), REVEL.
party pooper *n.* —*See* KILLJOY.
pass *v.* **1.** To move along a particular course ▸ go, proceed, push on, wend. *Idiom:* make (*or* wend) one's way. [*Compare* ADVANCE, ROVE.] **2.** To catch up with and move past ▸ outpace, outrun, outstrip, overhaul, overtake. [*Compare* OVERTAKE.] **3.** To use time in a particular way ▸ put in, spend. [*Compare* IDLE.] **4.** To come to one as by lot or inheritance ▸ devolve, fall. **5.** To come to an end ▸ go away, pass away. **6.** To be accepted or approved ▸ adopt, affiliate, carry, clear. *Informal:* sign off. —*See also* COMMUNICATE (1), COMMUNICATE (2), CONFIRM (3), CROSS (1), DECLINE, DIE, ELAPSE, HAPPEN (1), JOURNEY, LEAD, LEAVE[1] (1), PLUNGE, SURPASS.
pass away *v.* To come to an end ▸ go away, pass. —*See also* DIE.
pass for *v.* —*See* IMPERSONATE.
pass off *v.* To offer or put into circulation an inferior or fraudulent item ▸ foist, fob off, palm off, put off. [*Compare* DUMP.]
pass on *v.* —*See* CONDUCT (3), DIE.
pass out *v.* To suffer temporary lack of consciousness ▸ black out, faint, keel over, swoon. *Idioms:* drop (*or* faint *or* fall) dead away, see stars. [*Compare* COLLAPSE.]
pass over *v.* —*See* BLINK AT, NEGLECT (2).
pass through *v.* —*See* EXPERIENCE.
pass up *v.* —*See* LOSE (2).
pass *n.* A free ticket entitling one to transportation or admission ▸ *Informal:* comp. *Slang:* freebie. —*See also* CRISIS, WAY (2).
passable *adj.* Capable of being passed, traversed, or crossed ▸ navigable, negotiable, penetrable, surmountable, traversable. [*Compare* CLEAR.] —*See also* ACCEPTABLE (2).
passage *n.* A particular subdivision of a written work ▸ chapter, part, section, segment. —*See also* CONFIRMATION (1), JOURNEY, TRANSITION, WAY (2).
passageway *n.* —*See* WAY (2).
passé *adj.* —*See* OLD-FASHIONED.
passel *n.* —*See* HEAP (2).
passing *adj.* —*See* TRANSITORY.
passing *n.* —*See* DEATH (1).
passion *n.* Powerful, intense emotion ▸ ardor, fervency, fervor, fire, heat, warmth, zeal. *Slang:* sizzle. [*Compare* INTENSITY.] —*See also* DESIRE (2), EMOTION, ENTHUSIASM (1), ENTHUSIASM (2), LOVE (1), LOVE (2), TEMPER (2).
passionate *adj.* Fired with intense feeling ▸ ardent, blazing, burning, dithyrambic, fervent, fervid, feverish, fiery, flaming, glowing, heated, hot-blooded, impassioned, perfervid, red-hot, scorching, torrid. [*Compare* ENTHUSIASTIC, LIVELY.] —*See also* LASCIVIOUS.
passionless *adj.* —*See* COLD (2), FRIGID.

pas·sive (păsʹĭv) ▸ *adj.* **1.** Receiving or subjected to an action without acting in return. **2.** Accepting or submitting without resistance; compliant. **3.** Not participating, acting, or operating; inactive. **4.** *Gram.* Of or being a verb form or voice used to indicate that the grammatical subject is the object of the action. ▸ *n. Gram.* **1.** The passive voice. **2.** A verb or construction in the passive voice. **—pasʹsive·ly** *adv.* **—pasʹsive·ness** *n.* **—pas·sivʹi·ty** *n.*

passive restraint ▸ *n.* An automatic safety device, such as an air bag, in a motor vehicle that protects a person during a crash.

pass·key (păsʹkēʹ) ▸ *n.* **1.** See **master key**. **2.** See **skeleton key**.

Pass·o·ver (păsʹōʹvər) ▸ *n. Judaism* A holiday celebrated in the spring to commemorate the exodus of the Jews from Egypt.

pass·port (păsʹpôrtʹ) ▸ *n.* An official government document that certifies one's identity and citizenship and permits a citizen to travel abroad.

pass·word (păsʹwûrdʹ) ▸ *n.* **1.** A secret word or phrase that one uses to gain admittance or access to information. **2.** A sequence of characters that one must input to access a file, application, or computer system.

past (păst) ▸ *adj.* **1.** No longer current; over. **2.** Having existed or occurred in an earlier time; bygone. **3a.** Earlier than the present time; ago: *40 years past.* **b.** Just gone by or elapsed: *in the past few days.* **4.** Having served formerly in a given capacity: *a past president.* **5.** *Gram.* Of or being a verb tense or form used to express an action or a condition prior to the time it is expressed. ▸ *n.* **1.** The time before the present. **2.** Previous background, experiences, and activities. **3.** *Gram.* **a.** The past tense. **b.** A verb form in the past tense. ▸ *adv.* So as to pass by or go beyond: *He waved as he walked past.* ▸ *prep.* **1.** Beyond in time, position, extent, or amount. **2.** Beyond in position; farther than.

pas·ta (päsʹtə) ▸ *n.* **1.** Unleavened dough, made of wheat flour, water, and sometimes eggs, molded into any of a variety of shapes and boiled. **2.** A prepared dish of pasta.

paste (pāst) ▸ *n.* **1.** A smooth viscous mixture, as of flour and water, that is used as an adhesive. **2.** A soft, smooth, thick mixture, as: **a.** A smooth dough used in making pastry. **b.** A food that has been pounded until smooth: *anchovy paste.* **3.** The moist clay or clay mixture used in making porcelain or pottery. **4.** A hard, brilliant glass used in making artificial gems. ▸ *v.* **past·ed, past·ing. 1.** To cause to adhere by or as if by applying paste. **2.** *Comp. Sci.* To insert (e.g., text or a graphic) into a document or file.

paste·board (pāstʹbôrdʹ) ▸ *n.* A thin, firm board made of sheets of paper pasted together or pressed paper pulp.

pas·tel (pă-stĕlʹ) ▸ *n.* **1a.** A drawing medium of dried paste made of ground pigments and a water-based binder. **b.** A crayon of this material. **2a.** A picture or sketch drawn with this type of crayon. **b.** The art of drawing with pastels. **3.** A soft, delicate hue; a pale color. **—pas·telʹ** *adj.*

pas·tern (păsʹtərn) ▸ *n.* The part of a horse's foot between the fetlock and hoof.

Pas·ter·nak (păsʹtər-năkʹ), **Boris Leonidovich** (1890–1960) ▸ Russian writer; forced to decline a 1958 Nobel.

Pas·teur (păs-tûrʹ, pä-stœrʹ), **Louis** (1822–95) ▸ French chemist. **—Pas·teurʹi·an** *adj.*

pas·teur·i·za·tion (păsʹchər-ĭ-zāʹshən, păsʹtər-) ▸ *n.* The process of heating a beverage or other food, such as milk or beer, in order to kill microorganisms that could cause disease, spoilage, or undesired fermentation. **—pasʹteur·izeʹ** *v.* **—pasʹteur·izʹer** *n.*

pas·tiche (pă-stēshʹ, pä-) ▸ *n.* A dramatic, literary, or musical piece openly imitating the works of other artists.

pas·tille (pă-stēlʹ) also **pas·til** (păsʹtĭl) ▸ *n.* **1.** A small medicated or flavored tablet. **2.** A tablet containing aromatic substances that is burned to fumigate or deodorize the air.

pas·time (păsʹtīmʹ) ▸ *n.* An activity that occupies one's spare time pleasantly.

pas·tor (păsʹtər) ▸ *n.* A Christian minister or priest who is the leader of a congregation.

pas·tor·al (păsʹtər-əl) ▸ *adj.* **1.** Of or relating to shepherds or herders. **2a.** Of or relating to rural life. **b.** Charmingly simple and serene; idyllic. **3.** Of or relating to a pastor or the duties of a pastor. ▸ *n.* A literary or other artistic work that portrays or evokes rural life, usu. in an idealized manner. **—pasʹtor·al·ly** *adv.*

pas·to·rale (păsʹtə-rälʹ, -rălʹ, päʹstə-) ▸ *n.* A musical composition with a pastoral theme.

past participle ▸ *n.* A verb form indicating past or completed action or time that is used as an adjective and with auxiliaries to form the passive voice or perfect and pluperfect tenses.

past perfect ▸ *n.* See **pluperfect** 1.

pas·tra·mi (pə-sträʹmē) ▸ *n.* A highly seasoned smoked cut of beef, usu. from the shoulder.

pas·try (pāʹstrē) ▸ *n., pl.* **-tries. 1.** Dough or paste of flour, water, and shortening that is baked and used as a crust for foods such as pies. **2a.** Baked foods made with pastry. **b.** One of these foods.

pas·tur·age (păsʹchər-ĭj) ▸ *n.* **1.** The grass or other vegetation eaten by grazing animals. **2.** Land suitable for grazing animals.

pas·ture (păsʹchər) ▸ *n.* **1.** Grass or other vegetation eaten by grazing animals. **2.** Ground set aside for use by grazing animals. ▸ *v.* **-tured, -tur·ing. 1.** To herd (animals) into a pasture to graze. **2.** To graze.

past·y (pāʹstē) ▸ *adj.* **-i·er, -i·est. 1.** Resembling paste in consistency. **2.** Having a pale, lifeless appearance; pallid.

pat[1] (păt) ▸ *v.* **pat·ted, pat·ting. 1a.** To tap gently with the open hand or with something flat. **b.** To stroke lightly as a gesture of affection. **2.** To mold by tapping gently with the hands or a flat implement. ▸ *n.* **1.** A light stroke or tap. **2.** The sound made by a pat. **3.** A small mass: *a pat of butter.* ***—idiom:*** **pat on the back** A word or gesture of praise or approval.

pat[2] (păt) ▸ *adj.* **1.** Trite or glib: *pat answer.* **2a.** Timely or opportune. **b.** Suitable; fitting. ▸ *adv. Informal* Completely, exactly, or perfectly: *has the lesson down pat.* **—patʹly** *adv.* **—patʹness** *n.*

pa·ta·ca (pə-täʹkə) ▸ *n.* See **currency** table in Appendix.

Pat·a·go·ni·a (pătʹə-gōʹnē-ə, -gōnʹyə) ▸ A region of South America in S Argentina and Chile extending from the Río Colorado to the Straits of Magellan and from the Andes to the Atlantic. **—Patʹa·goʹni·an** *adj. & n.*

patch (păch) ▸ *n.* **1a.** A small piece of material affixed to another, larger piece to conceal, reinforce, or repair a worn area, hole, or tear. **b.** A small piece of cloth used for patchwork. **2.** A cloth badge affixed to a garment as a decoration or an insignia, as of a military unit. **3a.** A

THESAURUS

passive *adj.* Submitting without objection or resistance ▸ acquiescent, nonresistant, resigned, submissive, yielding. [*Compare* OBEDIENT.]

passport *n.* —*See* LICENSE (3).

past *adj.* Just gone by or elapsed ▸ ago, antecedent, anterior, bygone, bypast, earlier, foregoing, former, lapsed, precedent, preceding, previous, prior. [*Compare* LAST[1], OLD.] —*See also* LATE (2).

past *n.* The time before the present ▸ auld lang syne, old, yesterday, yesteryear, yore. *Idioms:* bygone days, days gone by, days of yore, long ago, the good old days, the old (*or* olden) days, water under the bridge. [*Compare* ANTIQUITY.] —*See also* HISTORY (2).

paste *v.* —*See* HIT.

paste *n.* —*See* BLOW[2].

pastel *adj.* —*See* PALE (1).

pastime *n.* —*See* AMUSEMENT.

past master *n.* One who has had long experience in a given activity or capacity ▸ old hand, vet, veteran. *Informal:* old-timer. —*See also* EXPERT.

pastor *n.* —*See* CLERIC.

pastoral *adj.* Charmingly simple and carefree ▸ arcadian, idyllic. [*Compare* FRESH, STILL.] —*See also* CLERICAL, COUNTRY.

pasture *n.* An area of open land ▸ clearing, field, meadow. [*Compare* LOT.]

pasture *v.* —*See* BROWSE (2).

pasty *adj.* —*See* PALE (1).

pat *v.* —*See* CARESS, TAP[1] (1).

pat down *v.* To examine a person or someone's personal effects in order to find something lost or concealed ▸ frisk, inspect, search. *Slang:* shake down. *Idiom:* do a body search of.

patch *v.* —*See* FIX (1).

patch *n.* —*See* LOT (1).

dressing or covering applied to a wound. **b.** A pad or shield of cloth, esp. one worn over an injured eye. **4a.** A small area that differs from the whole. **b.** A small plot or piece of land: *a bean patch.* **5.** A temporary, removable electronic connection. ▸ *v.* **1.** To put a patch or patches on. **2.** To make by sewing scraps of material together: *patch a quilt.* **3.** To mend, repair, or put together, esp. hastily. **4.** *Electron.* To connect temporarily. ***—phrasal verb:* patch up** To settle: *patch up a quarrel.*

patch test ▸ *n.* A test for allergic sensitivity in which a suspected allergen is applied to the skin on a small surgical pad.

patch·work (păch′wûrk′) ▸ *n.* Needlework consisting of varicolored patches of material sewn together, as in a quilt.

patch·y (păch′ē) ▸ *adj.* **-i·er, -i·est. 1.** Made up of or marked by patches. **2.** Uneven in quality or performance: *patchy work.* **—patch′i·ness** *n.*

pate (pāt) ▸ *n.* The human head, esp. the top of the head.

pâ·té (pä-tā′) ▸ *n.* A meat paste.

pa·tel·la (pə-tĕl′ə) ▸ *n., pl.* **-tel·lae** (-tĕl′ē). A flat triangular bone located at the front of the knee joint. **—pa·tel′lar** *adj.*

pat·en (păt′n) ▸ *n.* **1.** A plate used to hold the host during the celebration of the Eucharist. **2.** A thin disk of or resembling metal.

pat·ent (păt′nt) ▸ *n.* **1.** A grant made by a government that confers upon the creator of an invention the sole right to make, use, and sell that invention for a set period of time. **2.** An invention protected by such a grant. ▸ *adj.* **1a.** Protected or conferred by a patent. **b.** Of or relating to patents: *patent law.* **2.** (*also* pāt′nt) Obvious; plain. **3.** (*also* pāt′nt) *Archaic* Open to general inspection: *letters patent.* ▸ *v.* **1.** To obtain a patent on. **2.** To grant a patent to. **—pat′ent·ee′** *n.* **—pat′ent·ly** *adv.*

patent leather ▸ *n.* Black leather finished to a hard, glossy surface.

pa·ter·fa·mil·i·as (pā′tər-fə-mĭl′ē-əs, pä′-) ▸ *n., pl.* **pa·tres·fa·mil·i·as** (pā′trēz-, pä′-). A man who is the head of a household or the father of a family.

pa·ter·nal (pə-tûr′nəl) ▸ *adj.* **1.** Relating to or characteristic of a father or fatherhood; fatherly. **2.** Inherited from or related through one's father. **—pa·ter′nal·ly** *adv.*

pa·ter·nal·ism (pə-tûr′nə-lĭz′əm) ▸ *n.* A policy or practice of treating or governing people in a fatherly manner, esp. by providing for their needs without giving them rights or responsibilities. **—pa·ter′nal·is′tic** *adj.*

pa·ter·ni·ty (pə-tûr′nĭ-tē) ▸ *n.* The state of being a father; fatherhood.

path (păth) ▸ *n., pl.* **paths** (păthz, păths). **1.** A trodden track or way. **2.** A course; route.

pa·thet·ic (pə-thĕt′ĭk) ▸ *adj.* **1.** Arousing sympathetic sadness and compassion. **2.** Arousing scornful pity. **—pa·thet′i·cal·ly** *adv.*

path·find·er (păth′fīn′dər, päth′-) ▸ *n.* One that discovers a new course or way, esp. through or into unexplored regions.

patho– or **path–** ▸ *pref.* Disease; suffering: *pathogen.*

path·o·gen (păth′ə-jən) ▸ *n.* An agent that causes disease, esp. a living microorganism such as a bacterium or fungus. **—path′o·gen′ic** (-jĕn′ĭk) *adj.* **—path′o·ge·nic′i·ty** (-jə-nĭs′ĭ-tē) *n.*

path·o·gen·e·sis (păth′ə-jĕn′ĭ-sĭs) ▸ *n.* The development of a diseased or morbid condition.

pa·thol·o·gy (pă-thŏl′ə-jē) ▸ *n., pl.* **-gies. 1.** The scientific study of the nature of disease. **2.** The anatomic or functional manifestations of a disease. **3.** A departure or deviation from a normal condition. **—path′o·log′i·cal** (păth′ə-lŏj′ĭ-kəl) *adj.* **—path′o·log′i·cal·ly** *adv.* **—pa·thol′o·gist** *n.*

pa·thos (pā′thŏs′, -thôs′) ▸ *n.* A quality, as of an experience or a work of art, that arouses feelings of pity, sympathy, tenderness, or sorrow.

path·way (păth′wā′, päth′-) ▸ *n.* A path.

–pathy ▸ *suff.* **1.** Feeling; perception: *telepathy.* **2a.** Disease: *idiopathy.* **b.** A system of treating disease: *homeopathy.*

pa·tience (pā′shəns) ▸ *n.* **1.** The capacity, quality, or fact of being patient. **2.** *Chiefly Brit.* The game solitaire.

pa·tient (pā′shənt) ▸ *adj.* **1.** Enduring pain or difficulty with calmness. **2.** Tolerant; understanding. **3.** Persevering; constant. **4.** Capable of calmly awaiting an outcome; not hasty or impulsive. ▸ *n.* One who receives medical treatment. **—pa′tient·ly** *adv.*

pat·i·na (păt′n-ə, pə-tē′nə) ▸ *n.* **1.** A thin greenish layer that forms on copper or copper alloys as a result of corrosion. **2.** The sheen on any surface, produced by age and use.

pat·i·o (păt′ē-ō′) ▸ *n., pl.* **-os. 1.** An outdoor space for dining or recreation that adjoins a residence and is often paved. **2.** A roofless inner courtyard.

pat·ois (păt′wä′, pă-twä′) ▸ *n., pl.* **pat·ois** (păt′wäz′, pă-twä′). **1.** A regional dialect. **2a.** A creole language. **b.** Nonstandard speech. **3.** Jargon; cant.

patri– or **patr–** ▸ *pref.* Father, paternal: *patrilineal.*

pa·tri·arch (pā′trē-ärk′) ▸ *n.* **1.** A man who rules a family, clan, or tribe. **2.** A leading or venerable man. **3.** A bishop of high rank, esp. in an eastern Christian church. **—pa′tri·ar′chal, pa′tri·ar′chic** *adj.*

pa·tri·ar·chy (pā′trē-är′kē) ▸ *n., pl.* **-chies.** A social system in which the father is the head of the family.

pa·tri·cian (pə-trĭsh′ən) ▸ *n.* A person of high rank; aristocrat. **—pa·tri′cian** *adj.*

pat·ri·cide (păt′rĭ-sīd′) ▸ *n.* **1.** The act of murdering one's father. **2.** One who commits this act. **—pat′ri·cid′al** (-sīd′l) *adj.*

Pat·rick (păt′rĭk), Saint (A.D. 389?–461?) ▸ Christian missionary and patron saint of Ireland.

pat·ri·lin·e·al (păt′rə-lĭn′ē-əl) ▸ *adj.* Relating to, based on, or tracing ancestral descent through the paternal line.

pat·ri·mo·ny (păt′rə-mō′nē) ▸ *n., pl.* **-nies.** An inheritance, esp. from a father or other ancestor. **—pat′ri·mo′ni·al** *adj.*

pa·tri·ot (pā′trē-ət, -ŏt′) ▸ *n.* One who loves, supports, and defends one's country. **—pa′tri·ot′ic** (-ŏt′ĭk) *adj.* **—pa′tri·ot′i·cal·ly** *adv.* **—pa′tri·ot·ism** (-ə-tĭz′əm) *n.*

pa·tris·tic (pə-trĭs′tĭk) also **pa·tris·ti·cal** (-tĭ-kəl) ▸ *adj.* Of or relating to the fathers of the early Christian church or their writings.

pa·trol (pə-trōl′) ▸ *n.* **1.** The act of moving about an area for observation, inspection, or security. **2.** A person or group of persons who perform such an act. **3.** A military unit sent out on a reconnaissance or combat mission. ▸ *v.* **-trolled, -trol·ling.** To engage in a patrol (of).

pa·trol·man (pə-trōl′mən) ▸ *n.* A policeman who patrols or polices an assigned area.

patrol wagon ▸ *n.* An enclosed police truck used to convey prisoners.

pa·trol·wom·an (pə-trōl′wo͝om′ən) ▸ *n.* A policewoman who patrols or polices an assigned area.

THESAURUS

patchwork *n.* *—See* ASSORTMENT.

patchy *adj.* *—See* UNEVEN.

pate *n.* *—See* HEAD (1).

patent *adj.* *—See* APPARENT (1), OBVIOUS.

paterfamilias *n.* *—See* FATHER.

paternal *adj.* Like a father, especially in caring ▸ fatherlike, fatherly, patriarchal. [*Compare* BENEVOLENT.]

path *n.* *—See* WAY (1), WAY (2).

pathetic *adj.* *—See* PITIFUL, TERRIBLE.

pathogen *n.* *—See* GERM (1).

pathology *n.* *—See* DISEASE.

patience *n.* The capacity of enduring hardship or inconvenience without complaint ▸ acceptance, forbearance, longanimity, long-suffering, resignation, stoicism, sufferance, tolerance. [*Compare* ENDURANCE, TOLERANCE.]

patient *adj.* Enduring or capable of enduring hardship or inconvenience without complaint ▸ accepting, enduring, forbearing, long-suffering, resigned, stoic, tolerant. [*Compare* PASSIVE.]

patio *n.* *—See* COURT (1).

patois *n.* *—See* DIALECT, LANGUAGE (2).

patriarch *n.* *—See* FATHER, ORIGINATOR.

patriarchal *adj.* Like a father, especially in caring ▸ fatherlike, fatherly, paternal. [*Compare* BENEVOLENT.]

patrician *adj.* *—See* NOBLE.

patriciate *n.* *—See* SOCIETY (1).

patrimonial *adj.* *—See* ANCESTRAL.

patrimony *n.* Any special privilege accorded a firstborn ▸ birthright, heritage, inheritance, legacy. [*Compare* RIGHT.]

patrol *v.* *—See* POLICE.

patrol *n.* *—See* DETACHMENT (3), FORCE (3).

patrolman or **patrolwoman** *n.* *—See* POLICE OFFICER.

pa·tron (pā′trən) ▸ *n.* 1. One that supports, protects, or champions someone or something; sponsor or benefactor. 2. A customer, esp. a regular customer.
pa·tron·age (pā′trə-nĭj, păt′rə-) ▸ *n.* 1. Support from a patron. 2. The trade given to a commercial establishment by its customers. 3. Customers considered as a group; clientele. 4. The power to appoint people to political positions.
pa·tron·ess (pā′trə-nĭs) ▸ *n.* A woman who supports, protects, or champions someone or something; sponsor or benefactor.
pa·tron·ize (pā′trə-nīz′, păt′rə-) ▸ *v.* **-ized, -iz·ing.** 1. To act as a patron to; support or sponsor. 2. To go to as a customer, esp. on a regular basis. 3. To treat in a condescending manner. **—pa′tron·iz′ing·ly** *adv.*
patron saint ▸ *n.* A saint who is regarded as the advocate in heaven of a nation, place, craft, activity, class, or person.
pat·ro·nym·ic (păt′rə-nĭm′ĭk) ▸ *n.* A name derived from the name of one's father or a paternal ancestor. **—pat′ro·nym′ic** *adj.*
pa·troon (pə-tro͞on′) ▸ *n.* A landholder in New York under Dutch colonial rule who was granted proprietary rights to a large tract of land.
pat·sy (păt′sē) ▸ *n., pl.* **-sies.** *Slang* A person easily taken advantage of, blamed, or ridiculed.
pat·ter[1] (păt′ər) ▸ *v.* To make a quick succession of light, soft tapping sounds. ▸ *n.* A quick succession of light, soft tapping sounds.
pat·ter[2] (păt′ər) ▸ *v.* To speak or chatter glibly or mechanically. ▸ *n.* 1. The jargon of a particular group; cant. 2. Glib, rapid speech, as of an auctioneer.
pat·tern (păt′ərn) ▸ *n.* 1a. A model or an original used as an archetype. b. A person or thing considered worthy of imitation. 2. A plan, diagram, or model to be followed in making things. 3. A representative sample; specimen or ideal. 4. An artistic or decorative design. 5. A composite of traits or features. ▸ *v.* To make, mold, or design by following a pattern.
Pat·ton (păt′n), **George Smith, Jr.** (1885–1945) ▸ Amer. general.
pat·ty (păt′ē) ▸ *n., pl.* **-ties.** 1. A small rounded, flattened cake of food, esp. chopped food. 2. A small pie.
pau·ci·ty (pô′sĭ-tē) ▸ *n.* 1. Smallness of number. 2. Scarcity.
Paul (pôl), Saint (A.D. 5?–67?) ▸ Apostle to the Gentiles. **—Paul′ine** (-īn, -ēn) *adj.*
Paul VI (1897–1978) ▸ Pope (1963–78).
Pau·ling (pô′lĭng), **Linus Carl** (1901–94) ▸ Amer. chemist; 1954 Nobel.
paunch (pônch, pänch) ▸ *n.* 1. The belly, esp. a protuding one; potbelly. 2. See **rumen.** **—paunch′y** *adj.*
pau·per (pô′pər) ▸ *n.* One who is extremely poor, esp. one on public charity. **—pau′per·ism** *n.* **—pau′per·ize** *v.*
pause (pôz) ▸ *v.* **paused, paus·ing.** To cease or suspend an action temporarily; linger or hesitate. ▸ *n.* 1. A temporary cessation. 2. A hesitation. 3. *Mus.* A sign indicating that a note or rest is to be held. 4. Reason for hesitation.
pave (pāv) ▸ *v.* **paved, pav·ing.** To cover with pavement. ***—idiom:* pave the way** To make progress easier.
pave·ment (pāv′mənt) ▸ *n.* 1. A hard smooth surface, esp. of a thoroughfare, that will bear travel. 2. The material with which such a surface is made.
pa·vil·ion (pə-vĭl′yən) ▸ *n.* 1. An ornate tent. 2. A light, often open structure, used for amusement or shelter. 3. An annex of a building. 4. One of a group of related buildings forming a complex.
pav·ing (pā′vĭng) ▸ *n.* 1. The act or technique of laying pavement. 2. Pavement.
Pav·lov (păv′lôv′, päv′ləf), **Ivan Petrovich** (1849–1936) ▸ Russian physiologist; 1904 Nobel.
paw (pô) ▸ *n.* 1. The clawed foot esp. of a quadruped animal. 2. *Informal* A human hand. ▸ *v.* 1. To strike with the paw. 2. To scrape (e.g., the ground) with a paw or foot. 3. To handle clumsily, rudely, or with too much familiarity.
pawl (pôl) ▸ *n.* A hinged or pivoted device adapted to fit into a notch of a ratchet wheel to impart forward motion or prevent backward motion.
pawn[1] (pôn) ▸ *n.* 1. Something given as security for a loan; pledge. 2. The condition of being held as a pledge. ▸ *v.* To give or deposit (personal property) as security for money borrowed.
pawn[2] (pôn) ▸ *n.* 1. A chess piece of lowest value. 2. One used to further the purposes of another.
pawn·bro·ker (pôn′brō′kər) ▸ *n.* One that lends money at interest in exchange for personal property deposited as security.
Paw·nee (pô-nē′) ▸ *n., pl.* **-nee** or **-nees.** 1. A member of a Native American people formerly of Kansas and Nebraska, now of Oklahoma. 2. Their Caddoan language.
pawn·shop (pôn′shŏp′) ▸ *n.* The shop of a pawnbroker.
paw·paw (pô′pô) ▸ *n.* Var. of **papaw.**
pay (pā) ▸ *v.* **paid** (pād), **pay·ing.** 1. To recompense for goods or services. 2. To discharge or settle (a debt or obligation). 3. To requite. 4. To bear (a cost or penalty): *pay the price for nonconformity.* 5. To yield as a return. 6. To give or bestow: *pay compliments.* 7. To make (a visit or call). 8. To be profitable or worthwhile: *Crime doesn't pay.* ***—phrasal verb:* pay off** 1. To pay the full amount on (a debt). 2. To be profitable. 3. *Informal* To bribe. ▸ *adj.* Requiring payment to operate: *a pay telephone.* ▸ *n.* 1. The act of paying or state of being paid. 2. Something paid, as a salary or wages. ***—idiom:* pay the piper** To bear the consequences of something. **—pay′a·ble** *adj.* **—pay·ee′** *n.* **—pay′er** *n.*

THESAURUS

patron *n.* One who supports or champions an activity, cause, or institution ▸ backer, benefactor, benefactress, contributor, friend, philanthropist, sponsor, supporter. *Informal:* angel. [*Compare* ADVOCATE, FOLLOWER.] *—See also* CONSUMER, DONOR.
patronage *n.* 1. Aid or support given by a patron ▸ advocacy, aegis, auspices, backing, championship, encouragement, financing, furtherance, patronization, promotion, sponsorship. [*Compare* DONATION, HELP.] 2. The commercial transactions of customers with a supplier ▸ business, custom, trade, traffic. [*Compare* BUSINESS, DEAL.] 3. Customers or patrons collectively ▸ clientage, clientele, constituency, custom, trade. 4. The political appointments or jobs that are at the disposal of those in power ▸ pork, spoils.
patroness *n.* *—See* DONOR.
patronization *n.* *—See* CONDESCENSION, PATRONAGE (1).
patronize *v.* 1. To act as a patron to ▸ back, sponsor, support. [*Compare* DONATE, FINANCE, SUPPORT.] 2. To treat in a superciliously indulgent manner ▸ condescend. *Informal:* high-hat. *Idioms:* lord it over, queen it, speak (*or* talk) down to. [*Compare* INSULT, SNUB.]
patsy *n.* *—See* DUPE, SCAPEGOAT.
patter *v.* *—See* CHATTER (1).
patter *n.* *—See* CHATTER.
pattern *n.* *—See* EPITOME, FORM (1), METHOD, MODEL, ORIGINAL, USUAL.
pattern *v.* *—See* FOLLOW (5), MAKE.
paucity *n.* *—See* SHORTAGE.
paunchy *adj.* *—See* FAT (1).
pauper *n.* An impoverished person ▸ bankrupt, beggar, bum, derelict, down-and-out, down-and-outer, have-not, indigent, insolvent, tramp, vagabond. *Slang:* bag lady, skell. [*Compare* BEGGAR, HOBO.]
pauperism *n.* *—See* POVERTY.
pauperize *v.* *—See* RUIN.
pause *v.* To stop for an indefinite period ▸ interrupt, suspend. *Idiom:* put on hold. [*Compare* REST[1].] *—See also* HESITATE, REMAIN.
pause *n.* *—See* BREAK, HESITATION.
pave *v.* *—See* COVER (1).
pawl *n.* *—See* FASTENER.
pawn[1] *n.* Something given to guarantee the repayment of a loan or the fulfillment of an obligation ▸ bail, bond, collateral, earnest, gage, guaranty, hostage, pledge, recognizance, security, token, warrant, warranty. [*Compare* GUARANTEE, PROMISE.]
pawn *v.* To give or deposit as a pawn ▸ bond, collateralize, deposit, hypothecate, mortgage, pledge. *Slang:* hock.
pawn[2] *n.* A person who is used or controlled by others ▸ cat's-paw, dupe, instrument, puppet, stooge, tool. [*Compare* DUPE.]
pay *v.* *—See* COMPENSATE, RETURN (3), SETTLE (3), SPEND (1).
pay back *v.* *—See* AVENGE.
pay off *v.* *—See* AVENGE, BRIBE.
pay *n.* *—See* WAGE.
payable *adj.* *—See* DUE (1).

pay·check (pā′chĕk′) ▸ *n.* **1.** A check issued to an employee in payment of salary or wages. **2.** Salary or wages.
pay dirt ▸ *n.* **1.** Earth, ore, or gravel that is profitable to mine. **2.** *Informal* A profitable discovery or venture.
pay·load (pā′lōd′) ▸ *n.* **1.** The revenue-producing part of a cargo. **2.** The total weight of passengers and cargo that can be carried by an aircraft or spacecraft. **3.** The warhead of a missile.
pay·mas·ter (pā′măs′tər) ▸ *n.* A person in charge of paying wages and salaries.
pay·ment (pā′mənt) ▸ *n.* **1.** The act of paying. **2.** An amount paid.
pay·off (pā′ôf′, -ŏf′) ▸ *n.* **1.** Full payment of a salary or wages. **2.** *Informal* **a.** A final settlement or reckoning. **b.** The climax of a narrative or sequence of events. **3.** Final retribution or revenge. **4.** *Informal* A bribe.
pay·roll (pā′rōl′) ▸ *n.* **1.** A list of employees with the wages due to each. **2.** The total sum of wages paid during a pay period.
Pb ▸ The symbol for the element **lead**.
PC ▸ *abbr.* personal computer
PCB (pē′sē-bē′) ▸ *n.* An industrial compound and environmental pollutant.
PCP (pē′sē-pē′) ▸ *n.* A drug, $C_{17}H_{25}N$, used in veterinary medicine as an anesthetic and illegally as a hallucinogen.
pct. ▸ *abbr.* percent
Pd ▸ The symbol for the element **palladium**.
PE ▸ *abbr.* **1.** physical education **2.** Prince Edward Island
pea (pē) ▸ *n.* **1.** A vine having edible seeds enclosed in green pods. **2.** The round seed of this plant. **3.** Any of several related or similar plants.
peace (pēs) ▸ *n.* **1.** The absence of war or other hostilities. **2.** An agreement or treaty to end hostilities. **3.** Freedom from quarrels and disagreement; harmony. **4.** Public security and order: *disturbing the peace.* **5.** Serenity: *peace of mind.* **—peace′a·ble, peace′ful** *adj.* **—peace′a·bly, peace′ful·ly** *adv.* **—peace′ful·ness** *n.*
peace·keep·ing (pēs′kē′pĭng) ▸ *n.* The preservation of peace, esp. the supervision by international forces of a truce between hostile nations. **—peace′keep′ing** *adj.*
peace·mak·er (pēs′mā′kər) ▸ *n.* One who makes peace, esp. by settling disputes. **—peace′mak′ing** *adj. & n.*
peace officer ▸ *n.* A law enforcement officer responsible for maintaining civil peace.
peace pipe ▸ *n.* A calumet.
peace·time (pēs′tīm′) ▸ *n.* A time free from war. **—peace′time′** *adj.*
peach (pēch) ▸ *n.* **1.** A small tree having pink flowers and edible fruit. **2.** The soft juicy fruit of this tree, having yellow flesh and downy, red-tinted yellow skin. **—peach′y** *adj.*
pea·cock (pē′kŏk′) ▸ *n.* A male peafowl, having brilliant blue or green plumage and long back feathers that can be spread in a fanlike form.
pea·fowl (pē′foul′) ▸ *n.* A large Asian pheasant.
pea·hen (pē′hĕn′) ▸ *n.* A female peafowl.
peak (pēk) ▸ *n.* **1.** A tapering, projecting point. **2a.** The pointed summit of a mountain. **b.** The mountain itself. **3.** The point of greatest development, value, or intensity. ▸ *v.* **1.** To bring to or form a peak. **2.** To achieve a maximum of development or intensity.
peak·ed (pē′kĭd) ▸ *adj.* Having a sickly appearance.
peal (pēl) ▸ *n.* **1.** A ringing of bells. **2.** A set of tuned bells. **3.** A loud burst of noise: *peals of laughter.* ▸ *v.* To ring, as bells.
pea·nut (pē′nŭt′) ▸ *n.* **1.** A widely cultivated plant having seed pods that ripen underground. **2.** The edible, nutlike, oily seed of this plant. **3. peanuts** *Informal* A very small amount of money.
peanut butter ▸ *n.* A paste made from ground roasted peanuts.
pear (pâr) ▸ *n.* **1.** A widely cultivated tree having white flowers and edible fruit. **2.** The fruit of this tree, spherical at the base and narrow at the stem.
pearl (pûrl) ▸ *n.* **1.** A smooth, lustrous, variously colored deposit formed in the shells of certain mollusks and valued as a gem. **2.** Mother-of-pearl. **3.** One highly valued or esteemed. **4.** A yellowish white. **—pearl′y** *adj.*
Pearl Harbor ▸ An inlet of the Pacific on the S coast of Oahu, HI, W of Honolulu.
peas·ant (pĕz′ənt) ▸ *n.* **1.** A member of a class made up of agricultural workers, including small or tenant farmers and laborers on the land. **2.** A country person; rustic. **3.** An uncouth, crude, or ill-bred person; boor. **—peas′ant·ry** *n.*
peat (pēt) ▸ *n.* Partially carbonized vegetable matter, usu. mosses, found in bogs and used as fertilizer and fuel.
peat moss ▸ *n.* Any of various wetland mosses used as mulch and plant food.
peb·ble (pĕb′əl) ▸ *n.* A small stone, esp. one worn smooth by erosion. ▸ *v.* **-bled, -bling. 1.** To pave with pebbles. **2.** To impart a rough grainy surface to (leather or paper). **—peb′bly** *adj.*
pe·can (pĭ-kän′, -kăn′, pē′kăn) ▸ *n.* **1.** A tree of the central and S US, having deeply furrowed bark and edible nuts. **2.** The smooth oval nut of this tree.
pec·ca·dil·lo (pĕk′ə-dĭl′ō) ▸ *n., pl.* **-loes** or **-los.** A minor sin or fault.
pec·ca·ry (pĕk′ə-rē) ▸ *n., pl.* **-ries.** Any of several piglike American mammals having long, dark, dense bristles.
peck[1] (pĕk) ▸ *v.* **1.** To strike or make strokes with the beak or a pointed instrument. **2.** To pick up with the beak. **3.** *Informal* To kiss briefly and casually. **4.** To eat sparingly: *pecked at his dinner.* ▸ *n.* **1.** A stroke or mark made with the beak. **2.** *Informal* A light, quick kiss.
peck[2] (pĕk) ▸ *n.* **1.** See **measurement** table in Appendix. **2.** A unit of dry volume or capacity equal to 8 quarts or approx. 554.8 cubic inches.
peck·ing order (pĕk′ĭng) ▸ *n.* **1.** A hierarchy among a group, as of people, classes, or nations. **2.** The social hierarchy in a flock of domestic fowl in which each bird pecks subordinate birds and submits to being pecked by dominant birds.
pec·tin (pĕk′tĭn) ▸ *n.* Any of a group of water-soluble colloids found in ripe fruits and used to jell various foods, drugs, and cosmetics. **—pec′tic, pec′tin·ous** *adj.*
pec·to·ral (pĕk′tər-əl) ▸ *adj.* Of or situated in the breast or chest.
pec·u·late (pĕk′yə-lāt′) ▸ *v.* **-lat·ed, -lat·ing.** To embezzle. **—pec′u·la′tion** *n.*
pe·cu·liar (pĭ-kyo͞ol′yər) ▸ *adj.* **1.** Unusual or eccentric; odd. **2.** Distinct from all others. **3.** Belonging distinctively to one

THESAURUS

payment *n.* —*See* COMPENSATION, COST (1), DUE, PUNISHMENT, WAGE.
payoff *n.* —*See* BRIBE, CLIMAX.
payola *n.* —*See* BRIBE.
PDQ *adv.* —*See* IMMEDIATELY (1).
peace *n.* —*See* CALM, STILLNESS, TRUCE.
peaceable *adj.* Inclined or disposed to peace; not quarrelsome or unruly ▸ conciliatory, dovish, irenic, nonviolent, pacific, pacifical, pacifist, pacifistic, peaceful. [*Compare* AMIABLE.]
peaceful *adj.* —*See* CALM, PEACEABLE, STILL.
peacefulness *n.* —*See* CALM, STILLNESS.
peace officer *n.* —*See* POLICE OFFICER.
peacock *v.* —*See* STRUT.
peacock *n.* A man who is vain about his clothes ▸ beau, coxcomb, dandy, fop, swell.
peak[1] *n.* —*See* BILL[2] (2), CLIMAX.
peak *v.* —*See* CLIMAX.
peak *adj.* Of or constituting a climax ▸ climactic, crowning, culminating. [*Compare* LAST[1].] —*See also* MAXIMUM.
peak[2] *v.* —*See* PALE.
peaked *adj.* —*See* SICK (1).
peal *v.* —*See* RING[2].
peanuts *n. Informal* A small or trifling amount of money ▸ pocket money, small change. *Slang:* chicken feed, two bits
pearl *n.* —*See* TREASURE.
peccancy *n.* —*See* CRIME (2), EVIL (1).
peccant *adj.* —*See* EVIL.
peck[1] *v.* —*See* KISS.
peck at *v.* —*See* NAG.
peck *n.* —*See* KISS.
peck[2] *n.* —*See* ABUNDANCE, HEAP (2).
Pecksniffian *adj.* —*See* HYPOCRITICAL.
peculiar *adj.* —*See* ECCENTRIC, FUNNY (3), SPECIAL.

person, group, or kind; unique. **—pe·cu′li·ar′i·ty** (-kyo͞o′lē-ăr′ĭ-tē, -kyo͞ol-yăr′-) *n.*

pe·cu·ni·ar·y (pĭ-kyo͞o′nē-ĕr′ē) ► *adj.* Of or relating to money.

ped– ► *pref.* Var. of **pedo–.**

–ped or **–pede** ► *suff.* Foot: *biped.*

ped·a·gogue (pĕd′ə-gŏg′, -gôg′) ► *n.* A schoolteacher; educator.

ped·a·go·gy (pĕd′ə-gō′jē, -gŏj′ē) ► *n.* The art or profession of teaching. **—ped′a·gog′ic** (-gŏj′ĭk, -gō′jĭk), **ped′a·gog′i·cal** *adj.* **—ped′a·gog′i·cal·ly** *adv.*

ped·al (pĕd′l) ► *n.* A foot-operated lever, as on a piano or bicycle. ► *adj.* Of or relating to a foot or footlike part. ► *v.* **-aled, -al·ing** or **-alled, -al·ling. 1.** To use or operate a pedal or pedals. **2.** To ride a bicycle.

ped·ant (pĕd′nt) ► *n.* **1.** One who stresses trivial details of learning. **2.** One who exhibits learning ostentatiously.

pe·dan·tic (pə-dăn′tĭk) ► *adj.* Marked by a narrow, often ostentatious concern for book learning and formal rules. **—pe·dan′ti·cal·ly** *adv.* **—ped′ant·ry** (pĕd′n-trē) *n.*

ped·dle (pĕd′l) ► *v.* **-dled, -dling.** To travel about selling (wares). **—ped′dler** *n.*

ped·er·ast (pĕd′ə-răst′) ► *n.* A man who has sexual relations with a boy. **—ped′er·as′ty** *n.*

ped·es·tal (pĕd′ĭ-stəl) ► *n.* A support or base, as for a column or statue.

pe·des·tri·an (pə-dĕs′trē-ən) ► *n.* A person traveling on foot. ► *adj.* **1.** Going or performed on foot. **2.** Dull; ordinary: *pedestrian prose.*

pe·di·at·rics (pē′dē-ăt′rĭks) ► *n. (takes sing. v.)* The branch of medicine that deals with the care of infants and children and the treatment of their diseases. **—pe′di·at′ric** *adj.* **—pe′di·a·tri′cian** (-ə-trĭsh′ən) *n.*

ped·i·cure (pĕd′ĭ-kyo͝or′) ► *n.* A cosmetic treatment of the feet and toenails. **—ped′i·cur′ist** *n.*

ped·i·gree (pĕd′ĭ-grē′) ► *n.* **1.** A line of ancestors; ancestry or lineage. **2.** A list of ancestors, as of a purebred animal. **—ped′i·greed′** *adj.*

ped·i·ment (pĕd′ə-mənt) ► *n.* A gablelike, usu. triangular architectural or decorative element, as above a façade.

pedo– or **ped–** ► *pref.* Child; children: *pediatrics.*

pe·dom·e·ter (pĭ-dŏm′ĭ-tər) ► *n.* An instrument that gauges the approximate distance traveled on foot by registering the number of steps taken.

pe·dun·cle (pĭ-dŭng′kəl, pē′dŭng′kəl) ► *n.* **1.** *Bot.* A stalk bearing a flower. **2.** *Zool.* A stalklike part or structure.

peek (pēk) ► *v.* **1.** To glance quickly. **2.** To look or peer furtively, as from a place of concealment. **—peek** *n.*

peel (pēl) ► *n.* The skin or rind of certain fruits and vegetables. ► *v.* **1.** To strip or cut away the skin, rind, or bark from; pare. **2.** To strip away; pull off. **3.** To lose or shed skin, bark, or other covering. **4.** To come off in thin strips or pieces, as paint. **—peel′er** *n.*

peen (pēn) ► *n.* The end of a hammerhead opposite the flat striking surface, often wedge-shaped or ball-shaped.

peep[1] (pēp) ► *v.* To cheep or chirp, as a frog or baby bird. **—peep** *n.* **—peep′er** *n.*

peep[2] (pēp) ► *v.* **1.** To peek furtively, as through a small aperture. **2.** To become partly visible. ► *n.* **1.** A quick or furtive look. **2.** A first glimpse or appearance. **—peep′er** *n.*

peep·hole (pēp′hōl′) ► *n.* A small hole or crevice through which one may peep.

peer[1] (pîr) ► *v.* **1.** To look intently, searchingly, or with difficulty. **2.** To be partially visible; show.

peer[2] (pîr) ► *n.* **1.** One who has equal standing with another. **2a.** A nobleman. **b.** A British duke, marquis, earl, viscount, or baron.

peer·age (pîr′ĭj) ► *n.* The rank or title of a peer or peeress.

peer·ess (pîr′ĭs) ► *n.* A British duchess, marchioness, countess, viscountess, or baroness.

peer·less (pîr′lĭs) ► *adj.* Having no match or equal; incomparable. **—peer′less·ly** *adv.*

peeve (pēv) ► *v.* **peeved, peev·ing.** To annoy or vex. ► *n.* **1.** A vexation; grievance. **2.** A resentful mood.

pee·vish (pē′vĭsh) ► *adj.* **1.** Querulous or discontented. **2.** Ill-tempered. **—pee′vish·ly** *adv.* **—pee′vish·ness** *n.*

pee·wee (pē′wē) ► *n. Informal* One that is relatively or unusually small.

peg (pĕg) ► *n.* **1a.** A small cylindrical or tapered pin, as of wood, used to fasten things or plug a hole. **b.** A projection used as a support or boundary marker. **2.** A degree or notch. **3.** A straight throw of a ball. **4.** A pretext or occasion. ► *v.* **pegged, peg·ging. 1.** To fasten or plug with a peg or pegs. **2.** To mark with a peg or pegs. **3.** To fix (a price) at a certain level. **4.** *Informal* To classify; categorize. **5.** To throw. **6.** To work steadily; plug.

peg·ma·tite (pĕg′mə-tīt′) ► *n.* A coarse-grained granite.

P.E.I. ► *abbr.* Prince Edward Island

pei·gnoir (pān-wär′, pĕn-) ► *n.* A woman's loose-fitting dressing gown.

pe·jor·a·tive (pĭ-jôr′ə-tĭv, -jŏr′-, pĕj′ə-rā′tĭv) ► *adj.* **1.** Tending to make or become worse. **2.** Disparaging; belittling. ► *n.* A disparaging word or expression. **—pe·jor′a·tive·ly** *adv.*

Pe·king (pē′kĭng′, pā′-) ► See **Beijing.**

Pe·king·ese (pē′kĭng-ēz′, -ēs′) also **Pe·kin·ese** (pē′kə-nēz′, -nēs′) ► *n., pl.* **-ese. 1.** A native or resident of Peking (Beijing). **2.** The Chinese dialect of Peking. **3.** (pē′kə-nēz′, -nēs′) A small, short-legged, long-haired dog with a flat nose.

pe·koe (pē′kō) ► *n.* Black tea made of the leaves around the buds.

pe·lag·ic (pə-lăj′ĭk) ► *adj.* Of or relating to open oceans or seas.

pelf (pĕlf) ► *n.* Wealth or riches.

pel·i·can (pĕl′ĭ-kən) ► *n.* A large, web-footed bird with an expandable pouch under the lower bill used for catching and holding fish.

pel·lag·ra (pə-lăg′rə, -lā′grə, -lä′-) ► *n.* A disease caused by a deficiency of niacin and protein in the diet and marked by skin eruptions and digestive and nervous system disturbances. **—pel·lag′rous** *adj.*

pel·let (pĕl′ĭt) ► *n.* **1.** A small, solid or densely packed ball or mass, as of medicine. **2.** A bullet or piece of small shot.

THESAURUS

peculiarity *n.* —*See* ECCENTRICITY, IDENTITY (1), QUALITY (1).

peculiarly *adv.* —*See* UNUSUALLY.

pecuniary *adj.* Of or relating to money or finances ► financial, fiscal, monetary.

pedagogic or **pedagogical** *adj.* —*See* EDUCATIONAL (1), PEDANTIC.

pedagogue *n.* —*See* EDUCATOR.

pedagogy or **pedagogics** *n.* —*See* EDUCATION (1).

pedantic *adj.* Characterized by a narrow concern for book learning and formal rules ► academic, bookish, donnish, formalistic, inkhorn, literal, literary, pedagogic, pedantical, purist, scholastic. [*Compare* EDUCATED.]

peddle *v.* **1.** To travel about selling goods ► hawk, huckster, vend. **2.** To engage in the illicit sale of narcotics ► deal. *Slang:* push. —*See also* SELL.

peddler *n.* —*See* PUSHER, SELLER.

pedestal *n.* —*See* BASE[1] (2).

pedestrian *adj.* —*See* DULL (1).

pedigree *n.* A written record of ancestry ► family tree, genealogy. —*See also* ANCESTRY.

pedigreed *adj.* —*See* THOROUGHBRED.

peek *v.* To look briefly and quickly ► glance, glimpse, peep. ***Idiom:*** steal a glance (*or* look). [*Compare* LOOK.]

peek *n.* —*See* GLANCE (1).

peel *n.* —*See* SKIN (3).

peel *v.* —*See* BARE, FLAKE, SKIN.

peep *v.* To look briefly and quickly ► glance, glimpse, peek. ***Idiom:*** steal a glance (*or* look). [*Compare* LOOK.]

peep *n.* —*See* GLANCE (1).

peer[1] *v.* —*See* GAZE.

peer[2] *n.* One that is very similar to another in rank or position ► coequal, colleague, compeer, equal, equivalent, fellow, match, rival. [*Compare* ASSOCIATE, PARALLEL.]

peerless *adj.* —*See* UNIQUE.

peerlessness *n.* —*See* UNIQUENESS.

peeve *v.* —*See* ANNOY.

peeve *n.* —*See* ANNOYANCE (2).

peevish *adj.* —*See* ILL-TEMPERED.

peevishness *n.* —*See* TEMPER (1).

peewee *adj.* —*See* TINY.

peg *n.* —*See* DEGREE (1), NAIL, PLUG, THROW.

peg *v.* —*See* THROW.

pejorative *adj.* —*See* DISPARAGING.

pelagic *adj.* —*See* MARINE (1).

pelf *n.* —*See* WEALTH.

pell-mell also **pell·mell** (pĕl′mĕl′) ▸ *adv.* **1.** In a jumbled, confused manner. **2.** In frantic, disorderly haste; headlong.

pel·lu·cid (pə-lo͞o′sĭd) ▸ *adj.* **1.** Transparent or translucent. **2.** Very clear in style or meaning. **—pel·lu′cid·ly** *adv.*

Pel·o·pon·ne·sus (pĕl′ə-pə-nē′səs) ▸ A peninsula forming the S part of Greece S of the Gulf of Corinth. **—Pel′o·pon·ne′sian** (-nē′zhən, -shən) *adj. & n.*

pelt[1] (pĕlt) ▸ *n.* The skin of an animal with the fur or hair still on it.

pelt[2] (pĕlt) ▸ *v.* To strike repeatedly with or as if with blows or missiles.

pel·vis (pĕl′vĭs) ▸ *n., pl.* **-vis·es** or **-ves** (-vēz). A basin-shaped structure of the vertebrate skeleton that rests on the lower limbs and supports the spinal column. **—pel′vic** *adj.*

pem·mi·can also **pem·i·can** (pĕm′ĭ-kən) ▸ *n.* A food prepared from dried meat that is pounded into paste and mixed with fat.

pen[1] (pĕn) ▸ *n.* An instrument for writing or drawing with ink. ▸ *v.* **penned, pen·ning.** To write, esp. with a pen.

pen[2] (pĕn) ▸ *n.* **1.** A fenced enclosure for animals. **2.** A confining room or space. ▸ *v.* **penned** or **pent** (pĕnt), **pen·ning.** To confine in or as if in a pen.

pen[3] (pĕn) ▸ *n. Informal* A prison.

pe·nal (pē′nəl) ▸ *adj.* Of or relating to punishment, esp. for breaking the law. **—pe′nal·ly** *adv.*

pe·nal·ize (pē′nə-līz′, pĕn′ə-) ▸ *v.* **-ized, -iz·ing. 1.** To subject to a penalty. **2.** To hinder; handicap. **—pe′nal·i·za′tion** *n.*

pen·al·ty (pĕn′əl-tē) ▸ *n., pl.* **-ties. 1.** A punishment for a crime or offense. **2.** Something, esp. a sum of money, required as a forfeit for an offense. **3.** *Sports* A punishment, handicap, or loss of advantage imposed for infraction of a rule.

pen·ance (pĕn′əns) ▸ *n.* **1.** A voluntary act of contrition for a sin or other wrongdoing. **2.** A sacrament in some Christian churches for the forgiveness of one's sins.

Pe·na·tes (pə-nā′tēz, -nä′-) ▸ *pl.n.* The ancient Roman gods of the household.

pence (pĕns) ▸ *n. Chiefly Brit.* Pl. of **penny.**

pen·chant (pĕn′chənt) ▸ *n.* A definite liking; strong inclination.

pen·cil (pĕn′səl) ▸ *n.* **1.** A writing or drawing implement consisting of a thin rod esp. of graphite encased in wood or held in a mechanical holder. **2.** Something shaped or used like a pencil: *an eyebrow pencil.* ▸ *v.* **-ciled, -cil·ing** also **-cilled, -cil·ling.** To write, draw, or mark with a pencil.

pen·dant also **pen·dent** (pĕn′dənt) ▸ *n.* Something suspended from something else, esp. an ornament. ▸ *adj.* Var. of **pendent.**

pen·dent also **pen·dant** (pĕn′dənt) ▸ *adj.* **1.** Hanging down; dangling. **2.** Projecting; overhanging. **3.** Awaiting settlement; pending. ▸ *n.* Var. of **pendant.**

pend·ing (pĕn′dĭng) ▸ *adj.* **1.** Not yet decided or settled. **2.** Impending; imminent. ▸ *prep.* **1.** While in the process of; during. **2.** While awaiting; until.

pen·du·lar (pĕn′jə-lər, pĕn′dyə-, -də-) ▸ *adj.* Swinging back and forth like a pendulum.

pen·du·lous (pĕn′jə-ləs, pĕn′dyə-, -də-) ▸ *adj.* Hanging loosely; sagging.

pen·du·lum (pĕn′jə-ləm, pĕn′dyə-, pĕn′də-) ▸ *n.* A body suspended from a fixed support so that it swings freely back and forth under the influence of gravity.

pe·ne·plain also **pe·ne·plane** (pē′nə-plān′) ▸ *n.* A nearly flat land surface resulting from long erosion.

pen·e·trate (pĕn′ĭ-trāt′) ▸ *v.* **-trat·ed, -trat·ing. 1.** To enter or force a way into; pierce. **2.** To permeate. **3.** To grasp the inner significance of; understand. **4.** To see through. **5.** To affect deeply. **—pen′e·tra·ble** (-trə-bəl) *adj.* **—pen′e·trant** (-trənt) *n.* **—pen′e·tra′tion** *n.*

pen·e·trat·ing (pĕn′ĭ-trā′tĭng) ▸ *adj.* **1.** Able or seeming to penetrate; piercing. **2.** Keenly perceptive or understanding; acute: *a penetrating mind.* **—pen′e·trat′ing·ly** *adv.*

pen·guin (pĕng′gwĭn, pĕn′-) ▸ *n.* Any of various stout flightless marine birds of cool regions of the Southern Hemisphere, having flipperlike wings, webbed feet, and gen. black-and-white plumage.

pen·i·cil·lin (pĕn′ĭ-sĭl′ĭn) ▸ *n.* Any of a group of antibiotic drugs obtained from molds or produced synthetically and used in the treatment of various infections and diseases.

pen·in·su·la (pə-nĭn′syə-lə, -sə-lə) ▸ *n.* A piece of land that projects into a body of water. **—pen·in′su·lar** *adj.*

pe·nis (pē′nĭs) ▸ *n., pl.* **-nis·es** or **-nes** (-nēz). The male organ of copulation and, in mammals, of urination. **—pe′nile′** (-nīl′, -nəl) *adj.*

pen·i·tence (pĕn′ĭ-təns) ▸ *n.* The condition or quality of being penitent.

pen·i·tent (pĕn′ĭ-tənt) ▸ *adj.* Feeling or expressing remorse for one's misdeeds or sins. ▸ *n.* One who is penitent. **—pen′i·ten′tial** (-tĕn′shəl) *adj.* **—pen′i·tent·ly** *adv.*

pen·i·ten·tia·ry (pĕn′ĭ-tĕn′shə-rē) ▸ *n., pl.* **-ries.** A prison for those convicted of major crimes. ▸ *adj.* Of or resulting in imprisonment in a penitentiary.

pen·knife (pĕn′nīf′) ▸ *n.* A small pocketknife.

pen·man (pĕn′mən) ▸ *n.* **1.** A copyist; scribe. **2.** An expert in penmanship. **3.** An author.

pen·man·ship (pĕn′mən-shĭp′) ▸ *n.* The art, skill, or style of handwriting.

Penn (pĕn), **William** (1644–1718) ▸ English Quaker colonizer in America.

Penn. ▸ *abbr.* Pennsylvania

pen name also **pen·name** (pĕn′nām′) ▸ *n.* A pseudonym used by a writer.

pen·nant (pĕn′ənt) ▸ *n.* **1.** A long, tapering, usu. triangular flag, used on ships for signaling or identification. **2.** A flag or emblem similar to a pennant. **3.** *Sports* A flag that symbolizes the championship of a league.

pen·ne (pĕn′ā) ▸ *n., pl.* **penne.** Pasta in small short tubes with diagonally cut ends.

pen·ni·less (pĕn′ē-lĭs, pĕn′ə-) ▸ *adj.* Entirely without money; very poor.

pen·non (pĕn′ən) ▸ *n.* A long narrow banner borne on a lance.

THESAURUS

pellucid *adj.* —*See* CLEAR (1).

pellucidity or **pellucidness** *n.* —*See* CLARITY.

pelt[1] *n.* The skin of an animal, sometimes including fur, hair or feathers ▸ fur, hide, leather.

pelt[2] *v.* —*See* BARRAGE, BEAT (1), RUSH, THROW.

pen[1] *v.* —*See* COMPOSE (1), PUBLISH (2), WRITE.

pen[2] *n.* An enclosure for livestock ▸ corral, fold, paddock, sty, yard. [*Compare* CAGE.] —*See also* JAIL.

pen *v.* —*See* ENCLOSE (1).

penal *adj.* —*See* PUNISHING.

penalize *v.* To impose a fine on ▸ amerce, fine, mulct. —*See also* PUNISH.

penalty *n.* **1.** A coercive measure intended to ensure compliance or conformity ▸ interdict, interdiction, sanction. [*Compare* FORBIDDANCE, RESTRICTION.] **2.** A sum of money levied as punishment for an offense ▸ amercement, fine, mulct. —*See also* PUNISHMENT.

penance *n.* The act of making amends ▸ atonement, expiation, reconciliation, reparation. [*Compare* COMPENSATION, PURIFICATION.] —*See also* PUNISHMENT.

penchant *n.* —*See* INCLINATION (1).

pendent *adj.* —*See* HANGING.

pendulous *adj.* —*See* HANGING, HESITANT.

penetrable *adj.* —*See* PASSABLE.

penetrate *v.* To pass into or through by overcoming resistance ▸ break (through), enter, jab, perforate, pierce, poke, punch, puncture. [*Compare* CUT.] —*See also* ENTER (1).

penetrating *adj.* Having the quality or tendency to pervade or permeate ▸ permeating, pervading, pervasive, suffusive. [*Compare* GENERAL, PREVAILING, RECURRENT.] —*See also* BITTER (2), CRITICAL (2).

penetration *n.* —*See* DISCERNMENT, ENTRANCE[1], INSTINCT.

penitence or **penitency** *n.* A feeling of regret for one's sins or misdeeds ▸ attrition, compunction, contriteness, contrition, guilt, regret, remorse, remorsefulness, repentance, rue, self-reproach, shame.

penitent *adj.* —*See* SORRY.

penitentiary *n.* —*See* JAIL.

penmanship *n.* —*See* SCRIPT (1).

pennant *n.* —*See* FLAG[1].

penniless *adj.* —*See* POOR.

pennilessness *n.* —*See* POVERTY.

pennon *n.* —*See* FLAG[1].

Penn·syl·va·nia (pĕn′səl-vān′yə, -vā′nē-ə) ▸ A state of the E US. Cap. Harrisburg.

Pennsylvania Dutch ▸ *n.* **1.** The descendants of German and Swiss immigrants who settled in Pennsylvania in the 17th and 18th cent. **2.** The dialect of High German spoken by the Pennsylvania Dutch.

Penn·syl·va·nian (pĕn′səl-vān′yən, -vā′nē-ən) *Geol.* ▸ *adj.* Of or being the 6th period of the Paleozoic Era, marked by the formation of coal-bearing rock. ▸ *n.* The Pennsylvanian Period.

pen·ny (pĕn′ē) ▸ *n., pl.* **-nies. 1.** A US or Canadian coin worth one cent. **2.** *pl.* **pence** (pĕns). A coin used in Great Britain since 1971, worth 1/100 of a pound. **3.** Any of various coins of small denomination. ***—idiom:* pretty penny** A considerable sum of money.

penny pincher ▸ *n. Informal* A very stingy person. **—pen′ny-pinch′ing** *adj. & n.*

pen·ny·roy·al (pĕn′ē-roi′əl) ▸ *n.* Either of two plants whose leaves yield an aromatic oil.

pen·ny·weight (pĕn′ē-wāt′) ▸ *n.* A unit of troy weight equal to 24 grains, 1/20 of a troy ounce or approx. 1.555 grams.

pen·ny-wise (pĕn′ē-wīz′) ▸ *adj.* Careful in dealing with small sums of money or small matters.

Pe·nob·scot (pə-nŏb′skət, -skŏt′) ▸ *n., pl.* **-scot** or **-scots. 1.** A member of a Native American people inhabiting central Maine. **2.** Their Algonquian language.

pe·nol·o·gy (pē-nŏl′ə-jē) ▸ *n.* The study, theory, and practice of prison management and criminal rehabilitation. **—pe·nol′o·gist** *n.*

pen pal ▸ *n.* A person with whom one becomes acquainted through correspondence.

pen·sion (pĕn′shən) ▸ *n.* A sum of money paid regularly, esp. as a retirement benefit. ▸ *v.* To grant a pension to.

pen·sion·er (pĕn′shə-nər) ▸ *n.* One who receives a pension.

pen·sive (pĕn′sĭv) ▸ *adj.* Deeply, often wistfully or dreamily thoughtful. **—pen′sive·ness** *n.*

pent (pĕnt) ▸ *v.* P.t. and p.part of **pen**[2]. ▸ *adj.* Penned or shut up; closely confined.

penta– or **pent–** ▸ *pref.* Five: *pentameter.*

pen·ta·cle (pĕn′tə-kəl) ▸ *n.* A five-pointed star formed by five straight lines connecting the vertices of a pentagon.

pen·ta·gon (pĕn′tə-gŏn′) ▸ *n.* **1.** A polygon having five sides. **2. Pentagon** The US military establishment. **—pen·tag′o·nal** (pĕn-tăg′ə-nəl) *adj.*

pen·tam·e·ter (pĕn-tăm′ĭ-tər) ▸ *n.* A line of verse composed of five metrical feet.

Pen·ta·teuch (pĕn′tə-to͞ok′, -tyo͞ok′) ▸ *n.* The first five books of the Hebrew Scriptures.

pen·tath·lon (pĕn-tăth′lən, -lŏn′) ▸ *n.* An athletic contest in which each participant competes in five track and field events.

Pen·te·cost (pĕn′tĭ-kôst′, -kŏst′) ▸ *n.* A Christian festival celebrated the 7th Sunday after Easter to commemorate the descent of the Holy Spirit upon the disciples.

pent·house (pĕnt′hous′) ▸ *n.* **1.** An apartment or dwelling on the top floor or roof of a building. **2.** A shed or sloping roof attached to the side of a building or wall.

pent-up (pĕnt′ŭp′) ▸ *adj.* Not given expression; repressed: *pent-up emotions.*

pe·nul·ti·mate (pĭ-nŭl′tə-mĭt) ▸ *adj.* Next to last. **—pe·nul′ti·mate** *n.*

pe·num·bra (pĭ-nŭm′brə) ▸ *n., pl.* **-brae** (-brē) or **-bras.** A partial shadow, as in an eclipse, between regions of complete shadow and complete illumination.

pe·nu·ri·ous (pə-no͝or′ē-əs, -nyo͝or′-) ▸ *adj.* **1.** Miserly; stingy. **2.** Poverty-stricken; destitute.

pen·u·ry (pĕn′yə-rē) ▸ *n.* Extreme poverty; destitution.

Pe·nu·ti·an (pə-no͞o′tē-ən, -shən) ▸ *n.* A proposed stock of North American Indian languages spoken in Pacific coastal areas.

pe·on (pē′ŏn′, pē′ən) ▸ *n.* **1a.** An unskilled laborer or farm worker, esp. of Latin America. **b.** Such a worker bound in servitude to a landlord creditor. **2.** A menial worker. **—pe′on·age** (-ə-nĭj) *n.*

pe·o·ny (pē′ə-nē) ▸ *n., pl.* **-nies.** A garden plant having large, variously colored flowers.

peo·ple (pē′pəl) ▸ *n., pl.* **-ple. 1.** Humans collectively. **2.** A body of persons living in the same country under one national government; nationality. **3.** *pl.* **-ples.** A body of persons sharing a common religion, culture, language, or inherited condition of life. **4. the people a.** The mass of ordinary persons; populace. **b.** The citizens of a political unit; electorate. **5.** Family, relatives, or ancestors. ▸ *v.* **-pled, -pling.** To populate.

pep (pĕp) *Informal* ▸ *n.* Energy; vim. ▸ *v.* **pepped, pep·ping.** To impart pep to; invigorate. **—pep′py** *adj.*

pep·per (pĕp′ər) ▸ *n.* **1a.** A tropical Asian vine bearing small berrylike fruit. **b.** A peppercorn. **c.** A pungent spice made from whole or ground peppercorns. **2a.** Any of several tropical American plants, such as the bell pepper, having podlike, variously colored fruit. **b.** The mild to pungent fruit of any of these plants. ▸ *v.* **1.** To season or sprinkle with or as if with pepper. **2.** To shower with or as if with small missiles.

pep·per·corn (pĕp′ər-kôrn′) ▸ *n.* The small, dark, berrylike fruit of the pepper vine.

pep·per·mint (pĕp′ər-mĭnt′) ▸ *n.* **1.** An aromatic plant having leaves that yield a pungent oil. **2.** A candy flavored with this oil.

pep·per·y (pĕp′ə-rē) ▸ *adj.* **1.** Of, containing, or like pepper; pungent. **2.** Sharp-tempered; feisty. **3.** Fiery: *a peppery speech.*

pep·sin (pĕp′sĭn) ▸ *n.* **1.** A digestive enzyme found in gastric juice that catalyzes the breakdown of protein to peptides. **2.** A substance containing pepsin and used as a digestive aid.

pep talk ▸ *n. Informal* A speech meant to instill enthusiasm or bolster morale.

pep·tic (pĕp′tĭk) ▸ *adj.* **1.** Of or assisting digestion. **2.** Induced by or associated with the action of digestive secretions: *a peptic ulcer.*

pep·tide (pĕp′tīd′) ▸ *n.* Any of various natural or synthetic compounds consisting of two or more amino acids linked end to end.

Pe·quot (pē′kwŏt′) ▸ *n., pl.* **-quot** or **-quots. 1.** A member of a Native American people of E Connecticut. **2.** The Algonquian language of the Pequot.

per (pûr) ▸ *prep.* **1.** To, for, or by each. **2.** According to. **3.** By means of; through.

per– ▸ *pref.* Containing a large or the largest possible proportion of an element: *peroxide.*

per·am·bu·late (pə-răm′byə-lāt′) ▸ *v.* **-lat·ed, -lat·ing.** To walk about; stroll. **—per·am′bu·la′tion** *n.*

per·am·bu·la·tor (pə-răm′byə-lā′tər) ▸ *n. Chiefly Brit.* A baby carriage.

per an·num (pər ăn′əm) ▸ *adv.* By the year; annually.

per·cale (pər-kāl′) ▸ *n.* A closely woven cotton fabric used for sheets and clothing.

per cap·i·ta (pər kăp′ĭ-tə) ▸ *adv. & adj.* Per person.

THESAURUS

penny pincher *n.* —*See* MISER.

penny-pinching *adj.* —*See* STINGY.

pensile *adj.* —*See* HANGING.

pension *v.* To withdraw or remove from business or active life ▸ retire, step down, superannuate. *Idioms:* call it quits, hang up one's spurs, put out to pasture, turn in one's badge. [*Compare* DISMISS, QUIT.]

pensive *adj.* —*See* THOUGHTFUL.

penumbra *n.* Comparative darkness that results from the blocking of light rays ▸ shade, shadiness, shadow, umbra. [*Compare* DARK, TWILIGHT.]

penurious *adj.* —*See* POOR, STINGY.

penuriousness *n.* —*See* POVERTY.

penury *n.* —*See* DEPRIVATION, POVERTY.

people *n.* —*See* KIN, PUBLIC (1).

people *v.* To live in a place, as does a people ▸ inhabit, occupy, populate. [*Compare* LIVE[1], SETTLE.]

pep *n.* —*See* ENERGY, SPIRIT (1).

pep up *v.* —*See* ENERGIZE.

pepper *v.* —*See* BARRAGE, SPECKLE, SPRINKLE.

peppery *adj.* —*See* SPICY, TESTY.

peppiness *n.* —*See* ENERGY, SPIRIT (1).

peppy *adj.* —*See* ENERGETIC, LIVELY.

pep talk *n.* —*See* ENCOURAGEMENT.

perambulate *v.* —*See* STROLL.

perambulation *n.* —*See* WALK (1).

per·ceive (pər-sēv′) ► *v.* **-ceived, -ceiv·ing.** 1. To become aware of through the senses. 2. To achieve understanding of; apprehend. **—per·ceiv′a·ble** *adj.*

per·cent also **per cent** (pər-sĕnt′) ► *adv.* Out of each hundred; per hundred. ► *n., pl.* **percent** also **per cent.** 1. One part in a hundred. 2. A percentage or portion.

per·cent·age (pər-sĕn′tĭj) ► *n.* 1. A fraction or ratio with 100 understood as the denominator. 2. A proportion or share in relation to a whole; part. 3. *Informal* Advantage.

per·cen·tile (pər-sĕn′tīl′) ► *n.* One of a set of points on a scale arrived at by dividing a group into parts in order of magnitude.

per·cep·ti·ble (pər-sĕp′tə-bəl) ► *adj.* Capable of being perceived. **—per·cep′ti·bil′i·ty** *n.*

per·cep·tion (pər-sĕp′shən) ► *n.* 1. The process, act, or result of perceiving. 2a. Insight or knowledge gained by perceiving. b. The capacity for such insight.

per·cep·tive (pər-sĕp′tĭv) ► *adj.* 1. Of or relating to perception. 2a. Having the ability to perceive. b. Marked by discernment; insightful. **—per·cep′tive·ly** *adv.*

per·cep·tu·al (pər-sĕp′cho͞o-əl) ► *adj.* Of or involving perception.

perch[1] (pûrch) ► *n.* 1. A rod or branch serving as a roost for a bird. 2a. A place for resting or sitting. b. A secure position. **—perch** *v.*

perch[2] (pûrch) ► *n., pl.* **perch** or **-es.** 1. An edible freshwater fish. 2. Any of various similar or related fishes.

per·chance (pər-chăns′) ► *adv.* Perhaps.

per·cip·i·ent (pər-sĭp′ē-ənt) ► *adj.* Having the power of perceiving. **—per·cip′i·ence** *n.*

per·co·late (pûr′kə-lāt′) ► *v.* **-lat·ed, -lat·ing.** 1. To pass or cause to pass through a porous substance. 2. To make (coffee) in a percolator. **—per′co·la′tion** *n.*

per·co·la·tor (pûr′kə-lā′tər) ► *n.* A coffeepot in which boiling water is filtered repeatedly through a basket of ground coffee.

per·cus·sion (pər-kŭsh′ən) ► *n.* 1. The striking together of two bodies, esp. when noise is produced. 2. The sound, vibration, or shock caused by percussion. 3. The act of detonating a percussion cap in a firearm. 4. *Mus.* Percussion instruments or their players. **—per·cus′sive** *adj.*

percussion cap ► *n.* A thin metal cap containing gunpowder or another detonator that explodes on being struck.

percussion instrument ► *n.* An instrument, such as a drum, piano, or maraca, in which sound is produced by one object striking another or by being scraped or shaken. **—per·cus′sion·ist** *n.*

per di·em (pər dē′əm, dī′əm) ► *adv.* Per day. ► *n.* An allowance for daily expenses.

per·di·tion (pər-dĭsh′ən) ► *n.* 1. Eternal damnation. 2. Hell.

per·e·gri·nate (pĕr′ĭ-grə-nāt′) ► *v.* **-nat·ed, -nat·ing.** To journey or travel from place to place. **—per′e·gri·na′tion** *n.*

per·e·grine falcon (pĕr′ə-grĭn, -grēn′) ► *n.* A large, widely distributed falcon much used in falconry.

per·emp·to·ry (pə-rĕmp′tə-rē) ► *adj.* 1. Precluding further debate or action: *a peremptory decree.* 2. Not allowing contradiction or refusal; imperative. 3. Imperious; dictatorial. **—per·emp′to·ri·ly** *adv.* **—per·emp′to·ri·ness** *n.*

per·en·ni·al (pə-rĕn′ē-əl) ► *adj.* 1. Lasting through the year or many years. 2a. Lasting indefinitely; enduring. b. Recurring regularly. 3. *Bot.* Living three or more years. ► *n.* *Bot.* A perennial plant. **—per·en′ni·al·ly** *adv.*

per·fect (pûr′fĭkt) ► *adj.* 1. Lacking nothing essential. 2. Being without defect or blemish: *a perfect specimen.* 3. Completely suited for a particular purpose; ideal. 4. Accurate; exact. 5. Complete; utter: *a perfect fool.* 6. *Gram.* Of or constituting a verb form expressing action completed prior to a fixed point of reference in time. ► *n.* *Gram.* 1. The perfect tense. 2. A verb in this tense. ► *v.* (pər-fĕkt′) To bring to perfection or completion. **—per·fect′i·bil′i·ty** *n.* **—per·fect′i·ble** *adj.* **—per′fect·ly** *adv.* **—per′fect·ness** *n.*

per·fec·tion (pər-fĕk′shən) ► *n.* 1. The quality or condition of being perfect. 2. The act or process of perfecting. 3. One considered perfect.

per·fec·tion·ism (pər-fĕk′shə-nĭz′əm) ► *n.* A propensity for being displeased with anything not perfect or not meeting very high standards. **—per·fec′tion·ist** *adj. & n.*

per·fi·dy (pûr′fĭ-dē) ► *n., pl.* **-dies.** Deliberate breach of faith; treachery. **—per·fid′i·ous** (pər-fĭd′ē-əs) *adj.* **—per·fid′i·ous·ly** *adv.*

per·fo·rate (pûr′fə-rāt′) ► *v.* **-rat·ed, -rat·ing.** 1. To pierce, punch, or bore a hole or holes in. 2. To pierce or stamp with rows of holes to allow easy separation. **—per′fo·ra′tion** *n.*

per·force (pər-fôrs′) ► *adv.* By necessity; by force of circumstance.

per·form (pər-fôrm′) ► *v.* 1. To begin and carry through to completion; do. 2. To carry out; fulfill. 3. To give a public performance (of). **—per·form′er** *n.*

per·for·mance (pər-fôr′məns) ► *n.* 1. The act or manner of performing. 2. A presentation, as of a play or dance, before an audience. 3. Something performed; accomplishment.

per·fume (pûr′fyo͞om′, pər-fyo͞om′) ► *n.* 1. A fragrant substance, esp. a volatile liquid distilled from flowers or prepared synthetically. 2. A pleasing scent or odor. ► *v.* (pər-fyo͞om′) **-fumed, -fum·ing.** To fill with fragrance.

THESAURUS

perceivable *adj.* —*See* PERCEPTIBLE.

perceive *v.* To be intuitively aware of ► apprehend, feel, intuit, sense. *Idioms:* feel in one's bones, get vibrations. [*Compare* UNDERSTAND.] —*See also* SEE (1).

percentage *n.* —*See* PART (1).

perceptibility *n.* —*See* VISIBILITY.

perceptible *adj.* Capable of being perceived by the senses or the mind ► appreciable, cognizable, detectable, discernible, distinguishable, noticeable, observable, palpable, perceivable, ponderable, recognizable, sensible. [*Compare* APPARENT, PHYSICAL, UNDERSTANDABLE.]

perception *n.* —*See* AWARENESS, DISCERNMENT, IDEA, SENSATION (1).

perceptive *adj.* —*See* CRITICAL (2), VISIONARY.

perceptiveness *n.* —*See* DISCERNMENT.

perch *v.* —*See* BALANCE (3).

perch *n.* A place providing support for the foot in climbing ► foothold, footing, purchase, toehold.

perchance *adv.* —*See* MAYBE.

percipience or **percipiency** *n.* —*See* DISCERNMENT, DISCRIMINATION (1).

percipient *adj.* —*See* DISCRIMINATING.

percolate *v.* —*See* BOIL, OOZE.

percussion *n.* —*See* COLLISION.

perdition *n.* —*See* HELL.

perdurable *adj.* —*See* CONTINUING.

perdure *v.* —*See* ENDURE (2).

peregrinate *v.* —*See* JOURNEY, ROVE.

peregrination *n.* —*See* JOURNEY.

peregrinator *n.* —*See* HOBO.

peremptory *adj.* —*See* DICTATORIAL.

perennial *adj.* —*See* CONTINUAL, CONTINUING.

perfect *adj.* Free from flaws or blemishes ► absolute, clean, clear, consummate, faultless, flawless, impeccable, indefectible, regular, unblemished, unflawed, unmarked. *Idiom:* in mint condition. —*See also* COMPLETE (1), GOOD (2), IDEAL, PURE, UTTER[2].

perfect *v.* To bring to perfection or completion ► complement, complete, fill in (*or* out), hone, polish, refine, round off (*or* out), smooth. *Idiom:* smooth off the rough edges. [*Compare* CLIMAX, COMPLETE, SATISFY.]

perfection *n.* —*See* SOUNDNESS.

perfectly *adv.* —*See* COMPLETELY (1).

perfervid *adj.* —*See* PASSIONATE.

perfidious *adj.* —*See* DISHONEST, FAITHLESS.

perfidy or **perfidiousness** *n.* Willful betrayal of fidelity, confidence, or trust ► treacherousness, treachery, treason. —*See also* FAITHLESSNESS.

perforate *v.* —*See* BREACH, PENETRATE.

perforation *n.* —*See* PRICK.

perforce *adv.* —*See* HELPLESSLY.

perform *v.* 1. To begin and carry through to completion ► accomplish, achieve, discharge, do, effect, execute, fulfill, prosecute, transact. *Informal:* pull off. [*Compare* ACCOMPLISH, EFFECT.] 2. To make music ► concertize, play, render. —*See also* ACT (3), FULFILL, FUNCTION, STAGE.

performance *n.* The act of beginning and carrying through to completion ► discharge, effectuation, execution, prosecution, transaction. [*Compare* ACCOMPLISHMENT, FULFILLMENT.] —*See also* ACT (1), BEHAVIOR (2), INTERPRETATION.

performer *n.* —*See* PLAYER (2).

perfume *n.* —*See* FRAGRANCE.

perfume *v.* To fill with a pleasant odor ► aromatize, scent.

per·fum·er·y (pər-fyo͞o′mə-rē) ▸ *n., pl.* **-ies. 1.** Perfumes. **2.** An establishment that makes or sells perfume.
per·func·to·ry (pər-fŭngk′tə-rē) ▸ *adj.* Done routinely and with little care. **—per·func′to·ri·ly** *adv.* **—per·func′to·ri·ness** *n.*
per·go·la (pûr′gə-lə) ▸ *n.* An arbor or passageway of columns supporting a roof of trelliswork.
per·haps (pər-hăps′) ▸ *adv.* Maybe; possibly.
peri– ▸ *pref.* **1.** Around; about; enclosing: *periodontal.* **2.** Near: *perigee.*
per·i·anth (pĕr′ē-ănth′) ▸ *n.* The outer envelope of a flower.
per·i·car·di·um (pĕr′ĭ-kär′dē-əm) ▸ *n., pl.* **-di·a** (-dē-ə). The membranous sac that encloses the heart. **—per′i·car′di·al** *adj.*
Per·i·cles (pĕr′ĭ-klēz′) (d. 429 B.C.) ▸ Athenian leader.
per·i·gee (pĕr′ə-jē) ▸ *n.* The point nearest the earth's center in the orbit of the moon or a satellite.
per·i·he·li·on (pĕr′ə-hē′lē-ən, -hēl′yən) ▸ *n., pl.* **-he·li·a** (-hē′lē-ə, -hēl′yə). The point nearest the sun in the orbit of a planet or other celestial body.
per·il (pĕr′əl) ▸ *n.* **1.** Danger. **2.** Something that endangers or involves risk. **—per′il·ous** *adj.*
pe·rim·e·ter (pə-rĭm′ĭ-tər) ▸ *n.* **1.** *Math.* A closed curve bounding a plane area. **2.** The outer limits of an area.
per·i·ne·um (pĕr′ə-nē′əm) ▸ *n., pl.* **-ne·a** (-nē′ə). The portion of the body extending from the anus to the genitals.
pe·ri·od (pîr′ē-əd) ▸ *n.* **1.** An interval of time characterized by the occurrence of a certain condition or event. **2.** An interval regarded as a distinct evolutionary or developmental phase. **3.** *Geol.* A unit of time, longer than an epoch and shorter than an era. **4.** An arbitrary unit of time, as of an academic day. **5.** An instance of menstruation. **6.** A point at which something is ended; completion. **7.** The full pause at the end of a spoken sentence. **8.** A punctuation mark (.) indicating a full stop, placed esp. at the end of declarative sentences. ▸ *adj.* Of or representing a historical time.
pe·ri·od·ic (pîr′ē-ŏd′ĭk) ▸ *adj.* **1.** Having or marked by repeated cycles. **2.** Happening or appearing at regular intervals. **3.** Occasional; intermittent. **—pe′ri·od′i·cal·ly** *adv.* **—pe′ri·o·dic′i·ty** (-ə-dĭs′ĭ-tē) *n.*
pe·ri·od·i·cal (pîr′ē-ŏd′ĭ-kəl) ▸ *adj.* **1.** Periodic. **2a.** Published at regular intervals of more than one day. **b.** Of a publication issued at such intervals. ▸ *n.* A periodical publication.
periodical cicada ▸ *n.* A cicada of the E US whose 17- or 13-year life cycle consists almost entirely of a nymphal stage spent underground.
periodic table ▸ *n.* A tabular arrangement of the elements according to their atomic numbers.
per·i·o·don·tal (pĕr′ē-ə-dŏn′tl) ▸ *adj.* Of or being tissue and structures surrounding and supporting teeth. **—per′i·o·don′tist** *n.*
per·i·pa·tet·ic (pĕr′ə-pə-tĕt′ĭk) ▸ *adj.* Walking about from place to place.
pe·riph·er·al (pə-rĭf′ər-əl) ▸ *adj.* **1.** Of or on an outer boundary or periphery. **2.** Of minor relevance or importance. ▸ *n. Comp. Sci.* An auxiliary device, such as a printer or modem, that works in conjunction with a computer. **—pe·riph′er·al·ly** *adv.*
pe·riph·er·y (pə-rĭf′ə-rē) ▸ *n., pl.* **-ies. 1.** A line that forms the boundary of an area; perimeter. **2a.** The outermost part or region within a precise boundary. **b.** A zone constituting an imprecise boundary.
pe·riph·ra·sis (pə-rĭf′rə-sĭs) ▸ *n., pl.* **-ses** (-sēz′). Circumlocution. **—per′i·phras′tic** (pĕr′ə-frăs′tĭk) *adj.*
per·i·scope (pĕr′ĭ-skōp′) ▸ *n.* An optical instrument in which mirrors or prisms allow observation of objects not in a direct line of sight. **—per′i·scop′ic** (-skŏp′ĭk) *adj.*
per·ish (pĕr′ĭsh) ▸ *v.* **1.** To die, esp. in a violent or untimely manner. **2.** To disappear gradually.
per·ish·a·ble (pĕr′ĭ-shə-bəl) ▸ *adj.* Subject to decay or spoilage. ▸ *n.* Something, esp. foodstuff, that is perishable. **—per′ish·a·bil′i·ty** *n.* **—per′ish·a·bly** *adv.*
per·i·stal·sis (pĕr′ĭ-stôl′sĭs, -stăl′-) ▸ *n., pl.* **-ses** (-sēz). The wavelike muscular contractions of the alimentary canal or other tubular structures by which contents are forced onward toward the opening. **—per′i·stal′tic** *adj.*
per·i·style (pĕr′ĭ-stīl′) ▸ *n.* A series of columns surrounding a building or enclosing a court.
per·i·to·ne·um (pĕr′ĭ-tn-ē′əm) ▸ *n., pl.* **-to·ne·a** (-tn-ē′ə). The membrane that lines the walls of the abdominal cavity.
per·i·to·ni·tis (pĕr′ĭ-tn-ī′tĭs) ▸ *n.* Inflammation of the peritoneum.
per·i·wig (pĕr′ĭ-wĭg′) ▸ *n.* A wig; peruke.
per·i·win·kle[1] (pĕr′ĭ-wĭng′kəl) ▸ *n.* A small, often edible marine snail having a cone-shaped shell.
per·i·win·kle[2] (pĕr′ĭ-wĭng′kəl) ▸ *n.* A trailing evergreen plant having glossy, dark green leaves and blue flowers.
per·jure (pûr′jər) ▸ *v.* **-jured, -jur·ing.** *Law* To deliberately testify falsely under oath. **—per′jur·er** *n.* **—per′ju·ry** *n.*
perk[1] (pûrk) ▸ *v.* To raise (e.g., the head or ears) smartly or attentively. ***—phrasal verb:* perk up 1.** To regain or cause to regain one's good spirits or liveliness. **2.** To add to or refresh the appearance of. **—perk′i·ness** *n.* **—perk′y** *adj.*
perk[2] (pûrk) ▸ *n. Informal* A perquisite.
perk[3] (pûrk) ▸ *v.* To percolate.
per·lite (pûr′līt′) ▸ *n.* A natural volcanic glass used in a fluffy heat-expanded form for fire-resistant insulation and in soil for potting plants.
perm (pûrm) *Informal* ▸ *n.* A permanent. ▸ *v.* To give (hair) a permanent.
per·ma·frost (pûr′mə-frôst′, -frŏst′) ▸ *n.* Permanently frozen subsoil occurring in perennially frigid areas.
per·ma·nent (pûr′mə-nənt) ▸ *adj.* Lasting or fixed. ▸ *n.* A long-lasting hair wave. **—per′ma·nence, per′ma·nen·cy** *n.* **—per′ma·nent·ly** *adv.*
permanent press ▸ *n.* A chemical process in which fabrics are permanently shaped and treated for wrinkle resistance. **—per′ma·nent-press′** *adj.*
per·me·a·ble (pûr′mē-ə-bəl) ▸ *adj.* Capable of being permeated, esp. by liquids or gases. **—per′me·a·bil′i·ty** *n.*
per·me·ate (pûr′mē-āt′) ▸ *v.* **-at·ed, -at·ing. 1.** To spread or flow throughout; pervade. **2.** To pass through openings or small gaps of. **—per′me·a′tion** *n.* **—per′me·a′tive** *adj.*
Per·mi·an (pûr′mē-ən, pĕr′-) *Geol.* ▸ *adj.* Of or being the 7th and last period of the Paleozoic Era, ending with the largest known mass extinction in the history of life. ▸ *n.* The Permian Period.
per·mis·si·ble (pər-mĭs′ə-bəl) ▸ *adj.* Permitted or allow-

THESAURUS

perfumy *adj.* —*See* FRAGRANT.
perfunctory *adj.* Done routinely and impersonally ▸ automatic, cursory, mechanical, routine. [*Compare* APATHETIC, CARELESS.]
perhaps *adv.* —*See* MAYBE.
periapt *n.* —*See* CHARM.
peril *n.* —*See* DANGER.
peril *v.* —*See* ENDANGER.
perilous *adj.* —*See* DANGEROUS.
perimeter *n.* —*See* BORDER (1), CIRCUMFERENCE, LIMITS.
period *n.* **1.** A specific length of time characterized by the occurrence of certain conditions or events ▸ duration, season, session, space, span, stretch, term, time. [*Compare* BIT[1].] **2.** An interval regarded as a distinct evolutionary or developmental unit ▸ phase, stage. [*Compare* DEGREE.] —*See also* AGE (2), END (1).
periodic or **periodical** *adj.* Happening or appearing at regular intervals ▸ cyclic, cyclical, isochronal, isochronous. *Idiom:* like clockwork. [*Compare* RECURRENT.] —*See also* INTERMITTENT.
periodically *adv.* —*See* INTERMITTENTLY.
peripatetic *adj.* —*See* NOMADIC.
peripatetic *n.* —*See* HOBO.
periphery *n.* —*See* BORDER (1), CIRCUMFERENCE, LIMITS.
periphrastic *adj.* —*See* WORDY (1).
perish *v.* —*See* DIE, DISAPPEAR (2).
perjure *v.* —*See* LIE[2].
perjurer *n.* —*See* LIAR.
perjury *n.* —*See* MENDACITY.
perk *n.* —*See* GRATUITY.
perk up *v.* To make lively or animated ▸ animate, brighten, enliven, light (up). —*See also* ENCOURAGE (2), RECOVER (2).
perky *adj.* —*See* LIVELY.
permanence *n.* —*See* CHANGELESSNESS, CONTINUATION (1).
permanent *adj.* —*See* CONTINUING, UNCHANGING.
permanently *adv.* —*See* FOREVER.
permeable *adj.* —*See* ABSORBENT.
permeate *v.* —*See* CHARGE (1).
permissible *adj.* —*See* ACCEPTABLE (1), OPTIONAL.

able. **—per·mis′si·bil′i·ty, per·mis′si·ble·ness** *n.*

per·mis·sion (pər-mĭsh′ən) ► *n.* Consent, esp. formal consent.

per·mis·sive (pər-mĭs′ĭv) ► *adj.* Granting permission; tolerant or lenient. **—per·mis′sive·ly** *adv.* **—per·mis′sive·ness** *n.*

per·mit (pər-mĭt′) ► *v.* **-mit·ted, -mit·ting.** 1. To allow the doing of; consent to. 2. To afford opportunity or possibility (for). ► *n.* (pûr′mĭt, pər-mĭt′) A document or certificate granting permission. **—per′mit·tee′** *n.* **—per·mit′ter** *n.*

per·mu·ta·tion (pûr′myo͞o-tā′shən) ► *n.* 1. A transformation. 2. The act of altering a given set of objects in a group. 3. *Math.* An ordered arrangement of the elements of a set. **—per′mu·ta′tion·al** *adj.*

per·ni·cious (pər-nĭsh′əs) ► *adj.* 1. Deadly. 2. Destructive. **—per·ni′cious·ness** *n.*

pernicious anemia ► *n.* A severe anemia caused by failure to absorb vitamin B_{12} and marked by abnormally large red blood cells and gastrointestinal disturbances.

per·o·rate (pĕr′ə-rāt′) ► *v.* **-rat·ed, -rat·ing.** 1. To conclude a speech, esp. with a formal recapitulation. 2. To speak at great length; declaim. **—per′o·ra′tion** *n.*

per·ox·ide (pə-rŏk′sīd′) ► *n.* 1. A compound containing oxygen that yields hydrogen peroxide when treated with an acid. 2. Hydrogen peroxide. ► *v.* **-id·ed, -id·ing.** To treat or bleach with peroxide.

per·pen·dic·u·lar (pûr′pən-dĭk′yə-lər) ► *adj.* 1. Intersecting at or forming right angles. 2. At right angles to the horizontal; vertical. **—per′pen·dic′u·lar** *n.* **—per′pen·dic′u·lar′i·ty** (-lăr′ĭ-tē) *n.*

per·pe·trate (pûr′pĭ-trāt′) ► *v.* **-trat·ed, -trat·ing.** To be guilty of or responsible for; commit. **—per′pe·tra′tion** *n.* **—per′pe·tra′tor** *n.*

per·pet·u·al (pər-pĕch′o͞o-əl) ► *adj.* 1. Lasting for eternity. 2. Lasting for an indefinitely long time. 3. Continuing without interruption. **—per·pet′u·al·ly** *adv.*

per·pet·u·ate (pər-pĕch′o͞o-āt′) ► *v.* **-at·ed, -at·ing.** 1. To make perpetual. 2. To prolong the existence of. **—per·pet′u·ance, per·pet′u·a′tion** *n.* **—per·pet′u·a′tor** *n.*

per·pe·tu·i·ty (pûr′pĭ-to͞o′ĭ-tē, -tyo͞o′-) ► *n., pl.* **-ties.** The quality or condition of being perpetual. ***—idiom:* in perpetuity** Always.

per·plex (pər-plĕks′) ► *v.* To confuse or puzzle; bewilder. **—per·plex′ing·ly** *adv.* **—per·plex′i·ty** *n.*

per·qui·site (pûr′kwĭ-zĭt) ► *n.* 1. A payment or profit received in addition to a regular wage or salary. 2. A tip; gratuity. 3. Something claimed as an exclusive right.

Per·ry (pĕr′ē), **Oliver Hazard** (1785–1819) ► Amer. naval officer.

pers. ► *abbr.* person

per se (pər sā′, sē′) ► *adv.* In or by itself or oneself; as such.

per·se·cute (pûr′sĭ-kyo͞ot′) ► *v.* **-cut·ed, -cut·ing.** 1. To oppress or harass with ill-treatment, esp. because of race, religion, or beliefs. 2. To annoy persistently. **—per′se·cu′tion** *n.* **—per′se·cu′tor** *n.*

per·se·vere (pûr′sə-vîr′) ► *v.* **-vered, -ver·ing.** To persist in or remain constant to a purpose, idea, or task in spite of obstacles. **—per′se·ver′ance** *n.*

Per·shing (pûr′shĭng, -zhĭng), **John Joseph.** "Black Jack" (1860–1948) ► Amer. general.

Per·sia (pûr′zhə, -shə) ► 1. also **Persian Empire** An ancient empire of SW Asia. 2. See **Iran.**

Per·sian (pûr′zhən, -shən) ► *n.* 1. A native or inhabitant of Persia or Iran. 2. Any of the W Iranian dialects or languages of ancient or medieval Persia and modern Iran.

Persian cat ► *n.* A domestic cat having long silky fur and short legs.

Persian Gulf ► An arm of the Arabian Sea between Arabia and SW Iran.

Persian lamb ► *n.* The glossy, tightly curled fur of a young lamb of the karakul sheep of Asia.

per·si·flage (pûr′sə-fläzh′) ► *n.* Light good-natured talk; banter.

per·sim·mon (pər-sĭm′ən) ► *n.* 1. A tropical tree having hard wood and orange-red fruit edible only when fully ripe. 2. The fruit of a persimmon tree.

per·sist (pər-sĭst′, -zĭst′) ► *v.* 1. To be obstinately repetitious, insistent, or tenacious. 2. To hold firmly and steadfastly to a purpose or undertaking despite obstacles. 3. To continue in existence; last. **—per·sis′tence** *n.* **—per·sis′tent** *adj.* **—per·sis′tent·ly** *adv.*

per·snick·e·ty (pər-snĭk′ĭ-tē) ► *adj.* Very particular about details; fastidious.

per·son (pûr′sən) ► *n.* 1. A human. 2. An individual of specified character: *a person of importance.* 3. The personality of a human; self. 4. The living body of a human. 5. *Gram.* Any of three groups of pronouns with corresponding verb inflections that distinguish the speaker (first person), the individual addressed (second person), and the individual or thing spoken of (third person).

per·so·na (pər-sō′nə) ► *n., pl.* **-nas** or **-nae** (-nē). 1. A voice or character representing the speaker or narrator in a literary work. 2. *pl.* **-nas.** One's public image or personality.

THESAURUS

permission *n.* The approving of an action, especially when done by one in authority ► allowance, approbation, approval, assent, authority, authorization, consent, endorsement, imprimatur, leave, license, nod, permit, rubber stamp, sanction, thumbs-up. *Informal:* go-ahead, green light, OK. *Idioms:* seal of approval, stamp of approval. [*Compare* ACCEPTANCE, ADMISSION.]

permissive *adj.* *—See* TOLERANT.

permissiveness *n.* *—See* TOLERANCE.

permit *v.* 1. To neither forbid nor prevent ► allow, have, let, suffer, tolerate. 2. To give one's consent to ► allow, approbate, approve, authorize, consent, endorse, let, license, sanction. *Informal:* green-light, OK. [*Compare* ASSENT, GRANT, LEGALIZE.] 3. To afford an opportunity for ► admit, allow, give, let. 4. To give the means, ability, or opportunity to do ► empower, enable. *Idioms:* clear the path (*or* road *or* way) for, smooth the way for. [*Compare* EASE, PERMIT.]

permit *n.* *—See* LICENSE (3), PERMISSION.

permitted *adj.* *—See* LAWFUL.

permutable *adj.* *—See* CHANGEABLE (1).

permutation *n.* *—See* CHANGE (1), VARIATION.

pernicious *adj.* *—See* HARMFUL, POISONOUS.

perorate *v.* *—See* RANT.

perp *n.* *—See* CRIMINAL.

perpendicular *adj.* *—See* VERTICAL.

perpetrate *v.* To be responsible for or guilty of an error or crime ► carry out, commit, do. *Informal:* pull off. [*Compare* PERFORM.]

perpetrator *n.* *—See* CRIMINAL.

perpetual *adj.* *—See* CONTINUAL, ENDLESS (2).

perpetually *adv.* *—See* FOREVER.

perpetuate *v.* To cause to last endlessly ► eternalize, eternize, immortalize. ***Idiom:*** cast (*or* etch *or* fix *or* set) in stone. [*Compare* HONOR, MEMORIALIZE.]

perpetuity *n.* The totality of time without beginning or end ► eternity, infinity, sempiternity. [*Compare* FOREVER.] *—See also* ENDLESSNESS.

perplex *v.* *—See* BAFFLE, COMPLICATE, CONFUSE (1).

perplexed *adj.* *—See* CONFUSED (1).

perplexing *adj.* *—See* AMBIGUOUS (1).

perplexity *n.* *—See* COMPLEXITY, DAZE, MYSTERY.

perquisite *n.* *—See* GRATUITY, RIGHT.

persecute *v.* *—See* ABUSE (1), HARASS.

persecution *n.* *—See* HELL, OPPRESSION.

perseverance *n.* The state or quality of being insistent ► insistence, insistency, persistence, persistency. [*Compare* DECISION.] *—See also* DILIGENCE.

perseverate *v.* *—See* ENDURE (2).

persevere *v.* *—See* ENDURE (1), INSIST, SURVIVE (1).

persist *v.* *—See* ENDURE (1), ENDURE (2), INSIST, SURVIVE (1).

persistence or **persistency** *n.* The state or quality of being insistent ► insistence, insistency, perseverance. [*Compare* DECISION.] *—See also* CONTINUATION (1), DILIGENCE.

persistent *adj.* 1. Firm or obstinate, as in making a demand or maintaining a stand ► importunate, importune, insistent, urgent. [*Compare* FIRM[1], STUBBORN.] 2. Difficult to alleviate or cure ► obstinate, pertinacious, stubborn. *—See also* CHRONIC (2), CONTINUAL, CONTINUING, DILIGENT.

persnickety *adj.* *—See* FUSSY.

person *n.* *—See* HUMAN BEING.

persona *n.* A person portrayed in fiction or drama ► character, part, personage, role.

per·son·a·ble (pûr′sə-nə-bəl) ▸ *adj.* Pleasing in personality or appearance. **—per′son·a·ble·ness** *n.* **—per′son·a·bly** *adv.*

per·son·age (pûr′sə-nĭj) ▸ *n.* A person of distinction.

per·son·al (pûr′sə-nəl) ▸ *adj.* **1.** Of a particular person; private. **2.** Done in person: *a personal appearance.* **3.** Aimed pointedly at an individual, esp. in a critical or hostile manner. **4.** Of the body or physical being. **5.** *Law* Relating to a person's movable property. **6.** Indicating grammatical person. ▸ *n.* A personal item or notice in a newspaper. **—per′son·al·ly** *adv.*

personal computer ▸ *n.* A computer built around a microprocessor for use by an individual.

personal effects ▸ *pl.n.* Privately owned items, such as keys or a wallet or watch, regularly worn or carried on one's person.

per·son·al·i·ty (pûr′sə-năl′ĭ-tē) ▸ *n., pl.* **-ties. 1.** The quality or condition of being a person. **2.** The totality of distinctive traits of a specific person. **3.** The personal traits that make one socially appealing. **4.** *Informal* A celebrity.

per·son·al·ize (pûr′sə-nə-līz) ▸ *v.* **-ized, -iz·ing. 1.** To personify. **2.** To have printed, engraved, or monogrammed with one's name or initials. **—per′son·al·i·za′tion** *n.*

personal property ▸ *n. Law* Temporary or movable property.

personal watercraft ▸ *n. (takes pl. v.)* A motorized recreational water vehicle usu. ridden by straddling a seat.

persona non gra·ta (nŏn grä′tə, grăt′ə) ▸ *adj.* Unacceptable or unwelcome, esp. to a foreign government.

per·son·i·fy (pər-sŏn′ə-fī′) ▸ *v.* **-fied, -fy·ing. 1.** To think of or represent (e.g., an inanimate object) as a person. **2.** To be the embodiment or perfect example of. **—per·son′i·fi·ca′tion** *n.* **—per·son′i·fi′er** *n.*

per·son·nel (pûr′sə-nĕl′) ▸ *n.* **1.** The body of persons employed by or active in an organization, business, or service. **2.** An administrative division of an organization concerned with this body of persons.

per·spec·tive (pər-spĕk′tĭv) ▸ *n.* **1.** The technique of representing three-dimensional objects and depth relationships on a two-dimensional surface. **2a.** The relationship of aspects of a subject to each other and to a whole. **b.** A point of view. **—per·spec′tive·ly** *adv.*

per·spi·cac·i·ty (pûr′spĭ-kăs′ĭ-tē) ▸ *n.* Acuteness of perception or understanding. **—per·spi·ca′cious** (-kā-shəs) *adj.*

per·spic·u·ous (pər-spĭk′yo͞o-əs) ▸ *adj.* Clearly expressed or presented; easy to understand; lucid. **—per′spi·cu′i·ty** (-kyo͞o′ĭ-tē) *n.* **—per·spic′u·ous·ness** *n.*

per·spi·ra·tion (pûr′spə-rā′shən) ▸ *n.* **1.** The saline moisture excreted through the pores of the skin by the sweat glands; sweat. **2.** The act or process of perspiring.

per·spire (pər-spīr′) ▸ *v.* **-spired, -spir·ing.** To excrete through the pores of the skin.

per·suade (pər-swād′) ▸ *v.* **-suad·ed, -suad·ing.** To induce to undertake a course of action or embrace a point of view by means of argument, reasoning, or entreaty. **—per·suad′a·ble** *adj.* **—per·suad′er** *n.* **—per·sua′sive** *adj.* **—per·sua′sive·ly** *adv.* **—per·sua′sive·ness** *n.*

per·sua·sion (pər-swā′zhən) ▸ *n.* **1.** The act of persuading or state of being persuaded. **2.** The ability to persuade. **3.** A strongly held opinion. **4.** A body of religious beliefs.

pert (pûrt) ▸ *adj.* **-er, -est. 1.** Trim and stylish; jaunty. **2.** High-spirited. **3.** Impudently bold. **—pert′ly** *adv.* **—pert′ness** *n.*

per·tain (pər-tān′) ▸ *v.* **1.** To have reference; relate. **2.** To belong as an adjunct or accessory. **3.** To be suitable.

Perth (pûrth) ▸ A city of SW Australia near the Indian Ocean.

per·ti·na·cious (pûr′tn-ā′shəs) ▸ *adj.* **1.** Holding tenaciously to a purpose, belief, opinion, or course of action. **2.** Stubbornly persistent. **—per′ti·na′cious·ly** *adv.* **—per′ti·na′cious·ness** *n.* **—per′ti·nac′i·ty** (-ăs′ĭ-tē) *n.*

per·ti·nent (pûr′tn-ənt) ▸ *adj.* Relating to a specific matter; relevant. **—per′ti·nence, per′ti·nen·cy** *n.*

per·turb (pər-tûrb′) ▸ *v.* To disturb greatly; make uneasy or anxious. **—per·turb′a·ble** *adj.* **—per·tur·ba′tion** *n.*

per·tus·sis (pər-tŭs′ĭs) ▸ *n.* See **whooping cough. —per·tus′sal** *adj.*

Pe·ru (pə-ro͞o′) ▸ A country of W South America on the Pacific. **—Pe·ru′vi·an** (-vē-ən) *adj. & n.*

pe·ruke (pə-ro͝ok′) ▸ *n.* A wig, esp. one worn by men in the 17th and 18th cent.; periwig.

pe·ruse (pə-ro͞oz′) ▸ *v.* **-rused, -rus·ing.** To read or examine, esp. with great care. **—pe·rus′al** *n.*

per·vade (pər-vād′) ▸ *v.* **-vad·ed, -vad·ing.** To spread throughout; permeate. **—per·va′sion** (-vā′zhən) *n.* **—per·va′sive** (-vā′sĭv, -zĭv) *adj.* **—per·va′sive·ness** *n.*

per·verse (pər-vûrs′, pûr′vûrs′) ▸ *adj.* **1.** Directed away from what is right or good; perverted. **2.** Obstinately persisting in an error or fault. **3.** Cranky; peevish. **—per·verse′ness, per·ver′si·ty** *n.*

per·ver·sion (pər-vûr′zhən, -shən) ▸ *n.* **1.** The act of perverting or the state of being perverted. **2.** A sexual practice considered deviant.

per·vert (pər-vûrt′) ▸ *v.* **1.** To corrupt or debase. **2.** To

THESAURUS

personage *n.* A person portrayed in fiction or drama ▸ character, part, persona, role. *—See also* CELEBRITY, DIGNITARY, HUMAN BEING.

personal *adj.* **1.** Belonging to, relating to, or affecting a particular person ▸ individual, intimate, private. **2.** Belonging or confined to a particular person or group as opposed to the public or the government ▸ closed-door, private, privy. [*Compare* SECRET.] *—See also* ARBITRARY, BODILY, CONFIDENTIAL (2).

personal effects *n.* *—See* EFFECTS.

personality *n.* *—See* CELEBRITY, CHARACTER (1).

personalization *n.* *—See* EMBODIMENT.

personalize *v.* *—See* EMBODY (1).

personal property *n.* *—See* EFFECTS.

persona non grata *n.* *—See* OUTCAST.

personification *n.* *—See* EMBODIMENT.

personify *v.* *—See* EMBODY (1), REPRESENT (1).

perspective *n.* *—See* POSTURE (2), VIEW (2), VIEWPOINT.

perspicacious *adj.* *—See* DISCRIMINATING, SHREWD.

perspicacity *n.* *—See* DISCERNMENT, DISCRIMINATION (1).

perspicuity or **perspicuousness** *n.* *—See* CLARITY.

perspiration *n.* Moisture accumulated on a surface through sweating or condensation ▸ condensation, lather, sweat, transudation.

perspire *v.* To excrete moisture through a porous skin or layer ▸ lather, sweat, transude.

perspiring *adj.* Producing or covered with sweat ▸ sudoriferous, sweaty, sweating. [*Compare* DAMP, STICKY.]

persuade *v.* To succeed in causing a person to act or think in a certain way ▸ argue into, bring around (*or* round), coax, convince, get to, induce, move, prevail on (*or* upon), sell (on), talk into. [*Compare* COAX, INFLUENCE.] *—See also* CONVINCE.

persuasion *n.* Urgent solicitation ▸ insistence, insistency, pressing, urging. [*Compare* DEMAND.] *—See also* BELIEF (1), KIND^2, RELIGION.

persuasive *adj.* *—See* CONVINCING.

persuasiveness *n.* *—See* COGENCY.

pert *adj.* *—See* IMPUDENT, LIVELY.

pertain *v.* *—See* APPLY (2).

pertinacious *adj.* Difficult to alleviate or cure ▸ obstinate, persistent, stubborn. *—See also* DILIGENT, STUBBORN (1).

pertinacity or **pertinaciousness** *n.* *—See* DILIGENCE, STUBBORNNESS.

pertinence or **pertinency** *n.* *—See* RELEVANCE.

pertinent *adj.* *—See* RELEVANT.

pertness *n.* *—See* IMPUDENCE, SPIRIT (1).

perturb *v.* *—See* AGITATE (2).

perturbation *n.* *—See* AGITATION (2).

perturbing *adj.* *—See* DISTURBING.

perusal *n.* *—See* EXAMINATION (1).

peruse *v.* *—See* EXAMINE (1).

pervade *v.* *—See* CHARGE (1).

pervasive *adj.* Having the quality or tendency to pervade or permeate ▸ penetrating, permeating, pervading, suffusive. [*Compare* GENERAL, PREVAILING, RECURRENT.]

perverse *adj.* *—See* CONTRARY, CORRUPT (1), STUBBORN (1).

perversion *n.* *—See* ABUSE (1), CORRUPTION (1).

perversity or **perverseness** *n.* *—See* STUBBORNNESS.

pervert *v.* *—See* ABUSE (2), CORRUPT, DISTORT.

pervert *n.* One whose sexual behavior differs from the accepted norm ▸

misuse. **3.** To interpret incorrectly. ► *n.* (pûr′vûrt′) One who practices sexual perversion. **—per·vert′ed** *adj.*
per·vi·ous (pûr′vē-əs) ► *adj.* **1.** Open to passage; permeable. **2.** Open to arguments, ideas, or change. **—per′vi·ous·ly** *adv.* **—per′vi·ous·ness** *n.*
pe·se·ta (pə-sā′tə) ► *n.* The primary unit of currency in Spain and Andorra before the adoption of the euro.
pes·ky (pĕs′kē) ► *adj.* **-ki·er, -ki·est.** *Informal* Troublesome; annoying. **—pes′ki·ly** *adv.* **—pes′ki·ness** *n.*
pe·so (pā′sō) ► *n., pl.* **-sos.** See **currency** table in Appendix.
pes·si·mism (pĕs′ə-mĭz′əm) ► *n.* **1.** A tendency to take the gloomiest possible view of a situation. **2.** The doctrine or belief that the evil in the world outweighs the good. **—pes′si·mist** *n.* **—pes′si·mis′tic** *adj.*
pest (pĕst) ► *n.* **1.** An annoying person or thing; nuisance. **2.** An injurious plant or animal.
pes·ter (pĕs′tər) ► *v.* To harass with petty annoyances; bother. **—pes′ter·er** *n.*
pes·ti·cide (pĕs′tĭ-sīd′) ► *n.* A chemical used to kill pests, esp. insects.
pes·tif·er·ous (pĕ-stĭf′ər-əs) ► *adj.* **1.** Producing, causing, or contaminated with an infectious disease. **2.** Bothersome or annoying. **—pes·tif′er·ous·ly** *adv.* **—pes·tif′er·ous·ness** *n.*
pes·ti·lence (pĕs′tə-ləns) ► *n.* A usu. fatal epidemic disease, esp. bubonic plague.
pes·ti·lent (pĕs′tə-lənt) ► *adj.* **1.** Tending to cause death. **2.** Likely to cause an epidemic disease. **—pes′ti·len′tial** (-lĕn′shəl) *adj.*
pes·tle (pĕs′əl, pĕs′təl) ► *n.* A club-shaped, hand-held tool for grinding or mashing substances in a mortar.
pes·to (pĕs′tō) ► *n.* A sauce made of usu. fresh basil, garlic, pine nuts, olive oil, and grated cheese.
pet[1] (pĕt) ► *n.* **1.** An animal kept for amusement or companionship. **2.** An object of the affections. **3.** A favorite: *the teacher's pet.* ► *adj.* **1.** Kept as a pet. **2.** Particularly cherished or indulged. ► *v.* **pet·ted, pet·ting.** **1.** To stroke or caress gently. **2.** To engage in amorous fondling and caressing. **—pet′ter** *n.*
pet[2] (pĕt) ► *n.* Bad temper or pique.
pet·al (pĕt′l) ► *n.* A segment of a flower corolla, usu. showy and colored. **—pet′aled, pet′alled** *adj.*
pe·tard (pĭ-tärd′) ► *n.* A small bell-shaped bomb used to breach a gate or wall.
pet·cock (pĕt′kŏk′) ► *n.* A small valve used to drain pipes.
pe·ter (pē′tər) ► *v.* **1.** To come to an end slowly; diminish: *Their enthusiasm soon petered out.* **2.** To become exhausted.
Peter ► *n.* See **Bible** table in Appendix.
Peter, Saint (d. c. A.D. 67) ► The chief of the 12 Apostles.
Peter I. "Peter the Great" (1672–1725) ► Russian czar (1682–1725).
Peter Principle ► *n.* The theory that an employee within an organization will advance to his or her level of incompetence and remain there.
pet·i·ole (pĕt′ē-ōl′) ► *n.* *Bot.* The stalk by which a leaf is attached to a stem; leafstalk.
pet·it also **pet·ty** (pĕt′ē) ► *adj.* *Law* Lesser; minor: *petit larceny.*
pe·tite (pə-tēt′) ► *adj.* Small, slender, and trim.
petit four ► *n., pl.* **pe·tits fours** or **pet·it fours** (pĕt′ē). A small, square-cut, frosted tea cake.
pe·ti·tion (pə-tĭsh′ən) ► *n.* **1.** A solemn request; entreaty. **2.** A formal document containing such a request. ► *v.* **1.** To address a petition to. **2.** To request formally. **3.** To make a request, esp. formally: *petitioned for retrial.* **—pe·ti′tion·ar′y** (-tĭsh′ə-nĕr′ē) *adj.* **—pe·ti′tion·er** *n.*
petit jury also **petty jury** ► *n.* A jury that sits at civil and criminal trials.
petit mal (mäl, măl) ► *n.* A mild form of epilepsy marked by frequent but transient lapses of consciousness and only rare spasms or falling.
petit point ► *n.* Needlepoint that is done with a small stitch.
pe·tri dish (pē′trē) ► *n.* A shallow dish with a loose cover, used to culture microorganisms.
pet·ri·fy (pĕt′rə-fī′) ► *v.* **-fied, -fy·ing.** **1.** To convert (wood or other organic matter) into a stony replica by structural impregnation with dissolved minerals. **2.** To cause to become stonelike; deaden. **3.** To stun or paralyze with terror. **—pet′ri·fac′tion** (-făk′shən), **pet′ri·fi·ca′tion** *n.*
petro– or **petri–** or **petr–** ► *pref.* **1.** Rock; stone: *petroglyph.* **2.** Petroleum: *petrochemical.*
pet·ro·chem·i·cal (pĕt′rō-kĕm′ĭ-kəl) ► *n.* A chemical derived from petroleum or natural gas. **—pet′ro·chem′i·cal** *adj.*
pet·ro·glyph (pĕt′rə-glĭf′) ► *n.* *Archaeol.* A carving or line drawing on rock, esp. one made by prehistoric people. **—pet′ro·glyph′ic** *adj.*
pe·trog·ra·phy (pə-trŏg′rə-fē) ► *n.* The description and classification of rocks. **—pe·trog′ra·pher** *n.*
pet·rol (pĕt′rəl) ► *n.* *Chiefly Brit.* Gasoline.
pet·ro·la·tum (pĕt′rə-lā′təm, -lä′təm) ► *n.* See **petroleum jelly.**
pe·tro·le·um (pə-trō′lē-əm) ► *n.* A thick, flammable, yellow-to-black liquid hydrocarbon mixture that occurs naturally beneath the earth's surface and is processed for fractions including natural gas, gasoline, naphtha, kerosene, paraffin wax, and asphalt.
petroleum jelly ► *n.* A colorless-to-amber gelatinous semisolid, obtained from petroleum and used in lubricants and medicinal ointments.
pe·trol·o·gy (pə-trŏl′ə-jē) ► *n.* The study of the origin, composition, structure, and alteration of rocks. **—pe·trol′o·gist** *n.*
pet·ti·coat (pĕt′ē-kōt′) ► *n.* A woman's slip or underskirt.
pet·ti·fog·ger (pĕt′ē-fŏg′ər, -fô′gər) ► *n.* A petty, quibbling, unscrupulous lawyer. **—pet′ti·fog′** *v.* **—pet′ti·fog′ger·y** *n.*
pet·tish (pĕt′ĭsh) ► *adj.* Petulant or ill-tempered.
pet·ty (pĕt′ē) ► *adj.* **-ti·er, -ti·est.** **1.** Of small importance; trivial. **2.** Marked by narrowness of mind or views. **3.** Marked by meanness; spiteful. **4.** Secondary in importance or rank. **5.** *Law* Var. of **petit.** **—pet′ti·ly** *adv.* **—pet′ti·ness** *n.*
petty cash ► *n.* A small fund of money for incidental expenses, as in an office.
petty jury ► *n.* Var. of **petit jury.**
petty officer ► *n.* A noncommissioned naval officer, esp. in the three lower ranks.

THESAURUS

deviant, deviate, *Slang:* freak.
perverted *adj.* —*See* CORRUPT (1).
pesky *adj.* —*See* TROUBLESOME (2).
pessimist *n.* **1.** A person who expects only the worst from people ► cynic, misanthrope, misanthropist. [*Compare* SKEPTIC.] **2.** A prophet of misfortune or disaster ► apocalypticist, Cassandra, crapehanger, croaker, doomsayer, worrywart.
pessimistic *adj.* —*See* BLEAK (2).
pest *n.* —*See* ANNOYANCE (2).
pester *v.* —*See* ANNOY, HARASS.
pestering *n.* —*See* ANNOYANCE (1).
pestilence *n.* —*See* CONTAMINANT.
pestilent or **pestilential** *adj.* —*See* CONTAGIOUS, DEADLY, POISONOUS.
pestle *v.* —*See* CRUSH (2).
pet[1] *n.* One liked or preferred above all others ► darling, favorite. *Idiom:* apple of one's eye.
pet *adj.* —*See* DOMESTIC (2), FAVORITE.
pet *v.* —*See* CARESS, NECK.
pet[2] *v.* To be sullenly aloof or withdrawn, as in silent resentment or protest ► mope, pout, sulk. [*Compare* BROOD.]
petcock *n.* —*See* FAUCET.
peter out *v.* —*See* DECREASE, FADE.
petite *adj.* —*See* LITTLE.
petition *v.* **1.** To bring an appeal or request to the attention of ► address, appeal, apply, approach. [*Compare* REQUEST.] **2.** To ask for employment, acceptance, or admission ► apply, put in. —*See also* APPEAL (1).
petition *n.* —*See* APPEAL.
petitioner *n.* One that asks a higher authority for something, as a favor or redress ► appealer, appellant, suitor. —*See also* APPLICANT.
pet name *n.* —*See* NAME (1).
petrified *adj.* —*See* AFRAID.
petrify *v.* —*See* FRIGHTEN, HARDEN (2), PARALYZE.
petroleum *n.* —*See* OIL.
pettifog *v.* —*See* QUIBBLE.
pettifogger *n.* —*See* CRITIC (2), LAWYER.
pettifoggery *n.* —*See* QUIBBLING.
pettiness *n.* —*See* TRIFLE.
petty *adj.* —*See* MINOR (1), NARROW (1), STINGY, TRIVIAL.

pet·u·lant (pĕch′ə-lənt) ▸ *adj.* Unreasonably irritable or ill-tempered; peevish. **—pet′u·lance, pet′u·lan·cy** *n.* **—pet′u·lant·ly** *adv.*
pe·tu·nia (pĭ-tōōn′yə, -tyōōn′-) ▸ *n.* A garden plant having funnel-shaped, variously colored flowers.
pew (pyōō) ▸ *n.* A bench for the congregation in a church.
pe·wee (pē′wē) ▸ *n.* A small brownish North American flycatcher.
pew·ter (pyōō′tər) ▸ *n.* An alloy of tin with various amounts of antimony, copper, and lead, used for kitchen utensils and tableware. **—pew′ter** *adj.*
pe·yo·te (pā-ō′tē) ▸ *n.* **1.** A spineless, dome-shaped cactus of Mexico and the SW US, having buttonlike tubercles that are the source of mescaline. **2.** See **mescaline.**
pfen·nig (fĕn′ĭg) ▸ *n.* A former subunit of German currency, equal to 1/100 of a deutsche mark.
PG (pē′jē′) ▸ A trademark for a movie rating granting admission to persons of all ages but advising parental guidance in the case of children.
pg. ▸ *abbr.* page
PG-13 (pē′jē′thûr-tēn′) ▸ A trademark for a movie rating granting admission to persons of all ages but advising parental guidance in the case of children under 13.
pH (pē′āch′) ▸ *n.* A measure of the acidity or alkalinity of a solution, numerically equal to 7 for neutral solutions, increasing with increasing alkalinity and decreasing with increasing acidity.
pha·e·ton (fā′ĭ-tn) ▸ *n.* A light, four-wheeled open carriage, usu. drawn by a pair of horses.
-phage ▸ *suff.* One that eats: *bacteriophage.*
phago– ▸ *pref.* Eating; consuming: *phagocyte.*
phag·o·cyte (făg′ə-sīt′) ▸ *n.* A cell, such as a white blood cell, that engulfs and absorbs foreign bodies in the bloodstream and tissues. **—phag′o·cyt′ic** (-sĭt′ĭk) *adj.*
pha·lanx (fā′lăngks′, făl′ăngks′) ▸ *n., pl.* **-es** or **pha·lan·ges** (fə-lăn′jēz, fā-). **1.** A compact or close-knit group. **2.** A formation of infantry carrying overlapping shields and long spears, developed in Greece in the 4th cent. B.C. **3.** *pl.* **phalanges.** *Anat.* A bone of a finger or toe.
phal·a·rope (făl′ə-rōp′) ▸ *n.* Any of several small wading shore birds.
phal·lus (făl′əs) ▸ *n., pl.* **phal·li** (făl′ī′) or **-es. 1.** The penis. **2.** A representation or symbol of it. **—phal′lic** *adj.*
Phan·e·ro·zo·ic (făn′ər-ə-zō′ĭk) ▸ *n.* Of or being the geologic time period from approx. 570 million years ago to the present, including the Paleozoic, Mesozoic, and Cenozoic eras.
phan·tasm (făn′tăz′əm) ▸ *n.* A phantom. **—phan·tas′mal** (făn-tăz′məl), **phan·tas′mic** (-tăz′mĭk) *adj.*
phan·tas·ma·go·ri·a (făn-tăz′mə-gôr′ē-ə) ▸ *n.* A fantastic sequence of haphazardly associative imagery, as in dreams. **—phan·tas′ma·gor′ic** *adj.*
phan·tom (făn′təm) ▸ *n.* **1.** Something apparently seen, heard, or sensed, but having no physical reality; a ghost or apparition. **2.** An illusory mental image. ▸ *adj.* Resembling or being a phantom; illusive.
Phar·aoh also **phar·aoh** (fâr′ō, fā′rō) ▸ *n.* A king of ancient Egypt. **—Phar′a·on′ic** (fâr′ā-ŏn′ĭk) *adj.*
phar·i·see (făr′ĭ-sē) ▸ *n.* **1. Pharisee** A member of an ancient Jewish group that emphasized strict interpretation and observance of the Mosaic law. **2.** A hypocritical, self-righteous person. **—phar′i·sa′ic** (-sā′ĭk) *adj.*
phar·ma·ceu·ti·cal (fär′mə-sōō′tĭ-kəl) also **phar·ma·ceu·tic** (-tĭk) ▸ *adj.* Of pharmacy or pharmacists. ▸ *n.* A medicinal drug.
phar·ma·cist (fär′mə-sĭst) ▸ *n.* A person trained in pharmacy; druggist.
pharmaco– ▸ *pref.* Drug: *pharmacology.*
phar·ma·col·o·gy (fär′mə-kŏl′ə-jē) ▸ *n.* The science of drugs, including their composition, uses, and effects. **—phar′ma·co·log′ic** (-kə-lŏj′ĭk), **phar′ma·co·log′i·cal** *adj.* **—phar′ma·col′o·gist** *n.*
phar·ma·co·poe·ia also **phar·ma·co·pe·ia** (fär′mə-kə-pē′ə) ▸ *n.* **1.** A book containing an official list of medicinal drugs together with articles on their preparation and use. **2.** A collection or stock of drugs.
phar·ma·cy (fär′mə-sē) ▸ *n., pl.* **-cies. 1.** The art of preparing and dispensing drugs. **2.** A drugstore; apothecary.
pharyngo– or **pharyng–** ▸ *pref.* Pharynx: *pharyngoscope.*
phar·yn·gol·o·gy (făr′ĭn-gŏl′ə-jē, făr′ĭng-) ▸ *n.* The medical study of the pharynx and its diseases.
pha·ryn·go·scope (fə-rĭng′gə-skōp′) ▸ *n.* An instrument used in examining the pharynx. **—phar′yn·gos′co·py** (făr′ĭn-gŏs′kə-pē) *n.*
phar·ynx (făr′ĭngks) ▸ *n., pl.* **pha·ryn·ges** (fə-rĭn′jēz) or **-ynx·es.** The section of the alimentary canal that extends from the nasal cavities to the larynx, where it becomes continuous with the esophagus. **—pha·ryn′ge·al** (fə-rĭn′jē-əl, făr′ĭn-jē′əl) *adj.*
phase (fāz) ▸ *n.* **1.** A distinct stage of development. **2.** A temporary pattern of behavior: *just a passing phase.* **3.** An aspect or facet; part: *every phase of the operation.* **4.** One of the cyclically recurring apparent forms of the moon or a planet. ▸ *v.* **phased, phas·ing.** To plan or carry out systematically in phases. ***—phrasal verbs:* phase in** To introduce in stages. **phase out** To eliminate in stages. **—pha′sic** (fā′zĭk) *adj.*
phase-in (fāz′ĭn′) ▸ *n.* A gradual introduction.
phase-out (fāz′out′) ▸ *n.* A gradual discontinuation.
PhD ▸ *abbr. Lat.* Philosophiae Doctor (Doctor of Philosophy)
pheas·ant (fĕz′ənt) ▸ *n., pl.* **-ants** or **-ant.** Any of various chickenlike birds having long tails and, in the males, often brilliantly colored plumage.
phe·nix (fē′nĭks) ▸ *n.* Var. of **phoenix.**
pheno– or **phen–** ▸ *pref.* **1.** Showing; displaying: *phenotype.* **2.** Derived from benzene: *phenol.*
phe·no·bar·bi·tal (fē′nō-bär′bĭ-tôl′, -tăl′) ▸ *n.* A shiny white crystalline compound, $C_{12}H_{12}N_2O_3$, used medicinally as a sedative, hypnotic, and anticonvulsant.
phe·nol (fē′nôl′, -nōl′, -nŏl′) ▸ *n.* A caustic, poisonous, white crystalline compound, C_6H_5OH, derived from benzene and used in plastics, disinfectants, and drugs. **—phe·no′lic** (-nô′lĭk, -nō′-, -nŏl′ĭk) *adj.*
phe·nom·e·non (fĭ-nŏm′ə-nŏn′, -nən) ▸ *n., pl.* **-na** (-nə). **1.** An occurrence or fact that is perceptible by the senses. **2.** *pl.* **-nons. a.** An unusual fact or occurrence; marvel. **b.** A remarkable or outstanding person; paragon. **—phe·nom′e·nal** *adj.* **—phe·nom′e·nal·ly** *adv.*
phe·no·type (fē′nə-tīp′) ▸ *n.* **1.** The environmentally and genetically determined observable appearance of an organism. **2.** An individual or group of organisms exhibiting a particular phenotype. **—phe′no·typ′ic** (-tĭp′ĭk), **phe′no·typ′i·cal** *adj.*
pher·o·mone (fĕr′ə-mōn′) ▸ *n.* A chemical secreted by an animal that influences the behavior or development of others of the same species.
phi (fī) ▸ *n.* The 21st letter of the Greek alphabet.
phi·al (fī′əl) ▸ *n.* A vial.
Phi Beta Kappa ▸ *n.* An honorary society, founded in 1776, of college students and graduates whose members are chosen on the basis of high academic standing.
Phil·a·del·phi·a (fĭl′ə-dĕl′fē-ə) ▸ A city of SE PA on the Delaware R. **—Phil′a·del′phi·an** *adj. & n.*

THESAURUS

petulance *n.* —*See* TEMPER (1).
petulant *adj.* —*See* ILL-TEMPERED.
phantasm or **phantasma** *n.* —*See* DREAM (1), GHOST, ILLUSION.
phantasmagoria or **phantasmagory** *n.* An experience of things or events that are not real ▸ hallucination. *Slang:* trip. —*See also* DREAM (1), ILLUSION.
phantasmagoric *adj.* —*See* ILLUSIVE.
phantasmal *adj.* —*See* ILLUSIVE.
phantasmic *adj.* —*See* ILLUSIVE.
phantom *n.* —*See* GHOST.
pharisaic *adj.* —*See* HYPOCRITICAL.
pharisaism *n.* —*See* HYPOCRISY.
pharisee *n.* —*See* HYPOCRITE.
pharmaceutical *n.* —*See* DRUG (1).
phase *n.* An interval regarded as a distinct evolutionary or developmental unit ▸ period, stage. [*Compare* DEGREE.] —*See also* VIEWPOINT.
phenomenal *adj.* —*See* ASTONISHING, PHYSICAL.
phenomenon *n.* Something demonstrated to exist or known to have existed ▸ actuality, event, fact, reality. *Idiom:* hard (*or* cold *or* plain) fact. [*Compare* INFORMATION.] —*See also* EVENT (1), MARVEL.
phenomenonally *adv.* —*See* UNUSUALLY.

phi·lan·der (fĭ-lăn′dər) ▸ *v.* To engage in love affairs frivolously or casually. **—phi·lan′der·er** *n.*

phil·an·throp·ic (fĭl′ən-thrŏp′ĭk) also **phil·an·throp·i·cal** (-ĭ-kəl) ▸ *adj.* 1. Marked by philanthropy; humanitarian. 2. Providing charitable assistance. **—phil′an·throp′i·cal·ly** *adv.*

phi·lan·thro·py (fĭ-lăn′thrə-pē) ▸ *n., pl.* **-pies.** 1. The effort to increase the well-being of humankind, as by charitable donations. 2. Love of humankind in general. 3. A charitable activity or institution. **—phi·lan′thro·pist** *n.*

phi·lat·e·ly (fĭ-lăt′l-ē) ▸ *n.* The collection and study of postage stamps, postmarks, and related materials. **—phil′a·tel′ic** (fĭl′ə-tĕl′ĭk) *adj.* **—phi·lat′e·list** *n.*

—phile or **—phil** ▸ *suff.* One that loves or has a strong affinity or preference for: *audiophile.*

Phi·le·mon (fĭ-lē′mən, fī-) ▸ *n.* See **Bible** table in Appendix.

phil·har·mon·ic (fĭl′här-mŏn′ĭk, fĭl′ər-) ▸ *n.* A symphony orchestra or group that supports it.

—philia ▸ *suff.* Tendency toward: *hemophilia.*

Phil·ip (fĭl′ĭp) Prince Duke of Edinburgh (b. 1921) ▸ Husband of Elizabeth II of Great Britain.

Phi·lip·pi·ans (fĭ-lĭp′ē-ənz) ▸ *pl.n. (takes sing. v.)* See **Bible** table in Appendix.

phi·lip·pic (fĭ-lĭp′ĭk) ▸ *n.* A passionate speech intended to arouse opposition; tirade.

Phil·ip·pines (fĭl′ə-pēnz′, fĭl′ə-pēnz′) ▸ A country of E Asia consisting of the **Philippine Islands,** an archipelago in the W Pacific. **—Phil′ip·pine′** *adj.*

Phil·is·tine (fĭl′ĭ-stēn′, fĭ-lĭs′tĭn, -tēn′) ▸ *n.* 1. A member of an ancient people in Palestine. 2. often **philistine** One who is indifferent or antagonistic to artistic and cultural values. ▸ *adj.* 1. Of the ancient Philistines. 2. often **philistine** Boorish or uncultured.

phil·o·den·dron (fĭl′ə-dĕn′drən) ▸ *n., pl.* **-drons** or **-dra** (-drə). Any of various climbing tropical American plants often cultivated as houseplants.

phi·lol·o·gy (fĭ-lŏl′ə-jē) ▸ *n.* 1. Literary study or classical scholarship. 2. The study of linguistic change over time. **—phil′o·log′i·cal** (fĭl′ə-lŏj′ĭ-kəl) *adj.* **—phil′o·log′i·cal·ly** *adv.* **—phi·lol′o·gist** *n.*

phi·los·o·pher (fĭ-lŏs′ə-fər) ▸ *n.* 1. A specialist in philosophy. 2. One who lives by a particular philosophy. 3. One who takes a calm and rational approach toward life.

phi·los·o·phize (fĭ-lŏs′ə-fīz′) ▸ *v.* **-phized, -phiz·ing.** To speculate in a philosophical manner. **—phi·los′o·phiz′er** *n.*

phi·los·o·phy (fĭ-lŏs′ə-fē) ▸ *n., pl.* **-phies.** 1a. Investigation of the nature, causes, or principles of reality, knowledge, or values, based on logical reasoning rather than empirical methods. b. A system of thought based on or involving such inquiry. 2. The sciences and liberal arts, except medicine, law, and theology. 3. A system of values by which one lives. 4. A basic theory concerning a particular subject. **—phil′o·soph′i·cal** (fĭl′ə-sŏf′ĭ-kəl), **phil′o·soph′ic** *adj.*

phil·ter also **phil·tre** (fĭl′tər) ▸ *n.* 1. A love potion. 2. A magic potion or charm.

phle·bi·tis (flĭ-bī′tĭs) ▸ *n.* Inflammation of a vein. **—phle·bit′ic** (-bĭt′ĭk) *adj.*

phlebo— or **phleb—** ▸ *pref.* Vein: *phlebotomy.*

phle·bot·o·my (flĭ-bŏt′ə-mē) ▸ *n., pl.* **-mies.** The therapeutic practice of opening a vein by incision or puncture to draw blood.

phlegm (flĕm) ▸ *n.* Thick, sticky, stringy mucus produced in the respiratory tract.

phleg·mat·ic (flĕg-măt′ĭk) also **phleg·mat·i·cal** (-ĭ-kəl) ▸ *adj.* Having or suggesting a calm, stolid temperament; unemotional.

phlo·em (flō′ĕm′) ▸ *n.* The food-conducting tissue of vascular plants.

phlox (flŏks) ▸ *n., pl.* **phlox** or **-es.** A plant having clusters of white, red, pink, or purple flowers.

—phobe ▸ *suff.* One who fears or is averse to a specified thing: *Anglophobe.*

pho·bi·a (fō′bē-ə) ▸ *n.* A persistent, abnormal, or irrational fear of a specific thing or situation. **—pho′bic** (-bĭk) *adj.*

—phobia ▸ *suff.* An intense, abnormal, or illogical fear: *claustrophobia.*

phoe·be (fē′bē) ▸ *n.* A medium-sized North American flycatcher.

Phoe·ni·cia (fĭ-nĭsh′ə, -nē′shə) ▸ An ancient maritime country of SW Asia consisting of city-states along the E Mediterranean.

Phoe·ni·cian (fĭ-nĭsh′ən, -nē′shən) ▸ *n.* 1. A native or inhabitant of ancient Phoenicia. 2. The Semitic language of ancient Phoenicia.

phoe·nix also **phe·nix** (fē′nĭks) ▸ *n.* A bird in Egyptian mythology that consumed itself by fire after 500 years and rose renewed from its ashes.

Phoenix ▸ The capital of AZ, in the S-central part NW of Tucson.

phone (fōn) *Informal* ▸ *n.* A telephone. ▸ *v.* **phoned, phon·ing.** To telephone.

—phone ▸ *suff.* 1. Sound: *homophone.* 2. Device that receives or emits sound: *megaphone.* 3. Speaker of a language: *Anglophone.*

phone card ▸ *n.* A prepaid or credit card used to pay for telephone calls.

pho·neme (fō′nēm′) ▸ *n.* The smallest unit of speech that is capable of conveying a distinction in meaning, as the *m* of *mat* and the *b* of *bat* in English. **—pho·ne′mic** (fə-nē′mĭk, fō-) *adj.* **—pho·ne′mi·cal·ly** *adv.*

pho·net·ic (fə-nĕt′ĭk) ▸ *adj.* 1. Of or relating to phonetics. 2. Representing the sounds of speech with a set of distinct symbols, each designating a single sound. **—pho·net′i·cal·ly** *adv.*

pho·net·ics (fə-nĕt′ĭks) ▸ *n. (takes sing. v.)* The branch of linguistics that deals with the study of the sounds of speech. **—pho′ne·ti′cian** (fō′nĭ-tĭsh′ən) *n.*

phon·ics (fŏn′ĭks) ▸ *n. (takes sing. v.)* 1. A method of teaching reading and spelling based on phonetics. 2. Phonetics.

phono— or **phon—** ▸ *pref.* Sound; voice; speech: *phonology.*

pho·no·graph (fō′nə-grăf′) ▸ *n.* A machine that reproduces sound recorded on a grooved disk. **—pho′no·graph′ic** *adj.*

pho·nol·o·gy (fə-nŏl′ə-jē, fō-) ▸ *n.* The study of the distribution and pronunciation of speech sounds in a language. **—pho′no·log′ic** (fō′nə-lŏj′ĭk), **pho′no·log′i·cal** *adj.* **—pho·nol′o·gist** *n.*

pho·ny also **pho·ney** (fō′nē) ▸ *adj.* **-ni·er, -ni·est.** 1. Not genuine or real; fake. 2. Insincere or hypocritical. **—pho′ni·ness** *n.* **—pho′ny** *n.*

—phony ▸ *suff.* Sound: *telephony.*

—phore ▸ *suff.* Bearer; carrier: *semaphore.*

—phoresis ▸ *suff.* Transmission: *electrophoresis.*

THESAURUS

philander *v.* To be sexually unfaithful to another ▸ *Informal:* cheat, fool around, mess around, play around. *Slang:* two-time.

philanderer *n.* A man who philanders ▸ adulterer, Casanova, cheater, Don Juan, fornicator, lady's man, paramour, womanizer. *Slang:* lady-killer, wolf. *Idioms:* man on the make, skirt chaser. [*Compare* FLIRT, SEDUCER, WANTON.]

philanthropic *adj.* Of or concerned with charity ▸ altruistic, benevolent, charitable, eleemosynary. *—See also* HUMANITARIAN.

philanthropist *n.* *—See* DONOR, PATRON.

philanthropy *n.* *—See* BENEVOLENCE, FAVOR (1).

philippic *n.* *—See* TIRADE.

Philistine *n.* *—See* BOOR.

philistine *adj.* *—See* COARSE (1).

philosopher *n.* A person who seeks truth by thinking ▸ reasoner, theorist, thinker.

philosophizing *n.* *—See* THEORY (1).

philosophy *n.* *—See* POSTURE (2).

phlegm *n.* *—See* APATHY, SPIT.

phlegmatic *adj.* *—See* APATHETIC, COLD (2).

phobia *n.* An exaggerated concern ▸ anxiety, complex, neurosis. *Informal:* hang-up. [*Compare* ANXIETY, OBSESSION.]

phoenix *n.* A person or thing so excellent as to have no equal or match ▸ nonesuch, nonpareil, paragon. [*Compare* BEST, CELEBRITY, MODEL.]

phonate *v.* *—See* PRONOUNCE.

phone *v.* *—See* TELEPHONE.

phoniness *n.* *—See* HYPOCRISY, INSINCERITY.

phony *adj.* *—See* ARTIFICIAL (2), COUNTERFEIT, HYPOCRITICAL.

phony *n.* *—See* COUNTERFEIT, FAKE, HYPOCRITE.

phos·gene (fŏs′jēn′, fŏz′-) ▸ *n.* A colorless volatile liquid or gas, $COCl_2$, used as a poison gas and in making glass, dyes, resins, and plastics.
phos·phate (fŏs′fāt′) ▸ *n.* **1.** A salt or ester of phosphoric acid. **2.** A fertilizer containing phosphorus compounds. **—phos·phat′ic** (-făt′ĭk) *adj.*
phos·pho·lip·id (fŏs′fō-lĭp′ĭd) ▸ *n.* Any of various lipids that contain a phosphate group and one or more fatty acids.
phos·phor (fŏs′fər, -fôr′) ▸ *n.* **1.** A substance that exhibits phosphorescence. **2.** The phosphorescent coating on the inside of the screen of a cathode-ray tube.
phos·pho·res·cence (fŏs′fə-rĕs′əns) ▸ *n.* Persistent emission of light following exposure to and removal of incident radiation. **—phos′pho·resce′** *v.* **—phos′pho·res′cent** *adj.* **—phos′pho·res′cent·ly** *adv.*
phosphoric acid ▸ *n.* A clear colorless liquid, H_3PO_4, used in fertilizers, detergents, and food flavorings.
phos·pho·rus (fŏs′fər-əs) ▸ *n.* **1.** *Symbol* **P** A highly reactive, poisonous, nonmetallic element used in safety matches, pyrotechnics, incendiary shells, and fertilizers. At. no. 15. **2.** A phosphorescent substance. **—phos·phor′ic** (fŏs-fôr′ĭk, -fŏr′-) *adj.* **—phos′pho·rous** (fŏs′fər-əs, fŏs-fôr′əs) *adj.*
pho·tic (fō′tĭk) ▸ *adj.* **1.** Of or relating to light. **2.** Penetrated by light, esp. by sunlight: *the photic zone of the ocean.*
pho·to (fō′tō) ▸ *n., pl.* **-tos.** *Informal* A photograph. **—pho′to** *v.*
photo– or **phot–** ▸ *pref.* **1.** Light: *photosynthesis.* **2.** Photographic: *photomontage.* **3.** Photoelectric: *photoemission.*
pho·to·cell (fō′tō-sĕl′) ▸ *n.* A photoelectric cell.
pho·to·chem·is·try (fō′tō-kĕm′ĭ-strē) ▸ *n.* The study of the effects of light on chemical reactions. **—pho′to·chem′i·cal** *adj.*
pho·to·com·po·si·tion (fō′tō-kŏm′pə-zĭsh′ən) ▸ *n.* The preparation of manuscript for printing by the projection of images of type characters on photographic film. **—pho′to·com·pose′** *v.* **—pho′to·com·pos′er** *n.*
pho·to·cop·y (fō′tə-kŏp′ē) ▸ *v.* To make a photographic reproduction of (printed or pictorial material), esp. by xerography. ▸ *n.* A photographic reproduction. **—pho′to·cop′i·er** *n.*
pho·to·du·pli·cate (fō′tō-do͞o′plĭ-kāt′, -dyo͞o′-) ▸ *v.* To photocopy. **—pho′to·du′pli·cate** (-kĭt) *n.* **—pho′to·du′pli·ca′tion** *n.*
pho·to·e·lec·tric (fō′tō-ĭ-lĕk′trĭk) also **pho·to·e·lec·tri·cal** (-trĭ-kəl) ▸ *adj.* Of or relating to electric effects, esp. increased conductivity, caused by light. **—pho′to·e·lec′tri·cal·ly** *adv.*
photoelectric cell ▸ *n.* An electronic device having an electrical output that varies in response to the intensity of incident radiation; electric eye.
pho·to·e·lec·tron (fō′tō-ĭ-lĕk′trŏn′) ▸ *n.* An electron that is released in photoemission.
pho·to·e·mis·sion (fō′tō-ĭ-mĭsh′ən) ▸ *n.* Emission of photoelectrons from a metallic surface exposed to light or similar radiation.
pho·to·en·grav·ing (fō′tō-ĕn-grā′vĭng) ▸ *n.* **1.** The process of reproducing graphic material by photographing it on a metal plate and then etching the plate for printing. **2.** A reproduction made by this process. **—pho′to·en·grave′** *v.* **—pho′to·en·grav′er** *n.*
pho·to·es·say (fō′tō-ĕs′ā′) ▸ *n.* A story told chiefly through photographs usu. supplemented by a written commentary.
photo finish ▸ *n.* A race so closely contested that the winner must be determined by a photograph taken at the finish.
pho·to·flash (fō′tō-flăsh′) ▸ *n.* See **flashbulb.**
pho·to·gen·ic (fō′tə-jĕn′ĭk) ▸ *adj.* Attractive as a subject for photography.
pho·to·graph (fō′tə-grăf′) ▸ *n.* An image, esp. a positive print, recorded by a camera and reproduced chemically on a photosensitive surface. ▸ *v.* **1.** To take a photograph of. **2.** To be the subject for photographs. **—pho·tog′ra·pher** (fə-tŏg′rə-fər) *n.*
pho·to·graph·ic (fō′tə-grăf′ĭk) also **pho·to·graph·i·cal** (-ĭ-kəl) ▸ *adj.* **1.** Of or relating to photography or a photograph. **2.** Used in photography. **3.** Like a photograph, esp. in representing with accuracy and detail. **—pho′to·graph′i·cal·ly** *adv.*
pho·tog·ra·phy (fə-tŏg′rə-fē) ▸ *n.* **1.** The art or process of producing images on light-sensitive surfaces. **2.** The art, practice, or profession of taking and printing photographs.
pho·to·gra·vure (fō′tə-grə-vyo͝or′) ▸ *n.* The process of printing from an intaglio plate, etched according to a photographic image.
pho·to·jour·nal·ism (fō′tō-jûr′nə-lĭz′əm) ▸ *n.* Journalism in which pictorial matter, esp. photographs, takes precedence over written copy. **—pho′to·jour′nal·ist** *n.*
pho·tom·e·try (fō-tŏm′ĭ-trē) ▸ *n.* Measurement of the properties of light, esp. luminous intensity. **—pho′to·met′ric** (fō′tə-mĕt′rĭk), **pho′to·met′ri·cal** *adj.*
pho·to·mi·cro·graph (fō′tō-mī′krə-grăf′) ▸ *n.* A photograph made through a microscope. **—pho′to·mi′cro·graph′** *v.* **—pho′to·mi·crog′ra·phy** (-krŏg′rə-fē) *n.*
pho·to·mon·tage (fō′tō-mŏn-täzh′, -môn-) ▸ *n.* **1.** The technique of making a picture by assembling pieces of photographs, often with other graphic material. **2.** A composite picture produced by this technique.
pho·ton (fō′tŏn′) ▸ *n.* The quantum of electromagnetic energy, usu. regarded as a discrete particle having zero mass and no electric charge. **—pho·ton′ic** *adj.*
pho·ton·ics (fō-tŏn′ĭks) ▸ *n.* *(takes sing. v.)* The study or application of electromagnetic energy whose basic unit is the photon, including optics and information storage and processing.
pho·to·play (fō′tə-plā′) ▸ *n.* A play filmed or arranged for filming as a movie.
pho·to·re·cep·tor (fō′tō-rĭ-sĕp′tər) ▸ *n.* A nerve ending, cell, or group of cells specialized to sense or receive light.
pho·to·sen·si·tive (fō′tō-sĕn′sĭ-tĭv) ▸ *adj.* Sensitive to light. **—pho′to·sen′si·tiv′i·ty** *n.*
pho·to·sphere (fō′tə-sfîr′) ▸ *n.* The visible outer layer of a star, esp. of the sun.
Pho·to·stat (fō′tə-stăt′) ▸ A trademark for a device used to make positive or negative copies of graphic matter.
pho·to·syn·the·sis (fō′tō-sĭn′thĭ-sĭs) ▸ *n.* The process by which chlorophyll-containing cells in green plants use light as an energy source to synthesize carbohydrates from carbon dioxide and water. **—pho′to·syn′the·size** *v.* **—pho′to·syn·thet′ic** (-sĭn-thĕt′ĭk) *adj.* **—pho′to·syn·thet′i·cal·ly** *adv.*
pho·tot·ro·pism (fō-tŏt′rə-pĭz′əm, fō′tō-trō′-) ▸ *n.* *Biol.* Growth or movement in response to light. **—pho′to·tro′pic** (fō′tə-trō′pĭk) *adj.*
pho·to·vol·ta·ic (fō′tō-vŏl-tā′ĭk, -vōl-) ▸ *adj.* Capable of producing a voltage when exposed to radiant energy, esp. light.
photovoltaic cell ▸ *n.* See **solar cell.**
phrase (frāz) ▸ *n.* **1.** A sequence of words intended to have meaning. **2.** A brief, cogent expression. **3.** *Gram.* Two or more words in sequence that form a syntactic unit that is less than a complete sentence. **4.** *Mus.* A short passage, often consisting of four measures or forming part of a larger unit. ▸ *v.* **phrased, phras·ing. 1.** To express orally or in writing. **2.** *Mus.* To render in phrases. **—phras′al** *adj.*
phra·se·ol·o·gy (frā′zē-ŏl′ə-jē) ▸ *n., pl.* **-gies.** The way in which words and phrases are used in speech or writing; style. **—phra′se·o·log′i·cal** (-ə-lŏj′ĭ-kəl) *adj.*
phre·net·ic (frə-nĕt′ĭk) or **phre·net·i·cal** (-ĭ-kəl) ▸ *adj.* Vars. of **frenetic.**
–phrenia ▸ *suff.* Mental disorder: *schizophrenia.*
phre·nol·o·gy (frĭ-nŏl′ə-jē) ▸ *n.* The study of the shape and irregularities of the human skull, based on the now discredited belief that they reveal character and mental capacity. **—phren′o·log′ic** (frĕn′ə-lŏj′ĭk, frē′nə-), **phren′o·log′i·cal** *adj.* **—phre·nol′o·gist** *n.*
phy·la (fī′lə) ▸ *n.* Pl. of **phylum.**
phy·lac·ter·y (fĭ-lăk′tə-rē) ▸ *n., pl.* **-ies.** *Judaism* Either of

THESAURUS

photocopy *n.* —*See* COPY (1).
photocopy *v.* —*See* COPY.
photographic *adj.* —*See* GRAPHIC (1), GRAPHIC (4).
phrase *n.* —*See* EXPRESSION (3), WORDING.
phrase *v.* To convey in language or words of a particular form ▸ couch, express, formulate, frame, put, word. *Idiom:* put into words. [*Compare* SAY.]
phraseology *n.* —*See* WORDING.
phylactery *n.* —*See* CHARM.

two small leather boxes containing quotations from the Hebrew Scriptures, worn strapped to the forehead and the left arm esp. by orthodox Jewish men during weekday morning worship.

phyl·lo·tax·y (fĭl′ə-tăk′sē) also **phyl·lo·tax·is** (fĭl′ə-tăk′sĭs) ▸ *n., pl.* **-tax·ies** also **-tax·es**. The arrangement of leaves on a stem.

phy·log·e·ny (fī-lŏj′ə-nē) ▸ *n., pl.* **-nies**. The evolutionary development of an animal or plant species. **—phy′lo·ge·net′ic** (fī′lō-jə-nĕt′ĭk), **phy′lo·gen′ic** (-jĕn′ĭk) *adj.*

phy·lum (fī′ləm) ▸ *n., pl.* **-la** (-lə). **1.** *Biol.* The category ranking below a kingdom and above a class in the hierarchy of taxonomic classification. **2.** *Ling.* A large division of possibly genetically related families of languages or linguistic stocks.

phys– ▸ *pref.* Var. of **physio–**.

physi– ▸ *pref.* Var. of **physio–**.

phys·ic (fĭz′ĭk) ▸ *n.* A medicine or drug, esp. a cathartic. ▸ *v.* **-icked, -ick·ing. 1.** To act on as a cathartic. **2.** To cure or heal.

phys·i·cal (fĭz′ĭ-kəl) ▸ *adj.* **1.** Of or relating to the body. **2.** Of material things. **3.** Of or relating to matter and energy or the sciences dealing with them, esp. physics. ▸ *n.* A physical examination. **—phys′i·cal·ly** *adv.*

physical education ▸ *n.* Education in the care and development of the human body, stressing athletics and including hygiene.

physical examination ▸ *n.* A medical examination to determine the condition of a person's health or physical fitness.

physical geography ▸ *n.* The study of the natural features, structure, and phenomena of the earth's surface.

physical science ▸ *n.* Any of the sciences, such as physics, chemistry, astronomy, and geology, that analyze the nature and properties of energy and nonliving matter.

physical therapy ▸ *n.* The treatment of disease and injury by mechanical means such as exercise, heat, light, and massage. **—physical therapist** *n.*

phy·si·cian (fĭ-zĭsh′ən) ▸ *n.* A medical doctor.

phys·i·cist (fĭz′ĭ-sĭst) ▸ *n.* A scientist who specializes in physics.

phys·ics (fĭz′ĭks) ▸ *n.* **1.** *(takes sing. v.)* The science of matter and energy and of interactions between the two. **2.** *(takes pl. v.)* Physical properties, processes, or laws.

physio– or **physi–** or **phys–** ▸ *pref.* **1.** Nature: *physiography.* **2.** Physical: *physiotherapy.*

phys·i·og·no·my (fĭz′ē-ŏg′nə-mē, -ŏn′ə-mē) ▸ *n., pl.* **-mies**. **1.** The art of judging human character from facial features. **2.** Facial features; the face.

phys·i·og·ra·phy (fĭz′ē-ŏg′rə-fē) ▸ *n.* See **physical geography**. **—phys′i·og′ra·pher** *n.* **—phys′i·o·graph′ic** (-ə-grăf′ĭk), **phys′i·o·graph′i·cal** *adj.*

phys·i·ol·o·gy (fĭz′ē-ŏl′ə-jē) ▸ *n.* **1.** The biological science of the functions, activities, and processes of living organisms. **2.** All the functions of an organism. **—phys′i·o·log′i·cal** (-ə-lŏj′ĭ-kəl) *adj.* **—phys′i·o·log′i·cal·ly** *adv.* **—phys′i·ol′o·gist** *n.*

phys·i·o·ther·a·py (fĭz′ē-ō-thĕr′ə-pē) ▸ *n.* See **physical therapy**. **—phys′i·o·ther′a·peu′tic** (-ə-pyōō′tĭk) *adj.* **—phys′i·o·ther′a·pist** *n.*

phy·sique (fĭ-zēk′) ▸ *n.* The body considered with reference to its proportions, muscular development, and appearance. **—phy·siqued′** *adj.*

–phyte ▸ *suff.* A plant with a specified character or habitat: *epiphyte.*

phyto– or **phyt–** ▸ *pref.* Plant: *phytochemical.*

phy·to·plank·ton (fī′tō-plăngk′tən) ▸ *n.* Minute, free-floating aquatic plants.

pi[1] (pī) ▸ *n.* **1.** The 16th letter of the Greek alphabet. **2.** *Math.* A transcendental number, approx. 3.14159, expressing the ratio of the circumference to the diameter of a circle.

pi[2] also **pie** (pī) ▸ *n., pl.* **pis** also **pies**. *Print.* Jumbled type.

pi·a·nis·si·mo (pē′ə-nĭs′ə-mō′) ▸ *adv. & adj. Mus.* In a very soft or quiet tone.

pi·an·ist (pē-ăn′ĭst, pē′ə-nĭst) ▸ *n.* One who plays the piano.

pi·an·o[1] (pē-ăn′ō, pyăn′ō) ▸ *n., pl.* **-os**. A keyboard musical instrument with hammers that strike wire strings.

pi·a·no[2] (pē-ä′nō, pyä′-) ▸ *adv. & adj. Mus.* In a soft or quiet tone.

pi·an·o·for·te (pē-ăn′ō-fôr′tā, -tē, pē-ăn′ō-fôrt′) ▸ *n.* A piano.

pi·az·za (pē-ăz′ə, -ä′zə) ▸ *n.* **1.** (*also* pē-ät′sə, pyät′sä) A public square in an Italian town. **2.** *Regional* A verandah; porch.

pi·ca (pī′kə) ▸ *n. Print.* **1.** A printer's unit of type size, equal to 12 points or about 1/6 of an inch. **2.** A type size for typewriters, providing 10 characters to the inch.

pic·a·dor (pĭk′ə-dôr′) ▸ *n.* A horseman in a bullfight who lances the bull's neck muscles so as to weaken them.

pic·a·resque (pĭk′ə-rĕsk′, pē′kə-) ▸ *adj.* Of or involving clever rogues or adventurers, esp. in prose fiction.

Pi·cas·so (pĭ-kä′sō, -kăs′ō), **Pablo** (1881–1973) ▸ Spanish artist.

pic·a·yune (pĭk′ə-yōōn′) ▸ *adj.* **1.** Of little value or importance; paltry. **2.** Petty; mean.

pic·co·lo (pĭk′ə-lō′) ▸ *n., pl.* **-los**. A small flute pitched an octave above a regular flute.

pick[1] (pĭk) ▸ *v.* **1.** To select from a group. **2.** To gather in or from; harvest. **3a.** To remove the outer covering of; pluck. **b.** To tear off bit by bit. **4.** To poke at with the fingers. **5.** To break up, separate, or detach with a sharp instrument. **6.** To pierce with a sharp instrument. **7.** To steal the contents of (a pocket or purse). **8.** To open (a lock) without the use of a key. **9.** To provoke: *pick a fight.* **10.** *Mus.* To pluck (a string or stringed instrument). ***—phrasal verbs:* pick on** To tease or bully. **pick out** To choose or select. **pick up 1.** To take on (e.g., passengers or freight). **2.** To learn without great effort. **3.** To receive or intercept: *pick up a radio signal.* **4.** *Informal* To take into custody; arrest. **5.** *Informal* To improve in condition or activity. ▸ *n.* **1.** The act of selecting; choice. **2.** The best or choicest part. ***—idioms:* pick and choose** To select or decide with great care. **pick (one's) way** To make one's way carefully. **—pick′er** *n.*

pick[2] (pĭk) ▸ *n.* **1.** A tool for breaking hard surfaces, consisting of a curved bar sharpened at both ends and fitted to a long handle. **2.** *Mus.* A plectrum.

pick·ax or **pick·axe** (pĭk′ăks′) ▸ *n.* A pick, esp. with one end of the head pointed and the other end with a chisel edge.

pick·er·el (pĭk′ər-əl, pĭk′rəl) ▸ *n., pl.* **-el** or **-els**. A North American freshwater fish related to the pike.

pick·et (pĭk′ĭt) ▸ *n.* **1.** A pointed stake driven into the ground to support a fence, secure a tent, tether animals, mark surveying points, or serve as a defense. **2.** A detachment of one or more troops, ships, or aircraft on guard against an enemy's approach. **3.** A person or persons stationed outside a place of employment, usu. during a strike, to express grievance or protest. ▸ *v.* **1.** To enclose, secure, mark out, or fortify with pickets. **2.** *Military* To guard with a picket. **3.** To post a picket or pickets at a strike or demonstration. **4.** To act or serve as a picket. **—pick′et·er** *n.*

picket fence ▸ *n.* A fence of pointed pickets.

picket line ▸ *n.* A line or procession of people picketing a place of business or otherwise staging a public protest.

THESAURUS

physic *n.* —*See* CURE.

physic *v.* —*See* DRUG (1).

physical *adj.* Composed of or relating to things that occupy space and that can be perceived by the senses ▸ concrete, corporeal, material, objective, palpable, phenomenal, sensible, solid, substantial, tangible. [*Compare* PERCEPTIBLE, REAL.] —*See also* BODILY, SENSUAL (2).

physicality *n.* —*See* SENSUALITY (1), TANGIBILITY.

physiognomy *n.* —*See* FACE (1).

physique *n.* —*See* BRAWN, CONSTITUTION.

picayune *adj.* —*See* TRIVIAL.

picayune *n.* —*See* TRIFLE.

pick *v.* —*See* CHOOSE (1), GATHER, PULL (2).

pick at or **pick on** *v.* —*See* NAG.

pick off *v.* To wound or kill with a firearm ▸ gun (down), shoot. *Slang:* plug. *Idiom:* fill full of lead (*or* holes). [*Compare* KILL[1], MURDER.]

pick out *v.* —*See* DISCERN.

pick up *v.* —*See* ARREST, CONTINUE, CONTRACT (2), ELEVATE (1), GET (1), GLEAN, LEARN (1).

pick *n.* —*See* BEST (1), CHOICE, ELECT.

picket *n.* —*See* GUARD.

picket *v.* To cease working in support of demands made upon an employer ▸ strike, walk out. *Idioms:* go (*or* go out) on strike, stage a strike (*or* sickout *or* walkout), stop work. —*See also* ENCLOSE (2).

pick·ing (pĭk′ĭng) ▸ *n.* **1. pickings** Something that is or may be picked. **2.** often **pickings a.** Leftovers. **b.** A share of spoils.

pick·le (pĭk′əl) ▸ *n.* **1.** An edible product, such as a cucumber, preserved and flavored in a solution of brine or vinegar. **2.** A solution of brine or vinegar, often spiced, for preserving and flavoring food. **3.** *Informal* A disagreeable, difficult, or troublesome situation; plight. ▸ *v.* **-led, -ling.** To preserve or flavor in a solution of brine or vinegar.

pick-me-up (pĭk′mē-ŭp′) ▸ *n. Informal* A usu. alcoholic drink taken as a stimulant.

pick·pock·et (pĭk′pŏk′ĭt) ▸ *n.* One who steals from pockets or purses.

pick·up (pĭk′ŭp′) ▸ *n.* **1.** The act or process of picking up. **2.** Ability to accelerate rapidly. **3.** One that is picked up. **4.** A pickup truck. **5.** *Electron.* **a.** A device that converts the oscillations of a phonograph needle into electrical impulses for subsequent conversion into sound. **b.** The tone arm of a record player. **6a.** The reception of light or sound waves for conversion to electrical impulses. **b.** The apparatus used for such reception. **c.** A telecast originating outside a studio. **d.** The apparatus for transmitting a broadcast to a broadcasting station from outside.

pickup truck ▸ *n.* A light truck with an open body and low sides.

pick·y (pĭk′ē) ▸ *adj.* **-i·er, -i·est.** *Informal* Meticulous; fussy.

pic·nic (pĭk′nĭk) ▸ *n.* **1.** A meal eaten outdoors, as on an excursion. **2.** *Slang* An easy task. ▸ *v.* **-nicked, -nick·ing.** To go on a picnic. **—pic′nick·er** *n.*

pi·cot (pē′kō, pē-kō′) ▸ *n.* A small embroidered loop forming an edging, as on ribbon.

pic·to·graph (pĭk′tə-grăf′) ▸ *n.* **1.** A hieroglyph. **2.** A pictorial representation of numerical data or relationships. **—pic′to·graph′ic** *adj.*

pic·to·ri·al (pĭk-tôr′ē-əl) ▸ *adj.* **1.** Of or composed of pictures. **2.** Illustrated by pictures. ▸ *n.* An illustrated periodical. **—pic·to′ri·al·ly** *adv.*

pic·ture (pĭk′chər) ▸ *n.* **1.** A visual representation or image painted, drawn, photographed, or otherwise rendered on a flat surface. **2.** A vivid verbal description. **3.** One that bears a marked resemblance to another. **4.** One that typifies or embodies an emotion, state of mind, or mood. **5.** The chief circumstances of an event or time; situation. **6.** A movie. **7.** An image or series of images on a television or movie screen. ▸ *v.* **-tured, -tur·ing. 1.** To make a picture of. **2.** To visualize. **3.** To describe vividly in words.

pic·tur·esque (pĭk′chə-rĕsk′) ▸ *adj.* **1.** Of or suggesting a picture. **2.** Unusually or quaintly attractive. **3.** Strikingly expressive or vivid: *picturesque language.* **—pic′tur·esque′ly** *adv.* **—pic′tur·esque′ness** *n.*

picture tube ▸ *n.* A cathode-ray tube in a television receiver that translates received electrical signals into a visible picture on a luminescent screen.

picture window ▸ *n.* A large, usu. single-paned window that provides a broad view.

pid·dling (pĭd′lĭng) ▸ *adj.* Trifling or trivial.

pidg·in (pĭj′ən) ▸ *n.* A simplified mixture of two or more languages, used for communication between groups speaking different languages.

Pidgin English ▸ *n.* Any of several pidgins based on English and now spoken mostly in the Pacific islands.

pie[1] (pī) ▸ *n.* A baked pastry shell filled with fruit or other ingredients, and usu. covered with a crust. ***—idiom:* pie in the sky** An empty wish or promise.

pie[2] (pī) ▸ *n. Print.* Var. of **pi[2]**.

pie·bald (pī′bôld′) ▸ *adj.* Spotted or patched in color, esp. in black and white. ▸ *n.* A piebald animal, esp. a horse.

piece (pēs) ▸ *n.* **1.** A unit or element of a larger quantity or class; portion. **2.** An artistic or musical work. **3.** An instance; specimen. **4.** One's opinions or findings: *speak one's piece.* **5.** A coin or counter. **6.** A counter or figure used in a game. **7.** *Slang* A firearm, esp. a rifle. **8.** *Informal* A given distance: *down the road a piece.* ▸ *v.* **pieced, piec·ing. 1.** To mend by adding a piece to. **2.** To join the pieces of. ***—idiom:* of a piece** Of the same class or kind.

pièce de ré·sis·tance (pyĕs də rā-zē-stäɴs′) ▸ *n., pl.* **pièces de résistance** (pyĕs). **1.** An outstanding accomplishment. **2.** The principal dish of a meal.

piece·meal (pēs′mēl′) ▸ *adv.* By a small amount at a time; in stages. ▸ *adj.* Made or done in stages.

piece of eight ▸ *n., pl.* **pieces of eight.** An old Spanish silver coin.

piece·work (pēs′wûrk′) ▸ *n.* Work paid for by number of units made. **—piece′work′er** *n.*

pie chart ▸ *n.* A circular graph divided into sectors proportional to the relative size of the quantities represented.

pied (pīd) ▸ *adj.* Patchy in color; piebald.

pied-à-terre (pyā-dä-târ′) ▸ *n., pl.* **pieds-à-terre** (pyā-dä-târ′). A secondary or temporary place of lodging.

pied·mont (pēd′mŏnt′) ▸ *n.* An area of land at the foot of a mountain or mountain range.

Piedmont ▸ **1.** A historical region of NW Italy bordering on France and Switzerland. **2.** A plateau region of the E US extending from NY to AL between the Appalachian Mts. and the Atlantic coastal plain. **—Pied′mon·tese′** (-tēz′, -tēs′) *adj. & n.*

pier (pîr) ▸ *n.* **1.** A platform extending from a shore over water, used to secure, protect, and provide access to ships or boats. **2.** A supporting structure for the spans of a bridge. **3.** *Archit.* Any of various vertical supporting or reinforcing structures.

pierce (pîrs) ▸ *v.* **pierced, pierc·ing. 1.** To cut or pass through with or as if with a sharp instrument. **2.** To perforate. **3.** To make a way through. **—pierc′ing·ly** *adv.*

Pierce, Franklin (1804–69) ▸ The 14th US President (1853–57).

Pierre (pîr) ▸ The capital of SD, in the central part on the Missouri R.

pi·e·ty (pī′ĭ-tē) ▸ *n., pl.* **-ties. 1.** Devotion and reverence, esp. to God and family. **2.** A pious act or thought.

pi·e·zo·e·lec·tric·i·ty (pī-ē′zō-ĭ-lĕk-trĭs′ĭ-tē, -ē′lĕk-, pē-ā′zō-) ▸ *n.* Electricity or polarity induced in certain crystals, such as quartz, by mechanical stress. **—pi·e′zo·e·lec′tric, pi·e′zo·e·lec′tri·cal** *adj.*

pif·fle (pĭf′əl) ▸ *v.* **-fled, -fling.** To talk or act in a foolish, feeble, or futile way. ▸ *n.* Nonsense.

pig (pĭg) ▸ *n.* **1.** A mammal having short legs, cloven hooves, bristly hair, and a blunt snout used for digging, esp. one of a kind raised for meat. **2.** *Informal* A slovenly, greedy, or gross person. **3.** A crude oblong block of metal, chiefly iron or lead, poured from a smelting furnace. **4.** *Offensive Slang* A police officer. ▸ *v.* **pigged,**

THESAURUS

pickings *n.* —*See* BALANCE (4).
pickle *n.* —*See* PREDICAMENT.
pickle *v.* —*See* PRESERVE (1), STEEP[2].
pickled *adj.* —*See* DRUNK.
pick-me-up *n.* —*See* TONIC.
pickpocket *n.* —*See* THIEF.
pickup *n.* —*See* ARREST.
picky *adj.* —*See* FUSSY.
pictographic *adj.* —*See* GRAPHIC (4).
pictorial *adj.* —*See* GRAPHIC (4), GRAPHIC (1).
picture *n.* —*See* DOUBLE, VIEW (2).
picture *v.* —*See* IMAGINE, REPRESENT (2).
picturesque *adj.* Evoking strong mental images through distinctiveness ▸ colorful, graphic, striking, vivid. —*See also* GRAPHIC (1).
piddle *v.* —*See* IDLE (1).
piddling *adj.* —*See* TRIVIAL.
piece *n.* One's duty or responsibility in a common effort ▸ function, part, role, share. —*See also* BIT[1] (2), COMPOSITION (1), CUT (2), DISTANCE (1), ITEM, PART (1), SONG.
piecemeal *adj.* Proceeding steadily by degrees ▸ gradational, gradual, progressive, step-by-step. ***Idioms:*** one foot after another, one step at a time. [*Compare* CONSECUTIVE, METHODICAL, SLOW.]
piecemeal *adv.* —*See* GRADUALLY.
pie-eyed *adj.* —*See* DRUNK.
pie hole *n.* —*See* MOUTH (1).
pier *n.* —*See* COLUMN.
pierce *v.* —*See* BREACH, CUT (1), OVERWHELM (2), PENETRATE.
piercing *adj.* —*See* HIGH (3), LOUD, SHARP (3).
pietism *n.* —*See* DEVOTION.
pietistic *adj.* —*See* PIOUS.
pietistical *adj.* —*See* PIOUS.
piety *n.* —*See* DEVOTION, HYPOCRISY.
piffle *n.* —*See* NONSENSE.
pig *n.* A person who eats or consumes immoderate amounts of food and

pig·ging. To bear pigs; farrow. ***—phrasal verb:*** **pig out** *Slang* To eat ravenously; gorge.

pi·geon (pĭj′ən) ▸ *n.* **1.** Any of various doves having a deep-chested body, small head, and short legs, esp. a common, often domesticated species. **2.** *Slang* One easily swindled; dupe.

pi·geon·hole (pĭj′ən-hōl′) ▸ *n.* A small compartment, as in a desk. ▸ *v.* **-holed, -hol·ing. 1.** To place or file in a pigeonhole. **2.** To categorize. **3.** To put aside and ignore.

pi·geon-toed (pĭj′ən-tōd′) ▸ *adj.* Having the toes turned inward.

pig·gish (pĭg′ĭsh) ▸ *adj.* **1.** Greedy. **2.** Pigheaded. **3.** Dirty; slovenly.

pig·gy·back (pĭg′ē-băk′) ▸ *adv. & adj.* **1.** On the shoulders or back. **2.** By or of a method of transportation in which truck trailers are carried on trains.

pig·head·ed (pĭg′hĕd′ĭd) ▸ *adj.* Stubborn. **—pig′head′ed·ness** *n.*

pig iron ▸ *n.* Crude iron cast in blocks.

pig Latin ▸ *n.* A jargon formed by the transposition of the initial consonant to the end of the word and the suffixion of an additional syllable, as *igpay atinlay* for *pig Latin.*

pig·let (pĭg′lĭt) ▸ *n.* A young pig.

pig·ment (pĭg′mənt) ▸ *n.* **1.** A coloring substance or matter, usu. a powder to be mixed with water, oil, or other base. **2.** A substance, such as chlorophyll or melanin, that produces a characteristic color in plant or animal tissue. **—pig′men·tar′y** (-mən-tĕr′ē) *adj.*

pig·men·ta·tion (pĭg′mən-tā′shən) ▸ *n.* Coloration of animal or plant tissues by pigment.

Pig·my (pĭg′mē) ▸ *n. & adj.* Var. of **Pygmy.**

pig·pen (pĭg′pĕn′) ▸ *n.* **1.** A pen for pigs. **2.** *Slang* A dirty or very untidy place.

Pigs (pĭgz), **Bay of** ▸ A small inlet of the Caribbean Sea on the S coast of W Cuba.

pig·skin (pĭg′skĭn′) ▸ *n.* **1.** The skin of a pig or leather made from it. **2.** *Sports* A football.

pig·sty (pĭg′stī′) ▸ *n.* A pigpen.

pig·tail (pĭg′tāl′) ▸ *n.* A plait of braided hair. **—pig′tailed′** *adj.*

pi·ka (pī′kə, pē′-) ▸ *n.* A small, tailless, furry mammal of the mountains of North America and Eurasia.

pike[1] (pīk) ▸ *n.* A long spear formerly used by infantry. **—piked** *adj.*

pike[2] (pīk) ▸ *n., pl.* **pike** or **pikes**. A freshwater game and food fish having a narrow body and long snout.

pike[3] (pīk) ▸ *n.* A turnpike.

pike[4] (pīk) ▸ *n.* A spike or sharp point.

pik·er (pī′kər) ▸ *n. Slang* A petty or stingy person.

pi·laf or **pi·laff** (pĭ-läf′, pē′läf′) ▸ *n.* A steamed rice dish with bits of meat, shellfish, or vegetables.

pi·las·ter (pĭ-lăs′tər) ▸ *n.* A rectangular column projecting slightly from a wall as an ornamental motif.

Pi·late (pī′lət), **Pontius** (fl. 1st cent. A.D.) ▸ Roman prefect who ordered the crucifixion of Jesus.

pil·chard (pĭl′chərd) ▸ *n.* A small edible marine fish related to the herring.

pile[1] (pīl) ▸ *n.* **1.** A quantity of objects heaped or thrown together in a stack. **2.** *Informal* A large accumulation or quantity. **3.** A funeral pyre. **4.** A nuclear reactor. ▸ *v.* **piled, pil·ing. 1a.** To stack in or form a pile. **b.** To load with a pile: *pile a plate with food.* **2.** To move in a disorderly mass or group: *pile into a car.*

pile[2] (pīl) ▸ *n.* A heavy timber, concrete, or steel beam driven into the earth as a structural support.

pile[3] (pīl) ▸ *n.* Cut or uncut loops of yarn forming the surface of certain fabrics, such as velvet and carpeting. **—piled** *adj.*

pi·le·at·ed woodpecker (pī′lē-ā′tĭd) ▸ *n.* A large North American woodpecker having black and white plumage and a red crest.

pile driver ▸ *n.* A machine that drives piles into the ground.

piles (pīlz) ▸ *pl.n.* See **hemorrhoid** 2.

pile·up or **pile-up** (pīl′ŭp′) ▸ *n. Informal* A serious collision of several motor vehicles.

pil·fer (pĭl′fər) ▸ *v.* To steal or filch. **—pil′fer·age** (-ĭj) *n.*

pil·grim (pĭl′grəm) ▸ *n.* **1.** One who goes on a pilgrimage. **2.** A traveler. **3. Pilgrim** One of the English Puritans who migrated to New England in 1620.

pil·grim·age (pĭl′grə-mĭj) ▸ *n.* **1.** A journey to a sacred place. **2.** A long journey or search, esp. one of exalted purpose.

pil·ing (pī′lĭng) ▸ *n.* A number of piles supporting a structure.

Pil·i·pi·no (pĭl′ə-pē′nō) ▸ *n.* The Filipino language.

pill (pĭl) ▸ *n.* **1.** A small pellet or tablet of medicine. **2. the pill** *Informal* An oral contraceptive. **3.** Something that is both distasteful and necessary. **4.** *Slang* An ill-natured person.

pil·lage (pĭl′ĭj) ▸ *v.* **-laged, -lag·ing.** To rob of goods by force; plunder. ▸ *n.* **1.** The act of pillaging. **2.** Spoils.

pil·lar (pĭl′ər) ▸ *n.* **1.** A slender, freestanding, vertical support; column. **2.** One occupying a central or responsible position.

pill·box (pĭl′bŏks′) ▸ *n.* **1.** A small box for pills. **2.** A low-roofed concrete emplacement, esp. for a machine gun or antitank gun.

pil·lion (pĭl′yən) ▸ *n.* A seat for an extra rider behind the saddle on a horse or motorcycle.

pil·lo·ry (pĭl′ə-rē) ▸ *n., pl.* **-ries**. A wooden framework with holes for the head and hands, in which offenders were formerly locked to be exposed to public scorn as punishment. ▸ *v.* **-ried, -ry·ing. 1.** To expose to ridicule and abuse. **2.** To put in a pillory as punishment.

pil·low (pĭl′ō) ▸ *n.* **1.** A cloth case stuffed with soft material and used to cushion the head, esp. during sleep. **2.** A decorative cushion. ▸ *v.* To serve as a pillow for. **—pil′low·y** *adj.*

pil·low·case (pĭl′ō-kās′) ▸ *n.* A removable covering for a pillow.

pil·low·slip (pĭl′ō-slĭp′) ▸ *n.* See **pillowcase.**

pi·lose (pī′lōs) also **pi·lous** (-ləs) ▸ *adj.* Covered with fine soft hair. **—pi·los′i·ty** (-lŏs′ĭ-tē) *n.*

pi·lot (pī′lət) ▸ *n.* **1.** One who flies or is licensed to fly an aircraft. **2a.** A licensed specialist who conducts a ship in and out of port or through dangerous waters. **b.** A ship's helmsman. **3.** A guide or leader. **4.** A television program produced as a prototype of a prospective series. ▸ *v.* **1.** To serve as the pilot of. **2.** To steer or control the course of. ▸ *adj.* **1.** Serving as a small-scale experimental model. **2.** Serving or leading as guide. **—pi′lot·age** (-lə-tĭj) *n.*

pilot fish ▸ *n.* A small slender marine fish that often swims with larger fishes, esp. sharks and mantas.

pi·lot·house (pī′lət-hous′) ▸ *n. Naut.* An enclosed area, usu. on the bridge of a vessel, from which the vessel is controlled.

pilot light ▸ *n.* A small jet of gas kept burning in order to ignite a gas burner, as in a stove.

pils·ner (pĭlz′nər, pĭls′-) ▸ *n.* **1.** A light lager with a strong hops flavor. **2.** A tall, thin, footed beer glass.

Pilt·down man (pĭlt′doun′) ▸ *n.* An early species of human

THESAURUS

drink ▸ glutton, hog, overeater. [*Compare* SYBARITE.]

pig out *v.* —*See* GULP.

pigeon *n.* —*See* DUPE.

pigeonhole *v.* —*See* CLASSIFY.

piggish *adj.* —*See* GLUTTONOUS.

pigheaded *adj.* —*See* STUBBORN (1).

pigheadedness *n.* —*See* STUBBORNNESS.

pigment *n.* —*See* COLOR (2).

pigment *v.* —*See* COLOR (1).

pile *n.* Something built, especially for human use ▸ building, construction, edifice, erection, structure. —*See also* ABUNDANCE, FORTUNE, HEAP (1), HEAP (2).

pile *v.* —*See* CROWD, FILL (1), HEAP (1).

pile up *v.* —*See* ACCUMULATE, CRASH.

pileup *n.* —*See* CRASH (2).

pilfer *v.* —*See* STEAL.

pilferage *n.* —*See* LARCENY.

pilferer *n.* —*See* THIEF.

pilgrimage *n.* —*See* EXPEDITION.

pill *n.* —*See* DRIP (2), DRUG (1), KILLJOY.

pillage *v.* —*See* SACK[2].

pillage *n.* —*See* PLUNDER.

pillar *n.* —*See* COLUMN.

pillory *v.* —*See* DISGRACE.

pillow talk *n.* —*See* CONVERSATION.

pilose *adj.* —*See* HAIRY.

pilot *n.* A person who flies an airplane ▸ aviator, flier. *Slang:* flyboy. —*See also* GUIDE.

pilot *v.* —*See* DRIVE (1), GUIDE, MANEUVER (1).

pilot *adj.* Serving as a tentative model for future experiment or development ▸ experimental, probationary, probative, test, trial. [*Compare* INTRODUCTORY.]

postulated from a skull allegedly found about 1912 but proved in 1953 to be a fake.

Pi·ma (pē′mə) ▸ *n., pl.* **-ma** or **-mas.** 1. A member of a Native American people of S Arizona. 2. The Uto-Aztecan language of the Pima. **—Pi′man** *adj.*

pi·men·to (pĭ-mĕn′tō) ▸ *n., pl.* **-tos.** 1. See **allspice.** 2. Var. of **pimiento.**

pi·mien·to (pĭ-mĕn′tō, -myĕn′tō) also **pi·men·to** (-mĕn′tō) ▸ *n., pl.* **-tos.** A capsicum pepper having a mild-flavored red fruit.

pimp (pĭmp) ▸ *n.* One who procures customers for a prostitute. ▸ *v.* To be a pimp.

pim·per·nel (pĭm′pər-nĕl′, -nəl) ▸ *n.* A plant having small red, purple, or white flowers.

pim·ple (pĭm′pəl) ▸ *n.* A small inflamed swelling of the skin, usu. caused by acne. **—pim′pled, pim′ply** *adj.*

pin (pĭn) ▸ *n.* 1. A short, straight, stiff piece of wire with a blunt head and a sharp point, used esp. for fastening. 2. Something, such as a safety pin or hairpin, that resembles a pin in shape or use. 3. A slender, usu. cylindrical piece of wood or metal for holding, fastening, or supporting. 4. An ornament fastened to clothing by means of a clasp. 5. One of the clubs at which the ball is aimed in bowling. 6. The pole bearing a pennant to mark a hole in golf. 7. **pins** *Informal* The legs. ▸ *v.* **pinned, pin·ning.** 1. To fasten or secure with or as if with a pin. 2. To make completely dependent: *pinning all our hopes on winning.* 3. To hold fast; immobilize. ***—phrasal verbs:*** **pin down** 1. To fix or establish clearly. 2. To oblige to make a definite response. **pin on** To attribute (a wrongdoing or crime) to.

PIN ▸ *abbr.* personal identification number

pin·a·fore (pĭn′ə-fôr′) ▸ *n.* A sleeveless apronlike garment.

pi·ña·ta (pēn-yä′tə) ▸ *n.* A decorated container filled with candy and toys and hung from a height to be broken by blindfolded children with sticks.

pin·ball (pĭn′bôl′) ▸ *n.* A game in which the player operates a plunger to shoot a ball down or along a slanted surface having obstacles and targets.

pince-nez (păns′nā′, pĭns′-) ▸ *n., pl.* **pince-nez** (-nāz′, -nā′). Eyeglasses clipped to the bridge of the nose.

pin·cers (pĭn′sərz) also **pinch·ers** (pĭn′chərz) ▸ *pl.n. (takes sing. or pl. v.)* 1. A grasping tool having a pair of jaws and handles pivoted together to work in opposition. 2. The articulated, prehensile claws of certain arthropods, such as the lobster.

pinch (pĭnch) ▸ *v.* 1. To squeeze between the thumb and a finger, the jaws of a tool, or other edges. 2. To squeeze or bind (a part of the body) painfully. 3. To wither or shrivel. 4. To be miserly. 5. *Slang* To steal. 6. *Slang* To take into custody; arrest. ▸ *n.* 1. The act or an instance of pinching. 2. An amount that can be held between thumb and forefinger. 3. A difficult or straitened circumstance. 4. An emergency. **—pinch′er** *n.*

pinch-hit (pĭnch′hĭt′) ▸ *v.* 1. *Baseball* To bat in place of a scheduled player. 2. *Informal* To substitute for another. **—pinch hitter** *n.*

pin·cush·ion (pĭn′ko͝osh′ən) ▸ *n.* A cushion into which pins are stuck when not in use.

Pin·dar (pĭn′dər) (522?–443? B.C.) ▸ Greek lyric poet.

pine[1] (pīn) ▸ *n.* 1. Any of various cone-bearing evergreen trees having needle-shaped leaves in clusters. 2. The wood of any of these trees.

pine[2] (pīn) ▸ *v.* **pined, pin·ing.** 1. To feel longing; yearn. 2. To wither away from longing or grief.

pin·e·al gland (pĭn′ē-əl, pī′nē-) ▸ *n.* A small, cone-shaped organ in the brain of most vertebrates whose function in mammals is unclear.

pine·ap·ple (pīn′ăp′əl) ▸ *n.* 1. A tropical American plant having swordlike leaves and a large, fleshy, edible fruit. 2. The fruit of the pineapple.

pine needle ▸ *n.* The needle-shaped leaf of a pine tree.

pine nut ▸ *n.* The edible seed of certain pines.

pine·y (pī′nē) ▸ *adj.* Var. of **piny.**

pin·feath·er (pĭn′fĕth′ər) ▸ *n.* A growing feather, esp. one just emerging through the skin.

ping (pĭng) ▸ *n.* 1. A sharp, high-pitched sound, as that made by a bullet striking metal. 2. Engine knock. **—ping** *v.*

Ping-Pong (pĭng′pông′) ▸ A trademark for table tennis.

pin·head (pĭn′hĕd′) ▸ *n.* 1. The head of a pin. 2. Something small or insignificant. 3. *Slang* A stupid person. **—pin′head′ed** *adj.*

pin·hole (pĭn′hōl′) ▸ *n.* A tiny puncture made by or as if by a pin.

pin·ion[1] (pĭn′yən) ▸ *n.* A bird's wing. ▸ *v.* 1. To restrain or immobilize by binding the wings or arms. 2. To bind fast, hold down, or fix in one place.

pin·ion[2] (pĭn′yən) ▸ *n.* A small cogwheel that engages or is engaged by a larger cogwheel or a rack.

pink[1] (pĭngk) ▸ *n.* 1. A light or pale red. 2. Any of various plants related to the carnation, often cultivated for their showy, fragrant flowers. 3. The highest degree of excellence: *in the pink of health.* **—pink** *adj.* **—pink′ish** *adj.*

pink[2] (pĭngk) ▸ *v.* 1. To stab lightly; prick. 2. To decorate with a perforated pattern. 3. To cut with pinking shears.

pink·eye (pĭngk′ī′) ▸ *n.* An acute, very contagious form of conjunctivitis.

pink·ie also **pink·y** (pĭng′kē) ▸ *n., pl.* **-ies.** *Informal* The little finger.

pink·ing shears (pĭng′kĭng) ▸ *pl.n.* Shears with notched blades, used to finish edges of cloth with a zigzag cut for decoration or to prevent raveling or fraying.

pink·o (pĭng′kō) ▸ *n., pl.* **-os.** *Slang* One who holds moderately leftist political views.

pin money ▸ *n.* Money for incidental expenses.

pin·na·cle (pĭn′ə-kəl) ▸ *n.* 1. A small turret or spire on a roof or buttress. 2. A tall, pointed formation. 3. The highest point; acme.

pin·nate (pĭn′āt′) ▸ *adj.* Featherlike, as a compound leaf with leaflets along each side of a stalk.

pi·noch·le or **pi·noc·le** (pē′nŭk′əl, -nŏk′əl) ▸ *n.* A card game for two to four persons, played with a deck of 48 cards.

pi·ñon also **pin·yon** (pĭn′yōn′, -yən) ▸ *n.* Any of several pine trees bearing edible, nutlike seeds.

pin·point (pĭn′point′) ▸ *n.* An extremely small thing or spot; particle. ▸ *v.* To locate, identify, or target with precision.

pin·prick (pĭn′prĭk′) ▸ *n.* 1. A slight puncture made by or as if by a pin. 2. A minor annoyance.

pins and needles (pĭnz) ▸ *pl.n.* Tingling felt in a part of the body numbed from lack of circulation. ***—idiom:*** **on pins and needles** In a state of tense anticipation.

pin·stripe (pĭn′strīp′) ▸ *n.* 1. A thin stripe, esp. on a fabric. 2. A fabric with pinstripes.

pint (pīnt) ▸ *n.* 1. See **measurement** table in Appendix. 2. A unit of volume or capacity used in dry and liquid measure, equal to 0.568 liter.

pin·tail (pĭn′tāl′) ▸ *n., pl.* **-tail** or **-tails.** A duck of the Northern Hemisphere, having gray, brown, and white plumage and a sharply pointed tail.

pin·to (pĭn′tō) ▸ *n., pl.* **-tos** or **-toes.** A horse with patchy spots or markings.

pinto bean ▸ *n.* A form of the common string bean having mottled seeds.

pint-size (pīnt′sīz′) also **pint-sized** (-sīzd′) ▸ *adj. Informal* Diminutive.

THESAURUS

pin *n.* —*See* NAIL.
pin *v.* —*See* FASTEN, FIX (3).
pinafore *n.* —*See* DRESS (3).
pinch *v.* —*See* ARREST, SCRIMP, SQUEEZE (1), STEAL.
pinch *n.* —*See* ARREST, BIT[1] (1), EMERGENCY, PREDICAMENT.
pinchbeck *n.* —*See* COPY (2).
pinch-hit *v.* —*See* SUBSTITUTE.
pinch hitter *n.* —*See* SUBSTITUTE.
pinching *adj.* —*See* STINGY.
pinchpenny *n.* —*See* MISER.
pine *v.* —*See* DESIRE, LANGUISH.
pinheaded *adj.* —*See* STUPID.
pinheadedness *n.* —*See* STUPIDITY.
pink-slip *v.* —*See* DISMISS (1).
pinnacle *n.* —*See* CLIMAX.
pinpoint *v.* To look for and discover ▸ find, locate, spot. *Informal:* scare up. [*Compare* TRACE, UNCOVER.] —*See also* DESIGNATE, PLACE (1).
pinpoint *n.* —*See* POINT (2).
pintsize or **pintsized** *adj.* —*See* TINY.

pin·up (pĭn′ŭp′) ▸ *n.* A picture to be pinned up on a wall, esp. of an attractive person. **—pin′up′** *adj.*
pin·wheel (pĭn′hwēl′, -wēl′) ▸ *n.* **1.** A toy consisting of vanes of colored paper or plastic pinned to a stick so that they revolve when blown on. **2.** A firework that forms a rotating wheel of colored flames.
pin·worm (pĭn′wûrm′) ▸ *n.* Any of various small parasitic nematode worms, esp. one that infests the human intestines and rectum.
pin·y also **pine·y** (pī′nē) ▸ *adj.* **-i·er, -i·est.** Of or abounding in pines.
Pin·yin or **pin·yin** (pĭn′yĭn′, -yĭn) ▸ *n.* A system for transliterating Chinese characters into the Roman alphabet.
pin·yon (pĭn′yōn′, -yən) ▸ *n.* Var. of **piñon.**
pi·on (pī′ŏn′) ▸ *n.* A semistable subatomic particle in the meson family that exists in neutral, positively charged, or negatively charged forms.
pi·o·neer (pī′ə-nîr′) ▸ *n.* **1.** One who ventures into unknown or unclaimed territory to settle. **2.** An innovator, esp. in research and development. **—pi′o·neer′** *v.*
pi·ous (pī′əs) ▸ *adj.* **1.** Reverently observant of religion; devout. **2.** Solemnly hypocritical: *a pious fraud.* **3.** Devotional: *pious readings.* **4.** High-minded. **5.** Commendable; worthy. **—pi′ous·ly** *adv.* **—pi′ous·ness** *n.*
pip[1] (pĭp) ▸ *n.* A small fruit seed, as that of an apple or orange.
pip[2] (pĭp) ▸ *n.* **1.** A dot indicating numerical value on dice or dominoes. **2.** See **blip** 1.
pip[3] (pĭp) ▸ *n.* **1.** A disease of birds. **2.** *Slang* A minor, unspecified human ailment.
pipe (pīp) ▸ *n.* **1.** A hollow cylinder or tube used to conduct a liquid, gas, or finely divided solid. **2.** A device for smoking, consisting of a tube of wood, clay, or other material with a small bowl at one end and a mouthpiece at the other. **3.** *Informal* **a.** A tubular part or organ of the body. **b. pipes** The human respiratory system. **4a.** A tubular musical wind instrument, such as a fife. **b.** Any of the tubes in an organ. **5. pipes a.** A small wind instrument, consisting of tubes of different lengths bound together. **b.** A bagpipe. ▸ *v.* **piped, pip·ing. 1.** To convey or transmit by or as if by pipes. **2.** To play (a tune) on a pipe or pipes. **3.** To make a shrill sound. ***—phrasal verbs:* pipe down** *Slang* To be quiet. **pipe up** To speak up. **—pip′er** *n.*
pipe dream ▸ *n.* A fantastic notion or vain hope.
pipe fitter ▸ *n.* One that installs and repairs piping systems.
pipe·line (pīp′līn′) ▸ *n.* **1.** A conduit of pipe for the conveyance of water, gas, or petroleum products. **2.** A channel by which information is privately transmitted. **3.** A line of supply.
pipe organ ▸ *n. Mus.* See **organ** 1.
pipe·stone (pīp′stōn′) ▸ *n.* A red or pink clay stone used by Native American peoples for making tobacco pipes.
pi·pette also **pi·pet** (pī-pĕt′) ▸ *n.* A glass tube open at both ends and usu. graduated, used for transferring or measuring liquids.
pipe wrench ▸ *n.* A wrench with two serrated jaws, one adjustable, for gripping and turning pipe.
pip·ing (pī′pĭng) ▸ *n.* **1.** A system of pipes. **2.** Music made by a pipe or pipes. **3.** A narrow band of material, used for trimming a fabric. ***—idiom:* piping hot** Very hot.
pip·pin (pĭp′ĭn) ▸ *n.* Any of several varieties of apple.
pip-squeak (pĭp′skwēk′) ▸ *n. Informal* One that is small or insignificant.
pi·quant (pē′kənt, -känt′, pē-känt′) ▸ *adj.* **1.** Pleasantly pungent; spicy. **2.** Appealingly provocative. **—pi′quan·cy, pi′quant·ness** *n.*
pique (pēk) ▸ *n.* Resentment or vexation that results from wounded pride; huff. ▸ *v.* **piqued, piqu·ing. 1.** To cause to feel resentment. **2.** To provoke; arouse: *The box piqued her curiosity.*
pi·qué (pĭ-kā′, pē-) ▸ *n.* A fabric with various patterns of wales.
pi·ra·nha also **pi·ra·ña** (pĭ-rän′yə, -răn′yə) ▸ *n.* A sharp-toothed tropical American freshwater fish that often attacks and destroys living animals.
pi·rate (pī′rĭt) ▸ *n.* **1.** One who robs at sea or plunders the land from the sea. **2.** One who makes use of or reproduces the work of another illicitly or without authorization. **—pi′ra·cy** *n.* **—pi′rate** *v.* **—pi·rat′ic** (-răt′ĭk), **pi·rat′i·cal** *adj.*
pi·rogue (pĭ-rōg′, pîr′ō) ▸ *n.* A canoe made from a hollowed tree trunk.
pir·ou·ette (pĭr′o͞o-ĕt′) ▸ *n.* A full turn of the body on the tip of the toe or the ball of the foot, esp. in ballet. **—pir′ou·ette′** *v.*
pis·ca·to·ri·al (pĭs′kə-tôr′ē-əl) ▸ *adj.* Of or relating to fish or fishing. **—pis′ca·to′ri·al·ly** *adv.*
Pi·sces (pī′sēz) ▸ *pl.n. (takes sing. v.)* **1.** A constellation in the equatorial region of the Northern Hemisphere. **2.** The 12th sign of the zodiac.
pis·mire (pĭs′mīr′, pĭz′-) ▸ *n.* An ant.
pi·so (pē′sō) ▸ *n.* See **currency** table in Appendix.
pis·ta·chi·o (pĭ-stăsh′ē-ō′, -stä′shē-ō′) ▸ *n., pl.* **-os. 1.** An Asian tree bearing hard-shelled edible nuts with a green kernel. **2.** The nut of this tree.
pis·til (pĭs′təl) ▸ *n.* The seed-bearing reproductive organ of a flower.
pis·tol (pĭs′təl) ▸ *n.* A firearm designed to be held and fired with one hand.
pis·tol-whip (pĭs′təl-hwĭp′, -wĭp′) ▸ *v.* To beat with a pistol.
pis·ton (pĭs′tən) ▸ *n.* A solid cylinder or disk that fits snugly into a cylinder and moves back and forth under fluid pressure.
pit[1] (pĭt) ▸ *n.* **1.** A relatively deep hole in the ground. **2.** A trap or pitfall. **3a.** Hell. **b. the pits** *Slang* The worst. **4a.** A natural depression in the body or an organ. **b.** A small indented scar left in the skin by disease or injury; pockmark. **5.** An enclosed area in which animals are placed for fighting. **6.** The musicians' section directly in front of the stage of a theater. **7.** The section of an exchange where trading in a specific commodity is carried on. **8.** A refueling area beside an auto racecourse. ▸ *v.* **pit·ted, pit·ting. 1.** To mark or scar with pits. **2.** To set in opposition: *pitted brother against brother.*
pit[2] (pĭt) ▸ *n.* The single, hard-shelled seed of certain fruits, such as a peach or cherry; stone. ▸ *v.* **pit·ted, pit·ting.** To extract the pit from (a fruit).
pi·ta (pē′tə) ▸ *n.* A round, flat bread that opens to form a pocket for filling.
pit·a·pat (pĭt′ə-păt′) ▸ *v.* **-pat·ted, -pat·ting.** To make a repeated tapping sound. ▸ *n.* A series of quick steps, taps, or beats.
Pit·cairn Island (pĭt′kârn′) ▸ A volcanic island of the S Pacific ESE of Tahiti.
pitch[1] (pĭch) ▸ *n.* Any of various thick, dark, sticky substances obtained from the distillation residue of coal tar,

THESAURUS

pioneer *n.* —*See* DEVELOPER, FORERUNNER, SETTLER.
pioneer *v.* —*See* INTRODUCE (1).
pioneer *adj.* —*See* FIRST.
pious *adj.* Deeply concerned with God and the beliefs and practice of religion ▸ devoted, devotional, devout, godly, holy, pietistic, pietistical, prayerful, religious, saintlike, saintly, zealous. [*Compare* FAITHFUL, RIGHTEOUS, SPIRITUAL.] —*See also* DIVINE (2), HYPOCRITICAL, REVERENT.
piousness *n.* —*See* DEVOTION.
pip *n.* A fertilized plant ovule that is capable of germinating ▸ grain, kernel, pit, seed.
pipe dream *n.* —*See* DREAM (2).
piping *adj.* —*See* HIGH (3).
pip-squeak *n.* —*See* NONENTITY, SQUIRT (2).
piquant *adj.* —*See* SPICY.
pique *n.* —*See* OFFENSE.
pique *v.* —*See* INSULT, OFFEND (1), PRIDE, PROVOKE.
pirate *n.* One who reproduces another's work without permission ▸ cribber, plagiarist, plagiarizer. [*Compare* FORGER.]
pirate *v.* —*See* PLAGIARIZE.
pit[1] *n.* A place known for its great filth or corruption ▸ cesspit, cesspool, cloaca, den, gutter, hellhole, septic tank, sewer, sink, sump. *Slang:* armpit. —*See also* DEFORMITY, DEPRESSION (1), TRAP (1).
pit *v.* —*See* DEFORM, OPPOSE.
pit[2] *n.* A fertilized plant ovule capable of germinating ▸ grain, kernel, pip, seed.

wood tar, or petroleum and used for waterproofing, roofing, caulking, and paving.

pitch² (pĭch) ► *v.* **1.** To throw, usu. with careful aim. **2.** To throw (a baseball) from the mound to the batter. **3.** To put up or in position: *pitched a tent; pitch camp.* **4.** To set firmly; implant. **5.** To fix the level of. **6.** *Mus.* To set at a specified pitch or key. **7.** To hit (a golf ball) in a high arc with backspin. **8.** To fall headlong; plunge. **9.** To dip bow and stern alternately, as a ship in rough seas. ***—phrasal verb:*** **pitch in** *Informal* To set to work vigorously, esp. in cooperation with others. ► *n.* **1.** The act or an instance of pitching. **2a.** A downward slant. **b.** The degree of such a slant, as of the angle of a roof. **3.** A level or degree, as of intensity or development. **4.** Lowness or highness of a complex sound, such as a musical tone, that is dependent primarily on frequency. **5.** *Informal* A line of talk designed to persuade.

pitch-black (pĭch′blăk′) ► *adj.* Extremely black.

pitch·blende (pĭch′blĕnd′) ► *n.* A brownish-black mineral, the principal ore of uranium.

pitch-dark (pĭch′därk′) ► *adj.* Extremely dark.

pitch·er¹ (pĭch′ər) ► *n.* *Baseball* The player who pitches.

pitch·er² (pĭch′ər) ► *n.* A container for liquids, usu. having a handle and a lip or spout for pouring.

pitcher plant ► *n.* Any of various insectivorous plants having pitcherlike leaves that attract and trap insects.

pitch·fork (pĭch′fôrk′) ► *n.* A large, long-handled fork with widely spaced prongs for lifting and pitching hay.

pitch pipe ► *n.* A small pipe sounded to give the pitch for a piece of music or for tuning an instrument.

pit·e·ous (pĭt′ē-əs) ► *adj.* Arousing pity; pathetic. **—pit′e·ous·ness** *n.*

pit·fall (pĭt′fôl′) ► *n.* **1.** An unapparent difficulty or danger. **2.** A concealed hole in the ground that serves as a trap.

pith (pĭth) ► *n.* **1.** The soft, spongelike substance in the center of stems and branches of many plants. **2.** The essential or central part; heart. **3.** Strength; force.

pith helmet ► *n.* A lightweight hat of dried pith worn for protection from the sun.

pith·y (pĭth′ē) ► *adj.* **-i·er, -i·est.** **1.** Precise and meaningful. **2.** Of or resembling pith. **—pith′i·ly** *adv.* **—pith′i·ness** *n.*

pit·i·a·ble (pĭt′ē-ə-bəl) ► *adj.* Arousing pity. **—pit′i·a·ble·ness** *n.* **—pit′i·a·bly** *adv.*

pit·i·ful (pĭt′ĭ-fəl) ► *adj.* **1.** Inspiring, arousing, or deserving pity. **2.** Arousing contemptuous pity, as through ineptitude, inadequacy, or inferiority. **—pit′i·ful·ly** *adv.* **—pit′i·ful·ness** *n.*

pit·i·less (pĭt′ĭ-lĭs) ► *adj.* Having no pity; merciless. **—pit′i·less·ness** *n.*

pi·ton (pē′tŏn′) ► *n.* A spike with an eye or ring for securing a support rope in mountain climbing.

pit stop ► *n.* **1.** A stop at a pit for refueling or service during an automobile race. **2.** *Informal* A rest stop during a trip.

Pitt (pĭt), **William.** 1st Earl of Chatham (1708–78) ► British political leader and orator.

pit·tance (pĭt′ns) ► *n.* A small amount or portion, esp. of money.

pit·ter-pat·ter (pĭt′ər-păt′ər) ► *n.* Repeated light, tapping sounds.

Pitts·burgh (pĭts′bûrg′) ► A city of SW PA at the point where the confluence of the Allegheny and Monongahela rivers forms the Ohio R.

pi·tu·i·tar·y (pĭ-to͞o′ĭ-tĕr′ē, -tyo͞o′-) ► *n., pl.* **-ies.** A small oval endocrine gland attached to the base of the vertebrate brain, the secretions of which control the other endocrine glands and influence growth, metabolism, and maturation. **—pi·tu′i·tar′y** *adj.*

pit viper ► *n.* Any of various venomous snakes, such as the rattlesnake, having a small sensory pit below each eye.

pit·y (pĭt′ē) ► *n., pl.* **-ies.** **1.** Sympathy and sorrow aroused by the misfortune or suffering of another. **2.** A matter of regret: *It's a pity she can't go.* ► *v.* **-ied, -y·ing.** To feel pity (for).

Pi·us XII (pī′əs) (1876–1958) ► Pope (1939–58).

piv·ot (pĭv′ət) ► *n.* **1.** A short rod or shaft on which a related part rotates or swings. **2.** One that determines the direction or effect of something. **3.** The act of turning on or as if on a pivot. ► *v.* To turn or cause to turn on or as if on a pivot. **—piv′ot·al** *adj.* **—piv′ot·al·ly** *adv.*

pix (pĭks) ► *n.* Var. of **pyx.**

pix·el (pĭk′səl, -sĕl′) ► *n.* The basic compositional unit of an image on a television screen or computer monitor.

pix·ie or **pix·y** (pĭk′sē) ► *n., pl.* **-ies.** A fairylike or elfin creature. **—pix′y·ish** *adj.*

Pi·zar·ro (pĭ-zär′ō, -sär′-), **Francisco** (1475?–1541) ► Spanish explorer.

piz·za (pēt′sə) ► *n.* An Italian baked pie consisting of a crust covered usu. with seasoned tomato sauce and cheese.

piz·zazz or **piz·zaz** (pĭ-zăz′) ► *n.* *Slang* **1.** Dazzling style; flamboyance. **2.** Energy or excitement.

piz·ze·ri·a (pēt′sə-rē′ə) ► *n.* A place where pizzas are made and sold.

piz·zi·ca·to (pĭt′sĭ-kä′tō) ► *adj.* *Mus.* Played by plucking the strings. **—piz′zi·ca′to** *adv.*

pkg. ► *abbr.* package

pl. ► *abbr.* plural

plac·ard (plăk′ärd′, -ərd) ► *n.* **1.** A sign or notice for public display. **2.** A nameplate, as on a door. **—plac′ard** *v.*

pla·cate (plā′kāt′, plăk′āt′) ► *v.* **-cat·ed, -cat·ing.** To allay the anger of; appease. **—plac′a·ble** *adj.* **—pla·ca′tion** *n.*

place (plās) ► *n.* **1.** An area with or without definite boundaries; a portion of space. **2.** An area occupied by or allocated to a person or thing. **3.** A definite location. **4.** often **Place** A public square or short street in a town. **5.** A table setting. **6.** A position regarded as belonging to someone or something else; stead: *She was chosen in his place.* **7.** Relative position in a series; standing: *fourth place.* ► *v.* **placed, plac·ing.** **1.** To put in or as if in a particular position; set. **2.** To put or rank in a specified relation, order,

THESAURUS

pitch *v.* To move vigorously from side to side or up and down ► heave, rock, roll, toss. *—See also* DROP (2), ERECT, FALL (1), LURCH (1), PROMOTE (3), THROW.

pitch into *v.* *—See* ATTACK (1).

pitch *n.* *—See* CLIMAX, DROP (3), FALL (1), INTENSITY, PUBLICITY, THROW, TONE (2).

pitch-black or **pitch-dark** or **pitchy** *adj.* *—See* BLACK (1).

piteous *adj.* *—See* PITIFUL.

pitfall *n.* *—See* DANGER, TRAP (1).

pith *n.* *—See* HEART (1).

pithy *adj.* Precisely meaningful and tersely cogent ► aphoristic, compact, epigrammatic, gnomic, marrowy, pointed, proverbial, pungent, sententious, succinct. *Informal:* brass-tacks. *Idioms:* down to brass tacks (*or* the nitty-gritty), short and sweet, to the point. [*Compare* BRIEF, CRITICAL.] *—See also* PREGNANT (2).

pitiable *adj.* *—See* PITIFUL.

pitiful *adj.* Arousing or deserving pity ► forlorn, lamentable, pathetic, piteous, pitiable, poor, rueful, ruthful, sorry. [*Compare* AFFECTING, DEPLORABLE.] *—See also* TERRIBLE.

pitiless *adj.* *—See* CALLOUS, CRUEL.

pity *n.* **1.** Sympathetic, sad concern for someone in misfortune ► commiseration, compassion, condolence, empathy, heart, softheartedness, sympathy. [*Compare* MERCY.] **2.** A great disappointment or regrettable fact ► crime, shame. *Slang:* bummer. *Idiom:* a crying shame.

pity *v.* To feel pity for someone ► ache for, bleed for, commiserate with, feel for, sympathize with. *Idioms:* feel sorry for, have pity on, take pity on. [*Compare* COMFORT, FEEL.]

pitying *adj.* *—See* SYMPATHETIC.

pivot *v.* To turn in place, as on a fixed point ► slue, swing, swivel, wheel. *—See also* TURN (1).

pivot *n.* *—See* CENTER (3).

pivotal *adj.* *—See* PRIMARY (1).

pixilated *adj.* *—See* DRUNK.

placard *n.* *—See* SIGN (2).

placate *v.* *—See* PACIFY.

place *n.* **1.** Positioning of one individual vis-à-vis others ► condition, echelon, footing, level, position, rank, situation, standing, station, status. [*Compare* CLASS.] **2.** The function or position customarily occupied by another ► lieu, stead. **3.** The proper or designated location ► niche. *—See also* HOME (1), LOCALITY, POSITION (1), POSITION (3).

place *v.* **1.** To establish the identity of ► identify, know, pinpoint, recognize. *Slang:* finger. *Idiom:* put one's finger on. [*Compare* DISCERN.] **2.** To complete a race or competition in a specified position ► come in, finish,

or sequence. 3. To appoint to a post. 4a. To give an order for: *place a bet.* b. To arrange for; make: *place a telephone call.* 5. To arrive among the first three finishers in a race, esp. to finish second. *—idiom:* **in place of** Instead of.

pla·ce·bo (plə-sē′bō) ▸ *n., pl.* **-bos** or **-boes.** 1. A substance containing no medication, administered for its psychological effect on a patient. 2. An inactive substance used as a control in an experiment.

place kick ▸ *n. Football* A kick, as for a field goal, for which the ball is held or propped up in a fixed position. **—place′kick′** *v.*

place mat ▸ *n.* A table mat for a single setting of dishes and flatware.

place·ment (plās′mənt) ▸ *n.* 1a. The act of placing or arranging. b. The state of being placed or arranged. 2. The finding of jobs, lodgings, or other positions for applicants.

pla·cen·ta (plə-sĕn′tə) ▸ *n., pl.* **-tas** or **-tae** (-tē). A membranous vascular organ that develops in female mammals during pregnancy, lining the uterine wall and partially enveloping the fetus, to which it is attached by the umbilical cord. **—pla·cen′tal** *adj.*

plac·er (plăs′ər) ▸ *n.* A sand or gravel deposit left by a river or glacier, containing particles of valuable minerals.

plac·id (plăs′ĭd) ▸ *adj.* Undisturbed by tumult or disorder; calm or composed. **—pla·cid′i·ty** (plə-sĭd′ĭ-tē), **plac′id·ness** *n.* **—plac′id·ly** *adv.*

plack·et (plăk′ĭt) ▸ *n.* A slit in a dress, blouse, or skirt.

pla·gia·rize (plā′jə-rīz′) ▸ *v.* **-rized, -riz·ing.** To use and pass off as one's own (the ideas or writings of another). **—pla′gia·rism, pla′gia·ry** *n.* **—pla′gia·rist, pla′gia·riz′er** *n.*

plague (plāg) ▸ *n.* 1. A widespread affliction or calamity. 2. A cause of annoyance; nuisance. 3. A highly infectious, usu. fatal epidemic disease, esp. bubonic plague. ▸ *v.* **plagued, plagu·ing.** To harass, pester, or annoy.

plaid (plăd) ▸ *n.* 1. A rectangular woolen scarf of a checked or tartan pattern worn over the left shoulder by Scottish Highlanders. 2. A pattern of this kind, esp. in cloth. **—plaid** *adj.*

plain (plān) ▸ *adj.* **-er, -est.** 1. Free from obstructions; open to view; clear. 2. Easily understood; clearly evident. 3. Uncomplicated; simple. 4. Straightforward. 5. Not mixed with other substances; pure. 6. Common in rank or station; ordinary. 7. Not pretentious or affected. 8. Having little or no ornamentation or decoration. 9. Unattractive. ▸ *n.* An extensive, level, usu. treeless area of land. ▸ *adv. Informal* Clearly; simply. **—plain′ly** *adv.* **—plain′ness** *n.*

plain·clothes (plān′klōz′, -klōthz′) ▸ *adj.* Wearing civilian clothes while on duty to avoid being identified as police or security.

plain·clothes man or **plain·clothes·man** (plān′klōz′mən, -klōthz′-) ▸ *n.* A member of a police force, esp. a detective, who wears civilian clothes on duty.

Plains Indian (plānz) ▸ *n.* A member of any of the Native American peoples of the Great Plains of North America.

plain·song (plān′sông′, -sŏng′) ▸ *n.* Medieval liturgical music traditionally sung without accompaniment.

plain·spo·ken (plān′spō′kən) ▸ *adj.* Frank; straightforward. **—plain′spo′ken·ness** *n.*

plaint (plānt) ▸ *n.* 1. A complaint. 2. A lamentation.

plain·tiff (plān′tĭf) ▸ *n. Law* The party instituting a suit in a court.

plain·tive (plān′tĭv) ▸ *adj.* Expressing sorrow; mournful or melancholy. **—plain′tive·ly** *adv.* **—plain′tive·ness** *n.*

plait (plāt, plăt) ▸ *n.* A braid, esp. of hair. ▸ *v.* To braid.

plan (plăn) ▸ *n.* 1. A detailed scheme or method for the accomplishment of an objective. 2. A proposed or tentative project or goal. 3. An outline or sketch, esp. a drawing or diagram made to scale. ▸ *v.* **planned, plan·ning.** 1. To formulate, draw up, or make a plan or plans. 2. To intend. **—plan′ner** *n.*

pla·nar (plā′nər, -när′) ▸ *adj.* 1. Of or in a plane. 2. Flat.

Planck (plängk), **Max Karl Ernst Ludwig** (1858–1947) ▸ German physicist; 1918 Nobel.

plane[1] (plān) ▸ *n.* 1. A surface containing all the straight lines that connect any two points on it. 2. A flat or level surface. 3. A level of development. 4. An airplane. 5. A supporting surface of an airplane. ▸ *adj.* Of or being a figure lying in a plane.

plane[2] (plān) ▸ *n.* A carpenter's tool for smoothing and leveling wood. **—plane** *v.* **—plan′er** *n.*

plane geometry ▸ *n.* The geometry of two-dimensional figures.

plan·et (plăn′ĭt) ▸ *n.* 1. In the traditional model of solar systems, a nonluminous celestial body that revolves around a star. 2. A celestial body that orbits the sun, has sufficient mass to assume a nearly round shape, cleans out debris from the neighborhood around its orbit, and is not a satellite of another planet.

plan·e·tar·i·um (plăn′ĭ-târ′ē-əm) ▸ *n., pl.* **-i·ums** or **-i·a** (-ē-ə). 1. An apparatus or model representing the solar system. 2a. A device for projecting images of celestial bodies onto the inner surface of a dome. b. A building housing such a device.

plan·e·tar·y (plăn′ĭ-tĕr′ē) ▸ *adj.* 1. Of or resembling a planet. 2. Worldwide; global.

plan·gent (plăn′jənt) ▸ *adj.* 1. Loud and resounding. 2. Plaintive. **—plan′gen·cy** *n.*

plank (plăngk) ▸ *n.* 1. A thick piece of lumber. 2. One of the articles of a political platform. ▸ *v.* 1. To cover with planks. 2. To bake or broil and serve (fish or meat) on a board. 3. To put or set down with force.

plank·ton (plăngk′tən) ▸ *n.* Small or microscopic plant or animal organisms that float in bodies of water.

plant (plănt) ▸ *n.* 1. *Bot.* a. An organism characteristically having cellulose cell walls, growing by synthesis of inorganic substances, and lacking the power of locomotion. b. A plant having no permanent woody stem, as distinguished from a tree or shrub. 2. A factory. 3. The buildings, equipment, and fixtures of an institution. ▸ *v.* 1. To place in the ground to grow. 2. To sow or supply with or as if with seeds or plants. 3. To fix or set firmly in position. 4. To establish or found. 5. To implant in the

THESAURUS

run. —*See also* CLASSIFY, ESTIMATE (2), FIX (3), POSITION.

placement *n.* —*See* ARRANGEMENT (1), POSITION (1).

placid *adj.* —*See* CALM, STILL.

placidity or **placidness** *n.* —*See* CALM, STILLNESS.

plagiarist or **plagiarizer** *n.* One who reproduces another's work without permission ▸ cribber, pirate. [*Compare* FORGER.]

plagiarize *v.* To reproduce another's work without permission ▸ appropriate, borrow, crib, pirate, poach. *Informal:* lift. [*Compare* ADOPT, COPY, COUNTERFEIT.]

plague *n.* —*See* ANNOYANCE (2), CURSE (3), ERUPTION.

plague *v.* —*See* AFFLICT, HARASS.

plaguy *adj.* —*See* DISTURBING.

plain *adj.* —*See* APPARENT (1), BARE (1), FRANK, GENUINE, MODEST (1), OBVIOUS, ORDINARY, PURE, STRAIGHT, UGLY, UTTER[2].

plainclothesman *n.* —*See* DETECTIVE.

plain-Jane *adj.* —*See* BARE (1).

plainness *n.* —*See* CLARITY, MODESTY (2), UGLINESS.

plainspoken *adj.* —*See* FRANK.

plainspokenness *n.* —*See* HONESTY.

plaint *n.* —*See* CRY (1).

plaintiff *n.* One that makes a formal complaint, especially in court ▸ accuser, claimant, complainant.

plaintive *adj.* —*See* SORROWFUL.

plait *v.* —*See* FOLD, WEAVE.

plait *n.* —*See* FOLD (1).

plan *n.* —*See* APPROACH (1), METHOD.

plan *v.* To set the time for an event or occasion ▸ schedule, set, time. —*See also* ARRANGE (2), DESIGN (1), DESIGN (2), DRAFT (1), INTEND, PLOT (1).

planar *adj.* —*See* EVEN (1).

plane *adj.* —*See* EVEN (1).

plane *v.* —*See* EVEN.

planet *n.* The celestial body where humans live ▸ earth, globe, orb, world.

planetary *adj.* —*See* UNIVERSAL (1).

plangent *adj.* —*See* RESONANT.

plans *n.* Steps taken in preparation for an undertaking ▸ accommodations, arrangements, preparations, provisions.

plant *v.* To put seeds or young plants in soil ▸ broadcast, pot, root, scatter, seed, set (out), sow, transplant. [*Compare*

mind. **6.** To (place) for the purpose of spying, deception, or influencing behavior. **—plant′a·ble** *adj.*

plan·tain¹ (plăn′tən) ► *n.* A weedy plant with a dense spike of small greenish or whitish flowers.

plan·tain² (plăn′tən) ► *n.* A bananalike tropical plant or its fruit.

plan·ta·tion (plăn-tā′shən) ► *n.* **1.** A group of cultivated trees or plants. **2.** A large estate or farm on which crops are raised and harvested, often by resident workers.

plant·er (plăn′tər) ► *n.* **1.** One that plants. **2.** The owner or manager of a plantation. **3.** A decorative container for a plant.

plaque (plăk) ► *n.* **1.** An ornamented or engraved plate, slab, or disk used for decoration or on a monument for information. **2.** A small ornament or badge of membership. **3.** A deposit that builds up on a tooth or the inner lining of a blood vessel.

plash (plăsh) ► *n.* A light splash or the sound it makes.

–plasm ► *suff.* Material forming cells or tissue: *cytoplasm.*

plas·ma (plăz′mə) ► *n.* **1.** The clear yellowish fluid portion of blood, lymph, or intramuscular fluid in which cells are suspended. **2.** Protoplasm or cytoplasm. **3.** Whey. **4.** *Phys.* An electrically neutral, highly ionized gas composed of ions, electrons, and neutral particles. **—plas·mat′ic** (-măt′ĭk), **plas′mic** *adj.*

plas·min (plăz′mĭn) ► *n.* An enzyme in plasma that dissolves fibrin and other blood clotting factors.

plasmo– or **plasm–** ► *pref.* Plasma: *plasmin.*

plas·mol·y·sis (plăz-mŏl′ĭ-sĭs) ► *n., pl.* **-ses** (-sēz′). Shrinkage or contraction of the protoplasm in a cell, esp. a plant cell, caused by loss of water through osmosis. **—plas′mo·lyt′ic** (-mə-lĭt′ĭk) *adj.*

plas·ter (plăs′tər) ► *n.* **1.** A paste that hardens to a smooth solid and is used for coating walls and ceilings. **2.** Plaster of Paris. **3.** A pastelike mixture applied to a part of the body, as for healing. ► *v.* **1.** To cover with or as if with plaster. **2.** To cover conspicuously or to excess. **—plas′ter·er** *n.*

plas·ter·board (plăs′tər-bôrd′) ► *n.* A rigid board made of layers of fiberboard or paper bonded to a plaster core, used in construction to form walls.

plaster of Paris ► *n.* A quick-setting paste of white gypsum powder and water, used esp. for casts and statuary molds.

plas·tic (plăs′tĭk) ► *adj.* **1.** Capable of being shaped or formed: *plastic material such as clay.* **2.** Relating to or dealing with shaping or modeling. **3.** Made of a plastic. ► *n.* **1.** Any of various complex organic compounds produced by polymerization, capable of being molded, extruded, cast into various shapes and films, or drawn into filaments used as textile fibers. **2.** *Informal* A credit card or credit cards. **—plas′ti·cal·ly** *adv.* **—plas·tic′i·ty** (plă-tĭs′ĭ-tē) *n.* **—plas′ti·cize** (-tĭ-sīz′) *v.*

plastic surgery ► *n.* Surgery to remodel, repair, or restore injured or defective tissue or body parts. **—plastic surgeon** *n.*

plas·tid (plăs′tĭd) ► *n.* Any of several pigmented organelles found in plant cells and having various functions, such as the synthesis and storage of food.

Pla·ta (plä′tə, -tä), **Río de la** ► A wide estuary of SE South America between Argentina and Uruguay formed by the Paraná and Uruguay rivers.

plate (plāt) ► *n.* **1.** A smooth, flat, relatively thin, rigid body of uniform thickness. **2a.** A sheet of hammered, rolled, or cast metal. **b.** A flat piece of metal on which something is engraved. **3.** *Print.* **a.** A sheet of material converted into a printing surface, such as an electrotype. **b.** An impression taken from such a surface. **c.** A full-page book illustration, often in color. **4.** A light-sensitive sheet of glass or metal on which a photographic image can be recorded. **5.** A thin metallic or plastic support fitted to the gums to anchor artificial teeth. **6.** *Baseball* Home plate. **7.** A shallow dish from which food is served or eaten. **8.** Service and food for one person at a meal. **9.** Household articles or utensils made of or with a precious metal. **10.** *Geol.* In plate tectonics, one of the large sections into which the earth's crust is divided. ► *v.* **plat·ed, plat·ing. 1.** To cover with a thin layer of metal. **2.** To armor. **—plat′ed** *adj.*

pla·teau (plă-tō′) ► *n., pl.* **-teaus** or **-teaux** (-tōz′). **1.** An elevated, level expanse of land; tableland. **2.** A stable level, period, or state.

plate glass ► *n.* A strong rolled and polished glass used for mirrors and large windows.

plate·let (plāt′lĭt) ► *n.* A protoplasmic disk found in the blood plasma of mammals that promotes blood clotting.

plat·en (plăt′n) ► *n.* **1.** The roller on a typewriter or computer printer. **2.** A flat metal plate in a printing press that positions the paper and holds it against the inked type.

plate tectonics ► *n.* A theory that the earth's crust is made up of semirigid sections whose movement has resulted in seismic and volcanic activity and continental drift.

plat·form (plăt′fôrm′) ► *n.* **1.** A horizontal surface higher than an adjacent area. **2.** A formal declaration of the policy of a group, as of a political party. **3.** The basic technology of a computer system's hardware and software that defines how a computer is operated.

Plath (plăth), **Sylvia** (1932–63) ► Amer. writer.

plat·ing (plā′tĭng) ► *n.* **1.** A thin layer or coating of metal, such as gold or silver. **2.** A covering or layer of metal plates.

plat·i·num (plăt′n-əm) ► *n.* **1.** *Symbol* **Pt** A malleable, silver-white, corrosion-resistant metallic element used in electrical components, jewelry, and dentistry. At. no. 78. **2.** A medium to light gray.

plat·i·tude (plăt′ĭ-to͞od′, -tyo͞od′) ► *n.* A trite remark or idea. **—plat′i·tu′di·nous** *adj.*

Pla·to (plā′tō) (427?–347? B.C.) ► Greek philosopher.

Pla·ton·ic (plə-tŏn′ĭk, plā-) ► *adj.* **1.** Of or characteristic of Plato or his philosophy. **2.** often **platonic** Transcending physical desire; spiritual. **—Pla·ton′i·cal·ly** *adv.*

pla·toon (plə-to͞on′) ► *n.* **1.** A subdivision of a military company usu. consisting of two or more squads. **2.** A group of people working together.

plat·ter (plăt′ər) ► *n.* **1.** A large shallow dish or plate. **2.** *Slang* A phonograph record.

plat·y·pus (plăt′ĭ-pəs) ► *n., pl.* **-pus·es.** A semiaquatic, egg-laying Australian mammal with webbed feet and a snout like a duck's bill.

plau·dit (plô′dĭt) ► *n.* An expression of praise or approval.

plau·si·ble (plô′zə-bəl) ► *adj.* Apparently true or likely. **—plau′si·bil′i·ty, plau′si·ble·ness** *n.*

Plau·tus (plô′təs), **Titus Maccius** (254?–184 B.C.) ► Roman comic playwright.

play (plā) ► *v.* **1.** To occupy oneself in amusement, sport, or other recreation. **2.** To act in jest. **3.** To behave carelessly; toy. **4.** To act in a specified way: *play fair.* **5a.** To engage in (a game or sport). **b.** To compete against in a game or sport. **c.** To occupy (a position) in a game or sport. **d.** To use (a card, piece, or ball) in a game or sport. **6a.** To act or perform (a role). **b.** To pretend to be: *play cowboy.* **7.** To be performed, as a theatrical work. **8.**

THESAURUS

GROW, TILL.] —*See also* FIX (2), HIDE¹.

plant *n.* A building or complex in which an industry is located ► factory, mill, works.

plant life *n.* The plants of an area or region ► flora, vegetation, verdure.

plaster *n.* —*See* FINISH.

plaster *v.* —*See* DRESS (2), FINISH (2), SMEAR.

plastered *adj.* —*See* DRUNK.

plastic *adj.* Changing easily, as in expression ► changeable, fluid, mobile. [*Compare* CHANGEABLE, UNSTABLE.] —*See also* FLEXIBLE (1), FLEXIBLE (3), MALLEABLE.

plasticity *n.* —*See* FLEXIBILITY (1).

plat *n.* —*See* LOT (1).

plate *v.* —*See* COVER (1).

plateau *n.* A natural, flat land elevation ► mesa, table. [*Compare* HILL.]

platform *n.* A temporary framework with a floor, used by laborers ► scaffold, scaffolding, stage, staging.

platitude *n.* —*See* CLICHÉ.

platitudinal or **platitudinous** *adj.* —*See* TRITE.

platoon *n.* —*See* FORCE (3).

plaudit *n.* Approval expressed by clapping ► applause, hand, ovation. *Idiom:* round of applause. —*See also* PRAISE (1).

plausibility *n.* —*See* VERISIMILITUDE.

plausible or **plausibleness** *adj.* —*See* BELIEVABLE.

play *v.* **1.** To occupy oneself with amusement or diversion ► disport,

Mus. **a.** To perform on (an instrument). **b.** To perform (a piece). **9.** To perform or put into effect: *play a joke.* **10.** To manipulate: *played the rivals against each other.* **11.** To cause (e.g., a recorded tape) to emit sound. **12.** To move lightly or irregularly: *The breeze played on the water.* **13.** To bet or wager. ***—phrasal verbs:*** **play back** To replay (e.g., a recorded tape). **play down** To minimize the importance of. **play on (**or **upon)** To take advantage of (another's feelings). **play up** To emphasize or publicize. ▸ *n.* **1a.** A literary work for the stage. **b.** The performance of such a work. **2.** Activity engaged in for enjoyment or recreation. **3.** Fun. **4.** The act or manner of playing a game or sport. **5.** A move in a game: *a close play.* **6.** Manner or conduct: *fair play.* **7.** Action or use: *the play of the imagination.* **8.** Freedom for action; scope. **9.** Free movement, as of mechanical parts. ***—idioms:*** **in play** *Sports* In a position to be legitimately played. **play ball** *Slang* To cooperate. **play both ends against the middle** To set opponents against one another so as to advance one's goals. **play fast and loose** To behave irresponsibly or deceitfully. **play up to** To curry favor with. **play with fire** To take part in a dangerous or risky undertaking. **—play′a·ble** *adj.*

pla·ya (plī′ə) ▸ *n.* A flat area at the bottom of a desert basin, sometimes temporarily covered with water.

play-act (plā′ăkt′) ▸ *v.* **1.** To play a role in a dramatic performance. **2.** To make believe. **3.** To behave affectedly or artificially.

play·back (plā′băk′) ▸ *n.* The act or process of replaying a recording.

play·bill (plā′bĭl′) ▸ *n.* A poster announcing a theatrical performance.

play·boy (plā′boi′) ▸ *n.* A man devoted to the pursuit of pleasure.

play-by-play (plā′bī-plā′) ▸ *adj.* Being a detailed running commentary, as of the action of a sports event. **—play′-by-play′** *n.*

play·er (plā′ər) ▸ *n.* **1.** One who participates in a game or sport. **2.** An actor. **3.** A musician. **4.** A device for playing recorded sound or images.

player piano ▸ *n.* A mechanically operated piano that uses a perforated paper roll to actuate and control the keys.

play·ful (plā′fəl) ▸ *adj.* **1.** Full of fun; frolicsome. **2.** Humorous; jesting. **—play′ful·ly** *adv.* **—play′ful·ness** *n.*

play·girl (plā′gûrl′) ▸ *n.* A woman devoted to the pursuit of pleasure.

play·go·er (plā′gō′ər) ▸ *n.* One who attends the theater. **—play′go′ing** *n.*

play·ground (plā′ground′) ▸ *n.* An outdoor area for recreation and play.

play·ing card (plā′ĭng) ▸ *n.* A card marked with its rank and suit belonging to a deck and used in playing various games.

play·mate (plā′māt′) ▸ *n.* A companion in play.

play·off also **play-off** (plā′ôf′, -ŏf′) ▸ *n.* A final game or series of games played to determine a championship or break a tie.

play·pen (plā′pĕn′) ▸ *n.* A portable enclosure in which a baby can be left to play.

play·room (plā′ro͞om′, -ro͝om′) ▸ *n.* A room designed for recreation or play.

play·thing (plā′thĭng′) ▸ *n.* A toy.

play·wright (plā′rīt′) ▸ *n.* One who writes plays.

pla·za (plä′zə, plăz′ə) ▸ *n.* **1.** A public square or similar open area in a town or city. **2.** A parking or service area next to a highway. **3.** A shopping center.

plea (plē) ▸ *n.* **1.** An earnest request; appeal. **2.** An excuse; pretext. **3.** *Law* The answer of the accused to a charge or indictment.

plea-bar·gain (plē′bär′gən) ▸ *v. Law* To make an agreement to plead guilty to a lesser charge so as to avoid being tried for a more serious one. **—plea′-bar′gain·ing** *n.*

plead (plēd) ▸ *v.* **plead·ed** or **pled** (plĕd), **plead·ing. 1.** To appeal earnestly; beg. **2.** To argue for or against something. **3.** To put forward a plea in a court of law. **4.** To assert or submit as an excuse or defense. **5.** To argue or present (a case) in a court of law. **—plead′er** *n.* **—plead′ing·ly** *adv.*

pleas·ant (plĕz′ənt) ▸ *adj.* **-er, -est. 1.** Pleasing or agreeable; delightful. **2.** Pleasing in manner; amiable. **—pleas′ant·ness** *n.*

pleas·ant·ry (plĕz′ən-trē) ▸ *n., pl.* **-ries.** A pleasant or humorous remark.

please (plēz) ▸ *v.* **pleased, pleas·ing. 1.** To give enjoyment or satisfaction (to). **2.** To be the will or desire of: *may it please the court.* **3.** To be willing to. **4.** To like; wish. **—pleas′ing** *adj.*

pleas·ur·a·ble (plĕzh′ər-ə-bəl) ▸ *adj.* Agreeable; gratifying. **—pleas′ur·a·bly** *adv.*

pleas·ure (plĕzh′ər) ▸ *n.* **1.** Enjoyment or satisfaction. **2.** A source of enjoyment. **3.** One's preference, wish, or choice.

pleat (plēt) ▸ *n.* A fold in cloth made by doubling the material upon itself. **—pleat** *v.*

plebe (plēb) ▸ *n.* A freshman at a military academy.

ple·be·ian (plĭ-bē′ən) ▸ *adj.* Common or vulgar: *plebeian tastes.* ▸ *n.* One who is common and crude.

pleb·i·scite (plĕb′ĭ-sīt′, -sĭt) ▸ *n.* A direct vote by the entire electorate on an important issue.

plebs (plĕbz) ▸ *n., pl.* **ple·bes** (plē′bēz). **1.** The common

THESAURUS

frolic, recreate, sport. *Informal:* horse around. [*Compare* GAMBOL, IDLE, JOKE.] 2. To make a bet ▸ bet, gamble, game, lay, wager. *Idiom:* put one's money on something. 3. To treat lightly or flippantly ▸ dally, flirt, toy, trifle. 4. To make music ▸ concertize, perform, render. 5. To be performed ▸ run, show. *—See also* ACT (3), COMPETE, FIDDLE, INFLICT, INTERPRET (2), MANIPULATE (1).

play around *v. Informal* To be sexually unfaithful to another ▸ philander. *Informal:* cheat, fool around, mess around. *Slang:* two-time. *—See also* PUTTER.

play down *v. Informal* To make less emphatic or obvious ▸ de-emphasize, soft-pedal, tone down. *—See also* MODERATE (1).

play off *v.* To place in opposition or be in opposition to ▸ match, pit.

play out *v. —See* CONCLUDE, DRY UP (2), EXHAUST (1), UNWIND.

play over *v.* To do or perform an act again ▸ duplicate, do over, redo, repeat, replay. [*Compare* COPY.]

play up *v. —See* EMPHASIZE.

play *n.* Actions that are taken as a joke ▸ fun, game, jest, sport. *Idioms:* fun and games, in fun. *—See also* AMUSEMENT, EXERCISE (1), LICENSE (1), SCRIPT (2).

play-act *v. —See* ACT (3), ACT (2).

play-acting *n. —See* THEATRICS (2).

playbill *n. —See* PROGRAM (2).

player *n.* 1. A theatrical performer ▸ actor, actress, thespian, trouper. [*Compare* FAKE, LEAD, MIMIC.] 2. One who plays a musical instrument ▸ bandsman, instrumentalist, musician, performer, virtuosa, virtuoso. [*Compare* VOCALIST.] *—See also* GAMBLER (1), PARTICIPANT.

playful *adj. —See* MISCHIEVOUS.

plaything *n.* An object for children to play with ▸ game, toy. [*Compare* AMUSEMENT.]

plaza *n. —See* COMMON.

plea *n. —See* APOLOGY (1), APPEAL, EXCUSE (1).

pleach *v. —See* WEAVE.

plead *v. —See* APPEAL (1), ARGUE (2).

pleasant *adj.* Giving or affording pleasure, enjoyment, or entertainment ▸ agreeable, amusing, congenial, diverting, enjoyable, entertaining, favorable, feel-good, fun, good, grateful, gratifying, lovely, nice, pleasing, pleasurable, satisfying, welcome. *Idiom:* not half bad. [*Compare* ATTRACTIVE, DELIGHTFUL, INVIGORATING.] *—See also* AMIABLE.

pleasantness *n. —See* AMIABILITY.

pleasantry *n. —See* AMENITIES (2).

please *v. —See* CHOOSE (2), DELIGHT (1), SATISFY (1).

pleased *adj. —See* WILLING.

pleasing or **pleasurable** *adj. —See* DELIGHTFUL, PLEASANT.

pleasure *n.* Unrestricted freedom to choose ▸ convenience, discretion, leisure, will. [*Compare* LICENSE.] *—See also* AMUSEMENT, DELIGHT, LIKING.

pleasure *v.* To feel or take joy or pleasure ▸ delight, exult, rejoice. [*Compare* ENJOY, LUXURIATE.] *—See also* DELIGHT (1).

pleat *n. —See* FOLD (1).

pleat *v. —See* FOLD.

plebeian *adj. —See* COARSE (1), LOWLY (1).

plebeians or **plebs** *n. —See* COMMONALTY.

people of ancient Rome. **2.** The populace.

plec·trum (plĕkʹtrəm) ▸ *n., pl.* **-trums** or **-tra** (-trə). A thin piece of metal, plastic, or similar material, used to pluck the strings of certain musical instruments, such as the guitar or harpsichord.

pled (plĕd) ▸ *v.* P.t. and p.part of **plead.**

pledge (plĕj) ▸ *n.* **1.** A formal promise. **2.** Something considered as security to guarantee payment of a debt or obligation. **3.** One who has been accepted for membership in a club, fraternity, or sorority. ▸ *v.* **pledged, pledg·ing. 1.** To promise solemnly. **2.** To bind by or as if by a pledge. **3.** To deposit as security. **4.** To promise to join (e.g., a club). **—pledgʹer** *n.*

Ple·ia·des (plēʹə-dēzʹ, plīʹ-) ▸ *pl.n.* An open star cluster in the constellation Taurus, consisting of several hundred stars, of which six are visible to the naked eye.

Pleis·to·cene (plīʹstə-sēnʹ) *Geol.* ▸ *adj.* Of or being the 1st epoch of the Quaternary Period, marked by the appearance of humans. ▸ *n.* The Pleistocene Epoch.

ple·na·ry (plēʹnə-rē, plĕnʹə-) ▸ *adj.* **1.** Unlimited or full: *a diplomat with plenary powers.* **2.** Fully attended by all qualified members. **—pleʹna·ri·ly** *adv.*

plen·i·po·ten·ti·ar·y (plĕnʹə-pə-tĕnʹshē-ĕrʹē, -shə-rē) ▸ *adj.* Invested with full powers. ▸ *n., pl.* **-ies.** A diplomatic agent fully authorized to represent his or her government.

plen·i·tude (plĕnʹĭ-to͞odʹ, -tyo͞odʹ) ▸ *n.* An abundance; fullness.

plen·te·ous (plĕnʹtē-əs) ▸ *adj.* **1.** Abundant; copious. **2.** Producing or yielding in abundance.

plen·ti·ful (plĕnʹtĭ-fəl) ▸ *adj.* **1.** Existing in great quantity or ample supply. **2.** Providing or producing an abundance. **—plenʹti·ful·ly** *adv.* **—plenʹti·ful·ness** *n.*

plen·ty (plĕnʹtē) ▸ *n.* **1.** A full or more than adequate amount: *plenty of time; goods in plenty.* **2.** A condition of general abundance or prosperity. ▸ *adv. Informal* Sufficiently: *It's plenty hot.*

ple·si·o·saur (plēʹsē-ə-sôrʹ, plēʹzē-) also **ple·si·o·sau·rus** (plēʹsē-ə-sôrʹəs, plēʹzē-) ▸ *n.* A large extinct marine reptile of the Mesozoic Era having paddlelike limbs.

pleth·o·ra (plĕthʹər-ə) ▸ *n.* A superabundance; excess.

pleu·ri·sy (plo͝orʹĭ-sē) ▸ *n.* Inflammation of the membranous sacs that enclose the lungs.

Plex·i·glas (plĕkʹsĭ-glăsʹ) ▸ A trademark for a light, transparent, strong thermoplastic.

plex·us (plĕkʹsəs) ▸ *n., pl.* **-us** or **-us·es.** A structure in the form of a network, esp. of nerves, blood vessels, or lymphatics.

pli·a·ble (plīʹə-bəl) ▸ *adj.* **1.** Easily bent or shaped. **2.** Easily influenced, persuaded, or swayed. **3.** Easily alterable; adaptable. **—pliʹa·bilʹi·ty, pliʹa·ble·ness** *n.* **—pliʹa·bly** *adv.*

pli·ant (plīʹənt) ▸ *adj.* **1.** Easily bent or flexed. **2.** Receptive to change; adaptable. **—pliʹan·cy** *n.*

pli·ers (plīʹərz) ▸ *pl.n.* A tool having a pair of pivoted jaws, used for holding, bending, or cutting.

plight¹ (plīt) ▸ *n.* A difficult or adverse situation.

plight² (plīt) ▸ *v.* To promise or bind by a solemn pledge, esp. to betroth. **—plightʹer** *n.*

plinth (plĭnth) ▸ *n.* A block or slab on which a pedestal, column, or statue is placed.

Plin·y¹ (plĭnʹē) "the Elder" (A.D. 23–79) ▸ Roman scholar and naturalist.

Plin·y² (plĭnʹē) "the Younger" (A.D. 62?–113?) ▸ Roman consul and writer.

Pli·o·cene (plīʹə-sēnʹ) *Geol.* ▸ *adj.* Of or being the 5th and last epoch of the Tertiary Period, marked by the appearance of modern animals. ▸ *n.* The Pliocene Epoch.

plod (plŏd) ▸ *v.* **plod·ded, plod·ding. 1.** To walk heavily or laboriously; trudge. **2.** To work or act in a persevering or monotonous way; drudge. **—plodʹder** *n.*

plop (plŏp) ▸ *v.* **plopped, plop·ping. 1.** To fall with a sound like that of an object falling into water without splashing. **2.** To drop or set heavily. **—plop** *n. & adv.*

plot (plŏt) ▸ *n.* **1.** A small piece of ground. **2.** The pattern of events or main story in a narrative or drama. **3.** A secret plan; scheme. ▸ *v.* **plot·ted, plot·ting. 1.** To represent graphically, as on a chart. **2.** To conspire. **—plotʹter** *n.*

plough (plou) ▸ *n. & v.* Var. of **plow.**

plov·er (plŭvʹər, plōʹvər) ▸ *n., pl.* **-er** or **-ers.** Any of various smallish, short-billed wading birds.

plow also **plough** (plou) ▸ *n.* **1.** A farm implement used for breaking up soil and cutting furrows. **2.** An implement of similar function, such as a snowplow. ▸ *v.* **1.** To break and turn over (earth) with a plow. **2.** To move or progress with driving force: *plowed through the crowd.* ***—phrasal verbs:*** **plow back** To reinvest (e.g., profits) in one's business. **plow into** *Informal* To strike with force. **plow under** To overwhelm. **—plowʹa·ble** *adj.* **—plowʹer** *n.*

plow·share (plouʹshârʹ) ▸ *n.* The cutting blade of a plow.

ploy (ploi) ▸ *n.* A strategem to gain an advantage.

pluck (plŭk) ▸ *v.* **1.** To pull off or out; pick. **2.** To pull out the hair or feathers of. **3.** *Mus.* To sound (the strings of an instrument) by pulling and releasing them. ▸ *n.* **1.** The act or an instance of plucking. **2.** Resourceful courage; spirit.

pluck·y (plŭkʹē) ▸ *adj.* **-i·er, -i·est.** Courageous; brave. **—pluckʹi·ness** *n.*

plug (plŭg) ▸ *n.* **1.** An object used to fill a hole tightly; stopper. **2a.** A fitting, usu. with metal prongs for insertion in a fixed socket, used to make electrical connections.

THESAURUS

pledge *n.* The act of drinking to someone ▸ health, toast. *—See also* DONATION, PAWN¹, PROMISE (1).

pledge *v.* **1.** To guarantee by a solemn promise ▸ betroth, covenant, engage, plight, promise, swear, troth, vow. *Idioms:* cross one's heart and hope to die, give one's word of honor. [*Compare* CONFIRM, CONTRACT, GUARANTEE.] **2.** To assume an obligation ▸ commit, contract, engage, promise, undertake. *—See also* COMMIT (2), DEVOTE, DONATE, DRINK (4), PAWN¹.

plenitude or **plenteousness** *n.* *—See* PLENTY.

plenitudinous or **plenteous** or **plentiful** *adj.* *—See* GENEROUS (2).

plenty *n.* Prosperity and a sufficiency of life's necessities ▸ abundance, ampleness, bounteousness, bountifulness, copiousness, cornucopia, horn of plenty, muchness, plenitude, plenteousness, plentifulness. *—See also* ABUNDANCE.

pleonasm *n.* *—See* WORDINESS.

pleonastic *adj.* *—See* WORDY (1).

plethora *n.* *—See* ABUNDANCE, EXCESS (1).

pliability or **pliableness** *n.* *—See* FLEXIBILITY (1).

pliable *adj.* *—See* ADAPTABLE, FLEXIBLE (3), MALLEABLE.

pliancy or **pliantness** *n.* *—See* FLEXIBILITY (1).

pliant *adj.* *—See* ADAPTABLE, FLEXIBLE (3), MALLEABLE, OBEDIENT.

plica or **plication** *n.* *—See* FOLD (1).

plight¹ *n.* *—See* DIFFICULTY, PREDICAMENT.

plight² *v.* *—See* PLEDGE (1).

plight *n.* *—See* PROMISE (1).

plighted *adj.* *—See* ENGAGED.

plod *v.* *—See* GRIND (2), TRUDGE.

plodder *n.* *—See* DRUDGE (2).

plodding *adj.* *—See* DULL (1), PONDEROUS, SLOW (1).

plop *v.* To drop or sink heavily and noisily ▸ flop, plump, plunk. [*Compare* FALL.]

plot *n.* **1.** The series of events and relationships forming the basis of a composition ▸ action, movement, scenario, story, story line. **2.** A secret plan to achieve an evil or illegal end ▸ cabal, collusion, connivance, conspiracy, designs, intrigue, machination, scheme. [*Compare* TRICK.] *—See also* LOT (1).

plot *v.* **1.** To show graphically the direction or location of, as by using coordinates ▸ chart, graph, lay out, map (out), plan. **2.** To work out a secret plan to achieve an evil or illegal end ▸ cabal, collude, connive, conspire, hatch, intrigue, machinate, scheme. [*Compare* DESIGN.] *—See also* DRAFT (1).

plow *v.* *—See* TILL.

ploy *n.* *—See* TRICK (1).

pluck *v.* *—See* GATHER, PULL (2).

pluck or **pluckiness** *n.* *—See* COURAGE.

plucky *adj.* *—See* BRAVE.

plug *n.* Something used to fill a hole, space, or container ▸ bung, choke, cork, filling, peg, spigot, spile, stop, stopper, stopple, tap, wad. [*Compare* COVER.] *—See also* ENDORSEMENT, OUTLET (1), PUBLICITY.

plug *v.* *Slang* To wound or kill with a

b. A spark plug. 3. A hydrant. 4. A piece of chewing tobacco. 5. *Informal* A favorable public mention, esp. of a person or product. 6. *Slang* An old, worn-out horse. 7. An artificial fishing lure. ▸ *v.* **plugged, plug·ging.** 1. To fill (a hole) tightly with or as if with a plug. 2. *Slang* To hit with a bullet. 3. *Informal* To make favorable public mention of (e.g., a product). 4. *Informal* To work doggedly and persistently. ***—phrasal verb:* plug in** To connect to an electrical outlet by means of a plug.

plug-in (plŭg′ĭn′) ▸ *n.* See **add-in** 2.

plum (plŭm) ▸ *n.* 1a. A smooth-skinned, fleshy, edible fruit with a hard-shelled pit. b. A tree bearing such fruit. 2. An especially desirable position, assignment, or reward.

plum·age (plo͞o′mĭj) ▸ *n.* The feathers of a bird.

plumb (plŭm) ▸ *n.* 1. A weight on the end of a line, used to determine water depth. 2. Such a device used to establish true vertical. ▸ *adv.* 1. Straight up and down. 2. *Informal* Directly; squarely. 3. *Informal* Utterly; completely: *plumb worn out.* ▸ *adj.* 1. Exactly vertical. 2. *Informal* Utter; sheer: *a plumb fool.* ▸ *v.* 1. To determine the depth of; sound. 2. To test the alignment or angle of with a plumb. **—plumb′a·ble** *adj.*

plumb·er (plŭm′ər) ▸ *n.* One who installs and repairs pipes and plumbing.

plumb·ing (plŭm′ĭng) ▸ *n.* 1. The pipes, fixtures, and other apparatus of a water or sewage system in a building. 2. The work or trade of a plumber.

plumb line ▸ *n.* A line from which a weight is suspended to determine verticality or depth.

plume (plo͞om) ▸ *n.* 1. A feather, esp. a large and showy one. 2. Something that resembles a long feather: *a plume of smoke.* ▸ *v.* **plumed, plum·ing.** 1. To decorate with or as if with plumes. 2. To pride (oneself) in a self-satisfied way.

plum·met (plŭm′ĭt) ▸ *v.* To fall or drop straight down.

plump[1] (plŭmp) ▸ *adj.* **-er, -est.** Well-rounded and full in form; chubby. ▸ *v.* To make or become plump.

plump[2] (plŭmp) ▸ *v.* 1. To drop abruptly or heavily. 2. To give full support or praise. ▸ *n.* 1. A heavy or abrupt fall. 2. The sound of such a fall. ▸ *adv.* 1. With a heavy or abrupt drop. 2. Straight down.

plun·der (plŭn′dər) ▸ *v.* To rob of goods by force, esp. in time of war; pillage. ▸ *n.* Property stolen by fraud or force. **—plun′der·er** *n.*

plunge (plŭnj) ▸ *v.* **plunged, plung·ing.** 1. To thrust or throw forcefully into a substance or place. 2. To enter or cast suddenly into a given state, situation, or activity. 3. To descend steeply or suddenly. 4. To speculate or gamble extravagantly. **—plunge** *n.*

plung·er (plŭn′jər) ▸ *n.* 1. A device consisting of a rubber suction cup attached to the end of a stick, used to unclog drains and pipes. 2. A machine part that operates with a thrusting or plunging movement.

plunk (plŭngk) ▸ *v.* 1. To throw, place, or drop heavily or abruptly. 2. To strum or pluck (a stringed instrument). 3. To emit a hollow, twanging sound. **—plunk** *n.*

plu·per·fect (plo͞o-pûr′fĭkt) ▸ *adj.* Of or relating to a verb tense used to express action completed before a specified or implied past time. ▸ *n.* 1. The pluperfect tense. 2. A verb or form in this tense.

plu·ral (plo͝or′əl) ▸ *adj.* Of or being a grammatical form that designates more than one of the things specified. ▸ *n.* 1. The plural number or form. 2. A word or term in the plural form. **—plu′ral·ize′** *v.* **—plu′ral·i·za′tion** *n.*

plu·ral·ism (plo͝or′ə-lĭz′əm) ▸ *n.* A condition of society in which numerous distinct ethnic, religious, or cultural groups coexist within one nation. **—plu′ral·ist** *n.* **—plu′ral·is′tic** *adj.*

plu·ral·i·ty (plo͞o-răl′ĭ-tē) ▸ *n., pl.* **-ties.** 1a. In a contest of more than two choices, the number of votes cast for the winner if this number is not more than one half of the total votes cast. b. The number by which the vote of a winning choice in such a contest exceeds that of the closest opponent. 2. The larger or greater part.

plus (plŭs) ▸ *conj.* 1. *Math.* Increased by: *Two plus two is four.* 2. Added to; along with. ▸ *adj.* 1. Positive or on the positive part of a scale. 2. Added or extra. ▸ *n., pl.* **plus·es** or **plus·ses.** 1. *Math.* A symbol (+) used to indicate addition or a positive quantity. 2. A favorable factor.

plush (plŭsh) ▸ *n.* A fabric having a thick, deep pile. ▸ *adj.* **-er, -est.** Luxurious. **—plush′i·ly, plush′ly** *adv.* **—plush′i·ness, plush′ness** *n.* **—plush′y** *adj.*

Plu·tarch (plo͞o′tärk′) (A.D. 46?–120?) ▸ Greek biographer and philosopher.

Plu·to (plo͞o′tō) ▸ *n.* 1. *Gk. Myth.* The god of the dead and the ruler of the underworld. 2. A dwarf planet, having an orbit around the sun that is 4.4 billion km (2.8 billion mi) distant at perihelion and 7.4 billion km (4.6 billion mi) at aphelion, with a diameter less than half that of Earth. Until 2006, Pluto was classified as the ninth planet in the solar system.

plu·toc·ra·cy (plo͞o-tŏk′rə-sē) ▸ *n., pl.* **-cies.** 1. Government by the wealthy. 2. A wealthy class that controls a government. **—plu′to·crat′** (plo͞o′tə-krăt′) *n.* **—plu′to·crat′ic, plu′to·crat′i·cal** *adj.*

plu·ton·ic (plo͞o-tŏn′ĭk) ▸ *adj.* Of deep igneous or magmatic origin: *plutonic rocks.*

plu·to·ni·um (plo͞o-tō′nē-əm) ▸ *n.* *Symbol* **Pu** A naturally radioactive, silvery metallic element used as a reactor fuel and in nuclear weapons. At. no. 94.

plu·vi·al (plo͞o′vē-əl) ▸ *adj.* Of or caused by rain.

ply[1] (plī) ▸ *v.* **plied** (plīd), **ply·ing.** 1. To join together, as by molding or twisting. 2. To double over (e.g., cloth). ▸ *n., pl.* **plies.** 1. A layer, as of cloth or wood. 2. One of the strands twisted together to make yarn, rope, or thread.

ply[2] (plī) ▸ *v.* **plied** (plīd), **ply·ing.** 1. To use diligently; wield. 2. To engage in (e.g., a trade); practice. 3. To traverse or sail over regularly. 4. To continue supplying: *plied their guests with food.*

Plym·outh (plĭm′əth) ▸ 1. A borough of SW England on **Plymouth Sound,** an inlet of the English Channel. 2. A town of SE MA on **Plymouth Bay,** an inlet of the Atlantic SE of Boston; founded (1620) by Pilgrims from the *Mayflower.*

ply·wood (plī′wo͝od′) ▸ *n.* A structural material made of layers of wood glued together.

Pm ▸ The symbol for the element **promethium.**

P.M. also **p.m.** or **P.M.** ▸ *abbr.* post meridiem

pneu·mat·ic (no͞o-măt′ĭk, nyo͞o-) also **pneu·mat·i·cal** (-ĭ-kəl) ▸ *adj.* 1. Of or relating to air or other gases. 2. Filled

THESAURUS

firearm ▸ gun (down), pick off, shoot. *Idiom:* fill full of lead (*or* holes). [*Compare* KILL[1], MURDER.] *—See also* FILL (2), PROMOTE (3).

plug-ugly *n.* *—See* THUG.

plum *n.* A person or thing worth catching ▸ prize. *Informal:* catch. *Slang:* brass ring. *—See also* REWARD, TREASURE.

plumb *adj.* *—See* VERTICAL.

plumb *adv.* *—See* DIRECTLY (3).

plumb *v.* *—See* EXPLORE.

plume *v.* *—See* PRIDE.

plummet *v.* *—See* FALL (1), FALL (4).

plump[1] or **plumpish** *adj.* *—See* FAT (1).

plump[2] *v.* To drop or sink heavily and noisily ▸ flop, plop, plunk. [*Compare* FALL.]

plump for *v.* *—See* SUPPORT (1).

plunder *n.* Goods or property seized unlawfully ▸ booty, graft, loot, pillage, prize, spoils. *Slang:* boodle, swag.

plunder *v.* *—See* SACK[2].

plunge *v.* To penetrate into a substance or place with force ▸ dig, dive, drive, lunge, pass, ram, run, sink, stab, stick, strike, thrust. [*Compare* CUT.] *—See also* FALL (1), FALL (4).

plunge into *v.* *—See* ATTACK (2).

plunge *n.* The act of swimming ▸ dip, duck, dunk, swim. *—See also* DESCENT, FALL (1), FALL (3), GAMBLE.

plunging *adj.* *—See* DESCENDING, LOW (2).

plunk *v.* To drop or sink heavily and noisily ▸ flop, plop, plump. [*Compare* FALL.] *—See also* THUD.

plush or **plushy** *adj.* *—See* LUXURIOUS.

ply[1] *v.* *—See* FOLD.

ply[2] *v.* 1. To use with or as if with the hands ▸ handle, manipulate, wield. 2. To bring to bear steadily or forcefully, as influence ▸ exercise, exert, wield. ***Idiom:*** throw one's weight around.

pneuma *n.* *—See* SPIRIT (2).

pneumatic *adj.* Of or relating to air ▸ aerial, airy, atmospheric.

with or operated by compressed air.

pneu·mo·coc·cus (no͞o′mə-kŏk′əs, nyo͞o′-) ▸ *n., pl.* **-coc·ci** (-kŏk′sī′, -kŏk′ī′). A bacterium that causes pneumonia. **—pneu′mo·coc′cal** *adj.*

pneu·mo·nia (no͞o-mōn′yə, nyo͞o-) ▸ *n.* An acute or chronic disease marked by inflammation of the lungs and caused by viruses, bacteria, and physical and chemical irritants. **—pneu·mon′ic** (-mŏn′ĭk) *adj.*

Po[1] (pō) ▸ A river of N Italy flowing about 652 km (405 mi) to the Adriatic Sea.

Po[2] ▸ The symbol for the element **polonium.**

poach[1] (pōch) ▸ *v.* To cook in a simmering liquid.

poach[2] (pōch) ▸ *v.* **1.** To trespass on another's property in order to take fish or game. **2.** To take (fish or game) illegally. **—poach′er** *n.*

Po·ca·hon·tas (pō′kə-hŏn′təs) (1595?–1617) ▸ Powhatan princess.

pock (pŏk) ▸ *n.* **1.** A pustule caused by smallpox or a similar eruptive disease. **2.** A mark or scar left in the skin by such a pustule; pockmark. **—pock** *v.*

pock·et (pŏk′ĭt) ▸ *n.* **1.** A pouch with an open edge sewn into or onto a garment and used to carry small items. **2.** A receptacle or cavity. **3.** Financial means. **4.** A small isolated or protected area or group. ▸ *adj.* **1.** Suitable for being carried in one's pocket. **2.** Small; miniature. ▸ *v.* **1.** To place in or as if in a pocket. **2.** To take possession of for oneself, esp. dishonestly. **—pock′et·ful′** *n.*

pock·et·book (pŏk′ĭt-bo͝ok′) ▸ *n.* **1.** A wallet; billfold. **2.** A handbag. **3.** Financial means.

pock·et·knife (pŏk′ĭt-nīf′) ▸ *n.* A small knife with a blade or blades that fold into the handle when not in use.

pocket veto ▸ *n.* An executive's indirect veto of a bill by retaining the bill unsigned until the legislature adjourns.

pock·mark (pŏk′märk′) ▸ *n.* A pitlike scar left on the skin by smallpox or another eruptive disease. **—pock′mark′** *v.*

po·co (pō′kō) ▸ *adv. Mus.* To a slight degree; somewhat.

pod[1] (pŏd) ▸ *n.* **1.** *Bot.* A seed vessel, as of the pea, that splits open. **2.** An external or detachable housing, as for instruments or personnel, forming part of a vehicle.

pod[2] (pŏd) ▸ *n.* A school of marine mammals, such as seals or whales.

–pod or **–pode** ▸ *suff.* Foot; footlike part: *gastropod.*

po·di·a·try (pə-dī′ə-trē) ▸ *n.* The branch of medicine that deals with diseases of the foot. **—po′di·at′ric** (pō′dē-ăt′rĭk) *adj.* **—po·di′a·trist** *n.*

po·di·um (pō′dē-əm) ▸ *n., pl.* **-di·a** (-dē-ə) or **-di·ums.** An elevated platform, as for a speaker or orchestra conductor.

Poe (pō), **Edgar Allan** (1809–49) ▸ Amer. writer.

po·em (pō′əm) ▸ *n.* A verbal composition characterized by the use of condensed language chosen for its sound and suggestive power and by the use of literary techniques such as meter and metaphor.

po·e·sy (pō′ĭ-zē, -sē) ▸ *n.* Poetry.

po·et (pō′ĭt) ▸ *n.* A writer of poems.

po·et·as·ter (pō′ĭt-ăs′tər) ▸ *n.* An inferior poet.

po·et·ess (pō′ĭ-tĭs) ▸ *n.* A woman who writes poems.

po·et·ic (pō-ĕt′ĭk) also **po·et′i·cal** ▸ *adj.* Of or characteristic of poetry or poets.

poetic justice ▸ *n.* The rewarding of virtue and the punishment of vice, often in an appropriate or ironic manner.

poetic license ▸ *n.* The liberty taken by an artist or a writer in deviating from conventional form or fact to achieve a desired effect.

poet laureate ▸ *n., pl.* **poets laureate** or **poet laureates. 1.** A poet appointed for life by a British monarch as chief poet of the kingdom. **2.** A poet appointed to a similar honorary position.

po·et·ry (pō′ĭ-trē) ▸ *n.* **1.** The art or work of a poet. **2a.** Poems regarded as forming a division of literature. **b.** The poetic works of a given author, group, or kind.

po·grom (pə-grŏm′, pō′grəm) ▸ *n.* An organized massacre of a minority group, esp. Jews.

poi (poi) ▸ *n.* A food made from cooked taro root pounded to a paste and fermented.

poign·ant (poin′yənt) ▸ *adj.* **1.** Keenly distressing to the mind or feelings: *poignant anxiety.* **2.** Profoundly moving; touching: *a poignant memory.* **—poign′ance, poign′an·cy** *n.*

poi·kil·o·therm (poi-kĭl′ə-thûrm′) ▸ *n.* An organism, such as a reptile, having a body temperature that varies with the temperature of its surroundings. **—poi′ki·lo·ther′mic** (-kə-lō-thûr′mĭk) *adj.*

poin·ci·an·a (poin′sē-ăn′ə, -ä′nə) ▸ *n.* A tropical and semitropical tree having scarlet flowers and long pods.

poin·set·ti·a (poin-sĕt′ē-ə, -sĕt′ə) ▸ *n.* A tropical American shrub that has showy, usu. scarlet bracts beneath the small yellow flowers.

point (point) ▸ *n.* **1a.** A sharp or tapered end. **b.** A mark formed by or as if by a sharp end. **2.** A tapering extension of land projecting into water. **3.** *Math.* A dimensionless geometric object having no properties except location. **4.** A place or position. **5.** A specified degree, condition, or limit. **6.** A specific moment in time. **7.** An objective or purpose to be achieved. **8.** A significant or outstanding idea or suggestion. **9.** A distinctive quality or characteristic. **10.** A single unit, as in counting, rating, or measuring. **11.** An electrical contact, esp. one in the distributor of an automobile engine. ▸ *v.* **1.** To direct or aim. **2.** To bring to notice: *point out an error.* **3.** To indicate the position or direction of. **4.** To give emphasis to; stress: *pointed up the difference between them.* ***—idioms:*** **beside the point** Irrelevant. **in point of** With reference to. **stretch a point** To make an exception. **to the point** Closely concerning the matter at hand. **—point′y** *adj.*

point-and-click (point′ənd-klĭk′) ▸ *adj.* Allowing the activation of a selected computer command by clicking a pointing device.

point-blank (point′blăngk′) ▸ *adj.* **1a.** Aiming straight at a target. **b.** So close that missing the target is unlikely. **2.** Straightforward; blunt. **—point′-blank′** *adv.*

point·ed (poin′tĭd) ▸ *adj.* **1.** Having a point. **2.** Sharp; incisive. **3.** Obviously directed at a particular thing: *a pointed comment.* **4.** Clearly evident; marked: *a pointed lack of interest.* **—point′ed·ly** *adv.*

point·er (poin′tər) ▸ *n.* **1.** An indicator, as on a watch or scale. **2.** A long, tapered stick for indicating objects, as on a chart or blackboard. **3.** A usu. short-haired hunting dog bred to indicate game with an immobile stance. **4.** A piece of advice; suggestion.

THESAURUS

poach[1] *v.* —*See* COOK.

poach[2] *n.* —*See* PLAGIARIZE.

pock *v.* —*See* DEFORM.

pock *n.* —*See* DEFORMITY, WELT.

pocket *n.* —*See* HOLE (1).

pocketbook *n.* —*See* PURSE.

pocket money *n.* —*See* PEANUTS.

podium *n.* —*See* STAGE (1).

poem *n.* **1.** A poetic work ▸ poesy, poetry, rhyme, song, verse. **2.** A creation or experience having beauty suggestive of poetry ▸ lyricism, poetry.

poet *n.* One who writes poetry ▸ bard, jongleur, minstrel, muse, poetess, rhymer, rhymester, troubadour, versifier.

poetic or **poetical** *adj.* Relating to the characteristics of poetry ▸ lyric, lyrical, poetical. [*Compare* MELODIOUS, RHYTHMICAL.]

poetry *n.* A creation or experience having beauty suggestive of poetry ▸ lyricism, poem. —*See also* POEM (1).

poignant *adj.* —*See* AFFECTING.

point *n.* **1.** A sharp or tapered end ▸ acicula, acumination, apex, cusp, mucro, mucronation, neb, nib, tip. [*Compare* SPIKE.] **2.** A very small mark ▸ dash, dot, fleck, pinpoint, speck, speckle, spot. [*Compare* IMPRESSION.] —*See also* DEGREE (1), ELEMENT (2), INTENTION, MEANING, OCCASION (1), POSITION (1), REASON (1), SUBJECT, USE (2).

point *v.* —*See* AIM (1).

point out *v.* —*See* DESIGNATE, REFER (1).

point to *v.* —*See* IMPLY, INDICATE (1), NAME (2).

point up *v.* —*See* EMPHASIZE.

point-blank *adv.* —*See* FLATLY.

pointed *adj.* Having an end that tapers to a point ▸ acicular, aciculate, aciculated, acuminate, acute, barbed, cultrate, cuspate, cuspated, cuspidate, cuspidated, fine, keen, mucronate, pointy, pronged, spiked, spined, sharp, tined. [*Compare* SHARP, THORNY.] —*See also* NOTICEABLE, PITHY.

pointer *n.* —*See* ADVICE, TIP[3].

poin·til·lism (pwăɴ′tē-ĭz′əm, point′l-ĭz′-) ▸ *n.* A painting technique characterized by the application of paint in small dots and brush strokes. **—poin′til·list** *adj. & n.* **—poin′til·lis′tic** *adj.*

point·ing device (poin′tĭng) ▸ *n. Comp. Sci.* An input device, such as a mouse, for manipulating a cursor or pointer on a GUI.

point·less (point′lĭs) ▸ *adj.* Meaningless; irrelevant. **—point′less·ness** *n.*

point-of-sale (point′əv-sāl′) ▸ *adj.* Of or being the place where an item is purchased.

point of view ▸ *n.* **1.** A manner of viewing things; attitude. **2.** A position from which something is observed or considered.

poise (poiz) ▸ *v.* **poised, pois·ing.** To balance or be balanced. ▸ *n.* **1.** Balance; stability. **2.** Composure. **3.** Dignity of manner.

poi·son (poi′zən) ▸ *n.* A substance that causes injury, illness, or death, esp. by chemical means. ▸ *v.* **1.** To kill or harm with poison. **2.** To put poison on or into. **3a.** To pollute. **b.** To have a harmful influence on; corrupt. **—poi′son·er** *n.* **—poi′son·ous** *adj.* **—poi′son·ous·ly** *adv.*

poison hemlock ▸ *n.* A deadly poisonous European plant, widely naturalized in North America, having small white flowers.

poison ivy ▸ *n.* **1.** A North American plant having compound leaves with three leaflets and causing a rash on contact. **2.** The rash itself.

poison oak ▸ *n.* **1.** Either of two plants of the SE and W US related to poison ivy and causing a rash on contact. **2.** The rash itself.

poison sumac ▸ *n.* **1.** A swamp shrub of the SE US, having compound leaves and causing a rash on contact. **2.** The rash itself.

poke[1] (pōk) ▸ *v.* **poked, pok·ing.** **1.** To push or jab at, as with a finger; prod. **2.** To make (a hole or pathway) by or as if by prodding or jabbing. **3.** To push; thrust. **4.** To pry or meddle. **5.** To search curiously; rummage. ▸ *n.* A push, thrust, or jab. ***—idiom:*** **poke fun at** To ridicule; tease.

poke[2] (pōk) ▸ *n. Regional* A sack.

pok·er[1] (pō′kər) ▸ *n.* A metal rod used to stir a fire.

pok·er[2] (pō′kər) ▸ *n.* Any of various card games played by two or more players who bet on the value of their hands.

poke·weed (pōk′wēd′) ▸ *n.* A tall North American plant having small white flowers, blackish-red berries and a poisonous root.

po·key also **po·ky** (pō′kē) ▸ *n., pl.* **-keys** also **-kies.** *Slang* A jail.

pok·y also **poke·y** (pō′kē) ▸ *adj.* **-i·er, -i·est.** *Informal* Dawdling; slow. **—pok′i·ly** *adv.* **—pok′i·ness** *n.*

pol (pôl) ▸ *n. Informal* A politician.

Po·land (pō′lənd) ▸ A country of central Europe bordering on the Baltic Sea.

po·lar (pō′lər) ▸ *adj.* **1.** Of, measured from, or referred to a pole. **2.** Of or near the North or South Pole. **3.** Occupying or characterized by opposite extremes.

polar bear ▸ *n.* A large white bear of Arctic regions.

Po·lar·is (pə-lăr′ĭs) ▸ *n.* A star at the end of the handle of the Little Dipper and almost at the north celestial pole.

po·lar·i·ty (pō-lăr′ĭ-tē, pə-) ▸ *n., pl.* **-ties.** **1.** Intrinsic polar separation, alignment, or orientation, esp. of a physical property. **2.** An indicated polar extreme. **3.** The manifestation of two opposing tendencies.

po·lar·ize (pō′lə-rīz′) ▸ *v.* **-ized, -iz·ing.** **1.** To impart polarity to. **2.** To acquire polarity. **3.** To cause to concentrate about two conflicting positions. **—po′lar·i·za′tion** *n.*

Po·lar·oid (pō′lə-roid′) ▸ **1.** A trademark for a transparent plastic capable of polarizing light, used in glare-reducing optical devices. **2.** A trademark for an instant camera.

Polar Regions ▸ The lands and waters surrounding the North and South Poles, known respectively as the **North Polar Region** and the **South Polar Region.**

pole[1] (pōl) ▸ *n.* **1.** Either extremity of an axis through a sphere. **2.** *Geog.* The North Pole or the South Pole. **3.** *Phys.* A magnetic pole. **4.** Either of two oppositely charged terminals, as in an electric cell or battery. **5.** Either of two opposing forces.

pole[2] (pōl) ▸ *n.* A long slender piece of wood or other material. ▸ *v.* **poled, pol·ing.** **1.** To propel (e.g., a boat) with a pole. **2.** To use ski poles to maintain or gain speed.

Pole ▸ *n.* **1.** A native or inhabitant of Poland. **2.** A person of Polish descent.

pole·ax or **pole·axe** (pōl′ăks′) ▸ *n.* A long-handled battle-ax.

pole·cat (pōl′kăt′) ▸ *n.* **1.** A weasellike European mammal. **2.** See **skunk** 1.

po·lem·ic (pə-lĕm′ĭk) ▸ *n.* **1.** A controversy or refutation. **2.** **polemics** *(takes sing. or pl. v.)* The art or practice of debate or controversy. **—po·lem′ic, po·lem′i·cal** *adj.* **—po·lem′i·cist** *n.*

po·len·ta (pō-lĕn′tə) ▸ *n.* A thick mush made of coarse cornmeal.

pole·star (pōl′stär′) ▸ *n.* See **Polaris.**

pole vault ▸ *n.* A field event in which the contestant jumps or vaults over a high crossbar with the aid of a long pole. **—pole′-vault′** *v.* **—pole′-vault′er** *n.*

po·lice (pə-lēs′) ▸ *n., pl.* **-lice.** **1.** The governmental department established to maintain order, enforce the law, and detect and prevent crime. **2a.** A body of persons making up such a department. **b.** A body of persons having similar organization and function: *campus police.* **3.** The soldiers assigned to a specified maintenance duty. ▸ *v.* **-liced, -lic·ing.** **1.** To regulate, control, or keep in order with or as if with police. **2.** To make (e.g., a military area) neat in appearance.

police dog ▸ *n.* **1.** A guard dog. **2.** See **German shepherd.**

police force ▸ *n.* See **police** 2.

po·lice·man (pə-lēs′mən) ▸ *n.* A man who is a member of a police force.

police state ▸ *n.* A state in which the government exercises

THESAURUS

pointless *adj.* —*See* AIMLESS, FUTILE, MINDLESS.

pointlessness *n.* —*See* FUTILITY.

point of view *n.* —*See* VIEWPOINT.

pointy *adj.* —*See* POINTED.

poise *v.* To remain stationary over a place or object ▸ hang, hover. —*See also* BALANCE (1), BALANCE (3).

poise *n.* —*See* BALANCE (1), BALANCE (2), BEARING (1), EASE (1).

poised *adj.* —*See* CALM, CONFIDENT.

poison *n.* Anything that is injurious, destructive, or fatal ▸ bane, canker, contagion, toxicant, toxin, venom, virus. —*See also* CONTAMINANT.

poison *v.* To harm with poison ▸ canker, envenom, infect, intoxicate. [*Compare* HURT.] —*See also* CONTAMINATE, CORRUPT.

poison *adj.* —*See* POISONOUS.

poisonous *adj.* Capable of injuring or killing by poison ▸ malignant, mephitic, mephitical, miasmic, noxious, pernicious, pestiferous, pestilent, pestilential, poison, toxic, toxicant, venomous, virulent. [*Compare* DEADLY, HARMFUL.] —*See also* MALEVOLENT, UNWHOLESOME (2).

poisonousness *n.* —*See* MALEVOLENCE.

poke[1] *v.* **1.** To look into or inquire about curiously, inquisitively, or in a meddlesome fashion ▸ pry, snoop. *Informal:* nose (around), sniff about (*or* around). *Idiom:* stick one's nose into. [*Compare* MEDDLE.] **2.** To advance slowly ▸ crawl, creep, drag, inch. *Idiom:* go at a snail's pace. [*Compare* TRUDGE.] —*See also* DELAY (2), GROPE, PENETRATE, PUSH (1).

poke *n.* —*See* DIG, LAGGARD.

poke[2] *n.* —*See* BAG.

pokerfaced *adj.* —*See* EXPRESSIONLESS.

pokey *n.* —*See* JAIL.

poky *adj.* —*See* SLOW (1).

polar *adj.* —*See* COLD (1), OPPOSITE.

polarity *n.* —*See* OPPOSITION (1).

pole *n.* —*See* STICK (2).

polemic *n.* —*See* ARGUMENT.

polemic or **polemical** *adj.* —*See* ARGUMENTATIVE.

police *v.* To maintain or keep in order with or as if with police ▸ monitor, patrol, regulate, secure. *Idioms:* keep the peace, keep watch, pound a beat. [*Compare* DEFEND.] —*See also* TIDY (1).

policeman or **policewoman** *n.* —*See* POLICE OFFICER.

police officer *n.* A member of a law-enforcement agency ▸ bluecoat, constable, finest, marshal, officer, patrolman, patrolwoman, peace officer, policeman, policewoman, sheriff, trooper. *Informal:* cop, law. *Slang:* bull, copper, flatfoot, fuzz, gendarme, heat, man, narc. [*Compare* DETECTIVE.]

rigid and repressive controls, esp. by means of a secret police force.

police station ▸ *n.* The headquarters of a police force.

po·lice·wom·an (pə-lēs′wŏŏm′ən) ▸ *n.* A woman who is a member of a police force.

pol·i·cy[1] (pŏl′ĭ-sē) ▸ *n., pl.* **-cies.** 1. A plan or course of action, as of a government or business, intended to influence and determine decisions, actions, and other matters. 2. Prudence or sagacity in practical matters.

pol·i·cy[2] (pŏl′ĭ-sē) ▸ *n., pl.* **-cies.** A written contract or certificate of insurance. **—pol′i·cy·hol′der** *n.*

pol·i·cy·mak·ing (pŏl′ĭ-sē-mā′kĭng) ▸ *n.* High-level development of policy, esp. government policy. **—pol′i·cy·mak′er** *n.*

po·li·o (pō′lē-ō′) ▸ *n.* Poliomyelitis.

po·li·o·my·e·li·tis (pō′lē-ō-mī′ə-lī′tĭs) ▸ *n.* An infectious viral disease that chiefly affects children and in its acute forms attacks the central nervous system, leading to paralysis, muscular atrophy, and often deformity. **—po′li·o·my′e·lit′ic** (-lĭt′ĭk) *adj.*

pol·ish (pŏl′ĭsh) ▸ *v.* 1. To make smooth and shiny by rubbing or chemical action. 2. To remove the outer layers from (grains of rice). 3. To free from coarseness; refine. ***—phrasal verb:* polish off** *Informal* To finish or dispose of quickly. ▸ *n.* 1. Smoothness or shininess of surface. 2. A substance used to shine a surface. 3. Elegance of style or manner. **—pol′ish·er** *n.*

Po·lish (pō′lĭsh) ▸ *adj.* Of or relating to Poland or its people or language. ▸ *n.* The Slavic language of the Poles.

pol·it·bu·ro (pŏl′ĭt-byŏŏr′ō, pə-lĭt′-) ▸ *n., pl.* **-ros.** The chief political and executive committee of a Communist party.

po·lite (pə-līt′) ▸ *adj.* **-lit·er, -lit·est.** 1. Marked by consideration, tact, and courtesy. 2. Refined; elegant. **—po·lite′ly** *adv.* **—po·lite′ness** *n.*

pol·i·tesse (pŏl′ĭ-tĕs′, pô′lē-) ▸ *n.* Courteous formality.

pol·i·tic (pŏl′ĭ-tĭk) ▸ *adj.* 1. Shrewd; artful. 2. Prudent; judicious.

po·lit·i·cal (pə-lĭt′ĭ-kəl) ▸ *adj.* 1. Of or relating to the affairs of government, politics, or the state. 2. Characteristic of politics, parties, or politicians. **—po·lit′i·cal·ly** *adv.*

politically correct ▸ *adj.* Of or relating to broad social, political, and educational change, esp. to redress historical injustices in matters such as race and gender. **—political correctness** *n.*

political science ▸ *n.* The study of the processes, principles, and structure of government and political institutions.

pol·i·ti·cian (pŏl′ĭ-tĭsh′ən) ▸ *n.* 1. One actively involved in politics. 2. One who holds or seeks a political office.

po·lit·i·cize (pə-lĭt′ĭ-sīz′) ▸ *v.* **-cized, -ciz·ing.** To make political. **—po·lit′i·ci·za′tion** *n.*

pol·i·tick (pŏl′ĭ-tĭk) ▸ *v.* To engage in or discuss politics. **—pol′i·tick′er** *n.*

po·lit·i·co (pə-lĭt′ĭ-kō′) ▸ *n., pl.* **-cos.** A politician.

pol·i·tics (pŏl′ĭ-tĭks) ▸ *n.* 1. *(takes sing. v.)* The art or science of government or governing. 2. *(takes sing. or pl. v.)* The activities or affairs engaged in by a government. 3. *(takes sing. or pl. v.)* Intrigue or maneuvering within a group: *office politics.* 4. *(takes sing. or pl. v.)* Political positions.

pol·i·ty (pŏl′ĭ-tē) ▸ *n., pl.* **-ties.** An organized society, such as a nation, having a specific form of government.

Polk (pōk), **James Knox** (1795–1849) ▸ The 11th US President.

pol·ka (pōl′kə, pō′kə) ▸ *n.* 1. A lively dance performed by couples. 2. Music for this dance, having duple meter. **—pol′ka** *v.*

polka dot ▸ *n.* One of a number of dots forming a pattern on cloth.

poll (pōl) ▸ *n.* 1. The casting and registering of votes in an election. 2. The number of votes cast or recorded. 3. often **polls** The place where votes are cast and registered. 4. A survey of the public or of a sample of public opinion to acquire information. ▸ *v.* 1. To receive (a given number of votes). 2. To receive or record the votes of. 3. To question in a survey; canvass. 4. To cut off or trim (e.g., hair or horns). **—poll′er** *n.*

pol·lack (pŏl′ək) also **-lock** ▸ *n., pl.* **-lack** or **-lacks** also **-lock** or **-locks.** A marine food fish of N Atlantic waters.

pol·len (pŏl′ən) ▸ *n.* The powderlike material produced by the anthers of seed plants and functioning as the male agent in fertilization.

pol·li·nate (pŏl′ə-nāt′) ▸ *v.* **-li·nat·ed, -li·nat·ing.** To fertilize by transferring pollen from an anther to the stigma of (a flower). **—pol′li·na′tion** *n.* **—pol′li·na′tor** *n.*

pol·li·no·sis (pŏl′ə-nō′sĭs) ▸ *n.* See **hay fever.**

pol·li·wog also **pol·ly·wog** (pŏl′ē-wŏg′, -wôg′) ▸ *n.* See **tadpole.**

poll·ster (pōl′stər) ▸ *n.* One that takes public-opinion surveys.

poll tax ▸ *n.* A tax levied on people rather than on property, often as a voting requirement.

pol·lute (pə-lōōt′) ▸ *v.* **-lut·ed, -lut·ing.** 1. To make unfit for or harmful to living things, esp. by the addition of waste matter. 2. To render impure; corrupt. **—pol·lut′ant** *n.* **—pol·lut′er** *n.* **—pol·lu′tion** *n.*

Pol·lux (pŏl′əks) ▸ *n.* A bright star in the constellation Gemini.

po·lo (pō′lō) ▸ *n.* A game played by two teams on horseback equipped with long-handled mallets for driving a wooden ball.

Polo, Marco (1254–1324) ▸ Venetian traveler in Asia.

pol·o·naise (pŏl′ə-nāz′, pō′lə-) ▸ *n.* 1. A stately Polish dance in triple meter. 2. Music for this dance.

po·lo·ni·um (pə-lō′nē-əm) ▸ *n.* *Symbol* **Po** A radioactive metallic element that occurs naturally as a product of radium decay and is also produced artificially. At. no. 84.

polo shirt ▸ *n.* A knitted pullover sport shirt.

pol·ter·geist (pōl′tər-gīst′) ▸ *n.* A noisy, usu. mischievous ghost.

pol·troon (pŏl-trōōn′) ▸ *n.* A base coward. **—pol·troon′er·y** *n.*

poly– ▸ *pref.* 1. More than one; many; much: *polyatomic.* 2. More than usual; excessive; abnormal: *polydipsia.* 3. Polymer; polymeric: *polyethylene.*

pol·y·an·dry (pŏl′ē-ăn′drē) ▸ *n.* The condition or practice of having more than one husband at one time. **—pol′y·an′drous** *adj.*

pol·y·chrome (pŏl′ē-krōm′) ▸ *adj.* Having or decorated in many colors. **—pol′y·chro·mat′ic** (-krō-măt′ĭk), **pol′y·chro′mic, pol′y·chro′mous** *adj.*

pol·y·clin·ic (pŏl′ē-klĭn′ĭk) ▸ *n.* A clinic that treats various diseases and injuries.

pol·y·dip·si·a (pŏl′ē-dĭp′sē-ə) ▸ *n.* Excessive or abnormal thirst. **—pol′y·dip′sic** *adj.*

pol·y·es·ter (pŏl′ē-ĕs′tər, pŏl′ē-ĕs′tər) ▸ *n.* Any of numerous synthetic resins used esp. in fabric and molded parts.

pol·y·eth·yl·ene (pŏl′ē-ĕth′ə-lēn′) ▸ *n.* A synthetic resin,

THESAURUS

policy *n.* —*See* DOCTRINE.

polish *v.* To improve by making minor changes or additions ▸ remodel, retouch, touch up. [*Compare* FIX, RENEW.] —*See also* FINISH (2), GLOSS[1], PERFECT.

polish off *v.* —*See* CONSUME (1), EAT (1), EXHAUST (1).

polish *n.* —*See* ELEGANCE, FINISH, GLOSS[1].

polished *adj.* Proficient as a result of practice and study ▸ accomplished, finished, practiced. [*Compare* ABLE, EXPERT.] —*See also* CULTURED, GLOSSY.

polite *adj.* —*See* ATTENTIVE, COURTEOUS (1), DEFERENTIAL.

politeness *n.* —*See* AMENITIES (2), COURTESY.

politesse *n.* —*See* COURTESY.

politic *adj.* —*See* ADVISABLE, DELICATE (2).

political *adj.* —*See* GOVERNMENTAL.

polity *n.* —*See* STATE (1).

poll *n.* A gathering of information or opinion from a variety of sources or individuals ▸ count, poll, survey. —*See also* HEAD (1).

poll *v.* To cast a vote ▸ ballot, vote. *Idioms:* exercise one's civic duty, go to the polls.

pollinate *v.* To make fertile ▸ enrich, fecundate, fertilize. [*Compare* IMPREGNATE, PREGNANT.]

pollutant *n.* —*See* CONTAMINANT.

pollute *v.* —*See* CONTAMINATE, CORRUPT, VIOLATE (3).

polluted *adj.* —*See* IMPURE (2), DRUNK.

pollution *n.* —*See* CONTAMINANT, CONTAMINATION.

Pollyanna *n.* One who expects a favorable outcome or dwells on hopeful aspects ▸ optimist, Pangloss, positivist. [*Compare* DREAMER.]

poltroon *n.* —*See* COWARD.

polychromatic or **polychrome** *adj.* —*See* MULTICOLORED.

used esp. in the form of films and sheets.

po·lyg·a·my (pə-lĭg′ə-mē) ▸ *n.* The condition or practice of having more than one spouse at one time. **—po·lyg′a·mist** *n.* **—po·lyg′a·mous** *adj.* **—po·lyg′a·mous·ly** *adv.*

pol·y·glot (pŏl′ē-glŏt′) ▸ *n.* One with a speaking, reading, or writing knowledge of several languages.

pol·y·gon (pŏl′ē-gŏn′) ▸ *n.* A closed plane figure bounded by three or more line segments. **—po·lyg′o·nal** (pə-lĭg′ə-nəl) *adj.*

pol·y·graph (pŏl′ē-grăf′) ▸ *n.* An instrument that records changes in physiological processes such as heartbeat, blood pressure, and respiration, often used as a lie detector.

po·lyg·y·ny (pə-lĭj′ə-nē) ▸ *n.* The condition or practice of having more than one wife at one time. **—po·lyg′y·nous** *adj.*

pol·y·he·dron (pŏl′ē-hē′drən) ▸ *n., pl.* **-drons** or **-dra** (-drə). A solid whose faces are polygons. **—pol′y·he′dral** *adj.*

pol·y·math (pŏl′ē-măth′) ▸ *n.* A person of great or varied learning. **—pol′y·math′, pol′y·math′ic** *adj.*

pol·y·mer (pŏl′ə-mər) ▸ *n.* Any of numerous natural and synthetic compounds of usu. high molecular weight consisting of repeated linked units, each a relatively light and simple molecule. **—pol′y·mer′ic** (-mĕr′ĭk) *adj.*

pol·y·mer·ase (pə-lĭm′ə-rās′, -rāz′) ▸ *n.* Any of various enzymes that catalyze the formation of DNA or RNA.

pol·y·mer·ize (pŏl′ə-mə-rīz′, pə-lĭm′ə-) ▸ *v.* **-ized, -iz·ing.** To bond two or more monomers to form a polymer. **—po·lym′er·i·za′tion** *n.*

Pol·y·ne·sia (pŏl′ə-nē′zhə, -shə) ▸ A division of Oceania including islands of the central and S Pacific roughly between New Zealand, Hawaii, and Easter I.

Pol·y·ne·sian (pŏl′ə-nē′zhən, -shən) ▸ *n.* **1.** A native or inhabitant of Polynesia. **2.** A subfamily of the Austronesian language family spoken in Polynesia.

pol·y·no·mi·al (pŏl′ē-nō′mē-əl) ▸ *adj.* Of or consisting of more than two names or terms. ▸ *n. Math.* An algebraic function of one or more summed terms, each term consisting of a constant multiplier and one or more variables raised to integral powers.

pol·yp (pŏl′ĭp) ▸ *n.* **1.** An organism, such as a hydra or coral, having a cylindrical body and an oral opening usu. surrounded by tentacles. **2.** *Pathol.* A growth protruding from the mucous lining of an organ. **—pol′yp·oid′** *adj.*

pol·y·pep·tide (pŏl′ē-pĕp′tīd′) ▸ *n.* A peptide containing many molecules of amino acids.

po·lyph·o·ny (pə-lĭf′ə-nē) ▸ *n., pl.* **-nies.** Music with two or more independent melodic parts sounded together. **—pol′y·phon′ic** (pŏl′ē-fŏn′ĭk), **po·lyph′o·nous** *adj.*

pol·y·sac·cha·ride (pŏl′ē-săk′ə-rīd′) ▸ *n.* Any of a class of carbohydrates, such as starch and cellulose, consisting of a number of monosaccharides.

pol·y·sty·rene (pŏl′ē-stī′rēn) ▸ *n.* A rigid, clear thermoplastic polymer used esp. in molded parts or as an insulating foam.

pol·y·syl·la·ble (pŏl′ē-sĭl′ə-bəl) ▸ *n.* A word of more than three syllables. **—pol′y·syl·lab′ic** (-sĭ-lăb′ĭk) *adj.*

pol·y·tech·nic (pŏl′ē-tĕk′nĭk) ▸ *adj.* Offering or dealing with instruction in many industrial arts and applied sciences. ▸ *n.* A school specializing in such subjects.

pol·y·the·ism (pŏl′ē-thē-ĭz′əm, pŏl′ē-thē′ĭz-əm) ▸ *n.* The worship of or belief in more than one god. **—pol′y·the′ist** *n.*

pol·y·un·sat·u·rat·ed (pŏl′ē-ŭn-săch′ə-rā′tĭd) ▸ *adj.* Relating to long-chain carbon compounds, esp. fats, having many unsaturated bonds.

pol·y·u·re·thane (pŏl′ē-yo͝or′ə-thān′) ▸ *n.* Any of various resins used in tough chemical-resistant coatings, adhesives, and foams.

pol·y·va·lent (pŏl′ē-vā′lənt) ▸ *adj.* **1.** Involving more than one kind of antigen, antibody, toxin, or microorganism. **2.** *Chem.* **a.** Having more than one valence. **b.** Having a valence of 3 or higher. **—pol′y·va′lence, pol′y·va′len·cy** *n.*

pol·y·vi·nyl chloride (pŏl′e-vī′nəl) ▸ *n.* PVC.

po·made (pō-mād′, pŏ-) ▸ *n.* A perfumed hair ointment. **—po′made** *v.*

pom·e·gran·ate (pŏm′ĭ-grăn′ĭt) ▸ *n.* **1.** A shrub or small tree widely cultivated for its edible fruit. **2.** The fruit of this tree, having a tough reddish rind and many seeds.

Pom·er·a·ni·an (pŏm′ə-rā′nē-ən, -rān′yən) ▸ *adj.* Of or relating to Pomerania or its people. ▸ *n.* **1.** A native or inhabitant of Pomerania. **2.** Any of a breed of small dog having long silky hair and a foxlike face.

pom·mel (pŭm′əl, pŏm′-) ▸ *v.* **-meled, -mel·ing** also **-melled, -mel·ling.** To beat; pummel. ▸ *n.* **1.** The upper front part of a saddle. **2.** A knob on the hilt of a sword.

pommel horse ▸ *n.* A padded apparatus for gymnastic exercises having two handles on top and adjustable legs.

pomp (pŏmp) ▸ *n.* **1.** Magnificent display; splendor. **2.** Ostentatious display.

pom·pa·dour (pŏm′pə-dôr′) ▸ *n.* A hairstyle formed by sweeping the hair up from the forehead.

pom·pa·no (pŏm′pə-nō′) ▸ *n., pl.* **-no** or **-nos.** A food fish of tropical and temperate Atlantic waters.

Pom·pe·ii (pŏm-pā′, -pā′ē) ▸ An ancient city of S Italy SE of Naples; destroyed by an eruption of Mount Vesuvius (A.D. 79). **—Pom·pe′ian, Pom·pei′ian** *adj. & n.*

pom·pon (pŏm′pŏn′) also **pom·pom** (-pŏm′) ▸ *n.* **1.** A tuft or ball of wool, feathers, or other material used as a decoration. **2.** A buttonlike flower of some chrysanthemums and dahlias.

pom·pous (pŏm′pəs) ▸ *adj.* **1.** Self-important; pretentious. **2.** Marked by pomp or stately display. **—pom·pos′i·ty** (-pŏs′ĭ-tē), **pom′pous·ness** *n.* **—pom′pous·ly** *adv.*

Ponce de Le·ón (pŏns′ də lē-ōn′, pōn′sĕ), **Juan** (1460–1521) ▸ Spanish explorer.

pon·cho (pŏn′chō) ▸ *n., pl.* **-chos.** **1.** A blanketlike cloak having a hole in the center for the head. **2.** A similar hooded garment used as a raincoat.

pond (pŏnd) ▸ *n.* A still body of water smaller than a lake.

pon·der (pŏn′dər) ▸ *v.* **1.** To weigh carefully in the mind. **2.** To reflect on; meditate. **—pon′der·a·ble** *adj.*

pon·der·o·sa pine (pŏn′də-rō′sə) ▸ *n.* A tall timber tree of W North America, having long, dark green needles.

pon·der·ous (pŏn′dər-əs) ▸ *adj.* **1.** Having great weight. **2.** Lacking fluency; dull. **—pon′der·ous·ly** *adv.* **—pon′der·ous·ness, pon′der·os′i·ty** (-ŏs′ĭ-tē) *n.*

pon·gee (pŏn-jē′, pŏn′jē) ▸ *n.* A soft thin silk cloth.

pon·iard (pŏn′yərd) ▸ *n.* A dagger.

pons (pŏnz) ▸ *n., pl.* **pon·tes** (pŏn′tēz). A slender tissue joining two parts of an organ.

Pon·ti·ac (pŏn′tē-ăk′) (1720?–69) ▸ Ottawa leader.

pon·tiff (pŏn′tĭf) ▸ *n.* **1.** The pope. **2.** A bishop.

pon·tif·i·cal (pŏn-tĭf′ĭ-kəl) ▸ *adj.* **1.** Of or suitable for a pontiff. **2.** Pompously dogmatic; pretentious. ▸ *n.* **pontificals** The vestments and insignia of a pontiff.

pon·tif·i·cate (pŏn-tĭf′ĭ-kĭt, -kāt′) ▸ *n.* The office or term of office of a pontiff. ▸ *v.* (-kāt′) **-cat·ed, -cat·ing.** **1.** To express opinions or judgments in a dogmatic way. **2.** To

THESAURUS

polysyllabic *adj.* Having many syllables ▸ sesquipedal, sesquipedalian.

polyurethane *n.* —*See* FINISH.

polyurethane *v.* —*See* FINISH (2).

pomp *n.* —*See* ARRAY, GLITTER (2).

pomposity or **pompousness** *n.* —*See* ARROGANCE, PRETENTIOUSNESS.

pompous *adj.* Characterized by an exaggerated show of dignity or self-importance ▸ grandiose, hoity-toity, pontifical, pretentious, puffed-up, puffy, self-important. *Informal:* high-talutin. [*Compare* ARROGANT, BOASTFUL, SNOBBISH.]

ponder *v.* To think or think about carefully and at length ▸ chew on (*or* over), cogitate, consider, contemplate, deliberate, entertain, excogitate, meditate, mull, muse, reflect, revolve, ruminate, study, think, think out, think over, think through, turn over, weigh. *Idioms:* cudgel one's brains, put on one's thinking cap, rack one's brain. [*Compare* BROOD, THINK.]

ponderable *adj.* —*See* PERCEPTIBLE.

pondering *n.* —*See* THOUGHT.

ponderosity or **ponderousness** *n.* —*See* HEAVINESS.

ponderous *adj.* Lacking fluency or grace ▸ elephantine, ham-handed, heavy, heavy-footed, heavy-handed, labored, leaden, lumbering, plodding. [*Compare* AWKWARD.] —*See also* BULKY (1), HEAVY (1).

pontifical *adj.* —*See* POMPOUS.

pontificate *v.* To indulge in moral

administer the office of a pontiff. **—pon·tif′i·ca′tion** *n.*

pon·toon (pŏn-to͞on′) ▸ *n.* **1.** A flat-bottomed boat or other structure used to support a floating bridge. **2.** A float on a seaplane.

po·ny (pō′nē) ▸ *n., pl.* **-nies. 1.** A small horse. **2.** A word-for-word translation of a foreign language text, esp. one used secretly in studying or test-taking.

po·ny·tail (pō′nē-tāl′) ▸ *n.* A hairstyle in which the hair is drawn back and fastened so as to hang down like a horse's tail.

pooch (po͝och) ▸ *n. Slang* A dog.

poo·dle (po͞od′l) ▸ *n.* A dog bred in various sizes and having thick curly hair.

pooh (po͞o) ▸ *interj.* Used to express disdain.

Pooh-Bah or **pooh-bah** (po͞o′bä′) ▸ *n.* **1.** A pompous ineffectual official. **2.** A person in high office.

pooh-pooh (po͞o′po͞o′) ▸ *v. Informal* To express contempt for; make light of.

pool[1] (po͞ol) ▸ *n.* **1.** A small pond. **2.** A puddle. **3.** A deep or still place in a stream. **4.** A swimming pool. **—pool** *v.*

pool[2] (po͞ol) ▸ *n.* **1.** A fund containing all the money bet in a game of chance or on the outcome of an event. **2.** A grouping of resources for the common advantage of the participants. **3.** An agreement between competing business concerns to establish certain controls for common profit. **4.** Any of several games played on a six-pocket billiard table. ▸ *v.* **1.** To put into a fund for use by all. **2.** To join or form a pool.

pool·room (po͞ol′ro͞om′, -ro͝om′) ▸ *n.* A place for the playing of pool or billiards.

pool table ▸ *n.* A six-pocket billiards table on which pool is played.

poop[1] (po͞op) ▸ *n. Naut.* **1.** A superstructure at the stern of a ship. **2.** A poop deck.

poop[2] (po͞op) ▸ *v. Slang* To become or cause to become fatigued.

poop[3] (po͞op) ▸ *n. Slang* Inside information.

poop deck ▸ *n.* The aftermost deck of a ship.

poor (po͝or) ▸ *adj.* **-er, -est. 1.** Having little or no wealth. **2.** Lacking a specified resource or quality. **3.** Inferior: *a poor performance.* **4.** Lacking in value; insufficient: *poor wages.* **5.** Humble. **6.** Pitiable. **—poor′ly** *adv.* **—poor′ness** *n.*

poor box ▸ *n.* A box in a church used for collecting alms.

poor boy ▸ *n. Regional* See **submarine** 2.

poor·house (po͝or′hous′) ▸ *n.* An establishment maintained at public expense as housing for the homeless.

poor-mouth (po͝or′mouth′, -mou*th*′) ▸ *v.* To claim poverty as an excuse or defense.

pop[1] (pŏp) ▸ *v.* **popped, pop·ping. 1.** To make or cause to make a short, sharp, explosive sound. **2.** To burst open with such a sound. **3.** To appear abruptly. **4.** To open wide suddenly. **5.** To shoot a firearm, such as a pistol. **6.** To put or thrust suddenly. ▸ *n.* **1.** A sudden sharp, explosive sound. **2.** A shot with a firearm. **3.** *Regional* See **soft drink.**

pop[2] (pŏp) ▸ *n. Informal* Father.

pop[3] (pŏp) ▸ *adj. Informal* **1.** Of or for the general public; popular: *pop psychology.* **2.** Of or specializing in popular music: *a pop singer.* **3.** Suggestive of pop art. **—pop** *n.*

pop. ▸ *abbr.* population

pop art ▸ *n.* A form of art that depicts objects from everyday life and employs techniques of commercial art.

pop·corn (pŏp′kôrn′) ▸ *n.* A variety of corn having hard kernels that burst to form small white puffs when heated.

pope (pōp) ▸ *n.* often **Pope** The bishop of Rome and head of the Roman Catholic Church.

Pope, Alexander (1688–1744) ▸ English writer.

pop-eyed (pŏp′īd′) ▸ *adj.* **1.** Having bulging eyes. **2.** Amazed.

pop fly ▸ *n. Baseball* A short high fly ball.

pop·gun (pŏp′gŭn′) ▸ *n.* A toy gun that makes a popping noise.

pop·in·jay (pŏp′ĭn-jā′) ▸ *n.* A vain, talkative person.

pop·lar (pŏp′lər) ▸ *n.* **1.** Any of several trees having unisexual flowers borne in catkins. **2.** See **tulip tree.**

pop·lin (pŏp′lĭn) ▸ *n.* A ribbed fabric used in making clothing and upholstery.

pop·o·ver (pŏp′ō′vər) ▸ *n.* A very light, hollow muffin made with eggs, milk, and flour.

pop·py (pŏp′ē) ▸ *n., pl.* **-pies.** Any of numerous plants having showy red, orange, or white flowers and a milky juice.

pop·py·cock (pŏp′ē-kŏk′) ▸ *n.* Senseless talk.

pop-top (pŏp′tŏp′) ▸ *adj.* Having a tab that can be pulled up or off to make an opening in a container. **—pop′-top′** *n.*

pop·u·lace (pŏp′yə-lĭs) ▸ *n.* **1.** The general public; masses. **2.** A population.

pop·u·lar (pŏp′yə-lər) ▸ *adj.* **1.** Widely liked or appreciated. **2.** Of, representing, or carried on by the people at large. **3.** Accepted by or prevalent among the people in general. **—pop′u·lar′i·ty** (-lăr′ĭ-tē) *n.* **—pop′u·lar·ly** *adv.*

popular front ▸ *n.* A political coalition of leftist parties against fascism.

pop·u·lar·ize (pŏp′yə-lə-rīz′) ▸ *v.* **-ized, -iz·ing.** To make popular. **—pop′u·lar·i·za′tion** *n.* **—pop′u·lar·iz′er** *n.*

pop·u·late (pŏp′yə-lāt′) ▸ *v.* **-lat·ed, -lat·ing. 1.** To supply with inhabitants. **2.** To inhabit.

pop·u·la·tion (pŏp′yə-lā′shən) ▸ *n.* **1.** All of the people inhabiting a specified area. **2.** *Ecol.* All the organisms of the same kind living in a specified habitat. **3.** The set of individuals, items, or data from which a statistical sample is taken.

population explosion ▸ *n.* Great expansion of a biological population, esp. the unchecked growth in human population resulting from a decrease in infant mortality and an increase in longevity.

pop·u·lism (pŏp′yə-lĭz′əm) ▸ *n.* A political philosophy opposing the concentration of power in the hands of corporations, the government, and the rich. **—pop′u·list** *n.*

pop·u·lous (pŏp′yə-ləs) ▸ *adj.* Containing many inhabitants; having a large population. **—pop′u·lous·ness** *n.*

pop-up (pŏp′ŭp′) ▸ *n.* **1.** A device or illustration that pops up. **2.** *Baseball* See **pop fly.**

por·ce·lain (pôr′sə-lĭn) ▸ *n.* **1.** A hard white translucent ceramic. **2.** An object made of porcelain.

porch (pôrch) ▸ *n.* **1.** A covered platform, usu. having a separate roof, at an entrance to a building. **2.** An open or enclosed gallery or room attached to the outside of a building.

THESAURUS

reflection, usually pompously ▸ edify, moralize, preach, sermonize. [*Compare* CHASTISE.]

pony *n.* —*See* TRANSLATION.

pool *n.* —*See* ALLIANCE, BET.

poop[1] *v.* —*See* TIRE (1).

poop out *v.* —*See* MALFUNCTION, TIRE (2).

poop[2] *n.* —*See* DRIP (2).

pooped *adj.* —*See* TIRED (1).

poor *adj.* Having little or no money or wealth ▸ bankrupt, beggarly, busted, destitute, down-and-out, impecunious, impoverished, indigent, insolvent, mendicant, necessitous, needy, penniless, penurious, poverty-stricken. *Informal:* broke, strapped. *Idioms:* flat stone broke, hard up, on one's uppers, on the skids, on welfare. [*Compare* UNFORTUNATE.] —*See also* BAD (1), DEPRESSED (2), MEAGER, PITIFUL, SHODDY.

poorly *adj.* —*See* SICK (1).

poorness *n.* —*See* POVERTY.

pop[1] *v.* **1.** To come open or fly apart suddenly and violently, as from internal pressure ▸ blow (out), burst, explode. *Slang:* bust. **2.** To discharge a gun or firearm ▸ blast (away), fire (away *or* off), pop off, shoot (away *or* off). *Idioms:* go bang-bang, open fire, take a shot (*or* potshot). —*See also* CRACK (2), HIT.

pop in *v.* —*See* VISIT.

pop off *v.* —*See* DIE.

pop *n.* —*See* CRACK (1).

pop[2] *n.* —*See* FATHER.

poppycock *n.* —*See* NONSENSE.

populace *n.* —*See* COMMONALTY.

popular *adj.* Of, representing, or carried on by people at large ▸ civic, civil, communal, democratic, general, national, public, social, societal. [*Compare* COMMON.] —*See also* ACCEPTABLE (2), FAMOUS, FAVORITE, GENERAL (2), PREVAILING.

popularize *v.* —*See* INTRODUCE (1), PROMOTE (3).

popularity *n.* —*See* FAME.

populate *v.* To live in a place, as does a people ▸ inhabit, occupy, people. [*Compare* LIVE, SETTLE.]

por·cine (pôr′sīn′) ▸ *adj.* Of or resembling swine or a pig.
por·cu·pine (pôr′kyə-pīn′) ▸ *n.* Any of various rodents having long sharp quills.
pore[1] (pôr) ▸ *v.* **pored, por·ing.** 1. To read or study carefully and attentively. 2. To gaze intently; stare. 3. To meditate deeply; ponder.
pore[2] (pôr) ▸ *n.* A minute opening, as in an animal's skin or a plant leaf, for the passage of fluid.
pork (pôrk) ▸ *n.* The flesh of a pig or hog used as food.
pork barrel ▸ *n. Slang* A government project or appropriation that benefits a specific locale and a legislator's constituents.
pork·er (pôr′kər) ▸ *n.* A fattened young pig.
porn (pôrn) also **por·no** (pôr′nō) ▸ *n. Slang* Pornography. **—porn** *adj.*
por·nog·ra·phy (pôr-nŏg′rə-fē) ▸ *n.* Pictures, writing, or other material that is sexually explicit and intended to arouse sexual passion. **—por·nog′ra·pher** *n.* **—por′no·graph′ic** (-nə-grăf′ĭk) *adj.*
po·rous (pôr′əs) ▸ *adj.* 1. Full of or having pores. 2. Admitting the passage of gas or liquid through pores or interstices. **—po·ros′i·ty** (pə-rŏs′ĭ-tē) *n.* **—po′rous·ly** *adv.* **—po′rous·ness** *n.*
por·phy·ry (pôr′fə-rē) ▸ *n., pl.* **-ries.** A fine-grained igneous rock containing relatively large crystals, esp. of feldspar.
por·poise (pôr′pəs) ▸ *n., pl.* **-poise** or **-pois·es.** Any of several toothed whales of oceanic waters, characterized by a blunt snout and a triangular dorsal fin.
por·ridge (pôr′ĭj, pŏr′-) ▸ *n.* A soft food made by boiling oatmeal or another meal in water or milk.
por·rin·ger (pôr′ĭn-jər, pŏr′-) ▸ *n.* A shallow cup or bowl with a handle.
port[1] (pôrt) ▸ *n.* 1. A city or town on a waterway with facilities for loading and unloading ships. 2. A harbor. 3. *Comp. Sci.* A connection point for a peripheral device.
port[2] (pôrt) ▸ *n.* The left-hand side of a ship or aircraft facing forward. ▸ *adj.* Of or relating to the port.
port[3] (pôrt) ▸ *n.* 1. A porthole. 2. An opening, as in a cylinder, for the passage of steam or fluid.
port[4] also **Port** (pôrt) ▸ *n.* A rich sweet fortified wine.
por·ta·ble (pôr′tə-bəl) ▸ *adj.* Carried or moved with ease. **—por′ta·bil′i·ty, por′ta·ble·ness** *n.* **—por′ta·ble** *n.* **—por′ta·bly** *adv.*
port·age (pôr′tĭj, pôr-täzh′) ▸ *n.* 1. The carrying of boats and supplies overland between two waterways. 2. A track or route used for such carrying. ▸ *v.* **-aged, -ag·ing.** To transport or travel by portage.
por·tal (pôr′tl) ▸ *n.* 1. A doorway or entrance, esp. a large and imposing one. 2. *Comp. Sci.* A website considered as an entry point to other websites, often by being or providing access to a search engine.
Port-au-Prince (pôrt′ō-prĭns′) ▸ The capital of Haiti, in the SW part.
port·cul·lis (pôrt-kŭl′ĭs) ▸ *n.* A grating suspended in the gateway of a fortified place and lowered to block passage.
porte-co·chère or **porte-co·chere** (pôrt′kō-shâr′) ▸ *n.* An enclosure over a driveway at the entrance of a building to provide shelter.
por·tend (pôr-tĕnd′) ▸ *v.* 1. To serve as an omen or warning of; presage. 2. To indicate; forecast.
por·tent (pôr′tĕnt′) ▸ *n.* 1. An indication of something about to occur; omen. 2. Something amazing or marvelous; prodigy.
por·ten·tous (pôr-tĕn′təs) ▸ *adj.* 1. Of or constituting a portent. 2. Exciting wonder and awe. 3. Pompous; pretentiously weighty. **—por·ten′tous·ness** *n.*
por·ter[1] (pôr′tər) ▸ *n.* 1. A person employed to carry travelers' baggage. 2. A railroad employee who waits on passengers. 3. A maintenance worker.
por·ter[2] (pôr′tər) ▸ *n. Chiefly Brit.* One in charge of a gate or door.
por·ter[3] (pôr′tər) ▸ *n.* A dark beer made from browned or charred malt.
por·ter·house (pôr′tər-hous′) ▸ *n.* A cut of beef having a T-bone and a sizable piece of tenderloin.
port·fo·li·o (pôrt-fō′lē-ō′) ▸ *n., pl.* **-os.** 1. A portable case for holding loose papers or drawings. 2. The office or post of a cabinet member or minister of state. 3. A group of investments.
port·hole (pôrt′hōl′) ▸ *n.* A small, usu. circular window in a ship's side.
por·ti·co (pôr′tĭ-kō′) ▸ *n., pl.* **-coes** or **-cos.** A porch or walkway with a roof supported by columns, often leading to the entrance of a building.
por·tière or **por·tiere** (pôr-tyâr′) ▸ *n.* A heavy curtain hung across a doorway.
por·tion (pôr′shən) ▸ *n.* 1. A part of a whole. 2. A part allotted to a person or group. 3. A person's lot or fate. ▸ *v.* 1. To distribute in portions. 2. To provide with a share.
Port·land (pôrt′lənd) ▸ 1. A city of SW ME S of Lewiston. 2. A city of NW OR on the Columbia R. **—Port′land·er** *n.*
Portland cement or **portland cement** ▸ *n.* A hydraulic cement made by heating and pulverizing a mixture of limestone and clay.
port·ly (pôrt′lē) ▸ *adj.* **-li·er, -li·est.** Comfortably stout; corpulent. **—port′li·ness** *n.*
port·man·teau (pôrt-măn′tō, pôrt′măn-tō′) ▸ *n., pl.* **-teaus** or **-teaux** (-tōz, -tōz′). A large leather suitcase with two hinged compartments.
port of call ▸ *n.* A port where ships dock in the course of voyages to load or unload cargo, obtain supplies, or undergo repairs.
port of entry ▸ *n.* A place where travelers or goods may enter or leave a country under official supervision.
por·trait (pôr′trĭt, -trāt′) ▸ *n.* A likeness of a person, esp. one showing the face, created by a painter or photographer. **—por′trait·ist** *n.*
por·trai·ture (pôr′trĭ-chŏŏr′) ▸ *n.* The art or practice of making portraits.
por·tray (pôr-trā′) ▸ *v.* 1. To depict pictorially. 2. To describe in words. 3. To represent dramatically, as on the stage. **—por·tray′al** *n.* **—por·tray′er** *n.*
Port Stanley ▸ See **Stanley.**
Por·tu·gal (pôr′chə-gəl) ▸ A country of SW Europe on the W Iberian Peninsula.
Por·tu·guese (pôr′chə-gēz′, -gēs′) ▸ *n., pl.* **-guese.** 1. A native or inhabitant of Portugal. 2. The Romance language of Portugal and Brazil. **—Por′tu·guese′** *adj.*
Portuguese man-of-war ▸ *n.* A complex marine organism of warm seas, having a bluish, bladderlike float from which hang numerous long stinging tentacles.
por·tu·lac·a (pôr′chə-lăk′ə) ▸ *n.* A fleshy South American plant having showy flowers.
pose (pōz) ▸ *v.* **posed, pos·ing.** 1. To assume or cause to assume a particular position or posture, as in sitting for a portrait. 2. To affect a particular attitude. 3. To represent

THESAURUS

porcine *adj.* —*See* FAT (1).
pork *n.* The political appointments or jobs that are at the disposal of those politicians who are in power ▸ patronage, spoils.
porky *adj.* —*See* FAT (1).
pornography *n.* —*See* OBSCENITY (2).
port *n.* —*See* COVER (1), HARBOR.
portable *adj.* —*See* MOBILE (1).
portend *v.* —*See* FORESHADOW, PREDICT, THREATEN (1).
portent *n.* —*See* OMEN.
portentous *adj.* —*See* FATEFUL (1).
portion *n.* 1. A right or legal share in something ▸ claim, interest, stake, title. [*Compare* RIGHT.] 2. That which is inevitably destined ▸ destiny, fate, fortune, kismet, lot, predestination. —*See also* ALLOTMENT, CUT (2), FATE (2), PART (1), QUANTITY (2), SERVING.
portion *v.* —*See* DISTRIBUTE.
portly *adj.* —*See* FAT (1).
portrait *n.* —*See* DOUBLE.
portray *v.* —*See* ACT (3), REPRESENT (2).
portrayal *n.* —*See* INTERPRETATION, REPRESENTATION.
pose *v.* 1. To assume a particular position, as for a portrait ▸ attitudinize, model, posture, sit. *Idiom:* strike an attitude. 2. To seek an answer to a question ▸ ask, put, raise. [*Compare* SAY.] —*See also* ACT (2), PROPOSE.
pose as *v.* —*See* IMPERSONATE.
pose *n.* The way in which one is placed or arranged ▸ arrangement, attitude, position, posture. —*See also*

oneself falsely. 4. To place in a specific position. 5. To put forward; present: *pose a threat.* ▸ *n.* 1. A bodily attitude or position, esp. one assumed for an artist. 2. A studied attitude assumed for effect. **—pos′a·ble** *adj.*

Po·sei·don (pō-sīd′n, pə-) ▸ *n. Gk. Myth.* The god of the sea and brother of Zeus.

pos·er[1] (pō′zər) ▸ *n.* One who poses.

pos·er[2] (pō′zər) ▸ *n.* A baffling problem.

po·seur (pō-zœr′) ▸ *n.* One who affects a particular attitude or manner to impress others.

posh (pŏsh) ▸ *adj.* Fashionable. **—posh′ly** *adv.* **—posh′ness** *n.*

pos·it (pŏz′ĭt) ▸ *v.* To affirm or assume the existence of; postulate.

po·si·tion (pə-zĭsh′ən) ▸ *n.* 1. A place or location. 2. The right or appropriate place. 3. The way in which something or someone is placed. 4. A situation relative to circumstances: *in a position to bargain.* 5. A point of view. 6. Status; rank. 7. A post of employment; job. ▸ *v.* To put in position. **—po·si′tion·al** *adj.* **—po·si′tion·er** *n.*

pos·i·tive (pŏz′ĭ-tĭv) ▸ *adj.* 1. Marked by or displaying certainty or affirmation: *a positive answer.* 2. Explicitly expressed: *a positive demand.* 3. Admitting of no doubt; irrefutable. 4. Very sure; confident. 5. Real. 6. *Math.* Of or designating: a. A quantity greater than zero. b. A quantity, number, angle, or direction opposite to another designated as negative. 7. *Phys.* Of or designating electric charge of a sign opposite to that of an electron. 8. Having the areas of light and dark in their original and normal relationship, as in a photographic print. 9. *Gram.* Of or being the simple uncompared degree of an adjective or adverb. ▸ *n.* 1. A photographic image in which the lights and darks appear as they do in nature. 2. *Gram.* The positive degree of an adjective or adverb. **—pos′i·tive·ly** *adv.* **—pos′i·tive·ness, pos′i·tiv′i·ty** *n.*

pos·i·tron (pŏz′ĭ-trŏn′) ▸ *n.* The antiparticle of the electron.

pos·se (pŏs′ē) ▸ *n.* A group of people summoned by a sheriff to aid in law enforcement.

pos·sess (pə-zĕs′) ▸ *v.* 1. To have as property; own. 2. To have as an attribute. 3. To exert influence or control over; dominate. **—pos·ses′sor** *n.*

pos·sessed (pə-zĕst′) ▸ *adj.* 1. Controlled by or as if by a spirit or other force. 2. Calm; collected.

pos·ses·sion (pə-zĕsh′ən) ▸ *n.* 1a. The act or fact of possessing. b. The state of being possessed. 2. Something owned or possessed. 3. **possessions** Wealth or property. 4. A territory subject to foreign control. 5. Self-control. 6. The state of being dominated by evil spirits. 7. *Sports* Physical control of the ball or puck.

pos·ses·sive (pə-zĕs′ĭv) ▸ *adj.* 1. Having or manifesting a desire to control or dominate: *a possessive parent.* 2. *Gram.* Of or being a noun or pronoun case that indicates possession. ▸ *n. Gram.* 1. The possessive case. 2. A possessive form or construction. **—pos·ses′sive·ly** *adv.* **—pos·ses′sive·ness** *n.*

pos·si·ble (pŏs′ə-bəl) ▸ *adj.* 1. Capable of happening, existing, or being true. 2. Capable of occurring or being done. 3. Potential. **—pos′si·bil′i·ty** *n.* **—pos′si·bly** *adv.*

pos·sum (pŏs′əm) ▸ *n.* An opossum.

post[1] (pōst) ▸ *n.* 1. A stake set upright into the ground to serve as a marker or support. 2. Something similar to a post. 3. *Comp. Sci.* An electronic message sent to a newsgroup. ▸ *v.* 1. To display in a place of public view. 2. To announce by or as if by posters. 3. To put up signs on (property) warning against trespassing. 4. To publish (a name) on a list. 5. *Comp. Sci.* To send (an electronic message) to a newsgroup.

post[2] (pōst) ▸ *n.* 1. A military base. 2. An assigned station, as of a sentry. 3. A position of employment. 4. A trading post. ▸ *v.* 1. To assign to a position or station. 2. To put forward; present: *post bail.*

post[3] (pōst) ▸ *n.* 1. A delivery of mail. 2. *Chiefly Brit.* a. A governmental system for transporting and delivering the mail. b. A post office. ▸ *v.* 1. To mail (a letter or package). 2. To inform of the latest news. 3. To make entries in (a ledger). 4. To travel with speed.

post– ▸ *pref.* 1. After; later: *postdate.* 2. Behind; posterior to: *postnasal.*

post·age (pō′stĭj) ▸ *n.* The charge for mailing an item.

post·al (pō′stəl) ▸ *adj.* Of or relating to a post office or mail service. **—post′al·ly** *adv.*

postal card ▸ *n.* An unadorned card printed with the image of a postage stamp, issued by a government.

post card also **post·card** (pōst′kärd′) ▸ *n.* 1. A commercially printed card used for sending a short message through the mail. 2. See **postal card.**

post chaise ▸ *n.* A closed, four-wheeled, horse-drawn carriage.

post·date (pōst-dāt′, pōst′-) ▸ *v.* 1. To put a date on (e.g., a check) that is later than the actual date. 2. To occur later than.

post·doc·tor·al (pōst-dŏk′tər-əl) also **post·doc·tor·ate** (-ĭt) ▸ *adj.* Of or engaged in academic study beyond the doctorate.

post·er (pō′stər) ▸ *n.* A large, usu. printed placard, bill, or announcement posted to advertise or publicize something.

pos·te·ri·or (pŏ-stîr′ē-ər, pō-) ▸ *adj.* 1. Located behind a part or toward the rear of a structure. 2. Relating to the hind or back part of a body. 3. Following in time; subsequent. ▸ *n.* The buttocks. **—pos·te′ri·or·ly** *adv.*

pos·ter·i·ty (pŏ-stĕr′ĭ-tē) ▸ *n.* 1. Future generations. 2. All of a person's descendants.

THESAURUS

AFFECTATION, FAÇADE (2), POSTURE (1).

poser *n.* —*See* HYPOCRITE.

posh *adj.* —*See* EXCLUSIVE (3).

posit *v.* —*See* SUPPOSE (1).

position *n.* 1. The place where a person or thing is located ▸ emplacement, location, locus, place, placement, point, site, situation, spot. 2. The way in which one is placed or arranged ▸ arrangement, attitude, pose, posture. 3. A post of employment ▸ appointment, berth, billet, job, office, place, situation, slot, spot, work. *Slang:* gig. [*Compare* BUSINESS.] —*See also* BEARING (3), BELIEF (1), DOCTRINE, PLACE (1), POSTURE (2), VIEWPOINT.

position *v.* To put in a certain position or location ▸ base, deposit, emplace, install, lay, locate, place, put, set, site, situate, spot, stick. [*Compare* STATION.]

positioning *n.* —*See* ARRANGEMENT (1).

positive *adj.* —*See* CERTAIN (2), DEFINITE (1), DEFINITE (3), FAVORABLE (2), OPTIMISTIC, SURE (1), UTTER[2].

positively *adv.* —*See* ABSOLUTELY, FLATLY, REALLY.

positivity or **positiveness** *n.* —*See* SURENESS.

possess *v.* To dominate the mind or thoughts of ▸ fixate, obsess, preoccupy. [*Compare* ABSORB, GRIP.] —*See also* BEAR (3), CARRY (2), COMMAND (2).

possessed *adj.* —*See* CALM.

possession *n.* An area subject to rule by an outside power ▸ colony, dependency, mandate, protectorate, province, satellite, settlement, territory. —*See also* OWNERSHIP.

possessions *n.* —*See* EFFECTS, HOLDINGS.

possessive *adj.* Fearful of the loss of position or affection ▸ clinging, clutching, green-eyed, jealous. [*Compare* ENVIOUS.]

possessor *n.* —*See* OWNER.

possibility *n.* 1. Something that may occur or be done ▸ contingency, eventuality, potential, potentiality. [*Compare* EXPECTATION.] 2. Indication of future success or development ▸ makings, potential, promise, prospects. [*Compare* MATERIAL.] —*See also* CHANCE (3).

possible *adj.* Capable of occurring or being done ▸ achievable, attainable, doable, feasible, performable, practicable, viable, workable. *Idiom:* within reach. —*See also* CONCEIVABLE, LATENT, OPTIONAL, PROBABLE.

possibly *adv.* —*See* MAYBE.

post[1] *v.* To gain a point or points in a game or contest ▸ score, tally. *Informal:* notch. *Idiom:* make a goal (*or* point).

post[2] *n.* —*See* BASE[1] (1), COLUMN, LOOKOUT (2).

post *v.* To appoint and send to a particular place ▸ assign, set, station. [*Compare* POSITION.] —*See also* GAMBLE (2).

post[3] *v.* —*See* LIST[1], SEND (1).

poster *n.* —*See* SIGN (2).

posterior *adj.* Following something else in time ▸ after, later, subsequent, ulterior. [*Compare* FOLLOWING.] —*See also* BACK.

posterior *n.* —*See* BUTTOCKS.

posterity *n.* —*See* PROGENY.

pos·tern (pō′stərn, pŏs′tərn) ▸ *n.* A rear gate, esp. in a fort or castle.

Post Exchange ▸ A service mark for a store on a military base that sells goods to military personnel and their families.

post·grad·u·ate (pōst-grăj′o͞o-ĭt, -āt′) ▸ *adj.* Of or relating to advanced study after graduation from college. ▸ *n.* One engaged in postgraduate study.

post·haste (pōst′hāst′) ▸ *adv.* With great speed; rapidly.

post·hu·mous (pŏs′chə-məs) ▸ *adj.* **1.** Occurring or continuing after one's death. **2.** Published after the writer's death. **—post′hu·mous·ly** *adv.*

post·hyp·not·ic suggestion (pōst′hĭp-nŏt′ĭk) ▸ *n.* A suggestion made to a hypnotized person that specifies an action to be performed after awakening.

pos·til·ion also **pos·til·lion** (pō-stĭl′yən, pŏ-) ▸ *n.* One who rides the near horse of the leaders to guide the horses drawing a coach.

Post-it (pōst′ĭt′) ▸ A trademark for a slip of notepaper with an adhesive edge.

post·lude (pōst′lo͞od′) ▸ *n.* An organ voluntary played at the end of a church service.

post·man (pōst′mən) ▸ *n.* See **mailman**.

post·mark (pōst′märk′) ▸ *n.* An official mark stamped on mail that cancels the stamp and records the date and place of mailing. **—post′mark′** *v.*

post·mas·ter (pōst′măs′tər) ▸ *n.* A man in charge of a post office.

postmaster general ▸ *n., pl.* **postmasters general**. The executive head of a national postal service.

post me·rid·i·em (mə-rĭd′ē-əm) ▸ *adv. & adj.* After noon. Used chiefly in the abbreviated form to specify the hour: *10:30* **P.M.**; *a* **P.M.** *appointment.*

post·mis·tress (pōst′mĭs′trĭs) ▸ *n.* A woman in charge of a post office.

post·mor·tem (pōst-môr′təm) ▸ *adj.* **1.** Occurring or done after death. **2.** Of or relating to a postmortem. ▸ *n.* **1.** See **autopsy**. **2.** *Informal* An analysis or review of a completed event. **—post mor′tem** *adv.*

post·na·sal (pōst-nā′zəl) ▸ *adj.* Located or occurring posterior to the nose.

post·na·tal (pōst-nāt′l) ▸ *adj.* Of or occurring after birth. **—post·na′tal·ly** *adv.*

post office ▸ *n.* **1.** The public department responsible for the transportation and delivery of the mails. **2.** A local office where mail is processed and stamps are sold.

post·op·er·a·tive (pōst-ŏp′ər-ə-tĭv, -ŏp′rə-, -ŏp′ə-rā′-) ▸ *adj.* Happening or done after surgery. **—post·op′er·a·tive·ly** *adv.*

post·paid (pōst′pād′) ▸ *adj.* With the postage paid in advance.

post·par·tum (pōst-pär′təm) ▸ *adj.* Of or occurring after childbirth.

post·pone (pōst-pōn′, pōs-pōn′) ▸ *v.* **-poned, -pon·ing**. To delay until a future time; put off. **—post·pone′ment** *n.*

post·script (pōst′skrĭpt′, pōs′skrĭpt′) ▸ *n.* A message added to a letter after the writer's signature.

pos·tu·lant (pŏs′chə-lənt) ▸ *n.* A candidate for admission into a religious order.

pos·tu·late (pŏs′chə-lāt′) ▸ *v.* **-lat·ed, -lat·ing**. To assume or assert the truth or reality of, esp. as a basis of an argument. ▸ *n.* (pŏs′chə-lĭt, -lāt′) Something assumed without proof as being self-evident or generally accepted. **—pos′tu·la′tion** *n.*

pos·ture (pŏs′chər) ▸ *n.* **1a.** A position or attitude of the body or of body parts. **b.** An attitude; pose: *assumed a posture of defiance.* **2.** A stance with regard to something. **3.** A frame of mind; attitude. ▸ *v.* **-tured, -tur·ing**. To assume an exaggerated or unnatural pose or mental attitude. **—pos′tur·al** *adj.* **—pos′tur·er, pos′tur·ist** *n.*

po·sy (pō′zē) ▸ *n., pl.* **-sies**. A flower or bunch of flowers.

pot[1] (pŏt) ▸ *n.* **1.** A round cooking vessel with a handle. **2.** Something resembling a pot in appearance or function. **3.** *Games* The total amount staked by all the players in one hand at cards. **4.** *Informal* A common fund. ▸ *v.* **pot·ted, pot·ting**. **1.** To place or plant in a pot. **2.** To cook or preserve in a pot.

pot[2] (pŏt) ▸ *n. Slang* Marijuana.

po·ta·ble (pō′tə-bəl) ▸ *adj.* Fit to drink.

pot·ash (pŏt′ăsh′) ▸ *n.* **1.** See **potassium carbonate**. **2.** See **potassium hydroxide**. **3.** Any of several compounds containing potassium, esp. soluble compounds used chiefly in fertilizers.

po·tas·si·um (pə-tăs′ē-əm) ▸ *n. Symbol* **K** A soft, silver-white, highly or explosively reactive metallic element found naturally only in compounds and used in fertilizers and soaps. At. no. 19. **—po·tas′sic** *adj.*

potassium bromide ▸ *n.* A white crystalline solid or powder, KBr, used as a sedative and in lithography.

potassium carbonate ▸ *n.* A granular powder used in making glass, enamels, and soaps.

potassium cyanide ▸ *n.* An extremely poisonous white compound used in electroplating, photography, and as an insecticide.

potassium hydroxide ▸ *n.* A caustic white solid used as a bleach and in making soaps, dyes, and alkaline batteries; lye.

potassium nitrate ▸ *n.* A white crystalline compound used to pickle meat and in making explosives and fertilizers; saltpeter.

po·ta·tion (pō-tā′shən) ▸ *n.* **1.** The act of drinking. **2.** A drink, esp. an alcoholic beverage.

po·ta·to (pə-tā′tō) ▸ *n., pl.* **-toes**. **1.** A South American plant widely cultivated for its starchy edible tubers. **2.** A tuber of this plant.

potato chip ▸ *n.* A thin slice of potato fried in deep fat until crisp and then salted.

Pot·a·wat·o·mi (pŏt′ə-wŏt′ə-mē) ▸ *n., pl.* **-mi** or **-mis**. **1.** A member of a Native American people with populations in Oklahoma, Kansas, Michigan, and Ontario. **2.** The Algonquian language of the Potawatomi.

pot·bel·ly (pŏt′bĕl′ē) ▸ *n.* A protruding belly. **—pot′bel′lied** *adj.*

pot·boil·er (pŏt′boi′lər) ▸ *n.* A literary or artistic work of poor quality, produced quickly for profit.

pot cheese ▸ *n.* See **cottage cheese**.

po·tent (pōt′nt) ▸ *adj.* **1.** Possessing strength; powerful. **2.** Exerting or capable of exerting strong effects. **3.** Able to perform sexual intercourse. Used of a male. **—po′ten·cy** *n.* **—po′tent·ly** *adv.*

po·ten·tate (pōt′n-tāt′) ▸ *n.* One who has the power and position to rule over others; monarch.

po·ten·tial (pə-tĕn′shəl) ▸ *adj.* Capable of being but not yet in existence; latent. ▸ *n.* **1.** Capacity for growth, development, or coming into being. **2.** *Symbol* **V** *Elect.* The potential energy of a unit charge measured with respect to

THESAURUS

posthaste *adv.* —*See* FAST.

posting *n.* —*See* ENTRY.

postpone *v.* —*See* DEFER[1].

postponement *n.* —*See* DELAY (1).

postulant *n.* An entrant who has not yet taken the final vows of a religious order ▸ neophyte, novice, novitiate.

postulate *v.* —*See* CLAIM, SUPPOSE (1).

postulate *n.* —*See* ASSUMPTION.

postulated *adj.* —*See* THEORETICAL (2).

posture *n.* **1.** A way of holding or carrying one's body ▸ attitude, carriage, pose, stance. [*Compare* BEARING.] **2.** A frame of mind affecting one's thoughts or behavior ▸ attitude, mindset, outlook, perspective, philosophy, position, stance. [*Compare* MOOD, VIEWPOINT.] **3.** The way in which one is placed or arranged ▸ arrangement, attitude, pose, position.

posture *v.* —*See* IMPERSONATE, POSE (1).

posy *n.* —*See* BOUQUET, FLOWER.

pot *n.* —*See* BET.

pot *v.* —*See* PLANT, PRESERVE (1).

potable *n.* —*See* DRINK (1).

potation *n.* —*See* DRINK (1), DRINK (2).

potbellied *adj.* —*See* FAT (1).

potency *n.* —*See* EFFECT (2), ENERGY, KICK, STRENGTH.

potent *adj.* **1.** Having a high concentration of the distinguishing ingredient ▸ concentrated, stiff, strong. [*Compare* STRAIGHT.] **2.** Having great physical strength ▸ mighty, powerful, strong. [*Compare* ENERGETIC, MUSCULAR.] —*See also* FORCEFUL.

potentate *n.* —*See* CHIEF.

potential *n.* Indication of or capacity for future success or development ▸ makings, possibility, promise, prospects. [*Compare* MATERIAL.] —*See also* POSSIBILITY (1).

potential *adj.* —*See* LATENT, PROBABLE.

a specified reference point; voltage. **—po·ten′ti·al′i·ty** (-shē-ăl′ĭ-tē) *n.* **—po·ten′tial·ly** *adv.*

potential energy ▸ *n.* The energy of a body or system derived from position or condition rather than motion.

pot·head (pŏt′hĕd′) ▸ *n. Slang* One who habitually smokes marijuana.

poth·er (pŏ*th*′ər) ▸ *n.* **1.** A commotion; disturbance. **2.** A fuss.

pot·hold·er (pŏt′hōl′dər) ▸ *n.* A small fabric pad used to handle hot cooking utensils.

pot·hole (pŏt′hōl′) ▸ *n.* A large hole, esp. in a road surface. **—pot′holed′** *adj.*

po·tion (pō′shən) ▸ *n.* A liquid dose, esp. of medicinal, magic, or poisonous content.

pot·luck (pŏt′lŭk′) ▸ *n.* **1.** Whatever food happens to be available for a meal. **2.** A meal at which each guest brings food that is then shared by all.

Po·to·mac River (pə-tō′mək) ▸ A river of the E-central US rising in NE WV and flowing about 459 km (285 mi) to Chesapeake Bay.

pot·pie (pŏt′pī′) ▸ *n.* Meat or poultry and vegetables covered with a pastry crust and baked in a deep dish.

pot·pour·ri (pō′po͝o-rē′) ▸ *n., pl.* **-ris. 1.** A combination of incongruous things. **2.** A mixture of dried flower petals and spices.

pot roast ▸ *n.* Beef that is browned and then cooked until tender in a covered pot.

pot·sherd (pŏt′shûrd′) also **pot·shard** (-shärd′) ▸ *n.* A fragment of broken pottery.

pot·shot also **pot shot** (pŏt′shŏt′) ▸ *n.* **1.** A random or easy shot. **2.** A criticism made without careful thought and aimed at a handy target.

pot·tage (pŏt′ĭj) ▸ *n.* A thick soup or stew of vegetables and sometimes meat.

pot·ted (pŏt′ĭd) ▸ *adj.* **1.** Placed or grown in a pot. **2.** *Slang* Intoxicated; drunk.

pot·ter¹ (pŏt′ər) ▸ *n.* A maker of pottery.

pot·ter² (pŏt′ər) ▸ *v. Chiefly Brit.* Var. of **putter²**.

Potter, Beatrix (1866–1943) ▸ British writer and illustrator.

pot·ter·y (pŏt′ə-rē) ▸ *n., pl.* **-ies. 1.** Ware, such as vases, pots, bowls, or plates, shaped from moist clay and hardened by heat. **2.** The craft or occupation of a potter. **3.** The place where a potter works.

pouch (pouch) ▸ *n.* **1.** A small bag used esp. for carrying loose items. **2.** A bag used to carry mail or diplomatic dispatches. **3.** A sealed container used in packaging frozen or dehydrated food. **4.** *Zool.* A saclike structure, such as the external abdominal pocket in which marsupials carry their young.

poul·tice (pōl′tĭs) ▸ *n.* A soft, moist, usu. heated mass spread on cloth and applied to a sore or inflamed part of the body. **—poul′tice** *v.*

poul·try (pōl′trē) ▸ *n.* Domestic fowls, such as chickens, turkeys, ducks, or geese, raised for meat or eggs.

pounce (pouns) ▸ *v.* **pounced, pounc·ing.** To spring or swoop suddenly so as to seize someone or something. **—pounce** *n.* **—pounc′er** *n.*

pound¹ (pound) ▸ *n., pl.* **pound** or **pounds. 1a.** See **measurement** table in Appendix. **b.** A unit of apothecary weight equal to 12 oz. (373.242 gr). **2.** A unit of weight differing in various countries and times. **3.** See **currency** table in Appendix. **4.** The primary unit of currency in Ireland before the adoption of the euro.

pound² (pound) ▸ *v.* **1.** To strike repeatedly and forcefully. **2.** To beat to a powder or pulp; pulverize or crush. **3.** To instill by persistent, emphatic repetition. **4.** To pulsate rapidly and heavily. **—pound′er** *n.*

pound³ (pound) ▸ *n.* A public enclosure for confining stray animals.

pound·age (poun′dĭj) ▸ *n.* Weight measured in pounds.

pound cake ▸ *n.* A rich yellow cake containing eggs, flour, butter, and sugar.

pound sign ▸ *n.* **1.** The symbol (£) for a unit of currency, esp. the pound sterling. **2.** The symbol (#) for a pound as a unit of weight.

pour (pôr) ▸ *v.* **1.** To flow or cause to flow in a steady stream. **2.** To send forth or produce copiously, as if in a stream or flood. **3.** To rain heavily. **—pour′er** *n.*

pout (pout) ▸ *v.* **1.** To exhibit displeasure or disappointment; sulk. **2.** To protrude the lips in an expression of displeasure. **—pout** *n.* **—pout′y** *adj.*

pov·er·ty (pŏv′ər-tē) ▸ *n.* **1.** The state of being poor; lack of money or material goods. **2.** Deficiency in amount; scantiness. **3.** Unproductiveness.

pov·er·ty-strick·en (pŏv′ər-tē-strĭk′ən) ▸ *adj.* Destitute; miserably poor.

POW (pē′ō-dŭb′əl-yo͞o, -yo͞o) ▸ *n.* A prisoner of war.

pow·der (pou′dər) ▸ *n.* **1.** A substance consisting of ground, pulverized, or otherwise finely dispersed solid particles. **2.** Any of various preparations in the form of powder, as certain cosmetics and medicines. **3.** An explosive mixture, such as gunpowder. **4.** Light dry snow. ▸ *v.* **1.** To pulverize. **2.** To dust or cover with or as if with powder. **—pow′der·y** *adj.*

powder keg ▸ *n.* **1.** A small cask for holding gunpowder or other explosives. **2.** A potentially explosive situation.

powder puff ▸ *n.* A soft pad for applying powder to the skin.

powder room ▸ *n.* A lavatory for women.

pow·er (pou′ər) ▸ *n.* **1.** The ability or capacity to perform or act effectively. **2.** often **powers** A specific capacity, faculty, or aptitude: *her powers of concentration.* **3.** Strength or force exerted or capable of being exerted; might. **4.** The ability or official capacity to exercise control; authority. **5.** A person, group, or nation having influence or control over others. **6.** Forcefulness; effectiveness. **7.** The energy or motive force by which a physical system or machine is operated. **8.** Electricity. **9.** *Phys.* The rate at which work is done, commonly measured in units such as the watt and horsepower. **10.** *Math.* See **exponent** 2. **11.** A measure of the magnification of an optical instrument. ▸ *v.* To supply with power, esp. mechanical power. **—pow′er·ful** *adj.* **—pow′er·ful·ly** *adv.* **—pow′er·ful·ness** *n.* **—pow′er·less** *adj.* **—pow′er·less·ly** *adv.*

pow·er·boat (pou′ər-bōt′) ▸ *n.* See **motorboat**.

pow·er·house (pou′ər-hous′) ▸ *n.* **1.** See **power plant** 2. **2.**

THESAURUS

potentiality *n.* —*See* POSSIBILITY (1).

pother *n.* —*See* BOTHER.

potion *n.* —*See* DRINK (1).

potpourri *n.* —*See* ASSORTMENT.

potted *adj.* —*See* DRUGGED, DRUNK.

pouch *v.* —*See* BULGE.

pouch *n.* —*See* BAG.

pounce *v.* —*See* JUMP (1).

pounce *n.* The act of jumping ▸ jump, leap, spring, vault. [*Compare* FALL.]

pound¹ *v.* —*See* BEAT (1), BEAT (3), BEAT (5), CRUSH (2), INSTILL.

pound *n.* —*See* BEAT (1), BLOW².

pound² *n.* —*See* CAGE.

pour *v.* To cause a liquid to flow in a steady stream ▸ decant, discharge, drain, draw (off), effuse, empty, flow, issue, run. —*See also* CROWD, FLOW (2), RAIN (2).

pour *n.* —*See* RAIN.

pout *v.* To be sullenly aloof or withdrawn, as in silent resentment or protest ▸ mope, pet, sulk. [*Compare* BROOD.]

pout *n.* A contorted facial expression showing pain, contempt, or disgust ▸ face, grimace, moue. *Informal:* mug. [*Compare* FROWN, GLARE, SNEER.]

poverty *n.* The condition of being extremely poor ▸ beggary, destitution, impecuniosity, impecuniousness, impoverishment, indigence, need, neediness, pauperism, pennilessness, penuriousness, penury, poorness, privation, straits, want. [*Compare* BANKRUPTCY, BEGGARY.] —*See also* DEPRIVATION, SHORTAGE.

poverty-stricken *adj.* —*See* POOR.

powder *v.* —*See* CRUSH (2), SPRINKLE.

powdery *adj.* —*See* FINE¹ (1).

power *n.* —*See* AUTHORITY, DOMINANCE, ENERGY, FORCE (1), INFLUENCE, STRENGTH.

powerful *adj.* Having great physical strength ▸ mighty, potent, strong. [*Compare* ENERGETIC, MUSCULAR.] —*See also* DEEP (3), FORCEFUL, INFLUENTIAL, SEVERE (2).

powerfully *adv.* —*See* HARD (1).

powerfulness *n.* —*See* STRENGTH.

One that possesses great force or energy.
power of attorney ▸ *n.* A legal instrument authorizing one to act as another's attorney or agent.
power plant ▸ *n.* **1.** All the equipment that constitutes a unit power source. **2.** A complex of structures and machinery for generating electric energy from another source of energy.
power train ▸ *n.* An assembly of gears and associated parts by which power is transmitted from an engine to a driving axle.
Pow·ha·tan (pou′ə-tăn′, pou-hăt′n) ▸ *n., pl.* **-tan** or **-tans**. **1.** A member of a confederacy of Native American peoples formerly inhabiting E Virginia. **2.** The Algonquian language of the Powhatan.
pow·wow (pou′wou′) ▸ *n.* **1.** A council or meeting with or of Native Americans. **2.** A ceremony during which a shaman performs healing or hunting rituals. **3.** *Informal* A conference or gathering. **—pow′wow′** *v.*
pox (pŏks) ▸ *n.* A disease such as smallpox, marked by purulent skin eruptions.
pp. ▸ *abbr.* pages
p.p. ▸ *abbr.* past participle
PQ ▸ *abbr.* Quebec
Pr ▸ The symbol for the element **praseodymium.**
PR ▸ *abbr.* **1.** public relations **2.** or **P.R.** Puerto Rico
pr. ▸ *abbr.* **1.** present **2.** pronoun
prac·ti·ca·ble (prăk′tĭ-kə-bəl) ▸ *adj.* **1.** Capable of being effected, done, or put into practice; feasible. **2.** Usable. **—prac′ti·ca·bil′i·ty** *n.* **—prac′ti·ca·bly** *adv.*
prac·ti·cal (prăk′tĭ-kəl) ▸ *adj.* **1.** Of or acquired through practice or action, rather than theory or speculation: *practical experience.* **2.** Manifested in or involving practice: *practical applications.* **3.** Capable of being used or put into effect; useful. **4.** Intended to serve a purpose without elaboration: *practical shoes.* **5.** Level-headed, efficient, and unspeculative. **6.** Being almost actually so; virtual. **—prac′ti·cal′i·ty** (-kăl′ĭ-tē), **prac′ti·cal·ness** *n.*
practical joke ▸ *n.* A prank played on a person, esp. one that embarrasses the victim.
prac·ti·cal·ly (prăk′tĭk-lē) ▸ *adv.* **1.** In a practical way. **2.** Nearly; almost.
practical nurse ▸ *n.* A licensed practical nurse.
prac·tice (prăk′tĭs) ▸ *v.* **-ticed, -tic·ing. 1.** To do or perform habitually or customarily; make a habit of: *practice restraint.* **2.** To do or perform repeatedly in order to acquire or polish a skill. **3.** To work at, esp. as a profession: *practice law.* **4.** To carry out; observe. ▸ *n.* **1.** A habitual or customary action or way of doing something. **2a.** Repeated performance of an activity in order to learn or perfect a skill. **b.** Proficiency gained through repeated exercise. **3.** The act or process of doing something; performance. **4.** Exercise of an occupation or profession. **5.** The business of a professional person. **6.** A habitual action. **—prac′tic·er** *n.*
prac·ti·tion·er (prăk-tĭsh′ə-nər) ▸ *n.* One who practices an occupation, profession, or technique.
prae·tor (prē′tər) ▸ *n.* An ancient Roman magistrate below a consul. **—prae·to′ri·an** (-tôr′ē-ən) *adj. & n.*
prag·mat·ic (prăg-măt′ĭk) ▸ *adj.* **1.** Concerned with facts or actual events; practical. **2.** Relating to pragmatism. **—prag·mat′i·cal·ly** *adv.*
prag·ma·tism (prăg′mə-tĭz′əm) ▸ *n.* A practical, matter-of-fact way of approaching or assessing situations or of solving problems. **—prag′ma·tist** *n.*
Prague (präg) ▸ The capital of the Czech Republic, in the W part.
prai·rie (prâr′ē) ▸ *n.* An extensive area of flat or rolling grassland, esp. in central North America.
prairie dog ▸ *n.* A burrowing rodent of W-central North America, having light brown fur and a barklike call.
prairie schooner ▸ *n.* A covered wagon used by pioneers crossing the North American plains.
praise (prāz) ▸ *n.* **1.** Expression of approval, commendation, or admiration. **2.** The extolling or exaltation of a deity, ruler, or hero. **—praise** *v.*
praise·wor·thy (prāz′wûr′thē) ▸ *adj.* Meriting praise; highly commendable.
pra·line (prä′lēn′, prā′-) ▸ *n.* A crisp confection made of nut kernels stirred in boiling sugar syrup.
pram (prăm) ▸ *n. Chiefly Brit.* A perambulator.
prance (prăns) ▸ *v.* **pranced, pranc·ing. 1.** To spring forward on the hind legs, as a spirited horse. **2.** To move about in a spirited manner; strut. **—pranc′er** *n.* **—pranc′ing·ly** *adv.*
prank (prăngk) ▸ *n.* A mischievous trick. **—prank′ster** *n.*
pra·se·o·dym·i·um (prā′zē-ō-dĭm′ē-əm, prā′sē-) ▸ *n. Symbol* **Pr** A soft, silvery, malleable, rare-earth element used to color glass yellow and in metallic alloys. At. no. 59.
prate (prāt) ▸ *v.* **prat·ed, prat·ing.** To talk idly and at length; chatter.
prat·fall (prăt′fôl′) ▸ *n.* A fall on the buttocks.
prat·tle (prăt′l) ▸ *v.* **-tled, -tling.** To talk idly; babble. **—prat′tle** *n.*
prawn (prôn) ▸ *n.* An edible crustacean similar to but larger than the shrimps.
prax·is (prăk′sĭs) ▸ *n., pl.* **-es** (-sēz′). Practical application of a branch of learning.

THESAURUS

powerless *adj.* Lacking power or strength ▸ helpless, impotent, unable. —*See also* INEFFECTUAL (2).
powerlessness *n.* —*See* INABILITY, INEFFECTUALITY.
powwow *n.* —*See* CONFERENCE (1).
powwow *v.* —*See* CONFER (1).
practicable *adj.* —*See* ADVISABLE, OPEN (4), POSSIBLE, PRACTICAL.
practical *adj.* Serving or capable of serving a useful purpose ▸ functional, handy, no-nonsense, practicable, serviceable, useful, utilitarian. [*Compare* BENEFICIAL, USABLE.] —*See also* REALISTIC (1).
practicality *n.* —*See* USE (2).
practical joke *n.* —*See* PRANK[1].
practically *adv.* —*See* APPROXIMATELY.
practice *v.* **1.** To do or perform repeatedly so as to master ▸ exercise, go over (*or* through), rehearse, run through, walk through. [*Compare* INDOCTRINATE.] **2.** To work at, especially as a profession ▸ do, follow, pursue. *Idiom:* hang out one's shingle. [*Compare* LABOR.] **3.** To engage in activities in order to strengthen or condition ▸ drill, exercise, train, work out. —*See also* USE.
practice *n.* Repetition of an action so as to develop or maintain one's skill ▸ conditioning, drill, exercise, regimen, rehearsal, routine, study, training, workout. —*See also* BUSINESS (2), CUSTOM.
practiced *adj.* Proficient as a result of practice and study ▸ accomplished, finished, polished. [*Compare* ABLE, EXPERT.] —*See also* EXPERIENCED.
praetorian *adj.* —*See* CORRUPT (2).
pragmatic or **pragmatical** *adj.* —*See* REALISTIC (1).
praise *n.* **1.** An expression of warm approval ▸ acclaim, acclamation, accolade, applause, approbation, celebration, cheer, commendation, compliment, encomium, eulogy, kudos, laud, laudation, paean, panegyric, plaudit. [*Compare* APPLAUSE, EXALTATION.] **2.** The honoring of a deity, as in worship ▸ exaltation, extolment, glory, glorification, laudation, magnification, prostration. [*Compare* ADORATION, HONOR.] —*See also* COMPLIMENT.
praise *v.* **1.** To express warm approval of ▸ acclaim, accolade, applaud, cheer, commend, compliment, extol, laud. **2.** To pay a compliment to ▸ commend, compliment, congratulate, felicitate. *Idioms:* pay tribute to, raise a glass to, take off one's hat to. **3.** To honor a deity in religious worship ▸ exalt, extol, glorify, hymn, laud, magnify. [*Compare* REVERE.] —*See also* DISTINGUISH (3), HONOR (1).
praiseworthy *adj.* —*See* ADMIRABLE.
prance *v.* —*See* STRUT.
prank[1] *n.* A mischievous act ▸ antic, caper, frolic, gag, joke, lark, practical joke, trick. *Informal:* shenanigan. *Slang:* monkeyshine, put-on. [*Compare* MISCHIEF.]
prank[2] *v.* —*See* DRESS UP.
prankish *adj.* —*See* MISCHIEVOUS.
prankishness or **pranks** *n.* —*See* MISCHIEF.
prankster *n.* —*See* RASCAL.
prate *v.* —*See* BABBLE, CHATTER (1).
prate *n.* —*See* BABBLE, CHATTER.
prattle *v.* —*See* BABBLE, CHATTER (1), GOSSIP.
prattle *n.* —*See* BABBLE, CHATTER, GOSSIP (1).
praxis *n.* —*See* CUSTOM.

pray (prā) ▸ *v.* **1.** To address a prayer to a deity. **2.** To make a fervent request for something. **3.** To beseech; implore. **—pray′er** (prā′ər) *n.*

prayer (prâr) ▸ *n.* **1.** A reverent petition made to a deity. **2.** An act of praying. **3.** A specially worded form of praying. **4. prayers** A religious observance in which praying predominates. **5.** A fervent request. **6.** The slightest chance or hope.

prayer·ful (prâr′fəl) ▸ *adj.* **1.** Inclined to praying frequently. **2.** Typical of prayer, as a mannerism. **—prayer′ful·ly** *adv.*

pray·ing mantis (prā′ĭng) ▸ *n.* A green or brownish predatory insect that while at rest folds its front legs as if in prayer.

pre– ▸ *pref.* **1a.** Earlier; before: *prehistoric.* **b.** Preparatory; preliminary: *premedical.* **c.** In advance: *prepay.* **2.** Anterior; in front of: *premolar.*

preach (prēch) ▸ *v.* **1.** To proclaim or deliver in a sermon. **2.** To advocate or urge: *preach tolerance.* **3.** To give moral instruction, esp. in a tedious manner. **—preach′er** *n.* **—preach′y** *adj.*

pre·ad·o·les·cence (prē′ăd-l-ĕs′əns) ▸ *n.* The period between childhood and puberty. **—pre′ad·o·les′cent** *adj. & n.*

pre·am·ble (prē′ăm′bəl, prē-ăm′-) ▸ *n.* A preliminary statement, esp. to a formal document, explaining its purpose.

pre·am·pli·fi·er (prē-ăm′plə-fī′ər) ▸ *n.* An electronic circuit or device that detects and strengthens weak signals, as from a radio receiver, for subsequent amplification.

pre·ap·prove (prē′ə-pro͞ov′) ▸ *v.* To approve or qualify (e.g., an application) without formalities.

preb·end (prĕb′ənd) ▸ *n.* **1.** A cleric's stipend drawn from the endowment or revenues of an Anglican cathedral or church. **2.** The property or tithe providing a prebend.

preb·en·dar·y (prĕb′ən-dĕr′ē) ▸ *n., pl.* **-ies.** An Anglican cleric who receives a prebend.

Pre·cam·bri·an (prē-kăm′brē-ən) ▸ *adj.* Of or being the 1st geologic era and oldest and largest division of geologic time, marked by the appearance of early forms of life. ▸ *n.* The Precambrian Era.

pre·car·i·ous (prĭ-kâr′ē-əs) ▸ *adj.* **1.** Dangerously lacking in stability. **2.** Subject to chance or unknown conditions. **—pre·car′i·ous·ly** *adv.* **—pre·car′i·ous·ness** *n.*

pre·cau·tion (prĭ-kô′shən) ▸ *n.* An action taken to protect against possible danger or failure. **—pre·cau′tion·ar′y** (-shə-nĕr′ē) *adj.*

pre·cede (prĭ-sēd′) ▸ *v.* **-ced·ed, -ced·ing.** To come or be before in time, place, or rank.

prec·e·dence (prĕs′ĭ-dəns, prĭ-sēd′ns) ▸ *n.* The fact, state, or right of preceding; priority.

prec·e·dent (prĕs′ĭ-dənt) ▸ *n.* **1.** An act or instance that may be used as an example in dealing with later similar instances. **2.** Convention or custom. ▸ *adj.* (prĭ-sēd′nt, prĕs′ĭ-dənt) Preceding.

pre·ced·ing (prĭ-sē′dĭng) ▸ *adj.* Existing or coming before; previous.

pre·cen·tor (prĭ-sĕn′tər) ▸ *n.* A cleric who directs the choir of a church.

pre·cept (prē′sĕpt′) ▸ *n.* A rule or principle prescribing a particular course of action or conduct.

pre·cep·tor (prĭ-sĕp′tər, prē′sĕp′tər) ▸ *n.* A teacher; instructor. **—pre′cep·to′ri·al** (prē′sĕp-tôr′ē-əl) *adj.*

pre·cinct (prē′sĭngkt′) ▸ *n.* **1.** A district of a city patrolled by a specific unit of its police force. **2.** An election district of a city or town. **3.** often **precincts** A place or enclosure marked off by definite limits. **4. precincts** Neighborhood; environs.

pre·ci·os·i·ty (prĕsh′ē-ŏs′ĭ-tē, prĕs′-) ▸ *n., pl.* **-ties.** Extreme meticulousness or overrefinement.

pre·cious (prĕsh′əs) ▸ *adj.* **1.** Of high cost or worth; valuable. **2.** Dear; beloved. **3.** Affectedly dainty or overrefined. **—pre′cious·ness** *n.*

prec·i·pice (prĕs′ə-pĭs) ▸ *n.* **1.** An overhanging or extremely steep cliff. **2.** The brink of a dangerous situation.

pre·cip·i·tant (prĭ-sĭp′ĭ-tənt) ▸ *adj.* **1.** Rushing or falling headlong. **2.** Impulsive in thought or action; rash. **3.** Abrupt or unexpected; sudden. **—pre·cip′i·tance, pre·cip′i·tan·cy** *n.*

pre·cip·i·tate (prĭ-sĭp′ĭ-tāt′) ▸ *v.* **-tat·ed, -tat·ing. 1.** To hurl downward. **2.** To cause to happen, esp. suddenly or prematurely. **3.** To condense and fall as rain or snow. **4.** *Chem.* To cause (a solid substance) to be separated from a solution. ▸ *adj.* (-tĭt) **1.** Moving rapidly and heedlessly; speeding headlong. **2.** Impetuous; reckless. **3.** Occurring suddenly or unexpectedly. ▸ *n.* (-tāt′, -tĭt) *Chem.* A solid or solid phase separated from a solution. **—pre·cip′i·tate·ly** (-tĭt-lē) *adv.* **—pre·cip′i·tate·ness** *n.* **—pre·cip′i·ta′tive** *adj.* **—pre·cip′i·ta′tor** *n.*

pre·cip·i·ta·tion (prĭ-sĭp′ĭ-tā′shən) ▸ *n.* **1.** A headlong fall or rush. **2.** Abrupt or impulsive haste. **3a.** Water that falls as rain or snow. **b.** The quantity of such water falling in a specific area within a specific period. **4.** *Chem.* The production of precipitation.

pre·cip·i·tous (prĭ-sĭp′ĭ-təs) ▸ *adj.* **1.** Resembling a precipice; extremely steep. **2.** Having precipices: *a precipitous bluff.* **3.** *Informal* Headlong, precipitate. **—pre·cip′i·tous·ly** *adv.* **—pre·cip′i·tous·ness** *n.*

pré·cis (prā′sē, prā-sē′) ▸ *n., pl.* **pré·cis** (prā′sēz, prā-sēz′). A concise summary of a text; abstract. **—pré′cis** *v.*

pre·cise (prĭ-sīs′) ▸ *adj.* **1.** Clearly expressed or delineated; definite. **2.** Exact, as in performance or amount; correct. **3.** Strictly distinguished from others; very: *at that precise moment.* **4.** Conforming strictly to rule or proper form. **—pre·cise′ly** *adv.* **—pre·cise′ness** *n.*

pre·ci·sion (prĭ-sĭzh′ən) ▸ *n.* The state or quality of being precise.

THESAURUS

pray *v.* To offer a reverent petition to God or a god ▸ invoke, supplicate. *—See also* APPEAL (1).

prayer[1] *n.* **1.** The act of praying ▸ benediction, invocation, supplication. **2.** A formula of words used in praying ▸ collect, devotions, litany, orison, rogations. [*Compare* GRACE.] *—See also* APPEAL.

prayer[2] *n.* One who humbly entreats ▸ beggar, petitioner, suitor, suppliant, supplicant.

prayerful *adj.* *—See* PIOUS.

preach *v.* **1.** To deliver a sermon, especially as a vocation ▸ evangelize, sermonize. [*Compare* ADDRESS.] **2.** To indulge in moral reflection, usually pompously ▸ edify, moralize, pontificate, sermonize. [*Compare* CHASTISE.]

preacher *n.* *—See* CLERIC.

preachy *adj.* *—See* DIDACTIC (2), MORAL.

preadolescence *n.* The stage of life between birth and puberty ▸ childhood, early years, innocence, pubescence. [*Compare* YOUTH.]

preadolescent *n.* *—See* CHILD (1).

preamble *n.* *—See* INTRODUCTION.

prearrangement *n.* *—See* PREPARATION.

precarious *adj.* *—See* DELICATE (3), INSECURE (2).

precariousness *n.* *—See* INSTABILITY.

precaution *n.* *—See* CAUTION, PRUDENCE.

precautionary *adj.* *—See* PRESERVATIVE, PREVENTIVE (2).

precede *v.* To come, exist, or occur before in time ▸ antecede, antedate, forerun, predate, preexist. *—See also* INTRODUCE (3).

precedence *n.* The act, condition, or right of preceding or coming before ▸ antecedence, precedency, precession, priority, right of way.

precedent *n.* *—See* CUSTOM, MODEL.

precedent *adj.* *—See* ADVANCE, PAST.

preceding *adj.* Next before the present one ▸ foregoing, last, latter, previous. *—See also* ADVANCE, PAST.

precept *n.* *—See* DOCTRINE, LAW (1).

precession *n.* *—See* PRECEDENCE.

precincts *n.* *—See* ENVIRONMENT (1), LIMITS.

precious *adj.* *—See* COSTLY, DARLING.

precious *n.* *—See* DARLING (1).

precipitance *n.* *—See* HASTE (2).

precipitant *adj.* *—See* ABRUPT (2), RASH[1].

precipitate *v.* To put down, especially in layers, by a natural process ▸ deposit. *—See also* CAUSE, RAIN (2).

precipitate *adj.* *—See* ABRUPT (2), RASH[1].

precipitate *n.* *—See* DEPOSIT (2), EFFECT (1).

precipitateness *n.* *—See* HASTE (2).

precipitation *n.* *—See* DEPOSIT (2), HASTE (2), RAIN.

precipitous *adj.* *—See* STEEP[1] (1).

precise *adj.* Strictly distinguished from others ▸ exact, very. *—See also* ACCURATE, DEFINITE (1), DEFINITE (2), DELICATE (4).

precisely *adv.* *—See* DIRECTLY (3), EXACTLY.

precision or **preciseness** *n.* *—See* ACCURACY, CLARITY.

pre·clude (prĭ-klo͞od′) ► *v.* **-clud·ed, -clud·ing. 1.** To make impossible; prevent. **2.** To exclude; debar. **—pre·clu′sion** (-klo͞o′zhən) *n.* **—pre·clu′sive** (-klo͞o′sĭv, -zĭv) *adj.* **—pre·clu′sive·ly** *adv.*

pre·co·cious (prĭ kō′shəs) ► *adj.* Marked by unusually early development or maturity, esp. in mental aptitude. **—pre·co′cious·ly** *adv.* **—pre·coc′ity** (-kŏs′ĭ-tē), **pre·co′cious·ness** *n.*

pre·cog·ni·tion (prē′kŏg-nĭsh′ən) ► *n.* Knowledge of something before it occurs; clairvoyance. **—pre·cog′ni·tive** *adj.*

pre-Co·lum·bi·an (prē′kə-lŭm′bē-ən) ► *adj.* Of or originating in the Americas before the arrival of Christopher Columbus.

pre·con·ceive (prē′kən-sēv′) ► *v.* **-ceived, -ceiv·ing.** To form an opinion or a conception of before having adequate knowledge. **—pre′con·cep′tion** (-sĕp′shən) *n.*

pre·con·di·tion (prē′kən-dĭsh′ən) ► *n.* A prerequisite. ► *v.* To condition, train, or accustom in advance.

pre·cur·sor (prĭ-kûr′sər, prē′kûr′sər) ► *n.* **1.** One that precedes and indicates or announces another. **2.** One that precedes another; predecessor.

pre·da·cious (prĭ-dā′shəs) ► *adj.* Predatory.

pre·date (prē-dāt′) ► *v.* Antedate.

pre·da·tion (prĭ-dā′shən) ► *n.* **1.** The act of plundering or marauding. **2.** The capturing of prey as a means of maintaining life.

pred·a·to·ry (prĕd′ə-tôr′ē) ► *adj.* **1.** Living by preying on other organisms. **2.** Of or marked by plundering or marauding. **—pred′a·tor** (-tər, -tôr′) *n.* **—pred′a·to′ri·ness** *n.*

pred·e·ces·sor (prĕd′ĭ-sĕs′ər, prē′dĭ-) ► *n.* One who precedes another, esp. in an office or position.

pre·des·ti·na·tion (prē-dĕs′tə-nā′shən) ► *n.* **1.** *Theol.* **a.** The doctrine that God has foreordained all things. **b.** The divine decree foreordaining all souls to either salvation or damnation. **2.** Destiny; fate.

pre·des·tine (prē-dĕs′tĭn) ► *v.* To decide or decree in advance.

pre·de·ter·mine (prē′dĭ-tûr′mĭn) ► *v.* To determine or decide in advance. **—pre′de·ter′mi·nate** (-mə-nĭt) *adj.* **—pre′de·ter′mi·na′tion** *n.*

pred·i·ca·ble (prĕd′ĭ-kə-bəl) ► *adj.* That can be stated or predicated.

pre·dic·a·ment (prĭ-dĭk′ə-mənt) ► *n.* A troublesome or unpleasant situation.

pred·i·cate (prĕd′ĭ-kāt′) ► *v.* **-cat·ed, -cat·ing. 1.** To base or establish: *predicate an argument on the facts.* **2.** To affirm as an attribute or quality: *predicate the perfectibility of humankind.* ► *n.* (-kĭt) *Gram.* The part of a sentence or clause, including the verb, that expresses what the subject is or does. **—pred′i·ca′tion** *n.* **—pred′i·ca′tive** *adj.*

pre·dict (prĭ-dĭkt′) ► *v.* To state, tell about, or make known in advance; foretell. **—pre·dict′a·bil′i·ty** *n.* **—pre·dict′a·ble** *adj.* **—pre·dic′tion** *n.* **—pre·dic′tive** *adj.* **—pre·dic′tor** *n.*

pre·di·gest (prē′dī-jĕst′, -dĭ-) ► *v.* To subject to partial digestion. **—pre′di·ges′tion** *n.*

pred·i·lec·tion (prĕd′l-ĕk′shən, prēd′-) ► *n.* A disposition in favor of something; preference.

pre·dis·pose (prē′dĭ-spōz′) ► *v.* **-posed, -pos·ing. 1.** To make (someone) inclined to something in advance. **2.** To make susceptible or liable. **—pre′dis·po·si′tion** (-dĭs-pə-zĭsh′ən) *n.*

pre·dom·i·nant (prĭ-dŏm′ə-nənt) ► *adj.* **1.** Having greatest importance or authority. **2.** Most common or conspicuous; prevalent. **—pre·dom′i·nance, pre·dom′i·nan·cy** *n.* **—pre·dom′i·nant·ly** *adv.*

pre·dom·i·nate (prĭ-dŏm′ə-nāt′) ► *v.* **-nat·ed, -nat·ing. 1.** To have controlling power or influence; prevail. **2.** To be of or have greater quantity or importance. **—pre·dom′i·nate·ly** (-nĭt-lē) *adv.* **—pre·dom′i·na′tion** *n.* **—pre·dom′i·na′tor** *n.*

pree·mie (prē′mē) ► *n.* *Informal* A prematurely born infant.

pre·em·i·nent or **pre-em·i·nent** (prē-ĕm′ə-nənt) ► *adj.* Superior to all others; outstanding. **—pre·em′i·nence** *n.* **—pre·em′i·nent·ly** *adv.*

pre·empt or **pre-empt** (prē-ĕmpt′) ► *v.* **1.** To appropriate or seize for oneself before others. **2.** To take the place of; displace. **3.** To settle on (public land) so as to obtain the right to buy before others. **—pre·emp′tion** *n.* **—pre·emp′tive** *adj.* **—pre·emp′tor′** (-ĕmp′tôr′) *n.*

preen (prēn) ► *v.* **1.** To smooth or clean (feathers) with the beak or bill. **2.** To dress or groom (oneself) with care; primp. **3.** To take pride or satisfaction in (oneself).

pre·ex·ist or **pre-ex·ist** (prē′ĭg-zĭst′) ► *v.* To exist before. **—pre′ex·is′tence** *n.* **—pre′ex·is′tent** *adj.*

pref. ► *abbr.* **1.** preface **2.** prefix

pre·fab (prē′făb′) ► *n.* *Informal* Something prefabricated, esp. a building or section of a building. **—pre′fab′** *adj. & v.*

pre·fab·ri·cate (prē-făb′rĭ-kāt′) ► *v.* To manufacture in advance, esp. in standard sections that can be easily shipped and assembled. **—pre·fab′ri·ca′tion** *n.*

pref·ace (prĕf′ĭs) ► *n.* A preliminary statement introducing a book, usu. written by the author. ► *v.* **-aced, -ac·ing.** To introduce by or provide with a preface.

pref·a·to·ry (prĕf′ə-tôr′ē) ► *adj.* Of or being a preface; introductory.

pre·fect (prē′fĕkt′) ► *n.* **1.** A high administrative official, as in ancient Rome. **2.** A student monitor, esp. in a private school. **—pre′fec′ture** *n.*

pre·fer (prĭ-fûr′) ► *v.* **-ferred, -fer·ring. 1.** To choose as more desirable. **2.** *Law* To file before a legal authority: *prefer charges.*

pref·er·a·ble (prĕf′ər-ə-bəl, prĕf′rə-) ► *adj.* More desirable. **—pref′er·a·bly** *adv.*

pref·er·ence (prĕf′ər-əns, prĕf′rəns) ► *n.* **1.** The exercise of choice. **2.** One so chosen. **3.** The state or condition of

THESAURUS

preclude *v.* *—See* PREVENT.

preclusion *n.* *—See* PREVENTION.

preclusive *adj.* *—See* PREVENTIVE (1).

precocious *adj.* Developing, occurring, or appearing before the expected time ► early, premature, untimely. *—See also* GIFTED, PROGRESSIVE (1).

preconception *n.* *—See* BIAS.

precondition *n.* *—See* CONDITION (2), PROVISION.

precursor *n.* *—See* ANCESTOR (2), FORERUNNER.

predate *v.* *—See* PRECEDE.

predecessor *n.* *—See* ANCESTOR (2).

predestination *n.* *—See* FATE (1).

predetermine *v.* *—See* DESIGN (1).

predetermined *adj.* *—See* CALCULATED.

predicament *n.* A difficult, often embarrassing situation or condition ► box, corner, deep water, difficulty, dilemma, Dutch, fix, hole, hot spot, hot water, impasse, jam, mess, pinch, plight, quagmire, quandary, scrape, soup, straits, tightrope, trouble. *Informal:* bind, pickle, spot. *Idiom:* pretty kettle of fish. [*Compare* CRISIS, DIFFICULTY, ENTANGLEMENT.]

predicate *v.* *—See* BASE[1].

predict *v.* To tell about or make known in advance, especially by means of special knowledge ► call, forecast, foretell, portend, presage, prognosticate, project. [*Compare* FORESEE, FORESHADOW, PROPHESY.]

prediction *n.* The act of predicting ► forecast, outlook, prescience, prevision, prognosis, prognostication, projection. [*Compare* OMEN, PROPHECY.]

predictive *adj.* Of or relating to prediction ► prescient, previsionary, prognostic, prognosticative. [*Compare* PROPHETIC.]

predilection *n.* *—See* INCLINATION (1).

predispose *v.* *—See* INFLUENCE.

predisposed *adj.* *—See* INCLINED.

predisposition *n.* *—See* INCLINATION (1).

predominance *n.* *—See* DOMINANCE.

predominant *adj.* *—See* DOMINANT (1), PREVAILING.

predominate *v.* *—See* DOMINATE (1).

preeminence *n.* *—See* DOMINANCE, EXCELLENCE, FAME.

preeminent *adj.* *—See* BEST (1), DOMINANT (1), EXCEPTIONAL, FAMOUS.

preempt *v.* *—See* SEIZE (1).

preemption *n.* *—See* SEIZURE (2).

preen *v.* *—See* DRESS UP, PRIDE.

preexist *v.* *—See* PRECEDE.

preface *n.* *—See* INTRODUCTION.

preface *v.* *—See* INTRODUCE (3).

prefatory *adj.* *—See* INTRODUCTORY.

prefer *v.* To show partiality toward someone ► favor. *Idioms:* be partial, play favorites. [*Compare* ADVANCE, BABY.] *—See also* CHOOSE (2).

preferable *adj.* Of greater excellence than another ► better, superior.

preference *n.* Preferential treatment or bias ► favor, favoritism, partiality, partialness. [*Compare* BIAS, PREJUDICE.]

being preferred. **—pref′er·en′tial** (-ə-rĕn′shəl) *adj.*

pre·fer·ment (prĭ-fûr′mənt) ▸ *n.* Selection for promotion or favored treatment.

pre·fig·ure (prē-fĭg′yər) ▸ *v.* **1.** To presage; foreshadow. **2.** To imagine in advance. **—pre·fig′ur·a·tive** (-fĭg′yər-ə-tĭv) *adj.* **—pre·fig′ure·ment** *n.*

pre·fix (prē′fĭks′) ▸ *v.* To put or attach before. ▸ *n. Gram.* An affix attached to the front of a word to produce a derivative word or an inflected form.

pre·fron·tal (prē-frŭn′tl) ▸ *adj.* Of or situated in the anterior part of the frontal lobe.

preg·na·ble (prĕg′nə-bəl) ▸ *adj.* Vulnerable to seizure or capture: *a pregnable fort.* **—preg′na·bil′i·ty** *n.*

preg·nant (prĕg′nənt) ▸ *adj.* **1.** Carrying developing offspring within the body. **2.** Weighty or significant; full of meaning. **—preg′nan·cy** *n.*

pre·hen·sile (prē-hĕn′səl, -sīl′) ▸ *adj.* Adapted for seizing or holding, esp. by wrapping around: *a prehensile tail.* **—pre′hen·sil′i·ty** (-sĭl′ĭ-tē) *n.*

pre·his·tor·ic (prē′hĭ-stôr′ĭk, -stŏr′-) also **pre·his·tor·i·cal** (-ĭ-kəl) ▸ *adj.* Of or belonging to an era before recorded history. **—pre·his′to·ry** (-hĭs′tə-rē) *n.*

prej·u·dice (prĕj′ə-dĭs) ▸ *n.* **1.** An adverse judgment or opinion formed beforehand without knowledge of the facts. **2.** Irrational suspicion or hatred of a particular group, race, or religion. **3.** Harm or injury. ▸ *v.* **-diced, -dic·ing. 1.** To cause (someone) to have a prejudice. **2.** To do harm to: *a mistake that prejudiced the outcome.* **—prej′u·di′cial** (-dĭsh′əl) *adj.*

prel·ate (prĕl′ĭt) ▸ *n.* A high-ranking member of the clergy, esp. a bishop. **—prel′a·cy** (-ə-sē) *n.*

pre·lim·i·nar·y (prĭ-lĭm′ə-nĕr′ē) ▸ *adj.* Prior to the main matter, action, or business; introductory. ▸ *n., pl.* **-ies.** Something that precedes, prepares for, or introduces the main matter or action. **—pre·lim′i·nar′i·ly** (-nâr′ə-lē) *adv.*

prel·ude (prĕl′yo͞od′, prā′lo͞od′, prē′-) ▸ *n.* **1.** An introductory performance, event, or action. **2.** *Mus.* A piece or movement serving as an introduction to another section or composition.

pre·mar·i·tal (prē-măr′ĭ-tl) ▸ *adj.* Taking place or existing before marriage.

pre·ma·ture (prē′mə-tyo͝or′, -to͝or′, -cho͝or′) ▸ *adj.* Occurring, growing, or existing before the customary, correct, or assigned time; early. **—pre′ma·ture′ly** *adv.*

pre·med (prē′mĕd′) *Informal* ▸ *adj.* Premedical. ▸ *n.* A premedical student.

pre·med·i·cal (prē-mĕd′ĭ-kəl) ▸ *adj.* Preparing for or leading to the study of medicine.

pre·med·i·tate (prē-mĕd′ĭ-tāt′) ▸ *v.* To plan, arrange, or plot in advance. **—pre·med′i·ta′tion** *n.* **—pre·med′i·ta′tive** *adj.*

pre·men·stru·al (prē-mĕn′stro͞o-əl) ▸ *adj.* Of or occurring in the period just before menstruation. **—pre·men′stru·al·ly** *adv.*

pre·mier (prĭ-mîr′, -myîr′, prē′mîr) ▸ *adj.* **1.** First in status or importance; chief. **2.** First to occur or exist; earliest. ▸ *n.* (prĭ-mîr′) A prime minister. **—pre·mier′ship′** *n.*

pre·miere or **pre·mière** (prĭ-mîr′, -myâr′) ▸ *n.* The first public performance, as of a play. ▸ *v.* **-miered, -mier·ing** or **-mièred, -mièr·ing.** To present or receive a first public performance.

prem·ise (prĕm′ĭs) ▸ *n.* **1.** A proposition upon which an argument is based or from which a conclusion is drawn. **2. premises** Land and the buildings on it. **—prem′ise** *v.*

pre·mi·um (prē′mē-əm) ▸ *n.* **1.** A prize or award. **2.** A sum of money paid in addition to a regular amount. **3.** The amount paid, often in installments, for an insurance policy. **4.** An unusual or high value: *put a premium on honesty.* ▸ *adj.* Of superior quality or value: *premium gasoline.* **—*idiom:* at a premium** More valuable than usual, as from scarcity.

pre·mo·lar (prē-mō′lər) ▸ *n.* One of eight bicuspid teeth located in pairs between the canines and molars. **—pre·mo′lar** *adj.*

pre·mo·ni·tion (prē′mə-nĭsh′ən, prĕm′ə-) ▸ *n.* **1.** A presentiment of the future; foreboding. **2.** An advance warning; forewarning. **—pre·mon′i·to′ry** (-mŏn′ĭ-tôr′ē) *adj.*

pre·na·tal (prē-nāt′l) ▸ *adj.* Existing or occurring before birth. **—pre·na′tal·ly** *adv.*

pre·oc·cu·py (prē-ŏk′yə-pī′) ▸ *v.* **1.** To occupy completely the mind or attention of; engross. **2.** To occupy or take possession of in advance or before another. **—pre·oc′cu·pa′tion** (-pā′shən) *n.*

pre·op·er·a·tive (prē-ŏp′ər-ə-tĭv, -ŏp′rə-, -ŏp′ə-rā′-) ▸ *adj.* Happening or done before surgery.

prep. ▸ *abbr.* preposition

pre·pack·age (prē-păk′ĭj) ▸ *v.* To wrap or package (a product) before marketing.

prep·a·ra·tion (prĕp′ə-rā′shən) ▸ *n.* **1.** The act or process of preparing. **2.** Readiness. **3.** often **preparations** A preliminary measure or measures. **4.** A prepared substance, such as a medicine.

pre·par·a·to·ry (prĭ-păr′ə-tôr′ē, -pâr′-, prĕp′ər-ə-) ▸ *adj.* Serving to make ready or prepare.

preparatory school ▸ *n.* A usu. private secondary school that prepares students for college.

pre·pare (prĭ-pâr′) ▸ *v.* **-pared, -par·ing. 1.** To make ready. **2.** To put together or make by combining various ele-

THESAURUS

—*See also* CHOICE, TASTE (1).

preferential *adj.* Disposed to favor one over another ▸ favorable, partial. [*Compare* BIASED.] —*See also* UNFAIR.

preferment *n.* —*See* ADVANCEMENT.

preferred *adj.* —*See* FAVORITE.

prefigure *v.* —*See* FORESHADOW.

prefigurement *n.* —*See* OMEN.

pregnability *n.* —*See* EXPOSURE.

pregnable *adj.* —*See* VULNERABLE.

pregnancy *n.* The condition of carrying a developing fetus within the uterus ▸ gestation, gravidity, gravidness, parturiency.

pregnant *adj.* **1.** Carrying a developing fetus within the uterus ▸ big, enceinte, expectant, expecting, gestating, gravid, parturient. *Slang:* gone, knocked-up, preggers, preggo. *Idioms:* having a bun in the oven, in a family way, with child. **2.** Conveying hidden or unexpressed meaning ▸ consequential, meaningful, meaty, pithy, significant, suggestive, weighty. [*Compare* IMPORTANT.]

prehistoric *adj.* —*See* EARLY (1).

prehistory *n.* —*See* ANTIQUITY.

prejudge *v.* To make a mistake in judging ▸ misestimate, misjudge, mistake. [*Compare* MISUNDERSTAND, SUPPOSE.]

prejudice *n.* Irrational suspicion or hatred of a particular group, race, or religion ▸ bigotry, discrimination, intolerance. [*Compare* HATE.] —*See also* BIAS, INCLINATION (1).

prejudice *v.* —*See* BIAS (1), DAMAGE.

prejudiced or **prejudicial** *adj.* —*See* BIASED.

prelate *n.* —*See* CLERIC.

prelect *v.* To talk to an audience formally ▸ lecture, sermonize, speak. [*Compare* CONVERSE.]

prelection *n.* —*See* SPEECH (2).

preliminary *adj.* —*See* INTRODUCTORY, ROUGH (4).

prelude *n.* —*See* INTRODUCTION.

premature *adj.* Developing, occurring, or appearing before the expected time ▸ early, precocious, untimely.

premeditate *v.* —*See* DESIGN (1).

premeditated *adj.* —*See* CALCULATED, DELIBERATE (1).

premier *adj.* —*See* FIRST, PRIMARY (1).

premise *n.* —*See* ASSUMPTION.

premise *v.* —*See* SUPPOSE (1).

premium *n.* —*See* REWARD.

premium *adj.* —*See* CHOICE (1).

premonition *n.* —*See* FEELING (1).

preoccupation *n.* —*See* ABSORPTION (2), ATTENTION.

preoccupied *adj.* —*See* ABSENT-MINDED, RAPT.

preoccupy *v.* To dominate the mind or thoughts of ▸ fixate, obsess, possess. [*Compare* GRIP.] —*See also* ABSORB (1).

pre-owned *adj.* —*See* USED (2).

prep *v.* —*See* PREPARE.

preparation *n.* The condition of being made ready beforehand ▸ mobilization, prearrangement, preparedness, readiness. *Idiom:* made ready.

preparations *n.* Steps taken in preparation for an undertaking ▸ accommodations, arrangements, plans, provisions.

preparatory *adj.* —*See* INTRODUCTORY.

prepare *v.* To cause to be ready, as for use, consumption, or a special purpose ▸ cure, fit, fix, make, prime, ready. *In-*

ments or ingredients. 3. To fit out; equip.
pre·par·ed·ness (prĭ-pâr′ĭd-nĭs) ► *n.* The state of being prepared, esp. for combat.
pre·pon·der·ate (prĭ-pŏn′də-rāt′) ► *v.* **-at·ed, -at·ing.** To be greater than something else, as in power, weight, or importance. **—pre·pon′der·ance** *n.* **—pre·pon′der·ant** *adj.*
prep·o·si·tion (prĕp′ə-zĭsh′ən) ► *n.* In some languages, a word placed before a substantive indicating its relation to a verb, an adjective, or another substantive, as English *at, by, in, to, from,* and *with.* **—prep′o·si′tion·al** *adj.*
pre·pos·sess (prē′pə-zĕs′) ► *v.* 1. To influence beforehand; prejudice. 2. To impress favorably in advance.
pre·pos·sess·ing (prē′pə-zĕs′ĭng) ► *adj.* Serving to impress favorably; pleasing: *a prepossessing appearance.*
pre·pos·ter·ous (prĭ-pŏs′tər-əs) ► *adj.* Contrary to reason or common sense; absurd. **—pre·pos′ter·ous·ness** *n.*
prep·py or **prep·pie** (prĕp′ē) ► *n., pl.* **-pies.** *Informal* A student of a preparatory school. **—prep′pi·ness** *n.* **—prep′py** *adj.*
prep school ► *n.* *Informal* A preparatory school.
pre·puce (prē′pyo͞os′) ► *n.* See **foreskin. —pre·pu′tial** (-pyo͞o′shəl) *adj.*
pre·re·cord (prē′rĭ-kôrd′) ► *v.* To record (a radio or television program) for later presentation or use.
pre·req·ui·site (prē-rĕk′wĭ-zĭt) ► *adj.* Required as a prior condition. **—pre·req′ui·site** *n.*
pre·rog·a·tive (prĭ-rŏg′ə-tĭv) ► *n.* An exclusive right or privilege.
pres. ► *abbr.* 1. present 2. or **Pres.** president
pres·age (prĕs′ĭj) ► *n.* 1. An indication or warning of a future occurrence; omen. 2. A presentiment; foreboding. ► *v.* (prĭ-sāj′, prĕs′ĭj) **-saged, -sag·ing.** 1. To indicate or warn of in advance; portend. 2. To have a presentiment of.
pres·by·ter (prĕz′bĭ-tər, prĕs′-) ► *n.* 1. A priest in various hierarchical churches. 2. An elder in the Presbyterian Church.
pres·by·te·ri·an (prĕz′bĭ-tîr′ē-ən, prĕs′-) ► *adj.* 1. Relating to ecclesiastical government by presbyters. 2. **Presbyterian** Of or relating to a Protestant church governed by presbyters and traditionally Calvinist in doctrine. **—Pres′by·te′ri·an** *n.* **—pres′by·te′ri·an·ism** *n.*
pres·by·ter·y (prĕz′bĭ-tĕr′ē, prĕs′-) ► *n., pl.* **-ies.** 1. A court composed of Presbyterian Church ministers and representative elders of a particular locality. 2. The section of a church reserved for the clergy.
pre·school (prē′sko͞ol′) ► *adj.* Of or intended for the years of childhood that precede elementary school. **—pre′school′er** *n.*
pre·science (prĕsh′əns, -ē-əns, prē′shəns, -shē-əns) ► *n.* Knowledge of actions or events before they occur. **—pre′scient** *adj.*
pre·scribe (prĭ-skrīb′) ► *v.* **-scribed, -scrib·ing.** 1. To set down as a rule or guide. 2. To order the use of (a medicine or other treatment). **—pre·scrib′er** *n.* **—pre·scrip′tive** (-skrĭp′tĭv) *adj.* **—pre·scrip′tive·ness** *n.*
pre·scrip·tion (prĭ-skrĭp′shən) ► *n.* 1. The act of prescribing. 2a. A written order, esp. by a physician, for the preparation and administration of a medicine. b. A prescribed medicine.
pres·ence (prĕz′əns) ► *n.* 1. The state or fact of being present. 2. The area immediately surrounding someone. 3. A person who is present. 4a. A person's bearing. b. The quality of self-assurance and effectiveness.
pres·ent[1] (prĕz′ənt) ► *n.* 1. A moment or period in time intermediate between past and future; now. 2. *Gram.* The present tense. 3. **presents** *Law* The document or instrument in question. ► *adj.* 1. Existing or happening now: *present trends.* 2. Being at hand. 3. *Gram.* Designating a verb tense or form that expresses current time. **—pres′ent·ness** *n.*
pre·sent[2] (prĭ-zĕnt′) ► *v.* 1. To introduce, esp. formally. 2. To bring before the public. 3a. To make a gift or award of. b. To make a gift to. 4. To offer for examination or consideration. 5. To salute with (a weapon). 6. *Law* To bring a charge or indictment against. ► *n.* **pres·ent** (prĕz′ənt) Something presented; gift. **—pre·sent′a·ble** *adj.* **—pres′en·tation** (prĕz′ən-tā′shən, prē′zən-) *n.*
pres·ent-day (prĕz′ənt-dā′) ► *adj.* Current.
pre·sen·tient (prē-sĕn′shənt, -shē-ənt) ► *adj.* Having a presentiment.
pre·sen·ti·ment (prĭ-zĕn′tə-mənt) ► *n.* A sense that something is about to occur; premonition.
pres·ent·ly (prĕz′ənt-lē) ► *adv.* 1. In a short time; soon. 2. Currently.
pres·ent participle (prĕz′ənt) ► *n.* A participle expressing present action, in English formed by adding *-ing* to the infinitive and used to express present action, to form progressive tenses, and to function as a verbal adjective.
present per·fect (pûr′fĭkt) ► *n.* The verb tense expressing action completed at the present time, formed in English by combining the present tense of *have* with a past participle, as in *He has spoken.*
pres·er·va·tion·ist (prĕz′ər-vā′shə-nĭst) ► *n.* One who advocates preservation, esp. of natural areas or endangered species. **—pres′er·va′tion·ism** *n.*
pre·ser·va·tive (prĭ-zûr′və-tĭv) ► *n.* Something used to preserve, esp. a chemical added to foods to inhibit spoilage. **—pre·ser′va·tive** *adj.*
pre·serve (prĭ-zûrv′) ► *v.* **-served, -serv·ing.** 1. To protect

THESAURUS

formal: prep. *—See also* ARRANGE (2).
prepared *adj.* In a state of preparedness ► ready, set. *Informal:* go. *Slang:* together. *Idioms:* all set, in working order, on deck, ready (*or* raring) to go.
preparedness *n.* *—See* PREPARATION.
preponderance or **preponderancy** *n.* The greatest part or portion ► bulk, mass, weight. [*Compare* CENTER.] *—See also* DOMINANCE.
preponderant *adj.* *—See* DOMINANT (1).
preponderate *v.* *—See* DOMINATE (1).
prepossess *v.* *—See* BIAS (1).
prepossessed *adj.* *—See* BIASED.
prepossession *n.* *—See* ABSORPTION (2), BIAS.
preposterous *adj.* *—See* FOOLISH, OUTRAGEOUS.
preposterousness *n.* *—See* FOOLISHNESS.
prepotency *n.* *—See* DOMINANCE.
prepotent *adj.* *—See* DOMINANT (1).
prepubescence *n.* The stage of life between birth and puberty ► childhood, early years, innocence, preadolescence. [*Compare* YOUTH.]
prerequisite *n.* *—See* CONDITION (2), PROVISION, RIGHT.
prerequisite *adj.* *—See* ESSENTIAL (1).
prerogative *n.* *—See* AUTHORITY, RIGHT.
prerogative *adj.* *—See* EXCLUSIVE (1).
presage *n.* *—See* OMEN.
presage *v.* *—See* FORESHADOW, PREDICT.
presager *n.* *—See* FORERUNNER.
prescience *n.* *—See* PREDICTION, VISION (2).
prescient *adj.* *—See* PREDICTIVE, VISIONARY.
prescribe *v.* *—See* ADMINISTER (3), DICTATE.
prescribed *adj.* *—See* REQUIRED.
prescript *n.* *—See* RULE.
prescription *n.* *—See* DRUG (1), LAW (1).
prescriptive *adj.* *—See* DIDACTIC (2).
presence *n.* The condition or fact of being present ► attendance, occurrence. [*Compare* EXISTENCE.] *—See also* BEARING (1).
present[1] *n.* *—See* NOW.
present *adj.* In existence now ► contemporary, current, existent, existing, immediate, new, now, present-day. *—See also* CONTEMPORARY (2).
present *v.* *—See* DONATE.
present[2] *v.* To make known socially ► acquaint, familiarize, introduce. *—See also* CITE, CONFER (2), INTERPRET (2), OFFER (1), OFFER (2), STAGE.
present *n.* Something bestowed voluntarily ► bequest, gift, presentation. *Slang:* freebie. [*Compare* GRANT.] *—See also* DONATION.
presentable *adj.* *—See* DECENT (7).
presentation *n.* 1. Something bestowed voluntarily ► bequest, gift, present. *Slang:* freebie. [*Compare* GRANT.] 2. The instance or occasion of being presented for the first time to society ► coming-out, debut. *—See also* CONFERMENT, DISPLAY, INTERPRETATION, OFFER.
present-day *adj.* *—See* PRESENT[1].
presentiment *n.* *—See* FEELING (1).
preservation *n.* *—See* CONSERVATION, DEFENSE, MAINTENANCE.
preservative *adj.* Tending to or capable of preserving ► conservational, conservative, curatorial, precautionary, protective.
preserve *v.* 1. To prepare food for storage and future use ► brine, can, conserve, cure, dehydrate, dry, freeze, jerk,

from injury or peril. **2.** To keep or maintain intact. **3.** To treat fruit or other foods so as to prevent decay. ▸ *n.* **1.** often **preserves** Fruit cooked with sugar to protect against decay or fermentation. **2.** An area maintained for the protection of wildlife or natural resources. **—pres′er·va′tion** (prĕz′ər-vā′shən) *n.* **—pre·serv′er** *n.*

pre·shrunk also **pre-shrunk** (prē′shrŭngk′) ▸ *adj.* Shrunk during manufacture to minimize subsequent shrinkage.

pre·side (prĭ-zīd′) ▸ *v.* **-sid·ed, -sid·ing. 1.** To hold the position of authority; act as chairperson. **2.** To possess or exercise authority or control.

pres·i·dent (prĕz′ĭ-dənt, -dĕnt′) ▸ *n.* **1.** One appointed or elected to preside over an assembly or meeting. **2.** often **President** The chief executive of a republic, esp. of the US. **3.** The chief officer of an organization, as a corporation. **—pres′i·den·cy** *n.* **—pres′i·den′tial** (-dĕn′shəl) *adj.* **—pres′i·dent·ship′** *n.*

Pres·i·dents' Day (prĕz′ĭ-dənts, -dĕnts) ▸ *n.* The 3rd Monday in Feb. a US legal holiday commemorating the birthdays of George Washington and Abraham Lincoln.

press (prĕs) ▸ *v.* **1.** To exert steady weight or force against; bear down on. **2.** To squeeze the juice or other contents from. **3a.** To reshape or make compact by applying steady force. **b.** To iron (e.g., clothing). **4.** To try to influence, as by insistent arguments. **5.** To place in trying circumstances; harass. **6.** To advance or carry on vigorously. **7.** To put forward insistently. **8.** To assemble in large numbers; crowd. ▸ *n.* **1.** Any of various machines or devices that apply pressure. **2.** A printing press. **3.** A place or establishment where matter is printed. **4.** The art, method, or business of printing. **5a.** The collecting and publishing or broadcasting of news; journalism in general. **b.** The entirety of media that collect, publish, transmit, or broadcast the news. **c.** The people involved in the media, as news reporters and broadcasters. **6.** A large gathering; throng. **7.** The act of applying pressure. **8.** The urgency of business or matters. **9.** The set of proper creases in a garment or fabric, formed by ironing.

press agent ▸ *n.* A person employed to arrange advertising and publicity, as for a performer or business. **—press a′gent·ry** *n.*

press conference ▸ *n.* An interview held for news reporters by a political figure or famous person.

press·ing (prĕs′ĭng) ▸ *adj.* Demanding immediate attention; urgent. **—press′ing·ly** *adv.*

press·room (prĕs′ro͞om′, -ro͝om′) ▸ *n.* The room in a printing or newspaper publishing establishment that contains the presses.

pres·sure (prĕsh′ər) ▸ *n.* **1.** The act of pressing or the condition of being pressed. **2.** The application of continuous force by one body on another that it is touching. **3.** *Phys.* Force applied uniformly over a surface, measured as force per unit of area. **4.** A constraining influence: *pressure to conform.* **5.** Urgent claim or demand: *under the pressure of business.* ▸ *v.* **-sured, -sur·ing.** To exert pressure on.

pressure group ▸ *n.* A group that endeavors to influence public policy.

pressure suit ▸ *n.* A garment worn in high-altitude aircraft or in spacecraft to compensate for low-pressure conditions.

pres·sur·ize (prĕsh′ə-rīz′) ▸ *v.* **-ized, -iz·ing.** To maintain normal air pressure in (an enclosure, as an aircraft or submarine). **—pres′sur·i·za′tion** *n.* **—pres′sur·iz′er** *n.*

pres·ti·dig·i·ta·tion (prĕs′tĭ-dĭj′ĭ-tā′shən) ▸ *n.* Sleight of hand. **—pres′ti·dig′i·ta′tor** *n.*

pres·tige (prĕ-stēzh′, -stēj′) ▸ *n.* **1.** The level of respect at which one is regarded by others; standing. **2.** Prominence, honor, or distinction. **—pres·ti′gious** (-stē′jəs, -stĭj′əs) *adj.*

pres·to (prĕs′tō) ▸ *adv.* **1.** *Mus.* In rapid tempo. **2.** Suddenly; right away. **—pres′to** *adj.*

pre·sume (prĭ-zo͞om′) ▸ *v.* **-sumed, -sum·ing. 1.** To take for granted; assume. **2.** To act overconfidently; take liberties. **3.** To take unwarranted advantage of something. **—pre·sum′a·ble** *adj.* **—pre·sum′a·bly** *adv.*

pre·sump·tion (prĭ-zŭmp′shən) ▸ *n.* **1.** Behavior or attitude that is boldly arrogant or offensive; effrontery. **2.** Belief based on reasonable evidence; assumption or supposition. **3.** A condition or basis for accepting or presuming. **—pre·sump′tive** *adj.*

pre·sump·tu·ous (prĭ-zŭmp′cho͞o-əs) ▸ *adj.* Going beyond what is right or proper; excessively forward. **—pre·sump′tu·ous·ly** *adv.* **—pre·sump′tu·ous·ness** *n.*

pre·sup·pose (prē′sə-pōz′) ▸ *v.* **-posed, -pos·ing. 1.** To believe or suppose in advance. **2.** To require or involve necessarily as an antecedent condition. **—pre·sup′po·si′tion** (-sŭp′ə-zĭsh′ən) *n.*

pre·teen (prē′tēn′) ▸ *adj.* Of or designed for preadolescent children. **—pre′teen′** *n.*

pre·tend (prĭ-tĕnd′) ▸ *v.* **1.** To give a false appearance of; feign. **2.** To claim or allege insincerely or falsely; profess. **3.** To make believe. **4.** To make pretensions: *pretends to gourmet tastes.* **—pre·tend′er** *n.*

pre·tense (prē′tĕns′, prĭ-tĕns′) ▸ *n.* **1.** A false appearance or action intended to deceive. **2.** A studied show; affectation. **3.** A feigned reason or excuse; pretext. **4.** An outward appearance. **5.** A claim, esp. one without foundation. **6.** Pretentiousness; ostentation.

pre·ten·sion (prĭ-tĕn′shən) ▸ *n.* **1.** A specious allegation; pretext. **2.** A claim, esp. one without foundation. **3.** Ostentation; pretentiousness.

THESAURUS

keep, kipper, pickle, pot, put up, refrigerate, salt, season, smoke, souse. **2.** To protect an asset from loss or destruction ▸ conserve, husband, save. [*Compare* DEFEND.] **3.** To keep in a condition of good repair, efficiency, or use ▸ keep up, maintain, sustain. —*See also* DEFEND (1).

preserve *n.* Public land kept for a special purpose ▸ park, reservation, reserve, sanctuary. [*Compare* COMMON.]

press *v.* **1.** To extract from by applying pressure ▸ crush, express, squeeze. **2.** To smooth by applying heat or pressure ▸ calender, iron, mangle, roll. [*Compare* EVEN.] —*See also* ADVANCE (2), CROWD, EMBRACE (1), PUSH (1), RUB, TOUCH, URGE.

press *n.* A person or group of persons whose occupation is journalism ▸ anchor, anchorman, anchorperson, anchorwoman, columnist, commentator, correspondent, editor, editorialist, fourth estate, journalist, mass media, media, newscaster, newshound, newsman, newspaperman, newspaperwoman, newsperson, newswoman, reporter, stringer. *Informal:* legman. —*See also* CROWD, PUSH.

pressing *adj.* —*See* URGENT (1).

pressing *n.* Urgent solicitation ▸ insistence, insistency, persuasion, urging. [*Compare* DEMAND.]

pressure *n.* An oppressive condition of distress ▸ strain, stress, tautness, tenseness, tension. *Informal:* heat. [*Compare* ANXIETY.] —*See also* FORCE (1).

pressure *v.* —*See* FORCE (1).

prestidigitation *n.* —*See* MAGIC (2).

prestidigitator *n.* —*See* WIZARD.

prestige *n.* —*See* FACE (6), FAME, HONOR (2).

prestigious *adj.* —*See* FAMOUS.

presumable *adj.* —*See* PRESUMPTIVE.

presume *v.* To take advantage of unfairly ▸ abuse, exploit, impose, use. —*See also* SUPPOSE (1), VENTURE.

presuming *adj.* —*See* IMPUDENT.

presumption *n.* —*See* ARROGANCE, ASSUMPTION.

presumptive *adj.* Based on probability or presumption ▸ assumptive, given, likely, presumable, probable, prospective, supposable. *Idiom:* taken for granted. [*Compare* DUE, SUPPOSED.]

presumptuous *adj.* —*See* IMPUDENT.

presumptuousness *n.* —*See* IMPUDENCE.

presuppose *v.* —*See* SUPPOSE (1).

presupposition *n.* —*See* ASSUMPTION.

preteen *n.* —*See* CHILD (1).

pretend *v.* To claim or allege insincerely or falsely ▸ feign, pretext, profess, purport. —*See also* ACT (2), VENTURE.

pretend *adj.* —*See* ARTIFICIAL (1).

pretended *adj.* Being fictitious and not real, as a name ▸ assumed, made-up, pseudonymous. [*Compare* FALSE, FICTITIOUS.] —*See also* ARTIFICIAL (2).

pretender *n.* —*See* FAKE.

pretense *n.* A professed but feigned reason or excuse ▸ pretension, pretext. [*Compare* EXCUSE.] —*See also* ACT (2), AFFECTATION, CLAIM (1), FAÇADE (2), INSINCERITY.

pretension *n.* A professed but feigned reason or excuse ▸ pretense, pretext. [*Compare* EXCUSE.] —*See also* CLAIM (1), PRETENTIOUSNESS.

pre·ten·tious (prĭ-tĕn′shəs) ▸ *adj.* **1.** Claiming or demanding distinction or merit, esp. when unjustified. **2.** Showing or betraying an attitude of superiority. **3.** Extravagantly showy; ostentatious. **—pre·ten′tious·ly** *adv.* **—pre·ten′tious·ness** *n.*

pret·er·ite or **pret·er·it** (prĕt′ər-ĭt) ▸ *adj.* Of or being the verb tense that describes a past action or state. **—pret′er·ite** *n.*

pre·ter·nat·u·ral (prē′tər-năch′ər-əl, -năch′rəl) ▸ *adj.* **1.** Beyond the normal course of nature. **2.** Supernatural. **—pre′ter·nat′u·ral·ly** *adv.* **—pre′ter·nat′u·ral·ness** *n.*

pre·text (prē′tĕkst′) ▸ *n.* An ostensible or professed purpose; excuse.

Pre·to·ri·a (prĭ-tôr′ē-ə) ▸ The administrative capital of South Africa, in the NE part N of Johannesburg.

pret·ti·fy (prĭt′ĭ-fī′) ▸ *v.* **-fied, -fy·ing.** To make pretty. **—pret′ti·fi·ca′tion** *n.*

pret·ty (prĭt′ē) ▸ *adj.* **-ti·er, -ti·est. 1.** Pleasing or attractive in a graceful or delicate way. **2.** Clever; adroit: *a pretty maneuver.* **3.** Very bad; terrible: *in a pretty predicament.* **4.** Superficially attractive but lacking substance: *full of pretty phrases.* **5.** *Informal* Considerable in size or extent: *a pretty fortune.* ▸ *adv.* To a fair degree; moderately: *a pretty good student.* ▸ *v.* **-tied, -ty·ing.** To make pretty: *We prettied up the spare room for our guests.* **—pret′ti·ly** *adv.* **—pret′ti·ness** *n.*

pret·zel (prĕt′səl) ▸ *n.* A glazed, often salted biscuit usu. baked in the form of a loose knot or stick.

pre·vail (prĭ-vāl′) ▸ *v.* **1.** To be victorious; triumph. **2.** To win out. **3.** To be most common or frequent. **4.** To use persuasion or inducement successfully. **—pre·vail′er** *n.* **—pre·vail′ing** *adj.* **—pre·vail′ing·ly** *adv.*

prev·a·lent (prĕv′ə-lənt) ▸ *adj.* Widely or commonly occurring or practiced. **—prev′a·lence** *n.*

pre·var·i·cate (prĭ-văr′ĭ-kāt′) ▸ *v.* **-cat·ed, -cat·ing.** To stray from or evade the truth; equivocate. **—pre·var′i·ca′tion** *n.* **—pre·var′i·ca′tor** *n.*

pre·vent (prĭ-vĕnt′) ▸ *v.* **1.** To keep from happening: *took steps to prevent the strike.* **2.** To keep (someone) from doing something; impede: *prevented us from winning.* **—pre·vent′a·ble, pre·vent′i·ble** *adj.* **—pre·ven′tion** *n.*

pre·ven·tive (prĭ-vĕn′tĭv) also **pre·ven·ta·tive** (-tə-tĭv) ▸ *adj.* **1.** Intended or used to prevent or hinder; acting as an obstacle. **2.** Preventing or slowing the course of illness or disease; prophylactic. **—pre·ven′tive** *n.*

pre·view also **pre·vue** (prē′vyo͞o′) ▸ *n.* **1.** An advance showing, as of a movie, before public presentation begins. **2.** The presentation of several scenes advertising a forthcoming movie. **3.** An introductory sample or overview; foretaste. **—pre′view′** *v.*

pre·vi·ous (prē′vē-əs) ▸ *adj.* Existing or occurring before something else; prior. **—pre′vi·ous·ly** *adv.* **—pre′vi·ous·ness** *n.*

pre·vi·sion (prĭ-vĭzh′ən) ▸ *n.* **1.** A knowing in advance; foresight. **2.** A prediction.

prey (prā) ▸ *n.* **1.** An animal hunted or caught for food; quarry. **2.** A victim. **3.** The act or practice of preying. ▸ *v.* **1.** To hunt, catch, or eat as prey. **2.** To victimize. **3.** To exert an injurious effect.

price (prīs) ▸ *n.* **1.** The sum of money asked or given for something. **2.** The cost at which something is obtained. **3.** The cost of bribing someone: *everyone has a price.* ▸ *v.* **priced, pric·ing. 1.** To fix or establish a price for. **2.** To find out the price of.

price·less (prīs′lĭs) ▸ *adj.* Of inestimable worth; invaluable.

price war ▸ *n.* A period of intense competition in which each competitor tries to cut retail prices below those of the others.

pric·ey also **pric·y** (prī′sē) ▸ *adj.* **-i·er, -i·est.** *Informal* Expensive.

prick (prĭk) ▸ *n.* **1a.** The act of pricking. **b.** The sensation of being pricked. **2.** A small mark or puncture made by a pointed object. **3.** A pointed object, such as a thorn. ▸ *v.* **1.** To puncture lightly. **2.** To affect with a mental or emotional pang, as of remorse. **3.** To mark or delineate on a surface by means of small punctures. ***—idiom:*** **prick up (one's) ears** To listen with attentive interest.

prick·er (prĭk′ər) ▸ *n.* A prickle or thorn.

prick·le (prĭk′əl) ▸ *n.* **1.** A small sharp spine or thorn. **2.** A tingling sensation. ▸ *v.* **-led, -ling. 1.** To prick, as with a thorn. **2.** To tingle.

prick·ly (prĭk′lē) ▸ *adj.* **-li·er, -li·est. 1.** Having prickles. **2.** Marked by tingling. **3.** Causing trouble; thorny. **—prick′li·ness** *n.*

prickly heat ▸ *n.* See **heat rash.**

prickly pear ▸ *n.* **1.** Any of various cacti having bristly, flattened or cylindrical joints and showy, usu. yellow flowers. **2.** The edible fruit of a prickly pear.

pride (prīd) ▸ *n.* **1.** A sense of one's proper dignity or value; self-respect. **2.** Pleasure or satisfaction taken in achievement, possession, or association. **3.** Arrogance; conceit. **4.** The best of a group or class. **5.** A group of lions. ▸ *v.* **prid·ed, prid·ing.** To indulge (oneself) in a feeling of

THESAURUS

pretentious *adj.* —*See* POMPOUS, SHOWY.

pretentiousness *n.* Boastful self-importance or display ▸ grandioseness, grandiosity, loftiness, ostentation, pomposity, pompousness, pretension. [*Compare* ARROGANCE, EGOTISM.]

preternatural *adj.* Greatly exceeding or departing from the normal course of nature ▸ supernatural, unnatural. —*See also* ABNORMAL, SUPERNATURAL (1).

preternaturalness *n.* —*See* ABNORMALITY.

pretext *n.* A professed but feigned reason or excuse ▸ pretense, pretension. —*See also* EXCUSE (1), FAÇADE (2).

pretext *v.* To claim or allege insincerely or falsely ▸ feign, pretend, profess, purport.

pretty *adj.* —*See* ATTRACTIVE, BEAUTIFUL.

pretty *adv.* —*See* FAIRLY (2).

pretty penny *n.* —*See* FORTUNE.

prevail *v.* —*See* DOMINATE (1).

prevail on or **upon** *v.* —*See* PERSUADE.

prevail over *v.* —*See* DEFEAT.

prevailing *adj.* Most generally existing or encountered at a given time ▸ current, epidemic, general, pandemic, popular, predominant, prevalent, rampant, regnant, reigning, rife, ruling, widespread. [*Compare* COMMON, PERVASIVE.] —*See also* DOMINANT (1).

prevalence *n.* —*See* USUALNESS.

prevalent *adj.* —*See* PREVAILING.

prevaricate *v.* —*See* EQUIVOCATE (2), LIE[2].

prevarication *n.* —*See* EQUIVOCATION, LIE[2], MENDACITY.

prevaricator *n.* —*See* LIAR.

prevent *v.* To prohibit from occurring by advance planning or action ▸ anticipate, avert, forerun, forestall, forfend, head off, obviate, preclude, prohibit, rule out, stave off, ward (off). ***Idiom:*** nip in the bud. [*Compare* FORBID, FRUSTRATE, STOP.]

prevention *n.* The act of preventing ▸ determent, deterrence, exclusion, forestallment, frustration, obviation, preclusion, prohibition. [*Compare* FORBIDDANCE, STOP.]

preventive or **preventative** *adj.* **1.** Intended to prevent ▸ deterrent, exclusive, interdictive, preclusive, prohibitive, proscriptive. **2.** Defending against disease ▸ defensive, precautionary, prophylactic, protective.

previous *adj.* Next before the present one ▸ foregoing, last, latter, preceding. —*See also* ADVANCE, LATE (2), PAST.

previously *adv.* —*See* EARLIER.

prevision *n.* —*See* PREDICTION.

previsionary *adj.* —*See* PREDICTIVE.

prey *n.* —*See* VICTIM.

price *n.* The expenditure at which something is obtained ▸ cost, price, sacrifice, toll. *Informal:* damage. —*See also* COST (1).

priceless *adj.* —*See* COSTLY, FUNNY (1).

pricey *adj.* —*See* COSTLY.

prick *n.* A small mark or hole made by a sharp, pointed object ▸ nick, notch, perforation, puncture, stab. [*Compare* CUT, SCRAPE.] —*See also* PAIN, SPIKE.

prick *v.* —*See* CUT (1), PROVOKE.

prickle *n.* —*See* PAIN, SPIKE.

prickliness *n.* —*See* TEMPER (1).

prickly *adj.* Full of irritating difficulties or controversies ▸ nettlesome, spiny, thorny. [*Compare* COMPLEX, DELICATE, DISTURBING, TROUBLESOME.] —*See also* THORNY (1).

pricky *adj.* —*See* THORNY (1).

pride *n.* A sense of one's own dignity or worth ▸ amour-propre, ego, proudness, self-contentment, self-esteem, self-regard, self-respect, self-satisfaction. —*See also* ARROGANCE, EGOTISM, FLOCK.

pride *v.* To be proud of oneself, as

satisfaction. **—pride′ful** *adj.* **—pride′ful·ly** *adv.* **—pride′ful·ness** *n.*

prie-dieu (prē-dyœ′) ► *n., pl.* **-dieus** or **-dieux** (-dyœz′). A narrow, desklike kneeling bench for use at prayer.

priest (prēst) ► *n.* **1.** In many Christian churches, a member of the clergy ranking below a bishop but above a deacon. **2.** A person having the authority to perform and administer religious rites. **—priest′hood′** *n.* **—priest′li·ness** *n.* **—priest′ly** *adj.*

priest·ess (prē′stĭs) ► *n.* A woman who presides over rites, esp. in paganism.

prig (prĭg) ► *n.* A smugly proper or prudish person. **—prig′ger·y** *n.* **—prig′gish** *adj.* **—prig′gish·ness** *n.*

prim (prĭm) ► *adj.* **prim·mer, prim·mest.** Precise or proper to the point of affectation. **—prim′ly** *adv.* **—prim′ness** *n.*

pri·ma·cy (prī′mə-sē) ► *n., pl.* **-cies. 1.** The state of being first or foremost. **2.** *Eccles.* The office or rank of primate.

pri·ma don·na (prē′mə dŏn′ə, prĭm′ə) ► *n.* **1.** The leading woman soloist in an opera company. **2.** A temperamental, conceited person.

pri·ma fa·cie (prī′mə fā′shē, -shē-ē, fā′shə) ► *adv.* At first sight; before closer inspection. **—pri′ma fa′cie** *adj.*

pri·mal (prī′məl) ► *adj.* **1.** Being first in time; original. **2.** Of first importance; primary.

pri·mar·i·ly (prī-mâr′ə-lē, -mĕr′-) ► *adv.* **1.** Chiefly; mainly. **2.** At first; originally.

pri·mar·y (prī′mĕr′ē, -mə-rē) ► *adj.* **1.** First in rank, quality, or importance. **2.** Occurring first in time or sequence; earliest. **3.** Being the first of a kind. **4.** Being an essential component; basic. **5.** Immediate; direct. ► *n., pl.* **-ies. 1.** One that is first in time, order, or importance. **2.** A preliminary election in which voters nominate candidates for office.

primary care ► *n.* Medical care received upon first contact with the health care system, before referral elsewhere within the system.

primary color ► *n.* Any of a group of colors, such as red, yellow, and blue, which can be regarded as generating all colors.

primary school ► *n.* **1.** A school including the first three or four grades and sometimes kindergarten. **2.** See **elementary school.**

pri·mate (prī′mĭt, -māt′) ► *n.* **1.** (prī′māt′) One of the group of mammals which includes monkeys, apes, and humans. **2.** A bishop of highest rank in a province or country.

prime (prīm) ► *adj.* **1.** First in quality, importance, rank, or time. **2.** *Math.* Of or being a prime number. ► *n.* **1.** The earliest or beginning stage of something. **2.** Springtime. **3.** The period or phase of ideal or peak condition. **4.** *Math.* A prime number. ► *v.* **primed, prim·ing. 1.** To make ready; prepare. **2.** To load (a gun or mine) for firing. **3.** To prepare for operation, as by pouring water into a pump. **4.** To prepare (a surface) for painting by covering with an undercoat. **5.** To instruct beforehand; coach. **—prime′ness** *n.*

prime meridian ► *n.* The zero meridian from which longitude east and west is measured. It passes through Greenwich, England.

prime minister ► *n.* **1.** A chief minister appointed by a ruler. **2.** The chief executive of a parliamentary democracy. **—prime ministership, prime ministry** *n.*

prime number ► *n.* A positive integer that has itself and one as its only factors.

prim·er[1] (prĭm′ər) ► *n.* **1.** An elementary reading textbook. **2.** A book that covers the basic elements of a subject.

prim·er[2] (prī′mər) ► *n.* **1.** A device used to detonate an explosive charge. **2.** An undercoat of paint or size applied to prepare a surface.

prime rate ► *n.* The lowest rate of interest on bank loans at a given time and place, offered to preferred borrowers.

prime time ► *n.* The hours between 7 and 11 P.M. when the largest television audience is available. **—prime′-time′** *adj.*

pri·me·val (prī-mē′vəl) ► *adj.* Belonging to the first or earliest age or ages; original.

prim·i·tive (prĭm′ĭ-tĭv) ► *adj.* **1.** Of or relating to an earliest or original stage or state; primeval. **2.** Simple or crude; unsophisticated. **3.** *Anthro.* Of a nonindustrial, often tribal culture. **4.** Of or created by an artist without formal training. ► *n.* **1.** *Anthro.* A person belonging to a nonindustrial society. **2a.** A self-taught artist. **b.** A work of art by a primitive artist. **—prim′i·tive·ly** *adv.* **—prim′i·tive·ness** *n.*

prim·i·tiv·ism (prĭm′ĭ-tĭ-vĭz′əm) ► *n.* The style characteristic of a primitive artist. **—prim′i·tiv·ist** *adj. & n.*

pri·mo·gen·i·tor (prī′mō-jĕn′ĭ-tər) ► *n.* The earliest ancestor.

pri·mo·gen·i·ture (prī′mō-jĕn′ĭ-chŏŏr′) ► *n.* **1.** The state of being the firstborn or eldest child of the same parents. **2.** *Law* The right of the eldest child, esp. a son, to inherit the entire estate of one or both parents.

pri·mor·di·al (prī-môr′dē-əl) ► *adj.* Being or happening first in sequence of time; original. **—pri·mor′di·al·ly** *adv.*

primp (prĭmp) ► *v.* To dress or groom (oneself) with excessive care.

prim·rose (prĭm′rōz′) ► *n.* Any of numerous plants having tubular, variously colored flowers.

prince (prĭns) ► *n.* **1.** A boy or man in a royal family. **2.** A hereditary ruler; king. **3.** An outstanding man in a group or class: *a merchant prince.* **—prince′dom** *n.* **—prince′li·ness** *n.* **—prince′ly** *adj.*

Prince Edward Island ► A province of SE Canada consisting of **Prince Edward Island** in the S Gulf of St. Lawrence. Cap. Charlottetown.

prin·cess (prĭn′sĭs, -sĕs′, prĭn-sĕs′) ► *n.* **1.** A female member of a royal family. **2.** The wife of a prince.

prin·ci·pal (prĭn′sə-pəl) ► *adj.* First or foremost in importance; chief. ► *n.* **1.** The head of an elementary school or high school. **2.** A main participant. **3.** A person having a leading or starring role. **4a.** The capital of a financial holding as distinguished from the revenue from it. **b.** A sum of money owed as a debt, upon which interest is calculated. **5.** *Law* **a.** A person who empowers another to act as his or her representative. **b.** One primarily responsible for an obligation. **—prin′ci·pal·ly** *adv.* **—prin′ci·pal·ship′** *n.*

prin·ci·pal·i·ty (prĭn′sə-păl′ĭ-tē) ► *n., pl.* **-ties.** A territory, position, or jurisdiction of a prince.

principal parts ► *pl.n.* In traditional grammars, the forms of the verb from which all other forms are derived.

prin·ci·ple (prĭn′sə-pəl) ► *n.* **1.** A basic truth, law, or assumption. **2a.** A rule or standard, esp. of good behavior. **b.** Moral or ethical standards or judgments. **3.** A fixed or

THESAURUS

for an accomplishment or achievement ► gloat, pique, plume, preen.

prideful *adj.* —*See* ARROGANT, PROUD.

pridefulness *n.* —*See* ARROGANCE.

prier or **pryer** *n.* A person who snoops ► pry, snoop, snooper. [*Compare* BUSYBODY.]

priest *n.* —*See* CLERIC.

priestly *adj.* —*See* CLERICAL.

prig *n.* One who despises people or things regarded as inferior, especially because of social or intellectual pretension ► elitist, snob. *Informal:* snoot. —*See also* PRUDE.

priggish *adj.* —*See* ARROGANT, PRUDISH.

prim *adj.* —*See* NEAT, PRUDISH.

prima donna *n.* —*See* LEAD.

primal *adj.* —*See* EARLY (1), ELEMENTAL.

primary *adj.* **1.** Most important, influential, or significant ► capital, cardinal, central, chief, crucial, first, foremost, head, key, leading, main, major, number one, paramount, pivotal, premier, prime, principal, staple, top, vital. [*Compare* ELEMENTAL, ESSENTIAL, IMPORTANT.] **2.** Marked by the absence of any intervention ► direct, firsthand, immediate. —*See also* DOMINANT (1), FIRST, ORIGINAL, RADICAL.

prime *adj.* —*See* CHOICE (1), DOMINANT (1), EXCELLENT, FIRST, ORIGINAL, PRIMARY (1).

prime *n.* —*See* BLOOM[1] (1).

prime *v.* To put explosive material into a weapon ► charge, load, ready. —*See also* PREPARE.

primeval *adj.* —*See* EARLY (1).

primitive *adj.* —*See* EARLY (1), ELEMENTAL, IGNORANT (2), ORIGINAL, RADICAL, RUDE (1), UNCIVILIZED.

primogenitor *n.* —*See* ANCESTOR (1).

primordial *adj.* —*See* EARLY (1), FIRST.

primp *v.* —*See* DRESS UP.

princely *adj.* —*See* GENEROUS (1), GRAND.

principal *adj.* —*See* DOMINANT (1), PRIMARY (1).

principal *n.* —*See* CAPITAL (1), LEAD.

principle *n.* —*See* CHARACTER (2), DOCTRINE, LAW (3), MORAL.

predetermined policy. 4. A rule or law concerning the functioning of natural phenomena or mechanical processes. 5. A basic source.

prin·ci·pled (prĭn′sə-pəld) ▸ *adj.* Based on, marked by, or manifesting principle.

prink (prĭngk) ▸ *v.* To primp. **—prink′er** *n.*

print (prĭnt) ▸ *n.* 1. A mark or impression made by pressure. 2. Something marked with an impression. 3a. Lettering or other impressions produced in ink. b. Matter so produced; printed material. c. Printed state or form. 4. A design or picture reproduced by printing. 5. A photographic image transferred to a surface, usu. from a negative. 6. A copy of a film made from a negative. 7. A fabric with a stamped dyed pattern. ▸ *v.* 1. To press (e.g., a mark or design) onto a surface. 2. To make an impression on or in (a surface). 3. To produce by means of pressed type, an electronic printer, or similar means, on a paper surface. 4. To publish. 5. To write in characters similar to those commonly used in print. 6. To produce a photographic image from by passing light through film onto sensitized paper.

print·a·ble (prĭn′tə-bəl) ▸ *adj.* 1. Capable of being printed or of producing a print. 2. Fit for publication.

print·ed circuit (prĭn′tĭd) ▸ *n.* An electric circuit in which the conducting connections have been printed in predetermined patterns on an insulating base.

print·er (prĭn′tər) ▸ *n.* 1. One whose occupation is printing. 2. A device that prints text or graphics on paper.

print·ing (prĭn′tĭng) ▸ *n.* 1. The art, process, or business of producing printed material. 2. Matter that is printed. 3. All the copies of a publication, such as a book, that are printed at one time.

printing press ▸ *n.* A machine that transfers images onto paper or similar material.

print·mak·ing (prĭnt′mā′kĭng) ▸ *n.* The artistic design and making of prints, such as woodcuts. **—print′mak′er** *n.*

print·out (prĭnt′out′) ▸ *n.* *Comp. Sci.* Printed output.

pri·or[1] (prī′ər) ▸ *adj.* 1. Preceding in time or order. 2. Preceding in importance or value.

pri·or[2] (prī′ər) ▸ *n.* A monastic officer in charge of a priory.

pri·or·ess (prī′ər-ĭs) ▸ *n.* A nun in charge of a priory.

pri·or·i·tize (prī-ôr′ĭ-tīz′, -ŏr′-) ▸ *v.* **-tized, -tiz·ing.** To arrange or deal with in order of importance. **—pri·or′i·ti·za′tion** *n.*

pri·or·i·ty (prī-ôr′ĭ-tē, -ŏr′-) ▸ *n., pl.* **-ties.** 1. Precedence, esp. by order of importance. 2. An established right to precedence. 3. Something deserving prior attention.

prior to ▸ *prep.* Before.

pri·or·y (prī′ə-rē) ▸ *n., pl.* **-ies.** A monastery governed by a prior or a convent governed by a prioress.

prism (prĭz′əm) ▸ *n.* 1. A polyhedron with parallel, congruent polygons as ends and parallelograms as sides. 2. A transparent solid, usu. with triangular ends, used for separating white light passed into a spectrum. 3. A cut-glass object, such as a pendant of a chandelier. **—pris·mat′ic** (prĭz-măt′ĭk) *adj.* **—pris·mat′i·cal·ly** *adv.*

pris·on (prĭz′ən) ▸ *n.* A place where persons convicted or accused of crimes are confined; jail.

pris·on·er (prĭz′ə-nər, prĭz′nər) ▸ *n.* 1. A person held in custody or captivity, esp. in a prison. 2. One deprived of freedom of expression or action.

prisoner of war ▸ *n., pl.* **prisoners of war.** A person taken by or surrendering to enemy forces in wartime.

pris·sy (prĭs′ē) ▸ *adj.* **-si·er, -si·est.** Excessively prim and proper. **—pris′si·ness** *n.*

pris·tine (prĭs′tēn′, prĭ-stēn′) ▸ *adj.* 1. Remaining in a pure state; uncorrupted. 2. Of or typical of the earliest time or condition; primitive or original.

prith·ee (prĭth′ē, prĭth′ē) ▸ *interj.* *Archaic* Please.

pri·va·cy (prī′və-sē) ▸ *n.* 1. The condition of being secluded from others. 2. Secrecy.

pri·vate (prī′vĭt) ▸ *adj.* 1. Secluded from the sight, presence, or intrusion of others. 2. Of or confined to the individual; personal. 3. Not available for public use, control, or participation. 4. Belonging to a particular person or persons. 5. Not holding an official or public position. 6. Intimate; secret. ▸ *n.* Any of the lowest enlisted ranks, as in the US Army. **—pri′vate·ly** *adv.* **—pri′vate·ness** *n.*

pri·va·teer (prī′və-tîr′) ▸ *n.* 1. A ship privately owned and manned but authorized to attack and capture enemy vessels. 2. Such a ship's commander or one of its crew.

pri·va·tion (prī-vā′shən) ▸ *n.* 1. Lack of the basic necessities or comforts of life. 2. The condition resulting from such lack.

pri·va·tize (prī′və-tīz′) ▸ *v.* **-tized, -tiz·ing.** To change (e.g., an industry) from governmental or public ownership or control to private enterprise. **—pri′va·ti·za′tion** *n.*

priv·et (prĭv′ĭt) ▸ *n.* A shrub having opposite leaves and clusters of white flowers, widely used for hedges.

priv·i·lege (prĭv′ə-lĭj, prĭv′lĭj) ▸ *n.* A special advantage, immunity, or benefit granted to or enjoyed by an individual, class, or caste. ▸ *v.* **-leged, -leg·ing.** To grant a privilege to.

priv·i·leged (prĭv′ə-lĭjd, prĭv′lĭjd) ▸ *adj.* 1. Having privileges. 2. Confined to a chosen group of individuals: *privileged information.*

priv·y (prĭv′ē) ▸ *adj.* 1. Made a participant in something secret. 2. Belonging to a person, such as the British sovereign, in a private rather than official capacity. ▸ *n., pl.* **-ies.** An outhouse.

prize[1] (prīz) ▸ *n.* 1. Something offered or won as an award for superiority or victory, as in a contest or competition. 2. Something worth striving for or aspiring to. ▸ *adj.* 1. Offered or given as a prize. 2. Given or worthy of a prize. 3. Outstanding. ▸ *v.* **prized, priz·ing.** To value highly; esteem.

prize[2] (prīz) ▸ *n.* Something, esp. an enemy ship captured during wartime.

prize[3] (prīz) ▸ *v.* **prized, priz·ing.** To move with a lever; pry.

prize·fight (prīz′fīt′) ▸ *n.* A match fought between professional boxers for money. **—prize′fight′er** *n.* **—prize′fight′ing** *n.*

prize·win·ner (prīz′wĭn′ər) ▸ *n.* One that wins a prize. **—prize′win′ning** *adj.*

pro[1] (prō) ▸ *n., pl.* **pros.** 1. An argument in favor of something. 2. One who takes an affirmative position. ▸ *adv.* In favor; affirmatively.

pro[2] (prō) *Informal* ▸ *n., pl.* **pros.** 1. A professional. 2. An expert. ▸ *adj.* Professional.

pro–[1] ▸ *pref.* 1. Acting in place of: *pronoun.* 2. Supporting; favoring: *prorevolutionary.*

THESAURUS

principled *adj.* —*See* ETHICAL.

principles *n.* —*See* ETHICS (2).

print *n.* —*See* IMPRESSION (1), TRACK.

print *v.* —*See* PUBLISH (1).

printing *n.* The entire number of copies of a publication printed from a single typesetting ▸ impression —*See also* PUBLICATION (1).

prior *adj.* —*See* ADVANCE, PAST.

priority *n.* —*See* PRECEDENCE.

prison *n.* —*See* JAIL.

priss *n.* —*See* PRUDE.

prissy *adj.* —*See* PRUDISH.

pristine *adj.* —*See* FRESH (1), ORIGINAL.

privacy *n.* —*See* SOLITUDE.

private *adj.* 1. Belonging to, relating to, or affecting a particular person ▸ individual, intimate, personal. 2. Belonging or confined to a particular person or group as opposed to the public or the government ▸ closed-door, personal, privy. [*Compare* SECRET.] —*See also* CONFIDENTIAL (1), EXCLUSIVE (1).

privation *n.* —*See* DEPRIVATION, POVERTY.

privilege *n.* —*See* LICENSE (1), RIGHT.

privileged *adj.* —*See* CONFIDENTIAL (3).

privy *adj.* Belonging or confined to a particular person or group as opposed to the public or the government ▸ closed-door, personal, private. [*Compare* SECRET.] —*See also* CONFIDENTIAL (1).

prize[1] *n.* 1. A memento that is received as a symbol of excellence or victory ▸ accolade, cup, award, trophy. [*Compare* MEDAL.] 2. A person or thing that is worth catching ▸ *Informal:* catch, plum. *Slang:* brass ring. —*See also* BEST (1), DISTINCTION (2), REWARD, TREASURE.

prize *v.* —*See* VALUE.

prize *adj.* —*See* EXCELLENT.

prize[2] *n.* —*See* PLUNDER.

prizefighter *n.* A contestant in a boxing match ▸ boxer, fighter, pugilist. [*Compare* FIGHTER.]

prizewinner *n.* —*See* WINNER.

pro *n.* —*See* EXPERT, PROSTITUTE.

pro *adj.* —*See* EXPERT.

pro–² ▸ *pref.* 1. Precursor of: *procaine.* 2. Anterior; in front of: *prognathous.*
prob·a·bil·i·ty (prŏb′ə-bĭl′ĭ-tē) ▸ *n., pl.* **-ties.** 1. The quality or condition of being probable; likelihood. 2. A probable situation, condition, or event. 3. *Statistics* A number expressing the likelihood that a specific event will occur.
prob·a·ble (prŏb′ə-bəl) ▸ *adj.* 1. Likely to happen or to be true. 2. Likely but uncertain; plausible. **—prob′a·bly** *adv.*
pro·bate (prō′bāt′) *Law* ▸ *n.* The process of establishing the validity of a will. ▸ *v.* **-bat·ed, -bat·ing.** To establish the validity of (a will).
pro·ba·tion (prō-bā′shən) ▸ *n.* 1. A trial period in which a person's fitness, as for membership in a group, is tested. 2. *Law* The release of a convicted offender on the condition of good behavior. **—pro·ba′tion·al** *adj.* **—pro·ba′tion·ar′y** *adj.*
pro·ba·tion·er (prō-bā′shə-nər) ▸ *n.* A person on probation.
pro·ba·tive (prō′bə-tĭv) ▸ *adj.* 1. Serving to test or prove. 2. Furnishing evidence or proof.
probe (prōb) ▸ *n.* 1. An exploratory action, expedition, or device, esp. one designed to investigate an unknown region. 2. A slender, flexible instrument used to explore a wound or body cavity. 3. A thorough examination or investigation. ▸ *v.* **probed, prob·ing.** 1. To explore with or as if with a probe. 2. To delve into; investigate.
pro·bi·ty (prō′bĭ-tē) ▸ *n.* Integrity; honesty.
prob·lem (prŏb′ləm) ▸ *n.* 1. A question to be considered, solved, or answered. 2. A situation, matter, or person that presents perplexity or difficulty. ▸ *adj.* Difficult to deal with or control: *a problem child.*
prob·lem·at·ic (prŏb′lə-măt′ĭk) also **prob·lem·at·i·cal** (-ĭ-kəl) ▸ *adj.* 1. Posing a problem. 2. Open to doubt; dubious or unsettled. **—prob′lem·at′i·cal·ly** *adv.*
pro bo·no (prō bō′nō) ▸ *adj.* Done for the public good without compensation.
pro·bos·cis (prō-bŏs′ĭs) ▸ *n., pl.* **-cis·es** or **-bos·ci·des** (-bŏs′ĭ-dēz′). A long flexible snout or trunk, as of an elephant.
pro·caine (prō′kān′) ▸ *n.* A white crystalline powder, $C_{13}H_{20}N_2O_2$, used chiefly in its hydrochloride form as a local anesthetic.
pro·ce·dure (prə-sē′jər) ▸ *n.* 1. A way of doing something. 2. A series of steps to an end. 3. A set of established forms or methods for conducting legal or business affairs. **—pro·ce′dur·al** *adj.* **—pro·ce′dur·al·ly** *adv.*
pro·ceed (prō-sēd′, prə-) ▸ *v.* 1. To continue, esp. after an interruption. 2. To begin to carry on an action or a process. 3. To progress in an orderly manner. 4. To come from a source; originate. 5. To institute and conduct legal action. ▸ *n.* **pro·ceeds** (prō′sēdz′) The amount of money derived from a commercial or fundraising venture.
pro·ceed·ing (prō-sē′dĭng, prə-) ▸ *n.* 1. A course of action; procedure. 2. **proceedings a.** Events; doings. **b.** A record of business carried on by an organization. 3. often **proceedings** Legal action; litigation.
proc·ess¹ (prŏs′ĕs′, prō′sĕs′) ▸ *n.* 1. A series of actions, changes, or functions bringing about a result. 2. Progress; passage: *the process of time.* 3. *Law* **a.** The entire course of a judicial proceeding. **b.** A summons or writ ordering a defendant to appear in court. 4. *Biol.* An outgrowth of tissue: *a bony process.* ▸ *v.* 1. To put through the steps of a prescribed procedure. 2. To prepare, treat, or convert by subjecting to a special process. 3. *Comp. Sci.* To perform operations on (data).
pro·cess² (prə-sĕs′) ▸ *v.* To move along in or as if in a procession.
pro·ces·sion (prə-sĕsh′ən) ▸ *n.* A group of persons, vehicles, or objects moving along in an orderly, formal manner.
pro·ces·sion·al (prə-sĕsh′ə-nəl) ▸ *n.* Music intended to be played or sung during a procession, esp. a church procession.
proc·es·sor (prŏs′ĕs′ər, prō′sĕs′-) ▸ *n.* 1. One that processes, esp. an apparatus for preparing, treating, or converting material. 2. *Comp. Sci.* **a.** A computer. **b.** A central processing unit.
pro·claim (prō-klām′, prə-) ▸ *v.* To announce officially and publicly; declare. **—proc′la·ma′tion** (prŏk′lə-mā′shən) *n.*
pro·cliv·i·ty (prō-klĭv′ĭ-tē) ▸ *n., pl.* **-ties.** A natural propensity or inclination.
pro·con·sul (prō-kŏn′səl) ▸ *n.* 1. An ancient Roman provincial governor of consular rank. 2. A high administrator in certain modern colonial empires. **—pro·con′su·lar** (-sə-lər) *adj.*
pro·cras·ti·nate (prō-krăs′tə-nāt′, prə-) ▸ *v.* **-nat·ed, -nat·ing.** To put off doing something, esp. out of habitual carelessness or laziness. **—pro·cras′ti·na′tion** *n.* **—pro·cras′ti·na′tor** *n.*
pro·cre·ate (prō′krē-āt′) ▸ *v.* **-at·ed, -at·ing.** To beget offspring; reproduce. **—pro′cre·a′tion** *n.* **—pro′cre·a′tive** *adj.* **—pro′cre·a′tor** *n.*
Pro·crus·te·an also **pro·crus·te·an** (prō-krŭs′tē-ən) ▸ *adj.* Showing no regard for individual differences or special circumstances; ruthlessly inflexible.
proc·tor (prŏk′tər) ▸ *n.* A dormitory and examination supervisor in a school. ▸ *v.* To supervise (an examination). **—proc·to′ri·al** (-tôr′ē-əl) *adj.*
proc·u·ra·tor (prŏk′yə-rā′tər) ▸ *n.* An administrator, esp. a civil or provincial administrator of ancient Rome.
pro·cure (prō-kyo͝or′, prə-) ▸ *v.* **-cured, -cur·ing.** 1. To get by special effort; obtain or acquire. 2. To bring about; effect. 3. To obtain (a sexual partner) for another. **—pro·cur′a·ble** *adj.* **—pro·cure′ment** *n.* **—pro·cur′er** *n.*
prod (prŏd) ▸ *v.* **prod·ded, prod·ding.** 1. To jab or poke, as with a pointed object. 2. To goad to action; incite. ▸ *n.*

THESAURUS

probability *n.* —*See* CHANCE (3).
probable *adj.* Having a good chance of happening or being true ▸ contingent, likely, possible, potential. *Idiom:* in the cards. [*Compare* BELIEVABLE, INCLINED, LIABLE.] —*See also* PRESUMPTIVE.
probably *adv.* More likely than not ▸ believably, likely, presumably, reasonably, seemingly. *Idioms:* all things being equal, in all likelihood (*or* probability). [*Compare* MAYBE.]
probationary or **probative** *adj.* —*See* PILOT.
probe *n.* 1. The act or an instance of exploring or investigating ▸ exploration, investigation, reconnaissance. 2. Something, as a remark, that is used to determine another person's attitude ▸ feeler. *Idiom:* trial balloon. [*Compare* ADVANCES, INTRODUCTION.] —*See also* EXAMINATION (1), EXAMINATION (2).
probe *v.* To test the attitude of ▸ feel out, sound (out). *Idioms:* put out feelers, run something up the flagpole, send up a trial balloon. —*See also* EXPLORE.
probing *adj.* —*See* CRITICAL (2).
probity *n.* —*See* CHARACTER (2), GOOD (1).
problem *n.* A situation that presents difficulty, uncertainty, or perplexity ▸ case, hornets' nest, issue, matter, question. *Informal:* bind, can of worms, tight spot. [*Compare* PREDICAMENT.] —*See also* DIFFICULTY, DISADVANTAGE, QUALM.
problematic *adj.* —*See* AMBIGUOUS (1), DEBATABLE, DOUBTFUL (1).
pro bono *adj.* —*See* UNPAID.
proboscis *n.* —*See* NOSE (1).
procedure *n.* An action calculated to achieve an end ▸ maneuver, measure, move, step, tactic. —*See also* APPROACH (1).
proceed *v.* To move along a particular course ▸ go, pass, push on, wend. *Idiom:* make (*or* wend) one's way. [*Compare* HIKE, JOURNEY, ROVE.] —*See also* ADVANCE (2), CONTINUE, STEM.
process *n.* —*See* APPROACH (1), METHOD.
procession *n.* —*See* ADVANCE, SERIES.
proclaim *v.* To make known the presence or arrival of ▸ announce, herald, introduce, usher in. —*See also* ANNOUNCE, SHOW (1).
proclamation *n.* —*See* ANNOUNCEMENT, MESSAGE.
proclivity *n.* —*See* INCLINATION (1).
procrastinate *v.* —*See* DELAY (2).
procrastination *n.* —*See* DELAY (1).
procrastinator *n.* —*See* LAGGARD.
procreant *adj.* Of or relating to reproduction ▸ generative, procreative, reproductive.
procreate *v.* —*See* BREED.
procreation *n.* —*See* REPRODUCTION.
procreative *adj.* Of or relating to reproduction ▸ generative, procreant, reproductive.
procumbent *adj.* —*See* FLAT (1).
procurable *adj.* —*See* AVAILABLE.
procure *v.* —*See* GET (1).
prod *v.* —*See* PROVOKE, PUSH (1).

1. A pointed object used to prod. 2. An incitement; stimulus. **—prod′der** *n.*

prod·i·gal (prŏd′ĭ-gəl) ▸ *adj.* 1. Rashly or wastefully extravagant. 2. Profuse; lavish. **—prod′i·gal** *n.* **—prod′i·gal′i·ty** (-găl′ĭ-tē) *n.* **—prod′i·gal·ly** *adv.*

pro·di·gious (prə-dĭj′əs) ▸ *adj.* 1. Impressively great in size, force, or extent; enormous. 2. Extraordinary; marvelous. **—pro·di′gious·ly** *adv.*

prod·i·gy (prŏd′ə-jē) ▸ *n., pl.* **-gies.** 1. A person with exceptional talents or powers. 2. Something extraordinary or rare; marvel.

pro·duce (prə-dōōs′, -dyōōs′, prō-) ▸ *v.* **-duced, -duc·ing.** 1. To bring forth; yield. 2a. To create by physical or mental effort. b. To manufacture. 3. To cause; give rise to. 4. To bring forth; exhibit. 5. To supervise and finance the making of: *produce a play.* 6. *Math.* To extend (an area or volume) or lengthen (a line). ▸ *n.* (prŏd′ōōs, prō′dōōs) Something produced, esp. fresh farm products. **—pro·duc′er** *n.*

prod·uct (prŏd′əkt) ▸ *n.* 1. Something produced naturally or by human effort. 2. A direct result; consequence. 3. *Math.* The result obtained by performing multiplication.

pro·duc·tion (prə-dŭk′shən, prō-) ▸ *n.* 1. The act or process of producing. 2. Something produced; product. 3. An amount or quantity produced; output. 4. A presentation of a theatrical work.

pro·duc·tive (prə-dŭk′tĭv, prō-) ▸ *adj.* 1. Producing or capable of producing. 2. Producing abundantly. **—pro·duc′tive·ly** *adv.* **—pro′duc·tiv′i·ty** (prō′dŭk-tĭv′ĭ-tē, prŏd′ək-), **pro·duc′tive·ness** *n.*

pro·em (prō′ĕm′) ▸ *n.* An introduction; preface.

pro·fane (prō-fān′, prə-) ▸ *adj.* 1. Marked by contempt or irreverence for what is sacred. 2. Nonreligious; secular. 3. Vulgar; coarse. ▸ *v.* **-faned, -fan·ing.** 1. To treat with irreverence. 2. To put to an improper, unworthy, or degrading use; abuse. **—prof′a·na′tion** (prŏf′ə-nā′shən) *n.* **—pro·fan′a·to′ry** (-făn′ə-tôr′ē) *adj.* **—pro·fane′ness** *n.*

pro·fan·i·ty (prō-făn′ĭ-tē, prə-) ▸ *n., pl.* **-ties.** 1. The condition or quality of being profane. 2. Obscene or irreverent language.

pro·fess (prə-fĕs′, prō-) ▸ *v.* 1. To affirm openly; declare. 2. To make a pretense of. 3. To claim skill in or knowledge of. 4. To affirm belief in. **—pro·fess′ed·ly** *adv.*

pro·fes·sion (prə-fĕsh′ən) ▸ *n.* 1. An occupation requiring training and specialized study. 2. The body of qualified persons in an occupation or field: *the teaching profession.* 3. An act of professing; declaration. 4. An avowal of faith or belief.

pro·fes·sion·al (prə-fĕsh′ə-nəl) ▸ *adj.* 1. Of or engaged in a profession. 2. Engaging in a given activity as a source of livelihood. ▸ *n.* A person following a profession. **—pro·fes′sion·al·ly** *adv.*

pro·fes·sion·al·ism (prə-fĕsh′ə-nə-lĭz′əm) ▸ *n.* Professional status, methods, character, or standards.

pro·fes·sion·al·ize (prə-fĕsh′ə-nə-līz′) ▸ *v.* **-ized, -iz·ing.** To make professional. **—pro·fes′sion·al·i·za′tion** *n.*

pro·fes·sor (prə-fĕs′ər) ▸ *n.* 1. A college or university teacher of the highest rank. 2. A teacher or instructor. **—pro′fes·so′ri·al** (prō′fĭ-sôr′ē-əl, prŏf′ĭ-) *adj.* **—pro′fes·so′ri·al·ly** *adv.* **—pro·fes′sor·ship′** *n.*

prof·fer (prŏf′ər) ▸ *v.* To offer for acceptance. **—prof′fer** *n.*

pro·fi·cient (prə-fĭsh′ənt) ▸ *adj.* Expert in an art, vocation, or area of learning. **—pro·fi′cien·cy** *n.*

pro·file (prō′fīl′) ▸ *n.* 1. A side view of an object or a structure, esp. of the human head. 2. An outline; silhouette. 3. Degree of exposure to public notice; visibility: *kept a low profile.* 4. A brief biographical essay. **—pro′file** *v.*

prof·it (prŏf′ĭt) ▸ *n.* 1. An advantageous gain or return; benefit. 2. often **profits** The return received on an investment or a business undertaking after all charges or expenses have been paid. ▸ *v.* 1. To make a gain or profit. 2. To derive advantage; benefit. **—prof′it·a·bil′i·ty** *n.* **—prof′it·a·ble** *adj.* **—prof′it·a·bly** *adv.*

prof·it·eer (prŏf′ĭ-tîr′) ▸ *n.* One who makes excessive profits on goods in short supply. **—prof′it·eer′** *v.*

prof·li·gate (prŏf′lĭ-gĭt, -gāt′) ▸ *adj.* 1. Given over to immorality; dissolute. 2. Recklessly wasteful; extravagant. ▸ *n.* A profligate person. **—prof′li·ga·cy** (-gə-sē) *n.*

pro for·ma (prō fôr′mə) ▸ *adj.* Done as a formality; perfunctory.

pro·found (prə-found′, prō-) ▸ *adj.* **-er, -est.** 1. Extending to or coming from a great depth; deep. 2. Coming as if from the depths of one's being: *profound contempt.* 3. Thoroughgoing; far-reaching. 4. Penetrating beyond what is superficial or obvious. 5. Unqualified: *a profound*

THESAURUS

prod *n.* —*See* DIG, PROVOCATION (1), STIMULUS.

prodigal *adj.* —*See* EXTRAVAGANT, GENEROUS (1), PROFUSE.

prodigal *n.* —*See* WASTREL (1).

prodigality *n.* —*See* EXTRAVAGANCE.

prodigious *adj.* —*See* ASTONISHING, ENORMOUS.

prodigiousness *n.* —*See* ENORMOUSNESS.

prodigy *n.* —*See* MARVEL.

produce *v.* 1. To bring into existence ▸ bear, bring forth, create, develop, engender, generate, give, give forth, make, originate, provide, spawn, yield. *Idiom:* give birth (*or* rise) to. [*Compare* BREED, GIVE, OFFER.] 2. To bring (a product or idea, for example) into being ▸ develop, generate. —*See also* CITE, COMPOSE (1), MAKE, RETURN (3), STAGE.

produce *n.* Something produced by human effort ▸ product, production, manufacture, work. [*Compare* COMPOSITION, GOOD.]

producer *n.* —*See* DEVELOPER, MAKER.

product *n.* Something produced by human effort ▸ produce, production, manufacture, work. [*Compare* COMPOSITION, GOOD.]

production *n.* 1. Something produced by human effort ▸ produce, product, manufacture, work. [*Compare* GOOD.] 2. The amount or quantity produced ▸ garner, output, yield. —*See also* COMPOSITION (1).

productive *adj.* 1. Capable of reproducing ▸ fertile, fecund, fruitful, prolific. 2. Acting effectively with minimal waste ▸ efficient, streamlined, well-oiled. [*Compare* DILIGENT, METHODICAL.] —*See also* EFFECTIVE (1), FERTILE (1).

productivity or **productiveness** *n.* The quality of being efficient ▸ efficiency. [*Compare* ABILITY, DILIGENCE.] —*See also* FERTILITY.

profanation *n.* —*See* SACRILEGE.

profane *adj.* 1. Showing irreverence and contempt for something sacred ▸ blasphemous, impious, sacrilegious. 2. Not religious in subject matter, form, or use ▸ civil, lay, nonecclesiastical, nonreligious, nonspiritual, secular, temporal, worldly. [*Compare* EARTHLY.] —*See also* OBSCENE.

profane *v.* —*See* VIOLATE (3).

profaneness *n.* —*See* OBSCENITY (1).

profanity *n.* —*See* OBSCENITY (1), OBSCENITY (2), SWEARWORD.

profess *v.* To claim or allege insincerely or falsely ▸ feign, pretend, pretext, purport. —*See also* ASSERT.

profession *n.* —*See* ASSERTION, BUSINESS (2), RELIGION.

professional *adj.* —*See* EXPERT.

professional *n.* —*See* EXPERT.

proffer *v.* —*See* OFFER (1), PROPOSE.

proffer *n.* —*See* OFFER.

proficiency *n.* —*See* ABILITY (1).

proficient *adj.* —*See* EXPERT.

proficient *n.* —*See* EXPERT.

profile *n.* —*See* FORM (1).

profit *n.* Something earned, won, or otherwise acquired ▸ earnings, gain, return. [*Compare* INCREASE.] —*See also* ADVANTAGE (2), INTEREST (1), USE (2).

profit *v.* 1. To make a large profit ▸ batten, cash in. *Slang:* clean up. *Idioms:* make a killing, make out like a bandit. 2. To be an advantage to ▸ advantage, avail, benefit, help, serve. *Idioms:* do someone good, serve someone well, stand someone in good stead. —*See also* BENEFIT.

profitable *adj.* Affording profit ▸ advantageous, bankable, fat, gainful, lucrative, moneymaking, remunerative, rewarding. —*See also* BENEFICIAL.

profitless *adj.* —*See* FUTILE.

profitlessness *n.* —*See* FUTILITY.

profligacy *n.* —*See* EXTRAVAGANCE, LICENSE (2).

profligate *adj.* —*See* ABANDONED (2), EXTRAVAGANT.

profligate *n.* —*See* WANTON, WASTREL (1).

profound *adj.* —*See* DEEP (1), DEEP (2), DEEP (3).

silence. **—pro·found′ly** *adv.* **—pro·fun′di·ty** (fŭn′dĭ-tē) *n.*

pro·fuse (prə-fyo͞os′, prō-) ▸ *adj.* **1.** Plentiful; copious. **2.** Giving or given freely and abundantly; extravagant. **—pro·fuse′ly** *adv.* **—pro·fuse′ness** *n.* **—pro·fu′sion** (-fyo͞o′zhən) *n.*

pro·gen·i·tor (prō-jĕn′ĭ-tər) ▸ *n.* **1.** A direct ancestor. **2.** An originator of a line of descent. **3.** An originator; founder.

prog·e·ny (prŏj′ə-nē) ▸ *n.* Offspring or descendants.

pro·ges·ter·one (prō-jĕs′tə-rōn′) ▸ *n.* A steroid hormone secreted by the ovary before implantation of the fertilized ovum.

prog·na·thous (prŏg′nə-thəs, prŏg-nā′-) ▸ *adj.* Having jaws that project forward to a marked degree. **—prog′na·thism** *n.*

prog·no·sis (prŏg-nō′sĭs) ▸ *n., pl.* **-ses** (-sēz). A prediction, esp. of the probable course and outcome of a disease.

prog·nos·tic (prŏg-nŏs′tĭk) ▸ *adj.* Of or useful in prognosis. ▸ *n.* **1.** A forecast or prediction. **2.** A portent; omen.

prog·nos·ti·cate (prŏg-nŏs′tĭ-kāt′) ▸ *v.* **-cat·ed, -cat·ing.** To predict according to present indications or signs; foretell. **—prog·nos′ti·ca′tion** *n.* **—prog·nos′ti·ca′tor** *n.*

pro·gram (prō′grăm′, -grəm) ▸ *n.* **1a.** A listing of the order of events and other information for a public presentation. **b.** The presentation itself. **2.** A scheduled radio or television show. **3.** An ordered list of events or procedures to be followed; schedule. **4.** *Comp. Sci.* A set of coded instructions that enables a machine, especially a computer, to perform a desired sequence of operations. ▸ *v.* **-grammed, -gram·ming** or **-gramed, -gram·ing. 1.** To include or schedule in a program. **2.** To design a program for. **3.** To provide (a computer) with a set of instructions. **—pro′gram′ma·ble** *adj.* **—pro′gram·mat′ic** (-grə-măt′ĭk) *adj.*

pro·gramme (prō′grăm′, -grəm) ▸ *n. & v. Chiefly Brit.* Var. of **program.**

pro·gram·mer or **pro·gram·er** (prō′grăm′ər) ▸ *n.* One who programs, esp. one who writes computer programs.

pro·gram·ming language (prō′grăm′ĭng, -grə-mĭng) ▸ *n.* An artificial language that can be translated into machine language and executed by a computer.

prog·ress (prŏg′rĕs′, -rəs, prō′grĕs′) ▸ *n.* **1.** Movement, as toward a goal. **2.** Development or growth. **3.** Steady improvement, as of a society or civilization. ▸ *v.* **pro·gress** (prə-grĕs′) **1.** To advance; proceed. **2.** To move toward a higher or better stage.

pro·gres·sion (prə-grĕsh′ən) ▸ *n.* **1.** Movement forward; advance. **2.** A continuous series; sequence. **3.** *Math.* A series of numbers or quantities in which there is always the same relation between each quantity and the one succeeding it.

pro·gres·sive (prə-grĕs′ĭv) ▸ *adj.* **1.** Moving forward; advancing. **2.** Proceeding in steps. **3.** Favoring progress toward better conditions or new policies. **4.** Increasing in rate as the taxable amount increases. **5.** *Pathol.* Tending to spread or become more severe. **6.** *Gram.* Designating a verb form that expresses an action or condition in progress. ▸ *n.* A person who favors progress toward better conditions. **—pro·gres′sive·ly** *adv.* **—pro·gres′sive·ness** *n.* **—pro′gres·siv′i·ty** (prō′grĕ-sĭv′ĭ-tē, prŏg′rə-) *n.*

pro·hib·it (prō-hĭb′ĭt) ▸ *v.* **1.** To forbid by authority. **2.** To prevent; preclude.

pro·hi·bi·tion (prō′ə-bĭsh′ən) ▸ *n.* **1.** The act of prohibiting. **2.** The forbidding by law of making, transporting, or selling alcoholic beverages. **—pro′hi·bi′tion·ist** *n.*

pro·hib·i·tive (prō-hĭb′ĭ-tĭv) also **pro·hib·i·to·ry** (-tôr′ē) ▸ *adj.* **1.** Prohibiting; forbidding. **2.** So high or burdensome as to discourage purchase or use. **—pro·hib′i·tive·ly** *adv.*

proj·ect (prŏj′ĕkt′, -ĭkt) ▸ *n.* **1.** A plan or proposal; scheme. **2.** An undertaking requiring concerted effort. ▸ *v.* **pro·ject** (prə-jĕkt′) **1.** To thrust or extend outward or forward. **2.** To throw forward; hurl. **3.** To cause (light or an image) to appear on a surface. **4.** To direct (one's voice) so as to be heard clearly at a distance. **5.** To estimate based on present data: *project next year's expenses.* **—pro·jec′tion** *n.*

pro·jec·tile (prə-jĕk′təl, -tīl′) ▸ *n.* **1.** A fired, thrown, or otherwise propelled object, such as a bullet. **2.** A self-propelled missile, such as a rocket.

pro·jec·tor (prə-jĕk′tər) ▸ *n.* A machine for projecting an image onto a screen. **—pro·jec′tion·ist** *n.*

pro·kar·y·ote (prō-kăr′ē-ōt′) ▸ *n.* A single-celled organism that lacks a nuclear membrane, such as a bacterium. **—pro·kar′y·ot′ic** (-ŏt′ĭk) *adj.*

pro·lapse (prō-lăps′) ▸ *v.* **-lapsed, -laps·ing.** *Medic.* To fall or slip out of place, as a bodily organ. **—pro′lapse′** *n.*

pro·le·gom·e·non (prō′lĭ-gŏm′ə-nŏn′, -nən) ▸ *n., pl.* **-na** (-nə). An introductory essay or remark.

pro·le·tar·i·an (prō′lĭ-târ′ē-ən) ▸ *n.* A member of the proletariat. **—pro′le·tar′i·an** *adj.* **—pro′le·tar′i·an·ism** *n.*

pro·le·tar·i·at (prō′lĭ-târ′ē-ĭt) ▸ *n.* The class of industrial wage earners who must earn their living by selling their labor.

pro·lif·er·ate (prə-lĭf′ə-rāt′) ▸ *v.* **-at·ed, -at·ing. 1.** To grow

THESAURUS

profoundness *n.* Intellectual penetration or range ▸ deepness, depth, profundity, weightiness. [*Compare* DISCERNMENT, INTELLIGENCE, WISDOM.]

profundity *n.* Intellectual penetration or range ▸ deepness, depth, profoundness, weightiness. [*Compare* DISCERNMENT, INTELLIGENCE.] *—See also* WISDOM (1).

profuse *adj.* Given to or marked by unrestrained abundance ▸ extravagant, exuberant, lavish, lush, luxuriant, opulent, prodigal, riotous, superabundant. [*Compare* GENEROUS.] *—See also* EXTRAVAGANT, THICK (3).

profuseness *n.* *—See* EXTRAVAGANCE.

profusion *n.* *—See* ABUNDANCE, EXTRAVAGANCE.

progenitor *n.* *—See* ANCESTOR (1), ANCESTOR (2).

progeny *n.* A person or group descended directly from the same parents or ancestors ▸ brood, child, children, descendant, fruit, generation, get, issue, offspring, posterity, scion, seed, spawn. [*Compare* ANCESTRY, FAMILY.]

prognosis *n.* *—See* PREDICTION.

prognostic *adj.* *—See* PREDICTIVE.

prognostic *n.* *—See* OMEN.

prognosticate *v.* *—See* FORESHADOW, PREDICT.

prognostication *n.* *—See* OMEN, PREDICTION.

prognosticative *adj.* *—See* PREDICTIVE.

prognosticator *n.* *—See* PROPHET.

program *n.* **1.** An organized list, as of procedures, activities, or events ▸ agenda, calendar, catalog, docket, lineup, orders of the day, schedule, timetable. [*Compare* APPROACH, LIST[1].] **2.** A document that complements a public performance, presentation, or offering ▸ bill, card, catalog, playbill, prospectus, syllabus. **3.** A show that is aired on television or radio ▸ airing, broadcast.

program *v.* To enter on a schedule ▸ calendar, docket, schedule, slate. [*Compare* LIST[1], POST[3].] *—See also* INDOCTRINATE (2).

progress *n.* Steady improvement, as of an individual or society ▸ advancement, amelioration, betterment, development, headway, improvement, melioration. [*Compare* IMPROVEMENT.] *—See also* ADVANCE, DEVELOPMENT, JOURNEY.

progress *v.* *—See* ADVANCE (2), RISE (3).

progression *n.* *—See* ADVANCE, SERIES, TRANSITION.

progressive *adj.* **1.** Ahead of current trends or customs ▸ advanced, avant-garde, forward, forward-looking, forward-thinking, futuristic, precocious, revolutionary. *Idiom:* ahead of the times. [*Compare* INVENTIVE, NEW.] **2.** Proceeding steadily by degrees ▸ gradational, gradual, piecemeal, step-by-step. *Idioms:* one foot after another, one step at a time. [*Compare* CONSECUTIVE, METHODICAL, SLOW.] *—See also* BROAD-MINDED, LIBERAL.

progressive *n.* *—See* LIBERAL.

prohibit *v.* *—See* FORBID, PREVENT.

prohibited *adj.* *—See* FORBIDDEN.

prohibition *n.* *—See* FORBIDDANCE, PREVENTION.

prohibitive *adj.* *—See* PREVENTIVE (1).

project *n.* Something undertaken, especially something requiring extensive planning and work ▸ endeavor, enterprise, undertaking, venture. *—See also* APPROACH (1), TASK (1).

project *v.* *—See* BULGE, DESIGN (1), INTEND, PREDICT, SHED[1] (1), SHOOT (3).

projection *n.* A part that protrudes or extends outward ▸ bulb, bulge, jut, knob, knot, lip, overhang, protrusion, protuberance, salient. [*Compare* BUMP.] *—See also* INTENTION, PREDICTION.

prolegomenon *n.* *—See* INTRODUCTION.

proliferate *v.* *—See* BREED, INCREASE.

proliferation *n.* *—See* BUILDUP (2), EX-

or multiply by rapidly producing new parts, cells, or offspring. **2.** To increase or spread. **—pro·lif′er·a′tion** *n.*

pro·lif·ic (prə-lĭf′ĭk) ► *adj.* **1.** Producing offspring or fruit in abundance. **2.** Producing abundant works or results.

pro·lix (prō-lĭks′, prō′lĭks′) ► *adj.* Tediously long and wordy. **—pro·lix′i·ty** *n.*

pro·logue (prō′lôg′, -lŏg′) ► *n.* An introduction or preface, as to a play.

pro·long (prə-lông′, -lŏng′) ► *v.* **1.** To lengthen in duration; protract. **2.** To lengthen in extent. **—pro′lon·ga′tion** (prō′lông-gā′shən, -lŏng-) *n.*

prom (prŏm) ► *n.* A formal dance held for a high-school or college class.

prom·e·nade (prŏm′ə-nād′, -näd′) ► *n.* **1a.** A leisurely walk; stroll. **b.** A public place for such walking. **2.** A march of all the guests at the opening of a ball. **—prom′e·nade′** *v.*

Pro·me·the·us (prə-mē′thē-əs, -thyo͞os′) ► *n.* *Gk. Myth.* A Titan who stole fire from Olympus and gave it to humankind.

pro·me·thi·um (prə-mē′thē-əm) ► *n.* *Symbol* **Pm** A radioactive rare-earth element. At. no. 61.

prom·i·nence (prŏm′ə-nəns) ► *n.* **1.** The quality or condition of being prominent. **2.** Something prominent; projection.

prom·i·nent (prŏm′ə-nənt) ► *adj.* **1.** Projecting outward or upward. **2.** Immediately noticeable; conspicuous. **3.** Widely known; eminent.

pro·mis·cu·ous (prə-mĭs′kyo͞o-əs) ► *adj.* **1.** Indiscriminate in the choice of sexual partners. **2.** Lacking standards of selection; indiscriminate. **3.** Consisting of miscellaneous parts or members. **—prom′is·cu′i·ty** (prŏm′ĭs-kyo͞o′ĭ-tē, prō′mĭ-) *n.* **—pro·mis′cu·ous·ly** *adv.*

prom·ise (prŏm′ĭs) ► *n.* **1a.** A declaration assuring that one will or will not do something; vow. **b.** Something promised. **2.** Indication of something favorable to come, esp. future excellence or success. ► *v.* **-ised, -is·ing. 1.** To commit oneself by a promise to do or give; pledge. **2.** To afford a basis for expecting: *clouds that promise rain.* **—prom′is·er** *n.*

prom·is·ing (prŏm′ĭ-sĭng) ► *adj.* Likely to develop favorably. **—prom′is·ing·ly** *adv.*

prom·is·so·ry (prŏm′ĭ-sôr′ē) ► *adj.* Containing or involving a promise.

promissory note ► *n.* A written promise to pay or repay a specified sum of money at a stated time or on demand.

prom·on·to·ry (prŏm′ən-tôr′ē) ► *n., pl.* **-ries.** A high ridge of land or rock jutting out into a body of water.

pro·mote (prə-mōt′) ► *v.* **-mot·ed, -mot·ing. 1.** To raise in position or rank. **2.** To contribute to the progress or growth of; further. **3.** To advocate: *promote a constitutional amendment.* **4.** To attempt to sell or popularize: *promote a new product.* **—pro·mo′tion** *n.* **—pro·mo′tion·al** *adj.*

pro·mot·er (prə-mō′tər) ► *n.* **1.** An active supporter or advocate. **2.** A financial and publicity organizer, as of a boxing match.

prompt (prŏmpt) ► *adj.* **-er, -est. 1.** On time; punctual. **2.** Done without delay. ► *v.* **1.** To move to act; spur or incite. **2.** To give rise to; inspire. **3.** To give a cue to, as in a theatrical performance. ► *n.* **1.** A reminder or cue. **2.** *Comp. Sci.* A symbol that appears on a monitor to indicate that the computer is ready to receive input. **—prompt′er** *n.* **—promp′ti·tude′** (prŏmp′tĭ-to͞od′, -tyo͞od′), **prompt′ness** *n.*

prom·ul·gate (prŏm′əl-gāt′, prō-mŭl′gāt′) ► *v.* **-gat·ed, -gat·ing. 1.** To make known (e.g., a decree) by public declaration. **2.** To put (a law) into effect by formal public announcement. **—prom′ul·ga′tion** *n.* **—prom′ul·ga′tor** *n.*

pron. ► *abbr.* pronoun

prone (prōn) ► *adj.* **1.** Lying with the front or face downward. **2.** Having a tendency; inclined. **—prone** *adv.* **—prone′ness** *n.*

prong (prông, prŏng) ► *n.* **1.** A thin, pointed, projecting part. **2.** A branch or division.

prong·horn (prông′hôrn′, prŏng′-) ► *n., pl.* **-horn** or **-horns.** A small mammal resembling an antelope and having small forked horns, found on W North American plains.

pro·noun (prō′noun′) ► *n.* One of a class of words that function as substitutes for nouns or noun phrases.

pro·nounce (prə-nouns′) ► *v.* **-nounced, -nounc·ing. 1.** To utter or articulate (a word or speech sound). **2.** To declare officially or formally. **—pro·nounce′a·ble** *adj.* **—pro·nun′ci·a′tion** (-nŭn′sē-ā′shən) *n.*

pro·nounced (prə-nounst′) ► *adj.* Strongly marked; distinct. **—pro·nounc′ed·ly** (-noun′sĭd-lē) *adv.*

pro·nounce·ment (prə-nouns′mənt) ► *n.* A formal or authoritative declaration or statement.

pron·to (prŏn′tō) ► *adv.* *Informal* Without delay; quickly.

pro·nun·ci·a·men·to (prō-nŭn′sē-ə-mĕn′tō) ► *n., pl.* **-tos** or **-toes.** An official declaration; proclamation.

proof (pro͞of) ► *n.* **1.** The evidence or argument that establishes an assertion as true. **2.** Convincing demonstration of something. **3.** Determination of the quality of something by testing; trial. **4.** The alcoholic strength of a liquor, expressed as twice the percentage of alcoholic content. **5a.** A trial sheet of printed material. **b.** A trial impression, as of an engraved plate. **6.** A trial photographic print. ► *adj.* **1.**

THESAURUS

PANSION, INCREASE (1), REPRODUCTION.

prolific *adj.* Capable of reproducing ► fertile, fecund, fruitful, productive. *—See also* FERTILE (1).

prolificacy or **prolificness** *n.* *—See* FERTILITY.

prolix *adj.* *—See* WORDY (1).

prolixity *n.* *—See* WORDINESS.

prologue *n.* *—See* INTRODUCTION.

prolong or **prolongate** *v.* *—See* LENGTHEN.

prolongation *n.* *—See* EXTENSION (1).

prolonged *adj.* *—See* CHRONIC (2), LONG[1] (1), LONG[1] (2).

prom *n.* *—See* DANCE.

promenade *n.* *—See* DANCE, WALK (1).

promenade *v.* *—See* DISPLAY, STROLL.

prominence *n.* *—See* FAME, HILL.

prominency *n.* *—See* FAME.

prominent *adj.* *—See* FAMOUS, NOTICEABLE.

promiscuous *adj.* *—See* WANTON (1).

promise *n.* **1.** A declaration that one will or will not do a certain thing ► assurance, commitment, covenant, engagement, guarantee, guaranty, oath, pledge, plight, solemn word, vow, warrant, word, word of honor. [*Compare* PAWN[1].] **2.** Indication of future success or development ► makings, possibility, potential, prospects. [*Compare* MATERIAL.] **3.** Something expected ► anticipation, expectation, likelihood, prospect. [*Compare* CHANCE, THEORY.]

promise *v.* *—See* PLEDGE (2), PLEDGE (1).

promised *adj.* *—See* ENGAGED.

promising *adj.* Showing great promise ► coming, up-and-coming. *Idiom:* on the way up. *—See also* ENCOURAGING.

promote *v.* **1.** To raise in rank ► advance, elevate, exalt, jump, raise, up, upgrade. *Idioms:* kick upstairs, move up. **2.** To help bring about ► abet, cultivate, encourage, facilitate, feed, foster, nourish, nurture. [*Compare* SUPPORT.] **3.** To attempt to sell or popularize by advertising or publicity ► advertise, ballyhoo, boost, build up, cry up, market, popularize, publicize, puff (up), purvey, sell, talk up, tout. *Informal:* pitch, plug. *Slang:* hype, push. *Idioms:* beat the drum for, make a plug for. [*Compare* EMPHASIZE.] *—See also* ADVANCE (1).

promotion *n.* *—See* ADVANCEMENT, ADVERTISING, PATRONAGE (1), PUBLICITY.

prompt *adj.* Occurring, acting, or performed exactly at the time appointed ► punctual, timely.

prompt *v.* *—See* CAUSE, PROVOKE.

promptly *adv.* *—See* IMMEDIATELY (1), SOON.

promulgate *v.* *—See* ANNOUNCE, ESTABLISH (2).

promulgation *n.* *—See* ANNOUNCEMENT.

prone *adj.* *—See* FLAT (1), INCLINED, LIABLE (2).

proneness *n.* *—See* INCLINATION (1).

prong *n.* *—See* SPIKE.

pronounce *v.* To produce or make speech sounds ► articulate, enounce, enunciate, phonate, say, sound, utter, vocalize, voice. [*Compare* SAY.]

pronounced *adj.* *—See* APPARENT (1), DECIDED, NOTICEABLE, ORAL.

pronouncement *n.* *—See* MESSAGE, RULING.

pronto *adv.* *—See* FAST, IMMEDIATELY (1), SOON.

pronunciation *n.* *—See* EXPRESSION (1), VOICING.

proof *n.* *—See* CONFIRMATION (2), REASON (1), TEST (1).

proof *adj.* *—See* RESISTANT.

Fully resistant; impervious: *proof against temptation; bulletproof.* **2.** Of standard alcoholic strength. ► *v.* **1.** To make a trial impression of. **2.** To proofread (copy).

proof·read (pro͞of′rēd′) ► *v.* To read (copy or proof) in order to find errors and mark corrections. **—proof′read′er** *n.*

prop[1] (prŏp) ► *n.* A support, esp. one placed under or against something to keep it from falling. **—prop** *v.*

prop[2] (prŏp) ► *n.* A theatrical property.

prop[3] (prŏp) ► *n.* *Informal* A propeller.

prop·a·gan·da (prŏp′ə-găn′də) ► *n.* **1.** The systematic propagation of a doctrine or cause. **2.** Material disseminated by the advocates of a doctrine or cause. **—prop′a·gan′dist** *n.* **—prop′a·gan′dize′** *v.*

prop·a·gate (prŏp′ə-gāt′) ► *v.* **-gat·ed, -gat·ing. 1.** To reproduce or cause to reproduce; breed. **2.** To make known; publicize. **3.** *Phys.* To cause (e.g., a wave) to move in some direction or through a medium. **—prop′a·ga′tion** *n.* **—prop′a·ga′tive** *adj.* **—prop′a·ga′tor** *n.*

pro·pane (prō′pān′) ► *n.* A colorless gas, C_3H_8, found in natural gas and petroleum and widely used as a fuel.

pro·pel (prə-pĕl′) ► *v.* **-pelled, -pel·ling.** To cause to move forward or onward.

pro·pel·lant also **pro·pel·lent** (prə-pĕl′ənt) ► *n.* Something, such as an explosive charge or a rocket fuel, that propels. **—pro·pel′lant** *adj.*

pro·pel·ler also **pro·pel·lor** (prə-pĕl′ər) ► *n.* A machine for propelling an aircraft or boat, consisting of a revolving power-driven shaft with radiating blades.

pro·pen·si·ty (prə-pĕn′sĭ-tē) ► *n., pl.* **-ties.** An innate inclination; tendency.

prop·er (prŏp′ər) ► *adj.* **1.** Suitable; appropiate. **2.** Called for by rules or conventions; correct. **3.** Strictly following rules or conventions; seemly. **4.** Characteristically belonging to a person or thing: *regained its proper shape.* **5.** Strictly speaking: *the city proper.* **—prop′er·ly** *adv.* **—prop′er·ness** *n.*

proper fraction ► *n.* A fraction in which the numerator is less than the denominator.

proper noun ► *n.* A noun that is the name of a particular person, place, or thing.

prop·er·tied (prŏp′ər-tēd) ► *adj.* Owning land or securities as a principal source of revenue.

prop·er·ty (prŏp′ər-tē) ► *n., pl.* **-ties. 1a.** Something owned; a possession. **b.** A piece of real estate. **2.** The right of ownership; title. **3.** An article, except costumes and scenery, that is used in a play or movie. **4.** A characteristic trait, quality, or attribute.

proph·e·cy (prŏf′ĭ-sē) ► *n., pl.* **-cies. 1.** An inspired utterance of a prophet. **2.** A prediction.

proph·e·sy (prŏf′ĭ-sī′) ► *v.* **-sied, -sy·ing. 1.** To reveal by divine inspiration. **2.** To predict. **—proph′e·si′er** *n.*

proph·et (prŏf′ĭt) ► *n.* **1.** A person who speaks by or as if by divine inspiration. **2.** A predictor; soothsayer. **3.** The chief spokesperson of a movement or cause. **4. Prophets** See **Bible** table in Appendix. **5. Prophet** *Islam* Muhammad. Used with *the.*

proph·et·ess (prŏf′ĭ-tĭs) ► *n.* **1.** A woman who speaks by or as if by divine inspiration. **2.** A woman predictor. **3.** The chief spokeswoman of a movement or cause.

pro·phet·ic (prə-fĕt′ĭk) also **pro·phet·i·cal** (-ĭ-kəl) ► *adj.* Of or characteristic of a prophet or prophecy. **—pro·phet′i·cal·ly** *adv.*

pro·phy·lac·tic (prō′fə-lăk′tĭk, prŏf′ə-) ► *adj.* Acting to defend against or prevent something, esp. disease; protective. ► *n.* A prophylactic agent or device, such as a condom. **—pro′phy·lac′ti·cal·ly** *adv.*

pro·phy·lax·is (prō′fə-lăk′sĭs, prŏf′ə-) ► *n., pl.* **-lax·es** (-lăk′sēz′). Prevention of or protective treatment for disease.

pro·pin·qui·ty (prə-pĭng′kwĭ-tē) ► *n.* Proximity; nearness.

pro·pi·ti·ate (prō-pĭsh′ē-āt′) ► *v.* **-at·ed, -at·ing.** To conciliate; appease. **—pro·pi′ti·a′tion** *n.* **—pro·pi′ti·a′tor** *n.*

pro·pi·tious (prə-pĭsh′əs) ► *adj.* **1.** Favorable; auspicious. **2.** Kindly; gracious. **—pro·pi′tious·ly** *adv.*

pro·po·nent (prə-pō′nənt) ► *n.* One who argues in support of something; advocate.

pro·por·tion (prə-pôr′shən) ► *n.* **1.** A part considered in relation to the whole. **2.** A relationship between things or parts of things with respect to comparative magnitude, quantity, or degree. **3.** A relationship between quantities such that if one varies then another varies as a multiple of the first. **4.** Harmonious relation; symmetry. **5.** often **proportions** Dimensions; size. ► *v.* **1.** To adjust so that proper relations between parts are attained. **2.** To form with symmetry. **—pro·por′tion·al** *adj.* **—pro·por′tion·al·ly** *adv.* **—pro·por′tion·ate** *adj.*

pro·pose (prə-pōz′) ► *v.* **-posed, -pos·ing. 1.** To put forward for consideration; suggest. **2.** To nominate (a person) for a position, office, or membership. **3.** To offer (a toast to be drunk). **4.** To make known as one's intention. **5.** To make an offer, esp. of marriage. **—pro·pos′al** *n.*

prop·o·si·tion (prŏp′ə-zĭsh′ən) ► *n.* **1.** A plan suggested for acceptance; proposal. **2.** *Informal* A matter to be dealt

THESAURUS

prop *n.* —*See* SUPPORT.

prop *v.* —*See* SUPPORT (2).

propaganda *n.* The systematic widespread promotion of a particular doctrine or idea ► brainwashing, disinformation, evangelism, indoctrination, propagandism, proselytism. [*Compare* ADVERTISING, PUBLICITY.]

propagandist *n.* One who disseminates or engages in propaganda ► brainwasher, disseminator, evangelist, indoctrinator, missionary, missioner, pamphleteer, proselytizer. [*Compare* ADVOCATE.]

propagandize *v.* —*See* INDOCTRINATE (2).

propagate *v.* —*See* ANNOUNCE, BREED, GROW.

propagation *n.* —*See* REPRODUCTION.

propel *v.* —*See* ADVANCE (1), DRIVE (2), PROVOKE, SHOOT (3).

propensity *n.* —*See* INCLINATION (1).

proper *adj.* —*See* APPROPRIATE, CONVENIENT (1), ETHICAL, JUST, PRUDISH.

properly *adv.* —*See* FAIR[1].

properness *n.* —*See* DECENCY (2), DECENCY (1).

property *n.* —*See* EFFECTS, HOLDINGS, LAND, QUALITY (1).

prophecy *n.* Something that is foretold by or as if by supernatural means ► augury, divination, oracle, soothsaying, vaticination, vision. [*Compare* OMEN, PREDICTION.]

prophesier *n.* —*See* PROPHET.

prophesy *v.* To tell about or make known by or as if by supernatural means ► augur, divine, forebode, foretell, soothsay, vaticinate. [*Compare* FORESHADOW, PREDICT.]

prophet *n.* A person who foretells future events by or as if by supernatural means ► augur, auspex, clairvoyant, diviner, foreteller, fortuneteller, haruspex, oracle, palmist, prognosticator, prophesier, prophetess, seer, sibyl, soothsayer, vaticinator.

prophetic or **prophetical** *adj.* Of or relating to the foretelling of events by or as if by supernatural means ► augural, divinitory, fatidic, fatidical, mantic, oracular, sibylline, vatic, vatical, vaticinal, visionary. [*Compare* PREDICTIVE.]

prophylactic *adj.* —*See* PREVENTIVE (2).

propitiate *v.* —*See* PACIFY.

propitious *adj.* —*See* BENEFICIAL, FAVORABLE (1), OPPORTUNE.

proponent *n.* —*See* ADVOCATE.

proportion *n.* Satisfying arrangement marked by even distribution of elements, as in a design ► balance, harmony, symmetry. [*Compare* AGREEMENT.] —*See also* DEGREE (2).

proportion *v.* —*See* HARMONIZE (1).

proportional or **proportionate** *adj.* **1.** Properly or correspondingly related in size, amount, or scale ► commensurable, commensurate, corresponding, equivalent. *Idiom:* in proportion. [*Compare* EQUAL.] **2.** Characterized by or displaying symmetry, especially correspondence in scale or measure ► balanced, regular, symmetric, symmetrical. [*Compare* EVEN, PARALLEL.]

proportions *n.* —*See* SIZE (1).

proposal *n.* **1.** Something that is put forward for consideration ► motion, nomination, proposition, submission, suggestion. **2.** Something offered ► bid, offer, proffer, tender. —*See also* THEORY (2).

propose *v.* To state for consideration or debate ► advance, move, offer, pose, proffer, propound, put forward, set forth, submit, suggest, throw out. [*Compare* BROACH, NAME, OFFER, REFER.] —*See also* INTEND.

proposition *n.* —*See* ADVANCES, DOCTRINE, PROPOSAL (1).

with; task. **3.** *Informal* An offer of a private bargain, esp. a request for sexual relations. **4.** A subject for discussion or analysis. **—prop′o·si′tion·al** *adj.*

pro·pound (prə-pound′) ▸ *v.* To put forward for consideration; set forth.

pro·pri·e·tar·y (prə-prī′ĭ-tĕr′ē) ▸ *adj.* **1.** Of or befitting a proprietor. **2.** Exclusively owned; private. **3.** Owned by a private individual or corporation under a trademark or patent: *a proprietary drug.* **—pro·pri′e·tar′i·ly** *adv.*

pro·pri·e·tor (prə-prī′ĭ-tər) ▸ *n.* An owner, as of a business. **—pro·pri′e·tor·ship′** *n.*

pro·pri·e·tress (prə-prī′ĭ-trĭs) ▸ *n.* A woman who is an owner, as of a business.

pro·pri·e·ty (prə-prī′ĭ-tē) ▸ *n., pl.* **-ties. 1.** The quality of being proper; appropriateness. **2.** Conformity to prevailing customs and usages. **3. proprieties** The usages and customs of polite society.

pro·pul·sion (prə-pŭl′shən) ▸ *n.* **1.** The process of driving or propelling. **2.** A driving or propelling force. **—pro·pul′sive** *adj.*

pro ra·ta (prō rā′tə, răt′ə, rä′tə) ▸ *adv.* In proportion.

pro·rate (prō-rāt′, prō′rāt′) ▸ *v.* **-rat·ed, -rat·ing.** To divide, distribute, or assess proportionately. **—pro·ra′tion** *n.*

pro·rogue (prō-rōg′) ▸ *v.* **-rogued, -rogu·ing.** To discontinue a session of (e.g., a parliament). **—pro′ro·ga′tion** *n.*

pro·sa·ic (prō-zā′ĭk) ▸ *adj.* **1.** Matter-of-fact; straightforward. **2.** Lacking in imagination and spirit; dull. **—pro·sa′i·cal·ly** *adv.*

pro·sce·ni·um (prō-sē′nē-əm, prə-) ▸ *n.* The area of a modern theater located between the curtain and the orchestra.

pro·sciut·to (prō-shoo͞′tō) ▸ *n., pl.* **-ti** (-tē) **-tos.** An aged, dry-cured, spiced Italian ham.

pro·scribe (prō-skrīb′) ▸ *v.* **-scribed, -scrib·ing. 1.** To denounce or condemn. **2.** To prohibit. **3.** To outlaw (a person). **—pro·scrip′tion** (-skrĭp′shən) *n.*

prose (prōz) ▸ *n.* Ordinary speech or writing, without metrical structure.

pros·e·cute (prŏs′ĭ-kyo͞ot′) ▸ *v.* **-cut·ed, -cut·ing. 1.** To initiate court action against. **2.** To pursue (e.g., a task) until completion. **—pros′e·cu′tion** *n.* **—pros′e·cu′tor** *n.*

pros·e·lyte (prŏs′ə-līt′) ▸ *n.* A new convert to a doctrine or religion. ▸ *v.* **-lyt·ed, -lyt·ing.** To proselytize.

pros·e·ly·tize (prŏs′ə-lĭ-tīz′) ▸ *v.* **-tized, -tiz·ing.** To convert (a person) from one belief or faith to another. **—pros′e·ly·ti·za′tion** *n.* **—pros′e·ly·tiz′er** *n.*

pro·sim·i·an (prō-sĭm′ē-ən) ▸ *adj.* Of or belonging to a suborder of primates that includes the lemurs.

pros·o·dy (prŏs′ə-dē) ▸ *n.* The study of the metrical structure of verse. **—pro·sod′ic** (prə-sŏd′ĭk) *adj.*

pros·pect (prŏs′pĕkt′) ▸ *n.* **1.** Something expected; possibility. **2. prospects** Chances, esp. of success. **3a.** A potential customer or purchaser. **b.** A candidate likely to succeed. **4.** The direction in which an object faces. **5.** Something presented to the eye; scene. ▸ *v.* To search about or explore (a region) for mineral deposits or oil. **—pros′pec′tor** *n.*

pro·spec·tive (prə-spĕk′tĭv) ▸ *adj.* Likely to happen or become. **—pro·spec′tive·ly** *adv.*

pro·spec·tus (prə-spĕk′təs) ▸ *n.* A formal summary of a proposed venture or project, sent out to prospective buyers, investors, or participants.

pros·per (prŏs′pər) ▸ *v.* To be successful, esp. financially.

pros·per·i·ty (prŏ-spĕr′ĭ-tē) ▸ *n.* The condition of being prosperous.

pros·per·ous (prŏs′pər-əs) ▸ *adj.* **1.** Successful. **2.** Well-to-do; well-off. **3.** Propitious; favorable. **—pros′per·ous·ly** *adv.*

pros·tate (prŏs′tāt′) ▸ *n.* A gland in male mammals at the base of the bladder that controls release of urine and secretes a fluid which is a major constituent of semen.

pros·the·sis (prŏs-thē′sĭs) ▸ *n., pl.* **-ses** (-sēz). An artificial device used to replace a missing body part, such as a limb. **—pros·thet′ic** (-thĕt′ĭk) *adj.*

pros·ti·tute (prŏs′tĭ-to͞ot′, -tyo͞ot′) ▸ *n.* One who solicits and accepts payment for sex acts. ▸ *v.* **-tut·ed, -tut·ing. 1.** To offer (oneself or another) for sexual hire. **2.** To sell (oneself or one's talent) for an unworthy purpose. **—pros′ti·tu′tion** *n.*

pros·trate (prŏs′trāt′) ▸ *adj.* **1.** Lying face down, as in submission or adoration. **2.** Stretched at full length. **3.** Physically or emotionally incapacitated; overcome. ▸ *v.* **-trat·ed, -trat·ing. 1.** To place (oneself) in a prostrate position. **2.** To throw down flat. **3.** To crush or enervate; overcome. **—pros·tra′tion** *n.*

pros·y (prō′zē) ▸ *adj.* **-i·er, -i·est. 1.** Prosaic. **2.** Dull; commonplace. **—pros′i·ness** *n.*

prot– ▸ *pref.* Var. of **proto–.**

pro·tac·tin·i·um (prō′tăk-tĭn′ē-əm) ▸ *n. Symbol* **Pa** A rare radioactive element chemically similar to uranium. At. no. 91.

pro·tag·o·nist (prō-tăg′ə-nĭst) ▸ *n.* **1.** The main character in a drama or other literary work. **2.** A leading or principal figure, as of a cause.

Pro·tag·o·ras (prō-tăg′ər-əs) (fl. 5th cent. B.C.) ▸ Greek philosopher.

pro·te·an (prō′tē-ən, prō-tē′-) ▸ *adj.* Readily taking on varied shapes, forms, or meanings.

pro·tect (prə-tĕkt′) ▸ *v.* To keep from damage, attack, theft, or injury. **—pro·tec′tive** *adj.*

pro·tec·tion (prə-tĕk′shən) ▸ *n.* **1.** The act of protecting or the condition of being protected. **2.** One that protects. **3.** A system of protectionist tariffs.

pro·tec·tion·ism (prə-tĕk′shə-nĭz′əm) ▸ *n.* The protection of domestic producers by impeding or limiting, as by tariffs, the

THESAURUS

propound *v.* —*See* PROPOSE.
proprieties *n.* —*See* AMENITIES (2).
proprietor *n.* —*See* OWNER.
proprietorship *n.* —*See* OWNERSHIP.
propriety *n.* —*See* DECENCY (1), DECENCY (2), ETHICS (1), MANNERS.
prosaic *adj.* —*See* DULL (1), REALISTIC (1).
proscenium *n.* —*See* STAGE (1).
proscribe *v.* —*See* CONDEMN, FORBID.
proscription *n.* —*See* EXILE, FORBIDDANCE.
proscriptive *adj.* —*See* PREVENTIVE (1).
prosecute *v.* To institute or subject to legal proceedings ▸ law, litigate, sue. *Idioms:* bring suit, haul into court. —*See also* ENFORCE, PERFORM (1).
prosecution *n.* —*See* PERFORMANCE, PURSUIT (2).
proselytism *n.* —*See* PROPAGANDA.
proselytizer *n.* —*See* PROPAGANDIST.
prosopopeia *n.* —*See* EMBODIMENT.
prospect *n.* Something expected ▸ anticipation, expectation, likelihood, promise. [*Compare* CHANCE, THEORY.] —*See also* VIEW (2).
prospect *adj.* —*See* COMER (2).
prospective *adj.* —*See* PRESUMPTIVE.
prospects *n.* **1.** Chance of success or advancement ▸ outlook, future. **2.** Indication of future success or development ▸ makings, possibility, potential, promise. [*Compare* MATERIAL.] —*See also* CHANCE (3).
prospectus *n.* —*See* PROGRAM (2).
prosper *v.* To do or fare well ▸ batten, boom, flourish, go, thrive. *Slang:* score. *Idioms:* do right for oneself, get (*or* go) somewhere, go great guns, go strong. [*Compare* SUCCEED.]
prospering *adj.* —*See* FLOURISHING.
prosperity *n.* **1.** A state of health, happiness, and prospering ▸ weal, welfare, well-being. [*Compare* CONDITION, HAPPINESS.] **2.** Steady good fortune or financial security ▸ comfort, ease, luxuriance, luxury, prosperousness, wealth. *Informal:* easy street. *Idioms:* comfortable (*or* easy) circumstances, the good life. [*Compare* SUCCESS, WEALTH.]
prosperous *adj.* Enjoying steady good fortune or financial security ▸ comfortable, easy, successful, well-heeled, well-off, well-to-do. *Informal:* well-fixed. *Idioms:* comfortably off, in clover, on easy street, on top of the world. [*Compare* RICH.] —*See also* FLOURISHING, OPPORTUNE.
prosperousness *n.* —*See* PROSPERITY (2).
prostitute *n.* A person who engages in sex for payment ▸ sex worker, streetwalker, whore. *Slang:* hustler, pro. [*Compare* HARLOT, SLUT.]
prostrate *v.* —*See* DROP (3), OVERWHELM (2).
prostrate *adj.* —*See* FLAT (1).
prostration *n.* —*See* EXHAUSTION, PRAISE (2).
protagonist *n.* —*See* LEAD.
protean *adj.* —*See* VERSATILE.
protect *v.* —*See* DEFEND (1).
protection *n.* —*See* BRIBE, CARE (2), CONSERVATION, COVER (1), DEFENSE, GUARD.
protective *adj.* —*See* PRESERVATIVE, PREVENTIVE (2).

importation of foreign goods and services. **—pro·tec′tion·ist** *n.*

pro·tec·tor (prə-tĕk′tər) ► *n.* **1.** One that protects; guard or guardian. **2. Protector** One who rules a kingdom during the minority of a sovereign. **—pro·tec′tor·ship′** *n.*

pro·tec·tor·ate (prə-tĕk′tər-ĭt) ► *n.* **1a.** A relationship of protection and partial control by a superior power over a dependent country or region. **b.** The protected country or region. **2. Protectorate** The government, office, or term of a protector.

pro·té·gé (prō′tə-zhā′, prō′tə-zhā′) ► *n.* One whose welfare, training, or career is promoted by an influential person.

pro·tein (prō′tēn′, -tē-ĭn) ► *n.* Any of a group of complex organic compounds that are composed of amino acids, occur in all living cells, and are essential for the growth and repair of animal tissue.

pro tem (prō tĕm′) ► *adv.* Pro tempore.

pro tem·po·re (tĕm′pə-rē) ► *adv.* For the time being.

pro·test (prə-tĕst′, prō-, prō′tĕst′) ► *v.* **1.** To object to, esp. in a formal statement. **2.** To promise or affirm with earnest solemnity. ► *n.* (prō′tĕst′) **1.** A formal declaration of disapproval or objection issued by a person or group. **2.** An individual or collective display of disapproval. **—prot′es·ta′tion** (prŏt′ĭ-stā′shən, prō′tĭ-) *n.* **—pro·test′er** *n.* **—pro·test′ing·ly** *adv.*

Prot·es·tant (prŏt′ĭ-stənt) ► *n.* **1.** A Christian belonging to a denomination descending from those that broke away from the Roman Catholic Church in the 16th cent. **2.** (*also* prə-tĕs′tənt) **protestant** One who makes a declaration or avowal. **—Prot′es·tant·ism** *n.*

Pro·te·us (prō′tē-əs, -tyo͞os′) ► *n.* *Gk. Myth.* A sea god able to change his shape at will.

proto– or **prot–** ► *pref.* Earliest; original: *prototype.*

pro·to·col (prō′tə-kôl′, -kōl′, -kŏl′) ► *n.* **1a.** The forms of ceremony and etiquette observed by diplomats and heads of state. **b.** A code of correct conduct. **2.** The first copy of a treaty or other such document before its ratification. **3.** A preliminary draft or record of a transaction. **4.** The plan for a course of medical treatment or for a scientific experiment. **5.** A standard procedure for regulating data transmission between computers.

Pro·to-In·do-Eur·o·pe·an (prō′tō-ĭn′dō-yo͝or′ə-pē′ən) ► *n.* The earliest reconstructed stage of Indo-European.

pro·ton (prō′tŏn′) ► *n.* A stable, positively charged subatomic particle found in all atomic nuclei.

pro·to·plasm (prō′tə-plăz′əm) ► *n.* The complex, semifluid substance that constitutes the living matter of plant and animal cells. **—pro′to·plas′mic** (-plăz′mĭk) *adj.*

pro·to·type (prō′tə-tīp′) ► *n.* An original type or form that serves as a model on which later stages or examples are based or judged. **—pro′to·typ′al** (-tī′pəl), **pro′to·typ′ic** (-tĭp′ĭk), **pro′to·typ′i·cal** *adj.*

pro·to·zo·an (prō′tə-zō′ən) ► *n., pl.* **-zo·ans** or **-zo·a** (-zō′ə). Any of a large group of single-celled, usu. microscopic organisms, such as amoebas. **—pro′to·zo′an, pro′to·zo′ic** *adj.*

pro·tract (prō-trăkt′, prə-) ► *v.* To draw out or lengthen; prolong. **—pro·trac′tion** *n.*

pro·trac·tile (prō-trăk′təl, -tīl′, prə-) ► *adj.* That can be protracted; extensible.

pro·trac·tor (prō-trăk′tər, prə-) ► *n.* A semicircular instrument for measuring and constructing angles.

pro·trude (prō-tro͞od′) ► *v.* **-trud·ed, -trud·ing.** To push or jut outward; project. **—pro·tru′sion** *n.* **—pro·tru′sive** *adj.*

pro·tu·ber·ance (prō-to͞o′bər-əns, -tyo͞o′-, prə-) ► *n.* Something, such as a bulge, knob, or swelling, that protrudes. **—pro·tu′ber·ant** *adj.*

proud (proud) ► *adj.* **-er, -est. 1.** Feeling pleasurable satisfaction. **2.** Occasioning pride. **3.** Feeling or showing self-respect. **4.** Filled with or showing excessive self-esteem. **5.** Of great dignity; honored. **6.** Majestic; magnificent. **—proud′ly** *adv.* **—proud′ness** *n.*

prove (pro͞ov) ► *v.* **proved** or **prov·en** (pro͞o′vən), **prov·ing. 1.** To establish the truth or validity of by argument or evidence. **2.** To determine the quality of by testing; try out. **3.** To be shown to be such; turn out. **—prov′a·ble** *adj.*

prov·e·nance (prŏv′ə-nəns, -näns′) ► *n.* Place of origin.

Pro·ven·çal (prō′vən-säl′, -vän-, prŏv′ən-) ► *n.* **1.** A native or inhabitant of Provence. **2.** The Romance language of Provence. **—Pro′ven·çal′** *adj.*

Pro·vence (prə-väns′, prô-väɴs′) ► A historical region and former province of SE France bordering the Mediterranean Sea.

prov·en·der (prŏv′ən-dər) ► *n.* **1.** Dry food, such as hay, for livestock. **2.** Food or provisions.

pro·ve·nience (prə-vēn′yəns, -vē′nē-əns) ► *n.* A source or origin.

prov·erb (prŏv′ûrb′) ► *n.* **1.** A short pithy saying in widespread use that expresses a basic truth or practical precept. **2. Proverbs** *(takes sing. v.)* See **Bible** table in Appendix. **—pro·ver′bi·al** (prə-vûr′bē-əl) *adj.*

pro·vide (prə-vīd′) ► *v.* **-vid·ed, -vid·ing. 1.** To furnish; supply. **2.** To make available; afford. **3.** To set down as a stipulation. **4.** To take measures in preparation: *provide against emergencies.* **5.** To supply means of subsistence: *provide for one's family.* **—pro·vid′er** *n.*

pro·vid·ed (prə-vī′dĭd) ► *conj.* On the condition; if.

prov·i·dence (prŏv′ĭ-dəns, -dĕns′) ► *n.* **1.** Care or preparation in advance; foresight. **2.** Prudent management; economy. **3.** Divine care and guardianship. **4. Providence** God.

Providence ► The capital of RI, in the NE part on Narragansett Bay.

prov·i·dent (prŏv′ĭ-dənt, -dĕnt′) ► *adj.* **1.** Providing for future needs or events. **2.** Frugal; economical. **—prov′i·dent·ly** *adv.*

prov·i·den·tial (prŏv′ĭ-dĕn′shəl) ► *adj.* **1.** Of or resulting from divine providence. **2.** Fortunate; opportune.

pro·vid·ing (prə-vī′dĭng) ► *conj.* On the condition; provided.

THESAURUS

protector *n.* —*See* GUARD.

protectorate *n.* —*See* POSSESSION.

pro tem *adj.* —*See* TEMPORARY (1).

protest *v.* —*See* OBJECT.

protest or **protestation** *n.* —*See* OBJECTION.

protocol *n.* —*See* CEREMONY (2).

protohistory *n.* —*See* ANTIQUITY.

protoplast *n.* —*See* ORIGINAL.

prototypal *adj.* —*See* TYPICAL.

prototype *n.* —*See* ANCESTOR (2), EPITOME, ORIGINAL.

prototypical or **prototypic** *adj.* —*See* ORIGINAL, TYPICAL.

protract *v.* —*See* LENGTHEN.

protracted *adj.* —*See* CHRONIC (2), LONG[1] (2).

protractile *adj.* —*See* EXTENSIBLE.

protraction *n.* —*See* EXTENSION (1).

protrude *v.* —*See* BULGE.

protrusion *n.* —*See* PROJECTION.

protuberance *n.* —*See* BUMP (1), PROJECTION.

protuberate *v.* —*See* BULGE.

proud *adj.* Properly valuing oneself, one's honor, or one's dignity ► prideful, self-content, self-regarding, self-respecting, self-satisfied. —*See also* ARROGANT, GLORIOUS.

proudness *n.* —*See* ARROGANCE, PRIDE.

prove *v.* To establish as true, valid, or genuine through evidence ► authenticate, bear out, circumstantiate, confirm, corroborate, demonstrate, document, establish, evidence, justify, show, substantiate, sustain, validate, verify. *Idiom:* go to show. [*Compare* BACK, CONFIRM, DEFEND, SHOW.] —*See also* TEST (1).

prove out *v.* To prove valid under scrutiny ► hold up, stand up. *Informal:* wash. *Idioms:* hold water, pass muster, ring true.

provenance *n.* —*See* ORIGIN.

provender *n.* —*See* FOOD.

provenience *n.* —*See* ORIGIN.

proverb *n.* A usually pithy and familiar statement generally accepted as wise or true ► adage, aphorism, apothegm, axiom, byword, maxim, motto, saw, saying. [*Compare* DOCTRINE, EXPRESSION, LORE.]

proverbial *adj.* —*See* PITHY.

provide *v.* —*See* GIVE (1), OFFER (2), PRODUCE (1).

provide for *v.* **1.** To supply with the necessities of life ► keep, maintain, support. *Idioms:* put a roof over someone's head, put food on the table, take care of. [*Compare* NOURISH.] **2.** To state specifically ► detail, particularize, specify, stipulate. [*Compare* ASSERT, DESCRIBE, DESIGNATE, DICTATE.] —*See also* NURTURE.

providence *n.* —*See* ECONOMY, PRUDENCE.

provident *adj.* —*See* ECONOMICAL.

providential *adj.* Characterized by luck or good fortune ► fortuitous, fortunate, happy, lucky. [*Compare* OPPORTUNE.]

provider *n.* —*See* DONOR.

prov·ince (prŏv′ĭns) ▸ *n.* **1.** A territory governed as an administrative or political unit of a country or empire. **2. provinces** Areas of a country situated away from the capital or population center. **3.** A comprehensive area of knowledge, activity, or interest.

pro·vin·cial (prə-vĭn′shəl) ▸ *adj.* **1.** Of or relating to a province. **2.** Limited in perspective; narrow and self-centered. **—pro·vin′cial·ism** *n.* **—pro·vin′cial·ly** *adv.*

prov·ing ground (pro͞o′vĭng) ▸ *n.* A place for testing new devices or theories.

pro·vi·sion (prə-vĭzh′ən) ▸ *n.* **1.** The act of supplying or fitting out. **2.** Something provided. **3.** A preparatory action or measure. **4. provisions** A stock of necessary supplies, esp. food. **5.** A stipulation or qualification, esp. a clause in a document. ▸ *v.* To supply with provisions. **—pro·vi′sion·er** *n.*

pro·vi·sion·al (prə-vĭzh′ə-nəl) ▸ *adj.* Provided or serving only for the time being.

pro·vi·so (prə-vī′zō) ▸ *n., pl.* **-sos** or **-soes.** A clause in a document making a qualification, condition, or restriction.

prov·o·ca·tion (prŏv′ə-kā′shən) ▸ *n.* **1.** The act of provoking or inciting. **2.** Something that provokes.

pro·voc·a·tive (prə-vŏk′ə-tĭv) ▸ *adj.* Tending to provoke. **—pro·voc′a·tive·ness** *n.*

pro·voke (prə-vōk′) ▸ *v.* **-voked, -vok·ing. 1.** To incite to anger or resentment. **2.** To stir to action or feeling.

pro·vo·lo·ne (prō′və-lō′nē) ▸ *n.* A hard, usu. smoked Italian cheese.

pro·vost (prō′vōst′, -vəst, prŏv′əst) ▸ *n.* A high administrative officer, as of a university.

pro·vost marshal (prō′vō) ▸ *n.* The head of a unit of military police.

prow (prou) ▸ *n.* The forward part of a ship's hull; bow.

prow·ess (prou′ĭs) ▸ *n.* **1.** Superior skill or ability. **2.** Superior strength and courage, esp. in battle.

prowl (proul) ▸ *v.* To roam (through) stealthily, as in search of prey. **—prowl** *n.* **—prowl′er** *n.*

prowl car ▸ *n.* See **squad car.**

prox·i·mate (prŏk′sə-mĭt) ▸ *adj.* **1.** Close in space, time, or order; near. **2.** Approximate.

prox·im·i·ty (prŏk-sĭm′ĭ-tē) ▸ *n.* Nearness; closeness.

prox·y (prŏk′sē) ▸ *n., pl.* **-ies. 1.** A person authorized to act for another. **2.** Authority or written authorization to act for another.

Pro·zac (prō′zăk′) ▸ A trademark for a brand of antidepressant.

prude (pro͞od) ▸ *n.* One who is too concerned with being or seeming to be proper, modest, or righteous. **—prud′er·y** *n.* **—prud′ish** *adj.* **—prud′ish·ly** *adv.* **—prud′ish·ness** *n.*

pru·dent (pro͞od′nt) ▸ *adj.* **1.** Wise in practical matters. **2.** Careful for one's own interests; provident. **3.** Careful about one's conduct; circumspect. **—pru′dence** *n.* **—pru·den′tial** (pro͞o-dĕn′shəl) *adj.* **—pru′dent·ly** *adv.*

prune[1] (pro͞on) ▸ *n.* A partially dried plum.

prune[2] (pro͞on) ▸ *v.* **pruned, prun·ing. 1.** To cut off parts or branches of (a plant) to improve shape or growth. **2.** To remove or cut out as superfluous.

pru·ri·ent (pro͝or′ē-ənt) ▸ *adj.* Appealing to or arousing immoderate sexual desire. **—pru′ri·ence** *n.*

Prus·sia (prŭsh′ə) ▸ A historical region and former kingdom of N-central Europe including present-day N Germany and Poland. **—Prus′sian** *adj. & n.*

pry[1] (prī) ▸ *v.* **pried** (prīd), **pry·ing.** To look or inquire closely or curiously; snoop. **—pry′ing·ly** *adv.*

pry[2] (prī) ▸ *v.* **pried** (prīd), **pry·ing. 1.** To raise, move, or force open with a lever. **2.** To obtain with difficulty. ▸ *n., pl.* **pries** (prīz). A tool, as a crowbar, for prying.

PS ▸ *abbr.* postscript

psalm (säm) ▸ *n.* **1.** A sacred song; hymn. **2. Psalms** *(takes sing. v.)* See **Bible** table in Appendix. **—psalm′ist** *n.*

psalm·o·dy (sä′mə-dē, săl′mə-) ▸ *n., pl.* **-dies. 1.** The singing of psalms in divine worship. **2.** A collection of psalms.

Psal·ter also **psal·ter** (sôl′tər) ▸ *n.* A book containing the Book of Psalms or a particular version of, musical setting for, or selection from it.

pseudo– or **pseud–** ▸ *pref.* False; deceptive; sham: *pseudonym.*

pseu·do·nym (so͞od′n-ĭm′) ▸ *n.* A fictitious name assumed by an author; pen name. **—pseu·don′y·mous** (so͞o-dŏn′ə-məs) *adj.*

psi (sī, psī) ▸ *n.* The 23rd letter of the Greek alphabet.

psit·ta·co·sis (sĭt′ə-kō′sĭs) ▸ *n.* An infectious disease of parrots and related birds that is communicable to humans.

pso·ri·a·sis (sə-rī′ə-sĭs) ▸ *n.* A skin disease marked by recurring inflammation and scaly patches.

psych (sīk) *Informal* ▸ *n.* Psychology. ▸ *v.* **1.** To put into the right frame of mind. **2.** To undermine psychologically.

psy·che (sī′kē) ▸ *n.* **1.** The spirit or soul. **2.** In psychoanalysis, the mind functioning as the center of thought, emotion, and behavior.

psy·che·del·ic (sī′kĭ-dĕl′ĭk) ▸ *adj.* Marked by or generating

THESAURUS

province *n.* —*See* AREA (1), POSSESSION.

provincial *adj.* —*See* COUNTRY, NARROW (1).

provision *n.* A restricting or modifying element ▸ condition, limitation, qualification, precondition, prerequisite, proviso, reservation, specification, stipulation, term. *Informal:* string. [*Compare* RESTRICTION.] —*See also* HOARD.

provisional *adj.* —*See* CONDITIONAL, TEMPORARY (1), TEMPORARY (2).

provisions *n.* Steps taken in preparation for an undertaking ▸ arrangements, accommodations, plans, preparations. —*See also* FOOD.

proviso *n.* —*See* PROVISION.

provisory *adj.* —*See* CONDITIONAL.

provocation *n.* **1.** Something that causes others to feel angry or resentful ▸ goad, incitation, incitement, instigation, prod, stimulus, trigger. **2.** An act of taunting another to do something bold or rash ▸ challenge, dare, gauntlet. —*See also* ANNOYANCE (1), DEFIANCE (1).

provocative *adj.* —*See* RACY.

provoke *v.* To stir to action or feeling ▸ egg on, excite, foment, galvanize, goad, heat up, impel, incent, incentivize, incite, inflame, inspire, instigate, motivate, move, pique, prick, prod, prompt, propel, set off, spark, spur, stimulate, touch off, trigger, work up. [*Compare* AROUSE, ENERGIZE, MOVE, URGE.] —*See also* ANGER (1), ANNOY, CAUSE, COURT (1), OFFEND (1).

provoker *n.* —*See* AGGRESSOR.

provoking *adj.* —*See* DISTURBING.

prowess *n.* —*See* COURAGE, DEXTERITY.

prowl *v.* —*See* LURK, SNEAK.

prowler *n.* One who behaves in a stealthy, furtive way ▸ skulker, sneak, sneaker, weasel. [*Compare* CREEP, BETRAYER.]

proximate *adj.* —*See* CLOSE (1), IMMINENT.

proxy *n.* —*See* REPRESENTATIVE, SUBSTITUTE.

prude *n.* One excessively concerned with being proper, modest, or righteous ▸ bluenose, Mrs. Grundy, prig, priss, puritan, schoolmarm, Victorian. *Informal:* old maid. [*Compare* SQUARE.]

prudence *n.* The exercise of good judgment or common sense in practical matters ▸ caution, circumspection, discretion, forehandedness, foresight, foresightedness, forethought, forethoughtfulness, precaution, providence. [*Compare* CARE, CAUTION, COMMON SENSE.] —*See also* ECONOMY.

prudent *adj.* —*See* DELIBERATE (3), ECONOMICAL, SENSIBLE, WARY.

prudish *adj.* Marked by excessive concern for modesty or propriety ▸ bluenosed, genteel, mannered, mincing, overnice, overrefined, priggish, prim, prissy, proper, puritanical, schoolmarmish, strait-laced, stuffy, Victorian. *Informal:* old-maidish. *Idiom:* prim and proper. [*Compare* CEREMONIOUS, FUSSY, STIFF.]

prune *v.* —*See* CUT (3), DROP (5).

pruner *n.* —*See* SHEARS.

prurience or **pruriency** *n.* —*See* DESIRE (2).

prurient *adj.* —*See* LASCIVIOUS.

pry *v.* To look into or inquire about curiously, inquisitively, or in a meddlesome fashion ▸ poke, snoop. *Informal:* nose (around), sniff about (*or* around). *Idiom:* stick one's nose into. [*Compare* MEDDLE.]

pry *n.* A person who snoops ▸ prier, snoop, snooper. [*Compare* BUSYBODY.]

prying *adj.* —*See* CURIOUS (1).

prying *n.* —*See* CURIOSITY (2).

p's and q's *n.* —*See* MANNERS.

pseudonymous *adj.* Being fictitious and not real, as a name ▸ assumed, made-up, pretended. [*Compare* FALSE, FICTITIOUS.]

psyche *n.* —*See* PSYCHOLOGY, SPIRIT (2).

psyched *adj.* —*See* THRILLED.

hallucinations and distortions of perception. **—psy′che·del′ic** *n.*

psy·chi·a·try (sĭ-kī′ə-trē, sī-) ▸ *n.* The branch of medicine that deals with the diagnosis, treatment, and prevention of mental and emotional disorders. **—psy′chi·at′ric** (sī′kē-ăt′rĭk) *adj.* **—psy·chi′a·trist** *n.*

psy·chic (sī′kĭk) ▸ *n.* See **medium** 5. ▸ *adj.* **1.** Of the human mind or psyche: *psychic trauma.* **2.** Of or possessing extraordinary mental powers, such as ESP or mental telepathy. **—psy′chi·cal·ly** *adv.*

psycho– or **psych–** ▸ *pref.* Mind; mental: *psychology.*

psy·cho·ac·tive (sī′kō-ăk′tĭv) ▸ *adj.* Affecting the mind or mental processes.

psy·cho·a·nal·y·sis (sī′kō-ə-năl′ĭ-sĭs) ▸ *n.* **1.** A method of psychiatric therapy in which free association, dream interpretation, and analysis of feelings and behavior are used to investigate mental and emotional disorders. **2.** Psychiatric treatment incorporating the techniques of psychoanalysis. **—psy′cho·an′a·lyst** (-ăn′ə-lĭst) *n.* **—psy′cho·an′a·lyt′ic** (-ăn′ə-lĭt′ĭk), **psy′cho·an′a·lyt′i·cal** *adj.* **—psy′cho·an′a·lyze′** (-līz′) *v.*

psy·cho·dra·ma (sī′kə-drä′mə, -drăm′ə) ▸ *n.* A psychotherapeutic and analytic technique in which people are assigned roles to be played spontaneously in a drama.

psy·cho·gen·ic (sī′kə-jĕn′ĭk) ▸ *adj.* Originating in the mind or in mental or emotional processes. **—psy′cho·gen′i·cal·ly** *adv.*

psy·chol·o·gist (sī-kŏl′ə-jĭst) ▸ *n.* A person trained and educated to perform psychological research, testing, and therapy.

psy·chol·o·gy (sī-kŏl′ə-jē) ▸ *n., pl.* **-gies**. **1.** The science that deals with mental processes and behavior. **2.** The emotional and behavioral characteristics of an individual or group. **—psy′cho·log′i·cal** (sī′kə-lŏj′ĭ-kəl) *adj.* **—psy′cho·log′i·cal·ly** *adv.*

psy·cho·met·rics (sī′kə-mĕt′rĭks) ▸ *n.* *(takes sing. v.)* The branch of psychology that deals with testing and measuring psychological variables such as intelligence.

psy·cho·mo·tor (sī′kō-mō′tər) ▸ *adj.* Of or relating to movement or muscular activity associated with mental processes.

psy·cho·path (sī′kə-păth′) ▸ *n.* A person with an antisocial personality disorder, esp. one manifested in aggressive, perverted, or criminal behavior. **—psy′cho·path′ic** *adj.* **—psy′cho·path′i·cal·ly** *adv.* **—psy·chop′a·thy** (sī-kŏp′ə-thē) *n.*

psy·cho·pa·thol·o·gy (sī′kō-pə-thŏl′ə-jē, -pă-) ▸ *n.* The study of the origin, growth, and symptoms of mental or behavioral disorders. **—psy′cho·path′o·log′i·cal** (-păth′ə-lŏj′ĭ-kəl), **psy′cho·path′o·log′ic** *adj.* **—psy′cho·pa·thol′o·gist** *n.*

psy·cho·phys·i·ol·o·gy (sī′kō-fĭz′ē-ŏl′ə-jē) ▸ *n.* The study of correlations between the mind, behavior, and bodily mechanisms. **—psy′cho·phys′i·o·log′i·cal** (-fĭz′ē-ə-lŏj′ĭ-kəl), **psy′cho·phys′i·o·log′ic** *adj.* **—psy′cho·phys′i·ol′o·gist** *n.*

psy·cho·sex·u·al (sī′kō-sĕk′shōō-əl) ▸ *adj.* Of or relating to the mental and emotional aspects of sexuality.

psy·cho·sis (sī-kō′sĭs) ▸ *n., pl.* **-ses** (-sēz). A mental disorder marked by derangement of personality, loss of contact with reality, and deterioration of normal social functioning. **—psy·chot′ic** (-kŏt′ĭk) *adj. & n.*

psy·cho·so·mat·ic (sī′kō-sō-măt′ĭk) ▸ *adj.* **1.** Of or relating to a disorder having physical symptoms but originating from mental or emotional causes. **2.** Of or concerned with the influence of the mind on the body, esp. with respect to disease.

psy·cho·ther·a·py (sī′kō-thĕr′ə-pē) ▸ *n.* The treatment of mental and emotional disorders through the use of psychological techniques. **—psy′cho·ther′a·peu′tic** (-pyōō′tĭk) *adj.* **—psy′cho·ther′a·pist** *n.*

psy·cho·tro·pic (sī′kə-trō′pĭk, -trŏp′ĭk) ▸ *adj.* Having an altering effect on perception, emotion, or behavior. Used esp. of a drug.

Pt ▸ The symbol for the element **platinum**.

pt. ▸ *abbr.* **1.** pint **2.** point **3.** also **Pt.** port

ptar·mi·gan (tär′mĭ-gən) ▸ *n., pl.* **-gan** or **-gans**. A grouse of northern regions having feathered legs and feet.

PT boat (pē-tē′) ▸ *n.* A fast, lightly armed vessel used to torpedo enemy shipping.

pter·o·dac·tyl (tĕr′ə-dăk′təl) ▸ *n.* An extinct flying reptile.

pter·o·saur (tĕr′ə-sôr′) ▸ *n.* Any of an order of extinct flying reptiles that includes the pterodactyls.

Ptol·e·ma·ic system (tŏl′ə-mā′ĭk) ▸ *n.* The astronomical system of Ptolemy, in which Earth is at the center of the universe.

Ptol·e·my[1] (tŏl′ə-mē) ▸ An Egyptian dynasty of Macedonian kings (323–30 B.C.), including **Ptolemy I** (367?–283?) and **Ptolemy XV** (47–30).

Ptol·e·my[2] (tŏl′ə-mē) (fl. 2nd cent. A.D.) ▸ Alexandrian astronomer, mathematician, and geographer.

pto·maine (tō′mān′, tō-mān′) ▸ *n.* A basic nitrogenous organic compound produced by bacterial putrefaction of protein.

ptomaine poisoning ▸ *n.* Food poisoning, erroneously ascribed to ptomaine ingestion.

Pu ▸ The symbol for the element **plutonium**.

pub (pŭb) ▸ *n.* A tavern; bar.

pu·ber·ty (pyōō′bər-tē) ▸ *n.* The stage of adolescence in which an individual becomes physiologically capable of sexual reproduction. **—pu′ber·tal** *adj.*

pu·bes·cent (pyōō-bĕs′ənt) ▸ *adj.* **1.** Reaching or having reached puberty. **2.** Covered with short hairs or soft down. **—pu·bes′cence** *n.*

pu·bic (pyōō′bĭk) ▸ *adj.* Of or located in the region of the pubis or the pubes.

pu·bis (pyōō′bĭs) ▸ *n., pl.* **-bes** (-bēz). The forward portion of either of the hipbones, at the juncture forming the front arch of the pelvis.

pub·lic (pŭb′lĭk) ▸ *adj.* **1.** Of or affecting the community or the people. **2.** Maintained for or used by the people or community. **3.** Participated in or attended by the people or community: *public worship.* **4.** Connected with or acting on behalf of the people, community, or government: *public office.* **5.** Generally or widely known. **6.** Noncommercial: *public television.* ▸ *n.* **1.** The community or the people as a whole. **2.** A group of people sharing a common interest: *the reading public.* **—pub′lic·ly** *adv.*

pub·lic-ad·dress system (pŭb′lĭk-ə-drĕs′) ▸ *n.* An electronic amplification apparatus used for broadcasting in public areas.

pub·li·can (pŭb′lĭ-kən) ▸ *n.* **1.** *Chiefly Brit.* The keeper of a public house or tavern. **2.** A tax collector in the Roman Empire.

pub·li·ca·tion (pŭb′lĭ-kā′shən) ▸ *n.* **1.** The act or process of publishing. **2.** An issue of printed material.

public defender ▸ *n.* An attorney, usu. publicly appointed, responsible for the defense of those unable to afford legal assistance.

public domain ▸ *n.* **1.** Land owned and controlled by the state or federal government. **2.** The status of publications, products, and processes unprotected by patent or copyright.

public house ▸ *n.* *Chiefly Brit.* A licensed tavern or bar.

pub·li·cist (pŭb′lĭ-sĭst) ▸ *n.* One who publicizes, esp. a press or publicity agent.

pub·lic·i·ty (pŭ-blĭs′ĭ-tē) ▸ *n.* **1.** Information disseminated to

THESAURUS

psychic *adj.* —*See* MENTAL.

psycho *adj.* —*See* INSANE.

psychological *adj.* —*See* MENTAL.

psychology *n.* The thought processes characteristic of an individual or group ▸ ethos, mentality, mind, mindset, psyche. *Idiom:* what makes someone tick. [*Compare* CHARACTER, IDENTITY.]

psychopathy *n.* —*See* INSANITY.

psychotropic *n.* —*See* DRUG (2).

pub *n.* —*See* BAR (2).

puberty or **pubescence** *n.* —*See* YOUTH (1).

public *adj.* —*See* COMMON (2), OPEN (3), POPULAR.

public *n.* **1.** Persons as an organized body ▸ bloc, community, people, society. [*Compare* CIRCLE.] **2.** The body of persons who admire a public personality, especially an entertainer ▸ audience, following. [*Compare* FAN[2].] —*See also* COMMONALTY.

public assistance *n.* —*See* RELIEF (2).

publication *n.* **1.** The act or process of publishing printed matter ▸ circulation, issue, printing, publishing, release. **2.** An issue of printed material offered for sale or distribution ▸ edition, opus, organ, paper, title, volume, work. [*Compare* ADVISORY, BOOK.] —*See also* ANNOUNCEMENT.

public house *n.* —*See* BAR (2).

publicity *n.* Information disseminated

attract public notice. **2.** Public interest, notice, or notoriety.
pub·li·cize (pŭb′lĭ-sīz′) ▸ *v.* **-cized, -ciz·ing.** To give publicity to.
public relations ▸ *pl.n.* **1.** The methods and activities employed to establish a favorable relationship with the public. **2.** *(takes sing. or pl. v.)* The degree of success obtained in achieving favor with the public.
public school ▸ *n.* **1.** A tax-supported school in the US providing free education for children of a community or district. **2.** A private boarding school in Great Britain for pupils between the ages of 13 and 18.
pub·lic-spir·it·ed (pŭb′lĭk-spĭr′ĭ-tĭd) ▸ *adj.* Motivated by or showing devotion to the public welfare.
pub·lish (pŭb′lĭsh) ▸ *v.* **1.** To prepare and issue (a book, music, or other material) for public distribution, esp. for sale. **2.** To bring to the public attention; announce. **—pub′lish·a·ble** *adj.* **—pub′lish·er** *n.*
puck (pŭk) ▸ *n.* A hard rubber disk used in ice hockey.
Puck ▸ *n.* A mischievous sprite in English folklore.
puck·er (pŭk′ər) ▸ *v.* To gather into small wrinkles or folds. ▸ *n.* A wrinkle or fold.
puck·ish (pŭk′ĭsh) ▸ *adj.* Mischievous; impish.
pud·ding (po͝od′ĭng) ▸ *n.* A sweet dessert, usu. with a soft smooth consistency, that has been boiled, steamed, or baked.
pud·dle (pŭd′l) ▸ *n.* A small pool of liquid, esp. rainwater.
pud·dling (pŭd′lĭng) ▸ *n.* Purification of impure metal, esp. pig iron, by heating and stirring in an oxidizing atmosphere.
pu·den·dum (pyo͞o-dĕn′dəm) ▸ *n., pl.* **-da** (-də). The human external genitalia, esp. of a woman.
pudg·y (pŭj′ē) ▸ *adj.* **-i·er, -i·est.** Short and fat; chubby. **—pudg′i·ness** *n.*
Pueb·lo (pwĕb′lō) ▸ *n., pl.* **Pueblo** or **-los. 1.** A member of certain Native American peoples, such as the Hopi or Zuni, living in pueblos in N and W New Mexico and NE Arizona. **2. pueblo** *pl.* **-los.** A permanent community of a Pueblo people, typically consisting of multilevel adobe dwellings built around a central plaza.
puer·ile (pyo͝or′ĭl′, pwĕr′-, pyo͞o′ər-, -əl) ▸ *adj.* Immature; childish. **—puer·il′i·ty** (-ĭl′ĭ-tē) *n.*
pu·er·per·al (pyo͞o-ûr′pər-əl) ▸ *adj.* Relating to or occurring during or immediately after childbirth.
Puer·to Ri·co (pwĕr′tə rē′kō, pôrt′ə, pwĕr′tō) ▸ A self-governing US commonwealth in the Caribbean Sea E of Hispaniola. Cap. San Juan. **—Puer′to Ri′can** *adj. & n.*
puff (pŭf) ▸ *n.* **1a.** A short forceful discharge, as of air or smoke. **b.** A short sibilant sound produced by a puff. **2.** An act of drawing in and expelling the breath, as in smoking tobacco. **3.** A swelling or rounded protuberance. **4.** A light flaky pastry. **5.** A soft pad for applying powder or lotion. **6.** An expression of exaggerated praise. ▸ *v.* **1.** To blow in puffs. **2.** To breathe forcefully and rapidly. **3.** To emit puffs. **4.** To take puffs on smoking material. **5.** To swell or seem to swell. **6.** To fill with pride or conceit. **7.** To publicize with exaggerated praise. **—puff′i·ness** *n.* **—puff′y** *adj.*
puff·ball (pŭf′bôl′) ▸ *n.* A ball-shaped fungus that when pressed or struck releases the enclosed spores in puffs of dust.
puff·er (pŭf′ər) ▸ *n.* Any of various prickly, often poisonous, chiefly marine fishes capable of puffing up with water or air.
puff·er·y (pŭf′ə-rē) ▸ *n.* Flattering, often exaggerated praise and publicity.
puf·fin (pŭf′ĭn) ▸ *n.* A black and white sea bird of northern regions having a flattened triangular bill.
pug[1] (pŭg) ▸ *n.* **1.** A small dog having a snub nose, a wrinkled face, and a curled tail. **2.** A short, turned-up nose.
pug[2] (pŭg) ▸ *n.* *Slang* A boxer.
pu·gi·lism (pyo͞o′jə-lĭz′əm) ▸ *n.* *Sports* Boxing. **—pu′gi·list** *n.* **—pu′gi·lis′tic** *adj.*
pug·na·cious (pŭg-nā′shəs) ▸ *adj.* Combative in nature; belligerent. **—pug·na′cious·ness, pug·nac′i·ty** (-năs′ĭ-tē) *n.*
puis·sance (pwĭs′əns, pyo͞o′ĭ-səns) ▸ *n.* Power; might. **—puis′·sant** *adj.*
puke (pyo͞ok) ▸ *v.* **puked, puk·ing.** *Slang* To vomit. **—puke** *n.*
pu·la (po͞o′lä) ▸ *n.* See **currency** table in Appendix.
pul·chri·tude (pŭl′krĭ-to͞od′, -tyo͞od′) ▸ *n.* Physical beauty. **—pul′chri·tu′di·nous** (-to͞od′n-əs, -tyo͞od′-) *adj.*
pule (pyo͞ol) ▸ *v.* **puled, pul·ing.** To whine; whimper. **—pul′er** *n.*
Pu·lit·zer (po͝ol′ĭt-sər, pyo͞o′lĭt-), **Joseph** (1847–1911) ▸ Hungarian-born Amer. newspaper publisher.
pull (po͝ol) ▸ *v.* **1.** To apply force to so as to cause motion toward the source of the force. **2.** To remove from a fixed position; extract. **3.** To tug at; jerk or tweak. **4.** To rip or tear; rend. **5.** To stretch (e.g., taffy) repeatedly. **6.** To strain (e.g., a muscle) injuriously. **7.** *Informal* To attract; draw: *pull a large crowd.* **8.** *Slang* To draw out (a weapon). **9.** *Informal* To remove. **10.** To row a boat. ***—phrasal verbs:* pull off** *Informal* To do or accomplish in spite of difficulties. **pull out** To leave or depart. **pull through** To come or bring successfully through difficulty. **pull up** To bring or come to a halt. ▸ *n.* **1.** The act or process of pulling. **2.** Force exerted in pulling. **3.** Something, such as a knob, that is used for pulling. **4.** A deep inhalation or draft, as of smoke or liquor. **5.** *Slang* A means of gaining special advantage; influence. **6.** *Informal* Ability to draw or attract; appeal. **—pull′er** *n.*
pull·back (po͝ol′băk′) ▸ *n.* An orderly troop withdrawal.
pul·let (po͝ol′ĭt) ▸ *n.* A young domestic hen.
pul·ley (po͝ol′ē) ▸ *n., pl.* **-leys. 1.** A simple machine consisting essentially of a wheel with a grooved rim in which a pulled rope or chain can run to change the direction of the pull and thereby lift a load. **2.** A wheel turned by or driving a belt.
Pull·man (po͝ol′mən) ▸ *n.* **1.** A railroad parlor car or sleeping car. **2.** A large suitcase.
pull·out (po͝ol′out′) ▸ *n.* A withdrawal, esp. of troops.
pull·o·ver (po͝ol′ō′vər) ▸ *n.* A garment that is put on by being drawn over the head.

THESAURUS

through various media to attract public notice ▸ advertisement, advertising, ballyhoo, buildup, exposure, promotion, puff, puffery. *Informal:* hoopla, pitch, plug. *Slang:* hype. [*Compare* PROPAGANDA.] *—See also* ADVERTISING.
publicize *v.* *—See* PROMOTE (3).
publish *v.* **1.** To present for circulation, exhibit, or sale ▸ bring out, issue, print, put out, release, run off. [*Compare* SPREAD.] **2.** To be the author of a published work or works ▸ author, compose, pen, write. [*Compare* COMPOSE, WRITE.] *—See also* ANNOUNCE.
publishing *n.* *—See* PUBLICATION (1).
pucker *n.* *—See* FOLD (1).
pucker *v.* *—See* DRY (1), FOLD.
puckish *adj.* *—See* MISCHIEVOUS.
pudgy *adj.* *—See* FAT (1).
puerile *adj.* *—See* CHILDISH, YOUNG.
puff *n.* *—See* BREEZE (1), PUBLICITY, PULL (2).
puff *v.* *—See* BLOW[1] (1), BOAST, EXAGGERATE, PANT, PROMOTE (3), SWELL.
puffed-up or **puffy** *adj.* *—See* POMPOUS.
puffery *n.* *—See* PUBLICITY.
pugilist *n.* A contestant in a boxing match ▸ boxer, fighter, prizefighter. [*Compare* FIGHTER.]
pugnacious *adj.* *—See* AGGRESSIVE.
pugnacity or **pugnaciousness** *n.* *—See* AGGRESSION, FIGHT (2).
puke *v.* *—See* VOMIT.
pulchritudinous *adj.* *—See* BEAUTIFUL.
pule *v.* *—See* CRY.
pull *v.* **1.** To exert force so as to move something toward the source of the force ▸ drag, draw, haul, lug, tow, tug, yank. [*Compare* TRAIL.] **2.** To remove from a fixed position ▸ extract, pick, pluck, rend, tear, wrench, wrest, yank. [*Compare* REMOVE.] *—See also* ATTRACT, LIFT (3).
pull back *v.* *—See* RETREAT.
pull down *v.* *—See* DESTROY (2), EARN (2).
pull in *v.* *—See* ARRIVE (1), EARN (2), RESTRAIN.
pull off *v.* *Informal* To be responsible for or guilty of an error or crime ▸ carry out, commit, do, perpetrate. *—See also* PERFORM (1).
pull on *v.* *—See* DON, DRINK (1).
pull out *v.* To withdraw from an association or federation ▸ break off, secede, splinter (off), withdraw. *Informal:* split (away). [*Compare* QUIT.] *—See also* GO (1), RETREAT.
pull through *v.* *—See* SURVIVE (1).
pull *n.* **1.** The act of drawing or pulling a load ▸ draft, drag, draw, haul, tow, traction, yank. [*Compare* JERK.] **2.** An inhalation, as of a cigar, pipe, or cigarette ▸ draft, drag, draw, puff. *Slang:* hit. *—See also* ATTRACTION, DRINK (2), INFLUENCE.
pullback *n.* *—See* RETREAT.
pullout *n.* *—See* RETREAT.
pullulate *v.* *—See* TEEM[1].

pul·mo·nar·y (po͝ol′mə-nĕr′ē, pŭl′-) ► *adj.* Of or involving the lungs.

pulp (pŭlp) ► *n.* **1.** A soft, moist, shapeless mass of matter. **2.** The soft, moist part of a vegetable or fruit. **3.** A mixture of cellulose material, such as wood, paper, and rags, ground up and moistened to make paper. **4.** The soft inner structure of a tooth, containing nerves and blood vessels. **5.** A publication, such as a magazine, containing lurid subject matter. ► *v.* To reduce to pulp. **—pulp′i·ness** *n.* **—pulp′y** *adj.*

pul·pit (po͝ol′pĭt, pŭl′-) ► *n.* An elevated platform, lectern, or stand used in preaching or conducting a religious service.

pulp·wood (pŭlp′wo͝od′) ► *n.* Soft wood used in making paper.

pul·sar (pŭl′sär′) ► *n.* Any of several celestial radio sources emitting short intense bursts, as of radio waves or x-rays.

pul·sate (pŭl′sāt′) ► *v.* **-sat·ed, -sat·ing. 1.** To expand and contract rhythmically; beat. **2.** To quiver; vibrate. **—pul·sa′tion** *n.*

pulse (pŭls) ► *n.* **1.** The rhythmical throbbing of arteries produced by the regular contractions of the heart. **2.** *Phys.* A brief sudden change in a normally constant quantity: *a pulse of current.* ► *v.* **pulsed, puls·ing.** To pulsate.

pul·ver·ize (pŭl′və-rīz′) ► *v.* **-ized, -iz·ing. 1.** To reduce or be reduced to a powder or dust. **2.** To demolish.

pu·ma (po͞o′mə, pyo͞o′-) ► *n.* See **mountain lion.**

pum·ice (pŭm′ĭs) ► *n.* A light porous lava, used in solid form as an abrasive and in powdered form as a polish. **—pum′ice** *v.*

pum·mel (pŭm′əl) ► *v.* **-meled, -mel·ing** also **-melled, -mel·ling.** To beat, as with the fists; pommel.

pump¹ (pŭmp) ► *n.* A device for raising, compressing, or transferring fluids. ► *v.* **1.** To raise or cause to flow by means of a pump. **2.** To draw, deliver, or pour forth as if with a pump. **3.** To remove the water from. **4.** To cause to move with the up-and-down motion of a pump handle. **5.** To propel, eject, or insert with or as if with a pump. **6.** To question closely or persistently. ***—phrasal verb:* pump up 1.** To inflate with gas by means of a pump. **2.** *Slang* To fill with enthusiasm and energy. ***—idiom:* pump iron** To lift weights. **—pump′er** *n.*

pump² (pŭmp) ► *n.* A low-cut woman's shoe with no fastenings.

pum·per·nick·el (pŭm′pər-nĭk′əl) ► *n.* A dark coarse rye bread.

pump·kin (pŭmp′kĭn, pŭm′-, pŭng′-) ► *n.* **1.** A trailing vine cultivated for its fruit. **2.** The large round fruit of this plant, having a thick, orange-yellow rind and numerous seeds.

pun (pŭn) ► *n.* A play on words, sometimes on different senses of the same word and sometimes on the similar sense or sound of different words. **—pun** *v.*

punch¹ (pŭnch) ► *n.* **1.** A tool for piercing or stamping. **2.** A tool for forcing a pin, bolt, or rivet in or out of a hole. **—punch** *v.*

punch² (pŭnch) ► *v.* **1.** To hit with a sharp blow of the fist. **2a.** To poke or prod with a stick. **b.** To herd (cattle). **3.** To depress (e.g., a key or button). ► *n.* **1.** A blow with the fist. **2.** Vigor or drive. **—punch′er** *n.*

punch³ (pŭnch) ► *n.* A beverage of fruit juices, often spiced and mixed with wine or liquor.

punch card ► *n.* A card punched with holes or notches to represent data for a computer.

pun·cheon¹ (pŭn′chən) ► *n.* **1.** A short wooden upright used in structural framing. **2.** A piece of broad, roughly dressed timber.

pun·cheon² (pŭn′chən) ► *n.* A cask with a capacity of from 72 to 120 gal. (273 to 454 l).

punch line ► *n.* The climax of a joke or humorous story.

punch·y (pŭn′chē) ► *adj.* **-i·er, -i·est. 1.** Marked by vigor or drive. **2.** Groggy or dazed from or as if from a blow.

punc·til·i·o (pŭngk-tĭl′ē-ō′) ► *n., pl.* **-os. 1.** A fine point of etiquette. **2.** Precise observance of formalities. **—punc·til′i·ous** *adj.* **—punc·til′i·ous·ly** *adv.* **—punc·til′i·ous·ness** *n.*

punc·tu·al (pŭngk′cho͞o-əl) ► *adj.* Acting or arriving exactly at the time appointed; prompt. **—punc′tu·al′i·ty** (-ăl′ĭ-tē) *n.* **—punc′tu·al·ly** *adv.*

punc·tu·ate (pŭngk′cho͞o-āt′) ► *v.* **-at·ed, -at·ing. 1.** To provide (a text) with punctuation marks. **2.** To interrupt periodically. **3.** To emphasize.

punc·tu·a·tion (pŭngk′cho͞o-ā′shən) ► *n.* **1.** The use of standard marks and signs in writing and printing to separate words into sentences, clauses, and phrases in order to clarify meaning. **2.** The marks so used.

punc·ture (pŭngk′chər) ► *v.* **-tured, -tur·ing. 1.** To pierce with a pointed object. **2.** To deflate by or as if by piercing. ► *n.* **1.** The act or an instance of puncturing. **2.** A hole made by a sharp object.

pun·dit (pŭn′dĭt) ► *n.* A learned person; authority.

pun·gent (pŭn′jənt) ► *adj.* **1.** Having a sharp, acrid taste or smell. **2.** Penetrating, biting, or caustic: *pungent satire.* **—pun′gen·cy** *n.* **—pun′gent·ly** *adv.*

Pu·nic (pyo͞o′nĭk) ► *adj.* Of or relating to ancient Carthage. ► *n.* The dialect of Phoenician spoken in Carthage.

pun·ish (pŭn′ĭsh) ► *v.* **1.** To subject to a penalty for an offense or fault. **2.** To inflict a penalty for (an offense). **3.** To handle roughly; hurt. **—pun′ish·a·ble** *adj.*

pun·ish·ment (pŭn′ĭsh-mənt) ► *n.* **1a.** The act of punishing. **b.** The condition of being punished. **2.** A penalty for wrongdoing. **3.** Rough handling; mistreatment.

pu·ni·tive (pyo͞o′nĭ-tĭv) ► *adj.* Inflicting or aiming to inflict punishment.

Pun·jab (pŭn′jăb′, pŭn-jäb′) ► A historical region of NW India and N Pakistan.

Pun·ja·bi also **Pan·ja·bi** (pŭn-jä′bē, -jăb′ē) ► *n., pl.* **-bis. 1.** A native or inhabitant of the Punjab. **2.** An Indic language spoken in the Punjab. **—Pun·ja′bi** *adj.*

punk (pŭngk) ► *n.* **1.** *Slang* **a.** A young hoodlum or tough. **b.** An inexperienced young man. **2.** *Mus.* **a.** Punk rock. **b.** A punk rocker. **3.** Dry decayed wood, used as tinder. **4.** A substance that smolders when ignited. ► *adj. Slang* **1.** Of or relating to punk rock. **2.** Of poor quality; worthless.

punk rock ► *n.* A form of hard-driving rock 'n' roll marked by harsh, often angry lyrics. **—punk rocker** *n.*

pun·ster (pŭn′stər) ► *n.* A maker of puns.

punt¹ (pŭnt) ► *n.* An open, flat-bottomed boat with squared ends, propelled by a long pole. ► *v.* To propel (a boat) with a pole.

THESAURUS

pulp *v.* —*See* CRUSH (1).
pulpit *n.* —*See* STAGE (1).
pulpy or **pulpous** *adj.* —*See* SOFT (1).
pulsate *v.* —*See* BEAT (5).
pulsation *n.* —*See* BEAT (3).
pulse *n.* —*See* BEAT (3).
pulse *v.* —*See* BEAT (5), GLARE (2).
pulverize *v.* —*See* CRUSH (2), DESTROY (2).
pulverous or **pulverulent** *adj.* —*See* FINE¹ (1).
pummel *v.* —*See* BEAT (1).
pump *v.* —*See* ASK (1), DRAIN (1).
pump up *v.* —*See* ELEVATE (2), ENERGIZE.
punch *v.* —*See* BREACH, CUT (1), HIT, PENETRATE.
punch *n.* —*See* BLOW², DIG, DRIVE (2), ENERGY, KICK.
punch-drunk *adj.* —*See* CONFUSED (1).
punctilious *adj.* —*See* CAREFUL (2), CEREMONIOUS.
punctiliousness *n.* —*See* CEREMONY (2), THOROUGHNESS.
punctual *adj.* Occurring, acting, or performed exactly at the time appointed ► prompt, timely. *Idioms:* on the dot (*or* nose), on schedule, on time.
puncture *v.* —*See* BREACH, CUT (1), DISCREDIT, HUMBLE, PENETRATE.
puncture *n.* —*See* PRICK.
pundit *n.* —*See* CRITIC (1), SAGE.
pungent *adj.* —*See* BITING, BITTER (1), PITHY, SPICY.
puniness *n.* —*See* INFIRMITY.
punish *v.* To subject one to a penalty for a wrong ► castigate, chastise, correct, discipline, penalize, sentence. [*Compare* CHASTISE, CONDEMN, FINE².]
punishing *adj.* Inflicting or aiming to inflict punishment ► correctional, disciplinary, penal, punitive, punitory. —*See also* BITTER (2).
punishment *n.* Something, such as loss, pain, or confinement, imposed for wrongdoing ► castigation, chastisement, correction, deserts, discipline, infliction, payment, penalty, penance, rap, retribution, sentence. [*Compare* FINE, RULING.]
punitive or **punitory** *adj.* —*See* PUNISHING.
punk *n.* —*See* NONENTITY, SQUIRT (2), THUG.
punk *v.* —*See* DECEIVE.

punt[2] (pŭnt) ▸ *n. Football* A kick in which the ball is dropped from the hands and kicked before it touches the ground. **—punt** *v.*

pu·ny (pyo͞o′nē) ▸ *adj.* **-ni·er, -ni·est.** Of inferior size, strength, or significance; weak.

pup (pŭp) ▸ *n.* **1.** A puppy. **2.** The young of certain other animals, such as the seal.

pu·pa (pyo͞o′pə) ▸ *n., pl.* **-pae** (-pē) or **-pas.** The nonfeeding stage between the larva and adult in the metamorphosis of an insect. **—pu′pal** *adj.*

pu·pil[1] (pyo͞o′pəl) ▸ *n.* A student under the supervision of a teacher or professor.

pu·pil[2] (pyo͞o′pəl) ▸ *n.* The dark circular opening in the center of the iris of the eye.

pup·pet (pŭp′ĭt) ▸ *n.* **1.** A figure of a person or animal that can be animated by a performer, esp. a small figure designed to fit over the hand. **2.** A marionette. **3.** A doll. **4.** One whose behavior is determined by the will of others.

pup·pet·eer (pŭp′ĭ-tîr′) ▸ *n.* One who operates and entertains with puppets. **—pup′pet·ry** *n.*

pup·py (pŭp′ē) ▸ *n., pl.* **-pies.** A young dog; pup.

pur·blind (pûr′blīnd′) ▸ *adj.* **1.** Nearly or partly blind. **2.** Slow in understanding or discernment; dull. **—pur′blind′ness** *n.*

pur·chase (pûr′chĭs) ▸ *v.* **-chased, -chas·ing.** To obtain in exchange for money or its equivalent; buy. ▸ *n.* **1a.** The act or an instance of buying. **b.** Something bought. **2.** A secure grasp or hold. **3.** A position or device affording means to move or secure a weight. **—pur′chas·a·ble** *adj.* **—pur′chas·er** *n.*

pur·dah (pûr′də) ▸ *n.* The Hindu or Muslim system of sex segregation, esp. of keeping women in seclusion.

pure (pyo͝or) ▸ *adj.* **pur·er, pur·est. 1.** Having a uniform composition; not mixed: *pure oxygen.* **2.** Free from adulterants or impurities. **3.** Free of dirt, defilement, or pollution. **4.** Complete; utter: *pure folly.* **5.** Having no faults; perfect. **6.** Chaste; virgin. **7.** Of unmixed blood or ancestry. **8.** Theoretical: *pure science.* **—pure′ly** *adv.* **—pu′ri·ty** *n.*

pure·bred (pyo͝or′brĕd′) ▸ *adj.* Of a strain established by breeding many generations of unmixed stock. **—pure′bred′** *n.*

pu·rée (pyo͝o-rā′, pyo͝or′ā) ▸ *v.* **-réed, -rée·ing.** To rub (food) through a strainer or process in a blender to a thick pulpy consistency. ▸ *n.* Food prepared by puréeing.

pur·ga·tion (pûr-gā′shən) ▸ *n.* The act of purging or purifying.

pur·ga·tive (pûr′gə tĭv) ▸ *adj.* Tending to cleanse or purge, esp. causing evacuation of the bowels. **—pur′ga·tive** *n.*

pur·ga·to·ry (pûr′gə-tôr′ē) ▸ *n., pl.* **-ries. 1.** In certain Christian doctrines, a temporary state in which the souls of those who have died in grace must expiate their sins. **2.** A place or condition of suffering, expiation, or remorse. **—pur′ga·to′ri·al** (-tôr′ē-əl) *adj.*

purge (pûrj) ▸ *v.* **purged, purg·ing. 1.** To purify, esp. of sin, guilt, or defilement. **2.** To rid of undesirable people. **3.** To undergo or cause evacuation of (the bowels). ▸ *n.* **1.** The act of purging. **2.** Something that purges, esp. a medicinal purgative.

pu·ri·fy (pyo͝or′ə-fī′) ▸ *v.* **-fied, -fy·ing.** To make or become pure. **—pu′ri·fi·ca′tion** *n.* **—pu′ri·fi′er** *n.*

Pu·rim (po͝or′ĭm, po͞o-rēm′) ▸ *n. Judaism* The 14th of Adar, observed in commemoration of Esther's deliverance of the Jews of Persia from massacre.

pu·rine (pyo͝or′ēn′) ▸ *n.* **1.** A colorless crystalline organic base, $C_5H_4N_4$. **2.** Any of a group of organic compounds derived from or structurally related to purine, including uric acid and guanine.

pur·ism (pyo͝or′ĭz′əm) ▸ *n.* Strict observance of correctness, esp. of language. **—pur′ist** *n.* **—pu·ris′tic** *adj.*

Pu·ri·tan (pyo͝or′ĭ-tn) ▸ *n.* **1.** A member of a group of English Protestants who in the 16th and 17th cent. advocated strict discipline and simplification of religious ceremonies. **2. puritan** One who regards pleasure or luxury as sinful. **—pu′ri·tan′i·cal** (-tăn′ĭ-kəl) *adj.*

purl[1] (pûrl) ▸ *v.* To flow or ripple with a murmuring sound. ▸ *n.* The sound made by rippling water.

purl[2] (pûrl) ▸ *n.* An inverted knitting stitch. **—purl** *v.*

pur·lieu (pûrl′yo͞o, pûr′lo͞o) ▸ *n.* **1.** An outlying or neighboring area. **2. purlieus** Outskirts; environs.

pur·loin (pər-loin′, pûr′loin′) ▸ *v.* To commit theft; steal.

pur·ple (pûr′pəl) ▸ *n.* **1.** Any of a group of colors with a hue between violet and red. **2.** Purple cloth worn as a symbol of royalty or high office. ▸ *adj.* **1.** Of the color purple. **2.** Elaborate and ornate: *purple prose.* **—pur′ple** *v.* **—pur′plish** *adj.*

pur·port (pər-pôrt′) ▸ *v.* To profess to be, often falsely. ▸ *n.* (pûr′pôrt′) **1.** Meaning; import. **2.** Intention; purpose.

pur·pose (pûr′pəs) ▸ *n.* **1.** An aim or goal. **2.** A result or effect that is intended or desired; intention. **3.** Determination; resolution: *a man of purpose.* ▸ *v.* **-posed, -pos·ing.** To intend or resolve to perform or accomplish. ***—idiom:* on purpose** Intentionally; deliberately. **—pur′pose·ful** *adj.* **—pur′pose·less** *adj.* **—pur′pose·ly** *adv.*

purr (pûr) ▸ *n.* A soft vibrant sound like that made by a contented cat. **—purr** *v.*

purse (pûrs) ▸ *n.* **1.** A woman's bag for carrying personal items; handbag. **2.** A small bag or pouch for carrying money. **3.** Available wealth or resources; money. **4.** A

THESAURUS

puny *adj.* *—See* MEAGER, WEAK (1).

pup *n.* *—See* SQUIRT (2).

pupil *n.* *—See* STUDENT.

puppet *n.* *—See* PAWN[2].

puppy *n.* *—See* SQUIRT (2).

purblind *adj.* *—See* BLIND (3).

purchase *v.* *—See* BUY.

purchase *n.* **1.** Something bought or capable of being bought ▸ buy. [*Compare* EFFECTS, GOOD.] **2.** A place providing support for the foot in climbing ▸ foothold, footing, perch, toehold.

purchaser *n.* *—See* CONSUMER.

pure *adj.* Free from extraneous elements ▸ absolute, clear, genuine, perfect, plain, sheer, simple, unadulterated, undefiled, undiluted, unmixed. [*Compare* PERFECT.] *See also* CHASTE, FRESH (1), INNOCENT (1), STRAIGHT, UTTER[2].

pureblood or **pureblooded** or **purebred** *adj.* *—See* THOROUGHBRED.

purely *adv.* *—See* COMPLETELY (1).

pureness *n.* *—See* PURITY.

purgation *n.* *—See* PURIFICATION (2).

purgative *n.* *—See* PURIFIER.

purgative or **purgatorial** *adj.* Serving to purify of sin ▸ expiatory, lustral, lustrative, purificatory. *—See also* ELIMINATIVE.

purge *v.* *—See* CLEAR (3), ELIMINATE, PURIFY (1).

purge *n.* *—See* ELIMINATION.

purification *n.* **1.** The act or process of removing physical impurities ▸ catharsis, clarification, cleaning, cleansing, lavation, refinement. **2.** A freeing from sin, guilt, or defilement ▸ ablution, catharsis, lustration, pardoning, purgation, redemption. [*Compare* ATONEMENT.]

purificatory *adj.* *—See* PURGATIVE.

purifier *n.* Something that purifies or cleans ▸ antiseptic, cathartic, clarifier, cleaner, cleanser, disinfectant, purgative, refiner, refinery.

purify *v.* **1.** To free from sin, guilt, or defilement ▸ atone, cleanse, expiate, lustrate, pardon, purge, redeem. **2.** To remove impurities from ▸ clarify, clean, cleanse, refine. [*Compare* CLEAN.]

purist *adj.* *—See* PEDANTIC.

puritan *n.* *—See* PRUDE.

puritan *adj.* *—See* ASCETIC.

puritanical *adj.* *—See* ASCETIC, INTOLERANT (1), PRUDISH.

purity *n.* The condition of being clean and free of contaminants ▸ clarity, cleanliness, cleanness, disinfection, immaculacy, immaculateness, pureness, taintlessness. [*Compare* STERILITY.] *—See also* CHASTITY.

purl *v.* *—See* BURBLE, FLOW (1).

purl *n.* *—See* BURBLE.

purloin *v.* *—See* STEAL.

purloiner *n.* *—See* THIEF.

purport *n.* *—See* IMPORT, MEANING, THRUST.

purport *v.* To claim or allege insincerely or falsely ▸ feign, pretend, pretext, profess.

purported *adj.* *—See* SUPPOSED.

purpose *n.* *—See* DECISION (2), FUNCTION (1), INTENTION.

purpose *v.* *—See* INTEND.

purposeful *adj.* *—See* DELIBERATE (1).

purposefulness *n.* *—See* DECISION (2).

purposeless *adj.* *—See* AIMLESS, MINDLESS.

purr *v.* *—See* HUM.

purr *n.* *—See* HUM.

purring *adj.* *—See* ACTIVE.

purse *n.* A closeable container for carrying money and personal items ▸

sum of money collected as a present or offered as a prize. ▸ *v.* **pursed, purs·ing.** To pucker.

purs·er (pûr′sər) ▸ *n.* The officer in charge of money matters on board a ship or commercial aircraft.

purs·lane (pûrs′lĭn, -lān′) ▸ *n.* A trailing Asian weed having small yellow flowers and fleshy leaves that are cooked as a vegetable or used in salads.

pur·su·ance (pər-so͞o′əns) ▸ *n.* A carrying out or putting into effect.

pur·su·ant to (pər-so͞o′ənt) ▸ *prep.* In accordance with.

pur·sue (pər-so͞o′) ▸ *v.* **-sued, -su·ing. 1.** To follow so as to overtake or capture. **2.** To strive to accomplish. **3.** To proceed along the course of; follow: *pursue a course.* **4.** To be engaged in (e.g., a hobby). **—pur·su′er** *n.*

pur·suit (pər-so͞ot′) ▸ *n.* **1.** The act of pursuing. **2.** An activity, such as a hobby, engaged in regularly.

pu·ru·lent (pyo͝or′ə-lənt, pyo͝or′yə-) ▸ *adj.* Containing or secreting pus. **—pu′ru·lence** *n.*

pur·vey (pər-vā′, pûr′vā′) ▸ *v.* To supply (e.g., food); furnish. **—pur·vey′ance** *n.* **—pur·vey′or** *n.*

pur·view (pûr′vyo͞o′) ▸ *n.* **1.** The extent of function, power, or competence; scope. **2.** Range of vision, comprehension, or experience; outlook.

pus (pŭs) ▸ *n.* A usu. viscous, yellowish-white fluid formed in infected tissue, consisting of white blood cells, cellular debris, and necrotic tissue.

Pu·san (po͞o′sän′) ▸ A city of extreme SE South Korea on Korea Strait SE of Seoul.

push (po͝osh) ▸ *v.* **1.** To apply pressure against for the purpose of moving. **2.** To move (an object) by exerting force against it; thrust or shove. **3.** To force (one's way). **4.** To urge forward insistently; pressure: *push a child to study harder.* **5.** To bear hard upon; press. **6.** *Slang* **a.** To promote or sell (a product). **b.** To sell (a narcotic) illegally. ▸ *n.* **1.** The act of pushing; thrust. **2.** A vigorous or insistent effort; drive. **3.** A provocation to action; stimulus.

push·but·ton or **push button** (po͝osh′bŭt′n) ▸ *n.* A small button that activates an electric circuit when pushed.

push-but·ton (po͝osh′bŭt′n) ▸ *adj.* Equipped with or operated by a push button.

push·cart (po͝osh′kärt′) ▸ *n.* A light cart pushed by hand.

push·er (po͝osh′ər) ▸ *n.* *Slang* One who sells drugs illegally.

push·o·ver (po͝osh′ō′vər) ▸ *n.* **1.** One easily defeated or deceived. **2.** Something easily done.

Push·tu (pŭsh′to͞o) ▸ *n.* Var. of **Pashto.**

push·up (po͝osh′ŭp′) ▸ *n.* An exercise performed by lying face down with the palms on the floor and pushing the body up and down with the arms.

push·y (po͝osh′ē) ▸ *adj.* **-i·er, -i·est.** Disagreeably aggressive or forward. **—push′i·ly** *adv.* **—push′i·ness** *n.*

pu·sil·lan·i·mous (pyo͞o′sə-lăn′ə-məs) ▸ *adj.* Lacking courage; cowardly. **—pu′sil·lan′i·mous·ly** *adv.* **—pu′sil·la·nim′i·ty** (-lə-nĭm′ĭ-tē) *n.*

puss[1] (po͝os) ▸ *n.* *Informal* A cat.

puss[2] (po͝os) ▸ *n.* *Slang* The human face.

puss·y[1] (po͝os′ē) ▸ *n., pl.* **-ies.** *Informal* A cat.

pus·sy[2] (pŭs′ē) ▸ *adj.* **-si·er, -si·est.** Containing or resembling pus.

puss·y·cat (po͝os′ē-kăt′) ▸ *n.* **1.** A cat. **2.** *Informal* An easygoing, amiable person.

puss·y·foot (po͝os′ē-fo͝ot′) ▸ *v.* **1.** To move stealthily or cautiously. **2.** *Informal* To avoid committing oneself.

puss·y willow (po͝os′ē) ▸ *n.* A North American shrub or small tree with silky catkins.

pus·tule (pŭs′cho͞ol, pŭs′tyo͞ol) ▸ *n.* A small inflammation of the skin filled with pus. **—pus′tu·lar** *adj.*

put (po͝ot) ▸ *v.* **put, put·ting. 1.** To place in a specified position; set. **2.** To cause to be in a specified condition. **3.** To subject: *put him to a lot of trouble.* **4.** To attribute: *put a false interpretation on events.* **5.** To estimate: *put the time at five o'clock.* **6.** To impose or levy (a tax). **7.** To hurl with an overhand pushing motion: *put the shot.* **8.** To bring up for consideration or judgment: *put a question.* **9.** To express; state. **10.** To render in a specified language; translate. **11.** To adapt. **12.** To apply: *put our minds to it.* **13.** To proceed: *The ship put into the harbor.* ***—phrasal verbs:*** **put across** To state so as to be understood or accepted. **put down 1.** To write down. **2.** To suppress: *put down a rebellion.* **3.** *Slang* To criticize or belittle. **put off 1.** To delay or postpone. **2.** To offend or repel. **put on 1.** To clothe oneself with. **2.** *Slang* To tease or mislead. **put out 1.** To extinguish. **2.** To inconvenience. **3.** To anger or irritate. ***—idiom:*** **put up with** To endure.

pu·ta·tive (pyo͞o′tə-tĭv) ▸ *adj.* Generally regarded as such.

put·down (po͝ot′doun′) ▸ *n.* *Slang* A critical or slighting remark.

THESAURUS

bag, clutch, handbag, pocketbook, reticule.

pursuance *n.* *—See* PURSUIT (2).

pursue *v.* **1.** To follow another with the intent of overtaking and capturing ▸ chase (down), gun for, hunt, run after. ***Idioms:*** be (*or* go) in pursuit, give chase. [*Compare* FOLLOW, SEEK.] **2.** To work at, especially as a profession ▸ do, follow, practice. ***Idiom:*** hang out one's shingle. [*Compare* LABOR.] *—See also* COURT (2), LEAD.

pursuing *n.* *—See* PURSUIT (2).

pursuit *n.* **1.** The following of another in an attempt to overtake and capture ▸ chase, hot pursuit, hunt. **2.** An attempt to accomplish or attain ▸ hunt, prosecution, pursuance, pursuing, quest, search. [*Compare* EXPEDITION, EXPLORATION.] *—See also* BUSINESS (2).

purvey *v.* *—See* PROMOTE (3).

purview *n.* *—See* KEN, RANGE (1).

push *v.* **1.** To apply pressure on, against, or with ▸ bear (down), butt, crowd, crush, depress, dig, elbow, jab, jam, jog, jostle, nudge, poke, press, prod, ram, shoulder, shove, thrust. **2.** *Slang* To engage in the illicit sale of narcotics ▸ deal, peddle. [*Compare* SELL.] **3.** To force to work hard ▸ drive, task, tax, work. ***Idiom:*** crack the whip. [*Compare* FORCE.] *—See also* ADVANCE (1), ADVANCE (2), DRIVE (2), DRIVE (3), MUSCLE, PROMOTE (3).

push off *v.* *—See* GO (1).

push on *v.* To move along a particular course ▸ go, pass, proceed, wend. ***Idiom:*** make (*or* wend) one's way. [*Compare* ADVANCE, JOURNEY, ROVE.]

push *n.* An act or instance of pushing ▸ butt, jam, jostle, press, shove, thrust. [*Compare* DIG.] *—See also* DRIVE (1), DRIVE (2), STIMULUS.

pusher *n.* *Slang* A person who sells narcotics illegally ▸ dealer, peddler, trafficker. *Slang:* connection.

pushiness *n.* *—See* IMPUDENCE.

pushover *n.* *—See* BREEZE (2), DUPE, WEAKLING.

pushy *adj.* *—See* IMPUDENT.

pusillanimity *n.* *—See* COWARDICE.

pusillanimous *adj.* *—See* COWARDLY.

puss *n.* *—See* FACE (1), MOUTH (1).

pussyfoot *v.* *—See* EQUIVOCATE (1), SNEAK.

put *v.* **1.** To establish and apply as compulsory ▸ assess, exact, impose, levy. **2.** To seek an answer to a question ▸ ask, pose, raise. [*Compare* SAY.] **3.** To have or put in a customary place ▸ cache, keep, store. *—See also* AIR (2), ESTIMATE (2), GAMBLE (2), PHRASE, POSITION, TRANSLATE.

put away *v.* *—See* CONSUME (1), EAT (1), IMPRISON, MURDER.

put by *v.* *—See* SAVE (1).

put down *v.* *—See* BELITTLE, CRITICIZE (1), HUMBLE, SUPPRESS.

put forth *v.* *—See* BROACH.

put forward *v.* *—See* OFFER (1), PROPOSE.

put in *v.* **1.** To ask for employment, acceptance, or admission ▸ apply, petition. **2.** To spend or complete time, as a prison term ▸ serve. *Informal:* do. **3.** To use time in a particular way ▸ pass, spend. [*Compare* IDLE.] *—See also* INTRODUCE (2).

put off *v.* To offer or put into circulation an inferior or fraudulent item ▸ foist, fob off, palm off, pass off. [*Compare* DUMP.] *—See also* DEFER[1], DISSUADE, OFFEND (2).

put on *v.* *—See* ACT (2), DON, IMPOSE ON, STAGE.

put out *v.* *—See* ANNOY, EXTINGUISH, INCONVENIENCE, OFFEND (1), PUBLISH (1).

put through *v.* *—See* EFFECT.

put together *v.* *—See* MAKE.

put up *v.* *—See* BUILD, ERECT, LODGE, OFFER (1), PRESERVE (1).

putative *adj.* *—See* SUPPOSED.

putdown *n.* *—See* INDIGNITY, SNUB.

put-on (po͝ot′ŏn′, -ôn′) ▸ *adj.* Pretended; feigned. ▸ *n.* *Slang* **1.** The act of teasing or misleading someone, esp. for amusement. **2.** Something intended as a hoax or joke.

pu·tre·fy (pyo͞o′trə-fī′) ▸ *v.* **-fied, -fy·ing. 1.** To decay or cause to decay and have a foul odor. **2.** To make or become gangrenous. **—pu′tre·fac′tion** (-făk′shən) *n.* **—pu′tre·fac′tive** (-făk′tĭv) *adj.*

pu·tres·cent (pyo͞o-trĕs′ənt) ▸ *adj.* Becoming putrid; putrefying. **—pu·tres′cence** *n.*

pu·trid (pyo͞o′trĭd) ▸ *adj.* **1.** Decomposed and foul-smelling. **2.** Vile; corrupt. **3.** Extremely objectionable. **—pu·trid′i·ty** (-trĭd′ĭ-tē), **pu′trid·ness** *n.*

putsch (po͝och) ▸ *n.* A sudden attempt by a group to overthrow a government.

putt (pŭt) ▸ *n.* A light golf stroke made in an effort to place the ball into the hole. **—putt** *v.*

put·tee (pŭ-tē′, pŭt′ē) ▸ *n.* **1.** A strip of cloth wound spirally around the lower leg. **2.** A gaiter covering the lower leg.

put·ter[1] (pŭt′ər) ▸ *n.* A short golf club used for putting.

put·ter[2] (pŭt′ər) ▸ *v.* To occupy oneself in an aimless or ineffective manner.

put·ty (pŭt′ē) ▸ *n., pl.* **-ties. 1.** A doughlike cement made by mixing whiting and linseed oil, used to fill holes in woodwork and secure panes of glass. **2.** A substance with a similar consistency or function. **—put′ty** *v.*

puz·zle (pŭz′əl) ▸ *v.* **-zled, -zling. 1.** To baffle or confuse by presenting a difficult problem or matter. **2.** To clarify or solve by reasoning or study: *puzzled out the answer.* **3.** To ponder over a problem in an effort to solve or understand it. ▸ *n.* **1.** Something, such as a toy or game, that tests one's ingenuity. **2.** Something that baffles or confuses. **3.** Bewilderment. **—puz′zle·ment** *n.*

PVC (pē′vē-sē′) ▸ *n.* A common thermoplastic resin, used in a wide variety of manufactured products.

Pyg·my also **Pig·my** (pĭg′mē) ▸ *n., pl.* **-mies. 1.** also **pygmy** A member of any of several African or Asian peoples of gen. short stature. **2. pygmy** One of unusually small size or of little importance. **—Pyg′my, pyg′my** *adj.*

py·ja·mas (pə-jä′məz, -jăm′əz) ▸ *pl.n.* *Chiefly Brit.* Var. of **pajamas.**

py·lon (pī′lŏn′) ▸ *n.* **1.** A steel tower supporting high-tension wires. **2.** A monumental gateway, esp. a pair of truncated pyramids serving as the entrance to an Egyptian temple.

Pyong·yang (pyŭng′yăng′, -yăng′, pyông′-) ▸ The capital of North Korea, in the SW-central part.

py·or·rhe·a or **py·or·rhoe·a** (pī′ə-rē′ə) ▸ *n.* **1.** Inflammation of the gums and tooth sockets, often leading to loosening of the teeth. **2.** A discharge of pus.

pyr·a·mid (pĭr′ə-mĭd) ▸ *n.* **1.** A solid figure with a polygonal base and triangular faces that meet at a common point. **2a.** A massive monument of ancient Egypt having a rectangular base and four triangular faces meeting at an apex, built over or around a tomb. **b.** A flat-topped Mesoamerican temple of similar shape. ▸ *v.* **1.** To place or build in the shape of a pyramid. **2.** To increase rapidly and on a widening base. **—py·ram′i·dal** (pĭ-răm′ĭ-dl) *adj.*

pyre (pīr) ▸ *n.* A combustible pile for burning a corpse as a funeral rite.

Pyr·e·nees (pîr′ə-nēz′) ▸ A mountain range of SW Europe extending from the Bay of Biscay to the Mediterranean.

py·re·thrum (pī-rē′thrəm, -rĕth′rəm) ▸ *n.* **1.** Any of several Old World plants cultivated for their showy flowers. **2.** An insecticide made from the dried flowers of these plants.

Py·rex (pī′rĕks′) ▸ A trademark for any of various types of heat-resistant and chemical-resistant glass.

py·rim·i·dine (pī-rĭm′ĭ-dēn′, pĭ-) ▸ *n.* **1.** A crystalline organic base, $C_4H_4N_2$. **2.** Any of several basic compounds derived from or structurally related to pyrimidine, esp. uracil, cytosine, and thymine.

py·rite (pī′rīt′) ▸ *n.* A brass-colored mineral, FeS_2, used as an iron ore and in producing sulfuric acid. **—py·rit′ic** (-rĭt′ĭk) *adj.*

py·ri·tes (pī-rī′tēz, pī′rīts′) ▸ *n., pl.* **pyrites.** Any of various natural metallic sulfide minerals, esp. of iron.

pyro– or **pyr–** ▸ *pref.* Fire; heat: *pyromania.*

py·rol·y·sis (pī-rŏl′ĭ-sĭs) ▸ *n.* Decomposition or transformation of a compound caused by heat. **—py′ro·lyt′ic** (-rə-lĭt′ĭk) *adj.*

py·ro·ma·ni·a (pī′rō-mā′nē-ə, -mān′yə) ▸ *n.* An uncontrollable impulse to start fires. **—py′ro·ma′ni·ac′** (-mā′nē-ăk′) *n.*

py·rom·e·ter (pī-rŏm′ĭ-tər) ▸ *n.* A thermometer used for measuring high temperatures.

py·ro·tech·nics (pī′rə-tĕk′nĭks) ▸ *n. (takes sing. v.)* **1.** A fireworks display. **2.** A brilliant display, as of wit. **—py′ro·tech′nic, py′ro·tech′ni·cal** *adj.*

Pyr·rhic victory (pĭr′ĭk) ▸ *n.* A victory offset by excessive losses.

Py·thag·o·ras (pĭ-thăg′ər-əs) (fl. 6th cent. B.C.) ▸ Greek philosopher and mathematician.

Py·thag·o·re·an theorem (pĭ-thăg′ə-rē′ən) ▸ *n.* The theorem that the sum of the squares of the lengths of the sides of a right triangle is equal to the square of the length of the hypotenuse.

py·thon (pī′thŏn′, -thən) ▸ *n.* Any of various nonvenomous snakes found chiefly in Asia, Africa, and Australia, that coil around and suffocate their prey.

pyx also **pix** (pĭks) ▸ *n.* **1.** A container in which wafers for the Eucharist are kept. **2.** A container in which the Eucharist is carried to the sick.

THESAURUS

put-on *n.* —*See* FAÇADE (2), PRANK[1].

putrefaction or **putrescence** *n.* —*See* DECAY.

putrefy *v.* —*See* DECAY.

putrid or **putrescent** *adj.* —*See* BAD (2).

putridness *n.* —*See* DECAY.

putter *v.* To waste time by engaging in aimless activity ▸ dawdle (about), doodle, fiddle (around), fool. *Informal:* fool around, mess around, play around. *Slang:* screw around (*or* off). [*Compare* DELAY, IDLE.]

puzzle *v.* —*See* CONFUSE (1).

puzzle out *v.* —*See* DECIPHER.

puzzle *n.* —*See* MYSTERY.

puzzled *adj.* —*See* CONFUSED (1).

puzzlement *n.* —*See* DAZE.

puzzler *n.* —*See* MYSTERY.

puzzling *adj.* —*See* MYSTERIOUS.

pygmy *adj.* —*See* TINY.

pythonic *adj.* —*See* ENORMOUS.

Q

q[1] or **Q** (kyo͞o) ► *n., pl.* **q's** or **Q's** also **qs** or **Qs**. The 17th letter of the English alphabet.
q[2] ► *Phys.* The symbol for **charge** 11.
Q ► *abbr.* quarter (of a year)
Qa·tar (kä′tär′, KHŭt′ər) ► A country of E Arabia on a peninsula in the SW Persian Gulf. **—Qa·tar′i** *adj. & n.*
QED ► *abbr. Lat.* quod erat demonstrandum (which was to be demonstrated)
Qing·dao (chĭng′dou′) also **Tsing·tao** (tsĭng′tou′) ► A city of E China on the Yellow Sea NNW of Shanghai.
qt. or **qt** ► *abbr.* quart
quack[1] (kwăk) ► *n.* The characteristic sound of a duck. **—quack** *v.*
quack[2] (kwăk) ► *n.* **1.** An untrained person who pretends to have medical knowledge. **2.** A charlatan. **—quack′er·y** *n.*
quad[1] (kwŏd) ► *n.* A quadrangle.
quad[2] (kwŏd) ► *n.* A quadruplet.
quad·ran·gle (kwŏd′răng′gəl) ► *n.* **1.** A quadrilateral. **2.** A rectangular area surrounded on all four sides by buildings. **—quad·ran′gu·lar** (-răng′gyə-lər) *adj.*
quad·rant (kwŏd′rənt) ► *n.* **1.** *Math.* **a.** A circular arc of 90°; one fourth of the circumference of a circle. **b.** The plane area bounded by such an arc and two perpendicular radii. **c.** Any of the four areas into which a plane is divided by the reference axes in a Cartesian coordinate system. **2.** An early instrument for measuring altitude of celestial bodies.
quad·ra·phon·ic also **quad·ri·phon·ic** (kwŏd′rə-fŏn′ĭk) ► *adj.* Of or for a four-channel sound system.
quad·rat·ic (kwŏ-drăt′ĭk) ► *adj. Math.* Of or containing quantities of the second degree. **—quad·rat′ic** *n.*
quad·ren·ni·al (kwŏ-drĕn′ē-əl) ► *adj.* **1.** Happening once in four years. **2.** Lasting for four years. **—quad·ren′ni·al·ly** *adv.*
quadri– or **quadru–** or **quadr–** ► *pref.* Four: *quadrilateral.*
quad·ri·ceps (kwŏd′rĭ-sĕps′) ► *n.* The large four-part extensor muscle at the front of the thigh.
quad·ri·lat·er·al (kwŏd′rə-lăt′ər-əl) ► *n.* A plane figure with four sides and four angles. ► *adj.* Having four sides.
qua·drille (kwŏ-drĭl′, kwə-, kə-) ► *n.* **1.** A square dance of French origin, performed by four couples. **2.** Music for this dance.
quad·ril·lion (kwŏ-drĭl′yən) ► *n.* **1.** The cardinal number equal to 10^{15}. **2.** *Chiefly Brit.* The cardinal number equal to 10^{24}. **—quad·ril′lion** *adj.* **—quad·ril′lionth** *n. & adj.*
quad·ri·par·tite (kwŏd′rə-pär′tīt′) ► *adj.* **1.** Consisting of or divided into four parts. **2.** Involving four participants.
quad·ri·ple·gi·a (kwŏd′rə-plē′jē-ə, -jə) ► *n.* Complete paralysis of the body from the neck down. **—quad′ri·ple′gic** *adj. & n.*
quad·ru·ped (kwŏd′rə-pĕd′) ► *n.* A four-footed animal. ► *adj.* Four-footed.
quad·ru·ple (kwŏ-dro͞o′pəl, -drŭp′əl, kwŏd′ro͞o-pəl) ► *adj.* **1.** Having four parts. **2.** Four times as many or as much. ► *n.* A fourfold amount or number. ► *v.* **-pled, -pling.** To multiply or be multiplied by four.
quad·ru·plet (kwŏ-drŭp′lĭt, -dro͞o′plĭt, kwŏd′rə-plĭt) ► *n.* **1.** One of four offspring born in a single birth. **2.** A group or combination of four.
quad·ru·pli·cate (kwŏ-dro͞o′plĭ-kĭt) ► *adj.* **1.** Multiplied by four; quadruple. **2.** Fourth in a group of four identical things. ► *n.* One of a group of four identical items. ► *v.* (-kāt′) **-cat·ed, -cat·ing.** To quadruple. **—quad·ru′pli·ca′tion** *n.*
quaff (kwŏf, kwăf, kwôf) ► *v.* To drink heartily. **—quaff** *n.*
quag·mire (kwăg′mīr′, kwŏg′-) ► *n.* **1.** Land with a soft muddy surface. **2.** A difficult or precarious situation; predicament.
qua·hog (kō′hôg′, -hŏg′, kwô′-, kwō′-) ► *n.* An edible clam of the Atlantic coast of North America, having a hard rounded shell.
quail[1] (kwāl) ► *n., pl.* **quail** or **quails.** Any of various small chickenlike game birds having brown plumage and a short tail.
quail[2] (kwāl) ► *v.* To shrink back in fear; cower.
quaint (kwānt) ► *adj.* **-er, -est. 1.** Odd, esp. in an old-fashioned way. **2.** Unfamiliar or unusual; strange. **—quaint′ly** *adv.* **—quaint′ness** *n.*
quake (kwāk) ► *v.* **quaked, quak·ing. 1.** To shake or tremble. **2.** To shiver, as with cold or from fear. ► *n.* **1.** An instance of quaking. **2.** An earthquake. **—quak′y** *adj.*
Quak·er (kwā′kər) ► *n.* A member of the Society of Friends. **—Quak′er·ism** *n.*
qual·i·fi·ca·tion (kwŏl′ə-fĭ-kā′shən) ► *n.* **1.** The act of qualifying or the condition of being qualified. **2.** A quality or an ability that makes a person suitable for a particular position or task. **3.** A restriction or modification.
qual·i·fy (kwŏl′ə-fī′) ► *v.* **-fied, -fy·ing. 1.** To describe; characterize. **2.** To make competent or eligible for an office, position, or task. **3.** To declare competent or capable; certify. **4.** To modify, limit, or restrict. **5.** To make less harsh or severe. **6.** *Gram.* To modify the meaning of (e.g., a noun). **—qual′i·fi′er** *n.*
qual·i·ta·tive (kwŏl′ĭ-tā′tĭv) ► *adj.* Of or concerning quality. **—qual′i·ta′tive·ly** *adv.*
qual·i·ty (kwŏl′ĭ-tē) ► *n., pl.* **-ties. 1.** A trait or characteristic; property. **2.** Essential character; nature. **3.** Degree or grade of excellence. **4.** High social position. **—qual′i·ty** *adj.*
qualm (kwäm, kwôm) ► *n.* **1.** A sudden feeling of sickness, faintness, or nausea. **2.** A sudden disturbing feeling. **3.** A

THESAURUS

quack *n.* —*See* FAKE.
quad or **quadrangle** *n.* —*See* COURT (1).
quaff *v.* —*See* DRINK (1).
quaff *n.* —*See* DRINK (2).
quag *n.* —*See* SWAMP.
quaggy *adj.* —*See* SOFT (1).
quagmire *n.* —*See* PREDICAMENT, SWAMP.
quail *v.* —*See* FLINCH.
quaint *adj.* Agreeably curious, especially in an old-fashioned or unusual way ► curious, funny, odd. —*See also* ECCENTRIC.
quake *v.* —*See* SHAKE (1), SWAY.
quake *n.* A shaking of the earth ► earthquake, seism, temblor, tremor. *Informal:* shake. —*See also* TREMOR (2).
quaking or **quaky** *adj.* —*See* TREMULOUS.
qualification *n.* **1.** The quality or state of being eligible ► correctness, eligibility, fitness, suitability, suitableness, worthiness. **2.** A quality that makes a person suitable for a particular position or task ► attainment, credential, endowment, skill. **3.** The act or process of ascertaining dimensions, quantity, or capacity ► determination, measure, measurement, mensuration. [*Compare* COMPUTATION, ESTIMATION.] —*See also* PROVISION.
qualified *adj.* Not total, unlimited, or wholehearted ► conditioned, limited, modified, reserved, restricted. —*See also* ELIGIBLE.
qualify *v.* —*See* AUTHORIZE, MODERATE (1).
quality *n.* **1.** A distinctive element ► attribute, character, characteristic, feature, mark, peculiarity, property, savor, trait. [*Compare* ESSENCE.] **2.** Degree of excellence ► caliber, class, grade. [*Compare* DEGREE.] —*See also* ELEGANCE, MERIT, SOCIETY (1).
quality *adj.* —*See* EXCELLENT.
qualm *n.* A feeling of uncertainty about the fitness or correctness of an action ► compunction, concern, mis-

pang of conscience about a course of action.

quan·da·ry (kwŏn′də-rē, -drē) ► *n., pl.* **-ries.** A state of uncertainty or perplexity.

quan·ti·fy (kwŏn′tə-fī′) ► *v.* **-fied, -fy·ing.** To determine or express the quantity of. **—quan′ti·fi′a·ble** *adj.*

quan·ti·ta·tive (kwŏn′tĭ-tā′tĭv) ► *adj.* Relating to or expressed as a quantity. **—quan′ti·ta′tive·ly** *adv.*

quan·ti·ty (kwŏn′tĭ-tē) ► *n., pl.* **-ti·ties.** **1.** A specified or indefinite number or amount. **2.** A considerable amount or number.

quan·tum (kwŏn′təm) ► *n., pl.* **-ta** (-tə). **1.** A quantity or amount. **2.** *Phys.* A discrete quantity of electromagnetic radiation.

quantum physics ► *n. (takes sing. v.)* The branch of physics that uses quantum theory to describe and predict the properties of a physical system.

quantum theory ► *n. Phys.* The theory that radiant energy is transmitted in the form of discrete units.

quar·an·tine (kwôr′ən-tēn′, kwŏr′-) ► *n.* **1a.** A period of time during which one suspected of carrying a contagious disease is detained. **b.** A place for such detention. **2.** A condition of enforced isolation. ► *v.* **-tined, -tin·ing.** To isolate in or as if in quarantine. **—quar′an·tin′a·ble** *adj.*

quark (kwôrk, kwärk) ► *n.* Any of a group of hypothetical elementary particles with fractional electric charges, regarded as constituents of all hadrons.

quar·rel (kwôr′əl, kwŏr′-) ► *n.* **1.** An angry dispute; altercation. **2.** A cause of a dispute or argument. ► *v.* **-reled, -rel·ing** or **-relled, -rel·ling.** **1.** To engage in a quarrel; argue. **2.** To find fault. **—quar′rel·er, quar′rel·ler** *n.*

quar·rel·some (kwôr′əl-səm, kwŏr′-) ► *adj.* Given to quarreling; contentious.

quar·ry[1] (kwôr′ē, kwŏr′ē) ► *n., pl.* **-ries.** **1.** A hunted animal; prey. **2.** An object of pursuit.

quar·ry[2] (kwôr′ē, kwŏr′ē) ► *n., pl.* **-ries.** An open excavation or pit from which stone is obtained. **—quar′ri·er** *n.* **—quar′ry** *v.*

quart (kwôrt) ► *n.* **1.** A unit of volume or capacity in both liquid and dry measure. See **measurement** table in Appendix. **2.** A container having a capacity of one quart.

quar·ter (kwôr′tər) ► *n.* **1.** One of four equal parts. **2.** A coin equal to one fourth of the dollar of the US and Canada. **3.** One fourth of an hour; 15 minutes. **4a.** One fourth of a year; three months: *Sales were up in the second quarter.* **b.** An academic term lasting approximately three months. **5.** One leg of an animal's carcass. **6. quarters** A place of residence. **7.** often **Quarter** A specific district or section, as of a city. **8.** often **quarters** An unspecified direction, person, or group: *information from the highest quarters.* **9.** Mercy or clemency. ► *adj.* Equal to or being a quarter. ► *v.* **1.** To divide into four equal or equivalent parts. **2.** To dismember (a human body) into four parts. **3.** To furnish with housing.

quar·ter·back (kwôr′tər-băk′) ► *n. Football* The offensive backfield player who usu. calls the signals for the plays. **—quar′ter·back′** *v.*

quar·ter·deck (kwôr′tər-dĕk′) ► *n.* The after part of the upper deck of a ship.

quarter horse ► *n.* One of a breed of strong saddle horses developed in the W US.

quar·ter·ly (kwôr′tər-lē) ► *adj.* Occurring at three-month intervals: *a quarterly magazine; a quarterly payment.* ► *n., pl.* **-lies.** A publication issued regularly every three months.

quar·ter·mas·ter (kwôr′tər-măs′tər) ► *n.* **1.** An officer responsible for the food, clothing, and equipment of troops. **2.** A petty officer responsible for the navigation of a ship.

quarter note ► *n. Mus.* A note having one-fourth the time value of a whole note.

quar·tet also **quar·tette** (kwôr-tĕt′) ► *n.* **1.** *Mus.* A composition for four voices or instruments. **2.** A group or set of four.

quar·tile (kwôr′tīl′, -tĭl) ► *n. Statistics* The portion of a frequency distribution containing one fourth of the total sample.

quar·to (kwôr′tō) ► *n., pl.* **-tos.** **1.** The page size obtained by folding a whole sheet into four leaves. **2.** A book composed of pages of this size.

quartz (kwôrts) ► *n.* A hard mineral composed of silica, SiO_2, found worldwide in many different types of rocks, including sandstone and granite.

quartz·ite (kwôrt′sīt′) ► *n.* A rock formed from the metamorphism of quartz sandstone.

qua·sar (kwā′zär′, -sär′, -zər, -sər) ► *n.* A starlike object that emits powerful blue light and often radio waves.

quash[1] (kwŏsh) ► *v.* To set aside or annul, esp. by judicial action.

quash[2] (kwŏsh) ► *v.* To put down or suppress (e.g., a rebellion).

qua·si (kwā′zī′, -sī′, kwä′zē, -sē) ► *adj.* Having a likeness to something; resembling.

quasi– ► *pref.* Almost; somewhat: *quasi-stellar object.*

qua·si-stel·lar object (kwā′zī-stĕl′ər, -sī′-, kwä′zē-, -sē-) ► *n.* A quasar.

Quaternary (kwŏt′ər-nĕr′ē, kwə-tûr′nə-rē) *Geol.* ► *adj.* Of or being the 2nd period of the Cenozoic Era, including the Pleistocene and Holocene epochs. ► *n.* The Quaternary Period.

quat·rain (kwŏt′rān′, kwŏ-trān′) ► *n.* A stanza or poem of four lines.

quat·re·foil (kăt′ər-foil′, kăt′rə-) ► *n.* A representation of a flower with four petals or a leaf with four leaflets.

qua·ver (kwā′vər) ► *v.* **1.** To quiver, as from weakness; tremble. **2.** To speak in a shaky or tremulous voice. **—qua′ver** *n.* **—qua′ver·y** *adj.*

quay (kē, kā) ► *n.* A wharf.

quea·sy (kwē′zē) ► *adj.* **-si·er, -si·est.** **1.** Experiencing nausea; nauseated. **2.** Uneasy; troubled. **3.** Ill at ease; squeamish. **—quea′si·ly** *adv.* **—quea′si·ness** *n.*

Que·bec (kwĭ-bĕk′) or **Qué·bec** (kā-) ► **1.** A province of E Canada. Cap. Quebec. **2.** also **Quebec City** The capital of Quebec, Canada, in the S part on the St. Lawrence R. **—Que·beck′er, Que·bec′er** *n.*

Qué·be·cois (kā′bĕ-kwä′) ► *n., pl.* **-cois.** A native or inhabitant of Quebec, esp. a French-speaking one. **—Qué′be·cois′** *adj.*

Quech·ua (kĕch′wə, -wä′) ► *n., pl.* **-ua** or **-uas.** **1.** The Quechuan language of the Inca empire, now widely spoken in the Andes highlands. **2.** A speaker of the Quechua language.

Quech·uan (kĕch′wən) ► *n.* A subgroup of languages, the most important being Quechua. ► *adj.* Of the Quechua or their language or culture.

queen (kwēn) ► *n.* **1a.** The wife or widow of a king. **b.** A woman sovereign. **2.** Something eminent or supreme in a given domain and personified as a woman: *Paris is the*

THESAURUS

giving, reservation, scruple, worry. *Informal:* problem, trouble. *—See also* DOUBT.

quandary *n.* *—See* PREDICAMENT.

quantify or **quantitate** *v.* To ascertain the dimensions, quantity, or capacity of ► gauge, measure. *Idiom:* take the dimensions (*or* measure) of. [*Compare* ESTIMATE.]

quantity *n.* **1.** An amount that is represented in numerals ► figure, number. [*Compare* TOTAL.] **2.** An indefinite amount or extent ► bunch, deal, measure, number, portion. **3.** A measurable whole ► amount, body, budget, bulk, corpus, quantum. [*Compare* HOARD.]

quantum *n.* *—See* ALLOTMENT, QUANTITY (3).

quarantine *n.* *—See* DETENTION.

quarrel *n.* *—See* ARGUMENT.

quarrel *v.* *—See* ARGUE (1).

quarrelsome *adj.* *—See* AGGRESSIVE, ARGUMENTATIVE.

quarry *n.* *—See* VICTIM.

quarter *n.* **1.** One of four equal parts of something ► one-fourth, quartern. **2.** A coin equal to one-fourth of the dollar of the United States and Canada ► two bits, quarter-dollar. *—See also* AREA (2), NEIGHBORHOOD (1).

quarter *v.* *—See* CUT (2), LODGE.

quartern *n.* One of four equal parts of something ► one-fourth, quarter.

quarters *n.* Usually temporary living accommodations ► barracks, lodgings, rooms. *Slang:* crash-pad. [*Compare* APARTMENT, HOME.] *See also* NEIGHBORHOOD (1).

quash *v.* *—See* LIFT (3), SUPPRESS.

quaver *v.* *—See* SHAKE (1), TREMOR (2).

queasiness *n.* *—See* DISGUST.

queasy *adj.* *—See* SICK (1).

queen *n.* *—See* CHIEF.

queen of cities. **3.** *Games* **a.** The most powerful chess piece. **b.** A playing card bearing the figure of a queen. **4.** The fertile, fully developed female in a colony of social bees, ants, or termites. **—queen′li·ness** *n.* **—queen′ly** *adj.*

queen mother ▸ *n.* A dowager queen who is the mother of a reigning monarch.

Queens (kwēnz) ▸ A borough of New York City in SE NY on W Long I.

Queen's English ▸ *n.* English speech or usage that is considered standard or accepted.

queer (kwîr) ▸ *adj.* **-er, -est. 1.** Deviating from the expected or normal; strange. **2.** Eccentric. **3.** *Offensive Slang* Gay; homosexual. ▸ *n.* *Offensive Slang* A gay or homosexual person. ▸ *v.* *Slang* To ruin or thwart. **—queer′ly** *adv.* **—queer′ness** *n.*

quell (kwĕl) ▸ *v.* **1.** To put down forcibly; suppress. **2.** To pacify; quiet.

quench (kwĕnch) ▸ *v.* **1.** To put out; extinguish. **2.** To suppress; squelch. **3.** To slake (thirst). **4.** To cool (hot metal) by thrusting into liquid. **—quench′a·ble** *adj.*

quer·u·lous (kwĕr′ə-ləs, kwĕr′yə-) ▸ *adj.* **1.** Given to complaining; peevish. **2.** Expressing a complaint or grievance. **—quer′u·lous·ly** *adv.* **—quer′u·lous·ness** *n.*

que·ry (kwîr′ē) ▸ *n., pl.* **-ries. 1.** A question; inquiry. **2.** A doubt in the mind; reservation. **3.** A notation, usu. a question mark. ▸ *v.* **-ried, -ry·ing.** To question.

que·sa·dil·la (kā′sə-dē′yə) ▸ *n.* A flour tortilla folded over a filling, then fried or toasted.

quest (kwĕst) ▸ *n.* **1.** The act or an instance of seeking; search. **2.** An expedition undertaken in medieval romance by a knight. ▸ *v.* To search; seek. **—quest′er** *n.*

ques·tion (kwĕs′chən) ▸ *n.* **1.** An expression of inquiry that invites or calls for a reply. **2.** A subject open to controversy; issue. **3.** A difficult matter; problem: *a question of ethics.* **4.** A point or subject under discussion or consideration. **5.** Uncertainty; doubt. ▸ *v.* **1.** To put a question to; ask. **2.** To examine (e.g., a witness); interrogate. **3.** To express doubt about; dispute. ***—idiom:*** **out of the question** Not to be considered; impossible. **—ques′tion·er** *n.* **—ques′tion·ing·ly** *adv.*

ques·tion·a·ble (kwĕs′chə-nə-bəl) ▸ *adj.* **1.** Open to doubt; uncertain. **2.** Of dubious morality or respectability. **—ques′tion·a·bil′i·ty** *n.* **—ques′tion·a·bly** *adv.*

question mark ▸ *n.* A punctuation symbol (?) written at the end of a sentence or phrase to indicate a direct question.

ques·tion·naire (kwĕs′chə-nâr′) ▸ *n.* A set of questions usu. intended to gather information for a survey.

quet·zal (kĕt-säl′) ▸ *n., pl.* **quet·zals** or **quet·za·les** (-sä′lās). **1.** A Central American bird with brilliant bronze-green and red plumage. **2.** See **currency** table in Appendix.

queue (kyōō) ▸ *n.* **1.** A line of waiting people or vehicles. **2.** A long braid of hair worn hanging down the back of the neck. **3.** *Comp. Sci.* A sequence of stored data awaiting processing. ▸ *v.* **queued, queu·ing.** To get in line: *queue up for tickets.*

Que·zon City (kā′sôn′, -sōn′) ▸ A city of central Luzon, Philippines, adjoining Manila.

quib·ble (kwĭb′əl) ▸ *v.* **-bled, -bling.** To raise trivial distinctions and objections, esp. so as to evade an issue. **—quib′ble** *n.* **—quib′bler** *n.*

quiche (kēsh) ▸ *n.* A rich unsweetened custard pie, often with other ingredients.

quick (kwĭk) ▸ *adj.* **-er, -est. 1.** Moving or functioning rapidly; speedy. **2.** Learning, thinking, or understanding with speed and dexterity; bright. **3.** Hasty or sharp in reacting. **4.** Occurring or achieved in a brief period of time. ▸ *n.* **1.** Sensitive flesh, as under the fingernails. **2.** The most personal and sensitive aspect: *an insult that cut to the quick.* **3.** The living. **4.** The vital core; essence. ▸ *adv.* Quickly. **—quick′ly** *adv.* **—quick′ness** *n.*

quick·en (kwĭk′ən) ▸ *v.* **1.** To make more rapid; accelerate. **2.** To come to life; revive. **3.** To excite and stimulate; stir.

quick·ie (kwĭk′ē) ▸ *n.* *Informal* Something made or done rapidly.

quick·lime (kwĭk′līm′) ▸ *n.* Calcium oxide.

quick·sand (kwĭk′sănd′) ▸ *n.* A bed of loose sand mixed with water forming a soft shifting mass that yields easily to pressure and tends to engulf any object resting on its surface.

quick·sil·ver (kwĭk′sĭl′vər) ▸ *n.* See **mercury.**

quick·step (kwĭk′stĕp′) ▸ *n.* A march for accompanying quick time.

quick-tem·pered (kwĭk′tĕm′pərd) ▸ *adj.* Easily aroused to anger.

quick time ▸ *n.* A military marching pace of 120 steps per minute.

quick-wit·ted (kwĭk′wĭt′ĭd) ▸ *adj.* Mentally alert and sharp; keen. **—quick′-wit′ted·ly** *adv.*

quid[1] (kwĭd) ▸ *n.* A cut, as of chewing tobacco.

quid[2] (kwĭd) ▸ *n., pl.* **quid** or **quids.** *Chiefly Brit* A pound sterling.

quid pro quo (kwĭd′ prō kwō′) ▸ *n.* An equal exchange or substitution.

qui·es·cent (kwē-ĕs′ənt, kwī-) ▸ *adj.* Still or dormant; inactive. **—qui·es′cence** *n.* **—qui·es′cent·ly** *adv.*

qui·et (kwī′ĭt) ▸ *adj.* **-er, -est. 1.** Making no noise; silent. **2.** Unmoving; still. **3.** Peaceful; untroubled. **4.** Understated; restrained. ▸ *n.* The quality or condition of being quiet. ▸ *v.* To become or cause to become quiet. **—qui′et·ly** *adv.* **—qui′et·ness** *n.*

THESAURUS

queer *adj.* *—See* ECCENTRIC, FUNNY (3).

quell *v.* *—See* RELIEVE (1), SUPPRESS.

quench *v.* *—See* EXTINGUISH, REPRESS, SUPPRESS.

querier *n.* *—See* INQUIRER.

querulous *adj.* *—See* ILL-TEMPERED.

query *n.* A request for data ▸ inquiry, interrogation, question, questioning. [*Compare* DEMAND, PROBLEM.] *—See also* DOUBT.

query *v.* *—See* ASK (1), DOUBT.

quest *n.* *—See* EXPEDITION, PURSUIT (2).

quest *v.* To try to find something ▸ cast about, hunt, look, search, seek.

quester *n.* One who seeks adventure ▸ adventurer, daredevil, venturer. [*Compare* BUILDER.] *—See also* INQUIRER.

question *n.* A request for data ▸ inquiry, interrogation, query, questioning. [*Compare* DEMAND, PROBLEM.] *—See also* DOUBT, PROBLEM.

question *v.* *—See* ASK (1), DISBELIEVE, DISTRUST, DOUBT.

questionable *adj.* *—See* AMBIGUOUS (1), DEBATABLE, DOUBTFUL (1), SHADY (1).

questioner *n.* *—See* INQUIRER.

questioning *adj.* *—See* CURIOUS (2), INCREDULOUS.

questioning *n.* A request for data ▸ inquiry, interrogation, query, question. [*Compare* DEMAND, PROBLEM.]

questioningly *adv.* *—See* SKEPTICALLY.

queue *n.* *—See* LINE.

queue *v.* *—See* LINE.

quibble *v.* To raise unnecessary or trivial objections ▸ carp, cavil, niggle, nitpick, pettifog, squabble. *Idiom:* pick apart (*or* to pieces). [*Compare* COMPLAIN, NAG, OBJECT.] *—See also* ARGUE (1).

quibbler *n.* *—See* CRITIC (2).

quibbling *n.* The act of making trivial objections or distinctions ▸ caviling, hairsplitting, niggling, nitpicking, pettifoggery, trichoschistism.

quick *adj.* Accomplished or experienced in very little time ▸ brief, expeditious, fast, fleeting, flying, hasty, hurried, rapid, short, speedy, swift. [*Compare* INSTANT, LITTLE, TRANSITORY.] *—See also* CLEVER (1), FAST (1).

quick *n.* *—See* CENTER (3).

quick *adv.* *—See* FAST.

quicken *v.* To make alive ▸ animate, enliven, vitalize, vivify. [*Compare* ELATE, ENERGIZE, PROVOKE.] *—See also* SPEED.

quickening *adj.* *—See* INVIGORATING.

quickly *adv.* *—See* FAST, SOON.

quickness *n.* *—See* AGILITY, DEXTERITY, HASTE (1).

quick-tempered *adj.* *—See* TESTY.

quick-witted *adj.* *—See* CLEVER (1).

quiddity *n.* *—See* ESSENCE.

quidnunc *n.* *—See* BUSYBODY.

quiescence *n.* *—See* ABEYANCE.

quiescent *adj.* *—See* LATENT.

quiet *adj.* *—See* MODEST (1), SILENT (1), SOFT (2), STILL, TACITURN.

quiet *n.* *—See* SILENCE (1), STILLNESS.

quiet *v.* *—See* PACIFY, SILENCE.

quiet down *v.* *—See* FADE AWAY.

quieten *v.* *—See* SILENCE.

quietness *n.* *—See* MODESTY (2), SILENCE (1), STILLNESS.

qui·e·tude (kwī′ĭ-to͞od′, -tyo͞od′) ▸ *n.* Tranquillity.
qui·e·tus (kwī-ē′təs) ▸ *n.* **1.** Death. **2.** A final discharge, as of a debt.
quill (kwĭl) ▸ *n.* **1.** The hollow main shaft of a feather. **2.** A large stiff feather. **3.** A writing pen made from a quill. **4.** A sharp hollow spine, as of a porcupine.
quilt (kwĭlt) ▸ *n.* A coverlet made by stitching two layers of fabric with padding in between. **—quilt** *v.* **—quilt′ed** *adj.* **—quilt′er** *n.* **—quilt′ing** *n.*
quince (kwĭns) ▸ *n.* A tree with white flowers and hard applelike fruit that is edible only when cooked.
qui·nine (kwī′nīn′) ▸ *n.* A bitter, colorless, amorphous powder or crystalline alkaloid derived from certain cinchona barks and used to treat malaria.
quin·quen·ni·al (kwĭn-kwĕn′ē-əl, kwĭng-) ▸ *adj.* **1.** Happening once every five years. **2.** Lasting for five years. **—quin·quen′ni·al** *n.* **—quin·quen′ni·al·ly** *adv.*
quin·sy (kwĭn′zē) ▸ *n.* Acute inflammation of the tonsils and the surrounding tissue.
quint (kwĭnt) ▸ *n.* A quintuplet.
quin·tal (kwĭnt′l) ▸ *n.* **1.** A metric unit of mass equal to 100 kg. **2.** See **hundredweight** 2.
quin·tes·sence (kwĭn-tĕs′əns) ▸ *n.* **1.** The purest, most essential element of a thing. **2.** The purest or most typical instance. **—quin′tes·sen′tial** (kwĭn′tə-sĕn′shəl) *adj.*
quin·tet also **quin·tette** (kwĭn-tĕt′) ▸ *n.* **1.** *Mus.* A composition for five voices or instruments. **2.** A group or set of five.
quin·tile (kwĭn′tīl′, kwĭnt′l) ▸ *n.* *Statistics* The portion of a frequency distribution containing one fifth of the total sample.
quin·til·lion (kwĭn-tĭl′yən) ▸ *n.* **1.** The cardinal number equal to 10^{18}. **2.** *Chiefly Brit.* The cardinal number equal to 10^{30}. **—quin·til′lion** *adj.* **—quin·til′lionth** *n. & adj.*
quin·tu·ple (kwĭn-to͞o′pəl, -tyo͞o′-, -tŭp′əl, kwĭn′tə-pəl) ▸ *adj.* **1.** Consisting of five parts. **2.** Five times as much or as many. ▸ *n.* A fivefold amount or number. ▸ *v.* **-pled, -pling.** To multiply by five.
quin·tu·plet (kwĭn-tŭp′lĭt, -to͞o′plĭt, -tyo͞o′-, kwĭn′tə-plĭt) ▸ *n.* **1.** One of five offspring born in a single birth. **2.** A group or combination of five.
quin·tu·pli·cate (kwĭn-to͞o′plĭ-kĭt, -tyo͞o′-) ▸ *adj.* **1.** Multiplied by five; fivefold. **2.** Fifth in a group of five identical things. ▸ *n.* One of a set of five identical things. ▸ *v.* (-kāt′) **-cat·ed, -cat·ing.** To quintuple.
quip (kwĭp) ▸ *n.* A clever, witty, often sarcastic remark. ▸ *v.* **quipped, quip·ping.** To make quips or a quip.
quire (kwīr) ▸ *n.* A set of 24 or sometimes 25 sheets of paper of the same size and stock.
quirk (kwûrk) ▸ *n.* **1.** A peculiarity of behavior; idiosyncrasy. **2.** A sudden sharp turn or twist. **—quirk′i·ness** *n.* **—quirk′y** *adj.*
quirt (kwûrt) ▸ *n.* A riding whip with a short handle and a lash of braided rawhide.
quis·ling (kwĭz′lĭng) ▸ *n.* A traitor who serves as the puppet of the enemy occupying his or her country.
quit (kwĭt) ▸ *v.* **quit** or **quit·ted, quit·ting. 1.** To depart from; leave. **2.** To give up; relinquish. **3.** To cease performing an action.
quit·claim (kwĭt′klām′) ▸ *n.* *Law* The transfer of a title, right, or claim to another. **—quit′claim′** *v.*
quite (kwīt) ▸ *adv.* **1.** Altogether; completely. **2.** Actually; really. **3.** To a degree; rather: *quite tasty.*
quits (kwĭts) ▸ *adj.* On even terms with, as by payment.
quit·tance (kwĭt′ns) ▸ *n.* **1.** Release from a debt or an obligation. **2.** Something given as recompense.
quit·ter (kwĭt′ər) ▸ *n.* One who gives up easily.
quiv·er[1] (kwĭv′ər) ▸ *v.* To shake with a tremulous movement. **—quiv′er** *n.* **—quiv′er·y** *adj.*
quiv·er[2] (kwĭv′ər) ▸ *n.* A case for holding arrows.
qui vive (kē vēv′) ▸ *n.* A sentinel's challenge. ***—idiom:* on the qui vive** On the alert; vigilant.
quix·ot·ic (kwĭk-sŏt′ĭk) ▸ *adj.* **1.** Idealistic or romantic without regard to practicality. **2.** Capricious; impulsive. **—quix·ot′i·cal·ly** *adv.*
quiz (kwĭz) ▸ *v.* **quizzed, quiz·zing.** To question closely; interrogate. ▸ *n., pl.* **quiz·zes.** A short oral or written test.
quiz·zi·cal (kwĭz′ĭ-kəl) ▸ *adj.* **1.** Suggesting puzzlement; questioning. **2.** Teasing; mocking. **3.** Eccentric; odd. **—quiz′zi·cal′i·ty** (-kăl′ĭ-tē) *n.* **—quiz′zi·cal·ly** *adv.*
quoin (koin, kwoin) ▸ *n.* **1a.** An exterior angle of a wall or building. **b.** A stone forming a quoin; cornerstone. **2.** A keystone.
quoit (kwoit, koit) ▸ *n.* **1. quoits** *(takes sing. v.)* A game in which flat rings of iron or rope are pitched at a stake. **2.** One of the rings used in this game.
quon·dam (kwŏn′dəm, -dăm′) ▸ *adj.* That once was; former.
quo·rum (kwôr′əm) ▸ *n.* The minimum number of members of a committee or an organization needed for valid transaction of business.
quo·ta (kwō′tə) ▸ *n.* **1.** A proportional share; allotment. **2.** A production assignment. **3.** The maximum number, esp. of people, that may be admitted to a nation, group, or institution.
quot·a·ble (kwō′tə-bəl) ▸ *adj.* Worth quoting.
quo·ta·tion (kwō-tā′shən) ▸ *n.* **1.** The act of quoting. **2.** A passage quoted. **3.** The quoting of current prices and bids for securities and goods.
quotation mark ▸ *n.* Either of a pair of punctuation marks (" " or ' ') used to mark the beginning and end of a passage attributed to another and repeated word for word.
quote (kwōt) ▸ *v.* **quot·ed, quot·ing. 1.** To repeat or copy the words of (another), usu. with acknowledgment of the source. **2.** To cite for illustration or proof. **3.** To state (a price) for securities, goods, or services. ▸ *n.* **1.** *Informal* A quotation. **2.** A quotation mark. **—quot′er** *n.*
quoth (kwōth) ▸ *v.* *Archaic* Uttered; said.
quo·tid·i·an (kwō-tĭd′ē-ən) ▸ *adj.* **1.** Everyday; commonplace. **2.** Recurring daily.
quo·tient (kwō′shənt) ▸ *n.* The number obtained by dividing one quantity by another.
Qur·'an (kə-răn′, -rän′, kô-, kō-) ▸ *n.* Var. of **Koran.**
q.v. ▸ *abbr.* *Lat.* quod vide (which see)

THESAURUS

quietude *n.* —*See* CALM.
quietus *n.* —*See* DEATH (1).
quill *n.* —*See* SPIKE.
quintessence *n.* —*See* ESSENCE, HEART (1).
quintessential *adj.* —*See* ESSENTIAL (2), IDEAL, TYPICAL.
quip *n.* —*See* CRACK (3), JOKE (1).
quip *v.* To make jokes; behave playfully ▸ jest, joke (around). *Informal:* clown (around), fool around, horse around. *Idioms:* crack wise, play the fool. [*Compare* PLAY.]
quipster *n.* —*See* JOKER.
quirk or **quirkiness** *n.* —*See* ECCENTRICITY.
quirky *adj.* —*See* ECCENTRIC.
quit *v.* To relinquish one's engagement in or occupation with ▸ demit, leave, resign, terminate. *Idioms:* hang it up, throw in the towel. [*Compare* BREAK, RETIRE.] —*See also* ABANDON (1), ABANDON (2), ACT (1), DEFECT, DROP (4), GO (1), STOP (1).
quit *adj.* Owing or being owed nothing ▸ even, quits, square. *Informal:* even-steven.
quitclaim *n.* —*See* ABANDONMENT (1).
quitclaim *v.* —*See* ABANDON (1).
quite *adv.* —*See* COMPLETELY (1), CONSIDERABLY, FAIRLY (2).
quits *adj.* Owing or being owed nothing ▸ even, quit, square. *Informal:* even-steven.
quittance *n.* —*See* COMPENSATION.
quiver *v.* —*See* SHAKE (1).
quiver *n.* —*See* TREMOR (2).
quivering or **quivery** *adj.* —*See* TREMULOUS.
quixotic *adj.* —*See* IDEALISTIC.
quiz *v.* To subject to a test of knowledge or skill ▸ catechize, examine, quiz. —*See also* ASK (1).
quiz *n.* —*See* TEST (2).
quondam *adj.* —*See* LATE (2).
quota *n.* —*See* ALLOTMENT.
quote-unquote *adj.* —*See* SUPPOSED.
quotidian *adj.* —*See* EVERYDAY.

R

r[1] or **R** (är) ▸ *n., pl.* **r's** or **R's** also **rs** or **Rs**. The 18th letter of the English alphabet.
r[2] ▸ *abbr.* radius
R[1] (är) ▸ A trademark for a movie rating granting admission only to persons of or over a certain age, usu. 17, unless accompanied by a parent or guardian.
R[2] ▸ *Chem.* The symbol for **radical**.
R[3] ▸ *abbr.* **1.** registered trademark **2.** Republican **3.** right **4.** *Baseball* run
R. ▸ *abbr.* river
Ra[1] (rä) ▸ *n. Myth.* The ancient Egyptian sun god.
Ra[2] ▸ The symbol for the element **radium**.
Ra·bat (rə-bät′, rä-) ▸ The capital of Morocco, on the Atlantic NE of Casablanca.
rab·bet (răb′ĭt) ▸ *n.* **1.** A cut or groove along or near the edge of a piece of wood that allows another piece to fit into it to form a joint. **2.** A joint so made. ▸ *v.* **1.** To cut a rabbet in. **2.** To join by a rabbet.
rab·bi (răb′ī) ▸ *n., pl.* **-bis**. **1.** A person ordained for leadership of a Jewish congregation. **2.** A scholar qualified to interpret Jewish law. **—rab·bin′i·cal** (rə-bĭn′ĭ-kəl), **rab·bin′ic** *adj.*
rab·bin·ate (răb′ə-nāt′, -nĭt) ▸ *n.* **1.** The office or function of a rabbi. **2.** Rabbis collectively.
rab·bit (răb′ĭt) ▸ *n., pl.* **-bits** or **-bit**. **1.** A long-eared, short-tailed, burrowing mammal with soft fur. **2.** A hare. **3.** The fur of a rabbit or hare.
rab·ble (răb′əl) ▸ *n.* **1.** A tumultuous crowd; mob. **2.** The lowest or coarsest class of people.
rab·ble-rous·er (răb′əl-rou′zər) ▸ *n.* One who stirs up the passions of the masses; demagogue.
Ra·bi (rŭ′bē) also **Ra·bi·a** (rə-bē′ə) ▸ *n.* Either the 3rd or 4th month of the Muslim calendar.
rab·id (răb′ĭd) ▸ *adj.* **1.** Of or affected by rabies. **2.** Raging; uncontrollable: *rabid thirst.* **3.** Extremely zealous; fanatical. **—ra·bid′i·ty** (rə-bĭd′ĭ-tē, ră-), **rab′id·ness** *n.* **—rab′id·ly** *adv.*
ra·bies (rā′bēz) ▸ *n.* An acute, infectious, often fatal viral disease of most mammals that attacks the central nervous system and is transmitted by the bite of infected animals.
rac·coon (ră-ko͞on′) ▸ *n., pl.* **-coons** or **-coon**. **1.** A carnivorous North American mammal having black masklike facial markings and a black-ringed bushy tail. **2.** The fur of this mammal.
race[1] (rās) ▸ *n.* **1.** A local geographic or global human population distinguished by genetically transmitted physical characteristics. **2.** A group of people united by a common history, nationality, or tradition. **3.** A genealogical line; lineage. **4.** A subspecies, breed, or strain of a plant or animal.
race[2] (rās) ▸ *n.* **1.** A competition of speed. **2.** A contest for supremacy: *the presidential race.* **3.** Rapid onward movement: *the race of time.* **4a.** A strong or swift current of water. **b.** The channel of such a current. ▸ *v.* **raced, rac·ing. 1.** To compete in a race. **2.** To move rapidly or at top speed. **3.** To cause (an engine) to run too rapidly. **—rac′er** *n.*
race·course (rās′kôrs′) ▸ *n.* A course laid out for racing.
race·horse (rās′hôrs′) ▸ *n.* A horse that is bred and trained to race.
ra·ceme (rā-sēm′, rə-) ▸ *n.* An inflorescence having flowers arranged singly along a common stem.
race·track (rās′trăk′) ▸ *n.* A usu. oval course on which races are held.
ra·chi·tis (rə-kī′tĭs) ▸ *n.* See **rickets**. **—ra·chit′ic** (-kĭt′ĭk) *adj.*
Rach·ma·ni·noff (räk-mä′nə-nôf′), **Sergei Vasilievich** (1873–1943) ▸ Russian-born composer and pianist.
ra·cial (rā′shəl) ▸ *adj.* **1.** Of or determined by race. **2.** Between or among distinct human racial groups: *racial discrimination.* **—ra′cial·ly** *adv.*
rac·ism (rā′sĭz′əm) ▸ *n.* **1.** The belief that a particular race is superior to others. **2.** Discrimination or prejudice based on race. **—rac′ist** *adj. & n.*
rack[1] (răk) ▸ *n.* **1.** A framework or stand in or on which to hold, hang, or display something. **2.** *Slang* A bed. **3.** A toothed bar that meshes with a gearwheel or pinion. **4.** An instrument of torture for slowly stretching the victim's body. ▸ *v.* **1.** To place (e.g., billiard balls) in a rack. **2.** To torment. **3.** To torture on a rack. **4.** To strain to the utmost: *rack one's brains.* ***—phrasal verb:*** **rack up** *Informal* To accumulate or score: *rack up points.*
rack[2] (răk) ▸ *n.* A rib cut of lamb or veal.
rack·et[1] also **rac·quet** (răk′ĭt) ▸ *n.* **1.** A light bat with a tight network of strings stretched across an oval frame and a handle, used to strike a ball or shuttlecock. **2.** A table tennis paddle.
rack·et[2] (răk′ĭt) ▸ *n.* **1.** A loud distressing noise. **2.** A fraudulent or dishonest business or practice.
rack·et·eer (răk′ĭ-tîr′) ▸ *n.* A person who engages in extortion or other illegal business activities. **—rack′et·eer′** *v.*
rac·on·teur (răk′ŏn-tûr′) ▸ *n.* One who tells stories with skill and wit.
rac·quet·ball (răk′ĭt-bôl′) ▸ *n.* **1.** A court game similar to handball but played with short-handled rackets and a softer, larger ball. **2.** The ball used in this game.
rac·y (rā′sē) ▸ *adj.* **-i·er, -i·est. 1.** Strong and sharp in flavor or odor. **2.** Risqué; ribald. **—rac′i·ly** *adv.* **—rac′i·ness** *n.*
rad (răd) ▸ *n.* A unit of energy absorbed from ionizing radiation, equal to 0.01 joule per kilogram.
ra·dar (rā′där) ▸ *n.* A device used for detecting distant objects and determining such features as position or velocity by analysis of radio waves reflected from their surfaces.
ra·dar·scope (rā′där-skōp′) ▸ *n.* The viewing screen of a radar receiver.
ra·di·al (rā′dē-əl) ▸ *adj.* **1a.** Of or arranged like rays or radii. **b.** Having or marked by parts radiating from a common center. **2.** Moving or directed along a radius. **—ra′di·al·ly** *adv.*
radial symmetry ▸ *n.* Symmetrical arrangement of constituents, esp. of radiating parts, about a central point.
radial tire ▸ *n.* A pneumatic tire in which the ply cords are laid at right angles to the center line of the tread.
ra·di·an (rā′dē-ən) ▸ *n.* A unit of angular measure equal to approx. 57°17′44.6″.

THESAURUS

rabble *n.* —*See* RIFFRAFF.
rabble-rouser *n.* —*See* AGITATOR.
rabid *adj.* —*See* ANGRY, ENTHUSIASTIC, EXTREME (2).
race[1] *n.* —*See* ANCESTRY.
race[2] *n.* —*See* COMPETITION (1).
race *v.* —*See* COMPETE, RUSH.
racism *n.* Discrimination that is based on race ▸ discrimination, intolerance, prejudice. [*Compare* HATE.]
racist *adj.* ▸ bigoted, discriminatory, prejudiced. [*Compare* INTOLERANT.]
rack *v.* To subject another to extreme physical cruelty, as in punishing ▸ crucify, harrow, torment, torture. *Idioms:* put on the rack (*or* wheel), put the screws to. [*Compare* PUNISH.] —*See also* AFFLICT.
racket *n.* —*See* BUSINESS (2), NOISE (1).
racy *adj.* Bordering on indelicacy or impropriety ▸ blue, earthy, off-color, provocative, risqué, salty, scabrous, spicy, suggestive. *Slang:* funky. [*Compare* EROTIC, OBSCENE, RUDE.] —*See also* SPICY.
raddle *v.* —*See* WEAVE.
radiance *n.* —*See* BRILLIANCE (1).

ra·di·ant (rā′dē-ənt) ▸ *adj.* **1.** Emitting heat or light. **2.** Consisting of or emitted as radiation. **3a.** Filled with light; bright. **b.** Glowing; beaming. **—ra′di·ance, ra′di·an·cy** *n.*

radiant energy ▸ *n.* Energy transferred by radiation, esp. by an electromagnetic wave.

ra·di·ate (rā′dē-āt′) ▸ *v.* **-at·ed, -at·ing. 1.** To send out or issue in rays or waves. **2.** To spread out in straight lines from a center. **3.** To irradiate. **4.** To manifest glowingly: *radiate confidence.* ▸ *adj.* (-ĭt) **1.** *Bot.* Having rays or raylike parts. **2.** Marked by radial symmetry. **—ra′di·a′tive** *adj.*

ra·di·a·tion (rā′dē-ā′shən) ▸ *n.* **1.** The act or process of radiating. **2.** *Phys.* **a.** Emission of energy in the form of electromagnetic waves or photons. **b.** Energy traveling in this form. **c.** A stream of particles. **3.** Radiotherapy.

radiation sickness ▸ *n.* An often fatal illness induced by overexposure to ionizing radiation, marked by nausea, diarrhea, and loss of hair and teeth.

ra·di·a·tor (rā′dē-ā′tər) ▸ *n.* A device that radiates heat, esp.: **a.** A heating device through which steam or hot water is circulated. **b.** A cooling device that dissipates engine heat.

rad·i·cal (răd′ĭ-kəl) ▸ *adj.* **1.** Fundamental; basic. **2.** Departing markedly from the usual; extreme. **3.** Advocating fundamental or revolutionary changes. ▸ *n.* **1.** One who advocates fundamental or revolutionary changes. **2.** *Math.* The root of a quantity as indicated by the radical sign. **3.** *Symbol* **R** An atom or group of atoms with at least one unpaired electron. **—rad′i·cal·ness** *n.*

rad·i·cal·ism (răd′ĭ-kə-lĭz′əm) ▸ *n.* The doctrines or practices of political radicals.

rad·i·cal·ize (răd′ĭ-kə-līz′) ▸ *v.* **-ized, -iz·ing.** To make radical or more radical. **—rad′i·cal·i·za′tion** *n.*

radical sign ▸ *n.* The sign $\surd$ placed before a quantity, indicating either the square root or the root designated by a raised integer.

ra·di·i (rā′dē-ī′) ▸ *n.* Pl. of **radius.**

ra·di·o (rā′dē-ō) ▸ *n., pl.* **-os. 1.** The wireless transmission through space of electromagnetic waves in the radio frequency range. **2.** Communication of audible signals encoded in electromagnetic waves. **3.** An apparatus used to transmit or receive radio signals. **4.** Transmission of radio broadcast, esp. as an industry. ▸ *v.* **1.** To transmit by radio. **2.** To communicate with by radio.

radio– or **radi–** ▸ *pref.* **1.** Radiation; radiant energy: *radiometer.* **2.** Radioactive: *radiocarbon.* **3.** Radio: *radiotelephone.*

ra·di·o·ac·tiv·i·ty (rā′dē-ō-ăk-tĭv′ĭ-tē) ▸ *n.* **1.** Spontaneous emission of radiation, as from unstable atomic nuclei. **2.** The radiation, such as alpha particles, emitted by a radioactive source. **—ra′di·o·ac′tive** *adj.*

radio astronomy ▸ *n.* The study of celestial objects and phenomena by observation and analysis of emitted or reflected radio waves. **—radio astronomer** *n.*

ra·di·o·car·bon (rā′dē-ō-kär′bən) ▸ *n.* A radioactive isotope of carbon, esp. carbon 14.

radiocarbon dating ▸ *n.* The estimation of the age of an ancient object, such as a fossil, by measuring its content of carbon 14.

radio frequency ▸ *n.* A frequency in the range within which radio waves may be transmitted, from about 3 kilohertz to about 300,000 megahertz.

ra·di·o·gram (rā′dē-ō-grăm′) ▸ *n.* A message transmitted by wireless telegraphy.

ra·di·o·graph (rā′dē-ō-grăf′) ▸ *n.* An image produced, as on photographic film, by radiation other than visible light, esp. by x-rays. ▸ *v.* To make a radiograph of. **—ra′di·og′ra·pher** (-ŏg′rə-fər) *n.* **—ra′di·o·graph′ic** *adj.* **—ra′di·og′ra·phy** *n.*

ra·di·o·i·so·tope (rā′dē-ō-ī′sə-tōp′) ▸ *n.* A radioactive isotope.

ra·di·o·lo·ca·tion (rā′dē-ō-lō-kā′shən) ▸ *n.* Detection of distant objects by radar.

ra·di·ol·o·gy (rā′dē-ŏl′ə-jē) ▸ *n.* The use of radioactive substances or ionizing radiation, esp. x-rays, in medicine. **—ra′di·o·log′i·cal** (-ə-lŏj′ĭ-kəl), **ra′di·o·log′ic** *adj.* **—ra′di·ol′o·gist** *n.*

ra·di·om·e·ter (rā′dē-ŏm′ĭ-tər) ▸ *n.* A device that measures the intensity of radiant energy. **—ra′di·om′e·try** *n.*

ra·di·o·paque (rā′dē-ō-pāk′) ▸ *adj.* Not allowing the passage of x-rays or other radiation. **—ra′di·o·pac′i·ty** (-ō-păs′ĭ-tē) *n.*

ra·di·o·phone (rā′dē-ō-fōn′) ▸ *n.* A radiotelephone. **—ra′di·o·phon′ic** (-fŏn′ĭk) *adj.*

ra·di·o·sonde (rā′dē-ō-sŏnd′) ▸ *n.* An instrument carried aloft, as by balloon, to gather and transmit meteorological data.

ra·di·o·tel·e·graph (rā′dē-ō-tĕl′ĭ-grăf′) ▸ *n.* Radio transmission of telegraphic messages. **—ra′di·o·tel′e·graph′ic** *adj.* **—ra′di·o·te·leg′ra·phy** (-tə-lĕg′rə-fē) *n.*

ra·di·o·tel·e·phone (rā′dē-ō-tĕl′ə-fōn′) ▸ *n.* A telephone that sends and receives messages by radio. **—ra′di·o·tel′e·phon′ic** (-fŏn′ĭk) *adj.* **—ra′di·o·te·leph′o·ny** (-tə-lĕf′ə-nē) *n.*

radio telescope ▸ *n.* A device used for detecting and recording radio waves coming from celestial objects.

ra·di·o·ther·a·py (rā′dē-ō-thĕr′ə-pē) ▸ *n.* Treatment of disease with radiation.

radio wave ▸ *n.* An electromagnetic wave within the range of radio frequencies.

rad·ish (răd′ĭsh) ▸ *n.* **1.** A Eurasian plant having an edible root. **2.** The pungent root of this plant.

ra·di·um (rā′dē-əm) ▸ *n. Symbol* **Ra** A rare, white, highly radioactive metallic element, used in cancer radiotherapy and as a neutron source. At. no. 88.

ra·di·us (rā′dē-əs) ▸ *n., pl.* **-di·i** (-dē-ī′) or **-es. 1a.** A line segment that joins the center of a circle with any point on its circumference. **b.** A line segment that joins the center of a sphere with any point on its surface. **c.** The length of any such line segment. **2.** A circular area measured by a given radius. **3.** The shorter and thicker of the two forearm bones.

ra·don (rā′dŏn) ▸ *n. Symbol* **Rn** A radioactive, inert gaseous element formed by radium decay, used in radiotherapy. At. no. 86.

raf·fi·a (răf′ē-ə) ▸ *n.* **1.** An African palm tree having large fibrous leaves. **2.** The leaf fibers of this plant, used esp. for mats and baskets.

raff·ish (răf′ĭsh) ▸ *adj.* **1.** Vulgar; tawdry. **2.** Jaunty; rakish. **—raff′ish·ly** *adv.* **—raff′ish·ness** *n.*

raf·fle (răf′əl) ▸ *n.* A lottery in which a number of persons buy chances to win a prize. ▸ *v.* **-fled, -fling.** To award as a prize in a raffle: *raffle off a new car.*

raft[1] (răft) ▸ *n.* **1.** A floating platform, as of planks or logs fastened together, used for transport, travel, or recreation. **2.** A flat-bottomed inflatable boat. **—raft** *v.*

raft[2] (răft) ▸ *n. Informal* A great number or amount.

raf·ter (răf′tər) ▸ *n.* One of the sloping beams that support a pitched roof.

rag[1] (răg) ▸ *n.* **1.** A scrap of cloth. **2. rags** Threadbare or tattered clothing. **3.** *Slang* A newspaper.

rag[2] (răg) ▸ *v.* **ragged, rag·ging.** *Slang* **1.** To tease or taunt. **2.** To scold.

rag[3] (răg) ▸ *n.* A ragtime jazz composition.

rag·a·muf·fin (răg′ə-mŭf′ĭn) ▸ *n.* A dirty, shabbily clothed child.

rage (rāj) ▸ *n.* **1.** Violent, explosive anger. **2.** Furious intensity. **3.** A fad or craze. ▸ *v.* **raged, rag·ing. 1.** To speak or act in violent anger. **2.** To move or spread with violent force.

rag·ged (răg′ĭd) ▸ *adj.* **1.** Tattered, frayed, or torn. **2.** Dressed in tattered clothes. **3.** Having an uneven surface or edge. **4.** Imperfect; uneven: *a ragged performance.* **—rag′ged·ness** *n.* **—rag′ged·y** *adj.*

THESAURUS

radiant *adj.* —*See* BRIGHT, GLORIOUS.

radiate *v.* —*See* BEAM, BRANCH, SHED[1] (1), SPREAD (2).

radical *adj.* Arising from or going to the root or source ▸ basal, basic, foundational, fundamental, original, primary, primitive, underlying. [*Compare* DEEP, ELEMENTAL, FIRST, ORIGINAL.] —*See also* EXTREME (2).

radical *n.* —*See* EXTREMIST, THEME (1).

rafter *n.* —*See* BEAM (2).

rag *v.* —*See* HARASS, JOKE (2).

ragamuffin *n.* A person wearing ragged or tattered clothing ▸ tatterdemalion. [*Compare* HOBO.] —*See also* ORPHAN.

rage *n.* —*See* ANGER, ENTHUSIASM (2), FASHION.

rage *v.* —*See* ANGER (2).

ragged *adj.* —*See* HOARSE, ROUGH (1), SHABBY.

raggedness *n.* —*See* IRREGULARITY.

raggedy *adj.* —*See* SHABBY.

raging *adj.* —*See* ROUGH (2).

rag·lan (răg′lən) ► *adj.* Having or being a sleeve with slanted seams and extending in one piece to the neckline. **—rag′lan** *n.*

ra·gout (ră-go͞o′) ► *n.* A spicy meat or fish stew.

rag·tag (răg′tăg′) ► *adj.* **1.** Unkempt; ragged. **2.** Diverse and disorderly.

rag·time (răg′tīm′) ► *n.* A style of jazz in which a syncopated melody is played against a steadily accented accompaniment.

rag·weed (răg′wēd′) ► *n.* Any of various weeds whose abundant pollen is one of the chief causes of hay fever.

raid (rād) ► *n.* A surprise attack, invasion, or forcible entry. ► *v.* To make a raid on. **—raid′er** *n.*

rail[1] (rāl) ► *n.* **1.** A bar extending horizontally between supports, as in a fence. **2.** A steel bar used as a track for railroad cars or other vehicles. **3.** The railroad: *goods transported by rail.* ► *v.* To supply or enclose with rails or a rail.

rail[2] (rāl) ► *n.* A marsh bird having brownish plumage and short wings.

rail[3] (rāl) ► *v.* To complain bitterly or abusively. **—rail′er** *n.*

rail·ing (rā′lĭng) ► *n.* A structure, such as a fence, made of rails and upright members.

rail·ler·y (rā′lə-rē) ► *n., pl.* **-ies.** Good-natured teasing or ridicule.

rail·road (rāl′rōd′) ► *n.* **1.** A road composed of parallel steel rails supported by ties and providing a track for trains. **2.** A system of railroad track, together with the land, stations, rolling stock, and other assets. ► *v.* **1.** To transport by railroad. **2.** *Informal* **a.** To push through quickly in order to prevent careful consideration: *railroad a bill through Congress.* **b.** To convict without a fair trial or on false charges. **—rail′road′er** *n.*

rail·way (rāl′wā′) ► *n.* **1.** A railroad. **2.** A track providing a runway for wheeled equipment.

rai·ment (rā′mənt) ► *n.* Clothing; garments.

rain (rān) ► *n.* **1a.** Water condensed from atmospheric vapor and falling in drops. **b.** A rainfall. **2.** A heavy or abundant fall. ► *v.* **1.** To fall as or like rain. **2.** To release rain. ***—phrasal verb:* rain out** To postpone or interrupt because of rain. **—rain′i·ness** *n.* **—rain′y** *adj.*

rain·bow (rān′bō′) ► *n.* An arc of color appearing opposite the sun as a result of the refraction of sunlight in rain or mist.

rain check ► *n.* **1.** A ticket stub entitling the holder to admission to a future event if the scheduled event is canceled because of rain. **2.** An assurance that an offer will be honored or renewed at a later date.

rain·coat (rān′kōt′) ► *n.* A waterproof or water-resistant coat.

rain·drop (rān′drŏp′) ► *n.* A drop of rain.

rain·fall (rān′fôl′) ► *n.* **1.** A shower or fall of rain. **2.** The quantity of water that falls over a specified area during a given time.

rain forest ► *n.* A dense evergreen forest in a tropical region with an annual rainfall of at least 2.5 m (100 in.).

Rai·nier (rə-nîr′, rā-), **Mount** ► A peak, 4,395.1 m (14,410 ft), of the Cascade Range in W-central WA.

rain·mak·ing (rān′mā′kĭng) ► *n.* The process of producing or attempting to produce rain, as through magical or ritual actions. **—rain′mak′er** *n.*

rain·storm (rān′stôrm′) ► *n.* A storm accompanied by rain.

rain·wa·ter (rān′wô′tər, -wŏt′ər) ► *n.* Water that has fallen as rain.

raise (rāz) ► *v.* **raised, rais·ing. 1.** To move to a higher position; elevate. **2.** To erect or build. **3.** To cause to arise or exist. **4.** To increase, as in size or worth. **5.** To improve in rank or status. **6a.** To grow or breed, esp. in quantity. **b.** To bring up; rear: *raise children.* **7.** To put forward for consideration. **8.** To voice; utter: *raise a shout.* **9.** To arouse or stir up. **10.** To collect: *raise money.* **11.** To cause (dough) to puff up. **12.** To end (a siege). **13.** To bet more than (a preceding bettor in poker). ► *n.* **1.** The act of raising or increasing. **2.** An increase in salary. ***—idioms:* raise Cain** To behave in a rowdy or disruptive fashion. **raise eyebrows** To cause surprise or mild disapproval. **—rais′er** *n.*

rai·sin (rā′zĭn) ► *n.* A dried sweet grape.

rai·son d' ·tre (rā′zōn dĕt′rə, rĕ-zôN) ► *n., pl.* **rai·sons d' tre** (rā′zōn, rĕ-zôN). Reason for existing.

raj (räj) ► *n.* Dominion or rule, esp. the British rule over India (1757–1947).

Raj·ab (rŭj′əb) ► *n.* The 7th month of the Muslim calendar.

ra·jah or **ra·ja** (rä′jə) ► *n.* A prince or ruler in India or the East Indies.

rake[1] (rāk) ► *n.* A long-handled tool with a row of projecting teeth at its head. ► *v.* **raked, rak·ing. 1.** To gather, smooth, loosen, or move with or as if with a rake. **2.** *Informal* To acquire in abundance: *raking in money.* **3.** To conduct a thorough search: *raked through the files.* **4.** To aim heavy gunfire along the length of. ***—phrasal verb:* rake up** To revive or bring to light: *rake up old gossip.* **—rak′er** *n.*

rake[2] (rāk) ► *n.* An immoral or dissolute person.

rake[3] (rāk) ► *v.* **raked, rak·ing.** To slant or cause to incline from the perpendicular. **—rake** *n.*

rake-off (rāk′ôf′, -ŏf′) ► *n.* *Informal* A share of the profits of an enterprise, esp. one accepted as a bribe.

rak·ish[1] (rā′kĭsh) ► *adj.* **1.** Having a trim, streamlined appearance. **2.** Dashing or sporting; jaunty.

rak·ish[2] (rā′kĭsh) ► *adj.* Morally corrupt; dissolute.

Ra·leigh (rô′lē, rä′-) ► The capital of NC, in the E-central part SE of Durham.

Raleigh (rô′lē, rä′-), Sir **Walter** (1552?–1618) ► English navigator and colonizer.

ral·ly (răl′ē) ► *v.* **-lied, -ly·ing. 1.** To call or come together for a common purpose; assemble. **2.** To restore to order. **3.** To rouse or recover from inactivity or decline. **4.** *Sports* To engage in a rally. ► *n., pl.* **-lies. 1.** The act of rallying. **2.** A mass gathering, esp. to inspire enthusiasm: *a political rally.* **3.** A notable rise in stock market prices and trading volume after a decline. **4.** *Sports* **a.** An ex-

THESAURUS

ragtag and bobtail *n.* —*See* RIFFRAFF.

raid *n.* An act of invading, especially by military forces ► foray, incursion, inroad, invasion. [*Compare* ATTACK.] —*See also* CHARGE (1).

raid *v.* —*See* AMBUSH, INVADE (1).

rail[1] *n.* A string of railroad cars led by a locomotive ► railroad train, railway, train. *Informal:* choo-choo, choo-choo train.

rail[2] *v.* —*See* REVILE.

railing *n.* —*See* VITUPERATION.

raillery *n.* —*See* RIBBING.

railway *n.* A string of railroad cars led by a locomotive ► rail, railroad train, train. *Informal:* choo-choo, choo-choo train.

raiment *n.* —*See* DRESS (1).

rain *v.* **1.** To give in great abundance ► heap, lavish, shower. [*Compare* CONFER, DONATE, GIVE.] **2.** To fall in drops of water from clouds ► drizzle, mist, mizzle, pour, precipitate, shower, spatter, spit, sprinkle, teem. *Idioms:* come down in buckets, come down in sheets, come down in torrents, rain cats and dogs. [*Compare* SPLASH, STORM.]

rain *n.* Water condensed from atmospheric vapor and falling in drops ► cloudburst, deluge, downfall, downpour, drizzle, mist, mizzle, pour, precipitation, rainfall, shower, spit, sprinkle, torrent. [*Compare* STORM.] —*See also* BARRAGE.

raincoat *n.* —*See* COAT (1).

rainfall *n.* —*See* RAIN.

rainless *adj.* —*See* DRY (2).

rainy *adj.* Characterized by rain or drizzle ► damp, drizzly, misty, soft, wet. [*Compare* STORMY.]

raise *v.* **1.** To increase in amount ► boost, hike, jack (up), jump, up. [*Compare* INCREASE.] **2.** To take care of and educate a child ► bring up, rear. **3.** To seek an answer to a question ► ask, pose, put. [*Compare* SAY.] —*See also* AROUSE, BROACH, BUILD, ELEVATE (1), ELEVATE (2), ERECT, GROW, PROMOTE (1).

raise *n.* —*See* ADVANCEMENT, INCREASE (1), INCREASE (2).

raised *adj.* —*See* ELEVATED (1), ELEVATED (2), ERECT.

rake[1] *n.* —*See* WANTON.

rake[2] *v.* —*See* INCLINE.

rake *n.* —*See* INCLINATION (2).

rake[3] *v.* —*See* TILL.

rakehell *n.* —*See* WANTON.

rakish *adj.* —*See* ABANDONED (2).

rally *v.* —*See* MOBILIZE, RECOVER (2).

rally *n.* The process or period of a

tended volley, as in tennis. **b.** A race in which vehicles are driven over public roads.
ram (răm) ▸ *n.* **1.** A male sheep. **2.** A device used to drive, batter, or crush by forceful impact. ▸ *v.* **rammed, ram·ming.** **1.** To strike or drive against with a heavy impact. **2.** To force into place. **3.** To cram; stuff.
RAM (răm) ▸ *n. Comp. Sci.* A memory device in which information can be accessed in any order.
Ra·ma (rä′mə) ▸ *n. Hinduism* A deified hero worshiped as an incarnation of Vishnu.
Ram·a·dan (răm′ə-dän′, răm′ə-dän′) ▸ *n.* **1.** The 9th month of the Muslim calendar. **2.** The fast held from sunrise to sunset during this period.
ram·ble (răm′bəl) ▸ *v.* **-bled, -bling.** **1.** To wander aimlessly. **2.** To digress at length. ▸ *n.* A leisurely stroll. **—ram′bler** *n.*
ram·bunc·tious (răm-bŭngk′shəs) ▸ *adj.* Boisterous and disorderly. **—ram·bunc′tious·ness** *n.*
ra·men (rä′mən) ▸ *n.* **1.** A Japanese dish of noodles in broth. **2.** A thin white noodle.
ram·ie (răm′ē, rā′mē) ▸ *n.* A flaxlike fiber obtained from the stem of a tropical Asian plant and used in textiles.
ram·i·fy (răm′ə-fī′) ▸ *v.* **-fied, -fy·ing.** **1.** To have complicating consequences or developments. **2.** To branch out; divide. **—ram′i·fi·ca′tion** *n.*
ram·jet (răm′jĕt′) ▸ *n.* A jet engine that propels aircraft by igniting fuel mixed with air taken in and compressed by the engine.
ramp (rămp) ▸ *n.* An inclined surface or roadway connecting different levels.
ram·page (răm′pāj′) ▸ *n.* A course of violent, frenzied action or behavior. ▸ *v.* (*also* răm-pāj′) **-paged, -pag·ing.** To move about wildly or violently. **—ram·pa′geous** *adj.* **—ram·pag′er** *n.*
ram·pant (răm′pənt) ▸ *adj.* Growing or spreading unchecked. **—ram′pan·cy** *n.* **—ram′pant·ly** *adv.*
ram·part (răm′pärt′, -pərt) ▸ *n.* A defensive embankment, often with a parapet on top.
ram·rod (răm′rŏd′) ▸ *n.* **1.** A rod used to force the charge into a muzzleloading firearm. **2.** A rod used to clean the barrel of a firearm.
ram·shack·le (răm′shăk′əl) ▸ *adj.* Poorly constructed; rickety.
ran (răn) ▸ *v.* P.t. of **run.**
ranch (rănch) ▸ *n.* **1.** A large farm, esp. one on which cattle, sheep, or horses are raised. **2.** A ranch house. ▸ *v.* To manage or work on a ranch. **—ranch′er** *n.*
ranch house ▸ *n.* **1.** The main house on a ranch. **2.** A rectangular, one-story house with a low-pitched roof.
ran·cid (răn′sĭd) ▸ *adj.* Having the disagreeable odor or taste of decomposing oils or fats; rank. **—ran·cid′i·ty, ran′cid·ness** *n.*
ran·cor (răng′kər) ▸ *n.* Bitter, long-lasting resentment. **—ran′cor·ous** *adj.* **—ran′cor·ous·ly** *adv.*
rand (rănd, ränd) ▸ *n.* See **currency** table in Appendix.
ran·dom (răn′dəm) ▸ *adj.* **1.** Having no specific pattern or purpose. **2.** *Statistics* Of or relating to equal probability of selection or occurrence for each member of a group. **—ran′dom·ly** *adv.* **—ran′dom·ness** *n.*
ran·dom-ac·cess memory (răn′dəm-ăk′sĕs) ▸ *n.* RAM.
ran·dom·ize (răn′də-mīz′) ▸ *v.* **-ized, -iz·ing.** To make random in arrangement. **—ran′dom·i·za′tion** *n.*
ran·dy (răn′dē) ▸ *adj.* **-di·er, -di·est.** Lascivious; lecherous.
rang (răng) ▸ *v.* P.t. of **ring**[2].
range (rānj) ▸ *n.* **1a.** Extent of perception, knowledge, experience, or ability. **b.** The area or sphere of an activity or occurrence. **2.** An amount or extent of variation: *a wide price range.* **3.** The maximum extent or distance of operation, action, or effectiveness. **4.** A place for shooting at targets. **5.** Open land on which livestock wander and graze. **6.** The act of wandering or roaming. **7.** An extended group or series, esp. a chain of mountains. **8.** A stove for cooking. ▸ *v.* **ranged, rang·ing.** **1.** To arrange in a particular order, esp. in rows or lines. **2.** To classify. **3.** To determine the distance of (a target). **4.** To vary within limits. **5.** To extend in a direction. **6.** To wander freely; roam.
rang·er (rān′jər) ▸ *n.* **1.** A wanderer; rover. **2.** A warden employed to maintain and protect a forest or other natural area. **3. Ranger** A member of a group of US soldiers trained for making raids.
rang·y (rān′jē) ▸ *adj.* **-i·er, -i·est.** Having long slender limbs.
ra·ni also **ra·nee** (rä′nē) ▸ *n., pl.* **-nis** also **-nees.** **1.** The wife of a rajah. **2.** A princess or queen in India or the East Indies.
rank[1] (răngk) ▸ *n.* **1a.** A relative position or status in a group. **b.** An official position or grade. **c.** High station or position. **2.** A row, line, or series. **3a.** A line esp. of soldiers standing side by side in close order. **b. ranks** Personnel, esp. enlisted military personnel. **4. ranks** A body of people classed together; numbers. ▸ *v.* **1.** To place in a row or rows. **2.** To classify. **3.** To take precedence over. **4.** To hold a particular rank: *ranked first in the class.*
rank[2] (răngk) ▸ *adj.* **-er, -est.** **1.** Growing profusely or with excessive vigor. **2.** Strong and offensive in odor or flavor. **3.** Absolute; complete: *a rank amateur.* **—rank′ly** *adv.* **—rank′ness** *n.*
rank and file ▸ *n.* **1.** The common soldiers of an army. **2.** The ordinary members of a group, excluding the leaders and officers.
rank·ing (răng′kĭng) ▸ *adj.* Of a high or the highest rank.
ran·kle (răng′kəl) ▸ *v.* **-kled, -kling.** **1.** To cause irritation or resentment. **2.** To become sore or inflamed; fester.
ran·sack (răn′săk′) ▸ *v.* **1.** To search thoroughly. **2.** To pillage.
ran·som (răn′səm) ▸ *n.* **1.** The release of a captive in return for payment of a demanded price. **2.** The price demanded or paid for such release. **—ran′som** *v.* **—ran′som·er** *n.*
rant (rănt) ▸ *v.* To speak violently or vehemently. **—rant′er** *n.*

THESAURUS

return to health ▸ convalescence, recovery, recuperation. —*See also* ASSEMBLY.
rallying cry *n.* —*See* CRY (2).
ram *v.* —*See* DRIVE (2), PLUNGE, PUSH (1).
ramble *v.* —*See* DIGRESS, ROVE, STROLL.
ramble on *v.* —*See* CHATTER (1).
ramble *n.* —*See* WALK (1).
rambling *adj.* —*See* AIMLESS, DIGRESSIVE, ERRANT (1), INDIRECT (1).
ramification *n.* —*See* BRANCH (1), EFFECT (1).
ramify *v.* —*See* BRANCH.
rampage *n.* —*See* BINGE.
rampant *adj.* —*See* ERECT, PREVAILING.
rampart *n.* —*See* BULWARK.
ramshackle *adj.* —*See* SHABBY.
ranch *v.* —*See* GROW.
rancid *adj.* —*See* BAD (2), MOLDY.
rancor *n.* —*See* ENMITY, HATE (1), RESENTMENT.
rancorous *adj.* —*See* RESENTFUL.
rancorousness *n.* —*See* RESENTMENT.
random *adj.* Having no particular pattern, purpose, organization, or structure ▸ chance, desultory, haphazard, hit-or-miss, indiscriminate, spot, unplanned, unpredictable. [*Compare* CONFUSED, SPONTANEOUS.]
R and R *n.* —*See* REST[1] (2).
range *n.* **1.** An area or set of parameters within which something or someone exists, acts, or has influence ▸ ambit, circle, compass, extension, extent, orbit, purview, reach, realm, scope, spectrum, sphere, sweep, swing, territory. [*Compare* AREA, BEAT, LIMIT.] **2.** The ability or power to seize or attain ▸ capacity, compass, grasp, reach, scope. [*Compare* INFLUENCE.] **3.** Approximate size or amount ▸ *Informal:* neighborhood. *Slang:* ballpark. vicinity. —*See also* CLASS (2), DEGREE (2), DISTANCE (1), EXPANSE (1), HABITAT, KEN, SERIES.
range *v.* —*See* ARRANGE (1), CLASSIFY, GO (4), LINE, ROVE.
rangy *adj.* —*See* GANGLING.
rank[1] *n.* —*See* CLASS (2), DEGREE (1), LINE, PLACE (1).
rank *v.* —*See* CLASSIFY.
rank[2] *adj.* Conspicuously bad or offensive ▸ egregious, flagrant, glaring, gross. [*Compare* OFFENSIVE, OUTRAGEOUS, SHAMELESS.] —*See also* MOLDY, THICK (3).
rank and file *n.* —*See* COMMONALTY.
ranking *n.* —*See* ARRANGEMENT (1).
rankle *v.* —*See* ANNOY.
rankness *n.* The quality or state of being flagrant ▸ egregiousness, flagrancy, glaringness, grossness. [*Compare* IMPUDENCE, OUTRAGEOUSNESS.]
ransack *v.* —*See* SACK[2], SCOUR[2].
rant *v.* To speak in a loud, pompous, or prolonged manner ▸ declaim, harangue, mouth (off), orate, perorate, rave. [*Compare* REVILE.] —*See also* BABBLE.
rant *n.* —*See* BOMBAST.

rap[1] (răp) ▸ *v.* **rapped, rap·ping.** 1. To hit sharply and swiftly. 2. To utter sharply. 3. To criticize or blame. ▸ *n.* 1. A quick sharp blow. 2. A knocking or tapping sound. 3. *Slang* a. A reprimand. b. A prison sentence.
rap[2] (răp) ▸ *n.* 1. *Slang* A talk or conversation. 2. A form of popular music marked by spoken or chanted rhyming lyrics with a rhythmic accompaniment. ▸ *v.* **rap·ped, rap·ping.** 1. *Slang* To discuss freely. 2. To perform rap music.
ra·pa·cious (rə-pā′shəs) ▸ *adj.* 1. Greedy; ravenous. 2. Subsisting on live prey. **—ra·pac′i·ty** (rə-păs′ĭ-tē), **ra·pa′cious·ness** *n.*
rape[1] (rāp) ▸ *n.* 1. The crime of forcing a person to submit to sexual intercourse. 2. Seizing and carrying off by force; abduction. 3. Violation: *a rape of justice.* **—rape** *v.* **—rap′ist** *n.*
rape[2] (rāp) ▸ *n.* A plant cultivated as fodder and for its seed oil.
Raph·a·el (răf′ē-əl, rä′fē-ĕl′) (1483–1520) ▸ Italian painter.
rap·id (răp′ĭd) ▸ *adj.* **-er, -est.** Very fast; swift. ▸ *n.* often **rapids** A fast-moving part of a river. **—ra·pid′i·ty** (rə-pĭd′ĭ-tē), **rap′id·ness** *n.* **—rap′id·ly** *adv.*
rapid eye movement ▸ *n.* REM.
rapid transit ▸ *n.* An urban passenger rail system.
ra·pi·er (rā′pē-ər, rāp′yər) ▸ *n.* A long slender sword with a double-edged blade.
rap·ine (răp′ĭn) ▸ *n.* Forcible seizure of property; plunder.
rap·pel (ră-pĕl′) ▸ *v.* **-pelled, -pel·ling.** To descend from a steep height by means of a belayed rope that is passed under one thigh and over the opposite shoulder. **—rap·pel′** *n.*
rap·port (ră-pôr′, rə-) ▸ *n.* A relationship, esp. one of mutual trust or affinity.
rap·proche·ment (rä′prôsh-mäɴ′) ▸ *n.* 1. The establishment of cordial relations, as between two countries. 2. Cordial relations.
rap·scal·lion (răp-skăl′yən) ▸ *n.* A rascal; scamp.
rapt (răpt) ▸ *adj.* 1. Deeply moved or delighted; enraptured. 2. Deeply absorbed; engrossed. **—rapt·ly** *adv.*
rap·tor (răp′tər) ▸ *n.* A bird of prey. **—rap·to′ri·al** (-tôr′ē-əl) *adj.*
rap·ture (răp′chər) ▸ *n.* A state of ecstasy. **—rap′tur·ous** *adj.*
ra·ra a·vis (râr′ə ā′vĭs) ▸ *n., pl.* **ra·ra a·vis·es** or **ra·rae a·ves** (râr′ē ā′vēz). A rare person or thing.
rare[1] (râr) ▸ *adj.* **rar·er, rar·est.** 1. Infrequently occurring; uncommon. 2. Excellent; extraordinary. 3. Thin in density; rarefied. **—rare′ness** *n.* **—rar′i·ty** *n.*
rare[2] (râr) ▸ *adj.* **rar·er, rar·est.** Cooked a short time: *a rare steak.*
rare-earth element (râr′ûrth′) ▸ *n.* Any of the metallic elements of atomic number 57 through 71.
rar·e·fied also **rar·i·fied** (râr′ə-fīd′) ▸ *adj.* 1. Of or reserved for a small, select group; esoteric. 2. Elevated in character; lofty.
rar·e·fy also **rar·i·fy** (râr′ə-fī′) ▸ *v.* **-fied, -fy·ing.** 1. To make or become thin, less compact, or less dense. 2. To purify or refine. **—rar′e·fac′tion** *n.* **—rar′e·fi′a·ble** *adj.*
rare·ly (râr′lē) ▸ *adv.* 1. Not often; infrequently. 2. With uncommon excellence.
ras·cal (răs′kəl) ▸ *n.* 1. One that is playfully mischievous. 2. An unscrupulous person; scoundrel. **—ras·cal′i·ty** (-kăl′ĭ-tē) *n.*
rash[1] (răsh) ▸ *adj.* **-er, -est.** Imprudently hasty or bold. **—rash′ness** *n.*
rash[2] (răsh) ▸ *n.* 1. A skin eruption. 2. An outbreak of many instances within a brief period: *a rash of burglaries.*
rash·er (răsh′ər) ▸ *n.* 1. A thin slice of fried or broiled bacon. 2. A serving of thin slices of bacon.
rasp (răsp) ▸ *v.* 1. To file or scrape with a coarse file having sharp projections. 2. To utter in a grating voice. 3. To grate on (e.g., nerves). **—rasp** *n.*
rasp·ber·ry (răz′bĕr′ē) ▸ *n.* 1. A shrubby, usu. prickly plant in the rose family that bears edible fruit. 2. The fruit of this plant, consisting of many small, fleshy, usu. red drupelets.
Ras·pu·tin (răs-pyo͞o′tĭn, rə-spo͞o′tyĭn), **Grigori Efimovich** (1872?–1916) ▸ Russian mystic; assassinated.
rasp·y (răs′pē) ▸ *adj.* **-i·er, -i·est.** Rough; grating.
rat (răt) ▸ *n.* 1. Any of various long-tailed rodents similar to but larger than mice. 2. *Informal* A despicable person, esp. one who betrays or informs on associates. ▸ *v.* **rat·ted, rat·ting.** 1. To hunt for or catch rats. 2. *Slang* To betray one's associates by giving information.
ra·ta·tou·ille (răt′ə-to͞o′ē, rä′tä-) ▸ *n.* A vegetable stew made with eggplant, tomatoes, zucchini, peppers, onions, and spices.
ratch·et (răch′ĭt) ▸ *n.* A mechanism consisting of a pawl that engages the sloping teeth of a wheel or bar, permitting motion in one direction only. ▸ *v.* To increase or decrease by increments.
rate[1] (rāt) ▸ *n.* 1. A quantity measured with respect to another measured quantity. 2. A measure of a part with respect to a whole; proportion. 3. A charge or payment calculated in relation to a sum or quantity. 4. Level of quality. ▸ *v.* **rat·ed, rat·ing.** 1. To estimate the value of; appraise. 2. To place or be placed in a rank or grade. 3. To regard or consider. 4. *Informal* To merit or deserve. 5. *Informal* To have status or importance. ***—idiom:*** **at any rate** 1. Whatever the case may be. 2. At least.
rate[2] (rāt) ▸ *v.* **rat·ed, rat·ing.** To berate.
rate of exchange ▸ *n.* The ratio at which the unit of cur-

THESAURUS

rap[1] *v.* —*See* BANG (1), CHASTISE, CRITICIZE (1), TAP[1] (1).
rap out *v.* —*See* EXCLAIM.
rap *n.* The sound made by a light blow ▸ knock, rapping, tap, tapping. [*Compare* BEAT.] —*See also* BEAT (1), BLAME, PUNISHMENT, REBUKE.
rap[2] *n.* *Slang* An exchanging of views ▸ conference, discussion, ventilation. —*See also* CONVERSATION.
rap *v.* —*See* DISCUSS.
rapacious *adj.* —*See* VORACIOUS.
rapaciousness *n.* —*See* VORACITY.
rapacity *n.* —*See* GREED, VORACITY.
rape *v.* To compel another to participate in or submit to a sexual act ▸ assault, force, molest, ravish, violate. —*See also* SACK[2].
rapid *adj.* —*See* FAST (1), QUICK.
rapidity *n.* —*See* HASTE (1).
rapidly *adv.* —*See* FAST.
rapidness *n.* —*See* HASTE (1).
rapport *n.* —*See* AGREEMENT (2).
rapprochement *n.* A reestablishment of friendship or harmony ▸ conciliation, reconcilement, reconciliation, settlement. [*Compare* AGREEMENT, ATONEMENT, COMPROMISE.]
rap session *n.* —*See* CONFERENCE (1).
rapt *adj.* Having one's thoughts fully occupied ▸ absorbed, engrossed, immersed, intent, involved, preoccupied, riveted. *Idiom:* wrapped (*or* caught) up in. [*Compare* BUSY.]
rapture *n.* —*See* HEAVEN.
rare *adj.* Marked by great diffusion of component particles ▸ attenuate, attenuated, rarefied, thin. —*See also* EXCEPTIONAL, INFREQUENT.
rarefied *adj.* Marked by great diffusion of component particles ▸ attenuate, attenuated, rare, thin.
rarefy *v.* To become diffuse ▸ attenuate, thin.
rarely *adv.* —*See* INFREQUENTLY.
raring *adj.* —*See* EAGER.
rarity *n.* —*See* LUXURY, NOVELTY (1).
rascal *n.* One who causes minor trouble or damage ▸ devil, imp, mischief, mischief-maker, prankster, rogue, scamp, scoundrel. *Informal:* cutup, scalawag. [*Compare* AGITATOR, EVILDOER, URCHIN.]
rascality *n.* —*See* MISCHIEF.
rascally *adj.* —*See* MISCHIEVOUS.
rash[1] *adj.* Characterized by unthinking boldness and haste ▸ brash, foolhardy, harum-scarum, hasty, headlong, hotheaded, ill-considered, impetuous, improvident, impulsive, incautious, madcap, precipitant, precipitate, reckless, slapdash, temerarious, unconsidered. [*Compare* ABRUPT, CALLOUS, SPONTANEOUS, UNWISE.]
rash[2] *n.* —*See* ERUPTION.
rashness *n.* —*See* HASTE (2), TEMERITY.
rasp *v.* —*See* GASP, SCRAPE (1).
raspberry *n.* —*See* HISS (2).
raspberry *v.* —*See* HISS (2).
rasping *adj.* —*See* HARSH.
raspy or **rasping** *adj.* —*See* HARSH.
rat *n.* —*See* BETRAYER, CREEP (2), DEFECTOR, INFORMER.
rat *v.* —*See* BETRAY (1), DEFECT, INFORM (2).
rat-a-tat-tat *n.* —*See* CRACK (1).
rate *v.* —*See* CLASSIFY, EARN (1), ESTIMATE (1).
rate *n.* —*See* TOLL[1] (1).

rency of one country may be exchanged for the unit of currency of another country.

rath·er (răth′ər, rä′thər) ▸ *adv.* **1.** Preferably. **2.** With more reason. **3.** More exactly or accurately. **4.** Somewhat: *rather cold.* **5.** On the contrary.

raths·kel·ler (rät′skĕl′ər, răt′-, răth′-) ▸ *n.* A restaurant, usu. below street level, that serves beer.

rat·i·fy (răt′ə-fī′) ▸ *v.* **-fied, -fy·ing.** To approve and give formal sanction to. **—rat′i·fi·ca′tion** *n.*

rat·ing (rā′tĭng) ▸ *n.* **1.** A position assigned on a scale; a standing. **2.** An evaluation of financial status.

ra·tio (rā′shō, rā′shē-ō′) ▸ *n., pl.* **-tios.** **1.** Relation in degree or number between two things. **2.** *Math.* The relation between two quantities expressed as the quotient of one divided by the other.

ra·ti·oc·i·nate (răsh′ē-ŏs′ə-nāt′) ▸ *v.* **-nat·ed, -nat·ing.** To reason methodically and logically. **—ra′ti·oc′i·na′tion** *n.* **—ra′ti·oc′i·na·tive** *adj.* **—ra′ti·oc′i·na′tor** *n.*

ra·tion (răsh′ən, rā′shən) ▸ *n.* **1.** A fixed portion, esp. of food. **2. rations** Food issued or available to group members. ▸ *v.* **1.** To supply with rations. **2.** To distribute as rations.

ra·tion·al (răsh′ə-nəl) ▸ *adj.* **1.** Having or exercising the ability to reason. **2.** Of sound mind; sane. **3.** Consistent with or based on reason. **4.** *Math.* Capable of being expressed as a quotient of integers. **—ra′tion·al·ly** *adv.* **—ra′tion·al·ness** *n.*

ra·tion·ale (răsh′ə-năl′) ▸ *n.* **1.** A fundamental reason; rational basis. **2.** An exposition of principles or reasons.

ra·tion·al·ism (răsh′ə nə-lĭz′əm) ▸ *n.* Reliance on reason as the best guide for belief and action. **—ra′tion·al·ist** *n.*

ra·tion·al·i·ty (răsh′ə-năl′ĭ-tē) ▸ *n., pl.* **-ties.** The quality or condition of being rational.

ra·tion·al·ize (răsh′ə-nə-līz′) ▸ *v.* **-ized, -iz·ing.** **1.** To make rational. **2.** To interpret from a rational standpoint. **3.** To devise self-satisfying but false reasons for (one's behavior). **—ra′tion·al·i·za′tion** *n.*

rational number ▸ *n.* A number capable of being expressed as an integer or a quotient of integers, excluding zero as a denominator.

rat·line also **rat·lin** (răt′lĭn) ▸ *n.* Any of the small ropes fastened horizontally to the shrouds of a ship and forming a ladder for going aloft.

rat race ▸ *n.* *Informal* A frantic, often competitive activity or routine.

rat·tan (ră-tăn′, rə-) ▸ *n.* **1.** Any of various climbing palms of tropical Asia, having long, tough, slender stems. **2.** The stems of any of these palms, used to make wickerwork, canes, and furniture.

rat·tle (răt′l) ▸ *v.* **-tled, -tling.** **1.** To make or cause to make a quick succession of short percussive sounds. **2.** To speak rapidly, usu. at length and without much thought or effort. **3.** *Informal* To fluster; unnerve. ▸ *n.* **1.** A rapid succession of short percussive sounds. **2.** A device, such as a baby's toy, that rattles when shaken. **3.** The series of horny segments at the end of a rattlesnake's tail.

rat·tler (răt′lər) ▸ *n.* **1.** One that rattles. **2.** A rattlesnake.

rat·tle·snake (răt′l-snāk′) ▸ *n.* Any of various venomous New World snakes having a series of horny segments at the end of the tail that can be vibrated to produce a rattling or buzzing sound.

rat·tle·trap (răt′l-trăp′) ▸ *n.* A rickety, worn-out vehicle.

rat·ty (răt′ē) ▸ *adj.* **-ti·er, -ti·est.** **1.** Characteristic of or infested with rats. **2.** Dilapidated; shabby.

rau·cous (rô′kəs) ▸ *adj.* **1.** Rough-sounding; harsh. **2.** Boisterous and disorderly. **—rau′cous·ness** *n.*

raun·chy (rôn′chē, rän′-) ▸ *adj.* **-chi·er, -chi·est.** *Slang* **1.** Obscene, lewd, or vulgar. **2.** Grimy; unkempt. **—raun′chi·ly** *adv.* **—raun′chi·ness** *n.*

rav·age (răv′ĭj) ▸ *v.* **-aged, -ag·ing.** **1.** To destroy; devastate. **2.** To pillage; sack. ▸ *n.* **1.** The act or practice of ravaging. **2.** Grievous damage; havoc.

rave (rāv) ▸ *v.* **raved, rav·ing.** **1.** To speak wildly or irrationally. **2.** To roar; rage. **3.** To speak with wild enthusiasm. ▸ *n.* **1.** The act or an instance of raving. **2.** *Informal* An extravagantly enthusiastic opinion or review. ▸ *adj.* *Informal* Extravagantly enthusiastic: *a rave review.*

rav·el (răv′əl) ▸ *v.* **-eled, -el·ing** also **-elled, -el·ling.** **1.** To separate the fibers or threads of (e.g., cloth); unravel. **2.** To tangle or complicate. ▸ *n.* **1.** A raveling. **2.** A loose thread. **3.** A tangle. **—rav′el·er** *n.*

rav·el·ing also **rav·el·ling** (răv′ə-lĭng) ▸ *n.* A thread or fiber that has become separated from a woven material.

ra·ven (rā′vən) ▸ *n.* A large bird having black plumage and a croaking cry. ▸ *adj.* Black and shiny.

rav·en·ous (răv′ə-nəs) ▸ *adj.* **1.** Extremely hungry. **2.** Predatory. **3.** Greedy for gratification. **—rav′en·ous·ness** *n.*

ra·vine (rə-vēn′) ▸ *n.* A deep narrow valley, esp. one worn by running water.

rav·i·o·li (răv′ē-ō′lē) ▸ *n., pl.* **ravioli** or **-lis.** A small casing of pasta with a filling, such as chopped meat or cheese.

rav·ish (răv′ĭsh) ▸ *v.* **1.** To seize and carry away by force. **2.** To rape; violate. **3.** To overwhelm with emotion. **—rav′ish·er** *n.* **—rav′ish·ment** *n.*

rav·ish·ing (răv′ĭ-shĭng) ▸ *adj.* Extremely attractive; entrancing. **—rav′ish·ing·ly** *adv.*

raw (rô) ▸ *adj.* **-er, -est.** **1.** Uncooked: *raw meat.* **2a.** In a natural condition; not refined or finished: *raw wool.* **b.** Not subjected to adjustment, treatment, or analysis: *raw data.* **3.** Untrained and inexperienced. **4.** Having subcutaneous tissue exposed: *a raw wound.* **5.** Inflamed; sore. **6.** Unpleasantly damp and chilly: *raw weather.* **7.** Cruel and unfair: *a raw deal.* **8.** Outspoken; crude. ***—idiom:* in the raw** **1.** In a crude or unrefined state. **2.** Nude; naked. **—raw′ness** *n.*

raw·boned (rô′bōnd′) ▸ *adj.* Having a lean, gaunt frame with prominent bones.

raw·hide (rô′hīd′) ▸ *n.* **1.** The untanned hide of cattle or other animals. **2.** A whip or rope made of rawhide.

Raw·lings (rô′lĭngz), **Marjorie Kinnan** (1896–1953) ▸ Amer. writer.

ray[1] (rā) ▸ *n.* **1.** A thin line or narrow beam of light or other radiant energy. **2.** A small amount; trace: *a ray of*

THESAURUS

rather *adv.* —*See* FAIRLY (2).

ratification *n.* —*See* CONFIRMATION (1).

ratify *v.* —*See* CONFIRM (3).

ratiocinate *v.* —*See* THINK (1).

ratiocination *n.* —*See* LOGIC.

ratiocinative *adj.* —*See* LOGICAL (1).

ration *n.* —*See* ALLOTMENT.

ration *v.* —*See* DISTRIBUTE.

rational *adj.* Mentally healthy ▸ compos mentis, lucid, normal, sane. ***Idioms:*** all there, in one's right mind, of sound mind. [*Compare* HEALTHY.] —*See also* LOGICAL (1), LOGICAL (2), SENSIBLE.

rationale *n.* —*See* ACCOUNT (1), EXCUSE (1).

rationality *n.* —*See* LOGIC, SANITY, SENSE.

rationalization *n.* —*See* ACCOUNT (1), EXCUSE (1).

rationalize *v.* **1.** To show to be just, right, or valid ▸ excuse, justify, vindicate. ***Idiom:*** make a case for. **2.** To offer reasons for or a cause of ▸ account for, explain, justify. [*Compare* CLARIFY, RESOLVE.]

rationalness *n.* —*See* [illegible]

rations *n.* —*See* FOOD.

rattle *v.* To make or cause to make a succession of short, sharp sounds ▸ brattle, chatter, clack, clank, clatter. [*Compare* KNOCK, SHAKE.] —*See also* AGITATE (2), BUMP, CHATTER (1).

ratty *adj.* —*See* SHABBY.

raucous *adj.* —*See* HARSH.

raunch *n.* —*See* OBSCENITY (1), OBSCENITY (2).

raunchiness *n.* —*See* OBSCENITY (1).

raunchy *adj.* —*See* OBSCENE.

ravage *v.* —*See* BATTER, CONSUME (1), DEFORM, DESTROY (1), SACK[2].

rave *v.* To express great enthusiasm ▸ carry on, enthuse, gush, rhapsodize. *Informal:* boom. ***Idiom:*** wax poetic. [*Compare* ADORE, DROOL.] —*See also* BABBLE, RANT.

ravel *v.* —*See* COMPLICATE.

ravenous *adj.* —*See* GLUTTONOUS, HUNGRY (1), VORACIOUS.

ravenousness *n.* —*See* VORACITY.

ravish *v.* To compel another to participate in or submit to a sexual act ▸ assault, force, molest, rape, violate. —*See also* ENRAPTURE.

ravishing *adj.* —*See* BEAUTIFUL.

raw *adj.* Not cooked ▸ uncooked. —*See also* BLEAK (1), CRUDE, HOARSE, INEXPERIENCED, PAINFUL, RUDE (1).

rawboned *adj.* —*See* THIN (1).

raw deal *n.* —*See* INJUSTICE (1).

rawness *n.* —*See* INEXPERIENCE.

ray *n.* —*See* BEAM (1).

hope. 3a. A straight line extending from a point. b. A structure or part having the form of such a line.

ray² (rā) ▸ *n.* Any of an order of marine fishes having horizontally flattened bodies and narrow tails.

ray·on (rā′ŏn) ▸ *n.* 1. Any of several synthetic textile fibers produced by forcing a cellulose solution through fine spinnerets and solidifying the resulting filaments. 2. A fabric woven or knit with this fiber.

raze (rāz) ▸ *v.* **razed, raz·ing.** To level to the ground; demolish.

ra·zor (rā′zər) ▸ *n.* A sharp-edged cutting instrument used esp. for shaving.

razor clam ▸ *n.* Any of various clams having long narrow shells.

razz (răz) ▸ *v. Slang* To deride, heckle, or tease.

Rb ▸ The symbol for the element **rubidium.**

RBI ▸ *abbr. Baseball* runs batted in

Rd. ▸ *abbr.* road

re¹ (rā) ▸ *n. Mus.* The 2nd tone of the diatonic scale.

re² (rē) ▸ *prep.* In reference to; concerning.

Re ▸ The symbol for the element **rhenium.**

re– ▸ *pref.* 1. Again: *rebuild.* 2. Back: *react.* 3. Used as an intensive: *refine.*

reach (rēch) ▸ *v.* 1. To stretch out (a body part); extend. 2. To touch or grasp by extending. 3. To arrive at or get to. 4. To succeed in communicating with. 5. To extend or carry as far as. 6. To aggregate or amount to. ▸ *n.* 1. The act of stretching or thrusting out. 2. The extent something can reach. 3. An unbroken expanse.

re·act (rē-ăkt′) ▸ *v.* 1. To act in response to a stimulus or prompting. 2. To act in opposition to a former condition or act. 3. To undergo a chemical reaction.

re·ac·tance (rē-ăk′təns) ▸ *n. Symbol* **X** Opposition to the flow of alternating electric current caused by the inductance and capacitance in a circuit.

re·ac·tant (rē-ăk′tənt) ▸ *n.* A substance participating in a chemical reaction.

re·ac·tion (rē-ăk′shən) ▸ *n.* 1a. A response to a stimulus. b. The state resulting from such a response. 2. A reverse or opposing action. 3. Opposition to progress or liberalism. 4. A chemical change or transformation. 5. A nuclear reaction.

re·ac·tion·ar·y (rē-ăk′shə-nĕr′ē) ▸ *adj.* Opposed to progress or liberalism. ▸ *n., pl.* **-ar·ies.** An opponent of progress or liberalism.

re·ac·tive (rē-ăk′tĭv) ▸ *adj.* 1. Tending to be responsive or to react to a stimulus. 2. Marked by reaction. 3. Tending to participate readily in chemical or physical reactions.

re·ac·tor (rē-ăk′tər) ▸ *n.* 1. One that reacts. 2. *Electron.* A circuit element, such as a coil, used to introduce reactance. 3. A nuclear reactor.

read (rēd) ▸ *v.* **read** (rĕd), **read·ing.** 1. To comprehend the meaning of (written or printed characters, words, or symbols). 2. To speak aloud (written or printed material). 3. To determine the intent or mood of. 4. To attribute a certain interpretation or meaning to. 5. To foretell or predict. 6. To receive or comprehend (e.g., a radio message). 7. To study: *read law.* 8. To learn by reading. 9. To indicate or register: *The dial reads 32°.* 10. *Comp. Sci.* To obtain information from (a storage medium). 11. To have a particular wording. 12. To contain a specific meaning. *—idiom:* **read between the lines** To perceive an implicit or unexpressed meaning. **—read′a·bil′i·ty, read′a·ble·ness** *n.* **—read′a·ble** *adj.* **—read′er** *n.* **—read′er·ship′** *n.*

read·i·ly (rĕd′ə-lē, rĕd′l-ē) ▸ *adv.* 1. Promptly. 2. Willingly. 3. Easily.

read·ing (rē′dĭng) ▸ *n.* 1. The act or activity of a reader. 2. An official or public recitation of written material. 3. The specific form of a particular passage in a text. 4. A personal interpretation or appraisal. 5. Written or printed material. 6. The information indicated by a gauge.

read-on·ly memory (rēd′ōn′lē) ▸ *n.* ROM.

read·out or **read-out** (rēd′out′) ▸ *n.* Presentation of computer data, from calculations or storage.

read·y (rĕd′ē) ▸ *adj.* **-i·er, -i·est.** 1. Prepared or available for service or action. 2. Inclined; willing. 3. Prompt in apprehending or reacting. ▸ *v.* **read·ied, read·y·ing.** To make ready. **—read′i·ness** *n.*

read·y-made (rĕd′ē-mād′) ▸ *adj.* Already made or available: *ready-made clothes.*

Rea·gan (rā′gən), **Ronald Wilson** (1911–2004) ▸ The 40th US President (1981–89).

re·a·gent (rē-ā′jənt) ▸ *n.* A substance used in a chemical reaction to detect, measure, examine, or produce other substances.

re·al¹ (rē′əl, rēl) ▸ *adj.* 1. Being or occurring in fact or actuality; not imaginary or ideal. 2. Genuine; not artificial. 3. Serious: *in real trouble.* 4. *Law* Of or relating to stationary or fixed property. **—real′ness** *n.*

re·al² (rā-äl′) ▸ *n., pl.* **re·ais** (-ĭsh′). See **currency** table in Appendix.

re·al estate (rē′əl, rēl) ▸ *n.* Land, including all the natural resources and permanent buildings on it. **—re′al-es·tate′** *adj.*

re·al·ism (rē′ə-lĭz′əm) ▸ *n.* 1. An inclination toward objective truth and pragmatism. 2. The representation in art or literature of objects, actions, or social conditions as they actually are. **—re′al·ist** *n.*

re·al·is·tic (rē′ə-lĭs′tĭk) ▸ *adj.* 1. Tending to or expressing an awareness of things as they are. 2. Relating to the representation of objects, actions, or social conditions as they are: *a realistic novel.* **—re′al·is′ti·cal·ly** *adv.*

THESAURUS

raze *v.* —*See* DESTROY (2).

razz *n.* —*See* HISS (2).

razz *v.* —*See* HISS (2), JOKE (2).

razzle-dazzle *n.* —*See* GLITTER (2).

reach *v.* 1. To put forward, especially an appendage ▸ extend, outstretch, stretch (out). 2. To succeed in communicating with ▸ contact. *Informal:* catch, get. ***Idioms:*** catch up with, get hold of, get in touch with, get through to, get to, make contact with. [*Compare* FIND, RELATE.] —*See also* ACCOMPLISH, AMOUNT, ARRIVE (1), EXTEND (1).

reach *n.* The ability or power to seize or attain ▸ capacity, compass, grasp, range, scope. [*Compare* INFLUENCE.] —*See also* DISTANCE (1), EXPANSE (1), EXTENT, KEN, RANGE (1).

react *v.* To act in return to something, as a stimulus ▸ counter, respond. ***Idiom:*** act in response. [*Compare* RETALIATE.]

reactant *n.* —*See* CATALYST.

reaction *n.* An action elicited by a stimulus ▸ response, retroaction. [*Compare* RETALIATION.] —*See also* BEHAVIOR (2).

reactionary *adj.* Clinging to obsolete ideas ▸ backward, unprogressive. —*See also* ULTRACONSERVATIVE.

reactionary *n.* —*See* ULTRACONSERVATIVE.

reactivate *v.* —*See* REVIVE (1).

reactivation *n.* —*See* REVIVAL (1).

read *v.* To understand in a particular way ▸ construe, interpret, take. ***Idioms:*** read between the lines, see in a special light, take to mean. —*See also* SHOW (2), UNDERSTAND (1).

readiness *n.* —*See* EASE (2), PREPARATION.

reading *n.* —*See* INTERPRETATION.

ready *adj.* In a state of preparedness ▸ prepared, set. *Informal:* go. *Slang:* together. ***Idioms:*** all set, in working order, on deck, ready to go, raring to go. —*See also* CONVENIENT (2), WILLING.

ready *v.* —*See* GIRD, MOBILIZE, PREPARE.

real *adj.* 1. Having physical or verifiable existence ▸ concrete, objective, solid, substantial, substantive, tangible. [*Compare* PHYSICAL.] 2. Occurring or existing in act or fact ▸ actual, extant, existent, true. [*Compare* PHYSICAL.] —*See also* AUTHENTIC (1), GENUINE.

realistic *adj.* 1. Having or indicating an awareness of how things really are or what should be done ▸ down-to-earth, hard, hardheaded, matter-of-fact, objective, practical, pragmatic, pragmatical, prosaic, sober, straight, tough-minded, unromantic. [*Compare* APPROPRIATE, FRANK, GENUINE.] 2. Accurately representing what is depicted or described ▸ factual, lifelike, natural, naturalistic, true, true-life, true-to-life, truthful. [*Compare* ACCURATE.] —*See also* GRAPHIC (1).

re·al·i·ty (rē-ăl′ĭ-tē) ▸ *n., pl.* **-ties.** **1.** The quality or state of being actual or true. **2.** One that exists objectively.

re·al·ize (rē′ə-līz′) ▸ *v.* **-ized, -iz·ing.** **1.** To comprehend completely or correctly. **2.** To make real; fulfill. **3.** To obtain or achieve as gain or profit. **—re′al·iz′a·ble** *adj.* **—re′al·i·za′tion** *n.*

re·al·ly (rē′ə-lē′, rē′lē) ▸ *adv.* **1.** In truth or fact. **2.** Truly; genuinely. **3.** Indeed.

realm (rĕlm) ▸ *n.* **1.** A kingdom. **2.** A field or sphere: *the realm of science.*

re·al number (rē′əl, rēl) ▸ *n.* A number that is rational or irrational, not imaginary.

re·al·po·li·tik (rā-äl′pō′lĭ-tēk′) ▸ *n.* Politics based upon practical, not theoretical or ethical, considerations.

re·al time (rē′əl, rēl) ▸ *n.* **1.** The actual time in which a physical process under computer study or control occurs. **2.** The time required for a computer to solve a problem.

Re·al·tor (rē′əl-tər, -tôr′) ▸ A service mark for a real-estate agent affiliated with the National Association of Realtors.

re·al·ty (rē′əl-tē) ▸ *n., pl.* **-ties.** Real estate.

ream[1] (rēm) ▸ *n.* **1.** A quantity of paper, usu. 500 or 516 sheets. **2.** often **reams** A large amount.

ream[2] (rēm) ▸ *v.* **1.** To form, shape, taper, or enlarge (a hole) with or as if with a reamer. **2.** To remove (material) with a reamer.

ream·er (rē′mər) ▸ *n.* A tool used to shape or enlarge holes.

reap (rēp) ▸ *v.* **1.** To cut and gather (grain or a similar crop). **2.** To harvest a crop (from). **3.** To obtain as a result of effort: *reap profits.*

reap·er (rē′pər) ▸ *n.* One that reaps, esp. a machine for harvesting grain.

rear[1] (rîr) ▸ *n.* **1.** A back or hind part. **2.** The part of a military deployment farthest from the fighting front. ▸ *adj.* Of, at, or located in the rear.

rear[2] (rîr) ▸ *v.* **1.** To care for (children or a child) during the early stages of life. **2.** To lift upright. **3.** To build; erect. **4.** To breed or raise: *reared cattle.* **5.** To rise on the hind legs, as a horse.

rear admiral ▸ *n.* A rank, as in the US Navy, above commodore and below vice admiral.

rear guard ▸ *n.* A detachment of troops that protects the rear of a military force.

rear·most (rîr′mōst′) ▸ *adj.* Farthest in the rear; last.

rear·ward (rîr′wərd) also **rear·wards** (-wərdz) ▸ *adv.* Toward, to, or at the rear. **—rear′ward** *adj.*

rea·son (rē′zən) ▸ *n.* **1.** The basis or motive for an action, decision, or conviction. **2.** An underlying fact or cause that provides logical sense for a premise or occurrence. **3.** The capacity for logical, rational, and analytic thought. **4.** A normal mental state; sanity: *lost his reason.* ▸ *v.* **1.** To use the faculty of reason; think logically. **2.** To talk or argue logically and persuasively. **3.** To determine or conclude by logical thinking. ***—idioms:*** **by reason of** Because of. **within reason** Within the bounds of good sense or practicality. **—rea′son·er** *n.* **—rea′son·ing** *n.*

rea·son·a·ble (rē′zə-nə-bəl) ▸ *adj.* **1.** Capable of reasoning; rational. **2.** In accordance with reason or sound thinking. **3.** Not excessive or extreme. **—rea′son·a·bil′i·ty, rea′son·a·ble·ness** *n.*

re·as·sure (rē′ə-shŏŏr′) ▸ *v.* **-sured, -sur·ing.** **1.** To restore confidence to. **2.** To assure again. **—re′as·sur′ance** *n.*

re·bate (rē′bāt′) ▸ *n.* A deduction from an amount to be paid or a return of part of an amount paid. ▸ *v.* (rē′bāt′, rĭ-bāt′) **-bat·ed, -bat·ing.** To deduct or return (an amount) from a payment or bill. **—re′bat·er** *n.*

Re·bec·ca (rĭ-bĕk′ə) ▸ In the Bible, the wife of Isaac and the mother of Jacob and Esau.

re·bel (rĭ-bĕl′) ▸ *v.* **-belled, -bel·ling.** **1.** To refuse allegiance to and oppose by force an established government or ruling authority. **2.** To resist or defy an authority or a convention. **3.** To feel or express strong unwillingness or repugnance. ▸ *n.* **reb·el** (rĕb′əl) One who rebels.

re·bel·lion (rĭ-bĕl′yən) ▸ *n.* **1.** Open, armed, and organized resistance to a government. **2.** An act or a show of defiance toward an authority or convention. **—re·bel′lious** *adj.* **—re·bel′lious·ness** *n.*

THESAURUS

reality *n.* Something demonstrated to exist or known to have existed ▸ actuality, event, fact, phenomenon. ***Idiom:*** hard (*or* cold *or* plain) fact. [*Compare* INFORMATION.] *—See also* CERTAINTY, EXISTENCE.

realization *n.* The condition of being in full force or operation ▸ actualization, being, effect, force. [*Compare* EXERCISE.] *—See also* ACCOMPLISHMENT, FULFILLMENT (1), INTERPRETATION.

realize *v.* To make real or actual ▸ actualize, bring about, make happen, materialize. ***Idioms:*** bring to pass, carry (*or* put) into effect. [*Compare* EFFECT, PRODUCE.] *—See also* ACCOMPLISH, BRING (2), DISCOVER, RETURN (3).

really *adv.* In truth or fact ▸ actually, fairly, genuinely, indeed, positively, truly, truthfully, verily, veritably. ***Idioms:*** as a matter of fact, beyond (*or* without) a doubt, beyond a reasonable (*or* shadow of a) doubt, for fair (*or* real *or* sure *or* true), in point of fact. [*Compare* ABSOLUTELY, COMPLETELY, CONSIDERABLY, UNUSUALLY, VERY.]

realm *n.* *—See* AREA (1), RANGE (1).

realness *n.* *—See* VERACITY.

ream *n.* *—See* HEAP (2).

ream *v.* *—See* CUT (1).

reanimate *v.* *—See* REVIVE (1).

reap *v.* *—See* CUT (3), GATHER, GET (1), RETURN (3).

reappear *v.* To happen again or repeatedly ▸ iterate, recur, reoccur, repeat.

reappearance *n.* *—See* REPETITION.

reappoint *v.* REINSTALL.

rear[1] *n.* The part or area farthest from the front ▸ back, rearward. *—See also* BACK, BUTTOCKS.

rear *adj.* *—See* BACK.

rear[2] *v.* To take care of and educate a child ▸ bring up, foster, parent, raise. [*Compare* NURTURE.] *—See also* BUILD, ELEVATE (1), ERECT.

rear-end *v.* *—See* CRASH.

rear-guard *adj.* *—See* ULTRACONSERVATIVE.

rearmost *adj.* *—See* LAST[1] (2).

rearrange *v.* *—See* SHUFFLE.

rearrangement *n.* *—See* DISPLACEMENT.

rearward *adv.* *—See* BACKWARD.

rearward *adj.* *—See* BACK, BACKWARD (3).

reason *n.* **1.** A fact or circumstance that gives logical support to an assertion, claim, or proposal ▸ argument, case, grounds, point, proof, wherefore, why. ***Idiom:*** why and wherefore. [*Compare* ACCOUNT, EXPLANATION.] **2.** That which produces an effect ▸ antecedent, cause, determinant, occasion. [*Compare* IMPACT, ORIGIN, STIMULUS.] *—See also* ACCOUNT (1), BASIS (2), CAUSE (2), COMMON SENSE, LOGIC, SANITY, SENSE.

reason *v.* *—See* DISCUSS, INFER, THINK (1).

reasonable *adj.* *—See* ACCEPTABLE (2), BELIEVABLE, CONSERVATIVE (2), LOGICAL (2), SENSIBLE.

reasoning *n.* *—See* THEORY (1).

reasoner *n.* A person who seeks truth by thinking ▸ philosopher, theorist, thinker.

reassume *v.* *—See* RESUME.

reassurance *n.* A consoling in time of grief or pain ▸ comfort, consolation, solace, succor. [*Compare* HELP, PITY.]

reassure *v.* *—See* COMFORT.

reawaken *v.* *—See* REVIVE (1).

rebate *n.* *—See* DEDUCTION (1).

rebate *v.* *—See* DECREASE, DEDUCT.

rebel *v.* To vehemently defy and break allegiance with ▸ mutiny, revolt, rise (up). [*Compare* DEFECT, DEFY.] *—See also* DISOBEY.

rebel *n.* **1.** A person who rebels ▸ insurgent, insurrectionary, insurrectionist, mutineer, revolutionary, revolutionist, subversive, transgressor. [*Compare* SEPARATIST.] **2.** Someone with unconventional opinions or approaches ▸ avant-gardist, dissenter, freethinker, iconoclast, independent, maverick, nonconformist, original, rule-breaker, visionary.

rebellion *n.* Organized opposition intended to change or overthrow existing authority ▸ insurgence, insurgency, insurrection, mutiny, revolt, revolution, sedition, uprising. [*Compare* COMPETITION, BATTLE.] *—See also* DEFIANCE (1).

rebellious *adj.* Participating in open revolt against a government or ruling authority ▸ insurgent, insurrectionary, mutinous, revolutionary, seditionary, subversive. *—See also* DEFIANT.

rebelliousness *n.* *—See* DEFIANCE (2).

re·birth (rē-bûrth′, rē′bûrth′) ► *n.* **1.** A second or new birth. **2.** A revival.
re·born (rē-bôrn′) ► *adj.* Born again; revived.
re·bound (rē′bound′, rĭ-) ► *v.* **1.** To spring or bounce back after hitting or colliding with something. **2.** To recover, as from disappointment. **3.** *Basketball* To retrieve the ball as it bounces off the backboard or rim after an unsuccessful shot. ► *n.* (rē′bound′, rĭ-bound′) **1.** A springing or bounding back; recoil. **2a.** A rebounding or caroming ball or hockey puck. **b.** *Basketball* The act or an instance of taking possession of a rebounding ball. **3.** A recovery, as from a disappointment.
re·buff (rĭ-bŭf′) ► *n.* A blunt or abrupt repulse or refusal. ► *v.* **1.** To reject bluntly, often disdainfully; snub. **2.** To repel or drive back.
re·buke (rĭ-byo͞ok′) ► *v.* **-buked, -buk·ing.** To criticize sharply; reprimand. **—re·buke′** *n.*
re·bus (rē′bəs) ► *n., pl.* **-bus·es.** A representation of words in the form of pictures or symbols, often presented as a puzzle.
re·but (rĭ-bŭt′) ► *v.* **-but·ted, -but·ting.** To refute by offering opposing evidence or arguments. **—re·but′tal** *n.*
rec (rĕk) ► *n. Informal* Recreation.
re·cal·ci·trant (rĭ-kăl′sĭ-trənt) ► *adj.* Stubbornly resistant to and defiant of authority or guidance. **—re·cal′ci·trance, re·cal′ci·tran·cy** *n.*
re·call (rĭ-kôl′) ► *v.* **1.** To ask or order to return; call back. **2.** To remember; recollect. **3.** To cancel, take back, or revoke. **4.** To bring back; restore. ► *n.* (*also* rē′kôl′) **1.** The act of recalling. **2.** The ability to remember information or experiences. **3.** The act of revoking. **4.** The procedure by which a public official may be removed from office by popular vote.
re·cant (rĭ-kănt′) ► *v.* To make a formal denial of (e.g., an earlier statement). **—re′can·ta′tion** *n.*
re·cap¹ (rē-kăp′) ► *v.* **1.** To cap again. **2.** To restore (a used automobile tire) by bonding new rubber onto the worn tread. ► *n.* (rē′kăp′) A recapped tire.
re·cap² (rē′kăp′) *Informal* ► *v.* **-capped, -cap·ping.** To recapitulate. ► *n.* A recapitulation.
re·ca·pit·u·late (rē′kə-pĭch′ə-lāt′) ► *v.* **-lat·ed, -lat·ing.** To repeat in concise form; summarize. **—re′ca·pit′u·la′tion** *n.*
re·cap·ture (rē-kăp′chər) ► *v.* **1.** To capture again. **2.** To recall: *recapture the past.* **—re·cap′ture** *n.*
re·cede (rĭ-sēd′) ► *v.* **-ced·ed, -ced·ing.** **1.** To move back or away from a limit or point. **2.** To slope backward. **3.** To become or seem to become more distant.
re·ceipt (rĭ-sēt′) ► *n.* **1.** The act of receiving or being received. **2.** often **receipts** A quantity or amount received: *cash receipts.* **3.** A written acknowledgment that a specified article has been received. **4.** A recipe. ► *v.* **1.** To mark (a bill) as having been paid. **2.** To give a receipt for.
re·ceiv·a·ble (rĭ-sē′və-bəl) ► *adj.* **1.** Suitable for being received. **2.** Awaiting or requiring payment. **—re·ceiv′a·ble** *n.*
re·ceive (rĭ-sēv′) ► *v.* **-ceived, -ceiv·ing.** **1.** To take or acquire (something given, offered, or transmitted); get. **2.** To meet with; experience. **3.** To hear or see: *receive bad news.* **4.** To take in, hold, or contain. **5.** To greet or welcome: *receive guests.* **6.** To convert incoming electromagnetic waves into visible or audible signals.
re·ceiv·er (rĭ-sē′vər) ► *n.* **1.** One that receives something. **2.** A device, as part of a radio or telephone, that receives incoming electromagnetic signals and converts them to perceptible forms. **3.** A person appointed by a court to hold and administer the property of others pending litigation.
re·ceiv·er·ship (rĭ-sē′vər-shĭp′) ► *n. Law* **1.** The office or functions of a receiver. **2.** The state of being held by a receiver.
re·cent (rē′sənt) ► *adj.* **1.** Of or occurring at a time immediately before the present. **2.** Modern; new. **—re′cen·cy, re′cent·ness** *n.* **—re′cent·ly** *adv.*
re·cep·ta·cle (rĭ-sĕp′tə-kəl) ► *n.* **1.** Something that holds or contains. **2.** *Electron.* A fitting connected to a power supply and equipped to receive a plug.
re·cep·tion (rĭ-sĕp′shən) ► *n.* **1.** The act of receiving or of being received. **2.** A welcome or acceptance: *a friendly reception.* **3.** A social function: *a wedding reception.* **4a.** The receiving of electromagnetic signals. **b.** The quality of the waves or signals received.
re·cep·tion·ist (rĭ-sĕp′shə-nĭst) ► *n.* One employed chiefly to receive visitors and answer the telephone.
re·cep·tive (rĭ-sĕp′tĭv) ► *adj.* **1.** Capable of receiving. **2.** Ready or willing to receive favorably: *receptive to the proposal.* **—re′cep·tiv′i·ty, re·cep′tive·ness** *n.*
re·cep·tor (rĭ-sĕp′tər) ► *n.* **1.** A specialized cell or group of nerve endings that responds to sensory stimuli. **2.** A site on or in a cell that binds with substances such as drugs.
re·cess (rē′sĕs′, rĭ-sĕs′) ► *n.* **1a.** A temporary cessation of customary activities. **b.** The period of such cessation. **2.** often **recesses** A remote, secret, or secluded place. **3a.** An indentation or hollow. **b.** An alcove. ► *v.* **1.** To create a recess in: *recessed a portion of the wall.* **2.** To suspend (e.g., a session) for a recess.

THESAURUS

rebirth *n.* A fundamental change in one's beliefs ► conversion, metanoia, regeneration. *—See also* REVIVAL (1).
rebound *v.* **1.** To spring back or up after colliding with something ► bounce (back), bound, hop. **2.** To jerk backward, as a gun upon firing ► recoil. **3.** To reverse direction after striking something ► bounce, reflect, snap back, spring back. [*Compare* BEND, GLANCE.] *—See also* ECHO.
rebound *n.* A bouncing movement ► bounce, bound, hop.
rebuff *n.* *—See* SNUB.
rebuff *v.* *—See* DECLINE, REPEL, SNUB.
rebuild *v.* *—See* RESTORE (2).
rebuke *v.* *—See* CHASTISE.
rebuke *n.* Words expressive of strong disapproval ► admonishment, admonition, berating, chiding, dressing-down, lecture, opprobrium, remonstrance, reprimand, reproach, reproof, reproval, scolding, slap, upbraiding. *Informal:* tongue-lashing. *Slang:* chewing-out, rap, slam. *Idiom:* trip to the woodshed. [*Compare* CRITICISM, SNUB, VITUPERATION.]
rebut *v.* *—See* REFUTE.
recalcitrance or **recalcitrancy** *n.* *—See* DEFIANCE (2), UNRULINESS.
recalcitrant *adj.* *—See* DEFIANT, UNRULY.
recall *v.* To cause one to remember or think of ► hark back, suggest. *Idioms:* bring to mind, put one in mind of, take one back, remind one of. [*Compare* REFER, REMIND.] *—See also* LIFT (3), REMEMBER (1), RETRACT (1).
recall *n.* *—See* MEMORY (1), REPEAL.
recant *v.* *—See* RETRACT (1).
recantation *n.* *—See* RETRACTION.
recap *v.* *—See* REPEAT (1), REVIEW (1).
recap *n.* *—See* SUMMARY.
recapitulate *v.* *—See* REPEAT (1), REVIEW (1).
recapitulation *n.* *—See* SUMMARY.
recede *v.* To move back or away from a point, limit, or mark ► ebb, retract, retreat, retrocede, retrograde, retrogress, step back. [*Compare* BACK, WANE, WITHDRAW.]
receipts *n.* The amount of money collected as admission ► box office, gate, take.
receivable *adj.* *—See* DUE (1).
receive *v.* To admit to one's possession, presence, or awareness ► accept, have, take. [*Compare* ABSORB.] *—See also* ACCEPT (3), DERIVE (1), GET (1).
received *adj.* *—See* ACCEPTED, CONVENTIONAL.
receiver *n.* *—See* OBJECT (2).
recension *n.* *—See* REVISION.
recent *adj.* *—See* CONTEMPORARY (2).
recently *adv.* *—See* LATELY.
receptacle *n.* An object, such as a carton, can, or jar, in which material is held or carried ► container, holder, repository, vessel. [*Compare* DEPOSITORY, PACKAGE.]
receptive *adj.* Ready and willing to receive favorably, as new ideas ► acceptant, amenable, friendly, open, open-minded, responsive. [*Compare* ALERT, ATTENTIVE, FAIR, NEUTRAL.]
receptivity or **receptiveness** *n.* *—See* OPENNESS.
recess *n.* *—See* DEPRESSION (1), REST¹ (1).
recess *v.* To interrupt regular activity for a short period ► break. *Informal:* knock off. *Idioms:* take a break, take a breather, take five (*or* ten). [*Compare* REST¹.]

re·ces·sion (rĭ-sĕsh′ən) ► *n.* **1.** The act of withdrawing. **2.** An extended, moderate decline in general business activity. **3.** A ceremonial exit, esp. of clerics and choir members after a church service.

re·ces·sion·al (rĭ-sĕsh′ə-nəl) ► *n.* A hymn that accompanies a church recession.

re·ces·sive (rĭ-sĕs′ĭv) ► *adj.* **1.** Tending to go backward or recede. **2.** *Genet.* Incapable of being manifested when occurring with a dominant form of a gene. **—re·ces′sive·ly** *adv.* **—re·ces′sive·ness** *n.*

re·cid·i·vism (rĭ-sĭd′ə-vĭz′əm) ► *n.* A tendency to lapse into a previous pattern of behavior, esp. a tendency to return to criminal activity. **—re·cid′i·vist** *n.* **—re·cid′i·vis′tic, re·cid′i·vous** *adj.*

rec·i·pe (rĕs′ə-pē′) ► *n.* A set of directions for making or preparing something, esp. food.

re·cip·i·ent (rĭ-sĭp′ē-ənt) ► *adj.* Receptive. ► *n.* One that receives.

re·cip·ro·cal (rĭ-sĭp′rə-kəl) ► *adj.* **1.** Given or shown in return: *reciprocal trade concessions.* **2.** Performed or felt by both sides; mutual. **3.** Complementary. ► *n.* **1.** Something reciprocal to something else. **2.** *Math.* Either of a pair of numbers whose product is 1. **—re·cip′ro·cal′i·ty** (-kăl′ĭ-tē), **re·cip′ro·cal·ness** *n.* **—re·cip′ro·cal·ly** *adv.*

re·cip·ro·cate (rĭ-sĭp′rə-kāt′) ► *v.* **-cat·ed, -cat·ing. 1.** To give or take mutually; interchange. **2.** To show or give in return. **3.** To make a return for something given or done. **—re·cip′ro·ca′tion** *n.* **—re·cip′ro·ca′tive** *adj.* **—re·cip′ro·ca′tor** *n.*

rec·i·proc·i·ty (rĕs′ə-prŏs′ĭ-tē) ► *n., pl.* **-ties. 1.** A reciprocal condition or relationship. **2.** A mutual or cooperative interchange of favors, esp. the exchange of rights or privileges of trade between nations.

re·cit·al (rĭ-sīt′l) ► *n.* **1.** The act of reciting publicly. **2.** A detailed account of something. **3.** A performance of music or dance, esp. by a solo performer. **—re·ci′tal·ist** *n.*

rec·i·ta·tion (rĕs′ĭ-tā′shən) ► *n.* **1.** The act of reciting. **2.** Oral delivery of prepared lessons by a pupil.

rec·i·ta·tive (rĕs′ĭ tə tēv′, rĕch′-) ► *n.* **1.** A style used in operas, oratorios, and cantatas in which the text is declaimed in the rhythm of natural speech. **2.** A passage rendered in this style.

re·cite (rĭ-sīt′) ► *v.* **-cit·ed, -cit·ing. 1.** To repeat or utter aloud (something prepared or memorized), esp. before an audience. **2.** To relate in detail. **—re·cit′er** *n.*

reck·less (rĕk′lĭs) ► *adj.* **1.** Heedless or careless. **2.** Headstrong; rash. **—reck′less·ly** *adv.* **—reck′less·ness** *n.*

reck·on (rĕk′ən) ► *v.* **1.** To count or compute: *reckon the cost.* **2.** To regard as. **3.** *Informal* To think or assume. ***—phrasal verb:* reckon with** To settle accounts with.

reck·on·ing (rĕk′ə-nĭng) ► *n.* **1.** The act of counting or computing. **2.** A statement of a sum due. **3.** A settlement of accounts: *a day of reckoning.* **4.** The calculation of the position of a ship or aircraft.

re·claim (rĭ-klām′) ► *v.* **1.** To make (e.g., land) suitable for cultivation or habitation. **2.** To procure (usable substances) from waste products. **3.** To reform. **—re·claim′a·ble** *adj.* **—re·claim′ant, re·claim′er** *n.* **—rec′la·ma′tion** (rĕk′lə-mā′shən) *n.*

re·cline (rĭ-klīn′) ► *v.* **-clined, -clin·ing.** To assume or cause to assume a leaning or prone position.

re·clin·er (rĭ-klī′nər) ► *n.* An armchair with an adjustable backrest and footrest.

re·cluse (rĕk′lo͞os′, rĭ-klo͞os′) ► *n.* One who lives in seclusion. **—re·clu′sive** (-sĭv, -zĭv) *adj.* **—re·clu′sive·ness** *n.*

rec·og·ni·tion (rĕk′əg-nĭsh′ən) ► *n.* **1.** The act of recognizing or condition of being recognized. **2.** An acknowledgment, as of a claim. **3.** Attention or favorable notice.

re·cog·ni·zance (rĭ-kŏg′nĭ-zəns, -kŏn′ĭ-) ► *n.* *Law* An obligation of record that commits a person to perform a particular act, such as making a court appearance. **—re·cog′ni·zant** *adj.*

rec·og·nize (rĕk′əg-nīz′) ► *v.* **-nized, -niz·ing. 1.** To know or identify from past experience or knowledge. **2.** To acknowledge or accept. **3.** To approve of or appreciate. **—rec′og·niz′a·ble** *adj.*

re·coil (rĭ-koil′) ► *v.* **1.** To spring back, as a gun upon firing. **2.** To shrink back, as in fear. **—re′coil′** (rē′koil′) *n.* **—re·coil′er** *n.*

rec·ol·lect (rĕk′ə-lĕkt′) ► *v.* To recall to mind; remember. **—rec′ol·lec′tion** *n.*

re·com·bi·nant DNA (rē-kŏm′bə-nənt) ► *n.* Genetically engineered DNA prepared by transplanting or splicing genes from one species into the cells of a different species.

re·com·bi·na·tion (rē′kŏm-bə-nā′shən) ► *n.* The natural formation in offspring of genetic combinations not present in parents.

rec·om·mend (rĕk′ə-mĕnd′) ► *v.* **1.** To commend to another as worthy or desirable; endorse. **2.** To advise or counsel. **—rec′om·men·da′tion** *n.*

rec·om·pense (rĕk′əm pĕns′) ► *v.* **pensed, -pens·ing.** To award compensation to or for. ► *n.* **1.** Amends made, as for damage or loss. **2.** Payment in return for something.

rec·on·cile (rĕk′ən-sīl′) ► *v.* **-ciled, -cil·ing. 1.** To reestablish a close relationship between. **2.** To settle or resolve. **3.** To bring (oneself) to accept. **4.** To make compatible or consistent: *reconcile opposing views.* **—rec′on·cil′a·bil′i·ty** *n.*

THESAURUS

recession *n.* A period of decreased business activity and high unemployment ► depression, downturn, slowdown, slump.

recidivism *n.* *—See* RELAPSE.

recipient *n.* *—See* OBJECT (2).

reciprocal *adj.* *—See* COMPLEMENTARY, MUTUAL.

reciprocate *v.* To give or take mutually ► requite, return. ***Idiom:*** respond in kind. [*Compare* EXCHANGE, RESPOND.] *—See also* RETALIATE.

reciprocation *n.* *—See* CHANGE (2), RETALIATION.

reciprocative *adj.* *—See* MUTUAL.

reciprocity *n.* *—See* CHANGE (2).

recite *v.* *—See* DESCRIBE.

reckless *adj.* *—See* CARELESS, RASH[1], WANTON (2).

recklessness *n.* *—See* TEMERITY.

reckon *v.* *—See* CALCULATE, COUNT (2), ESTIMATE (2), REGARD, SUPPOSE (1).

reckon on or **upon** *v.* *—See* DEPEND ON (1).

reckoning *n.* The act, process, or result of calculating ► calculation, cast, computation, figuring. *—See also* ACCOUNT (2), COUNT (1).

reclaim *v.* *—See* RESCUE, RESTORE (2).

re-claim *v.* *—See* RESUME.

recline *v.* To take repose, as by sleeping or lying quietly ► curl up, lie (down), repose, rest, stretch (out). [*Compare* NAP, SLEEP.] *—See also* LIE[1] (1).

reclining *adj.* *—See* FLAT (1).

reclusion *n.* *—See* SECLUSION.

reclusive *adj.* *—See* SOLITARY.

recognition *n.* *—See* ACCEPTANCE (2), ACKNOWLEDGMENT (1).

recognizable *adj.* *—See* PERCEPTIBLE.

recognizance *n.* *—See* PAWN[1].

recognize *v.* To express recognition of ► acknowledge, admit. [*Compare* CONFIRM.] *—See also* DISCERN, NOTICE, PLACE (1).

recognized *adj.* *—See* ACCEPTED, FAMOUS.

recoil *v.* *—See* FLINCH.

recoil *n.* An act of drawing back in an involuntary or instinctive fashion ► cringe, flinch, jerk (back), shrink, wince. [*Compare* START.]

recollect *v.* *—See* REMEMBER (1).

recollection *n.* An act or instance of remembering ► memory, mental image, remembrance, reminiscence. [*Compare* IDEA.] *—See also* MEMORY (1).

recommend *v.* *—See* ADVISE, SUPPORT (1).

recommendable *adj.* *—See* ADVISABLE.

recommendation *n.* A statement attesting to personal qualifications, character, and dependability ► character, reference, testimonial. [*Compare* ENDORSEMENT.] *—See also* ADVICE, ENDORSEMENT.

recommendatory *adj.* *—See* [illegible]

recompense *v.* *—See* COMPENSATE.

recompense *n.* *—See* COMPENSATION, DUE, WAGE.

reconcile *v.* **1.** To reestablish friendship between ► conciliate, make up, reunite. [*Compare* PACIFY.] **2.** To bring oneself to accept ► resign. ***Idiom:*** get used to. **3.** To make or become suitable to a particular situation or use ► acclimate, acclimatize, accommodate, adapt, adjust, conform, fashion, fit, square, suit, tailor. *—See*

—rec′on·cil′a·ble *adj.* —rec′on·cile′ment, rec′on·cil′i·a′tion (-sĭl′ē-ā′shən) *n.* —rec′on·cil′er *n.*

rec·on·dite (rĕk′ən-dīt′, rĭ-kŏn′dīt′) ▸ *adj.* **1.** Not easily understood; abstruse. **2.** Concealed; hidden. —rec′on·dite′ness *n.*

re·con·nais·sance (rĭ-kŏn′ə-səns, -zəns) ▸ *n.* An inspection or exploration of an area, esp. to gather military information.

re·con·noi·ter (rē′kə-noi′tər, rĕk′ə-) ▸ *v.* To make a preliminary inspection of, esp. to gather military information. —re′con·noi′ter·er *n.*

re·con·sid·er (rē′kən-sĭd′ər) ▸ *v.* To consider again, esp. with intent to modify a previous decision. —re′con·sid′er·a′tion *n.*

re·con·struct (rē′kən-strŭkt′) ▸ *v.* To construct again; make over. —re′con·struct′i·ble *adj.* —re′con·struc′tive *adj.*

re·con·struc·tion (rē′kən-strŭk′shən) ▸ *n.* **1.** The act or result of reconstructing. **2. Reconstruction** The period (1865–77) during which the states of the Confederacy were controlled by the federal government before being readmitted to the Union.

re·cord (rĭ-kôrd′) ▸ *v.* **1.** To set down for preservation, esp. in writing. **2.** To register or indicate. **3.** To register (sound or images) in permanent form, as on a record or tape. ▸ *n.* **rec·ord** (rĕk′ərd) **1a.** A usu. written account of events or facts. **b.** Something on which such an account is made. **2.** Information on a particular subject collected and preserved: *the coldest day on record.* **3.** The known history of performance: *your academic record.* **4.** An unsurpassed measurement: *a world record in weightlifting.* **5.** A disk designed for a phonograph. —*idioms:* **off the record** Not for publication. **on record** Known to have taken a certain position.

re·cord·er (rĭ-kôr′dər) ▸ *n.* **1.** One that records: *a video recorder.* **2.** A flute with eight finger holes and a whistlelike mouthpiece.

re·cord·ing (rĭ-kôr′dĭng) ▸ *n.* **1.** Something on which sound or images have been recorded. **2.** A recorded sound or picture.

re·count (rĭ-kount′) ▸ *v.* To narrate the facts or particulars of.

re-count (rē-kount′) ▸ *v.* To count again. ▸ *n.* (*also* rē′kount′) An additional count, as of votes.

re·coup (rĭ-ko͞op′) ▸ *v.* **1.** To receive an equivalent for (e.g., a loss). **2.** To reimburse.

re·course (rē′kôrs′, rĭ-kôrs′) ▸ *n.* **1.** A turning or applying to a person or thing for aid or security: *have recourse to the courts.* **2.** One that is turned to for aid or security.

re·cov·er (rĭ-kŭv′ər) ▸ *v.* **1.** To get back; regain. **2.** To regain a usual condition, as of health. **3.** To procure (usable substances) from unusable substances, such as waste. **4.** To receive a favorable judgment in a lawsuit. —re·cov′er·a·ble *adj.* —re·cov′er·y *n.*

rec·re·ant (rĕk′rē-ənt) ▸ *adj.* **1.** Unfaithful or disloyal. **2.** Craven or cowardly. ▸ *n.* **1.** A faithless or disloyal person. **2.** A coward. —rec′re·ance, rec′re·an·cy *n.*

re-cre·ate (rē′krē-āt′) ▸ *v.* To create anew. —re′-cre·a′tion *n.*

rec·re·a·tion (rĕk′rē-ā′shən) ▸ *n.* Refreshment of one's mind or body through activity that amuses or stimulates; play. —rec′re·ate′ *v.* —rec′re·a′tion·al *adj.*

recreational vehicle ▸ *n.* A vehicle, such as a motor home, used for recreation.

re·crim·i·nate (rĭ-krĭm′ə-nāt′) ▸ *v.* **-nat·ed, -nat·ing.** To counter one accusation with another. —re·crim′i·na′tion *n.* —re·crim′i·na′tive, re·crim′i·na·to′ry (-nə-tôr′ē) *adj.*

re·cru·desce (rē′kro͞o-dĕs′) ▸ *v.* **-desced, -desc·ing.** To break out anew, as after an inactive period. —re′cru·des′cence *n.* —re′cru·des′cent *adj.*

re·cruit (rĭ-kro͞ot′) ▸ *v.* **1.** To seek out and engage (persons), as for work or military service. **2.** To strengthen or raise (an armed force) by enlistment. ▸ *n.* A newly engaged member of a military force or other organization. —re·cruit′er *n.* —re·cruit′ment *n.*

rec·tal (rĕk′təl) ▸ *adj.* Of or situated near the rectum. —rec′tal·ly *adv.*

rec·tan·gle (rĕk′tăng′gəl) ▸ *n.* A parallelogram with four right angles. —rec·tan′gu·lar *adj.* —rec·tan′gu·lar′i·ty (-lăr′ĭ-tē) *n.*

rec·ti·fy (rĕk′tə-fī′) ▸ *v.* **-fied, -fy·ing.** To set right; correct. —rec′ti·fi′a·ble *adj.* —rec′ti·fi·ca′tion *n.*

rec·ti·lin·e·ar (rĕk′tə-lĭn′ē-ər) ▸ *adj.* Moving in, bounded by, or characterized by a straight line or lines.

rec·ti·tude (rĕk′tĭ-to͞od′, -tyo͞od′) ▸ *n.* Moral uprightness.

rec·to (rĕk′tō) ▸ *n., pl.* **-tos.** A right-hand page.

rec·tor (rĕk′tər) ▸ *n.* **1.** A cleric in charge of a parish. **2.** A Roman Catholic priest serving as managerial and spiritual head of a church or other institution. **3.** The principal of certain schools, colleges, and universities.

rec·to·ry (rĕk′tə-rē) ▸ *n., pl.* **-ries.** The house in which a rector lives.

rec·tum (rĕk′təm) ▸ *n., pl.* **-tums** or **-ta** (-tə). The terminal portion of the large intestine, extending from the colon to the anal canal.

re·cum·bent (rĭ-kŭm′bənt) ▸ *adj.* Lying down; reclining.

re·cu·per·ate (rĭ-ko͞o′pə-rāt′, -kyo͞o′-) ▸ *v.* **-at·ed, -at·ing. 1.** To return to health or strength; recover. **2.** To regain: *recuperate losses.* —re·cu′per·a′tion *n.* —re·cu′per·a′tive (-pə-rā′tĭv, -pər-ə-tĭv) *adj.*

THESAURUS

also HARMONIZE (1), SETTLE (2).

reconcilement *n.* A reestablishment of friendship or harmony ▸ conciliation, rapprochement, reconciliation, settlement. [*Compare* AGREEMENT, ATONEMENT, COMPROMISE.]

reconciliation *n.* **1.** A reestablishment of friendship or harmony ▸ conciliation, rapprochement, reconcilement, settlement. [*Compare* AGREEMENT, ATONEMENT, COMPROMISE.] **2.** The act of making amends ▸ atonement, expiation, penance, reparation. [*Compare* COMPENSATION, PURIFICATION.]

recondite *adj.* —*See* AMBIGUOUS (1), DEEP (2), OBSCURE (1).

recondition *v.* —*See* RENEW (1), RESTORE (2).

reconfigure *v.* —*See* OVERHAUL, SHUFFLE.

reconnaissance *n.* The act or an instance of exploring or investigating ▸ exploration, investigation, probe. [*Compare* EXAMINATION.]

reconnoiter *v.* —*See* EXPLORE.

reconsider *v.* To consider again, especially with the possibility of change ▸ reevaluate, reexamine, rethink, reweigh, review. [*Compare* CONSIDER, DOUBT.]

reconstruct *v.* —*See* RESTORE (2).

record *v.* —*See* LIST[1], SHOW (2).

record *n.* —*See* ENTRY, HISTORY (2), STORY (1), TRACE.

recount *v.* —*See* DESCRIBE.

recoup *v.* —*See* COMPENSATE, RECOVER (1).

recoup *n.* The act of getting back or regaining ▸ recovery, repossession, retrieval.

recoupment *n.* —*See* COMPENSATION.

recourse *n.* That to which one turns for help when in desperation ▸ refuge, resort, resource. [*Compare* HELP, SUPPORT.] —*See also* EXERCISE (1).

recover *v.* **1.** To get back ▸ make up, recoup, regain, repossess, retrieve. **2.** To regain one's health ▸ bounce back, come around (*or* round), convalesce, gain, get better, get well, improve, mend, perk up, rally, recuperate. *Idiom:* be on the mend. [*Compare* REVIVE.] —*See also* RESCUE.

recovery *n.* **1.** The act of getting back or regaining ▸ recoup, repossession, retrieval. **2.** The process or period of a return to health ▸ convalescence, rally, recuperation. **3.** A return to former prosperity or status ▸ comeback, reestablishment, restoration. [*Compare* RENEWAL, REVIVAL.]

recreance or **recreancy** *n.* —*See* DEFECTION.

recreant *adj.* —*See* COWARDLY, FAITHLESS.

recreant *n.* —*See* COWARD, DEFECTOR.

recreate *v.* —*See* AMUSE, PLAY (1).

re-create *v.* —*See* RENEW (1).

recreation *n.* —*See* AMUSEMENT.

recriminate *v.* —*See* ACCUSE.

recrimination *n.* —*See* ACCUSATION.

recriminator *n.* One that accuses ▸ accuser, arraigner, denouncer, indicter.

recrudesce *v.* —*See* RETURN (1).

recruit *v.* —*See* EMPLOY (1).

rectify *v.* —*See* CORRECT (1), SETTLE (2).

rectitude *n.* —*See* ETHICS (1), GOOD (1).

rector *n.* —*See* CLERIC.

recumbent *adj.* —*See* FLAT (1).

recuperate *v.* —*See* RECOVER (2).

recuperation *n.* The process or period of a return to health ▸ convalescence, rally, recovery.

re·cur (rĭ-kûr′) ► *v.* **-curred, -cur·ring.** To happen, come up, or show up again or repeatedly. **—re·cur′rence** *n.* **—re·cur′rent** *adj.* **—re·cur′rent·ly** *adv.*

re·curve (rē-kûrv′) ► *v.* To curve backward or downward.

re·cy·cle (rē-sī′kəl) ► *v.* **-cled, -cling. 1.** To put or pass through a cycle again, as for further treatment. **2.** To reprocess and use again: *recycle aluminum cans.* **—re·cy′cla·ble** *adj. & n.* **—re·cy′cler** *n.*

red (rĕd) ► *n.* **1a.** Any of a group of colors whose hue resembles that of blood. **b.** The hue of the long-wave end of the visible spectrum. **2.** often **Red** A revolutionary, esp. a Communist. ► *adj.* **red·der, red·dest. 1.** Of the color red. **2a.** Having a red or reddish color: *red hair.* **b.** Ruddy or flushed: *red with embarrassment.* **3.** often **Red** Communist. *—idiom:* **in the red** Operating at a loss; in debt. **—red′ness** *n.*

red blood cell ► *n.* A cell in the blood of vertebrates that transports oxygen and carbon dioxide to and from the tissues.

red-blood·ed (rĕd′blŭd′ĭd) ► *adj.* Strong and highly spirited.

red·breast (rĕd′brĕst′) ► *n.* A bird, such as the robin, with a red or reddish breast.

Red Cloud (1822–1909) ► Oglala Sioux leader.

red·coat (rĕd′kōt′) ► *n.* A British soldier, esp. during the American Revolution.

red·den (rĕd′n) ► *v.* To make or become red.

red·dish (rĕd′ĭsh) ► *adj.* Mixed or tinged with red; somewhat red. **—red′dish·ness** *n.*

re·deem (rĭ-dēm′) ► *v.* **1.** To recover ownership of by paying a specified sum. **2.** To pay off (e.g., a promissory note). **3.** To turn in (e.g., coupons) and receive something in exchange. **4.** To set free; rescue. **5.** To save from sinfulness. **6.** To make up for: *redeem an earlier mistake.* **—re·deem′a·ble** *adj.* **—re·deem′er** *n.*

re·demp·tion (rĭ-dĕmp′shən) ► *n.* The act of redeeming or state of being redeemed. **—re·demp′tion·al, re·demp′tive** *adj.*

red-faced (rĕd′fāst′) ► *adj.* Embarrassed.

red flag ► *n.* **1.** A warning signal. **2.** Something that provokes an irritated reaction.

red giant ► *n.* A star of great size and brightness with a relatively low surface temperature.

red-hand·ed (rĕd′hăn′dĭd) ► *adv. & adj.* In the act of committing something wrong.

red·head (rĕd′hĕd′) ► *n.* A person with red hair.

red herring ► *n.* Something that draws attention away from the central issue.

red-hot (rĕd′hŏt′) ► *adj.* **1.** Glowing hot; very hot. **2.** Very recent: *red-hot information.*

re·dis·trict (rē-dĭs′trĭkt) ► *v.* To divide again into administrative or election districts.

red-let·ter (rĕd′lĕt′ər) ► *adj.* Memorably happy: *a red-letter day.*

red·line (rĕd′līn′) ► *v.* **-lined, -lin·ing.** To refuse home mortgages or home insurance to areas or neighborhoods deemed poor financial risks.

red·o·lent (rĕd′l-ənt) ► *adj.* **1.** Strongly scented; aromatic. **2.** Suggestive; reminiscent: *a campaign that was redolent of machine politics.* **—red′o·lence** *n.*

re·doubt (rĭ-dout′) ► *n.* A small, often temporary defensive fortification.

re·doubt·a·ble (rĭ-dou′tə-bəl) ► *adj.* **1.** Arousing fear or awe; formidable. **2.** Worthy of respect or honor. **—re·doubt′a·bly** *adv.*

re·dound (rĭ-dound′) ► *v.* **1.** To have an effect or consequence. **2.** To contribute; accrue.

red pepper ► *n.* **1.** The pungent red fruit of certain pepper plants. **2.** See **cayenne pepper.**

re·dress (rĭ-drĕs′) ► *v.* **1.** To set right; remedy or rectify. **2.** To make amends to or for. ► *n.* (*also* rē′drĕs) **1.** Satisfaction for wrong or injury; reparation. **2.** Correction or reformation.

Red Sea ► A sea between NE Africa and the Arabian Peninsula.

red·shift (rĕd′shĭft′) ► *n.* An increase in the wavelength of radiation emitted by a celestial body due to the Doppler effect.

red snapper ► *n.* Any of several marine food fishes with red or reddish bodies.

red tape ► *n.* Official forms and procedures, esp. when oppressively complex and time consuming.

red tide ► *n.* A reddish discoloration of coastal ocean waters caused by a proliferation of red, single-celled organisms that produce toxins harmful to fish and shellfish.

re·duce (rĭ-do͞os′, -dyo͞os′) ► *v.* **-duced, -duc·ing. 1.** To bring down, as in extent, amount, or degree; diminish. **2.** To bring to a humbler, weaker, or more difficult state or condition. **3.** To lower in rank or grade; demote. **4.** To put in order systematically. **5.** To separate into orderly components by analysis. **6.** *Chem.* **a.** To decrease the valence of (an atom) by adding electrons. **b.** To remove oxygen from. **c.** To add hydrogen to. **d.** To change to a metallic state; smelt. **7.** *Math.* To simplify the form of (e.g., a fraction) without changing the value. **8.** To lose weight, as by dieting. **—re·duc′i·bil′i·ty** *n.* **—re·duc′i·ble** *adj.* **—re·duc′tion** (-dŭk′shən) *n.* **—re·duc′tive** *adj.*

re·dun·dan·cy (rĭ-dŭn′dən-sē) ► *n., pl.* **-cies. 1.** The state of being redundant. **2.** An excess. **3.** Unnecessary repetition.

re·dun·dant (rĭ-dŭn′dənt) ► *adj.* **1.** Exceeding what is necessary or natural; superfluous. **2.** Needlessly repetitive; verbose. **—re·dun′dant·ly** *adv.*

re·du·pli·cate (rĭ-do͞o′plə-kāt′, -dyo͞o′-) ► *v.* **-cat·ed, -cat·ing. 1.** To redouble. **2.** *Ling.* To double (the initial syllable or all of a root word) to form a new word. **—re·du′pli·ca′tion** *n.*

red·wood (rĕd′wo͝od′) ► *n.* **1.** A very tall evergreen coniferous tree of S Oregon and N California. **2.** Its soft reddish wood.

reed (rēd) ► *n.* **1a.** Any of various tall, hollow-stemmed aquatic grasses. **b.** The stalk of a reed. **2a.** A flexible strip of cane or metal used in the mouthpiece of certain musical instruments to produce tone by vibrating in response to a stream of air. **b.** An instrument fitted with a reed. **—reed′i·ness** *n.* **—reed′y** *adj.*

reef¹ (rēf) ► *n.* A strip or ridge of rocks, sand, or coral at or near the surface of a body of water.

reef² (rēf) ► *n.* A portion of a sail rolled and tied down to

THESAURUS

recur *v.* To happen again or repeatedly ► iterate, reappear, reoccur, repeat. *—See also* RETURN (1).

recurrence *n.* *—See* REPETITION.

recurrent *adj.* Happening or appearing consistently or repeatedly ► episodic, regular, repeating, repetitive. [*Compare* PERIODIC, PERIODICAL, RHYTHMIC.]

redaction *n.* *—See* REVISION.

red-blooded *adj.* *—See* LUSTY.

redden *v.* *—See* BLUSH.

redecorate *v.* *—See* RENEW (1).

redeem *v.* *—See* CANCEL (2), PURIFY (1), RESCUE.

redeemer *n.* *—See* RESCUER.

redemption *n.* *—See* PURIFICATION (2).

red-hot *adj. Informal* Relating to great current interest ► hot, live. [*Compare* FASHIONABLE, IMPORTANT.] *—See also* HOT (1), PASSIONATE.

redo *v.* To do or perform an act again ► do over, duplicate, play over, repeat, replay. [*Compare* COPY.]

redolence *n.* *—See* FRAGRANCE.

redolent *adj.* *—See* FRAGRANT, SPICY.

redouble *v.* To make or become twice as great ► double, duplicate, geminate, twin. *—See also* INTENSIFY.

redoubt *n.* *—See* FORT.

redoubtable *adj.* *—See* FAMOUS, FEARFUL.

red-pencil *v.* *—See* CENSOR (1).

redraft *v.* *—See* REVISE.

redraft *n.* *—See* REVISION.

redress *v.* *—See* AVENGE, COMPENSATE, CORRECT (1).

redress *n.* *—See* COMPENSATION.

red tape *n.* *—See* BOTHER.

reduce *v.* **1.** To lose body weight, as by dieting ► slim (down), thin (down), trim down. *Idioms:* get the weight off, lose weight, shed some pounds. **2.** To make thick or thicker, especially through evaporation or condensation ► condense, inspissate, thicken. [*Compare* COAGULATE.] *—See also* ANALYZE, DECREASE, DEMOTE, DEPRECIATE, SHORTEN.

reduction *n.* The act or an instance of demoting ► demotion, degradation, downgrade. *—See also* ANALYSIS, DECREASE, DEDUCTION (1), DEPRECIATION.

redundancy or **redundance** *n.* *—See* WORDINESS.

redundant *adj.* *—See* SUPERFLUOUS, WORDY (1).

reduplication *n.* *—See* COPY (1).

reecho *v.* *—See* ECHO.

lessen the area exposed to the wind. ▸ *v.* To reduce the size of (a sail) by tucking in a part.

reef·er (rē′fər) ▸ *n. Slang* Marijuana, esp. a marijuana cigarette.

reek (rēk) ▸ *v.* **1.** To smoke, steam, or fume. **2.** To be pervaded by something unpleasant. **3.** To give off a strong, unpleasant odor. ▸ *n.* **1.** A stench. **2.** Vapor; steam.

reel[1] (rēl) ▸ *n.* **1.** A device, such as a spool, that turns on an axis and is used for winding rope, tape, or similar materials. **2.** The quantity of material wound on one reel. ▸ *v.* **1.** To wind on a reel. **2.** To recover by winding on a reel: *reel in a fish.* **—*phrasal verb:* reel off** To recite fluently: *reeled off a list of names.*

reel[2] (rēl) ▸ *v.* **1.** To be thrown off balance or fall back. **2.** To stagger or sway, as from drunkenness. **3.** To feel dizzy, as with confusion. ▸ *n.* **1.** A staggering or whirling movement. **2a.** A moderately fast dance of Scottish origin. **b.** The music for this dance.

re·en·try also **re-en·try** (rē-ĕn′trē) ▸ *n.* **1.** The act of reentering. **2.** The return of a missile or spacecraft into Earth's atmosphere.

re·fec·to·ry (rĭ-fĕk′tə-rē) ▸ *n., pl.* **-ries.** A room where meals are served.

re·fer (rĭ-fûr′) ▸ *v.* **-ferred, -fer·ring. 1.** To direct to a source for help or information. **2.** To direct the attention of. **3.** To pertain; concern. **4.** To make mention or reference. **5.** To have recourse; turn: *refer to a dictionary.* **—ref′er·a·ble** (rĕf′ər-ə-bəl, rĭ-fûr′-) *adj.* **—re·fer′ral** *n.*

ref·e·ree (rĕf′ə-rē′) ▸ *n.* **1.** One to whom something is referred, esp. for settlement or decision. **2.** *Sports* An official who supervises play. ▸ *v.* **-reed, -ree·ing.** To act as referee (at or for).

ref·er·ence (rĕf′ər-əns, rĕf′rəns) ▸ *n.* **1.** An act of referring. **2.** Regard; respect: *with reference to.* **3.** A mention or an allusion. **4.** A note in a publication referring the reader to another passage or source. **5.** A work frequently used as a source. **6a.** A person who is in a position to recommend another, as for a job. **b.** A statement about a person's qualifications and character. **—ref′er·en′tial** (-ə-rĕn′shəl) *adj.*

ref·er·en·dum (rĕf′ə-rĕn′dəm) ▸ *n., pl.* **-dums** or **-da** (-də). **1.** The submission of a proposed public measure or actual statute to a direct popular vote. **2.** Such a vote.

re·fill (rē-fĭl′) ▸ *v.* To fill again. ▸ *n.* (rē′fĭl′) **1.** A replacement for the used contents of a container. **2.** An additional filling.

re·fine (rĭ-fīn′) ▸ *v.* **-fined, -fin·ing. 1.** To reduce to a pure state; purify. **2.** To free from coarse characteristics: *tried to refine his manners.* **—re·fin′er** *n.*

re·fined (rĭ-fīnd′) ▸ *adj.* **1.** Free from coarseness or vulgarity. **2.** Free of impurities. **3.** Precise to a fine degree.

re·fine·ment (rĭ-fīn′mənt) ▸ *n.* **1.** The act of refining or the condition of being refined. **2.** An improvement. **3.** Fineness, as of expression or taste. **4.** A subtle distinction.

re·fin·er·y (rĭ-fī′nə-rē) ▸ *n., pl.* **-ies.** An industrial plant for purifying a crude substance, such as petroleum or sugar.

re·flect (rĭ-flĕkt′) ▸ *v.* **1.** To throw or bend back (e.g., light) from a surface. **2.** To form an image of; mirror. **3.** To manifest; show: *Her work reflects intelligence.* **4.** To think seriously. **—re·flec′tion** *n.* **—re·flec′tive** *adj.* **—re·flec′tive·ly** *adv.*

re·flec·tor (rĭ-flĕk′tər) ▸ *n.* Something, such as a surface, that reflects.

re·flex (rē′flĕks′) ▸ *adj.* **1.** Bent, turned, or thrown back. **2.** Involuntary or automatic: *a reflex response.* ▸ *n.* **1a.** Something reflected. **b.** An image produced by reflection. **2.** An involuntary, unlearned, or instinctive response to a stimulus.

re·flex·ive (rĭ-flĕk′sĭv) ▸ *adj.* **1.** Directed back on itself. **2.** *Gram.* **a.** Of or being a verb having an identical subject and direct object, as *dressed* in the sentence *She dressed herself.* **b.** Of or being the pronoun used as the direct object of a reflexive verb, as *herself* in *She dressed herself.* **3.** Of or relating to a reflex. **4.** Elicited automatically; spontaneous. **—re·flex′ive** *n.* **—re·flex′ive·ly** *adv.* **—re·flex′ive·ness, re′flex·iv′i·ty** (rē′flĕk-sĭv′ĭ-tē) *n.*

re·for·est (rē-fôr′ĭst, -fŏr′ĭst) ▸ *v.* To replant (an area) with trees. **—re′for·es·ta′tion** *n.*

re·form (rĭ-fôrm′) ▸ *v.* **1.** To improve by correcting errors, or removing defects. **2.** To abolish abuse or malpractice in. **3.** To give up harmful or immoral practices. ▸ *n.* **1.** A change for the better; an improvement. **2.** Action to improve social or economic conditions. ▸ *adj.* **Reform** Of a branch of Judaism that does not require strict observance of traditional religious law and ritual. **—re·form′a·ble** *adj.* **—re·for′ma·tive** *adj.* **—re·formed′** *adj.* **—re·form′er** *n.*

ref·or·ma·tion (rĕf′ər-mā′shən) ▸ *n.* **1.** The act of reforming or the state of being reformed. **2. Reformation** A 16th-cent. movement in Western Europe for the reform of the Roman Catholic Church that resulted in the establishment of the Protestant and other churches. **—ref′or·ma′tion·al** *adj.*

re·for·ma·to·ry (rĭ-fôr′mə-tôr′ē) ▸ *n., pl.* **-ries.** A penal institution for young offenders.

re·fract (rĭ-frăkt′) ▸ *v.* To deflect from a straight path by refraction.

THESAURUS

reek *v.* To have or give off a foul odor ▸ smell, stink. ***Idiom:*** stink to high heaven.

reek *n.* —*See* STENCH.

reeking or **reeky** *adj.* —*See* SMELLY.

reel *v.* To have the sensation of turning in circles ▸ spin, swim, swirl, whirl. ***Idiom:*** go round and round. —*See also* STAGGER (1), TURN (1).

reeling *adj.* —*See* DIZZY (1).

reengineer *v.* —*See* OVERHAUL.

reengineering *n.* A thorough or drastic reorganization ▸ overhaul, reshuffling, shakeup. *Informal:* housecleaning. [*Compare* RENEWAL, REVOLUTION.]

reestablish *v.* To bring back into existence or use ▸ reinstate, reintroduce, renew, restore, return, revive. [*Compare* RESTORE.]

reestablishment *n.* A return to former prosperity or status ▸ comeback, recovery, restoration. [*Compare* RENEWAL, REVIVAL.]

reevaluate *v.* —*See* RECONSIDER.

ref *n.* —*See* JUDGE (2).

refer *v.* **1.** To make reference to something ▸ advert, allude (to), bring up, mention, note, point to (*or* out), touch (on *or* upon). ***Idiom:*** call (*or* direct) attention to. [*Compare* CITE, DESIGNATE, PROPOSE, RECALL.] **2.** To direct a person elsewhere for help or information ▸ send, transfer, turn over. —*See also* APPLY (2), ATTRIBUTE, RESORT.

refer to *v.* —*See* NAME (2).

referee *n.* —*See* JUDGE (2).

referee *v.* —*See* JUDGE.

reference *n.* **1.** The act of referring ▸ citation, naming, pointing out, referral, signification, signifying. [*Compare* MEANING, SIGN.] **2.** An object referred to ▸ referent, signified. [*Compare* MEANING.] **3.** A statement attesting to personal qualifications, character, and dependability ▸ character, recommendation, testimonial. [*Compare* ENDORSEMENT.]

referent *n.* An object referred to ▸ reference, signified. [*Compare* MEANING.]

referral *n.* —*See* REFERENCE (1).

refine *v.* To remove impurities from ▸ clarify, clean, cleanse, purify. [*Compare* CLEAN.] —*See also* PERFECT.

refined *adj.* Exhibiting refined, tasteful beauty of manner, form, or style ▸ exquisite, graceful. —*See also* CULTURED, DELICATE (4).

refinement *n.* —*See* CULTURE (3), DISCRIMINATION (1), ELEGANCE, IMPROVEMENT (1), MANNERS, PURIFICATION (1).

refinery or **refiner** *n.* —*See* PURIFIER.

refining *adj.* —*See* CULTURAL.

reflect *v.* **1.** To send back or form an image of ▸ image, mirror. [*Compare* REPRESENT.] **2.** To reverse direction after striking something ▸ bound (back), rebound, snap back, spring back. [*Compare* BEND, GLANCE.] —*See also* BEND (2), COMMENT, ECHO, MIMIC, PONDER, THINK (1).

reflection *n.* **1.** An image caused by reflection ▸ image, likeness. [*Compare* COPY.] **2.** Light that is reflected ▸ glare, highlight. [*Compare* FLASH.] **3.** An act of reflection ▸ deflection, glance, scattering. [*Compare* BOUNCE.] **4.** An implied criticism ▸ imputation, slur. [*Compare* CRACK, LIBEL.] —*See also* COMMENT, ECHO (1), THOUGHT.

reflective *adj.* —*See* THOUGHTFUL.

reflex *adj.* —*See* SPONTANEOUS.

reflex *n.* —*See* ECHO (1).

reflexive *adj.* —*See* SPONTANEOUS.

reform *v.* —*See* CORRECT (1).

reformative or **reformatory** *adj.* —*See* CORRECTIVE.

refract *v.* —*See* BEND (2).

re·frac·tion (rĭ-frăk′shən) ▸ *n.* The turning or bending of wave when it passes from one medium into another of different density. **—re·frac′tion·al, re·frac′tive** *adj.* **—re·frac′tive·ly** *adv.* **—re·frac′tive·ness, re′frac·tiv′i·ty** (rē′frăk-tĭv′ĭ-tē) *n.*

re·frac·to·ry (rĭ-frăk′tə-rē) ▸ *adj.* **1.** Resistant to authority or control; obstinate. **2.** Difficult to melt or work. ▸ *n., pl.* **-ries.** A material that has a high melting point. **—re·frac′to·ri·ly** *adv.* **—re·frac′to·ri·ness** *n.*

re·frain[1] (rĭ-frān′) ▸ *v.* To hold oneself back; forbear: *refrained from swearing.*

re·frain[2] (rĭ-frān′) ▸ *n.* A phrase or verse repeated at intervals throughout a song or poem.

re·fresh (rĭ-frĕsh′) ▸ *v.* **1.** To revive with or as if with rest or food. **2.** To make cool, clean, or moist; freshen up. **3.** To renew by stimulation: *refresh one's memory.* **4.** To replenish: *refresh a drink.* **—re·fresh′er** *n.* **—re·fresh′ing** *adj.*

re·fresh·ment (rĭ-frĕsh′mənt) ▸ *n.* **1.** The act of refreshing or the state of being refreshed. **2.** Something that refreshes. **3. refreshments** A snack or light meal.

re·frig·er·ant (rĭ-frĭj′ər-ənt) ▸ *n.* A substance, such as air, ammonia, water, or carbon dioxide, used to provide cooling.

re·frig·er·ate (rĭ-frĭj′ə-rāt′) ▸ *v.* **-at·ed, -at·ing.** **1.** To cool or chill (a substance). **2.** To preserve (food) by chilling. **—re·frig′er·a′tion** *n.*

re·frig·er·a·tor (rĭ-frĭj′ə-rā′tər) ▸ *n.* A cabinet for storing food or other substances at a low temperature.

ref·uge (rĕf′yo͞oj) ▸ *n.* **1.** Protection or shelter, as from danger or hardship. **2.** A place providing protection or shelter; sanctuary.

ref·u·gee (rĕf′yo͞o-jē′) ▸ *n.* One who flees in search of refuge, as from war or political oppression.

re·ful·gent (rĭ-fo͝ol′jənt, -fŭl′-) ▸ *adj.* Shining radiantly; resplendent. **—re·ful′gence** *n.*

re·fund (rĭ-fŭnd′, rē′fŭnd′) ▸ *v.* To give back, (esp. money); repay. ▸ *n.* (rē′fŭnd′) **1.** A repayment of funds. **2.** An amount repaid. **—re·fund′a·ble** *adj.*

re·fur·bish (rē-fûr′bĭsh) ▸ *v.* To make clean, bright, or fresh again; restore. **—re·fur′bish·ment** *n.*

re·fuse[1] (rĭ-fyo͞oz′) ▸ *v.* **-fused, -fus·ing.** To decline to do, accept, give, or allow. **—re·fus′al** *n.*

ref·use[2] (rĕf′yo͞os) ▸ *n.* Anything discarded or rejected as useless or worthless; trash.

re·fute (rĭ-fyo͞ot′) ▸ *v.* **-fut·ed, -fut·ing.** To prove to be false or erroneous. **—re·fut′a·ble** (rĭ-fyo͞o′tə-bəl, rĕf′yə-tə-) *adj.* **—re·fut′a·bly** *adv.* **—ref′u·ta′tion** *n.* **—re·fut′er** *n.*

re·gain (rē-gān′) ▸ *v.* **1.** To recover possession of. **2.** To reach again.

re·gal (rē′gəl) ▸ *adj.* Of a monarch; royal. **—re′gal·ly** *adv.*

re·gale (rĭ-gāl′) ▸ *v.* **-galed, -gal·ing.** **1.** To delight or entertain. **2.** To entertain sumptuously.

re·ga·lia (rĭ-gāl′yə, -gā′lē-ə) ▸ *pl.n.* *(takes sing. or pl. v.)* **1.** The emblems and symbols of royalty. **2.** The distinguishing symbols of a rank, office, order, or society. **3.** Magnificent attire; finery.

re·gard (rĭ-gärd′) ▸ *v.* **1.** To look at attentively; observe. **2.** To look upon or consider: *I regard him as my best friend.* **3.** To hold in esteem or respect. **4.** To relate or refer to; concern. **5.** To take into account. ▸ *n.* **1.** A look or gaze. **2.** Careful thought or attention; heed. **3a.** Respect, affection, or esteem. **b. regards** Good wishes: *Give her my regards.* **4.** Respect: *lucky in that regard.* **5.** Reference or relation: *in regard to her.* **—re·gard′ful** *adj.*

re·gard·ing (rĭ-gär′dĭng) ▸ *prep.* In reference to; concerning.

re·gard·less (rĭ-gärd′lĭs) ▸ *adv.* In spite of everything; anyway. ▸ *adj.* Heedless; unmindful. **—re·gard′less·ly** *adv.*

re·gat·ta (rĭ-gä′tə, -găt′ə) ▸ *n.* A boat race or a series of boat races.

re·gen·cy (rē′jən-se) ▸ *n., pl.* **-cies.** **1.** A person or group governing in place of a monarch who is absent, disabled, or still in minority. **2.** The period during which a regent governs. **3.** The office, region, or government of regents or a regent.

re·gen·er·ate (rĭ-jĕn′ə-rāt′) ▸ *v.* **-at·ed, -at·ing.** **1.** To reform spiritually or morally. **2.** To form, construct, or create anew. **3.** To give new life or energy to; revitalize. ▸ *adj.* (-ər-ĭt) **1.** Spiritually or morally reformed. **2.** Formed or created anew. **3.** Refreshed or renewed. **—re·gen′er·a′tion** *n.* **—re·gen′er·a′tive** *adj.* **—re·gen′er·a′tor** *n.*

re·gent (rē′jənt) ▸ *n.* **1.** One who rules during the minority, absence, or disability of a monarch. **2.** One acting as a ruler or governor. **3.** A member of a governing board of an institution.

reg·gae (rĕg′ā) ▸ *n.* Popular music of Jamaican origin having a strongly accentuated offbeat.

reg·i·cide (rĕj′ĭ-sīd′) ▸ *n.* **1.** The killing of a king. **2.** One who kills a king. **—reg′i·cid′al** *adj.*

re·gime (rā-zhēm′, rĭ-) ▸ *n.* **1.** A government in power; administration. **2.** A regulated system, as of diet and exercise; regimen.

reg·i·men (rĕj′ə-mən, -mĕn′) ▸ *n.* **1.** Governmental rule or control. **2.** A system or course, as of diet or exercise.

reg·i·ment (rĕj′ə-mənt) ▸ *n.* A military unit of ground troops consisting of at least two battalions. ▸ *v.* (rĕj′ə-mĕnt′) **1.** To put into order; systematize. **2.** To subject to uniformity and rigid order. **—reg′i·men′tal** *adj.* **—reg′i·men·ta′tion** *n.*

Re·gi·na (rĭ-jī′nə) ▸ The capital of Saskatchewan, Canada, in the S part.

THESAURUS

refractoriness *n.* —*See* UNRULINESS.

refractory *adj.* —*See* UNRULY.

refrain *v.* To hold oneself back ▸ abstain, forbear, hold off, keep, withhold. *Informal:* sit out. [*Compare* AVOID, HESITATE.]

refrain from *v.* —*See* AVOID.

refresh *v.* To impart renewed energy and strength to a person ▸ freshen, reinvigorate, rejuvenate, renew, restore, revitalize, revivify. [*Compare* ENERGIZE.] —*See also* RENEW (1).

refreshing *adj.* —*See* [illegible]

refreshment *n.* A light meal ▸ collation, snack. *Informal:* bite, nosh. *Slang:* munchies. [*Compare* APPETIZER.] —*See also* DRINK (1).

refuge *n.* **1.** Protection or shelter, as from danger or hardship ▸ asylum, harborage, safety, sanctuary, shelter. *Idiom:* safe haven. [*Compare* DEFENSE.] **2.** A person or thing to which one turns for help when in desperation ▸ recourse, resort, resource. [*Compare* HELP, SUPPORT.] —*See also* COVER (1).

refugee *n.* One who flees, as from confinement or the police ▸ escapee, fugitive, outlaw, runaway. [*Compare* CRIMINAL.] —*See also* ÉMIGRÉ.

refulgent *adj.* —*See* BRIGHT.

refund *v.* To give back, especially money ▸ reimburse, repay, restitute. [*Compare* COMPENSATE, RETURN.]

refund *n.* A quantity of money that is returned ▸ reimbursement, repayment. [*Compare* DEDUCTION, RETURN.]

refurbish *v.* —*See* RENEW (1).

refurbishment *n.* —*See* RENEWAL (1).

refusal *n.* A turning down of a request ▸ denial, disallowance, nonacceptance, rejection, turndown. [*Compare* FORBIDDANCE.] —*See also* NO (1).

refuse[1] *v.* —*See* DECLINE.

refuse[2] *n.* —*See* GARBAGE.

refute *v.* To prove or show to be false ▸ belie, confute, disprove, rebut. [*Compare* CANCEL, DISCREDIT, REPUDIATE.]

regain *v.* —*See* RECOVER (1).

regal *adj.* —*See* GRAND, NOBLE.

regale *v.* To sustain with food ▸ feast, feed, nourish. *Idiom:* wine and dine. [*Compare* SUPPORT.] —*See also* AMUSE.

regalia *n.* —*See* ATTIRE.

regard *v.* To look upon in a particular way ▸ account, consider, deem, esteem, look upon, reckon, see, think of, view. [*Compare* BELIEVE.] —*See also* VALUE, WATCH (1).

regard *n.* An act of directing the eyes on an object ▸ contemplation, look, sight, view. [*Compare* GAZE, WATCH.] —*See also* [illegible] (1), [illegible] (1), CONSIDERATION (1), CURIOSITY (1), ESTEEM, NOTICE (1), VIEWPOINT.

regardful *adj.* —*See* ALERT, ATTENTIVE, CAREFUL (1).

regards *n.* Friendly greetings or acknoweldgment ▸ best, greetings, respects. [*Compare* HELLO.]

regenerate *v.* —*See* REVIVE (2).

regeneration *n.* A fundamental change in one's beliefs ▸ conversion, metanoia, rebirth. [*Compare* REVIVAL.]

regime *n.* —*See* GOVERNMENT (2).

regimen *n.* —*See* PRACTICE, TREATMENT.

regiment *v.* —*See* ARRANGE (1).

re·gion (rē′jən) ▸ *n.* **1.** A large, usu. continuous segment of a surface or space; area. **2.** A specified district or territory. **3.** An area of the body: *the abdominal region.*
re·gion·al (rē′jə-nəl) ▸ *adj.* **1.** Of or relating to a large geographic region. **2.** Of or characteristic of a particular region: *a regional accent.* **—re′gion·al·ly** *adv.*
reg·is·ter (rĕj′ĭ-stər) ▸ *n.* **1a.** An official recording of items, names, or actions. **b.** A book for such entries. **2.** A device that automatically records a quantity or number. **3.** A grill-like device through which heated or cooled air is released into a room. **4.** A state of proper alignment or adjustment. **5.** *Mus.* The range or part of the range of an instrument or voice. ▸ *v.* **1a.** To enter in an official register. **b.** To enroll; esp. in order to vote or attend classes. **2.** To indicate on an instrument or a scale. **3.** To reveal; express: *Her face registered surprise.* **4.** To cause (mail) to be officially recorded by payment of a fee. **5.** To make an impression in the mind: *The warning failed to register.* **—reg′is·tra·ble** (-ĭ-strə-bəl) *adj.* **—reg′is·trant** *n.*
reg·is·tered nurse (rĕj′ĭ-stərd) ▸ *n.* A graduate trained nurse who has passed a state registration examination and has been licensed to practice nursing.
reg·is·trar (rĕj′ĭ-strär′, rĕj′ĭ-strär′) ▸ *n.* An official, as of a university or corporation, who is in charge of keeping records.
reg·is·tra·tion (rĕj′ĭ-strā′shən) ▸ *n.* **1.** The act or process of registering. **2.** The number of persons registered; enrollment. **3.** A document certifying registering.
reg·is·try (rĕj′ĭ-strē) ▸ *n., pl.* **-tries. 1.** Registration. **2.** A place where official records are kept.
reg·nant (rĕg′nənt) ▸ *adj.* Reigning; ruling.
re·gress (rĭ-grĕs′) ▸ *v.* **1.** To go back; move backward. **2.** To return to a previous, usu. worse or less developed state. **—re′gress′** *n.*
re·gres·sion (rĭ-grĕsh′ən) ▸ *n.* **1.** Backward movement. **2.** Relapse to a less perfect or developed state.
re·gres·sive (rĭ-grĕs′ĭv) ▸ *adj.* **1.** Tending to regress. **2.** Marked by regression. **3.** Decreasing proportionately as the amount taxed increases. **—re·gres′sive·ly** *adv.* **—re·gres′sive·ness** *n.*
re·gret (rĭ-grĕt′) ▸ *v.* **-gret·ted, -gret·ting. 1.** To feel sorry, disappointed, or distressed about. **2.** To mourn. ▸ *n.* **1.** A sense of loss and longing for someone or something gone. **2.** Distress about something that one wishes could be different. **3. regrets** A courteous refusal of an invitation. **—re·gret′ful** *adj.* **—re·gret′ful·ly** *adv.* **—re·gret′ful·ness** *n.* **—re·gret′ta·ble** *adj.* **—re·gret′ta·bly** *adv.* **—re·gret′ter** *n.*
re·group (rē-gro͞op′) ▸ *v.* **1.** To arrange in a new grouping. **2.** To reorganize for renewed effort, as after a setback.
reg·u·lar (rĕg′yə-lər) ▸ *adj.* **1.** Customary, usual, or normal. **2.** Orderly, even, or symmetrical. **3.** Conforming to a fixed procedure, principle, or discipline. **4.** Well-ordered; methodical. **5.** Occurring at fixed or normal intervals; periodic. **6.** Not varying; constant. **7.** Formally correct; proper. **8.** *Informal* Complete; thorough: *a regular scoundrel.* **9.** *Informal* Good; nice: *a regular guy.* **10.** *Gram.* Conforming to the usual pattern of inflection, derivation, or word formation. **11.** *Math.* **a.** Having equal sides and angles. **b.** Having faces that are congruent regular polygons and congruent polyhedral angles. **12.** Belonging to or constituting the permanent army of a nation. ▸ *n.* **1.** A soldier in a regular army. **2.** A dependable, loyal person. **3.** A habitual customer. **—reg′u·lar′i·ty** (-lăr′ĭ-tē) *n.* **—reg′u·lar·ly** *adv.*
reg·u·lar·ize (rĕg′yə-lə-rīz′) ▸ *v.* **-ized, -iz·ing.** To make regular. **—reg′u·lar·i·za′tion** *n.*
reg·u·late (rĕg′yə-lāt′) ▸ *v.* **-lat·ed, -lat·ing. 1.** To control or direct according to rule, principle, or law. **2.** To adjust to a specification or requirement: *regulate temperature.* **3.** To adjust for accurate and proper functioning. **—reg′u·la′tive, reg′u·la·to′ry** (-lə-tôr′ē) *adj.* **—reg′u·la′tor** *n.*
reg·u·la·tion (rĕg′yə-lā′shən) ▸ *n.* **1.** The act of regulating or the state of being regulated. **2.** A principle, rule, or law for controlling or governing conduct. **3.** A governmental order having the force of law.
re·gur·gi·tate (rē-gûr′jĭ-tāt′) ▸ *v.* **-tat·ed, -tat·ing.** To vomit. **—re·gur′gi·ta′tion** *n.*
re·ha·bil·i·tate (rē′hə-bĭl′ĭ-tāt′) ▸ *v.* **-tat·ed, -tat·ing. 1.** To restore to health or useful life, as through therapy and education. **2.** To restore the former rank, privileges, or good name of. **—re′ha·bil′i·ta′tion** *n.* **—re′ha·bil′i·ta′tive** *adj.*
re·hash (rē-hăsh′) ▸ *v.* To repeat, rework, rewrite: *rehash old ideas.* **—re′hash′** *n.*
re·hears·al (rĭ-hûr′səl) ▸ *n.* **1.** The act of practicing in preparation for a public performance. **2.** A session of practice for a performance, as of a play.
re·hearse (rĭ-hûrs′) ▸ *v.* **-hearsed, -hears·ing. 1.** To practice in preparation for a public performance. **2.** To perfect (an action) by repetition. **3.** To retell or recite.
Rehn·quist (rĕn′kwĭst′), **William Hubbs** (1924–2005) ▸ Amer. jurist; associate justice of the US Supreme Court (1972–86) and chief justice (1986–2005).
reign (rān) ▸ *n.* **1.** Exercise of sovereign power, as by a monarch. **2.** The period during which a monarch rules. **3.** Dominance or widespread influence. **—reign** *v.*
re·im·burse (rē′ĭm-bûrs′) ▸ *v.* **-bursed, -burs·ing.** To pay back. **—re′im·burs′a·ble** *adj.* **—re′im·burse′ment** *n.*
rein (rān) ▸ *n.* **1.** often **reins** A long, narrow leather strap attached to each end of the bit of a bridle and used by a rider or driver to control a horse or other animal. **2.** A means of restraint, check, or guidance. ▸ *v.* **1.** To check or hold back

THESAURUS

region *n.* —*See* AREA (2), TERRITORY.
regional *adj.* Relating to or restricted to a particular territory ▸ sectional, territorial. [*Compare* LOCAL.] —*See also* INDIGENOUS, LOCAL.
register *n.* To come as a realization ▸ dawn on (*or* upon), sink in, soak in. [*Compare* DISCOVER, STRIKE, UNDERSTAND.] —*See also* LIST[1].
register *v.* —*See* LIST[1], SHOW (2).
regnant *adj.* —*See* DOMINANT (1), PREVAILING.
regress *v.* —*See* RELAPSE.
regression *n.* —*See* RELAPSE.
regret *v.* To feel or express sorrow for ▸ deplore, repent, rue, sorrow (over). [*Compare* FEEL, GRIEVE.]
regret *n.* —*See* DISAPPOINTMENT (1), PENITENCE.
regretful *adj.* —*See* SORRY.
regrets *n.* A statement of acknowledgment expressing regret or asking pardon ▸ apology, excuse, mea culpa. [*Compare* ACKNOWLEDGMENT.]
regrettable *adj.* —*See* SORROWFUL.
regular *adj.* **1.** Characterized by or displaying symmetry, especially correspondence in scale or measure ▸ balanced, proportional, proportionate, symmetric, symmetrical. [*Compare* EVEN, PARALLEL.] **2.** Happening or appearing consistently or repeatedly ▸ episodic, recurrent, repeating, repetitive. [*Compare* PERIODIC, PERVASIVE, THEMATIC.] —*See also* COMMON (1), CONVENTIONAL, METHODICAL, PERFECT, UNCHANGING.
regularity *n.* —*See* CHANGELESSNESS, USUALNESS.
regularize *v.* —*See* CONVENTIONALIZE.
regularly *adv.* —*See* USUALLY.
regulate *v.* —*See* ADJUST, ARRANGE (1), GOVERN, POLICE.
regulated *adj.* —*See* RESTRICTED.
regulation *n.* —*See* LAW (1), RULE.
regulatory *adj.* —*See* GOVERNMENTAL.
rehab *n.* —*See* TREATMENT.
rehabilitate *v.* —*See* CURE, RESTORE (2).
rehabilitation *n.* —*See* IMPROVEMENT (1), TREATMENT.
rehash *v.* —*See* PARAPHRASE.
rehearsal *n.* —*See* PRACTICE.
rehearse *v.* —*See* DESCRIBE, PRACTICE (1).
reification *n.* —*See* EMBODIMENT.
reign *n.* —*See* DOMINATION.
reign *v.* —*See* ADMINISTER (1), DOMINATE (1).
reigning *adj.* —*See* DOMINANT (1), PREVAILING.
reimbursable *adj.* Affording compensation ▸ compensative, compensatory, remunerative.
reimburse *v.* To give back, especially money ▸ refund, repay, restitute. [*Compare* RETURN.] —*See also* COMPENSATE.
reimbursement *n.* A quantity of money that is returned ▸ refund, repayment. [*Compare* DEDUCTION, RETURN.] —*See also* COMPENSATION.
rein *v.* —*See* RESTRAIN.
rein *n.* —*See* BRAKE.

by or as if by the use of reins. **2.** To restrain or control. ***—idiom:* give (free) rein to** To release from restraints.

re·in·car·na·tion (rē′ĭn-kär-nā′shən) ▸ *n.* **1.** Rebirth of the soul in another body. **2.** A new embodiment. **—re′in·car′nate** *v.*

rein·deer (rān′dîr′) ▸ *n., pl.* **-deer** or **-deers**. A large deer of arctic regions, having branched antlers.

re·in·force (rē′ĭn-fôrs′) ▸ *v.* **-forced, -forc·ing**. **1.** To strengthen or support. **2.** To strengthen with additional personnel or equipment. **3.** *Psychol.* To reward (e.g., a desired response) in order to encourage its repetition. **—re′in·force′ment** *n.* **—re′in·forc′er** *n.*

re·in·state (rē′ĭn-stāt′) ▸ *v.* **-stat·ed, -stat·ing**. To restore to a previous condition or position. **—re′in·state′ment** *n.*

re·it·er·ate (rē-ĭt′ə-rāt′) ▸ *v.* **-at·ed, -at·ing**. To say again or repeatedly. **—re·it′er·a′tion** *n.* **—re·it′er·a′tive** (-ə-rā′tĭv, -ər-ə-tĭv) *adj.*

re·ject (rĭ-jĕkt′) ▸ *v.* **1.** To refuse to accept, submit to, believe, or make use of. **2.** To refuse to consider or grant; deny. **3.** To discard as defective or useless. ▸ *n.* (rē′jĕkt) One that has been rejected. **—re·jec′tion** *n.*

re·joice (rĭ-jois′) ▸ *v.* **-joiced, -joic·ing**. To feel joyful or be delighted. **—re·joic′ing** *n.*

re·join[1] (rĭ-join′) ▸ *v.* To say in reply; answer.

re·join[2] (rē-join′) ▸ *v.* To come or join together again.

re·join·der (rĭ-join′dər) ▸ *n.* An answer, esp. to a reply.

re·ju·ve·nate (rĭ-jo͞o′və-nāt′) ▸ *v.* **-nat·ed, -nat·ing**. To restore to youthful vigor or appearance. **—re·ju′ve·na′tion** *n.* **—re·ju′ve·na′tor** (-tər) *n.*

re·lapse (rĭ-lăps′) ▸ *v.* **-lapsed, -laps·ing**. **1.** To fall or slide back into a former state. **2.** To regress after partial recovery from illness. ▸ *n.* (rē′lăps, rĭ-lăps′) A falling back into a former state, esp. after improvement.

re·late (rĭ-lāt′) ▸ *v.* **-lat·ed, -lat·ing**. **1.** To narrate or tell. **2.** To bring into logical or natural association. **3.** To establish or demonstrate a connection between. **4.** To have connection, relation, or reference. **5.** To interact with others. **—re·lat′a·ble** *adj.*

re·lat·ed (rĭ-lā′tĭd) ▸ *adj.* **1.** Connected; associated. **2.** Connected by kinship, common origin, or marriage. **—re·lat′ed·ness** *n.*

re·la·tion (rĭ-lā′shən) ▸ *n.* **1.** A logical or natural association between two or more things. **2.** The connection of people by blood or marriage; kinship. **3.** A relative. **4. relations a.** Mutual dealings or connections, as among persons, groups, or nations. **b.** Sexual intercourse. **5.** Reference; regard. **6.** The act of telling or narrating. **—re·la′tion·ship′** *n.*

rel·a·tive (rĕl′ə-tĭv) ▸ *adj.* **1.** Connected or related. **2.** Considered in comparison to or dependent on something else. **3.** *Gram.* Referring to or qualifying an antecedent, as the pronoun *who* in *the man who was on TV.* ▸ *n.* **1.** One related by kinship or marriage. **2.** Something related or connected to something else. **—rel′a·tive·ly** *adv.* **—rel′a·tive·ness** *n.*

relative clause ▸ *n.* A dependent clause introduced by a relative pronoun, as *which is downstairs* in *The dining room, which is downstairs, is too dark.*

relative humidity ▸ *n.* The ratio of the amount of water vapor in the air at a specific temperature to the maximum capacity of the air at that temperature.

rel·a·tiv·ism (rĕl′ə-tĭ-vĭz′əm) ▸ *n. Philos.* A theory that conceptions of truth and moral values are not absolute but are relative to the persons holding them.

rel·a·tiv·ist (rĕl′ə-tĭ-vĭst) ▸ *n.* **1.** *Philos.* A proponent of relativism. **2.** A physicist who specializes in the theories of relativity.

rel·a·tiv·i·ty (rĕl′ə-tĭv′ĭ-tē) ▸ *n.* **1.** The quality or state of being relative. **2.** *Phys.* **a.** Special relativity. **b.** General relativity.

re·lax (rĭ-lăks′) ▸ *v.* **1.** To make or become less tight. **2.** To make or become less severe or strict. **3.** To relieve from tension or strain. **4.** To take one's ease; rest. **—re′lax·a′tion** (rē′lăk-sā′shən) *n.* **—re·lax′er** *n.*

re·lax·ant (rĭ-lăk′sənt) ▸ *n.* Something, such as a medicament, that relieves muscular or nervous tension. **—re·lax′ant** *adj.*

re·lay (rē′lā) ▸ *n.* **1.** An act of passing something along, as from one person to another. **2.** A relay race. **3.** *Electron.* A device that responds to a small current or voltage change by activating switches or other devices in an electric circuit. **4.** A fresh team or crew that relieves another. ▸ *v.* (rē′lā, rĭ-lā′) **1.** To pass or send along. **2.** To supply with fresh relays.

relay race ▸ *n.* A race between two or more teams in which each team member runs part of the race and is then relieved by a teammate.

re·lease (rĭ-lēs′) ▸ *v.* **-leased, -leas·ing**. **1.** To set free from

THESAURUS

reinforce *v.* To make firmer in a particular conviction or habit ▸ confirm, fortify, harden, strengthen. [*Compare* BACK, ESTABLISH.] *—See also* SUPPLEMENT, SUPPORT (2).

reinforcement *n.* *—See* SUPPORT.

reinstall *v.* To put someone in the possession of a prior position or office ▸ give back, reappoint, reinstate, replace, restore, return.

reinstate *v.* To bring back into existence or use ▸ reestablish, reintroduce, renew, restore, return, revive. *—See also* REINSTALL, RESTORE (2).

reintroduce *v.* To bring back into existence or use ▸ reestablish, reinstate, renew, restore, return, revive. [*Compare* RESTORE.]

reinvigorate *v.* *—See* REFRESH.

reinvigorating *adj.* *—See* INVIGORATING.

reiterate *v.* *—See* REPEAT (1).

reiteration *n.* *—See* REPETITION.

reiterative *adj.* Characterized by repetition ▸ iterative, repetitious, repetitive. [*Compare* BORING, SUPERFLUOUS, WORDY.]

reject *v.* *—See* DECLINE, DISAPPROVE, DISBELIEVE, DISMISS (3), EXCLUDE, REPUDIATE.

reject *n.* *—See* OUTCAST.

rejected *adj.* *—See* ABANDONED (1), UNWELCOME.

rejection *n.* A turning down of a request ▸ denial, disallowance, nonacceptance, refusal, turndown. [*Compare* FORBIDDANCE.] *—See also* DENIAL (1), DISAPPROVAL, DISBELIEF, NO (1).

rejoice *v.* To feel or take joy or pleasure ▸ delight, exult, pleasure. [*Compare* ENJOY, LUXURIATE.] *—See also* CELEBRATE (2).

rejoicing *n.* *—See* CELEBRATION (3).

rejoin *v.* *—See* ANSWER.

rejoinder *n.* *—See* ANSWER (1).

rejuvenate *v.* *—See* REFRESH, RENEW (1), RESTORE (2).

rejuvenation *n.* *—See* RENEWAL (1).

rekindle *v.* *—See* REVIVE (1).

relapse *v.* To slip from a higher or better condition to a former, usually lower or poorer one ▸ backslide, fall back, lapse, regress, retrogress, revert. [*Compare* DETERIORATE.]

relapse *n.* A slipping from a higher or better condition to a former, usually lower or poorer one ▸ backslide, backsliding, lapse, recidivation, recidivism, regression, retrogradation, retrogression. [*Compare* DETERIORATION, REVERSE.]

relate *v.* **1.** To associate or affiliate oneself closely with a person or group ▸ empathize, identify, sympathize. [*Compare* UNDERSTAND.] **2.** To interact with another or others in a harmonious fashion ▸ communicate, connect, get along (on), harmonize. *Informal:* cotton (to). *Slang:* click. *Idioms:* be in synch, be on the same wavelength, hit it off, make a good fit (*or* match). [*Compare* AGREE.] *—See also* APPLY (2), ASSOCIATE (1), DESCRIBE, LIKEN.

related *adj.* *—See* KINDRED.

relation *n.* **1.** A logical or natural association between two or more things ▸ connection, correlation, interconnection, interdependence, interrelationship, link, linkage, relationship, tie-in. *Informal:* hookup. [*Compare* BOND, RELEVANCE.] **2.** A person who is connected to another person by blood or marriage ▸ kinsman, kinswoman, relative. [*Compare* ANCESTRY, FAMILY, KIN.]

relationship *n.* *—See* RELATION (1).

relative *adj.* Estimated by comparison ▸ comparable, comparative. *—See also* CONDITIONAL.

relative *n.* A person connected to another person by blood or marriage ▸ kinsman, kinswoman, relation. [*Compare* ANCESTRY, FAMILY, KIN.]

relax *v.* *—See* EASE (1), EVEN, REST[1] (1).

relaxation *n.* *—See* REST[1] (2).

relaxed *adj.* *—See* EASYGOING, LOOSE (1).

release *v.* *—See* DISCHARGE, DISMISS (1), DISMISS (2), EMIT, EXCUSE (1), EX-

confinement or restraint. **2.** To free or unfasten; let go. **3.** To dismiss, as from a job. **4.** To issue for performance, sale, publication, or distribution. **5.** To relinquish (e.g., a right). ▸ *n.* **1.** An act of releasing. **2.** A device or catch for locking or releasing a mechanism. **3.** Something issued or made public. **4.** The document authorizing the relinquishment of a right or claim. **—re·leas′a·ble** *adj.* **—re·leas′er** *n.*

rel·e·gate (rĕl′ĭ-gāt′) ▸ *v.* **-gat·ed, -gat·ing. 1.** To assign to an obscure place or position. **2.** To assign to a category; classify. **3.** To refer or assign (e.g., a task) for decision or action. **4.** To exile; banish. **—rel′e·ga′tion** *n.*

re·lent (rĭ-lĕnt′) ▸ *v.* To become more lenient or forgiving.

re·lent·less (rĭ-lĕnt′lĭs) ▸ *adj.* **1.** Unyielding; pitiless. **2.** Steady and persistent. **—re·lent′less·ly** *adv.* **—re·lent′less·ness** *n.*

rel·e·vant (rĕl′ə-vənt) ▸ *adj.* Having to do with the matter at hand. **—rel′e·vance, rel′e·van·cy** *n.* **—rel′e·vant·ly** *adv.*

re·li·a·ble (rĭ-lī′ə-bəl) ▸ *adj.* Capable of being relied on; dependable. **—re·li′a·bil′i·ty, re·li′a·ble·ness** *n.* **—re·li′a·bly** *adv.*

re·li·ant (rĭ-lī′ənt) ▸ *adj.* Having or exhibiting trust in or dependence on something. **—re·li′ance** *n.* **—re·li′ant·ly** *adv.*

rel·ic (rĕl′ĭk) ▸ *n.* **1.** Something that has survived from an extinct culture or bygone period. **2.** A memento; keepsake. **3.** An object of religious veneration. **4.** or **relics** A corpse; remains.

re·lief (rĭ-lēf′) ▸ *n.* **1.** The easing of a burden or distress. **2.** Something that alleviates pain or distress. **3.** Aid, as given to the needy or disaster victims. **4a.** Release from a post or duty. **b.** One who releases another by taking over a post or duty. **5.** The projection of figures or forms from a flat background, as in sculpture. **6.** The variations in elevation of an area of the earth's surface.

relief map ▸ *n.* A map that depicts land configuration, usu. with contour lines.

re·lieve (rĭ-lēv′) ▸ *v.* **-lieved, -liev·ing. 1.** To lessen or alleviate. **2.** To free from pain, anxiety, or distress. **3.** To assist; aid. **4.** To free from a specified duty or obligation, esp. by providing a substitute. **5.** To make less tedious or unpleasant. **6.** To make distinct by contrast; set off. **—re·liev′er** *n.*

re·li·gion (rĭ-lĭj′ən) ▸ *n.* **1a.** Belief in and reverence for a supernatural power or powers regarded as creator or governor of the universe. **b.** A personal or institutionalized system grounded in such belief. **2.** A cause or activity pursued with zeal or conscientious devotion.

re·li·gious (rĭ-lĭj′əs) ▸ *adj.* **1.** Having belief in and reverence for a deity. **2.** Of or relating to religion. **3.** Scrupulous or conscientious. ▸ *n., pl.* **-gious.** A member of a monastic order. **—re·li′gious·ly** *adv.* **—re·li′gious·ness** *n.*

re·lin·quish (rĭ-lĭng′kwĭsh) ▸ *v.* **1.** To retire from; give up or abandon. **2.** To put aside or desist from. **3.** To surrender. **4.** To release. **—re·lin′quish·er** *n.* **—re·lin′quish·ment** *n.*

rel·i·quar·y (rĕl′ĭ-kwĕr′ē) ▸ *n., pl.* **-ies.** A receptacle for keeping or displaying sacred relics.

rel·ish (rĕl′ĭsh) ▸ *n.* **1.** An appetite for something. **2a.** Hearty enjoyment. **b.** Something that lends pleasure or zest. **3.** A spicy or savory condiment, as of chopped sweet pickles. **4.** The flavor of a food, esp. when appetizing. ▸ *v.* **1.** To take keen or zestful pleasure in. **2.** To enjoy the flavor of.

re·live (rē-lĭv′) ▸ *v.* To undergo or experience again, esp. in the imagination.

re·luc·tant (rĭ-lŭk′tənt) ▸ *adj.* **1.** Unwilling; disinclined: *reluctant to help.* **2.** Hesitant; grudging: *a reluctant smile.* **—re·luc′tance** *n.* **—re·luc′tant·ly** *adv.*

re·ly (rĭ-lī′) ▸ *v.* **-lied, -ly·ing. 1.** To depend: *relies on her parents for tuition.* **2.** To have faith or confidence: *relied on them to tell the truth.*

rem (rĕm) ▸ *n. Phys.* The amount of ionizing radiation required to produce the same biological effect as one rad of high-penetration x-rays.

REM (rĕm) ▸ *n.* The rapid, periodic, jerky movement of the eyes during certain stages of the sleep cycle when dreaming takes place.

re·main (rĭ-mān′) ▸ *v.* **1.** To continue in the same state, condition, or place. **2.** To be left after the removal, loss, passage, or destruction of others. **3.** To be left as still to be dealt with: *A cure remains to be found.* **4.** To endure or persist.

re·main·der (rĭ-mān′dər) ▸ *n.* **1.** Something left over after other parts have been taken away. **2a.** The number that is left over when one integer is divided by another. **b.** The number that is obtained when one number is subtracted from another; difference. **3.** A book that remains with a publisher after sales have fallen off. ▸ *v.* To sell (books)

THESAURUS

TRICATE, FREE (1), OPEN (1), PUBLISH (1), RID, UNDO.

release *n.* —*See* PUBLICATION (1), RESCUE.

relegate *v.* —*See* ENTRUST (1).

relent *v.* —*See* WEAKEN.

relentless *adj.* —*See* BITTER (2), CONTINUAL, STUBBORN (1).

relentlessness *n.* —*See* STUBBORNNESS.

relevance or **relevancy** *n.* The relationship of something to the matter at hand ▸ applicability, application, appositeness, bearing, germaneness, materiality, pertinence, pertinency, relevancy. [*Compare* IMPORTANCE, INFLUENCE, INTEREST.]

relevant *adj.* Related to or affecting the matter at hand ▸ applicable, apposite, apropos, germane, material, pertinent. *Idiom:* to the point. [*Compare* INFLUENTIAL, IMPORTANT.]

reliability *n.* —*See* HONESTY, VERACITY.

reliable *adj.* —*See* DEPENDABLE.

reliance *n.* The state or relation of being determined or controlled ▸ dependence, dependency. [*Compare* AUTHORITY, DOMINANCE, NEED, RELATION.] —*See also* TRUST.

relic *n.* —*See* REMEMBRANCE (1), TRACE.

relief *n.* **1.** Reduction of pain or distress, or a cause of that reduction ▸ alleviation, assuagement, ease, mitigation, palliation, succor. [*Compare* COMFORT, DECREASE, WANING.] **2.** Assistance, especially money, food, and other necessities, given to the needy or dispossessed ▸ aid, handout, public assistance, welfare. *Informal:* dole. [*Compare* DONATION.] —*See also* HELP, SCULPTURE, SUBSTITUTE.

relieve *v.* **1.** To make less severe or more bearable ▸ allay, alleviate, assuage, ease, lessen, lighten, mitigate, palliate, quell. [*Compare* COMFORT, HELP.] **2.** To free from a specific duty by acting as a substitute ▸ spell, take over. [*Compare* SUBSTITUTE.] —*See also* EXCUSE (1), HELP, RID.

reliever *n.* —*See* ASSISTANT.

religion *n.* A system of religious belief, worship, or ritual ▸ confession, creed, cult, denomination, faith, persuasion, profession, sect. [*Compare* DEVOTION, DOCTRINE.]

religiosity or **religionism** *n.* —*See* DEVOTION.

religious *adj.* Of or relating to a church or to an established religion ▸ church, churchly, ecclesiastical, spiritual. [*Compare* CLERICAL, DIVINE, HOLY, RITUAL.] —*See also* DIVINE (2), PIOUS.

religiousness *n.* —*See* DEVOTION.

relinquish *v.* To yield oneself unrestrainedly, as to an impulse ▸ abandon, deliver, surrender. *Idiom:* give oneself up (*or* over). —*See also* ABANDON (1), DROP (4), LOSE (2).

relinquished *adj.* —*See* ABANDONED (1).

relish *n.* Spirited enjoyment ▸ gusto, zest. [*Compare* ENTHUSIASM.] —*See also* FLAVOR (1), TASTE (1).

relish *v.* To be avidly interested in ▸ devour, feast on. *Slang:* eat up. —*See also* ENJOY.

relocate *v.* **1.** To change one's residence or place of business, for example ▸ move, remove, transfer. *Idiom:* pull up stakes. [*Compare* EMIGRATE, GO.] **2.** To move to a place and reside there ▸ locate, settle. *Idioms:* fix one's residence, make one's home, put down roots, take up residence. [*Compare* LIVE[1].]

relocation *n.* The act of moving from one place to another ▸ move, removal. *Idiom:* change of address (*or* residence). [*Compare* DEPARTURE.] —*See also* DISPLACEMENT.

reluctance *n.* —*See* INDISPOSITION.

reluctant *adj.* —*See* INDISPOSED.

rely on or **upon** *v.* —*See* DEPEND ON (1).

remain *v.* To continue to be in a place ▸ abide, bide, linger, pause, stay, tarry, wait. *Informal:* hang around, stick around. *Idioms:* cool one's heels (*or* jets), stay put. [*Compare* DELAY.] —*See also* ENDURE (2).

remainder *n.* —*See* BALANCE (4), TRACE.

remaining *adj.* Being what remains,

as a remainder, usu. at a reduced price.

re·mains (rĭ-mānz′) ▸ *pl.n.* **1.** All that is left after other parts have been taken away, used up, or destroyed. **2.** A corpse.

re·mand (rĭ-mănd′) ▸ *v.* To send back to prison, to a lower court, or to another agency for further proceedings. **—re·mand′ment** *n.*

re·mark (rĭ-märk′) ▸ *v.* **1.** To express briefly and casually as a comment. **2.** To take notice of; observe. ▸ *n.* **1.** The act of noticing or observing. **2.** A casual or brief statement.

re·mark·a·ble (rĭ-mär′kə-bəl) ▸ *adj.* **1.** Worthy of notice. **2.** Unusual; extraordinary. **—re·mark′a·bly** *adv.*

Rem·brandt van Rijn or **Rem·brandt van Ryn** (rĕm′brănt′ văn rīn′, -bränt′) (1606–69) ▸ Dutch painter.

re·me·di·a·ble (rĭ-mē′dē-ə-bəl) ▸ *adj.* Possible to remedy.

re·me·di·al (rĭ-mē′dē-əl) ▸ *adj.* Intended to correct or improve something, esp. deficient skills. **—re·me′di·al·ly** *adv.*

rem·e·dy (rĕm′ĭ-dē) ▸ *n., pl.* **-dies.** **1.** Something that relieves pain, cures disease, or corrects a disorder. **2.** Something that corrects an evil, a fault, or an error. ▸ *v.* **-died, -dy·ing.** **1.** To relieve or cure. **2.** To set right; rectify.

re·mem·ber (rĭ-mĕm′bər) ▸ *v.* **1.** To recall to the mind; think of again. **2.** To retain in the memory. **3.** To keep (someone) in mind. **4.** To give greetings from. **—re·mem′ber·a·ble** *adj.*

re·mem·brance (rĭ-mĕm′brəns) ▸ *n.* **1.** The act of remembering or the state of being remembered. **2.** A memorial. **3.** The length of time over which one's memory extends. **4.** Something remembered. **5.** A souvenir.

re·mind (rĭ-mīnd′) ▸ *v.* To cause (someone) to remember. **—re·mind′er** *n.*

rem·i·nisce (rĕm′ə-nĭs′) ▸ *v.* **-nisced, -nisc·ing.** To recollect and tell of the past.

rem·i·nis·cence (rĕm′ə-nĭs′əns) ▸ *n.* **1.** The act or process of recalling the past. **2.** A memory. **3.** often **reminiscences** A narration of past experiences.

rem·i·nis·cent (rĕm′ə-nĭs′ənt) ▸ *adj.* **1.** Of or containing reminiscence. **2.** Suggestive of something in the past.

re·miss (rĭ-mĭs′) ▸ *adj.* Lax in attending to duty.

re·mis·si·ble (rĭ-mĭs′ə-bəl) ▸ *adj.* Able to be forgiven. **—re·mis′si·bil′i·ty** *n.* **—re·mis′si·bly** *adv.*

re·mis·sion (rĭ-mĭsh′ən) ▸ *n.* **1.** The act of remitting or the condition of being remitted. **2.** A lessening of intensity or seriousness, as of a disease.

re·mit (rĭ-mĭt′) ▸ *v.* **-mit·ted, -mit·ting.** **1.** To transmit (money) in payment. **2a.** To cancel (e.g., a tax or penalty). **b.** To pardon; forgive. **3.** To slacken. **4.** To diminish; abate. **—re·mit′ta·ble** *adj.* **—re·mit′tal** *n.* **—re·mit′ter** *n.*

re·mit·tance (rĭ-mĭt′ns) ▸ *n.* Credit or money sent to someone.

re·mit·tent (rĭ-mĭt′nt) ▸ *adj.* Marked by temporary abatement in severity.

re·mix (rē-mĭks′) ▸ *v.* To recombine recorded audio tracks or channels so as to produce a new recording. ▸ *n.* (rē′mĭks′) A recording produced by remixing.

rem·nant (rĕm′nənt) ▸ *n.* **1.** Something left over; remainder. **2.** A surviving trace or vestige.

re·mod·el (rē-mŏd′l) ▸ *v.* To make over in structure or style; renovate. **—re·mod′el·er** *n.*

re·mon·strance (rĭ-mŏn′strəns) ▸ *n.* The act or an instance of remonstrating.

re·mon·strate (rĭ-mŏn′strāt′) ▸ *v.* **-strat·ed, -strat·ing.** To say or plead in protest, objection, or reproof. **—re′mon·stra′tion** (rē′mŏn-strā′shən, rĕm′ən-) *n.*

rem·o·ra (rĕm′ər-ə) ▸ *n.* Any of a family of marine fishes having a sucking disk on the head with which they attach themselves to sharks, whales, sea turtles, or the hulls of ships.

re·morse (rĭ-môrs′) ▸ *n.* Bitter regret for past misdeeds. **—re·morse′ful** *adj.* **—re·morse′ful·ly** *adv.* **—re·morse′ful·ness** *n.*

re·morse·less (rĭ-môrs′lĭs) ▸ *adj.* Having no pity or compassion. **—re·morse′less·ly** *adv.* **—re·morse′less·ness** *n.*

re·mote (rĭ-mōt′) ▸ *adj.* **-mot·er, -mot·est.** **1.** Located far away. **2.** Distant in time. **3.** Faint; slight: *a remote possibility.* **4.** Distantly related: *a remote cousin.* **5.** Distant in manner; aloof. **6.** Operating or controlled from a distance. ▸ *n.* **1.** A radio or television broadcast from outside a studio. **2.** Remote control. **—re·mote′ly** *adv.* **—re·mote′ness** *n.*

remote control ▸ *n.* **1.** The control of an activity, process, or machine from a distance, as by radioed instructions or coded signals. **2.** A device used to control an apparatus from a distance.

re·mo·val (rĭ-mo͞o′vəl) ▸ *adj.* **1.** The act of being removed. **2.** The fact of being removed.

THESAURUS

especially after a part has been removed ▸ extra, leftover, stray. *Idiom:* left behind. [*Compare* SUPERFLUOUS.]

remains *n.* The substance of the body, especially after decay or cremation ▸ ashes, clay, cremains, dust. *—See also* BALANCE (4), BODY (2), RUIN (2), TRACE.

remand *v.* *—See* ENTRUST (1).

remark *v.* *—See* COMMENT, NOTICE.

remark *n.* *—See* COMMENT, NOTICE (1).

remarkable *adj.* *—See* EXCELLENT, EXCEPTIONAL, NOTICEABLE.

remarkably *adv.* *—See* UNUSUALLY.

remedial *adj.* *—See* CORRECTIVE, CURATIVE.

remedy *n.* *—See* CURE.

remedy *v.* *—See* CORRECT (1), CURE.

remember *v.* **1.** To renew an image or a thought in the mind ▸ bethink, mind, recall, recollect, remind oneself, reminisce, retain, retrieve, revive. *Idioms:* bring to mind, call to mind. [*Compare* IMAGINE, MEMORIZE, THINK.] **2.** To care enough to keep someone in mind ▸ cherish, think about, think of.

remembrance *n.* **1.** Something that causes one to remember ▸ favor, forget-me-not, keepsake, memento, relic, reminder, souvenir, token, trophy. [*Compare* MEMORIAL, NOVELTY.] **2.** An act or instance of remembering ▸ memory, mental image, recollection, reminiscence. [*Compare* IDEA.] **3.** Something, as a structure or custom, serving to honor or keep alive a memory ▸ commemoration, memorial, monument. [*Compare* TESTIMONIAL.] *—See also* MEMORY (1).

remind *n.* To cause to remember ▸ bring back to. *Idiom:* make think of. [*Compare* RECALL, SUGGEST.]

reminder *n.* *—See* NOTE, REMEMBRANCE (1).

reminisce *v.* *—See* REMEMBER (1).

reminiscence *n.* An act or instance of remembering ▸ memory, mental image, recollection, remembrance. [*Compare* IDEA.] *—See also* MEMORY (1).

reminiscences *n.* *—See* MEMOIR.

reminiscent *adj.* Tending to bring a memory, mood, or image, for example, subtly or indirectly to mind ▸ allusive, connotative, evocative, impressionistic, suggestive. [*Compare* DESIGNATIVE, SYMBOLIC.]

remise *v.* *—See* EXCUSE (1).

remiss *adj.* *—See* NEGLIGENT.

remissible *adj.* *—See* PARDONABLE.

remission *n.* *—See* ABEYANCE, EXCULPATION, FORGIVENESS, WANING.

remissness *n.* *—See* NEGLIGENCE.

remit *v.* *—See* ABANDON (2), COMPENSATE, DEFER[1], ENTRUST (1), EXCUSE (1), FORGIVE, SUBSIDE.

remnant *n.* *—See* BALANCE (4), TRACE.

remodel *v.* *—See* ADAPT.

remonstrance *n.* *—See* OBJECTION, REBUKE.

remonstrate *v.* *—See* OBJECT.

remorse *n.* *—See* PENITENCE.

remorseful *adj.* *—See* SORRY.

remorsefulness *n.* *—See* PENITENCE.

remorseless *adj.* Devoid of remorse ▸ impenitent, unrepentant. *—See also* CALLOUS, STUBBORN (1).

remorselessness *n.* *—See* STUBBORNNESS.

remote *adj.* **1.** Far from centers of human population ▸ back, insular, isolated, lonely, lonesome, outlying, out-of-the-way, removed, secluded, solitary. *Slang:* backwater. *Idioms:* centrally isolated, in the middle of nowhere, off the beaten path (*or* track). [*Compare* INACCESSIBLE, LONELY, OBSCURE.] **2.** Small in degree, especially of probability ▸ faint, narrow, negligible, outside, slender, slight, slim. [*Compare* DOUBTFUL, TINY.] *—See also* COOL, DETACHED (1), DISTANT.

remoteness *n.* The fact or condition of being far removed or apart ▸ distance, farness, separateness, separation. *—See also* DETACHMENT (2).

removal *n.* The act of moving from one place to another ▸ move, relocation, remotion. *Idiom:* change of address, change of residence. [*Compare* DEPARTURE.] *—See also* DISPOSAL, EJECTION, ELIMINATION, RETREAT.

re·move (rĭ-mo͞ov′) ▸ *v.* **-moved, -mov·ing.** **1.** To move from a place or position occupied. **2.** To take off: *removed her jewelry.* **3.** To take away; eliminate. **4.** To dismiss from office. **5.** To change one's residence; move. ▸ *n.* **1.** The act of removing. **2.** Distance or degree of separation. **—re·mov′a·ble** *adj.* **—re·mov′a·bly** *adv.* **—re·mov′er** *n.*

re·moved (rĭ-mo͞ovd′) ▸ *adj.* **1.** Distant in space, time, or nature; remote. **2.** Separated in relationship by a given degree of descent: *first cousin once removed.*

re·mu·ner·ate (rĭ-myo͞o′nə-rāt′) ▸ *v.* **-at·ed, -at·ing.** To pay for goods provided, services rendered, or losses incurred. **—re·mu′ner·a′tion** *n.* **—re·mu′ner·a·tive** (-nər-ə-tĭv, -nə-rā′tĭv) *adj.*

ren·ais·sance (rĕn′ĭ-säns′, -zäns′, rĭ-nā′səns) ▸ *n.* **1.** A rebirth or revival. **2. Renaissance a.** The humanistic revival of classical art, architecture, literature, and learning in Europe. **b.** The period of this revival, roughly the 14th through the 16th cent. **3.** often **Renaissance** A revival of intellectual or artistic achievement.

re·nal (rē′nəl) ▸ *adj.* Relating to or near the kidneys.

re·nas·cent (rĭ-năs′ənt, -nā′sənt) ▸ *adj.* Showing renewed growth or vigor. **—re·nas′cence** *n.*

rend (rĕnd) ▸ *v.* **rent** (rĕnt) or **rend·ed, rend·ing.** **1.** To tear or split apart or into pieces violently. **2.** To tear away forcibly; wrest. **3.** To pierce or disturb with sound. **4.** To cause pain or distress to.

ren·der (rĕn′dər) ▸ *v.* **1.** To submit or present. **2.** To give; provide: *render assistance.* **3.** To give what is due. **4.** To represent in verbal or artistic form; depict. **5.** To translate. **6.** To make: *The news rendered her speechless.* **7.** To liquefy (fat) by heating. **—ren′der·er** *n.*

ren·dez·vous (rän′dā-vo͞o′, -də-) ▸ *n., pl.* **-vous** (-vo͞oz′). **1.** A meeting at a set time and place. **2.** A set meeting place. **3.** A popular gathering place. ▸ *v.* To meet at a set time and place.

ren·di·tion (rĕn-dĭsh′ən) ▸ *n.* **1.** The act of rendering. **2.** An interpretation or performance of a musical or dramatic work. **3.** A translation.

ren·e·gade (rĕn′ĭ-gād′) ▸ *n.* **1.** A person who rejects a religion, cause, allegiance, or group for another; deserter. **2.** An outlaw. **—ren′e·gade′** *adj.*

re·nege (rĭ-nĭg′, -nĕg′) ▸ *v.* **-neged, -neg·ing.** **1.** To fail to carry out a promise or commitment. **2.** To fail to follow suit in card games when able and required to do so. **—re·neg′er** *n.*

re·new (rĭ-no͞o′, -nyo͞o′) ▸ *v.* **1.** To make new or as if new again; restore. **2.** To take up again; resume. **3.** To repeat so as to reaffirm: *renew a promise.* **4.** To arrange for the extension of: *renew a contract.* **—re·new′a·ble** *adj.* **—re·new′al** *n.*

ren·net (rĕn′ĭt) ▸ *n.* A dried extract from the stomach lining of a ruminant, used in cheesemaking to curdle milk.

ren·nin (rĕn′ĭn) ▸ *n.* A milk-coagulating enzyme produced from rennet.

Ren·oir (rĕn′wär′, rən-wär′), **Pierre Auguste** (1841–1919) ▸ French painter.

re·nounce (rĭ-nouns′) ▸ *v.* **-nounced, -nounc·ing.** **1.** To give up, esp. by formal announcement. **2.** To reject; disown. **—re·nounce′ment** *n.*

ren·o·vate (rĕn′ə-vāt′) ▸ *v.* **-vat·ed, -vat·ing.** To restore to an earlier state. **—ren′o·va′tion** *n.* **—ren′o·va′tor** *n.*

re·nown (rĭ-noun′) ▸ *n.* Widespread honor and acclaim; fame. **—re·nowned′** *adj.*

rent[1] (rĕnt) ▸ *n.* Periodic payment made by a tenant in return for the right to use the property of another. ▸ *v.* **1.** To use (another's property) in return for regular payments. **2.** To be for rent. **—rent′a·ble** *adj.* **—rent′er** *n.*

rent[2] (rĕnt) ▸ *v.* P.t. and p.part. of **rend.** ▸ *n.* An opening made by rending; rip.

rent·al (rĕn′tl) ▸ *n.* **1.** An amount paid out or taken in as rent. **2.** Property available for renting. **3.** The act of renting. **—rent′al** *adj.*

rent control ▸ *n.* Governmental regulation of the amounts charged for rented housing.

re·nun·ci·a·tion (rĭ-nŭn′sē-ā′shən) ▸ *n.* The act or an instance of renouncing. **—re·nun′ci·a′tive, re·nun′ci·a·to′ry** (-ə-tôr′ē) *adj.*

re·or·der (rē-ôr′dər) ▸ *v.* **1.** To order (the same goods) again. **2.** To rearrange. **—re·or′der** *n.*

rep[1] (rĕp) ▸ *n.* A ribbed or corded fabric.

rep[2] (rĕp) ▸ *n.* *Informal* A representative.

rep[3] (rĕp) ▸ *n.* *Informal* Reputation.

THESAURUS

remove *v.* **1.** To move something from a position occupied ▸ carry (off *or* away), pick out, pluck out, rip out, take, take away, take off, take out, tear out, uproot, withdraw. *Idiom:* pluck (*or* pull) out by the roots. [*Compare* CARRY, DROP, PULL.] **2.** To change one's residence or place of business, for example ▸ move, relocate, transfer. *Idiom:* pull up stakes. [*Compare* EMIGRATE, GO.] **3.** To take from one's own person ▸ cast off, doff, pull off, slip off, slough off, take off. *Idiom:* slip (*or* step) out of. [*Compare* BARE.] **4.** To rid of obstructions ▸ clear, free, open, unblock. [*Compare* RID.] *—See also* DEDUCT, ELIMINATE, GO (1), MOVE (2), RETREAT.

removed *adj.* *—See* DISTANT, REMOTE (1), SOLITARY.

remunerate *v.* *—See* COMPENSATE.

remuneration *n.* *—See* COMPENSATION, WAGE.

remunerative *adj.* Affording compensation ▸ compensative, compensatory, reimbursable. *—See also* PROFITABLE.

renaissance *n.* *—See* REVIVAL (1).

rend *v.* *—See* PULL (2), TEAR[1].

render *v.* **1.** To make music ▸ concertize, perform, play. **2.** To deliver an indictment or verdict, for example ▸ hand down, return. *—See also* ABANDON (1), GIVE (1), INTERPRET (2), OFFER (1), OFFER (2), PARAPHRASE, REPRESENT (2), TRANSLATE.

rendering *n.* *—See* INTERPRETATION, PARAPHRASE, REPRESENTATION, TRANSLATION.

rendezvous *n.* *—See* ENGAGEMENT (1), HAUNT.

rendezvous *v.* To come together by arrangement ▸ connect, hook up, get together, meet (up).

rendition *n.* *—See* INTERPRETATION, PARAPHRASE.

renege *v.* To abandon a former position or commitment ▸ back down, back away, back out, backpedal, blink, retreat, skip out, walk out. *Slang:* cop out, fink out. *Idioms:* beat a (hasty) retreat, cut and run. [*Compare* ABANDON, ESCAPE, RETREAT, SURRENDER.]

renegade *n.* *—See* DEFECTOR.

renegade *v.* *—See* DEFECT.

renew *v.* **1.** To make new or as if new again ▸ do over, fix up, furbish, recondition, re-create, redecorate, redo, refresh, refurbish, regenerate, rejuvenate, renovate, restore, revamp, smarten up, spruce up. *Idioms:* give a facelift to, give a new look to. [*Compare* FIX[1], MODERNIZE, OVERHAUL, RESTORE, STREAMLINE.] **2.** To bring back into existence or use ▸ reestablish, reinstate, reintroduce, restore, return, revive. [*Compare* RESTORE.] *—See also* CONTINUE, REFRESH, REVIVE (1).

renewal *n.* **1.** The act of making new or as if new again ▸ face-lift, facelifting, furbishment, reconditioning, redecorating, refurbishment, regeneration, rejuvenation, renovation, restoration, revampment. **2.** A continuing after interruption ▸ continuation, resumption, resurgence, revival. *—See also* COMEBACK, REVIVAL (1).

renewing *adj.* *—See* INVIGORATING.

renounce *v.* *—See* ABANDON (1), BREAK (5), DEFECT, DENY, REPUDIATE.

renouncement *n.* *—See* DEFECTION.

renovate *v.* *—See* RENEW (1), RESTORE (2), REVIVE (1).

renovation *n.* *—See* RENEWAL (1).

renown *n.* Wide recognition for one's deeds ▸ celebrity, fame, famousness, notoriety, popularity, reputation, repute. *—See also* FAME.

renowned *adj.* *—See* FAMOUS.

rent[1] *v.* To engage the temporary use of something for a fee ▸ charter, hire, lease. *—See also* LEASE (1).

rent[2] *n.* A hole made by tearing ▸ rip, run, tear. [*Compare* CRACK.] *—See also* BREACH (2).

renunciation *n.* *—See* ABANDONMENT (1), DENIAL (1).

reoccupy *v.* *—See* RESUME.

reoccur *v.* To happen again or repeatedly ▸ iterate, reappear, recur, repeat. *—See also* RETURN (1).

reoccurrence *n.* *—See* REPETITION.

reopen *v.* *—See* CONTINUE.

reorder *v.* *—See* SHUFFLE.

rep *n.* *Informal* Public estimation of

Rep. ► *abbr.* 1. representative 2. republic 3. Republican

re·pair¹ ► *v.* **1.** To restore to sound condition after damage or injury; fix. **2.** To set right; remedy. **3.** To renew or revitalize. ► *n.* **1.** The work or act of repairing. **2.** General condition after use or repairing: *in good repair.* **—re·pair′a·ble** *adj.* **—re·pair′man** *n.* **—re·pair′wom′an** *n.*

re·pair² (rĭ-pâr′) ► *v.* To betake oneself; go.

rep·a·ra·ble (rĕp′ər-ə-bəl) ► *adj.* Possible to repair. **—rep′a·ra·bly** *adv.*

rep·a·ra·tion (rĕp′ə-rā′shən) ► *n.* **1.** The act or process of making amends. **2.** Something done or paid to make amends. **3. reparations** Compensation, esp. that required from a defeated nation as indemnity for war damages. **—re·par′a·tive** (rĭ-păr′ə-tĭv), **re·par′a·to′ry** (-tôr′ē) *adj.*

rep·ar·tee (rĕp′ər-tē′, -tā′, -är-) ► *n.* **1.** A swift, witty reply. **2.** Conversation marked by witty retorts.

re·past (rĭ-păst′) ► *n.* A meal or the food eaten or provided at a meal. ► *v.* To eat or feast.

re·pa·tri·ate (rē-pā′trē-āt′) ► *v.* **-at·ed, -at·ing.** To return (a person) to the country of birth, citizenship, or origin. ► *n.* (-ĭt, -āt′) One who has been repatriated. **—re·pa′tri·a′tion** *n.*

re·pay (rĭ-pā′) ► *v.* **1.** To pay back: *repaid a debt.* **2.** To give in return for. **—re·pay′a·ble** *adj.* **—re·pay′ment** *n.*

re·peal (rĭ-pēl′) ► *v.* To revoke or rescind, esp. by an official or formal act. **—re·peal′** *n.* **—re·peal′er** *n.*

re·peat (rĭ-pēt′, rē′pēt′) ► *v.* **1.** To say or do again. **2.** To tell to another. **3.** To manifest or express (oneself) in the same way or words. ► *n.* **1.** An act of repeating. **2.** Something repeated. **—re·peat′a·ble** *adj.* **—re·peat′er** *n.*

re·peat·ed (rĭ-pē′tĭd) ► *adj.* Said, done, or occurring again and again. **—re·peat′ed·ly** *adv.*

re·peat·ing decimal (rĭ-pē′tĭng) ► *n.* A decimal in which a pattern of one or more digits is repeated indefinitely.

re·pel (rĭ-pĕl′) ► *v.* **-pelled, -pel·ling.** **1.** To ward off or keep away: *repel insects.* **2.** To drive back: *repel an invasion.* **3.** To cause aversion or distaste in. **4.** To be incapable of absorbing or mixing with: *Oil repels water.* **5.** To present an opposing force to: *Electric charges of the same sign repel one another.*

re·pel·lent also **re·pel·lant** (rĭ-pĕl′ənt) ► *adj.* **1.** Serving or tending to repel. **2.** Repulsive. **3.** Resistant or impervious to a substance. ► *n.* **1.** A substance used to repel insects. **2.** A substance for making a surface resistant to something. **—re·pel′lence, re·pel′len·cy** *n.*

re·pent (rĭ-pĕnt′) ► *v.* **1.** To feel regret or self-reproach for what one has done or failed to do. **2.** To change for the better as a result of remorse or contrition for one's sins. **—re·pent′er** *n.*

re·pen·tance (rĭ-pĕn′təns) ► *n.* Remorse or contrition for past conduct or sin. **—re·pen′tant** *adj.* **—re·pen′tant·ly** *adv.*

re·per·cus·sion (rē′pər-kŭsh′ən, rĕp′ər-) ► *n.* **1.** An often indirect effect of an event or action. **2.** A reciprocal motion after impact. **3.** A reflection, esp. of sound. **—re′per·cus′sive** *adj.*

rep·er·toire (rĕp′ər-twär′) ► *n.* **1.** The stock of songs, plays, or other works that a player or company is prepared to perform. **2.** The range of skills, aptitudes, or accomplishments of a person or group.

rep·er·to·ry (rĕp′ər-tôr′ē) ► *n., pl.* **-ries.** **1.** A repertoire. **2.** A theater in which a resident company presents works from a specified repertoire, usu. in alternation. **—rep′er·to′ri·al** *adj.*

rep·e·tend (rĕp′ĭ-tĕnd′, rĕp′ĭ-tĕnd′) ► *n.* The digit or group of digits that repeats infinitely in a repeating decimal.

rep·e·ti·tion (rĕp′ĭ-tĭsh′ən) ► *n.* **1.** The act or an instance of repeating. **2.** Something repeated.

rep·e·ti·tious (rĕp′ĭ-tĭsh′əs) ► *adj.* Filled esp. with needless repetition. **—rep′e·ti′tious·ly** *adv.* **—rep′e·ti′tious·ness** *n.*

re·pet·i·tive (rĭ-pĕt′ĭ-tĭv) ► *adj.* Given to or marked by repetition. **—re·pet′i·tive·ly** *adv.* **—re·pet′i·tive·ness** *n.*

repetitive strain injury ► *n.* Damage to soft tissue, esp. tendons or nerves, caused by excessive repetition of certain movements.

re·pine (rĭ-pīn′) ► *v.* **-pined, -pin·ing.** To be discontented or low in spirits; fret. **—re·pin′er** *n.*

re·place (rĭ-plās′) ► *v.* **1.** To put back in place. **2.** To take the place of. **—re·place′a·ble** *adj.* **—re·place′ment** *n.* **—re·plac′er** *n.*

re·play (rē-plā′) ► *v.* To play (e.g., a game or recording) over again. **—re′play′** *n.*

re·plen·ish (rĭ-plĕn′ĭsh) ► *v.* To fill or make complete again. **—re·plen′ish·er** *n.* **—re·plen′ish·ment** *n.*

re·plete (rĭ-plēt′) ► *adj.* **1.** Abundantly supplied; abounding: *a report replete with errors.* **2.** Filled to satiation; gorged. **—re·ple′tion, re·plete′ness** *n.*

rep·li·ca (rĕp′lĭ-kə) ► *n.* A copy or close reproduction.

rep·li·cate (rĕp′lĭ-kāt′) ► *v.* **-cat·ed, -cat·ing.** **1.** To duplicate, copy, reproduce, or repeat. **2.** To fold over or bend back. **—rep′li·ca′tion** *n.*

re·ply (rĭ-plī′) ► *v.* **-plied, -ply·ing.** **1.** To say or give as an answer. **2.** To respond by an action or gesture. ► *n., pl.* **-plies.** A response; answer. **—re·pli′er** *n.*

THESAURUS

someone ► character, name, report, reputation, repute. [*Compare* IMAGE, PLACE.]

repair¹ *v.* *—See* CORRECT (1), FIX (1).

repair *n.* *—See* SHAPE.

repair² *v.* *—See* FREQUENT, RESORT.

repairs *n.* *—See* MAINTENANCE.

reparation *n.* The act of making amends ► atonement, expiation, penance, reconciliation. [*Compare* COMPENSATION, PURIFICATION.] *—See also* COMPENSATION, MAINTENANCE.

reparative *adj.* *—See* CORRECTIVE.

repartee *n.* *—See* ANSWER (1).

repay *v.* To give back, especially money ► refund, reimburse, restitute. [*Compare* COMPENSATE, RETURN.] *—See also* AVENGE, COMPENSATE, RETURN (3).

repayment *n.* A quantity of money that is returned ► refund, reimbursement. [*Compare* DEDUCTION, RETURN.] *—See also* COMPENSATION.

repeal *v.* *—See* LIFT (3).

repeal *n.* The act of reversing or annulling ► recall, rescindment, rescission, retraction, reversal, revocation. [*Compare* ABOLITION.]

repeat *v.* **1.** To state again ► iterate, recapitulate, reiterate, restate, retell, reutter. *Informal:* recap. [*Compare* SAY, TELL.] **2.** To do or perform an act again ► do over, duplicate, play over, redo, replay. [*Compare* COPY.] **3.** To happen again or repeatedly ► iterate, reappear, recur, reoccur. *—See also* ECHO, MIMIC.

repeat *n.* *—See* REPETITION.

repel *v.* To turn aside or drive away ► beat off, check, deflect, fend (off), fight off, keep off, parry, rebuff, repulse, resist, stave off, ward off, withstand. [*Compare* SUPPRESS.] *—See also* DISGUST, OFFEND (2).

repellence or **repellency** *n.* *—See* HATE (1).

repellent *adj.* *—See* OFFENSIVE (1), RESISTANT.

repent *v.* To feel or express sorrow for ► deplore, regret, rue, sorrow (over). [*Compare* FEEL, GRIEVE.]

repentance *n.* *—See* PENITENCE.

repentant *adj.* *—See* SORRY.

repercussion *n.* Repetition of sound via reflection from a surface ► echo, reverberation. *—See also* IMPACT.

repetition *n.* The act or process of repeating ► echo, iteration, reappearance, recurrence, reiteration, reoccurrence, repeat, restatement, return. [*Compare* REPRODUCTION.] *—See also* ECHO (1), MONOTONY.

repetitious *adj.* Characterized by repetition ► iterative, reiterative, repetitive. [*Compare* BORING, SUPERFLUOUS, WORDY.]

repetitive *adj.* **1.** Characterized by repetition ► iterative, reiterative, repetitious. [*Compare* BORING, SUPERFLUOUS, WORDY.] **2.** Happening or appearing consistently or repeatedly ► episodic, recurrent, regular, repeating. [*Compare* PERIODIC, PERVASIVE, THEMATIC.]

rephrase *v.* *—See* PARAPHRASE.

repine *v.* *—See* COMPLAIN.

replace *v.* **1.** To substitute for or fill the place of ► displace, supersede, supplant, surrogate. ***Idioms:*** fill someone's shoes, take over from, take the reins from. [*Compare* SUBSTITUTE.] *—See also* REINSTALL, RETURN (2).

replacement *n.* *—See* SUBSTITUTE.

replay *v.* To do or perform an act again ► do over, duplicate, play over, redo, repeat. [*Compare* COPY.]

replete *adj.* *—See* FULL (1), FULL (2).

repletion *n.* *—See* SATIATION.

replica *n.* *—See* COPY (1).

replicate *v.* *—See* COPY.

replication *n.* *—See* COPY (1).

reply *v.* *—See* ANSWER.

reply *n.* *—See* ANSWER (1).

re·port (rĭ-pôrt′) ▸ *n.* **1.** An account, esp. one presented formally and in detail. **2.** Common talk; rumor. **3.** Reputation: *a person of bad report.* **4.** An explosive noise. ▸ *v.* **1.** To make or present an account of. **2.** To relate or present: *report one's findings.* **3.** To make known, esp. to an authority: *reported the incident to the police.* **4.** To serve as a reporter. **5.** To present oneself: *report for duty.*

report card ▸ *n.* A periodic report of a student's progress.

re·port·ed·ly (rĭ-pôr′tĭd-lē) ▸ *adv.* By report; supposedly.

re·port·er (rĭ-pôr′tər) ▸ *n.* A writer or investigator of news stories. **—rep′or·to′ri·al** (rĕp′ər-tôr′ē-əl, rē′pər-) *adj.*

re·pose[1] (rĭ-pōz′) ▸ *n.* **1.** The act of resting or the state of being at rest. **2.** Calmness; tranquillity. ▸ *v.* **-posed, -pos·ing. 1.** To lie at rest; relax. **2.** To lie supported by something. **—re·pose′ful** *adj.* **—re·pose′ful·ly** *adv.*

re·pose[2] (rĭ-pōz′) ▸ *v.* **-posed, -pos·ing.** To put or place: *Reposed our hopes in a single man.*

re·pos·i·to·ry (rĭ-pŏz′ĭ-tôr′ē) ▸ *n., pl.* **-ries. 1.** A place where things may be put esp. for safekeeping. **2.** One possessing or entrusted with something.

re·pos·sess (rē′pə-zĕs′) ▸ *v.* To regain possession of (property). **—re′pos·ses′sion** *n.*

rep·re·hend (rĕp′rĭ-hĕnd′) ▸ *v.* To reprove or blame; censure. **—rep′re·hen′sion** *n.*

rep·re·hen·si·ble (rĕp′rĭ-hĕn′sə-bəl) ▸ *adj.* Deserving rebuke or censure. **—rep′re·hen′si·bil′i·ty** *n.* **—rep′re·hen′si·bly** *adv.*

rep·re·sent (rĕp′rĭ-zĕnt′) ▸ *v.* **1.** To stand for; symbolize. **2.** To depict; portray. **3.** To describe (a person or thing) as having a specified quality. **4.** To serve as the delegate, spokesperson, or agent for. **5.** To serve as an example of. **—rep′re·sent′a·ble** *adj.*

rep·re·sen·ta·tion (rĕp′rĭ-zĕn-tā′shən, -zən-) ▸ *n.* **1.** The act of representing or the state of being represented. **2.** Something that represents. **3.** A statement, as of facts or arguments.

rep·re·sen·ta·tion·al (rĕp′rĭ-zĕn-tā′shə-nəl, -zən-) ▸ *adj.* Of or relating to realistic graphic representation.

rep·re·sen·ta·tive (rĕp′rĭ-zĕn′tə-tĭv) ▸ *n.* **1.** A typical example, esp. of a class or group. **2.** A delegate or agent acting on behalf of another. **3a.** A member of a legislative body chosen by popular vote. **b.** A member of the US House of Representatives or of the lower house of a state legislature. ▸ *adj.* **1.** Of or based on political representation: *representative government.* **2.** Serving as a typical example. **—rep′re·sen′ta·tive·ly** *adv.* **—rep′re·sen′ta·tive·ness** *n.*

re·press (rĭ-prĕs′) ▸ *v.* **1.** To hold back: *repress a laugh.* **2.** To put down by force: *repress a rebellion.* **3.** *Psychol.* To exclude from the conscious mind. **—re·press′i·ble** *adj.* **—re·pres′sion** *n.* **—re·pres′sive** *adj.* **—re·pres′sive·ly** *adv.* **—re·pres′sor** *n.*

re·prieve (rĭ-prēv′) ▸ *v.* **-prieved, -priev·ing.** To postpone or cancel the punishment of. ▸ *n.* **1.** Postponement or cancellation of a punishment. **2.** Temporary relief, as from pain.

rep·ri·mand (rĕp′rə-mănd′) ▸ *v.* To reprove severely; admonish. ▸ *n.* A severe or formal rebuke.

re·print (rē′prĭnt′) ▸ *n.* **1.** A new or additional printing of a book. **2.** A printed excerpt; offprint. **—re·print′** *v.* **—re·print′er** *n.*

re·pri·sal (rĭ-prī′zəl) ▸ *n.* Retaliation for an injury with the intent of inflicting at least as much injury in return.

re·prise (rĭ-prēz′) ▸ *n.* **1.** *Mus.* A repetition of a theme or verse. **2.** A recurrence or resumption.

re·proach (rĭ-prōch′) ▸ *v.* To express disapproval or criticism. ▸ *n.* **1.** Blame; rebuke. **2.** Disgrace; shame. **—re·proach′a·ble** *adj.* **—re·proach′ful** *adj.* **—re·proach′ful·ly** *adv.*

rep·ro·bate (rĕp′rə-bāt′) ▸ *n.* A morally unprincipled person. **—rep′ro·bate′** *adj.* **—rep′ro·ba′tion** *n.*

re·pro·duce (rē′prə-do͞os′, -dyo͞os′) ▸ *v.* **-duced, -duc·ing. 1.** To produce a counterpart, image, or copy of. **2.** To produce offspring. **3.** To produce again or anew; re-create. **4.** To undergo copying: *graphics that reproduce well.* **—re′pro·duc′er** *n.* **—re′pro·duc′i·ble** *adj.* **—re′pro·duc′tion** (-dŭk′shən) *n.* **—re′pro·duc′tive** (-dŭk′tĭv) *adj.* **—re′pro·duc′tive·ly** *adv.*

re·proof (rĭ-pro͞of′) ▸ *n.* Censure; rebuke.

THESAURUS

report *n.* Public estimation of someone ▸ character, name, reputation, repute. *Informal:* rep. [*Compare* IMAGE, PLACE.] —*See also* CRACK (1), GOSSIP (1), NEWS, STORY (1).

report *v.* —*See* COMMUNICATE (1), DESCRIBE, INFORM (2).

repose *n.* —*See* CALM, REST[1] (2).

repose *v.* To take repose, as by sleeping or lying quietly ▸ curl up, lie (down), recline, rest[1], stretch (out). [*Compare* NAP, SLEEP.] —*See also* CONSIST, LIE[1] (1).

repository *n.* **1.** One in whom secrets are confided ▸ confessor, confidant, confidante, intimate. **2.** An object, such as a carton, can, or jar, in which material is held or carried ▸ container, holder, receptacle, vessel. [*Compare* PACKAGE.] —*See also* DEPOSITORY.

repossess *v.* —*See* RECOVER (1), RESUME.

repossession *n.* The act of getting back or regaining ▸ recoup, recovery, retrieval.

reprehend *v.* —*See* DEPLORE (1).

reprehensible *adj.* —*See* BLAMEWORTHY, DEPLORABLE, OUTRAGEOUS.

reprehension *n.* —*See* CRITICISM.

represent *v.* **1.** To serve as an example, image, or symbol of ▸ epitomize, exemplify, illustrate, personify, stand for, symbolize, typify. [*Compare* DESIGNATE, EMBODY, EQUAL, MEAN.] **2.** To present a lifelike image of ▸ characterize, delineate, depict, describe, draw, express, illustrate, image, limn, picture, portray, render, show. [*Compare* ACT, INTERPRET.] **3.** To serve as an official delegate of ▸ act (as *or* for), answer for, speak for, stand for. ***Idioms:*** be spokesperson (*or* representative) for, be the voice of. [*Compare* SUBSTITUTE.] —*See also* ACT (3), INTERPRET (2).

representation *n.* The act or process of describing in lifelike imagery ▸ characterization, delineation, depiction, description, drawing, expression, illustration, portrayal, rendering. —*See also* INTERPRETATION.

representational *adj.* —*See* SYMBOLIC.

representative *n.* One who represents the interests of another ▸ advocate, ambassador, consul, delegate, deputy, emissary, envoy, factor, lieutenant, minister, proxy, steward. [*Compare* AGENT, SPEAKER, SUBSTITUTE.] —*See also* EXAMPLE (1).

representative *adj.* —*See* DESCRIPTIVE, SYMBOLIC, TYPICAL.

repress *v.* To hold something requiring an outlet in check ▸ bottle up, burke, choke (back), gag, hold back, hold down, hold in, hush (up), keep back (in), muffle, muzzle, quench, smother, squelch, stifle, strangle, subdue, suppress, throttle. *Informal:* sit on (*or* upon). ***Idiom:*** hold (*or* keep) in check. [*Compare* CENSOR, HINDER, RESTRAIN, SUPPRESS.]

repression *n.* Forceful subjugation, as against an uprising ▸ clampdown, crackdown, lockdown, suppression. [*Compare* RESTRAINT.] —*See also* DOMINATION, OPPRESSION.

repressive *adj.* Serving to restrain forcefully ▸ inhibitive, inhibitory, restraining, restrictive, stifling, suppressive. [*Compare* ABSOLUTE, AUTHORITARIAN.]

reprieve *n.* Temporary immunity from penalties ▸ exemption, grace, immunity, respite. [*Compare* DELAY.]

reprimand *v.* —*See* CHASTISE.

reprimand *n.* —*See* REBUKE.

reprint *n.* —*See* COPY (2).

reprint *v.* —*See* COPY.

reprisal *n.* —*See* RETALIATION.

reproach *v.* To cause to feel embarrassment, dishonor, and often guilt ▸ brand, mortify, shame, stigmatize. ***Idioms:*** put to shame, put to the blush. [*Compare* BELITTLE, DENIGRATE, EMBARRASS, HUMBLE.] —*See also* CHASTISE.

reproach *n.* —*See* DISAPPROVAL, DISGRACE, REBUKE.

reproachable *adj.* —*See* DISGRACEFUL.

reproachful *adj.* —*See* CRITICAL (1).

reprobate *adj.* —*See* CONDEMNED, EVIL, WANTON (1).

reprobate *v.* —*See* DEPLORE (1), DISAPPROVE.

reprobate *n.* —*See* WANTON.

reprobation *n.* —*See* CRITICISM.

reproduce *v.* —*See* BREED, COPY.

reproduction *n.* The process by which an organism produces others of its kind ▸ breeding, generation, multiplication, procreation, proliferation, propagation, spawning. —*See also* COPY (1), ECHO (1).

reproductive *adj.* Of or relating to reproduction ▸ generative, procreant, procreative.

reproof *n.* —*See* DISAPPROVAL, REBUKE.

re·prove (rĭ-pro͞ov′) ▸ *v.* **-proved, -prov·ing.** **1.** To voice or convey disapproval of; rebuke. **2.** To find fault with. **—re·prov′ing·ly** *adv.*

rep·tile (rĕp′tīl′, -tĭl) ▸ *n.* Any of various cold-blooded, usu. egg-laying vertebrates, such as a snake, crocodile, or turtle, having scales or horny plates. **—rep·til′i·an** (-tĭl′ē-ən, -tĭl′yən) *adj. & n.*

re·pub·lic (rĭ-pŭb′lĭk) ▸ *n.* **1.** A government whose head of state is not a monarch and is usu. a president. **2.** A country governed by the elected representatives of its people.

re·pub·li·can (rĭ-pŭb′lĭ-kən) ▸ *adj.* **1.** Of or advocating a republic. **2. Republican** Of or belonging to the Republican Party. ▸ *n.* **1.** One who favors a republican form of government. **2. Republican** A member of the Republican Party. **—re·pub′li·can·ism** *n.*

Republican Party ▸ *n.* One of the two major US political parties.

re·pu·di·ate (rĭ-pyo͞o′dē-āt′) ▸ *v.* **-at·ed, -at·ing.** **1.** To reject the validity of. **2.** To refuse to recognize, acknowledge, or pay. **—re·pu′di·a′tion** *n.*

re·pug·nant (rĭ-pŭg′nənt) ▸ *adj.* **1.** Arousing disgust or aversion; repulsive. **2.** *Logic* Contradictory. **—re·pug′nance** *n.*

re·pulse (rĭ-pŭls′) ▸ *v.* **-pulsed, -puls·ing.** **1.** To drive back; repel. **2.** To reject with rudeness, coldness, or denial. **3.** *Informal* To cause repulsion in. ▸ *n.* **1.** The act of repulsing. **2.** Rejection; refusal.

re·pul·sion (rĭ-pŭl′shən) ▸ *n.* **1.** The act of repulsing. **2.** Extreme aversion.

re·pul·sive (rĭ-pŭl′sĭv) ▸ *adj.* **1.** Causing repugnance or disgust. **2.** Tending to repel or drive off. **—re·pul′sive·ly** *adv.* **—re·pul′sive·ness** *n.*

rep·u·ta·ble (rĕp′yə-tə-bəl) ▸ *adj.* Having a good reputation. **—rep′u·ta·bly** *adv.*

rep·u·ta·tion (rĕp′yə-tā′shən) ▸ *n.* **1.** The general estimation of a person or thing held by the public. **2.** The state of being held in high esteem.

re·pute (rĭ-pyo͞ot′) ▸ *v.* **-put·ed, -put·ing.** To consider; suppose. ▸ *n.* Reputation; esteem.

re·put·ed (rĭ-pyo͞o′tĭd) ▸ *adj.* Generally supposed. **—re·put′ed·ly** *adv.*

re·quest (rĭ-kwĕst′) ▸ *v.* **1.** To ask for. **2.** To ask (a person) to do something. ▸ *n.* **1.** The act of asking. **2.** Something asked for. ***—idiom:* on (** or **upon) request** When asked for: *References are available on request.*

req·ui·em (rĕk′wē-əm, rē′kwē-) ▸ *n.* **1. Requiem** *Rom. Cath. Ch.* **a.** A mass for a deceased person. **b.** A musical composition for such a mass. **2.** A hymn, composition, or service for the dead.

re·quire (rĭ-kwīr′) ▸ *v.* **-quired, -quir·ing.** **1.** To need. **2.** To insist upon; demand. **—re·quire′ment** *n.*

re·quired (rĭ-kwīrd′) ▸ *adj.* **1.** Needed; essential. **2.** Obligatory: *required reading.*

req·ui·site (rĕk′wĭ-zĭt) ▸ *adj.* Required; essential. ▸ *n.* A necessity.

req·ui·si·tion (rĕk′wĭ-zĭsh′ən) ▸ *n.* **1.** A formal request for something needed. **2.** The state of being needed or in use. ▸ *v.* To demand, as for military needs.

re·quite (rĭ-kwīt′) ▸ *v.* **-quit·ed, -quit·ing.** **1.** To make repayment or return for. **2.** To avenge. **—re·quit′a·ble** *adj.* **—re·quit′al** *n.* **—re·quit′er** *n.*

re·run (rē′rŭn′) ▸ *n.* A second or subsequent presentation of a movie or television program. **—re·run′** *v.*

re·scind (rĭ-sĭnd′) ▸ *v.* To repeal or annul. **—re·scind′a·ble** *adj.* **—re·scis′sion** (-sĭzh′ən) *n.*

res·cue (rĕs′kyo͞o) ▸ *v.* **-cued, -cu·ing.** To save, as from danger. **—res′cue** *n.* **—res′cu·er** *n.*

re·search (rĭ-sûrch′, rē′sûrch′) ▸ *n.* Careful investigation or study, esp. of a scholarly or scientific nature. **—re·search′** *v.* **—re·search′er** *n.*

re·sec·tion (rĭ-sĕk′shən) ▸ *n.* Surgical removal of part of an organ or structure.

re·sem·blance (rĭ-zĕm′bləns) ▸ *n.* A similarity, esp. in appearance.

re·sem·ble (rĭ-zĕm′bəl) ▸ *v.* **-bled, -bling.** To exhibit similarity or likeness to.

re·sent (rĭ-zĕnt′) ▸ *v.* To feel angry or bitter about. **—re·sent′ful** *adj.* **—re·sent′ful·ly** *adv.* **—re·sent′ment** *n.*

res·er·va·tion (rĕz′ər-vā′shən) ▸ *n.* **1.** The act of reserving. **2.** A limiting qualification or condition. **3.** A tract of public land set apart for a special purpose, esp. one for the use of a Native American people. **4.** An arrangement by which accommodations are secured in advance.

THESAURUS

reprove *v.* —*See* CHASTISE, CRITICIZE (1).

reptile *n.* —*See* CREEP (2).

repudiate *v.* To refuse to recognize or acknowledge ▸ deny, disacknowledge, disavow, disclaim, disown, reject, renounce. ***Idioms:*** turn one's back on, turn up one's nose at. [*Compare* DENY, DISBELIEVE, RETRACT.] —*See also* DISMISS (3).

repudiation *n.* —*See* DENIAL (1).

repugnance *n.* —*See* DISGUST, HATE (1).

repugnancy *n.* —*See* HATE (1).

repugnant *adj.* —*See* OFFENSIVE (1).

repulse *v.* —*See* DISGUST, OFFEND (2), REPEL.

repulsion *n.* —*See* HATE (1).

repulsive *adj.* —*See* OFFENSIVE (1), UNPALATABLE.

repulsiveness *n.* —*See* UGLINESS.

reputable *adj.* —*See* ADMIRABLE, FAMOUS.

reputation or **repute** *n.* Public estimation of someone ▸ character, name, report, repute. *Informal:* rep. [*Compare* IMAGE, PLACE.] —*See also* FAME, HONOR (2).

reputed *adj.* —*See* SUPPOSED.

request *v.* —*See* APPEAL (1).

requiem *n.* —*See* FUNERAL.

require *v.* **1.** To be without what is needed, required, or essential ▸ lack, need, want. [*Compare* DEMAND.] **2.** To oblige to do or not do by force of authority, propriety, or custom ▸ expect, oblige, obligate, suppose. [*Compare* MUST.] —*See also* DEMAND (1), DEMAND (2).

required *adj.* Imposed on one by authority, command, or convention ▸ compulsory, dictated, imperative, mandatory, necessary, obligatory, prescribed, requisite. —*See also* ESSENTIAL (1), OBLIGED (2).

requirement *n.* —*See* CONDITION (2), DEMAND (2), DUTY (1).

requisite *adj.* —*See* ESSENTIAL (1), REQUIRED.

requisite *n.* —*See* CONDITION (2).

requisition *n.* —*See* APPEAL, DEMAND (1).

requisition *v.* —*See* DEMAND (1).

requital *n.* —*See* COMPENSATION, RETALIATION.

requite *v.* To give or take mutually ▸ reciprocate, return. ***Idiom:*** respond in kind. —*See also* AVENGE, COMPENSATE, RETALIATE.

requited *adj.* —*See* MUTUAL.

rescind *v.* —*See* LIFT (3).

rescission *n.* —*See* REPEAL.

rescue *v.* To set free, as from danger or confinement ▸ bail out, deliver, reclaim, recover, redeem, salvage, save. ***Idioms:*** save by the bell, save someone's bacon (*or* neck), come to the rescue of. [*Compare* FREE, HELP.]

rescue *n.* Extrication from danger or confinement ▸ deliverance, delivery, emancipation, freeing, liberation, release, salvage, salvation, saving. [*Compare* FREEDOM.]

rescuer *n.* One who frees someone from danger or confinement ▸ angel, deliverer, liberator, lifesaver, redeemer, savior. [*Compare* GUARD, PATRON.]

research *n.* —*See* EXAMINATION (1).

research *v.* —*See* EXAMINE (1).

researcher *n.* —*See* INQUIRER.

resemblance *n.* —*See* LIKENESS (1).

resemble *v.* To be similar especially in appearance ▸ be like, look like, match, mimic, take after. *Chiefly Regional:* favor. ***Idioms:*** be a dead ringer for, be like as two peas in a pod, be the spitting (*or* spit and) image of. [*Compare* AGREE, APPEAR, EQUAL.]

resentful *adj.* Bitingly hostile ▸ acrimonious, bitter, embittered, hard, rancorous, virulent. [*Compare* ANGRY, HOSTILE.]

resentfulness *n.* —*See* RESENTMENT.

resentment *n.* The quality or state of feeling bitter ▸ acrimony, bitterness, embitterment, gall, rancor, rancorousness, resentfulness, virulence, virulency. [*Compare* ENMITY, HATE.] —*See also* ANGER, OFFENSE.

reservation *n.* Public land kept for a special purpose ▸ park, preserve, reserve, sanctuary. [*Compare* COMMON.] —*See also* DOUBT, PROVISION, QUALM.

re·serve (rĭ-zûrv′) ► *v.* **-served, -serv·ing.** **1.** To keep back, as for future use. **2.** To set apart for a particular person or use. **3.** To retain; defer: *reserve judgment.* ► *n.* **1.** Something kept back, as for future use. **2.** The condition of being reserved: *funds held in reserve.* **3.** Self-restraint; reticence. **4.** A reservation of public land. **5.** An amount of a resource known to exist in a particular location: *oil reserves.* **6.** often **reserves** The part of a country's armed forces not on active duty but subject to call in an emergency. **—re·serv′a·ble** *adj.*

re·served (rĭ-zûrvd′) ► *adj.* **1.** Set aside, as for a particular person or use. **2.** Marked by self-restraint and reticence. **—re·serv′ed·ly** (-zûr′vĭd-lē) *adv.* **—re·serv′ed·ness** *n.*

re·serv·ist (rĭ-zûr′vĭst) ► *n.* A member of a military reserve.

res·er·voir (rĕz′ər-vwär′, -vwôr′, -vôr′) ► *n.* **1.** A body of water stored for public use. **2.** A chamber for storing a fluid. **3.** A large or extra supply.

re·side (rĭ-zīd′) ► *v.* **-sid·ed, -sid·ing.** **1.** To live in a place; dwell. **2.** To be inherently present: *the power that resides in the electorate.* **—re·sid′er** *n.*

res·i·dence (rĕz′ĭ-dəns, -dĕns′) ► *n.* **1.** The place in which one lives. **2.** The act or a period of residing in a place.

res·i·den·cy (rĕz′ĭ-dən-sē, -dĕn′-) ► *n., pl.* **-cies.** A period of specialized clinical training for a physician.

res·i·dent (rĕz′ĭ-dənt, -dĕnt′) ► *n.* **1.** One who resides in a particular place. **2.** A physician serving a period of residency. **—res′i·dent** *adj.*

res·i·den·tial (rĕz′ĭ-dĕn′shəl) ► *adj.* **1.** Of or having residence. **2.** Of or limited to homes: *residential zoning.* **—res′i·den′tial·ly** *adv.*

re·sid·u·al (rĭ-zĭj′o͞o-əl) ► *adj.* Of or remaining as a residue. ► *n.* **1.** A residue; remainder. **2.** A payment made, as to a performer, for each rerun of a television show. **—re·sid′u·al·ly** *adv.*

res·i·due (rĕz′ĭ-do͞o′, -dyo͞o′) ► *n.* The remainder of something after removal of parts or a part.

re·sign (rĭ-zīn′) ► *v.* **1.** To submit (oneself) passively. **2.** To give up (a position); quit. **3.** To relinquish (a privilege, right, or claim).

res·ig·na·tion (rĕz′ĭg-nā′shən) ► *n.* **1.** The act of resigning. **2.** A formal statement that one is resigning. **3.** Acceptance; submission.

re·signed (rĭ-zīnd′) ► *adj.* Acquiescent; accepting. **—re·sign′ed·ly** (-zī′nĭd-lē) *adv.*

re·sil·ient (rĭ-zĭl′yənt) ► *adj.* **1.** Marked by the ability to recover readily, as from misfortune. **2.** Capable of returning to an original shape or position, as after having been compressed. **—re·sil′ience, re·sil′ien·cy** *n.* **—re·sil′ient·ly** *adv.*

res·in (rĕz′ĭn) ► *n.* **1.** A viscous substance of plant origin, such as rosin or amber, used in varnishes, adhesives, synthetic plastics, and pharmaceuticals. **2.** Any of various synthetic substances similar to natural resins, used in plastics. ► *v.* To treat with resin. **—res′in·ous** *adj.*

re·sist (rĭ-zĭst′) ► *v.* **1.** To strive or work against. **2.** To remain firm against; withstand. **—re·sist′er** *n.* **—re·sist′i·ble** *adj.*

re·sis·tance (rĭ-zĭs′təns) ► *n.* **1.** The act of resisting or the capacity to resist. **2.** A force that opposes or retards motion. **3.** *Elect.* The opposition of a body or substance to current passing through it. **—re·sis′tant** *adj.*

re·sis·tor (rĭ-zĭs′tər) ► *n.* A device used to provide resistance in an electric circuit.

res·o·lute (rĕz′ə-lo͞ot′, rĕz′ə-lo͞ot′) ► *adj.* Firm or determined; unwavering. **—res′o·lute′ly** *adv.* **—res′o·lute′ness** *n.*

res·o·lu·tion (rĕz′ə-lo͞o′shən) ► *n.* **1.** The state or quality of being resolute. **2.** A course of action determined or decided on. **3.** A formal statement of a decision, as by a legislature. **4.** An explanation, as of a problem; solution. **5.** The fineness of detail that can be distinguished in an image.

re·solve (rĭ-zŏlv′) ► *v.* **-solved, -solv·ing.** **1.** To make a firm decision about. **2.** To decide or express by formal vote. **3.** To separate (something) into constituent parts. **4.** To find a solution to. **5.** To dispel: *resolve a doubt.* ► *n.* **1.** Firmness of purpose; resolution. **2.** A determination or decision. **—re·solv′a·ble** *adj.*

res·o·nance (rĕz′ə-nəns) ► *n.* **1.** The quality or condition of being resonant. **2.** *Phys.* The increase in amplitude of oscillation of an electric or mechanical system exposed to a periodic force whose frequency is equal or very close to the natural frequency of the system. **3.** Intensification of sound, esp. of a musical tone, by sympathetic vibration.

res·o·nant (rĕz′ə-nənt) ► *adj.* **1a.** Strong and deep in tone; resounding. **b.** Continuing to sound; echoing: *resonant words.* **2.** Producing, exhibiting, or resulting from resonance. **—res′o·nant·ly** *adv.*

res·o·nate (rĕz′ə-nāt′) ► *v.* **-nat·ed, -nat·ing.** **1.** To exhibit or produce resonance. **2.** To resound.

res·o·na·tor (rĕz′ə-nā′tər) ► *n.* A hollow chamber designed to permit internal resonant oscillation of electromagnetic or acoustical waves of specific frequencies.

THESAURUS

reserve *v.* *—See* BOOK, HOLD (1).

reserve *n.* **1.** The keeping of one's thoughts and emotions to oneself ► constraint, control, guardedness, introversion, remoteness, reservedness, restraint, reticence, self-control, self-restraint, taciturnity, uncommunicativeness, unresponsiveness. [*Compare* BALANCE, INHOSPITALITY, SILENCE.] **2.** Public land kept for a special purpose ► park, preserve, reservation, sanctuary. [*Compare* COMMON.] *—See also* HOARD.

reserve *adj.* *—See* AUXILIARY (2).

reserved *adj.* Tending to keep one's thoughts and emotions to oneself ► constrained, controlled, guarded, inhibited, introverted, noncommittal, remote, restrained, self-controlled, self-restrained, unresponsive. *—See also* COOL, QUALIFIED, TACITURN.

reservoir *n.* *—See* HOARD.

resettle *v.* To leave one's native land and settle in another ► emigrate (from), immigrate (to), migrate, transmigrate. [*Compare* MOVE, SETTLE.]

reshape *v.* *—See* CONVERT.

reshuffle *v.* *—See* OVERHAUL.

reshuffling *n.* A thorough or drastic reorganization ► overhaul, reengineering, shakeup. *Informal:* housecleaning. [*Compare* RENEWAL, REVOLUTION.]

reside *v.* *—See* CONSIST, LIVE[1].

residence *n.* *—See* HOME (1).

resident *n.* *—See* INHABITANT.

residential *adj.* *—See* DOMESTIC (1).

residual *adj.* Being what remains, especially after a part has been removed ► extra, leftover, remaining, stray. ***Idiom:*** left behind. [*Compare* SUPERFLUOUS.]

residue *n.* *—See* BALANCE (4).

resign *v.* **1.** To bring oneself to accept ► reconcile. ***Idiom:*** get used to. **2.** To relinquish one's engagement in or occupation with ► demit, leave, quit, terminate. ***Idioms:*** hang it up, throw in the sponge, throw in the towel. [*Compare* BREAK.] *—See also* ABANDON (1).

resignation *n.* *—See* ABANDONMENT (1), PATIENCE.

resigned *adj.* *—See* PASSIVE, PATIENT.

resilience or **resiliency** *n.* The ability to recover quickly from depression or discouragement ► bounce, buoyancy, elasticity, flexibility, resiliency. *—See also* FLEXIBILITY (1).

resilient *adj.* *—See* FLEXIBLE (1).

resist *v.* To take a stand against ► buck, challenge, contest, dispute, oppose, traverse. *—See also* DISOBEY, OPPOSE, REPEL.

resistance *n.* **1.** The capacity to withstand ► immunity, imperviousness, insusceptibility, unsusceptibility. [*Compare* ENDURANCE, STABILITY.] **2.** A clandestine organization of freedom fighters in an oppressed land ► opposition, underground. *—See also* DEFIANCE (1), INDISPOSITION.

resistant *adj.* Having the capacity to withstand ► immune, impervious, insusceptible, proof, repellent, resisting, resistive, unsusceptible. [*Compare* DEFIANT, STABLE, STRONG, STUBBORN.] *—See also* INDISPOSED, OPPOSING.

resister *n.* *—See* OPPONENT.

resisting *adj.* *—See* RESISTANT.

resolute *adj.* *—See* FIRM[1] (3), INTENT.

resoluteness *n.* *—See* DECISION (2).

resolution *n.* *—See* ANSWER (2), DECISION (1), DECISION (2), RULING.

resolve *v.* *—See* ANALYZE, DECIDE, SETTLE (2), SOLVE (1).

resolve *n.* *—See* DECISION (2).

resonance *n.* *—See* TONE (2).

resonant *adj.* Having or producing a full, deep, or rich sound ► mellow, orotund, plangent, resounding, ringing, rotund, round, sonorous, vibrant. [*Compare* LOUD.]

re·sort (rĭ-zôrt′) ▸ *v.* **1.** To have recourse: *resorted to violence.* **2.** To go customarily or frequently. ▸ *n.* **1.** A place frequented by people for relaxation or recreation. **2.** Recourse. **3.** One turned to for aid or relief.

re·sound (rĭ-zound′) ▸ *v.* **1.** To be filled with sound; reverberate. **2.** To sound loudly; ring. **3.** To send back (sound). **—re·sound′ing** *adj.* **—re·sound′ing·ly** *adv.*

re·source (rē′sôrs′, -zôrs′) ▸ *n.* **1.** A source of support or help. **2.** often **resources** An available supply. **3.** The ability to deal with a situation effectively. **4.** often **resources** Means; assets. **5.** A natural resource.

re·source·ful (rĭ-sôrs′fəl, -zôrs′-) ▸ *adj.* Clever and imaginative, esp. in dealing with difficult situations. **—re·source′ful·ly** *adv.* **—re·source′ful·ness** *n.*

re·spect (rĭ-spĕkt′) ▸ *v.* **1.** To have regard for; esteem. **2.** To avoid violation of. **3.** To concern. ▸ *n.* **1.** High, often deferential regard; esteem. **2. respects** Expressions of consideration or deference: *pay one's respects.* **3.** A particular aspect, feature, or detail. **4.** Relation; reference. **—re·spect′er** *n.* **—re·spect′ful** *adj.* **—re·spect′ful·ly** *adv.* **—re·spect′ful·ness** *n.*

re·spect·a·ble (rĭ-spĕk′tə-bəl) ▸ *adj.* **1.** Meriting respect or esteem. **2.** Good or proper in behavior or conventional conduct. **3.** Of moderately good quality. **4.** Considerable in amount, number, or size: *a respectable sum of money.* **5.** Acceptable in appearance; presentable. **—re·spect′a·bil′i·ty** *n.* **—re·spect′a·bly** *adv.*

re·spec·tive (rĭ-spĕk′tĭv) ▸ *adj.* Individual; particular: *They took their respective seats.*

re·spec·tive·ly (rĭ-spĕk′tĭv-lē) ▸ *adv.* Singly in the order designated or mentioned.

res·pi·ra·tion (rĕs′pə-rā′shən) ▸ *n.* **1.** The act or process of inhaling and exhaling. **2.** The act or process by which a cell or organism without lungs exchanges gases with its environment. **—res′pi·ra·to′ry** (-pər-ə-tôr′ē, rĭ-spīr′ə-) *adj.*

res·pi·ra·tor (rĕs′pə-rā′tər) ▸ *n.* **1.** A device for artificial respiration. **2.** A screenlike device worn over the mouth and nose to protect the respiratory tract.

respiratory system ▸ *n.* The system of organs involved in the intake and exchange of oxygen and carbon dioxide between an organism and the environment.

re·spire (rĭ-spīr′) ▸ *v.* **-spired, -spir·ing. 1.** To breathe in and out. **2.** To engage in respiration.

res·pite (rĕs′pĭt) ▸ *n.* **1.** A short interval of rest or relief. **2.** A reprieve.

re·splen·dent (rĭ-splĕn′dənt) ▸ *adj.* Splendid or dazzling in appearance. **—re·splen′dence, re·splen′den·cy** *n.* **—re·splen′dent·ly** *adv.*

re·spond (rĭ-spŏnd′) ▸ *v.* **1.** To reply; answer. **2.** To act in return. **3.** To react positively or favorably.

re·spon·dent (rĭ-spŏn′dənt) ▸ *n.* One who responds, esp. a defendant in a divorce or equity case. **—re·spon′dent** *adj.*

re·sponse (rĭ-spŏns′) ▸ *n.* **1.** The act of responding. **2.** A reply; answer. **3.** A reaction to a specific stimulus.

re·spon·si·bil·i·ty (rĭ-spŏn′sə-bĭl′ĭ-tē) ▸ *n., pl.* **-ties. 1.** The state or fact of being responsible. **2.** Something for which one is responsible.

re·spon·si·ble (rĭ-spŏn′sə-bəl) ▸ *adj.* **1.** Liable to be required to give account for something. **2.** Involving personal accountability: *a responsible position.* **3.** Being a source or cause. **4.** Dependable; reliable. **—re·spon′si·ble·ness** *n.* **—re·spon′si·bly** *adv.*

re·spon·sive (rĭ-spŏn′sĭv) ▸ *adj.* **1.** Readily reacting. **2.** Containing responses: *responsive liturgy.* **—re·spon′sive·ly** *adv.* **—re·spon′sive·ness** *n.*

rest[1] (rĕst) ▸ *n.* **1.** Cessation or absence of work, motion, or activity. **2.** A period of inactivity, sleep, or quiet activity. **3.** *Mus.* **a.** An interval of silence having a specified length. **b.** The symbol indicating such a pause. **4.** A device used as a support: *a back rest.* ▸ *v.* **1.** To stop motion or work. **2.** To lie down, esp. to sleep. **3.** To be or cause to be temporarily quiet or inactive. **4a.** To be supported or based: *The ladder rests against the wall.* **b.** To place, lay, or lean. **5.** To be imposed as a responsibility: *The decision rests with you.* **6.** To depend or rely. **—rest′er** *n.*

rest[2] (rĕst) ▸ *n.* **1.** Something left over; remainder. **2.** That or those remaining: *The rest are arriving later.* ▸ *v.* To remain: *Rest assured that we'll be there.*

res·tau·rant (rĕs′tər-ənt, -tə-ränt′) ▸ *n.* A place where meals are served to the public.

res·tau·ra·teur (rĕs′tər-ə-tûr′) also **res·tau·ran·teur** (-tə-rän-tûr′) ▸ *n.* The manager or owner of a restaurant.

THESAURUS

resort *v.* To look to when in need ▸ apply, go, refer, repair, run, turn. *Idioms:* fall back on, fall back upon, have recourse to. *—See also* FREQUENT.

resort *n.* That to which one turns for help when in desperation ▸ recourse, refuge, resource. [*Compare* HELP, SUPPORT.] *—See also* EXERCISE (1), HAUNT, MAKESHIFT.

resound *v.* *—See* ECHO, RUMBLE (1).

resounding *adj.* *—See* RESONANT.

resource *n.* That to which one turns for help when in desperation ▸ recourse, refuge, resort. [*Compare* HELP, SUPPORT.]

resourceful *adj.* *—See* CLEVER (1), INVENTIVE.

resourcefulness *n.* *—See* INVENTION (1).

resources *n.* Things, such as money, property, or goods, having economic value ▸ assets, capital, fortune, means, wealth, wherewithal. [*Compare* FUNDS, MONEY.] *—See also* AMENITIES (1), CAPITAL (1).

respect *v.* *—See* VALUE.

respect *n.* The particular angle from which something is considered ▸ angle, aspect, facet, frame of reference, hand, light, phase, regard, side. *—See also* ESTEEM, HONOR (2).

respectability or **respectableness** *n.* *—See* DECENCY (2).

respectable *adj.* *—See* ACCEPTABLE (2), ADMIRABLE, APPROPRIATE, BIG, DECENT (7), HONEST.

respectful *adj.* *—See* ATTENTIVE, DEFERENTIAL.

respects *n.* *—See* REGARDS.

respiration *n.* *—See* BREATH.

respire *v.* *—See* BREATHE (1).

respite *n.* Temporary immunity from penalties ▸ exemption, grace, immunity, reprieve. [*Compare* DELAY.] *—See also* REST[1] (1).

resplendence *n.* *—See* GLITTER (2).

resplendent *adj.* *—See* GLORIOUS, ORNATE, SPARKLING.

respond *v.* To act in return to something, as a stimulus ▸ counter, react. *Idiom:* act in response. [*Compare* RETALIATE.] *—See also* ANSWER.

respondent *n.* A person against whom an action is brought ▸ accused, defendant.

response *n.* An action elicited by a stimulus ▸ reaction, retroaction. [*Compare* RETALIATION.] *—See also* ANSWER (1).

responsibility *n.* The state of being responsible ▸ accountability, amenability, amenableness, answerability, liability. [*Compare* BLAME, BURDEN[1].] *—See also* DUTY (1).

responsible *adj.* *—See* DEPENDABLE, LIABLE (1).

responsive *adj.* Easily approached ▸ accessible, approachable, welcoming. [*Compare* CONVENIENT.] *—See also* RECEPTIVE, SENSITIVE (1).

responsiveness *n.* *—See* OPENNESS.

rest[1] *n.* **1.** A pause or interval, as from work or duty ▸ break, breathing spell, downtime, hiatus, intermission, recess, respite, time-out. *Informal:* breather. [*Compare* ABEYANCE, GAP, STOP.] **2.** Freedom from labor, responsibility, or strain ▸ ease, leisure, relaxation, repose, time-out. *Informal:* R and R. [*Compare* CALM, INACTION, SLEEP.] *—See also* DEATH (1).

rest *v.* **1.** To take repose by ceasing work or other effort for an interval of time ▸ chill out, kick back, lounge, mellow out, relax, sit back, unbend, unwind. *Idioms:* lead (*or* live) the life of Riley, put one's feet up, take a load off one's feet, take it easy. **2.** To take repose, as by sleeping or lying quietly ▸ lay up, lie (down), recline, repose, stretch (out). [*Compare* NAP, SLEEP.] **3.** To be in a certain position; have a location ▸ be located, be situated, sit, stand. *—See also* BASE[1], CONSIST.

rest on or **upon** *v.* *—See* DEPEND ON (2).

rest[2] *n.* *—See* BALANCE (4).

restart *v.* *—See* CONTINUE.

restate *v.* *—See* PARAPHRASE, REPEAT (1).

restatement *n.* *—See* PARAPHRASE, REPETITION.

rest·ful (rĕst′fəl) ► *adj.* Affording, marked by, or suggesting rest; tranquil. **—rest′ful·ly** *adv.* **—rest′ful·ness** *n.*

rest home ► *n.* An establishment where the elderly or frail are housed and cared for.

res·ti·tu·tion (rĕs′tĭ-to͞o′shən, -tyo͞o′-) ► *n.* **1.** The act of restoring something to the rightful owner. **2.** The act of compensating for loss, damage, or injury.

res·tive (rĕs′tĭv) ► *adj.* **1.** Impatiently restless; uneasy. **2.** Difficult to control. **—res′tive·ly** *adv.* **—res′tive·ness** *n.*

rest·less (rĕst′lĭs) ► *adj.* **1.** Marked by a lack of quiet, repose, or rest. **2.** Not able to rest, relax, or be still. **3.** Never still: *the restless sea.* **—rest′less·ly** *adv.* **—rest′less·ness** *n.*

res·to·ra·tion (rĕs′tə-rā′shən) ► *n.* **1.** An act of restoring or the state of being restored. **2.** Something that has been restored.

re·stor·a·tive (rĭ-stôr′ə-tĭv) ► *adj.* Tending or having the power to restore. ► *n.* Something that restores health or strength.

re·store (rĭ-stôr′) ► *v.* **-stored, -stor·ing. 1.** To bring back into existence or use. **2.** To bring back to an original condition. **3.** To make restitution of; give back. **—re·stor′er** *n.*

re·strain (rĭ-strān′) ► *v.* **1.** To hold back. **2.** To deprive of freedom. **3.** To limit or restrict. **—re·strain′a·ble** *adj.* **—re·strain′er** *n.*

re·straint (rĭ-strānt′) ► *n.* **1.** The act of restraining or the condition of being restrained. **2.** Something that restrains. **3.** Control or repression of feelings.

re·strict (rĭ-strĭkt′) ► *v.* To keep or confine within limits. **—re·stric′tion** *n.*

re·stric·tive (rĭ-strĭk′tĭv) ► *adj.* **1.** Tending or serving to restrict. **2.** *Gram.* Of or being a subordinate clause that restricts the meaning of the noun, phrase, or clause it modifies, as the clause *who live in glass houses* in *People who live in glass houses shouldn't throw stones.* **—re·stric′tive·ly** *adv.* **—re·stric′tive·ness** *n.*

rest·room (rĕst′ro͞om′, -ro͝om′) ► *n.* A room with toilets and sinks for public use.

re·sult (rĭ-zŭlt′) ► *v.* **1.** To come about as a consequence. **2.** To end in a particular way. ► *n.* **1.** A consequence; outcome. **2.** *Math.* The quantity or expression obtained by calculation. **—re·sul′tant** *adj. & n.*

re·sume (rĭ-zo͞om′) ► *v.* **-sumed, -sum·ing. 1.** To begin or take up again after interruption. **2.** To take or occupy again. **—re·sum′a·ble** *adj.* **—re·sump′tion** (-zŭmp′shən) *n.*

re·su·mé or **re·su·me** or **ré·su·mé** (rĕz′o͝o-mā′, rĕz′o͝o-mā′) ► *n.* A summary of one's work experience and qualifications, often submitted when applying for a job.

re·sur·gent (rĭ-sûr′jənt) ► *adj.* **1.** Experiencing or bringing about renewal or revival. **2.** Sweeping or surging back again. **—re·sur′gence** *n.*

res·ur·rect (rĕz′ə-rĕkt′) ► *v.* **1.** To raise from the dead. **2.** To bring back, as into notice or use.

res·ur·rec·tion (rĕz′ə-rĕk′shən) ► *n.* **1.** A revival; rebirth. **2. Resurrection** *Christianity* **a.** The rising of Jesus on the third day after the Crucifixion. **b.** The rising of the dead at the Last Judgment.

re·sus·ci·tate (rĭ-sŭs′ĭ-tāt′) ► *v.* **-tat·ed, -tat·ing.** To return or bring back to consciousness or life. **—re·sus′ci·ta′tion** *n.* **—re·sus′ci·ta′tive** *adj.* **—re·sus′ci·ta′tor** *n.*

re·tail (rē′tāl′) ► *n.* The sale of goods directly to consumers. **—re′tail′** *adj. & adv. & v.* **—re′tail′er** *n.*

re·tain (rĭ-tān′) ► *v.* **1.** To maintain possession of. **2.** To keep or hold in a particular place, condition, or position. **3.** To keep in mind; remember. **4.** To hire (e.g., a lawyer) by paying a fee. **5.** To keep in one's service or pay. **—re·tain′a·ble** *adj.* **—re·tain′ment** *n.*

re·tain·er¹ (rĭ-tā′nər) ► *n.* **1.** One that retains. **2.** A servant or attendant, esp. in a noble or wealthy household.

re·tain·er² (rĭ-tā′nər) ► *n.* A fee paid to retain a professional adviser.

re·take (rē-tāk′) ► *v.* **1.** To take back or again. **2.** To recapture. **3.** To photograph, film, or record again. **—re′take′** *n.*

re·tal·i·ate (rĭ-tăl′ē-āt′) ► *v.* **-at·ed, -at·ing.** To return like for like; take revenge. **—re·tal′i·a′tion** *n.* **—re·tal′i·a′tive, re·tal′i·a·to′ry** (-ə-tôr′ē) *adj.*

THESAURUS

restful *adj.* —*See* COMFORTABLE.

restitute *v.* To give back, especially money ► reimburse, refund, repay. [*Compare* COMPENSATE, RETURN.] —*See also* RESTORE (2), RETURN (2).

restitution *n.* —*See* COMPENSATION.

restive *adj.* —*See* EDGY.

restiveness *n.* —*See* RESTLESSNESS.

restless *adj.* Affording no quiet, repose, or rest ► uneasy, unquiet, unsettled. [*Compare* WAKEFUL.] —*See also* BUSY (2), EDGY.

restlessness *n.* An uneasy or nervous state ► disquiet, disquietude, edginess, inquietude, jumpiness, nervousness, restiveness, skittishness, tenseness, twitchiness, unease, uneasiness, unrest. [*Compare* AGITATION, ANXIETY, EXCITEMENT.]

restoration *n.* A return to former prosperity or status ► comeback, reestablishment, renewal. —*See also* RENEWAL (1), REVIVAL (1).

restorative *adj.* —*See* CURATIVE, INVIGORATING.

restorative *n.* —*See* CURE, TONIC.

restore *v.* **1.** To bring back into existence or use ► reestablish, reinstate, reintroduce, renew, return, revive. **2.** To bring back to a previous normal condition ► rebuild, reclaim, recondition, reconstruct, rehabilitate, reinstate, rejuvenate, renovate, restitute. —*See also* REFRESH, REINSTALL, RENEW (1), RETURN (2), REVIVE (2).

restrain *v.* To control, restrict, or arrest ► bit, bottle (up), brake, bridle, check, constrain, curb, harness, hold, hold back, hold down, hold in, inhibit, keep, keep back, pull in, rein (back *or* in *or* up). ***Idioms:*** hold in leash, keep in check, keep under control, keep within bounds, put a lid on. [*Compare* HINDER, LIMIT, REPRESS, STOP.]

restrained *adj.* —*See* CONSERVATIVE (2), MODEST (1), RESERVED, RESTRICTED.

restraint *n.* Something that limits or holds back ► check, circumscription, constraint, control, cramp, curb, deterrent, drag, inhibition, limit, limitation, restriction, stay, stricture. —*See also* BOND (1), BRAKE, MODESTY (2), RESERVE (1), RESTRICTION.

restrict *v.* —*See* DETERMINE, LIMIT.

restricted *adj.* Kept within certain limits ► bridled, checked, circumscribed, confined, controlled, held back, limited, regulated, reined in, restrained. [*Compare* LOCAL.] —*See also* CONFIDENTIAL (3), QUALIFIED.

restriction *n.* The act of limiting or condition of being limited ► circumscription, confinement, constraint, limitation, restraint, stranglehold, throttlehold. [*Compare* PROVISION.] —*See also* RESTRAINT.

restrictive *adj.* —*See* REPRESSIVE, TIGHT (4).

restyle *v.* —*See* REVISE.

result *v.* To occur as a consequence ► attend, ensue, follow. [*Compare* STEM.]

result in *v.* —*See* CAUSE.

result *n.* —*See* ANSWER (2), DISCOVERY, EFFECT (1).

resultant *n.* —*See* EFFECT (1).

resume *v.* To occupy or take again ► reassume, re-claim, reoccupy, repossess, retake, take back. —*See also* CONTINUE.

resumé *v.* —*See* HISTORY (2).

resumption *n.* A continuing after interruption ► continuation, renewal, resurgence, revival.

resurgence *n.* A continuing after interruption ► continuation, renewal, resumption, revival. —*See also* REVIVAL (1).

resurrect *v.* —*See* REVIVE (1).

resurrection *n.* —*See* REVIVAL (1).

resuscitate *v.* —*See* REVIVE (1), REVIVE (2).

resuscitation *n.* —*See* REVIVAL (1).

retail *v.* —*See* SELL.

retailer *n.* —*See* SELLER.

retain *v.* —*See* EMPLOY (1), HOLD (1), KEEP (5), REMEMBER (1).

retained *adj.* —*See* EMPLOYED.

retake *v.* —*See* RESUME.

retaliate *v.* To return like for like, especially to return an unfriendly or hostile action with a similar one ► counter, counterattack, hit back, reciprocate, requite, retort, strike back. [*Compare* AVENGE, EXCHANGE.]

retaliation *n.* The act of retaliating ► counteraction, counterattack, counterblow, reciprocation, reprisal, requital, retribution, revenge, tit for tat, vengeance. ***Idioms:*** an eye for an eye, a tooth for a tooth, like for like, measure for measure.

re·tard (rĭ-tärd′) ▸ *v.* To cause to move or develop slowly; delay or impede.

re·tar·dant (rĭ-tär′dnt) ▸ *adj.* Acting or tending to retard. **—re·tar′dant** *n.*

re·tar·da·tion (rē′tär-dā′shən) ▸ *n.* **1.** The act or process of delaying or holding back. **2.** The extent to which something is held back or delayed. **3.** *Often Offensive* Impaired mental development.

re·tard·ed (rĭ-tär′dĭd) ▸ *adj.* **1.** *Often Offensive* Affected with impaired mental development. **2.** Delayed.

retch (rĕch) ▸ *v.* To vomit or try to vomit. **—retch** *n.*

re·ten·tion (rĭ-tĕn′shən) ▸ *n.* **1.** The act of retaining or the state of being retained. **2.** Capacity or power of retaining. **—re·ten′tive** *adj.* **—re·ten′tive·ness** *n.*

ret·i·cent (rĕt′ĭ-sənt) ▸ *adj.* **1.** Inclined to keep one's personal affairs to oneself. **2.** Restrained or reserved in style. **3.** Reluctant; unwilling. **—ret′i·cence** *n.* **—ret′i·cent·ly** *adv.*

ret·i·na (rĕt′n-ə) ▸ *n., pl.* **-nas** or **-nae** (rĕt′n-ē′). A multilayered, light-sensitive membrane lining the inner eyeball and connected by the optic nerve to the brain. **—ret′i·nal** *adj.*

ret·i·nue (rĕt′n-o͞o′, -yo͞o′) ▸ *n.* The attendants accompanying a high-ranking person.

re·tire (rĭ-tīr′) ▸ *v.* **-tired, -tir·ing. 1.** To withdraw, as for rest or seclusion. **2.** To go to bed. **3.** To withdraw from business or public life. **4.** To take out of use or circulation. **5.** *Baseball* To put out (a batter). **—re·tire′ment** *n.*

re·tired (rĭ-tīrd′) ▸ *adj.* **1.** Withdrawn from business or public life. **2.** Withdrawn; secluded.

re·tir·ee (rĭ-tīr′ē′) ▸ *n.* One who has retired from active working life.

re·tir·ing (rĭ-tīr′ĭng) ▸ *adj.* Shy and reserved; modest. **—re·tir′ing·ness** *n.*

re·tool (rē-to͞ol′) ▸ *v.* **1.** To provide (e.g., a factory) with new machinery and tools. **2.** To revise and reorganize.

re·tort[1] (rĭ-tôrt′) ▸ *v.* **1.** To reply or answer, esp. in a quick, caustic, or witty manner. **2.** To return in kind; pay back. ▸ *n.* A quick, witty reply.

re·tort[2] (rĭ-tôrt′, rē′tôrt′) ▸ *n.* A closed laboratory vessel with an outlet tube, used for distillation or decomposition by heat.

re·touch (rē-tŭch′) ▸ *v.* **1.** To add new details or touches to. **2.** To improve or change (a photograph) as by removing flaws. **—re′touch′** *n.*

re·trace (rē-trās′) ▸ *v.* To trace again or back. **—re·trace′a·ble** *adj.*

re·tract (rĭ-trăkt′) ▸ *v.* **1.** To take back. **2.** To draw back or in. **—re·tract′a·ble, re·tract′i·ble** *adj.* **—re′trac′tion** *n.*

re·trac·tile (rĭ-trăk′tĭl, -tīl′) ▸ *adj.* That can be drawn back or in.

re·tread (rē-trĕd′) ▸ *v.* To fit (a worn tire) with a new tread. ▸ *n.* (rē′trĕd′) A tire that has been retreaded.

re·treat (rĭ-trēt′) ▸ *n.* **1.** The act or process of withdrawing, esp. from difficulty or danger. **2.** A place affording peace, privacy, or security. **3.** A period of retirement or solitude, esp. for prayer or meditation. **4a.** Withdrawal of a military force from an enemy attack. **b.** The signal for such withdrawal. **c.** A bugle call or drumbeat signaling the lowering of the flag at sunset. ▸ *v.* To fall or draw back; withdraw.

re·trench (rĭ-trĕnch′) ▸ *v.* **1.** To cut down; reduce. **2.** To curtail expenses; economize. **—re·trench′ment** *n.*

ret·ri·bu·tion (rĕt′rə-byo͞o′shən) ▸ *n.* Something given or demanded in repayment, esp. punishment. **—re·trib′u·tive** (rĭ-trĭb′yə-tĭv), **re·trib′u·to′ry** (-tôr′ē) *adj.*

re·trieve (rĭ-trēv′) ▸ *v.* **-trieved, -triev·ing. 1.** To get or bring back; regain. **2.** To find and carry back; fetch. **—re·triev′a·ble** *adj.* **—re·triev′al** *n.*

re·triev·er (rĭ-trē′vər) ▸ *n.* One that retrieves, esp. any of several breeds of dog developed and trained to retrieve game.

ret·ro (rĕt′rō) ▸ *adj.* **1.** Retroactive. **2.** Involving or reminiscent of things past.

retro– ▸ *pref.* Backward; back: *retroactive.*

ret·ro·ac·tive (rĕt′rō-ăk′tĭv) ▸ *adj.* Applying to a period before enactment. **—ret′ro·ac′tive·ly** *adv.*

ret·ro·fire (rĕt′rō-fīr′) ▸ *v.* To fire (a retrorocket).

ret·ro·fit (rĕt′rō-fĭt′) ▸ *v.* To provide with parts or equipment unavailable at the time of original manufacture. **—ret′ro·fit′** *n.*

ret·ro·grade (rĕt′rə-grād′) ▸ *adj.* **1.** Moving or tending backward. **2.** Reverting to an earlier or inferior condition. ▸ *v.* **-grad·ed, -grad·ing. 1.** To move backward. **2.** To deteriorate; degenerate.

ret·ro·gress (rĕt′rə-grĕs′, rĕt′rə-grĕs′) ▸ *v.* **1.** To return to an earlier, inferior, or less complex condition. **2.** To go or move backward. **—ret′ro·gres′sion** *n.* **—ret′ro·gres′sive** *adj.* **—re′tro·gres′sive·ly** *adv.*

ret·ro·rock·et (rĕt′rō-rŏk′ĭt) ▸ *n.* A rocket used to retard, arrest, or reverse motion.

ret·ro·spect (rĕt′rə-spĕkt′) ▸ *n.* A review or contemplation of things in the past. **—ret′ro·spec′tion** *n.* **—ret′ro·spec′tive** *n. & adj.*

ret·ro·vi·rus (rĕt′rō-vī′rəs, rĕt′rə-vī′-) ▸ *n.* A virus, such as

THESAURUS

retard *v.* —*See* DELAY (1), HINDER.

retardation *n.* —*See* DELAY (2).

retch *v.* —*See* VOMIT.

retell *v.* —*See* REPEAT (1).

retention *n.* The act of employing for wages ▸ employment, engagement, hire, hiring. —*See also* MEMORY (1).

retentive *adj.* —*See* ABSORBENT.

rethink *v.* —*See* RECONSIDER.

reticence *n.* Reserve in speech, behavior, or dress ▸ demureness, diffidence, modesty, self-effacement. —*See also* RESERVE (1).

reticent *adj.* —*See* COOL, TACITURN.

retinue *n.* A group of attendants or followers ▸ entourage, following, suite, train. [*Compare* CIRCLE, FOLLOWING, PUBLIC.]

retire *v.* **1.** To go to bed ▸ bed (down). *Informal:* turn in. *Slang:* crash, flop. *Idioms:* call it a night, go beddy-bye (*or* night-night), hit the hay (*or* sack). [*Compare* SLEEP.] **2.** To withdraw or remove from business or active life ▸ pension (off), step down, superannuate. *Idioms:* call it quits, hang up one's spurs, put out to pasture, turn in one's badge. [*Compare* DISMISS, QUIT.] —*See also* GO (1), RETREAT.

retirement *n.* —*See* DEPARTURE, RETREAT, SECLUSION, SOLITUDE.

retiring *adj.* —*See* SHY[1].

retiringness *n.* —*See* SHYNESS.

retort *v.* **retort** —*See* ANSWER, RETALIATE.

retort *n.* —*See* ANSWER (1).

retouch *v.* To improve by making minor changes or additions ▸ polish, remodel, touch up. [*Compare* FIX, RENEW.]

retract *v.* **1.** To disavow something previously written or said irrevocably and usually formally ▸ abjure, countermand, forswear, recall, recant, take back, unsay, withdraw. [*Compare* LIFT.] **2.** To pull back in ▸ draw in, withdraw. —*See also* RECEDE.

retraction *n.* A formal statement of disavowal ▸ abjuration, countermand, palinode, recantation, retractation, withdrawal. —*See also* REPEAL.

retreat *n.* The moving back of a military force in the face of enemy attack or after a defeat ▸ evacuation, fallback, pullback, pullout, removal, retirement, withdrawal. [*Compare* ESCAPE.] —*See also* COVER (1), SOLITUDE.

retreat *v.* To move back in the face of enemy attack or after a defeat ▸ draw back, evacuate, fall back, pull back, pull out, remove, retire, turn back, withdraw. *Idioms:* beat a retreat, give ground (*or* way). [*Compare* ESCAPE.] —*See also* BACK (1), RECEDE, RENEGE.

retribution *n.* —*See* PUNISHMENT, RETALIATION.

retrieval *n.* The act of getting back or regaining ▸ recoup, recovery, repossession.

retrieve *v.* —*See* RECOVER (1), REMEMBER (1), REVIVE (1).

retroaction *n.* An action elicited by a stimulus ▸ reaction, response. [*Compare* RETALIATION.]

retrocede *v.* —*See* BACK (1), RECEDE.

retrogradation *n.* —*See* DETERIORATION (1), RELAPSE.

retrograde *adj.* —*See* BACKWARD (3).

retrograde *v.* —*See* BACK (1), DETERIORATE, RECEDE.

retrogress *v.* —*See* BACK (1), RECEDE, RELAPSE.

retrogression *n.* —*See* RELAPSE.

retrogressive *adj.* —*See* BACKWARD (3).

retrospective *n.* —*See* EXHIBITION.

the one causing AIDS, that contains RNA and an enzyme that can create DNA using RNA as a template.

re·turn (rĭ-tûrn′) ▸ *v.* **1.** To go or come back, as to an earlier condition or place. **2.** To answer or respond. **3.** To send, put, or carry back. **4.** To give in reciprocation. **5.** To yield (profit or interest). **6.** *Law* To deliver (e.g., a verdict) to a court of law. **7.** To reelect to an office. ▸ *n.* **1.** The act of returning. **2.** Something returned. **3.** A periodic recurrence. **4.** Something exchanged for that received; repayment. **5.** A reply; response. **6.** A profit or yield. **7.** An official report: *a tax return.* ▸ *adj.* **1.** Of or bringing about a return. **2.** Given, sent, or done in reciprocation: *return mail.* **—re·turn′a·ble** *adj. & n.* **—re·turn′er** *n.*

re·turn·ee (rĭ-tûr′nē′) ▸ *n.* One who returns, as from military duty overseas.

re·un·ion (rē-yo͞on′yən) ▸ *n.* **1.** The act of reuniting or the state of being reunited. **2.** A gathering of the members of a group who have been separated.

Ré·un·ion (rē-yo͞on′yən, rā-ü-nyôɴ′) ▸ An island of France in the W Indian Ocean SW of Mauritius.

rev (rĕv) *Informal* ▸ *n.* A revolution, as of a motor. ▸ *v.* **revved, rev·ving. 1.** To increase the speed of (e.g., a motor). **2.** To make livelier or more productive.

re·vamp (rē-vămp′) ▸ *v.* To make over; revise. **—re·vamp′** *n.*

re·veal (rĭ-vēl′) ▸ *v.* **1.** To make known. **2.** To bring to view; show.

rev·eil·le (rĕv′ə-lē) ▸ *n.* A signal, as on a bugle, given in the morning to awaken soldiers.

rev·el (rĕv′əl) ▸ *v.* **-eled, -el·ing** also **-elled, -el·ling. 1.** To take great pleasure or delight. **2.** To engage boisterous festivities. ▸ *n.* A boisterous festivity or celebration. **—rev′el·er, rev′el·ler** *n.* **—rev′el·ry** *n.*

rev·e·la·tion (rĕv′ə-lā′shən) ▸ *n.* **1a.** An act of revealing. **b.** Something that is revealed, esp. a dramatic disclosure. **2. Revelation** See **Bible** table in Appendix. **—rev′e·la·to′ry** (-lə-tôr′ē) *adj.*

re·venge (rĭ-vĕnj′) ▸ *v.* **-venged, -veng·ing.** To inflict punishment in return for (injury or insult); avenge. ▸ *n.* **1.** The act of revenging. **2.** A desire for revenge. **3.** An opportunity to retaliate or get even. **—re·venge′ful** *adj.* **—re·veng′er** *n.*

rev·e·nue (rĕv′ə-no͞o, -nyo͞o) ▸ *n.* **1.** The income of a government. **2.** Yield from property or investment.

re·ver·ber·ate (rĭ-vûr′bə-rāt′) ▸ *v.* **-at·ed, -at·ing.** To echo repeatedly; resound. **—re·ver′ber·a′tion** *n.*

re·vere (rĭ-vîr′) ▸ *v.* **-vered, -ver·ing.** To regard with deference and devotion.

Revere, Paul (1735–1818) ▸ Amer. Revolutionary hero.

rev·er·ence (rĕv′ər-əns) ▸ *n.* **1.** Profound awe and respect. **2.** An act of respect, esp. a bow or curtsy. **3. Reverence** Used as a form of address for certain members of the Christian clergy. ▸ *v.* **-enced, -enc·ing.** To consider or treat with reverence.

rev·er·end (rĕv′ər-ənd) ▸ *adj.* **1.** Deserving reverence. **2. Reverend** A title of respect for certain Christian clerics. ▸ *n. Informal* A cleric or minister.

rev·er·ent (rĕv′ər-ənt) ▸ *adj.* Feeling or expressing reverence. **—rev′er·ent·ly** *adv.*

rev·er·en·tial (rĕv′ə-rĕn′shəl) ▸ *adj.* **1.** Reverent. **2.** Inspiring reverence.

rev·er·ie (rĕv′ə-rē) ▸ *n.* **1.** A state of abstracted musing. **2.** A daydream.

re·ver·sal (rĭ-vûr′səl) ▸ *n.* **1.** The act or an instance of reversing. **2.** A usu. adverse change in fortune.

re·verse (rĭ-vûrs′) ▸ *adj.* **1.** Turned backward in position, direction, or order. **2.** Moving, acting, or organized in a manner contrary to the usual. **3.** Causing backward movement: *a reverse gear.* ▸ *n.* **1.** The opposite or contrary. **2.** The back or rear part. **3.** A change to an opposite position, condition, or direction esp. for the worse. **4.** A mechanism, such as a gear in a motor vehicle, used to reverse movement. ▸ *v.* **-versed, -vers·ing. 1.** To turn around to the opposite direction or position. **2.** To exchange the positions of; transpose. **3.** *Law* To revoke or annul. **4.** To turn or move in the opposite direction. **5.** To reverse the action of an engine. **—re·vers′er** *n.* **—re·vers′i·ble** *adj. & n.*

THESAURUS

return *v.* **1.** To come back to a former condition or place ▸ come back, go back, recrudesce, recur, reoccur, revert, revisit, turn back. [*Compare* RELAPSE.] **2.** To send, put, or carry back to a former location ▸ give back, replace, restitute, restore, take back. [*Compare* REFUND.] **3.** To make as income or profit ▸ bring in, clear, draw, earn, gain, gross, net, pay, produce, realize, reap, repay, yield. *Informal:* pull in, rake in. [*Compare* EARN.] **4.** To bring back into existence or use ▸ reestablish, reinstate, reintroduce, renew, restore, revive. [*Compare* RESTORE.] **5.** To give or take mutually ▸ reciprocate, requite. *Idiom:* respond in kind. [*Compare* EXCHANGE, RESPOND.] **6.** To deliver an indictment or verdict, for example ▸ hand down, render. *—See also* ANSWER, REINSTALL.

return *n.* Something earned, won, or otherwise acquired ▸ earnings, gain, profit. [*Compare* INCREASE.] *—See also* ANSWER (1), REPETITION.

reunite *v.* To reestablish friendship between ▸ conciliate, make up, reconcile. [*Compare* PACIFY.]

reutter *v.* *—See* REPEAT (1).

revamp *v.* *—See* FIX (1), RENEW (1), REVISE.

revampment *n.* *—See* RENEWAL (1).

reveal *v.* To make visible or known ▸ bare, disclose, display, expose, show, unclothe, uncover, unmask, unveil. *Idioms:* bring to light (*or* view), lay open (*or* bare), make plain (*or* public). [*Compare* ANNOUNCE, DISPLAY.] *—See also* BETRAY (2), COMMUNICATE (1), SHOW (1).

revel *v.* To behave riotously ▸ carouse, frolic, party, riot, roister, romp. *Informal:* hell (around). *Idioms:* blow off steam, cut loose, kick over the traces, kick up one's heels, let go, let loose, make merry, make whoopee, paint the town red, raise Cain (*or* the devil *or* hell), whoop it up. *—See also* CELEBRATE (2), LUXURIATE.

revel *n.* *—See* CELEBRATION (1).

revelation *n.* Something disclosed, especially something not previously known or realized ▸ apocalypse, disclosure, divulgence, exposé, exposure. *Informal:* eye opener. [*Compare* ACKNOWLEDGMENT, NEWS.]

revelry *n.* *—See* CELEBRATION (3), MERRIMENT (2).

revels *n.* *—See* CELEBRATION (1), MERRIMENT (2).

revenant *n.* *—See* GHOST.

revenge *n.* The quality or condition of being vindictive ▸ spite, spitefulness, vengefulness, vindictiveness. [*Compare* RESENTMENT.] *—See also* RETALIATION.

revengeful *adj.* *—See* VINDICTIVE.

reverberate *v.* *—See* ECHO.

reverberation *n.* Repetition of sound via reflection from a surface ▸ echo, repercussion. *—See also* BLAST (1), IMPACT.

revere *v.* To regard with deep respect, deference, and esteem ▸ adore, hallow, idolize, reverence, venerate, worship. [*Compare* DISTINGUISH, PRAISE, HONOR, VALUE.]

reverence *n.* The act of adoring, especially reverently ▸ adoration, idolization, veneration, worship. [*Compare* DEVOTION, HONOR, PRAISE.] *—See also* DEVOTION, HONOR (1).

reverence *v.* *—See* REVERE.

reverend *n.* *—See* CLERIC.

reverent or **reverential** *adj.* Feeling or showing reverence ▸ devout, pious, venerational, worshipful. [*Compare* DEFERENTIAL.]

reverie *n.* *—See* DREAM (1), TRANCE.

reversal *n.* **1.** The act of changing or being changed from one position, direction, or course to the opposite ▸ about-face, change of heart, flip-flop, inversion, transposition, turnabout, turnaround, U-turn. **2.** A change from better to worse ▸ backset, reverse, setback. [*Compare* MISFORTUNE, RELAPSE.] *—See also* ACCIDENT, REPEAL.

reverse *adj.* *—See* OPPOSITE.

reverse *n.* A change from better to worse ▸ backset, reversal, setback. [*Compare* MISFORTUNE, RELAPSE.] *—See also* OPPOSITE.

reverse *v.* **1.** To change to the opposite position, direction, or course ▸ flip-flop, invert, transpose, turn (about *or* around *or* over *or* round). **2.** To turn sharply around ▸ about-face, double (back). *Idiom:* turn on one's heels. *—See also* BACK (1), LIFT (3).

reverse osmosis ▸ *n.* A method of purifying water with a membrane across which salts or impurities cannot pass.
re·vert (rĭ-vûrt′) ▸ *v.* **1.** To return to a former condition, practice, or belief. **2.** *Law* To return to the former owner or to the rightful heirs. **—re·ver′sion** *n.* **—re·ver′sion·ar·y** *adj.*
re·view (rĭ-vyo͞o′) ▸ *v.* **1.** To look over, study, or examine again. **2.** To look back on. **3.** To examine critically or for correction. **4.** To write or give a critical report on. **5.** *Law* To reexamine judicially, esp. in a higher court. **6.** To subject to a formal inspection. ▸ *n.* **1.** A reexamination or reconsideration. **2.** A restudying of subject matter. **3.** An inspection or examination for evaluation. **4a.** A critical estimate of a work or performance. **b.** A periodical devoted esp. to critical articles and essays. **5.** A formal military inspection. **6.** *Law* A judicial reexamination, esp. by a higher court.
re·view·er (rĭ-vyo͞o′ər) ▸ *n.* One who reviews, esp. one who writes critical reviews.
re·vile (rĭ-vīl′) ▸ *v.* **-viled, -vil·ing.** To assail with or use abusive language. **—re·vile′ment** *n.* **—re·vil′er** *n.*
re·vise (rĭ-vīz′) ▸ *v.* **-vised, -vis·ing. 1.** To prepare a new edition of (a text). **2.** To reconsider and modify. **—re·vis′er, re·vi′sor** *n.* **—re·vi′sion** (-vĭzh′ən) *n.*
re·vi·sion·ism (rĭ-vĭzh′ə-nĭz′əm) ▸ *n.* Advocacy of the revision of an accepted, usu. long-standing view, theory, or doctrine. **—re·vi′sion·ist** *adj. & n.*
re·viv·al (rĭ-vī′vəl) ▸ *n.* **1.** The act of reviving or the state of being revived. **2.** A new presentation, as of a play. **3.** A meeting or series of meetings for reawakening religious faith.
re·vive (rĭ-vīv′) ▸ *v.* **-vived, -viv·ing. 1.** To return or bring back to life or consciousness. **2.** To impart new health, vigor, or spirit to. **3.** To restore to use, currency, or notice. **4.** To present (e.g., an old play) again. **—re·viv′a·ble** *adj.* **—re·viv′er** *n.*
re·viv·i·fy (rē-vĭv′ə-fī′) ▸ *v.* **-fied, -fy·ing.** To give new life to. **—re·viv′i·fi·ca′tion** *n.*
rev·o·ca·ble (rĕv′ə-kə-bəl) also **re·vok·a·ble** (rĭ-vō′-) ▸ *adj.* That can be revoked.
re·voke (rĭ-vōk′) ▸ *v.* **-voked, -vok·ing.** To void or annul by recalling or withdrawing. **—rev′o·ca′tion** (rĕv′ə-kā′shən) *n.* **—re·vok′er** *n.*
re·volt (rĭ-vōlt′) ▸ *v.* **1.** To attempt to overthrow the authority of the state; rebel. **2.** To oppose or refuse to accept something. **3.** To fill with disgust or abhorrence; repel. ▸ *n.* An uprising, esp. against state authority; rebellion.
re·volt·ing (rĭ-vōl′tĭng) ▸ *adj.* Causing abhorrence or disgust.
rev·o·lu·tion (rĕv′ə-lo͞o′shən) ▸ *n.* **1a.** Orbital motion about a point, esp. as distinguished from axial rotation. **b.** A turning or rotation about an axis. **c.** A single complete cycle of such orbital or axial motion. **2.** The overthrow of one government and its replacement with another. **3.** A sudden or momentous change in a situation.
rev·o·lu·tion·ar·y (rĕv′ə-lo͞o′shə-nĕr′ē) ▸ *adj.* **1.** Of or relating to a revolution: *revolutionary war.* **2.** Marked by or resulting in radical change. ▸ *n., pl.* **-ies.** One who supports or engages in revolution.
rev·o·lu·tion·ist (rĕv′ə-lo͞o′shə-nĭst) ▸ *n.* A revolutionary. **—rev′o·lu′tion·ist** *adj.*
rev·o·lu·tion·ize (rĕv′ə-lo͞o′shə-nīz′) ▸ *v.* **-ized, -iz·ing.** To bring about a radical change in.
re·volve (rĭ-vŏlv′) ▸ *v.* **-volved, -volv·ing. 1.** To orbit a central point. **2.** To turn on an axis; rotate. **3.** To recur periodically. **—re·volv′a·ble** *adj.*
re·volv·er (rĭ-vŏl′vər) ▸ *n.* A pistol having a revolving cylinder with several cartridge chambers that may be fired in succession.
re·vue (rĭ-vyo͞o′) ▸ *n.* A musical show consisting of often satirical skits, songs, and dances.
re·vul·sion (rĭ-vŭl′shən) ▸ *n.* **1.** A sudden strong feeling of disgust or loathing. **2.** A withdrawing or turning away from something.
re·ward (rĭ-wôrd′) ▸ *n.* **1.** Something given or received for worthy behavior. **2.** Money offered or given for some special service, such as the return of a lost article. ▸ *v.* To give a reward to or for.
re·word (rē-wûrd′) ▸ *v.* To state or express again in different words.

THESAURUS

reversible *adj.* —*See* CHANGEABLE (1).
reversion *n.* —*See* RELAPSE.
revert *v.* —*See* RELAPSE, RETURN (1).
review *v.* **1.** To give a recapitulation of the salient facts of ▸ abstract, epitomize, go over, recapitulate, run down, run through, summarize, sum up, synopsize, wrap up. *Informal:* recap. [*Compare* PARAPHRASE.] **2.** To write a critical report on ▸ criticize, critique. [*Compare* COMMENT, ESTIMATE.] —*See also* EXAMINE (1), RECONSIDER.
review *n.* A formal military inspection ▸ parade. —*See also* COMMENTARY, EXAMINATION (1).
reviewer *n.* —*See* CRITIC (1).
revile *v.* To attack with harsh, often insulting language ▸ abuse, assail, blaspheme, execrate, fulminate against, rail (at), spit on, vilify, vituperate (against). *Idioms:* call names, vent one's spleen at. [*Compare* CHASTISE, DESPISE, DISLIKE, HATE.]
revilement or **reviling** *n.* —*See* VITUPERATION.
revisal *n.* —*See* REVISION.
revise *v.* To prepare a new version of ▸ amend, edit, emend, emendate, redraft, restyle, revamp, rework, rewrite, work over. [*Compare* CHANGE.] —*See also* CORRECT (1).
revision *n.* The act or process of revising ▸ amendment, emendation, recension, redaction, redraft, revisal, rewrite. [*Compare* IMPROVEMENT.]
revisit *v.* —*See* RETURN (1).
revitalization *n.* —*See* REVIVAL (1).
revitalize *v.* —*See* REFRESH, REVIVE (1).
revival *n.* **1.** The act of reviving or condition of being revived ▸ reactivation, rebirth, renaissance, renascence, renewal, restoration, resurgence, resurrection, resuscitation, revitalization, revivification. [*Compare* COMEBACK, RENEWAL.] **2.** A continuing after interruption ▸ continuation, renewal, resumption, resurgence. —*See also* COMEBACK.
revive *v.* **1.** To rouse from a state of inactivity or quiescence ▸ reactivate, reanimate, reawaken, rekindle, renew, renovate, resurrect, resuscitate, retrieve, revitalize, revivify. [*Compare* REFRESH.] **2.** To cause to come back to life or consciousness ▸ bring around (*or* round), regenerate, restore, resuscitate, revivify. [*Compare* CURE, EVOKE, RECOVER.] **3.** To bring back into existence or use ▸ reestablish, reinstate, reintroduce, renew, restore, return. [*Compare* RESTORE.] —*See also* [illegible] (1).
revivification *n.* —*See* REVIVAL (1).
revivify *v.* —*See* REFRESH, REVIVE (1), REVIVE (2).
revocation *n.* —*See* REPEAL.
revoke *v.* —*See* LIFT (3).
revolt *v.* To vehemently defy and break allegiance with ▸ mutiny, rebel, rise (up). [*Compare* DEFECT, DEFY.] —*See also* DISGUST.
revolt *n.* —*See* REBELLION.
revolting *adj.* —*See* OFFENSIVE (1).
revolution *n.* **1.** A circular movement around a point or about an axis ▸ circle, circuit, circulation, circumvolution, gyration, orbit, rotation, spin, swirl, turn, twirl, wheel, whirl. **2.** A momentous or sweeping change ▸ cataclysm, convulsion, metamorphosis, transformation, upheaval. [*Compare* CHANGE, SHAKEUP.] —*See also* REBELLION.
revolutionary *adj.* —*See* EXTREME (2), PROGRESSIVE (1), REBELLIOUS.
revolutionary or **revolutionist** *n.* —*See* EXTREMIST, REBEL (1).
revolutionize *v.* To bring about a radical change in ▸ make over, metamorphose, remake, transform. *Idioms:* stand on its ear (*or* head), turn inside-out (*or* topsy-turvy *or* upside-down). [*Compare* CHANGE, OVERHAUL.]
revolve *v.* —*See* PONDER, TURN (1).
revolve around *v.* —*See* DEPEND ON (2).
revulsion *n.* —*See* [illegible], HATE (1).
reward *n.* Something given in return for a service or accomplishment ▸ accolade, award, bonus, bounty, guerdon, honorarium, plum, premium, prize. *Idiom:* token of appreciation (*or* esteem). [*Compare* DISTINCTION, GRATUITY, TROPHY.] —*See also* COMPENSATION, DUE.
reward *v.* To bestow a reward on ▸ award, guerdon, honor. [*Compare* CONFER.] —*See also* COMPENSATE.
rewarding *adj.* —*See* PROFITABLE.
reword *v.* —*See* PARAPHRASE.
rework *v.* —*See* REVISE.

re·write (rē-rīt′) ► *v.* To write again, esp. in a different or improved form. **—re′write′** *n.*
Rf ► The symbol for the element **rutherfordium.**
Rh[1] (är′āch′) ► *adj.* Of or relating to the Rh factor: *an Rh antigen.*
Rh[2] ► The symbol for the element **rhodium.**
Rhae·to-Ro·mance (rē′tō-rō-măns′) ► *n.* A group of Romance dialects spoken in S Switzerland, N Italy, and the Tyrol.
rhap·so·dy (răp′sə-dē) ► *n., pl.* **-dies. 1.** Exalted or excessively enthusiastic expression of feeling. **2.** *Mus.* A usu. instrumental composition of irregular form, often incorporating improvisation. **—rhap·sod′ic** (-sŏd′ĭk) *adj.* **—rhap·sod′i·cal·ly** *adv.* **—rhap′so·dize** *v.*
rhe·a (rē′ə) ► *n.* A flightless, three-toed South American bird resembling the ostrich.
rhe·ni·um (rē′nē-əm) ► *n. Symbol* **Re** A rare, dense, silvery-white metallic element used for electrical contacts and high-temperature thermocouples. At. no. 75.
rhe·o·stat (rē′ə-stăt′) ► *n.* A variable electrical resistor used to regulate current. **—rhe′o·stat′ic** *adj.*
rhe·sus monkey (rē′səs) ► *n.* A brownish monkey of India, often used in scientific research.
rhet·o·ric (rĕt′ər-ĭk) ► *n.* **1.** The art or study of using language effectively and persuasively. **2.** A style of speaking or writing: *political rhetoric.* **3.** Language that is pretentious or insincere. **—rhe·tor′i·cal** (rĭ-tôr′ĭ-kəl) *adj.* **—rhe·tor′i·cal·ly** *adv.* **—rhet′o·ri′cian** (rĕt′ə-rĭsh′ən) *n.*
rhetorical question ► *n.* A question to which no answer is expected.
rheum (ro͞om) ► *n.* A watery mucous discharge from the eyes or nose. **—rheum′y** *adj.*
rheu·mat·ic (ro͞o-măt′ĭk) ► *adj.* Of or suffering from rheumatism. ► *n.* One who is affected by rheumatism.
rheumatic fever ► *n.* A severe infectious disease occurring chiefly in children, marked by fever and painful inflammation of the joints and frequently resulting in permanent damage to the heart valves.
rheu·ma·tism (ro͞o′mə-tĭz′əm) ► *n.* **1.** Any of several pathological conditions of the muscles, tendons, joints, bones, or nerves, marked by pain and disability. **2.** Rheumatoid arthritis.
rheu·ma·toid arthritis (ro͞o′mə-toid′) ► *n.* A chronic disease marked by stiffness, inflammation, and deformity of the joints.
Rh factor ► *n.* Any of several substances on the surface of red blood cells that induce a strong antigenic response in individuals lacking the substance.
Rhine (rīn) ► A river of W Europe rising in E Switzerland and flowing about 1,319 km (820 mi) through Germany and the Netherlands to the North Sea.
rhine·stone (rīn′stōn′) ► *n.* A colorless artificial gem of paste or glass. **—rhine′stoned′** *adj.*
rhi·ni·tis (rī-nī′tĭs) ► *n.* Inflammation of the nasal mucous membranes.
rhi·no (rī′nō) ► *n., pl.* **-nos.** A rhinoceros.
rhi·noc·er·os (rī-nŏs′ər-əs) ► *n., pl.* **-os** or **-os·es.** A large, thick-skinned, herbivorous mammal of Africa and Asia, having one or two upright horns on the snout.
rhi·zome (rī′zōm′) ► *n.* A horizontal, usu. underground stem that often sends out roots and shoots.
Rh-neg·a·tive (är′āch-nĕg′ə-tĭv) ► *adj.* Lacking an Rh factor.
rho (rō) ► *n.* The 17th letter of the Greek alphabet.
Rhode Island (rōd) ► A state of the NE US on the Atlantic. Cap. Providence. **—Rhode Is′land·er** *n.*
Rhodes (rōdz) ► The largest of the Dodecanese Is. of SE Greece, in the Aegean off SW Turkey.
Rho·de·sia (rō-dē′zhə) ► See **Zimbabwe. —Rho·de′sian** *adj. & n.*
rho·di·um (rō′dē-əm) ► *n. Symbol* **Rh** A hard, durable, silvery-white metallic element used to form high-temperature alloys with platinum. At. no. 45.
rho·do·den·dron (rō′də-dĕn′drən) ► *n.* A usu. evergreen ornamental shrub having clusters of variously colored, often bell-shaped flowers.
rhom·boid (rŏm′boid′) ► *n.* A parallelogram with unequal adjacent sides.
rhom·bus (rŏm′bəs) ► *n., pl.* **-bus·es** or **-bi** (-bī). An equilateral parallelogram.
Rhone or **Rhône** (rōn) ► A river of SW Switzerland and SE France, flowing about 813 km (505 mi) to the Mediterranean Sea.
Rh-pos·i·tive (är′āch-pŏz′ĭ-tĭv) ► *adj.* Containing an Rh factor.
rhu·barb (ro͞o′bärb′) ► *n.* **1.** A plant with long reddish leafstalks that are edible when cooked. **2.** *Informal* A heated dispute; fray.
rhyme also **rime** (rīm) ► *n.* **1.** Correspondence of terminal sounds of words or of lines of verse. **2.** A poem or poems having such correspondence. **3.** A word that corresponds with another in terminal sound. ► *v.* **rhymed** also **rimed, rhym·ing rim·ing. 1.** To form a rhyme. **2.** To compose rhymes or verse. **3.** To use as a rhyme.
rhythm (rĭth′əm) ► *n.* **1.** Movement or action marked by the regular recurrence of different quantities or conditions. **2.** The patterned, recurring alternations of contrasting elements of sound. **3.** *Mus.* The pattern of musical movement through time. **4.** Metrical movement as regulated by the alternation of long and short or accented and unaccented syllables. **—rhyth′mic, rhyth′mi·cal** *adj.* **—rhyth′mi·cal·ly** *adv.*
rhythm and blues ► *pl.n. (takes sing. or pl. v.)* A kind of music that combines blues and jazz, marked by a strong backbeat.
rhythm method ► *n.* A birth-control method based on abstinence during ovulation.
RI or **R.I.** ► *abbr.* Rhode Island
ri·al (rē-ôl′, -äl′) ► *n.* See **currency** table in Appendix.
rib (rĭb) ► *n.* **1.** One of a series of long, curved bones extending from the spine to or toward the sternum in most vertebrates. **2.** Something similar to a rib and serving to shape or support. **3.** A cut of meat with one or more rib bones. **4.** A raised ridge or wale in fabric. ► *v.* **ribbed, rib·bing. 1.** To shape, support, or provide with a rib or ribs. **2.** To make with ridges. **3.** *Informal* To tease or make fun of.
rib·ald (rĭb′əld, rī′bôld′) ► *adj.* Marked by vulgar, lewd humor. ► *n.* A vulgar, lewdly funny person. **—rib′ald·ry** *n.*
rib·bing (rĭb′ĭng) ► *n.* **1.** An arrangement of ribs, as in a boat. **2.** *Informal* The act or an instance of joking or teasing.
rib·bon (rĭb′ən) ► *n.* **1.** A narrow strip or band of fabric, finished at the edges and used for trimming or tying. **2.** Something resembling a ribbon in shape. **3. ribbons** Tattered or ragged strips. **4.** An inked band used for making an impression, as in a typewriter.
rib cage ► *n.* The structure formed by the ribs and the bones to which they are attached.
ri·bo·fla·vin (rī′bō-flā′vĭn, -bə-) ► *n.* An orange-yellow crystalline compound, the principal growth-promoting factor in the vitamin B complex, found in milk, leafy vegetables, fresh meat, and egg yolks.

THESAURUS

rewrite *v.* —*See* REVISE.
rewrite *n.* —*See* REVISION.
rhapsodize *v.* —*See* DROOL, RAVE.
rhetoric *n.* —*See* ELOQUENCE, ORATORY.
rhetorical *adj.* —*See* ORATORICAL.
rhetorician *n.* —*See* SPEAKER (1).
rhinestone *n.* A small sparkling decoration ► diamond, glitter, sequin, spangle.
rhubarb *n.* —*See* ARGUMENT.
rhyme *n.* —*See* POEM (1).
rhymer or **rhymester** *n.* —*See* POET.
rhythm *n.* The patterned, recurring alternation of contrasting elements, such as stressed and unstressed notes in music ► beat, cadence, cadency, measure, meter, swing. [*Compare* BEAT.]
rhythmical or **rhythmic** *adj.* Marked by a regular rhythm ► cadenced, measured, metrical. [*Compare* POETIC.]
rib *v.* —*See* JOKE (2).
ribald *adj.* —*See* OBSCENE.
ribaldry *n.* —*See* OBSCENITY (2).
riband *n.* —*See* BAND[1].
ribbing *n. Informal* Good-natured teasing ► badinage, banter, chaff, joking, kidding, raillery, taunt, teasing. [*Compare* TAUNT.]
ribbon *n.* —*See* BAND[1], DECORATION, DISTINCTION (2).

ri·bo·nu·cle·ic acid (rī′bō-no͞o-klē′ĭk, -klā′-, -nyo͞o-) ▸ *n.* See **RNA**.

ri·bose (rī′bōs′) ▸ *n.* A crystalline sugar, occurring as a component of riboflavin, nucleotides, and nucleic acids.

ri·bo·some (rī′bə-sōm′) ▸ *n.* A minute, round particle composed of RNA and protein found in cytoplasm and active in the synthesis of proteins. **—ri′bo·so′mal** *adj.*

rice (rīs) ▸ *n.* **1.** A cereal grass cultivated extensively in warm climates. **2.** The starchy edible grain of this plant.

rich (rĭch) ▸ *adj.* **-er, -est. 1.** Possessing great material wealth. **2.** Having great worth or value: *a rich harvest.* **3.** Magnificent; sumptuous. **4a.** Abundant: *rich in ideas.* **b.** Abounding, esp. in natural resources: *a rich land.* **5.** Very productive: *rich soil.* **6a.** Containing a large amount of choice ingredients, such as butter, sugar, or eggs. **b.** Strongly aromatic. **7a.** Pleasantly full and mellow. **b.** Warm and strong in color. **8.** Containing a large proportion of fuel to air: *a rich gas mixture.* **9.** *Informal* Highly amusing. **—rich′ly** *adv.* **—rich′ness** *n.*

Rich·ard I (rĭch′ərd). "the Lion-Hearted" (1157–99) ▸ King of England (1189–99).

Ri·che·lieu (rĭsh′ə-lo͞o′, rē-shə-lyœ′), Duc de (1585–1642) ▸ French prelate and politician.

rich·es (rĭch′ĭz) ▸ *pl.n.* Valuable or precious possessions.

Rich·mond (rĭch′mənd) ▸ The capital of VA, in the E-central part on the James R.

Rich·ter scale (rĭk′tər) ▸ *n.* A logarithmic scale usu. ranging from 1 to 9, used to express an earthquake's magnitude.

rick (rĭk) ▸ *n.* A stack, as of hay or straw, esp. when covered.

rick·ets (rĭk′ĭts) ▸ *n. (takes sing. or pl. v.)* A disease occurring chiefly in children, resulting from a lack of vitamin D or calcium, and marked by defective bone growth.

rick·et·y (rĭk′ĭ-tē) ▸ *adj.* **-i·er, -i·est. 1.** Likely to break or fall apart; shaky. **2.** Of, having, or resembling rickets. **—rick′et·i·ness** *n.*

rick·ey (rĭk′ē) ▸ *n., pl.* **-eys.** A drink of soda water, lime or lemon juice, sugar, and usu. gin.

rick·sha or **rick·shaw** (rĭk′shô) ▸ *n.* A jinriksha.

ric·o·chet (rĭk′ə-shā′, rĭk′ə-shā′) ▸ *v.* **-cheted** (-shād′), **-chet·ing** (-shā′ĭng). To rebound from a surface. **—ric′o·chet′** *n.*

ri·cot·ta (rĭ-kŏt′ə) ▸ *n.* A soft Italian cheese that resembles cottage cheese.

rid (rĭd) ▸ *v.* **rid** or **rid·ded, rid·ding.** To free from. **—rid′dance** *n.*

rid·dle¹ (rĭd′l) ▸ *v.* **-dled, -dling. 1.** To pierce with numerous holes; perforate. **2.** To spread throughout.

rid·dle² (rĭd′l) ▸ *n.* **1.** A puzzling question or statement requiring thought to answer or understand. **2.** One that is perplexing; enigma. ▸ *v.* **-dled, -dling.** To solve or explain. **—rid′dler** *n.*

ride (rīd) ▸ *v.* **rode** (rōd), **rid·den** (rĭd′n), **rid·ing. 1.** To be carried or conveyed, as in a vehicle or on horseback. **2.** To travel over a surface: *This car rides well.* **3.** To move on or as if on water. **4.** To be sustained or supported as on a pivot or an axle. **5.** To be contingent; depend. **6.** To continue without interference: *Let the matter ride.* **7.** To sit on and move in a given direction: *rode my bike to town.* **8.** To take part in or do by riding: *He rode his last race.* **9.** To cause to be carried. ***—phrasal verb:* ride out** to survive or outlast: *rode out the storm.* ▸ *n.* **1.** The act or an instance of riding. **2.** A path made for riding. **3.** A device, as at an amusement park, that one rides for pleasure or excitement. **4.** A means of transportation: *waiting for my ride to come.*

rid·er (rī′dər) ▸ *n.* **1.** One that rides. **2.** An amendment or addition, esp. a clause added to a legislative bill.

rid·er·ship (rī′dər-shĭp′) ▸ *n.* The number of people who ride a public transport system.

ridge (rĭj) ▸ *n.* **1.** A long narrow upper section or crest: *the ridge of a wave.* **2.** A long narrow chain of hills or mountains. **3.** A long, narrow, or crested part of the body: *the ridge of the nose.* **4.** The horizontal line formed by the juncture of two sloping planes, esp. the line formed by the surfaces at the top of a roof. **5.** A narrow, raised strip, as in cloth or on plowed ground. ▸ *v.* **ridged, ridg·ing.** To mark with, form into, or provide with ridges.

ridge·pole (rĭj′pōl′) ▸ *n.* A horizontal beam at the ridge of a roof to which the rafters are attached.

rid·i·cule (rĭd′ĭ-kyo͞ol′) ▸ *n.* Words or actions intended to evoke contemptuous laughter at a person or thing. ▸ *v.* **-culed, -cul·ing.** To make fun of.

ri·dic·u·lous (rĭ-dĭk′yə-ləs) ▸ *adj.* Deserving or inspiring ridicule; absurd or preposterous. **—ri·dic′u·lous·ly** *adv.* **—ri·dic′u·lous·ness** *n.*

ri·el (rē-ĕl′) ▸ *n.* See **currency** table in Appendix.

rife (rīf) ▸ *adj.* **rif·er, rif·est. 1.** Widespread; prevalent. **2.** Abounding; full.

riff (rĭf) ▸ *n. Mus.* A short rhythmic phrase, esp. one repeated in improvisation.

riff·raff (rĭf′răf′) ▸ *n.* **1.** Disreputable or worthless people. **2.** Rubbish; trash.

ri·fle¹ (rī′fəl) ▸ *n.* A firearm with a rifled bore, designed to be fired from the shoulder. ▸ *v.* **-fled, -fling.** To cut spiral grooves within.

ri·fle² (rī′fəl) ▸ *v.* **-fled, -fling. 1.** To search with intent to steal. **2.** To rob: *rifle a safe.* **—ri′fler** *n.*

ri·fle·ry (rī′fəl-rē) ▸ *n.* The skill and practice of shooting a rifle.

ri·fling (rī′flĭng) ▸ *n.* Grooves cut in a rifle barrel.

rift (rĭft) ▸ *n.* **1.** A narrow fissure in rock. **2.** A break in friendly relations. ▸ *v.* To split or cause to split open.

rig (rĭg) ▸ *v.* **rigged, rig·ging. 1.** To equip; fit out. **2.** To equip (a ship) with rigging. **3.** *Informal* To dress, clothe, or adorn. **4.** To make or construct in a makeshift manner. **5.** To manipulate dishonestly for personal gain: *rig a prizefight.* ▸ *n.* **1.** The arrangement of masts, spars, and sails on a sailing vessel. **2.** Gear used for a particular purpose. **3a.** A truck, tractor, or tractor-trailer. **b.** A vehicle

THESAURUS

rib-tickler *n.* —*See* JOKE (1).

rich *adj.* **1.** Possessing a large amount of money, land, or other material possessions ▸ affluent, flush, moneyed, wealthy. *Slang:* loaded. *Idioms:* having money to burn, in the money, made of money, rolling in money (*or* dough). [*Compare* LUXURIOUS, PROSPEROUS.] **2.** Not readily digested because of richness ▸ filling, heavy. —*See also* COLORFUL (1), COSTLY, FERTILE (1), FUNNY (1).

riches *n.* —*See* WEALTH.

richness *n.* —*See* FERTILITY.

ricketiness *n.* —*See* UNSTEADINESS.

rickety *adj.* —*See* INSECURE (2).

ricochet *v.* —*See* GLANCE (1).

rid *v.* To relieve a burden ▸ clear, disburden, discharge, disembarrass, disencumber, dump, empty, release, relieve, shake off, throw off, unburden, unlade, unload. *Slang:* shake. [*Compare* CLEAR, ELIMINATE.]

riddance *n.* —*See* DISPOSAL, ELIMINATION.

riddle *n.* —*See* MYSTERY.

ride *v.* —*See* HARASS, JOKE (2).

ride out *v.* —*See* SURVIVE (1).

ride *n.* —*See* DRIVE (3).

ridicule *n.* Words or actions intended to evoke contemptuous laughter ▸ derision, mockery. [*Compare* SARCASM, TAUNT.]

ridicule *v.* To subject to ridicule ▸ deride, gibe (at), jeer (at), jest (at), lampoon, laugh at, mock (at), pillory, scoff (at), scout (at), sneer at, taunt, twit. *Idioms:* make a laughingstock out of, make fun (*or* sport) of, poke fun at, thumb one's nose at. [*Compare* BELITTLE, DENIGRATE, DISGRACE.]

ridiculous *adj.* Causing or deserving laughter or derision ▸ farcical, laughable, ludicrous, risible. —*See also* FOOLISH, OUTRAGEOUS.

ridiculousness *n.* —*See* FOOLISHNESS, HUMOR.

rife *adj.* —*See* PREVAILING.

rifle *v.* —*See* BROWSE (1), SHUFFLE.

riffraff *n.* A person or group of persons regarded as worthless or contemptible ▸ dregs, good-for-nothing, lumpenproletariat, rabble, ragtag and bobtail, trash, vermin. *Slang:* scum. *Idioms:* scum of the earth, tag and rag, the great unwashed. [*Compare* COMMONALTY, NONENTITY.]

rift *n.* —*See* BREACH (2), CRACK (2).

rift *v.* —*See* BREAK (1), CRACK (1).

rig *v.* To prearrange the outcome of a contest ▸ fix, tamper. *Idiom:* stack the deck. —*See also* FURNISH.

rig up *v.* —*See* IMPROVISE (2).

with one or more horses harnessed to it.

rig·a·ma·role (rĭg′ə-mə-rōl′) ► *n.* Var. of **rigmarole.**

rig·ging (rĭg′ĭng) ► *n.* **1.** The system of ropes, chains, and tackle used to support and control the masts, sails, and yards of a sailing vessel. **2.** The supporting material for construction work.

right (rīt) ► *adj.* **-er, -est. 1.** Conforming with justice or morality. **2.** In accordance with fact, reason, or truth; correct. **3.** Fitting, proper, or appropriate. **4.** Favorable, desirable, or convenient. **5.** In or into a satisfactory state or condition. **6.** Intended to be worn or positioned facing outward: *the right side of the medallion.* **7.** Of, located on, or corresponding to the side of the body to the south when one is facing east. **8.** often **Right** Of or belonging to the political right. **9.** *Math.* **a.** Formed by or in reference to a line or plane that is perpendicular to another line or plane. **b.** Having a right angle: *a right triangle.* ► *n.* **1.** That which is just, morally good, legal, proper, or fitting. **2a.** The direction or position on the right side. **b.** A turn in this direction: *make a right.* **c.** The right side. **d.** The right hand. **3.** often **Right** The people and groups who pursue conservative or reactionary political goals. **4.** Something due to a person or governmental body by law, tradition, or nature. ► *adv.* **1.** Toward or on the right. **2.** In a straight line; directly. **3.** In the proper or desired manner. **4.** Exactly; just: *right over there.* **5.** Immediately: *right after dinner.* **6.** Used as an intensive: *kept right on going.* **7.** Used in titles: *The Right Reverend Pat Smith.* ► *v.* **1.** To put in or restore to an upright or proper position. **2.** To put in order or set right; correct. **3.** To redress: *right a wrong.* ***—idioms:*** **by rights** In a just or proper manner; justly. **to rights** In a satisfactory or orderly condition. **—right′er** *n.* **—right′ness** *n.*

right angle ► *n.* An angle of 90° formed by two intersecting perpendicular lines. **—right′-an′gled** *adj.*

right·eous (rī′chəs) ► *adj.* Morally upright; just. **—right′eous·ly** *adv.* **—right′eous·ness** *n.*

right field ► *n. Baseball* The third of the outfield that is to the right as viewed from home plate. **—right field′er** *n.*

right·ful (rīt′fəl) ► *adj.* **1.** Right or proper; just. **2.** Having or held by a rightful claim. **—right′ful·ly** *adv.* **—right′ful·ness** *n.*

right-hand (rīt′hănd′) ► *adj.* **1.** Relating to or located on the right. **2.** Designed for or done with the right hand. **3.** Indispensible; reliable.

right-hand·ed (rīt′hăn′dĭd) ► *adj.* **1.** Using the right hand more skillfully or easily than the left. **2.** Done with or made for the right hand. **3.** Clockwise. ► *adv.* With the right hand. **—right′-hand′ed·ly** *adv.* **—right′-hand′ed·ness** *n.*

right-hand·er (rīt′hăn′dər) ► *n.* One who is right-handed.

right·ism also **Right·ism** (rī′tĭz′əm) ► *n.* The ideology of the political right. **—right′ist** *n.*

right·ly (rīt′lē) ► *adv.* **1.** In a correct manner; properly. **2.** With honesty; justly.

right of way also **right-of-way** (rīt′əv-wā′) ► *n., pl.* **rights of way** or **right of ways. 1a.** The right to pass over property owned by another. **b.** The path or thoroughfare on which such passage is made. **2.** The strip of land over which facilities such as highways, railroads, or power lines are built. **3.** The customary or legal right of a person, vessel, or vehicle to pass in front of another.

right-on (rīt′ŏn′, -ôn′) ► *adj. Slang* **1.** Up-to-date and sophisticated. **2.** Absolutely right.

right whale ► *n.* Any of several whales with a large head, whalebone plates in the mouth, and no dorsal fin.

right wing ► *n.* **1.** The conservative or reactionary faction of a group. **2.** See **right** 3. **—right′-wing′** *adj.* **—right′-wing′er** *n.*

rig·id (rĭj′ĭd) ► *adj.* **1.** Not flexible or pliant; stiff. **2.** Not moving; fixed. **3.** Rigorous and exacting. **—rig′id·ly** *adv.* **—ri·gid′i·ty, rig′id·ness** *n.*

rig·ma·role (rĭg′mə-rōl′) also **rig·a·ma·role** (-ə-mə-rōl′) ► *n.* **1.** Confused or rambling discourse; nonsense. **2.** A complicated, petty procedure.

rig·or (rĭg′ər) ► *n.* **1.** Strictness or severity. **2.** A harsh or trying circumstance; hardship. **3.** Shivering or trembling, as caused by a chill. **—rig′or·ous** *adj.* **—rig′or·ous·ly** *adv.*

rigor mor·tis (môr′tĭs) ► *n.* Muscular stiffening after death.

rile (rīl) ► *v.* **riled, ril·ing.** To stir to anger; irritate.

rill (rĭl) ► *n.* A small brook.

rim (rĭm) ► *n.* **1.** The border or edge of an object. **2.** The circular outer part of a wheel. ► *v.* **rimmed, rim·ming.** To furnish with a rim.

rime[1] (rīm) ► *n.* Frost or a coating of granular ice, as on grass and trees. **—rime** *v.* **—rim′y** *adj.*

rime[2] (rīm) ► *n. & v.* Var. of **rhyme.**

rind (rīnd) ► *n.* A tough outer covering such as bark or the skin of some fruits.

ring[1] (rĭng) ► *n.* **1.** A circular object, form, or arrangement with a vacant circular center. **2.** A small circular band, often of precious metal, worn on the finger. **3.** An enclosed area in which exhibitions or contests take place. **4.** A group of people acting to advance their interests. ► *v.* **1.** To surround with or as if with a ring; encircle. **2.** To form into a ring or rings.

ring[2] (rĭng) ► *v.* **rang** (răng), **rung** (rŭng), **ring·ing. 1.** To give forth a clear, resonant sound. **2.** To cause something to ring. **3.** To sound a bell to summon someone. **4.** To have a character suggestive of a particular quality: *a story that rings true.* **5.** To be filled with sound; resound. **6.** To hear a persistent humming or buzzing: *My ears were ringing from the blast.* **7.** To call (someone) on the telephone. ***—phrasal verb:*** **ring up** To record, esp. by means of a cash register: *ring up a sale.* ► *n.* **1.** The sound created by or as

THESAURUS

rig *n.* —*See* DRESS (2), OUTFIT.

rigamarole *n.* —*See* RIGMAROLE.

right *adj.* Conforming to accepted standards ► becoming, befitting, comely, comme il faut, correct, decent, decorous, de rigueur, nice, proper, respectable, seemly. —*See also* ACCURATE, APPROPRIATE, CONSERVATIVE (1), ETHICAL, HEALTHY, JUST.

right *n.* A benefit granted to a person by law, nature, or custom ► birthright, civil liberty, droit, due, entitlement, franchise, freedom, perquisite, prerogative, privilege. [*Compare* AUTHORITY, CLAIM, PERMISSION.]

right *adv.* —*See* DIRECTLY (1), DIRECTLY (3), YES.

right *v.* —*See* CORRECT (1), FIX (1).

right away *adv.* —*See* IMMEDIATELY (1).

righteous *adj.* —*See* ETHICAL, HONEST.

righteousness *n.* —*See* ETHICS (1), GOOD (1), HONESTY.

rightful *adj.* **1.** In accordance with principles of right or good conduct ► ethical, moral, principled, proper, right, righteous, right-minded, virtuous. **2.** Being so legitimately ► legitimate, true. —*See also* JUST, LAWFUL.

rightfulness *n.* —*See* GOOD (1), LEGALITY.

rightist *n.* —*See* CONSERVATIVE.

rightist *adj.* —*See* CONSERVATIVE (1).

right-minded *adj.* —*See* ETHICAL.

rightness *n.* —*See* ACCURACY, ETHICS (1), GOOD (1).

right off *adv.* —*See* IMMEDIATELY (1).

right of way *n.* —*See* PRECEDENCE.

right on *adv.* —*See* YES.

right-wing *adj.* —*See* CONSERVATIVE (1).

right-winger *n.* —*See* CONSERVATIVE.

rigid *adj.* Not changing shape or not bending ► inelastic, inflexible, stiff, unbending, unyielding. [*Compare* FIRM[1], TAUT.] —*See also* IMMUTABLE, MOTIONLESS, SEVERE (1), STUBBORN (1).

rigidity or **rigidness** *n.* —*See* SEVERITY, STUBBORNNESS.

rigmarole or **rigamarole** *n.* —*See* BOTHER, NONSENSE.

rigor *n.* —*See* DIFFICULTY, SEVERITY.

rigorous *adj.* —*See* ACCURATE, BITTER (2), BURDENSOME, CLOSE (2), SEVERE (1).

rigorousness *n.* —*See* SEVERITY.

rile *v.* —*See* ANGER (1), ANNOY.

rim *n.* —*See* BORDER (1).

rim *v.* —*See* BORDER.

rimple *n.* —*See* FOLD (1).

rimple *v.* —*See* FOLD, WRINKLE.

rind *n.* —*See* SKIN (3).

ring[1] *n.* An organized group of criminals, hoodlums, or wrongdoers ► band, gang, pack. *Informal:* mob. —*See also* ALLIANCE, CIRCLE (1), LOOP.

ring *v.* —*See* ENCIRCLE, SURROUND.

ring in *v.* —*See* INTRODUCE (3).

ring[2] *v.* To give forth or cause to give forth a clear resonant sound ► bell, bong, chime, ding, knell, peal, sound, strike, toll. —*See also* TELEPHONE.

if by a bell. **2.** A loud sound that is repeated or continued. **3.** A telephone call. **4.** A suggestion of a quality: *His offer has a suspicious ring.* **—*idiom:* ring a bell** *Informal* To arouse an often indistinct memory.

ring·er (rĭng′ər) ▸ *n.* **1.** One that rings, esp. one that sounds a bell or chime. **2.** *Slang* A contestant entered dishonestly into a competition. **3.** *Slang* One who bears a striking resemblance to another.

ring·git (rĭng′gĭt) ▸ *n.* See **currency** table in Appendix.

ring·lead·er (rĭng′lē′dər) ▸ *n.* A leader, esp. of a group involved in illicit activities.

ring·let (rĭng′lĭt) ▸ *n.* **1.** A curled lock of hair. **2.** A small circle or ring.

ring·mas·ter (rĭng′măs′tər) ▸ *n.* A person in charge of the performances in a circus ring.

ring·side (rĭng′sīd′) ▸ *n.* The area or seats immediately outside an arena or a ring.

ring·worm (rĭng′wûrm′) ▸ *n.* A contagious skin disease caused by a fungi and marked by ring-shaped, scaly, itching patches.

rink (rĭngk) ▸ *n.* **1.** An area surfaced with smooth ice for skating. **2.** A smooth floor suited for roller-skating.

rinse (rĭns) ▸ *v.* **rinsed, rins·ing.** **1.** To wash lightly, as with water. **2.** To remove (e.g., soap) by flushing with water. ▸ *n.* **1.** The act of rinsing. **2.** The liquid used in rinsing. **3.** A solution used in coloring or conditioning the hair.

Ri·o de Ja·nei·ro (rē′ō dā zhə-nâr′ō, dē-) ▸ A city of SE Brazil on Guanabara Bay, an arm of the Atlantic.

Ri·o Grande (rē′ō grănd′, grăn′dē) ▸ A river, about 3,033 km (1,885 mi), rising in SW CO and flowing to the Gulf of Mexico, forming much of the US-Mexican border.

ri·ot (rī′ət) ▸ *n.* **1.** A public uproar or disturbance. **2.** An unrestrained outbreak, as of laughter or passions. **3.** A profusion. **4.** *Slang* An irresistibly funny person or thing. ▸ *v.* **1.** To take part in a riot. **2.** To engage in uncontrolled revelry. **—ri′ot·er** *n.*

ri·ot·ous (rī′ət-əs) ▸ *adj.* **1.** Of or resembling a riot. **2.** Participating in or inciting to riot. **3.** Uproarious; boisterous. **4.** Dissolute; wanton. **5.** Abundant or luxuriant. **—ri′ot·ous·ly** *adv.* **—ri′ot·ous·ness** *n.*

rip (rĭp) ▸ *v.* **ripped, rip·ping.** **1.** To tear apart or become torn apart esp. roughly or energetically. **2.** To split or saw (wood) along the grain. **3.** *Informal* To move quickly or violently. **—*phrasal verb:* rip off** *Slang* **1.** to steal or steal from. **2.** To exploit, swindle, or defraud. ▸ *n.* **1.** The act of ripping. **2.** A torn or split place; tear. **—rip′per** *n.*

RIP ▸ *abbr. Lat.* requiescat in pace (may he rest in peace; may she rest in peace)

ri·par·i·an (rĭ-pâr′ē-ən) ▸ *adj.* Of or relating to the banks of a natural course of water.

rip·cord (rĭp′kôrd′) ▸ *n.* A cord pulled to release a parachute from its pack.

ripe (rīp) ▸ *adj.* **rip·er, rip·est.** **1.** Fully developed; mature: *ripe peaches.* **2.** Fully prepared; ready. **3.** Sufficiently advanced; opportune. **—ripe′ly** *adv.* **—rip′en** *v.* **—ripe′ness** *n.*

rip-off (rĭp′ôf′, -ŏf′) ▸ *n. Slang* **1.** A theft. **2.** An act of exploitation. **3.** Something clearly imitative of or based on something else.

ri·poste (rĭ-pōst′) ▸ *n.* **1.** A quick thrust given after parrying an opponent's lunge in fencing. **2.** A retaliatory action or retort. **—ri·poste** *v.*

rip·ple (rĭp′əl) ▸ *v.* **-pled, -pling.** **1.** To form or display small waves on the surface. **2.** To rise and fall gently in tone or volume. ▸ *n.* **1.** A small wave or wavelike motion. **2.** A sound like that made by rippling water: *a ripple of laughter.*

rip·saw (rĭp′sô′) ▸ *n.* A coarse-toothed saw used for cutting wood along the grain.

rip tide ▸ *n.* A strong surface current flowing away from shore.

rise (rīz) ▸ *v.* **rose** (rōz), **ris·en** (rĭz′ən), **ris·ing.** **1.** To stand up after lying, sitting, or kneeling. **2.** To get out of bed. **3.** To move from a lower to a higher position. **4.** To increase in size, volume, or level. **5.** To increase in number, amount, or value. **6.** To increase in intensity, force, or speed. **7.** To increase in pitch or volume. **8.** To appear above the horizon. **9.** To slope or extend upward. **10.** To come into existence; originate. **11.** To attain a higher status. **12.** To return to life. **13.** To rebel. ▸ *n.* **1.** The act of rising; ascent. **2.** The appearance of the sun or other celestial body above the horizon. **3.** An increase in height, as of the level of water. **4.** A gently sloped hill. **5.** An origin, beginning, or source. **6.** An increase in price, worth, quantity, or degree. **7.** An increase in intensity, volume, or pitch. **8.** Elevation in status, prosperity, or importance. **9.** *Informal* An angry or irritated reaction.

ris·er (rī′zər) ▸ *n.* **1.** One who rises, esp. from sleep. **2.** The vertical part of a stair step.

ris·i·bil·i·ty (rĭz′ə-bĭl′ĭ-tē) ▸ *n.* **1.** The ability or tendency to laugh. **2.** Laughter; hilarity.

ris·i·ble (rĭz′ə-bəl) ▸ *adj.* **1.** Eliciting laughter; ludicrous. **2.** Capable of laughing or inclined to laugh. **—ris′i·bly** *adv.*

risk (rĭsk) ▸ *n.* **1.** The possibility of suffering harm or loss; danger. **2.** A factor, element, or course involving uncertain danger. ▸ *v.* **1.** To expose to a chance of loss or damage. **2.** To incur the risk of: *His action risked a sharp reprisal.* **—risk′i·ness** *n.* **—risk′y** *adj.*

ri·sot·to (rē-zōt′tō) ▸ *n., pl.* **-tos.** A dish of rice cooked in broth, often flavored with saffron.

ris·qué (rĭs-kā′) ▸ *adj.* Suggestive of or bordering on indelicacy or impropriety.

rite (rīt) ▸ *n.* **1.** The prescribed form for conducting a

THESAURUS

ring *n.* A telephone communication ▸ buzz, call.
ringer *n.* —*See* DOUBLE, SUBSTITUTE.
ringing *adj.* —*See* DEFINITE (1), RESONANT.
ringleader *n.* —*See* CHIEF.
ringlet *n.* —*See* LOOP.
rinky-dink *adj.* —*See* TRIVIAL.
rinse *v.* —*See* CLEAN (1).
riot *n.* —*See* BINGE, DISORDER (2), FIGHT (1), SCREAM (2).
riot *v.* —*See* REVEL.
riotous *adj.* —*See* DISORDERLY, PROFUSE.
rip *v.* —*See* RUSH, TEAR[1].
rip into *v.* —*See* SLAM (1).
rip off *v.* —*See* CHEAT (1), STEAL.
rip up *v.* —*See* SHRED.
rip *n.* A hole made by tearing ▸ rent, run, tear. [*Compare* CRACK.]
rip[2] *n.* —*See* WANTON.
ripe *adj.* Brought to full flavor and richness by aging ▸ aged, mellow. [*Compare* MATURE.] —*See also* MATURE.
ripen *v.* —*See* MATURE.
rip-off *n.* —*See* LARCENY.
riposte *n.* —*See* ANSWER (1).
riposte *v.* —*See* ANSWER.
ripped *adj.* —*See* DRUGGED.
ripping *adj.* —*See* MARVELOUS.
ripple *v.* —*See* BURBLE, FLOW (1), WAVE (1).
ripple *n.* —*See* BURBLE, WAVE.
rippled *adj.* —*See* WAVY.
rise *v.* **1.** To leave one's bed ▸ arise, get up, roll out. *Informal:* turn out. *Slang:* hit the deck. ***Idioms:*** jump (*or* leap *or* pile *or* spring) out of bed, rise and shine. [*Compare* WAKE[1].] **2.** To move from a lower to a higher position ▸ arise, ascend, climb, lift, mount, soar, tower. [*Compare* ASCEND, SOAR.] **3.** To attain a higher status, rank, or condition ▸ advance, ascend, climb, get ahead, mount, progress. ***Idiom:*** go up the ladder. [*Compare* ADVANCE.] **4.** To gain success ▸ arrive, get ahead, get on, succeed. ***Idioms:*** go far, go places, make good, make it. **5.** To refuse allegiance to and oppose by force a government or ruling authority ▸ mutiny, rebel, revolt, rise up. [*Compare* DEFECT, DEFY.] —*See also* BLOW[1] (1), INCREASE, STAND (1), STEM.
rise *n.* —*See* ADVANCEMENT, ASCENT (1), ASCENT (2), HILL, INCREASE (1), INCREASE (2), ORIGIN.
risible *adj.* Causing or deserving laughter or derision ▸ farcical, laughable, ludicrous, ridiculous. [*Compare* FOOLISH.] —*See also* FUNNY (1).
rising *n.* —*See* ASCENT (1).
rising star *n.* —*See* COMER (2).
risk *n.* A possibility of danger or harm ▸ chance, gamble, hazard. *Informal:* shaky ground, thin ice. —*See also* DANGER, GAMBLE.
risk *v.* —*See* ENDANGER, GAMBLE (2), VENTURE.
risk capital *n.* —*See* CAPITAL (1).
risky *adj.* —*See* DANGEROUS.
risqué *adj.* —*See* IMPROPER (1), RACY.
rite *n.* —*See* CEREMONY (1).

religious or other solemn ceremony. 2. A ceremonial act.
rit·u·al (rĭch′o͞o-əl) ▸ *n.* 1. The prescribed form of a ceremony. 2. A system of ceremonies or rites. 3. **rituals** A ceremonial act or a series of such acts. 4. A customary or regular procedure. **—rit′u·al·ism** *n.* **—rit′u·al·is′tic** *adj.* **—rit′u·al·ize′** *v.* **—rit′u·al·ly** *adv.*
ritz·y (rĭt′sē) ▸ *adj.* **-i·er, -i·est.** *Informal* Elegant; fancy.
ri·val (rī′vəl) ▸ *n.* 1. One who attempts to equal or surpass another; competitor. 2. One that equals another in a particular respect. ▸ *v.* **-valed, -val·ing** or **-valled, -val·ling.** 1. To attempt to equal or surpass. 2. To be the equal of; match. **—ri′val** *adj.* **—ri′val·ry** *n.*
rive (rīv) ▸ *v.* **rived, riv·en** (rĭv′ən) also **rived, riv·ing.** 1. To rend or tear apart. 2. To cleave or split into pieces.
riv·er (rĭv′ər) ▸ *n.* A large natural stream of water.
riv·er·boat (rĭv′ər-bōt′) ▸ *n.* A boat for use on a river.
riv·er·side (rĭv′ər-sīd′) ▸ *n.* The bank or area alongside a river. **—riv′er·side** *adj.*
riv·et (rĭv′ĭt) ▸ *n.* A metal bolt or pin having a head on one end, inserted through the pieces to be joined and then hammered on the plain end to form a second head. ▸ *v.* 1. To fasten or secure with or as if with a rivet. 2. To engross or hold (e.g., the attention). **—riv′et·er** *n.*
Riv·i·er·a (rĭv′ē-ĕr′ə, rē-vyĕ′rä) ▸ A coastal region between the Alps and the Mediterranean from SE France to NW Italy.
riv·u·let (rĭv′yə-lĭt) ▸ *n.* A small brook or stream.
Ri·yadh (rē-yäd′) ▸ The capital of Saudi Arabia, in the E-central part.
ri·yal (rē-ôl′, -äl′) ▸ *n.* See **currency** table in Appendix.
Rn ▸ The symbol for the element **radon.**
RN ▸ *abbr.* registered nurse
RNA (är′ĕn-ā′) ▸ *n.* A nucleic acid that is involved in protein synthesis, consisting of a long, usu. single-stranded chain of nucleotides.
roach[1] (rōch) ▸ *n., pl.* **roach** or **-es.** A freshwater fish of N Europe.
roach[2] (rōch) ▸ *n., pl.* **roach·es.** A cockroach.
road (rōd) ▸ *n.* 1. An open, usu. public way for the passage of vehicles, people, and animals. 2. A course or path. ***—idiom:* on the road** Traveling.
road·bed (rōd′bĕd′) ▸ *n.* 1. The foundation upon which railroad tracks are laid. 2. The foundation and surface of a road.
road·block (rōd′blŏk′) ▸ *n.* 1. A blockade set across a road. 2. Something that prevents progress; obstacle.
road·house (rōd′hous′) ▸ *n.* An inn, restaurant, or nightclub located on a road outside a city.
road·run·ner (rōd′rŭn′ər) ▸ *n.* A swift-running, crested bird of SW North America, with streaked brownish plumage and a long tail.
road show ▸ *n.* A show that is presented by traveling performers.
road·side (rōd′sīd′) ▸ *n.* The area bordering a road. **—road′side′** *adj.*
road·ster (rōd′stər) ▸ *n.* An open automobile having a single seat in the front for two or three people.
road·way (rōd′wā′) ▸ *n.* A road, esp. the part over which vehicles travel.
road·work (rōd′wûrk′) ▸ *n.* 1. Outdoor long-distance running as a form of exercise or conditioning. 2. Highway construction.
roam (rōm) ▸ *v.* To move about without purpose; wander. **—roam′er** *n.*
roan (rōn) ▸ *adj.* Having a chestnut, bay, or sorrel coat thickly sprinkled with white or gray: *a roan horse.* ▸ *n.* A roan animal.
Ro·a·noke (rō′ə-nōk′) ▸ An independent city of SW VA WSW of Richmond.
Roanoke Island ▸ An island off the NE coast of NC, where Sir Walter Raleigh attempted to found the first English settlement in North America (1585).
roar (rôr) ▸ *v.* 1. To utter a loud, deep, prolonged sound, as in rage or excitement. 2. To laugh loudly or excitedly. **—roar** *n.*
roast (rōst) ▸ *v.* 1. To cook with dry heat, as in an oven. 2. To expose to great or excessive heat. 3. To heat (ores) in order to dehydrate, purify, or oxidize. 4. *Informal* To ridicule or criticize harshly. ▸ *n.* 1. A cut of meat suitable for roasting. 2. An outing at which food is roasted. ▸ *adj.* Roasted. **—roast′er** *n.*
rob (rŏb) ▸ *v.* **robbed, rob·bing.** 1. To steal (from) esp. by using or threatening to use force. 2. To deprive of something. **—rob′ber** *n.* **—rob′ber·y** *n.*
robe (rōb) ▸ *n.* 1. A long, loose, flowing outer garment, esp. one worn to show office or rank. 2. A dressing gown or bathrobe. 3. A blanket or covering for the lap or legs. ▸ *v.* **robed, rob·ing.** To dress in or as if in a robe.
rob·in (rŏb′ĭn) ▸ *n.* 1. A North American songbird having a rust-red breast and gray and black upper plumage. 2. A small Old World bird having an orange breast and a brown back.
Rob·in·son (rŏb′ĭn-sən), **Jack Roosevelt.** "Jackie" (1919–72) ▸ Amer. baseball player.
ro·bot (rō′bŏt′) ▸ *n.* 1. A mechanical device, sometimes resembling a human, capable of performing often complex tasks. 2. A device that operates automatically or by remote control. 3. A person who works or follows orders mechanically. **—ro·bot′ic** *adj.*
ro·bot·ics (rō-bŏt′ĭks) ▸ *n.* *(takes sing. v.)* The science and technology of robotic design.
ro·bust (rō-bŭst′, rō′bŭst′) ▸ *adj.* 1. Full of health and strength; vigorous. 2. Marked by richness and fullness: *a robust wine.* **—ro·bust′ly** *adv.* **—ro·bust′ness** *n.*
rock[1] (rŏk) ▸ *n.* 1. Relatively hard, naturally formed mineral or petrified matter. 2. A fragment or body of such material. 3. A naturally formed aggregate of mineral matter making up much of the earth's crust. 4. One that is stable, firm, or dependable. 5. *Slang* A large gem, esp. a diamond. ***—idiom:* on the rocks** 1. In a state of difficulty or ruin. 2. Served over ice cubes.
rock[2] (rŏk) ▸ *v.* 1. To move back and forth or from side to side, esp. gently or rhythmically. 2. To shake or cause to

THESAURUS

ritual *n.* A conventional social gesture or act without intrinsic purpose ▸ ceremony, form, formality, mummery, nicety. [*Compare* CUSTOM, MANNERS.] *—See also* CEREMONY (1).
ritual *adj.* Of or characterized by ceremony ▸ ceremonial, ceremonious, formal, liturgical, ritualistic. [*Compare* CEREMONIOUS, SPIRITUAL.]
ritualistic *adj.* *—See* RITUAL.
ritzy *adj.* *—See* EXCLUSIVE (3), LUXURIOUS.
rival *n.* *—See* COMPETITOR, PEER[2].
rival *v.* To attempt to equal or surpass, as in quality or amount ▸ approach, approximate, border on (*or* upon), challenge, verge on. *—See also* COMPETE.
rivalrous *adj.* *—See* COMPETITIVE.
rivalry *n.* *—See* COMPETITION (1).
rive *v.* *—See* BREAK (1), TEAR[1].
river *n.* A relatively large natural flow of water ▸ estuary, stream, tributary, watercourse, waterway. [*Compare* BROOK[1].]
rivet *n.* *—See* NAIL.
rivet *v.* *—See* FASTEN, GRIP.
riveted *adj.* *—See* RAPT.
road *n.* *—See* WAY (2).
roam *v.* *—See* ROVE.
roamer *n.* *—See* HOBO.
roaming *adj.* *—See* ERRANT (1).
roar *v.* *—See* BLAST (1), BURN (2), LAUGH, SHOUT.
roar *n.* A loud, deep, prolonged sound ▸ bawl, bellow, bluster, clamor, roll, rumble. *—See also* BLAST (1), LAUGH, SHOUT.
roaring *adj.* *—See* FLOURISHING, LOUD.
roast *v.* *—See* BURN (3), COOK, SLAM (1).
roasting *adj.* *—See* HOT (1).
rob *v.* To take property or possessions from someone unlawfully and usually forcibly ▸ burglarize, hold up, mug, stick up. *Slang:* heist, knock off. [*Compare* SACK[2], STEAL.] *—See also* DEPRIVE.
robber *n.* *—See* THIEF.
robbery *n.* *—See* LARCENY.
robe *n.* Clothing worn by members of a religious order ▸ habit, vestment.
robe *v.* *—See* CLOTHE.
roborant *adj.* *—See* INVIGORATING.
roborant *n.* *—See* TONIC.
robust *adj.* *—See* HEALTHY, LUSTY, MUSCULAR.
rock *v.* To move vigorously from side

shake violently. 3. To play or dance to rock 'n' roll. ▸ *n.* 1. A rocking motion. 2. Rock 'n' roll.

rock-and-roll (rŏk′ən-rōl′) ▸ *n.* Var. of **rock 'n' roll.**

rock bottom ▸ *n.* The lowest possible level.

rock·bound also **rock-bound** (rŏk′bound′) ▸ *adj.* Hemmed in by or bordered with rocks.

rock·er (rŏk′ər) ▸ *n.* 1. A rocking chair. 2. One of the two curved pieces upon which something rocks. 3. A rock 'n' roll song, fan, or musician. ***—idiom:* off (one's) rocker** *Slang* Out of one's mind; crazy.

rock·et[1] (rŏk′ĭt) ▸ *n.* 1. An engine that propels by the ejection of matter, esp. by the high-velocity ejection of gaseous combustion products. 2. A device, such as a craft or projectile weapon, propelled by one or more rocket engines. ▸ *v.* To move swiftly and powerfully, as a rocket.

rock·et[2] (rŏk′ĭt) ▸ *n.* A Mediterranean plant having yellowish flowers and leaves that are used in salads.

rock·et·ry (rŏk′ĭ-trē) ▸ *n.* The science and technology of rocket design, construction, and flight.

rocket ship ▸ *n.* A spacecraft propelled by rockets.

rock·ing chair (rŏk′ĭng) ▸ *n.* A chair mounted on rockers or springs.

rocking horse ▸ *n.* A toy horse mounted on rockers or springs.

rock 'n' roll or **rock-and-roll** (rŏk′ən-rōl′) ▸ *n.* A form of popular music arising esp. from rhythm and blues, country music, and gospel and marked by amplified instrumentation and a heavily accented beat.

rock salt ▸ *n.* Common salt in large chunks.

rock·y[1] (rŏk′ē) ▸ *adj.* **-i·er, -i·est.** 1. Consisting of or abounding in rocks. 2. Resembling or suggesting rock; unyielding. 3. Marked by difficulties. **—rock′i·ness** *n.*

rock·y[2] (rŏk′ē) ▸ *adj.* **-i·er, -i·est.** 1. Inclined to sway or totter; unsteady or shaky. 2. Weak, dizzy, or nauseated.

Rocky Mountains ▸ A mountain system of W North America extending more than 4,827 km (3,000 mi) from NW Alaska to the Mexican border.

ro·co·co also **Ro·co·co** (rə-kō′kō, rō′kə-kō′) ▸ *n.* A style of art, esp. architecture and decorative art, originating in France in the early 18th cent. and marked by elaborate and fanciful ornamentation. ▸ *adj.* 1. Of the rococo. 2. Overly elaborate or complicated.

rod (rŏd) ▸ *n.* 1. A thin straight stick or bar, such as: a. A fishing rod. b. A lightning rod. c. A stick used for measuring. 2a. A stick used to punish by whipping. b. Punishment. 3. A scepter or wand symbolizing authority. 4. See **measurement** table in Appendix. 5. A rod-shaped cell in the retina that responds to dim light. 6. *Slang* A handgun.

rode (rōd) ▸ *v.* P.t. of **ride.**

ro·dent (rōd′nt) ▸ *n.* Any of an order of mammals, such as a mouse, rat, squirrel, or beaver, with large incisors adapted for gnawing or nibbling.

ro·de·o (rō′dē-ō′, rō-dā′ō) ▸ *n., pl.* **-os.** 1. A competition or exhibition of skills such as riding broncos or roping calves. 2. A cattle roundup.

roe[1] (rō) ▸ *n.* The eggs or the egg-laden ovary of a fish.

roe[2] (rō) ▸ *n., pl.* **roe** or **roes.** A rather small, delicately formed Eurasian deer.

roent·gen (rĕnt′gən, -jən, rŭnt′-) ▸ *n.* A unit of exposure to ionizing radiation, such as x-rays or gamma rays. **—roent′gen** *adj.*

Roentgen, Wilhelm Konrad (1845–1923) ▸ German physicist; 1901 Nobel.

roent·gen·i·um (rĕnt-gĕn′ē-əm) ▸ *n. Symbol* **Rg** A synthetic radioactive element. At. no. 111.

rog·er (rŏj′ər) ▸ *interj.* Used esp. in radio communications to indicate receipt of a message.

rogue (rōg) ▸ *n.* 1. An unprincipled person; scoundrel. 2. One who is playfully mischievous. **—rogu′ish** *adj.*

roil (roil) ▸ *v.* 1. To make muddy or cloudy by stirring up sediment. 2. To displease or disturb; vex.

role also **rôle** (rōl) ▸ *n.* 1. A character or part played by a performer. 2. A function: *his role in the coup.*

role model ▸ *n.* A person whose behavior serves as a model for another person.

roll (rōl) ▸ *v.* 1. To move or cause to move by repeatedly turning over. 2. To move or push on wheels or rollers. 3. To start to move or operate: *The cameras were rolling.* 4. To gain momentum: *The campaign is finally rolling.* 5. To turn around; revolve or rotate. 6. To advance with a rising and falling motion, as waves. 7. To move or rock from side to side, as a ship. 8. To make a deep rumbling sound, as thunder. 9. To pronounce with a trill: *roll one's r's.* 10. To wrap something around itself or something else: *roll up a rug.* 11. To envelop or enfold in a covering. 12. To spread or flatten by applying pressure with a roller. 13. *Games* To throw (dice), as in craps. ***—phrasal verb:* roll back** To reduce (e.g., prices or wages) to a previous level. ▸ *n.* 1. The act or an instance of rolling. 2. Something rolled up: *a roll of tape.* 3. A quantity, as of cloth, rolled into a cylinder. 4. A piece of parchment or paper that can be or is rolled up; scroll. 5. A list of names of persons belonging to a group. 6a. A small rounded portion of bread. b. A portion of food shaped like a tube with a filling. 7. A rolling, swaying, or rocking motion. 8. A gentle undulation of a surface. 9. A deep reverberation or rumble. 10. A rapid succession of short sounds: *a drum roll.* ***—idiom:* on a roll** *Informal* Having sustained success.

roll·back (rōl′băk′) ▸ *n.* A reduction, esp. in prices or wages, to a previous level.

roll call ▸ *n.* The reading aloud of a list of names to determine who is present.

roll·er (rō′lər) ▸ *n.* 1. One that rolls. 2. A small spokeless wheel, as on a caster. 3. An elongated cylinder on which something is wound. 4. A heavy cylinder used to level, crush, or smooth. 5. A cylinder used to apply ink or paint to a surface. 6. A heavy, breaking wave.

roller coaster ▸ *n.* A steep, sharply banked elevated railway with open cars, operated as a ride.

roller skate ▸ *n.* A shoe or boot with two or four wheels attached to its sole for skating on hard surfaces. **—rol′ler-skate′** *v.*

rol·lick (rŏl′ĭk) ▸ *v.* To romp or frolic boisterously. **—rol′lick·ing** *adj.*

roll·ing pin (rō′lĭng) ▸ *n.* A smooth cylinder used for rolling out dough.

ro·ly-po·ly (rō′lē-pō′lē) ▸ *adj.* Short and plump.

Rom (rōm) ▸ *n., pl.* **Rom** or **Ro·ma** (rō′mə). A Romani, esp. a Romani man or boy.

ROM (rŏm) ▸ *n.* Computer hardware that holds permanently stored data but prevents modification of the data.

Ro·ma (rō′mə) ▸ *n., pl.* **Roma** or **Ro·mas.** A Romani, esp. a member of a Romani people of central and E Europe.

ro·maine (rō-mān′) ▸ *n.* A variety of lettuce having a slender head of long leaves.

THESAURUS

to side or up and down ▸ heave, pitch, roll, toss. [*Compare* LURCH.] *—See also* AGITATE (1), AGITATE (2), SWAY

rock bottom *n.* A very low or lowest level, position, or degree ▸ bottom, low, minimum, nadir.

rocket *v.* *—See* RUSH, SOAR.

rococo *adj.* *—See* ORNATE.

rod *n.* A straight, rigid piece of metal or other solid material ▸ bar, bloom, shaft, stem. [*Compare* STICK.]

rogations *n.* *—See* PRAYER[1] (2).

roger *adv.* *—See* YES.

rogue *n.* *—See* RASCAL.

roguery *n.* *—See* MISCHIEF.

roguish *adj.* *—See* MISCHIEVOUS.

roguishness *n.* *—See* MISCHIEF.

roiled or **roily** *adj.* *—See* MURKY (1), ROUGH (2).

roister *v.* *—See* REVEL.

role *n.* 1. One's duty or responsibility in a common effort ▸ function, part, piece, share. 2. A person portrayed in fiction or drama ▸ character, part, persona, personage. *—See also* FUNCTION (1).

role model *n.* *—See* MODEL.

roll *v.* To move vigorously from side to side or up and down ▸ heave, pitch, rock, toss. [*Compare* LURCH.] *—See also* LURCH (1), LUXURIATE, PRESS (2), RUMBLE (1), TEEM[1], THROW, WRAP (1).

roll about or **around** *v.* To move about in an indolent or clumsy manner ▸ flounder, wallow, welter.

roll out *v.* *—See* EVEN, RISE (1).

roll up *v.* *—See* ACCUMULATE.

roll *n.* *—See* LIST[1], ROAR, THROW.

rollick *v.* *—See* GAMBOL, LUXURIATE.

roly-poly *adj.* *—See* FAT (1).

Ro·man (rō′mən) ▸ *adj.* **1a.** Of or relating to Rome or its people or culture. **b.** Of the Roman Empire. **2.** Of or relating to Latin. **3.** Of the Roman Catholic Church. **4.** **roman** Of or being a style of printing type with upright letters having serifs. ▸ *n.* **1.** A native or inhabitant of ancient or modern Rome. **2.** **roman** Roman print or typestyle. **3.** **Romans** *(takes sing. v.)* See **Bible** table in Appendix.

Roman candle ▸ *n.* A cylindrical firework that emits balls of fire.

Roman Catholic ▸ *adj.* Relating to the Roman Catholic Church. ▸ *n.* A member of the Roman Catholic Church. **—Roman Catholicism** *n.*

Roman Catholic Church ▸ *n.* The Christian church having the Bishop of Rome as its head.

ro·mance (rō-măns′, rō′măns′) ▸ *n.* **1a.** A love affair. **b.** Romantic involvement; love. **2.** A mysterious or fascinating quality or appeal, as of something adventurous. **3a.** A medieval narrative telling of the adventures of chivalric heroes. **b.** A long fictitious tale of heroes and extraordinary or mysterious events. **4.** A story or film dealing with a love affair. **5.** **Romance** The Romance languages. ▸ *adj.* **Romance** Of or being any of the languages that developed from Latin, including Italian, French, Portuguese, Romanian, and Spanish. ▸ *v.* (rō-măns′) **-manced, -manc·ing.** *Informal* To have a love affair with; woo. **—ro·manc′er** *n.*

Roman Empire ▸ An empire (27 B.C.– A.D. 395) stretching from Britain and Germany to North Africa and the Persian Gulf.

Ro·man·esque (rō′mə-nĕsk′) ▸ *adj.* Of or being a style of European architecture containing both Roman and Byzantine elements, prevalent esp. in the 11th and 12th cent. **—Ro′man·esque′** *n.*

Rom·a·ni or **Rom·a·ny** (rŏm′ə-nē, rō′mə-) ▸ *n., pl.* **Romani** or **-nis** also **Romany** or **-nies.** **1.** A member of a nomadic people orig. migrating from N India to Europe around the 14th cent. **2.** The language of the Romani, related to Hindi. **—Rom′a·ni** *adj.*

Ro·ma·ni·a (rō-mā′nē-ə, -mān′yə) or **Ru·ma·ni·a** (ro͞o-) ▸ A country of SE Europe with a short coastline on the Black Sea.

Ro·ma·ni·an (rō-mā′nē-ən, -mān′yən) also **Ru·ma·ni·an** (ro͞o-) ▸ *n.* **1.** A native or inhabitant of Romania. **2.** Their Romance language. **—Ro·ma′ni·an** *adj.*

Roman numeral ▸ *n.* Any of the numerical symbols formed with the Roman letters I, V, X, L, C, D, and M, representing respectively the numbers 1, 5, 10, 50, 100, 500, and 1000.

Ro·mansch (rō-mänsh′, -mănsh′) ▸ *n.* The Rhaeto-Romance dialect that is an official language of Switzerland.

ro·man·tic (rō-măn′tĭk) ▸ *adj.* **1.** Of or characteristic of romance. **2.** Given to thoughts or feelings of romance. **3.** Expressive of or conducive to love. **4.** Imaginative but impractical. **5.** often **Romantic** Of or relating to romanticism in the arts. ▸ *n.* **1.** A romantic person. **2.** often **Romantic** A romanticist. **—ro·man′ti·cal·ly** *adv.*

ro·man·ti·cism (rō-măn′tĭ-sĭz′əm) ▸ *n.* often **Romanticism** An artistic and intellectual movement originating in Europe in the late 18th cent. and marked by emphasis on emotion and imagination, departure from classical forms, and rebellion against social conventions. **—ro·man′ti·cist** *n.*

ro·man·ti·cize (rō-măn′tĭ-sīz′) ▸ *v.* **-cized, -ciz·ing.** **1.** To view or interpret romantically. **2.** To think in a romantic way.

Rom·a·ny (rŏm′ə-nē, rō′mə-) ▸ *n.* Variant of **Romani.** **—Rom′a·ny** *adj.*

Rome (rōm) ▸ The capital of Italy, in the W-central part.

Ro·me·o (rō′mē-ō′) ▸ *n., pl.* **-os.** A man devoted to the pursuit of love.

romp (rŏmp) ▸ *v.* **1.** To play or frolic boisterously. **2.** *Slang* To win a race or game easily. **—romp** *n.*

romp·er (rŏm′pər) ▸ *n.* **1.** One that romps. **2.** **rompers** A loosely fitted, one-piece garment worn esp. by small children for play.

ron·do (rŏn′dō, rŏn-dō′) ▸ *n., pl.* **-dos.** A musical work with a recurring main theme.

rood (ro͞od) ▸ *n.* **1.** A crucifix or cross. **2.** A measure of land equal to 1/4 acre, or 40 square rods (0.10 hectare).

roof (ro͞of, ro͝of) ▸ *n.* **1.** The exterior top surface of a building and its supporting structures. **2.** The top covering of something: *the roof of a car.* **3.** The upper surface of the mouth. **4.** The highest point or limit. ▸ *v.* To cover with a roof. **—roof′er** *n.*

roof·ing (ro͞o′fĭng, ro͝of′ĭng) ▸ *n.* **1.** Materials used in building a roof. **2.** A roof.

rook[1] (ro͝ok) ▸ *n.* An Old World bird resembling the crow. ▸ *v.* To swindle; cheat.

rook[2] (ro͝ok) ▸ *n.* A chess piece that may move in a rank or file over any number of empty squares.

rook·er·y (ro͝ok′ə-rē) ▸ *n., pl.* **-ies.** **1.** A place where rooks nest or breed. **2.** The breeding ground of certain other birds or animals.

rook·ie (ro͝ok′ē) ▸ *n.* **1.** A first-year professional athlete. **2.** *Slang* A beginner; a novice.

room (ro͞om, ro͝om) ▸ *n.* **1.** Space that is or can be occupied. **2a.** An interior area of a building set off by walls or partitions. **b.** The people present in such an area: *The whole room laughed.* **3.** **rooms** Living quarters. **4.** Opportunity or scope: *no room for error.* ▸ *v.* To occupy a room; lodge. **—room′ful** *n.* **—room′y** *adj.*

room·er (ro͞o′mər, ro͝om′ər) ▸ *n.* A lodger.

room·ing house (ro͞o′mĭng, ro͝om′ĭng) ▸ *n.* A house where lodgers may rent rooms.

room·mate (ro͞om′māt′, ro͝om′-) ▸ *n.* A person with whom one shares a room or rooms.

room·y (ro͞o′mē, ro͝om′ē) ▸ *adj.* **-i·er, -i·est.** Having plenty of room; spacious. **—room′i·ness** *n.*

Roo·se·velt (rō′zə-vĕlt′, ro͞o′-), **(Anna) Eleanor** (1884–1962) ▸ Amer. diplomat, writer, and First Lady of the US (1933–45).

Roosevelt, Franklin Delano (1882–1945) ▸ The 32nd US President (1933–45).

Roosevelt, Theodore (1858–1919) ▸ The 26th US President (1901–09); 1906 Nobel Peace Prize.

roost (ro͞ost) ▸ *n.* **1.** A perch on which birds rest. **2.** A place where birds perch. ▸ *v.* To perch for the night.

roost·er (ro͞o′stər) ▸ *n.* An adult male chicken.

root[1] (ro͞ot, ro͝ot) ▸ *n.* **1.** The usu. underground portion of a plant that serves as support, draws minerals and water from the soil, and sometimes stores food. **2.** A similar underground plant part, such as a rhizome. **3.** The part of an organ or structure, such as a hair, that is embedded in other tissue. **4.** A base or support. **5.** An essential part; core. **6.** A source; origin. **7.** often **roots** The condition of belonging to a particular place or society. **8.** *Ling.* The element that carries the meaning in a word and provides the base for inflection. **9.** *Math.* A number that when multiplied by itself an indicated number of times forms a specified product. ▸ *v.* **1.** To grow roots or a root. **2.** To become firmly established or settled. **3.** To remove by or as if by the roots. **—root′er** *n.* **—root′less** *adj.*

root[2] (ro͞ot, ro͝ot) ▸ *v.* **1.** To dig with or as if with the snout or nose. **2.** To rummage for something. **—root′er** *n.*

root[3] (ro͞ot, ro͝ot) ▸ *v.* To encourage by applause; cheer. **—root′er** *n.*

THESAURUS

romance *n.* A narrative not based on fact ▸ fable, fiction, novel, story. [*Compare* YARN.] —*See also* LOVE (1), LOVE (2), LOVE (3).

romance *v.* —*See* COURT (2).

romantic *adj.* —*See* IDEALISTIC, SENTIMENTAL.

romantic *n.* —*See* DREAMER (1).

romp *v.* —*See* BREEZE, GAMBOL, REVEL.

romp *n.* —*See* RUNAWAY (1).

roof *n.* —*See* CLIMAX.

rook *n.* —*See* CHEAT (2).

rook *v.* —*See* CHEAT (1).

rookie *n.* —*See* BEGINNER.

room *n.* —*See* LICENSE (1).

room *v.* —*See* LODGE.

roomy *adj.* Having plenty of room ▸ ample, capacious, commodious, spacious. [*Compare* BIG, BROAD.]

roost *v.* —*See* BALANCE (3).

root[1] *n.* —*See* BASIS (1), CENTER (3), HEART (1), ORIGIN, THEME (1).

root *v.* —*See* ANNIHILATE, BASE[1], FIX (2), PLANT.

root[2] *v.* To express approval audibly, as by clapping ▸ applaud, cheer, clap. *Idioms:* give a big hand (*or* welcome), give an ovation, give someone a hand, put one's hands together.

root beer ▸ *n.* A carbonated soft drink made from extracts of plant roots and herbs.

root canal ▸ *n.* **1.** A pulp-filled channel in the root of a tooth. **2.** A treatment in which diseased tissue from the root canal is removed.

root cellar ▸ *n.* An underground pit or cellar used for storing vegetables.

root·stock (ro͞ot′stŏk′, ro͝ot′-) ▸ *n.* **1.** See **rhizome**. **2.** A root used as a stock for plant propagation.

rope (rōp) ▸ *n.* **1.** A flexible heavy cord of tightly intertwined hemp or other fiber. **2.** A string of items attached in one line by or as if by twisting or braiding: *a rope of onions.* **3. ropes** *Informal* Specialized procedures or details: *learn the ropes.* ▸ *v.* **roped, rop·ing. 1.** To tie or fasten with or as if with rope. **2.** To enclose with a rope: *rope off the area.* **3.** To lasso. ***—idioms:* on the ropes** On the verge of defeat or collapse. **the end of (one's) rope** The limit of one's patience, endurance, or resources.

Roque·fort (rōk′fərt) ▸ A trademark for a sheep's milk cheese ripened in caves.

ror·qual (rôr′kwəl) ▸ *n.* Any of a family of baleen whales with a grooved throat and a small, pointed dorsal fin.

Ror·schach test (rôr′shäk′, -shäkh′) ▸ *n. Psychol.* A projective test in which a subject's interpretations of ten standard inkblots are used to measure emotional and intellectual functioning and integration.

ro·sa·ry (rō′zə-rē) ▸ *n., pl.* **-ries.** *Rom. Cath. Ch.* **1.** A series of prayers dedicated to the Virgin Mary. **2.** A string of beads on which these prayers are counted.

rose[1] (rōz) ▸ *n.* **1a.** Any of a genus of shrubs or vines having prickly stems and variously colored, often fragrant flowers. **b.** The flower of any of these plants. **2.** A rosette. **3.** A dark pink. **—rose** *adj.*

rose[2] (rōz) ▸ *v.* P.t. of **rise.**

ro·sé (rō-zā′) ▸ *n.* A light pink wine made from purple grapes.

ro·se·ate (rō′zē-ĭt, -āt′) ▸ *adj.* **1.** Rose-colored. **2.** Cheerful or bright; optimistic.

rose·bud (rōz′bŭd′) ▸ *n.* The bud of a rose.

rose·bush (rōz′bo͝osh′) ▸ *n.* A shrub that bears roses.

rose-col·ored (rōz′kŭl′ərd) ▸ *adj.* Cheerfully, often unduly optimistic.

rose·mar·y (rōz′mâr′ē) ▸ *n., pl.* **-ies.** An aromatic evergreen shrub having grayish-green leaves that are used in cooking and perfumery.

ro·sette (rō-zĕt′) ▸ *n.* An ornament, as of ribbon or silk, that resembles a rose.

rose water ▸ *n.* A fragrant preparation made by steeping or distilling rose petals in water, used in cosmetics and cookery.

rose window ▸ *n.* A circular window with radiating tracery suggesting a rose.

rose·wood (rōz′wo͝od′) ▸ *n.* **1.** Any of various tropical trees having hard reddish wood. **2.** The wood itself, used in cabinetwork.

Rosh Ha·sha·nah (rôsh′ hə-shô′nə, hä-shä-nä′) ▸ *n.* The Jewish New Year, observed on the 1st or 1st and 2nd days of Tishri.

Ro·si·cru·cian (rō′zĭ-kro͞o′shən, rŏz′ĭ-) ▸ *n.* A member of an international organization devoted to the study of ancient mysticism and its application to modern life. **—Ro′si·cru′cian·ism** *n.*

ros·in (rŏz′ĭn) ▸ *n.* A brownish translucent resin derived from pine sap, used on the bows of stringed instruments, to prevent slipping, and as an ingredient in varnishes, inks, and adhesives. ▸ *v.* To coat or rub with rosin. **—ros′in·y** *adj.*

Ross (rôs, rŏs), **Betsy Griscom** (1752–1836) ▸ Amer. patriot.

ros·ter (rŏs′tər, rô′stər) ▸ *n.* **1.** A list of names. **2.** A list of military personnel enrolled for active duty.

ros·trum (rŏs′trəm, rô′strəm) ▸ *n., pl.* **-trums** or **-tra** (-trə). An elevated platform for public speaking.

ros·y (rō′zē) ▸ *adj.* **-i·er, -i·est. 1a.** Having a rose color. **b.** Flushed: *rosy cheeks.* **2.** Bright; optimistic. **—ros′i·ness** *n.*

rot (rŏt) ▸ *v.* **rot·ted, rot·ting. 1.** To decompose; decay. **2.** To languish: *rot in jail.* ▸ *n.* **1.** The process of rotting or the condition of being rotten. **2.** A plant or animal disease marked by the breakdown of tissue. **3.** Foolish talk; nonsense.

ro·ta·ry (rō′tə-rē) ▸ *adj.* Of, causing, or marked by rotation, esp. axial rotation. ▸ *n., pl.* **-ries. 1.** A rotary part or device. **2.** A traffic circle.

ro·tate (rō′tāt) ▸ *v.* **-tat·ed, -tat·ing. 1.** To turn on an axis. **2.** To alternate in sequence. **—ro′ta′tor** *n.* **—ro′ta·to′ry** (-tə-tôr′ē) *adj.*

ro·ta·tion (rō-tā′shən) ▸ *n.* **1a.** The act or process of turning around a center or an axis **b.** A single complete cycle of such motion. **2.** Regular and uniform variation in a sequence or series. **—ro·ta′tion·al** *adj.*

ROTC ▸ *abbr.* Reserve Officer's Training Corps

rote (rōt) ▸ *n.* **1.** Memorization through repetition, often without understanding. **2.** Mechanical routine. **—rote** *adj.*

ro·tis·se·rie (rō-tĭs′ə-rē) ▸ *n.* A device with a rotating spit on which meat or other food is roasted.

ro·to·gra·vure (rō′tə-grə-vyo͝or′) ▸ *n.* **1.** An intaglio printing process in which the impression is transferred from an etched copper cylinder in a rotary press. **2.** Material produced by this process.

ro·tor (rō′tər) ▸ *n.* **1.** A rotating part of a machine or device. **2.** An assembly of rotating airfoils, as of a helicopter.

ro·to·till·er (rō′tə-tĭl′ər) ▸ *n.* A motorized rotary cultivator. **—ro′to·till′** *v.*

rot·ten (rŏt′n) ▸ *adj.* **-er, -est. 1.** Being in a state of decay; decomposed. **2.** Having a foul odor; putrid. **3.** Morally corrupt or despicable. **4.** Very bad; wretched. **—rot′ten·ness** *n.*

Rot·ter·dam (rŏt′ər-dăm′) ▸ A city of SW Netherlands on the Rhine-Meuse delta SSE of The Hague.

rott·wei·ler (rŏt′wī′lər, rôt′-) ▸ *n.* A breed of dog having a stocky body, short black fur, and tan face markings.

ro·tund (rō-tŭnd′) ▸ *adj.* Rounded in figure; plump. **—ro·tun′di·ty** *n.*

ro·tun·da (rō-tŭn′də) ▸ *n.* **1.** A circular building, esp. one with a dome. **2.** A large, often round room with a high ceiling.

rou·ble (ro͞o′bəl) ▸ *n.* Var. of **ruble.**

rou·é (ro͞o-ā′) ▸ *n.* A lecherous, dissipated man.

rouge (ro͞ozh) ▸ *n.* **1.** A red or pink cosmetic for coloring the cheeks or lips. **2.** A reddish powder used to polish metals or glass. **—rouge** *v.*

rough (rŭf) ▸ *adj.* **-er, -est. 1.** Having a bumpy or irregular surface; not smooth. **2.** Coarse or shaggy to the touch. **3.** Stormy; turbulent: *rough seas.* **4.** Marked by violence or

THESAURUS

rooted *adj.* —*See* CONFIRMED (1), FIXED.

roots *n.* —*See* ANCESTRY.

rootstock *n.* —*See* ORIGIN.

rope *n.* —*See* CORD.

roseate or **rose-colored** *adj.* —*See* OPTIMISTIC.

roster *n.* —*See* LIST[1].

rostrum *n.* —*See* STAGE (1).

rosy *adj.* —*See* OPTIMISTIC, RUDDY.

rot *v.* —*See* DECAY.

rot *n.* —*See* DECAY, NONSENSE.

rotate *v.* To take turns ▸ alternate, interchange, shift. —*See also* TURN (1).

rotation *n.* Occurrence in successive turns ▸ alternation, interchange, shift. —*See also* REVOLUTION (1).

rote *n.* —*See* ROUTINE.

rotten *adj.* —*See* BAD (2), CORRUPT (1), MOLDY, OFFENSIVE (1), SHODDY, TERRIBLE, WORTHLESS.

rottenness *n.* —*See* DECAY.

rotund *adj.* —*See* FAT (1), RESONANT.

roué *n.* —*See* LECHER.

rough *adj.* **1.** Having a surface that is not smooth ▸ abrasive, bumpy, coarse, cragged, craggy, harsh, ironbound, jagged, ragged, rugged, scabrous, scraggy, scratchy, uneven. **2.** Violently disturbed or agitated, as by storms ▸ blustery, dirty, heavy, raging, roiled, roily, rugged, stormy, tempestuous, tumultuous, turbulent, ugly, violent, wild. [*Compare* INTENSE.] **3.** Marked by vigorous physical exertion ▸ arduous, knockabout, rough-and-tumble, rugged, strenuous, tough. [*Compare* BURDENSOME, DIFFICULT.] **4.** Not perfected, elaborated, or completed ▸ crude, imperfect, incomplete, preliminary, sketchy, tentative, unfinished, unperfected, unpolished. —*See also* BITTER (2), BURDENSOME, COARSE (1), COARSE (2), CRUDE, HARSH, LOOSE (3), RUDE (1), WILD (1).

force; harsh: *rough handling.* **5.** Difficult or unpleasant; taxing. **6.** Uncouth or rowdy: *a rough crowd.* **7.** Not polished or refined. **8.** Harsh to the ear. **9.** Not complete, exact, or perfect: *a rough drawing.* ▸ *n.* **1a.** Rugged, overgrown terrain. **b.** The part of a golf course left unmowed and uncultivated. **2.** An unrefined or imperfect state: *a diamond in the rough.* **3.** A rowdy; tough. ▸ *v.* **1.** To roughen. **2.** To treat roughly or with physical violence. **3.** To prepare or make in an unfinished form: *rough out a house plan.* ▸ *adv.* In a rough manner. *—idiom:* **rough it** To live without comforts and conveniences. **—rough′ly** *adv.* **—rough′ness** *n.*

rough·age (rŭf′ĭj) ▸ *n.* See **fiber** 6.

rough·en (rŭf′ən) ▸ *v.* To make or become rough.

rough-hew (rŭf′hyo͞o′) ▸ *v.* **1.** To hew or shape (e.g., timber) roughly, without finishing. **2.** To make in rough form. **—rough′hewn′** *adj.*

rough·house (rŭf′hous′) ▸ *n.* Rowdy, rough behavior. **—rough′house′** (-houz′) *v.*

rough·neck (rŭf′nĕk′) ▸ *n.* A rowdy; tough.

rough·shod (rŭf′shŏd′) ▸ *adj.* Shod with horseshoes having projecting points to prevent slipping. *—idiom:* **ride roughshod over** To treat with brutal force.

rou·lade (ro͞o-läd′) ▸ *n.* A slice of meat rolled around a filling and cooked.

rou·lette (ro͞o-lĕt′) ▸ *n.* A gambling game in which the players bet on which slot of a rotating disk a small ball will come to rest in.

round (round) ▸ *adj.* **-er, -est. 1a.** Spherical; ball-shaped. **b.** Circular or curved. **c.** Cylindrical. **2.** Complete; full: *a round dozen.* **3.** *Math.* Expressed or designated as a whole number or integer; not fractional. **4.** Not exact; approximate: *a round estimate.* ▸ *n.* **1.** Something round, such as a circle, disk, globe, or ring. **2.** A cut of beef between the rump and the shank. **3a.** A complete course, succession, or series: *a round of negotiations.* **b.** often **rounds** A course of customary or prescribed actions, duties, or places: *physicians' rounds.* **4.** One drink for each person in a gathering. **5.** A single outburst, as of applause or cheering. **6a.** A single shot or volley. **b.** A single cartridge or shell. **7.** An interval of play or action in various sports and games. **8.** *Mus.* A composition in which the melody is repeated by successive overlapping voices. ▸ *v.* **1.** To make or become round. **2.** To surround. **3.** To fill out; make plump. **4.** To bring to completion or perfection; finish. **5.** To express as a round number. **6.** To go or pass around. **7.** To make a turn about or to the other side of: *rounded a bend in the road.* *—phrasal verb:* **round up 1.** To bring together. **2.** To herd (cattle) in a roundup. ▸ *adv. & prep.* Around. *—idiom:* **in the round 1.** With the stage in the center of the audience. **2.** Fully shaped and freestanding, as a sculpture. **—round′ish** *adj.* **—round′ness** *n.*

round·a·bout (round′ə-bout′) ▸ *adj.* Indirect; circuitous. ▸ *n.* A traffic circle.

roun·de·lay (roun′də-lā′) ▸ *n.* A poem or song with a recurring refrain.

round·house (round′hous′) ▸ *n.* **1.** A circular building for housing and switching locomotives. **2.** *Slang* A sweeping sidearm punch.

round·ly (round′lē) ▸ *adv.* Fully; thoroughly.

round robin ▸ *n.* A tournament in which each contestant is matched in turn against every other contestant.

round·ta·ble (round′tā′bəl) ▸ *n.* **1.** often **round table** A conference or discussion involving several participants. **2. Round Table** In Arthurian legend, the circular table of King Arthur and his knights.

round-the-clock (round′*th*ə-klŏk′) ▸ *adj.* Twenty-four hours a day; continuous.

round·trip also **round trip** (round′trĭp′) ▸ *n.* A trip to a place and back.

round·up (round′ŭp′) ▸ *n.* **1.** A herding together of cattle. **2.** A gathering up, as of suspects by the police. **3.** A summary.

round·worm (round′wûrm′) ▸ *n.* See **nematode**.

rouse (rouz) ▸ *v.* **roused, rous·ing. 1.** To arouse from sleep, apathy, or depression. **2.** To excite, as to anger or action; stir up.

rous·ing (rou′zĭng) ▸ *adj.* Inducing enthusiasm or excitement; stirring.

roust (roust) ▸ *v.* To rout, esp. out of bed.

roust·a·bout (rous′tə-bout′) ▸ *n.* An unskilled laborer, as in an oil field.

rout[1] (rout) ▸ *n.* **1.** A disorderly retreat or flight following defeat. **2.** An overwhelming defeat. ▸ *v.* **1.** To put to disorderly flight or retreat. **2.** To defeat overwhelmingly.

rout[2] (rout) ▸ *v.* **1.** To dig with the snout; root. **2.** To rummage. **3.** To gouge out. **4.** To drive or force out: *rout out an informant.* **—rout′er** *n.*

route (ro͞ot, rout) ▸ *n.* **1.** A road or way from one place to another. **2.** A customary line of travel. **3.** A means of reaching a goal. ▸ *v.* **rout·ed, rout·ing.** To send by a route.

rou·tine (ro͞o-tēn′) ▸ *n.* **1.** A prescribed and detailed course of action. **2.** A set of customary and often mechanically performed procedures or activities. **3.** A set piece of entertainment. **4.** *Comp. Sci.* A set of programming instructions for a specific task. ▸ *adj.* **1.** In accord with established procedure. **2.** Not special; ordinary. **—rou·tine′ly** *adv.*

roux (ro͞o) ▸ *n., pl.* **roux.** A mixture of flour and fat cooked together, used as a thickening.

rove (rōv) ▸ *v.* **roved, rov·ing.** To wander about at random; roam. **—rov′er** *n.*

row[1] (rō) ▸ *n.* **1.** A series of objects or persons placed next to each other, usu. in a straight line. **2.** A continuous line of buildings along a street.

row[2] (rō) ▸ *v.* **1.** To propel (a boat) with oars. **2.** To travel

THESAURUS

rough in or **out** *v.* —*See* DRAFT (1).
rough up *v.* —*See* BATTER, MANHANDLE.
rough *n.* —*See* DRAFT (1).
rough-and-tumble *adj.* —*See* ROUGH (3).
roughly *adv.* —*See* APPROXIMATELY.
roughneck *n.* —*See* THUG.
roughness *n.* —*See* IRREGULARITY.
round *adj.* **1.** Having the shape of a curve everywhere equidistant from a fixed point ▸ annular, circular, globoid, globular, orbicular, spheric, spherical. **2.** No less than; at least ▸ full, good, whole. —*See also* COMPLETE (1), FAT (1), RESONANT.
round *n.* A stage of a competition ▸ heat, stage. [*Compare* COMPETITION, TURN.] —*See also* BEAT (2), BEND, CIRCLE (1), CIRCLE (2), SERIES.
round *v.* —*See* BEND (1), DULL.
round off *v.* —*See* PERFECT.
round up *v.* —*See* ASSEMBLE.
roundabout *adj.* —*See* INDIRECT (1).
rounded *adj.* —*See* BENT.
rounder *n.* —*See* WANTON.
roundlet *n.* —*See* CIRCLE (1).
rounds *n.* —*See* ROUTINE.
roundtable *n.* —*See* CONFERENCE (1).
round-the-clock *adj.* —*See* CONTINUAL.
rouse *v.* —*See* AROUSE, EVOKE, FIRE (1), WAKE[1].
rousing *adj.* —*See* INVIGORATING.
roustabout *n.* —*See* LABORER.
rout *n.* —*See* CROWD, DEFEAT, FLOCK, RUNAWAY (1).
rout *v.* —*See* OVERWHELM (1).
route *n.* A means or method of entering into or achieving something desirable ▸ formula, key, secret. *Informal:* ticket. [*Compare* TICKET.] —*See also* BEAT (2), DIRECTION, WAY (2).
route *v.* —*See* GUIDE, SEND (1).
routine *n.* A course of action to be followed regularly ▸ method, rote, rounds, rut, track, treadmill. *Informal:* grind. *Slang:* groove. —*See also* BIT[1] (4), CUSTOM, PRACTICE, USUAL.
routine *adj.* Subject to a habit or pattern of behavior ▸ accustomed, chronic, habitual. —*See also* COMMON (1), ORDINARY, PERFUNCTORY.
routinely *adv.* —*See* USUALLY.
routineness *n.* —*See* USUALNESS.
routinism *n.* —*See* DULLNESS.
rove *v.* To move about at random, especially over a wide area ▸ drift, gad, gallivant, meander, peregrinate, ramble, range, roam, stray, traipse, tramp, wander. [*Compare* HIKE, JOURNEY, WALK.]
rover *n.* —*See* HOBO.
roving *adj.* —*See* ERRANT (1).
row[1] *n.* —*See* LINE.
row[2] *n.* —*See* ARGUMENT, FIGHT (1), NOISE (1).

or carry by rowboat. ▸ *n.* A trip by rowboat. **—row′er** *n.*

row[3] (rou) ▸ *n.* **1.** A noisy fight or quarrel. **2.** An uproar. **—row** *v.*

row·boat (rō′bōt′) ▸ *n.* A small boat propelled by oars.

row·dy (rou′dē) ▸ *n., pl.* **-dies.** A rough, disorderly person. ▸ *adj.* **-di·er, -di·est.** Disorderly; rough. **—row′di·ly** *adv.* **—row′di·ness** *n.* **—row′dy·ism** *n.*

row·el (rou′əl) ▸ *n.* A sharp-toothed wheel inserted into the end of the shank of a spur. **—row′el** *v.*

row house (rō) ▸ *n.* One of a series of similar or identical houses built side by side and joined by common walls.

roy·al (roi′əl) ▸ *adj.* **1.** Of or relating to a monarch. **2.** Befitting royalty; stately. **—roy′al·ly** *adv.*

royal blue ▸ *n.* A deep to strong blue. **—roy′al-blue′** *adj.*

roy·al·ist (roi′ə-lĭst) ▸ *n.* A supporter of government by a monarch.

royal poinciana ▸ *n.* A tree native to Madagascar and having clusters of large scarlet flowers.

roy·al·ty (roi′əl-tē) ▸ *n., pl.* **-ties. 1a.** A person of royal rank or lineage. **b.** Monarchs and their families collectively. **2.** The power, status, or authority of a monarch. **3.** Royal quality or bearing. **4a.** A share paid to a writer or composer out of the proceeds resulting from the sale or performance of his or her work. **b.** A share paid to an inventor or a proprietor for the right to use his or her invention or services.

rpm ▸ *abbr.* revolutions per minute

RR ▸ *abbr.* **1.** railroad **2.** rural route

-rrhea or **-rrhoea** ▸ *suff.* Flow; discharge: *pyorrhea.*

RSVP ▸ *abbr. French* répondez s'il vous plaît (please reply)

Rte. ▸ *abbr.* route

Ru ▸ The symbol for the element **ruthenium.**

rub (rŭb) ▸ *v.* **rubbed, rub·bing. 1a.** To apply friction and pressure to (a surface), as with a back and forth motion. **b.** To move or cause to move along a surface with friction and pressure. **2a.** To irritate; annoy. **b.** To chafe. **3.** To be transferred: *Her luck rubbed off on me.* **—*phrasal verbs:*** **rub down** To massage. **rub out 1.** To obliterate by or as if by rubbing. **2.** *Slang* To murder. ▸ *n.* **1.** The act of rubbing. **2.** A difficulty or obstacle.

rub·ber[1] (rŭb′ər) ▸ *n.* **1.** A yellowish elastic material obtained from the milky sap of various tropical plants and used in products such as electric insulation, elastic bands, and tires. **2.** Any of numerous synthetic materials similar to natural rubber. **3.** A low overshoe made of rubber. **4.** An eraser. **5.** *Slang* A condom. **—rub·ber·y** *adj.*

rub·ber[2] (rŭb′ər) ▸ *n. Games* **1.** A series of games of which a majority must be won to terminate the play. **2.** An odd game played to break a tie.

rubber band ▸ *n.* An elastic loop of rubber used to hold objects together.

rubber cement ▸ *n.* An adhesive of nonvulcanized rubber.

rub·ber·ize (rŭb′ə-rīz′) ▸ *v.* **-ized, -iz·ing.** To coat, treat, or impregnate with rubber.

rub·ber·neck (rŭb′ər-nĕk′) ▸ *v. Slang* To stare or gawk. **—rub′ber·neck′er** *n.*

rubber stamp ▸ *n.* A piece of rubber with raised letters or designs, used to make ink impressions.

rub·ber-stamp (rŭb′ər-stămp′) ▸ *v.* To endorse or approve without question or deliberation.

rub·bing (rŭb′ĭng) ▸ *n.* An image of a raised or indented surface made by placing paper over the surface and rubbing the paper gently with a marking agent.

rub·bish (rŭb′ĭsh) ▸ *n.* **1.** Refuse; garbage. **2.** Foolish discourse; nonsense.

rub·ble (rŭb′əl) ▸ *n.* **1.** Fragments of rock or masonry. **2.** Irregular pieces of rock used in masonry. **—rub′bly** *adj.*

rub·down (rŭb′doun′) ▸ *n.* A massage.

rube (ro͞ob) ▸ *n. Slang* An unsophisticated rustic.

ru·bel (ro͞o′bəl) ▸ *n.* See **currency** table in Appendix.

ru·bel·la (ro͞o-bĕl′ə) ▸ *n.* A mild, contagious viral disease capable of producing congenital defects in infants born to mothers infected during early pregnancy.

ru·bi·cund (ro͞o′bĭ-kənd) ▸ *adj.* Rosy in complexion; ruddy.

ru·bid·i·um (ro͞o-bĭd′ē-əm) ▸ *n. Symbol* **Rb** A soft, alkali metallic element used in photocells. At. no. 37.

ru·ble also **rou·ble** (ro͞o′bəl) ▸ *n.* See **currency** table in Appendix.

ru·bric (ro͞o′brĭk) ▸ *n.* **1a.** A class or category. **b.** A title or heading, as of a chapter in a code of law. **2.** A heading or initial letter printed distinctively, usu. in red lettering.

ru·by (ro͞o′bē) ▸ *n., pl.* **-bies. 1.** A deep red, translucent corundum, highly valued as a precious stone. **2.** A deep purplish red. **—ru′by** *adj.*

ruck·sack (rŭk′săk′, ro͝ok′-) ▸ *n.* A knapsack.

ruck·us (rŭk′əs) ▸ *n.* A disturbance; commotion.

rud·der (rŭd′ər) ▸ *n.* **1.** A vertically hinged plate mounted at the stern of a vessel or aircraft for steering. **2.** A controlling agent or influence.

rud·dy (rŭd′ē) ▸ *adj.* **-di·er, -di·est. 1.** Having a healthy reddish color. **2.** Reddish; rosy. **—rud′di·ness** *n.*

rude (ro͞od) ▸ *adj.* **rud·er, rud·est. 1.** Relatively undeveloped; primitive. **2.** Crudely or roughly made. **3.** Ill-mannered; discourteous. **4.** Abrupt and unpleasant: *a rude shock.* **—rude′ly** *adv.* **—rude′ness** *n.*

ru·di·ment (ro͞o′də-mənt) ▸ *n.* **1.** A fundamental element, principle, or skill. **2.** often **rudiments** Something in an incipient or undeveloped form. **—ru′di·men′ta·ry** (-mĕn′tə-rē, -mĕn′trē) *adj.*

rue[1] (ro͞o) ▸ *v.* **rued, ru·ing.** To feel regret, remorse, or sorrow for. **—rue′ful** *adj.* **—rue′ful·ness** *n.*

rue[2] (ro͞o) ▸ *n.* Any of various aromatic Eurasian plants that yield an acrid oil formerly used in medicine.

ruff (rŭf) ▸ *n.* **1.** A stiffly starched circular collar worn in

THESAURUS

row *v.* —*See* ARGUE (1).

rowdy *n.* —*See* THUG.

rowdy *adj.* —*See* DISORDERLY.

royal *adj.* —*See* GRAND, NOBLE.

royalty *n.* —*See* NOBILITY.

rub *v.* To move over or along with pressure ▸ knead, manipulate, massage, press, rub down, stroke, work (over). [*Compare* BRUSH[1], TOUCH.] —*See also* CANCEL (1), CHAFE.

rub against *v.* —*See* BRUSH[1].

rub along *v.* —*See* BRUSH[1].

rub away or **off** *v.* To remove an outer layer or something adherent from an object by friction ▸ scour, scrape, scrub. [*Compare* CHAFE, SCRAPE.]

rub out *v.* —*See* ANNIHILATE, MURDER.

rub *n. Informal* A tricky or unsuspected condition ▸ catch, hitch, snag. [*Compare* BAR, DISADVANTAGE, TRICK.] —*See also* BRUSH[1].

rubber stamp *n.* —*See* PERMISSION.

rubbish *n.* —*See* GARBAGE, NONSENSE.

rubble *n.* —*See* RUIN (2).

rube *n.* —*See* CLODHOPPER.

rubicund *adj.* —*See* RUDDY.

rubric *n.* —*See* RULE.

ruck[1] *n.* —*See* COMMONALTY, CROWD.

ruck[2] *v.* —*See* FOLD.

ruck *n.* —*See* FOLD (1).

ruckus *n.* —*See* DISORDER (2).

ruction *n.* —*See* FIGHT (1).

rudderless *adj.* —*See* AIMLESS.

ruddy *adj.* Of a healthy reddish color ▸ blooming, blushing, florid, flush, flushed, full-blooded, glowing, red, rosy, rubicund, sanguine.

rude *adj.* **1.** Lacking expert, careful craftsmanship ▸ crude, homemade, primitive, raw, rough, rough-hewn, unpolished. [*Compare* SHODDY.] **2.** Lacking good manners ▸ discourteous, disrespectful, foul-mouthed, ill-bred, ill-mannered, impolite, rugged, uncivil, ungracious, unmannered, unmannerly, unpolished. [*Compare* DISRESPECTFUL, TACTLESS, THOUGHTLESS.] **3.** Characterized by unpleasant discordance of sound ▸ cacophonous, discordant, disharmonious, dissonant, inharmonic, inharmonious, unharmonious, unmusical. —*See also* COARSE (1), CRUDE, DISRESPECTFUL, OFFENSIVE (2), UNCIVILIZED.

rudeness *n.* —*See* DISRESPECT, IMPUDENCE.

rudiment *n.* —*See* BASIS (1), ELEMENT (1).

rudimentary *adj.* —*See* ELEMENTARY (2).

rue *v.* To feel or express sorrow for ▸ deplore, regret, repent, sorrow (over). [*Compare* FEEL, GRIEVE.]

rue *n.* —*See* PENITENCE.

rueful *adj.* —*See* PITIFUL, SORROWFUL, SORRY.

the 16th and 17th cent. 2. A collarlike projection around the neck, as of feathers on a bird. **—ruffed** *adj.*

ruf·fi·an (rŭf′ē-ən, rŭf′yən) ▸ *n.* A tough or rowdy person.

ruf·fle (rŭf′əl) ▸ *n.* 1. A strip of frilled or closely pleated fabric used for trimming or decoration. 2. A ruff on a bird. 3. A ripple. ▸ *v.* **-fled, -fling.** 1. To disturb the smoothness or regularity of. 2. To pleat or gather (fabric) into a ruffle. 3. To erect (the feathers). 4. To discompose; fluster. 5. To annoy.

ru·fi·yaa (ro͞o′fē-yä′) ▸ *n.* See **currency** table in Appendix.

ru·fous (ro͞o′fəs) ▸ *adj.* Reddish to reddish-orange.

rug (rŭg) ▸ *n.* A heavy fabric used to cover a floor.

Rug·by (rŭg′bē) ▸ *n.* A form of football in which forward passing, substitution of players, and time-outs are not permitted.

rug·ged (rŭg′ĭd) ▸ *adj.* 1. Having a rough, irregular surface. 2. Strong and sturdy. 3. Foul; stormy. 4. Demanding great effort or endurance. **—rug′ged·ly** *adv.* **—rug′ged·ness** *n.*

Ruhr (ro͝or) ▸ A region of NW Germany along and N of the **Ruhr River,** which flows about 233 km (145 mi) to the Rhine R.

ru·in (ro͞o′ĭn) ▸ *n.* 1. Total destruction or disintegration. 2. A cause of such destruction. 3. often **ruins** The remains of something destroyed, disintegrated, or decayed. ▸ *v.* 1. To destroy completely; demolish. 2. To harm irreparably. 3. To reduce to poverty or bankruptcy. **—ru′in·a·ble** *adj.* **—ru′in·a′tion** *n.* **—ru′in·ous** *adj.*

rule (ro͞ol) ▸ *n.* 1. Governing power; authority. 2. An authoritative direction for conduct or procedure. 3. A usual or customary course of action or behavior. 4. A statement that describes what is true in most or all cases. 5. A standard method or procedure. 6. See **ruler** 2. ▸ *v.* **ruled, rul·ing.** 1. To exercise control (over); govern. 2. To dominate by powerful influence. 3. To decide judicially; decree. 4. To mark with straight parallel lines. ***—phrasal verb:* rule out** To exclude.

rule of thumb ▸ *n., pl.* **rules of thumb.** A useful principle having wide application but not intended to be strictly accurate.

rul·er (ro͞o′lər) ▸ *n.* 1. One that rules or governs. 2. A straightedged strip for drawing straight lines and measuring lengths.

rul·ing (ro͞o′lĭng) ▸ *adj.* 1. Exercising control or authority. 2. Predominant. ▸ *n.* An official decision: *a court ruling.*

rum (rŭm) ▸ *n.* An alcoholic liquor distilled from fermented molasses or sugar cane.

Ru·ma·ni·a (ro͞o-mā′nē-ə, -mān′yə) ▸ See **Romania. —Ru·ma′ni·an** *adj. & n.*

rum·ba (rŭm′bə, ro͝om′-, ro͞om′-) ▸ *n.* A complex rhythmical dance of Cuban origin. **—rum′ba** *v.*

rum·ble (rŭm′bəl) ▸ *v.* **-bled, -bling.** 1. To make a deep long rolling sound. 2. To move or proceed with a rumble. 3. *Slang* To engage in a gang fight. ▸ *n.* 1. A deep long rolling sound. 2. *Slang* a. Murmurous discontent. b. A gang fight. **—rum′bler** *n.* **—rum′bly** *adj.*

ru·men (ro͞o′mən) ▸ *n., pl.* **-mi·na** (-mə-nə) or **-mens.** The first division of the stomach of a ruminant. **—ru′mi·nal** *adj.*

ru·mi·nant (ro͞o′mə-nənt) ▸ *n.* Any of various hoofed, usu. horned mammals, such as cattle, sheep, and deer, having a divided stomach and chewing a cud. ▸ *adj.* 1. Chewing cud. 2. Meditative; contemplative.

ru·mi·nate (ro͞o′mə-nāt′) ▸ *v.* **-nat·ed, -nat·ing.** 1. To consider a matter at length. 2. To chew cud. **—ru′mi·na′tion** *n.* **—ru′mi·na′tive** *adj.* **—ru′mi·na′tor** *n.*

rum·mage (rŭm′ĭj) ▸ *v.* **-maged, -mag·ing.** To make a thorough, often disorderly search (of).

rummage sale ▸ *n.* A sale of assorted secondhand objects.

rum·my (rŭm′ē) ▸ *n.* A card game in which the object is to obtain sets of three or more cards of the same rank or suit.

ru·mor (ro͞o′mər) ▸ *n.* A report of uncertain origin and accuracy; hearsay. **—ru′mor** *v.*

rump (rŭmp) ▸ *n.* 1. The fleshy hindquarters of an animal. 2. A cut of beef from the rump. 3. The buttocks. 4. The last or inferior part.

rum·ple (rŭm′pəl) ▸ *v.* **-pled, -pling.** To wrinkle or form into folds or creases. **—rum′ply** *adj.*

rum·pus (rŭm′pəs) ▸ *n.* A noisy ruckus.

rumpus room ▸ *n.* A play or family room.

run (rŭn) ▸ *v.* **ran** (răn), **run, run·ning.** 1. To move on foot at a pace faster than a walk. 2. To flee. 3. To move without hindrance or restraint. 4. To make a short, quick trip. 5. To cause to move quickly: *ran her finger along the keyboard.* 6. To hurry; hasten. 7a. To take part in a race. b. To compete for elected office: *ran for mayor.* 8. To swim in large numbers, as in migrating. 9. To move freely, as by rolling or sliding. 10a. To function or cause to function. b. To control or manage. 11. To cause to collide or penetrate. 12. To go regularly. 13. *Naut.* To sail or steer before the wind or on an indicated coursea. 14a. To flow in a steady stream. b. To discharge or leak. 15. To cause to flow: *run the water into the tub.* 16. To spread and dissolve, as dye in fabric. 17. To extend: *This road runs into the next town.* 18. To spread or climb, as a vine. 19. To spread rapidly, as a disease. 20. To unravel, as a nylon stocking. 21. To continue in effect or operation. 22. To pass; elapse. 23. To persist or recur. 24. To accumulate or accrue. 25. To have a particular form or expression. 26. To tend or incline. 27. To exist in a certain range: *sizes run from small to large.* 28. To pass into a specified

THESAURUS

ruffian *n.* —*See* THUG.

ruffle *v.* —*See* AGITATE (2), ANNOY.

ruffled feathers *n.* —*See* OFFENSE.

rugged *adj.* —*See* HARD (2), MUSCULAR, ROUGH (1), ROUGH (2), ROUGH (3).

ruin *n.* 1. Something that causes total loss or severe impairment ▸ bane, destroyer, destruction, downfall, ruination, undoing, wrecker. [*Compare* BREAKDOWN, CURSE.] 2. The remains of something destroyed, disintegrated, or decayed ▸ debris, remains, rubble, wrack, wreck, wreckage. [*Compare* TRACE.] —*See also* BANKRUPTCY, DESTRUCTION.

ruin *v.* To reduce to the point of financial insolvency ▸ bankrupt, break, bust, do in, impoverish, pauperize. *Slang:* clean out. —*See also* BREAK (2), DESTROY (1).

ruination *n.* —*See* BANKRUPTCY, DESTRUCTION, RUIN (1).

ruinous *adj.* —*See* DISASTROUS, HARMFUL, SHABBY.

rulable *adj.* Capable of being governed ▸ administrable, controllable, governable, manageable. [*Compare* LOYAL, OBEDIENT.]

rule *n.* A code or set of codes governing action or procedure, for example ▸ dictate, guideline, law, prescript, regulation, rubric. [*Compare* STANDARD.] —*See also* AUTHORITY, DOMINANCE, DOMINATION, GOVERNMENT (1), LAW (1), USUAL.

rule *v.* —*See* ADMINISTER (1), BOSS, DOMINATE (1), JUDGE.

rule out *v.* —*See* DICTATE, EXCLUDE, PREVENT.

ruler *n.* —*See* CHIEF.

ruling *adj.* —*See* DOMINANT (1), PREVAILING.

ruling *n.* An authoritative or official decision, especially one made by a court ▸ adjudication, decision, dictum, decree, determination, edict, finding, judgment, opinion, pronouncement, resolution, sentence, verdict. [*Compare* COMMAND, LAW.]

rumble *v.* 1. To make a continuous deep reverberating sound ▸ boom, growl, grumble, resound, roll. 2. *Slang* To exchange blows with another person ▸ fight. *Idioms:* duke it out, mix it up, slug it out. [*Compare* WRESTLE.] —*See also* BLAST (1).

rumble *n.* —*See* BLAST (1), FIGHT (1), ROAR.

ruminate *v.* —*See* CHEW, PONDER.

rumination *n.* —*See* THOUGHT.

ruminative *adj.* —*See* THOUGHTFUL.

rummage *v.* —*See* SCOUR[2].

rummy *n.* —*See* DRUNKARD.

rumor *n.* —*See* GOSSIP (1).

rumor *v.* —*See* GOSSIP.

rumormonger *n.* —*See* GOSSIP (2).

rump *n.* —*See* BUTTOCKS.

rumple *v.* —*See* FOLD, TOUSLE.

rumpus *n.* —*See* NOISE (1), VOCIFERATION.

run *v.* 1. To move on foot at a pace faster than a walk ▸ canter, gallop, jog, lope, scamper, scurry, scuttle, shin, sprint, trot. [*Compare* BOUND[1], RUSH.] 2. To leave hastily ▸ bolt, get out. *Informal:* clear out, get, hotfoot, skedaddle. *Slang:* hightail, scram, take off, vamoose. *Idioms:* beat it,

condition: *run into debt.* **29.** *Comp. Sci.* To process or execute (a program or instruction). ***—phrasal verbs:*** **run along** To go away; leave. **run down 1.** To stop because of lack of force or power. **2.** To become tired. **3.** To collide with and knock down. **4.** To chase and capture. **5.** To trace the source of. **6.** To disparage. **run out** To become used up. **run over 1.** To collide with and knock down. **2.** To go beyond a limit. **run through 1.** To pierce. **2.** To use up. **3.** To examine or rehearse quickly. ▸ *n.* **1a.** A pace faster than a walk. **b.** A fast gallop. **2.** An act of running. **3.** A distance covered by or as if by running. **4.** A quick trip or visit. **5a.** A running race. **b.** A campaign for public office. **6.** *Baseball* A point scored by reaching home plate safely. **7.** The migration of fish, esp. in order to spawn. **8.** Unrestricted freedom or use: *the run of the library.* **9.** A continuous period of operation, as by a machine or factory. **10.** A movement or flow. **11a.** A conduit or channel. **b.** *Regional* See **creek**. **12.** A continuous length or extent. **13.** The direction, configuration, or lie of something. **14.** An outdoor enclosure for domestic animals or poultry. **15.** A length of unraveled stitches in a knitted fabric. **16.** An unbroken series or sequence, as of theatrical performances. **17.** A series of unexpected and urgent demands, as by customers: *a run on a bank.* **18a.** A continuous set or sequence, as of playing cards. **b.** A successful sequence of shots or points. **19.** A sustained state or condition: *a run of good luck.* **20.** A trend or tendency. **21.** An average type or category: *the broad run of voters.* ***—idioms:*** **in the long run** In the final analysis or outcome. **in the short run** In the immediate future. **on the run 1.** In rapid retreat. **2.** In hiding. **3.** Hurrying busily from place to place. **run out of** To exhaust the supply of.

run·a·bout (rŭn′ə-bout′) ▸ *n.* A small open automobile, carriage, or motorboat.

run·a·round (rŭn′ə-round′) ▸ *n.* *Informal* Deception, usu. in the form of evasive excuses.

run·a·way (rŭn′ə-wā′) ▸ *n.* **1.** One who has run away. **2.** *Informal* An easy victory. ▸ *adj.* **1.** Escaping or having escaped confinement. **2.** Out of control. **3.** Easily won.

run·down (rŭn′doun′) ▸ *n.* A point-by-point summary. ▸ *adj.* also **run-down** (rŭn′doun′) **1a.** Weak or exhausted. **b.** Dirty and dilapidated. **2.** Unwound and not running.

rune (ro͞on) ▸ *n.* **1.** One of the letters of an alphabet used by ancient Germanic peoples. **2.** A magic charm.

rung¹ (rŭng) ▸ *n.* **1.** A bar forming a step of a ladder. **2.** A crosspiece between the legs of a chair. **3.** A spoke of a wheel.

rung² (rŭng) ▸ *v.* P.part. of **ring²**.

run-in (rŭn′ĭn′) ▸ *n.* A quarrel or argument.

run·nel (rŭn′əl) ▸ *n.* **1.** A rivulet; brook. **2.** A narrow channel, as for water.

run·ner (rŭn′ər) ▸ *n.* **1.** One who runs, as in a race. **2a.** *Baseball* One who runs the bases. **b.** *Football* One who carries the ball. **3.** A messenger. **4.** A smuggler. **5.** A vessel engaged in smuggling. **6.** A device in or on which a mechanism slides or moves, as the blade of a skate. **7.** A long narrow carpet. **8.** A slender creeping stem that roots at intervals along its length.

run·ner-up (rŭn′ər-ŭp′) ▸ *n., pl.* **run·ners-up** (rŭn′ərz-). One that takes second place.

run·ning (rŭn′ĭng) ▸ *n.* The act or sport of running. ▸ *adj.* Ongoing; continuous. ▸ *adv.* Consecutively.

running board ▸ *n.* A narrow footboard extending under and along the doors of some vehicles.

running light ▸ *n.* One of several lights on a ship or aircraft to indicate position and size.

run·ny (rŭn′ē) ▸ *adj.* **-ni·er, -ni·est.** Inclined to run or flow: *a runny nose.*

Run·ny·mede (rŭn′ē-mēd′) ▸ A meadow in SE England on the Thames R.; site of royal acceptance of the Magna Carta (1215).

run·off (rŭn′ôf′, -ŏf′) ▸ *n.* **1.** An overflow of fluid. **2.** A competition held to break a tie.

run-of-the-mill (rŭn′əv-*th*ə-mĭl′) ▸ *adj.* Not special; average.

runt (rŭnt) ▸ *n.* **1.** An undersized animal, esp. the smallest of a litter. **2.** *Slang* A short person. **—runt′y** *adj.*

run-through (rŭn′thro͞o′) ▸ *n.* A complete but rapid review or rehearsal.

run·way (rŭn′wā′) ▸ *n.* **1.** A usu. paved strip of level ground on which aircraft take off and land. **2.** A path, channel, or track over which something runs. **3.** A narrow walkway from a stage into an auditorium.

ru·pee (ro͞o-pē′, ro͞o′pē) ▸ *n.* See **currency** table in Appendix.

ru·pi·ah (ro͞o-pē′ə) ▸ *n., pl.* **ru·pi·ah** or **ru·pi·ahs**. See **currency** table in Appendix.

rup·ture (rŭp′chər) ▸ *n.* **1a.** The process of breaking open or bursting. **b.** The state of being broken. **2.** A hernia. **—rup′ture** *v.*

ru·ral (ro͝or′əl) ▸ *adj.* Of or relating to the country as opposed to the city. **—ru′ral·ly** *adv.*

ruse (ro͞os, ro͞oz) ▸ *n.* An action or device meant to mislead or confuse; deception.

rush¹ (rŭsh) ▸ *v.* **1.** To move or cause to move swiftly; hurry. **2.** To attack suddenly. **3.** To perform with haste. **4.** To transport with urgent speed. ▸ *n.* **1.** A sudden forward motion. **2a.** Urgent movement to or from a place. **b.** A sudden generalized demand: *a rush for gold coins.* **3.** General haste

THESAURUS

hightail it, hotfoot it, make tracks, take a powder. 3. To move or proceed away from a place ▸ depart, exit, get away, get off, go, go away, leave, pull out, quit, retire, run along, withdraw. *Informal:* cut out, push off, shove off. *Slang:* blow, split, take off. 4. To complete a race or competition in a specified position ▸ come in, finish, place. 5. To be performed ▸ play, show. *—See also* ADMINISTER (1), ASSOCIATE (2), AMOUNT, CONDUCT (1), DRIVE (3), EXTEND (1), FLOW (1), FLOW (2), FUNCTION, GO (4), HUNT, MELT, OPERATE, PLUNGE, POUR, RESORT, RUSH, SMUGGLE, TEAR¹.

run across *v.* *—See* ENCOUNTER (1).

run after *v.* *—See* COURT (2), PURSUE (1).

run along or **away** *v.* *—See* GO (1).

run away *v.* *—See* ESCAPE (1).

run down *v.* *—See* BELITTLE, REVIEW (1), TRACE (1).

run in *v.* *—See* ARREST, VISIT.

run into *v.* *—See* COLLIDE, ENCOUNTER (1).

run off *v.* *—See* PUBLISH (1).

run on *v.* *—See* CHATTER (1).

run out *v.* To prove deficient or insufficient ▸ fail, give out. *Idioms:* fall short, run dry, run short. [*Compare* DECREASE.] *—See also* DISMISS (2), DRY UP (2), LAPSE.

run through *v.* *—See* BROWSE (1), EXHAUST (1), PRACTICE (1), REVIEW (1).

run up *v.* *—See* INCREASE.

run *n.* 1. A pace faster than a walk ▸ canter, dash, gallop, jog, lope, sprint, trot. [*Compare* HIKE, WALK.] 2. A length of torn or unraveled stitches in knitted fabric ▸ rent, rip, tear. *—See also* BROOK¹, CAGE, DRIVE (1), [illegible]

runagate *n.* *—See* DEFECTOR.

runaway *n.* 1. An easy victory ▸ cakewalk, rout, walkaway, walkover. *Slang:* romp. *Idiom:* clean sweep. [*Compare* BREEZE, DEFEAT.] 2. One who flees, as from confinement or the police ▸ escapee, fugitive, outlaw, refugee. [*Compare* CRIMINAL.]

runaway *adj.* 1. Fleeing or having fled, as from confinement or the police ▸ escaped, fugitive, fleeing. *Idiom:* on the lam (*or* loose *or* run). 2. Out of control ▸ amuck, unbridled, uncontrolled. *Idioms:* out of hand, running wild. [*Compare* ABANDONED, LOOSE.]

rundown *n.* *—See* SUMMARY.

rundown *adj.* *—See* SHABBY, TIRED (1), WEAK (1).

rung *n.* *—See* DEGREE (1).

run-in *n.* *—See* ARGUMENT.

runner *n.* A person who engages in smuggling ▸ bootlegger, contrabandist, smuggler. *Slang:* mule. *—See also* MESSENGER, SHOOT.

running *adj.* *—See* ACTIVE.

run-of-the-mill *adj.* *—See* ORDINARY.

run-through *n.* *—See* SUMMARY.

runt *n.* *—See* SQUIRT (2).

runty *adj.* *—See* LITTLE.

rupture *n.* An opening, especially in a solid structure ▸ breach, break, gap, hole, perforation. *—See also* BREACH (2).

rupture *v.* *—See* CRACK (1).

rural *adj.* *—See* COUNTRY.

ruse *n.* *—See* TRICK (1).

rush *v.* To move swiftly ▸ bolt, bucket,

or busyness. **4.** A sudden attack. **5.** A rapid, often noisy flow. **6.** A sudden brief exhilaration. ▸ *adj.* Performed with or requiring great haste or urgency. **—rush′er** *n.*

rush² (rŭsh) ▸ *n.* **1.** A marsh plant having pliant hollow or pithy stems. **2.** The stem itself, used in wickerwork.

Rush·more (rŭsh′môr′), **Mount** ▸ A mountain, 1,708 m (5,600 ft), in the Black Hills of W SD; site of a national memorial.

rusk (rŭsk) ▸ *n.* Sweet raised bread dried and browned in an oven.

rus·set (rŭs′ĭt) ▸ *n.* **1.** A reddish brown. **2.** A brown homespun cloth. **3.** A winter apple with a reddish-brown skin. **—rus′set** *adj.*

Rus·sia (rŭsh′ə) ▸ A country of E Europe and N Asia extending from the Gulf of Finland to the Pacific and reaching N to the Arctic Ocean.

Rus·sian (rŭsh′ən) ▸ *n.* **1.** A native or inhabitant of Russia. **2.** The Slavic language of the Russians. **—Rus′sian** *adj.*

rust (rŭst) ▸ *n.* **1.** Any of various reddish-brown oxides formed on iron and iron-containing materials by low-temperature oxidation in the presence of water. **2.** Any of various metallic coatings formed by corrosion. **3.** A plant disease caused by various fungi, marked by reddish or brownish spots on leaves and stems. **4.** A strong brown. ▸ *v.* **1.** To corrode. **2.** To deteriorate through inactivity or neglect. **—rust** *adj.* **—rust′i·ness** *n.* **—rust′y** *adj.*

rus·tic (rŭs′tĭk) ▸ *adj.* **1.** Typical of country life. **2.** Unsophisticated; simple; crude. ▸ *n.* **1.** A rural person. **2.** A crude, coarse, or simple person. **—rus·tic′i·ty** (-tĭs′ĭ-tē) *n.*

rus·ti·cate (rŭs′tĭ-kāt′) ▸ *v.* **-cat·ed, -cat·ing.** To go to or live in the country. **—rus′ti·ca′tion** *n.*

rus·tle (rŭs′əl) ▸ *v.* **-tled, -tling. 1.** To move or cause to move with soft fluttering or crackling sounds. **2.** To obtain in an enterprising manner: *rustle up supper.* **3.** To steal (livestock). **—rus′tler** *n.*

rut¹ (rŭt) ▸ *n.* **1.** A sunken track or groove made by the passage of vehicles. **2.** A fixed, usu. boring routine. ▸ *v.* **rut·ted, rut·ting.** To furrow. **—rut′ty** *adj.*

rut² (rŭt) ▸ *n.* An annually recurring condition of sexual activity, as in male deer. **—rut** *v.*

ru·ta·ba·ga (ro͞o′tə-bā′gə, ro͝ot′ə-) ▸ *n.* A turniplike plant having a thick, bulbous, edible root.

Ruth (ro͞oth) ▸ *n.* See **Bible** table in Appendix.

Ruth, George Herman. "Babe" (1895–1948) ▸ Amer. baseball player.

Ru·the·nia (ro͞o-thēn′yə, -thē′nē-ə) ▸ A region of W Ukraine S of the Carpathian Mts. **—Ru·the′ni·an** *adj. & n.*

ru·the·ni·um (ro͞o-thē′nē-əm) ▸ *n. Symbol* **Ru** A hard, white, acid-resistant metallic element used to harden platinum and palladium. At. no. 44.

ruth·er·for·di·um (rŭth′ər-fôr′dē-əm) ▸ *n. Symbol* **Rf** A short-lived, synthetic radioactive element. At. no. 104.

ruth·less (ro͞oth′lĭs) ▸ *adj.* Having no compassion or pity; merciless. **—ruth′less·ly** *adv.* **—ruth′less·ness** *n.*

RV ▸ *abbr.* recreational vehicle

R-val·ue (är′văl′yo͞o) ▸ *n.* A measure of the capacity of a material, such as insulation, to impede heat flow.

Rwan·da (ro͞o-än′də) ▸ A country of E-central Africa. **—Rwan′dan** *adj. & n.*

Rx (är′ĕks′) ▸ *n.* A medical prescription.

-ry ▸ *suff.* Var. of **-ery.**

rye (rī) ▸ *n.* **1.** A widely cultivated cereal grass. **2.** The grain of this plant, used in making flour and whiskey and for livestock feed. **3.** Whiskey made from this grain.

Ryu·kyu Islands (rē-o͞o′kyo͞o′, ryo͞o′kyo͞o) ▸ An island group of SW Japan extending between Kyushu and Taiwan.

THESAURUS

bustle, dart, dash, festinate, flash, fleet, flit, fly, haste, hasten, hurry, hustle, pelt, race, rocket, run, sail, sally, scoot, scour, shoot, speed, sprint, tear, trot, whirl, whisk, whiz, wing, zing, zip, zoom. *Informal:* rip. *Slang:* barrel, highball. ***Idioms:*** get a move on, get cracking, go like lightning, go like the wind, hotfoot it, make haste, make time, make tracks, run like the wind, shake a leg, step (*or* jump) on it. [*Compare* RUN.] *—See also* ATTACK (1), FLOW (2).

rush *n.* *—See* CHARGE (1), FLOW, HASTE (2), HASTE (1).

rush *adj.* Designed to meet emergency needs as quickly as possible ▸ *Informal:* crash, hurry-up.

rustic *adj.* Of a charmingly plain and unsophisticated nature ▸ artless, homely, homespun, natural, simple, unadorned, unpolished. [*Compare* COARSE.] *—See also* COUNTRY.

rustic *n.* *—See* CLODHOPPER.

rustle *n.* *—See* HISS (1), MURMUR.

rustle *v.* To make a low, continuous, and indistinct sound ▸ murmur, sigh, sough, whisper. [*Compare* BURBLE, HUM.] *—See also* HISS (1).

rut *n.* *—See* FURROW, ROUTINE.

ruthful *adj.* *—See* PITIFUL.

ruthless *adj.* *—See* CRUEL, UNSCRUPULOUS

S

s[1] or **S** (ĕs) ▸ *n., pl.* **s's** or **S's** also **ss** or **Ss**. The 19th letter of the English alphabet.
s[2] ▸ *abbr.* **1.** second (unit of time) **2.** *Math.* second (of arc)
S[1] ▸ The symbol for the element **sulfur.**
S[2] ▸ *abbr.* **1.** satisfactory **2.** small **3.** soprano **4.** south **5.** *Baseball* strike
s. ▸ *abbr.* **1.** singular **2.** son
–s[1] or **–es** ▸ *suff.* Used to form plural nouns: *letters; ashes.*
–s[2] or **–es** ▸ *suff.* Used to form the 3rd person singular present tense of all regular and most irregular verbs: *looks; goes.*
–s[3] ▸ *suff.* Used to form adverbs: *caught unawares.*
–'s ▸ *suff.* Used to form the possessive case: *nation's.*
Sab·bath (săb′əth) ▸ *n.* **1.** The 7th day of the week, Saturday, observed as the day of rest and worship by Jews and some Christians. **2.** The 1st day of the week, Sunday, observed as the day of rest and worship by most Christians.
sab·bat·i·cal year also **sab·bat·i·cal** (sə-băt′ĭ-kəl) ▸ *n.* An often paid leave of absence, usu. granted every 7th year, as to a professor, for travel, research, or rest.
sa·ber (sā′bər) ▸ *n.* **1.** A heavy cavalry sword with a one-edged, slightly curved blade. **2.** A light dueling or fencing sword having a tapered flexible blade.
Sa·bin (sā′bĭn), **Albert Bruce** (1906–93) ▸ Amer. microbiologist and physician.
Sa·bine (sā′bīn′) ▸ *n.* **1.** A member of an ancient people of central Italy. **2.** The Italic language of the Sabines. **—Sa′bine′** *adj.*
Sabin vaccine ▸ *n.* An oral vaccine used to immunize against poliomyelitis.
sa·ble (sā′bəl) ▸ *n.* **1a.** A weasellike mammal of N Eurasia, having soft dark fur. **b.** The fur of this animal. **2a.** The color black. **b. sables** Black garments worn in mourning. **—sa′ble** *adj.*
sab·o·tage (săb′ə-täzh′) ▸ *n.* **1.** Destruction of property or obstruction of normal operations, as by civilians or enemy agents in time of war. **2.** Treacherous action to hinder an endeavor; deliberate subversion. **—sab′o·tage′** *v.*
sab·o·teur (săb′ə-tûr′) ▸ *n.* One who commits sabotage.
sa·bra (sä′brə) ▸ *n.* A native-born Israeli.
sac (săk) ▸ *n.* A pouchlike plant or animal structure.
Sac (săk, sôk) ▸ *n.* Var. of **Sauk.**
Sac·a·ga·we·a (săk′ə-gə-wē′ə, sä-kä′gä-wē′ä) or **Sac·a·ja·we·a** (săk′ə-jə-wē′ə) (1787?–1812) ▸ Shoshone guide and interpreter for the Lewis and Clark Expedition.
sacchar– ▸ *pref.* Sugar: *saccharine.*
sac·cha·rin (săk′ər-ĭn) ▸ *n.* A very sweet, white crystalline powder, $C_7H_5NO_3S$, used as a calorie-free sweetener.
sac·cha·rine (săk′ər-ĭn, -ə-rēn′, -ə-rīn′) ▸ *adj.* **1.** Of or characteristic of sugar or saccharin; sweet. **2.** Cloyingly sweet.
sac·er·do·tal (săs′ər-dōt′l, săk′-) ▸ *adj.* Of or relating to priests or the priesthood.
sa·chem (sā′chəm) ▸ *n.* A chief of a Native American, esp. Algonquian tribe or confederation.
sa·chet (să-shā′) ▸ *n.* A packet of perfumed powder used to scent clothes.
sack[1] (săk) ▸ *n.* **1a.** A large bag of strong coarse material. **b.** A similar container of paper or plastic. **2.** A short, loose-fitting garment. **3.** *Slang* Dismissal from employment. **4.** *Informal* A bed. ▸ *v.* **1.** To place into a sack. **2.** *Slang* To dismiss; fire.
sack[2] (săk) ▸ *v.* To plunder; pillage. **—sack** *n.*
sack·cloth (săk′klôth′, -klŏth′) ▸ *n.* **1.** Sacking. **2a.** A rough coarse cloth. **b.** Garments made of sackcloth, worn as a symbol of mourning or penitence.
sack·ing (săk′ĭng) ▸ *n.* A coarse woven cloth used for making sacks.
sa·cra (sā′krə, săk′rə) ▸ *n.* Pl. of **sacrum.**
sac·ra·ment (săk′rə-mənt) ▸ *n.* *Christianity* **1.** A rite instituted by Jesus that confers sanctifying grace. **2.** often **Sacrament** The consecrated elements of the Eucharist. **—sac′ra·men′tal** (-mĕn′tl) *n. & adj.*
Sac·ra·men·to (săk′rə-mĕn′tō) ▸ The capital of CA, in the N-central part on the Sacramento R.
sa·cred (sā′krĭd) ▸ *adj.* **1.** Dedicated to or set apart for worship. **2.** Worthy of religious veneration. **3.** Made or declared holy. **4.** Dedicated or devoted exclusively to a single use or person. **5.** Worthy of respect; venerable. **6.** Of or relating to religious objects or practices. **—sa′cred·ly** *adv.* **—sa′cred·ness** *n.*
sacred cow ▸ *n.* One immune from criticism.
sac·ri·fice (săk′rə-fīs′) ▸ *n.* **1.** The offering of something to a deity. **2a.** Forfeiture of something highly valued for the sake of one considered to have a greater value or claim. **b.** Something so forfeited. **3.** Relinquishment of something at less than its presumed value. ▸ *v.* **-ficed, -fic·ing. 1.** To offer as a sacrifice. **2.** To forfeit (one thing) for another thing considered of greater value. **3.** To sell or give away at a loss. **—sac′ri·fic′er** *n.* **—sac′ri·fi′cial** (-fĭsh′əl) *adj.* **—sac′ri·fi′cial·ly** *adv.*
sac·ri·lege (săk′rə-lĭj) ▸ *n.* Desecration, profanation, misuse, or theft of something sacred.
sac·ri·le·gious (săk′rə-lĭj′əs, -lē′jəs) ▸ *adj.* Grossly irreverent toward what is sacred. **—sac′ri·le′gious·ly** *adv.*

THESAURUS

sabbatical *n.* A regularly scheduled period spent away from work or duty, often in recreation ▸ furlough, holiday, leave, vacation. ***Idiom:*** time (or day) off. [*Compare* BREAK, TRIP.]
saber-rattling *n.* —*See* AGGRESSION.
sable *adj.* —*See* BLACK (1).
sabotage *n.* Treacherous action to defeat or do harm to an endeavor ▸ subversion, undermining. [*Compare* DEFEAT, DESTRUCTION.]
sabotage *v.* To damage, destroy, or defeat by sabotage ▸ subvert, undermine. [*Compare* DESTROY, DISORDER.]
sabulous *adj.* —*See* COARSE (2).
saccharine *adj.* Having or suggesting the taste of sugar ▸ honeyed, sugary, sweet. —*See also* FLATTERING.
sacerdotal *adj.* —*See* CLERICAL.
sachem *n.* —*See* CHIEF.
sack[1] *n.* —*See* BAG, DISMISSAL.
sack *v.* —*See* DISMISS (1).
sack out *v. Slang* To be asleep ▸ sleep, slumber. ***Idioms:*** be in the land of Nod, catch some shuteye, catch (*or* cop) some z's, saw logs (*or* wood), sleep like a log (*or* baby *or* rock *or* top), sleep tight. [*Compare* NAP, REST[1].]
sack[2] *v.* To rob of goods by force, especially in time of war ▸ depredate, despoil, loot, pillage, plunder, ransack, rape, ravage, strip. [*Compare* ATTACK, INVADE.]
sacrarium *n.* A sacred or holy place ▸ sanctorium, sanctuary, sanctum, shrine.
sacred *adj.* —*See* DIVINE (2), HOLY, UNSPEAKABLE (2).
sacredness *n.* —*See* HOLINESS.
sacrifice *n.* The expenditure by which something is obtained ▸ cost, expense, price, toll. *Informal:* damage. —*See also* ABANDONMENT (1), OFFERING.
sacrifice *v.* To offer as a sacrifice ▸ immolate, offer up, victimize. —*See also* ABANDON (1), DEVOTE.
sacrilege *n.* An act of disrespect or impiety toward something regarded as sacred ▸ blasphemy, desecration, impiety, profanation, violation.
sacrilegious *adj.* Showing irreverence and contempt for something sacred ▸ blasphemous, impious, profane.

sac·ris·tan (săk′rĭ-stən) ► *n.* **1.** One in charge of a sacristy. **2.** A sexton.

sac·ris·ty (săk′rĭ-stē) ► *n., pl.* **-ties.** A room in a church housing the sacred vessels and vestments.

sac·ro·il·i·ac (săk′rō-ĭl′ē-ăk′, sā′krō-) ► *n.* The region of the lower back in which the sacrum and ilium join. **—sac′ro·il′i·ac′** *adj.*

sac·ro·sanct (săk′rō-săngkt′) ► *adj.* Inviolably sacred. **—sac′ro·sanc′ti·ty** *n.*

sa·crum (sā′krəm, săk′rəm) ► *n., pl.* **sa·cra** (sā′krə, săk′rə). A triangular bone that forms the posterior section of the pelvis. **—sa′cral** *adj.*

sad (săd) ► *adj.* **sad·der, sad·dest.** **1.** Sorrowful; unhappy. **2.** Causing sorrow or gloom. **3.** Deplorable; sorry. **—sad′ly** *adv.* **—sad′ness** *n.*

sad·den (săd′n) ► *v.* To make or become sad.

sad·dle (săd′l) ► *n.* **1a.** A leather seat for a rider, secured on an animal's back. **b.** The seat of a bicycle or similar vehicle. **2.** A cut of meat consisting of part of the backbone and both loins. ► *v.* **-dled, -dling.** **1.** To put a saddle onto. **2.** To load or burden; encumber. **—*idiom:* in the saddle** In control; dominant.

sad·dle·bag (săd′l-băg′) ► *n.* **1.** A pouch that hangs across the back of a horse. **2.** A similar pouch on a motorcycle or bicycle.

Sad·du·cee (săj′ə-sē′, săd′yə-) ► *n.* A member of a priestly Jewish sect (2nd cent. B.C.–1st cent. A.D.) that accepted only the written Mosaic law. **—Sad′du·ce′an** (-sē′ən) *adj.*

sa·dism (sā′dĭz′əm, săd′ĭz′-) ► *n.* **1.** *Psychol.* The association of sexual gratification with infliction of pain on others. **2.** Delight in cruelty. **—sa′dist** *n.* **—sa·dis′tic** (sə-dĭs′tĭk) *adj.* **—sa·dis′ti·cal·ly** *adv.*

sa·do·mas·o·chism (sā′dō-măs′ə-kĭz′əm, săd′ō-) ► *n. Psychol.* Deriving esp. sexual pleasure from both sadism and masochism. **—sa′do·mas′o·chist** *n.* **—sa′do·mas′o·chis′tic** *adj.*

Sa·far also **Sa·phar** (sə-fär′) ► *n.* The 2nd month of the Muslim calendar.

sa·fa·ri (sə-fär′ē) ► *n., pl.* **-ris.** An overland expedition, esp. in E Africa.

safe (sāf) ► *adj.* **saf·er, saf·est.** **1.** Secure from danger, harm, or evil. **2.** Unhurt: *safe and sound.* **3.** Free from risk: *a safe bet.* **4.** Affording protection: *a safe place.* **5.** *Baseball* Reaching a base without being put out. ► *n.* A strong container for storing valuables. **—safe′ly** *adv.*

safe-con·duct (sāf′kŏn′dŭkt) ► *n.* A document or an escort assuring unmolested passage, as through enemy territory.

safe·crack·er (sāf′krăk′ər) ► *n.* One who breaks into safes. **—safe′crack′ing** *n.*

safe-de·pos·it box (sāf′dĭ-pŏz′ĭt) ► *n.* A fireproof box, usu. in a bank vault, for the safe storage of valuables.

safe·guard (sāf′gärd′) ► *n.* A precautionary measure or device. ► *v.* To ensure the safety of; protect.

safe·keep·ing (sāf′kē′pĭng) ► *n.* Protection; care.

safe·light (sāf′līt′) ► *n.* A lamp that allows darkroom illumination without affecting photosensitive film or paper.

safe sex ► *n.* Sexual activity in which safeguards, such as the use of a condom, are taken to reduce the risk of acquiring or spreading a sexually transmitted disease. **—safe′-sex′** *adj.*

safe·ty (sāf′tē) ► *n., pl.* **-ties.** **1.** Freedom from danger, risk, or injury. **2.** A protective device, as a lock on a firearm. **3.** *Football* A play in which the offensive team downs the ball behind its own goal line, resulting in two points for the defensive team.

safety belt ► *n.* A strap or belt worn as a safety precaution, esp. a seat belt.

safety glass ► *n.* Glass that resists shattering, esp. a composite of two sheets of glass with an intermediate layer of plastic.

safety match ► *n.* A match that can be lighted only by being struck against a chemically prepared friction surface.

safety pin ► *n.* A pin in the form of a clasp, with a sheath to cover and hold the point.

safety razor ► *n.* A razor with guards around the blade to prevent deep cuts.

safety valve ► *n.* A valve, as in a steam boiler, that automatically opens when pressure reaches a dangerous level.

saf·flow·er (săf′lou′ər) ► *n.* A plant with flowers yielding a dyestuff and seeds that yield a cooking oil.

saf·fron (săf′rən) ► *n.* **1.** The dried stigmas of a kind of crocus, used to color and flavor food and as a dye. **2.** A moderate or strong orange yellow.

sag (săg) ► *v.* **sagged, sag·ging.** **1.** To sink, droop, or settle from pressure or weight. **2.** To lose vigor, firmness, or resilience. **3.** To decline, as in value or price. **—sag** *n.*

sa·ga (sä′gə) ► *n.* **1.** An Icelandic prose narrative written between the 12th and 14th cent. **2.** A long heroic narrative.

sa·ga·cious (sə-gā′shəs) ► *adj.* Shrewd and wise. **—sa·ga′cious·ly** *adv.* **—sa·gac′i·ty** (-găs′ĭ-tē) *n.*

sage[1] (sāj) ► *n.* A venerated, wise person. ► *adj.* **sag·er, sag·est.** Judicious; wise. **—sage′ly** *adv.* **—sage′ness** *n.*

sage[2] (sāj) ► *n.* **1.** An aromatic plant with grayish-green leaves used as a seasoning. **2.** Sagebrush.

sage·brush (sāj′brŭsh′) ► *n.* An aromatic shrub of arid regions of W North America.

Sag·it·tar·i·us (săj′ĭ-târ′ē-əs) ► *n.* **1.** A constellation in the Southern Hemisphere. **2.** The 9th sign of the zodiac in astrology.

sa·go (sā′gō) ► *n., pl.* **-gos.** A powdery edible starch obtained from the trunks of an Asian palm.

sa·gua·ro (sə-gwär′ō, -wär′ō) also **sa·hua·ro** (sə-wär′ō) ► *n., pl.* **-ros.** **1.** A large branching cactus of the SW US and N Mexico. **2.** Its edible fruit.

Sa·hap·tin (sä-hăp′tĭn) ► *n., pl.* **-tin** or **-tins.** **1.** A member of a Native American people of Idaho, Washington, and Oregon. **2.** The dialectally diverse language of the Sahaptin.

Sa·har·a (sə-hâr′ə, -hăr′ə, -hä′rə) ► A desert of N Africa extending from the Atlantic coast to the Nile Valley and S from the Atlas Mts. to the Sudan. **—Sa·har′an** *adj.*

Sa·hel (sə-hāl′, -hēl′) ► A semiarid region of N-central Africa S of the Sahara Desert. **—Sa·hel′i·an** *adj.*

sa·hib (sä′ĭb, -ēb, -hĭb) ► *n.* Used as a form of respectful address for a European man in colonial India.

THESAURUS

sacrosanct *adj.* —*See* DIVINE (2), HOLY.

sacrosanctity *n.* —*See* HOLINESS.

sad *adj.* —*See* DEPRESSED (1), SORROWFUL.

sadden *v.* —*See* DEPRESS.

saddle *v.* —*See* BURDEN[1].

saddle with *v.* —*See* IMPOSE ON.

sadism *n.* —*See* CRUELTY.

sadistic *adj.* —*See* CRUEL.

sadness *n.* —*See* DEPRESSION (2).

safari *n.* —*See* EXPEDITION.

safe *adj.* **1.** Free from danger, injury, or the threat of harm ► unharmed, unhurt, uninjured, unscathed. *Idioms:* out of danger, out of harm's way, safe and sound. [*Compare* GOOD, HEALTHY.] **2.** Affording protection ► defended, guarded, immune, impenetrable, impregnable, invulnerable, secure, unassailable, unconquerable. [*Compare* INVINCIBLE.] —*See also* HARMLESS.

safe *n.* —*See* DEPOSITORY.

safeguard *n.* —*See* CARE (2), DEFENSE.

safeguard *v.* —*See* DEFEND (1).

safe house *n.* —*See* COVER (1).

safekeeping *n.* —*See* CARE (2).

safeness *n.* —*See* SAFETY.

safety *n.* The quality or state of being safe ► assurance, immunity, impenetrability, impregnability, invulnerability, safeness, security, unassailability, unconquerability. [*Compare* DEFENSE.] —*See also* REFUGE (1).

sag *v.* —*See* BEND (3), DROP (1), FALL (4), SLOUCH (2), WILT.

sag *n.* —*See* DEPRESSION (1).

saga *v.* —*See* STORY (1).

sagacious *adj.* Possessing deep knowledge and understanding ► knowing, sage, sapient, wise. —*See also* SENSIBLE, SHREWD.

sagacity or **sagaciousness** *n.* —*See* DISCERNMENT, WISDOM (1).

sagamore *n.* —*See* CHIEF.

sage *n.* A person noted for wisdom, knowledge, and judgment ► guru, pundit, savant, scholar, wise man, wise woman. [*Compare* EXPERT, MIND.]

sage *adj.* Possessing deep knowledge and understanding ► knowing, sagacious, sapient, wise. —*See also* SENSIBLE.

sageness *n.* —*See* DISCERNMENT, WISDOM (1).

said (sĕd) ▸ *v.* P.t. and p.part. of **say.** ▸ *adj. Law* Aforementioned.

Sai·gon (sī-gŏn′) ▸ See **Ho Chi Minh City.**

sail (sāl) ▸ *n.* **1.** A piece of shaped fabric that catches the wind and propels or aids in maneuvering a vessel. **2.** A sailing vessel. **3.** A trip in a sailing craft. **4.** Something resembling a sail. ▸ *v.* **1a.** To move across the surface of water, esp. by means of a sail. **b.** To travel by water in a vessel. **c.** To start out on such a voyage. **2.** To navigate or manage (a vessel). **3.** To glide through the air.

sail·board (sāl′bôrd′) ▸ *n.* A modified surfboard having a sail mounted on a pivoting mast, ridden while standing up. **—sail′board′** *v.* **—sail′board′er** *n.*

sail·boat (sāl′bōt′) ▸ *n.* A relatively small boat propelled by a sail or sails.

sail·fish (sāl′fĭsh′) ▸ *n.* A large marine fish with a high dorsal fin and a spearlike projection from the upper jaw.

sail·or (sā′lər) ▸ *n.* One who sails, esp. one who serves in a navy or works on a ship.

sail·plane (sāl′plān′) ▸ *n.* A light glider used esp. for soaring. **—sail′plane′** *v.*

saint (sānt) ▸ *n.* **1.** A person considered holy and worthy of public veneration, esp. one who has been canonized. **2.** An extremely virtuous person. **—saint′dom** *n.* **—saint′ed** *adj.* **—saint′hood′** *n.* **—saint′li·ness** *n.* **—saint′ly** *adj.*

Saint Au·gus·tine (ô′gə-stēn′) ▸ A city of NE FL on the Atlantic; the oldest permanent European settlement in the US.

Saint Ber·nard (bər-närd′) ▸ *n.* A large strong dog orig. used in the Swiss Alps to rescue lost travelers.

Saint Chris·to·pher-Ne·vis (krĭs′tə-fər-nē′vĭs, -nĕv′ĭs) ▸ See **Saint Kitts and Nevis.**

Saint Croix (kroi) ▸ An island of the US Virgin Is. in the West Indies E of Puerto Rico.

Saint El·mo's fire (ĕl′mōz) ▸ *n.* A visible electric discharge on a pointed object during an electrical storm.

Saint He·le·na (hə-lē′nə) ▸ A volcanic island in the S Atlantic W of Angola; part of the British dependency of **Saint Helena.**

Saint Hel·ens (hĕl′ənz), **Mount** ▸ An active volcanic peak of the Cascade Range in SW WA.

Saint John's (jŏnz) ▸ The capital of Newfoundland, Canada, on the SE coast.

Saint John's wort *n.* Any of a genus of herbs or shrubs used in medicinal preparations esp. as an antidepressant.

Saint Kitts and Ne·vis (kĭts; nē′vĭs, nĕv′ĭs) also **Saint Chris·to·pher-Ne·vis** (krĭs′tə-fər-nē′vĭs, -nĕv′ĭs) ▸ An island country in the Leeward Is. of the West Indies ESE of Puerto Rico comprising **Saint Kitts** and the islands of Nevis and Sombrero.

Saint Lawrence River ▸ A river of SE Canada flowing about 1,207 km (750 mi) from Lake Ontario to the Gulf of St. Lawrence.

Saint Lawrence Seaway ▸ A waterway, about 3,781 km (2,350 mi), consisting of a system of canals, dams, and locks in the St. Lawrence R. and connecting channels through the Great Lakes.

Saint Lou·is (lo͞o′ĭs) ▸ A city of E MO on the Mississippi R.

Saint Lu·cia (lo͞o′shə, lo͞o-sē′ə) ▸ An island country of the West Indies in the Windward Is. S of Martinique.

Saint Mar·tin or **Saint Maar·ten** (mär′tn) ▸ An island of the West Indies in the W Leeward Is.

Saint Paul ▸ The capital of MN, in the SE part on the Mississippi R. adjacent to Minneapolis.

Saint Pe·ters·burg (pē′tərz-bûrg′). Formerly **Leningrad** ▸ A city of NW Russia on the Neva R.

Saint Pi·erre and Mi·que·lon (pîr′, pē-âr′; mĭk′ə-lŏn′) ▸ A French island group and overseas department in the N Atlantic Ocean S of Newfoundland, Canada.

Saint Thomas (sānt) ▸ An island of the US Virgin Is. in the West Indies E of Puerto Rico.

Saint Valentine's Day ▸ *n.* See **Valentine's Day.**

Saint Vincent and the Grenadines ▸ An island country in the central Windward Is. of the West Indies.

Sai·pan (sī-păn′, -pän′, sī′păn) ▸ An island of the W Pacific in the S Mariana Is. **—Sai′pa·nese′** (-nēz′, -nēs′) *adj. & n.*

saith (sĕth, sā′ĭth) ▸ *v. Archaic* 3rd pers. sing. pr.t. of **say.**

sake¹ (sāk) ▸ *n.* **1.** Purpose: *for the sake of argument.* **2.** Advantage; good: *for the sake of your health.*

sa·ke² also **sa·ki** (sä′kē, -kĕ) ▸ *n.* A Japanese liquor made from fermented rice.

sal (săl) ▸ *n.* Salt.

sa·laam (sə-läm′) ▸ *n.* An act of deference or obeisance, esp. a low bow performed while placing the right palm on the forehead. **—sa·laam′** *v.*

sa·la·cious (sə-lā′shəs) ▸ *adj.* Prurient; lascivious. **—sa·la′cious·ly** *adv.* **—sa·la′cious·ness** *n.*

sal·ad (săl′əd) ▸ *n.* A dish usu. made of leafy greens or raw vegetables served with a dressing.

sal·a·man·der (săl′ə-măn′dər) ▸ *n.* A small lizardlike amphibian.

sa·la·mi (sə-lä′mē) ▸ *n.* A highly spiced sausage.

sal·a·ry (săl′ə-rē, săl′rē) ▸ *n., pl.* **-ries.** Fixed compensation for services, paid to a person on a regular basis. **—sal′a·ried** *adj.*

sale (sāl) ▸ *n.* **1.** The exchange of goods or services for money. **2.** An instance of selling. **3.** Availability for purchase. **4.** An auction. **5.** A special disposal of goods at lowered prices. **—sal′a·bil′i·ty** *n.* **—sal′a·ble, sale′a·ble** *adj.*

Sa·lem (sā′ləm) ▸ The capital of OR, in the NW part on the Willamette R.

sales·clerk (sālz′klûrk′) ▸ *n.* One employed to sell goods in a store.

sales·man (sālz′mən) ▸ *n.* A man employed to sell merchandise in a store or designated territory. **—sales′man·ship′** *n.*

sales·per·son (sālz′pûr′sən) ▸ *n.* A salesman or saleswoman. **—sales′peo′ple** *pl.n.*

sales tax (sālz) ▸ *n.* A tax levied on the price of goods and services.

sales·wom·an (sālz′wo͝om′ən) ▸ *n.* A woman employed to sell merchandise in a store or territory.

sal·i·cyl·ic acid (săl′ĭ-sĭl′ĭk) ▸ *n.* A white crystalline acid used in making aspirin.

sa·li·ent (sā′lē-ənt, sāl′yənt) ▸ *adj.* **1.** Projecting or jutting beyond a line or surface. **2.** Strikingly conspicuous. **—sa′li·ence, sa′li·en·cy** *n.*

sa·line (sā′lēn′, -līn′) ▸ *adj.* Of or containing salt. **—sa·lin′i·ty** (sə-lĭn′ĭ-tē) *n.*

Sa·lish (sā′lĭsh) also **Sa·lish·an** (-lĭ-shən) ▸ *n.* **1.** A family of Native American languages of the NW US and British Columbia. **2.** The group of Native American peoples speaking languages of this family. **—Sa′lish·an** *adj.*

sa·li·va (sə-lī′və) ▸ *n.* The watery mixture of secretions from glands in the mouth that aids in swallowing and digestion. **—sal′i·var′y** (săl′ə-vĕr′ē) *adj.*

sal·i·vate (săl′ə-vāt′) ▸ *v.* **-vat·ed, -vat·ing.** To secrete or produce saliva. **—sal′i·va′tion** *n.*

Salk (sôlk), **Jonas Edward** (1914–95) ▸ Amer. microbiologist.

Salk vaccine ▸ *n.* A vaccine consisting of inactivated polioviruses, used to immunize against poliomyelitis.

THESAURUS

sail *v.* *—See* BLOW¹ (2), BREEZE, FLY (1), FLY (2), RUSH.

sail into *v.* *—See* ATTACK (1).

sailor *n.* A person engaged in sailing or working on a ship ▸ boatman, Jack, Jack-tar, mariner, navigator, sea dog, seafarer, seaman. *Informal:* salt, tar. *Slang:* gob.

saintliness *n.* *—See* HOLINESS.

saintly *adj.* *—See* PIOUS.

salaam *v.* *—See* BOW¹ (1).

salaam *n.* *—See* BOW¹.

salability or **salableness** *n.* Market appeal ▸ marketability, sell.

salacious *adj.* *—See* EROTIC.

salad days *n.* *—See* YOUTH (1).

salary *n.* *—See* WAGE.

sale *n.* *—See* DEAL (1).

salesclerk or **salesperson** *n.* *—See* SELLER.

salesman or **saleswoman** *n.* *—See* SELLER.

salient *adj.* *—See* NOTICEABLE.

salient *n.* *—See* PROJECTION.

saline *adj.* Containing salt ▸ brackish, briny, salty.

saliva *n.* *—See* SPIT.

salivate *v.* *—See* DROOL.

salivation *n.* Saliva running from the mouth ▸ drivel, drool, slaver, slobber.

sal·low (săl′ō) ▸ *adj.* **-er, -est.** Of a sickly yellowish color. **—sal′low·ly** *adv.* **—sal′low·ness** *n.*

sal·ly (săl′ē) ▸ *n., pl.* **-lies.** **1.** A sudden assault from a defensive position. **2.** A quick witticism; quip. **3.** A venturing forth; jaunt. **—sal′ly** *v.*

salm·on (săm′ən) ▸ *n., pl.* **-on** or **-ons.** **1.** Any of various large food and game fishes of northern waters, usu. with pinkish flesh. **2.** A yellowish pink to reddish orange. **—salm′on** *adj.*

sal·mo·nel·la (săl′mə-nĕl′ə) ▸ *n., pl.* **-nel·lae** (-nĕl′ē) or **-las** or **-la.** Any of various rod-shaped bacteria, many of which cause food poisoning or other diseases in warm-blooded animals.

sa·lon (sə-lŏn′, să-lôɴ′) ▸ *n.* **1.** A large room, such as a drawing room, used for receiving and entertaining guests. **2.** A periodic gathering of people of social or intellectual distinction. **3.** A commercial establishment offering a product or service related to fashion: *a beauty salon.*

sa·loon (sə-lo͞on′) ▸ *n.* **1.** A bar; tavern. **2.** A large social lounge on a passenger ship.

sal·sa (säl′sə) ▸ *n.* **1.** A spicy sauce usu. made of tomatoes, onions, and chili peppers. **2.** A popular form of Latin-American dance music.

salt (sôlt) ▸ *n.* **1.** A colorless or white crystalline solid, chiefly sodium chloride, used extensively as a food seasoning and preservative. **2.** A chemical compound formed by replacing all or part of the hydrogen ions of an acid with metal ions or electropositive radicals. **3. salts** Any of various mineral salts used as laxatives or cathartics. **4.** An element that gives flavor or zest. **5.** Sharp, lively wit. **6.** *Informal* A veteran sailor. ▸ *adj.* **1.** Salty. **2.** Preserved in salt. ▸ *v.* **1.** To add salt to. **2.** To preserve with salt. ***—phrasal verb:* salt away** To put aside; save. ***—idiom:* worth (one's) salt** Efficient and capable. **—salt′i·ly** *adv.* **—salt′i·ness** *n.* **—salt′y** *adj.*

salt·cel·lar (sôlt′sĕl′ər) ▸ *n.* A small dish for dispensing salt.

sal·tine (sôl-tēn′) ▸ *n.* A thin salted cracker.

Salt Lake City ▸ The capital of UT, in the N-central part near Great Salt Lake.

salt lick ▸ *n.* A block or deposit of exposed salt that animals lick.

salt marsh ▸ *n.* Low coastal grassland frequently overflowed by the tide.

salt·pe·ter (sôlt′pē′tər) ▸ *n.* **1.** See **potassium nitrate.** **2.** See **sodium nitrate.** **3.** See **niter.**

salt·shak·er (sôlt′shā′kər) ▸ *n.* A container for sprinkling table salt.

salt·wa·ter (sôlt′wô′tər, -wŏt′ər) ▸ *adj.* Consisting of or inhabiting salt water.

sa·lu·bri·ous (sə-lo͞o′brē-əs) ▸ *adj.* Conducive or favorable to health or well-being. **—sa·lu′bri·ty** (-brĭ-tē) *n.*

sal·u·tar·y (săl′yə-tĕr′ē) ▸ *adj.* **1.** Beneficial: *salutary advice.* **2.** Wholesome. **—sal′u·tar′i·ly** (-târ′ə-lē) *adv.* **—sal′u·tar′i·ness** *n.*

sal·u·ta·tion (săl′yə-tā′shən) ▸ *n.* An expression of greeting, goodwill, or courtesy.

sa·lu·ta·to·ri·an (sə-lo͞o′tə-tôr′ē-ən) ▸ *n.* The student with the second highest academic rank in a class who delivers the opening address at graduation.

sa·lute (sə-lo͞ot′) ▸ *v.* **-lut·ed, -lut·ing.** **1.** To greet. **2.** To recognize (a military superior) with a prescribed gesture. **3.** To honor formally. **—sa·lute′** *n.*

Sal·va·dor (săl′və-dôr′) ▸ A city of E Brazil on the Atlantic SSW of Recife.

Sal·va·do·ran (săl′və-dôr′ən) or **Sal·va·do·ri·an** (-dôr′ē-ən) ▸ *n.* A native or inhabitant of El Salvador. **—Sal′va·do′ran, Sal′va·do′ri·an** *adj.*

sal·vage (săl′vĭj) ▸ *n.* **1a.** The rescue of a ship. **b.** Compensation given to those who aid in such a rescue. **2a.** The act of saving imperiled property from loss. **b.** The property so saved. **3.** Something saved from destruction or waste and put to further use. ▸ *v.* **-vaged, -vag·ing.** To save from loss or destruction. **—sal′vage·a·ble** *adj.* **—sal′vag·er** *n.*

sal·va·tion (săl-vā′shən) ▸ *n.* **1a.** Preservation or deliverance from difficulty or evil. **b.** A means or cause of such deliverance. **2.** Deliverance from sin; redemption. **—sal·va′tion·al** *adj.*

salve (săv, säv) ▸ *n.* An ointment that soothes or heals. ▸ *v.* **salved, salv·ing.** To soothe or heal with or as if with salve.

sal·ver (săl′vər) ▸ *n.* A serving tray.

sal·vi·a (săl′vē-ə) ▸ *n.* Any of various plants having opposite leaves, a two-lipped corolla, and two stamens.

sal·vo (săl′vō) ▸ *n., pl.* **-vos** or **-voes.** **1.** A simultaneous discharge of firearms. **2.** A sudden outburst.

Sa·mar·i·a (sə-măr′ē-ə, -mâr′-) ▸ An ancient city of Palestine in present-day NW Jordan.

Sa·mar·i·tan (sə-măr′ĭ-tn) ▸ *n.* **1.** A native or inhabitant of Samaria. **2.** often **samaritan** A Good Samaritan. **—Sa·mar′i·tan** *adj.*

sa·mar·i·um (sə-mâr′ē-əm, -măr′-) ▸ *n.* *Symbol* **Sm** A silvery or pale gray metallic rare-earth element used in laser materials, in infrared absorbing glass, and as a neutron absorber. At. no. 62.

sam·ba (săm′bə, säm′-) ▸ *n.* **1.** A Brazilian ballroom dance of African origin. **2.** Music for this dance. **—sam′ba** *v.*

same (sām) ▸ *adj.* **1.** Being the very one; identical. **2.** Similar or corresponding. ▸ *adv.* In the same way. ▸ *pron.* **1.** One identical with another. **2.** The one previously mentioned. **—same′ness** *n.*

same-sex (sām′sĕks′) ▸ *adj.* **1.** Involving or restricted to members of the same sex: *same-sex schools.* **2.** Of or involving gay men or lesbians: *same-sex couples.*

Sa·mo·a[1] (sə-mō′ə) ▸ An island group of the S Pacific ENE of Fiji, divided between **Samoa**, a sovereign nation, and **American Samoa. —Sa·mo′an** *adj. & n.*

Sa·mo·a[2] (sə-mō′ə). Formerly **Western Samoa** ▸ An island country of the S Pacific comprising the W Samoa Is.

Sam·o·set (săm′ə-sĕt′) (d. c. 1653) ▸ Native American leader and friend of the early colonists.

sam·o·var (săm′ə-vär′) ▸ *n.* A metal urn with a spigot, used to boil water for tea.

Sam·o·yed (săm′oi-ĕd′, sə-moi′ĭd) ▸ *n.* **1.** A member of a nomadic people of NW Siberia. **2.** The Uralic language of the Samoyed. **3.** A working dog of a breed orig. developed in N Eurasia. **—Sam′o·yed′** *adj.*

sam·pan (săm′păn′) ▸ *n.* A flat-bottomed Asian skiff.

sam·ple (săm′pəl) ▸ *n.* **1.** A portion, piece, or segment representative of a whole. **2.** *Statistics* A set of elements

THESAURUS

sallow *adj.* —*See* PALE (1).
sallow *v.* —*See* PALE.
sally *v.* —*See* RUSH.
sally *n.* —*See* JOKE (1).
salmagundi *n.* —*See* ASSORTMENT.
salon *n.* —*See* EXHIBITION.
saloon *n.* —*See* BAR (2).
salt *n.* —*See* SAILOR.
salt *v.* —*See* PRESERVE (1).
salt away *v.* —*See* BANK[2], SAVE (1).
salty *adj.* Containing salt ▸ brackish, briny, saline. —*See also* MARINE (1), RACY.
salutary or **salubrious** *adj.* —*See* BENEFICIAL, HEALTHFUL.
salutation *n.* An expression, in words or gestures, marking a meeting of persons ▸ hail, greeting, greetings, salute, welcome. *Informal:* hello.
salutations *interj.* —*See* HELLO.
salute *v.* **1.** To address in a friendly and respectful way ▸ greet, hail, welcome. **2.** To approach for the purpose of speech ▸ accost, greet, hail. [*Compare* ENCOUNTER, INTERRUPT, WELCOME.] —*See also* DRINK (4).
salute *n.* An expression, in words or gestures, marking a meeting of persons ▸ hail, greeting, salutation, welcome. *Informal:* hello. —*See also* TESTIMONIAL (2).
salvage *n.* —*See* RESCUE.
salvage *v.* —*See* RESCUE.
salvation *n.* —*See* RESCUE.
salve *n.* —*See* OINTMENT.
salve *v.* —*See* CURE.
salvo *n.* —*See* BARRAGE, TESTIMONIAL (2).
same *adj.* Being the one and not another; not different in nature or identity ▸ identical, selfsame, very. [*Compare* LIKE[2].] —*See also* EQUAL, UNCHANGING.
sameness *n.* The quality or condition of being exactly the same as something else ▸ identicalness, identity, oneness, selfsameness. [*Compare* LIKENESS.] —*See also* CHANGELESSNESS, EQUIVALENCE, MONOTONY.
sample *n.* A limited or anticipatory experience ▸ foretaste, sampling, taste. [*Compare* GLANCE.] —*See also* EXAMPLE (1).
sample *v.* —*See* EXPERIENCE.

drawn from and analyzed to estimate the characteristics of a population. ▸ *v.* **-pled, -pling.** To take a sample of, esp. in order to test or examine.
sam·pler (săm′plər) ▸ *n.* **1.** One employed to appraise samples. **2.** A piece of cloth embroidered with various designs.
sam·pling (săm′plĭng) ▸ *n.* See **sample** 2.
Sam·son (săm′sən) ▸ In the Bible, a warrior betrayed to the Philistines by Delilah.
Sam·u·el (săm′yo͞o-əl) ▸ *n.* **1.** Hebrew judge and prophet of the 11th cent. B.C. **2.** See **Bible** table in Appendix.
sam·u·rai (săm′ə-rī′) ▸ *n., pl.* **-rai** or **-rais.** The Japanese feudal military aristocracy or one of its members.
San (sän) ▸ *n., pl.* **San** or **Sans. 1.** A member of a nomadic hunting people of SW Africa. **2.** Any of the Khoisan languages of the San.
San An·to·ni·o (săn ăn-tō′nē-ō′) ▸ A city of S-central TX SW of Austin.
san·a·to·ri·um (săn′ə-tôr′ē-əm) also **san·a·tar·i·um** (-târ′-) ▸ *n., pl.* **-to·ri·ums** or **-to·ri·a** (-tôr′ē-ə) also **-tar·i·ums** or **-tar·i·a** (-târ′ē-ə). **1.** An institution for the treatment of chronic diseases. **2.** A resort for improvement of health, esp. for convalescents.
sanc·ti·fy (săngk′tə-fī′) ▸ *v.* **-fied, -fy·ing. 1.** To set apart for sacred use; consecrate. **2.** To make holy; purify. **—sanc′ti·fi·ca′tion** *n.*
sanc·ti·mo·ny (săngk′tə-mō′nē) ▸ *n.* Hypocritical piety. **—sanc′ti·mo′ni·ous** *adj.* **—sanc′ti·mo′ni·ous·ly** *adv.*
sanc·tion (săngk′shən) ▸ *n.* **1.** Authoritative permission or approval. **2.** A penalty intended to enforce compliance or conformity. **3.** A coercive measure adopted usu. by several nations against a nation violating international law. ▸ *v.* To authorize, approve, or encourage.
sanc·ti·ty (săngk′tĭ-tē) ▸ *n., pl.* **-ties. 1.** Holiness of life; saintliness. **2.** Sacredness or inviolability.
sanc·tu·ar·y (săngk′cho͞o-ĕr′ē) ▸ *n., pl.* **-ies. 1.** A sacred place, such as a church, temple, or mosque. **2.** A place of refuge, asylum, or protection.
sanc·tum (săngk′təm) ▸ *n., pl.* **-tums** or **-ta** (-tə). **1.** A sacred or holy place. **2.** A private room or study.
sand (sănd) ▸ *n.* Small loose grains of worn or disintegrated rock, finer than a granule and coarser than silt. ▸ *v.* To polish or scrape with sand or sandpaper. **—sand′er** *n.* **—sand′i·ness** *n.* **—sand′y** *adj.*
san·dal (săn′dl) ▸ *n.* **1.** A shoe consisting of a sole fastened to the foot by thongs or straps. **2.** A low-cut shoe with an ankle strap. **—san′daled** *adj.*
san·dal·wood (săn′dl-wo͝od′) ▸ *n.* **1.** An Asian tree with aromatic wood used in carving and perfumery. **2.** The wood of this tree.
sand·bag (sănd′băg′) ▸ *n.* A bag filled with sand and used esp. to form protective walls. ▸ *v.* **1.** To put sandbags in or around. **2.** *Slang* **a.** To deal a heavy blow to. **b.** To coerce.
sand·bar (sănd′bär′) ▸ *n.* A ridge of sand formed in a river or along a shore.
sand·blast (sănd′blăst′) ▸ *n.* A blast of air carrying sand at high velocity, as for cleaning stone or glass. **—sand′blast′** *v.*
sand·box (sănd′bŏks′) ▸ *n.* A box filled with sand for children to play in.
sand dollar ▸ *n.* Any of various thin circular echinoderms of sandy ocean bottoms of the N Atlantic and Pacific.
sand·hog (sănd′hôg′, -hŏg′) ▸ *n.* *Slang* One who works in a caisson, as in the construction of underwater tunnels.
San Di·e·go (dē-ā′gō) ▸ A city of S CA on **San Diego Bay,** an inlet of the Pacific near the Mexican border.
sand·lot (sănd′lŏt′) ▸ *n.* A vacant lot used esp. by children for games. **—sand′lot′** *adj.*
sand·man (sănd′măn′) ▸ *n.* A character in folklore who puts children to sleep by sprinkling sand in their eyes.
sand·pa·per (sănd′pā′pər) ▸ *n.* Heavy paper coated on one side with an abrasive material, used for smoothing surfaces. **—sand′pa′per** *v.*
sand·pi·per (sănd′pī′pər) ▸ *n.* Any of various small, usu. long-billed shore birds.
sand·stone (sănd′stōn′) ▸ *n.* A sedimentary rock formed by the compaction of sand with a natural cement, such as silica.
sand·storm (sănd′stôrm′) ▸ *n.* A strong wind carrying clouds of sand and dust.
sand trap ▸ *n.* A sand-filled depression serving as a hazard on a golf course.
sand·wich (sănd′wĭch, săn′-) ▸ *n.* Two or more slices of bread with a filling placed between them. ▸ *v.* To insert (one thing) tightly between two other things.
sane (sān) ▸ *adj.* **san·er, san·est. 1.** Mentally healthy. **2.** Having or showing good judgment; reasonable. **—sane′ly** *adv.* **—sane′ness** *n.*
San Fran·cis·co (frən-sĭs′kō) ▸ A city of W CA on a peninsula between the Pacific and **San Francisco Bay,** an inlet of the Pacific. **—San Fran·cis′can** *n.*
sang (săng) ▸ *v.* P.t. of **sing.**
sang-froid (säɴ-frwä′) ▸ *n.* Coolness and composure.
san·gri·a (săng-grē′ə, săn-) ▸ *n.* A cold drink usu. made of wine, brandy, sugar, fruit juice, and soda water.
san·gui·nar·y (săng′gwə-nĕr′ē) ▸ *adj.* **1.** Accompanied by bloodshed. **2.** Bloodthirsty. **—san′gui·nar′i·ly** (-nâr′ə-lē) *adv.*
san·guine (săng′gwĭn) ▸ *adj.* **1a.** Of the color of blood; red. **b.** Ruddy: *a sanguine complexion.* **2.** Cheerful; optimistic. **—san′guine·ly** *adv.* **—san′guine·ness, san·guin′i·ty** *n.* **—san·guin′e·ous** *adj.*
san·i·tar·i·um (săn′ĭ-târ′ē-əm) ▸ *n., pl.* **-i·ums** or **-i·a** (-ē-ə). See **sanatorium.**
san·i·tar·y (săn′ĭ-tĕr′ē) ▸ *adj.* **1.** Relating to health. **2.** Clean; hygienic. **—san′i·tar′i·ly** (-târ′ə-lē) *adv.*
sanitary napkin ▸ *n.* A disposable pad of absorbent material worn to absorb menstrual flow.
san·i·ta·tion (săn′ĭ-tā′shən) ▸ *n.* **1.** Formulation and application of public health measures. **2.** Disposal of sewage and garbage.
san·i·tize (săn′ĭ-tīz′) ▸ *v.* **-tized, -tiz·ing. 1.** To make sanitary. **2.** To remove unpleasant or offensive features from: *sanitized the language in the novel for television.*
san·i·ty (săn′ĭ-tē) ▸ *n.* The quality or condition of being sane.
San Jo·se (hō-zā′) ▸ A city of W CA SE of San Francisco.
San Juan (săn wän′, hwän′) ▸ The capital of Puerto Rico, in the NE part on the Atlantic.
sank (săngk) ▸ *v.* P.t. of **sink.**
San Ma·ri·no (săn mə-rē′nō) ▸ A country within N-central Italy in the Apennines.
sans (sănz, säɴ) ▸ *prep.* Without.

THESAURUS

sanctified *adj.* —*See* DIVINE (2), HOLY.
sanctify *v.* To make sacred by a religious rite ▸ bless, consecrate, hallow. [*Compare* EXALT.]
sanctimonious *adj.* —*See* HYPOCRITICAL.
sanctimony or **sanctimoniousness** *n.* —*See* HYPOCRISY.
sanction *n.* A coercive measure intended to ensure compliance or conformity ▸ interdict, interdiction, penalty. [*Compare* FORBIDDANCE, RESTRAINT, PUNISHMENT.] —*See also* CONFIRMATION (1), PERMISSION.
sanction *v.* —*See* CONFIRM (3), PERMIT (2).
sanctioned *adj.* [illegible] THORITATIVE (1).
sanctity *n.* —*See* HOLINESS.
sanctuary *n.* **1.** A sacred or holy place ▸ sacrarium, sanctorium, sanctum, shrine. **2.** Public land kept for a special purpose ▸ park, preserve, reserve, reservation. [*Compare* COMMON.] —*See also* COVER (1), REFUGE (1).
sandy *adj.* —*See* COARSE (2).
sane *adj.* Mentally healthy ▸ compos mentis, lucid, normal, rational. *Idioms:* all there, in one's right mind, of sound mind. [*Compare* HEALTHY.] —*See also* SENSIBLE.
saneness *n.* —*See* SANITY.
sang-froid *n.* —*See* BALANCE (2).
sanguinary *adj.* —*See* MURDEROUS.
sanguine *adj.* —*See* OPTIMISTIC, RUDDY.
sanguineous *adj.* —*See* MURDEROUS.
sanguinity or **sanguineness** *n.* —*See* OPTIMISM.
sanitary *adj.* —*See* STERILE (1).
sanitize *v.* To render free of microorganisms ▸ decontaminate, disinfect, irradiate, sterilize. [*Compare* CLEAN.] —*See also* CENSOR (1).
sanitized *adj.* —*See* STERILE (1).
sanity *n.* A healthy mental state ▸ lucidity, lucidness, mind, rationality, reason, saneness, sense (*or* senses), soundness, wits. *Slang:* marbles.

San·skrit (săn′skrĭt′) ▸ *n.* An ancient Indic language that is the classical language of India. **—San′skrit′ist** *n.*
San·ta An·a (săn′tə ăn′ə) ▸ *n.* A hot desert wind of S California blowing toward the Pacific coast usu. in winter.
San·ta An·na or **San·ta An·a** (săn′tə ăn′ə), **Antonio López de** (1795?–1876) ▸ Mexican military and political leader.
Santa Claus (klôz′) ▸ *n.* The personification of the spirit of Christmas, usu. represented as a jolly, fat old man with a white beard and red suit.
San·ta Fe (săn′tə fā′) ▸ The capital of NM, in the N-central part NE of Albuquerque.
San·tee (săn-tē′) ▸ *n., pl.* **-tee** or **-tees**. A member of the eastern branch of the Sioux, with populations in Nebraska, Minnesota, the Dakotas, and Canada.
San·te·ri·a (săn′tə-rē′ə, sän′-) ▸ *n.* A religion originating in Cuba and Brazil that combines worship of traditional Yoruban deities with worship of Roman Catholic saints.
San·ti·a·go (săn′tē-ä′gō, sän′-) ▸ The capital of Chile, in the central part ESE of Valparaiso.
São Pau·lo (pou′lō) ▸ A city of SE Brazil WSW of Rio de Janeiro.
São Tomé and Prín·ci·pe (tə-mā′; prĭn′sə-pə) ▸ An island country in the Gulf of Guinea off W Africa.
sap[1] (săp) ▸ *n.* **1.** The watery fluid that circulates through a plant, carrying food and other substances to the tissues. **2.** Health and energy; vitality. **3.** *Slang* A gullible person; dupe. ▸ *v.* **sapped, sap·ping.** To drain of sap.
sap[2] (săp) ▸ *v.* **sapped, sap·ping. 1.** To undermine the foundations of (a fortification). **2.** To deplete or weaken gradually.
Sa·phar (sə-fär′) ▸ *n.* Var. of **Safar.**
sa·pi·ent (sā′pē-ənt) ▸ *adj.* Wise and discerning. **—sa′pi·ence** *n.* **—sa′pi·ent·ly** *adv.*
sap·ling (săp′lĭng) ▸ *n.* A young tree.
sap·o·dil·la (săp′ə-dĭl′ə, -dē′yə) ▸ *n.* **1.** An evergreen tree of Mexico and Central America having an edible fruit. **2.** The fruit of this plant.
sa·pon·i·fi·ca·tion (sə-pŏn′ə-fĭ-kā′shən) ▸ *n.* A reaction in which an ester is heated with an alkali, producing a free alcohol and an acid salt, esp. alkaline hydrolysis of a fat or oil to make soap.
sa·pon·i·fy (sə-pŏn′ə-fī′) ▸ *v.* **-fied, -fy·ing. 1.** To convert (an ester) by saponification. **2.** To convert (a fat or oil) into soap.
sap·per (săp′ər) ▸ *n.* A military engineer.
sap·phire (săf′īr′) ▸ *n.* **1.** A clear, hard, usu. blue variety of corundum used as a gemstone. **2.** A corundum gem. **3.** The blue color of a gem sapphire.
Sap·pho (săf′ō) (fl. c. 600 B.C.) ▸ Greek lyric poet. **—Sap′phic** *adj.*
sap·py (săp′ē) ▸ *adj.* **-pi·er, -pi·est. 1.** Full of sap; juicy. **2.** *Slang* Silly; foolish.
sap·ro·phyte (săp′rə-fīt′) ▸ *n.* An organism that grows on and derives its nourishment from dead or decaying organic matter. **—sap′ro·phyt′ic** (-fĭt′ĭk) *adj.*
sap·suck·er (săp′sŭk′ər) ▸ *n.* A small American woodpecker that drills holes in trees to feed on sap and insects.
Sar·a·cen (săr′ə-sən) ▸ *n.* **1.** A member of a pre-Islamic nomadic people of the Syrian-Arabian deserts. **2.** An Arab. **3.** A Muslim, esp. of the time of the Crusades.
Sar·ah (sâr′ə) ▸ In the Bible, the wife of Abraham and mother of Isaac.
Sa·ra·je·vo (săr′ə-yā′vō) ▸ The capital of Bosnia and Herzegovina, in the S-central part.
sa·ran (sə-răn′) ▸ *n.* Any of various thermoplastic resins used to make packaging films and in various heavy fabrics.
sa·ra·pe (sə-rä′pē, -răp′ē) ▸ *n.* Var. of **serape.**
Sa·ra·wak (sə-rä′wäk, -wä) ▸ A region of Malaysia on NW Borneo.
sar·casm (sär′kăz′əm) ▸ *n.* **1.** A cutting, often ironic remark. **2.** The use of sarcasm. **—sar·cas′tic** (-kăs′tĭk) *adj.* **—sar·cas′ti·cal·ly** *adv.*
sar·co·ma (sär-kō′mə) ▸ *n., pl.* **-mas** also **-ma·ta** (-mə-tə). A malignant tumor arising from connective tissues.
sar·coph·a·gus (sär-kŏf′ə-gəs) ▸ *n., pl.* **-gi** (-jī′) or **-gus·es.** A stone coffin.
sar·dine (sär-dēn′) ▸ *n.* A small herring or related fish, often canned in oil.
Sar·din·i·a (sär-dĭn′ē-ə) ▸ An island of Italy in the Mediterranean S of Corsica. **—Sar·din′i·an** *adj. & n.*
sar·don·ic (sär-dŏn′ĭk) ▸ *adj.* Scornfully mocking. **—sar·don′i·cal·ly** *adv.*
sar·gas·so (sär-găs′ō) ▸ *n., pl.* **-sos.** See **gulfweed.**
Sar·gas·so Sea (sär-găs′ō) ▸ A part of the N Atlantic between the West Indies and the Azores.
sa·ri (sä′rē) ▸ *n., pl.* **-ris.** A lightweight, wrapped outer garment worn chiefly by women of India and Pakistan.
sa·rong (sə-rông′, -rŏng′) ▸ *n.* A length of brightly colored cloth wrapped about the waist, worn by men and women in Malaysia, Indonesia, and the Pacific islands.
sar·sa·pa·ril·la (săs′pə-rĭl′ə, särs′-) ▸ *n.* **1.** The dried roots of a tropical American plant, used as a flavoring. **2.** A sweet soft drink flavored with these roots.
sar·to·ri·al (sär-tôr′ē-əl) ▸ *adj.* Of or relating to tailors or tailoring. **—sar·to′ri·al·ly** *adv.*
Sar·tre (sär′trə, särt), **Jean Paul** (1905–80) ▸ French writer and philosopher; declined a 1957 Nobel.
sash[1] (săsh) ▸ *n.* A band or ribbon worn about the waist or over the shoulder.
sash[2] (săsh) ▸ *n.* A frame in which the panes of a window or door are set.
sa·shay (să-shā′) ▸ *v.* *Informal* To strut or flounce in a showy manner.
Sask. ▸ *abbr.* Saskatchewan
Sas·katch·e·wan (să-skăch′ə-wän′, -wən) ▸ A province of S-central Canada. Cap. Regina.
Sas·ka·toon (săs′kə-to͞on′) ▸ A city of S-central Saskatchewan, Canada, NW of Regina.
Sas·quatch (săs′kwŏch, -kwăch) ▸ *n.* See **Bigfoot.**
sass (săs) ▸ *n.* *Informal* Impertinence; back talk. **—sass** *v.*
sas·sa·fras (săs′ə-frăs′) ▸ *n.* **1.** A North American tree with irregularly lobed leaves and aromatic bark. **2.** The dried root bark of this plant, used as a flavoring.
sas·sy (săs′ē) ▸ *adj.* **-si·er, -si·est.** Rude and disrespectful; impudent. **—sas′si·ly** *adv.* **—sas′si·ness** *n.*
sat (săt) ▸ *v.* P.t. and p.part. of **sit.**
SAT (ĕs′ā-tē′) ▸ A trademark used for a set of standardized college entrance examinations.
Sat. ▸ *abbr.* Saturday
Sa·tan (sāt′n) ▸ *n.* The Devil.
sa·tan·ic (sə-tăn′ĭk, sā-) or **sa·tan·i·cal** (-ĭ-kəl) ▸ *adj.* **1.** Relating to or suggestive of Satan. **2.** Fiendishly cruel or evil. **—sa·tan′i·cal·ly** *adv.*
satch·el (săch′əl) ▸ *n.* A small bag for carrying books or clothing.
sate (sāt) ▸ *v.* **sat·ed, sat·ing. 1.** To satisfy (an appetite) fully. **2.** To satisfy to excess.

THESAURUS

sap[1] *n.* —*See* DUPE.
sap[2] *v.* —*See* ENERVATE, EXHAUST (1).
sapience *n.* —*See* WISDOM (1).
sapient *adj.* Possessing deep knowledge and understanding ▸ knowing, sagacious, sage, wise. —*See also* SENSIBLE.
sappiness *n.* —*See* SENTIMENTALITY.
sappy *adj.* —*See* SENTIMENTAL.
sarcasm *n.* The use of irony to ridicule or express contempt ▸ acerbity, acidity, acridity, bitterness, causticity, corrosiveness, cynicism, irony, mordacity, mordancy, trenchancy. [*Compare* MOCKERY, RIDICULE.]
sarcastic *adj.* Contemptuous or ironic in manner or wit ▸ cynical, derisive, ironic, ironical, jeering, mocking, sardonic, satiric, satirical, scoffing, sneering, snide, wry. [*Compare* BITING.]
sardonic *adj.* —*See* SARCASTIC.
sash *n.* —*See* BAND[1].
sashay *v.* —*See* STRUT.
sass *v.* *Informal* To utter an impertinent rejoinder ▸ talk back, talk up. *Informal:* sauce. ***Idiom:*** give someone lip (*or* mouth *or* sass).
sass *n.* *Informal* Insolent talk ▸ back talk, mouth. *Informal:* lip. [*Compare* IMPUDENCE, TAUNT.]
sassiness *n.* —*See* IMPUDENCE.
sassy *adj.* —*See* IMPUDENT, LIVELY.
satanic *adj.* —*See* FIENDISH.
satchel *n.* —*See* SUITCASE.
sate *v.* —*See* SATIATE.

sa·teen (să-tēn′) ▸ *n.* A cotton fabric with a satinlike finish.

sat·el·lite (săt′l-īt′) ▸ *n.* **1.** *Astron.* A celestial body that orbits a planet; moon. **2.** An object launched to orbit a celestial body. **3.** A subservient follower; sycophant. **4.** A nation dominated politically and economically by another. **5.** A community located near a big city.

satellite dish ▸ *n.* A dish antenna that receives and transmits satellite signals.

sa·ti·ate (sā′shē-āt′) ▸ *v.* **-at·ed, -at·ing. 1.** To satisfy fully. **2.** To satisfy to excess. ▸ *adj.* (-ĭt) Filled to satisfaction. **—sa′ti·a′tion** *n.*

sa·ti·e·ty (sə-tī′ĭ-tē) ▸ *n.* The condition of being sated.

sat·in (săt′n) ▸ *n.* A smooth glossy fabric. **—sat′in·y** *adj.*

sat·in·wood (săt′n-wo͝od′) ▸ *n.* A tree of India and Sri Lanka with hard yellow wood.

sat·ire (săt′īr′) ▸ *n.* **1.** An artistic work in which human vice or folly is attacked through irony, derision, or wit. **2.** Irony or caustic wit used to expose or attack human folly. **—sa·tir′i·cal** (sə-tĭr′ĭ-kəl), **sa·tir′ic** *adj.* **—sa·tir′i·cal·ly** *adv.* **—sat′ir·ist** (săt′ər-ĭst) *n.*

sat·i·rize (săt′ə-rīz′) ▸ *v.* **-rized, -riz·ing.** To ridicule or attack by satire.

sat·is·fac·tion (săt′ĭs-făk′shən) ▸ *n.* **1a.** The gratification of a desire, need, or appetite. **b.** Pleasure derived from such gratification. **2.** Compensation for injury or loss; reparation.

sat·is·fac·to·ry (săt′ĭs-făk′tə-rē) ▸ *adj.* Giving satisfaction; adequate. **—sat′is·fac′to·ri·ly** *adv.* **—sat′is·fac′to·ri·ness** *n.*

sat·is·fy (săt′ĭs-fī′) ▸ *v.* **-fied, -fy·ing. 1.** To gratify or fulfill (a need or desire). **2.** To free from doubt or question; assure. **3.** To fulfill or discharge (an obligation). **4.** To conform to the requirements of. **5.** To give satisfaction.

sa·trap (sā′trăp′, săt′răp′) ▸ *n.* A subordinate ruler.

sat·u·rate (săch′ə-rāt′) ▸ *v.* **-rat·ed, -rat·ing. 1.** To imbue or impregnate thoroughly. **2.** To soak, fill, or load to capacity. **3.** *Chem.* To cause (a substance) to unite with the greatest possible amount of another substance. ▸ *adj.* (-rĭt) Saturated. **—sat′u·ra·ble** (săch′ər-ə-bəl) *adj.* **—sat′u·ra′tion** *n.*

sat·u·rat·ed fat (săch′ə-rā′tĭd) ▸ *n.* A fat, usu. of animal origin, composed predominantly of fatty acids having only single bonds in the carbon chain.

Sat·ur·day (săt′ər-dē, -dā′) ▸ *n.* The 7th day of the week.

Saturday night special ▸ *n. Informal* A cheap handgun easily obtained and concealed.

Sat·urn (săt′ərn) ▸ *n.* **1.** *Rom. Myth.* The god of agriculture. **2.** The 2nd largest planet in the solar system and the 6th from the sun at a mean distance of about 1,425,000,000 km (886,000,000 mi), and having a mean diameter of approx. 119,000 km (74,000 mi).

sat·ur·nine (săt′ər-nīn′) ▸ *adj.* Morose and sardonic.

sa·tyr (sā′tər, săt′ər) ▸ *n.* **1.** often **Satyr** *Gk. Myth.* A woodland creature that is usually depicted as having the ears, legs, and horns of a goat. **2.** A lecher.

sauce (sôs) ▸ *n.* **1.** A liquid dressing served with food. **2.** Stewed fruit. **3.** *Informal* Impudence. **4.** *Slang* Alcoholic liquor. ▸ *v.* **sauced, sauc·ing. 1.** To flavor with sauce. **2.** To add zest to. **3.** *Informal* To be impudent to.

sauce·pan (sôs′păn′) ▸ *n.* A deep cooking pan with a handle.

sau·cer (sô′sər) ▸ *n.* **1.** A small shallow dish for holding a cup. **2.** An object resembling a saucer.

sauc·y (sô′sē) ▸ *adj.* **-i·er, -i·est. 1.** Impertinent or disrespectful. **2.** Pert. **—sau′ci·ly** *adv.* **—sau′ci·ness** *n.*

Sau·di Arabia (sou′dē, sô′dē, sä-o͞o′dē) ▸ A country occupying most of the Arabian Peninsula. **—Sau′di, Sau′di Arabian** *adj. & n.*

sau·er·bra·ten (sour′brät′n) ▸ *n.* A pot roast of beef marinated in vinegar, water, wine, and spices before cooking.

sau·er·kraut (sour′krout′) ▸ *n.* Shredded cabbage salted and fermented in its own juice.

Sauk (sôk) also **Sac** (săk, sôk) ▸ *n., pl.* **Sauk** or **Sauks** also **Sac** or **Sacs. 1.** A member of a Native American people formerly of Wisconsin, Illinois, and Iowa, now mainly in Oklahoma. **2.** Their Algonquian language.

Saul (sôl) (fl. 11th cent. B.C.) ▸ The first king of Israel.

sau·na (sô′nə, sou′-) ▸ *n.* **1.** A steam bath in which the steam is produced by pouring water over heated rocks. **2.** A dry heat bath.

saun·ter (sôn′tər) ▸ *v.* To walk at a leisurely pace. ▸ *n.* A leisurely stroll. **—saun′ter·er** *n.*

sau·sage (sô′sĭj) ▸ *n.* Finely chopped and seasoned meat stuffed into a casing.

sau·té (sō-tā′, sô-) ▸ *v.* **-téed, -té·ing.** To fry lightly in fat.

Sau·ternes (sō-tûrn′, sô-) ▸ *n., pl.* **-ternes.** A delicate, sweet white wine.

sav·age (săv′ĭj) ▸ *adj.* **1.** Not domesticated or cultivated; wild. **2.** Not civilized; barbaric. **3.** Ferocious; fierce. ▸ *n.* **1.** A primitive or uncivilized person. **2.** A brutal person. **3.** A rude person. ▸ *v.* **-aged, -ag·ing.** To assault ferociously. **—sav′age·ly** *adv.* **—sav′age·ry** *n.*

sa·van·na also **sa·van·nah** (sə-văn′ə) ▸ *n.* A flat grassland of tropical or subtropical regions.

sa·vant (să-vänt′) ▸ *n.* A learned person.

save[1] (sāv) ▸ *v.* **saved, sav·ing. 1a.** To rescue from danger. **b.** To deliver from sin. **2.** To pressure or safeguard. **3.** To prevent waste. **4.** To set aside for future use; store. **5.** To keep from harm; spare: *save one's eyesight.* **6.** *Comp. Sci.* To copy (a file) from main memory to a storage medium. **—sav′er** *n.*

save[2] (sāv) ▸ *prep.* With the exception of; except. ▸ *conj.* Except; but.

sav·ing (sā′vĭng) ▸ *n.* **1.** Preservation or rescue. **2.** Economy. **3. savings** Money saved. ▸ *prep.* With the exception of. ▸ *conj.* Except; save.

THESAURUS

satellite *n.* —*See* FOLLOWER, POSSESSION.

satiate *v.* To satisfy to the full or to excess ▸ cloy, engorge, glut, gorge, sate, surfeit. [*Compare* PACIFY, RELIEVE, SATISFY.]

satiation or **satiety** *n.* The condition of being full to or beyond satisfaction ▸ engorgement, fullness, repletion, surfeit. [*Compare* FULFILLMENT.]

satiny *adj.* Smooth and lustrous as if polished ▸ silken, silky, sleek. [*Compare* EVEN, GLOSSY, SLICK.]

satire *n.* An artistic work that exposes folly by the use of humor, irony, or comic imitation ▸ burlesque, caricature, farce, imitation, impersonation, lampoon, parody, spoof. *Informal:* send-up, takeoff.

satirical or **satiric** *adj.* —*See* SARCASTIC.

satisfaction *n.* The condition of being satisfied ▸ contentedness, contentment, fulfillment, gratification. [*Compare* HAPPINESS, SATIATION.] —*See also* COMPENSATION, DUE.

satisfactory *adj.* —*See* ACCEPTABLE (2), CONVINCING, SUFFICIENT.

satisfied *adj.* Having achieved satisfaction, as of one's goal ▸ content, fulfilled, gratified, happy.

satisfy *v.* **1.** To be suitable or sufficient to fulfill a need, demand, or purpose ▸ answer, do, fill, fulfill, meet, please, serve, suffice, suit. *Idioms:* fill the bill, pass muster. **2.** To grant or have what is demanded by a need or desire ▸ appease, content, fulfill, gratify, indulge. [*Compare* DELIGHT, PACIFY, RELIEVE, SATIATE.] —*See also* CONVINCE, SETTLE (3).

satisfying *adj.* —*See* PLEASANT.

saturate *v.* —*See* CHARGE (1), WET (1).

saturated *adj.* —*See* WET.

saturnine *adj.* —*See* GLUM.

sauce *n.* —*See* IMPUDENCE.

sauce *v. Informal:* To utter an impertinent rejoinder ▸ talk back, talk up. *Informal:* sass. *Idiom:* give someone lip.

saucebox *n.* —*See* SMART ALECK.

sauciness *n.* —*See* IMPUDENCE.

saucy *adj.* —*See* IMPUDENT.

saunter *v.* —*See* STROLL.

saunter *n.* —*See* WALK (1).

sauté *v.* —*See* COOK.

savage *adj.* —*See* CRUEL, UNCIVILIZED, WILD (2).

savage *n.* —*See* FIEND.

savagery *n.* —*See* CRUELTY.

savant *n.* —*See* SAGE.

save *v.* **1.** To keep or accumulate for future use ▸ hoard, keep, lay aside (away *or* by), lay in (*or* up), put by, salt away, save up, set aside, set by, squirrel away, stockpile, store (up), stow, treasure, warehouse. *Informal:* sock away. *Slang:* stash. [*Compare* ACCUMULATE, BANK[2], HIDE[1].] **2.** To protect an asset from loss or destruction ▸ conserve, husband, preserve. [*Compare* DEFEND.] —*See also* RESCUE, SCRIMP.

saving *adj.* —*See* ECONOMICAL.

sav·ings account (sā′vĭngz) ▸ *n.* A bank account that draws interest.
savings and loan association ▸ *n.* A financial institution that invests deposits chiefly in home mortgage loans.
savings bank ▸ *n.* A bank that invests and pays interest on savings accounts.
sav·ior (sāv′yər) ▸ *n.* A person who rescues another from harm, danger, or loss.
sa·voir-faire (săv′wär-fâr′) ▸ *n.* Social skill or tact.
sa·vor (sā′vər) ▸ *n.* **1.** Taste or aroma. **2.** A specific taste or smell. **3.** A distinctive quality. ▸ *v.* **1.** To have a particular savor. **2.** To appreciate fully; relish. **—sa′vor·er** *n.*
sa·vor·y[1] (sā′və-rē) ▸ *adj.* **1.** Appetizing to the taste or smell. **2.** Piquant, pungent, or salty to the taste. **—sa′vor·i·ness** *n.*
sa·vor·y[2] (sā′və-rē) ▸ *n., pl.* **-ies.** An aromatic herb used as a seasoning.
sav·vy (săv′ē) *Informal* ▸ *adj.* **-vi·er, -vi·est.** Well informed and perceptive; shrewd. ▸ *n.* Practical understanding. ▸ *v.* **sav·vied** (săv′ēd), **sav·vy·ing.** To understand.
saw[1] (sô) ▸ *n.* A cutting tool having a thin metal blade or disk with a sharp-toothed edge. ▸ *v.* **sawed, sawed** or **sawn** (sôn), **saw·ing.** To cut or divide with a saw. **—saw′er** *n.*
saw[2] (sô) ▸ *n.* A familiar and often trite saying.
saw[3] (sô) ▸ *v.* P.t. of **see**[1].
saw·buck (sô′bŭk′) ▸ *n.* A sawhorse, esp. one with x-shaped legs.
saw·dust (sô′dŭst′) ▸ *n.* The small waste particles that result from sawing.
sawed-off (sôd′ôf′, -ŏf′) ▸ *adj.* **1.** Having one end sawed off: *a sawed-off shotgun.* **2.** *Slang* Short; runty.
saw·fish (sô′fĭsh′) ▸ *n.* A fish related to the rays and skates and having a bladelike snout with teeth along both sides.
saw·horse (sô′hôrs′) ▸ *n.* A frame used to support pieces of wood being sawed.
saw·mill (sô′mĭl′) ▸ *n.* A mill where timber is sawed into boards.
sawn (sôn) ▸ *v.* P.part. of **saw**[1].
saw·yer (sô′yər) ▸ *n.* One employed in sawing wood.
sax (săks) ▸ *n.* A saxophone.
sax·i·frage (săk′sə-frĭj, -frāj′) ▸ *n.* Any of a genus of plants with flowers and leaves that often form a basal rosette.
Sax·on (săk′sən) ▸ *n.* **1.** A member of a Germanic tribal group that invaded Britain in the 5th cent. A.D. **2.** A native or inhabitant of Saxony. **3.** The Germanic language of any of the Saxons. **—Sax′on** *adj.*
Sax·ony (săk′sə-nē) ▸ A historical region of N Germany.
sax·o·phone (săk′sə-fōn′) ▸ *n.* A woodwind instrument with a single-reed mouthpiece and a usu. curved conical metal tube. **—sax′o·phon′ist** *n.*
say (sā) ▸ *v.* **said** (sĕd), **say·ing.** **1.** To utter aloud. **2.** To express in words. **3.** To state; declare. **4.** To recite. **5.** To allege. **6.** To indicate; show: *The clock says noon.* **7.** To suppose; assume. ▸ *n.* A turn or chance to speak. ▸ *adv.* **1.** Approximately. **2.** For instance. **—say′er** *n.*
say·ing (sā′ĭng) ▸ *n.* An adage or maxim.
sa·yo·na·ra (sī′ə-när′ə) ▸ *interj.* Good-bye.
say-so (sā′sō′) ▸ *n., pl.* **-sos.** *Informal* **1.** An unsupported statement or assurance. **2.** An authoritative expression of permission or approval. **3.** The authority to decide.
Sb ▸ The symbol for the element **antimony.**
Sc ▸ The symbol for the element **scandium.**
SC ▸ *abbr.* **1.** Security Council **2.** or **S.C.** South Carolina **3.** Supreme Court
scab (skăb) ▸ *n.* **1.** A crust discharged from and covering a healing wound. **2.** A person who takes the place of a striking worker. ▸ *v.* **scabbed, scab·bing.** **1.** To become covered with a scab. **2.** To work as a scab.
scab·bard (skăb′ərd) ▸ *n.* A sheath, as for a dagger or sword.
scab·by (skăb′ē) ▸ *adj.* **-bi·er, -bi·est.** **1.** Having or covered with scabs. **2.** Affected with scabies. **—scab′bi·ness** *n.*
sca·bies (skā′bēz) ▸ *n.* A contagious skin disease caused by a mite and characterized by intense itching. **—sca′bi·et′ic** (-ĕt′ĭk) *adj.*
scab·rous (skăb′rəs, skā′brəs) ▸ *adj.* Rough or harsh.
scads (skădz) ▸ *pl.n. Informal* A large number or amount.
scaf·fold (skăf′əld, -ōld′) ▸ *n.* **1.** A temporary platform on which workers perform tasks at heights above the ground. **2.** A platform used in the execution of condemned prisoners.
sca·lar (skā′lər, -lär′) ▸ *n.* A quantity, such as length, that is completely specified by its magnitude and has no direction.
scal·a·wag (skăl′ə-wăg′) ▸ *n. Informal* A scoundrel; rascal.
scald (skôld) ▸ *v.* **1.** To burn with or as if with hot liquid or steam. **2.** To subject to or treat with boiling water. **3.** To heat (e.g., milk) almost to the boiling point. ▸ *n.* An injury caused by scalding.
scale[1] (skāl) ▸ *n.* **1a.** One of the small platelike structures forming the external covering of fishes, reptiles, and certain mammals. **b.** A similar structure or part. **2.** A dry thin flake of epidermis shed from the skin. **3.** A small thin piece. **4.** A scale insect. **5.** A flaky oxide film formed on a metal. ▸ *v.* **scaled, scal·ing.** **1.** To clear or strip of scale or scales. **2.** To remove or come off in layers or scales. **3.** To become encrusted. **—scal′i·ness** *n.* **—scal′y** *adj.*
scale[2] (skāl) ▸ *n.* **1a.** A system of ordered marks at fixed intervals used in measurement. **b.** An instrument or device bearing such marks. **2.** A progressive classification, as of size, importance, or rank. **3.** A relative level or degree. **4.** *Mus.* An ascending or descending series of tones proceeding by a specified scheme of intervals. ▸ *v.* **scaled, scal·ing.** **1.** To climb up or over; ascend. **2.** To make in accord with a particular proportion or scale. **3.** To adjust in calculated amounts: *scaled down their demands.* **—scal′a·ble** *adj.*
scale[3] (skāl) ▸ *n.* often **scales** An instrument or machine for weighing.
scale insect ▸ *n.* A destructive insect that sucks the juices of plants and secretes and remains under waxy scales on plant tissue.
sca·lene (skā′lēn′, skā-lēn′) ▸ *adj.* Having three unequal sides. Used of triangles.
scal·lion (skăl′yən) ▸ *n.* A young onion before the development of the bulb.
scal·lop (skŏl′əp, skăl′-) ▸ *n.* **1a.** A bivalve marine mollusk with a fan-shaped ridged shell. **b.** The edible muscle of a

THESAURUS

savior *n.* *—See* RESCUER.
savoir-faire *n.* *—See* TACT.
savor *n.* A distinctive yet intangible quality ▸ aroma, atmosphere, flavor, smack. *—See also* FLAVOR (1), QUALITY (1).
savor *v.* **1.** To have a particular flavor or suggestion of something ▸ smack, smell, suggest, taste. [*Compare* HINT.] **2.** To undergo an emotional reaction ▸ experience, feel, have, know, taste. *—See also* ENJOY.
savory *adj.* *—See* DELICIOUS, FRAGRANT, SPICY.
savvy *adj.* *—See* SHREWD.
savvy *n.* *—See* ABILITY (1).
savvy *v.* *—See* UNDERSTAND (1).
saw *n.* *—See* CLICHÉ, PROVERB.
saw-toothed *adj.* Having a notched edge like a saw ▸ dentate, notched, serrate, serrated, toothed. [*Compare* ROUGH.]
say *v.* To put into words ▸ articulate, communicate, convey, declare, deliver, express, state, talk, tell, utter, vent, verbalize, vocalize, voice. ***Idiom:*** give tongue (*or* vent *or* voice) to. [*Compare* AIR, BELIEVE, DESCRIBE, SPEAK.] *—See also* ASSERT, PRONOUNCE.
say *n.* The right or chance to express an opinion or participate in a decision ▸ input, suffrage, voice, vote. *Informal:* say-so.
saying *n.* Something said ▸ statement, utterance, word. [*Compare* LANGUAGE, SPEECH.] *—See also* PROVERB, VOICING.
say-so *n.* *Informal* The right or chance to express an opinion or participate in a decision ▸ input, say, suffrage, voice, vote. *—See also* AUTHORITY.
scabrous *adj.* *—See* RACY, ROUGH (1).
scad *n.* *—See* HEAP (2).
scaffolding or **scaffold** *n.* A temporary framework with a floor, used by laborers ▸ platform, stage, staging. [*Compare* BASE[1].]
scalawag *n.* *—See* RASCAL.
scalding *adj.* *—See* HOT (1).
scale[1] *n.* Scaly pieces of dry shedded skin ▸ dander, dandruff, furfur, scurf. [*Compare* FLAKE.] *—See also* FLAKE.
scale *v.* *—See* FLAKE, SKIN.
scale[2] *v.* *—See* ASCEND.
scale *n.* *—See* SERIES.

scallop. **2.** One of a series of curved projections forming an ornamental border. **3.** A thin, boneless slice of meat. ▸ *v.* **-loped, -lop·ing. 1.** To edge (e.g., cloth) with scallops. **2.** To bake in a casserole with milk or a sauce and often with bread crumbs. **—scal′lop·er** *n.*

scalp (skălp) ▸ *n.* The skin covering the top of the human head. ▸ *v.* **1.** To cut or tear the scalp from. **2.** *Slang* To resell (tickets) at an excessively high price. **—scalp′er** *n.*

scal·pel (skăl′pəl) ▸ *n.* A small surgical knife with a thin sharp blade.

scam (skăm) ▸ *n. Slang* A fraudulent business scheme; swindle. **—scam** *v.*

scamp (skămp) ▸ *n.* A rogue; rascal.

scam·per (skăm′pər) ▸ *v.* To run nimbly. **—scam′per** *n.* **—scam′per·er** *n.*

scan (skăn) ▸ *v.* **scanned, scan·ning. 1.** To examine closely. **2.** To look over quickly. **3.** To analyze (verse) into metrical patterns. **4.** *Electron.* To move a finely focused beam of light or electrons in a systematic pattern over (a surface) to reproduce or sense and subsequently transmit an image. **5.** *Comp. Sci.* To search (stored data) automatically for specific data. **6.** *Medic.* To examine (e.g., a body part) with a scanner. **—scan** *n.*

scan·dal (skăn′dl) ▸ *n.* **1.** Public disgrace. **2.** A person, thing, or circumstance that causes disgrace or outrage. **3.** Malicious gossip. **—scan′dal·ous** *adj.* **—scan′dal·ous·ly** *adv.*

scan·dal·ize (skăn′dl-īz′) ▸ *v.* **-ized, -iz·ing.** To offend the moral sensibilities of. **—scan′dal·i·za′tion** *n.* **—scan′dal·iz′er** *n.*

scandal sheet ▸ *n.* A newspaper that habitually prints scandalous stories.

Scan·di·na·vi·a (skăn′də-nā′vē-ə, -nāv′yə) ▸ A region of N Europe consisting of Norway, Sweden, and Denmark, and sometimes Finland, Iceland, and the Faeroe Is.

Scan·di·na·vi·an (skăn′də-nā′vē-ən, -nāv′yən) ▸ *n.* **1.** A native or inhabitant of Scandinavia. **2.** A branch of Germanic including Norwegian, Swedish, Danish, and Icelandic. **—Scan′di·na′vi·an** *adj.*

scan·di·um (skăn′dē-əm) ▸ *n. Symbol* **Sc** A silvery-white metallic element found in various rare minerals and in certain uranium ores. At. no. 21.

scan·ner (skăn′ər) ▸ *n.* **1.** One that scans. **2.** A receiver that broadcasts signals from specified radio frequencies. **3.** A device that converts printed images and text into digital information stored as computer file. **4.** A device, such as a CAT scanner, for observing internal body structures.

scan·sion (skăn′shən) ▸ *n.* Analysis of verse into metrical patterns.

scant (skănt) ▸ *adj.* **-er, -est. 1.** Barely sufficient: *paid scant attention to me.* **2.** Falling just short of a specific measure. ▸ *v.* **1.** To skimp. **2.** To limit, as in amount; stint. **—scant′ly** *adv.*

scant·y (skăn′tē) ▸ *adj.* **-i·er, -i·est. 1.** Barely sufficient or adequate. **2.** Insufficient. **—scant′i·ly** *adv.* **—scant′i·ness** *n.*

scape·goat (skāp′gōt′) ▸ *n.* One bearing blame for others. ▸ *v.* To make a scapegoat of.

scap·u·la (skăp′yə-lə) ▸ *n., pl.* **-las** or **-lae** (-lē′). Either of two large, flat bones forming the back part of the shoulder; shoulder blade. **—scap′u·lar** *adj.*

scar (skär) ▸ *n.* **1.** A mark left on the skin after a surface injury or wound has healed. **2.** A lingering sign of damage or injury. ▸ *v.* **scarred, scar·ring.** To mark with or form a scar.

scar·ab (skăr′əb) ▸ *n.* **1.** A large black beetle regarded as sacred by the ancient Egyptians. **2.** A representation of this beetle.

scarce (skârs) ▸ *adj.* **scarc·er, scarc·est. 1.** Insufficient to meet a demand or requirement; short in supply. **2.** Hard to find; absent or rare. **—scarce′ness, scar′ci·ty** *n.*

scarce·ly (skârs′lē) ▸ *adv.* **1.** By a small margin; barely. **2.** Almost not; hardly. **3.** Certainly not.

scare (skâr) ▸ *v.* **scared, scar·ing.** To frighten or become frightened. ▸ *n.* **1.** A fright. **2.** A panic.

scare·crow (skâr′krō′) ▸ *n.* A crude figure set up in a cultivated area to scare birds away.

scarf[1] (skärf) ▸ *n., pl.* **scarfs** or **scarves** (skärvz). **1.** A piece of cloth worn about the head, neck, or shoulders. **2.** A runner, as for a bureau.

scarf[2] (skärf) ▸ *n., pl.* **scarfs** (skärfs). A joint made by cutting the ends of two pieces correspondingly and strapping or bolting them together. **—scarf** *v.*

scar·i·fy (skăr′ə-fī′) ▸ *v.* **-fied, -fy·ing. 1.** To make shallow cuts in (the skin). **2.** To distress deeply, as with severe criticism. **—scar′i·fi·ca′tion** *n.*

scar·la·ti·na (skär′lə-tē′nə) ▸ *n.* See **scarlet fever.**

scar·let (skär′lĭt) ▸ *n.* A strong to vivid red or reddish orange. **—scar′let** *adj.*

scarlet fever ▸ *n.* An acute contagious bacterial disease occurring predominantly among children and marked by a scarlet skin eruption and high fever.

scarp (skärp) ▸ *n.* An escarpment.

scar·y (skâr′ē) ▸ *adj.* **-i·er, -i·est. 1.** Frightening. **2.** Easily scared; very timid. **—scar′i·ly** *adv.* **—scar′i·ness** *n.*

scat[1] (skăt) ▸ *v.* **scat·ted, scat·ting.** *Informal* To go away hastily.

scat[2] (skăt) ▸ *n.* Jazz singing in which improvised, meaningless syllables are sung to a melody. **—scat** *v.*

scath·ing (skā′*th*ĭng) ▸ *adj.* **1.** Harshly critical. **2.** Harmful or painful; injurious. **—scath′ing·ly** *adv.*

sca·tol·o·gy (skă-tŏl′ə-jē, skə-) ▸ *n.* An obsession with excrement or obscenity, esp. in literature. **—scat′o·log′i·cal** (skăt′l-ŏj′ĭ-kəl), **scat′o·log′ic** *adj.*

scat·ter (skăt′ər) ▸ *v.* **1.** To disperse. **2.** To distribute loosely by or as if by sprinkling; strew. **3.** *Phys.* To deflect

THESAURUS

scalp *v.* —*See* CHEAT (1).

scam *v.* —*See* CHEAT (1).

scam *n.* —*See* CHEAT (1).

scammer *n.* —*See* CHEAT (2).

scamp *n.* —*See* RASCAL, URCHIN.

scamper *v.* —*See* RUN (1).

scan *v.* To view broadly or from a height ▸ look over, overlook, survey. [*Compare* LOOK.] —*See also* BROWSE (1).

scan *n.* —*See* GLANCE (1).

scandal *n.* —*See* GOSSIP (1), LIBEL.

scandalize *v.* —*See* OFFEND (1).

scandalmonger *n.* —*See* GOSSIP (2).

scandalous *adj.* —*See* LIBELOUS, OUTRAGEOUS.

scandalousness *n.* —*See* OUTRAGEOUSNESS.

scant *adj.* Just sufficient ▸ bare, mere, scanty. [*Compare* INSUFFICIENT.] —*See also* MEAGER.

scantiness or **scantness** *n.* —*See* SHORTAGE.

scanty *adj.* Just sufficient ▸ bare, mere, scant. [*Compare* INSUFFICIENT.] —*See also* MEAGER.

scapegoat *n.* One who is made an object of blame ▸ goat, whipping boy. *Slang:* fall guy, patsy. [*Compare* DUPE, VICTIM.]

scapegoat *v.* —*See* CRITICIZE (1).

scar *v.* —*See* DEFORM.

scar *n.* —*See* DEFORMITY.

scarce *adj.* —*See* INFREQUENT, INSUFFICIENT.

scarce or **scarcely** *adv.* By a very little; almost not ▸ barely, hardly, just, scarcely. *Idioms:* by a hair (*or* whisker), by the skin of one's teeth. [*Compare* APPROXIMATELY, MERELY, ONLY.]

scarcity or **scarceness** *n.* —*See* SHORTAGE.

scare *v.* —*See* FRIGHTEN.

scare up *v.* To look for and discover ▸ find, locate, pinpoint, spot. [*Compare* TRACE, UNCOVER.]

scared *adj.* —*See* AFRAID.

scaredy-cat *n.* —*See* COWARD.

scaremonger *n.* One who needlessly alarms others ▸ alarmist, Chicken Little, panicmonger. *Idiom:* one who cries wolf. [*Compare* PESSIMIST.]

scarf *n.* A long piece of cloth worn about the head, neck, or shoulders ▸ ascot, cravat, fichu, headscarf, kerchief, muffler, rebozo. [*Compare* WRAP.]

scarify[1] *v.* —*See* CUT (1), SLIT (1).

scarify[2] *v.* —*See* FRIGHTEN.

scarlet woman *n.* —*See* HARLOT.

scary *adj.* —*See* FEARFUL.

scathe *v.* —*See* SLAM (1).

scathing *adj.* —*See* BITING.

scatological or **scatologic** *adj.* —*See* OBSCENE.

scatology *n.* —*See* OBSCENITY (2).

scatter *v.* **1.** To cause to separate and go in various directions ▸ dispel, disperse, dissipate. [*Compare* DIVIDE, SEPARATE.] **2.** To move apart and go in various directions ▸ break up, disband, disperse, move apart, separate, split up. [*Compare* BRANCH, DIVIDE.] —*See*

(radiation or particles). **—scat′ter·er** *n.*

scat·ter·brain (skăt′ər-brān′) ▸ *n.* A flighty or disorganized person. **—scat′ter·brained′** *adj.*

scatter rug ▸ *n.* A small rug.

scat·ter·shot (skăt′ər-shŏt′) ▸ *adj.* Wide-ranging and indiscriminate: *scattershot criticism.*

scav·en·ger (skăv′ən-jər) ▸ *n.* **1.** One who searches, as through refuse, for food or useful material. **2.** An animal that feeds on dead or decaying matter. **—scav′enge** *v.*

sce·nar·i·o (sĭ-nâr′ē-ō′, -när′-, -năr′-) ▸ *n., pl.* **-os. 1.** A script or outline of a motion picture. **2.** An outline of possible future events. **—sce·nar′ist** *n.*

scene (sēn) ▸ *n.* **1.** A prospect; view. **2.** The setting of an action. **3.** A subdivision of an act of a play. **4.** A shot or series of related shots in a movie. **5.** The scenery for a dramatic presentation. **6.** A public display of passion or temper. **7.** A sphere of activity: *the arts scene.*

scen·er·y (sē′nə-rē) ▸ *n., pl.* **-ies. 1.** A landscape. **2.** The painted backdrops on a theatrical stage. **—sce′nic** *adj.* **—sce′ni·cal·ly** *adv.*

sce·nog·ra·phy (sē-nŏg′rə-fē) ▸ *n.* The art of representing objects in perspective, esp. in theatrical scenery. **—sce·nog′raph·er** *n.*

scent (sĕnt) ▸ *n.* **1.** A distinctive odor. **2.** A perfume. **3.** The trail of a hunted animal or fugitive. ▸ *v.* **1.** To smell, esp. to hunt by smell. **2.** To detect as if by smelling: *scented danger.* **3.** To fill with a scent. **—scent′ed** *adj.*

scep·ter (sĕp′tər) ▸ *n.* A staff held by a sovereign as an emblem of authority.

scep·tic (skĕp′tĭk) ▸ *n.* Var. of **skeptic.**

scep·ti·cism (skĕp′tĭ-sĭz′əm) ▸ *n.* Var. of **skepticism.**

sched·ule (skĕj′o͞ol, -o͞o-əl, skĕj′əl) ▸ *n.* **1.** A timetable. **2.** A production plan. **3.** A list of items. **4.** A program of events or appointments. ▸ *v.* **-uled, -ul·ing. 1.** To enter on a schedule. **2.** To make up a schedule for. **3.** To plan for a certain time. **—sched′u·ler** *n.*

sche·ma (skē′mə) ▸ *n., pl.* **sche·ma·ta** (skē-mä′tə, skĭ-măt′ə) or **-mas.** A diagrammatic representation; outline; model.

sche·mat·ic (skē-măt′ĭk, skĭ-) ▸ *adj.* Relating to or in the form of a scheme or diagram. ▸ *n.* A structural diagram, esp. of an electrical or mechanical system. **—sche·mat′i·cal·ly** *adv.*

scheme (skēm) ▸ *n.* **1.** A systematic plan or design. **2.** A plot. **3.** An orderly combination of elements: *a color scheme.* ▸ *v.* **schemed, schem·ing. 1.** To contrive a plan or scheme for. **2.** To plot. **—schem′er** *n.*

scher·zo (skĕr′tsō) ▸ *n., pl.* **-zos** or **-zi** (-tsē). *Mus.* A lively movement commonly in 3/4 time.

Schick test (shĭk) ▸ *n.* A skin test to determine immunity to diphtheria.

schil·ling (shĭl′ĭng) ▸ *n.* The primary unit of currency in Austria before the adoption of the euro.

schism (skĭz′əm, sĭz′-) ▸ *n.* A separation or division into factions, esp. within a religious body. **—schis·mat′ic** *adj.* **—schis·mat′i·cal·ly** *adv.*

schist (shĭst) ▸ *n.* A metamorphic rock composed of laminated, often flaky parallel layers.

schis·to·so·mi·a·sis (shĭs′tə-sə-mī′ə-sĭs) ▸ *n.* A severe tropical disease caused by infestation with parasitic worms.

schizo– or **schiz–** ▸ *pref.* **1.** Split: *schizophrenia.* **2.** Schizophrenia: *schizoid.*

schiz·oid (skĭt′soid′) ▸ *adj.* **1.** Relating to a personality disorder marked by extreme shyness and reclusiveness. **2.** Schizophrenic. Not in scientific use. ▸ *n.* A schizoid person.

schiz·o·phre·ni·a (skĭt′sə-frē′nē-ə, -frĕn′ē-ə) ▸ *n.* A psychosis usu. marked by withdrawal from reality and by variable emotional, behavioral, or intellectual disturbances. **—schiz′o·phren′ic** (-frĕn′ĭk) *adj. & n.*

schle·miel (shlə-mēl′) ▸ *n. Slang* A habitual bungler; dolt.

schlep (shlĕp) ▸ *v.* **schlepped, schlep·ping.** *Slang* To carry clumsily or with difficulty; lug. **—schlep** *n.*

schlock (shlŏk) ▸ *n. Slang* Something that is inferior or shoddy. **—schlock, shlock′y** *adj.*

schmaltz also **schmalz** (shmälts) ▸ *n. Informal* Excessively sentimental art or music. **—schmaltz′y** *adj.*

schmuck (shmŭk) ▸ *n. Slang* An insignificant or contemptible person.

schnapps (shnäps, shnăps) ▸ *n., pl.* **schnapps.** Any of various strong, often flavored liquors.

schnau·zer (shnou′zər, shnou′tsər) ▸ *n.* A dog with a wiry gray coat and blunt muzzle.

schol·ar (skŏl′ər) ▸ *n.* **1.** A learned person. **2.** A pupil or student. **3.** A student holding a scholarship. **—schol′ar·li·ness** *n.* **—schol′ar·ly** *adj.*

schol·ar·ship (skŏl′ər-shĭp′) ▸ *n.* **1.** The methods and attainments of a scholar. **2.** A grant awarded to a student.

scho·las·tic (skə-lăs′tĭk) ▸ *adj.* **1.** Of or relating to schools or scholarship. **2.** Showing narrow concern for scholarly detail. **—scho·las′ti·cal·ly** *adv.*

school¹ (sko͞ol) ▸ *n.* **1.** An institution for instruction and learning. **2.** The student body of an educational institution. **3.** The process of being educated. **4.** A group of people under a common influence or sharing a unifying belief. ▸ *v.* **1.** To educate. **2.** To train or discipline. **—school′boy′** *n.* **—school′girl′** *n.*

school² (sko͞ol) ▸ *n.* A large group of aquatic animals, esp. fish, swimming together. **—school** *v.*

school·ing (sko͞o′lĭng) ▸ *n.* **1.** Instruction given at school. **2.** Education obtained through experience.

school·marm (sko͞ol′märm′) ▸ *n.* A woman teacher, esp. a strict or old-fashioned one.

school·mas·ter (sko͞ol′măs′tər) ▸ *n.* **1.** A man who teaches school. **2.** One who educates, guides, or instructs.

THESAURUS

also DISORDER, LIFT (2), PLANT, SPREAD (2).

scatterbrained *adj.* *—See* ABSENT-MINDED, GIDDY (2).

scattergood *n.* *—See* WASTREL (1).

scattering *n.* An act of reflection ▸ deflection, glance, reflection. [*Compare* BOUNCE.] *—See also* DISTRIBUTION (2).

scenario *n.* *—See* PLOT (1), SCRIPT (2).

scene *n.* **1.** The place where an action or event occurs ▸ backdrop, locale, setting, site, stage. [*Compare* ENVIRONMENT, LOCALITY.] **2.** The properties, objects, and accessories arranged for a dramatic presentation ▸ backdrop, background, mise en scène, props, scenery, set, setting, staging. [*Compare* STAGE.] *—See also* AGITATION (1), AREA (1), CONDITIONS, VIEW (2).

scenery *n.* *—See* SCENE (2), VIEW (2).

scent *n.* **1.** The quality of something that may be perceived by the olfactory sense ▸ aroma, odor, smell. [*Compare* FRAGRANCE, STENCH.] **2.** The sense by which odors are perceived ▸ nose, olfaction, smell. *—See also* FRAGRANCE, TIP³, TRACK.

scent *v.* To fill with a pleasant odor ▸ aromatize, perfume. *—See also* SMELL (1).

schedule *n.* *—See* LIST¹, PROGRAM (1).

schedule *v.* **1.** To enter on a schedule ▸ calendar, docket, program, slate. [*Compare* LIST¹.] **2.** To set the time for an event or occasion ▸ plan, set, time. *—See also* ARRANGE (2).

scheduled *adj.* *—See* DUE (2).

schema *n.* *—See* APPROACH (1).

scheme *n.* *—See* APPROACH (1), METHOD, PLOT (2).

scheme *v.* *—See* DESIGN (1), PLOT (2).

scheming *adj.* Coldly planning to achieve selfish aims ▸ calculating, conniving, designing, manipulative. *—See also* ARTFUL.

schism *n.* *—See* BREACH (2), CONFLICT, DIVISION (2).

schismatic *n.* *—See* SEPARATIST.

schlep *v.* *—See* CARRY (1), TRUDGE.

schlep *n.* *—See* OAF.

schlocky *adj.* *—See* SHODDY.

schmaltz or **schmaltziness** *n.* *—See* SENTIMENTALITY.

schmaltzy *adj.* *—See* SENTIMENTAL.

schmuck or **schmo** *n.* *—See* DRIP (2), FOOL.

schnoz *n.* *—See* NOSE (1).

schnozzle *n.* *—See* NOSE (1).

scholar *n.* *—See* SAGE, STUDENT.

scholarly *adj.* Devoted to study or reading ▸ bookish, studious. [*Compare* INTELLECTUAL.] *—See also* EDUCATED.

scholarship *n.* *—See* EDUCATION (2).

scholastic *adj.* *—See* EDUCATIONAL (1), PEDANTIC.

school *v.* *—See* EDUCATE.

school *n.* *—See* CLASS (2), FLOCK.

schooling *n.* *—See* EDUCATION (1).

schoolmaster or **schoolmistress** *n.* *—See* EDUCATOR.

school·mis·tress (sko͞ol′mĭs′trĭs) ► *n.* **1.** A woman who teaches school. **2.** A headmistress.
school·room (sko͞ol′ro͞om′, -ro͝om′) ► *n.* A classroom.
school·teach·er (sko͞ol′tē′chər) ► *n.* One who teaches in a school below the college level.
schoo·ner (sko͞o′nər) ► *n.* **1.** A fore-and-aft rigged sailing vessel with at least two masts. **2.** A large beer glass, usu. holding a pint or more.
Schu·bert (sho͞o′bərt, -bĕrt′), **Franz Peter** (1797–1828) ► Austrian composer.
schuss (sho͝os, sho͞os) ► *v.* To ski a fast straight downhill course. **—schuss** *n.*
schwa (shwä) ► *n.* **1.** A neutral vowel sound typically occurring in unstressed syllables, as the final vowel of English *sofa.* **2.** The symbol (ə) used to represent schwa.
sci·at·i·ca (sī-ăt′ĭ-kə) ► *n.* Chronic neuralgic pain in the area of the hip or thigh.
sci·ence (sī′əns) ► *n.* **1.** The observation, identification, description, experimental investigation, and theoretical explanation of phenomena. **2.** Methodological activity, discipline, or study. **3.** An activity regarded as requiring study and method. **4.** Knowledge gained through experience. **—sci′en·tif′ic** (sī′ən-tĭf′ĭk) *adj.* **—sci′en·tif′i·cal·ly** *adv.*
science fiction ► *n.* Fiction in which the plot is based on speculative scientific discoveries, drastic environmental changes, or space travel. **—sci′ence-fic′tion** *adj.*
scientific notation ► *n.* A method of writing or displaying numbers in terms of a decimal number between 1 and 10 multiplied by a power of 10.
sci·en·tist (sī′ən-tĭst) ► *n.* A person having expert knowledge of one or more sciences.
sci-fi (sī′fī′) ► *n. Informal* Science fiction.
scim·i·tar (sĭm′ĭ-tər, -tär′) ► *n.* A broad curved sword with the edge on the convex side.
scin·til·la (sĭn-tĭl′ə) ► *n.* A minute amount; trace. **—scin′til·lant** *adj.*
scin·til·late (sĭn′tl-āt′) ► *v.* **-lat·ed, -lat·ing. 1.** To throw off sparks; flash. **2.** To be animated and brilliant. **—scin′til·la′tion** *n.*
sci·on (sī′ən) ► *n.* **1.** A descendant or heir. **2.** A detached plant shoot used in grafting.
scis·sors (sĭz′ərz) ► *n. (takes sing. or pl. v.)* A cutting implement of two blades joined by a swivel pin that allows the cutting edges to be opened and closed. **—scis′sor** *v.*
scissors kick ► *n.* A swimming kick in which the legs are opened and closed like scissors.
scle·ra (sklîr′ə) ► *n.* The tough fibrous tissue covering all of the eyeball except the cornea. **—scle′ral** *adj.*
scle·ro·sis (sklə-rō′sĭs) ► *n., pl.* **-ses** (-sēz). A thickening or hardening of a body part, as of an artery, esp. from tissue overgrowth or disease. **—scle·rot′ic** (-rŏt′ĭk) *adj.*
scoff (skŏf, skôf) ► *v.* To express derision or scorn: *scoffed at their threats.* **—scoff** *n.* **—scoff′er** *n.*
scoff·law (skŏf′lô′, skôf′-) ► *n.* One who habitually violates the law.
scold (skōld) ► *v.* To reprimand harshly. ► *n.* A persistent nag or critic. **—scold′er** *n.*
sco·li·o·sis (skō′lē-ō′sĭs, skŏl′ē-) ► *n.* Abnormal lateral curvature of the spine. **—sco′li·ot′ic** (-ŏt′ĭk) *adj.*
sconce (skŏns) ► *n.* A wall bracket for candles or lights.
scone (skōn, skŏn) ► *n.* A small, rich, biscuitlike pastry.
scoop (sko͞op) ► *n.* **1.** A small shovellike serving utensil. **2.** The bucket or shovel, as of a dredge or backhoe. **3.** *Informal* An exclusive news story acquired by luck or initiative. ► *v.* **1.** To take up or dip into with or as if with a scoop. **2.** To hollow out. **3.** *Informal* To top or outmaneuver (a competitor) in acquiring a news story. **—scoop′er** *n.*
scoot (sko͞ot) ► *v.* To go suddenly and speedily.
scoot·er (sko͞o′tər) ► *n.* **1.** A child's vehicle consisting of a long footboard between two end wheels, controlled by an upright steering handle. **2.** A motor scooter.
scope (skōp) ► *n.* **1.** The range of one's perceptions, thoughts, or actions. **2.** Breadth or opportunity to function. **3.** The area covered by a given activity or subject. **4.** *Informal* A telescope.
-scope ► *suff.* An instrument for observing: *telescope.*
Scopes (skōps), **John Thomas** (1900–70) ► Amer. teacher; convicted (1925) for teaching evolution.
scor·bu·tic (skôr-byo͞o′tĭk) also **scor·bu·ti·cal** (-tĭ-kəl) ► *adj.* Of, resembling, or affected by scurvy.
scorch (skôrch) ► *v.* **1.** To burn superficially. **2.** To wither or parch with intense heat. ► *n.* **1.** A slight burn. **2.** Discoloration caused by heat. **—scorch′er** *n.*
score (skôr) ► *n.* **1.** A notch or incision. **2.** A record of points made in a competitive event. **3.** A result of a test or examination. **4.** A debt. **5.** A ground; reason. **6.** A group of 20 items. **7.** The written form of a musical composition. ► *v.* **scored, scor·ing. 1.** To mark with lines or notches. **2.** To gain (a point) in a game or contest. **3.** To keep the score of a game or contest. **4.** To achieve; win. **5.** To evaluate and assign a grade to. **6.** *Mus.* **a.** To orchestrate. **b.** To arrange for a specific instrument. **—score′less** *adj.* **—scor′er** *n.*
sco·ri·a (skôr′ē-ə) ► *n.* **1.** *Geol.* Porous cinderlike fragments of dark lava. **2.** *Metall.* The refuse of a smelted metal or ore; slag.
scorn (skôrn) ► *n.* **1a.** Contempt or disdain. **b.** Derision. **2.** One spoken of or treated with contempt. ► *v.* **1.** To consider or treat as contemptible or unworthy. **2.** To reject or refuse with derision. **—scorn′ful** *adj.* **—scorn′ful·ly** *adv.* **—scorn′ful·ness** *n.*
Scor·pi·o (skôr′pē-ō′) ► *n.* **1.** Var. of **Scorpius. 2.** The 8th sign of the zodiac.
scor·pi·on (skôr′pē-ən) ► *n.* Any of various arachnids with an erectile tail tipped with a venomous sting.
Scor·pi·us (skôr′pē-əs) also **Scor·pi·o** (-pē-ō′) ► *n.* A constellation in the Southern Hemisphere.
Scot (skŏt) ► *n.* **1.** A native or inhabitant of Scotland. **2.** A member of a Gaelic tribe that migrated to N Britain from Ireland in about the 6th cent. A.D.
scotch (skŏch) ► *v.* **1.** To put an abrupt end to. **2.** To injure so as to render harmless. **3.** To cut or score.
Scotch ► *n.* **1.** The people of Scotland. **2.** Scots English. **3.** Scotch whisky. ► *adj.* Scottish. **—Scotch′man** *n.* **—Scotch′wom′an** *n.*
Scotch-I·rish (skŏch′ī′rĭsh) ► *n.* The people of Scotland who settled in N Ireland or their descendants. **—Scotch′-I′rish** *adj.*

THESAURUS

schoolteacher *n.* —*See* EDUCATOR.
science *n.* —*See* EDUCATION (2).
scilicet *adv.* —*See* NAMELY.
scintillate *v.* —*See* GLITTER.
scintillating *adj.* —*See* CLEVER (2), SPARKLING.
scintillation *n.* —*See* FLASH (1), GLITTER (1).
scion *n.* —*See* PROGENY.
scissors *n.* —*See* SHEARS.
scoff *v.* —*See* RIDICULE.
scoff *n.* —*See* TAUNT.
scoffing *adj.* —*See* SARCASTIC.
scofflaw *n.* —*See* CRIMINAL.
scold *v.* —*See* CHASTISE.
scold *n.* A person, traditionally a woman, who persistently nags or criticizes ► fishwife, fury, harpy, harridan, nag, shrew, termagant, virago, vixen, *Informal:* battle-ax. [*Compare* CRITIC, GROUCH.]
scolding *n.* —*See* REBUKE.
scoop *n.* —*See* NEWS.
scoop *v.* —*See* DIG, DIP (2).
scoot *v.* —*See* RUSH.
scope *n.* The ability or power to seize or to attain ► capacity, compass, grasp, range, reach. [*Compare* INFLUENCE.] —*See also* DEGREE (2), KEN, LICENSE (1), RANGE (1).
scope out *v.* —*See* EXAMINE (1).
scorch *v.* —*See* BLAST (2), BURN (1), SLAM (1).
scorch *n.* —*See* BURN.
scorched *adj.* —*See* DRY (2).
scorching *adj.* —*See* BITING, HOT (1), PASSIONATE.
score *n.* —*See* COUNT (1), CUT (1), DEBT (1).
score *v.* **1.** To gain a point or points in a game or contest ► post, tally. *Informal:* notch. *Idiom:* make a goal (*or* point). **2.** To evaluate and assign a grade to ► correct, grade, mark. —*See also* ACCOMPLISH, BUY, COMPOSE (1), COUNT (2), PROSPER, SLAM (1).
scores *n.* —*See* CROWD.
scorn *n.* —*See* DESPISAL, DISGRACE.
scorn *v.* —*See* DESPISE.
scornful *adj.* —*See* DISDAINFUL, DISRESPECTFUL.

Scotch whisky ▸ *n.* A whiskey distilled in Scotland from malted barley.

scot-free (skŏt′frē′) ▸ *adv. & adj.* Free from obligation or penalty.

Scot·land (skŏt′lənd) ▸ A constituent country of the United Kingdom, in N Great Britain. **—Scots′man** *n.* **—Scots′wom′an** *n.*

Scott (skŏt), **Dred** (1795?–1858) ▸ Amer. slave; subject of a US Supreme Court decision supporting slavery (1857).

Scot·tish (skŏt′ĭsh) ▸ *adj.* Of or relating to Scotland or its people or language. ▸ *n.* **1.** Scots English. **2.** The people of Scotland.

Scottish Gaelic ▸ *n.* The Celtic language of Scotland.

scoun·drel (skoun′drəl) ▸ *n.* A villain; rogue. **—scoun′drel·ly** *adj.*

scour[1] (skour) ▸ *v.* **1.** To clean by scrubbing vigorously, as with an abrasive. **2.** To scrub something in order to clean or polish it.

scour[2] (skour) ▸ *v.* **1.** To search through or over thoroughly. **2.** To move swiftly; scurry.

scourge (skûrj) ▸ *n.* **1.** A source of great suffering or harm. **2.** A means of inflicting severe suffering or punishment. **3.** A whip. ▸ *v.* **scourged, scourg·ing. 1.** To devastate; ravage. **2.** To chastise severely. **3.** To whip or flog.

scout (skout) ▸ *v.* **1.** To reconnoiter. **2.** To observe and evaluate (a talented person) for possible hiring. ▸ *n.* **1.** One that is sent out to gather information. **2.** A sentinel. **3.** One who seeks out talented persons, esp. in sports and entertainment. **4.** often **Scout a.** A Boy Scout. **b.** A Girl Scout. **—scout′er** *n.*

scout·mas·ter (skout′măs′tər) ▸ *n.* The adult leader of a troop of Boy Scouts.

scow (skou) ▸ *n.* A large flat-bottomed boat with square ends.

scowl (skoul) ▸ *v.* To wrinkle or contract the brow as in anger or disapproval. ▸ *n.* A look of anger or strong disapproval. **—scowl′er** *n.* **—scowl′ing·ly** *adv.*

scrab·ble (skrăb′əl) ▸ *v.* **-bled, -bling. 1.** To grope or scratch frantically. **2.** To struggle. **3.** To clamber. **4.** To scribble. **—scrab′ble** *n.*

scrag·gly (skrăg′lē) ▸ *adj.* **-gli·er, -gli·est.** Ragged; unkempt.

scrag·gy (skrăg′ē) ▸ *adj.* **-gi·er, -gi·est. 1.** Jagged; rough. **2.** Bony and lean. **—scrag′gi·ness** *n.*

scram (skrăm) ▸ *v.* **scrammed, scram·ming.** *Slang* To leave at once.

scram·ble (skrăm′bəl) ▸ *v.* **-bled, -bling. 1.** To move or climb hurriedly. **2.** To compete frantically. **3.** To mix haphazardly. **4.** To take off with all possible haste. Used of a warplane. **5.** To cook (beaten eggs) while stirring. **6.** *Electron.* To distort (a signal) so as to render it unintelligible without a special receiver. **—scram′ble** *n.* **—scram′bler** *n.*

scrap[1] (skrăp) ▸ *n.* **1.** A small bit or fragment. **2. scraps** Leftover food. **3.** Discarded waste material, esp. metal suitable for reprocessing. ▸ *v.* **scrapped, scrap·ping. 1.** To break down into parts for disposal or salvage. **2.** To discard as worthless. **—scrap′py** *adj.*

scrap[2] (skrăp) ▸ *v.* **scrapped, scrap·ping.** To fight, often with the fists. ▸ *n.* A fight or scuffle. **—scrap′per** *n.*

scrap·book (skrăp′bo͝ok′) ▸ *n.* A book with blank pages for mounting pictures, clippings, or other mementos.

scrape (skrāp) ▸ *v.* **scraped, scrap·ing. 1.** To rub (a surface) with considerable pressure. **2.** To draw (a hard or abrasive object) forcefully over a surface. **3.** To abrade, smooth, injure, or remove by this procedure. **4.** To come into abrasive contact. **5.** To rub or move with a harsh grating noise. **6.** To amass or produce with difficulty: *scrape together some cash.* ▸ *n.* **1.** The act or sound of scraping. **2.** An abrasion on the skin. **3a.** A predicament. **b.** A scuffle. **—scrap′er** *n.*

scrap·py (skrăp′ē) ▸ *adj.* **-pi·er, -pi·est. 1.** Quarrelsome; contentious. **2.** Full of fighting spirit. **—scrap′pi·ly** *adv.* **—scrap′pi·ness** *n.*

scratch (skrăch) ▸ *v.* **1.** To make a shallow cut or mark with something sharp. **2.** To use the nails or claws to dig or scrape at. **3.** To rub (the skin) to relieve itching. **4.** To strike out or cancel (e.g., a word) by or as if by drawing lines through. ▸ *n.* A mark or wound produced by scratching. ▸ *adj.* **1.** Done haphazardly or by chance. **2.** Assembled hastily or at random. ***—idioms:*** **from scratch** From the very beginning. **up to scratch** *Informal* Meeting the requirements. **—scratch′er** *n.* **—scratch′i·ly** *adv.* **—scratch′i·ness** *n.* **—scratch′y** *adj.*

scrawl (skrôl) ▸ *v.* To write hastily or illegibly. **—scrawl** *n.* **—scrawl′y** *adj.*

scraw·ny (skrô′nē) ▸ *adj.* **-ni·er, -ni·est.** Gaunt and bony. **—scraw′ni·ness** *n.*

scream (skrēm) ▸ *v.* **1.** To utter a long loud piercing cry, as from pain or fear. **2.** To produce a startling effect. ▸ *n.* **1.** A long loud piercing cry or sound. **2.** *Informal* One that is hilariously or ridiculously funny. **—scream′er** *n.*

scree (skrē) ▸ *n.* Loose rock debris covering a slope.

THESAURUS

scoundrel *n.* —*See* EVILDOER, RASCAL.

scour[1] *v.* To remove an outer layer or something adherent from an object by friction ▸ rub away, rub off, scrape, scrub. [*Compare* CHAFE, SCRAPE.]

scour[2] *v.* To search through or over thoroughly ▸ comb, forage, ransack, rummage, search. *Slang:* shake down. ***Idioms:*** beat the bushes, leave no stone unturned, look (*or* search) high and low, look (*or* search) up and down, turn inside out, turn upside down. [*Compare* EXAMINE, EXPLORE, SEEK.] —*See also* RUSH.

scourge *n.* —*See* CURSE (3).

scourge *v.* —*See* AFFLICT, BEAT (2), SLAM (1).

scout[1] *v.* —*See* EXPLORE.

scout[2] *v.* —*See* DESPISE, RIDICULE.

scowl *v.* **1.** To wrinkle one's brow, as in thought, puzzlement, or displeasure ▸ frown, glower, lower. ***Idioms:*** knit one's brow, look black, turn one's mouth down. [*Compare* GRIMACE.] **2.** To stare fixedly and angrily ▸ glare, glower, lower. ***Idioms:*** give the evil eye, look daggers. [*Compare* GAZE, SNEER.]

scowl *n.* A fixed angry stare ▸ glare, glower, lower. [*Compare* FACE, SNEER.] —*See also* FROWN.

scrabble *v.* —*See* GROPE.

scraggy *adj.* —*See* ROUGH (1).

scram *v.* —*See* RUN (2).

scramble *v.* —*See* ASCEND, CONFUSE (3), SHUFFLE.

scramble *n.* —*See* DISORDER (1).

scrap[1] *n.* —*See* BIT[1] (1), BIT[1] (2), END (3).

scrap *v.* *Slang* To decide not to continue ▸ call off, cancel. *Slang:* scratch, scrub. [*Compare* DEFER[1], DROP.] —*See also* DISCARD.

scrap[2] *n.* —*See* FIGHT (1).

scrape *v.* **1.** To bring or come into abrasive contact, often with a harsh sound ▸ abrade, file, grate, rasp, scratch. [*Compare* CHAFE.] **2.** To remove an outer layer or something adherent from an object by friction ▸ rub away, rub off, scour, scrub. [*Compare* CHAFE.] —*See also* SCRIMP.

scrape *n.* A mark or shallow cut made by contact with an object ▸ abrasion, scratch, scuff, striation. [*Compare* CUT, FURROW, IMPRESSION.] —*See also* PREDICAMENT.

scrappy *adj.* —*See* AGGRESSIVE, ARGUMENTATIVE.

scratch *v.* *Slang* To decide not to continue ▸ call off, cancel. *Slang:* scrap, scrub. [*Compare* DEFER[1], DROP.] —*See also* CANCEL (1), SCRAPE (1).

scratch *n.* A mark or shallow cut made by contact with an object ▸ abrasion, scrape, scuff, striation. [*Compare* CUT, FURROW, IMPRESSION.] —*See also* MONEY (1).

scratchy *adj.* —*See* HARSH, ROUGH (1).

scrawny *adj.* —*See* THIN (1).

screak *n.* A long, loud, piercing cry, as in fright ▸ scream, screech, shriek. [*Compare* HOWL.]

screak *v.* To utter a long, loud, piercing cry, as of fright ▸ scream, screech, shriek, shrill. [*Compare* HOWL.]

scream *v.* To utter a long, loud, piercing cry, as in fright ▸ screak, screech, shriek, shrill. [*Compare* HOWL.] —*See also* SHOUT.

scream *n.* **1.** A long, loud, piercing cry, as of fright ▸ screak, screech, shriek. [*Compare* HOWL.] **2.** *Informal* Something or someone uproariously funny or absurd ▸ absurdity. *Informal:* hoot, joke, laugh. *Slang:* gas, howl, panic, riot. ***Idiom:*** a laugh a minute. [*Compare* FOOLISHNESS.] —*See also* SHOUT.

screech (skrēch) ▸ *n.* **1.** A high shrill cry. **2.** A similar sound, as of scraping metal. **—screech** *v.* **—screech′y** *adj.*

screech owl ▸ *n.* Any of various small North American owls with ear tufts and a quavering, whistlelike call.

screen (skrēn) ▸ *n.* **1.** Something serving to divide, conceal, or protect, such as a movable room partition. **2.** A coarse sieve. **3.** A window or door insertion of framed mesh used to keep out insects. **4a.** The surface on which a picture is projected for viewing. **b.** The movie industry. **5.** The phosphorescent surface on which an image is displayed in a cathode-ray tube. ▸ *v.* **1.** To provide with a screen. **2.** To conceal or protect. **3a.** To separate or sift out by means of a sieve or screen. **b.** To test or examine, as for suitability. **4.** To show (e.g., a movie) on a screen. **—screen′er** *n.*

screen·play (skrēn′plā′) ▸ *n.* The script for a movie.

screen test ▸ *n.* A brief movie sequence filmed to test the ability of an aspiring performer. **—screen′-test′** *v.*

screen·writ·er (skrēn′rī′tər) ▸ *n.* A writer of screenplays. **—screen′writ′ing** *n.*

screw (skro͞o) ▸ *n.* **1.** A cylindrical rod with incised threads, having a slotted head so that it can be driven as a fastener by turning it with a screwdriver. **2.** A propeller. ▸ *v.* **1.** To fasten, tighten, or attach by or as if by means of a screw. **2.** To turn or twist. ***—phrasal verb:* screw up** *Slang* To make a mess of.

screw·ball (skro͞o′bôl′) ▸ *n.* **1.** *Baseball* A pitched ball curving in the direction opposite to a normal curve ball. **2.** *Slang* An eccentric or irrational person.

screw·driv·er (skro͞o′drī′vər) ▸ *n.* **1.** A tool used for turning screws. **2.** A cocktail of vodka and orange juice.

screw·y (skro͞o′ē) ▸ *adj.* **-i·er, -i·est.** *Slang* **1.** Eccentric; crazy. **2.** Ludicrously odd.

scrib·ble (skrĭb′əl) ▸ *v.* **-bled, -bling.** To write hastily or carelessly. **—scrib′ble** *n.* **—scrib′bler** *n.*

scribe (skrīb) ▸ *n.* **1.** A public clerk. **2.** A professional copyist of manuscripts. **3.** A writer or journalist. **—scrib′al** *adj.*

scrim·mage (skrĭm′ĭj) ▸ *n.* **1.** *Football* The contest between two teams from the time the ball is snapped until it is declared dead. **2.** *Sports* A practice game. **3.** A rough-and-tumble struggle; tussle. **—scrim′mage** *v.*

scrimp (skrĭmp) ▸ *v.* To economize severely. **—scrimp′er** *n.*

scrim·shaw (skrĭm′shô′) ▸ *n., pl.* **-shaw** or **-shaws.** **1.** The art of carving on whalebone or whale ivory. **2.** An article made in this way.

scrip[1] (skrĭp) ▸ *n.* Paper money issued for temporary emergency use.

scrip[2] (skrĭp) ▸ *n.* A provisional certificate entitling the holder to a fractional share of stock or of other property.

script (skrĭpt) ▸ *n.* **1a.** Handwriting. **b.** A style of writing in cursive. **2.** The text of a play, broadcast, or movie. **3.** *Comp. Sci.* A simple program, esp. in an application's proprietary language. ▸ *v.* To prepare (a text) for filming or broadcasting. **—script′writ′er** *n.* **—script′writ′ing** *n.*

Scrip·ture (skrĭp′chər) ▸ *n.* **1a.** A sacred writing or book. **b.** A passage from such a writing or book. **2.** often **Scriptures** The Bible. **3. scripture** An authoritative statement. **—Scrip′tur·al, scrip′tur·al** *adj.*

scriv·en·er (skrĭv′ə-nər, skrĭv′nər) ▸ *n.* A scribe or author.

scrod (skrŏd) ▸ *n., pl.* **scrod.** A young cod or haddock.

scroll (skrōl) ▸ *n.* **1.** A roll, as of papyrus, used esp. for writing a document. **2.** Ornamentation that resembles a scroll. **3.** *Mus.* The curved head on an instrument, esp. a violin. ▸ *v.* *Comp. Sci.* To cause displayed text or graphics to move up, down, or across the screen.

Scrooge also **scrooge** (skro͞oj) ▸ *n.* A mean-spirited miserly person; skinflint.

scro·tum (skrō′təm) ▸ *n., pl.* **-ta** (-tə) or **-tums.** The external sac of skin enclosing the testes. **—scro′tal** (skrōt′l) *adj.*

scrounge (skrounj) ▸ *v.* **scrounged, scroung·ing.** *Slang* **1.** To beg; mooch. **2.** To obtain by salvaging or foraging. **—scroung′er** *n.*

scrub[1] (skrŭb) ▸ *v.* **scrubbed, scrub·bing.** **1.** To rub hard in order to clean. **2.** To clean or wash something by hard rubbing. **3.** *Slang* To cancel. **—scrub** *n.* **—scrub′ber** *n.*

scrub[2] (skrŭb) ▸ *n.* **1.** A growth of stunted vegetation. **2.** An undersized, poorly developed plant or animal. **3.** *Sports* A player not on the first team. **—scrub′by** *adj.*

scruff (skrŭf) ▸ *n.* The back of the neck; the nape.

scruff·y (skrŭf′ē) ▸ *adj.* **-i·er, -i·est.** Shabby; untidy. **—scruff′i·ly** *adv.* **—scruff′i·ness** *n.*

scrump·tious (skrŭmp′shəs) ▸ *adj.* Delicious; delectable.

scrunch (skrŭnch, skro͝onch) ▸ *v.* **1.** To crush or crunch. **2.** To hunch. **3.** To make a crunching sound. **—scrunch** *n.*

scru·ple (skro͞o′pəl) ▸ *n.* **1.** An uneasy feeling arising from conscience or principle. **2.** A unit of apothecary weight equal to about 1.3 grams, or 20 grains. **—scru′ple** *v.*

scru·pu·lous (skro͞o′pyə-ləs) ▸ *adj.* **1.** Conscientious; painstaking. **2.** Having scruples; principled. **—scru′pu·los′i·ty** (-lŏs′ĭ-tē), **scru′pu·lous·ness** *n.* **—scru′pu·lous·ly** *adv.*

scru·ti·nize (skro͞ot′n-īz′) ▸ *v.* **-nized, -niz·ing.** To examine carefully.

scru·ti·ny (skro͞ot′n-ē) ▸ *n., pl.* **-nies.** A close, careful examination.

scu·ba (sko͞o′bə) ▸ *n.* An apparatus containing compressed air and used for breathing under water.

scud (skŭd) ▸ *v.* **scud·ded, scud·ding.** To skim along swiftly and easily: *dark clouds scudding by.* ▸ *n.* Wind-driven clouds, mist, or rain.

scuff (skŭf) ▸ *v.* **1.** To scrape with the feet. **2.** To scrape and roughen the surface of. ▸ *n.* **1.** The act or sound of scuffing. **2.** A flat, backless slipper.

THESAURUS

screech *n.* A long, loud, piercing cry, as of fright ▸ screak, scream, shriek. [*Compare* HOWL.] *—See also* SHOUT.

screech *v.* To utter a long, loud, piercing cry, as in fright ▸ screak, scream, shriek, shrill. [*Compare* HOWL.] *—See also* SHOUT.

screed *n.* *—See* TIRADE.

screen *v.* **1.** To shelter, especially from light ▸ shade, shadow. **2.** To separate with or as if with a wall ▸ fence, partition, wall. *—See also* BLOCK, CENSOR (1), CONCEAL.

screen *n.* A solid structure that separates one area from another ▸ barrier, partition, wall. [*Compare* BORDER.] *—See also* COVER (1), VEIL.

screened *adj.* Concealed from view ▸ blind, hidden, secluded, secret. *Idioms:* out of sight, out of view. [*Compare* HIDDEN.]

screenplay *n.* *—See* SCRIPT (2).

screw *v.* *—See* FASTEN.

screw *n.* *—See* NAIL.

screw around or **off** *v.* *—See* PUTTER.

screw up *v.* *—See* BOTCH, ERR.

screwball *n.* *—See* CRACKPOT.

screwball *adj.* *—See* ECCENTRIC.

screwup *n.* *—See* BLUNDERER, MESS (1).

screwy *adj.* *—See* INSANE.

scribble *v.* *—See* WRITE.

scrimp *v.* To be frugal or sparing ▸ conserve, economize, pinch, save, scrape, skimp, spare, stint. *Idioms:* pinch pennies, tighten one's belt.

scrimpy *adj.* *—See* MEAGER.

script *n.* **1.** Writing done with the hand ▸ calligraphy, cursive, handwriting, longhand, penmanship. **2.** The text of a play, movie, opera, or similar work ▸ book, dialogue, libretto, manuscript, play, screenplay, scenario.

scriptural *adj.* Of or relating to representation by means of writing ▸ calligraphic, graphic, written.

Scrooge *n.* *—See* MISER.

scrounge *v.* *—See* BEG.

scrub *v.* **1.** To remove an outer layer or something adherent from an object by friction ▸ rub away, rub off, scour, scrape. [*Compare* CHAFE, SCRAPE.] **2.** *Slang* To decide not to continue ▸ call off, cancel. *Slang:* scrap, scratch. [*Compare* DEFER, DROP.]

scrub *n.* *—See* NONENTITY, SQUIRT (2).

scrubby *adj.* *—See* SHABBY.

scruffy *adj.* *—See* SHABBY.

scrumptious *adj.* *—See* DELICIOUS.

scrunch *v.* *—See* SQUEEZE (1), STOOP.

scruple *n.* *—See* BIT[1] (1), QUALM.

scrupulous *adj.* *—See* CAREFUL (2), ETHICAL.

scrupulousness *n.* *—See* THOROUGHNESS.

scrutinize *v.* *—See* EXAMINE (1), WATCH (1).

scrutiny *n.* The act of observing, often for an extended time ▸ observance, observation, watch, watching. *—See also* EXAMINATION (1).

scuff *v.* *—See* BATTER, TRUDGE.

scuff *n.* A mark or shallow cut made by contact with an object ▸ abrasion, scrape, scratch, striation. [*Compare* CUT, FURROW, IMPRESSION.]

scuf·fle (skŭf′əl) ▸ *v.* **-fled, -fling.** **1.** To fight confusedly at close quarters. **2.** To shuffle. ▸ *n.* A disorderly struggle at close quarters. **—scuf′fler** *n.*

scull (skŭl) ▸ *n.* **1.** An oar used for rowing a boat from the stern. **2.** One of a pair of short-handled oars used by a single rower. **3.** A small light boat for racing. **—scull** *v.* **—scull′er** *n.*

scul·ler·y (skŭl′ə-rē) ▸ *n., pl.* **-ies.** A room adjoining a kitchen for dishwashing and other chores.

sculpt (skŭlpt) ▸ *v.* To sculpture.

sculp·tor (skŭlp′tər) ▸ *n.* One who sculptures.

sculp·tress (skŭlp′trĭs) ▸ *n.* A woman who sculptures.

sculp·ture (skŭlp′chər) ▸ *n.* **1.** The art or practice of shaping three-dimensional figures or forms, as by chiseling marble, modeling clay, or casting in metal. **2.** A work of art created by sculpture. ▸ *v.* **-tured, -tur·ing.** **1.** To fashion (e.g., stone or clay) into sculpture. **2.** To represent in sculpture. **3.** To ornament with sculpture. **—sculp′tur·al** *adj.*

scum (skŭm) ▸ *n.* **1.** A filmy layer of impure matter on the surface of a liquid. **2.** Refuse or worthless matter. **3.** *Slang* A worthless or disreputable person or element of society. **—scum′my** *adj.*

scup·per (skŭp′ər) ▸ *n.* A deck-level opening in the side of a ship to allow water to run off.

scurf (skûrf) ▸ *n.* Scaly or shredded dry skin, such as dandruff. **—scurf′i·ness** *n.* **—scurf′y** *adj.*

scur·ri·lous (skûr′ə-ləs, skŭr′-) ▸ *adj.* Vulgar; abusive. **—scur′ri·lous·ly** *adv.* **—scur·ril′i·ty** (skə-rĭl′ĭ-tē), **scur′ri·lous·ness** *n.*

scur·ry (skûr′ē, skŭr′ē) ▸ *v.* **-ried, -ry·ing.** **1.** To scamper. **2.** To flurry or swirl about.

scur·vy (skûr′vē) ▸ *n.* A disease caused by deficiency of vitamin C, marked by bleeding gums, subcutaneous bleeding, and weakness. ▸ *adj.* **-vi·er, -vi·est.** Contemptible. **—scur′vi·ness** *n.*

scut·tle[1] (skŭt′l) ▸ *n.* A small hatch in a ship's deck or hull. ▸ *v.* **-tled, -tling.** **1.** To sink (a ship) by cutting or opening holes in the hull. **2.** To scrap; discard.

scut·tle[2] (skŭt′l) ▸ *n.* A metal pail for carrying coal.

scut·tle[3] (skŭt′l) ▸ *v.* **-tled, -tling.** To run hastily; scurry. **—scut′tle** *n.*

scut·tle·butt (skŭt′l-bŭt′) ▸ *n.* *Slang* Gossip; rumor.

scythe (sīth) ▸ *n.* A tool with a long curved blade and a bent handle, used for mowing or reaping. **—scythe** *v.*

SD or **S.D.** ▸ *abbr.* South Dakota

Se ▸ The symbol for the element **selenium.**

SE ▸ *abbr.* **1.** southeast **2.** southeastern

sea (sē) ▸ *n.* **1a.** The continuous body of salt water covering most of the earth's surface. **b.** A tract of water within an ocean. **c.** A large body of water completely or partially enclosed by land. **2.** The condition of the ocean's surface: *a high sea.* **3.** Something that suggests the ocean in its vastness: *a sea of controversy.* ***—idiom:*** **at sea** **1.** On the ocean. **2.** At a loss; perplexed.

sea anemone ▸ *n.* Any of various marine organisms with a flexible cylindrical body and numerous tentacles.

sea·board (sē′bôrd′) ▸ *n.* **1.** A seacoast. **2.** Land near the sea.

sea·bor·gi·um (sē-bôr′gē-əm) ▸ *n.* *Symbol* **Sg** A synthetic radioactive element. At. no. 106.

sea·coast (sē′kōst′) ▸ *n.* Land bordering the sea.

sea·far·er (sē′fâr′ər) ▸ *n.* A sailor. **—sea′far′ing** *adj.*

sea·food (sē′fo͞od′) ▸ *n.* Edible fish or shellfish from the sea.

sea·go·ing (sē′gō′ĭng) ▸ *adj.* Made or used for ocean voyages.

sea·gull also **sea gull** (sē′gŭl′) ▸ *n.* A gull, especially one that is found near areas along the coast.

sea horse ▸ *n.* A small marine fish with a prehensile tail, a horselike head, and a body covered with bony plates.

seal[1] (sēl) ▸ *n.* **1a.** A die or signet with a raised or incised emblem used to stamp an impression on a substance such as wax or lead. **b.** The impression so made. **c.** A small disk or wafer bearing such an imprint and affixed to a document to prove authenticity or to secure it. **2.** Something that authenticates or confirms. **3.** A sealant. **4.** An airtight closure. **5.** A small decorative paper sticker. ▸ *v.* **1.** To affix a seal to, esp. in order to prove authenticity or attest to accuracy or quality. **2a.** To close with or as if with a seal. **b.** To apply sealant to. **3.** To determine irrevocably: *His fate was sealed.* **—seal′er** *n.*

seal[2] (sēl) ▸ *n.* **1.** Any of various aquatic mammals with a sleek, torpedo-shaped body and limbs in the form of flippers. **2.** The pelt or fur of a seal. ▸ *v.* To hunt seals. **—seal′er** *n.*

sea-lane (sē′lān′) ▸ *n.* A sea route.

seal·ant (sē′lənt) ▸ *n.* A substance used to seal a surface to prevent passage of a liquid or gas.

sea level ▸ *n.* The level of the ocean's surface, esp. the level halfway between mean high and low tide.

sea lion ▸ *n.* A large seal of the N Pacific with relatively long neck and limbs.

seam (sēm) ▸ *n.* **1a.** A line formed by sewing together two pieces of material. **b.** A similar line, ridge, or groove. **2.** A line across a surface, as a crack or wrinkle. **3.** A thin layer or stratum, as of coal. ▸ *v.* **1.** To join with or as if with a seam. **2.** To mark with a wrinkle or crack: *a face seamed with age.*

sea·man (sē′mən) ▸ *n.* **1.** A sailor. **2.** Any of the three lowest ranks in the US Navy or Coast Guard.

sea·man·ship (sē′mən-shĭp′) ▸ *n.* Skill in navigating or managing a boat or ship.

seam·stress (sēm′strĭs) ▸ *n.* A woman who sews, esp. as an occupation.

seam·y (sē′mē) ▸ *adj.* **-i·er, -i·est.** **1.** Sordid; base. **2.** Having a seam. **—seam′i·ness** *n.*

sé·ance (sā′äns′) ▸ *n.* A meeting of people to receive spiritualistic messages.

sea otter ▸ *n.* A large marine otter of N Pacific coastal waters.

sea·plane (sē′plān′) ▸ *n.* An aircraft equipped with floats for landing on or taking off from water.

sea·port (sē′pôrt′) ▸ *n.* A port with facilities for seagoing ships.

sea power ▸ *n.* **1.** A nation having significant naval strength. **2.** Naval strength.

sea·quake (sē′kwāk′) ▸ *n.* An earthquake originating under the sea floor.

sear[1] (sîr) ▸ *v.* **1.** To scorch or burn the surface of. **2.** To wither or parch.

sear[2] (sîr) ▸ *adj.* Var. of **sere.**

search (sûrch) ▸ *v.* **1.** To make a thorough examination of in order to find something; explore. **2.** To look into or investigate; probe: *search one's conscience.* **3.** *Law* To make a thorough check of: *search a title.* **—search** *n.* **—search′er** *n.*

search engine ▸ *n.* A software program that searches a database for information about specified terms.

search·light (sûrch′līt′) ▸ *n.* **1.** A powerful light source with a reflector for projecting a high-intensity beam. **2.** The beam itself.

THESAURUS

scuffle *v.* —*See* CONTEND, TRUDGE.
scuffle *n.* —*See* FIGHT (1).

scullion *n.* —*See* DRUDGE (1).

sculpt *v.* —*See* FORM (1).

sculpture *n.* A work of art created by shaping a solid material ▸ bust, carving, cast, figure, figurine, relief, statue, statuette. [*Compare* FORM.]

scum *n.* —*See* RIFFRAFF.

scurf *n.* Scaly pieces of dry shedded skin ▸ dander, dandruff, furfur, scale. [*Compare* FLAKE.]

scurrility or **scurrilousness** *n.* —*See* OBSCENITY (1), VITUPERATION.

scurrilous *adj.* —*See* ABUSIVE, OBSCENE.

scurry or **scuttle** *v.* —*See* RUN (1).

scuttlebutt *n.* —*See* GOSSIP (1).

scythe *v.* —*See* CUT (3).

sea *n.* —*See* OCEAN.
sea *adj.* —*See* MARINE (1).

seafarer or **seadog** *n.* —*See* SAILOR.

seal *v.* To move a door, for example, in order to cover an opening ▸ close, clench, shut, slam. —*See also* FILL (2).

seam *n.* —*See* JOINT (1).

seaman *n.* —*See* SAILOR.

seamy *adj.* —*See* SORDID.

sear *v.* —*See* BURN (1), COOK, DRY (1).
sear *n.* —*See* BURN.

search *v.* To examine a person or someone's personal effects in order to find something lost or concealed ▸ frisk, inspect, pat down. *Slang:* shake down. *Idiom:* do a body search of. —*See also* SCOUR[2].
search for *v.* —*See* SEEK (1).
search *n.* A thorough search of a place or persons ▸ body search, frisk, patdown. *Slang:* shakedown. —*See also* EXAMINATION (1), PURSUIT (2).

search warrant ▸ *n.* A warrant giving legal authorization for a search.
sea·scape (sē′skāp′) ▸ *n.* A view of the sea.
sea·shell (sē′shĕl′) ▸ *n.* The shell of a marine mollusk.
sea·shore (sē′shôr′) ▸ *n.* Land by the sea.
sea·sick·ness (sē′sĭk′nĭs) ▸ *n.* Nausea and dizziness resulting from the motion of a vessel at sea. **—sea′sick′** *adj.*
sea·side (sē′sīd′) ▸ *n.* The seashore.
sea snake ▸ *n.* Any of various venomous tropical saltwater snakes.
sea·son (sē′zən) ▸ *n.* **1a.** One of the four natural divisions of the year, spring, summer, fall, and winter. **b.** The two divisions of the year, rainy and dry, in some tropical regions. **2.** A recurrent period marked by certain occurrences or festivities: *the holiday season; tomato season.* ▸ *v.* **1.** To enhance the flavor of (food) by adding salt or other flavorings. **2.** To add zest or interest to. **3.** To treat or dry (e.g., lumber) until usable; cure. **4.** To render competent through experience. **5.** To inure.
sea·son·a·ble (sē′zə-nə-bəl) ▸ *adj.* **1.** In keeping with the time or the season. **2.** Occurring at the proper time. **—sea′son·a·bly** *adv.*
sea·son·al (sē′zə-nəl) ▸ *adj.* Of or dependent on a particular season. **—sea′son·al·ly** *adv.*
sea·son·ing (sē′zə-nĭng) ▸ *n.* Something used to flavor food.
seat (sēt) ▸ *n.* **1.** Something, such as a chair or bench, on which one may sit. **2.** A place in which one may sit. **3.** The part on which one rests in sitting: *a bicycle seat.* **4a.** The buttocks. **b.** The part of a garment covering the buttocks. **5a.** The place where something is located or based: *the seat of intelligence.* **b.** A center of authority; capital. **6.** Membership, as in a legislature. ▸ *v.* **1.** To place in or on a seat. **2.** To have or provide seats for.
seat belt ▸ *n.* A safety strap that holds a person securely in a seat, as in a car.
seat·ing (sē′tĭng) ▸ *n.* **1.** The act of providing with seats. **2.** The seats so provided.
Se·at·tle (sē-ăt′l) ▸ A city of W-central WA on Puget Sound.
sea urchin ▸ *n.* Any of various marine organisms having a spiny globular shell.
sea·wall also **sea wall** (sē′wôl′) ▸ *n.* An embankment to prevent erosion of a shoreline.
sea·ward (sē′wərd) ▸ *adv. & adj.* Toward or at the sea. **—sea′wards** (-wərdz) *adv.*
sea·wa·ter (sē′wô′tər, -wŏt′ər) ▸ *n.* The salt water of the ocean.
sea·way (sē′wā′) ▸ *n.* **1.** A sea route. **2.** An inland waterway for ocean shipping.
sea·weed (sē′wēd′) ▸ *n.* Any of numerous marine algae, such as kelp or gulfweed.
sea·wor·thy (sē′wûr′thē) ▸ *adj.* Fit to traverse the seas. **—sea′wor′thi·ness** *n.*
se·ba·ceous (sĭ-bā′shəs) ▸ *adj. Physiol.* Of or secreting oil.
seb·or·rhe·a also **seb·or·rhoe·a** (sĕb′ə-rē′ə) ▸ *n.* A disease of the sebaceous glands of the skin marked by excessive secretion of oil. **—seb′or·rhe′ic** *adj.*
sec[1] (sĕk) ▸ *adj.* Dry. Used of wines.
sec[2] ▸ *abbr.* secant
sec. ▸ *abbr.* second
se·cant (sē′kănt′, -kənt) ▸ *n.* The reciprocal of the cosine of an angle in a right triangle.
se·cede (sĭ-sēd′) ▸ *v.* **-ced·ed, -ced·ing.** To withdraw formally from membership in an organization, association, or alliance.
se·ces·sion (sĭ-sĕsh′ən) ▸ *n.* The act of seceding. **—se·ces′sion·ism** *n.* **—se·ces′sion·ist** *n.*
se·clude (sĭ-klo͞od′) ▸ *v.* **-clud·ed, -clud·ing. 1.** To set apart from others. **2.** To screen from view. **—se·clu′sion** *n.* **—se·clu′sive** *adj.*
sec·ond[1] (sĕk′ənd) ▸ *n.* **1.** A unit of time equal to $1/60$ of a minute. **2.** A brief interval of time. **3.** *Math.* A unit of angular measure equal to $1/60$ of a minute.
sec·ond[2] (sĕk′ənd) ▸ *adj.* **1.** Coming next after the first. **2.** Inferior to another; subordinate. ▸ *n.* **1a.** The ordinal number matching the number 2 in a series. **b.** One of two equal parts. **2.** One that is next after the first. **3.** often **seconds** Merchandise of inferior quality. **4.** The official attendant of a contestant in a duel or boxing match. **5.** The second lowest forward gear in a motor vehicle. ▸ *v.* **1.** To attend as an aide or assistant. **2.** To promote or encourage. **3.** To endorse (a motion or nomination). **—sec′ond, sec′ond·ly** *adv.*
sec·ond·ar·y (sĕk′ən-dĕr′ē) ▸ *adj.* **1a.** Of the second rank; not primary. **b.** Inferior; minor. **2.** Derived from what is original: *a secondary source.* **3.** Of or relating to education between elementary school and college. ▸ *n., pl.* **-ies.** One that acts in an auxiliary or subordinate capacity. **—sec′ond·ar′i·ly** (-dâr′ə-lē) *adv.* **—sec′ond·ar′i·ness** *n.*
secondary sex characteristic ▸ *n.* Any of various genetically transmitted physiological or behavioral characteristics, such as growth of facial hair or breast development, that differentiate between the sexes without having a direct reproductive function.
second base ▸ *n. Baseball* The 2nd base to be reached by a runner. **—second baseman** *n.*
second class ▸ *n.* **1.** The class or category ranking below the first or best. **2.** A class of mail consisting of newspapers and periodicals. **—sec′ond-class′** *adj.*
sec·ond-de·gree burn (sĕk′ənd-dĭ-grē′) ▸ *n.* A burn that blisters the skin.
second fiddle ▸ *n. Informal* A secondary role.
sec·ond-gen·er·a·tion (sĕk′ənd-jĕn′ə-rā′shən) ▸ *adj.* Of or relating to one whose parents are first-generation immigrants or citizens.
sec·ond-guess (sĕk′ənd-gĕs′) ▸ *v.* **1.** To criticize (a decision) after an outcome is known. **2.** To outguess. **—sec′ond-guess′er** *n.*
sec·ond·hand (sĕk′ənd-hănd′) ▸ *adj.* **1.** Previously used; not new. **2.** Dealing in used merchandise. **3.** Not primary or original. **—sec′ond·hand′** *adv.*
second lieutenant ▸ *n.* The lowest commissioned rank, as in the US Army.
second nature ▸ *n.* A deeply ingrained behavior or trait.
second person ▸ *n.* The form of a pronoun or verb used in referring to the person addressed.
sec·ond-rate (sĕk′ənd-rāt′) ▸ *adj.* Inferior.
sec·ond-string (sĕk′ənd-strĭng′) ▸ *adj.* Of or being a substitute, as on a sports team.
second thought ▸ *n.* A reconsideration of a decision or opinion.

THESAURUS

searing *adj.* —*See* BITING, HOT (1).
season *n.* —*See* PERIOD (1).
season *v.* To impart flavor to ▸ flavor, spice (up), zest. —*See also* HARDEN (1).
seasonable *adj.* —*See* OPPORTUNE.
seasonal *adj.* —*See* MIGRATORY (1).
seasoned *adj.* —*See* EXPERIENCED, SPICY.
seasoning or **seasoner** *n.* —*See* FLAVORING.
seat *n.* —*See* BASE[1] (2), BUTTOCKS, CENTER (1).
seat *v.* —*See* ESTABLISH (1).
sec *n.* —*See* FLASH (2).
secede *v.* To sever one's association with an alliance or federation ▸ break away, pull out, splinter (off), withdraw. *Informal:* split (away). [*Compare* QUIT.] —*See also* DEFECT.
secession *n.* —*See* DEFECTION.
seclude *v.* To put into solitude ▸ cloister, isolate, sequester, sequestrate. [*Compare* ENCLOSE, IMPRISON.] —*See also* ISOLATE (1).
secluded *adj.* Concealed from view ▸ blind, hidden, screened, secret. *Idioms:* out of sight, out of view. [*Compare* HIDDEN.] —*See also* REMOTE (1).
seclusion *n.* The act of secluding or the state of being secluded ▸ isolation, reclusion, retirement, separateness, sequestration. —*See also* SOLITUDE.
second[1] *n.* —*See* FLASH (2).
second[2] *n.* —*See* ASSISTANT, DOUBLE.
secondary *adj.* Stemming from an original source ▸ derivational, derivative, derived. —*See also* AUXILIARY (2), MINOR (1).
secondary *n.* —*See* SUBORDINATE.
second-class *adj.* —*See* BAD (1), MINOR (1).
second fiddle *n.* —*See* SUBORDINATE.
secondhand *adj.* —*See* USED (2).
second-rate *adj.* —*See* BAD (1).

second wind (wĭnd) ▸ *n.* Restored energy or strength.
se·cre·cy (sē′krĭ-sē) ▸ *n., pl.* **-cies**. 1. The quality or condition of being secret. 2. The ability or habit of keeping secrets.
se·cret (sē′krĭt) ▸ *adj.* 1. Concealed from knowledge or view. 2. Operating covertly: *a secret agent.* 3. Beyond ordinary understanding; mysterious. ▸ *n.* 1. Something concealed from others. 2. Something beyond understanding or explanation; mystery. **—se′cret·ly** *adv.*
sec·re·tar·i·at (sĕk′rĭ-târ′ē-ĭt) ▸ *n.* 1. The department administered by a governmental secretary. 2. The position of a governmental secretary.
sec·re·tar·y (sĕk′rĭ-tĕr′ē) ▸ *n., pl.* **-ies**. 1. One employed to handle correspondence and do clerical work. 2. An officer in charge of records, minutes of meetings, and correspondence, as for a company. 3. An official presiding over an administrative department of state. 4. A desk with a small bookcase on top. **—sec′re·tar′i·al** (-târ′ē-əl) *adj.*
sec·re·tar·y-gen·er·al (sĕk′rĭ-tĕr′ē-jĕn′ər-əl) ▸ *n., pl.* **sec·re·tar·ies-gen·er·al**. A principal executive officer, as in the United Nations.
se·crete[1] (sĭ-krēt′) ▸ *v.* **-cret·ed, -cret·ing**. To generate and separate (a substance) from cells or bodily fluids. **—se·cre′tion** *n.* **—se·cre′tion·ar′y** *adj.* **—se·cre′to·ry** *adj.*
se·crete[2] (sĭ-krēt′) ▸ *v.* **-cret·ed, -cret·ing**. To conceal; hide. **—se·cre′tion** *n.*
se·cre·tive (sē′krĭ-tĭv, sĭ-krē′tĭv) ▸ *adj.* Inclined to secrecy. **—se′cre·tive·ly** *adv.* **—se′cre·tive·ness** *n.*
secret service ▸ *n.* 1. A government agency engaged in intelligence-gathering activities. 2. **Secret Service** A branch of the US Treasury Department concerned esp. with protection of the President.
sect (sĕkt) ▸ *n.* 1. A group of people forming a distinct unit within a larger group by virtue of common beliefs. 2. A religious body, esp. one that has separated from a larger denomination.
-sect ▸ *suff.* To cut; divide: *trisect.*
sec·tar·i·an (sĕk-târ′ē-ən) ▸ *adj.* 1. Of a sect. 2. Partisan. 3. Narrow-minded; parochial. ▸ *n.* 1. A member of a sect. 2. One who is narrow-minded. **—sec·tar′i·an·ism** *n.*
sec·tion (sĕk′shən) ▸ *n.* 1. One of several components; a piece or part. 2. Representation of a solid object as it would appear if cut by an intersecting plane, so that the internal structure is displayed. ▸ *v.* To divide into parts.
sec·tion·al (sĕk′shə-nəl) ▸ *adj.* 1. Of or relating to a particular district. 2. Composed of or divided into component sections. **—sec′tion·al·ly** *adv.*
sec·tion·al·ism (sĕk′shə-nə-lĭz′əm) ▸ *n.* Excessive devotion to local interests and customs. **—sec′tion·al·ist** *n.*
sec·tor (sĕk′tər, -tôr′) ▸ *n.* 1. *Math.* The part of a circle bounded by two radii and the included arc. 2. A military zone of action. 3. A division, as of a city or economy. **—sec·to′ri·al** (-tôr′ē-əl) *adj.*
sec·u·lar (sĕk′yə-lər) ▸ *adj.* 1. Worldly rather than spiritual. 2. Not related to religion. 3. *Eccles.* Not belonging to a religious order. Used of the clergy. **—sec′u·lar′i·ty** (-lăr′ĭ-tē) *n.* **—sec′u·lar·ly** *adv.*
sec·u·lar·ize (sĕk′yə-lə-rīz′) ▸ *v.* **-ized, -iz·ing**. 1. To transfer from ecclesiastical to civil use or ownership. 2. To make secular. **—sec′u·lar·i·za′tion** *n.*
se·cure (sĭ-kyŏŏr′) ▸ *adj.* **-cur·er, -cur·est**. 1. Free from danger; safe. 2. Free from fear or doubt. 3. Reliable; dependable. 4. Assured; certain. ▸ *v.* **-cured, -cur·ing**. 1. To guard from danger or risk of loss. 2. To make firm. 3. To make certain; guarantee. 4. To acquire. **—se·cure′ly** *adv.* **—se·cure′ment** *n.*
se·cu·ri·ty (sĭ-kyŏŏr′ĭ-tē) ▸ *n., pl.* **-ties**. 1. Safety. 2. Confidence. 3. Something that gives or assures safety. 4. Something deposited or given as assurance of the fulfillment of an obligation; pledge. 5. A stock or bond. 6. Measures adopted to guard against attack, theft, or disclosure.
se·dan (sĭ-dăn′) ▸ *n.* 1. A closed car with two or four doors and a front and rear seat. 2. also **sedan chair** An enclosed chair carried on poles by two bearers.
se·date[1] (sĭ-dāt′) ▸ *adj.* Serenely deliberate in character or manner. **—se·date′ly** *adv.* **—se·date′ness** *n.*
se·date[2] (sĭ-dāt′) ▸ *v.* **-dat·ed, -dat·ing**. To administer a sedative to. **—se·da′tion** *n.*
sed·a·tive (sĕd′ə-tĭv) ▸ *adj.* Having a soothing, calming, or tranquilizing effect. ▸ *n.* A sedative drug.
sed·en·tar·y (sĕd′n-tĕr′ē) ▸ *adj.* Marked by or requiring little physical activity.
Se·der (sā′dər) ▸ *n. Judaism* The feast commemorating the exodus of the Jews from Egypt, celebrated on the first night or the first two nights of Passover.
sedge (sĕj) ▸ *n.* Any of numerous grasslike plants found esp. in wet places.
sed·i·ment (sĕd′ə-mənt) ▸ *n.* Material that settles to the bottom of a liquid; lees. **—sed′i·men·ta′tion** *n.*
sed·i·men·ta·ry (sĕd′ə-mĕn′tə-rē, -mĕn′trē) ▸ *adj.* 1. Of or resembling sediment. 2. *Geol.* Of rocks formed from sediment.
se·di·tion (sĭ-dĭsh′ən) ▸ *n.* 1. Conduct or language inciting rebellion against the state. 2. Insurrection; rebellion. **—se·di′tious** *adj.* **—se·di′tious·ly** *adv.* **—se·di′tious·ness** *n.*
se·duce (sĭ-dōōs′, -dyōōs′) ▸ *v.* **-duced, -duc·ing**. 1. To lead away from proper conduct. 2. To induce to engage in sex. 3. To entice or beguile; win over. **—se·duc′er** *n.* **—se·duc′tion**

THESAURUS

secrecy *n.* The habit, practice, or policy of keeping secrets ▸ clandestineness, clandestinity, concealment, covertness, huggermugger, huggermuggery, secretiveness, secretness. [*Compare* STEALTH.]
secret *adj.* 1. Operating in a way so as to ensure concealment and confidentiality ▸ backstairs, clandestine, cloak-and-dagger, covert, huggermugger, sub-rosa, undercover. *Informal:* hush-hush. [*Compare* ARTFUL, ULTERIOR.] 2. Concealed from view ▸ blind, hidden, screened, secluded. *Idioms:* out of sight, out of view. [*Compare* HIDDEN.] *—See also* CONFIDENTIAL (1), HIDDEN (1).
secret *n.* A means or method of entering into or achieving something desirable ▸ formula, key, route. *Informal:* ticket. [*Compare* TRICK.]
secrete *v.* *—See* HIDE[1].
secretive *adj.* *—See* STEALTHY.
secretiveness *n.* *—See* SECRECY, STEALTH.
secretly *adv.* In a secret way ▸ clandestinely, covertly, huggermugger, sub rosa. *Idioms:* behind closed doors, by stealth, on the q.t., on the sly, under cover (*or* wraps), under the radar.
secretness *n.* *—See* SECRECY.
sect *n.* *—See* RELIGION.
sectarian *n.* *—See* SEPARATIST.
sectary *n.* *—See* DEVOTEE, SEPARATIST.
section *n.* A particular subdivision of a written work ▸ chapter, part, passage, segment. *—See also* AREA (2), BRANCH (3), PART (1).
section *v.* *—See* DIVIDE.
sectional *adj.* Relating to or restricted to a particular territory ▸ regional, territorial. [*Compare* LOCAL.]
sector *n.* *—See* AREA (2), PART (1).
secular *adj.* *—See* EARTHLY, PROFANE (2).
secure *adj.* *—See* CONFIDENT, FIRM[1] (2), SAFE (2), SURE (2), TIGHT (1).
secure *v.* To make fast or firmly fixed, as by means of a cord or rope ▸ bind, fasten, knot, tie, tie up. *—See also* ATTACH (1), CAPTURE, CAUSE, DEFEND (1), FASTEN, GET (1), GUARANTEE (2), POLICE.
security *n.* A partial or initial payment ▸ deposit, down payment, installment. *—See also* DEFENSE, PAWN[1], SAFETY, STABILITY.
sedate[1] *adj.* *—See* SERIOUS (1).
sedate[2] *v.* *—See* DRUG (1).
sedateness *n.* *—See* SERIOUSNESS (1).
sedative *adj.* *—See* SOPORIFIC.
sedative *n.* *—See* DRUG (2), SOPORIFIC.
sediment *n.* *—See* DEPOSIT (2).
sedimentary *adj.* *—See* MURKY (1).
sedition *n.* Willful violation of allegiance to one's country ▸ lese majesty, seditiousness, traitorousness, treason. [*Compare* FAITHLESSNESS.] *—See also* REBELLION.
seditious *adj.* Involving, relating to, or constituting treason ▸ traitorous, treasonable, treasonous. [*Compare* FAITHLESS.]
seditiousness *n.* Willful violation of allegiance to one's country ▸ lese majesty, sedition, traitorousness, treason. [*Compare* FAITHLESSNESS.]
seduce *v.* To beguile or lure into a wrong or foolish course of action, especially a sexual act ▸ allure, entice, inveigle, lure, tempt. *Idiom:* lead

(-dŭk′shən) *n.* **—se·duc′tive** *adj.* **—se·duc′tive·ly** *adv.*

sed·u·lous (sĕj′ə-ləs) ▸ *adj.* Persevering; assiduous. **—sed′u·lous·ly** *adv.* **—sed′u·lous·ness** *n.*

see[1] (sē) ▸ *v.* **saw** (sô), **seen** (sēn), **see·ing.** **1.** To perceive with the eye. **2.** To understand; comprehend. **3.** To regard; view. **4.** To believe possible; imagine. **5.** To foresee. **6.** To undergo. **7.** To find out; ascertain. **8.** To take note of. **9.** To meet regularly, as in dating. **10a.** To visit socially. **b.** To visit for consultation: *see a doctor.* **11.** To escort; attend: *I'll see you home.* **12.** To make sure: *Please see that it gets done.* ***—phrasal verb:*** **see through** To understand the true character of.

see[2] (sē) ▸ *n.* The seat or jurisdiction of a bishop.

seed (sēd) ▸ *n., pl.* **seeds** or **seed.** **1.** A ripened plant ovule containing an embryo. **2.** Seeds collectively. **3.** A source or germ. **4.** Offspring. ▸ *v.* **1.** To plant seeds in. **2.** To remove seeds from. ***—idiom:*** **go** (or **run**) **to seed 1.** To pass into the seed-bearing stage. **2.** To deteriorate.

seed·ling (sēd′lĭng) ▸ *n.* A young plant grown from a seed.

seed·pod (sēd′pŏd′) ▸ *n.* See **pod**[1] 1.

seed·y (sē′dē) ▸ *adj.* **-i·er, -i·est.** **1.** Having many seeds. **2.** Shabby; run-down. **—seed′i·ly** *adv.* **—seed′i·ness** *n.*

see·ing (sē′ĭng) ▸ *conj.* Inasmuch as.

seek (sēk) ▸ *v.* **sought** (sôt), **seek·ing.** **1.** To search for. **2.** To try to obtain or reach. **3.** To try; endeavor: *seek to do good.* **—seek′er** *n.*

seem (sēm) ▸ *v.* **1.** To give the impression of being. **2.** To appear to one's own mind. **3.** To appear to be true or evident. **4.** To appear to exist.

seem·ing (sē′mĭng) ▸ *adj.* Apparent; ostensible. **—seem′ing** *n.* **—seem′ing·ly** *adv.*

seem·ly (sēm′lē) ▸ *adj.* **-li·er, -li·est.** **1.** Proper; suitable. **2.** Of pleasing appearance. **—seem′li·ness** *n.*

seen (sēn) ▸ *v.* P.part. of **see**[1].

seep (sēp) ▸ *v.* **1.** To pass slowly through small openings. **2.** To enter, depart, or spread gradually. **—seep′age** *n.*

seer (sîr) ▸ *n.* **1.** A clairvoyant. **2.** A prophet.

seer·suck·er (sîr′sŭk′ər) ▸ *n.* A light thin fabric with a crinkled surface and a usu. striped pattern.

see·saw (sē′sô′) ▸ *n.* **1.** A long plank balanced on a central fulcrum so that with a person riding on each end, one end goes up as the other goes down. **2.** The game of riding a seesaw. **3.** A back-and-forth or up-and-down movement. **—see′saw′** *v.*

seethe (sēth) ▸ *v.* **seethed, seeth·ing.** **1.** To churn and foam as if boiling. **2.** To be violently agitated.

seg·ment (sĕg′mənt) ▸ *n.* A part into which something can be divided; section. ▸ *v.* (sĕg-mĕnt′) To divide into segments. **—seg·men′tal** *adj.* **—seg′men·ta′tion** *n.*

seg·re·gate (sĕg′rĭ-gāt′) ▸ *v.* **-gat·ed, -gat·ing.** **1.** To separate or isolate from others or from a main body or group. **2.** To impose the separation of (a race or class) from the rest of society. **—seg′re·ga′tion** *n.* **—seg′re·ga′tion·ist** *adj. & n.* **—seg′re·ga′tor** *n.*

se·gue (sĕg′wā′, sā′gwā′) ▸ *v.* **-gued, -gue·ing.** **1.** *Mus.* To make a transition directly from one section or theme to another. **2.** To move smoothly from one situation or element to another.

seign·ior (sān-yôr′, sān′yôr′) ▸ *n.* A feudal lord. **—sei·gnio′ri·al** *adj.*

seine (sān) ▸ *n.* A large fishing net made to hang vertically in the water by weights and floats. ▸ *v.* **seined, sein·ing.** To fish with a seine. **—sein′er** *n.*

Seine (sān, sĕn) ▸ A river of N France flowing about 772 km (480 mi) to the English Channel near Le Havre.

seis·mic (sīz′mĭk) ▸ *adj.* Of or caused by an earthquake. **—seis′mi·cal·ly** *adv.* **—seis·mic′i·ty** (-mĭs′ĭ-tē) *n.*

seismo– or **seism–** ▸ *pref.* Earthquake: *seismograph.*

seis·mo·graph (sīz′mə-grăf′) ▸ *n.* An instrument for automatically detecting and recording the intensity and duration of ground movements, esp. of earthquakes. **—seis·mog′ra·pher** (-mŏg′rə-fər) *n.* **—seis′mo·graph′ic** *adj.* **—seis·mog′ra·phy** *n.*

seis·mol·o·gy (sīz-mŏl′ə-jē) ▸ *n.* The geophysical science of earthquakes and the mechanical properties of the earth. **—seis′mo·log′ic** (-mə-lŏj′ĭk), **seis′mo·log′i·cal** *adj.* **—seis·mol′o·gist** *n.*

sei·tan (sā′tăn′) ▸ *n.* A chewy, protein-rich food made from wheat gluten and used as a meat substitute.

seize (sēz) ▸ *v.* **seized, seiz·ing.** **1.** To grasp suddenly and forcibly. **2.** To have a sudden forceful effect on. **3.** To take into custody; confiscate.

sei·zure (sē′zhər) ▸ *n.* **1.** The act of seizing or being seized. **2.**

THESAURUS

astray. [*Compare* CHARM, CORRUPT, FLIRT, PHILANDER.]

seducer *n.* **1.** A person who beguiles or seduces ▸ allurer, beguiler, charmer, enticer, inveigler, lurer, tempter. **2.** A man who seduces women ▸ debaucher, Don Juan, Lothario. [*Compare* FLIRT, LECHER, PHILANDERER.]

seduction *n.* *—See* LURE (1).

seductive *adj.* Tending to seduce ▸ alluring, beguiling, bewitching, come-hither, enthralling, enticing, entrancing, inviting, luring, sexy, siren, tantalizing, tempting, witching. [*Compare* ATTRACTIVE, BEAUTIFUL.]

seductress *n.* A woman who seduces or exploits men ▸ enchantress, femme fatale, siren, temptress. *Informal:* vamp, witch. [*Compare* FLIRT.]

sedulous *adj.* *—See* DILIGENT.

see *v.* **1.** To perceive with the eyes ▸ behold, catch, descry, detect, discern, espy, perceive, spot, spy. *Idioms:* cast one's eyes on, catch sight of, get a load of, get a look at, lay (*or* clap) eyes on. [*Compare* GLIMPSE, LOOK.] **2.** To be with another person socially on a regular basis ▸ date, go out (with), go with. *Informal:* take out. *Idioms:* go steady, go together. *—See also* ENCOUNTER (1), EXPERIENCE, FORESEE, IMAGINE, NOTICE, REGARD, UNDERSTAND (1), VISIT, WATCH (1).

see through *v.* *—See* CONCLUDE.

see to *v.* *—See* TEND[2].

seeable *adj.* *—See* VISIBLE.

seed *n.* A fertilized plant ovule capable of germinating ▸ grain, kernel, pip, pit. *—See also* ANCESTRY, GERM (2), PROGENY.

seed *v.* *—See* PLANT.

seedtime *n.* The season of the year during which the weather becomes warmer and plants revive ▸ spring, springtide, springtime.

seedy *adj.* *—See* SHABBY.

seeing *n.* *—See* VISION (1).

seeing *adj.* Serving, resulting from, or relating to the sense of sight ▸ ocular, optic, optical, visual.

seek *v.* **1.** To try to find something ▸ cast about (*or* around), ferret (around), fish for, hunt for, look for, search for, sniff about (*or* around). [*Compare* PURSUE, SCOUR[2].] **2.** To strive toward a goal ▸ aspire, seek. *Idioms:* go (*or* grab) for the brass ring, keep one's eyes on the prize, set one's sights on. *—See also* APPEAL (1), ATTEMPT.

seeker *n.* One who aspires ▸ aspirant, aspirer, dreamer, hopeful. *Informal:* wannabe. *—See also* APPLICANT.

seem *v.* To give the impression of being ▸ appear, feel, look, sound. *Idioms:* have all the earmarks of being, give the idea (*or* impression) of being, strike one as being. [*Compare* RESEMBLE.]

seeming *adj.* *—See* APPARENT (2).

seemingly *adv.* *—See* APPARENTLY.

seemliness *n.* *—See* DECENCY (2).

seemly *adj.* *—See* APPROPRIATE.

seep *v.* *—See* OOZE.

seer *n.* Someone who sees something occur ▸ audience, eyewitness, viewer, witness. *—See also* PROPHET.

seesaw *v.* *—See* LURCH (1).

seethe *v.* *—See* ANGER (2), BOIL.

see-through *adj.* *—See* CLEAR (1).

segment *n.* A particular subdivision of a written work ▸ chapter, part, passage, section. *—See also* PART (1).

segment *v.* *—See* DIVIDE.

segmentation *n.* *—See* DIVISION (1).

segregate *v.* *—See* ISOLATE (1).

segregation *n.* *—See* ISOLATION.

seism *n.* A shaking of the earth ▸ earthquake, quake, temblor, tremor. *Informal:* shake.

seize *v.* **1.** To lay claim to or take possession of ▸ appropriate, arrogate, assume, commandeer, confiscate, expropriate, grab, hijack, impound, preempt, take (over), snatch, usurp. *Idiom:* help oneself to. [*Compare* STEAL.] **2.** To have a sudden overwhelming effect on ▸ catch, strike, take. [*Compare* MOVE.] *—See also* ARREST, CATCH (2), GRASP, OCCUPY (2).

seizure *n.* **1.** A sudden and often acute manifestation of a disease ▸ apoplexy, attack, convulsion, fit, paroxysm.

A sudden attack or spasm, as in epilepsy or another disorder.

sel·dom (sĕl′dəm) ▸ *adv.* Not often; rarely. **—sel′dom·ness** *n.*

se·lect (sĭ-lĕkt′) ▸ *v.* To choose from among several; pick out. ▸ *adj.* **1.** Singled out; chosen. **2.** Of special quality; choice. **—se·lec′tive** *adj.* **—se·lec′tive·ly** *adv.* **—se·lec′tiv′i·ty** *n.* **—se·lect′ness** *n.* **—se·lec′tor** *n.*

se·lect·ee (sĭ-lĕk′tē′) ▸ *n.* One selected.

se·lec·tion (sĭ-lĕk′shən) ▸ *n.* **1a.** The act of selecting or the fact of being selected. **b.** One selected. **2.** A carefully chosen collection. **3.** A literary or musical text chosen for reading or performance. **4.** *Biol.* A process that favors survival and perpetuation of one organism over others.

selective service ▸ *n.* A system for calling up people for compulsory military service.

se·lect·man (sĭ-lĕkt′măn′, -mən) ▸ *n.* One of a board of town officers chosen annually in New England communities.

se·lect·wom·an (sĭ-lĕkt′wo͝om′ən) ▸ *n.* A woman who is a selectman.

se·le·ni·um (sĭ-lē′nē-əm) ▸ *n. Symbol* **Se** A nonmetallic element resembling sulfur, used as a semiconductor and in photocells. At. no. 34.

self (sĕlf) ▸ *n., pl.* **selves** (sĕlvz). **1.** One's total being. **2.** Individuality. **3.** One's own interests or advantage. **4.** *Immunol.* That which the immune system identifies as belonging to the body. ▸ *pron.* Myself, yourself, himself, or herself.

self– ▸ *pref.* **1.** Oneself: *self-control.* **2.** Automatic; automatically: *self-loading.*

self-ab·sorbed (sĕlf′əb-sôrbd′, -zôrbd′) ▸ *adj.* Excessively self-involved. **—self′-ab·sorp′tion** *n.*

self-ad·dressed (sĕlf′ə-drĕst′) ▸ *adj.* Addressed to oneself.

self-ap·point·ed (sĕlf′ə-poin′tĭd) ▸ *adj.* Designated by oneself.

self-as·ser·tion (sĕlf′ə-sûr′shən) ▸ *n.* Determined advancement of one's own personality, wishes, or views. **—self′-as·ser′tive** *adj.* **—self-as·ser′tive·ness** *n.*

self-as·sured (sĕlf′ə-sho͝ord′) ▸ *adj.* Confident and poised. **—self′-as·sur′ance** *n.*

self-cen·tered (sĕlf′sĕn′tərd) ▸ *adj.* Engrossed in oneself; selfish. **—self′-cen′tered·ly** *adv.* **—self′-cen′tered·ness** *n.*

self-con·scious (sĕlf′kŏn′shəs) ▸ *adj.* **1.** Aware of oneself as an individual. **2.** Socially ill at ease. **—self′-con′scious·ly** *adv.* **—self′-con′scious·ness** *n.*

self-con·tained (sĕlf′kən-tānd′) ▸ *adj.* **1.** Complete in itself. **2a.** Self-sufficient. **b.** Reserved. **—self′-con·tain′ment** *n.*

self-con·trol (sĕlf′kən-trōl′) ▸ *n.* Control of one's emotions, desires, or actions. **—self′-con·trolled′** *adj.*

self-de·fense (sĕlf′dĭ-fĕns′) ▸ *n.* **1.** Defense of oneself, one's property, or one's reputation. **2.** *Law* The right to protect oneself against violence or threatened violence with whatever means reasonably necessary.

self-de·ni·al (sĕlf′dĭ-nī′əl) ▸ *n.* Sacrifice of one's own desires or interests. **—self′-de·ny′ing** *adj.* **—self′-de·ny′ing·ly** *adv.*

self-de·struct (sĕlf′dĭ-strŭkt′) ▸ *n.* A mechanism for causing a device to destroy itself. ▸ *v.* To destroy oneself or itself.

self-de·struc·tion (sĕlf′dĭ-strŭk′shən) ▸ *n.* The act of destroying oneself, esp. suicide. **—self′-de·struc′tive** *adj.* **—self′-de·struc′tive·ly** *adv.* **—self′-de·struc′tive·ness** *n.*

self-de·ter·mi·na·tion (sĕlf′dĭ-tûr′mə-nā′shən) ▸ *n.* **1.** Determination of one's course of action without compulsion. **2.** Freedom of the people to determine their political status; independence.

self-dis·ci·pline (sĕlf′dĭs′ə-plĭn) ▸ *n.* Training and control of oneself, usu. for personal improvement.

self-ef·fac·ing (sĕlf′ĭ-fā′sĭng) ▸ *adj.* Not drawing attention to oneself; modest. **—self′-ef·face′ment** *n.*

self-es·teem (sĕlf′ĭ-stēm′) ▸ *n.* Confidence; self-respect.

self-ev·i·dent (sĕlf′ĕv′ĭ-dənt) ▸ *adj.* Requiring no proof or explanation. **—self′-ev′i·dence** *n.* **—self′-ev′i·dent·ly** *adv.*

self-ex·plan·a·to·ry (sĕlf′ĭk-splăn′ə-tôr′ē) ▸ *adj.* Needing no explanation.

self-ex·pres·sion (sĕlf′ĭk-sprĕsh′ən) ▸ *n.* Expression of one's own personality, as through speech or art. **—self′-ex·pres′sive** *adj.*

self-fer·til·i·za·tion (sĕlf′fûr′tl-ĭ-zā′shən) ▸ *n.* Fertilization of a plant or animal by itself.

self-ful·fill·ing (sĕlf′fo͝ol-fĭl′ĭng) ▸ *adj.* **1.** Achieving fulfillment as a result of having been expected or foretold: *a self-fulfilling prophecy.* **2.** Achieving self-fulfillment.

self-ful·fill·ment (sĕlf′fo͝ol-fĭl′mənt) ▸ *n.* Fulfillment of one's goals and potential.

self-gov·ern·ment (sĕlf′gŭv′ərn-mənt) ▸ *n.* **1.** Political independence; autonomy. **2.** Democracy. **—self′-gov′erned** *adj.* **—self′-gov′ern·ing** *adj.*

self-hard·en·ing (sĕlf′här′dn-ĭng) ▸ *adj.* Of or relating to materials that harden without special treatment.

self-im·age (sĕlf′ĭm′ĭj) ▸ *n.* One's conception of oneself.

self-im·por·tance (sĕlf′ĭm-pôr′tns) ▸ *n.* Excessively high regard for one's own importance. **—self′-im·por′tant** *adj.* **—self′-im·por′tant·ly** *adv.*

self-im·posed (sĕlf′ĭm-pōzd′) ▸ *adj.* Imposed by oneself on oneself; voluntarily assumed.

self-in·crim·i·na·tion (sĕlf′ĭn-krĭm′ə-nā′shən) ▸ *n.* Incrimination of oneself, esp. by one's own testimony in a criminal prosecution. **—self′-in·crim′i·nat′ing** *adj.* **—self′-in·crim′i·na·to′ry** (-nə-tôr′ē) *adj.*

self-in·duced (sĕlf′ĭn-do͞ost′, -dyo͞ost′) ▸ *adj.* **1.** Induced by oneself. **2.** *Elect.* Produced by self-induction.

self-in·duc·tion (sĕlf′ĭn-dŭk′shən) ▸ *n.* The generation by a changing current of an electromotive force in the same circuit. **—self′-in·duc′tive** *adj.*

self-in·dul·gence (sĕlf′ĭn-dŭl′jəns) ▸ *n.* Excessive indulgence of one's own appetites and desires. **—self′-in·dul′gent** *adj.* **—self′-in·dul′gent·ly** *adv.*

self-in·ter·est (sĕlf′ĭn′trĭst, -ĭn′tər-ĭst) ▸ *n.* **1.** Selfish regard for one's own advantage or interest. **2.** Personal advantage or interest. **—self′-in′ter·est·ed** *adj.*

self·ish (sĕl′fĭsh) ▸ *adj.* Concerned chiefly or only with one-

THESAURUS

Informal: spell. **2.** The act of taking possession of something ▸ appropriation, arrogation, assumption, commandeering, confiscation, expropriation, grab, hijacking, impoundment, preemption, seizing, snatch, takeover, taking, usurpation. [*Compare* LARCENY.] *—See also* ARREST, CATCH (1).

seldom *adv.* *—See* INFREQUENTLY.

select *v.* *—See* CHOOSE (1).

select *adj.* Singled out in preference ▸ choice, chosen, elect, exclusive. [*Compare* EXCELLENT, FAVORITE.] *—See also* CHOICE (1), DISCRIMINATING.

select *n.* *—See* ELECT.

selection *n.* *—See* CHOICE.

selective *adj.* *—See* DISCRIMINATING, EXCLUSIVE (3).

selective service *n.* *—See* DRAFT (2).

selectivity or **selectiveness** *n.* *—See* DISCRIMINATION (1).

self *n.* *—See* HUMAN BEING.

self-absorbed *adj.* *—See* EGOTISTIC (2).

self-absorption *n.* *—See* EGOTISM.

self-assurance *n.* *—See* CONFIDENCE.

self-assured *adj.* *—See* CONFIDENT.

self-centered *adj.* *—See* EGOTISTIC (2).

self-centeredness *n.* *—See* EGOTISM.

self-confidence *n.* *—See* CONFIDENCE.

self-confident *adj.* *—See* CONFIDENT.

self-conscious *adj.* *—See* AWKWARD (3).

self-contained *adj.* *—See* INDEPENDENT (1).

self-containment *n.* *—See* INDEPENDENCE.

self-content *adj.* *—See* PROUD.

self-contentment *n.* *—See* PRIDE.

self-contradictory *adj.* *—See* FALLACIOUS (1).

self-control *n.* *—See* RESERVE (1).

self-controlled *adj.* *—See* RESERVED.

self-denial *n.* *—See* TEMPERANCE (1).

self-denying *adj.* *—See* ASCETIC, SELFLESS.

self-determination *n.* *—See* FREEDOM, INDEPENDENCE.

self-determined or **self-directed** *adj.* *—See* INDEPENDENT (1).

self-effacement *n.* *—See* SHYNESS.

self-effacing *adj.* *—See* SHY[1].

self-esteem *n.* *—See* PRIDE.

self-evident *adj.* *—See* APPARENT (1).

self-forgetful or **self-forgetting** *adj.* *—See* SELFLESS.

self-governing *adj.* *—See* FREE (1).

self-government *n.* *—See* FREEDOM.

selfhood *n.* *—See* IDENTITY (1).

self-importance *n.* *—See* ARROGANCE, EGOTISM.

self-important *adj.* *—See* ARROGANT, POMPOUS.

self-involved *adj.* *—See* EGOTISTIC (2).

self-involvement *n.* *—See* EGOTISM.

selfish *adj.* *—See* EGOTISTIC (2).

self. **—self′-ish·ly** *adv.* **—self′ish·ness** *n.*

self·less (sĕlf′lĭs) ► *adj.* Having no concern for oneself; unselfish. **—self′less·ly** *adv.* **—self′less·ness** *n.*

self-made (sĕlf′măd′) ► *adj.* Successful as a result of one's own efforts.

self-mail·er (sĕlf′mā′lər) ► *n.* A folder that can be mailed without being enclosed in an envelope. **—self′-mail′ing** *adj.*

self-pit·y (sĕlf′pĭt′ē) ► *n.* Exaggerated pity for oneself. **—self′-pit′y·ing** *adj.*

self-pol·li·na·tion (sĕlf′pŏl′ə-nā′shən) ► *n.* Transfer of pollen from an anther to a stigma of the same flower. **—self′-pol′li·nate′** *v.*

self-pos·ses·sion (sĕlf′pə-zĕsh′ən) ► *n.* Full command of one's faculties, feelings, and behavior. **—self′-pos·sessed′** *adj.*

self-pres·er·va·tion (sĕlf′prĕz′ər-vā′shən) ► *n.* Protection of oneself from harm or destruction.

self-pro·claimed (sĕlf′prō-klāmd′, -prə-) ► *adj.* Self-styled.

self-re·al·i·za·tion (sĕlf′rē′ə-lĭ-zā′shən) ► *n.* Complete development of one's own potential.

self-ref·er·en·tial (sĕlf′rĕf′ə-rĕn′shəl) ► *adj.* Referring to oneself. **—self′-ref′er·ence** *n.*

self-re·spect (sĕlf′rĭ-spĕkt′) ► *n.* Due respect for oneself. **—self′-re·spect′ing** *adj.*

self-right·eous (sĕlf′rī′chəs) ► *adj.* Piously sure of one's own righteousness; moralistic. **—self′-right′eous·ly** *adv.* **—self′-right′eous·ness** *n.*

self-ris·ing flour (sĕlf′rī′zĭng) ► *n.* A packaged mixture of flour and leavening.

self-sac·ri·fice (sĕlf′săk′rə-fīs′) ► *n.* Sacrifice of one's own interests or well-being for the sake of others. **—self′-sac′ri·fic′ing** *adj.*

self·same (sĕlf′sām′) ► *adj.* Being the very same; identical.

self-sat·is·fac·tion (sĕlf′săt′ĭs-făk′shən) ► *n.* Smug satisfaction with oneself. **—self′-sat′is·fied′** *adj.*

self-seal·ing (sĕlf′sē′lĭng) ► *adj.* **1.** Capable of sealing itself. **2.** Sealable without moisture: *a self-sealing envelope.*

self-search·ing (sĕlf′sûr′chĭng) ► *n.* Examination of one's feelings and actions and their motivation. **—self′-search′ing** *adj.*

self-seek·ing (sĕlf′sē′kĭng) ► *adj.* Pursuing only one's own ends or interests. **—self′-seek′ing** *n.*

self-ser·vice (sĕlf′sûr′vĭs) ► *adj.* Requiring customers or users to help themselves: *a self-service elevator.* **—self′-ser′vice** *n.*

self-serv·ing (sĕlf′sûr′vĭng) ► *adj.* Serving one's own interests, esp. without concern for others. **—self′-serv′ing·ly** *adv.*

self-start·er (sĕlf′stär′tər) ► *n.* One who displays an unusual amount of initiative. **—self′-start′ing** *adj.*

self-styled (sĕlf′stīld′) ► *adj.* As characterized by oneself, often without justification.

self-suf·fi·cient (sĕlf′sə-fĭsh′ənt) ► *adj.* Able to provide for oneself without help. **—self′-suf·fi′cien·cy** *n.*

self-will (sĕlf′wĭl′) ► *n.* Willfulness; obstinacy. **—self′-willed′** *adj.*

sell (sĕl) ► *v.* **sold** (sōld), **sell·ing.** **1.** To exchange for money or its equivalent. **2.** To offer for sale: *a firm that sells textiles.* **3.** To promote successfully. **4.** To convince: *They sold me on the idea.* **5.** To be sold or be on sale. ***—phrasal verb:* sell out** *Slang* To betray. **—sell′er** *n.*

sell·off (sĕl′ôf′, -ŏf′) ► *n.* The sale of a large number of stocks, bonds, or commodities that causes a sharp decline in prices.

sell·out (sĕl′out′) ► *n.* **1.** An event for which all the tickets are sold. **2.** *Slang* One who has betrayed one's principles.

selt·zer (sĕlt′sər) ► *n.* **1.** A natural effervescent spring water of high mineral content. **2.** See **soda water** 1.

sel·vage also **sel·vedge** (sĕl′vĭj) ► *n.* The edge of a fabric woven to prevent raveling.

selves (sĕlvz) ► *n.* Pl. of **self.**

se·man·tic (sĭ-măn′tĭk) ► *adj.* Of or relating to meaning, esp. in language. **—se·man′ti·cal·ly** *adv.*

se·man·tics (sĭ-măn′tĭks) ► *n.* *(takes sing. or pl. v.)* The study of meaning in language.

sem·a·phore (sĕm′ə-fôr′) ► *n.* **1.** A visual signaling apparatus with flags, lights, or mechanically moving arms. **2.** A system for alphabetic signaling using hand-held flags. ► *v.* **-phored, -phor·ing.** To send (a message) by semaphore.

sem·blance (sĕm′bləns) ► *n.* **1.** An outward or token appearance. **2.** A likeness. **3.** The barest trace.

se·men (sē′mən) ► *n.* A whitish secretion of the male reproductive organs, containing spermatozoa.

se·mes·ter (sə-mĕs′tər) ► *n.* One of two divisions of 15 to 18 weeks each of an academic year.

sem·i (sĕm′ī, sĕm′ē) ► *n., pl.* **sem·is.** *Informal* **1.** A semitrailer. **2.** A semifinal.

semi– ► *pref.* **1.** Half: *semicircle.* **2.** Partial; partially: *semiconscious.* **3.** Occurring twice during: *semimonthly.*

sem·i·an·nu·al (sĕm′ē-ăn′yo͞o-əl, sĕm′ī-) ► *adj.* Occurring or issued twice a year. **—sem′i·an′nu·al·ly** *adv.*

sem·i·cir·cle (sĕm′ĭ-sûr′kəl) ► *n.* A half of a circle as divided by a diameter. **—sem′i·cir′cu·lar** (-kyə-lər) *adj.*

semicircular canal ► *n.* Any of three tubular and looped structures of the inner ear, together functioning in maintenance of the sense of balance in the body.

sem·i·co·lon (sĕm′ĭ-kō′lən) ► *n.* A mark of punctuation (;) used to connect independent clauses and indicating a closer relationship between the clauses than a period does.

sem·i·con·duc·tor (sĕm′ē-kən-dŭk′tər, sĕm′ī-) ► *n.* Any of various solid crystalline substances, such as germanium or silicon, having electrical conductivity greater than insulators but less than good conductors. **—sem′i·con·duct′ing** *adj.*

sem·i·fi·nal (sĕm′ē-fī′nəl, sĕm′ī-) ► *n.* A competition or examination that precedes the final one. **—sem′i·fi′nal** *adj.* **—sem′i·fi′nal·ist** *n.*

sem·i·month·ly (sĕm′ē-mŭnth′lē, sĕm′ī-) ► *adj.* Occurring or issued twice a month.

THESAURUS

selfishness *n.* —*See* EGOTISM.

selfless *adj.* Without concern for oneself ► self-denying, self-forgetful, self-forgetting, self-sacrificing, unselfish. [*Compare* BENEVOLENT, GENEROUS, HUMANITARIAN.]

self-possessed *adj.* —*See* CONFIDENT.

self-possession *n.* —*See* BALANCE (2), CONFIDENCE.

self-regard *n.* —*See* PRIDE.

self-reliance *n.* —*See* INDEPENDENCE.

self-reliant *adj.* —*See* INDEPENDENT (1).

self-reproach *n.* —*See* PENITENCE.

self-respect *n.* —*See* PRIDE.

self-respecting *adj.* —*See* PROUD.

self-restrained *adj.* —*See* RESERVED.

self-restraint *n.* —*See* RESERVE (1).

self-righteous *adj.* Piously or overly sure of one's own righteousness ► holier-than-thou, moralistic. [*Compare* ARROGANT, HYPOCRITICAL, MORAL.]

self-rule *n.* —*See* FREEDOM.

self-ruling *adj.* —*See* FREE (1).

self-sacrificing *adj.* —*See* SELFLESS.

selfsame *adj.* —*See* SAME.

selfsameness *n.* The quality or condition of being exactly the same as something else ► identicalness, identity, oneness, sameness. [*Compare* LIKENESS.]

self-satisfaction *n.* —*See* ARROGANCE, PRIDE.

self-satisfied *n.* —*See* ARROGANT, PROUD.

self-seeking *adj.* —*See* EGOTISTIC (2).

self-serving *adj.* —*See* EGOTISTIC (2).

self-sufficiency *n.* —*See* INDEPENDENCE.

self-sufficient *adj.* Able to support oneself financially ► independent, self-supporting. —*See also* INDEPENDENT (1).

self-supporting *adj.* Able to support oneself financially ► independent, self-sufficient.

sell *v.* To offer for sale ► deal (in), handle, market, merchandise, merchant, peddle, retail, trade (in), vend. ***Idioms:*** put up for sale, put on the block. [*Compare* CARRY, OFFER.] —*See also* CONVINCE, PERSUADE, PROMOTE (3).

sell for *v.* To require a specified price ► cost, go for. ***Idiom:*** set someone back. [*Compare* DEMAND.] —*See also* BRING (2).

sell off or **out** *v.* To get rid of by selling ► close out, dispose of, dump, unload.

sell *n.* *Slang* Market appeal ► marketability, marketableness, salability, salableness.

seller *n.* One who sells ► barker, clerk, crier, hawker, peddler, retailer, salesclerk, salesman, salesperson, saleswoman, vendor. [*Compare* DEALER.]

sellout *n.* —*See* BETRAYAL.

semblance *n.* —*See* APPEARANCE (1), FAÇADE (2), SHADE (2).

sem·i·nal (sĕm′ə-nəl) ▸ *adj.* **1.** Of or relating to semen. **2.** Creative. **3.** Providing a basis or stimulus for further development: *seminal research in a new field.* **—sem′i·nal·ly** *adv.*
sem·i·nar (sĕm′ə-när′) ▸ *n.* **1.** A small group of advanced students engaged in original research or intensive study. **2.** A conference.
sem·i·nar·y (sĕm′ə-nĕr′ē) ▸ *n., pl.* **-ies.** A school for the training of priests, ministers, or rabbis. **—sem′i·nar′i·an** (-nâr′ē-ən) *n.*
Sem·i·nole (sĕm′ə-nōl′) ▸ *n., pl.* **-nole** or **-noles. 1.** A member of a Native American people of primarily Creek origin, now living in Oklahoma and S Florida. **2.** Either of the Muskogean languages of the Seminole.
se·mi·ot·ics (sē′mē-ŏt′ĭks, sĕm′ē-, sē′mī-) ▸ *n. (takes sing. v.)* The theory and study of signs and symbols, esp. as elements of language. **—se′mi·o·ti′cian** (-ə-tĭsh′ən) *n.*
sem·i·pre·cious stone (sĕm′ē-prĕsh′əs) ▸ *n.* A gem, such as an opal, that is not as rare or expensive as a precious stone.
sem·i·pri·vate (sĕm′ē-prī′vĭt, sĕm′ī-) ▸ *adj.* Shared with other hospital patients.
sem·i·pro (sĕm′ē-prō′, sĕm′ī-) ▸ *adj. Informal* Semiprofessional. **—sem′i·pro′** *n.*
sem·i·pro·fes·sion·al (sĕm′ē-prə-fĕsh′ə-nəl, sĕm′ī-) ▸ *adj. Sports* **1.** Playing a sport for pay but not on a full-time basis. **2.** Composed of or engaged in by semiprofessional players. **—sem′i·pro·fes′sion·al** *n.*
sem·i·skilled (sĕm′ē-skĭld′, sĕm′ī-) ▸ *adj.* Possessing or requiring intermediate skills.
sem·i·sol·id (sĕm′ē-sŏl′ĭd, sĕm′ī-) ▸ *adj.* Intermediate in properties, esp. in rigidity, between solids and liquids. ▸ *n.* (sĕm′ē-sŏl′ĭd, sĕm′ī-) A semisolid substance.
Sem·ite (sĕm′īt′) ▸ *n.* **1.** A member of a group of Semitic-speaking peoples of the Near East and N Africa, including the Arabs and Jews. **2.** A Jew.
Se·mit·ic (sə-mĭt′ĭk) ▸ *adj.* **1.** Of or relating to the Semites. **2.** Of or relating to a subgroup of the Afro-Asiatic languages that includes Arabic and Hebrew. ▸ *n.* **1.** The Semitic languages. **2.** Any of the Semitic languages.
Sem·i·tism (sĕm′ĭ-tĭz′əm) ▸ *n.* Semitic traits or customs.
sem·i·tone (sĕm′ē-tōn′, sĕm′ī-) ▸ *n. Mus.* An interval equal to a half tone in the standard diatonic scale. **—sem′i·ton′ic** (-tŏn′ĭk) *adj.*
sem·i·trail·er (sĕm′ē-trā′lər, sĕm′ī-) ▸ *n.* A trailer having rear wheels only, with the forward portion supported by the truck tractor.
sem·i·vow·el (sĕm′ĭ-vou′əl) ▸ *n.* A sound having the quality of a vowel but functioning as a consonant, as the initial sounds of *yell* and *well.*
sem·i·week·ly (sĕm′ē-wēk′lē, sĕm′ī-) ▸ *adj.* Issued or occurring twice a week.
sem·i·year·ly (sĕm′ē-yîr′lē, sĕm′ī-) ▸ *adj.* Issued or occurring twice a year.
sem·o·li·na (sĕm′ə-lē′nə) ▸ *n.* Gritty coarse particles of wheat left after bolting and used for pasta.
sen·ate (sĕn′ĭt) ▸ *n.* **1a.** often **Senate** The upper house in a bicameral legislature, such as the US Congress. **b.** The supreme council of state of the ancient Roman Republic and Empire. **2.** The building in which a senate meets. **3.** A governing or advisory body of some colleges.
sen·a·tor (sĕn′ə-tər) ▸ *n.* A member of a senate. **—sen′a·to′ri·al** (-tôr′ē-əl) *adj.*
send (sĕnd) ▸ *v.* **sent** (sĕnt), **send·ing. 1.** To cause to be conveyed to a destination. **2.** To dispatch, as by a communications medium: *send a message by radio.* **3a.** To direct to go on a mission. **b.** To enable to go: *sent her kid to college.* **4.** To emit. **5.** To direct or propel with force. **6.** To cause to take place or occur. **7.** To put into a given state or condition. **—send′er** *n.*
send·off (sĕnd′ôf′, -ŏf′) ▸ *n.* A demonstration of affection and good wishes, as for a person beginning a journey.
Sen·e·ca (sĕn′ĭ-kə) ▸ *n., pl.* **-ca** or **-cas. 1.** A member of a Native American people of W New York, now also in SE Ontario. **2.** The Iroquoian language of the Seneca.
Seneca, Lucius Amaeus. "the Younger" (4 B.C.?– A.D. 65) ▸ Roman Stoic philosopher and writer.
Sen·e·gal (sĕn′ĭ-gôl′, -gäl′) ▸ A country of W Africa on the Atlantic. **—Sen′e·ga·lese′** (-gô-lēz′, -lēs′) *adj. & n.*
se·nes·cent (sĭ-nĕs′ənt) ▸ *adj.* Growing old; aging. **—se·nes′cence** *n.*
se·nile (sē′nīl′, sĕn′īl′) ▸ *adj.* **1.** Of or characteristic of old age. **2.** Relating to mental impairment associated with aging. **—se′nile′ly** *adv.* **—se·nil′i·ty** (sĭ-nĭl′ĭ-tē) *n.*
sen·ior (sēn′yər) ▸ *adj.* **1.** Of or being the older of two persons having the same name. **2.** Above others of the same set or class. **3.** Of the fourth and last year of a US high school or college. ▸ *n.* **1.** A person who is older than another. **2.** A senior citizen. **3.** A fourth-year student in a US high school or college.
senior chief petty officer ▸ *n.* A rank, as in the US Navy, below master chief petty officer.
senior citizen ▸ *n.* A person of or over the age of retirement. **—sen′ior-cit′i·zen** *adj.*
senior high school ▸ *n.* A high school usu. comprising grades 10, 11, and 12.
sen·ior·i·ty (sēn-yôr′ĭ-tē, -yŏr′-) ▸ *n.* **1.** The state of being senior. **2.** Precedence over others because of length of service.
senior master sergeant ▸ *n.* A rank in the US Air Force below chief master sergeant.
sen·na (sĕn′ə) ▸ *n.* **1.** Any of various plants having compound leaves and yellow flowers. **2.** The dried leaves of a senna, used as a cathartic.
se·ñor (sĕ-nyôr′) ▸ *n., pl.* **se·ño·res** (sĕ-nyō′rĕs). A Spanish courtesy title for a man.
se·ño·ra (sĕ-nyō′rä) ▸ *n.* A Spanish courtesy title for a married woman.
se·ño·ri·ta (sĕ′nyō-rē′tä) ▸ *n.* A Spanish courtesy title for a girl or unmarried woman.
sen·sa·tion (sĕn-sā′shən) ▸ *n.* **1.** A perception associated with stimulation of a sense organ. **2.** An indefinite, generalized body feeling. **3a.** A state of heightened interest or emotion. **b.** A cause of such interest and excitement. **—sen·sa′tion·al** *adj.* **—sen·sa′tion·al·ly** *adv.*

THESAURUS

seminal *adj.* —*See* INFLUENTIAL, INVENTIVE, ORIGINAL.
seminar *n.* —*See* CONFERENCE (1).
sempiternal *adj.* —*See* ENDLESS (2).
sempiternity *n.* The totality of time without beginning or end ▸ eternity, infinity, perpetuity. [*Compare* FOREVER.]
send *v.* **1.** To cause something to be conveyed to a destination ▸ address, consign, dispatch, express, forward, mail, post, route, ship, transmit. [*Compare* CONVEY, PASS.] **2.** To direct or allow to leave ▸ dismiss, send away. ***Idioms:*** send about one's business, send packing, show someone the door. **3.** To direct a person elsewhere for help or information ▸ refer, transfer, turn over. —*See also* ENRAPTURE.
send away *v.* —*See* DISMISS (2).
send for *v.* —*See* ASSEMBLE.
send forth *v.* —*See* EMIT, SHED[1] (1).
send up *v.* —*See* COMMIT.
send-up *n.* —*See* SATIRE.
senescence or **senectitude** *n.* —*See* AGE (1).
senescent *adj.* —*See* OLD (2).
senile *adj.* Relating to the mental deterioration that often accompanies old age ▸ doddering, doting. [*Compare* OLD, INFIRM.]
senility *n.* The condition of being senile ▸ anecdotage, anility, caducity, dotage. [*Compare* AGE.]
senior *adj.* Being at a rank or level above another ▸ greater, higher, superior, upper. —*See also* OLD (2).
senior *n.* **1.** One who stands above another in rank ▸ better, elder, superior. *Informal:* higher-up. [*Compare* CHIEF.] **2.** An elderly person ▸ ancient, elder, golden ager, senior citizen. *Informal:* oldster, old-timer.
senior citizen *n.* —*See* SENIOR (2).
seniority *n.* —*See* AGE (1).
sensation *n.* **1.** The capacity for or an act of responding to a stimulus ▸ feeling, impression, perception, sense, sensibility, sensitiveness, sensitivity. [*Compare* AWARENESS, EMOTION.] **2.** A condition of intense public interest or excitement ▸ ado, brouhaha, bustle, stir, uproar. *Informal:* to-do. *Slang:* hoo-hah. [*Compare* AGITATION.] —*See also* MARVEL.
sensational *adj.* Of or relating to sensation or the senses ▸ sensitive, sensorial, sensory, sensual, sensuous. —*See also* DRAMATIC (2), MARVELOUS.

sen·sa·tion·al·ism (sĕn-sāʹshə-nə-lĭzʹəm) ▸ *n.* The use of lurid or exaggerated matter, esp. in writing, journalism, or politics. **—sen·saʹtion·al·ist** *n.* **—sen·saʹtion·al·isʹtic** *adj.* **—sen·saʹtion·al·ize** *v.*

sense (sĕns) ▸ *n.* **1.** Any of the faculties of hearing, sight, smell, touch, taste, and equilibrium. **2. senses** The faculties of sensation as means of providing physical gratification and pleasure. **3.** Intuitive or acquired perception. **4.** often **senses** Correct judgment. **5a.** A meaning; signification. **b.** One of the meanings of a word or phrase. ▸ *v.* **sensed, sens·ing. 1.** To become aware of; perceive. **2.** To understand. **3.** To detect automatically: *sense radioactivity.*

sense·less (sĕnsʹlĭs) ▸ *adj.* **1.** Lacking sense or meaning; meaningless. **2.** Foolish. **3.** Unconscious. **—senseʹless·ly** *adv.* **—senseʹless·ness** *n.*

sen·si·ble (sĕnʹsə-bəl) ▸ *adj.* **1.** Perceptible by the senses or the mind. **2.** Readily perceived; appreciable. **3.** Able to feel or perceive. **4.** Aware; cognizant. **5.** Acting with or showing good sense: *a sensible choice.* **—senʹsi·ble·ness** *n.* **—senʹsi·bly** *adv.*

sen·si·tive (sĕnʹsĭ-tĭv) ▸ *adj.* **1.** Capable of perceiving. **2.** Responsive to external conditions or stimulation. **3.** Susceptible to the attitudes, feelings, or circumstances of others. **4.** Quick to take offense; touchy. **5.** Easily irritated. **6.** Readily altered: *film that is sensitive to light.* **7.** Registering very slight differences or changes. **8.** Of or relating to classified information. **—senʹsi·tive·ly** *adv.* **—senʹsi·tive·ness, senʹsi·tivʹi·ty** *n.*

sen·si·tize (sĕnʹsĭ-tīzʹ) ▸ *v.* **-tized, -tiz·ing.** To make or become sensitive or more sensitive. **—senʹsi·ti·zaʹtion** *n.*

sen·sor (sĕnʹsər, -sôrʹ) ▸ *n.* A device, such as a photoelectric cell, that receives and responds to a signal or stimulus.

sen·so·ry (sĕnʹsə-rē) ▸ *adj.* Of the senses.

sen·su·al (sĕnʹsho͞o-əl) ▸ *adj.* **1.** Of or affecting the senses. **2a.** Relating to gratification of the physical appetites. **b.** Suggesting sexuality. **c.** Physical rather than intellectual. **—senʹsu·al·ness, senʹsu·alʹi·ty** (-ălʹĭ-tē) *n.* **—senʹsu·al·ize** *v.*

sen·su·ous (sĕnʹsho͞o-əs) ▸ *adj.* **1.** Of, derived from, or gratifying the senses. **2.** Highly appreciative of the pleasures of sensation. **—senʹsu·osʹi·ty** (-ŏsʹĭ-tē), **senʹsu·ous·ness** *n.* **—senʹsu·ous·ly** *adv.*

sent (sĕnt) ▸ *v.* P.t. and p.part. of **send.**

sen·tence (sĕnʹtəns) ▸ *n.* **1.** An independent grammatical unit that has a subject and a predicate with a finite verb. **2.** *Law* **a.** A court judgment, esp. a decision of the punishment to be inflicted on one found guilty. **b.** The penalty imposed. ▸ *v.* **-tenced, -tenc·ing.** *Law* To pronounce sentence upon. **—sen·tenʹtial** (sĕn-tĕnʹshəl) *adj.* **—sen·tenʹtial·ly** *adv.*

sen·ten·tious (sĕn-tĕnʹshəs) ▸ *adj.* **1.** Terse and energetic in expression; pithy. **2.** Given to pompous moralizing. **—sen·tenʹtious·ness** *n.*

sen·tient (sĕnʹshənt, -shē-ənt) ▸ *adj.* **1.** Having sense perception; conscious. **2.** Experiencing sensation. **—senʹtience** *n.* **—senʹtient·ly** *adv.*

sen·ti·ment (sĕnʹtə-mənt) ▸ *n.* **1a.** A cast of mind; general mental disposition. **b.** An opinion about a specific matter; view. **2.** A thought or attitude based on emotion instead of reason. **3.** The emotional import of a passage.

sen·ti·men·tal (sĕnʹtə-mĕnʹtl) ▸ *adj.* **1a.** Characterized or swayed by sentiment. **b.** Affectedly or extravagantly emotional. **2.** Appealing to the sentiments, esp. to romantic feelings. **—senʹti·menʹtal·ism, senʹti·men·talʹi·ty** (-tălʹĭ-tē) *n.* **—senʹti·menʹtal·izeʹ** *v.* **—senʹti·menʹtal·ly** *adv.*

sen·ti·nel (sĕnʹtə-nəl) ▸ *n.* A guard; sentry.

sen·try (sĕnʹtrē) ▸ *n., pl.* **-tries. 1.** A guard, esp. a soldier posted to prevent the passage of unauthorized persons. **2.** The duty of a sentry.

Seoul (sōl) ▸ The capital and largest city of South Korea, in the NW part E of Inchon.

se·pal (sēʹpəl) ▸ *n.* *Bot.* One of the leaflike segments of a

THESAURUS

sense *n.* What is sound or reasonable ▸ logic, rationality, rationalness, reason, reasonableness. *—See also* AWARENESS, COMMON SENSE, INTELLIGENCE, MEANING, SANITY, SENSATION (1).

sense *v.* To view in a certain way ▸ believe, hold, think. [*Compare* BELIEVE, REGARD.] *—See also* PERCEIVE, UNDERSTAND (1).

senseless *adj.* *—See* FOOLISH, MINDLESS, UNCONSCIOUS.

senselessness *n.* *—See* FOOLISHNESS, NONSENSE.

sensibility *n.* The quality or condition of being emotionally and intuitively sensitive ▸ feeling, sensibility, sensitiveness. [*Compare* PITY, SYMPATHY.] *—See also* SENSATION (1).

sensible *adj.* Proceeding from or exhibiting good judgment and prudence ▸ balanced, commonsensible, commonsensical, judicious, levelheaded, prudent, rational, reasonable, sagacious, sage, sane, sapient, sober, sound, well-founded, well-grounded, wise. [*Compare* ADVISABLE, LOGICAL.] *—See also* AWARE, PERCEPTIBLE, PHYSICAL, SENSITIVE (1).

sensitive *adj.* **1.** Able to receive and respond to external stimuli ▸ impressible, impressionable, responsive, sensible, sentient, susceptible, susceptive. [*Compare* AWARE.] **2.** Readily stirred by emotion ▸ emotional, feeling. [*Compare* PASSIONATE.] *—See also* CONFIDENTIAL (3), CRITICAL (2), DELICATE (2), DELICATE (3), FINE[1] (2), GENTLE (1), OVERSENSITIVE, SENSATIONAL.

sensitiveness *n.* The quality or condition of being emotionally and intuitively sensitive ▸ feeling, sensibility, sensitivity. [*Compare* PITY, SYMPATHY.] *—See also* SENSATION (1).

sensitivity *n.* The quality or condition of being emotionally and intuitively sensitive ▸ feeling, sensibility, sensitiveness. [*Compare* PITY, SYMPATHY.] *—See also* DISCERNMENT, OVERSENSITIVITY, SENSATION (1), SUBTLETY, TACT.

sensory or **sensorial** *adj.* *—See* SENSATIONAL.

sensual *adj.* **1.** Relating to, suggestive of, or appealing to sense gratification ▸ epicurean, sensuous, sensualistic, voluptuous. [*Compare* SYBARITIC.] **2.** Relating to the desires and appetites of the body, especially sexual desire ▸ animal, carnal, fleshly, fleshy, physical, sexual, sexy, voluptuous. **3.** Of or preoccupied with material rather than spiritual or intellectual things ▸ material, materialistic. [*Compare* EARTHLY, GREEDY, SUPERFICIAL.] *—See also* EROTIC, SENSATIONAL.

sensualism *n.* The quality or condition of being sensuous ▸ sensuality, sensuousness, voluptuousness. *—See also* EROTICISM.

sensualist *n.* *—See* SYBARITE.

sensualistic *adj.* Relating to, suggestive of, or appealing to sense gratification ▸ epicurean, sensual, sensuous, voluptuous. [*Compare* SYBARITIC.]

sensuality *n.* **1.** The quality or condition of being sensual or being preoccupied with bodily desires ▸ animalism, animality, carnality, eroticism, fleshliness, physicality, sexiness, sexuality, suggestiveness, voluptuousness. [*Compare* DESIRE.] **2.** The quality or condition of being sensuous ▸ sensuousness, sensualism, voluptuousness. *—See also* EROTICISM.

sensuous *adj.* Relating to, suggestive of, or appealing to sense gratification ▸ epicurean, sensual, sensualistic, voluptuous. [*Compare* SYBARITIC.] *—See also* EROTIC, SENSATIONAL.

sensuousness *n.* The quality or condition of being sensuous ▸ sensualism, sensuality, voluptuousness. *—See also* EROTICISM.

sentence *n.* *—See* RULING.

sentence *v.* *—See* CONDEMN, PUNISH.

sentenced *adj.* *—See* CONDEMNED.

sententious *adj.* *—See* PITHY.

sentient *adj.* *—See* AWARE, SENSITIVE (1).

sentiment *n.* A general cast of mind with regard to something ▸ attitude, feeling. [*Compare* IDEA.] *—See also* BELIEF (1), EMOTION, SENTIMENTALITY.

sentimental *adj.* Affectedly or extravagantly emotional ▸ bathetic, bleeding-heart, corny, gushy, maudlin, mawkish, misty, misty-eyed, namby-pamby, romantic, romanticized, slushy, sobby, soft, soppy, syrupy, treacly. *Informal:* gooey, mushy, schmaltzy, sloppy, soft-boiled, soupy. *Slang:* drippy, hokey, sappy, tear-jerking.

sentimentality or **sentimentalism** *n.* The quality or condition of being affectedly or overly emotional ▸ bathos, corniness, maudlinism, mawkishness, romanticism, sentiment, treacle. *Informal:* mush, mushiness, sloppiness, schmaltz, schmaltziness. *Slang:* hokiness, sappiness.

sentry or **sentinel** *n.* *—See* GUARD.

calyx. **—se′paled, sep′a·lous** (sĕp′ə-ləs) *adj.*
sep·a·ra·ble (sĕp′ər-ə-bəl, sĕp′rə-) ▸ *adj.* Possible to separate. **—sep′a·ra·bil′i·ty** *n.*
sep·a·rate (sĕp′ə-rāt′) ▸ *v.* **-rat·ed, -rat·ing.** 1a. To set, keep, or come apart; scatter; disunite. b. To sort. 2. To differentiate between; distinguish. 3. To remove from a mixture or combination; isolate. 4. To stop living together as spouses. 5. To part company; disperse. ▸ *adj.* (sĕp′ər-ĭt, sĕp′rĭt) 1. Set apart; disunited. 2. Existing as an independent entity. 3. Dissimilar; distinct. 4. Not shared; individual: *separate rooms.* **—sep′a·rate·ly** *adv.* **—sep′a·rate·ness** *n.*
sep·a·ra·tion (sĕp′ə-rā′shən) ▸ *n.* 1a. The act or process of separating. b. The condition of being separated. 2. The place at which a division or parting occurs. 3. *Law* A formal agreement terminating a spousal relationship.
sep·a·ra·tist (sĕp′ər-ə-tĭst, sĕp′rə-, sĕp′ə-rā′-) ▸ *n.* One who advocates political or religious separation. **—sep′a·ra·tism** *n.* **—sep′a·ra·tist** *adj.*
sep·a·ra·tor (sĕp′ə-rā′tər) ▸ *n.* One that separates, as a device for separating cream from milk.
Se·phar·di (sə-fär′dē) ▸ *n., pl.* **-dim** (-dĭm). A descendent of the Jews who lived in Spain and Portugal during the Middle Ages. **—Se·phar′dic** (-dĭk) *adj.*
se·pi·a (sē′pē-ə) ▸ *n.* 1. A dark brown pigment. 2. A drawing or photograph in a brown tint. **—se′pi·a** *adj.*
sep·pu·ku (sĕp′o͞o-ko͞o, sĕ-po͞o′-) ▸ *n.* Ritual suicide by disembowelment.
sep·sis (sĕp′sĭs) ▸ *n., pl.* **-ses** (-sēz). The presence of pathogenic organisms or their toxins in the blood or tissues.
Sept. ▸ *abbr.* September
Sep·tem·ber (sĕp-tĕm′bər) ▸ *n.* The 9th month of the Gregorian calendar.
sep·tic (sĕp′tĭk) ▸ *adj.* Of or causing sespis.
sep·ti·ce·mi·a (sĕp′tĭ-sē′mē-ə) ▸ *n.* A systemic disease resulting from sepsis of the bloodstream. **—sep′ti·ce′mic** (-mĭk) *adj.*
septic tank ▸ *n.* A sewage-disposal tank in which waste material is decomposed by anaerobic bacteria.
sep·til·lion (sĕp-tĭl′yən) ▸ *n.* 1. The cardinal number equal to 10^{24}. 2. *Chiefly Brit.* The cardinal number equal to 10^{42}. **—sep·til′lion** *adj.* **—sep·til′lionth** *n. & adj.*
Sep·tu·a·gint (sĕp′to͞o-ə-jĭnt′, sĕp-to͞o′ə-jənt, -tyo͞o′-) ▸ *n.* A Greek translation of the Hebrew Bible made in the 3rd cent. B.C.
sep·tum (sĕp′təm) ▸ *n., pl.* **-ta** (-tə). A thin partition or membrane between two cavities or soft masses of tissue in an organism.
sep·tu·plet (sĕp-tŭp′lĭt, -to͞o′plĭt, -tyo͞o′-) ▸ *n.* One of seven offspring born in a single birth.
sep·ul·cher (sĕp′əl-kər) ▸ *n.* 1. A burial vault. 2. A receptacle for sacred relics. ▸ *v.* **-chered, -cher·ing.** To place into a sepulcher; inter. **—se·pul′chral** (sə-pŭl′krəl, -po͝ol′-) *adj.*
se·quel (sē′kwəl) ▸ *n.* 1. Something that follows; continuation. 2. A literary work that continues an earlier narrative. 3. A consequence.
se·quence (sē′kwəns, -kwĕns′) ▸ *n.* 1. A following of one thing after another; succession. 2. An order of succession; arrangement. 3. A related or continuous series. **—se′quence** *v.* **—se·quen′tial** (sĭ-kwĕn′shəl) *adj.* **—se·quen′tial·ly** *adv.*
se·ques·ter (sĭ-kwĕs′tər) ▸ *v.* 1. To cause to withdraw into seclusion. 2. To set apart; segregate. 3. *Law* To confiscate (property) as security against legal claims. **—se′ques·tra′tion** *n.*
se·quin (sē′kwĭn) ▸ *n.* A small shiny ornamental disk, usu. sewn on cloth; spangle. **—se′quined** *adj.*
se·quoi·a (sĭ-kwoi′ə) ▸ *n.* 1. A very large cone-bearing evergreen tree of the mountains of California. 2. A redwood.
Se·quoy·a or **Se·quoy·ah** (sĭ-kwoi′ə) (1770?–1843) ▸ Cherokee scholar.
se·ra (sîr′ə) ▸ *n.* Pl. of **serum.**
se·ra·glio (sə-răl′yō, -räl′-) ▸ *n., pl.* **-glios.** 1. A harem. 2. A sultan's palace.
se·ra·pe also **sa·ra·pe** (sə-rä′pē, -răp′ē) ▸ *n.* A long often brightly colored shawl resembling a blanket, worn esp. by Mexican men.
ser·aph (sĕr′əf) ▸ *n., pl.* **-a·phim** (-ə-fĭm) or **-aphs.** *Christianity* An angel of the highest order. **—se·raph′ic** (sə-răf′ĭk), **se·raph′i·cal** *adj.*
Serb (sûrb) ▸ *n.* A native or inhabitant of Serbia.
Ser·bi·a (sûr′bē-ə) ▸ A country of SE Europe.
Ser·bi·an (sûr′bē-ən) ▸ *n.* 1. A Serb. 2. The Slavic language of Serbia. **—Ser′bi·an** *adj.*
Ser·bo-Cro·a·tian (sûr′bō-krō-ā′shən) ▸ *n.* The closely related Slavic languages of Croatia, Bosnia and Herzegovina, Montenegro, and Serbia when considered a single language. **—Ser′bo-Cro·a′tian** *adj.*
sere also **sear** (sîr) ▸ *adj.* Withered; dry.
ser·e·nade (sĕr′ə-nād′, sĕr′ə-nād′) ▸ *n.* A musical performance given to honor or express love for someone. ▸ *v.* **-nad·ed, -nad·ing.** To perform a serenade (for). **—ser′e·nad′er** *n.*
ser·en·dip·i·ty (sĕr′ən-dĭp′ĭ-tē) ▸ *n.* The faculty of making fortunate discoveries by accident. **—ser′en·dip′i·tous** *adj.* **—ser′en·dip′i·tous·ly** *adv.*
se·rene (sə-rēn′) ▸ *adj.* 1. Calm and unruffled; tranquil. 2. Unclouded; fair. **—se·rene′ly** *adv.* **—se·rene′ness, se·ren′i·ty** (-rĕn′ĭ-tē) *n.*
serf (sûrf) ▸ *n.* 1. A member of a feudal class of people in Europe, bound to the land and owned by a lord. 2. A slave. **—serf′dom** *n.*
serge (sûrj) ▸ *n.* A twilled cloth of worsted or worsted and wool.
ser·geant (sär′jənt) ▸ *n.* 1. Any of several ranks of noncommissioned officers in the US Army, Air Force, or Marine Corps. 2. A police officer ranking next below a captain, lieutenant, or inspector.
sergeant at arms ▸ *n., pl.* **sergeants at arms.** An officer appointed to keep order within an organization, such as a legislature.
sergeant first class ▸ *n., pl.* **sergeants first class.** A rank in the US Army below master sergeant.
sergeant major ▸ *n., pl.* **sergeants major** or **sergeant majors.** 1. Any of the highest noncommissioned ranks in the US Army and Marine Corps. 2. *Chiefly Brit.* A noncommissioned officer of the highest rank.
se·ri·al (sîr′ē-əl) ▸ *adj.* 1. Of, forming, or arranged in a series. 2. Published or produced in installments. ▸ *n.* A work

THESAURUS

separate *v.* 1. To end an association by or as if by leaving one another ▸ break off, break up, divorce, part. *Informal:* split (up). *Idioms:* call it quits, come to a parting of the ways, part company. 2. To set apart one kind or type from others ▸ sift, sort, winnow. *Idiom:* separate the sheep from the goats. *—See also* CLASSIFY, DETACH, DISCHARGE, DISTINGUISH (1), DIVIDE, ISOLATE (1), SCATTER (2), SLIP (2).
separate *adj.* *—See* DIFFERENT, DISTINCT, INDIVIDUAL (2), LONE.
separately *adv.* As a separate unit ▸ apart, discretely, independently, individually, singly. *Idioms:* one at a time, one by one. [*Compare* ALONE.]
separateness *n.* *—See* DIFFERENCE, INDIVIDUALITY, SECLUSION.
separation *n.* *—See* DETACHMENT (1), DISTINCTION (1), DIVISION (1), GAP (1), ISOLATION.
separatist or **separationist** *n.* A person who dissents from the doctrine of an established church ▸ dissenter, dissident, heretic, nonconformist, schismatic, sectarian, sectary. [*Compare* REBEL.]
sepulcher *n.* *—See* GRAVE[1].
sepulcher *v.* *—See* BURY.
sepulture *n.* *—See* BURIAL, GRAVE[1].
sequel *n.* *—See* EFFECT (1).
sequence *n.* *—See* ARRANGEMENT (1), EFFECT (1), SERIES.
sequent *adj.* *—See* CONSECUTIVE.
sequent *n.* *—See* EFFECT (1).
sequential *adj.* *—See* CONSECUTIVE.
sequester or **sequestrate** *v.* To put into solitude ▸ cloister, isolate, seclude. [*Compare* ENCLOSE, IMPRISON.] *—See also* ISOLATE (1).
sequestration *n.* *—See* ISOLATION, SECLUSION.
sequin *n.* A small sparkling decoration ▸ diamond, glitter, rhinestone, spangle.
sere *adj.* *—See* DRY (1).
serendipitous *adj.* *—See* ACCIDENTAL.
serendipity *n.* *—See* CHANCE (2).
serene *adj.* *—See* CALM, STILL.
serenity *n.* *—See* CALM, STILLNESS.
serf *n.* *—See* SLAVE.
serfdom *n.* *—See* SLAVERY.
serial *adj.* *—See* CONSECUTIVE.

published or produced in installments. **—se′ri·al·i·za′tion** *n.* **—se′ri·al·ize′** *v.* **—se′ri·al·ly** *adv.*

se·ries (sîr′ēz) ▸ *n., pl.* **series.** **1.** A number of objects or events arranged one after the other in succession; set. **2.** A succession of regularly aired radio or television programs. **3.** *Sports* A number of games played in succession by the same opposing teams.

ser·if (sĕr′ĭf) ▸ *n. Print.* A fine line finishing off the main strokes of a letter.

se·ri·o·com·ic (sîr′ē-ō-kŏm′ĭk) ▸ *adj.* Both serious and comic.

se·ri·ous (sîr′ē-əs) ▸ *adj.* **1.** Grave in quality or manner. **2.** Carried out in earnest. **3.** Concerned with important rather than trivial matters. **4.** Causing great concern; critical. **—se′ri·ous·ly** *adv.* **—se′ri·ous·ness** *n.*

ser·mon (sûr′mən) ▸ *n.* **1.** A homily delivered as part of a liturgy. **2.** A lengthy and tedious reproof or exhortation. **—ser′mon·ize′** *v.* **—ser′mon·iz′er** *n.*

se·rol·o·gy (sĭ-rŏl′ə-jē) ▸ *n.* The medical study of serum. **—se′ro·log′ic** (sîr′ə-lŏj′ĭk), **se′ro·log′i·cal** *adj.* **—se·rol′o·gist** *n.*

se·ro·neg·a·tive (sîr′ō-nĕg′ə-tĭv) ▸ *adj.* Showing a negative reaction to a test on blood serum for a disease, esp. syphilis or AIDS.

se·ro·pos·i·tive (sîr′ō-pŏz′ĭ-tĭv) ▸ *adj.* Showing a positive reaction to a test on blood serum for a disease.

se·ro·to·nin (sĕr′ə-tō′nĭn, sîr′-) ▸ *n.* A hormone found in plants and animals that acts as a neurotransmitter and vasoconstrictor in humans.

se·rous (sîr′əs) ▸ *adj.* Containing, secreting, or resembling serum.

ser·pent (sûr′pənt) ▸ *n.* A snake.

ser·pen·tine (sûr′pən-tēn′, -tīn′) ▸ *adj.* Of or like a serpent, as in form or movement.

ser·rate (sĕr′āt′) or **ser·rat·ed** (sĕr′ā′tĭd, sə-rā′-) ▸ *adj.* Edged with sharp toothlike projections. **—ser·ra′tion** (sə-rā′shən) *n.* **—ser′rate′** *v.*

ser·ried (sĕr′ēd) ▸ *adj.* Pressed together in rows.

se·rum (sîr′əm) ▸ *n., pl.* **se·rums** or **se·ra** (sîr′ə). **1.** The clear yellowish fluid obtained upon separating whole blood into its solid and liquid components. **2.** Blood serum from the tissues of immunized animals, used to transfer immunity to another individual.

ser·vant (sûr′vənt) ▸ *n.* One employed to perform domestic services.

serve (sûrv) ▸ *v.* **served, serv·ing.** **1.** To work for; be a servant to. **2.** To place food before (someone); wait on. **3.** To provide goods and services for (customers). **4.** To be of assistance to. **5.** To spend or complete (time). **6.** To undergo military service for. **7.** To give homage to. **8.** To requite. **9.** To meet the needs of; satisfy. **10.** *Law* To present (a writ or summons). **11.** *Sports* To put (a ball) in play, as in tennis. ▸ *n. Sports* The right or act of serving in many court games.

serv·er (sûr′vər) ▸ *n.* **1.** One who serves. **2.** Something, as a tray, that is used in serving food and drink. **3.** *Comp. Sci.* **a.** A file server. **b.** A computer that processes HTML requests.

ser·vice (sûr′vĭs) ▸ *n.* **1a.** Employment in work for another, esp. for a government. **b.** A government branch or department and its employees. **2.** The armed forces of a nation, or any branch thereof. **3.** The occupation or duties of a servant. **4.** Work done for others as an occupation. **5.** Installation or repairs provided by a dealer or manufacturer. **6.** A set of dishes or utensils. **7.** *Sports* A serve. ▸ *v.* **-viced, -vic·ing.** **1.** To repair or maintain: *service a car.* **2.** To provide services to.

ser·vice·a·ble (sûr′vĭ-sə-bəl) ▸ *adj.* **1.** Ready for service; usable. **2.** Able to give long service; durable. **—ser′vice·a·bil′i·ty, ser′vice·a·ble·ness** *n.* **—ser′vice·a·bly** *adv.*

ser·vice·man (sûr′vĭs-măn′, -mən) ▸ *n.* **1.** A man who is a member of the armed forces. **2.** also **service man** A man whose work is the maintenance and repair of equipment.

service mark ▸ *n.* A mark used in the sale or advertising of services to identify and distinguish them.

service station ▸ *n.* A retail establishment at which motor vehicles are refueled, serviced, and sometimes repaired.

ser·vice·wom·an (sûr′vĭs-wo͝om′ən) ▸ *n.* A woman member of the armed forces.

ser·vile (sûr′vəl, -vīl′) ▸ *adj.* Abjectly submissive; slavish. **—ser′vile·ly** *adv.* **—ser′vile·ness, ser·vil′i·ty** (sər-vĭl′ĭ-tē) *n.*

serv·ing (sûr′vĭng) ▸ *n.* A helping of food or drink.

ser·vi·tor (sûr′vĭ-tər, -tôr′) ▸ *n.* An attendant.

ser·vi·tude (sûr′vĭ-to͞od′, -tyo͞od′) ▸ *n.* **1.** Subjection to an owner or master. **2.** Forced labor imposed as a punishment.

ser·vo·mech·a·nism (sûr′vō-mĕk′ə-nĭz′əm) ▸ *n.* A feedback system used in the automatic control of a mechanical device.

ser·vo·mo·tor (sûr′vō-mō′tər) ▸ *n.* A motor that controls the action of the mechanical device in a servomechanism.

ses·a·me (sĕs′ə-mē) ▸ *n.* **1.** A tropical Asian plant bearing small, edible, oil-rich seeds. **2.** The seed of this plant.

ses·qui·cen·ten·ni·al (sĕs′kwĭ-sĕn-tĕn′ē-əl) ▸ *adj.* Relating to a period of 150 years. ▸ *n.* A 150th anniversary or its celebration.

ses·qui·pe·da·lian (sĕs′kwĭ-pĭ-dāl′yən) ▸ *n.* A long word. ▸ *adj.* **1.** Given to the use of long words. **2.** Polysyllabic.

ses·sile (sĕs′īl′, -əl) ▸ *adj.* **1.** *Bot.* Attached directly at the

THESAURUS

series *n.* A number of things placed or occurring one after the other ▸ chain, concatenation, consecution, course, gamut, order, procession, progression, range, round, run, scale, sequence, string, succession, suite, train. *Informal:* streak. [*Compare* GROUP, LINE.]

serious *adj.* **1.** Characterized by careful thought and a lack of frivolity or exaggeration ▸ businesslike, dignified, earnest, [illegible] sober, sobersided, solemn, somber, staid. *Idiom:* in earnest. [*Compare* CEREMONIOUS, [illegible], FRANK, SEVERE.] **2.** Having or threatening severe negative consequences ▸ dire, grave, grievous, severe. [*Compare* DISASTROUS, FATEFUL.] *—See also* DIFFICULT (1), GRAVE[2] (1).

seriousness *n.* **1.** The quality of being dignified and serious, as in manner or bearing ▸ dignity, earnestness, graveness, gravitas, gravity, sedateness, sobersidedness, sobriety, solemnness, solemnity, somberness, staidness. [*Compare* CEREMONY, SEVERITY.] **2.** The condition of being grave and of involving serious consequences ▸ graveness, gravity, heaviness, momentousness, weightiness. [*Compare* SEVERITY.]

sermon *n.* *—See* SPEECH (2).

sermonize *v.* **1.** To deliver a sermon, especially as a vocation ▸ evangelize, preach. [*Compare* ADDRESS.] **2.** To indulge in moral reflection, usually pompously ▸ edify, moralize, pontificate, preach. [*Compare* CHASTISE.] **3.** To talk to an audience formally ▸ lecture, prelect, speak. [*Compare* CONVERSE.]

serpentine *adj.* *—See* WINDING.

serrated *adj.* *—See* SAW-TOOTHED.

servant *n.* *—See* SLAVE.

serve *v.* **1.** To work and care for ▸ attend, do for, minister to, wait on (*or* upon). [*Compare* HELP, TEND[2], WORK.] **2.** To place food before someone ▸ wait on (*or* upon). [*Compare* GIVE, DISTRIBUTE.] **3.** To spend or complete time, as a prison term ▸ put in. *Informal:* do. *—See also* OBLIGE (1), PROFIT (2), SATISFY (1).

service *n.* The state of being employed ▸ employ, employment, hire. *—See also* CEREMONY (1), DUTY (2), FAVOR (1).

service *v.* *—See* FIX (1).

serviceable *adj.* *—See* PRACTICAL, USABLE.

serviceman or **servicewoman** *n.* *—See* [illegible].

services *n.* *—See* AMENITIES (1).

servile *adj.* Excessively eager to serve or obey ▸ bootlicking, cringing, fawning, grovelling, menial, obsequious, slavish, subservient, sycophantic, toadying. [*Compare* HUMBLE, LOWLY, UNCTUOUS.]

servility *n.* *—See* SLAVERY.

serving *n.* An individual quantity of food ▸ bowlful, helping, mess, plateful, portion. [*Compare* ALLOTMENT.]

servitude *n.* *—See* SLAVERY.

sesquipedalian or **sesquipedal** *adj.* Having many syllables ▸ polysyllabic.

base: *sessile leaves.* 2. *Zool.* Permanently attached, as a barnacle.

ses·sion (sĕsh′ən) ▸ *n.* 1a. A meeting of a legislative or judicial body. b. A series of such meetings. c. The duration of such a series of meetings. 2. The part of a year or of a day during which a school holds classes.

ses·tet (sĕ-stĕt′) ▸ *n.* The last six lines of a sonnet.

set[1] (sĕt) ▸ *v.* **set, set·ting.** 1. To put in a specified position or state. 2. To put into a stable position; fix. 3. To restore to a proper and normal state. 4. To adjust for proper functioning. 5. To arrange properly for use: *set a table.* 6. To apply curlers and clips to (hair) in order to style. 7. To arrange (type) into words and sentences preparatory to printing; compose. 8. To prescribe or establish: *set a precedent.* 9. To assign to a duty. 10. To establish as a model: *set a good example.* 11. To put in a mounting; mount. 12. To cause to sit. 13. To sit on eggs, as a hen. 14. To determine (a price or value). 15. To disappear below the horizon. 16. To diminish or decline; wane. 17. To become fixed; harden; coagulate. ***—phrasal verbs:*** **set about** To begin. **set aside** 1. To reserve for a special purpose. 2. To annul. **set back** To slow down the progress of. **set down** To put in writing. **set forth** 1. To present for consideration. 2. To express in words. 3. To begin a journey. **set off** 1. To cause to occur. 2. To cause to explode. 3. To distinguish. 4. To direct attention to by contrast. 5. To start a journey. **set out** 1. To start a journey. 2. To undertake or begin something. **set up** 1. To place in an upright position. 2. To invest with power. 3. To assemble and erect. 4. To establish; found. ▸ *adj.* 1. Fixed or established. 2. Established by convention. 3. Fixed and rigid. 4. Unwilling to change. 5. Ready. ▸ *n.* 1. The act or process of setting. 2. The condition resulting from setting. ***—idioms:*** **set sail** To begin a voyage on water. **set the stage for** To provide the basis for.

set[2] (sĕt) ▸ *n.* 1. A group of persons or things of the same kind that belong together: *a chess set.* 2. A group of books or periodicals published as a unit. 3a. The scenery constructed for a theatrical performance. b. The enclosure in which a movie is filmed. 4. The receiving apparatus assembled to operate a radio or television. 5. *Math.* A collection of distinct elements. 6. *Sports* A group of tennis games constituting one division or unit of a match.

set·back (sĕt′băk′) ▸ *n.* 1. An unanticipated check in progress; reverse. 2. A steplike recession, as in a wall or in the rise of a tall building.

Se·ton (sēt′n), Saint **Elizabeth Ann Bayley.** "Mother Seton" (1774–1821) ▸ Amer. religious leader.

set piece ▸ *n.* 1. A piece of freestanding stage scenery. 2. An artistic or literary work marked by a formal pattern. 3. A carefully planned and executed military operation.

set·screw (sĕt′skro͞o′) ▸ *n.* A usu. headless screw used to hold two parts together.

set·tee (sĕ-tē′) ▸ *n.* 1. A long wooden bench with a back. 2. A small sofa.

set·ter (sĕt′ər) ▸ *n.* Any of several breeds of long-haired hunting dogs.

set theory ▸ *n. Math.* The study of the properties of sets.

set·ting (sĕt′ĭng) ▸ *n.* 1. The position in which something, such as an automatic control, is set. 2. A context or background. 3. A mounting, as for a gem.

set·tle (sĕt′l) ▸ *v.* **-tled, -tling.** 1. To put into order; arrange or fix definitely as desired. 2. To establish residence (in). 3. To restore calmness or comfort to. 4a. To sink, become compact, or come to rest: *Dust settled on the road.* b. To cause (a liquid) to become clear by forming a sediment. 5. To stabilize. 6a. To make compensation for (a claim). b. To pay (a debt). 7. To conclude (a dispute). 8. To decide (a lawsuit) by mutual agreement without court action. **—set′tler** *n.*

set·tle·ment (sĕt′l-mənt) ▸ *n.* 1. The act or process of settling. 2a. Establishment, as of a person in a business or of people in a new region. b. A newly colonized region. 3. A small community. 4. An adjustment or other understanding reached. 5. also **settlement house** A center providing community services in an underprivileged area.

set-to (sĕt′to͞o′) ▸ *n., pl.* **-tos.** A brief, usu. heated conflict.

set·up (sĕt′ŭp′) ▸ *n.* 1. An arrangement or plan, esp. an initial organization. 2. often **setups** *Informal* The collective ingredients for serving alcoholic drinks. 3. *Slang* a. A contest prearranged to result in an easy or faked victory. b. A deceptive scheme, such as a fraud.

sev·en (sĕv′ən) ▸ *n.* 1. The cardinal number equal to 6 + 1. 2. The 7th in a set or sequence. **—sev′en** *adj. & pron.*

sev·en·teen (sĕv′ən-tēn′) ▸ *n.* 1. The cardinal number equal to 16 + 1. 2. The 17th in a set or sequence. **—sev′en·teen′** *adj. & pron.*

sev·en·teenth (sĕv′ən-tēnth′) ▸ *n.* 1. The ordinal number matching the number 17 in a series. 2. One of 17 equal parts. **—sev′en·teenth′** *adv. & adj.*

sev·enth (sĕv′ənth) ▸ *n.* 1. The ordinal number matching the number 7 in a series. 2. One of seven equal parts. 3. *Mus.* A tone seven degrees above or below a given tone in a diatonic scale. **—sev′enth** *adv. & adj.*

seventh heaven ▸ *n.* A state of great joy.

sev·en·ti·eth (sĕv′ən-tē-ĭth) ▸ *n.* 1. The ordinal number

THESAURUS

session *n.* *—See* CONVENTION, PERIOD (1).

set[1] *v.* 1. To arrange tableware upon a table in preparation for a meal ▸ lay, spread. 2. To set the time for an event or occasion ▸ plan, schedule, time. [*Compare* ARRANGE.] 3. To appoint and send to a particular place ▸ assign, post, station. [*Compare* POSITION.] *—See also* ADJUST, AIM (1), COAGULATE, ESTIMATE (2), HARDEN (2), LIMIT, POSITION, SETTLE (2).

set about *v.* *—See* START (1).

set apart *v.* *—See* APPROPRIATE, DISTINGUISH (2), ISOLATE (1).

set aside *v.* *—See* ABOLISH, APPROPRIATE, SAVE (1).

set back *v.* *—See* DELAY (1).

set by *v.* *—See* SAVE (1).

set down *v.* *—See* LAND (2), LIST[1].

set forth *v.* *—See* GO (1), PROPOSE.

set in *v.* To manifest strong winds and precipitation ▸ blow (up), squall, storm. [*Compare* RAIN.]

set off *v.* To endow with beauty and elegance ▸ beautify, embellish, enhance, grace. [*Compare* ADORN.] *—See also* BALANCE (2), CANCEL (2), CAUSE, GO (1), PROVOKE.

set out *v.* *—See* ARRANGE (2), BEAR (5), DESIGN (2), GO (1), PLANT, START (1).

set to *v.* *—See* START (1).

set up *v.* *—See* ERECT, ESTABLISH (1), FOUND, TREAT (2).

set *adj.* In a state of preparedness ▸ prepared, ready. *Informal:* go. *Slang:* together. ***Idioms:*** all set, in working order, on deck, ready (*or* raring) to go. *—See also* CONFIRMED (1), DECIDED, INTENT, SPECIAL, UNCHANGING.

set[2] *n.* *—See* CIRCLE (3), CLASS (1), GROUP, SCENE (2).

setback *n.* A change from better to worse ▸ backset, reverse, reversal. [*Compare* MISFORTUNE, RELAPSE.] *—See also* ACCIDENT.

setoff *n.* *—See* COMPENSATION.

setting *n.* *—See* CONDITIONS, SCENE (1), SCENE (2).

settle *v.* 1. To put into correct or conclusive form ▸ arrange, conclude, dispose of, finalize, fix. [*Compare* CONCLUDE.] 2. To bring something into a state of agreement or accord ▸ arrange, conclude, fix, negotiate, reconcile, rectify, resolve, set, settle upon, smooth over, straighten out. [*Compare* COMPROMISE, DECIDE, JUDGE.] 3. To set right by giving what is due ▸ clear, discharge, liquidate, pay (off *or* up), satisfy, square. [*Compare* SATISFY.] 4. To move to a place and reside there ▸ locate, relocate. ***Idioms:*** fix one's residence, make one's home, put down roots, take up residence. [*Compare* EMIGRATE, LIVE[1], MOVE.] *—See also* DECIDE, ESTABLISH (1), LAND (2), PACIFY, SINK (1).

settled *adj.* *—See* CONFIRMED (1), DECIDED.

settlement *n.* A reestablishment of friendship or harmony ▸ conciliation, rapprochement, reconcilement, reconciliation. [*Compare* AGREEMENT, ATONEMENT, COMPROMISE.] *—See also* COMPENSATION, COMPROMISE, POSSESSION, VILLAGE.

settler *n.* One who settles in a new region ▸ colonial, colonist, colonizer, homesteader, pioneer.

setup *n.* *—See* ARRANGEMENT (1).

seventh heaven *n.* *—See* HEAVEN.

matching the number 70 in a series. **2.** One of 70 equal parts. **—sev′en·ti·eth** *adv. & adj.*

sev·en·ty (sĕv′ən-tē) ▸ *n., pl.* **-ties.** The cardinal number equal to 7 × 10. **—sev′en·ty** *adj. & pron.*

sev·er (sĕv′ər) ▸ *v.* **1.** To divide or separate. **2.** To cut off (a part) from a whole. **3.** To break up (e.g., a relationship); dissolve.

sev·er·al (sĕv′ər-əl, sĕv′rəl) ▸ *adj.* **1.** Being of a number more than two or three but not many. **2.** Respectively different; various: *They parted and went their several ways.* ▸ *pron. (takes pl. v.)* An indefinite but small number; a few. **—sev′er·al·ly** *adv.*

sev·er·al·ty (sĕv′ər-əl-tē, sĕv′rəl-) ▸ *n., pl.* **-ties.** *Law* **1.** A separate and individual right to possession or ownership. **2.** Property owned in severalty.

sev·er·ance (sĕv′ər-əns, sĕv′rəns) ▸ *n.* **1a.** The act or process of severing. **b.** The condition of being severed. **2.** Extra pay given an employee upon leaving a position.

se·vere (sə-vîr′) ▸ *adj.* **-ver·er, -ver·est. 1.** Unsparing or harsh, as in treatment of others; strict. **2.** Marked by rigorous standards. **3.** Austere or dour; forbidding. **4.** Extremely plain in substance or style. **5.** Extremely violent or intense: *a severe storm.* **6.** Extremely difficult; trying. **—se·vere′ly** *adv.* **—se·vere′ness, se·ver′i·ty** (-vĕr′ĭ-tē) *n.*

sew (sō) ▸ *v.* **sewed, sewn** (sōn) or **sewed, sew·ing. 1.** To make, repair, or fasten by stitching, as with a needle and thread. **2.** To close, fasten, or attach with stitches. ***—phrasal verb:* sew up** *Informal* **1.** To complete successfully. **2.** To monopolize. **—sew′er** *n.*

sew·age (so͞o′ĭj) ▸ *n.* Liquid and solid waste carried off in sewers or drains.

sew·er (so͞o′ər) ▸ *n.* An artificial, usu. underground conduit for carrying off sewage or rainwater.

sew·er·age (so͞o′ər-ĭj) ▸ *n.* **1.** A system of sewers. **2.** Removal of waste materials by sewers. **3.** Sewage.

sew·ing (sō′ĭng) ▸ *n.* **1.** The act of one who sews. **2.** An article being sewn.

sewing machine ▸ *n.* A machine for sewing.

sex (sĕks) ▸ *n.* **1a.** The property or quality by which organisms are classified on the basis of their reproductive organs. **b.** Either of the two divisions, designated female and male, of this classification. **2.** Females or males collectively. **3.** The condition or character of being female or male. **4.** Sexual intercourse.

sex·a·ge·nar·i·an (sĕk′sə-jə-nâr′ē-ən) ▸ *n.* A person between the ages of 60 and 70. **—sex′a·ge·nar′i·an** *adj.*

sex·a·ges·i·mal (sĕk′sə-jĕs′ə-məl) ▸ *adj.* Of or based on the number 60.

sex chromosome ▸ *n.* Either of a pair of chromosomes, usu. designated X or Y, in the germ cells of most animals and some plants, that combine to determine the sex of an individual, XX resulting in a female and XY in a male.

sex hormone ▸ *n.* Any of various hormones affecting the growth or function of the reproductive organs.

sex·ism (sĕk′sĭz′əm) ▸ *n.* Discrimination based on gender, esp. discrimination against women. **—sex′ist** *adj. & n.*

sex·less (sĕks′lĭs) ▸ *adj.* **1.** Lacking sexual characteristics; neuter. **2.** Lacking in sexual activity. **—sex′less·ness** *n.*

sex-linked (sĕks′lĭngkt′) ▸ *adj.* **1.** Carried by a sex chromosome, esp. an X chromosome: *a sex-linked gene.* **2.** Sexually determined. **—sex linkage** *n.*

sex·tant (sĕk′stənt) ▸ *n.* A navigational instrument used to measure the altitudes of celestial bodies.

sex·tet (sĕk-stĕt′) ▸ *n.* **1a.** A group composed of six musicians. **b.** A composition written for six performers. **2.** A group of six persons or things.

sex·til·lion (sĕk-stĭl′yən) ▸ *n.* **1.** The cardinal number equal to 10^{21}. **2.** *Chiefly Brit.* The cardinal number equal to 10^{36}. **—sex·til′lion** *adj. & pron.* **—sex·til′lionth** *n. & adj.*

sex·ton (sĕk′stən) ▸ *n.* One responsible for the care and upkeep of church property.

sex·tu·ple (sĕk-sto͞o′pəl, -styo͞o′-, -stŭp′əl) ▸ *v.* **-pled, -pling.** To multiply or be multiplied by six. ▸ *adj.* **1.** Having six parts. **2.** Multiplied by six; sixfold. ▸ *n.* A sixfold amount or number. **—sex·tu′ply** *adv.*

sex·tup·let (sĕk-stŭp′lĭt, -sto͞o′plĭt, -styo͞o′-) ▸ *n.* One of six offspring born in a single birth.

sex·u·al (sĕk′sho͞o-əl) ▸ *adj.* **1.** Of sex, sexuality, the sexes, or the sex organs and their functions. **2.** Implying or symbolizing erotic desires or activity. **3.** Of or involving the union of male and female gametes: *sexual reproduction.* **—sex′u·al·ly** *adv.*

sexual harassment ▸ *n.* The making of unwanted and offensive sexual advances, remarks, or acts, esp. by one in a supervisory position.

sexual intercourse ▸ *n.* Sexual union between humans, gen. involving physical union of the sexual organs.

sex·u·al·i·ty (sĕk′sho͞o-ăl′ĭ-tē) ▸ *n.* **1.** The condition of being characterized and distinguished by sex. **2.** Concern with sex. **3.** Sexual character or potency.

sexually transmitted disease ▸ *n.* Any of several diseases, such as syphilis and gonorrhea, that are transmitted by sexual contact.

sexual orientation ▸ *n.* The direction of one's sexual interest toward members of the same, opposite, or both sexes.

sex·y (sĕk′sē) ▸ *adj.* **-i·er, -i·est. 1.** Arousing sexual desire or interest. **2.** *Slang* Highly appealing or interesting. **—sex′i·ly** *adv.* **—sex′i·ness** *n.*

Sey·chelles (sā-shĕl′, -shĕlz′) ▸ An island country in the W Indian Ocean N of Madagascar.

Sg ▸ The symbol for the element **seaborgium**.

SGML (ĕs′jē-ĕm-ĕl′) ▸ *n.* A markup language for describing the logical structure of a computer document.

Sha'·ban also **Shaa·ban** (shə-bän′, shä-, shô-) ▸ *n.* The 8th month of the Muslim calendar.

Shab·bat (shə-bät′, shä′bəs) ▸ *n.* *Judaism* The Sabbath.

shab·by (shăb′ē) ▸ *adj.* **-bi·er, -bi·est. 1.** Wearing threadbare clothing. **2a.** Threadbare or worn-out. **b.** Dilapidated or

THESAURUS

sever *v.* —*See* CUT (2).

several *adj.* Consisting of a number more than two or three but less than many ▸ certain, divers, few, some, sundry, various. —*See also* DISTINCT.

several *pron.* A number more than two or three but less than many ▸ few, handful, small number, some, smattering, sprinkling. [*Compare* COUPLE.]

severance *n.* —*See* DIVISION (1).

severe *adj.* **1.** Rigorous and unsparing in treating others ▸ demanding, draconian, exacting, hard, harsh, rigid, rigorous, stern, strict, stringent, tough, uncompromising, unyielding. [*Compare* CRUEL, FIRM[1], FORBIDDING, STUBBORN.] **2.** Conveying great physical force ▸ hard, heavy, hefty, powerful. [*Compare* FORCEFUL, INTENSE.] **3.** Having or threatening severe negative consequences ▸ dire, grave, grievous, serious. [*Compare* DISASTROUS, FATEFUL.] —*See also* BARE (1), BITTER (2), BLEAK (1), BURDENSOME, GRAVE[2] (1).

severity *n.* The fact or condition of being rigorous and unsparing ▸ austerity, hardness, harshness, rigidity, rigidness, rigor, rigorousness, sternness, strictness, stringency, toughness. [*Compare* CRUELTY, SERIOUSNESS, STUBBORNNESS.] —*See also* INTENSITY.

sewer *n.* —*See* PIT[1].

sexiness *n.* —*See* EROTICISM, SENSUALITY (1).

sexism *n.* Discrimination based on gender ▸ discrimination, intolerance, prejudice. [*Compare* HATE.]

sexist *adj.* ▸ bigoted, discriminatory, prejudiced. [*Compare* INTOLERANT.]

sexless *adj.* —*See* ANDROGYNOUS.

sexlessness *n.* The quality of being androgynous ▸ androgyny, epicenism, gender-neutrality. [*Compare* EFFEMINACY, MASCULINITY.]

sexual *adj.* Employed in reproduction ▸ reproductive. —*See also* EROTIC, SENSUAL (2).

sexuality *n.* —*See* EROTICISM, SENSUALITY (1).

sexy *adj.* —*See* DESIRABLE, EROTIC, LASCIVIOUS, SEDUCTIVE, SENSUAL (2).

shabby *adj.* Showing signs of wear and tear or neglect ▸ bedraggled, broken-down, decayed, decaying, decrepit, deteriorated, dilapidated, dingy, down-at-heel, faded, frayed, mangy, ragged, raggedy, ramshackle, ruinous, rundown, scrubby, scruffy, seedy, shoddy, sleazy, tatterdemalion, tattered, tatty, threadbare, tumbledown, worn, worn-out. *Informal:* tacky. *Slang:* ratty. *Idioms:* all the worse for wear, gone to pot (*or* seed),

deteriorated; seedy. 3. Disgraceful; mean: *shabby treatment.* **—shab′bi·ly** *adv.* **—shab′bi·ness** *n.*

shack (shăk) ▸ *n.* A small, crudely built cabin.

shack·le (shăk′əl) ▸ *n.* 1. A metal fastening, usu. one of a pair, for encircling and confining the ankle or wrist of a prisoner or captive; fetter; manacle. 2. Something that confines or restrains. ▸ *v.* **-led, -ling.** 1. To confine with shackles. 2. To restrict.

shad (shăd) ▸ *n., pl.* **shad** or **shads.** A herringlike food fish that swims up streams from marine waters to spawn.

shade (shād) ▸ *n.* 1. Light diminished in intensity; partial darkness. 2. An area or space of partial darkness. 3. Cover or shelter from the sun or its rays. 4. Any of various devices used to screen light or heat. 5. **shades** *Slang* Sunglasses. 6. The degree to which a color is mixed with black or is decreasingly illuminated. 7. A slight variation; nuance. 8. A small amount; trace. 9. A disembodied spirit; ghost. ▸ *v.* **shad·ed, shad·ing.** 1. To screen from light or heat. 2. To represent degrees of shade or shadow in. 3. To vary by slight degrees.

shad·ow (shăd′ō) ▸ *n.* 1. An area that is partially or totally unilluminated because of the interception of radiation by an opaque object. 2. The rough image cast by an object blocking rays of illumination. 3. A cause or feeling of gloom or unhappiness. 4. A shaded area in a picture. 5. A phantom; ghost. 6. A constant companion. 7. A faint indication. 8. A remnant. 9. A trace. ▸ *v.* 1. To cast a shadow on; shade. 2. To make gloomy or dark. 3. To represent vaguely or mysteriously. 4. To shade (a painting). 5. To follow, esp. in secret; trail. ▸ *adj.* Not having official status: *a shadow government.* **—shad′ow·er** *n.* **—shad′ow·i·ness** *n.* **—shad′ow·y** *adj.*

shad·ow·box (shăd′ō-bŏks′) ▸ *v.* To spar with an imaginary opponent. **—shad′ow·box′ing** *n.*

shad·y (shā′dē) ▸ *adj.* **-i·er, -i·est.** 1. Full of shade. 2. Of dubious character or honesty; questionable. **—shad′i·ly** *adv.* **—shad′i·ness** *n.*

shaft (shăft) ▸ *n.* 1a. The long narrow body of a spear or arrow. b. A spear or arrow. 2. A satirical barb. 3. A ray or beam of light. 4. A long handle, as of certain tools. 5. A column or columnlike part. 6a. A long cylindrical bar or pole. b. A drive shaft. 7. A long, often vertical passage or duct: *an elevator shaft.* ▸ *v. Slang* To treat in a harsh, unfair way.

shag (shăg) ▸ *n.* 1. A tangle or mass, esp. of matted hair. 2. Cloth having a coarse, long nap. 3. A rug with a thick, rough pile.

shag·gy (shăg′ē) ▸ *adj.* **-gi·er, -gi·est.** 1. Having long rough hair or wool. 2. Bushy and matted. 3. Poorly groomed; unkempt. **—shag′gi·ness** *n.*

shah (shä) ▸ *n.* Used formerly as a title for the hereditary monarch of Iran.

shake (shāk) ▸ *v.* **shook** (shŏŏk), **shak·en** (shā′kən), **shak·ing.** 1. To move or cause to move to and fro with short jerky movements. 2. To tremble, vibrate, or rock. 3. To cause to waver or become unstable. 4. To remove or dislodge by or as if by jerky movements. 5. To brandish or wave. 6. To clasp (hands) in greeting or leave-taking or as a sign of agreement. ***—phrasal verbs:*** **shake down** *Slang* 1. To extort money from. 2. *Slang* To make a thorough search of. **shake off** To free oneself from. **shake up** 1. To unnerve; shock. 2. To rearrange drastically. ▸ *n.* 1. The act or an instance of shaking. 2. See **milk shake.** 3. **shakes** *Informal* Uncontrollable trembling. ***—idioms:*** **no great shakes** *Slang* Unexceptional; ordinary. **shake a leg** *Informal* To hurry.

shake·down (shāk′doun′) ▸ *n.* 1. *Slang* Extortion of money, as by blackmail. 2. *Slang* A thorough search. 3. A period of appraisal followed by adjustments to improve efficiency or functioning. ▸ *adj.* Serving to test performance: *a shakedown cruise.*

shak·er (shā′kər) ▸ *n.* 1. One that impels or encourages action. 2. A container used for shaking. 3. **Shaker** A member of a Christian group practicing communal living and observing celibacy.

Shake·speare (shāk′spîr), **William** (1564–1616) ▸ English playwright and poet. **—Shake·spear′e·an, Shake·spear′i·an** *adj. & n.*

shake·up (shāk′ŭp′) ▸ *n.* A thorough reorganization.

shak·o (shăk′ō, shā′kō, shä′-) ▸ *n., pl.* **-os** or **-oes.** A stiff cylindrical military dress hat with a short visor and a plume.

shak·y (shā′kē) ▸ *adj.* **-i·er, -i·est.** 1. Trembling or quivering. 2. Unsteady or weak. 3. Precarious: *a shaky existence.* **—shak′i·ly** *adv.* **—shak′i·ness** *n.*

shale (shāl) ▸ *n.* A rock composed of layers of claylike, fine-grained sediments. **—shal′ey** *adj.*

shale oil ▸ *n.* A crude oil obtained from oil shale by heating and distillation.

shall (shăl) ▸ *aux.v., p.t.* **should** (shŏŏd). Used before a

THESAURUS

past cure (*or* hope). [*Compare* MISERABLE, SHODDY, TERRIBLE.] *—See also* BAD (1), OFFENSIVE (1).

shack *n.* *—See* HUT.

shackle *n.* *—See* BOND (1).

shackle *v.* *—See* HAMPER[1].

shade *n.* 1. A slight variation between nearly identical entities ▸ gradation, hue, nicety, nuance, subtlety. 2. A slight amount or indication ▸ breath, dash, ghost, hair, hint, intimation, semblance, shadow, soupçon, streak, suggestion, suspicion, taste, tinge, touch, trace, whiff, whisper. *Informal:* whisker. [*Compare* BIT[1].] 3. Comparative darkness that results from the blocking of light rays ▸ penumbra, shadiness, shadow, umbra. [*Compare* DARK, TWILIGHT.] *—See also* COLOR (1), GHOST.

shade *v.* 1. To shelter, especially from light ▸ screen, shadow. 2. To make dark or darker ▸ adumbrate, darken, gloom, overcast, overshadow, shadow. [*Compare* OBSCURE.] 3. To make a slight reduction in a price ▸ shave, trim. *—See also* CHANGE (1).

shaded *adj.* *—See* SHADY (2).

shadiness *n.* Comparative darkness that results from the blocking of light rays ▸ penumbra, shade, shadow, umbra. [*Compare* DARK, TWILIGHT.] *—See also* DISHONESTY (2).

shadow *n.* 1. Comparative darkness that results from the blocking of light rays ▸ penumbra, shade, shadiness, umbra. [*Compare* DARK, TWILIGHT.] 2. An agent assigned to observe and report on another ▸ watcher. *Informal:* tail. [*Compare* DETECTIVE.] *—See also* GHOST, SHADE (2).

shadow *v.* To shelter, especially from light ▸ screen, shade. *—See also* FOLLOW (3), OBSCURE, SHADE (2).

shadowy *adj.* *—See* DARK (1), SHADY (2), UNCLEAR.

shady *adj.* 1. Of doubtful honesty or character ▸ doubtful, dubious, equivocal, left-handed, questionable, suspect, suspicious, uncertain, untrustworthy. *Informal:* fishy. [*Compare* DISHONEST, ILLEGAL, UNDERHAND.] 2. Full of or affording shade ▸ dappled, leafy, shaded, shadowy, umbrageous. [*Compare* GLOOMY.] *—See also* DARK (1).

shaft *n.* *—See* BEAM (1), COLUMN, ROD.

shaggy *adj.* *—See* HAIRY.

shake *v.* 1. To move to and fro in short, jerky movements ▸ quake, quaver, quiver, shiver, shudder, switch, tremble, twitter, vibrate. [*Compare* BUMP.] 2. To cause to move to and fro with short, jerky movements ▸ jar, jiggle, joggle. [*Compare* JERK.] *—See also* AGITATE (1), DISMAY, DISTURB, LOSE (3), RID, SWAY.

shake down *v. Slang* To examine a person or someone's personal effects in order to find something lost or concealed ▸ frisk, inspect, pat down, search. *Idiom:* do a body search of. *—See also* EXTORT.

shake off *v.* *—See* LOSE (3), RID.

shake up *v.* *—See* AGITATE (2), OVERHAUL.

shake *n. Informal* A shaking of the earth ▸ earthquake, quake, seism, temblor, tremor. *—See also* TREMOR (2).

shakedown *n. Slang* A thorough search of a place or persons ▸ frisk, search. *—See also* TEST (1).

shaken or **shaken-up** *adj.* *—See* ANXIOUS.

shakes *n.* *—See* JITTERS.

shakeup *n.* A thorough or drastic reorganization ▸ overhaul, reengineering, reshuffling. *Informal:* housecleaning. [*Compare* RENEWAL, REVOLUTION.]

shakiness *n.* *—See* INSTABILITY.

shaky *adj.* *—See* IMPLAUSIBLE, INSECURE (2), TREMULOUS.

verb in the infinitive to show: **a.** Simple futurity: *We shall arrive tomorrow.* **b.** An order, promise, or obligation: *You shall leave now.* **c.** Inevitability: *That day shall come.*

shal·lot (shăl′ət, shə-lŏt′) ▸ *n.* **1.** A type of onion with pear-shaped bulbs. **2.** The mild-flavored edible bulb of this plant.

shal·low (shăl′ō) ▸ *adj.* **-er, -est.** **1.** Measuring little from bottom to top or surface; lacking physical depth. **2.** Lacking depth of intellect, emotion, or knowledge. ▸ *n.* often **shallows** A part of a body of water of little depth; shoal. **—shal′low·ly** *adv.* **—shal′low·ness** *n.*

sha·lom (shä-lōm′, shə-) ▸ *interj.* Used as a greeting or farewell.

shalt (shălt) ▸ *aux.v. Archaic* 2nd pers. sing. pr.t. of **shall.**

sham (shăm) ▸ *n.* **1.** Something false or empty purported to be genuine. **2.** One who assumes a false character; impostor. ▸ *adj.* Not genuine; fake. ▸ *v.* **shammed, sham·ming.** To put on a false appearance; feign. **—sham′mer** *n.*

sha·man (shä′mən, shā′-) ▸ *n.* A member of certain tribal societies who mediates between the visible and the spirit worlds for purposes of healing, divination, and control over natural events. **—sha′man·ism** *n.* **—sha′man·is′tic** *adj.*

sham·ble (shăm′bəl) ▸ *v.* **-bled, -bling.** To walk in an awkward, lazy, or unsteady manner, shuffling the feet. **—sham′ble** *n.*

sham·bles (shăm′bəlz) ▸ *pl.n. (takes sing. v.)* A scene or condition of complete disorder or ruin.

shame (shām) ▸ *n.* **1a.** A painful emotion caused by a strong sense of guilt, embarrassment, unworthiness, or disgrace. **b.** Capacity for such a feeling: *Have you no shame?* **2.** One that brings dishonor, disgrace, or condemnation. **3.** Disgrace; ignominy. **4.** A great disappointment. ▸ *v.* **shamed, sham·ing.** **1.** To cause to feel shame. **2.** To bring dishonor or disgrace on. **3.** To force by making ashamed: *He was shamed into an apology.* **—shame′ful** *adj.* **—shame′ful·ly** *adv.* **—shame′ful·ness** *n.*

shame·faced (shām′fāst′) ▸ *adj.* **1.** Indicative of shame: *a shamefaced excuse.* **2.** Shy; bashful. **—shame′fac′ed·ly** (-fā′sĭd-lē) *adv.* **—shame′fac′ed·ness** *n.*

shame·less (shām′lĭs) ▸ *adj.* **1.** Feeling no shame or disgrace. **2.** Brazen; blatant: *a shameless lie.* **—shame′less·ly** *adv.* **—shame′less·ness** *n.*

sham·my (shăm′ē) ▸ *n.* Var. of **chamois** 2.

sham·poo (shăm-po͞o′) ▸ *n., pl.* **-poos.** **1.** A preparation of soap or detergent used to wash the hair and scalp. **2.** Any of various cleaning agents for rugs or upholstery. **3.** The act or process of washing or cleaning with shampoo. **—sham·poo′** *v.*

sham·rock (shăm′rŏk′) ▸ *n.* A plant, such as a clover, having leaves with three leaflets, considered the national emblem of Ireland.

Shan·dong (shän′dông′) also **Shan·tung** (shăn′tŭng′, shän′to͝ong′) ▸ A province of E China bordered by the Bo Hai and the Yellow Sea.

shang·hai (shăng-hī′, shăng′hī′) ▸ *v.* **-haied, -hai·ing.** **1.** To kidnap (a man) for service aboard a ship, esp. after drugging him. **2.** To compel (someone) to do something, esp. by fraud or force.

Shang·hai (shăng-hī′, shäng′-) ▸ A city of E China at the mouth of the Chang Jiang R. SE of Nanjing.

Shan·gri-la (shăng′grĭ-lä′) ▸ *n.* An imaginary, remote paradise on earth.

shank (shăngk) ▸ *n.* **1.** The part of the human leg between the knee and ankle or the corresponding part in other vertebrates. **2.** A cut of meat from the leg of an animal. **3.** The section of a tool or instrument connecting the functioning part and handle. **4.** A long narrow part; shaft.

shan't (shănt, shänt) ▸ Shall not.

shan·ty (shăn′tē) ▸ *n., pl.* **-ties.** A shack.

shape (shāp) ▸ *n.* **1.** The characteristic surface configuration of a thing; form. **2.** The contour of a person's body; figure. **3.** A definite, distinctive form. **4.** A form or condition in which something may exist or appear. ▸ *v.* **shaped, shap·ing.** **1.** To give a particular form to. **2.** To take a definite form; develop. ***—phrasal verb:*** **shape up 1.** *Informal* To turn out; develop. **2.** To improve. **—shaped** *adj.* **—shap′er** *n.*

shape·less (shāp′lĭs) ▸ *adj.* Lacking a definite shape. **—shape′less·ly** *adv.* **—shape′less·ness** *n.*

shape·ly (shāp′lē) ▸ *adj.* **-li·er, -li·est.** Having a pleasing shape. **—shape′li·ness** *n.*

shard (shärd) ▸ *n.* **1.** A piece of broken pottery, esp. one found in an archaeological dig. **2.** A fragment.

share[1] (shâr) ▸ *n.* **1.** A part or portion belonging to a person or group. **2.** An equitable portion. **3.** Any of the equal parts into which the capital stock of a corporation or company is divided. ▸ *v.* **shared, shar·ing.** **1.** To divide and parcel out in shares; apportion. **2.** To use or experience in common. **—shar′er** *n.*

share[2] (shâr) ▸ *n.* A plowshare.

share·crop·per (shâr′krŏp′ər) ▸ *n.* A tenant farmer who gives a share of the crops raised to the landlord as rent.

share·hold·er (shâr′hōl′dər) ▸ *n.* One that owns or holds shares of stock; stockholder. **—share′hold′ing** *n.*

share·ware (shâr′wâr′) ▸ *n.* Copyrighted software that is available free of charge on a trial basis.

shark (shärk) ▸ *n.* **1.** Any of numerous often large and voracious marine fishes having a cartilaginous skeleton and tough skin covered with small toothlike scales. **2.** A ruthless, greedy, or dishonest person.

shark·skin (shärk′skĭn′) ▸ *n.* **1.** A shark's skin or leather made from it. **2.** A synthetic fabric having a smooth shiny surface.

sharp (shärp) ▸ *adj.* **-er, -est.** **1.** Having a thin edge or a fine point. **2a.** Having clear form and distinct detail. **b.** Not rounded or blunt; pointed: *a sharp nose.* **3.** Abrupt or acute: *a sharp turn.* **4.** Shrewd; astute. **5.** Crafty or deceitful. **6.** Alert: *a sharp eye.* **7.** Harsh or biting. **8.** Intense; severe: *a*

THESAURUS

shallow *adj.* —*See* SUPERFICIAL.

sham *n.* —*See* ACT (2), COUNTERFEIT, FAKE, MOCKERY (2).

sham *adj.* —*See* COUNTERFEIT.

sham *v.* —*See* ACT (2).

shamble *v.* —*See* TRUDGE.

shambles *n.* —*See* [illegible] (1).

shame *n.* A great disappointment or regrettable fact ▸ crime, pity. *Slang:* bummer. *Idiom:* a crying shame. —*See also* DISGRACE, PENITENCE.

shame *v.* To cause to feel embarrassment, dishonor, and often guilt ▸ brand, mortify, reproach, stigmatize. *Idioms:* put to shame, put to the blush. [*Compare* BELITTLE, DENIGRATE, EMBARRASS, HUMBLE.] —*See also* DISGRACE.

shameful *adj.* —*See* DEPLORABLE, DISGRACEFUL.

shamefulness *n.* —*See* INFAMY.

shameless *adj.* —*See* IMPUDENT, UNSCRUPULOUS.

shamelessness *n.* —*See* IMPUDENCE.

shanty *n.* —*See* HUT.

shape *n.* A state of sound readiness ▸ condition, fettle, fitness, form, kilter, order, repair, trim. —*See also* CONSTITUTION, FORM (1).

shape *v.* —*See* ADAPT, FORM (1), MAKE.

shapeless *adj.* Having no distinct shape ▸ amorphous, formless, inchoate, unformed, unshaped, unstructured.

shapely *adj.* Having a full, voluptuous figure ▸ big-bosomed, bosomy, buxom, curvaceous, curvy, full-bosomed, full-figured, well-developed, well-endowed, zaftig. *Informal:* built. *Slang:* stacked.

shard *n.* —*See* BIT[1] (1), END (3).

share *n.* One's duty or responsibility in a common effort ▸ function, part, piece, role. [*Compare* FUNCTION.] —*See also* ALLOTMENT.

share *v.* To tell in confidence ▸ breathe, confide, unbosom, whisper. [*Compare* COMMUNICATE, REVEAL, SAY.] —*See also* CONTRIBUTE (2), DISTRIBUTE.

shared *adj.* —*See* COMMON (2), MUTUAL.

sharing *n.* The act or fact of participating ▸ engagement, involvement, partaking, participation. —*See also* DISTRIBUTION (1).

sharp *adj.* **1.** Having a fine edge, as for cutting ▸ honed, keen, keen-edged, knife-edged, razor-edged, razor-sharp, sharpened, whetted. **2.** Clearly defined; not ambiguous ▸ clear, distinct, unambiguous, unequivocal, unmistakable, well-defined. [*Compare* APPARENT, DEFINITE.] **3.** Marked by pain that is severe or intense ▸ acute, biting,

sharp pain. **9.** Sudden and shrill. **10.** *Mus.* **a.** Raised in pitch by a semitone: *a C sharp.* **b.** Being above the proper pitch. **11.** *Informal* Attractive or stylish. ▸ *adv.* **1.** In a sharp manner. **2.** Punctually; exactly. **3.** *Mus.* Above the proper pitch. ▸ *n.* **1.** *Mus.* **a.** A note or tone raised one semitone above its normal pitch. **b.** A sign (#) indicating this. **2.** A shrewd cheater. **—sharp′ly** *adv.* **—sharp′ness** *n.*

sharp·en (shär′pən) ▸ *v.* To make or become sharp or sharper. **—sharp′en·er** *n.*

sharp·shoot·er (shärp′sho͞o′tər) ▸ *n.* One who is highly proficient at shooting.

Shas·ta (shăs′tə), **Mount** ▸ A volcanic peak, 4,319.4 m (14,162 ft), of the Cascade Range in N CA.

shat·ter (shăt′ər) ▸ *v.* **1.** To break or burst suddenly into pieces, as with a violent blow. **2.** To disable or destroy.

shat·ter·proof (shăt′ər-pro͞of′) ▸ *adj.* Resistant to shattering.

shave (shāv) ▸ *v.* **shaved, shaved** or **shav·en** (shā′vən), **shav·ing. 1.** To remove the beard or other body hair (from) with a razor or shaver. **2.** To remove thin slices of or from. **3.** To come close to or graze in passing. ▸ *n.* The act, process, or result of shaving.

shav·er (shā′vər) ▸ *n.* **1.** A device, esp. an electric razor, used in shaving. **2.** *Informal* A small child, esp. a boy.

shav·ing (shā′vĭng) ▸ *n.* A thin slice or sliver, as of wood.

Shaw (shô), **George Bernard** (1856–1950) ▸ Irish-born British playwright; 1925 Nobel.

shawl (shôl) ▸ *n.* A piece of cloth worn as a covering for the head, neck, and shoulders.

Shaw·nee (shô-nē′) ▸ *n., pl.* **-nee** or **-nees. 1.** A member of a Native American people formerly of the central Ohio Valley, now in Oklahoma. **2.** Their Algonquian language.

Shaw·wal (shə-wäl′) ▸ *n.* The 10th month of the Muslim calendar.

she (shē) ▸ *pron.* **1.** Used to refer to the female previously mentioned or implied. **2.** Used in place of *it* to refer to certain inanimate things, such as ships and nations. ▸ *n.* A female animal or person: *Is the cat a she?*

sheaf (shēf) ▸ *n., pl.* **sheaves** (shēvz). **1.** A bound bundle of cut stalks, esp. of grain. **2.** A collection of items held or bound together.

shear (shîr) ▸ *v.* **sheared, sheared** or **shorn** (shôrn), **shear·ing. 1.** To remove (fleece or hair) by cutting or clipping. **2.** To remove the hair or fleece from. **3.** To cut with or as if with shears: *shear a hedge.* **4.** To divest or deprive. ▸ *n.* also **shears 1.** A pair of scissors. **2.** Any of various implements or machines that cut with a scissorlike action. **—shear′er** *n.*

sheath (shēth) ▸ *n., pl.* **sheaths** (shē*th*z, shēths). **1a.** A case for a blade, as of a sword or knife. **b.** Any of various similar coverings. **2.** *Biol.* An enveloping tubular structure, as the base of a grass leaf. **3.** A close-fitting dress. **—sheath** *v.*

sheathe (shē*th*) ▸ *v.* **sheathed, sheath·ing.** To insert into or provide with a sheath.

sheath·ing (shē′*th*ĭng) ▸ *n.* A layer esp. of boards applied to a building to serve as a base for weatherproof cladding.

she·bang (shə-băng′) ▸ *n.* *Slang* A situation or organization: *ran the whole shebang.*

She·bat (shə-bät′, -vät′) ▸ *n.* Var. of **Shevat.**

shed[1] (shĕd) ▸ *v.* **shed, shed·ding. 1.** To pour forth: *shed tears.* **2.** To radiate; cast: *shed light.* **3.** To repel without allowing penetration: *shed water.* **4.** To lose by natural process: *a snake shedding its skin.* ***—idiom:* shed blood** To kill. **—shed′der** *n.*

shed[2] (shĕd) ▸ *n.* A small roofed structure for storage or shelter.

she'd (shēd) ▸ **1.** She had. **2.** She would.

sheen (shēn) ▸ *n.* Glistening brightness; luster.

sheep (shēp) ▸ *n., pl.* **sheep. 1.** Any of various usu. horned ruminant mammals raised for wool, meat, or skin. **2.** One who is easily swayed or led.

sheep·dog also **sheep dog** (shēp′dôg′, -dŏg′) ▸ *n.* A dog bred or trained to herd sheep.

sheep·ish (shē′pĭsh) ▸ *adj.* Embarrassed, as by consciousness of a fault: *a sheepish grin.* **—sheep′ish·ly** *adv.*

sheep·skin (shēp′skĭn′) ▸ *n.* **1.** The tanned skin of a sheep, with or without the fleece. **2.** *Informal* A diploma.

sheer[1] (shîr) ▸ *v.* To swerve from a course. **—sheer** *n.*

sheer[2] (shîr) ▸ *adj.* **-er, -est. 1.** Thin and transparent: *sheer curtains.* **2.** Undiluted; pure: *sheer happiness.* **3.** Almost perpendicular: *a sheer cliff.*

sheet[1] (shēt) ▸ *n.* **1.** A rectangular piece of fabric serving as a basic article of bedding. **2.** A broad, thin, usu. rectangular piece, as of paper or metal.

sheet[2] (shēt) ▸ *n.* *Naut.* **1.** A rope or chain attached to a lower corner of a sail, serving to move or extend it. **2. sheets** The spaces at either end of an open boat in front of and behind the seats.

sheet metal ▸ *n.* Metal rolled into a relatively thin sheet. **—sheet′-met′al** *adj.*

sheet music ▸ *n.* Musical compositions printed on unbound sheets of paper.

Sheet·rock (shēt′rŏk′) ▸ A trademark for plasterboard.

sheik also **sheikh** (shēk, shāk) ▸ *n.* The leader of an Arab or Muslim tribe, village, or family. **—sheik′dom** *n.*

shek·el (shĕk′əl) ▸ *n.* **1a.** Any of several ancient units of weight, esp. a Hebrew unit equal to about a half ounce. **b.** The chief silver coin of the ancient Hebrews. **2. shekels** *Slang* Money.

shelf (shĕlf) ▸ *n., pl.* **shelves** (shĕlvz). **1.** A flat, usu. rectangular structure, as of wood or metal, fixed horizontally to a wall or in a frame and used to hold or store objects. **2.** Something, such as a projecting ledge of rock, that resembles a shelf.

shelf life ▸ *n.* The length of time a product may be stored without deteriorating.

shell (shĕl) ▸ *n.* **1a.** The usu. hard outer covering that encases certain organisms, such as mollusks and insects. **b.** A similar outer covering on an egg, fruit, or nut. **2.** Something resembling a shell, esp.: **a.** An external, usu. hard, protective cover. **b.** A framework or exterior, as of a building. **c.** A thin layer of pastry. **3.** A long narrow racing boat propelled by rowers. **4.** A projectile or piece of ammunition. **5.** *Phys.* **a.** Any of the hypothetical spherical surfaces centered on the nucleus of an atom containing electrons. **b.** An analogous pattern of protons and neutrons within a nucleus. **6.** *Comp. Sci.* A program that works with the operating system as a command processor. ▸ *v.* **1.**

THESAURUS

gnawing, knifelike, piercing, shooting, stabbing, throbbing. [*Compare* BITTER, INTENSE, SEVERE.] *—See also* ABRUPT (2), ARTFUL, BITING, CLEVER (1), CRITICAL (2), FASHIONABLE, POINTED, SOUR, SPICY, STEEP[1] (1).

sharpen *v.* To give a sharp edge to ▸ edge, file, grind, hone, strop, whet. *—See also* INTENSIFY.

sharper *n.* *—See* CHEAT (2).

sharpness *n.* *—See* DISCERNMENT, EDGE.

sharp-tongued *adj.* *—See* ABUSIVE, BITING.

sharp-witted *adj.* *—See* CLEVER (1).

shatter *v.* *—See* BREAK (1), BREAK (2), DESTROY (1).

shave *v.* To make a slight reduction in a price ▸ shade, trim. *—See also* BRUSH[1], CUT (3).

shaving *n.* *—See* FLAKE.

shawl *n.* WRAP.

shawl *v.* *—See* CLOTHE.

shear *v.* *—See* CUT (3).

shears *n.* An implement used for cutting or pruning ▸ clippers, cutters, loppers, nippers, pruner, scissors, snips, snippers.

sheath or **sheathing** *n.* *—See* SKIN (2).

sheathe *v.* *—See* FACE (2).

shed[1] *v.* **1.** To send out heat, light, or energy ▸ cast (out), emit, irradiate, project, radiate, send forth, send out, throw (out). [*Compare* BEAM, EMIT.] **2.** To cast off by a natural process ▸ exuviate, molt, slough, throw off. *—See also* DISCARD, FLAKE.

shed[2] *n.* *—See* HUT.

sheen *n.* *—See* GLOSS[1].

sheer[1] *v.* *—See* SWERVE.

sheer[2] *adj.* Thin, fine, and light ▸ airy, diaphanous, ethereal, filmy, gauzy, gossamer, gossamery, transparent, vaporous, vapory. *—See also* PURE, STEEP[1] (1), UTTER[2].

sheet *n.* A document used in applying, as for a job ▸ application, form, paper. *—See also* COAT (2), SKIN (2).

sheik *n.* *—See* CHIEF.

shell *n.* *—See* FRAME, SKIN (3).

shell *v.* *—See* BARRAGE, SKIN.

To remove the shell of; shuck. **2.** To fire shells at; bombard. ***—phrasal verb:*** **shell out** *Informal* To pay (money).

she'll (shēl) ▸ **1.** She will. **2.** She shall.

shel·lac (shə-lăk′) ▸ *n.* **1.** A purified lac formed into flakes and used in varnishes, paints, inks, and sealants. **2.** A thin varnish made by dissolving this substance in denatured alcohol. ▸ *v.* **-lacked, -lack·ing. 1.** To coat or finish with shellac. **2.** *Slang* To defeat decisively.

Shel·ley (shĕl′ē), **Mary Wollstonecraft Godwin** (1797–1851) ▸ British writer.

Shelley, Percy Bysshe (1792–1822) ▸ British romantic poet.

shell·fire (shĕl′fīr′) ▸ *n.* The shooting of artillery shells.

shell·fish (shĕl′fĭsh′) ▸ *n.* An aquatic animal, such as a mollusk, having a shell or shell-like covering. **—shell′fish′ing** *n.*

shell shock ▸ *n.* Any of various acute neuroses due to trauma suffered under fire in modern warfare. **—shell′-shocked′** *adj.*

shel·ter (shĕl′tər) ▸ *n.* **1a.** Something that provides cover or protection, as from the weather. **b.** A refuge; haven. **c.** An establishment that provides temporary housing for homeless people. **2.** The state of being covered or protected. ▸ *v.* **1.** To provide shelter for. **2.** To take cover or refuge.

shelve (shĕlv) ▸ *v.* **shelved, shelv·ing. 1.** To place on a shelf. **2.** To put aside; postpone.

shelves (shĕlvz) ▸ *n.* Pl. of **shelf.**

shelv·ing (shĕl′vĭng) ▸ *n.* A set of shelves.

Shen·an·do·ah Valley (shĕn′ən-dō′ə) ▸ A valley of N VA between the Allegheny Mts. and the Blue Ridge.

she·nan·i·gan (shə-năn′ĭ-gən) ▸ *n.* *Informal* **1.** An underhanded act. **2.** often **shenanigans** Mischief.

Shen·yang (shŭn′yäng′) ▸ A city of NE China ENE of Beijing.

shep·herd (shĕp′ərd) ▸ *n.* One who herds, guards, and tends sheep. ▸ *v.* To guard or tend as or like a shepherd.

shep·herd·ess (shĕp′ər-dĭs) ▸ *n.* A girl or woman who herds or guards sheep.

shep·herd's pie (shĕp′ərdz) ▸ *n.* A meat pie baked under a crust of mashed potatoes.

sheq·el (shĕk′əl) ▸ *n., pl.* **sheq·al·im** (shĕk′ə-lĭm). See **currency** table in Appendix.

sher·bet (shûr′bĭt) also **sher·bert** (-bûrt′) ▸ *n.* A frozen dessert made of fruit juice, sugar, and water with milk, egg white, or gelatin.

sher·iff (shĕr′ĭf) ▸ *n.* The chief law enforcement officer in a US county.

Sher·man (shûr′mən), **Roger** (1721–93) ▸ Amer. Revolutionary patriot and politician.

Sherman, William Tecumseh (1820–91) ▸ Amer. Union general.

Sher·pa (shûr′pə) ▸ *n., pl.* **-pa** or **-pas.** A member of a Tibetan people living in Nepal and Sikkim.

sher·ry (shĕr′ē) ▸ *n., pl.* **-ries.** A fortified Spanish wine.

Sher·wood Forest (shûr′wo͝od′) ▸ A forest of central England; site of the legendary exploits of Robin Hood.

Shet·land (shĕt′lənd) ▸ *n.* A fine yarn made from the wool of sheep raised in the Shetland Islands.

Shetland Islands ▸ An archipelago of N Scotland in the Atlantic NE of the Orkney Is.

Shetland pony ▸ *n.* A small sturdy pony of a breed originating in the Shetland Islands.

She·vat (shə-vät′) also **She·bat** (shə-bät′, -vät′) ▸ *n.* A month of the Jewish calendar.

shi·at·su (shē-ät′so͞o) ▸ *n.* Therapeutic massage with the thumbs and palms of those areas of the body used in acupuncture.

shib·bo·leth (shĭb′ə-lĭth, -lĕth′) ▸ *n.* A word or phrase closely identified with a particular group or cause.

shied[1] (shīd) ▸ *v.* P.t. and p.part. of **shy**[1].

shied[2] (shīd) ▸ *v.* P.t. and p.part. of **shy**[2].

shield (shēld) ▸ *n.* **1.** A broad piece of armor strapped to the arm for protection against weapons. **2.** A protective device or structure. **3.** Something that resembles a shield. ▸ *v.* **1.** To protect or defend with or as if with a shield; guard. **2.** To cover up; conceal. **—shield′er** *n.*

shi·er (shī′ər) ▸ *adj.* Comp. of **shy**[1].

shi·est (shī′ĭst) ▸ *adj.* Superl. of **shy**[1].

shift (shĭft) ▸ *v.* **1.** To exchange (one thing) for another: *shifted assignments.* **2.** To move or transfer from one place or position to another. **3.** To change position, direction, or place. **4.** To change (gears), as in an automobile. **5.** To provide for one's own needs; get along. ▸ *n.* **1.** A change from one person or configuration to another; substitution. **2a.** A group of workers that relieve another on a regular schedule. **b.** The working period of such a group: *the night shift.* **3.** A change in direction or position. **4.** A gearshift. **5a.** A loosely fitting dress that hangs straight from the shoulder. **b.** A woman's undergarment; slip or chemise. **—shift′er** *n.*

shift·less (shĭft′lĭs) ▸ *adj.* Lacking ambition or purpose. **—shift′less·ness** *n.*

shift·y (shĭf′tē) ▸ *adj.* **-i·er, -i·est.** Suggestive of deceitful character; evasive or untrustworthy. **—shift′i·ly** *adv.* **—shift′i·ness** *n.*

Shi·ite also **Shi·'ite** (shē′īt′) ▸ *n.* A member of the branch of Islam that regards the caliph Ali and his descendants as the legitimate successors to Muhammad. **—Shi′ism** *n.* **—Shi′ite′** *adj.*

shil·in (shĭl′ĭn) ▸ *n.* See **currency** table in Appendix.

shill (shĭl) ▸ *n.* *Slang* One who poses as a satisfied customer to dupe bystanders into participating in a swindle. **—shill** *v.*

shil·le·lagh (shə-lā′lē, -lə) ▸ *n.* A cudgel of oak or other hardwood.

shil·ling (shĭl′ĭng) ▸ *n.* See **currency** table in Appendix.

shil·ly-shal·ly (shĭl′ē-shăl′ē) ▸ *v.* **-lied** (-lēd), **-ly·ing. 1.** To procrastinate; dawdle. **2.** To vacillate. **—shil′ly-shal′li·er** *n.*

shim (shĭm) ▸ *n.* A thin piece or wedge used to make something level or to adjust something to fit properly. **—shim** *v.*

shim·mer (shĭm′ər) ▸ *v.* To shine with a flickering light. ▸ *n.* A flickering or tremulous light; glimmer. **—shim′mer·ing·ly** *adv.* **—shim′mer·y** *adj.*

shim·my (shĭm′ē) ▸ *n., pl.* **-mies. 1.** Abnormal vibration or wobbling, as of the wheels of an automobile. **2.** A chemise. ▸ *v.* **-mied, -my·ing.** To vibrate or wobble.

shin (shĭn) ▸ *n.* The front part of the leg between the knee and the ankle. ▸ *v.* **shinned, shin·ning.** To climb (e.g., a pole) by gripping and pulling alternately with the hands and legs.

shin·dig (shĭn′dĭg′) ▸ *n.* A festive party or celebration.

shine (shīn) ▸ *v.* **shone** (shōn) or **shined, shin·ing. 1.** To emit light. **2.** To reflect light; glint or glisten. **3.** To distinguish

THESAURUS

shell out *v.* —*See* SPEND (1).

shellac *v.* —*See* FINISH (1), OVERWHELM (1).

shellac *n.* —*See* FINISH.

shellacking *n.* —*See* DEFEAT.

shelter *n.* Dwellings in general ▸ housing, lodging. *Idiom:* a roof over one's head. [*Compare* HOME, HUT.] —*See also* COVER (1), HOME (3), REFUGE (1).

shelter *v.* To give refuge to ▸ harbor, haven, house, take in. [*Compare* DEFEND.]

shelve *v.* —*See* DEFER[1].

shenanigan *n.* —*See* PRANK[1], TRICK (1).

shenanigans *n.* —*See* MISCHIEF.

shepherd *n.* —*See* GUIDE.

shepherd *v.* —*See* GUIDE.

sheriff *n.* —*See* POLICE OFFICER.

sherlock *n.* —*See* DETECTIVE.

shield *n.* —*See* DEFENSE.

shield *v.* —*See* DEFEND (1).

shift *v.* **1.** To move or cause to move slightly ▸ budge, move, stir. **2.** To take turns ▸ alternate, interchange, rotate. —*See also* CHANGE (3), DISTURB, MOVE (2), TURN (2).

shift *n.* **1.** Occurrence in successive turns ▸ alternation, interchange, shift. **2.** An often sudden change or departure, as in a trend ▸ tack, turn, twist. [*Compare* DEVIATION.] —*See also* CHANGE (1), CHANGE (2), CONVERSION (1), DISPLACEMENT, DRESS (3), MAKESHIFT, TRANSITION, TURN (1).

shiftiness *n.* —*See* DECEIT, DISHONESTY (2).

shiftless *adj.* —*See* LAZY.

shiftlessness *n.* —*See* LAZINESS.

shifty *adj.* —*See* CAPRICIOUS, UNDERHAND.

shill *n.* —*See* CHEAT (2).

shilly-shally *v.* —*See* HESITATE.

shilly-shally *adj.* —*See* HESITANT.

shilly-shally *n.* —*See* HESITATION.

shimmer *v.* —*See* GLITTER.

shimmer *n.* —*See* GLITTER (1).

shin *v.* —*See* RUN (1).

shindig or **shindy** *n.* —*See* BLAST (3).

shine *v.* To be in one's prime ▸ flourish, flower. *Idioms:* cut a figure, have one's day in the sun, make a splash.

oneself; excel. **4.** To aim or cast the beam of (a light). **5.** To make glossy or bright by polishing. ▸ *n.* **1.** Brightness; radiance. **2.** A shoeshine. **3.** Fair weather: *rain or shine.* ***—idiom:*** **take a shine to** *Informal* To like spontaneously.

shin·er (shī′nər) ▸ *n.* **1.** *Slang* A black eye. **2.** Any of numerous small silvery fishes.

shin·gle[1] (shĭng′gəl) ▸ *n.* **1.** A thin oblong piece of material, such as wood, laid in overlapping rows to cover the roofs or sides of a house. **2.** *Informal* A small signboard, as one indicating a professional office. ▸ *v.* **1.** To cover (e.g., a roof) with shingles. **2.** To cut (hair) short and close to the head. **—shin′gler** *n.*

shin·gle[2] (shĭng′gəl) ▸ *n.* **1.** Beach gravel consisting of large smooth pebbles. **2.** A beach covered with such gravel.

shin·gles (shĭng′gəlz) ▸ *pl.n. (takes sing. or pl. v.)* An acute viral infection marked by skin eruption along a nerve path on one side of the body.

shin·ny (shĭn′ē) ▸ *v.* **-nied** (-nēd), **-ny·ing.** To shin: *shinny up a pole.*

Shin·to (shĭn′tō) ▸ *n.* A religion native to Japan, marked by worship of nature spirits and ancestors. **—Shin′to** *adj.* **—Shin′to·ism** *n.* **—Shin′to·ist** *adj. & n.*

shin·y (shī′nē) ▸ *adj.* **-i·er, -i·est.** Bright; glistening. **—shin′i·ness** *n.*

ship (shĭp) ▸ *n.* **1.** A large vessel built for deep-water navigation. **2.** A sailing vessel having three or more square-rigged masts. **3.** An aircraft or spacecraft. ▸ *v.* **shipped, ship·ping. 1.** To place or receive on board a ship. **2.** To cause to be transported; send. **3.** To take in (water) over the side of a ship. **—ship′per** *n.*

-ship ▸ *suff.* **1.** Quality or condition: *friendship.* **2.** Rank, status, or office: *professorship.* **3.** Art or skill: *penmanship.*

ship·board (shĭp′bôrd′) ▸ *n.* A ship.

ship·build·ing (shĭp′bĭl′dĭng) ▸ *n.* The business of designing and constructing ships. **—ship′build′er** *n.*

ship·mas·ter (shĭp′măs′tər) ▸ *n.* The officer in command of a merchant ship.

ship·mate (shĭp′māt′) ▸ *n.* A fellow sailor.

ship·ment (shĭp′mənt) ▸ *n.* **1.** The act of shipping goods. **2.** A quantity of goods or cargo shipped together.

ship·ping (shĭp′ĭng) ▸ *n.* **1.** The act or business of transporting goods. **2.** The body of ships belonging to one port or country.

ship·shape (shĭp′shāp′) ▸ *adj.* Orderly and neat; tidy. **—ship′-shape′** *adv.*

ship·wreck (shĭp′rĕk′) ▸ *n.* **1.** The destruction of a ship, as by storm or collision. **2.** The remains of a wrecked ship. ▸ *v.* To cause to suffer shipwreck.

ship·yard (shĭp′yärd′) ▸ *n.* A yard where ships are built or repaired.

shire (shīr) ▸ *n.* A division of Great Britain, equivalent to a county.

shirk (shûrk) ▸ *v.* To avoid or neglect (a duty or responsibility). **—shirk′er** *n.*

shirr (shûr) ▸ *v.* **1.** To gather (cloth) into parallel rows. **2.** To cook (eggs) by baking until set.

shirt (shûrt) ▸ *n.* **1.** A garment for the upper part of the body, usu. having a collar, sleeves, and a front opening. **2.** An undershirt.

shirt·waist (shûrt′wāst′) ▸ *n.* A woman's blouse or bodice that is styled like a tailored shirt.

shish ke·bab also **shish ke·bob** or **shish ka·bob** (shĭsh′ kə-bŏb′) ▸ *n.* A dish of pieces of seasoned meat and often vegetables roasted and served on skewers.

Shi·va (shē′və) ▸ *n.* A principal Hindu god, the destroyer and restorer of worlds.

shiv·er[1] (shĭv′ər) ▸ *v.* To shake, as with cold or fear; tremble. **—shiv′er** *n.* **—shiv′er·y** *adj.*

shiv·er[2] (shĭv′ər) ▸ *v.* To break into fragments or splinters.

Sho·ah (shō′ə) ▸ *n.* The mass murder of European Jews by the Nazis during World War II.

shoal[1] (shōl) ▸ *n.* **1.** A shallow. **2.** A sandbank or sandbar.

shoal[2] (shōl) ▸ *n.* **1.** A large group; crowd. **2.** A large school of fish.

shoat (shōt) ▸ *n.* A young pig.

shock[1] (shŏk) ▸ *n.* **1.** A violent collision or impact. **2.** A violent, unexpected disturbance of mental or emotional balance. **3.** A severe offense to one's sense of propriety or decency; outrage. **4.** A gen. temporary physiological reaction to severe trauma, usu. marked by loss of blood pressure and depression of vital processes. **5.** The sensation caused by an electric current passing through the body. ▸ *v.* **1.** To strike with sudden forceful impact. **2.** To disgust; offend. **3.** To induce a state of shock in (a person). **4.** To subject to an electric shock.

shock[2] (shŏk) ▸ *n.* **1.** A number of sheaves of grain stacked upright in a field for drying. **2.** A thick heavy mass: *a shock of white hair.*

shock absorber ▸ *n.* A device used to absorb mechanical shocks, esp. in a motor vehicle.

shock·er (shŏk′ər) ▸ *n.* One that startles or horrifies, as a sensational story.

shock·ing (shŏk′ĭng) ▸ *adj.* **1.** Highly disturbing emotionally. **2.** Highly offensive; distasteful. **—shock′ing·ly** *adv.*

shock therapy ▸ *n.* A treatment for mental disorders in which a convulsion is induced by electric current or drugs.

shock troops ▸ *pl.n.* Soldiers specially chosen, trained, and armed to lead an attack.

shock wave ▸ *n.* A large-amplitude compression wave, as that produced by an explosion or by supersonic motion of a body in a medium.

shod·dy (shŏd′ē) ▸ *adj.* **-di·er, -di·est. 1.** Made of or containing inferior material. **2.** Dishonest or unscrupulous. **3.** Cheaply imitative. **—shod′di·ly** *adv.* **—shod′di·ness** *n.*

shoe (sho͞o) ▸ *n.* **1.** A durable covering for the human foot. **2.** A horseshoe. **3.** The casing of a pneumatic tire. **4.** The part of a brake that presses against the wheel or drum to retard motion. ▸ *v.* **shod** (shŏd), **shod** or **shod·den** (shŏd′n), **shoe·ing.** To furnish or fit with shoes.

shoe·horn (sho͞o′hôrn′) ▸ *n.* A curved implement inserted at the heel to help put on a shoe. **—shoe′horn′** *v.*

shoe·lace (sho͞o′lās′) ▸ *n.* A string or cord used for lacing and fastening shoes.

shoe·mak·er (sho͞o′mā′kər) ▸ *n.* One that makes or repairs shoes. **—shoe′mak′ing** *n.*

shoe·string (sho͞o′strĭng′) ▸ *n.* **1.** See **shoelace. 2.** A small sum of money or capital used to launch a venture. ▸ *adj.* Cut long and slender: *shoestring potatoes.*

shoe·tree (sho͞o′trē′) ▸ *n.* A form made of inflexible material inserted into a shoe to preserve its shape.

THESAURUS

—See also BEAM, GLOSS[1].

shine *n.* *—See* GLOSS[1].

shiner *n. Slang* A bruise surrounding the eye ▸ black eye. *Informal:* mouse. [*Compare* BRUISE.]

shining *adj.* *—See* BRIGHT, GLORIOUS, GLOSSY.

shiny *adj.* *—See* BRIGHT, GLOSSY.

ship *n.* A conveyance that travels over water ▸ bark, barque, boat, craft, vessel, watercraft.

ship *v.* *—See* SEND (1).

shipment *n.* *—See* DELIVERY.

shipping *n.* *—See* TRANSPORTATION.

shipshape *adj.* *—See* NEAT.

shipwreck *v.* To damage, disable, or destroy a seacraft ▸ run aground, sink, wreck. [*Compare* SINK.]

shirk *v.* *—See* CUT (4), IDLE (1), NEGLECT (2).

shirker *n.* *—See* WASTREL (2).

shirking *n.* *—See* FAILURE (2).

shiver[1] *v.* *—See* SHAKE (1).

shiver *n.* *—See* TREMOR (2).

shiver[2] *v.* *—See* BREAK (1).

shivering *adj.* *—See* TREMULOUS.

shivers *n.* *—See* JITTERS.

shivery *adj.* *—See* COLD (1), TREMULOUS.

shock[1] *n.* Something that stuns or jars the mind ▸ blow, bombshell, jolt, rude awakening, surprise, trauma, wake-up call. *Idiom:* bolt from the blue. *—See also* COLLISION.

shock *v.* *—See* DISMAY, STAGGER (2), STARTLE.

shock[2] *n.* *—See* HEAP (1).

shocking *adj.* *—See* OUTRAGEOUS, TERRIBLE.

shoddy *adj.* Of decidedly inferior quality ▸ base, cheap, junky, lousy, miserable, paltry, poor, rotten, sleazy, sorry, trashy, worthless. *Informal:* cheesy. *Slang:* crappy, crummy, schlocky, stinko. [*Compare* BAD, RUDE, TERRIBLE.] *—See also* SHABBY.

sho·gun (shō′gən) ▸ *n.* The hereditary commander of the Japanese army who until 1867 exercised absolute rule.
shone (shōn) ▸ *v.* P.t. and p.part. of **shine.**
shoo (sho͞o) ▸ *interj.* Used to frighten away animals. **—shoo** *v.*
shoo-in (sho͞o′ĭn′) ▸ *n. Informal* A sure winner.
shook (sho͝ok) ▸ *v.* P.t. of **shake.**
shook-up (sho͝ok-ŭp′) ▸ *adj. Slang* Emotionally upset; shaken.
shoot (sho͞ot) ▸ *v.* **shot** (shŏt), **shoot·ing. 1.** To hit, wound, or kill with a missile. **2.** To fire (a missile) from a weapon. **3.** To discharge (a weapon). **4.** To send forth swiftly. **5.** To pass over or through swiftly: *shooting the rapids.* **6.** To record on film. **7.** To project or cause to project or protrude. **8.** To begin to grow or produce; put forth. **9.** *Sports & Games* To propel (e.g., a ball) toward its objective. **10.** *Informal* To spend, exhaust, or waste: *shot their savings on a new boat.* ***—phrasal verb:*** **shoot up 1.** *Informal* To grow or get taller rapidly. **2.** *Slang* To inject a drug with a hypodermic syringe. ▸ *n.* **1.** The young growth arising from a germinating seed; sprout. **2.** An organized shooting activity, such as a hunt. **—shoot′er** *n.*
shoot·ing star (sho͞o′tĭng) ▸ *n.* See **meteor.**
shop (shŏp) ▸ *n.* **1.** A small retail store. **2.** A place for manufacturing or repairing goods or machinery. **3.** A commercial or industrial establishment. ▸ *v.* **shopped, shop·ping.** To visit stores to buy or examine goods. **—shop′per** *n.*
shop·keep·er (shŏp′kē′pər) ▸ *n.* One who owns or manages a shop.
shop·lift (shŏp′lĭft′) ▸ *v.* To steal merchandise on display in a store. **—shop′lift′er** *n.* **—shop′lift′ing** *n.*
shop·ping center (shŏp′ĭng) ▸ *n.* A group of retail stores and other businesses having a common parking lot.
shopping mall ▸ *n.* **1.** An urban shopping area limited to pedestrians. **2.** A shopping center with stores facing enclosed walkways for pedestrians.
shop steward ▸ *n.* A union member elected to represent coworkers in dealings with management.
shop·talk (shŏp′tôk′) ▸ *n.* Talk or conversation concerning one's work or business.
shop·worn (shŏp′wôrn′) ▸ *adj.* **1.** Frayed, faded, or defective from being on display in a store. **2.** Hackneyed; trite.
shore[1] (shôr) ▸ *n.* The land along the edge of an ocean, sea, lake, or river; coast.
shore[2] (shôr) ▸ *v.* **shored, shor·ing.** To support by or as if by a prop: *shore up a sagging wall.*
shore·line (shôr′līn′) ▸ *n.* The edge of a body of water.
shorn (shôrn) ▸ *v.* P.part. of **shear.**
short (shôrt) ▸ *adj.* **-er, -est. 1.** Having little length. **2.** Having little height. **3.** Lasting a brief time. **4.** Not lengthy; succinct. **5.** Rudely brief; abrupt. **6.** Inadequate; insufficient: *oil in short supply.* **7.** Lacking in length or amount. **8.** Containing shortening; flaky: *a short pie crust.* **9.** *Ling.* Of or being a speech sound of relatively brief duration, as the sound of (ă) in *pat.* ▸ *adv.* **1.** Abruptly; quickly. **2.** At a point before a given limit or goal. **3.** At a disadvantage: *caught short.* ▸ *n.* **1.** Anything short. **2a. shorts** Short trousers extending to the knee or above. **b. shorts** Men's undershorts. **3.** A short circuit. **4.** A short subject. ▸ *v.* To cause a short circuit in. **—short′ness** *n.*
short·age (shôr′tĭj) ▸ *n.* A deficiency in amount.
short·bread (shôrt′brĕd′) ▸ *n.* A cookie made with much butter or other shortening.
short·cake (shôrt′kāk′) ▸ *n.* A cake made with rich biscuit dough and usu. served with fruit.
short·change (shôrt′chānj′) ▸ *v.* **1.** To give less than the correct change to. **2.** *Informal* To treat deceitfully; cheat.
short circuit ▸ *n.* A low-resistance connection accidentally established between two points in an electric circuit. **—short′-cir′cuit** *v.*
short·com·ing (shôrt′kŭm′ĭng) ▸ *n.* A deficiency; flaw.
short·cut (shôrt′kŭt′) ▸ *n.* **1.** A more direct route than the customary one. **2.** A means of saving time or effort. **—short′cut′** *v.*
short·en (shôr′tn) ▸ *v.* To make or become short or shorter. **—short′en·er** *n.*
short·en·ing (shôr′tn-ĭng, shôrt′nĭng) ▸ *n.* A fat, such as butter or lard, used to make cake or pastry light and flaky.
short·fall (shôrt′fôl′) ▸ *n.* **1.** A shortage. **2.** The amount by which a supply falls short of expectation, need, or demand.
short·hand (shôrt′hănd′) ▸ *n.* A system of rapid handwriting employing symbols to represent words, phrases, and letters.
short-hand·ed (shôrt′hăn′dĭd) ▸ *adj.* Lacking the necessary number of workers.
short·list (shôrt′lĭst′) ▸ *n.* A list of preferable items or candidates selected for final consideration. **—short′-list′** *v.*
short-lived (shôrt′līvd′, -lĭvd′) ▸ *adj.* Living or lasting only a short time.
short·ly (shôrt′lē) ▸ *adv.* **1.** Soon. **2.** In a few words; concisely. **3.** Rudely; curtly.
short order ▸ *n.* Food prepared and served quickly. **—short′-or′der** *adj.*
short-range (shôrt′rānj′) ▸ *adj.* **1.** Designed for short distances: *a short-range missile.* **2.** Relating to the near future: *short-range goals.*
short shrift ▸ *n.* **1.** Careless treatment. **2.** Quick work.
short·sight·ed (shôrt′sī′tĭd) ▸ *adj.* **1.** Nearsighted; myopic. **2.** Lacking foresight. **—short′sight′ed·ness** *n.*
short·stop (shôrt′stŏp′) ▸ *n. Baseball* **1.** The field position between 2nd and 3rd base. **2.** The infielder who plays this position.
short story ▸ *n.* A relatively short piece of prose fiction, having few characters and aiming at unity of effect.
short subject ▸ *n.* A brief film shown before a feature-length film.

THESAURUS

shoo-in *n. Informal* A leading contestant or sure winner ▸ favorite, front-runner, leader, number one, vanguard.
shoot *v.* **1.** To wound or kill with a firearm ▸ gun (down), pick off. *Slang:* plug. *Idiom:* fill full of lead (*or* holes). [*Compare* KILL[1], MURDER.] **2.** To discharge a gun or firearm ▸ blast (away), fire (away *or* off), pop (off), shoot away, shoot off. ***Idioms:*** go bang-bang, open fire, take a shot (*or* potshot). **3.** To launch with great force ▸ fire, hurtle, loose, project, propel. *Idiom:* let fly. *—See also* FLY (2), RUSH, THROW.
shoot down *v.* *—See* DISCREDIT.
shoot for or **at** *v.* *—See* ATTEMPT.
shoot up *v.* *—See* SOAR.
shoot *n.* A young stemlike growth arising from a plant ▸ bine, offshoot, runner, sprig, sprout, sucker, tendril.
shooting *adj.* *—See* SHARP (3).
shop *n.* A retail establishment where merchandise is sold ▸ boutique, emporium, outlet, store.
shopper *n.* *—See* CONSUMER.
shopworn *adj.* *—See* TRITE.
shore *n.* *—See* [illegible]
shore *v.* *—See* SUPPORT (2).
short *adj.* *—See* ABRUPT (1), BRIEF, INSUFFICIENT, LITTLE, QUICK, TRANSITORY.
short *adv.* Without adequate preparation ▸ aback, unawarely, unawares. *Idioms:* by surprise, off guard.
shortage *n.* The condition or fact of being deficient ▸ defect, deficit, deficiency, inadequacy, insufficiency, lack, paucity, poverty, scantiness, scantness, scant supply, scarceness, scarcity, shortcoming, shortfall, underage. [*Compare* ABSENCE, NEED.]
shortchange *v.* *—See* CHEAT (1).
shortcoming *n.* *—See* DEFECT, DISADVANTAGE, SHORTAGE, WEAKNESS.
shorten *v.* To make short or shorter ▸ abbreviate, abridge, boil down, condense, curtail, reduce, shrink, truncate. [*Compare* CONSTRICT, CUT, DECREASE.]
shortfall *n.* *—See* SHORTAGE.
short fuse *n.* *—See* TEMPER (1).
short-handed *adj.* Having fewer workers or participants than are needed ▸ short-staffed, undermanned, understaffed.
short-lived *adj.* *—See* TRANSITORY.
short-range *adj.* Designed or implemented so as to gain a temporary limited advantage ▸ tactical. *—See also* TEMPORARY (2).
short-spoken *adj.* *—See* ABRUPT (1).
short-staffed *adj.* Having fewer workers or participants than are needed ▸ short-handed, undermanned, understaffed.

short-tem·pered (shôrt′tĕm′pərd) ▸ *adj.* Easily moved to anger.

short-term (shôrt′tûrm′) ▸ *adj.* **1.** Involving or lasting a relatively brief time. **2.** Payable or reaching maturity within a relatively brief time, such as a year.

short ton ▸ *n.* See **measurement** table in Appendix.

short wave ▸ *n.* An electromagnetic wave with a wavelength of approx. 200 m or less. **—short′wave′** *adj.*

Sho·sho·ne also **Sho·sho·ni** (shō-shō′nē) ▸ *n., pl.* **-ne** or **-nes** also **-ni** or **-nis**. **1.** A member of a Native American people inhabiting an area from W Wyoming and SE Idaho to S Nevada. **2.** Any of their languages. **—Sho·sho′ne·an** *adj.*

shot[1] (shŏt) ▸ *n.* **1.** The firing or discharge of a weapon. **2.** The distance over which something is shot; range. **3.** *Sports* A throw, hit, or drive in any of several games. **4.** *Informal* **a.** An attempt; try. **b.** A guess. **c.** An opportunity. **5.** *pl.* **shot**. **a.** A projectile designed to be discharged from a gun. **b.** One of a group of pellets discharged esp. from a shotgun. **6.** *Sports* A shot put. **7a.** A photograph. **b.** A single cinematic take. **8.** A hypodermic injection. **9.** A drink of liquor.

shot[2] (shŏt) ▸ *v.* P.t. and p.part. of **shoot**.

shot·gun (shŏt′gŭn′) ▸ *n.* A smooth-bore gun that fires shot over short ranges.

shot put ▸ *n.* **1.** An athletic event in which a heavy metal ball is thrown for distance. **2.** The ball used in this competition. **—shot′-put′ter** *n.*

should (sho͝od) ▸ *aux.v.* P.t. of **shall**. Used to express obligation, necessity, probability, or contingency.

shoul·der (shōl′dər) ▸ *n.* **1a.** The joint connecting the arm with the torso. **b.** The part of the human body between the neck and upper arm. **2.** often **shoulders** The area of the back from one shoulder to the other. **3.** The edge along either side of a roadway. ▸ *v.* **1.** To carry or place on the shoulders. **2.** To take on; assume. **3.** To push with or as if with the shoulder.

shoulder blade ▸ *n.* See **scapula**.

should·n't (sho͝od′nt) ▸ Should not.

shout (shout) ▸ *n.* A loud cry. ▸ *v.* To utter a shout. **—shout′er** *n.*

shove (shŭv) ▸ *v.* **shoved, shov·ing**. **1.** To push forward or along. **2.** To push rudely or roughly. ***—phrasal verb:* shove off** **1.** To push (a boat) away from shore in leaving. **2.** *Informal* To leave. **—shove** *n.* **—shov′er** *n.*

shov·el (shŭv′əl) ▸ *n.* **1.** A tool with a handle and scoop for digging and moving material, such as dirt or snow. **2.** A large mechanical device for heavy digging or excavation. ▸ *v.* **-eled, -el·ing** also **-elled, -el·ling**. **1.** To move or remove with a shovel. **2.** To convey roughly or hastily: *shoveled his food down.*

show (shō) ▸ *v.* **showed, shown** (shōn) or **showed, show·ing**. **1.** To cause or allow to be seen; display. **2.** To conduct; guide. **3.** To point out. **4.** To manifest; reveal. **5.** To demonstrate by reasoning or procedure. **6.** To grant; bestow. **7.** To be visible or evident. **8.** *Sports* To finish third or better, as in a horserace. ***—phrasal verb:* show off** To behave or display in an ostentatious or boasting manner. ▸ *n.* **1.** A display; manifestation. **2.** A false appearance; pretense. **3.** A striking display; spectacle. **4.** A public exhibition or entertainment. **5.** *Informal* An undertaking: *ran the whole show.* **6.** *Sports* Third place esp. in a horserace.

show·boat (shō′bōt′) ▸ *n.* A river steamboat having a troupe of performers and a theater. ▸ *v.* To show off.

show business ▸ *n.* The entertainment industry.

show·case (shō′kās′) ▸ *n.* **1.** A display case, as in a store or museum. **2.** A setting for advantageous display. ▸ *v.* **-cased, -cas·ing**. To display or feature prominently.

show·down (shō′doun′) ▸ *n.* An event that forces an issue to a conclusion.

show·er (shou′ər) ▸ *n.* **1.** A brief fall of rain, hail, or sleet. **2.** An outpouring: *a shower of praise.* **3.** A party held to honor and present gifts to someone. **4.** A bath in which the water is sprayed on the bather. ▸ *v.* **1.** To pour down in a shower. **2.** To bestow abundantly or liberally. **3.** To take a shower.

show·ing (shō′ĭng) ▸ *n.* **1.** A presentation or display. **2.** Performance: *a poor showing.*

show·man (shō′mən) ▸ *n.* **1.** A theatrical producer. **2.** One with a flair for dramatic behavior. **—show′man·ship′** *n.*

show·off (shō′ôf′, -ŏf′) ▸ *n.* **1.** The act of showing off. **2.** One who shows off.

show·piece (shō′pēs′) ▸ *n.* Something exhibited as an outstanding example of its kind.

show place also **show·place** (shō′plās′) ▸ *n.* A place viewed and frequented for its beauty or historical noteworthiness.

show room ▸ *n.* A large room in which merchandise is displayed.

show·stop·per (shō′stŏp′ər) ▸ *n.* *Informal* A performance that evokes so much applause from the audience that the show is temporarily interrupted.

show·y (shō′ē) ▸ *adj.* **-i·er, -i·est**. **1.** Making an imposing display; striking. **2.** Ostentatious; flashy. **—show′i·ly** *adv.* **—show′i·ness** *n.*

shrank (shrăngk) ▸ *v.* P.t. of **shrink**.

shrap·nel (shrăp′nəl) ▸ *n., pl.* **-nel**. **1.** An artillery shell containing metal balls fused to explode in the air above enemy troops. **2.** Shell fragments from a high-explosive shell.

shred (shrĕd) ▸ *n.* **1.** A long irregular strip cut or torn off. **2.** A small amount; particle: *not a shred of evidence.* ▸ *v.* **shred·ded** or **shred, shred·ding**. To cut or tear into shreds. **—shred′der** *n.*

THESAURUS

short-tempered *adj.* *—See* ILL-TEMPERED, TESTY.

short-term *adj.* *—See* TEMPORARY (2).

shorty *n.* *—See* SQUIRT (2).

shot *n.* *Informal* A brief trial ▸ crack, go, stab, try. *Informal:* fling, whack, whirl. *—See also* ATTEMPT, DROP (4), OPPORTUNITY.

should *v.* *—See* MUST.

shoulder *v.* *—See* ASSUME, BEAR (1), MUSCLE, PUSH (1).

shout *v.* To speak or say in a loud cry ▸ bawl, bellow, blare, bluster, call (out), clamor, cry (out), halloo, holler, howl, roar, scream, screech, shriek, squawk, vociferate, wail, whoop, yell. [*Compare* EXCLAIM, HOWL, YELP.]

shout *n.* A loud call or cry ▸ bellow, call, cry, ejaculation, exclamation, halloo, holler, howl, outcry, roar, scream, screech, shriek, squawk, wail, whoop, yell. [*Compare* VOCIFERATION, YELP.]

shove *v.* *—See* DRIVE (2), MUSCLE, PUSH (1).

shove off *v.* *—See* GO (1).

shove *n.* *—See* PUSH.

shovel *v.* *—See* DIG.

show *v.* **1.** To make manifest or apparent ▸ demonstrate, display, evidence, evince, exhibit, manifest, proclaim, reveal. [*Compare* CLARIFY, EXPLAIN.] **2.** To give a precise indication of, as on a register or scale ▸ indicate, mark, read, record, register. **3.** To be performed ▸ play, run. *—See also* APPEAR (1), DISPLAY, GUIDE, PROVE, REPRESENT (2), REVEAL.

show off *v.* To behave in an ostentatious manner or perform dangerous stunts ▸ *Slang:* hot-dog, showboat. [*Compare* BOAST, SWAGGER.] *—See also* DISPLAY.

show up *v.* *—See* ARRIVE (1).

show *n.* *—See* ACT (2), ARRAY, DISPLAY, EXHIBITION, FAÇADE (2).

showboat *n.* A person who behaves in an ostentatious manner or performs dangerous stunts ▸ *Slang:* hotdog, showoff. [*Compare* BRAGGART.]

showboat *v.* To behave in an ostentatious manner or perform dangerous stunts ▸ *Slang:* hot-dog, show off. [*Compare* BOAST, SWAGGER.]

showcase *v.* *—See* DISPLAY.

showdown *n.* *—See* CONFRONTATION.

shower *n.* *—See* BARRAGE, RAIN.

shower *v.* To give in great abundance ▸ heap, lavish, rain. [*Compare* CONFER, DONATE, GIVE.] *—See also* BARRAGE, RAIN (2).

showiness *n.* *—See* GLITTER (2).

showoff *n.* A person who behaves in an ostentatious manner or performs dangerous stunts ▸ *Slang:* hotdog, showboat. [*Compare* BRAGGART.]

showy *adj.* Marked by outward, often extravagant display ▸ flamboyant, ostentatious, pretentious, splashy, splurgy. [*Compare* GAUDY, ORNATE.]

shred *n.* *—See* BIT[1] (1).

shred *v.* To pull or cut into many pieces ▸ cut up, grate, rip up, slice up, tear up.

shreds *n.* Torn and ragged clothing ▸ rags, tatters.

shrew (shro͞o) ▸ *n.* **1.** A small, mouselike, chiefly insectivorous mammal having a pointed snout. **2.** A nagging or scolding woman. **—shrew′ish** *adj.* **—shrew′ish·ly** *adv.* **—shrew′ish·ness** *n.*

shrewd (shro͞od) ▸ *adj.* **-er, -est. 1.** Marked by keen awareness and a sense of the practical. **2.** Artful; cunning. **—shrewd′ly** *adv.* **—shrewd′ness** *n.*

shriek (shrēk) ▸ *n.* A shrill, often frantic cry. **—shriek** *v.*

shrift (shrĭft) ▸ *n.* *Archaic* The act of shriving.

shrike (shrīk) ▸ *n.* A carnivorous bird having a strong hooked bill and often impaling its prey on thorns.

shrill (shrĭl) ▸ *adj.* **-er, -est.** High-pitched and piercing. ▸ *v.* To produce a shrill sound. **—shrill′ness** *n.* **—shril′ly** *adv.*

shrimp (shrĭmp) ▸ *n., pl.* **shrimp** or **shrimps. 1.** Any of various small, often edible marine crustaceans. **2.** *Slang* A small or unimportant person. **—shrimp′er** *n.*

shrine (shrīn) ▸ *n.* **1.** A container for sacred relics. **2.** The tomb of a saint. **3.** A site or object revered for its associations.

shrink (shrĭngk) ▸ *v.* **shrank** (shrăngk) or **shrunk** (shrŭngk), **shrunk** or **shrunk·en** (shrŭng′kən), **shrink·ing. 1.** To contract from heat, moisture, or cold. **2.** To dwindle. **3.** To draw back; recoil. ▸ *n.* *Slang* A psychotherapist. **—shrink′a·ble** *adj.* **—shrink′age** *n.* **—shrink′er** *n.*

shrink-wrap (shrĭngk′răp′) ▸ *n.* A protective plastic film wound about articles of merchandise and then shrunk by heat to form a sealed package. **—shrink′-wrap′** *v.*

shrive (shrīv) ▸ *v.* **shrove** (shrōv) or **shrived, shriv·en** (shrĭv′ən) or **shrived, shriv·ing.** To hear the confession of and give absolution to (a penitent).

shriv·el (shrĭv′əl) ▸ *v.* **-eled, -el·ing** or **-elled, -el·ling. 1.** To become or make shrunken and wrinkled, often by drying. **2.** To lose or cause to lose vitality.

shroud (shroud) ▸ *n.* **1.** A cloth used to wrap a body for burial. **2.** Something that conceals, protects, or screens. **3.** One of a set of ropes or cables stretched from the masthead to a vessel's sides to support the mast. ▸ *v.* **1.** To wrap (a corpse) in burial clothing. **2.** To shut off from sight; screen.

shrub (shrŭb) ▸ *n.* A low woody plant having several stems but no single trunk. **—shrub′bi·ness** *n.* **—shrub′by** *adj.*

shrub·ber·y (shrŭb′ə-rē) ▸ *n., pl.* **-ies.** A group or planting of shrubs.

shrug (shrŭg) ▸ *v.* **shrugged, shrug·ging.** To raise (the shoulders) as a gesture of doubt, disdain, or indifference. ***—phrasal verb:*** **shrug off 1.** To minimize. **2.** To get rid of. **—shrug** *n.*

shrunk (shrŭngk) ▸ *v.* P.t. and p.part. of **shrink.**

shrunk·en (shrŭng′kən) ▸ *v.* P.part. of **shrink.**

shuck (shŭk) ▸ *n.* A husk or shell. ▸ *v.* **1.** To remove the husk or shell from. **2.** *Informal* To cast off. ▸ *interj.*

shucks (shŭks) Used to express mild disappointment, disgust, or annoyance. **—shuck′er** *n.*

shud·der (shŭd′ər) ▸ *v.* **1.** To shiver convulsively, as from fear or revulsion. **2.** To vibrate; quiver. **—shud′der** *n.* **—shud′der·ing·ly** *adv.*

shuf·fle (shŭf′əl) ▸ *v.* **-fled, -fling. 1.** To slide (the feet) along the floor or ground while walking. **2.** To move (something) from one place to another. **3.** To mix together; jumble. **4.** *Games* To mix together (playing cards, tiles, or dominoes) in random order. **—shuf′fle** *n.* **—shuf′fler** *n.*

shuf·fle·board (shŭf′əl-bôrd′) ▸ *n.* A game in which disks are pushed along a smooth level surface toward numbered scoring areas.

shun (shŭn) ▸ *v.* **shunned, shun·ning.** To avoid deliberately.

shunt (shŭnt) ▸ *n.* **1.** The act of turning aside or moving to an alternate course. **2.** A railroad switch. **3.** *Elect.* A low-resistance alternative path for a portion of the current. ▸ *v.* **1.** To turn onto another course: *shunting traffic around an accident.* **2.** To evade by putting aside or ignoring. **3.** *Elect.* To provide or divert (current) by means of a shunt.

shush (shŭsh) ▸ *interj.* Used to demand silence. ▸ *v.* To silence by saying "shush."

shut (shŭt) ▸ *v.* **shut, shut·ting. 1.** To move or be moved so as to block an opening: *Shut the window. The door shut by itself.* **2.** To block entrance to or exit from. **3.** To confine. **4.** To stop or cause to stop operating: *shut down a club.* ***—phrasal verbs:*** **shut off** To stop the flow of. **shut out 1.** To prevent (a team) from scoring any points or runs. **2.** To keep from entering. **shut up 1.** To become or cause to become silent. **2.** To confine.

shut·down (shŭt′doun′) ▸ *n.* A cessation of operations, as at a factory.

shut·eye (shŭt′ī′) ▸ *n.* *Slang* Sleep.

shut-in (shŭt′ĭn′) ▸ *n.* One confined indoors by illness or disability. **—shut-in′** *adj.*

shut·out (shŭt′out′) ▸ *n.* **1.** See **lockout. 2.** *Sports* A game in which one side does not score.

shut·ter (shŭt′ər) ▸ *n.* **1.** A hinged cover or screen for a window. **2.** A device that opens and closes the lens aperture of a camera. ▸ *v.* To furnish or close with shutters.

shut·ter·bug (shŭt′ər-bŭg′) ▸ *n.* *Informal* An enthusiastic amateur photographer.

shut·tle (shŭt′l) ▸ *n.* **1.** A device used in weaving to carry the woof thread back and forth. **2.** A device for holding the thread in tatting or in a sewing machine. **3.** A vehicle used for regular travel between two points. **4.** A space shuttle. ▸ *v.* **-tled, -tling.** To move or travel back and forth by or as if by a shuttle.

shut·tle·cock (shŭt′l-kŏk′) ▸ *n.* A small rounded piece of

THESAURUS

shrew *n.* —*See* SCOLD.

shrewd *adj.* Having or showing a clever awareness and resourcefulness in practical matters ▸ astute, cagey, canny, knowing, perspicacious, sagacious, slick, smart, street-smart, wise. *Informal:* savvy. [*Compare* SOPHISTICATED.] —*See also* ARTFUL, CLEVER (1).

shrewdness *n.* —*See* ART, DISCERNMENT.

shriek *n.* A long, loud, piercing cry, as of fright ▸ screak, scream, screech. [*Compare* HOWL.] —*See also* SHOUT.

shriek *v.* To utter a long, loud, piercing cry, as in fright ▸ screak, scream, screech, shrill. [*Compare* HOWL.] —*See also* SHOUT.

shrieky *adj.* —*See* HIGH (3).

shrill *adj.* —*See* HARSH, HIGH (3), LOUD.

shrill *v.* To utter a long, loud, piercing cry, as of fright ▸ screak, scream, screech, shriek. [*Compare* HOWL.]

shrilly *adj.* —*See* HIGH (3).

shrimp *n.* —*See* NONENTITY, SQUIRT (2).

shrine *n.* A sacred or holy place ▸ sacrarium, sanctorium, sanctuary, sanctum.

shrink *v.* —*See* CONSTRICT (1), DECREASE, FLINCH, SHORTEN.

shrink *n.* —*See* RECOIL.

shrinkage *n.* —*See* CONSTRICTION, DECREASE, DEPRECIATION.

shrivel *v.* —*See* BLAST (2), DRY (1), [illegible]

shroud *v.* —*See* BLOCK, CONCEAL, WRAP (2).

shroud *n.* A cloth or garment in which a corpse is buried ▸ cerecloth, cerement, cerements, grave clothes, winding sheet. —*See also* VEIL.

shrubbery *n.* —*See* BRUSH².

shrunken *adj.* —*See* HAGGARD.

shuck *v.* —*See* DISCARD, SKIN.

shudder *v.* —*See* SHAKE (1).

shudder *n.* —*See* TREMOR (2).

shuddering *adj.* —*See* TREMULOUS.

shuffle *v.* To mix together so as to change the order of arrangement ▸ jumble, rearrange, reconfigure, reorder, riffle, scramble. *Informal:* rejigger. —*See also* EQUIVOCATE (1), EQUIVOCATE (2), MUDDLE, TRUDGE.

shuffle *n.* —*See* EQUIVOCATION.

shun *v.* —*See* AVOID, SNUB.

shunt *v.* —*See* TURN (2).

shush *v.* —*See* SILENCE.

shut *v.* To move a door, for example, in order to cover an opening ▸ close, [illegible]

shut away or **in** or **up** *v.* —*See* ENCLOSE (1), IMPRISON.

shut off [illegible]

shut out *v.* —*See* DISMISS (3), EXCLUDE.

shut up *v.* To enclose so as to hinder or prohibit escape ▸ closet, confine, imprison. —*See also* SILENCE.

shutdown *n.* —*See* END (1).

shuteye *n.* The natural recurring condition of suspended consciousness by which the body rests ▸ dreamland, slumber. *Slang:* z's. *Idioms:* land of Nod, the arms of Morpheus. [*Compare* NAP, REST.]

cork or rubber with a crown of feathers or plastic, used in badminton.

shy[1] (shī) ▸ *adj.* **shi·er** (shī′ər), **shi·est** (shī′ĭst) or **shy·er, shy·est.** **1.** Easily startled; timid. **2.** Drawing back from contact with others; reserved. **3.** Distrustful; wary. **4.** Short; lacking. ▸ *v.* **shied** (shīd), **shy·ing. 1.** To move suddenly, as if startled. **2.** To draw back, as from fear. **—shy′ly** *adv.* **—shy′ness** *n.*

shy[2] (shī) ▸ *v.* **shied** (shīd), **shy·ing.** To throw with a swift motion; fling.

shy·ster (shī′stər) ▸ *n. Slang* An unethical, unscrupulous practitioner, esp. of law.

Si ▸ The symbol for the element **silicon.**

SI ▸ *abbr. French* Système International [d'Unités] (International System [of Units])

Si·am (sī-ăm′) ▸ See **Thailand. —Si′a·mese′** (-ə-mēz′, -mēs′) *adj. & n.*

Siamese cat ▸ *n.* A short-haired cat having blue eyes and a pale coat with darker ears, tail, and feet.

Siamese twin ▸ *n.* Either of a pair of twins born with their bodies joined at some point.

Si·an (sē′än′, shē′-) ▸ See **Xi'an.**

Siang Kiang (syäng′ kyäng′, shyäng′) ▸ See **Xiang Jiang.**

Si·be·ri·a (sī-bîr′ē-ə) ▸ A region of central and E Russia stretching from the Urals to the Pacific. **—Si·be′ri·an** *adj. & n.*

sib·i·lant (sĭb′ə-lənt) *Ling.* ▸ *adj.* Of or producing a hissing sound. ▸ *n.* A sibilant speech sound, such as English (s) or (z). **—sib′i·lance, sib′i·lan·cy** *n.* **—sib′i·lant·ly** *adv.*

sib·ling (sĭb′lĭng) ▸ *n.* One of two or more individuals having one or both parents in common; a brother or sister.

sib·yl (sĭb′əl) ▸ *n.* A woman prophet.

sic[1] (sĭk) ▸ *adv.* Thus; so. Used in written texts to indicate that a surprising or paradoxical word or fact is not a mistake and is to be read as it stands.

sic[2] also **sick** (sĭk) ▸ *v.* **sicced, sic·cing** also **sicked, sick·ing.** To urge (e.g., a dog) to attack or chase.

Si·chuan also **Sze·chwan** or **Sze·chuan** (sĕch′wän′) ▸ A province of S-central China.

Si·ci·ly (sĭs′ə-lē) ▸ An island of S Italy in the Mediterranean off the S end of the Italian peninsula. **—Si·cil′ian** (sĭ-sĭl′yən) *adj. & n.*

sick (sĭk) ▸ *adj.* **-er, -est. 1a.** Suffering from a physical illness. **b.** Of or for sick persons: *sick wards.* **c.** Nauseated. **2a.** Mentally ill or disturbed. **b.** Unwholesome; morbid: *a sick joke.* **3.** Defective; unsound. **4a.** Deeply distressed; upset. **b.** Disgusted; revolted. **c.** Weary; tired: *sick of it all.* **d.** Pining; longing. **—sick′ness** *n.*

sick·bay (sĭk′bā′) ▸ *n.* The hospital and dispensary of a ship.

sick·bed (sĭk′bĕd′) ▸ *n.* A sick person's bed.

sick·en (sĭk′ən) ▸ *v.* To make or become sick.

sick·en·ing (sĭk′ə-nĭng) ▸ *adj.* **1.** Revolting or disgusting. **2.** Causing sickness. **—sick′en·ing·ly** *adv.*

sick·le (sĭk′əl) ▸ *n.* A tool having a curved blade attached to a short handle, used for cutting grain or tall grass.

sickle cell anemia ▸ *n.* A hereditary, usu. fatal anemia marked by the presence of crescent-shaped red blood cells and by episodic pain in the joints, fever, leg ulcers, and jaundice.

sick·ly (sĭk′lē) ▸ *adj.* **-li·er, -li·est. 1.** Prone to sickness. **2.** Of or associated with sickness: *a sickly pallor.* **3.** Causing nausea; nauseating. **4.** Feeble or weak. **—sick′li·ness** *n.*

sick·out (sĭk′out′) ▸ *n.* An organized job action in which employees absent themselves from work on the pretext of illness.

side (sīd) ▸ *n.* **1.** A surface of an object, esp. a surface joining a top and bottom. **2.** Either of the two surfaces of a flat object, such as a piece of paper. **3.** The left or right half in reference to a vertical axis, as of the body. **4.** The space immediately next to someone or something: *stood at her father's side.* **5.** An area separated from another area by an intervening feature, such as a line or barrier: *on this side of the Atlantic.* **6.** One of two or more opposing individuals, groups, teams, or sets of opinions. **7.** A distinct aspect: *showed his kinder side.* **8.** Line of descent. ▸ *adj.* **1.** Located on a side: *a side door.* **2.** From or to one side; oblique: *a side view.* **3.** Minor; incidental: *a side interest.* **4.** Supplementary: *a side benefit.* ▸ *v.* **sid·ed, sid·ing.** To align oneself in a disagreement: *sided with the liberals.* **—*idioms:* on the side** In addition to the main portion, occupation, or activity. **side by side** Next to each other. **this side of** *Informal* Verging on: *just this side of criminal.*

side·arm (sīd′ärm′) ▸ *adj.* Thrown with a sideways motion of the arm between shoulder and hip height. **—side′arm′** *adv.*

side arm ▸ *n.* A small weapon, such as a pistol, carried at the side or waist.

side·board (sīd′bôrd′) ▸ *n.* A piece of dining room furniture having drawers for linens and tableware.

side·burns (sīd′bûrnz′) ▸ *pl.n.* Growths of hair down the sides of a man's face in front of the ears.

side·car (sīd′kär′) ▸ *n.* A one-wheeled passenger car attached to the side of a motorcycle.

side effect ▸ *n.* A secondary, usu. undesirable effect, esp. of a drug or therapy.

side·kick (sīd′kĭk′) ▸ *n. Slang* A close companion.

side·light (sīd′līt′) ▸ *n.* Incidental information.

side·line (sīd′līn′) ▸ *n.* **1.** *Sports* A line along either side of a playing court or field, marking its limits. **2.** A secondary job, activity, or line of merchandise. ▸ *v. Informal* To remove from active participation.

side·long (sīd′lông′, -lŏng′) ▸ *adj.* Directed to one side; sideways: *a sidelong glance.* **—side′long′** *adv.*

side·man (sīd′măn′) ▸ *n.* A member of a jazz band who is not the leader.

si·de·re·al (sī-dîr′ē-əl) ▸ *adj.* **1.** Of or concerned with the stars. **2.** Measured in reference to the apparent motion of the stars: *sidereal time.*

side·sad·dle (sīd′săd′l) ▸ *n.* A saddle designed so that the rider sits with both legs on one side of the horse. **—side′sad·dle** *adv.*

side·show (sīd′shō′) ▸ *n.* **1.** A minor show offered in addition to the main attraction. **2.** An incidental spectacle.

side·step (sīd′stĕp′) ▸ *v.* **1.** To step out of the way of. **2.** To evade; skirt.

THESAURUS

shy[1] *adj.* Awkward or unconfident in the presence of others ▸ backward, bashful, coy, demure, diffident, introverted, modest, nonassertive, retiring, self-effacing, timid, unassuming. [*Compare* COOL, RESERVED, TACITURN.] *—See also* INSUFFICIENT.

shy *v.* *—See* FLINCH.

shy[2] *v.* *—See* THROW.

shy *n.* *—See* THROW.

shyness *n.* An awkwardness or lack of self-confidence in the presence of others ▸ backwardness, bashfulness, coyness, demureness, diffidence, modesty, retiringness, self-effacement, timidity, timidness. [*Compare* RESERVE.]

sibilant *n.* *—See* HISS (1).

sibilate *v.* *—See* HISS (1).

sibyl *n.* *—See* PROPHET.

sibylline *adj.* *—See* PROPHETIC.

sick *adj.* **1.** Suffering from or appearing to suffer from an illness ▸ ailing, anemic, down, ill, indisposed, low, nauseated, nauseous, off-color, peaked, queasy, sickly, unhealthy, unwell. *Informal:* laid up. *Chiefly Regional:* poorly. ***Idioms:*** green around the gills, under the weather. [*Compare* FEVERISH, INFIRM, PALE, WEAK.] **2.** Out of patience ▸ disgusted, fed up, tired, weary. *Idiom:* sick and tired. [*Compare* ANGRY.] *—See also* INSANE, MORBID.

sicken *v.* *—See* CONTRACT (2), DISGUST.

sickening *adj.* Producing dizziness or vertigo ▸ dizzy, dizzying, giddy, vertiginous. [*Compare* STEEP.] *—See also* OFFENSIVE (1), UNPALATABLE.

sickle *v.* *—See* CUT (3).

sickly *adj.* *—See* PALE (2), SICK (1).

sickness *n.* The condition of being sick ▸ affliction, ailment, bug, complaint, failing health, ill health, illness, indisposition, infirmity, malady, malaise, poor health, unhealthiness. [*Compare* DISTRESS.] *—See also* DISEASE.

side *n.* **1.** An outer surface, layer, or part of an object ▸ face, facet, surface. [*Compare* BACK, BOTTOM, FRONT.] **2.** One of two or more contrasted parts or places identified by its location with respect to a center ▸ flank, hand. *—See also* FORCE (3), VIEWPOINT.

side *v.* *—See* FACE (2).

side with *v.* *—See* SUPPORT (1).

sidekick *n.* *—See* ASSOCIATE (2), FRIEND.

sidesplitting *adj.* *—See* FUNNY (1).

sidestep *v.* *—See* EVADE (1).

side·stroke (sīd′strōk′) ▸ *n.* A swimming stroke in which a person swims on one side and thrusts the arms forward alternately while performing a scissors kick. **—side′stroke′** *v.*
side·swipe (sīd′swīp′) ▸ *v.* To strike along the side in passing. ▸ *n.* A glancing blow.
side·track (sīd′trăk′) ▸ *v.* **1.** To divert from a main issue or course. **2.** To switch (a railroad car) to a siding. ▸ *n.* A railroad siding.
side·walk (sīd′wôk′) ▸ *n.* A paved walkway along the side of a street.
side·wall (sīd′wôl′) ▸ *n.* A side surface of an automobile tire.
side·ways (sīd′wāz′) ▸ *adv. & adj.* **1.** Toward or from one side. **2.** With one side forward: *turned sideways to the camera.*
side·wind·er (sīd′wīn′dər) ▸ *n.* A small rattlesnake that moves by a lateral looping motion of its body.
sid·ing (sī′dĭng) ▸ *n.* **1.** Material, such as shingles, used for surfacing a frame building. **2.** A short section of railroad track connected by switches with a main track.
si·dle (sīd′l) ▸ *v.* **-dled, -dling.** **1.** To move sideways. **2.** To advance in a furtive or coy way.
SIDS ▸ *abbr.* sudden infant death syndrome
siege (sēj) ▸ *n.* **1.** The surrounding and blockading of a city, town, or fortress by an army attempting to capture it. **2.** A prolonged period, as of illness. ▸ *v.* **sieged, sieg·ing.** To lay siege to.
si·er·ra (sē-ĕr′ə) ▸ *n.* A rugged range of mountains having a jagged profile. **—si·er′ran** *adj.*
Sierra Le·one (lē-ōn′, -ō′nē) ▸ A country of W Africa on the Atlantic coast.
Sierra Ma·dre (mä′drā) ▸ *n.* A mountain system of Mexico comprising three ranges: **Sierra Madre del Sur,** in the S along the Pacific; **Sierra Madre Occidental,** running parallel to the Pacific coastline; and **Sierra Madre Oriental,** roughly paralleling the Gulf of Mexico.
si·es·ta (sē-ĕs′tə) ▸ *n.* A rest after the midday meal.
sieve (sĭv) ▸ *n.* A utensil of wire mesh or closely perforated metal, used for straining, sifting, or puréeing. **—sieve** *v.*
sift (sĭft) ▸ *v.* **1.** To put through a sieve to separate fine from coarse particles. **2.** To pass through or as if through a sieve. **3.** To examine and sort carefully: *sift the evidence.* **—sift′er** *n.*
sigh (sī) ▸ *v.* **1.** To exhale audibly in a long deep breath, as in weariness or relief. **2.** To feel longing or grief. ▸ *n.* The act or sound of sighing. **—sigh′er** *n.*
sight (sīt) ▸ *n.* **1.** The ability to see. **2.** The act or fact of seeing. **3.** A view. **4.** Something worth seeing. **5.** *Informal* Something unsightly. **6.** A device used to assist aim by guiding the eye, as on a firearm. ▸ *v.* **1.** To perceive with the eyes: *sighted land after 40 days at sea.* **2.** To take aim (with).
sight·ed (sī′tĭd) ▸ *adj.* Having sight.
sight·less (sīt′lĭs) ▸ *adj.* Unable to see; blind. **—sight′less·ly** *adv.* **—sight′less·ness** *n.*
sight·ly (sīt′lē) ▸ *adj.* **-li·er, -li·est.** Pleasing to see; attractive. **—sight′li·ness** *n.*
sight-read (sīt′rēd′) ▸ *v.* To read or perform (e.g., music) without preparation or prior acquaintance. **—sight′-read′er** *n.*
sight·see·ing (sīt′sē′ĭng) ▸ *n.* The act of visiting sights of interest.
sig·ma (sĭg′mə) ▸ *n.* The 18th letter of the Greek alphabet.
sign (sīn) ▸ *n.* **1.** Something that suggests the existence of a fact, condition, or quality. **2.** An act or gesture used to convey an idea. **3.** A posted notice bearing a designation, direction, or command. **4.** A figure or device that stands for a word, phrase, or operation: *a minus sign.* **5.** A portentous event; omen. **6.** One of the 12 divisions of the zodiac. ▸ *v.* **1.** To affix one's signature to. **2.** To write (one's signature). **3.** To approve or ratify (a document) by affixing a signature or seal. **4.** To hire by obtaining a signature on a contract. **5.** To relinquish or transfer title to by signature. **6.** To communicate with a sign or by sign language. ***—phrasal verb:* sign up** To enlist. **—sign′er** *n.*
sig·nal (sĭg′nəl) ▸ *n.* **1.** An indicator that serves as a means of communication: *a traffic signal; a smoke signal.* **2.** *Electron.* **a.** An impulse or fluctuating electric quantity whose variations represent coded information. **b.** The sound, image, or message transmitted by such coded information. ▸ *adj.* Notable; remarkable. ▸ *v.* **-naled, -nal·ing** or **-nalled, -nal·ling.** **1.** To make a signal (to). **2.** To relate or make known by signals: *signaled their approval.* **—sig′nal·er, sig′nal·ler** *n.* **—sig′nal·ly** *adv.*
sig·nal·ize (sĭg′nə-līz′) ▸ *v.* **-ized, -iz·ing.** **1.** To make remarkable or conspicuous. **2.** To point out particularly.
sig·na·to·ry (sĭg′nə-tôr′ē) ▸ *adj.* Bound by signed agreement. ▸ *n., pl.* **-ries.** One that has signed a treaty or document.
sig·na·ture (sĭg′nə-chər) ▸ *n.* **1.** One's name as written by oneself. **2.** A distinctive mark, characteristic, or sound. **3.** *Mus.* A sign used to indicate tempo or key.
sign·board (sīn′bôrd′) ▸ *n.* A board bearing a sign.
sig·net (sĭg′nĭt) ▸ *n.* A seal, esp. one used officially to mark documents.
sig·nif·i·cance (sĭg-nĭf′ĭ-kəns) ▸ *n.* **1.** The state or quality of being significant. **2.** The meaning of something; import. **3.** An implied meaning.
sig·nif·i·cant (sĭg-nĭf′ĭ-kənt) ▸ *adj.* **1.** Having or expressing a meaning; meaningful. **2.** Insinuating; suggestive: *a significant glance.* **3.** Having a major effect; important. **4.** Fairly large; substantial: *significant losses.* **—sig·nif′i·cant·ly** *adv.*
sig·ni·fi·ca·tion (sĭg′nə-fĭ-kā′shən) ▸ *n.* **1.** The established meaning of a word. **2.** The act of signifying; indication.
sig·ni·fi·er (sĭg′nə-fī′ər) *n.* One that signifies.

THESAURUS

sideswipe *v.* —*See* CRASH.
sideswipe *n.* —*See* CRASH (2).
sidle *v.* To advance carefully and gradually ▸ ease, edge. [*Compare* CRAWL, SNEAK.]
siege *n.* A prolonged encirclement of an objective by hostile troops or forces ▸ beleaguerment, besiegement, blockade, investment. [*Compare* ATTACK.]
siege *v.* —*See* BESIEGE.
siesta *n.* —*See* NAP.
sift *v.* To set apart one kind or type from others ▸ separate, sort, winnow. *Idiom:* separate the sheep from the goats.
sigh *v.* To make a low, continuous, and indistinct sound ▸ murmur, rustle, sough, whisper. [*Compare* BURBLE, HUM.]
sigh *n.* —*See* MURMUR.
sight *n.* An act of directing the eyes on an object ▸ contemplation, look, regard, view. [*Compare* GAZE, WATCH.] —*See also* MESS (2), VIEW (2), VISION (1).
sightless *adj.* —*See* BLIND (1).
sightlessness *n.* The condition of not being able to see ▸ blindness, darkness, legal blindness, visual impairment.
sightseer *n.* —*See* TOURIST.
sign *n.* **1.** Something visible or evident that gives grounds for believing in the existence or presence of something else ▸ badge, emblem, evidence, index, indication, indicator, mark, manifestation, note, signification, stamp, symbol, symptom, token, witness. [*Compare* HINT, SYMBOL, TRACE, TRACK.] **2.** A usually public posting that conveys a message ▸ bill, billboard, notice, placard, poster. —*See also* CHARACTER (7), EXPRESSION (2), GESTURE, OMEN.
sign *v.* To affix one's signature to ▸ autograph, endorse, inscribe, subscribe, undersign. ***Idioms:*** put one's John Hancock on, set one's hand to. —*See also* EMPLOY (1), GESTURE.
sign off *v.* —*See* PASS (6).
sign on *v.* —*See* JOIN (1).
sign over *v.* —*See* TRANSFER (1).
sign up *v.* —*See* JOIN (1).
signal *n.* —*See* GESTURE.
signal *adj.* —*See* NOTICEABLE.
signal *v.* —*See* DESIGNATE, GESTURE.
signalize *v.* —*See* DISTINGUISH (2), DISTINGUISH (3), GESTURE.
significance or **significancy** *n.* —*See* IMPORTANCE, MEANING.
significant *adj.* —*See* BIG, DESIGNATIVE, EXPRESSIVE, IMPORTANT, PREGNANT (2).
significantly *adv.* —*See* CONSIDERABLY.
signification *n.* —*See* MEANING, REFERENCE (1), SIGN (1).
signifier *n.* An object or expression associated with and serving to identify something else ▸ attribute, emblem, metaphor, symbol, token. [*Compare* EXPRESSION, SIGN, TERM.]

sig·ni·fy (sĭg′nə-fī′) ▸ *v.* **-fied, -fy·ing.** 1. To denote; mean. 2. To make known; signal. 3. To be significant; matter.

sign language ▸ *n.* A language that uses a system of manual, facial, and other body movements as the means of communication.

sign·post (sīn′pōst′) ▸ *n.* 1. A post supporting a sign. 2. An indication; guide.

Sikh (sēk) ▸ *n.* An adherent of a monotheistic religion of India combining elements of Hinduism and Islam. **—Sikh** *adj.* **—Sikh′ism** *n.*

si·lage (sī′lĭj) ▸ *n.* Green fodder prepared by storing and fermenting in a silo.

si·lence (sī′ləns) ▸ *n.* 1. The absence of sound; stillness. 2. A period of time without speech or noise. 3. Refusal or failure to speak out. ▸ *v.* **-lenced, -lenc·ing.** 1. To make silent. 2. To suppress.

si·lenc·er (sī′lən-sər) ▸ *n.* A device attached to a firearm to muffle the sound of firing.

si·lent (sī′lənt) ▸ *adj.* 1. Marked by absence of sound; still. 2. Not inclined to speak; reticent. 3. Unable to speak. 4. Not voiced or expressed; unspoken: *offered a silent prayer.* 5. *Ling.* Unpronounced, as the *b* in *subtle.* **—si′lent·ly** *adv.*

sil·hou·ette (sĭl′o͞o-ĕt′) ▸ *n.* 1. A drawing consisting of the outline of something, esp. a human profile, filled in with a solid color. 2. An outline. ▸ *v.* **-et·ted, -et·ting.** To cause to be seen as a silhouette; outline.

sil·i·ca (sĭl′ĭ-kə) ▸ *n.* A crystalline compound, SiO_2, occurring abundantly as quartz, sand, and other minerals. **—si·li′ceous** (sĭ-lĭsh′əs) *adj.*

sil·i·cate (sĭl′ĭ-kāt′, -kĭt) ▸ *n.* A compound containing silicon, oxygen, and a metal.

sil·i·con (sĭl′ĭ-kən, -kŏn′) ▸ *n.* *Symbol* **Si** A nonmetallic element occurring extensively in the earth's crust and used in glass, semiconductors, and concrete. At. no. 14.

sil·i·cone (sĭl′ĭ-kōn′) ▸ *n.* Any of a group of semi-inorganic polymers containing chains of alternate silicon and oxygen atoms, characterized by wide-range thermal stability and used in adhesives, lubricants, protective coatings, and synthetic rubber.

sil·i·co·sis (sĭl′ĭ-kō′sĭs) ▸ *n.* A lung disease caused by continued inhalation of silica dust and marked by progressive fibrosis.

silk (sĭlk) ▸ *n.* 1a. A fine lustrous fiber produced by a silkworm to form its cocoon. b. Thread or fabric made from this fiber. 2. A silky, filamentous material, such as the webbing spun by spiders.

silk-cot·ton tree (sĭlk′kŏt′n) ▸ *n.* A spiny tropical tree cultivated for its leathery fruit that contain the silklike fiber kapok.

silk·en (sĭl′kən) ▸ *adj.* 1. Made of silk. 2. Smooth and lustrous.

silk-screen also **silk·screen** (sĭlk′skrēn′) ▸ *n.* A stencil method in which ink is forced through a design-bearing screen of silk or other fine mesh onto the printing surface. **—silk′-screen′** *v.*

silk·worm (sĭlk′wûrm′) ▸ *n.* Any of various moth caterpillars that produce silk cocoons.

silk·y (sĭl′kē) ▸ *adj.* **-i·er, -i·est.** 1. Resembling silk; lustrous. 2. Silken. **—silk′i·ly** *adv.* **—silk′i·ness** *n.*

sill (sĭl) ▸ *n.* The horizontal member that bears the upright portion of a frame, esp. the base of a window.

sil·ly (sĭl′ē) ▸ *adj.* **-li·er, -li·est.** 1. Lacking good sense; foolish. 2. Frivolous. 3. Dazed. **—sil′li·ness** *n.*

si·lo (sī′lō) ▸ *n., pl.* **-los.** 1. A tall cylindrical structure in which fodder is stored. 2. An underground shelter for a missile.

silt (sĭlt) ▸ *n.* A fine sediment intermediate in size between sand and clay. ▸ *v.* To fill or become filled with silt. **—silt·a′tion** *n.* **—silt′y** *adj.*

Si·lu·ri·an (sĭ-lo͝or′ē-ən, sī-) *Geol.* ▸ *adj.* Of or being the 3rd period of the Paleozoic Era, marked by the development of early invertebrate land animals. ▸ *n.* The Silurian Period.

sil·van (sĭl′vən) ▸ *adj.* Var. of **sylvan.**

sil·ver (sĭl′vər) ▸ *n.* 1. *Symbol* **Ag** A lustrous white malleable metallic element highly valued for jewelry, tableware, and other ornamental use and used in coinage, photography, dental and soldering alloys, electrical contacts, and printed circuits. At. no. 47. 2. Coins made of silver. 3. Tableware and other articles made of or plated with silver. 4. A lustrous medium gray. ▸ *adj.* 1. Of the color silver. 2. Eloquent: *a silver voice.* 3. Of a 25th anniversary. ▸ *v.* 1. To cover, plate, or adorn with silver or a silvery substance. 2. To give a silver color to. **—sil′ver·i·ness** *n.* **—sil′ver·y** *adj.*

silver bromide ▸ *n.* A pale yellow crystalline compound, AgBr, used as the light-sensitive component on photographic film.

sil·ver·fish (sĭl′vər-fĭsh′) ▸ *n., pl.* **-fish** or **-fish·es.** A silvery wingless insect that often damages bookbindings and clothing.

silver iodide ▸ *n.* A yellow powder, AgI, used in photography, rainmaking, and medicine.

silver nitrate ▸ *n.* A poisonous colorless crystalline compound, $AgNO_3$, used in making photographic film, silvering mirrors, dyeing hair, plating silver, and medicine.

sil·ver·smith (sĭl′vər-smĭth′) ▸ *n.* One that makes or replates articles of silver.

sil·ver·ware (sĭl′vər-wâr′) ▸ *n.* Articles made of or plated with silver, esp. tableware.

sim·i·an (sĭm′ē-ən) ▸ *n.* An ape or monkey. **—sim′i·an** *adj.*

sim·i·lar (sĭm′ə-lər) ▸ *adj.* Related in appearance or nature; alike though not identical. **—sim′i·lar·ly** *adv.*

sim·i·lar·i·ty (sĭm′ə-lăr′ĭ-tē) ▸ *n., pl.* **-ties.** The quality or condition of being similar.

sim·i·le (sĭm′ə-lē) ▸ *n.* A figure of speech in which two essentially unlike things are compared, often using *like* or *as,* as in *eyes like stars.*

si·mil·i·tude (sĭ-mĭl′ĭ-to͞od′, -tyo͞od′) ▸ *n.* Similarity; resemblance.

sim·mer (sĭm′ər) ▸ *v.* 1. To be cooked gently just at or below the boiling point. 2. To be filled with pent-up emotion; seethe. ***—phrasal verb:* simmer down** To become calm after excitement or anger. **—sim′mer** *n.*

si·mo·ny (sī′mə-nē, sĭm′ə-) ▸ *n.* The buying or selling of ecclesiastical pardons or offices.

sim·pa·ti·co (sĭm-pä′tĭ-kō′, -păt′ĭ-) ▸ *adj.* 1. Compatible. 2. Attractive; pleasing.

sim·per (sĭm′pər) ▸ *v.* To smile in a silly or self-conscious manner. **—sim′per** *n.* **—sim′per·er** *n.*

sim·ple (sĭm′pəl) ▸ *adj.* **-pler, -plest.** 1. Having only one thing, element, or part. 2. Not involved or complicated;

THESAURUS

signify *v.* —*See* COUNT (1), DESIGNATE, MEAN[1].

silence *n.* 1. The absence of sound or noise ▸ hush, noiselessness, quiet, quietness, soundlessness, still, stillness. [*Compare* CALM, STILLNESS.] 2. The avoidance of speech ▸ dumbness, muteness, speechlessness, wordlessness. [*Compare* RESERVE.]

silence *v.* To cause to become silent ▸ hush, quiet, quieten, shush, shut up, still. [*Compare* REPRESS, SUPPRESS.] —*See also* CENSOR (2).

silent *adj.* 1. Marked by, done with, or making no sound or noise ▸ hushed, inaudible, noiseless, quiet, soundless, still. 2. Not voiced or expressed ▸ tacit, undeclared, unexpressed, unsaid, unspoken, unuttered, unvoiced, wordless. [*Compare* IMPLICIT, ULTERIOR.] —*See also* MUTE, SPEECHLESS, TACITURN.

silhouette *n.* —*See* FORM (1).

silky or **silken** *adj.* Smooth and lustrous as if polished ▸ satiny, sleek. [*Compare* EVEN, GLOSSY, SLICK.]

silliness *n.* —*See* FOOLISHNESS, NONSENSE.

silly *adj.* —*See* FOOLISH, GIDDY (2).

silver-tongued *adj.* —*See* ELOQUENT.

similar *adj.* —*See* LIKE[2].

similarity *n.* —*See* LIKENESS (1).

similarly *adj.* In a similar manner ▸ likewise, so. *Idioms:* by the same token, in like fashion, in like manner, in the same way.

similitude *n.* —*See* LIKENESS (1).

simmer *v.* —*See* BOIL, COOK.

simmer down *v.* —*See* COMPOSE (4).

simper *v.* —*See* SMILE.

simper *n.* A facial expression marked by an upward curving of the lips ▸ grin, smile, smirk. [*Compare* SNEER.]

simple *adj.* Of little distinction ▸ humble, lowly, mean. [*Compare*

easy. 3. Bare; mere: *a simple "yes" or "no."* 4. Not embellished or adorned: *a simple dress.* 5. Not elaborate or luxurious. 6. Unassuming or unpretentious. 7. Simple-minded. 8. Straightforward; sincere. 9. Humble or lowly in condition or rank. 10. Insignificant; trivial. **—sim′ple·ness** *n.*

simple fraction ► *n.* A fraction in which both the numerator and the denominator are whole numbers.

simple interest ► *n.* Interest paid only on the original principal, not on the interest accrued.

sim·ple-mind·ed (sĭm′pəl-mīn′dĭd) ► *adj.* 1. Lacking in sophistication; naive. 2. Stupid or silly. 3. Mentally impaired. **—sim′ple-mind′ed·ly** *adv.* **—sim′ple-mind′ed·ness** *n.*

simple sentence ► *n.* A sentence having only one clause, as *The cat purred.*

sim·ple·ton (sĭm′pəl-tən) ► *n.* A person deficient in judgment or intelligence; fool.

sim·plic·i·ty (sĭm-plĭs′ĭ-tē) ► *n., pl.* **-ties.** 1. The property, condition, or quality of being simple. 2. Absence of luxury or showiness; plainness. 3. Absence of affectation or pretense. 4. Foolishness.

sim·pli·fy (sĭm′plə-fī′) ► *v.* **-fied, -fy·ing.** To make simple or simpler. **—sim′pli·fi·ca′tion** *n.* **—sim′pli·fi′er** *n.*

sim·ply (sĭm′plē) ► *adv.* 1. In a plain and unadorned way. 2. Merely; only. 3. Absolutely; altogether: *simply delicious.*

sim·u·late (sĭm′yə-lāt′) ► *v.* **-lat·ed, -lat·ing.** 1. To take on the appearance or form of. 2. To pretend; feign. 3. To create a model of. **—sim′u·la′tion** *n.* **—sim′u·la′tive** *adj.* **—sim′u·la′tor** *n.*

si·mul·cast (sī′məl-kăst′, sĭm′əl-) ► *v.* To broadcast simultaneously by FM and AM radio or by radio and television. **—si′mul·cast′** *n.*

si·mul·ta·ne·ous (sī′məl-tā′nē-əs, sĭm′əl-) ► *adj.* Happening, existing, or done at the same time. **—si′mul·ta′ne·ous·ly** *adv.* **—si′mul·ta′ne·ous·ness, si′mul·ta·ne′i·ty** (-tə-nē′ĭ-tē, -nā′-) *n.*

sin[1] (sĭn) ► *n.* 1. A transgression of a religious or moral law. 2. Something shameful or wrong. **—sin** *v.* **—sin′ful** *adj.* **—sin′ful·ness** *n.* **—sin′ner** *n.*

sin[2] ► *abbr.* sine

Si·nai (sī′nī′), **Mount** ► A mountain, about 2,288 m (7,500 ft), of the S Sinai Peninsula.

Sinai Peninsula ► A peninsula between the gulfs of Suez and Aqaba.

since (sĭns) ► *adv.* 1. From then until now or between then and now: *They left town and haven't been here since.* 2. Before now; ago: *long since forgotten.* ► *prep.* From the time of: *friends since school.* ► *conj.* 1. From the time when or after which: *hasn't worked since the accident.* 2. Inasmuch as; because: *Since you asked, I'll tell you.*

sin·cere (sĭn-sîr′) ► *adj.* **-cer·er, -cer·est.** Not feigned or affected; true. **—sin·cer′i·ty** (-sĕr′ĭ-tē) *n.* **—sin·cere′ly** *adv.* **—sin·cere′ness** *n.*

sine (sīn) ► *n.* In a right triangle, the ratio of the side opposite an acute angle to the hypotenuse.

si·ne·cure (sī′nĭ-kyo͝or′, sĭn′ĭ-) ► *n.* A salaried position requiring little or no work.

si·ne di·e (sī′nĭ dī′ē, sĭn′ā dē′ā′) ► *adv.* Without a future time specified; indefinitely.

si·ne qua non (sĭn′ĭ kwä nōn′, nŏn′, sī′nĭ) ► *n.* An essential element or condition.

sin·ew (sĭn′yo͞o) ► *n.* 1. A tendon. 2. Vigorous strength.

sin·ew·y (sĭn′yo͞o-ē) ► *adj.* 1. Stringy and tough, as meat. 2. Lean and muscular.

sing (sĭng) ► *v.* **sang** (săng) or **sung** (sŭng), **sung, sing·ing.** 1. To utter a series of words or sounds in musical tones. 2. To make melodious sounds. 3. To bring to a specified state by singing: *sang the baby to sleep.* 4. To proclaim or extol something in verse. 5. *Slang* To give evidence against someone. ► *n.* A gathering of people for group singing. **—sing′a·ble** *adj.* **—sing′er** *n.*

sing. ► *abbr.* singular

Sin·ga·pore (sĭng′gə-pôr′, sĭng′ə-) ► A country of SE Asia comprising **Singapore Island** and adjacent smaller islands. **—Sin′ga·por′e·an** *adj. & n.*

singe (sĭnj) ► *v.* **singed, singe·ing.** 1. To burn superficially; scorch. 2. To burn off the feathers or bristles of. **—singe** *n.*

Sing·ha·lese (sĭng′gə-lēz′, -lēs′) ► *n. & adj.* Var. of **Sinhalese.**

sin·gle (sĭng′gəl) ► *adj.* 1. Not accompanied by another or others; solitary. 2. Consisting of one part or section. 3. Separate; individual: *Every single one of you.* 4. Designed to accommodate one person: *a single bed.* 5. Unmarried. ► *n.* 1. One that is separate and individual. 2. An accommodation for one person, as in a hotel. 3. An unmarried person. 4. A one-dollar bill. 5. *Baseball* A one-base hit. 6. **singles** *Sports* A match between two players in tennis and other games. ► *v.* **-gled, -gling.** 1. To choose or distinguish from others: *singled her out for praise.* 2. *Baseball* To make a one-base hit. **—sin′gle·ness** *n.*

sin·gle-breast·ed (sĭng′gəl-brĕs′tĭd) ► *adj.* Closing with a narrow overlap and fastened with a single row of buttons.

single file ► *n.* A line of people or things standing or moving one behind the other.

sin·gle-hand·ed (sĭng′gəl-hăn′dĭd) ► *adj.* 1. Working or done without help; unassisted. 2. Using only one hand. **—sin′gle-hand′ed·ly** *adv.* **—sin′gle-hand′ed·ness** *n.*

sin·gle-mind·ed (sĭng′gəl-mīn′dĭd) ► *adj.* 1. Having one overriding purpose or goal. 2. Steadfast. **—sin′gle-mind′ed·ly** *adv.* **—sin′gle-mind′ed·ness** *n.*

sin·gles bar (sĭng′gəlz) ► *n.* A bar patronized esp. by unmarried men and women.

sin·gly (sĭng′glē) ► *adv.* 1. Alone. 2. One by one; individually.

sing·song (sĭng′sông′, -sŏng′) ► *n.* A monotonous rising and falling of the voice. **—sing′song′** *adj.*

sin·gu·lar (sĭng′gyə-lər) ► *adj.* 1. Being only one; individual. 2. Unique. 3. Being beyond what is usual; remarkable. 4.

THESAURUS

MODEST.] *—See also* ARTLESS, BACKWARD (1), BARE (1), EASY (1), GULLIBLE, MODEST (1), PURE, RUSTIC.

simple *n.* *—See* FOOL.

simple-minded *adj.* *—See* BACKWARD (1).

simpleness *n.* *—See* ARTLESSNESS, MODESTY (2).

simpleton *n.* *—See* DULLARD, FOOL.

simplex *n.* *—See* THEME (1).

simplicity *n.* *—See* ARTLESSNESS, CLARITY, MODESTY (2), STUPIDITY.

simplify *v.* To reduce in complexity or scope ► boil down, pare (down), streamline. *Idiom:* reduce to the basics (*or* essentials *or* bare bones). [*Compare* EXPLAIN.] *—See also* CLARIFY (1).

simply *adv.* Nothing more than ► but, just, merely, only. [*Compare* BARELY, SOLELY.]

simulacrum *n.* *—See* COPY (1).

simulate *v.* *—See* ACT (2), COPY, IMITATE.

simulated *adj.* *—See* ARTIFICIAL (1).

simulation *n.* *—See* ACT (2), AFFECTATION, COPY (2).

simultaneous *adj.* *—See* CONCURRENT.

simultaneously *adv.* At the same time ► concurrently, synchronously, together. *Idioms:* all at once, all together.

sin *n.* *—See* CRIME (2), EVIL (1).

sin *v.* *—See* OFFEND (3).

since *conj.* *—See* BECAUSE.

sincere *adj.* *—See* GENUINE.

sincerity *n.* *—See* HONESTY.

sine qua non *n.* *—See* CONDITION (2), ESSENCE.

sinew *n.* *—See* STRENGTH.

sinewy *adj.* Containing or consisting of fibers ► fibrous, stringy, threadlike. *—See also* MUSCULAR.

sinful *adj.* *—See* EVIL.

sing *v.* To utter words or sounds in musical tones ► carol, chant, croon, intone, trill, vocalize, warble. *Slang:* belt (out). *—See also* INFORM (2).

singe *v.* *—See* BURN (1).

singe *n.* *—See* BURN.

singer *n.* *—See* VOCALIST.

single *adj.* Not married or involved in a committed relationship ► available, eligible, fancy-free, footloose, lone, marriageable, nubile, sole, spouseless, unattached, [illegible]. *Idioms:* footloose and fancy-free, in the market. *—See also* EXCLUSIVE (1), INDIVIDUAL (2), LONE, SOLITARY.

single *v.* *—See* CHOOSE (1).

single out *v.* *—See* DISTINGUISH (1), DISTINGUISH (2), NAME (2).

single-handedly *adv.* *—See* ALONE.

single-minded *adj.* *—See* FIRM[1] (3), INTENT.

singleness *n.* The condition of being one ► oneness, singularity, unity. [*Compare* COMPLETENESS.] *—See also* SOLITUDE, UNIQUENESS.

singly *adv.* *—See* ALONE, SEPARATELY.

singular *adj.* *—See* ECCENTRIC,

Deviating from the expected; odd. 5. *Gram.* Of or being a single person or thing or several entities considered as a unit. ▸ *n. Gram.* The singular number or a form designating it. **—sin′gu·lar′i·ty** (-lăr′ĭ-tē), **sin′gu·lar·ness** *n.* **—sin′gu·lar·ly** *adv.*

Sin·ha·lese (sĭn′hə-lēz′, -lēs′) or **Sing·ha·lese** (sĭng′gə-lēz′, -lēs′) ▸ *n., pl.* **-lese.** 1. A member of a people constituting the majority of the population of Sri Lanka. 2. The Indic language of the Sinhalese. **—Sin′ha·lese′** *adj.*

sin·is·ter (sĭn′ĭ-stər) ▸ *adj.* 1. Suggesting or threatening evil. 2. Presaging trouble; ominous.

sink (sĭngk) ▸ *v.* **sank** (săngk) or **sunk** (sŭngk), **sunk, sink·ing.** 1a. To descend to the bottom. b. To cause to descend beneath a surface. 2. To fall or drop to a lower level. 3. To force into or penetrate a substance. 4. To dig or drill (e.g., a well) in the earth. 5. To pass into a specified condition: *sank into a deep sleep.* 6. To deteriorate in quality or condition. 7. To diminish or decline. 8. To become weaker, quieter, or less forceful. 9. To become felt or understood: *The lesson sank in.* 10. To invest. 11. *Sports* To get (a ball) into a hole or basket. ▸ *n.* 1. A basin fixed to a wall or floor and having a drainpipe and a piped water supply. 2. A sinkhole. **—sink′a·ble** *adj.*

sink·er (sĭng′kər) ▸ *n.* A weight used for sinking fishing lines or nets.

sink·hole (sĭngk′hōl′) ▸ *n.* A natural depression in a land surface, usu. occurring in limestone regions and formed by solution or collapse of a cavern roof.

sink·ing fund (sĭng′kĭng) ▸ *n.* A fund accumulated to pay off a corporate or public debt.

Sino– ▸ *pref.* Chinese: *Sinology.*

Si·nol·o·gy (sī-nŏl′ə-jē, sĭ-) ▸ *n.* The study of Chinese language, literature, or civilization. **—Si′no·log′i·cal** (sī′nə-lŏj′ĭ-kəl, sĭn′ə-) *adj.* **—Si·nol′o·gist** *n.*

Si·no-Ti·bet·an (sī′nō-tĭ-bĕt′n, sĭn′ō-) ▸ *n.* A language family that includes Chinese and Tibeto-Burman. **—Si′no-Ti·bet′an** *adj.*

sin·u·ous (sĭn′yo͞o-əs) ▸ *adj.* 1. Twisting; winding. 2. Supple and lithe: *the sinuous grace of a dancer.* 3. Not direct; devious. **—sin′u·os′i·ty** (-ŏs′ĭ-tē), **sin′u·ous·ness** *n.* **—sin′u·ous·ly** *adv.*

si·nus (sī′nəs) ▸ *n.* 1. Any of various air-filled cavities in the bones of the skull, esp. one communicating with the nostrils. 2. A bodily channel containing chiefly venous blood.

si·nus·i·tis (sī′nə-sī′tĭs) ▸ *n.* Inflammation of a sinus, esp. in the nasal region.

Si·on (sī′ən) ▸ *n.* Var. of **Zion.**

Siou·an (so͞o′ən) ▸ *n.* A large North American Indian language family spoken from Lake Michigan to the Rocky Mountains.

Sioux (so͞o) ▸ *n., pl.* **Sioux** (so͞o, so͞oz). 1. A member of a group of Native American peoples of the N Great Plains, now mainly in North and South Dakota. 2. Any of their Siouan languages. **—Sioux** *adj.*

sip (sĭp) ▸ *v.* **sipped, sip·ping.** To drink in small quantities. ▸ *n.* 1. The act of sipping. 2. A small quantity of liquid sipped. **—sip′per** *n.*

si·phon also **sy·phon** (sī′fən) ▸ *n.* A bent tube through which a fluid can be drawn over the edge of one container into a lower container by means of air pressure. ▸ *v.* To draw off or drain with or as if with a siphon.

sir (sûr) ▸ *n.* 1. **Sir** Used as an honorific title for baronets and knights. 2. Used as a form of polite address for a man. 3. Used as a salutation in a letter: *Dear Sir.*

sire (sīr) ▸ *n.* 1. A father. 2. *Archaic* Used as a form of address for a male superior, esp. a king. ▸ *v.* **sired, sir·ing.** To beget.

si·ren (sī′rən) ▸ *n.* A device for making a loud, usu. wailing sound as a signal or warning.

Siren ▸ *n.* 1. *Gk. Myth.* One of a group of sea nymphs whose sweet singing lured mariners to destruction. 2. **siren** A beautiful or alluring woman.

Sir·i·us (sĭr′ē-əs) ▸ *n.* A star in Canis Major, the brightest star in the sky.

sir·loin (sûr′loin′) ▸ *n.* A cut of meat from the upper part of the loin.

si·roc·co (sə-rŏk′ō) ▸ *n., pl.* **-cos.** A hot, humid southerly wind of S Europe originating in the Sahara.

sir·up (sĭr′əp, sûr′-) ▸ *n.* Var. of **syrup.**

sis (sĭs) ▸ *n. Informal* Sister.

si·sal (sī′səl) ▸ *n.* The fiber of a Mexican and Central American plant, used for cordage and rope.

sis·sy (sĭs′ē) ▸ *n., pl.* **-sies.** 1. A boy or man who does not fit the masculine stereotype. 2. A timid person. **—sis′sy·ish** *adj.*

sis·ter (sĭs′tər) ▸ *n.* 1. A female having one or both parents in common with another person. 2. A female who shares a common ancestry or allegiance with another, esp.: a. A kinswoman. b. A close female friend. c. A fellow African-American female. 3. **Sister** A nun. ▸ *adj.* Closely related or associated: *sister ships.* **—sis′ter·li·ness** *n.* **—sis′ter·ly** *adj.*

sis·ter·hood (sĭs′tər-ho͝od′) ▸ *n.* 1. The relationship of being a sister or sisters. 2. The quality of being sisterly. 3. Association of women in a common cause.

sis·ter-in-law (sĭs′tər-ĭn-lô′) ▸ *n., pl.* **sis·ters-in-law** (-tərz-). 1. The sister of one's husband or wife. 2. The wife of one's brother. 3. The wife of the brother of one's spouse.

sit (sĭt) ▸ *v.* **sat** (săt), **sit·ting.** 1. To rest with the body supported on the buttocks or hindquarters. 2. To perch, as a bird. 3. To cover eggs for hatching; brood. 4. To maintain a seated position on (a horse). 5. To be situated or located. 6. To pose for an artist or photographer. 7. To be in session. 8. To remain inactive or unused. 9. To please: *The idea didn't sit well with me.* 10. To baby-sit. ***—phrasal verbs:*** **sit down** To take a seat. **sit in on** To attend as a visitor. **sit on** *Informal* To suppress: *sat on the evidence.* **sit up** 1. To rise to a sitting position. 2. To become suddenly alert. ***—idiom:*** **sit tight** *Informal* To patiently await the next move. **—sit′ter** *n.*

si·tar (sĭ-tär′) ▸ *n.* A stringed instrument of India, having a track of 20 movable frets with 6 or 7 metal playing strings above and usu. 13 sympathetic resonating strings below. **—si·tar′ist** *n.*

sit·com (sĭt′kŏm′) ▸ *n.* A situation comedy.

THESAURUS

EXCEPTIONAL, INDIVIDUAL (2), LONE, UNIQUE.

singularity *n.* The condition of being one ▸ oneness, singleness, unity. [*Compare* COMPLETENESS.] *—See also* DETAIL, ECCENTRICITY, IDENTITY (1), INDIVIDUALITY, UNIQUENESS.

singularize *v.* *—See* DISTINGUISH (2).

singularly *adv.* *—See* UNUSUALLY.

sinister *adj.* *—See* FATEFUL (1).

sink *v.* 1. To go beneath the surface or to the bottom of a liquid ▸ founder, go down, go under, gravitate, settle, submerge, submerse, subside. 2. To undergo moral deterioration ▸ degenerate, fall, slip. [*Compare* DETERIORATE.] 3. To damage, disable, or destroy a seacraft ▸ run aground, shipwreck, wreck. *—See also* CONDESCEND (1), DESTROY (1), DETERIORATE, DROP (1), DROP (2), FADE, FALL (1), FALL (4), LOWER[2], PLUNGE.

sink in *v.* To come as a realization ▸ dawn on (*or* upon), register, soak in. [*Compare* DISCOVER, STRIKE, UNDERSTAND.]

sink *n.* *—See* DEPRESSION (1), PIT[1].

sinkhole *n.* *—See* DEPRESSION (1).

sinless *adj.* *—See* INNOCENT (1).

sinner *n.* *—See* EVILDOER.

sinuate *v.* *—See* CRAWL (1).

sinuous *adj.* *—See* WINDING.

sip *v.* *—See* DRINK (1).

sip *n.* *—See* DRINK (2), DROP (4).

sire *n.* *—See* FATHER.

sire *v.* To be the biological father of ▸ beget, father, get. *—See also* BREED.

siren *n.* *—See* SEDUCTRESS.

siren *adj.* *—See* SEDUCTIVE.

sis *n.* *—See* GIRL.

sissified *adj.* *—See* EFFEMINATE.

sissy *adj.* *—See* COWARDLY.

sissy *n.* *—See* COWARD.

sissyish *adj.* *—See* EFFEMINATE.

sister *n.* *—See* FRIEND, GIRL.

sisterhood *n.* *—See* COMPANY (3).

sit *v.* 1. To assume a position resting on the buttocks with the torso upright ▸ be seated, seat oneself, sit down. *Informal:* park oneself. *Idioms:* take a load off (one's feet), take a seat. [*Compare* SQUAT.] 2. To be in a certain position; have a location ▸ be located, be situated, rest, stand. *—See also* POSE (1).

sit back *v.* *—See* REST[1] (1).

sit on or **upon** *v.* *—See* REPRESS.

sit out *v.* *—See* REFRAIN.

sit through *v.* *—See* ENDURE (1).

sit-down (sĭt′doun′) ► *n.* **1.** A work stoppage in which the workers refuse to leave their place of employment until their demands are met. **2.** An obstruction of normal activity by the act of a large group sitting down to express a grievance or protest.

site (sīt) ► *n.* **1.** The place where something was, is, or is to be located. **2.** A website. ► *v.* **sit·ed, sit·ing.** To situate or locate.

sit-in (sĭt′ĭn′) ► *n.* **1.** See **sit-down** 1. **2.** An organized protest in which participants sit down in a place and refuse to move.

sit·ting (sĭt′ĭng) ► *n.* **1.** A period during which one is seated and occupied with a single activity. **2.** A session, as of a legislature. ► *adj.* Incumbent: *a sitting governor.*

Sitting Bull (1834?–90) ► Sioux leader.

sit·u·ate (sĭch′o͞o-āt′) ► *v.* **-at·ed, -at·ing.** To place in a certain spot; locate.

sit·u·a·tion (sĭch′o͞o-ā′shən) ► *n.* **1.** Position; location. **2.** A state of affairs. **3.** A job. **—sit′u·a′tion·al** *adj.*

situation comedy ► *n.* A humorous television series having a regular cast of characters.

sit-up (sĭt′ŭp′) ► *n.* A physical exercise in which one uses the abdominal muscles to raise the torso to a sitting position without moving the legs.

Si·van (sĭv′ən) ► *n.* A month of the Jewish calendar.

six (sĭks) ► *n.* **1.** The cardinal number equal to 5 + 1. **2.** The 6th in a set or sequence. **—six** *adj. & pron.*

six-gun (sĭks′gŭn′) ► *n.* A six-chambered revolver.

Six Nations ► *pl.n.* The Iroquois confederacy after the Tuscarora joined it in 1722.

six-pack (sĭks′păk′) ► *n.* Six units of a commodity, esp. six containers of a beverage sold in a pack.

six-shoot·er (sĭks′sho͞o′tər) ► *n.* A six-gun.

six·teen (sĭk-stēn′) ► *n.* **1.** The cardinal number equal to 15 + 1. **2.** The 16th in a set or sequence. **—six·teen′** *adj. & pron.*

six·teenth (sĭk-stēnth′) ► *n.* **1.** The ordinal number matching the number 16 in a series. **2.** One of 16 equal parts. **—six·teenth′** *adv. & adj.*

sixth (sĭksth) ► *n.* **1.** The ordinal number matching the number 6 in a series. **2.** One of six equal parts. **3.** *Mus.* A tone six degrees above or below a given tone in a diatonic scale. **—sixth** *adv. & adj.*

six·ti·eth (sĭk′stē-ĭth) ► *n.* **1.** The ordinal number matching the number 60 in a series. **2.** One of 60 equal parts. **—six′ti·eth** *adv. & adj.*

six·ty (sĭks′tē) ► *n., pl.* **-ties.** The cardinal number equal to 6 × 10. **—six′ty** *adj. & pron.*

siz·a·ble also **size·a·ble** (sī′zə-bəl) ► *adj.* Of considerable size; fairly large. **—siz′a·ble·ness** *n.* **—siz′a·bly** *adv.*

size[1] (sīz) ► *n.* **1.** The physical dimensions, magnitude, or extent of an object. **2.** Any of a series of graduated dimensions whereby manufactured articles are classified. ► *v.* **sized, siz·ing.** To arrange according to size. ***—phrasal verb:* size up** To make an estimate or judgment of.

size[2] (sīz) ► *n.* A gluey substance used as a glaze or filler for materials such as paper, cloth, or wall surfaces. **—size** *v.*

siz·ing (sī′zĭng) ► *n.* A glaze or filler; size.

siz·zle (sĭz′əl) ► *v.* **-zled, -zling. 1.** To make the hissing sound of frying fat. **2.** To seethe with anger. **3.** To be very hot. **—siz′zle** *n.* **—siz′zling·ly** *adv.*

SK ► *abbr.* Saskatchewan

ska (skä) ► *n.* Popular music of Jamaican origin having a fast tempo and a strongly accentuated offbeat.

skate[1] (skāt) ► *n.* **1.** An ice skate. **2.** A roller skate. ► *v.* **skat·ed, skat·ing.** To glide along on or as if on skates. **—skat′er** *n.*

skate[2] (skāt) ► *n.* A saltwater ray having a flattened body and winglike fins that extend around the head.

skate·board (skāt′bôrd′) ► *n.* A short narrow board mounted on roller skate wheels and usu. ridden standing or crouching. **—skate′board′** *v.* **—skate′board′er** *n.*

skeet (skēt) ► *n.* A form of trapshooting in which clay targets are thrown from traps to simulate birds in flight.

skein (skān) ► *n.* **1.** A length of thread or yarn wound in a loose long coil. **2.** A flock of geese in flight.

skel·e·ton (skĕl′ĭ-tn) ► *n.* **1a.** The internal supporting structure of a vertebrate, composed of bone and cartilage. **b.** The hard external supporting and protecting structure in many invertebrates, such as crustaceans. **2.** A supporting structure or framework. **3.** An outline or sketch. **—skel′e·tal** *adj.*

skeleton key ► *n.* A key designed or adapted to open many different locks.

skep·tic also **scep·tic** (skĕp′tĭk) ► *n.* **1.** One who habitually doubts, questions, or disagrees. **2.** One inclined to skepticism in religion or philosophy. **—skep′ti·cal** *adj.* **—skep′ti·cal·ly** *adv.*

skep·ti·cism also **scep·ti·cism** (skĕp′tĭ-sĭz′əm) ► *n.* **1.** A doubting or questioning attitude. **2.** *Philos.* The doctrine that absolute knowledge is impossible. **3.** Doubt or disbelief esp. of religious tenets.

sketch (skĕch) ► *n.* **1.** A hasty or undetailed drawing or painting. **2.** A brief outline. **3.** A short, often satirical scene or play; skit. ► *v.* To make a sketch (of). **—sketch′er** *n.* **—sketch′i·ly** *adv.* **—sketch′i·ness** *n.* **—sketch′y** *adj.*

skew (skyo͞o) ► *v.* **1.** To turn or place at an angle. **2.** To distort. ► *adj.* Turned to one side. ► *n.* A slant.

skew·er (skyo͞o′ər) ► *n.* A long pointed rod for impaling and holding food during cooking. **—skew′er** *v.*

ski (skē) ► *n., pl.* **skis.** One of a pair of long flat runners for gliding over snow or water. ► *v.* **skied, ski·ing.** To go or glide on skis, esp. as a sport. **—ski′a·ble** *adj.* **—ski′er** *n.* **—ski′ing** *n.*

skid (skĭd) ► *n.* **1.** The act of sliding or slipping over a surface. **2a.** A plank or log used for sliding or rolling heavy objects. **b.** A pallet for loading or handling goods. **3.** A device applying pressure to a wheel to brake a vehicle. **4.** A runner in the landing gear of certain aircraft, such as helicopters. **5. skids** *Slang* A path to ruin or failure: *His career hit the skids.* ► *v.* **skid·ded, skid·ding. 1.** To slide sideways while moving due to loss of traction. **2.** To slide without revolving: *wheels skidding on oily pavement.*

skid row (rō) ► *n.* *Slang* A squalid district inhabited by derelicts.

THESAURUS

site *n.* —*See* POSITION (1), SCENE (1).
site *v.* —*See* POSITION.
situate *v.* —*See* POSITION.
situation *n.* —*See* BEARING (3), CONDI-[illegible]TION (3).
sixth sense *n.* —*See* INSTINCT.
sizable *adj.* —*See* BIG.
sizableness *n.* —*See* SIZE (2).
sizably *adv.* —*See* CONSIDERABLY.
size *n.* **1.** The amount of space occupied by something ► area, dimensions, extent, magnitude, measure, measurements, proportions, volume. [*Compare* RANGE.] **2.** The quality or state of being large in amount, extent, or importance ► amplitude, bigness, greatness, largeness, magnitude, sizableness, voluminousness. [*Compare* ENORMOUSNESS, HEAVINESS.] —*See also* BULK (1).
size *v.* —*See* CLASSIFY.
size up *v.* —*See* ESTIMATE (1).
sizzle *v.* —*See* HISS (1).
sizzle *n.* —*See* EROTICISM, HISS (1), PASSION.
sizzling *adj.* —*See* DESIRABLE, EROTIC, HOT (1).
skate *v.* —*See* BREEZE, GLIDE (1).
skedaddle *v.* —*See* RUN (2).
skein *n.* —*See* TANGLE.
skeletal *adj.* —*See* HAGGARD.
skeleton *n.* —*See* DRAFT (1), FRAME.
skell *n.* —*See* PAUPER.
skeptic *n.* One who habitually or instinctively doubts or questions ► agnostic, doubter, doubting Thomas, nonbeliever, unbeliever.
skeptical *adj.* —*See* DISTRUSTFUL, DOUBTFUL (2), INCREDULOUS.
skeptically *adv.* With skepticism ► askance, distrustfully, distrustingly, doubtfully, doubtingly, dubiously, leerily, mistrustfully, questioningly, suspiciously, untrustingly. *Idioms:* with a grain of salt, with reservations.
skepticism *n.* —*See* DISBELIEF, DISTRUST, DOUBT.
sketch *n.* A short theatrical piece within a larger production ► act, skit. [*Compare* SATIRE.] —*See also* DRAFT (1), SYNOPSIS.
sketch *v.* —*See* DESIGN (2), DRAFT (1).
sketchy *adj.* —*See* DEFICIENT, ROUGH (4), SUPERFICIAL.
skew *v.* —*See* BIAS (2), SWERVE, TEND[1].
skid *n.* —*See* FALL (3).
skid *v.* —*See* FALL (4), STUMBLE.

skiff (skĭf) ▸ *n.* A small, flat-bottomed open boat.
ski lift ▸ *n.* A power-driven conveyor used to carry skiers to the top of a slope.
skill (skĭl) ▸ *n.* **1.** Proficiency; dexterity. **2.** An art, trade, or technique, esp. one requiring use of the hands or body. **—skilled** *adj.*
skil·let (skĭl′ĭt) ▸ *n.* See **frying pan.**
skill·ful also **skil·ful** (skĭl′fəl) ▸ *adj.* **1.** Possessing or exercising skill. **2.** Marked by or requiring skill. **—skill′ful·ly** *adv.* **—skill′ful·ness** *n.*
skim (skĭm) ▸ *v.* **skimmed, skim·ming. 1a.** To remove floating matter from (a liquid). **b.** To remove (floating matter): *skimmed the cream off the milk.* **c.** To take away the choicest parts from. **2.** To glide or pass quickly and lightly over. **3.** To read or glance through quickly or superficially.
skim milk ▸ *n.* Milk from which the cream has been removed.
skimp (skĭmp) ▸ *v.* **1.** To deal with hastily or carelessly. **2.** To be stingy or sparing; scrimp.
skimp·y (skĭm′pē) ▸ *adj.* **-i·er, -i·est. 1.** Inadequate in size or amount; scanty. **2.** Stingy or niggardly. **—skimp′i·ly** *adv.* **—skimp′i·ness** *n.*
skin (skĭn) ▸ *n.* **1.** The membranous tissue forming the outer covering of an animal. **2.** An animal hide or pelt. **3.** A usu. thin, closely adhering outer layer: *a peach skin; the skin of an aircraft.* ▸ *v.* **skinned, skin·ning. 1.** To remove skin from. **2.** To injure the skin of. **3.** *Slang* To cheat; swindle. ***—idioms:*** **by the skin of (one's) teeth** By the smallest margin. **get under (one's) skin** To provoke. **—skin′less** *adj.*
skin diving ▸ *n.* Underwater swimming, often with flippers, a face mask, and usu. a snorkel. **—skin′-dive′** *v.* **—skin diver** *n.*
skin·flint (skĭn′flĭnt′) ▸ *n.* A miser.
Skin·ner (skĭn′ər), **B(urrhus) F(rederick)** (1904–90) ▸ Amer. psychologist.
skin·ny (skĭn′ē) ▸ *adj.* **-ni·er, -ni·est.** Very thin. **—skin′ni·ness** *n.*
skin·ny-dip (skĭn′ē-dĭp′) ▸ *v. Informal* To swim in the nude. **—skin′ny-dip′ping** *n.*
skip (skĭp) ▸ *v.* **skipped, skip·ping. 1a.** To move by stepping and hopping on one foot and then the other. **b.** To leap or jump lightly (over). **2.** To ricochet. **3.** To pass from point to point omitting what intervenes. **4.** To pass over, omit, or disregard. **5.** To be promoted beyond (the next grade or level). **6.** *Informal* To leave hastily: *skipped town.* ▸ *n.* **1.** A skipping gait. **2.** A gap or omission. **—skip′per** *n.*
skip·per (skĭp′ər) ▸ *n.* The master of a ship. **—skip′per** *v.*
skir·mish (skûr′mĭsh) ▸ *n.* **1.** A minor battle in war. **2.** A minor conflict or dispute. **—skir′mish** *v.*
skirt (skûrt) ▸ *n.* **1.** The part of a garment, such as a dress or coat, that hangs from the waist down. **2.** A separate garment hanging from the waist down. ▸ *v.* **1.** To lie along the edge (of); border. **2.** To pass around the edge or border (of). **3.** To evade or avoid.
skit (skĭt) ▸ *n.* A short, usu. comic theatrical sketch.
skit·ter (skĭt′ər) ▸ *v.* To skip, glide, or move rapidly or lightly along a surface.
skit·tish (skĭt′ĭsh) ▸ *adj.* **1.** Excitable or nervous. **2.** Inconstant; capricious. **—skit′tish·ly** *adv.* **—skit′tish·ness** *n.*
skoal (skōl) ▸ *interj.* Used as a drinking toast.
skulk (skŭlk) ▸ *v.* **1.** To lie in hiding; lurk. **2.** To move about stealthily. **—skulk′er** *n.*
skull (skŭl) ▸ *n.* The bony framework of the head; cranium.
skull·cap (skŭl′kăp′) ▸ *n.* **1.** A light, close-fitting, brimless cap. **2.** A yarmulke.
skull·dug·ger·y or **skul·dug·ger·y** (skŭl-dŭg′ə-rē) ▸ *n.* Crafty deception or trickery.
skunk (skŭngk) ▸ *n.* **1.** A New World mammal having a bushy tail and black and white fur and ejecting a foul-smelling secretion if startled. **2.** *Slang* A despicable person. ▸ *v. Slang* To defeat overwhelmingly.
skunk cabbage ▸ *n.* A North American swamp plant having ill-smelling minute flowers in a mottled greenish or purplish spathe.
sky (skī) ▸ *n., pl.* **skies** (skīz). **1.** The upper atmosphere, seen as a hemisphere above the earth. **2.** often **skies** Atmospheric conditions: *fair skies.* **3.** The celestial regions.
sky·cap (skī′kăp′) ▸ *n.* An airport porter.
sky·dive (skī′dīv′) ▸ *v.* To jump from an airplane, performing various maneuvers before opening a parachute. **—sky′div′er** *n.* **—sky′div′ing** *n.*
sky-high (skī′hī′) ▸ *adv.* **1.** To a very high level: *garbage piled sky-high.* **2.** In or to pieces: *blew the bridge sky-high.* ▸ *adj.* Exorbitantly high in cost or value.
sky·jack (skī′jăk′) ▸ *v.* To hijack (an aircraft in flight). **—sky′jack′er** *n.* **—sky′jack′ing** *n.*
sky·lark (skī′lärk′) ▸ *n.* An Old World lark with brownish plumage, noted for its singing while in flight. ▸ *v.* To romp or frolic.
sky·light (skī′līt′) ▸ *n.* An overhead window, as in a roof, admitting daylight.
sky·line (skī′līn′) ▸ *n.* **1.** The horizon. **2.** An outline, as of buildings, against the sky.
sky·rock·et (skī′rŏk′ĭt) ▸ *n.* A firework that rises into the air and explodes brilliantly. ▸ *v.* To rise rapidly and suddenly.
sky·scrap·er (skī′skrā′pər) ▸ *n.* A very tall building.
sky·ward (skī′wərd) ▸ *adv. & adj.* At or toward the sky. **—sky′wards** *adv.*
sky·writ·ing (skī′rī′tĭng) ▸ *n.* The process of writing in the sky by releasing a visible vapor from a flying airplane. **—sky′writ′er** *n.*
slab (slăb) ▸ *n.* **1.** A broad, flat, thick piece or slice. **2.** An outside piece cut from a log when squaring it for lumber.
slack (slăk) ▸ *adj.* **-er, -est. 1.** Moving slowly; sluggish. **2.** Lacking in activity; not busy. **3.** Not tense, firm, or taut. **4.** Lacking in diligence, care, or concern. ▸ *v.* **1.** To make or become slack. **2.** To slake (lime). ***—phrasal verb:*** **slack off (or up)** To decrease in activity or intensity. ▸ *n.* **1.** Some-

THESAURUS

skill *n.* A quality that makes a person suitable for a particular position or task ▸ attainment, credential, endowment, qualification. *—See also* ABILITY (1), DEXTERITY.
skilled *adj.* *—See* ABLE, EXPERT.
skillful *adj.* *—See* ABLE, DEXTEROUS, EXPERT.
skim *v.* *—See* BROWSE (1), BRUSH[1], FLY (2), GLANCE (1), GLIDE (1).
skim *n.* *—See* BRUSH[1].
skimp *v.* *—See* SCRIMP.
skimpy *adj.* *—See* MEAGER.
skin *n.* **1.** The tissue forming the external covering of the body ▸ epidermis, integument. **2.** A thin outer covering of an object ▸ film, lamina, membrane, sheath, sheathing, sheet. [*Compare* COAT.] **3.** The outer covering of a fruit or similar plant part ▸ hull, husk, peel, rind, shell, zest.
skin *v.* To remove the skin of ▸ decorticate, hull, husk, pare, peel, scale, shell, shuck, strip. *—See also* CHEAT (1).
skin-deep *adj.* *—See* SUPERFICIAL.
skinflint *n.* *—See* MISER.
skinny *adj.* *—See* THIN (1).
skip *v. Informal* To fail to attend on purpose ▸ duck, shirk. *Idiom:* go AWOL. [*Compare* CUT (4).] *—See also* BOUND[1], DROP (4), ESCAPE (1), GLANCE (1).
skip out *v.* *—See* RENEGE.
skip *n.* *—See* BOUND[1].
skipper *n.* ▸ captain, commander, shipmaster.
skirmish *n.* *—See* BATTLE.
skirt *v.* To pass around but not through ▸ bypass, circumnavigate, circumvent, detour, go around. [*Compare* AVOID.] *—See also* EVADE (1).
skit *n.* A short theatrical piece within a larger production ▸ act, sketch. [*Compare* SATIRE.]
skitter *v.* *—See* BOUND[1].
skittish *adj.* *—See* EDGY.
skulk *v.* *—See* LURK, SNEAK.
skull *n.* The bony framework of the head ▸ braincase, brainpan, cranium. [*Compare* HEAD.]
skunk *v.* *—See* OVERWHELM (1).
skunk *n.* *—See* CREEP (2).
sky *n.* The celestial regions as seen from the earth ▸ air, firmament, heavens. *Idiom:* wild blue yonder.
sky *v.* *—See* SOAR.
sky-high *adj.* *—See* HIGH (1), STEEP[1] (2).
skyrocket *v.* *—See* SOAR.
slab *n.* *—See* CUT (2), LUMP[1].
slack *adj.* *—See* LOOSE (1), NEGLIGENT, SLOW (2).
slack *v.* To avoid the fulfillment of ▸ disregard, neglect, shirk. *Idiom:* let slide. *—See also* EASE (1).
slack off *v.* *—See* IDLE (1), SUBSIDE.

thing slack or loose. 2. A period of little activity. 3. **slacks** Trousers for informal wear. **—slack′ly** *adv.* **—slack′ness** *n.*

slack·en (slăk′ən) ▸ *v.* To make or become slower, looser, or less intense or severe.

slack·er (slăk′ər) ▸ *n.* One who shirks work or duty, esp. military service in wartime.

slag (slăg) ▸ *n.* The glassy mass left after smelting metallic ore.

slain (slān) ▸ *v.* P.part. of **slay**.

slake (slāk) ▸ *v.* **slaked, slak·ing**. 1. To cause to lessen or subside; moderate or quench. 2. To combine (lime) chemically with water or moist air.

sla·lom (slä′ləm) ▸ *n.* A skiing race along a downhill zigzag course.

slam[1] (slăm) ▸ *v.* **slammed, slam·ming**. 1. To shut with force and loud noise. 2. To put, throw, or hit so as to produce a loud noise. ▸ *n.* 1. A loud forceful impact. 2. A noise so produced.

slam[2] (slăm) ▸ *n.* The winning of all the tricks or all but one during the play of one hand in bridge and other card games.

slam dunk ▸ *n.* *Basketball* A dramatic forceful dunk. **—slam′-dunk′** *v.*

slam·mer (slăm′ər) ▸ *n.* *Slang* A jail.

slan·der (slăn′dər) ▸ *n.* A false and malicious, usu. oral statement injurious to a person's reputation. **—slan′der** *v.* **—slan′der·er** *n.* **—slan′der·ous** *adj.* **—slan′der·ous·ly** *adv.*

slang (slăng) ▸ *n.* A vocabulary of casual or playful, often short-lived expressions used esp. for humor, irreverence, or striking effect. **—slang′i·ness** *n.* **—slang′y** *adj.*

slant (slănt) ▸ *v.* 1. To slope or cause to slope. 2. To present in a way that conforms with a particular bias. ▸ *n.* 1. A sloping plane, direction, or course. 2. A particular bias. **—slant′ing·ly** *adv.* **—slant′wise′** *adv. & adj.*

slap (slăp) ▸ *n.* 1a. A sharp blow made with the open hand or a flat object. b. The sound so made. 2. An insult. ▸ *v.* **slapped, slap·ping**. 1. To give a slap to. 2. To strike or cause to strike sharply and loudly. 3. To insult sharply. **—*idiom:* slap on the wrist** A token punishment.

slap·dash (slăp′dăsh′) ▸ *adj.* Hasty and careless. **—slap′dash′** *adv.*

slap·hap·py (slăp′hăp′ē) ▸ *adj.* *Slang* Dazed, giddy, or silly, as if from blows to the head.

slap·stick (slăp′stĭk′) ▸ *n.* Comedy marked by loud and boisterous farce.

slash (slăsh) ▸ *v.* 1. To cut with forceful sweeping strokes. 2. To make a gash or slit in. 3. To reduce drastically. ▸ *n.* 1a. A sweeping stroke made with a sharp instrument. b. A cut made by slashing. 2. A virgule. **—slash′er** *n.*

slat (slăt) ▸ *n.* A flat narrow strip, as of metal or wood.

slate (slāt) ▸ *n.* 1a. A fine-grained rock that splits into thin, smooth-surfaced layers. b. A piece of this rock cut for use as roofing or surfacing material or as a writing surface. 2. A list of the candidates of a political party running for various offices. 3. A dark or bluish gray. ▸ *v.* **slat·ed, slat·ing**. 1. To cover with slate. 2. To schedule. **—slat′y** *adj.*

slath·er (slăth′ər) ▸ *v.* *Informal* To spread thickly or lavishly.

slat·tern (slăt′ərn) ▸ *n.* A slovenly woman. **—slat′tern·li·ness** *n.* **—slat′tern·ly** *adj.*

slaugh·ter (slô′tər) ▸ *n.* 1. The killing of animals for food. 2. The killing of a large number of people; massacre. ▸ *v.* 1. To butcher (animals) for food. 2. To kill brutally or in large numbers. **—slaugh′ter·er** *n.*

slaugh·ter·house (slô′tər-hous′) ▸ *n.* A place where animals are butchered.

Slav (släv) ▸ *n.* A member of one of the Slavic-speaking peoples of E Europe.

slave (slāv) ▸ *n.* 1. One bound in servitude as the property of a person or household. 2. One who is abjectly subservient to a specified person, emotion, or influence. ▸ *v.* **slaved, slav·ing**. To work very hard or doggedly; toil.

slav·er[1] (slăv′ər) ▸ *v.* 1. To slobber; drool. 2. To fawn. **—slav′er** *n.*

slav·er[2] (slā′vər) ▸ *n.* One, such as a person or ship, engaged in the trafficking of slaves.

slav·er·y (slā′və-rē, slāv′rē) ▸ *n.*, *pl.* **-ies**. 1. The state of being a slave; bondage. 2. The practice of owning slaves. 3. A condition of hard work and subjection.

Slav·ic (slä′vĭk) ▸ *adj.* Of or relating to the Slavs or their languages. ▸ *n.* A branch of Indo-European including Bulgarian, Czech, Polish, Russian, Serbo-Croatian, Slovak, and Slovenian.

slav·ish (slā′vĭsh) ▸ *adj.* 1. Of or like a slave; servile: *slavish devotion.* 2. Showing no originality: *a slavish copy of the original.* **—slav′ish·ly** *adv.* **—slav′ish·ness** *n.*

Sla·von·ic (slə-vŏn′ĭk) ▸ *n.* Slavic. **—Sla·von′ic** *adj.*

slaw (slô) ▸ *n.* Coleslaw.

slay (slā) ▸ *v.* **slew** (slo͞o), **slain** (slān), **slay·ing**. To kill violently. **—slay′er** *n.*

slea·zy (slē′zē) ▸ *adj.* **-zi·er, -zi·est**. 1a. Shabby and dirty; tawdry. b. Dishonest or corrupt. 2. Cheap or shoddy. **—sleaze** *n.* **—slea′zi·ly** *adv.* **—slea′zi·ness** *n.*

sled (slĕd) ▸ *n.* 1. A vehicle mounted on runners, used for

THESAURUS

slacken *v.* —*See* DELAY (1), EASE (1), SUBSIDE, WEAKEN.

slackening *n.* —*See* WANING.

slacker *n.* —*See* WASTREL (2).

slackness *n.* —*See* LICENSE (2), NEGLIGENCE.

slam *v.* 1. *Slang* To criticize harshly and devastatingly ▸ blast, blister, drub, excoriate, flay, lacerate, lash, rip into, scarify, scathe, scorch, score, scourge, slap, slash, tear into, wither. *Informal:* bash, cut up, lambaste, light into, roast. *Slang:* trash. *Idioms:* burn someone's ears, crawl (*or* jump) all over someone, jump down someone's throat, let someone have it, pin someone's ears back, put someone on the griddle, put someone on the hot seat, rake over the coals, read the riot act to. [*Compare* CHASTISE, CRITICIZE, MALIGN.] 2. To move a door, for example, in order to cover an opening ▸ close, clench, seal, shut. —*See also* BANG (1), COLLIDE, DRIVE (2), HIT.

slam *n.* A forceful movement causing a loud noise ▸ bang, crash, smash, wham. —*See also* REBUKE.

slammer *n.* —*See* JAIL.

slander *n.* —*See* GOSSIP (1), LIBEL.

slander *v.* —*See* MALIGN.

slanderous *adj.* —*See* LIBELOUS.

slant *v.* —*See* BIAS (2), DISTORT, INCLINE, SWERVE, TEND[1].

slant *n.* —*See* ASCENT (2), BIAS, INCLINATION (2), VIEWPOINT.

slanted *adj.* —*See* BIASED, OBLIQUE.

slanting *adj.* —*See* OBLIQUE.

slap *n.* A sharp blow, especially with the open hand ▸ box, cuff, smack, smacker, spank, swat, whack. *Informal:* spat. [*Compare* BLOW[2].] —*See also* CLASH, REBUKE.

slap *v.* To hit with a sharp blow, especially with the open hand ▸ box, clap, cuff, smack, spank, swat, whack. *Informal:* spat. [*Compare* BEAT, HIT.] —*See also* SLAM (1).

slap around *v.* —*See* MANHANDLE.

slapdash *adj.* —*See* MESSY (1), RASH[1].

slash *v.* —*See* CUT (1), CUT (3), SLAM (1).

slash *n.* —*See* CUT (1), DECREASE.

slashing *adj.* —*See* BITING.

slate *n.* A list of candidates proposed or endorsed by a political party ▸ ballot, lineup, ticket.

slate *v.* To enter on a schedule ▸ calendar, docket, program, schedule. [*Compare* LIST[1], POST[3].]

slated *adj.* —*See* DUE (2).

slattern *n.* —*See* SLUT.

slaughter *n.* —*See* MASSACRE.

slaughter *v.* —*See* MASSACRE.

slaughterer *n.* —*See* MURDERER.

slaughterous *adj.* —*See* MURDEROUS.

slave *n.* One bound to serve another person or influence ▸ bondservant, chattel, helot, serf, servant, vassal. [*Compare* SUBORDINATE.] —*See also* DRUDGE (1), SYCOPHANT.

slave *v.* —*See* GRIND (2), LABOR.

slaver *v.* —*See* DROOL, FAWN.

slaver *n.* Saliva running from the mouth ▸ drivel, drool, salivation, slobber.

slavery *n.* A state of subjugation to an owner or master ▸ bondage, enslavement, helotry, involuntary servitude, serfdom, servileness, servility, servitude, thrall, thralldom, villeinage, yoke.

slavish *adj.* —*See* IMITATIVE (1), SERVILE.

slay *v.* —*See* KILL[1], MURDER.

slayer *n.* —*See* MURDERER.

sleaze *n.* —*See* OBSCENITY (2).

sleazy *adj.* —*See* SHABBY, SHODDY.

sled or **sledge** *v.* To ride or be pulled

moving over ice and snow. **2.** A light wooden frame on runners, used by children for coasting over snow or ice. ▸ *v.* **sled·ded, sled·ding.** To ride or convey by a sled.

sledge (slĕj) ▸ *n.* A large sled drawn by work animals, used for transporting loads across ice and snow.

sledge·ham·mer (slĕj′hăm′ər) ▸ *n.* A long heavy hammer usu. wielded with both hands.

sleek (slēk) ▸ *adj.* **-er, -est. 1.** Smooth and lustrous as if polished. **2.** Well-groomed and neatly tailored. **3.** Healthy or well-fed; thriving. **4.** Polished or smooth in behavior. **—sleek** *v.* **—sleek′ly** *adv.* **—sleek′ness** *n.*

sleep (slēp) ▸ *n.* **1.** A natural, periodic state of rest in which consciousness is lost and bodily movement and responsiveness to external stimuli decrease. **2.** A state, as of inactivity or unconsciousness, similar to sleep. ▸ *v.* **slept** (slĕpt), **sleep·ing. 1.** To be in or as if in a state of sleep. **2.** To pass by sleeping. ***—phrasal verb:* sleep with** To have sexual relations with.

sleep·er (slē′pər) ▸ *n.* **1.** One that sleeps. **2.** A sleeping car. **3.** One that achieves unexpected recognition, popularity, or success.

sleep·ing bag (slē′pĭng) ▸ *n.* A lined, usu. zippered bag for sleeping, esp. outdoors.

sleeping car ▸ *n.* A railroad car having accommodations for sleeping.

sleeping pill ▸ *n.* A sedative in the form of a pill or capsule used to relieve insomnia.

sleeping sickness ▸ *n.* An often fatal infectious disease of tropical Africa transmitted by the tsetse fly and marked by fever and lethargy.

sleep·less (slēp′lĭs) ▸ *adj.* **1a.** Marked by a lack of sleep. **b.** Unable to sleep. **2.** Always alert or in motion. **—sleep′less·ly** *adv.* **—sleep′less·ness** *n.*

sleep·walk·ing (slēp′wô′kĭng) ▸ *n.* The act of walking or performing other activities while asleep or in a sleeplike state; somnambulism. **—sleep′walk′** *v.*

sleep·y (slē′pē) ▸ *adj.* **-i·er, -i·est. 1.** Ready for sleep; drowsy. **2.** Inactive; quiet. **—sleep′i·ly** *adv.* **—sleep′i·ness** *n.*

sleet (slēt) ▸ *n.* **1.** Precipitation consisting of frozen or partially frozen raindrops. **2.** An icy glaze. ▸ *v.* To shower sleet. **—sleet′y** *adj.*

sleeve (slēv) ▸ *n.* **1.** A part of a garment that covers the arm. **2.** A case into which an object fits. ***—idiom:* up (one's) sleeve** Hidden but ready to be used. **—sleeved** *adj.* **—sleeve′less** *adj.*

sleigh (slā) ▸ *n.* A light vehicle on runners, usu. drawn by a horse over snow or ice. **—sleigh** *v.*

sleight (slīt) ▸ *n.* **1.** Dexterity. **2.** A trick or stratagem.

sleight of hand ▸ *n.* **1.** A trick or set of tricks performed so quickly that the manner of execution cannot be observed; legerdemain. **2.** Performance of such tricks.

slen·der (slĕn′dər) ▸ *adj.* **-er, -est. 1.** Having little width in proportion to height or length. **2.** Small in amount or extent; meager. **—slen′der·ly** *adv.* **—slen′der·ness** *n.*

slen·der·ize (slĕn′də-rīz′) ▸ *v.* **-ized, -iz·ing.** To make or become slender.

slept (slĕpt) ▸ *v.* P.t. and p.part. of **sleep.**

sleuth (slo͞oth) ▸ *n.* A detective. **—sleuth** *v.*

sleuth·hound (slo͞oth′hound′) ▸ *n.* **1.** A dog used for tracking or pursuing. **2.** A detective.

slew[1] also **slue** (slo͞o) ▸ *n.* *Informal* A large amount or number.

slew[2] (slo͞o) ▸ *v.* P.t. of **slay.**

slew[3] (slo͞o) ▸ *v. & n.* Var. of **slue**[1].

slice (slīs) ▸ *n.* **1.** A thin broad piece cut from a larger amount. **2.** A portion or share. **3.** *Sports* A stroke that causes a ball to curve off course to the right or, if the player is left-handed, to the left. ▸ *v.* **sliced, slic·ing. 1.** To cut or divide into slices. **2.** To cut or remove from a larger piece. **3.** *Sports* To hit (a ball) with a slice. **—slice′a·ble** *adj.* **—slic′er** *n.*

slick (slĭk) ▸ *adj.* **-er, -est. 1.** Smooth, glossy, and slippery. **2.** Deftly executed; adroit. **3.** Shrewd; wily. **4.** Superficially attractive but lacking depth; glib. ▸ *n.* A smooth or slippery surface or area: *an oil slick.* ▸ *v.* To make smooth or glossy. **—slick′ly** *adv.* **—slick′ness** *n.*

slick·er (slĭk′ər) ▸ *n.* **1.** A long loose raincoat made of a glossy material. **2.** *Informal* A person with stylish clothing and manners.

slide (slīd) ▸ *v.* **slid** (slĭd), **slid·ing. 1.** To move over a surface while maintaining continuous contact. **2.** To pass smoothly and quietly; glide. **3.** To slip or skid. **4.** To return to a less favorable or worthy condition. ▸ *n.* **1.** A sliding movement or action. **2.** A smooth surface or track for sliding. **3.** A playground apparatus for sliding down. **4.** A part that operates by sliding, as the bolt in a lock. **5.** A usu. photographic image on a transparent base for projection on a screen. **6.** A small glass plate for mounting specimens for a microscope. **7.** A fall of a mass of rock, earth, or snow down a slope.

slid·er (slī′dər) ▸ *n.* **1.** One that slides. **2.** *Baseball* A fast pitch that breaks in the same direction as a curve ball at the last moment.

slide rule ▸ *n.* A device consisting of two logarithmically scaled rules arranged to slide along each other, used in performing mathematical operations.

slid·ing scale (slī′dĭng) ▸ *n.* A scale in which indicated prices, taxes, or wages vary in accordance with another factor, as wages with the cost-of-living index.

sli·er (slī′ər) ▸ *adj.* Comp. of **sly.**

sli·est (slī′ĭst) ▸ *adj.* Superl. of **sly.**

slight (slīt) ▸ *adj.* **-er, -est. 1.** Small in size, degree, or amount. **2.** Frail or delicate. **3.** Of small importance; trifling. ▸ *v.* **1.** To treat as if of small importance. **2.** To snub

THESAURUS

on a sled in the snow ▸ coast, sleigh-ride, slide. ***Idiom:*** go sledding (*or* coasting *or* sleigh-riding).

sleek *adj.* **1.** Smooth and lustrous as if polished ▸ satiny, silken, silky. [*Compare* EVEN, GLOSSY, SLICK.] **2.** Having slender and graceful lines ▸ streamlined, trim. *—See also* UNCTUOUS.

sleek *v.* *—See* GLOSS[1].

sleek over *v.* *—See* EXTENUATE.

sleekness *n.* *—See* GLOSS[1].

sleep *n.* The natural recurring condition of suspended consciousness by which the body rests ▸ dreamland, slumber. *Slang:* shuteye, z's. ***Idioms:*** land of Nod, the arms of Morpheus. [*Compare* NAP, REST.]

sleep *v.* To be asleep ▸ slumber. *Slang:* sack out. ***Idioms:*** be in the land of Nod, catch some shuteye, catch (*or* cop) some z's, saw logs (*or* wood), sleep like a log (*or* baby *or* rock *or* top), sleep tight. [*Compare* NAP, REST.]

sleeper *n.* *—See* HIT.

sleeping *adj.* In a state of sleep ▸ asleep, snoozing, unawake. *Slang:* conked out, sacked out, zonked. ***Idioms:*** catching (*or* copping) some z's, dead to the world, in dreamland, fast (*or* sound) asleep, in a sound (*or* wakeless) sleep, in the arms of Morpheus, in the land of Nod, out like a light, sawing logs (*or* wood). *—See also* LATENT.

sleepless *adj.* Marked by an absence of sleep ▸ slumberless, wakeful. [*Compare* WAKEFUL.]

sleepwalking *n.* *—See* TRANCE.

sleepy *adj.* Ready for or needing sleep ▸ dozy, drowsy, nodding, slumberous, slumbery, somnolent, soporific. *—See also* LANGUID, SOPORIFIC.

sleight *n.* *—See* DEXTERITY, TRICK (1).

sleight of hand *n.* *—See* MAGIC (2).

slender *adj.* *—See* REMOTE (2), THIN (1).

sleuth *n.* *—See* DETECTIVE.

slew or **slue** *n.* *—See* HEAP (2).

slice *n.* *—See* BIT[1] (2), CUT (1), CUT (2), FLAKE.

slice *v.* *—See* CUT (2).

slice up *v.* *—See* SHRED.

slick *adj.* So smooth and glassy as to offer insecure hold or footing ▸ lubricious, oily, slippery, slithery. ***Idiom:*** slippery as an eel. [*Compare* SLEEK.] *—See also* DEXTEROUS, GLIB, SHREWD.

slick up *v.* *—See* TIDY (2).

slicker *n.* *—See* COAT (1).

slide *v.* **1.** To ride or be pulled on a sled in the snow ▸ coast, sled, sledge, sleigh-ride. ***Idiom:*** go sledding (*or* coasting *or* sleigh-riding). **2.** To maneuver gently and slowly into place ▸ ease, glide, slip. [*Compare* EASE.] *—See also* CRAWL (1), GLIDE (1), SNEAK, STUMBLE.

slide *n.* *—See* DESCENT, FALL (3).

slight *adj.* *—See* GENTLE (2), LIGHT[2] (2), MINOR (1), REMOTE (2).

slight *v.* *—See* BELITTLE, NEGLECT (1), SNUB.

slight *n.* *—See* INDIGNITY, NEGLECT.

or insult. **3.** To neglect. ▸ *n.* An act of deliberate discourtesy or disrespect; snub. **—slight′ly** *adv.* **—slight′ness** *n.*

slim (slĭm) ▸ *adj.* **slim·mer, slim·mest. 1.** Small in girth or thickness; slender. **2.** Scanty or meager. ▸ *v.* **slimmed, slim·ming.** To make or become slim. **—slim′ly** *adv.* **—slim′ness** *n.*

slime (slīm) ▸ *n.* **1.** A moist, foul, gen. slippery or sticky substance. **2.** A mucous secretion, as of fish or slugs. **—slim′y** *adj.*

sling (slĭng) ▸ *n.* **1.** A weapon made of a looped strap in which a stone is hurled. **2.** A looped belt, rope, strap, or chain for supporting, cradling, or hoisting loads. **3.** A cloth band suspended from the neck to support an injured arm or hand. ▸ *v.* **slung** (slŭng), **sling·ing. 1.** To hurl with a swinging motion; fling. **2.** To place, carry, or move in a sling. **—sling′er** *n.*

sling·shot (slĭng′shŏt′) ▸ *n.* A Y-shaped stick having an elastic strap attached to the prongs, used for shooting stones or pellets.

slink (slĭngk) ▸ *v.* **slunk** (slŭngk), **slink·ing.** To move furtively.

slink·y (slĭng′kē) ▸ *adj.* **-i·er, -i·est. 1.** Stealthy; furtive. **2.** Sinuous and sleek.

slip[1] (slĭp) ▸ *v.* **slipped, slip·ping. 1.** To move quietly and stealthily. **2.** To slide involuntarily and lose one's balance. **3.** To slide out of place or from one's grasp. **4.** To leave or escape unnoticed. **5a.** To decline from a former or standard level; fall off. **b.** To make a mistake. **6.** To place or insert smoothly and quietly. **7.** To put on or remove easily or quickly: *slip on a sweater.* ▸ *n.* **1.** The act of slipping. **2.** A slight error or oversight. **3.** A docking place for a ship between two piers. **4.** A woman's undergarment of dress length. **5.** A pillowcase. ***—idioms:*** **give (someone) the slip** *Slang* To escape the company or pursuit of. **let slip** To say inadvertently or thoughtlessly. **slip one over on** *Informal* To hoodwink; trick. **—slip′page** *n.*

slip[2] (slĭp) ▸ *n.* **1.** A plant cutting used for propagation. **2.** A slender, youthful person. **3.** A small piece of paper.

slip·cov·er (slĭp′kŭv′ər) ▸ *n.* A fitted, removable, usu. cloth cover for a piece of upholstered furniture. **—slip′cov′er** *v.*

slip·knot (slĭp′nŏt′) ▸ *n.* A knot made with a loop so that it slips easily along the rope or cord around which it is tied.

slipped disk (slĭpt) ▸ *n.* An injury due to the shifting out of position of a cushioning disk between the spinal vertebrae.

slip·per (slĭp′ər) ▸ *n.* A light low shoe that can be slipped on and off easily.

slip·per·y (slĭp′ə-rē) ▸ *adj.* **-i·er, -i·est. 1.** Causing or tending to cause sliding or slipping. **2.** Not trustworthy; elusive or tricky. **—slip′per·i·ness** *n.*

slip·shod (slĭp′shŏd′) ▸ *adj.* **1.** Careless; sloppy; slovenly. **2.** Shabby or seedy.

slip-up (slĭp′ŭp′) ▸ *n.* An error; oversight.

slit (slĭt) ▸ *n.* A long straight narrow cut or opening. **—slit** *v.*

slith·er (slĭth′ər) ▸ *v.* **1.** To slip and slide. **2.** To move along by gliding, as a snake does. **—slith′er·y** *adj.*

sliv·er (slĭv′ər) ▸ *n.* A thin sharp-ended piece; splinter. **—sliv′er** *v.*

slob (slŏb) ▸ *n.* *Informal* A crude or slovenly person.

slob·ber (slŏb′ər) ▸ *v.* **1.** To let saliva or food dribble from the mouth; drool. **2.** To express emotion effusively. **—slob′ber** *n.* **—slob′ber·er** *n.*

sloe (slō) ▸ *n.* **1.** See **blackthorn**. **2.** The tart, blue-black, plumlike fruit of the blackthorn.

slog (slŏg) ▸ *v.* **slogged, slog·ging. 1.** To walk with a slow, labored gait. **2.** To work diligently for long hours; toil.

slo·gan (slō′gən) ▸ *n.* **1.** A phrase expressing the aims or nature of an enterprise, team, or other group; motto. **2.** A catchword used in advertising or promotion.

sloop (slo͞op) ▸ *n.* A single-masted, fore-and-aft rigged sailing boat with a mainsail and a jib.

slop (slŏp) ▸ *n.* **1.** Spilled or splashed liquid. **2.** Soft mud or slush. **3.** Unappetizing watery food. **4.** often **slops** Waste food used esp. to feed pigs. ▸ *v.* **slopped, slop·ping. 1.** To spill or splash messily. **2.** To feed slops to.

slope (slōp) ▸ *v.* **sloped, slop·ing.** To incline upward or downward. ▸ *n.* **1.** An inclined line, surface, plane, or stretch of ground. **2a.** A deviation from the horizontal. **b.** The amount of such deviation.

slop·py (slŏp′ē) ▸ *adj.* **-pi·er, -pi·est. 1.** Untidy or messy. **2.** Carelessly done. **3.** Muddy or slushy. **—slop′pi·ly** *adv.* **—slop′pi·ness** *n.*

slosh (slŏsh) ▸ *v.* **1.** To splash or flounder, as in water. **2.** To splash (a liquid) copiously. **—slosh′y** *adj.*

slot (slŏt) ▸ *n.* **1.** A narrow groove or opening. **2.** A suitable place, position, or niche, as in a sequence. ▸ *v.* **slot·ted, slot·ting. 1.** To make a slot in. **2.** To put into or assign to a slot.

sloth (slôth, slōth, slŏth) ▸ *n.* **1.** Laziness or indolence. **2.** Any of a family of slow-moving, arboreal mammals of tropical America.

sloth·ful (slôth′fəl, slōth′-, slŏth′-) ▸ *adj.* Indolent; lazy. **—sloth′ful·ly** *adv.* **—sloth′ful·ness** *n.*

slot machine ▸ *n.* A coin-operated vending or gambling machine.

slouch (slouch) ▸ *n.* **1.** An awkward, drooping posture or gait. **2.** *Slang* A lazy or incompetent person. **—slouch** *v.*

THESAURUS

slighting *adj.* *—See* DISDAINFUL, DISPARAGING.

slim *adj.* *—See* REMOTE (2), THIN (1).

slim *v.* To lose body weight, as by dieting ▸ reduce, slim down, thin, trim down. ***Idioms:*** get the weight off, lose weight, shed some pounds.

slime *n.* A viscous, usually dirty substance ▸ mire, muck, ooze, slop, sludge, slush. *Informal:* goo, gunk. *Slang:* goop. [*Compare* OIL.]

slimy *adj.* Relating to or covered with slime ▸ miry, mucky, oozy, sludgy, slushy. *Informal:* gooey, gunky. *Slang:* goopy. [*Compare* FATTY.]

sling *n.* *—See* THROW.

sling *v.* *—See* HURL (1), THROW.

slink *v.* *—See* SNEAK.

slinkiness *n.* *—See* STEALTH.

slinky *adj.* *—See* STEALTHY.

slip *v.* **1.** To maneuver gently and slowly into place ▸ ease, glide, slide. [*Compare* EASE.] **2.** To displace a bone from a socket or joint ▸ dislocate, separate, throw out. ***Idiom:*** throw out of joint. **3.** To undergo moral deterioration ▸ degenerate, fall, sink. [*Compare* DETERIORATE.] *—See also* ELAPSE, ERR, FALL (4), GLIDE (1), LOSE (3), SNEAK, STUMBLE, UNDO.

slip into or **on** *v.* *—See* DON.

slip up *v.* *—See* ERR.

slip *n.* A minor mistake ▸ lapse, slip-up. *Informal:* fluff. *—See also* ERROR.

slippery *adj.* Inclined or intended to evade ▸ elusive, evasive, fugitive. [*Compare* UNDERHAND.] *—See also* SLICK.

slipshod *adj.* *—See* MESSY (1), NEGLIGENT.

slip-up *n.* A minor mistake ▸ lapse, slip. *Informal:* fluff. *—See also* ERROR.

slit *n.* *—See* CUT (1).

slit *v.* *—See* CUT (1), CUT (2).

slither *v.* *—See* CRAWL (1), GLIDE (1), STUMBLE.

slithery *adj.* *—See* SLICK.

sliver *n.* *—See* BIT[1] (2), CUT (2), FLAKE.

slob *n.* *—See* BOOR.

slobber *n.* Saliva running from the mouth ▸ drivel, drool, salivation, slaver.

slobber *v.* *—See* DROOL.

slobber over *v.* *Informal* To make an excessive show of desire for or interest in ▸ *Informal:* drool over, ogle. [*Compare* ADORE, DESIRE, LUST, RAVE.]

slog *v.* *—See* GRIND (2), HIT, TRUDGE.

slog *n.* *—See* TASK (2).

slogan *n.* *—See* CRY (2).

slop *n.* *—See* SLIME.

slop *v.* *—See* SPLASH (1), TRUDGE.

slope *v.* *—See* INCLINE.

slope *n.* *—See* ASCENT (2), INCLINATION (2).

sloppiness *n.* *—See* DISORDERLINESS, SENTIMENTALITY.

sloppy *adj.* *—See* MESSY (1), NEGLIGENT, SENTIMENTAL.

slosh *v.* *—See* SPLASH (1).

sloshed *adj.* *—See* DRUNK.

slot *n.* *—See* HOLE (2), POSITION (3).

sloth *n.* *—See* LAZINESS, WASTREL (2).

slothful *adj.* *—See* LAZY, LETHARGIC.

slothfulness *n.* *—See* LAZINESS, LETHARGY.

slouch *v.* **1.** To take on or move with an awkward, slovenly posture ▸ loll, slump. [*Compare* BOW[1], STOOP.] **2.** To hang limply and loosely ▸ droop, flop, loll, lop, sag, wilt.

slouch *n.* *—See* WASTREL (2).

slough[1] (slo͞o, slou) ▸ *n.* **1.** A hollow, usu. filled with mud. **2.** A stagnant swamp. **3.** A state of deep despair.

slough[2] (slŭf) ▸ *n.* **1.** Dead tissue separated from surrounding living tissue, as in a wound. **2.** An outer layer that is shed. ▸ *v.* To shed or cast off.

Slo·vak (slō′väk′, -văk′) also **Slo·va·ki·an** (slō-vä′kē-ən, -văk′ē-ən) ▸ *n.* **1.** A member of a Slavic people living in Slovakia. **2.** The Slavic language of the Slovaks. **—Slo′vak, Slo·va′ki·an** *adj.*

Slo·va·ki·a (slō-vä′kē-ə, -văk′ē-ə) ▸ A country of central Europe; formerly part of Czechoslovakia.

slov·en (slŭv′ən) ▸ *n.* One who is habitually untidy or careless.

Slo·vene (slō′vēn′) also **Slo·ve·ni·an** (slō-vē′nē-ən, -vēn′yən) ▸ *n.* **1.** A member of a Slavic people living in Slovenia. **2.** The Slavic language of the Slovenes. **—Slo′vene, Slo·ve′ni·an** *adj.*

Slo·ve·ni·a (slō-vē′nē-ə, -vēn′yə) ▸ A country of central Europe.

slov·en·ly (slŭv′ən-lē) ▸ *adj.* **1.** Untidy or messy. **2.** Marked by carelessness; slipshod: *slovenly work.* **—slov′en·li·ness** *n.*

slow (slō) ▸ *adj.* **-er, -est. 1a.** Not moving or able to move quickly. **b.** Marked by a low speed or tempo: *a slow waltz.* **2.** Taking or requiring a long time. **3.** Registering a time or rate behind or below the correct one. **4.** Marked by low sales or activity. **5.** Dull or boring. **6.** Not having or showing mental quickness. ▸ *adv.* **-er, -est.** Slowly. ▸ *v.* **1.** To make or become slow or slower. **2.** To delay; retard. **—slow′ly** *adv.* **—slow′ness** *n.*

slow·down (slō′doun′) ▸ *n.* A slackening of pace: *a production slowdown.*

slow motion ▸ *n.* A filmmaking technique in which the action as projected is slower than the original action. **—slow′-mo′tion** *adj.*

slow·poke (slō′pōk′) ▸ *n. Informal* One who moves, works, or acts slowly.

sludge (slŭj) ▸ *n.* **1.** Semisolid material such as that precipitated by sewage treatment. **2.** Mud, mire, or ooze. **—sludg′y** *adj.*

slue[1] also **slew** (slo͞o) ▸ *v.* **slued, slu·ing** also **slewed, slew·ing.** To turn or twist to the side. ▸ *n.* The act of sluing.

slue[2] (slo͞o) ▸ *n.* Var. of **slew**[1].

slug[1] (slŭg) ▸ *n.* **1.** A round bullet larger than buckshot. **2.** *Informal* A shot of liquor. **3.** A small metal disk used in place of a coin. **4.** A lump of metal.

slug[2] (slŭg) ▸ *n.* A terrestrial gastropod mollusk having a slow-moving elongated body with no shell.

slug[3] (slŭg) ▸ *v.* **slugged, slug·ging.** To strike heavily, esp. with the fist or a bat. **—slug** *n.* **—slug′ger** *n.*

slug·gard (slŭg′ərd) ▸ *n.* A lazy person; idler. **—slug′gard·ly** *adj.*

slug·gish (slŭg′ĭsh) ▸ *adj.* **1.** Slow; inactive. **2.** Lazy or indolent. **3.** Slow to perform or respond. **—slug′gish·ly** *adv.* **—slug′gish·ness** *n.*

sluice (slo͞os) ▸ *n.* **1a.** An artificial channel for water, with a gate to regulate the flow. **b.** The gate itself. **2.** A sluiceway. **3.** A long inclined trough, as for floating logs or separating gold ore. ▸ *v.* **sluiced, sluic·ing. 1.** To wash with or as if with a sudden flow of water; flush. **2.** To draw off by a sluice. **3.** To send down a sluice.

sluice·way (slo͞os′wā′) ▸ *n.* An artificial channel, esp. one for carrying off excess water.

slum (slŭm) ▸ *n.* A poor, squalid, densely populated urban area. ▸ *v.* **slummed, slum·ming.** To visit a slum, esp. from curiosity. **—slum′my** *adj.*

slum·ber (slŭm′bər) ▸ *v.* **1.** To sleep or doze. **2.** To be dormant. **—slum′ber** *n.* **—slum′ber·er** *n.*

slum·ber·ous (slŭm′bər-əs) or **slum·brous** (-brəs) ▸ *adj.* **1.** Sleepy; drowsy. **2.** Quiet; tranquil. **3.** Causing or inducing sleep.

slum·lord (slŭm′lôrd′) ▸ *n.* An owner of slum property, esp. one who allows the property to deteriorate.

slump (slŭmp) ▸ *v.* **1.** To fall, decline, or sink suddenly. **2.** To droop, as in sitting; slouch. **—slump** *n.*

slung (slŭng) ▸ *v.* P.t. and p.part. of **sling.**

slunk (slŭngk) ▸ *v.* P.t. and p.part. of **slink.**

slur (slûr) ▸ *v.* **slurred, slur·ring. 1.** To pronounce indistinctly. **2.** To disparage. **3.** To pass over lightly or carelessly. **4.** *Mus.* To glide over (a series of notes) smoothly without a break. ▸ *n.* **1.** A disparaging remark; aspersion. **2.** A slurred sound. **3.** *Mus.* A curved line connecting notes to indicate that they are to be played or sung legato.

slurp (slûrp) ▸ *v.* To eat or drink noisily. **—slurp** *n.*

slush (slŭsh) ▸ *n.* **1.** Partially melted snow or ice. **2.** Soft mud; slop. **3.** Sentimental drivel. **4.** A drink made of flavored syrup and crushed ice. **—slush′i·ly** *adv.* **—slush′i·ness** *n.* **—slush′y** *adj.*

slush fund ▸ *n.* A fund for undesignated purposes, esp. one used to finance a corrupt practice, such as bribery.

slut (slŭt) ▸ *n.* **1a.** A sexually promiscuous woman. **b.** A

THESAURUS

slough[1] *n.* —*See* SWAMP.

slough[2] *v.* —*See* DISCARD, SHED[1] (2).

slovenliness *n.* —*See* DISORDERLINESS.

slovenly *adj.* —*See* MESSY (1).

slow *adj.* **1.** Proceeding at a rate less than usual or desired ▸ crawling, creeping, delaying, dilatory, glacial, laggard, laboring, plodding, procrastinating, slow-footed, slow-going, slow-paced, sluggish, snaillike, tardy. *Informal:* poky. ***Idiom:*** slow as molasses in January. [*Compare* DELIBERATE, LANGUID, LETHARGIC.] **2.** Characterized by reduced economic activity ▸ down, dull, off, slack, sluggish, soft, stagnant. —*See also* BACKWARD (1), LATE (1).

slow *adv.* —*See* LATE.

slow *v.* —*See* DELAY (1).

slowdown *n.* A period of decreased business activity and high unemployment ▸ depression, downturn, recession, slump. —*See also* DECREASE.

slow-going or **slow-footed** *adj.* —*See* SLOW (1).

slow motion *n.* A very slow rate of speed ▸ crawl, creep, footpace. ***Idiom:*** snail's pace.

slowness *n.* The quality or condition of not being on time ▸ belatedness, lateness, tardiness, unpunctuality.

slow-paced *adj.* —*See* SLOW (1).

slowpoke *n.* —*See* LAGGARD.

slow-witted *adj.* —*See* BACKWARD (1).

sludge *n.* —*See* SLIME.

sludgy *adj.* —*See* SLIMY.

slue or **slew** *v.* To turn in place, as on a fixed point ▸ pivot, swing, swivel, wheel. [*Compare* TURN.] —*See also* SWERVE.

slug[1] *n.* —*See* DROP (4).

slug[2] *n.* —*See* WASTREL (2).

slug[3] *v.* —*See* HIT.

slug *n.* —*See* BLOW[2].

slugabed *n.* —*See* WASTREL (2).

slugfest *n.* —*See* FIGHT (1).

sluggard *n.* —*See* WASTREL (2).

sluggard *adj.* —*See* LAZY.

sluggardness *n.* —*See* LAZINESS.

sluggish *adj.* —*See* LAZY, LETHARGIC, SLOW (1), SLOW (2).

sluggishness *n.* —*See* DULLNESS, LAZINESS, LETHARGY.

slumber *v.* To be asleep ▸ sleep. *Slang:* sack out. ***Idioms:*** be in the land of Nod, catch some shuteye, catch (*or* cop) some z's, saw logs (*or* wood), sleep like a log (*or* baby *or* rock *or* top), sleep tight. [*Compare* NAP, REST[1].]

slumber *n.* The natural recurring condition of suspended consciousness by which the body rests ▸ dreamland, sleep. *Slang:* shuteye, z's. ***Idioms:*** land of Nod, the arms of Morpheus. [*Compare* NAP, REST[1].]

slumberless *adj.* Marked by an absence of sleep ▸ sleepless, wakeful. [*Compare* WAKEFUL.]

slumberous or **slumbrous** *adj.* —*See* SLEEPY, SOPORIFIC.

slumbery *adj.* —*See* SLEEPY.

slump *v.* To take on or move with an awkward, slovenly posture ▸ loll, slouch. [*Compare* BOW[1], STOOP.] —*See also* DROP (1), FALL (4).

slump *n.* A period of decreased business activity and high unemployment ▸ depression, downturn, recession, slowdown. —*See also* FALL (3).

slur *v.* —*See* MALIGN.

slur *n.* An implied criticism ▸ imputation, reflection. [*Compare* CRACK, LIBEL.]

slurp *v.* —*See* DRINK (1).

slush *n.* —*See* SLIME.

slush *v.* —*See* DIRTY.

slushy *adj.* —*See* SENTIMENTAL, SLIMY.

slut *n.* A person, typically a woman, who is sexually promiscuous ▸ baggage, hussy, jade, slattern, tart, tramp, wanton, wench, whore. *Slang:* floozy.

prostitute. 2. A slovenly woman. **—slut′tish** *adj.*

sly (slī) ▸ *adj.* **sli·er, sli·est** also **sly·er, sly·est.** 1. Adept in craft or cunning. 2. Secretive. 3. Underhand or deceitful. 4. Playfully mischievous. ***—idiom:* on the sly** Secretly. **—sly′ly** *adv.* **—sly′ness** *n.*

Sm ▸ The symbol for the element **samarium.**

smack[1] (smăk) ▸ *v.* 1. To make a sound by pressing the lips together and pulling them apart quickly. 2. To kiss or slap noisily. ▸ *n.* 1. The loud sharp sound of smacking the lips. 2. A noisy kiss. 3. A sharp blow or loud slap. ▸ *adv.* Directly; straight: *was hit smack in the face.*

smack[2] (smăk) ▸ *n.* 1. A distinctive flavor. 2. A suggestion or trace. ▸ *v.* 1. To have a distinct flavor. 2. To suggest: *This smacks of foul play.*

smack[3] (smăk) ▸ *n.* A sloop-rigged boat used chiefly in fishing.

smack[4] (smăk) ▸ *n. Slang* Heroin.

small (smôl) ▸ *adj.* **-er, -est.** 1. Being below the average in size, quantity, or extent. 2. Insignificant or trivial. 3. Limited in degree or scope: *a small farmer.* 4. Not fully grown. 5. Narrow in outlook; petty: *a small mind.* 6. Belittled; humiliated. 7. Lacking force or volume: *a small voice.* ▸ *adv.* 1. In small pieces: *Cut the meat up small.* 2. Softly. 3. In a small manner. ▸ *n.* Something smaller than the rest: *the small of the back.* **—small′ness** *n.*

small arm ▸ *n.* A firearm that can be carried in the hand.

small calorie ▸ *n.* See **calorie** 1.

small capital ▸ *n.* A letter having the form of a capital letter but smaller.

small fry ▸ *n.* 1. Small children. 2. Persons or things regarded as unimportant.

small intestine ▸ *n.* The part of the alimentary canal between the outlet of the stomach and the large intestine.

small-mind·ed (smôl′mīn′dĭd) ▸ *adj.* Having a narrow or petty attitude. **—small′-mind′ed·ly** *adv.* **—small′-mind′ed·ness** *n.*

small·pox (smôl′pŏks′) ▸ *n.* An acute, highly infectious viral disease marked by high fever and pustules that form pockmarks.

small talk ▸ *n.* Casual or light conversation.

small·time or **small-time** (smôl′tīm′) ▸ *adj. Informal* Insignificant or minor. **—small′tim′er** *n.*

smarm·y (smär′mē) ▸ *adj.* **-i·er, -i·est.** Hypocritically or exaggeratedly earnest.

smart (smärt) ▸ *adj.* **-er, -est.** 1a. Intelligent; bright. b. Amusingly clever; witty. c. Impertinent or insolent. 2. Quick and energetic: *a smart pace.* 3. Canny and sharp in dealings; shrewd. 4. Fashionable; elegant: *a smart restaurant.* 5. Having a built-in computational ability: *a smart bomb.* ▸ *v.* 1. To cause or feel a sharp stinging pain. 2. To feel mental distress. **—smart′ly** *adv.* **—smart′ness** *n.*

smart al·eck (ăl′ĭk) ▸ *n. Informal* One who is offensively arrogant. **—smart′-al′eck·y** *adj.*

smart·en (smär′tn) ▸ *v.* 1. To make or become more brisk or lively. 2. To make or become smart or smarter.

smash (smăsh) ▸ *v.* 1. To break or be broken into pieces. 2. To throw or dash violently so as to crush or shatter. 3. To strike with a heavy blow; hit. ▸ *n.* 1. The act or sound of smashing or the condition of having been smashed. 2. Total destruction; ruin. 3. A collision or crash. 4. *Sports* A powerful overhand stroke, as in tennis. 5. *Informal* A resounding success. ▸ *adj. Informal* Very successful. **—smash′er** *n.*

smash·up (smăsh′ŭp′) ▸ *n.* 1. A total defeat. 2. A serious collision between vehicles.

smat·ter·ing (smăt′ər-ĭng) ▸ *n.* 1. Superficial or piecemeal knowledge. 2. A small, scattered amount.

smear (smîr) ▸ *v.* 1. To spread, cover, or stain with a sticky dirty substance. 2. To smudge or soil. 3. To slander or vilify. ▸ *n.* 1. A smudge or blot. 2. Vilification or slander. 3. A sample, as of blood, spread on a slide for microscopic examination. **—smear′y** *adj.*

smell (smĕl) ▸ *v.* **smelled** or **smelt** (smĕlt), **smell·ing.** 1. To perceive the odor of by the sense organs of the nose. 2. To have or emit an odor. 3. To suggest evil or corruption. ▸ *n.* 1. The olfactory sense. 2. The odor of something. 3. The act of smelling. 4. A distinctive quality; aura.

smell·ing salts (smĕl′ĭng) ▸ *pl.n.* A preparation based on an ammonia compound, sniffed esp. to relieve faintness.

smell·y (smĕl′ē) ▸ *adj.* **-i·er, -i·est.** *Informal* Having an unpleasant odor.

smelt[1] (smĕlt) ▸ *v.* To melt or fuse (ores) to separate the metallic constituents.

smelt[2] (smĕlt) ▸ *n., pl.* **smelts** or **smelt.** A small silvery food fish.

THESAURUS

[*Compare* HARLOT, PROSTITUTE.]

sluttish *adj.* —*See* WANTON (1).

sly *adj.* —*See* ARTFUL, STEALTHY.

slyness *n.* —*See* ART, DISHONESTY (2), STEALTH.

smack[1] *v.* —*See* BANG (1), KISS, SLAP.

smack *n.* —*See* BEAT (1), CLASH, KISS, SLAP.

smack *adv.* —*See* DIRECTLY (3).

smack[2] *n.* A distinctive yet intangible quality ▸ aroma, atmosphere, flavor, savor. [*Compare* QUALITY.] —*See also* FLAVOR (1).

smack *v.* To have a particular flavor or suggestion of something ▸ savor, smell, suggest, taste. [*Compare* HINT.]

smack-dab *adv.* —*See* DIRECTLY (3).

smacker *n.* —*See* KISS, MOUTH (1), SLAP.

small *adj.* —*See* [illegible] NARROW (1), SOFT (2), TRIVIAL.

small change *n.* —*See* PEANUTS, TRIFLE.

smallest *adj.* —*See* MINIMAL.

small fry *n.* —*See* NONENTITY, SQUIRT (2).

smallish *adj.* —*See* LITTLE.

small-minded *adj.* —*See* NARROW (1), TRIVIAL.

smallness *n.* —*See* TRIFLE.

small potatoes *n.* —*See* TRIFLE.

small talk *n.* —*See* CHATTER.

smalltime or **small-time** *adj.* —*See* MINOR (1).

small-town *adj.* —*See* NARROW (1).

smarmy *adj.* —*See* UNCTUOUS.

smart *adj.* —*See* CLEVER (1), CLEVER (2), EXCLUSIVE (3), FASHIONABLE, IMPUDENT, INTELLIGENT, SHREWD.

smart *v.* —*See* HURT (2).

smart *n.* —*See* PAIN.

smart aleck *n. Informal* One who is obnoxiously self-assertive and arrogant ▸ *Informal:* know-it-all, saucebox, smarty, smarty-pants, wisenheimer. *Slang:* wiseacre, wisecracker, wise guy. [*Compare* BOASTER, JOKER.]

smart-alecky *adj.* —*See* IMPUDENT.

smarten *v.* —*See* RENEW (1).

smarting *adj.* —*See* PAINFUL.

smarts *n.* —*See* INTELLIGENCE.

smarty or **smarty-pants** *n.* —*See* SMART ALECK.

smash *v.* —*See* BANG (1), BEAT (1), BREAK (1), CRASH, CRUSH (1), CRUSH (2), DESTROY (1), HIT, OVERWHELM (1).

smash *n.* A forceful movement causing a loud noise ▸ bang, crash, slam, wham. —*See also* CLASH, COLLAPSE (2), COLLISION, CRASH (2), HIT.

smashed *adj.* —*See* DRUNK.

smash hit *n.* —*See* HIT.

smashup *n.* —*See* COLLAPSE (2), CRASH (2).

smatterer *n.* —*See* AMATEUR.

smear *v.* To spread with a greasy, sticky, or dirty substance ▸ bedaub, besmear, dab, daub, plaster, smirch, smudge. [*Compare* DIRTY, FINISH, OIL, STAIN.] —*See also* DENIGRATE, OVERWHELM (1).

smear *n.* A discolored mark made by smearing or soiling ▸ blot, blotch, daub, smirch, smudge, smutch, splotch, spot, stain. —*See also* LIBEL.

smell *v.* 1. To perceive with the olfactory sense ▸ nose, scent, sniff, snuff, whiff. *Idiom:* catch (*or* get) a whiff of. [*Compare* BREATHE.] 2. To have or give off a foul odor ▸ reek, stink. *Idiom:* stink to high heaven. 3. To have a particular flavor or suggestion of something ▸ savor, smack, suggest, taste. [*Compare* HINT.]

smell out *v.* To follow the traces of, as in hunting ▸ [illegible] track (down), trail. *Idiom:* be hot on the trail of. [*Compare* HUNT.]

smell *n.* 1. The [illegible] by which odors are perceived ▸ nose, olfaction, scent. 2. The quality of something that may be perceived by smelling ▸ aroma, odor, scent. [*Compare* FRAGRANCE, STENCH.] —*See also* AIR (3).

smelly *adj. Informal* Having an unpleasant odor ▸ fetid, foul, foul-smelling, malodorous, mephitic, mephitical, noisome, odoriferous, odorous, overpowering, reeking, reeky, stinking. [*Compare* BAD, FRAGRANT, MOLDY, OFFENSIVE.]

smelt³ (smĕlt) ▸ *v.* P.t. and p.part. of **smell**.
smelt·er (smĕl′tər) ▸ *n.* **1.** also **smelt·er·y** (-tə-rē) *pl.* **-ies**. An establishment for smelting. **2.** A worker who smelts ore.
smid·gen or **smid·gin** (smĭj′ən) ▸ *n.* A very small quantity or portion; bit.
smi·lax (smī′lăks′) ▸ *n.* A slender, glossy-leaved climbing vine used in floral decoration.
smile (smīl) ▸ *n.* A facial expression formed by an upward curving of the corners of the mouth and indicating pleasure, affection, or amusement. ▸ *v.* **smiled, smil·ing. 1.** To have or form a smile. **2.** To express approval. **3.** To express with a smile. **—smil′ing·ly** *adv.*
smil·ey (smī′lē) ▸ *n., pl.* **-eys**. An emoticon, esp. one indicating a smiling face :-).
smirch (smûrch) ▸ *v.* **1.** To soil or stain. **2.** To dishonor. **—smirch** *n.*
smirk (smûrk) ▸ *v.* To smile in an affected, often offensively self-satisfied manner. **—smirk** *n.* **—smirk′er** *n.*
smite (smīt) ▸ *v.* **smote** (smōt), **smit·ten** (smĭt′n) or **smote, smit·ing. 1.** To inflict a heavy blow on. **2.** To kill by or as if by blows. **3.** To afflict.
smith (smĭth) ▸ *n.* **1.** A metalworker, esp. one who works with hot metal. **2.** A blacksmith.
Smith, Adam (1723–90) ▸ Scottish economist and philosopher.
Smith, Joseph (1805–44) ▸ Amer. founder (1830) of the Church of Jesus Christ of Latter-day Saints.
smith·er·eens (smĭth′ə-rēnz′) ▸ *pl.n. Informal* Pieces; bits.
smith·y (smĭth′ē, smĭth′ē) ▸ *n., pl.* **-ies**. A blacksmith's shop; forge.
smock (smŏk) ▸ *n.* A loose outer garment worn to protect the clothes. ▸ *v.* To decorate (fabric) with stitched gathers in a honeycomb pattern.
smog (smŏg, smôg) ▸ *n.* **1.** Fog polluted with smoke. **2.** Air pollution produced when sunlight causes hydrocarbons and nitrogen oxides, esp. from automotive exhaust, to combine. **—smog′gy** *adj.*
smoke (smōk) ▸ *n.* **1.** The vapor made up of small particles of matter from incomplete burning of materials such as wood or coal. **2.** A cloud of fine particles. **3.** The act of smoking a form of tobacco. **4.** *Informal* A cigarette or cigar. ▸ *v.* **smoked, smok·ing. 1.** To draw in and exhale smoke from a cigarette, cigar, or pipe. **2.** To emit smoke. **3.** To emit smoke excessively. **4.** To preserve (meat or fish) by exposure to smoke. **5.** To fumigate. **6.** *Slang* To perform at the utmost capacity. **7.** *Slang* To kill. ***—phrasal verb:* smoke out** To force out of hiding by or as if by the use of smoke. **—smoke′less** *adj.* **—smok′er** *n.* **—smok′i·ness** *n.* **—smok′y** *adj.*
smoke·house (smōk′hous′) ▸ *n.* A structure where meat or fish is smoked.
smoke screen ▸ *n.* **1.** Dense smoke used to conceal military operations. **2.** Something used to conceal plans or intentions.
smoke·stack (smōk′stăk′) ▸ *n.* A large vertical pipe through which combustion gases and smoke are discharged.
smol·der also **smoul·der** (smōl′dər) ▸ *v.* **1.** To burn with little smoke and no flame. **2.** To exist in a suppressed state. ▸ *n.* Thick smoke resulting from a slow fire.
smooch (smo͞och) *Slang* ▸ *n.* A kiss. ▸ *v.* To kiss.
smooth (smo͞o*th*) ▸ *adj.* **-er, -est. 1.** Free from irregularities, roughness, or projections. **2.** Having a fine texture or consistency. **3.** Having an even or gentle motion. **4.** Having no obstructions or difficulties. **5.** Ingratiating: *smooth talk.* ▸ *v.* **1.** To make or become smooth. **2.** To rid of obstructions, hindrances, or difficulties. **3.** To make calm; soothe. **—smooth′er** *n.* **—smooth′ly** *adv.* **—smooth′ness** *n.*
smooth·bore (smo͞o*th*′bôr′) ▸ *adj.* Having no rifling within the barrel. Used of a firearm. **—smooth′bore′** *n.*
smor·gas·bord (smôr′gəs-bôrd′) ▸ *n.* A buffet meal featuring a varied number of dishes.
smote (smōt) ▸ *v.* P.t. and p.part. of **smite**.
smoth·er (smŭ*th*′ər) ▸ *v.* **1.** To kill or extinguish by depriving of oxygen. **2.** To conceal or suppress. **3.** To cover thickly.
smudge (smŭj) ▸ *v.* **smudged, smudg·ing.** To smear or blur. ▸ *n.* **1.** A blotch or smear. **2.** A smoky fire used to protect against insects or frost. **—smudg′y** *adj.*
smug (smŭg) ▸ *adj.* **smug·ger, smug·gest.** Self-satisfied or complacent. **—smug′ly** *adv.* **—smug′ness** *n.*
smug·gle (smŭg′əl) ▸ *v.* **-gled, -gling. 1.** To import or export without paying lawful customs charges or duties. **2.** To convey illicitly or by stealth. **—smug′gler** *n.*
smut (smŭt) ▸ *n.* **1.** A particle of dirt. **2.** Obscene or pornographic speech or printed matter. **3.** Any of various plant diseases caused by fungi that form black powdery masses. **—smut′ti·ness** *n.* **—smut′ty** *adj.*
Sn ▸ The symbol for the element **tin**.
snack (snăk) ▸ *n.* **1.** A light meal. **2.** Food eaten between meals. **—snack** *v.*
snaf·fle (snăf′əl) ▸ *n.* A jointed bit for a horse.
sna·fu (snă-fo͞o′) ▸ *n., pl.* **-fus.** *Slang* A chaotic or confused situation.
snag (snăg) ▸ *n.* **1.** A sharp or jagged protuberance. **2.** A tree or limb that protrudes above a water surface. **3.** A break, pull, or tear in fabric. **4.** An unforeseen obstacle. ▸ *v.* **snagged, snag·ging. 1.** To get caught by or as if by a snag. **2.** *Informal* To catch or get unexpectedly or quickly. **3.** To hinder; impede.
snail (snāl) ▸ *n.* An aquatic or terrestrial mollusk having a spirally coiled shell and distinct head.
snake (snāk) ▸ *n.* **1.** Any of numerous scaly, legless, some-

THESAURUS

smidgen *n.* —*See* BIT[1] (1).
smile *n.* A facial expression marked by an upward curving of the lips ▸ grin, simper, smirk. [*Compare* SNEER.]
smile *v.* To curve the lips upward in expressing amusement, pleasure, or happiness ▸ beam, grin, simper, smirk. *Idioms:* break into a smile, crack (*or* flash *or* give) a smile.
smile on or **upon** *v.* To lend supportive approval to ▸ countenance, encourage, favor. [*Compare* APPROVE, SUPPORT.]
smirch *v.* —*See* SMEAR.
smirch *n.* —*See* SMEAR.
smirk *v.* —*See* SMILE.
smirk *n.* A facial expression marked by an upward curving of the lips ▸ grin, simper, smile. [*Compare* SNEER.]
smite *v.* —*See* AFFLICT, HIT.
smitten *adj.* —*See* INFATUATED.
smock *n.* —*See* DRESS (3).
smog *n.* —*See* HAZE.
smoggy *adj.* Heavy, dark, or dense, especially with impurities ▸ hazy, murky, turbid. [*Compare* DIRTY.]
smoke *v.* —*See* SMOLDER.
smolder *v.* To undergo partial or unsteady combustion ▸ flicker, gutter, smoke, sputter. [*Compare* BURN.] —*See also* BOIL.
smooch *n.* —*See* KISS.
smooch *v.* —*See* KISS.
smooth *adj.* Gracious and tactful in social manner ▸ debonair, suave, urbane. [*Compare* COURTEOUS, CULTURED, SOPHISTICATED.] —*See also* EASY (1), EVEN (1), FLUENT, GENTLE (2), GLIB.
smooth *v.* —*See* EVEN, PERFECT.
smooth over *v.* —*See* SETTLE (2).
smooth-spoken *adj.* —*See* ELOQUENT.
smooth-talking or **smooth-tongued** *adj.* —*See* GLIB.
smother *v.* —*See* CHOKE, EXTINGUISH, REPRESS.
smudge *v.* —*See* DENIGRATE, DIRTY, SMEAR.
smudge *n.* —*See* HAZE, SMEAR.
smug *adj.* —*See* ARROGANT.
smuggle *v.* To bring in or take out secretly and illegally ▸ bootleg, run, sneak, spirit. *Idiom:* run contraband.
smuggler *n.* A person who engages in smuggling ▸ bootlegger, contrabandist, runner. *Slang:* mule.
smut *n.* —*See* OBSCENITY (2).
smut *v.* —*See* DENIGRATE, STAIN.
smutch *v.* —*See* DIRTY.
smuttiness *n.* —*See* DIRTINESS, OBSCENITY (1).
smutty *adj.* —*See* DIRTY, OBSCENE.
snack *n.* —*See* REFRESHMENT.
snack *v.* —*See* EAT (2).
snaffle *n.* —*See* BRAKE.
snafu *n.* —*See* DISORDER (1), MESS (1).
snafu *v.* —*See* BOTCH, CONFUSE (3).
snafu *adj.* —*See* CONFUSED (2).
snag *n. Informal* A tricky or unsuspected condition ▸ catch, hitch, rub. [*Compare* DISADVANTAGE, TRICK.] —*See also* BAR (1), SPIKE.
snag *v.* —*See* CATCH (2), CATCH (3).
snail *n.* —*See* LAGGARD.
snake *v.* —*See* CRAWL (1), SNEAK, WIND[2].

times poisonous reptiles having a long, tapering, cylindrical body. **2.** A treacherous person. **3.** A long flexible wire used for cleaning drains and sewers. ▸ *v.* **snaked, snak·ing.** To move, drag, or pull in a snakelike manner. **—snak′i·ly** *adv.* **—snak′y** *adj.*

snake oil ▸ *n.* A worthless preparation fraudulently peddled as a cure for many ills.

snap (snăp) ▸ *v.* **snapped, snap·ping. 1.** To make or cause to make a sharp cracking sound. **2.** To break suddenly with a sharp sound. **3.** To give way abruptly. **4.** To bite or seize with a snatching motion. **5.** To speak abruptly or sharply: *snapped at the child.* **6.** To move swiftly and smartly. **7.** To flash or sparkle. **8.** *Football* To pass the ball so as to initiate a play. **9.** To open or close with a click. **10a.** To take (a photograph). **b.** To photograph (a subject). ▸ *n.* **1.** A sharp cracking sound. **2.** A sudden breaking or release of something under pressure. **3.** A clasp, catch, or other fastening device. **4.** A sudden attempt to bite or snatch. **5.** A thin crisp cookie. **6.** *Informal* Briskness or energy. **7.** A spell of cold weather. **8.** Something accomplished without effort. **9.** *Football* The act of snapping the ball. **—snap′pish** *adj.* **—snap′py** *adj.*

snap bean ▸ *n.* A string bean cultivated for its crisp edible pods.

snap·drag·on (snăp′drăg′ən) ▸ *n.* A cultivated plant having showy clusters of two-lipped, variously colored flowers.

snap·per (snăp′ər) ▸ *n.* **1.** One that snaps. **2.** *pl.* **-per** or **-pers.** Any of numerous marine fishes prized as food and game fishes.

snap·ping turtle (snăp′ĭng) ▸ *n.* Any of a family of freshwater turtles having a rough shell and powerful hooked jaws.

snap·shot (snăp′shŏt′) ▸ *n.* A photograph taken with a small camera.

snare[1] (snâr) ▸ *n.* **1.** A trap, often consisting of a noose, used for capturing birds and small animals. **2.** Something that entangles the unwary. ▸ *v.* **snared, snar·ing.** To trap with or as if with a snare.

snare[2] (snâr) ▸ *n.* Any of the wires or cords stretched across the lower head of a drum so as to vibrate against it.

snarl[1] (snärl) ▸ *v.* **1.** To growl while baring the teeth. **2.** To speak angrily or threateningly. **—snarl** *n.* **—snarl′er** *n.*

snarl[2] (snärl) ▸ *n.* A tangle. ▸ *v.* **1.** To tangle or knot. **2.** To confuse.

snatch (snăch) ▸ *v.* **1.** To try to grasp or seize. **2.** To seize or grab. ▸ *n.* **1.** The act of snatching. **2.** A brief period. **3.** A bit or fragment: *a snatch of dialogue.* **—snatch′er** *n.*

snaz·zy (snăz′ē) ▸ *adj.* **-zi·er, -zi·est.** *Slang* Fashionable and flashy or showy.

sneak (snēk) ▸ *v.* **sneaked** also **snuck** (snŭk), **sneak·ing.** To move, give, or take in a quiet, stealthy way. ▸ *n.* **1.** One who is stealthy or underhanded. **2.** An instance of sneaking. **—sneak′i·ly** *adv.* **—sneak′i·ness** *n.* **—sneak′y** *adj.*

sneak·er (snē′kər) ▸ *n.* A sports shoe usu. made of canvas and having rubber soles.

sneer (snîr) ▸ *n.* A slight raising of one corner of the upper lip, expressive of contempt. **—sneer** *v.*

sneeze (snēz) ▸ *v.* **sneezed, sneez·ing.** To expel air forcibly from the mouth and nose in an explosive involuntary spasm. **—sneeze** *n.*

snick·er (snĭk′ər) ▸ *v.* To utter a nasty, partly stifled laugh. **—snick′er** *n.*

snide (snīd) ▸ *adj.* **snid·er, snid·est.** Slyly derogatory. **—snide′ly** *adv.*

sniff (snĭf) ▸ *v.* **1.** To inhale a short audible breath through the nose. **2.** To indicate ridicule, contempt, or doubt. **3.** To detect by or as if by sniffing. **—sniff** *n.* **—sniff′er** *n.*

snif·fle (snĭf′əl) ▸ *v.* **-fled, -fling. 1.** To breathe audibly through a congested nose. **2.** To whimper. **—snif′fle** *n.*

snif·ter (snĭf′tər) ▸ *n.* A pear-shaped goblet with a narrow top, used esp. in serving brandy.

snig·ger (snĭg′ər) ▸ *v.* To snicker. **—snig′ger** *n.*

snip (snĭp) ▸ *v.* **snipped, snip·ping.** To cut or clip with short quick strokes. ▸ *n.* **1a.** A small cut made with scissors or shears. **b.** A small piece clipped off. **2.** *Informal* A small person.

snipe (snīp) ▸ *n.* **1.** *pl.* **snipe** or **snipes.** Any of various long-billed, brownish wading birds. **2.** A shot, esp. a gunshot, from a concealed place. ▸ *v.* **sniped, snip·ing. 1.** To shoot at people from a concealed place. **2.** To make nasty remarks. **—snip′er** *n.*

THESAURUS

snake *n.* —*See* BETRAYER, CREEP (2).

snaky *adj.* —*See* WINDING.

snap *v.* **1.** To make a light, sharp noise ▸ clack, click. [*Compare* CRACKLE.] **2.** To try to bite something quickly or eagerly ▸ nip, snatch, strike. **3.** To speak abruptly and sharply ▸ bark, growl, snarl. ***Idioms:*** bite someone's head off, snap someone's head (*or* nose) off. [*Compare* CHASTISE, REVILE, SAY, SHOUT.] **4.** To move or cause to move with a sudden abrupt motion ▸ jerk, lurch, twitch, wrench, yank. [*Compare* MOVE.] —*See also* BREAK (3), CRACK (2).

snap back *v.* To reverse direction after striking something ▸ bounce (back), rebound, reflect, spring back. [*Compare* BEND, GLANCE.]

snap *n.* A light, sharp noise ▸ clack, click, crackle. —*See also* BREEZE (2), CRACK (1), ENERGY, FASTENER, JERK.

snap *adj.* —*See* EASY (1), EXTEMPORANEOUS.

snappish *adj.* —*See* ILL-TEMPERED.

snappy *adj.* —*See* ENERGETIC, FASHIONABLE, ILL-TEMPERED, LIVELY.

snare *n.* —*See* TRAP (1).

snare *v.* —*See* CATCH (1).

snarl[1] *v.* —*See* SNAP (3).

snarl[2] *n.* —*See* TANGLE.

snarl *v.* —*See* COMPLICATE, CONFUSE (3), ENTANGLE.

snatch *v.* **1.** To try to bite something quickly or eagerly ▸ nip, snap, strike. **2.** To seize and detain a person unlawfully ▸ abduct, kidnap, spirit away, take hostage. —*See also* CATCH (2), SEIZE (1), STEAL.

snatch *n.* —*See* CATCH (1), SEIZURE (2).

snazzy *adj.* —*See* FASHIONABLE.

sneak *v.* To move silently and furtively ▸ creep, glide, lurk, mouse, prowl, pussyfoot, skulk, slide, slink, slip, snake, steal. *Slang:* gumshoe. [*Compare* LAY[1].] —*See also* SMUGGLE.

sneak or **sneaker** *n.* One who behaves in a stealthy, furtive way ▸ prowler, skulker, sneaker, weasel. [*Compare* CREEP, BETRAYER.]

sneakiness *n.* —*See* DISHONESTY (2), STEALTH.

sneaking *adj.* —*See* [illegible]

sneaky *adj.* —*See* STEALTHY, UNDERHAND.

sneer *n.* A facial expression or laugh conveying scorn or derision ▸ fleer, snicker, snigger. [*Compare* FACE, GRIMACE, LAUGH, SMILE.]

sneer *v.* To smile or laugh scornfully or derisively ▸ fleer, snicker, snigger. *Idiom:* curl one's lip. [*Compare* GRIMACE, LAUGH, SMILE.]

sneer at *v.* —*See* DESPISE, RIDICULE.

sneering *adj.* —*See* DISDAINFUL, SARCASTIC.

snicker *v.* To smile or laugh scornfully or derisively ▸ fleer, sneer, snigger. *Idiom:* curl one's lip. [*Compare* GRIMACE, SMILE.] —*See also* LAUGH.

snicker *n.* A facial expression or laugh conveying scorn or derision ▸ fleer, sneer, snigger. [*Compare* SMILE.] —*See also* LAUGH.

snide *adj.* —*See* SARCASTIC.

sniff *v.* To breathe audibly through the nose ▸ sniffle, snort, snuff, snuffle. —*See also* SMELL (1).

sniff about or **around** *v.* *Informal* To look into or inquire about curiously, inquisitively, or in a meddlesome fashion ▸ poke, pry, snoop. *Informal:* nose (around). ***Idiom:*** stick one's nose into. [*Compare* MEDDLE.] —*See also* SEEK (1).

sniff at *v.* —*See* DESPISE, DISAPPROVE.

sniff out *v.* To follow the traces of, as in hunting ▸ smell out, trace, track, trail. ***Idiom:*** be hot on the trail of. [*Compare* HUNT.]

sniffle *v.* To breathe audibly through the nose ▸ sniff, snort, snuff, snuffle. —*See also* CRY.

snigger *n.* A facial expression or laugh conveying scorn or derision ▸ fleer, sneer, snicker. [*Compare* SMILE.] —*See also* LAUGH.

snigger *v.* To smile or laugh scornfully or derisively ▸ fleer, sneer, snicker. *Idiom:* curl one's lip. [*Compare* GRIMACE, SMILE.] —*See also* LAUGH.

snip *n.* —*See* BIT[1] (1), CUT (2).

snip *v.* —*See* CUT (2), CUT (3).

snip·pet (snĭp′ĭt) ▸ *n.* A tidbit or morsel.

snip·py (snĭp′ē) ▸ *adj.* **-pi·er, -pi·est.** *Informal* Sharp-tongued; impertinent.

snit (snĭt) ▸ *n. Informal* An agitated state.

snitch (snĭch) ▸ *v. Slang* **1.** To steal. **2.** To turn informer. **—snitch** *n.*

sniv·el (snĭv′əl) ▸ *v.* **-eled, -el·ing** or **-elled, -el·ling. 1.** To complain or whine tearfully. **2.** To run at the nose, esp. while crying. **—sniv′el** *n.*

snob (snŏb) ▸ *n.* One who affects an offensive air of superiority, as in matters of taste or intellect. **—snob′ber·y** *n.* **—snob′bish** *adj.* **—snob′bish·ly** *adv.*

snoop (sno͞op) ▸ *v.* To pry furtively. ▸ *n.* One who snoops. **—snoop′er** *n.* **—snoop′i·ly** *adv.* **—snoop′i·ness** *n.* **—snoop′y** *adj.*

snoot (sno͞ot) ▸ *n. Informal* A snout or nose.

snoot·y (sno͞o′tē) ▸ *adj.* **-i·er, -i·est.** *Informal* Snobbishly aloof; haughty. **—snoot′i·ness** *n.*

snooze (sno͞oz) ▸ *v.* **snoozed, snooz·ing.** To take a light nap; doze. **—snooze** *n.*

snore (snôr) ▸ *v.* **snored, snor·ing.** To breathe with harsh snorting noises while sleeping. **—snore** *n.* **—snor′er** *n.*

snor·kel (snôr′kəl) ▸ *n.* **1.** A breathing apparatus used by skin divers, consisting of a long tube held in the mouth. **2.** A retractable tube in a submarine that contains air-intake and exhaust pipes. **—snor′kel** *v.*

snort (snôrt) ▸ *n.* **1.** A loud rough sound made by breathing forcefully through the nostrils. **2.** *Slang* A drink of liquor, esp. a small one. ▸ *v.* **1.** To make a snort. **2.** To make an abrupt noise expressive of scorn or anger. **3.** *Slang* To ingest (e.g., a drug) by sniffing. **—snort′er** *n.*

snot (snŏt) ▸ *n. Slang* **1.** Nasal mucus; phlegm. **2.** An annoying, arrogant, or impertinent person. **—snot′ti·ly** *adv.* **—snot′ti·ness** *n.* **—snot′ty** *adj.*

snout (snout) ▸ *n.* **1.** The projecting nose or facial part of an animal's muzzle. **2.** *Slang* The human nose.

snow (snō) ▸ *n.* **1.** Frozen precipitation in the form of translucent ice crystals that fall in soft white flakes. **2.** A fall of snow. ▸ *v.* **1.** To fall to the earth as snow. **2.** To cover or close off with snow. **3.** *Slang* To overwhelm with insincere talk, esp. with flattery. **—snow′y** *adj.*

snow·ball (snō′bôl′) ▸ *n.* A mass of soft wet snow packed into a ball. ▸ *v.* **1.** To grow or cause to grow rapidly in significance, importance, or size. **2.** To throw snowballs (at).

snow·board (snō′bôrd′) ▸ *n.* A board resembling a small surfboard and equipped with bindings, used to descend snow-covered slopes on one's feet without ski poles. **—snow′board′** *v.* **—snow′board′er** *n.*

snow·bound (snō′bound′) ▸ *adj.* Confined in one place by heavy snow.

snow·drift (snō′drĭft′) ▸ *n.* A mass or bank of snow piled up by the wind.

snow·drop (snō′drŏp′) ▸ *n.* A bulbous plant having nodding white spring flowers.

snow·fall (snō′fôl′) ▸ *n.* **1.** A fall of snow. **2.** The amount of snow that falls in a given period and area.

snow·flake (snō′flāk′) ▸ *n.* A single flake or crystal of snow.

snow leopard ▸ *n.* A large cat of central Asia, having grayish fur with dark markings.

snow·man (snō′măn′) ▸ *n.* A figure of a person made from packed snow.

snow·mo·bile (snō′mō-bēl′, -mə-) ▸ *n.* A small vehicle with skis in front and tanklike treads, used for traveling on snow.

snow pea ▸ *n.* A variety of the common pea having a soft thick edible pod.

snow·plow (snō′plou′) ▸ *n.* A plowlike device or vehicle used to remove snow.

snow·shoe (snō′sho͞o′) ▸ *n.* A racket-shaped frame with interlaced strips attached to the shoe to prevent sinking into deep snow. **—snow′shoe′** *v.*

snow·storm (snō′stôrm′) ▸ *n.* A storm marked by heavy snowfall.

snow tire ▸ *n.* A tire with a deep tread or studs for traction on snow-covered surfaces.

snub (snŭb) ▸ *v.* **snubbed, snub·bing. 1.** To ignore or behave coldly toward; slight. **2.** To dismiss or turn down in a decisive way. **3.** *Naut.* To check the movement of (e.g., a rope) by turning it quickly about a post. ▸ *n.* A deliberate slight.

snub-nosed (snŭb′nōzd′) ▸ *adj.* Having a short, turned-up nose.

snuck (snŭk) ▸ *v. Informal* P.t. and p.part. of **sneak.**

snuff[1] (snŭf) ▸ *v.* **1.** To inhale audibly through the nose. **2.** To sniff (at).

snuff[2] (snŭf) ▸ *v.* **1.** To put out; extinguish. **2.** To cut off the charred portion of (a candlewick). **—snuff′er** *n.*

snuff[3] (snŭf) ▸ *n.* A preparation of finely pulverized tobacco for ingesting by sniffing. ***—idiom:* up to snuff** *Informal* Up to standard.

snuf·fle (snŭf′əl) ▸ *v.* **-fled, -fling. 1.** To breathe noisily, as through a blocked nose. **2.** To sniffle. **—snuf′fle** *n.* **—snuf′fler** *n.*

snug (snŭg) ▸ *adj.* **snug·ger, snug·gest. 1.** Comfortably sheltered; cozy. **2.** Small but well arranged: *a snug apartment.* **3.** Close-fitting; tight. **—snug, snug′ly** *adv.* **—snug′ness** *n.*

snug·gle (snŭg′əl) ▸ *v.* **-gled, -gling.** To nestle or cuddle.

so[1] (sō) ▸ *adv.* **1.** In the manner expressed or indicated;

THESAURUS

snippet *n.* —*See* BIT[1] (1), CUT (2).

snippety or **snippy** *adj.* —*See* IMPUDENT.

snit *n.* —*See* STATE (2).

snitch or **snitcher** *v.* —*See* INFORM (2), STEAL.

snitch *n.* —*See* INFORMER.

snivel *v.* —*See* COMPLAIN, CRY.

snob *n.* One who despises people or things regarded as inferior, especially because of social or intellectual pretension ▸ elitist, prig. *Informal:* snoot.

snobbery *n.* —*See* CONDESCENSION.

snobbish or **snobby** *adj.* Characteristic of or resembling a snob ▸ elitist. *Informal:* high-hat, snooty, stuck-up, uppish, uppity. [*Compare* ARROGANT, POMPOUS.]

snoop *v.* To look into or inquire about curiously, inquisitively, or in a meddlesome fashion ▸ poke, pry. *Informal:* nose (around), sniff about (*or* around). ***Idiom:*** stick one's nose into. [*Compare* MEDDLE.]

snoop or **snooper** *n.* A person who snoops ▸ prier, pry. [*Compare* BUSYBODY.] —*See also* GOSSIP (2).

snoopiness *n.* —*See* CURIOSITY (2).

snoopy *adj.* —*See* CURIOUS (1).

snoot *n. Informal* One who despises people or things regarded as inferior, especially because of social or intellectual pretension ▸ elitist, prig, snob. —*See also* NOSE (1).

snootiness *n.* —*See* CONDESCENSION.

snooty *adj.* —*See* ARROGANT, SNOBBISH.

snooze *v.* —*See* NAP.

snooze *n.* —*See* NAP.

snort *n.* —*See* DROP (4).

snort *v.* To breathe audibly through the nose ▸ sniff, sniffle, snuff, snuffle. —*See also* GASP.

snotty *adj.* —*See* IMPUDENT.

snout *n.* —*See* NOSE (1).

snow *v.* —*See* DECEIVE.

snowball *v.* To increase or expand suddenly, rapidly, or without control ▸ balloon, explode, mushroom. —*See also* INCREASE.

snow job *n.* —*See* TRICK (1).

snub *v.* To slight someone deliberately ▸ cut, disregard, ignore, neglect, rebuff, shun, slight, spurn. *Informal:* coldshoulder. ***Idioms:*** give someone the cold shoulder, give someone the go-by, turn one's back on, turn up one's nose at, close (*or* shut) the door on. [*Compare* BELITTLE, BLACKBALL, NEGLECT.]

snub *n.* A deliberate slight or affront ▸ cut, putdown, rebuff, spurning. *Informal:* cold shoulder, go-by. [*Compare* REBUKE.]

snuff *v.* To breathe audibly through the nose ▸ sniff, sniffle, snort, snuffle. —*See also* SMELL (1).

snuff out *v.* —*See* ANNIHILATE, EXTINGUISH, MURDER.

snuffle *v.* To breathe audibly through the nose ▸ sniff, sniffle, snort, snuff.

snug *adj.* —*See* COMFORTABLE, NEAT, TIGHT (4).

snug *v.* —*See* SNUGGLE.

snuggle *v.* To lie or press close together, usually with another person or another thing ▸ cuddle, nestle, nuzzle, snug. [*Compare* EMBRACE, NECK.]

so *adj.* In a similar manner ▸ likewise, similarly. ***Idioms:*** by the same token,

thus: *Hold the brush so.* **2.** To such an extent: *She was so weary that she fell.* **3.** To a great extent: *It's so cold.* **4.** As a result; consequently. **5.** Afterward; then: *to the store and so home.* **6.** Thereabouts: *only $10 or so.* **7.** Likewise. **8.** Apparently; then: *So you think you've got troubles?* **9.** In truth; indeed. ▸ *adj.* True or factual. ▸ *conj.* **1.** With the result or consequence that: *He quit, so I took his place.* **2.** In order that: *I stayed so I could see you.* ▸ *interj.* Used to express surprise or comprehension. *—idioms:* **so as to** In order to: *Shop early so as to beat the rush.* **so that** In order that.

so² (sō) ▸ *n. Mus.* Var. of **sol¹**.

so. or **So.** ▸ *abbr.* **1.** south **2.** southern

soak (sōk) ▸ *v.* **1.** To make thoroughly wet by or as if by being immersed in liquid; steep. **2.** To absorb. **3.** To be immersed. **4.** To penetrate or permeate; seep. ▸ *n.* **1.** The act or process of soaking. **2.** *Slang* A drunkard. **—soak′er** *n.*

soap (sōp) ▸ *n.* **1.** A cleansing agent made from an alkali acting on natural oils and fats. **2.** A metallic salt of a fatty acid. **3.** *Slang* A soap opera. **—soap** *v.* **—soap′i·ly** *adv.* **—soap′i·ness** *n.* **—soap′y** *adj.*

soap·box (sōp′bŏks′) ▸ *n.* **1.** A box in which soap is packed. **2.** A temporary platform used for impromptu public speaking.

soap opera ▸ *n.* A serial drama, usu. performed on daytime television or radio, characterized by melodrama and sentimentality.

soap·stone (sōp′stōn′) ▸ *n.* A soft metamorphic rock composed mostly of talc.

soar (sôr) ▸ *v.* **1.** To rise, fly, or glide high in the air. **2.** To climb swiftly or powerfully.

sob (sŏb) ▸ *v.* **sobbed, sob·bing.** To weep aloud with convulsive gasping. **—sob** *n.* **—sob′bing·ly** *adv.*

so·ba (sō′bə) ▸ *n.* A Japanese noodle made with buckwheat flour.

so·ber (sō′bər) ▸ *adj.* **-er, -est. 1.** Abstemious or temperate. **2.** Not intoxicated. **3.** Devoid of frivolity, excess, or exaggeration. **4.** Serious; solemn. **5.** Marked by circumspection and self-restraint. ▸ *v.* To make or become sober. **—so′ber·ly** *adv.* **—so′ber·ness** *n.*

so·bri·e·ty (sə-brī′ĭ-tē, sō-) ▸ *n.* **1.** Seriousness or gravity; solemnity. **2.** Absence of alcoholic intoxication.

so·bri·quet (sō′brĭ-kā′, -kĕt′) ▸ *n.* **1.** A nickname. **2.** An assumed name.

so-called (sō′kôld′) ▸ *adj.* So named, called, or designated, often incorrectly.

soc·cer (sŏk′ər) ▸ *n.* A game in which two 11-member teams propel a ball into the opposing team's goal by kicking or butting or by using any part of the body except the arms and hands.

so·cia·ble (sō′shə-bəl) ▸ *adj.* **1.** Fond of the company of others. **2.** Marked by or affording occasion for agreeable conversation and conviviality. **3.** Pleasant and affable. ▸ *n.* A social. **—so′cia·bil′i·ty, so′cia·ble·ness** *n.* **—so′cia·bly** *adv.*

so·cial (sō′shəl) ▸ *adj.* **1a.** Living together in communities or groups: *social insects.* **b.** Of or typical of communal or group living. **c.** Of or relating to human society and its organization: *social classes.* **2.** Of or in fashionable society. **3.** Seeking out or enjoying the company of others. **4.** Marked by friendly relations or companionship. **5.** Of or occupied with human welfare: *social programs.* ▸ *n.* An informal social gathering. **—so′cial·ly** *adv.*

social disease ▸ *n.* A venereal disease.

so·cial·ism (sō′shə-lĭz′əm) ▸ *n.* A social system in which the means of producing and distributing goods are owned collectively and political power is exercised by the whole community. **—so′cial·ist** *n.* **—so′cial·is′tic** *adj.*

so·cial·ite (sō′shə-līt′) ▸ *n.* One prominent in fashionable society.

so·cial·ize (sō′shə-līz′) ▸ *v.* **-ized, -iz·ing. 1.** To place under public ownership or control. **2.** To convert or adapt to social needs. **3.** To take part in social activities. **—so′cial·i·za′tion** *n.* **—so′cial·iz′er** *n.*

so·cial·ized medicine (sō′shə-līzd′) ▸ *n.* A system for providing medical and hospital care for all at nominal cost through government regulation of health services and tax subsidies.

social science ▸ *n.* A science, such as sociology, psychology, or anthropology, that studies society and individual relationships in and to society. **—social scientist** *n.*

social security ▸ *n.* A government program that provides monthly payments to the elderly and the disabled, financed by assessment of employers and employees.

social studies ▸ *pl.n.* *(takes sing. or pl. v.)* A course of study including geography, history, government, and sociology, taught in elementary and secondary schools.

social work ▸ *n.* Organized public work to aid the disadvantaged and counsel those with special problems. **—social worker** *n.*

so·ci·e·ty (sə-sī′ĭ-tē) ▸ *n., pl.* **-ties. 1.** Humans collectively. **2.** A group of people having mutual interests, shared institutions, and a common culture. **3.** An association of people uniting in a common interest. **4.** The rich and fashionable social class. **5.** Companionship; company. **6.** *Biol.* A community of organisms. **—so·ci′e·tal** *adj.*

Society of Friends ▸ *n.* A Christian denomination, founded in the mid-17th cent. in England, that rejects ritual, formal sacraments, a formal creed, a priesthood, and violence; Quakers.

socio– ▸ *pref.* **1.** Society: *sociology.* **2.** Social: *socioeconomic.*

so·ci·o·ec·o·nom·ic (sō′sē-ō-ĕk′ə-nŏm′ĭk, -ē′kə-, -shē-) ▸ *adj.* Both social and economic.

so·ci·ol·o·gy (sō′sē-ŏl′ə-jē, -shē-) ▸ *n.* The study of the origins, organization, institutions, and development of human society. **—so′ci·o·log′ic** (-ə-lŏj′ĭk), **so′ci·o·log′i·cal** *adj.* **—so′ci·o·log′i·cal·ly** *adv.* **—so′ci·ol′o·gist** *n.*

so·ci·o·path (sō′sē-ə-păth′, -shē-) ▸ *n.* One affected with a personality disorder marked by antisocial behavior. **—so′ci·o·path′ic** *adj.*

THESAURUS

in like fashion, in like manner, in the same way.

soak *v.* *—See* CHEAT (1), DRINK (3), DRINK (2), STEEP², WET (1).

soak in *v.* To come as a realization ▸ dawn on (or upon), register, sink in. [*Compare* DISCOVER, STRIKE, UNDERSTAND.]

soak up *v.* *—See* ABSORB (2).

soaked or **soaking** *adj.* *—See* WET.

soar *v.* To rise steeply and abruptly ▸ rocket, sky, skyrocket. *Informal:* shoot up. *—See also* FLY (2), INCREASE, RISE (2).

soaring *adj.* *—See* ELEVATED (4), HIGH (1).

sob *v.* *—See* CRY.

sobbing *n.* *—See* CRY (1).

sobby *adj.* *—See* SENTIMENTAL.

sober *adj.* *—See* DELIBERATE (3), REALISTIC (1), SENSIBLE, SERIOUS (1), TEMPERATE (2).

soberness *n.* *—See* TEMPERANCE (2).

sobersided *adj.* *—See* SERIOUS (1).

sobersidedness *n.* *—See* SERIOUSNESS (1).

sobriety *n.* *—See* MODERATION, SERIOUSNESS (1), TEMPERANCE (1), TEMPERANCE (2).

sobriquet *n.* *—See* NAME (1).

so-called *adj.* *—See* SUPPOSED.

sociability *n.* *—See* AMIABILITY.

sociable *adj.* *—See* AMIABLE, SOCIAL.

sociableness *n.* *—See* AMIABILITY.

social *adj.* Enjoying company ▸ companionable, convivial, gregarious, sociable. [*Compare* AMIABLE, OUTGOING, TALKATIVE.] *—See also* POPULAR.

social *n.* *—See* PARTY.

socialize *v.* **1.** To take part in social activities ▸ mingle, mix. **2.** To place under government or group ownership or control ▸ communalize, nationalize. **3.** To fit for companionship with others, especially in attitude or manners ▸ acculturate, civilize, humanize.

societal *adj.* *—See* POPULAR.

society *n.* **1.** People of the highest social level ▸ aristocracy, blue blood, crème de la crème, elite, flower, gentility, gentry, high society, jet set, nobility, patriciate, quality, smart set, upper class, who's who. *Informal:* upper crust. **2.** The total product of human creativity and intellect ▸ civilization, culture, Kultur. *—See also* COMPANY (3), CULTURE (2), PUBLIC (1), UNION (1).

sock[1] (sŏk) ► *n., pl.* **socks** or **sox** (sŏks). A short stocking.
sock[2] (sŏk) ► *v.* To strike forcefully; punch. **—sock** *n.*
sock·et (sŏk′ĭt) ► *n.* An opening or cavity into which something fits.
Soc·ra·tes (sŏk′rə-tēz′) (470?–399 B.C.) ► Greek philosopher.
So·crat·ic (sə-krăt′ĭk, sō-) ► *adj.* Of Socrates or his method of trying to arrive at the truth by asking questions.
sod (sŏd) ► *n.* Grass-covered surface soil held together by matted roots. ► *v.* **sod·ded, sod·ding.** To cover with sod.
so·da (sō′də) ► *n.* **1a.** Any of various forms of sodium carbonate. **b.** Chemically combined sodium. **2a.** Soda water. **b.** See **soft drink**. **3.** A drink made from carbonated water, ice cream, and usu. flavoring.
soda fountain ► *n.* **1.** An apparatus for dispensing soda water. **2.** A counter where soft drinks, ice-cream dishes, or sandwiches are served.
soda pop ► *n.* See **soft drink.**
soda water ► *n.* **1.** Effervescent water charged under pressure with carbon dioxide; club soda. **2.** See **soft drink.**
sod·den (sŏd′n) ► *adj.* **1.** Thoroughly soaked; saturated. **2.** Soggy and heavy. **3.** Stupid or dull, esp. from drink.
so·di·um (sō′dē-əm) ► *n.* *Symbol* **Na** A soft, light, extremely malleable metallic element that is naturally abundant in various compounds, esp. in common salt. At. no. 11.
sodium bicarbonate ► *n.* See **baking soda.**
sodium chloride ► *n.* A colorless crystalline compound, NaCl, used in the manufacture of chemicals and as a food preservative and seasoning; salt.
sodium hydroxide ► *n.* An alkaline compound, NaOH, used in chemicals and soaps and in petroleum refining; lye.
sodium nitrate ► *n.* A white crystalline compound, $NaNO_3$, used in fertilizers, pyrotechnics, and glass.
Sod·om (sŏd′əm) ► A city of ancient Palestine.
sod·om·y (sŏd′ə-mē) ► *n.* Any of various forms of sexual intercourse held to be unnatural or abnormal, esp. anal intercourse or copulation with an animal. **—sod′o·mize′** (-mīz′) *v.*
so·fa (sō′fə) ► *n.* A long upholstered seat usu. with a back and arms; couch.
soft (sôft, sŏft) ► *adj.* **-er, -est. 1.** Not hard or firm; yielding readily to pressure or weight. **2.** Out of condition; flabby. **3.** Smooth or fine to the touch. **4a.** Not loud, harsh, or irritating. **b.** Not brilliant or glaring; subdued. **5.** Mild; balmy: *a soft breeze.* **6a.** Of a gentle disposition; yielding. **b.** Affectionate. **c.** Not stern; lenient. **7.** *Informal* Simple; feeble. **8.** *Informal* Easy: *a soft job.* **9.** Apt to change, fluctuate, or devalue. **10.** Having low dissolved mineral content: *soft water.* ► *adv.* In a soft manner; gently. **—soft′en** *v.* **—soft′en·er** *n.* **—soft′ly** *adv.* **—soft′ness** *n.*
soft·ball (sôft′bôl′, sŏft′-) ► *n.* *Sports* **1.** A variation of baseball played with a larger, softer ball. **2.** The ball used in this game.
soft-boiled (sôft′boild′, sŏft′-) ► *adj.* Boiled in the shell to a soft consistency. Used of an egg.
soft coal ► *n.* See **bituminous coal.**
soft-core (sôft′kôr′, sŏft′-) ► *adj.* Being less explicit than hard-core material in depicting or describing sexual activity.
soft drink ► *n.* A sweetened, nonalcoholic carbonated beverage.
soft·heart·ed (sôft′här′tĭd, sŏft′-) ► *adj.* Easily moved; tender; merciful. **—soft′heart′ed·ly** *adv.* **—soft′heart′ed·ness** *n.*
soft landing ► *n.* The landing of a space vehicle in such a way as to prevent damage.
soft palate ► *n.* The movable fold that hangs from the rear of the hard palate and closes off the nasal cavity from the oral cavity during swallowing.
soft-ped·al (sôft′pĕd′l, sŏft′-) ► *v.* *Informal* To make less emphatic or obvious.
soft sell ► *n.* *Informal* A subtly persuasive method of selling or advertising.
soft-shell clam (sôft′shĕl′, sŏft′-) ► *n.* An edible clam having a thin elongated shell.
soft soap ► *n.* *Informal* Flattery; cajolery. **—soft′-soap′** *v.*
soft·ware (sôft′wâr′, sŏft′-) ► *n.* *Comp. Sci.* The programs, routines, and symbolic languages that control the functioning of the hardware and direct its operation.
soft·wood (sôft′wo͝od′, sŏft′-) ► *n.* A coniferous tree or its wood.
soft·y or **soft·ie** (sôf′tē, sŏf′-) ► *n., pl.* **-ies.** *Informal* One who is overly sentimental, trusting, or lenient.
sog·gy (sŏg′ē, sô′gē) ► *adj.* **-gi·er, -gi·est.** Saturated with moisture; soaked. **—sog′gi·ly** *adv.* **—sog′gi·ness** *n.*
soil[1] (soil) ► *n.* **1.** The top layer of the earth's surface, suitable for the growth of plant life. **2.** A particular kind of earth or ground. **3.** Country; land: *one's native soil.*
soil[2] (soil) ► *v.* **1.** To make or become dirty. **2.** To disgrace; tarnish. **3.** To corrupt; defile. ► *n.* **1a.** The state of being soiled. **b.** A stain. **2.** Manure, esp. human excrement, used as fertilizer.
soi·ree also **soi·rée** (swä-rā′) ► *n.* An evening party or reception.
so·journ (sō′jûrn′, sō-jûrn′) ► *v.* To stay for a time. ► *n.* A temporary stay. **—so′journ′er** *n.*
sol[1] (sōl) also **so** (sō) ► *n.* *Mus.* The 5th tone of the diatonic scale.
sol[2] (sōl) ► *n., pl.* **so·les** (sō′lĕs). See **currency** table in Appendix.
sol·ace (sŏl′ĭs) ► *n.* **1.** Comfort in sorrow or distress; consolation. **2.** A source of comfort or consolation. ► *v.* **-aced, -ac·ing.** To comfort or console in time of trouble or sorrow.
so·lar (sō′lər) ► *adj.* **1.** Of or proceeding from the sun: *solar rays.* **2.** Powered by the energy of sunlight. **3.** Measured in reference to the sun: *a solar year.*
solar battery ► *n.* An electric battery consisting of a number of connected solar cells.
solar cell ► *n.* A semiconductor device that converts solar radiation to electric energy.
solar flare ► *n.* A temporary eruption of hydrogen gas from the sun's surface.
so·lar·i·um (sō-lâr′ē-əm, sə-) ► *n., pl.* **-i·a** (-ē-ə) or **-i·ums.** A room or glassed-in porch exposed to the sun.
solar plexus ► *n.* **1.** The large network of nerves located behind the stomach. **2.** The pit of the stomach.
solar system ► *n.* The sun together with the eight planets and all other celestial bodies that orbit the sun.
solar wind (wĭnd) ► *n.* The stream of charged atomic particles that radiates from the sun.

THESAURUS

sock *v.* —*See* HIT.
sock *n.* —*See* BLOW[2].
sock away *v.* —*See* BANK[2], SAVE (1).
socket *n.* —*See* OUTLET (1).
sock-hop *n.* —*See* DANCE.
sod *n.* —*See* EARTH (1).
sodden *adj.* —*See* DRUNK, WET.
sodden *v.* —*See* WET (1).
soft *adj.* **1.** Yielding easily to pressure or weight ► doughy, mushy, pappy, pulpous, pulpy, quaggy, spongy, squashy, squishy, yielding. *Informal:* squooshy. **2.** Not irritating, strident, or loud ► hushed, low, low-key, low-keyed, muffled, muted, quiet, small, subdued, whispery. [*Compare* FAINT, LOW.] —*See also* COMFORTABLE, GENTLE (1), GENTLE (2), LIGHT[2] (2), LIMP, RAINY, SENTIMENTAL, SLOW (2), TOLERANT.
soften *v.* —*See* MODERATE (1), PACIFY, WEAKEN.
softhead *n.* —*See* DULLARD, FOOL.
softheaded *adj.* —*See* STUPID.
softheadedness *n.* —*See* STUPIDITY.
softhearted *adj.* —*See* GENTLE (1), SYMPATHETIC.
soft-pedal *v.* *Informal* To make less emphatic or obvious ► de-emphasize, play down, tone down. [*Compare* MODERATE.]
soft soap *n.* —*See* FLATTERY.
soft-soap *v.* —*See* COAX, FLATTER (1).
soft spot *n.* —*See* LIKING.
softy *n.* —*See* BABY (2), WEAKLING.
soggy *adj.* —*See* STICKY (2), WET.
soil *n.* —*See* EARTH (1).
soil *v.* —*See* CORRUPT, DENIGRATE, DIRTY.
soiled *adj.* —*See* DIRTY.
soiree or **soireé** *n.* —*See* PARTY.
sojourn *v.* —*See* LODGE.
sojourn *n.* A remaining in a place as a guest or lodger ► stay, stop, stopover, visit.
sojourner *n.* —*See* TOURIST.
solace *n.* A consoling in time of grief or pain ► comfort, consolation, reassurance, succor. [*Compare* HELP, PITY.]
solace *v.* —*See* COMFORT.

sold (sōld) ▸ *v.* P.t. and p.part. of **sell.**

sol·der (sŏd′ər) ▸ *n.* **1.** Any of various alloys, usu. tin and lead, used in the molten state to join metallic parts. **2.** Something that joins or cements. **—sol′der** *v.* **—sol′der·er** *n.*

sol·dier (sōl′jər) ▸ *n.* **1.** One who serves in an army. **2.** An enlisted person or a noncommissioned officer. **3.** An active follower. ▸ *v.* To be or serve as a soldier. **—sol′dier·ly** *adj.*

soldier of fortune ▸ *n.* One who will serve in any army for pay or love of adventure.

sol·dier·y (sōl′jə-rē) ▸ *n.* **1.** Soldiers collectively. **2.** The profession of soldiering.

sole[1] (sōl) ▸ *n.* **1.** The underside of the foot. **2.** The underside of a shoe or boot. ▸ *v.* **soled, sol·ing.** To furnish (a shoe or boot) with a sole.

sole[2] (sōl) ▸ *adj.* Being the only one; single. **—sole′ly** *adv.*

sole[3] (sōl) ▸ *n., pl.* **sole** or **soles.** Any of various chiefly marine flatfishes valued as food fishes.

sol·e·cism (sŏl′ĭ-sĭz′əm, sō′lĭ-) ▸ *n.* **1.** A nonstandard usage or grammatical construction. **2.** A violation of etiquette.

sol·emn (sŏl′əm) ▸ *adj.* **1.** Deeply earnest; grave. **2.** Performed with full ceremony. **3.** Gloomy; somber. **—so·lem′ni·ty** (sə-lĕm′nĭ-tē), **sol′emn·ness** *n.* **—sol′emn·ly** *adv.*

sol·em·nize (sŏl′əm-nīz′) ▸ *v.* **-nized, -niz·ing. 1.** To celebrate or observe with dignity and gravity. **2.** To perform with formal ceremony. **—sol′em·ni·za′tion** *n.*

so·le·noid (sō′lə-noid′) ▸ *n.* A coil of insulated wire in which a magnetic field is established when an electric current passes through it.

so·lic·it (sə-lĭs′ĭt) ▸ *v.* **1.** To seek to obtain: *solicit votes.* **2.** To petition persistently; entreat. **3.** To entice or tempt. **—so·lic′i·ta′tion** *n.*

so·lic·i·tor (sə-lĭs′ĭ-tər) ▸ *n.* **1.** One who solicits. **2.** The chief law officer of a city, town, or government department. **3.** *Chiefly Brit.* An attorney who is not a member of the bar and who may be heard only in the lower courts.

so·lic·i·tous (sə-lĭs′ĭ-təs) ▸ *adj.* **1.** Anxious or concerned; attentive. **2.** Eager. **—so·lic′i·tous·ly** *adv.* **—so·lic′i·tous·ness** *n.*

so·lic·i·tude (sə-lĭs′ĭ-to͞od′, -tyo͞od′) ▸ *n.* The state of being solicitous.

sol·id (sŏl′ĭd) ▸ *adj.* **-er, -est. 1a.** Of definite shape and volume; not liquid or gaseous. **b.** Firm or compact in substance. **2.** Not hollowed out. **3.** Being the same substance or color throughout. **4.** Of three-dimensional geometric figures or bodies. **5.** Of good quality and substance. **6.** Sound; reliable. **7.** Financially sound. **8.** Upstanding and dependable. **9.** Acting together; unanimous. ▸ *n.* **1.** A solid substance. **2.** A geometric figure having three dimensions. **—so·lid′i·ty** (sə-lĭd′ĭ-tē), **sol′id·ness** *n.* **—sol′id·ly** *adv.*

sol·i·dar·i·ty (sŏl′ĭ-dăr′ĭ-tē) ▸ *n.* A unity of interests or sympathies among a group.

so·lid·i·fy (sə-lĭd′ə-fī′) ▸ *v.* **-fied, -fy·ing.** To make or become solid or united. **—so·lid′i·fi·ca′tion** *n.*

sol·id-state (sŏl′ĭd-stāt′) ▸ *adj.* **1.** Of or relating to the physical properties of solid materials, esp. crystalline solids. **2.** Based on or using transistors or other semiconducting materials or devices.

so·lil·o·quy (sə-lĭl′ə-kwē) ▸ *n., pl.* **-quies. 1.** A dramatic discourse in which a character reveals his or her thoughts when alone or unaware of the presence of other characters. **2.** The act of speaking to oneself. **—so·lil′o·quize′** *v.*

sol·ip·sism (sŏl′ĭp-sĭz′əm, sō′lĭp-) ▸ *n. Philos.* The theory that the self is the only reality. **—sol′ip·sist** *n.* **—sol′ip·sis′tic** *adj.*

sol·i·taire (sŏl′ĭ-târ′) ▸ *n.* **1.** A gemstone set alone, as in a ring. **2.** A card game played by one person.

sol·i·tar·y (sŏl′ĭ-tĕr′ē) ▸ *adj.* **1.** Existing or living alone. **2.** Happening or done alone. **3.** Remote or secluded. **4.** Single; sole. **—sol′i·tar′i·ly** (-târ′ə-lē) *adv.* **—sol′i·tar′i·ness** *n.*

sol·i·tude (sŏl′ĭ-to͞od′, -tyo͞od′) ▸ *n.* **1.** The state of being alone; isolation. **2.** A lonely or secluded place.

so·lo (sō′lō) ▸ *n., pl.* **-los. 1.** *Mus.* A composition for an individual voice or instrument, with or without accompaniment. **2.** A performance or accomplishment by a single individual. ▸ *v.* To perform a solo. **—so′lo** *adj. & adv.* **—so′lo·ist** *n.*

Sol·o·mon (sŏl′ə-mən) (fl. 10th cent. B.C.) ▸ King of Israel famous for his wisdom.

Solomon Islands[1] ▸ An island group of the W Pacific E of New Guinea divided between Papua New Guinea and the independent Solomon Is.

Solomon Islands[2] ▸ A country comprising the Solomon Is. SE of Bougainville.

So·lon (sō′lən, -lŏn′) (638?–559? B.C.) ▸ Athenian lawgiver and poet.

sol·stice (sŏl′stĭs, sōl′-, sôl′-) ▸ *n.* Either of two times of the year when the sun reaches an extreme of its northward or southward motion. **—sol·sti′tial** (-stĭsh′əl) *adj.*

sol·u·ble (sŏl′yə-bəl) ▸ *adj.* **1.** Capable of being dissolved. **2.** Possible to solve or explain. **—sol′u·bil′i·ty** *n.* **—sol′u·bly** *adv.*

sol·ute (sŏl′yo͞ot, sō′lo͞ot) ▸ *n.* A substance dissolved in another substance. ▸ *adj.* Being in solution; dissolved.

so·lu·tion (sə-lo͞o′shən) ▸ *n.* **1a.** A homogeneous mixture of two or more substances, which may be solids, liquids, gases, or a combination of these. **b.** The process of forming such a mixture. **2.** The method or process of solving a problem. **3.** The answer to or disposition of a problem.

solve (sŏlv, sôlv) ▸ *v.* **solved, solv·ing.** To find a solution to. **—solv′a·ble** *adj.* **—solv′er** *n.*

THESAURUS

soldier *n.* **1.** One who engages in a combat or struggle ▸ belligerent, combatant, fighter, warrior. [*Compare* AGGRESSOR.] **2.** An enlisted person ▸ GI, legionnaire, legionary, military man, military woman, militiaman, serviceman, serviceperson, servicewoman, trooper. *Slang:* GI Jane, GI Joe, grunt. [*Compare* MERCENARY.]

soldier *v.* —*See* ENDURE (1).

soldier of fortune *n.* A freelance fighter ▸ adventurer, mercenary. [*Compare* FIGHTER, SOLDIER.]

sole *adj.* —*See* EXCLUSIVE (1), INDIVIDUAL (2), LONE, SINGLE.

solecism *n.* —*See* BLUNDER, CORRUPTION (3), IMPROPRIETY (2).

solely *adv.* To the exclusion of anyone or anything else ▸ alone, exclusively, just, only. [*Compare* COMPLETELY, MERELY.] *See also* ALONE.

solemn *adj.* —*See* CEREMONIOUS, SERIOUS (1).

solemnity *n.* —*See* CELEBRATION (2), CEREMONY (1), SERIOUSNESS (1).

solemnization *n.* —*See* CELEBRATION (2).

solemnize *v.* To mark a day or an event with ceremonies of respect, festivity, or rejoicing ▸ celebrate, commemorate, keep, observe. [*Compare* SANCTIFY.]

solemnness *n.* —*See* SERIOUSNESS (1).

solicit *v.* —*See* APPEAL (1), BILL[1], COURT (1).

solicitous *adj.* —*See* ANXIOUS, ATTENTIVE, CAREFUL (2), EAGER.

solicitude *n.* —*See* ANXIETY (1), CONSIDERATION (1).

solid *adj.* Unyielding to pressure ▸ firm, hard, incompressible. —*See also* DEPENDABLE, FIRM[1] (2), INTIMATE[1] (1), PHYSICAL, REAL (1), SOUND[2], UNANIMOUS.

solidarity *n.* An identity or coincidence of interests, purposes, or sympathies among the members of a group ▸ concord, oneness, union, unity. [*Compare* ALLIANCE, UNION.]

solidify *v.* —*See* HARDEN (2).

solidity *n.* The quality, condition, or degree of being thick ▸ compactness, density, thickness. —*See also* STABILITY.

solipsistic *adj.* Holding the philosophical view that the self is the center and norm of existence ▸ egocentric, egoistic, egoistical, individualistic. [*Compare* EGOTISTIC.]

solitarily *adv.* —*See* ALONE.

solitariness *n.* —*See* SOLITUDE.

solitary *adj.* Set away from or lacking the company of all others ▸ alone, apart, cloistered, companionless, detached, friendless, isolate, isolated, lone, lonely, lonesome, recluse, reclusive, removed, sequestered, single, unaccompanied. *Idiom:* by one's lonesome. [*Compare* ABANDONED, LONELY.] —*See also* COOL, LONE, REMOTE (1).

solitude *n.* The quality or state of being alone ▸ aloneness, isolation, loneliness, privacy, retirement, retreat, seclusion, singleness, solitariness. [*Compare* CALM, STILLNESS.]

solemn word *n.* —*See* PROMISE (1).

solo *adv.* —*See* ALONE.

solution *n.* —*See* ANSWER (2).

solve *v.* **1.** To find a solution for ▸ answer, clear up, decipher, divine,

sol·vent (sŏl′vənt, sôl′-) ▸ *adj.* **1.** Able to meet financial obligations. **2.** Capable of dissolving another substance. ▸ *n.* A substance, usu. a liquid, capable of dissolving another substance. **—sol′ven·cy** *n.*

som (sōm) ▸ *n., pl.* **som.** See **currency** table in Appendix.

So·ma·li (sō-mä′lē) ▸ *n., pl.* **-li** or **-lis.** **1.** A native or inhabitant of Somalia. **2.** The Cushitic language of Somalia. **—So·ma′li** *adj.*

So·ma·li·a (sō-mä′lē-ə, -mäl′yə) ▸ A country of extreme E Africa on the Gulf of Aden and the Indian Ocean. **—So·ma′li·an** *adj. & n.*

so·mat·ic (sō-măt′ĭk) ▸ *adj.* Of the body, esp. as distinguished from a body part, the mind, or the environment; physical.

somatic cell ▸ *n.* Any cell of a plant or animal other than a germ cell.

som·ber (sŏm′bər) ▸ *adj.* **1.** Dark; gloomy. **2.** Melancholy; dismal. **—som′ber·ly** *adv.*

som·bre (sŏm′bər) ▸ *adj. Chiefly Brit.* Var. of **somber.**

som·bre·ro (sŏm-brâr′ō, səm-) ▸ *n., pl.* **-ros.** A large, broad-brimmed hat.

some (sŭm) ▸ *adj.* **1.** Being an unspecified number or quantity: *some people; some sugar.* **2.** Unknown or unspecified by name: *Some man called.* **3.** *Informal* Remarkable: *She is some skier.* ▸ *pron.* An indefinite or unspecified number, quantity, or portion. ▸ *adv.* **1.** Approximately; about. **2.** *Informal* Somewhat.

-some[1] ▸ *suff.* Characterized by a specified quality, condition, or action: *loathsome.*

-some[2] ▸ *suff.* A group of a specified number of members: *threesome.*

-some[3] ▸ *suff.* Body: *centrosome.*

some·bod·y (sŭm′bŏd′ē, -bŭd′ē, -bə-dē) ▸ *pron.* An unspecified or unknown person. ▸ *n. Informal* A person of importance.

some·day (sŭm′dā′) ▸ *adv.* At an indefinite time in the future.

some·how (sŭm′hou′) ▸ *adv.* In a way not specified, understood, or known.

some·one (sŭm′wŭn′, -wən) ▸ *pron.* An unspecified or unknown person; somebody. ▸ *n. Informal* A somebody.

some·place (sŭm′plās′) ▸ *adv. & n.* Somewhere.

som·er·sault (sŭm′ər-sôlt′) ▸ *n.* An acrobatic stunt in which the body rolls in a complete circle, heels over head. **—som′er·sault′** *v.*

some·thing (sŭm′thĭng) ▸ *pron.* An unspecified or not definitely known thing. ▸ *n. Informal* A remarkable or important thing or person. ▸ *adv.* Somewhat. ***—idiom:* something else** *Informal* One that is special or remarkable.

some·time (sŭm′tīm′) ▸ *adv.* **1.** At an indefinite or unstated time. **2.** At an indefinite time in the future. ▸ *adj.* Former.

some·times (sŭm′tīmz′) ▸ *adv.* Now and then.

some·way (sŭm′wā′) also **some·ways** (-wāz′) ▸ *adv.* In some way or another.

some·what (sŭm′hwŏt′, -wŏt′, -hwət, -wət) ▸ *adv.* To some extent or degree; rather.

some·where (sŭm′hwâr′, -wâr′) ▸ *adv.* **1.** At, in, or to a place not specified or known. **2.** To a place or state of further development or progress. ▸ *n.* An unspecified place.

som·me·lier (sŭm′əl-yā′, sô′mə-lyā′) ▸ *n.* A restaurant employee who orders and maintains the wines sold in the restaurant.

som·nam·bu·late (sŏm-năm′byə-lāt′) ▸ *v.* **-lat·ed, -lat·ing.** To walk while asleep.

som·nam·bu·lism (sŏm-năm′byə-lĭz′əm) ▸ *n.* See **sleepwalking. —som·nam′bu·list** *n.*

som·no·lent (sŏm′nə-lənt) ▸ *adj.* Drowsy; sleepy. **—som′no·lence** *n.* **—som′no·lent·ly** *adv.*

so·mo·ni (sô-mô-nē′) ▸ *n.* See **currency** table in Appendix.

son (sŭn) ▸ *n.* **1.** One's male child. **2.** A male descendant. **3.** A man considered as if in a relationship of child to parent: *a son of the soil.* **—son′ly** *adj.*

so·nar (sō′när′) ▸ *n.* A system or apparatus using transmitted and reflected sound waves to detect and locate underwater objects.

so·na·ta (sə-nä′tə) ▸ *n. Mus.* A composition for one or more solo instruments, usu. written in three or four movements.

song (sông, sŏng) ▸ *n.* **1a.** A brief composition written for singing. **b.** The act or art of singing: *broke into song.* **2.** A melodious utterance, as of a bird. **3a.** Poetry. **b.** A lyric poem. ***—idiom:* for a song** *Informal* At a low price.

song·bird (sông′bûrd′, sŏng′-) ▸ *n.* A bird having a melodious song or call.

Song of Solomon ▸ *n.* Song of Songs.

Song of Songs ▸ *n.* See **Bible** table in Appendix.

song·ster (sông′stər, sŏng′-) ▸ *n.* **1.** One who sings. **2.** See **songwriter.**

song·writ·er (sông′rī′tər, sŏng′-) ▸ *n.* One who writes song lyrics or tunes.

son·ic (sŏn′ĭk) ▸ *adj.* Of or relating to sound or its speed in air.

sonic barrier ▸ *n.* The sudden sharp increase in aerodynamic drag experienced by aircraft approaching the speed of sound.

sonic boom ▸ *n.* An explosive sound caused by the shock wave preceding an aircraft traveling at a supersonic speed.

son-in-law (sŭn′ĭn-lô′) ▸ *n., pl.* **sons-in-law** (sŭnz′-). The husband of one's daughter.

son·net (sŏn′ĭt) ▸ *n.* A 14-line poetic verse form usu. in iambic pentameter, with a fixed rhyme pattern.

son·o·gram (sŏn′ə-grăm′, sō′nə-) ▸ *n.* An image, as of an unborn fetus or an internal body organ, produced by ultrasonography.

son·o·rous (sŏn′ər-əs, sə-nôr′-) ▸ *adj.* **1.** Having or producing sound. **2.** Having or producing a full, deep, or rich sound. **3.** Impressive in style of speech: *a sonorous oration.* **—so·nor′i·ty** (sə-nôr′ĭ-tē, -nŏr′-) *n.* **—son′o·rous·ly** *adv.*

soon (so͞on) ▸ *adv.* **-er, -est.** **1.** In the near future. **2.** Within a short time; quickly. **3.** Early. **4.** Willingly; gladly: *I'd as soon leave right now.* ***—idiom:* sooner or later** Eventually.

soot (so͝ot, so͞ot) ▸ *n.* The fine black particles, chiefly carbon, produced by incomplete combustion of coal, oil, wood, or other fuel. **—soot′i·ness** *n.* **—soot′y** *adj.*

sooth (so͞oth) ▸ *n. Archaic* Truth; reality.

soothe (so͞o*th*) ▸ *v.* **soothed, sooth·ing.** **1.** To calm or quiet. **2.** To ease or relieve the pain of. **—sooth′er** *n.* **—sooth′ing·ly** *adv.*

sooth·say·er (so͞oth′sā′ər) ▸ *n.* One who foretells events; seer.

THESAURUS

explain, reason out, resolve, think out (through), unravel, untangle. *Informal:* dope out, figure out. *Idioms:* get to the bottom of, hit on the answer (*or* solution), put two and two together. [*Compare* ANALYZE, DECIPHER.] **2.** To arrive at an answer to a mathematical problem ▸ work out. *Informal:* figure out. [*Compare* CALCULATE.]

somatic *adj.* —*See* BODILY.

somber *adj.* —*See* GLOOMY, SERIOUS (1).

some *adj.* —*See* SEVERAL.

some *adv.* —*See* APPROXIMATELY.

some *pron.* —*See* SEVERAL.

somebody or **someone** *n.* —*See* DIGNITARY.

something *n.* —*See* OBJECT (1), THING (1).

sometime *adj.* —*See* LATE (2).

sometimes *adv.* —*See* INTERMITTENTLY.

somnifacient *adj.* —*See* SOPORIFIC.

somnifacient *n.* —*See* SOPORIFIC.

somniferous or **somnific** *adj.* —*See* SOPORIFIC.

somnolent *adj.* —*See* SLEEPY, SOPORIFIC.

sonance *n.* Vibrations detected by the ear ▸ noise, sound. [*Compare* TONE.]

song *n.* A brief composition written or adapted for singing ▸ ballad, carol, ditty, hymn, jingle, lyrics, number, piece, tune. [*Compare* MELODY.] —*See also* POEM (1).

sonorous *adj.* —*See* ORATORICAL, RESONANT.

soon *adv.* In the near future ▸ before long, by and by, imminently, presently, promptly, quickly, shortly, without delay. *Informal:* pronto. *Idioms:* before long, in a bit (*or* jiffy *or* minute *or* moment), in short order. [*Compare* IMMEDIATELY.]

soothe *v.* —*See* COMFORT, PACIFY.

soothing *adj.* —*See* COMFORTABLE, GENTLE (2).

soothsayer *n.* —*See* PROPHET.

soothsaying *n.* —*See* PROPHECY.

sop (sŏp) ▸ *v.* **sopped, sop·ping.** **1.** To dip, soak, or drench in a liquid. **2.** To take up by absorption. ▸ *n.* Something yielded to placate or soothe; bribe. **—sop′py** *adj.*

soph·ism (sŏf′ĭz′əm) ▸ *n.* **1.** A plausible but fallacious argument. **2.** Deceptive or fallacious argumentation. **—soph′ist** *n.* **—so·phis′tic, so·phis′ti·cal** *adj.* **—so·phis′ti·cal·ly** *adv.*

so·phis·ti·cate (sə-fĭs′tĭ-kāt′) ▸ *v.* **-cat·ed, -cat·ing.** **1.** To cause to become less naive and more worldly. **2.** To refine. ▸ *n.* (-kĭt) A sophisticated person. **—so·phis′ti·ca′tion** *n.*

so·phis·ti·cat·ed (sə-fĭs′tĭ-kā′tĭd) ▸ *adj.* **1.** Having acquired worldly knowledge or refinement. **2.** Very complex or complicated. **3.** Appealing to refined tastes.

soph·is·try (sŏf′ĭ-strē) ▸ *n., pl.* **-tries.** Plausible but faulty or misleading argumentation.

Soph·o·cles (sŏf′ə-klēz′) (496?–406 B.C.) ▸ Greek dramatist.

soph·o·more (sŏf′ə-môr′, sŏf′môr′) ▸ *n.* A second-year student in a US high school or college.

soph·o·mor·ic (sŏf′ə-môr′ĭk, -mŏr′-) ▸ *adj.* **1.** Of or like a sophomore. **2.** Exhibiting immaturity and lack of judgment.

sop·o·rif·ic (sŏp′ə-rĭf′ĭk, sō′pə-) ▸ *adj.* **1.** Inducing sleep. **2.** Drowsy. ▸ *n.* A drug that induces sleep.

so·pran·o (sə-prăn′ō, -prä′nō) ▸ *n., pl.* **-os.** **1.** The highest singing voice of a woman or young boy. **2.** The tonal range characteristic of a soprano. **3.** A singer, voice, or instrument having this range.

sor·bi·tol (sôr′bĭ-tôl′, -tōl′, -tŏl′) ▸ *n.* A white sweetish crystalline alcohol that is found in fruits, used esp. as a sugar substitute.

sor·cer·y (sôr′sə-rē) ▸ *n.* Use of supernatural power over others through the assistance of spirits. **—sor′cer·er** *n.* **—sor′cer·ess** *n.*

sor·did (sôr′dĭd) ▸ *adj.* **1.** Filthy; foul. **2.** Depressingly squalid; wretched. **3.** Morally degraded; base. **—sor′did·ly** *adv.* **—sor′did·ness** *n.*

sore (sôr) ▸ *adj.* **sor·er, sor·est.** **1.** Painful or tender. **2.** Feeling pain; hurting. **3.** Causing sorrow or distress; grievous. **4.** *Informal* Angry; offended. ▸ *n.* **1.** An open skin lesion, wound, or ulcer. **2.** A source of pain or distress. **—sore′ly** *adv.* **—sore′ness** *n.*

sor·ghum (sôr′gəm) ▸ *n.* An Old World grass cultivated as grain and forage or as a source of syrup.

so·ror·i·ty (sə-rôr′ĭ-tē, -rŏr′-) ▸ *n., pl.* **-ties.** **1.** A chiefly social organization of women college students. **2.** An association or society of women.

sor·rel[1] (sôr′əl, sŏr′-) ▸ *n.* Any of several plants with acid-flavored leaves.

sor·rel[2] (sôr′əl, sŏr′-) ▸ *n.* **1.** A yellowish to reddish brown. **2.** A sorrel-colored horse.

sor·row (sŏr′ō, sôr′ō) ▸ *n.* **1.** Mental suffering caused by loss or despair. **2.** Something causing sadness or grief. ▸ *v.* To feel or express sorrow. **—sor′row·ful** *adj.* **—sor′row·ful·ly** *adv.* **—sor′row·ful·ness** *n.*

sor·ry (sŏr′ē, sôr′ē) ▸ *adj.* **-ri·er, -ri·est.** **1.** Feeling or expressing sympathy or regret. **2.** Poor or wretched: *a sorry excuse.* **3.** Grievous or sad. **—sor′ri·ness** *n.*

sort (sôrt) ▸ *n.* **1.** A group of similar persons or things; kind. **2.** Type, character, or quality. **3.** A way of acting or behaving. ▸ *v.* To arrange according to class, kind, or size. ***—idioms:*** **out of sorts** **1.** Slightly ill. **2.** Irritable or cross. **sort of** *Informal* Somewhat.

sor·tie (sôr′tē, sôr-tē′) ▸ *n.* **1.** An armed attack made from a place surrounded by enemy forces. **2.** A flight of a combat aircraft on a mission.

SOS (ĕs′ō-ĕs′) ▸ *n.* A call or signal for help or rescue.

so-so (sō′sō′) ▸ *adj.* Mediocre. **—so′-so′** *adv.*

sot (sŏt) ▸ *n.* A drunkard. **—sot′tish** *adj.* **—sot′tish·ly** *adv.*

sou·brette (so͞o-brĕt′) ▸ *n.* A saucy maid in comic drama or opera.

souf·flé (so͞o-flā′) ▸ *n.* A light fluffy baked dish made with egg yolks and beaten egg whites.

sough (sŭf, sou) ▸ *v.* To make a soft murmuring sound. **—sough** *n.*

sought (sôt) ▸ *v.* P.t. and p.part. of **seek**.

soul (sōl) ▸ *n.* **1.** The animating and vital principle in humans often conceived as an immaterial entity that survives death. **2.** A spirit or ghost. **3.** A human. **4.** The central or vital part of something. **5.** A person considered as the perfect embodiment of an intangible quality: *the very soul of discretion.* **6.** A person's emotional or moral nature. **7.** A sense of ethnic pride among African Americans. **8.** A strong, deeply felt emotion conveyed by a speaker, performer, or artist.

soul·ful (sōl′fəl) ▸ *adj.* Filled with or expressing deep feeling. **—soul′ful·ly** *adv.* **—soul′ful·ness** *n.*

sound[1] (sound) ▸ *n.* **1a.** A vibratory disturbance, with frequencies in the approximate range of 20 to 20,000 hertz, capable of being heard. **b.** The sensation stimulated in the organs of hearing by such a disturbance. **c.** Such sensations collectively. **2.** A distinctive noise. **3.** *Ling.* An articulation

THESAURUS

sooty *adj.* —*See* BLACK (1).

sop *v.* —*See* WET (1).

sop up *v.* —*See* DRINK (3).

sop *n.* —*See* BRIBE.

sophism *n.* —*See* FALLACY (1).

sophistic *adj.* —*See* FALLACIOUS (1).

sophisticate *v.* —*See* CONTAMINATE.

sophisticated *adj.* Experienced in the ways of the world; lacking natural simplicity ▸ cosmopolitan, worldly, worldly-wise. [*Compare* EXPERIENCED, SHREWD, SUAVE.] —*See also* COMPLEX (1), CULTURED, EXCLUSIVE (3), IMPURE (2), INTELLECTUAL.

sophistication *n.* —*See* CONTAMINATION, [illegible]

sophistry *n.* —*See* FALLACY (2).

sophomoric *adj.* —*See* CHILDISH.

soporific *adj.* Inducing sleep or sedation ▸ hypnotic, narcotic, opiate, sedative, sleepy, slumberous, somnifacient, somniferous, somnific, somnolent, stupefacient, stupefying, tranquilizing. —*See also* SLEEPY.

soporific *n.* Something that induces sleep or sedation ▸ hypnotic, narcotic, opiate, sedative, somnifacient, stupefacient, tranquilizer. [*Compare* DRUG.]

sopping *adj.* —*See* WET.

soppy *adj.* —*See* SENTIMENTAL, WET.

sorcerer *n.* —*See* WIZARD.

sorceress *n.* A woman who practices magic ▸ enchantress, hag, lamia, witch. [*Compare* WIZARD.]

sorcery *n.* —*See* MAGIC (1).

sordid *adj.* Having or proceeding from low moral standards ▸ base, ignoble, low, low-down, mean, seamy, squalid, vile. [*Compare* CORRUPT, DISGRACEFUL.]

sore *adj.* —*See* ANGRY, PAINFUL.

sorehead *n.* —*See* GROUCH.

soreness *n.* —*See* IRRITATION, PAIN.

sorority *n.* —*See* UNION (1).

sorrow *n.* —*See* CURSE (3), DEPRESSION [illegible]

sorrow *v.* To feel or express sorrow for ▸ deplore, regret, repent, rue. [*Compare* FEEL.] —*See also* GRIEVE.

sorrowful *adj.* Causing or expressing sadness, sorrow, or regret ▸ blue, cheerless, deplorable, depressing, discouraging, disheartening, dismal, dispiriting, doleful, dolorous, gloomy, grievous, heartbreaking, heart-rending, joyless, lamentable, lugubrious, melancholy, mournful, plaintive, regrettable, rueful, sad, saddening, woebegone, woeful. [*Compare* AFFECTING, GLOOMY, PITIFUL.] —*See also* DEPRESSED (1).

sorry *adj.* Feeling or expressing sympathy, pity, or regret ▸ apologetic, compunctious, contrite, penitent, penitential, regretful, remorseful, repentant, rueful. *Idiom:* down on one's knees. —*See also* DISAPPOINTING, PITIFUL, SHODDY.

sort *n.* —*See* KIND[2].

sort *v.* To set apart one kind or type from others ▸ separate, sift, winnow. *Idiom:* separate the sheep from the goats. —*See also* ARRANGE (1), CLASSIFY.

sortie *n.* —*See* BATTLE, EXPEDITION.

so-so *adj.* —*See* ORDINARY.

sot *n.* —*See* DRUNKARD.

sottish *adj.* —*See* DRUNK.

sough *n.* —*See* MURMUR.

sough *v.* To make a low, continuous, and indistinct sound ▸ murmur, rustle, sigh, whisper. [*Compare* BURBLE, HUM.]

soul *n.* The seat of a person's innermost emotions and feelings ▸ bosom, breast, heart. *Idioms:* the bottom (*or* cockles) of one's heart, one's heart of hearts. —*See also* GHOST, HEART (1), HUMAN BEING, SPIRIT (2).

soulless *adj.* —*See* CALLOUS.

soul mate *n.* —*See* FRIEND.

sound[1] *n.* **1.** Vibrations detected by

made by the vocal apparatus. 4. A conveyed impression; implication. 5. Auditory material that is recorded, as for a movie. ▸ *v.* 1. To make or cause to make a sound. 2. To convey an impression: *sounds reasonable.* 3. To summon or signal by a sound. 4. *Medic.* To examine by auscultation. **—sound′er** *n.* **—sound′less** *adj.* **—sound′less·ly** *adv.*

sound² (sound) ▸ *adj.* **-er, -est.** 1. Free from defect or damage. 2. Solid. 3. Financially secure or safe. 4. Based on valid reasoning. 5. Thorough; complete: *a sound thrashing.* 6. Deep and undisturbed: *fell into a sound sleep.* 7. *Law* Legally valid: *sound title.* **—sound′ly** *adv.* **—sound′ness** *n.*

sound³ (sound) ▸ *n.* A long body of water, wider than a strait, usu. connecting larger bodies of water.

sound⁴ (sound) ▸ *v.* 1. To measure the depth of (water). 2. To try to learn the attitudes or opinions of. 3. To dive swiftly downward, as a whale. **—sound′er** *n.* **—sound′ing** *n.*

sound barrier ▸ *n.* See **sonic barrier**.

sound box ▸ *n.* *Mus.* A hollow chamber, as of a violin or guitar, that intensifies resonance.

sound effect ▸ *n.* An imitative sound, as of thunder, produced for film, stage, or radio.

sound·ing board (soun′dĭng) ▸ *n.* 1. A thin board forming the upper portion of the resonant chamber in an instrument, such as a violin or piano. 2. A structure placed so as to amplify a speaker's voice. 3. A means serving to spread or popularize opinions.

sound·proof (sound′pro͝of′) ▸ *adj.* Not penetrable by audible sound. **—sound′proof′** *v.*

sound·track (sound′trăk′) ▸ *n.* 1. The narrow strip at one side of a movie film that carries the sound recording. 2. A recording of the music from a movie.

soup (so͞op) ▸ *n.* 1. A liquid food prepared from meat, fish, or vegetable stock combined with various other ingredients. 2. Dense fog. ***—phrasal verb:*** **soup up** *Slang* To modify so as to enhance power or performance. ***—idiom:*** **in the soup** *Slang* In trouble or difficulties.

soup·çon (so͞op-sôN′, so͞op′sŏn′) ▸ *n.* A very small amount; trace.

soup kitchen ▸ *n.* A place where food is offered to the needy.

soup·y (so͞o′pē) ▸ *adj.* **-i·er, -i·est.** 1. Having the appearance or consistency of soup. 2. *Slang* Foggy.

sour (sour) ▸ *adj.* **-er, -est.** 1. Having a sharp or acid taste. 2. Spoiled or rancid. 3a. Bad-tempered. b. Displeased, disagreeable, or disenchanted. ▸ *v.* To make or become sour. **—sour′ish** *adj.* **—sour′ly** *adv.* **—sour′ness** *n.*

sour·ball (sour′bôl′) ▸ *n.* A round piece of hard tart candy.

source (sôrs) ▸ *n.* 1. A point of origin. 2. The beginning of a stream of water, such as a spring or river. 3. One that supplies information.

sour cream ▸ *n.* Cream soured esp. by lactic-acid bacteria and used in cooking.

sour·dough (sour′dō′) ▸ *n.* Sour fermented dough used as leaven in making bread.

sour·sop (sour′sŏp′) ▸ *n.* A tropical American tree bearing spiny tart fruit.

Sou·sa (so͞o′zə, -sə), **John Philip** (1854–1932) ▸ Amer. bandmaster and composer.

souse (sous) ▸ *v.* **soused, sous·ing.** 1. To plunge into a liquid. 2. To drench or become drenched. 3. To steep. 4. *Slang* To make intoxicated. ▸ *n.* 1. The act or process of sousing. 2a. Food steeped in pickle, esp. pork trimmings. b. Brine. 3. *Slang* A drunkard.

south (south) ▸ *n.* 1a. The direction along a meridian 90° clockwise from east. b. The compass point 180° clockwise from north. 2. often **South** a. The southern part of the earth. b. The southern part of a region or country. ▸ *adj.* 1. To, toward, of, or in the south. 2. Coming from the south: *a south wind.* ▸ *adv.* In, from, or toward the south. **—south′ward** (south′wərd, sŭth′ərd) *adj. & adv.* **—south′ward·ly** *adj. & adv.* **—south′wards** *adv.*

South Africa ▸ A country of S Africa on the Atlantic and Indian oceans. Caps. Pretoria, Cape Town, and Bloemfontein. **—South African** *adj. & n.*

South America ▸ A continent of the S Western Hemisphere SE of North America between the Atlantic and Pacific oceans. **—South American** *adj. & n.*

South Car·o·li·na (kăr′ə-lī′nə) ▸ A state of the SE US bordering on the Atlantic. Cap. Columbia. **—South Car′o·lin′i·an** (-lĭn′ē-ən) *adj. & n.*

South Dakota ▸ A state of the N-central US. Cap. Pierre. **—South Dakotan** *adj. & n.*

south·east (south-ēst′, sou-ēst′) ▸ *n.* 1. The direction that is 45° clockwise from east and 45° counterclockwise from south. 2. often **Southeast** An area or region lying to the southeast of a particular point. **—south·east′** *adj. & adv.* **—south·east′er·ly** *adj. & adv.* **—south·east′ern** *adj.* **—south·east′ward** *adv. & adj.* **—south·east′ward·ly** *adv. & adj.* **—south·east′wards** *adv.*

Southeast Asia ▸ A region of Asia including Indochina, the Malay Peninsula, and the Malay Archipelago. **—Southeast Asian** *adj. & n.*

south·east·er (south-ē′stər, sou-ē′-) ▸ *n.* A storm or gale blowing from the southeast.

south·east·er·ly (south-ē′stər-lē, sou-ē′-) ▸ *adj.* 1. Situated toward the southeast. 2. Coming or being from the southeast. **—south·east′er·ly** *adv.*

south·er·ly (sŭth′ər-lē) ▸ *adj.* 1. In or toward the south. 2. From the south: *southerly winds.* **—south′er·ly** *adv.*

south·ern (sŭth′ərn) ▸ *adj.* 1. Of, in, or toward the south. 2. From the south: *southern breezes.* **—south′ern·most′** *adj.*

south·ern·er also **South·ern·er** (sŭth′ər-nər) ▸ *n.* A native or inhabitant of a southern region.

Southern Hemisphere ▸ *n.* The half of the earth south of the equator.

southern lights ▸ *pl.n.* See **aurora australis**.

Southern Yemen ▸ A former country of SW Asia on the Arabian Peninsula; united with North Yemen (1990) to form the new country of Yemen.

South Korea ▸ A country of E Asia on the S Korean peninsula. **—South Korean** *adj. & n.*

south·paw (south′pô′) ▸ *n.* *Slang* A left-handed person, esp. a left-handed baseball pitcher.

South Pole ▸ *n.* 1. The southern end of the earth's axis of rotation, a point in Antarctica. 2. The celestial zenith of the heavens as viewed from the south terrestrial pole.

THESAURUS

the ear ▸ noise, sonance. [*Compare* NOISE, TONE.] 2. Range of audibility ▸ earshot, hearing. [*Compare* RANGE.]

sound *v.* To give the impression of being ▸ appear, feel, look, seem. ***Idioms:*** have all the earmarks of being, give the idea (*or* impression) of being, strike one as being. [*Compare* RESEMBLE.] —*See also* EXPLORE, PRONOUNCE, RING².

sound² *adj.* Based on good judgment, reasoning, or evidence ▸ cogent, just, solid, tight, valid, well-considered, well-founded, well-grounded. [*Compare* CONVINCING, LOGICAL.] —*See also* DEPENDABLE, FIRM¹ (2), GOOD (2), HEALTHY, SENSIBLE.

sound³ *v.* To test the attitude of someone ▸ feel (out), probe, sound out. ***Idioms:*** put out feelers, run something up the flagpole, send up a trial balloon.

sound⁴ *n.* A body of water partly enclosed by land but having a wide outlet to the sea ▸ bay, bight, gulf. [*Compare* CHANNEL, HARBOR, INLET.]

soundless *adj.* —*See* SILENT (1).

soundlessness *n.* —*See* SILENCE (1).

soundness *n.* The condition of being free from defects or flaws ▸ flawlessness, intactness, integrity, perfection, wholeness. ***Idiom:*** mint condition. —*See also* HEALTH (1), LEGALITY, SANITY, STABILITY.

soup *n.* —*See* PREDICAMENT.

soupçon *n.* —*See* SHADE (2).

soupy *adj.* —*See* SENTIMENTAL.

sour *adj.* Having a taste characteristic of that produced by acids ▸ acerbic, acetous, acid, acidic, acidulous, dry, green, sharp, tangy, tart, unripe, vinegary. [*Compare* BITTER (1).] —*See also* GLUM.

sour *v.* —*See* DISAPPOINT.

source *n.* An acquaintance who is in a position to help ▸ connection, contact. —*See also* INFORMER, ORIGIN.

sourpuss *n.* —*See* GROUCH.

souse *v.* —*See* DIP (1), STEEP², WET (1).

souse *n.* —*See* BENDER, DRUNKARD.

soused *adj.* —*See* DRUNK.

South Sudan ► A country of NE Africa S of Sudan. **—South Sudanese** *adj. & n.*

South Vietnam ► A former country of SE Asia (1954–75); now part of Vietnam. **—South Vietnamese** *adj. & n.*

south·west (south-wĕst′, sou-wĕst′) ► *n.* **1.** The direction 45° clockwise from south and 45° counterclockwise from west. **2.** often **Southwest** An area or region lying in the southwest. **—south·west′** *adj. & adv.* **—south·west′er·ly** *adj. & adv.* **—south·west′ern** *adj.* **—south·west′ward** *adv. & adj.* **—south·west′ward·ly** *adv. & adj.* **—south·west′wards** *adv.*

south·west·er (south-wĕs′tər, sou-wĕs′-) also **sou′·west·er** (sou-wĕs′-) ► *n.* **1.** A storm or gale from the southwest. **2.** A waterproof hat with a broad brim in back.

sou·ve·nir (so͞o′və-nîr′, so͞o′və-nîr′) ► *n.* A token of remembrance; memento.

sov·er·eign (sŏv′ər-ĭn, sŏv′rĭn) ► *n.* **1.** The chief of state in a monarchy. **2.** A gold coin formerly used in Great Britain. ► *adj.* **1.** Independent: *a sovereign state.* **2.** Having supreme rank or power. **3.** Paramount; supreme. **4a.** Excellent. **b.** Unmitigated: *sovereign contempt.*

sov·er·eign·ty (sŏv′ər-ĭn-tē, sŏv′rĭn-) ► *n., pl.* **-ties. 1.** Supremacy of authority or rule. **2.** Royal rank, authority, or power. **3.** Complete independence and self-government. **4.** A territory existing as a sovereign state.

so·vi·et (sō′vē-ĕt′, -ĭt, sŏv′ē-) ► *n.* **1.** One of the popularly elected legislative assemblies of the former Soviet Union. **2. Soviets** The people and government of the former Soviet Union.

Soviet Union ► See **Union of Soviet Socialist Republics. —Soviet** *adj.*

sow^{1} (sō) ► *v.* **sowed, sown** (sōn) or **sowed, sow·ing. 1.** To plant (seeds) to produce a crop. **2.** To propagate or disseminate; spread. **3.** To scatter with or as if with seed. **—sow′er** *n.*

sow^{2} (sou) ► *n.* An adult female hog.

So·we·to (sə-wĕt′ō, -wā′tō) ► A city of NE South Africa SW of Johannesburg.

sox (sŏks) ► *n.* Pl. of **sock^{1}**.

soy (soi) ► *n.* **1.** The soybean. **2.** A salty brown liquid condiment made from soybeans.

soy·bean (soi′bēn′) ► *n.* An Asian bean cultivated for forage and for its nutritious seeds.

soy·milk (soi′mĭlk′) ► *n.* A milk substitute made from soybeans, often supplemented with vitamins.

soy sauce ► *n.* A salty brown sauce made by fermenting soybeans and wheat.

spa (spä) ► *n.* **1.** A resort providing therapeutic baths. **2.** A resort area having mineral springs.

space (spās) ► *n.* **1a.** *Math.* A set of elements or points satisfying specified geometric postulates. **b.** The infinite extension of the three-dimensional region in which all matter exists. **2a.** The expanse in which the solar system, stars, and galaxies exist; universe. **b.** The region of this expanse beyond Earth's atmosphere. **3.** A blank or empty area. **4.** A particular area, such as an accommodation on a train. **5a.** A period or interval of time. **b.** A little while. ► *v.* **spaced, spac·ing. 1.** To organize or arrange with spaces between. **2.** *Slang* To become disoriented from or as if from a drug: *space out.* **—spac′er** *n.*

space bar ► *n.* A bar of a typewriter or computer keyboard that when pressed introduces a blank space, as between words.

space·craft (spās′krăft′) ► *n., pl.* **-craft.** A vehicle designed to be launched into space.

space heater ► *n.* A small, usu. portable appliance that warms a small enclosed area.

space·ship (spās′shĭp′) ► *n.* See **spacecraft**.

space shuttle ► *n.* A reusable spacecraft designed to transport astronauts between Earth and an orbiting space station and to deploy and retrieve satellites.

space station ► *n.* A large satellite equipped to support a human crew and designed to remain in extended orbit around Earth.

space suit ► *n.* A protective pressure suit permitting an astronaut relatively free movement in space, esp. outside a spacecraft.

space-time (spās′tīm′) ► *n. Phys.* The four-dimensional continuum of one temporal and three spatial coordinates in which any event or physical object is located.

space walk ► *n.* Extravehicular activity. **—space walk** *v.* **—space walker** *n.*

spa·cious (spā′shəs) ► *adj.* Large in range, extent, or scope. **—spa′cious·ly** *adv.* **—spa′cious·ness** *n.*

spac·y or **spac·ey** (spā′sē) ► *adj.* **-i·er, -i·est.** *Slang* **1.** Disoriented from or as if from drug use. **2.** Eccentric; offbeat.

spade^{1} (spād) ► *n.* A digging tool with a long handle and a flat blade. ► *v.* **spad·ed, spad·ing.** To dig with a spade.

spade^{2} (spād) ► *n.* Any of a suit of playing cards marked with a black, leaf-shaped figure.

spade·work (spād′wûrk′) ► *n.* Preparatory work necessary for a project or activity.

spa·dix (spā′dĭks) ► *n., pl.* **-di·ces** (-dĭ-sēz′). A clublike stalk bearing tiny flowers, usu. enclosed in a sheathlike spathe.

spa·ghet·ti (spə-gĕt′ē) ► *n.* Pasta in long, often thick strands.

Spain (spān) ► A country of SW Europe comprising most of the Iberian Peninsula and the Balearic and Canary Is.

spake (spāk) ► *v. Archaic* P.t. of **speak**.

spam (spăm) ► *n.* Unsolicited e-mail, usu. of a commercial nature. ► *v.* **spammed, spam·ming.** To send unsolicited e-mail to.

span (spăn) ► *n.* **1.** The distance or extent between two points or extremities. **2.** The distance between vertical supports of a horizontal structural part. **3.** The section between two intermediate supports of a bridge. **4.** A unit of measure equal to about 9 in. (23 cm). **5.** A period of time: *a span of life.* ► *v.* **spanned, span·ning. 1.** To measure by or as if by the extended hand. **2.** To extend across in space or time.

span·dex (spăn′dĕks) ► *n.* An elastic synthetic fiber or fabric made from a polymer containing polyurethane.

span·gle (spăng′gəl) ► *n.* A small piece of shiny metal or plastic used esp. on garments for decoration. **—span′gle** *v.* **—span′gly** *adj.*

Span·iard (spăn′yərd) ► *n.* A native or inhabitant of Spain.

span·iel (spăn′yəl) ► *n.* A dog usu. having drooping ears, short legs, and a wavy, silky coat.

Span·ish (spăn′ĭsh) ► *n.* **1.** The Romance language of the largest part of Spain and most of Central and South America. **2.** The people of Spain. **—Span′ish** *adj.*

Spanish America ► The former Spanish possessions in the New World.

Spanish American ► *n.* **1.** A native or inhabitant of Spanish America. **2.** A US citizen or resident of Hispanic descent. ► *adj.* **Span·ish-A·mer·i·can** (spăn′ĭsh-ə-mĕr′ĭ-kən) **1.** Of Spanish America. **2.** Of Spain and America, esp. the United States.

Spanish moss ► *n.* A plant of the SE US and tropical America that grows on trees in long gray tangled clusters.

Spanish Sahara ► See **Western Sahara**.

spank (spăngk) ► *v.* To slap on the buttocks with the open hand. **—spank** *n.*

spank·ing (spăng′kĭng) ► *adj.* **1.** *Informal* Exceptional; remarkable. **2.** Brisk and fresh: *a spanking breeze.* ► *adv.* Used as an intensive: *a spanking clean shirt.* ► *n.* A number of slaps on the buttocks in rapid succession.

THESAURUS

souvenir *n.* —*See* REMEMBRANCE (1).

sovereign *adj.* —*See* FREE (1).

sovereign *n.* —*See* CHIEF.

sovereignty *n.* —*See* AUTHORITY, FREEDOM.

sow *v.* —*See* PLANT.

space *n.* —*See* BIT^{1} (3), DISTANCE (1), EXPANSE (1), HOLE (1), PERIOD (1).

spaced-out *adj.* —*See* ABSENT-MINDED, DRUGGED.

spacious *adj.* Having plenty of room ► ample, capacious, commodious, roomy. [*Compare* BIG.] —*See also* BROAD (1).

spade *v.* —*See* DIG, TILL.

span^{1} *n.* —*See* DISTANCE (1), EXTENT, LIFE, PERIOD (1).

span *v.* —*See* CROSS (1).

span^{2} *n.* —*See* COUPLE.

spangle *n.* A small decoration that sparkles ► diamond, glitter, rhinestone, sequin.

spangle *v.* —*See* GLITTER.

spank *v.* —*See* SLAP.

spank *n.* —*See* SLAP.

spar[1] (spär) ▸ *n.* A wooden or metal pole used to support sail rigging.
spar[2] (spär) ▸ *v.* **sparred, spar·ring.** **1.** To box, esp. for practice. **2.** To bandy words about; wrangle.
spare (spâr) ▸ *v.* **spared, spar·ing.** **1.** To treat mercifully; deal with leniently. **2.** To refrain from harming or destroying. **3.** To save from experiencing or doing something; exempt. **4.** To use with restraint or frugality. **5.** To do without. ▸ *adj.* **spar·er, spar·est.** **1a.** Kept in reserve: *a spare part.* **b.** Extra: *spare cash.* **c.** Free for other use; unoccupied: *spare time.* **2a.** Without excess; meager. **b.** Lean and trim. **3.** Not profuse or copious. ▸ *n.* **1.** A replacement, esp. a tire, reserved for future need. **2.** The knocking down of all ten bowling pins with two successive rolls of the ball. **—spare′ly** *adv.* **—spare′ness** *n.*
spare·ribs (spâr′rĭbz′) ▸ *pl.n.* Pork ribs with most of the meat trimmed off.
spar·ing (spâr′ĭng) ▸ *adj.* Thrifty or frugal. **—spar′ing·ly** *adv.*
spark[1] (spärk) ▸ *n.* **1.** A glowing particle, esp. one thrown off from a burning substance or resulting from friction. **2a.** A brief flash of light, esp. one produced by electric discharge. **b.** A short pulse or flow of electric current. **3.** A quality or factor with latent potential; seed: *the spark of genius.* ▸ *v.* **1.** To give off sparks. **2.** To set in motion; spur: *spark a controversy.*
spark[2] (spärk) ▸ *n.* **1.** A young dandy. **2.** A male suitor; beau. ▸ *v.* To court or woo. **—spark′er** *n.*
spar·kle (spär′kəl) ▸ *v.* **-kled, -kling.** **1.** To give off sparks. **2.** To give off or reflect flashes of light; glitter. **3.** To be brilliant or witty. **4.** To release gas bubbles; effervesce. **—spar′kle** *n.* **—spar′kler** *n.*
spark plug ▸ *n.* A device in a cylinder of an internal-combustion engine that ignites the fuel mixture by an electric spark.
spar·row (spăr′ō) ▸ *n.* Any of various small brownish or grayish New World finches.
sparrow hawk ▸ *n.* **1.** A small Old World hawk that preys on small birds. **2.** A small North American falcon.
sparse (spärs) ▸ *adj.* **spars·er, spars·est.** Occurring, growing, or settled at widely spaced intervals. **—sparse′ly** *adv.* **—sparse′ness, spar′si·ty** *n.*
Spar·ta (spär′tə) ▸ A city-state of ancient Greece in the SE Peloponnesus.
Spar·ta·cus (spär′tə-kəs) (d. 71 B.C.) ▸ Thracian slave who led a revolt against Rome.
Spar·tan (spär′tn) ▸ *adj.* **1.** Of Sparta or its people. **2a.** Rigorously self-disciplined. **b.** Simple, frugal, or austere. ▸ *n.* **1.** A citizen of Sparta. **2.** One of Spartan character.
spasm (spăz′əm) ▸ *n.* **1.** A sudden involuntary muscular contraction. **2.** A sudden burst of energy, activity, or emotion. **—spas·mod′ic** (spăz-mŏd′ĭk) *adj.* **—spas·mod′i·cal·ly** *adv.*
spas·tic (spăs′tĭk) ▸ *adj.* Of or affected by muscular spasms. ▸ *n.* A person affected with chronic muscular spasms. **—spas′ti·cal·ly** *adv.*
spat[1] (spăt) ▸ *v.* P.t. and p.part. of **spit[1]**.
spat[2] (spăt) ▸ *n., pl.* **spat** or **spats.** The larval stage of a bivalve mollusk, such as an oyster.
spat[3] (spăt) ▸ *n.* A gaiter covering the upper shoe and the ankle.
spat[4] (spăt) ▸ *n.* A brief quarrel. ▸ *v.* **spat·ted, spat·ting.** To engage in a spat.
spate (spāt) ▸ *n.* A sudden flood, rush, or outpouring.
spathe (spā*th*) ▸ *n. Bot.* A leaflike organ that encloses or spreads from the base of the spadix, as in the jack-in-the-pulpit and the calla lily.
spa·tial (spā′shəl) ▸ *adj.* Relating to space. **—spa′tial·ly** *adv.*
spat·ter (spăt′ər) ▸ *v.* To scatter or be scattered in drops or small splashes; splatter. ▸ *n.* **1.** The act or sound of spattering. **2.** A drop or splash of something spattered.
spat·u·la (spăch′ə-lə) ▸ *n.* An implement with a flexible blade used esp. to mix, spread, or lift material.
spav·in (spăv′ĭn) ▸ *n.* A condition in which the hock joint becomes swollen or painful. **—spav′ined** *adj.*
spawn (spôn) ▸ *n.* **1.** The eggs of aquatic animals such as fishes, oysters, or frogs. **2.** Offspring, esp. when produced in large numbers; brood. ▸ *v.* **1.** To produce offspring. **2.** To produce offspring in large numbers. **3.** To give rise to; engender.
spay (spā) ▸ *v.* To remove the ovaries of (an animal).
speak (spēk) ▸ *v.* **spoke** (spōk), **spo·ken** (spō′kən), **speak·ing.** **1.** To utter words; talk. **2.** To converse. **3.** To deliver a public speech. **4.** To act as spokesperson. **5.** To converse in or be able to converse in (a language). ***—phrasal verb:*** **speak out (or up)** To speak without fear or hesitation. **—speak′a·ble** *adj.*
speak·eas·y (spēk′ē′zē) ▸ *n., pl.* **-ies.** A place for the illegal sale and consumption of alcoholic drinks.
speak·er (spē′kər) ▸ *n.* **1.** One who speaks. **2.** One who delivers a public speech. **3.** The presiding officer of a legislative assembly. **4.** A loudspeaker.
spear[1] (spîr) ▸ *n.* **1.** A weapon consisting of a long shaft with a sharply pointed end. **2.** A barbed shaft for spearing fish. ▸ *v.* To pierce or stab with or as if with a spear.
spear[2] (spîr) ▸ *n.* A slender stalk, as of asparagus or grass.
spear·fish (spîr′fĭsh′) ▸ *v.* To fish with a spear or spear gun. **—spear′fish′er** *n.* **—spear′fish′ing** *n.*
spear gun ▸ *n.* A device for mechanically shooting a spearlike missile under water, as in spearfishing.
spear·head (spîr′hĕd′) ▸ *n.* **1.** The sharpened head of a spear. **2.** The leading forces in a military attack. **3.** The driving force in an action or endeavor. **—spear′head** *v.*
spear·mint (spîr′mĭnt′) ▸ *n.* A common mint yielding an oil used widely as a flavoring.
spe·cial (spĕsh′əl) ▸ *adj.* **1.** Surpassing what is common or usual; exceptional. **2.** Distinct among others of a kind; singular. **3.** Peculiar to a specific person or thing; particular. **4.** Having a limited or specific function, application, or scope. **5.** Additional or extra. ▸ *n.* **1.** One that is special. **2.** Something arranged, issued, or produced for a particular service or

THESAURUS

spar *v.* —*See* ARGUE (1), CONTEND.
spare *v.* —*See* EXCUSE (1), SCRIMP.
spare *adj.* —*See* BARE (1), MEAGER, SUPERFLUOUS, THIN (1), TIGHT (3).
sparing *adj.* —*See* ECONOMICAL.
spark[1] *n.* —*See* FLASH (1), GERM (2).
spark *v.* To set in motion ▸ activate, actuate, start, turn on. [*Compare* ENERGIZE.] —*See also* PROVOKE.
spark[2] *v.* —*See* COURT (2).
sparkle *v.* —*See* GLITTER.
sparkle *n.* —*See* GLITTER (1), GLITTER (2), SPIRIT (1).
sparkling *adj.* Full of bright shifting or flickering light ▸ coruscating, flashing, gleaming, glinting, glistening, glittering, resplendent, scintillating, shimmering, twinkling, twinkly. [*Compare* BRIGHT, BRILLIANT, GLOSSY.] —*See also* CLEVER (2), LIVELY.
sparkly *adj.* —*See* LIVELY.
sparse *adj.* —*See* MEAGER.
spartan *adj.* —*See* BARE (1), MEAGER, TEMPERATE (2).
spasm *n.* —*See* PAIN, TREMOR (2).
spasmodic *adj.* —*See* UNEVEN.
spat *n.* —*See* ARGUMENT, SLAP.
spat *v.* —*See* ARGUE (1), SLAP.
spate *n.* —*See* FLOOD, FLOW.
spatter *v.* —*See* DENIGRATE, RAIN (2), SPLASH (1), STAIN.
spawn *v.* —*See* BREED, PRODUCE (1).
spawn *n.* The offspring, as of an animal or bird, for example, that are the result of one breeding season ▸ brood, litter, young. —*See also* PROGENY.
spawning *n.* —*See* REPRODUCTION.
spay *v.* —*See* STERILIZE (2).
speak *v.* **1.** To express oneself in speech ▸ talk, verbalize, vocalize. *Idioms:* bend someone's ear, open one's mouth (*or* lips), put in (*or* into) words, wag one's tongue. [*Compare* BABBLE, CHATTER, SAY.] **2.** To direct speech to ▸ address, talk. **3.** To talk to an audience formally ▸ lecture, prelect, sermonize. —*See also* CONVERSE[1].
speak for *v.* To serve as an official delegate of ▸ act (as *or* for), answer for, represent, stand for. *Idioms:* be spokesperson (*or* representative) for, be the voice of. [*Compare* SUBSTITUTE.]
speak up *v.* —*See* OBJECT.
speaker *n.* **1.** One who delivers a public speech ▸ declaimer, lecturer, orator, rhetorician, speechifier, speechmaker. **2.** A person who speaks on behalf of another or others ▸ mouth, spokesman, spokesperson, spokeswoman. *Informal:* mouthpiece. [*Compare* REPRESENTATIVE.]
spear *v.* —*See* CUT (1).
special *adj.* Relating to, identifying,

occasion: *a television special.* **3.** A featured attraction, such as a reduced price: *a special on salmon.* **—spe′cial·ly** *adv.*

special delivery ▸ *n.* Delivery of mail at an unscheduled time for an additional fee.

special education ▸ *n.* Instruction designed for students whose learning needs cannot be met by a standard school curriculum.

special effect ▸ *n.* A visual effect added to a movie or a taped television show during processing.

Special Forces ▸ *pl.n.* A division of the US Army composed of soldiers specially trained in guerrilla fighting.

spe·cial·ist (spĕsh′ə-lĭst) ▸ *n.* **1.** One who is devoted to a particular occupation or branch of study. **2.** A physician whose practice is limited to a particular branch of medicine or surgery. **3.** Any of several noncommissioned ranks in the US Army.

spe·cial·ize (spĕsh′ə-līz′) ▸ *v.* **-ized, -iz·ing. 1.** To pursue a special activity, occupation, or field of study. **2.** *Biol.* To adapt or become adapted to a specific function or environment. **—spe′cial·i·za′tion** *n.*

special relativity ▸ *n.* The physical theory of space and time developed by Albert Einstein.

spe·cial·ty (spĕsh′əl-tē) ▸ *n., pl.* **-ties. 1.** A special pursuit, occupation, aptitude, or skill. **2.** A branch of medicine in which a physician specializes. **3.** A special feature; peculiarity.

spe·cie (spē′shē, -sē) ▸ *n.* Coined money; coin.

spe·cies (spē′shēz, -sēz) ▸ *n., pl.* **spe·cies. 1.** *Biol.* **a.** The category ranking below a genus in the hierarchy of taxonomic classification, usu. the narrowest group to which an organism can be assigned. **b.** The group of organisms assigned to such a category. **2.** A kind, variety, or type.

spe·cif·ic (spĭ-sĭf′ĭk) ▸ *adj.* **1.** Explicitly set forth; definite. **2.** Of, characterizing, or distinguishing a species. **3.** Intended for or acting on a particular thing, esp. effective in the treatment of a particular disease. ▸ *n.* **1.** A remedy for a particular ailment or disorder. **2. specifics** Distinct items or details; particulars. **—spe·cif′i·cal·ly** *adv.* **—spec′i·fic′i·ty** (spĕs′ə-fĭs′ĭ-tē) *n.*

spec·i·fi·ca·tion (spĕs′ə-fĭ-kā′shən) ▸ *n.* **1.** Something that is specified. **2. specifications** A detailed statement of particulars, esp. one prescribing materials, dimensions, and quality of work for something to be built, installed, or manufactured.

specific gravity ▸ *n.* The ratio of the mass of a solid or liquid to the mass of an equal volume of distilled water at 4°C (39°F) or of a gas to an equal volume of air or hydrogen under prescribed conditions of temperature and pressure.

spec·i·fy (spĕs′ə-fī′) ▸ *v.* **-fied, -fy·ing.** To state explicitly, unambiguously, or in detail.

spec·i·men (spĕs′ə-mən) ▸ *n.* An individual, item, or part representative of an entire set or whole; sample.

spe·cious (spē′shəs) ▸ *adj.* **1.** Seemingly true but actually fallacious: *a specious argument.* **2.** Deceptively attractive. **—spe′cious·ly** *adv.* **—spe′cious·ness** *n.*

speck (spĕk) ▸ *n.* **1.** A small spot or mark. **2.** A tiny amount; bit. ▸ *v.* To mark with specks.

speck·le (spĕk′əl) ▸ *n.* A small spot, esp. a natural dot of color on skin, plumage, or foliage. **—speck′le** *v.* **—speck′led** *adj.*

spec·ta·cle (spĕk′tə-kəl) ▸ *n.* **1a.** A remarkable or impressive sight. **b.** A lavish public performance or display. **2. spectacles** A pair of eyeglasses. **—spec′ta·cled** *adj.*

spec·tac·u·lar (spĕk-tăk′yə-lər) ▸ *adj.* Of the nature of a spectacle; sensational. ▸ *n.* A lavish spectacle. **—spec·tac′u·lar·ly** *adv.*

spec·ta·tor (spĕk′tā′tər) ▸ *n.* An observer of an event.

spec·ter (spĕk′tər) ▸ *n.* **1.** A ghostly apparition; phantom. **2.** A haunting or disturbing prospect: *the specter of nuclear war.*

spec·tra (spĕk′trə) ▸ *n.* Pl. of **spectrum.**

spec·tral (spĕk′trəl) ▸ *adj.* **1.** Resembling a specter; ghostly. **2.** Of or produced by a spectrum.

spectro– ▸ *pref.* Spectrum: *spectrograph.*

spec·tro·gram (spĕk′trə-grăm′) ▸ *n.* A graph or photograph of a spectrum.

spec·tro·graph (spĕk′trə-grăf′) ▸ *n.* **1.** A spectroscope equipped to photograph spectra. **2.** A spectrogram. **—spec′tro·graph′ic** *adj.* **—spec′tro·graph′i·cal·ly** *adv.* **—spec·trog′ra·phy** (-trŏg′rə-fē) *n.*

spec·trom·e·ter (spĕk-trŏm′ĭ-tər) ▸ *n.* A spectroscope equipped to measure wavelengths or indexes of refraction. **—spec′tro·met′ric** (-trə-mĕt′rĭk) *adj.* **—spec·trom′e·try** *n.*

spec·tro·scope (spĕk′trə-skōp′) ▸ *n.* An instrument for producing, observing, or recording spectra. **—spec′tro·scop′ic** (-skŏp′ĭk), **spec′tro·scop′i·cal** *adj.* **—spec·tros′co·pist** (-trŏs′kə-pĭst) *n.* **—spec·tros′co·py** *n.*

spec·trum (spĕk′trəm) ▸ *n., pl.* **-tra** (-trə) or **-trums. 1.** *Phys.* The distribution of a characteristic of a physical system or phenomenon, esp. the distribution of energy emitted by a radiant source, as by an incandescent body, arranged in order of wavelengths. **2.** A broad range: *the whole spectrum of modern thought.*

spec·u·late (spĕk′yə-lāt′) ▸ *v.* **-lat·ed, -lat·ing. 1.** To meditate on a subject; reflect. **2.** To engage in risky business ventures that offer the chance of large profits. **—spec′u·la′tion** *n.* **—spec′u·la·tive** *adj.* **—spec′u·la′tor** *n.*

spec·u·lum (spĕk′yə-ləm) ▸ *n., pl.* **-la** (-lə) or **-lums. 1.** A mirror used in optical instruments. **2.** An instrument for dilating a body cavity for medical examination.

speech (spēch) ▸ *n.* **1a.** The act of speaking. **b.** The capacity to speak. **2.** Vocal communication; conversation. **3.** A talk or public address. **4.** One's manner of speaking. **5.** The language or dialect of a nation or region.

speech·less (spēch′lĭs) ▸ *adj.* **1.** Lacking the faculty of

THESAURUS

or setting apart an individual or group ▸ characteristic, distinctive, distinguishing, especial, express, individual, particular, peculiar, set, specific, typical, vintage. [*Compare* DEFINITE, DISTINCT.] —*See also* EXCEPTIONAL.

specialist *n.* [illegible]

specialty *n.* An area of academic study that is part of a larger body of learning ▸ branch, discipline, field. [*Compare* AREA.] —*See also* BUSINESS (2), DETAIL, FORTE.

species *n.* —*See* KIND².

specific *adj.* —*See* DEFINITE (1), DEFINITE (2), SPECIAL.

specifically *adv.* —*See* NAMELY.

specification *n.* —*See* PROVISION.

specify *v.* To state specifically ▸ detail, particularize, provide, stipulate. [*Compare* ASSERT, DESCRIBE, DICTATE.] —*See also* DESIGNATE, NAME (2).

specimen *n.* —*See* EXAMPLE (1).

specious *adj.* —*See* FALLACIOUS (1), FALSE.

speciousness *n.* —*See* FALLACY (2).

speck *n.* —*See* BIT¹ (1), POINT (2).

speck *v.* —*See* SPECKLE.

speckle *v.* To mark with many small spots ▸ bespeckle, besprinkle, dapple, [illegible], pepper, speck, spot, sprinkle, stipple. [*Compare* STREAK.]

speckle *n.* —*See* POINT (2).

spectacle *n.* —*See* ARRAY, VIEW (2).

spectacular *adj.* —*See* DRAMATIC (2), MARVELOUS.

spectator *n.* —*See* WATCHER (1).

specter *n.* —*See* GHOST.

spectral *adj.* —*See* GHASTLY (2).

spectrum *n.* —*See* RANGE (1).

speculate *v.* To formulate as a tentative explanation ▸ hypothesize, theorize. [*Compare* SUPPOSE.] —*See also* GAMBLE (3), GUESS, THINK (1).

speculation *n.* —*See* ASSUMPTION, GAMBLE, GUESS, THEORY (1), THOUGHT.

speculative *adj.* —*See* CURIOUS (2), THEORETICAL (1), THOUGHTFUL.

speculator *n.* One who speculates for quick profits ▸ adventurer, gambler, operator.

speech *n.* **1.** The faculty, act, or product of speaking ▸ [illegible], talk, utterance, verbalization, vocalization. [*Compare* BABBLE, CHATTER, EXPRESSION.] **2.** A usually formal spoken communication to an audience ▸ address, allocution, declamation, homily, lecture, oration, prelection, sermon, talk. [*Compare* DISCOURSE, TIRADE.] —*See also* CONVERSATION, LANGUAGE (1), ORATORY.

speechless *adj.* Temporarily unable or unwilling to speak, as from shock or fear ▸ dumb, dumbstruck, inarticulate, mum, mute, silent, tongue-tied, voiceless, wordless. —*See also* MUTE.

speech. 2. Temporarily unable to speak, as from astonishment. **—speech′less·ly** *adv.* **—speech′less·ness** *n.*

speed (spēd) ▸ *n.* 1. The rate or a measure of the rate of motion. 2. A rate of action, activity, or performance. 3a. The act of moving rapidly. b. Rapidity or swiftness. 4. A transmission gear in a motor vehicle. 5. *Slang* An amphetamine drug. ▸ *v.* **sped** (spĕd) or **speed·ed, speed·ing.** 1. To move or cause to move rapidly. 2. To increase the speed or rate of; accelerate. 3. To drive at a speed exceeding a legal limit. **—speed′er** *n.* **—speed′i·ly** *adv.* **—speed′i·ness** *n.* **—speed′y** *adj.*

speed·boat (spēd′bōt′) ▸ *n.* A fast motorboat.

speed·om·e·ter (spĭ-dŏm′ĭ-tər, spē-) ▸ *n.* 1. An instrument for indicating speed, as of an automobile. 2. An odometer.

speed·up (spēd′ŭp′) ▸ *n.* Acceleration of production without an increase in pay.

speed·way (spēd′wā′) ▸ *n.* 1. *Sports* A course for automobile or motorcycle racing. 2. A road designed for fast-moving traffic.

speed·well (spēd′wĕl′) ▸ *n.* A plant with clusters of small, usu. blue flowers.

spell[1] (spĕl) ▸ *v.* **spelled** or **spelt** (spĕlt), **spell·ing.** 1. To name or write in order the letters of (a word). 2. To mean; signify: *an event that spells trouble.* ***—phrasal verb:*** **spell out** To make explicit; specify.

spell[2] (spĕl) ▸ *n.* 1. A word or formula believed to have magic power. 2. A bewitched state; trance. 3. Allure; fascination.

spell[3] (spĕl) ▸ *n.* 1. A short, indefinite period of time. 2. *Informal* A period of weather: *a cold spell.* 3. One's turn at work; shift. 4. *Informal* A period of illness or indisposition. ▸ *v.* To relieve (someone) from work temporarily.

spell·bind (spĕl′bīnd′) ▸ *v.* To hold under or as if under a spell; enchant. **—spell′bind′er** *n.*

spell·er (spĕl′ər) ▸ *n.* 1. One who spells words. 2. A book used to teach spelling.

spell·ing (spĕl′ĭng) ▸ *n.* 1. The forming of words with letters in an accepted order. 2. The way in which a word is spelled.

spe·lunk·er (spĭ-lŭng′kər, spē′lŭng′-) ▸ *n.* One who explores and studies caves; a caver. **—spe′lunk′ing** *n.*

spend (spĕnd) ▸ *v.* **spent** (spĕnt), **spend·ing.** 1. To use up or put out; expend. 2. To pay out (money); disburse. 3. To wear out; exhaust. 4. To pass (time). 5. To waste or squander. **—spend′er** *n.*

spend·thrift (spĕnd′thrĭft′) ▸ *n.* One who spends money recklessly or wastefully.

Spen·ser (spĕn′sər), **Edmund** (1552?–1599) ▸ English poet.

spent (spĕnt) ▸ *v.* P.t. and p.part. of **spend.** ▸ *adj.* Depleted of energy, force, or strength; exhausted.

sperm (spûrm) ▸ *n., pl.* **sperm** or **sperms.** 1. A spermatozoon. 2. Semen. **—sper·mat′ic** (spər-măt′ĭk) *adj.*

sper·ma·ce·ti (spûr′mə-sē′tē, -sĕt′ē) ▸ *n., pl.* **-tis.** A white waxy substance obtained from the sperm whale and used for making candles, ointments, and cosmetics.

sper·mat·o·zo·on (spər-măt′ə-zō′ŏn′, -ən, spûr′mə-tə-) ▸ *n., pl.* **-zo·a** (-zō′ə). The fertilizing gamete of a male animal.

sper·mi·cide (spûr′mĭ-sīd′) ▸ *n.* A contraceptive agent that kills spermatozoa. **—sper′mi·cid′al** (-sīd′l) *adj.*

sperm whale ▸ *n.* A large toothed whale with a long narrow jaw and a massive head.

spew (spyōō) ▸ *v.* 1. To force out in or as if in a stream. 2. To vomit.

sphag·num (sfăg′nəm) ▸ *n.* Any of a genus of mosses whose decomposed remains form peat.

sphere (sfîr) ▸ *n.* 1. *Math.* A three-dimensional surface, all points of which are equidistant from a fixed point. 2. A spherical object or figure; ball. 3. A planet, star, or other heavenly body. 4. An area of power, control, or influence; domain. **—spher′i·cal** (sfîr′ĭ-kəl, sfĕr′-) *adj.* **—spher′i·cal·ly** *adv.*

spher·oid (sfîr′oid′, sfĕr′-) ▸ *n.* A three-dimensional geometric surface generated by revolving an ellipse around one of its axes. **—sphe·roi′dal** *adj.*

sphinc·ter (sfĭngk′tər) ▸ *n.* A ringlike muscle that normally maintains constriction of a body passage or orifice.

sphinx (sfĭngks) ▸ *n., pl.* **sphinx·es** or **sphin·ges** (sfĭn′jēz′). 1. A figure in Egyptian myth having the body of a lion and the head of a man, ram, or hawk. 2. A winged creature in Greek myth having the head of a woman and the body of a lion, noted for killing those who could not answer its riddle. 3. A puzzling or mysterious person.

spice (spīs) ▸ *n.* 1. A pungent, aromatic plant substance, as nutmeg or pepper, used as flavoring. 2. Something that adds zest or interest. **—spice** *v.* **—spic′y** *adj.*

spick-and-span also **spic-and-span** (spĭk′ən-spăn′) ▸ *adj.* 1. Neat and clean; spotless. 2. Brand-new; fresh.

spic·ule (spĭk′yōōl) ▸ *n.* *Biol.* A small needlelike structure or part.

spi·der (spī′dər) ▸ *n.* 1. Any of an order of eight-legged arachnids having a body divided into two parts and often spinning webs to trap insects. 2. See **frying pan.** **—spi′der·y** *adj.*

spider monkey ▸ *n.* A tropical American monkey having long legs and a long prehensile tail and lacking a thumb.

spiel (spēl, shpēl) ▸ *n.* *Informal* A lengthy, usu. extravagant speech or argument intended to persuade. **—spiel** *v.*

spiff·y (spĭf′ē) ▸ *adj.* **-i·er, -i·est.** *Informal* Smart in appearance or dress. **—spiff′i·ly** *adv.*

spig·ot (spĭg′ət) ▸ *n.* A faucet.

spike[1] (spīk) ▸ *n.* 1a. A long, thick, sharp-pointed piece of wood or metal, such as one along the top of a fence or wall. b. A large heavy nail. 2. A sharp-pointed projection such as one in the sole of a shoe for traction. ▸ *v.* **spiked, spik·ing.** 1. To secure or provide with a spike. 2. To pierce or injure with a spike. 3. *Informal* To put an end to; block: *spike a rumor.* 4. *Informal* To add liquor to. **—spik′y** *adj.*

spike[2] (spīk) ▸ *n.* 1. An ear of grain. 2. *Bot.* A usu. elongated cluster of stalkless flowers.

spike·let (spīk′lĭt) ▸ *n.* A small or secondary spike, characteristic of grasses and sedges.

spike·nard (spīk′närd′) ▸ *n.* An aromatic plant from which a fragrant ointment was obtained in ancient times.

THESAURUS

speechlessness *n.* —*See* SILENCE (2).

speechmaker *n.* —*See* SPEAKER (1).

speed *v.* To increase the speed of ▸ accelerate, expedite, hasten, hurry, hustle, quicken, speed up, step up. —*See also* RUSH.

speed *n.* Rate of motion or performance ▸ pace, tempo, velocity. *Informal:* clip. —*See also* HASTE (1).

speediness *n.* —*See* HASTE (1).

speedy *adj.* —*See* FAST (1), QUICK.

spell[1] *v.* —*See* MEAN[1].

spell out *v.* —*See* EXPLAIN (1).

spell[2] *n.* A word or formula believed to have magic powers ▸ abracadabra, charm, enchantment, incantation, magic. [*Compare* CURSE.]

spell *v.* —*See* CHARM (2).

spell[3] *n.* —*See* BIT[1] (3), SEIZURE (1), TURN (1).

spell *v.* To free from a specific duty by acting as a substitute ▸ relieve, take over. [*Compare* SUBSTITUTE.]

spellbind *v.* —*See* CHARM (2), GRIP.

spend *v.* 1. To give money as payment ▸ disburse, expend, give, lay out, outlay, pay (out). *Informal:* fork out (over *or* up), shell out. [*Compare* WASTE.] 2. To use time in a particular way ▸ pass, put in. [*Compare* IDLE.] 3. To be depleted ▸ consume, exhaust, go. ***Idiom:*** go down the drain. —*See also* EXHAUST (1), LEAD.

spendthrift *n.* —*See* WASTREL (1).

spendthrift *adj.* —*See* EXTRAVAGANT.

spent *adj.* —*See* TIRED (1).

spew *v.* —*See* ERUPT, VOMIT.

sphere *n.* —*See* BALL, RANGE (1).

spherical or **spheric** *adj.* —*See* ROUND (1).

spheroid *n.* —*See* BALL.

spice *n.* —*See* FLAVORING.

spice *v.* To impart flavor to ▸ flavor, season.

spice up *v.* —*See* CHANGE (1).

spick-and-span *adj.* —*See* CLEAN (1), NEAT.

spicy *adj.* Having a sharp, penetrating flavor or aroma ▸ aromatic, fiery, hot, peppery, piquant, pungent, racy, redolent, savory, seasoned, sharp, zesty. [*Compare* DELICIOUS.] —*See also* EROTIC, RACY.

spiel *v.* —*See* CHATTER (1).

spigot *n.* —*See* FAUCET, PLUG.

spike *n.* A sharp protuberance or projection ▸ barb, jag, needle, prick, prickle, prong, quill, snag, spine, spinule, spur, sticker, thorn, tine, tooth. [*Compare* POINT.] —*See also* NAIL.

spill (spĭl) ▸ *v.* **spilled** or **spilt** (spĭlt), **spill·ing.** **1.** To cause or allow to run, flow, or fall out. **2.** To shed (blood). **3.** To fall or cause to fall, as from a horse. ▸ *n.* **1.** The act or an instance of spilling. **2.** An amount spilled. **3.** A fall. **—spill′age** *n.*

spill·way (spĭl′wā′) ▸ *n.* A channel for an overflow of water, as from a reservoir.

spin (spĭn) ▸ *v.* **spun** (spŭn), **spin·ning.** **1a.** To draw out and twist (fibers) into thread. **b.** To form (thread or yarn) by spinning. **2.** To form (e.g., a web or cocoon) by extruding viscous threads. **3.** To tell, esp. imaginatively: *spin tales.* **4.** To rotate or cause to rotate swiftly; twirl. **5.** To reel; whirl. **6.** To ride or drive rapidly. **7.** To interpret or distort, esp. so as to sway public opinion. ▸ *n.* **1.** A swift whirling motion. **2.** A state of confusion. **3.** *Informal* A short drive in a vehicle. **4.** An interpretation or distortion. **—spin′ner** *n.*

spin·ach (spĭn′ĭch) ▸ *n.* A plant cultivated for its dark-green edible leaves.

spi·nal (spī′nəl) ▸ *adj.* Of or near the spine or spinal cord. ▸ *n.* An anesthetic injected into the spinal cord. **—spi′nal·ly** *adv.*

spinal column ▸ *n.* The series of vertebrae encasing the spinal cord and forming the main support of the body; spine.

spinal cord ▸ *n.* The part of the central nervous system that extends from the brain through the spinal column.

spin·dle (spĭn′dl) ▸ *n.* **1.** A slender rod or pin on which fibers are twisted into thread and then wound. **2.** Any of various slender revolving mechanical parts. **3.** A dragonfly.

spin·dly (spĭnd′lē) ▸ *adj.* **-dli·er, -dli·est.** Slender, elongated, and often weak.

spin·drift (spĭn′drĭft′) ▸ *n.* Windblown sea spray.

spine (spīn) ▸ *n.* **1.** The spinal column of a vertebrate. **2.** A sharp-pointed, projecting plant or animal part such as a thorn or quill. **3.** Courage or willpower; backbone. **—spine′less** *adj.* **—spin′y** *adj.*

spin·et (spĭn′ĭt) ▸ *n.* **1.** A small upright piano. **2.** A small harpsichord with a single keyboard.

spin·na·ker (spĭn′ə-kər) ▸ *n.* A large triangular sail set on a spar that swings out opposite the mainsail.

spin·ner·et (spĭn′ə-rĕt′) ▸ *n.* A structure from which spiders and silkworms secrete silk threads to form webs or cocoons.

spin·ning jenny (spĭn′ĭng) ▸ *n.* An early spinning machine having several spindles.

spinning wheel ▸ *n.* A device for making yarn or thread, consisting of a foot-driven or hand-driven wheel and a single spindle.

spin·off or **spin-off** (spĭn′ôf′, -ŏf′) ▸ *n.* Something, such as a product or enterprise, derived from something larger or more complex; byproduct.

spin·ster (spĭn′stər) ▸ *n.* A woman who has remained single beyond the conventional age for marrying. **—spin′ster·hood′** *n.*

spir·a·cle (spĭr′ə-kəl, spī′rə-) ▸ *n.* **1.** A small respiratory opening, esp. in the exoskeleton of an insect. **2.** A blowhole.

spi·ral (spī′rəl) ▸ *n.* **1.** A curve on a plane that continuously winds around a fixed point at an increasing or decreasing distance. **2.** A three-dimensional curve that turns around an axis; helix. **3.** Something having the form of such a curve. ▸ *adj.* **1.** Of or resembling a spiral. **2.** Coiling in a constantly changing plane; helical. ▸ *v.* **-raled, -ral·ing** also **-ralled, -ral·ling.** **1.** To take or cause to take a spiral form or course. **2.** To rise or fall with steady acceleration. **—spi′ral·ly** *adv.*

spiral galaxy ▸ *n.* A galaxy having a spiral structure.

spi·rant (spī′rənt) ▸ *n.* See **fricative.** **—spi′rant** *adj.*

spire (spīr) ▸ *n.* **1.** A top part or point that tapers upward. **2.** A structure, such as a steeple, that tapers to a point.

spi·re·a also **spi·rae·a** (spī-rē′ə) ▸ *n.* Any of various shrubs having clusters of white or pink flowers.

spir·it (spĭr′ĭt) ▸ *n.* **1.** The animating force within living beings; soul. **2.** **Spirit** The Holy Spirit. **3.** A supernatural being; ghost. **4.** The part of a human associated with the mind, will, and feelings. **5.** A person as marked by a stated quality: *He is a proud spirit.* **6.** **spirits** A mood or emotional state. **7.** Vivacity, vigor, or courage. **8.** Strong loyalty or dedication. **9.** A predominant mood or attitude: *a spirit of rebellion.* **10.** The actual though unstated sense or significance of something: *the spirit of the law.* **11.** often **spirits** *(takes sing. v.)* An alcohol solution of an essential or volatile substance. **12.** **spirits** An alcoholic beverage. ▸ *v.* To carry off mysteriously or secretly. **—spir′it·less** *adj.*

spir·it·ed (spĭr′ĭ-tĭd) ▸ *adj.* Marked by animation, vigor, or courage. **—spir′it·ed·ly** *adv.*

spir·i·tu·al (spĭr′ĭ-cho͞o-əl) ▸ *adj.* **1.** Relating to or consisting of spirit. **2.** Ecclesiastical; sacred. ▸ *n.* A religious song of African-American origin. **—spir′i·tu·al′i·ty** (-ăl′ĭ-tē) *n.* **—spir′i·tu·al·ize′** *v.* **—spir′i·tu·al·ly** *adv.*

spir·i·tu·al·ism (spĭr′ĭ-cho͞o-ə-lĭz′əm) ▸ *n.* The belief that the dead communicate with the living, as through a medium. **—spir′i·tu·al·ist** *n.* **—spir′i·tu·al·is′tic** *adj.*

spir·i·tu·ous (spĭr′ĭ-cho͞o-əs) ▸ *adj.* Of or containing alcohol; alcoholic.

spi·ro·chete (spī′rə-kēt′) ▸ *n.* Any of an order of slender spiral microorganisms, including those causing syphilis.

spit¹ (spĭt) ▸ *n.* **1.** Saliva, esp. when expectorated. **2.** The act of spitting. ▸ *v.* **spat** (spăt) or **spit, spit·ting.** **1.** To eject (e.g., saliva) from the mouth. **2.** To eject as if by spitting. ***—phrasal verb:* spit up** To vomit.

spit² (spĭt) ▸ *n.* **1.** A slender pointed rod on which meat is impaled for roasting. **2.** A narrow point of land extending into a body of water. ▸ *v.* **spit·ted, spit·ting.** To impale on or as if on a spit.

spit·ball (spĭt′bôl′) ▸ *n.* **1.** A chewed lump of paper to be used as a projectile. **2.** *Baseball* An illegal pitch in which the ball is moistened on one side, as if with saliva.

spite (spīt) ▸ *n.* Malicious ill will prompting an urge to hurt. ▸ *v.* **spit·ed, spit·ing.** To treat with malice. ***—idiom:* in**

THESAURUS

spiky *adj.* —*See* THORNY (1).

spile *n.* —*See* PLUG.

spill *v.* —*See* BETRAY (2), FALL (1), SPREAD (2).

spill *n.* —*See* FALL (1).

spin *v.* To have the sensation of turning in circles ▸ reel, swim, swirl, whirl. *Idiom:* go round and round. —*See also* LENGTHEN, TURN (1).

spin *n.* —*See* DRIVE (3), EXPLANATION, REVOLUTION (1).

spindling or **spindly** *adj.* —*See* GANGLING.

spine *n.* —*See* COURAGE, SPIKE.

spineless *adj.* —*See* COWARDLY.

spinning *adj.* —*See* DIZZY (1).

spinoff *n.* —*See* DERIVATIVE.

spinule *n.* —*See* SPIKE.

spiny *adj.* Full of irritating difficulties or controversies ▸ nettlesome, prickly, thorny. [*Compare* COMPLEX, DELICATE, DISTURBING, TROUBLESOME.] —*See also* THORNY (1).

spiral *v.* —*See* WIND².

spiral *n.* —*See* CURL.

spiral *adj.* —*See* CURLY.

spirit *n.* **1.** A lively, emphatic, eager quality or manner ▸ animation, bounce, brio, dash, élan, esprit, life, liveliness, pertness, sparkle, verve, vigor, vim, vivaciousness, vivacity, zing, zip. *Informal:* ginger, pep, peppiness. *Slang:* oomph. [*Compare* ENERGY.] **2.** The vital principle or animating force within living beings ▸ anima, breath, consciousness, divine spark, élan vital, life force, pneuma, psyche, soul, vital force, vitality. —*See also* COURAGE, GHOST, HEART (1), HUMAN BEING, TEMPER (3).

spirit *v.* —*See* SMUGGLE.

spirit away *v.* To seize and detain a person unlawfully ▸ abduct, kidnap, snatch, take hostage. [*Compare* SEIZE, STEAL.] —*See also* STEAL.

spirited *adj.* —*See* BRAVE, LIVELY.

spiritless *adj.* —*See* DEPRESSED (1), DULL (1), LANGUID.

spirits *n.* —*See* MOOD.

spiritual *adj.* Of or relating to a church or to an established religion ▸ church, churchly, ecclesiastical, religious. [*Compare* CLERICAL, DIVINE, HOLY, RITUAL.] —*See also* IMMATERIAL, SUPERNATURAL (1).

spirituality *n.* —*See* DEVOTION.

spirituous *adj.* —*See* HARD (3).

spit *n.* Saliva or other liquid ejected from the mouth ▸ expectorate, mucus, phlegm, saliva, spittle, sputum. [*Compare* DROOL.] —*See also* RAIN.

spit *v.* To expel a small amount of saliva or mucus from the mouth ▸ expectorate, hawk. [*Compare* DROOL.] —*See also* RAIN (2).

spit up *v.* —*See* VOMIT.

spite *n.* The quality or condition of

spite of Regardless of; despite. **—spite′ful** *adj.* **—spite′ful·ly** *adv.* **—spite′ful·ness** *n.*

spit·tle (spĭt′l) ▸ *n.* Spit; saliva.

spit·tle·bug (spĭt′l-bŭg′) ▸ *n.* Any of a family of insects whose nymphs form frothy masses of liquid on plant stems.

spit·toon (spĭ-to͞on′) ▸ *n.* A bowl-shaped vessel for spitting into; cuspidor.

splash (splăsh) ▸ *v.* **1.** To propel, dash, or scatter (a fluid) about in masses. **2.** To scatter fluid upon. **3.** To fall into or move through fluid with the sound of splashing. ▸ *n.* **1.** The act or sound of splashing. **2.** A flying mass of fluid. **3.** A mark made by or as if by splashing. **4.** A sensation; stir. **—splash′er** *n.*

splash·down (splăsh′doun′) ▸ *n.* The landing of a spacecraft or missile in water.

splash·y (splăsh′ē) ▸ *adj.* **-i·er, -i·est. 1.** Making a splash or splashes. **2.** Ostentatious. **—splash′i·ness** *n.*

splat[1] (splăt) ▸ *n.* A slat of wood, as one in the middle of a chair back.

splat[2] (splăt) ▸ *n.* A smacking noise.

splat·ter (splăt′ər) ▸ *v.* To spatter. **—splat′ter** *n.*

splay (splā) ▸ *adj.* **1.** Spread or turned out. **2.** Clumsy or awkward. ▸ *v.* **1.** To spread or be spread out or apart, esp. clumsily. **2.** To slant or slope or make slanting or sloping. **—splay** *n.*

splay·foot (splā′fo͝ot′) ▸ *n.* A deformity marked by abnormally flat and turned-out feet. **—splay′foot′ed** *adj.*

spleen (splēn) ▸ *n.* **1.** A large lymphoid organ, lying on the left side of the human body below the diaphragm, that filters and stores blood and produces lymphocytes. **2.** Ill temper.

splen·did (splĕn′dĭd) ▸ *adj.* **1.** Brilliant with light or color; radiant. **2.** Magnificent. **3.** Glorious; illustrious. **4.** Excellent. **—splen′did·ly** *adv.*

splen·dif·er·ous (splĕn-dĭf′ər-əs) ▸ *adj.* Splendid.

splen·dor (splĕn′dər) ▸ *n.* **1.** Great light or luster; brilliance. **2.** Magnificent appearance or display.

splen·dour (splĕn′dər) ▸ *n.* *Chiefly Brit.* Var. of **splendor.**

sple·net·ic (splĭ-nĕt′ĭk) ▸ *adj.* **1.** Of the spleen. **2.** Ill-humored; irritable.

splen·ic (splĕn′ĭk) ▸ *adj.* Of or near the spleen.

splice (splīs) ▸ *v.* **spliced, splic·ing. 1a.** To join (e.g., two pieces of film) at the ends. **b.** To join (e.g., ropes) by interweaving strands. **2.** To join (pieces of wood) by overlapping and binding. **3.** To join together or insert (segments of DNA or RNA) so as to form new genetic combinations. **—splice** *n.*

splint (splĭnt) ▸ *n.* **1.** A rigid device used to prevent motion of a joint or the ends of a fractured bone. **2.** A thin flexible wooden strip, such as one used in making baskets. **—splint** *v.*

splin·ter (splĭn′tər) ▸ *n.* A sharp slender piece, as of wood or metal, split or broken off from a main body. ▸ *v.* To form or cause to form splinters.

split (splĭt) ▸ *v.* **split, split·ting. 1.** To divide or become divided, esp. into lengthwise sections. **2.** To break, burst, or rip apart with force; rend. **3.** To separate; disunite: *a quarrel that split the family.* **4.** To divide and share: *split a dessert.* **5.** To separate into layers or sections. **6.** *Slang* To leave, esp. abruptly. ▸ *n.* **1.** The act or a result of splitting. **2.** A breach or rupture in a group. **—split′ter** *n.*

split-lev·el (splĭt′lĕv′əl) ▸ *adj.* Having the floor levels of adjoining rooms separated by about half a story: *a split-level ranch house.*

split personality ▸ *n.* **1.** Multiple personality. **2.** Schizophrenia.

split second ▸ *n.* An instant; flash.

split·ting (splĭt′ĭng) ▸ *adj.* Very severe: *a splitting headache.*

splotch (splŏch) ▸ *n.* An irregularly shaped spot, stain, or blotch. **—splotch** *v.* **—splotch′y** *adj.*

splurge (splûrj) ▸ *v.* **splurged, splurg·ing.** To indulge in an extravagant expense or display. **—splurge** *n.*

splut·ter (splŭt′ər) ▸ *v.* **1.** To make a spitting sound. **2.** To speak or utter incoherently, as when confused or angry. **—splut′ter** *n.*

spoil (spoil) ▸ *v.* **spoiled** or **spoilt** (spoilt), **spoil·ing. 1.** To impair the value or quality of; damage. **2.** To impair the completeness, perfection, or unity of; disrupt; disturb. **3.** To overindulge (someone) so as to harm the character of. **4.** To become tainted or rotten; decay. **5.** To pillage or plunder. ***—phrasal verb:* spoil for** To be eager for: *spoiling for a fight.* ▸ *n.* **spoils 1.** Goods or property seized by force; plunder. **2.** Political patronage enjoyed by a successful party or candidate. **—spoil′age** *n.* **—spoil′er** *n.*

spoil·sport (spoil′spôrt′) ▸ *n.* One who spoils or mars the pleasure of others.

spoke[1] (spōk) ▸ *n.* **1.** One of the rods connecting the hub and rim of a wheel. **2.** A rung of a ladder.

spoke[2] (spōk) ▸ *v.* **1.** P.t. of **speak. 2.** *Archaic* P.part. of **speak.**

spo·ken (spō′kən) ▸ *v.* P.part. of **speak.**

spokes·man (spōks′mən) ▸ *n.* A man who speaks on behalf of another or others.

spokes·per·son (spōks′pûr′sən) ▸ *n.* A spokesman or spokeswoman.

spokes·wom·an (spōks′wo͝om′ən) ▸ *n.* A woman who speaks on behalf of another or others.

spo·li·a·tion (spō′lē-ā′shən) ▸ *n.* **1.** The act of plundering. **2.** The state of being plundered.

sponge (spŭnj) ▸ *n.* **1a.** A primitive marine animal with a porous skeleton. **b.** The flexible, absorbent skeleton of the sponge, used for bathing, cleaning, and other purposes. **c.** A material with similar qualities and uses. **2.** A

THESAURUS

being vindictive ▸ revenge, spitefulness, vengefulness, vindictiveness. [*Compare* RESENTMENT.] *—See also* MALEVOLENCE.

spiteful *adj.* *—See* MALEVOLENT, VINDICTIVE.

spitefulness *n.* The quality or condition of being vindictive ▸ revenge, spite, vengefulness, vindictiveness. [*Compare* RESENTMENT.] *—See also* MALEVOLENCE.

spitting image *n.* *—See* DOUBLE.

spittle *n.* *—See* SPIT.

splash *v.* **1.** To hurl or scatter liquid ▸ bespatter, dash, slop, slosh, spatter, splatter, spray, sprinkle, swash. [*Compare* RAIN, SQUIRT.] **2.** To make the sound of moving or disturbed water ▸ lap, swash, wash. [*Compare* BURBLE, SWISH.]

splash *n.* *—See* DROP (4).

splashy *adj.* *—See* SHOWY.

splatter *v.* *—See* SPLASH (1), STAIN.

splay *v.* *—See* SPREAD (1).

spleen *n.* *—See* TEMPER (1).

splendid *adj.* *—See* EXCELLENT, GLORIOUS, GRAND, MARVELOUS.

splendor *n.* *—See* GLORY.

splendorous or **splendrous** *adj.* *—See* GLORIOUS.

splenetic *adj.* *—See* ILL-TEMPERED.

splice *v.* *—See* WEAVE.

splinter *v.* To withdraw from an association or federation ▸ pull out, secede, splinter off, withdraw. *Informal:* split (away). [*Compare* QUIT.] *—See also* BREAK (1).

split *v.* *Informal* To withdraw from an association or federation ▸ pull out, secede, splinter (off), withdraw. *Informal:* split (away). [*Compare* QUIT.] *—See also* BRANCH, CRACK (1), CUT (2), DIVIDE, GO (1), SEPARATE (1), TEAR[1].

split up *v.* *—See* SCATTER (2).

split *n.* *—See* ALLOTMENT, BREACH (2), CRACK (2), CUT (1), DIVISION (1).

splotch *n.* *—See* SMEAR.

splotch *v.* *—See* STAIN.

splurge *n.* *—See* BINGE.

splurge *v.* *—See* LUXURIATE, WASTE.

splurgy *adj.* *—See* SHOWY.

splutter *v.* To make a series of short, sharp noises ▸ crackle, crepitate, sputter. [*Compare* CRACK, HISS, SNAP.] *—See also* STAMMER.

spoil *v.* To overindulge with affection or attention ▸ dote on. [*Compare* RAVE.] *—See also* BABY, BOTCH, DECAY, DESTROY (1).

spoilage *n.* *—See* DECAY.

spoiled *adj.* *—See* BAD (2).

spoils *n.* The political appointments or jobs that are at the disposal of those in power ▸ patronage, pork. *—See also* PLUNDER.

spoilsport *n.* *—See* KILLJOY.

spoken *adj.* *—See* ORAL.

spokesman or **spokeswoman** *n.* *—See* SPEAKER (2).

sponge *n.* *—See* DRUNKARD, PARASITE.

sponge *v.* To take advantage of the generosity of others ▸ leech, live off. *Slang:* freeload. [*Compare* BEG.]

sponge up *v.* *—See* ABSORB (2), DRINK (3).

gauze pad used to absorb blood and other fluids, as in surgery. ▸ *v.* **sponged, spong·ing.** 1. To moisten, wipe, or clean with a sponge. 2. *Informal* To live by relying on another's generosityl; freeload. **—spong′er** *n.* **—spong′y** *adj.*

sponge cake ▸ *n.* A light, porous cake containing no shortening.

sponge rubber ▸ *n.* A soft porous rubber used in cushions, gaskets, and weather stripping.

spon·sor (spŏn′sər) ▸ *n.* 1. One who assumes responsibility for another person or a group. 2. A godparent. 3. A business enterprise that pays for radio or television programming, usu. in return for advertising time. **—spon′sor** *v.* **—spon′sor·ship′** *n.*

spon·ta·ne·ous (spŏn-tā′nē-əs) ▸ *adj.* 1. Happening or arising without apparent external cause; self-generated. 2. Voluntary or unpremeditated: *spontaneous applause.* **—spon′ta·ne′i·ty** (-tə-nē′ĭ-tē, -nā′-) *n.* **—spon·ta′ne·ous·ly** *adv.*

spontaneous abortion ▸ *n.* See **miscarriage** 1.

spontaneous combustion ▸ *n.* The breaking into flame of combustible material, such as oily rags or hay, due to heat generated within the material by slow oxidation.

spoof (spo͞of) ▸ *n.* 1. A hoax. 2. A gentle satirical imitation; light parody. **—spoof** *v.*

spook (spo͝ok) ▸ *n.* 1. *Informal* A ghost. 2. *Slang* A secret agent; spy. ▸ *v.* *Informal* 1. To haunt. 2. To frighten. **—spook′i·ly** *adv.* **—spook′i·ness** *n.* **—spook′y** *adj.*

spool (spo͞ol) ▸ *n.* 1. A cylinder on which yarn, wire, thread, or string is wound. 2. A reel for magnetic tape. **—spool** *v.*

spoon (spo͞on) ▸ *n.* 1. A utensil consisting of a small shallow bowl on a handle, used in preparing, serving, or eating food. 2. A shiny, curved, metallic fishing lure. ▸ *v.* 1. To lift, scoop up, or carry with or as if with a spoon. 2. To engage in amorous kissing or caressing. **—spoon′ful′** *n.*

spoon·bill (spo͞on′bĭl′) ▸ *n.* Any of several long-legged wading birds having a long flat bill with a broad tip.

spoon·er·ism (spo͞o′nə-rĭz′əm) ▸ *n.* A transposition of sounds of two or more words, such as *Let me sew you to your sheet* for *Let me show you to your seat.*

spoon-feed (spo͞on′fēd′) ▸ *v.* 1. To feed (another) with a spoon. 2. To treat (another) in a way that discourages independent thought or action.

spoor (spo͝or) ▸ *n.* The track or trail of an animal, esp. a wild animal.

Spor·a·des (spôr′ə-dēz′, spô-rä′*th*ēs) ▸ Two island groups of Greece in the Aegean, the **Northern Sporades** off the central mainland and the **Southern Sporades** off Turkey.

spo·rad·ic (spə-răd′ĭk, spô-) ▸ *adj.* Occurring at irregular intervals; having no pattern in time. **—spo·rad′i·cal·ly** *adv.*

spore (spôr) ▸ *n.* A usu. one-celled reproductive body or resting stage, as of a fern, fungus, or bacterium.

spor·ran (spôr′ən, spŏr′-) ▸ *n.* A pouch worn at the front of the kilt by Scottish Highlanders.

sport (spôrt) ▸ *n.* 1. An activity usu. involving physical exertion and having a set form and body of rules; game. 2. An active pastime; diversion. 3. Light mockery. 4. One known for the manner of one's acceptance of defeat or criticism: *a poor sport.* 5. *Informal* One who lives a jolly, extravagant life. 6. *Biol.* A mutation. ▸ *v.* 1. To play or frolic. 2. To joke or trifle. 3. To display or show off. ▸ *adj.* also **sports** Of or appropriate for sport: *sport fishing.* **—sport′i·ness** *n.* **—sport′y** *adj.*

sport·ing (spôr′tĭng) ▸ *adj.* 1. Used in or appropriate for sports: *sporting goods.* 2. Marked by sportsmanship. 3. Of or associated with gambling. **—sport′ing·ly** *adv.*

spor·tive (spôr′tĭv) ▸ *adj.* Playful or frolicsome.

sports·cast (spôrts′kăst′) ▸ *n.* A radio or television broadcast of a sports event or of sports news. **—sports′cast′er** *n.*

sports·man (spôrts′mən) ▸ *n.* 1. A man who is active in sports. 2. One who exhibits sportsmanship. **—sports′man·like′** *adj.*

sports·man·ship (spôrts′mən shĭp′) ▸ *n.* Conduct and attitude appropriate to sports, esp. fair play and courtesy.

sports·wom·an (spôrts′wo͝om′ən) ▸ *n.* A woman who is active in sports.

sports·writ·er (spôrts′rī′tər) ▸ *n.* One who writes about sports, esp. for a newspaper or magazine.

sport-u·til·i·ty vehicle (spôrt′yo͞o-tĭl′ĭ-tē) ▸ *n.* A large four-wheel-drive vehicle designed for off-road travel.

spot (spŏt) ▸ *n.* 1. A position; location. 2. A mark, such as a stain, on a surface differing sharply in color from its surroundings. 3. *Informal* A situation, esp. a troublesome one. ▸ *v.* **spot·ted, spot·ting.** 1. To mark or become marked with spots. 2. To locate precisely. 3. To detect or discern, esp. visually. ▸ *adj.* Made, paid, or delivered immediately: *a spot sale.* ***—idiom:* on the spot** Under pressure. **—spot′ted** *adj.*

spot check ▸ *n.* An inspection conducted at random or limited to a few instances. **—spot′-check′** *v.*

spot·less (spŏt′lĭs) ▸ *adj.* 1. Perfectly clean. 2. Impeccable. **—spot′less·ly** *adv.* **—spot′less·ness** *n.*

spot·light (spŏt′līt′) ▸ *n.* 1a. A strong beam of light that illuminates only a small area, used esp. on a stage. b. A lamp that produces such a light. 2. Public attention, notoriety, or prominence. **—spot′light′** *v.*

spot·ter (spŏt′ər) ▸ *n.* One that looks for, locates, and reports something, esp. a military lookout.

spot·ty (spŏt′ē) ▸ *adj.* **-ti·er, -ti·est.** Lacking consistency; uneven, as in quality.

spou·sal (spou′zəl, -səl) ▸ *adj.* Of a spouse. ▸ *n.* often **spousals** Marriage; nuptials.

spouse (spous, spouz) ▸ *n.* One's husband or wife; marriage partner.

THESAURUS

spongy *adj.* —*See* ABSORBENT, SOFT (1).

sponsor *n.* One who assumes financial responsibility for another ▸ backer, guarantor, guaranty, surety, underwriter. *Informal:* angel. [*Compare* ADVOCATE, DONOR.] —*See also* PATRON.

sponsor *v.* To act as a patron to ▸ back, patronize, support. [*Compare* DONATE, FINANCE, SUPPORT.]

sponsorship *n.* —*See* PATRONAGE (1).

spontaneity *n.* The absence of forethought, prompting, or planning in action ▸ automaticity, impulsiveness, impulsivity, instinctiveness, involuntariness, reflexiveness, reflexivity. [*Compare* IMPROVISATION, TEMERITY.] —*See also* EASE (1).

spontaneous *adj.* Acting or happening without apparent forethought, prompting, or planning ▸ automatic, impulsive, instinctive, involuntary, natural, reflex, reflexive, unplanned, unpremeditated, unprompted, unrehearsed. [*Compare* EXTEMPORANEOUS, INSTINCTIVE, RASH[1], UNINTENTIONAL.] —*See also* EASYGOING, VOLUNTARY.

spontaneously *adv.* 1. Without apparent forethought, prompting, or planning ▸ automatically, impulsively, instinctively, involuntarily, reflexively. 2. Of one's own free will ▸ by choice, freely, voluntarily, willfully, willingly. *Idioms:* of one's own accord, on one's own volition.

spoof *n.* —*See* SATIRE.

spook *n.* —*See* GHOST, SPY.

spook *v.* —*See* FRIGHTEN.

spooked *adj.* —*See* AFRAID.

spooky *adj.* —*See* WEIRD.

spoon *v.* —*See* DIP (2), NECK.

spoor *n.* —*See* TRACK.

sporadic *adj.* —*See* INFREQUENT, INTERMITTENT.

sporadically *adv.* —*See* INFREQUENTLY, INTERMITTENTLY.

sport *n.* —*See* AMUSEMENT, PLAY.

sport *v.* —*See* DISPLAY, PLAY (1).

sport coat or **sports coat** or **sport jacket** or **sports jacket** *n.* —*See* COAT (1).

sporting *adj.* According to the rules ▸ clean, fair, sportsmanlike, sportsmanly.

sportingly *adv.* —*See* FAIR[1].

sportive *adj.* —*See* MISCHIEVOUS.

sportsmanlike or **sportsmanly** *adj.* According to the rules ▸ clean, fair, sporting.

spot *n.* —*See* POINT (2), POSITION (1), POSITION (3), PREDICAMENT, SMEAR, STAIN.

spot *v.* To look for and discover ▸ find, locate, pinpoint. *Informal:* scare up. [*Compare* TRACE, UNCOVER.] —*See also* DISCERN, POSITION, SEE (1), SPECKLE, STAIN.

spot *adj.* —*See* RANDOM.

spotless *adj.* —*See* CLEAN (1).

spotlight *v.* —*See* EMPHASIZE.

spotty *adj.* —*See* UNEVEN.

spousal *adj.* —*See* MARITAL.

spousals *n.* —*See* WEDDING.

spouse *n.* A person who is married to

spout (spout) ► *v.* **1.** To gush forth or discharge in a rapid stream or in spurts. **2.** *Informal* To utter loudly and pompously: *spout nonsense.* ► *n.* **1.** A tube, mouth, or pipe through which liquid is discharged. **2.** A continuous stream of liquid. **—spout′er** *n.*

spp. ► *abbr.* species (plural)

sprain (sprān) ► *n.* A painful wrenching or laceration of the ligaments of a joint. ► *v.* To cause a sprain to (a joint or ligament).

sprang (sprăng) ► *v.* P.t. of **spring.**

sprat (sprăt) ► *n.* **1.** A small food fish of NE Atlantic waters, often canned as a sardine. **2.** A young herring.

sprawl (sprôl) ► *v.* **1.** To sit or lie with the limbs spread out awkwardly. **2.** To spread out haphazardly. **—sprawl** *n.*

spray[1] (sprā) ► *n.* **1.** Liquid moving in a mass of dispersed droplets or mist, as from a wave. **2a.** A fine jet of liquid discharged from a pressurized container. **b.** A pressurized container; atomizer. ► *v.* **1.** To disperse (a liquid) in a spray. **2.** To apply a spray to (a surface). **—spray′er** *n.*

spray[2] (sprā) ► *n.* A small branch bearing buds, flowers, or berries.

spread (sprĕd) ► *v.* **spread, spread·ing. 1.** To open or be extended more fully; stretch. **2.** To separate or become separated more widely; open out. **3.** To distribute over a surface in a layer; apply. **4.** To distribute widely: *The tornado spread destruction.* **5.** To become or cause to become widely known. ► *n.* **1.** The act or process of spreading. **2.** An open area of land; expanse. **3.** The extent or limit to which something is or can be spread; range. **4.** A cloth covering for a bed or table. **5.** *Informal* An abundant meal laid out on a table. **6.** A food to be spread on bread or crackers. **7.** Two facing pages of a magazine or newspaper, often with related matter extending across the fold. **8.** A difference, as between two totals. **—spread′a·ble** *adj.* **—spread′er** *n.*

spread eagle ► *n.* **1.** The figure of an eagle with wings and legs spread. **2.** A posture or design resembling a spread eagle. **—spread′ ea′gle** *adj.*

spread·sheet (sprĕd′shēt′) ► *n.* An accounting or bookkeeping program that displays data in rows and columns on a screen.

spree (sprē) ► *n.* Overindulgence in an activity.

spri·er (sprī′ər) ► *adj.* Comp. of **spry.**

spri·est (sprī′ĭst) ► *adj.* Superl. of **spry.**

sprig (sprĭg) ► *n.* A small shoot or twig of a plant.

spright·ly (sprīt′lē) ► *adj.* **-li·er, -li·est.** Lively and brisk; animated.

spring (sprĭng) ► *v.* **sprang** (sprăng) or **sprung** (sprŭng), **sprung, spring·ing. 1.** To move upward or forward suddenly; leap. **2.** To move suddenly on or as if on a spring. **3.** To emerge suddenly. **4.** To arise from a source; develop. **5.** To come loose, as parts of a mechanism. **6.** To release from a checked or held position; actuate: *spring a trap.* **7.** To present unexpectedly or suddenly: *spring a surprise.* ► *n.* **1.** An elastic device, esp. a coil of wire, that regains its original shape after being compressed or extended. **2.** Elasticity; resilience. **3.** The act of springing. **4.** A natural fountain or stream of water. **5.** A source or origin. **6.** The season of the year that is between winter and summer. **—spring′i·ly** *adv.* **—spring′i·ness** *n.* **—spring′y** *adj.*

spring·board (sprĭng′bôrd′) ► *n.* **1.** A flexible board used by gymnasts. **2.** See **diving board.**

spring fever ► *n.* A feeling of languor or yearning brought on by the coming of spring.

Spring·field (sprĭng′fēld′) ► The capital of IL, in the central part.

spring-load·ed (sprĭng′lō′dĭd) ► *adj.* Secured or loaded by means of a spring.

spring tide ► *n.* The exceptionally high and low tides that occur at the time of the new moon or the full moon.

spring·time (sprĭng′tīm′) ► *n.* The season of spring.

sprin·kle (sprĭng′kəl) ► *v.* **-kled, -kling.** To scatter or fall in drops or small particles. ► *n.* **1.** A light rainfall. **2.** A small amount. **—sprin′kler** *n.*

sprinkler system ► *n.* A network of overhead pipes that release water to extinguish fires.

sprin·kling (sprĭng′klĭng) ► *n.* A small or scattered amount.

sprint (sprĭnt) ► *n.* A short race at top speed. **—sprint** *v.* **—sprint′er** *n.*

sprite (sprīt) ► *n.* **1.** An elf or pixie. **2.** A specter or ghost.

spritz·er (sprĭt′sər, shprĭt′-) ► *n.* A drink made of wine and carbonated water.

sprock·et (sprŏk′ĭt) ► *n.* Any of various toothlike projections arranged on a wheel rim to engage the links of a chain.

sprout (sprout) ► *v.* **1.** To begin to grow; give off shoots or buds. **2.** To emerge and develop rapidly. ► *n.* A young plant growth, such as a bud or shoot.

spruce[1] (spro͞os) ► *n.* **1.** Any of various cone-bearing evergreen trees with short pointed needles and soft wood. **2.** The wood of a spruce.

spruce[2] (spro͞os) ► *adj.* **spruc·er, spruc·est.** Neat and trim

THESAURUS

another ► consort, helpmate, helpmeet, husband, mate, partner, wife. *Informal:* better half, hubby, missis, other half. *Slang:* old lady, old man. [*Compare* LOVER.]

spouseless *adj.* —*See* SINGLE.

spout *v.* To eject or be ejected in a sudden thin, swift stream ► jet, spray, spurt, squirt. [*Compare* ERUPT, FLOW.]

spout *n.* A sudden swift stream of ejected liquid ► jet, spray, spurt, squirt. [*Compare* FLOW.]

sprain *v.* To injure a bodily part by twisting ► strain, twist, turn, wrench. [*Compare* HURT.]

sprawl *v.* To sit or lie with the limbs spread out awkwardly ► drape, loll, lounge, spread-eagle, straddle. [*Compare* LIE[1], SLOUCH.] —*See also* SPREAD (2).

sprawl *n.* —*See* BUILDUP (2).

spray *n.* A sudden swift stream of ejected liquid ► jet, spout, spurt, squirt. [*Compare* FLOW.]

spray *v.* To eject or be ejected in a sudden thin, swift stream ► jet, spout, spurt, squirt. [*Compare* ERUPT, FLOW.] —*See also* SPLASH (1).

spread *v.* **1.** To move or arrange so as to cover a larger area ► expand, extend, fan (out), open (out *or* up), outstretch, splay, stretch, unfold, unfurl, unroll. **2.** To extend or distribute over a wide area ► circulate, diffuse, disperse, disseminate, distribute, radiate, scatter, spill, sprawl, straggle, strew. [*Compare* DISTRIBUTE.] **3.** To become known far and wide ► circulate, get around, go around, travel. ***Idiom:*** go (*or* make) the rounds. **4.** To arrange tableware upon a table in preparation for a meal ► lay, set. —*See also* BROADEN, COMMUNICATE (2), COVER (1).

spread *n. Informal* A large, elaborately prepared meal ► banquet, feast, junket. *Informal:* feed. —*See also* BUILDUP (2), EXPANSE (1), EXPANSION.

spread *adj.* —*See* OPEN (2).

spread-eagle *v.* —*See* SPRAWL.

spree *n.* —*See* BENDER, BINGE.

sprig *n.* —*See* SHOOT.

sprightliness *n.* —*See* ENERGY.

sprightly *adj.* —*See* ENERGETIC.

spring *v.* —*See* BOUND[1], DESCEND, FREE (1), JUMP (1), STEM.

spring back *v.* To reverse direction after striking something ► bounce, bounce back, rebound, reflect, snap back. [*Compare* BEND, GLANCE.]

spring for *v.* —*See* TREAT (2).

spring *n.* **1.** The act of jumping ► jump, pounce, leap, vault. [*Compare* FALL.] **2.** The season of the year during which the weather becomes warmer and plants revive ► seedtime, springtide, springtime. —*See also* BIRTH (2), BOUND[1] (2), CAUSE (2), FLEXIBILITY (1), ORIGIN, YOUTH (1).

springiness *n.* —*See* FLEXIBILITY (1).

springtime *n.* The season of the year during which the weather becomes warmer and plants revive ► seedtime, spring, springtide. —*See also* YOUTH (1).

springy *adj.* —*See* FLEXIBLE (1).

sprinkle *v.* To scatter or release in drops or small particles ► besprinkle, dust, pepper, powder. [*Compare* SPREAD.] —*See also* RAIN (2), SPECKLE, SPLASH (1).

sprinkle *n.* —*See* RAIN.

sprint *v.* —*See* RUN (1), RUSH.

sprint *n.* —*See* RUN (1).

sprite *n.* —*See* FAIRY.

sprout *n.* —*See* SHOOT.

spruce *adj.* —*See* NEAT.

spruce *v.* —*See* RENEW (1), TIDY (1), TIDY (2).

in appearance. ▸ *v.* **spruced, spruc·ing**. To neaten.
sprung (sprŭng) ▸ *v.* A p.t. and the p.part. of **spring**.
spry (sprī) ▸ *adj.* **spri·er** (sprī′ər), **spri·est** (sprī′ĭst) or **spry·er, spry·est**. Active; nimble. **—spry′ly** *adv.* **—spry′ness** *n.*
spud (spŭd) ▸ *n.* **1.** *Slang* A potato. **2.** A sharp spadelike tool.
spume (spyo͞om) ▸ *n.* Foam or froth on a liquid. **—spu′mous, spum′y** *adj.*
spu·mo·ni or **spu·mo·ne** (spo͞o-mō′nē) ▸ *n.* Ice cream in layers of different colors or flavors, often with fruits and nuts.
spun (spŭn) ▸ *v.* P.t. and p.part. of **spin**.
spun glass ▸ *n.* See **fiberglass**.
spunk (spŭngk) ▸ *n.* *Informal* Spirit; pluck. **—spunk′y** *adj.*
spur (spûr) ▸ *n.* **1.** A spiked device attached to a rider's heel and used to urge a horse forward. **2.** An incentive. **3.** A spurlike attachment or projection, as on the back of a bird's leg or on certain flowers. **4.** A lateral ridge projecting from a mountain or mountain range. **5.** A short side track connecting with the main railroad track. ▸ *v.* **spurred, spur·ring**. **1.** To urge (a horse) on by the use of spurs. **2.** To incite or stimulate.
spurge (spûrj) ▸ *n.* Any of various plants with milky juice and small flowers.
spu·ri·ous (spyo͝or′ē-əs) ▸ *adj.* Lacking authenticity or validity; false. **—spu′ri·ous·ly** *adv.* **—spu′ri·ous·ness** *n.*
spurn (spûrn) ▸ *v.* To reject or refuse disdainfully; scorn. **—spurn′er** *n.*
spurt (spûrt) ▸ *n.* **1.** A sudden forcible gush or jet. **2.** A sudden short burst of energy or activity. ▸ *v.* **1.** To gush forth. **2.** To make a brief intense effort.
sput·nik (spŭt′nĭk, spo͝ot′nyĭk) ▸ *n.* A Soviet artificial earth satellite.
sput·ter (spŭt′ər) ▸ *v.* **1.** To spit out small particles in noisy bursts. **2.** To utter in an excited or confused manner. **—sput′ter** *n.* **—sput′ter·er** *n.*
spu·tum (spyo͞o′təm) ▸ *n., pl.* **-ta** (-tə). Expectorated matter including saliva and substances such as phlegm from the respiratory tract.
spy (spī) ▸ *n., pl.* **spies** (spīz). **1.** An agent employed by a state to obtain secret information concerning its potential or actual enemies or rivals. **2.** One who secretly keeps watch on others. ▸ *v.* **spied** (spīd), **spy·ing**. **1.** To observe secretly with hostile intent. **2.** To catch sight of. **3.** To investigate intensively.
spy·glass (spī′glăs′) ▸ *n.* A small telescope.
sq. or **Sq.** ▸ *abbr.* square
squab (skwŏb) ▸ *n.* A young or unfledged pigeon.
squab·ble (skwŏb′əl) ▸ *v.* **-bled, -bling**. To engage in an argument, usu. over a trivial matter; wrangle. ▸ *n.* A noisy, usu. trivial quarrel.
squad (skwŏd) ▸ *n.* **1.** A small group of people organized in a common activity. **2.** The smallest tactical military unit. **3.** A small police unit. **4.** An athletic team.
squad car ▸ *n.* A police automobile connected by radio with headquarters.
squad·ron (skwŏd′rən) ▸ *n.* **1.** A naval unit consisting of two or more divisions of a fleet. **2.** A basic tactical air force unit.
squal·id (skwŏl′ĭd) ▸ *adj.* **1.** Dirty and wretched. **2.** Morally repulsive; sordid. **—squal′id·ly** *adv.* **—squal′id·ness** *n.*
squall¹ (skwôl) ▸ *n.* A loud harsh cry. **—squall** *v.*
squall² (skwôl) ▸ *n.* A brief sudden violent windstorm, often with rain or snow. **—squall′y** *adj.*
squal·or (skwŏl′ər) ▸ *n.* A filthy and wretched condition.
squa·mous (skwā′məs, skwä′-) ▸ *adj.* Covered with or resembling scales.
squan·der (skwŏn′dər) ▸ *v.* To spend or use extravagantly.
Squan·to (skwŏn′tō) (d. 1622) ▸ Native American who helped the English colonists in Massachusetts.
square (skwâr) ▸ *n.* **1.** A plane figure having four equal sides. **2.** Something having an equal-sided rectangular form. **3.** An instrument for drawing or testing right angles. **4.** *Math.* The product of a number or quantity multiplied by itself. **5a.** An open area at the intersection of two or more streets. **b.** A rectangular space enclosed by streets; block. **6.** *Slang* A dull, rigidly conventional person. ▸ *adj.* **squar·er, squar·est**. **1.** Having four equal sides and four right angles. **2.** Forming a right angle. **3a.** Expressed in units measuring area: *square feet.* **b.** Having a specified length in each of two equal dimensions. **4.** Like a square in form: *a square house.* **5.** Honest; direct: *a square answer.* **6.** Just; equitable: *a square deal.* **7.** Paid up; settled. **8.** Even; tied. **9.** *Slang* Rigidly conventional. ▸ *v.* **squared, squar·ing**. **1.** To cut to a square or rectangular shape. **2.** To conform; agree: *a story that did not square with the facts.* **3.** To bring into balance; settle: *square a debt.* **4.** *Math.* To multiply a number or quantity by itself. **—square′ly** *adv.* **—square′ness** *n.*
square bracket ▸ *n.* See **bracket** 3.
square dance ▸ *n.* A dance in which sets of four couples form squares. **—square′-dance′** *v.* **—square dancer** *n.*
square knot ▸ *n.* A double knot in which the loose ends are parallel to the standing parts, usu. used to join the ends of two lines.
square meal ▸ *n.* A substantial nourishing meal.
square-rigged (skwâr′rĭgd′) ▸ *adj.* *Naut.* Fitted with square sails as the principal sails.
square-rig·ger (skwâr′rĭg′ər) ▸ *n.* *Naut.* A square-rigged vessel.
square root ▸ *n.* *Math.* A divisor of a quantity that when squared gives the quantity.
squash¹ (skwŏsh, skwôsh) ▸ *n.* **1.** Any of various plants related to the pumpkins and gourds. **2.** The fleshy fruit of a squash, eaten as a vegetable.
squash² (skwŏsh, skwôsh) ▸ *v.* **1.** To beat, squeeze, or flatten into a pulp. **2.** To suppress; quash. ▸ *n.* **1.** The impact

THESAURUS

spry *adj.* —*See* ENERGETIC.
spryness *n.* —*See* AGILITY.
spume *n.* —*See* FOAM.
spume *v.* —*See* FOAM.
spumous or **spumy** *adj.* —*See* FOAMY.
spunk or **spunkiness** *n.* —*See* COURAGE.
spunky *adj.* —*See* BRAVE.
spur *n.* —*See* SPIKE, [illegible]
spur *v.* —*See* PROVOKE.
spurious *adj.* —*See* COUNTERFEIT, FALLACIOUS (1), FALSE, [illegible]
spuriousness *n.* —*See* FALLACY (2).
spurn *v.* —*See* DECLINE, SNUB.
spur-of-the-moment *adj.* —*See* EXTEMPORANEOUS.
spurt *n.* A sudden swift stream of ejected liquid ▸ jet, spout, spray, squirt. [*Compare* FLOW.]
spurt *v.* To eject or be ejected in a sudden thin, swift stream ▸ jet, spout, spray, squirt. [*Compare* ERUPT, FLOW.]
sputter *v.* To make a series of short, sharp noises ▸ crackle, crepitate, splutter. [*Compare* CRACK, HISS, SNAP.] —*See also* SMOLDER, STAMMER.
sputum *n.* —*See* SPIT.
spy *n.* A person who secretly observes others to obtain information ▸ agent, [illegible], operative, secret agent, undercover agent. *Informal:* spook.
spy *v.* —*See* SEE (1).
squabble *v.* —*See* ARGUE (1), QUIBBLE.
squabble *n.* —*See* ARGUMENT.
squad *n.* —*See* DETACHMENT (3), FORCE (3).
squadron *n.* —*See* FORCE (3).
squalid *adj.* Heavily soiled; very dirty or unclean ▸ filthy, foul, nasty, vile. —*See also* DIRTY, SORDID.
squall¹ *v.* —*See* BAWL, CRY.
squall² *n.* —*See* STORM.
squall *v.* To manifest strong winds and precipitation ▸ blow (up), set in, storm. [*Compare* RAIN.]
squalor *n.* —*See* DIRTINESS.
squander *v.* —*See* LOSE (2), WASTE.
squander *n.* —*See* EXTRAVAGANCE.
square *n.* *Slang* An old-fashioned person who is reluctant to [illegible] innovate ▸ fogy, fossil, fuddy-duddy, mossback. *Informal:* stick-in-the-mud, stuffed shirt. [*Compare* DRIP, DULLARD, FOOL.] *See also* COMMON.
square *adj.* Owing or being owed nothing ▸ even, quit, quits. *Informal:* even-steven. —*See also* CONVENTIONAL, EVEN (2), FAIR¹ (1).
square *v.* —*See* AGREE (1), EQUALIZE, SETTLE (3).
square *adv.* —*See* DIRECTLY (3).
squarely *adv.* —*See* DIRECTLY (3), FAIRLY (1).
squash *v.* —*See* CRUSH (1), SUPPRESS.

or sound of squashing. 2. A crush or press, as of people. 3. A game played in a closed walled court with rackets and a hard rubber ball. **—squash′i·ness** *n.* **—squash′y** *adj.*

squat (skwŏt) ▸ *v.* **squat·ted, squat·ting.** 1. To sit in a crouching position with the hams resting on or near the heels. 2. To settle on unoccupied land without legal claim. 3. To occupy a given piece of public land in order to acquire title to it. ▸ *adj.* **squat·ter, squat·test.** 1. Short and thick. 2. Crouched in a squatting position. ▸ *n.* The act or posture of squatting. **—squat′ter** *n.*

squaw (skwô) ▸ *n.* *Offensive* A Native American woman.

squawk (skwôk) ▸ *v.* 1. To utter a harsh cry; screech. 2. *Informal* To complain noisily or peevishly. **—squawk** *n.*

squeak (skwēk) ▸ *v.* To utter or give forth a thin, high-pitched cry or sound. **—squeak** *n.* **—squeak′i·ly** *adv.* **—squeak′i·ness** *n.* **—squeak′y** *adj.*

squeal (skwēl) ▸ *v.* 1. To utter with or produce a loud shrill cry or sound. 2. *Slang* To turn informer. **—squeal** *n.* **—squeal′er** *n.*

squea·mish (skwē′mĭsh) ▸ *adj.* 1a. Easily nauseated or sickened. b. Nauseated. 2. Easily shocked or disgusted. 3. Excessively fastidious. **—squea′mish·ly** *adv.* **—squea′mish·ness** *n.*

squee·gee (skwē′jē) ▸ *n.* A tool with a rubber or leather blade set perpendicular to a handle, used to remove water from a flat surface, as a window. **—squee′gee** *v.*

squeeze (skwēz) ▸ *v.* **squeezed, squeez·ing.** 1. To press together; compress. 2. To press gently, as in affection: *squeezed her hand.* 3. To exert pressure. 4. To extract by applying pressure: *squeeze juice from a lemon.* 5. To force by pressure; cram. ▸ *n.* 1. An act of squeezing. 2. An amount squeezed. **—squeez′er** *n.*

squelch (skwĕlch) ▸ *v.* 1. To crush by or as if by trampling; squash. 2. To put down or silence, as with a crushing retort. 3. To produce a splashing, squishing, or sucking sound. **—squelch** *n.*

squib (skwĭb) ▸ *n.* 1a. A small firecracker. b. A firecracker that burns but does not explode. 2. A brief witty writing or speech.

squid (skwĭd) ▸ *n., pl.* **squids** or **squid.** A marine mollusk with a long body and ten arms surrounding the mouth.

squig·gle (skwĭg′əl) ▸ *n.* A small wiggly mark or scrawl. ▸ *v.* **-gled, -gling.** To squirm and wriggle. **—squig′gly** *adj.*

squint (skwĭnt) ▸ *v.* 1a. To look with the eyes partly closed, as in bright sunlight. b. To close (the eyes) partly. 2. To be affected with strabismus. **—squint** *n.* **—squint′y** *adj.*

squire (skwīr) ▸ *n.* 1. A man who attends or escorts a woman; gallant. 2. An English country gentleman. 3. A judge or other local dignitary. 4. A young nobleman attendant upon and ranked next below a knight. ▸ *v.* **squired, squir·ing.** To attend as a squire; escort.

squirm (skwûrm) ▸ *v.* 1. To twist about in a wriggling motion; writhe. 2. To feel or exhibit signs of humiliation or embarrassment. 3. To fidget. **—squirm** *n.* **—squirm′er** *n.* **—squirm′y** *adj.*

squir·rel (skwûr′əl, skwŭr′-) ▸ *n.* 1. Any of various arboreal rodents with gray or reddish-brown fur and a long bushy tail. 2. The fur of a squirrel.

squirt (skwûrt) ▸ *v.* To eject (liquid) in a thin swift stream or jet. ▸ *n.* 1. A device for squirting. 2. A squirted jet. 3. A small or young person; pipsqueak.

squish (skwĭsh) ▸ *v.* 1. To crush or squash. 2. To emit the gurgling or sucking sound of soft mud being walked on. **—squish** *n.* **—squish′y** *adj.*

Sr ▸ The symbol for the element **strontium.**

Sr. ▸ *abbr.* 1. or **sr.** senior 2. señor 3. *Eccles.* sister (title)

Sri Lan·ka (srē läng′kə). Formerly **Cey·lon** (sĭ-lŏn′, sā-) ▸ An island country in the Indian Ocean off SE India. **—Sri Lan′kan** *adj. & n.*

SSE ▸ *abbr.* south-southeast

SSN ▸ *abbr.* Social Security number

SSW ▸ *abbr.* south-southwest

St. ▸ *abbr.* 1. saint 2. state 3. strait 4. street

-st ▸ *suff.* Var. of **-est**[2].

stab (stăb) ▸ *v.* **stabbed, stab·bing.** 1. To pierce or wound with or as if with a pointed weapon. 2. To thrust with or as if with a pointed weapon. ▸ *n.* 1. An act of stabbing. 2. A wound inflicted with a pointed weapon. 3. A sudden piercing pain. 4. An attempt; try.

sta·bi·lize (stā′bə-līz′) ▸ *v.* **-lized, -liz·ing.** 1. To make or become stable. 2. To maintain the stability of. **—sta′bi·li·za′tion** *n.* **—sta′bi·liz′er** *n.*

sta·ble[1] (stā′bəl) ▸ *adj.* **-bler, -blest.** 1a. Resistant to change of position or condition. b. Maintaining equilibrium. 2. Long-lasting; enduring. 3a. Consistently dependable. b. Not subject to mental illness or irrationality. **—sta·bil′i·ty** *n.* **—sta′bly** *adv.*

sta·ble[2] (stā′bəl) ▸ *n.* 1. A building for the shelter and feeding of domestic animals, esp. horses. 2. All the racehorses of a single owner. ▸ *v.* **-bled, -bling.** To put or keep in a stable.

stac·ca·to (stə-kä′tō) ▸ *adj.* 1. *Mus.* Cut short crisply; detached. 2. Made up of short, sharp sounds: *staccato gunfire.* **—stac·ca′to** *n. & adv.*

stack (stăk) ▸ *n.* 1. A large, usu. conical pile, as of straw. 2. An orderly pile, esp. one arranged in layers. 3. A chimney or flue. 4. A vertical exhaust pipe, as on a ship or locomotive. 5. often **stacks** The area of a library in which most of the books are shelved. 6. *Informal* A large quantity. ▸ *v.* 1. To arrange in a stack; pile. 2. *Games* To prearrange the order of (a deck of cards) so as to cheat. ***—phrasal verb:*** **stack up** *Informal* To measure up; compare. **—stack′er** *n.*

sta·di·um (stā′dē-əm) ▸ *n., pl.* **-di·ums** or **-di·a** (-dē-ə). A large, usu. open structure for sports events.

THESAURUS

squashy *adj.* —*See* SOFT (1).

squat *v.* —*See* STOOP.

squat *adj.* —*See* STOCKY.

squawk *v.* —*See* COMPLAIN, OBJECT, SHOUT.

squawk *n.* —*See* COMPLAINT, SHOUT.

squawky *adj.* —*See* HARSH.

squeal *v.* To utter a shrill, short cry ▸ yap, yawp, yelp, yip. [*Compare* CRY, SHOUT.] —*See also* INFORM (2).

squeal *n.* A shrill, short cry ▸ yap, yawp, yelp, yip.

squealer *n.* —*See* INFORMER.

squeamish *adj.* —*See* FUSSY.

squeeze *v.* 1. To subject to compression ▸ compact, compress, constrict, constringe, pinch, scrunch. [*Compare* CRUSH, WRENCH.] 2. To extract from by applying pressure ▸ crush, express, press. 3. To handle in a way so as to mix, form, and shape ▸ knead, manipulate, work. —*See also* CROWD, EMBRACE (1), EXTORT.

squeeze *n.* —*See* CONSTRICTION, EMBRACE.

squelch *v.* —*See* REPRESS, SUPPRESS.

squib *n.* —*See* ITEM.

squiggle *v.* —*See* CRAWL (1).

squint *v.* To peer with the eyes partly closed ▸ squinch. ***Idiom:*** screw up one's eyes. [*Compare* GAZE, GLIMPSE.] —*See also* TEND[1].

squint-eyed or **squinty** *adj.* Marked by or affected with a squint ▸ cross-eyed, strabismal, strabismic.

squirm *v.* To twist agitatedly, as in pain, struggle, or embarrassment ▸ toss, twist, writhe. [*Compare* SHAKE.] —*See also* CRAWL (1).

squirrel away *v.* —*See* HIDE[1], SAVE (1).

squirt *v.* To eject or be ejected in a sudden thin, swift stream ▸ jet, spout, spray, spurt. [*Compare* ERUPT, FLOW.]

squirt *n.* 1. A sudden swift stream of ejected liquid ▸ jet, spout, spurt, spray. [*Compare* FLOW.] 2. *Informal* A small or young person ▸ pup, puppy, scrub, small fry. *Informal:* pipsqueak, shorty. *Slang:* half-pint, punk, runt, shrimp. —*See also* NONENTITY.

squishy *adj.* —*See* SOFT (1).

stab *v.* —*See* CUT (1), PLUNGE.

stab *n.* —*See* ATTEMPT, DIG, PAIN, PRICK.

stabbing *adj.* —*See* PAINFUL, SHARP (3).

stability *n.* Reliability in withstanding pressure, force, or stress ▸ fastness, firmness, hardness, security, solidity, soundness, stableness, steadiness, strength, sturdiness, sureness. [*Compare* BALANCE.]

stabilize *v.* —*See* BALANCE (1), SUPPORT (2).

stable *adj.* —*See* DEPENDABLE, FIRM[1] (2).

stable *n.* —*See* CROWD, FLOCK.

stableness *n.* —*See* STABILITY.

stack *n.* —*See* HEAP (1).

stack *v.* —*See* HEAP (1).

stack up *v.* —*See* EQUAL (1).

staff (stăf) ▶ *n., pl.* **staffs** or **staves** (stāvz). **1.** A stick or cane used as an aid in walking, as a weapon, or as a symbol of authority. **2.** *pl.* **staffs. a.** A group of assistants to a person in authority. **b.** The personnel of an enterprise. **3.** A set of horizontal lines on which musical notes are written. ▶ *v.* To provide with a staff of employees.

staff·er (stăf′ər) ▶ *n. Informal* A member of a staff.

staff sergeant ▶ *n.* A rank in the US Army, Air Force, and Marine Corps above sergeant.

stag (stăg) ▶ *n.* An adult male deer. ▶ *adj.* **1.** Of or for men only: *a stag party.* **2.** Pornographic: *stag films.* ▶ *adv.* Unaccompanied: *went to the dance stag.*

stage (stāj) ▶ *n.* **1.** A raised and level floor or platform. **2a.** A raised platform on which theatrical performances are presented. **b.** The acting profession: *The stage is her life.* **3.** The scene of a noteworthy event. **4.** A resting place on a journey. **5.** A stagecoach. **6.** A level, degree, or period of time in the course of a process; step. **7.** One of the successive propulsion units of a rocket. ▶ *v.* **staged, stag·ing. 1.** To exhibit or present on or as if on a stage. **2.** To produce or direct (a theatrical performance). **3.** To arrange and carry out: *stage an invasion.* **—idiom: stage left (**or **right)** The area of a stage to one's left (or right) when facing the audience.

stage·coach (stāj′kōch′) ▶ *n.* A four-wheeled horse-drawn vehicle formerly used to transport mail and passengers.

stage·craft (stāj′krăft′) ▶ *n.* Skill in the techniques and devices of the theater.

stag·ger (stăg′ər) ▶ *v.* **1.** To move or cause to move unsteadily; totter. **2.** To cause to falter. **3.** To overwhelm, as with emotion or misfortune. **4.** To arrange in alternating or overlapping times or positions. ▶ *n.* A tottering or reeling motion. **—stag′ger·er** *n.* **—stag′ger·ing·ly** *adv.*

stag·ing (stā′jĭng) ▶ *n.* **1.** A temporary platform; scaffolding. **2.** The process of putting on a play.

stag·nant (stăg′nənt) ▶ *adj.* **1.** Not moving or flowing. **2.** Foul from standing: *stagnant ponds.* **3.** Lacking vitality; sluggish. **4.** Failing to change or develop. **—stag′nan·cy** *n.* **—stag′nant·ly** *adv.*

stag·nate (stăg′nāt′) ▶ *v.* **-nat·ed, -nat·ing.** To be or become stagnant. **—stag·na′tion** *n.*

stag·y also **stag·ey** (stā′jē) ▶ *adj.* **-i·er, -i·est.** Overly theatrical or dramatic. **—stag′i·ly** *adv.* **—stag′i·ness** *n.*

staid (stād) ▶ *adj.* **1.** Sedate and dignified; proper. **2.** Stodgy; stuffy. **—staid′ly** *adv.*

stain (stān) ▶ *v.* **1.** To discolor, soil, or spot. **2.** To corrupt; taint. **3.** To color with a penetrating liquid dye or tint. ▶ *n.* **1.** A discolored or soiled spot or smudge. **2.** A blemish on one's character or reputation. **3.** A liquid substance, as a dye, used to stain. **—stain′less** *adj.*

stained glass (stānd) ▶ *n.* Glass that is colored esp. for use in windows.

stainless steel ▶ *n.* Any of various steels alloyed with sufficient chromium to be resistant to corrosion or rusting.

stair (stâr) ▶ *n.* **1.** often **stairs** A staircase. **2.** One of a flight of steps.

stair·case (stâr′kās′) ▶ *n.* A flight of steps and its supporting structure.

stair·way (stâr′wā′) ▶ *n.* See **staircase.**

stair·well (stâr′wĕl′) ▶ *n.* A vertical shaft around which a staircase has been built.

stake (stāk) ▶ *n.* **1.** A pointed piece of wood or metal driven into the ground as a marker, barrier, or support. **2a.** A post to which an offender is bound for execution by burning. **b.** Execution by burning. **3.** often **stakes a.** Money or property risked in a wager or gambling game. **b.** The prize awarded the winner of a contest or race. **4.** A share or interest in an enterprise. ▶ *v.* **staked, stak·ing. 1.** To mark the location or limits of with or as if with stakes. **2.** To fasten with or to a stake. **3.** To gamble; risk. **4.** To provide working capital for; finance.

stake·out (stāk′out′) ▶ *n.* Surveillance of an area, building, or person, esp. by police.

sta·lac·tite (stə-lăk′tīt′, stăl′ək-) ▶ *n.* An icicle-shaped mineral deposit hanging from the roof of a cavern.

sta·lag·mite (stə-lăg′mīt′, stăl′əg-) ▶ *n.* A conical mineral deposit built up on the floor of a cavern.

stale (stāl) ▶ *adj.* **stal·er, stal·est. 1.** Having lost freshness or flavor: *stale bread.* **2.** Lacking originality or spontaneity; trite. **—stale** *v.* **—stale′ly** *adv.* **—stale′ness** *n.*

stale·mate (stāl′māt′) ▶ *n.* A situation in which further action is blocked; deadlock. **—stale′mate′** *v.*

Sta·lin (stä′lĭn), **Joseph** (1879–1953) ▶ Soviet politician. **—Sta′lin·ism** *n.*

stalk[1] (stôk) ▶ *n.* A stem that supports a plant or plant part.

stalk[2] (stôk) ▶ *v.* **1.** To walk with a stiff or haughty gait. **2.** To move threateningly or menacingly. **3.** To track (game). **4.** To pursue stealthily. **—stalk′er** *n.*

stall[1] (stôl) ▶ *n.* **1.** A compartment for one animal in a barn or shed. **2a.** A booth or stand for selling wares. **b.** A small compartment: *a shower stall.* **3.** A pew in a church. ▶ *v.* **1.** To cause (an engine) accidentally to stop running. **2.** To come to a standstill: *Negotiations stalled.*

stall[2] (stôl) ▶ *v.* To employ delaying tactics (against). **—stall** *n.*

THESAURUS

staff *n.* —*See* STICK (2).

staffer *n.* —*See* EMPLOYEE.

stage *n.* **1.** A raised platform on which theatrical performances or speeches are given ▶ boards, dais, podium, proscenium, pulpit, rostrum, soapbox. **2.** The art and occupation of an actor ▶ acting, dramatics, theater, theatrics. **3.** A temporary framework with a floor, used by laborers ▶ platform, scaffold, scaffolding, staging. [*Compare* BASE[1].] **4.** An interval regarded as a distinct evolutionary or developmental unit ▶ period, phase. [*Compare* AGE.] **5.** A stage of a competition ▶ [illegible] round. [*Compare* COMPETITION, TURN.] —*See also* DEGREE (1), OCCASION (1), SCENE (1).

stage *v.* To produce on the stage ▶ act (out), direct, do, dramatize, enact, give, mount, perform, present, produce, put on. [*Compare* CONDUCT.] —*See also* HAVE (3).

stagger *v.* **1.** To walk unsteadily ▶ careen, dodder, falter, halt, hitch, hobble, limp, lurch, reel, stumble, sway, teeter, totter, weave, wobble. [*Compare* BLUNDER, SWAY, TRUDGE.] **2.** To overwhelm with surprise, wonder, or bewilderment ▶ boggle, bowl over, dumbfound, flabbergast, floor, shock, stun. *Informal:* knock out (*or* over). *Idioms:* be thunderstruck at, strike dumb (*or* speechless), take someone's breath away. [*Compare* STARTLE, SURPRISE.] —*See also* DAZE (1), HESITATE, MUDDLE.

staggering *adj.* —*See* ASTONISHING.

staginess *n.* —*See* THEATRICALISM.

stagnant *adj.* —*See* AIRLESS (2), SLOW (2).

stagnation *n.* —*See* INACTION.

staid *adj.* —*See* SERIOUS (1).

staidness *n.* —*See* SERIOUSNESS (1).

stain *v.* To mark or soil with foreign matter ▶ bespatter, bestain, blotch, discolor, smut, spatter, splatter, splotch, spot. [*Compare* DIRTY, SMEAR.] —*See also* COLOR (1), CORRUPT, DENIGRATE, FINISH (2).

stain *n.* A mark of discredit or disgrace ▶ black eye, blemish, blot, onus, spot, stigma, taint, tarnish. *Idiom:* a blot on one's name (*or* escutcheon). [*Compare* DISGRACE, REFLECTION.] —*See also* COLOR (2), FINISH, SMEAR.

stainless *adj.* —*See* CLEAN (1).

stake *n.* A right or legal share in something ▶ claim, interest, portion, title. [*Compare* CUT, RIGHT.] —*See also* BET, CAPITAL (1), STICK (1).

stake *v.* —*See* FINANCE, GAMBLE (2).

v. To pay regular and close attention to ▶ follow, monitor, observe, survey, watch. *Idioms:* have one's (*or* keep an) eye on, keep tabs on, keep track of, ride herd on.

stakeout *n.* —*See* LOOKOUT (1).

stale *adj.* —*See* AIRLESS (1), FLAT (2), MOLDY, TRITE.

stalemate *n.* An equality of scores, [illegible] in a contest ▶ dead heat, deadlock, draw, standoff, tie.

staleness *n.* —*See* DULLNESS.

stalk[1] *n.* The main ascending part of a plant, which supports the other parts ▶ stem, stock, trunk. [*Compare* SHOOT.]

stalk[2] *v.* —*See* HUNT.

stall[1] *v.* —*See* STOP (1), STOP (2).

stall *n.* A small, often makeshift structure for the display and sale of goods ▶ booth, counter, stand. [*Compare* STORE.] —*See also* CAGE.

stall[2] *v.* —*See* DEFER[1], DELAY (2), DELAY (1).

stal·lion (stăl′yən) ▸ *n.* An uncastrated adult male horse.

stal·wart (stôl′wərt) ▸ *adj.* **1.** Physically strong; sturdy. **2.** Firm and resolute; stout.

sta·men (stā′mən) ▸ *n., pl.* **-mens** or **sta·mi·na** (stā′mə-nə, stăm′ə-). The pollen-producing reproductive organ of a flower.

stam·i·na (stăm′ə-nə) ▸ *n.* Physical or moral power of endurance.

sta·mi·nate (stā′mə-nĭt, -nāt′, stăm′ə-) ▸ *adj.* Having stamens but lacking pistils.

stam·mer (stăm′ər) ▸ *v.* To speak with involuntary pauses or repetitions. **—stam′mer** *n.* **—stam′mer·er** *n.*

stamp (stămp) ▸ *v.* **1.** To bring down (the foot) forcibly. **2.** To step on heavily, esp. so as to crush or extinguish. **3.** To shape or cut out with a mold, form, or die. **4.** To imprint or impress with a mark, design, or seal. **5.** To affix an adhesive stamp to. **6.** To mark; characterize. ▸ *n.* **1.** The act of stamping. **2a.** An implement or device used to stamp. **b.** The impression or shape stamped. **3.** A mark, design, or seal indicating ownership, approval, or completion. **4.** A postage stamp. **5.** A characterizing mark or quality.

stam·pede (stăm-pēd′) ▸ *n.* A sudden frenzied rush of panic-stricken animals or people. ▸ *v.* **-ped·ed, -ped·ing.** To participate in or cause a stampede.

stance (stăns) ▸ *n.* **1.** The position of a standing person or animal. **2.** Point of view.

stanch[1] (stônch, stänch, stănch) also **staunch** (stônch, stänch) ▸ *v.* To stop or check the flow of a bodily fluid, esp. blood.

stanch[2] (stônch, stänch, stănch) ▸ *adj.* Var. of **staunch**[1].

stan·chion (stăn′chən, -shən) ▸ *n.* An upright pole or post.

stand (stănd) ▸ *v.* **stood** (stŏŏd), **stand·ing. 1.** To rise to an upright position. **2.** To assume or maintain an upright position. **3.** To place upright. **4.** To be placed or situated. **5.** To remain stable, valid, or intact. **6.** To be in a specific state or condition: *stands in awe of the achievement.* **7.** To remain motionless or inactive. **8.** To tolerate; endure. **9.** To undergo: *stand trial.* ***—phrasal verbs:*** **stand for 1.** To represent; symbolize. **2.** To tolerate. **stand out** To be prominent or outstanding. **stand up** To remain valid, sound, or durable. ▸ *n.* **1.** The act of standing. **2.** A halt; standstill. **3.** A stop on a performance tour. **4.** A place designated for standing: *a witness stand.* **5.** A booth or counter for the display of goods for sale. **6.** A parking space reserved for taxis. **7.** A position or opinion one is prepared to uphold: *take a stand.* **8. stands** A grandstand; bleachers. **9.** A rack or prop for holding things upright. **10.** A growth of tall plants or trees. ***—idioms:*** **stand up for** To side with; defend. **stand up to** To confront fearlessly.

stan·dard (stăn′dərd) ▸ *n.* **1.** A flag, banner, or ensign. **2.** An acknowledged basis for comparing or measuring; criterion. **3.** A degree or level of requirement, excellence, or attainment. **4.** A pedestal, stand, or base. **—stan′dard** *adj.*

stan·dard-bear·er (stăn′dərd-bâr′ər) ▸ *n.* One who is in the vanguard of a political or religious movement.

standard deviation ▸ *n.* A statistic used as a measure of the dispersion or variation in a distribution.

stan·dard·ize (stăn′dər-dīz′) ▸ *v.* **-ized, -iz·ing.** To cause to conform to a standard. **—stan′dard·i·za′tion** *n.*

standard of living ▸ *n.* A measure of the goods and services affordable by and available to a person or country.

standard time ▸ *n.* The time in any of 24 global time zones, usu. the mean solar time at the central meridian of each zone.

stand·by (stănd′bī′) ▸ *n., pl.* **-bys. 1.** One that can always be relied on, as in an emergency. **2.** One kept in readiness as a substitute. ▸ *adj.* Waiting to be assigned unfilled travel space, as on an airline. ▸ *adv.* On a standby basis: *flew standby to Seattle.*

stand·ee (stăn-dē′) ▸ *n.* One who stands, as in a theater.

stand-in (stănd′ĭn′) ▸ *n.* **1.** One who substitutes for a movie actor, as during technical adjustments. **2.** A substitute.

stand·ing (stăn′dĭng) ▸ *n.* **1.** A relative position in a group; rank. **2.** Status; reputation. **3.** Continuance in time; duration. ▸ *adj.* **1.** Remaining upright. **2.** Performed from a standing position: *a standing jump.* **3.** Permanent: *a standing army.* **4.** Remaining in force indefinitely: *a standing invitation.*

standing stone ▸ *n.* A prehistoric monument consisting of a single tall upright megalith.

Stan·dish (stăn′dĭsh′), **Miles** or **Myles** (1584?–1656) ▸ English colonist in America.

stand·off (stănd′ôf′, -ŏf′) ▸ *n.* A tie or draw, as in a contest.

stand·off·ish (stănd-ô′fĭsh, -ŏf′ĭsh) ▸ *adj.* Aloof or reserved. **—stand·off′ish·ness** *n.*

stand·out (stănd′out′) ▸ *n. Informal* One that is outstanding or excellent.

stand·pipe (stănd′pīp′) ▸ *n.* A large vertical pipe into which water is pumped in order to produce a desired pressure.

stand·point (stănd′point′) ▸ *n.* A position from which things are considered; point of view.

stand·still (stănd′stĭl′) ▸ *n.* A halt.

stand·up or **stand-up** (stănd′ŭp′) ▸ *adj.* **1.** Standing erect. **2.** Of or being a performer who works solo and without props: *a standup comedian.*

stank (stăngk) ▸ *v.* P.t. of **stink.**

Stan·ton (stăn′tən), **Elizabeth Cady** (1815–1902) ▸ Amer. feminist and social reformer.

stan·za (stăn′zə) ▸ *n.* One of the divisions of a poem,

THESAURUS

stalwart *adj.* —*See* STRONG (2).

stamina *n.* —*See* ENDURANCE.

stammer *v.* To speak with involuntary repetitions or pauses; speak hesitatingly or clumsily ▸ falter, splutter, sputter, stumble, stutter. [*Compare* BABBLE, CHATTER, HESITATE.]

stammer *n.* A way of speaking marked by involuntary repetitions and pauses ▸ stammering, stutter, stuttering.

stamp *v.* To step on heavily and repeatedly so as to crush, injure, or destroy ▸ stomp, tramp, trample, tread, tromp. [*Compare* CRUSH.] —*See also* BEAT (3), ENGRAVE (2), TRUDGE.

stamp out *v.* —*See* ANNIHILATE.

stamp *n.* —*See* APPEARANCE (1), IMPRESSION (1), KIND[2], SIGN (1).

stance *n.* —*See* POSTURE (1), POSTURE (2).

stand *v.* **1.** To adopt a standing posture ▸ arise, get up, jump up, rise, stand up, uprise. ***Idioms:*** get (*or* jump *or* leap *or* spring) to one's feet, take one's feet. **2.** To be in a certain position; have a location ▸ be located, be situated, rest, sit. —*See also* ENDURE (1), ENDURE (2), TREAT (2).

stand against *v.* —*See* OPPOSE.

stand behind *v.* —*See* GUARANTEE (1), SUPPORT (1).

stand by *v.* —*See* SUPPORT (1).

stand for *v.* To serve as an official delegate of ▸ act (as *or* for), answer for, represent, speak for. ***Idioms:*** be spokesperson (*or* representative) for, be the voice of. [*Compare* SUBSTITUTE.] —*See also* REPRESENT (1).

stand in *v.* —*See* SUBSTITUTE.

stand out *v.* To be obtrusively conspicuous ▸ glare, stick out. ***Idioms:*** stare someone in the face, stick out like a sore thumb. —*See also* BULGE.

stand up *v.* To prove valid under scrutiny ▸ hold up, prove out. *Informal:* wash. ***Idioms:*** hold water, pass muster, ring true. —*See also* BEAR.

stand *n.* A small, often makeshift structure for the display and sale of goods ▸ booth, counter, stall. [*Compare* STORE.] —*See also* BASE[1] (2), VIEWPOINT.

standard *n.* A means by which individuals or things are compared and judged ▸ benchmark, criterion, gauge, mark, measure, norm, test, touchstone, yardstick. [*Compare* CONDITION, LAW, RULE.] —*See also* FLAG[1], MODEL, ORIGINAL.

standard *adj.* —*See* AUTHORITATIVE (1), CONVENTIONAL, ORDINARY.

standardize *v.* —*See* CONVENTIONALIZE.

standards *n.* —*See* ETHICS (2).

standby *adj.* —*See* AUXILIARY (2).

stand-in *n.* —*See* SUBSTITUTE.

standing *n.* —*See* BASIS (3), FACE (6), PLACE (1).

standing *adj.* —*See* VERTICAL.

standoff *n.* An equality of scores, votes, or performances in a contest ▸ dead heat, deadlock, draw, stalemate, tie.

standoffish *adj.* —*See* COOL.

standout *adj.* —*See* EXCEPTIONAL.

standpat *adj.* —*See* ULTRACONSERVATIVE.

standpoint *n.* —*See* VIEWPOINT.

standstill *n.* —*See* STOP (2).

composed of two or more lines.

sta·pes (stā′pēz) ▸ *n., pl.* **-pes** or **sta·pe·des** (stā′pĭ-dēz′). A small bone of the middle ear, shaped somewhat like a stirrup.

staph·y·lo·coc·cus (stăf′ə-lō-kŏk′əs) ▸ *n., pl.* **-coc·ci** (-kŏk′sī, -kŏk′ī). A spherical parasitic bacterium usu. occurring in grapelike clusters and causing septicemia and other infections. **—staph′y·lo·coc′cal, staph′y·lo·coc′cic** (-kŏk′sĭk, -kŏk′ĭk) *adj.*

sta·ple[1] (stā′pəl) ▸ *n.* **1.** A principal raw material or commodity. **2.** A major part, element, or feature. **3.** A basic dietary item. **4.** The fiber of cotton, wool, or flax, graded as to length and fineness. ▸ *adj.* **1.** Produced or stocked in large quantities. **2.** Principal; main.

sta·ple[2] (stā′pəl) ▸ *n.* **1.** A U-shaped metal loop with pointed ends, driven into a surface to hold something, as a bolt or wire. **2.** A thin piece of wire in the shape of a square bracket, used to fasten thin material, as paper. **—sta′ple** *v.* **—sta′pler** *n.*

star (stär) ▸ *n.* **1a.** A luminous celestial body consisting of a mass of hot gas held together by its own gravity. **b.** A celestial body visible at night as a relatively stationary point of light. **2.** A graphic design having five or more radiating points. **3a.** An outstanding performer, esp. a leading actor or actress. **b.** A celebrity; luminary. **4.** An asterisk (*). **5. stars** The future; destiny. ▸ *v.* **starred, star·ring.** **1.** To ornament or mark with stars. **2.** To mark with an asterisk. **3.** To play the leading role in a theatrical or film production. **—star′dom** *n.* **—star′ry** *adj.*

star·board (stär′bərd) ▸ *n.* The right-hand side of a ship or aircraft as one faces forward. **—star′board** *adj. & adv.*

starch (stärch) ▸ *n.* **1.** A nutrient carbohydrate, $(C_6H_{10}O_5)_n$, found notably in corn, potatoes, wheat, and rice and commonly prepared as a white tasteless powder. **2.** Any of various substances, such as natural starch, used to stiffen cloth, as in laundering. **3.** A food having a high starch content. ▸ *v.* To stiffen with starch. **—starch′i·ness** *n.* **—starch′y** *adj.*

stare (stâr) ▸ *v.* **stared, star·ing.** To look directly and fixedly, often with a wide-eyed gaze. ▸ *n.* An intent gaze. **—star′er** *n.*

star·fish (stär′fĭsh′) ▸ *n.* Any of various, often spiny marine animals having five arms extending from a central disk.

star·gaze (stär′gāz′) ▸ *v.* **1.** To observe the stars. **2.** To daydream. **—star′gaz′er** *n.*

stark (stärk) ▸ *adj.* **-er, -est.** **1.** Bare; blunt: *stark truth.* **2.** Complete or utter; extreme: *stark poverty.* **3.** Harsh; grim. ▸ *adv.* Utterly: *stark naked.* **—stark′ly** *adv.* **—stark′ness** *n.*

star·let (stär′lĭt) ▸ *n.* A young film actress publicized as a future star.

star·light (stär′līt′) ▸ *n.* The light from the stars.

star·ling (stär′lĭng) ▸ *n.* An Old World bird with dark, often iridescent plumage, widely naturalized in North America.

star·lit (stär′lĭt′) ▸ *adj.* Illuminated by starlight.

star·ry-eyed (stär′ē-īd′) ▸ *adj.* Naively enthusiastic, overoptimistic, or romantic.

Stars and Stripes (stärz) ▸ *n. (takes sing. or pl. v.)* The flag of the US.

start (stärt) ▸ *v.* **1.** To commence; begin. **2.** To move suddenly or involuntarily: *started at the noise.* **3.** To set into motion, operation, or activity. **4.** To introduce; originate. **5.** To enter in a race or game. **6.** To establish: *start a business.* ▸ *n.* **1.** A beginning. **2.** A place or time of beginning. **3.** A startled reaction or movement. **—start′er** *n.*

star·tle (stär′tl) ▸ *v.* **-tled, -tling.** **1.** To cause to make a quick involuntary movement, as in fright. **2.** To alarm or surprise. **—star′tling·ly** *adv.*

start-up or **start·up** (stärt′ŭp′) ▸ *n.* **1.** The act of setting into operation or motion. **2.** A business that has recently begun operation.

starve (stärv) ▸ *v.* **starved, starv·ing.** **1.** To die or cause to die from prolonged lack of food. **2.** *Informal* To be hungry. **3.** To suffer from deprivation: *starving for love.* **—star·va′tion** *n.*

starve·ling (stärv′lĭng) ▸ *n.* One that is starving or being starved.

stash (stăsh) *Slang* ▸ *v.* To hide or store away in a secret place. ▸ *n.* A hidden or secret supply.

-stasis ▸ *suff.* **1.** Stable state: *homeostasis.* **2.** Position: *metastasis.*

-stat ▸ *suff.* One that stabilizes: *rheostat.*

state (stāt) ▸ *n.* **1.** A condition of being. **2.** A mental or emotional condition. **3.** Social position or rank. **4.** The supreme public power within a sovereign political entity. **5.** A body politic, esp. one constituting a nation. **6.** One of the semiautonomous territorial and political subdivisions of a federated country, such as the US. ▸ *v.* **stat·ed, stat·ing.** To set forth in words; declare. **—state′hood′** *n.*

state·craft (stāt′krăft′) ▸ *n.* The art of leading a country.

state·house (stāt′hous′) ▸ *n.* A building in which a state legislature holds sessions.

state·less (stāt′lĭs) ▸ *adj.* Not having citizenship in a state or nation.

state·ly (stāt′lē) ▸ *adj.* **-li·er, -li·est.** **1.** Dignified; formal. **2.** Majestic; lofty.

state·ment (stāt′mənt) ▸ *n.* **1.** The act of stating. **2.** Something stated. **3.** An abstract of a financial account. **4.** A monthly report sent to a debtor or bank depositor.

Stat·en Island (stăt′n). Formerly **Richmond** ▸ A borough of New York City coextensive with **Staten Island** in New York Bay SW of Manhattan I.

state·room (stāt′ro͞om′, -ro͝om′) ▸ *n.* A private compartment on a ship or train.

state·side (stāt′sīd′) ▸ *adj.* Of or in esp. the continental US. **—state′side′.**

THESAURUS

star *n.* —*See* CELEBRITY, LEAD.

starch *n.* —*See* ENERGY.

staple *adj.* —*See* PRIMARY (1).

starchy *adj.* Rigidly constrained or formal; lacking grace and spontaneity ▸ buckram, stiff, stilted, wooden. [*Compare* COOL, FORCED, PRUDISH.]

star-crossed *adj.* —*See* UNFORTUNATE (1).

stare [illegible]

stare *n.* An intent fixed look ▸ gape, gaze. [*Compare* LOOK.]

stargaze [illegible]

stargazer *n.* —*See* DREAMER (1).

stark *adj.* —*See* BARE (1), BLEAK (1), UTTER[2].

starry-eyed *adj.* —*See* DREAMY, IDEALISTIC.

start *v.* **1.** To go about the initial step in doing something ▸ approach, begin, commence, embark on (*or* upon), enter (on *or* upon), get off, inaugurate, initiate, institute, launch, lead off, open, set about, set out, set to, take on, take up, undertake. *Informal:* kick off. *Idioms:* get cracking, get going, get the ball rolling, get the show on the road, take the plunge. [*Compare* CAUSE, INTRODUCE, PRODUCE.] **2.** To set in motion ▸ activate, actuate, spark, turn on. [*Compare* ENERGIZE, PROVOKE.] **3.** To move suddenly and involuntarily ▸ bolt, jump. [*Compare* BUMP, JERK.] [illegible] BEGIN, FLINCH, FOUND.

start out *v.* —*See* BEAR (5).

start *n.* A sudden and involuntary movement ▸ bolt, jump, startle. [*Compare* JERK, RECOIL.] —*See also* ADVANTAGE (1), BEGINNING, BIRTH (2).

starter *n.* —*See* APPETIZER.

startle *v.* To cause to experience a sudden momentary shock ▸ electrify, jolt, shock. *Idioms:* give someone a start, make someone jump, make someone's heart skip a beat (*or* stand still). [*Compare* STAGGER.] —*See also* FRIGHTEN, SURPRISE.

startle *n.* A sudden and involuntary movement ▸ bolt, jump, start. [*Compare* JERK, RECOIL.]

start-up or **startup** *n.* —*See* FOUNDATION.

starving *adj.* —*See* HUNGRY (1).

stash *v.* —*See* HIDE[1], SAVE (1).

stash *n.* —*See* HOARD.

stasis *n.* —*See* BALANCE (1).

[illegible] organized geopolitical unit ▸ body politic, country, land, nation, polity. **2.** *Informal* A condition [illegible] distress ▸ fume. *Informal:* snit, sweat, swivet. *Slang:* tizzy. [*Compare* AGITATION, DISTRESS.] —*See also* CONDITION (1), GOVERNMENT (2).

state *v.* —*See* AIR (2), ASSERT, SAY.

stately *adj.* —*See* CEREMONIOUS, GRACIOUS (2), GRAND.

statement *n.* Something said ▸ saying, utterance, word. [*Compare* LANGUAGE, SPEECH.] —*See also* ACCOUNT (2), ASSERTION, EXPRESSION (1), MESSAGE, STORY (1).

state of mind *n.* —*See* MOOD.

states·man (stāts′mən) ▸ *n.* **1.** A man who is a leader in national or international affairs. **2.** A man noted for disinterested public service. **—states′man·like′** *adj.* **—states′man·ship′** *n.*

states·wom·an (stāts′wo͝om′ən) ▸ *n.* **1.** A woman who is a leader in national or international affairs. **2.** A woman noted for disinterested public service.

stat·ic (stăt′ĭk) ▸ *adj.* **1.** Having no motion; being at rest. **2.** *Phys.* Relating to bodies at rest or forces that balance each other. **3.** Of or producing stationary electrical charges; electrostatic. **4.** Of or caused by random radio noise. ▸ *n.* **1.** Random noise, as crackling in a receiver or specks on a video screen, caused by atmospheric disturbance of the signal. **2.** *Informal* **a.** Interference. **b.** Angry criticism. **—stat′i·cal·ly** *adv.*

sta·tion (stā′shən) ▸ *n.* **1.** The place where a person or thing stands or is assigned to stand; post. **2.** The place from which a service is provided or operations are directed: *a police station.* **3.** A stopping place along a route, esp. a depot. **4.** Social position; rank. **5.** An establishment equipped for radio or television transmission. ▸ *v.* To assign to a position.

sta·tion·ar·y (stā′shə-nĕr′ē) ▸ *adj.* **1.** Not moving; fixed. **2.** Unchanging.

station break ▸ *n.* An intermission in a radio or television program for identification of the network or station.

sta·tion·er (stā′shə-nər) ▸ *n.* One who sells stationery.

sta·tion·er·y (stā′shə-nĕr′ē) ▸ *n.* Writing materials, such as paper and envelopes.

station wagon ▸ *n.* An automobile having an extended interior with a third seat or luggage platform and a tailgate.

sta·tis·tic (stə-tĭs′tĭk) ▸ *n.* A numerical datum. **—sta·tis′ti·cal** *adj.* **—sta·tis′ti·cal·ly** *adv.*

sta·tis·tics (stə-tĭs′tĭks) ▸ *n.* **1.** *(takes sing. v.)* The mathematics of the collection, organization, and interpretation of numerical data. **2.** *(takes pl. v.)* Numerical data. **—stat′is·ti′cian** (stăt′ĭ-stĭsh′ən) *n.*

stat·u·ar·y (stăch′o͞o-ĕr′ē) ▸ *n., pl.* **-ies.** Statues collectively.

stat·ue (stăch′o͞o) ▸ *n.* A form or likeness sculpted, modeled, or cast in material such as stone, clay, or bronze.

stat·u·esque (stăch′o͞o-ĕsk′) ▸ *adj.* Suggestive of a statue, as in grace or dignity.

stat·u·ette (stăch′o͞o-ĕt′) ▸ *n.* A small statue.

stat·ure (stăch′ər) ▸ *n.* **1.** The natural height of a human or animal in an upright position. **2.** An achieved level; status.

stat·us (stăt′əs, stā′təs) ▸ *n.* **1.** Position relative to that of others; standing. **2.** High standing; prestige. **3.** The legal character or condition of a person or thing: *the status of a minor.* **4.** A state of affairs; situation.

status quo (kwō) ▸ *n.* The existing state of affairs.

stat·ute (stăch′o͞ot) ▸ *n.* **1.** A law enacted by a legislature. **2.** A bylaw or decree.

statute mile ▸ *n.* The standard mile, 5,280 ft.

stat·u·to·ry (stăch′ə-tôr′ē) ▸ *adj.* Enacted, regulated, or authorized by statute.

staunch¹ (stônch, stänch) also **stanch** (stônch, stänch, stănch) ▸ *adj.* **-er, -est.** **1.** Firm and steadfast; true. **2.** Strong; solid. **—staunch′ly** *adv.* **—staunch′ness** *n.*

staunch² (stônch, stänch) ▸ *v.* Var. of **stanch¹**.

stave (stāv) ▸ *n.* **1.** A narrow strip of wood forming part of the sides of a barrel, tub, or similar structure. **2.** A staff or cudgel. **3.** See **staff** 3. **4.** A stanza. ▸ *v.* **staved** or **stove** (stōv), **stav·ing.** **1.** To break in or puncture the staves of. **2.** To break or smash a hole in. **—*phrasal verb:* stave off** To keep or hold off.

staves (stāvz) ▸ *n.* Pl. of **staff.**

stay¹ (stā) ▸ *v.* **1.** To continue to be in a place or condition. **2.** To stop moving; halt. **3.** To wait; pause. **4.** To endure or persist: *stay with a plan.* **5.** To postpone; delay. **6.** To satisfy or appease temporarily. ▸ *n.* **1.** A stop or pause. **2.** A brief period of residence or visiting.

stay² (stā) ▸ *v.* To brace, support, or prop up. ▸ *n.* **1.** A support or brace. **2.** A strip of bone, plastic, or metal, used to stiffen a garment or part. **3. stays** A corset.

STD ▸ *abbr.* sexually transmitted disease

stead (stĕd) ▸ *n.* **1.** The place, position, or function of another person. **2.** Advantage: *stood them in good stead.*

stead·fast (stĕd′făst′, -fəst) ▸ *adj.* **1.** Fixed or unchanging; steady. **2.** Firmly loyal or constant. **—stead′fast′ly** *adv.* **—stead′fast′ness** *n.*

stead·y (stĕd′ē) ▸ *adj.* **-i·er, -i·est.** **1.** Firm in position or place; fixed. **2.** Direct and unfaltering; sure. **3.** Not changing or fluctuating; uniform. **4.** Not easily excited or upset. **5.** Reliable; dependable. ▸ *v.* **stead·ied, stead·y·ing.** To make or become steady. **—stead′i·ly** *adv.* **—stead′i·ness** *n.*

steak (stāk) ▸ *n.* **1.** A slice or slab of meat, esp. beef, usu. grilled or broiled. **2.** A thick slice of a large fish cut across the body.

steal (stēl) ▸ *v.* **stole** (stōl), **sto·len** (stō′lən), **steal·ing.** **1.** To take (the property of another) without right or permission. **2.** To get or effect surreptitiously or artfully: *steal a kiss.* **3.** To move, carry, or place stealthily. **4.** *Baseball* To advance safely to (another base) during the delivery of a pitch. ▸ *n.* **1.** The act of stealing. **2.** *Slang* A bargain. **—steal′er** *n.*

stealth (stĕlth) ▸ *n.* **1.** The act of moving, proceeding, or acting in a covert way. **2.** Furtiveness. **—stealth′i·ly** *adv.* **—stealth′i·ness** *n.* **—stealth′y** *adj.*

steam (stēm) ▸ *n.* **1a.** The vapor phase of water. **b.** A mist of cooling water vapor. **2.** Pressurized water vapor used for heating, cooking, or to provide mechanical power. **3.** Power; energy. ▸ *v.* **1.** To produce or emit steam. **2.** To become or rise up as steam. **3.** To become misted or covered with steam. **4.** To move by means of steam power.

THESAURUS

static *adj.* —*See* MOTIONLESS.

station *n.* A stopping place along a route for picking up or dropping off passengers ▸ depot, stop, terminal, terminus. —*See also* BASE¹ (1), PLACE (1).

station *v.* To appoint and send to a particular place ▸ assign, post, set. [*Compare* POSITION.]

stationary *adj.* —*See* FIXED, MOTIONLESS.

statue or **statuette** *n.* —*See* SCULPTURE.

statuesque *adj.* —*See* BEAUTIFUL.

stature *n.* —*See* MERIT.

status *n.* —*See* BASIS (3), CONDITION (1), FACE (6), HONOR (2), PLACE (1).

statute *n.* —*See* LAW (2).

staunch *adj.* —*See* FAITHFUL.

stave *n.* —*See* STICK (2).

stave off *v.* —*See* PREVENT, REPEL.

stay¹ *v.* —*See* DEFER¹, ENDURE (2), LIVE¹, LODGE, REMAIN, STOP (2), VISIT (1).

stay with *v.* —*See* KEEP (5).

stay *n.* A remaining in a place as a guest or lodger ▸ sojourn, stop, stopover, visit. —*See also* DELAY (1), RESTRAINT, STOP (1).

stay² *n.* —*See* SUPPORT.

staying power *n.* —*See* ENDURANCE.

stead *n.* The function or position customarily occupied by another ▸ lieu, place.

steadfast *adj.* —*See* DEPENDABLE, FAITHFUL, FIRM¹ (3), FIXED.

steadfastness *n.* —*See* FIDELITY.

steadiness *n.* —*See* BALANCE (2), CHANGELESSNESS, STABILITY.

steady *adj.* —*See* DEPENDABLE, FIRM¹ (2), FIRM¹ (3), FIXED, GRADUAL (2), UNCHANGING.

steady *v.* —*See* BALANCE (1), SUPPORT (2).

steady *n.* —*See* LOVER.

steady-going *adj.* —*See* DEPENDABLE.

steal *v.* To take another's property without permission ▸ abscond with, carry off, crib, embezzle, filch, mooch, pilfer, purloin, snatch, spirit away, thieve. *Informal:* lift, swipe. *Slang:* boost, cop, dip, heist, hook, nip, pinch, rip off, snitch. *Idioms:* make (*or* walk) off with, run off (*or* away) with. [*Compare* KIDNAP, ROB, SACK², SEIZE.] —*See also* SNEAK.

steal *n.* *Slang* Something offered or bought at a low price ▸ bargain, find. *Informal:* buy, deal. —*See also* LARCENY.

stealer *n.* —*See* THIEF.

stealth *n.* The act of proceeding so as to escape observation ▸ furtiveness, secretiveness, slinkiness, slyness, sneakiness, stealthiness, surreptitiousness. [*Compare* ART, SECRECY.]

stealthy *adj.* Moving or acting so as to escape observation ▸ catlike, feline, furtive, secretive, slinky, sly, sneaking, sneaky, surreptitious. [*Compare* ARTFUL, SECRET, UNDERHAND.]

steam *n.* —*See* ENERGY, HAZE.

steam *v.* —*See* ANGER (2), BURN (3), EVAPORATE.

5. *Informal* To become very angry; fume. **6.** To expose to steam, as in cooking. **—steam′y** *adj.*

steam·boat (stēm′bōt′) ▸ *n.* A steamship.

steam engine ▸ *n.* An engine that converts the heat energy of pressurized steam into mechanical energy, esp. one in which steam drives a piston in a closed cylinder.

steam·er (stē′mər) ▸ *n.* **1.** A steamship. **2.** A container in which something is steamed. **3.** See **soft-shell clam.**

steam·fit·ter (stēm′fĭt′ər) ▸ *n.* One who installs and repairs heating, ventilating, refrigerating, and air-conditioning systems.

steam·roll·er (stēm′rō′lər) ▸ *n.* A machine equipped with a heavy roller for smoothing road surfaces. ▸ *v.* **1.** To smooth or level (a road) with a steamroller. **2.** To overwhelm or suppress ruthlessly; crush.

steam·ship (stēm′shĭp′) ▸ *n.* A large vessel propelled by steam-driven screws or paddles.

steam shovel ▸ *n.* **1.** A large, steam-driven machine for digging. **2.** See **power shovel.**

ste·a·tite (stē′ə-tīt′) ▸ *n.* See **soapstone.**

steed (stēd) ▸ *n.* A horse, esp. a spirited one.

steel (stēl) ▸ *n.* **1.** A hard, strong, durable, malleable alloy of iron and carbon. **2.** Something, such as a sword, made of steel. **3.** A quality suggestive of steel: *nerves of steel.* ▸ *v.* **1.** To cover, plate, edge, or point with steel. **2.** To make hard or strong; brace. **—steel′i·ness** *n.* **—steel′y** *adj.*

steel drum ▸ *n.* A tuned metal percussion instrument fashioned from an oil barrel.

steel wool ▸ *n.* Fine fibers of steel matted or woven together to form an abrasive.

steep[1] (stēp) ▸ *adj.* **-er, -est. 1.** Having a sharp inclination; precipitous. **2.** Excessive; stiff: *a steep price.* **—steep′en** *v.* **—steep′ly** *adv.* **—steep′ness** *n.*

steep[2] (stēp) ▸ *v.* **1.** To soak or be soaked in liquid in order to cleanse, soften, or extract a given property from. **2.** To saturate: *steeped in history.*

stee·ple (stē′pəl) ▸ *n.* **1.** A tall tower rising from the roof of a building, such as a church. **2.** A spire.

stee·ple·chase (stē′pəl-chās′) ▸ *n.* A horserace across open country or over an obstacle course. **—stee′ple·chas′er** *n.*

stee·ple·jack (stē′pəl-jăk′) ▸ *n.* A worker on very high structures, such as steeples.

steer[1] (stîr) ▸ *v.* **1.** To guide by a device such as a rudder or wheel. **2.** To direct the course or progress of. **3.** To follow or move in a set course. **—steer′er** *n.* **—steers′man** *n.*

steer[2] (stîr) ▸ *n.* A young ox, esp. one castrated before sexual maturity and raised for beef.

steer·age (stîr′ĭj) ▸ *n.* **1.** The act or practice of steering. **2.** The section of a passenger ship providing the cheapest accommodations.

steg·o·saur (stĕg′ə-sôr′) also **steg·o·sau·rus** (stĕg′ə-sôr′əs) ▸ *n.* A herbivorous dinosaur having a double row of upright bony plates along the back.

stein (stīn) ▸ *n.* A mug, esp. for beer.

Stein·beck (stīn′bĕk′), **John Ernst** (1902–68) ▸ Amer. writer; 1962 Nobel.

stel·lar (stĕl′ər) ▸ *adj.* **1.** Of or consisting of stars. **2a.** Of a star performer. **b.** Outstanding.

stem[1] (stĕm) ▸ *n.* **1a.** The main ascending axis of a plant; stalk. **b.** A stalk supporting another plant part, such as a leaf or flower. **2.** A connecting or supporting part, such as the tube of a tobacco pipe or the slender upright support of a wineglass. **3.** The main line of descent of a family. **4.** *Ling.* The main part of a word to which affixes are added. **5.** *Naut.* The prow. ▸ *v.* **stemmed, stem·ming. 1.** To derive or originate. **2.** To make progress against (a force or flow).

stem[2] (stĕm) ▸ *v.* **stemmed, stem·ming.** To stop or hold back by or as if by damming.

stem·ware (stĕm′wâr′) ▸ *n.* Glassware mounted on a stem.

stench (stĕnch) ▸ *n.* A strong, foul odor; stink.

sten·cil (stĕn′səl) ▸ *n.* A sheet, as of plastic, in which a letter or design has been cut so that ink or paint applied to the sheet will reproduce the pattern on the surface beneath. ▸ *v.* **-ciled, -cil·ing** or **-cilled, -cil·ling.** To mark or produce with a stencil.

ste·nog·ra·phy (stə-nŏg′rə-fē) ▸ *n.* The art or process of writing or transcribing in shorthand. **—ste·nog′ra·pher** *n.* **—sten′o·graph′ic** (stĕn′ə-grăf′ĭk) *adj.* **—sten′o·graph′i·cal·ly** *adv.*

sten·to·ri·an (stĕn-tôr′ē-ən) ▸ *adj.* Extremely loud.

step (stĕp) ▸ *n.* **1a.** The single complete movement of raising one foot and putting it down in another spot, as in walking. **b.** A manner of walking; gait. **c.** A fixed rhythm or pace, as in marching. **2.** A short distance. **3a.** A rest for the foot in ascending or descending. **b. steps** Stairs. **4a.** One of a series of actions or measures taken to achieve a goal. **b.** A stage in a process. **5.** A degree in progress or a grade or rank in a scale. ▸ *v.* **stepped, step·ping. 1.** To put or press the foot down. **2.** To shift or move by or as if by taking a step. **3.** To walk a short distance. **4.** To measure by pacing. ***—phrasal verb:* step up 1.** To increase, esp. in stages: *step up production.* **2.** To come forward. ***—idioms:* in step 1.** Moving in rhythm. **2.** In conformity with one's environment: *in step with the times.* **out of step 1.** Not moving in rhythm. **2.** Not in conformity with one's environment.

step– ▸ *pref.* Related through remarriage rather than by blood: *stepparent.*

step·broth·er (stĕp′brŭ*th*′ər) ▸ *n.* A son of one's stepparent.

step·child (stĕp′chīld′) ▸ *n.* A spouse's child by a previous marriage.

step·daugh·ter (stĕp′dô′tər) ▸ *n.* A spouse's daughter by a previous marriage.

step·fa·ther (stĕp′fä′*th*ər) ▸ *n.* The husband of one's mother and not one's natural father.

step·lad·der (stĕp′lăd′ər) ▸ *n.* A portable ladder with a hinged supporting frame.

step·moth·er (stĕp′mŭ*th*′ər) ▸ *n.* The wife of one's father and not one's natural mother.

step·par·ent (stĕp′pâr′ənt, -păr′-) ▸ *n.* A stepfather or stepmother.

steppe (stĕp) ▸ *n.* A vast semiarid grass-covered plain, as found in SE Europe and Siberia.

step·ping·stone (stĕp′ĭng-stōn′) ▸ *n.* An advantageous position for advancement toward a goal.

step·sis·ter (stĕp′sĭs′tər) ▸ *n.* A daughter of one's stepparent.

THESAURUS

steamroller *v.* —*See* EVEN, OVERWHELM (1).

steamy *adj.* —*See* EROTIC.

steel *v.* —*See* GIRD.

steep[1] *adj.* **1.** Having a sharp inclination; almost perpendicular ▸ abrupt, bold, precipitous, sharp, sheer, sudden. [*Compare* VERTICAL.] **2.** Exceeding a normal limit, especially in price ▸ exorbitant, extortionate, overpriced, sky-high, stiff, stratospheric, unconscionable. [*Compare* COSTLY, EXCESSIVE.]

steep[2] *v.* To cause something to become thoroughly wet or saturated by immersion in a liquid ▸ infuse, macerate, marinate, pickle, soak, souse, suffuse. [*Compare* CHARGE, DIP, WET.]

steer *v.* —*See* CONDUCT (1), DRIVE (1), GUIDE, MANEUVER (1).

steer *n.* —*See* TIP[3].

stem *v.* To have as a source ▸ arise, come, derive, emanate, flow, issue, originate, proceed, rise, spring, upspring. [*Compare* APPEAR, BEGIN.] —*See also* HINDER.

stem *n.* The main ascending part of a plant, which supports the other parts ▸ stalk, stock, trunk. [*Compare* SHOOT.] —*See also* ROD, THEME (1).

stench *n.* A strong, foul odor ▸ fetor, malodor, reek, stink. [*Compare* FRAGRANCE, SMELL.]

stentorian *adj.* —*See* LOUD, VOCIFEROUS.

step *n.* An action calculated to achieve an end ▸ maneuver, measure, move, procedure, tactic. —*See also* DEGREE (1), WALK (1).

step *v.* —*See* DANCE, WALK.

step back *v.* —*See* RECEDE.

step down *v.* To withdraw or remove from business or active life ▸ pension (off), retire, superannuate. *Idioms:* call it quits, hang up one's spurs, put out to pasture, turn in one's badge. [*Compare* DISMISS, QUIT.]

step up *v.* —*See* INCREASE, INTENSIFY, SPEED.

step-by-step *adj.* Proceeding steadily by degrees ▸ gradational, gradual, piecemeal, progressive. *Idioms:* one foot after another, one step at a time. [*Compare* CONSECUTIVE, METHODICAL, SLOW.]

step·son (stĕp′sŭn′) ► *n.* A spouse's son by a previous marriage.

–ster ► *suff.* **1.** One that is associated with, participates in, makes, or does: *songster.* **2.** One that is: *youngster.*

stere (stîr) ► *n.* A unit of volume equal to one cubic meter.

ster·e·o (stĕr′ē-ō′, stîr′-) ► *n., pl.* **-os.** **1.** A stereophonic sound-reproduction system. **2.** Stereophonic sound. **—ste′re·o′** *adj.*

stereo– ► *pref.* **1.** Solid: *stereotype.* **2.** Three-dimensional: *stereoscope.*

ster·e·o·phon·ic (stĕr′ē-ə-fŏn′ĭk, stîr′-) ► *adj.* Of or used in a sound-reproduction system that uses two or more separate channels to give a more natural distribution of sound. **—ster′e·o·phon′i·cal·ly** *adv.*

ster·e·o·scope (stĕr′ē-ə-skōp′, stîr′-) ► *n.* An optical instrument with two eyepieces used to impart a three-dimensional effect to two photographs of the same scene taken at slightly different angles. **—ster′e·o·scop′ic** *adj.*

ster·e·os·co·py (stĕr′ē-ŏs′kə-pē, stîr′-) ► *n.* The viewing of objects as three-dimensional.

ster·e·o·type (stĕr′ē-ə-tīp′, stîr′-) ► *n.* **1.** A conventional, oversimplified conception, opinion, or image. **2.** One regarded as embodying or conforming to a set image or type. **3.** A metal printing plate cast from a matrix that is molded from a raised printing surface. ► *v.* **1.** To make a stereotype of or from. **2.** To characterize by a conventional stereotype. **—ster′e·o·typ′ic** (-tĭp′ĭk), **ster′e·o·typ′i·cal** *adj.*

ster·ile (stĕr′əl, -īl′) ► *adj.* **1.** Incapable of producing offspring. **2.** Producing little or no vegetation. **3.** Free from microorganisms. **4.** Not productive or effective. **—ste·ril′i·ty** (stə-rĭl′ĭ-tē) *n.*

ster·il·ize (stĕr′ə-līz′) ► *v.* **-ized, -iz·ing.** To make sterile. **—ster′il·i·za′tion** *n.*

ster·ling (stûr′lĭng) ► *n.* **1.** British money. **2.** Sterling silver. ► *adj.* **1.** Of or consisting of British money. **2.** Made of sterling silver. **3.** Of the highest quality.

sterling silver ► *n.* An alloy of 92.5% silver with copper or another metal.

stern[1] (stûrn) ► *adj.* **-er, -est.** **1.** Hard or severe in manner or character. **2.** Firm or unyielding; uncompromising. **3.** Inexorable; relentless. **—stern′ly** *adv.* **—stern′ness** *n.*

stern[2] (stûrn) ► *n.* The rear part of a ship or boat.

ster·num (stûr′nəm) ► *n., pl.* **-nums** or **-na** (-nə). A long flat bone that is situated along the center of the chest and articulates with the ribs; breastbone.

ster·oid (stîr′oid′, stĕr′-) ► *n.* Any of numerous fat-soluble organic compounds having as a basis 17 carbon atoms arranged in 4 rings and including the sterols and many hormones.

ster·ol (stîr′ôl′, stĕr′-) ► *n.* Any of a group of predominantly unsaturated solid alcohols of the steroid group, such as cholesterol, present in the fatty tissues of plants and animals.

stet (stĕt) ► *v.* **stet·ted, stet·ting.** *Print.* To nullify (a correction or deletion) in printed matter.

steth·o·scope (stĕth′ə-skōp′) ► *n.* An instrument used for listening to sounds produced within the body.

ste·ve·dore (stē′vĭ-dôr′) ► *n.* A worker who loads or unloads ships.

Ste·ven·son (stē′vən-sən), **Robert Louis Balfour** (1850–94) ► British writer.

stew (sto͞o, styo͞o) ► *v.* **1.** To cook (food) by simmering or boiling slowly. **2.** *Informal* To be in a state of anxiety or agitation. ► *n.* **1.** A dish, as of meat and vegetables, cooked by stewing. **2.** *Informal* Mental agitation.

stew·ard (sto͞o′ərd, styo͞o′-) ► *n.* **1.** One who manages another's property, finances, or other affairs. **2.** One in charge of the household affairs of a large estate, club, hotel, or resort. **3.** A ship's officer in charge of provisions and dining arrangements. **4.** An attendant on a ship or airplane. **—stew′ard·ship′** *n.*

stew·ard·ess (sto͞o′ər-dĭs, styo͞o′-) ► *n.* A woman flight attendant.

stick (stĭk) ► *n.* **1.** A long slender piece of wood, esp. a branch cut from a tree or shrub. **2.** A sticklike implement, such as a cane or baton, used for a particular purpose. **3.** Something slender and often cylindrical in form: *a stick of dynamite.* **4.** A poke or thrust. **5. sticks** *Informal* A remote area; backwoods. **6.** *Informal* A stiff, boring, or spiritless person. ► *v.* **stuck** (stŭk), **stick·ing.** **1.** To pierce, puncture, or penetrate with a pointed instrument. **2.** To fasten by forcing an end or point into something. **3.** To fasten or attach with an adhesive, such as glue or tape. **4.** To fix or impale on a pointed object. **5.** To put, thrust, or push. **6.** To be or become fixed or embedded in place. **7.** To persist, endure, or persevere. **8.** To be or become blocked, checked, or obstructed: *stuck in the mud.* **9.** To confuse or puzzle. **10.** To project or protrude. ***—phrasal verbs:*** **stick around** *Informal* To remain; linger. **stick up** To rob, esp. at gunpoint.

stick·er (stĭk′ər) ► *n.* **1.** One that sticks, as an adhesive label. **2.** A thorn or prickle.

stick·ler (stĭk′lər) ► *n.* One who insists on something unyieldingly.

stick shift ► *n.* An automotive transmission with a shift lever operated by hand.

stick-to-it·ive·ness (stĭk-to͞o′ĭ-tĭv-nĭs) ► *n.* *Informal* Unwavering tenacity.

stick·up (stĭk′ŭp′) ► *n.* *Slang* A robbery, esp. at gunpoint.

stick·y (stĭk′ē) ► *adj.* **-i·er, -i·est.** **1.** Sticking or tending to stick to a surface; adhesive. **2.** Warm and humid; muggy.

THESAURUS

stereotype *n.* —*See* CLICHÉ.
stereotype *v.* —*See* CLASSIFY, CONVENTIONALIZE.

stereotyped *adj.* —*See* CONVENTIONAL, TRITE.

stereotypical or **stereotypic** *adj.* —*See* TRITE.

sterile *adj.* **1.** Free or freed from microorganisms ► antiseptic, aseptic, disinfected, germ-free, germless, hygienic, sanitary, sanitized, sterilized. [*Compare* CLEAN.] **2.** Lacking originality ► uncreative, unimaginative, uninspired, uninventive, unoriginal. [*Compare* BORING, TRITE.] —*See also* BARREN (1), BARREN (2), DULL (1).

sterileness *n.* —*See* DULLNESS.

sterility *n.* **1.** The state or condition of being free from microorganisms ► asepsis, germlessness, sanitization, sterilization. [*Compare* PURITY.] **2.** The state or condition of being unable to reproduce ► barrenness, fruitlessness, impotence, infertility, unfruitfulness. —*See also* DULLNESS.

sterilization *n.* The state or condition of being free from microorganisms ► asepsis, germlessness, sanitization, sterility.

sterilize *v.* **1.** To render free of microorganisms ► decontaminate, disinfect, irradiate, sanitize. **2.** To render incapable of reproducing ► alter, castrate, fix, geld, neuter, spay, unsex.

sterilized *adj.* —*See* STERILE (1).

sterling *adj.* —*See* CHOICE (1).

stern[1] *adj.* —*See* FORBIDDING, SEVERE (1).

stern[2] *n.* —*See* BACK.

sternness *n.* —*See* SEVERITY.

stew *v.* —*See* BROOD, COOK.
stew *n.* —*See* AGITATION (2).

steward *n.* —*See* REPRESENTATIVE.

stewardship *n.* —*See* MANAGEMENT.

stewed *adj.* —*See* DRUNK.

stick *n.* **1.** A short straight piece of wood ► baton, branch, lath, stake, switch, twig, wand. [*Compare* ROD.] **2.** A fairly long, straight piece of solid material used especially as a support in walking ► cane, crook, pole, staff, stave, walking stick.

stick *v.* —*See* BAFFLE, BOND, CATCH (3), CHEAT (1), CUT (1), PLUNGE, POSITION.
stick around *v.* —*See* REMAIN.
stick in *v.* —*See* INTRODUCE (2).
stick out *v.* To be obtrusively conspicuous ► glare, stand out. ***Idioms:*** stare someone in the face, stick out like a sore thumb. —*See also* BULGE, ENDURE (1).
stick to *v.* —*See* KEEP (5).
stick up *v.* —*See* ROB.
stick with *v.* —*See* HOLD (1), IMPOSE ON, KEEP (5).

sticker *n.* —*See* SPIKE.

sticking power *n.* —*See* ENDURANCE.

stick-in-the-mud *n.* —*See* KILLJOY, SQUARE.

stick-to-itiveness *n.* —*See* DILIGENCE.

stickup *n.* —*See* LARCENY.

sticky *adj.* **1.** Having the property of adhering ► adhesive, gluey, glutinous, gooey, gummy, mucilaginous, tacky.

3. *Informal* Painful or difficult: *a sticky situation.* **—stick′i·ly** *adv.* **—stick′i·ness** *n.*

stiff (stĭf) ▸ *adj.* **-er, -est. 1.** Difficult to bend; rigid. **2.** Not moving or operating easily or freely: *stiff joints.* **3.** Drawn tightly; taut. **4a.** Rigidly formal. **b.** Lacking ease or grace. **5.** Not loose or fluid; thick: *stiff dough.* **6.** Blowing with strong steady force: *a stiff breeze.* **7.** Potent or strong: *a stiff drink.* **8.** Difficult; arduous. **9.** Harsh or severe: *a stiff penalty.* ▸ *n. Slang* A corpse. ▸ *v. Slang* To cheat (someone) of something owed. **—stiff′en** *v.* **—stiff′ly** *adv.* **—stiff′ness** *n.*

stiff-necked (stĭf′nĕkt′) ▸ *adj.* Stubborn and arrogant or aloof.

sti·fle (stī′fəl) ▸ *v.* **-fled, -fling. 1.** To extinguish or cut off: *stifle dissent.* **2.** To keep in or hold back; supress. **3.** To smother or suffocate. **—sti′fling·ly** *adv.*

stig·ma (stĭg′mə) ▸ *n., pl.* **stig·ma·ta** (stĭg-mä′tə, -măt′ə, stĭg′mə-) or **-mas. 1.** A mark or token of infamy or disgrace. **2. stigmata** Marks or sores corresponding to the crucifixion wounds of Jesus. **3.** *Bot.* The apex of a flower pistil, on which pollen is deposited. **—stig·mat′ic** (-măt′ĭk) *adj.*

stig·ma·tize (stĭg′mə-tīz′) ▸ *v.* **-tized, -tiz·ing. 1.** To characterize as disgraceful; brand. **2.** To mark with stigmata or a stigma. **—stig′ma·ti·za′tion** *n.*

stile (stīl) ▸ *n.* A set or series of steps for crossing a fence or wall.

sti·let·to (stĭ-lĕt′ō) ▸ *n., pl.* **-tos** or **-toes.** A small dagger with a slender tapering blade.

still[1] (stĭl) ▸ *adj.* **-er, -est. 1.** Free of sound. **2.** Low in sound; hushed or subdued. **3.** Not moving or in motion. **4.** Free from disturbance, agitation, or commotion. ▸ *n.* **1.** Silence; quiet. **2.** A still photograph, esp. one from a scene of a movie. ▸ *adv.* **1.** Without movement: *stand still.* **2.** Now as before; yet: *still unfinished.* **3.** In increasing amount or degree: *and still further complaints.* **4.** All the same; nevertheless. ▸ *v.* **1.** To make or become still. **2.** To allay; calm. **—still′ness** *n.*

still[2] (stĭl) ▸ *n.* **1.** An apparatus for distilling liquids, such as alcohols. **2.** A distillery.

still·birth (stĭl′bûrth′) ▸ *n.* The birth of a dead child or fetus. **—still′born** *adj.*

still life ▸ *n., pl.* **still lifes.** A painting, picture, or photograph of inanimate objects.

stilt (stĭlt) ▸ *n.* **1.** Either of a pair of long slender poles, each equipped with a raised footrest to enable the user to walk elevated above the ground. **2.** A tall supporting post, as for a dock.

stilt·ed (stĭl′tĭd) ▸ *adj.* Stiffly or artificially formal; stiff. **—stilt′ed·ly** *adv.*

stim·u·lant (stĭm′yə-lənt) ▸ *n.* **1.** An agent, esp. a drug, that temporarily arouses or accelerates physiological activity. **2.** A stimulus or incentive. **3.** An alcoholic drink. **—stim′u·lant** *adj.*

stim·u·late (stĭm′yə-lāt′) ▸ *v.* **-lat·ed, -lat·ing.** To rouse to activity or heightened action; excite. **—stim′u·la′tion** *n.* **—stim′u·la′tive** *adj.*

stim·u·lus (stĭm′yə-ləs) ▸ *n., pl.* **-li** (-lī′). Something that stimulates.

sting (stĭng) ▸ *v.* **stung** (stŭng), **sting·ing. 1.** To pierce or wound painfully with or as if with a sharp-pointed structure or organ. **2.** To cause to feel a sharp, smarting pain. **3.** To cause to suffer keenly. ▸ *n.* **1.** The act of stinging. **2.** The wound or pain caused by or as if by stinging. **3.** A sharp, piercing organ or part, as of a bee or wasp. **—sting′er** *n.*

sting·ray (stĭng′rā′) ▸ *n.* A ray having a whiplike tail armed with one or more venomous spines.

stin·gy (stĭn′jē) ▸ *adj.* **-gi·er, -gi·est. 1.** Giving or spending reluctantly. **2.** Scanty or meager. **—stin′gi·ly** *adv.* **—stin′gi·ness** *n.*

stink (stĭngk) ▸ *v.* **stank** (stăngk) or **stunk** (stŭngk), **stunk, stink·ing. 1.** To emit a strong foul odor. **2.** To be offensive or abhorrent. **3.** *Slang* To be extremely bad. ▸ *n.* **1.** A stench. **2.** *Slang* A fuss; uproar. **—stink′er** *n.*

stink·bug (stĭngk′bŭg′) ▸ *n.* Any of numerous insects that emit a foul odor.

stint (stĭnt) ▸ *v.* **1.** To restrict or limit, as in amount or number. **2.** To be frugal or sparing. ▸ *n.* **1.** A fixed or allotted amount of work. **2.** A limitation or restriction. **3.** A period of time spent in an activity. **—stint′er** *n.*

sti·pend (stī′pĕnd′, -pənd) ▸ *n.* A fixed and regular payment, such as a salary or allowance.

stip·ple (stĭp′əl) ▸ *v.* **-pled, -pling. 1.** To draw, engrave, or paint in dots or short strokes. **2.** To apply (e.g., paint) in dots or short strokes. **—stip′ple** *n.*

stip·u·late (stĭp′yə-lāt′) ▸ *v.* **-lat·ed, -lat·ing. 1.** To lay down as a condition of an agreement. **2.** To guarantee or promise

THESAURUS

[*Compare* VISCOUS.] 2. Damp and warm ▸ humid, muggy, soggy, sultry. [*Compare* DAMP, HOT, RAINY, WET.] 3. *Informal* Hard to deal with or get out of ▸ rough, tight, tricky. [*Compare* DELICATE.]

sticky-fingered *adj.* —*See* THIEVISH.

stiff *adj.* 1. Rigidly constrained or formal; lacking grace and spontaneity ▸ buckram, starchy, stilted, wooden. [*Compare* COOL, FORCED, PRUDISH.] 2. Having a high concentration of the distinguishing ingredient ▸ concentrated, potent, strong. [*Compare* STRAIGHT.] —*See also* FIRM[1] (3), RIGID, STEEP[1] (2).

stiff *n.* —*See* BODY (2), DRUNKARD, HARD (3), MISER.

stiffen *v.* —*See* COAGULATE, HARDEN (2), TENSE.

stiff-necked *adj.* —*See* STUBBORN (1).

stifle *v.* —*See* CENSOR (2), CHOKE, MUFFLE, REPRESS.

stifling *adj.* —*See* AIRLESS (1), REPRESSIVE.

stigma *n.* —*See* STAIN.

stigmatize *v.* To cause to feel embarrassment, dishonor, and often guilt ▸ brand, mortify, reproach, shame. ***Idioms:*** put to shame, put to the blush. [*Compare* BELITTLE, DENIGRATE, EMBARRASS, HUMBLE.] —*See also* DISGRACE.

still *adj.* Free from disturbance, agitation, or commotion ▸ calm, halcyon, pacific, peaceful, placid, quiet, serene, tranquil, untroubled. [*Compare* CALM, IDYLLIC.] —*See also* AIRLESS (2), MOTIONLESS, SILENT (1).

still *n.* —*See* SILENCE (1).

still *adv.* 1. In spite of a preceding event or consideration ▸ all the same, anyway, however, nevertheless, nonetheless, yet. *Informal:* still and all. ***Idiom:*** be that as it may. 2. To a more extreme degree ▸ even, ever more so, yet. —*See also* ADDITIONALLY.

still *v.* —*See* PACIFY, SILENCE.

stillness *n.* An absence of motion or disturbance ▸ calm, calmness, hush, lull, peace, peacefulness, placidity, placidness, quiet, quietness, serenity, tranquillity, untroubledness. —*See also* SILENCE (1).

stilted *adj.* Rigidly constrained or formal; lacking grace and spontaneity ▸ buckram, starchy, stiff, wooden. [*Compare* COOL, FORCED, PRUDISH.]

stimulant *n.* —*See* DRUG (2), STIMULUS, TONIC.

stimulate *v.* —*See* ENERGIZE, PROVOKE.

stimulating *adj.* —*See* INVIGORATING.

stimulation *n.* —*See* ENCOURAGEMENT, STIMULUS.

stimulator *n.* —*See* STIMULUS.

stimulus *n.* Something that causes and encourages an action or response ▸ catalyst, encouragement, fillip, goad, impetus, impulse, incentive, inducement, motivation, prod, push, spur, stimulant, stimulation, stimulator. [*Compare* CAUSE, IMPACT.] —*See also* PROVOCATION (1).

sting *v.* —*See* CHEAT (1), CUT (1), HURT (2).

sting *n.* —*See* CHEAT (1), EDGE, KICK, PAIN.

stinging *adj.* —*See* BITING, BITTER (2), PAINFUL.

stingy *adj.* Ungenerously or pettily reluctant to spend money ▸ cheap, close, close-fisted, costive, hard-fisted, mean, miserly, niggard, niggardly, parsimonious, penny-pinching, penurious, petty, pinching, tight, tightfisted. [*Compare* GREEDY.] —*See also* MEAGER.

stink *v.* To have or give off a foul odor ▸ reek, smell. ***Idiom:*** stink (*or* smell) to high heaven.

stink *n.* —*See* COMPLAINT, STENCH.

stinking *adj.* —*See* DRUNK, SMELLY.

stinko *adj.* —*See* DRUNK, SHODDY.

stint *v.* —*See* SCRIMP.

stint *n.* —*See* TASK (1), TURN (1).

stipend *n.* —*See* WAGE.

stipple *v.* —*See* SPECKLE.

stipulate *v.* To state specifically ▸ detail,

(something) in an agreement. **—stip′u·la′tion** *n.*

stir[1] (stûr) ▸ *v.* **stirred, stir·ring. 1.** To pass an implement through in circular motions so as to mix or cool the contents. **2.** To change or cause to change position slightly. **3a.** To rouse, as from indifference, and prompt to action. **b.** To provoke: *stir up trouble.* **4.** To excite strong feelings in. ▸ *n.* **1.** An act of stirring. **2.** A slight movement. **3.** A disturbance or commotion. **—stir′rer** *n.*

stir[2] (stûr) ▸ *n. Slang* Prison.

stir-fry (stûr′frī′) ▸ *v.* To fry quickly in a small amount of oil while stirring continuously.

stir·ring (stûr′ĭng) ▸ *adj.* **1.** Exciting; rousing. **2.** Active; lively. **—stir′ring·ly** *adv.*

stir·rup (stûr′əp, stĭr′-) ▸ *n.* A loop or ring hung from either side of a horse's saddle to support the rider's foot.

stitch (stĭch) ▸ *n.* **1.** A link, loop, or knot formed by a threaded needle in sewing or surgical suturing. **2.** A single loop of yarn around a knitting needle. **3.** A method of sewing, knitting, or crocheting: *a purl stitch.* **4.** A sudden sharp pain. ▸ *v.* **1.** To fasten, join, or ornament with or as if with stitches. **2.** To sew. **—stitch′er** *n.* **—stitch′er·y** *n.*

stoat (stōt) ▸ *n., pl.* **stoat** or **stoats.** *Chiefly Brit.* The ermine, esp. in its brown color phase.

sto·chas·tic (stō-kăs′tĭk) ▸ *adj. Math.* Involving or containing random variables.

stock (stŏk) ▸ *n.* **1.** A supply accumulated for future use; store. **2.** The total merchandise kept on hand by a commercial establishment. **3.** Domestic animals; livestock. **4a.** The capital or fund that a corporation raises through the sale of shares. **b.** The number of shares that each stockholder possesses. **5.** *Bot.* A trunk or main stem. **6a.** The original progenitor of a family line. **b.** The descendants of a common ancestor. **c.** Ancestry or lineage. **d.** A group of related languages. **7.** The raw material out of which something is made. **8.** The broth in which meat, fish, bones, or vegetables are simmered, used in preparing soup or sauces. **9.** A supporting structure, block, or frame: *a gun stock.* **10. stocks** A wooden device with holes for confining the ankles and sometimes the wrists, formerly used for punishment. **11.** A company of actors and technicians attached to a single theater and performing in repertory. **12.** Confidence or credence. ▸ *v.* **1.** To provide with stock. **2.** To keep and store for future sale or use. ▸ *adj.* **1.** Kept regularly in stock. **2.** Routine: *a stock answer.*

stock·ade (stŏ-kād′) ▸ *n.* A defensive barrier made of strong posts or timbers driven upright side by side into the ground.

stock·bro·ker (stŏk′brō′kər) ▸ *n.* One that acts as an agent in buying and selling stocks or other securities.

stock car ▸ *n.* An automobile of a standard make modified for racing.

stock exchange ▸ *n.* **1.** A place where stocks, bonds, or other securities are bought and sold. **2.** An association of stockbrokers.

stock·hold·er (stŏk′hōl′dər) ▸ *n.* A shareholder.

Stock·holm (stŏk′hōlm′, -hōm′) ▸ The capital of Sweden, in the E part on the Baltic Sea.

stock·ing (stŏk′ĭng) ▸ *n.* A close-fitting, usu. knitted covering for the foot and leg.

stocking cap ▸ *n.* A long tapering knitted cap.

stock market ▸ *n.* **1.** See **stock exchange. 2.** The buying and selling of stocks.

stock·pile (stŏk′pīl′) ▸ *n.* A supply stored for future use. **—stock′pile′** *v.*

stock-still (stŏk′stĭl′) ▸ *adj.* Completely still; motionless.

stock·y (stŏk′ē) ▸ *adj.* **-i·er, -i·est.** Solidly built; thickset. **—stock′i·ness** *n.*

stock·yard (stŏk′yärd′) ▸ *n.* A large enclosed yard in which livestock are kept until slaughtered or sold.

stodg·y (stŏj′ē) ▸ *adj.* **-i·er, -i·est. 1a.** Dull, unimaginative, and commonplace. **b.** Prim or pompous; stuffy. **2.** Indigestible; heavy. **—stodg′i·ly** *adv.* **—stodg′i·ness** *n.*

sto·ic (stō′ĭk) ▸ *n.* **1.** One who is seemingly indifferent to or unaffected by pleasure or pain. **2. Stoic** A member of a Greek school of philosophy advocating the calm acceptance of all occurrences. ▸ *adj.* also **sto·i·cal** (-ĭ-kəl) Seemingly indifferent to or unaffected by pleasure or pain; impassive. **—sto′i·cal·ly** *adv.* **—sto′i·cism** *n.*

stoke (stōk) ▸ *v.* **stoked, stok·ing. 1.** To stir up and feed (a fire or furnace). **2.** To tend a furnace, as on a steamship or steam locomotive. **—stok′er** *n.*

stole[1] (stōl) ▸ *n.* **1.** A long scarf worn by some members of the Christian clergy while officiating. **2.** A woman's long scarf of cloth or fur worn about the shoulders.

stole[2] (stōl) ▸ *v.* P.t. of **steal.**

sto·len (stō′lən) ▸ *v.* P.part. of **steal.**

stol·id (stŏl′ĭd) ▸ *adj.* **-er, -est.** Having or revealing little emotion; impassive. **—sto·lid′i·ty** *n.*

sto·ma (stō′mə) ▸ *n., pl.* **-ma·ta** (-mə-tə) or **-mas.** A small opening, esp. one of the minute pores in a leaf through which gases and water vapor pass.

stom·ach (stŭm′ək) ▸ *n.* **1.** A large saclike digestive organ of the alimentary canal, located in vertebrates between the esophagus and the small intestine. **2.** The abdomen or belly. **3.** An appetite for food. **4.** Desire; inclination. ▸ *v.* To bear; tolerate.

stom·ach·ache (stŭm′ək-āk′) ▸ *n.* Pain in the stomach or abdomen.

stom·ach·er (stŭm′ə-kər) ▸ *n.* A decorative garment formerly worn over the chest and stomach, esp. by women.

sto·mach·ic (stə-măk′ĭk) ▸ *adj.* Beneficial to or stimulating digestion in the stomach. **—sto·mach′ic** *n.*

stomp (stŏmp, stômp) ▸ *v.* To tread or trample heavily or violently (on).

stone (stōn) ▸ *n.* **1.** Hardened earthy or mineral matter; rock. **2.** A small piece of rock. **3.** A gem or precious stone. **4.** The hard covering enclosing the seed in certain fruits, such as the cherry. **5.** A mineral concretion in an organ, such as the kidney. **6.** *pl.* **stone.** A unit of weight in Great Britain, 14 lbs. (6.4 kg). ▸ *v.* **stoned, ston·ing.** To pelt or kill with stones.

Stone Age ▸ *n.* **1.** The earliest known period of human culture, marked by the use of stone tools. **2.** *Slang* An extremely backward era or state.

stoned (stōnd) ▸ *adj. Slang* Drunk or intoxicated.

stone·wall (stōn′wôl′) ▸ *v. Informal* To refuse to answer or cooperate (with).

stone·ware (stōn′wâr′) ▸ *n.* A heavy, nonporous pottery.

THESAURUS

particularize, provide, specify. [*Compare* ASSERT, DESCRIBE, DESIGNATE, DICTATE.] —*See also* CONTRACT (1).

stipulation *n.* —*See* PROVISION.

stir[1] *v.* To move or cause to move slightly ▸ budge, move, shift. —*See also* AROUSE, BEAT (6), BLOW[1] (1), CAUSE, FIRE (1), MIX (1), WAKE[1].

stir *n.* —*See* AGITATION (1), AGITATION (3), MOTION, SENSATION (2).

stir[2] *n.* —*See* JAIL.

stir-fry *v.* —*See* COOK.

stirring *adj.* —*See* AFFECTING.

stitch *n.* —*See* PAIN.

stock *n.* The main ascending part of a plant, which supports the other parts ▸ stalk, stem, trunk. [*Compare* SHOOT.] —*See also* ANCESTRY, FAMILY (2), GOOD (2), HOARD.

stock *v.* To have for sale ▸ carry, deal (in), keep, offer. [*Compare* SELL.]

stock *adj.* —*See* ORDINARY, TRITE.

stockpile *n.* —*See* HOARD.

stockpile *v.* —*See* SAVE (1).

stock-still *adj.* —*See* MOTIONLESS.

stocky *adj.* Short, heavy, and solidly built ▸ blocky, chunky, compact, dumpy, heavyset, squat, stodgy, stubby, stumpy, thick, thickset. [*Compare* BULKY, FAT.]

stodginess *n.* —*See* DULLNESS.

stodgy *adj.* —*See* DULL (1), STOCKY.

stoic *adj.* —*See* PATIENT.

stoicism *n.* —*See* PATIENCE.

stoked *adj.* —*See* THRILLED.

stole *n.* WRAP.

stolid *adj.* —*See* COLD (2).

stolidity or **stolidness** *n.* —*See* APATHY.

stomach *n.* —*See* APPETITE.

stomach *v.* —*See* ENDURE (1).

stomp *v.* To step on heavily and repeatedly so as to crush, injure, or destroy ▸ stamp, tramp, trample, tread, tromp. [*Compare* CRUSH.] —*See also* TRUDGE.

stomping ground *n.* —*See* HAUNT.

stoned *adj.* —*See* DRUGGED, DRUNK.

ston·y (stō′nē) ▸ *adj.* **-i·er, -i·est. 1.** Covered with or full of stones. **2.** Resembling stone. **3.** Cold; impassive: *a stony expression.* **—ston′i·ly** *adv.* **—ston′i·ness** *n.*

stood (stŏŏd) ▸ *v.* P.t. and p.part. of **stand**.

stooge (stōōj) ▸ *n.* **1.** The straight man to a comedian. **2.** A willing dupe. **3.** *Slang* A stool pigeon.

stool (stōōl) ▸ *n.* **1.** A backless and armless single seat. **2.** A low bench or support for the feet. **3.** A toilet. **4.** Waste excreted from the bowel.

stool pigeon ▸ *n.* **1.** *Slang* A person acting as a decoy or informer, esp. for the police. **2.** A pigeon used as a decoy.

stoop[1] (stōōp) ▸ *v.* **1.** To bend forward and down. **2.** To walk or stand with the head and upper back bent forward. **3a.** To lower or debase oneself. **b.** To condescend. ▸ *n.* The act, habit, or posture of stooping.

stoop[2] (stōōp) ▸ *n.* A small porch or staircase at the entrance of a house or building.

stop (stŏp) ▸ *v.* **stopped, stop·ping. 1.** To close (an opening) by covering, filling in, or plugging up. **2.** To obstruct or prevent the flow or passage of. **3.** To bring or come to an end or halt. **4.** To desist from; cease. **5.** To restrain; prevent. **6.** To adjust a vibrating medium to produce a desired pitch. **7.** To make a brief halt, visit, or stay. ▸ *n.* **1.** The act of stopping or the condition of being stopped. **2.** A finish; end. **3.** A stay or visit. **4.** A place stopped at: *a bus stop.* **5.** A stopper. **6.** An f-stop. **7.** A mark of punctuation, esp. a period. **8a.** The act of stopping a string or hole on an instrument. **b.** A tuned set of pipes, as in an organ. **—stop′page** (stŏp′ĭj) *n.*

stop·cock (stŏp′kŏk′) ▸ *n.* A valve that regulates the flow of fluid through a pipe.

stop·gap (stŏp′găp′) ▸ *n.* A temporary expedient.

stop·light (stŏp′līt′) ▸ *n.* See **traffic light.**

stop·o·ver (stŏp′ō′vər) ▸ *n.* A place visited briefly in the course of a journey.

stop·per (stŏp′ər) ▸ *n.* A device, such as a plug, inserted to close an opening.

stop·watch (stŏp′wŏch′) ▸ *n.* A watch that can be instantly started and stopped by pushing a button and used to measure an exact duration of time.

stor·age (stôr′ĭj) ▸ *n.* **1a.** The act of storing or the state of being stored. **b.** A space for storing. **2.** The price charged for keeping goods stored.

storage battery ▸ *n.* A group of reversible or rechargeable electric cells acting as a unit.

store (stôr) ▸ *n.* **1.** A place where merchandise is offered for sale; shop. **2.** A stock or supply reserved for future use. **3. stores** Supplies, esp. of food, clothing, or arms. **4.** A storehouse. ▸ *v.* **stored, stor·ing. 1.** To reserve or put away for future use. **2.** To fill, supply, or stock. **3.** To deposit in a storehouse for safekeeping. **4.** To copy (data) into memory or onto a storage device, such as a hard disk.

store·front (stôr′frŭnt′) ▸ *n.* **1.** The side of a store facing a street. **2.** A room in a commercial building that is at street level.

store·house (stôr′hous′) ▸ *n.* **1.** A building in which goods are stored; warehouse. **2.** An abundant source or supply.

store·keep·er (stôr′kē′pər) ▸ *n.* One who keeps a retail store or shop.

store·room (stôr′rōōm′, -rŏŏm′) ▸ *n.* A room in which things are stored.

sto·rey (stôr′ē) ▸ *n.* *Chiefly Brit.* Var. of **story**[2].

sto·ried (stôr′ēd) ▸ *adj.* Celebrated or famous in history or story.

stork (stôrk) ▸ *n.* A large, chiefly Old World wading bird with long legs and a long straight bill.

storm (stôrm) ▸ *n.* **1.** An atmospheric disturbance with strong winds accompanied by rain, snow, or other precipitation. **2.** A violent disturbance or upheaval: *a storm of protest.* **3.** A sudden overwhelming attack. ▸ *v.* **1a.** To blow forcefully. **b.** To rain, snow, hail, or sleet. **2.** To be extremely angry. **3.** To move or rush violently or angrily: *stormed into the room.* **4.** To assault or overwhelm with sudden force. **—storm′i·ness** *n.* **—storm′y** *adj.*

sto·ry[1] (stôr′ē) ▸ *n., pl.* **-ries. 1.** An account of an event or a series of events. **2.** A prose or verse narrative intended to entertain. **3.** A short story. **4.** A news report. **5.** An explanation: *What's the story on these bills?* **6.** A lie.

sto·ry[2] (stôr′ē) ▸ *n., pl.* **-ries. 1.** A complete horizontal division of a building. **2.** The set of rooms on the same level of a building.

sto·ry·tell·er (stôr′ē-tĕl′ər) ▸ *n.* One who tells stories. **—sto′ry·tell′ing** *n.*

stoup (stōōp) ▸ *n.* A basin for holy water at a church.

stout (stout) ▸ *adj.* **-er, -est. 1.** Resolute or bold in character; valiant. **2.** Strong in body; sturdy. **3.** Substantial; solid. **4.** Thickset; fat. ▸ *n.* A strong, very dark beer or ale. **—stout′ly** *adv.* **—stout′ness** *n.*

stout·heart·ed (stout′här′tĭd) ▸ *adj.* Brave; courageous. **—stout′heart′ed·ly** *adv.* **—stout′heart′ed·ness** *n.*

THESAURUS

stonyhearted *adj.* —*See* CALLOUS.

stooge *n.* —*See* PAWN[2].

stool *v.* —*See* INFORM (2).

stoolie or **stool pigeon** *n.* —*See* INFORMER.

stoop *v.* To bend or lower the body ▸ arch, bend (down), bow, crouch, huddle, hump, hunch, hunker (down), scrunch, squat. [*Compare* BOW[1], SLOUCH, SIT.] —*See also* CONDESCEND (1).

stop *v.* **1.** To come to a cessation ▸ cease, check, desist, discontinue, halt, leave off, quit, stall, surcease. *Idiom:* come to a halt (*or* standstill *or* stop). [*Compare* CONCLUDE.] **2.** To prevent the occurrence or continuation of a movement, action, or operation ▸ arrest, belay, cease, check, discontinue, forbear, halt, idle, immobilize, stall, stay, surcease, tie up. *Idioms:* bring to a standstill (*or* screeching halt), call a halt to, cut short, put a stop to. [*Compare* HINDER, RESTRAIN, SUSPEND.] —*See also* ABANDON (2), BREAK (5), DROP (4), FILL (2), VETO, VISIT.

stop *n.* **1.** The act of stopping ▸ cessation, check, cutoff, discontinuance, discontinuation, halt, idling, stay, stoppage, surcease. **2.** The condition of being stopped ▸ cease, cessation, discontinuance, discontinuation, gridlock, halt, idleness, immobilization, jam, standstill, stoppage, surcease, tie-up. [*Compare* BREAK.] **3.** A stopping place along a route for picking up or dropping off passengers ▸ depot, station, terminal, terminus. **4.** A remaining in a place as a guest or lodger ▸ sojourn, stay, stopover, visit. —*See also* BAR (1), END (1), PLUG, VISIT (1).

stopcock *n.* —*See* FAUCET.

stopgap *n.* —*See* MAKESHIFT.

stopgap *adj.* —*See* TEMPORARY (2).

stopover *n.* A remaining in a place as a guest or lodger ▸ sojourn, stay, stop, visit.

stoppage *n.* A cessation of normal activity, caused by an accident or strike, for example ▸ gridlock, immobilization, jam, tie-up. —*See also* STOP (1), STOP (2).

stopper *n.* —*See* PLUG.

stopping point *n.* —*See* END (1).

stopple *n.* —*See* PLUG.

store *n.* A retail establishment where merchandise is sold ▸ boutique, emporium, outlet, shop. —*See also* DEPOSITORY, HOARD.

store *v.* To have or put in a customary place ▸ cache, keep, put. —*See also* SAVE (1).

storehouse *n.* —*See* DEPOSITORY.

storied *adj.* —*See* FAMOUS.

storm *n.* An atmospheric disturbance characterized by strong winds and precipitation ▸ blizzard, blow, cyclone, electrical storm, gale, hurricane, ice storm, monsoon, rainstorm, snowstorm, squall, tempest, thunderstorm, typhoon. [*Compare* RAIN.] —*See also* BARRAGE.

storm *v.* To manifest strong winds and precipitation ▸ blow (up), set in, squall. [*Compare* RAIN.] —*See also* ANGER (2), ATTACK (1).

stormy *adj.* —*See* TROUBLED, ROUGH (2).

story *n.* **1.** A recounting of past events ▸ account, chronicle, description, history, narration, narrative, record, report, saga, statement, version. **2.** A narrative not based on fact ▸ fable, fiction, novel, romance. —*See also* ITEM, LIE[2], PLOT (1), YARN.

story line *n.* —*See* PLOT (1).

storyteller *n.* —*See* LIAR.

stout *adj.* —*See* BRAVE, BULKY (2), FAT (1), STRONG (2).

stouthearted *adj.* —*See* BRAVE.

stoutheartedness *n.* —*See* COURAGE.

stove[1] (stōv) ► *n.* An apparatus in which electricity or a fuel is used to furnish heat, as for cooking or heating.
stove[2] (stōv) ► *v.* P.t. and p.part. of **stave.**
stove·pipe (stōv′pīp′) ► *n.* **1.** A pipe used to conduct smoke from a stove into a chimney flue. **2.** A man's tall silk hat.
stow (stō) ► *v.* **1.** To put or store away compactly. **2.** To fill by packing tightly. ***—phrasal verb:*** **stow away** To be a stowaway.
stow·a·way (stō′ə-wā′) ► *n.* A person who hides aboard a vehicle, esp. a ship, to obtain free passage.
Stowe (stō), **Harriet (Elizabeth) Beecher** (1811–96) ► Amer. writer.
stra·bis·mus (strə-bĭz′məs) ► *n.* A visual defect in which one eye cannot focus with the other on an objective because of imbalance of the eye muscles. **—stra·bis′mal, stra·bis′mic** *adj.*
strad·dle (străd′l) ► *v.* **-dled, -dling. 1.** To stand or sit with a leg on each side of. **2.** To appear to favor both sides of (an issue). **—strad′dle** *n.* **—strad′dler** *n.*
strafe (strāf) ► *v.* **strafed, straf·ing.** To attack with machine-gun fire from a low-flying aircraft.
strag·gle (străg′əl) ► *v.* **-gled, -gling. 1.** To stray or fall behind. **2.** To spread out in a scattered group. **—strag′gler** *n.* **—strag′gly** *adj.*
straight (strāt) ► *adj.* **-er, -est. 1.** Extending continuously in the same direction without curving. **2.** Having no waves or bends. **3.** Erect; upright. **4.** Level or even. **5.** Direct and candid: *a straight answer.* **6a.** Honest; fair. **b.** Right; correct. **7.** Neatly arranged; orderly. **8.** Uninterrupted; consecutive: *five straight days.* **9.** Heterosexual. **10.** *Slang* Not being under the influence of alcohol or drugs. **11.** Not deviating from the normal or usual; conventional. **12.** Undiluted: *straight bourbon.* ► *adv.* In a straight course or manner. ► *n.* **1.** Something that is straight. **2.** A straightaway. **3.** *Games* A poker hand containing five cards of various suits in numerical sequence. **4a.** A conventional person. **b.** A heterosexual person. **—straight′ly** *adv.* **—straight′ness** *n.*
straight angle ► *n.* An angle of 180°.
straight·a·way (strāt′ə-wā′) ► *n.* A straight course, stretch, or track, esp. the stretch of a racecourse from the last turn to the finish. ► *adv.* (strāt′ə-wā′) At once; immediately.
straight·edge (strāt′ĕj′) ► *n.* A rigid flat rectangular bar with a straight edge for testing or drawing straight lines.
straight·en (strāt′n) ► *v.* To make or become straight or straighter. ***—phrasal verb:*** **straighten out** To reform or correct. **—straight′en·er** *n.*
straight·for·ward (strāt-fôr′wərd) ► *adj.* **1.** Direct. **2.** Honest; frank. ► *adv.* In a direct or frank manner. **—straight·for′ward·ly** *adv.* **—straight·for′ward·ness** *n.* **—straight·for′wards** *adv.*
straight man ► *n.* An actor who serves as a foil for a comedian.
straight razor ► *n.* A razor consisting of a blade hinged to a handle into which it slips when not in use.
straight·way (strāt′wā′, -wā′) ► *adv.* At once.
strain[1] (strān) ► *v.* **1.** To pull, draw, or stretch tight. **2.** To exert or tax to the utmost. **3.** To injure or impair by overuse or overexertion; wrench. **4.** To stretch or force beyond the proper or legitimate limit. **5.** To pass through a filtering agent such as a strainer. **6.** To strive hard. ► *n.* **1.** The act of straining. **2a.** A great effort, force, or tension. **b.** A great pressure, demand, or stress. **3.** A deformation produced by stress.
strain[2] (strān) ► *n.* **1.** The collective descendants of a common ancestor. **2.** Ancestry; lineage. **3.** *Biol.* A group of organisms of the same species, having distinctive characteristics but not usu. considered a separate breed or variety. **4.** A kind or sort. **5a.** An inborn tendency or character. **b.** A streak; trace. **6.** often **strains** *Mus.* A tune or air.
strain·er (strā′nər) ► *n.* **1.** One that strains. **2.** A device, such as a filter or sieve, used to separate liquids from solids.
strait (strāt) ► *n.* also **straits 1.** A narrow channel joining two larger bodies of water. **2.** A position of difficulty: *in desperate straits.* ► *adj.* **1.** *Archaic* Narrow. **2.** Strict, rigid, or righteous.
strait·en (strāt′n) ► *v.* **1.** To make narrow or restricted. **2.** To put into difficulties.
strait·jack·et also **straight·jack·et** (strāt′jăk′ĭt) ► *n.* A jacketlike garment used to bind the arms tightly as a means of restraining a violent patient or prisoner.
strait-laced (strāt′lāst′) ► *adj.* Excessively strict in behavior, morality, or opinions.
strand[1] (strănd) ► *n.* A shore; beach. ► *v.* **1.** To drive or be driven aground. **2.** To bring into or leave in a difficult or helpless position.
strand[2] (strănd) ► *n.* **1.** Any of a number of fibers or filaments that have been twisted together, as to form a cable or rope. **2.** A ropelike string, as of beads.
strange (strānj) ► *adj.* **strang·er, strang·est. 1.** Not previously known; unfamiliar. **2.** Out of the ordinary; unusual or striking. **3.** Not of one's own locality or kind; exotic. **4.** Not comfortable or at ease. **5.** Not accustomed or conditioned. **—strange′ly** *adv.* **—strange′ness** *n.*
strang·er (strān′jər) ► *n.* **1.** One who is neither a friend nor an acquaintance. **2.** A foreigner, newcomer, or outsider.
stran·gle (străng′gəl) ► *v.* **-gled, -gling. 1a.** To kill by choking or suffocating. **b.** To smother. **2.** To suppress or stifle. **—stran′gler** *n.*
stran·gu·late (străng′gyə-lāt′) ► *v.* **-lat·ed, -lat·ing. 1.** To strangle. **2.** *Pathol.* To constrict so as to cut off the flow of blood or other fluid. **—stran′gu·la′tion** *n.*
strap (străp) ► *n.* A long narrow strip of pliant material, such as leather, often with a fastener for binding or securing objects. ► *v.* **strapped, strap·ping. 1.** To fasten or secure with a strap. **2.** To beat with a strap. **3.** To strop (a razor).
strap·less (străp′lĭs) ► *adj.* Having no strap or straps. ► *n.* A strapless garment.
strapped (străpt) ► *adj.* *Informal* In financial need.
strap·ping (străp′ĭng) ► *adj.* Tall and sturdy; robust.

THESAURUS

stow *v.* —*See* SAVE (1).
strabismal or **strabismic** *adj.* Marked by or affected with a squint ► cross-eyed, squint-eyed, squinty.
straddle *v.* To sit or stand with a leg on each side of ► bestride, stride. —*See also* SPRAWL.
straggle *v.* —*See* SPREAD (2).
straggler *n.* —*See* LAGGARD.
straight *adj.* Not diluted or mixed with other substances ► full-strength, neat, plain, pure, unblended, undiluted, unmixed. [*Compare* STRONG.] —*See also* CONVENTIONAL, DIRECT (1), EVEN (1), FRANK, HONEST, REALISTIC (1).
straight *adv.* —*See* DIRECTLY (1), DIRECTLY (3).
straightaway *adv.* —*See* DIRECTLY (1), IMMEDIATELY (1).
straighten *v.* —*See* EVEN, TIDY (1).
straighten out *v.* —*See* SETTLE (2).
straightforward *adj.* —*See* DEFINITE (1), DIRECT (1), FRANK.
straight-from-the-shoulder *adj.* —*See* FRANK.
straight off *adv.* —*See* IMMEDIATELY (1).
straight-out *adj.* —*See* FRANK.
straight-shooting *adj.* —*See* FRANK, HONEST.
strain[1] *v.* To injure a bodily part by twisting ► sprain, turn, twist, wrench. [*Compare* HURT.] —*See also* BURDEN[1], DRAIN (1), LABOR, OVERDO.
strain *n.* —*See* BURDEN[1] (1), EFFORT, INTENSITY, PRESSURE.
strain[2] *n.* An inherent, contrasting, or unexpected quality, especially in a person's character ► streak, vein. [*Compare* DISPOSITION, INCLINATION.] —*See also* MELODY.
strained *adj.* Not natural or spontaneous ► contrived, effortful, forced, labored. [*Compare* AWKWARD, STIFF.]
strait *n.* —*See* CHANNEL.
strait-laced *adj.* —*See* PRUDISH.
straits *n.* —*See* EMERGENCY, POVERTY, PREDICAMENT.
strand *n.* Something suggesting the continuousness of a filament ► hairline, thread. [*Compare* THREAD.]
strange *adj.* —*See* ECCENTRIC, EXOTIC, FOREIGN (1), FUNNY (3), WEIRD.
strangely *adv.* —*See* UNUSUALLY.
stranger *n.* —*See* FOREIGNER.
strangle *v.* —*See* CHOKE, REPRESS.
strangulate *v.* —*See* CHOKE.
strap *n.* —*See* BAND[1].
strap *v.* —*See* BEAT (2), FASTEN.
strapped *adj.* —*See* POOR.
strapping *adj.* —*See* LUSTY, MUSCULAR.

stra·ta (strā′tə, străt′ə) ▸ *n.* Pl. of **stratum**.

strat·a·gem (străt′ə-jəm) ▸ *n.* **1.** A maneuver designed to deceive or surprise an enemy. **2.** A scheme for achieving an objective.

strat·e·gy (străt′ə-jē) ▸ *n., pl.* **-gies. 1.** The overall planning and conduct of large-scale military operations. **2.** A plan of action. **3.** The art or skill of using stratagems, as in politics and business. **—stra·te′gic** (strə-tē′jĭk) *adj.* **—stra·te′gi·cal·ly** *adv.* **—strat′e·gist** *n.*

Strat·ford-up·on-Av·on (străt′fərd-ə-pŏn-ā′vən, -pôn-) also **Strat·ford-on-Av·on** (-ŏn-, -ôn-) ▸ A municipal borough of central England; birthplace of William Shakespeare.

strat·i·fy (străt′ə-fī′) ▸ *v.* **-fied, -fy·ing. 1.** To form, arrange, or deposit in layers. **2.** To arrange or separate into social levels. **—strat′i·fi·ca′tion** *n.*

strat·o·sphere (străt′ə-sfîr′) ▸ *n.* The region of the atmosphere above the troposphere and below the mesosphere. **—strat′o·spher′ic** (-sfîr′ĭk, -sfĕr′-) *adj.*

stra·tum (strā′təm, străt′əm) ▸ *n., pl.* **-ta** (-tə) or **-tums. 1.** A horizontal layer of material, esp. one of several layers of sedimentary rock. **2.** A level of society composed of people with similar social or economic status.

strat·us (străt′əs, strā′təs) ▸ *n., pl.* **-i** (-ī). A low-altitude cloud formation consisting of a horizontal layer of gray clouds.

straw (strô) ▸ *n.* **1a.** Stalks of threshed grain. **b.** A single stalk of threshed grain. **2.** A slender tube used for sucking up a liquid. **3.** Something of little value.

straw·ber·ry (strô′bĕr′ē) ▸ *n.* **1.** A low-growing plant having white flowers and red, fleshy, edible fruit. **2.** The fruit itself.

straw boss ▸ *n. Informal* A temporary boss or crew leader.

straw vote ▸ *n.* An unofficial vote or poll.

stray (strā) ▸ *v.* **1a.** To move away from or go beyond established limits. **b.** To become lost. **2.** To wander about; roam. **3.** To go morally astray; err. **4.** To digress. ▸ *n.* One that has strayed, esp. a loose domestic animal. ▸ *adj.* **1.** Straying or having strayed; wandering or lost: *a stray cat.* **2.** Scattered or separate.

streak (strēk) ▸ *n.* **1.** A line, mark, or band differentiated by color or texture from its surroundings. **2.** A slight contrasting element; trace. **3.** *Informal* An unbroken stretch; run. ▸ *v.* **1.** To mark with or form streaks. **2.** To move at high speed; rush. **—streak′er** *n.* **—streak′y** *adj.*

stream (strēm) ▸ *n.* **1.** A flow of water in a channel or bed, as a brook. **2.** A steady current of a fluid. **3.** A steady flow or succession. ▸ *v.* **1.** To flow in or as if in a stream. **2.** To pour forth or give off a stream. **3.** To come or go in large numbers. **4.** To extend, wave, or float outward. **5.** To leave a continuous trail of light.

stream·er (strē′mər) ▸ *n.* **1a.** A long narrow flag or banner. **b.** A long narrow strip of material. **2.** A newspaper headline that runs across a full page.

stream·line (strēm′līn′) ▸ *v.* **1.** To construct so as to offer the least resistance to fluid flow. **2.** To improve the efficiency of. **—stream′lined′** *adj.*

street (strēt) ▸ *n.* **1.** A public thoroughfare in a city or town. **2.** The people living, working, or gathering along a street.

street·car (strēt′kär′) ▸ *n.* A public vehicle operated on rails along the streets of a city.

street·walk·er (strēt′wô′kər) ▸ *n.* A prostitute.

strength (strĕngkth, strĕngth, strĕnth) ▸ *n.* **1.** The quality of being strong. **2.** The power to resist attack; impregnability. **3.** The power to resist strain or stress; durability. **4.** Moral or intellectual power. **5.** Capacity or potential for action. **6.** Power or force, as of an army. **7.** Degree of intensity, force, or potency. **8.** Effective or binding force: *the strength of an argument.*

strength·en (strĕngk′thən, strĕng′-, strĕn′-) ▸ *v.* To make or become strong or stronger. **—strength′en·er** *n.*

stren·u·ous (strĕn′yo͞o-əs) ▸ *adj.* **1.** Requiring great effort, energy, or exertion. **2.** Vigorously active. **—stren′u·ous·ly** *adv.* **—stren′u·ous·ness** *n.*

strep throat (strĕp) ▸ *n.* A throat infection, often epidemic, caused by streptococci and characterized by fever and inflamed tonsils.

strep·to·coc·cus (strĕp′tə-kŏk′əs) ▸ *n., pl.* **-coc·ci** (-kŏk′sī, -kŏk′ī). Any of various rounded bacteria that occur in pairs or chains and cause various diseases. **—strep′to·coc′cal** *adj.*

strep·to·my·cin (strĕp′tə-mī′sĭn) ▸ *n.* An antibiotic used esp. to treat tuberculosis.

stress (strĕs) ▸ *n.* **1.** Importance, significance, or emphasis placed on something. **2.** The relative force with which a word or sound is spoken. **3.** *Mus.* Accent or a mark representing it. **4.** *Phys.* An applied force or system of forces that tends to strain or deform a body. **5.** A state of extreme difficulty, pressure, or strain. ▸ *v.* **1.** To place emphasis on. **2.** To pronounce with a stress. **3.** To subject to pressure or strain. **4.** To subject to mechanical stress. **—stress′ful** *adj.*

stres·sor (strĕs′ər) ▸ *n.* An agent or condition that causes stress.

stretch (strĕch) ▸ *v.* **1.** To lengthen, widen, or distend. **2.** To cause to extend across a given space. **3.** To make taut; tighten. **4.** To reach or put forth; extend: *stretched out his hand.* **5.** To extend (oneself) to full length. **6.** To wrench or strain (e.g., a muscle). **7.** To extend or enlarge beyond the usual or proper limits. **8.** To increase the quantity of by admixture or dilution: *stretch a meal.* **9.** To prolong. ▸ *n.* **1.** The act of stretching or the state of being stretched.

THESAURUS

stratagem *n.* A method of deploying troops and equipment in combat ▸ battle plan, maneuver, plan of attack, strategy, tactic. —*See also* TRICK (1).

strategize *v.* —*See* DESIGN (1).

strategy *n.* A method of deploying troops and equipment in combat ▸ battle plan, maneuver, plan of attack, stratagem, tactic. —*See also* APPROACH (1).

stratify *v.* —*See* CLASS (1).

stratospheric *adj.* —*See* STEEP[1] (2).

stratum *n.* —*See* CLASS (2).

straw boss *n.* —*See* BOSS.

stray *v.* —*See* DEVIATE, DIGRESS, ROVE.

stray *adj.* Being what remains, especially after a part has been removed ▸ extra, leftover, remaining. ***Idiom:*** left behind. [*Compare* SUPERFLUOUS.] —*See also* ERRANT (2), ERRATIC, LOST (1).

stray *n.* —*See* ORPHAN.

streak *n.* An inherent, contrasting, or unexpected quality, especially in a person's character ▸ strain, vein. [*Compare* DISPOSITION, INCLINATION.] —*See also* SERIES, SHADE (2), STRIPE.

streak *v.* To mark with a line or band, as of different color or texture ▸ band, bar, line, striate, stripe, variegate. [*Compare* SPECKLE.]

stream *n.* —*See* BEAM (1), FLOW, RIVER.

stream *v.* —*See* BLOW[1] (2), FLOW (1), FLOW (2).

streamer *n.* —*See* FLAG[1].

streamline *v.* **1.** To make modern in appearance or style ▸ modernize, update. ***Idiom:*** bring up to date. [*Compare* IMPROVE, RENEW.] **2.** To reduce in complexity or scope ▸ boil down, pare (down), simplify. ***Idiom:*** reduce to the basics (*or* essentials *or* bare bones). [*Compare* EXPLAIN.]

streamlined *adj.* **1.** Acting effectively with minimal waste ▸ efficient, productive, well-oiled. [*Compare* DILIGENT, METHODICAL.] **2.** Having slender and graceful lines ▸ sleek, trim.

street *n.* —*See* WAY (2).

street-smart *adj.* —*See* SHREWD.

streetwalker *n.* —*See* PROSTITUTE.

strength *n.* The state or quality of being physically strong ▸ brawn, might, muscle, potency, power, powerfulness, sinew, thews. [*Compare* ENDURANCE.] —*See also* ENERGY, FORCE (1), FORTE, STABILITY, VIRTUE.

strengthen *v.* To make firmer in a particular conviction or habit ▸ confirm, fortify, harden, reinforce. [*Compare* BACK, ESTABLISH.] —*See also* GIRD, HARDEN (1), SUPPLEMENT, SUPPORT (2).

strenuous *adj.* —*See* [illegible], ROUGH (3).

strenuously *adv.* —*See* HARD (1).

stress *n.* Special attention given to something considered important ▸ accent, accentuation, emphasis, weight. [*Compare* IMPORTANCE, NOTICE.] —*See also* ANXIETY (1), PRESSURE.

stress *v.* —*See* EMPHASIZE.

stressor *n.* A cause of distress or anxiety ▸ care, concern, trouble, worry. [*Compare* ANXIETY, BURDEN[1].]

stretch *v.* **1.** To put forward, especially an appendage ▸ extend, outstretch,

2. The extent to which something can be stretched. 3. A continuous length, area, or expanse. 4. A straight section of a racecourse or track. 5a. A continuous period of time. b. *Slang* A term of imprisonment. ▸ *adj.* Made of an elastic material. **—stretch′a·ble** *adj.* **—stretch′y** *adj.*

stretch·er (strĕch′ər) ▸ *n.* 1. A litter used to transport the sick, wounded, or dead. 2. One that stretches.

strew (stro͞o) ▸ *v.* **strewed, strewn** (stro͞on) or **strewed, strew·ing.** 1. To spread here and there; scatter. 2. To cover (a surface) with things scattered or sprinkled. 3. To be or become dispersed over.

stri·a (strī′ə) ▸ *n., pl.* **stri·ae** (strī′ē). 1. A thin narrow groove or channel. 2. A thin line or band. **—stri′at′ed** (-ā′tĭd) *adj.* **—stri·a′tion** *n.*

strick·en (strĭk′ən) ▸ *v.* P.part. of **strike.** ▸ *adj.* 1. Struck or wounded, as by a projectile. 2. Afflicted, as with disease.

strict (strĭkt) ▸ *adj.* **-er, -est.** 1. Precise; exact. 2. Complete; absolute: *strict loyalty.* 3. Kept within narrow limits: *a strict application of a law.* 4. Rigorous in the imposition of discipline. 5. Exacting; stringent. **—strict′ly** *adv.* **—strict′ness** *n.*

stric·ture (strĭk′chər) ▸ *n.* 1. A restraint, limit, or restriction. 2. An adverse criticism. 3. *Pathol.* An abnormal narrowing of a passage.

stride (strīd) ▸ *v.* **strode** (strōd), **strid·den** (strĭd′n), **strid·ing.** To walk with long steps. ▸ *n.* 1. The act of striding. 2. A single long step. 3. often **strides** An advance. **—strid′er** *n.*

stri·dent (strīd′nt) ▸ *adj.* Loud, harsh, grating, or shrill. **—stri′dence, stri′den·cy** *n.* **—stri′dent·ly** *adv.*

strife (strīf) ▸ *n.* 1. Heated, often violent dissension; bitter conflict. 2. Contention or competition between rivals.

strike (strīk) ▸ *v.* **struck** (strŭk), **struck** or **strick·en** (strĭk′ən), **strik·ing.** 1a. To hit sharply, as with the hand, the fist, or a weapon. b. To inflict (a blow). 2. To collide with or crash into. 3. To attack or begin an attack. 4. To afflict suddenly, as with a disease. 5. To impress by stamping or printing. 6. To produce by hitting some agent, as a key on a musical instrument. 7. To indicate by a percussive sound: *The clock struck nine.* 8. To produce (a flame or spark) by friction. 9. To eliminate: *strike a statement from the records.* 10. To discover. 11. To reach; fall upon. 12. To impress: *strikes me as a good idea.* 13. To cause (an emotion) to penetrate deeply. 14a. To make or conclude (a bargain). b. To achieve (a balance). 15. To take on or assume (a pose). 16. To set out: *strike out for new lands.* 17. To engage in a strike against an employer. ***—phrasal verbs:* strike out** *Baseball* 1. To pitch three strikes to (a batter), putting the batter out. 2. To be struck out. **strike up** 1. To start to play vigorously. 2. To initiate or begin. ▸ *n.* 1. An act of striking. 2. An attack. 3. A cessation of work by employees in support of demands made on their employer. 4. A sudden achievement or discovery. 5. *Baseball* A pitched ball counted against the batter, typically one swung at and missed or judged to have passed through the strike zone. 6. The knocking down of all the pins in bowling with the first bowl of a frame. **—strik′er** *n.*

strike·break·er (strīk′brā′kər) ▸ *n.* A person who works or is hired during a strike.

strike·out (strīk′out′) ▸ *n. Baseball* An act of striking out.

strike zone ▸ *n. Baseball* The area over home plate through which a pitch must pass to be called a strike.

strik·ing (strī′kĭng) ▸ *adj.* Arrestingly or vividly impressive. **—strik′ing·ly** *adv.*

string (strĭng) ▸ *n.* 1. A cord usu. made of fiber, used for fastening, tying, or lacing. 2. Something shaped into a long thin line. 3. A set of objects threaded together: *a string of beads.* 4. A series; sequence. 5. *Comp. Sci.* A set of consecutive characters. 6. *Mus.* a. A cord stretched on an instrument and struck, plucked, or bowed to produce tones. b. also **strings** Stringed instruments collectively. 7. also **strings** *Informal* A limiting or hidden condition. ▸ *v.* **strung** (strŭng), **string·ing.** 1. To fit or furnish with strings or a string: *string a guitar.* 2. To thread on a string. 3. To arrange in a series. 4. To fasten, tie, or hang with strings. 5. To stretch out or extend. **—string′i·ness** *n.* **—string′y** *adj.*

string bean ▸ *n.* 1. A tropical American plant having edible pods. 2. The narrow green pod of this plant.

strin·gent (strĭn′jənt) ▸ *adj.* 1. Imposing rigorous standards; severe. 2. Constricted; tight. 3. Characterized by scarcity of money or credit. **—strin′gen·cy** *n.* **—strin′gent·ly** *adv.*

string·er (strĭng′ər) ▸ *n.* 1. One that strings. 2. A heavy horizontal timber used as a support or connector. 3. A part-time or freelance news correspondent.

strip[1] (strĭp) ▸ *v.* **stripped, strip·ping.** 1a. To remove the covering from. b. To undress. 2. To deprive, as of honors or rank; divest. 3. To remove all excess detail from. 4. To dismantle piece by piece. 5. To damage or break the threads of (e.g., a screw) or the teeth of (a gear). 6. To rob or plunder. **—strip′per** *n.*

strip[2] (strĭp) ▸ *n.* 1. A long narrow piece. 2. A comic strip. 3. An airstrip. 4. A narrow space or area, as along a highway.

stripe (strīp) ▸ *n.* 1. A long narrow band distinguished, as by color or texture, from the surrounding material or surface.

THESAURUS

reach, stretch out. 2. To take repose, as by sleeping or lying quietly ▸ curl up, lie (down), recline, repose, rest. [*Compare* NAP, SLEEP.] *—See also* DISTORT, EXTEND (1), LENGTHEN, LIE[1] (1), OVERDO, SPREAD (1), TENSE.

stretch *n.* A prison term ▸ hitch, time. *—See also* DISTANCE (1), EXPANSE (1), EXTENT, PERIOD (1), TURN (1).

stretch *adj.* *—See* EXTENSIBLE.

stretchable *adj.* *—See* EXTENSIBLE.

stretching *n.* *—See* EXTENSION (1).

stretchy *adj.* *—See* EXTENSIBLE.

strew *v.* *—See* SPREAD (2).

striate *v.* *—See* STREAK.

striation *n.* A mark or shallow cut made by contact with an object ▸ abrasion, scrape, scratch, scuff. [*Compare* CUT, FURROW, IMPRESSION.] *—See also* STRIPE.

stricken *adj.* *—See* UNFORTUNATE (1).

strict *adj.* *—See* CLOSE (2), SEVERE (1).

strictly *adv.* *—See* EXACTLY.

strictness *n.* *—See* SEVERITY.

stricture *n.* *—See* RESTRAINT.

stride *v.* To sit or stand with a leg on each side of ▸ bestride, straddle. *—See also* WALK.

stride *n.* *—See* ADVANCE, WALK (2).

strident *adj.* *—See* HARSH, LOUD, VOCIFEROUS.

strife *n.* *—See* BATTLE, COMPETITION (1), CONFLICT.

strike *v.* 1. To try to bite something quickly or eagerly ▸ nip, snap, snatch. 2. To enter a person's mind ▸ come to, hit, impress, occur to. *Idioms:* come (*or* spring) to mind, cross (*or* enter) one's mind, dawn on. [*Compare* REGISTER.] 3. To have a sudden overwhelming effect on ▸ catch, seize, take. 4. To cease working in support of demands made upon an employer ▸ picket, walk out. *Idioms:* go on strike, go out on strike, stage a strike, stage a sickout, stage a walkout, stop work. *—See also* AFFLICT, ATTACK (1), CANCEL (1), COLLIDE, HIT, MOVE (1), PLUNGE, RING[2].

strike back *v.* *—See* RETALIATE.

strike down *v.* *—See* DROP (3).

strike out *v.* *—See* BEAR (5), FAIL (1).

strike *n.* A cessation of work by employees in support of demands made upon their employer ▸ job action, sickout, walkout, work stoppage, work to rule. *—See also* ATTACK, DISCOVERY.

striking *adj.* Evoking strong mental images through distinctiveness ▸ colorful, graphic, picturesque, vivid. *—See also* NOTICEABLE.

string *n.* *—See* CORD, LINE, PRESS, PROVISION, SERIES.

string *v.* To put objects onto a thread ▸ thread.

string out *v.* *—See* LENGTHEN.

string up *v.* *Informal* To execute by suspending by the neck ▸ gibbet, hang. *Slang:* swing.

stringency *n.* *—See* SEVERITY.

stringent *adj.* *—See* SEVERE (1).

stringy *adj.* Containing or consisting of fibers ▸ fibrous, sinewy, threadlike.

strip[1] *v.* *—See* BARE, DEPRIVE, EMPTY, SACK[2], SKIN.

strip[2] *n.* *—See* BAND[1], STRIPE.

stripe *n.* A long narrow area that has a different color or marking from what surrounds it ▸ band, bar, line, streak, striation, strip. *—See also* BAND[1], KIND[2].

stripe *v.* *—See* STREAK.

2. A strip of cloth or braid worn on a uniform to indicate rank, awards received, or length of service. 3. Sort; kind. ▸ *v.* **striped, strip·ing**. To mark with stripes or a stripe.

strip·ling (strĭp′lĭng) ▸ *n.* An adolescent youth.

strip mall ▸ *n.* A shopping complex containing a row of businesses that usu. open onto a common parking lot.

strip mine ▸ *n.* An open mine, esp. a coal mine, whose seams are exposed by the removal of topsoil. **—strip′-mine′** *v.*

strip search ▸ *n.* A bodily search in which a person is required to remove all clothing. **—strip′-search** *v.*

strip·tease (strĭp′tēz′) ▸ *n.* A burlesque act in which a person slowly removes clothing, usu. to musical accompaniment.

strive (strīv) ▸ *v.* **strove** (strōv), **striv·en** (strĭv′ən) or **strived, striv·ing**. 1. To exert much effort or energy. 2. To struggle; contend.

strobe (strōb) ▸ *n.* 1. A strobe light. 2. A stroboscope.

strobe light ▸ *n.* A flash lamp that produces high-intensity short-duration light pulses.

stro·bo·scope (strō′bə-skōp′) ▸ *n.* Any of various instruments used to observe moving objects by making them appear stationary, as by pulsed illumination. **—stro′bo·scop′ic** (-skŏp′ĭk) *adj.*

strode (strōd) ▸ *v.* P.t. of **stride**.

stroke[1] (strōk) ▸ *n.* 1. The act of striking; blow. 2. A sudden occurrence or result. 3. A sudden severe attack, as of paralysis. 4. A sudden loss of brain function caused by a blockage or rupture of a blood vessel to the brain. 5. An inspired or effective idea or act. 6a. A single completed movement, as in swimming or rowing. b. A movement of a piston from one end of the limit of its motion to another. 7. A single mark made by a writing implement, such as a pen.

stroke[2] (strōk) ▸ *v.* **stroked, strok·ing**. To rub lightly. ▸ *n.* A light caressing movement.

stroll (strōl) ▸ *v.* To go for a leisurely walk. **—stroll** *n.*

stroll·er (strō′lər) ▸ *n.* 1. One who strolls. 2. A light four-wheeled carriage for transporting small children.

strong (strông) ▸ *adj.* **-er, -est**. 1. Physically powerful. 2. In good or sound health. 3. Capable of withstanding force or wear. 4. Having force or rapidity of motion: *a strong current.* 5. Persuasive or forceful. 6. Extreme; drastic. 7. Intense in degree or quality. 8. Having a specified number of members. 9. Stressed or accented, as a syllable. **—strong′ly** *adv.*

strong-arm (strông′ärm′) ▸ *adj. Informal* Coercive: *strong-arm tactics.*

strong·box (strông′bŏks′) ▸ *n.* A stoutly made safe.

strong·hold (strông′hōld′) ▸ *n.* A fortress.

strong interaction ▸ *n.* A fundamental interaction between elementary particles that causes protons and neutrons to bind together in the atomic nucleus.

strong·man (strông′măn′) ▸ *n.* A political figure who exercises control by force.

stron·ti·um (strŏn′chē-əm, -tē-əm, -shəm) ▸ *n. Symbol* **Sr** A soft, silvery, easily oxidized metallic element, used in fireworks and various alloys. At. no. 38.

strontium 90 ▸ *n.* A strontium isotope with a half-life of 28 years, present as a radiation hazard in nuclear fallout.

strop (strŏp) ▸ *n.* A flexible strip of leather or canvas used to sharpen a razor. ▸ *v.* **stropped, strop·ping**. To sharpen (a razor) on a strop.

stro·phe (strō′fē) ▸ *n.* A stanza of a poem. **—stro′phic** (strō′fĭk, strŏf′ĭk) *adj.*

strove (strōv) ▸ *v.* P.t. of **strive**.

struck (strŭk) ▸ *v.* P.t. and p.part. of **strike**. ▸ *adj.* Affected or shut down by a labor strike.

struc·ture (strŭk′chər) ▸ *n.* 1. Something made up of parts that are put together in a particular way. 2. The way in which parts are arranged or put together to form a whole. 3. Something constructed, as a building. ▸ *v.* **-tured, -tur·ing**. To give form or arrangement to. **—struc′tur·al** *adj.* **—struc′tur·al·ly** *adv.*

stru·del (stro͞od′l) ▸ *n.* A pastry made with fruit or cheese rolled up in layers of thin sheets of dough and baked.

strug·gle (strŭg′əl) ▸ *v.* **-gled, -gling**. 1. To make a strenuous effort; strive. 2. To contend or compete. 3. To progress with difficulty. ▸ *n.* 1. Strenuous effort. 2. Combat; strife. **—strug′gler** *n.*

strum (strŭm) ▸ *v.* **strummed, strum·ming**. To play (e.g., a guitar) by stroking or brushing the strings. **—strum** *n.*

strum·pet (strŭm′pĭt) ▸ *n.* A prostitute.

strung (strŭng) ▸ *v.* P.t. and p.part. of **string**.

strung-out (strŭng′out′) ▸ *adj. Slang* Severely debilitated from long-term drug use.

strut (strŭt) ▸ *v.* **strut·ted, strut·ting**. To walk in an exaggerated, self-important manner. ▸ *n.* 1. A strutting gait. 2. A bar or rod used to brace a structure against forces applied from the side. **—strut′ter** *n.*

strych·nine (strĭk′nīn′, -nĭn, -nēn′) ▸ *n.* A poisonous white crystalline alkaloid, $C_{21}H_{22}O_2N_2$, derived from plants and used as a poison and medicinally as a stimulant.

stub (stŭb) ▸ *n.* 1. A short blunt remaining end. 2a. The part of a check or receipt retained as a record. b. The part of a ticket returned as a voucher of payment. ▸ *v.* **stubbed, stub·bing**. 1. To strike (one's toe or foot) against something. 2. To crush out (a lit cigarette).

stub·ble (stŭb′əl) ▸ *n.* 1. The short stiff stalks, as of grain, that remain on a field after harvesting. 2. Something, such as a short growth of beard, that resembles stubble. **—stub′bly** *adj.*

stub·born (stŭb′ərn) ▸ *adj.* 1. Unreasonably determined to exert one's will; obstinate. 2. Persistent. 3. Difficult to

THESAURUS

strive *v.* —*See* ATTEMPT, CONTEND, LABOR.

striving *n.* —*See* COMPETITION (1), EFFORT.

stroke *n.* —*See* BLOW[2], TOUCH (1).

stroke *v.* —*See* CARESS, RUB, TOUCH.

stroll *v.* To walk at a leisurely pace ▸ amble, perambulate, promenade, ramble, saunter, toddle, wander. *Informal:* mosey [*Compare* HIKE, STRUT, WALK.]

stroll *n.* —*See* WALK (1).

strong *adj.* 1. Having great physical strength ▸ mighty, potent, powerful. [*Compare* ENERGETIC, LUSTY, MUSCULAR.] 2. Capable of exerting considerable effort or of withstanding considerable stress or hardship ▸ hardy, stalwart, stout, sturdy, tough. 3. Having a high concentration of the distinguishing ingredient ▸ concentrated, potent, stiff. [*Compare* STRAIGHT.] —*See also* DEEP (3), DEFINITE (1), FIRM[1] (2), FORCEFUL, HARD (3), INTENSE.

strong-arm *adj. Informal* Accomplished by force ▸ coercive, forced, forcible, violent.

strong-arm *v.* —*See* COERCE, INTIMIDATE.

stronghold *n.* —*See* FORT.

strongman *n.* —*See* DICTATOR.

strong point or **strong suit** *n.* —*See* FORTE.

strop *n.* —*See* BAND[1].

strop *v.* —*See* SHARPEN.

structure *n.* Something built, especially for human use ▸ building, construction, edifice, erection, pile. —*See also* FORM (1).

structure *v.* —*See* MAKE.

struggle *v.* —*See* ATTEMPT, CONTEND, GRIND (2).

struggle *n.* —*See* BATTLE, COMPETITION (1), EFFORT.

strumpet *n.* —*See* HARLOT.

strut *v.* To walk with pompous bearing ▸ flounce, peacock, prance, swagger, swank, swash. *Informal:* sashay. [*Compare* HIKE, STROLL, WALK.] —*See also* DISPLAY.

stub *n.* —*See* END (3).

stubborn *adj.* 1. Firmly, often unreasonably immovable in purpose or will ▸ adamant, adamantine, brassbound, bullheaded, die-hard, dogged, grim, hardheaded, headstrong, implacable, incompliant, inexorable, inflexible, intransigent, iron, mulish, obdurate, obstinate, pertinacious, perverse, pigheaded, relentless, remorseless, rigid, stiff-necked, tenacious, unbendable, unbending, uncompliant, uncompromising, unrelenting, unyielding, willful. *Idiom:* stubborn as a mule (*or* ox). 2. Difficult to alleviate or cure ▸ obstinate, persistent, pertinacious.

stubbornness *n.* The quality or state of being immovable in purpose or will ▸ bullheadedness, die-hardism, doggedness, grimness, hardheadedness, implacability, implacableness, incompliance, incompliancy, inexorability, inexorableness, inflexibility, inflexibleness, intransigence, intransigency,

treat or deal with. **—stub′born·ly** *adv.* **—stub′born·ness** *n.*

stub·by (stŭb′ē) ▸ *adj.* **-bi·er, -bi·est.** Short and stocky. **—stub′bi·ness** *n.*

stuc·co (stŭk′ō) ▸ *n., pl.* **-coes** or **-cos.** A durable finish for exterior walls, usu. made of cement, sand, and lime. ▸ *v.* To finish or decorate with stucco.

stuck (stŭk) ▸ *v.* P.t. and p.part. of **stick.**

stuck-up (stŭk′ŭp′) ▸ *adj. Informal* Snobbish; conceited.

stud[1] (stŭd) ▸ *n.* **1.** An upright post in the framework of a wall for supporting sheets of lath or wallboard. **2.** A small knob or rivet slightly projecting from a surface. **3a.** A small ornamental button mounted on a short post. **b.** A mounted buttonlike earring. ▸ *v.* **stud·ded, stud·ding. 1.** To provide with studs. **2.** To strew: *Daisies studded the meadow.*

stud[2] (stŭd) ▸ *n.* **1.** A male animal, such as a bull or stallion, kept for breeding. **2.** *Slang* A virile man.

stud·book (stŭd′bo͝ok′) ▸ *n.* A book registering the pedigrees of thoroughbred animals.

stu·dent (sto͞od′nt, styo͞od′-) ▸ *n.* **1.** One who attends a school, college, or university. **2.** One who makes a study of something.

stud·ied (stŭd′ēd) ▸ *adj.* Carefully contrived; calculated.

stu·di·o (sto͞o′dē-ō, styo͞o′-) ▸ *n., pl.* **-os. 1.** An artist's workroom. **2.** A place where an art is taught: *a dance studio.* **3.** A room or building for audio, movie, television, or radio productions. **4.** A studio apartment.

studio apartment ▸ *n.* A small apartment usu. consisting of one main living space, a kitchen, and a bathroom.

stu·di·ous (sto͞o′dē-əs, styo͞o′-) ▸ *adj.* **1.** Given to diligent study. **2.** Earnest; purposeful. **—stu′di·ous·ly** *adv.* **—stu′di·ous·ness** *n.*

stud·y (stŭd′ē) ▸ *n., pl.* **-ies. 1.** The act or process of studying. **2.** Attentive scrutiny. **3.** A branch of knowledge. **4.** A room intended or equipped for studying or writing. ▸ *v.* **-ied, -y·ing. 1.** To apply one's mind purposefully to the acquisition of knowledge or understanding of (a subject). **2.** To take (a course) at a school. **3.** To inquire into; investigate. **4.** To examine closely; scrutinize.

stuff (stŭf) ▸ *n.* **1.** The material out of which something is made or formed; substance. **2.** *Informal* **a.** Unspecified material: *Put that stuff over there.* **b.** Worthless objects. **3.** *Slang* Foolish or empty words or ideas. **4.** *Chiefly Brit.* Woven material, esp. woolens. ▸ *v.* **1a.** To pack tightly. **b.** To block (a passage); plug. **2.** To fill with stuffing. **3.** To gorge: *stuffed myself on desserts.*

stuff·ing (stŭf′ĭng) ▸ *n.* **1.** Padding, as for cushions. **2.** Food used as a filling for meat or vegetables.

stuff·y (stŭf′ē) ▸ *adj.* **-i·er, -i·est. 1.** Lacking sufficient ventilation. **2.** Blocked: *a stuffy nose.* **3.** Stodgy. **—stuff′i·ness** *n.*

stul·ti·fy (stŭl′tə-fī′) ▸ *v.* **-fied, -fy·ing. 1.** To limit or stifle: *stultify free expression.* **2.** To cause to seem stupid or foolish. **—stul′ti·fi·ca′tion** *n.*

stum·ble (stŭm′bəl) ▸ *v.* **-bled, -bling. 1a.** To trip and almost fall. **b.** To proceed unsteadily; flounder. **c.** To act or speak falteringly or clumsily. **2.** To make a mistake. **3.** To come upon accidentally. **—stum′ble** *n.*

stum·bling block (stŭm′blĭng) ▸ *n.* An obstacle or impediment.

stump (stŭmp) ▸ *n.* **1.** The part of a tree trunk left in the ground after the tree has fallen or been felled. **2.** A part remaining after the main part has been cut off or worn away. **3.** A place or occasion used for political speeches. ▸ *v.* **1.** To clear stumps from. **2.** To traverse (a district) making political speeches. **3.** To walk in a stiff, heavy manner. **4.** To puzzle; baffle. **—stump′er** *n.* **—stump′y** *adj.*

stun (stŭn) ▸ *v.* **stunned, stun·ning. 1.** To daze or render senseless, as by a blow. **2.** To stupefy.

stung (stŭng) ▸ *v.* P.t. and p.part. of **sting.**

stunk (stŭngk) ▸ *v.* P.t. and p.part. of **stink.**

stun·ning (stŭn′ĭng) ▸ *adj.* **1.** Strikingly attractive. **2a.** Impressive. **b.** Surprising. **—stun′ning·ly** *adv.*

stunt[1] (stŭnt) ▸ *v.* To check the growth or development of.

stunt[2] (stŭnt) ▸ *n.* **1.** A feat displaying unusual skill or daring. **2.** Something unusual done for publicity.

stu·pa (sto͞o′pə) ▸ *n.* A dome-shaped Buddhist shrine or monument.

stu·pe·fy (sto͞o′pə-fī′, styo͞o′-) ▸ *v.* **-fied, -fy·ing. 1.** To dull the senses of. **2.** To amaze; astonish. **—stu′pe·fac′tion** (-făk′shən) *n.*

stu·pen·dous (sto͞o-pĕn′dəs, styo͞o-) ▸ *adj.* **1.** Of astounding force, volume, or degree. **2.** Amazingly large or great: *stupendous savings.* **—stu·pen′dous·ly** *adv.*

stu·pid (sto͞o′pĭd, styo͞o′-) ▸ *adj.* **-er, -est. 1.** Slow to learn or understand. **2.** Lacking intelligence. **3.** In a dazed or stunned state. **4.** Pointless; worthless. **—stu·pid′i·ty** *n.* **—stu′pid·ly** *adv.* **—stu′pid·ness** *n.*

THESAURUS

mulishness, obduracy, obdurateness, obstinacy, obstinateness, pertinaciousness, pertinacity, perverseness, perversity, pigheadedness, relentlessness, remorselessness, rigidity, rigidness, tenaciousness, tenacity, willfulness. [*Compare* CRUELTY, DECISION, SEVERITY.]

stubby *adj.* —*See* STOCKY.

stuck *adj.* —*See* CONFUSED (1).

stuck-up *adj.* —*See* EGOTISTIC (1), SNOBBISH.

stud *n.* —*See* BEAUTY, COLUMN, NAIL.

student *n.* One who is being educated ▸ apprentice, learner, pupil, scholar, trainee. [*Compare* FOLLOWER.]

studied *adj.* —*See* ARTIFICIAL (2), DELIBERATE (2).

studio *n.* An artist's workspace ▸ atelier, workroom, workshop. —*See also* APARTMENT.

studious *adj.* Devoted to study or reading ▸ bookish, scholarly. [*Compare* EDUCATED, INTELLECTUAL, LEARNED.] —*See also* DELIBERATE (2), DILIGENT.

studiousness *n.* —*See* DILIGENCE.

study *n.* Careful consideration ▸ advisement, consideration, deliberation. [*Compare* ATTENTION, SCRUTINY.] —*See also* EXAMINATION (1), PRACTICE, TRANCE.

study *v.* To apply one's mind to the acquisition of knowledge, especially when pressed for time ▸ lucubrate. *Informal:* bone up, cram, grind. *Idioms:* burn the midnight oil, hit the books. —*See also* EXAMINE (1), PONDER.

stuff *n.* A person considered to have qualities suitable for a particular activity ▸ material, timber. [*Compare* COMER, POTENTIAL.] —*See also* EFFECTS, HEART (1), MATERIAL (1).

stuff *v.* —*See* FILL (1).

stuffing *n.* —*See* FILLER (1).

stuffy *adj.* —*See* AIRLESS (1), BORING, PRUDISH.

stultify *v.* —*See* BORE[2].

stumble *v.* To lose one's balance and fall or almost fall ▸ skid, slide, slip, slither, trip. ***Idioms:*** go flying, have one's feet go out from under one, lose one's footing, make a false step, take a skid (*or* slide). [*Compare* FALL.] —*See also* BLUNDER, ERR, MUDDLE, STAGGER (1), STAMMER.

stumble on or **upon** *v.* —*See* ENCOUNTER (1).

stumble *n.* —*See* BLUNDER.

stumbling block *n.* —*See* DIFFICULTY.

stump *v.* —*See* BAFFLE, BLUNDER, FRUSTRATE.

stumpy *adj.* —*See* STOCKY.

stun *v.* —*See* DAZE (1), PARALYZE, STAGGER (2).

stunner *n.* —*See* BEAUTY, MARVEL.

stunning *adj.* —*See* ASTONISHING, BEAUTIFUL.

stunt *n.* A clever, dexterous act ▸ feat, trick. ***Idiom:*** sleight of hand. [*Compare* ACCOMPLISHMENT.]

stupefacient *adj.* —*See* SOPORIFIC.

stupefacient *n.* —*See* SOPORIFIC.

stupefaction *n.* —*See* DAZE, WONDER (1).

stupefy *v.* —*See* DAZE (1), DRUG (2), PARALYZE.

stupendous *adj.* —*See* ASTONISHING, ENORMOUS.

stupendousness *n.* —*See* ENORMOUSNESS.

stupid *adj.* Lacking in or showing a lack of intelligence ▸ birdbrained, blockheaded, brainless, cloddish, dense, doltish, dumb, hebetudinous, idiotic, imbecilic, mindless, moronic, obtuse, softheaded, thickheaded, thick-witted, unintelligent, witless. *Informal:* boneheaded, knuckleheaded, lamebrained, muttonheaded, thick. *Slang:* dimwitted, dopey, fatheaded, half-witted, lunkheaded, pinheaded. [*Compare* BACKWARD, FOOLISH, IGNORANT.] —*See also* LETHARGIC, WORTHLESS.

stupidity *n.* The state of being stupid ▸ brainlessness, cloddishness, density, doltishness, dumbness, idiocy, imbecility, mindlessness, obtuseness, simplicity, softheadedness, stupidness, witlessness. *Informal:* boneheadedness. *Slang:* dimwittedness, dopiness, fatheadedness, pinheadedness. [*Compare* FOOLISHNESS, LETHARGY.]

stu·por (sto͞o′pər, styo͞o′-) ▸ *n.* **1.** A state of reduced sensibility; daze. **2.** A state of mental numbness, as from shock. **—stu′por·ous** *adj.*

stur·dy (stûr′dē) ▸ *adj.* **-di·er, -di·est. 1.** Substantially built; strong. **2.** Healthy and vigorous; robust. **—stur′di·ly** *adv.* **—stur′di·ness** *n.*

stur·geon (stûr′jən) ▸ *n.* Any of various large food fishes valued as a source of caviar.

stut·ter (stŭt′ər) ▸ *v.* To speak with a spasmodic repetition or prolongation of sounds. ▸ *n.* The act or habit of stuttering. **—stut′ter·er** *n.*

Stuy·ve·sant (stī′vĭ-sənt), **Peter** (1592?–1672) ▸ Dutch colonial administrator.

sty[1] (stī) ▸ *n.*, *pl.* **sties** (stīz). **1.** An enclosure for swine. **2.** A filthy place.

sty[2] (stī) ▸ *n.*, *pl.* **sties** (stīz). Inflammation of one or more sebaceous glands of an eyelid.

style (stīl) ▸ *n.* **1.** The way in which something is said, done, expressed, or performed. **2.** Sort; type. **3.** Individuality expressed in one's actions and tastes. **4.** Elegance. **5a.** The fashion of the moment. **b.** A particular fashion. **6.** A customary manner of presenting printed material, including usage, punctuation, and spelling. **7.** A slender, pointed writing instrument. **8.** *Bot.* The usu. slender part of a pistil. ▸ *v.* **styled, styl·ing. 1.** To call or name; designate. **2.** To make consistent with rules of style. **3.** To arrange or design. **—sty·lis′tic** (stī-lĭs′tĭk) *adj.* **—sty·lis′ti·cal·ly** *adv.*

styl·ish (stī′lĭsh) ▸ *adj.* Conforming to the current fashion. **—styl′ish·ly** *adv.* **—styl′ish·ness** *n.*

styl·ist (stī′lĭst) ▸ *n.* **1.** One who cultivates an artful literary style. **2.** A designer of or consultant on styles. **3.** A hairdresser.

styl·ize (stī′līz′) ▸ *v.* **-ized, -iz·ing.** To restrict or make conform to a particular style.

sty·lus (stī′ləs) ▸ *n.*, *pl.* **-lus·es** or **-li** (-lī). **1a.** A sharp, pointed instrument used for writing, marking, or engraving. **b.** *Comp. Sci.* A pointed instrument for use on a pressure-sensitive screen. **2.** A phonograph needle.

sty·mie (stī′mē) ▸ *v.* **-mied, -mie·ing.** To thwart; stump.

styp·tic (stĭp′tĭk) ▸ *adj.* Contracting the tissues or blood vessels; astringent. **—styp′tic** *n.*

Sty·ro·foam (stī′rə-fōm′) ▸ A trademark used for a light resilient polystyrene plastic.

suave (swäv) ▸ *adj.* **suav·er, suav·est.** Smoothly agreeable and courteous. **—suave′ly** *adv.* **—suave′ness, suav′i·ty** *n.*

sub[1] (sŭb) ▸ *n.* *Informal* A submarine.

sub[2] (sŭb) *Informal* ▸ *n.* A substitute. ▸ *v.* **subbed, sub·bing.** To act as a substitute.

sub– ▸ *pref.* **1.** Below; beneath: *subsoil.* **2a.** Subordinate; secondary: *subhead.* **b.** Subdivision: *subatomic.* **3.** Less than; short of: *subnormal.*

sub·al·tern (sŭb-ôl′tərn, sŭb′əl-tûrn′) ▸ *n.* **1.** A subordinate. **2.** *Chiefly Brit.* An officer holding a military rank just below that of captain.

sub·a·tom·ic (sŭb′ə-tŏm′ĭk) ▸ *adj.* **1.** Of or relating to the constituents of the atom. **2.** Participating in reactions characteristic of these constituents.

subatomic particle ▸ *n.* Any of various units of matter below the size of an atom.

sub·com·mit·tee (sŭb′kə-mĭt′ē) ▸ *n.* A subordinate committee composed of members from a main committee.

sub·com·pact (sŭb-kŏm′păkt′) ▸ *n.* An automobile smaller than a compact.

sub·con·scious (sŭb-kŏn′shəs) ▸ *adj.* Beneath the threshold of conscious perception. ▸ *n.* The part of the mind below the level of conscious perception. **—sub·con′scious·ly** *adv.* **—sub·con′scious·ness** *n.*

sub·con·ti·nent (sŭb′kŏn′tə-nənt, sŭb-kŏn′-) ▸ *n.* A large landmass, such as India, that is part of a continent but is considered either geographically or politically separate.

sub·con·tract (sŭb-kŏn′trăkt′, sŭb′kŏn′trăkt) ▸ *n.* A contract that assigns some of the obligations of a prior contract to another party. **—sub·con′tract′** *v.* **—sub·con′trac′tor** *n.*

sub·cul·ture (sŭb′kŭl′chər) ▸ *n.* A cultural subgroup within a larger cultural group.

sub·cu·ta·ne·ous (sŭb′kyo͞o-tā′nē-əs) ▸ *adj.* Just beneath the skin. **—sub′cu·ta′ne·ous·ly** *adv.*

sub·di·vide (sŭb′dĭ-vīd′, sŭb′dĭ-vīd′) ▸ *v.* **1.** To divide into smaller parts. **2.** To divide into a number of parts, esp. to divide (land) into lots. **—sub′di·vid′er** *n.* **—sub′di·vi′sion** (-vĭzh′ən) *n.*

sub·due (səb-do͞o′, -dyo͞o′) ▸ *v.* **-dued, -du·ing. 1.** To conquer and subjugate; vanquish. **2.** To quiet or bring under control. **3.** To make less intense. **—sub·du′er** *n.*

sub·head (sŭb′hĕd′) ▸ *n.* **1.** The heading or title of a subdivision of a printed subject. **2.** A subordinate heading or title.

subj. ▸ *abbr.* **1.** subject **2.** subjunctive

sub·ject (sŭb′jĭkt) ▸ *adj.* **1.** Under the power or authority of another. **2.** Prone; disposed: *subject to colds.* **3.** Likely to incur or receive: *subject to misinterpretation.* **4.** Contingent or dependent: *subject to approval.* ▸ *n.* **1.** One who is under the rule of another, esp. one who owes allegiance to a government or ruler. **2a.** One about which something is said or done; topic. **b.** The main theme of a work of art. **3.** A course or area of study. **4a.** One that experiences or is subjected to something. **b.** One that is the object of study. **5.** *Gram.* The noun, noun phrase, or pronoun in a sentence or clause that denotes the doer of the action or what is described by the predicate. ▸ *v.* (səb-jĕkt′) **1.** To expose to something. **2.** To cause to experience. **3.** To subjugate. **—sub·jec′tion** (səb-jĕk′shən) *n.*

sub·jec·tive (səb-jĕk′tĭv) ▸ *adj.* **1a.** Proceeding from or taking place within a person's mind such as to be unaffected by the external world. **b.** Particular to a given person; personal: *subjective experience.* **2.** *Gram.* Of or being the nominative case. **—sub·jec′tive·ly** *adv.* **—sub·jec′tive·ness, sub′jec·tiv′i·ty** (sŭb′jĕk-tĭv′ĭ-tē) *n.*

sub·join (səb-join′) ▸ *v.* To add at the end; append.

sub·ju·gate (sŭb′jə-gāt′) ▸ *v.* **-gat·ed, -gat·ing. 1.** To bring under control; conquer. **2.** To make subservient. **—sub′ju·ga′tion** *n.* **—sub′ju·ga′tor** *n.*

THESAURUS

stupor *n.* *—See* DAZE, LETHARGY.

stuporous *adj.* *—See* DEAD (2), LETHARGIC.

sturdiness *n.* *—See* STABILITY.

sturdy *adj.* *—See* [illegible] LUSTY, MUSCULAR, STRONG (2).

Sturm und Drang *n.* *—See* AGITATION (1).

stutter *v.* *—See* STAMMER.

stutter *n.* A way of speaking marked by involuntary repetitions and pauses ▸ stammer, stammering, stuttering.

sty *n.* *—See* PEN[2].

style *n.* A distinctive way of expressing oneself ▸ fashion, manner, mode, tone, vein. *—See also* BEARING (1), BEHAVIOR (1), ELEGANCE, FASHION, NAME (1), WAY (1).

style *v.* *—See* CALL, NAME (1).

stylish *adj.* *—See* FASHIONABLE.

stylize *v.* *—See* CONVENTIONALIZE.

stymie *v.* *—See* FRUSTRATE.

suave *adj.* Gracious and tactful in social manner ▸ debonair, smooth, ur[illegible] [*Compare* [illegible], CULTURED, GLIB, SOPHISTICATED.]

sub *n.* *—See* SUBSTITUTE.

sub [illegible]

subaltern *adj.* *—See* MINOR (1).

subaltern *n.* *—See* SUBORDINATE.

subdivide *v.* *—See* ANALYZE, BRANCH.

subdivision *n.* *—See* ANALYSIS, BRANCH (1), PART (1).

subdue *v.* *—See* DEFEAT, MODERATE (1).

subdued *adj.* *—See* MODEST (1), SOFT (2).

subject *n.* What a speech, piece of writing, or artistic work is about ▸ argument, case, matter, point, subject matter, text, theme, topic. [*Compare* HEART, PROBLEM.] *—See also* AREA (1), CITIZEN, OBJECT (2).

subject *adj.* Subject to the authority [illegible] ▸ dependent, subordinate, subservient. [*Compare* AUXILIARY.] *—See also* CONDITIONAL, LIABLE (2).

subject *v.* To lay open, as to something undesirable or injurious ▸ expose, leave open. [*Compare* ENDANGER.] *—See also* ENSLAVE.

subjective *adj.* *—See* ARBITRARY.

subject matter *n.* *—See* SUBJECT.

subjoin *v.* *—See* ATTACH (2).

subjugate *v.* *—See* DEFEAT, ENSLAVE, OCCUPY (2).

subjugation *n.* *—See* CONQUEST, DOMINATION, OPPRESSION.

subjugator *n.* *—See* CONQUEROR.

sub·junc·tive (səb-jŭngk′tĭv) ► *adj.* Of or being a mood of a verb used to express an uncertainty, a wish, or an unlikely condition. **—sub·junc′tive** *n.*

sub·lease (sŭb′lēs′) ► *n.* A lease of property granted by a lessee. **—sub′lease′** *v.*

sub·let (sŭb′lĕt′) ► *v.* **1.** To rent (property one holds by lease) to another. **2.** To subcontract (work). ► *n.* (sŭb′lĕt′) Property rented by one tenant to another.

sub·li·mate (sŭb′lə-māt′) ► *v.* **-mat·ed, -mat·ing. 1.** *Chem.* To change from a solid to a gaseous state or from a gaseous to a solid state without becoming a liquid. **2.** *Psychol.* To modify the natural expression of (an instinctual impulse) in a socially acceptable manner. **—sub′li·ma′tion** *n.*

sub·lime (sə-blīm′) ► *adj.* **1.** Of high spiritual, moral, or intellectual worth. **2.** Exalted; lofty. **3.** Inspiring awe; impressive. ► *v.* **-limed, -lim·ing** *Chem.* To sublimate. **—sub·lime′ly** *adv.* **—sub·lime′ness, sub·lim′i·ty** (sə-blĭm′ĭ-tē) *n.*

sub·lim·i·nal (sŭb-lĭm′ə-nəl) ► *adj. Psychol.* Below the threshold of conscious perception or awareness. **—sub·lim′i·nal·ly** *adv.*

sub·lu·na·ry (sŭb-lo͞o′nə-rē, sŭb′lo͞o-nĕr′ē) ► *adj.* **1.** Situated beneath the moon. **2.** Of this world; earthly.

sub·ma·chine gun (sŭb′mə-shēn′) ► *n.* A lightweight automatic or semiautomatic gun fired from the shoulder or hip.

sub·ma·rine (sŭb′mə-rēn′, sŭb′mə-rēn′) ► *n.* **1.** A ship capable of operating under water. **2.** A large sandwich consisting of a long roll filled with layers of meat, cheese, tomatoes, lettuce, and condiments. ► *adj.* Beneath the surface of the water; undersea.

sub·merge (səb-mûrj′) ► *v.* **-merged, -merg·ing. 1.** To place under water. **2.** To cover with water. **3.** To go under or as if under water. **—sub·mer′gence** *n.* **—sub·mer′gi·ble** *adj.*

sub·merse (səb-mûrs′) ► *v.* **-mersed, -mers·ing.** To submerge. **—sub·mer′sion** (-mûr′zhən, -shən) *n.*

sub·mers·i·ble (səb-mûr′sə-bəl) ► *adj.* Submergible. ► *n.* A vessel capable of operating under water.

sub·mi·cro·scop·ic (sŭb′mī-krə-skŏp′ĭk) ► *adj.* Too small to be resolved by an optical microscope.

sub·mit (səb-mĭt′) ► *v.* **-mit·ted, -mit·ting. 1.** To yield or surrender (oneself) to the will or authority of another. **2.** To commit (something) to the consideration or judgment of another. **3.** To offer as a proposition or contention. **4.** To allow oneself to be subjected to something. **—sub·mis′sion** *n.* **—sub·mis′sive** *adj.* **—sub·mit′tal** *n.*

sub·nor·mal (sŭb-nôr′məl) ► *adj.* Less than normal; below the average. **—sub′nor·mal′i·ty** (-măl′ĭ-tē) *n.*

sub·or·bi·tal (sŭb-ôr′bĭ-tl) ► *adj.* Having a trajectory of less than one full orbit.

sub·or·di·nate (sə-bôr′dn-ĭt) ► *adj.* **1.** Of a lower or inferior class or rank. **2.** Subject to the authority or control of another. ► *n.* One that is subordinate. ► *v.* (sə-bôr′dn-āt′) **-nat·ed, -nat·ing. 1.** To put in a lower or inferior rank or class. **2.** To make subservient. **—sub·or′di·nate·ly** *adv.* **—sub·or′di·na′tion** *n.* **—sub·or′di·na′tive** *adj.*

sub·orn (sə-bôrn′) ► *v.* To induce to commit an unlawful act, esp. perjury. **—sub′or·na′tion** (sŭb′ôr-nā′shən) *n.* **—sub·orn′er** *n.*

sub·plot (sŭb′plŏt′) ► *n.* A plot subordinate to the main plot of a literary work or film.

sub·poe·na (sə-pē′nə) ► *n.* A writ requiring appearance in court to give testimony. ► *v.* To serve or summon with such a writ.

sub ro·sa (sŭb rō′zə) ► *adv.* In secret; privately. **—sub-ro′sa** *adj.*

sub-Sa·har·an (sŭb′sə-hâr′ən, -hăr′-, -här′-) ► *adj.* Of or relating to the region of Africa south of the Sahara.

sub·scribe (səb-scrīb′) ► *v.* **-scribed, -scrib·ing. 1.** To pledge or contribute (a sum of money). **2.** To sign (one's name). **3.** To sign one's name to in testimony or consent: *subscribe a will.* **4.** To contract to receive and pay for a subscription, as to a publication. **5.** To express approval or agreement: *subscribe to a belief.* **—sub·scrib′er** *n.*

sub·script (sŭb′skrĭpt′) ► *n.* A character or symbol written directly beneath or next to and slightly below a letter or number.

sub·scrip·tion (səb-skrĭp′shən) ► *n.* **1.** A purchase made by signed order, as for issues of a periodical or a series of events. **2.** The signing of one's name, as to a document.

sub·se·quent (sŭb′sĭ-kwĕnt′, -kwənt) ► *adj.* Following in time or order; succeeding. **—sub′se·quent′ly** *adv.*

sub·ser·vi·ent (səb-sûr′vē-ənt) ► *adj.* **1.** Subordinate. **2.** Obsequious; servile. **—sub·ser′vi·ence** *n.* **—sub·ser′vi·ent·ly** *adv.*

sub·set (sŭb′sĕt′) ► *n.* A set contained within a set.

sub·side (səb-sīd′) ► *v.* **-sid·ed, -sid·ing. 1.** To sink to a lower level. **2.** To sink to the bottom, as a sediment. **3.** To become less; abate. **—sub·si′dence** *n.*

sub·sid·i·ar·y (səb-sĭd′ē-ĕr′ē) ► *adj.* **1.** Serving to assist or supplement. **2.** Subordinate. **3.** Of or like a subsidy. ► *n., pl.* **-ar·ies.** One that is subsidiary to another, esp. a company owned by another company. **—sub·sid′i·ar′i·ly** (-âr′ə-lē) *adv.*

sub·si·dize (sŭb′sĭ-dīz′) ► *v.* **-dized, -diz·ing.** To assist or support with a subsidy. **—sub′si·di·za′tion** *n.*

sub·si·dy (sŭb′sĭ-dē) ► *n., pl.* **-dies.** Financial assistance given by one person or government to another.

sub·sist (səb-sĭst′) ► *v.* **1.** To exist; be. **2.** To maintain life, esp. at a meager level: *subsisted on one meal a day.*

sub·sis·tence (səb-sĭs′təns) ► *n.* **1.** The act or state of subsisting. **2.** A means of subsisting. **3.** Existence. **—sub·sis′tent** *adj.*

sub·soil (sŭb′soil′) ► *n.* The layer of earth beneath the topsoil.

sub·son·ic (sŭb-sŏn′ĭk) ► *adj.* **1.** Of less than audible frequency. **2.** Having a speed less than that of sound.

sub·stance (sŭb′stəns) ► *n.* **1a.** That which has mass and occupies space; matter. **b.** A material of a particular kind or constitution. **2.** The essence; gist. **3.** That which is

THESAURUS

sublet *v.* —*See* LEASE (1).

sublime *adj.* —*See* ELEVATED (3), EXCEPTIONAL, GRAND.

submerge or **submerse** *v.* —*See* DIP (1), FLOOD (1), SINK (1).

submission *n.* The act of submitting or surrendering to the power of another ► capitulation, giving up, surrender. —*See also* OBEDIENCE, PROPOSAL (1).

submissive *adj.* —*See* DEFERENTIAL, OBEDIENT, PASSIVE.

submissiveness *n.* —*See* OBEDIENCE.

submit *v.* To conform to the will or judgment of another ► bow, defer, yield. [*Compare* HUMOR.] —*See also* OFFER (1), PROPOSE, SUCCUMB, SURRENDER (1).

subordinate *adj.* Subject to the authority or control of another ► dependent, subject, subservient. [*Compare* AUXILIARY.] —*See also* MINOR (1).

subordinate *n.* One belonging to a lower class or rank ► inferior, junior, secondary, subaltern, underling. *Informal:* second fiddle. [*Compare* ASSISTANT, PAWN[2], SLAVE, SYCOPHANT.]

subordinate *v.* —*See* ENSLAVE.

suborn *v.* —*See* BRIBE, CORRUPT.

subpar *adj.* —*See* BAD (1).

sub rosa *adv.* —*See* SECRETLY.

sub-rosa *adj.* —*See* SECRET (1).

subscribe *v.* —*See* ASSENT, CONTRIBUTE (1), DONATE, SIGN.

subscriber *n.* —*See* DONOR.

subscription *n.* —*See* DONATION.

subsequent *adj.* Following something else in time ► after, later, posterior, ulterior. —*See also* FOLLOWING (1), FUTURE.

subsequently *adv.* —*See* LATER.

subservient *adj.* Subject to the authority or control of another ► dependent, subject, subordinate. [*Compare* AUXILIARY.] —*See also* SERVILE.

subside *v.* To become less active or intense ► abate, bate, die (away *or* down *or* off *or* out), diminish, ease (off *or* up), ebb, fall, fall off, lapse, let up, moderate, remit, slacken, slack off, wane, wind down. [*Compare* FALL, DEPRECIATE.] —*See also* DECREASE, SINK (1).

subsidence *n.* —*See* WANING.

subsidiary *adj.* —*See* AUXILIARY (1).

subsidiary *n.* —*See* BRANCH (3).

subsidize *v.* —*See* FINANCE.

subsidy *n.* Money or other resources granted for a particular purpose ► appropriation, budget, grant, subvention.

subsist *v.* To have being or actuality ► be, exist. —*See also* EXIST.

subsist on *v.* To include as part of one's diet by nature or preference ► eat, exist on, feed on, live on.

subsistence *n.* —*See* LIVING.

subsisting *adj.* —*See* ALIVE.

substance *n.* —*See* ESSENCE, HEART

solid and practical: *a plan without substance.* **4.** Density; body. **5.** Material possessions; wealth.

substance abuse ► *n.* Excessive use of addictive substances, esp. alcohol or narcotics.

sub·stan·dard (sŭb-stăn′dərd) ► *adj.* Failing to meet a standard; below standard.

sub·stan·tial (səb-stăn′shəl) ► *adj.* **1.** Of or having substance; material. **2.** Not imaginary; real. **3.** Solidly built; strong. **4.** Ample; sustaining. **5.** Considerable; large: *won by a substantial margin.* **6.** Possessing wealth; well-to-do. **—sub·stan′tial·ly** *adv.*

sub·stan·ti·ate (səb-stăn′shē-āt′) ► *v.* **-at·ed, -at·ing.** To support with proof or evidence. **—sub·stan′ti·a′tion** *n.*

sub·stan·tive (sŭb′stən-tĭv) ► *adj.* **1.** Substantial; considerable. **2.** Basic; essential. ► *n. Gram.* A word or group of words functioning as a noun. **—sub′stan·tive·ly** *adv.*

sub·sta·tion (sŭb′stā′shən) ► *n.* A branch station, as of a post office.

sub·sti·tute (sŭb′stĭ-to͞ot′, -tyo͞ot′) ► *n.* One that takes the place of another. ► *v.* **-tut·ed, -tut·ing.** **1.** To put or use in place of another. **2.** To take the place of another. **—sub′sti·tu′tion** *n.*

sub·strate (sŭb′strāt′) ► *n.* **1.** The substance on which an enzyme acts. **2.** An underlying layer; substratum.

sub·stra·tum (sŭb′strā′təm, -străt′əm) ► *n.* **1.** An underlying layer or foundation. **2.** Subsoil.

sub·struc·ture (sŭb′strŭk′chər) ► *n.* The supporting part of a structure; foundation.

sub·sume (səb-so͞om′) ► *v.* **-sumed, -sum·ing.** To place in a broader or more comprehensive category. **—sub·sum′a·ble** *adj.*

sub·tend (səb-tĕnd′) ► *v. Math.* To be opposite to and delimit: *The hypotenuse subtends a right angle.*

sub·ter·fuge (sŭb′tər-fyo͞oj′) ► *n.* A deceptive stratagem or device.

sub·ter·ra·ne·an (sŭb′tə-rā′nē-ən) ► *adj.* **1.** Situated or operating beneath the earth's surface; underground. **2.** Hidden; secret.

sub·text (sŭb′tĕkst′) ► *n.* The implicit meaning or theme of a literary text.

sub·ti·tle (sŭb′tīt′l) ► *n.* **1.** A secondary, usu. explanatory title, as of a literary work. **2.** A printed translation of the dialogue of a foreign-language film shown at the bottom of the screen. **—sub′ti′tle** *v.*

sub·tle (sŭt′l) ► *adj.* **-tler, -tlest.** **1a.** So slight as to be difficult to detect: *a subtle smile.* **b.** Not obvious; abstruse. **2.** Able to make fine distinctions: *a subtle mind.* **3a.** Skillful; clever. **b.** Crafty. **—sub′tle·ty, sub′tle·ness** *n.* **—sub′tly** *adv.*

sub·to·tal (sŭb′tōt′l) ► *n.* The total of part of a series of numbers. **—sub′to′tal** *v.*

sub·tract (səb-trăkt′) ► *v.* To take away or deduct, as one number from another. **—sub·trac′tion** *n.*

sub·tra·hend (sŭb′trə-hĕnd′) ► *n. Math.* A quantity to be subtracted from another.

sub·trop·i·cal (sŭb-trŏp′ĭ-kəl) ► *adj.* Of or being the geographic areas adjacent to the tropics.

sub·trop·ics (sŭb-trŏp′ĭks) ► *pl.n.* Subtropical regions.

sub·urb (sŭb′ûrb′) ► *n.* **1.** A usu. residential area near a city. **2. suburbs** The usu. residential region surrounding a major city. **—sub·ur′ban** (sə-bûr′bən) *adj.*

sub·ur·ban·ite (sə-bûr′bə-nīt′) ► *n.* One who lives in a suburb.

sub·ur·bi·a (sə-bûr′bē-ə) ► *n.* **1.** The suburbs. **2.** Suburbanites collectively.

sub·ven·tion (səb-vĕn′shən) ► *n.* An endowment or subsidy. **—sub·ven′tion·ar′y** *adj.*

sub·ver·sive (səb-vûr′sĭv, -zĭv) ► *adj.* Intended or serving to subvert, esp. an established government. ► *n.* One who advocates subversive means or policies. **—sub·ver′sive·ly** *adv.* **—sub·ver′sive·ness** *n.*

sub·vert (səb-vûrt′) ► *v.* **1.** To destroy completely; ruin. **2.** To undermine the character or morals of; corrupt. **3.** To overthrow completely. **—sub·ver′sion** (-vûr′zhən, -shən) *n.* **—sub·vert′er** *n.*

sub·way (sŭb′wā′) ► *n.* An underground railroad, usu. operated by electricity.

suc·ceed (sək-sēd′) ► *v.* **1.** To come next in time or succession, esp. to replace another in a position. **2.** To accomplish something attempted.

suc·cess (sək-sĕs′) ► *n.* **1.** The achievement of something attempted. **2.** The gaining of fame or prosperity. **3.** One that succeeds. **—suc·cess′ful** *adj.* **—suc·cess′ful·ly** *adv.*

suc·ces·sion (sək-sĕsh′ən) ► *n.* **1.** The act of following in order. **2.** A group of people or things following in order; sequence. **3.** The sequence, right, or act of succeeding to a title, throne, or estate. **—suc·ces′sion·al** *adj.* **—suc·ces′sion·al·ly** *adv.*

suc·ces·sive (sək-sĕs′ĭv) ► *adj.* Following in uninterrupted order; consecutive. **—suc·ces′sive·ly** *adv.*

suc·ces·sor (sək-sĕs′ər) ► *n.* One that succeeds or follows another.

suc·cinct (sək-sĭngkt′) ► *adj.* Brief and clear in expression; concise. **—suc·cinct′ly** *adv.* **—suc·cinct′ness** *n.*

suc·cor (sŭk′ər) ► *n.* Assistance in time of distress; relief. **—suc′cor** *v.*

suc·co·tash (sŭk′ə-tăsh′) ► *n.* A stew of kernels of corn, lima beans, and tomatoes.

THESAURUS

(1), IMPORT, MATERIAL (1), THRUST.

substance abuse *n.* —*See* ADDICTION.

substandard *adj.* —*See* BAD (1).

substantial *adj.* —*See* BIG, FIRM[1] (2), GENEROUS (2), IMPORTANT, PHYSICAL, REAL (1).

substantiality *n.* —*See* EXISTENCE.

substantially *adv.* —*See* CONSIDERABLY.

substantiate *v.* —*See* BACK (2), CONFIRM (1), EMBODY (1), PROVE.

substantiation *n.* —*See* CONFIRMATION (2), EMBODIMENT.

substantive *adj.* —*See* REAL (1).

substantiveness *n.* —*See* EXISTENCE.

substitute *n.* One that can take the place of another ► alternate, cover, double, proxy, relief, replacement, stand-in, surrogate. *Informal:* fill-in, pinch hitter, ringer, sub. [*Compare* AUXILIARY, COUNTERPART.]

substitute *v.* To act as a substitute ► cover for, fill in, function as, serve as, stand in, supply. *Informal:* pinch-hit, sub. *Idiom:* take the place of. —*See also* CHANGE (3).

substitute *adj.* —*See* TEMPORARY (1).

substitution *n.* —*See* CHANGE (2).

substratum *n.* —*See* BASE[1] (2).

substructure *n.* —*See* BASE[1] (2), FRAME.

subsume *v.* —*See* CONTAIN (1).

subterfuge *n.* —*See* TRICK (1).

subterranean or **subterrestrial** *adj.* —*See* UNDERGROUND.

subtle *adj.* —*See* DELICATE (4), DISCRIMINATING, FINE[1] (2), IMPERCEPTIBLE (1), UNDERHAND.

subtlety *n.* The ability to make or detect effects of great [illegible] cacy, fineness, niceness, sensitivity, subtleness. —*See also* DISCRIMINATION (1), SHADE (1).

subtract *v.* —*See* DEDUCT.

suburbs *n.* —*See* OUTSKIRTS.

subvent *v.* —*See* FINANCE.

subvention *n.* Money or other resources granted for a particular purpose ► appropriation, budget, grant, subsidy.

subversion *n.* Treacherous action to defeat or do harm to an endeavor ► sabotage, undermining. [*Compare* DEFEAT, DESTRUCTION.]

subversive *adj.* —*See* REBELLIOUS.

subversive *n.* —*See* REBEL (1).

subvert *v.* To damage, destroy, or defeat by sabotage ► sabotage, undermine. [*Compare* DESTROY, DISORDER.] —*See also* CORRUPT, OVERTHROW.

succeed *v.* **1.** To gain success ► arrive, get ahead, get on, rise. *Idioms:* go far, go places, make good, make it. **2.** To turn out well ► come off, go (over), pan out, work (out). *Slang:* click. *Idiom:* fall into place. [*Compare* EF[illegible]] [illegible] FOLLOW (1).

succeeding *adj.* —*See* FOLLOWING (1).

success or **successfulness** *n.* —*See* ACCOMPLISHMENT.

successful *adj.* —*See* FLOURISHING, PROSPEROUS.

succession *n.* —*See* SERIES.

successive or **successional** *adj.* —*See* CONSECUTIVE.

succinct *adj.* —*See* BRIEF, PITHY.

succor *n.* A consoling in time of grief or pain ► comfort, consolation, reassurance, solace. [*Compare* PITY.] —*See also* HELP, RELIEF (1).

succor *v.* —*See* COMFORT, HELP.

succorer *n.* —*See* ASSISTANT.

Suc·coth also **Suk·koth** (so͝ok′əs, so͞o-kôt′) ▸ *n.* A Jewish harvest festival celebrated in Tishri.

suc·cu·bus (sŭk′yə-bəs) ▸ *n., pl.* **-bus·es** or **-bi** (-bī′, -bē′). An evil spirit supposed to have sexual intercourse with a sleeping man.

suc·cu·lent (sŭk′yə-lənt) ▸ *adj.* **1.** Full of juice or sap; juicy. **2.** Having thick fleshy leaves or stems. ▸ *n.* A succulent plant, such as a cactus. **—suc′cu·lence** *n.* **—suc′cu·lent·ly** *adv.*

suc·cumb (sə-kŭm′) ▸ *v.* **1.** To submit or yield to something overwhelming. **2.** To die, esp. from disease or injury.

such (sŭch) ▸ *adj.* Of this or that kind or extent. ▸ *adv.* **1.** To so extreme a degree; so: *such beautiful flowers.* **2.** Very; especially. ▸ *pron.* **1.** Such a one or ones. **2.** Someone or something implied or indicated: *Such are the fortunes of war.* **3.** The like: *pins, needles, and such.* ***—idiom:*** **such as** For example.

such·like (sŭch′līk′) ▸ *adj.* Similar. ▸ *pron.* One or ones of such a kind.

Sü·chow (so͞o′chou′, sü′jō′) ▸ See **Xuzhou.**

suck (sŭk) ▸ *v.* **1.** To draw (liquid) into the mouth by movements that create suction. **2.** To draw something in by suction. **3.** To suckle. ▸ *n.* The act or sound of sucking.

suck·er (sŭk′ər) ▸ *n.* **1.** One that sucks. **2.** *Informal* One who is easily deceived. **3.** A lollipop. **4.** A freshwater fish with a thick-lipped mouth adapted for feeding by suction. **5.** An organ or other structure adapted for sucking nourishment or for clinging by suction. **6.** *Bot.* A secondary shoot produced from the base or roots of a woody plant. ▸ *v. Informal* To trick; dupe.

suck·le (sŭk′əl) ▸ *v.* **-led, -ling. 1.** To give or take milk at the breast or udder; nurse. **2.** To nourish; nurture.

suck·ling (sŭk′lĭng) ▸ *n.* A young unweaned mammal. **—suck′ling** *adj.*

su·crose (so͞o′krōs′) ▸ *n.* A sugar found in many plants, notably sugar cane and sugar beets.

suc·tion (sŭk′shən) ▸ *n.* **1.** The act or process of sucking. **2.** A force that causes a fluid or solid to be drawn into a space or to adhere to a surface because of the difference between the external and internal pressures. **—suc′tion** *v.*

Su·dan (so͞o-dăn′) ▸ **1.** A region of N Africa S of the Sahara and N of the equator. **2.** A country of NE Africa S of Egypt. **—Su′da·nese′** (so͞od′n-ēz′, -ēs′) *adj. & n.*

sud·den (sŭd′n) ▸ *adj.* **1.** Happening without warning; unforeseen. **2.** Hasty; abrupt. **3.** Rapid; swift. **—sud′den·ly** *adv.* **—sud′den·ness** *n.*

sudden infant death syndrome ▸ *n.* A fatal syndrome of infants marked by sudden cessation of breathing.

Su·de·ten·land (so͞o-dāt′n-lănd′, zo͞o-) ▸ A historical region of N Czech Republic along the Polish border.

suds (sŭdz) ▸ *pl.n.* A foam or lather, esp. of soapy water. **—suds′sy** *adj.*

sue (so͞o) ▸ *v.* **sued, su·ing. 1.** To institute legal proceedings; bring suit against (a person) for redress of grievances. **2.** To make an appeal or entreaty: *sue for peace.* **—su′er** *n.*

suede also **suède** (swād) ▸ *n.* **1.** Leather with a soft napped surface. **2.** Fabric made to resemble suede.

su·et (so͞o′ĭt) ▸ *n.* The hard fat around the kidneys of cattle and sheep, used in cooking and making tallow.

Su·ez (so͞o-ĕz′, so͞o′ĕz′) ▸ A city of NE Egypt at the head of the **Gulf of Suez,** an arm of the Red Sea W of the Sinai Peninsula.

Suez Canal ▸ A ship canal, about 166 km (103 mi), linking the Red Sea with the Mediterranean.

suff. ▸ *abbr.* suffix

suf·fer (sŭf′ər) ▸ *v.* **1.** To feel pain or distress; sustain loss or harm. **2.** To tolerate or endure: *suffered death for her beliefs.* **3.** To appear at a disadvantage: *suffer by comparison.* **4.** To endure or bear. **5.** To permit; allow. **—suf′fer·a·ble** *adj.* **—suf′fer·a·bly** *adv.* **—suf′fer·er** *n.*

suf·fer·ance (sŭf′ər-əns, sŭf′rəns) ▸ *n.* **1.** Patient endurance. **2.** Sanction or permission implied by failure to prohibit; tacit consent.

suf·fer·ing (sŭf′ər-ĭng, sŭf′rĭng) ▸ *n.* Physical or mental pain or distress.

suf·fice (sə-fīs′) ▸ *v.* **-ficed, -fic·ing. 1.** To be sufficient (for). **2.** To be capable or competent.

suf·fi·cient (sə-fĭsh′ənt) ▸ *adj.* Being as much as is needed. **—suf·fi′cien·cy** *n.* **—suf·fi′cient·ly** *adv.*

suf·fix (sŭf′ĭks) ▸ *n.* An affix added to the end of a word or stem, serving to form a new word or an inflectional ending. **—suf′fix** *v.* **—suf·fix′ion** (sə-fĭk′shən) *n.*

suf·fo·cate (sŭf′ə-kāt′) ▸ *v.* **-cat·ed, -cat·ing. 1.** To kill or destroy by preventing access to oxygen. **2.** To suppress; stifle. **—suf′fo·ca′tion** *n.*

suf·frage (sŭf′rĭj) ▸ *n.* **1.** The right or privilege of voting. **2.** A vote.

suf·fra·gette (sŭf′rə-jĕt′) ▸ *n. Chiefly Brit.* A woman advocating suffrage for women.

suf·fra·gist (sŭf′rə-jĭst) ▸ *n.* An advocate of the extension of voting rights, esp. to women. **—suf′fra·gism** *n.*

suf·fuse (sə-fyo͞oz′) ▸ *v.* **-fused, -fus·ing.** To spread through or over, as with liquid, color, or light. **—suf·fu′sion** *n.* **—suf·fu′sive** *adj.*

Su·fi (so͞o′fē) ▸ *n. Islam* A Muslim mystic. **—Su′fism** (-fĭz′əm) *n.*

sug·ar (sho͝og′ər) ▸ *n.* **1.** Any of a class of water-soluble crystalline carbohydrates with a characteristically sweet taste. **2.** Crystalline or powdered sucrose, used as a sweetener; table sugar. ▸ *v.* **1.** To coat, cover, or sweeten with sugar. **2.** To make less distasteful.

sugar beet ▸ *n.* A beet with fleshy white roots from which sugar is obtained.

sugar cane ▸ *n.* A tall tropical grass with thick stems that yield sugar.

sug·ar·coat (sho͝og′ər-kōt′) ▸ *v.* **1.** To cause to seem more appealing or pleasant. **2.** To cover with sugar.

sug·ar·less (sho͝og′ər-lĭs) ▸ *adj.* **1.** Containing no sugar. **2.** Sweetened with a substance other than sucrose.

sugar maple ▸ *n.* A maple tree of E North America, with sap that is the source of maple syrup and maple sugar.

sug·ar·plum (sho͝og′ər-plŭm′) ▸ *n.* A small ball of candy.

sug·ar·y (sho͝og′ə-rē) ▸ *adj.* **-i·er, -i·est. 1.** Tasting of or re-

THESAURUS

succumb *v.* To give in from or as if from a gradual loss of strength ▸ bow, buckle, capitulate, fold, submit, surrender, yield. *—See also* COLLAPSE (1), DIE.

suck *v.* *—See* INVOLVE (1).
suck up *v.* *—See* FAWN.

sucker *n.* *—See* DUPE, SHOOT.
sucker *v.* *—See* DECEIVE.

sudden *adj.* *—See* ABRUPT (2), STEEP[1] (1).

sudoriferous *adj.* Producing or covered with sweat ▸ perspiring, sweating, sweaty. [*Compare* DAMP, STICKY.]

suds *n.* *—See* FOAM.

sudsy *adj.* *—See* FOAMY.

sue *v.* To institute or subject to legal proceedings ▸ law, litigate, prosecute. *Idioms:* bring suit, haul (*or* drag *or* hale) into court. *—See also* APPEAL (1).

suet *n.* Adipose tissue ▸ blubber, fat, lard, tallow. [*Compare* OIL.]

suffer *v.* *—See* ENDURE (1), EXPERIENCE, GRIEVE, PERMIT (1).

sufferable *adj.* *—See* BEARABLE.

sufferance *n.* *—See* PATIENCE.

sufferer *n.* *—See* VICTIM.

suffering *n.* *—See* MISERY.
suffering *adj.* *—See* MISERABLE.

suffice *v.* *—See* SATISFY (1).

sufficiency *n.* An adequate quantity ▸ adequacy, enough.

sufficient *adj.* Being what is needed without being in excess ▸ adequate, ample, comfortable, competent, decent, enough, satisfactory. *—See also* ACCEPTABLE (2).

suffocate *v.* *—See* CHOKE.

suffocating *adj.* *—See* AIRLESS (1).

suffrage *n.* The right or chance to express an opinion or participate in a decision ▸ input, say, voice, vote. *Informal:* say-so.

suffuse *v.* *—See* CHARGE (1), STEEP[2].

suffusive *adj.* Having the quality or tendency to pervade or permeate ▸ penetrating, permeating, pervading, pervasive. [*Compare* GENERAL, PREVAILING, RECURRENT.]

sugar *v.* *—See* SWEETEN.
sugar *n.* *—See* DARLING (1).

sugarcoat *v.* *—See* COLOR (2), SWEETEN.

sugary *adj.* Having or suggesting the taste of sugar ▸ honeyed, saccharine, sweet. *—See also* FLATTERING.

sembling sugar. 2. Excessively or cloyingly sweet.

sug·gest (səg-jĕst′, sə-jĕst′) ▸ *v.* **1.** To offer for consideration or action; propose. **2.** To bring or call to mind by association. **3.** To imply.

sug·gest·i·ble (səg-jĕs′tə-bəl, sə-jĕs′-) ▸ *adj.* Readily influenced by suggestion.

sug·ges·tion (səg-jĕs′chən, sə-jĕs′-) ▸ *n.* **1.** The act of suggesting. **2.** Something suggested. **3.** A hint or trace.

sug·ges·tive (səg-jĕs′tĭv, sə-jĕs′-) ▸ *adj.* **1.** Tending to suggest thoughts or ideas; provocative. **2.** Tending to suggest something improper or indecent. **—sug·ges′tive·ly** *adv.* **—sug·ges′tive·ness** *n.*

su·i·cide (so͞o′ĭ-sīd′) ▸ *n.* **1.** The act or an instance of intentionally killing oneself. **2.** One who commits suicide. **—su′i·cid′al** *adj.*

su·i ge·ne·ris (so͞o′ī′ jĕn′ər-ĭs, so͞o′ē) ▸ *adj.* Unique; singular.

suit (so͞ot) ▸ *n.* **1a.** A set of matching outer garments, esp. a coat with trousers or a skirt. **b.** A costume for a special activity: *a diving suit.* **2.** A group of related things. **3.** Any of the four sets of playing cards that constitute a deck. **4.** *Law* A proceeding to recover a right or claim. **5.** The act or an instance of courtship. ▸ *v.* **1.** To meet the requirements of. **2.** To make appropriate; adapt. **3.** To be appropriate for; befit: *That color suits you.* **4.** To please; satisfy.

suit·a·ble (so͞o′tə-bəl) ▸ *adj.* Appropriate to a purpose or occasion. **—suit′a·bil′i·ty, suit′a·ble·ness** *n.* **—suit′a·bly** *adv.*

suit·case (so͞ot′kās′) ▸ *n.* A usu. rectangular and flat piece of luggage.

suite (swēt) ▸ *n.* **1.** A staff of attendants; retinue. **2.** (*also* so͞ot) A set of matching furniture. **3.** A series of connected rooms used as a unit. **4.** *Mus.* An instrumental composition consisting of a succession of dances.

suit·or (so͞o′tər) ▸ *n.* **1.** A man who is courting a woman. **2.** A petitioner.

su·ki·ya·ki (so͞o′kē-yä′kē) ▸ *n.* A Japanese dish of sliced meat, bean curd, and vegetables fried together.

Suk·koth (so͝ok′əs, so͞o-kôt′) ▸ *n.* Var. of **Succoth.**

Su·la·we·si (so͞o′lä-wā′sē) also **Cel·e·bes** (sĕl′ə-bēz′, sə-lē′bēz′, sĕ-lā′bĕs) ▸ An island of central Indonesia on the equator E of Borneo.

sul·fa drug (sŭl′fə) ▸ *n.* Any of a group of synthetic organic compounds used to inhibit bacterial growth and activity.

sul·fa·nil·a·mide (sŭl′fə-nĭl′ə-mīd′, -mĭd) ▸ *n.* A white odorless compound used to treat various bacterial infections.

sul·fate (sŭl′fāt′) ▸ *n.* A chemical compound containing the bivalent group SO_4.

sul·fide (sŭl′fīd′) ▸ *n.* A compound of sulfur with another element, esp. a metal.

sul·fur also **sul·phur** (sŭl′fər) ▸ *n.* *Symbol* **S** A pale yellow nonmetallic element occurring widely in nature and used in gunpowder, insecticides, pharmaceuticals, and compounds such as sulfuric acid. At. no. 16.

sulfur dioxide ▸ *n.* A colorless, extremely irritating gas or liquid, SO_2, used in the manufacture of sulfuric acid.

sul·fu·ric (sŭl-fyo͝or′ĭk) ▸ *adj.* Of or containing sulfur.

sulfuric acid ▸ *n.* A highly corrosive, dense oily liquid, H_2SO_4, used to manufacture a wide variety of chemicals and materials.

sul·fur·ous (sŭl′fər-əs, -fyər-, sŭl-fyo͝or′əs) ▸ *adj.* **1.** Of or containing sulfur. **2.** Characteristic of burning sulfur, as in odor.

sulk (sŭlk) ▸ *v.* **sulked, sulk·ing.** To be sullenly aloof or withdrawn. ▸ *n.* A mood or display of sulking.

sulk·y[1] (sŭl′kē) ▸ *adj.* **-i·er, -i·est.** Sullenly aloof. **—sulk′i·ly** *adv.* **—sulk′i·ness** *n.*

sulk·y[2] (sŭl′kē) ▸ *n., pl.* **-ies.** A light two-wheeled vehicle carrying only the driver and drawn by one horse.

sul·len (sŭl′ən) ▸ *adj.* **-er, -est. 1.** Showing a brooding ill humor or silent resentment. **2.** Gloomy or somber. **—sul′len·ly** *adv.* **—sul′len·ness** *n.*

sul·ly (sŭl′ē) ▸ *v.* **-lied, -ly·ing. 1.** To mar the cleanness or luster of. **2.** To defile; taint.

sul·phur (sŭl′fər) ▸ *n.* Var. of **sulfur.**

sul·tan (sŭl′tən) ▸ *n.* A ruler of a Muslim country, esp. of the former Ottoman Empire.

sul·tan·a (sŭl-tăn′ə, -tä′nə) ▸ *n.* **1.** The wife, mother, sister, or daughter of a sultan. **2.** A small yellow seedless raisin.

sul·tan·ate (sŭl′tə-nāt′) ▸ *n.* **1.** The office, power, or reign of a sultan. **2.** A country ruled by a sultan.

sul·try (sŭl′trē) ▸ *adj.* **-tri·er, -tri·est. 1a.** Very humid and hot. **b.** Hot; torrid. **2.** Sensual; voluptuous. **—sul′tri·ness** *n.*

sum (sŭm) ▸ *n.* **1a.** The result obtained by addition. **b.** An arithmetic problem. **2.** The whole quantity; aggregate. **3.** An amount of money. **4.** A summary. **5.** The gist. ▸ *v.* **summed, sum·ming.** To add. ***—phrasal verb:*** **sum up** To summarize.

su·mac also **su·mach** (so͞o′măk, sho͞o′-) ▸ *n.* Any of various shrubs or small trees with compound leaves, greenish flowers, and usu. red fruit.

Su·ma·tra (so͞o-mä′trə) ▸ An island of W Indonesia in the Indian Ocean S of the Malay Peninsula. **—Su·ma′tran** *adj. & n.*

Su·mer (so͞o′mər) ▸ An ancient country of S Mesopotamia in present-day S Iraq. **—Su·me′ri·an** (-mîr′ē-ən, -mĕr′-) *adj. & n.*

sum·ma·rize (sŭm′ə-rīz′) ▸ *v.* **-rized, -riz·ing.** To make a summary of. **—sum′ma·ri·za′tion** *n.*

sum·ma·ry (sŭm′ə-rē) ▸ *adj.* **1.** Presented in condensed form; concise. **2.** Performed speedily and without ceremony: *summary justice.* ▸ *n., pl.* **-ries.** A condensed statement of the substance or principal points of a larger work.

THESAURUS

suggest *v.* **1.** To cause one to remember or think of ▸ hark back, recall. ***Idioms:*** bring to mind, put one in mind of, take one back, remind one of. [*Compare* REFER, REMIND.] **2.** To have a particular flavor or suggestion of something ▸ savor, smack, smell, taste. *—See also* HINT, IMPLY, PROPOSE.

suggested *adj.* *—See* IMPLICIT (1).

suggestible *adj.* *—See* FLEXIBLE (3).

suggestion *n.* Something, such as a feeling or idea, associated with a specific person or thing ▸ association, connection, connotation, impression. *—See also* ADVICE, HINT (2), PROPOSAL (1), SHADE (2).

suggestive *adj.* Tending to bring a memory, mood, or image, for example, subtly or indirectly to mind ▸ allusive, connotative, evocative, impressionistic, reminiscent. [*Compare* DESIGNATIVE, SYMBOLIC.] *—See also* EROTIC, INSINUATING, PREGNANT (2), RACY.

suggestiveness *n.* *—See* EROTICISM, SENSUALITY (1).

suit *v.* **1.** To be suitable to or in keeping with ▸ become, befit, fit, go with, match. ***Idioms:*** be one's cup of tea, be right down one's alley, suit one to a T. [*Compare* AGREE.] **2.** To look good on or with ▸ become, enhance, flatter. ***Idiom:*** put in the best light. *—See also* ADAPT, SATISFY (1).

suit *n.* *—See* LAWSUIT.

suitability or **suitableness** *n.* *—See* QUALIFICATION.

suitable *adj.* *—See* CONVENIENT (1), ELIGIBLE, JUST.

suitcase *n.* A container or piece of luggage for carrying clothing and other items ▸ bag, carryall, carryon, duffle (bag), flight bag, grip, kit, overnight bag, portmanteau, satchel, shoulder bag, valise.

suit coat or **suit jacket** *n.* *—See* COAT (1).

suite *n.* *—See* APARTMENT, RETINUE, SERIES.

suitor *n.* **1.** One that asks a higher authority for something, as a favor or redress ▸ appealer, appellant, petitioner. **2.** One who humbly entreats ▸ beggar, petitioner, prayer, suppliant, supplicant. *—See also* BEAU (1).

sulk *v.* To be sullenly aloof or withdrawn, as in silent resentment or protest ▸ mope, pet, pout. [*Compare* BROOD.]

sulky *adj.* *—See* GLUM.

sullen *adj.* *—See* FATEFUL (1), GLUM.

sully *v.* *—See* DENIGRATE, DIRTY, DISGRACE.

sultry *adj.* *—See* HOT (1), STICKY (2).

sum *n.* *—See* SUMMARY, SYSTEM, TOTAL, WHOLE.

sum *v.* *—See* ADD.

sum up *v.* *—See* AMOUNT, REVIEW (1).

summarize *v.* *—See* REVIEW (1).

summary *n.* A review of the essential points or consequences of something ▸ recap, recapitulation, rundown, run-through, sum, summation, summing-up, wrap-up. [*Compare* ESSENCE, STORY, SYNOPSIS.]

summary *adj.* *—See* BRIEF.

—**sum·mar′i·ly** (sə-mĕr′ə-lē) *adv.*
sum·ma·tion (sə-mā′shən) ▸ *n.* A concluding statement summarizing the principal points, esp. of a case before a court of law.
sum·mer (sŭm′ər) ▸ *n.* The usu. warmest season of the year, occurring between spring and autumn. ▸ *v.* To pass the summer. —**sum′mer·y** *adj.*
sum·mer·house (sŭm′ər-hous′) ▸ *n.* A small roofed structure in a park or garden.
sum·mer·time (sŭm′ər-tīm′) ▸ *n.* The summer season.
sum·mit (sŭm′ĭt) ▸ *n.* **1.** The highest point. **2.** The highest degree of achievement or status. **3.** A summit conference.
sum·mon (sŭm′ən) ▸ *v.* **1.** To call together; convene. **2.** To request to appear; send for. **3.** To order to appear in court. **4.** To call forth; rouse or evoke.
sum·mons (sŭm′ənz) ▸ *n., pl.* **-mons·es. 1.** A call to appear or do something. **2.** *Law* A notice summoning a person to report to court. —**sum′mons** *v.*
su·mo (sōō′mō) ▸ *n.* A Japanese form of wrestling.
sump (sŭmp) ▸ *n.* **1.** A pit or hole that receives drainage. **2.** A cesspool.
sump·tu·ous (sŭmp′chōō-əs) ▸ *adj.* Of a size or splendor suggesting great expense; lavish. —**sump′tu·ous·ly** *adv.* —**sump′tu·ous·ness** *n.*
sun (sŭn) ▸ *n.* **1.** often **Sun** A star that is the center of the solar system, sustains life on Earth with its light and heat, and has a mean distance from Earth of about 150 million km (93 million mi). **2.** A star that is the center of a planetary system. **3.** The radiant energy, esp. heat and visible light, emitted by the sun; sunshine. ▸ *v.* **sunned, sun·ning.** To expose to or bask in the sun's rays. —**sun′less** *adj.*
Sun. ▸ *abbr.* Sunday
sun·baked (sŭn′bākt′) ▸ *adj.* Baked, dried, or hardened by exposure to sunlight.
sun·bathe (sŭn′bāth′) ▸ *v.* To expose the body to the sun. —**sun′bath′er** *n.*
sun·beam (sŭn′bēm′) ▸ *n.* A ray of sunlight.
Sun·belt also **Sun Belt** (sŭn′bĕlt′) ▸ The S and SW US.
sun·block (sŭn′blŏk′) ▸ *n.* A sunscreen.
sun·bon·net (sŭn′bŏn′ĭt) ▸ *n.* A woman's wide-brimmed bonnet for shading the face and neck from the sun.
sun·burn (sŭn′bûrn′) ▸ *n.* Inflammation or blistering of the skin caused by overexposure to direct sunlight. —**sun′burn′** *v.*
sun·burst (sŭn′bûrst′) ▸ *n.* A design having a central sunlike disk with radiating spires.
sun·dae (sŭn′dē, -dā′) ▸ *n.* A dish of ice cream with a topping such as syrup, fruits, nuts, or whipped cream.
Sun·day (sŭn′dē, -dā′) ▸ *n.* **1.** The 1st day of the week. **2.** The Sabbath for many Christians.
sun·der (sŭn′dər) ▸ *v.* To break or wrench apart; sever. —**sun′der·ance** *n.*
sun·di·al (sŭn′dī′əl) ▸ *n.* An instrument that indicates the time of day by the shadow cast by a central projecting pointer on a calibrated dial.
sun·down (sŭn′doun′) ▸ *n.* Sunset.
sun·dries (sŭn′drēz) ▸ *pl.n.* Small miscellaneous items.
sun·dry (sŭn′drē) ▸ *adj.* Various; miscellaneous.
sun·fish (sŭn′fĭsh′) ▸ *n.* **1.** Any of various flat-bodied North American freshwater fishes. **2.** Any of various large, round-bodied salt water fishes.
sun·flow·er (sŭn′flou′ər) ▸ *n.* Any of various plants with large yellow-rayed flower heads that produce edible seeds rich in oil.
sung (sŭng) ▸ *v.* A p.t. and the p.part. of **sing.**
sun·glass·es (sŭn′glăs′ĭz) ▸ *pl.n.* Eyeglasses with tinted lenses to protect the eyes from the sun's glare.
sunk (sŭngk) ▸ *v.* A p.t. and the p.part. of **sink.**
sunk·en (sŭng′kən) ▸ *adj.* **1.** Depressed, fallen in, or hollowed: *sunken cheeks.* **2.** Submerged: *a sunken reef.* **3.** Below a surrounding level.
sun·lamp or **sun lamp** (sŭn′lămp′) ▸ *n.* A lamp that radiates ultraviolet rays used in therapeutic and cosmetic treatments.
sun·light (sŭn′līt′) ▸ *n.* The light of the sun.
sun·lit (sŭn′lĭt′) ▸ *adj.* Illuminated by the sun.
Sun·na also **Sun·nah** (sōōn′ə) ▸ *n.* The way of life prescribed as normative in Islam, based on the teachings and practices of Muhammad and on the Koran.
Sun·ni (sōōn′ē) ▸ *n., pl.* **-ni** or **-nis.** A member of the branch of Islam that accepts the first four caliphs as rightful successors of Muhammad. —**Sun′ni** *adj.* —**Sun′nite′** *n.*
sun·ny (sŭn′ē) ▸ *adj.* **-ni·er, -ni·est. 1.** Exposed to or abounding in sunshine. **2.** Cheerful; genial. —**sun′ni·ness** *n.*
sun·rise (sŭn′rīz′) ▸ *n.* The appearance of the sun above the eastern horizon.
sun·roof (sŭn′rōōf′, -rŏŏf′) ▸ *n.* A roof panel on a motor vehicle that can be slid back or raised.
sun·screen (sŭn′skrēn′) ▸ *n.* A preparation used to protect skin from the damaging rays of the sun.
sun·set (sŭn′sĕt′) ▸ *n.* The disappearance of the sun below the western horizon.
sun·shade (sŭn′shād′) ▸ *n.* Something, as a parasol, used as a protection from the sun.
sun·shine (sŭn′shīn′) ▸ *n.* **1.** The light or the direct rays from the sun. **2.** Cheerfulness; geniality. —**sun′shin′y** *adj.*
sun·spot (sŭn′spŏt′) ▸ *n.* Any of the relatively cool dark spots appearing in groups on the surface of the sun.
sun·stroke (sŭn′strōk′) ▸ *n.* Heat stroke caused by exposure to the sun.
sun·tan (sŭn′tăn′) ▸ *n.* A darkening of the skin resulting from exposure to the sun. —**sun′tanned′** *adj.*
sun·up (sŭn′ŭp′) ▸ *n.* The time of sunrise.
sup (sŭp) ▸ *v.* **supped, sup·ping.** To have supper; dine.
su·per (sōō′pər) *Informal* ▸ *n.* A superintendent in an apartment or office building. ▸ *adj.* **1.** Very large or great. **2.** Excellent.
super– ▸ *pref.* **1.** Above; over; upon: *superimpose.* **2.** Superior in size, quality, number, or degree: *superfine.* **3.** Exceeding a norm: *supersaturate.*
su·per·a·ble (sōō′pər-ə-bəl) ▸ *adj.* Possible to overcome; surmountable.
su·per·a·bun·dant (sōō′pər-ə-bŭn′dənt) ▸ *adj.* Abundant to excess. —**su′per·a·bun′dance** *n.*
su·per·an·nu·at·ed (sōō′pər-ăn′yōō-ā′tĭd) ▸ *adj.* **1.** Retired or ineffective because of advanced age. **2.** Outmoded; obsolete.
su·perb (sōō-pûrb′) ▸ *adj.* **1.** First-rate; excellent. **2.** Majestic; imposing. —**su·perb′ly** *adv.*

THESAURUS

summation *n.* The act or process of adding ▸ addition, totalization. [*Compare* CALCULATION.] —*See also* SUMMARY, TOTAL.
summer or **summertime** *n.* The season occurring between spring and autumn ▸ dog days.
summing-up *n.* —*See* SUMMARY.
summit *n.* —*See* CLIMAX, CONFERENCE (1).
summon *v.* To request that someone take part in or be present at a particular occasion ▸ ask, bid, invite. *Idioms:* extend an invitation to, request the presence of. [*Compare* APPEAL, REQUEST.] —*See also* ASSEMBLE, COMMAND (1), EVOKE.
summons *n.* A spoken or written request for someone to take part or be present ▸ bid, call, invitation. *Informal:* invite. [*Compare* REQUEST.]
sump *n.* —*See* PIT[1].
sumptuous *adj.* —*See* LUXURIOUS.
sumptuousness *n.* —*See* GLITTER (2).
sum total *n.* —*See* TOTAL.
sunder *v.* —*See* BREAK (1).
sundown *n.* —*See* EVENING.
sundries *n.* —*See* ODDS AND ENDS.
sundry *adj.* —*See* SEVERAL, VARIOUS.
sunken *adj.* —*See* HOLLOW (2).
sunny *adj.* —*See* CHEERFUL, CLEAR (2).
sunrise *n.* —*See* DAWN.
sunset *n.* —*See* EVENING.
sunup *n.* —*See* DAWN.
sup *v.* —*See* DRINK (1), EAT (2).
sup *n.* —*See* DRINK (2).
super *adj.* —*See* MARVELOUS.
super *adv.* —*See* UNDULY.
superabundance *n.* —*See* EXCESS (1).
superabundant *adj.* —*See* PROFUSE.
superannuate *v.* To withdraw or remove from business or active life ▸ pension (off), retire, step down. *Idioms:* call it quits, hang up one's spurs, put out to pasture, turn in one's badge. [*Compare* DISMISS, QUIT.]
superannuated *adj.* —*See* OBSOLETE.
superb *adj.* —*See* EXCELLENT, GRAND, MARVELOUS.
superbness *n.* —*See* EXCELLENCE.

su·per·car·go (so͞o′pər-kär′gō) ▸ *n., pl.* **-goes** or **-gos**. An officer on a merchant ship who has charge of the cargo.

su·per·charge (so͞o′pər-chärj′) ▸ *v.* To increase the power of (e.g., an engine).

su·per·charg·er (so͞o′pər-chär′jər) ▸ *n.* A blower or compressor for supplying air under high pressure to the cylinders of an internal-combustion engine.

su·per·cil·i·ous (so͞o′pər-sĭl′ē-əs) ▸ *adj.* Feeling or showing haughty disdain. **—su′per·cil′i·ous·ly** *adv.* **—su′per·cil′i·ous·ness** *n.*

su·per·col·lid·er (so͞o′pər-kə-lĭd′ər) ▸ *n.* A high-energy particle accelerator.

su·per·con·duc·tiv·i·ty (so͞o′pər-kŏn′dŭk-tĭv′ĭtē) ▸ *n.* The flow of electric current without resistance in certain metals, alloys, and ceramics, usu. at temperatures near absolute zero. **—su′per·con·duc′tive** *adj.* **—su′per·con·duc′tor** *n.*

su·per·cool (so͞o′pər-ko͞ol′) ▸ *v.* To cool (a liquid) below the freezing point without solidification.

su·per·e·go (so͞o′pər-ē′gō) ▸ *n., pl.* **-gos**. In psychoanalysis, the part of the psyche formed through the internalization of moral standards of parents and society.

su·per·e·rog·a·to·ry (so͞o′pər-ĭ-rŏg′ə-tôr′ē) ▸ *adj.* Superfluous; unnecessary.

su·per·fi·cial (so͞o′pər-fĭsh′əl) ▸ *adj.* **1.** Of, affecting, or being on the surface. **2.** Concerned with or comprehending only the obvious; shallow. **3.** Apparent rather than actual or substantial. **4.** Trivial. **—su′per·fi′ci·al′i·ty** (-fĭsh′ē-ăl′ĭ-tē) *n.* **—su′per·fi′cial·ly** *adv.*

su·per·fine (so͞o′pər-fīn′) ▸ *adj.* **1.** Of exceptional quality. **2.** Overly delicate or refined. **3.** Of extra fine texture.

su·per·flu·i·ty (so͞o′pər-flo͞o′ĭ-tē) ▸ *n., pl.* **-ties**. **1.** The quality or condition of being superfluous. **2.** Something superfluous. **3.** Overabundance; excess.

su·per·flu·ous (so͞o-pûr′flo͞o-əs) ▸ *adj.* Beyond what is required or sufficient. **—su·per′flu·ous·ly** *adv.*

su·per·gal·ax·y (so͞o′pər-găl′ək-sē) ▸ *n.* A very large group of galaxies.

su·per·gi·ant (so͞o′pər-jī′ənt) ▸ *n.* A very large star with a luminosity thousands of times that of the sun.

su·per·he·ro (so͞o′pər-hîr′ō) ▸ *n.* A figure, esp. in a comic strip or cartoon, of superhuman powers and usu. portrayed as fighting evil or crime.

su·per·high·way (so͞o′pər-hī′wā′) ▸ *n.* A broad highway for high-speed traffic.

su·per·hu·man (so͞o′pər-hyo͞o′mən) ▸ *adj.* **1.** Divine; supernatural. **2.** Beyond ordinary or normal human ability, power, or experience. **—su′per·hu′man·ly** *adv.*

su·per·im·pose (so͞o′pər-ĭm-pōz′) ▸ *v.* **-posed, -pos·ing**. To lay or place on or over something else. **—su′per·im′po·si′tion** (-ĭm′pə-zĭsh′ən) *n.*

su·per·in·tend (so͞o′pər-ĭn-tĕnd′, so͞o′prĭn-) ▸ *v.* **1.** To oversee and direct; supervise. **2.** To take care of; manage. **—su′per·in·ten′dence** *n.* **—su′per·in·ten′dent** *n.*

su·pe·ri·or (so͞o-pîr′ē-ər) ▸ *adj.* **1.** High or higher in order, degree, rank, quality, or estimation. **2.** Situated above or over. **3.** Arrogant; haughty. **4.** Indifferent or immune. ▸ *n.* **1.** One who surpasses another in rank or quality. **2.** The head of a religious order or house. **—su·pe′ri·or′i·ty** (-ôr′ĭ-tē, -ŏr′-) *n.* **—su·pe′ri·or·ly** *adv.*

Superior, Lake ▸ The largest of the Great Lakes, between the N-central US and S Ontario, Canada.

su·per·la·tive (so͞o-pûr′lə-tĭv) ▸ *adj.* **1.** Of the highest order, quality, or degree. **2.** Excessive or exaggerated. **3.** *Gram.* Expressing or involving the extreme degree of comparison of an adjective or adverb. ▸ *n.* **1.** Something superlative. **2.** *Gram.* **a.** The superlative degree. **b.** An adjective, such as *biggest,* or adverb, such as *most highly,* expressing this degree. **—su·per′la·tive·ly** *adv.*

su·per·man (so͞o′pər-măn′) ▸ *n.* A man with more than human powers.

su·per·mar·ket (so͞o′pər-mär′kĭt) ▸ *n.* A large self-service retail market selling food and household goods.

su·per·nal (so͞o-pûr′nəl) ▸ *adj.* **1.** Celestial; heavenly. **2.** Of or from the sky. **—su·per′nal·ly** *adv.*

su·per·nat·u·ral (so͞o′pər-năch′ər-əl) ▸ *adj.* **1.** Of or relating to existence outside the natural world. **2.** Attributed to divine power. **—su′per·nat′u·ral·ly** *adv.*

su·per·no·va (so͞o′pər-nō′və) ▸ *n., pl.* **-vae** (-vē) or **-vas**. A rare celestial phenomenon in which a star explodes, resulting in an extremely bright, short-lived object.

su·per·nu·mer·ar·y (so͞o′pər-no͞o′mə-rĕr′ē, -nyo͞o′-) ▸ *adj.* **1.** Exceeding a fixed or prescribed number; extra. **2.** Superfluous. ▸ *n., pl.* **-ies**. **1.** One that is supernumerary. **2.** An actor or actress without a speaking part; extra.

su·per·phos·phate (so͞o′pər-fŏs′fāt′) ▸ *n.* **1.** An acid phosphate. **2.** A fertilizer made by the action of sulfuric acid on phosphate rock.

su·per·pow·er (so͞o′pər-pou′ər) ▸ *n.* A powerful and dominant nation, esp. the leader of an international power bloc.

su·per·sat·u·rate (so͞o′pər-săch′ə-rāt′) ▸ *v.* To cause (a chemical solution) to be more highly concentrated than is normally possible under given conditions of temperature and pressure. **—su′per·sat′u·ra′tion** *n.*

su·per·scribe (so͞o′pər-skrīb′) ▸ *v.* **-scribed, -scrib·ing**. To write (something) on the outside or upper part, as of a letter. **—su′per·scrip′tion** (-skrĭp′shən) *n.*

su·per·script (so͞o′pər-skrĭpt′) ▸ *n.* A character placed above and immediately to one side of another. **—su′per·script** *adj.*

su·per·sede (so͞o′pər-sēd′) ▸ *v.* **-sed·ed, -sed·ing**. **1.** To take the place of; succeed. **2.** To displace; supplant.

THESAURUS

supercilious *adj.* —*See* ARROGANT, DISDAINFUL.

superciliousness *n.* —*See* ARROGANCE.

supererogatory or **supererogative** *adj.* —*See* SUPERFLUOUS, WANTON (2).

superficial *adj.* Lacking in intellectual depth or thoroughness ▸ cursory, naive, one-dimensional, shallow, sketchy, skin-deep, surface, uncritical. [*Compare* TRITE.] —*See also* APPARENT (3).

superficially *adv.* —*See* APPARENTLY.

superfluity *n.* —*See* EXCESS (1), SURPLUS.

superfluous *adj.* Being more than is needed, desired, or appropriate ▸ de trop, excess, extra, leftover, redundant, spare, supererogatory, supernumerary, surplus. [*Compare* EXCESSIVE, REMAINING, UNNECESSARY.]

superfluousness *n.* —*See* EXCESS (1).

superhighway *n.* —*See* WAY (2).

superhuman *adj.* —*See* SUPERNATURAL (1).

superintend *v.* —*See* SUPERVISE.

superintendence *n.* —*See* CARE (2), MANAGEMENT.

superintendent *n.* —*See* BOSS.

superior *adj.* **1.** Of greater excellence than another ▸ better, preferable. **2.** Being at a rank or level above another ▸ greater, higher, senior, upper. —*See also* ARROGANT, CHOICE (1), DISDAINFUL, EXCELLENT.

superior *n.* One who stands above another in rank ▸ better, elder, senior. *Informal:* higher-up. [*Compare* CHIEF.] —*See also* BOSS.

superiority *n.* —*See* ADVANTAGE (3), ARROGANCE, AUTHORITY, EXCELLENCE.

superlative *adj.* —*See* BEST (1).

supernal *adj.* —*See* DIVINE (1), HEAVENLY (1), HEAVENLY (2).

supernatural *adj.* **1.** Of or relating to existence outside the natural world ▸ extramundane, extrasensory, metaphysical, miraculous, mystic, mystical, numinous, otherworldly, paranormal, preternatural, spiritual, superhuman, superphysical, supersensible, transcendental, unearthly, unworldly. [*Compare* DIVINE, HEAVENLY, IMMATERIAL, WEIRD.] **2.** Greatly exceeding or departing from the normal course of nature ▸ preternatural, unnatural. [*Compare* ABNORMAL.]

supernormal *adj.* —*See* ELEVATED [illegible].

supernumerary *adj.* —*See* SUPERFLUOUS.

supernumerary *n.* —*See* SURPLUS.

superphysical *adj.* —*See* SUPERNATURAL (1).

superscribe *v.* ▸ address, direct. [*Compare* TICKET.]

supersede *v.* To substitute for or fill the place of ▸ displace, replace, supplant, surrogate. *Idioms:* fill someone's shoes, take over from, take the reins from. [*Compare* SUBSTITUTE.]

superseded *adj.* —*See* OBSOLETE.

supersensible *adj.* —*See* SUPERNATURAL (1).

su·per·son·ic (so͞o′pər-sŏn′ĭk) ▸ *adj.* Of, caused by, or having a speed greater than the speed of sound. **—su′per·son′i·cal·ly** *adv.*

su·per·star (so͞o′pər-stär′) ▸ *n.* A widely acclaimed star, as in movies or sports, who has great popular appeal.

su·per·sti·tion (so͞o′pər-stĭsh′ən) ▸ *n.* **1.** A belief that an object, action, or circumstance not logically related to a course of events influences its outcome. **2.** A belief or practice irrationally maintained by ignorance or by faith in magic or chance. **—su′per·sti′tious** *adj.* **—su′per·sti′tious·ly** *adv.*

su·per·struc·ture (so͞o′pər-strŭk′chər) ▸ *n.* A physical or conceptual structure built on top of something else, esp. a ship's structure above the main deck.

su·per·tank·er (so͞o′pər-tăng′kər) ▸ *n.* A very large ship used esp. to transport oil.

su·per·vene (so͞o′pər-vēn′) ▸ *v.* **-vened, -ven·ing.** To come or occur as something additional or unexpected.

su·per·vise (so͞o′pər-vīz′) ▸ *v.* **-vised, -vis·ing.** To have the charge and direction of; superintend. **—su′per·vi′sor** *n.* **—su′per·vi′so·ry** *adj.*

su·per·vi·sion (so͞o′pər-vĭzh′ən) ▸ *n.* The act or function of supervising.

su·pine (so͞o-pīn′, so͞o′pīn′) ▸ *adj.* **1.** Lying on the back or having the face upward. **2.** Lethargic; passive. **3.** Cravenly submissive. **—su·pine′ly** *adv.*

sup·per (sŭp′ər) ▸ *n.* An evening meal, esp. a light meal when dinner is taken at midday.

sup·plant (sə-plănt′) ▸ *v.* To take the place of; supercede.

sup·ple (sŭp′əl) ▸ *adj.* **-pler, -plest.** **1.** Readily bent; pliant. **2.** Agile; limber. **3.** Yielding readily; compliant or adaptable. **—sup′ple·ness** *n.* **—sup′ply, sup′ple·ly** *adv.*

sup·ple·ment (sŭp′lə-mənt) ▸ *n.* Something added to complete a thing or to make up for a deficiency. ▸ *v.* (-mĕnt′) To provide or form a supplement to. **—sup′ple·men′ta·ry** (-mĕn′tə-rē, -trē), **sup′ple·men′tal** *adj.* **—sup′ple·men·ta′tion** (-mĕn-tā′shən) *n.*

sup·pli·ant (sŭp′lē-ənt) ▸ *adj.* Asking humbly and earnestly; beseeching. ▸ *n.* A supplicant. **—sup′pli·ance** *n.* **—sup′pli·ant·ly** *adv.*

sup·pli·cant (sŭp′lĭ-kənt) ▸ *n.* One who beseeches or supplicates. ▸ *adj.* Supplicating.

sup·pli·cate (sŭp′lĭ-kāt′) ▸ *v.* **-cat·ed, -cat·ing.** **1.** To make a humble, earnest petition; beg. **2.** To beseech. **—sup′pli·ca′tion** *n.*

sup·ply (sə-plī′) ▸ *v.* **-plied, -ply·ing.** **1.** To make available for use; provide. **2.** To furnish or equip with. **3.** To fill sufficiently; satisfy: *supply a need.* ▸ *n., pl.* **-plies.** **1.** The act of supplying. **2.** An amount available; stock. **3.** often **supplies** Materials or provisions stored and dispensed when needed. **4.** *Econ.* The amount of a commodity available for meeting a demand or for purchase at a given price. **—sup·pli′er** *n.*

sup·port (sə-pôrt′) ▸ *v.* **1.** To bear the weight of. **2.** To maintain in position; hold up. **3.** To be capable of bearing; withstand. **4.** To keep from weakening or failing. **5.** To provide for or maintain by supplying with money or necessities. **6.** To furnish corroborating evidence for. **7.** To aid the cause or interests of. ▸ *n.* **1.** The act of supporting or the condition of being supported. **2.** One that supports. **3.** Financial maintenance. **—sup·port′a·ble** *adj.* **—sup·port′er** *n.* **—sup·por′tive** *adj.*

sup·pose (sə-pōz′) ▸ *v.* **-posed, -pos·ing.** **1.** To assume to be true for the sake of argument. **2a.** To believe, esp. on uncertain grounds. **b.** To consider to be probable or likely. **3.** To imply as an antecedent condition; presuppose.

sup·posed (sə-pōzd′, -pō′zĭd) ▸ *adj.* Presumed or considered to be true, often mistakenly. **—sup·pos′ed·ly** *adv.*

sup·pos·ing (sə-pō′zĭng) ▸ *conj.* Assuming that: *Supposing I'm right, what can we do?*

sup·po·si·tion (sŭp′ə-zĭsh′ən) ▸ *n.* **1.** The act of supposing. **2.** An assumption.

sup·pos·i·to·ry (sə-pŏz′ĭ-tôr′ē) ▸ *n., pl.* **-ries.** A small plug

THESAURUS

superstar *n.* —*See* CELEBRITY.

superstition *n.* —*See* LORE (1).

supervene *v.* —*See* FOLLOW (1).

supervening *adj.* —*See* FOLLOWING (1).

supervenient *adj.* Not part of the real or essential nature of a thing ▸ adscititious, adventitious, incidental, inessential. [*Compare* IRRELEVANT, UNNECESSARY.]

supervise *v.* To direct and watch over the work and performance of others ▸ boss, monitor, overlook, oversee, superintend, watch over. [*Compare* ARRANGE, CONDUCT.]

supervision *n.* —*See* CARE (2), MANAGEMENT.

supervisor *n.* —*See* BOSS.

supervisory *adj.* —*See* ADMINISTRATIVE.

supine *adj.* —*See* APATHETIC, COWARDLY, FLAT (1).

supplant *v.* **1.** To take the place of another against the other's will ▸ cut out, displace, force out, usurp. [*Compare* ASSUME, OCCUPY, SEIZE.] **2.** To substitute for or fill the place of ▸ displace, replace, supersede, surrogate. *Idioms:* fill someone's shoes, take over from, take the reins from. [*Compare* SUBSTITUTE.]

supple *adj.* —*See* ADAPTABLE, FLEXIBLE (1), FLEXIBLE (2), FLEXIBLE (3), MALLEABLE, OBEDIENT.

supplement *v.* To add to or make whole ▸ accompany, augment, complement, complete, enhance, enrich, reinforce, strengthen. [*Compare* INCREASE, SUPPORT.]

supplement *n.* —*See* ATTACHMENT, ENHANCEMENT.

supplemental or **supplementary** *adj.* —*See* ADDITIONAL, AUXILIARY (2), COMPLEMENTARY.

suppleness *n.* —*See* FLEXIBILITY (1).

supplicant or **suppliant** *n.* One who humbly entreats ▸ beggar, petitioner, prayer, suitor.

supplicate *v.* To offer a reverent petition to God or a god ▸ invoke, pray. —*See also* APPEAL (1).

supplication *n.* The act of praying ▸ benediction, invocation, prayer. —*See also* APPEAL.

supplier *n.* —*See* DONOR.

supply *v.* —*See* GIVE (1), OFFER (2), SUBSTITUTE.

supply *n.* —*See* HOARD.

support *v.* **1.** To aid the cause of by approving or favoring ▸ advocate, back, champion, endorse, get behind, plump for, recommend, side with, stand behind, stand by, uphold. *Idioms:* align oneself with, go to bat for, throw one's weight behind. **2.** To make stronger or more resistant ▸ bolster, brace, bracket, buoy (up), buttress, hold (up), prop (up), reinforce, shore (up), stabilize, steady, strengthen, sustain, tighten, undergird, underpin, underprop, uphold. [*Compare* BALANCE, FASTEN.] **3.** To supply with the necessities of life ▸ keep, maintain, provide for. *Idioms:* put a roof over someone's head, put food on the table, take care of. [*Compare* NOURISH.] **4.** To act as a patron to ▸ back, patronize, sponsor. [*Compare* DONATE, FINANCE.] —*See also* BACK (2), BEAR (1), ENDURE (1).

support *n.* A means or device that keeps something erect, stable, or secure ▸ brace, bracket, buttress, crutch, prop, reinforcement, shore, stay, underpinning. —*See also* ENDORSEMENT, HELP, LIVING.

supportable *adj.* —*See* BEARABLE.

supporter *n.* —*See* ADVOCATE, FOLLOWER, PATRON.

supportive *adj.* —*See* AUXILIARY (1), SYMPATHETIC.

supposable *adj.* —*See* PRESUMPTIVE.

suppose *v.* **1.** To consider to be true without proof ▸ assume, imagine, posit, postulate, premise, presume, presuppose. *Informal:* expect, reckon. *Idiom:* take for granted (*or* as a given). [*Compare* BELIEVE, INFER.] **2.** To oblige to do or not do by force of authority, propriety, or custom ▸ expect, oblige, obligate, require. [*Compare* MUST.] —*See also* GUESS.

supposed *adj.* Presumed to be true, real, or genuine, especially on inconclusive grounds ▸ alleged, conjectural, hypothetic, hypothetical, hypothesized, inferential, presumed, purported, putative, reputed, so-called, suppositional, suppositious, supposititious, suppositive. *Informal:* quote-unquote. [*Compare* AMBIGUOUS, PRESUMPTIVE.]

supposition *n.* —*See* ASSUMPTION, GUESS.

suppositional or **suppositive** *adj.* —*See* SUPPOSED.

supposititious or **suppositious** *adj.* —*See* COUNTERFEIT, SUPPOSED.

of medication designed to melt within a body cavity other than the mouth.

sup·press (sə-prĕs′) ▸ *v.* **1.** To put an end to forcibly; subdue. **2.** To keep from being revealed, published, or circulated. **3.** To inhibit the expression of; check: *suppress a smile.* **—sup·press′ion** *n.* **—sup·press′ive** *adj.*

sup·pu·rate (sŭp′yə-rāt′) ▸ *v.* **-rat·ed, -rat·ing.** To form or discharge pus. **—sup′pu·ra′tion** *n.*

su·pra·na·tion·al (so͞o′prə-năsh′ə-nəl, -năsh′nəl) ▸ *adj.* Of or extending beyond the boundaries or authority of a nation.

su·prem·a·cist (so͞o-prĕm′ə-sĭst) ▸ *n.* One who believes that a certain group is or should be supreme.

su·prem·a·cy (so͞o-prĕm′ə-sē) ▸ *n.* **1.** The quality or condition of being supreme. **2.** Supreme power.

su·preme (so͞o-prēm′) ▸ *adj.* **1.** Greatest in power, authority, or rank. **2.** Greatest in importance, degree, or achievement. **3.** Ultimate; final: *the supreme sacrifice.* **—su·preme′ly** *adv.* **—su·preme′ness** *n.*

Supreme Court ▸ *n.* **1.** The highest US federal court. **2. supreme court** The highest court in most US states.

sur– ▸ *pref.* **1.** Over; above; upon: *surpass.* **2.** Additional: *surtax.*

sur·cease (sûr′sēs′, sər-sēs′) ▸ *n.* Cessation.

sur·charge (sûr′chärj′) ▸ *n.* **1.** An additional sum added to the usual cost. **2.** An overcharge, esp. when unlawful. ▸ *v.* **1.** To charge an extra sum. **2.** To overcharge.

sure (sho͝or, shûr) ▸ *adj.* **sur·er, sur·est. 1.** Impossible to doubt or dispute; certain. **2.** Strong; firm: *sure convictions.* **3.** Confident: *sure of victory.* **4a.** Bound to happen; inevitable: *sure defeat.* **b.** Destined: *sure to succeed.* **5.** Trustworthy; reliable. ***—idioms:*** **for sure** *Informal* Certainly; unquestionably. **make sure** Make certain. **to be sure** Indeed; certainly. **—sure′ness** *n.*

sure-fire (sho͝or′fīr′) ▸ *adj. Informal* Bound to be successful.

sure-foot·ed or **sure·foot·ed** (sho͝or′fo͝ot′ĭd) ▸ *adj.* Not liable to stumble or fall. **—sure′-foot′ed·ly** *adv.*

sure·ly (sho͝or′lē) ▸ *adv.* **1.** With confidence; unhesitatingly. **2.** Undoubtedly; certainly.

sur·e·ty (sho͝or′ĭ-tē) ▸ *n., pl.* **-ties. 1.** The condition of being sure. **2.** Something beyond doubt. **3.** A guarantee or security. **4.** One who has contracted to be responsible for another. **—sur′e·ty·ship′** *n.*

surf (sûrf) ▸ *n.* The waves of the sea as they break upon a shore or reef. ▸ *v.* To engage in surfing. **—surf′er** *n.*

sur·face (sûr′fəs) ▸ *n.* **1.** The outer or the topmost boundary of an object. **2.** The superficial or external aspect. ▸ *adj.* **1.** Of or on the surface. **2.** Superficial. ▸ *v.* **-faced, -fac·ing. 1.** To form the surface of. **2.** To rise or come to the surface. **3.** To emerge from concealment.

surf·board (sûrf′bôrd′) ▸ *n.* A narrow, somewhat rounded board used for surfing.

sur·feit (sûr′fĭt) ▸ *v.* To feed or supply to excess; satiate. ▸ *n.* **1a.** Overindulgence in food or drink. **b.** The result of such overindulgence; satiety or disgust. **2.** An excessive amount.

surf·ing (sûr′fĭng) ▸ *n.* The sport of riding on the crest or along the tunnel of a wave, esp. while on a surfboard.

surge (sûrj) ▸ *v.* **surged, surg·ing. 1.** To move in a billowing or swelling manner. **2.** To increase suddenly. ▸ *n.* **1.** A swelling motion like that of great waves. **2.** A sudden onrush: *a surge of joy.* **3.** *Elect.* A sudden increase in current or voltage.

sur·geon (sûr′jən) ▸ *n.* A physician specializing in surgery.

sur·ger·y (sûr′jə-rē) ▸ *n., pl.* **-ies. 1.** The diagnosis and treatment of injury, deformity, and disease by manual and instrumental means. **2.** A surgical procedure, esp. the removal of a diseased part. **3.** A surgical operating room or laboratory. **—sur′gi·cal** *adj.* **—sur′gi·cal·ly** *adv.*

Su·ri·na·me (so͞o′rə-nä′mə) also **Su·ri·nam** (so͞or′ə-năm′, -näm′) ▸ A country of NE South America on the Atlantic. **—Su′ri·na·mese′** (-nä-mēz′, -mēs′) *adj. & n.*

sur·ly (sûr′lē) ▸ *adj.* **-li·er, -li·est.** Sullenly ill-humored; gruff. **—sur′li·ly** *adv.* **—sur′li·ness** *n.*

sur·mise (sər-mīz′) ▸ *v.* **-mised, -mis·ing.** To infer with little evidence; guess. ▸ *n.* An idea or opinion based on little evidence; conjecture.

sur·mount (sər-mount′) ▸ *v.* **1.** To overcome; conquer: *surmount an obstacle.* **2.** To ascend to the top of. **3.** To be above or on top of. **—sur·mount′a·ble** *adj.* **—sur·mount′er** *n.*

sur·name (sûr′nām′) ▸ *n.* A name shared in common to identify the members of a family; last name.

sur·pass (sər-păs′) ▸ *v.* **1.** To be beyond the limit, powers, or capacity of; transcend: *surpass comprehension.* **2.** To be greater or better than; exceed.

sur·pass·ing (sər-păs′ĭng) ▸ *adj.* Exceptional; exceeding. **—sur·pass′ing·ly** *adv.*

sur·plice (sûr′plĭs) ▸ *n.* A loose-fitting white ecclesiastical gown worn over a cassock.

sur·plus (sûr′pləs, -plŭs′) ▸ *adj.* Being in excess of what is needed. ▸ *n.* A surplus amount or quantity.

sur·prise (sər-prīz′) ▸ *v.* **-prised, -pris·ing. 1.** To encounter suddenly or unexpectedly. **2.** To attack or capture suddenly and without warning. **3.** To astonish by the unanticipated.

THESAURUS

suppress *v.* To overcome opposition or uprising with overwhelming force ▸ choke off, crush, extinguish, put down, quash, quell, quench, squash, squelch. *Idiom:* put the lid on. [*Compare* ABOLISH, DEFEAT, FRUSTRATE.] —*See also* CENSOR (2), REPRESS.

suppression *n.* Forceful subjugation, as against an uprising ▸ clampdown, crackdown, lockdown, repression. [*Compare* OPPRESSION, RESTRAINT.] —*See also* DOMINATION.

suppressive *adj.* —*See* REPRESSIVE.

supremacy *n.* —*See* AUTHORITY, DOMINANCE.

supreme *adj.* —*See* AUTHORITATIVE (1), BEST (1), DOMINANT (1), IDEAL.

surcease *v.* —*See* STOP (1), STOP (2).

surcease *n.* —*See* STOP (1), STOP (2).

sure *adj.* **1.** Having no doubt ▸ assured, certain, confident, convinced, doubtless, positive, undoubting. **2.** Certain not to fail, miss, or err ▸ certain, fail-safe, foolproof, infallible, secure, unerring, unfailing. *Informal:* sure-fire. *Slang:* idiot-proof. [*Compare* DEPENDABLE.] —*See also* CERTAIN (1), CERTAIN (2), DEFINITE (3), FIRM[1] (2).

sure-fire *adj.* —*See* SURE (2).

surely *adv.* —*See* ABSOLUTELY.

sureness *n.* The fact or condition of being without doubt ▸ assurance, assuredness, certainty, certitude, confidence, conviction, doubtlessness, indubitability, positiveness, positivity, surety. [*Compare* IMPUDENCE.] —*See also* STABILITY.

sure thing *n.* —*See* CERTAINTY.

surety *n.* An assumption of responsibility, as one given by a manufacturer, for the quality, worth, or durability of a product ▸ certification, guarantee, guaranty, warrant, warranty. —*See also* SPONSOR, SURENESS.

surface *n.* An outer surface, layer, or part of an object ▸ face, facet, side. [*Compare* BACK, BOTTOM, FRONT.] —*See also* FACE (3), FINISH.

surface *v.* —*See* FACE (2), FINISH (2).

surface *adj.* —*See* SUPERFICIAL.

surfeit *v.* —*See* SATIATE.

surfeit *n.* —*See* EXCESS (1), EXCESS (2), SATIATION, SURPLUS.

surge *v.* —*See* FLOW (2), INCREASE.

surge *n.* —*See* ERUPTION, FLOW.

surly *adj.* —*See* GLUM, ILL-TEMPERED.

surmise *v.* —*See* GUESS.

surmise *n.* —*See* GUESS.

surmised *adj.* —*See* UNTRIED.

surmount *v.* To pass by or over successfully ▸ clear, hurdle, negotiate. —*See also* DEFEAT.

surmountable *adj.* —*See* PASSABLE.

surpass *v.* To be greater or better than ▸ best, better, exceed, excel, one-up, outdo, outmatch, outrun, outshine, outstrip, pass, top, transcend. *Informal:* beat. ***Idioms:*** go beyond, go one better. [*Compare* DOMINATE.] —*See also* EXCEED.

surplus *n.* A thing, amount, or quantity beyond what is needed, desired, or appropriate ▸ excess, extra, fat, glut, leftover, overage, overflow, overmuch, overrun, overstock, oversupply, superfluity, supernumerary, surfeit, surplusage. *Idiom:* fifth wheel. [*Compare* EXCESS.]

surplus *adj.* —*See* SUPERFLUOUS.

surprise *v.* To impress strongly by what is unexpected or unusual ▸ amaze, astonish, astound, awe, startle. *Idioms:* catch (*or* take) unawares, take aback, throw for a loop. [*Compare* STAGGER, STARTLE.] —*See also* AMBUSH.

► *n.* **1.** The act of surprising or the condition of being surprised. **2.** Something that surprises. **—sur·pris′ing** *adj.* **—sur·pris′ing·ly** *adv.*

sur·re·al·ism (sə-rē′ə-lĭz′əm) ► *n.* A 20th-cent. literary and artistic movement that attempts to express the workings of the subconscious by fantastic imagery and incongruous juxtaposition of subject matter. **—sur·re′al, sur·re′al·is′tic** *adj.* **—sur·re′al·ist** *n.* **—sur·re′al·is′ti·cal·ly** *adv.*

sur·ren·der (sə-rĕn′dər) ► *v.* **1.** To relinquish possession or control of to another because of demand or compulsion. **2.** To give (oneself) up, as to an emotion: *surrendered himself to grief.* **3.** To give oneself up to another. ► *n.* The act of surrendering.

sur·rep·ti·tious (sûr′əp-tĭsh′əs) ► *adj.* Secret and stealthy. **—sur′rep·ti′tious·ly** *adv.*

sur·rey (sûr′ē, sŭr′ē) ► *n., pl.* **-reys.** A four-wheeled horse-drawn carriage having two or four seats.

sur·ro·gate (sûr′ə-gĭt, -gāt′, sŭr′-) ► *n.* **1.** A substitute. **2.** *Law* A judge in some US states having jurisdiction over the settlement of estates. **—sur′ro·gate** (-gĭt, gāt′) *adj.*

sur·round (sə-round′) ► *v.* **1.** To extend on all sides of simultaneously; encircle. **2.** To enclose or confine on all sides.

sur·round·ings (sə-roun′dĭngz) ► *pl.n.* The external circumstances that surround one.

sur·tax (sûr′tăks′) ► *n.* **1.** An additional tax. **2.** A tax levied after net income has exceeded a certain level.

sur·veil·lance (sər-vā′ləns) ► *n.* Close observation of a person or group, esp. one under suspicion.

sur·vey (sər-vā′, sûr′vā′) ► *v.* **1.** To examine or look at comprehensively. **2.** To determine the boundaries, area, or elevations of (part of the earth's surface) by means of measuring angles and distances. ► *n.* (sûr′vā′) *pl.* **-veys.** **1.** A detailed inspection or investigation. **2.** A comprehensive view. **3a.** The process of surveying. **b.** A report on or map of what has been surveyed. **—sur·vey′or** *n.*

sur·vey·ing (sər-vā′ĭng) ► *n.* The act, practice, or occupation of a surveyor.

sur·vive (sər-vīv′) ► *v.* **-vived, -viv·ing.** **1.** To remain alive or in existence; endure. **2.** To live longer than; outlive. **—sur·viv′a·ble** *adj.* **—sur·viv′al** *n.* **—sur·vi′vor** *n.*

sus·cep·ti·ble (sə-sĕp′tə-bəl) ► *adj.* **1.** Easily influenced or affected. **2.** Likely to be affected with: *susceptible to colds.* **3.** Capable of accepting or permitting: *susceptible of proof.* **—sus·cep′ti·bil′i·ty** *n.* **—sus·cep′ti·bly** *adv.*

su·shi (so͞o′shē) ► *n.* Cold rice shaped into small pieces and topped with raw or cooked fish.

sus·pect (sə-spĕkt′) ► *v.* **1.** To surmise to be true or probable; imagine. **2.** To distrust or doubt: *I suspect his motives.* **3.** To think guilty without proof. ► *n.* (sŭs′pĕkt′) One who is suspected, esp. of a crime. ► *adj.* (sŭs′pĕkt′, sə-spĕkt′) Open to or viewed with suspicion.

sus·pend (sə-spĕnd′) ► *v.* **1.** To bar for a period from a privilege, office, or position. **2.** To cause to stop for a period; interrupt. **3a.** To hold in abeyance; defer: *suspend judgment.* **b.** To render temporarily ineffective: *suspend a jail sentence.* **4.** To hang so as to allow free movement. **5.** To support or keep from falling without apparent attachment.

sus·pend·ers (sə-spĕn′dərz) ► *n.* A pair of often elastic straps worn over the shoulders to support trousers.

sus·pense (sə-spĕns′) ► *n.* **1.** The state or quality of being undecided. **2.** Anxiety or apprehension resulting from uncertainty. **—sus·pense′ful** *adj.*

sus·pen·sion (sə-spĕn′shən) ► *n.* **1.** The act of suspending or the condition of being suspended, esp.: **a.** A temporary deferment. **b.** A postponement of judgment or decision. **2.** A device from which a mechanical part is suspended. **3.** The system of springs and other devices that insulates the chassis of a vehicle from shocks. **4.** *Chem.* A relatively coarse, noncolloidal dispersion of solid particles in a liquid.

suspension bridge ► *n.* A bridge having the roadway suspended from cables that are usu. supported at intervals by towers.

sus·pi·cion (sə-spĭsh′ən) ► *n.* **1.** The act of suspecting something, esp. something wrong, on little evidence or proof. **2.** A hint or trace.

sus·pi·cious (sə-spĭsh′əs) ► *adj.* **1.** Arousing or apt to arouse suspicion; questionable. **2.** Tending to suspect; distrustful. **3.** Expressing suspicion. **—sus·pi′cious·ly** *adv.* **—sus·pi′cious·ness** *n.*

sus·tain (sə-stān′) ► *v.* **1.** To keep in existence; maintain. **2.** To supply with necessities or nourishment. **3.** To keep from falling or sinking; prop. **4.** To support the spirits or resolution of; encourage. **5.** To endure or withstand: *sustain hardships.* **6.** To suffer: *sustained a fatal injury.* **7.** To affirm the validity of: *The judge sustained the objection.* **8.** To prove; confirm. **—sus·tain′a·ble** *adj.*

sus·te·nance (sŭs′tə-nəns) ► *n.* **1.** The act of sustaining or condition of being sustained. **2.** Something, esp. food, that sustains life or health. **3.** Means of livelihood.

su·tra (so͞o′trə) ► *n.* **1.** *Hinduism* Any of various aphoris-

THESAURUS

surprise *n.* —*See* MARVEL, SHOCK[1], WONDER (1).

surprisingly *adv.* —*See* UNUSUALLY.

surrender *v.* **1.** To give up in favor of another ► acquiesce, blink, bow, capitulate, concede, give in, give up, submit, yield. *Idiom:* bend one's knee. **2.** To yield oneself unrestrainedly, as to an impulse ► abandon, deliver, relinquish. *Idiom:* give oneself up (*or* over). —*See also* ABANDON (1), SUCCUMB.

surrender *n.* The act of submitting or surrendering to the power of another ► capitulation, giving up, submission. [*Compare* OBEDIENCE.] —*See also* ABANDONMENT (1), DELIVERY.

surreptitious *adj.* —*See* STEALTHY.

surrogate *n.* —*See* SUBSTITUTE.

surrogate *v.* To substitute for or fill the place of ► displace, replace, supersede, supplant. *Idioms:* fill someone's shoes, take over from, take the reins from. [*Compare* SUBSTITUTE.]

surround *v.* To shut in on all sides ► beset, circle, compass, embrace, encircle, encompass, environ, hedge, hedge in, hem, hem in, ring. [*Compare* ENCLOSE, WRAP.] —*See also* ENCIRCLE.

surroundings *n.* —*See* CONDITIONS, ENVIRONMENT (1), ENVIRONMENT (2).

surveillance *n.* —*See* LOOKOUT (1).

survey *v.* **1.** To pay regular and close attention to ► follow, monitor, observe, stake out, watch. *Idioms:* have one's (*or* keep an) eye on, keep tabs on, keep track of, ride herd on. **2.** To view broadly or from a height ► look over, overlook, scan. [*Compare* LOOK.] —*See also* EXAMINE (1), WATCH (1).

survey *n.* **1.** A gathering of information or opinion from a variety of sources or individuals ► canvass, count, poll. **2.** A general or comprehensive view or treatment ► overview. [*Compare* SYNOPSIS.] —*See also* EXAMINATION (1).

survival *n.* —*See* CONTINUATION (1).

survive *v.* **1.** To exist in spite of adversity ► come through, get through, last, make it, outride, persevere, persist, pull through, ride out, weather. [*Compare* ENDURE.] **2.** To live, exist, or remain longer than ► outlast, outlive, outwear.

susceptibility *n.* —*See* EXPOSURE.

susceptible or **susceptive** *adj.* —*See* GULLIBLE, LIABLE (2), SENSITIVE (1), VULNERABLE.

susceptibleness *n.* —*See* EXPOSURE.

suspect *v.* —*See* DISTRUST, GUESS.

suspect *adj.* —*See* DEBATABLE, SHADY (1).

suspend *v.* **1.** To stop for an indefinite period ► interrupt, pause. *Idiom:* put on hold. [*Compare* REST.] **2.** To bring an activity or relationship to an end suddenly ► break off, cease, discontinue, interrupt, terminate. —*See also* DEFER[1], HANG (1).

suspenseful *adj.* —*See* DRAMATIC (2).

suspension *n.* —*See* ABEYANCE, BREAK, DELAY (1).

suspicion *n.* —*See* DISTRUST, DOUBT, FEELING (1), HINT (1), SHADE (2).

suspicious *adj.* —*See* DISTRUSTFUL, DOUBTFUL (2), SHADY (1).

suspiciously *adv.* —*See* SKEPTICALLY.

sustain *v.* To keep in a condition of good repair, efficiency, or use ► keep up, maintain, preserve. —*See also* BACK (2), BEAR (1), CONFIRM (1), DEVELOP (1), ENDURE (1), KEEP (5), NURTURE, PROVE, SUPPORT (2).

sustained *adj.* —*See* LONG[1] (2).

sustenance *n.* —*See* FOOD, LIVING, MAINTENANCE.

susurration or **susurrus** *n.* —*See* MURMUR.

tic doctrinal summaries recorded between 500 and 200 B.C. **2.** *Buddhism* A scriptural narrative, esp. a text traditionally regarded as a discourse of the Buddha.

su·ture (so͞o′chər) ▸ *n.* **1a.** The act of joining together by or as if by sewing. **b.** The material used in this procedure. **2.** The line of junction or an immovable joint between two bones, esp. of the skull. ▸ *v.* **-tured, -tur·ing.** To join by means of sutures.

SUV ▸ *abbr.* sport-utility vehicle

su·ze·rain (so͞o′zər-ən, -zə-rān′) ▸ *n.* **1.** A nation that controls another nation in international affairs but allows it domestic sovereignty. **2.** A feudal lord. **—su′ze·rain** *adj.* **—su′ze·rain·ty** *n.*

svelte (svĕlt) ▸ *adj.* **svelt·er, svelt·est.** Slender and graceful in figure or outline.

SW ▸ *abbr.* **1.** southwest **2.** southwestern

swab (swŏb) ▸ *n.* **1.** Absorbent material attached to the end of a stick or wire and used for cleansing or applying medicine. **2.** A mop used for cleaning floors or decks. **3.** *Slang* A sailor. ▸ *v.* **swabbed, swab·bing.** To clean or treat with a swab.

swad·dle (swŏd′l) ▸ *v.* **-dled, -dling.** **1.** To swathe. **2.** To wrap (a baby) in strips of cloth.

swag (swăg) ▸ *n.* *Slang* Stolen property; loot.

swag·ger (swăg′ər) ▸ *v.* **1.** To walk or behave with an insolent air; strut. **2.** To brag. **—swag′ger** *n.*

swagger stick ▸ *n.* A short cane carried esp. by military officers.

Swa·hi·li (swä-hē′lē) ▸ *n., pl.* **-li** or **-lis.** **1.** A member of a predominantly Muslim people of the coast and islands of E Africa. **2.** The Bantu language of the Swahili, widely used as a lingua franca in E and E-central Africa.

swain (swān) ▸ *n.* **1.** A country lad, esp. a young shepherd. **2.** A beau.

swal·low[1] (swŏl′ō) ▸ *v.* **1.** To cause to pass through the mouth and throat into the stomach. **2.** To bear humbly or passively: *swallowed the insults.* **3.** To consume or devour. **4.** *Slang* To believe without question. ▸ *n.* **1.** The act of swallowing. **2.** An amount swallowed.

swal·low[2] (swŏl′ō) ▸ *n.* Any of a family of birds with long pointed wings and a usu. notched or forked tail.

swal·low-tail (swŏl′ō-tāl′) ▸ *n.* **1.** A deeply forked tail, as of a swallow. **2.** Any of a family of butterflies with a tail-like extension at the end of each hind wing.

swam (swăm) ▸ *v.* P.t. of **swim.**

swa·mi (swä′mē) ▸ *n., pl.* **-mis.** **1.** A Hindu religious teacher. **2.** A mystic.

swamp (swŏmp, swômp) ▸ *n.* **1.** A wetland, esp. one that is forested and seasonally flooded. **2.** A tangle; morass. ▸ *v.* **1.** To drench in or cover with liquid. **2.** To overwhelm. **3.** To fill or sink (a ship) with water. **—swamp′i·ness** *n.* **—swamp′y** *adj.*

swan (swŏn) ▸ *n.* Any of a family of large aquatic birds with webbed feet, a long slender neck, and usu. white plumage.

swan dive ▸ *n.* A dive with the legs straight together, the back arched, and the arms stretched out from the sides.

swank (swăngk) ▸ *adj.* **-er, -est.** **1.** Imposingly fashionable or elegant; grand. **2.** Ostentatious. **—swank′i·ness** *n.* **—swank′y** *adj.*

swan's-down also **swans·down** (swŏnz′doun′) ▸ *n.* **1.** The soft down of a swan. **2.** A soft woolen fabric.

swan song ▸ *n.* A farewell appearance, action, or work.

swap (swŏp) *Informal* ▸ *v.* **swapped, swap·ping.** To trade one thing for another. ▸ *n.* An exchange; trade.

sward (swôrd) ▸ *n.* Land covered with grassy turf.

swarm (swôrm) ▸ *n.* **1.** A large number of insects or other small organisms, esp. when in motion. **2.** A multitude; throng. ▸ *v.* **1a.** To move in a swarm. **b.** To leave a hive as a swarm. Used of bees. **2.** To move or gather in large numbers. **3.** To be overrun; teem: *a riverbank swarming with insects.*

swarth·y (swôr′thē) ▸ *adj.* **-i·er, -i·est.** Having a dark complexion or color. **—swarth′i·ness** *n.*

swash (swŏsh, swôsh) ▸ *v.* To strike, move, or wash with a splashing sound. **—swash** *n.*

swash·buck·ler (swŏsh′bŭk′lər, swôsh′-) ▸ *n.* A flamboyant soldier or adventurer. **—swash′buck′ling** *adj.*

swas·ti·ka (swŏs′tĭ-kə) ▸ *n.* **1.** The emblem of Nazi Germany. **2.** An ancient cosmic or religious symbol formed by a Greek cross with the ends of the arms bent at right angles.

swat (swŏt) ▸ *v.* **swat·ted, swat·ting.** To deal a sharp blow to; slap. **—swat** *n.* **—swat′ter** *n.*

swatch (swŏch) ▸ *n.* A sample strip cut from a piece of material.

swath (swŏth, swôth) ▸ *n.* **1.** The width of a scythe stroke or a mowing-machine blade. **2.** A path left in mowing. ***—idiom:*** **cut a swath** To create a great stir or impression.

swathe (swŏ*th*, swô*th*, swā*th*) ▸ *v.* **swathed, swath·ing.** To wrap with or as if with bandages. **—swathe** *n.*

sway (swā) ▸ *v.* **1.** To move or cause to move back and forth with a swinging motion. **2.** To incline or bend to one side. **3.** To vacillate. **4.** To exert influence on or control over. ▸ *n.* **1.** The act of swaying. **2.** Power; influence. **3.** Dominion or control.

sway·back (swā′băk′) ▸ *n.* Excessive inward or downward curvature of the spine. **—sway′backed′** *adj.*

Swa·zi (swä′zē) ▸ *n., pl.* **-zi** or **-zis.** **1.** A member of a SE African people of Swaziland. **2.** The Bantu language of this people.

Swa·zi·land (swä′zē-lănd′) ▸ A country of SE Africa between South Africa and Mozambique.

swear (swâr) ▸ *v.* **swore** (swôr), **sworn** (swôrn), **swear·ing.** **1.** To make a solemn declaration. **2.** To promise; vow. **3.** To use profane oaths; curse. **4.** To assert under oath. **5.** To declare or affirm with great conviction. **6.** To administer a

THESAURUS

suzerain *n.* —*See* CHIEF.

svelte *adj.* —*See* THIN (1).

swaddle *v.* —*See* WRAP (1).

swag *n.* —*See* PLUNDER.

swagger *v.* —*See* BOAST, STRUT.

swagman *n.* —*See* HOBO.

swain *n.* —*See* BEAU (1).

swale *n.* —*See* SWAMP, VALLEY.

swallow *v.* To cause to pass from the mouth into the stomach ▸ ingest, take. [*Compare* DRINK, EAT, GULP.] —*See also* BELIEVE (1), ENDURE (1).

swallow up *v.* —*See* CONSUME (1).

swallow *n.* An act of swallowing ▸ gulp, ingestion, swig. —*See also* BIT[1] (2), DRINK (2).

swamp or **swampland** *n.* A usually low-lying area of soft waterlogged ground and standing water ▸ bog, fen, marsh, marshland, mire, moor, morass, muskeg, quag, quagmire, slough, swale, wetland.

swamp *v.* To affect as if by an outpouring of water ▸ deluge, flood, inundate, overwhelm.

swank *adj.* —*See* EXCLUSIVE (3), FASHIONABLE.

swank *v.* —*See* STRUT.

swanky *adj.* —*See* EXCLUSIVE (3), FASHIONABLE.

swap *v.* —*See* CHANGE (3), EXCHANGE.

swap *n.* —*See* CHANGE (2).

swarm *n.* —*See* CROWD, FLOCK.

swarm *v.* —*See* CROWD, TEEM[1].

swarming *adj.* —*See* BUSY (2), OVERCROWDED.

swarthy *adj.* —*See* DARK (2).

swash *v.* To make the sound of moving or disturbed water ▸ lap, splash, wash. [*Compare* BURBLE, SWISH.] —*See also* SPLASH (1), STRUT.

swat *v.* —*See* HIT, SLAP.

swat *n.* —*See* BLOW[2], SLAP.

swatch *n.* —*See* BAND[1].

swath *n.* —*See* BAND[1].

swathe *v.* —*See* DRESS (2), WRAP (1).

sway *v.* To move back and forth or from side to side ▸ fluctuate, oscillate, quake, rock, shake, swing, switch, teeter, totter, tremble, undulate, vacillate, vibrate, wag, waggle, wave, waver, weave, wobble. [*Compare* SHAKE.] —*See also* INFLUENCE, STAGGER (1).

sway *n.* —*See* AUTHORITY, DOMINANCE, DOMINATION, INFLUENCE.

swear *v.* To use profane or obscene language ▸ blaspheme, curse, damn. *Informal:* cuss. —*See also* ASSERT, PLEDGE (1), TESTIFY.

swear at *v.* To hurl strong deprecations, curses, or insults at ▸ *Informal:* cuss at (*or* out), mouth off at. [*Compare* CURSE, INSULT, REVILE.]

swear off *v.* —*See* ABANDON (2), BREAK (5).

legal oath to. **—phrasal verbs: swear in** To administer an oath of office to. **swear off** *Informal* To renounce; give up.

sweat (swĕt) ▸ *v.* **sweat·ed** or **sweat, sweat·ing. 1.** To excrete perspiration through the pores in the skin; perspire. **2.** To exude or become moist with surface droplets. **3.** To condense atmospheric moisture. **4.** *Informal* To work or cause to work long and hard. **5.** *Informal* To fret or worry. **—phrasal verb: sweat out** *Slang* To endure anxiously. ▸ *n.* **1.** Perspiration. **2.** Condensation of moisture in the form of droplets on a surface. **3.** The process of sweating or the condition of being sweated. **4.** *Informal* An anxious, fretful condition. **—sweat′i·ness** *n.* **—sweat′y** *adj.*

sweat·er (swĕt′ər) ▸ *n.* A knitted or crocheted garment worn on the upper body.

sweat gland ▸ *n.* Any of the numerous small glands in the skin of humans that secrete perspiration externally through pores.

sweat·shirt (swĕt′shûrt′) ▸ *n.* A usu. long-sleeved pullover made usu. of heavy cotton jersey.

sweat·shop (swĕt′shŏp′) ▸ *n.* A shop or factory in which employees work long hours at low wages under poor conditions.

Swede (swēd) ▸ *n.* A native or inhabitant of Sweden.

Swe·den (swēd′n) ▸ A country of N Europe on the E Scandinavian Peninsula.

Swed·ish (swē′dĭsh) ▸ *adj.* Of or relating to Sweden, the Swedes, or their language. ▸ *n.* The Germanic language of Sweden.

sweep (swēp) ▸ *v.* **swept** (swĕpt), **sweep·ing. 1.** To clean or clear with or as if with a broom or brush. **2.** To touch or brush lightly. **3.** To clear, drive, or convey with relentless force, as by wind or rain. **4.** To move swiftly or with great intensity: *The news swept through the country.* **5a.** To win all the stages of (a game or contest). **b.** To win overwhelmingly in. **6.** To extend gracefully, esp. in a long curve. ▸ *n.* **1.** An act or instance of sweeping. **2a.** A wide curving motion. **b.** The range or scope encompassed by sweeping. **3.** A broad reach or extent. **4.** A curve or contour. **5.** A chimney sweep. **6a.** The winning of all stages of a contest. **b.** An overwhelming victory. **—sweep′er** *n.*

sweep·ing (swē′pĭng) ▸ *adj.* **1.** Having wide-ranging influence or effect. **2.** Curving; contoured. ▸ *n.* **sweepings** Things swept up; refuse. **—sweep′ing·ly** *adv.*

sweep·stakes (swēp′stāks′) ▸ *pl.n.* *(takes sing. or pl. v.)* **1.** A lottery in which the participants' contributions form a fund awarded as a prize to one or several winners. **2.** An event or a contest, esp. a horserace, the result of which determines the winner of such a lottery.

sweet (swēt) ▸ *adj.* **-er, -est. 1.** Having the taste of sugar. **2.** Pleasing to the senses, mind, or feelings. **3.** Having a pleasing disposition; lovable. **4.** Not saline or salted: *sweet butter.* **5.** Not spoiled, sour, or decaying. ▸ *n.* **1.** Something sweet to the taste. **2. sweets** Sweet foods, esp. candy. **3.** A dear or beloved person. **—sweet′ly** *adv.* **—sweet′ness** *n.*

sweet alyssum ▸ *n.* A garden plant grown for its small, fragrant, varicolored flowers.

sweet·bread (swēt′brĕd′) ▸ *n.* The thymus gland or pancreas of a young animal used for food.

sweet·bri·er also **sweet·bri·ar** (swēt′brī′ər) ▸ *n.* A rose having prickly stems, fragrant leaves, and bright pink flowers.

sweet corn ▸ *n.* The common table corn, with kernels that are sweet when young.

sweet·en (swēt′n) ▸ *v.* **1.** To make sweet or sweeter. **2.** To make more valuable or agreeable. **—sweet′en·er** *n.*

sweet·en·ing (swēt′n-ĭng) ▸ *n.* **1.** The act or process of making sweet. **2.** Something that sweetens; sweetener.

sweet·heart (swēt′härt′) ▸ *n.* **1.** A beloved. **2.** *Informal* A generous or dear person.

sweet·meat (swēt′mēt′) ▸ *n.* A sweet delicacy, as a piece of candy or candied fruit.

sweet pea ▸ *n.* A climbing plant of the pea family, cultivated for its fragrant flowers.

sweet potato ▸ *n.* **1.** A tropical American vine cultivated for its fleshy, tuberous orange root. **2.** The root of this vine, eaten cooked as a vegetable.

sweet-talk (swēt′tôk′) ▸ *v.* *Informal* To coax or cajole with flattery. **—sweet talk** *n.*

sweet tooth ▸ *n.* *Informal* A fondness or craving for sweets.

sweet William ▸ *n.* A widely cultivated plant with flat-topped dense clusters of varicolored flowers.

swell (swĕl) ▸ *v.* **swelled, swelled** or **swol·len** (swō′lən), **swell·ing. 1.** To increase in size or volume. **2.** To increase in force, size, number, or intensity. **3.** To bulge out, as a sail. **4.** To be or become filled or puffed up, as with pride. ▸ *n.* **1.** A swollen part. **2.** A long wave on water that moves continuously without breaking. **3.** *Informal* One who is fashionably dressed or socially prominent. ▸ *adj.* **-er, -est.** *Informal* **1.** Fashionably elegant; stylish. **2.** Excellent; wonderful.

swell·ing (swĕl′ĭng) ▸ *n.* **1.** The state of being swollen. **2.** Something swollen.

swel·ter (swĕl′tər) ▸ *v.* To suffer from oppressive heat.

swept (swĕpt) ▸ *v.* P.t. and p.part. of **sweep**.

swerve (swûrv) ▸ *v.* **swerved, swerv·ing.** To turn aside or be turned aside from a straight course. ▸ *n.* The act of swerving.

swift (swĭft) ▸ *adj.* **-er, -est. 1.** Moving or capable of moving with great speed; fast. **2.** Occurring or accomplished quickly. ▸ *n.* Any of various small dark birds noted for their long narrow wings and darting flight. **—swift′ly** *adv.* **—swift′ness** *n.*

Swift, Jonathan (1667–1745) ▸ Irish-born English writer.

swig (swĭg) ▸ *n.* *Informal* A deep swallow or draft, esp. of liquor; gulp. **—swig** *v.*

swill (swĭl) ▸ *v.* **1.** To drink greedily or grossly. **2.** To feed

THESAURUS

swearword *n.* A profane or obscene term ▸ blasphemy, curse, epithet, expletive, oath, obscenity, profanity. *Informal:* cuss. ***Idioms:*** bad (*or* dirty) word, four-letter word.

sweat *v.* To excrete moisture through a porous skin or layer ▸ lather, perspire, transude. *—See also* LABOR, OOZE.

sweat out *v.* *—See* ENDURE (1).

sweat *n.* Moisture accumulated on a surface through sweating or condensation ▸ condensation, lather, perspiration, transudation. *—See also* LABOR, STATE (2), TASK (2).

sweaty or **sweating** *adj.* Producing or covered with sweat ▸ perspiring, sudoriferous. [*Compare* DAMP, STICKY.]

sweep *v.* *—See* BLOW[1] (1), FLOURISH, FLOW (1).

sweep *n.* *—See* EXPANSE (1), RANGE (1).

sweeping *adj.* *—See* GENERAL (2).

sweet *adj.* **1.** Having or suggesting the taste of sugar ▸ honeyed, saccharine, sugary. **2.** Not sour or salted ▸ fresh, uncured, unsalted. *—See also* AMIABLE, ATTRACTIVE, DELIGHTFUL.

sweet *n.* *—See* DARLING (1).

sweeten *v.* To make superficially more acceptable or appealing ▸ candy, gild, honey, sugar, sugarcoat. [*Compare* MODERATE.] *—See also* PACIFY.

sweetheart *n.* *—See* DARLING (1).

sweetmeat *n.* *—See* DELICACY.

sweet-sounding *adj.* *—See* MELODIOUS.

sweet talk *n.* *—See* FLATTERY.

sweet-talk *v.* *—See* COAX, FLATTER (1).

swell *v.* To expand from or as if from internal pressure ▸ balloon, bloat, blow up, bulge (out), distend, inflate, puff (up *or* out), tumefy, tumesce. [*Compare* BULGE.] *—See also* BOAST, INCREASE.

swell *n.* A man who is vain about his clothes ▸ beau, coxcomb, dandy, fop, peacock. *—See also* INCREASE (1), WAVE.

swell *adj.* *—See* EXCELLENT, MARVELOUS.

swellheaded *adj.* *—See* ARROGANT, EGOTISTIC (1).

swelling *n.* *—See* BUMP (2).

swelter *v.* *—See* BURN (3).

sweltering *adj.* *—See* HOT (1).

swerve *v.* To turn aside sharply from a straight course ▸ angle, cut, sheer, skew, slant, slue, tack, veer, zag, zig, zigzag. [*Compare* BEND, GLANCE.] *—See also* DEVIATE.

swift *adj.* *—See* FAST (1), QUICK.

swiftly *adv.* *—See* FAST.

swiftness *n.* *—See* AGILITY, HASTE (1).

swig *n.* An act of swallowing ▸ gulp, ingestion, swallow. *—See also* DRINK (2).

swig *v.* *—See* DRINK (1).

swill *v.* *—See* DRINK (1), GULP.

swill *n.* *—See* DRINK (2).

(animals) with swill. ▸ *n.* **1.** A mixture of liquid and solid food fed to animals, esp. pigs; slop. **2.** Kitchen waste; garbage. **3.** Nonsense; rubbish.

swim (swĭm) ▸ *v.* **swam** (swăm), **swum** (swŭm), **swim·ming.** **1.** To move through water by means of the limbs, fins, or tail. **2.** To move as though gliding through water. **3.** To cross by swimming. **4.** To be covered with or as if with a liquid. **5.** To feel dizzy. **6.** To appear to spin or reel. ▸ *n.* The act or a period of swimming. ***—idiom:*** **in the swim** Active in the general current of affairs. **—swim′mer** *n.*

swim·ming·ly (swĭm′ĭng-lē) ▸ *adv.* Splendidly; excellently.

swim·suit (swĭm′so͞ot′) ▸ *n.* A garment worn while swimming; bathing suit.

swin·dle (swĭn′dl) ▸ *v.* **-dled, -dling.** To cheat or defraud of money or property. ▸ *n.* The act or an instance of swindling. **—swin′dler** *n.*

swine (swīn) ▸ *n., pl.* **swine.** **1.** Any of various hoofed mammals of the family that includes pigs, hogs, and boars. **2.** A brutish or contemptible person.

swing (swĭng) ▸ *v.* **swung** (swŭng), **swing·ing.** **1.** To move or cause to move back and forth. **2.** To hit at something with a sweeping motion. **3.** To turn in place, as on a hinge or pivot. **4.** To walk or move with a swaying motion. **5.** To hang freely. **6.** *Slang* To be put to death by hanging. **7.** *Informal* To manage or arrange successfully. **8.** To have a compelling or infectious rhythm. **9.** *Slang* **a.** To be lively, trendy, and exciting. **b.** To be sexually promiscuous. ▸ *n.* **1.** The act of swinging. **2.** The sweep or scope of something that swings. **3.** A seat suspended from above on which one can ride back and forth. **4.** A popular dance music based on jazz but usu. employing a larger band and simpler harmonic and rhythmic patterns.

swing·er (swĭng′ər) ▸ *n.* **1.** One that swings. **2.** *Slang* **a.** A sophisticated, socially active person. **b.** One who is sexually promiscuous.

swipe (swīp) ▸ *n.* **1.** A sweeping blow or stroke. **2.** *Informal* A critical remark. ▸ *v.* **swiped, swip·ing.** **1.** To hit with a sweeping motion. **2.** *Informal* To steal.

swirl (swûrl) ▸ *v.* **1.** To move with a spinning or whirling motion. **2.** To arrange in a spiral or whorl. **—swirl** *n.* **—swirl′y** *adj.*

swish (swĭsh) ▸ *v.* **1.** To move with a hissing sound. **2.** To rustle. **—swish** *n.*

Swiss (swĭs) ▸ *n.* **1.** *pl.* **Swiss.** A native or inhabitant of Switzerland. **2.** A firm white or pale yellow cheese with many holes. **—Swiss** *adj.*

Swiss chard ▸ *n.* A variety of beet having large succulent leaves used as a vegetable.

switch (swĭch) ▸ *n.* **1.** A slender flexible rod, stick, or twig. **2.** A blow given with a switch. **3.** A device used to break or open an electric circuit. **4.** A device used to transfer rolling stock from one track to another. **5.** A change or shift from one thing to another. ▸ *v.* **1.** To whip with or as if with a switch. **2.** To shift, transfer, or divert. **3.** To exchange: *switch seats.* **4.** To connect or disconnect by operating a switch. **—switch′er** *n.*

switch·blade (swĭch′blād′) ▸ *n.* A pocketknife with a spring-operated blade.

switch·board (swĭch′bôrd′) ▸ *n.* **1.** A panel with apparatus for operating electric circuits. **2.** See **telephone exchange.**

switch hitter ▸ *n.* *Baseball* A player who can bat either right-handed or left-handed.

switch·man (swĭch′mən) ▸ *n.* One who operates railroad switches.

Swit·zer·land (swĭt′sər-lənd) ▸ A country of W-central Europe.

swiv·el (swĭv′əl) ▸ *n.* A link, pivot, or other fastening that permits free turning of attached parts. ▸ *v.* **-eled, -el·ing** or **-elled, -el·ling.** To turn or rotate on or as if on a swivel.

swiz·zle stick (swĭz′əl) ▸ *n.* A small thin rod for stirring mixed drinks.

swol·len (swō′lən) ▸ *v.* P.part. of **swell.** ▸ *adj.* Puffed up; distended.

swoon (swo͞on) ▸ *v.* To faint. ▸ *n.* A fainting spell.

swoop (swo͞op) ▸ *v.* To move in a sudden sweep, as a bird descending on its prey. **—swoop** *n.*

sword (sôrd) ▸ *n.* **1.** A weapon having a long blade with one or two cutting edges. **2.** An instrument of death or destruction. **3.** The use of force, as in war.

sword·fish (sôrd′fĭsh′) ▸ *n.* A large marine food and game fish having a long swordlike extension of the upper jaw.

sword·play (sôrd′plā′) ▸ *n.* The act or art of using a sword.

swords·man (sôrdz′mən) ▸ *n.* One skilled in the use of swords. **—swords′man·ship′** *n.*

swore (swôr) ▸ *v.* P.t. of **swear.**

sworn (swôrn) ▸ *v.* P.part. of **swear.**

swum (swŭm) ▸ *v.* P.part. of **swim.**

swung (swŭng) ▸ *v.* P.t. and p.part. of **swing.**

syb·a·rite (sĭb′ə-rīt′) ▸ *n.* A person devoted to pleasure and luxury; voluptuary. **—syb′a·rit′ic** (-rĭt′ĭk) *adj.*

syc·a·more (sĭk′ə-môr′) ▸ *n.* **1.** A deciduous tree, esp. of North America, having palmately lobed leaves and balllike fruit clusters. **2.** A Eurasian maple tree.

syc·o·phant (sĭk′ə-fənt, sī′kə-) ▸ *n.* A servile self-seeker who attempts to win favor by flattering influential people. **—syc′o·phan·cy** *n.* **—syc′o·phan′tic** (-făn′tĭk) *adj.*

THESAURUS

swim *v.* To have the sensation of turning in circles ▸ reel, spin, swirl, whirl. *Idiom:* go round and round. *—See also* TEEM[1].

swim *n.* *—See* PLUNGE.

swindle *v.* *—See* CHEAT (1), DECEIVE.

swindle *n.* *—See* CHEAT (1).

swindler *n.* *—See* CHEAT (2).

swing *v.* **1.** To turn in place, as on a fixed point ▸ pivot, slue, swivel, wheel. **2.** To shift from one attitude, interest, condition, or emotion to another ▸ dilly-dally, vacillate, waver. **3.** *Slang* To execute by suspending by the neck ▸ gibbet, hang. *Informal:* string up. *—See also* EFFECT, HANG (1), SWAY, TURN (2).

swing at *v.* *—See* HIT.

swing *n.* *—See* BLOW[2], RANGE (1), RHYTHM.

swinger *n.* *—See* WANTON.

swipe *v.* *—See* STEAL.

swipe *n.* *—See* BLOW[2], TAUNT.

swirl *v.* **1.** To move or cause to move like a rapidly rotating current of liquid ▸ eddy, whirl. **2.** To rotate rapidly ▸ spin, twirl, whirl. **3.** To have the sensation of turning in circles ▸ reel, spin, swim, whirl. *Idiom:* go round and round. *—See also* TURN (1).

swirl *n.* *—See* CURL, REVOLUTION (1), WHIRLPOOL.

swish *v.* *—See* HISS (1).

swish *adj.* *—See* FASHIONABLE.

swish *n.* *—See* HISS (1).

switch *v.* **1.** To move to and fro vigorously and usually repeatedly ▸ wag, waggle, wave. **2.** To leave or discard for another ▸ change, shift. *—See also* CHANGE (3), SHAKE (1), TURN (2).

switch *n.* *—See* CHANGE (2), STICK (1).

swivel *v.* To turn in place, as on a fixed point ▸ pivot, slue, swing, wheel. [*Compare* TURN.]

swivet *n.* *—See* STATE (2).

swollen *adj.* Expanded from or as if from internal pressure ▸ bloated, blown up, bulging, distended, inflated, puffed (up *or* out), tumescent. [*Compare* INFLATED.] *—See also* BOASTFUL.

swoon *v.* To suffer temporary lack of consciousness ▸ black out, faint, keel over, pass out. *Idioms:* drop (*or* faint *or* fall) dead away, see stars. [*Compare* COLLAPSE.]

swoon *n.* A temporary lack of consciousness ▸ blackout, faint, fainting spell, syncope.

sword of Damocles *n.* *—See* DANGER.

sybarite *n.* A person devoted to pleasure and luxury ▸ epicure, epicurean, hedonist, pagan, pleasure-seeker, sensualist, voluptuary.

sybaritic *adj.* Characterized by or devoted to pleasure and luxury as a lifestyle ▸ epicurean, hedonic, hedonistic, voluptuary, voluptuous. [*Compare* LUXURIOUS, SENSUAL.]

sycophant *n.* One who flatters another or behaves obsequiously in an attempt to win favor ▸ adulator, bootlicker, courtier, fawner, flatterer, groveler, lackey, minion, slave, toady, truckler, yes man. *Informal:* apple-polisher, brownnose, brownnoser. [*Compare* FOLLOWER, PARASITE, SLAVE, SUBORDINATE.]

sycophantic *adj.* *—See* SERVILE.

Syd·ney (sĭd′nē) ▸ A city of SE Australia on an inlet of the Tasman Sea.

syl·lab·i·fy (sĭ-lăb′ĭ-fī′) or **syl·lab·i·cate** (-kāt′) ▸ *v.* **-fied, -fy·ing** or **-cat·ed, -cat·ing**. To form or divide into syllables. **—syl·lab′i·fi·ca′tion, syl·lab′i·ca′tion** *n.*

syl·la·ble (sĭl′ə-bəl) ▸ *n.* **1.** A unit of spoken language consisting of a single uninterrupted sound forming a word, such as *wit*, or part of a word, such as *per-* in *person*. **2.** One or more letters or phonetic symbols representing a spoken syllable. **—syl·lab′ic** (sĭ-lăb′ĭk) *adj.*

syl·la·bus (sĭl′ə-bəs) ▸ *n., pl.* **-bus·es** or **-bi** (-bī′). An outline or summary of the main points of a text, lecture, or course of study.

syl·lo·gism (sĭl′ə-jĭz′əm) ▸ *n.* A form of deductive reasoning consisting of a major premise, a minor premise, and a conclusion. **—syl′lo·gis′tic** *adj.* **—syl′lo·gis′ti·cal·ly** *adv.*

sylph (sĭlf) ▸ *n.* **1.** A slim graceful woman or girl. **2.** An imaginary being believed to inhabit the air.

syl·van also **sil·van** (sĭl′vən) ▸ *adj.* **1.** Of or characteristic of woods or forest regions. **2.** Abounding in trees.

sym·bi·o·sis (sĭm′bē-ō′sĭs, -bī-) ▸ *n. Biol.* A close association between two or more different organisms, esp. when mutually beneficial. **—sym′bi·ot′ic** (-ŏt′ĭk) *adj.* **—sym′bi·ot′i·cal·ly** *adv.*

sym·bol (sĭm′bəl) ▸ *n.* **1.** Something that represents something else by association, resemblance, or convention. **2.** A printed or written sign used to represent an operation, element, quantity, quality, or relation, as in mathematics or music. **—sym·bol′ic** (-bŏl′ĭk) *adj.* **—sym·bol′i·cal·ly** *adv.*

symbolic language ▸ *n.* A high-level programming language.

sym·bol·ism (sĭm′bə-lĭz′əm) ▸ *n.* The representation of things by means of symbols.

sym·bol·ize (sĭm′bə-līz′) ▸ *v.* **-ized, -iz·ing. 1.** To serve as a symbol of. **2.** To represent by a symbol. **—sym′bol·i·za′tion** *n.*

sym·me·try (sĭm′ĭ-trē) ▸ *n., pl.* **-tries. 1.** Exact correspondence of form and configuration on opposite sides of a dividing line or plane or about a center or axis. **2.** An arrangement with balanced or harmonious proportions. **—sym·met′ri·cal** (sĭ-mĕt′rĭ-kəl), **sym·met′ric** *adj.* **—sym·met′ri·cal·ly** *adv.*

sym·pa·thet·ic (sĭm′pə-thĕt′ĭk) ▸ *adj.* **1.** Of, expressing, feeling, or resulting from sympathy. **2.** Favorably inclined; agreeable. **3.** Produced in one body by transmission of vibrations of the same frequency from another body. **—sym′pa·thet′i·cal·ly** *adv.*

sympathetic nervous system ▸ *n.* The part of the autonomic nervous system that in general inhibits or opposes the parasympathetic nervous system, as by reducing digestive secretions, speeding up the heart, and contracting blood vessels.

sym·pa·thize (sĭm′pə-thīz′) ▸ *v.* **-thized, -thiz·ing. 1.** To feel or express compassion; commiserate. **2.** To understand or be sensitive to the feelings or ideas of another. **—sym′pa·thiz′er** *n.*

sym·pa·thy (sĭm′pə-thē) ▸ *n., pl.* **-thies. 1a.** A relationship between people or things in which whatever affects one correspondingly affects the other. **b.** Mutual understanding or affection. **2.** A feeling or expression of pity or sorrow for the distress of another. **3.** Harmonious agreement; accord.

sym·phon·ic (sĭm-fŏn′ĭk) ▸ *adj.* **1.** Relating to or having the form of a symphony. **2.** Harmonious in sound.

sym·pho·ny (sĭm′fə-nē) ▸ *n., pl.* **-nies. 1.** An extended piece for a symphony orchestra. **2.** A symphony orchestra. **3.** Harmony, esp. of sound.

symphony orchestra ▸ *n.* A large orchestra composed of string, wind, and percussion sections.

sym·po·si·um (sĭm-pō′zē-əm) ▸ *n., pl.* **-si·ums** or **-si·a** (-zē-ə). **1.** A meeting or conference for discussion of a particular topic. **2.** A collection of writings on a particular topic.

symp·tom (sĭm′təm, sĭmp′-) ▸ *n.* **1.** An indication; sign. **2.** A sign or indication of disorder or disease, esp. a change from normal function, sensation, or appearance. **—symp′to·mat′ic** *adj.* **—symp′to·mat′i·cal·ly** *adv.*

syn. ▸ *abbr.* synonym

syn·a·gogue (sĭn′ə-gŏg′, -gôg′) ▸ *n.* **1.** A building or place of meeting for worship and religious instruction in the Jewish faith. **2.** A congregation of Jews for the purpose of worship.

syn·apse (sĭn′ăps′, sĭ-năps′) ▸ *n.* The junction across which a nerve impulse passes to a neuron or other cell. ▸ *v.* **-apsed, -aps·ing.** To form a synapse. **—syn·ap′tic** *adj.*

sync or **synch** (sĭngk) *Informal* ▸ *n.* **1.** Synchronization. **2.** Harmony; accord. ▸ *v.* To synchronize.

syn·chro·nize (sĭng′krə-nīz′, sĭn′-) ▸ *v.* **-nized, -niz·ing. 1.** To occur or cause to occur at the same time. **2.** To operate in unison. **3.** To cause to agree exactly in time or rate. **4.** To arrange so as to indicate parallel occurrence. **—syn′chro·ni·za′tion** *n.* **—syn′chro·niz′er** *n.*

syn·chro·nous (sĭng′krə-nəs, sĭn′-) ▸ *adj.* **1.** Occurring or existing at the same time. **2.** Moving or operating at the same rate. **—syn′chro·nous·ly** *adv.* **—syn′chro·ny** *n.*

syn·co·pate (sĭng′kə-pāt′, sĭn′-) ▸ *v.* **-pat·ed, -pat·ing.** To modify (rhythm) by syncopation.

syn·co·pa·tion (sĭng′kə-pā′shən, sĭn′-) ▸ *n. Mus.* A shift of accent when a normally weak beat is stressed.

THESAURUS

syllabus *n.* —*See* PROGRAM (2).

symbiotic *adj.* —*See* COMPLEMENTARY.

symbol *n.* An object or expression associated with and serving to identify something else ▸ attribute, emblem, metaphor, signifier, token. [*Compare* EXPRESSION, TERM.] —*See also* CHARACTER (7), SIGN (1).

symbolic *adj.* Serving as a symbol ▸ emblematic, emblematical, figurative, metaphoric, metaphorical, representational, representative, symbolical. [*Compare* DESIGNATIVE.] —*See also* GRAPHIC (4).

symbolize *v.* —*See* REPRESENT (1).

symmetrical or **symmetric** *adj.* **1.** Characterized by or displaying symmetry, especially correspondence in scale or measure ▸ balanced, proportional, proportionate, regular. [*Compare* EVEN, PARALLEL.] **2.** Having components that are pleasingly combined ▸ balanced, concordant, congruous, harmonious.

symmetry *n.* Satisfying arrangement marked by even distribution of elements, as in a design ▸ balance, harmony, proportion. [*Compare* AGREEMENT.]

sympathetic *adj.* Feeling or expressing sympathy or pity ▸ bleeding-heart, comforting, commiserative, compassionate, concerned, condolatory, empathetic, empathic, feeling, loving, pitying, softhearted, supportive, tender, understanding, warm-hearted. [*Compare* ATTENTIVE, GENEROUS, GENTLE.]

sympathize *v.* **1.** To experience or express compassion ▸ ache, commiserate, condole, feel. ***Idioms:*** be (*or* feel) sorry, have one's heart bleed for someone, have one's heart go out to someone. [*Compare* COMFORT, PITY.] **2.** To understand or be sensitive to another's feelings or ideas ▸ empathize, understand. ***Idioms:*** feel someone's pain, put oneself (*or* walk) in someone else's shoes. **3.** To associate or affiliate oneself closely with a person or group ▸ empathize, identify, relate. [*Compare* UNDERSTAND.]

sympathy *n.* **1.** A very close understanding between persons ▸ empathy, understanding. **2.** A relationship or an affinity between people or things in which many properties are shared ▸ harmony, synch, synchronization, synchrony. [*Compare* AGREEMENT.] —*See also* PITY (1).

symphonic or **symphonious** *adj.* —*See* HARMONIOUS (2).

symphony *n.* —*See* HARMONY (1).

symposium *n.* —*See* CONFERENCE (1).

symptom *n.* —*See* SIGN (1).

synch *n.* A relationship or an affinity between people or things in which many properties are shared ▸ harmony, sympathy, synchronization, synchrony. [*Compare* AGREEMENT.]

synchronic *adj.* — *See* CONCURRENT, CONTEMPORARY (1).

synchronize *v.* To occur at the same time ▸ coincide, concur, harmonize.

synchronous *adj.* —*See* CONCURRENT, CONTEMPORARY (1).

synchronously *adv.* At the same time ▸ concurrently, simultaneously, together. ***Idioms:*** all at once, all together.

synchrony or **synchronization** *n.* A relationship or an affinity between people or things in which many properties are shared ▸ harmony, sympathy,

syn·co·pe (sĭng′kə-pē, sĭn′-) ▸ *n. Pathol.* A brief loss of consciousness; swoon.

syn·di·cate (sĭn′dĭ-kĭt) ▸ *n.* **1.** An association of people or firms authorized to undertake a duty or transact specific business. **2.** An agency that sells articles or photographs for publication in a number of newspapers or periodicals simultaneously. ▸ *v.* (-kāt′) **-cat·ed, -cat·ing. 1.** To organize into a syndicate. **2.** To sell or publish through a syndicate. **—syn′di·ca′tion** *n.*

syn·drome (sĭn′drōm′) ▸ *n.* A group of symptoms that collectively characterize a disease or disorder.

syn·er·gy (sĭn′ər-jē) also **syn·er·gism** (-jĭz′əm) ▸ *n.* The interaction of two or more agents or forces so that their combined effect is greater than the sum of their individual effects. **—syn′er·gist′ic** *adj.* **—syn′er·gist′ic·al·ly** *adv.*

syn·fu·el (sĭn′fyo͞o′əl) ▸ *n.* A fuel derived from coal, shale, or tar sand, or obtained by fermentation, as of grain.

syn·od (sĭn′əd) ▸ *n.* **1.** A council or assembly of Christian church officials. **2.** A council; assembly. **—syn·od′ic** (sĭ-nŏd′ĭk), **syn·od′i·cal** *adj.*

syn·o·nym (sĭn′ə-nĭm′) ▸ *n.* A word having the same or nearly the same meaning as another word in a language. **—syn′o·nym′i·ty** *n.* **—syn·on′y·mous** (sĭ-nŏn′ə-məs) *adj.* **—syn·on′y·mous·ly** *adv.*

syn·on·y·my (sĭ-nŏn′ə-mē) ▸ *n.* The quality of being synonymous.

syn·op·sis (sĭ-nŏp′sĭs) ▸ *n., pl.* **-ses** (-sēz). A brief outline or general view, as of a written work.

syn·tax (sĭn′tăks′) ▸ *n.* The way in which words or other elements of sentence structure are combined to form grammatical sentences. **—syn·tac′tic** (-tăk′tĭk), **syn·tac′ti·cal** *adj.* **—syn·tac′ti·cal·ly** *adv.*

syn·the·sis (sĭn′thĭ-sĭs) ▸ *n., pl.* **-ses** (-sēz′). **1.** The combining of separate elements or substances to form a coherent whole. **2.** The complex whole so formed. **3.** *Chem.* Formation of a compound from simpler compounds or elements. **—syn′the·size′** *v.*

syn·the·siz·er (sĭn′thĭ-sī′zər) ▸ *n.* An electronic instrument that combines simple waveforms to produce more complex sounds, such as those of various other instruments.

syn·thet·ic (sĭn-thĕt′ĭk) ▸ *adj.* **1.** Of or produced by synthesis. **2.** Not natural or genuine; artificial. ▸ *n.* A synthetic chemical compound. **—syn·thet′i·cal·ly** *adv.*

syph·i·lis (sĭf′ə-lĭs) ▸ *n.* A chronic infectious disease caused by a spirochete, usu. transmitted in sexual intercourse, and progressing through three stages of increasing severity. **—syph′i·lit′ic** *adj.*

sy·phon (sī′fən) ▸ *n. & v.* Var. of **siphon.**

Syr·i·a (sîr′ē-ə) ▸ A country of SW Asia on the E Mediterranean coast. **—Syr′i·an** *adj. & n.*

sy·ringe (sə-rĭnj′, sîr′ĭnj) ▸ *n.* **1.** A medical instrument used to inject fluids into the body or draw them from it. **2.** A hypodermic syringe.

syr·up also **sir·up** (sĭr′əp, sûr′-) ▸ *n.* **1.** A thick, sweet, sticky liquid consisting of sugar, flavorings, and water. **2.** The concentrated juice of a fruit or plant. **—syr′up·y** *adj.*

sys·tem (sĭs′təm) ▸ *n.* **1.** A group of interacting elements forming a complex whole. **2.** The human body regarded as a functional physiological unit. **3.** A network of structures and channels, as for communication. **4.** A condition of harmonious, orderly interaction. **5.** An organized method; procedure. **—sys′tem·at′ic** *adj.* **—sys′tem·at′i·cal·ly** *adv.*

sys·tem·a·tize (sĭs′tə-mə-tīz′) ▸ *v.* **-tized, -tiz·ing.** To formulate into or reduce to a system. **—sys′tem·a·ti·za′tion** *n.*

sys·tem·ic (sĭ-stĕm′ĭk) ▸ *adj.* **1.** Of or relating to systems or a system. **2.** Of or affecting the entire body. **—sys·tem′i·cal·ly** *adv.*

sys·tem·ize (sĭs′tə-mīz′) ▸ *v.* **-ized, -iz·ing.** To systematize.

sys·tems analysis (sĭs′təmz) ▸ *n.* The study of an activity or procedure to determine the desired end and the most efficient method of obtaining it. **—systems analyst** *n.*

sys·to·le (sĭs′tə-lē) ▸ *n.* The rhythmic contraction of the heart, esp. of the ventricles. **—sys·tol′ic** (sĭ-stŏl′ĭk) *adj.*

Sze·chuan or **Sze·chwan** (sĕch′wän′) ▸ See **Sichuan.**

THESAURUS

synch. [*Compare* AGREEMENT.]

syncope *n.* A temporary lack of consciousness ▸ blackout, faint, fainting spell, swoon.

syndicate *n.* *—See* ALLIANCE.

syndrome *n.* *—See* COMPLEX (1).

synergistic or **synergetic** *adj.* *—See* COOPERATIVE.

synergy *n.* *—See* COOPERATION.

synod *n.* *—See* CONVENTION.

synopsis *n.* A shortened version or summary ▸ abridgment, abstract, brief, condensation, digest, epitome, outline, sketch. [*Compare* SUMMARY.]

synopsize *v.* *—See* REVIEW (1).

synthesize *v.* *—See* HARMONIZE (2).

synthetic *adj.* *—See* ARTIFICIAL (1).

syrupy *adj.* *—See* VISCOUS.

system *n.* An organized array of individual elements and parts forming and working as a unit ▸ arrangement, body, entity, integral, machine, organization, sum, totality, whole. *—See also* COMPLEX (1), METHOD, WAY (1).

systematic or **systematical** *adj.* *—See* METHODICAL.

systematization or **systemization** *n.* *—See* METHOD.

systematize *v.* *—See* ARRANGE (1).

systemize *v.* *—See* ARRANGE (1).

T

t[1] or **T** (tē) ▸ *n., pl.* **t's** or **T's** also **ts** or **Ts.** The 20th letter of the English alphabet. **—*idiom:* to a T** Perfectly; precisely.
t[2] ▸ *abbr.* Troy (system of weights)
T ▸ *abbr.* **1.** temperature **2.** tenor **3.** Thursday **4.** Tuesday
t. ▸ *abbr.* **1.** teaspoon **2.** time **3.** transitive
T. ▸ *abbr.* tablespoon
Ta ▸ The symbol for the element **tantalum.**
tab[1] (tăb) ▸ *n.* A projection attached to an object to facilitate opening, handling, or identification.
tab[2] (tăb) ▸ *n.* **1.** *Informal* A bill or check. **2.** A key on a computer keyboard or typewriter used esp. in indenting text. **—*idiom:* keep tabs on** *Informal* To observe carefully.
tab·bou·leh or **ta·bou·leh** (tə-bo͞o′lə) ▸ *n.* A Lebanese salad of bulgur, scallions, tomatoes, mint, and parsley.
tab·by (tăb′ē) ▸ *n., pl.* **-bies. 1.** A domestic cat with black and grayish striped or mottled fur. **2.** A domestic cat, esp. a female.
tab·er·na·cle (tăb′ər-năk′əl) ▸ *n.* **1.** often **Tabernacle** The portable sanctuary in which the Jews carried the Ark of the Covenant through the desert. **2.** often **Tabernacle** A case or box on a church altar containing the consecrated elements of the Eucharist. **3.** A place of worship.
ta·ble (tā′bəl) ▸ *n.* **1.** An article of furniture having a flat horizontal surface supported by legs. **2.** An orderly display of data, usu. arranged in rows and columns. **3.** An abbreviated list, as of contents; synopsis. **4.** A slab or tablet bearing an inscription or a device. ▸ *v.* **-bled, -bling. 1.** To put or place on a table. **2.** To postpone consideration of; shelve.
tab·leau (tăb′lō′, tă-blō′) ▸ *n., pl.* **tab·leaux** or **tab·leaus** (tăb′lōz′, tă-blōz′). **1.** A vivid or graphic description. **2.** A stage technique in which the performers freeze in position simultaneously.
ta·ble·cloth (tā′bəl-klôth′, -klŏth′) ▸ *n.* A cloth to cover a table, esp. during a meal.
ta·ble d'hôte (tä′bəl dōt′, tä′blə) ▸ *n., pl.* **ta·bles d'hôte** (tä′bəl, tä′blə). A full-course meal served at a fixed price in a restaurant or hotel.
ta·ble·land (tā′bəl-lănd′) ▸ *n.* A plateau or mesa.
ta·ble·spoon (tā′bəl-spo͞on′) ▸ *n.* **1.** A large spoon used for serving food. **2.** A household cooking measure equal to 3 teaspoons or 1/2 fl. oz. (15 ml). **—ta′ble·spoon·ful′** *n.*
tab·let (tăb′lĭt) ▸ *n.* **1.** A slab or plaque, as of stone or ivory, bearing an inscription. **2.** A pad of writing paper glued together along one edge. **3.** A small flat pellet of oral medication.
table tennis ▸ *n.* A game similar to lawn tennis, played on a table with wooden paddles and a small plastic ball.
ta·ble·top (tā′bəl-tŏp′) ▸ *n.* The flat surface of a table. ▸ *adj.* Designed or made for use on the top of a table.
ta·ble·ware (tā′bəl-wâr′) ▸ *n.* Dishes, glassware, and silverware used in setting a table for a meal.
tab·loid (tăb′loid′) ▸ *n.* A newspaper of small format giving the news in condensed form, often with sensational material.
ta·boo also **ta·bu** (tə-bo͞o′, tă-) ▸ *n., pl.* **-boos** also **-bus. 1.** A ban attached to something by social custom. **2.** A prohibition, esp. among certain South Pacific peoples, excluding something from use, approach, or mention because of its sacred and inviolable nature. **—ta·boo′** *adj.* **—ta·boo′** *v.*
ta·bor (tā′bər) ▸ *n.* A small drum used to accompany a fife.
ta·bou·leh (tə-bo͞o′lə) ▸ *n.* Var. of **tabbouleh.**
tab·u·lar (tăb′yə-lər) ▸ *adj.* Organized as a table or list.
tab·u·late (tăb′yə-lāt′) ▸ *v.* **-lat·ed, -lat·ing.** To arrange in tabular form; condense and list. **—tab′u·la′tion** *n.* **—tab′u·la′tor** *n.*
ta·chom·e·ter (tă-kŏm′ĭ-tər, tə-) ▸ *n.* An instrument used to measure speed, esp. rotational speed. **—tach′o·met′ric** (tăk′ə-mĕt′rĭk) *adj.* **—ta·chom′e·try** *n.*
tac·it (tăs′ĭt) ▸ *adj.* **1.** Not spoken: *tacit approval.* **2.** Implied by or inferred from actions or statements. **—tac′it·ly** *adv.* **—tac′it·ness** *n.*
tac·i·turn (tăs′ĭ-tûrn′) ▸ *adj.* Habitually untalkative or silent. **—tac′i·tur′ni·ty** *n.* **—tac′i·turn·ly** *adv.*
tack[1] (tăk) ▸ *n.* **1.** A short light nail with a sharp point and a flat head. **2.** The position of a vessel relative to the trim of its sails. **3.** A course of action. **4.** A loose, temporary stitch. ▸ *v.* **1.** To fasten or attach with a tack. **2.** To add as an extra item: *tacked on a hefty surcharge.* **3.** To change the course of a vessel. **—tack′er** *n.*
tack[2] (tăk) ▸ *n.* The harness for a horse, including the bridle and saddle.
tack·le (tăk′əl) ▸ *n.* **1.** The equipment used in a sport or occupation, esp. in fishing; gear. **2.** (tăk′əl, tā′kəl) A system of ropes and blocks for raising and lowering weights. **3.** *Sports* **a.** The act of stopping a player carrying the ball, esp. by forcing the player to the ground, as in football. **b.** The act of obstructing a player so as to cause loss of possession of the ball, as in soccer. **c.** In football, either of the two line players positioned between guard and end. ▸ *v.* **-led, -ling. 1.** To take on and wrestle with (e.g., an opponent or problem). **2.** To stop or obstruct (an opponent) by means of a tackle. **—tack′ler** *n.*
tack·y[1] (tăk′ē) ▸ *adj.* **-i·er, -i·est.** Gummy; sticky. **—tack′i·ness** *n.*
tack·y[2] (tăk′ē) ▸ *adj.* **-i·er, -i·est.** *Informal* **1.** Rundown; shabby. **2a.** Lacking style or good taste: *tacky clothes.* **b.** Vulgar; tasteless: *a tacky remark.* **—tack′i·ly** *adv.* **—tack′i·ness** *n.*
ta·co (tä′kō) ▸ *n., pl.* **-cos.** A corn tortilla folded around a filling, as of meat or cheese.
tac·o·nite (tăk′ə-nīt′) ▸ *n.* A variety of chert mined as an iron ore.
tact (tăkt) ▸ *n.* Sensitivity in dealing with others. **—tact′ful** *adj.* **—tact′less** *adj.*
tac·tic (tăk′tĭk) ▸ *n.* **1.** An expedient for achieving a goal; ma-

THESAURUS

tab *n.* —*See* ACCOUNT (2), COST (1), TICKET (1).
tabby *n.* —*See* GOSSIP (2).
table *n.* **1.** A natural, flat land elevation ▸ mesa, plateau. [*Compare* HILL.] **2.** An orderly columnar display of data ▸ chart, tabulation. —*See also* LIST[1].
table *v.* —*See* DEFER[1].
tableau *n.* —*See* VIEW (2).
taboo *n.* —*See* FORBIDDANCE.
taboo *adj.* —*See* FORBIDDEN.
taboo *v.* —*See* FORBID.
tabulate *v.* —*See* LIST[1].
tabulation *n.* An orderly columnar display of data ▸ chart, table. [*Compare* LIST[1].]
tacit *adj.* —*See* IMPLICIT (1), SILENT (2).
taciturn *adj.* Habitually untalkative ▸ close, close-mouthed, incommunicable, incommunicative, laconic, quiet, reserved, reticent, silent, tightlipped, uncommunicable, uncommunicative, untalkative. [*Compare* BRIEF.]
taciturnity *n.* —*See* RESERVE (1).
tack *n.* An often sudden change or departure, as in a trend ▸ shift, turn, twist. [*Compare* CHANGE, DEVIATION.] —*See also* APPROACH (1), NAIL.
tack *v.* —*See* FASTEN, SWERVE.
tackle *n.* —*See* OUTFIT.
tackle *v.* —*See* ASSUME, ATTACK (2).
tacky *adj.* —*See* COARSE (1), GAUDY, SHABBY, STICKY (1).
tact *n.* The ability to say and do the right thing at the right time ▸ address, delicacy, diplomacy, discretion, savoir-faire, sensitivity, tactfulness. [*Compare* CONSIDERATION, DECENCY.]
tactful *adj.* —*See* DELICATE (2).
tactfulness *n.* —*See* TACT.
tactic *n.* **1.** An action calculated to achieve an end ▸ maneuver, measure,

neuver. **2. tactics** *(takes sing. v.)* The military science of securing objectives set by strategy. **—tac′ti·cal** *adj.* **—tac·ti′cian** (-tĭsh′ən) *n.*

tac·tile (tăk′təl, -tīl′) ▸ *adj.* Of, perceptible to, or proceeding from the sense of touch. **—tac′tile·ly** *adv.* **—tac·til′i·ty** (-tĭl′ĭ-tē) *n.*

tad (tăd) ▸ *n. Informal* **1.** A small boy. **2.** A small amount or degree.

tad·pole (tăd′pōl′) ▸ *n.* The limbless aquatic larval stage of a frog or toad, with gills and a long flat tail.

tae kwon do (tī′ kwŏn′ dō′) ▸ *n.* A Korean art of self-defense.

taf·fe·ta (tăf′ĭ-tə) ▸ *n.* A crisp, lustrous, plain-woven fabric of silk, rayon, or nylon.

taf·fy (tăf′ē) ▸ *n., pl.* **-fies.** A sweet chewy candy of molasses or brown sugar.

Taft (tăft), **William Howard** (1857–1930) ▸ The 27th US President (1909–13); chief justice of the US Supreme Court (1921–30).

tag¹ (tăg) ▸ *n.* **1.** A strip of paper, metal, or plastic attached to something to identify, classify, or label. **2.** The plastic or metal tip at the end of a shoelace. **3.** A designation or epithet. **4.** *Comp. Sci.* A character sequence in a markup language that gives information, esp. formatting specifications. ▸ *v.* **tagged, tag·ging. 1.** To label or identify with a tag. **2.** To follow closely. **3.** To mark or vandalize (a surface) with graffiti. **—tag′ger** *n.*

tag² (tăg) ▸ *n.* **1.** A children's game in which one player pursues the others until he or she touches one of them, who in turn becomes the pursuer. **2.** *Baseball* The act of tagging a player out. ▸ *v.* **tagged, tag·ging. 1.** To touch (another player) in the game of tag. **2.** *Baseball* To touch (a runner) with the ball in order to put that player out.

Ta·ga·log (tə-gä′lôg, -ləg) ▸ *n., pl.* **-log** or **-logs. 1.** A member of a people native to the Philippines. **2.** The Austronesian language of the Tagalog.

ta·hi·ni (tə-hē′nē) ▸ *n.* A paste made from ground sesame seeds.

Ta·hi·ti (tə-hē′tē) ▸ An island of the S Pacific in the Society Is. of French Polynesia.

Ta·hi·tian (tə-hē′shən) ▸ *n.* **1.** A native or inhabitant of Tahiti. **2.** The Polynesian language of Tahiti. **—Ta·hi′tian** *adj.*

Ta·hoe (tä′hō), **Lake** ▸ A lake on the CA-NV border W of Carson City, NV.

Tai (tī) ▸ *n., pl.* **Tai** or **Tais. 1.** A family of languages of SE Asia and S China that includes Thai and Lao. **2.** A member of a Tai-speaking people. **3.** Thai. **—Tai** *adj.*

tai chi or **Tai Chi** (tī′ chē′, jē′) ▸ *n.* A Chinese system of physical exercise designed esp. for self-defense and meditation.

tai·ga (tī′gə) ▸ *n.* The subarctic evergreen forest of N Eurasia just south of the tundra.

tail (tāl) ▸ *n.* **1.** The hind part of an animal, esp. when extending beyond the main part of the body. **2.** The bottom, rear, or hindmost part of something. **3a.** The rear of an aircraft. **b.** An assembly of stabilizing planes and control surfaces in this rear portion. **4.** An appendage to the rear or bottom: *the tail of a kite.* **5.** often **tails** *(takes sing. v.)* The reverse side of a coin. **6. tails** A formal evening costume worn by men. ▸ *adj.* Posterior; hindmost. ▸ *v. Informal* To follow and keep under surveillance. **—tail′less** *adj.*

tail·gate (tāl′gāt′) ▸ *n.* A hinged part that extends across the rear of a pickup truck or other vehicle and can be folded down. ▸ *v.* **-gat·ed, -gat·ing.** To drive too closely behind (another vehicle). **—tail′gat′er** *n.*

tail·ings (tā′lĭngz) ▸ *pl.n.* Refuse or dross remaining after ore has been processed.

tail·light (tāl′līt′) ▸ *n.* A red light mounted on the rear of a vehicle.

tai·lor (tā′lər) ▸ *n.* One who makes, repairs, and alters garments. ▸ *v.* **1.** To make (a garment). **2.** To make or adapt for a particular purpose.

tai·lor-made (tā′lər-măd′) ▸ *adj.* Made or as if made to order.

tail·pipe (tāl′pīp′) ▸ *n.* The pipe through which exhaust gases from an engine are discharged.

tail·spin (tāl′spĭn′) ▸ *n.* **1.** The rapid descent of an aircraft in a nose-down spiral spin. **2.** A sudden steep decline or slump.

Tai·no (tī′nō) ▸ *n., pl.* **-no** or **-nos. 1.** A member of an Arawak people of the West Indies who became extinct under Spanish colonization. **2.** The language of this people.

taint (tānt) ▸ *v.* **1.** To affect with or as if with a disease. **2.** To affect with decay or putrefaction; spoil. ▸ *n.* **1.** A moral defect considered as a stain or spot. **2.** An infecting touch, influence, or tinge.

Tai·pei (tī′pā′, -bā′) ▸ The capital of Taiwan, in the N part.

Tai·wan (tī′wän′). Officially **Republic of China.** Formerly **For·mo·sa** (fôr-mō′sə) ▸ A country off SE China comprising the island of **Taiwan** and other smaller islands. **—Tai′wan·ese′** (-wä-nēz′, -nēs′) *adj. & n.*

Ta·jik (tä-jĭk′, tə-) ▸ *n., pl.* **-jik** or **-jiks. 1.** A member of a people inhabiting Tajikistan and neighboring areas. **2.** Their Iranian language.

Ta·jik·i·stan (tä-jĭk′ĭ-stăn′, -stän′) ▸ A country of W-central Asia bordering on Afghanistan and China.

ta·ka (tä′kə) ▸ *n.* See **currency** table in Appendix.

take (tāk) ▸ *v.* **took** (to͝ok), **tak·en** (tā′kən), **tak·ing. 1.** To get possession of; capture; seize. **2.** To grasp with the hands. **3.** To carry, convey, or lead to another place. **4.** To remove from a place. **5.** To charm; captivate. **6.** To eat, drink, consume, or inhale. **7.** To assume upon oneself; commit oneself to. **8.** *Gram.* To govern: *Intransitive verbs take no*

THESAURUS

move, procedure, step. **2.** A method of deploying troops and equipment in combat ▸ battle plan, maneuver, plan of attack, stratagem, strategy. *—See also* APPROACH (1).

tactile *adj.* **1.** Discernible by touch ▸ palpable, tangible, touchable. **2.** Relating to the sense of touch ▸ tactual.

tactility *n.* The faculty or ability to perceive tactile stimulation ▸ feel, feeling, touch. [illegible] [*Compare* SENSATION.] *—See also* TANGIBILITY.

taction *n.* A coming together or touching ▸ contact, contingence, touch. [*Compare* BRUSH¹, TOUCH.]

tactless *adj.* Lacking sensitivity and skill in dealing with others ▸ brash, clumsy, gauche, impolitic, indelicate, insensitive, maladroit, undiplomatic, unpolitic, untactful. [*Compare* ABRUPT, RUDE.]

tactlessness *n.* *—See* THOUGHTLESSNESS (2).

tactual *adj.* Relating to the sense of touch ▸ tactile.

tad *n.* *—See* BIT¹ (1).

tag *v.* To attach a ticket to ▸ earmark, flag, label, mark, ticket. *—See also* CALL, FOLLOW (3), MARK (1).

tag *n.* *—See* NAME (1), TICKET (1).

tag end *n.* *—See* BACK.

tail *n.* **1.** Something that follows or is drawn along behind ▸ trail, train, wake. [*Compare* STREAM.] **2.** *Informal* An agent assigned to observe and report on another ▸ shadow, watcher. [*Compare* [illegible]] *—See also* BACK, BUTTOCKS.

tail *adj.* *—See* LAST¹ (2).

tail *v.* *—See* FOLLOW (3).

tail away or **off** *v.* *—See* DECREASE.

tail end *n.* *—See* BACK.

tailor *v.* *—See* ADAPT, BIAS (2).

tailored *adj.* *—See* CUSTOM.

tailor-made *adj.* *—See* APPROPRIATE, CONVENIENT (1), CUSTOM.

taint *v.* *—See* CONTAMINATE, CORRUPT, DECAY, DENIGRATE.

taint *n.* *—See* CONTAMINANT, STAIN.

tainted *adj.* *—See* IMPURE (2).

taintlessness *n.* *—See* PURITY.

take *v.* **1.** To have a sudden overwhelming effect on ▸ catch, seize, strike. **2.** To cause to pass from the mouth into the stomach ▸ ingest, swallow. [*Compare* DRINK, EAT, GULP.] **3.** To admit to one's possession, presence, or awareness ▸ accept, have, receive. [*Compare* ABSORB.] **4.** To receive something given or offered willingly and gladly ▸ accept, embrace, take up, welcome. **5.** To go [illegible] catch. *Informal:* hop. **6.** To understand in a particular way ▸ construe, interpret, read. **7.** To take away a quantity from another quantity ▸ abate, deduct, discount, rebate, subtract, take off. *Informal:* knock off. *—See also* ATTRACT, BRING (1), CAPTURE, CHEAT (1), CHOOSE (1), CONTRACT (2), DEMAND (2), DERIVE (1), ENDURE (1), FUNCTION, GET (1), REMOVE (1), SEIZE (1), UNDERSTAND (1).

take after *v.* *—See* RESEMBLE.

take apart *v.* *—See* DISASSEMBLE.

take away *v.* To move something from a position occupied ▸ remove,

direct object. **9.** To pick out; choose. **10.** To use as a means of conveyance or transportation. **11.** To use as a means of safety: *take shelter.* **12.** To occupy: *take a seat.* **13.** To require: *It takes money to do that.* **14.** To determine through measurement or observation. **15.** To write down: *take notes.* **16.** To make by photography: *take a picture.* **17.** To accept (e.g., something given). **18.** To endure: *take criticism.* **19.** To follow (e.g., a suggestion). **20.** To make or perform: *take a decision.* **21.** To let in; admit. **22.** To interpret or react in a certain manner: *take literally.* **23.** To subtract. **24.** To commit oneself to the study of: *take a course.* **25.** To have the intended effect; work. **26.** To become: *take sick.* ***—phrasal verbs:*** **take after** To follow as an example. **take back** To retract (something stated or written). **take for** To regard as or mistake for: *took him for the boss.* **take in 1.** To include or constitute. **2.** To understand. **3.** To view: *She took in the scene.* **take off 1.** To remove, as clothing. **2.** To rise up in flight, as an airplane. **3.** *Slang* To depart. **take out 1.** To extract; remove. **2.** *Informal* To escort, as a date. **take over** To assume the control or management of. **take to 1.** To become fond of. **2.** To develop as a habit. **take up 1.** To begin again. **2.** To develop an interest in. ▸ *n.* **1a.** The act or process of taking. **b.** The amount taken, esp. at one time. **2.** The money collected as admission to an event. **3.** The uninterrupted running of a camera or a set of recording equipment, as in filming a movie. ***—idioms:*** **take effect 1.** To become operative, as a law. **2.** To produce the desired reaction. **take place** To happen; occur. **—tak′er** *n.*

take·off (tāk′ôf′, -ŏf′) ▸ *n.* **1.** The act of leaving the ground. **2.** *Informal* An imitative caricature or burlesque.

take·out also **take-out** (tāk′out′) ▸ *adj.* Intended to be eaten off the premises: *takeout pizza.* **—take′-out′** *n.*

take·o·ver also **take-o·ver** (tāk′ō′vər) ▸ *n.* The act of assuming control.

ta·la (tä′lə) ▸ *n.* See **currency** table in Appendix.

talc (tălk) ▸ *n.* A fine-grained mineral used in making talcum powder.

tal·cum powder (tăl′kəm) ▸ *n.* A fine powder made from purified talc, for use on the skin.

tale (tāl) ▸ *n.* **1.** A recital of events or happenings. **2.** A narrative of imaginary events; story. **3.** A deliberate lie.

tale·bear·er (tāl′bâr′ər) ▸ *n.* One who spreads malicious gossip. **—tale′bear′ing** *adj. & n.*

tal·ent (tăl′ənt) ▸ *n.* **1.** A natural or acquired ability; aptitude. **2.** Natural endowment or ability of a superior quality. **3.** A person with such ability. **4.** Any of various ancient units of weight and money. **—tal′ent·ed** *adj.*

tal·is·man (tăl′ĭs-mən, -ĭz-) ▸ *n.* An object believed to protect or give supernatural powers to its bearer. **—tal′is·man′ic** (-măn′ĭk) *adj.*

talk (tôk) ▸ *v.* **1.** To articulate words. **2a.** To converse by means of spoken language. **b.** To converse about: *talk politics.* **3.** To speak: *talk Arabic.* **4.** To gossip. **5.** To parley or negotiate. **6.** To consult or confer. **7.** To persuade with arguments: *talked them into joining.* ***—phrasal verbs:*** **talk back** To reply rudely. **talk down** To address someone with insulting condescension. **talk over** To discuss. ▸ *n.* **1.** The act of talking; conversation. **2.** A speech or lecture. **3.** Hearsay, rumor, or speculation. **4.** A subject of conversation. **5.** often **talks** A conference or negotiation. **—talk′er** *n.*

talk·a·tive (tô′kə-tĭv) ▸ *adj.* Inclined to talk or converse. **—talk′a·tive·ness** *n.*

talk·ing-to (tô′kĭng-to͞o′) ▸ *n., pl.* **-tos.** *Informal* A scolding; dressing-down.

talk show ▸ *n.* A television or radio show in which people participate in discussions or are interviewed.

tall (tôl) ▸ *adj.* **-er, -est. 1.** Having greater than ordinary height. **2.** Having a specified height: *a plant three feet tall.* **3.** *Informal* Fanciful or boastful. **4.** Impressively great or difficult: *a tall order to fill.* ▸ *adv.* With proud bearing; straight: *stand tall.* **—tall′ness** *n.*

Tal·la·has·see (tăl′ə-hăs′ē) ▸ The capital of FL, in the NW part.

tal·low (tăl′ō) ▸ *n.* Hard fat obtained from cattle, sheep, or horses and used in candles, soaps, and lubricants. **—tal′low·y** *adj.*

tal·ly (tăl′ē) ▸ *n., pl.* **-lies. 1.** A reckoning or score. **2.** A stick on which notches are made to keep a count. ▸ *v.* **-lied, -ly·ing. 1.** To reckon or count. **2.** To correspond or agree.

tal·ly·ho (tăl′ē-hō′) ▸ *interj.* Used to urge hounds on during a fox hunt.

Tal·mud (täl′mo͝od, tăl′məd) ▸ *n. Judaism* The collection of ancient Rabbinic writings constituting the basis of religious authority in Orthodox Judaism. **—Tal·mu′dic** (-mo͞o′dĭk, -myo͞o′-), **Tal·mu′di·cal** *adj.* **—Tal′mud·ist** *n.*

tal·on (tăl′ən) ▸ *n.* The long curved claw esp. of a bird of prey.

THESAURUS

take (off *or* out), withdraw. *—See also* DEDUCT.

take back *v.* *—See* RESUME, RETRACT (1), RETURN (2).

take down *v.* *—See* DISASSEMBLE, LOWER[2].

take in *v.* *—See* ACCEPT (3), CONTAIN (1), DECEIVE, OUTWIT, UNDERSTAND (1).

take off *v.* To rise up in flight ▸ lift off. *—See also* DEDUCT, GO (1), REMOVE (3), REMOVE (1), RUN (2).

take on *v.* *—See* ADOPT, ASSUME, CONTEND, EMPLOY (1), START (1).

take out *v. Informal* To be with another person socially on a regular basis ▸ date, go out (with), go with, see. *Idioms:* go steady, go together. *—See also* MURDER, REMOVE (1).

take over *v.* To free from a specific duty by acting as a substitute ▸ relieve, spell. [*Compare* SUBSTITUTE.] *—See also* ASSUME, OCCUPY (2).

take to *v.* *—See* LIKE[1].

take up *v.* *—See* ABSORB (2), ADOPT, CONTINUE, DEAL (1), DRINK (3), ELEVATE (1), START (1).

take *n.* The amount of money collected as admission ▸ box office, gate, receipts. *—See also* ATTEMPT.

take-in *n.* *—See* TRICK (1).

takeoff *n.* The act of rising in flight ▸ liftoff. *—See also* SATIRE.

taking *adj.* *—See* ATTRACTIVE, CONTAGIOUS.

tale *n.* *—See* LIE[2], YARN.

talebearer *n.* *—See* GOSSIP (2), INFORMER.

talebearing *n.* *—See* GOSSIP (1).

talebearing *adj.* Inclined to gossip ▸ blabby, gossipy, taletelling.

talent *n.* An innate capability ▸ aptitude, aptness, bent, faculty, flair, genius, gift, head, instinct, knack, turn. [*Compare* ABILITY.]

talented *adj.* *—See* GIFTED.

taleteller *n.* *—See* GOSSIP (2).

taletelling *adj.* Inclined to gossip ▸ blabby, gossipy, talebearing.

talisman *n.* *—See* CHARM.

talismanic *adj.* *—See* MAGIC.

talk *v.* **1.** To express oneself in speech ▸ speak, verbalize, vocalize. [*Compare* BABBLE, CHATTER.] **2.** To direct speech to ▸ address, speak. *—See also* CONFER (1), CONVERSE[1], GOSSIP, INFORM (2), SAY.

talk back *v.* To utter an impertinent rejoinder ▸ talk up. *Informal:* sass, sauce. *Idiom:* give someone lip.

talk down *v.* *—See* BELITTLE.

talk into *v.* *—See* PERSUADE.

talk over *v.* *—See* DISCUSS.

talk up *v.* To utter an impertinent rejoinder ▸ talk back. *Informal:* sass, sauce. *Idiom:* give someone lip. *—See also* PROMOTE (3).

talk *n.* The act or process of dealing with another to reach an agreement ▸ negotiation, parley. *—See also* CONVERSATION, DISCOURSE, GOSSIP (1), SPEECH (1), SPEECH (2).

talkative *adj.* Given to conversation ▸ chatty, conversational, garrulous, loquacious, talky, voluble. *Slang:* gabby. [*Compare* WORDY.]

talker *n.* *—See* CONVERSATIONALIST.

talkfest *n.* *—See* CONVERSATION.

talky *adj.* *—See* TALKATIVE.

tall *adj.* *—See* DIFFICULT (1), HIGH (1).

tallow *n.* Adipose tissue ▸ blubber, fat, lard, suet. [*Compare* OIL.]

tall tale *n.* *—See* EXAGGERATION, LIE[2], YARN.

tall talk *n.* *—See* EXAGGERATION.

tally *n.* The total number of points made by a contestant, side, or team in a game or contest ▸ score. *—See also* ACCOUNT (2), COUNT (1).

tally *v.* To gain a point or points in a game or contest ▸ post, score. *Informal:* notch. *Idiom:* make a goal (*or* point). *—See also* AGREE (1), COUNT (2).

ta·lus (tā′ləs) ▸ *n., pl.* **-li** (-lī). The bone that articulates with the tibia and fibula to form the ankle joint.

ta·ma·le (tə-mä′lē) ▸ *n.* A Mexican dish of fried chopped meat and crushed peppers, wrapped in cornmeal dough and cornhusks and steamed.

ta·ma·ri (tə-mä′rē) ▸ *n.* Soy sauce made with little or no wheat.

tam·a·rind (tăm′ə-rĭnd′) ▸ *n.* **1.** A tropical Asian tree with pods containing an edible acid pulp. **2.** The fruit of this tree.

tam·a·risk (tăm′ə-rĭsk′) ▸ *n.* A shrub or small tree with scalelike leaves and white, pink, or red flowers.

tam·bou·rine (tăm′bə-rēn′) ▸ *n.* A musical instrument consisting of a small drumhead with jingling disks fitted into the rim.

tame (tām) ▸ *adj.* **tam·er, tam·est. 1.** Brought from wildness into a domesticated or tractable state. **2.** Gentle; docile. **3.** Insipid; flat. **—tam′a·ble, tame′a·ble** *adj.* **—tame** *v.* **—tame′ly** *adv.* **—tame′ness** *n.* **—tam′er** *n.*

Tam·er·lane (tăm′ər-lān′) (1336–1405) ▸ Mongol conqueror.

Tam·il (tăm′əl, tŭm′-, tä′məl) ▸ *n., pl.* **-il** or **-ils. 1.** A member of a people of S India and N Sri Lanka. **2.** The Dravidian language of the Tamil. **—Tam′il** *adj.*

Tam·muz (tä′mo͝oz) ▸ *n.* A month of the Jewish calendar.

tam-o'-shan·ter (tăm′ə-shăn′tər) ▸ *n.* A flat-topped, tight-fitting Scottish cap.

tamp (tămp) ▸ *v.* To pack down tightly by a succession of blows or taps.

tam·per (tăm′pər) ▸ *v.* **1.** To interfere harmfully; meddle. **2.** To make improper or secret arrangements: *tamper with a jury.* **—tam′per·er** *n.*

tam·pon (tăm′pŏn′) ▸ *n.* A plug of absorbent material inserted into a body cavity or wound.

tan[1] (tăn) ▸ *v.* **tanned, tan·ning. 1.** To convert (hide) into leather, as by treating with tannin. **2.** To make brown by exposure to the sun. **3.** *Informal* To thrash; beat. ▸ *n.* **1.** A light brown. **2.** The brown color that sun rays impart to the skin. ▸ *adj.* **tan·ner, tan·nest. 1.** Of the color tan. **2.** Having a suntan.

tan[2] ▸ *abbr. Math.* tangent

tan·a·ger (tăn′ĭ-jər) ▸ *n.* Any of a family of small New World birds often having brightly colored plumage.

tan·bark (tăn′bärk′) ▸ *n.* **1.** Tree bark used as a source of tannin. **2.** Shredded bark used to cover a surface such as a circus arena.

tan·dem (tăn′dəm) ▸ *n.* **1.** A bicycle built for two riders. **2.** Two or more persons or objects placed one behind the other. ▸ *adv.* One behind the other: *rode tandem on the bike.* **—tan′dem** *adj.*

tang (tăng) ▸ *n.* **1.** A distinctively sharp taste, flavor, or odor. **2.** A projection by which a tool is attached to its handle. **—tang′i·ness** *n.* **—tang′y** *adj.*

Tan·gan·yi·ka (tăn′gən-yē′kə, tăng′-) ▸ A former country of E-central Africa; joined with Zanzibar (1964) to form Tanzania. **—Tan′gan·yi′kan** *adj. & n.*

Tanganyika, Lake ▸ A lake of E-central Africa between Dem. Rep. of the Congo and Tanzania.

tan·ge·lo (tăn′jə-lō′) ▸ *n., pl.* **-los. 1.** A hybrid citrus tree derived from grapefruit and tangerine. **2.** The fruit of this tree.

tan·gent (tăn′jənt) ▸ *adj.* **1.** Making contact at a single point or along a line; touching but not intersecting. **2.** Irrelevant. ▸ *n.* **1.** A line, curve, or surface touching but not intersecting another line, curve, or surface. **2.** In a right triangle, the ratio of the sine of an acute angle to its cosine. **3.** A sudden digression. **—tan′gen·cy** *n.* **—tan·gen′tial** (-jĕn′shəl) *adj.* **—tan·gen′tial·ly** *adv.*

tan·ger·ine (tăn′jə-rēn′, tăn′jə-rēn′) ▸ *n.* A mandarin orange with a red-orange skin.

tan·gi·ble (tăn′jə-bəl) ▸ *adj.* **1.** Discernible by the touch; palpable. **2.** Possible to understand or realize. **3.** Real or concrete. ▸ *n.* **1.** Something palpable or concrete. **2. tangibles** Material assets. **—tan′gi·bil′i·ty, tan′gi·ble·ness** *n.* **—tan′gi·bly** *adv.*

Tan·gier (tăn-jîr′) also **Tan·giers** (-jîrz′) ▸ A city of N Morocco at the W end of the Strait of Gibraltar.

tan·gle (tăng′gəl) ▸ *v.* **-gled, -gling. 1.** To intertwine in a confused mass; snarl. **2.** To be or become entangled. **3.** To snare; entrap. **4.** *Informal* To enter into dispute or conflict: *tangled with the law.* **—tan′gle** *n.*

tan·go (tăng′gō) ▸ *n., pl.* **-gos.** A Latin American ballroom dance in 2/4 or 4/4 time. **—tan′go** *v.*

tank (tăngk) ▸ *n.* **1.** A large container for liquids or gases. **2.** An enclosed, heavily armored combat vehicle mounted with cannon and guns and moving on caterpillar treads. **—tank′ful′** *n.*

tank·ard (tăng′kərd) ▸ *n.* A large drinking cup, usu. with a handle and a hinged cover.

tank·er (tăng′kər) ▸ *n.* A ship, plane, or truck constructed to transport liquids, such as oil, in bulk.

tank top ▸ *n.* A sleeveless shirt with wide shoulder straps.

tan·ner (tăn′ər) ▸ *n.* One who tans hides.

tan·ner·y (tăn′ə-rē) ▸ *n., pl.* **-ies.** An establishment where hides are tanned.

tan·nic acid (tăn′ĭk) ▸ *n.* A white or yellowish powder derived from certain plants and used in tanning hides and as a medicine.

tan·nin (tăn′ĭn) ▸ *n.* Tannic acid or another substance having similar uses.

Ta·no·an (tä′nō-ən) ▸ *n.* An American Indian language family of New Mexico and NE Arizona. **—Ta′no·an** *adj.*

tan·sy (tăn′zē) ▸ *n., pl.* **-sies.** A plant with buttonlike yellow flower heads and aromatic leaves that are sometimes used medicinally.

tan·ta·lize (tăn′tə-līz′) ▸ *v.* **-lized, -liz·ing.** To excite (another) by exposing something desirable while keeping it out of reach. **—tan′ta·li·za′tion** *n.* **—tan′ta·liz′er** *n.* **—tan′ta·liz′ing·ly** *adv.*

tan·ta·lum (tăn′tə-ləm) ▸ *n. Symbol* **Ta** A very hard, heavy, gray metallic element that is used to make light-bulb filaments, nuclear reactor parts, and surgical instruments. At. no. 73.

tan·ta·mount (tăn′tə-mount′) ▸ *adj.* Equivalent in effect or value.

tan·tra (tŭn′trə, tăn′-) ▸ *n.* Any of a comparatively recent body of Hindu or Buddhist religious literature. **—tan′tric** *adj.*

tan·trum (tăn′trəm) ▸ *n.* A fit of bad temper.

Tan·za·ni·a (tăn′zə-nē′ə) ▸ A country of E-central Africa on the Indian Ocean. Cap. Dodoma. **—Tan·za′ni·an** *adj. & n.*

Tao (dou, tou) ▸ *n.* **1.** In Taoism, the basic, eternal principle of the universe. **2.** In Confucianism, the right manner of human activity and virtuous conduct.

Tao·ism (dou′ĭz′əm, tou′-) ▸ *n.* A Chinese philosophy and system of religion based on the teachings of Lao-tzu in the 6th cent. B.C. **—Tao′ist** *n.* **—Tao·is′tic** *adj.*

tap[1] (tăp) ▸ *v.* **tapped, tap·ping. 1.** To strike gently; rap. **2.** To make light clicking sounds. **3.** To select, as for membership

THESAURUS

tame *adj.* —*See* DOMESTIC (2), GENTLE (3).

tame *v.* —*See* DOMESTICATE, GENTLE, MODERATE (1).

tameness *n.* —*See* DULLNESS.

tamper *v.* To prearrange the outcome of a contest ▸ fix, rig. *Idiom:* stack the deck. —*See also* TINKER.

tang *n.* —*See* FLAVOR (1).

tangent *n.* —*See* DIGRESSION.

tangential *adj.* —*See* DIGRESSIVE.

tangibility *n.* The quality or condition of being tangible ▸ corporeality, palpability, physicality, tactility, tangibleness, touchableness. [*Compare* MATTER.]

tangible *adj.* Discernible by touch ▸ palpable, tactile, touchable. —*See also* PHYSICAL, REAL (1).

tangle *n.* Something that is intricately or bewilderingly complex ▸ cat's cradle, entanglement, imbroglio, jungle, knot, labyrinth, maze, mesh, morass, skein, snarl, web. —*See also* ARGUMENT.

tangle *v.* —*See* ARGUE (1), CATCH (1), COMPLICATE, ENTANGLE.

tangled *adj.* —*See* COMPLEX (1).

tangy *adj.* —*See* SOUR.

tank *n.* —*See* VAT.

tanked *adj.* —*See* DRUNK.

tank up *v.* —*See* DRINK (2).

tantalize *v.* To excite by exposing something desirable while keeping it out of reach ▸ bait, tease. *Idiom:* make one's mouth water. [*Compare* CHARM, FLIRT.]

tantalizing *adj.* —*See* SEDUCTIVE.

tantamount *adj.* —*See* EQUAL.

tantrum *n.* —*See* TEMPER (2).

tap[1] *v.* **1.** To strike lightly or gently ▸

in an organization. ▸ *n.* 1a. A gentle blow. b. The sound made by such a blow. 2. A metal plate attached to the toe or heel of a shoe.

tap² (tăp) ▸ *n.* 1. A faucet; spigot. 2. Liquor drawn from a spigot. 3. A tool for cutting an internal screw thread. 4. A makeshift terminal in an electric circuit. ▸ *v.* **tapped, tap·ping.** 1. To furnish with a spigot or tap. 2. To pierce in order to draw off liquid. 3. To draw (liquid) from a vessel or container. 4. To open outlets from: *tap a water main.* 5a. To wiretap. b. To establish an electric connection in (a power line). 6. To cut screw threads in.

tap dance ▸ *n.* A dance in which the rhythm is sounded out by the clicking taps on the heels and toes of a dancer's shoes. **—tap′-dance′** *v.* **—tap dancer** *n.*

tape (tāp) ▸ *n.* 1. A narrow strip of strong woven fabric. 2. A continuous narrow flexible strip of material such as adhesive tape or magnetic tape. 3. A string stretched across the finish line of a racetrack. 4. A tape recording. ▸ *v.* **taped, tap·ing.** 1. To fasten, secure, or wrap with tape. 2. To tape-record.

tape deck ▸ *n.* A tape recorder and player with no amplifier or speaker, used as a component in an audio system.

tape measure ▸ *n.* A tape marked off in a scale, used for taking measurements.

tape player ▸ *n.* A self-contained machine for playing tape recordings.

ta·per (tā′pər) ▸ *n.* 1. A slender candle or waxed wick. 2. A gradual decrease in thickness or width of an elongated object. ▸ *v.* 1. To make or become gradually narrower or thinner toward one end. 2. To diminish gradually; slacken off. **—ta′per·ing·ly** *adv.*

tape recorder ▸ *n.* A device for recording and playing back sound on magnetic tape.

tape recording ▸ *n.* 1a. A magnetic tape on which sound or images have been recorded. b. The material recorded. 2. The act of recording on this tape. **—tape′-re·cord′** *v.*

tap·es·try (tăp′ĭ-strē) ▸ *n., pl.* **-tries.** A heavy cloth woven with varicolored designs, usu. hung on walls.

tape·worm (tāp′wûrm′) ▸ *n.* A long ribbonlike worm that is parasitic in the intestines of vertebrates.

tap·i·o·ca (tăp′ē-ō′kə) ▸ *n.* A beady starch obtained from the cassava root and used for puddings.

ta·pir (tā′pər, tə-pîr′) ▸ *n.* A tropical American or Asian mammal with a heavy body, short legs, and a long fleshy upper lip.

tap·room (tăp′ro͞om′, -ro͝om′) ▸ *n.* A barroom.

tap·root (tăp′ro͞ot′, -ro͝ot′) ▸ *n.* The main root of a plant, growing straight downward from the stem.

taps (tăps) ▸ *pl.n. (takes sing. or pl. v.)* A military bugle call sounded at night as an order to put out lights and at funerals and memorial services.

tar¹ (tär) ▸ *n.* 1. A dark, oily, viscous material, consisting mainly of hydrocarbons, produced by the destructive distillation of organic substances such as wood, coal, or peat. 2. A solid residue of tobacco smoke. ▸ *v.* **tarred, tar·ring.** To coat or surface with tar.

tar² (tär) ▸ *n.* A sailor.

tar·an·tel·la (tăr′ən-tĕl′ə) ▸ *n.* 1. A lively, whirling southern Italian dance. 2. The music for this dance.

ta·ran·tu·la (tə-răn′chə-lə) ▸ *n., pl.* **-las** or **-lae** (-lē′). Any of various large, hairy, chiefly tropical spiders capable of inflicting a painful bite.

tar·dy (tär′dē) ▸ *adj.* **-di·er, -di·est.** 1. Not on time. 2. Slow; sluggish. **—tar′di·ly** *adv.* **—tar′di·ness** *n.*

tare¹ (târ) ▸ *n.* Any of several weeds that grow in grain fields.

tare² (târ) ▸ *n.* A deduction from gross weight made to allow for the weight of a container.

tar·get (tär′gĭt) ▸ *n.* 1a. An object with a marked surface that is shot at to test accuracy. b. Something aimed or fired at. 2. An object of criticism or attack. 3. A goal. **—tar′get** *v.*

tar·iff (tăr′ĭf) ▸ *n.* 1a. A list or system of duties imposed on imported or exported goods. b. A duty of this kind. 2. A schedule of prices or fees.

tar·mac (tär′măk′) ▸ *n.* A bituminous road or surface, esp. an airport runway.

tarn (tärn) ▸ *n.* A small mountain lake.

tar·nish (tär′nĭsh) ▸ *v.* 1. To make or become dull or discolored. 2. To sully or taint. **—tar′nish** *n.*

ta·ro (tär′ō, tăr′ō) ▸ *n., pl.* **-ros.** A tropical Asian plant with broad leaves and a large, starchy, edible tuber.

tar·ot (tăr′ō, tə-rō′) ▸ *n.* Any of a set of playing cards used in fortunetelling.

tarp (tärp) ▸ *n. Informal* A tarpaulin.

tar·pa·per (tär′pā′pər) ▸ *n.* Heavy paper impregnated with tar, used as a waterproof building material.

tar·pau·lin (tär-pô′lĭn, tär′pə-) ▸ *n.* Material, such as waterproofed canvas, used to cover and protect things.

tar·pon (tär′pən) ▸ *n., pl.* **-pon** or **-pons.** A large silvery game fish of Atlantic coastal waters.

tar·ra·gon (tăr′ə-gŏn′, -gən) ▸ *n.* An aromatic Eurasian herb with leaves used in seasoning.

tar·ry (tăr′ē) ▸ *v.* **-ried, -ry·ing.** 1. To linger or be late. 2. To wait. 3. To stay temporarily; sojourn. **—tar′ri·er** *n.*

tar·sus (tär′səs) ▸ *n., pl.* **-si** (-sī, -sē). The section of the vertebrate foot between the leg and the metatarsus. **—tar′sal** *adj.*

tart¹ (tärt) ▸ *adj.* **-er, -est.** 1. Having a sharp pungent taste; sour. 2. Caustic; cutting. **—tart′ly** *adv.* **—tart′ness** *n.*

tart² (tärt) ▸ *n.* 1. A pastry shell with shallow sides, no top crust, and any of various fillings. 2. A prostitute.

tar·tan (tär′tn) ▸ *n.* Any of numerous textile patterns of Scottish origin consisting of stripes of varying widths and colors crossed at right angles against a solid background.

tar·tar (tär′tər) ▸ *n.* 1. *Dentistry* A hard yellowish deposit on the teeth. 2. A reddish acid compound deposited on the sides of casks during winemaking.

Tartar ▸ *n.* 1. also **Ta·tar** (tä′tər) A member of any of the Turkic and Mongolian peoples of central Asia who invaded W Asia and E Europe in the Middle Ages. 2. often **tartar** A ferocious or violent person.

tartar sauce ▸ *n.* Mayonnaise mixed with chopped onion, pickles, and capers and served as a sauce with fish.

Tar·ta·ry (tär′tə-rē) ▸ A region of E Europe and N Asia controlled by the Mongols in the 13th and 14th cent.

task (tăsk) ▸ *n.* 1. A piece of assigned work. 2. A difficult or tedious undertaking. **—*idiom:* take to task** To reprimand or censure.

task·bar (tăsk′bär′) ▸ *n.* A row of buttons on a computer screen that represent programs that are running.

THESAURUS

dab, flick, pat, rap. [*Compare* BRUSH¹, DIG.] 2. To indicate time or rhythm ▸ beat, count. *Idioms:* keep time, mark time. *—See also* APPOINT, BEAT (5).

tap *n.* The sound made by a light blow ▸ knock, rap, rapping, tapping. [*Compare* BEAT.]

tap² *v.* To monitor telephone calls with a concealed device connected to the circuit ▸ bug, wiretap. *—See also* DRAIN (1).

tap *n.* *—See* FAUCET, PLUG.

tape *n.* *—See* BAND¹.

taper *n.* *—See* DECREASE.

taper *v.* *—See* DECREASE.

tar *n.* *—See* SAILOR.

tardily *adv.* *—See* LATE.

tardiness *n.* The quality or condition of not being on time ▸ belatedness, lateness, slowness, unpunctuality.

tardy *adj.* *—See* LATE (1), SLOW (1).

target *n.* One that is fired at, attacked, or abused ▸ butt, mark. *—See also* INTENTION, OBJECT (2).

target *v.* To make a target of ▸ mark. *Idioms:* draw (*or* get) a bead on, get in one's sights. *—See also* INTEND.

tariff *n.* *—See* TAX, TOLL¹ (1).

tarnish *v.* *—See* DAMAGE, DENIGRATE, DISGRACE.

tarnish *n.* *—See* STAIN.

tarrier *n.* *—See* LAGGARD.

tarry *v.* *—See* DELAY (2), REMAIN.

tart¹ *adj.* *—See* SOUR.

tart² *n.* *—See* HARLOT, SLUT.

tartuffe *n.* *—See* HYPOCRITE.

tartuffery *n.* *—See* HYPOCRISY.

task *n.* 1. A piece of work that has been assigned ▸ assignment, chore, duty, job, office, project, stint. 2. A difficult or tedious undertaking ▸ chore, effort, grind, slog, sweat. *Informal:* job. [*Compare* LABOR.] *—See also* FUNCTION (1).

task *v.* To force to work hard ▸ drive, push, tax, work. *Idiom:* crack the whip. [*Compare* FORCE.]

task force ▸ *n.* A temporary grouping of forces for achieving a specific goal.

task·mas·ter (tăsk′măs′tər) ▸ *n.* One who imposes heavy work.

Tas·ma·ni·a (tăz-mā′nē-ə, -mān′yə) ▸ An island of SE Australia separated from the mainland by Bass Strait. **—Tas·ma′ni·an** *adj. & n.*

tas·sel (tăs′əl) ▸ *n.* **1.** A bunch of loose threads or cords bound at one end and hanging free at the other, used as an ornament. **2.** Something resembling this, esp. the pollen-bearing inflorescence of a corn plant. ▸ *v.* **-seled, -sel·ing** or **-selled, -sel·ling. 1.** To fringe or decorate with tassels. **2.** To put forth a tassellike blossom.

taste (tāst) ▸ *v.* **tast·ed, tast·ing. 1.** To distinguish the flavor of by taking into the mouth. **2.** To eat or drink a small quantity of. **3.** To experience, esp. for the first time. **4.** To have a distinct flavor: *The stew tastes salty.* ▸ *n.* **1.** The sense that distinguishes the sweet, sour, salty, and bitter qualities of something placed in the mouth. **2.** The sensation produced by or as if by something in the mouth; flavor. **3.** A small quantity eaten or tasted. **4.** A limited or first experience. **5.** A personal preference. **6.** The faculty of discerning what is aesthetically appropriate: *a room furnished with superb taste.* **—tast′a·ble** *adj.* **—tast′er** *n.*

taste bud ▸ *n.* Any of numerous clusters of cells on the tongue that are primarily responsible for the sense of taste.

taste·ful (tāst′fəl) ▸ *adj.* Having, showing, or in keeping with good taste. **—taste′ful·ly** *adv.* **—taste′ful·ness** *n.*

taste·less (tāst′lĭs) ▸ *adj.* **1.** Lacking flavor; insipid. **2.** Having or showing poor taste. **—taste′less·ly** *adv.* **—taste′less·ness** *n.*

tast·y (tā′stē) ▸ *adj.* **-i·er, -i·est.** Having a pleasing flavor. **—tast′i·ly** *adv.* **—tast′i·ness** *n.*

tat (tăt) ▸ *v.* **tat·ted, tat·ting.** To do or make by tatting. **—tat′ter** *n.*

ta·ta·mi (tä-tä′mē, tə-) ▸ *n., pl.* **-mi** or **-mis.** Straw matting used as a floor covering esp. in a Japanese house.

Ta·tar (tä′tər) ▸ *n.* Var. of **Tartar** 1.

tat·ter (tăt′ər) ▸ *n.* **1.** A torn and hanging piece of cloth; shred. **2. tatters** Torn and ragged clothing; rags. ▸ *v.* To make or become ragged.

tat·ter·de·mal·ion (tăt′ər-dĭ-māl′yən, -mā′lē-ən) ▸ *n.* A ragamuffin. ▸ *adj.* Ragged; tattered.

tat·ting (tăt′ĭng) ▸ *n.* **1.** Handmade lace made by looping and knotting a single strand of heavy thread on a small hand shuttle. **2.** The art of making such lace.

tat·tle (tăt′l) ▸ *v.* **-tled, -tling. 1.** To tell the secrets of another. **2.** To prattle; prate. **—tat′tler** *n.*

tat·tle·tale (tăt′l-tāl′) ▸ *n.* One who tells or tattles on others.

tat·too[1] (tă-tōō′) ▸ *n., pl.* **-toos. 1.** A call sounded to summon soldiers or sailors to quarters at night. **2.** A rhythmic tapping. **—tat·too′** *v.*

tat·too[2] (tă-tōō′) ▸ *n., pl.* **-toos.** A permanent mark or design made on the skin by a process of pricking and ingraining an indelible pigment. ▸ *v.* To mark (the skin) with a tattoo. **—tat·too′er** *n.*

tau (tou, tô) ▸ *n.* The 19th letter of the Greek alphabet.

taught (tôt) ▸ *v.* P.t. and p.part. of **teach.**

taunt (tônt) ▸ *v.* To provoke or deride in a jeering manner. ▸ *n.* A jeer or gibe. **—taunt′er** *n.* **—taunt′ing·ly** *adv.*

taupe (tōp) ▸ *n.* A brownish gray. **—taupe** *adj.*

Tau·rus (tôr′əs) ▸ *n.* **1.** A constellation in the Northern Hemisphere. **2.** The 2nd sign of the zodiac.

taut (tôt) ▸ *adj.* **-er, -est. 1.** Tight; not slack. **2.** Strained; tense. **3.** Trim; tidy. **—taut′ly** *adv.* **—taut′ness** *n.*

tau·tol·o·gy (tô-tŏl′ə-jē) ▸ *n., pl.* **-gies. 1.** Needless repetition of the same sense in different words; redundancy. **2.** *Logic* A statement that includes all logical possibilities and is therefore always true. **—tau′to·log′i·cal** (tôt′l-ŏj′ĭ-kəl), **tau′to·log′ic** *adj.*

tav·ern (tăv′ərn) ▸ *n.* **1.** A saloon; bar. **2.** A roadside inn.

taw·dry (tô′drē) ▸ *adj.* **-dri·er, -dri·est. 1.** Gaudy and cheap. **2.** Shameful; indecent. **—taw′dri·ly** *adv.* **—taw′dri·ness** *n.*

taw·ny (tô′nē) ▸ *n.* A light brown to brownish orange. **—taw′ni·ness** *n.* **—taw′ny** *adj.*

tax (tăks) ▸ *n.* **1.** A contribution for the support of a government required of persons, groups, or businesses within the domain of that government. **2.** An excessive demand; strain. ▸ *v.* **1.** To place a tax on (e.g., property). **2.** To exact a tax from. **3.** To make heavy demands upon. **4.** To charge; accuse. **—tax′a·ble** *adj.* **—tax·a′tion** *n.* **—tax′er** *n.*

tax·i (tăk′sē) ▸ *n., pl.* **-is** or **-ies.** A taxicab. ▸ *v.* **tax·ied** (tăk′sēd), **tax·i·ing** or **tax·y·ing. 1.** To transport or be transported by taxi. **2.** To move slowly on the ground or water before takeoff or after landing.

tax·i·cab (tăk′sē-kăb′) ▸ *n.* An automobile that carries passengers for a fare.

tax·i·der·my (tăk′sĭ-dûr′mē) ▸ *n.* The art or operation of stuffing and mounting animal skins in a lifelike state. **—tax′i·der′mist** *n.*

tax·ing (tăk′sĭng) ▸ *adj.* Burdensome.

taxo– or **taxi–** or **tax–** ▸ *pref.* Order; arrangement: *taxonomy.*

tax·on·o·my (tăk-sŏn′ə-mē) ▸ *n., pl.* **-mies. 1.** The classification of organisms in an ordered system that indicates natural relationships. **2.** The science or principles of classification. **—tax′o·nom′ic** (tăk′sə-nŏm′ĭk) *adj.* **—tax′o·nom′i·cal·ly** *adv.* **—tax·on′o·mist** *n.*

tax·pay·er (tăks′pā′ər) ▸ *n.* One who pays taxes.

tax shelter ▸ *n.* A financial operation that reduces taxes on current earnings.

Tay·lor (tā′lər), **Zachary** (1784–1850) ▸ The 12th US President (1849–50).

Tb ▸ The symbol for the element **terbium.**

TB ▸ *abbr.* tuberculosis

T-bone (tē′bōn′) ▸ *n.* A thick steak taken from the small

THESAURUS

taskmaster or **taskmistress** *n.* —*See* BOSS.

taste *v.* **1.** To have a particular flavor or suggestion of something ▸ savor, smack, smell, suggest. [*Compare* HINT.] **2.** To undergo an emotional reaction ▸ experience, feel, have, know, savor. —*See also* EXPERIENCE.

taste *n.* **1.** A liking for something ▸ fondness, partiality, preference, relish, weakness. [*Compare* INCLINATION.] **2.** A limited or anticipatory experience ▸ foretaste, sample, sampling. [*Compare* GLANCE.] —*See also* APPETITE, BIT[1] (2), DISCRIMINATION (1), DRINK (2), DROP (4), ELEGANCE, FLAVOR (1), SHADE (2).

tasteful *adj.* —*See* DECENT (7), DELICIOUS, ELEGANT, MODEST (1).

tastefulness *n.* —*See* ELEGANCE, MODESTY (2).

tasteless *adj.* —*See* COARSE (1), FLAT (2).

tasty *adj.* —*See* DELICIOUS.

tatter *n.* To wear away along the edges ▸ fray, frazzle. [*Compare* ERODE, SHRED.]

tatterdemalion *n.* A person wearing ragged or tattered clothing ▸ ragamuffin. [*Compare* HOBO.]

tatterdemalion *adj.* —*See* SHABBY.

tattered *adj.* —*See* SHABBY.

tatters *n.* Torn and ragged clothing ▸ rags, shreds.

tattle *v.* —*See* CHATTER (1), GOSSIP, INFORM (2).

tattle *n.* —*See* CHATTER, GOSSIP (1), GOSSIP (2).

tattler or **tattletale** *n.* —*See* GOSSIP (2), INFORMER.

tatty *adj.* —*See* SHABBY.

taunt *n.* An instance of mockery or derision ▸ cut, fleer, gibe, insult, jeer, scoff, twit. *Informal:* swipe. *Slang:* dig. [*Compare* INDIGNITY, LIBEL.] —*See also* RIBBING.

taunt *v.* —*See* HARASS, RIDICULE.

taut *adj.* Stretched tightly ▸ strained, tense, tight. [*Compare* RIGID.] —*See also* EDGY, NEAT, TIGHT (3).

tauten *v.* —*See* TENSE.

tautness *n.* —*See* PRESSURE.

tautological *adj.* —*See* WORDY (1).

tavern *n.* —*See* BAR (2).

tawdry *adj.* —*See* FLASHY.

tawny *adj.* —*See* DARK (2).

tax *n.* A compulsory contribution, usually of money, that is required for the support of an authority ▸ assessment, customs, duty, impost, levy, tariff, tithe, tribute. —*See also* BURDEN[1] (1), TOLL[1] (1).

tax *v.* To force to work hard ▸ drive, push, task, work. *Idiom:* crack the whip. [*Compare* FORCE.] —*See also* ACCUSE, BURDEN[1], CHASTISE.

tax with *v.* —*See* IMPOSE ON.

taxi *v.* —*See* DRIVE (1).

taxing *adj.* —*See* BURDENSOME.

taxpayer *n.* —*See* CITIZEN.

end of the loin and containing a T-shaped bone.

tbs. or **tbsp.** ▸ *abbr.* tablespoon

Tc ▸ The symbol for the element **technetium.**

T cell ▸ *n.* A principal type of white blood cell that has various roles in the immune system, including recognition of foreign antigens and activation of other immune cells.

Tchai·kov·sky (chī-kôf′skē), **Peter Ilich** (1840–93) ▸ Russian composer.

Te ▸ The symbol for the element **tellurium.**

tea (tē) ▸ *n.* **1a.** An Asian evergreen shrub with glossy leaves. **b.** The dried processed leaves of this plant, steeped in boiling water to make a beverage. **2.** The beverage thus made. **3.** Any similar drink prepared from the leaves of other plants. **4.** An afternoon reception or social gathering at which tea is served. **5.** *Slang* Marijuana.

tea bag ▸ *n.* A small porous sack holding enough tea leaves to make an individual serving of tea.

teach (tēch) ▸ *v.* **taught** (tôt), **teach·ing. 1.** To impart knowledge or skill (to). **2.** To instruct in. **3.** To cause to learn by example or experience. **—teach′a·bil′i·ty, teach′a·ble·ness** *n.* **—teach′a·ble** *adj.*

teach·er (tē′chər) ▸ *n.* One who teaches, esp. one hired to teach.

teach·ing (tē′chĭng) ▸ *n.* **1.** The work of a teacher. **2.** A precept or doctrine.

teak (tēk) ▸ *n.* **1.** An Asian tree with hard, durable yellowish-brown wood. **2.** The wood of this tree.

tea·ket·tle (tē′kĕt′l) ▸ *n.* A covered kettle with a spout and handle, used for boiling water, as for tea.

teal (tēl) ▸ *n., pl.* **teal** or **teals. 1.** Any of several small wild ducks. **2.** A moderate bluish green. **—teal** *adj.*

team (tēm) ▸ *n.* **1.** A group on the same side, as in a game. **2.** A group organized to work together. **3.** Two or more harnessed draft animals. ▸ *v.* **1.** To harness together to form a team. **2.** To form a team.

team·mate (tēm′māt′) ▸ *n.* A fellow member of a team.

team·ster (tēm′stər) ▸ *n.* **1.** A truck driver. **2.** One who drives a team of draft animals.

team·work (tēm′wûrk′) ▸ *n.* Cooperative effort.

tea·pot (tē′pŏt′) ▸ *n.* A covered pot with a spout, used for making and serving tea.

tear[1] (târ) ▸ *v.* **tore** (tôr), **torn** (tôrn), **tear·ing. 1.** To pull apart or into pieces; rend. **2.** To make (an opening) by ripping. **3.** To lacerate. **4.** To separate forcefully; wrench. **5.** To divide or disrupt. **6.** To rush headlong. ***—phrasal verb:* tear down** To demolish. ▸ *n.* A rip or rent. ***—idiom:* tear (one's) hair** To be greatly upset or distressed.

tear[2] (tîr) ▸ *n.* **1.** A drop of the clear salty liquid that lubricates the surface between the eyeball and eyelid. **2. tears** The act of weeping. ▸ *v.* To fill with tears. **—tear′ful** *adj.* **—tear′ful·ly** *adv.* **—tear′i·ly** *adv.* **—tear′i·ness** *n.* **—tear′y** *adj.*

tear·drop (tîr′drŏp′) ▸ *n.* A single tear.

tear gas (tîr) ▸ *n.* Any of various agents that irritate the eyes and cause blinding tears.

tear·jerk·er (tîr′jûr′kər) ▸ *n.* *Slang* A very sad or sentimental story, drama, or performance.

tea·room (tē′ro͞om′, -ro͝om′) ▸ *n.* A restaurant or shop serving tea and other light refreshments.

tease (tēz) ▸ *v.* **teased, teas·ing. 1.** To annoy; vex. **2.** To make fun of. **3.** To arouse hope, desire, or curiosity without affording satisfaction. **4.** To coax. **5.** To disentangle and dress the fibers of (wool). **6.** To raise the nap of (cloth). **7.** To brush or comb (the hair) toward the scalp for a bouffant effect. **—teas′er** *n.* **—teas′ing·ly** *adv.*

tea·sel (tē′zəl) ▸ *n.* **1.** A plant with thistlelike flowers surrounded by stiff bristles. **2.** Its bristly flower head, used to raise a nap on fabrics.

tea·spoon (tē′spo͞on′) ▸ *n.* **1.** The common small spoon used esp. with tea, coffee, and desserts. **2.** A household cooking measure equal to 1/3 tablespoon (about 5 ml). **—tea′spoon·ful** *n.*

teat (tēt, tĭt) ▸ *n.* A nipple of the mammary gland.

tech (tĕk) *Informal* ▸ *n.* **1.** A technician. **2.** Technology. **3.** Technical work. ▸ *adj.* Technical.

tech·ne·ti·um (tĕk-nē′shē-əm, -shəm) ▸ *n.* *Symbol* **Tc** A silvery-gray radioactive metal, the first synthetically produced element. At. no. 43.

tech·ni·cal (tĕk′nĭ-kəl) ▸ *adj.* **1.** Of or derived from technique. **2.** Specialized. **3.** Of the practical, mechanical, or industrial arts: *a technical school.* **4a.** Abstract or theoretical. **b.** Scientific. **5.** Formal rather than practical: *a technical distinction.* **6.** Technological. **—tech′ni·cal·ly** *adv.*

tech·ni·cal·i·ty (tĕk′nĭ-kăl′ĭ-tē) ▸ *n., pl.* **-ties. 1.** The quality or condition of being technical. **2a.** Something meaningful only to a specialist. **b.** A fine point, as of law.

technical sergeant ▸ *n.* A rank in the US Air Force above staff sergeant.

tech·ni·cian (tĕk-nĭsh′ən) ▸ *n.* An expert in a technical field or process.

Tech·ni·col·or (tĕk′nĭ-kŭl′ər) ▸ A trademark for a method of making color movies.

tech·nique (tĕk-nēk′) ▸ *n.* **1.** The systematic procedure by which a complex or scientific task is accomplished. **2.** also **tech·nic** (tĕk′nĭk) The degree of skill shown in any performance.

tech·noc·ra·cy (tĕk-nŏk′rə-sē) ▸ *n., pl.* **-cies.** Government by technicians or technical experts. **—tech′no·crat** *n.* **—tech′no·crat′ic** *adj.*

tech·nol·o·gy (tĕk-nŏl′ə-jē) ▸ *n., pl.* **-gies. 1.** The application of science, esp. in industry or commerce. **2.** The scientific methods and materials thus used. **—tech′no·log′i·cal** (-nə-lŏj′ĭ-kəl) *adj.* **—tech′no·log′i·cal·ly** *adv.* **—tech′nol′o·gist** *n.*

tec·ton·ics (tĕk-tŏn′ĭks) ▸ *n.* *(takes sing. v.)* **1.** The geology of the earth's structural features. **2.** The art of large-scale construction. **—tec·ton′ic** *adj.*

Te·cum·seh (tĭ-kŭm′sə) (1768–1813) ▸ Shawnee leader.

ted·dy bear also **Ted·dy bear** (tĕd′ē) ▸ *n.* A child's toy bear.

te·di·ous (tē′dē-əs) ▸ *adj.* Tiresomely long or dull; boring. **—te′di·ous·ly** *adv.* **—te′di·ous·ness** *n.*

te·di·um (tē′dē-əm) ▸ *n.* Boredom; monotony.

tee (tē) ▸ *n.* **1.** A small peg with a concave top for holding a golf ball for an initial drive. **2.** The area of each golf hole from which the initial drive is made. ▸ *v.* To place (a golf ball) on a tee. ***—phrasal verb:* tee off 1.** To drive a golf ball from the tee. **2.** *Slang* To start.

THESAURUS

tea *n.* —*See* PARTY.

teach *v.* —*See* EDUCATE.

teachable *adj.* Capable of being educated ▸ docile, educable, trainable. [*Compare* OBEDIENT.]

teacher *n.* —*See* EDUCATOR.

teaching *n.* —*See* DOCTRINE, EDUCATION (1).

teaching *adj.* —*See* EDUCATIONAL (1).

team *n.* —*See* FORCE (3).

teamwork *n.* —*See* COOPERATION.

tear[1] *v.* To separate or pull apart by force ▸ rend, rip, rive, run, split. [*Compare* CUT, SHRED.] —*See also* PULL (2), RUSH.

tear down *v.* —*See* DENIGRATE, DESTROY (2), MALIGN.

tear into *v.* —*See* ATTACK (1), SLAM (1).

tear up *v.* —*See* SHRED.

tear *n.* A hole made by tearing ▸ rent, rip, run. [*Compare* CRACK.] —*See also* BENDER.

tear[2] *n.* —*See* DROP (1).

tear *v.* To fill with tears ▸ tear (up), water, well (up). [*Compare* FLOW.] —*See also* DRIP.

teardrop *n.* —*See* DROP (1).

tearful *adj.* Filled with or shedding tears ▸ lachrymose, teary, weeping, weepy. ***Idioms:*** in tears, with tears in one's eyes. [*Compare* DEPRESSED, SORROWFUL.]

tear-jerking *adj.* —*See* SENTIMENTAL.

tears *n.* —*See* CRY (1).

teary *adj.* —*See* TEARFUL.

tease *v.* To arouse hope or desire without affording satisfaction ▸ bait, tantalize. ***Idiom:*** make one's mouth water. [*Compare* CHARM, FLIRT.] —*See also* HARASS.

tease *n.* A woman who is given to flirting ▸ coquette, flirt. *Informal:* vamp. [*Compare* SEDUCTRESS.] —*See also* BULLY.

technicality *n.* —*See* DETAIL.

technique *n.* —*See* ABILITY (1), APPROACH (1).

tedious *adj.* —*See* BORING.

tedium or **tediousness** *n.* —*See* BOREDOM, DULLNESS, MONOTONY.

tee-hee *v.* —*See* LAUGH.

tee-hee *n.* —*See* LAUGH.

teem (tēm) ► *v.* To abound or swarm. **—teem′ing·ly** *adv.*

teen (tēn) ► *n.* **1. teens a.** The numbers 13 through 19. **b.** The years of life between ages 13 and 19. **2.** A teenager. ► *adj.* Teenage.

teen·age or **teen-age** (tēn′āj′) also **teen·aged** or **teen-aged** (-ājd′) ► *adj.* Of, for, or involving those aged 13 through 19. **—teen′ag′er** *n.*

tee·ny (tē′nē) also **teen·sy** (tēn′sē) ► *adj.* **-ni·er, -ni·est** also **-si·er, -si·est.** *Informal* Tiny.

tee·pee (tē′pē) ► *n.* Var. of **tepee.**

tee shirt ► *n.* Var. of **T-shirt.**

tee·ter (tē′tər) ► *v.* **1.** To move unsteadily; totter. **2.** To seesaw; vacillate.

tee·ter-tot·ter (tē′tər-tŏt′ər) ► *n.* See **seesaw** 1.

teeth (tēth) ► *n.* Pl. of **tooth.**

teethe (tē*th*) ► *v.* **teethed, teeth·ing.** To grow or cut one's teeth.

tee·to·tal·er (tē′tōt′l-ər) ► *n.* One who abstains completely from alcoholic beverages. **—tee·to′tal·ism** *n.*

Tef·lon (tĕf′lŏn′) ► A trademark for a nonstick material used to coat cooking utensils.

Teh·ran or **Te·he·ran** (tĕ′ə-răn′, -rän′, tĕ-răn′, -rän′) ► The capital of Iran, in the N-central part.

tek·tite (tĕk′tīt′) ► *n.* A dark glassy rock of possibly meteoric origin.

tel. ► *abbr.* telephone

Tel A·viv–Ya·fo (tĕl′ä-vēv′yä′fō) or **Tel A·viv–Jaf·fa** (-jăf′ə, -yä′fə) ► A city of W-central Israel on the Mediterranean WNW of Jerusalem.

tele– or **tel–** ► *pref.* **1.** Distance; distant: *telepathy.* **2a.** Telegraph; telephone: *telegram.* **b.** Television: *telecast.*

tel·e·cast (tĕl′ĭ-kăst′) ► *v.* To broadcast by television. **—tel′e·cast′** *n.*

tel·e·com·mu·ni·ca·tion (tĕl′ĭ-kə-myōō′nĭ-kā′shən) ► *n.* often **telecommunications** *(takes sing. v.)* The science and technology of sending messages by electrical or electronic means.

tel·e·com·mute (tĕl′ĭ-kə-myōōt′) ► *v.* **-mut·ed, -mut·ing.** To work at home using a computer connected to the network of one's employer. **—tel′e·com·mut′er** *n.*

tel·e·con·fer·ence (tĕl′ĭ-kŏn′fər-əns, -frəns) ► *n.* A conference held among people in different locations with telecommunications equipment.

tel·e·gen·ic (tĕl′ə-jĕn′ĭk) ► *adj.* Presenting an appealing appearance on television.

tel·e·gram (tĕl′ĭ-grăm′) ► *n.* A message sent by telegraph.

tel·e·graph (tĕl′ĭ-grăf′) ► *n.* **1.** A communications system that transmits coded messages by means of unmodulated electric impulses, esp. one in which the transmission and reception stations are connected by wires. **2.** A telegram. ► *v.* To transmit (a message) by telegraph. **—te·leg′ra·pher** (tə-lĕg′rə-fər), **te·leg′ra·phist** *n.* **—tel′e·graph′ic** *adj.* **—tel′e·graph′i·cal·ly** *adv.* **—te·leg′ra·phy** *n.*

tel·e·ki·ne·sis (tĕl′ĭ-kĭ-nē′sĭs, -kī-) ► *n.* The movement of objects by scientifically inexplicable means. **—tel′e·ki·net′ic** (-nĕt′ĭk) *adj.*

tel·e·mar·ket·ing (tĕl′ə-mär′kĭ-tĭng) ► *n.* The business of marketing goods or services by telephone. **—tel′e·mar′ket·er** *n.*

tel·e·med·i·cine (tĕl′ĭ-mĕd′ĭ-sĭn) ► *n.* The use of telecommunications to provide health care services, as by accessing off-site databases.

te·lem·e·try (tə-lĕm′ĭ-trē) ► *n.* The automatic measurement and transmission of data from remote sources to receiving stations for recording and analysis. **—tel′e·me′ter** (tĕl′ə-mē′tər) *n.* **—tel′e·met′ric** (tĕl′ə-mĕt′rĭk), **tel′e·met′ri·cal** *adj.*

te·lep·a·thy (tə-lĕp′ə-thē) ► *n.* Communication through means other than the senses. **—tel′e·path′ic** (tĕl′ə-păth′ĭk) *adj.* **—tel′e·path′i·cal·ly** *adv.* **—te·lep′a·thist** *n.*

tel·e·phone (tĕl′ə-fōn′) ► *n.* An instrument that converts voice and other sound signals into a form that can be transmitted to remote locations. ► *v.* **-phoned, -phon·ing.** To speak with (a person) by telephone.

telephone exchange ► *n.* A central system of switches and other equipment that establishes connections between telephones.

te·leph·o·ny (tə-lĕf′ə-nē) ► *n.* The transmission of sound between distant stations, esp. by radio or telephone. **—tel′e·phon′ic** (tĕl′ə-fŏn′ĭk) *adj.*

tel·e·pho·to (tĕl′ə-fō′tō) ► *adj.* Of or relating to a photographic lens or lens system used to produce a large image of a distant object.

tel·e·play (tĕl′ə-plā′) ► *n.* A play written or adapted for television.

tel·e·scope (tĕl′ĭ-skōp′) ► *n.* **1.** An arrangement of lenses or mirrors or both that gathers visible light, permitting direct observation or photographic recording of distant objects. **2.** Any of various devices used to detect and observe distant objects by their emission or reflection of invisible radiation. ► *v.* **-scoped, -scop·ing. 1.** To slide inward or outward in overlapping sections, as the cylindrical sections of a small hand telescope do. **2.** To condense. **—tel′e·scop′ic** (-skŏp′ĭk) *adj.*

tel·e·thon (tĕl′ə-thŏn′) ► *n.* A lengthy television program to raise funds for a charity.

tel·e·type·writ·er (tĕl′ĭ-tīp′rī′tər) ► *n.* An electromechanical typewriter that either transmits or receives messages coded in electrical signals.

tel·e·vise (tĕl′ə-vīz′) ► *v.* **-vised, -vis·ing.** To broadcast by television.

tel·e·vi·sion (tĕl′ə-vĭzh′ən) ► *n.* **1.** The transmission of visual images, usu. with accompanying sound, as electromagnetic waves. **2.** An electronic apparatus that receives such waves and displays the reconverted images on a screen. **3.** The industry of producing and broadcasting television programs.

tel·ex (tĕl′ĕks′) ► *n.* **1.** A communications system consisting of teletypewriters connected to a telephonic network. **2.** A message sent or received by telex. **—tel′ex′** *v.*

tell (tĕl) ► *v.* **told** (tōld), **tell·ing. 1.** To give an account of; narrate. **2.** To express with words. **3.** To notify; inform. **4.** To give instructions to; direct. **5.** To discover by observation; discern. **6.** To have an effect or impact: *In this game every move tells.* **—*phrasal verb:* tell off** *Informal* To rebuke severely; reprimand.

tell·er (tĕl′ər) ► *n.* A bank employee who receives and pays out money.

tell·ing (tĕl′ĭng) ► *adj.* Having force or effect; striking. **—tell′ing·ly** *adv.*

tell·tale (tĕl′tāl′) ► *n.* **1.** A tattletale; talebearer. **2.** An indicator; sign.

tel·lu·ri·um (tĕ-lŏŏr′ē-əm) ► *n.* *Symbol* **Te** A brittle, silvery-white metallic element used to alloy stainless steel and lead, in ceramics, and in thermoelectric devices. At. no. 52.

te·mer·i·ty (tə-mĕr′ĭ-tē) ► *n.* Audacity; nerve.

THESAURUS

teem[1] *v.* To be abundantly filled or richly supplied ► abound, bristle, crawl, flow, overflow, pullulate, roll, swarm, swim.

teem[2] *v.* —*See* RAIN (2).

teeming *adj.* —*See* BUSY (2), OVERCROWDED.

teen *n.* —*See* TEENAGER.

teenager *n.* A young person, usually between the ages of 13 and 19 ► adolescent, teen, youth. *Informal:* kid, teener. *Slang:* teenybopper. [*Compare* MINOR.]

teeny or **teensy** or **teeny-weeny** or **teensy-weensy** *adj.* —*See* TINY.

teenybopper *n.* —*See* TEENAGER.

tee off *v.* —*See* ANGER (1).

teeter *v.* —*See* BALANCE (3), STAGGER (1), SWAY.

teetering *adj.* —*See* INSECURE (2).

teetotalism *n.* —*See* TEMPERANCE (2).

telephone *v.* To communicate with someone by telephone ► buzz, call (up), dial, phone, ring (up). *Idioms:* get someone on the horn, give someone a buzz (*or* call *or* ring).

tell *v.* —*See* BETRAY (2), COMMAND (1), COMMUNICATE (1), COUNT (2), DESCRIBE, DISTINGUISH (1), INFORM (1), SAY.

tell off *v.* —*See* CHASTISE.

telling *adj.* —*See* CONVINCING.

telltale *n.* —*See* GOSSIP (2).

tellurian or **telluric** *adj.* —*See* EARTHLY.

temblor *n.* A shaking of the earth ► earthquake, quake, seism, tremor. *Informal.* shake.

temerarious *adj.* —*See* RASH[1].

temerity *n.* Foolhardy boldness or disregard of danger ► brashness, foolhardiness, incautiousness, rashness, recklessness, temerariousness. [*Compare* COURAGE, DARING.]

temp. ▸ *abbr.* **1.** temperature **2.** temporary **3.** *Lat.* tempore (in the time of)

tem·peh (tĕm′pā′) ▸ *n.* A high-protein food made from partially cooked, fermented soybeans.

tem·per (tĕm′pər) ▸ *v.* **1.** To soften or moderate. **2.** To harden or strengthen (e.g., metal), as by alternate heating and cooling. **3.** To adjust finely; attune. ▸ *n.* **1.** A state of mind or emotions; mood. **2.** Calmness; composure. **3a.** A tendency to become angry or irritable. **b.** An outburst of rage. **4.** The degree of hardness of a metal.

tem·per·a (tĕm′pər-ə) ▸ *n.* **1.** A painting medium in which pigment is mixed with water-soluble glutinous materials such as size or egg yolk. **2.** Painting done in this medium.

tem·per·a·ment (tĕm′prə-mənt, tĕm′pər-ə-) ▸ *n.* **1.** The manner of thinking, behaving, or reacting characteristic of a particular person. **2.** Excessive irritability or sensitiveness. **—tem′per·a·men′tal** *adj.* **—tem′per·a·men′tal·ly** *adv.*

tem·per·ance (tĕm′pər-əns, -prəns) ▸ *n.* **1.** Moderation and self-restraint. **2.** Abstinence from alcoholic liquors.

tem·per·ate (tĕm′pər-ĭt, -prĭt) ▸ *adj.* **1.** Exercising moderation and self-restraint. **2.** Moderate; restrained. **3.** Not subject to extreme hot or cold weather. **—tem′per·ate·ly** *adv.* **—tem′per·ate·ness** *n.*

Temperate Zone ▸ Either of two latitude zones of the earth, the **North Temperate Zone,** between the Arctic Circle and the tropic of Cancer, or the **South Temperate Zone,** between the Antarctic Circle and the tropic of Capricorn.

tem·per·a·ture (tĕm′pər-ə-cho͝or′, -chər, tĕm′prə-) ▸ *n.* **1.** The hotness or coldness of a body or environment. **2.** Abnormally high body heat caused by illness; fever.

tem·pered (tĕm′pərd) ▸ *adj.* Having a specified temper or disposition.

tem·pest (tĕm′pĭst) ▸ *n.* A violent windstorm.

tem·pes·tu·ous (tĕm-pĕs′cho͞o-əs) ▸ *adj.* Tumultuous; stormy. **—tem·pes′tu·ous·ly** *adv.* **—tem·pes′tu·ous·ness** *n.*

tem·plate (tĕm′plĭt) ▸ *n.* A pattern or gauge, such as a thin metal plate, used as a guide in making something accurately.

tem·ple[1] (tĕm′pəl) ▸ *n.* **1.** A building dedicated to religious ceremonies or worship. **2.** *Judaism* A synagogue, esp. of a Reform congregation.

tem·ple[2] (tĕm′pəl) ▸ *n.* **1.** The flat region on either side of the forehead. **2.** The sidepiece of an eyeglass frame.

tem·po (tĕm′pō) ▸ *n., pl.* **-pos** or **-pi** (-pē). **1.** The speed at which music is to be played. **2.** A pace.

tem·po·ral[1] (tĕm′pər-əl, -prəl) ▸ *adj.* **1.** Of or limited by time. **2.** Worldly; secular. **—tem′po·ral·ly** *adv.*

tem·po·ral[2] (tĕm′pər-əl, -prəl) ▸ *adj.* Of or near the temples of the skull.

temporal bone ▸ *n.* Either of two bones that form the sides and base of the skull.

tem·po·rar·y (tĕm′pə-rĕr′ē) ▸ *adj.* Lasting or used for a limited time. ▸ *n., pl.* **-ies.** *Informal* One that works or serves for a limited time. **—tem′po·rar′i·ly** *adv.*

tem·po·rize (tĕm′pə-rīz′) ▸ *v.* **-rized, -riz·ing. 1.** To gain time, as by postponing an action or decision. **2.** To yield to current conditions; compromise. **—tem′po·ri·za′tion** *n.*

tempt (tĕmpt) ▸ *v.* **1.** To try to get (someone) to do wrong, esp. by a promise of reward. **2.** To be attractive to. **3.** To risk provoking: *tempt fate.* **4.** To incline or dispose: *I'm tempted to go.* **—temp·ta′tion** *n.* **—tempt′er** *n.*

tempt·ress (tĕmp′trĭs) ▸ *n.* An alluring, bewitching woman.

tem·pu·ra (tĕm′po͝o-rə, tĕm-po͝or′ə) ▸ *n.* A Japanese dish of deep-fried batter-dipped vegetables and shrimp or other seafood.

ten (tĕn) ▸ *n.* **1.** The cardinal number equal to 9 + 1. **2.** The 10th in a set or sequence. **—ten** *adj. & pron.*

ten·a·ble (tĕn′ə-bəl) ▸ *adj.* Defensible: *a tenable theory.* **—ten′a·bil′i·ty, ten′a·ble·ness** *n.* **—ten′a·bly** *adv.*

te·na·cious (tə-nā′shəs) ▸ *adj.* **1.** Holding firmly, as to a belief; stubborn. **2.** Clinging; adhesive. **3.** Tending to retain; retentive. **—te·na′cious·ly** *adv.* **—te·nac′i·ty** (-năs′ĭ-tē), **te·na′cious·ness** *n.*

ten·an·cy (tĕn′ən-sē) ▸ *n., pl.* **-cies. 1.** Possession or occupancy of land or building by title, lease, or rent. **2.** The period of a tenant's occupancy or possession.

ten·ant (tĕn′ənt) ▸ *n.* **1.** One that pays rent to use or occupy property owned by another. **2.** An occupant.

Ten Commandments ▸ *pl.n. Bible* The ten laws given by God to Moses on Mount Sinai.

tend[1] (tĕnd) ▸ *v.* **1.** To have a tendency. **2.** To be likely. **3.** To move or extend in a certain direction.

tend[2] (tĕnd) ▸ *v.* **1.** To take care of. **2.** To serve at: *tend bar.* **3.** To apply one's attention; attend.

ten·den·cy (tĕn′dən-sē) ▸ *n., pl.* **-cies. 1.** Prevailing movement; trend. **2.** An inclination to think, act, or behave in a particular way.

ten·den·tious (tĕn-dĕn′shəs) ▸ *adj.* Promoting a particular point of view; biased.

THESAURUS

temper *n.* **1.** A tendency to become angry or irritable ▸ bile, biliousness, cantankerousness, crankiness, disagreeability, hotheadedness, irascibility, irascibleness, irritability, orneriness, peevishness, petulance, petulancy, prickliness, spleen, temperament, testiness, tetchiness, waspishness. *Informal:* dander, meanness. *Slang:* short fuse. ***Idiom:*** low boiling point. [*Compare* OVERSENSITIVITY.] **2.** An angry outburst ▸ fit, huff, passion, tantrum. *Informal:* conniption, conniption fit, hissy, hissy fit. [*Compare* STATE.] **3.** A prevailing quality, as of thought, behavior, or attitude ▸ climate, mood, spirit, timbre, tone. —*See also* DISPOSITION, MOOD.

temper *v.* —*See* ADJUST, MODERATE (1).

temperament *n.* —*See* CHARACTER (1), DISPOSITION, TEMPER (1).

temperamental *adj.* Given to changeable emotional states, especially of anger or gloom ▸ mercurial, moody. [*Compare* TESTY.] —*See also* CAPRICIOUS.

temperance *n.* **1.** Moderation or restraint of one's behavior or desires ▸ abstinence, continence, self-denial, sobriety. **2.** The practice of refraining from use of alcoholic liquors ▸ abstinence, dryness, soberness, sobriety, teetotalism. —*See also* MODERATION.

temperate *adj.* **1.** Free from extremes in temperature ▸ balmy, clement, mild, moderate. [*Compare* PLEASANT.] **2.** Characterized by self-restraint in appetites and behavior ▸ abstemious, continent, sober, spartan, unindulgent. [*Compare* ASCETIC.] —*See also* CONSERVATIVE (2).

tempest *n.* —*See* AGITATION (1), STORM.

tempestuous *adj.* —*See* AGITATED, ROUGH (2).

tempo *n.* Rate of motion or performance ▸ pace, speed, velocity. *Informal:* clip.

temporal *adj.* —*See* EARTHLY, PROFANE (2), TRANSITORY.

temporary *adj.* **1.** Temporarily assuming the duties of another ▸ acting, ad interim, interim, pro tem, provisional, substitute. *Informal:* fill-in. **2.** Intended, used, or present for a limited time ▸ ad hoc, impermanent, interim, make-do, makeshift, provisional, short-range, short-term, stopgap. —*See also* TRANSITORY.

tempt *v.* —*See* COURT (1), SEDUCE.

temptation *n.* —*See* LURE (1).

tempter *n.* —*See* SEDUCER (1).

tempting *adj.* —*See* ATTRACTIVE, SEDUCTIVE.

temptress *n.* —*See* SEDUCTRESS.

tenable *adj.* **1.** Capable of being justified ▸ defensible, excusable, justifiable. [*Compare* LOGICAL, SOUND[2].] **2.** Capable of being defended against armed attack ▸ defendable, defensible. [*Compare* SAFE.]

tenacious *adj.* —*See* STUBBORN (1), TIGHT (1).

tenacity or **tenaciousness** *n.* —*See* STUBBORNNESS.

tenant *n.* —*See* INHABITANT.

tend[1] *v.* To have a tendency or inclination ▸ incline, lean, skew, slant, squint, trend. [*Compare* INCLINED.]

tend[2] *v.* To have the care and supervision of ▸ attend, baby-sit, care for, look after, mind, minister to, see to, watch (over). ***Idioms:*** keep an eye on, look out for, take care (*or* charge) of, take under one's wing. [*Compare* ADMINISTER, SERVE, SUPERVISE.] —*See also* GROW, NURTURE.

tendency *n.* —*See* INCLINATION (1), THRUST.

tendentious *adj.* —*See* BIASED.

tendentiousness *n.* —*See* BIAS.

ten·der[1] (tĕn′dər) ▸ *adj.* **-er, -est.** **1a.** Delicate; fragile. **b.** Easily chewed. **2.** Young and vulnerable. **3.** Sensitive or sore. **4.** Gentle and loving. **5.** Sentimental; soft. **—ten′der·ly** *adv.* **—ten′der·ness** *n.*

ten·der[2] (tĕn′dər) ▸ *n.* **1.** A formal offer. **2.** Money: *legal tender.* ▸ *v.* To offer formally. **—ten′der·er** *n.*

tend·er[3] (tĕn′dər) ▸ *n.* **1.** One who tends something. **2.** *Naut.* A vessel attendant on other vessels. **3.** A railroad car attached to the locomotive, carrying fuel and water.

ten·der·foot (tĕn′dər-fo͝ot′) ▸ *n., pl.* **-foots** or **-feet.** An inexperienced person; novice.

ten·der·heart·ed (tĕn′dər-här′tĭd) ▸ *adj.* Compassionate. **—ten′der·heart′ed·ly** *adv.* **—ten′der·heart′ed·ness** *n.*

ten·der·ize (tĕn′də-rīz′) ▸ *v.* **-ized, -iz·ing.** To make (meat) tender. **—ten′der·iz′er** *n.*

ten·der·loin (tĕn′dər-loin′) ▸ *n.* The tenderest part of a loin of beef or pork.

ten·di·ni·tis also **ten·do·ni·tis** (tĕn′də-nī′tĭs) ▸ *n.* Inflammation of a tendon.

ten·don (tĕn′dən) ▸ *n.* A band of tough fibrous tissue that connects a muscle with its bony attachment.

ten·dril (tĕn′drəl) ▸ *n.* **1.** A twisting threadlike structure by which a twining plant clings to a support. **2.** Something resembling this.

ten·e·ment (tĕn′ə-mənt) ▸ *n.* **1.** A building to live in, esp. one rented to tenants. **2.** A rundown, low-rental apartment building whose facilities and upkeep barely meet minimum standards.

ten·et (tĕn′ĭt) ▸ *n.* A doctrine or principle held to be true.

ten-gal·lon hat (tĕn′găl′ən) ▸ *n.* A hat with an exceptionally tall crown and a wide brim.

ten·ge (tĕn-gĕ′) ▸ *n., pl.* **tenge.** See **currency** table in Appendix.

Ten·nes·see (tĕn′ĭ-sē′, tĕn′ĭ-sē′) ▸ A state of the SE US. Cap. Nashville. **—Ten′nes·se′an** *adj. & n.*

ten·nis (tĕn′ĭs) ▸ *n.* A game played with rackets and a light ball by two players or two pairs of players on a court divided by a net.

tennis shoe ▸ *n.* See **sneaker.**

Ten·ny·son (tĕn′ĭ-sən), **Alfred.** 1st Baron Tennyson (1809–92) ▸ British poet.

ten·on (tĕn′ən) ▸ *n.* A projection on a piece of wood shaped for insertion into a mortise to make a joint.

ten·or (tĕn′ər) ▸ *n.* **1.** A continuous course. **2.** General sense; drift or purport. **3.** *Mus.* **a.** The highest natural adult male voice. **b.** The range between alto and bass. **c.** A singer, voice, or instrument having this range.

ten·pin (tĕn′pĭn′) ▸ *n.* **1.** One of the bottle-shaped pins used in bowling. **2. tenpins** *(takes sing. v.)* See **bowling** 1.

tense[1] (tĕns) ▸ *adj.* **tens·er, tens·est.** **1.** Tightly stretched; taut. **2.** Feeling mental or nervous tension. **3.** Nerve-racking; suspenseful. ▸ *v.* **tensed, tens·ing.** To make or become tense. **—tense′ly** *adv.* **—tense′ness** *n.*

tense[2] (tĕns) ▸ *n.* Any of the inflected forms of a verb that indicate the time and continuance or completion of the action or state.

ten·sile (tĕn′səl, -sīl′) ▸ *adj.* **1.** Of or relating to tension. **2.** Capable of being stretched or extended. **—ten·sil′i·ty** (tĕn-sĭl′ĭ-tē) *n.*

ten·sion (tĕn′shən) ▸ *n.* **1.** The act of stretching or the condition of being stretched. **2.** A force tending to stretch or elongate something. **3a.** Mental strain. **b.** A strained relationship between people or groups. **c.** Uneasy suspense. **4.** Voltage.

ten·sor (tĕn′sər, -sôr′) ▸ *n.* A muscle that tenses a body part.

tent (tĕnt) ▸ *n.* A portable shelter, as of canvas, stretched over a supporting framework of poles with ropes and pegs.

ten·ta·cle (tĕn′tə-kəl) ▸ *n.* An elongated, flexible, unjointed appendage, as of an octopus or squid. **—ten·tac′u·lar** (-tăk′yə-lər) *adj.*

ten·ta·tive (tĕn′tə-tĭv) ▸ *adj.* **1.** Not fully worked out or concluded; provisional. **2.** Uncertain; hesitant. **—ten′ta·tive·ly** *adv.* **—ten′ta·tive·ness** *n.*

ten·ter·hook (tĕn′tər-ho͝ok′) ▸ *n.* A hooked nail for securing cloth on a drying framework. ***—idiom:* on tenterhooks** In a state of suspense or anxiety.

tenth (tĕnth) ▸ *n.* **1.** The ordinal number matching the number 10 in a series. **2.** One of ten equal parts. **—tenth** *adv. & adj.*

ten·u·ous (tĕn′yo͞o-əs) ▸ *adj.* **1.** Long and thin; slender. **2.** Rarefied. **3.** Slight; flimsy. **—ten′u·ous·ly** *adv.* **—ten′u·ous·ness, te·nu′i·ty** (tĕ-no͞o′ĭ-tē, -nyo͞o′-) *n.*

ten·ure (tĕn′yər, -yo͝or′) ▸ *n.* **1a.** The holding of something, as an office or real estate. **b.** A period during which something is held. **2.** The status of holding one's position on a permanent basis.

te·pee also **tee·pee** or **ti·pi** (tē′pē) ▸ *n.* A portable dwelling of certain Native American peoples, consisting of a conical framework of poles covered with skins or bark.

tep·id (tĕp′ĭd) ▸ *adj.* Moderately warm; lukewarm. **—te·pid′i·ty, tep′id·ness** *n.* **—tep′id·ly** *adv.*

te·qui·la (tə-kē′lə) ▸ *n.* An alcoholic liquor distilled from an agave.

tera– ▸ *pref.* One trillion (10^{12}): *terabyte.*

ter·a·byte (tĕr′ə-bīt′) ▸ *n.* A unit of computer memory equal to 1,024 gigabytes (2^{40} bytes).

te·rat·o·gen (tə-răt′ə-jən, tĕr′ə-tə-) ▸ *n.* An agent, such as a drug, that causes malformation of an embryo or fetus. **—ter′a·to·gen′ic** *adj.*

ter·bi·um (tûr′bē-əm) ▸ *n. Symbol* **Tb** A soft, silvery-gray rare-earth element, used in x-ray and color television tubes. At. no. 65.

ter·cen·ten·a·ry (tûr′sĕn-tĕn′ə-rē, tər-sĕn′tə-nĕr′ē) ▸ *n., pl.* **-ries.** A 300th anniversary. **—ter′cen·ten′a·ry** *adj.*

Te·re·sa (tə-rē′sə, -zə, -rā′-), Mother (1910–97) ▸ Albanian-born Indian nun; 1979 Nobel Peace Prize.

ter·i·ya·ki (tĕr′ē-yä′kē) ▸ *n.* A Japanese dish of grilled or broiled slices of marinated meat or shellfish.

term (tûrm) ▸ *n.* **1a.** A limited period of time. **b.** An assigned period for a person to serve. **c.** A period when a school or court is in session. **2a.** An end or termination. **b.** The end of a normal gestation period: *carried the fetus to term.* **c.** A deadline, as for making a payment. **3a.** A word or phrase having a particular meaning. **b. terms** Language of a certain kind: *praised him in glowing terms.* **4.** often **terms** A stipulation or condition: *peace terms.* **5. terms** The relationship between persons or groups: *on*

THESAURUS

tender[1] *adj.* *—See* AFFECTIONATE, GENTLE (1), PAINFUL, SYMPATHETIC.

tender[2] *n.* *—See* OFFER.

tender *v.* *—See* OFFER (1).

tenderfoot *n.* *—See* BEGINNER.

tenderhearted *adj.* *—See* GENTLE (1).

tenderness *n.* *—See* CONSIDERATION (1), IRRITATION, LOVE (1).

tending *adj.* *—See* INCLINED.

tendril *n.* *—See* SHOOT.

tenebrific *adj.* *—See* GLOOMY.

tenet *n.* *—See* DOCTRINE, LAW (1).

tenor *n.* *—See* IMPORT, THRUST.

tense *v.* To make or become tense ▸ brace, stiffen, stretch, tauten, tighten.

tense *adj.* Stretched tightly ▸ taut, tight. [*Compare* RIGID.] *—See also* DRAMATIC (2), EDGY.

tenseness *n.* *—See* PRESSURE, RESTLESSNESS.

tension *n.* *—See* PRESSURE.

ten-strike *n.* *—See* HIT.

tentative *adj.* *—See* CONDITIONAL, DOUBTFUL (2), HESITANT, ROUGH (4).

tentativeness *n.* *—See* HESITATION.

tenuous *adj.* *—See* IMPLAUSIBLE.

tenure *n.* The holding of a position ▸ incumbency, occupancy, occupation. [*Compare* PERIOD.]

tepid *adj.* Lacking warmth, interest, enthusiasm, or involvement ▸ halfhearted, Laodicean, lukewarm, unenthusiastic. [*Compare* APATHETIC, COLD, COOL.]

tergiversate *v.* *—See* DEFECT, EQUIVOCATE (1).

tergiversation *n.* *—See* AMBIGUITY, DEFECTION, EQUIVOCATION.

tergiversator *n.* *—See* DEFECTOR.

term *n.* A sound or combination of sounds that symbolizes and communicates a meaning ▸ expression, lexical item, lexeme, locution, vocable, word. [*Compare* SPEECH.] *—See also* LIFE, PERIOD (1), PROVISION.

term *v.* *—See* CALL, NAME (1).

good terms. **6.** *Math.* One of the quantities in a fraction, equation, or series. ▸ *v.* To designate; call.
ter·ma·gant (tûr′mə-gənt) ▸ *n.* A scolding woman; shrew.
ter·mi·nal (tûr′mə-nəl) ▸ *adj.* **1.** Of or forming a limit, boundary, or end. **2.** Concluding; final. **3.** Of or occurring in a term or each term. **4.** Ending in death; fatal. ▸ *n.* **1.** A point or part that forms the end. **2.** *Elect.* A position in a circuit at which a connection is normally established or broken. **3.** A railroad or bus station, esp. a terminus. **4.** A device, usu. having a keyboard and video display, through which data can be entered or displayed. **—ter′mi·nal·ly** *adv.*
ter·mi·nate (tûr′mə-nāt′) ▸ *v.* **-nat·ed, -nat·ing.** To bring or come to an end; conclude. **—ter′mi·na·ble** *adj.* **—ter′mi·na′tion** *n.* **—ter′mi·na′tive** *adj.* **—ter′mi·na′tor** *n.*
ter·mi·nol·o·gy (tûr′mə-nŏl′ə-jē) ▸ *n., pl.* **-gies. 1.** The technical terms of a particular field, science, or art; nomenclature. **2.** The study of nomenclature. **—ter′mi·no·log′i·cal** (-nə-lŏj′ĭ-kəl) *adj.*
ter·mi·nus (tûr′mə-nəs) ▸ *n., pl.* **-nus·es** or **-ni** (-nī′). **1.** The final point; end. **2.** An end point on a transportation line.
ter·mite (tûr′mīt′) ▸ *n.* Any of numerous antlike social insects that often feed on wood.
tern (tûrn) ▸ *n.* Any of various sea birds resembling gulls but usu. smaller and having a forked tail.
ter·na·ry (tûr′nə-rē) ▸ *adj.* **1.** Composed of three or arranged in threes. **2.** *Math.* **a.** Having the base three. **b.** Involving three variables.
terp·si·cho·re·an (tûrp′sĭ-kə-rē′ən, -kôr′ē-ən) ▸ *adj.* Of dancing. ▸ *n.* A dancer.
terr. ▸ *abbr.* **1.** terrace **2.** territory
ter·race (tĕr′ĭs) ▸ *n.* **1.** A porch or balcony. **2.** An open area adjacent to a house serving as an outdoor living space. **3.** A raised bank of earth having vertical or sloping sides and a flat top. **4.** A row of buildings on raised or sloping ground. **5.** A residential street, esp. along the top or slope of a hill. ▸ *v.* **-raced, -rac·ing.** To form into terraces.
ter·ra cot·ta (tĕr′ə kŏt′ə) ▸ *n.* **1.** A hard ceramic clay used in pottery and construction. **2.** A brownish orange. **—ter′ra-cot′ta** *adj.*
terra fir·ma (fûr′mə) ▸ *n.* Dry land.
ter·rain (tə-rān′) ▸ *n.* **1.** An area of land; ground. **2.** Topography: *rugged terrain.*
ter·ra·pin (tĕr′ə-pĭn) ▸ *n.* Any of various North American aquatic turtles.
ter·rar·i·um (tə-râr′ē-əm) ▸ *n., pl.* **-i·ums** or **-i·a** (-ē-ə). A closed container in which plants and sometimes small animals, such as turtles and lizards, are kept.
ter·res·tri·al (tə-rĕs′trē-əl) ▸ *adj.* **1.** Of Earth or its inhabitants. **2.** Of or consisting of land. **3.** Living or growing on land. ▸ *n.* An inhabitant of Earth.
ter·ri·ble (tĕr′ə-bəl) ▸ *adj.* **1.** Causing great fear or alarm; dreadful. **2.** Extreme or severe. **3.** Very bad. **—ter′ri·bly** *adv.*
ter·ri·er (tĕr′ē-ər) ▸ *n.* Any of several small dogs orig. bred to hunt burrowing animals.
ter·rif·ic (tə-rĭf′ĭk) ▸ *adj.* **1.** Fine; splendid: *a terrific party.* **2.** Awesome; astounding. **3.** Terrifying. **4.** Terrible; severe. **—ter·rif′i·cal·ly** *adv.*
ter·ri·fy (tĕr′ə-fī′) ▸ *v.* **-fied, -fy·ing.** To fill with terror.
ter·ri·to·ri·al (tĕr′ĭ-tôr′ē-əl) ▸ *adj.* **1.** Of or relating to the geographic area under a given jurisdiction. **2.** Of a particular territory; regional. **—ter′ri·to′ri·al·ly** *adv.*
ter·ri·to·ry (tĕr′ĭ-tôr′ē) ▸ *n., pl.* **-ries. 1.** An area of land; region. **2.** The land and waters under the jurisdiction of a government. **3.** often **Territory** A usu. self-governing part of a nation not accorded statehood or provincial status. **4.** An area for which a person is responsible. **5.** A sphere of activity.
ter·ror (tĕr′ər) ▸ *n.* **1.** Intense, overpowering fear. **2.** One that instills intense fear. **3.** Violence committed esp. by a group for political purposes. **4.** *Informal* A nuisance; pest.
ter·ror·ism (tĕr′ə-rĭz′əm) ▸ *n.* The political use of violence or intimidation. **—ter′ror·ist** *n.* **—ter′ror·is′tic** *adj.*
ter·ror·ize (tĕr′ə-rīz′) ▸ *v.* **-ized, -iz·ing. 1.** To terrify. **2.** To coerce by intimidation or fear. **—ter′ror·i·za′tion** *n.* **—ter′ror·iz′er** *n.*
ter·ry (tĕr′ē) ▸ *n.* An absorbent pile fabric, usu. of cotton, with uncut loops on both sides.
terse (tûrs) ▸ *adj.* **ters·er, ters·est.** Brief and to the point; concise. **—terse′ly** *adv.* **—terse′ness** *n.*
ter·ti·ar·y (tûr′shē-ĕr′ē) ▸ *adj.* **1.** Third in order, degree, or rank. **2. Tertiary** *Geol.* Of or being the 1st period of the Cenozoic Era, including the Pliocene, Miocene, Oligocene, Eocene, and Paleocene epochs. ▸ *n.* **Tertiary** The Tertiary Period.
Tes·la (tĕs′lə), **Nikola** (1856–1943) ▸ Serbian-born Amer. engineer and physicist.
tes·sel·late (tĕs′ə-lāt′) ▸ *v.* **-lat·ed, -lat·ing.** To form into a mosaic pattern. **—tes′sel·la′tion** *n.*
test (tĕst) ▸ *n.* **1.** A procedure for critical evaluation of the presence, quality, or truth of something; trial. **2.** A series of questions or problems designed to determine knowledge, intelligence, or ability. **3.** A basis for evaluation or judgment. **—test′er** *n.*

THESAURUS

termagant *n.* —*See* SCOLD.
terminal *adj.* Of or relating to a terminative condition, stage, or point ▸ final, last, latter, ultimate. [*Compare* CLIMACTIC.] —*See also* LAST[1] (1).
terminal *n.* A stopping place along a route for picking up or dropping off passengers ▸ depot, station, stop, terminus. —*See also* JUNCTION, OUTLET (1).
terminate *v.* **1.** To bring an activity or relationship to an end suddenly ▸ break off, cease, discontinue, interrupt, suspend. **2.** To relinquish one's engagement in or occupation with ▸ demit, leave, quit, resign. ***Idioms:*** hang it up, throw in the towel. [*Compare* BREAK.] —*See also* CONCLUDE, DISMISS (1), LAPSE.
termination *n.* —*See* DISMISSAL, END (1), END (2).
terminology *n.* —*See* LANGUAGE (2).
terminus *n.* A stopping place along a route for picking up or dropping off passengers ▸ depot, station, stop, terminal. —*See also* END (1).
terms *n.* —*See* BASIS (3).
terpsichorean *n.* A person who dances, especially professionally ▸ chorine, chorus boy, chorus girl, dancer. *Slang:* hoofer.
terrain *n.* The character, natural features, and configuration of land ▸ topography. ***Idiom:*** the lay of the land. —*See also* AREA (1), EARTH (1), TERRITORY.
terrene *adj.* —*See* EARTHLY.
terrestrial *adj.* Consisting of or resembling soil ▸ earthen, earthlike, earthy. —*See also* EARTHLY.
terrible *adj.* Very bad ▸ abysmal, appalling, awful, dreadful, fearful, frightful, ghastly, horrendous, horrible, lousy, pathetic, pitiful, rotten, shocking, woebegone, wretched. *Slang:* crappy. ***Idiom:*** for the birds. [*Compare* BAD, DEPLORABLE, SHODDY.] —*See also* FEARFUL, INTENSE.
terrific *adj.* —*See* EXCELLENT, HORRIBLE, MARVELOUS.
terrified *adj.* —*See* AFRAID.
terrify *v.* —*See* FRIGHTEN.
territorial *adj.* Relating to or restricted to a particular territory ▸ regional, sectional. [*Compare* LOCAL.]
territory *n.* A particular area used for or associated with a specific individual or activity ▸ belt, country, district, region, terrain, zone. *Slang:* turf. [*Compare* ENVIRONMENT.] —*See also* AREA (1), BEAT (2), HABITAT, POSSESSION, RANGE (1).
terror *n.* —*See* FEAR.
terrorize *v.* —*See* FRIGHTEN.
terse *adj.* —*See* BRIEF.
test *n.* **1.** A procedure that ascertains effectiveness, value, proper function, or other quality ▸ assay, dry run, essay, evaluation, experiment, experimentation, proof, shakedown, trial, tryout. [*Compare* ESTIMATE.] **2.** A set of questions or exercises designed to determine knowledge or skill ▸ catechism, catechization, exam, examination, quiz. [*Compare* INQUIRY.] —*See also* STANDARD.
test *v.* **1.** To subject to a test of effectiveness, value, function, or other quality ▸ appraise, assay, check, essay, evaluate, examine, prove, try (out). ***Idioms:*** bring to the test, feel the cloth, kick the tires, make trial of, put to the proof (*or* test). **2.** To subject to a test of knowledge or skill ▸ catechize, examine, quiz. [*Compare* ASK.]
test *adj.* —*See* PILOT.

tes·ta·ment (tĕs′tə-mənt) ► *n.* **1.** Proof; evidence. **2.** A statement of belief. **3.** A legal document providing for the disposition of a person's property after death; will. **4. Testament** Either of the two main divisions of the Christian Bible. **—tes′ta·men′tar·y** (-mĕn′tə-rē, -mĕn′trē) *adj.*

tes·tate (tĕs′tāt′) ► *adj.* Having made a legally valid will.

tes·ta·tor (tĕs′tā′tər, tĕ-stā′tər) ► *n.* One who has made a legally valid will.

tes·ta·trix (tĕ-stā′trĭks) ► *n., pl.* **-tri·ces** (-trĭ-sēz′). A woman who has made a legally valid will.

tes·ti·cle (tĕs′tĭ-kəl) ► *n.* A testis, esp. together with the scrotum.

tes·ti·fy (tĕs′tə-fī′) ► *v.* **-fied, -fy·ing. 1.** To make a declaration under oath; submit testimony. **2.** To serve as evidence. **3.** To declare publicly. **—tes′ti·fi′er** *n.*

tes·ti·mo·ni·al (tĕs′tə-mō′nē-əl) ► *n.* **1.** A statement in support of a particular truth or fact. **2.** A written affirmation of another's character or worth. **3.** A tribute. **—tes′ti·mo′ni·al** *adj.*

tes·ti·mo·ny (tĕs′tə-mō′nē) ► *n., pl.* **-nies. 1a.** A declaration by a witness under oath, as that given before a court. **b.** All such declarations offered in a legal case or hearing. **2.** Supportive evidence; proof. **3.** A public declaration.

tes·tis (tĕs′tĭs) ► *n., pl.* **-tes** (-tēz). The male reproductive gland.

tes·tos·ter·one (tĕs-tŏs′tə-rōn′) ► *n.* A steroid hormone responsible for the development of male secondary sex characteristics.

test tube ► *n.* A clear cylindrical glass tube used in laboratory experimentation.

tes·ty (tĕs′tē) ► *adj.* **-ti·er, -ti·est.** Irritable; touchy. **—tes′ti·ly** *adv.* **—tes′ti·ness** *n.*

Tet (tĕt) ► *n.* The lunar New Year as celebrated in Southeast Asia.

tet·a·nus (tĕt′n-əs) ► *n.* An often fatal infectious disease marked by spasmodic contraction of voluntary muscles, esp. of the neck and jaw.

tête-à-tête (tāt′ə-tāt′, tĕt′ə-tĕt′) ► *adv. & adj.* Without the intrusion of a third person. ► *n.* A private conversation between two persons.

teth·er (tĕth′ər) ► *n.* **1.** A rope or chain for an animal, allowing it a short radius in which to move about. **2.** The limit of one's resources or endurance. ► *v.* To fasten with or as if with a tether.

Te·ton (tē′tŏn′) ► *n., pl.* **-ton** or **-tons.** A member of the largest and westernmost of the Sioux peoples.

Teton Range ► A range of the Rocky Mts. in NW WY and SE ID.

tetra– or **tetr–** ► *pref.* Four: *tetrahedron.*

tet·ra·cy·cline (tĕt′rə-sī′klēn′, -klĭn) ► *n.* A yellow crystalline compound used as an antibiotic.

tet·ra·he·dron (tĕt′rə-hē′drən) ► *n., pl.* **-drons** or **-dra** (-drə). A polyhedron with four faces. **—tet′ra·he′dral** *adj.*

te·tram·e·ter (tĕ-trăm′ĭ-tər) ► *n.* A line of verse consisting of four metrical feet.

Teu·ton (to͞ot′n, tyo͞ot′n) ► *n.* **1.** A member of an ancient people, probably of Germanic or Celtic origin, who lived in Jutland until about 100 B.C. **2.** A member of a Germanic-speaking people, esp. a German.

Teu·ton·ic (to͞o-tŏn′ĭk, tyo͞o-) ► *adj.* **1.** Of or relating to the Teutons. **2.** Of the Germanic languages. ► *n.* Germanic.

Te·vet (ta′vas, tē-vĕt′) ► *n.* A month of the Jewish calendar.

Tex·as (tĕk′səs) ► A state of the S-central US on the Gulf of Mexico. Cap. Austin. **—Tex′an** *adj. & n.*

text (tĕkst) ► *n.* **1.** The wording or words of something written or printed. **2.** The body of a printed work as distinct from a preface, footnote, or appendix. **3.** A Scriptural passage to be read and expounded upon in a sermon. **4.** A subject; topic. **5.** A textbook. **—tex′tu·al** *adj.*

text·book (tĕkst′bo͝ok′) ► *n.* A book used for the study of a subject.

tex·tile (tĕks′tīl′, -təl) ► *n.* **1.** A cloth or fabric, esp. when woven or knitted. **2.** Fiber or yarn for weaving cloth.

tex·ture (tĕks′chər) ► *n.* **1.** A structure of interwoven fibers or other elements. **2.** The basic structure or composition of a substance. **3.** The appearance and feel of a surface. **—tex′tur·al** *adj.* **—tex′tured** *adj.*

Th ► The symbol for the element **thorium.**

Th. ► *abbr.* Thursday

–th[1] ► *suff.* Var. of **–eth**[1].

–th[2] also **–eth** ► *suff.* Used to form ordinal numbers: *millionth.*

Thai (tī) ► *n., pl.* **Thai** or **Thais. 1.** A native or inhabitant of Thailand. **2.** The Tai language of Thailand. **3.** Tai. **—Thai** *adj.*

Thai·land (tī′lănd′, -lənd). Formerly **Siam** ► A country of SE Asia on the **Gulf of Thailand** (formerly the Gulf of Siam), an arm of the South China Sea.

thal·a·mus (thăl′ə-məs) ► *n., pl.* **-mi** (-mī′). A large mass of gray matter that relays sensory impulses to the cerebral cortex. **—tha·lam′ic** (thə-lăm′ĭk) *adj.*

tha·lid·o·mide (thə-lĭd′ə-mīd′) ► *n.* A sedative drug found to cause severe birth defects when taken during pregnancy.

thal·li·um (thăl′ē-əm) ► *n. Symbol* **Tl** A soft, malleable, highly toxic metallic element used in photocells and infrared detectors. At. no. 81.

Thames (tĕmz) ► A river of S England flowing about 338 km (210 mi) eastward through London to a wide estuary on the North Sea.

than (*th*ăn, *th*ən) ► *conj.* Used to introduce the second element or clause of an unequal comparison: *She is a better athlete than I.* ► *prep. Informal* In comparison with: *valued no one more than her.*

thane (thān) ► *n.* **1.** A freeman granted land by the king in Anglo-Saxon England. **2.** A feudal lord in Scotland.

thank (thăngk) ► *v.* **1.** To express gratitude to. **2.** To credit.

thank·ful (thăngk′fəl) ► *adj.* Grateful. **—thank′ful·ly** *adv.* **—thank′ful·ness** *n.*

thank·less (thăngk′lĭs) ► *adj.* **1.** Ungrateful. **2.** Not likely to be appreciated: *a thankless job.* **—thank′less·ly** *adv.* **—thank′less·ness** *n.*

thanks (thăngks) ► *pl.n.* Grateful feelings or thoughts; gratitude. ► *interj.* Used to express thanks. ***idiom:* thanks to** On account of; because of.

THESAURUS

testament *n.* —*See* CONFIRMATION (2).

testifier *n.* One who testifies, especially in court ► attestant, attester, deponent, witness.

testify *v.* To give evidence or testimony under oath ► attest, depone, depose, swear, witness. *Idioms:* bear witness, take the stand. —*See also* CERTIFY, CONFIRM (1), INDICATE (1).

testimonial *n.* **1.** A statement attesting to personal qualifications, character, and dependability ► character, recommendation, reference. [*Compare* ENDORSEMENT.] **2.** A formal token of appreciation and admiration for a person's high achievements ► ovation, salute, salvo, tribute. [*Compare* HONOR, MEMORIAL, TOAST[2].] —*See also* CONFIRMATION (2).

testimony *n.* A formal declaration of truth or fact given under oath ► affidavit, deposition, witness. —*See also* CONFIRMATION (2).

testiness *n.* —*See* TEMPER (1).

testy *adj.* Easily moved to anger ► choleric, irascible, peppery, quick-tempered, short-tempered, tetchy, touchy. —*See also* ILL-TEMPERED.

tetchiness *n.* —*See* TEMPER (1).

tetchy *adj.* —*See* TESTY.

tete-a-tete *n.* —*See* CONVERSATION.

text *n.* —*See* SUBJECT.

texture *n.* A distinctive, complex underlying pattern or structure ► contexture, fabric, fiber, grain, warp and woof, weave, web. [*Compare* CHARACTER, FORM, QUALITY.] —*See also* ESSENCE.

thalassic *adj.* —*See* MARINE (1).

thankful *adj.* Showing or feeling gratitude ► appreciative, grateful. —*See also* OBLIGED (1).

thankfulness *n.* —*See* APPRECIATION.

thankless *adj.* **1.** Not showing or feeling gratitude ► unappreciative, ungrateful, unthankful, unthanking. **2.** Not apt to be appreciated ► unappreciated, ungrateful, unthankful.

thanks *n.* A short prayer said at meals ► benediction, blessing, grace, thanksgiving. [*Compare* PRAYER[1].] —*See also* APPRECIATION.

thanks·giv·ing (thăngks-gĭv′ĭng) ▸ *n.* An act of giving thanks, esp. to God.
Thanksgiving Day ▸ *n.* The 4th Thursday of Nov., a legal holiday in the US.
that (*th*ăt, *th*ət) ▸ *pron., pl.* **those** (*th*ōz). **1a.** The one designated or implied: *What kind of soup is that?* **b.** The one, thing, or type specified: *The relics found were those of an earlier time.* **2.** Used to introduce a clause, esp. a restrictive clause: *the car that has the flat tire.* **3.** In, on, by, or with which: *She called the day that she arrived.* ▸ *adj., pl.* **those. 1.** Being the one indicated or implied: *that place.* **2.** Being the one further removed or less obvious: *That route is shorter than this one.* ▸ *adv.* To such an extent: *Is it that difficult?* ▸ *conj.* **1.** Used to introduce a subordinate clause: *I doubt that you are right.* **2.** Used to introduce an exclamation of desire: *Oh, that I were rich!*
thatch (thăch) ▸ *n.* Plant stalks or foliage used for roofing. ▸ *v.* To cover with or as if with thatch.
Thatch·er (thăch′ər), **Margaret Hilda** (1925–2013) ▸ British prime minister (1979–90).
thaw (thô) ▸ *v.* **1.** To change from a frozen solid to a liquid by gradual warming. **2.** To lose stiffness or numbness by being warmed. **3.** To become warm enough for snow and ice to melt. **4.** To become less reserved. ▸ *n.* **1.** The process of thawing. **2.** A period during which ice and snow melt. **3.** A relaxation of restraint or tension.
THC (tē′āch-sē′) ▸ *n.* The primary intoxicant in marijuana and hashish.
the[1] (*th*ē *before a vowel; th*ə *before a consonant*) ▸ *def.art.* **1.** Used before singular or plural nouns and noun phrases that denote particular, specified persons or things: *the shoes I bought.* **2.** Used before a noun or an adjective with generic force: *an animal such as the wolf; the rich.*
the[2] (*th*ē *before a vowel; th*ə *before a consonant*) ▸ *adv.* **1.** Because of that: *thinks the worse of me.* **2.** To that extent; by that much: *the sooner the better.*
the·a·ter or **the·a·tre** (thē′ə-tər) ▸ *n.* **1.** A building for the presentation of plays, films, or other dramatic performances. **2.** A room with tiers of seats used for lectures or demonstrations. **3.** Dramatic literature or performance. **4.** A setting, as for military operations.
the·at·ri·cal (thē-ăt′rĭ-kəl) ▸ *adj.* **1.** Of or suitable for the theater. **2.** Affectedly dramatic. ▸ *n.* often **theatricals** Stage performances, esp. by amateurs. **—the·at′ri·cal′i·ty** (-kăl′ĭ-tē), **the·at′ri·cal·ness** *n.* **—the·at′ri·cal·ly** *adv.*
the·at·rics (thē-ăt′rĭks) ▸ *n.* **1.** *(takes sing. v.)* The art of the theater. **2.** *(takes pl. v.)* Theatrical effects or mannerisms.
Thebes (thēbz) ▸ **1.** An ancient city of Upper Egypt on the Nile R. in present-day central Egypt. **2.** An ancient city of Greece NW of Athens. **—The′ban** (thē′bən) *adj. & n.*
thee (*th*ē) ▸ *pron.* The objective case of **thou**[1].
theft (thĕft) ▸ *n.* The act of stealing; larceny.
their (*th*âr) ▸ *adj.* The possessive form of **they**. Used as a modifier before a noun: *their house.*
theirs (*th*ârz) ▸ *pron. (takes sing. or pl. v.)* The one or ones belonging to them: *The red house is theirs.*
the·ism (thē′ĭz′əm) ▸ *n.* Belief in the existence of a god or gods. **—the′ist** *n.* **—the·is′tic, the·is′ti·cal** *adj.*
them (*th*ĕm, *th*əm) ▸ *pron.* The objective case of **they**. **1.** Used as the direct or indirect object of a verb. **2.** Used as the object of a preposition.
the·mat·ic (thĭ-măt′ĭk) ▸ *adj.* Of or being a theme. **—the·mat′i·cal·ly** *adv.*
theme (thēm) ▸ *n.* **1.** A topic of discourse or discussion. **2.** The subject of an artistic work. **3.** An implicit or recurrent idea; motif. **4.** A short written composition. **5.** *Mus.* The principal melodic phrase in a composition.
them·selves (*th*ĕm-sĕlvz′, *th*əm-) ▸ *pron.* **1.** Those ones identical with them. **2.** Used reflexively as the direct or indirect object of a verb or as the object of a preposition. **3.** Used for emphasis: *We ourselves have heard nothing.*
then (*th*ĕn) ▸ *adv.* **1.** At that time. **2.** Next in time, space, or order. **3.** In addition; moreover; besides. **4.** In that case: *If it snows, then bring your skis.* **5.** As a consequence: *The case, then, is closed.* ▸ *n.* That time or moment. ▸ *adj.* Being so at that time.
thence (*th*ĕns, thĕns) ▸ *adv.* **1.** From there. **2.** From that circumstance or source. **3.** *Archaic* Thenceforth.
thence·forth (*th*ĕns-fôrth′, thĕns-) ▸ *adv.* From that time forward; thereafter.
thence·for·ward (*th*ĕns-fôr′wərd, thĕns-) also **thence·for·wards** (-wərdz) ▸ *adv.* From that time or place onward; thenceforth.
theo– or **the–** ▸ *pref.* God: *theocracy.*
the·oc·ra·cy (thē-ŏk′rə-sē) ▸ *n., pl.* **-cies. 1.** A government ruled by or subject to religious authority. **2.** A state so governed. **—the′o·crat′** (thē′ə-krăt′) *n.* **—the′o·crat′ic** *adj.* **—the′o·crat′i·cal·ly** *adv.*
the·ol·o·gy (thē-ŏl′ə-jē) ▸ *n., pl.* **-gies. 1.** The study of the nature of God and religious truth. **2.** A system or school of opinions concerning God and religious questions. **—the′o·lo′gi·an** (-ə-lō′jən) *n.* **—the′o·log′i·cal** (-ə-lŏj′ĭ-kəl) *adj.* **—the′o·log′i·cal·ly** *adv.*
the·o·rem (thē′ər-əm, thîr′əm) ▸ *n.* **1.** An idea that is demonstrably true or is assumed to be so. **2.** *Math.* A proposition that has been or is to be proved.
the·o·ret·i·cal (thē′ə-rĕt′ĭ-kəl) also **the·o·ret·ic** (-rĕt′ĭk) ▸ *adj.* Of or based on theory. **—the′o·ret′i·cal·ly** *adv.*
the·o·re·ti·cian (thē′ər-ĭ-tĭsh′ən, thîr′ĭ-) ▸ *n.* One who formulates, studies, or is expert in the theory of a science or an art.
the·o·rize (thē′ə-rīz′, thîr′īz) ▸ *v.* **-rized, -riz·ing.** To formulate theories or a theory. **—the′o·riz′er, the′o·rist** *n.*
the·o·ry (thē′ə-rē, thîr′ē) ▸ *n., pl.* **-ries. 1.** A set of statements or principles devised to explain a group of facts or

THESAURUS

thanksgiving *n.* A short prayer said at meals ▸ benediction, blessing, grace, thanks. [*Compare* PRAYER[1].]
thaumaturgic or **thaumaturgical** *adj.* —*See* MAGIC.
thaumaturgy *n.* —*See* MAGIC (1).
thaw *v.* —*See* MELT.
theater *n.* The art and occupation of an actor ▸ acting, dramatics, stage, theatrics.
theatric or **theatrical** *adj.* —*See* DRAMATIC (1), DRAMATIC (2).
theatricalism or **theatricality** *n.* Showy mannerisms and behavior ▸ campiness, exhibitionism, staginess, theatricalness. [*Compare* AFFECTATION, THEATRICS.]
theatricals *n.* —*See* THEATRICS (2).
theatricism *n.* —*See* AFFECTATION.
theatrics *n.* **1.** The art and occupation of an actor ▸ acting, dramatics, stage, theater. **2.** Overemotional, exaggerated behavior calculated for effect ▸ dramatics, histrionics, melodrama, melodramatics, play-acting, theatricals. [*Compare* THEATRICALISM.]
theft *n.* —*See* LARCENY.
thematic *adj.* Of, constituting, or relating to a theme or themes ▸ motivic, topical.
theme *n.* **1.** The main part of a word to which affixes are attached ▸ base, radical, root, simplex, stem. **2.** A relatively brief discourse written especially as an exercise ▸ composition, essay, paper. —*See also* MELODY, SUBJECT.
theorem *n.* —*See* LAW (3), THEORY (2).
theoretical or **theoretic** *adj.* **1.** Concerned primarily with theories rather than practical matters ▸ abstract, academic, armchair, conceptual, ideological, impractical, ivory-tower, moot, speculative. [*Compare* IDEALISTIC.] **2.** Existing only in concept and not in reality ▸ abstract, conceptual, hypothetic, hypothetical, hypothesized, ideal, impractical, notional, postulated, virtual. [*Compare* IMAGINARY, SUPPOSED.] —*See also* UNTRIED.
theoretics *n.* —*See* THEORY (1).
theorist or **theoretic** *n.* A person who seeks truth by thinking ▸ philosopher, reasoner, thinker. —*See also* DREAMER (1).
theorization *n.* —*See* THEORY (1).
theorize *v.* To formulate as a tentative explanation ▸ hypothesize, speculate. [*Compare* SUPPOSE.]
theorizer *n.* —*See* DREAMER (1).
theory *n.* **1.** Abstract reasoning, as opposed to experience ▸ conceptualization, conjecture, philosophizing, reasoning, speculating, speculation, theoretics, theorization, theorizing. [*Compare* THOUGHT.] **2.** A proposition maintained by argument or empirical evidence ▸ contention, hypothesis, proposal, theorem, thesis. [*Compare* ASSUMPTION, REASON.] —*See also* DOCTRINE.

phenomena, esp. one that has been repeatedly tested or is widely accepted. **2.** The branch of a science or art consisting of its explanatory statements, accepted principles, and methods of analysis, as opposed to practice. **3.** Abstract reasoning; speculation. **4.** An assumption; conjecture.

the·os·o·phy (thē-ŏs′ə-fē) ▸ *n., pl.* **-phies.** Religious philosophy or speculation about the nature of the soul based on mystical insight into the nature of God. **—the′o·soph′ic** (-ə-sŏf′ĭk), **the′o·soph′i·cal** *adj.* **—the·os′o·phist** *n.*

ther·a·peu·tic (thĕr′ə-pyōō′tĭk) ▸ *adj.* Having healing or curative powers. **—ther′a·peu′ti·cal·ly** *adv.*

ther·a·peu·tics (thĕr′ə-pyōō′tĭks) ▸ *n. (takes sing. v.)* Medical treatment of disease. **—ther′a·peu′tist** *n.*

ther·a·py (thĕr′ə-pē) ▸ *n., pl.* **-pies. 1.** Treatment of illness or disability. **2.** Psychotherapy. **—ther′a·pist** *n.*

there (*th*âr) ▸ *adv.* **1.** At or in that place. **2.** To, into, or toward that place. **3.** At that stage, moment, or point. ▸ *pron.* Used to introduce a clause or sentence: *There is hope.* ▸ *n.* That place or point.

there·a·bouts (*th*âr′ə-bouts′) also **there·a·bout** (-bout′) ▸ *adv.* **1.** Near that place. **2.** Approximately.

there·af·ter (*th*âr-ăf′tər) ▸ *adv.* From a specified time onward; from then on.

there·at (*th*âr-ăt′) ▸ *adv.* **1.** At that place; there. **2.** At that event; on account of that.

there·by (*th*âr-bī′) ▸ *adv.* By that means.

there·fore (*th*âr′fôr′) ▸ *adv.* For that reason; consequently.

there·from (*th*âr-frŭm′, -frŏm′) ▸ *adv.* From that place, time, or thing.

there·in (*th*âr-ĭn′) ▸ *adv.* **1.** In that place, time, or thing. **2.** In that respect.

there·in·af·ter (*th*âr′ĭn-ăf′tər) ▸ *adv.* In a later part.

there·of (*th*âr-ŭv′, -ŏv′) ▸ *adv.* **1.** Of this, that, or it. **2.** From that cause or origin.

there·on (*th*âr-ŏn′, -ôn′) ▸ *adv.* On or upon this, that, or it.

there·to (*th*âr-tōō′) ▸ *adv.* To that, this, or it.

there·to·fore (*th*âr′tə-fôr′) ▸ *adv.* Until that time.

there·un·to (*th*âr′ŭn-tōō′) ▸ *adv. Archaic* To that, this, or it; thereto.

there·up·on (*th*âr′ə-pŏn′, -pôn′) ▸ *adv.* **1.** Concerning that matter; upon that. **2.** Directly following that. **3.** In consequence of that; therefore.

there·with (*th*âr-wĭ*th*′, -wĭth′) ▸ *adv.* With that, this, or it.

there·with·al (*th*âr′wĭ*th*-ôl′, -wĭth-) ▸ *adv.* With all that, this, or it; besides.

ther·mal (thûr′məl) ▸ *adj.* Of, using, producing, or caused by heat. ▸ *n.* A rising current of warm air. **—ther′mal·ly** *adv.*

thermo– or **therm–** ▸ *pref.* Heat: *thermodynamics.*

ther·mo·cou·ple (thûr′mə-kŭp′əl) ▸ *n.* A device used to measure temperatures, consisting of two dissimilar metals joined at the ends so that an electric current flows when the contacts are at different temperatures.

ther·mo·dy·nam·ics (thûr′mō-dī-năm′ĭks) ▸ *n. (takes sing. v.)* Physics that deals with the relationships between heat and other forms of energy. **—ther′mo·dy·nam′ic** *adj.* **—ther′mo·dy·nam′i·cal·ly** *adv.*

ther·mom·e·ter (thər-mŏm′ĭ-tər) ▸ *n.* An instrument for measuring temperature. **—ther′mo·met′ric** (thûr′mō-mĕt′rĭk) *adj.* **—ther·mom′e·try** *n.*

ther·mo·nu·cle·ar (thûr′mō-nōō′klē-ər, -nyōō′-) ▸ *adj.* **1.** Of or derived from the fusion of atomic nuclei at high temperatures. **2.** Of atomic weapons based on fusion.

ther·mo·plas·tic (thûr′mə-plăs′tĭk) ▸ *adj.* Becoming soft when heated and hard when cooled. ▸ *n.* A thermoplastic material.

ther·mos (thûr′məs) ▸ *n.* A vacuum bottle.

ther·mo·set·ting (thûr′mō-sĕt′ĭng) ▸ *adj.* Permanently hardening or solidifying on being heated.

ther·mo·sphere (thûr′mə-sfîr′) ▸ *n.* The outermost shell of the atmosphere, between the mesosphere and outer space, where temperatures increase steadily with altitude. **—ther′mo·spher′ic** (-sfîr′ĭk, -sfĕr′-) *adj.*

ther·mo·stat (thûr′mə-stăt′) ▸ *n.* A device, as in a heating system or an appliance, that senses temperature changes and activates switches controlling the equipment. **—ther′mo·stat′ic** *adj.*

the·sau·rus (thĭ-sôr′əs) ▸ *n., pl.* **-sau·ri** (-sôr′ī′) or **-rus·es.** A book of selected words, esp. a dictionary of synonyms and related words.

these (*th*ēz) ▸ *pron. & adj.* Pl. of **this.**

the·sis (thē′sĭs) ▸ *n., pl.* **-ses** (-sēz). **1.** A proposition maintained by argument. **2.** A dissertation advancing an original point of view as a result of research.

thes·pi·an (thĕs′pē-ən) ▸ *adj.* Of or relating to drama; dramatic. ▸ *n.* An actor or actress.

Thes·pis (thĕs′pĭs) (6th cent. B.C.) ▸ Greek poet.

Thes·sa·lo·ni·ans (thĕs′ə-lō′nē-ənz) ▸ *pl.n. (takes sing. v.)* See **Bible** table in Appendix.

Thes·sa·ly (thĕs′ə-lē) ▸ A region of E-central Greece along the Aegean Sea. **—Thes·sa′lian** (thĕ-sā′lē-ən, -sāl′yən), **Thes′sa·lo′ni·an** *adj. & n.*

the·ta (thā′tə, thē′-) ▸ *n.* The 8th letter of the Greek alphabet.

thew (thyōō) ▸ *n.* often **thews** Sinew or muscle.

they (*th*ā) ▸ *pron.* The ones previously mentioned or implied.

they'd (*th*ād) ▸ **1.** They had. **2.** They would.

they'll (*th*āl) ▸ **1.** They will. **2.** They shall.

they're (*th*âr) ▸ They are.

they've (*th*āv) ▸ They have.

thi·a·mine (thī′ə-mĭn, -mēn′) also **thi·a·min** (-mĭn) ▸ *n.* A vitamin of the vitamin B complex, found in yeast, meat, and bran and necessary for carbohydrate metabolism.

thick (thĭk) ▸ *adj.* **-er, -est. 1a.** Relatively great in extent from one surface to the opposite; not thin. **b.** Measuring in this dimension: *two inches thick.* **2.** Thickset. **3.** Dense; concentrated. **4.** Having a heavy or viscous consistency. **5.** Having a great number; abounding. **6.** Indistinctly articulated. **7.** Noticeable; conspicuous. **8.** *Informal* Lacking mental agility; stupid. **9.** *Informal* Very friendly; intimate. **10.** *Informal* Excessive. ▸ *n.* **1.** The thickest part. **2.** The most intense part: *in the thick of the fighting.* **—*idiom:* thick and thin** Good and bad times. **—thick′ly** *adv.* **—thick′ness** *n.*

thick·en (thĭk′ən) ▸ *v.* To make or become thick or thicker. **—thick′en·er** *n.* **—thick′en·ing** *n.*

thick·et (thĭk′ĭt) ▸ *n.* A dense growth of shrubs or underbrush.

thick·set (thĭk′sĕt′) ▸ *adj.* **1.** Having a short wide body; stocky. **2.** Placed closely together.

thick-skinned (thĭk′skĭnd′) ▸ *adj.* **1.** Having a thick skin. **2.** Not easily offended.

thief (thēf) ▸ *n., pl.* **thieves** (thēvz). One who steals.

therapeutic *adj.* —*See* CURATIVE.

therapy or **therapeutics** *n.* —*See* TREATMENT.

thesis *n.* —*See* DISCOURSE, DOCTRINE, THEORY (2).

thespian *n.* A theatrical performer ▸ actor, actress, player, trouper. [*Compare* FAKE, LEAD, MIMIC.]

thespian *adj.* —*See* DRAMATIC (1).

theurgic or **theurgical** *adj.* —*See* MAGIC.

theurgy *n.* —*See* MAGIC (1).

thick *adj.* 1. Relatively great in extent from one surface to the opposite ▸ fat. [*Compare* BULKY.] 2. Having all parts near to each other ▸ close, compact, compressed, consolidated crowded, dense, packed, tight. [*Compare* FULL.] 3. Growing profusely ▸ dense, heavy, lush, luxuriant, overgrown, profuse, rank. —*See also* INTIMATE[1] (1), STOCKY, STUPID, VISCOUS.

thick *n.* The most intensely active central part ▸ eye, midst. [*Compare* CENTER.]

thicken *v.* To make thick or thicker, especially through evaporation or condensation ▸ condense, inspissate, reduce. [*Compare* COAGULATE.]

thicket *n.* —*See* BRUSH[2].

thickhead *n.* —*See* DULLARD.

thickheaded *adj.* —*See* STUPID.

thickness *n.* The condition or degree of being dense or close together ▸ closeness, compaction, compactness, denseness, density. —*See also* VISCOSITY.

thickset *adj.* —*See* STOCKY.

thick-witted *adj.* —*See* BACKWARD (1), STUPID.

thief *n.* A person who steals ▸ bandit, brigand, burglar, highwayman, housebreaker, larcener, larcenist, looter, pickpocket, pilferer, purloiner, robber, stealer.

thieve (thēv) ▸ *v.* **thieved, thiev·ing.** To steal. **—thiev′er·y** *n.*

thigh (thī) ▸ *n.* The portion of the leg between the hip and the knee.

thigh·bone (thī′bōn′) ▸ *n.* See **femur.**

thim·ble (thĭm′bəl) ▸ *n.* A small cup, as of metal or plastic, worn to protect the finger in sewing. **—thim′ble·ful′** *n.*

thin (thĭn) ▸ *adj.* **thin·ner, thin·nest.** **1a.** Relatively small in extent from one surface to the opposite. **b.** Not great in diameter or cross section; fine. **2.** Lean or slender. **3.** Not dense or concentrated; sparse. **4.** Not rich or heavy in consistency. **5.** Lacking force or substance; flimsy. ▸ *v.* **thinned, thin·ning.** To make or become thin or thinner. **—thin′ly** *adv.* **—thin′ness** *n.*

thine (*th*īn) ▸ *pron. (takes sing. or pl. v.)* Used to indicate the one or ones belonging to thee. ▸ *adj.* A possessive form of **thou.** Used instead of *thy* before an initial vowel or *h*: *thine enemy.*

thing (thĭng) ▸ *n.* **1.** Something that exists; entity. **2a.** A tangible object. **b.** An inanimate object. **3.** A creature. **4a. things** Possessions; belongings. **b.** An article of clothing. **5.** An act, deed, or work. **6.** A thought or notion. **7.** A piece of information. **8.** A matter of concern. **9.** A turn of events. **10. things** The general state of affairs; conditions. **11.** *Slang* A uniquely suitable and satisfying activity: *doing his own thing.*

think (thĭngk) ▸ *v.* **thought** (thôt), **think·ing.** **1.** To have or formulate in the mind. **2a.** To ponder. **b.** To reason. **3.** To believe; suppose. **4.** To call to mind; remember. **5.** To visualize; imagine. **6.** To devise or invent: *think up a plan.* **7.** To consider. **—think′a·ble** *adj.* **—think′er** *n.*

think tank ▸ *n.* A research group organized esp. by a government for solving complex problems.

thin·ner (thĭn′ər) ▸ *n.* A liquid, as turpentine, mixed with paint to reduce viscosity.

thin-skinned (thĭn′skĭnd′) ▸ *adj.* **1.** Having a thin rind or skin. **2.** Oversensitive.

third (thûrd) ▸ *n.* **1.** The ordinal number matching the number 3 in a series. **2.** One of three equal parts. **3.** *Mus.* A tone three degrees above or below a given tone in a diatonic scale. **4.** The transmission gear next higher to second in a motor vehicle. **—third** *adv. & adj.* **—third′ly** *adv.*

third base ▸ *n.* *Baseball* The third base to be reached by a runner. **—third baseman** *n.*

third class ▸ *n.* **1.** A class of mail including all unsealed printed matter except newspapers and magazines. **2.** Accommodations of the third and usu. lowest order of luxury and price. **—third′-class′** *adv. & adj.*

third-de·gree burn (thûrd′dĭ-grē′) ▸ *n.* A severe burn in which the skin and underlying tissues are destroyed and sensitive nerve endings are exposed.

third person ▸ *n.* The form of a verb or pronoun used in referring to a person or thing other than the speaker or the one spoken to.

Third World ▸ *n.* The developing nations of Africa, Asia, and Latin America.

thirst (thûrst) ▸ *n.* **1a.** A sensation of dryness in the mouth related to a desire to drink. **b.** The desire to drink. **2.** An insistent desire; craving. ▸ *v.* **1.** To feel a need to drink. **2.** To yearn. **—thirst′i·ly** *adv.* **—thirst′y** *adj.*

thir·teen (thûr-tēn′) ▸ *n.* **1.** The cardinal number equal to 12 + 1. **2.** The 13th in a set or sequence. **—thir·teen′** *adj. & pron.*

thir·teenth (thûr-tēnth′) ▸ *n.* **1.** The ordinal number matching the number 13 in a series. **2.** One of 13 equal parts. **—thir·teenth′** *adv. & adj.*

thir·ti·eth (thûr′tē-ĭth) ▸ *n.* **1.** The ordinal number matching the number 30 in a series. **2.** One of 30 equal parts. **—thir′ti·eth** *adv. & adj.*

thir·ty (thûr′tē) ▸ *n., pl.* **-ties.** The cardinal number equal to 3 × 10. **—thir′ty** *adj. & pron.*

this (*th*ĭs) ▸ *pron., pl.* **these** (*th*ēz). **1a.** The person or thing present, nearby, or just mentioned. **b.** What is about to be said. **c.** The present event, action, or time. **2.** The nearer or the more immediate one. ▸ *adj., pl.* **these.** **1.** Being just mentioned or present. **2.** Being nearer or more immediate. **3.** Being about to be stated or described. ▸ *adv.* To this extent; so: *never stayed out this late.*

this·tle (thĭs′əl) ▸ *n.* Any of numerous weedy plants having prickly leaves and bracts and usu. purplish flowers.

this·tle·down (thĭs′əl-doun′) ▸ *n.* The silky down attached to the seeds of a thistle.

thith·er (thĭ*th*′ər, *th*ĭ*th*′-) ▸ *adv.* To or toward that place; there. ▸ *adj.* Being on the more distant side; farther.

thole pin (thōl) ▸ *n.* A peg set in pairs in the gunwales of a boat to serve as an oarlock.

Thor (thôr) ▸ *n.* *Myth.* The Norse god of thunder.

tho·rax (thôr′ăks′) ▸ *n., pl.* **-es** or **tho·ra·ces** (thôr′ə-sēz′). **1.** The part of the vertebrate body between the neck and the diaphragm, partially encased by the ribs; chest. **2.** The middle region of the arthropod body. **—tho·rac′ic** (thə-răs′ĭk) *adj.*

Tho·reau (thə-rō′, thôr′ō), **Henry David** (1817–62) ▸ Amer. writer.

tho·ri·um (thôr′ē-əm) ▸ *n.* *Symbol* **Th** A radioactive, silvery-white metallic element used in magnesium alloys. At. no. 90.

thorn (thôrn) ▸ *n.* **1a.** A sharp woody spine protruding from a plant stem. **b.** Any of various shrubs, trees, or

THESAURUS

thieve *v.* *—See* STEAL.

thievery *n.* *—See* LARCENY.

thievish or **thieving** *adj.* Given to committing theft ▸ larcenous, light-fingered, sticky-fingered.

thin *adj.* **1.** Having little flesh or fat on the body ▸ angular, bony, fleshless, gaunt, gracile, lank, lanky, lean, meager, rawboned, scrawny, skinny, slender, slim, spare, stringy, svelte, twiggy, weedy, willowy. ***Idioms:*** all skin and bones, skinny as a rail (*or* post *or* beanpole). [*Compare* GANGLING.] **2.** Marked by great diffusion of component particles ▸ attenuate, attenuated, rare, rarefied. *—See also* DILUTE, IMPLAUSIBLE, MEAGER, PALE (2).

thin *v.* **1.** To lose body weight, as by dieting ▸ slim (down), trim down. ***Idioms:*** get the weight off, lose weight, shed some pounds. **2.** To become diffuse ▸ attenuate, rarefy. *—See also* DILUTE.

thin out *v.* *—See* LIFT (2).

thing *n.* **1.** One that exists independently ▸ being, entity, existence, existent, individual, object, something. **2.** Something to be done, considered, or dealt with ▸ affair, business, matter. [*Compare* BUSINESS, PROBLEM, TASK.] **3.** An extravagant, short-lived romantic attachment ▸ *Informal:* crush, infatuation. ***Idiom:*** passing fancy. [*Compare* LOVE, OBSESSION.] *—See also* ACT (1), CIRCUMSTANCE (1), EVENT (1), FASHION, FORTE, GADGET, OBJECT (1), OBSESSION.

thingamabob or **thingamajig** *n.* *—See* GADGET, OBJECT (1).

things *n.* *—See* EFFECTS, ODDS AND ENDS.

think *v.* **1.** To use the powers of the mind, as in conceiving ideas, drawing inferences, and making judgments ▸ cerebrate, cogitate, conceptualize, deliberate, ideate, ratiocinate, reason, reflect, speculate. ***Idioms:*** put on one's thinking cap, use one's head. [*Compare* REMEMBER.] **2.** To view in a certain way ▸ believe, feel, hold, sense. [*Compare* PERCEIVE, REGARD.] *—See also* BELIEVE (3), GUESS, IMAGINE, PONDER.

think about or **of** *v.* **1.** To receive an idea and think about it in order to form an opinion about it ▸ consider, entertain, hear of. **2.** To care enough to keep someone in mind ▸ remember. *—See also* REGARD.

think out or **through** *v.* *—See* PONDER, SOLVE (1).

think over *v.* *—See* PONDER.

think up *v.* *—See* INVENT.

thinkable *adj.* *—See* CONCEIVABLE.

thinker *n.* A person who seeks truth by thinking ▸ philosopher, reasoner, theorist. *—See also* MIND (2).

thinking *adj.* *—See* THOUGHTFUL.

thinking *n.* *—See* THOUGHT.

third estate *n.* *—See* COMMONALTY.

thirst *v.* To have a greedy, obsessive desire ▸ crave, hunger, itch, lust. [*Compare* DESIRE.]

thirst *n.* *—See* APPETITE, DESIRE (1).

thirsting *adj.* *—See* EAGER.

thirsty *adj.* Needing or desiring drink ▸ dry, parched. ***Idiom:*** dry as a bone (*or* whistle). *—See also* DRY (2), EAGER.

thistly *adj.* *—See* THORNY (1).

thong *n.* *—See* CORD.

thorn *n.* *—See* ANNOYANCE (2), SPIKE.

woody plants bearing such spines. 2. One that causes pain, irritation, or discomfort. **—thorn′i·ness** *n.* **—thorn′y** *adj.*

thor·ough (thûr′ō, thŭr′ō) ▸ *adj.* 1. Complete in all respects. 2. Painstakingly careful. **—thor′ough·ly** *adv.* **—thor′ough·ness** *n.*

thor·ough·bred (thûr′ō-brĕd′, thûr′ə-, thŭr′-) ▸ *n.* 1. A purebred or pedigreed animal. 2. **Thoroughbred** Any of a breed of horses originating from a cross between Arabian stallions and English mares. ▸ *adj.* Bred of pure stock; purebred.

thor·ough·fare (thûr′ō-fâr′, thûr′ə-, thŭr′-) ▸ *n.* A main road or public highway.

thor·ough·go·ing (thûr′ō-gō′ĭng, thûr′ə-, thŭr′-) ▸ *adj.* 1. Very thorough; complete. 2. Absolute; unqualified.

those (*th*ōz) ▸ *pron. & adj.* Pl. of **that**.

thou (*th*ou) ▸ *pron.* Used to indicate the one being addressed, esp. in a religious context.

though (*th*ō) ▸ *conj.* 1. Although; while. 2. Even if. ▸ *adv.* However; nevertheless.

thought (thôt) ▸ *v.* P.t. and p.part. of **think**. ▸ *n.* 1. The process or power of thinking. 2. An idea. 3. A body of ideas. 4. Consideration; attention. 5. Intention; expectation.

thought·ful (thôt′fəl) ▸ *adj.* 1. Engrossed in thought. 2. Showing careful thought. 3. Showing regard for others; considerate. **—thought′ful·ly** *adv.* **—thought′ful·ness** *n.*

thought·less (thôt′lĭs) ▸ *adj.* 1. Careless; unthinking. 2. Inconsiderate. **—thought′less·ly** *adv.* **—thought′less·ness** *n.*

thou·sand (thou′zənd) ▸ *n.* The cardinal number equal to 10×100 or 10^3. **—thou′sand** *adj. & pron.*

thou·sandth (thou′zəndth, -zənth) ▸ *n.* 1. The ordinal number matching the number 1,000 in a series. 2. One of 1,000 equal parts. **—thou′sandth** *adv. & adj.*

Thrace (thrās) ▸ A region and ancient country of the SE Balkan Peninsula N of the Aegean Sea. **—Thra′cian** (thrā′shən) *adj. & n.*

thrall (thrôl) ▸ *n.* 1. One held in bondage; slave. 2. Servitude; bondage. **—thrall′dom, thral′dom** *n.*

thrash (thrăsh) ▸ *v.* 1. To beat with or as if with a whip or flail. 2. To defeat utterly; vanquish. 3. To move wildly or violently. **—thrash′er** *n.*

thrash·er (thrăsh′ər) ▸ *n.* Any of various long-tailed New World songbirds.

thread (thrĕd) ▸ *n.* 1. A fine cord made of fibers or filaments twisted together, used in needlework and in weaving cloth. 2. Something like a thread, as in fineness or length. 3. A helical or spiral ridge on a screw, nut, or bolt. ▸ *v.* 1a. To pass one end of a thread through (e.g., a needle). b. To pass a tape or film into or through. 2. To pass cautiously through. 3. To machine a thread on (a screw, nut, or bolt). **—thread′er** *n.* **—thread′y** *adj.*

thread·bare (thrĕd′bâr′) ▸ *adj.* 1. Having the nap worn down so that the threads show through. 2. Shabby; seedy. 3. Hackneyed.

threat (thrĕt) ▸ *n.* 1. An expression of an intention to inflict pain, injury, or evil. 2. One regarded as a possible danger.

threat·en (thrĕt′n) ▸ *v.* 1. To express a threat against. 2. To be a source of danger to; menace. 3. To portend. 4. To indicate danger or harm. **—threat′en·ing·ly** *adv.*

three (thrē) ▸ *n.* 1. The cardinal number equal to 2 + 1. 2. The 3rd in a set or sequence. 3. Something having three parts, units, or members. **—three** *adj. & pron.*

three-di·men·sion·al (thrē′dĭ-mĕn′shə-nəl, -dī-) ▸ *adj.* 1. Of, having, or existing in three dimensions. 2. Having or appearing to have extension in depth.

three·score (thrē′skôr′) ▸ *adj.* Sixty. **—three′score′** *n. & pron.*

three·some (thrē′səm) ▸ *n.* A group of three.

thren·o·dy (thrĕn′ə-dē) ▸ *n., pl.* **-dies**. A poem or song of lamentation. **—thren′o·dist** *n.*

thresh (thrĕsh) ▸ *v.* 1. To beat (e.g., cereal plants) with a machine or flail to separate the grains or seeds from the straw. 2. To thrash. **—thresh′er** *n.*

thresh·old (thrĕsh′ōld′, -hōld′) ▸ *n.* 1. A piece of wood or stone placed beneath a door. 2. An entrance. 3. The beginning; outset. 4. The lowest level or intensity at which a stimulus can be perceived or can produce a given effect.

threw (thro͞o) ▸ *v.* P.t. of **throw**.

thrice (thrīs) ▸ *adv.* Three times.

thrift (thrĭft) ▸ *n.* 1. Wise economy in managing money and other resources; frugality. 2. A savings and loan association, credit union, or savings bank. **—thrift′i·ly** *adv.* **—thrift′i·ness** *n.* **—thrift′y** *adj.*

THESAURUS

thorny *adj.* 1. Covered with sharp protuberances ▸ aculeate, barbed, brambly, briery, bristled, bristly, echinate, glochidiate, muricate, prickly, pricky, spiky, spiny, thistly. 2. Full of irritating difficulties or controversies ▸ nettlesome, prickly, spiny. [*Compare* COMPLEX, DELICATE, DISTURBING, TROUBLESOME.] *—See also* UNCOMFORTABLE.

thorough *adj.* Covering all aspects with painstaking accuracy ▸ complete, exhaustive, full-dress, thoroughgoing, thoroughpaced. [*Compare* DILIGENT.] *—See also* DETAILED, UTTER[2].

thoroughbred *adj.* Of pure breeding stock ▸ full-blooded, highbred, pedigreed, pureblood, pureblooded, purebred. *—See also* NOBLE.

thoroughfare *n.* *—See* WAY (2).

thoroughgoing *adj.* *—See* THOROUGH, UTTER[2].

thoroughly *adv.* *—See* COMPLETELY (1), [illegible] (2).

thoroughness *n.* Attentiveness to detail ▸ care, carefulness, fastidiousness, meticulousness, pains, painstaking, punctiliousness, scrupulousness.

thoroughpaced *adj.* *—See* THOROUGH.

thought *n.* The act or process of thinking ▸ brainstorming, brainwork, cerebration, cogitation, conceptualization, conceptualizing, contemplation, deliberation, excogitation, headwork, ideation, intellection, meditation, musing, pondering, reflection, rumination, speculation, thinking. [*Compare* THEORY.] *—See also* IDEA.

thoughtful *adj.* Of, characterized by, or disposed to thought ▸ cogitative, contemplative, deliberative, excogitative, meditative, pensive, reflective, ruminative, speculative, thinking. *Idiom:* in a brown study. [*Compare* DREAMY, RAPT, SERIOUS.] *—See also* ATTENTIVE, INTELLECTUAL.

thoughtfulness *n.* *—See* CONSIDERATION (1).

thoughtless *adj.* Devoid of consideration for others' feelings ▸ disregardful, inconsiderate, insensitive, unthinking, unthoughtful. [*Compare* RUDE, TACTLESS.] *—See also* CARELESS.

thoughtlessness *n.* 1. A careless, often reckless disregard for consequences ▸ abandon, blitheness, carelessness, heedlessness. [*Compare* TEMERITY.] 2. A lack of consideration for others' feelings ▸ disregard, inconsiderateness, inconsideration, insensitivity, tactlessness, unthoughtfulness. [*Compare* DISRESPECT.]

thought out *adj.* *—See* DELIBERATE (2).

thrall or **thralldom** or **thraldom** *n.* *—See* SLAVERY.

thrash *v.* 1. To beat plants to separate the grain from the straw ▸ flail, thresh. 2. To swing about or strike at wildly ▸ flail, thresh, toss. *Idiom:* toss and turn. [*Compare* STAGGER, SWAY.] *—See also* BEAT (1), BEAT (2), OVERWHELM (1).

thrash out or **over** *v.* *—See* DISCUSS.

thrashing *n.* *—See* BEATING, DEFEAT.

thread *n.* 1. A very fine continuous strand ▸ fiber, fibril, filament, microfiber. [*Compare* CORD.] 2. Something suggesting the continuousness of a filament ▸ hairline, strand.

thread *v.* To put objects onto a thread ▸ string.

threadbare *adj.* *—See* SHABBY, TRITE.

threadlike *adj.* Containing or consisting of fibers ▸ fibrous, sinewy, stringy.

threads *n.* *—See* DRESS (1).

threat *n.* An expression of intent to hurt or punish another ▸ intimidation, menace. *—See also* DANGER.

threaten *v.* 1. To give warning signs of ▸ bode, forebode, forewarn, portend. [*Compare* FORESHADOW.] 2. To be imminent ▸ brew, hang over, hover, impend, loom, lower, menace, overhang. *Idiom:* breathe down one's neck. [*Compare* APPROACH.] *—See also* ENDANGER, INTIMIDATE.

threatening *adj.* *—See* DANGEROUS, FATEFUL (1).

three or **threesome** *n.* *—See* TRIO.

thresh *v.* 1. To beat plants to separate the grain from the straw ▸ flail, thrash. 2. To swing about or strike at wildly ▸ flail, thrash, toss. *Idiom:* toss and turn. [*Compare* STAGGER, SWAY.] *—See also* BEAT (1).

thresh out or **over** *v.* *—See* DISCUSS.

threshold *n.* *—See* BORDER (1).

thrift or **thriftiness** *n.* *—See* ECONOMY.

thriftless *adj.* *—See* EXTRAVAGANT.

thrift shop ► *n.* A shop that sells used articles, esp. clothing, as to benefit a charity.

thrill (thrĭl) ► *v.* **1.** To feel or cause to feel a sudden intense sensation. **2.** To enrapture; delight. **3.** To quiver; tremble. ► *n.* **1.** A quivering or trembling. **2.** A source or cause of excitement or rapture. **—thrill′er** *n.* **—thrill′ing·ly** *adv.*

thrive (thrīv) ► *v.* **thrived** or **throve** (thrōv), **thrived** or **thriv·en** (thrĭv′ən), **thriv·ing.** **1.** To make steady progress; prosper. **2.** To flourish. **—thriv′er** *n.*

throat (thrōt) ► *n.* **1.** The anterior portion of the neck. **2.** The portion of the digestive tract that lies between the rear of the mouth and the esophagus.

throat·y (thrō′tē) ► *adj.* **-i·er, -i·est.** Uttered or sounding as if uttered deep in the throat. **—throat′i·ly** *adv.* **—throat′i·ness** *n.*

throb (thrŏb) ► *v.* **throbbed, throb·bing.** **1.** To beat rapidly or violently; pound. **2.** To vibrate rhythmically; pulsate. **—throb** *n.* **—throb′bing·ly** *adv.*

throe (thrō) ► *n.* **1.** A severe pang or spasm of pain. **2. throes** Agonizing struggle or effort.

throm·bo·sis (thrŏm-bō′sĭs) ► *n., pl.* **-ses** (-sēz). The formation or presence of a thrombus.

throm·bus (thrŏm′bəs) ► *n., pl.* **-bi** (-bī). A blood clot formed in a blood vessel or in a chamber of the heart.

throne (thrōn) ► *n.* **1.** A chair occupied by a sovereign or bishop on state or ceremonial occasions. **2.** Sovereign power or rank.

throng (thrông, thrŏng) ► *n.* A large group of people or things crowded together. ► *v.* **1.** To crowd into or around. **2.** To move in a throng.

throt·tle (thrŏt′l) ► *n.* **1.** A valve that regulates the flow of a fluid, such as the valve in an internal-combustion engine that controls the amount of vaporized fuel entering the cylinders. **2.** A lever or pedal controlling such a valve. ► *v.* **-tled, -tling.** **1.** To regulate the speed of (an engine) with a throttle. **2.** To suppress: *tried to throttle the press.* **3.** To strangle; choke. **—throt′tler** *n.*

through (thro͞o) ► *prep.* **1.** In one side and out another side of. **2.** In the midst of. **3.** By way of. **4.** By the means or agency of. **5.** Here and there in; around. **6.** From the beginning to the end of. **7.** Done or finished with. ► *adv.* **1.** From one end or side to another end or side. **2.** From beginning to end. **3.** Throughout the whole extent or thickness. **4.** To a conclusion. ► *adj.* **1.** Allowing continuous passage; unobstructed. **2.** Passing or extending from one end, side, or surface to another. **3.** Finished; done. ***—idiom:*** **through and through** **1.** In every part; throughout. **2.** Completely.

through·out (thro͞o-out′) ► *prep.* In, to, through, or during every part of: *throughout the entire year.* ► *adv.* **1.** Everywhere. **2.** During the entire time or extent.

throve (thrōv) ► *v.* P.t. of **thrive.**

throw (thrō) ► *v.* **threw** (thro͞o), **thrown** (thrōn), **throw·ing.** **1.** To propel through the air with a swift motion of the hand or arm; fling. **2.** To put with force; hurl. **3.** *Informal* To confuse; perplex. **4.** To put on or off hastily or carelessly. **5.** To form on a potter's wheel. **6.** To cast: *throw a shadow.* **7.** To arrange or give (e.g., a party). **8.** To activate (a lever or switch). **9.** *Informal* To lose (e.g., a contest) purposely. ***—phrasal verbs:*** **throw away (or out)** To discard. **throw over** To desert; abandon. **throw up** To vomit. ► *n.* **1.** The act or an instance of throwing. **2.** The distance or height to which something is or can be thrown. **3.** A light coverlet. ***—idiom:*** **throw up (one's) hands** To give up in despair. **—throw′er** *n.*

throw·back (thrō′băk′) ► *n.* A reversion to a former type or ancestral characteristic.

thru (thro͞o) ► *prep. & adv. & adj. Informal* Through.

thrum (thrŭm) ► *v.* **thrummed, thrum·ming.** To play (a stringed instrument) idly or monotonously. **—thrum** *n.*

thrush (thrŭsh) ► *n.* Any of various songbirds usu. having brownish upper plumage and a spotted breast.

thrust (thrŭst) ► *v.* **thrust, thrust·ing.** **1.** To push or drive forcibly. **2.** To force into a specified state or condition. **3.** To interject. ► *n.* **1.** A forceful shove. **2a.** A driving force or pressure. **b.** The forward-directed force developed in a jet or rocket engine as a reaction to the rearward ejection of exhaust gases. **3.** A stab. **4.** The essence; point. **5.** Outward or lateral stress in a structure.

thru·way also **through·way** (thro͞o′wā′) ► *n.* See **expressway.**

Thu·cyd·i·des (tho͞o-sĭd′ĭ-dēz′) (460?–400? B.C.) ► Greek historian.

thud (thŭd) ► *n.* **1.** A dull sound. **2.** A blow or fall causing such a sound. **—thud** *v.*

thug (thŭg) ► *n.* A cutthroat or ruffian; hoodlum. **—thug′ger·y** *n.* **—thug′gish** *adj.*

thu·li·um (tho͞o′lē-əm) ► *n. Symbol* **Tm** A bright, silvery rare-earth element, one isotope of which is used in small portable x-ray units. At. no. 69.

thumb (thŭm) ► *n.* **1.** The short, thick first digit of the human hand, opposable to the other four digits. **2.** The part of a glove or mitten that covers the thumb. ► *v.* **1.** To scan by turning over pages with the thumb. **2.** To soil or wear by handling. **3.** *Informal* To hitchhike. ***—idiom:*** **all thumbs** Clumsy.

thumb·nail (thŭm′nāl′) ► *n.* **1.** The nail of the thumb. **2.** *Comp. Sci.* A reduced image of a graphic or a document page. ► *adj.* Brief: *a thumbnail sketch.*

THESAURUS

thrifty *adj.* *—See* ECONOMICAL.

thrill *n.* A strong, pleasant feeling of excitement or stimulation ► lift. *Informal:* wallop. *Slang:* bang, boot, buzz, high, jollies, kick. *Idiom:* kick in the pants. *—See also* TREMOR (2).

thrill *v.* *—See* DELIGHT (1), ENRAPTURE.

thrilled *adj.* Feeling strong pleasure or excitement ► atingle, excited, fired up, worked up. *Informal:* psyched. *Slang:* stoked, turned-on, wired. [*Compare* ELATED, PASSIONATE.]

thrilling *adj.* *—See* DRAMATIC (2).

thrive *v.* To grow rapidly ► bloom, blossom, flourish. [*Compare* INCREASE.] *—See also* PROSPER.

thriving *adj.* *—See* FLOURISHING, HEALTHY.

throb *v.* *—See* BEAT (5), GLARE (2).

throb *n.* *—See* BEAT (3).

throbbing *adj.* *—See* BRILLIANT, SHARP (3).

throe *n.* *—See* PAIN.

throes *n.* A condition of agonizing struggle or trouble ► convulsion, paroxysm, spasm.

throng *n.* *—See* CROWD.

throng *v.* *—See* CROWD.

throttle *v.* *—See* CHOKE, REPRESS.

through *adj.* **1.** Having no further relationship ► done, finished. **2.** No longer effective, capable, or valuable ► done, done for, finished, washed-up. *Informal:* kaput. *Idioms:* at the end of one's line (*or* road), over the hill, past one's prime. [*Compare* GONER.] *—See also* COMPLETE (3), DIRECT (1).

through *prep.* *—See* BECAUSE OF.

throw *v.* To send through the air with a motion of the hand or arm ► bowl, cast, dart, dash, fling, heave, hurl, hurtle, launch, lob, pelt, pitch, roll, shoot, shy, sling, toss. *Informal:* chuck, fire, peg. *—See also* BAFFLE, CONFUSE (1), DROP (3), HAVE (3), SHED[1] (1).

throw away *v.* *—See* DISCARD, WASTE.

throw in *v.* *—See* INTRODUCE (2).

throw off *v.* *—See* EMIT, LOSE (3), RID, SHED[1] (2).

throw out *v.* *—See* DISCARD, EJECT (1), PROPOSE, SLIP (2).

throw over *v.* *—See* ABANDON (1).

throw up *v.* *—See* VOMIT.

throw *n.* An act of throwing ► bowl, cast, fling, heave, hurl, launch, lob, peg, pitch, roll, shy, sling, toss. *Informal:* chuck.

thrust *n.* The current of thought that unites all elements of a text or discourse ► aim, burden, drift, gist, intent, purport, substance, tendency, tenor. [*Compare* HEART, MEANING.] *—See also* PUSH.

thrust *v.* *—See* DRIVE (2), PLUNGE, PUSH (1).

thruway *n.* *—See* WAY (2).

thud *v.* To make a dull sound by or as if by striking a surface with a heavy object ► clomp, clump, clunk, plunk, thump, whomp. [*Compare* BANG.]

thud *n.* *—See* BEAT (1).

thug *n.* A person who treats others violently or roughly, especially for hire ► hoodlum, hooligan, mug, roughneck, rowdy, ruffian, tough. *Informal:* bruiser, toughie. *Slang:* gangsta, goon, gorilla, gunsel, hood, plug-ugly, punk. [*Compare* CRIMINAL.]

thumb *v.* *—See* BROWSE (1).

thumb·screw (thŭm′skrōō′) ► *n.* A screw designed so that it can be turned with the thumb and fingers.

thumb·tack (thŭm′tăk′) ► *n.* A smooth-headed tack that can be pressed into place with the thumb. **—thumb′tack′** *v.*

thump (thŭmp) ► *n.* **1.** A heavy resounding blow. **2.** The muffled sound produced by such a blow. ► *v.* **1.** To beat with or as if with a blunt object so as to produce a muffled sound. **2.** To pound.

thun·der (thŭn′dər) ► *n.* **1.** The booming sound produced by rapidly expanding air along the path of the electrical discharge of lightning. **2.** A sound resembling thunder. ► *v.* **1.** To produce thunder or similar sounds. **2.** To utter loud remarks or threats. **—thun′der·ous** *adj.*

thun·der·bolt (thŭn′dər-bōlt′) ► *n.* A discharge of lightning accompanied by thunder.

thun·der·clap (thŭn′dər-klăp′) ► *n.* A single sharp crash of thunder.

thun·der·cloud (thŭn′dər-kloud′) ► *n.* A large dark cloud that produces thunder and lightning.

thun·der·head (thŭn′dər-hĕd′) ► *n.* The swollen upper portion of a thundercloud.

thun·der·show·er (thŭn′dər-shou′ər) ► *n.* A brief rainstorm accompanied by thunder and lightning.

thun·der·storm (thŭn′dər-stôrm′) ► *n.* An electrical storm with heavy rain.

thun·der·struck (thŭn′dər-strŭk′) ► *adj.* Astonished; stunned.

Thur. ► *abbr.* Thursday

Thurs·day (thûrz′dē, -dā′) ► *n.* The 5th day of the week.

thus (*th*ŭs) ► *adv.* **1.** In this manner. **2.** To a stated degree or extent; so. **3.** Therefore; consequently.

thwack (thwăk) ► *v.* To strike resoundingly with a flat object. **—thwack** *n.*

thwart (thwôrt) ► *v.* To block or hinder; frustrate. ► *n.* A seat across a boat on which a rower may sit. ► *adj.* Transverse.

thy (*th*ī) ► *adj.* The possessive form of **thou**.

thyme (tīm) ► *n.* An aromatic plant with leaves used as seasoning.

thy·mine (thī′mēn′) ► *n.* A pyrimidine base that is an essential constituent of DNA.

thy·mus (thī′məs) ► *n., pl.* **-mus·es.** A small glandular organ, situated behind the top of the breastbone, that plays some part in building resistance to disease but is usu. vestigial after puberty.

thy·roid (thī′roid′) ► *n.* **1.** The thyroid gland. **2.** A dried powdered preparation of the thyroid gland of certain domestic animals, used in medicine.

thyroid gland ► *n.* A two-lobed endocrine gland located in front of and on either side of the trachea in humans and producing various hormones.

thy·self (*th*ī-sĕlf′) ► *pron. Archaic* Yourself.

ti (tē) ► *n. Mus.* The 7th tone of the diatonic scale.

Ti ► The symbol for the element **titanium**.

Tian Shan (tyän′ shän′) ► A mountain range of central Asia extending about 2,414 km (1,500 mi).

ti·ar·a (tē-ăr′ə, -âr′ə, -är′ə) ► *n.* **1.** A bejeweled crownlike ornament worn on the head by women. **2.** The triple crown worn by the pope.

Ti·ber (tī′bər) ► A river of central Italy flowing about 406 km (252 mi) through Rome to the Tyrrhenian Sea at Ostia.

Ti·bet (tə-bĕt′) ► **1.** A historical region of central Asia that is between the Himalaya and Kunlun mountains. **2.** See **Xizang**. **—Ti·bet′an** *adj. & n.*

Ti·bet·o-Bur·man (tĭ-bĕt′ō-bûr′mən) ► *n.* A branch of the Sino-Tibetan language family that includes Tibetan and Burmese.

tib·i·a (tĭb′ē-ə) ► *n., pl.* **-i·ae** (-ē-ē′) or **-i·as.** The inner and larger of the two bones of the lower leg, extending from the knee to the ankle. **—tib′i·al** *adj.*

tic (tĭk) ► *n.* A spasmodic muscular contraction, usu. of the face or extremities.

tick[1] (tĭk) ► *n.* **1.** A clicking sound made repeatedly by a machine, such as a clock. **2.** A light mark used to check off or call attention to an item. **—tick** *v.*

tick[2] (tĭk) ► *n.* Any of numerous bloodsucking parasitic arachnids or louselike insects, many of which transmit diseases.

tick[3] (tĭk) ► *n.* **1.** A cloth case for a mattress or pillow. **2.** Ticking.

tick·er (tĭk′ər) ► *n.* **1.** A telegraphic instrument that receives news reports and prints them on paper tape. **2.** *Slang* The heart.

ticker tape ► *n.* The paper strip on which a ticker prints.

tick·et (tĭk′ĭt) ► *n.* **1.** A paper slip or card indicating that its holder has paid for admission or a service. **2.** A certificate or license. **3.** An identifying tag; label. **4.** A list of candidates endorsed by a political party; slate. **5.** A summons, esp. for a traffic violation. ► *v.* **1.** To serve with a legal summons. **2.** To tag; label.

tick·ing (tĭk′ĭng) ► *n.* A strong, tightly woven fabric used to make pillow and mattress coverings.

tick·le (tĭk′əl) ► *v.* **-led, -ling.** **1.** To touch (the body) lightly so as to cause laughter or twitching movements. **2.** To feel a light tingling on the skin. **3a.** To tease or excite pleasurably. **b.** To please; delight. **—tick′le** *n.*

tick·lish (tĭk′lĭsh) ► *adj.* **1.** Sensitive to tickling. **2.** Easily offended or upset. **3.** Requiring tactful handling; delicate. **—tick′lish·ly** *adv.* **—tick′lish·ness** *n.*

tic-tac-toe also **tick-tack-toe** (tĭk′tăk′tō′) ► *n.* A game for two, each trying to make a line of three X's or three O's in a boxlike figure with nine spaces.

tid·al (tīd′l) ► *adj.* Of or affected by tides.

tidal wave ► *n.* **1.** An unusual rise or incursion of water along the seashore. **2.** A tsunami. **3.** An overwhelming manifestation, as of opinion; flood.

tid·bit (tĭd′bĭt′) ► *n.* A choice morsel.

tid·dly·winks (tĭd′lē-wĭngks′) ► *pl.n. (takes sing. v.)* A game in which players try to snap small disks into a cup by pressing them on the edge with a larger disk.

tide (tīd) ► *n.* **1a.** The periodic variation in the surface level of the oceans, seas, and other open waters of the earth, caused by gravitational attraction of the moon and sun. **b.** A specific occurrence of such a variation. **c.** The water that moves in such a variation. **2.** An onrush; flow: *a tide of immigration.* **3.** A time or season. ► *v.* **tid·ed, tid·ing.** To drift with the tide. ***—phrasal verb:*** **tide over** To support through a difficult period.

tide·land (tīd′lănd′) ► *n.* Coastal land submerged during high tide.

tide·wa·ter (tīd′wô′tər, -wŏt′ər) ► *n.* **1.** Water that inundates land at flood tide. **2.** Water affected by the tides, esp. tidal streams. **3.** Low coastal land drained by tidal streams.

THESAURUS

thumbs-down *n.* —*See* NO (1).

thumbs-up *n.* —*See* PERMISSION.

thump *n.* —*See* BEAT (1), BLOW[2].

thump *v.* —*See* BANG (1), BEAT (1), BEAT (5), THUD.

thunder *n.* —*See* BLAST (1).

thunder *v.* —*See* BLAST (1).

thundercloud *n.* An indication of impending danger or harm ► foreboding, forewarning, threat. —*See also* OMEN.

thunderous *adj.* —*See* LOUD.

thwack *v.* —*See* BANG (1), HIT.

thwack *n.* —*See* BLOW[2].

thwart *v.* —*See* FRUSTRATE.

thwart *adj.* —*See* TRANSVERSE.

tic *n.* —*See* TREMOR (2).

tick *n.* —*See* BEAT (3).

tick *v.* —*See* BEAT (5).

tick away *v.* —*See* ELAPSE.

tick off *v.* —*See* ANGER (1), ENUMERATE.

ticker *n.* *Slang* The circulatory organ of the body ► blood pump, heart.

ticket *n.* **1.** An identifying or descriptive slip ► earmark, flag, label, tab, tag. **2.** A list of candidates proposed or endorsed by a political party ► ballot, lineup, slate. **3.** *Informal* A means or method of entering into or achieving something desirable ► formula, key, route, secret [Compare TRICK.] **4.** A written or printed notification of a legal infraction ► citation. —*See also* LICENSE (3).

ticket *v.* To attach a ticket to ► earmark, flag, label, mark, tag.

ticking *adj.* —*See* ACTIVE.

tickle *v.* —*See* DELIGHT (1).

tickled *adj.* —*See* WILLING.

ticklish *adj.* —*See* CAPRICIOUS, DELICATE (3), OVERSENSITIVE.

tidbit *n.* —*See* BIT[1] (2), DELICACY.

tide *n.* —*See* FLOW.

tid·ings (tī′dĭngz) ▸ *pl.n.* Information; news.
ti·dy (tī′dē) ▸ *adj.* **-di·er, -di·est. 1.** Orderly and neat. **2.** *Informal* Substantial; considerable. ▸ *v.* **-died, -dy·ing.** To put (things) in order. **—ti′di·ly** *adv.* **—ti′di·ness** *n.*
tie (tī) ▸ *v.* **tied, ty·ing** (tī′ĭng). **1.** To fasten or secure with a cord, rope, or strap. **2.** To draw together and knot with strings or laces. **3.** To make (a knot or bow). **4.** To bring or hold together; unite. **5.** To equal (an opponent) in a contest. ***—phrasal verbs:* tie in** To coordinate; connect. **tie up 1.** To obstruct. **2.** To keep occupied; engage. **3.** To moor; dock. ▸ *n.* **1.** A length, as of cord or string, used for tying. **2.** A necktie. **3.** Something that unites; bond. **4.** An equality, as of votes or scores. **5.** A beam or rod that gives structural support. **6.** A timber laid crosswise to support railway tracks.
tie-dye (tī′dī′) ▸ *v.* To dye (fabric) after tying parts of the fabric so that they will not absorb dye, creating a mottled or streaked look. **—tie′-dye′** *n.*
tie-in (tī′ĭn′) ▸ *n.* A connection; link.
tier (tîr) ▸ *n.* One of a series of rows placed one above another. **—tier** *v.*
Ti·er·ra del Fue·go (tē-ĕr′ə dĕl fwā′gō) ▸ **1.** An archipelago off S South America separated from the mainland by the Strait of Magellan. **2.** The main island of this archipelago.
tie-up (tī′ŭp′) ▸ *n.* A temporary stoppage.
tiff (tĭf) ▸ *n.* **1.** A fit of irritation. **2.** A petty quarrel. **—tiff** *v.*
ti·ger (tī′gər) ▸ *n.* A large carnivorous Asian cat having a tawny coat with black stripes. **—ti′gress** *n.*
tiger lily ▸ *n.* An E Asian plant with large black-spotted reddish-orange flowers.
tight (tīt) ▸ *adj.* **-er, -est. 1.** Fixed or fastened firmly in place. **2.** Stretched or drawn out fully. **3.** Of such close construction as to be impermeable. **4.** Compact. **5.** Fitting close or too close to the skin; snug. **6.** *Slang* Personally close; intimate. **7.** Constricted. **8.** Stingy. **9.** Difficult: *a tight spot.* **10.** Closely contested. **11.** *Slang* Drunk. ▸ *adv.* **-er, -est. 1.** Firmly; securely. **2.** Soundly: *sleep tight.* **—tight′en** *v.* **—tight′ly** *adv.* **—tight′ness** *n.*
tight·fist·ed (tīt′fĭs′tĭd) ▸ *adj.* Stingy.
tight·lipped also **tight-lipped** (tīt′lĭpt′) ▸ *adj.* **1.** Having the lips pressed together. **2.** Loath to speak; close-mouthed.
tight·rope (tīt′rōp′) ▸ *n.* A tightly stretched rope on which acrobats perform.
tights (tīts) ▸ *pl.n.* A snug stretchable garment covering the body from the waist or neck down.
tight·wad (tīt′wŏd′) ▸ *n. Slang* A miser.
Ti·gris (tī′grĭs) ▸ A river of SW Asia rising in E Turkey and flowing about 1,850 km (1,150 mi) through Iraq to the Euphrates R.
Ti·jua·na (tē′ə-wä′nə, tē-hwä′nä) ▸ A city of extreme NW Mexico on the US border S of San Diego.
til·de (tĭl′də) ▸ *n.* A diacritical mark (~) placed over the letter *n* in Spanish and over a vowel in Portuguese to indicate nasalization.
tile (tīl) ▸ *n.* **1.** A slab, as of baked clay, laid in rows to cover walls, floors, and roofs. **2.** A short length of clay or concrete pipe, used in sewers and drains. **3.** A marked playing piece, as in mahjong. ▸ *v.* **tiled, til·ing.** To cover or provide with tiles. **—til′er** *n.*
till[1] (tĭl) ▸ *v.* To cultivate (land or soil). **—till′a·ble** *adj.*
till[2] (tĭl) ▸ *prep. & conj.* Until.
till[3] (tĭl) ▸ *n.* A drawer or compartment for money, as in a store.
till·age (tĭl′ĭj) ▸ *n.* Cultivation of land.
till·er[1] (tĭl′ər) ▸ *n.* One that tills land.
til·ler[2] (tĭl′ər) ▸ *n.* A lever used to turn a boat's rudder.
tilt (tĭlt) ▸ *v.* **1.** To slope or cause to slope, as by raising one end; incline. **2.** To thrust (a lance) in a joust. ▸ *n.* **1.** A slant; slope. **2.** A joust. **3.** A bias. ***—idiom:* at full tilt** *Informal* At full speed. **—tilt′er** *n.*
tim·ber (tĭm′bər) ▸ *n.* **1a.** Trees or wooded land considered as a source of wood. **b.** Wood used as a building material. **2a.** A dressed piece of wood, esp. a structural beam. **b.** A rib in a ship's frame. **—tim′bered** *adj.*
tim·ber·line (tĭm′bər-līn′) ▸ *n.* The elevation in a mountainous region above which trees do not grow.
timber wolf ▸ *n.* See **gray wolf.**
tim·bre (tăm′bər, tĭm′-) ▸ *n.* The quality of a sound that distinguishes it from others of the same pitch and volume.
time (tīm) ▸ *n.* **1a.** A nonspatial continuum in which events occur in apparently irreversible succession. **b.** An interval separating two points on this continuum; duration. **c.** A number, as of years, days, or minutes, representing such an interval. **d.** A similar number representing a specific point on this continuum, reckoned in hours and minutes. **e.** A system by which such intervals are measured or such numbers are reckoned. **2.** often **times** A period; era: *hard times.* **3.** A suitable or opportune moment. **4.** A period designated for a given activity: *harvest time.* **5.** One of several instances. **6.** *Informal* A prison sentence. **7.** The rate of speed of a measured activity: *marching in double time.* **8.** The characteristic beat of musical rhythm. ▸ *adj.* **1.** Of or relating to time. **2.** Constructed to operate at a particular moment: *a time release.* **3.** Of or relating to installment buying. ▸ *v.* **timed, tim·ing. 1.** To set the time for (e.g., an event). **2.** To adjust to keep accurate time. **3.** To adjust the timing of. **4.** To record, set, or maintain the speed, tempo, or duration of. ***—idioms:* for the time being** Temporarily. **from**

THESAURUS

tidings *n.* —*See* NEWS.
tidy *v.* **1.** To make or keep an area clean and orderly ▸ clean (up), clear (up), neaten (up), police, spruce (up), straighten (up). **2.** To make neat, trim, or presentable ▸ clean (up), freshen (up), groom, neaten (up), slick up, spruce (up), tidy up, trig (out), trim.
tidy *adj.* —*See* ACCEPTABLE (2), BIG, NEAT.
tidy sum *n.* —*See* FORTUNE.
tie *v.* To do or make something equal to ▸ equal, match, meet. —*See also* FASTEN, HAMPER[1].
tie up *v.* —*See* ABSORB (1), FASTEN, STOP (2).
tie *n.* An equality of scores, votes, or performances in a contest ▸ dead heat, deadlock, draw, stalemate, standoff. —*See also* BOND (2).
tie beam *n.* —*See* BEAM (2).
tie-in *n.* —*See* RELATION (1).
tier *n.* —*See* CLASS (2), LINE.
tie-up *n.* —*See* STOP (2).
tiff *n.* —*See* ARGUMENT.
tiff *v.* —*See* ARGUE (1).
tight *adj.* **1.** Persistently holding to something ▸ clinging, fast, firm, secure, tenacious. [*Compare* FIXED.] **2.** Stretched tightly ▸ taut, tense. [*Compare* RIGID.] **3.** Characterized by an economy of artistic expression ▸ lean, minimalist, spare, taut. [*Compare* BARE.] **4.** Affording little room for movement ▸ close, confining, cramped, crowded, narrow, restrictive, snug. **5.** Difficult to deal with or get out of ▸ rough, tricky. *Informal:* sticky. [*Compare* DELICATE.] **6.** Almost even ▸ nip and tuck. *Idiom:* neck and neck. —*See also* DRUNK, INTIMATE[1] (1), SOUND[2], STINGY, THICK (2).
tighten *v.* —*See* CONSTRICT (1), SUPPORT (2), TENSE.
tightfisted *adj.* —*See* STINGY.
tightlipped *adj.* —*See* TACITURN.
tightrope *n.* —*See* PREDICAMENT.
tightwad *n.* —*See* MISER.
till *v.* To prepare soil for the planting and raising of crops ▸ cultivate, culture, dig, fork, harrow, hoe, plow, rake, spade, turn (over), work. [*Compare* FERTILIZE, GROW, PLANT.]
tilt *n.* A competition or test of opposing wills suggesting the sport fought by mounted knights with lances ▸ joust, tournament, tourney. [*Compare* BATTLE, COMPETITION.] —*See also* INCLINATION (2).
tilt *v.* —*See* CONTEND, INCLINE.
timber *n.* A person considered to have qualities suitable for a particular activity ▸ material, stuff. [*Compare* COMER, POTENTIAL.] —*See also* BEAM (2).
timberland *n.* A dense growth of trees and underbrush covering an area ▸ backwoods, forest, woodland, woods. [*Compare* COUNTRY, WILDERNESS.]
timbre *n.* The distinct quality or character of a sound ▸ tonality, tone, tone color. —*See also* TEMPER (3).
time *n.* A prison or jail term ▸ hitch, stretch. —*See also* AGE (2), BIT[1] (3), LIFE, OCCASION (1), PERIOD (1), TURN (1).
time *v.* **1.** To set the time for an event or occasion ▸ plan, schedule, set. [*Compare* ARRANGE.] **2.** To

time to time Once in a while. **on time 1.** According to schedule. **2.** By paying in installments. **—tim′er** *n.*

time bomb ▸ *n.* **1.** A bomb that can be set to detonate at a particular time. **2.** Something that threatens eventual disaster.

time clock ▸ *n.* A clock that records the starting and quitting times of employees.

time deposit ▸ *n.* A bank deposit that cannot be withdrawn before a specified date.

time-hon·ored (tīm′ŏn′ərd) ▸ *adj.* Respected because of age or age-old observance.

time·keep·er (tīm′kē′pər) ▸ *n.* One who records time, as in a sports event.

time-lapse (tīm′lăps′) ▸ *adj.* Of or being a technique that photographs a slow process at intervals, so that serial projection of the frames gives an accelerated view of the process.

time·less (tīm′lĭs) ▸ *adj.* **1.** Eternal. **2.** Unaffected by time; ageless. **—time′less·ly** *adv.* **—time′less·ness** *n.*

time·line (tīm′līn′) ▸ *n.* **1.** A timetable. **2.** A chronology, esp. a representation of key events in a given time period.

time·ly (tīm′lē) ▸ *adj.* **-li·er, -li·est.** Occurring at a suitable or opportune time; well-timed. **—time′li·ness** *n.*

time-out also **time out** (tīm′out′) ▸ *n.* A brief cessation of play during a game.

time·piece (tīm′pēs′) ▸ *n.* An instrument that measures, registers, or records time.

times (tīmz) ▸ *prep. Math.* Multiplied by: *Five times two is ten.*

time-shar·ing (tīm′shâr′ĭng) ▸ *n.* **1.** A technique permitting many users simultaneous access to a central computer through remote terminals. **2.** also **time-share** (-shâr′) Joint ownership of vacation property allowing individual use for fixed periods.

times sign ▸ *n. Math.* The symbol × used to indicate multiplication.

time·ta·ble (tīm′tā′bəl) ▸ *n.* A schedule of the expected times of events, such as arrivals and departures at a railroad station.

time·worn (tīm′wôrn′) ▸ *adj.* **1.** Showing the effects of long use or wear. **2.** Trite.

time zone ▸ *n.* Any of the 24 longitudinal divisions of the earth's surface in which a standard time is kept.

tim·id (tĭm′ĭd) ▸ *adj.* **-er, -est. 1.** Shy. **2.** Fearful and hesitant. **—ti·mid′i·ty, tim′id·ness** *n.* **—tim′id·ly** *adv.*

tim·ing (tī′mĭng) ▸ *n.* The regulation of occurrence, pace, or coordination to achieve the most desirable effects.

Ti·mor (tē′môr, tē-môr′) ▸ Island in the Malay Archipelago E of Java, divided between Indonesia and East Timor.

tim·or·ous (tĭm′ər-əs) ▸ *adj.* Fearful; timid. **—tim′or·ous·ly** *adv.* **—tim′or·ous·ness** *n.*

Timor Sea ▸ An arm of the Indian Ocean between Timor and Australia.

tim·o·thy (tĭm′ə-thē) ▸ *n.* A grass widely cultivated for hay.

Timothy ▸ *n.* See **Bible** table in Appendix.

tim·pa·ni also **tym·pa·ni** (tĭm′pə-nē) ▸ *pl.n.* A set of kettledrums. **—tim′pa·nist** *n.*

tin (tĭn) ▸ *n.* **1.** *Symbol* **Sn** A malleable, silvery metallic element used to coat other metals to prevent corrosion and in alloys such as soft solder, pewter, type metal, and bronze. At. no. 50. **2.** A tin container or box. **3.** *Chiefly Brit.* A can for preserved food. ▸ *v.* **tinned, tin·ning. 1.** To plate or coat with tin. **2.** *Chiefly Brit.* To pack in tins; can.

tinc·ture (tĭngk′chər) ▸ *n.* **1.** A dyeing substance; pigment. **2.** An imparted color; tint. **3.** A trace or vestige. **4.** An alcohol solution of a nonvolatile medicine: *tincture of iodine.* ▸ *v.* **-tured, -tur·ing.** To stain or tint with a color.

tin·der (tĭn′dər) ▸ *n.* Readily combustible material used for kindling.

tin·der·box (tĭn′dər-bŏks′) ▸ *n.* **1.** A box for holding tinder. **2.** A potentially explosive situation.

tine (tīn) ▸ *n.* A point or prong, as on a fork. **—tined** (tīnd) *adj.*

tin·foil also **tin foil** (tĭn′foil′) ▸ *n.* A thin pliable sheet of aluminum, tin, or a tin alloy.

tinge (tĭnj) ▸ *v.* **tinged** (tĭnjd), **tinge·ing** or **ting·ing. 1.** To color slightly; tint. **2.** To affect slightly. **—tinge** *n.*

tin·gle (tĭng′gəl) ▸ *v.* **-gled, -gling.** To have a prickling, stinging sensation, as from cold or excitement. **—tin′gle** *n.* **—tin′gler** *n.* **—tin′gly** *adj.*

tin·ker (tĭng′kər) ▸ *n.* **1.** A traveling mender of metal household utensils. **2.** A clumsy worker; meddler. ▸ *v.* **1.** To work as a tinker. **2.** To make aimless or experimental efforts at repair; fiddle.

tin·kle (tĭng′kəl) ▸ *v.* **-kled, -kling.** To make or cause to make light metallic sounds, as those of a small bell. **—tin′kle** *n.* **—tin′kly** *adj.*

tin·ny (tĭn′ē) ▸ *adj.* **-ni·er, -ni·est. 1.** Of, containing, or suggesting tin. **2.** Having a thin metallic sound. **—tin′ni·ness** *n.*

tin·sel (tĭn′səl) ▸ *n.* **1.** Very thin sheets or strips of a glittering material used as a decoration. **2.** Something showy but basically valueless. **—tin′sel** *adj.*

tin·smith (tĭn′smĭth′) ▸ *n.* One who works with light metal, such as tin.

tint (tĭnt) ▸ *n.* **1.** A shade of a color, esp. a pale or delicate variation. **2.** A slight coloration. **3.** A trace. **4.** A hair dye. ▸ *v.* To give a tint to. **—tint′er** *n.*

tin·tin·nab·u·la·tion (tĭn′tĭ-năb′yə-lā′shən) ▸ *n.* The ringing or sounding of bells.

tin·type (tĭn′tīp′) ▸ *n.* See **ferrotype.**

ti·ny (tī′nē) ▸ *adj.* **-ni·er, -ni·est.** Extremely small; minute. **—ti′ni·ness** *n.*

tip[1] (tĭp) ▸ *n.* **1.** The end of a pointed or projecting object. **2.** A piece meant to be fitted to the end of something. ▸ *v.* **tipped, tip·ping. 1.** To furnish with a tip. **2.** To cover, decorate, or remove the tip of.

tip[2] (tĭp) ▸ *v.* **tipped, tip·ping. 1.** To push or knock over; topple. **2.** To tilt. **3.** To raise (one's hat) in greeting. **—tip** *n.*

tip[3] (tĭp) ▸ *v.* **tipped, tip·ping.** To strike gently; tap. **—tip** *n.*

tip[4] (tĭp) ▸ *n.* **1.** An extra sum of money given to someone for services rendered; gratuity. **2.** A piece of useful advice or information. **—tip** *v.* **—tip′per** *n.*

ti·pi (tē′pē) ▸ *n.* Var. of **tepee.**

THESAURUS

record the speed or duration of ▸ clock. [*Compare* MEASURE.]

time-honored *adj.* —*See* ACCEPTED, TRADITIONAL.

timeless *adj.* Existing unchanged forever ▸ ageless, eternal. [*Compare* ENDLESS.] —*See also* CONTINUAL, VINTAGE.

timely *adj.* Occurring, acting, or performed exactly at the time appointed ▸ prompt, punctual. *Idioms:* on the dot (*or* nose), on schedule, on time. —*See also* OPPORTUNE.

time-out *n.* —*See* REST[1] (1), REST[1] (2).

timetable *n.* —*See* PROGRAM (1).

timeworn *adj.* —*See* OLD (1), TRITE.

timid *adj.* —*See* AFRAID, HESITANT, SHY[1].

timidity or **timidness** *n.* —*See* HESITATION, SHYNESS.

timorous *adj.* —*See* AFRAID.

tinct *n.* —*See* COLOR (1).

tincture *n.* —*See* COLOR (2).

tincture *v.* —*See* COLOR (1).

tine *n.* —*See* SPIKE.

tinge *n.* —*See* COLOR (1), SHADE (2).

tinge *v.* —*See* COLOR (1).

tingle *n.* A feeling of pervasive emotional warmth ▸ flush, glow.

tinker *v.* To handle something in an attempt to adjust or improve it ▸ fiddle, fool, meddle, mess (around), tamper. *Informal:* monkey. [*Compare* ADJUST, FIX.] —*See also* FIDDLE.

tinsel *adj.* —*See* GAUDY.

tint *n.* —*See* COLOR (1).

tint *v.* —*See* COLOR (1).

tiny *adj.* Extremely small ▸ diminutive, dwarf, Lilliputian, microscopic, midget, mini, miniature, minuscule, minute, pygmy, wee. *Informal:* eensy, peewee, pintsize, pintsized, teensy, teensy-weensy, teeny, teeny-weeny, weeny. [*Compare* IMPERCEPTIBLE, LITTLE.]

tip[1] *n.* —*See* POINT (1).

tip *v.* To put a topping on ▸ cap, crest, crown, top, top off. [*Compare* COVER.]

tip[2] *v.* —*See* INCLINE.

tip over *v.* —*See* FALL (2), OVERTURN.

tip *n.* —*See* INCLINATION (2).

tip[3] *n.* An item of advance or inside information given as a guide to action ▸ clue, hint, lead, pointer, scent, steer. *Informal:* tip-off. [*Compare* HINT.] —*See also* ADVICE, GRATUITY.

tip *v.* —*See* INFORM (2).

tip-off (tĭp′ôf′, -ŏf′) ▸ *n. Informal* A piece of inside information; hint or warning.

tip·pet (tĭp′ĭt) ▸ *n.* A covering for the shoulders with long ends that hang in front.

tip·ple (tĭp′əl) ▸ *v.* **-pled, -pling.** To drink (alcoholic liquor), esp. habitually. **—tip′pler** *n.*

tip·ster (tĭp′stər) ▸ *n. Informal* One who sells tips to bettors or speculators.

tip·sy (tĭp′sē) ▸ *adj.* **-si·er, -si·est.** Slightly drunk. **—tip′si·ly** *adv.* **—tip′si·ness** *n.*

tip·toe (tĭp′tō′) ▸ *v.* To walk or move quietly or stealthily on one's toes. ▸ *adv.* On one's toes. **—tip′toe′** *n.*

tip·top (tĭp′tŏp′) ▸ *n.* The highest point; summit. ▸ *adj.* Excellent; first-rate.

ti·rade (tī′rād′, tī-rād′) ▸ *n.* An angry, often denunciatory speech; diatribe.

tire[1] (tīr) ▸ *v.* **tired, tir·ing. 1.** To make or become weary. **2.** To make or become bored or impatient.

tire[2] (tīr) ▸ *n.* **1.** A covering for a wheel, usu. of hollow rubber filled with compressed air. **2.** A hoop of metal or rubber fitted around a wheel.

tired (tīrd) ▸ *adj.* **1a.** Fatigued. **b.** Impatient; bored. **2.** Trite: *the same tired rhetoric as always.* **—tired′ly** *adv.* **—tired′ness** *n.*

tire·less (tīr′lĭs) ▸ *adj.* Not tiring easily; indefatigable. **—tire′less·ly** *adv.*

tire·some (tīr′səm) ▸ *adj.* Tedious; wearisome. **—tire′some·ly** *adv.* **—tire′some·ness** *n.*

'tis (tĭz) ▸ It is.

Tish·ri (tĭsh′rē, -rā) ▸ *n.* A month of the Jewish calendar.

tis·sue (tĭsh′o͞o, -yo͞o) ▸ *n.* **1.** A fine, very thin fabric, such as gauze. **2.** Thin translucent paper used esp. for packing or wrapping. **3.** A soft absorbent piece of paper used as toilet paper or a handkerchief. **4.** A web; network. **5.** *Biol.* **a.** A group of cells that are similar in form or function. **b.** Cellular matter in general.

tit[1] (tĭt) ▸ *n.* **1.** A titmouse. **2.** Any of various similar small birds.

tit[2] (tĭt) ▸ *n.* A teat.

Ti·tan (tīt′n) ▸ *n.* **1.** *Gk. Myth.* One of a family of giants who were overthrown by the family of Zeus. **2. titan** A person of colossal size, strength, or achievement.

ti·tan·ic (tī-tăn′ĭk) ▸ *adj.* Of enormous size or strength; colossal. **—ti·tan′i·cal·ly** *adv.*

ti·ta·ni·um (tī-tā′nē-əm, tĭ-) ▸ *n. Symbol* **Ti** A strong, low-density, highly corrosion-resistant, lustrous white metallic element used to alloy metals for low weight, strength, and high-temperature stability. At. no. 22.

tithe (tīth) ▸ *n.* **1.** A tenth part of one's income, contributed esp. to a church. **2.** A tenth part. ▸ *v.* **tithed, tith·ing.** To pay a tithe. **—tith′er** *n.*

Ti·ti·ca·ca (tē′tē-kä′kä), **Lake** ▸ A freshwater lake of South America in the Andes on the Bolivia-Peru border.

tit·il·late (tĭt′l-āt′) ▸ *v.* **-lat·ed, -lat·ing.** To excite pleasurably; arouse. **—tit′il·lat′ing·ly** *adv.* **—tit′il·la′tion** *n.*

ti·tle (tīt′l) ▸ *n.* **1.** An identifying name given to a book, film, or other work. **2.** *Law* **a.** Just cause of possession or control. **b.** The evidence of a right of possession. **c.** The instrument, such as a deed, that constitutes this evidence. **3.** A claim or right. **4a.** A formal appellation, as of rank or office. **b.** Such an appellation used to indicate nobility. **5.** *Sports* A championship. ▸ *v.* **-tled, -tling.** To give a title to.

ti·tled (tīt′ld) ▸ *adj.* Having a title, esp. of nobility.

tit·mouse (tĭt′mous′) ▸ *n., pl.* **-mice** (-mīs′). A small grayish crested North American bird.

ti·tra·tion (tī-trā′shən) ▸ *n.* Determination of the concentration of a solute by measuring the amount of an added reagent needed to complete a reaction. **—ti′trate′** *v.*

tit·ter (tĭt′ər) ▸ *v.* To laugh in a restrained, nervous giggle. **—tit′ter** *n.*

tit·tle (tĭt′l) ▸ *n.* The tiniest bit; iota.

tit·u·lar (tĭch′ə-lər) ▸ *adj.* **1.** Of or constituting a title. **2.** In name only; nominal.

Ti·tus (tī′təs) ▸ *n.* See **Bible** table in Appendix.

tiz·zy (tĭz′ē) ▸ *n., pl.* **-zies.** *Slang* A state of nervous confusion; dither.

TKO ▸ *abbr.* technical knockout

Tl ▸ The symbol for the element **thallium.**

Tlin·git (tlĭng′gĭt, -kĭt, klĭng′kĭt) ▸ *n., pl.* **-git** or **-gits. 1.** A member of a Native American people of the coastal and island areas of SE Alaska. **2.** The language of the Tlingit.

Tm ▸ The symbol for the element **thulium.**

TM ▸ *abbr.* trademark

TN ▸ *abbr.* Tennessee

TNT (tē′ĕn-tē′) ▸ *n.* A yellow crystalline compound used as an explosive.

to (to͞o; *when unstressed* tə) ▸ *prep.* **1.** In a direction toward. **2.** Reaching as far as. **3.** Toward or reaching a given state. **4.** In contact with; against: *cheek to cheek.* **5.** In front of: *face to face.* **6.** For or of: *the top to the jar.* **7.** Concerning; regarding: *no answer to my letter.* **8.** In a relation with: *parallel to the road.* **9.** As an accompaniment for. **10.** Composing; constituting: *two cups to a pint.* **11.** In accord with: *not to my liking.* **12.** As compared with: *a book superior to his others.* **13a.** Before: *The time is ten to five.* **b.** Up till; until: *worked from nine to five.* **14.** For the purpose of: *went out to lunch.* **15.** Used before a verb to indicate the infinitive: *I'd like to go.* ▸ *adv.* **1.** Into a shut or closed position: *pushed the door to.* **2.** Into a state of consciousness: *The patient came to.* **3.** Into a state of action: *sat down for lunch and fell to.* **4.** *Naut.* Into the wind.

toad (tōd) ▸ *n.* A froglike, mostly land-dwelling amphibian with rough warty skin.

toad·stool (tōd′sto͞ol′) ▸ *n.* An inedible or poisonous mushroom.

THESAURUS

tip-off *n.* —*See* TIP[3].

tipple *v.* —*See* DRINK (2).

tippler *n.* —*See* DRUNKARD.

tipsiness *n.* —*See* DRUNKENNESS.

tipster *n.* —*See* INFORMER.

tipsy *adj.* —*See* DRUNK.

tiptop *adj.* —*See* EXCELLENT.

tirade *n.* A long, violent, or blustering speech, usually of censure or denunciation ▸ berating, diatribe, fulmination, harangue, jeremiad, onslaught, philippic, screed, tongue-lashing, upbraiding. [*Compare* VITUPERATION.]

tire *v.* **1.** To make weary ▸ drain, exhaust, fatigue, frazzle, jade, tire out, wear down, wear out, weary. *Informal:* knock out, tucker (out). *Slang:* do in, poop (out). *Idioms:* run ragged, take it out of. [*Compare* ENERVATE.] **2.** To grow weary ▸ burn out, droop, flag, give out, wear down, wear out, wilt. *Slang:* poop (out). [*Compare* COLLAPSE, FADE, LABOR.] —*See also* BORE[2].

tired *adj.* **1.** Depleted of energy ▸ bleary, dead, drained, exhausted, fatigued, jaded, rundown, spent, tired-out, wearied, weariful, weary, worn-down, worn-out. *Informal:* beat, bushed, knocked-out, tuckered (out). *Slang:* done in, pooped (out), wiped, wiped-out. *Idioms:* all in, ready to drop. **2.** Out of patience ▸ disgusted, fed up, sick, weary. *Idiom:* sick and tired. [*Compare* ANGRY.] —*See also* TRITE.

tiredness *n.* —*See* EXHAUSTION.

tired-out *adj.* —*See* TIRED (1).

tireless *adj.* Having or showing a capacity for protracted effort, regardless of difficulty or frustration ▸ indefatigable, inexhaustible, unfailing, unflagging, untiring, unwearied, unwearying, weariless. [*Compare* FIRM, STUBBORN.]

tiresome *adj.* —*See* BORING.

tiring *adj.* Causing fatigue ▸ draining, exhausting, fatiguing, wearing, wearying. [*Compare* BURDENSOME.]

tissue *n.* —*See* COMPLEX (1).

titan *n.* —*See* GIANT.

titanic *adj.* —*See* ENORMOUS.

tit for tat *n.* —*See* RETALIATION.

tithe *n.* —*See* TAX.

title *n.* A right or legal share in something ▸ claim, interest, portion, stake. [*Compare* CUT, RIGHT.] —*See also* CLAIM (1), NAME (1), OWNERSHIP, PUBLICATION (2).

title *v.* —*See* CALL, NAME (1).

titleholder *n.* —*See* OWNER, WINNER.

titter *v.* —*See* LAUGH.

titter *n.* —*See* LAUGH.

tittle *n.* —*See* BIT[1] (1).

tittle-tattle *n.* —*See* GOSSIP (1).

tittle-tattle *v.* —*See* GOSSIP.

tizzy *n.* —*See* STATE (2).

toad·y (tō′dē) ▸ *n., pl.* **-ies.** A servile flatterer; sycophant. ▸ *v.* **-ied, -y·ing.** To be a toady to.
toast[1] (tōst) ▸ *v.* **1.** To heat and brown (e.g., bread). **2.** To warm thoroughly. ▸ *n.* Sliced bread heated and browned.
toast[2] (tōst) ▸ *n.* **1.** The act of raising a glass and drinking in honor of a person or thing. **2.** The person or thing honored in this way. ▸ *v.* To drink to or propose a toast (to).
toast·er (tō′stər) ▸ *n.* A mechanical device used to toast bread.
toast·y (tō′stē) ▸ *adj.* **-i·er, -i·est.** Pleasantly warm.
to·bac·co (tə-băk′ō) ▸ *n., pl.* **-cos** or **-coes. 1.** A plant native to tropical America, having broad leaves used chiefly for smoking. **2.** The leaves of this plant processed chiefly for use in cigarettes, cigars, snuff, or pipes. **3.** Such products collectively.
to·bac·co·nist (tə-băk′ə-nĭst) ▸ *n.* A dealer in tobacco and smoking supplies.
To·ba·go (tə-bā′gō) ▸ An island of Trinidad and Tobago in the SE West Indies NE of Trinidad.
To·bit (tō′bĭt) ▸ *n.* See **Bible** table in Appendix.
to·bog·gan (tə-bŏg′ən) ▸ *n.* A long, narrow, runnerless sled constructed of thin boards curled upward at the front end. ▸ *v.* **1.** To travel on a toboggan. **2.** *Slang* To decline or fall rapidly. **—to·bog′gan·er, to·bog′gan·ist** *n.*
toc·ca·ta (tə-kä′tə) ▸ *n. Mus.* A virtuoso, freestyle composition, usu. for the organ, with brilliant runs and scales.
toc·sin (tŏk′sĭn) ▸ *n.* A warning bell.
to·day (tə-dā′) ▸ *n.* The present day, time, or age. ▸ *adv.* **1.** During or on the present day. **2.** At the present time.
tod·dle (tŏd′l) ▸ *v.* **-dled, -dling.** To walk with short unsteady steps. **—tod′dler** *n.*
to-do (tə-dōō′) ▸ *n., pl.* **-dos** (-dōōz′). *Informal* A commotion or stir.
toe (tō) ▸ *n.* **1.** One of the digits of the foot. **2.** The forward part of something worn on the foot. **3.** Something resembling a toe in form, function, or location. ▸ *v.* **toed, toe·ing.** To touch, kick, or reach with the toe.
toe·a (toi′ə) ▸ *n., pl.* **toea.** See **currency** table in Appendix.
toed (tōd) ▸ *adj.* Having a toe, esp. of a specified number or kind: *an even-toed ungulate.*
toe·hold (tō′hōld′) ▸ *n.* **1.** A space to support the toe in climbing. **2.** A slight or initial advantage.
toe·nail (tō′nāl′) ▸ *n.* The nail on a toe.
tof·fee (tô′fē, tŏf′ē) ▸ *n.* A chewy candy of brown sugar or molasses and butter.
to·fu (tō′fōō) ▸ *n.* A protein-rich food made from an extract of soybeans and used in salads and cooked foods.
tog (tŏg, tôg) *Informal* ▸ *n.* **togs** Clothes. ▸ *v.* **togged, tog·ging.** To dress or clothe.
to·ga (tō′gə) ▸ *n.* A loose one-piece outer garment worn in public by male citizens in ancient Rome. **—to′gaed** (tō′gəd) *adj.*
to·geth·er (tə-gĕ*th*′ər) ▸ *adv.* **1.** In or into a single group or place. **2.** In or into contact. **3a.** In relationship to one another. **b.** By joint or cooperative effort. **4.** Regarded collectively. **5.** Simultaneously. **6.** In harmony or accord. **—to·geth′er·ness** *n.*
tog·gle switch (tŏg′əl) ▸ *n.* A switch in which a projecting lever with a spring is used to open or close an electric circuit.
To·go (tō′gō′) ▸ A country of W Africa on the Gulf of Guinea.
To·ho·no O'o·dham (tō-hō′no ō′ə-däm) ▸ *n., pl.* **-dham** or **-dhams.** See **Papago.**
toil[1] (toil) ▸ *v.* **1.** To work strenuously. **2.** To proceed with difficulty. ▸ *n.* Exhausting labor or effort. **—toil′er** *n.*
toil[2] (toil) ▸ *n.* often **toils** Something that entangles: *in the toils of despair.*
toi·let (toi′lĭt) ▸ *n.* **1a.** A disposal fixture for defecation and urination. **b.** A room or booth containing such a fixture. **2.** The act of dressing or grooming oneself.
toilet paper ▸ *n.* Thin absorbent paper for cleaning oneself after defecation or urination.
toi·let·ry (toi′lĭ-trē) ▸ *n., pl.* **-ries.** An article used in personal grooming or dressing.
toi·lette (twä-lĕt′) ▸ *n.* **1.** The process of dressing or grooming oneself; toilet. **2.** A person's dress or style of dress.
toilet water ▸ *n.* A scented liquid with a high alcohol content used in bathing or applied as a skin freshener.
to·ken (tō′kən) ▸ *n.* **1.** Something serving as an indication or representation; sign. **2.** Something that signifies or evidences authority, validity, or identity. **3.** One that represents a group. **4.** A keepsake. **5.** A piece of stamped metal used as a substitute for currency. ▸ *adj.* Done as an indication or a pledge: *a token payment.*
to·ken·ism (tō′kə-nĭz′əm) ▸ *n.* Symbolic gestures rather than effective action toward a goal.
To·ky·o (tō′kē-ō′, -kyō) ▸ The capital of Japan, in E-central Honshu on **Tokyo Bay,** an inlet of the Pacific.
told (tōld) ▸ *v.* P.t. and p.part. of **tell.**
tol·er·a·ble (tŏl′ər-ə-bəl) ▸ *adj.* **1.** Capable of being tolerated; endurable. **2.** Fairly good; passable. **—tol′er·a·bil′i·ty, tol′er·a·ble·ness** *n.* **—tol′er·a·bly** *adv.*
tol·er·ance (tŏl′ər-əns) ▸ *n.* **1.** The capacity for respecting the beliefs or practices of others. **2.** Leeway for variation from a standard. **3.** The capacity to endure hardship or pain. **4.** Resistance, as to a drug. **—tol′er·ant** *adj.* **—tol′er·ant·ly** *adv.*
tol·er·ate (tŏl′ə-rāt′) ▸ *v.* **-at·ed, -at·ing. 1.** To allow without prohibiting or opposing; permit. **2.** To recognize and respect (the rights, beliefs, or practices of others). **3.** To put up with; endure. **—tol′er·a′tion** *n.*
Tol·kien (tōl′kēn′, tŏl′-), **J(ohn) R(onald) R(euel)** (1892–1973) ▸ British writer.
toll[1] (tōl) ▸ *n.* **1.** A fixed tax for a privilege, esp. for passage across a bridge. **2.** A charge for a service, such as a long-distance telephone call. **3.** The amount or extent of loss or destruction, as in a disaster.

THESAURUS

toady *n.* —*See* SYCOPHANT.
toady *v.* —*See* FAWN.
to-and-fro *n.* —*See* HESITATION.
toast[1] *v.* —*See* COOK.
toast *n.* *Slang* One that is ruined or doomed ▸ dead duck, dead meat, goner. [*Compare* THROUGH.]
toast[2] *n.* The act of drinking to someone ▸ health, pledge
toast *v.* —*See* DRINK (4).
today *n.* —*See* NOW.
today *adv.* At the present; these days ▸ now, nowadays. *Idioms:* in our time, in this day and age.
toddle *v.* —*See* STROLL.
toddler *n.* —*See* BABY (1).
to-do *n.* —*See* AGITATION (1), SENSATION (2).
toehold *n.* A place providing support for the foot in climbing ▸ foothold, footing, perch, purchase. —*See also* ADVANTAGE (1).
tog *v.* —*See* DRESS (1).
together *adv.* **1.** In, into, or as a single body ▸ jointly. *Idioms:* all together, as one, in one breath, in the same breath, in unison, with one accord, with one voice. **2.** At the same time ▸ concurrently, simultaneously, synchronously. *Idioms:* all at once, all together.
together *adj.* *Slang* In a state of preparedness ▸ prepared, ready, set. *Informal:* go. *Idioms:* all set, in working order, on deck, ready (*or* raring) to go.
togs *n.* —*See* DRESS (1).
toil *v.* —*See* LABOR, TRUDGE.
toil *n.* —*See* LABOR.
toiler *n.* —*See* LABORER.
toilette *n.* —*See* DRESS (2).
token *n.* An object or expression associated with and serving to identify something else ▸ attribute, emblem, metaphor, signifier, symbol. [*Compare* TERM.] —*See also* EXPRESSION (2), PAWN[1], REMEMBRANCE (1), SIGN (1).
tolerable *adj.* —*See* ACCEPTABLE (2), AVERAGE, BEARABLE.
tolerance *n.* Forbearing or lenient treatment ▸ charitableness, charity, forbearance, indulgence, lenience, leniency, lenity, permissiveness, toleration. [*Compare* FORGIVENESS.] —*See also* PATIENCE.
tolerant *adj.* Not strict or severe ▸ charitable, clement, easy, forbearing, indulgent, lax, lenient, merciful, permissive, soft. —*See also* BROAD-MINDED, PATIENT.
tolerate *v.* —*See* ENDURE (1), PERMIT (1).
toleration *n.* —*See* TOLERANCE.
toll[1] *n.* **1.** A fixed amount of money charged for a privilege or service ▸ charge, dues, exaction, exactment, fare, fee, rate, tariff, tax. [*Compare* COST.] **2.** The expenditure at which

toll² (tōl) ► *v.* **1.** To sound (a large bell) slowly at regular intervals. **2.** To announce or summon by tolling. ► *n.* The sound of a bell being struck.

toll·booth (tōl′bo͞oth′) ► *n.* A booth where a toll is collected.

toll·gate (tōl′gāt′) ► *n.* A gate barring passage until a toll is collected.

Tol·stoy (tōl′stoi, tŏl′-), Count **Leo** (1828–1910) ► Russian writer.

Tol·tec (tōl′tĕk′, tŏl′-) ► *n., pl.* **-tec** or **-tecs.** A member of a Nahuatl-speaking people of central and S Mexico whose empire flourished from the 10th to the 12th cent. **—Tol′tec, Tol′tec′an** *adj.*

tom (tŏm) ► *n.* The male of various animals, esp. a cat or turkey.

tom·a·hawk (tŏm′ə-hôk′) ► *n.* A light ax formerly used as a tool or weapon by certain Native American peoples. **—tom′a·hawk′** *v.*

to·ma·to (tə-mā′tō, -mä′-) ► *n., pl.* **-toes. 1.** A fleshy, smooth-skinned reddish fruit, eaten as a vegetable. **2.** A plant bearing such fruit.

tomb (to͞om) ► *n.* **1.** A place of burial. **2.** A vault or chamber for burial of the dead.

tom·boy (tŏm′boi′) ► *n.* A girl considered boyish or masculine in behavior or manner.

tomb·stone (to͞om′stōn′) ► *n.* A gravestone.

tom·cat (tŏm′kăt′) ► *n.* A male cat.

tome (tōm) ► *n.* A book, esp. a large or scholarly one.

tom·fool·er·y (tŏm-fo͞o′lə-rē) ► *n., pl.* **-ies. 1.** Foolish behavior. **2.** Nonsense.

to·mog·ra·phy (tō-mŏg′rə-fē) ► *n.* A technique for making detailed x-rays of a predetermined plane section of a solid object. **—to′mo·gram′** (tō′mə-grăm′) *n.* **—to′mo·graph′** *n.* **—to′mo·graph′ic** *adj.*

to·mor·row (tə-môr′ō, -mŏr′ō) ► *n.* **1.** The day following today. **2.** The near future. ► *adv.* On or for the day following today.

tom-tom (tŏm′tŏm′) ► *n.* Any of various small-headed drums that are beaten with the hands.

-tomy ► *suff.* Cutting; incision: *lobotomy.*

ton (tŭn) ► *n.* **1a.** A short ton. **b.** A long ton. **c.** A metric ton. **2.** *Informal* A very large quantity: *tons of fan mail.*

to·nal·i·ty (tō-năl′ĭ-tē) ► *n., pl.* **-ties.** *Mus.* The arrangement of the tones and chords of a composition in relation to a tonic.

tone (tōn) ► *n.* **1.** *Mus.* **a.** A sound of distinct pitch, quality, and duration; note. **b.** The largest interval between adjacent notes in the diatonic scale. **2.** The quality of sound. **3.** The pitch of a word or phrase. **4.** Manner of expression: *an angry tone of voice.* **5.** A general quality or atmosphere: *a room with an elegant tone.* **6a.** A color or shade of color. **b.** Quality of color. **7.** *Physiol.* **a.** The tension in resting muscles. **b.** Normal tissue firmness. ► *v.* **toned, ton·ing. 1.** To give a particular tone or inflection to. **2.** *Physiol.* To give tone to. ***—phrasal verbs:* tone down** To make less harsh or severe; moderate. **tone up** To make or become brighter or more vigorous. **—ton′al** *adj.* **—ton′al·ly** *adv.*

tone arm ► *n.* The arm of a phonograph turntable that holds the cartridge.

ton·er (tō′nər) ► *n.* One that tones, esp. a powdery ink that is used dry or is suspended in a liquid to produce a photocopy.

Ton·ga (tŏng′gə) ► A country in the SW Pacific E of Fiji comprising about 150 islands. **—Ton′gan** *adj. & n.*

tongs (tôngz, tŏngz) ► *pl.n. (takes sing. or pl. v.)* A grasping device consisting of two arms joined at one end by a pivot or hinge.

tongue (tŭng) ► *n.* **1.** The fleshy, movable, muscular organ in the mouth that functions in tasting, chewing, swallowing, and speech. **2.** The tongue of an animal, such as a cow, used as food. **3.** A spoken language. **4.** Quality of utterance: *his sharp tongue.* **5.** Anything resembling a tongue in shape or function.

tongue-in-cheek (tŭng′ĭn-chēk′) ► *adj.* Meant ironically or facetiously.

tongue-tied (tŭng′tīd′) ► *adj.* Speechless or confused in expression, as from shyness, embarrassment, or astonishment.

tongue twister ► *n.* **1.** A word or group of words difficult to articulate rapidly. **2.** Something difficult to pronounce.

ton·ic (tŏn′ĭk) ► *n.* **1.** An invigorating, refreshing, or restorative agent or influence. **2.** *Regional* See **soft drink. 3.** *Mus.* The first note of a diatonic scale; keynote. ► *adj.* **1.** Stimulating physical or mental vigor. **2.** *Mus.* Of or based on the tonic or keynote.

to·night (tə-nīt′) ► *adv.* On or during the present or coming night. ► *n.* This night or the night of this day.

Ton·kin (tŏn′kĭn′, tŏng′-) ► A historical region of SE Asia on the **Gulf of Tonkin,** an arm of the South China Sea, now forming most of N Vietnam.

ton·nage (tŭn′ĭj) ► *n.* **1.** The number of tons of water a ship displaces when afloat. **2.** The capacity of a merchant ship in units of 100 cu. ft. **3.** A charge per ton on cargo. **4.** The total shipping of a country or port, figured in tons. **5.** Weight measured in tons.

ton·sil (tŏn′səl) ► *n.* A mass of lymphoid tissue, esp. either of two such masses embedded at the back of the mouth. **—ton′sil·lar** *adj.*

ton·sil·lec·to·my (tŏn′sə-lĕk′tə-mē) ► *n., pl.* **-mies.** Surgical removal of tonsils or a tonsil.

ton·sil·li·tis (tŏn′sə-lī′tĭs) ► *n.* Inflammation of the tonsils. **—ton′sil·lit′ic** (-lĭt′ĭk) *adj.*

ton·so·ri·al (tŏn-sôr′ē-əl) ► *adj.* Of barbering or a barber.

ton·sure (tŏn′shər) ► *n.* **1.** The act of shaving the head, esp. as a preliminary to becoming a priest. **2.** The part of the head so shaved. ► *v.* **-sured, -sur·ing.** To shave the head of.

ton·y (tō′nē) ► *adj.* **-i·er, -i·est.** *Informal* Expensive, luxurious, or exclusive.

too (to͞o) ► *adv.* **1.** In addition; also. **2.** More than enough; excessively: *She worries too much.* **3.** *Informal* Indeed; so: *You will too do it!*

took (to͝ok) ► *v.* P.t. of **take.**

tool (to͞ol) ► *n.* **1.** A device, such as a saw, used to perform manual or mechanical work. **2.** A machine, such as a lathe, used to cut and shape machine parts. **3.** A means or instrument. **4.** *Comp. Sci.* An application program, esp. one that creates or edits other programs. **5.** A dupe. ► *v.* **1.** To form, work, or decorate with a tool. **2.** *Slang* To drive or ride in a vehicle. ***—phrasal verb:* tool up** To furnish tools or machinery for (an industry or factory).

tool·bar (to͞ol′bär′) ► *n.* A row of icons on a computer screen for activating commands or functions.

toot (to͞ot) ► *v.* To sound a horn or whistle in short blasts.

THESAURUS

something is obtained ► cost, expense, price, sacrifice. *Informal:* damage.

toll² *v.* *—See* RING².

tomb *n.* *—See* GRAVE¹.

tome *n.* *—See* BOOK.

tomfoolery *n.* *—See* FOOLISHNESS, MISCHIEF, NONSENSE.

tomorrow *n.* Time that is yet to be ► by-and-by, future, futurity, hereafter. *Idiom:* time to come. [*Compare* APPROACH, POSSIBILITY.]

ton *n.* *—See* HEAP (2).

tonality *n.* The distinct quality or character of a sound ► timbre, tone, tone color.

tone *n.* **1.** The distinct quality or character of a sound ► timbre, tonality, tone color. **2.** An expressive vocal quality ► accent, edge, inflection, intonation, lilt, pitch, resonance, sonority, sonorousness. *Idiom:* tone of voice. *—See also* AIR (3), COLOR (1), STYLE, TEMPER (3).

tone down *v.* *Informal* To make less emphatic or obvious ► de-emphasize, mute, play down, soft-pedal. [*Compare* MODERATE.] *—See also* MODERATE (1).

tongue *n.* *—See* LANGUAGE (1).

tongue-lashing *n.* *—See* TIRADE.

tongueless or **tongue-tied** *adj.* *—See* MUTE.

tonic *n.* An agent, such as a medicine or drink, that restores vigor or energy ► energizer, restorative, roborant, stimulant. *Informal:* bracer, pick-me-up. *Idiom:* shot in the arm. [*Compare* CURE, DRUG.]

tonic *adj.* *—See* INVIGORATING.

tony *adj.* *—See* EXCLUSIVE (3).

too *adv.* *—See* ADDITIONALLY.

tool *n.* A device used to do work or perform a task ► implement, instrument, utensil. [*Compare* AGENT, DEVICE, GADGET.] *—See also* DUPE, PAWN².

tool *v.* *—See* DRIVE (1).

▸ *n.* A blast, as of a horn. **—toot′er** *n.*

tooth (to͞oth) ▸ *n., pl.* **teeth** (tēth). **1.** One of a set of hard, bonelike structures rooted in sockets in the jaws, used to bite and chew. **2.** A projecting part resembling a tooth in shape or function, as on a comb. ***—idiom:* to the teeth** Lacking nothing; completely: *armed to the teeth.* **—toothed** *adj.* **—tooth′less** *adj.*

tooth·ache (to͞oth′āk′) ▸ *n.* An aching pain in or near a tooth.

tooth·brush (to͞oth′brŭsh′) ▸ *n.* A brush for cleaning teeth.

tooth·paste (to͞oth′pāst′) ▸ *n.* A paste for cleaning teeth.

tooth·pick (to͞oth′pĭk′) ▸ *n.* A small stick for removing food from between the teeth.

tooth·some (to͞oth′səm) ▸ *adj.* Delicious; luscious. **—tooth′some·ness** *n.*

top[1] (tŏp) ▸ *n.* **1.** The uppermost part, point, surface, or end. **2.** A lid or cap. **3a.** The highest position or rank. **b.** The highest degree or pitch; acme; zenith. ▸ *v.* **topped, top·ping. 1.** To form, furnish with, or serve as a top. **2.** To reach or go over the top of. **3.** To exceed or surpass. ***—idioms:* off the top of (one's) head** *Informal* In an impromptu way. **on top of** *Informal* **1.** In control of. **2.** Fully informed about. **3.** In addition to. **4.** Following closely on.

top[2] (tŏp) ▸ *n.* A toy made to spin on the pointed end.

to·paz (tō′păz′) ▸ *n.* **1.** A mineral consisting largely of aluminum silicate and valued as a gem. **2.** Any of various yellow gemstones, esp. a yellow variety of sapphire.

top·coat (tŏp′kōt′) ▸ *n.* A lightweight overcoat.

top dog ▸ *n. Slang* One who has the dominant position or highest authority.

top-drawer (tŏp′drôr′) ▸ *adj.* Of the highest importance, rank, or merit.

To·pe·ka (tə-pē′kə) ▸ The capital of KS, in the NE part W of Kansas City.

top·er (tō′pər) ▸ *n.* A chronic drinker.

top·flight (tŏp′flīt′) ▸ *adj. Informal* First-rate; excellent.

top hat ▸ *n.* A man's formal hat with a narrow brim and a tall cylindrical crown.

top-heav·y (tŏp′hĕv′ē) ▸ *adj.* Likely to topple because overloaded at the top.

to·pi·ar·y (tō′pē-ĕr′ē) ▸ *n., pl.* **-ies. 1.** The art of trimming live shrubs or trees into decorative shapes. **2.** A plant so trimmed.

top·ic (tŏp′ĭk) ▸ *n.* The subject of a speech, essay, thesis, or conversation.

top·i·cal (tŏp′ĭ-kəl) ▸ *adj.* **1.** Local. **2.** Currently of interest; contemporary. **3.** *Medic.* Of or applied to a localized area of the body. **—top′i·cal′i·ty** (-kăl′ĭ-tē) *n.* **—top′i·cal·ly** *adv.*

top·knot (tŏp′nŏt′) ▸ *n.* **1.** A crest or knot of hair or feathers on the crown of the head. **2.** A decorative ribbon or bow worn as a headdress.

top·less (tŏp′lĭs) ▸ *adj.* **1.** Having no top. **2.** Not covering the breasts.

top·most (tŏp′mōst′) ▸ *adj.* Highest; uppermost.

top-notch or **top·notch** (tŏp′nŏch′) ▸ *adj. Informal* First-rate; excellent.

topo– ▸ *pref.* Place: *topography.*

to·pog·ra·phy (tə-pŏg′rə-fē) ▸ *n.* **1.** The physical features of a region. **2.** Detailed description or representation of such features. **—to·pog′ra·pher** *n.* **—top′o·graph′ic** (tŏp′ə-grăf′ĭk), **top′o·graph′i·cal** *adj.* **—top′o·graph′i·cal·ly** *adv.*

top·ping (tŏp′ĭng) ▸ *n.* A sauce, frosting, or garnish for food.

top·ple (tŏp′əl) ▸ *v.* **-pled, -pling. 1.** To push or throw over; overturn. **2.** To totter and fall.

tops (tŏps) ▸ *adj. Slang* First-rate; excellent.

top·sail (tŏp′səl, -sāl′) ▸ *n. Naut.* A square sail set above the lowest sail on the mast of a square-rigged ship.

top-se·cret (tŏp′sē′krĭt) ▸ *adj.* Of the highest level of security classification.

top·side (tŏp′sīd′) ▸ *adv. & adj.* On or to the upper parts of a ship; on deck.

top·soil (tŏp′soil′) ▸ *n.* The upper part of soil.

top·sy-tur·vy (tŏp′sē-tûr′vē) ▸ *adv.* **1.** Upside-down. **2.** In utter disorder or confusion. ▸ *adj.* In a disordered state. **—top′sy-tur′vi·ly** *adv.* **—top′sy-tur′vi·ness** *n.*

toque (tōk) ▸ *n.* A woman's small, brimless, close-fitting hat.

tor (tôr) ▸ *n.* A rocky peak or hill.

To·rah also **to·rah** (tôr′ə) ▸ *n. Judaism* **1.** The entire body of religious law and learning. **2.** The first five books of the Hebrew Scriptures. See **Bible** table in Appendix. **3.** The scroll on which these scriptures are written, used in a synagogue during services.

torch (tôrch) ▸ *n.* **1a.** A portable light produced by the flame of a burning material wound about the end of a stick. **b.** *Chiefly Brit.* A flashlight. **2.** Something that serves to illuminate or guide. **3.** *Slang* An arsonist. **4.** A portable apparatus that produces a very hot flame by the combustion of gases, used in welding. ▸ *v. Slang* To set on fire.

tore (tôr) ▸ *v.* P.t. of **tear**[1].

tor·e·a·dor (tôr′ē-ə-dôr′) ▸ *n.* A bullfighter.

tor·ment (tôr′mĕnt′) ▸ *n.* **1.** Great physical pain or mental anguish. **2.** A source of harassment or pain. ▸ *v.* (tôr-mĕnt′, tôr′mĕnt′) **1.** To cause to undergo torment. **2.** To pester; annoy. **—tor·ment′ing·ly** *adv.* **—tor·men′tor, tor·ment′er** *n.*

torn (tôrn) ▸ *v.* P.part. of **tear**[1].

tor·na·do (tôr-nā′dō) ▸ *n., pl.* **-does** or **-dos.** A rotating column of air, usu. accompanied by a funnel-shaped downward extension of a cumulonimbus cloud and moving destructively over a narrow path.

To·ron·to (tə-rŏn′tō) ▸ The capital of Ontario, Canada, in the S part on Lake Ontario.

tor·pe·do (tôr-pē′dō) ▸ *n., pl.* **-does. 1.** A cigar-shaped, self-propelled underwater projectile, designed to detonate on contact with or in the vicinity of a target. **2.** Any of various explosive devices. ▸ *v.* **-doed, -do·ing.** To attack or destroy with or as if with a torpedo.

tor·pid (tôr′pĭd) ▸ *adj.* **1.** Deprived of the power of motion or feeling. **2.** Dormant; hibernating. **3.** Lethargic; apathetic. **—tor·pid′i·ty** *n.*

tor·por (tôr′pər) ▸ *n.* **1.** A state of inactivity or insensibility.

THESAURUS

tooth *n.* —*See* SPIKE.

toothed *adj.* —*See* SAW-TOOTHED.

toothsome *adj.* —*See* DELICIOUS.

top *n.* Something that covers, especially to prevent contents from spilling ▸ cap, cover, covering, lid [*Compare* PLUG.] —*See also* BEST (1), CLIMAX, MAXIMUM.

top *adj.* Of, being, located at, or forming the top ▸ highest, loftiest, topmost, upmost, uppermost. [*Compare* CLIMACTIC.] —*See also* BEST (1), EXCELLENT, MAXIMUM, PRIMARY (1).

top *v.* To put a topping on ▸ cap, crest, crown, tip, top off. [*Compare* COVER.] —*See also* CLIMAX, SURPASS.

top off *v.* —*See* FILL (1).

top-drawer *adj.* —*See* CHOICE (1).

toper *n.* —*See* DRUNKARD.

topflight *adj.* —*See* EXCELLENT.

topic *n.* —*See* SUBJECT.

topical *adj.* Of, constituting, or relating to a theme or themes ▸ motivic, thematic. —*See also* CONTEMPORARY (2).

topmost *adj.* Of, being, located at, or forming the top ▸ highest, loftiest, top, upmost, uppermost [*Compare* CLIMACTIC.] —*See also* MAXIMUM.

topnotch *adj.* —*See* EXCELLENT.

topography *n.* The character, natural features, and configuration of land ▸ terrain. *Idiom:* the lay of the land.

topple *v.* To undergo capture, defeat, or ruin ▸ collapse, fall, go down, go under. [*Compare* SUCCUMB, SURRENDER.] *See also* FALL (2), OVERTHROW, OVERTURN.

top secret *n.* —*See* CONFIDENTIAL (3).

topsy-turviness *n.* —*See* DISORDER (1), DISORDERLINESS.

topsy-turvy *adj.* —*See* CONFUSED (2), UPSIDE-DOWN.

torch *v.* —*See* BURN (1), LIGHT[1] (1).

torment *v.* **1.** To subject another to extreme physical cruelty, as in punishing ▸ crucify, harrow, rack, torture. *Idioms:* put on the rack (*or* wheel), put the screws to. [*Compare* PUNISH.] **2.** To come to mind continually ▸ haunt, obsess, trouble, weigh on (*or* upon). —*See also* AFFLICT, HARASS.

torment *n.* —*See* ANNOYANCE (2), DISTRESS, GRIEF, HELL.

tormenting *adj.* Extraordinarily painful or distressing ▸ agonizing, anguishing, atrocious, excruciating, harrowing, torturous. [*Compare* BITTER, TERRIBLE, UNBEARABLE.]

tormentor *n.* —*See* BULLY.

torpedo *v.* —*See* DESTROY (1).

torpid *adj.* —*See* DEAD (2), LATENT, LETHARGIC.

torpor or **torpidity** *n.* —*See* LETHARGY.

2. Lethargy; apathy. **—tor′po·rif′ic** (-pə-rĭf′ĭk) *adj.*
torque (tôrk) ► *n.* The tendency of a force to produce rotation about an axis. **—torque** *v.*
tor·rent (tôr′ənt, tŏr′-) ► *n.* 1. A turbulent, swift-flowing stream. 2. A deluge. 3. An overwhelming outpouring; flood. **—tor·ren′tial** (tô-rĕn′shəl, tə-) *adj.*
tor·rid (tôr′ĭd, tŏr′-) ► *adj.* **-er, -est.** 1. Very dry and hot. 2. Passionate. **—tor·rid′i·ty, tor′rid·ness** *n.* **—tor′rid·ly** *adv.*
Torrid Zone ► The central latitude zone of the earth, between the tropic of Cancer and the tropic of Capricorn.
tor·sion (tôr′shən) ► *n.* 1. A twisting or turning. 2. The stress caused when one end of an object is twisted in one direction and the other end is held motionless. **—tor′sion·al** *adj.*
tor·so (tôr′sō) ► *n., pl.* **-sos.** The trunk of the human body.
tort (tôrt) ► *n. Law* Any wrongful act that does not involve a breach of contract and for which a civil suit can be brought.
torte (tôrt, tôr′tə) ► *n.* A rich cake made with many eggs, flour, and usu. chopped nuts.
tor·til·la (tôr-tē′yə) ► *n.* A thin disk of unleavened bread made from cornmeal or wheat flour.
tor·toise (tôr′tĭs) ► *n.* Any of various terrestrial turtles.
tor·toise·shell (tôr′tĭs-shĕl′) ► *n.* The translucent brownish outer covering of certain turtles, used to make combs and jewelry.
Tor·to·la (tôr-tō′lə) ► An island of the British Virgin Is. in the West Indies E of Puerto Rico.
Tor·tu·ga (tôr-to͞o′gə) ► An island in the West Indies off N Haiti.
tor·tu·ous (tôr′cho͞o-əs) ► *adj.* 1. Winding or twisting. 2. Not straightforward; devious. 3. Complex. **—tor′tu·ous·ly** *adv.* **—tor′tu·ous·ness** *n.*
tor·ture (tôr′chər) ► *n.* 1. Infliction of severe pain as a means of punishment or coercion. 2. Pain or mental anguish. ► *v.* **-tured, -tur·ing.** 1. To subject to torture. 2. To afflict with great pain or anguish. 3. To twist or distort. **—tor′tur·er** *n.* **—tor′tur·ous** *adj.* **—tor′tur·ous·ly** *adv.*
To·ry (tôr′ē) ► *n., pl.* **-ries.** 1. A member of the Conservative Party in Great Britain. 2. An American who favored the British side during the American Revolution. **—To′ry** *adj.* **—To′ry·ism** *n.*
toss (tôs, tŏs) ► *v.* 1. To throw lightly. 2. To throw or be thrown to and fro. 3. To mix (a salad). 4. To move or lift (the head) with a sudden motion. 5. To flip (a coin) to decide something. ► *n.* 1. An act of tossing. 2. An abrupt upward movement, as of the head.
toss·up (tôs′ŭp′, tŏs′-) ► *n. Informal* An even chance or choice.
tot[1] (tŏt) ► *n.* 1. A small child. 2. A small amount.
tot[2] (tŏt) ► *v.* **tot·ted, tot·ting.** To total: *totted up the bill.*
to·tal (tōt′l) ► *n.* 1. An amount obtained by addition; sum. 2. A whole quantity; entirety. ► *adj.* 1. Constituting the whole; entire. 2. Complete; utter. ► *v.* **-taled, -tal·ing** or **-talled, -tal·ling.** 1. To determine the sum of. 2. To amount to. 3. *Slang* To destroy: *totaled the car.* **—to′tal·ly** *adv.*
to·tal·i·tar·i·an (tō-tăl′ĭ-târ′ē-ən) ► *adj.* Of or being a form of government in which the political authority exercises absolute control over all aspects of life and opposition is outlawed. ► *n.* A practitioner or supporter of such a government. **—to·tal′i·tar′i·an·ism** *n.*
to·tal·i·ty (tō-tăl′ĭ-tē) ► *n., pl.* **-ties.** 1. The quality or state of being total. 2. An aggregate amount.
tote (tōt) ► *v.* **tot·ed, tot·ing.** *Informal* To haul; lug.
to·tem (tō′təm) ► *n.* 1. *Anthro.* a. An animal, plant, or natural object serving as a emblem of a clan or family. b. A representation of this. 2. A venerated symbol. **—to·tem′ic** (-tĕm′ĭk) *adj.*
totem pole ► *n.* A post carved and painted with a series of family or clan crests, as among certain Native American peoples.
tot·ter (tŏt′ər) ► *v.* 1. To sway as if about to fall. 2. To walk unsteadily. **—tot′ter** *n.* **—tot′ter·y** *adj.*
tou·can (to͞o′kăn′, -kän′) ► *n.* A tropical American bird with brightly colored plumage and a very large bill.
touch (tŭch) ► *v.* 1. To cause or permit a part of the body, esp. the hand or fingers, to come in contact with so as to feel. 2. To be or bring into contact with. 3. To tap or nudge lightly. 4. To partake of: *didn't touch her food.* 5. To disturb or move by handling. 6a. To adjoin or border. b. To come up to; equal. 7. To treat briefly or allusively: *remarks touching recent events.* 8. To be pertinent to. 9. To affect emotionally; move. ***—phrasal verbs:*** **touch down** To land. **touch off** 1. To cause to explode. 2. To initiate; trigger. **touch up** To improve by making minor changes. ► *n.* 1. The act or an instance of touching. 2. The physiological sense by which bodily contact is perceived. 3. A sensation from a specific contact. 4. A light push; tap. 5. A mark or effect left by contact with something. 6. A small amount; trace. 7. A characteristic way of doing things. 8. A facility; knack. 9. Contact or communica-

THESAURUS

torrent *n.* —*See* FLOOD, OUTBURST, RAIN.
torrid *adj.* —*See* HOT (1), PASSIONATE.
torridity or **torridness** *n.* —*See* HEAT (1).
tort *n.* —*See* CRIME (1).
tortuous *adj.* —*See* COMPLEX (1), INDIRECT (1), WINDING.
torture *v.* To subject another to extreme physical cruelty, as in punishing ► crucify, harrow, rack, torment. ***Idioms:*** put on the rack (*or* wheel), put the screws to. [*Compare* PUNISH.] —*See also* AFFLICT.
torture *n.* —*See* DISTRESS, HELL.
torturous *adj.* —*See* TORMENTING.
Tory *n.* —*See* CONSERVATIVE.
Tory *adj.* —*See* CONSERVATIVE (1).
toss *v.* 1. To move vigorously from side to side or up and down ► heave, pitch, rock, roll. [*Compare* LURCH.] 2. To swing about or strike at wildly ► flail, thrash, thresh. ***Idiom:*** toss and turn. [*Compare* STAGGER, SWAY.] 3. To twist agitatedly, as in pain, struggle, or embarrassment ► squirm, twist, writhe. [*Compare* SHAKE.] 4. To throw a coin in order to decide something ► flip. ***Idiom:*** call heads or tails. —*See also* AGITATE (2), DISCARD, THROW.
toss around *v.* —*See* DISCUSS.
toss back or **down** *v.* —*See* DRINK (1).
toss *n.* —*See* THROW.
tot[1] *n.* —*See* BABY (1), CHILD (1), DRINK (2), DROP (4).
tot[2] *v.* —*See* ADD.
total *n.* A number or quantity obtained as a result of addition ► aggregate, amount, sum, summation, sum total, totality. [*Compare* ACCOUNT, COUNT.] —*See also* WHOLE.
total *adj.* —*See* COMPLETE (1), GENERAL (1), UTTER[2].
total *v.* —*See* ADD, AMOUNT, CRASH, DESTROY (1).
totalitarian *adj.* —*See* ABSOLUTE, AUTHORITARIAN.
totalitarian *n.* —*See* AUTHORITARIAN, DICTATOR.
totalitarianism *n.* —*See* ABSOLUTISM (1), TYRANNY.
totality *n.* —*See* COMPLETENESS, SYSTEM, TOTAL, WHOLE.
totalization *n.* The act or process of adding ► addition, summation. [*Compare* CALCULATION.]
totalize *v.* —*See* ADD.
totally *adv.* —*See* COMPLETELY (1).
tote *v.* —*See* CARRY (1).
tote *n.* —*See* BAG.
totter *v.* —*See* STAGGER (1), SWAY.
tottering or **tottery** *adj.* —*See* INSECURE (2).
touch *v.* To bring especially the hands or fingers into contact with ► feel, finger, handle, manipulate, palpate, press, stroke. [*Compare* CARESS, BRUSH[1], RUB.] —*See also* ADJOIN, EQUAL (1), MOVE (1).
touch down *v.* —*See* LAND (2).
touch off *v.* —*See* CAUSE, EXPLODE (1), LIGHT[1] (1), PROVOKE.
touch on or **upon** *v.* —*See* REFER (1).
touch up *v.* To improve by making minor changes or additions ► polish, remodel, retouch. [*Compare* FIX, RENEW.]
touch *n.* 1. An act of touching ► feel, feeling, manipulation, palpation, stroke. 2. A coming together so as to be touching ► contact, contingence. 3. The faculty or ability to perceive tactile stimulation ► feel, feeling, tactility. ***Idiom:*** sense of touch. [*Compare* SENSATION.] 4. A particular sensation conveyed by means of physical contact ► feel, feeling. [*Compare* CONTACT, BRUSH.] 5. A situation allowing exchange of ideas or messages ► communication, contact, correspondence, intercommunication. [*Compare* COM-

tion: *Please keep in touch.* **—touch′a·ble** *adj.*

touch-and-go (tŭch′ən-gō′) ▸ *adj.* Precarious and uncertain in nature or outcome.

touch·down (tŭch′doun′) ▸ *n.* **1.** *Football* A score of six points, made by moving the ball across the opponent's goal line. **2.** The contact of a landing aircraft or spacecraft with the landing surface.

tou·ché (to͞o-shā′) ▸ *interj.* Used to acknowledge a hit in fencing or a successful criticism in an argument.

touch·ing (tŭch′ĭng) ▸ *adj.* Eliciting sympathy or tenderness. **—touch′ing·ly** *adv.*

touch·screen (tŭch′skrēn′) ▸ *n.* A monitor screen that is responsive to pressure, esp. from a finger or stylus.

touch·stone (tŭch′stōn′) ▸ *n.* **1.** A hard stone used to test the quality of gold or silver. **2.** A test of authenticity or value; standard.

touch·y (tŭch′ē) ▸ *adj.* **-i·er, -i·est. 1.** Easily offended or annoyed; oversensitive. **2.** Delicate; difficult: *a touchy situation.* **—touch′i·ly** *adv.* **—touch′i·ness** *n.*

tough (tŭf) ▸ *adj.* **-er, -est. 1.** Strong and resilient. **2.** Hard to cut or chew. **3.** Physically rugged. **4.** Severe; harsh. **5.** Aggressive; pugnacious. **6.** Demanding; difficult. **7.** Strong-minded; resolute. **8.** *Slang* Unfortunate; too bad: *a tough break.* ▸ *n.* A hoodlum. **—tough′ly** *adv.* **—tough′ness** *n.*

tough·en (tŭf′ən) ▸ *v.* To make or become tough.

tou·pee (to͞o-pā′) ▸ *n.* A hairpiece worn to cover a bald spot.

tour (to͝or) ▸ *n.* **1.** A trip with visits to places of interest for business, pleasure, or instruction. **2.** A brief trip to or through a place to see or inspect it. **3.** A journey to fulfill a round of engagements in several places: *a concert tour.* **4.** A period of duty at a single place or job. ▸ *v.* To make a tour (of).

tour de force (to͝or′ də fôrs′) ▸ *n., pl.* **tours de force** (to͝or′). A feat of great virtuosity or strength.

tour·ism (to͝or′ĭz′əm) ▸ *n.* Tourist travel and accommodation.

tour·ist (to͝or′ĭst) ▸ *n.* One who travels for pleasure. **—tour′ist·y** *adj.*

tour·ma·line (to͝or′mə-lĭn, -lēn′) ▸ *n.* A mineral valued, esp. in its green, clear, and blue varieties, as a gemstone.

tour·na·ment (to͝or′nə-mənt, tûr′-) ▸ *n.* **1.** A contest composed of a series of elimination games or trials. **2.** A medieval jousting or tilting match.

tour·ney (to͝or′nē, tûr′-) ▸ *n., pl.* **-neys.** A tournament.

tour·ni·quet (to͝or′nĭ-kĭt, tûr′-) ▸ *n.* A device, usu. a tightly encircling bandage, used to check bleeding in an injured limb.

tou·sle (tou′zəl) ▸ *v.* **-sled, -sling.** To disarrange or rumple; dishevel.

tout (tout) ▸ *v.* **1.** To promote or publicize energetically. **2.** To deal in information on racehorses. ▸ *n.* One who touts. **—tout′er** *n.*

tow[1] (tō) ▸ *v.* To draw or pull behind by a chain or line. ▸ *n.* **1.** An act of towing. **2.** Something that tows or is towed. ***—idiom:* in tow 1.** Following closely. **2.** Under one's charge. **—tow′age** *n.* **—tow′er** *n.*

tow[2] (tō) ▸ *n.* Coarse broken flax or hemp fiber prepared for spinning.

to·ward (tôrd, tə-wôrd′) also **to·wards** (tôrdz, tə-wôrdz′) ▸ *prep.* **1.** In the direction of. **2.** In a position facing. **3.** Somewhat before in time. **4.** With regard to. **5.** In partial fulfillment of: *a payment toward the house.*

tow·el (tou′əl) ▸ *n.* An absorbent cloth or paper used for wiping or drying. ▸ *v.* **-eled, -el·ing** or **-elled, -el·ling.** To wipe or dry with a towel.

tow·er (tou′ər) ▸ *n.* **1.** A tall building or part of a building. **2.** A tall slender structure used for observation, signaling, or pumping. ▸ *v.* To rise to a conspicuous height.

tow·er·ing (tou′ər-ĭng) ▸ *adj.* **1.** Of imposing height. **2.** Outstanding; preeminent. **3.** Very great or intense. **—tow′er·ing·ly** *adv.*

tow·head (tō′hĕd′) ▸ *n.* A person with white-blond hair. **—tow′head′ed** *adj.*

tow·hee (tō′hē, tō-hē′) ▸ *n.* A North American bird with black, white, and rust-colored plumage in the male.

town (toun) ▸ *n.* **1.** A population center larger than a village and usu. smaller than a city. **2.** *Informal* A city. **3.** The commercial district of an area.

town·house or **town house** (toun′hous′) ▸ *n.* A row house, esp. a fashionable one.

town meeting ▸ *n.* A legislative assembly of townspeople.

town·ship (toun′shĭp′) ▸ *n.* **1.** A subdivision of a county in most northeast and Midwest US states. **2.** A public land surveying unit of 36 square miles.

towns·peo·ple (tounz′pē′pəl) ▸ *pl.n.* The inhabitants or citizens of a town or city.

tow·path (tō′păth′) ▸ *n.* A path along a canal or river used by animals towing boats.

tox·e·mi·a (tŏk-sē′mē-ə) ▸ *n.* A condition in which toxins produced by body cells at a local source of infection are contained in the blood. **—tox·e′mic** *adj.*

toxi- or **tox-** ▸ *pref.* Poison: *toxemia.*

tox·ic (tŏk′sĭk) ▸ *adj.* **1.** Of or caused by a toxin or poison. **2.** Poisonous. ▸ *n.* A toxic chemical or other substance. **—tox′i·cal·ly** *adv.* **—tox·ic′i·ty** (-sĭs′ĭ-tē) *n.*

tox·i·col·o·gy (tŏk′sĭ-kŏl′ə-jē) ▸ *n.* The study of poisons and the treatment of poisoning. **—tox′i·co·log′i·cal** (-kə-lŏj′ĭ-kəl), **tox′i·co·log′ic** *adj.* **—tox′i·col′o·gist** *n.*

tox·in (tŏk′sĭn) ▸ *n.* A poisonous substance, esp. a protein, produced by living cells or organisms and capable of causing disease when introduced into the body, but also capable of stimulating production of an antitoxin.

toy (toi) ▸ *n.* **1.** An object for children to play with. **2.** A trifle or bauble. **3.** A very small breed of dog. ▸ *v.* **1.** To amuse oneself idly. **2.** To treat something casually; flirt: *toyed with the idea.*

tr. ▸ *abbr.* **1.** transitive **2.** translated

trace[1] (trās) ▸ *n.* **1.** A visible mark or sign of the former presence or passage of some person, thing, or event. **2.** A barely perceivable indication; touch. **3.** A minute amount. ▸ *v.*

THESAURUS

MUNICATION.] *—See also* SHADE (2).

touchable *adj.* Discernible by touch ▸ palpable, tactile, tangible.

touchableness *n.* *—See* TANGIBILITY.

touch-and-go *adj.* *—See* DELICATE (3).

touched *adj.* *—See* INSANE.

touching *adj.* *—See* AFFECTING.

touchstone *n.* *—See* STANDARD.

touchy *adj.* *—See* DELICATE (3), OVERSENSITIVE, TESTY.

tough *adj.* *—See* BITTER (2), BURDENSOME, DIFFICULT (1), FIRM[1] (3), HARD (2), ROUGH (3), SEVERE (1), STRONG (2).

tough *n.* *—See* THUG.

tough out *v.* *—See* ENDURE (1).

toughen *v.* *—See* HARDEN (1), HARDEN (2).

toughie *n.* *—See* THUG.

tough-minded *adj.* *—See* REALISTIC (1).

toughness *n.* *—See* DECISION (2), ENDURANCE, SEVERITY.

tour *n.* *—See* CIRCLE (2), EXPEDITION, TURN (1).

tour *v.* *—See* JOURNEY.

tour de force *n.* *—See* ACCOMPLISHMENT.

tourist *n.* One who travels for pleasure ▸ day-tripper, excursionist, globetrotter, jet-setter, sightseer, sojourner, traveler, vacationer, visitor.

tournament or **tourney** *n.* Any competition or test of opposing wills likened to the sport in which knights fought with lances ▸ joust, tilt. [*Compare* BATTLE.] *—See also* COMPETITION (2).

tousle *v.* To put something into a state of disarray, such as the hair or clothes ▸ disarrange, dishevel, disorder, disorganize, mess (up), muss (up), rumple. [*Compare* DIRTY.]

tout *v.* *—See* PROMOTE (3).

tow *v.* *—See* PULL (1).

tow *n.* *—See* PULL (1).

toward *adj.* *—See* BENEFICIAL.

tower *v.* *—See* RISE (2).

tower above *v.* *—See* DOMINATE (2).

towering *adj.* *—See* EXCEPTIONAL, HIGH (1).

towheaded *adj.* *—See* FAIR[1] (2).

town *n.* *—See* CITY.

townsman or **townswoman** *n.* *—See* INHABITANT.

toxic *adj.* *—See* HARMFUL, POISONOUS.

toxicant *adj.* *—See* POISONOUS.

toxicant *n.* *—See* POISON.

toxin *n.* *—See* POISON.

toy *n.* An object for children to play with ▸ game, plaything. [*Compare* AMUSEMENT.] *—See also* NOVELTY (3).

toy *v.* To treat lightly or flippantly ▸ dally, flirt, play, trifle. *—See also* FIDDLE, FLIRT (2).

trace *n.* A mark or remnant that in-

traced, trac·ing. 1. To follow the course or trail of. 2. To ascertain the successive stages in the development of. 3. To locate or discover through inquiry. 4. To draw (a line or figure). 5. To form (letters) with special care. 6. To copy by following lines seen through transparent paper. **—trace′a·bil′i·ty** *n.* **—trace′a·ble** *adj.* **—trac′er** *n.*

trace² (trās) ► *n.* One of two side straps or chains connecting a harnessed draft animal to a vehicle.

tracer bullet ► *n.* A bullet that leaves a luminous or smoky trail.

trac·er·y (trā′sə-rē) ► *n., pl.* **-ies.** Ornamental work of interlaced and branching lines.

tra·che·a (trā′kē-ə) ► *n., pl.* **-che·ae** (-kē-ē′) or **-che·as.** A thin-walled tube of cartilaginous and membranous tissue descending from the larynx to the bronchi and carrying air to the lungs; windpipe. **—tra′che·al** *adj.*

tra·che·ot·o·my (trā′kē-ŏt′ə-mē) ► *n., pl.* **-mies.** The surgical incision into the trachea through the neck.

track (trăk) ► *n.* 1. A mark, such as a footprint, left in passing. 2. A path or course; trail. 3a. A course laid out for running or racing. b. Track and field. 4. A rail or set of parallel rails upon which a train or trolley runs. 5. A groove, ridge, or rail for a moving device or part. ► *v.* 1. To follow the tracks of; trail. 2. To locate by searching diligently: *track down a story.* 3. To carry on the shoes and deposit: *tracked mud on the rug.* 4. To observe or monitor, as by radar. ***—idioms:*** **keep track of** To remain informed about. **lose track of** To fail to keep informed about. **—track′a·ble** *adj.* **—track′er** *n.* **—track′less** *adj.*

track and field ► *n.* Athletic events performed on a running track and the adjacent field. **—track′-and-field′** *adj.*

track·ball (trăk′bôl′) ► *n.* A ball mounted in a stationary housing and rotated to control a pointer on a computer screen.

track·ing (trăk′ĭng) ► *n.* The placing of students in a course of study according to ability, achievement, or needs.

tract¹ (trăkt) ► *n.* 1a. An expanse of land. b. A specified area of land. 2. *Anat.* A system of organs and tissues that together perform a specialized function.

tract² (trăkt) ► *n.* A propaganda pamphlet, esp. one put out by a religious or political group.

trac·ta·ble (trăk′tə-bəl) ► *adj.* 1. Easily managed or controlled; governable. 2. Easily worked, as metals; malleable. **—trac′ta·bil′i·ty, trac′ta·ble·ness** *n.* **—trac′ta·bly** *adv.*

tract house ► *n.* One of numerous houses of similar or complementary design constructed on a tract of land. **—tract housing** *n.*

trac·tion (trăk′shən) ► *n.* 1. The act of drawing or pulling or the condition of being drawn or pulled. 2. Pulling power, as of an engine. 3. Adhesive friction, as of a wheel on a road.

trac·tor (trăk′tər) ► *n.* 1. An automotive vehicle designed for pulling machinery. 2. A truck having a cab and no body, used for pulling large vehicles.

trac·tor-trail·er (trăk′tər-trā′lər) ► *n.* A truck consisting of a tractor attached to a semitrailer or trailer, used for transporting loads.

trade (trād) ► *n.* 1. The business of buying and selling commodities; commerce. 2. Customers; clientele. 3. An exchange of one thing for another. 4. An occupation, esp. one requiring skilled labor; craft. ► *v.* **trad·ed, trad·ing.** 1. To engage in buying and selling. 2. To exchange one thing for another. 3. To shop regularly at a particular store. **—trad′er** *n.*

trade-in (trād′ĭn′) ► *n.* Merchandise accepted as partial payment for a new purchase.

trade·mark (trād′märk′) ► *n.* A name, symbol, or other device identifying a product, legally restricted to the use of the owner or manufacturer. ► *v.* 1. To label (a product) with a trademark. 2. To register (a name or device) as a trademark.

trade name ► *n.* 1. A name used to identify a commercial product or service. 2. The name under which a business firm operates.

trade·off or **trade-off** (trād′ôf′, -ŏf′) ► *n.* An exchange in which something desirable, as a benefit or advantage, is given up for another regarded as more desirable.

trades·man (trādz′mən) ► *n.* 1. One engaged in retail trade. 2. A skilled worker.

trade union ► *n.* A labor union. **—trade unionism** *n.* **—trade unionist** *n.*

trade wind (wĭnd) ► *n.* Any of a system of winds occupying most of the tropics, blowing northeasterly in the Northern Hemisphere and southeasterly in the Southern Hemisphere.

trad·ing post (trā′dĭng) ► *n.* A store in a sparsely settled area offering supplies in exchange for local products.

tra·di·tion (trə-dĭsh′ən) ► *n.* 1. The passing down of a culture from generation to generation, esp. orally. 2a. A custom handed down. b. A set of such customs viewed as a coherent body of precedents influencing the present. **—tra·di′tion·al** *adj.* **—tra·di′tion·al·ist** *adj. & n.* **—tra·di′tion·al·ly** *adv.*

tra·duce (trə-do͞os′, -dyo͞os′) ► *v.* **-duced, -duc·ing.** To slander; defame. **—tra·duce′ment** *n.*

traf·fic (trăf′ĭk) ► *n.* 1. The commercial exchange of goods; trade. 2a. The passage of persons, vehicles, or messages through routes of transportation or communication. b. The amount, as of vehicles, in transit. 3. Dealings; communication. ► *v.* **-ficked, -fick·ing.** To carry on trade; deal in. **—traf′fick·er** *n.*

traffic circle ► *n.* A circular one-way road at a junction of thoroughfares, facilitating an uninterrupted flow of traffic.

traffic light ► *n.* A road signal for directing vehicular traffic by means of colored lights.

trag·e·dy (trăj′ĭ-dē) ► *n., pl.* **-dies.** 1. A drama or literary work in which the main character is brought to ruin or suffers extreme sorrow. 2. A disastrous event. **—tra·ge′di·an** (trə-jē′dē-ən) *n.* **—tra·ge′di·enne′** (-ĕn′) *n.*

trag·ic (trăj′ĭk) ► *adj.* 1. Of or having the nature of tragedy. 2. Writing or performing in tragedy. 3. Calamitous; disastrous. **—trag′i·cal·ly** *adv.*

trag·i·com·e·dy (trăj′ĭ-kŏm′ĭ-dē) ► *n., pl.* **-dies.** A drama combining elements of tragedy and comedy. **—trag′i·com′ic** (-kŏm′ĭk), **trag′i·com′i·cal** *adj.*

trail (trāl) ► *v.* 1. To drag or allow to drag or stream be-

THESAURUS

dicates the former presence of something ► record, relic, remainder, remains, remnant, vestige. [*Compare* SIGN.] *—See also* SHADE (2), TRACK.

trace *v.* 1. To pursue and locate ► hunt down, nose out, run down, track down. *Idiom:* run to earth (*or* ground). 2. To follow the traces or scent of, as in hunting ► smell out, sniff out, track, trail. *Idiom:* be hot on the trail of. [*Compare* HUNT.]

track *n.* A visible sign or mark of the passage of someone or something ► footmarks, footprints, marks, odor, print, scent, spoor, trace, trail. [*Compare* LEAD, SIGN.] *—See also* ROUTINE.

track *v.* To follow the traces or scent of, as in hunting ► smell out, sniff out, trace, trail. *Idiom:* be hot on the trail of (*or* after). [*Compare* HUNT.] *—See also* CROSS (1), FOLLOW (3).

track down *v.* *—See* TRACE (1).

tract¹ *n.* *—See* AREA (2), EXPANSE (1), LOT (1).

tract² *n.* *—See* DISCOURSE.

tractability or **tractableness** *n.* *—See* FLEXIBILITY (1), OBEDIENCE.

tractable *adj.* *—See* MALLEABLE, OBEDIENT.

traction *n.* *—See* PULL (1).

trade *n.* *—See* BUSINESS (1), BUSINESS (2), CHANGE (2), DEAL (1), PATRONAGE (2), PATRONAGE (3).

trade *v.* *—See* CHANGE (3), EXCHANGE, SELL.

trademark *n.* *—See* MARK (1).

trademark *v.* *—See* MARK (1).

tradeoff *n.* *—See* COMPROMISE.

trader or **tradesman** *n.* *—See* DEALER.

trading *n.* *—See* BUSINESS (1).

tradition *n.* Something immaterial, as a style or philosophy, that is passed from one generation to another ► heritage, inheritance, legacy. *—See also* CEREMONY (1), CULTURE (2), LORE (1).

traditional *adj.* *—See* ACCEPTED, CONVENTIONAL.

traditionalist *n.* *—See* CONSERVATIVE.

traditionalist or **traditionalistic** *adj.* *—See* CONSERVATIVE (1).

traditionalize *v.* *—See* CONVENTIONALIZE.

traduce *v.* *—See* MALIGN.

traducement *n.* *—See* LIBEL.

traffic *n.* *—See* BUSINESS (1), PATRONAGE (2).

trafficker *n.* *—See* DEALER, PUSHER.

tragedy *n.* *—See* DISASTER.

trail *v.* 1. To hang down and be pulled along behind ► drag, draggle, train.

hind, as along the ground. **2.** To follow the traces or scent of; track. **3.** To lag behind (an opponent). **4.** To extend or grow along the ground or over a surface. **5.** To drift in a thin stream. **6.** To become gradually fainter: *Her voice trailed off.* ▸ *n.* **1.** Something that hangs loose and long. **2.** Something that follows behind. **3.** A mark or trace left by a moving body. **4.** A marked or beaten path.

trail bike ▸ *n.* A small motorcycle designed for off-road riding.

trail·blaz·er (trāl′blā′zər) ▸ *n.* **1.** One who blazes a trail. **2.** An innovative leader in a field; pioneer. **—trail′blaz′ing** *adj.*

trail·er (trā′lər) ▸ *n.* **1.** A large transport vehicle hauled by a truck or tractor. **2.** A van drawn by a truck or automobile and used as a dwelling or office.

trailer park ▸ *n.* An area in which parking space for house trailers is rented.

trail·ing arbutus (trā′lĭng) ▸ *n.* A low-growing evergreen shrub of E North America.

train (trān) ▸ *n.* **1.** A series of connected railroad cars. **2.** A long line of moving people, animals, or vehicles. **3.** A part of a gown that trails behind the wearer. **4.** A staff of people following in attendance. **5.** An orderly succession of related events or thoughts. ▸ *v.* **1.** To coach in or accustom to a mode of behavior or performance. **2.** To make or become proficient with specialized instruction and practice. **3.** To prepare physically, as with a regimen. **4.** To cause (e.g., a plant) to take a desired course or shape. **5.** To focus; aim. **—train′a·ble** *adj.* **—train·ee′** *n.* **—train′er** *n.* **—train′ing** *n.*

traipse (trāps) ▸ *v.* **traipsed, traips·ing.** To walk or tramp about.

trait (trāt) ▸ *n.* **1.** A distinguishing feature, as of character. **2.** A genetically determined characteristic or condition.

trai·tor (trā′tər) ▸ *n.* One who betrays one's country, a cause, or a trust, esp. one who commits treason. **—trai′tor·ous** *adj.*

tra·jec·to·ry (trə-jĕk′tə-rē) ▸ *n., pl.* **-ries.** The path of a projectile or other moving body through space.

tram (trăm) ▸ *n.* **1.** *Chiefly Brit.* A streetcar. **2.** A cable car, esp. one suspended from an overhead cable. **3.** An open wagon run on tracks in a coal mine.

tram·mel (trăm′əl) ▸ *n.* **1.** A shackle used in teaching horses. **2.** A hindrance or restraint. ▸ *v.* **-meled, -mel·ing** or **-melled, -mel·ling. 1.** To trap or enmesh. **2.** To hinder. **—tram′mel·er** *n.*

tramp (trămp) ▸ *v.* **1.** To walk with a firm heavy step. **2.** To travel on foot; hike. **3.** To tread down; trample. ▸ *n.* **1.** The sound of heavy walking or marching. **2.** A walking trip. **3.** One who travels aimlessly about; vagrant. **4.** A prostitute. **5.** A cargo vessel that has no regular schedule but takes on freight whenever it can. **—tramp′er** *n.*

tram·ple (trăm′pəl) ▸ *v.* **-pled, -pling. 1.** To beat down with the feet so as to injure or destroy. **2.** To treat harshly or ruthlessly. **—tram′ple** *n.*

tram·po·line (trăm′pə-lēn′, -lĭn) ▸ *n.* A sheet of strong canvas attached with springs to a metal frame and used for gymnastic springing and tumbling. **—tram′po·lin′er, tram′po·lin′ist** *n.*

trance (trăns) ▸ *n.* **1.** A hypnotic, cataleptic, or ecstatic state. **2.** Detachment from one's physical surroundings, as in contemplation or daydreaming. **3.** A dazed state.

tran·quil (trăng′kwəl, trăn′-) ▸ *adj.* Free from agitation; calm. **—tran·quil′li·ty, tran·quil′i·ty** *n.* **—tran′quil·ly** *adv.*

tran·quil·ize also **tran·quil·lize** (trăng′kwə-līz′, trăn′-) ▸ *v.* **-ized** also **-lized, -iz·ing -liz·ing. 1.** To make or become tranquil. **2.** To sedate. **—tran′quil·i·za′tion** *n.*

tran·quil·iz·er (trăng′kwə-līz′ər, trăn′-) ▸ *n.* A tranquilizing or depressant drug.

trans. ▸ *abbr.* **1.** transitive **2.** translation

trans– ▸ *pref.* **1.** Across; beyond: *transatlantic.* **2.** Change; transfer: *transliterate.*

trans·act (trăn-săkt′, -zăkt′) ▸ *v.* To carry out or conduct (business or affairs). **—trans·ac′tor** *n.*

trans·ac·tion (trăn-săk′shən, -zăk′-) ▸ *n.* **1.** The act or process of transacting. **2.** Something transacted. **—trans·ac′tion·al** *adj.*

trans·at·lan·tic (trăns′ət-lăn′tĭk, trănz′-) ▸ *adj.* **1.** On the other side of the Atlantic. **2.** Spanning or crossing the Atlantic.

trans·ax·le (trăns-ăk′səl, trănz-) ▸ *n.* An automotive part that combines the transmission and the differential, used on vehicles with front-wheel drive.

Trans·cau·ca·sia (trăns′kô-kā′zhə, -zhē-ə, trănz′-) ▸ A region of Georgia, Armenia, and Azerbaijan between the Caucasus Mts. and the borders of Turkey and Iran. **—Trans′cau·ca′sian** *adj. & n.*

tran·scend (trăn-sĕnd′) ▸ *v.* **1.** To go beyond; exceed. **2.** To surpass. **3.** To exist above and independent of. **—tran·scen′dence** *n.* **—tran·scen′dent** *adj.*

tran·scen·den·tal (trăn′sĕn-dĕn′tl) ▸ *adj.* **1.** Rising above common thought or ideas; exalted; mystical. **2.** *Math.* Of or relating to a real or complex number that is not the root of any polynomial that has positive degree and rational coefficients. **—tran′scen·den′tal·ly** *adv.*

tran·scen·den·tal·ism (trăn′sĕn-dĕn′tl-ĭz′əm) ▸ *n.* A belief or doctrine asserting the existence of an ideal spiritual reality

THESAURUS

[*Compare* PULL.] 2. To follow the traces of, as in hunting ▸ smell out, sniff out, trace, track. ***Idiom:*** be hot on the trail of. [*Compare* HUNT.] 3. To follow closely or persistently ▸ dog, heel, tag. *—See also* DELAY (2), FOLLOW (3), TRUDGE.

trail *n.* Something that follows or is drawn along behind ▸ tail, train, wake. [*Compare* STREAM.] *—See also* TRACK, WAY (2).

trailblazer *n.* *—See* FORERUNNER.

train *n.* 1. A string of railroad cars led by a locomotive ▸ rail, railroad train, railway. *Informal:* choo-choo, choo-choo train. 2. Something that follows or is drawn along behind ▸ tail, trail, wake. [*Compare* STREAM.] *—See also* RETINUE, SERIES.

train *v.* 1. To hang down and be pulled along behind ▸ drag, draggle, trail. [*Compare* PULL.] 2. To engage in activities to strengthen or condition ▸ drill, exercise, practice, work out. *—See also* AIM (1), EDUCATE.

trainable *adj.* Capable of being educated ▸ docile, educable, teachable. [*Compare* OBEDIENT.]

trained *adj.* *—See* EDUCATED.

trainee *n.* *—See* STUDENT.

trainer *n.* *—See* EDUCATOR.

training *n.* *—See* EDUCATION (1), PRACTICE.

traipse *v.* *—See* ROVE.

trait *n.* *—See* QUALITY (1).

traitor *n.* *—See* BETRAYER, DEFECTOR.

traitorous *adj.* Involving or constituting treason ▸ seditious, treasonable, treasonous. *—See also* FAITHLESS.

traitorousness *n.* Willful violation of allegiance to one's country ▸ lese majesty, sedition, seditiousness, treason. *—See also* FAITHLESSNESS.

trammel *n.* *—See* BOND (1).

trammel *v.* *—See* CATCH (1), HAMPER[1].

tramp *v.* 1. To travel about or journey on foot ▸ hike, backpack, march, trek. [*Compare* JOURNEY, WALK.] 2. To step on heavily and repeatedly so as to crush, injure, or destroy ▸ stamp, stomp, trample, tread, tromp. [*Compare* CRUSH.] *—See also* ROVE, TRUDGE.

tramp *n.* *—See* HOBO, PAUPER, SLUT, WALK (1).

trample *v.* 1. To step on heavily and repeatedly so as to crush, injure, or destroy ▸ stamp, stomp, tramp, tread, tromp. [*Compare* CRUSH, TRUDGE.] 2. To treat arbitrarily or cruelly ▸ grind (down), oppress. [*Compare* ABUSE, ENSLAVE, SUPPRESS.]

trampy *v.* *—See* WANTON (1).

trance *n.* The condition of being so lost in solitary thought that one is unaware of one's surroundings ▸ absent-mindedness, abstraction, bemusement, brown study, daydreaming, dream, half-conscious state, hypnotic state, muse, reverie, sleepwalking, study. *—See also* DAZE.

tranquil *adj.* *—See* CALM, STILL.

tranquilize *v.* *—See* DRUG (1), PACIFY.

tranquilizer *n.* *—See* SOPORIFIC.

tranquillity or **tranquility** *n.* *—See* CALM, STILLNESS.

transact *v.* *—See* PERFORM (1).

transaction *n.* *—See* DEAL (1), PERFORMANCE.

transcend *v.* *—See* EXCEED, SURPASS.

transcendence *n.* *—See* EXCELLENCE.

transcendent *adj.* *—See* MAXIMUM.

transcendental *adj.* *—See* SUPERNATURAL (1).

that transcends the empirical and scientific and is knowable through intuition. **—tran′scen·den′tal·ist** *n.*

trans·con·ti·nen·tal (trăns′kŏn-tə-nĕn′tl) ► *adj.* Spanning or crossing a continent.

tran·scribe (trăn-skrīb′) ► *v.* **-scribed, -scrib·ing. 1.** To write or type a copy of. **2.** To write out fully, as from notes. **3.** To adapt or arrange (a musical composition). **4.** To record for broadcast at a later date. **—tran·scrib′er** *n.*

tran·script (trăn′skrĭpt′) ► *n.* Something transcribed; a written or printed copy.

tran·scrip·tion (trăn-skrĭp′shən) ► *n.* **1.** The act or process of transcribing. **2.** Something transcribed, esp.: **a.** An adaptation of a musical composition. **b.** A recorded radio or television program.

trans·duc·er (trăns-do͞o′sər, -dyo͞o′-, trănz-) ► *n.* A substance or device, such as a microphone, that converts input energy of one form into output energy of another.

tran·sept (trăn′sĕpt′) ► *n.* Either of the two lateral arms of a cruciform church.

trans fatty acid (trăns) ► *n.* An unsaturated fatty acid produced by the partial hydrogenation of vegetable oils.

trans·fer (trăns-fûr′, trăns′fər) ► *v.* **-ferred, -fer·ring. 1.** To convey, shift, or change from one place, person, or thing to another. **2.** *Law* To make over the possession or legal title of. **3.** To convey (e.g., a design) from one surface to another. **4.** To change from one public conveyance to another. ► *n.* (trăns′fər) **1.** also **trans·fer·al** (trăns-fûr′əl) The conveyance of something from one place or person to another. **2.** One who transfers or is transferred. **3.** A design conveyed by contact from one surface to another. **4.** A ticket entitling a passenger to change from one public conveyance to another. **5.** also **transferal** *Law* A conveyance of title or property from one person to another. **—trans·fer′a·ble, trans·fer′ra·ble** *adj.* **—trans·fer′ence** *n.* **—trans·fer′rer** *n.*

trans·fig·ure (trăns-fĭg′yər) ► *v.* **-ured, -ur·ing. 1.** To alter the outward appearance of; transform. **2.** To exalt or glorify. **—trans·fig′u·ra′tion** *n.*

trans·fix (trăns-fĭks′) ► *v.* **1.** To pierce with or as with a pointed weapon; impale. **2.** To render motionless, as with terror. **—trans·fix′ion** *n.*

trans·form (trăns-fôrm′) ► *v.* **1.** To change markedly in appearance or form. **2.** To change in nature or condition. **—trans·form′a·ble** *adj.* **—trans′for·ma′tion** *n.*

trans·form·er (trăns-fôr′mər) ► *n.* A device used to transfer electric energy from one circuit to another.

trans·fuse (trăns-fyo͞oz′) ► *v.* **-fused, -fus·ing. 1.** To transfer (liquid) from one vessel into another. **2.** To permeate; instill. **3.** To administer a transfusion of or to. **—trans·fus′er** *n.*

trans·fu·sion (trăns-fyo͞o′zhən) ► *n.* **1.** The act or process of transfusing. **2.** The transfer of whole blood or blood products from one individual to another.

trans·gen·der (trăns-jĕn′dər, trănz-) ► *adj.* Identifying as or having undergone surgery to become a member of the opposite sex. ► *n.* A person who is transgender.

trans·gress (trăns-grĕs′, trănz-) ► *v.* **1.** To go beyond or over (a limit). **2.** To act in violation of (a law or commandment). **—trans·gress′ion** *n.* **—trans·gres′sor** *n.*

tran·ship (trăn-shĭp′) ► *v.* Var. of **transship.**

tran·si·ent (trăn′zē-ənt, -zhənt, -shənt) ► *adj.* **1.** Passing with time; transitory. **2.** Remaining in a place only a brief time. ► *n.* One that is transient, esp. a person staying a single night at a hotel. **—tran′si·ence, tran′si·en·cy** *n.* **—tran′si·ent·ly** *adv.*

tran·sis·tor (trăn-zĭs′tər, -sĭs′-) ► *n.* **1.** A semiconductor device with at least three terminals, used in a circuit as an amplifier, detector, or switch. **2.** A small portable radio using transistors. **—tran·sis′tor·ize′** *v.*

tran·sit (trăn′sĭt, -zĭt) ► *n.* **1.** The act of passing over, across, or through; passage. **2.** Conveyance of people or goods from one place to another, esp. on a local public transportation system. **3.** A surveying instrument that measures angles.

tran·si·tion (trăn-zĭsh′ən, -sĭsh′-) ► *n.* Passage from one form, state, style, or place to another. **—tran·si′tion·al, tran·si′tion·ar′y** *adj.* **—tran·si′tion·al·ly** *adv.*

tran·si·tive (trăn′sĭ-tĭv, -zĭ-) ► *adj.* Being or using a verb that requires a direct object to complete its meaning. **—tran′si·tive·ly** *adv.* **—tran′si·tive·ness, tran′si·tiv′i·ty** *n.*

tran·si·to·ry (trăn′sĭ-tôr′ē, trăn′zĭ-) ► *adj.* Existing only briefly. **—tran′si·to′ri·ly** *adv.* **—tran′si·to′ri·ness** *n.*

trans·late (trăns′lāt′, trănz′-, trăns-lāt′, trănz-) ► *v.* **-lat·ed, -lat·ing. 1.** To render in another language. **2.** To put into simpler terms; explain or interpret. **3.** To convey from one form or style to another. **4.** *Phys.* To move from one place to another without rotation. **—trans·lat′a·bil′i·ty, trans·lat′a·ble·ness** *n.* **—trans·lat′a·ble** *adj.* **—trans·la′tion** *n.* **—trans′la′tor** *n.*

trans·lit·er·ate (trăns-lĭt′ə-rāt′, trănz-) ► *v.* **-at·ed, -at·ing.** To represent (letters or words) in the corresponding characters of another alphabet. **—trans·lit′er·a′tion** *n.*

trans·lu·cent (trăns-lo͞o′sənt, trănz-) ► *adj.* Transmitting light but diffusing it sufficiently to cause images to be blurred. **—trans·lu′cence, trans·lu′cen·cy** *n.*

trans·mi·grate (trăns-mī′grāt′, trănz-) ► *v.* **-grat·ed, -grat·ing.** To pass into another body after death. Used of the soul. **—trans′mi·gra′tion** *n.* **—trans·mi′gra′tor** *n.* **—trans·mi′gra·to′ry** (-grə-tôr′ē) *adj.*

trans·mis·sion (trăns-mĭsh′ən, trănz-) ► *n.* **1.** The act or process of transmitting. **2.** Something transmitted. **3.** An automotive assembly of gears that links an engine to a

THESAURUS

transcribe *v.* *—See* TRANSLATE.

transfer *v.* **1.** To change the ownership of property by means of a legal document ► assign, cede, convey, deed, grant, make over, sign over, transmit. **2.** To change one's residence or place of business, for example ► move, relocate, remove. ***Idiom:*** pull up stakes. [*Compare* EMIGRATE, GO.] **3.** To direct a person elsewhere for help or information ► refer, send, turn over. *—See also* COMMUNICATE (2), CONDUCT (3), GIVE (1), MOVE (2).

transfer *n.* *—See* DELIVERY, GRANT.

transferable *adj.* *—See* CONTAGIOUS.

transferal *n.* *—See* GRANT.

transfiguration *n.* *—See* CONVERSION (1).

transfigure *v.* *—See* CONVERT.

transfix *v.* *—See* CUT (1), GRIP.

transform *v.* *—See* CONVERT, REVOLUTIONIZE.

transformable *adj.* *—See* CHANGEABLE (1).

transformation *n.* *—See* CONVERSION (1), REVOLUTION (2).

transfuse *v.* *—See* CHARGE (1).

transgress *v.* *—See* DISOBEY, EXCEED, OFFEND (3), VIOLATE (1).

transgression *n.* *—See* BREACH (1), TRESPASS (2).

transgressor *n.* *—See* CRIMINAL, REBEL (1).

transient *adj.* *—See* MIGRATORY (1), TRANSITORY.

transient *n.* *—See* HOBO.

transit *n.* *—See* JOURNEY, TRANSITION, TRANSPORTATION.

transit *v.* *—See* CROSS (1).

transition *n.* Passage from one form, state, or stage to another ► change, flux, move, passage, progression, shift, transit, turn. ***Idiom:*** change of course. [*Compare* CHANGE, CONVERSION.]

transitory *adj.* Lasting or existing only for a short time ► brief, ephemeral, evanescent, fleet, fleeting, fugacious, fugitive, momentary, passing, short, short-lived, temporal, temporary, transient. [*Compare* TEMPORARY.]

translate *v.* To express in another language ► construe, interpret, metaphrase, put, render, transcribe, transliterate, transpose. [*Compare* CONVERT.] *—See also* CONVERT, PARAPHRASE.

translation *n.* The act or process of translating ► construe, crib, interpretation, metaphrase, pony, rendering, transliteration, trot. *—See also* CONVERSION (1), PARAPHRASE.

transliterate *v.* *—See* TRANSLATE.

transliteration *n.* *—See* TRANSLATION.

translucent *adj.* *—See* CLEAR (1).

transmigrant *n.* One who emigrates ► emigrant, immigrant, migrant.

transmigrate *v.* **1.** To leave one's native land and settle in another ► emigrate (from), immigrate (to), migrate, resettle. [*Compare* MOVE, SETTLE.] **2.** To change habitat seasonally ► migrate.

transmigration *n.* Settling in a country to which one is not native ► immigration, migration. *—See also* EMIGRATION.

transmigratory *adj.* *—See* MIGRATORY (1).

transmission *n.* *—See* DELIVERY.

driving axle. 4. The sending of a signal from a transmitter. **—trans·mis′sive** (-mĭs′ĭv) *adj.*

trans·mit (trăns-mĭt′, trănz-) ▸ *v.* **-mit·ted, -mit·ting.** 1. To send from one person, thing, or place to another. 2. To cause to spread, as an infection. 3. To impart by heredity. 4. To send (a signal), as by radio. 5. To convey (e.g., force) from one part of a mechanism to another. **—trans·mis′si·ble, trans·mit′ta·ble** *adj.* **—trans·mit′tal** *n.*

trans·mit·ter (trăns-mĭt′ər, trănz-) ▸ *n.* 1. One that transmits. 2. Any of various electrical devices used to originate signals, as in radio or telegraphy.

trans·mog·ri·fy (trăns-mŏg′rə-fī′, trănz-) ▸ *v.* **-fied** (-fīd′), **-fy·ing.** To change into a different shape or form, esp. one that is fantastic or bizarre.

trans·mute (trăns-myo͞ot′, trănz-) ▸ *v.* **-mut·ed, -mut·ing.** 1. To change from one form, nature, substance, or state into another; transform. 2. To transfer (an element) into another by nuclear reactions. **—trans·mut′a·bil′i·ty** *n.* **—trans·mut′a·ble** *adj.* **—trans·mut′a·bly** *adv.* **—trans′mu·ta′tion** *n.*

trans·na·tion·al (trăns-năsh′ə-nəl, trănz-) ▸ *adj.* 1. Reaching beyond national boundaries. 2. Of or involving several nations or nationalities.

trans·o·ce·an·ic (trăns′ō-shē-ăn′ĭk, trănz′-) ▸ *adj.* 1. Situated beyond the ocean. 2. Spanning or crossing the ocean.

tran·som (trăn′səm) ▸ *n.* 1. A small hinged window above a door. 2. A horizontal crosspiece over a door or in a window.

trans·pa·cif·ic (trăns′pə-sĭf′ĭk, trănz′-) ▸ *adj.* 1. Situated on the other side of the Pacific Ocean. 2. Crossing the Pacific Ocean.

trans·par·ent (trăns-pâr′ənt, -păr′-) ▸ *adj.* 1. Capable of transmitting light so that objects on the other side can be seen clearly. 2. So fine in texture that it can be seen through; sheer. 3a. Easily detected; obvious: *transparent lies.* b. Free from guile; candid or open. **—trans·par′en·cy** *n.* **—trans·par′ent·ly** *adv.*

tran·spire (trăn-spīr′) ▸ *v.* **-spired, -spir·ing.** 1. *Biol.* To give off (vapor containing waste products) through pores or stomata. 2. To become known. 3. *Informal* To happen; occur. **—tran′spi·ra′tion** (-spə-rā′shən) *n.*

trans·plant (trăns-plănt′) ▸ *v.* 1. To uproot and replant (a growing plant). 2. To transfer from one place or residence to another. 3. *Medic.* To transfer (tissue or an organ) from one body or body part to another. **—trans′plant′** *n.* **—trans′plan·ta′tion** *n.*

trans·port (trăns-pôrt′) ▸ *v.* 1. To carry from one place to another. 2. To move to strong emotion; enrapture. 3. To send abroad to a penal colony. ▸ *n.* (trăns′pôrt′) 1. The act of transporting; conveyance. 2. Rapture. 3. A ship or aircraft used to transport troops or military equipment. 4. A vehicle, as an aircraft, used to transport passengers or freight. **—trans·port′a·bil′i·ty** *n.* **—trans·port′a·ble** *adj.* **—trans′por·ta′tion** *n.* **—trans·port′er** *n.*

trans·pose (trăns-pōz′) ▸ *v.* **-posed, -pos·ing.** 1. To reverse or change the order or place of. 2. *Mus.* To write or perform (a composition) in a key other than the original. **—trans·pos′er** *n.* **—trans′po·si′tion** (-pə-zĭsh′ən) *n.*

trans·sex·u·al (trăns-sĕk′sho͞o-əl) ▸ *n.* 1. One whose primary sexual identification is with the opposite sex. 2. One who has undergone a sex change. **—trans·sex′u·al** *adj.* **—trans·sex′u·al·ism, trans·sex′u·al′i·ty** *n.*

trans·ship (trăns-shĭp′) also **tran·ship** (trăn-shĭp′) ▸ *v.* To transfer (cargo) from one conveyance to another for reshipment. **—trans·ship′ment** *n.*

tran·sub·stan·ti·ate (trăn′səb-stăn′shē-āt′) ▸ *v.* **-at·ed, -at·ing.** 1. To change (one substance) into another; transmute. 2. *Christianity* To change the substance of (the Eucharistic bread and wine) into the body and blood of Jesus. **—tran′sub·stan′ti·a′tion** *n.*

trans·u·ran·ic (trăns′yo͞o-răn′ĭk, -rā′nĭk, trănz′-) also **trans·u·ra·ni·um** (-rā′nē-əm) ▸ *adj.* Having an atomic number greater than 92.

Trans·vaal (trăns-väl′, trănz-) ▸ A region of NE South Africa.

trans·ver·sal (trăns-vûr′səl, trănz-) ▸ *adj.* Transverse. ▸ *n. Math.* A line that intersects a system of other lines.

trans·verse (trăns-vûrs′, trănz-, trăns′vûrs′, trănz′-) ▸ *adj.* Situated or lying across; crosswise. **—trans·verse′** *n.* **—trans·verse′ly** *adv.*

trans·ves·tite (trăns-vĕs′tīt′, trănz-) ▸ *n.* A person who dresses and acts in a style or manner of the opposite sex. **—trans·ves′tism** *n.*

Tran·syl·va·nia (trăn′sĭl-vān′yə, -vā′nē-ə) ▸ A historical region of W Romania bounded by the Transylvanian Alps and the Carpathian Mts. **—Tran′syl·va′ni·an** *adj. & n.*

Transylvanian Alps ▸ A range of the S Carpathian Mts. across central Romania.

trap (trăp) ▸ *n.* 1. A device for catching and holding animals. 2. Any stratagem for betraying, tricking, or exposing an unsuspecting person or group. 3. A device, such as a U-shaped bend in a drainpipe, for sealing a passage against the escape of foul gases. 4. A sand trap. 5. **traps** *Mus.* Percussion instruments. 6. *Slang* The human mouth. ▸ *v.* **trapped, trap·ping.** 1. To catch in or as if in a trap. 2. To trap furbearing animals. **—trap′per** *n.*

trap·door (trăp′dôr′) ▸ *n.* A hinged or sliding door in a floor, roof, or ceiling.

tra·peze (tră-pēz′, trə-) ▸ *n.* A short horizontal bar suspended from two parallel ropes, used for acrobatics.

trap·e·zoid (trăp′ĭ-zoid′) ▸ *n.* A quadrilateral with two parallel sides. **—trap′e·zoi′dal** *adj.*

trap·pings (trăp′ĭngz) ▸ *pl.n.* 1. An ornamental covering for a horse. 2a. Articles of dress or adornment. b. Outward signs; appearance.

trap·shoot·ing (trăp′sho͞o′tĭng) ▸ *n. Sports* Shooting at clay pigeons hurled into the air.

trash (trăsh) ▸ *n.* 1. Discarded material; refuse. 2. Literary or artistic matter of little merit. 3. A person or group held in contempt. ▸ *v. Slang* 1. To discard. 2. To wreck or destroy, as by vandalism. **—trash′y** *adj.*

THESAURUS

transmit *v.* —*See* COMMUNICATE (1), COMMUNICATE (2), CONDUCT (3), LEAVE[1] (1), SEND (1), TRANSFER (1).

transmittable *adj.* —*See* CONTAGIOUS.

transmogrification *n.* —*See* CONVERSION (1).

transmogrify *v.* —*See* CONVERT.

transmutable *adj.* —*See* CHANGEABLE (1).

transmutation *n.* —*See* CONVERSION (1).

transmute *v.* —*See* CONVERT.

transparent *adj.* —*See* CLEAR (1), OBVIOUS, SHEER[2].

transpire *v.* To be made public ▸ break, come out, get out, out. *Informal:* leak (out). [*Compare* AIR, ANNOUNCE, APPEAR.] —*See also* HAPPEN (1), OOZE.

transplant *v.* —*See* PLANT.

transport *v.* —*See* BANISH, BRING (1), CARRY (1), ENRAPTURE.

transport *n.* —*See* HEAVEN, TRANSPORTATION.

transportable *adj.* —*See* MOBILE (1).

transportation *n.* The moving of persons or goods from one place to another ▸ carriage, carrying, conveyance, conveying, freight, hauling, shipping, transit, transport. —*See also* EXILE.

transpose *v.* —*See* CHANGE (3), CONVERT, REVERSE (1), TRANSLATE.

transposition *n.* —*See* CHANGE (2), REVERSAL (1)

transubstantiate *v.* —*See* CONVERT.

transubstantiation *n.* —*See* CONVERSION (1).

transude *v.* To excrete moisture through a porous skin or layer ▸ lather, perspire, sweat. —*See also* OOZE.

transversal *adj.* —*See* TRANSVERSE.

transverse *adj.* Situated or lying across ▸ across, crossing, crossways, crosswise, thwart, transversal, traverse. [*Compare* OBLIQUE.]

trap *n.* 1. A device or stratagem for catching or tricking a person or animal ▸ booby trap, deadfall, gin, noose, pit, pitfall, snare, springe, trip wire. [*Compare* LURE, TRICK.] 2. An attack or stratagem for capturing or tricking an unsuspecting person ▸ ambuscade, ambush. [*Compare* DECEIT.] —*See also* MOUTH (1).

trap *v.* —*See* CATCH (1).

trash *n.* —*See* GARBAGE, NONSENSE, RIFFRAFF.

trash *v. Slang* To injure or destroy property maliciously ▸ wreck, vandalize. [*Compare* DESTROY.] —*See also* SLAM (1).

trashy *adj.* —*See* SHODDY.

trau·ma (trô′mə, trou′-) ► *n., pl.* **-mas.** **1.** A serious injury or shock to the body. **2.** An emotional shock that causes lasting psychological damage. **—trau·mat′ic** (-măt′ĭk) *adj.* **—trau′ma·tize′** *v.*

tra·vail (trə-vāl′, trăv′āl′) ► *n.* **1.** Strenuous work; toil. **2.** Tribulation or agony; anguish. **3.** The labor of childbirth. **—tra·vail′** *v.*

trav·el (trăv′əl) ► *v.* **-eled, -el·ing** or **-elled, -el·ling. 1.** To go from one place to another; journey. **2.** To be transmitted, as light or sound. **3.** To advance or proceed. **4.** To associate. **5.** To move swiftly. ► *n.* **1.** The act of traveling. **2. travels** A series of journeys. **—trav′el·er, trav′el·ler** *n.*

trav·e·logue also **trav·e·log** (trăv′ə-lôg′, -lŏg′) ► *n.* A film or illustrated lecture on travel.

tra·verse (trə-vûrs′, trăv′ərs) ► *v.* **-versed, -vers·ing. 1.** To travel or pass across, over, or through. **2.** To move to and fro over. **3.** To cross (a slope) diagonally, as in skiing. **4.** To swivel (e.g., a mounted gun) laterally on a pivot. **5.** To extend across. ► *n.* **trav·erse** (trăv′ərs, trə-vûrs′) **1.** The act of traversing. **2.** Something, such as a beam, lying crosswise. ► *adj.* **trav·erse** (trăv′ərs, trə-vûrs′) Transverse. **—tra·vers′a·ble** *adj.* **—tra·vers′al** *n.* **—tra·vers′er** *n.*

trav·er·tine (trăv′ər-tēn′, -tĭn) ► *n.* A porous calcite deposited from solution in ground or surface waters.

trav·es·ty (trăv′ĭ-stē) ► *n., pl.* **-ties.** A grotesque imitation or likeness. **—trav′es·ty** *v.*

trawl (trôl) ► *n.* A large tapered fishing net that is towed along the sea bottom. ► *v.* To fish with a trawl.

trawl·er (trô′lər) ► *n.* A boat equipped for trawling.

tray (trā) ► *n.* A shallow flat receptacle with a raised edge, used for carrying, holding, or displaying articles.

treach·er·ous (trĕch′ər-əs) ► *adj.* **1.** Betraying a trust or confidence; traitorous. **2.** Unreliable. **3.** Marked by unforeseen hazards; dangerous or deceptive. **—treach′er·ous·ly** *adv.* **—treach′er·ous·ness** *n.*

treach·er·y (trĕch′ə-rē) ► *n., pl.* **-ies.** Willful betrayal of trust; perfidy.

trea·cle (trē′kəl) ► *n.* **1.** Cloying speech or sentiment. **2.** *Chiefly Brit.* Molasses. **—trea′cly** (-klē) *adj.*

tread (trĕd) ► *v.* **trod** (trŏd), **trod·den** (trŏd′n) or **trod, tread·ing. 1.** To walk on, over, or along. **2.** To press beneath the feet; trample. **3.** To walk or dance: *tread a measure.* ► *n.* **1.** The act, manner, or sound of treading. **2.** The horizontal part of a step in a staircase. **3.** The grooved face of a tire. **4.** The part of a shoe sole that touches the ground. **—tread′er** *n.*

tread·le (trĕd′l) ► *n.* A pedal operated by the foot to drive a wheel, as in a sewing machine. **—tread′le** *v.*

tread·mill (trĕd′mĭl′) ► *n.* **1.** A device operated by walking on an endless belt or on a set of moving steps attached to a wheel. **2.** A monotonous routine.

trea·son (trē′zən) ► *n.* The betrayal of one's country, esp. by aiding an enemy. **—trea′son·a·ble** *adj.* **—trea′son·ous** *adj.*

treas·ure (trĕzh′ər) ► *n.* **1.** Accumulated or stored wealth in the form of money, jewels, or other valuables. **2.** One considered esp. precious or valuable. ► *v.* **-ured, -ur·ing. 1.** To value highly. **2.** To store away; hoard. **—treas′ur·a·ble** *adj.*

treas·ur·er (trĕzh′ər-ər) ► *n.* One in charge of funds or revenues, as of a government, corporation, or club.

treas·ure-trove (trĕzh′ər-trōv′) ► *n.* **1.** Treasure found hidden. **2.** A discovery of great value.

treas·ur·y (trĕzh′ə-rē) ► *n., pl.* **-ies. 1.** A place where treasure is kept. **2.** A place where funds are received, kept, managed, and disbursed. **3.** Such funds or revenues. **4. Treasury** A governmental department in charge of the public revenue.

treat (trēt) ► *v.* **1.** To act or behave toward: *treated me fairly.* **2.** To regard and handle in a certain way: *treated the matter as a joke.* **3.** To deal with, handle, or cover. **4.** To provide with food, entertainment, or gifts at one's own expense. **5.** To subject to a process. **6.** To give medical aid to (someone). ► *n.* **1.** Something paid for by someone else. **2.** A special delight or pleasure. **—treat′a·ble** *adj.*

trea·tise (trē′tĭs) ► *n.* A systematic, usu. extensive written discourse on a subject.

treat·ment (trēt′mənt) ► *n.* **1.** The act or manner of handling or dealing with someone or something. **2.** The application of remedies to relieve or cure a disease or disorder.

trea·ty (trē′tē) ► *n., pl.* **-ties.** A formal agreement between two or more states.

treb·le (trĕb′əl) ► *adj.* **1.** Triple. **2.** *Mus.* Of or having the highest part, voice, or range. **3.** High-pitched; shrill. ► *n.* **1.** *Mus.* The highest part, voice, instrument, or range. **2.** A high shrill sound or voice. ► *v.* **-led, -ling.** To triple. **—treb′ly** *adv.*

treble clef ► *n. Mus.* A symbol centered on the second line from the bottom of a staff to indicate G above middle C.

tree (trē) ► *n.* **1.** A perennial woody plant with a main trunk and usu. a distinct crown. **2.** Something resembling a tree: *a clothes tree.* **3.** A diagram showing family lineage. ► *v.* To chase and force up a tree. **—tree′less** *adj.*

tree frog ► *n.* A small arboreal frog with long toes terminating in adhesive disks.

tree line ► *n.* **1.** The limit of northern or southern latitude beyond which trees will not grow. **2.** See **timberline.**

tree-of-heav·en (trē′əv-hĕv′ən) ► *n.* A deciduous, rapidly growing tree widely planted as a street tree.

THESAURUS

trauma *n.* Marked tissue damage, especially when produced by physical injury ► laceration, lesion, traumatism, wound. *—See also* EMERGENCY, HARM, SHOCK[1].

traumatize *v.* To cause bodily damage to a living thing ► hurt, injure, wing, wound. [*Compare* CUT, BREAK.] *—See also* DISTRESS.

travail *n.* *—See* BIRTH (1), LABOR.

travail *v.* *—See* LABOR.

travel *v.* To become known far and wide ► circulate, get around, go around, spread. *Idiom:* go (*or* make) the rounds. *—See also* JOURNEY, MOVE (2).

travel *n.* *—See* JOURNEY.

traveler *n.* *—See* TOURIST.

traveling *adj.* *—See* MOBILE (1), NOMADIC.

traversable *adj.* *—See* PASSABLE.

traversal *n.* *—See* DENIAL (1), JOURNEY.

traverse *v.* *—See* CONTEST, COVER (2), CROSS (1), DENY, EXAMINE (1).

traverse *adj.* *—See* TRANSVERSE.

travesty *n.* *—See* MOCKERY (2).

travesty *v.* *—See* IMITATE.

trawl *v.* *—See* FISH (1).

treacherous *adj.* *—See* DANGEROUS, FAITHLESS.

treacherousness *n.* *—See* FAITHLESSNESS.

treachery *n.* *—See* BETRAYAL, FAITHLESSNESS.

treacle *n.* *—See* SENTIMENTALITY.

tread *v.* To step on heavily and repeatedly so as to crush, injure, or destroy ► stamp, stomp, tramp, trample, tromp. [*Compare* CRUSH, TRUDGE.] *—See also* WALK.

tread *n.* *—See* WALK (2).

treadmill *n.* *—See* ROUTINE.

treason *n.* Willful violation of allegiance to one's country ► lese majesty, sedition, seditiousness, traitorousness. *—See also* FAITHLESSNESS.

treasonous or **treasonable** *adj.* Involving or constituting treason ► seditious, traitorous. [*Compare* FAITHLESS.]

treasure *n.* Someone or something considered exceptionally precious ► find, gem, pearl, plum, prize. *Informal:* catch. *Idioms:* apple of one's eye, pride and joy. [*Compare* MASTERPIECE.] *—See also* HOARD, WEALTH.

treasure *v.* *—See* SAVE (1), VALUE.

treasury or **treasure house** *n.* *—See* DEPOSITORY.

treat *v.* **1.** To behave in a specified way toward someone ► cope with, handle. **2.** To pay for the food, drink, or entertainment of another ► *Informal:* set up, stand. *Slang:* blow, spring for. *Idioms:* pick up the check (*or* tab), stand treat. [*Compare* AMUSE.] *—See also* ADMINISTER (3), DEAL (1).

treat *n.* *—See* AMUSEMENT, DELICACY, LUXURY.

treatise *n.* *—See* DISCOURSE.

treatment *n.* The systematic application of remedies to effect a cure ► care, doctoring, medical care, nursing, regimen, rehabilitation, therapeutics, therapy. *Informal:* rehab. [*Compare* DRUG.] *—See also* CURE.

treaty *n.* A formal agreement between two or more states or nations ► accord, agreement, concord, concordat, convention, entente, pact. [*Compare* AGREEMENT, BARGAIN, COMPROMISE, TRUCE.]

treble *adj.* *—See* HIGH (3).

tre·foil (trē′foil′, trĕf′oil′) ▸ *n.* **1.** A plant, such as a clover, having compound leaves with three leaflets. **2.** An ornament resembling such a leaf.

trek (trĕk) ▸ *v.* **trekked, trek·king.** To make a long difficult journey. **—trek** *n.* **—trek′ker** *n.*

trel·lis (trĕl′ĭs) ▸ *n.* An open latticework used for training climbing plants. **—trel′lised** *adj.*

trem·a·tode (trĕm′ə-tōd′) ▸ *n.* Any of numerous parasitic flatworms having external suckers or hooks.

trem·ble (trĕm′bəl) ▸ *v.* **-bled, -bling. 1.** To shake involuntarily, as from excitement, fear, or frailty; quake. **2.** To feel or express fear or anxiety. **—trem′ble** *n.* **—trem′bler** *n.*

tre·men·dous (trĭ-mĕn′dəs) ▸ *adj.* **1a.** Extremely large; enormous. **b.** *Informal* Marvelous; wonderful. **2.** Capable of making one tremble; awesome or terrible. **—tre·men′dous·ly** *adv.*

trem·o·lo (trĕm′ə-lō′) ▸ *n., pl.* **-los.** *Mus.* A tremulous effect produced either by the rapid repetition of a single tone or by the rapid alternation of two tones.

trem·or (trĕm′ər) ▸ *n.* **1.** A shaking or vibrating movement, as of the earth. **2.** An involuntary trembling or quivering, as from nervous agitation or disease.

trem·u·lous (trĕm′yə-ləs) ▸ *adj.* **1.** Vibrating or quivering; trembling. **2.** Timid; fearful. **—trem′u·lous·ly** *adv.*

trench (trĕnch) ▸ *n.* **1.** A deep furrow. **2.** A ditch embanked with its own soil and used for concealment and protection in warfare. **3.** A steep-sided valley on the ocean floor. ▸ *v.* **1.** To cut a trench in. **2.** To fortify with trenches.

trench·ant (trĕn′chənt) ▸ *adj.* **1.** Keen; incisive: *a trenchant argument.* **2.** Caustic; cutting. **—trench′an·cy** *n.*

trench coat ▸ *n.* A belted raincoat with straps on the shoulders and deep pockets.

trench·er (trĕn′chər) ▸ *n.* A wooden serving board.

trench fever ▸ *n.* An acute infectious disease caused by a microorganism and transmitted by a louse.

trench foot ▸ *n.* A foot disorder resembling frostbite, often affecting soldiers who must stand in cold flooded trenches.

trench mouth ▸ *n.* A painful bacterial infection of the mouth and throat.

trend (trĕnd) ▸ *n.* **1.** A general direction of movement. **2.** A general tendency or inclination. **3.** Current style; vogue: *the latest trend in fashion.* ▸ *v.* To have a certain direction or tendency.

trend·y (trĕn′dē) ▸ *adj.* **-i·er, -i·est.** *Informal* In accord with the latest fashion. **—trend′i·ly** *adv.* **—trend′i·ness** *n.*

Tren·ton (trĕn′tən) ▸ The capital of New Jersey, in the W-central part on the Delaware R.

tre·pan (trĭ-păn′) ▸ *n.* A trephine. ▸ *v.* **-panned, -pan·ning.** To trephine.

tre·phine (trĭ-fīn′) ▸ *n.* A surgical saw for cutting out disks of bone, usu. from the skull. ▸ *v.* **-phined, -phin·ing.** To operate on with a trephine. **—treph′i·na′tion** (trĕf′ə-nā′shən) *n.*

trep·i·da·tion (trĕp′ĭ-dā′shən) ▸ *n.* Dread; apprehension.

tres·pass (trĕs′pəs, -păs′) ▸ *v.* **1.** To commit an offense or sin; transgress or err. **2.** To invade the property or rights of another without consent. **3.** To infringe on the privacy or time of another. **—tres′pass** *n.* **—tres′pass·er** *n.*

tress (trĕs) ▸ *n.* A lock of hair.

tres·tle (trĕs′əl) ▸ *n.* **1.** A horizontal bar held up by two pairs of divergent legs and used as a support. **2.** A framework of vertical slanted supports and horizontal crosspieces supporting a bridge.

trey (trā) ▸ *n., pl.* **treys.** A card or die with three pips.

tri– ▸ *pref.* **1.** Three: *trisect.* **2a.** Occurring at intervals of three: *trimonthly.* **b.** Occurring three times during: *triweekly.*

tri·ad (trī′ăd′, -əd) ▸ *n.* A group of three. **—tri·ad′ic** *adj.*

tri·age (trē-äzh′, trē′äzh′) ▸ *n.* **1.** A process for sorting injured people into groups based on their need for medical treatment. **2.** A system used to allocate a scarce commodity, esp. in an emergency.

tri·al (trī′əl) ▸ *n.* **1.** Examination of evidence and applicable law to determine the issue of specified charges or claims. **2.** The act or process of testing or trying. **3.** An effort or attempt. **4.** A test of patience or endurance. **5.** A nuisance; pain. **6.** A qualifying competition, as in a sport. ▸ *adj.* **1.** Of a trial. **2.** Provisional; experimental. **3.** Made or done during a test. ***—idiom:* on trial** In the process of being tried, as in a court of law.

tri·an·gle (trī′ăng′gəl) ▸ *n.* **1a.** The plane figure formed by connecting three points not in a straight line by straight line segments. **b.** Something shaped like a triangle. **2.** A musical percussion instrument formed of a metal bar in the shape of a triangle. **—tri·an′gu·lar** *adj.*

tri·an·gu·late (trī-ăng′gyə-lāt′) ▸ *v.* **-lat·ed, -lat·ing.** To measure by using trigonometry. **—tri·an′gu·la′tion** *n.*

Tri·as·sic (trī-ăs′ĭk) *Geol.* ▸ *adj.* Of or being the 1st period of the Mesozoic Era, marked by the rise of dinosaurs and the appearance of the earliest mammals. ▸ *n.* The Triassic Period.

tri·ath·lon (trī-ăth′lən, -lŏn′) ▸ *n.* An athletic contest consisting of three successive events, usu. long-distance swimming, bicycling, and running. **—tri·ath′lete** *n.*

tribe (trīb) ▸ *n.* **1.** A unit of social organization consisting of a number of families, clans, or other groups who share a common ancestry, culture, and typically impermanent leadership. **2.** A group sharing a common distinguishing characteristic. **—trib′al** *adj.* **—trib′al·ly** *adv.* **—tribes′man** *n.* **—tribes′wom·an** *n.*

trib·u·la·tion (trĭb′yə-lā′shən) ▸ *n.* **1.** Great affliction or distress. **2.** An experience that tests one's endurance, patience, or faith.

THESAURUS

trek *v.* To travel about or journey on foot ▸ backpack, hike, march, tramp. [*Compare* ROVE, WALK.] *—See also* JOURNEY.

trek *n.* *—See* EXPEDITION.

tremble *v.* *—See* SHAKE (1), SWAY.

tremble *n.* *—See* TREMOR (2).

trembles *n.* *—See* JITTERS.

trembling *adj.* *—See* TREMULOUS.

trembling *n.* *—See* TREMOR (2).

tremendous *adj.* *—See* ENORMOUS, MARVELOUS.

tremendousness *n.* *—See* ENORMOUSNESS.

tremor *n.* **1.** A shaking of the earth ▸ earthquake, quake, seism, temblor. *Informal:* shake. **2.** A nervous shaking of the body ▸ jerk, paroxysm, quake, quaver, quiver, shake, shaking, shiver, shudder, spasm, thrill, tic, tremble, trembling, twitch, vibrating, vibration. [*Compare* SHAKE.]

tremulant *adj.* *—See* TREMULOUS.

tremulous *adj.* Marked by or affected with tremors ▸ aquiver, jerky, quaking, quaky, quavering, quivering, quivery, shaky, shivering, shivery, shuddering, trembling, tremulant, twittery, vibrating. *—See also* AFRAID.

trench *n.* *—See* FURROW.

trenchancy *n.* *—See* SARCASM.

trenchant *adj.* *—See* [illegible], CRITICAL (2).

trench coat *n.* *—See* COAT (1).

trend *n.* *—See* FASHION, INCLINATION (1).

trend *v.* *—See* TEND[1].

trendy *adj.* *—See* FASHIONABLE.

trepidation *n.* *—See* FEAR.

trespass *v.* To enter forcibly or illegally ▸ break in, burglarize, invade. [*Compare* ROB, STEAL.] *—See also* INTRUDE, OFFEND (3).

trespass *n.* **1.** The act of entering a building or room with the intent to commit theft ▸ break-in, breaking and entering, burglary, forced entry. [*Compare* LARCENY.] **2.** An advance beyond proper or legal limits ▸ encroachment, entrenchment, impingement, infringement, intrusion, obtrusion, overstepping, transgression. [*Compare* INVASION.] *—See also* BREACH (1).

trestle *n.* *—See* BEAM (2).

triad *n.* *—See* TRIO.

trial *n.* **1.** A state of pain or anguish that tests one's resiliency and character ▸ affliction, crucible, ordeal, tribulation, visitation. [*Compare* DIFFICULTY.] **2.** The examination of evidence, charges, and claims in court ▸ court case, hearing, inquest, inquiry. [*Compare* EXAMINATION.] **3.** An operation employed to resolve an uncertainty ▸ experiment, experimentation, test. *—See also* ANNOYANCE (2), ATTEMPT, BURDEN[1] (1), COMPETITION (2), TEST (1).

trial *adj.* *—See* PILOT.

tribe *n.* *—See* FAMILY (2).

tribulation *n.* *—See* BURDEN[1] (1), TRIAL (1).

tri·bu·nal (trī-byo͞o′nəl, trĭ-) ▸ *n.* **1.** *Law* A seat or court of justice. **2.** A committee or board appointed to adjudicate in a particular matter.

trib·une (trĭb′yo͞on′, trĭ-byo͞on′) ▸ *n.* **1.** An officer of ancient Rome elected by the plebeians to protect their rights. **2.** A protector or champion of the people. **—trib′u·nar′y** (trĭb′yə-nĕr′ē) *adj.*

trib·u·tar·y (trĭb′yə-tĕr′ē) ▸ *adj.* **1.** Contributory. **2.** Paid in tribute. **3.** Paying tribute. ▸ *n., pl.* **-ies. 1.** A stream that flows into a larger body of water. **2.** One that pays tribute.

trib·ute (trĭb′yo͞ot) ▸ *n.* **1.** A gift or other acknowledgment of gratitude, respect, or admiration. **2a.** A payment made by one ruler or nation to another in acknowledgment of submission or as the price of protection or security. **b.** A forced payment.

trice (trīs) ▸ *n.* A very short period of time; instant.

tri·cen·ten·ni·al (trī′sĕn-tĕn′ē-əl) ▸ *adj.* Tercentenary. ▸ *n.* A tercentenary event or celebration.

tri·ceps (trī′sĕps′) ▸ *n., pl.* **-ceps·es** (-sĕp′sĭz) also **-ceps.** A large muscle running along the back of the upper arm and serving to extend the forearm.

tri·cer·a·tops (trī-sĕr′ə-tŏps′) ▸ *n.* A herbivorous dinosaur with three facial horns and a bony plate covering the neck.

trich·i·no·sis (trĭk′ə-nō′sĭs) ▸ *n.* A disease caused by eating undercooked pork infested with parasitic worms, causing intestinal disorders, fever, nausea, muscular pain, and edema of the face.

trick (trĭk) ▸ *n.* **1.** An act or plan intended to achieve an end by deceptive or fraudulent means. **2.** A mischievous action; prank. **3a.** A peculiar trait; mannerism. **b.** A deceptive or illusive appearance: *a trick of sunlight.* **4a.** A feat requiring special knowledge. **b.** A specialized skill: *the tricks of the trade.* **5.** A feat of magic or legerdemain. **6.** A clever act. **7.** *Games* All the cards played in a single round. ▸ *v.* To cheat or deceive. ▸ *adj.* **1.** Involving tricks; tricky. **2.** Weak, defective, or liable to fail: *a trick knee.* ***—idiom:*** **not miss a trick** To be extremely alert. **—trick′er** *n.*

trick·er·y (trĭk′ə-rē) ▸ *n., pl.* **-ies.** The practice or use of tricks; deception.

trick·le (trĭk′əl) ▸ *v.* **-led, -ling. 1.** To flow or fall in drops or in a thin stream. **2.** To proceed slowly or bit by bit. ▸ *n.* **1.** The act or condition of trickling. **2.** A slow, small, or irregular quantity.

trick·ster (trĭk′stər) ▸ *n.* One who plays clever or deceptive tricks.

trick·y (trĭk′ē) ▸ *adj.* **-i·er, -i·est. 1.** Crafty; sly. **2.** Requiring caution or skill. **—trick′i·ly** *adv.* **—trick′i·ness** *n.*

tri·col·or (trī′kŭl′ər) ▸ *n.* A flag having three colors. ▸ *adj.* also **tri·col·ored** (-ərd) Having three colors.

tri·corn also **tri·corne** (trī′kôrn′) ▸ *n.* A hat with the brim turned up on three sides.

tri·cot (trē′kō) ▸ *n.* **1.** A fabric knitted so as to resist runs. **2.** A soft ribbed woolen cloth.

tri·cy·cle (trī′sĭk′əl, -sĭ-kəl) ▸ *n.* A three-wheeled vehicle usu. propelled by pedals.

tri·dent (trīd′nt) ▸ *n.* A long, three-pronged fishing spear or weapon.

tried (trīd) ▸ *v.* P.t. and p.part. of **try.** ▸ *adj.* Tested and proved to be trustworthy.

tri·en·ni·al (trī-ĕn′ē-əl) ▸ *adj.* **1.** Occurring every third year. **2.** Lasting three years. ▸ *n.* A third anniversary. **—tri·en′ni·al·ly** *adv.*

tri·fle (trī′fəl) ▸ *n.* **1.** Something of little importance or value. **2.** A small amount. ▸ *v.* **-fled, -fling. 1.** To deal with something as if it were of little significance or value. **2.** To play or toy with something. **—tri′fler** (trī′flər) *n.*

tri·fling (trī′flĭng) ▸ *adj.* **1.** Of slight worth or importance. **2.** Frivolous or idle.

tri·fo·cal (trī-fō′kəl, trī′fō′-) ▸ *adj.* Having three focal lengths. ▸ *n.* **trifocals** Eyeglasses having trifocal lenses.

trig (trĭg) ▸ *adj.* **1.** Smart and trim, as in appearance. **2.** In good condition.

trig·ger (trĭg′ər) ▸ *n.* **1a.** The lever pressed by the finger to discharge a firearm. **b.** A similar device used to release or activate a mechanism. **2.** An event that precipitates other events. **—trig′ger** *v.*

tri·glyc·er·ide (trī-glĭs′ə-rīd′) ▸ *n.* A naturally occurring ester of three fatty acids and glycerol that is the chief constituent of fats and oils.

trig·o·nom·e·try (trĭg′ə-nŏm′ĭ-trē) ▸ *n.* The study of relationships between the sides and the angles of triangles. **—trig′o·no·met′ric** (-nə-mĕt′rĭk), **trig′o·no·met′ri·cal** *adj.*

trill (trĭl) ▸ *n.* **1.** A fluttering or tremulous sound; warble. **2.** *Mus.* The rapid alternation of two tones either a whole or a half tone apart. **3.** *Ling.* **a.** A rapid vibration of one speech organ against another. **b.** A speech sound so pronounced. **—trill** *v.*

tril·lion (trĭl′yən) ▸ *n.* **1.** The cardinal number equal to 10^{12}. **2.** *Chiefly Brit.* The cardinal number equal to 10^{18}. **—tril′lion** *adj.* **—tril′lionth** *n. & adj.*

tri·lo·bite (trī′lə-bīt′) ▸ *n.* An extinct three-lobed marine arthropod of the Paleozoic Era.

tril·o·gy (trĭl′ə-jē) ▸ *n., pl.* **-gies.** A group of three related artistic works.

trim (trĭm) ▸ *v.* **trimmed, trim·ming. 1.** To make neat or tidy by clipping, smoothing, or pruning. **2.** To rid of excess or remove by cutting. **3.** To ornament; decorate. **4.** *Naut.* **a.** To adjust (the sails and yards) so that they receive the wind properly. **b.** To balance (a ship) by shifting its cargo or contents. **5.** To balance (an aircraft) in flight. ▸ *n.* **1a.** State of order or appearance; condition. **b.** A condition of good health or fitness. **2.** Ornamentation. **3.** Excised

THESAURUS

tribunal *n.* —*See* COURT (2).

tributary *n.* —*See* BRANCH (1), BROOK[1], RIVER.

tribute *n.* —*See* COMPLIMENT, TAX, TESTIMONIAL (2).

trice *n.* —*See* FLASH (2).

trick *n.* **1.** An indirect, usually cunning means of gaining an end ▸ artifice, deception, device, dodge, feint, gimmick, hustle, imposture, jig, maneuver, ploy, ruse, sleight, stratagem, subterfuge, wile. *Informal:* con game, fast one, shenanigan, take-in. *Slang:* snow job. [*Compare* MOVE, PLOT, TRAP.] **2.** The proper method for doing, using, or handling something ▸ feel, knack. *Informal:* hang. **3.** A clever, dexterous act ▸ feat, stunt. *Idiom:* sleight of hand. [*Compare* ACCOMPLISHMENT.] —*See also* PRANK[1], TURN (1), WRINKLE (2).

trick *v.* —*See* DECEIVE.

trick out or **up** *v.* —*See* DRESS UP.

trick *adj.* So weak or defective as to be liable to fail ▸ undependable, unreliable. [*Compare* DEFECTIVE, WEAK.]

trickery *n.* —*See* DECEIT, DISHONESTY (2).

trickiness *n.* —*See* DISHONESTY (2).

trickle *v.* —*See* DRIP.

trickle *n.* The process or sound of dripping ▸ dribble, drip, drizzle, mizzle.

tricks *n.* —*See* MISCHIEF.

trickster *n.* —*See* CHEAT (2).

tricky *adj.* —*See* ARTFUL, DELICATE (3).

tried *adj.* —*See* EXPERIENCED.

trifle *n.* Something or things of little importance ▸ fiddle-faddle, frippery, frivolity, froth, inconsequence, inconsequentiality, inconsequentialness, inconsiderableness, indifference, insignificance, insignificancy, levity, lightness, minutia, negligibility, negligibleness, nonsense, paltriness, pettiness, picayune, small change, smallness, triviality, trivialness, unimportance. *Informal:* small potatoes. —*See also* BIT[1] (1), NOVELTY (3).

trifle *v.* To treat lightly or flippantly ▸ dally, flirt, play, toy. —*See also* FIDDLE, FLIRT (2).

trifle away *v.* —*See* IDLE (2), WASTE.

trifling *adj.* —*See* TRIVIAL.

trig *adj.* —*See* NEAT.

trig *v.* —*See* TIDY (2).

trigger *n.* —*See* PROVOCATION (1).

trigger *v.* —*See* CAUSE, PROVOKE.

triggerman *n.* —*See* MURDERER.

trillion *n.* —*See* HEAP (2).

trim *v.* To make a slight reduction in prices ▸ shade, shave. —*See also* ADORN (1), BEAT (2), CHEAT (1), CUT (3), DEFEAT, TIDY (2).

trim down *v.* To lose body weight, as by dieting ▸ reduce, slim (down), thin (down). *Idioms:* get the weight off, lose weight, shed some pounds.

trim *n.* —*See* ADORNMENT, SHAPE.

trim *adj.* Having slender and graceful lines ▸ sleek, streamlined. —*See also* NEAT.

or rejected material. **4a.** The readiness of a vessel for sailing. **b.** The balance of a ship. ▸ *adj.* **trim·mer, trim·mest. 1.** In good or neat order. **2.** Having lines of neat and pleasing simplicity. ▸ *adv.* In a trim manner. **—trim′ly** *adv.* **—trim′mer** *n.* **—trim′ness** *n.*

tri·mes·ter (trī-mĕs′tər, trī′mĕs′-) ▸ *n.* **1.** A period of three months. **2.** One of three terms into which an academic year is sometimes divided.

trim·e·ter (trĭm′ĭ-tər) ▸ *n.* A line of verse consisting of three metrical feet. **—tri·met′ric** (trī-mĕt′rĭk), **tri·met′ri·cal** *adj.*

trim·ming (trĭm′ĭng) ▸ *n.* **1.** The act of one that trims. **2.** Something added as decoration. **3. trimmings** Accessories; extras.

trine (trīn) ▸ *adj.* Threefold; triple. ▸ *n.* A group of three.

Trin·i·dad (trĭn′ĭ-dăd′) ▸ An island of Trinidad and Tobago in the Atlantic off NE Venezuela. **—Trin′i·dad′i·an** *adj. & n.*

Trinidad and Tobago ▸ A country of the SE West Indies in the Atlantic off NE Venezuela, comprising the islands of Trinidad and Tobago.

trin·i·ty (trĭn′ĭ-tē) ▸ *n., pl.* **-ties. 1.** A group of three closely related members. **2. Trinity** In Christian theology, the union of the three divine persons in one God.

trin·ket (trĭng′kĭt) ▸ *n.* **1.** A small ornament or piece of jewelry. **2.** A trifle.

tri·o (trē′ō) ▸ *n., pl.* **-os. 1.** A group of three. **2.** *Mus.* **a.** A composition for three performers. **b.** The group performing such a composition.

trip (trĭp) ▸ *n.* **1.** A going from one place to another; journey. **2.** A stumble or fall. **3.** A maneuver causing someone to stumble or fall. **4.** *Slang* An exciting or hallucinatory experience. **5.** A device for triggering a mechanism. ▸ *v.* **tripped, trip·ping. 1.** To stumble or cause to stumble. **2.** To move nimbly with light rapid steps; skip. **3.** To make or cause to make an error. **4.** To release or be released, as a catch, trigger, or switch. **—trip′per** *n.*

tri·par·tite (trī-pär′tīt) ▸ *adj.* **1.** Composed of or divided into three parts. **2.** Of or executed by three parties: *a tripartite agreement.*

tripe (trīp) ▸ *n.* **1.** The stomach lining of cattle or other ruminants, used as food. **2.** *Informal* Something of no value; rubbish.

tri·ple (trĭp′əl) ▸ *adj.* **1.** Having three parts. **2.** Three times as many or as much. **3.** *Mus.* Having three beats in a measure. ▸ *n.* **1.** A number or quantity three times as great as another. **2.** A group or set of three; a triad. **3.** *Baseball* A hit that enables the batter to reach third base safely. ▸ *v.* **-pled, -pling. 1.** To make or become three times as great in number or amount. **2.** *Baseball* To make a triple. **—tri′ply** *adv.*

triple play ▸ *n.* *Baseball* A play in which three players are put out.

trip·let (trĭp′lĭt) ▸ *n.* **1.** A group or set of three. **2.** One of three children born at one birth.

tri·plex (trĭp′lĕks′, trī′plĕks′) ▸ *adj.* Having three parts or divisions: *a triplex cinema.* **—tri′plex′** *n.*

trip·li·cate (trĭp′lĭ-kĭt) ▸ *n.* One of a set of three identical objects or copies. ▸ *v.* (-kāt′) **-cat·ed, -cat·ing.** To make three identical copies of. **—trip′li·ca′tion** *n.*

tri·pod (trī′pŏd′) ▸ *n.* **1.** A three-legged object, such as a cauldron, stool, or table. **2.** An adjustable three-legged stand, as for supporting a camera or telescope.

Trip·o·li (trĭp′ə-lē) ▸ The capital of Libya, in the NW part on the Mediterranean Sea.

trip·tych (trĭp′tĭk) ▸ *n.* A three-paneled work of art.

tri·sect (trī′sĕkt′, trī-sĕkt′) ▸ *v.* To divide into three equal parts. **—tri′sec′tion** *n.*

trite (trīt) ▸ *adj.* **trit·er, trit·est.** Overused and commonplace; lacking originality. **—trite′ly** *adv.* **—trite′ness** *n.*

trit·i·um (trĭt′ē-əm, trĭsh′ē-) ▸ *n.* A rare radioactive hydrogen isotope with atomic mass 3.

tri·umph (trī′əmf) ▸ *v.* **1.** To be victorious or successful; win. **2.** To rejoice; exult. ▸ *n.* **1.** The fact or an instance of being victorious; victory. **2.** Exultation. **—tri·um′phal** *adj.* **—tri·um′phant** *adj.*

tri·um·vir (trī-ŭm′vər) ▸ *n., pl.* **-virs** or **-vi·ri** (-və-rī′). One of three men sharing civil authority in ancient Rome. **—tri·um′vi·ral** *adj.* **—tri·um′vi·rate** (-vər-ĭt) *n.*

triv·et (trĭv′ĭt) ▸ *n.* **1.** A stand with short feet, used under a hot dish on a table. **2.** A three-legged stand.

triv·i·a (trĭv′ē-ə) ▸ *pl.n.* *(takes sing. or pl. v.)* Insignificant or inessential matters.

triv·i·al (trĭv′ē-əl) ▸ *adj.* **1.** Of little significance or value. **2.** Commonplace. **—triv′i·al′i·ty** (-ăl′ĭ-tē) *n.* **—triv′i·al·ly** *adv.*

triv·i·al·ize (trĭv′ē-ə-līz′) ▸ *v.* **-ized, -iz·ing.** To reduce to triviality. **—triv′i·al·i·za′tion** *n.*

-trix ▸ *suff.* A woman who is connected with a specified thing: *testatrix.*

tro·chee (trō′kē) ▸ *n.* A metrical foot consisting of a stressed syllable followed by an unstressed syllable. **—tro·cha′ic** (-kā′ĭk) *adj.*

trod (trŏd) ▸ *v.* P.t. and p.part. of **tread.**

trod·den (trŏd′n) ▸ *v.* P.part. of **tread.**

trog·lo·dyte (trŏg′lə-dīt′) ▸ *n.* **1.** A member of a fabulous or prehistoric race that lived in caves. **2.** A reclusive, reactionary, or brutish person. **—trog′lo·dyt′ic** (-dĭt′ĭk) *adj.*

troi·ka (troi′kə) ▸ *n.* A Russian carriage drawn by three horses abreast.

Tro·jan (trō′jən) ▸ *n.* **1.** A native or inhabitant of ancient Troy. **2.** A person of courageous determination. **—Tro′jan** *adj.*

Trojan War ▸ *n.* *Gk. Myth.* The ten-year war waged against Troy by the Greeks, resulting in the destruction of Troy.

troll[1] (trōl) ▸ *v.* **1.** To fish by trailing a baited line from behind a slowly moving boat. **2a.** To sing in succession the parts of (a round). **b.** To sing heartily. ▸ *n.* **1.** The act of trolling for fish. **2.** A musical round. **—troll′er** *n.*

troll[2] (trōl) ▸ *n.* A supernatural creature of Scandinavian folklore, often described as living in caves or under bridges.

trol·ley also **trol·ly** (trŏl′ē) ▸ *n., pl.* **-leys** also **-lies. 1.** A streetcar. **2.** A device that collects electric current and transmits

THESAURUS

trimming *n.* —*See* ADORNMENT, BEATING, DEFEAT.

trine or **trinity** *n.* —*See* TRIO.

trinket *n.* —*See* NOVELTY (3).

trio *n.* A group of three individuals ▸ three, threesome, triad, trine, trinity, triple, triumvirate, triune, triunity, troika. [*Compare* GROUP.]

trip *n.* **1.** A usually short journey taken for pleasure ▸ excursion, jaunt, junket, outing. [*Compare* EXPEDITION.] **2.** *Slang* A temporary concentration of interest ▸ *Slang:* kick. **3.** *Slang* An experience of things or events that are not real ▸ hallucination, phantasmagoria, phantasmagory. —*See also* ERROR, JOURNEY.

trip *v.* —*See* BOUND[1], JOURNEY, STUMBLE.

trip up *v.* —*See* ERR.

triple *n.* —*See* TRIO.

tripping *adj.* —*See* DRUGGED.

tristful *adj.* —*See* DEPRESSED (1).

trite *adj.* Without freshness or appeal because of overuse ▸ banal, bromidic, clichéd, commonplace, corny, hackneyed, musty, overused, overworked, platitudinal, platitudinous, shopworn, stale, stereotyped, stereotypic, stereotypical, stock, threadbare, timeworn, tired, unimaginative, uninspired, unoriginal, warmed-over, well-worn, worn-out. [*Compare* BORING, DULL.]

triturate *v.* —*See* CRUSH (2).

triumph *v.* —*See* EXULT (1).

triumph over *v.* —*See* DEFEAT.

triumph *n.* —*See* ACCOMPLISHMENT, CONQUEST, EXULTATION.

triumphal *adj.* —*See* VICTORIOUS.

triumphant *adj.* Feeling or expressing an uplifting joy over a success or victory ▸ exultant, gloating, jubilant. [*Compare* BOASTFUL.] —*See also* VICTORIOUS.

triumvirate *n.* —*See* TRIO.

triune or **triunity** *n.* —*See* TRIO.

trivia *n.* —*See* DETAIL, TRIFLE.

trivial *adj.* Of little importance or seriousness ▸ fluffy, frivolous, frothy, inconsequent, inconsequential, inconsiderable, insignificant, light, lightweight, little, negligible, niggling, nugatory, paltry, petty, picayune, piddling, small, small-minded, trifling, unimportant. *Slang:* measly, rinky-dink, two-bit. *Idiom:* of no account. [*Compare* SUPERFICIAL, WORTHLESS.]

triviality or **trivialness** *n.* —*See* TRIFLE.

troika *n.* —*See* TRIO.

troll *v.* —*See* FISH (1).

it to the motor of an electric vehicle. **3.** A wheeled carriage or basket suspended from an overhead track.

trolley bus ► *n.* A bus that is powered by electricity from an overhead wire.

trolley car ► *n.* A streetcar.

trol·lop (trŏl′əp) ► *n.* **1.** A slovenly woman. **2.** A strumpet.

trom·bone (trŏm-bōn′, trəm-, trŏm′bōn′) ► *n.* A brass musical instrument with a movable U-shaped slide for producing different pitches. **—trom·bon′ist** *n.*

tromp (trŏmp) ► *v.* **1.** To tramp. **2.** To trample underfoot. **3.** To trounce.

trompe l'oeil (trômp′ loi′) ► *n.* A detailed style of painting that gives an illusion of photographic reality.

–tron ► *suff.* Device for manipulating subatomic particles: *betatron.*

troop (tro͞op) ► *n.* **1.** A group or company of people, animals, or things. **2a.** A group of soldiers. **b. troops** Military units; soldiers. ► *v.* To move or go as a throng.

troop·er (tro͞o′pər) ► *n.* **1a.** A member of a cavalry unit. **b.** A cavalry horse. **2a.** A mounted police officer. **b.** A state police officer.

trope (trōp) ► *n.* A figure of speech using words in nonliteral ways.

tro·phy (trō′fē) ► *n., pl.* **-phies.** A prize or memento received as a symbol of victory.

–trophy ► *suff.* Nutrition; growth: *hypertrophy.*

trop·ic (trŏp′ĭk) ► *n.* **1.** Either of two parallels of latitude, the tropic of Cancer or the tropic of Capricorn, representing the farthest north and south at which the sun can shine directly overhead. **2. tropics** The region of the earth's surface bounded by these latitudes. ► *adj.* Of or concerning the tropics; tropical.

–tropic ► *suff.* Changing in a specified way or in response to a specified stimulus: *phototropic.*

trop·i·cal (trŏp′ĭ-kəl) ► *adj.* **1.** Of or characteristic of the tropics. **2.** Hot and humid; torrid. **—trop′i·cal·ly** *adv.*

tropical year ► *n.* The time interval between two successive passages of the sun through the vernal equinox; solar year.

tropic of Cancer ► *n.* The parallel of latitude 23°27' north of the equator.

tropic of Capricorn ► *n.* The parallel of latitude 23°27' south of the equator.

tro·pism (trō′pĭz′əm) ► *n.* The turning or bending movement of an organism toward or away from an external stimulus.

tro·po·sphere (trō′pə-sfîr′, trŏp′ə-) ► *n.* The lowest region of the earth's atmosphere, marked by decreasing temperature with increasing altitude. **—tro′po·spher′ic** (-sfîr′ĭk, -sfĕr′-) *adj.*

–tropy ► *suff.* The state of turning in a specified way or from a specified stimulus: *phototropy.*

trot (trŏt) ► *n.* **1.** The gait of a four-footed animal in which diagonal pairs of legs move forward together. **2.** A gait of a person, faster than a walk; jog. ► *v.* **trot·ted, trot·ting. 1.** To go or move at a trot. **2.** To hurry. **—trot′ter** *n.*

troth (trôth, trŏth, trōth) ► *n.* **1a.** Betrothal. **b.** One's pledged fidelity. **2.** Good faith; fidelity.

Trot·sky or **Trot·ski** (trŏt′skē, trôt′-), **Leon** (1879–1940) ► Russian revolutionary theoretician.

trou·ba·dour (tro͞o′bə-dôr′, -do͝or′) ► *n.* **1.** One of a class of 12th and 13th cent. lyric poets in S France, N Italy, and N Spain. **2.** A strolling minstrel.

trou·ble (trŭb′əl) ► *n.* **1.** A state of distress, affliction, danger, or need. **2.** A source of distress or difficulty. **3.** Inconvenience or bother. **4.** A condition of pain or malfunction. ► *v.* **-bled, -bling. 1.** To agitate; stir up. **2.** To afflict with pain or discomfort. **3.** To distress; worry. **4.** To inconvenience; bother. **—trou′bler** *n.* **—trou′ble·some** *adj.*

trou·ble·mak·er (trŭb′əl-mā′kər) ► *n.* One who stirs up trouble or strife.

trou·ble·shoot·er (trŭb′əl-sho͞o′tər) ► *n.* One who locates and eliminates sources of trouble.

trough (trôf, trŏf) ► *n.* **1.** A long, narrow, usu. shallow receptacle, esp. for holding water or feed for animals. **2.** A gutter under the eaves of a roof. **3.** A long narrow depression, as between waves. **4.** A low point in a cycle or on a graph.

trounce (trouns) ► *v.* **trounced, trounc·ing. 1.** To thrash; beat. **2.** To defeat decisively.

troupe (tro͞op) ► *n.* A company or group, esp. of touring performers. ► *v.* **trouped, troup·ing.** To tour with a theatrical company. **—troup′er** *n.*

trou·sers (trou′zərz) ► *pl.n.* A garment covering the body from the waist to the ankles, divided into sections to fit each leg separately.

trous·seau (tro͞o′sō, tro͞o-sō′) ► *n., pl.* **-seaux** (-sōz, -sōz′) or **-seaus.** The special wardrobe a bride assembles for her marriage.

trout (trout) ► *n., pl.* **trout** or **trouts.** Any of various edible, chiefly freshwater fishes related to the salmon.

trove (trōv) ► *n.* A treasure-trove.

trow·el (trou′əl) ► *n.* **1.** A flat-bladed hand tool for leveling, spreading, or shaping substances such as cement. **2.** A small digging tool with a scoop-shaped blade. **—trow′el** *v.*

troy (troi) ► *adj.* Of or expressed in troy weight.

Troy ► An ancient city of NW Asia Minor near the Dardanelles.

troy weight ► *n.* A system of units of weight in which the grain is the same as in the avoirdupois system and the pound contains 12 ounces, 240 pennyweights, or 5,760 grains.

tru·ant (tro͞o′ənt) ► *n.* **1.** One absent without permission, esp. from school. **2.** One who shirks work or duty. **—tru′ant** *adj.* **—tru′an·cy** *n.*

truce (tro͞os) ► *n.* A temporary cessation of hostilities by agreement; armistice.

truck[1] (trŭk) ► *n.* **1.** A heavy motor vehicle for carrying loads. **2.** A two-wheeled barrow for moving heavy objects by hand. **3.** One of the swiveling frames of wheels under each end of a railroad car or trolley car. ► *v.* **1.** To transport by truck. **2.** To drive a truck. **—truck′er** *n.*

truck[2] (trŭk) ► *v.* **1.** To exchange; barter. **2.** To have dealings or commerce; traffic. ► *n.* **1.** Garden produce raised

THESAURUS

tromp *v.* To step on heavily and repeatedly so as to crush, injure, or destroy ► stamp, stomp, tramp, trample, tread. [*Compare* CRUSH.] *—See also* TRUDGE.

troop *n.* *—See* ASSEMBLY, BAND[2], CROWD, FLOCK.

trooper *n.* *—See* POLICE OFFICER, SOLDIER (2).

trophy *n.* A memento received as a symbol of excellence or victory ► accolade, award, cup, prize. [*Compare* MEDAL, REWARD.] *—See also* DISTINCTION (2), REMEMBRANCE (1).

tropical *adj.* *—See* HOT (1).

trot *n.* *—See* RUN (1), TRANSLATION.

trot *v.* *—See* RUN (1), RUSH.

troth *n.* The act or condition of being pledged to marry ► betrothal, engagement, espousal.

troth *v.* *—See* PLEDGE (1).

troubadour *n.* *—See* POET.

trouble *n.* A cause or source of distress or anxiety ► care, concern, stressor, worry. [*Compare* ANXIETY, BURDEN[1].] *—See also* DIFFICULTY, EFFORT, EMERGENCY, INCONVENIENCE, PREDICAMENT, QUALM.

trouble *v.* To come to mind continually ► haunt, obsess, torment, weigh on (*or* upon). *—See also* DISTRESS, INCONVENIENCE, WORRY.

troublemaker *n.* *—See* AGITATOR.

troubleshooter *n.* *—See* GO-BETWEEN.

troublesome *adj.* **1.** Causing difficulty, trouble, or discomfort ► difficult, incommodious, inconvenient. **2.** Hard to treat, manage, or cope with ► demanding, difficult, trying, wicked. *Informal:* pesky. *Slang:* mean. [*Compare* FUSSY, UNRULY.] *—See also* DISTURBING.

troubling or **troublous** *adj.* *—See* DISTURBING.

trough *n.* *—See* FURROW.

trounce *v.* *—See* OVERWHELM (1).

trouncing *n.* *—See* DEFEAT.

troupe *n.* *—See* BAND[2].

trouper *n.* A theatrical performer ► actor, actress, player, thespian. [*Compare* FAKE, LEAD, MIMIC.]

truancy or **truantry** *n.* *—See* ABSENCE (1).

truant *v.* *—See* CUT (4).

truant *adj.* *—See* ABSENT.

truce *n.* A temporary cessation of hostilities by mutual agreement ► armistice, cease-fire, peace, white flag. *Idioms:* cooling-off period, peace agreement, suspension of hostilities. [*Compare* BREAK.]

for the market. **2.** *Informal* Worthless goods; rubbish. **3.** Barter; exchange. **4.** *Informal* Dealings; business.

truck·age (trŭk′ĭj) ▸ *n.* **1.** Transportation of goods by truck. **2.** A charge for this service.

truck·le (trŭk′əl) ▸ *n.* A small wheel or roller; caster. ▸ *v.* **-led, -ling.** To be servile or submissive.

truc·u·lent (trŭk′yə-lənt) ▸ *adj.* **1.** Disposed to fight; pugnacious. **2.** Savage and cruel; fierce. **—truc′u·lence** *n.*

Tru·deau (tro͞o-dō′), **Pierre Elliott** (1919–2000) ▸ Canadian prime minister (1968–79 and 1980–84).

trudge (trŭj) ▸ *v.* **trudged, trudg·ing.** To walk in a laborious, heavy-footed way; plod. **—trudge** *n.* **—trudg′er** *n.*

true (tro͞o) ▸ *adj.* **tru·er, tru·est. 1a.** Consistent with fact or reality; not false or erroneous. **b.** Truthful. **2.** Real; genuine. **3.** Reliable; accurate. **4.** Faithful; loyal. **5.** Sincerely felt or expressed. **6.** Rightful; legitimate. **7.** Exactly conforming to a rule, standard, or pattern. **8.** Determined with reference to the earth's axis, not the magnetic poles: *true north.* ▸ *adv.* **1.** Rightly; truthfully. **2.** Unswervingly; exactly. **3.** So as to conform to a type, standard, or pattern. ▸ *v.* **trued, tru·ing** or **true·ing.** To position (something) so as to make it balanced, level, or square. ▸ *n.* **1. the true** Truth or reality. **2.** Proper alignment or adjustment: *out of true.* **—true′ness** *n.*

true-blue (tro͞o′blo͞o′) ▸ *adj.* Loyal or faithful; staunch.

true·love (tro͞o′lŭv′) ▸ *n.* One's beloved.

truf·fle (trŭf′əl) ▸ *n.* **1.** An underground fungus valued as a delicacy. **2.** A rich chocolate confection.

tru·ism (tro͞o′ĭz′əm) ▸ *n.* A self-evident truth. **—tru·is′tic** *adj.*

Truk Islands (trŭk, tro͝ok) ▸ See **Chuuk Islands.**

tru·ly (tro͞o′lē) ▸ *adv.* **1.** Sincerely; genuinely. **2.** Truthfully; accurately. **3.** Indeed.

Tru·man (tro͞o′mən), **Harry S.** (1884–1972) ▸ The 33rd US President (1945–53).

trump (trŭmp) ▸ *n.* **1.** often **trumps** A suit in card games that outranks all other suits for the duration of a hand. **2.** A card of such a suit. ▸ *v.* To play a trump. ***—phrasal verb:* trump up** To devise fraudulently.

trump·er·y (trŭm′pə-rē) ▸ *n., pl.* **-ies. 1.** Showy but worthless finery. **2.** Nonsense. **3.** Trickery.

trum·pet (trŭm′pĭt) ▸ *n.* **1a.** A soprano brass wind instrument consisting of a long metal tube ending in a flared bell. **b.** Something shaped or sounding like a trumpet. **2.** A resounding call. ▸ *v.* To sound or proclaim loudly. **—trum′pet·er** *n.*

trun·cate (trŭng′kāt′) ▸ *v.* **-cat·ed, -cat·ing.** To shorten by or as if by cutting off the end or top. **—trun·ca′tion** *n.*

trun·cheon (trŭn′chən) ▸ *n.* A short stick carried by police; billy club. **—trun′cheon** *v.*

trun·dle (trŭn′dl) ▸ *v.* **-dled, -dling.** To push on wheels or rollers.

trundle bed ▸ *n.* A low bed on casters that can be rolled under another bed for storage when not in use.

trunk (trŭngk) ▸ *n.* **1.** The main woody axis of a tree. **2.** The human body excluding the head and limbs; torso. **3.** A proboscis, esp. the long prehensile proboscis of an elephant. **4.** A main body, apart from tributaries or appendages. **5a.** A covered compartment for luggage and storage, usu. at the rear of an automobile. **b.** A large packing case or box that clasps shut, used as luggage or for storage. **6. trunks** Shorts worn esp. for swimming.

trunk line ▸ *n.* A direct line between two telephone switchboards.

truss (trŭs) ▸ *n.* **1.** A supportive device worn to prevent enlargement of a hernia or the return of a reduced hernia. **2.** A wooden or metal framework designed to support a structure, such as a roof. ▸ *v.* **1.** To tie up or bind tightly. **2.** To bind the wings or legs of (a fowl) before cooking. **3.** To support or brace with a truss.

trust (trŭst) ▸ *n.* **1.** Firm reliance on the integrity or ability of a person or thing. **2.** Custody; care. **3.** Something committed into the care of another; charge. **4a.** The condition and obligation of having confidence placed in one. **b.** One in which confidence is placed. **5.** Reliance on something in the future; hope. **6.** A legal title to property held by one party for the benefit of another. **7.** A combination of firms or corporations for the purpose of reducing competition. ▸ *v.* **1.** To rely or depend (on); have confidence (in). **2.** To be confident; hope. **3.** To expect with assurance; assume. **4.** To believe. **5.** To entrust. **6.** To grant discretion to confidently. **7.** To extend credit to. ***—idiom:* in trust** In the possession or care of a trustee. **—trust′er** *n.*

trus·tee (trŭ-stē′) ▸ *n.* **1.** A person or agent holding legal title to and administering property for a beneficiary. **2.** A member of a board that directs the funds and policy of an institution. **—trus·tee′ship′** *n.*

trust·ful (trŭst′fəl) ▸ *adj.* Full of trust. **—trust′ful·ly** *adv.* **—trust′ful·ness** *n.*

trust·wor·thy (trŭst′wûr′*th*ē) ▸ *adj.* Warranting trust; reliable. **—trust′wor′thi·ness** *n.*

trust·y (trŭs′tē) ▸ *adj.* **-i·er, -i·est.** Meriting trust; dependable. ▸ *n., pl.* **-ies.** A trusted person, esp. a convict granted special privileges. **—trust′i·ly** *adv.* **—trust′i·ness** *n.*

truth (tro͞oth) ▸ *n., pl.* **truths** (tro͞o*th*z, tro͞oths). **1.** Conformity to fact or actuality. **2.** A statement proven to be or accepted as true. **3.** Sincerity; honesty. **4.** Reality; actuality.

Truth, Sojourner (1797?–1883) ▸ Amer. abolitionist and feminist.

truth·ful (tro͞oth′fəl) ▸ *adj.* **1.** Consistently telling the truth; honest. **2.** Corresponding to reality. **—truth′ful·ly** *adv.* **—truth′ful·ness** *n.*

try (trī) ▸ *v.* **tried** (trīd), **try·ing. 1.** To make an effort (to do something); attempt. **2.** To test in order to determine

THESAURUS

truckle *v.* —*See* FAWN.

truckler *n.* —*See* SYCOPHANT.

truculence or **truculency** *n.* —*See* AGGRESSION, CRUELTY, FIGHT (2).

truculent *adj.* —*See* AGGRESSIVE, BITING, CRUEL.

trudge *v.* To walk in a laborious way ▸ forge, plod, scuff, scuffle, shamble, shuffle, slog, slop, stamp, stomp, toil, trail, tramp, trample, wade. *Informal:* tromp. *Slang:* schlep. [*Compare* CRAWL, TRAMPLE, WALK.]

true *adj.* **1.** Occurring or existing in act or fact ▸ actual, existent, extant, real. [*Compare* PHYSICAL.] **2.** Marked by uprightness in principle and action ▸ good, honest, honorable, incorruptible, righteous, upright, upstanding. *Informal:* straight-shooting. *Idiom:* on the up-and-up. **3.** Being so legitimately ▸ legitimate, rightful. [*Compare* LAWFUL.] —*See also* ACCURATE, AUTHENTIC (1), AUTHENTIC (2), FAITHFUL, GENUINE, HONEST, REALISTIC (2).

true-life *adj.* —*See* REALISTIC (2).

truelove *n.* —*See* DARLING (1).

truism *n.* —*See* CLICHÉ, LAW (3).

truly *adv.* —*See* REALLY.

trump *v.* To outmaneuver an opponent ▸ finesse. *Informal:* one-up. *Idioms:* play gotcha, pull (*or* put over) a fast one. [*Compare* DECEIVE, MANEUVER, OUTWIT.]

trump or **trump card** *n.* A key resource to be used at an opportune moment ▸ ace. *Informal:* [illegible] *Idiom:* ace in the hole.

trumpet *v.* —*See* ANNOUNCE.

truncate *v.* —*See* CUT (3), SHORTEN.

trunk *n.* **1.** The human body excluding the head and limbs ▸ body, midsection, torso. **2.** The main ascending part of a plant, which supports the other parts ▸ stalk, stem, stock. [*Compare* SHOOT.]

truss *v.* —*See* DRESS (2).

trust *n.* Absolute certainty that a person or thing will not fail ▸ belief, confidence, dependence, faith, reliance. —*See also* ALLIANCE, CARE (2).

trust *v.* **1.** To have confidence in the truthfulness of ▸ believe, credit. *Idioms:* give credence to, have faith (*or* trust *or* confidence) in, take at one's word. **2.** To place a trust upon ▸ charge, entrust. [*Compare* AUTHORIZE.] —*See also* DEPEND ON (1), ENTRUST (1).

trusting *adj.* —*See* GULLIBLE.

trustworthiness *n.* —*See* HONESTY.

trustworthy *adj.* —*See* [illegible] DEPENDABLE.

trusty *adj.* —*See* DEPENDABLE.

truth *n.* —*See* CERTAINTY, HONESTY, VERACITY.

truthful *adj.* —*See* HONEST, REALISTIC (2).

truthfully *adv.* —*See* REALLY.

truthfulness *n.* —*See* VERACITY.

truthless *adj.* —*See* FALSE.

truthlessness *n.* —*See* MENDACITY.

try *v.* —*See* ATTEMPT, BURDEN[1], TEST (1).

try *n.* —*See* ATTEMPT.

strength, effect, worth, or desirability. **3a.** To examine or hear (e.g., a case) by judicial process. **b.** To put (a defendant) on trial. **4.** To subject to strain or hardship; tax. **5.** To render (fat). **6.** To smooth, fit, or align accurately. ▸ *n., pl.* **tries** (trīz). An attempt; effort.

try·ing (trī′ĭng) ▸ *adj.* Causing strain, hardship, or distress. **—try′ing·ly** *adv.*

try·out (trī′out′) ▸ *n.* A test to ascertain the skills of applicants, as for a sports team.

tryst (trĭst) ▸ *n.* **1.** An agreement between lovers to meet. **2.** A meeting or meeting place so arranged. **—tryst** *v.* **—tryst′er** *n.*

tsar (zär, tsär) ▸ *n.* Var. of **czar** 1.

tset·se fly (tsĕt′sē, tsē′tsē) ▸ *n.* A bloodsucking African fly that transmits microorganisms causing diseases such as sleeping sickness.

T-shirt also **tee shirt** (tē′shûrt′) ▸ *n.* A short-sleeved, collarless shirt.

tsp. ▸ *abbr.* teaspoon

T-square (tē′skwâr′) ▸ *n.* A T-shaped ruler used for drawing parallel lines.

tsu·na·mi (tso͝o-nä′mē) ▸ *n., pl.* **-mis.** A very large ocean wave caused by an underwater earthquake or volcanic eruption.

Tswa·na (tswä′nə, swä′-) ▸ *n., pl.* **-na** or **-nas.** **1.** A member of a Bantu people of Botswana and W South Africa. **2.** The Bantu language of the Tswana.

Tu. ▸ *abbr.* Tuesday

tub (tŭb) ▸ *n.* **1.** A round, open, flat-bottomed vessel used for washing, packing, or storing. **2.** A bathtub.

tu·ba (to͞o′bə, tyo͞o′-) ▸ *n.* A large, valved, brass wind instrument with a bass pitch.

tu·bal ligation (to͞o′bəl, tyo͞o′-) ▸ *n.* A method of female sterilization in which the fallopian tubes are surgically tied.

tub·by (tŭb′ē) ▸ *adj.* **-bi·er, -bi·est.** Short and fat. **—tub′bi·ness** *n.*

tube (to͞ob, tyo͞ob) ▸ *n.* **1.** A hollow cylinder, esp. one that conveys a fluid or functions as a passage. **2.** A flexible cylindrical container sealed at one end and having a screw cap at the other, for pigments, toothpaste, or other substances. **3a.** An electron tube. **b.** A vacuum tube. **4.** *Chiefly Brit.* A subway. **5.** often **the tube** *Slang* Television. **—tube′less** *adj.*

tu·ber (to͞o′bər, tyo͞o′-) ▸ *n.* **1.** A swollen, usu. underground stem, such as the potato, bearing buds from which new plants sprout. **2.** *Biol.* A tubercle. **—tu′ber·ous** *adj.*

tu·ber·cle (to͞o′bər-kəl, tyo͞o′-) ▸ *n.* **1.** The characteristic lesion of tuberculosis. **2.** *Biol.* A small rounded prominence on the roots of some plants or in the skin or on a bone.

tu·ber·cu·lar (to͝o-bûr′kyə-lər, tyo͝o-) ▸ *adj.* **1.** Of or covered with tubercles. **2.** Of or affected with tuberculosis.

tu·ber·cu·lin (to͝o-bûr′kyə-lĭn, tyo͝o-) ▸ *n.* A liquid derived from tubercle bacilli and used in tests for tuberculosis.

tu·ber·cu·lo·sis (to͝o-bûr′kyə-lō′sĭs, tyo͝o-) ▸ *n.* An infectious disease of humans and animals caused by a bacillus and characterized by the formation of tubercles, esp. in the lungs. **—tu·ber′cu·lous** *adj.*

tube·rose (to͞ob′rōz′, tyo͞ob′-, to͞o′bə-) ▸ *n.* A tuberous Mexican plant cultivated for its fragrant white flowers.

Tub·man (tŭb′mən), **Harriet** (1820?–1913) ▸ Amer. abolitionist.

tu·bu·lar (to͞o′byə-lər, tyo͞o′-) ▸ *adj.* Of or having the form of a tube.

tuck (tŭk) ▸ *v.* **1.** To make one or more folds in. **2.** To turn under the end or edge of in order to secure. **3.** To put in a snug, safe, or concealed place. **4.** To draw in; contract. ***—phrasal verb:*** **tuck in** To make one secure in bed for sleep, esp. by tucking bedclothes into the bed. ▸ *n.* A flattened pleat or fold, esp. one stitched in place.

tuck·er (tŭk′ər) ▸ *v. Informal* To weary; exhaust.

-tude ▸ *suff.* Condition, state, or quality: *exactitude.*

Tues. ▸ *abbr.* Tuesday

Tues·day (to͞oz′dē, -dā′, tyo͞oz′-) ▸ *n.* The 3rd day of the week.

tuff (tŭf) ▸ *n.* A rock composed of compacted volcanic ash.

tuft (tŭft) ▸ *n.* A short cluster of strands, as of hair or grass, attached at the base or growing close together. **—tuft′ed** *adj.*

tug (tŭg) ▸ *v.* **tugged, tug·ging.** **1.** To pull vigorously (at). **2.** To move by pulling with great effort or exertion. **3.** To tow by tugboat. ▸ *n.* **1.** A strong pull or pulling force. **2.** A tugboat.

tug·boat (tŭg′bōt′) ▸ *n.* A small powerful boat designed for towing or pushing larger vessels.

tug of war ▸ *n.* **1.** A contest in which two teams tug on opposite ends of a rope, each trying to pull the other across a dividing line. **2.** A struggle for supremacy.

tu·grik (to͞o′grĭk) ▸ *n.* See **currency** table in Appendix.

tu·i·tion (to͞o-ĭsh′ən, tyo͞o-) ▸ *n.* **1.** A fee for instruction, esp. at a school. **2.** Instruction; teaching. **—tu·i′tion·al, tu·i′tion·ar′y** *adj.*

tu·lip (to͞o′lĭp, tyo͞o′-) ▸ *n.* A bulbous plant widely cultivated for its showy, variously colored flowers.

tulip tree ▸ *n.* A tall tree with tuliplike green and orange flowers.

tulle (to͞ol) ▸ *n.* A fine starched net of silk, rayon, or nylon, used esp. for veils, tutus, or gowns.

tum·ble (tŭm′bəl) ▸ *v.* **-bled, -bling.** **1.** To perform acrobatic feats, such as somersaults. **2a.** To fall or roll end over end. **b.** To spill or roll out in disorder. **c.** To pitch headlong; fall. **3.** To decline or collapse suddenly. **4.** To cause to fall; bring down. **5.** To toss or whirl in a drum or tumbler. **—tum′ble** *n.*

tum·ble·down (tŭm′bəl-doun′) ▸ *adj.* Dilapidated or rickety.

tum·bler (tŭm′blər) ▸ *n.* **1.** An acrobat or gymnast. **2.** A drinking glass without a handle or stem. **3.** The part in a lock that releases the bolt when moved by a key. **4.** The drum of a clothes dryer.

tum·ble·weed (tŭm′bəl-wēd′) ▸ *n.* A densely branched plant that when withered breaks off from the roots and is rolled about by the wind.

tum·brel or **tum·bril** (tŭm′brəl) ▸ *n.* A two-wheeled cart, esp. one that can be tilted to dump a load.

tu·mes·cence (to͞o-mĕs′əns, tyo͞o-) ▸ *n.* A swelling or enlarging. **—tu·mes′cent** *adj.*

tu·mid (to͞o′mĭd, tyo͞o′-) ▸ *adj.* **1.** Swollen; distended. **2.** Overblown; bombastic. **—tu·mid′i·ty** *n.*

tum·my (tŭm′ē) ▸ *n., pl.* **-mies.** *Informal* The human stomach.

tu·mor (to͞o′mər, tyo͞o′-) ▸ *n.* **1.** An abnormal growth of tissue due to uncontrolled, progressive multiplication of cells and serving no physiological function; neoplasm. **2.** A swollen part; swelling. **—tu′mor·ous** *adj.*

tu·mult (to͞o′mŭlt′, tyo͞o′-) ▸ *n.* **1.** The din and commotion of a great crowd. **2.** Agitation of the mind or emotions. **—tu·mul′tu·ous** (to͝o-mŭl′cho͞o-əs, tyo͝o-) *adj.* **—tu·mul′tu·ous·ness** *n.*

tu·mu·lus (to͞o′myə-ləs, tyo͞o′-) ▸ *n., pl.* **-li** (-lī′). An ancient grave mound; barrow.

tun (tŭn) ▸ *n.* A large cask.

tu·na (to͞o′nə, tyo͞o′-) ▸ *n., pl.* **-na** or **-nas.** **1.** Any of various often large marine food fishes. **2.** also **tuna fish** The canned or processed flesh of tuna.

tun·dra (tŭn′drə) ▸ *n.* A treeless area of Arctic regions with

THESAURUS

trying *adj.* —*See* BURDENSOME, TROUBLESOME (2).
tryout *n.* —*See* TEST (1).
tryst *n.* —*See* ENGAGEMENT (1).
tub *n.* —*See* VAT.
tubby *adj.* —*See* FAT (1).
tucker *v.* —*See* TIRE (1).
tuckered *adj.* —*See* TIRED (1).
tug *v.* —*See* LABOR, PULL (1).
tug *n.* —*See* JERK.
tug of war *n.* —*See* COMPETITION (1).
tuition *n.* —*See* EDUCATION (1).
tumble *v.* To bring about the downfall of ▸ bring down, overthrow, overturn, subvert, topple, unhorse. —*See also* DISORDER, FALL (1), FALL (2), FALL (4).
tumble on *v.* —*See* ENCOUNTER (1).
tumble *n.* —*See* DESCENT, DISORDER (1), FALL (1), FALL (3), HEAP (1).
tumbledown *adj.* —*See* SHABBY.
tumesce *v.* —*See* SWELL.
tumescent *adj.* —*See* INFLATED, SWOLLEN.
tumid *adj.* —*See* INFLATED.
tumult *n.* —*See* AGITATION (1), AGITATION (2), DISORDER (2), FIGHT (1), NOISE (1).
tumultuous *adj.* —*See* AGITATED, ROUGH (2).
tundra *n.* —*See* DESERT[1].

a permanently frozen subsoil and low-growing vegetation.

tune (tōōn, tyōōn) ▸ *n.* **1.** *Mus.* **a.** A melody, esp. a simple one. **b.** A song. **c.** The state of being in correct pitch: *sang out of tune all night long.* **2.** Concord or agreement; harmony: *in tune with the times.* **3.** *Electron.* Adjustment of a receiver or circuit for maximum response to a given signal or frequency. ▸ *v.* **tuned, tun·ing. 1.** *Mus.* To put into tune. **2.** To adjust for maximum performance. **3.** *Electron.* To adjust (a receiver) to a desired frequency. **—tun′a·ble, tune′a·ble** *adj.* **—tune′less** *adj.* **—tune′less·ly** *adv.* **—tune′less·ness** *n.*

tune·ful (tōōn′fəl, tyōōn′-) ▸ *adj.* Melodious. **—tune′ful·ly** *adv.* **—tune′ful·ness** *n.*

tun·er (tōō′nər, tyōō′-) ▸ *n.* **1.** One that tunes. **2.** A device for tuning, esp. an electronic device used to select signals for amplification and conversion to video, sound, or both.

tune-up (tōōn′ŭp′, tyōōn′-) ▸ *n.* An adjustment of a motor or engine to improve working order or efficiency.

tung·sten (tŭng′stən) ▸ *n.* *Symbol* **W** A hard, brittle, corrosion-resistant gray to white metallic element used in high-temperature structural materials and in electrical elements. At. no. 74.

Tun·gus·ic (tŏŏng-gōō′zĭk, tŭn-) ▸ *n.* A subfamily of the Altaic languages of E Siberia and N Manchuria. **—Tun·gus′ic** *adj.*

tu·nic (tōō′nĭk, tyōō′-) ▸ *n.* **1.** A loose-fitting, knee-length garment worn by the ancient Greeks and Romans. **2a.** A long, plain, close-fitting military jacket. **b.** A long plain blouse.

tun·ing fork (tōō′nĭng, tyōō′-) ▸ *n.* A small two-pronged metal device that when struck produces a sound of fixed pitch, used for tuning musical instruments.

Tu·nis (tōō′nĭs, tyōō′-) ▸ The capital of Tunisia, in the N part on the **Gulf of Tunis,** an inlet of the Mediterranean.

Tu·ni·sia (tōō-nē′zhə, -shə, tyōō-) ▸ A country of N Africa bordering on the Mediterranean. **—Tu·ni′sian** *adj. & n.*

tun·nel (tŭn′əl) ▸ *n.* An underground or underwater passage. ▸ *v.* **-neled, -nel·ing** or **-nelled, -nel·ling. 1.** To make a tunnel (through or under). **2.** To dig in the form of a tunnel.

tunnel vision ▸ *n.* An extremely narrow outlook; narrow-mindedness.

tu·pe·lo (tōō′pə-lō′, tyōō′-) ▸ *n., pl.* **-los.** A tree of the SE US having soft light wood.

Tu·pi (tōō′pē, tōō pē′) ▸ *n., pl.* **-pi** or **-pis. 1.** A member of any of a group of Indian peoples living along the coast of Brazil, in the Amazon River valley, and in Paraguay. **2.** The language of the Tupi. **—Tu′pi·an** *adj.*

tur·ban (tûr′bən) ▸ *n.* A headdress consisting of a long piece of cloth wound around a small cap or directly around the head.

tur·bid (tûr′bĭd) ▸ *adj.* **1.** Having sediment or foreign particles stirred up or suspended: *turbid water.* **2.** Heavy or dense, as smoke. **3.** In turmoil: *turbid feelings.* **—tur′bid·ly** *adv.* **—tur′bid·ness, tur·bid′i·ty** *n.*

tur·bine (tûr′bĭn, -bīn′) ▸ *n.* A machine in which the kinetic energy of a moving fluid is converted to mechanical power as the fluid turns a series of buckets, paddles, or blades arrayed about the circumference of a wheel or cylinder.

tur·bo·jet (tûr′bō-jĕt′) ▸ *n.* A jet engine with a turbine-driven compressor.

tur·bo·prop (tûr′bō-prŏp′) ▸ *n.* A turbojet engine used to drive an external propeller.

tur·bot (tûr′bət) ▸ *n., pl.* **-bot** or **-bots.** An edible European flatfish.

tur·bu·lent (tûr′byə-lənt) ▸ *adj.* **1.** Violently agitated or disturbed. **2.** Marked by unrest or disturbance. **—tur′bu·lence** *n.* **—tur′bu·lent·ly** *adv.*

tu·reen (tŏŏ-rēn′, tyŏŏ-) ▸ *n.* A broad, deep, usu. covered dish used esp. for serving soups or stews.

turf (tûrf) ▸ *n.* **1.** Surface earth containing grass and its matted roots; sod. **2.** A piece of cut turf. **3.** A piece of peat burned as fuel. **4.** *Informal* **a.** The range of one's authority or influence. **b.** The area claimed by a gang. **5.** A racetrack for horses.

tur·gid (tûr′jĭd) ▸ *adj.* **1.** Excessively ornate or complex: *turgid prose.* **2.** Swollen or distended, as from fluid. **—tur·gid′i·ty, tur′gid·ness** *n.*

Tu·rin (tŏŏr′ĭn, tyŏŏr′-) ▸ A city of NW Italy on the Po R.

Turk (tûrk) ▸ *n.* **1.** A native or inhabitant of Turkey. **2.** An Ottoman. **3.** A member of a Turkic-speaking people.

tur·key (tûr′kē) ▸ *n., pl.* **-keys. 1.** A large, widely domesticated North American bird having brownish plumage and a bare wattled head and neck. **2.** *Slang* **a.** A disliked person. **b.** A failure; flop.

Turkey ▸ A country of SW Asia and SE Europe between the Mediterranean and Black seas.

turkey vulture ▸ *n.* A New World vulture with dark plumage and a bare red head and neck.

Turk·ic (tûr′kĭk) ▸ *n.* A subfamily of the Altaic languages including Turkish. **—Turk′ic** *adj.*

Turk·ish (tûr′kĭsh) ▸ *adj.* Of or relating to Turkey, the Turks, or the Turkish language. ▸ *n.* The Turkic language of Turkey.

Turkish bath ▸ *n.* A steam bath followed by a shower and massage.

Turk·men·i·stan (tûrk′mĕn-ĭ-stăn′, -stän′) ▸ A country of W-central Asia E of the Caspian Sea. **—Turk′men** (tûrk′mən) *n. & adj.*

Turks and Cai·cos Islands (tûrks; kā′kəs, kī′kōs) ▸ Two island groups of the British West Indies in the Atlantic in the SE Bahamas.

tur·mer·ic (tûr′mər-ĭk) ▸ *n.* An Indian plant with yellow flowers and a rhizome that when powdered is used as a condiment and as a yellow dye.

tur·moil (tûr′moil′) ▸ *n.* A state of extreme confusion or agitation.

turn (tûrn) ▸ *v.* **1.** To move or cause to move around an axis or center; rotate or revolve. **2.** To change the position of so as to show the other side. **3.** To shape on a lathe. **4.** To give distinctive form to: *turn a phrase.* **5.** To injure by twisting: *turn an ankle.* **6.** To nauseate; upset. **7a.** To change the direction or course of: *turn the car left.* **b.** To direct or change one's way or course. **8.** To make a course around or about: *turn the corner.* **9.** To set in a specified way or direction. **10.** To antagonize or become antagonistic. **11.** To direct (e.g., the attention or interest) toward or away from something. **12.** To send, drive, or let: *turn the dog loose.* **13.** To have recourse; resort. **14.** To depend on something for success or failure; hinge. **15.** To become: *a lawyer turned novelist.* **16.** To transform or become transformed; change. **17.** To become sour. **18.** To change color. ***—phrasal verbs:* turn down 1.** To diminish, as the volume of. **2.** To reject. **turn in 1.** To hand in. **2.** To inform on or deliver: *The thief turned himself in.* **3.** *Informal* To go to bed. **turn off 1.** To stop the operation of. **2.** *Slang* To displease or disgust. **turn on 1.** To start the operation of:

THESAURUS

tune *n.* —*See* AGREEMENT (2), HARMONY (1), MELODY, SONG.
 tune *v.* —*See* HARMONIZE (1).
 tune up *v.* —*See* ADJUST.
tuneful *adj.* —*See* MELODIOUS.
tunnel *n.* —*See* CAVE, HOLE (2).
turbid *adj.* Heavy, dark, or dense, especially with impurities ▸ hazy, murky, smoggy. [*Compare* DIRTY.] —*See also* CONFUSED (1), MURKY (1).
turbulence *n.* —*See* AGITATION (1).
turbulent *adj.* —*See* AGITATED, DISORDERLY, ROUGH (2).
turf *n.* —*See* AREA (1), EARTH (1), TERRITORY.
turgid *adj.* —*See* INFLATED.
turgidity *n.* —*See* BOMBAST.
turkey *n.* —*See* DRIP (2), FAILURE (1), FOOL.
turmoil *n.* —*See* AGITATION (1), AGITATION (2), DISORDER (2).
turn *v.* **1.** To move in circles or around an axis ▸ circle, circumvolve, go around (*or* round), gyrate, orbit, pivot, reel, revolve, rotate, spin, swirl, twirl, wheel, whirl. [*Compare* INCLINE.] **2.** To change the direction or course of ▸ avert, deflect, deviate, divert, redirect, shift, shunt, sidetrack, swing, switch, turn aside, veer. [*Compare* SWERVE.] **3.** To change to the opposite position, direction, or course ▸ invert, reverse, transpose, turn (about *or* around *or* over *or* round). **4.** To injure a bodily part by twisting ▸ sprain, strain, twist, wrench. [*Compare* HURT.] —*See also* AIM (1), APPLY (1), BEAR (5), BECOME (1), BEND (1), BEND (2), CHANGE (1), CHANGE (2),

Turn on the light. **2.** *Slang* To please or excite. **turn out 1.** To shut off. **2.** To arrive or assemble. **3.** To produce; make. **4.** To result; end up. **turn over 1.** To think about; consider. **2.** To transfer to another. **turn up 1.** To increase, as the volume of. **2.** To find or be found. **3.** To arrive; appear. ▸ *n.* **1.** The act of turning; rotation; revolution. **2.** A change of direction: *a left turn.* **3.** A departure or deviation, as in a trend. **4.** A chance or opportunity to do something. **5.** Natural inclination: *a speculative turn of mind.* **6.** A deed or action: *a good turn.* **7.** A short excursion. **8.** A single wind or convolution, as of wire on a spool. **9.** A rendering: *a turn of phrase.* **10.** A momentary shock or scare. ***—idioms:*** **by turns** Alternately. **in turn** In the proper order. **out of turn** Not in the proper order. **turn over a new leaf** To change for the better. **turn the tables** To reverse a situation and gain the upper hand. **—turn′er** *n.*

turn·a·bout (tûrn′ə-bout′) ▸ *n.* A shift or reversal in fortune, allegiance, or direction.

turn·a·round (tûrn′ə-round′) ▸ *n.* A turnabout.

turn·buck·le (tûrn′bŭk′əl) ▸ *n.* A metal coupling device consisting of an oblong piece internally threaded at both ends into which two pieces of threaded rod are screwed.

turn·coat (tûrn′kōt′) ▸ *n.* One who traitorously switches allegiance.

Turner, Nat (1800–31) ▸ Amer. slave leader.

turn·ing point (tûr′nĭng) ▸ *n.* A decisive moment.

tur·nip (tûr′nĭp) ▸ *n.* **1.** A cultivated plant with a large edible yellow or white root. **2.** The root of this plant.

turn·key (tûrn′kē′) ▸ *n., pl.* **-keys.** A jailer.

turn·off (tûrn′ôf′, -ŏf′) ▸ *n.* **1.** An exit on a highway. **2.** *Slang* Something distasteful.

turn-on (tûrn′ŏn′, -ôn′) ▸ *n.* *Slang* Something that causes pleasure or excitement.

turn·out (tûrn′out′) ▸ *n.* **1.** The number of people at a gathering; attendance. **2.** An array of equipment. **3.** A widening in a road.

turn·o·ver (tûrn′ō′vər) ▸ *n.* **1.** The act of turning over; an upset. **2.** An abrupt change; reversal. **3.** A pastry made by covering half of a piece of dough with filling and folding the other half over it. **4a.** The number of times a particular stock of goods is sold and restocked during a given period. **b.** The amount of business transacted during a given period. **5.** The rate of replacement of personnel.

turn·pike (tûrn′pīk′) ▸ *n.* A toll road, esp. an expressway with tollgates.

turn·stile (tûrn′stīl′) ▸ *n.* A device for controlling passage from one area to another, usu. consisting of several revolving horizontal arms projecting from a central post.

turn·ta·ble (tûrn′tā′bəl) ▸ *n.* **1.** The circular rotating platform of a phonograph on which the record is placed. **2.** A circular rotating platform for turning locomotives.

tur·pen·tine (tûr′pən-tīn′) ▸ *n.* A thin volatile oil, $C_{10}H_{16}$, obtained from certain pine trees and used as a paint thinner, solvent, and medicinally as a liniment.

tur·pi·tude (tûr′pĭ-to͞od′, -tyo͞od′) ▸ *n.* Depravity; baseness: *moral turpitude.*

tur·quoise (tûr′kwoiz′, -koiz′) ▸ *n.* **1.** A blue to blue-green mineral of aluminum and copper, prized as a gemstone. **2.** A light bluish green. **—tur′quoise′** *adj.*

tur·ret (tûr′ĭt, tŭr′-) ▸ *n.* **1.** A small tower-shaped projection on a building. **2.** A projecting armored structure, usu. rotating horizontally, containing mounted guns and their gunners, as on a warship or tank. **—tur′ret·ed** *adj.*

tur·tle[1] (tûr′tl) ▸ *n.* Any of an order of aquatic or terrestrial reptiles having beaklike jaws and the body enclosed in a bony or leathery shell.

tur·tle[2] (tûr′tl) ▸ *n.* *Archaic* A turtledove.

tur·tle·dove (tûr′tl-dŭv′) ▸ *n.* **1.** An Old World dove with a soft purring call. **2.** See **mourning dove.**

tur·tle·neck (tûr′tl-nĕk′) ▸ *n.* **1.** A high, close-fitting, turned-down collar. **2.** A garment with such a collar.

Tus·ca·ny (tŭs′kə-nē′) ▸ A region of W-central Italy between the N Apennines and the Ligurian and Tyrrhenian seas. **—Tus′can** *adj. & n.*

Tus·ca·ro·ra (tŭs′kə-rôr′ə) ▸ *n., pl.* **-ra** or **-ras. 1.** A member of a Native American people formerly of North Carolina, now in W New York and SE Ontario. **2.** The Iroquoian language of the Tuscarora.

tusk (tŭsk) ▸ *n.* A long pointed tooth, as of an elephant, extending outside the mouth. **—tusked** *adj.*

tus·sle (tŭs′əl) ▸ *v.* **-sled, -sling.** To struggle roughly; scuffle or wrestle. **—tus′sle** *n.*

tus·sock (tŭs′ək) ▸ *n.* A clump or tuft, as of grass.

tu·te·lage (to͞ot′l-ĭj, tyo͞ot′-) ▸ *n.* **1.** The function or role of a guardian; guardianship. **2.** The function or role of a tutor; instruction. **3.** The state of being under a guardian or tutor. **—tu′te·lar′y** (-ĕr′ē) *adj.*

tu·tor (to͞o′tər, tyo͞o′-) ▸ *n.* A private instructor, esp. one giving additional or remedial instruction. **—tu′tor** *v.* **—tu·to′ri·al** (-tôr′ē-əl) *adj. & n.*

Tut·si (to͞ot′sē) ▸ *n., pl.* **-si** or **-sis.** A member of a Bantu-speaking people of Rwanda and Burundi.

tut·ti-frut·ti (to͞o′tē-fro͞o′tē) ▸ *n.* A confection or flavoring that contains a variety of chopped candied fruits.

tu·tu (to͞o′to͞o) ▸ *n.* A short ballet skirt, usu. having layers of gathered sheer fabric.

Tu·va·lu (to͞o-vä′lo͞o, to͞o′və-lo͞o′) ▸ An island country of the W Pacific N of Fiji.

tux (tŭks) ▸ *n.* *Informal* A tuxedo.

tux·e·do (tŭk-sē′dō) ▸ *n., pl.* **-dos** or **-does.** A man's formal or semiformal suit, usu. black with a tailless jacket and a black bow tie.

TV (tē′vē′) ▸ *n.* Television.

TVA ▸ *abbr.* Tennessee Valley Authority

TV dinner ▸ *n.* A frozen precooked meal that needs only to be heated before serving.

twad·dle (twŏd′l) ▸ *n.* Idle talk; nonsense. **—twad′dle** *v.*

twain (twān) ▸ *n. & adj. & pron.* Two.

Twain, Mark ▸ See **Samuel Langhorne Clemens.**

twang (twăng) ▸ *n.* **1.** A sharp vibrating sound, as of the plucked string of a banjo or guitar. **2.** A strongly nasal tone of voice. **—twang** *v.* **—twang′y** *adj.*

THESAURUS

CONVINCE, DECAY, DEFECT, DULL, RESORT, UPSET.

turn back *v.* *—See* RETREAT, RETURN (1).

turn down *v.* *—See* DECLINE, VETO.

turn in *v.* *—See* BETRAY (1), OFFER (1), RETIRE (1).

turn off *v.* *—See* DISGUST, ESTRANGE, OFFEND (2).

turn on *v.* To set in motion ▸ activate, actuate, spark, start. [*Compare* ENERGIZE, PROVOKE.] *—See also* DEPEND ON (2), GRIP.

turn out *v.* *—See* FURNISH, HAPPEN (1), RISE (1).

turn over *v.* To direct a person elsewhere for help or information ▸ refer, send, transfer. *—See also* ENTRUST (1), GIVE (1), OVERTURN, PONDER, TILL.

turn up *v.* *—See* APPEAR (1), ARRIVE (1), DISCOVER, UNCOVER.

turn *n.* **1.** A limited, often assigned period of activity, duty, or opportunity ▸ bout, go, hitch, inning, shift, spell, stint, stretch, time, tour, trick, watch. *Informal:* crack, shot, whack. [*Compare* OPPORTUNITY, TRY.] **2.** An often sudden change or departure, as in a trend ▸ shift, tack, twist. [*Compare* CHANGE, DEVIATION.] *—See also* BEND, CIRCLE (2), DRIVE (3), INCLINATION (1), REVOLUTION (1), TALENT, TRANSITION, WALK (1).

turnabout or **turnaround** *n.* *—See* REVERSAL (1).

turncoat *n.* *—See* DEFECTOR.

turndown *n.* A turning down of a request ▸ denial, disallowance, nonacceptance, refusal, rejection. [*Compare* FORBIDDANCE.]

turned-on *adj.* *—See* DRUGGED, THRILLED.

turnkey *n.* A guard or keeper of a prison ▸ jailer, warden. *Slang:* screw. [*Compare* GUARD, POLICE OFFICER.]

turnout *n.* *—See* DRESS (2), OUTFIT.

turnpike *n.* *—See* WAY (2).

turpitude *n.* *—See* CORRUPTION (1).

tush *n.* *—See* BUTTOCKS.

tussle *v.* *—See* CONTEND.

tussle *n.* *—See* FIGHT (1).

tutelage *n.* *—See* CARE (2), EDUCATION (1).

tutor *n.* *—See* EDUCATOR.

tutor *v.* *—See* EDUCATE.

tutoring *n.* *—See* EDUCATION (1).

twaddle *n.* *—See* BABBLE, NONSENSE.

tweak (twēk) ▸ *v.* To pinch or twist sharply. **—tweak** *n.*
tweed (twēd) ▸ *n.* **1.** A coarse woolen fabric usu. woven of several colors. **2. tweeds** Clothing made of tweed. **—tweed′y** *adj.*
tweet (twēt) ▸ *n.* A high chirping sound, as of a young or small bird. **—tweet** *v.*
tweet·er (twē′tər) ▸ *n.* A loudspeaker designed to reproduce high-pitched sounds in a high-fidelity audio system.
tweez·ers (twē′zərz) ▸ *pl.n. (takes sing. or pl. v.)* Small pincers, usu. of metal, used for plucking or handling small objects. **—tweeze** *v.*
twelfth (twĕlfth) ▸ *n.* **1.** The ordinal number matching the number 12 in a series. **2.** One of 12 equal parts. **—twelfth** *adv. & adj.*
Twelfth Night ▸ *n.* Jan. 5, the eve of Epiphany.
twelve (twĕlv) ▸ *n.* **1.** The cardinal number equal to the sum of 11 + 1. **2.** The 12th in a set or sequence. **—twelve** *adj. & pron.*
twelve·month (twĕlv′mŭnth′) ▸ *n.* A year.
twen·ti·eth (twĕn′te-ĭth) ▸ *n.* **1.** The ordinal number matching the number 20 in a series. **2.** One of 20 equal parts. **—twen′ti·eth** *adv. & adj.*
twen·ty (twĕn′tē) ▸ *n., pl.* **-ties**. The cardinal number equal to 2 × 10. **—twen′ty** *adj. & pron.*
twen·ty-twen·ty or **20/20** (twĕn′tē-twĕn′tē) ▸ *adj.* Having normal visual acuity.
twerp (twûrp) ▸ *n. Slang* An insignificant and contemptible person.
Twi (chwē, chē) ▸ *n.* A language of Ghana.
twice (twīs) ▸ *adv.* **1.** In two cases or on two occasions; two times. **2.** In doubled degree or amount.
twid·dle (twĭd′l) ▸ *v.* **-dled, -dling. 1.** To turn over or around lightly. **2.** To play with; trifle. ***—idiom:* twiddle (one's) thumbs** To do little or nothing; be idle. **—twid′dler** *n.*
twig (twĭg) ▸ *n.* A small slender branch. **—twig′gy** *adj.*
twi·light (twī′līt′) ▸ *n.* **1.** The time of the day when the sun is below the horizon but is casting diffuse light. **2.** The soft indistinct light of this time, esp. after sunset. **3.** A period or condition of decline.
twill (twĭl) ▸ *n.* A fabric with diagonal parallel ribs.
twin (twĭn) ▸ *n.* **1.** One of two offspring born at the same birth. **2.** One of two identical or similar things; counterpart. ▸ *adj.* **1.** Born at the same birth. **2.** Being two or one of two identical or like things. **3.** Consisting of two identical or like parts.
twin bed ▸ *n.* One of a matching pair of single beds.
twine (twīn) ▸ *v.* **twined, twin·ing. 1.** To twist together; intertwine. **2.** To form by twisting. **3.** To encircle or coil about. **4.** To go in a winding course. ▸ *n.* A strong string or cord made of two or more threads twisted together.
twinge (twĭnj) ▸ *n.* A sudden sharp physical or emotional pain. ▸ *v.* **twinged, twing·ing.** To feel or cause to feel a sharp pain.
twin·kle (twĭng′kəl) ▸ *v.* **-kled, -kling. 1.** To shine with slight intermittent gleams. **2.** To be bright or sparkling: *Their eyes twinkled.* **3.** To wink. ▸ *n.* **1.** An intermittent gleam of light. **2.** A sparkle of merriment or delight in the eye. **3.** A brief interval. **—twink′ly** *adj.*
twin·kling (twĭng′klĭng) ▸ *n.* A brief interval.
twirl (twûrl) ▸ *v.* **1.** To rotate or revolve briskly; spin. **2.** To twist or wind (around). **—twirl** *n.* **—twirl′er** *n.*
twist (twĭst) ▸ *v.* **1.** To entwine (several threads) to produce a single strand. **2.** To wind or coil about something: *twisted the reins around her hand.* **3.** To impart a spiral or coiling shape to. **4a.** To turn or open by turning. **b.** To break by turning: *twist off a small branch.* **5.** To wrench or sprain. **6.** To distort the intended meaning of. **7.** To move in a winding course. **8.** To rotate or revolve. ▸ *n.* **1.** Something twisted or formed by twisting. **2.** The act of twisting; a spin or twirl. **3.** A sprain or wrench, as of an ankle. **4.** An unexpected turn of events. **—twist′er** *n.*
twit (twĭt) ▸ *v.* **twit·ted, twit·ting.** To taunt or tease. ▸ *n. Slang* An annoying person.
twitch (twĭch) ▸ *v.* To move or cause to move jerkily or spasmodically. ▸ *n.* **1.** A sudden involuntary muscular movement. **2.** A sudden jerk or tug. **—twitch′y** *adj.*
twit·ter (twĭt′ər) ▸ *v.* To utter a series of light chirping or tremulous sounds. **—twit′ter** *n.* **—twit′ter·y** *adj.*
twixt also **'twixt** (twĭkst) ▸ *prep.* Betwixt.
two (to͞o) ▸ *n.* **1.** The cardinal number equal to the sum of 1 + 1. **2.** The 2nd in a set or sequence. **—two** *adj. & pron.*
two-bit (to͞o′bĭt′) ▸ *adj. Slang* Worth very little; cheap; insignificant.
two bits ▸ *pl.n.* **1.** *Informal* Twenty-five cents. **2.** *Slang* A petty sum.
two-by-four (to͞o′bī-fôr′) ▸ *n.* A length of lumber that is 2 inches thick and 4 inches wide or that is trimmed to slightly smaller dimensions.
two-di·men·sion·al (to͞o′dĭ-mĕn′shə-nəl, -dī-) ▸ *adj.* **1.** Having only two dimensions, esp. length and width. **2.** Lacking depth: *a movie with two-dimensional characters.*
two-faced (to͞o′fāst′) ▸ *adj.* **1.** Having two faces. **2.** Hypocritical or double-dealing; deceitful. **—two′-fac′ed·ly** (-fā′sĭd-lē, -fāst′lē) *adv.* **—two′-fac′ed·ness** *n.*
two-ply (to͞o′plī′) ▸ *adj.* Made of two layers, thicknesses, or strands.
two·some (to͞o′səm) ▸ *n.* Two people together; a couple.
two-step (to͞o′stĕp′) ▸ *n.* A ballroom dance in 2/4 time with long sliding steps.
two-time (to͞o′tīm′) ▸ *v. Slang* **1.** To be unfaithful to. **2.**

THESAURUS

tweak *v.* —*See* ADJUST.
twelvemonth *n.* A period of time of approximately 12 months, especially that period during which the earth completes a single revolution around the sun ▸ calendar year, season cycle, year.
24-7 *adv.* —*See* CONTINUALLY.
twerp *n.* —*See* DRIP (2), NONENTITY.
twiddle *v.* —*See* FIDDLE.
twig *n.* —*See* STICK (1).
twiggy *adj.* —*See* THIN (1).
twilight *n.* —*See* [illegible].
twill *v.* —*See* WEAVE.
twin *adj.* Consisting of two identical or similar related things, parts, or elements ▸ double, dual, matched, paired. [*Compare* EQUAL.]
twin *n.* —*See* DOUBLE, MATE.
twin *v.* To make or become twice as great ▸ double, duplicate, geminate, redouble.
twine *v.* —*See* WEAVE, WIND².
twinge *n.* —*See* PAIN.
twinge *v.* —*See* HURT (2), HURT (3).
twinkle *v.* —*See* BLINK, GLITTER.
twinkle *n.* —*See* FLASH (1), FLASH (2), GLITTER (1).
twinkling *n.* —*See* FLASH (2), SPARKLING.
twirl *v.* —*See* TURN (1).
twirl *n.* —*See* REVOLUTION (1).
twist *v.* **1.** To injure a bodily part by twisting ▸ sprain, strain, turn, wrench. [*Compare* HURT.] **2.** To alter the position of by a sharp, forcible twisting or turning movement ▸ wrench, wrest, wring. **3.** To twist agonizingly, as in pain, struggle, or embarrassment ▸ squirm, toss, writhe. [*Compare* SHAKE.] —*See also* DEFORM, DISTORT, WEAVE, WIND².
twist *n.* An often sudden change or departure, as in a trend ▸ shift, tack, turn. [*Compare* CHANGE, DEVIATION.] —*See also* CURL, WRINKLE (2).
twisting *adj.* —*See* INDIRECT (1), WINDING.
twit *v.* —*See* RIDICULE.
twit *n.* —*See* DRIP (2), FOOL, TAUNT.
twitch *v.* To move or cause to move with a sudden abrupt motion ▸ jerk, lurch, snap, wrench, yank. [*Compare* MOVE.]
twitch *n.* —*See* JERK, TREMOR (2).
twitchy *adj.* —*See* EDGY.
twitter *v.* —*See* SHAKE (1).
twitter *n.* —*See* AGITATION (2).
twittery *adj.* —*See* TREMULOUS.
two *n.* —*See* COUPLE.
two bits *n.* A coin equal to one-fourth of the dollar of the United States and Canada ▸ quarter, quarter-dollar. —*See also* PEANUTS.
two-edged *adj.* —*See* AMBIGUOUS (2).
two-faced *adj.* Of or practicing hypocrisy ▸ Janus-faced, Pecksniffian, phony. —*See also* DISHONEST.
two-facedness *n.* —*See* HYPOCRISY.
two-fisted *adj.* *Informal* Indulging in drink to an excessive degree ▸ hard, heavy.
twofold *adj.* Twice as much or as large ▸ double. —*See also* DOUBLE (2).
twosome *n.* —*See* COUPLE.
two-time *v.* *Informal* To be sexually

To deceive; double-cross. **—two′-tim′er** *n.*

two-way (to͞o′wā′) ▸ *adj.* Affording passage or communication in two directions.

TX ▸ *abbr.* Texas

–ty ▸ *suff.* Condition; quality: *novelty.*

ty·coon (tī-ko͞on′) ▸ *n.* A wealthy and powerful businessperson; magnate.

tyke (tīk) ▸ *n.* **1.** A small child, esp. a boy. **2.** A mongrel or cur.

Ty·ler (tī′lər), **John** (1790–1862) ▸ The 10th US President (1841–45).

tym·pa·ni (tĭm′pə-nē) ▸ *pl.n.* Var. of **timpani —tym′pa·nist** *n.*

tym·pan·ic membrane (tĭm-păn′ĭk) ▸ *n.* See **eardrum.**

tym·pa·num (tĭm′pə-nəm) ▸ *n., pl.* **-na** (-nə) or **-nums. 1.** See **middle ear. 2.** See **eardrum.**

type (tīp) ▸ *n.* **1.** A number of people or things sharing common traits; class; category. **2.** One having the features of a group or class: *a type of cactus.* **3.** An example or model; embodiment. **4.** *Print.* **a.** A small block bearing a raised character that leaves a printed impression when inked and pressed on paper. **b.** Such pieces collectively. **c.** Printed or typewritten characters; print. ▸ *v.* **typed, typ·ing. 1.** To typewrite. **2.** To classify according to a particular system. **3.** To typecast. **4.** To represent or typify.

type·cast (tīp′kăst′) ▸ *v.* To assign (a performer) repeatedly to the same kind of part.

type·face (tīp′fās′) ▸ *n. Print.* **1.** The surface of a block of type that makes the impression. **2.** The size or style of type.

type·script (tīp′skrĭpt′) ▸ *n.* A typewritten copy, as of a book.

type·set (tīp′sĕt′) ▸ *v.* To set (written material) into type; compose. **—type′set′ter** *n.* **—type′set′ting** *n.*

type·write (tīp′rīt′) ▸ *v.* To write (something) with a typewriter; type.

type·writ·er (tīp′rī′tər) ▸ *n.* A machine that prints characters by means of a manually operated keyboard that moves a set of raised types, which strike the paper through an inked ribbon.

ty·phoid (tī′foid′) ▸ *n.* Typhoid fever. **—ty′phoid′** *adj.*

typhoid fever ▸ *n.* An acute, highly infectious disease caused by a bacillus transmitted by contaminated food or water and marked by high fever, coughing, and red rashes.

ty·phoon (tī-fo͞on′) ▸ *n.* A tropical cyclone of the W Pacific or Indian Oceans.

ty·phus (tī′fəs) ▸ *n.* Any of several infectious diseases caused by microorganisms and marked by severe headache, sustained high fever, delirium, and red rashes. **—ty′phous** (-fəs) *adj.*

typ·i·cal (tĭp′ĭ-kəl) ▸ *adj.* **1.** Exhibiting the characteristics peculiar to a kind, group, or category; representative. **2.** Conforming to or serving as a type. **3.** Usual; ordinary: *a typical day at the office.* **—typ′i·cal·ly** *adv.* **—typ′i·cal·ness, typ′i·cal′i·ty** (-kăl′ĭ-tē) *n.*

typ·i·fy (tĭp′ə-fī′) ▸ *v.* **-fied** (-fīd′), **-fy·ing. 1.** To serve as a typical example of. **2.** To represent by an image, form, or model; symbolize. **—typ′i·fi′er** *n.*

typ·ist (tī′pĭst) ▸ *n.* One who operates a typewriter.

ty·po (tī′pō) ▸ *n., pl.* **-pos.** *Informal* A typographical error.

typographical error ▸ *n.* A mistake in printed copy, esp. one caused by striking an incorrect key on a keyboard.

ty·pog·ra·phy (tī-pŏg′rə-fē) ▸ *n., pl.* **-phies. 1.** The composition of printed material from movable type. **2.** The arrangement and appearance of printed matter. **—ty·pog′ra·pher** *n.* **—ty′po·graph′i·cal** (tī′pə-grăf′ĭ-kəl), **ty′po·graph′ic** *adj.*

ty·ran·ni·cal (tĭ-răn′ĭ-kəl, tī-) also **ty·ran·nic** (-răn′ĭk) ▸ *adj.* Of or relating to a tyrant or tyranny; despotic. **—ty·ran′ni·cal·ly** *adv.*

tyr·an·nize (tĭr′ə-nīz′) ▸ *v.* **-nized, -niz·ing. 1.** To treat tyrannically; oppress. **2.** To rule as a tyrant. **—tyr′an·niz′er** *n.*

ty·ran·no·saur (tĭ-răn′ə-sôr′, tī-) also **ty·ran·no·saur·us** (tĭ-răn′ə-sôr′əs, tī-) ▸ *n.* A large carnivorous dinosaur with small forelimbs and a large head.

tyr·an·nous (tĭr′ə-nəs) ▸ *adj.* Despotic; tyrannical. **—tyr′an·nous·ly** *adv.*

tyr·an·ny (tĭr′ə-nē) ▸ *n., pl.* **-nies. 1.** A government in which a single ruler is vested with absolute power. **2.** Absolute power, esp. when exercised unjustly or cruelly. **3.** A tyrannical act. **4.** Extreme harshness or severity; rigor.

ty·rant (tī′rənt) ▸ *n.* **1.** An absolute ruler, esp. an oppressive or cruel one. **2.** A harsh or domineering person.

tyre (tīr) ▸ *n. Chiefly Brit.* Var. of **tire**[2].

ty·ro (tī′rō) ▸ *n., pl.* **-ros.** A beginner.

Ty·rol or **Ti·rol** (tə-rōl′, tī-, tī′rōl′) ▸ A region of the E Alps in W Austria and N Italy.

Tyr·rhe·ni·an Sea (tə-rē′nē-ən) ▸ An arm of the Mediterranean between the Italian peninsula and the islands of Corsica, Sardinia, and Sicily.

tzar (zär, tsär) ▸ *n.* Var. of **czar** 1.

THESAURUS

unfaithful to another ▸ philander. *Informal:* cheat, fool around, mess around, play around.

type *n.* —*See* EMBODIMENT, KIND[2].

typical or **typic** *adj.* Having the nature of, constituting, or serving as a type ▸ archetypal, archetypic, archetypical, classic, classical, model, paradigmatic, prototypal, prototypic, prototypical, quintessential, representative. [*Compare* EPITOME, MODEL.] —*See also* COMMON (1), CONVENTIONAL, SPECIAL.

typically *adv.* —*See* USUALLY.

typification *n.* —*See* EMBODIMENT.

typify *v.* —*See* REPRESENT (1).

tyrannical or **tyrannic** *adj.* —*See* ABSOLUTE, AUTHORITARIAN.

tyrannize *v.* To treat arbitrarily or cruelly ▸ grind (down), oppress, trample. [*Compare* ABUSE, ENSLAVE, SUPPRESS.] —*See also* BOSS.

tyrannous *adj.* —*See* ABSOLUTE.

tyranny *n.* Absolute power, especially when exercised unjustly or cruelly ▸ authoritarianism, autocracy, despotism, dictatorship, fascism, imperiousness, oppression, totalitarianism. *Idiom:* reign of terror. [*Compare* OPPRESSION.] —*See also* ABSOLUTISM (2).

tyrant *n.* —*See* AUTHORITARIAN, DICTATOR.

tyro *n.* —*See* BEGINNER.

U

u or **U** (yo͞o) ▸ *n., pl.* **u's** or **U's** also **us** or **Us**. The 21st letter of the English alphabet.

U ▸ The symbol for the element **uranium**.

UAE ▸ *abbr.* United Arab Emirates

u·biq·ui·tous (yo͞o-bĭk′wĭ-təs) ▸ *adj.* Being or seeming to be everywhere at the same time; omnipresent. **—u·biq′ui·tous·ly** *adv.* **—u·biq′ui·ty** *n.*

U-boat (yo͞o′bōt′) ▸ *n.* A German submarine.

U-bolt (yo͞o′bōlt′) ▸ *n.* A U-shaped bolt, fitted with threads and a nut at each end.

ud·der (ŭd′ər) ▸ *n.* A baglike mammary organ of female cows, sheep, and goats.

UFO (yo͞o′ĕf-ō′) ▸ *n.* An unidentified flying object.

U·gan·da (yo͞o-găn′də, o͞o-găn′dä) ▸ A country of E-central Africa. **—U·gan′dan** *adj. & n.*

ug·ly (ŭg′lē) ▸ *adj.* **-li·er, -li·est.** 1. Displeasing to the eye; unsightly. 2. Repulsive or offensive; objectionable. 3. Morally reprehensible; bad. 4. Threatening or ominous: *ugly black clouds.* 5. Cross or disagreeable: *an ugly temper.* **—ug′li·ness** *n.*

U·gric (o͞o′grĭk, yo͞o′-) ▸ *n.* The branch of the Finno-Ugric subfamily of languages that includes Hungarian. **—U′gric** *adj.*

UHF ▸ *abbr.* ultrahigh frequency

UK ▸ *abbr.* United Kingdom

u·kase (yo͞o-kās′, -kāz′, yo͞o′kās′, -kāz′) ▸ *n.* An authoritative decree; edict.

U·kraine (yo͞o-krān′) ▸ A country of E Europe.

U·krain·i·an (yo͞o-krā′nē-ən) ▸ *n.* 1. A native or inhabitant of Ukraine. 2. Their Slavic language. **—U·krain′i·an** *adj.*

u·ku·le·le or **u·ke·le·le** (yo͞o′kə-lā′lē, o͞o′kə-) ▸ *n.* A small four-stringed guitar popularized in Hawaii.

ul·cer (ŭl′sər) ▸ *n.* 1. A lesion of the skin or a mucous membrane accompanied by formation of pus and necrosis of surrounding tissue. 2. A corrupting condition or influence. **—ul′cer·ous** *adj.*

ul·cer·ate (ŭl′sə-rāt′) ▸ *v.* **-at·ed, -at·ing.** To develop or cause to develop an ulcer. **—ul′cer·a′tion** *n.* **—ul′cer·a′tive** (-sə-rā′tĭv, -sər-ə-tĭv) *adj.*

–ule ▸ *suff.* Small: *ovule.*

ul·na (ŭl′nə) ▸ *n., pl.* **-nas** or **-nae** (-nē). The bone extending from the elbow to the wrist on the side opposite to the thumb. **—ul′nar** *adj.*

ul·ster (ŭl′stər) ▸ *n.* A loose, long, often belted overcoat.

Ulster ▸ A historical region of N Ireland.

ult. ▸ *abbr.* 1. ultimately 2. ultimo

ul·te·ri·or (ŭl-tîr′ē-ər) ▸ *adj.* 1. Beyond or outside what is evident or admitted: *an ulterior motive.* 2. Lying beyond or outside of a certain area.

ul·ti·mate (ŭl′tə-mĭt) ▸ *adj.* 1. Completing a series, process, or progression. 2. Fundamental; elemental. 3. Greatest; extreme. 4. Farthest; remotest. 5. Eventual: *hoped for ultimate victory.* ▸ *n.* 1. The basic or fundamental fact, element, or principle. 2. The final point; the conclusion. 3. The maximum: *the ultimate in sophistication.* **—ul′ti·mate·ly** *adv.*

ul·ti·ma·tum (ŭl′tə-mā′təm, -mä′-) ▸ *n., pl.* **-tums** or **-ta** (-tə). A statement of terms that expresses or implies the threat of serious penalties if the terms are not accepted.

ul·ti·mo (ŭl′tə-mō′) ▸ *adv.* In or of the month before the present one.

ul·tra (ŭl′trə) ▸ *adj.* Going beyond the normal limit; extreme.

ultra– ▸ *pref.* 1. Beyond: *ultraviolet.* 2. Extreme; excessive: *ultraconservative.*

ul·tra·con·ser·va·tive (ŭl′trə-kən-sûr′və-tĭv) ▸ *adj.* Extremely conservative; reactionary.

ul·tra·high frequency (ŭl′trə-hī′) ▸ *n.* A band of radio frequencies from 300 to 3,000 megahertz.

ul·tra·lib·er·al (ŭl′trə-lĭb′ər-əl, -lĭb′rəl) ▸ *adj.* Extremely liberal; radical.

ul·tra·ma·rine (ŭl′trə-mə-rēn′) ▸ *n.* 1. A blue pigment. 2. A bright deep blue. ▸ *adj.* 1. Of the color ultramarine. 2. Of or from a place beyond the sea.

ul·tra·mi·cro·scope (ŭl′trə-mī′krə-skōp′) ▸ *n.* A microscope with high-intensity illumination used to study very minute objects.

ul·tra·mi·cro·scop·ic (ŭl′trə-mī′krə-skŏp′ĭk) ▸ *adj.* Too minute to be seen with an ordinary microscope.

ul·tra·mod·ern (ŭl′trə-mŏd′ərn) ▸ *adj.* Extremely modern in ideas or style. **—ul′tra·mod′ern·ism** *n.* **—ul′tra·mod′ern·ist** *n.*

THESAURUS

ubiquitous *adj.* Ever present in all places ▸ omnipresent, universal. [*Compare* RAMPANT.]

ugliness *n.* The quality or condition of being ugly ▸ frightfulness, hideousness, homeliness, loathsomeness, monstrosity, monstrousness, odiousness, plainness, repulsiveness, unattractiveness, uncomeliness, unloveliness, unsightliness, vileness. —*See also* MESS (2).

ugly *adj.* Displeasing to the eye ▸ hideous, homely, ill-favored, monstrous, plain, unattractive, uncomely, unlovely, unsightly. *Idioms:* not much for looks, not much to look at, short on looks, ugly as sin. —*See also* ILL-TEMPERED, OFFENSIVE (1), ROUGH (2).

ugly *n.* —*See* MESS (2).

uh-huh *adv.* —*See* YES.

ulterior *adj.* 1. Lying beyond what is obvious or avowed ▸ buried, concealed, covert, hidden, obscured, undisclosed, unrevealed. *Idiom:* under cover (*or* wraps). [*Compare* HIDDEN, SECRET, SILENT.] 2. Following something else in time ▸ after, later, posterior, subsequent. [*Compare* FOLLOWING.]

ulteriorly *adv.* —*See* LATER.

ultimate *adj.* Of or relating to a terminative condition, stage, or point ▸ final, last, latter, terminal. [*Compare* CLIMACTIC.] —*See also* DEFINITIVE, ELEMENTAL, EXTREME (1), LAST[1] (1), MAXIMUM.

ultimate *n.* —*See* MAXIMUM.

ultimately *adv.* 1. After a considerable length of time, usually after a delay ▸ eventually, finally. *Idioms:* at last (*or* long last), at the end of the day, in due course, in good (*or* due) time, in the end (*or* long run), in the fullness of time, when all is said and done. 2. In conclusion ▸ conclusively, finally, last, lastly. *Idioms:* at last, in the end.

ultra *adj.* —*See* EXTREME (2).

ultra *n.* —*See* EXTREMIST.

ultraconservative *adj.* Extremely or stubbornly conservative ▸ archconservative, die-hard, fossilized, mossbacked, old-line, old-school, reactionary, rearguard, standpat. [*Compare* CONSERVATIVE, EXTREME, STUBBORN.]

ultraconservative *n.* One who is extremely or stubbornly conservative ▸ archconservative, die-hard, fossil, mossback, reactionary, standpatter. [*Compare* EXTREMIST.]

ultraist *n.* —*See* EXTREMIST.

ultraliberal *adj.* Extremely or stubbornly liberal ▸ archliberal, bleeding-heart, do-good, Jacobinical, radical. *Slang:* crunchy-granola, goo-goo, pink. [*Compare* EXTREME, LIBERAL, STUBBORN.]

ultraliberal *n.* One who is extremely or stubbornly liberal ▸ archliberal, bleeding-heart, do-gooder, Jacobin, radical, yippie. *Informal:* tree-hugger. *Slang:* pinko. [*Compare* EXTREMIST.]

ultramodern *adj.* —*See* CONTEMPORARY (2).

ul·tra·mon·tane (ŭl′trə-mŏn′tān′, -mŏn-tān′) ▸ *adj.* **1.** Of or relating to peoples or regions lying beyond the mountains. **2.** Supporting the authority of the pope in ecclesiastical and political matters. **—ul′tra·mon′tane′** *n.*

ul·tra·son·ic (ŭl′trə-sŏn′ĭk) ▸ *adj.* **1.** Relating to acoustic frequencies above the range of human hearing, or above approx. 20,000 hertz. **2.** Of or involving ultrasound.

ul·tra·so·nog·ra·phy (ŭl′trə-sə-nŏg′rə-fē) ▸ *n.* Diagnostic imaging in which ultrasound is used to visualize an internal body structure or a developing fetus. **—ul′tra·son′o·graph** *n.* **—ul′tra·so·nog′ra·pher** *n.*

ul·tra·sound (ŭl′trə-sound′) ▸ *n.* **1.** Ultrasonic sound. **2.** The use of ultrasonic waves for medical diagnosis or therapy.

ul·tra·vi·o·let (ŭl′trə-vī′ə-lĭt) ▸ *adj.* Of the range of invisible radiation wavelengths shorter than violet in the visible spectrum and on the border of the x-ray region. ▸ *n.* Ultraviolet light or the ultraviolet part of the spectrum.

ul·u·late (ŭl′yə-lāt′, yo͞ol′-) ▸ *v.* **-lat·ed, -lat·ing.** To howl, wail, or lament loudly. **—ul′u·la′tion** *n.*

U·lys·ses (yo͞o-lĭs′ēz′) ▸ *n. Myth.* Odysseus.

um·bel (ŭm′bəl) ▸ *n.* A flat-topped or rounded flower cluster in which the individual flower stalks arise from about the same point.

um·ber (ŭm′bər) ▸ *n.* **1.** A natural brown earth containing ferric and manganese oxides, used as pigment. **2.** Any of the shades of brown produced by umber. ▸ *adj.* Brownish.

um·bil·i·cal (ŭm-bĭl′ĭ-kəl) ▸ *adj.* Of or located near the navel or umbilical cord. ▸ *n.* An umbilical cord.

umbilical cord ▸ *n.* The flexible cordlike structure connecting a fetus at the navel with the placenta and containing blood vessels that transport nourishment to the fetus and remove its wastes.

um·bil·i·cus (ŭm-bĭl′ĭ-kəs, ŭm′bə-lī′kəs) ▸ *n., pl.* **-ci** (-sī′). See **navel.**

um·bra (ŭm′brə) ▸ *n., pl.* **-bras** or **-brae** (-brē). **1.** A dark area, esp. the darkest part of a shadow. **2.** The completely dark portion of the shadow cast by one body onto another during an eclipse. **—um′bral** *adj.*

um·brage (ŭm′brĭj) ▸ *n.* **1.** Offense; resentment: *took umbrage at their rudeness.* **2.** Shadow or shade.

um·brel·la (ŭm-brĕl′ə) ▸ *n.* **1.** A device for protection from the weather consisting of a collapsible canopy mounted on a central rod. **2.** Something that covers or protects. **3.** Something that encompasses many different elements or groups.

Um·bri·a (ŭm′brē-ə) ▸ A region of central Italy. **—Um′bri·an** *adj. & n.*

u·mi·ak (o͞o′mē-ăk′) ▸ *n.* A large open Inuit or Eskimo boat made of skins stretched on a wooden frame.

um·laut (o͝om′lout′) ▸ *n.* **1.** A change in a vowel sound caused by partial assimilation to a sound in the following syllable. **2.** The diacritic mark (¨) placed over a vowel to indicate an umlaut, esp. in German.

um·pire (ŭm′pīr′) ▸ *n.* **1.** One appointed to rule on plays in various sports, esp. baseball. **2.** One appointed to settle a dispute between other persons or groups. **—um′pire′** *v.*

ump·teen (ŭmp′tēn′, ŭm′-) ▸ *adj. Informal* Large but unspecified in number. **—ump′teenth′** *adj.*

UN ▸ *abbr.* United Nations

un-¹ ▸ *pref.* Not: *unhappy.*

un-² ▸ *pref.* **1.** To reverse an action: *unbind.* **2.** To deprive of: *unfrock.* **3.** Used as an intensive: *unloose.*

un·a·ble (ŭn-ā′bəl) ▸ *adj.* **1.** Lacking the necessary power, authority, or means. **2.** Incompetent.

un·ac·com·pa·nied (ŭn′ə-kŭm′pə-nēd) ▸ *adj.* **1.** Going or acting without a companion. **2.** *Mus.* Performed or scored without accompaniment.

un·ac·count·a·ble (ŭn′ə-koun′tə-bəl) ▸ *adj.* **1.** Impossible to account for; inexplicable. **2.** Not responsible. **—un′ac·count′a·bly** *adv.*

un·ac·cus·tomed (ŭn′ə-kŭs′təmd) ▸ *adj.* **1.** Not common or usual. **2.** Not habituated: *unaccustomed to a life of stress.*

un·a·dul·ter·at·ed (ŭn′ə-dŭl′tə-rā′tĭd) ▸ *adj.* Not mingled or diluted; pure.

un·ad·vised (ŭn′əd-vīzd′) ▸ *adj.* **1.** Not informed. **2.** Rash; imprudent. **—un′ad·vis′ed·ly** (-vī′zĭd-lē) *adv.*

un·af·fect·ed (ŭn′ə-fĕk′tĭd) ▸ *adj.* **1.** Not changed or affected. **2.** Sincere; genuine. **—un′af·fect′ed·ness** *n.*

un·al·loyed (ŭn′ə-loid′) ▸ *adj.* **1.** Not in mixture with other metals; pure. **2.** Complete; unqualified. **—un′al·loy′ed·ly** *adv.*

u·nan·i·mous (yo͞o-năn′ə-məs) ▸ *adj.* **1.** Sharing the same opinions or views. **2.** Based on complete agreement. **—u′na·nim′i·ty** (yo͞o′nə-nĭm′ĭ-tē) *n.* **—u·nan′i·mous·ly** *adv.* **—u·nan′i·mous·ness** *n.*

un·armed (ŭn-ärmd′) ▸ *adj.* Lacking weapons; defenseless.

un·as·sail·a·ble (ŭn′ə-sā′lə-bəl) ▸ *adj.* **1.** Impossible to dispute or disprove; undeniable. **2.** Impregnable. **—un′as·sail′a·bil′i·ty** *n.*

un·as·sist·ed (ŭn′ə-sĭs′tĭd) ▸ *adj.* **1.** Not having assistance; unaided. **2.** *Baseball* Designating a play handled by only one fielder.

un·as·sum·ing (ŭn′ə-so͞o′mĭng) ▸ *adj.* Not pretentious; modest.

un·at·tached (ŭn′ə-tăcht′) ▸ *adj.* **1.** Not attached or joined. **2.** Not engaged, married, or involved in a serious relationship.

un·a·vail·ing (ŭn′ə-vā′lĭng) ▸ *adj.* Not availing; useless. **—un′a·vail′ing·ly** *adv.*

THESAURUS

ululate *v.* —*See* GRIEVE, HOWL.

ululation *n.* —*See* HOWL.

umbra *n.* Comparative darkness that results from the blocking of light rays ▸ penumbra, shade, shadow, shadiness. [*Compare* DARK, TWILIGHT.]

umbrage *n.* —*See* OFFENSE.

umbrageous *adj.* —*See* SHADY (2).

umpire *n.* —*See* JUDGE (2).

umpteen *adj.* —*See* MANY.

unabashed *adj.* —*See* IMPUDENT.

unabbreviated *adj.* —*See* COMPLETE (2).

unable *adj.* Lacking power or strength ▸ helpless, impotent, powerless. —*See also* INEFFECTUAL (2), INEFFICIENT.

unabridged *adj.* —*See* COMPLETE (2).

unacceptable *adj.* —*See* OBJECTIONABLE, UNBEARABLE.

unaccompanied *adj.* —*See* SOLITARY.

unaccountable *adj.* That cannot be explained ▸ inexplicable, unexplainable. [*Compare* MYSTERIOUS.]

unachievable *adj.* —*See* IMPOSSIBLE.

unacquainted *adj.* —*See* IGNORANT (3).

unadorned *adj.* —*See* BARE (1), RUSTIC.

unadulterated *adj.* —*See* NATURAL (1), PURE.

unadvantageous *adj.* —*See* UNFAVORABLE (1).

unaffected *adj.* —*See* ARTLESS, COLD (2), GENUINE.

unafraid *adj.* —*See* BRAVE.

unalterable *adj.* That cannot be revoked or undone ▸ irretrievable, irreversible, irrrevocable. ***Idiom:*** beyond recall. [*Compare* UNCHANGEABLE.] —*See also* IMMUTABLE.

unambiguous *adj.* —*See* DEFINITE (2), DEFINITE (1), SHARP (2).

unambitious *adj.* Having or expressing feelings of humility ▸ humble, lowly, meek, modest. [*Compare* DEFERENTIAL.]

unanimity *n.* —*See* AGREEMENT (2).

unanimous *adj.* Being in or characterized by complete agreement ▸ accordant, agreeing, assenting, concordant, consensual, consonant, harmonious, like-minded, solid, undivided, unified, universal. ***Idioms:*** as one, at one, of one mind, with one voice. [*Compare* AGREEABLE, COMMON, COOPERATIVE.]

unanimousness *n.* —*See* AGREEMENT (2).

unanticipated *adj.* —*See* ACCIDENTAL.

unapparent *adj.* —*See* HIDDEN (1).

unappeasable *adj.* —*See* VORACIOUS.

unappetizing *adj.* —*See* UNPALATABLE.

unappreciated *adj.* Not apt to be appreciated ▸ thankless, ungrateful, unthankful.

unappreciative *adj.* —*See* THANKLESS (1).

unapproachable *adj.* —*See* COOL, INACCESSIBLE (1).

unapt *adj.* —*See* DOUBTFUL (1), IMPROPER (2).

unassailability *n.* —*See* SAFETY.

unassailable *adj.* —*See* CERTAIN (2), SAFE (2).

unassuming *adj.* —*See* INCONSPICUOUS, MODEST (1), SHY[1].

unassumingness *n.* —*See* MODESTY (1), MODESTY (2).

unattached *adj.* —*See* SINGLE.

unattainable *adj.* —*See* IMPOSSIBLE, INACCESSIBLE (1).

unattractive *adj.* —*See* UGLY.

unattractiveness *n.* —*See* UGLINESS.

unavailable *adj.* —*See* INACCESSIBLE (1).

unavailing *adj.* —*See* FUTILE.

un·a·void·a·ble (ŭn′ə-voi′də-bəl) ► *adj.* Impossible to avoid; inevitable. **—un′a·void′a·bil′i·ty** *n.* **—un′a·void′a·bly** *adv.*

un·a·ware (ŭn′ə-wâr′) ► *adj.* Not aware or cognizant. ► *adv.* Unawares.

un·a·wares (ŭn′ə-wârz′) ► *adv.* **1.** By surprise; unexpectedly. **2.** Without forethought or plan.

un·bal·anced (ŭn-băl′ənst) ► *adj.* **1.** Not in balance or not in proper balance. **2.** Mentally deranged. **3.** *Accounting* Not adjusted so that debit and credit correspond.

un·bar (ŭn-bär′) ► *v.* To open.

un·bear·a·ble (ŭn-bâr′ə-bəl) ► *adj.* Unendurable; intolerable. **—un·bear′a·bly** *adv.*

un·beat·a·ble (ŭn-bē′tə-bəl) ► *adj.* Impossible to defeat or surpass.

un·beat·en (ŭn-bēt′n) ► *adj.* **1.** Never defeated. **2.** Untrodden. **3.** Not beaten or pounded.

un·be·com·ing (ŭn′bĭ-kŭm′ĭng) ► *adj.* **1.** Not appropriate, attractive, or flattering. **2.** Not proper; indecorous.

un·be·known (ŭn′bĭ-nōn′) ► *adj.* Occurring or existing without one's knowledge: *a crisis unbeknown to us.*

un·be·lief (ŭn′bĭ-lēf′) ► *n.* Lack of belief or faith, esp. in religious matters. **—un′be·liev′er** *n.* **—un′be·liev′ing** *adj.*

un·bend (ŭn-bĕnd′) ► *v.* **1.** To make or become less tense; relax. **2.** To straighten.

un·bend·ing (ŭn-bĕn′dĭng) ► *adj.* **1.** Not yielding; inflexible. **2.** Aloof and often antisocial. **—un·bend′ing·ly** *adv.*

un·bid·den (ŭn-bĭd′n) also **un·bid** (-bĭd′) ► *adj.* Not invited, asked, or requested.

un·blink·ing (ŭn-blĭng′kĭng) ► *adj.* **1.** Without blinking. **2.** Without visible emotion. **3.** Fearless in facing reality. **—un·blink′ing·ly** *adv.*

un·blush·ing (ŭn-blŭsh′ĭng) ► *adj.* Without shame or embarrassment. **—un·blush′ing·ly** *adv.*

un·bolt (ŭn-bōlt′) ► *v.* To release the bolts of (a door or gate); unlock.

un·born (ŭn-bôrn′) ► *adj.* Not yet born.

un·bos·om (ŭn-bo͝oz′əm, -bo͞o′zəm) ► *v.* **1.** To confide (one's thoughts). **2.** To relieve (oneself) of thoughts or feelings.

un·bound·ed (ŭn-boun′dĭd) ► *adj.* Having no boundaries or limits.

un·bowed (ŭn-boud′) ► *adj.* **1.** Not bowed; unbent. **2.** Not subdued.

un·bri·dled (ŭn-brīd′ld) ► *adj.* **1.** Unrestrained; uncontrolled. **2.** Not fitted with a bridle.

un·bro·ken (ŭn-brō′kən) ► *adj.* **1.** Not broken; intact. **2.** Uninterrupted; continuous. **3.** Not tamed or broken to harness.

un·bur·den (ŭn-bûr′dn) ► *v.* To free from a burden or trouble.

un·but·ton (ŭn-bŭt′n) ► *v.* **1.** To unfasten the buttons (of). **2.** To open or expose as if by unbuttoning.

un·called-for (ŭn-kôld′fôr′) ► *adj.* **1.** Not required or requested. **2.** Not justified or deserved; unwarranted.

un·can·ny (ŭn-kăn′ē) ► *adj.* **-ni·er, -ni·est. 1.** Peculiarly unsettling; eerie. **2.** So keen and perceptive as to seem preternatural. **—un·can′ni·ly** *adv.* **—un·can′ni·ness** *n.*

un·cer·e·mo·ni·ous (ŭn-sĕr′ə-mō′nē-əs) ► *adj.* **1.** Without the due formalities; abrupt. **2.** Informal. **—un·cer′e·mo′ni·ous·ly** *adv.*

un·cer·tain (ŭn-sûr′tn) ► *adj.* **1.** Not known or established; questionable. **2.** Not determined; undecided. **3.** Not having sure knowledge. **4.** Subject to change. **—un·cer′tain·ly** *adv.* **—un·cer′tain·ness** *n.*

un·cer·tain·ty (ŭn-sûr′tn-tē) ► *n.* **1.** Lack of certainty. **2.** Something uncertain.

un·char·i·ta·ble (ŭn-chăr′ĭ-tə-bəl) ► *adj.* **1.** Not generous or tolerant. **2.** Unfair or unkind. **—un·char′i·ta·bly** *adv.*

un·chart·ed (ŭn-chär′tĭd) ► *adj.* Not recorded on a map or plan; unexplored; unknown.

un·chaste (ŭn-chāst′) ► *adj.* Not chaste or modest. **—un·chaste′ly** *adv.*

un·chris·tian (ŭn-krĭs′chən) ► *adj.* **1.** Not in accord with the spirit or principles of Christianity. **2.** Not Christian.

un·cial also **Un·cial** (ŭn′shəl, -sē-əl) ► *adj.* Of a style of writing characterized by somewhat rounded capital letters and found esp. in Greek and Latin manuscripts of the 4th to the 8th cent. A.D. **—un′cial** *n.*

un·civ·il (ŭn-sĭv′əl) ► *adj.* Discourteous; rude. **—un·civ′il·ly** *adv.*

un·civ·i·lized (ŭn-sĭv′ə-līzd′) ► *adj.* Not civilized; barbarous.

un·clad (ŭn-klăd′) ► *adj.* Naked.

un·clasp (ŭn-klăsp′) ► *v.* **1.** To release or loosen the clasp of. **2.** To release from a grip or embrace.

un·cle (ŭng′kəl) ► *n.* **1.** The brother of one's mother or father.

THESAURUS

unavoidable *adj.* —*See* CERTAIN (1).

unawake *adj.* —*See* SLEEPING.

unaware *adj.* —*See* IGNORANT (3).

unawareness *n.* —*See* IGNORANCE (2).

unawares *adv.* Without adequate preparation ► aback, short, unawarely. *Idioms:* by surprise, off guard, with one's pants down.

unbalance *v.* —*See* DERANGE.

unbalance *n.* —*See* INSANITY.

unbalanced *adj.* —*See* INSANE.

unbarred *adj.* —*See* CLEAR (3).

unbearable *adj.* So unpleasant or painful as not to be endured or tolerated ► impossible, insufferable, insupportable, intolerable, unacceptable, unendurable, unsufferable, unsupportable. [*Compare* TORMENTING.]

unbecoming *adj.* —*See* COARSE (1), IMPROPER (1), IMPROPER (2).

unbecomingness *n.* —*See* IMPROPRIETY (1).

unbefitting *adj.* —*See* IMPROPER (1), IMPROPER (2).

unbelief *n.* —*See* ATHEISM, DISBELIEF.

unbelievable *adj.* —*See* ASTONISHING, IMPLAUSIBLE, INCREDIBLE.

unbeliever *n.* —*See* SKEPTIC.

unbelieving *adj.* —*See* INCREDULOUS.

unbend *v.* —*See* REST[1] (1).

unbendable *adj.* —*See* STUBBORN (1).

unbending *adj.* —*See* FIRM[1] (3), RIGID, STUBBORN (1).

unbiased *adj.* —*See* FAIR[1] (1), NEUTRAL (1).

unbind *v.* —*See* UNDO.

unblamable *adj.* —*See* EXEMPLARY, INNOCENT (2).

unblemished *adj.* —*See* GOOD (2), INNOCENT (1), PERFECT.

unblended *adj.* —*See* STRAIGHT.

unblock *v.* To rid of obstructions ► clear, free, open, remove. [*Compare* RID.]

unblocked *adj.* —*See* CLEAR (3).

unblushing *adj.* —*See* IMPUDENT.

unbodied *adj.* —*See* IMMATERIAL.

unbosom *v.* To tell in confidence ► breathe, confide, share, whisper. [*Compare* COMMUNICATE, REVEAL, SAY.]

unbound *adj.* —*See* LOOSE (1).

unbounded *adj.* —*See* ENDLESS (1), UTTER[1].

unboundedness *n.* —*See* INFINITY (1).

unbridled *adj.* Out of control ► amuck, runaway, uncontrolled. *Idioms:* out of hand, running wild. —*See also* ABANDONED (2), EXCESSIVE, LOOSE (2).

unbroken *adj.* —*See* CONTINUAL, GOOD (2), WILD (2).

unburden *v.* —*See* RID.

uncalled-for *adj.* —*See* UNNECESSARY, WANTON (2).

uncanny *adj.* —*See* WEIRD.

uncaring *adj.* —*See* CALLOUS.

unceasing *adj.* —*See* CONTINUAL.

uncensored *adj.* —*See* COMPLETE (2).

unceremonious *adj.* —*See* EASYGOING.

unceremoniousness *n.* —*See* EASE (1).

uncertain *adj.* —*See* AMBIGUOUS (1), AMBIGUOUS (2), CAPRICIOUS, CHANGEABLE (1), DEBATABLE, DOUBTFUL (2), INDEFINITE (2), SHADY (1).

uncertainty *n.* —*See* DOUBT, VAGUENESS.

unchained *adj.* —*See* LOOSE (2).

unchangeable *adj.* —*See* IMMUTABLE.

unchanging *adj.* Having no change or variation; remaining unchanged ► changeless, consistent, constant, equable, even, firm, fixed, flat, immutable, invariable, invariant, permanent, regular, same, set, steady, unfailing, uniform, unvarying. *Idioms:* cast (or etched or fixed or set) in stone, steady as she goes. [*Compare* CONTINUAL, CONTINUING, ENDLESS.]

unchaste *adj.* —*See* IMPURE (1), WANTON (1).

unchecked *adj.* —*See* LOOSE (2).

uncivil *adj.* —*See* OFFENSIVE (2), RUDE (2).

uncivility *n.* —*See* INHOSPITALITY.

uncivilized *adj.* Not civilized ► barbarian, barbaric, barbarous, brutish, primitive, rude, savage, uncultivated, uncultured, untamed, wild. —*See also* COARSE (1).

unclad *adj.* —*See* NUDE.

unclasp *v.* —*See* UNDO.

2. The husband of one's aunt. *—idiom:* **cry uncle** *Informal* To surrender or submit.

un·clean (ŭn-klēn′) ► *adj.* **1.** Foul or dirty. **2.** Morally defiled; unchaste. **3.** Ceremonially impure. **—un·clean′ness** *n.*

un·clean·ly (ŭn-klĕn′lē) ► *adj.* Habitually unclean. **—un·clean′li·ness** *n.*

Uncle Sam (săm) ► *n.* The government of the US, often personified as a tall thin man with a white beard.

Uncle Tom ► *n. Offensive* A Black person regarded as being too deferential to white people.

un·cloak (ŭn-klōk′) ► *v.* **1.** To remove a cloak or cover from. **2.** To expose; reveal.

un·close (ŭn-klōz′) ► *v.* To open.

un·clothe (ŭn-klō*th*′) ► *v.* To remove the clothing or cover from.

un·coil (ŭn-koil′) ► *v.* To unwind or become unwound.

un·com·fort·a·ble (ŭn-kŭm′fər-tə-bəl, -kŭmf′tə-, -kŭmf′tər-) ► *adj.* **1.** Experiencing discomfort; uneasy. **2.** Causing anxiety; disquieting. **—un·com′fort·a·bly** *adv.*

un·com·mit·ted (ŭn′kə-mĭt′ĭd) ► *adj.* Not pledged to a specific cause or course.

un·com·mon (ŭn-kŏm′ən) ► *adj.* **1.** Not common; rare. **2.** Wonderful; remarkable. **—un·com′mon·ly** *adv.* **—un·com′mon·ness** *n.*

un·com·mu·ni·ca·tive (ŭn′kə-myōō′nĭ-kā′tĭv, -kə-tĭv) ► *adj.* Not communicative; reserved. **—un′com·mu′ni·ca′tive·ness** *n.*

un·com·pro·mis·ing (ŭn-kŏm′prə-mī′zĭng) ► *adj.* Not making concessions; inflexible.

un·con·cern (ŭn′kən-sûrn′) ► *n.* **1.** Lack of interest; indifference. **2.** Lack of worry or apprehensiveness.

un·con·cerned (ŭn′kən-sûrnd′) ► *adj.* **1.** Not interested; indifferent. **2.** Not anxious or apprehensive. **—un′con·cern′ed·ly** (-sûr′nĭd-lē) *adv.*

un·con·di·tion·al (ŭn′kən-dĭsh′ə-nəl) ► *adj.* Without conditions or limitations. **—un′con·di′tion·al·ly** *adv.*

un·con·di·tioned (ŭn′kən-dĭsh′ənd) ► *adj.* **1.** Unconditional. **2.** *Psychol.* Not resulting from conditioning; unlearned or natural.

un·con·scion·a·ble (ŭn-kŏn′shə-nə-bəl) ► *adj.* **1.** Not restrained or guided by conscience. **2.** Beyond prudence or reason; excessive. **—un·con′scion·a·bly** *adv.*

un·con·scious (ŭn-kŏn′shəs) ► *adj.* **1.** Lacking awareness and the capacity for sensory perception. **2.** Temporarily lacking consciousness. **3.** Occurring without conscious awareness: *unconscious resentment.* **4.** Involuntary: *an unconscious mannerism.* ► *n. Psychol.* The part of the mind that operates without conscious awareness or control. **—un·con′scious·ly** *adv.* **—un·con′scious·ness** *n.*

un·con·sti·tu·tion·al (ŭn′kŏn-stĭ-tōō′shə-nəl, -tyōō′-) ► *adj.* Not in accord with the constitution of a nation or state. **—un′con·sti·tu′tion·al′i·ty** (-năl′ĭ-tē) *n.* **—un′con·sti·tu′tion·al·ly** *adv.*

un·con·ven·tion·al (ŭn′kən-vĕn′shə-nəl) ► *adj.* Not adhering to convention; out of the ordinary. **—un′con·ven′tion·al′i·ty** (-năl′ĭ-tē) *n.* **—un′con·ven′tion·al·ly** *adv.*

un·cork (ŭn-kôrk′) ► *v.* **1.** To draw the cork from. **2.** To free from a constrained state.

un·cou·ple (ŭn-kŭp′əl) ► *v.* To disconnect.

un·couth (ŭn-kōōth′) ► *adj.* **1.** Crude; unrefined. **2.** Awkward or clumsy. **—un·couth′ly** *adv.*

un·cov·er (ŭn-kŭv′ər) ► *v.* **1.** To remove the cover from. **2.** To disclose; reveal. **3.** To remove the hat from (one's head) in respect.

un·cross (ŭn-krôs′, -krŏs′) ► *v.* To move (e.g., one's legs) from a crossed position.

unc·tion (ŭngk′shən) ► *n.* **1.** The act of anointing as part of a religious, ceremonial, or healing ritual. **2.** An ointment or oil; salve. **3.** Something that serves to soothe;

THESAURUS

unclean or **uncleanly** *adj.* —*See* DIRTY, IMPURE (1).

uncleanliness or **uncleanness** *n.* —*See* CONTAMINATION, DIRTINESS.

unclear *adj.* Not clearly perceptible; difficult to see clearly ► blear, bleary, blurry, cloudy, dim, faint, filmy, foggy, fuzzy, hazy, indefinite, indistinct, misty, murky, obscure, shadowy, undistinct, vague. —*See also* AMBIGUOUS (1), AMBIGUOUS (2).

unclose *v.* —*See* OPEN (1).

unclothe *v.* To remove the clothing or covering from ► disrobe, strip, undress. —*See also* REVEAL.

unclouded *adj.* —*See* CLEAR (2).

uncoil *v.* —*See* UNWIND.

uncomeliness *n.* —*See* UGLINESS.

uncomely *adj.* —*See* UGLY.

uncomfortable *adj.* Causing discomfort ► comfortless, thorny, uncomforting. *Informal:* uncomfy. [*Compare* DISTURBING, PAINFUL, TORMENTING.] —*See also* AWKWARD (3).

uncomfy *adj.* —*See* UNCOMFORTABLE.

uncommitted *adj.* —*See* NEUTRAL (1).

uncommon *adj.* —*See* EXCEPTIONAL, INFREQUENT.

uncommonly *adv.* —*See* INFREQUENTLY, UNUSUALLY.

uncommonness *n.* —*See* UNIQUENESS.

uncommunicative *adj.* —*See* COOL, TACITURN.

uncommunicativeness *n.* —*See* RESERVE (1).

uncompassionate *adj.* —*See* CALLOUS.

uncompelled *adj.* —*See* VOLUNTARY.

uncompensated *adj.* —*See* UNPAID.

uncompliant *adj.* —*See* STUBBORN (1).

uncomplimentary *adj.* —*See* DISPARAGING.

uncomprehending *adj.* —*See* BLIND (3).

uncomprehensible *adj.* —*See* INCOMPREHENSIBLE.

uncompromising *adj.* —*See* FIRM[1] (3), GRAPHIC (1), SEVERE (1), STUBBORN (1).

unconceivable *adj.* —*See* IMPLAUSIBLE.

unconcern *n.* —*See* APATHY, DETACHMENT (2).

unconcerned *adj.* —*See* APATHETIC, CARELESS, DETACHED (1).

unconditional *adj.* Without limitations or mitigating conditions ► absolute, full, unconditioned, unqualified, unreserved. [*Compare* UTTER[2].] —*See also* IMPLICIT (2).

unconditioned *adj.* —*See* UNCONDITIONAL.

unconfined *adj.* —*See* LOOSE (2).

unconfirmed *adj.* —*See* DEBATABLE.

uncongenial *adj.* —*See* INHARMONIOUS (1), UNPLEASANT.

uncongeniality *n.* —*See* INHOSPITALITY.

unconnected *adj.* —*See* IRRELEVANT.

unconquerability *n.* —*See* SAFETY.

unconquerable *adj.* **1.** Incapable of being conquered or subjugated ► indomitable, invincible, unbeatable, undefeatable. [*Compare* INSUPERABLE.] **2.** Incapable of being negotiated or overcome ► impassable, insuperable, insurmountable. [*Compare* IMPOSSIBLE.] —*See also* SAFE (2).

unconscionable *adj.* —*See* OUTRAGEOUS, STEEP[1] (2), UNSCRUPULOUS.

unconscious *adj.* Lacking consciousness ► cold, comatose, insensible, out, senseless. *Idioms:* blacked out, out like a light, out cold. [*Compare* DEAD, INANIMATE.] —*See also* IGNORANT (3).

unconsciousness *n.* —*See* IGNORANCE (2).

unconsidered *adj.* —*See* RASH[1].

unconspicuous *adj.* —*See* INCONSPICUOUS.

unconstrained *adj.* —*See* ABANDONED (2).

uncontaminated *adj.* —*See* FRESH (1).

uncontrollability or **uncontrollableness** *n.* —*See* UNRULINESS.

uncontrollable *adj.* —*See* UNRULY.

uncontrolled *adj.* Out of control ► amuck, runaway, unbridled. *Idioms:* out of hand, running wild. [*Compare* LOOSE.] —*See also* ABANDONED (2), ERRATIC.

unconventional *adj.* —*See* ECCENTRIC, UNUSUAL.

unconventionally *adv.* —*See* UNUSUALLY.

unconversant *adj.* —*See* INEXPERIENCED.

unconvinced *adj.* —*See* INCREDULOUS.

unconvincing *adj.* —*See* IMPLAUSIBLE.

uncooked *adj.* Not cooked ► raw.

uncool *adj.* —*See* CONVENTIONAL.

uncoordinated *adj.* —*See* AWKWARD (1).

uncorporal *adj.* —*See* IMMATERIAL.

uncorrupted *adj.* —*See* INNOCENT (1).

uncountable *adj.* —*See* INCALCULABLE.

uncouple *v.* —*See* DETACH, DIVIDE.

uncoupling *n.* —*See* DETACHMENT (1).

uncouth *adj.* —*See* COARSE (1).

uncover *v.* To find by investigation ► dig (up *or* out), disinter, exhume, turn up, unearth. *Idiom:* bring to light. [*Compare* DISCOVER.] —*See also* BARE, BETRAY (2), REVEAL.

uncovered *adj.* —*See* OPEN (2).

uncreative *adj.* —*See* STERILE (2).

uncritical *adj.* —*See* SUPERFICIAL.

unction *n.* —*See* OIL, OINTMENT.

balm. **4.** Affected or exaggerated earnestness.

unc·tu·ous (ŭngk′cho͞o-əs) ▸ *adj.* **1.** Marked by affected, exaggerated, or insincere earnestness. **2.** Greasy; oily. **—unc′tu·ous·ly** *adv.* **—unc′tu·ous·ness** *n.*

un·cut (ŭn-kŭt′) ▸ *adj.* **1.** Not cut. **2.** *Print.* Not slit or trimmed: *uncut pages.* **3.** Not shaped by cutting: *uncut gems.* **4.** Not condensed, abridged, or censored.

un·daunt·ed (ŭn-dôn′tĭd, -dän′-) ▸ *adj.* Not discouraged or disheartened; resolutely courageous. **—un·daunt′ed·ly** *adv.* **—un·daunt′ed·ness** *n.*

un·de·cid·ed (ŭn′dĭ-sī′dĭd) ▸ *adj.* **1.** Not yet determined or settled. **2.** Not having reached a decision; uncommitted.

un·de·mon·stra·tive (ŭn′dĭ-mŏn′strə-tĭv) ▸ *adj.* Not given to expressions of feeling; reserved. **—un′de·mon′stra·tive·ness** *n.*

un·der (ŭn′dər) ▸ *prep.* **1.** In a lower position or place than. **2.** Beneath the surface of. **3.** Beneath the guise of: *traveled under a false name.* **4.** Less than; smaller than: *under three years of age.* **5.** Less than the required amount or degree of: *under voting age.* **6.** Inferior to in status or rank. **7.** Subject to the authority of: *under a dictatorship.* **8.** Undergoing or receiving the effects of: *under constant care.* **9.** Subject to the obligation of: *under contract.* **10.** Within the group or classification of: *listed under biology.* **11.** In the process of: *under discussion.* **12.** Because of: *under these conditions.* ▸ *adv.* **1.** In or into a place below or beneath. **2.** Into a subordinate or inferior condition or position. **3.** So as to be covered or enveloped. **4.** So as to be less than the required amount or degree. ▸ *adj.* **1.** Lower. **2.** Subordinate; inferior. **3.** Less than is required or customary.

under– ▸ *pref.* **1.** Beneath; below: *underground.* **2.** Inferior; subordinate: *undersecretary.* **3.** Less than normal: *undersized.*

un·der·a·chieve (ŭn′dər-ə-chēv′) ▸ *v.* To perform worse or achieve less success than expected. **—un′der·a·chiev′er** *n.*

un·der·age[1] (ŭn′dər-ĭj) ▸ *n.* **1.** An amount, as of money, falling short of the listed amount in records of account. **2.** A deficient amount; shortfall.

un·der·age[2] (ŭn′dər-āj′) also **un·der·aged** (-ājd′) ▸ *adj.* Below the customary or legal age.

un·der·arm (ŭn′dər-ärm′) ▸ *adj.* **1.** Located, placed, or used under the arm. **2.** *Sports* Underhand. ▸ *adv.* With an underarm motion or delivery. ▸ *n.* The armpit.

un·der·bel·ly (ŭn′dər-bĕl′ē) ▸ *n.* **1.** The soft underside of an animal's body. **2.** The vulnerable or weak part.

un·der·bid (ŭn′dər-bĭd′) ▸ *v.* **1.** To bid lower than. **2.** *Games* To bid too low. **—un′der-bid′** *n.*

un·der·bite (ŭn′dər-bīt′) ▸ *n.* A condition of the teeth in which the lower teeth protrude beyond the upper teeth.

un·der·brush (ŭn′dər-brŭsh′) ▸ *n.* Small trees, shrubs, or similar plants growing beneath the taller trees in a forest.

un·der·car·riage (ŭn′dər-kăr′ĭj) ▸ *n.* **1.** A supporting framework, as of a motor vehicle. **2.** The landing gear of an aircraft.

un·der·charge (ŭn′dər-chärj′) ▸ *v.* To charge (someone) less than is customary or required. **—un′der·charge′** *n.*

un·der·class·man (ŭn′dər-klăs′mən) ▸ *n.* A student in the freshman or sophomore class at a secondary school or college.

un·der·clothes (ŭn′dər-klōz′, -klōthz′) ▸ *pl.n.* See **underwear.**

un·der·coat (ŭn′dər-kōt′) ▸ *n.* **1.** A coat worn beneath another coat. **2.** Short hairs or fur underneath the longer outer hairs of an animal's coat. **3.** also **un·der·coat·ing** (-kō′tĭng) **a.** A coat of sealing material applied before a final coat. **b.** A tarlike substance sprayed on the underside of a vehicle to prevent rusting. **—un′der·coat′** *v.*

un·der·cov·er (ŭn′dər-kŭv′ər) ▸ *adj.* Performed or occurring in secret.

un·der·cur·rent (ŭn′dər-kûr′ənt, -kŭr′-) ▸ *n.* **1.** A current below another current or a surface. **2.** An underlying tendency or force often contrary to what is superficially evident.

un·der·cut (ŭn′dər-kŭt′) ▸ *v.* **1.** To diminish or destroy the effectiveness of; undermine. **2.** To sell at a lower price or work for lower wages than (a competitor). **3.** To make a cut under or below. **4.** *Sports* **a.** To impart backspin to (a ball) by striking downward as well as forward. **b.** To slice (a ball) with an underarm stroke. **—un′der·cut′** *n.*

un·der·de·vel·oped (ŭn′dər-dĭ-vĕl′əpt) ▸ *adj.* **1.** Not adequately or normally developed; immature. **2.** Having a low level of economic and technological development. **—un′der·de·vel′op·ment** *n.*

un·der·dog (ŭn′dər-dôg′, -dŏg′) ▸ *n.* **1.** One who is expected to lose a contest or struggle. **2.** One who is at a disadvantage.

un·der·done (ŭn′dər-dŭn′) ▸ *adj.* Not sufficiently cooked.

un·der·dress (ŭn′dər-drĕs′) ▸ *n.* Underwear. ▸ *v.* (ŭn′dər-drĕs′) **1.** To dress too informally for the occasion. **2.** To dress without sufficient warmth.

un·der·es·ti·mate (ŭn′dər-ĕs′tə-māt′) ▸ *v.* To make too low an estimate of the quantity, degree, or worth of. ▸ *n.* (-mĭt) An estimate that is too low. **—un′der·es′ti·ma′tion** *n.*

un·der·ex·pose (ŭn′dər-ĭk-spōz′) ▸ *v.* To expose (film) to light for too short a time. **—un′der·ex·po′sure** *n.*

un·der·foot (ŭn′dər-fo͝ot′) ▸ *adv.* **1.** Below or under the feet. **2.** In the way.

un·der·gar·ment (ŭn′dər-gär′mənt) ▸ *n.* A garment worn under outer garments.

un·der·go (ŭn′dər-gō′) ▸ *v.* **1.** To pass through; experience. **2.** To endure; suffer.

un·der·grad·u·ate (ŭn′dər-grăj′o͞o-ĭt) ▸ *n.* A college or university student who has not yet received a degree.

un·der·ground (ŭn′dər-ground′) ▸ *adj.* **1.** Below the surface of the earth. **2.** Hidden or concealed; clandestine. **3.** Of or relating to avant-garde or experimental films, publications, and art. ▸ *n.* **1.** A clandestine, often nationalist, organization working against a government in power. **2.** *Chiefly Brit.* A subway system. **3.** An avant-garde movement. ▸ *adv.* (ŭn′dər-ground′) **1.** Below the surface of the earth. **2.** In secret; stealthily.

un·der·growth (ŭn′dər-grōth′) ▸ *n.* Low-growing plants, saplings, and shrubs beneath trees in a forest.

un·der·hand (ŭn′dər-hănd′) also **un·der·hand·ed** (ŭn′dər-hăn′dĭd) ▸ *adj.* **1.** Done slyly and secretly; sneaky. **2.** *Sports*

THESAURUS

unctuous *adj.* Affectedly and self-servingly earnest ▸ fulsome, oily, oleaginous, sleek, smarmy. [*Compare* FLATTERING, GLIB, SERVILE.] *—See also* FATTY.

uncultivated *adj.* *—See* COARSE (1), IGNORANT (1), UNCIVILIZED, WILD (1).

uncultured *adj.* *—See* COARSE (1), UNCIVILIZED.

uncut *adj.* *—See* COMPLETE (2).

undamaged *adj.* *—See* GOOD (2).

undaunted *adj.* *—See* BRAVE.

undauntedness *n.* *—See* COURAGE.

undeceive *v.* *—See* DISABUSE.

undecided *adj.* *—See* DOUBTFUL (2), INDEFINITE (2).

undeclared *adj.* *—See* SILENT (2).

undecorated *adj.* *—See* BARE (1).

undefended *adj.* *—See* INSECURE (1).

undefiled *adj.* *—See* INNOCENT (1).

undemanding *adj.* Requiring little effort or exertion ▸ easy, light, moderate. *Informal:* cushy, soft.

undemonstrated *adj.* *—See* UNTRIED.

undemonstrative *adj.* *—See* COOL.

undeniable *adj.* *—See* CERTAIN (2).

undependable *adj.* **1.** Not to be depended on ▸ fair-weather, irresponsible, unreliable, untrustworthy. [*Compare* CAPRICIOUS, CHANGEABLE.] **2.** So weak or defective as to be liable to fail ▸ trick, unreliable. [*Compare* DEFECTIVE, WEAK.]

under *adj.* *—See* INSUFFICIENT, MINOR (1).

underage[1] *n.* *—See* SHORTAGE.

underage[2] *adj.* Not yet a legal adult ▸ juvenile, minor.

underbrush *n.* *—See* BRUSH[2].

undercover *adj.* *—See* SECRET (1).

undercurrent *n.* *—See* HINT (1).

underdeveloped *adj.* *—See* BACKWARD (2).

underdog *n.* *—See* UNFORTUNATE.

underestimate *v.* *—See* MISCALCULATE.

undergird *v.* *—See* BASE[1], SUPPORT (2).

undergo *v.* *—See* EXPERIENCE.

underground *adj.* Located or operating beneath the earth's surface ▸ belowground, buried, hypogeal, hypogean, hypogeous, subterranean, subterrestrial.

underground *n.* A clandestine organization of freedom fighters in an oppressed land ▸ opposition, resistance.

underhand or **underhanded** *adj.* Marked by or done in a deceptive or

Executed with the hand brought forward and up from below the level of the shoulder; underarm. **—un′der·hand′** *n.* **—un′der·hand′, un′der·hand′ed** *adv.* **—un′der·hand′ed·ly** *adv.* **—un′der·hand′ed·ness** *n.*

un·der·lie (ŭn′dər-lī′) ▸ *v.* **-lay, -lain, -ly·ing.** **1.** To be located under or below. **2.** To be the support or basis of; account for.

un·der·line (ŭn′dər-līn′, ŭn′dər-līn′) ▸ *v.* **1.** To draw a line under; underscore. **2.** To emphasize. **—un′der·line′** *n.*

un·der·ling (ŭn′dər-lĭng) ▸ *n.* A subordinate.

un·der·ly·ing (ŭn′dər-lī′ĭng) ▸ *adj.* **1.** Lying under or beneath. **2.** Basic; fundamental. **3.** Present but not obvious; implicit.

un·der·mine (ŭn′dər-mīn′) ▸ *v.* **1.** To weaken by wearing away gradually or imperceptibly. **2.** To dig a mine or tunnel beneath.

un·der·most (ŭn′dər-mōst′) ▸ *adj.* Lowest in position, rank, or place; bottom. ▸ *adv.* Lowest.

un·der·neath (ŭn′dər-nēth′) ▸ *adv.* **1.** In or to a place beneath; below. **2.** On the lower face or underside. ▸ *prep.* **1.** Under; below; beneath. **2.** Under the power or control of. ▸ *adj.* Lower; under. ▸ *n.* The part or side below or under.

un·der·pants (ŭn′dər-pănts′) ▸ *pl.n.* Briefs or shorts worn as underwear.

un·der·pass (ŭn′dər-păs′) ▸ *n.* A passage underneath something, esp. a road under another road.

un·der·pin·ning (ŭn′dər-pĭn′ĭng) ▸ *n.* **1.** A supporting structure or part. **2.** often **underpinnings** *Informal* The legs.

un·der·play (ŭn′dər-plā′, ŭn′dər-plā′) ▸ *v.* **1.** To act (a role) subtly or with restraint. **2.** To minimize the importance of.

un·der·rate (ŭn′dər-rāt′) ▸ *v.* To rate too low; underestimate.

un·der·score (ŭn′dər-skôr′) ▸ *v.* **1.** To underline. **2.** To emphasize; stress. **—un′der·score′** *n.*

un·der·sea (ŭn′dər-sē′) ▸ *adj. & adv.* Beneath the surface of the sea. **—un′der·seas′** *adv.*

un·der·sec·re·tar·y (ŭn′dər-sĕk′rə-tĕr′ē) ▸ *n.* An official directly subordinate to a cabinet member. **—un′der·sec′re·tar′i·at** (-târ′ē-ĭt) *n.*

un·der·sell (ŭn′dər-sĕl′) ▸ *v.* **1.** To sell for a lower price than. **2.** To present in a way that minimizes the value.

un·der·shirt (ŭn′dər-shûrt′) ▸ *n.* An undergarment worn under a shirt.

un·der·shoot (ŭn′dər-sho͞ot′) ▸ *v.* **1.** To shoot a projectile short of (a target). **2.** To land an aircraft short of (a landing area).

un·der·shorts (ŭn′dər-shôrts′) ▸ *pl.n.* Underpants.

un·der·shot (ŭn′dər-shŏt′) ▸ *adj.* **1.** Driven by water passing from below, as a water wheel. **2.** Having the lower jaw or teeth projecting beyond the upper.

un·der·side (ŭn′dər-sīd′) ▸ *n.* The side or surface that is underneath.

un·der·signed (ŭn′dər-sīnd′) ▸ *n., pl.* **-signed.** A signer whose name is at the bottom or end of a document. **—un′der·signed′** *adj.*

un·der·sized (ŭn′dər-sīzd′) also **un·der·size** (-sīz′) ▸ *adj.* Smaller than normal or sufficient size.

un·der·slung (ŭn′dər-slŭng′) ▸ *adj.* Having springs attached to the axles from below, as on an auto chassis.

un·der·stand (ŭn′dər-stănd′) ▸ *v.* **-stood** (-sto͝od′, **-stand·ing.** **1.** To perceive and comprehend the nature and significance of; grasp. **2.** To know thoroughly by close contact or long experience with. **3.** To comprehend the language, sounds, form, or symbols of. **4.** To know and be tolerant or sympathetic toward. **5.** To learn indirectly, as by hearsay. **6.** To conclude; infer. **7.** To accept as an agreed fact: *It is understood that the fee will be 50 dollars.* **—un′der·stand′a·ble** *adj.* **—un′der·stand′a·bly** *adv.*

un·der·stand·ing (ŭn′dər-stăn′dĭng) ▸ *n.* **1.** The quality of discernment; comprehension. **2.** The faculty by which one understands; intelligence. **3.** Individual or specified judgment or outlook; opinion. **4.** An agreement between two or more people or groups. **5.** A reconciliation of differences. ▸ *adj.* Compassionate; sympathetic.

un·der·state (ŭn′dər-stāt′) ▸ *v.* **1.** To state with less completeness or truth than seems warranted by the facts. **2.** To express with restraint or lack of emphasis, esp. for rhetorical effect. **—un′der·state′ment** *n.*

un·der·stood (ŭn′dər-sto͝od′) ▸ *adj.* **1.** Agreed on; assumed. **2.** Implicit or implied.

un·der·sto·ry (ŭn′dər-stôr′ē) ▸ *n.* An underlying layer of vegetation, esp. beneath a forest's canopy.

un·der·stud·y (ŭn′dər-stŭd′ē) ▸ *v.* **1.** To study or know (a role) so as to be able to replace a regular performer. **2.** To act as an understudy to. ▸ *n.* A performer who understudies another.

un·der·take (ŭn′dər-tāk′) ▸ *v.* **1.** To take upon oneself, as a task. **2.** To pledge or commit (oneself) to.

un·der·tak·er (ŭn′dər-tā′kər) ▸ *n.* See **funeral director.**

un·der·tak·ing (ŭn′dər-tā′kĭng) ▸ *n.* **1.** Something undertaken; venture. **2.** A guaranty or promise. **3.** The profession of a funeral director.

un·der-the-count·er (ŭn′dər-*th*ə-koun′tər) ▸ *adv. & adj.* Transacted or sold illicitly.

un·der·tone (ŭn′dər-tōn′) ▸ *n.* **1.** An underlying or implied tendency or meaning; undercurrent. **2.** A tone of low pitch or volume. **3.** A pale or subdued color.

THESAURUS

secret manner ▸ devious, disingenuous, duplicitous, guileful, indirect, left-handed, lubricious, shifty, sneaky, subtle, unscrupulous. [*Compare* ARTFUL, SECRET, SHADY, STEALTHY.]

underhandedness *n.* —*See* DISHONESTY (2).

underline *v.* —*See* EMPHASIZE.

underling *n.* —*See* SUBORDINATE.

underlying *adj.* —*See* ELEMENTAL, RADICAL.

undermanned *adj.* Having fewer workers or participants than are needed ▸ short-handed, short-staffed, understaffed.

undermine *v.* To damage, destroy, or defeat by sabotage ▸ sabotage, subvert. [*Compare* DESTROY, DISORDER.] —*See also* ENERVATE.

undermining *n.* Treacherous action to defeat or do harm to an endeavor ▸ sabotage, subversion. [*Compare* DEFEAT, DESTRUCTION.]

undermost *adj.* —*See* BOTTOM.

underneath *n.* —*See* BOTTOM (1).

underpin *v.* —*See* BASE[1], SUPPORT (2).

underpinning *n.* —*See* BASE[1] (2), BASIS (1), SUPPORT.

underprivileged *adj.* —*See* DEPRESSED (2).

underprivileged *n.* —*See* UNFORTUNATE.

underprop *v.* —*See* SUPPORT (2).

underscore *v.* —*See* EMPHASIZE.

undersexed *adj.* —*See* FRIGID.

underside *n.* —*See* BOTTOM (1).

undersign *v.* —*See* SIGN.

undersized *adj.* —*See* LITTLE.

understaffed *adj.* Having fewer workers or participants than are needed ▸ short-handed, short-staffed, undermanned.

understand *v.* **1.** To perceive and recognize the meaning of ▸ accept, apprehend, catch (on), compass, comprehend, conceive, fathom, follow, get, grasp, make out, read, see, sense, take, take in. *Informal:* hear, savvy. *Slang:* dig. ***Idioms:*** get (*or* have) a handle on, get the picture. [*Compare* KNOW.] **2.** To understand or be sensitive to another's feelings or ideas ▸ empathize, sympathize. ***Idioms:*** feel someone's pain, put oneself (*or* walk) in someone else's shoes. —*See also* INFER.

understandable *adj.* Capable of being readily understood ▸ appreciable, apprehensible, coherent, comprehensible, fathomable, intelligible, knowable, lucid, unambiguous. —*See also* PARDONABLE.

understanding *n.* **1.** Intellectual hold ▸ apprehension, comprehension, grasp, grip, hold. [*Compare* KNOWLEDGE.] **2.** A very close understanding between persons ▸ empathy, sympathy. **3.** The sum of what has been perceived, discovered, or inferred ▸ knowledge, lore, wisdom. [*Compare* ACTUALITY.] —*See also* AGREEMENT (1), INTELLIGENCE.

understanding *adj.* —*See* SYMPATHETIC.

understood *adj.* —*See* IMPLICIT (1).

undersurface *n.* —*See* BOTTOM (1).

undertake *v.* —*See* ASSUME, PLEDGE (2), START (1).

undertaking *n.* Something undertaken, especially something requiring extensive planning and work ▸ endeavor, enterprise, project, venture. [*Compare* TASK.] —*See also* ATTEMPT, MISSION (1).

undertone *n.* —*See* COLOR (1), HINT (1).

un·der·tow (ŭn′dər-tō′) ▸ *n.* The seaward pull of receding waves after they break on a shore.
un·der·wa·ter (ŭn′dər-wô′tər, -wŏt′ər) ▸ *adj.* Used, done, or existing beneath the surface of water. **—un′der·wa′ter** *adv.*
un·der·wear (ŭn′dər-wâr′) ▸ *n.* Clothes worn next to the skin, beneath one's outer clothing.
un·der·weight (ŭn′dər-wāt′) ▸ *adj.* Weighing less than is normal, healthy, or required.
un·der·world (ŭn′dər-wûrld′) ▸ *n.* **1.** The part of society organized for and engaged in crime and vice. **2.** *Gk. & Rom. Myth.* The world of the dead; Hades.
un·der·write (ŭn′dər-rīt′) ▸ *v.* **1.** To assume financial responsibility for. **2.** To sign (an insurance policy) so as to assume liability in case of specified losses. **3.** To agree to buy the unsold part of (stock not yet sold publicly) at a fixed time and price. **4.** To write under, esp. to endorse (a document). **—un′der·writ′er** *n.*
un·de·sir·a·ble (ŭn′dĭ-zīr′ə-bəl) ▸ *adj.* Not wanted; objectionable. ▸ *n.* An undesirable person. **—un′de·sir′a·bly** *adv.*
un·dies (ŭn′dēz) ▸ *pl.n.* *Informal* Underwear.
un·dis·posed (ŭn′dĭ-spōzd′) ▸ *adj.* **1.** Not settled, removed, or resolved. **2.** Disinclined; unwilling.
un·do (ŭn-do͞o′) ▸ *v.* **1.** To reverse or erase; annul. **2.** To untie, disassemble, or loosen. **3.** To open; unwrap. **4a.** To cause the ruin or downfall of; destroy. **b.** To throw into confusion; unsettle.
un·do·ing (ŭn-do͞o′ĭng) ▸ *n.* **1.** The act of unfastening or loosening. **2a.** The act of bringing to ruin. **b.** A cause or source of ruin. **3.** The act of reversing or annulling something.
un·dress (ŭn-drĕs′) ▸ *v.* To remove the clothing (of); disrobe. ▸ *n.* **1.** Informal attire. **2.** Nakedness.
un·due (ŭn-do͞o′, -dyo͞o′) ▸ *adj.* **1.** Exceeding what is appropriate or normal. **2.** Not just, proper, or legal. **3.** Not yet payable or due.
un·du·lant (ŭn′jə-lənt, ŭn′dyə-, -də-) ▸ *adj.* Undulating.
un·du·late (ŭn′jə-lāt′, ŭn′dyə-, -də-) ▸ *v.* **-lat·ed, -lat·ing. 1.** To move or cause to move in a smooth wavelike motion. **2.** To have a wavelike appearance or form.
un·du·la·tion (ŭn′jə-lā′shən, ŭn′dyə-, -də-) ▸ *n.* **1.** A wavelike movement. **2.** A wavelike form, outline, or appearance. **3.** One of a series of waves or wavelike segments.
un·du·ly (ŭn-do͞o′lē, -dyo͞o′-) ▸ *adv.* Excessively; immoderately: *unduly fearful.*
un·dy·ing (ŭn-dī′ĭng) ▸ *adj.* Everlasting.
un·earned (ŭn-ûrnd′) ▸ *adj.* **1.** Not gained by work or service. **2.** Not deserved.
un·earth (ŭn-ûrth′) ▸ *v.* **1.** To dig up. **2.** To bring to public notice; uncover.
un·earth·ly (ŭn-ûrth′lē) ▸ *adj.* **1.** Not of the earth; supernatural. **2.** Unnaturally strange and frightening; eerie.
un·eas·y (ŭn-ē′zē) ▸ *adj.* **1.** Lacking ease, comfort, or a sense of security. **2.** Affording no ease or reassurance: *an uneasy calm.* **3.** Awkward or unsure in manner; constrained. **—un·ease′, un·eas′i·ness** *n.* **—un·eas′i·ly** *adv.*
un·em·ployed (ŭn′ĕm-ploid′, -ĭm-) ▸ *adj.* **1.** Not having work; jobless. **2.** Not being used; idle. **—un′em·ploy′ment** *n.*
un·e·qual (ŭn-ē′kwəl) ▸ *adj.* **1.** Not the same in any measurable aspect. **2.** Asymmetrical. **3.** Irregular; variable. **4.** Not having the required abilities; inadequate. **5.** Not fair. **—un·e′qual·ly** *adv.*
un·e·qualed also **un·e·qualled** (ŭn-ē′kwəld) ▸ *adj.* Not matched or paralleled; unrivaled.
un·e·quiv·o·cal (ŭn′ĭ-kwĭv′ə-kəl) ▸ *adj.* Open to no doubt or misunderstanding; clear. **—un′e·quiv′o·cal·ly** *adv.*
un·e·ven (ŭn-ē′vən) ▸ *adj.* **1.** Not equal, as in size, length, or quality. **2.** Not consistent or uniform. **3.** Not smooth or level. **4.** Not straight or parallel. **—un·e′ven·ly** *adv.* **—un·e′ven·ness** *n.*
un·e·vent·ful (ŭn′ĭ-vĕnt′fəl) ▸ *adj.* **1.** Lacking in significant events. **2.** Occurring without disruption. **—un′e·vent′ful·ness** *n.*
un·ex·am·pled (ŭn′ĭg-zăm′pəld) ▸ *adj.* Without precedent; unparalleled.
un·ex·cep·tion·a·ble (ŭn′ĭk-sĕp′shə-nə-bəl) ▸ *adj.* Beyond any reasonable objection.
un·ex·cep·tion·al (ŭn′ĭk-sĕp′shə-nəl) ▸ *adj.* **1.** Not varying

THESAURUS

underwhelming *adj.* —*See* DISAPPOINTING.
underwrite *v.* —*See* FINANCE.
underwriter *n.* —*See* SPONSOR.
undescribable *adj.* —*See* UNSPEAKABLE (1).
undesigned *adj.* —*See* UNINTENTIONAL.
undesirable *adj.* —*See* OBJECTIONABLE, UNWELCOME.
undesired *adj.* —*See* UNWELCOME.
undetected *adj.* Not found ▸ undiscovered, unexposed, unfound.
undetermined *adj.* —*See* INDEFINITE (1), INDEFINITE (2).
undeveloped *adj.* —*See* BACKWARD (2), FRESH (1).
undeviating *adj.* —*See* DIRECT (1), LITERAL.
undevised *adj.* —*See* UNINTENTIONAL.
undiluted *adj.* —*See* PURE, STRAIGHT.
undiplomatic *adj.* —*See* TACTLESS.
undirected *adj.* —*See* AIMLESS.
undisciplined *adj.* —*See* UNRULY.
undisclosed *adj.* —*See* ULTERIOR (1).
undiscovered *adj.* Not found ▸ undetected, unexposed, unfound.
undisputable *adj.* —*See* CERTAIN (2).
undistinct *adj.* —*See* UNCLEAR.
undistinguished *adj.* —*See* INCONSPICUOUS, OBSCURE (2), ORDINARY.
undivided *adj.* —*See* CONCENTRATED (1), UNANIMOUS.
undo *v.* To free from ties or fasteners ▸ disengage, loose, loosen, release, slip, unbind, unclasp, unfasten, unloose, unloosen, untie. —*See also* CANCEL (1), DESTROY (1), ENERVATE, OPEN (1).
undoing *n.* —*See* DESTRUCTION, RUIN (1).
undomesticated *adj.* —*See* WILD (1), WILD (2).
undoubted *adj.* —*See* AUTHENTIC (1).
undoubtedly *adv.* —*See* ABSOLUTELY, YES.
undoubting *adj.* —*See* IMPLICIT (2), SURE (1).
undress *v.* —*See* BARE.
undress *n.* —*See* NUDITY.
undue *adj.* —*See* EXCESSIVE.
undulate *v.* —*See* CRAWL (1), SWAY, WAVE (1).
unduly *adv.* Too much ▸ disproportionately, excessively, extravagantly, extremely, inordinately, overly, overmuch. *Informal:* super.
undying *adj.* Not being subject to death ▸ deathless, immortal. [*Compare* ENDLESS.] —*See also* CONTINUAL.
unearth *v.* —*See* DISCOVER, UNCOVER.
unearthly *adj.* —*See* SUPERNATURAL (1), WEIRD.
unease or **uneasiness** *n.* —*See* ANXIETY (1), RESTLESSNESS.
uneasy *adj.* Affording no quiet, repose, or rest ▸ restless, unquiet, unsettled. [*Compare* EDGY, WAKEFUL.] —*See also* ANXIOUS, AWKWARD (3).
uneconomical *adj.* —*See* EXTRAVAGANT.
unedited *adj.* —*See* COMPLETE (2).
uneducated *adj.* —*See* IGNORANT (1).
unemotional *adj.* —*See* COLD (2).
unemployable *adj.* —*See* UNWORKABLE.
unemployed *adj.* Having no job ▸ idle, jobless, unoccupied, workless. *Idiom:* out of a job (*or* employ *or* work). —*See also* IDLE (1).
unencouraging *adj.* —*See* BLEAK (2).
unending *adj.* —*See* CONTINUAL, ENDLESS (2), LONG[1] (2).
unendingly *adv.* —*See* FOREVER.
unendurable *adj.* —*See* UNBEARABLE.
unenlightened *adj.* —*See* IGNORANT (2), IGNORANT (3).
unenthusiastic *adj.* Lacking warmth, interest, enthusiasm, or involvement ▸ halfhearted, Laodicean, lukewarm, tepid. [*Compare* APATHETIC, COLD, COOL.]
unequal *adj.* —*See* INEFFICIENT, UNFAIR.
unequaled *adj.* —*See* UNIQUE.
unequivocal *adj.* —*See* DEFINITE (1), SHARP (2), UTTER[2].
unerring *adj.* —*See* SURE (2).
unessential *adj.* —*See* UNNECESSARY.
unethical *adj.* —*See* UNSCRUPULOUS.
uneven *adj.* Lacking consistency or regularity in quality or performance ▸ erratic, inconsistent, patchy, spasmodic, spotty, unsteady, variable. [*Compare* INTERMITTENT.] —*See also* ROUGH (1), UNFAIR.
unevenness *n.* —*See* IRREGULARITY.
unexampled *adj.* —*See* UNIQUE.
unexceptionable *adj.* —*See* ACCEPTABLE (1).
unexceptional *adj.* —*See* ORDINARY.

from a norm; usual. 2. Not subject to exceptions; absolute. **—un′ex·cep′tion·al·ly** *adv.*

un·ex·pect·ed (ŭn′ĭk-spĕk′tĭd) ▸ *adj.* Coming without warning; unforeseen. **—un′ex·pect′ed·ly** *adv.* **—un′ex·pect′ed·ness** *n.*

un·fail·ing (ŭn-fā′lĭng) ▸ *adj.* 1. Not failing or running out; inexhaustible. 2. Constant; unflagging. 3. Infallible. **—un·fail′ing·ly** *adv.*

un·fair (ŭn-fâr′) ▸ *adj.* 1. Not just or evenhanded; biased. 2. Contrary to laws or conventions, esp. in commerce; unethical. **—un·fair′ly** *adv.* **—un·fair′ness** *n.*

un·faith·ful (ŭn-fāth′fəl) ▸ *adj.* 1. Not faithful; disloyal. 2. Adulterous. 3. Not justly representing or reflecting the original; inaccurate. **—un·faith′ful·ly** *adv.* **—un·faith′ful·ness** *n.*

un·fa·mil·iar (ŭn′fə-mĭl′yər) ▸ *adj.* 1. Not within one's knowledge; strange. 2. Not acquainted; not conversant. **—un′fa·mil·iar′i·ty** (-mĭl-yăr′ĭ-tē, -mĭl′ē-ăr′ĭ-tē) *n.* **—un′fa·mil′iar·ly** *adv.*

un·feel·ing (ŭn-fē′lĭng) ▸ *adj.* 1. Having no sensation; insentient. 2. Not sympathetic; callous. **—un·feel′ing·ly** *adv.*

un·feigned (ŭn′fānd′) ▸ *adj.* Not pretended; genuine.

un·fet·ter (ŭn-fĕt′ər) ▸ *v.* To free from restrictions or bonds.

un·fit (ŭn-fĭt′) ▸ *adj.* 1. Inappropriate. 2. Unqualified. 3. In poor physical or mental health. ▸ *v.* To make unfit; disqualify. **—un·fit′ly** *adv.* **—un·fit′ness** *n.*

un·flag·ging (ŭn-flăg′ĭng) ▸ *adj.* Not flagging; untiring. **—un·flag′ging·ly** *adv.*

un·flap·pa·ble (ŭn-flăp′ə-bəl) ▸ *adj.* Not easily upset; cool. **—un·flap′pa·bil′i·ty** *n.*

un·fledged (ŭn-flĕjd′) ▸ *adj.* 1. Not having the feathers necessary to fly. Used of a young bird. 2. Inexperienced or immature.

un·flinch·ing (ŭn-flĭn′chĭng) ▸ *adj.* Steadfast; resolute. **—un·flinch′ing·ly** *adv.*

un·fold (ŭn-fōld′) ▸ *v.* 1. To open and spread out (something that is folded); extend. 2. To remove the coverings from. 3. To reveal or be revealed gradually.

un·for·get·ta·ble (ŭn′fər-gĕt′ə-bəl) ▸ *adj.* Permanently impressed on one's memory; memorable. **—un′for·get′ta·bly** *adv.*

un·formed (ŭn-fôrmd′) ▸ *adj.* 1. Having no definite shape or structure. 2. Immature; undeveloped.

un·for·tu·nate (ŭn-fôr′chə-nĭt) ▸ *adj.* 1. Unlucky. 2. Causing misfortune; disastrous. 3. Regrettable; deplorable. ▸ *n.* A victim of bad luck. **—un·for′tu·nate·ly** *adv.*

un·found·ed (ŭn-foun′dĭd) ▸ *adj.* Not based on fact or sound evidence; groundless.

un·fre·quent·ed (ŭn-frē′kwən-tĭd, ŭn′frē-kwĕn′tĭd) ▸ *adj.* Receiving few or no visitors.

un·friend·ly (ŭn-frĕnd′lē) ▸ *adj.* 1. Not disposed to friendship. 2. Unfavorable. **—un·friend′li·ness** *n.*

un·frock (ŭn-frŏk′) ▸ *v.* To defrock.

un·furl (ŭn-fûrl′) ▸ *v.* To spread or open (something) out.

un·gain·ly (ŭn-gān′lē) ▸ *adj.* **-li·er, -li·est.** 1. Awkward; clumsy. 2. Unwieldy. **—un·gain′li·ness** *n.*

Un·ga·va Bay (ŭn-gā′və, -gä′-) ▸ An inlet of Hudson Strait in NE Quebec, Canada, between N Labrador and **Ungava Peninsula** between Hudson and Ungava bays.

un·god·ly (ŭn-gŏd′lē) ▸ *adj.* 1. Not revering God; impious. 2. Sinful; wicked. 3. Outrageous: *an ungodly hour.* **—un·god′li·ness** *n.*

un·gov·ern·a·ble (ŭn-gŭv′ər-nə-bəl) ▸ *adj.* Incapable of being governed or controlled.

un·gra·cious (ŭn-grā′shəs) ▸ *adj.* 1. Lacking courtesy; rude. 2. Disagreeable. **—un·gra′cious·ly** *adv.* **—un·gra′cious·ness** *n.*

un·guard·ed (ŭn-gär′dĭd) ▸ *adj.* 1. Lacking protection; vulnerable. 2. Incautious; imprudent.

un·guent (ŭng′gwənt) ▸ *n.* A salve; ointment.

un·gu·late (ŭng′gyə-lĭt, -lāt′) ▸ *adj.* Hoofed. **—un′gu·late** *n.*

un·hal·lowed (ŭn-hăl′ōd) ▸ *adj.* 1. Not hallowed or consecrated. 2. Irreverent; impious.

THESAURUS

unexpected *adj.* —*See* ACCIDENTAL.

unexpectedly *adv.* —*See* UNUSUALLY.

unexplainable *adj.* That cannot be explained ▸ inexplicable, unaccountable. [*Compare* MYSTERIOUS.]

unexposed *adj.* Not found ▸ undetected, undiscovered, unfound.

unexpressed *adj.* —*See* IMPLICIT (1), SILENT (2).

unexpurgated *adj.* —*See* COMPLETE (2).

unfailing *adj.* —*See* CONTINUAL, SURE (2), TIRELESS, UNCHANGING.

unfair *adj.* Not fair, right, or just ▸ dirty, discriminatory, inequitable, preferential, unequal, uneven, unjust, wrong. [*Compare* BIASED, UNSCRUPULOUS.]

unfairness *n.* Lack of equality, as of opportunity, treatment, or status ▸ discrimination, inequality, unjustness. [*Compare* BIAS.] —*See also* INJUSTICE (2).

unfaithful *adj.* —*See* FAITHLESS.

unfaithfulness *n.* —*See* FAITHLESSNESS.

unfaltering *adj.* —*See* IMPLICIT (2).

unfamiliar *adj.* —*See* IGNORANT (3), NEW.

unfamiliarity *n.* —*See* IGNORANCE (2).

unfasten *v.* —*See* OPEN (1), UNDO.

unfastened *adj.* —*See* LOOSE (1).

unfathomable *adj.* —*See* INCALCULABLE, INCOMPREHENSIBLE.

unfavorable *adj.* 1. Tending to discourage, retard, or make more difficult ▸ adverse, antagonistic, disadvantageous, negative, unadvantageous, unsatisfactory, untoward. [*Compare* INHOSPITABLE.] 2. Not encouraging life or growth ▸ adverse, hostile, inhospitable. [*Compare* SEVERE.] —*See also* FATEFUL (1), OPPOSING.

unfeeling *adj.* —*See* CALLOUS, DEAD (2).

unfeigned *adj.* —*See* GENUINE.

unfettered *adj.* —*See* LOOSE (2).

unfinished *adj.* —*See* PARTIAL (1), ROUGH (4).

unfit *adj.* —*See* IMPROPER (2), INEFFICIENT.

unfit *v.* To make incapable, as of doing a job ▸ disable, disqualify.

unfitness *n.* —*See* IMPROPRIETY (1).

unflagging *adj.* —*See* DILIGENT, TIRELESS.

unflappability *n.* —*See* BALANCE (2).

unflappable *adj.* —*See* CALM.

unflawed *adj.* —*See* PERFECT.

unflinching *adj.* —*See* BRAVE, FIRM[1] (3).

unfold *v.* —*See* DEVELOP (2), SPREAD (1).

unfolding *n.* —*See* DEVELOPMENT.

unforbearing *adj.* Being unable or unwilling to endure irritation or opposition, for example ▸ impatient, intolerant, unindulgent. [*Compare* ILL-TEMPERED, INTOLERANT.] —*See also* VINDICTIVE.

unforced *adj.* —*See* VOLUNTARY.

unforgivable *adj.* —*See* INEXCUSABLE.

unforgiving *adj.* —*See* VINDICTIVE.

unformed *adj.* —*See* SHAPELESS.

unfortunate *adj.* 1. Involving or undergoing chance misfortune ▸ hapless, hexed, ill-fated, ill-starred, jinxed, luckless, star-crossed, stricken, unhappy, unlucky, untoward. 2. Characterized by inappropriateness and gracelessness, especially in expression ▸ awkward, ill-chosen, inappropriate, inept, infelicitous, unhappy. [*Compare* IMPROPER, INCONVENIENT, UNWISE.] —*See also* DEPLORABLE.

unfortunate *n.* A person living under very unhappy circumstances ▸ loser, miserable, underdog, underprivileged, wretch.

unfortunateness *n.* —*See* MISFORTUNE.

unfound *adj.* Not found ▸ undetected, undiscovered, unexposed.

unfounded *adj.* —*See* BASELESS.

unfoundedly *adv.* Without basis or foundation in fact ▸ baselessly, groundlessly, unwarrantedly.

unfrequented *adj.* —*See* LONELY (1).

unfriendliness *n.* —*See* INHOSPITALITY.

unfriendly *adj.* Feeling or showing unfriendliness ▸ hostile, inimical. [*Compare* MEAN[2].]

unfruitful *adj.* —*See* BARREN (1), BARREN (2).

unfurl *v.* —*See* DEVELOP (2), SPREAD (1).

ungainly *adj.* —*See* AWKWARD (1), AWKWARD (2).

ungodly *adj.* —*See* ATHEISTIC, OUTRAGEOUS.

ungovernable *adj.* —*See* UNRULY.

ungovernableness *n.* —*See* UNRULINESS.

ungoverned *adj.* —*See* ABANDONED (2).

ungraceful *adj.* —*See* AWKWARD (1).

ungracious *adj.* —*See* RUDE (2).

ungraciousness *n.* —*See* INHOSPITALITY.

ungrateful *adj.* Not apt to be appreciated ▸ thankless, unappreciated, unthankful. —*See also* THANKLESS (1).

ungrudging *adj.* —*See* GENEROUS (1).

unguarded *adj.* —*See* INSECURE (1).

unguent *n.* —*See* OINTMENT.

un·hand (ŭn-hănd′) ► *v.* To remove one's hand from; let go.

un·hap·py (ŭn-hăp′ē) ► *adj.* **1.** Not happy; sad. **2.** Not satisfied; discontented. **3.** Unlucky. **4.** Not suitable; inappropriate: *an unhappy choice of words.* **—un·hap′pi·ly** *adv.* **—un·hap′pi·ness** *n.*

un·health·y (ŭn-hĕl′thē) ► *adj.* **1a.** In ill health; sick. **b.** Symptomatic of ill health. **c.** Conducive to poor health; unwholesome. **2.** Harmful to character; corruptive. **—un′health′i·ly** *adv.* **—un·health′i·ness** *n.*

un·heard (ŭn-hûrd′) ► *adj.* **1.** Not heard. **2.** Not given a hearing.

un·heard-of (ŭn-hûrd′ŭv′, -ŏv′) ► *adj.* **1.** Not previously known. **2.** Without precedent.

un·hinge (ŭn-hĭnj′) ► *v.* **1.** To remove from hinges. **2.** To derange; unbalance.

un·ho·ly (ŭn-hō′lē) ► *adj.* **1.** Wicked; immoral. **2.** Not hallowed or consecrated. **3.** *Informal* Outrageous. **—un·ho′li·ness** *n.*

un·hook (ŭn-ho͝ok′) ► *v.* **1.** To remove from a hook. **2.** To unfasten the hooks of.

un·horse (ŭn-hôrs′) ► *v.* **1.** To cause to fall from a horse. **2.** To overthrow or dislodge.

uni– ► *pref.* One: *unicycle.*

u·ni·cam·er·al (yo͞o′nĭ-kăm′ər-əl) ► *adj.* Consisting of a single legislative chamber.

u·ni·cel·lu·lar (yo͞o′nĭ-sĕl′yə-lər) ► *adj.* Consisting of one cell: *unicellular organisms.*

u·ni·corn (yo͞o′nĭ-kôrn′) ► *n.* A fabled creature usu. represented as a horse with a single spiraled horn on its forehead.

u·ni·cy·cle (yo͞o′nĭ-sī′kəl) ► *n.* A single-wheeled vehicle usu. propelled by pedals.

un·i·den·ti·fied flying object (ŭn′ī-dĕn′tə-fīd′) ► *n.* A flying or apparently flying object of an unknown nature, esp. one presumed to be of extraterrestrial origin.

u·ni·form (yo͞o′nə-fôrm′) ► *adj.* **1.** Always the same; unvarying. **2.** Being the same as or consonant with another or others. ► *n.* A distinctive outfit intended to identify those who wear it as members of a specific group. **—u′ni·for′mi·ty, u′ni·form′ness** *n.* **—u′ni·form′ly** *adv.*

u·ni·fy (yo͞o′nə-fī′) ► *v.* **-fied, -fy·ing.** To make into or become a unit; consolidate. **—u′ni·fi·ca′tion** *n.*

u·ni·lat·er·al (yo͞o′nə-lăt′ər-əl) ► *adj.* Of, on, involving, or affecting only one side. **—u′ni·lat′er·al·ly** *adv.*

un·im·peach·a·ble (ŭn′ĭm-pē′chə-bəl) ► *adj.* Beyond doubt, question, or reproach. **—un′im·peach′a·bly** *adv.*

un·in·ter·est·ed (ŭn-ĭn′trĭ-stĭd, -tə-rĕs′tĭd) ► *adj.* **1.** Without an interest, esp. not having a financial interest. **2.** Not interested; indifferent. **—un·in′ter·est·ed·ly** *adv.*

un·ion (yo͞on′yən) ► *n.* **1a.** The act of uniting or the state of being united. **b.** A combination so formed, esp. a confederation of people, parties, or political entities for common interest. **2a.** The state of matrimony; marriage. **b.** Sexual intercourse. **3.** A labor union. **4.** A coupling device for connecting parts, such as pipes or rods. **5.** A design on a flag that signifies the union of two or more sovereignties. **6. Union** The United States of America, esp. during the Civil War.

un·ion·ism (yo͞on′yə-nĭz′əm) ► *n.* **1.** The principle or theory of forming a union. **2.** The principles, theory, or system of a union, esp. a labor union. **3. Unionism** Loyalty to the federal government during the Civil War. **—un′ion·ist** *n.*

un·ion·ize (yo͞on′yə-nīz′) ► *v.* **-ized, -iz·ing.** To organize into or cause to join a labor union. **—un′ion·i·za′tion** *n.* **—un′ion·iz′er** *n.*

union jack ► *n.* **1.** A flag consisting entirely of a union. **2. Union Jack** The flag of the United Kingdom.

Union of Soviet Socialist Republics. Commonly called **Soviet Union** ► A former country of E Europe and N Asia with coastlines on the Baltic and Black seas and the Arctic and Pacific oceans.

union shop ► *n.* A business or industrial establishment whose employees are required to be or become union members; closed shop.

u·nique (yo͞o-nēk′) ► *adj.* **1.** Being the only one of its kind.

THESAURUS

unhandy *adj.* Not accessible or handy ► inaccessible, unhandy. ***Idioms:*** beyond reach, out of reach, out of the way. [*Compare* REMOTE.] *—See also* AWKWARD (2).

unhappiness *n.* *—See* DEPRESSION (2).

unhappy *adj.* *—See* DEPRESSED (1), UNFORTUNATE (1), UNFORTUNATE (2).

unharmed *adj.* *—See* GOOD (2), SAFE (1).

unharmonious *adj.* *—See* INHARMONIOUS (1), INHARMONIOUS (2).

unhealthful *adj.* *—See* UNWHOLESOME (1).

unhealthy *adj.* *—See* CORRUPT (1), HARMFUL, MORBID, SICK (1), UNWHOLESOME (1), UNWHOLESOME (2).

unheard-of *adj.* *—See* OBSCURE (2).

unheeding *adj.* *—See* CARELESS.

unhesitating *adj.* *—See* IMPLICIT (2), INTENT.

unhindered *adj.* *—See* CLEAR (3), LOOSE (2).

unhinge *v.* *—See* DERANGE.

unhinged *adj.* *—See* INSANE.

unhorse *v.* *—See* OVERTHROW.

unhospitable *adj.* *—See* FORBIDDING.

unhurried *adj.* *—See* DELIBERATE (3).

unhurt *adj.* *—See* GOOD (2), SAFE (1).

unhygienic *adj.* *—See* UNWHOLESOME (1).

unidentified *adj.* *—See* ANONYMOUS.

unification *n.* A bringing together into a whole ► coalition, consolidation, union, unity. *—See also* COMBINATION.

unified *adj.* *—See* UNANIMOUS.

uniform *adj.* *—See* LIKE[2], UNCHANGING.

uniformity *n.* *—See* CHANGELESSNESS, CONSISTENCY, LIKENESS (1).

uniformness *n.* *—See* LIKENESS (1).

unify *v.* *—See* COMBINE (1), HARMONIZE (2).

unimaginable *adj.* *—See* IMPOSSIBLE, INCREDIBLE.

unimaginative *adj.* *—See* DULL (1), STERILE (2), TRITE.

unimpaired *adj.* *—See* GOOD (2).

unimpeachable *adj.* *—See* DEFINITE (3).

unimpeded *adj.* *—See* CLEAR (3).

unimportance *n.* *—See* OBSCURITY, TRIFLE.

unimportant *adj.* *—See* TRIVIAL.

unimpressionable *adj.* *—See* COLD (2).

unindulgent *adj.* Being unable or unwilling to endure irritation or opposition, for example ► impatient, intolerant, unforbearing. [*Compare* ILL-TEMPERED, INTOLERANT.]

uninformed *adj.* *—See* IGNORANT (2), IGNORANT (3).

uninhabited *adj.* *—See* LONELY (1), OPEN (4).

uninhibited *adj.* *—See* ABANDONED (2).

uninitiate *adj.* *—See* INEXPERIENCED.

uninitiate *n.* *—See* AMATEUR.

uninitiated *adj.* *—See* INEXPERIENCED.

uninjured *adj.* *—See* GOOD (2), SAFE (1).

uninspired *adj.* *—See* DULL (1), STERILE (2), TRITE.

uninstructed *adj.* *—See* IGNORANT (1).

unintelligent *adj.* *—See* STUPID.

unintelligible *adj.* *—See* INCOMPREHENSIBLE.

unintended *adj.* *—See* ACCIDENTAL, UNINTENTIONAL.

unintentional *adj.* Not intended ► accidental, inadvertent, involuntary, undesigned, undevised, unintended, unmeant, unplanned, unthinking, unwitting.

uninterest *n.* *—See* APATHY.

uninterested *adj.* *—See* APATHETIC, DETACHED (1).

uninteresting *adj.* *—See* BORING.

uninterrupted *adj.* *—See* CONTINUAL.

uninventive *adj.* *—See* STERILE (2).

uninvited *adj.* *—See* UNWELCOME.

uninviting *adj.* *—See* FORBIDDING.

uninvolved *adj.* *—See* DETACHED (1), NEUTRAL (1).

uninvolvment *n.* *—See* DETACHMENT (2).

union *n.* **1.** A group of people who are united in a relationship and having some interest, activity, or purpose in common ► association, club, confederation, congress, federation, fellowship, fraternity, guild, league, order, organization, society, sorority. [*Compare* GROUP.] **2.** An identity or coincidence of interests, purposes, or sympathies among the members of a group ► concord, oneness, solidarity, unity. *—See also* ALLIANCE, COMBINATION, JOINT (1), MARRIAGE, UNIFICATION.

uniplanar *adj.* *—See* EVEN (2).

unique *adj.* Without equal or rival ► alone, incomparable, matchless, nonpareil, only, peerless, singular, unequaled, unexampled, unexcelled, unmatched, unparalleled, unrivaled, unsurpassed. ***Idioms:*** beyond compare, in a class by itself, second to

2. Without an equal or equivalent; unparalleled. **—u·nique′ly** *adv.* **—u·nique′ness** *n.*

u·ni·sex (yo͞o′nĭ-sĕks′) ▸ *adj.* Designed for or suitable to both sexes.

u·ni·sex·u·al (yo͞o′nĭ-sĕk′sho͞o-əl) ▸ *adj.* **1.** Of or for only one sex. **2.** *Bot.* Having either stamens or pistils but not both.

u·ni·son (yo͞o′nĭ-sən, -zən) ▸ *n.* **1a.** Identity of musical pitch. **b.** The combination of parts at the same pitch or in octaves. **2.** A speaking of the same words simultaneously by two or more speakers. **3.** Agreement; concord. ***—idiom:* in unison** **1.** In complete agreement. **2.** At the same time.

u·nit (yo͞o′nĭt) ▸ *n.* **1.** One regarded as a constituent part of a whole. **2a.** A mechanical part or module. **b.** An entire apparatus that performs a specific function. **3.** A precisely specified quantity in terms of which the magnitudes of other quantities of the same kind can be stated.

U·ni·tar·i·an (yo͞o′nĭ-târ′ē-ən) ▸ *n.* A member of a Christian denomination that rejects the doctrine of the Trinity and emphasizes tolerance in religious belief. **—U′ni·tar′i·an** *adj.* **—U′ni·tar′i·an·ism** *n.*

u·ni·tar·y (yo͞o′nĭ-tĕr′ē) ▸ *adj.* **1.** Of or relating to a unit. **2.** Whole. **—u′ni·tar′i·ly** *adv.*

u·nite (yo͞o-nīt′) ▸ *v.* **u·nit·ed, u·nit·ing. 1.** To bring together so as to form a whole. **2.** To combine (people) in interest, attitude, or action. **3.** To become joined, formed, or combined into a unit.

U·nit·ed Arab Emirates (yo͞o-nī′tĭd) ▸ A country of E Arabia, a federation of seven sheikdoms on the Persian Gulf and the Gulf of Oman.

United Kingdom or **United Kingdom of Great Britain and Northern Ireland.** Commonly called **Great Britain** ▸ A country of W Europe comprising England, Scotland, Wales, and Northern Ireland.

United Nations ▸ An international organization founded in 1945 to promote peace, security, and development.

United States or **United States of America** ▸ A country of central and NW North America with coastlines on the Atlantic and Pacific. Cap. Washington DC.

unit pricing ▸ *n.* The pricing of goods on the basis of cost per unit of measure.

u·ni·ty (yo͞o′nĭ-tē) ▸ *n., pl.* **-ties. 1.** The state or quality of being one; singleness. **2.** The condition of being in accord; harmony. **3.** The combination or arrangement of parts into a whole; unification. **4.** Singleness of purpose or action; continuity. **5.** An ordering of all elements in a work of art or literature so that each contributes to a unified aesthetic effect. **6.** *Math.* The number 1.

univ. ▸ *abbr.* **1.** universal **2.** university

u·ni·va·lent (yo͞o′nĭ-vā′lənt) ▸ *adj. Chem.* **1.** Having valence 1. **2.** Having only one valence.

u·ni·valve (yo͞o′nĭ-vălv′) ▸ *n.* A mollusk having a shell consisting of a single valve or piece. **—u′ni·valve′** *adj.*

u·ni·ver·sal (yo͞o′nə-vûr′səl) ▸ *adj.* **1.** Extending to or affecting the entire world; worldwide. **2.** Of, including, or affecting all members of a class or group. **3.** Applicable or common to all purposes, conditions, or situations. **4.** Relating to the universe or cosmos. **5.** Knowledgeable about or constituting all or many subjects. **6.** Adapted or adjustable to many sizes or mechanical uses. **—u′ni·ver′sal·ly** *adv.* **—u′ni·ver·sal′i·ty** *n.*

universal donor ▸ *n.* A person with group O blood, which is compatible with all other groups in the ABO system.

U·ni·ver·sal·ism (yo͞o′nə-vûr′sə-lĭz′əm) ▸ *n.* The theological doctrine that everyone will be saved. **—U′ni·ver′sal·ist** *n. & adj.*

universal joint ▸ *n.* A joint or coupling that allows parts of a machine not in line with each other limited freedom of movement in any direction while transmitting rotary motion.

Universal Product Code ▸ *n.* A number and bar code that allow a scanner to identify a particular consumer product.

universal time ▸ *n.* The mean solar time for the meridian at Greenwich, England, used as a basis for calculating time throughout most of the world.

u·ni·verse (yo͞o′nə-vûrs′) ▸ *n.* **1.** All existing things regarded as a whole. **2a.** The earth. **b.** The human race.

u·ni·ver·si·ty (yo͞o′nə-vûr′sĭ-tē) ▸ *n., pl.* **-ties.** An institution for higher learning with teaching and research facilities constituting a graduate school, professional schools, and an undergraduate division.

un·kempt (ŭn-kĕmpt′) ▸ *adj.* **1a.** Not combed. **b.** Disorderly or untidy. **2.** Unpolished; rude.

un·lead·ed (ŭn-lĕd′ĭd) ▸ *adj.* Not containing lead: *unleaded gasoline.*

un·learn (ŭn-lûrn′) ▸ *v.* To put (something learned) out of the mind; forget.

un·learn·ed (ŭn-lûr′nĭd) ▸ *adj.* **1.** Not educated. **2.** (-lûrnd′) Not acquired by training or studying. **—un·learn′ed·ly** *adv.*

un·leash (ŭn-lēsh′) ▸ *v.* To release or loose from or as if from a leash.

un·less (ŭn-lĕs′) ▸ *conj.* Except on the condition that.

un·let·tered (ŭn-lĕt′ərd) ▸ *adj.* Not educated, esp. unable to read and write.

un·like (ŭn-līk′) ▸ *adj.* **1.** Not alike; different; dissimilar. **2.** Not equal. ▸ *prep.* **1.** Different from; not like. **2.** Not typical of: *It's unlike him not to call.* **—un·like′ness** *n.*

un·like·ly (ŭn-līk′lē) ▸ *adj.* **1.** Not likely; improbable. **2.** Likely to fail. **—un·like′li·hood′** *n.* **—un·like′li·ness** *n.*

un·lim·ber (ŭn-lĭm′bər) ▸ *v.* To make ready for action.

un·load (ŭn-lōd′) ▸ *v.* **1a.** To remove the load or cargo from. **b.** To discharge (cargo or a load). **2a.** To relieve (oneself) of something oppressive; unburden. **b.** To pour forth (one's troubles or feelings). **3a.** To remove the charge from (a firearm). **b.** To discharge (a firearm); fire. **4.** To dispose of,

THESAURUS

none. [*Compare* BEST, EXCEPTIONAL.] —*See also* LONE, UNUSUAL.

uniquely *adv.* —*See* UNUSUALLY.

uniqueness *n.* The quality or condition of being unique ▸ matchlessness, oneness, peerlessness, singleness, singularity, uncommonness. [*Compare* INDIVIDUALITY.] —*See also* IDENTITY (1), NOVELTY (1).

unison *n.* —*See* AGREEMENT (2).

unit *n.* —*See* BAND², DEGREE (1), FORCE (3).

unite *v.* To come together from different directions ▸ close, converge, join, meet. —*See also* BAND², COMBINE (1), COOPERATE, MARRY.

united *adj.* —*See* COOPERATIVE.

unity *n.* **1.** The condition of being one ▸ oneness, singleness, singularity. [*Compare* COMPLETENESS.] **2.** An identity or coincidence of interests, purposes, or sympathies among the members of a group ▸ concord, oneness, solidarity, union. [*Compare* ALLIANCE, UNION.] —*See also* AGREEMENT (2), COMBINATION, UNIFICATION.

universal *adj.* **1.** So pervasive and all-inclusive as to exist in or affect the whole world ▸ catholic, cosmic, cosmopolitan, ecumenical, global, pandemic, planetary, worldwide. **2.** Ever present in all places ▸ omnipresent, ubiquitous. [*Compare* RAMPANT.] —*See also* GENERAL (1), UNANIMOUS.

universal *n.* —*See* LAW (3).

universe *n.* The totality of all existing things ▸ cosmos, creation, macrocosm, nature, wide world, world. *Idiom:* sum of all things. [*Compare* ENVIRONMENT.] —*See also* HUMANKIND.

unjudicious *adj.* —*See* IMPROPER (1).

unjust *adj.* —*See* UNFAIR.

unjustifiable *adj.* —*See* INEXCUSABLE.

unjustness *n.* Lack of equality, as of opportunity, treatment, or status ▸ discrimination, inequality, unfairness. [*Compare* BIAS.] —*See also* INJUSTICE (2).

unkempt *adj.* —*See* MESSY (1).

unknowing *adj.* —*See* IGNORANT (3).

unknown *adj.* —*See* ANONYMOUS, OBSCURE (2).

unlade *v.* —*See* RID.

unlawful *adj.* Contrary to accepted, especially moral conventions ▸ criminal, illicit. [*Compare* FORBIDDEN.] —*See also* CRIMINAL (1), ILLEGAL, ILLEGITIMATE.

unlawfulness *n.* The state or quality of being illegal ▸ illegality, illegitimacy, illicitness, lawlessness.

unlearned *adj.* —*See* IGNORANT (1), INSTINCTIVE.

unlike *adj.* —*See* DIFFERENT.

unlikely *adj.* —*See* DOUBTFUL (1), IMPLAUSIBLE.

unlikeness *n.* —*See* DIFFERENCE.

unlimited *adj.* —*See* ENDLESS (1), UTTER².

unlimitedness *n.* —*See* INFINITY (1).

unlit *adj.* —*See* BLACK (2).

unload *v.* —*See* RID, UNLOAD.

esp. by selling in great quantity. **—un·load′er** *n.*

un·lock (ŭn-lŏk′) ▸ *v.* **1a.** To undo (a lock). **b.** To undo the lock of. **2.** To give access to; open. **3.** To provide a key to: *unlock a mystery.*

un·looked-for (ŭn-lo͝okt′fôr′) ▸ *adj.* Not expected; unforeseen: *unlooked-for riches.*

un·loose (ŭn-lo͞os′) ▸ *v.* **1.** To let loose or unfasten; release. **2.** To relax or ease.

un·luck·y (ŭn-lŭk′ē) ▸ *adj.* **1.** Subjected to or marked by misfortune. **2.** Inauspicious. **3.** Disappointing: *an unlucky choice.* **—un·luck′i·ly** *adv.* **—un·luck′i·ness** *n.*

un·make (ŭn-māk′) ▸ *v.* **1.** To deprive of position, rank, or authority. **2.** To ruin; destroy. **3.** To alter the nature of.

un·man·nered (ŭn-măn′ərd) ▸ *adj.* **1.** Lacking good manners; rude. **2.** Natural and unaffected. **—un·man′nered·ly** *adv.*

un·mask (ŭn-măsk′) ▸ *v.* **1.** To remove a mask from. **2.** To disclose the true character of; expose.

un·men·tion·a·ble (ŭn-mĕn′shə-nə-bəl) ▸ *adj.* Not fit to be mentioned.

un·mer·ci·ful (ŭn-mûr′sĭ-fəl) ▸ *adj.* **1.** Having no mercy; merciless. **2.** Excessive: *unmerciful heat.* **—un·mer′ci·ful·ly** *adv.* **—un·mer′ci·ful·ness** *n.*

un·mis·tak·a·ble (ŭn′mĭ-stā′kə-bəl) ▸ *adj.* Obvious; evident. **—un′mis·tak′a·bly** *adv.*

un·mit·i·gat·ed (ŭn-mĭt′ĭ-gā′tĭd) ▸ *adj.* **1.** Not diminished or moderated. **2.** Without qualification or exception; absolute.

un·mor·al (ŭn-môr′əl, -mŏr′-) ▸ *adj.* Amoral.

un·nat·u·ral (ŭn-năch′ər-əl) ▸ *adj.* **1.** In violation of a natural law. **2.** Contrived or constrained; artificial. **3.** In violation of natural feelings or normal or accepted standards. **—un·nat′u·ral·ly** *adv.* **—un·nat′u·ral·ness** *n.*

un·nerve (ŭn-nûrv′) ▸ *v.* **1.** To deprive of strength or firmness of purpose. **2.** To make nervous or upset. **—un·nerv′ing·ly** *adv.*

un·num·bered (ŭn-nŭm′bərd) ▸ *adj.* **1.** Innumerable; countless. **2.** Not marked with an identifying number.

un·or·gan·ized (ŭn-ôr′gə-nīzd′) ▸ *adj.* **1.** Lacking order or unity. **2.** Not unionized.

un·pack (ŭn-păk′) ▸ *v.* **1.** To remove the contents of. **2.** To remove (something) from a container.

un·par·al·leled (ŭn-păr′ə-lĕld′) ▸ *adj.* Without parallel; unequaled.

un·par·lia·men·ta·ry (ŭn′pär-lə-mĕn′tə-rē, -mĕn′trē) ▸ *adj.* Not in accord with parliamentary procedure.

un·peo·ple (ŭn-pē′pəl) ▸ *v.* To depopulate (an area).

un·per·son (ŭn′pûr′sən) ▸ *n.* A nonperson.

un·plug (ŭn-plŭg′) ▸ *v.* **1.** To remove a plug from. **2.** To disconnect (an electric appliance) by removing a plug from an outlet.

un·plugged (ŭn-plŭgd′) ▸ *adj.* Relating to music that is not electronically amplified or modified; acoustic. ▸ *adv.* Acoustically.

un·plumbed (ŭn-plŭmd′) ▸ *adj.* **1.** Not measured or sounded with a plumb. **2.** Not fully examined or explored.

un·prec·e·dent·ed (ŭn-prĕs′ĭ-dĕn′tĭd) ▸ *adj.* Having no previous example.

un·pre·pared (ŭn′prĭ-pârd′) ▸ *adj.* **1.** Not prepared or ready. **2.** Impromptu. **—un′pre·par′ed·ly** *adv.* **—un′pre·par′ed·ness** *n.*

un·pre·ten·tious (ŭn′prĭ-tĕn′shəs) ▸ *adj.* Lacking pretention or affectation; modest. **—un′pre·ten′tious·ly** *adv.* **—un′pre·ten′tious·ness** *n.*

un·print·a·ble (ŭn-prĭn′tə-bəl) ▸ *adj.* Not proper for publication.

un·pro·fes·sion·al (ŭn′prə-fĕsh′ə-nəl) ▸ *adj.* **1.** Not conforming

THESAURUS

unloose or **unloosen** *v.* —*See* UNDO.

unloveliness *n.* —*See* UGLINESS.

unlovely *adj.* —*See* UGLY.

unluckiness *n.* —*See* MISFORTUNE.

unlucky *adj.* —*See* DISAPPOINTING, FATEFUL (1), UNFORTUNATE (1).

unmanageability *n.* —*See* UNRULINESS.

unmanageable *adj.* —*See* AWKWARD (2), UNRULY.

unmanliness *n.* —*See* COWARDICE, EFFEMINACY.

unmanly *adj.* —*See* COWARDLY, EFFEMINATE.

unmannered or **unmannerly** *adj.* —*See* DISRESPECTFUL, RUDE.

unmarked *adj.* —*See* PERFECT.

unmarred *adj.* —*See* GOOD (2).

unmarried *adj.* —*See* SINGLE.

unmask *v.* —*See* REVEAL.

unmatched *adj.* —*See* UNIQUE.

unmeant *adj.* —*See* UNINTENTIONAL.

unmentionable *adj.* —*See* UNSPEAKABLE (2).

unmerciful *adj.* —*See* CALLOUS.

unmindful *adj.* —*See* CARELESS.

unmistakable *adj.* —*See* OBVIOUS, SHARP (2).

unmitigated *adj.* —*See* UTTER^{2}.

unmixed *adj.* —*See* PURE, STRAIGHT.

unmovable *adj.* —*See* FIXED.

unmoved *adj.* —*See* COLD (2).

unmoving *adj.* —*See* FIXED, MOTIONLESS.

unmusical *adj.* —*See* INHARMONIOUS (2).

unnamed *adj.* —*See* ANONYMOUS.

unnatural *adj.* Greatly exceeding or departing from the normal course of nature ▸ preternatural, supernatural. [*Compare* SUPERNATURAL.] —*See also* ABNORMAL, ECCENTRIC.

unnaturalness *n.* —*See* ABNORMALITY.

unnecessary *adj.* Not necessary ▸ dispensable, inessential, needless, nonessential, uncalled-for, unessential, unneeded, unrequired. [*Compare* EXTRA, IRRELEVANT.]

unneeded *adj.* —*See* UNNECESSARY.

unnegotiable *adj.* —*See* UNWORKABLE.

unnerve *v.* —*See* DISCOURAGE, DISMAY, ENERVATE, FRIGHTEN.

unnerving *adj.* —*See* FEARFUL.

unnoticeable *adj.* —*See* HIDDEN (1), IMPERCEPTIBLE (1), INCONSPICUOUS.

unobjectionable *adj.* —*See* ACCEPTABLE (1).

unobservable *adj.* —*See* IMPERCEPTIBLE (1).

unobstructed *adj.* —*See* CLEAR (3).

unobtainable *adj.* —*See* IMPOSSIBLE, INACCESSIBLE (1).

unobtrusive *adj.* —*See* INCONSPICUOUS, MODEST (1).

unoccupied *adj.* Having no job ▸ idle, jobless, unemployed, workless. *Idiom:* out of a job (*or* employment *or* work). —*See also* IDLE (1), OPEN (4).

unoffensive *adj.* —*See* HARMLESS.

unoriginal *adj.* —*See* STERILE (2), TRITE.

unorthodox *adj.* —*See* ECCENTRIC, EXOTIC.

unostentatious *adj.* —*See* MODEST (1).

unostentatiousness *n.* —*See* MODESTY (2).

unpaid *adj.* Contributing one's time without pay ▸ freewill, pro bono, uncompensated, unrecompensed, unremunerated, unsalaried, voluntary, volunteer. —*See also* DUE (1).

unpalatable *adj.* So unpleasant in flavor as to be inedible ▸ disgusting, distasteful, foul-tasting, inedible, nauseating, repulsive, sickening, unappetizing, uneatable, unsavory, untasteful, untasty. *Informal:* icky. *Slang:* gross, yucky. [*Compare* UNPLEASANT.] —*See also* BITTER (3).

unparalleled *adj.* —*See* UNIQUE.

unpardonable *adj.* —*See* INEXCUSABLE.

unpeopled *adj.* —*See* LONELY (1).

unperceptive *adj.* —*See* BLIND (3).

unperfected *adj.* —*See* ROUGH (4).

unpitying *adj.* —*See* CALLOUS.

unplanned *adj.* —*See* ACCIDENTAL, RANDOM, SPONTANEOUS, UNINTENTIONAL.

unpleasant *adj.* Not pleasant or agreeable ▸ bad, disagreeable, displeasing, offensive, uncongenial, unsympathetic. *Informal:* icky. *Slang:* yucky. [*Compare* OFFENSIVE.] —*See also* BITTER (3).

unplugged *adj.* —*See* CLEAR (3).

unpolished *adj.* —*See* COARSE (1), ROUGH (4), RUDE (1), RUDE (2), RUSTIC, UNSKILLFUL.

unpolitic *adj.* —*See* TACTLESS.

unpolluted *adj.* —*See* FRESH (1).

unpopulated *adj.* —*See* LONELY (1).

unpracticed *adj.* —*See* INEXPERIENCED, UNTRIED.

unprecedented *adj.* —*See* EXCEPTIONAL, NEW.

unpredictable *adj.* —*See* CAPRICIOUS, RANDOM.

unprejudiced *adj.* —*See* FAIR^{1} (1), NEUTRAL (1).

unpremeditated *adj.* —*See* SPONTANEOUS.

unpretentious *adj.* —*See* MODEST (1).

unpretentiousness *n.* —*See* MODESTY (1), MODESTY (2).

unprincipled *adj.* —*See* UNSCRUPULOUS.

unprocessed *adj.* —*See* CRUDE, NATURAL (1).

unproductive *adj.* —*See* BARREN (2).

unprofessional *adj.* —*See* AMATEURISH.

to the standards of a profession. **2.** Characteristic of an amateur; inexpert. **—un′pro·fes′sion·al·ly** *adv.*

un·prof·it·a·ble (ŭn-prŏf′ĭ-tə-bəl) ▸ *adj.* **1.** Bringing in no profit. **2.** Serving no useful purpose. **—un·prof′it·a·bly** *adv.*

un·qual·i·fied (ŭn-kwŏl′ə-fīd′) ▸ *adj.* **1.** Lacking the proper or required qualifications: *unqualified for the job.* **2.** Not modified by conditions or reservations.

un·quote (ŭn-kwōt′) ▸ *n.* Used by a speaker to indicate the end of a quotation.

un·rav·el (ŭn-răv′əl) ▸ *v.* **1.** To separate (entangled threads). **2.** To separate and clarify the elements of (something baffling); solve.

un·read (ŭn-rĕd′) ▸ *adj.* **1.** Not read or studied. **2.** Having read little; unlearned.

un·read·a·ble (ŭn-rē′də-bəl) ▸ *adj.* **1.** Illegible. **2.** Not interesting; dull. **3.** Incomprehensible.

un·re·al (ŭn-rē′əl, -rēl′) ▸ *adj.* **1.** Not real or substantial. **2.** *Slang* Too good to be true; fantastic. **—un′re·al′i·ty** *n.*

un·rea·son·a·ble (ŭn-rē′zə-nə-bəl) ▸ *adj.* **1.** Not governed by reason. **2.** Exceeding reasonable limits. **—un·rea′son·a·ble·ness** *n.* **—un·rea′son·a·bly** *adv.*

un·re·gen·er·ate (ŭn′rĭ-jĕn′ər-ĭt) ▸ *adj.* **1.** Not spiritually renewed or reformed; not repentant. **2.** Stubborn.

un·re·lent·ing (ŭn′rĭ-lĕn′tĭng) ▸ *adj.* **1.** Relentless; inexorable. **2.** Not diminishing in intensity, pace, or effort.

un·re·mit·ting (ŭn′rĭ-mĭt′ĭng) ▸ *adj.* Never slackening; persistent.

un·re·served (ŭn′rĭ-zûrvd′) ▸ *adj.* **1.** Not held back for a particular person. **2.** Given without reservation; unqualified. **—un′re·serv′ed·ly** (-zûr′vĭd-lē) *adv.*

un·rest (ŭn-rĕst′, ŭn′rĕst′) ▸ *n.* Uneasiness; disquiet: *social unrest.*

un·ri·valed or **un·ri·valled** (ŭn-rī′vəld) ▸ *adj.* Unequaled; incomparable.

un·roll (ŭn-rōl′) ▸ *v.* **1.** To unwind and open (something rolled up). **2.** To unfold; reveal.

un·ruf·fled (ŭn-rŭf′əld) ▸ *adj.* Not agitated; calm.

un·ru·ly (ŭn-ro͞o′lē) ▸ *adj.* Difficult or impossible to discipline, control, or rule. **—un·ru′li·ness** *n.*

un·sad·dle (ŭn-săd′l) ▸ *v.* **1.** To remove a saddle from. **2.** To unhorse.

un·sat·u·rat·ed (ŭn-săch′ə-rā′tĭd) ▸ *adj.* **1.** Not saturated. **2.** Of or being a fat, usu. of plant origin, composed predominantly of fatty acids having one or more double bonds in the carbon chain.

un·sa·vor·y (ŭn-sā′və-rē) ▸ *adj.* **1.** Distasteful or disagreeable. **2.** Not savory: *an unsavory meal.* **3.** Morally offensive.

un·scathed (ŭn-skāthd′) ▸ *adj.* Not injured or harmed: *escaped the hurricane unscathed.*

un·schooled (ŭn-sko͝old′) ▸ *adj.* **1.** Not educated or instructed. **2.** Not the result of training; natural: *unschooled talents.*

un·scram·ble (ŭn-skrăm′bəl) ▸ *v.* **1.** To disentangle; resolve. **2.** To restore (a scrambled message) to intelligible form.

un·screw (ŭn-skro͞o′) ▸ *v.* **1.** To take out the screw or screws from. **2.** To loosen, adjust, or remove by rotating.

un·scru·pu·lous (ŭn-skro͞o′pyə-ləs) ▸ *adj.* Devoid of scruples; not honorable. **—un·scru′pu·lous·ly** *adv.* **—un·scru′pu·lous·ness** *n.*

un·sea·son·a·ble (ŭn-sē′zə-nə-bəl) ▸ *adj.* **1.** Not character-

THESAURUS

unprofitable *adj.* —*See* FUTILE.

unprofitableness *n.* —*See* FUTILITY.

unprogressive *adj.* Clinging to obsolete ideas ▸ backward, reactionary. [*Compare* CONSERVATIVE.]

unpromising *adj.* —*See* BLEAK (2).

unpropitious *adj.* —*See* BLEAK (2), FATEFUL (1).

unprotected *adj.* —*See* INSECURE (1), OPEN (2), VULNERABLE.

unprotectedness *n.* —*See* EXPOSURE.

unproved *adj.* —*See* BASELESS, UNTRIED.

unqualified *adj.* —*See* INEFFICIENT, UNCONDITIONAL, UTTER[2].

unquestionable *adj.* —*See* AUTHENTIC (1), CERTAIN (2), DECIDED.

unquestionably *adv.* —*See* ABSOLUTELY, YES.

unquestioned *adj.* —*See* CERTAIN (2).

unquestioning *adj.* —*See* IMPLICIT (2).

unquiet *adj.* Affording no quiet, repose, or rest ▸ restless, uneasy, unsettled. [*Compare* EDGY, WAKEFUL.]

unravel *v.* —*See* DEVELOP (2), SOLVE (1), UNWIND.

unreachable *adj.* —*See* INACCESSIBLE (1).

unread *adj.* —*See* IGNORANT (1).

unreal *adj.* —*See* ILLUSIVE, IMAGINARY.

unrealistic *adj.* —*See* IDEALISTIC.

unrealizable *adj.* —*See* IMPOSSIBLE.

unreasonable *adj.* Not governed by or predicated on reason ▸ illogical, irrational, unreasoned. ***Idioms:*** out of bounds, without rhyme or reason. [*Compare* FALLACIOUS, FOOLISH.] —*See also* OUTRAGEOUS.

unreasonableness or **unreason** *n.* The absence of reason ▸ illogicality, illogicalness, irrationality. [*Compare* FALLACY, FOOLISHNESS.]

unreasoned *adj.* Not governed by or predicated on reason ▸ illogical, irrational, unreasonable. ***Idioms:*** out of bounds, without rhyme or reason. [*Compare* FALLACIOUS, FOOLISH.]

unreceptiveness *n.* —*See* INHOSPITALITY.

unrecompensed *adj.* —*See* UNPAID.

unreel *v.* —*See* UNWIND.

unrefined *adj.* —*See* COARSE (1), CRUDE.

unrehearsed *adj.* —*See* EXTEMPORANEOUS, SPONTANEOUS.

unrelated *adj.* —*See* IRRELEVANT.

unrelenting *adj.* —*See* STUBBORN (1).

unreliable *adj.* So weak or defective as to be liable to fail ▸ trick, undependable. [*Compare* DEFECTIVE, WEAK.] —*See also* UNDEPENDABLE (1).

unrelieved *adj.* —*See* UTTER[2].

unremarkable *adj.* —*See* ORDINARY.

unremitting *adj.* —*See* CONTINUAL, DILIGENT.

unremunerated *adj.* —*See* UNPAID.

unrepentant *adj.* Devoid of remorse ▸ impenitent, remorseless.

unrequired *adj.* —*See* UNNECESSARY.

unreserved *adj.* —*See* FRANK, IMPLICIT (2), OPEN (4), OUTGOING, UNCONDITIONAL, UTTER[2].

unresolved *adj.* —*See* INDEFINITE (2).

unresponsive *adj.* —*See* APATHETIC, COLD (2), DEAD (2), FRIGID.

unresponsiveness *n.* —*See* APATHY.

unrest *n.* —*See* AGITATION (1), DISORDER (2), RESTLESSNESS.

unrestrained *adj.* —*See* ABANDONED (2), EASYGOING, EXCESSIVE, LOOSE (2).

unrestraint *n.* —*See* ABANDON (1), EASE (1).

unrestricted *adj.* —*See* OPEN (3).

unrevealed *adj.* —*See* ULTERIOR (1).

unrivaled or **unrivalled** *adj.* —*See* UNIQUE.

unroll *v.* —*See* SPREAD (1), UNWIND.

unromantic *adj.* —*See* REALISTIC (1).

unruffled *adj.* —*See* CALM, EVEN (1).

unruliness *n.* The quality or condition of being unruly ▸ disorderliness, fractiousness, indocility, intractability, intractableness, lawlessness, obstinacy, obstinateness, obstreperousness, recalcitrance, recalcitrancy, refractoriness, uncontrollability, uncontrollableness, ungovernableness, unmanageability, untowardness, wildness. [*Compare* DEFIANCE, MISCHIEF.]

unruly *adj.* Not submitting to discipline or control ▸ bad, disorderly, fractious, froward, headstrong, ill-behaved, indocile, insubordinate, intractable, lawless, naughty, noncompliant, obstinate, obstreperous, recalcitrant, refractory, uncontrollable, undisciplined, ungovernable, unmanageable, untoward, wayward, wild. ***Idioms:*** out of control, out of line. [*Compare* MISCHIEVOUS, REBELLIOUS.]

unsafe *adj.* —*See* DANGEROUS, INSECURE (1).

unsaid *adj.* —*See* IMPLICIT (1), SILENT (2).

unsalaried *adj.* —*See* UNPAID.

unsalutary *adj.* —*See* UNWHOLESOME (1).

unsatisfactory *adj.* —*See* BAD (1), DISAPPOINTING, UNFAVORABLE (1).

unsatisfied *adj.* —*See* DUE (1).

unsatisfying *adj.* —*See* DISAPPOINTING.

unsavory *adj.* —*See* FLAT (2), UNPALATABLE.

unsay *adj.* —*See* RETRACT (1).

unscathed *adj.* —*See* SAFE (1).

unscholarly or **unschooled** *adj.* —*See* IGNORANT (1).

unscientific *adj.* —*See* ARBITRARY.

unscrupulous *adj.* Lacking scruples or principles ▸ amoral, conscienceless, debased, degraded, ruthless, shameless, unconscionable, unethical, unprincipled. [*Compare* DISHONEST, EVIL, SORDID.] —*See also* UNDERHAND.

unseasonable *adj.* Not suitable for

istic of the time of year: *unseasonable weather.* **2.** Poorly timed; inopportune. **—un·sea′son·a·bly** *adv.*

un·seat (ŭn-sēt′) ▸ *v.* **1.** To remove from a seat, esp. from a saddle. **2.** To dislodge from a position or office.

un·seem·ly (ŭn-sēm′lē) ▸ *adj.* **1.** Not in good taste; grossly improper. **2.** Inappropriate.

un·set·tle (ŭn-sĕt′l) ▸ *v.* To make unstable; disturb.

un·set·tled (ŭn-sĕt′ld) ▸ *adj.* **1.** Disordered; disturbed. **2.** Likely to change or vary; variable: *unsettled weather.* **3.** Not determined or resolved. **4.** Not paid or adjusted. **5.** Not populated; uninhabited. **6.** Not fixed or established: *an unsettled lifestyle.*

un·sight·ly (ŭn-sīt′lē) ▸ *adj.* Unpleasant or offensive to look at; unattractive. **—un′sight′li·ness** *n.*

un·skilled (ŭn-skĭld′) ▸ *adj.* **1.** Lacking skill or training. **2.** Requiring no training or skill. **3.** Exhibiting a lack of skill; inexpert.

un·so·cia·ble (ŭn-sō′shə-bəl) ▸ *adj.* Not disposed to seek the company of others. **—un·so′cia·bil′i·ty** *n.* **—un·so′cia·bly** *adv.*

un·sound (ŭn-sound′) ▸ *adj.* **1.** Not dependably strong or solid. **2.** Not physically or mentally healthy. **3.** Not logically valid; fallacious. **—un·sound′ly** *adv.* **—un·sound′ness** *n.*

un·spar·ing (ŭn-spâr′ĭng) ▸ *adj.* **1.** Unmerciful; severe. **2.** Not frugal; generous. **—un·spar′ing·ly** *adv.* **—un·spar′ing·ness** *n.*

un·speak·a·ble (ŭn-spē′kə-bəl) ▸ *adj.* **1.** Beyond description; inexpressible. **2.** Inexpressibly bad or objectionable. **—un·speak′a·bly** *adv.*

un·sta·ble (ŭn-stā′bəl) ▸ *adj.* **1.** Tending strongly to change: *unstable weather.* **2a.** Fickle. **b.** Lacking control of one's emotions. **3.** Unsteady: *an unstable ladder.* **4a.** Decaying with relatively short lifetime. Used of subatomic particles. **b.** Radioactive. **—un·sta′ble·ness** *n.* **—un·sta′bly** *adv.*

un·stead·y (ŭn-stĕd′ē) ▸ *adj.* **1.** Not securely in place; unstable. **2.** Fluctuating; inconstant. **3.** Not even; wavering. **—un·stead′i·ly** *adv.* **—un·stead′i·ness** *n.*

un·stick (ŭn-stĭk′) ▸ *v.* To free from being stuck.

un·stop (ŭn-stŏp′) ▸ *v.* **1.** To remove a stopper from. **2.** To remove an obstruction from.

un·stressed (ŭn-strĕst′) ▸ *adj.* **1.** *Ling.* Not stressed or accented. **2.** Not exposed or subjected to stress.

un·struc·tured (ŭn-strŭk′chərd) ▸ *adj.* **1.** Lacking structure. **2.** Not regulated or regimented.

un·strung (ŭn-strŭng′) ▸ *adj.* **1.** Having the strings loosened or removed. **2.** Emotionally upset.

un·stud·ied (ŭn-stŭd′ēd) ▸ *adj.* **1.** Not contrived; natural. **2.** Not gained by study or instruction.

un·sub·stan·tial (ŭn′səb-stăn′shəl) ▸ *adj.* **1.** Lacking material substance; not real. **2.** Flimsy. **3.** Lacking basis in fact.

un·sung (ŭn-sŭng′) ▸ *adj.* **1.** Not honored or praised; uncelebrated. **2.** Not sung.

un·tan·gle (ŭn-tăng′gəl) ▸ *v.* **1.** To disentangle. **2.** To clarify or resolve.

un·taught (ŭn-tôt′) ▸ *adj.* **1.** Not instructed. **2.** Not acquired by instruction; natural.

un·thank·ful (ŭn-thăngk′fəl) ▸ *adj.* **1.** Ungrateful. **2.** Unwelcome.

un·think·a·ble (ŭn-thĭng′kə-bəl) ▸ *adj.* Impossible to imagine; inconceivable.

un·think·ing (ŭn′thĭng′kĭng) ▸ *adj.* **1.** Thoughtless or heedless.

THESAURUS

or characteristic of the season ▸ ill-timed, inopportune, mistimed, untimely. *Idiom:* out of season. [*Compare* IMPROPER.]

unseasoned *adj.* *—See* INEXPERIENCED.

unseeing *adj.* *—See* BLIND (1), BLIND (3).

unseemliness *n.* *—See* IMPROPRIETY (1).

unseemly *adj.* *—See* IMPROPER (1), IMPROPER (2).

unseen *adj.* *—See* HIDDEN (1).

unselfish *adj.* *—See* GENEROUS (1), SELFLESS.

unselfishness *n.* *—See* GENEROSITY.

unserviceable *adj.* *—See* UNWORKABLE.

unsettle *v.* *—See* AGITATE (2), DISORDER, UPSET.

unsettled *adj.* Affording no quiet, repose, or rest ▸ restless, uneasy, unquiet. [*Compare* EDGY, WAKEFUL.] *—See also* ANXIOUS, CHANGEABLE (1), DEBATABLE, DUE (1), INDEFINITE (2).

unsettling *adj.* *—See* DISTURBING.

unsex *v.* *—See* STERILIZE (2).

unshakable *adj.* *—See* FIRM[1] (2).

unshaped *adj.* *—See* SHAPELESS.

unshielded *adj.* *—See* INSECURE (1).

unsightliness *n.* *—See* UGLINESS.

unsightly *adj.* *—See* UGLY.

unsigned *adj.* *—See* ANONYMOUS.

unskilled *adj.* *—See* AMATEURISH, INEFFICIENT.

unskillful *adj.* Clumsily lacking in the ability to do or perform ▸ awkward, bumbling, bungling, clumsy, floundering, fumbling, gauche, ham-fisted, ham-handed, heavy-handed, inept, maladroit, unpolished. [*Compare* AWKWARD.] *—See also* AMATEURISH, INEFFICIENT.

unsleeping *adj.* Not in a state of sleep or unable to sleep ▸ awake, wakeful, wide-awake. *Idiom:* tossing and turning. [*Compare* RESTLESS.]

unsoiled *adj.* *—See* CLEAN (1).

unsophisticated *adj.* *—See* ARTLESS.

unsought *adj.* *—See* UNWELCOME.

unsound *adj.* *—See* ERRONEOUS, FALLACIOUS (1), INSANE, UNWISE, WEAK (1).

unsoundness *n.* *—See* INFIRMITY.

unsparing *adj.* *—See* GENEROUS (1).

unsparingness *n.* *—See* GENEROSITY.

unspeakable *adj.* **1.** Beyond description ▸ incommunicable, indefinable, indescribable, ineffable, inexpressible, undescribable, unutterable. *Idioms:* beyond description (*or* words), defying description. [*Compare* INCREDIBLE.] **2.** That may not be spoken of or uttered ▸ eyes-only, sacred, unmentionable, unutterable. [*Compare* FORBIDDEN, HOLY, SECRET.] *—See also* OUTRAGEOUS.

unspecified *adj.* *—See* INDEFINITE (2).

unspoiled *adj.* *—See* FRESH (1).

unspoken *adj.* *—See* IMPLICIT (1), SILENT (2).

unstable *adj.* *—See* CAPRICIOUS, CHANGEABLE (1), ERRATIC, INSECURE (2).

unstableness *n.* *—See* INSTABILITY.

unstained *adj.* *—See* INNOCENT (1).

unsteadiness *n.* The quality or condition of being physically unsteady ▸ ricketiness, wiggling, wobbliness, wonkiness. *—See also* DIZZINESS, INSTABILITY.

unsteady *adj.* *—See* CAPRICIOUS, CHANGEABLE (1), DIZZY (1), INSECURE (2), UNEVEN.

unstinting *adj.* *—See* GENEROUS (1).

unstudied *adj.* *—See* ARTLESS.

unstudious *adj.* *—See* IGNORANT (1).

unsubstantial *adj.* *—See* IMMATERIAL, IMPLAUSIBLE, WEAK (1).

unsubstantiality *n.* *—See* INFIRMITY.

unsubtle *adj.* *—See* OBVIOUS.

unsuccessful *adj.* *—See* FUTILE.

unsufferable *adj.* *—See* UNBEARABLE.

unsuitability or **unsuitableness** *n.* *—See* IMPROPRIETY (1).

unsuitable *adj.* *—See* IMPROPER (2), OBJECTIONABLE.

unsuited *adj.* *—See* IMPROPER (2).

unsullied *adj.* *—See* CLEAN (1), INNOCENT (1).

unsupportable *adj.* *—See* UNBEARABLE.

unsure *adj.* *—See* AMBIGUOUS (1), DOUBTFUL (2), INDEFINITE (2), INSECURE (2).

unsureness *n.* *—See* INSTABILITY.

unsurpassable *adj.* *—See* MAXIMUM.

unsurpassed *adj.* *—See* BEST (1), UNIQUE.

unsusceptibility *n.* The capacity to withstand ▸ immunity, imperviousness, insusceptibility, resistance. [*Compare* ENDURANCE, STABILITY.]

unsusceptible *adj.* *—See* COLD (2), RESISTANT.

unswerving *adj.* *—See* CONCENTRATED (1), DIRECT (1).

unsympathetic *adj.* *—See* CALLOUS, UNPLEASANT.

unsystematic *adj.* *—See* CONFUSED (2).

untactful *adj.* *—See* TACTLESS.

untainted *adj.* *—See* INNOCENT (1).

untalkative *adj.* *—See* TACITURN.

untamed *adj.* *—See* UNCIVILIZED, WILD (2).

untangle *v.* *—See* EXTRICATE, SOLVE (1).

untasteful *adj.* *—See* UNPALATABLE.

untaught *adj.* *—See* IGNORANT (1), INSTINCTIVE.

untenable *adj.* *—See* FALLACIOUS (1).

untested *adj.* *—See* UNTRIED.

unthankful *adj.* Not apt to be appreciated ▸ thankless, unappreciated, ungrateful. *—See also* THANKLESS (1).

unthanking *adj.* *—See* THANKLESS (1).

unthinkable *adj.* *—See* IMPOSSIBLE, INCREDIBLE.

unthinking *adj.* *—See* CARELESS,

2. Not deliberate; inadvertent. **—un·think′ing·ly** *adv.*
un·tie (ŭn-tī′) ► *v.* **1.** To undo or loosen (e.g., a knot). **2.** To free from something that binds or restrains.
un·til (ŭn-tĭl′) ► *prep.* **1.** Up to the time of: *We danced until dawn.* **2.** Before (a specified time): *She can't leave until Friday.* ► *conj.* **1.** Up to the time that: *We walked until it got dark.* **2.** Before: *You cannot leave until your work is finished.* **3.** To the point or extent that: *I talked until I was hoarse.*
un·time·ly (ŭn-tīm′lē) ► *adj.* **1.** Occurring or done at an inappropriate time; inopportune. **2.** Occurring too soon; premature. **—un·time′li·ness** *n.* **—un·time′ly** *adv.*
un·to (ŭn′to͞o) ► *prep.* To.
un·told (ŭn-tōld′) ► *adj.* **1.** Not told or revealed. **2.** Beyond description or enumeration.
un·touch·a·ble (ŭn-tŭch′ə-bəl) ► *adj.* **1.** Not to be touched. **2.** Out of reach; unobtainable. **3.** Beyond criticism, impeachment, or attack. ► *n.* often **Untouchable** *Hinduism* A member of the class that is considered unclean and defiling by the four Hindu castes.
un·to·ward (ŭn-tôrd′) ► *adj.* **1.** Not favorable; unpropitious. **2.** Hard to control; unruly.
un·truth (ŭn-tro͞oth′) ► *n.* **1.** Something false; a lie. **2.** Lack of truth.
un·tu·tored (ŭn-to͞o′tərd, -tyo͞o′-) ► *adj.* **1.** Having had no formal education. **2.** Unsophisticated; unrefined.
un·twist (ŭn-twĭst′) ► *v.* To loosen or separate (something twisted) by turning in the opposite direction; unwind.
un·used (ŭn-yo͞ozd′, ŭn-yo͞ost′) ► *adj.* **1.** Not in use. **2.** Never having been used. **3.** Not accustomed: *unused to city traffic.*
un·u·su·al (ŭn-yo͞o′zho͞o-əl) ► *adj.* Not usual or ordinary. **—un·u′su·al·ly** *adv.*
un·ut·ter·a·ble (ŭn-ŭt′ər-ə-bəl) ► *adj.* **1.** That cannot or must not be uttered or expressed. **2.** Not capable of being pronounced. **—un·ut′ter·a·bly** *adv.*
un·var·nished (ŭn′vär′nĭsht) ► *adj.* **1.** Not varnished. **2.** Stated with no effort to soften or disguise; plain.
un·veil (ŭn-vāl′) ► *v.* **1.** To remove a veil or covering from. **2.** To disclose; reveal.
un·voiced (ŭn-voist′) ► *adj.* **1.** Not expressed or uttered. **2.** *Ling.* Voiceless.
un·war·rant·ed (ŭn-wôr′ən-tĭd, -wŏr′-) ► *adj.* Having no justification; groundless.
un·wea·ried (ŭn-wîr′ēd) ► *adj.* **1.** Not tired. **2.** Never wearying.
un·well (ŭn-wĕl′) ► *adj.* In poor health; sick.
un·whole·some (ŭn-hōl′səm) ► *adj.* **1.** Injurious to health; unhealthy. **2.** Offensive or loathsome. **—un·whole′some·ness** *n.*
un·wield·y (ŭn-wēl′dē) ► *adj.* Difficult to carry or manage because of bulk or shape.
un·will·ing (ŭn-wĭl′ĭng) ► *adj.* **1.** Not willing; hesitant. **2.** Done, given, or said reluctantly. **—un·will′ing·ly** *adv.* **—un·will′ing·ness** *n.*
un·wind (ŭn-wīnd′) ► *v.* **1.** To unroll; uncoil. **2.** To disentangle. **3.** To relax.
un·wit·ting (ŭn-wĭt′ĭng) ► *adj.* **1.** Not knowing; unaware. **2.** Not intended; unintentional. **—un·wit′ting·ly** *adv.*
un·wont·ed (ŭn-wôn′tĭd, -wōn′-, -wŭn′-) ► *adj.* Not habitual or ordinary; unusual.
un·world·ly (ŭn-wûrld′lē) ► *adj.* **1.** Not of this world; spiritual. **2.** Concerned with the spirit or soul. **3.** Not

THESAURUS

THOUGHTLESS, UNINTENTIONAL.
unthoughtful *adj.* —*See* THOUGHTLESS.
unthoughtfulness *n.* —*See* THOUGHTLESSNESS (2).
unthrifty *adj.* —*See* EXTRAVAGANT.
untidiness *n.* —*See* DISORDERLINESS.
untidy *adj.* —*See* MESSY (1).
untie *v.* —*See* OPEN (1), UNDO.
untighten *v.* —*See* EASE (1).
untimely *adj.* **1.** Not occurring at a favorable time ► ill-timed, inconvenient, inopportune. **2.** Developing, occurring, or appearing before the expected time ► early, precocious, premature. —*See also* UNSEASONABLE.
untiring *adj.* —*See* TIRELESS.
untouchable *n.* —*See* OUTCAST.
untouched *adj.* —*See* CALLOUS, FRESH (1).
untoward *adj.* —*See* IMPROPER (1), UNFAVORABLE (1), UNFORTUNATE (1), UNRULY.
untowardness *n.* —*See* MISFORTUNE, UNRULINESS.
untrammeled *adj.* —*See* LOOSE (2).
untried *adj.* Not tested or proved ► conjectured, hypothesized, hypothetical, surmised, theoretical, theorized, undemonstrated, unestablished, unpracticed, unproved, untested. [*Compare* NEW, PILOT.] —*See also* INEXPERIENCED.
untroubled *adj.* —*See* LIGHTHEARTED, STILL.
untroubledness *n.* —*See* STILLNESS.
untrue *adj.* —*See* ERRONEOUS, FAITHLESS, FALSE.
untrusting *adj.* —*See* DISTRUSTFUL.
untrustworthiness *n.* —*See* DISHONESTY (1).
untrustworthy *adj.* —*See* DISHONEST, SHADY (1), UNDEPENDABLE (1).
untruth *n.* —*See* FALLACY (1), LIE[2].
untruthful *adj.* —*See* DISHONEST, FALSE.
untruthfulness *n.* —*See* MENDACITY.
untwine *v.* —*See* UNWIND.
untwist *v.* —*See* UNWIND.
unusable *adj.* —*See* UNWORKABLE.
unused *adj.* —*See* IDLE (1).
unusual *adj.* Not usual or ordinary ► atypic, atypical, novel, unconventional, unique, unordinary, unwonted. *Slang:* offbeat. [*Compare* ABNORMAL, EXOTIC.] —*See also* ECCENTRIC, EXCEPTIONAL, INFREQUENT.
unusually *adv.* In a manner or to a degree that is unusual ► abnormally, atypically, bizarrely, curiously, exceptionally, extraordinarily, incredibly, oddly, peculiarly, phenomenally, remarkably, singularly, strangely, surprisingly, uncommonly, unconventionally, unexpectedly, uniquely. [*Compare* ABSOLUTELY, COMPLETELY, CONSIDERABLY, REALLY, VERY.]
unutterable *adj.* —*See* UNSPEAKABLE (1), UNSPEAKABLE (2).
unuttered *adj.* —*See* IMPLICIT (1), SILENT (2).
unvarnished *adj.* —*See* BARE (1), LITERAL.
unvarying *adj.* —*See* UNCHANGING.
unveil *v.* —*See* BETRAY (2), REVEAL.
unventilated *adj.* —*See* AIRLESS (1).
unversed *adj.* —*See* INEXPERIENCED.
unvoiced *adj.* —*See* SILENT (2).
unwanted *adj.* —*See* OBJECTIONABLE, UNWELCOME.
unwarranted *adj.* —*See* BASELESS, WANTON (2).
unwarrantedly *adv.* Without basis or foundation in fact ► baselessly, groundlessly, unfoundedly.
unwashed *adj.* —*See* LOWLY (1).
unwavering *adj.* —*See* FIRM[1] (3).
unwearied *adj.* —*See* TIRELESS.
unwed *adj.* —*See* SINGLE.
unwelcome *adj.* Not welcome or wanted ► banished, excluded, rejected, undesirable, undesired, uninvited, unsought, unwanted, unwished-for. —*See also* OBJECTIONABLE.
unwelcome or **unwelcomeness** *n.* —*See* INHOSPITALITY.
unwell *adj.* —*See* SICK (1).
unwholesome *adj.* **1.** Not sustaining or promoting health ► insalubrious, junk, unhealthful, unhealthy, unhygienic, unsalutary. **2.** Morally detrimental ► contaminative, corruptive, demoralizing, poisonous, unhealthy. [*Compare* EVIL.] —*See also* HARMFUL, MORBID, OFFENSIVE (1).
unwholesomeness *n.* —*See* CONTAMINATION.
unwieldy *adj.* —*See* AWKWARD (2).
unwilling *adj.* —*See* INDISPOSED.
unwillingness *n.* —*See* INDISPOSITION.
unwind *v.* To cause a line to become longer and less taut ► play out, uncoil, unravel, unreel, unroll, untwine, untwist. [*Compare* EXTRICATE, UNDO.] —*See also* REST[1] (1).
unwise *adj.* Not wise ► contraindicated, ill-advised, ill-considered, impolitic, impractical, imprudent, inadvisable, indiscreet, inexpedient, injudicious, unsound. [*Compare* FOOLISH, RASH, UNRULY.]
unwished-for *adj.* —*See* UNWELCOME.
unwitting *adj.* —*See* IGNORANT (3), UNINTENTIONAL.
unwonted *adj.* —*See* UNUSUAL.
unworkable *adj.* Incapable of being used or availed of to advantage ► impracticable, unemployable, unnegotiable, unserviceable, unusable, useless. —*See also* IMPOSSIBLE.
unworkmanlike *adj.* —*See* INEFFICIENT.
unworldly *adj.* —*See* ARTLESS, SUPERNATURAL (1).

worldly-wise; naive. **—un·world′li·ness** *n.*

un·wor·thy (ŭn-wûr′*th*ē) ▸ *adj.* **1.** Insufficient in worth; undeserving. **2.** Not suiting or befitting. **3.** Vile; despicable. **—un·wor′thi·ly** *adv.* **—un·wor′thi·ness** *n.*

un·writ·ten (ŭn-rĭt′n) ▸ *adj.* **1.** Not written or recorded. **2.** Forceful through custom; traditional.

up (ŭp) ▸ *adv.* **1.** In or to a higher position: *looking up.* **2.** In or to an upright position: *sat up in bed.* **3a.** Above a surface: *coming up for air.* **b.** Above the horizon: *as the sun came up.* **4.** Into consideration: *take up a new topic.* **5.** In or toward a position conventionally regarded as higher, as on a map: *up in Canada.* **6.** To or at a higher price: *stocks going up.* **7.** So as to advance, increase, or improve: *Our spirits went up.* **8.** With or to a greater pitch or volume. **9.** Into a state of excitement or turbulence. **10.** Completely; entirely: *drank it up in a gulp; fastened up the coat.* **11.** Used as an intensifier with certain verbs: *typed up a list.* ▸ *adj.* **1.** Above a former level; higher: *My grades are up.* **2a.** Out of bed: *was up by seven.* **b.** Standing; erect. **c.** Facing upward. **3.** Raised; lifted: *a switch in the up position.* **4.** Moving or directed upward: *an up elevator.* **5a.** Increasingly excited or agitated; aroused. **b.** *Informal* Cheerful; optimistic. **c.** *Slang* Happily excited; euphoric. **6.** *Informal* Taking place; going on: *wondered what was up back home.* **7.** Being considered; under study: *a contract up for renewal.* **8.** Running as a candidate. **9.** On trial; charged: *up for manslaughter.* ▸ *prep.* **1.** From a lower to or toward a higher point on: *up the hill.* **2.** Toward or at a point farther along: *up the road.* **3.** Toward the source of: *up the Nile.* ▸ *n.* **1.** An upward slope; rise. **2.** An upward movement or trend. **3.** *Slang* Excitement or euphoria. ▸ *v.* **upped, up·ping. 1.** To increase: *upped their fees.* **2.** To raise to a higher level. ***—idioms:*** **on the up-and-up** Open and honest. **up against** Confronted with; facing. **up to 1.** Occupied with, esp. devising or scheming. **2.** Able to do or deal with. **3.** Dependent on: *It's up to us.*

up– ▸ *pref.* **1.** Up; upward: *uphill.* **2.** Upper: *upland.*

up-and-com·ing (ŭp′ən-kŭm′ĭng) ▸ *adj.* Marked for future success; promising.

U·pan·i·shad (o͞o-pä′nĭ-shäd′) ▸ *n.* Any of a group of philosophical treatises contributing to the theology of ancient Hinduism, elaborating on the earlier Vedas.

up·beat (ŭp′bēt′) ▸ *n.* *Mus.* An unaccented beat occurring before the first beat of a measure. ▸ *adj.* *Informal* Optimistic; cheerful.

up·braid (ŭp-brād′) ▸ *v.* To reprove sharply; reproach.

up·bring·ing (ŭp′brĭng′ĭng) ▸ *n.* The rearing and training received during childhood.

UPC ▸ *abbr.* Universal Product Code

up·com·ing (ŭp′kŭm′ĭng) ▸ *adj.* Occurring soon; forthcoming.

up·coun·try (ŭp′kŭn′trē) ▸ *n.* An inland or upland region of a country. **—up′coun′try** *adj.* & *adv.*

up·date (ŭp-dāt′) ▸ *v.* To bring up to date. **—up′date′** *n.*

up·draft (ŭp′drăft′) ▸ *n.* An upward current of air.

up·end (ŭp-ĕnd′) ▸ *v.* **1.** To stand, set, or turn on one end. **2.** To overturn or overthrow.

up·front or **up·front** (ŭp′frŭnt′) ▸ *adj.* *Informal* **1.** Straightforward; frank. **2.** Paid or due in advance: *up-front cash.* **—up′front′** *adv.*

up·grade (ŭp′grād′) ▸ *v.* **1.** To raise to a higher grade or standard. **2.** *Comp. Sci.* To replace (software or hardware) with a newer or better product. ▸ *n.* **1.** An upward incline. **2.** *Comp. Sci.* A hardware or software product that is newer or performs better than an earlier version.

up·heav·al (ŭp-hē′vəl) ▸ *n.* **1.** The process of being heaved upward. **2.** A sudden violent disruption or upset. **3.** *Geol.* A raising of a part of the earth's crust.

up·hill (ŭp′hĭl′) ▸ *adj.* **1.** Going up a hill or slope. **2.** Difficult; laborious. ▸ *adv.* (ŭp′hĭl′) **1.** To or toward higher ground; up a slope. **2.** Against adversity; with difficulty.

up·hold (ŭp-hōld′) ▸ *v.* **1.** To hold aloft. **2.** To prevent from falling; support. **3.** To maintain against opposition. **—up·hold′er** *n.*

up·hol·ster (ŭp-hōl′stər, ə-pōl′-) ▸ *v.* To supply (furniture) with stuffing, springs, cushions, and covering fabric. **—up·hol′ster·er** *n.*

up·hol·ster·y (ŭp-hōl′stə-rē, -strē, ə-pōl′-) ▸ *n., pl.* **-ies. 1.** The materials used in upholstering. **2.** The business of upholstering.

up·keep (ŭp′kēp′) ▸ *n.* The act or cost of maintaining in proper operation and repair.

up·land (ŭp′lənd, -lănd′) ▸ *n.* An area of land of high elevation. **—up′land′** *adj.*

up·lift (ŭp-lĭft′) ▸ *v.* **1.** To raise; elevate. **2.** To raise to a higher social, intellectual, or moral level. **3.** To raise to spiritual or emotional heights; exalt. **—up′lift′** *n.*

up·load (ŭp′lōd′) ▸ *v.* To transfer (data or programs), usu. from a peripheral computer or device to a central computer.

up·most (ŭp′mōst′) ▸ *adj.* Uppermost.

up·on (ə-pŏn′, ə-pôn′) ▸ *prep.* On.

up·per (ŭp′ər) ▸ *adj.* **1.** Higher in place, position, or rank. **2. Upper** *Geol.* & *Archaeol.* Being a later division of the period named. ▸ *n.* **1.** The part of a shoe or boot above the sole. **2.** *Slang* A drug, esp. an amphetamine, used as a stimulant. **3.** An exhilarating or euphoric experience.

up·per·case (ŭp′ər-kās′) ▸ *adj.* Of or relating to capital letters as distinguished from small letters. **—up′per·case′** *n.* & *v.*

upper class ▸ *n.* The highest socioeconomic class in a society. **—up′per-class′** *adj.*

up·per·class·man (ŭp′ər-klăs′mən) ▸ *n.* A student in the junior or senior class of a secondary school or college.

upper crust ▸ *n.* *Informal* The highest social class or group. **—up′per-crust′** *adj.*

up·per·cut (ŭp′ər-kŭt′) ▸ *n.* *Sports* A swinging blow directed upward, as in boxing.

upper hand ▸ *n.* A position of control or advantage.

up·per·most (ŭp′ər-mōst′) ▸ *adv.* & *adj.* In the highest position, place, or rank.

THESAURUS

unwritten *adj.* *—See* ORAL.

unyielding *adj.* *—See* FIRM[1] (3), RIGID, SEVERE (1), STUBBORN (1).

up *adj.* *—See* ELATED.

up *v.* To increase in amount ▸ boost, hike, jack (up), jump, raise. *—See also* PROMOTE (1).

up-and-coming *adj.* Showing great promise ▸ coming, promising. ***Idiom:*** on the way up.

upbeat *adj.* *—See* OPTIMISTIC.

upbraid *v.* *—See* CHASTISE.

upbraiding *n.* *—See* TIRADE.

upbringing *n.* Training in the proper forms of social and personal conduct ▸ breeding, education. [*Compare* COURTESY, MANNERS.]

upchuck *v.* *—See* VOMIT.

upcoming *adj.* In the relatively near future ▸ approaching, coming, due, forthcoming. ***Idioms:*** around the corner, on the horizon. [*Compare* CLOSE, IMMINENT.]

update *v.* To make modern in appearance or style ▸ modernize, streamline. ***Idiom:*** bring up to date. [*Compare* IMPROVE, RENEW.]

upend *v.* *—See* OVERTURN.

upfront *adj.* *—See* FRANK.

upgrade *v.* *—See* IMPROVE, PROMOTE (1).

upgrade *n.* *—See* ADVANCEMENT, IMPROVEMENT (1).

upheaval *n.* *—See* REVOLUTION (2), UPSET.

uphill *adj.* *—See* DIFFICULT (1).

uphold *v.* *—See* BEAR (1), DEFEND (2), ELEVATE (1), SUPPORT (1), SUPPORT (2).

upkeep *n.* *—See* LIVING, MAINTENANCE.

uplift *v.* *—See* ELATE, ELEVATE (1), EXALT.

uplift *n.* *—See* ELATION, LIFT.

upmost *adj.* Of, being, located at, or forming the top ▸ highest, loftiest, top, topmost, uppermost. [*Compare* CLIMACTIC.]

up on *adj.* *—See* INFORMED.

upper *adj.* Being at a rank or level above another ▸ greater, higher, senior, superior.

upper class *n.* *—See* SOCIETY (1).

upper-class *adj.* *—See* NOBLE.

upper crust *n.* *—See* SOCIETY (1).

upper-crust *adj.* *—See* NOBLE.

upper hand *n.* *—See* ADVANTAGE (3).

uppermost *adj.* Of, being, located at, or forming the top ▸ highest, loftiest, top, topmost, upmost. [*Compare* CLIMACTIC.]

Upper Vol·ta (vŏl′tə, vōl′-) ► See **Burkina Faso.**

up·pi·ty (ŭp′ĭ-tē) ► *adj. Informal* Presumptuous.

up·raise (ŭp-rāz′) ► *v.* To raise or lift up.

up·right (ŭp′rīt′) ► *adj.* **1.** In a vertical position or direction. **2.** Moral; honorable. ► *adv.* Vertically: *walk upright.* ► *n.* Something, such as a goal post, that stands upright. **—up′right′ly** *adv.* **—up′right′ness** *n.*

upright piano ► *n.* A piano having the strings mounted vertically.

up·ris·ing (ŭp′rī′zĭng) ► *n.* A revolt against a constituted government.

up·roar (ŭp′rôr′) ► *n.* A condition of noisy excitement and confusion.

up·roar·i·ous (ŭp-rôr′ē-əs) ► *adj.* **1.** Causing or accompanied by an uproar. **2.** Hilarious. **—up·roar′i·ous·ly** *adv.*

up·root (ŭp-ro͞ot′, -ro͝ot′) ► *v.* To remove completely by or as if by pulling up the roots. **—up·root′ed·ness** *n.*

up·scale (ŭp′skāl′) ► *adj.* Intended for or relating to high-income consumers. **—up·scale′** *v.*

up·set (ŭp-sĕt′) ► *v.* **1.** To overturn or cause to overturn. **2.** To disturb the functioning, order, or course of. **3.** To distress mentally or emotionally. **4.** To overthrow; topple. ► *n.* (ŭp′sĕt′) **1.** The act of upsetting or the condition of being upset. **2.** A disturbance, disorder, or state of agitation. **3.** A game or contest in which the favorite is defeated. ► *adj.* **1.** Overturned; capsized. **2.** Showing symptoms of indigestion. **3.** Emotionally or mentally distressed.

up·shot (ŭp′shŏt′) ► *n.* The final result; outcome.

up·side down (ŭp′sīd′) ► *adv.* **1.** With the upper side down. **2.** In great disorder. **—up′side-down′** *adj.*

up·si·lon (ŭp′sə-lŏn′, yo͞op′-) ► *n.* The 20th letter of the Greek alphabet.

up·stage (ŭp′stāj′) ► *adv.* Toward, at, or on the rear part of a stage. ► *adj.* Of the rear part of a stage. ► *v.* (ŭp-stāj′) **1.** To make (another performer) face away from the audience by assuming a position upstage. **2.** To divert attention or praise from. **3.** To treat haughtily.

up·stairs (ŭp′stârz′) ► *adv.* **1.** Up the stairs. **2.** To or on a higher floor. ► *n.* (ŭp′stârz′) *(takes sing. v.)* The upper part of a building. **—up′stairs′** *adj.*

up·stand·ing (ŭp-stăn′dĭng, ŭp′stăn′-) ► *adj.* **1.** Standing erect or upright. **2.** Morally upright; honest.

up·start (ŭp′stärt′) ► *n.* A person who attains sudden wealth or importance, esp. one made immodest by the change; parvenu.

up·state (ŭp′stāt′) ► *n.* The northerly section of a US state. **—up′state′** *adv. & adj.*

up·stream (ŭp′strēm′) ► *adv. & adj.* Against the current of a stream.

up·stroke (ŭp′strōk′) ► *n.* An upward stroke.

up·surge (ŭp′sûrj′) ► *n.* A rapid or abrupt rise: *an upsurge in crime.* **—up·surge′** *v.*

up·sweep (ŭp′swēp′) ► *n.* An upward curve or sweep. **—up′sweep′** *v.*

up·swing (ŭp′swĭng′) ► *n.* An upward swing or trend; increase.

up·take (ŭp′tāk′) ► *n.* **1.** A passage for drawing up smoke or air. **2.** Understanding; comprehension: *quick on the uptake.*

up·tem·po also **up·tem·po** (ŭp′tĕm′pō) ► *n., pl.* **-pos.** A fast or lively tempo, as in jazz. **—up′-tem′po** *adj.*

up·tight (ŭp′tīt′) ► *adj. Slang* **1.** Tense; nervous. **2.** Outraged; angry. **3.** Rigidly conventional.

up-to-date (ŭp′tə-dāt′) ► *adj.* Informed of or reflecting the latest information or styles. **—up′-to-date′ness** *n.*

up·town (ŭp′toun′) ► *n.* The upper part of a town or city. ► *adv.* (ŭp′toun′) To, toward, or in the uptown. **—up′town′** *adj.*

up·turn (ŭp′tûrn′, ŭp-tûrn′) ► *v.* **1.** To turn up or over. **2.** To direct upward. ► *n.* (ŭp′tûrn′) An upward movement, curve, or trend, as in business.

up·ward (ŭp′wərd) ► *adv. & adj.* From a lower to a higher place, point, or level. ***—idiom:*** **upward (**or **upwards) of** More than; in excess of. **—up′ward·ly** *adv.* **—up′wards** *adv.*

up·wind (ŭp′wĭnd′) ► *adv.* In or toward the direction from which the wind blows. **—up′wind′** *adj.*

Ur (ûr, o͝or) ► A city of ancient Sumer in S Mesopotamia on a site in SE Iraq.

u·ra·cil (yo͝or′ə-sĭl) ► *n.* A pyrimidine base that is an essential constituent of RNA.

U·ral-Al·ta·ic (yo͝or′əl-ăl-tā′ĭk) ► *n.* A language group that comprises the Uralic and Altaic families. **—U′ral-Al·ta′ic** *adj.*

U·ral·ic (yo͞o-răl′ĭk) also **U·ra·li·an** (yo͞o-rā′lē-ən) ► *n.* A language family that comprises the Finno-Ugric and Samoyedic subfamilies. **—U·ral′ic** *adj.*

U·ral Mountains (yo͝or′əl) ► A range of W Russia forming the traditional boundary between Europe and Asia and extending about 2,414 km (1,500 mi) from the Arctic to Kazakhstan.

Ural River ► A river of W Russia and W Kazakhstan rising in the S Ural Mts. and flowing about 2,533 km (1,574 mi) to the Caspian Sea.

u·ra·ni·um (yo͞o-rā′nē-əm) ► *n. Symbol* **U** A heavy, radioactive, silvery-white metallic element, used in research, nuclear fuels, and nuclear weapons. At. no. 92.

U·ra·nus (yo͝or′ə-nəs, yo͞o-rā′nəs) ► *n.* **1.** *Gk. Myth.* The earliest supreme god, a personification of the sky. **2.** The 7th planet from the sun, at a distance of approx. 2,869 million km (1,790 million mi) and with a mean diameter of 52,290 km (32,480 mi).

ur·ban (ûr′bən) ► *adj.* Of, relating to, or located in a city.

ur·bane (ûr-bān′) ► *adj.* **-ban·er, -ban·est.** Polite and refined in manner; suave. **—ur·bane′ly** *adv.*

ur·ban·ite (ûr′bə-nīt′) ► *n.* A city dweller.

ur·ban·i·ty (ûr-băn′ĭ-tē) ► *n.* Refinement and elegance of manner.

ur·ban·ize (ûr′bə-nīz′) ► *v.* **-ized, -iz·ing.** To make urban in nature or character. **—ur′ban·i·za′tion** *n.*

ur·chin (ûr′chĭn) ► *n.* **1.** A playful or mischievous young-

THESAURUS

uppity or **uppish** *adj.* —*See* IMPUDENT, SNOBBISH.

uppityness or **uppishness** *n.* —*See* IMPUDENCE.

upraise or **uprear** *v.* —*See* ELEVATE (1), ERECT.

upraised *adj.* —*See* ELEVATED (1), ERECT.

upright *adj.* —*See* ERECT, ETHICAL, HONEST, VERTICAL.

uprightness *n.* —*See* CHARACTER (2), GOOD (1).

uprise *v.* —*See* STAND (1).

uprising *n.* —*See* REBELLION.

uproar *n.* —*See* AGITATION (1), DISORDER (2), NOISE (1), SENSATION (2), VOCIFERATION.

uproarious *adj.* —*See* FUNNY (1).

uproot *v.* —*See* ANNIHILATE.

upset *v.* To disturb the health or physiological functioning of ► derange, disconcert, disorder, turn, unsettle. [*Compare* DERANGE.] —*See also* AGITATE (2), DISORDER, DISRUPT, DISTURB, OFFEND (1), OFFEND (2), OVERTHROW, OVERTURN.

upset *n.* The act or an example of upsetting ► disordering, disorganization, disruption, overthrow, overturn, upheaval. [*Compare* DEFEAT, DISTURBANCE.] —*See also* AGITATION (2).

upset *adj.* —*See* ANXIOUS, UPSIDE-DOWN.

upsetting *adj.* —*See* DISTURBING.

upshot *n.* —*See* EFFECT (1).

upside-down *adj.* Turned over completely ► capsized, inverted, overturned, topsy-turvy, upended, upset, upturned. *Idiom:* bottom-side up. —*See also* CONFUSED (2).

upspring *v.* —*See* STEM.

upstanding *adj.* —*See* ERECT, HONEST.

upstandingness *n.* —*See* HONESTY.

upsurge *v.* —*See* INCREASE.

upsurge *n.* —*See* INCREASE (1).

upswing *n.* —*See* INCREASE (1).

uptight *adj.* —*See* EDGY.

up to *adj.* Having the necessary strength or ability ► equal. —*See also* ELIGIBLE.

up-to-date or **up-to-the-minute** *adj.* —*See* CONTEMPORARY (2).

upturn *n.* —*See* INCREASE (1).

upturn *v.* —*See* OVERTURN.

upturned *adj.* —*See* UPSIDE-DOWN.

urban *adj.* —*See* CITY.

urbane *adj.* Gracious and tactful in social manner ► debonair, smooth, suave. [*Compare* COURTEOUS, GLIB, SOPHISTICATED.] —*See also* CULTURED.

urbanity *n.* —*See* AMENITIES (2), ELEGANCE.

urchin *n.* A mischievous youngster ►

ster; scamp. **2.** A sea urchin. **3.** A hedgehog.

Ur·du (o͝or′do͞o, ûr′-) ▸ *n.* An Indic language that is an official language of Pakistan and is also widely used in India.

–ure ▸ *suff.* **1.** Act; process; condition: *erasure.* **2a.** Function; office: *judicature.* **b.** Body performing a function: *legislature.*

u·re·a (yo͞o-rē′ə) ▸ *n.* A water-soluble compound that is the chief nitrogenous component of the urine in mammals and other organisms.

u·re·mi·a (yo͞o-rē′mē-ə) ▸ *n.* A toxic condition resulting from kidney disease in which there is retention in the bloodstream of waste products normally excreted in the urine. **—u·re′mic** *adj.*

u·re·ter (yo͞o-rē′tər, yo͝or′ĭ-tər) ▸ *n.* The long narrow duct that conveys urine from the kidney to the urinary bladder or cloaca.

u·re·thra (yo͞o-rē′thrə) ▸ *n., pl.* **-thras** or **-thrae** (-thrē). The canal through which urine is discharged and through which semen is discharged in the male. **—u·re′thral** *adj.*

urge (ûrj) ▸ *v.* **urged, urg·ing. 1.** To force or drive forward or onward; impel. **2.** To entreat earnestly and often repeatedly; exhort. **3.** To advocate earnestly; press for. ▸ *n.* **1.** The act of urging. **2.** An impulse that prompts action or effort.

ur·gent (ûr′jənt) ▸ *adj.* **1.** Compelling immediate action; pressing. **2.** Insistent or importunate. **—ur′gen·cy** *n.* **—ur′gent·ly** *adv.*

–urgy ▸ *suff.* Technique; process: *metallurgy.*

u·ric (yo͝or′ĭk) ▸ *adj.* Relating to, contained in, or obtained from urine.

uric acid ▸ *n.* A semisolid compound, $C_5H_4N_4O_3$, that is the chief nitrogenous component of the urine in birds, terrestrial reptiles, and insects.

u·ri·nal (yo͝or′ə-nəl) ▸ *n.* **1.** A place for urinating. **2.** A receptacle for urine.

u·ri·nal·y·sis (yo͝or′ə-năl′ĭ-sĭs) ▸ *n.* Chemical analysis of urine.

u·ri·nar·y (yo͝or′ə-nĕr′ē) ▸ *adj.* Of urine or its production, function, or excretion.

urinary bladder ▸ *n.* A muscular sac in the anterior part of the pelvic cavity in which urine collects before excretion.

u·ri·nate (yo͝or′ə-nāt′) ▸ *v.* **-nat·ed, -nat·ing.** To excrete urine. **—u′ri·na′tion** *n.*

u·rine (yo͝or′ĭn) ▸ *n.* The waste product secreted by the kidneys that in mammals is a yellowish, slightly acid fluid discharged through the urethra.

urino– or **urin–** ▸ *pref.* Urine: *urinalysis.*

URL (yo͞o′är-ĕl′) ▸ *n.* An Internet address (e.g., *http://www.hmco.com/trade/*), usu. consisting of the access protocol (*http*), the domain name (*www.hmco.com*), and optionally the path to a file (*trade*).

urn (ûrn) ▸ *n.* **1.** A vase of varying size and shape, usu. having a footed base or pedestal. **2.** A closed metal vessel having a spigot and used for warming or serving tea or coffee.

uro– or **ur–** ▸ *pref.* **1.** Urine: *uric.* **2.** Urinary tract: *urology.* **3.** Urea: *polyurethane.*

u·ro·gen·i·tal (yo͝or′ō-jĕn′ĭ-tl) ▸ *adj.* Of or involving both the urinary and genital structures or functions.

u·rol·o·gy (yo͞o-rŏl′ə-jē) ▸ *n.* The branch of medicine that deals with the diseases of the urinary tract and urogenital system. **—ur′o·log′ic** (yo͝or′ə-lŏj′ĭk), **ur′o·log′i·cal** *adj.* **—u·rol′o·gist** *n.*

Ur·sa Major (ûr′sə) ▸ *n.* A constellation containing the seven stars that form the Big Dipper.

Ursa Minor ▸ *n.* A constellation having the shape of a ladle with Polaris at the tip of its handle.

ur·sine (ûr′sīn′) ▸ *adj.* Of or characteristic of a bear.

ur·ti·car·i·a (ûr′tĭ-kâr′ē-ə) ▸ *n.* See **hives.**

U·ru·guay (yo͝or′ə-gwī′, -gwā′) ▸ A country of SE South America on the Atlantic and the Río de la Plata. **—U′ru·guay′an** *adj. & n.*

Uruguay River ▸ A river of SE South America rising in S Brazil and flowing about 1,609 km (1,000 mi) to the Río de la Plata.

us (ŭs) ▸ *pron.* The objective case of **we. 1.** Used as the direct object of a verb: *She saw us.* **2.** Used as the indirect object of a verb: *They offered us free tickets.* **3.** Used as the object of a preposition: *This letter is addressed to us.* **4.** *Informal* Used as a predicate nominative: *It's us.*

US ▸ *abbr.* United States

USA ▸ *abbr.* **1.** United States Army **2.** United States of America

us·a·ble also **use·a·ble** (yo͞o′zə-bəl) ▸ *adj.* **1.** That can be used: *usable byproducts.* **2.** Fit for use; convenient to use: *a usable reference.* **—us′a·bil′i·ty** *n.* **—us′a·bly** *adv.*

USAF ▸ *abbr.* United States Air Force

us·age (yo͞o′sĭj, -zĭj) ▸ *n.* **1.** The act, manner, or amount of using. **2.** A usual, habitual, or accepted practice. **3.** The way in which words or phrases are actually used in a speech community.

USCG ▸ *abbr.* United States Coast Guard

USDA ▸ *abbr.* United States Department of Agriculture

use (yo͞oz) ▸ *v.* **used, us·ing. 1.** To put into service; employ. **2.** To avail oneself of; practice. **3.** To conduct oneself toward; treat. **4.** To exploit. **5.** To take habitually, as alcohol or tobacco. **6.** Used in the past tense with *to* to indicate a former state, habitual practice, or custom: *Mail service used to be faster.* ***—phrasal verb:* use up** To consume completely. ▸ *n.* (yo͞os) **1a.** The act of using; employment. **b.** The fact of being used. **2.** The manner of using. **3a.** The privilege of using something. **b.** The ability to use something. **4.** The need or occasion to employ: *have no use for these old clothes.* **5.** The quality of being suitable to an end; usefulness. **6.** A purpose for which something is used. **7.** Accustomed or usual practice. **8.** *Law* **a.** Enjoyment of property, as by occupying or exercising it. **b.** The benefit or profit of lands and tenements held in trust by another. **—us′er** *n.*

used (yo͞ozd) ▸ *adj.* **1.** Not new; secondhand. **2.** (also yo͞ost) Accustomed; habituated: *We aren't used to the cold.*

use·ful (yo͞os′fəl) ▸ *adj.* Having a beneficial use; serviceable. **—use′ful·ly** *adv.* **—use′ful·ness** *n.*

THESAURUS

brat, elf, gamin, gamine, imp, juvenile delinquent, minx, scamp, whelp. *Idiom:* holy terror. [*Compare* CHILD, RASCAL.]

urge *v.* To impel to action ▸ drive, exhort, induce, press. [*Compare* PROVOKE.]

urge *n.* —*See* DESIRE (2), INCLINATION (1).

urgency *n.* —*See* EMERGENCY.

urgent *adj.* **1.** Demanding immediate attention ▸ acute, burning, climacteric, compelling, critical, crucial, crying, desperate, dire, emergent, exigent, imperative, instant, pressing, vital. [*Compare* ESSENTIAL, IMPORTANT, PRIMARY.] **2.** Firm or obstinate, as in making a demand or maintaining a stand ▸ importunate, importune, insistent, persistent. [*Compare* FIRM[1], STUBBORN.]

urging *n.* Urgent solicitation ▸ insistence, insistency, persuasion, pressing. [*Compare* DEMAND.]

urinary *adj.* —*See* ELIMINATIVE.

usable *adj.* In a condition to be used ▸ applicable, employable, operational, serviceable, utilizable. [*Compare* ACTIVE, PRACTICAL.] *See also* OPEN (4).

usage *n.* The act of consuming ▸ consumption, depletion, expenditure, use, utilization. [*Compare* USE.] —*See also* CUSTOM, EXERCISE (1).

usance *n.* —*See* CUSTOM.

use *v.* To put into action or use ▸ actuate, adopt, apply, draw on, employ, exercise, exploit, harness, implement, practice, utilize, work. *Idioms:* avail oneself of, bring into play, bring to bear, make use of, put into practice, put to use. [*Compare* EXERCISE, HANDLE.] —*See also* ABUSE (1), MANIPULATE (1), OPERATE.

use up *v.* —*See* EXHAUST (1).

use *n.* **1.** The act of consuming ▸ consumption, depletion, expenditure, usage, utilization. **2.** The quality of being suitable or adaptable to an end ▸ account, advantage, avail, benefit, merit, point, practicality, profit, usefulness, utility. [*Compare* PURPOSE.] —*See also* CUSTOM, DUTY (2), EXERCISE (1), INTEREST (1).

used *adj.* **1.** In the habit ▸ accustomed, habituated, wont. **2.** Previously owned or made use of; not new ▸ hand-me-down, pre-owned, secondhand. [*Compare* OBSOLETE, OLD-FASHIONED.]

useful *adj.* —*See* BENEFICIAL, CONVENIENT (1), PRACTICAL.

usefulness *n.* —*See* USE (2).

use·less (yo͞os′lĭs) ▸ *adj.* **1.** Of no beneficial use; futile; ineffective. **2.** Incapable of functioning; ineffectual. **—use′less·ly** *adv.* **—use′less·ness** *n.*

Use·net or **USE·NET** (yo͞oz′nĕt′) ▸ *n.* A messaging system that uses a computer network, esp. the Internet, to transfer thematically organized messages.

us·er-friend·ly (yo͞o′zər-frĕnd′lē) ▸ *adj.* Easy to use or learn to use. **—us′er-friend′li·ness** *n.*

us·er·name (yo͞o′zər-nām′) ▸ *n.* A sequence of characters used as identification esp. for logging on to a multiuser computer system.

ush·er (ŭsh′ər) ▸ *n.* **1.** One who escorts people to their seats, as in a theater. **2.** An official doorkeeper, as in a courtroom. **3.** An official who precedes persons of rank in a procession. ▸ *v.* **1.** To serve as an usher to; escort. **2.** To lead or conduct. **3.** To precede and introduce; inaugurate: *events that ushered in a new era.*

USMC ▸ *abbr.* United States Marine Corps

USN ▸ *abbr.* United States Navy

USO ▸ *abbr.* United Service Organizations

USS ▸ *abbr.* United States ship

USSR ▸ *abbr.* Union of Soviet Socialist Republics

usu. ▸ *abbr.* usually

u·su·al (yo͞o′zho͞o-əl) ▸ *adj.* **1.** Common; ordinary; normal. **2.** Habitual or customary. **—u′su·al·ly** *adv.* **—u′su·al·ness** *n.*

u·su·fruct (yo͞o′zə-frŭkt′, -sə-) ▸ *n. Law* The right to use and enjoy the profits and advantages of something belonging to another as long as the property is not damaged or altered in any way.

u·su·rer (yo͞o′zhər-ər) ▸ *n.* One who lends money at interest, esp. at an exorbitant or unlawfully high rate.

u·su·ri·ous (yo͞o-zho͝or′ē-əs) ▸ *adj.* Relating to, practicing, or being usury. **—u·su′ri·ous·ly** *adv.* **—u·su′ri·ous·ness** *n.*

u·surp (yo͞o-sûrp′, -zûrp′) ▸ *v.* To seize and hold by force and without legal authority. **—u′sur·pa′tion** (yo͞o′sər-pā′shən, -zər-) *n.* **—u·surp′er** *n.*

u·su·ry (yo͞o′zhə-rē) ▸ *n., pl.* **-ries. 1.** The practice of lending money and charging the borrower interest, esp. at an exorbitant or illegally high rate. **2.** An excessive or illegally high interest rate.

UT or **Ut.** ▸ *abbr.* Utah

U·tah (yo͞o′tô′, -tä′) ▸ A state of the W US. Cap. Salt Lake City. **—U′tahn** *adj. & n.*

Ute (yo͞ot) ▸ *n., pl.* **Ute** or **Utes. 1.** A member of a Native American people of Utah, Colorado, and N New Mexico. **2.** The Uto-Aztecan language of the Ute.

u·ten·sil (yo͞o-tĕn′səl) ▸ *n.* An instrument or container, esp. one used in a kitchen.

u·ter·us (yo͞o′tər-əs) ▸ *n., pl.* **u·ter·i** (yo͞o′tə-rī′) or **-us·es. 1.** A hollow muscular organ located in the pelvic cavity of female mammals in which the fertilized egg develops. **2.** A corresponding part in other animals **—u′ter·ine** (-tər-ĭn, -tə-rīn′) *adj.*

u·tile (yo͞ot′l, yo͞o′tīl′) ▸ *adj.* Useful.

u·til·i·tar·i·an (yo͞o-tĭl′ĭ-târ′ē-ən) ▸ *adj.* **1.** Of or in the interests of utility. **2.** Stressing utility over beauty. **3.** Believing in or advocating utilitarianism. ▸ *n.* One who advocates utilitarianism.

u·til·i·tar·i·an·ism (yo͞o-tĭl′ĭ-târ′ē-ə-nĭz′əm) ▸ *n.* **1.** The belief that the value of a thing or action is determined by its utility. **2.** The ethical theory that all action should be directed toward achieving the greatest happiness for the greatest number of people.

u·til·i·ty (yo͞o-tĭl′ĭ-tē) ▸ *n., pl.* **-ties. 1.** The quality or condition of being useful; usefulness. **2.** A useful article or device. **3.** An organization, such as a power company, that provides a public service under government regulation. **4.** *Comp. Sci.* A program that performs a specific task related to the management of computer functions, resources, or files.

u·til·ize (yo͞ot′l-īz′) ▸ *v.* **-ized, -iz·ing.** To put to use. **—u′til·iz′a·ble** *adj.* **—u′til·i·za′tion** *n.* **—u′til·iz′er** *n.*

ut·most (ŭt′mōst′) ▸ *adj.* **1.** Being or at the most distant limit or point; farthest. **2.** Of the highest or greatest degree, amount, or intensity. **—ut′most′** *n.*

U·to-Az·tec·an (yo͞o′tō-ăz′tĕk′ən) ▸ *n.* **1.** A language family of North and Central America that includes Ute, Hopi, Nahuatl, and Shoshone. **2.** A member of a people speaking a Uto-Aztecan language. **—U′to-Az′tec·an** *adj.*

u·to·pi·a (yo͞o-tō′pē-ə) ▸ *n.* **1.** often **Utopia** An ideally perfect place, esp. in its social, political, and moral aspects. **2.** An impractical, idealistic scheme. **—u·to′pi·an** *adj.*

ut·ter[1] (ŭt′ər) ▸ *v.* **1.** To send forth with the voice: *uttered a cry.* **2.** To pronounce or speak. **—ut′ter·a·ble** *adj.*

ut·ter[2] (ŭt′ər) ▸ *adj.* Complete; absolute; entire: *utter darkness.*

ut·ter·ance (ŭt′ər-əns) ▸ *n.* **1a.** The act of uttering. **b.** The power of speaking; speech. **2.** Something expressed; statement.

ut·ter·ly (ŭt′ər-lē) ▸ *adv.* Completely; absolutely; entirely.

ut·ter·most (ŭt′ər-mōst′) ▸ *adj.* **1.** Utmost. **2.** Outermost. **—ut′ter·most′** *n.*

U-turn (yo͞o′tûrn′) ▸ *n.* A turn, as by a vehicle, reversing the direction of travel.

UV ▸ *abbr.* ultraviolet

u·vu·la (yo͞o′vyə-lə) ▸ *n.* A small, conical, fleshy mass of tissue suspended from the center of the soft palate.

ux·o·ri·ous (ŭk-sôr′ē-əs, ŭg-zôr′-) ▸ *adj.* Excessively submissive or devoted to one's wife. **—ux·o′ri·ous·ness** *n.*

Uz·bek (o͝oz′bĕk′, ŭz′-) ▸ *n., pl.* **-bek** or **-beks. 1.** A member of a Turkic people inhabiting Uzbekistan and neighboring areas. **2.** The Turkic language of the Uzbeks.

Uz·bek·i·stan (o͝oz-bĕk′ĭ-stăn′, -stän′, ŭz-) ▸ A country of W-central Asia.

THESAURUS

useless *adj.* —*See* FUTILE, INEFFECTUAL (1), INEFFECTUAL (2), UNWORKABLE.

uselessness *n.* —*See* FUTILITY, INEFFECTUALITY.

user *n.* —*See* CONSUMER.

usher *n.* —*See* GUIDE.

usher *v.* —*See* GUIDE.

usher in *v.* —*See* INTRODUCE (3), PROCLAIM.

usual *adj.* —*See* COMMON (1), CONVENTIONAL.

usual *n.* A regular or customary matter, condition, or course of events ▸ average, commonplace, everyday, form, norm, ordinary, pattern, routine, rule.

usually *adv.* In an expected or customary manner ▸ commonly, consistently, customarily, frequently, generally, habitually, mainly, mostly, naturally, normally, often, ordinarily, regularly, routinely, typically. *Idioms:* as usual, by and large, on the whole, per usual. [*Compare* APPROXIMATELY, FAIRLY.]

usualness *n.* The quality or condition of being usual ▸ averageness, commonness, customariness, habitualness, normalcy, normality, ordinariness, prevalence, regularity, routineness.

usurp *v.* To take the place of another against the other's will ▸ cut out, displace, force out, supplant. [*Compare* ASSUME, OCCUPY.] —*See also* SEIZE (1).

usurpation *n.* —*See* SEIZURE (2).

usurper *n.* —*See* DICTATOR.

utensil *n.* A device used to do work or perform a task ▸ implement, instrument, tool. [*Compare* AGENT, DEVICE, GADGET.]

utilitarian *adj.* —*See* PRACTICAL.

utility *n.* —*See* USE (2).

utilizable *adj.* —*See* OPEN (4), USABLE.

utilization *n.* —*See* CONSUMPTION, DUTY (2), EXERCISE (1).

utilize *v.* —*See* OPERATE, USE.

utmost *adj.* —*See* EXTREME (1), MAXIMUM.

utmost *n.* —*See* MAXIMUM.

utopian *adj.* —*See* IDEALISTIC.

utopian *n.* —*See* DREAMER (1).

utter[1] *v.* —*See* PRONOUNCE, SAY.

utter[2] *adj.* Completely such, without qualification or exception ▸ absolute, all-out, arrant, complete, consummate, crashing, damned, dead, downright, flat, full-fledged, out-and-out, outright, perfect, plain, pure, sheer, stark, thorough, thoroughgoing, total, unbounded, unequivocal, unlimited, unmitigated, unqualified, unrelieved, unreserved. *Informal:* flat out, positive. *Idiom:* out-and-out. [*Compare* MAXIMUM.]

utterance *n.* Something said ▸ saying, statement, word. [*Compare* LANGUAGE.] —*See also* EXPRESSION (1), SPEECH (1), VOICING.

uttered *adj.* —*See* ORAL.

utterly *adv.* —*See* COMPLETELY (1).

uttermost *adj.* —*See* EXTREME (1), MAXIMUM.

uttermost *n.* —*See* MAXIMUM.

U-turn *n.* —*See* REVERSAL (1).

V

v or **V** (vē) ► *n., pl.* **v's** or **V's** also **vs** or **Vs**. The 22nd letter of the English alphabet.

V[1] ► **1.** The symbol for the element **vanadium**. **2.** *Elect.* The symbol for **potential** 2. **3.** also **v** The symbol for the Roman numeral 5.

V[2] ► *abbr.* **1.** velocity **2.** victory **3.** volt **4.** volume **5.** vowel

v. ► *abbr.* **1.** verb **2.** verse **3.** version **4.** versus **5.** vide **6.** volume (book)

VA ► *abbr.* **1.** Veterans' Administration **2.** or **Va.** Virginia

va·can·cy (vā′kən-sē) ► *n., pl.* **-cies. 1.** The condition of being vacant; emptiness. **2.** An empty space; void. **3.** A position, office, or lodging that is unfilled or unoccupied.

va·cant (vā′kənt) ► *adj.* **1a.** Containing nothing; empty. **b.** Unoccupied. **2a.** Lacking intelligence. **b.** Lacking expression; blank. **3.** Free from activity; idle. **—va′cant·ly** *adv.*

va·cate (vā′kāt′, vā-kāt′) ► *v.* **-cat·ed, -cat·ing. 1.** To make vacant. **2.** *Law* To make void or annul.

va·ca·tion (vā-kā′shən, və-) ► *n.* A period of time devoted to rest or relaxation, as from work or study. ► *v.* To take or spend a vacation. **—va·ca′tion·er** *n.*

vac·ci·nate (văk′sə-nāt′) ► *v.* **-nat·ed, -nat·ing.** To inoculate with a vaccine in order to produce immunity to an infectious disease. **—vac′ci·na′tion** *n.*

vac·cine (văk-sēn′, văk′sēn′) ► *n.* A preparation of a weakened or killed pathogen, such as a bacterium or virus, used to vaccinate.

vac·il·late (văs′ə-lāt′) ► *v.* **-lat·ed, -lat·ing. 1.** To sway to and fro. **2.** To swing indecisively from one course of action or opinion to another; waver. **—vac′il·la′tion** *n.*

va·cu·i·ty (vă-kyōō′ĭ-tē, və-) ► *n., pl.* **-ties. 1.** Total absence of matter; emptiness. **2.** An empty space; vacuum. **3.** Emptiness of mind. **4.** Something, esp. a remark, that is vacuous.

vac·u·ole (văk′yōō-ōl′) ► *n.* A small, usu. fluid-filled cavity in the cytoplasm of a cell.

vac·u·ous (văk′yōō-əs) ► *adj.* **1.** Empty. **2.** Inane; stupid. **3.** Blank; vacant. **—vac′u·ous·ness** *n.*

vac·u·um (văk′yōō-əm, -yōōm, -yəm) ► *n., pl.* **-u·ums** or **-u·a** (-yōō-ə). **1a.** Absence of matter. **b.** A space relatively empty of matter. **2.** A state or feeling of emptiness; void. ► *v.* To clean with a vacuum cleaner.

vacuum bottle ► *n.* A bottle or flask having a vacuum between its inner and outer walls, designed to maintain the desired temperature of the contents.

vacuum cleaner ► *n.* An electrical appliance that cleans surfaces by suction.

vac·u·um-packed (văk′yōō-əm-păkt′, văk′yōōm-, văk′yəm-) ► *adj.* Packed in an airtight container.

vacuum tube ► *n.* An electron tube that has an internal vacuum sufficiently high to permit electrons to move with low interaction with any remaining gas molecules.

va·de me·cum (vā′dē mā′kəm) ► *n., pl.* **-cums.** A useful thing that one constantly carries about.

vag·a·bond (văg′ə-bŏnd′) ► *n.* **1.** A person without a permanent home who moves from place to place; wanderer. **2.** A tramp; vagrant. **—vag′a·bond′** *adj.* **—vag′a·bond′age** *n.*

va·ga·ry (vā′gə-rē, və-gâr′ē) ► *n., pl.* **-ries. 1.** An erratic or capricious happening. **2.** A whim.

va·gi·na (və-jī′nə) ► *n., pl.* **-nas** or **-nae** (-nē). The passage leading from the vulva to the uterus in female mammals. **—vag′i·nal** (văj′ə-nəl) *adj.*

va·grant (vā′grənt) ► *n.* **1.** One who wanders from place to place without a permanent home or livelihood. **2.** One who lives on the streets and constitutes a public nuisance. ► *adj.* **1.** Wandering from place to place; roving. **2.** Moving in a random fashion. **—va′gran·cy** *n.*

vague (vāg) ► *adj.* **vagu·er, vagu·est. 1.** Not clearly expressed or outlined. **2.** Lacking definite shape, form, or character; indistinct. **3.** Indistinctly perceived, understood, or recalled. **—vague′ly** *adv.* **—vague′ness** *n.*

vain (vān) ► *adj.* **-er, -est. 1.** Not successful; futile. **2.** Lacking substance or worth; hollow. **3.** Excessively proud of one's appearance or accomplishments; conceited. ***—idiom:* in vain 1.** To no avail; without success. **2.** Irreverently or disrespectfully. **—vain′ly** *adv.*

vain·glo·ry (vān′glôr′ē) ► *n., pl.* **-ries. 1.** Excessive pride and vanity. **2.** Vain and ostentatious display. **—vain·glo′ri·ous** *adj.*

val·ance (văl′əns, vā′ləns) ► *n.* **1.** An ornamental drapery hung across a top edge, as of a bed. **2.** A decorative frame mounted esp. across the top of a window.

vale (vāl) ► *n.* A valley; dale.

val·e·dic·tion (văl′ĭ-dĭk′shən) ► *n.* An act or expression of leave-taking.

val·e·dic·to·ri·an (văl′ĭ-dĭk-tôr′ē-ən) ► *n.* The student, usu. with the highest academic rank in a class, who delivers the valedictory at graduation.

val·e·dic·to·ry (văl′ĭ-dĭk′tə-rē) ► *n., pl.* **-ries.** A farewell address, esp. at graduation exercises. **—val′e·dic′to·ry** *adj.*

va·lence (vā′ləns) ► *n. Chem.* **1.** The capacity of an atom or group of atoms to combine in specific proportions with other atoms. **2.** An integer used to represent this capacity.

Va·len·ci·a (və-lĕn′shē-ə, -sē-ə) ► **1.** A city of E Spain on the **Gulf of Valencia,** a wide inlet of the Mediterranean Sea.

THESAURUS

vacancy *n.* —*See* EMPTINESS (2), NOTHINGNESS (2).

vacant *adj.* Lacking intelligent thought or content ► blank, empty, empty-headed, impassive, inane, lifeless, unreasoning, vacuous. [*Compare* ABSENT-MINDED, FOOLISH, STUPID.] —*See also* EMPTY (1), HOLLOW (1), IDLE (1), LONELY (1), OPEN (4).

vacate *v.* —*See* EMPTY.

vacation *n.* A regularly scheduled period spent away from work or duty, often in recreation ► furlough, holiday, leave, sabbatical. *Idiom:* time (or day) off. [*Compare* BREAK, TRIP.]

vacationer *n.* —*See* TOURIST.

vaccinate *v.* —*See* ADMINISTER (3).

vacillant *adj.* —*See* HESITANT.

vacillate *v.* To shift from one attitude, interest, condition, or emotion to another ► dilly-dally, swing, waver. —*See also* CHANGE (2), HESITATE, SWAY.

vacillating *adj.* —*See* DOUBTFUL (2).

vacillation *n.* —*See* HESITATION.

vacillatory *adj.* —*See* HESITANT.

vacuity *n.* —*See* EMPTINESS (2), HOLE (1), NOTHINGNESS (2).

vacuous *adj.* —*See* EMPTY (1), VACANT.

vacuousness *n.* —*See* EMPTINESS (2).

vacuum *n.* —*See* EMPTINESS (1), NOTHINGNESS (2).

vagabond *n.* —*See* HOBO, PAUPER.

vagabond *adj.* —*See* NOMADIC.

vagary *n.* —*See* FANCY.

vagrant *adj.* —*See* CAPRICIOUS, NOMADIC.

vagrant *n.* —*See* HOBO.

vague *adj.* —*See* AMBIGUOUS (2), INDEFINITE (2), UNCLEAR.

vagueness *n.* The quality or state of being imprecise or indefinite ► ambiguity, ambiguousness, cloudiness, equivocalness, fuzziness, imprecision, indefiniteness, indistinctness, inexactness, looseness, nebulousness, obscureness, obscurity, uncertainty, unclearness.

vain *adj.* —*See* EGOTISTIC (1), FUTILE, HOLLOW (1).

vainglorious *adj.* —*See* EGOTISTIC (1).

vainglory *n.* —*See* EGOTISM.

vainness *n.* —*See* EGOTISM, FUTILITY.

vale *n.* —*See* VALLEY.

valediction *n.* —*See* DEPARTURE.

valedictory *adj.* —*See* PARTING.

2. A city of N Venezuela WSW of Caracas on the W shore of **Lake Valencia.**

–valent ► *suff.* Having a specified valence or valences: *polyvalent.*

val·en·tine (văl′ən-tīn′) ► *n.* **1.** A usu. sentimental card sent to a sweetheart or friend on Valentine's Day. **2.** One's chosen sweetheart on Valentine's Day.

Valentine, Saint (fl. 3rd cent. A.D.) ► Roman Christian martyr.

Val·en·tine's Day or **Val·en·tines Day** (văl′ən-tīnz′) ► *n.* Feb. 14, celebrated in various countries by the exchange of valentines.

va·le·ri·an (və-lîr′ē-ən) ► *n.* A plant widely cultivated for its small fragrant flowers and for use in medicine as a sedative.

val·et (vă-lā′, văl′ā, văl′ĭt) ► *n.* **1.** A man's male servant, who takes care of his clothes and performs other personal services. **2.** An employee, as in a hotel, who performs personal services for guests.

val·e·tu·di·nar·i·an (văl′ĭ-to͞od′n-âr′ē-ən, -tyo͞od′-) ► *n.* A sickly or weak person who is constantly concerned with his or her health. **—val′e·tu′di·nar′i·an·ism** *n.*

Val·hal·la (văl-hăl′ə, väl-hä′lə) ► *n. Myth.* In Norse myth, the hall in which Odin received the souls of slain heroes.

val·iant (văl′yənt) ► *adj.* Possessing, showing, or acting with valor; brave. **—val′iance** *n.* **—val′iant·ly** *adv.*

val·id (văl′ĭd) ► *adj.* **1.** Founded on evidence or fact; sound: *a valid objection.* **2.** Having legal force; effective: *a valid passport.* **—va·lid′i·ty, val′id·ness** *n.* **—val′id·ly** *adv.*

val·i·date (văl′ĭ-dāt′) ► *v.* **-dat·ed, -dat·ing. 1.** To make legally valid. **2.** To substantiate; verify. **—val′i·da′tion** *n.*

va·lise (və-lēs′) ► *n.* A small piece of hand luggage.

Val·i·um (văl′ē-əm) ► A trademark for the drug diazepam.

Val·kyr·ie (văl-kîr′ē, -kī′rē, văl′kə-rē) ► *n. Myth.* In Norse myth, any of Odin's handmaidens who conducted the souls of the slain to Valhalla.

val·ley (văl′ē) ► *n., pl.* **-leys. 1.** A long narrow lowland between mountains or hills. **2.** An area drained by a river system. **3.** The area where two slopes of a roof form a drainage channel.

Valley Forge ► A village of SE PA; site of George Washington's winter headquarters (1777–78).

val·or (văl′ər) ► *n.* Courage and boldness, as in battle; bravery. **—val′or·ous** *adj.*

val·u·a·ble (văl′yo͞o-ə-bəl, văl′yə-) ► *adj.* **1.** Having high monetary or material value. **2.** Of great importance, use, or service. ► *n.* often **valuables** A valuable personal possession, such as a piece of jewelry.

val·u·ate (văl′yo͞o-āt′) ► *v.* **-at·ed, -at·ing.** To set a value for; appraise. **—val′u·a′tor** *n.*

val·u·a·tion (văl′yo͞o-ā′shən) ► *n.* **1.** The act of assessing value or price; appraisal. **2.** Assessed value or price.

val·ue (văl′yo͞o) ► *n.* **1.** A fair equivalent or return for something, as goods or services. **2.** Monetary or material worth. **3.** Worth as measured in usefulness or importance; merit. **4.** A principle, standard, or quality considered worthwhile or desirable. **5.** Precise meaning, as of a word. **6.** *Math.* An assigned or calculated numerical quantity. **7.** *Mus.* The relative duration of a tone or rest. **8.** The relative darkness or lightness of a color. **9.** *Ling.* The sound quality of a letter or diphthong. ► *v.* **-ued, -u·ing. 1.** To determine or estimate the value of; appraise. **2.** To regard highly; esteem. **3.** To rate according to relative worth or desirability; evaluate. **—val′ue·less** *adj.*

val·ue-add·ed tax (văl′yo͞o-ăd′ĭd) ► *n.* A tax on the estimated market value added to a product or material at each stage of manufacture or distribution.

valve (vălv) ► *n.* **1.** *Anat.* A membranous structure, as in a vein, that prevents the return flow of a fluid. **2a.** A device that regulates the flow of gases or liquids by blocking and opening passageways. **b.** The movable control element of such a device. **c.** A device in a brass wind instrument that permits change in pitch by a rapid varying of the air column in a tube. **3.** A paired or separable structure or part, as of a mollusk shell or seed pod. **—valved** *adj.*

va·moose (vă-mo͞os′, və-) ► *v.* **-moosed, -moos·ing.** *Slang* To leave hurriedly.

vamp[1] (vămp) ► *n.* **1.** The part of a boot or shoe covering the instep and often the toe. **2.** *Mus.* An improvised accompaniment. ► *v.* **1.** To provide with a new vamp. **2.** To patch up. **3.** To improvise. **—vamp′er** *n.*

vamp[2] (vămp) ► *n. Informal* A woman who exploits men esp. by seduction. **—vamp** *v.*

vam·pire (văm′pīr′) ► *n.* **1.** A reanimated corpse believed to rise from the grave at night to suck the blood of sleeping people. **2.** A person who preys on others. **3.** Any of various tropical American bats that bite mammals and birds to feed on their blood.

van[1] (văn) ► *n.* **1.** An enclosed truck or wagon, as for transporting goods or livestock. **2.** A roomy motor vehicle with rear doors and often side panels. **3.** *Chiefly Brit.* A railroad baggage or freight car.

van[2] (văn) ► *n.* The vanguard.

va·na·di·um (və-nā′dē-əm) ► *n. Symbol* **V** A bright white, ductile metallic element used in some steels and as a catalyst. At. no. 23.

Van Allen belt ► *n.* Either of two zones of highly energetic, charged particles trapped in Earth's magnetic field, surrounding the planet and serving as a source of high-intensity particulate radiation.

Van Bu·ren (byo͝or′ən), **Martin** (1782–1862) ► The 8th US President (1837–41).

Van·cou·ver (văn-ko͞o′vər) ► A city of SW British Columbia, Canada, opposite Vancouver Island.

Vancouver Island ► An island in the Pacific off SW British Columbia, Canada.

Van·dal (văn′dl) ► *n.* **1. vandal** One who commits vandalism. **2.** A member of a Germanic people that overran Gaul, Spain, and N Africa in the 4th and 5th cent. A.D. and sacked Rome in 455.

van·dal·ism (văn′dl-ĭz′əm) ► *n.* Willful or malicious destruction or defacement of public or private property. **—van′dal·ize′** *v.*

Van·dyke (văn-dīk′) ► *n.* A short pointed beard.

vane (vān) ► *n.* **1.** A weathervane. **2.** A usu. thin rigid surface radially mounted along an axis that is turned by or used to turn a fluid. **3.** A metal guidance or stabilizing fin attached to the tail of a bomb or other missile.

van Gogh (văn gō′, gôKH′), **Vincent** (1853–90) ► Dutch painter.

van·guard (văn′gärd) ► *n.* **1.** The foremost position in an

THESAURUS

valiance or **valiancy** or **valiantness** *n.* —*See* COURAGE.

valiant *adj.* —*See* BRAVE.

valid *adj.* —*See* AUTHENTIC (2), BELIEVABLE, LAWFUL, SOUND[2].

validate *v.* —*See* CONFIRM (1), PROVE.

validation *n.* —*See* CONFIRMATION (2).

validity *n.* —*See* LEGALITY, VERACITY.

valise *n.* —*See* SUITCASE.

valley *n.* An elongated lowland between mountains or hills ► canyon, dale, dell, glen, gorge, hollow, lowland, swale, vale.

valor *n.* —*See* COURAGE.

valorous *adj.* —*See* BRAVE.

valuable *adj.* —*See* BENEFICIAL, COSTLY.

valuate *v.* —*See* ESTIMATE (1).

valuation *n.* A measure of those qualities that determine merit, desirability, usefulness, or importance ► account, value, worth. [*Compare* COST, IMPORTANCE.] —*See also* ESTIMATE (1).

value *v.* To have a high opinion of or regard for ► admire, appreciate, cherish, consider, esteem, honor, prize, regard, respect, treasure. ***Idioms:*** hold dear, look up to, think highly (*or* much *or* well) of, set store by. [*Compare* REVERE, ENJOY, LIKE[1].] —*See also* ESTIMATE (1).

value *n.* A measure of those qualities that determine merit, desirability, usefulness, or importance ► account, valuation, worth. [*Compare* COST, IMPORTANCE.] —*See also* MEANING, MERIT.

valueless *adj.* —*See* WORTHLESS.

vamoose *v.* —*See* GO (1), RUN (2).

vamp *n. Informal* A woman who is given to flirting ► coquette, flirt, tease. —*See also* SEDUCTRESS.

vamp *v.* —*See* CHARM (2).

vandalize *v.* To injure or destroy property maliciously ► wreck. *Slang:* trash. [*Compare* DESTROY.]

vanguard *n.* A leading contestant or sure winner ► favorite, front-runner,

army or fleet. **2.** The foremost or leading position in a trend or movement.

va·nil·la (və-nĭl′ə) ▸ *n.* **1.** A tropical American vine of the orchid family, cultivated for its long narrow seedpods. **2.** The seedpod of this plant. **3.** A flavoring extract prepared from the seedpods of this plant.

va·nil·lin (və-nĭl′ĭn, văn′ə-lĭn) ▸ *n.* A crystalline compound found in vanilla beans and used in perfumes, flavorings, and pharmaceuticals.

van·ish (văn′ĭsh) ▸ *v.* **1.** To pass out of sight, esp. quickly. **2.** To pass out of existence. **—van′ish·er** *n.*

van·i·ty (văn′ĭ-tē) ▸ *n., pl.* **-ties. 1.** Excessive pride in one's appearance or accomplishments. **2.** Uselessness; worthlessness. **3a.** Something vain, futile, or worthless. **b.** Something about which one is vain. **4.** A vanity case. **5.** See **dressing table**.

vanity case ▸ *n.* **1.** A small handbag or case used for carrying cosmetics or toiletries. **2.** A woman's compact.

vanity plate ▸ *n.* A license plate for a motor vehicle bearing a combination of letters or numbers selected by the purchaser.

vanity press ▸ *n.* A publisher that publishes a book at the expense of the author.

van·quish (văng′kwĭsh, văn′-) ▸ *v.* **1.** To defeat, as in a battle or contest. **2.** To overcome or subdue. **—van′quish·er** *n.*

van·tage (văn′tĭj) ▸ *n.* **1.** An advantage in a competition or conflict. **2.** Something, as a strategic position, that provides superiority. **3.** A position affording a comprehensive view or perspective.

Va·nu·a·tu (vä′no͞o-ä′to͞o). Formerly **New Hebrides** ▸ An island country of the S Pacific E of N Australia. **—Va′nu·a′tu·an** *adj. & n.*

vap·id (văp′ĭd, vā′pĭd) ▸ *adj.* Lacking liveliness, zest, or interest; flat or dull. **—va·pid′i·ty, vap′id·ness** *n.*

va·por (vā′pər) ▸ *n.* **1.** Barely visible or cloudy diffused matter, such as mist, suspended in the air. **2.** The gaseous state of a substance that is liquid or solid under ordinary conditions. **3.** *Archaic* Something insubstantial or fleeting. **4. vapors** *Archaic* Depression or hysteria. ▸ *v.* **1.** To give off vapor. **2.** To evaporate.

va·por·ize (vā′pə-rīz′) ▸ *v.* **-ized, -iz·ing.** To convert or be converted into vapor. **—va′por·i·za′tion** *n.* **—va′por·iz′er** *n.*

vapor lock ▸ *n.* A pocket of vaporized gasoline in the fuel line of an internal-combustion engine that obstructs the flow of fuel.

va·por·ous (vā′pər-əs) ▸ *adj.* **1.** Of or resembling vapor. **2a.** Producing vapors; volatile. **b.** Giving off or full of vapors. **3.** Insubstantial, vague, or ethereal. **—va′por·ous·ness** *n.*

va·pour (vā′pər) ▸ *n. & v. Chiefly Brit.* Vapor.

va·que·ro (vä-kâr′ō) ▸ *n., pl.* **-ros.** *Regional* See **cowboy**.

var·i·a·ble (vâr′ē-ə-bəl, văr′-) ▸ *adj.* **1a.** Likely to vary; changeable. **b.** Inconstant; fickle. **2.** *Biol.* Tending to deviate, as from an established type; aberrant. ▸ *n.* **1.** Something that is variable. **2.** *Math.* **a.** A quantity capable of assuming any of a set of values. **b.** A symbol representing such a quantity. **—var′i·a·bil′i·ty, var′i·a·ble·ness** *n.* **—var′i·a·bly** *adv.*

var·i·ance (vâr′ē-əns, văr′-) ▸ *n.* **1a.** Variation; difference. **b.** The degree of such variation. **2.** A difference of opinion; dispute. **3.** *Law* License to engage in an act contrary to a usual rule.

var·i·ant (vâr′ē-ənt, văr′-) ▸ *adj.* **1.** Exhibiting variation; differing. **2.** Liable to vary; variable. ▸ *n.* Something exhibiting variation in form from another, as a different spelling of the same word.

var·i·a·tion (vâr′ē-ā′shən, văr′-) ▸ *n.* **1.** The act, process, or result of varying. **2.** The extent or degree to which something varies. **3.** Something differing from another of the same type. **4.** *Mus.* An altered version of a given theme, diverging from it by melodic ornamentation and by changes in harmony, rhythm, or key.

var·i·col·ored (vâr′ĭ-kŭl′ərd, văr′-) ▸ *adj.* Having a variety of colors; variegated.

var·i·cose (văr′ĭ-kōs′) ▸ *adj.* Abnormally swollen or knotted: *varicose veins.* **—var′i·cos′i·ty** *n.*

var·ied (vâr′ēd, văr′-) ▸ *adj.* **1.** Varying; diverse. **2.** Modified; altered. **3.** Varicolored.

var·i·e·gate (vâr′ē-ĭ-gāt′, vâr′ĭ-gāt′, văr′-) ▸ *v.* **-gat·ed, -gat·ing. 1.** To change the appearance of, esp. by marking with different colors. **2.** To give variety to. **—var′i·e·ga′tion** *n.*

va·ri·e·ty (və-rī′ĭ-tē) ▸ *n., pl.* **-ties. 1.** The quality or condition of being various. **2.** A number of different things; assortment. **3.** A group that is distinguished from other groups by a specific characteristic or set of characteristics. **4.** *Biol.* A subdivision of a species consisting of naturally occurring or selectively bred populations or individuals. **—va·ri′e·tal** *adj.*

variety show ▸ *n.* A theatrical entertainment consisting of successive unrelated acts.

variety store ▸ *n.* A retail store that carries a variety of usu. inexpensive merchandise.

var·i·o·rum (vâr′ē-ôr′əm, văr′-) ▸ *n.* An edition of a written work with notes by various scholars and often with various versions of the text.

var·i·ous (vâr′ē-əs, văr′-) ▸ *adj.* **1a.** Of diverse kinds. **b.** Unlike; different. **2.** Being more than one. **3.** Many-sided; versatile. **4.** Individual; separate. **—var′i·ous·ly** *adv.*

var·let (vär′lĭt) ▸ *n.* **1.** An attendant or servant. **2.** A rascal; knave.

var·mint (vär′mĭnt) ▸ *n. Informal* A person or animal considered undesirable or troublesome.

var·nish (vär′nĭsh) ▸ *n.* **1a.** A paint containing a solvent and a binder, used to coat a surface with a hard, glossy, transparent film. **b.** The smooth coating resulting from the application of this paint. **2.** A deceptively attractive external appearance; gloss. ▸ *v.* **1.** To cover with varnish. **2.** To gloss: *tried to varnish the truth.*

var·si·ty (vär′sĭ-tē) ▸ *n., pl.* **-ties. 1.** The principal team representing a university, college, or school, as in sports. **2.** *Chiefly Brit.* A university.

var·y (vâr′ē, văr′ē) ▸ *v.* **-ied** (-ēd), **-y·ing. 1.** To cause or undergo

THESAURUS

leader, number one. *Informal:* shoo-in. —*See also* FOREFRONT, FORERUNNER.

vanilla *adj.* —*See* BARE (1).

vanish *v.* —*See* DISAPPEAR (1).

vanished *adj.* —*See* LOST (2).

vanishment *n.* —*See* DISAPPEARANCE.

vanity *n.* —*See* EGOTISM, FUTILITY.

vanquish *v.* —*See* DEFEAT.

vanquisher *n.* —*See* CONQUEROR.

vanquishing *adj.* —*See* VICTORIOUS.

vanquishment *n.* —*See* DEFEAT.

vantage *n.* —*See* ADVANTAGE (1), ADVANTAGE (3), VIEWPOINT.

vapid *adj.* —*See* INSIPID.

vapidity or **vapidness** *n.* —*See* DULLNESS, INSIPIDITY.

vapor *n.* —*See* HAZE.

vaporize *v.* —*See* EVAPORATE.

vaporous or **vapory** *adj.* —*See* SHEER².

variable *adj.* —*See* CAPRICIOUS, CHANGEABLE (1), UNEVEN.

variance *n.* —*See* CONFLICT, DIFFERENCE, VARIETY.

variant *n.* —*See* VARIATION.

variant *adj.* —*See* CHANGEABLE (1), DIFFERENT.

variation *n.* One that is slightly different from others of the same kind or designation ▸ adaptation, alteration, alternative, development, form, modification, permutation, variant, variety, version. —*See also* CHANGE (1), DEVIATION, DIFFERENCE.

varicolored *adj.* —*See* MULTICOLORED.

varied *adj.* —*See* VARIOUS.

variegate *v.* —*See* STREAK.

variegated *adj.* —*See* MULTICOLORED, VARIOUS.

variegation *n.* —*See* VARIETY.

variety *n.* The quality of being made of many different elements, forms, kinds, or individuals ▸ disparateness, diverseness, diversification, diversity, heterogeneity, heterogeneousness, miscellaneousness, multifariousness, multiformity, multiplicity, variance, variegation, variousness. —*See also* ASSORTMENT, [illegible], VARIATION.

variform *adj.* —*See* IRREGULAR.

various *adj.* Consisting of a number of different kinds ▸ assorted, disparate, divers, diverse, diversified, heterogeneous, miscellaneous, mixed, motley, multifarious, multiform, sundry, varied, variegated. [*Compare* COMPLEX.] —*See also* DIFFERENT, DISTINCT, SEVERAL, VERSATILE.

variousness *n.* —*See* VARIETY.

varnish *v.* —*See* COLOR (2), FINISH (2), GLOSS¹.

varnish *n.* —*See* FINISH, GLOSS¹.

vary *v.* —*See* CHANGE (1), CHANGE (2), CONFLICT, DEVIATE, DIFFER, GO (4).

change; modify or alter. **2.** To give variety to; make diverse. **3.** To be different; deviate.
vas (văs) ▸ *n., pl.* **va·sa** (vā′zə). *Anat.* A vessel or duct.
vas·cu·lar (văs′kyə-lər) ▸ *adj.* Of, characterized by, or containing vessels that carry or circulate fluids, such as blood, lymph, or sap.
vas def·er·ens (văs′ dĕf′ər-ənz, -ə-rĕnz′) ▸ *n.* The duct through which sperm is carried from a testis to the ejaculatory duct.
vase (vās, vāz, väz) ▸ *n.* An open container, as of glass, used for holding flowers or for ornamentation.
va·sec·to·my (və-sĕk′tə-mē) ▸ *n., pl.* **-mies.** Surgical removal of all or part of the vas deferens, usu. as a means of sterilization.
vaso– or **vas–** ▸ *pref.* **1.** Blood vessel: *vasoconstriction.* **2.** Vas deferens: *vasectomy.*
va·so·con·stric·tion (vā′zō-kən-strĭk′shən) ▸ *n.* Constriction of a blood vessel. **—va′so·con·stric′tor** *n.*
va·so·dil·a·tion (vā′zō-dī-lā′shən, -dĭ-) also **va·so·dil·a·ta·tion** (-dĭl′ə-tā′shən, -dī′lə-) ▸ *n.* Dilation of a blood vessel. **—va′so·di·la′tor** *n.*
va·so·mo·tor (vā′zō-mō′tər) ▸ *adj.* Causing or regulating constriction or dilation of blood vessels.
vas·sal (văs′əl) ▸ *n.* **1.** A person who held land from a feudal lord and received protection in return for homage and allegiance. **2.** A subordinate or dependent.
vas·sal·age (văs′ə-lĭj) ▸ *n.* **1.** The condition of being a vassal. **2.** The service, homage, and fealty required of a vassal. **3.** Subordination or subjection; servitude.
vast (văst) ▸ *adj.* **-er, -est.** Very great in size, amount, intensity, degree, or extent. **—vast′ly** *adv.* **—vast′ness** *n.*
vat (văt) ▸ *n.* A large vessel, such as a tub, used to hold or store liquids.
vat·ic (văt′ĭk) ▸ *adj.* Of or characteristic of a prophet; oracular.
Vat·i·can (văt′ĭ-kən) ▸ *n.* **1.** The official residence of the pope in Vatican City. **2.** The papal government; papacy.
Vatican City ▸ An independent papal state on the Tiber River within Rome, Italy.
va·tu (vä′to͞o) ▸ *n.* See **currency** table in Appendix.
vaude·ville (vôd′vĭl′, vōd′-, vô′də-) ▸ *n.* Stage entertainment offering a variety of short acts such as comedy and song-and-dance routines. **—vaude·vil′lian** *n.*
vault[1] (vôlt) ▸ *n.* **1.** An arched structure, usu. of masonry, serving to cover a space. **2.** Something resembling a vault. **3.** A room, such as a storeroom, with arched walls and ceiling, esp. when underground. **4.** A room or compartment for the safekeeping of valuables. **5.** A burial chamber. ▸ *v.* To construct, supply, or cover with a vault.
vault[2] (vôlt) ▸ *v.* To jump or leap over, esp. with the aid of a support such as the hands or a pole. **—vault** *n.* **—vault′er** *n.*
vault·ing horse (vôl′tĭng) ▸ *n.* A piece of gymnastic equipment with an upholstered body used esp. for vaulting.
vaunt (vônt, vŏnt) ▸ *v.* To boast; brag. **—vaunt** *n.*
vb. ▸ *abbr.* verb
V-chip (vē′chĭp′) ▸ *n.* A computer chip installed in a television to control the display of esp. sexual or violent programs.
VCR (vē′sē-är′) ▸ *n.* An electronic device for recording and playing back video images and sound on a videocassette.
veal (vēl) ▸ *n.* The meat of a calf.
vec·tor (vĕk′tər) ▸ *n.* **1.** *Math.* A quantity completely specified by a magnitude and a direction. **2.** *Pathol.* An organism that carries disease-causing microorganisms from one host to another.
Ve·da (vā′də, vē′-) ▸ *n.* *Hinduism* Any of the oldest Hindu sacred texts, composed in Sanskrit. **—Ve′dic** *adj.*
Ve·dan·ta (vĭ-dän′tə, -dăn′-) ▸ *n.* *Hinduism* The system of philosophy that further develops the implications in the Upanishads that all reality is a single principle. **—Ve·dan′tic** *adj.*
veep (vēp) ▸ *n.* *Slang* A vice president.
veer (vîr) ▸ *v.* To turn aside from a course, direction, or purpose. **—veer** *n.*
veg (vĕj) ▸ *v.* **vegged, veg·ging.** *Informal* To engage in relaxing or passive activities. Often used with *out.*
ve·gan (vē′gən, vĕj′ən) ▸ *n.* A vegetarian who eats plant products only.
veg·e·ta·ble (vĕj′tə-bəl, vĕj′ĭ-tə-) ▸ *n.* **1a.** A usu. herbaceous plant cultivated for an edible part, such as roots, leaves, or flowers. **b.** The edible part of such a plant. **c.** An organism classified as a plant. **2a.** A dull or passive person. **b.** One who is severely incapacitated, as by coma. **—veg′e·ta·ble** *adj.*
veg·e·tal (vĕj′ĭ-tl) ▸ *adj.* **1.** Of or characteristic of plants. **2.** Relating to growth rather than to sexual reproduction; vegetative.
veg·e·tar·i·an (vĕj′ĭ-târ′ē-ən) ▸ *n.* One whose diet consists primarily or wholly of vegetables, grains, and plant products and who eats no meat. **—veg′e·tar′i·an** *adj.* **—veg′e·tar′i·an·ism** *n.*
veg·e·tate (vĕj′ĭ-tāt′) ▸ *v.* **-tat·ed, -tat·ing.** **1.** To grow or sprout as a plant. **2.** To be in a state of physical or mental inactivity or insensibility.
veg·e·ta·tion (vĕj′ĭ-tā′shən) ▸ *n.* **1.** The act or process of vegetating. **2.** The plants of an area or region; plant life.
veg·e·ta·tive (vĕj′ĭ-tā′tĭv) ▸ *adj.* **1.** Of or characteristic of plants or their growth. **2.** *Biol.* **a.** Of or capable of growth. **b.** Of or functioning in processes such as growth or nutrition rather than sexual reproduction. **c.** Of or relating to asexual reproduction.
ve·he·ment (vē′ə-mənt) ▸ *adj.* **1.** Characterized by forcefulness of expression or intensity of emotion; fervid. **2.** Marked by vigor or energy; strong. **—ve′he·mence** *n.* **—ve′he·ment·ly** *adv.*
ve·hi·cle (vē′ĭ-kəl) ▸ *n.* **1.** A device for transporting persons or things; conveyance. **2.** A medium through which something is transmitted, expressed, or accomplished. **3.** A substance used as the medium in which active ingredients are applied or administered. **—ve·hic′u·lar** (vē-hĭk′yə-lər) *adj.*
veil (vāl) ▸ *n.* **1.** A length of often sheer cloth worn by women over the head, shoulders, and often the face. **2.** The life or vows of a nun: *take the veil.* **3.** Something that conceals or obscures: *a veil of secrecy.* ▸ *v.* To cover, conceal, or disguise with or as if with a veil.
vein (vān) ▸ *n.* **1.** A vessel through which blood returns to the heart. **2.** One of the branching structures forming the framework of a leaf or an insect's wing. **3.** *Geol.* A long, regularly shaped deposit of an ore; lode. **4.** A long wavy strip of color, as in marble. **5.** A pervading character or quality; strain. **6.** A particular turn of mind: *spoke in a serious vein.* ▸ *v.* To mark, form, or decorate with or as if with veins. **—veined** *adj.*
ve·lar (vē′lər) ▸ *adj.* **1.** Of a velum, esp. the soft palate. **2.** *Ling.* Articulated with the back of the tongue touching or near the soft palate.

THESAURUS

varying *adj.* —*See* CHANGEABLE (1).
vassal *n.* —*See* SLAVE.
vast *adj.* —*See* ENORMOUS.
vastly *adv.* —*See* VERY.
vastness *n.* —*See* ENORMOUSNESS.
vat *n.* A large vessel used to hold or store liquids ▸ barrel, basin, cask, cistern, keg, tank, tub, vessel.
vatic or **vatical** or **vaticinal** *adj.* —*See* PROPHETIC.
vaticinate *v.* —*See* PROPHESY.
vaticination *n.* —*See* PROPHECY.
vaticinator *n.* —*See* PROPHET.
vault[1] *n.* —*See* DEPOSITORY, GRAVE[1].
vault[2] *v.* —*See* JUMP (1).
vault *n.* The act of jumping ▸ jump, pounce, leap, spring. [*Compare* FALL.]
vaunt *v.* —*See* BOAST.
vaunt *n.* —*See* BOAST.
vaunter *n.* —*See* BRAGGART.
vector *n.* The compass direction in which a ship or aircraft moves ▸ bearing, course, heading. [*Compare* DIRECTION.]
veer *v.* —*See* DEVIATE, DIGRESS, SWERVE, TURN (2).
vegetate *v.* —*See* IDLE (1).
vegetation *n.* The plants of an area or region ▸ flora, plant life, verdure.
vehemence or **vehemency** *n.* —*See* INTENSITY.
vehement *adj.* —*See* INTENSE.
veil *n.* A covering that obscures or hides something ▸ cloak, cover, mantle, screen, shroud. [*Compare* COVER, FAÇADE.] —*See also* DISGUISE.
veil *v.* —*See* CONCEAL, DISGUISE, WRAP (2).
vein *n.* An inherent, contrasting or unexpected quality, especially in a person's character ▸ strain, streak. [*Compare* DISPOSITION, INCLINATION.] —*See also* MOOD, STYLE, VESSEL (2).

Vel·cro (vĕl′krō) ▸ A trademark for a fastening tape used esp. on cloth products.

veld also **veldt** (vĕlt, fĕlt) ▸ *n.* Any of the open grazing areas of S Africa.

vel·lum (vĕl′əm) ▸ *n.* **1.** A fine parchment made from calfskin, lambskin, or kidskin and used in making books. **2.** A paper resembling vellum.

ve·loc·i·rap·tor (və-lŏs′ə-răp′tər) ▸ *n.* **1.** A small meat-eating dinosaur having short front legs, sharp curved claws, and a long flat snout with sharp teeth.

ve·loc·i·ty (və-lŏs′ĭ-tē) ▸ *n., pl.* **-ties.** **1.** Rapidity of motion; speed. **2.** *Phys.* The rate per unit of time at which a body moves in a specified direction.

ve·lour or **ve·lours** (və-lo͝or′) ▸ *n., pl.* **-lours** (-lo͝orz′). A closely napped fabric resembling velvet.

ve·lum (vē′ləm) ▸ *n., pl.* **-la** (-lə). **1.** A covering or partition of thin membranous tissue. **2.** The soft palate.

vel·vet (vĕl′vĭt) ▸ *n.* **1.** A soft fabric having a smooth dense pile and a plain underside. **2.** Something suggesting the smooth surface of velvet. **3.** The soft furry covering on the developing antlers of deer.

vel·vet·een (vĕl′vĭ-tēn′) ▸ *n.* A cotton pile fabric resembling velvet.

ve·na ca·va (vē′nə kā′və) ▸ *n., pl.* **ve·nae ca·vae** (vē′nē kā′vē). Either of two large veins that empty into the right atrium of the heart.

ve·nal (vē′nəl) ▸ *adj.* Open to, marked by, or susceptible to bribery; corrupt or corruptible. **—ve·nal′i·ty** (-năl′ĭ-tē) *n.* **—ve′nal·ly** *adv.*

ve·na·tion (vē-nā′shən, vĕ-) ▸ *n.* Distribution or arrangement of a system of veins.

vend (vĕnd) ▸ *v.* To sell, esp. by peddling.

ven·det·ta (vĕn-dĕt′ə) ▸ *n.* A bitter feud, esp. between two families.

vend·ing machine (vĕn′dĭng) ▸ *n.* A self-service machine that dispenses merchandise after payment is made.

vend·or or **ven·der** (vĕn′dər) ▸ *n.* **1.** One that sells or vends: *a vendor of fruit.* **2.** One that provides products or services to a business for a fee.

ve·neer (və-nîr′) ▸ *n.* **1.** A thin surface layer, as of finely grained wood, glued to a base of inferior material. **2.** A surface show; façade. ▸ *v.* To overlay with a veneer.

ven·er·a·ble (vĕn′ər-ə-bəl) ▸ *adj.* **1.** Commanding respect by virtue of age or position. **2.** Worthy of reverence, as by religious association. **—ven′er·a·bil′i·ty** *n.*

ven·er·ate (vĕn′ə-rāt′) ▸ *v.* To regard with great respect or reverence. **—ven′er·a′tion** *n.*

ve·ne·re·al (və-nîr′ē-əl) ▸ *adj.* Of or transmitted by sexual intercourse.

venereal disease ▸ *n.* A sexually transmitted disease.

ve·ne·tian blind (və-nē′shən) ▸ *n.* A window blind made of thin horizontal adjustable slats that overlap when closed.

Ven·e·zue·la (vĕn′ə-zwā′lə) ▸ A country of N South America on the Caribbean Sea. **—Ven′e·zue′lan** *adj. & n.*

ven·geance (vĕn′jəns) ▸ *n.* Infliction of punishment in return for a wrong committed; retribution.

venge·ful (vĕnj′fəl) ▸ *adj.* Desiring vengeance; vindictive. **—venge′ful·ly** *adv.* **—venge′ful·ness** *n.*

ve·ni·al (vē′nē-əl, vēn′yəl) ▸ *adj.* Easily excused or forgiven; pardonable; minor.

Ven·ice (vĕn′ĭs) ▸ A city of NE Italy on islets within a lagoon in the **Gulf of Venice,** a wide inlet of the N Adriatic. **—Ve·ne′tian** (və-nē′shən) *n. & adj.*

ve·ni·re (və-nī′rē, -nîr′ē) ▸ *n.* **1.** A writ summoning prospective jurors. **2.** A panel from which a jury is selected.

ve·ni·re·man (və-nī′rē-mən, -nîr′ē-) ▸ *n.* A person summoned to jury duty under a venire.

ven·i·son (vĕn′ĭ-sən, -zən) ▸ *n.* The flesh of a deer used as food.

ven·om (vĕn′əm) ▸ *n.* **1.** A poisonous secretion of an animal, such as a snake or spider, usu. transmitted by a bite or sting. **2.** Malice; spite.

ven·om·ous (vĕn′ə-məs) ▸ *adj.* **1.** Secreting venom: *a venomous snake.* **2.** Full of venom. **3.** Malicious; spiteful.

ve·nous (vē′nəs) ▸ *adj.* **1.** Of or relating to veins. **2.** Having numerous veins.

vent[1] (vĕnt) ▸ *n.* **1.** A means of escape or release; outlet. **2.** An opening permitting escape, as of fumes or a gas. ▸ *v.* **1.** To give expression to. **2.** To release or discharge through an opening. **3.** To provide with a vent.

vent[2] (vĕnt) ▸ *n.* A slit in a garment, as in the seam of a pocket.

ven·ti·late (vĕn′tl-āt′) ▸ *v.* **-lat·ed, -lat·ing.** **1.** To admit fresh air into to replace stale or noxious air. **2.** To circulate through and freshen. **3.** To provide with a vent, as for airing. **4.** To expose to public discussion or examination. **5.** To aerate or oxygenate (blood). **—ven′ti·la′tion** *n.* **—ven′ti·la′tor** *n.*

ven·tral (vĕn′trəl) ▸ *adj.* **1.** Of or relating to the abdomen; abdominal. **2.** Of or situated on or close to the anterior aspect of the human body or the lower surface of the body of an animal.

ven·tri·cle (vĕn′trĭ-kəl) ▸ *n.* A cavity or chamber within a body or an organ, esp.: **a.** Either of the chambers of the heart that contract to pump blood into arteries. **b.** Any of the interconnecting cavities of the brain. **—ven·tric′u·lar** (-trĭk′yə-lər) *adj.*

ven·tril·o·quism (vĕn-trĭl′ə-kwĭz′əm) also **ven·tril·o·quy** (-kwē) ▸ *n.* The art of projecting one's voice so that it seems to come from another source. **—ven·tril′o·quist** *n.*

ven·ture (vĕn′chər) ▸ *n.* **1.** An undertaking that is dangerous or of uncertain outcome. **2.** Something, such as money, at hazard in a risky enterprise. ▸ *v.* **-tured, -tur·ing.** **1.** To expose to danger or risk. **2.** To brave the dangers of. **3.** To express at the risk of denial, criticism, or censure. **4.** To take a risk; dare.

ven·ture·some (vĕn′chər-səm) ▸ *adj.* **1.** Inclined to take risks; daring. **2.** Risky; hazardous. **—ven′ture·some·ness** *n.*

ven·tur·ous (vĕn′chər-əs) ▸ *adj.* Venturesome. **—ven′tur·ous·ness** *n.*

ven·ue (vĕn′yo͞o) ▸ *n.* **1.** The locality where a crime is committed or a cause of legal action occurs. **2.** The locality from which a jury is called and in which a trial is held. **3.** A place where a gathering is held.

THESAURUS

velocity *n.* Rate of motion or performance ▸ pace, speed, tempo. *Informal:* clip.

venal *adj.* —*See* CORRUPT (1).

venality *n.* —*See* CORRUPTION (2).

vend *v.* To travel about selling goods ▸ hawk, huckster, peddle. —*See also* SELL.

vendor or **vender** *n.* —*See* SELLER.

veneer *n.* —*See* FAÇADE (2).

veneer *v.* —*See* COLOR (2), FACE (2).

venerability *n.* —*See* HOLINESS.

venerable *adj.* —*See* ADMIRABLE, EXALTED, HOLY, OLD (1).

venerate *v.* —*See* REVERE.

veneration *n.* The act of adoring, especially reverently ▸ adoration, idolization, reverence, worship. [*Compare* DEVOTION, PRAISE.] —*See also* HONOR (1).

venerational *adj.* —*See* REVERENT.

vengeance *n.* —*See* RETALIATION.

vengeful *adj.* —*See* VINDICTIVE.

vengefulness *n.* The quality or condition of being vindictive ▸ revenge, spite, spitefulness, vindictiveness. [*Compare* RESENTMENT.]

venial *adj.* —*See* PARDONABLE.

venom *n.* —*See* POISON.

venomous *adj.* —*See* BITING, MALEVOLENT, POISONOUS.

venomousness *n.* —*See* MALEVOLENCE.

vent *n.* —*See* HOLE (2).

vent *v.* —*See* AIR (2), EMIT, SAY.

ventilate *v.* To expose to circulating air ▸ aerate, air, freshen, wind. —*See also* AIR (2).

ventilated *adj.* —*See* AIRY (3).

ventilation *n.* —*See* EXPRESSION (1).

venture *v.* To express at the risk of rebuff or criticism ▸ adventure, brave, chance, dare, hazard, presume, pretend, risk. *Idioms:* make bold (*or* so bold), take the liberty. —*See also* GAMBLE (2), GAMBLE (3).

venture *n.* Something undertaken, especially something requiring extensive planning and work ▸ endeavor, enterprise, project, undertaking. [*Compare* TASK.] —*See also* ADVENTURE, BET, GAMBLE.

venture capital *n.* —*See* CAPITAL (1).

venturer *n.* One who seeks adventure ▸ adventurer, daredevil, quester. [*Compare* BUILDER.]

venturesome or **venturous** *adj.* —*See* ADVENTUROUS, DANGEROUS.

venturesomeness or **venturousness** *n.* —*See* DARING.

Ve·nus (vē′nəs) ▸ *n.* **1.** *Rom. Myth.* The goddess of love and beauty. **2.** The 2nd planet from the sun, at a mean distance of approx. 108.1 million km (67.2 million mi) and with an average radius of 6,052 km (3,760 mi). **—Ve·nu′sian** (vĭ-no͞o′zhən, -nyo͞o′-) *adj.*

Venus fly·trap (flī′trăp′) ▸ *n.* An insectivorous plant of the coastal Carolinas, having hinged leaf blades that close and entrap insects.

ve·ra·cious (və-rā′shəs) ▸ *adj.* **1.** Honest; truthful. **2.** Accurate; precise. **—ve·ra′cious·ness** *n.*

ve·rac·i·ty (və-răs′ĭ-tē) ▸ *n., pl.* **-ties. 1.** Adherence to the truth; truthfulness. **2.** Conformity to fact or truth; accuracy. **3.** Something that is true.

ve·ran·da or **ve·ran·dah** (və-răn′də) ▸ *n.* A usu. roofed porch or balcony extending along the outside of a building.

verb (vûrb) ▸ *n.* The part of speech that expresses existence, action, or occurrence in most languages.

ver·bal (vûr′bəl) ▸ *adj.* **1.** Of or associated with words. **2.** Concerned with words only rather than with content or ideas. **3.** Spoken rather than written; oral: *a verbal contract.* **4.** Word for word; literal. **5.** Of or derived from a verb. ▸ *n.* A noun or adjective derived from a verb. **—ver′bal·ly** *adv.*

ver·bal·ize (vûr′bə-līz′) ▸ *v.* **-ized, -iz·ing. 1.** To express in words. **2.** To convert to use as a verb. **3.** To be verbose. **—ver′bal·i·za′tion** *n.*

ver·ba·tim (vər-bā′tĭm) ▸ *adv. & adj.* In the same words; word for word.

ver·be·na (vər-bē′nə) ▸ *n.* Any of various plants cultivated for their showy spikes of variously colored flowers.

ver·bi·age (vûr′bē-ĭj, -bĭj) ▸ *n.* **1.** An excess of words for the purpose; wordiness. **2.** Wording; diction.

ver·bose (vər-bōs′) ▸ *adj.* Using more words than is necessary; wordy. **—ver·bos′i·ty** (-bŏs′ĭ-tē) *n.*

ver·bo·ten (vər-bōt′n, fĕr-) ▸ *adj.* Forbidden; prohibited.

ver·dant (vûr′dnt) ▸ *adj.* **1.** Green with vegetation. **2.** Of a green color. **—ver′dan·cy** *n.*

Verde (vûrd), **Cape** ▸ A peninsula of W Senegal projecting into the Atlantic; westernmost point of Africa.

Ver·di (vâr′dē), **Giuseppe** (1813–1901) ▸ Italian composer.

ver·dict (vûr′dĭkt) ▸ *n.* **1.** The finding of a jury in a trial. **2.** A judgment; conclusion.

ver·di·gris (vûr′dĭ-grēs′, -grĭs′, -grē′) ▸ *n.* A green patina formed on copper, brass, and bronze after long exposure to air or seawater.

ver·dure (vûr′jər) ▸ *n.* **1.** The lush greenness of flourishing vegetation. **2.** Green vegetation.

verge[1] (vûrj) ▸ *n.* **1.** An edge, rim, or margin. **2.** The point beyond which an action or a condition is likely to begin or occur; brink. **3.** A rod or staff carried as an emblem of authority or office. ▸ *v.* **verged, verg·ing.** To border on; approach.

verge[2] (vûrj) ▸ *v.* **verged, verg·ing. 1.** To slope or incline. **2.** To pass or merge gradually.

verg·er (vûr′jər) ▸ *n. Chiefly Brit.* **1.** One who carries a verge, as before a religious dignitary in a procession. **2.** One who takes care of the interior of a church.

Ver·gil (vûr′jəl) ▸ See **Virgil.**

ver·i·fy (vĕr′ə-fī′) ▸ *v.* **-fied** (-fīd′), **-fy·ing. 1.** To prove the truth of; substantiate. **2.** To determine or test the truth or accuracy of. **—ver′i·fi′a·ble** *adj.* **—ver′i·fi·ca′tion** *n.* **—ver′i·fi′er** *n.*

ver·i·ly (vĕr′ə-lē) ▸ *adv.* **1.** In truth; in fact. **2.** Surely; assuredly.

ver·i·si·mil·i·tude (vĕr′ə-sĭ-mĭl′ĭ-to͞od′, -tyo͞od′) ▸ *n.* **1.** The quality of appearing to be true or real. **2.** Something that appears to be true or real.

ver·i·ta·ble (vĕr′ĭ-tə-bəl) ▸ *adj.* Being truly so called; real or genuine. **—ver′i·ta·bly** *adv.*

ver·i·ty (vĕr′ĭ-tē) ▸ *n., pl.* **-ties. 1.** The quality or condition of being true, factual, or real. **2.** Something, such as a statement or belief, that is true.

ver·meil (vûr′məl, -māl′) ▸ *n.* **1.** Vermilion. **2.** (vĕr-mā′) Gilded silver, bronze, or copper.

ver·mi·cel·li (vûr′mĭ-chĕl′ē, -sĕl′ē) ▸ *n.* Pasta in long, very thin strands.

ver·mic·u·lite (vər-mĭk′yə-līt′) ▸ *n.* Any of a group of minerals resembling mica and used in heat-expanded form esp. as insulation.

ver·mi·form (vûr′mə-fôrm′) ▸ *adj.* Resembling or shaped like a worm.

vermiform appendix ▸ *n.* A narrow vestigial process projecting from the cecum in the lower right-hand part of the abdomen.

ver·mi·fuge (vûr′mə-fyo͞oj′) ▸ *n.* A medicine that expels intestinal worms.

ver·mil·ion also **ver·mil·lion** (vər-mĭl′yən) ▸ *n.* **1.** A bright red pigment. **2.** A vivid red to reddish orange. **—ver·mil′ion** *adj.*

ver·min (vûr′mĭn) ▸ *n., pl.* **vermin.** Various small animals or insects, such as rats or cockroaches, that are destructive, annoying, or injurious to health. **—ver′min·ous** *adj.*

Ver·mont (vər-mŏnt′) ▸ A state of the NE US bordering on Canada. Cap. Montpelier. **—Ver·mont′er** *n.*

ver·mouth (vər-mo͞oth′) ▸ *n.* A sweet or dry wine flavored with aromatic herbs.

ver·nac·u·lar (vər-năk′yə-lər) ▸ *n.* **1.** The standard native language of a country or locality, esp. as distinct from literary language. **2.** A jargon: *the legal vernacular.* **—ver·nac′u·lar** *adj.*

ver·nal (vûr′nəl) ▸ *adj.* Of or occurring in the spring. **—ver′nal·ly** *adv.*

Verne (vûrn, vĕrn), **Jules** (1828–1905) ▸ French writer.

ver·ni·er (vûr′nē-ər) ▸ *n.* A small scale attached to a main scale, calibrated to indicate fractional parts of the subdivisions of the larger scale.

vernier caliper ▸ *n.* An L-shaped caliper having a sliding attachment with a vernier.

ve·ron·i·ca (və-rŏn′ĭ-kə) ▸ *n.* Any of various plants that include the speedwells.

ver·sa·tile (vûr′sə-təl, -tīl′) ▸ *adj.* **1.** Capable of doing many things competently. **2.** Having varied uses or functions. **—ver′sa·til′i·ty** (-tĭl′ĭ-tē) *n.*

THESAURUS

veracious *adj.* —*See* ACCURATE, HONEST.

veracity or **veraciousness** *n.* Correspondence with fact or truth ▸ accuracy, accurateness, authenticity, correctness, credibility, exactitude, exactness, faithfulness, fidelity, genuineness, realness, reliability, truth, truthfulness, validity, veridicality, verity. [*Compare* CERTAINTY.]

verbal *adj.* Relating to, consisting of, or having the nature of words ▸ lexical, linguistic, wordy. —*See also* LITERAL, ORAL.

verbalism *n.* —*See* WORDING.

verbalization *n.* —*See* EXPRESSION (1), SPEECH (1).

verbalize *v.* To express oneself in speech ▸ speak, talk, vocalize. —*See also* SAY.

verbatim *adj.* —*See* LITERAL.

verbatim *adv.* —*See* EXACTLY.

verbiage *n.* —*See* WORDINESS.

verbose *adj.* —*See* WORDY (1).

verbosity or **verboseness** *n.* —*See* WORDINESS.

verboten *adj.* —*See* FORBIDDEN.

verdict *n.* —*See* RULING.

verdure *n.* The plants of an area or region ▸ flora, plant life, vegetation.

verge *n.* —*See* BORDER (1).

verge *v.* —*See* ADJOIN, BORDER.

verge on *v.* —*See* RIVAL.

veridical *adj.* —*See* ACCURATE.

veridicality *n.* —*See* VERACITY.

verification *n.* —*See* CONFIRMATION (1), CONFIRMATION (2).

verify *v.* —*See* CERTIFY, CONFIRM (1), PROVE.

verily *adv.* —*See* REALLY.

verisimilitude *n.* Appearance of truth or authenticity ▸ believability, color, credibility, credibleness, creditability, creditableness, plausibility, plausibleness. [*Compare* TRUTH, VERACITY.]

veritable *adj.* —*See* AUTHENTIC (1).

veritably *adv.* —*See* REALLY.

verity *n.* —*See* VERACITY.

vermin *n.* —*See* RIFFRAFF.

vernacular *n.* —*See* DIALECT, LANGUAGE (1), LANGUAGE (2).

versant *adj.* Having good knowledge of something ▸ aquainted, conversant, familiar, schooled, versed. *Idiom:* up on. [*Compare* ACCUSTOMED, INFORMED.]

versatile *adj.* Having many aspects, uses, or abilities ▸ all-around, all-purpose, all-round, many-sided, multifaceted, multipurpose, multitalented, protean, various. —*See also* ADAPTABLE.

verse (vûrs) ▸ *n.* **1.** Writing arranged according to a metrical pattern; poetry. **2a.** One line of poetry. **b.** A stanza. **3.** A specific type of metrical composition, such as blank verse. **4.** One of the numbered subdivisions of a chapter in the Bible.

versed (vûrst) ▸ *adj.* Practiced or skilled; knowledgeable.

ver·si·fy (vûr′sə-fī′) ▸ *v.* **-fied, -fy·ing. 1.** To change from prose into metrical form. **2.** To write verses. **—ver′si·fi·ca′tion** *n.* **—ver′si·fi′er** *n.*

ver·sion (vûr′zhən, -shən) ▸ *n.* **1.** A description or account from one point of view. **2.** A translation, esp. of the Bible or of a part of it. **3.** A form or variation of an earlier or original type. **4.** An adaptation of a work of art or literature into another medium or style.

vers li·bre (vĕr lē′brə) ▸ *n.* Free verse.

ver·so (vûr′sō) ▸ *n., pl.* **-sos.** A left-hand page.

ver·sus (vûr′səs, -səz) ▸ *prep.* **1.** Against: *the plaintiff versus the defendant.* **2.** In contrast with: *death versus dishonor.*

ver·te·bra (vûr′tə-brə) ▸ *n., pl.* **-brae** (-brā′, -brē′) or **-bras.** Any of the bones or cartilaginous segments forming the spinal column. **—ver′te·bral** *adj.*

ver·te·brate (vûr′tə-brĭt, -brāt′) ▸ *adj.* **1.** Having a backbone or spinal column. **2.** Of the vertebrates. ▸ *n.* Any of a group of animals, including the fishes, amphibians, reptiles, birds, and mammals, having a segmented spinal column.

ver·tex (vûr′tĕks′) ▸ *n., pl.* **-ti·ces** (-tĭ-sēz′) or **-tex·es. 1.** The highest point; apex or summit. **2a.** The point at which the sides of an angle intersect. **b.** The point on a triangle opposite to and farthest away from its base. **c.** A point on a polyhedron common to three or more sides.

ver·ti·cal (vûr′tĭ-kəl) ▸ *adj.* **1.** Being or situated at right angles to the horizon; upright. **2.** Situated at the vertex or highest point; directly overhead. ▸ *n.* **1.** Something vertical, as a line. **2.** A vertical position. **—ver′ti·cal·ly** *adv.*

ver·tig·i·nous (vər-tĭj′ə-nəs) ▸ *adj.* **1.** Turning about an axis. **2.** Affected by vertigo. **3.** Tending to produce vertigo; dizzying.

ver·ti·go (vûr′tĭ-gō′) ▸ *n., pl.* **-goes** or **-gos.** The sensation of dizziness; giddiness.

ver·vain (vûr′vān′) ▸ *n.* See **verbena.**

verve (vûrv) ▸ *n.* **1.** Energy and enthusiasm, as in artistic performance or composition. **2.** Vitality; liveliness.

ver·y (vĕr′ē) ▸ *adv.* **1.** In a high degree; extremely: *very happy.* **2.** Truly; absolutely: *the very best advice.* ▸ *adj.* **-i·er, -i·est. 1.** Complete; absolute: *the very end.* **2.** Identical; selfsame: *the very question she asked yesterday.* **3.** Used for emphasis: *the very mountains shook.* **4.** Precise; exact: *the very center of town.* **5.** Mere: *The very thought is frightening.* **6.** Actual: *caught in the very act.*

very high frequency ▸ *n.* A band of radio frequencies between 30 and 300 megahertz.

very low frequency ▸ *n.* A band of radio frequencies between 3 and 30 kilohertz.

ves·i·cant (vĕs′ĭ-kənt) ▸ *n.* A blistering agent, esp. mustard gas. **—ves′i·cant** *adj.*

ves·i·cle (vĕs′ĭ-kəl) ▸ *n.* **1.** A small bladderlike cell or cavity. **2.** A blister. **—ve·sic′u·lar** (vĕ-sĭk′yə-lər, və-) *adj.*

ves·per (vĕs′pər) ▸ *n.* **1.** A bell that summons worshipers to vespers. **2.** *Archaic* Evening.

ves·pers (vĕs′pərz) ▸ *pl.n.* *(takes sing. or pl. v.)* A worship service held in the late afternoon or evening.

ves·per·tine (vĕs′pər-tīn′) ▸ *adj.* **1.** Of or occurring in the evening. **2.** *Bot.* Opening or blooming in the evening.

Ves·puc·ci (vĕs-po͞o′chē, -pyo͞o′-), **Amerigo** (1454–1512) ▸ Italian explorer.

ves·sel (vĕs′əl) ▸ *n.* **1.** A hollow container, as a cup, vase, or pitcher; receptacle. **2.** A ship, large boat, or similar craft. **3.** *Anat.* A duct or other narrow tube that contains or conveys a body fluid. **4.** A person seen as the agent or embodiment, as of a quality.

vest (vĕst) ▸ *n.* **1.** A sleeveless garment, often having buttons down the front, worn over a shirt or as part of a three-piece suit. **2.** *Chiefly Brit.* An undershirt. ▸ *v.* **1.** To place in the control of a person or group: *vested his estate in his daughter.* **2.** To invest or endow with power or rights: *vested the council with broad powers.* **3.** To clothe or robe, as in ecclesiastical vestments.

Ves·ta (vĕs′tə) ▸ *n.* *Rom. Myth.* The goddess of the hearth.

ves·tal (vĕs′təl) ▸ *adj.* Chaste; pure. ▸ *n.* A woman who is a virgin.

vest·ed interest (vĕs′tĭd) ▸ *n.* **1.** A special interest in protecting or promoting that which is to one's own personal advantage. **2.** A group that has a vested interest.

ves·ti·bule (vĕs′tə-byo͞ol′) ▸ *n.* **1.** A small entrance hall or lobby. **2.** An enclosed area at the end of a passenger car on a train. **3.** *Anat.* A cavity, chamber, or channel that leads to another cavity.

ves·tige (vĕs′tĭj) ▸ *n.* **1.** A visible trace, evidence, or sign of something that no longer exists or appears. **2.** A remnant.

ves·tig·i·al (vĕ-stĭj′ē-əl, -stĭj′əl) ▸ *adj.* **1.** Of or constituting a vestige. **2.** *Biol.* Occurring or persisting as a rudimentary or degenerate structure. **—ves·tig′i·al·ly** *adv.*

vest·ment (vĕst′mənt) ▸ *n.* **1.** A garment, esp. a robe or gown worn as an indication of office. **2.** Any of the ritual robes worn by members of the clergy or assistants at ecclesiastical services or rites.

vest-pock·et (vĕst′pŏk′ĭt) ▸ *adj.* Small.

ves·try (vĕs′trē) ▸ *n., pl.* **-tries. 1.** A sacristy. **2.** A meeting room in a church. **3.** A committee elected to administer the temporal affairs of a parish.

ves·try·man (vĕs′trē-mən) ▸ *n.* A member of a vestry.

ves·ture (vĕs′chər) ▸ *n.* **1.** Clothing; apparel. **2.** Something that covers or cloaks.

Ve·su·vi·us (vĭ-so͞o′vē-əs), **Mount** ▸ An active volcano, 1,281 m (4,200 ft), of S Italy on the E shore of the Bay of Naples. **—Ve·su′vi·an** *adj.*

vet[1] (vĕt) ▸ *n.* *Informal* A veterinarian.

vet[2] (vĕt) ▸ *n.* *Informal* A veteran.

vetch (vĕch) ▸ *n.* A plant having featherlike leaves that end in tendrils and small, variously colored flowers.

vet·er·an (vĕt′ər-ən, vĕt′rən) ▸ *n.* **1.** A person of long experience in an activity or capacity. **2.** A person who has served in the armed forces.

THESAURUS

verse *n.* —*See* POEM (1).

versed *adj.* Having good knowledge of something ▸ acquainted, conversant, familiar, schooled, versant. *Idiom:* up on. [*Compare* ACCUSTOMED, INFORMED.] —*See also* EDUCATED, EXPERIENCED.

versicolor or **versicolored** *adj.* —*See* MULTICOLORED.

versifier *n.* —*See* POET.

version *n.* —*See* PARAPHRASE, STORY (1), VARIATION.

vertex *n.* —*See* CLIMAX.

vertical *adj.* At right angles to the horizon or to level ground ▸ on end, perpendicular, plumb, standing, upright. [*Compare* ERECT, STEEP.]

vertiginous *adj.* Producing dizziness or vertigo ▸ dizzy, dizzying, giddy, sickening. [*Compare* STEEP.] —*See also* DIZZY (1).

vertiginousness *n.* —*See* DIZZINESS.

vertigo *n.* —*See* DIZZINESS.

verve *n.* —*See* ENERGY, ENTHUSIASM (1), SPIRIT (1).

very *adv.* To a high degree ▸ acutely, awfully, decidedly, dreadfully, eminently, exceedingly, exceptionally, extra, extremely, greatly, highly, hugely, intensely, most, notably, particularly, vastly. *Informal:* awful, mighty. [*Compare* ABSOLUTELY, COMPLETELY, CONSIDERABLY, REALLY, UNUSUALLY.]

very *adj.* **1.** Strictly distinguished from others ▸ exact, precise. **2.** Considered apart from anything else ▸ mere. —*See also* SAME.

vessel *n.* **1.** A conveyance that travels over water ▸ bark, barque, boat, craft, ship, watercraft. **2.** A tube that contains a body fluid ▸ artery, blood vessel, canal, capillary, duct, vein. **3.** An object, such as a carton, can, or jar, in which material is held or carried ▸ container, holder, receptacle, repository. [*Compare* DEPOSITORY, PACKAGE.] —*See also* VAT.

vest *v.* —*See* CLOTHE.

vested *adj.* —*See* CONFIRMED (1).

vestige *n.* —*See* TRACE.

vestment *n.* Clothing worn by members of a religious order ▸ habit, robe.

veteran or **vet** *n.* One who has had long experience in a given activity or capacity ▸ old hand, past master, vet. *Informal:* old-timer. [*Compare* EXPERT.]

veteran *adj.* —*See* EXPERIENCED.

Vet·er·ans Day (vĕt′ər-ənz, vĕt′rənz) ▸ *n.* Nov. 11, observed in the US in honor of veterans of the armed services and in commemoration of the armistice that ended World War I in 1918.

vet·er·i·nar·i·an (vĕt′ər-ə-nâr′ē-ən, vĕt′rə-) ▸ *n.* A person who practices veterinary medicine.

vet·er·i·nar·y (vĕt′ər-ə-nĕr′ē, vĕt′rə-) ▸ *adj.* Of the medical or surgical treatment of animals. ▸ *n., pl.* **-ies.** A veterinarian.

ve·to (vē′tō) ▸ *n., pl.* **-toes.** **1a.** The vested power or constitutional right of a branch of government, esp. of a chief executive, to reject a bill passed by a legislative body and thus prevent or delay its enactment into law. **b.** Exercise of this right. **2.** An authoritative prohibition or rejection of a proposed or intended act. ▸ *v.* **-toed, -to·ing.** **1.** To prevent (a legislative bill) from becoming law by exercising the power of veto. **2.** To forbid or prohibit authoritatively.

vex (vĕks) ▸ *v.* **1.** To annoy; bother. **2.** To cause perplexity in; puzzle. **3.** To debate at length.

vex·a·tion (vĕk-sā′shən) ▸ *n.* **1.** The condition of being vexed; annoyance. **2.** One that vexes. **—vex·a′tious** *adj.*

VHF ▸ *abbr.* very high frequency

VHS (vē′āch-ĕs′) ▸ A trademark for a videotape format.

VI or **V.I.** ▸ *abbr.* Virgin Islands

vi·a (vī′ə, vē′ə) ▸ *prep.* By way of.

vi·a·ble (vī′ə-bəl) ▸ *adj.* **1.** Capable of living or developing under favorable conditions. **2.** Capable of living outside the uterus. **3.** Feasible; practicable. **—vi′a·bil′i·ty** *n.*

vi·a·duct (vī′ə-dŭkt′) ▸ *n.* A series of spans or arches used to carry a road or railroad over something, such as a valley or road.

vi·al (vī′əl) ▸ *n.* A small container for liquids.

vi·and (vī′ənd) ▸ *n.* **1.** An item of food. **2. viands** Provisions; victuals.

vi·at·i·cum (vī-ăt′ĭ-kəm, vē-) ▸ *n., pl.* **-ca** (-kə) or **-cums.** The Eucharist given to a dying person or one in danger of death.

vibes (vībz) ▸ *pl.n.* **1.** A vibraphone. **2.** *Slang* Vibrations.

vi·brant (vī′brənt) ▸ *adj.* **1.** Full of vigor or energy. **2.** Produced as a result of vibration; vibrating. **—vi′bran·cy** *n.* **—vi′brant·ly** *adv.*

vi·bra·phone (vī′brə-fōn′) ▸ *n. Mus.* An instrument similar to a marimba but having metal bars and rotating disks in the resonators to produce a vibrato. **—vi′bra·phon′ist** *n.*

vi·brate (vī′brāt′) ▸ *v.* **-brat·ed, -brat·ing.** **1.** To move or cause to move back and forth rapidly. **2.** To feel a quiver of emotion. **3.** To shake or tremble. **4.** To produce a sound; resonate. **—vi′bra′tor** *n.* **—vi′bra·to′ry** (-brə-tôr′ē) *adj.*

vi·bra·tion (vī-brā′shən) ▸ *n.* **1a.** The act of vibrating. **b.** The condition of being vibrated. **2.** *Phys.* A rapid linear motion of a particle or of an elastic solid about an equilibrium position. **3.** A single complete vibrating motion. **4. vibrations** *Slang* A distinctive emotional aura or atmosphere that is instinctively sensed or experienced.

vi·bra·to (və-brä′tō, vī-) ▸ *n., pl.* **-tos.** *Mus.* A tremulous or pulsating effect produced in an instrumental or vocal tone by slight rapid variations in pitch.

vi·bur·num (vī-bûr′nəm) ▸ *n.* Any of various shrubs or trees having clusters of small white or pink flowers and berrylike red or black fruit.

vic·ar (vĭk′ər) ▸ *n.* **1a.** A parish priest in the Church of England. **b.** A cleric in charge of a chapel in the Episcopal Church. **2.** *Rom. Cath. Ch.* A priest who acts for or represents another.

vic·ar·age (vĭk′ər-ĭj) ▸ *n.* The residence or benefice of a vicar.

vi·car·i·ous (vī-kâr′ē-əs, -kăr′-, vĭ-) ▸ *adj.* **1.** Felt or undergone as if one were taking part in the experience or feelings of another. **2.** Endured or done by one person substituting for another. **3.** Acting for another. **—vi·car′i·ous·ly** *adv.* **—vi·car′i·ous·ness** *n.*

vice[1] (vīs) ▸ *n.* **1a.** Evil; wickedness. **b.** Sexual immorality, esp. prostitution. **2.** A degrading or immoral practice or habit. **3a.** A personal failing; shortcoming. **b.** A defect; flaw.

vice[2] (vīs) ▸ *n.* Var. of **vise.**

vi·ce[3] (vī′sē, -sə) ▸ *prep.* In place of; replacing. ▸ *adj.* (vīs) Acting as a deputy or substitute for another: *a vice chairman.*

vice admiral (vīs) ▸ *n.* A rank, as in the US Navy, above rear admiral and below admiral.

vice president ▸ *n.* **1.** An officer ranking next below a president, usu. empowered to assume the president's duties under conditions such as absence, illness, or death. **2.** A deputy to a president, esp. in a corporation, in charge of a specific department or location. **—vice-pres′i·den·cy** *n.*

vice·re·gal (vīs-rē′gəl) ▸ *adj.* Of a viceroy.

vice·roy (vīs′roi′) ▸ *n.* The governor of a country, province, or colony, ruling as the representative of a sovereign. **—vice′roy′al·ty** *n.*

vi·ce ver·sa (vī′sə vûr′sə, vīs′) ▸ *adv.* With the order or meaning reversed; conversely.

vi·chys·soise (vĭsh′ē-swäz′, vē′shē-) ▸ *n.* A thick creamy potato soup flavored with leeks or onions, usu. served cold.

vi·cin·i·ty (vĭ-sĭn′ĭ-tē) ▸ *n., pl.* **-ties.** **1.** Nearness; proximity. **2.** A nearby or surrounding area; neighborhood. **3.** An approximate degree or amount.

vi·cious (vĭsh′əs) ▸ *adj.* **1.** Evil; wicked. **2.** Savage and dangerous. **3.** Spiteful; malicious. **4.** Violent; intense. **5.** Marked by a tendency to worsen. **—vi′cious·ly** *adv.* **—vi′cious·ness** *n.*

vi·cis·si·tude (vĭ-sĭs′ĭ-to͞od′, -tyo͞od′) ▸ *n.* **1.** The quality of being changeable; mutability. **2.** often **vicissitudes** A sudden or unexpected change or shift.

vic·tim (vĭk′tĭm) ▸ *n.* **1.** One who is harmed or killed, as by accident or disease. **2.** A living creature offered as a sacrifice during a religious rite. **3.** One who is tricked, swindled, or injured.

vic·tim·ize (vĭk′tə-mīz′) ▸ *v.* **-ized, -iz·ing.** To make a victim of. **—vic′tim·i·za′tion** *n.* **—vic′tim·iz′er** *n.*

vic·tim·less crime (vĭk′tĭm-lĭs) ▸ *n.* An illegal act having no direct victim.

vic·tor (vĭk′tər) ▸ *n.* The winner in a fight, battle, contest, or struggle.

vic·to·ri·a (vĭk-tôr′ē-ə) ▸ *n.* A low, four-wheeled carriage for two with a folding top and an elevated driver's seat in front.

Victoria[1] (1819–1901) ▸ Queen of Great Britain and Ireland (1837–1901) and empress of India (1876–1901).

Victoria[2] ▸ The capital of British Columbia, Canada, on SE Vancouver I.

Victoria, Lake. Also **Victoria Ny·an·za** (nī-ăn′zə, nyän′-) ▸ A lake of E-central Africa in Uganda, Kenya, and Tanzania.

Victoria Falls ▸ A waterfall, 108.3 m (355 ft), of S-central Africa in the Zambezi R. between SW Zambia and NW Zimbabwe.

THESAURUS

veto *v.* To prevent or forbid authoritatively ▸ blackball, block, negative, stop, turn down. *Slang:* nix. *Idiom:* turn thumbs down on. [*Compare* ABOLISH, DECLINE, FORBID, PREVENT, REFUSE[1].]

vex *v.* —*See* ANNOY, COMPLICATE, DISTRESS.

vexation *n.* —*See* ANNOYANCE (1), ANNOYANCE (2), DISTRESS.

vexatious or **vexing** *adj.* —*See* DISTURBING.

viable *adj.* —*See* POSSIBLE.

viands *n.* —*See* FOOD.

vibe *n.* —*See* AIR (3).

vibrancy *n.* —*See* ENERGY.

vibrant *adj.* —*See* COLORFUL (1), LIVELY, RESONANT.

vibrate *v.* —*See* GLARE (2), SHAKE (1), SWAY.

vibrating *adj.* —*See* TREMULOUS.

vibrating *n.* —*See* TREMOR (2).

vibration *n.* —*See* AIR (3), TREMOR (2).

vicar *n.* —*See* CLERIC.

vice *n.* —*See* CORRUPTION (1), EVIL (1).

vicinity *n.* Approximate size or amount ▸ range. *Informal:* neighborhood. *Slang:* ballpark. —*See also* ENVIRONMENT (1), LOCALITY.

vicious *adj.* —*See* CRUEL, EVIL, MALEVOLENT.

viciousness *n.* —*See* MALEVOLENCE.

vicissitude *n.* —*See* CHANGE (1), DIFFICULTY.

victim *n.* One that is made to suffer injury, loss, or death ▸ casualty, martyr, prey, quarry, statistic, sufferer, wounded. [*Compare* FATALITY, SCAPEGOAT, UNFORTUNATE.] —*See also* DUPE, OFFERING.

victimization *n.* —*See* CHEAT (1).

victimize *v.* To offer as a sacrifice ▸ immolate, offer up, sacrifice. —*See also* ABUSE (1), CHEAT (1).

victimizer *n.* —*See* CHEAT (2).

victor *n.* —*See* CONQUEROR, WINNER.

Vic·to·ri·an (vĭk-tôr′ē-ən) ▸ *adj.* **1.** Of or belonging to the period of the reign of Queen Victoria. **2.** Displaying the moral standards or ideals characteristic of this period. **3.** Being in the highly ornamented, massive style of architecture, decor, and furnishings popular in 19th-cent. England. ▸ *n.* A person of the Victorian period.

vic·to·ri·ous (vĭk-tôr′ē-əs) ▸ *adj.* **1.** Being the winner in a contest or struggle. **2.** Characteristic of or expressing victory. **—vic·to′ri·ous·ly** *adv.* **—vic·to′ri·ous·ness** *n.*

vic·to·ry (vĭk′tə-rē) ▸ *n., pl.* **-ries. 1.** Defeat of an enemy or opponent. **2.** Success in a struggle against difficulties; triumph.

vict·ual (vĭt′l) ▸ *n.* **1.** Food fit for human consumption. **2. victuals** Food supplies; provisions. ▸ *v.* **-ualed, -ual·ing** or **-ualled, -ual·ling. 1.** To provide with food. **2.** To lay in food supplies.

vi·cu·ña also **vi·cu·na** (vī-ko͞on′yə, -ko͞o′nə, -kyo͞o′nə, vĭ-) ▸ *n.* **1.** A llamalike mammal of the central Andes, having fine silky wool. **2.** The wool of the vicuña.

vi·de (vī′dē, wē′dā′) ▸ *v.* See. Used to direct a reader's attention: *vide page 47.*

vi·del·i·cet (vī-dĕl′ĭ-sĕt′, wĭ-dā′lĭ-kĕt′) ▸ *adv.* That is; namely. Used to introduce examples, lists, or items.

vid·e·o (vĭd′ē-ō′) ▸ *n., pl.* **-os. 1.** A sequence of images displayed in rapid succession on a screen to simulate continuous motion. **2.** A movie recorded electronically. **3.** The electronic medium in which movies are recorded. **4.** A videotaped rendition of a song. **—vid′e·o** *adj.*

video camera ▸ *n.* A camera that captures moving images and converts them into electronic signals so that they can be saved on a storage device, such as videotape or a memory card, and viewed on a monitor.

vid·e·o·cas·sette (vĭd′ē-ō-kə-sĕt′, -kă-) ▸ *n.* A cassette containing blank or prerecorded videotape.

videocassette recorder ▸ *n.* A VCR.

vid·e·o·disc also **vid·e·o·disk** (vĭd′ē-ō-dĭsk′) ▸ *n.* A disc on which sounds and images, such as of a movie, are recorded.

video display ▸ *n.* A device, such as a computer screen, that gives information in visual form.

video game ▸ *n.* An electronic or computerized game played by manipulating images on a video display.

vid·e·o·tape (vĭd′ē-ō-tāp′) ▸ *n.* A magnetic tape used to record visual images and associated sound for subsequent playback or broadcasting. **—vid′e·o·tape′** *v.*

vie (vī) ▸ *v.* **vied, vy·ing** (vī′ĭng). To strive for superiority; contend.

Vi·en·na (vē-ĕn′ə) ▸ The capital of Austria, in the NE part on the Danube R. **—Vi′en·nese′** (-ə-nēz′, -nēs′) *adj. & n.*

Vi·et·cong (vē-ĕt′kŏng′, -kông′, vyĕt′-) ▸ *n., pl.* **-cong.** A Vietnamese in or supporting the National Liberation Front of the former South Vietnam. **—Vi·et′cong′** *adj.*

Vi·et·nam (vē-ĕt′näm′, -năm′, vyĕt′-) ▸ A country of SE Asia in E Indochina on the South China Sea; divided (1954–1976) into **North Vietnam** and **South Vietnam.**

Vi·et·nam·ese (vē-ĕt′nə-mēz′, vē′ĭt-, vyĕt′-) ▸ *n., pl.* **-ese. 1.** A native or inhabitant of Vietnam. **2.** The language of Vietnam. **—Vi′et·nam·ese′** *adj.*

view (vyo͞o) ▸ *n.* **1.** An examination or inspection. **2.** An overview. **3.** An opinion; judgment: *my views on politics.* **4.** Field of vision: *disappeared from view.* **5.** A scene or vista. **6.** A picture of a landscape. **7.** A way of showing or seeing something, as from a particular position or angle: *a side view of the house.* **8.** An aim or intention: *laws enacted with a view to ending discrimination.* ▸ *v.* **1.** To look at; watch. **2a.** To examine or inspect. **b.** To regard; consider. **—view′er** *n.*

view·find·er (vyo͞o′fīn′dər) ▸ *n.* A device on a camera that indicates what will appear in the field of view of the lens.

view·point (vyo͞o′point′) ▸ *n.* A point of view.

vig·il (vĭj′əl) ▸ *n.* **1.** A watch kept during normal sleeping hours. **2.** The eve of a religious festival as observed by devotional watching. **3.** often **vigils** Ritual devotions observed on the eve of a holy day.

vig·i·lance (vĭj′ə-ləns) ▸ *n.* Alert watchfulness.

vig·i·lant (vĭj′ə-lənt) ▸ *adj.* On the alert; watchful. **—vig′i·lant·ly** *adv.*

vig·i·lan·te (vĭj′ə-lăn′tē) ▸ *n.* A person, especially a member of a group of volunteers, who without authority assumes law enforcement powers. **—vig′i·lan′tism, vig′i·lan′te·ism** *n.*

vi·gnette (vĭn-yĕt′) ▸ *n.* **1.** A decorative design that is placed at the beginning or end of a book or chapter or along the border of a page. **2.** A picture that shades off into the surrounding color at the edges. **3.** A brief literary or dramatic sketch.

vig·or (vĭg′ər) ▸ *n.* **1.** Physical or mental strength or energy. **2.** Strong feeling; enthusiasm or intensity. **3.** Legal effectiveness or validity.

vig·or·ous (vĭg′ər-əs) ▸ *adj.* **1.** Robust; hardy. **2.** Energetic; lively. **—vig′or·ous·ly** *adv.*

vig·our (vĭg′ər) ▸ *n. Chiefly Brit.* Var. of **vigor.**

Vi·king (vī′kĭng) ▸ *n.* One of a group of seafaring Scandinavian warriors and explorers who plundered the coasts of N and W Europe from the 8th through the 10th cent.

vile (vīl) ▸ *adj.* **vil·er, vil·est. 1.** Loathsome; disgusting. **2.** Unpleasant or objectionable. **3.** Miserably poor; wretched. **4.** Morally low; base. **—vile′ly** *adv.* **—vile′ness** *n.*

vil·i·fy (vĭl′ə-fī′) ▸ *v.* **-fied, -fy·ing.** To speak evil of; defame. **—vil′i·fi·ca′tion** *n.* **—vil′i·fi′er** *n.*

vil·la (vĭl′ə) ▸ *n.* **1.** An often large and luxurious country house. **2.** *Chiefly Brit.* A house in a middle-class suburb.

Vil·la (vē′ə), **Francisco.** "Pancho" (1877?–1923) ▸ Mexican revolutionary leader.

vil·lage (vĭl′ĭj) ▸ *n.* **1.** A usu. rural settlement smaller than a town. **2.** An incorporated community smaller in population than a town. **3.** The inhabitants of a village. **—vil′lag·er** *n.*

vil·lain (vĭl′ən) ▸ *n.* **1.** A wicked or evil person; scoundrel. **2.** (also vĭl′ān′, vĭ-lān′) Var. of **villein.**

THESAURUS

Victorian *adj.* —*See* PRUDISH.

victorious *adj.* Being the winner in a contest or struggle ▸ champion, conquering, triumphal, triumphant, vanquishing, winning.

victory *n.* —*See* CONQUEST.

victuals *n.* —*See* FOOD.

videlicet *adv.* —*See* NAMELY.

vie *v.* —*See* COMPETE.

view *n.* 1. An act of directing the eyes on an object ▸ contemplation, look, regard, sight. [*Compare* GAZE, WATCH.] 2. That which is or can be seen ▸ landscape, lookout, outlook, panorama, perspective, picture, prospect, scene, scenery, sight, spectacle, tableau, vista. —*See also* BELIEF (1), EXAMINATION (1), INTENTION, VIEWPOINT.

view *v.* —*See* EXAMINE (1), LOOK (1), REGARD.

viewable *adj.* —*See* VISIBLE.

viewer *n.* Someone who sees something occur ▸ audience, eyewitness, seer, witness.

viewpoint *n.* The position from which something is observed or considered ▸ angle, aspect, eye, facet, frame of reference, hand, light, outlook, part, perspective, phase, point of view, position, regard, respect, side, slant, stand, standpoint, vantage, view. [*Compare* BELIEF, POSTURE.]

viga *n.* —*See* BEAM (2).

vigil *n.* —*See* LOOKOUT (1).

vigilance *n.* —*See* ALERTNESS, LOOKOUT (1).

vigilant *adj.* —*See* ALERT.

vigor *n.* —*See* ENERGY, ENTHUSIASM (1), SPIRIT (1).

vigorous *adj.* —*See* ENERGETIC, FORCEFUL, HEALTHY, LUSTY.

vigorously *adv.* —*See* HARD (1).

vigorousness *n.* —*See* ENERGY.

vile *adj.* —*See* DIRTY, OFFENSIVE (1), SORDID.

vileness *n.* —*See* UGLINESS.

vilification *n.* —*See* LIBEL.

vilify *v.* —*See* MALIGN, REVILE.

villa *n.* A house in the country ▸ chalet, cottage, country home, country house, dacha, estate, manor. [*Compare* HOME.]

village *n.* A small group of dwellings, usually in a rural area ▸ community, hamlet, settlement, small town. [*Compare* CITY.]

villain *n.* A mean, worthless character in a story or play ▸ *Slang:* bad guy, heavy. —*See also* EVILDOER, FIEND.

vil·lain·ous (vĭl′ə-nəs) ▸ *adj.* 1. Befitting a villain; wicked. 2. Unpleasant; vile.
vil·lain·y (vĭl′ə-nē) ▸ *n., pl.* **-ies.** 1. Baseness of mind or character. 2. Viciousness of conduct or action. 3. A treacherous or vicious act.
vil·lein also **vil·lain** (vĭl′ən, -ān′, vĭ-lān′) ▸ *n.* One of a class of feudal serfs who held the legal status of freemen in their dealings with all people except their lord.
vim (vĭm) ▸ *n.* Ebullient vitality and energy.
vin·ai·grette (vĭn′ĭ-grĕt′) ▸ *n.* 1. A small decorative bottle or container used for holding an aromatic preparation such as smelling salts. 2. A dressing made of vinegar or lemon juice and oil.
vin·ci·ble (vĭn′sə-bəl) ▸ *adj.* Capable of being defeated.
vin·di·cate (vĭn′dĭ-kāt′) ▸ *v.* **-cat·ed, -cat·ing.** 1. To clear of accusation, blame, suspicion, or doubt with supporting proof. 2. To substantiate: *vindicate one's claim.* 3. To justify or prove the worth of, esp. in light of later developments. 4. To avenge. **—vin′di·ca′tion** *n.* **—vin′di·ca′tor** *n.*
vin·dic·tive (vĭn-dĭk′tĭv) ▸ *adj.* 1. Disposed to seek revenge; vengeful. 2. Intended to cause pain or harm; spiteful. **—vin·dic′tive·ly** *adv.* **—vin·dic′tive·ness** *n.*
vine (vīn) ▸ *n.* 1a. A weak-stemmed plant that derives its support from climbing, twining, or creeping along a surface. b. The stem of such a plant. 2. A grapevine.
vin·e·gar (vĭn′ĭ-gər) ▸ *n.* An impure dilute solution of acetic acid obtained by fermentation and used as a condiment and preservative.
vin·e·gar·y (vĭn′ĭ-gə-rē, -grē) ▸ *adj.* 1. Of or like vinegar; acid. 2. Unpleasant and irascible.
vine·yard (vĭn′yərd) ▸ *n.* Ground planted with cultivated grapevines.
vin·i·cul·ture (vĭn′ĭ-kŭl′chər, vī′nĭ-) ▸ *n.* Viticulture.
vin·tage (vĭn′tĭj) ▸ *n.* 1. The yield of wine or grapes from a vineyard or district during one season. 2. Wine, usu. of high quality, identified as to year and vineyard or district of origin. 3a. The harvesting of a grape crop. b. The initial stages of winemaking. 4. A year or period of origin: *a car of 1942 vintage.* ▸ *adj.* 1. Of or relating to a vintage. 2. Of very high quality. 3. Of the best or most distinctive.
vint·ner (vĭnt′nər) ▸ *n.* 1. A wine merchant. 2. One who makes wine.
vi·nyl (vī′nəl) ▸ *n.* Any of various typically tough, flexible, shiny plastics, often used for coverings and clothing.
vi·ol (vī′əl) ▸ *n.* Any of a family of stringed instruments, chiefly of the 16th and 17th cent. having a fretted fingerboard, usu. six strings, and played with a bow.
vi·o·la (vē-ō′lə) ▸ *n.* A stringed instrument of the violin family, slightly larger than a violin, tuned a fifth lower, and having a deeper, more sonorous tone. **—vi·o′list** *n.*
vi·o·la·ble (vī′ə-lə-bəl) ▸ *adj.* That can be violated.
vi·o·late (vī′ə-lāt′) ▸ *v.* **-lat·ed, -lat·ing.** 1. To break or disregard (e.g., a law). 2. To assault (a person) sexually. 3. To desecrate or defile. 4. To disturb; interrupt. **—vi′o·la′tive** *adj.* **—vi′o·la′tor** *n.*
vi·o·la·tion (vī′ə-lā′shən) ▸ *n.* The act or an instance of violating or the condition of being violated.
vi·o·lence (vī′ə-ləns) ▸ *n.* 1. Physical force exerted so as to cause damage, abuse, or injury. 2. An instance of violent action or behavior. 3. Intensity or severity: *the violence of a hurricane.* 4. Detriment to meaning, content, or intent: *do violence to a text.* 5. Vehemence; fervor.
vi·o·lent (vī′ə-lənt) ▸ *adj.* 1. Marked by or resulting from great force. 2. Having or showing great emotional force. 3. Intense; extreme. 4. Caused by unexpected force or injury rather than by natural causes: *a violent death.* **—vi′o·lent·ly** *adv.*
vi·o·let (vī′ə-lĭt) ▸ *n.* 1a. Any of various low-growing plants having spurred irregular flowers that are characteristically purplish-blue but sometimes yellow or white. b. Any of several plants similar to the violet. 2a. A reddish blue. b. The hue of the short-wave end of the visible spectrum.
vi·o·lin (vī′ə-lĭn′) ▸ *n.* A stringed instrument played with a bow, having four strings tuned at intervals of a fifth, an unfretted fingerboard, and a shallower body than the viol. **—vi′o·lin′ist** *n.*
vi·o·lon·cel·lo (vē′ə-lən-chĕl′ō, vī′ə-) ▸ *n., pl.* **-los.** A cello.
VIP (vē′ī-pē′) ▸ *n. Informal* A very important person.
vi·per (vī′pər) ▸ *n.* 1. Any of several venomous Old World snakes having a single pair of long hollow fangs. 2. A venomous or supposedly venomous snake. 3. A malicious or treacherous person. **—vi′per·ous** *adj.*
vi·ra·go (və-rä′gō, -rā′-, vîr′ə-gō′) ▸ *n., pl.* **-goes** or **-gos.** A noisy, domineering woman.
vi·ral (vī′rəl) ▸ *adj.* Of or caused by a virus. **—vi′ral·ly** *adv.*
vir·e·o (vîr′ē-ō′) ▸ *n., pl.* **-os.** Any of various small songbirds having grayish or greenish plumage.
Vir·gil also **Ver·gil** (vûr′jəl) (70–19 B.C.) ▸ Roman poet.
vir·gin (vûr′jĭn) ▸ *n.* 1. A person who has not experienced sexual intercourse. 2. An unmarried woman who has taken religious vows of chastity. 3. **Virgin** Mary, the mother of Jesus. ▸ *adj.* 1. Of or being a virgin; chaste. 2. In a pure or natural state. **—vir·gin′i·ty** *n.*
vir·gin·al[1] (vûr′jə-nəl) ▸ *adj.* 1. Of or befitting a virgin. 2. Untouched or unsullied; fresh.
vir·gin·al[2] (vûr′jə-nəl) ▸ *n.* A small legless harpsichord popular in the 16th and 17th cent.
Vir·gin·ia (vər-jĭn′yə) ▸ A state of the E US on Chesapeake Bay and the Atlantic. Cap. Richmond. **—Vir·gin′ian** *adj. & n.*
Virginia creeper ▸ *n.* A North American climbing vine having compound leaves with five leaflets and bluish-black berries.
Virginia reel ▸ *n.* An American country-dance in which couples perform various steps together to the instructions of a caller.
Virgin Islands ▸ 1. A group of islands of the NE West Indies E of Puerto Rico; divided politically into the **British Virgin Islands** to the NE and the Virgin Islands of the United States to the SW. 2. Officially **Virgin Islands of the United States** A US territory constituting the SW group of the Virgin Is. Cap. Charlotte Amalie.

THESAURUS

villainous *adj.* *—See* CORRUPT (1), FIENDISH.
villainy or **villainousness** *n.* *—See* CORRUPTION (1).
villeinage *n.* *—See* SLAVERY.
vim *n.* *—See* ENERGY, SPIRIT (1).
vincible *adj.* *—See* VULNERABLE.
vinculum *n.* *—See* BOND (2).
vindicate *v.* To show to be just, right, or valid ▸ excuse, justify, rationalize. *Idiom:* make a case for. *—See also* AVENGE, CLAIM, CLEAR (3), DEFEND (2).
vindication *n.* *—See* APOLOGY (1), EXCULPATION.
vindictive *adj.* Disposed to seek revenge ▸ avenging, implacable, revengeful, spiteful, unforbearing, unforgiving, vengeful. [*Compare* RESENTFUL.] *—See also* MALEVOLENT.
vindictiveness *n.* The quality or condition of being vindictive ▸ revenge, spite, spitefulness, vengefulness. [*Compare* RESENTMENT.] *—See also* MALEVOLENCE.
vintage *adj.* Characterized by enduring excellence, appeal, and importance ▸ ageless, antique, classic, classical, enduring, historic, timeless. [*Compare* OLD.] *—See also* SPECIAL.
vintage *n.* *—See* HARVEST.
violate *v.* 1. To fail to fulfill a promise or conform to a regulation ▸ breach, break, contravene, infringe, overstep, transgress. 2. To compel another to participate in or submit to a sexual act ▸ assault, force, molest, rape, ravish. 3. To spoil or mar the sanctity of ▸ defile, desecrate, despoil, pollute, profane. [*Compare* DEBASE, DIRTY, DISGRACE.] *—See also* DISOBEY.
violation *n.* *—See* BREACH (1), SACRILEGE.
violence *n.* *—See* FORCE (1), INTENSITY.
violent *adj.* Accomplished by force ▸ coercive, forced, forcible. *Informal:* strong-arm. *—See also* INTENSE, ROUGH (2).
violently *adv.* With force and violence ▸ coercively, forcibly. *Idioms:* against one's will, by force, under duress.
VIP *n.* *—See* DIGNITARY.
virago *n.* *—See* SCOLD.
virgin *adj.* *—See* CHASTE, CRUDE.
virgin *n.* *—See* INNOCENT (1).
virginal *adj.* *—See* CHASTE, INNOCENT (1).
virginity *n.* *—See* CHASTITY.

Vir·go (vûr′gō) ▸ *n.* **1.** A constellation in the region of the celestial equator between Leo and Libra. **2.** The 6th sign of the zodiac.

vir·gule (vûr′gyo͞ol) ▸ *n.* A diagonal mark (/) used esp. to separate alternatives, as in *and/or,* and to represent the word *per,* as in *miles/hour.*

vir·ile (vîr′əl, -īl′) ▸ *adj.* **1.** Of or having the characteristics of an adult male. **2.** Having or showing masculine spirit, strength, or power. **3.** Capable of performing sexually as a male; potent. **—vi·ril′i·ty** (və-rĭl′ĭ-tē) *n.*

vi·rol·o·gy (vī-rŏl′ə-jē) ▸ *n.* The study of viruses and viral diseases. **—vi·rol′o·gist** *n.*

vir·tu·al (vûr′cho͞o-əl) ▸ *adj.* **1.** Existing in essence or effect though not in actual fact or form. **2.** Created, simulated, or carried on by means of a computer or computer network. **—vir′tu·al′i·ty** (-ăl′ĭ-tē) *n.*

vir·tu·al·ly (vûr′cho͞o-ə-lē) ▸ *adv.* In fact or to all purposes; practically.

virtual reality ▸ *n.* A computer simulation of a real or imaginary system in real time.

vir·tue (vûr′cho͞o) ▸ *n.* **1a.** Moral excellence and righteousness; goodness. **b.** An example or kind of moral excellence. **2.** Chastity, esp. in a woman. **3.** A particularly efficacious or beneficial quality; advantage. **4.** Effective force or power. ***—idiom:* by virtue of** On the basis of.

vir·tu·os·i·ty (vûr′cho͞o-ŏs′ĭ-tē) ▸ *n., pl.* **-ties.** The technical skill, fluency, or style of a virtuoso.

vir·tu·o·so (vûr′cho͞o-ō′sō, -zō) ▸ *n., pl.* **-sos** or **-si** (-sē). **1.** A musician with masterly ability, technique, or style. **2.** A person with masterly skill or technique in any field, esp. the arts. **—vir′tu·o′sic** *adj.*

vir·tu·ous (vûr′cho͞o-əs) ▸ *adj.* **1.** Having or showing virtue, esp. moral excellence. **2.** Chaste; pure. **—vir′tu·ous·ly** *adv.*

vir·u·lent (vîr′yə-lənt, vîr′ə-) ▸ *adj.* **1.** Extremely infectious, harmful, or poisonous, as a disease or toxin. **2.** Bitterly hostile or antagonistic. **—vir′u·lence** *n.* **—vir′u·lent·ly** *adv.*

vi·rus (vī′rəs) ▸ *n.* **1a.** Any of various submicroscopic, often pathogenic parasites that consist essentially of a core of RNA or DNA surrounded by a protein coat and that are typically not considered living organisms. **b.** A disease caused by a virus. **2.** *Comp. Sci.* A self-replicating program that copies itself into other programs on a computer, usu. having negative effects.

vi·sa (vē′zə) ▸ *n.* An official authorization appended to a passport, permitting entry into and travel within a particular country or region.

vis·age (vĭz′ĭj) ▸ *n.* **1.** The face or facial expression of a person; countenance. **2.** Appearance; aspect.

vis-à-vis (vē′zə-vē′) ▸ *prep.* **1.** Compared with. **2.** In relation to. ▸ *adv.* Face to face. ▸ *n., pl.* **vis-à-vis** (-vēz′, -vē′). One opposite or corresponding to another; counterpart.

vis·cer·a (vĭs′ər-ə) ▸ *pl.n.* The internal body organs, esp. those contained within the abdomen and throrax.

vis·cer·al (vĭs′ər-əl) ▸ *adj.* **1.** Of, situated in, or affecting the viscera. **2.** Intensely emotional. **3.** Instinctive. **—vis′cer·al·ly** *adv.*

vis·cid (vĭs′ĭd) ▸ *adj.* Thick and adhesive. Used of a fluid. **—vis·cid′i·ty** *n.* **—vis′cid·ly** *adv.*

vis·cose (vĭs′kōs′) ▸ *n.* A thick, golden-brown viscous solution derived from cellulose, used in the manufacture of rayon and cellophane.

vis·cos·i·ty (vĭ-skŏs′ĭ-tē) ▸ *n., pl.* **-ties.** The condition or property of being viscous.

vis·count (vī′kount′) ▸ *n.* A nobleman ranking below an earl or count and above a baron.

vis·cous (vĭs′kəs) ▸ *adj.* **1.** Having relatively high resistance to flow. **2.** Viscid. **—vis′cous·ly** *adv.* **—vis′cous·ness** *n.*

vise also **vice** (vīs) ▸ *n.* A clamping device, usu. consisting of two jaws closed or opened by a screw or lever, used in carpentry or metalworking to hold a piece in position.

Vish·nu (vĭsh′no͞o) ▸ *n.* *Hinduism* A principal Hindu deity, often conceived as a member of the triad including Brahma and Shiva.

vis·i·bil·i·ty (vĭz′ə-bĭl′ĭ-tē) ▸ *n., pl.* **-ties.** **1.** The fact, state, or degree of being visible. **2.** The greatest distance under given weather conditions to which it is possible to see without instrumental assistance.

vis·i·ble (vĭz′ə-bəl) ▸ *adj.* **1.** Capable of being seen. **2.** Manifest; apparent. **—vis′i·bly** *adv.*

Vis·i·goth (vĭz′ĭ-gŏth′) ▸ *n.* A member of the western Goths that invaded the Roman Empire in the 4th cent. A.D. and settled in France and Spain.

vi·sion (vĭzh′ən) ▸ *n.* **1.** The faculty of sight; eyesight. **2.** Unusual foresight. **3.** A mental image produced by the imagination. **4.** The experience of seeing the supernatural as if with the eyes. **5.** One of extraordinary beauty.

vi·sion·ar·y (vĭzh′ə-nĕr′ē) ▸ *adj.* **1.** Marked by vision or foresight. **2.** Having the nature of fantasies or dreams. **3.** Given to impractical or fanciful ideas. **4.** Not practicable; utopian. ▸ *n., pl.* **-ies.** **1.** One given to speculative, often impractical ideas. **2.** A seer; prophet. **3.** One having unusual foresight.

vis·it (vĭz′ĭt) ▸ *v.* **1.** To go or come to see for reasons of business, duty, or pleasure. **2.** To stay with as a guest.

THESAURUS

virile *adj.* *—See* MANLY.

virility *n.* *—See* MASCULINITY.

virtual *adj.* *—See* THEORETICAL (2).

virtue *n.* A particularly good or beneficial quality ▸ asset, beauty, distinction, merit, strength. [*Compare* ADVANTAGE, EXCELLENCE, QUALITY.] *—See also* CHASTITY, GOOD (1), MERIT.

virtuoso or **virtuosa** *n.* *—See* PLAYER (2).

virtuous *adj.* *—See* CHASTE, ETHICAL, HOLY.

virtuousness *n.* *—See* CHASTITY, GOOD (1).

virulence or **virulency** *n.* *—See* RESENTMENT.

virulent *adj.* *—See* CONTAGIOUS, POISONOUS, RESENTFUL.

virus *n.* *—See* GERM (1), POISON.

visa *n.* *—See* LICENSE (3).

visage *n.* *—See* APPEARANCE (1), EXPRESSION (4), FACE (1).

vis-à-vis *n.* One that has the same functions and characteristics as another ▸ counterpart, equivalent, opposite number.

viscera *n.* Internal organs of the abdomen ▸ bowels, entrails, intestines. *Informal:* guts, insides.

visceral *adj.* *—See* INNER (2), INSTINCTIVE.

viscid *adj.* *—See* VISCOUS.

viscidity *n.* *—See* VISCOSITY.

viscose *adj.* *—See* VISCOUS.

viscosity *n.* The physical property of being viscous ▸ glutinousness, sliminess, stickiness, thickness, viscidity.

viscous *adj.* Having a heavy, gluey quality ▸ gelatinous, glutinous, heavy, mucilaginous, syrupy, thick, viscid, viscose. [*Compare* SLIMY, STICKY.]

vise *n.* *—See* [illegible]

visibility *n.* The quality or degree of being visible or providing a clear view ▸ clarity, clearness, observability, perceptibility, visuality, visualness. *Idiom:* range of vision.

visible *adj.* Capable of being seen ▸ discernible, observable, seeable, viewable, visual. *Idioms:* in sight (*or* view), on display (*or* view). [*Compare* NOTICEABLE, PERCEPTIBLE.] *—See also* APPARENT (1).

vision *n.* **1.** The faculty of seeing ▸ eye, eyesight, optics, seeing, sight. [*Compare* VIEW.] **2.** Discernment or perception which is unusually competent or creative ▸ farsightedness, foreknowledge, foresight, imagination, innovation, inspiration, prescience. *Idiom:* breadth (*or* depth) of view. [*Compare* BRILLIANCE, DISCERNMENT, INSTINCT, INVENTION.] *—See also* BEAUTY, DREAM (1), DREAM (3), PROPHECY.

vision *v.* *—See* IMAGINE.

visionary *adj.* Characterized by foresight or vision ▸ farsighted, foresighted, imaginative, inspired, insightful, intuitive, perceptive, prescient. [*Compare* INTELLIGENT, INVENTIVE.] *—See also* DREAMY, IDEALISTIC, ILLUSIVE, IMAGINARY, PROPHETIC.

visionary *n.* *—See* DREAMER (1).

visit *v.* To go to or seek out the company of someone in order to socialize ▸ call, come around, come by (*or* over), drop by (*or* in), go by (*or* over), look in (*or* up), pop in, run in, see, stop by (*or* in). *Idiom:* pay a visit (*or* a call). *—See also* CONVERSE[1], INFLICT, LODGE.

visit *n.* **1.** An act or an instance of going or coming to see another ▸ call, get-together, look-in, social call, stay, stop, visitation. **2.** A remaining in a

3a. To afflict or assail. **b.** To inflict punishment on or for; avenge. **4.** *Informal* To converse; chat. ► *n.* **1.** An act or instance of visiting. **2.** A stay as a guest. **3.** The act of visiting in an official capacity: *a doctor's visit.*

vis·i·tant (vĭz′ĭ-tənt) ► *n.* A visitor; guest.

vis·i·ta·tion (vĭz′ĭ-tā′shən) ► *n.* **1.** A visit, esp. an official inspection or examination. **2.** The right of a divorced or separated parent to visit a child. **3.** A visit of affliction or blessing regarded as being ordained by God. **—vis′i·ta′tion·al** *adj.*

vis·i·tor (vĭz′ĭ-tər) ► *n.* One that visits.

vi·sor also **vi·zor** (vī′zər) ► *n.* **1.** A projecting part, as on a cap or the windshield of a car, that protects the eyes from sun, wind, or rain. **2.** The movable front piece of a helmet.

vis·ta (vĭs′tə) ► *n.* **1.** A distant view, esp. one seen through an opening. **2.** A broad mental view, as of a series of events.

vi·su·al (vĭzh′o͞o-əl) ► *adj.* **1.** Of or relating to the sense of sight. **2.** Able to be seen; visible. **3.** Done or executed by sight only. **4.** Of a method of instruction involving sight. **—vi′su·al·ly** *adv.*

vi·su·al·ize (vĭzh′o͞o-ə-līz′) ► *v.* **-ized, -iz·ing.** To form a mental image or vision of. **—vi′su·al·i·za′tion** *n.* **—vi′su·al·iz′er** *n.*

vi·ta (vī′tə, vē′-) ► *n., pl.* **vi·tae** (vī′tē, vē′tī). **1.** A short biographical or autobiographical account. **2.** A curriculum vitae.

vi·tal (vīt′l) ► *adj.* **1.** Of or characteristic of life. **2.** Necessary to the continuation of life. **3.** Full of life; animated. **4.** Of great importance; essential. **—vi′tal·ly** *adv.*

vi·tal·i·ty (vī-tăl′ĭ-tē) ► *n., pl.* **-ties. 1.** The capacity to live, grow, or develop. **2.** Vigor; energy. **3.** The principle or force that distinguishes living from nonliving things.

vi·tal·ize (vīt′l-īz′) ► *v.* **-ized, -iz·ing.** To endow with life, vigor, or energy. **—vi′tal·i·za′tion** *n.* **—vi′tal·iz′er** *n.*

vi·tals (vīt′lz) ► *pl.n.* **1.** The vital body organs. **2.** Essential parts, as of a system.

vital signs ► *pl.n.* The pulse rate, temperature, and respiratory rate of an individual.

vital statistics ► *pl.n.* Statistics concerning births, deaths, marriages, and migrations.

vi·ta·min (vī′tə-mĭn) ► *n.* Any of various organic substances essential in minute amounts for normal growth and activity of the body and obtained naturally from plant and animal foods.

vitamin A ► *n.* A vitamin or mixture of vitamins found in fish-liver oils, milk, and some yellow and dark green vegetables, responsible in deficiency for hardening and roughening of the skin and night blindness.

vitamin B ► *n.* **1.** Vitamin B complex. **2.** A member of this complex, esp. thiamine.

vitamin B_1 ► *n.* See **thiamine.**

vitamin B_2 ► *n.* See **riboflavin.**

vitamin B_{12} ► *n.* A complex compound containing cobalt, found esp. in liver and widely used to treat pernicious anemia.

vitamin B complex ► *n.* A group of vitamins including thiamine, riboflavin, niacin, folic acid, biotin, and vitamin B_{12}, occurring chiefly in yeast, liver, eggs, and some vegetables.

vitamin C ► *n.* See **ascorbic acid.**

vitamin D ► *n.* A vitamin that is required for normal growth of teeth and bones and is produced by ultraviolet irradiation of sterols found in milk, fish, and eggs.

vitamin E ► *n.* A vitamin found in plant leaves, wheat germ oil, and milk and used to treat various abnormalities of the muscles, red blood cells, liver, and brain.

vitamin K ► *n.* A vitamin occurring in leafy green vegetables, tomatoes, and egg yolks, that promotes blood clotting and prevents hemorrhaging.

vi·ti·ate (vĭsh′ē-āt′) ► *v.* **-at·ed, -at·ing. 1.** To reduce the value or impair the quality of. **2.** To corrupt morally; debase. **3.** To invalidate. **—vi′ti·a′tion** *n.* **—vi′ti·a′tor** *n.*

vit·i·cul·ture (vĭt′ĭ-kŭl′chər, vī′tĭ-) ► *n.* The cultivation of grapes. **—vit′i·cul′tur·ist** *n.*

vit·re·ous (vĭt′rē-əs) ► *adj.* **1.** Of or resembling glass; glassy. **2.** Of or relating to the vitreous humor.

vitreous humor ► *n.* The clear gelatinous substance that fills the eyeball between the retina and the lens.

vit·ri·fy (vĭt′rə-fī′) ► *v.* **-fied, -fy·ing.** To change or make into glass or a glassy substance, esp. through heat fusion. **—vit′ri·fi·ca′tion** *n.*

vit·ri·ol (vĭt′rē-ōl′, -əl) ► *n.* **1a.** See **sulfuric acid. b.** Any of various sulfates of metals. **2.** Bitterly abusive feeling or expression.

vit·ri·ol·ic (vĭt′rē-ŏl′ĭk) ► *adj.* **1.** Of or derived from vitriol. **2.** Bitterly scathing; caustic.

vit·tles (vĭt′əlz) ► *pl.n. Nonstandard* Victuals.

vi·tu·per·ate (vī-to͞o′pə-rāt′, -tyo͞o′-, vĭ-) ► *v.* **-at·ed, -at·ing.** To rail against abusively; berate. **—vi·tu′per·a′tion** *n.* **—vi·tu′per·a·tive** *adj.*

vi·va (vē′və, -vä′) ► *interj.* Used to express acclamation, salute, or applause.

vi·va·ce (vē-vä′chā) ► *adv. & adj. Mus.* Lively; briskly. Used as a direction.

vi·va·cious (vĭ-vā′shəs, vī-) ► *adj.* Full of animation and spirit; lively. **—vi·va′cious·ly** *adv.* **—vi·vac′i·ty** (-văs′ĭ-tē), **vi·va′cious·ness** *n.*

viv·id (vĭv′ĭd) ► *adj.* **1.** Perceived as bright and distinct; brilliant. **2.** Having intensely bright colors. **3.** Full of the freshness of immediate experience. **4a.** Evoking lifelike mental images. **b.** Active in forming lifelike images: *a vivid imagination.* **—viv′id·ly** *adv.* **—viv′id·ness** *n.*

viv·i·fy (vĭv′ə-fī′) ► *v.* **-fied, -fy·ing. 1.** To give or bring life to; animate. **2.** To make more lively, intense, or striking; enliven.

vi·vip·a·rous (vī-vĭp′ər-əs, vĭ-) ► *adj.* Giving birth to living offspring that develop within the mother's body. **—vi′vi·par′i·ty** (vī′və-păr′ĭ-tē, vĭv′ə-) *n.* **—vi·vip′a·rous·ly** *adv.*

viv·i·sec·tion (vĭv′ĭ-sĕk′shən) ► *n.* The cutting into or operation upon living animals, esp. for scientific research. **—viv′i·sect′** *v.*

vix·en (vĭk′sən) ► *n.* **1.** A female fox. **2.** A quarrelsome, shrewish, or malicious woman. **—vix′en·ish** *adj.*

viz. ► *abbr. Lat.* videlicet (namely)

viz·ard (vĭz′ərd, -ärd′) ► *n.* A mask.

vi·zier (vĭ-zîr′, vĭz′yər) ► *n.* A high officer in a Muslim

THESAURUS

place as a guest or lodger ► sojourn, stay, stop, stopover.

visitant *n.* A person or persons visiting one ► caller, company, guest, visitor. *—See also* GHOST.

visitation *n. —See* TRIAL (1), VISIT (1).

visitor *n.* **1.** A person or persons visiting one ► caller, company, guest, visitant. **2.** One that arrives ► arrival, comer, newcomer. [*Compare* ADDITION, COMPANY.] *—See also* TOURIST.

visor *n. —See* BILL² (2).

vista *n. —See* EXPANSE (1), LOOKOUT (2), VIEW (2).

visual *adj.* Serving, resulting from, or relating to the sense of sight ► ocular, optic, optical, seeing. *—See also* VISIBLE.

visuality *n. —See* VISIBILITY.

visualize *v. —See* IMAGINE.

vital *adj. —See* ALIVE, ESSENTIAL (2), LUSTY, PRIMARY (1), URGENT (1).

vital force *n. —See* SPIRIT (2).

vitality *n. —See* ENERGY, SPIRIT (2).

vitalize *v.* To make alive ► animate, enliven, quicken, vivify. [*Compare* ELATE, PROVOKE.] *—See also* ENERGIZE.

vitalizing *adj. —See* INVIGORATING.

vitiate *v. —See* ABOLISH, CORRUPT, DAMAGE.

vitreous or **vitrescent** *adj.* Of or resembling glass ► glasslike, glassy, hyaline. [*Compare* TRANSLUCENT.]

vitriolic *adj. —See* BITING.

vituperate *v. —See* REVILE.

vituperation *n.* Sustained, harshly abusive language ► abuse, billingsgate, condemnation, contumely, denunciation, invective, obloquy, railing, revilement, reviling, scurrility, scurrilousness. [*Compare* BELITTLEMENT, CURSE, LIBEL, TIRADE.]

vituperative *adj. —See* ABUSIVE.

vivacious *adj. —See* LIVELY, SPIRIT (1).

vivacity or **vivaciousness** *n. —See* SPIRIT (1).

vivid *adj.* Evoking strong mental images through distinctiveness ► colorful, graphic, picturesque, striking. *—See also* COLORFUL (1), DESCRIPTIVE, DRAMATIC (2), GRAPHIC (1).

vivify *v.* To make alive ► animate, enliven, quicken, vitalize. [*Compare* ELATE, ENERGIZE, PROVOKE.]

vivifying *adj. —See* INVIGORATING.

vixen *n. —See* SCOLD.

viz. *adv. —See* NAMELY.

government, esp. in the Ottoman Empire.

vi·zor (vī′zər) ▸ *n.* Var. of **visor.**

Vla·di·vos·tok (vlăd′ə-və-stŏk′, -vŏs′tŏk′) ▸ A city of extreme SE Russia on an arm of the Sea of Japan.

vo·ca·ble (vo′kə-bəl) ▸ *n.* A word considered as a sequence of sounds or letters rather than as a unit of meaning.

vo·cab·u·lar·y (vō-kăb′yə-lĕr′ē) ▸ *n., pl.* **-ies.** **1.** All the words of a language. **2.** The sum of words used by a particular person or group. **3.** A list of words and often phrases, usu. arranged alphabetically and defined or translated; lexicon.

vo·cal (vō′kəl) ▸ *adj.* **1.** Of or for the voice. **2.** Uttered or produced by the voice. **3.** Capable of emitting sound or speech. **4.** Full of voices; resounding. **5.** Quick to speak or criticize; outspoken. ▸ *n.* **1.** A vocal sound. **2.** *Mus.* A singing part: *jazz vocals.* **—vo′cal·ly** *adv.*

vocal cords ▸ *pl.n.* A pair of bands or folds of mucous membrane in the larynx that vibrate when pulled together and when air is passed up from the lungs, thereby producing vocal sounds.

vo·cal·ic (vō-kăl′ĭk) ▸ *adj.* Relating to or having the nature of a vowel.

vo·cal·ist (vō′kə-lĭst) ▸ *n.* A singer.

vo·cal·ize (vō′kə-līz′) ▸ *v.* **-ized, -iz·ing.** **1.** To use the voice, esp. to sing. **2.** To give voice to. **3.** To articulate (a consonant) as a vowel. **—vo′cal·i·za′tion** *n.* **—vo′cal·iz′er** *n.*

vo·ca·tion (vō-kā′shən) ▸ *n.* **1.** An occupation, esp. one for which a person is particularly suited. **2.** A calling, esp. to a religious career. **—vo·ca′tion·al** *adj.*

vocational school ▸ *n.* A school that offers instruction in skilled trades such as mechanics or carpentry.

voc·a·tive (vŏk′ə-tĭv) ▸ *adj.* Of or being a grammatical case indicating the one being addressed. **—voc′a·tive** *n.*

vo·cif·er·ate (vō-sĭf′ə-rāt′) ▸ *v.* **-at·ed, -at·ing.** To cry out loudly and vehemently, esp. in protest.

vo·cif·er·ous (vō-sĭf′ər-əs) ▸ *adj.* Making an outcry; clamorous. **—vo·cif′er·ous·ly** *adv.* **—vo·cif′er·ous·ness** *n.*

vod·ka (vŏd′kə) ▸ *n.* A clear alcoholic liquor distilled from a mash of fermented wheat, rye, corn, or potatoes.

vogue (vōg) ▸ *n.* **1.** The prevailing fashion, practice, or style. **2.** Popular acceptance or favor; popularity. **—vogu′ish** *adj.*

voice (vois) ▸ *n.* **1a.** Sound produced by the vocal organs of a vertebrate, esp. a human. **b.** The ability to produce such sounds: *lost her voice.* **2.** A specified quality, condition, or pitch of vocal sound. **3.** *Ling.* Expiration of air through vibrating vocal cords, used in the production of vowels and voiced consonants. **4.** A sound resembling vocal utterance: *the voice of the wind.* **5.** *Mus. a.* Musical sound produced by vibration of the vocal cords. **b.** A singer: *a choir of 200 voices.* **c.** One of the individual parts or strands in a composition. **6a.** Expression; utterance. **b.** A medium or agency of expression. **c.** The right or opportunity to express a choice or opinion. **7.** *Gram.* A verb form indicating the relation between the subject and the action expressed by the verb. ▸ *v.* **voiced, voic·ing.** **1.** To give voice to; utter. **2.** *Ling.* To pronounce with vibration of the vocal cords. **3.** *Mus.* To regulate the tone of (e.g., the pipes of an organ).

voice box ▸ *n.* The larynx.

voiced (voist) ▸ *adj.* **1.** Having a voice or a specified kind of voice: *harsh-voiced.* **2.** *Ling.* Uttered with vibration of the vocal cords, as the consonant *b.*

voice·less (vois′lĭs) ▸ *adj.* **1.** Having no voice. **2.** *Ling.* Uttered without vibration of the vocal cords, as the consonant *t.* **—voice′less·ly** *adv.* **—voice′less·ness** *n.*

voice mail ▸ *n.* A computerized system for leaving and receiving telephone messages.

voice-o·ver or **voice·o·ver** (vois′ō′vər) ▸ *n.* The voice of an unseen narrator in a movie or a television broadcast.

voice·print (vois′prĭnt′) ▸ *n.* An electronically recorded graphic representation of a person's voice.

void (void) ▸ *adj.* **1.** Containing no matter; empty. **2.** Not occupied; vacant. **3.** Completely lacking; devoid. **4.** Ineffective; useless. **5.** Having no legal force or validity; null. ▸ *n.* **1.** An empty space; vacuum. **2.** A feeling of emptiness, loneliness, or loss. ▸ *v.* **1.** To empty. **2.** To excrete (body wastes). **3.** To leave; vacate. **4.** To make void; invalidate. **—void′a·ble** *adj.* **—void′er** *n.*

voile (voil) ▸ *n.* A sheer fabric of cotton, rayon, silk, or wool used for making lightweight dresses and curtains.

vol. ▸ *abbr.* volume

vol·a·tile (vŏl′ə-tl, -tīl′) ▸ *adj.* **1.** Evaporating readily at normal temperatures and pressures. **2a.** Tending to vary often. **b.** Inconstant; fickle. **c.** Ephemeral; fleeting. **3.** Tending to violence; explosive. **—vol′a·til′i·ty** (-tĭl′ĭ-tē) *n.*

vol·a·til·ize (vŏl′ə-tl-īz′) ▸ *v.* **-ized, -iz·ing.** **1.** To become or make volatile. **2.** To evaporate or cause to evaporate.

vol·can·ic (vŏl-kăn′ĭk, vôl-) ▸ *adj.* **1.** Of or resembling a volcano. **2.** Powerfully explosive: *a volcanic temper.*

vol·ca·nism (vŏl′kə-nĭz′əm) also **vul·ca·nism** (vŭl′-) ▸ *n.* Volcanic force or activity.

vol·ca·no (vŏl-kā′nō) ▸ *n., pl.* **-noes** or **-nos.** **1.** An opening in the earth's crust through which molten lava, ash, and gases are ejected. **2.** A mountain formed by the materials ejected from a volcano.

Volcano Islands ▸ A group of Japanese islands in the NW Pacific N of the Mariana Is.

vole (vōl) ▸ *n.* Any of various rodents resembling rats or mice but having a shorter tail.

Vol·ga (vŏl′gə) ▸ A river of W Russia rising NW of Moscow and flowing about 3,701 km (2,300 mi) to the Caspian Sea.

Vol·go·grad (vŏl′gə-grăd′). Formerly **Stalingrad** ▸ A city of SW Russia on the Volga R. E of Voroshilovgrad.

vo·li·tion (və-lĭsh′ən) ▸ *n.* **1.** The act of making a conscious choice or decision. **2.** A conscious choice or decision. **3.** The power or faculty of choosing; will. **—vo·li′tion·al** *adj.*

vol·ley (vŏl′ē) ▸ *n., pl.* **-leys.** **1a.** A simultaneous discharge of a number of shots or missiles. **b.** The missiles thus discharged. **2.** A bursting forth of many things together: *a*

THESAURUS

vocable *n.* —*See* TERM.

vocabulary *n.* **1.** All the words of a language ▸ lexicon, word-hoard. **2.** An alphabetical list of words often defined or translated ▸ dictionary, glossary, lexicon, wordbook. —*See also* LANGUAGE (2).

vocal *adj.* Characterized by, containing, or functioning as a vowel or vowels ▸ sonorant, vocalic, vowel. —*See also* FRANK, ORAL.

vocalism *n.* —*See* VOICING.

vocalist *n.* A person who sings ▸ singer, songster, songstress, voice. *Slang:* crooner, songbird. [*Compare* PLAYER.]

vocalization *n.* —*See* EXPRESSION (1), SPEECH (1), VOICING.

vocalize *v.* To express oneself in speech ▸ speak, talk, verbalize. —*See also* PRONOUNCE, SAY, SING.

vocation *n.* An inner urge to pursue an activity or perform a service ▸ calling, mission. [*Compare* DREAM, DUTY, FATE.] —*See also* BUSINESS (2).

vociferate *v.* —*See* SHOUT.

vociferation *n.* Loud and insistent utterance or noisemaking, usually expressing disapproval ▸ brouhaha, clamor, hullabaloo, katzenjammer, outcry, rumpus, uproar. *Idiom:* hue and cry. [*Compare* NOISE.]

vociferous or **vociferant** *adj.* Offensively loud and insistent ▸ blatant, boisterous, clamorous, obstreperous, stentorian, strident. *Informal:* loudmouthed. [*Compare* HARSH, LOUD.]

vogue *n.* —*See* FASHION.

voice *n.* The right or chance to express an opinion or participate in a decision ▸ input, say, suffrage, vote. *Informal:* say-so, two cents (worth). —*See also* EXPRESSION (1), VOCALIST.

voice *v.* —*See* AIR (2), PRONOUNCE, SAY.

voiced *adj.* —*See* ORAL.

voiceless *adj.* —*See* MUTE, SPEECHLESS.

voicing *n.* The use of the vocal organs to produce sound or speech ▸ articulation, enunciation, pronunciation, saying, utterance, vocalism, vocalization. [*Compare* SPEECH.]

void *adj.* —*See* EMPTY (1), EMPTY (2).

void *n.* —*See* EMPTINESS (1), GAP (2), HOLE (1), NOTHINGNESS (2).

void *v.* —*See* ABOLISH, EMPTY.

voidance *n.* —*See* ABOLITION.

volatile *adj.* —*See* CAPRICIOUS.

volatilize *v.* —*See* EVAPORATE.

volition *n.* The mental faculty by which one deliberately chooses or decides ▸ free will, will. [*Compare* SPIRIT.] —*See also* CHOICE.

volitional *adj.* —*See* VOLUNTARY.

volley *n.* —*See* BARRAGE.

volley of questions. 3. *Sports* An act of volleying, esp. in tennis. ► *v.* 1. To discharge or be discharged in or as if in a volley. 2. *Sports* To strike (a ball) before it touches the ground. **—vol′ley·er** *n.*

vol·ley·ball (vŏl′ē-bôl′) ► *n.* 1. A game played by two teams on a court divided by a high net, in which up to three hits are used to ground the ball on the opposing team's court. 2. The inflated ball used in this game.

volt (vōlt) ► *n.* The unit of electric potential and electromotive force equal to the difference in potential needed to cause a current of one ampere to flow through a resistance of one ohm.

Vol·ta (vŏl′tə) ► A river of W Africa, flowing about 467 km (290 mi) through Ghana to the Gulf of Guinea.

Vol·ta (vōl′tä), Count **Alessandro** (1745–1827) ► Italian physicist.

volt·age (vōl′tĭj) ► *n.* Electromotive force or potential difference, usu. expressed in volts.

vol·ta·ic (vŏl-tā′ĭk, vōl-, vôl-) ► *adj.* Of or producing electricity by chemical action; galvanic.

Vol·taire (vōl-târ′, vŏl-). François Marie Arouet. (1694–1778) ► French philosopher and writer.

volt·me·ter (vōlt′mē′tər) ► *n.* An instrument for measuring potential differences in volts.

vol·u·ble (vŏl′yə-bəl) ► *adj.* Marked by a ready flow of speech; fluent. **—vol′u·bil′i·ty** *n.* **—vol′u·bly** *adv.*

vol·ume (vŏl′yo͞om, -yəm) ► *n.* 1a. A collection of written or printed sheets bound together; book. **b.** One of the books of a set. **c.** A series of issues of a periodical, usu. covering one calendar year. 2a. The amount of space occupied by a three-dimensional object or region of space. **b.** The capacity of such a region or of a specified container. 3. Amount; quantity: *a low volume of business.* 4a. The amplitude or loudness of a sound.. **b.** A control for adjusting loudness.

vol·u·met·ric (vŏl′yo͞o-mĕt′rĭk) ► *adj.* Of or relating to measurement by volume.

vo·lu·mi·nous (və-lo͞o′mə-nəs) ► *adj.* 1. Having great volume, fullness, size, or number. 2. Filling or capable of filling many volumes. 3. Having many coils; winding. **—vo·lu′mi·nous·ly** *adv.* **—vo·lu′mi·nous·ness** *n.*

vol·un·tar·y (vŏl′ən-tĕr′ē) ► *adj.* 1. Arising from one's own free will. 2. Acting or done willingly and without constraint or expectation of reward. 3. Normally controlled by or subject to individual volition. 4. *Law* Done deliberately; intentional. ► *n., pl.* **-ies.** A piece for solo organ played before, during, or after a religious service. **—vol′un·tar′i·ly** (-târ′ə-lē) *adv.*

vol·un·teer (vŏl′ən-tîr′) ► *n.* A person who performs or offers a service of his or her own free will. ► *v.* 1. To give or offer of one's own accord. 2. To perform or offer to perform a service of one's own free will.

vol·un·teer·ism (vŏl′ən-tîr′ĭz′əm) ► *n.* Use of or reliance on volunteers.

vo·lup·tu·ar·y (və-lŭp′cho͞o-ĕr′ē) ► *n., pl.* **-ies.** One who is given over to luxury and sensual pleasures. **—vo·lup′tu·ar′y** *adj.*

vo·lup·tu·ous (və-lŭp′cho͞o-əs) ► *adj.* 1. Of, marked by, or giving sensual pleasure. 2. Devoted to or indulging in sensual pleasures. 3. Full and appealing in form. **—vo·lup′tu·ous·ly** *adv.* **—vo·lup′tu·ous·ness** *n.*

vo·lute (və-lo͞ot′) ► *n.* A spiral, scroll-like formation or decoration.

vom·it (vŏm′ĭt) ► *v.* 1. To eject part or all of the contents of the stomach through the mouth. 2. To eject or discharge in a gush; spew out. ► *n.* Matter ejected from the stomach through the mouth.

voo·doo (vo͞o′do͞o) ► *n.* 1. A religion practiced chiefly in Caribbean countries, esp. Haiti, in which a supreme God rules a pantheon of local deities, deified ancestors, and saints. 2. A fetish, spell, or curse holding magic power for adherents of voodoo. 3. A priest or priestess of voodoo. 4. Deceptive or delusive nonsense. **—voo′doo·ism** *n.*

vo·ra·cious (vô-rā′shəs, və-) ► *adj.* 1. Consuming or eager to consume great amounts of food; ravenous. 2. Exceedingly eager; insatiable. **—vo·ra′cious·ly** *adv.* **—vo·rac′i·ty** (-răs′ĭ-tē), **vo·ra′cious·ness** *n.*

-vorous ► *suff.* Eating; feeding on: *omnivorous.*

vor·tex (vôr′tĕks′) ► *n., pl.* **-es** or **-ti·ces** (-tĭ-sēz′). 1. A spiral motion of fluid, esp. a whirling mass of water or air; whirlpool or whirlwind. 2. Something regarded as drawing into its center all that surrounds it. **—vor′ti·cal** *adj.*

vo·ta·ry (vō′tə-rē) ► *n., pl.* **-ries.** 1a. One bound by religious vows. **b.** A devout worshiper. 2. One who is fervently devoted, as to a leader, activity, or ideal.

vote (vōt) ► *n.* 1a. A formal expression of preference for a candidate for office or for a proposed resolution of an issue. **b.** A means by which such a preference is made known, such as a raised hand or a marked ballot. 2. The number of votes cast in an election or to resolve an issue. 3. A group of voters: *the rural vote.* 4. The result of an election. 5. Suffrage. ► *v.* **vot·ed, vot·ing.** 1. To cast a vote. 2. To endorse, bring into existence, or make available by vote. 3. To declare by general consent: *voted the play a success.* **—vot′er** *n.*

vo·tive (vō′tĭv) ► *adj.* Given or dedicated in fulfillment of a vow.

THESAURUS

volubility *n.* —*See* ELOQUENCE.

voluble *adj.* —*See* ELOQUENT, TALKATIVE.

volume *n.* —*See* BOOK, BULK (1), PUBLICATION (2), SIZE (1).

voluminous *adj.* —*See* BULKY (1), FULL (3), GENEROUS (2).

voluntarily *adv.* Of one's own free will ► by choice, freely, spontaneously, willfully, willingly. *Idioms:* of one's own accord, on one's own (*or* own volition).

voluntary *adj.* Of or relating to free exercise of the will ► spontaneous, uncompelled, unforced, volitional, willed, willful, willing. [*Compare* FREE, INDEPENDENT.] —*See also* DELIBERATE (1), UNPAID.

voluntary *n.* Someone who offers his or her services freely ► volunteer.

volunteer *v.* —*See* OFFER (1).

volunteer *adj.* —*See* UNPAID.

volunteer *n.* Someone who offers his or her services freely ► voluntary.

voluptuary *n.* —*See* SYBARITE.

voluptuary *adj.* Characterized by or devoted to pleasure and luxury as a lifestyle ► epicurean, hedonic, hedonistic, sybaritic, voluptuous. [*Compare* LUXURIOUS, SENSUAL.]

voluptuous *adj.* 1. Characterized by or devoted to pleasure and luxury as a lifestyle ► epicurean, hedonic, hedonistic, sybaritic, voluptuary. [*Compare* LUXURIOUS.] 2. Relating to, suggestive of, or appealing to sense gratification ► epicurean, sensual, sensualistic, sensuous. —*See also* SENSUAL (2).

voluptuousness *n.* The quality or condition of being sensuous ► sensualism, sensuality, sensuousness. —*See also* SENSUALITY (1).

vomit *v.* To eject the contents of the stomach through the mouth ► heave, retch, spit up, throw up. *Informal:* puke. *Slang:* barf, boot, chuck, hurl, ralph, spew, upchuck, yack, yarf. *Idioms:* blow chunks, do the technicolor yawn, drive (ride) the porcelain bus, hug the throne, worship the porcelain god. —*See also* ERUPT.

voodoo *v.* —*See* CHARM (2).

n. —*See* MAGIC (1).

voracious *adj.* Having an insatiable appetite for an activity or pursuit ► avid, edacious, gluttonous, greedy, insatiable, obsessive, omnivorous, rapacious, ravenous, unappeasable, wolfish. [*Compare* ENTHUSIASTIC, GREEDY.] —*See also* GLUTTONOUS, HUNGRY (1).

voracity *n.* The quality or condition of being voracious ► avidity, avidness, edacity, insatiability, obsessiveness, omnivorousness, rapaciousness, rapacity, ravenousness, voraciousness. [*Compare* APPETITE, ENTHUSIASM, GREED, LUST.]

vortex *n.* —*See* WHIRLPOOL.

votary *n.* —*See* DEVOTEE.

vote *v.* 1. To select by vote for an office ► elect, vote in. [*Compare* CHOOSE.] 2. To cast a vote ► ballot, poll. *Idioms:* exercise one's civic duty, go to the polls. —*See also* CHOOSE (1).

vote down *v.* —*See* EXCLUDE.

vote *n.* The right or chance to express an opinion or participate in a decision ► input, say, suffrage, voice. *Informal:* say-so.

voter *n.* One who votes ► balloter, elector. *Idiom:* member of the electorate.

vouch (vouch) ▸ *v.* **1.** To give a personal assurance or guarantee: *I can vouch for his integrity.* **2.** To serve as a guarantee. **3.** To substantiate by supplying evidence.

vouch·er (vou′chər) ▸ *n.* **1.** One that vouches. **2.** A written record, as of an expenditure or transaction. **3.** A certificate representing a credit against future expenditures.

vouch·safe (vouch-sāf′, vouch′sāf′) ▸ *v.* **-safed, -saf·ing.** To condescend to grant or bestow.

vow[1] (vou) ▸ *n.* **1.** An earnest promise that binds one to a specified act or mode of behavior. **2.** A declaration or assertion. ▸ *v.* **1.** To promise solemnly; pledge. **2.** To make a vow. ***—idiom:* take vows** To enter a religious order. **—vow′er** *n.*

vow[2] (vou) ▸ *v.* To declare or assert.

vow·el (vou′əl) ▸ *n.* **1.** A speech sound created by the relatively free passage of breath through the larynx and mouth. **2.** A letter representing a vowel.

vox pop·u·li (vŏks pŏp′yə-lī′, -lē) ▸ *n.* Popular opinion.

voy·age (voi′ĭj) ▸ *n.* **1.** A long journey, esp. by sea, to foreign or distant parts. **2.** A journey through outer space. ▸ *v.* **-aged, -ag·ing.** To make a voyage. **—voy′ag·er** *n.*

voy·eur (voi-yûr′) ▸ *n.* A person who derives sexual gratification from observing the sexual acts of others. **—voy·eur′ism** *n.* **—voy′eur·is′tic** *adj.*

VP ▸ *abbr.* vice president

vs. ▸ *abbr.* versus

VT also **Vt.** ▸ *abbr.* Vermont

Vul·can (vŭl′kən) ▸ *n. Rom. Myth.* The god of fire and metalworking.

vul·ca·nism (vŭl′kə-nĭz′əm) ▸ *n.* Var. of **volcanism.**

vul·ca·nize (vŭl′kə-nīz′) ▸ *v.* **-nized, -niz·ing.** To improve the strength, resiliency, and texture of (e.g., rubber) by combining with sulfur or other additives under heat and pressure. **—vul′ca·ni·za′tion** *n.* **—vul′ca·niz′er** *n.*

vul·gar (vŭl′gər) ▸ *adj.* **1.** Of or associated with the common people. **2.** Of or expressed in language spoken by the common people; vernacular. **3.** Deficient in taste, cultivation, or refinement. **4.** Crudely indecent. **—vul′gar·ly** *adv.*

vul·gar·i·an (vŭl-gâr′ē-ən) ▸ *n.* A vulgar person.

vul·gar·ism (vŭl′gə-rĭz′əm) ▸ *n.* **1.** Vulgarity. **2a.** A crudely indecent word or phrase; obscenity. **b.** A word, phrase, or manner of expression used chiefly by uneducated people.

vul·gar·i·ty (vŭl-găr′ĭ-tē) ▸ *n., pl.* **-ties. 1.** The quality or condition of being vulgar. **2.** Something, such as an act or expression, that offends good taste or propriety.

vul·gar·ize (vŭl′gə-rīz′) ▸ *v.* **-ized, -iz·ing. 1.** To make vulgar; debase. **2.** To popularize. **—vul′gar·i·za′tion** *n.* **—vul′gar·iz′er** *n.*

Vulgar Latin ▸ *n.* The common speech of the ancient Romans, which is distinguished from standard literary Latin and is the ancestor of the Romance languages.

vul·gate (vŭl′gāt′, -gĭt) ▸ *n.* **1.** Common speech; vernacular. **2. Vulgate** The Latin edition of the Bible used as the Roman Catholic authorized version.

vul·ner·a·ble (vŭl′nər-ə-bəl) ▸ *adj.* **1a.** Not protected against harm or injury. **b.** Susceptible to attack; assailable. **c.** Easily affected or hurt, as by criticism. **2.** *Games* In a position to receive greater penalties or bonuses after winning one game of a rubber. **—vul′ner·a·bil′i·ty** *n.* **—vul′ner·a·bly** *adv.*

vul·pine (vŭl′pīn′) ▸ *adj.* **1.** Of a fox. **2.** Cunning.

vul·ture (vŭl′chər) ▸ *n.* **1.** Any of various large, usu. carrion-eating birds characteristically having dark plumage and a featherless head and neck. **2.** A greedy, opportunistic person.

vul·va (vŭl′və) ▸ *n., pl.* **-vae** (-vē). The external genital organs of the female. **—vul′val, vul′var** *adj.*

v.v. ▸ *abbr.* vice versa

THESAURUS

vouch *v.* To confirm formally as true, accurate, or genuine ▸ attest, certify, testify, vouch for, witness. *Idiom:* bear witness to. —*See also* BACK (2).

vouchsafe *v.* To let have as a favor, prerogative, or privilege ▸ accord, award, concede, give, grant. [*Compare* YIELD.] —*See also* CONDESCEND (1).

vow *n.* —*See* PROMISE (1).

vow *v.* —*See* PLEDGE (1).

vowel *adj.* Characterized by, containing, or functioning as a vowel or vowels ▸ sonorant, vocal, vocalic.

voyage *n.* —*See* EXPEDITION, JOURNEY.

voyage *v.* —*See* JOURNEY.

vulgar *adj.* —*See* COARSE (1), GAUDY, LOWLY (1), OBSCENE.

vulgarian *n.* —*See* BOOR.

vulgarity *n.* —*See* OBSCENITY (1), OBSCENITY (2).

vulgarness *n.* —*See* OBSCENITY (1).

vulnerability or **vulnerableness** *n.* —*See* EXPOSURE.

vulnerable *adj.* Susceptible to physical or emotional injury or attack ▸ assailable, attackable, defenseless, helpless, pregnable, susceptible, susceptive, unprotected, vincible. *Idioms:* like a sitting duck, open to attack. [*Compare* INSECURE, OPEN.] —*See also* LIABLE (2).

W

w¹ or **W** (dŭb′əl-yo͞o, -yo͞o) ▸ *n., pl.* **w's** or **W's** also **ws** or **Ws**. The 23rd letter of the English alphabet.
w² ▸ *abbr.* **1.** weight **2.** width
W¹ ▸ The symbol for the element **tungsten**.
W² ▸ *abbr.* **1.** watt **2.** Wednesday **3.** week **4a.** west **b.** western
w. ▸ *abbr.* **1.** wife **2.** also **w/** with
WA ▸ *abbr.* Washington
wack·y (wăk′ē) also **whack·y** (hwăk′ē, wăk′ē) ▸ *adj.* **-i·er, -i·est.** *Slang* **1.** Eccentric. **2.** Crazy; silly. **—wack′i·ly** *adv.* **—wack′i·ness** *n.*
wad (wŏd) ▸ *n.* **1.** A small mass of soft material. **2.** A compressed ball, roll, or lump, as of tobacco. **3.** A plug, as of cloth, used to hold a powder charge in place, as in a muzzleloading gun. **4.** *Informal* A large amount. **5.** *Informal* A sizable roll of paper money. ▸ *v.* **wad·ded, wad·ding. 1.** To compress into a wad. **2.** To pad, pack, line, or plug with wadding.
wad·ding (wŏd′ĭng) ▸ *n.* **1.** Wads collectively. **2.** A soft layer of fibrous cotton or wool used for padding. **3.** Material for gun wads.
wad·dle (wŏd′l) ▸ *v.* **-dled, -dling.** To walk with short steps that tilt the body from side to side, as a duck does. **—wad′dle** *n.* **—wad′dler** *n.*
wade (wād) ▸ *v.* **wad·ed, wad·ing. 1.** To walk in or through a substance, such as water, that impedes movement. **2.** To make one's way arduously: *waded through a boring report.*
wad·er (wā′dər) ▸ *n.* **1.** See **wading bird. 2. waders** Waterproof hip boots or trousers.
wa·di (wä′dē) ▸ *n., pl.* **-dis** also **-dies. 1.** A valley, gully, or streambed in N Africa and SW Asia that remains dry except during the rainy season. **2.** An oasis.
wad·ing bird (wā′dĭng) ▸ *n.* A long-legged bird that frequents shallow water.
wa·fer (wā′fər) ▸ *n.* **1.** A thin crisp cake, biscuit, or candy. **2.** *Eccles.* A small thin disk of unleavened bread used in the Eucharist. **3.** A small adhesive seal for papers. **4.** *Electron.* A thin semiconductor slice on which an integrated circuit can be formed.
waf·fle¹ (wŏf′əl) ▸ *n.* A light crisp batter cake baked in a waffle iron.
waf·fle² (wŏf′əl) ▸ *v.* **-fled, -fling.** *Informal* To speak or write evasively.
waffle iron ▸ *n.* An appliance having hinged indented plates that impress a grid pattern into waffle batter as it cooks.
waft (wäft, wăft) ▸ *v.* To carry or cause to go gently and smoothly through the air or over water. ▸ *n.* **1.** A whiff. **2.** A light breeze.
wag¹ (wăg) ▸ *v.* **wagged, wag·ging.** To move or cause to move briskly and repeatedly from side to side, to and fro, or up and down. **—wag** *n.*
wag² (wăg) ▸ *n.* A humorous or droll person; wit. **—wag′ger·y** *n.* **—wag′gish** *adj.* **—wag′gish·ly** *adv.*
wage (wāj) ▸ *n.* **1.** Payment for labor or services to a worker. **2. wages** *(takes sing. or pl. v.)* A suitable return or reward. ▸ *v.* **waged, wag·ing.** To engage in (e.g., a war or campaign).
wa·ger (wā′jər) ▸ *n.* Something staked on an uncertain outcome. ▸ *v.* To bet.
wag·gle (wăg′əl) ▸ *v.* **-gled, -gling.** To move or wave with short quick motions; wag. **—wag′gle** *v.* **—wag′gly** *adj.*
wag·on (wăg′ən) ▸ *n.* **1.** A large, four-wheeled vehicle drawn by draft animals or tractor and used esp. for transporting loads. **2a.** A station wagon. **b.** A police patrol wagon. **3.** A child's low, four-wheeled cart. ***—idiom:* on the wagon** *Slang* Abstaining from alcohol.
wagon train ▸ *n.* A line or train of wagons traveling cross-country.
wa·hoo (wä-ho͞o′, wä′ho͞o) ▸ *n., pl.* **-hoo** or **-hoos.** A tropical marine food and game fish of the mackerel family.
waif (wāf) ▸ *n.* **1.** A homeless or forsaken child. **2.** A stray animal.
Wai·ki·ki (wī′kĭ-kē′) ▸ A beach and resort district of Oahu I., HI, SE of Honolulu.
wail (wāl) ▸ *v.* **1.** To cry loudly and mournfully, as in grief or protest. **2.** To make a mournful, high-pitched sound: *The wind wailed through the trees.* **—wail** *n.* **—wail′er** *n.*
wain (wān) ▸ *n.* A large open farm wagon.
wain·scot (wān′skət, -skŏt′, -skōt′) ▸ *n.* **1.** A facing or paneling, usu. of wood, on the walls of a room. **2.** The lower part of an interior wall when finished in a material different from that of the upper part. **—wain′scot** *v.*
wain·wright (wān′rīt′) ▸ *n.* One who builds and repairs wagons.
waist (wāst) ▸ *n.* **1.** The part of the human trunk between the bottom of the rib cage and the pelvis. **2a.** The part of a garment that encircles the waist. **b.** A garment that extends from the shoulders to the waistline, as a blouse. **3.** The middle section or part of an object.
waist·band (wāst′bănd′) ▸ *n.* A band of material encircling the waist of a garment.
waist·coat (wĕs′kĭt, wāst′kōt′) ▸ *n.* *Chiefly Brit.* A vest.
waist·line (wāst′līn′) ▸ *n.* **1a.** The narrowest part of the waist. **b.** The measurement of this part. **2.** The line at which the skirt and bodice of a dress join.
wait (wāt) ▸ *v.* **1.** To remain in expectation: *waiting for the bus.* **2.** To be ready for use. **3.** To be in abeyance. **4.** To work as a waiter, waitress, or salesperson. ▸ *n.* The act of waiting or the time spent waiting.

THESAURUS

wackiness or **whackiness** *n.* —*See* FOOLISHNESS.
wacky or **whacky** *adj.* —*See* FOOLISH, INSANE.
wad *n.* —*See* FORTUNE, HEAP (2), LUMP¹, PLUG.
wadding *n.* —*See* FILLER (1).
wade *v.* —*See* TRUDGE.
wade in or **into** *v.* —*See* ATTACK (2).
waffle *v.* —*See* EQUIVOCATE (1).
waffle *n.* —*See* EQUIVOCATION.
waft *v.* —*See* BLOW¹ (2), GLIDE (1).
waft *n.* —*See* WIND¹.
wag¹ *v.* —*See* SWAY.
wag *n.* —*See* GESTURE.
wag² *n.* —*See* JOKER.
wage *n.* Payment for work done ▸ compensation, earnings, emolument, fee, hire, pay, payment, recompense, remuneration, salary, stipend.
wage *v.* To engage in (a war or campaign, for example) ▸ carry on, carry out, conduct. [*Compare* OPPOSE.]
wage earner *n.* —*See* EMPLOYEE.
wager *n.* —*See* BET, GAMBLE.
wager *v.* To make a bet ▸ bet, gamble, game, lay, play. ***Idiom:*** put one's money on something. —*See also* EXPECT (1), GAMBLE (2).
wages *n.* —*See* DUE.
wage slave *n.* —*See* LABORER.
waggish *adj.* —*See* MISCHIEVOUS.
waggle *v.* —*See* CRAWL (1), FLAP (1), SWAY.
waif *n.* —*See* ORPHAN.
wail *v.* —*See* BAWL, CRY, HOWL, SHOUT.
wail *n.* —*See* HOWL, SHOUT.
wailing *n.* —*See* CRY (1).
wait *v.* —*See* DEFER¹, EXPECT (1), REMAIN.
wait on or **upon** *v.* **1.** To work and care for ▸ attend, do for, minister to, serve. [*Compare* CATER, HELP, TEND², WORK.] **2.** To place food before someone ▸ cater, serve. [*Compare* GIVE, DISTRIBUTE.]

wait·er (wā′tər) ▸ *n.* A man who serves at a table, as in a restaurant.
wait·ing room (wā′tĭng) ▸ *n.* A room, as in a doctor's office, for the use of people waiting.
wait·ress (wā′trĭs) ▸ *n.* A woman who serves at a table, as in a restaurant.
waive (wāv) ▸ *v.* **waived, waiv·ing. 1.** To give up (a claim or right) voluntarily. **2.** To postpone.
waiv·er (wā′vər) ▸ *n.* **1.** Intentional relinquishment of a right, claim, or privilege. **2.** The document that waives a right or claim.
wake[1] (wāk) ▸ *v.* **woke** (wōk) or **waked** (wākt), **waked** or **wok·en** (wō′kən), **wak·ing. 1a.** To become awake: *woke late.* **b.** To stay awake. **c.** To make aware of; alert. **2.** To keep watch or guard, esp. over a corpse. ▸ *n.* A watch over a corpse before burial.
wake[2] (wāk) ▸ *n.* **1.** The visible track left by something, as a ship, moving through water. **2.** A track or condition left behind; aftermath.
wake·ful (wāk′fəl) ▸ *adj.* **1a.** Not sleeping. **b.** Without sleep; sleepless. **2.** Watchful; alert. **—wake′ful·ness** *n.*
wak·en (wā′kən) ▸ *v.* **1.** To rouse from sleep; awake. **2.** To rouse from an inactive state. **—wak′en·er** *n.*
wale (wāl) ▸ *n.* **1.** A mark raised on the skin, as by a whip; welt. **2.** A raised ridge in the surface of a fabric such as corduroy. **3.** One of the heavy planks extending along the sides of a wooden ship. ▸ *v.* **waled, wal·ing.** To raise wales on (the skin).
Wales (wālz) ▸ A principality of the United Kingdom on the W peninsula of the island of Great Britain. Cap. Cardiff.
walk (wôk) ▸ *v.* **1.** To move or cause to move on foot at a pace slower than a run. **2.** To pass over, on, or through on foot. **3.** *Informal* To quit one's job. **4.** *Informal* To be acquitted. **5.** *Baseball* To give or be given a base on balls. ***—phrasal verbs:*** **walk out** To go on strike. **walk over** *Informal* To treat badly or contemptuously. ▸ *n.* **1a.** A manner of walking. **b.** A gait, esp. a slow gait of a horse in which the feet touch the ground one after another. **2.** The act or an instance of walking. **3.** A distance covered in walking. **4.** A sidewalk or other walkway. **5.** *Baseball* A base on balls. **—walk′er** *n.* **—walk′a·ble** *adj.*
walk·a·way (wôk′ə-wā′) ▸ *n.* **1.** An easily won contest or victory. **2.** An easy task.
walk·ie-talk·ie (wô′kē-tô′kē) ▸ *n.* A portable two-way short-range radio.
walk·ing papers (wô′kĭng) ▸ *pl.n.* *Slang* A notice of discharge or dismissal.
walking stick ▸ *n.* **1.** A staff used as an aid in walking. **2.** Any of various insects that look like twigs or sticks.
walk-on (wôk′ŏn′, -ôn′) ▸ *n.* A minor, usu. nonspeaking role in a theatrical production.
walk·out (wôk′out′) ▸ *n.* **1.** A labor strike. **2.** The act of leaving or quitting a meeting or organization as a sign of protest.
walk·o·ver (wôk′ō′vər) ▸ *n.* **1.** A horserace with only one horse entered, won by merely walking the track. **2.** A walkaway.
walk·up also **walk-up** (wôk′ŭp′) ▸ *n.* **1.** A multistory building with no elevator. **2.** An apartment or office in a walkup.
walk·way (wôk′wā′) ▸ *n.* A passage for walking.
wall (wôl) ▸ *n.* **1.** A vertical structure or partition that encloses an area or separates two areas. **2.** A defensive embankment or rampart. **3.** Something resembling a wall in appearance or function: *the stomach wall.* ▸ *v.* To enclose, surround, or fortify with or as if with a wall.
wal·la·by (wŏl′ə-bē) ▸ *n., pl.* **-bies** or **-by.** Any of various Australian marsupials related to the kangaroos but gen. smaller.
wall·board (wôl′bôrd′) ▸ *n.* See **plasterboard.**
wal·let (wŏl′ĭt) ▸ *n.* A flat pocket-sized folding case for holding paper money, cards, or photographs.
wall·eye (wôl′ī′) ▸ *n.* **1a.** An eye with a white or opaque cornea. **b.** A disorder in which one eye deviates in orientation from the other. **2.** *pl.* **-eye** or **-eyes.** A North American freshwater food and game fish having large staring eyes. **—wall′eyed′** *adj.*
wall·flow·er (wôl′flou′ər) ▸ *n.* **1.** A cultivated plant with fragrant yellow, orange, or brownish flowers. **2.** One who does not participate in the activity at a social event because of shyness or unpopularity.
Wal·loon (wŏ-lo͞on′) ▸ *n.* **1.** One of a French-speaking people of Celtic descent inhabiting S and SE Belgium. **2.** Their dialect of French.
wal·lop (wŏl′əp) *Informal* ▸ *v.* **1.** To beat soundly; thrash. **2.** To strike with a hard blow; impact. **3.** To defeat thoroughly. ▸ *n.* **1.** A hard blow. **2.** The capacity to create a forceful effect; impact. **—wal′lop·er** *n.*
wal·low (wŏl′ō) ▸ *v.* **-lowed, -low·ing. 1.** To roll around in or as if in mud. **2.** To luxuriate; revel. **3.** To be plentifully supplied: *wallowing in money.* **4.** To move in a clumsy or rolling manner. ▸ *n.* A muddy pool where animals wallow.
wall·pa·per (wôl′pā′pər) ▸ *n.* Paper printed with designs or colors and pasted to a wall as a decorative covering. **—wall′pa′per** *v.*
wall-to-wall (wôl′tə-wôl′) ▸ *adj.* **1.** Completely covering a floor. **2.** *Informal* Present or spreading everywhere.
wal·nut (wôl′nŭt′, -nət) ▸ *n.* **1a.** Any of several deciduous trees with round sticky fruit that encloses an edible nut. **b.** The nut of a walnut. **2.** The hard, dark brown wood of a walnut.
wal·rus (wôl′rəs, wŏl′-) ▸ *n., pl.* **-rus** or **-rus·es.** A large Arctic marine mammal with two long tusks and tough wrinkled skin.
waltz (wôlts, wôls) ▸ *n.* **1.** A dance in triple time with a strong accent on the first beat. **2.** Music for this dance. ▸ *v.* **1.** To dance the waltz (with). **2.** *Slang* To move lightly and easily: *waltzed out of the room.* **3.** *Informal* To accomplish a task, chore, or assignment with little effort. **—waltz′er** *n.*

THESAURUS

waive *v.* —*See* ABANDON (1), DEFER[1].
waiver *n.* —*See* ABANDONMENT (1), DELAY (1).
wake[1] *v.* To cease or cause to cease sleeping ▸ arouse, awake, awaken, get up, [illegible] wake up, waken. [*Compare* RISE.]
wake *n.* A watch over the body of a dead person before burial ▸ watch.
wake[2] *n.* Something that follows or is drawn along behind ▸ tail, trail, train. [*Compare* STREAM.]
wakeful *adj.* **1.** Not in a state of sleep or unable to sleep ▸ awake, unsleeping, wide-awake. *Idiom:* tossing and turning. [*Compare* RESTLESS.] **2.** Marked by an absence of sleep ▸ sleepless, slumberless. —*See also* ALERT.
wakefulness *n.* —*See* ALERTNESS.
waken *v.* —*See* AROUSE, WAKE[1].
wale *n.* —*See* WELT.
walk *n.* **1.** An act of walking ▸ amble, constitutional, hike, march, perambulation, promenade, ramble, saunter, stroll, tramp, turn, wander. **2.** A manner of walking ▸ footfall, footstep, gait, pace, step, stride, tread.
walk *v.* To go on foot ▸ ambulate, foot, pace, step, stride, tread. *Slang:* hoof. *Idioms:* foot it, hoof it. [*Compare* HIKE, ROVE, STROLL, TRUDGE.]
walk out *v.* To cease working in support of demands made upon an employer ▸ picket, strike. *Idioms:* go (*or* go out on) strike, stage a strike (*or* sickout *or* walkout), stop work. —*See also* RENEGE.
walk through *v.* —*See* PRACTICE (1).
walkaway *n.* —*See* BREEZE (2), RUNAWAY (1).
walking stick *n.* —*See* STICK (2).
walk of life *n.* —*See* BUSINESS (2).
walkout *n.* A cessation of work by employees in support of demands made upon their employer ▸ job action, sickout, strike, work stoppage, work to rule.
walkover *n.* —*See* BREEZE (2), RUNAWAY (1).
wall *n.* A solid structure that separates one area from another ▸ barrier, partition, screen. [*Compare* BORDER.] —*See also* BAR (1).
wall *v.* To separate with or as if with a wall ▸ fence, partition, screen. —*See also* ENCLOSE (1).
wallop *v.* —*See* HIT, OVERWHELM (1).
wallop *n.* —*See* BLOW[2], KICK, THRILL.
walloping *adj.* —*See* ENORMOUS.
wallow *v.* To move about in an indolent or clumsy manner ▸ flounder, roll about, roll around, welter. —*See also* LUXURIATE.
waltz *v.* —*See* BREEZE.

Wam·pa·no·ag (wäm′pə-nō′ăg) ▸ *n., pl.* **-ag** or **-ags. 1.** A member of a Native American people of E Rhode Island and SE Massachusetts. **2.** Their Algonquian language.
wam·pum (wŏm′pəm, wôm′-) ▸ *n.* **1.** Small beads made from polished shells and fashioned into strings or belts, formerly used by certain Native American peoples as currency and jewelry. **2.** *Informal* Money.
wan (wŏn) ▸ *adj.* **wan·ner, wan·nest. 1.** Unnaturally pale; pallid. **2.** Weak or faint. **3.** Sad: *a wan smile.* **—wan′ly** *adv.* **—wan′ness** *n.*
wand (wŏnd) ▸ *n.* **1.** A slender rod carried as a symbol of office; scepter. **2.** A stick or baton used by a magician, conjurer, or diviner.
wan·der (wŏn′dər) ▸ *v.* **1.** To move about aimlessly. **2.** To go by an indirect route or at no set pace. **3.** To go astray. **4.** To lose clarity or coherence of thought or expression. **—wan′der·er** *n.* **—wan′der·ing·ly** *adv.*
wan·der·ing Jew (wŏn′dər-ĭng) ▸ *n.* A trailing plant with usu. variegated foliage, popular as a houseplant.
wan·der·lust (wŏn′dər-lŭst′) ▸ *n.* A strong or irresistible impulse to travel.
wane (wān) ▸ *v.* **waned, wan·ing. 1.** To decrease gradually in size, amount, intensity, or degree. **2.** To exhibit a decreasing illuminated area from full moon to new moon. **3.** To approach an end: *The old year is waning.* ▸ *n.* **1.** A gradual decrease or decline. **2.** The period of the moon's waning.
wan·gle (wăng′gəl) ▸ *v.* **-gled, -gling.** *Informal* **1.** To make, achieve, or get by contrivance. **2.** To manipulate, esp. fraudulently. **—wang′ler** *n.*
wan·na·be (wŏn′ə-bē′, wôn′-) *Informal* ▸ *n.* **1.** One who, aspiring to a position, imitates the customs of the one admired. **2.** An imitative product. ▸ *adj.* Wishing to be; would-be.
want (wŏnt, wônt) ▸ *v.* **1.** To wish for. **2.** To be without; lack. **3.** To be in need of; require. **4.** To have need. ▸ *n.* **1.** The condition of lacking something usual or necessary. **2.** Pressing need; destitution. **3.** Something desired. **4.** A defect; fault.
want ad ▸ *n.* A classified advertisement.
want·ing (wŏn′tĭng, wôn′-) ▸ *adj.* **1.** Absent; lacking. **2.** Not up to standards or expectations. ▸ *prep.* **1.** Without. **2.** Minus; less.
wan·ton (wŏn′tən) ▸ *adj.* **1.** Immoral or unchaste; lewd. **2.** Gratuitously cruel; merciless: *wanton killing.* **3.** Unrestrainedly excessive: *wanton spending.* **4.** Luxuriant; overabundant. **5.** Frolicsome; playful. **6.** Undisciplined. ▸ *n.* A wanton person, esp. an immoral one. **—wan′ton·ly** *adv.* **—wan′ton·ness** *n.*
wap·i·ti (wŏp′ĭ-tē) ▸ *n., pl.* **-ti** or **-tis.** A large North American deer having long branching antlers; elk.
war (wôr) ▸ *n.* **1a.** A state or period of armed conflict between nations, states, or parties. **b.** The techniques of war; military science. **2a.** A condition of antagonism or contention. **b.** A determined struggle or attack. ▸ *v.* **warred, war·ring. 1.** To wage war. **2.** To struggle, contend, or fight.
war·ble (wôr′bəl) ▸ *v.* **-bled, -bling.** To sing with trills, runs, or other melodic embellishments. ▸ *n.* The act or sound of warbling.
war·bler (wôr′blər) ▸ *n.* **1.** Any of various small, often yellowish New World songbirds. **2.** Any of various small, often brownish or grayish Old World songbirds.
war chest ▸ *n.* An accumulation of funds to finance a war effort.
war cry ▸ *n.* A battle cry.
ward (wôrd) ▸ *n.* **1.** An administrative division of a city or town, esp. an electoral district. **2.** A division in a hospital: *a maternity ward.* **3.** A division in a prison. **4.** A minor or incompetent person placed under the care or protection of a guardian or a court. **5.** The state of being under guard; custody. **6.** The act of guarding or protecting. **7.** A means of protection. ▸ *v.* **1.** To guard; protect. ***—phrasal verb:* ward off** To avert: *ward off disaster.*
-ward or **-wards** ▸ *suff.* Direction toward: *downward; backwards.*
war·den (wôrd′n) ▸ *n.* **1.** The chief administrative official of a prison. **2.** An official charged with the enforcement of certain regulations: *a game warden.* **3.** A churchwarden.
ward·er (wôr′dər) ▸ *n.* A guard or watcher of a gate or tower.
ward heel·er (hē′lər) ▸ *n.* A worker for the local organization of a political machine.
ward·robe (wôr′drōb′) ▸ *n.* **1.** A cabinet or closet built to hold clothes. **2.** Garments collectively, esp. all the clothing belonging to one person. **3.** The costumes belonging to a theater.
ward·room (wôrd′ro͞om′, -ro͝om′) ▸ *n.* The common recreation area and dining room for the commissioned officers on a warship.
ward·ship (wôrd′shĭp′) ▸ *n.* **1.** The condition of being a ward. **2.** Custody; guardianship.
-ware ▸ *suff.* **1.** Articles that are of the same general kind, material, or use: *silverware.* **2.** Software: *shareware.*
wares (wârz) ▸ *pl.n.* **1.** Articles of commerce; goods.
ware·house (wâr′hous′) ▸ *n.* A place in which goods or merchandise are stored. **—ware′house′** (-houz′) *v.*
war·fare (wôr′fâr′) ▸ *n.* **1.** The act of waging war. **2.** Conflict; strife.
war·fa·rin (wôr′fər-ĭn) ▸ *n.* A white crystalline compound used to kill rodents and medicinally as an anticoagulant.
war·head (wôr′hĕd′) ▸ *n.* A section in the forward part of a projectile, such as a guided missile, that contains the explosive charge.
war·horse (wôr′hôrs′) ▸ *n.* **1.** A horse used in combat; charger. **2.** *Informal* One who has been through many struggles.

THESAURUS

wampum *n.* —*See* MONEY (1).
wan *adj.* —*See* HAGGARD, PALE (1).
wan *v.* —*See* PALE.
wand *n.* —*See* STICK (1).
wander *v.* —*See* DIGRESS, ROVE, STROLL.
wander *n.* —*See* WALK (1).
wanderer *n.* —*See* HOBO.
wandering *adj.* —*See* AIMLESS, ERRANT (1), ERRATIC, INDIRECT (1), NOMADIC.
wane *v.* —*See* DECREASE, DETERIORATE, DISAPPEAR (1), FADE, SUBSIDE.
wane *n.* —*See* DECREASE, DETERIORATION (1), WANING.
wangle *v.* —*See* MANEUVER (2).
waning *n.* The process of becoming less active or intense ▸ abatement, diminishment, easing, ebb, falling off, lapsing, letup, moderation, remission, slackening, subsidence, wane. [*Compare* DECREASE.]
wannabe *n. Informal* One who aspires ▸ aspirant, aspirer, dreamer, hopeful, seeker.
want *v.* To be without what is needed, required, or essential ▸ lack, need, require. —*See also* CHOOSE (2), DEMAND (2), DESIRE.
want *n.* The condition of lacking something ▸ absence, dearth, lack. [*Compare* NEED, SHORTAGE.] —*See also* DEMAND (2), POVERTY.
wanting *adj.* —*See* DEFICIENT, EMPTY (2), INSUFFICIENT.
wanton *adj.* **1.** Sexually unrestrained ▸ easy, fast, libertine, light, loose, promiscuous, reprobate, sluttish, trampy, unchaste, whorish. **2.** Not required, necessary, or warranted by the circumstances of the case ▸ excessive, gratuitous, reckless, supererogative, supererogatory, uncalled-for, unwarranted. [*Compare* CARELESS, OBSCENE.] —*See also* ABANDONED (2), OUTRAGEOUS.
wanton *n.* An immoral or licentious person ▸ debauchee, debaucher, gigolo, libertine, profligate, rake, rakehell, reprobate, rip, rounder. *Slang:* swinger. [*Compare* LECHER, PHILANDERER.] —*See also* SLUT.
wantonness *n.* —*See* ABANDON (1).
war *n.* —*See* BATTLE, COMPETITION (1).
war *v.* —*See* CONTEND.
warble *v.* —*See* SING.
war cry *n.* —*See* CRY (2).
ward *n.* A person who relies on another for support ▸ charge, dependent. —*See also* CARE (2), DEFENSE, DETENTION, GUARD, NEIGHBORHOOD (1).
ward *v.* —*See* DEFEND (1), PREVENT.
ward off *v.* —*See* REPEL.
warden *n.* A guard or keeper of a prison ▸ jailer, turnkey. *Slang:* screw. [*Compare* GUARD, POLICE OFFICER.]
wardrobe *n.* —*See* DRESS (2).
ware *n.* —*See* GOOD (2).
warehouse *n.* —*See* DEPOSITORY.
warehouse *v.* —*See* SAVE (1).
warfare *n.* —*See* BATTLE, COMPETITION (1), CONFLICT.
wariness *n.* —*See* ALERTNESS, CARE (1), CAUTION, DISTRUST.

war·like (wôr′līk′) ▸ *adj.* **1.** Belligerent; hostile. **2.** Of or relating to war.
war·lock (wôr′lŏk′) ▸ *n.* A male witch, sorcerer, or wizard.
war·lord (wôr′lôrd′) ▸ *n.* A military commander exercising civil power in a region, usu. by force of arms.
warm (wôrm) ▸ *adj.* **-er, -est. 1.** Moderately hot. **2.** Preserving or imparting heat: *a warm overcoat.* **3.** Having a sensation of unusually high body heat, as from exercise. **4.** Marked by enthusiasm; ardent: *warm support.* **5.** Excited, animated, or emotional: *a warm debate.* **6.** Recently made; fresh: *a warm trail.* **7.** Close to discovering, guessing, or finding something, as in certain games. **8.** *Informal* Uncomfortable because of danger or annoyance: *Things are warm for the bookies.* ▸ *v.* **1.** To make or become warm. **2.** To make zealous or ardent; enliven. **3.** To fill with pleasant emotions: *warmed by the sight of home.* **4.** To become ardent, enthusiastic, or animated: *began to warm to the subject.* ***—phrasal verb:*** **warm up** To make or become ready for action, as by exercising or practicing beforehand. **—warm′er** *n.* **—warm′ish** *adj.* **—warm′ly** *adv.* **—warm′ness** *n.*
warm-blood·ed (wôrm′blŭd′ĭd) ▸ *adj.* Maintaining a relatively constant and warm body temperature independent of environmental temperature, as a mammal. **—warm′-blood′ed·ness** *n.*
warm-heart·ed (wôrm′här′tĭd) ▸ *adj.* Kind; friendly. **—warm′-heart′ed·ness** *n.*
war·mon·ger (wôr′mŭng′gər, -mŏng′-) ▸ *n.* One who advocates or attempts to stir up war. **—war′mon′ger·ing** *n.*
warmth (wôrmth) ▸ *n.* **1.** The quality or condition of being warm. **2.** Excitement or intensity.
warm-up (wôrm′ŭp′) ▸ *n.* The act, procedure, or period of warming up.
warn (wôrn) ▸ *v.* **1.** To make aware of present or potential danger; caution. **2.** To admonish as to action or manners. **3.** To notify to go or stay away. **4.** To notify or apprise in advance.
warn·ing (wôr′nĭng) ▸ *n.* **1.** An intimation, threat, or sign of impending danger. **2.** Advice to beware or desist. **3.** Something, such as a signal, that warns. ▸ *adj.* Acting or serving to warn.
warp (wôrp) ▸ *v.* **1.** To twist or bend or become twisted or bent out of shape. **2.** To turn or be turned from a proper course; pervert. **3.** To distort. **4.** *Naut.* To move (a vessel) by hauling on a line fastened to an anchor or pier. ▸ *n.* **1.** The state of being twisted or bent out of shape. **2.** A distortion or twist. **3.** The threads that run lengthwise in a woven fabric, crossed at right angles to the woof.
war·path (wôr′păth′, -päth′) ▸ *n.* **1.** A course that leads to warfare or battle. **2.** A hostile course or mood.
war·plane (wôr′plān′) ▸ *n.* A combat aircraft.
war·rant (wôr′ənt, wŏr′-) ▸ *n.* **1.** Authorization or certification; sanction. **2.** Something that assures, attests to, or guarantees; proof. **3.** An order that serves as authorization, esp. a judicial writ authorizing a search, seizure, or arrest. **4.** A certificate of appointment given to a warrant officer. ▸ *v.* **1.** To guarantee or attest to the quality, accuracy, or condition of. **2.** To vouch for. **3a.** To guarantee (a product). **b.** To guarantee (a purchaser) indemnification against damage or loss. **4.** To provide adequate grounds for; justify. **5.** To authorize or empower. **—war′rant·a·bil′i·ty** *n.* **—war′rant·a·ble** *adj.* **—war′ran·tee′** *n.* **—war′ran·tor** *n.*
warrant officer ▸ *n.* A military officer intermediate between a noncommissioned and a commissioned rank.
war·ran·ty (wôr′ən-tē, wŏr′-) ▸ *n., pl.* **-ties. 1.** Official authorization or sanction. **2.** Justification for an act or course of action. **3.** A legally binding guarantee.
war·ren (wôr′ən, wŏr′-) ▸ *n.* **1.** An area where small game animals, esp. rabbits, live and breed. **2.** An overcrowded living area.
war·ri·or (wôr′ē ər, wŏr′-) ▸ *n.* One engaged or experienced in battle.
War·saw (wôr′sô′) ▸ The capital of Poland, in the E-central part on the Vistula R.
war·ship (wôr′shĭp′) ▸ *n.* A combat ship.
wart (wôrt) ▸ *n.* **1.** A hard rough lump on the skin, caused by a virus. **2.** A similar growth, as on a plant. **3.** A flaw or imperfection. **—wart′y** *adj.*
wart hog ▸ *n.* A wild African hog having prominent upward-curving tusks and wartlike growths on the face.
war·time (wôr′tīm′) ▸ *n.* A time of war.
war·y (wâr′ē) ▸ *adj.* **-i·er, -i·est. 1.** On guard; watchful. **2.** Prudent; cautious. **—war′i·ly** *adv.* **—war′i·ness** *n.*
was (wŭz, wŏz; wəz *when unstressed*) ▸ *v.* 1st and 3rd pers. sing. p. indic. of **be**.
wa·sa·bi (wä′sə-bē, wə-sä′-) ▸ *n.* A pungent green Japanese horseradish, usu. used as a condiment.
Wa·satch Range (wô′săch′) ▸ A range of the Rocky Mts. extending about 402 km (250 mi) from SE ID to central UT.
wash (wŏsh, wôsh) ▸ *v.* **1.** To cleanse, using water or other liquid, usu. with soap, detergent, or bleach, by immersing, dipping, rubbing, or scrubbing. **2.** To cleanse oneself. **3.** To make moist or wet. **4.** To flow over, against, or past: *waves washed the beach.* **5.** To carry, erode, or destroy by moving water: *Rain washed the topsoil away.* **6.** To rid of corruption; purify. **7.** To separate constituents of (an ore) by immersion in or agitation with water. **8.** *Informal* To hold up under examination: *Your excuse won't wash.* ***—phrasal verbs:*** **wash down** To follow the swallowing of (food) with a drink. **wash up 1.** To clean one's hands. **2.** To ruin: *He's washed up as a ballplayer.* ▸ *n.* **1.** The act of washing. **2.** A quantity of articles that are to be or have just been washed. **3.** Waste liquid. **4.** A liquid used in washing or coating. **5.** A

THESAURUS

warlike *adj.* —*See* AGGRESSIVE, MILITARY (1).
warlock *n.* —*See* WIZARD.
warm *adj.* —*See* AMIABLE, ENTHUSIASTIC.
warmed-over *adj.* —*See* TRITE.
warm-hearted *adj.* —*See* AMIABLE, GENEROUS (1), SYMPATHETIC.
warmongering *n.* —*See* AGGRESSION.
warmonger *adj.* —*See* AGGRESSIVE, MILITARY (1).
warmth *n.* —*See* AMIABILITY, HEAT (1), PASSION.
warn *v.* To notify someone of imminent danger or risk ▸ admonish, alarm, alert, caution, forewarn. *Idiom:* put on (*or* on one's) guard. [*Compare* INFORM, THREATEN.]
warning *n.* Advice to beware, as of a person or thing ▸ alarum, admonishment, admonition, caution, caveat, monition. *Idiom:* shot across someone's bow. [*Compare* ADVICE.] —*See also* ALARM, EXAMPLE (2), OMEN.
warning *adj.* Giving warning ▸ admonishing, admonitory, cautionary, monitory.
warp *v.* —*See* BEND (2), BEND (3), BIAS (1), CORRUPT, DEFORM, DISTORT.
warp and woof *n.* —*See* TEXTURE.
warped *adj.* —*See* BENT.
warrant *n.* An assumption of responsibility, as one given by a manufacturer, for the quality, worth, or durability of a product ▸ certification, guarantee, guaranty, surety, warranty. —*See also* BASIS (2), CONFIRMATION (2), LICENSE (3), PAWN[1], PROMISE (1).
warrant *v.* —*See* CONFIRM (1), GUARANTEE (1), GUARANTEE (2), JUSTIFY (2), LEGALIZE.
warranted *adj.* —*See* LAWFUL.
warranty *n.* An assumption of responsibility, as one given by a manufacturer, for the quality, worth, or durability of a product ▸ certification, guarantee, guaranty, surety, warrant. —*See also* PAWN[1].
warrior *n.* One who engages in a combat or struggle ▸ belligerent, combatant, fighter, soldier. [*Compare* AGGRESSOR, SOLDIER.]
wart *n.* —*See* WELT, DEFECT.
wary *adj.* Trying attentively to avoid danger, risk, or error ▸ careful, cautious, chary, circumspect, forehanded, gingerly, prudent. —*See also* ALERT, DISTRUSTFUL.
wash *v.* **1.** To make moist ▸ bathe, dampen, moisten, wet. **2.** To flow against or along ▸ bathe, lap, lave, lip. [*Compare* FLOW.] **3.** To make the sound of moving or disturbed water ▸ lap, splash, swash. [*Compare* BURBLE, SWISH.] **4.** To move along with or be carried away by the action of water ▸ drift, float. **5.** *Informal* To prove valid under scrutiny ▸ hold up, prove out, stand up. *Idioms:* hold water, pass muster, ring true. —*See also* CLEAN (1), COLOR (1).
wash out *v.* —*See* FAIL (1), PALE.

thin layer of watercolor or India ink spread on a drawing. 6. A rush of water. 7. *Regional* The dry bed of a stream.

Wash. ▸ *abbr.* Washington

wash·a·ble (wŏsh′ə-bəl, wôsh′-) ▸ *adj.* Capable of being washed without damage.

wash-and-wear (wŏsh′ən-wâr′, wôsh′-) ▸ *adj.* Treated so as to require little or no ironing after being washed.

wash·ba·sin (wŏsh′bā′sən, wôsh′-) ▸ *n.* A washbowl.

wash·board (wŏsh′bôrd′, wôsh′-) ▸ *n.* A board having a corrugated surface on which clothes can be rubbed during laundering.

wash·bowl (wŏsh′bōl′, wôsh′-) ▸ *n.* A basin that can be filled with water for use in washing oneself.

wash·cloth (wŏsh′klôth′, -klŏth′, wôsh′-) ▸ *n.* A cloth used for washing the face or body.

washed-out (wŏsht′out′, wôsht′-) ▸ *adj.* **1.** Carried or eroded away by moving water: *a washed-out road.* **2.** Lacking color or intensity; faded. **3.** Exhausted.

washed-up (wŏsht′ŭp′, wôsht′-) ▸ *adj.* No longer successful, esp. in a public career.

wash·er (wŏsh′ər, wô′shər) ▸ *n.* **1.** One that washes, esp. a machine for washing. **2.** A flat disk, as of metal, placed beneath a nut or at an axle bearing to relieve friction, prevent leakage, or distribute pressure.

wash·ing (wŏsh′ĭng, wô′shĭng) ▸ *n.* **1.** Articles washed at one time. **2.** The residue after an ore has been washed.

washing soda ▸ *n.* A hydrated sodium carbonate used as a general cleanser.

Wash·ing·ton (wŏsh′ĭng-tən, wô′shĭng-) ▸ **1.** A state of the NW US on the Pacific Ocean. Cap. Olympia. **2.** The capital of the US, on the Potomac R. between VA and MD and coextensive with the District of Columbia. **—Wash′ing·to′ni·an** (-tō′nē-ən) *adj. & n.*

Washington, Booker T(aliaferro) (1856–1915) ▸ Amer. educator.

Washington, George (1732–99) ▸ Amer. military leader and 1st US President (1789–97).

wash·out (wŏsh′out′, wôsh′-) ▸ *n.* **1.** Erosion of a relatively soft surface, such as a roadbed, by a sudden gush of water. **2.** A total failure or disappointment.

wash·room (wŏsh′ro͞om′, -ro͝om′, wôsh′-) ▸ *n.* A bathroom, esp. one in a public place.

wash·stand (wŏsh′stănd′, wôsh′-) ▸ *n.* **1.** A stand designed to hold a basin and pitcher of water for washing. **2.** A bathroom sink.

wash·tub (wŏsh′tŭb′, wôsh′-) ▸ *n.* A tub used for washing clothes.

wash·y (wŏsh′ē, wô′shē) ▸ *adj.* **-i·er, -i·est.** **1.** Watery; diluted. **2.** Weak; insipid.

was·n't (wŭz′ənt, wŏz′-) ▸ Was not.

wasp (wŏsp, wôsp) ▸ *n.* Any of various social or solitary insects having a slender body with a constricted abdomen and often inflicting a painful sting.

WASP or **Wasp** (wŏsp, wôsp) ▸ *n.* A white Protestant of Anglo-Saxon ancestry.

wasp·ish (wŏs′pĭsh) ▸ *adj.* **1.** Of or suggestive of a wasp. **2.** Easily irritated or annoyed; snappish. **—wasp′ish·ly** *adv.*

wasp waist ▸ *n.* A very slender or tightly corseted waist. **—wasp′-waist′ed** *adj.*

was·sail (wŏs′əl, wŏ-sāl′) ▸ *n.* **1a.** A toast given in drinking someone's health. **b.** The drink used in such toasting. **2.** A festivity with much drinking and merriment. ▸ *v.* To drink to the health of; toast. **—was′sail·er** *n.*

Was·ser·mann test (wä′sər-mən) ▸ *n.* A diagnostic test for syphilis.

wast (wŏst; wəst *when unstressed*) ▸ *v. Archaic* 2nd pers. sing. p.t. of **be.**

wast·age (wā′stĭj) ▸ *n.* **1.** Loss by deterioration or wear. **2.** An amount wasted.

waste (wāst) ▸ *v.* **wast·ed, wast·ing.** **1.** To use, consume, or expend thoughtlessly or carelessly. **2.** To lose or cause to lose energy, strength, or vigor: *Disease wasted his body.* **3.** To fail to take advantage of; lose: *waste an opportunity.* **4.** To destroy completely. ▸ *n.* **1a.** The act or an instance of wasting. **b.** The state of being wasted. **2.** A barren or wild area or expanse. **3.** A useless byproduct. **4.** Garbage; trash. **5.** The undigested residue of food eliminated from the body; excrement.

waste·bas·ket (wāst′băs′kĭt) ▸ *n.* A container for rubbish.

waste·ful (wāst′fəl) ▸ *adj.* Marked by or inclined to waste. **—waste′ful·ly** *adv.*

waste·land (wāst′lănd′) ▸ *n.* Land that is desolate, barren, or ravaged.

waste·pa·per (wāst′pā′pər) ▸ *n.* Discarded paper.

wast·rel (wā′strəl) ▸ *n.* **1.** One who wastes. **2.** An idler or loafer.

watch (wŏch) ▸ *v.* **1.** To observe carefully or continuously. **2.** To look and wait expectantly or in anticipation: *watch for an opportunity.* **3.** To stay awake deliberately; keep vigil. **4.** To keep a watchful eye on; guard. **5.** To keep up on or informed about: *watch the price of gold.* **6.** To tend (e.g., a flock). ▸ *n.* **1.** The act of watching. **2.** A period of close observation. **3.** A person or group of people serving, esp. at night, to guard or protect. **4.** The post or period of duty of a guard or sentinel. **5.** *Naut.* **a.** Any of the periods of time into which a part of the crew is assigned to duty. **b.** The members of a ship's crew on duty during a specific watch. **6.** A small portable timepiece, esp. one worn on the wrist or carried in the pocket. **—watch′er** *n.*

watch·dog (wŏch′dôg′, -dŏg′) ▸ *n.* **1.** A dog trained to guard people or property. **2.** One serving as a guardian or protector.

THESAURUS

wash up *v.* —*See* DESTROY (1).

wash *n.* —*See* COLOR (1).

washed out *adj.* —*See* PALE (1).

washed-up *adj.* —*See* THROUGH (2).

washiness *n.* —*See* INSIPIDITY.

washout *n.* —*See* DISAPPOINTMENT (2), FAILURE (1).

washy *adj.* —*See* DILUTE, INSIPID.

waspish *adj.* —*See* BITING, ILL-TEMPERED.

waspishness *n.* —*See* TEMPER (1).

waste *v.* To use, consume, spend, or expend thoughtlessly or carelessly ▸ dissipate, fool away, fritter away, riot away, splurge, squander, throw away, trifle away. *Slang:* blow. [*Compare* CONSUME, GIVE.] —*See also* CONSUME (1), IDLE (2), KILL[1], LANGUISH, LOSE (2), MURDER.

waste away *v.* —*See* FADE.

waste *n.* A sad or tragic deprivation ▸ loss. [*Compare* DEPRIVATION.] —*See also* DESERT[1], EXTRAVAGANCE, GARBAGE.

waste *adj.* —*See* BARREN (2).

wasted *adj.* —*See* DRUGGED, HAGGARD.

wasteful *adj.* —*See* EXTRAVAGANT.

wastefulness *n.* —*See* EXTRAVAGANCE.

wasteland *n.* —*See* DESERT[1].

waster *n.* —*See* WASTREL (1).

wastrel *n.* **1.** A person who spends money or resources wastefully ▸ prodigal, profligate, scattergood, spendthrift, waster. **2.** A self-indulgent person who spends time avoiding work or other useful activity ▸ bum, drone, fainéant, idler, loafer, ne'er-do-well, shirker, slacker, sluggard. *Informal:* do-little, do-nothing, good-for-nothing, layabout, lazybones, lounger, no-good, sloth, slug. *Slang:* couch potato, deadbeat, slouch, slugabed.

watch *v.* **1.** To look at or on attentively or carefully ▸ eye, observe, regard, scrutinize, see, survey. [*Compare* LOOK.] **2.** To pay regular and close attention to ▸ follow, monitor, observe, stake out, survey. *Idioms:* have one's (*or* keep an) eye on, keep tabs on, keep track of, ride herd on. —*See also* TEND[2].

watch out *v.* To be careful ▸ beware, look out, mind. *Idioms:* be on guard, be on the lookout, keep an eye peeled, take care (*or* heed).

watch over *v.* —*See* SUPERVISE.

watch *n.* **1.** The act of observing, often for an extended time ▸ observance, observation, scrutiny, watching. [*Compare* LOOK.] **2.** A watch over the body of a dead person before burial ▸ wake. —*See also* GUARD, LOOKOUT (1), TURN (1).

watchdog *n.* —*See* GUARD.

watcher *n.* **1.** Someone who observes ▸ beholder, bystander, gaper, gawker, looker-on, observer, onlooker, spectator. *Slang:* rubbernecker. [*Compare* GUARD.] **2.** An agent assigned to observe and report on another ▸ shadow. *Informal:* tail. [*Compare* DETECTIVE.]

watch·ful (wŏch′fəl) ▸ *adj.* Closely observant or alert; vigilant. **—watch′ful·ly** *adv.* **—watch′ful·ness** *n.*

watch·mak·er (wŏch′mā′kər) ▸ *n.* One who makes or repairs watches.

watch·man (wŏch′mən) ▸ *n.* A man employed to stand guard or keep watch.

watch·tow·er (wŏch′tou′ər) ▸ *n.* An observation tower for a guard or lookout.

watch·word (wŏch′wûrd′) ▸ *n.* **1.** A prearranged reply to a challenge, as from a guard; password. **2.** A rallying cry; slogan.

wa·ter (wô′tər, wŏt′ər) ▸ *n.* **1.** A clear, colorless, odorless, and tasteless liquid, H_2O, essential for most plant and animal life and the most widely used of all solvents. **2a.** Any of various forms of water, as rain. **b.** often **waters** Naturally occurring mineral water, as at a spa. **3.** A body of water such as a sea, lake, river, or stream. **4.** A body fluid, such as urine, perspiration, or tears. **5.** An aqueous solution of a substance, esp. a gas: *ammonia water.* **6.** A wavy finish or sheen, as of a fabric. **7a.** The transparency and luster of a gem. **b.** A level of excellence: *of the first water.* ▸ *v.* **1.** To sprinkle, moisten, or supply with water. **2.** To give drinking water to. **3.** To dilute or weaken by or as if by adding water. **4.** To give a sheen to the surface of (silk, linen, or metal). **5.** To produce or discharge fluid, as from the eyes or mouth.

wa·ter·bed (wô′tər-bĕd′, wŏt′ər-) ▸ *n.* A bed whose mattress is a large water-filled plastic bag.

wa·ter·borne (wô′tər-bôrn′, wŏt′ər-) ▸ *adj.* Supported or transported by water: *waterborne freight.*

water buffalo ▸ *n.* A large, often domesticated Asian buffalo with large spreading horns.

water cannon ▸ *n.* A truck-mounted apparatus that fires water at high pressure, used esp. to disperse crowds.

water chestnut ▸ *n.* **1.** An Asian sedge having an edible corm and cylindrical leaves. **2.** The succulent corm of this plant.

water closet ▸ *n.* A room or booth containing a toilet and often a washbowl.

wa·ter·col·or (wô′tər-kŭl′ər, wŏt′ər-) ▸ *n.* **1.** A paint composed of a water-soluble pigment. **2.** A painting that is made with watercolors. **—wa′ter·col′or·ist** *n.*

wa·ter·course (wô′tər-kôrs′, wŏt′ər-) ▸ *n.* **1.** A channel through which water flows. **2.** A stream or river.

wa·ter·craft (wô′tər-krăft′, wŏt′ər-) ▸ *n.* A boat or ship.

wa·ter·cress (wô′tər-krĕs′, wŏt′ər-) ▸ *n.* A plant growing in freshwater ponds and streams and having pungent edible leaves.

wa·ter·fall (wô′tər-fôl′, wŏt′ər-) ▸ *n.* A steep descent of water from a height.

wa·ter·fowl (wô′tər-foul′, wŏt′ər-) ▸ *n.* **1.** A water bird, esp. a swimming bird. **2.** Swimming birds, such as ducks and geese, collectively.

wa·ter·front (wô′tər-frŭnt′, wŏt′ər-) ▸ *n.* **1.** Land abutting a body of water. **2.** The part of a town or city that abuts water.

water gap ▸ *n.* A cleft in a mountain ridge through which water flows.

water hyacinth ▸ *n.* A tropical American plant forming dense floating masses in ponds and streams.

wa·ter·ish (wô′tər-ĭsh, wŏt′ər-) ▸ *adj.* Watery.

water lily ▸ *n.* Any of various aquatic plants with broad floating leaves and showy, variously colored flowers.

water line ▸ *n.* Any of several parallel lines on the hull of a ship that indicate the depth to which the ship sinks under various loads.

wa·ter·logged (wô′tər-lôgd′, -lŏgd′, wŏt′ər-) ▸ *adj.* So soaked or saturated with water as to be heavy, sluggish, or unwieldy.

wa·ter·loo (wô′tər-lo͞o′, wŏt′ər-) ▸ *n., pl.* **-loos.** A final crushing defeat.

Waterloo ▸ A town of central Belgium near Brussels; site of Napoleon's final defeat (1815).

wa·ter·mark (wô′tər-märk′, wŏt′ər-) ▸ *n.* **1.** A mark showing the height to which water has risen. **2.** A translucent design impressed on paper during manufacture and visible when the paper is held to the light. ▸ *v.* To mark (paper) with a watermark.

wa·ter·mel·on (wô′tər-mĕl′ən, wŏt′ər-) ▸ *n.* **1.** An African vine cultivated for its large edible fruit. **2.** The fruit itself, having a hard green rind and sweet watery reddish flesh.

water moccasin ▸ *n.* A venomous snake of lowlands and swampy regions of the S US; cottonmouth.

water ou·zel (o͞o′zəl) ▸ *n.* See **dipper** 2.

water pipe ▸ *n.* **1.** A pipe that conducts water. **2.** An apparatus for smoking in which the smoke is drawn through a vessel of water.

water polo ▸ *n.* A water sport with two teams that try to pass a ball into the other's goal.

wa·ter·pow·er (wô′tər-pou′ər, wŏt′ər-) ▸ *n.* The energy produced by running or falling water that is used for driving machinery, esp. for generating electricity.

wa·ter·proof (wô′tər-pro͞of′, wŏt′ər-) ▸ *adj.* Impervious to or unaffected by water. ▸ *n.* *Chiefly Brit.* A raincoat. **—wa′ter·proof′** *v.*

wa·ter-re·pel·lent (wô′tər-rĭ-pĕl′ənt, wŏt′ər-) ▸ *adj.* Resistant to water but not entirely waterproof.

wa·ter-re·sis·tant (wô′tər-rĭ-zĭs′tənt, wŏt′ər-) ▸ *adj.* Water-repellent.

wa·ter·shed (wô′tər-shĕd′, wŏt′ər-) ▸ *n.* **1.** A ridge of high land dividing two areas drained by different river systems. **2.** The region draining into a body of water. **3.** A turning point.

wa·ter·side (wô′tər-sīd′, wŏt′ər-) ▸ *n.* Land bordering a body of water.

water ski ▸ *n.* A broad ski used for gliding over water while being towed by a motorboat. **—wa′ter-ski′** *v.* **—wa′ter-ski′er** *n.*

wa·ter·spout (wô′tər-spout′, wŏt′ər-) ▸ *n.* **1.** A tornado or lesser whirlwind occurring over water and resulting in a whirling column of air and spray. **2.** A hole or pipe from which water, esp. rainwater, is discharged.

water table ▸ *n.* The level below which the ground is saturated with water.

wa·ter·tight (wô′tər-tīt′, wŏt′ər-) ▸ *adj.* **1.** So tightly made that water cannot enter or escape. **2.** Unassailable: *a watertight alibi.*

water tower ▸ *n.* A standpipe or elevated tank used for storing water.

wa·ter·way (wô′tər-wā′, wŏt′ər-) ▸ *n.* A navigable body of water, as a river or canal.

water wheel ▸ *n.* A wheel driven by falling or running water, used to power machinery.

water wings ▸ *pl.n.* An inflatable device used to support the body of a person learning to swim.

wa·ter·works (wô′tər-wûrks′, wŏt′ər-) ▸ *pl.n.* **1.** The water system, including reservoirs, tanks, buildings, pumps, and pipes, of a city or town. **2.** *Informal* Tears.

wa·ter·y (wô′tə-rē, wŏt′ə-) ▸ *adj.* **-i·er, -i·est.** **1.** Filled with, consisting of, or soaked with water. **2.** Diluted: *watery soup.* **3.** Pale; washed out. **—wa′ter·i·ness** *n.*

watt (wŏt) ▸ *n.* A unit of power equal to one joule per second.

Watt, James (1736–1819) ▸ British engineer and inventor

THESAURUS

watchful *adj.* —*See* ALERT, CAREFUL (1).

watchfulness *n.* —*See* ALERTNESS, CARE (1).

watching *n.* The act of observing, often for an extended time ▸ observance, observation, scrutiny, watch.

watchman *n.* —*See* GUARD.

watchtower *n.* —*See* LOOKOUT (2).

watchword *n.* —*See* CRY (2).

water *v.* To fill with tears ▸ tear (up), well (up). [*Compare* FLOW.] —*See also* DILUTE.

watercourse *n.* —*See* BROOK[1], RIVER.

watercraft *n.* A conveyance that travels over water ▸ bark, barque, boat, craft, ship, vessel.

watered-down *adj.* —*See* DILUTE.

watering hole *n.* —*See* BAR (2).

waterish *adj.* —*See* DILUTE, INSIPID, PALE (2).

waterless *adj.* —*See* DRY (1).

waterlogged *adj.* —*See* WET.

waterloo *n.* A disastrous defeat or ruin ▸ collapse, fall, downfall. —*See also* DEFEAT.

watershed *n.* The region that is drained by a river system ▸ drainage basin, watershed.

watery *adj.* —*See* DILUTE, INSIPID, PALE (2).

watt·age (wŏt′ĭj) ▸ *n.* **1.** An amount of power, esp. electric power, expressed in watts or kilowatts. **2.** The electric power required by an appliance or device.
wat·tle (wŏt′l) ▸ *n.* **1.** A construction of poles that are intertwined with twigs, reeds, or branches, used for walls, fences, and roofs. **2.** A fleshy, often brightly colored fold of skin hanging from the throat of certain birds. **—wat′tled** *adj.*
Waugh (wô), **Evelyn (Arthur Saint John)** (1903–66) ▸ British writer.
wave (wāv) ▸ *v.* **waved, wav·ing. 1.** To move or cause to move back and forth or up and down in the air. **2.** To move or swing as in giving a signal. **3.** To curve or curl, as hair. ▸ *n.* **1.** A ridge or swell moving along the surface of a body of water. **2.** An undulating surface movement: *waves of wheat.* **3.** A slight curve or curl, as in the hair. **4.** A movement up and down or back and forth: *a wave of the hand.* **5.** A surge or rush: *a wave of nausea.* **6.** A persistent weather condition: *a heat wave.* **7.** *Phys.* **a.** A disturbance traveling through a medium. **b.** A graphic representation of the variation of such a disturbance with time.
wave·band (wāv′bănd′) ▸ *n.* A range of frequencies, esp. radio frequencies.
wave·form (wāv′fôrm′) ▸ *n.* The mathematical representation of a wave, esp. a graph obtained by plotting a characteristic of the wave against time.
wave·length (wāv′lĕngkth′, -lĕngth′, -lĕnth′) ▸ *n.* The distance between one peak or crest of a wave, as of light or sound, and the next corresponding peak or crest.
wave·let (wāv′lĭt) ▸ *n.* A small wave; ripple.
wa·ver (wā′vər) ▸ *v.* **1.** To move or swing back and forth. **2a.** To show or experience irresolution or indecision; vacillate. **b.** To falter or yield: *His resolve began to waver.* **3.** To tremble or quaver, as a voice. **4.** To flicker or glimmer, as light. **—wa′ver** *n.* **—wa′ver·ing·ly** *adv.*
wav·y (wā′vē) ▸ *adj.* **-i·er, -i·est. 1.** Abounding or rising in waves: *a wavy sea.* **2.** Marked by or moving in a wavelike form. **3.** Having curls, curves, or undulations: *wavy hair.* **—wav′i·ly** *adv.* **—wav′i·ness** *n.*
wax¹ (wăks) ▸ *n.* **1a.** Any of various natural, oily or greasy heat-sensitive substances, such as beeswax, consisting of hydrocarbons or fats. **b.** Cerumen. **2.** A preparation containing wax used for polishing. ▸ *v.* To treat or polish with wax.
wax² (wăks) ▸ *v.* **1.** To increase gradually in size, amount, intensity, or degree. **2.** To show an increasing illuminated area from new moon to full moon. **3.** To grow or become: *a speaker waxing eloquent.*
wax bean ▸ *n.* A variety of string bean having yellow pods.
wax·en (wăk′sən) ▸ *adj.* **1.** Made of wax. **2.** Pale or smooth as wax: *waxen skin.*
wax myrtle ▸ *n.* An aromatic evergreen shrub of the SE US, having small berrylike fruit with a waxy coating.
wax·wing (wăks′wĭng′) ▸ *n.* Any of several crested birds having grayish-brown plumage and waxy red tips on the wing feathers.
wax·work (wăks′wûrk′) ▸ *n.* **1.** A figure made of wax, esp. a life-size wax effigy of a famous person. **2. waxworks** *(takes sing. or pl. v.)* An exhibition of wax figures.
wax·y (wăk′sē) ▸ *adj.* **-i·er, -i·est. 1.** Resembling wax, as in texture. **2.** Full of or covered with wax. **—wax′i·ness** *n.*
way (wā) ▸ *n.* **1.** A road, route, path, or passage that leads from one place to another. **2.** Space to proceed. **3.** A usual or customary course of action or state of affairs. **4.** Progress or advancement in accomplishing a goal: *worked her way up.* **5.** A course of action: *the easy way out.* **6.** A manner or method of doing: *no way to reach him.* **7.** A habit, characteristic, or tendency: *Things have a way of happening.* **8.** also **ways** (wāz) *(takes sing. v.) Informal* Distance: *The travelers have come a long way.* **9.** A specific direction: *He glanced my way.* **10.** An aspect or feature: *resembles his father in many ways.* **11.** Freedom to do as one wishes: *if I had my way.* **12.** An aptitude or a facility: *has a way with words.* **13.** A condition: *in a bad way financially.* **14.** Vicinity: *out our way.* ***—idioms:* by the way** Incidentally. **by way of 1.** Through; via. **2.** As a means of: *by way of apology.*, **out of the way 1.** In a remote location. **2.** Improper; amiss., **under way** In progress.
way·bill (wā′bĭl′) ▸ *n.* A document giving details and instructions relating to a shipment of goods.
way·far·er (wā′fâr′ər) ▸ *n.* One who travels, esp. on foot. **—way′far′ing** *n. & adj.*
way·lay (wā′lā′) ▸ *v.* **-laid** (-lād′), **-lay·ing. 1.** To lie in wait for and attack from ambush. **2.** To accost or intercept.
-ways ▸ *suff.* Way, manner, direction, or position: *sideways.*
ways and means (wāz) ▸ *pl.n.* Methods and resources available to accomplish an end, esp. to meet expenses.
way·side (wā′sīd′) ▸ *n.* The side of a road.
way station ▸ *n.* A station between principal stations on a route, as of a railroad.
way·ward (wā′wərd) ▸ *adj.* **1.** Disobedient; willful: *a wayward child.* **2.** Capricious. **—way′ward·ly** *adv.* **—way′ward·ness** *n.*
WC ▸ *abbr.* water closet
we (wē) ▸ *pron.* **1.** Used to indicate the speaker or writer along with another or others as the subject. **2.** Used instead of *I*, esp. by a sovereign or by a writer.
weak (wēk) ▸ *adj.* **-er, -est. 1.** Lacking physical strength, energy, or vigor; feeble. **2.** Likely to fail under pressure, stress, or strain. **3.** Lacking strength of character or will. **4.** Lacking the proper strength or amount of ingredients: *weak coffee.* **5.** Unable to function normally or fully: *a weak heart.* **6.** Lacking aptitude or skill. **7.** Lacking persuasiveness: *a weak argument.* **8.** Lacking power or intensity: *weak light; a weak voice.* **9.** Unstressed or unaccented, as a syllable.
weak·en (wē′kən) ▸ *v.* To make or become weak or weaker.
weak·fish (wēk′fĭsh′) ▸ *n.* A marine food and game fish of North American Atlantic waters.

THESAURUS

wattle *v.* *—See* WEAVE.
wave *v.* **1.** To have or cause to have a curved or wavy surface ▸ corrugate, curl, curve, ripple, undulate. [*Compare* BEND, FOLD.] **2.** To move or cause to move about while being fixed at one edge ▸ flap, flutter, fly. **3.** To wield boldly and dramatically ▸ brandish, flourish, sweep. [*Compare* HANDLE.] *—See also* BLOW¹ (2), FLAP (1), GESTURE, SWAY.
wave *n.* A ridge or swell of water, or a shape suggestive of such a swell ▸ breaker, comber, ripple, roller, swell, undulation, whitecap. *Idiom:* peaks and troughs. *—See also* GESTURE.
waver *v.* To shift from one attitude, interest, condition, or emotion to another ▸ dilly-dally, swing, vacillate. *—See also* DOUBT, HESITATE, SWAY.
wavering *adj.* *—See* DOUBTFUL (2), INSECURE (2).
wavy *adj.* Having a curved or ridged surface ▸ corrugated, curly, curvy, rippled, sinusoidal, waggly, wiggly.
wax¹ *n.* *—See* FINISH.
wax *v.* *—See* FINISH (2).
wax² *v.* *—See* BECOME (1), INCREASE.
waxen or **waxy** *adj.* *—See* PALE (1).
way *n.* **1.** The approach used to do something ▸ fashion, formula, manner, method, mode, modus operandi, path, style, system, wise. [*Compare* APPROACH.] **2.** A course affording passage from one place to another ▸ alley, avenue, boulevard, canal, channel, course, drive, expressway, footpath, freeway, highway, lane, pass, passage, passageway, path, road, roadway, route, street, superhighway, thoroughfare, thruway, trail, turnpike. *—See also* BEHAVIOR (1), CUSTOM, DIRECTION, DISTANCE (1).
wayfaring *n.* *—See* JOURNEY.
waylay *v.* *—See* AMBUSH.
wayward *adj.* *—See* CAPRICIOUS, CONTRARY, ERRATIC, UNRULY.
weak *adj.* **1.** Not physically strong ▸ debilitated, decrepit, delicate, enervated, enfeebled, faint, feeble, flimsy, fragile, frail, infirm, insubstantial, puny, rundown, unsound, unsubstantial, weakly. [*Compare* INSECURE, PALE, SICK, TIRED.] **2.** So soft as to be barely audible ▸ faint, feeble. [*Compare* SOFT.] *—See also* DILUTE, IMPLAUSIBLE, INEFFECTUAL (2), INSECURE (2), PALE (2).
weaken *v.* To moderate or change a position or course of action as a result of pressure ▸ back down (*or* off), ease off, relent, slacken, soften, yield. *Idiom:* give way (*or* ground). [*Compare* ASSENT.] *—See also* DETERIORATE, DILUTE, ENERVATE, FADE.
weakening *n.* *—See* DEBILITATION, DETERIORATION (1).

weak interaction ▸ *n.* A fundamental interaction between elementary particles that is responsible for some particle and nuclear decay and for neutrino absorption and emission.

weak-kneed (wēk′nēd′) ▸ *adj.* Lacking strength of character or purpose.

weak·ling (wēk′lĭng) ▸ *n.* One of weak constitution or character.

weak·ly (wēk′lē) ▸ *adj.* **-li·er, -li·est.** Feeble; weak. ▸ *adv.* In a weak manner.

weak·ness (wēk′nĭs) ▸ *n.* **1.** The condition or quality of being weak. **2.** A personal defect or failing. **3.** A special fondness or liking: *a weakness for chocolate.*

weal[1] (wēl) ▸ *n.* Prosperity; well-being.

weal[2] (wēl) ▸ *n.* A welt or bump.

weald (wēld) ▸ *n. Chiefly Brit.* **1.** A woodland. **2.** An area of open rolling upland.

wealth (wĕlth) ▸ *n.* **1a.** An abundance of valuable material possessions or resources; riches. **b.** The state of being rich; affluence. **2.** All goods and resources having economic value.

wealth·y (wĕl′thē) ▸ *adj.* **-i·er, -i·est.** Having wealth; rich; prosperous.

wean (wēn) ▸ *v.* **1.** To accustom (the young of a mammal) to take nourishment other than by suckling. **2.** To rid of a habit or interest: *weaned herself from cigarettes.* **3.** *Informal* To be raised on: *weaned on good literature.*

weap·on (wĕp′ən) ▸ *n.* **1.** An instrument of attack or defense in combat. **2.** A means used to defend against or defeat another.

weap·on·ry (wĕp′ən-rē) ▸ *n.* Weapons collectively.

wear (wâr) ▸ *v.* **wore** (wôr), **worn** (wôrn), **wear·ing.** **1.** To carry or have on the person: *wear a jacket.* **2.** To have habitually on the person: *wear glasses; wear a beard.* **3.** To display in one's appearance: *wears a smile.* **4.** To bear or maintain in a particular manner: *wears her hair long.* **5a.** To damage, erode, or consume by long or hard use: *shoes worn down at the heels.* **b.** To show the effect of such use: *The tires are starting to wear.* **6.** To produce by constant use or exposure: *wore hollows in the steps.* **7.** To fatigue, weary, or exhaust: *criticism that wore her patience.* **8.** To last under continual or hard use: *a fabric that wears well.* **9.** To pass gradually or tediously: *The hours wore on.* ***—phrasal verbs:*** **wear down** To break down or exhaust by relentless pressure or resistance. **wear off** To diminish gradually in effect. **wear out** **1.** To make or become unusable through long or heavy use. **2.** To use up or consume gradually. ▸ *n.* **1.** The act of wearing or the state of being worn; use. **2.** Clothing, esp. of a particular kind or for a particular use: *men's wear; evening wear.* **3.** Gradual impairment or diminution resulting from use or attrition: *The rug is beginning to show wear.* **4.** The ability to withstand use; durability. **—wear′a·ble** *adj.* **—wear′er** *n.*

wear and tear (târ) ▸ *n.* Damage or depreciation resulting from ordinary use.

wea·ri·less (wîr′ē-lĭs) ▸ *adj.* Displaying or feeling no fatigue.

wea·ri·some (wîr′ē-səm) ▸ *adj.* Causing fatigue; tedious. **—wea′ri·some·ly** *adv.* **—wea′ri·some·ness** *n.*

wea·ry (wîr′ē) ▸ *adj.* **-ri·er, -ri·est.** **1.** Tired. **2.** Expressive of fatigue: *a weary smile.* **3.** Exhausted of tolerance; impatient: *weary of delays.* ▸ *v.* **wea·ried** (wîr′ēd), **wea·ry·ing.** To make or become weary. **—wea′ri·ly** *adv.* **—wea′ri·ness** *n.*

wea·sel (wē′zəl) ▸ *n.* **1.** Any of several carnivorous mammals having a long slender body, a long tail, and short legs. **2.** A sneaky or treacherous person. ▸ *v.* To be evasive; equivocate.

weath·er (wĕth′ər) ▸ *n.* **1.** The state of the atmosphere at a given time and place with respect to temperature, moisture, wind velocity, and barometric pressure. **2.** Bad, rough, or stormy atmospheric conditions. ▸ *v.* **1.** To expose to or withstand the action of the weather. **2.** To show the effects of exposure to the weather. **3.** To come through safely; survive. **—weath′ered** *adj.*

weath·er-beat·en (wĕth′ər-bēt′n) ▸ *adj.* **1.** Worn by exposure to the weather. **2.** Tanned and coarsened from being outdoors: *a weather-beaten face.*

weath·er·board (wĕth′ər-bôrd′) ▸ *n.* See **clapboard.**

weath·er-bound (wĕth′ər-bound′) ▸ *adj.* Delayed, halted, or kept indoors by bad weather.

weath·er·cock (wĕth′ər-kŏk′) ▸ *n.* **1.** A weathervane, esp. one in the form of a rooster. **2.** One that is fickle.

weath·er·ing (wĕth′ər-ĭng) ▸ *n.* Any of the chemical or mechanical processes by which rocks exposed to the weather break down.

weath·er·ize (wĕth′ə-rīz′) ▸ *v.* **-ized, -iz·ing.** To protect against cold weather, as with insulation.

weath·er·man (wĕth′ər-măn) ▸ *n.* A man who reports and forecasts the weather.

weath·er·proof (wĕth′ər-pro͞of′) ▸ *adj.* Capable of withstanding exposure to weather without damage. **—weath′er·proof′** *v.*

weather stripping ▸ *n.* A narrow piece of material installed around doors and windows to protect an interior from external extremes in temperature. **—weath′er-strip′** (wĕth′ər-strĭp′) *v.*

weath·er·vane (wĕth′ər-vān′) ▸ *n.* A device that pivots on a vertical spindle to indicate wind direction.

weave (wēv) ▸ *v.* **wove** (wōv), **wo·ven** (wō′vən), **weav·ing.** **1a.** To make (cloth) by interlacing the threads of the weft and the warp on a loom. **b.** To interlace (e.g., threads) into cloth. **2.** To construct by interlacing or interweaving strips or strands of material: *weave a basket.* **3.** To combine (elements) into a whole. **4.** To interpose (another element) throughout a complex whole: *wove folk tunes into the symphony.* **5.** To spin (a web). **6.** *p.t.* **weaved.** To move or progress by winding in and out or from side to side: *weaved through the traffic.* ▸ *n.* A pattern or method of weaving: *a twill weave.* **—weav′er** *n.*

web (wĕb) ▸ *n.* **1.** A woven fabric, esp. one on a loom or just removed from it. **2.** A latticed or woven structure. **3.** A

THESAURUS

weak-kneed *adj.* *—See* COWARDLY.

weakliness *n.* *—See* INFIRMITY.

weakling *n.* A weak or ineffectual person ▸ pushover. *Informal:* jellyfish, softy. *Slang:* cream puff, doormat, pantywaist, weenie, wimp. [*Compare* BABY, COWARD.]

weakly *adj.* *—See* WEAK (1).

weak-minded *adj.* *—See* BACKWARD (1).

weakness *n.* An imperfection of character ▸ Achilles' heel, failing, fault, foible, frailty, infirmity, shortcoming, weak point. *—See also* DEFECT, INFIRMITY, TASTE (1).

weak point *n.* *—See* WEAKNESS.

weal[1] *n.* A state of health, happiness, and prospering ▸ prosperity, welfare, well-being. [*Compare* CONDITION, HAPPINESS.]

weal[2] *n.* *—See* WELT.

wealth *n.* A great amount of accumulated money and precious possessions ▸ affluence, fortune, money, opulence, pelf, riches, treasure. [*Compare* CAPITAL.] *—See also* ABUNDANCE, PROSPERITY (2), RESOURCES.

wealthy *adj.* *—See* RICH (1).

wear *v.* *—See* BEAR (3), DISPLAY, ERODE.

wear down or **out** *v.* *—See* TIRE (1).

wearied *adj.* *—See* TIRED (1).

weariful *adj.* *—See* BORING, TIRED (1).

weariless *adj.* *—See* TIRELESS.

weariness *n.* *—See* DULLNESS, EXHAUSTION.

wearing *adj.* Causing fatigue ▸ draining, exhausting, fatiguing, tiring, wearying. [*Compare* BURDENSOME.]

wearisome *adj.* *—See* BORING.

weary *adj.* Out of patience ▸ disgusted, fed up, sick, tired. ***Idiom:*** sick and tired. [*Compare* ANGRY.] *—See also* BORING, TIRED (1).

weary *v.* *—See* BORE[2], TIRE (1).

wearying *adj.* Causing fatigue ▸ draining, exhausting, fatiguing, tiring, wearing. [*Compare* BURDENSOME.]

weasel *n.* One who behaves in a stealthy, furtive way ▸ prowler, skulker, sneak, sneaker. [*Compare* CREEP, BETRAYER.] *—See also* CREEP (2).

weasel *v.* *—See* EQUIVOCATE (1).

weasel word *n.* *—See* EQUIVOCATION.

weather *v.* *—See* SURVIVE (1).

weave *v.* To interlace strips or strands ▸ braid, enlace, entwine, interlace, intertwine, plait, pleach, raddle, splice, twill, twist, twine, wattle. *—See also* STAGGER (1), SWAY, WIND[2].

weave *n.* *—See* TEXTURE, WEB.

web *n.* An open and loosely connected structure, usually interlaced, woven, or knotted ▸ braid, lace, lacing, lattice, mesh, net, netting, network,

structure of threadlike filaments spun by spiders. **4.** Something intricately contrived, esp. something that ensnares or entangles: *a web of lies.* **5.** A complex network: *a web of telephone wires.* **6.** A membrane or fold of skin connecting the toes, as of certain amphibians and birds. **7.** The vane of a feather. **8.** often **Web** *Comp. Sci.* The World Wide Web. ▸ *v.* **webbed, web·bing. 1.** To provide or cover with a web. **2.** To ensnare in or as if in a web. **—webbed** *adj.*

web·bing (wĕb′ĭng) ▸ *n.* A strong, narrow, closely woven fabric used esp. for seat belts and harnesses or in upholstery.

web·cast (wĕb′kăst′) ▸ *n.* A broadcast of an event over the World Wide Web.

web-foot·ed (wĕb′fo͝ot′ĭd) ▸ *adj.* Having feet with webbed toes.

web·mas·ter (wĕb′măs′tər) ▸ *n.* A person who develops, markets, or maintains websites.

web·page or **Web page** (wĕb′pāj′) ▸ *n.* A document on the World Wide Web, often linked to other Web documents.

web·site or **Web site** (wĕb′sīt′) ▸ *n.* A set of interconnected webpages, gen. located on the same server, prepared as a collection of information by a person or organization.

Web·ster (wĕb′stər), **Daniel** (1782–1852) ▸ Amer. politician and orator.

Webster, Noah (1758–1843) ▸ Amer. lexicographer.

web·worm (wĕb′wûrm′) ▸ *n.* Any of various usu. destructive caterpillars that construct webs.

wed (wĕd) ▸ *v.* **wed·ded, wed** or **wed·ded, wed·ding. 1.** To take as a spouse; marry. **2.** To perform the marriage ceremony for. **3.** To unite closely.

Wed. ▸ *abbr.* Wednesday

wed·ding (wĕd′ĭng) ▸ *n.* **1.** The ceremony or celebration of a marriage. **2.** The anniversary of a marriage. **3.** A close association or union: *a wedding of ideas.*

wedge (wĕj) ▸ *n.* **1.** A piece of material, such as metal or wood, tapered for insertion in a narrow crevice and used for splitting, tightening, securing, or levering. **2a.** Something shaped like a wedge: *a wedge of pie.* **b.** *Regional* See **submarine** 2. **3.** Something that intrudes and causes division or disruption. ▸ *v.* **wedged, wedg·ing. 1.** To split or force apart with or as if with a wedge. **2.** To fix in place with a wedge. **3.** To crowd or squeeze into a limited space.

wed·lock (wĕd′lŏk′) ▸ *n.* The state of being married; matrimony.

Wednes·day (wĕnz′dē, -dā′) ▸ *n.* The 4th day of the week.

wee (wē) ▸ *adj.* **we·er, we·est. 1.** Very small; tiny. **2.** Very early: *the wee hours.*

weed[1] (wēd) ▸ *n.* A plant considered undesirable, unattractive, or troublesome, esp. one growing where it is not wanted, as in a garden. ▸ *v.* **1.** To clear of weeds. **2.** To eliminate as unsuitable or unwanted: *weed out unqualified applicants.* **—weed′er** *n.* **—weed′y** *adj.*

weed[2] (wēd) ▸ *n.* **1.** A token of mourning. **2. weeds** The black mourning clothes of a widow.

week (wēk) ▸ *n.* **1.** A period of seven days, esp. a period that begins on a Sunday and continues through the next Saturday. **2.** The part of a calendar week devoted to work, school, or business: *worked a four-day week.*

week·day (wēk′dā′) ▸ *n.* Any day of the week except Sunday, or often except Saturday and Sunday.

week·end (wēk′ĕnd′) ▸ *n.* The end of the week, esp. the period from Friday evening through Sunday evening. ▸ *v.* To spend the weekend.

week·ly (wēk′lē) ▸ *adv.* **1.** Once a week. **2.** Every week. **3.** By the week. ▸ *adj.* **1.** Occurring, appearing, or done once a week or every week. **2.** Computed by the week. ▸ *n., pl.* **-lies.** A publication issued once a week.

week·night (wēk′nīt′) ▸ *n.* A night of the week exclusive of Saturday and Sunday.

ween (wēn) ▸ *v.* *Archaic* To think; suppose.

weep (wēp) ▸ *v.* **wept** (wĕpt), **weep·ing. 1.** To shed (tears) as an expression of emotion, esp. grief; cry. **2.** To ooze or exude (moisture). **—weep′er** *n.* **—weep′y** *adj.*

weep·ing (wē′pĭng) ▸ *adj.* **1.** Shedding tears. **2.** Having slender drooping branches.

wee·vil (wē′vəl) ▸ *n.* Any of numerous beetles that characteristically have a downward-curving snout and are destructive to nuts, fruits, stems, and roots.

weft (wĕft) ▸ *n.* **1.** The woof in a woven fabric. **2.** Woven fabric.

weigh (wā) ▸ *v.* **1.** To determine the weight of by or as if by using a scale or balance. **2.** To consider or balance in the mind; ponder. **3.** *Naut.* To raise (anchor). **4.** To be of a specific weight. **5.** To have consequence or importance: *The decision weighed heavily against us.* **6.** To burden or be a burden on; oppress. ***—phrasal verb:* weigh in 1.** To be weighed before or after an athletic contest. **2.** *Slang* To contribute to a discussion.

weight (wāt) ▸ *n.* **1.** A measure of the heaviness of an object. **2a.** The force with which an object is attracted to Earth or another celestial body, equal to the product of the object's mass and the acceleration of gravity. **b.** A unit measure of this force. **c.** A system of such measures. **3.** An object used principally to exert a force by virtue of its gravitational attraction to Earth, esp.: **a.** A solid used as a standard in weighing. **b.** An object used to hold something down. **c.** *Sports* A heavy object, such as a dumbbell, used in weightlifting. **4.** Burden: *the weight of responsibility.* **5.** The greater part; preponderance. **6.** Influence; importance. ▸ *v.* **1.** To add heaviness or weight to. **2.** To load down; burden.

weight·less (wāt′lĭs) ▸ *adj.* **1.** Having little or no weight. **2.** Not experiencing the effects of gravity. **—weight′less·ness** *n.*

weight·lift·ing (wāt′lĭf′tĭng) ▸ *n.* The lifting of heavy weights as an exercise or in athletic competition. **—weight lifter** *n.*

weight·y (wā′tē) ▸ *adj.* **-i·er, -i·est. 1.** Heavy. **2.** Burdensome; oppressive. **3.** Of great consequence; momentous: *a weighty matter.* **4.** Having great power or influence: *a weighty argument.* **—weight′i·ly** *adv.* **—weight′i·ness** *n.*

weir (wîr) ▸ *n.* **1.** A fence placed in a stream to catch fish. **2.** A dam across a river or canal to raise, regulate, or divert the water.

weird (wîrd) ▸ *adj.* **-er, -est. 1.** Of or suggestive of the su-

THESAURUS

weave. —*See also* COMPLEX (1), TANGLE, TEXTURE.

web *v.* —*See* CATCH (1).

wed *v.* —*See* COMBINE (1), MARRY.

wedded *adj.* —*See* MARITAL.

wedding *n.* The act or ceremony by which two people are married ▸ bridal, espousal, marriage, nuptials, spousals.

wedge *n.* —*See* ANCHOR, CUT (2).

wedlock *n.* —*See* MARRIAGE.

wee *adj.* —*See* TINY.

weedy *adj.* —*See* THIN (1).

weeny *adj.* —*See* TINY.

weep *v.* —*See* CRY, DRIP, OOZE.

weeping *n.* —*See* CRY (1).

weeping or **weepy** *adj.* —*See* TEARFUL.

weigh *v.* —*See* CHOOSE (1), COMPARE, COUNT (1), ESTIMATE (1), PONDER.

weigh down *v.* —*See* DEPRESS.

weigh on or **upon** *v.* To come to mind continually ▸ haunt, obsess, torment, trouble.

weight *n.* **1.** The greatest part or portion ▸ bulk, mass, preponderance, preponderancy. [*Compare* CENTER.] **2.** Special attention given to something considered important ▸ accent, accentuation, emphasis, stress, weight. [*Compare* IMPORTANCE, NOTICE.] —*See also* BURDEN[1] (1), BURDEN[1] (2), COGENCY, IMPORTANCE, INFLUENCE, HEAVINESS.

weight *v.* —*See* BURDEN[1].

weightiness *n.* **1.** The condition of being grave and of involving serious consequences ▸ graveness, gravity, heaviness, momentousness, seriousness. [*Compare* SEVERITY.] **2.** Intellectual penetration or range ▸ deepness, depth, profoundness, profundity. [*Compare* DISCERNMENT, INTELLIGENCE, WISDOM.] —*See also* HEAVINESS, IMPORTANCE.

weightless *adj.* Having little weight; not heavy ▸ airy, fluffy, light, lightweight. ***Idiom:*** light as air (*or* a feather). [*Compare* IMMATERIAL, SHEER[2].]

weighty *adj.* —*See* BURDENSOME, FAT (1), GRAVE[2] (1), HEAVY (1), INFLUENTIAL, PREGNANT (2).

weird *adj.* Of an unnatural and usually frightening nature ▸ eerie, freakish, otherworldly, strange, uncanny, unearthly. *Informal:* crawly, creepy, spooky. [*Compare* MYSTERIOUS, SU-

pernatural; unearthly. 2. Of an odd or unusual character; strange. **—weird′ly** *adv.* **—weird′ness** *n.*

weird·o (wîr′dō) ▸ *n., pl.* **-oes.** *Slang* A strange or eccentric person.

wel·come (wĕl′kəm) ▸ *adj.* 1. Greeted, received, or accepted with pleasure. 2. Cordially permitted or invited: *You are welcome to join us.* 3. Freely granted one's courtesy: *"Thank you." "You're welcome."* ▸ *v.* **-comed, -com·ing.** 1. To greet or entertain cordially or hospitably. 2. To receive or accept gladly. **—wel′come** *interj. & n.*

weld (wĕld) ▸ *v.* 1. To join (metals) by applying heat and sometimes pressure. 2. To bring into close association or union. ▸ *n.* A union or joint produced by welding. **—weld′er** *n.*

wel·fare (wĕl′fâr′) ▸ *n.* 1. Health, happiness, or prosperity; well-being. 2. Organized efforts, as by an organization, for the betterment of people in need. 3. Financial or other aid provided, esp. by the government, to people in need.

welfare state ▸ *n.* A social system whereby the state assumes primary responsibility for the welfare of its citizens.

well[1] (wĕl) ▸ *n.* 1. A deep hole or shaft sunk into the earth to obtain water, oil, gas, or brine. 2. A container or reservoir for a liquid, such as ink. 3. A spring or fountain. 4. An abundant source: *a well of information.* 5. An open space extending vertically through the floors of a building, as for stairs. 6. An enclosure in a ship's hold for the pumps. ▸ *v.* 1. To rise up. 2. To pour forth.

well[2] (wĕl) ▸ *adv.* **bet·ter** (bĕt′ər), **best** (bĕst). 1. In a good or proper manner. 2. Skillfully: *dances well.* 3. Satisfactorily: *slept well.* 4. Successfully: *gets along well with people.* 5. In a comfortable or affluent manner: *lived well.* 6. Advantageously: *married well.* 7. With reason or propriety: *can't very well say no.* 8. In all likelihood: *You may well need a coat.* 9. Prudently: *You would do well to obey.* 10. In a close or familiar manner: *knew them well.* 11. Favorably: *spoke well of them.* 12. Thoroughly: *well cooked.* 13. Perfectly: *I well understand your fears.* 14. Considerably: *well past noon.* ▸ *adj.* **better, best.** 1. In a satisfactory condition: *All is well.* 2a. Healthy. b. Cured or healed. 3a. Advisable: *It would be well not to ask.* b. Fortunate: *It is well that you stayed.* ▸ *interj.* 1. Used to introduce a remark or fill a pause. 2. Used to express surprise. ***—idiom:* as well** 1. In addition. 2. With equal effect: *I might as well go.*

we'll (wēl) ▸ 1. We will. 2. We shall.

well-ap·point·ed (wĕl′ə-poin′tĭd) ▸ *adj.* Having a full array of suitable equipment or furnishings.

well-bal·anced (wĕl′băl′ənst) ▸ *adj.* 1. Evenly proportioned, balanced, or regulated. 2. Mentally stable; sensible or sound.

well-be·ing (wĕl′bē′ĭng) ▸ *n.* The state of being healthy, happy, or prosperous; welfare.

well·born (wĕl′bôrn′) ▸ *adj.* Of good lineage or stock.

well-bred (wĕl′brĕd′) ▸ *adj.* Of good upbringing; well-mannered and refined.

well-de·fined (wĕl′dĭ-fīnd′) ▸ *adj.* Having definite and distinct lines or features.

well-dis·posed (wĕl′dĭ-spōzd′) ▸ *adj.* Disposed to be kindly, friendly, or receptive.

well-fixed (wĕl′fĭkst′) ▸ *adj. Informal* Financially secure; well-to-do.

well-found·ed (wĕl′foun′dĭd) ▸ *adj.* Based on sound judgment, reasoning, or evidence.

well-groomed (wĕl′grōōmd′) ▸ *adj.* 1. Neat and clean in dress and personal appearance. 2. Carefully tended or cared for.

well-ground·ed (wĕl′groun′dĭd) ▸ *adj.* 1. Adequately versed in a subject. 2. Having a sound basis; well-founded.

well-heeled (wĕl′hēld′) ▸ *adj.* Wealthy.

Wel·ling·ton (wĕl′ĭng-tən) ▸ The capital of New Zealand, on S North I.

well-in·ten·tioned (wĕl′ĭn-tĕn′shənd) ▸ *adj.* Marked by or having good intentions.

well-knit (wĕl′nĭt′) ▸ *adj.* Strongly knit, esp. strongly and firmly constructed.

well-man·nered (wĕl′măn′ərd) ▸ *adj.* Polite.

well-mean·ing (wĕl′mē′nĭng) ▸ *adj.* Well-intentioned.

well·ness (wĕl′nĭs) ▸ *n.* The condition of good physical and mental health, esp. when maintained by proper diet and exercise.

well-nigh (wĕl′nī′) ▸ *adv.* Nearly; almost.

well-off (wĕl′ôf′, -ŏf′) ▸ *adj.* 1. Well-to-do. 2. In fortunate circumstances.

well-read (wĕl′rĕd′) ▸ *adj.* Knowledgeable through having read extensively.

well-round·ed (wĕl′roun′dĭd) ▸ *adj.* Well-balanced in a range or variety of aspects.

Wells (wĕlz), **H(erbert) G(eorge)** (1866–1946) ▸ British writer.

well-spo·ken (wĕl′spō′kən) ▸ *adj.* 1. Chosen or expressed with aptness or propriety. 2. Courteous in speech.

well·spring (wĕl′sprĭng′) ▸ *n.* 1. The source of a stream or spring. 2. A source; origin.

well-timed (wĕl′tīmd′) ▸ *adj.* Occurring at an opportune time.

well-to-do (wĕl′tə-dōō′) ▸ *adj.* Prosperous; affluent; well-off.

well-turned (wĕl′tûrnd′) ▸ *adj.* 1. Shapely: *a well-turned ankle.* 2. Concisely or aptly expressed: *a well-turned phrase.*

well-wish·er (wĕl′wĭsh′ər) ▸ *n.* One who extends good wishes to another.

well-worn (wĕl′wôrn′) ▸ *adj.* 1. Showing signs of much wear or use. 2. Trite.

welsh (wĕlsh, wĕlch) ▸ *v.* **welshed, welsh·ing.** *Informal* 1. To swindle a person by not paying a debt or wager. 2. To fail to fulfill an obligation. **—welsh′er** *n.*

Welsh ▸ *n.* 1. The people of Wales. 2. The Celtic language of Wales. **—Welsh** *adj.* **—Welsh′man** *n.* **—Welsh′wom′an** *n.*

Welsh cor·gi (kôr′gē) ▸ *n.* A dog of a breed originating in Wales, having a long body, short legs, and a foxlike head.

Welsh rabbit also **Welsh rare·bit** (râr′bĭt) ▸ *n.* A dish made of melted cheese and sometimes ale, served hot over toast or crackers.

welt (wĕlt) ▸ *n.* 1. A usu. leather strip stitched into a shoe

THESAURUS

PERNATURAL.] *—See also* ECCENTRIC, FUNNY (3).

weirdie *n.* *—See* CRACKPOT.

weirdo *n.* *—See* CRACKPOT.

weisenheimer *n.* *See* WISENHEIMER

welcome *n.* An expression, in words or gestures, marking a meeting of persons ▸ hail, greeting, salutation salute. *Informal:* hello. *—See also* ACCEPTANCE (2).

welcome *adj.* *—See* PLEASANT.

welcome *v.* 1. To address in a friendly and respectful way ▸ greet, hail, salute. 2. To receive something given or offered willingly and gladly ▸ accept, embrace, take (up).

welcoming *adj.* Easily approached ▸ accessible, approachable, responsive. [*Compare* CONVENIENT.]

welfare *n.* A state of health, happiness, and prospering ▸ prosperity, weal, well-being. [*Compare* CONDITION, HAPPINESS.] *—See also* RELIEF (2).

well[1] *n.* *—See* ORIGIN.

well *v.* To fill with [illegible] (up), water. *—See also* FLOW (2).

well[2] *adv.* *—See* COMPLETELY (1), CONSIDERABLY.

well *adj.* *—See* ADVISABLE, HEALTHY.

well-being *n.* A state of health, happiness, and prospering ▸ prosperity, weal, welfare. [*Compare* CONDITION, HAPPINESS.]

wellborn *adj.* *—See* NOBLE.

well-bred *adj.* *—See* COURTEOUS (1), CULTURED.

well-considered *adj.* *—See* SOUND[2].

well-defined *adj.* *—See* SHARP (2).

well-developed *adj.* *—See* SHAPELY.

well-fixed *adj.* *—See* PROSPEROUS.

well-founded *adj.* *—See* SENSIBLE, SOUND[2].

well-groomed *adj.* *—See* NEAT.

well-grounded *adj.* *—See* SENSIBLE, SOUND[2].

well-heeled *adj.* *—See* PROSPEROUS.

well-kept *adj.* *—See* NEAT.

well-known *adj.* *—See* FAMOUS.

well-liked *adj.* *—See* FAVORITE.

well-mannered *adj.* *—See* COURTEOUS (1).

wellness *n.* *—See* HEALTH (1).

well-off *adj.* *—See* PROSPEROUS.

well-read *adj.* *—See* EDUCATED.

well-spoken *adj.* *—See* COURTEOUS (1), ELOQUENT.

wellspring *n.* *—See* ORIGIN.

well-timed *adj.* *—See* OPPORTUNE.

well-to-do *adj.* *—See* PROSPEROUS.

well-worn *adj.* *—See* TRITE.

welt *n.* A ridge or bump raised on

between the sole and the upper. **2.** A tape or covered cord sewn into a seam as reinforcement or trimming. **3.** A ridge or bump on the skin caused by a blow or an allergic reaction. ▸ *v.* **1.** To reinforce or trim with a welt. **2.** To flog.

wel·ter (wĕl′tər) ▸ *n.* **1.** A confused mass; jumble. **2.** Confusion; turmoil. ▸ *v.* **1.** To wallow or toss about, as in mud or high seas. **2.** To lie soaked, as in blood. **3.** To roll and surge, as the sea.

wel·ter·weight (wĕl′tər-wāt′) ▸ *n.* A boxer weighing from 136 to 147 lbs., between a lightweight and a middleweight.

Wel·ty (wĕl′tē), **Eudora** (1909–2001) ▸ Amer. writer.

wen (wĕn) ▸ *n.* A harmless cyst containing sebaceous matter.

wench (wĕnch) ▸ *n.* **1.** A young woman or girl, esp. a peasant girl. **2.** A woman servant. **3.** A wanton woman.

wend (wĕnd) ▸ *v.* To proceed on or along (one's way).

went (wĕnt) ▸ *v.* P.t. of **go**[1].

wept (wĕpt) ▸ *v.* P.t. and p.part. of **weep**.

were (wûr) ▸ *v.* **1.** 2nd pers. sing. and pl. and 1st and 3rd pers. pl. p.t. of **be**. **2.** P. subjunctive of **be**.

we're (wîr) ▸ We are.

were·n't (wûrnt, wûr′ənt) ▸ Were not.

were·wolf also **wer·wolf** (wâr′wo͝olf′, wîr′-, wûr′-) ▸ *n.* In folklore, a person capable of assuming the form of a wolf.

wert (wûrt) ▸ *v.* *Archaic* 2nd pers. sing. p.t. of **be**.

Wes·ley (wĕs′lē, wĕz′-), **John** (1703–91) ▸ British founder of Methodism (1738).

west (wĕst) ▸ *n.* **1a.** The direction opposite to the earth's axial rotation; the general direction of sunset. **b.** The compass point 270° clockwise from due north. **2.** often **West** The western part of a region or country. **3.** often **West** Europe and the Western Hemisphere. ▸ *adj.* **1.** To, toward, of, or in the west. **2.** Coming from the west: *a west wind.* ▸ *adv.* In, from, or toward the west. **—west′ward** *adj. & adv.* **—west′ward·ly** *adj. & adv.* **—west′wards** *adv.*

West Bank ▸ A disputed territory of SW Asia between Israel and Jordan W of the Jordan R.; occupied by Israel since 1967.

west·er·ly (wĕs′tər-lē) ▸ *adj.* **1.** Situated toward the west. **2.** From the west: *westerly winds.* **—west′er·ly** *adv.*

west·ern (wĕs′tərn) ▸ *adj.* **1.** Of, in, or toward the west. **2.** From the west: *western breezes.* **3.** often **Western** Of or characteristic of western regions or the West. ▸ *n.* often **Western** A novel, film, or television or radio program having themes or settings characteristic of the American West.

west·ern·er also **West·ern·er** (wĕs′tər-nər) ▸ *n.* A native or inhabitant of the west, esp. the W US.

Western Hemisphere ▸ The half of the earth comprising North America, Central America, and South America.

west·ern·ize (wĕs′tər-nīz′) ▸ *v.* **-ized, -iz·ing.** To convert to the customs of Western civilization. **—west′ern·i·za′tion** *n.*

Western Sahara also **Spanish Sahara** ▸ A region of NW Africa on the Atlantic coast.

Western Samoa ▸ See **Samoa**[2].

West Germany ▸ A former country (1945–90) of central Europe bordering on the North Sea; reunified with East Germany to form Germany. **—West German** *adj. & n.*

West Indies ▸ An archipelago between SE North America and N South America, separating the Caribbean Sea from the Atlantic and including the Greater Antilles, the Lesser Antilles, and the Bahama Is. **—West Indian** *adj. & n.*

West·pha·lia (wĕst-fāl′yə, -fā′lē-ə) ▸ A historical region and former duchy of W-central Germany that is located east of the Rhine R. **—West·pha′lian** *adj. & n.*

West Virginia ▸ A state of the E-central US. Cap. Charleston. **—West Virginian** *adj. & n.*

wet (wĕt) ▸ *adj.* **wet·ter, wet·test.** **1.** Covered or soaked with a liquid, such as water. **2.** Not yet dry or firm: *wet paint.* **3.** Rainy or foggy. **4.** *Informal* Allowing the sale of alcoholic beverages: *a wet county.* ▸ *n.* **1.** Moisture. **2.** Rainy weather. ▸ *v.* **wet** or **wet·ted, wet·ting.** To make or become wet. ***—idiom:* all wet** *Slang* Entirely mistaken. **—wet′ly** *adv.* **—wet′ness** *n.*

wet blanket ▸ *n.* *Informal* One that discourages enjoyment or enthusiasm.

weth·er (wĕth′ər) ▸ *n.* A castrated ram.

wet·land (wĕt′lănd′) ▸ *n.* A lowland area, as a marsh, that is saturated with moisture.

wet nurse ▸ *n.* A woman who suckles another woman's child.

wet·suit also **wet suit** (wĕt′so͞ot′) ▸ *n.* A tight-fitting permeable suit worn in cold water to retain body heat.

we've (wēv) ▸ We have.

whack (hwăk, wăk) ▸ *v.* To strike with a sharp blow; slap. ▸ *n.* **1.** A sharp resounding blow. **2.** The sound made by a whack. ***—idiom:* out of whack** *Informal* Not functioning correctly.

whack·y (hwăk′ē, wăk′ē) ▸ *adj.* *Slang* Var. of **wacky.**

whale[1] (hwāl, wāl) ▸ *n.* **1.** Any of an order of often very large marine mammals having flippers, a tail with horizontal flukes, and one or two blowholes for breathing. **2.** *Informal* An impressive example: *a whale of a story.* ▸ *v.* **whaled, whal·ing.** To engage in the hunting of whales.

whale[2] (hwāl, wāl) ▸ *v.* **whaled, whal·ing.** To strike repeatedly; thrash.

whale·boat (hwāl′bōt′, wāl′-) ▸ *n.* A long rowboat, pointed at both ends and formerly used in whaling.

whale·bone (hwāl′bōn′, wāl′-) ▸ *n.* **1.** The elastic horny material forming the fringed plates that hang from the upper jaw of certain whales and strain plankton from the water. **2.** An object made of this material.

whal·er (hwā′lər, wā′-) ▸ *n.* **1.** One who hunts whales. **2.** A ship used in hunting whales. **3.** A whaleboat.

wham (hwăm, wăm) ▸ *n.* **1.** A forceful resounding blow. **2.** The sound of such a blow; thud. ▸ *v.* **whammed, wham·ming.** To strike with resounding impact.

wham·my (hwăm′ē, wăm′ē) ▸ *n., pl.* **-mies.** *Slang* A supernatural spell for causing misfortune; hex.

wharf (hwôrf, wôrf) ▸ *n., pl.* **wharves** (hwôrvz, wôrvz) or **wharfs.** A landing place or pier where ships may tie up and load or unload.

wharf·age (hwôr′fĭj, wôr′fĭj) ▸ *n.* **1.** The use of a wharf. **2.** The charges for this usage.

what (hwŏt, hwŭt, wŏt, wŭt; hwət, wət *when unstressed*) ▸ *pron.* **1a.** Which thing or which particular one of many: *What are you having for dinner?* **b.** Which kind, character, or designation: *What are these objects?* **c.** One of how much value or significance: *What are possessions to a dying man?* **2a.** That which; the thing that: *Listen to what I tell you.* **b.** Whatever thing that: *come what may.* **3.** *Informal* Something: *I'll tell you what.* ▸ *adj.* **1.** Which one or ones: *What train do I take?* **2.** Whatever: *They soon repaired what damage had been done.* **3.** How great: *What a fool!* ▸ *adv.* How much; how: *What does it matter?* ▸ *interj.* Used to express surprise or incredulity.

THESAURUS

the flesh as a result of irritation, infection, or injury ▸ blister, boil, pock, wale, wart, weal, wheal, whelk. [*Compare* BUMP.] *—See also* BLOW[2].

welter *v.* To move about in an indolent or clumsy manner ▸ flounder, roll about, roll around, wallow.

wench *n.* *—See* SLUT.

wend *v.* To move along a particular course ▸ go, pass, proceed, push on. *Idiom:* make (*or* wend) one's way. [*Compare* ADVANCE, JOURNEY, ROVE.]

wet *adj.* Covered with or full of liquid ▸ doused, drenched, dripping, saturated, soaked, soaking, sodden, soggy, sopping, soppy, waterlogged. [*Compare* DAMP, STICKY.] *—See also* RAINY.

wet *v.* **1.** To make thoroughly wet ▸ douse, drench, saturate, soak, sodden, sop, souse. **2.** To make moist ▸ bathe, dampen, moisten, wash.

wet blanket *n.* *—See* KILLJOY.

wetland *n.* *—See* SWAMP.

whack *v.* *—See* BANG (1), HIT, SLAP.

whack *n.* *Informal* A brief trial ▸ crack, go, stab, try. *Informal:* fling, shot, whirl. *—See also* BEAT (1), BLOW[2], CLASH, SLAP.

whack *adj.* *—See* INSANE.

whackiness *adj.* *See* WACKINESS.

whacky *adj.* *See* WACKY.

whale *v.* *—See* BEAT (1).

wham *n.* A forceful movement causing a loud noise ▸ bang, crash, slam, smash. *—See also* BLOW[2].

wham *v.* *—See* HIT.

whammy *n.* *—See* CURSE (1).

what·ev·er (hwŏt-ĕv′ər, hwŭt-, wŏt-, wŭt-) ▸ *pron.* **1.** Everything or anything that: *Do whatever you please.* **2.** No matter what: *Whatever happens, we'll meet here tonight.* **3.** *Informal* What: *Whatever does he mean?* ▸ *adj.* Of any number or kind; any: *Whatever requests you make will be granted.*

what·not (hwŏt′nŏt′, hwŭt′-, wŏt′-, wŭt′-) ▸ *n.* **1.** An unspecified object or article. **2.** A set of open shelves for ornaments.

what·so·ev·er (hwŏt′sō-ĕv′ər, hwŭt′-, wŏt′-, wŭt′-) ▸ *pron. & adj.* Whatever.

wheat (hwēt, wēt) ▸ *n.* **1.** A cereal grass widely cultivated for its commercially important edible grain. **2.** The grain of this plant, ground to produce flour. **—wheat′en** *adj.*

wheat germ ▸ *n.* The vitamin-rich embryo of the wheat kernel, used as a cereal or food supplement.

Wheat·ley (hwēt′lē, wēt′-), **Phillis** (1753?–84) ▸ African-born Amer. poet.

whee·dle (hwēd′l, wēd′l) ▸ *v.* **-dled, -dling.** To persuade, attempt to persuade, or obtain by flattery or guile; cajole. **—whee′dler** *n.* **—whee′dling·ly** *adv.*

wheel (hwēl, wēl) ▸ *n.* **1.** A solid disk or rigid circular ring connected by spokes to a hub, designed to turn around an axle passed through the center. **2.** Something resembling a wheel in appearance or movement. **3.** Something having a wheel as its principal part: *a steering wheel.* **4. wheels** Forces that provide energy, movement, or direction: *the wheels of commerce.* **5.** A revolution or rotation around an axis; turn. **6. wheels** *Slang* A motor vehicle. **7.** *Slang* One with power or influence: *A big wheel at the bank.* ▸ *v.* **1.** To roll, move, or transport on or as if on wheels. **2.** To turn around or as if around a central axis; revolve or rotate. **3.** To whirl around, changing direction; pivot.

wheel·bar·row (hwēl′băr′ō, wēl′-) ▸ *n.* A one- or two-wheeled vehicle with handles at the rear, used to carry small loads.

wheel·base (hwēl′bās′, wēl′-) ▸ *n.* The distance from front to rear axle in a motor vehicle, usu. expressed in inches.

wheel·chair (hwēl′châr′, wēl′-) ▸ *n.* A chair mounted on large wheels for the use of a sick or disabled person.

wheel·er (hwē′lər, wē′-) ▸ *n.* **1.** One that wheels. **2.** Something equipped with wheels: *a three-wheeler.*

wheel·er-deal·er (hwē′lər-dē′lər, wē′-) ▸ *n.* *Informal* An aggressive or unscrupulous operator, esp. in business.

wheel·house (hwēl′hous′, wēl′-) ▸ *n.* See **pilothouse**.

wheel·wright (hwēl′rīt′, wēl′-) ▸ *n.* One who builds and repairs wheels.

wheeze (hwēz, wēz) ▸ *v.* **wheezed, wheez·ing.** To breathe with difficulty, producing a hoarse whistling sound. ▸ *n.* **1.** A wheezing sound. **2.** *Informal* An old joke. **—wheez′er** *n.* **—wheez′i·ly** *adv.* **—wheez′i·ness** *n.* **—wheez′y** *adj.*

whelk (hwĕlk, wĕlk) ▸ *n.* Any of various large, mostly edible marine snails.

whelm (hwĕlm, wĕlm) ▸ *v.* **1.** To submerge. **2.** To overwhelm.

whelp (hwĕlp, wĕlp) ▸ *n.* **1.** A young offspring of an animal, such as a dog or wolf. **2.** An impudent youth. ▸ *v.* To give birth to whelps.

when (hwĕn, wĕn) ▸ *adv.* At what time: *When will we leave?* ▸ *conj.* **1.** At the time that: *in the spring, when the snow melts.* **2.** As soon as: *I'll call you when I get there.* **3.** Whenever: *When the wind blows, all the doors rattle.* **4.** Whereas; although: *playing when she should have been studying.* ▸ *pron.* What or which time: *Since when are you the expert?* ▸ *n.* The time or date: *the where and when of the [illegible]*

whence (hwĕns, wĕns) ▸ *adv.* **1.** From what place: *Whence came this traveler?* **2.** From what origin or source: *Whence comes this feast?* ▸ *conj.* By reason of which: *[illegible] the same name, whence the error.*

when·ev·er (hwĕn-ĕv′ər, wĕn-) ▸ *adv.* **1.** At whatever time. **2.** When. ▸ *conj.* **1.** At whatever time that. **2.** Every time that: *My knees hurt whenever it rains.*

when·so·ev·er (hwĕn′sō-ĕv′ər, wĕn′-) ▸ *adv. & conj.* Whenever.

where (hwâr, wâr) ▸ *adv.* **1.** At or in what place or position: *Where is the telephone?* **2.** From what place or source: *Where did you get this idea?* **3.** To what place or end: *Where is this argument leading?* ▸ *conj.* **1.** At what or which place: *moved to the city, where jobs are available.* **2a.** In or to a place in which: *Put it where it belongs. Let's go where it's quieter.* **b.** Wherever: *Where there's smoke, there's fire.* ▸ *n.* **1.** The place or occasion: *the where and when of the performance.* **2.** What place, source, or cause: *Where are you from?*

where·a·bouts (hwâr′ə-bouts′, wâr′-) ▸ *adv.* About where; in, at, or near what location: *Whereabouts do you live?* ▸ *n. (takes sing. or pl. v.)* Approximate location: *Her whereabouts are still unknown.*

where·as (hwâr-ăz′, wâr-) ▸ *conj.* **1.** It being the fact that; inasmuch as. **2.** While at the same time. **3.** While on the contrary.

where·at (hwâr-ăt′, wâr-) ▸ *conj.* **1.** Toward or at which. **2.** Whereupon.

where·by (hwâr-bī′, wâr-) ▸ *conj.* In accordance with which; by or through which.

where·fore (hwâr′fôr′, wâr′-) ▸ *adv.* **1.** For what reason; why. **2.** Therefore. ▸ *n.* A purpose or cause: *the whys and wherefores of your decision.*

where·in (hwâr-ĭn′, wâr-) ▸ *adv.* In what way; how: *Wherein have we sinned?* ▸ *conj.* **1.** In which location; where. **2.** During which.

where·of (hwâr-ŏv′, -ŭv′, wâr-) ▸ *conj.* **1.** Of what: *I know whereof I speak.* **2.** Of which or when: *ancient lore whereof much is lost.*

where·on (hwâr-ŏn′, -ôn′, wâr-) ▸ *adv.* *Archaic* On which or what.

where·so·ev·er (hwâr′sō-ĕv′ər, wâr′-) ▸ *conj.* Wherever.

where·to (hwâr′to͞o′, wâr′-) ▸ *adv.* To what place; toward what end. ▸ *conj.* To which.

where·up·on (hwâr′ə-pŏn′, -pôn′, wâr′-) ▸ *conj.* **1.** On which. **2.** Following which.

wher·ev·er (hwâr-ĕv′ər, wâr-) ▸ *adv.* **1.** In or to whatever place: *used red pencil wherever needed.* **2.** Where. ▸ *conj.* In or to whichever place or situation: *goes wherever I go.*

where·with (hwâr′wĭth′, -wĭth′, wâr′-) ▸ *conj.* By means of which.

where·with·al (hwâr′wĭth-ôl′, -wĭth-, wâr′-) ▸ *n.* The necessary means, esp. financial means.

whet (hwĕt, wĕt) ▸ *v.* **whet·ted, whet·ting.** **1.** To sharpen (e.g., a knife); hone. **2.** To make more keen; stimulate.

wheth·er (hwĕth′ər, wĕth′-) ▸ *conj.* **1.** Used to introduce: **a.** One alternative: *We should find out whether the museum is open.* **b.** Alternative possibilities: *Whether she wins or loses, she can be proud.* **2.** Either: *He passed the test, whether by skill or luck.*

whet·stone (hwĕt′stōn′, wĕt′-) ▸ *n.* A hard, fine-grained stone for honing tools.

whey (hwā, wā) ▸ *n.* The watery part of milk that separates from the curds, as in the process of making cheese.

which (hwĭch, wĭch) ▸ *pron.* **1.** What particular one or ones: *Which is your house?* **2.** The one or ones previously mentioned or implied: *my room, which is small and dark; the topic on which she spoke.* **3.** Whichever: *Choose which you like best.* **4.** A thing or circumstance that: *He left early, which was wise.* ▸ *adj.* **1.** What particular one or ones of a number of things or people: *Which part of town do you mean?* **2.** Any one of any number of; whichever: *Use which door you please.* **3.** Being the one or ones previously mentioned or implied: *It started to rain, at which point we ran.*

THESAURUS

whatnot *n.* —*See* NOVELTY (3).
wheal *n.* —*See* WELT.
wheedle *v.* —*See* COAX.
wheel *n.* —*See* CIRCLE (1), REVOLUTION (1).
wheel *v.* To turn in place, as on a fixed point ▸ pivot, slue, swing, swivel. —*See also* DRIVE (1), TURN (1).
wheeze *v.* —*See* GASP, PANT.
whelk *n.* —*See* WELT.
whelp *n.* —*See* CHILD (1), URCHIN.
whereabouts *n.* —*See* BEARING (3).
wherefore *n.* —*See* CAUSE (2), REASON (1).
wherewithal *n.* —*See* RESOURCES.
whet *v.* —*See* SHARPEN.
whey-faced *adj.* —*See* PALE (1).

which·ev·er (hwĭch-ĕv′ər, wĭch-) ▸ *pron.* Whatever one or ones. ▸ *adj.* Being any one or number: *Take whichever items you please.*

which·so·ev·er (hwĭch′sō-ĕv′ər, wĭch′-) ▸ *pron. & adj.* Whichever.

whiff (hwĭf, wĭf) ▸ *n.* **1.** A slight gentle gust of air. **2a.** A brief passing odor carried in the air: *a whiff of perfume.* **b.** A minute trace. **3.** An inhalation, as of air or smoke. ▸ *v.* **1.** To waft. **2.** To smell or sniff.

whif·fle·tree (hwĭf′əl-trē, wĭf′-) ▸ *n. Regional* The pivoted horizontal crossbar to which the harness traces of a draft animal are attached.

Whig (hwĭg, wĭg) ▸ *n.* **1.** A member of an 18th- and 19th-cent. British political party opposed to the Tories. **2.** A supporter of the war against England during the American Revolution. **3.** A member of a 19th-century American political party formed to oppose the Democratic Party. **—Whig′ger·y** *n.* **—Whig′gish** *adj.* **—Whig′gism** *n.*

while (hwīl, wīl) ▸ *n.* **1.** A period of time: *stay for a while.* **2.** The time, effort, or trouble taken in doing something: *It wasn't worth my while.* ▸ *conj.* **1.** As long as: *fun while it lasted.* **2.** Although: *While I like opera, I'm not a fanatic.* **3.** Whereas: *The soles are leather, while the uppers are canvas.* ▸ *v.* **whiled, whil·ing.** To spend (time) idly or pleasantly: *while away the hours.*

whi·lom (hwī′ləm, wī′-) ▸ *adj.* Former: *the whilom editor in chief.* ▸ *adv. Archaic* At a past time.

whilst (hwīlst, wīlst) ▸ *conj. Chiefly Brit.* While.

whim (hwĭm, wĭm) ▸ *n.* **1.** A sudden or capricious idea; fancy. **2.** Arbitrary thought or impulse: *governed by whim.*

whim·per (hwĭm′pər, wĭm′-) ▸ *v.* To make soft whining sounds. **—whim′per** *n.* **—whim′per·ing·ly** *adv.*

whim·si·cal (hwĭm′zĭ-kəl, wĭm′-) ▸ *adj.* **1.** Marked by playful whim or caprice; fanciful. **2.** Erratic in nature or behavior; capricious: *a whimsical personality.* **—whim′si·cal′i·ty** (-kăl′ĭ-tē) *n.* **—whim′si·cal·ly** *adv.*

whim·sy also **whim·sey** (hwĭm′zē, wĭm′-) ▸ *n., pl.* **-sies** also **-seys. 1.** An odd or fanciful idea; whim. **2.** A quaint or fanciful quality: *stories full of whimsy.*

whine (hwīn, wīn) ▸ *v.* **whined, whin·ing. 1.** To utter a plaintive, high-pitched sound, as in pain, fear, or supplication. **2.** To complain in a childish fashion. **3.** To make a steady, high-pitched noise: *jet engines whining.* **—whine** *n.* **—whin′er** *n.* **—whin′y** *adj.*

whin·ny (hwĭn′ē, wĭn′ē) ▸ *v.* **whin·nied** (hwĭn′ēd, wĭn′-), **whin·ny·ing.** To neigh softly, as a horse. **—whin′ny** *n.*

whip (hwĭp, wĭp) ▸ *v.* **whipped** or **whipt** (hwĭpt, wĭpt), **whip·ping. 1.** To strike with repeated strokes, as with a strap or rod; lash. **2.** To punish by or as if by whipping. **3.** To drive, force, or compel by or as if by whipping. **4.** To beat (e.g., cream or eggs) into a froth or foam. **5.** *Informal* To snatch or remove in a sudden manner: *He whipped off his cap.* **6.** To wrap or bind (e.g., a rope) with twine to prevent unraveling or fraying. **7.** *Informal* To defeat; beat. **8.** To move swiftly or nimbly. **9.** To move like a whip; thrash: *branches whipping in the wind.* ***—phrasal verb:* whip up 1.** To arouse; excite: *whip up enthusiasm.* **2.** *Informal* To prepare quickly: *whip up a light lunch.* ▸ *n.* **1.** A flexible instrument, esp. a rod or thong, used for driving animals or administering punishment. **2.** A whipping motion or stroke; lash. **3.** A member of a legislative body charged by his or her party with enforcing party discipline and ensuring attendance. **4.** A dessert made of sugar and stiffly beaten egg whites or cream, often with fruit. **—whip′per** *n.*

whip·cord (hwĭp′kôrd′, wĭp′-) ▸ *n.* **1.** A worsted fabric with a distinct diagonal rib. **2.** A strong twisted or braided cord sometimes used in making whiplashes. **3.** Catgut.

whip·lash (hwĭp′lăsh′, wĭp′-) ▸ *n.* **1.** The lash of a whip. **2.** An injury to the cervical spine caused by an abrupt jerking motion of the head, either backward or forward.

whip·per·snap·per (hwĭp′ər-snăp′ər, wĭp′-) ▸ *n.* An insignificant and pretentious person.

whip·pet (hwĭp′ĭt, wĭp′-) ▸ *n.* A swift, short-haired dog resembling the greyhound but smaller.

whip·ping boy (hwĭp′ĭng, wĭp′-) ▸ *n.* A scapegoat.

whip·poor·will (hwĭp′ər-wĭl′, wĭp′-) ▸ *n.* A brownish insect-eating nocturnal North American bird.

whip·saw (hwĭp′sô′, wĭp′-) ▸ *n.* A narrow two-person crosscut saw. ▸ *v.* **1.** To cut with a whipsaw. **2.** To defeat in two ways at once.

whip·stitch (hwĭp′stĭch′, wĭp′-) ▸ *v.* To sew with overcast stitches, as in finishing a fabric edge or binding two pieces of fabric together. **—whip′stitch′** *n.*

whipt (hwĭpt, wĭpt) ▸ *v.* P.t. and p.part. of **whip.**

whir (hwûr, wûr) ▸ *v.* **whirred, whir·ring.** To move so as to produce an airy vibrating sound. ▸ *n.* **1.** A whirring sound: *a whir of wings.* **2.** A flurry; bustle.

whirl (hwûrl, wûrl) ▸ *v.* **1.** To rotate or cause to rotate rapidly; spin. **2.** To wheel or pivot: *whirled around to face him.* **3.** To have the sensation of spinning; reel. **4.** To move or drive at high speed. ▸ *n.* **1.** A whirling or spinning motion. **2.** One that whirls or is whirled. **3.** A state of confusion; tumult. **4.** A swift succession or round of events: *the social whirl.* **5.** A state of giddiness or dizziness: *My head is in a whirl.* **6.** *Informal* **a.** A short trip or ride. **b.** A try: *give it a whirl.* **—whirl′er** *n.*

whirl·i·gig (hwûr′lĭ-gĭg′, wûr′-) ▸ *n.* **1.** A toy, such as a pinwheel, that whirls. **2.** A merry-go-round.

whirl·pool (hwûrl′po͞ol′, wûrl′-) ▸ *n.* **1.** A rapidly rotating current of water; vortex. **2.** A bathtub or pool having submerged jets of warm water.

whirl·wind (hwûrl′wĭnd′, wûrl′-) ▸ *n.* **1.** A rapidly rotating column of air, such as a tornado, dust devil, or waterspout. **2a.** A tumultuous rush. **b.** A destructive force. ▸ *adj.* Tumultuous or rapid: *a whirlwind campaign.*

whisk (hwĭsk, wĭsk) ▸ *v.* **1.** To move or cause to move with quick light sweeping motions. **2.** To whip (eggs or cream). **3.** To move lightly, nimbly, and rapidly. ▸ *n.* **1.** A quick light sweeping motion. **2.** A whiskbroom. **3.** A kitchen utensil for whipping foodstuffs.

whisk·broom (hwĭsk′bro͞om′, -bro͝om′, wĭsk′-) ▸ *n.* A small short-handled broom used esp. to brush clothes.

whisk·er (hwĭs′kər, wĭs′-) ▸ *n.* **1a. whiskers** The hair on a man's cheeks and chin. **b.** A single hair of a beard or mustache. **2.** One of the long stiff tactile bristles that grow near the mouth of most mammals. **3.** *Informal* A narrow margin: *lost by a whisker.* **—whisk′ered, whisk′er·y** *adj.*

whis·key also **-ky** (hwĭs′kē, wĭs′-) ▸ *n., pl.* **-keys** also **-kies. 1.** An alcoholic liquor distilled from grain, such as corn, rye, or barley. **2.** A drink of whiskey.

whis·per (hwĭs′pər, wĭs′-) ▸ *n.* **1.** Soft speech produced

THESAURUS

whiff *n.* —*See* BREEZE (1), SHADE (2).
whiff *v.* —*See* SMELL (1).

while *n.* —*See* BIT[1] (3), EFFORT.
while *v.* —*See* IDLE (2).

whilom *adj.* —*See* LATE (2).

whim *n.* —*See* FANCY.

whimper *v.* —*See* COMPLAIN, CRY.
whimper *n.* —*See* COMPLAINT.

whimsical *adj.* **1.** Showing invention or whimsy in design ▸ fanciful, fantastic, imaginative. [*Compare* ELABORATE, ORNATE.] **2.** Determined or marked by whim or caprice rather than reason ▸ arbitrary, capricious. —*See also* CAPRICIOUS.

whimsy *n.* —*See* FANCY.

whim-whams *n.* —*See* JITTERS.

whine *v.* —*See* COMPLAIN, CRY.
whine *n.* —*See* COMPLAINT.

whiner *n.* —*See* GROUCH.

whip *v.* —*See* AGITATE (1), BEAT (2), BEAT (6), OVERWHELM (1).

whippersnapper *n.* —*See* NONENTITY.

whipping *n.* —*See* BEATING, DEFEAT.

whipping boy *n.* —*See* SCAPEGOAT.

whir *v.* —*See* HUM.
whir *n.* —*See* HUM.

whirl *v.* **1.** To move or cause to move like a rapidly rotating current of liquid ▸ eddy, swirl. **2.** To have the sensation of turning in circles ▸ reel, spin, swim, swirl. *Idiom:* go round and round. —*See also* RUSH, TURN (1).
whirl *n. Informal* A brief trial ▸ crack, go, stab, try. *Informal:* fling, shot, whack. —*See also* AGITATION (3), DRIVE (3), REVOLUTION (1).

whirlpool *n.* A rotating, often concave current of liquid ▸ eddy, maelstrom, swirl, vortex. —*See also* AGITATION (3).

whisk *v.* —*See* BEAT (6), RUSH.

whisker *n.* —*See* SHADE (2).

whisper *n.* —*See* MURMUR, SHADE (2).
whisper *v.* **1.** To tell in confidence ▸

without full voice. 2. Something uttered very softly. 3. A rumor or hint: *whispers of scandal.* 4. A low rustling or sighing sound. ▸ *v.* 1. To speak softly. 2. To tell secretly or privately. 3. To make a soft rustling sound. **—whis′per·er** *n.* **—whis′per·y** *adj.*

whist (hwĭst, wĭst) ▸ *n.* A card game similar to bridge.

whis·tle (hwĭs′əl, wĭs′-) ▸ *v.* 1. **-tled, -tling.** To produce a clear, shrill or musical sound by forcing air through the teeth or pursed lips or by blowing on or through a device. 2. To make a high-pitched sound when moving swiftly through the air: *The stone whistled past my head.* 3. To produce by whistling: *whistle a tune.* ▸ *n.* 1. A device or instrument for making whistling sounds by means of breath, forced air, or steam. 2. A sound produced by a whistle or by whistling. ***—idiom:* blow the whistle** *Slang* To expose a wrongdoing in the hope of ending it. **—whis′tler** *n.*

Whis·tler (hwĭs′lər, wĭs′-), **James Abbott McNeill** (1834–1903) ▸ Amer. painter.

whistle stop ▸ *n.* 1. A town at which a train stops only if signaled. 2. An appearance of a political candidate in a small town, as on the rear platform of a train.

whit (hwĭt, wĭt) ▸ *n.* The least bit; iota.

white (hwīt, wīt) ▸ *n.* 1. The achromatic color of maximum lightness; the color of objects that reflect nearly all light of all visible wavelengths. 2. The white or whitish part, as of an egg. 3. **whites** White trousers or a white outfit. 4. also **White** A member of a racial group having light skin coloration, esp. one of European origin. ▸ *adj.* **whit·er, whit·est.** 1. Being of the color white. 2. Light-colored; pale. 3. also **White** Of or belonging to a racial group having light skin coloration, esp. one of European origin. 4. Not written on; blank. 5. Unsullied; pure. 6. Snowy: *a white Christmas.* 7. Incandescent. **—whit′en** *v.* **—whit′en·er** *n.* **—white′ness** *n.*

white ant ▸ *n.* See **termite.**

white·bait (hwīt′bāt′, wīt′-) ▸ *n.* The young of various fishes, esp. the herring, considered a delicacy when fried.

white blood cell ▸ *n.* Any of the whitish nucleated cells in the blood that help protect the body from infection and disease.

white·cap (hwīt′kăp′, wīt′-) ▸ *n.* A wave with a crest of foam.

white-col·lar (hwīt′kŏl′ər, wīt′-) ▸ *adj.* Of or relating to workers whose work does not involve manual labor.

white dwarf ▸ *n.* A whitish star of low luminosity, small size, and very great density.

white elephant ▸ *n.* 1. A rare, expensive possession that is a financial burden to maintain. 2. Something useless or no longer wanted. 3. A rare whitish form of the Asian elephant.

white feather ▸ *n.* A sign of cowardice.

white·fish (hwīt′fĭsh′, wīt′-) ▸ *n.* 1. Any of various silvery freshwater food fishes. 2. See **beluga** 2.

white flag ▸ *n.* A white cloth or flag signaling truce or surrender.

white gold ▸ *n.* An alloy of gold and nickel, sometimes also containing palladium or zinc, having a pale platinumlike color.

White·hall (hwīt′hôl′, wīt′-) ▸ *n.* The British civil service.

White·horse (hwīt′hôrs′, wīt′-) ▸ The capital of Yukon Terr., Canada, in the S part on the Yukon R.

White House ▸ *n.* 1. The executive branch of the US government. 2. The executive mansion of the US President.

white lead (lĕd) ▸ *n.* A heavy white poisonous compound of lead used in paint pigments.

white lie ▸ *n.* A trivial, harmless, or well-intentioned untruth.

white matter ▸ *n.* Whitish nerve tissue, esp. of the brain and spinal cord, consisting chiefly of nerve fibers with myelin sheaths.

White Mountains ▸ A section of the Appalachian Mts. in N NH.

White Nile ▸ A section of the Nile R. in E Africa flowing to Khartoum, where it joins the Blue Nile to form the Nile River proper.

white pine ▸ *n.* 1. A timber tree of E North America, having durable, easily worked wood. 2. The wood of this tree.

white sauce ▸ *n.* A sauce made with butter, flour, and milk, cream, or stock.

white slave ▸ *n.* A woman held unwillingly for prostitution. **—white slavery** *n.*

white·wash (hwīt′wŏsh′, -wôsh′, wīt′-) ▸ *n.* 1. A mixture of lime and water, often with whiting, size, or glue added, used to whiten walls and fences. 2. Concealment or palliation of flaws or failures. ▸ *v.* 1. To paint or coat with whitewash. 2. To conceal or gloss over (e.g., wrongdoing). **—white′wash′er** *n.*

white whale ▸ *n.* A small toothed whale usu. of northern waters that is white when mature.

whith·er (hwĭth′ər, wĭth′-) ▸ *adv.* To what place, result, or condition. ▸ *conj.* 1. To which specified place or position. 2. Wherever.

whit·ing[1] (hwī′tĭng, wī′-) ▸ *n.* A pure white chalk ground and washed for use in paints, ink, and putty.

whit·ing[2] (hwī′tĭng, wī′-) ▸ *n., pl.* **-ing** or **-ings.** A codlike food fish of European Atlantic waters.

whit·ish (hwī′tĭsh, wī′-) ▸ *adj.* Somewhat white.

Whit·man (hwĭt′mən, wĭt′-), **Walt** (1819–92) ▸ Amer. poet.

Whit·ney (hwĭt′nē, wĭt′-), **Eli** (1765–1825) ▸ Amer. inventor of the cotton gin (1793).

Whit·sun·day (hwĭt′sən-dē, -dā′, wĭt′-) ▸ *n.* See **Pentecost.**

whit·tle (hwĭt′l, wĭt′l) ▸ *v.* **-tled, -tling.** 1a. To cut small bits or pare shavings from (a piece of wood). b. To fashion in this way. 2. To reduce gradually: *whittled down my expenses.* **—whit′tler** *n.*

whiz also **whizz** (hwĭz, wĭz) ▸ *v.* **whizzed, whiz·zing.** 1. To make a whirring or hissing sound, as of an object speeding through air. 2. To rush past. ▸ *n., pl.* **whiz·zes.** 1. A whizzing sound. 2. *Informal* One who has remarkable skill: *a math whiz.*

who (ho͞o) ▸ *pron.* 1. What or which person or persons: *Who left?* 2. The person or persons that: *The boy who came yesterday has gone.*

WHO ▸ *abbr.* World Health Organization

whoa (hwō, wō) ▸ *interj.* Used as a command to stop, as to a horse.

who'd (ho͞od) ▸ 1. Who would. 2. Who had.

who·dun·it (ho͞o-dŭn′ĭt) ▸ *n.* *Informal* A detective story.

who·ev·er (ho͞o-ĕv′ər) ▸ *pron.* 1. Whatever person or persons. 2. Who.

whole (hōl) ▸ *adj.* 1. Containing all parts; complete: *whole milk.* 2. Not divided; in one unit: *a whole loaf.* 3. Constituting the full amount, extent, or duration: *cried the whole time.* 4. Not wounded, injured, or impaired. 5. *Math.* Not fractional; integral. ▸ *n.* 1. All of the component parts or elements of a thing. 2. A complete entity or system. ***—idiom:* on the whole** In general. **—whole′ness** *n.*

whole·heart·ed (hōl′här′tĭd) ▸ *adj.* Without reservation: *wholehearted approval.* **—whole′heart′ed·ly** *adv.*

whole note ▸ *n.* A musical note having, in common time, the value of four beats.

THESAURUS

breathe, confide, share, unbosom. [*Compare* COMMUNICATE, REVEAL, SAY.] 2. To make a low, continuous, and indistinct sound ▸ murmur, rustle, sigh, sough. [*Compare* BURBLE, HUM.] *—See also* GOSSIP, MUTTER.

whisperer *n.* *—See* GOSSIP (2).

whispery *adj.* *—See* SOFT (2).

whistleblower *n.* *—See* INFORMER.

whit *n.* *—See* BIT[1] (1).

whitecap *n.* *—See* WAVE.

white flag *n.* *—See* TRUCE.

whiten *v.* *—See* PALE.

white-tie *adj.* *—See* FORMAL.

whitewash *v.* *—See* COLOR (2), EXTENUATE.

whiz *v.* *—See* HISS (1), HUM, RUSH.

whiz *n.* *—See* EXPERT, HISS (1), HUM.

whole *n.* An amount or quantity from which nothing is left out or held back ▸ aggregate, all, entirety, everything, grand total, gross, sum, total, totality. *Informal:* works. *Idioms:* everything but (*or* except) the kitchen sink, lock, stock, and barrel, the lot, the whole ball of wax, the whole kit and caboodle, the whole lot, the whole megillah, the whole nine yards, the whole shebang (*or* schmeer), the works. [*Compare* COMPLETENESS.] *—See also* SYSTEM.

whole *adj.* No less than; at least ▸ full, good, round. *—See also* COMPLETE (1), CONCENTRATED (1), GOOD (2), HEALTHY.

wholehearted *adj.* *—See* IMPLICIT (2).

wholeness *n.* *—See* COMPLETENESS, HEALTH (1), SOUNDNESS.

whole number ▸ *n.* **1.** A member of the set of positive integers and zero. **2.** A positive integer. **3.** An integer.

whole·sale (hōl′sāl′) ▸ *n.* The sale of goods in large quantities, as for resale by a retailer. ▸ *adj.* **1.** Of or engaged in the sale of goods at wholesale. **2.** Performed extensively and indiscriminately: *wholesale destruction.* ▸ *v.* **-saled, -sal·ing.** To sell or be sold at wholesale. **—whole′sale′** *adv.* **—whole′sal′er** *n.*

whole·some (hōl′səm) ▸ *adj.* **-som·er, -som·est. 1.** Conducive to mental or physical well-being: *a wholesome diet.* **2.** Promoting mental, moral, or social health: *wholesome entertainment.* **3.** Healthy. **—whole′some·ly** *adv.* **—whole′some·ness** *n.*

whole-wheat (hōl′hwēt′, -wēt′) ▸ *adj.* Made from the entire grain of wheat.

who'll (ho͞ol) ▸ **1.** Who will. **2.** Who shall.

whol·ly (hō′lē, hōl′lē) ▸ *adv.* **1.** Completely; entirely. **2.** Exclusively; solely.

whom (ho͞om) ▸ *pron.* The objective case of **who**.

whom·ev·er (ho͞om-ĕv′ər) ▸ *pron.* The objective case of **whoever**.

whom·so·ev·er (ho͞om′sō-ĕv′ər) ▸ *pron.* The objective case of **whosoever**.

whoop (ho͞op, hwo͞op, wo͞op) ▸ *n.* **1.** A loud cry of exultation or excitement. **2.** The paroxysmal gasp typical of whooping cough. ▸ *v.* **1.** To utter with a whoop. **2.** To gasp as with whooping cough. **3.** To chase, call, urge on, or drive with a whoop.

whoop·ing cough (ho͞o′pĭng, hwo͞o′-, wo͞o′-) ▸ *n.* A highly contagious bacterial disease of the respiratory system, usu. affecting children and marked by spasms of coughing interspersed with deep noisy gasps.

whooping crane ▸ *n.* A large, very rare North American crane having black and white plumage and a whooping cry.

whoops (hwo͝ops, wo͝ops, hwo͞ops, wo͞ops) also **woops** (wo͝ops, wo͞ops) ▸ *interj.* Used to express apology or mild surprise.

whoosh (hwo͞osh, wo͞osh, hwo͝osh, wo͝osh) ▸ *n.* **1.** A soft rushing sound. **2.** A swift movement or flow; rush. **—whoosh** *v.*

whop (hwŏp, wŏp) ▸ *v.* **whopped, whop·ping. 1.** To strike with a thudding blow. **2.** To defeat soundly. **—whop** *n.*

whop·per (hwŏp′ər, wŏp′-) ▸ *n. Slang* **1.** Something exceptionally big or remarkable. **2.** A gross lie.

whop·ping (hwŏp′ĭng, wŏp′-) ▸ *adj. Slang* Exceptionally large.

whore (hôr) ▸ *n.* A prostitute. **—whor′ish** *adj.*

whorl (hwôrl, wôrl, hwûrl, wûrl) ▸ *n.* **1.** A form that coils or spirals; curl; swirl. **2.** *Bot.* An arrangement of three or more leaves, petals, or other organs radiating from a single node.

who's (ho͞oz) ▸ **1.** Who is. **2.** Who has.

whose (ho͞oz) ▸ *adj.* **1.** The possessive form of **who**. **2.** The possessive form of **which**.

who·so·ev·er (ho͞o′sō-ĕv′ər) ▸ *pron.* Whoever.

why (hwī, wī) ▸ *adv.* For what purpose, reason, or cause: *Why do birds sing?* ▸ *conj.* **1.** The reason, cause, or purpose for which: *I know why you left.* **2.** *Informal* For which: *told me the reason why he's angry.* ▸ *n., pl.* **whys.** The cause or reason. ▸ *interj.* Used to express mild surprise, indignation, or impatience.

WI ▸ *abbr.* Wisconsin

Wic·ca (wĭk′ə) ▸ *n.* A polytheistic Neo-Pagan nature religion whose central deity is a mother goddess. **—Wic′can** *adj. & n.*

wick (wĭk) ▸ *n.* A cord or strand of woven fibers, as in a candle, that draws up fuel to the flame by capillary action. **—wick** *v.*

wick·ed (wĭk′ĭd) ▸ *adj.* **-er, -est. 1.** Evil by nature and in practice. **2.** Playfully mischievous: *a wicked prank.* **3.** Severe and distressing. **—wick′ed·ly** *adv.* **—wick′ed·ness** *n.*

wick·er (wĭk′ər) ▸ *n.* **1.** A long flexible twig, as of a willow, used in weaving baskets or furniture. **2.** Wickerwork.

wick·er·work (wĭk′ər-wûrk′) ▸ *n.* Woven wicker.

wick·et (wĭk′ĭt) ▸ *n.* **1.** A small door or gate, esp. one built into or near a larger one. **2.** A small, often grated window or opening. **3.** In cricket, either of the two sets of three stumps forming the bowler's target. **4.** An arch through which players try to drive their ball in croquet.

wick·i·up (wĭk′ē-ŭp′) ▸ *n.* A frame hut covered with matting, as of bark or brush, used by certain nomadic Native Americans.

wide (wīd) ▸ *adj.* **wid·er, wid·est. 1a.** Measured from side to side: *a ribbon two inches wide.* **b.** Extending over a large area from side to side; broad: *a wide road.* **2.** Great in extent or range: *a wide selection.* **3.** Fully open: *look with wide eyes.* **4.** Far from a goal or point: *a shot wide of the mark.* ▸ *adv.* **-er, -est. 1.** Extensively: *traveled far and wide.* **2.** To the full extent; completely. **3.** So as to miss a target; astray. **—wide′ly** *adv.* **—wid′en** *v.* **—wide′ness** *n.*

wide-a·wake (wīd′ə-wāk′) ▸ *adj.* **1.** Completely awake. **2.** Alert; watchful.

wide-eyed (wīd′īd′) ▸ *adj.* **1.** With the eyes completely open, as in wonder. **2.** Innocent; credulous.

wide·spread (wīd′sprĕd′) ▸ *adj.* **1.** Fully opened or extended. **2.** Occurring widely.

wid·geon (wĭj′ən) ▸ *n., pl.* **-geon** or **-geons.** A wild freshwater duck having a brownish back and a light head patch.

wid·ow (wĭd′ō) ▸ *n.* A woman whose spouse has died and who has not remarried. ▸ *v.* To make a widow or widower of. **—wid′ow·hood′** *n.*

wid·ow·er (wĭd′ō-ər) ▸ *n.* A man whose spouse has died and who has not remarried.

width (wĭdth, wĭtth) ▸ *n.* **1.** The state, quality, or fact of being wide. **2.** The measurement of something from side to side.

wield (wēld) ▸ *v.* **1.** To handle (e.g., a weapon or tool), esp. capably. **2.** To exercise (e.g., power) effectively.

wie·ner (wē′nər) ▸ *n.* A frankfurter.

wife (wīf) ▸ *n., pl.* **wives** (wīvz). A female spouse. **—wife′hood′** *n.* **—wife′ly** *adj.*

wig (wĭg) ▸ *n.* A covering of human or synthetic hair worn on the head for personal adornment, as part of a costume, or to conceal baldness.

wig·gle (wĭg′əl) ▸ *v.* **-gled, -gling.** To move or cause to move from side to side with short irregular twisting motions. **—wig′gle** *n.* **—wig′gler** *n.* **—wig′gly** *adj.*

Wight (wīt), **Isle of** ▸ An island in the English Channel off S-central England.

wig·wam (wĭg′wŏm′) ▸ *n.* A Native American dwelling usu. having an arched or conical framework overlaid with bark, hides, or mats.

THESAURUS

wholesome *adj.* —*See* CLEAN (2), HEALTHFUL, HEALTHY.

wholly *adv.* —*See* COMPLETELY (1).

whomp *v.* —*See* THUD.

whoop *n.* —*See* SHOUT.

whoop *v.* —*See* SHOUT.

whoosh *v.* —*See* HISS (1).

whoosh *n.* —*See* HISS (1).

whop *v.* —*See* HIT.

whop *n.* —*See* BLOW[2].

whopper *n.* —*See* GIANT, LIE[2].

whopping *adj.* —*See* ENORMOUS.

whore *n.* —*See* PROSTITUTE, SLUT.

whorish *adj.* —*See* WANTON (1).

who's who *n.* —*See* SOCIETY (1).

why *n.* —*See* CAUSE (2), INTENTION, REASON (1).

wicked *adj.* —*See* EVIL, MALEVOLENT, TROUBLESOME (2).

wickedness *n.* —*See* CORRUPTION (1), CRIME (2), EVIL (1).

wide *adj.* —*See* BROAD (1), FULL (3), OPEN (1).

wide-awake *adj.* Not in a state of sleep or unable to sleep ▸ awake, unsleeping, wakeful. [*Compare* RESTLESS.] —*See also* ALERT.

widen *v.* —*See* BROADEN.

wideness *n.* The extent of something from side to side ▸ breadth, broadness, expanse, width. [*Compare* DISTANCE.]

wide-ranging or **wide-reaching** *adj.* —*See* GENERAL (2).

widespread *adj.* Spread out over a large area ▸ far-flung. [*Compare* BROAD.] —*See also* COMMON (1), GENERAL (2), PREVAILING.

widget *n.* —*See* GADGET.

width *n.* The extent of something from side to side ▸ breadth, broadness, expanse, wideness. [*Compare* DISTANCE.]

wield *v.* **1.** To use with or as if with the hands ▸ handle, manipulate, ply. **2.** To bring to bear steadily or forcefully, as influence ▸ exercise, exert, ply. ***Idiom:*** throw one's weight around. —*See also* OPERATE.

wife *v.* —*See* SPOUSE.

wiggle *v.* —*See* CRAWL (1).

wiggly *adj.* —*See* INSECURE (2), WAVY.

wild (wīld) ▸ *adj.* **-er, -est. 1.** Occurring or living in a natural state; not domesticated or cultivated: *wild geese, wild plants.* **2.** Not inhabited or farmed: *remote, wild country.* **3.** Uncivilized; savage. **4.** Unruly: *wild children.* **5.** Full or suggestive of uncontrolled emotion: *wild with jealousy.* **6.** Extravagant; fantastic: *a wild idea.* **7.** Erratic: *a wild pitch.* **8.** Having a value determined by the cardholder's choice: *deuces wild.* ▸ *adv.* In a wild manner: *roaming wild.* ▸ *n.* **1.** A natural or undomesticated state: *plants growing in the wild.* **2.** often **wilds** An uninhabited or uncultivated region. **—wild′ly** *adv.* **—wild′ness** *n.*

wild·cat (wīld′kăt′) ▸ *n.* **1.** Any of various wild felines of small to medium size, as the lynx. **2.** A quick-tempered person. **3.** An oil well that is drilled in an area not known to be productive. ▸ *adj.* **1.** Risky or unsound, esp. financially. **2.** Undertaken without official union approval: *a wildcat strike.*

Wilde (wīld), **Oscar (Fingal O'Flahertie Wills)** (1854–1900) ▸ Irish-born writer.

wil·de·beest (wĭl′də-bēst′, vĭl′-) ▸ *n., pl.* **-beests** or **-beest.** See **gnu.**

Wil·der (wĭl′dər), **Thornton (Niven)** (1897–1975) ▸ Amer. writer.

wil·der·ness (wĭl′dər-nĭs) ▸ *n.* **1.** An unsettled, uncultivated region left in its natural condition. **2.** A bewildering or threatening vastness.

wild-eyed (wīld′īd′) ▸ *adj.* Glaring in or as if in anger, terror, madness, or passion.

wild·fire (wīld′fīr′) ▸ *n.* A raging, rapidly spreading fire.

wild·fowl (wīld′foul′) ▸ *n.* A wild game bird, such as a duck or quail.

wild-goose chase (wīld′go͞os′) ▸ *n.* A futile pursuit or search.

wild·life (wīld′līf′) ▸ *n.* Wild animals and vegetation, esp. in a natural state.

wild rice ▸ *n.* **1.** A tall aquatic grass of North America, bearing edible grain. **2.** The grain of this plant.

wile (wīl) ▸ *n.* **1.** A deceitful stratagem or trick. **2.** A disarming or seductive manner, device, or procedure. ▸ *v.* **wiled, wil·ing. 1.** To lure; entice. **2.** To pass (time) agreeably.

will[1] (wĭl) ▸ *n.* **1.** The mental faculty by which one deliberately chooses a course of action; volition. **2.** Self-control; self-discipline. **3.** A desire, purpose, or determination, esp. of one in authority. **4.** Deliberate intention or wish: *against my will.* **5.** Bearing or attitude toward others; disposition: *full of good will.* **6.** A legal declaration of how a person wishes his or her possessions to be disposed of after death. ▸ *v.* **willed, will·ing. 1.** To decide on; choose. **2.** To yearn for; desire. **3.** To decree, dictate, or order. **4.** To grant in a legal will; bequeath. ***—idiom:*** **at will** Just as or when one wishes.

will[2] (wĭl) ▸ *aux.v., P.t.* **would** (wo͝od). **1.** Used to indicate: **a.** Simple futurity: *They will appear later.* **b.** Likelihood or certainty: *You will regret this.* **c.** Willingness: *Will you help me?* **d.** Requirement or command: *You will report to me now.* **e.** Intention: *I will if I feel like it.* **f.** Customary or habitual action: *They would get together on weekends.* **g.** Probability: *That will be Katie ringing.* **2.** To wish; desire: *Do what you will.*

will·ful also **wil·ful** (wĭl′fəl) ▸ *adj.* **1.** Deliberate; voluntary. **2.** Obstinate; stubborn. **—will′ful·ly** *adv.* **—will′ful·ness** *n.*

Wil·liam I (wĭl′yəm). "William the Conqueror" (1027?–87) ▸ King of England (1066–87).

Wil·liams (wĭl′yəmz), **Tennessee** (1911–83) ▸ Amer. playwright.

wil·lies (wĭl′ēz) ▸ *pl.n. Slang* Feelings of uneasiness; creeps.

will·ing (wĭl′ĭng) ▸ *adj.* **1.** Disposed or inclined; prepared. **2.** Acting or ready to act gladly. **3.** Done, given, or borne voluntarily. **—will′ing·ly** *adv.* **—will′ing·ness** *n.*

wil·li·waw (wĭl′ē-wô′) ▸ *n.* A violent gust of cold wind blowing seaward from a mountainous coast.

will-o'-the-wisp (wĭl′ə-*thə*-wĭsp′) ▸ *n.* **1.** See **ignis fatuus** 1. **2.** A delusive or misleading hope.

wil·low (wĭl′ō) ▸ *n.* **1.** Any of various trees or shrubs having usu. narrow leaves and slender flexible twigs. **2.** The wood of a willow.

wil·low·y (wĭl′ō-ē) ▸ *adj.* **-i·er, -i·est.** Slender and graceful: *a willowy figure.*

will·pow·er or **will pow·er** (wĭl′pou′ər) ▸ *n.* The strength of will to carry out one's decisions, wishes, or plans.

wil·ly-nil·ly (wĭl′ē-nĭl′ē) ▸ *adv. & adj.* **1.** Whether desired or not. **2.** Without order or plan.

Wil·son (wĭl′sən), **(Thomas) Woodrow** (1856–1924) ▸ The 28th US President (1913–21).

wilt[1] (wĭlt) ▸ *v.* **1.** To lose or cause to lose freshness; droop. **2.** To lose or deprive of energy or vigor; weaken; sap. ▸ *n.* Any of various plant diseases marked by collapse of terminal shoots, branches, or entire plants.

wilt[2] (wĭlt) ▸ *aux.v. Archaic* 2nd pers. sing. pr.t. of **will**[2].

wi·ly (wī′lē) ▸ *adj.* **-li·er, -li·est.** Full of wiles; cunning. **—wil′i·ness** *n.*

wim·ble (wĭm′bəl) ▸ *n.* A hand tool for boring holes. **—wim′ble** *v.*

wimp (wĭmp) ▸ *n. Slang* A weak, ineffectual person. **—wimp′y** *adj.*

wim·ple (wĭm′pəl) ▸ *n.* A cloth framing the face and drawn into folds beneath the chin, worn by women in medieval times and by certain nuns.

win (wĭn) ▸ *v.* **won** (wŭn), **win·ning. 1.** To achieve victory or finish first in a competition. **2.** To achieve success in an effort. **3.** To receive as a prize or reward. **4.** To obtain or earn. **5.** To succeed in gaining the favor or support of. ▸ *n.* A victory, esp. in a competition. **—win′ner** *n.*

wince (wĭns) ▸ *v.* **winced, winc·ing.** To shrink or start involuntarily, as in pain or distress; flinch. **—wince** *n.*

winch (wĭnch) ▸ *n.* **1.** A stationary hoisting machine having a drum around which is wound a rope or chain attached to

THESAURUS

wild *adj.* **1.** Unaltered by human intervention; not cultivated or developed ▸ native, natural, rough, uncultivated, undomesticated. **2.** Living outside of human control or intervention; not domesticated ▸ feral, savage, unbroken, undomesticated, untamed. *—See also* [illegible] ROUGH (2), UNCIVILIZED, UNRULY.

wild *n.* *—See* WILDERNESS.

wilderness *n.* An uninhabited region left in its natural state ▸ bush, jungle, outback, outdoors, wild, wildness, wilds. [*Compare* COUNTRY, DESERT[1].]

wildness *n.* *—See* ABANDON (1), UNRULINESS, WILDERNESS.

wilds *n.* *—See* WILDERNESS.

wile *n.* *—See* TRICK (1).

wile *v.* *—See* IDLE (2).

wiliness *n.* *—See* ART.

will *n.* **1.** The mental faculty by which one deliberately chooses or decides ▸ free will, volition. [*Compare* CHOICE, SPIRIT.] **2.** Unrestricted freedom to choose ▸ convenience, discretion, leisure, pleasure. *—See also* DECISION (2), LIKING.

will *v.* *—See* CHOOSE (1), CHOOSE (2), LEAVE[1] (1).

willful *adj.* *—See* DELIBERATE (1), STUB- [illegible]

willfully *adv.* Of one's own free will ▸ by choice, freely, spontaneously, voluntarily, willingly. *Idioms:* of one's own accord, on one's own volition.

willfulness *n.* *—See* STUBBORNNESS.

willies *n.* *—See* JITTERS.

willing *adj.* Disposed to accept, agree, or participate ▸ acquiescent, agreeable, amenable, delighted, eager, game, glad, happy, minded, pleased, ready, tickled. [*Compare* OBLIGING.] *—See also* VOLUNTARY.

willingly *adv.* Of one's own free will ▸ by choice, freely, spontaneously, voluntarily, willfully. *Idioms:* of one's own accord, on one's own volition. *—See also* YES.

will-o'-the-wisp *n.* *—See* ILLUSION.

willowy *adj.* *—See* THIN (1).

willpower *n.* *—See* DECISION (2).

willy-nilly *adv.* *—See* HELPLESSLY.

wilt *v.* To become limp, as from loss [illegible] *—See also* SLOUCH (2), TIRE (2).

wily *adj.* *—See* ARTFUL.

wimp *n.* *—See* WEAKLING.

wimpy *adj.* *—See* COWARDLY.

win *v.* To achieve victory ▸ be victorious. *Idioms:* claim the victory (*or* prize), come out on top, finish (*or* come in) first, take the laurels (*or* palm). [*Compare* DEFEAT.] *—See also* CAPTURE, EARN (1), EARN (2), GET (1).

win over *v.* *—See* CHARM (1), CONVINCE.

win *n.* *—See* CONQUEST.

wince *v.* *—See* FLINCH.

wince *n.* *—See* RECOIL.

the load being lifted. 2. A crank used to give rotary motion. **—winch** *v.*

wind[1] (wĭnd) ▸ *n.* 1. Moving air, esp. air moving along the ground. 2. Moving air carrying sound or a scent. 3a. Respiration: *had the wind knocked out of me.* b. Flatulence. 4. often **winds** *Mus.* a. The brass and woodwinds sections of an orchestra. b. Wind instruments or their players. 5. An agent of change or disruption: *the winds of war.* 6. Empty or boastful talk. ▸ *v.* 1. To detect the scent of. 2. To cause to be out of breath.

wind[2] (wīnd) ▸ *v.* **wound** (wound), **wind·ing.** 1. To wrap or be wrapped around a center or another object once or repeatedly. 2. To encircle or be encircled in coils; entwine. 3. To go along (a twisting course). 4. To turn (e.g., a crank) in circular motions. 5. To lift or haul by a windlass or winch. ***—phrasal verb:* wind up** 1. To finish; end. 2. To put in order; settle. 3. To arrive eventually in a place or situation: *wound up in debt.* ▸ *n.* A single turn, twist, or curve. **—wind′er** *n.*

wind[3] (wīnd, wĭnd) ▸ *v.* **wind·ed** (wīn′dĭd, wīn′-) or **wound** (wound), **wind·ing.** *Mus.* To sound by blowing (a wind instrument).

wind·bag (wĭnd′băg′) ▸ *n. Slang* A tiresomely talkative person.

wind·break (wĭnd′brāk′) ▸ *n.* A hedge, fence, or row of trees serving to lessen or break the force of the wind.

wind·burn (wĭnd′bûrn′) ▸ *n.* Skin irritation caused by exposure to the wind. **—wind′burned′** *adj.*

wind-chill factor (wĭnd′chĭl′) ▸ *n.* The temperature of still air that would have the same effect on exposed skin as a given combination of wind speed and air temperature.

wind·fall (wĭnd′fôl′) ▸ *n.* 1. A sudden, unexpected piece of good fortune. 2. A fruit blown down by the wind.

wind·flow·er (wĭnd′flou′ər) ▸ *n.* See **anemone** 1.

wind·ing (wīn′dĭng) ▸ *n.* 1. Something wound about a center or an object. 2. A curve or bend, as of a road. ▸ *adj.* 1. Twisting or turning; sinuous. 2. Spiral.

wind·ing-sheet (wīn′dĭng-shēt′) ▸ *n.* A sheet for wrapping a corpse; shroud.

wind instrument (wĭnd) ▸ *n. Mus.* 1. An instrument, such as an oboe or tuba, sounded by a column of air, esp. the breath. 2. A woodwind, as opposed to a brass instrument.

wind·jam·mer (wĭnd′jăm′ər) ▸ *n.* A large sailing ship.

wind·lass (wĭnd′ləs) ▸ *n.* Any of numerous hauling or lifting machines consisting essentially of a horizontal cylinder wound with rope and turned by a crank.

wind·mill (wĭnd′mĭl′) ▸ *n.* A machine that runs on the energy generated by a wheel of adjustable blades rotated by the wind.

win·dow (wĭn′dō) ▸ *n.* 1. An opening constructed in a wall or roof to admit light or air. 2. A framework enclosing a window. 3. A windowpane. 4. An opening that resembles a window. 5. A temporary period of a specified nature: *a window of opportunity.* 6. *Comp. Sci.* A rectangular area on a display screen that can be viewed independently of other such areas.

window box ▸ *n.* A usu. long narrow box for plants, placed on a windowsill or ledge.

win·dow-dress·ing also **win·dow dress·ing** (wĭn′dō-drĕs′ĭng) ▸ *n.* 1. Decorative exhibition of retail merchandise in store windows. 2. A means of improving appearances or creating a falsely favorable impression.

win·dow·pane (wĭn′dō-pān′) ▸ *n.* A piece of glass in a window.

win·dow-shop (wĭn′dō-shŏp′) ▸ *v.* To look at merchandise in store windows or showcases without buying. **—win′dow-shop′per** *n.*

win·dow·sill (wĭn′dō-sĭl′) ▸ *n.* The horizontal ledge at the base of a window opening.

wind·pipe (wĭnd′pīp′) ▸ *n. Anat.* See **trachea.**

wind·row (wĭnd′rō′) ▸ *n.* A row, as of leaves or snow, heaped up by the wind.

wind·shield (wĭnd′shēld′) ▸ *n.* A framed protective pane of transparent shielding located in front of the occupants of a vehicle.

wind·sock (wĭnd′sŏk′) ▸ *n.* A tapered, open-ended sleeve pivotally attached to a standard so as to indicate the direction of the wind blowing through it.

Wind·sor (wĭn′zər) ▸ A city of SE Ontario, Canada, on the Detroit R. opposite Detroit, MI.

wind·storm (wĭnd′stôrm′) ▸ *n.* A storm with high winds but little or no rain.

wind·surf·ing (wĭnd′sûrf′ĭng) ▸ *n.* The sport of sailing while standing on a sailboard. **—wind′surf′** *v.* **—wind′surf′er** *n.*

wind·swept (wĭnd′swĕpt′) ▸ *adj.* Exposed to or swept by winds.

wind tunnel (wĭnd) ▸ *n.* A chamber through which air is forced at controlled velocities to study its effect on an object.

wind-up or **wind·up** (wīnd′ŭp′) ▸ *n.* 1a. The act of bringing something to an end. b. A conclusion; finish. 2. The movements of a pitcher preparatory to pitching the ball. ▸ *adj.* Operated by a hand-wound spring.

wind·ward (wĭnd′wərd) ▸ *adv. & adj.* Toward the wind. **—wind′ward** *n.*

Windward Islands ▸ An island group of the SE West Indies, including the S group of the Lesser Antilles.

wind·y (wĭn′dē) ▸ *adj.* **-i·er, -i·est.** 1. Marked by or abounding in wind. 2. Open to the wind; unsheltered. 3. Tiresomely talkative. **—wind′i·ly** *adv.* **—wind′i·ness** *n.*

wine (wīn) ▸ *n.* 1. The fermented juice of grapes. 2. The fermented juice of other fruits or plants. ▸ *v.* **wined, win·ing.** To entertain with wine.

wine·glass (wīn′glăs′) ▸ *n.* A glass, usu. with a stem, from which wine is drunk.

wine·grow·er (wīn′grō′ər) ▸ *n.* One who owns a vineyard and produces wine.

wine·press (wīn′prĕs′) ▸ *n.* 1. A vat in which the juice is pressed from grapes. 2. A device that presses the juice from grapes.

win·er·y (wī′nə-rē) ▸ *n., pl.* **-ies.** An establishment at which wine is made.

wine·skin (wīn′skĭn′) ▸ *n.* A bag, as of goatskin, used for holding and dispensing wine.

wing (wĭng) ▸ *n.* 1. One of a pair of movable organs for flying, as of a bird, bat, or insect. 2. *Informal* A human arm. 3. An airfoil whose main function is providing lift, esp. either of two such airfoils positioned on each side of the fuselage of an aircraft. 4. **wings** The unseen backstage area on either side of a stage. 5. A structure attached to and connected with a main building. 6. Either of two groups with opposing views within a larger group; faction. 7a. Either the left or right flank of an army or a naval fleet. b. An air force unit larger than a group but smaller than a division. 8. *Sports* Either of the forward positions played near the sideline, esp. in hockey. ▸ *v.* 1. To move on or as if on wings; fly. 2. To furnish with wings. 3. To effect or accomplish by flying. 4. To wound

THESAURUS

wind[1] *n.* A natural movement or current of air ▸ air, blast, blow, gust, waft, zephyr. [*Compare* BREEZE.] *—See also* BREATH.

wind *v.* To expose to circulating air ▸ aerate, air, freshen, ventilate.

wind[2] *v.* To move or cause to lie along a repeatedly curving path ▸ coil, corkscrew, curl, entwine, meander, snake, spiral, twine, twist, weave, wrap, wreathe. [*Compare* TURN.] *—See also* INSINUATE.

wind up *v.* *—See* CONCLUDE.

wind down *v.* *—See* SUBSIDE.

windbreaker *n.* *—See* COAT (1).

windiness *n.* *—See* WORDINESS.

winding *adj.* Repeatedly curving in alternate directions ▸ anfractuous, convoluted, curvy, flexuous, meandering, meandrous, serpentine, sinuous, snaky, tortuous, twisting, windy. *—See also* INDIRECT (1).

winding *n.* *—See* CURL.

windless *adj.* *—See* AIRLESS (2).

window-dressing *n.* *—See* FAÇADE (2).

wind-up *n.* *—See* END (1), END (2).

windy *adj.* *—See* AIRY (3), INFLATED, WINDING.

wine bar *n.* *—See* BAR (2).

wing *n.* *—See* BRANCH (3), EXTENSION (2).

wing *v.* To cause bodily damage to a living thing ▸ hurt, injure, traumatize, wound. [*Compare* CUT, BREAK.] *—See also* FLY (1), RUSH.

superficially. ***—idioms:*** **on the wing** In flight; flying. **under (one's) wing** Under one's protection. **wing it** *Informal* To improvise; ad-lib. **—wing′less** *adj.*

wing·ding (wĭng′dĭng′) ► *n.* *Informal* A lavish or lively party or celebration.

winged (wĭngd, wĭng′ĭd) ► *adj.* **1.** Having wings or winglike appendages. **2.** Soaring with or as if with wings.

wing nut ► *n.* A nut with winglike projections for thumb and forefinger leverage in turning.

wing·span (wĭng′spăn′) ► *n.* Wingspread.

wing·spread (wĭng′sprĕd′) ► *n.* The distance between the tips of the extended wings, as of a bird, insect, or aircraft.

wink (wĭngk) ► *v.* **1.** To close and open one eye deliberately, as to convey a message, signal, or suggestion. **2.** To blink rapidly. **3.** To shine fitfully; twinkle. ***—phrasal verb:*** **wink at** To pretend not to notice: *wink at corruption.* ► *n.* **1.** The act of winking. **2.** An instant. **3.** *Informal* A brief period of sleep.

Win·ne·ba·go (wĭn′ə-bā′gō) ► *n., pl.* **-go** or **-gos** or **-goes. 1.** A member of a Native American people of Wisconsin, now also in Nebraska. **2.** Their Siouan language.

win·ning (wĭn′ĭng) ► *adj.* **1.** Successful; victorious. **2.** Attractive; charming. ► *n.* **1.** Victory. **2.** often **winnings** Something won, esp. money.

Win·ni·peg (wĭn′ə-pĕg′) ► The capital of Manitoba, Canada, in the SE part.

win·now (wĭn′ō) ► *v.* **1.** To separate the chaff from (grain) by means of a current of air. **2.** To sort into categories, esp. of good and bad. **3.** To separate or get rid of (an undesirable part). **—win′now·er** *n.*

win·o (wī′nō) ► *n., pl.* **-os.** *Slang* An indigent wine-drinking alcoholic.

win·some (wĭn′səm) ► *adj.* Charming, often in a childlike way. **—win′some·ly** *adv.* **—win′some·ness** *n.*

win·ter (wĭn′tər) ► *n.* The usu. coldest season of the year, occurring between autumn and spring. ► *v.* **1.** To spend the winter. **2.** To keep or feed (e.g., livestock) during the winter.

win·ter·green (wĭn′tər-grēn′) ► *n.* **1.** A low-growing evergreen plant of North America, with aromatic leaves and spicy scarlet berries. **2.** An oil or flavoring from this plant.

win·ter·ize (wĭn′tə-rīz′) ► *v.* **-ized, -iz·ing.** To prepare or equip (e.g., an automobile) for winter weather. **—win′ter·i·za′tion** *n.*

win·ter·kill (wĭn′tər-kĭl′) ► *v.* To kill by or die from exposure to cold winter weather. **—win′ter·kill′** *n.*

winter squash ► *n.* Any of several thick-rinded varieties of squash, such as the acorn squash, that can be stored for long periods.

win·ter·time (wĭn′tər-tīm′) ► *n.* The season of winter.

win·try (wĭn′trē) also **win·ter·y** (wĭn′tə-rē) ► *adj.* **-tri·er, -tri·est** also **-ter·i·er, -ter·i·est. 1.** Of or like winter; cold. **2.** Suggestive of winter; cheerless: *a wintry smile.*

wipe (wīp) ► *v.* **wiped, wip·ing. 1.** To rub, as with a cloth or paper, in order to clean or dry. **2.** To remove, clean, or dry by or as if by rubbing. **3.** To rub or pass (e.g., a cloth) over a surface. ***—phrasal verb:*** **wipe out 1.** To destroy completely. **2.** *Slang* To murder. **—wipe** *n.* **—wip′er** *n.*

wire (wīr) ► *n.* **1.** A usu. pliable metallic strand or rod, often electrically insulated, used esp. for structural support or to conduct electricity. **2.** A group of wire strands bundled or twisted together; cable. **3.** An open telephone connection. **4.** *Slang* A hidden microphone, as on a person's body. **5a.** A telegraph service. **b.** A telegram or cablegram. **6.** The finish line of a racetrack. ► *v.* **wired, wir·ing. 1.** To bind, connect, or attach with wires or a wire. **2.** To equip with a system of electrical wires. **3.** *Slang* To install electronic eavesdropping equipment in. **4.** To send by telegraph. **5.** To send a telegram to.

wire·haired (wīr′hârd′) ► *adj.* Having a coat of stiff wiry hair, as certain dogs.

wire·less (wīr′lĭs) ► *adj.* Having no wire or wires. ► *n.* **1.** A radiotelegraph or radiotelephone system. **2.** *Chiefly Brit.* Radio.

wire service ► *n.* A news-gathering organization that distributes syndicated copy electronically to subscribers.

wire·tap (wīr′tăp′) ► *n.* A concealed listening or recording device connected to a communications circuit. ► *v.* To monitor (a telephone line) by means of a wiretap.

wir·ing (wīr′ĭng) ► *n.* A system of electric wires.

wir·y (wīr′ē) ► *adj.* **-i·er, -i·est. 1.** Wirelike, esp. in stiffness; kinky. **2.** Sinewy and lean: *a wiry build.* **—wir′i·ness** *n.*

Wis·con·sin (wĭs-kŏn′sĭn) ► A state of the N-central US. Cap. Madison. **—Wis·con′sin·ite′** *n.*

wis·dom (wĭz′dəm) ► *n.* **1.** Understanding of what is true, right, or lasting. **2.** Common sense; good judgment. **3.** Scholarly learning.

Wisdom of Solomon ► *n.* See **Bible** table in Appendix.

wisdom tooth ► *n.* One of four rearmost molars on each side of both jaws in humans.

wise[1] (wīz) ► *adj.* **wis·er, wis·est. 1.** Having wisdom; judicious. **2.** Exhibiting common sense; prudent. **3.** Learned; erudite. **4.** Aware; informed: *wise to their tricks.* **5.** *Slang* Rude and disrespectful; impudent. **—wise′ly** *adv.*

wise[2] (wīz) ► *n.* Method or manner of doing; way: *in no wise.*

-wise ► *suff.* Manner, direction, or position: *clockwise.*

wise·a·cre (wīz′ā′kər) ► *n.* *Slang* A smart aleck.

wise·crack (wīz′krăk′) ► *n.* *Slang* A flippant, usu. sardonic remark. **—wise′crack′** *v.*

wish (wĭsh) ► *n.* **1.** A desire or longing for something. **2.** An expression of a wish. **3.** Something desired or longed for. ► *v.* **1.** To long for; want: *I wish that you could come.* **2.** To express wishes for; bid: *wished her good night.* **3.** To invoke upon: *I wish them luck.* **4.** To order or entreat: *I wish you to go.* **—wish′er** *n.*

wish·bone (wĭsh′bōn′) ► *n.* The forked bone in front of the breastbone of most birds.

wish·ful (wĭsh′fəl) ► *adj.* Having or expressing a wish or longing. **—wish′ful·ly** *adv.* **—wish′ful·ness** *n.*

wish·y-wash·y (wĭsh′ē-wŏsh′ē, -wô′shē) ► *adj.* **-i·er, -i·est.** *Informal* Lacking in strength or character; indecisive.

wisp (wĭsp) ► *n.* **1.** A small bunch or bundle, as of hair. **2.** One that is thin, frail, or slight. **3.** A faint streak, as of smoke or clouds. **—wisp′y** *adj.*

wis·ter·i·a (wĭ-stîr′ē-ə) also **wis·tar·i·a** (wĭ-stâr′-) ► *n.* A

THESAURUS

wink *v.* —*See* BLINK, GLITTER.
wink at *v.* —*See* BLINK AT.
wink *n.* —*See* BLINK, FLASH (1), FLASH (2), HINT (2).

winner *n.* One that wins a contest or competition ► champion, conqueror, medalist, prizewinner, titleholder, victor. *Informal:* champ. —*See also* CONQUEROR, HIT.

winning *adj.* —*See* ATTRACTIVE, VICTORIOUS.

winnow *v.* To set apart one kind or type from others ► separate, sift, sort. *Idiom:* separate the sheep from the goats.

wino *n.* —*See* DRUNKARD.

winsome *adj.* —*See* ATTRACTIVE.

wintriness *n.* —*See* COLD.

wintry *adj.* —*See* COLD (1).

wipe *v.* —*See* CANCEL (1).
wipe out *v.* —*See* ANNIHILATE, ELIMINATE, MASSACRE, MURDER.

wiped out *adj.* [illegible] (1).

wiretap *v.* To monitor telephone calls with a concealed device connected to the circuit ► bug, tap.

wisdom *n.* **1.** Deep, thorough, or mature understanding ► insight, intelligence, profundity, sagaciousness, sagacity, sageness, sapience. [*Compare* CULTURE, DISCERNMENT, ILLUMINATION, UNDERSTANDING.] **2.** The sum of what has been perceived, discovered, or inferred ► knowledge, lore, understanding. [*Compare* ACTUALITY.] —*See also* COMMON SENSE.

wise[1] *adj.* Possessing deep knowledge and understanding ► knowing, sagacious, sage, sapient. —*See also* [illegible], SENSIBLE, SHREWD.

wise[2] *n.* —*See* WAY (1).

wiseacre [illegible] ALECK.

wisecrack *n.* —*See* CRACK (3).

wise guy *n.* —*See* SMART ALECK.

wise man or **wise woman** *n.* —*See* SAGE.

wisenheimer or **weisenheimer** *n.* —*See* SMART ALECK.

wisest *adj.* —*See* ADVISABLE.

wish *n.* —*See* DESIRE (1), DREAM (3).
wish *v.* —*See* CHOOSE (2), DESIRE.

wishy-washiness *n.* —*See* INSIPIDITY.

wishy-washy *adj.* —*See* INSIPID.

climbing woody vine having racemes of showy purplish or white flowers.

wist·ful (wĭst′fəl) ▸ *adj.* 1. Full of wishful yearning. 2. Pensively sad; melancholy. **—wist′ful·ly** *adv.* **—wist′ful·ness** *n.*

wit (wĭt) ▸ *n.* 1. Perception and understanding; intelligence. 2a. often **wits** Keenness and quickness of perception or discernment. b. **wits** Sound mental faculties; sanity. 3a. The ability to perceive and humorously express the relationship between seemingly incongruous things. b. One noted for this ability. ***—idiom:* at (one's) wits' end** At the limit of one's mental resources; utterly at a loss.

witch (wĭch) ▸ *n.* 1a. A sorceress, esp. in folkore. b. A woman believed to practice sorcery. 2. A follower of Wicca. 3. A hag. 4. A spiteful or overbearing woman. 5. *Informal* A bewitching woman. **—witch′er·y** *n.* **—witch′y** *adj.*

witch·craft (wĭch′krăft′) ▸ *n.* Magic; sorcery.

witch doctor ▸ *n.* A shamanistic healer.

witch hazel ▸ *n.* 1. A deciduous shrub of E North America having yellow flowers. 2. An alcoholic solution containing an extract of this plant, used as a mild astringent.

witch-hunt (wĭch′hŭnt′) ▸ *n.* An investigation meant to identify and harass those with differing views.

witch·ing (wĭch′ĭng) ▸ *adj.* 1. Of or appropriate to witchcraft. 2. Enchanting.

with (wĭth, wĭth) ▸ *prep.* 1. In the company of: *Did you go with her?* 2. Next to: *stood with the rabbi.* 3. Having: *a man with a moustache.* 4. In a manner characterized by: *performed with skill.* 5. In the charge or keeping of: *left the cat with the neighbors.* 6. In the opinion of: *if it's all right with you.* 7. In support of; on the side of: *I'm with you all the way.* 8. By the means of: *eat with a fork.* 9. In spite of. 10. At the same time as: *gets up with the birds.* 11. In regard to: *pleased with her decision.* 12. In comparison or contrast to: *a dress identical with the one I had.* 13. Having received: *With her permission, he left.* 14. In opposition to; against: *wrestling with an opponent.* 15. As a result or consequence of: *sick with the flu.* 16. So as to be touching or joined to: *linked arms with their partners.* 17. So as to be free of or separated from: *parted with her husband.* 18. In the course of: *We grow older with the hours.* 19. In proportion to: *wines that improve with age.* 20. As well as: *sing with the best of them.*

with·al (wĭth-ôl′, wĭth-) ▸ *adv.* 1. In addition; besides. 2. Despite that; nevertheless. 3. *Archaic* Therewith.

with·draw (wĭth-drô′, wĭth-) ▸ *v.* **-drew** (-dro͞o′), **-drawn** (-drôn′), **-draw·ing.** 1. To take back or away; remove. 2. To recall or retract. 3. To move or draw back; retire. 4. To remove oneself from active participation.

with·draw·al (wĭth-drô′əl, wĭth-) ▸ *n.* 1. The act or process of withdrawing. 2. Detachment, as from social or emotional involvement. 3a. Discontinuation of the use of an addictive substance. b. The physiological and mental readjustment that accompanies such discontinuation.

with·drawn (wĭth-drôn′, wĭth-) ▸ *adj.* 1. Retiring; shy. 2. Emotionally unresponsive.

withe (wĭth, wĭth, wīth) ▸ *n.* A tough supple twig, esp. of willow, used for binding things together.

with·er (wĭth′ər) ▸ *v.* 1. To dry up or shrivel from or as if from loss of moisture. 2. To lose or cause to lose freshness. 3. To devastate; stun: *withered them with a glance.*

with·ers (wĭth′ərz) ▸ *pl.n.* The high part of the back of a horse, located between the shoulder blades.

with·hold (wĭth-hōld′, wĭth-) ▸ *v.* **-held** (-hĕld′), **-hold·ing.** 1. To keep in check; restrain. 2. To refrain from giving, granting, or permitting. 3. To deduct (withholding tax) from a salary.

with·hold·ing tax (wĭth-hōl′dĭng, wĭth-) ▸ *n.* A portion of an employee's wages or salary withheld by the employer as partial payment of the employee's income tax.

with·in (wĭth-ĭn′, wĭth-) ▸ *adv.* 1. Inside. 2. Inside the mind or body; inwardly. 3. Indoors. ▸ *prep.* 1. Inside. 2. Inside the limits or extent of. 3. Inside the fixed limits of: *within one's rights.* 4. In the scope or sphere of. ▸ *n.* An inner position, place, or area: *treachery from within.*

with-it (wĭth′ĭt′, wĭth-) ▸ *adj. Slang* Up-to-date.

with·out (wĭth-out′, wĭth-) ▸ *adv.* 1. On the outside. 2. Outdoors. ▸ *prep.* 1a. Not having; lacking. b. Not accompanied by. 2. At, on, to, or toward the outside or exterior of.

with·stand (wĭth-stănd′, wĭth-) ▸ *v.* **-stood** (-sto͝od′), **-stand·ing.** 1. To oppose with force or resolution. 2. To resist successfully.

wit·less (wĭt′lĭs) ▸ *adj.* Lacking intelligence or wit; foolish. **—wit′less·ly** *adv.*

wit·ness (wĭt′nĭs) ▸ *n.* 1. One who can give a firsthand account of something seen, heard, or experienced. 2. Something serving as evidence; sign. 3. *Law* a. One called on to testify in court. b. One called on to be present at a transaction to attest to what takes place. c. One who signs one's name to a document in attestation of its authenticity. 4. An attestation; testimony. ▸ *v.* 1. To be present at or have personal knowledge of. 2. To provide or serve as evidence of. 3. To testify to; bear witness. 4. To be the setting or site of. 5. To attest to the legality or authenticity of by signing one's name.

wit·ti·cism (wĭt′ĭ-sĭz′əm) ▸ *n.* A witty remark.

wit·ty (wĭt′ē) ▸ *adj.* **-ti·er, -ti·est.** Having or showing wit; cleverly humorous. **—wit′ti·ly** *adv.* **—wit′ti·ness** *n.*

wives (wīvz) ▸ *n.* Pl. of **wife.**

wiz·ard (wĭz′ərd) ▸ *n.* 1. A sorcerer or magician. 2. A skilled or clever person: *a wizard at math.* **—wiz′ard·ry** *n.*

wiz·ened (wĭz′ənd) ▸ *adj.* Withered; shriveled.

wk. ▸ *abbr.* week

WNW ▸ *abbr.* west-northwest

w/o ▸ *abbr.* without

woad (wōd) ▸ *n.* 1. An annual Old World plant with leaves that yield a blue dye. 2. The dye from this plant.

wob·ble (wŏb′əl) ▸ *v.* **-bled, -bling.** 1. To move or rotate with an uneven or rocking motion from side to side. 2. To tremble or quaver. 3. To waver or vacillate in one's opinions. **—wob′ble** *n.* **—wob′bli·ness** *n.* **—wob′bly** *adj.*

THESAURUS

wistful *adj.* —*See* DEPRESSED (1).

wit *n.* —*See* DISCERNMENT, HUMOR, INTELLIGENCE, JOKER.

witch *n.* 1. A woman who practices magic ▸ enchantress, hag, lamia, sorceress. [*Compare* WIZARD.] 2. An ugly, frightening woman, usually old ▸ beldam, crone, hag. *Slang:* battle-ax, biddy, crow. —*See also* SEDUCTRESS.

witch *v.* —*See* CHARM (2).

witchcraft *n.* —*See* MAGIC (1).

witchery *n.* —*See* ATTRACTION, MAGIC (1).

witching *adj.* —*See* MAGIC, SEDUCTIVE.

witching *n.* —*See* MAGIC (1).

withdraw *v.* To pull back in ▸ draw in, retract. —*See also* DEDUCT, DETACH, GO (1), LIFT (2), REMOVE (1), RETRACT (1), RETREAT.

withdrawal *n.* —*See* DEPARTURE, DETACHMENT (1), RETRACTION, RETREAT.

withdrawn *adj.* —*See* COOL.

wither *v.* —*See* BLAST (2), DRY (1), LANGUISH, PARALYZE, SLAM (1), WILT.

withering *adj.* —*See* BITING.

withhold *v.* —*See* CENSOR (2), DECLINE, DEPRIVE, HOLD (1), REFRAIN.

with-it *adj.* —*See* AWARE, FASHIONABLE.

withstand *v.* —*See* ENDURE (1), OPPOSE, REPEL.

witless *adj.* —*See* FOOLISH, STUPID.

witlessness *n.* —*See* STUPIDITY.

witness *n.* 1. Someone who sees something occur ▸ audience, eyewitness, seer, viewer. 2. One who testifies, especially in court ▸ attestant, attester, deponent, testifier. 3. A formal declaration of truth or fact given under oath ▸ affidavit, deposition, testimony. —*See also* SIGN (1).

witness *v.* —*See* CERTIFY, INDICATE (1), TESTIFY.

wits *n.* —*See* SANITY.

witticism *n.* —*See* JOKE (1).

wittiness *n.* —*See* HUMOR.

witting *adj.* —*See* DELIBERATE (1).

witty *adj.* —*See* CLEVER (2), FUNNY (1).

wizard *n.* One who practices sorcery or magic ▸ conjurer, enchanter, magician, necromancer, prestidigitator, sorcerer, warlock. [*Compare* WITCH.] —*See also* EXPERT.

wizardly *adj.* —*See* MAGIC.

wizardry *n.* —*See* MAGIC (1).

wizen *v.* —*See* DRY (1).

wobble *v.* —*See* HESITATE, STAGGER (1), SWAY.

wobbliness *n.* —*See* UNSTEADINESS.

wobbly *adj.* —*See* INSECURE (2).

woe (wō) ▸ *n.* **1.** Distress or misery, as from grief. **2.** Misfortune; calamity: *economic and political woes.* ▸ *interj.* Used to express sorrow or dismay.

woe·be·gone (wō′bĭ-gôn′, -gŏn′) ▸ *adj.* Wretched or pitiful, esp. in appearance.

woe·ful (wō′fəl) ▸ *adj.* **1.** Affected by woe; mournful. **2.** Causing woe. **3.** Deplorably bad or wretched: *woeful housing conditions.* **—woe′ful·ly** *adv.* **—woe′ful·ness** *n.*

wok (wŏk) ▸ *n.* A metal pan having a convex bottom, used esp. for frying and steaming in Asian cooking.

woke (wōk) ▸ *v.* P.t. of **wake**[1].

wok·en (wō′kən) ▸ *v.* P.part. of **wake**[1].

wolf (wo͝olf) ▸ *n., pl.* **wolves** (wo͝olvz). **1.** A carnivorous mammal, chiefly of northern regions, related to and resembling the dog. **2.** One regarded as predatory, rapacious, and fierce. **3.** *Slang* A man given to paying unwanted sexual attention to women. ▸ *v.* To eat greedily or voraciously. **—wolf′ish** *adj.* **—wolf′ish·ly** *adv.*

wolf·hound (wo͝olf′hound′) ▸ *n.* Any of various large dogs orig. trained to hunt wolves.

wolf·ram (wo͝ol′frəm) ▸ *n.* See **tungsten.**

wol·ver·ine (wo͝ol′və-rēn′) ▸ *n.* A carnivorous mammal of northern forest regions, related to the weasel.

wom·an (wo͝om′ən) ▸ *n., pl.* **wom·en** (wĭm′ĭn). **1.** An adult female human. **2.** Womankind. **3.** *Informal* A wife, lover, or sweetheart.

wom·an·hood (wo͝om′ən-ho͝od′) ▸ *n.* **1.** The state of being a woman. **2.** The qualities thought to be appropriate to or representative of women. **3.** Women collectively.

wom·an·ish (wo͝om′ə-nĭsh) ▸ *adj.* **1.** Characteristic of a woman. **2.** Effeminate.

wom·an·ize (wo͝om′ə-nīz′) ▸ *v.* **-ized, -iz·ing.** To pursue women lecherously. **—wom′an·iz′er** *n.*

wom·an·kind (wo͝om′ən-kīnd′) ▸ *n.* Women collectively.

wom·an·ly (wo͝om′ən-lē) ▸ *adj.* **-li·er, -li·est.** Having qualities usu. attributed to a woman. **—wom′an·li·ness** *n.*

womb (wo͞om) ▸ *n.* **1.** See **uterus. 2.** A place where something has its earliest development.

wom·bat (wŏm′băt′) ▸ *n.* An Australian marsupial somewhat resembling a small bear.

wom·en (wĭm′ĭn) ▸ *n.* Pl. of **woman.**

wom·en·folk (wĭm′ĭn-fōk′) ▸ *pl.n.* **1.** Women collectively. **2.** The women of a community.

won[1] (wôn) ▸ *n., pl.* **won.** See **currency** table in Appendix.

won[2] (wŭn) ▸ *v.* P.t. and p.part. of **win.**

won·der (wŭn′dər) ▸ *n.* **1a.** One that arouses awe, surprise, or admiration; marvel. **b.** The feeling thus aroused. **2.** A feeling of puzzlement or doubt. ▸ *v.* **1.** To have a feeling of awe or admiration; marvel. **2.** To be filled with curiosity or doubt. **3.** To be inquisitive or in doubt about.

won·der·ful (wŭn′dər-fəl) ▸ *adj.* **1.** Capable of eliciting wonder; astonishing. **2.** Admirable; excellent. **—won′der·ful·ly** *adv.*

won·der·land (wŭn′dər-lănd′) ▸ *n.* **1.** A marvelous imaginary realm. **2.** A marvelous real place or scene.

won·der·ment (wŭn′dər-mənt) ▸ *n.* **1.** Astonishment, awe, or surprise. **2.** A marvel. **3.** Puzzlement or curiosity.

won·drous (wŭn′drəs) ▸ *adj.* Wonderful. **—won′drous·ly** *adv.*

wonk (wŏngk) ▸ *n.* *Slang* **1.** A student who studies excessively. **2.** One who studies an issue or topic thoroughly or excessively.

wont (wônt, wōnt, wŭnt) ▸ *adj.* **1.** Accustomed or used: *was wont to give generously.* **2.** Likely. ▸ *n.* Customary practice; habit: *left early, as was her wont.*

won't (wont) ▸ Will not.

wont·ed (wôn′tĭd, wōn′-, wŭn′-) ▸ *adj.* Accustomed; usual: *ate with his wonted appetite.*

won ton or **won·ton** (wŏn′tŏn′) ▸ *n.* A noodle-dough dumpling filled usu. with spiced minced pork or other ground meat.

woo (wo͞o) ▸ *v.* **1.** To seek the affection of with intent to romance. **2.** To seek to achieve; try to gain. **3.** To entreat or importune. **—woo′er** *n.*

wood (wo͝od) ▸ *n.* **1a.** The tough fibrous supporting and water-conducting tissue beneath the bark of trees and shrubs, consisting largely of cellulose and lignin. **b.** This tissue, often cut and dried esp. for building material and fuel. **2.** often **woods** A forest.

wood alcohol ▸ *n.* See **methanol.**

wood·bine (wo͝od′bīn′) ▸ *n.* **1.** Any of various climbing vines, esp. a Mediterranean honeysuckle having yellowish flowers. **2.** See **Virginia creeper.**

wood·block (wo͝od′blŏk′) ▸ *n.* See **woodcut.**

wood·chuck (wo͝od′chŭk′) ▸ *n.* A common North American rodent having a short-legged, heavy-set body and brownish fur.

wood·cock (wo͝od′kŏk′) ▸ *n., pl.* **-cock** or **-cocks.** A game bird having brownish plumage, short legs, and a long bill.

wood·craft (wo͝od′krăft′) ▸ *n.* **1.** Skill in matters relating to the woods, as hunting or camping. **2.** Skill in working with wood.

wood·cut (wo͝od′kŭt′) ▸ *n.* **1.** A block of wood with an engraved design for printing. **2.** A print made from a woodcut.

wood·cut·ter (wo͝od′kŭt′ər) ▸ *n.* One who fells trees and chops wood, as for fuel.

wood duck ▸ *n.* A brightly colored American duck, the male of which has a large crest.

wood·ed (wo͝od′ĭd) ▸ *adj.* Covered with trees or woods.

wood·en (wo͝od′n) ▸ *adj.* **1.** Made of wood. **2.** Without spirit or liveliness. **3.** Clumsy and awkward. **—wood′en·ly** *adv.*

wood·land (wo͝od′lənd, -lănd′) ▸ *n.* Land covered with trees and shrubs.

wood·peck·er (wo͝od′pĕk′ər) ▸ *n.* Any of various usu. brightly colored birds that cling to and climb trees and have a chisellike bill for drilling through bark and wood.

wood·pile (wo͝od′pīl′) ▸ *n.* A pile of wood, esp. for fuel.

wood·ruff (wo͝od′rəf, -rŭf′) ▸ *n.* A fragrant herb with white flowers.

wood·shed (wo͝od′shĕd′) ▸ *n.* A shed in which firewood is stored.

woods·man (wo͝odz′mən) ▸ *n.* A man who works or lives in the woods or is versed in woodcraft; forester.

THESAURUS

woe *n.* —*See* CURSE (3), DISTRESS, MISERY.

woebegone *adj.* —*See* MISERABLE, SORROWFUL, TERRIBLE.

woeful *adj.* —*See* DEPLORABLE, MISERABLE, SORROWFUL.

wolf *n.* A man who is given to flirting ▸ flirt. *Slang:* masher. [*Compare* SEDUCER.] —*See also* PHILANDERER.

wolf *v.* —*See* GULP.

womanhood *n.* Women in general ▸ womankind, womenfolk.

womanish *adj.* Relating to or characteristic of women ▸ female, feminine, womanly. —*See also* EFFEMINATE.

womanishness *n.* —*See* EFFEMINACY.

womanizer *n.* —*See* PHILANDERER.

womankind *n.* Women in general ▸ womanhood, womenfolk.

womanliness *n.* The quality or condition of being feminine ▸ femaleness, feminineness, femininity.

womanly *adj.* Relating to or characteristic of women ▸ female, feminine, womanish.

womenfolk *n.* Women in general ▸ womanhood, womankind.

wonder *n.* **1.** The emotion aroused by something awe-inspiring or astounding ▸ amaze, amazement, astonishment, awe, marvel, stupefaction, surprise, wonderment. [*Compare* ENTHUSIASM, SURPRISE.] **2.** An event inexplicable by the laws of nature ▸ miracle. ***Idiom:*** act of God. —*See also* DOUBT, MARVEL.

wonder *v.* To have a feeling of great awe and rapt admiration ▸ admire, marvel. ***Idiom:*** be agog (*or* agape *or* awestruck). [*Compare* GAZE, STAGGER.] —*See also* DOUBT.

wonderful *adj.* —*See* ASTONISHING, GLORIOUS, MARVELOUS.

wonderment *n.* —*See* MARVEL, WONDER (1).

wondrous *adj.* —*See* ASTONISHING, GLORIOUS.

wonkiness *adj.* —*See* UNSTEADINESS.

wont *adj.* In the habit ▸ accustomed, habituated, used. —*See also* INCLINED.

wont *n.* —*See* CUSTOM.

wonted *adj.* —*See* COMMON (1).

woo *v.* —*See* COURT (2).

wooden *adj.* Rigidly constrained or formal; lacking grace and spontaneity ▸ buckram, starchy, stiff, stilted. [*Compare* COOL, FORCED, PRUDISH.]

woodland or **woods** *n.* A dense growth of trees and underbrush covering an area ▸ backwoods, forest, timberland. [*Compare* COUNTRY, WILDERNESS.]

woods·y (wŏŏd′zē) ▸ *adj.* **-i·er, -i·est**. Of or suggestive of the woods.
wood·wind (wŏŏd′wĭnd′) ▸ *n. Mus.* Any of a group of wind instruments that includes the bassoon, clarinet, flute, oboe, and saxophone.
wood·work (wŏŏd′wûrk′) ▸ *n.* Something made of wood, esp. wooden interior fittings in a house, as moldings or doors.
wood·y (wŏŏd′ē) ▸ *adj.* **-i·er, -i·est**. **1.** Forming or consisting of wood: *woody tissue.* **2.** Suggestive of wood. **3.** Wooded.
woof (wŏŏf, wōōf) ▸ *n.* **1.** The crosswise threads in a woven fabric at right angles to the warp threads. **2.** The texture of a fabric.
woof·er (wŏŏf′ər) ▸ *n.* A loudspeaker designed to reproduce bass frequencies.
wool (wŏŏl) ▸ *n.* **1a.** The dense, soft, often curly hair of sheep and certain other mammals, used as a textile fabric. **b.** A yarn or garment made of this hair. **2.** A covering or substance suggestive of the texture of true wool.
wool·en also **wool·len** (wŏŏl′ən) ▸ *adj.* Made or consisting of wool. ▸ *n.* often **woolens** Fabric or clothing made from wool.
Woolf (wŏŏlf), **(Adeline) Virginia (Stephen)** (1882–1941) ▸ British writer.
wool·gath·er·ing (wŏŏl′găth′ər-ĭng) ▸ *n.* Indulgence in fanciful daydreams.
wool·ly also **wool·y** (wŏŏl′ē) ▸ *adj.* **-li·er, -li·est** also **-i·er, -i·est**. **1a.** Made of or covered with wool. **b.** Resembling wool. **2.** Not sharp or clear: *woolly thinking.* **3.** Lawless and disorderly. ▸ *n., pl.* **-lies** also **-ies**. A garment made of wool. **—wool′li·ness** *n.*
woom·er·a (wŏŏm′ər-ə) ▸ *n.* A hooked wooden stick used for hurling a spear or dart.
woops (wŏŏps, wōōps) ▸ *interj.* Var. of **whoops**.
wooz·y (wōō′zē, wŏŏz′ē) ▸ *adj.* **-i·er, -i·est**. **1.** Dazed or confused. **2.** Dizzy or queasy. **—wooz′i·ness** *n.*
Worces·ter·shire (wŏŏs′tər-shîr, -shər) ▸ *n.* A piquant sauce of soy, vinegar, and spices.
word (wûrd) ▸ *n.* **1.** A meaningful sound or combination of sounds, or its representation in writing. **2.** Something said; a remark or comment. **3. words** Discourse or talk; speech. 4. **words** *Mus.* Lyrics; text. **5.** An assurance; promise. **6a.** A command or direction. **b.** A verbal signal; password. 7a. News. **b.** Rumor. **8. words** An angry argument. **9. Word** The Bible. ▸ *v.* To express in words. **—word′less** *adj.*
word·age (wûr′dĭj) ▸ *n.* **1.** Words collectively. **2.** The number of words used. **3.** Wording.
word·book (wûrd′bŏŏk′) ▸ *n.* A lexicon, vocabulary, or dictionary.
word·ing (wûr′dĭng) ▸ *n.* The way in which something is expressed in words.
word·play (wûrd′plā′) ▸ *n.* A witty or clever use of words.
word processing ▸ *n.* The creation, editing, and production of documents and texts by means of computer systems. **—word processor** *n.*
Words·worth (wûrdz′wûrth′), **William** (1770–1850) ▸ British poet.
word·y (wûr′dē) ▸ *adj.* **-i·er, -i·est**. Using more words than are necessary to convey meaning. **—word′i·ness** *n.*
wore (wôr) ▸ *v.* P.t. of **wear**.
work (wûrk) ▸ *n.* **1.** Physical or mental effort or activity. **2a.** A job; employment: *looking for work.* **b.** A profession or other means of livelihood. **3.** A duty or task. **4a.** The part of a day devoted to an occupation: *met her after work.* **b.** One's place of employment: *I'll call you at work.* **5a.** Something produced as the result of effort. **b.** An act; deed: *charitable works.* **c.** An artistic creation, such as a painting. **d. works** The output of a creative artist. **e. works** Engineering structures. **6. works** *(takes sing. or pl. v.)* A factory or industrial plant: *a steel works.* **7. works** Internal mechanism: *the works of a watch.* **8.** Workmanship: *sloppy work.* **9.** *Phys.* The transfer of energy from one physical system to another. **10. works** *Informal* Everything: *a pizza with the works.* ▸ *v.* **1.** To exert oneself physically or mentally. **2.** To be employed. **3.** To operate or cause to operate. **4.** To have an effect or influence. **5.** To reach a specified condition through gradual or repeated movement: *The stitches worked loose.* **6.** To proceed laboriously: *worked through the pile of unpaid bills.* **7.** To move in an agitated manner, as with emotion. **8.** To behave in a specified way when processed: *Gold works easily.* **9.** To bring about: *work miracles.* **10.** To shape or forge. **11.** To solve (a problem) by calculation. **12.** To bring to a specified condition by gradual or repeated effort: *worked the nail out of the board.* **13.** *Informal* To arrange or contrive. **14.** To excite or provoke: *worked the mob into a frenzy.* ***—phrasal verb:* work out** **1.** To solve: *worked out their differences.* **2.** To develop: *work out a plan.* **3.** To prove successful or effective. **4.** To engage in strenuous exercise. ***—idiom:* in the works** In preparation; under development.
work·a·ble (wûr′kə-bəl) ▸ *adj.* **1.** Capable of being worked. **2.** Capable of being put into effect; practicable. **—work′a·bil′i·ty** *n.*
work·a·day (wûr′kə-dā′) ▸ *adj.* **1.** Of or suited for working days. **2.** Mundane; commonplace.
work·a·hol·ic (wûr′kə-hô′lĭk, -hŏl′ĭk) ▸ *n.* One who has a

THESAURUS

wooer *n.* —*See* BEAU (1).
woolgather *v.* —*See* DREAM.
woolgathering *adj.* —*See* DREAMY.
woolly *adj.* —*See* AMBIGUOUS (1), HAIRY.
wooziness *n.* —*See* DIZZINESS.
woozy *adj.* —*See* DIZZY (1).
word *n.* Something said ▸ saying, statement, utterance. [*Compare* LANGUAGE, SPEECH.] —*See also* ARGUMENT, COMMAND (1), COMMENT, GOSSIP (1), MESSAGE, NEWS, PROMISE (1), TERM.
word *v.* —*See* PHRASE.
wordage *n.* —*See* WORDINESS, WORDING.
wordbook *n.* An alphabetical list of words often defined or translated ▸ dictionary, glossary, lexicon, vocabulary.
word-for-word *adj.* —*See* LITERAL.
word-hoard *n.* All the words of a language ▸ lexicon, vocabulary.
wordiness *n.* The use of words in excess of those needed for clarity or precision ▸ circumlocution, diffuseness, diffusion, long-windedness, pleonasm, prolixity, redundance, redundancy, verbiage, verboseness, verbosity, windiness, wordage. *Idiom:* verbal diarrhea. [*Compare* BOMBAST.]
wording *n.* Choice of words and the way in which they are used ▸ diction, locution, parlance, phrase, phraseology, phrasing, verbalism, wordage. *Idioms:* turn of phrase, way of putting it. [*Compare* EXPRESSION.]
wordless *adj.* —*See* IMPLICIT (1), MUTE, SILENT (2), SPEECHLESS.
wordlessness *n.* —*See* SILENCE (2).
word of honor *n.* —*See* PROMISE (1).
word-of-mouth *adj.* —*See* ORAL.
words *n.* —*See* ARGUMENT.
wordy *adj.* **1.** Using or containing an excessive number of words ▸ circumlocutionary, circumlocutory, diffuse, long-winded, periphrastic, pleonastic, prolix, redundant, tautological, verbose. [*Compare* INDIRECT, TALKATIVE.] **2.** Relating to, consisting of, or having the nature of words ▸ lexical, linguistic, wordy.
work *n.* **1.** The technique, style, and quality of working ▸ craft, craftsmanship, workmanship. [*Compare* APPROACH.] **2.** Something produced by human effort ▸ produce, product, production, manufacture. [*Compare* GOOD.] —*See also* ACT (1), BUSINESS (2), COMPOSITION (1), LABOR, POSITION (3), PUBLICATION (2).
work *v.* **1.** To handle in a way so as to mix, form, and shape ▸ knead, manipulate, squeeze. **2.** To force to work hard ▸ drive, push, task, tax. *Idiom:* crack the whip. [*Compare* FORCE.] —*See also* FUNCTION, INSINUATE, LABOR, OPERATE, RUB, SUCCEED (2), TILL, USE.
work out *v.* **1.** To arrive at an answer to a mathematical problem ▸ solve, work. *Informal:* figure out. [*Compare* CALCULATE.] **2.** To plan the details or arrangements of ▸ arrange, lay out, prepare, schedule. **3.** To engage in activities in order to strengthen or condition ▸ drill, exercise, practice, train. —*See also* DERIVE (2), DESIGN (1), SUCCEED (2).
work over *v.* —*See* BATTER, REVISE.
work up *v.* —*See* PROVOKE.
work on *v.* —*See* INFLUENCE.
workable *adj.* —*See* MALLEABLE, POSSIBLE.
workaday or **workday** *adj.* —*See* EVERYDAY.

compulsive and unrelenting need to work.

work·bench (wûrk′bĕnch′) ▸ *n.* A sturdy table or bench at which manual work is done, as by a machinist or carpenter.

work·book (wûrk′bo͝ok′) ▸ *n.* **1.** A booklet containing problems and exercises that a student works directly on the pages. **2.** An operating manual, as for an appliance. **3.** A book in which a record of work is kept.

work·day (wûrk′dā′) ▸ *n.* **1.** A day on which work is usually done. **2.** The part of the day during which one works.

work·er (wûr′kər) ▸ *n.* **1.** One who works. **2.** One who does manual or industrial labor. **3.** A member of a colony of social insects such as ants or bees, usu. a sterile female, that performs specialized work.

work·fare (wûrk′fâr′) ▸ *n.* A form of welfare in which aid recipients are required to perform public-service work.

work force ▸ *n.* **1.** The workers employed in a specific project or activity. **2.** All people working or available to work, as in a nation.

work·horse (wûrk′hôrs′) ▸ *n.* **1.** A horse used for labor rather than for racing or riding. **2.** *Informal* A person who works tirelessly.

work·house (wûrk′hous′) ▸ *n.* **1.** A prison in which limited sentences are served at manual labor. **2.** *Chiefly Brit.* A poorhouse.

work·ing (wûr′kĭng) ▸ *adj.* **1a.** Of, used for, or spent in work. **b.** Functioning. **2.** Sufficient or adequate for using: *a working knowledge of Spanish.* **3.** Serving as a basis for further work: *a working hypothesis.*

work·load (wûrk′lōd′) ▸ *n.* The amount of work assigned or done in a given time period.

work·man (wûrk′mən) ▸ *n.* **1.** A man who performs labor for wages. **2.** A craftsman.

work·man·like (wûrk′mən-līk′) ▸ *adj.* Befitting a skilled worker; skillfully done.

work·man·ship (wûrk′mən-shĭp′) ▸ *n.* **1.** The art of a skilled worker or craftsperson. **2.** The quality of something made.

work·out (wûrk′out′) ▸ *n.* **1.** A session of exercise or practice to improve fitness or athletic skill. **2.** A strenuous task.

work·place (wûrk′plās′) ▸ *n.* **1.** A place where people are employed. **2.** The work setting in general.

work·shop (wûrk′shŏp′) ▸ *n.* **1.** A room, area, or establishment where manual work is done. **2.** An educational seminar in a specified field.

work·space (wûrk′spās′) ▸ *n.* An area used or allocated for one's work, as in an office.

work·sta·tion (wûrk′stā′shən) ▸ *n.* **1.** An area, as in an office, equipped for one worker, usu. including a computer. **2.** A powerful computer usu. used for processing graphics.

work·ta·ble (wûrk′tā′bəl) ▸ *n.* A table designed for a specific activity, as sewing.

work·week (wûrk′wēk′) ▸ *n.* The hours or days worked in a week.

world (wûrld) ▸ *n.* **1.** The earth. **2.** The universe. **3.** The earth with its inhabitants. **4.** The human race. **5.** The public. **6.** often **World** A specified part of the earth. **7.** A realm or domain. **8.** A sphere of human activity or interest: *the world of sports.* **9.** A particular way of life. **10.** Secular life and its concerns: *a woman of the world.* **11.** A large amount: *did him a world of good.* **12.** A celestial body such as a planet.

world·ly (wûrld′lē) ▸ *adj.* **-li·er, -li·est.** **1.** Of or devoted to temporal rather than to religious or spiritual matters. **2.** Sophisticated; cosmopolitan. **—world′li·ness** *n.*

world·ly-wise (wûrld′lē-wīz′) ▸ *adj.* Experienced in the ways of the world.

world·wide (wûrld′wīd′) ▸ *adj.* Involving or extending throughout the world; universal. **—world′wide′** *adv.*

World Wide Web ▸ *n.* The complete set of documents on all Internet servers that use the HTTP protocol, accessible to users via a simple point-and-click system.

worm (wûrm) ▸ *n.* **1.** Any of various invertebrates, as an earthworm or tapeworm, having a long, flexible, rounded or flattened body. **2.** Any of various insect larvae having a soft elongated body. **3.** Something that resembles a worm. **4.** An insidiously tormenting or devouring force. **5.** A pitiable or contemptible person. **6. worms** Infestation of the intestines with worms or wormlike parasites. ▸ *v.* **1.** To move with or as if with the sinuous crawling motion of a worm. **2.** To elicit by artful or devious means: *wormed a confession out of the suspect.* **3.** To cure of intestinal worms. **—worm′y** *adj.*

worm-eat·en (wûrm′ēt′n) ▸ *adj.* **1.** Bored through or gnawed by worms: *worm-eaten apples.* **2.** Decayed; rotten. **3.** Antiquated; decrepit.

worm gear ▸ *n.* **1.** A gear consisting of a spirally threaded shaft and a wheel with teeth that mesh into it. **2.** A worm wheel.

worm wheel ▸ *n.* The toothed wheel of a worm gear.

worm·wood (wûrm′wo͝od′) ▸ *n.* An aromatic herb yielding a bitter extract used in making absinthe.

worn (wôrn) ▸ *v.* P.part. of **wear.** ▸ *adj.* **1.** Affected or impaired by wear or use. **2.** Showing the wearing effects of overwork, care, worry, or suffering.

worn-out (wôrn′out′) ▸ *adj.* **1.** Worn or used until no longer usable. **2.** Thoroughly exhausted; spent.

wor·ri·some (wûr′ē-səm, wŭr′-) ▸ *adj.* **1.** Causing worry or anxiety. **2.** Tending to worry.

wor·ry (wûr′ē, wŭr′ē) ▸ *v.* **-ried, -ry·ing.** **1.** To feel uneasy or troubled. **2.** To cause to feel anxious, distressed, or troubled. **3.** To bother or annoy. **4a.** To pull, bite, or tear at repeatedly. **b.** To touch, move, or handle idly. ▸ *n., pl.* **-ries.** **1.** Mental uneasiness or anxiety. **2.** A source of worry. **—wor′ri·er** *n.*

wor·ry·wart (wûr′ē-wôrt′, wŭr′-) ▸ *n.* One who worries excessively and needlessly.

THESAURUS

worked up *adj.* —*See* THRILLED.

worker *n.* —*See* EMPLOYEE, LABORER.

workhorse *n.* —*See* DRUDGE (2).

working *adj.* —*See* ACTIVE, BUSY (1), EMPLOYED.

working *n.* —*See* BEHAVIOR (2).

working girl *n.* —*See* HARLOT, LABORER.

workingman or **workingwoman** *n.* —*See* LABORER.

workless *adj.* Having no job ▸ idle, jobless, unemployed, unoccupied. *Idiom:* out of a job (*or* work).

workman or **workwoman** *n.* —*See* LABORER.

workmanship *n.* The technique, style, and quality of something that is made ▸ craft, craftsmanship, work. [*Compare* APPROACH.]

workout *n.* Energetic physical action ▸ activity, exercise, workout. —*See also* PRACTICE.

workroom *n.* An artist's workspace ▸ atelier, studio, workshop.

works *n.* A building or complex in which an industry is located ▸ factory, mill, plant. —*See also* WHOLE.

workshop *n.* An artist's workspace ▸ atelier, studio, workroom. —*See also* CONFERENCE (1).

workup *n.* —*See* EXAMINATION (2).

world *n.* The celestial body where humans live ▸ earth, globe, orb, planet. —*See also* ABUNDANCE, AREA (1), ENVIRONMENT (2), ENVIRONMENT (3), HUMANKIND, UNIVERSE.

worldly *adj.* Experienced in the ways of the world; lacking natural simplicity ▸ cosmopolitan, sophisticated, worldly-wise. [*Compare* EXPERIENCED, SHREWD, SUAVE.] —*See also* EARTHLY, PROFANE (2).

worldly-wise *adj.* Experienced in the ways of the world; lacking natural simplicity ▸ cosmopolitan, sophisticated, worldly. [*Compare* EXPERIENCED, SHREWD, SUAVE.]

worldwide *adj.* —*See* UNIVERSAL (1).

worm *v.* —*See* CRAWL (1), INSINUATE, MANEUVER (2).

worm *n.* —*See* CREEP (2).

worm-eaten or **wormy** *adj.* —*See* BAD (2).

worn *adj.* —*See* HAGGARD, SHABBY.

worn down *adj.* —*See* TIRED (1).

worn-out *adj.* —*See* SHABBY, TIRED (1), TRITE.

worried *adj.* —*See* ANXIOUS.

worrisome *adj.* —*See* DISTURBING.

worry *v.* To cause anxious uneasiness in ▸ ail, bother, concern, distress, trouble. —*See also* AGITATE (1), BROOD, HARASS.

worry *n.* A cause of distress or anxiety ▸ care, concern, stressor, trouble. [*Compare* BURDEN[1].] —*See also* ANXIETY (1), QUALM.

worrywart *n.* —*See* PESSIMIST (2).

worse (wûrs) ▸ *adj.* Comp. of **bad, ill.** In a worse manner. ▸ *adv.* Comp. of **badly, ill.**

wors·en (wûr′sən) ▸ *v.* To make or become worse.

wor·ship (wûr′shĭp) ▸ *n.* **1a.** Reverent love and devotion for a deity or sacred object. **b.** The ceremonies or prayers by which this love is expressed. **2.** Ardent devotion; adoration: *his worship of fame.* **3.** often **Worship** *Chiefly Brit.* Used as a form of address for magistrates and certain other dignitaries: *Your Worship.* ▸ *v.* **-shiped, -ship·ing** or **-shipped, -ship·ping. 1.** To honor and love as a deity. **2.** To love devotedly. **3.** To participate in religious worship. **—wor′ship·er** *n.*

wor·ship·ful (wûr′shĭp-fəl) ▸ *adj.* **1.** Given to or showing worship. **2.** *Chiefly Brit.* Used as a respectful form of address. **—wor′ship·ful·ly** *adv.*

worst (wûrst) ▸ *adj.* Superl. of **bad, ill. 1.** Most inferior, as in quality, condition, health, or effect. **2.** Most severe or unfavorable. ▸ *adv.* Superl. of **badly, ill.** In the worst manner or degree. ▸ *v.* To gain the advantage over; defeat. ▸ *n.* Something that is worst.

wor·sted (wŏŏs′tĭd, wûr′stĭd) ▸ *n.* **1.** Firm-textured, compactly twisted woolen yarn made from long-staple fibers. **2.** Fabric made from such yarn.

wort (wûrt, wôrt) ▸ *n.* A plant: *liverwort.*

worth (wûrth) ▸ *n.* **1.** The quality that renders something desirable, useful, or valuable. **2.** Material or market value. **3.** A quantity of something that may be purchased for a specified sum. **4.** Wealth; riches. ▸ *adj.* **1.** Equal in value to something specified. **2.** Deserving of; meriting: *a proposal worth considering.* **3.** Having wealth or riches amounting to.

worth·less (wûrth′lĭs) ▸ *adj.* **1.** Lacking worth; of no use or value. **2.** Low; despicable. **—worth′less·ness** *n.*

worth·while (wûrth′hwīl′, -wīl′) ▸ *adj.* Sufficiently valuable or important to be worth one's time or effort.

wor·thy (wûr′thē) ▸ *adj.* **-thi·er, -thi·est. 1.** Having worth, merit, or value. **2.** Honorable; admirable. **3.** Deserving: *worthy of acclaim.* ▸ *n., pl.* **-thies.** An eminent or distinguished person. **—wor′thi·ness** *n.*

would (wŏŏd) ▸ *aux.v.* P.t. of **will[2]**. **1.** Used after a statement of desire or request: *I wish you would stay.* **2.** Used for politeness: *Would you go with me?* **3.** Used to indicate uncertainty: *It would seem so.*

would-be (wŏŏd′bē′) ▸ *adj.* Desiring or attempting to be: *a would-be actor.*

would·n't (wŏŏd′nt) ▸ Would not.

wouldst (wŏŏdst) or **would·est** (wŏŏd′ĭst) ▸ *v. Archaic* 2nd pers. sing. p.t. of **will[2]**.

wound[1] (wōōnd) ▸ *n.* **1.** An injury, esp. one in which the skin is torn, pierced, cut, or otherwise broken. **2.** An injury to the feelings. ▸ *v.* To inflict a wound on.

wound[2] (wound) ▸ *v.* P.t. and p.part. of **wind[2]**.

Wound·ed Knee (wōōn′dĭd) ▸ A creek of SW SD, site of a Native American massacre by US troops (1890).

wove (wōv) ▸ *v.* P.t. of **weave.**

wo·ven (wō′vən) ▸ *v.* P.part. of **weave.**

wow (wou) *Informal* ▸ *interj.* Used to express wonder, amazement, or great pleasure. ▸ *n.* An outstanding success. ▸ *v.* To have a strong and usu. pleasurable effect on.

wrack (răk) ▸ *n.* **1.** Destruction or ruin. **2.** A remnant of something destroyed.

wraith (rāth) ▸ *n.* **1.** An apparition of a living person. **2.** The ghost of a dead person.

wran·gle (răng′gəl) ▸ *v.* **-gled, -gling. 1.** To quarrel noisily or angrily; bicker. **2.** To win or obtain by argument. **3.** To herd (horses or other livestock). ▸ *n.* An angry or noisy dispute. **—wran′gler** *n.*

wrap (răp) ▸ *v.* **wrapped** or **wrapt** (răpt), **wrap·ping. 1.** To draw, fold, or wind about in order to cover. **2.** To enclose within a covering; enfold. **3.** To encase and secure (an object), esp. with paper; package. **4.** To clasp, fold, or coil about something. **5.** To envelop or surround, esp. so as to obscure. **6.** To absorb; engross: *wrapped in thought.* ***—phrasal verb:*** **wrap up 1.** To finish; conclude. **2.** To summarize; recapitulate. ▸ *n.* **1.** An outer garment worn for warmth. **2.** A wrapping or wrapper. **3.** The completion of filming on a movie. ***—idiom:*** **under wraps** Secret or concealed.

wrap·a·round (răp′ə-round′) ▸ *n.* A garment, such as a skirt, that is open to the side and is wrapped around the body.

wrap·per (răp′ər) ▸ *n.* **1.** One that wraps. **2.** A material, such as paper, in which something is wrapped. **3.** The tobacco leaf covering a cigar. **4.** A loose robe or negligee.

wrap·ping (răp′ĭng) ▸ *n.* The material in which something is wrapped.

wrap-up (răp′ŭp′) ▸ *n.* A brief final summary, as of the news.

wrasse (răs) ▸ *n.* Any of numerous chiefly tropical, often brightly colored marine fishes.

wrath (răth) ▸ *n.* **1.** Furious, often vindictive anger; rage. **2a.** Punishment or vengeance as a manifestation of anger. **b.** Divine retribution. **—wrath′ful** *adj.* **—wrath′ful·ly** *adv.*

wreak (rēk) ▸ *v.* **1.** To inflict (e.g., vengeance). **2.** To vent (e.g., anger).

wreath (rēth) ▸ *n., pl.* **wreaths** (rē*th*z, rēths). **1.** A ring or circular band, as of flowers or leaves. **2.** A curling or circular form: *a wreath of smoke.*

wreathe (rē*th*) ▸ *v.* **wreathed, wreath·ing. 1.** To twist or entwine into a wreath. **2.** To coil or spiral. **3.** To encircle with or as if with a wreath.

THESAURUS

worse *n.* Whatever is destructive or harmful ▸ bad, badness, evil, ill. [*Compare* HARM.]

worsen *v.* *—See* DETERIORATE.

worship *n.* The act of adoring, especially reverently ▸ adoration, idolization, reverence, veneration. [*Compare* DEVOTION, HONOR, PRAISE.] *—See also* LOVE (1).

worship *v.* To feel deep devoted love for ▸ adore, love. *Idioms:* be soft (*or* stuck *or* sweet on), place (*or* put) on a pedestal, worship the ground someone walks on. *—See also* REVERE.

worshipful *adj.* *—See* REVERENT.

worst *v.* *—See* DEFEAT.

worth *n.* A measure of those qualities that determine merit, desirability, usefulness, or importance ▸ account, valuation, value. [*Compare* COST, IMPORTANCE.] *—See also* MERIT.

worthiness *n.* *—See* QUALIFICATION.

worthless *adj.* Lacking worth and value ▸ drossy, empty, good-for-nothing, no-good, useless, valueless. *Informal:* dumb, no-account, nothing, rotten, stupid. [*Compare* AIMLESS, TRIVIAL.] *—See also* SHODDY.

worthwhile *adj.* *—See* BENEFICIAL.

worthy *adj.* *—See* ADMIRABLE, COSTLY, ELIGIBLE, GOOD (1).

worthy *n.* *—See* DIGNITARY.

wound *n.* Marked tissue damage, especially when produced by physical injury ▸ laceration, lesion, trauma, traumatism. [*Compare* HARM.] *—See also* DISTRESS.

wound *v.* **1.** To cause bodily damage to a living thing ▸ hurt, injure, traumatize, wing. [*Compare* CUT, BREAK, HURT.] **2.** To inflict physical or mental injury or distress on ▸ shock, traumatize. *—See also* DISTRESS, OFFEND (1).

wounded *n.* *—See* VICTIM.

wow *n.* *—See* HIT.

wrack *n.* *—See* DESTRUCTION, RUIN (2).

wrack *v.* *—See* DESTROY (1).

wraith *n.* *—See* GHOST.

wrangle *v.* *—See* ARGUE (1), DRIVE (3), HAGGLE.

wrangle *n.* *—See* ARGUMENT.

wrap *v.* **1.** To cover completely and closely, as with clothing or bandages ▸ bundle, enfold, envelop, roll, swaddle, swathe. **2.** To surround and cover completely so as to obscure ▸ cloak, clothe, enfold, enshroud, envelop, enwrap, infold, invest, shroud, veil. [*Compare* CONCEAL, COVER, SURROUND.] *—See also* WIND[2].

wrap up *v.* To put on warm clothes ▸ bundle up, wrap. *—See also* CONCLUDE, INVOLVE (1).

wrap *n.* A garment worn wrapped about a person ▸ afghan, cloak, muffler, shawl, stole, throw, wrapper. [*Compare* SCARF.] *—See also* WRAPPER.

wrapper or **wrapping** *n.* The material in which something is wrapped ▸ case, casing, cover, covering, envelope, jacket, packaging, wrap. [*Compare* FRAME.] *—See also* WRAP.

wrap-up *n.* *—See* END (1), END (2), SUMMARY.

wrath or **wrathfulness** *n.* *—See* ANGER.

wrathful *adj.* *—See* ANGRY.

wreak *v.* *—See* INFLICT.

wreath *n.* *—See* BOUQUET, CIRCLE (1).

wreathe *v.* *—See* WIND[2].

wreck (rĕk) ► *v.* **1.** To destroy in or as if in a collision. **2.** To dismantle or tear down. **3.** To bring to a state of ruin. ► *n.* **1.** The act of wrecking or the state of being wrecked. **2.** A shipwreck. **3a.** The damaged remains, as of a wrecked ship or vehicle. **b.** Debris or cargo cast ashore after a shipwreck. **4.** One in a shattered, broken-down, or worn-out state.

wreck·age (rĕk′ĭj) ► *n.* **1.** The act of wrecking or the state of being wrecked. **2.** The debris of something wrecked.

wreck·er (rĕk′ər) ► *n.* **1.** One that wrecks. **2.** A member of a demolition crew. **3a.** A vehicle or piece of equipment employed in recovering or removing wrecks. **b.** One that salvages wrecked cargo or parts.

wren (rĕn) ► *n.* Any of various small brownish songbirds having a short, often erect tail.

wrench (rĕnch) ► *n.* **1.** A sudden forcible twist or turn. **2.** An injury produced by twisting or straining. **3.** A sudden surge of emotion. **4.** A tool with fixed or adjustable jaws for gripping, turning, or twisting an object such as a nut. ► *v.* **1a.** To twist or turn suddenly and forcibly. **b.** To twist and sprain: *wrenched my knee.* **2.** To free by pulling at; yank. **3.** To pull at the feelings or emotions of; distress. **4.** To distort; pervert.

wrest (rĕst) ► *v.* **1.** To obtain by or as if by pulling with violent twisting movements. **2.** To gain or take by force. ► *n.* The act of wresting. **—wrest′er** *n.*

wres·tle (rĕs′əl) ► *v.* **-tled, -tling. 1.** To fight by grappling and attempting to throw or immobilize one's opponent. **2.** To contend against in the sport of wrestling. **3.** To struggle to master something: *wrestle with a problem.* **—wres′tle** *n.* **—wres′tler** *n.*

wres·tling (rĕs′lĭng) ► *n.* A sport in which two competitors attempt to throw or immobilize each other by grappling.

wretch (rĕch) ► *n.* **1.** A miserable, unfortunate, or unhappy person. **2.** A base or despicable person.

wretch·ed (rĕch′ĭd) ► *adj.* **-er, -est. 1.** Woeful; miserable. **2.** Of a poor or mean character; dismal. **3.** Contemptible; vile. **4.** Of inferior quality. **—wretch′ed·ly** *adv.* **—wretch′ed·ness** *n.*

wri·er (rī′ər) ► *adj.* Comp. of **wry.**

wri·est (rī′ĭst) ► *adj.* Superl. of **wry.**

wrig·gle (rĭg′əl) ► *v.* **-gled, -gling. 1.** To turn or twist with sinuous motions; squirm. **2.** To proceed with sinuous motions. **3.** To insinuate or extricate oneself by sly or subtle means. **—wrig′gle** *n.* **—wrig′gly** *adj.*

wrig·gler (rĭg′lər) ► *n.* **1.** The larva of a mosquito. **2.** One that wriggles.

Wright (rīt), **Frank Lloyd** (1869–1959) ► Amer. architect.

Wright, Orville (1871–1948) ► Amer. aviation pioneer; with his brother **Wilbur** (1867–1912) invented the airplane.

wring (rĭng) ► *v.* **wrung** (rŭng), **wring·ing. 1.** To twist and squeeze, esp. to extract liquid. **2.** To extract by or as if by twisting or compressing; extort: *wring the truth out of a witness.* **3.** To wrench or twist forcibly or painfully: *wring someone's neck.* **4.** To twist or squeeze (one's hands) in distress. **5.** To anguish or aggrieve.

wring·er (rĭng′ər) ► *n.* One that wrings, esp. a device in which laundry is pressed between rollers to extract water.

wrin·kle (rĭng′kəl) ► *n.* **1.** A small furrow, ridge, or crease on a normally smooth surface, as cloth or the skin. **2.** An ingenious innovation. **3.** A problem or flaw. ► *v.* **-kled, -kling. 1.** To make a wrinkle or wrinkles in. **2.** To form wrinkles. **—wrin′kly** *adj.*

wrist (rĭst) ► *n.* **1.** The joint between the hand and forearm. **2.** The bones of this joint; carpus.

wrist·band (rĭst′bănd′) ► *n.* A band, as on a long sleeve, that encircles the wrist.

wrist·watch (rĭst′wŏch′) ► *n.* A watch worn on a band that fastens about the wrist.

writ (rĭt) ► *n.* **1.** A written order issued by a court, commanding the party to whom it is addressed to perform or cease performing a specified act. **2.** Writings: *holy writ.*

writ·a·ble also **write·a·ble** (rī′tə-bəl) ► *adj. Comp. Sci.* Capable of recording data: *writable compact disks.*

write (rīt) ► *v.* **wrote** (rōt), **writ·ten** (rĭt′n), **writ·ing. 1a.** To form (letters, words, or symbols) on a surface with an instrument such as a pen. **b.** To spell. **2.** To form (letters or words) in cursive style. **3.** To compose and set down, esp. in literary or musical form. **4.** To relate or communicate in writing. **5.** To send a letter or note to. **6.** To communicate by letter; correspond. **7.** *Comp. Sci.* To copy (data) to a storage device. ***—phrasal verbs:*** **write in** To cast a vote by inserting (a name not listed on a ballot). **write off 1.** To reduce the book value of. **2.** To cancel from accounts as a loss.

write-in (rīt′ĭn′) ► *n.* A vote cast by writing in the name of a candidate not on the ballot.

write-pro·tect (rīt′prə-tĕkt′) ► *v. Comp. Sci.* To modify (a file or disk) so that its data cannot be edited or erased.

writ·er (rī′tər) ► *n.* One who writes, esp. as an occupation.

write-up (rīt′ŭp′) ► *n.* A published account, review, or notice.

writhe (rīth) ► *v.* **writhed, writh·ing.** To twist or squirm, as in pain.

writ·ing (rī′tĭng) ► *n.* **1.** Written form: *Put it in writing.* **2.** Handwriting. **3.** Something written, esp. a literary composition. **4.** The activity, occupation, or style of a writer. **5. Writings** *(takes sing. or pl. v.) Bible* The third of the three divisions of the Hebrew Bible. See **Bible** table in Appendix.

wrong (rông, rŏng) ► *adj.* **1.** Not correct; erroneous. **2a.** Contrary to conscience, morality, law, or custom. **b.** Unfair; unjust. **3.** Not required, intended, or wanted. **4.** Not fitting; inappropriate. **5.** Not in accord with established usage, method, or procedure. **6.** Being the side, as of a garment, that is less finished and not intended to show. ► *adv.*

THESAURUS

wreck *n.* —*See* COLLAPSE (2), CRASH (2), DESTRUCTION, RUIN (2).

wreck *v.* **1.** To damage, disable, or destroy a seacraft ► shipwreck, sink, run aground. [*Compare* SINK.] **2.** To injure or destroy property maliciously ► vandalize. *Slang:* trash. —*See also* BLAST (2), BOTCH, CRASH, DESTROY (2), DESTROY (1).

wreckage *n.* —*See* DAMAGE, DESTRUCTION, RUIN (2).

wrecker *n.* —*See* RUIN (1).

wrench *v.* **1.** To injure a bodily part by twisting ► sprain, strain, turn, twist. [*Compare* HURT.] **2.** To move or cause to move with a sudden abrupt motion ► jerk, lurch, snap, twitch, yank. [*Compare* MOVE.] **3.** To alter the position of by a sharp, forcible twisting or turning movement ► twist, wrest, wring. —*See also* DISTORT, EXTORT, PULL (2).

wrench *n.* —*See* JERK.

wrest *v.* To alter the position of by a sharp, forcible twisting or turning movement ► twist, wrench, wring. —*See also* DISTORT, EXTORT, PULL (2).

wrestle *v.* —*See* CONTEND.

wretch *n.* —*See* UNFORTUNATE.

wretched *adj.* —*See* DEPLORABLE, DESPONDENT, MISERABLE, OFFENSIVE (1), TERRIBLE.

wretchedness *n.* —*See* DISTRESS, MISERY.

wriggle *v.* —*See* CRAWL (1).

wring *v.* To alter the position of by a sharp, forcible twisting or turning movement ► twist, wrench, wrest. —*See also* EXTORT.

wrinkle *n.* **1.** An indentation or seam on the skin, especially on the face ► crease, crinkle, crow's-foot, furrow, line. **2.** *Informal* A clever, unexpected new trick or method ► gimmick, trick, twist. *Informal:* kicker. *Slang:* angle, kick. —*See also* FOLD (1).

wrinkle *v.* To make irregular folds in, especially by pressing or twisting ► crimp, crinkle, crumple, rimple, rumple, wrinkle. —*See also* FOLD.

writ *n.* —*See* COMMAND (1).

write *v.* To form letters, characters, or words on a surface with an instrument ► chalk, engross, indite, ink, inscribe, pen, pencil, scratch (out), scrawl, scribe. *Informal:* scribble. —*See also* COMPOSE (1), PUBLISH (2).

write down *v.* —*See* DEPRECIATE, LIST[1].

write off *v.* —*See* DROP (4).

write-down *n.* —*See* DEPRECIATION.

write-up *n.* —*See* ITEM.

writhe *v.* To twist agitatedly, as in pain, struggle, or embarrassment ► squirm, toss, twist. [*Compare* SHAKE.] —*See also* CRAWL (1).

writing *n.* —*See* COMPOSITION (1).

written *adj.* Of or relating to representation by means of writing ► calligraphic, graphic, scriptural.

wrong *adj.* —*See* ERRONEOUS, EVIL, FALSE, INSANE, UNFAIR.

wrong *adv.* Not in the right way or

1. In a wrong manner; erroneously. 2. Immorally or unjustly. 3. In an unfavorable way; amiss. ▸ *n.* 1. Something that is wrong. 2. The condition of being in error or at fault: *in the wrong.* ▸ *v.* 1. To treat injuriously or dishonorably. 2. To discredit unjustly; malign. **—wrong′ly** *adv.*

wrong·do·er (rông′do͞o′ər, rŏng′-) ▸ *n.* One who does wrong. **—wrong′do′ing** *n.*

wrong·ful (rông′fəl, rŏng′-) ▸ *adj.* 1. Wrong; unjust. 2. Unlawful: *wrongful death.* **—wrong′ful·ly** *adv.* **—wrong′ful·ness** *n.*

wrong-head·ed (rông′hĕd′ĭd, rŏng′-) ▸ *adj.* Persistently and stubbornly wrong.

wrote (rōt) ▸ *v.* P.t. of **write.**

wroth (rôth) ▸ *adj.* Angry.

wrought (rôt) ▸ *adj.* 1. Fashioned; created. 2. Shaped by hammering: *wrought silver.*

wrought iron ▸ *n.* A purified form of iron that is easily shaped, forged, or welded.

wrought-up (rôt′ŭp′) ▸ *adj.* Agitated; excited.

wrung (rŭng) ▸ *v.* P.t. and p.part. of **wring.**

wry (rī) ▸ *adj.* **wri·er** (rī′ər), **wri·est** (rī′ĭst) or **wry·er, wry·est.** 1. Dryly humorous. 2. Temporarily twisted in an expression of distaste or displeasure: *made a wry face.* 3. Bent to one side; crooked. **—wry′ly** *adv.* **—wry′ness** *n.*

WSW ▸ *abbr.* west-southwest

wt. ▸ *abbr.* weight

WTO ▸ *abbr.* World Trade Organization

Wu·han (wo͞o′hän′) ▸ A city of E-central China on the Chang Jiang (Yangtze R.).

wurst (wûrst, wo͝orst) ▸ *n.* Sausage.

WV or **W.Va.** ▸ *abbr.* West Virginia

WWI ▸ *abbr.* World War I

WWII ▸ *abbr.* World War II

WWW ▸ *abbr.* World Wide Web

WY ▸ *abbr.* Wyoming

Wy·an·dot also **Wy·an·dotte** (wī′ən-dŏt′) ▸ *n., pl.* **-dot** or **-dots** also **-dotte** or **-dottes.** 1. A member of a Native American people of the former Huron confederacy, now in NE Oklahoma. 2. Their Iroquoian language.

Wy·o·ming (wī-ō′mĭng) ▸ A state of the W US. Cap. Cheyenne.

WYSIWYG (wĭz′ē-wĭg′) ▸ *adj.* Of or being a word-processing system in which the screen displays text exactly as it will be printed.

THESAURUS

on the proper course ▸ afield, amiss, astray, awry.

wrong *n.* —*See* CRIME (2), EVIL (1), INJUSTICE (1), INJUSTICE (2).

wrong *v.* —*See* ABUSE (1), OFFEND (1).

wrongdoer *n.* —*See* EVILDOER.

wrongdoing *n.* —*See* CRIME (2), MISBEHAVIOR.

wrongful *adj.* —*See* CRIMINAL (1), ILLEGAL.

wry *adj.* —*See* SARCASTIC.

X

x[1] or **X** (ĕks) ▸ *n., pl.* **x's** or **X's** also **xs** or **Xs**. **1.** The 24th letter of the English alphabet. **2.** A mark inscribed to represent the signature of an illiterate person. **3.** An unknown or unnamed factor, thing, or person. ▸ *v.* **x'd** or **X'd, x'ing** or **X'ing**. To delete or cancel with a series of X's: *x'd out the error.*

x[2] ▸ The symbol for **abscissa**.

X[1] (ĕks) ▸ *n.* A movie rating barring admission to anyone under the age of 17.

X[2] ▸ **1.** *Elect.* The symbol for **reactance**. **2.** also **x** The symbol for the Roman numeral 10.

Xa·vi·er (zā′vē-ər, zăv′ē-), Saint **Francis** (1506–52) ▸ Spanish Jesuit missionary.

x-ax·is (ĕks′ăk′sĭs) ▸ *n., pl.* **x-ax·es** (-ăk′sēz). **1.** The horizontal axis of a two-dimensional Cartesian coordinate system. **2.** One of three axes in a three-dimensional Cartesian coordinate system.

X-chro·mo·some (ĕks′krō′mə-sōm′) ▸ *n.* The sex chromosome associated with female characteristics, occurring paired in the female and single in the male sex-chromosome pair.

Xe ▸ The symbol for the element **xenon**.

xe·bec (zē′bĕk′) ▸ *n.* A small three-masted Mediterranean vessel with both square and triangular sails.

xe·non (zē′nŏn′) ▸ *n. Symbol* **Xe** A colorless, odorless, inert gaseous element found in minute quantities in the atmosphere. At. no. 54.

Xe·noph·a·nes (zə-nôf′ə-nēz′) (560?–478? B.C.) ▸ Greek philosopher.

xen·o·phobe (zĕn′ə-fōb′, zē′nə-) ▸ *n.* One unduly fearful or contemptuous of strangers or foreigners. **—xen′o·pho′bi·a** *n.* **—xen′o·pho′bic** *adj.*

xer·ic (zĕr′ĭk, zîr′-) ▸ *adj.* Of or adapted to an extremely dry habitat.

xe·rog·ra·phy (zĭ-rŏg′rə-fē) ▸ *n.* A dry photographic or photocopying process in which a negative image formed by a resinous powder on an electrically charged plate is transferred to and thermally fixed on a paper or other surface. **—xer′o·graph′ic** (zîr′ə-grăf′ĭk) *adj.*

xer·o·phyte (zîr′ə-fīt′) ▸ *n.* A plant adapted to living in a dry, arid habitat. **—xer′o·phyt′ic** (-fĭt′ĭk) *adj.*

Xer·ox (zîr′ŏks) ▸ A trademark for a photocopying process or machine employing xerography.

Xer·xes I (zûrk′sēz). "Xerxes the Great" (519?–465 B.C.) ▸ King of Persia (486–465).

Xho·sa also **Xo·sa** (kō′sä, -zə) ▸ *n., pl.* **-sa** or **-sas**. **1.** A member of a Bantu people of the E part of Cape Province, South Africa. **2.** The Bantu language of this people.

xi (zī, sī, ksē) ▸ *n.* The 14th letter of the Greek alphabet.

Xi'an (shē′än′, shyän) also **Si·an** (sē′än′, shē′-) ▸ A city of central China SW of Beijing.

Xiang Jiang (shyäng′ jyäng′) also **Siang Kiang** (syäng′ kyäng′, shyäng′) ▸ A river, about 1,150 km (715 mi), flowing generally northward from SE China.

Xin·gu (shĕng-go͞o′) ▸ A river of central and N Brazil flowing about 1,979 km (1,230 mi) to the Amazon R.

Xi·zang (shē′dzäng′) or **Ti·bet** (tə-bĕt′) ▸ An autonomous region of China in the SW part N and W of the Himalayas. Cap. Lhasa.

X·mas (krĭs′məs, ĕks′məs) ▸ *n.* Christmas.

x-ra·di·a·tion (ĕks′rā′dē-ā′shən) ▸ *n.* **1.** Treatment with or exposure to x-rays. **2.** Radiation composed of x-rays.

x-ray also **X-ray** (ĕks′rā′) ▸ *n.* **1a.** A relatively high-energy photon with a very short wavelength. **b.** A stream of such photons, used in radiography, radiology, radiotherapy, and scientific research. **2.** A photograph taken with x-rays. ▸ *v.* **1.** To irradiate with x-rays. **2.** To photograph with x-rays.

xy·lem (zī′ləm) ▸ *n.* The supporting and water-conducting tissue of vascular plants, consisting primarily of woody tissue.

xy·lo·phone (zī′lə-fōn′) ▸ *n.* A percussion instrument consisting of a mounted row of wooden bars graduated in length to sound a chromatic scale, played with two small mallets. **—xy′lo·phon′ist** *n.*

THESAURUS

x *v.* —*See* CANCEL (1).

Y

y[1] or **Y** (wī) ▸ *n., pl.* **y's** or **Y's** also **ys** or **Ys**. The 25th letter of the English alphabet.
y[2] ▸ The symbol for **ordinate.**
Y[1] ▸ The symbol for the element **yttrium.**
Y[2] ▸ *abbr.* year
–y[1] or **–ey** ▸ *suff.* **1.** Characterized by: *rainy.* **2a.** Like: *summery.* **3.** Inclined toward: *sleepy.*
–y[2] ▸ *suff.* **1.** Condition; quality: *jealousy.* **2a.** Activity: *cookery.* **b.** Instance of a specified action: *entreaty.* **3a.** Place for an activity: *cannery.* **b.** Result or product of an activity: *laundry.* **4.** Group: *soldiery.*
–y[3] or **–ie** ▸ *suff.* **1.** Small one: *doggy.* **2.** Dear one: *sweetie.* **3.** One having to do with or characterized by: *groupie.*
yacht (yät) ▸ *n.* A relatively small sailing or motor-driven vessel, usu. with smart, graceful lines, used for pleasure cruises or racing. **—yacht** *v.* **—yacht′ing** *n.* **—yachts′man** *n.* **—yachts′wom′an** *n.*
Ya·fo (yä′fō) also **Jaf·fa** (jăf′ə, yä′fə) ▸ A former city of W-central Israel on the Mediterranean Sea; part of Tel Aviv–Yafo since 1950.
ya·hoo (yä′ho͞o, yā′-) ▸ *n., pl.* **-hoos**. A crude or brutish person.
Yah·weh (yä′wā, -wĕ) also **Yah·veh** (-vā, -vĕ) ▸ *n.* In the Hebrew Bible, a name of God; Jehovah.
yak[1] (yăk) ▸ *n.* A shaggy-haired ox of the mountains of central Asia.
yak[2] (yăk) ▸ *v.* **yakked, yak·king.** *Slang* To talk or chatter persistently. **—yak** *n.*
y'all (yôl) ▸ *pron. Regional* Var. of **you-all.**
Yal·ta (yôl′tə) ▸ A city of SE Ukraine in the S Crimea on the Black Sea.
yam (yăm) ▸ *n.* **1.** The starchy edible root of a tropical vine. **2.** *Regional* See **sweet potato.**
yam·mer (yăm′ər) ▸ *v. Informal* **1.** To complain peevishly; whine. **2.** To jabber; chatter.
yang (yăng) ▸ *n.* The active, male cosmic principle in Chinese dualistic philosophy.
Yang·tze River (yăng′sē′, -tsē′) ▸ See **Chang Jiang.**
yank (yăngk) ▸ *v.* To pull or extract with or as if with a sudden forceful movement. ▸ *n.* A sudden vigorous pull.
Yank ▸ *n. Informal* A Yankee.
Yan·kee (yăng′kē) ▸ *n.* **1.** A native of a northern US state, esp. a New Englander. **2.** A US citizen; American.
yap (yăp) ▸ *v.* **yapped, yap·ping. 1.** To bark sharply or shrilly; yelp. **2.** *Slang* To talk noisily or stupidly; jabber. ▸ *n.* **1.** A bark; yelp. **2.** *Slang* Chatter; jabber. **3.** *Slang* The mouth. **—yap′per** *n.*
Ya·qui (yä′kē) ▸ *n., pl.* **-qui** or **-quis. 1.** A member of a Native American people of NW Mexico, now also in S Arizona. **2.** The Uto-Aztecan language of the Yaqui.
yard[1] (yärd) ▸ *n.* **1.** See **measurement** table in Appendix. **2.** *Naut.* A long tapering spar slung to a mast to support and spread a sail.
yard[2] (yärd) ▸ *n.* **1.** A tract of ground next to a building. **2.** A tract of ground, often enclosed, used for a specific activity. **3.** An area where railroad trains are made up and cars are switched, stored, and serviced. **4.** An enclosed area for livestock.
yard·age (yär′dĭj) ▸ *n.* An amount or length of something measured in yards.
yard·arm (yärd′ärm′) ▸ *n. Naut.* Either end of a yard of a square sail.
yard·stick (yärd′stĭk′) ▸ *n.* **1.** A graduated measuring stick one yard in length. **2.** A test or standard used in making a comparison or judgment.
yar·mul·ke (yär′məl-kə, yä′məl-) ▸ *n.* A skullcap worn by Jewish men and boys.
yarn (yärn) ▸ *n.* **1.** A continuous strand of twisted threads, as of wool or nylon, used in weaving or knitting. **2.** *Informal* A long, often elaborate story.
yar·row (yăr′ō) ▸ *n.* Any of several plants having finely dissected foliage and flat, usu. white or yellow flower heads.
yaw (yô) ▸ *v.* **1.** To swerve off course momentarily or temporarily, as a ship. **2.** To turn about the vertical axis, as a missile. **—yaw** *n.*
yawl (yôl) ▸ *n.* **1.** A two-masted fore-and-aft-rigged sailing vessel with the smaller mast abaft the rudder. **2.** A ship's small boat.
yawn (yôn) ▸ *v.* **1.** To open the mouth wide with a deep inhalation, as when sleepy or bored. **2.** To open wide; gape. ▸ *n.* The act of yawning. **—yawn′er** *n.*
yaws (yôz) ▸ *pl.n. (takes sing. or pl. v.)* A highly contagious tropical disease marked by multiple red sores.
y-ax·is (wī′ăk′sĭs) ▸ *n., pl.* **y-ax·es** (-ăk′sēz). **1.** The vertical axis of a two-dimensional Cartesian coordinate system. **2.** One of three axes in a three-dimensional Cartesian coordinate system.
Yb ▸ The symbol for the element **ytterbium.**
Y-chro·mo·some (wī′krō′mə-sōm′) ▸ *n.* The sex chromosome associated with male characteristics, occurring with one X-chromosome in the male sex-chromosome pair.
yd. ▸ *abbr.* yard (measurement)
ye[1] (thē) ▸ *def.art. Archaic* The.
ye[2] (yē) ▸ *pron. Archaic* You.
yea (yā) ▸ *adv.* **1.** Yes; aye. **2.** Indeed; truly. ▸ *n.* **1.** An affirmative statement or vote. **2.** One who votes affirmatively.
yeah (yĕ′ə, yă′ə, yā′ə) ▸ *adv. Informal* Yes.
year (yîr) ▸ *n.* **1a.** The period during which the earth com-

THESAURUS

yahoo *n.* —*See* BOOR.
yak *v.* —*See* CHATTER (1).
yammer *v.* —*See* CHATTER (1), COMPLAIN.
yammer *n.* —*See* CHATTER, COMPLAINT.
yank *v.* To move or cause to move with a sudden abrupt motion ▸ jerk, lurch, snap, twitch, wrench. [*Compare* MOVE.] —*See also* PULL (1), PULL (2).
yank *n.* —*See* JERK, PULL (1).
yap *v.* To utter a shrill, short cry ▸ squeal, yawp, yelp, yip. [*Compare* CRY, SHOUT.]
yap *n.* A shrill, short cry ▸ squeal, yawp, yelp, yip. [*Compare* CRY, SHOUT.] —*See also* MOUTH (1).
yard *n.* —*See* COURT (1), PEN[2].
yardstick *n.* —*See* STANDARD.
yarn *n. Informal* An entertaining and often oral account of a real or fictitious occurrence ▸ anecdote, fable, story, tale. *Informal:* tall tale.
yaw *v.* —*See* LURCH (1).
yawn *v.* **1.** To open the mouth wide with a deep breath, as when tired or bored ▸ gape. **2.** To open wide ▸ gap, gape. [*Compare* OPEN, WIDEN.]
yawning *adj.* Open wide ▸ abysmal, abyssal, cavernous, gaping. [*Compare* BROAD, OPEN.]
yawp *v.* To utter a shrill, short cry ▸ squeal, yap, yelp, yip. [*Compare* CRY, SHOUT.]
yawp *n.* A shrill, short cry ▸ squeal, yap, yelp, yip. [*Compare* CRY, SHOUT.]
yea *adv.* —*See* EVEN (2), YES.
yea *n.* An affirmative vote or voter ▸ aye, yes.
yeah *adv.* —*See* YES.
year *n.* A period of time of approximately 12 months, especially that pe-

pletes one revolution around the sun, equal to 365 days, 5 hours, 49 minutes, and 12 seconds. In the Gregorian calendar, the year begins on January 1 and ends on December 31 and is divided into 12 months, 52 weeks, and 365 days, or 366 days in a leap year. **b.** A corresponding period in other calendars. **2.** A year or part of a year devoted to a special activity: *the academic year.* **3.** **years** Age, esp. old age. **4.** **years** A long time.

year·book (yîr′bo͝ok′) ▸ *n.* **1.** A book published every year, containing information about the previous year. **2.** A yearly book published by the graduating class of a school or college.

year·ling (yîr′lĭng) ▸ *n.* An animal that is one year old or has not completed its second year.

year·long (yîr′lông′, -lŏng′) ▸ *adj.* Lasting one year.

year·ly (yîr′lē) ▸ *adj.* Occurring once a year; annual. ▸ *adv.* Once a year; annually.

yearn (yûrn) ▸ *v.* **1.** To have a strong or deep desire; long. **2.** To feel deep pity, sympathy, or tenderness.

yearn·ing (yûr′nĭng) ▸ *n.* A deep longing.

year-round (yîr′round′) ▸ *adj.* Existing, active, or continuous throughout the year.

yeast (yēst) ▸ *n.* **1.** Any of various unicellular fungi capable of fermenting carbohydrates. **2.** Froth consisting of yeast cells that is present in or added to fruit juices and other substances in the production of alcoholic beverages. **3.** A commercial preparation containing yeast cells and used esp. as a leavening agent. **4.** An agent of ferment or activity. **—yeast′y** *adj.*

Yeats (yāts), **William Butler** (1865–1939) ▸ Irish writer; 1923 Nobel. **—Yeats′i·an** *adj.*

yell (yĕl) ▸ *v.* To cry out or utter loudly, as in pain, fright, surprise, or enthusiasm. **—yell** *n.*

yel·low (yĕl′ō) ▸ *n.* **1a.** Any of a group of colors whose hue is that of ripe lemons. **b.** The hue of the visible spectrum lying between orange and green. **2.** *Regional* The yolk of an egg. ▸ *adj.* **-er, -est.** **1.** Of the color yellow. **2.** Having a yellow-brown skin color. **3.** *Slang* Cowardly. **4.** Exploiting, distorting, or exaggerating; sensational: *yellow journalism.* ▸ *v.* To make or become yellow. **—yel′low·ish** *adj.*

yellow card ▸ *n.* A yellow-colored card shown by a referee, esp. in soccer, to signal a flagrant foul.

yellow fever ▸ *n.* An infectious tropical disease transmitted by mosquitoes and marked by high fever, jaundice, and gastrointestinal hemorrhaging.

yellow jack ▸ *n.* **1.** A yellow flag hoisted on a ship to warn of disease on board. **2.** See **yellow fever.**

yellow jacket ▸ *n.* A small wasp with yellow and black markings.

Yel·low·knife (yĕl′ō-nīf′) ▸ The capital of Northwest Terrs., Canada, on the N shore of Great Slave Lake.

Yellow River ▸ See **Huang He.**

Yellow Sea ▸ An arm of the Pacific between China and the Korean Peninsula.

yelp (yĕlp) ▸ *v.* To utter a short sharp bark or cry. **—yelp** *n.*

Yem·en (yĕm′ən, yā′mən) ▸ A country of SW Asia at the S tip of the Arabian peninsula; formed when Yemen (or North Yemen) merged with Southern Yemen (1990). **—Yem′en·ite′, Yem′e·ni** (-ə-nē) *adj. & n.*

yen[1] (yĕn) ▸ *n.* A yearning or craving. **—yen** *v.*

yen[2] (yĕn) ▸ *n., pl.* **yen.** See **currency** table in Appendix.

yen·ta (yĕn′tə) ▸ *n. Slang* A meddlesome or gossipy person, esp. a woman.

yeo·man (yō′mən) ▸ *n.* **1.** An attendant, servant, or lesser official in a royal or noble household. **2.** A petty officer performing chiefly clerical duties in the US Navy. **3.** A small independent farmer, esp. a member of a former class of small freeholding farmers in England.

yeo·man·ry (yō′mən-rē) ▸ *pl.n.* The class of yeomen; small freeholding farmers.

yep (yĕp) ▸ *adv. Informal* Yes.

yer·ba ma·té (yâr′bə mä′tā, yûr′bə mä-tā′) ▸ *n.* See **maté.**

yes (yĕs) ▸ *adv.* Used to express affirmation, agreement, confirmation, or consent. ▸ *n., pl.* **yes·es.** An affirmative response or vote.

ye·shi·va or **ye·shi·vah** (yə-shē′və) ▸ *n. Judaism* **1.** A school where students study the Talmud. **2.** An elementary or secondary school with a curriculum that includes religion and culture.

yes man ▸ *n. Informal* One who slavishly agrees with a superior.

yes·ter·day (yĕs′tər-dā′, -dē) ▸ *n.* **1.** The day before the present day. **2.** also **yesterdays** Time in the past, esp. the recent past. ▸ *adv.* **1.** On the day before the present day. **2.** A short while ago.

yes·ter·year (yĕs′tər-yîr′) ▸ *n.* **1.** The year before the present year. **2.** Time past.

yet (yĕt) ▸ *adv.* **1.** At this time; for the present. **2.** Up to a specified time; thus far. **3.** At a future time; eventually. **4.** Besides; in addition. **5.** Still more; even: *a yet sadder tale.* **6.** Nevertheless: *young yet wise.* ▸ *conj.* And despite this; nevertheless. ***—idiom:* as yet** Up to the present time.

ye·ti (yĕt′ē) ▸ *n., pl.* **-tis.** See **abominable snowman.**

yew (yo͞o) ▸ *n.* **1.** A poisonous evergreen tree or shrub having scarlet cup-shaped seeds and flat, dark green needles. **2.** The durable, fine-grained wood of a yew.

Yid·dish (yĭd′ĭsh) ▸ *n.* The language historically of Jews of Central and Eastern Europe, derived principally from medieval German dialects. **—Yid′dish** *adj.*

yield (yēld) ▸ *v.* **1a.** To give forth by or as if by a natural process, esp. by cultivation. **b.** To furnish or give in return: *an investment that yields high returns.* **2a.** To give over possession of; surrender. **b.** To give up or concede. **3.** To give way to pressure, force, or persuasion. **4.** To give place, as to one that is superior. ▸ *n.* **1.** An amount yielded, as of a crop. **2.** A profit obtained from an investment; return.

yin (yĭn) ▸ *n.* The passive, female cosmic principle in Chinese dualistic philosophy.

yip (yĭp) ▸ *n.* A sharp, high-pitched bark; yelp. **—yip** *v.*

yip·pee (yĭp′ē) ▸ *interj. Informal* Used to express joy or elation.

THESAURUS

riod during which the earth completes a single revolution around the sun ▸ calendar year, season, cycle, twelvemonth.

yearn *v.* —*See* DESIRE.

yearning *n.* —*See* DESIRE (1).

years *n.* —*See* AGE (1), AGES.

yeast *n.* —*See* CATALYST, FOAM.

yeast *v.* —*See* FOAM.

yeasty *adj.* —*See* FOAMY.

yell *v.* —*See* SHOUT.

yell *n.* —*See* SHOUT.

yellow or **yellow-bellied** *adj.* —*See* COWARDLY.

yellow-belly *n.* —*See* COWARD.

yellow streak *n.* —*See* COWARDICE.

yelp *v.* To utter a shrill, short cry ▸ squeal, yap, yawp, yip. [*Compare* CRY, SHOUT.]

yelp *n.* A shrill, short cry ▸ squeal, yap, yawp, yip. [*Compare* CRY, SHOUT.]

yen *n.* —*See* DESIRE (1).

yenta *n.* —*See* GOSSIP (2).

yep *adv.* —*See* YES.

yes *adv.* It is so; as you say or ask ▸ absolutely, affirmative, agreed, all right, assuredly, aye, gladly, indeed, indubitably, naturally, right, roger, undoubtedly, unquestionably, willingly, yea. *Informal:* OK, uh-huh, yeah, yep, yup. *Slang:* for sure, right on, ten four. *Idioms:* you got it, you got that right. [*Compare* ACTUALLY, REALLY.]

yes *n.* An affirmative vote or voter ▸ aye, yea. —*See also* ACCEPTANCE (1).

yes *v.* —*See* ASSENT.

yes man *n.* —*See* SYCOPHANT.

yesterday or **yesteryear** *n.* —*See* PAST.

yet *adv.* To a more extreme degree ▸ even, ever more so, still. —*See also* ADDITIONALLY, EARLIER (2), STILL (1).

yield *v.* To conform to the will or judgment of another ▸ bow, defer, submit. *Idioms:* give ground, give way. [*Compare* HUMOR.] —*See also* ABANDON (1), PRODUCE (1), RETURN (3), SUCCUMB, SURRENDER (1), WEAKEN.

yield *n.* The amount or quantity produced ▸ garner, output, production. —*See also* HARVEST.

yielding *adj.* —*See* DEFERENTIAL, GENTLE (3), PASSIVE, SOFT (1).

yip *n.* A shrill, short cry ▸ squeal, yap, yawp, yelp. [*Compare* CRY, SHOUT.]

yip *v.* To utter a shrill, short cry ▸ squeal, yap, yawp, yelp. [*Compare* CRY, SHOUT.]

–yl ▸ *suff.* An organic acid radical: *methyl.*
YMCA ▸ *abbr.* Young Men's Christian Association
YMHA ▸ *abbr.* Young Men's Hebrew Association
yo·del (yōd′l) ▸ *v.* **-deled, -del·ing** or **-delled, -del·ling.** To sing so that the voice fluctuates between the normal chest voice and a falsetto. **—yo′del** *n.*
yo·ga (yō′gə) ▸ *n.* **1.** also **Yoga** A Hindu discipline for training the consciousness to attain perfect spiritual insight and tranquillity. **2.** A system of exercises practiced as part of this discipline.
yo·gi (yō′gē) ▸ *n., pl.* **-gis.** One who practices yoga.
yo·gurt also **yo·ghurt** (yō′gərt) ▸ *n.* A tart custardlike food prepared from milk curdled by bacteria.
yoke (yōk) ▸ *n.* **1a.** A crossbar with two U-shaped pieces that encircle the necks of draft animals. **b.** *pl.* **yoke** or **yokes.** A pair of draft animals joined by a yoke. **2.** A frame carried across a person's shoulders with equal loads suspended from each end. **3.** A clamp or vise that holds two parts together. **4.** A fitted part of a garment, esp. at the shoulders, to which another piece is attached. **5.** A bond or tie. **6.** Subjugation or bondage. ▸ *v.* **yoked, yok·ing. 1.** To fit or join with or as if with a yoke. **2.** To join or bind together.
yo·kel (yō′kəl) ▸ *n.* A rustic; bumpkin.
Yo·ko·ha·ma (yō′kə-hä′mə) ▸ A city of SE Honshu, Japan, on the W shore of Tokyo Bay.
yolk (yōk) ▸ *n.* The yellow portion of an egg of a bird or reptile, serving as nutriment for the developing young.
Yom Kip·pur (yôm′ kĭp′ər, kē-pŏŏr′) ▸ *n. Judaism* A holy day observed on the 10th day of Tishri and marked by fasting and prayer for the atonement of sins.
yon (yŏn) ▸ *adv. & adj.* Yonder.
yon·der (yŏn′dər) ▸ *adv.* In or at that indicated place. ▸ *adj.* Being at an indicated distance, usu. within sight.
yoo-hoo (yōō′hōō′) ▸ *interj.* Used to call someone at a distance.
yore (yôr) ▸ *n.* Time long past: *days of yore.*
York·town (yôrk′toun′) ▸ A village of SE VA; site of British surrender in the Revolutionary War (1781).
Yo·ru·ba (yôr′ə-bə, yō-rōō-bä′) ▸ *n., pl.* **-ba** or **-bas. 1.** A member of a West African people living chiefly in SW Nigeria. **2.** The language of the Yoruba. **—Yo′ru·ban** *adj.*
Yo·sem·i·te Valley (yō-sĕm′ĭ-tē) ▸ A valley of E-central CA; surrounded by **Yosemite National Park** and including **Yosemite Falls,** 739.6 m (2,425 ft) high.
you (yōō) ▸ *pron.* **1.** The one or ones being addressed: *Is that you?* **2.** One; anyone: *You can't win them all.*
you-all (yōō′ôl′) also **y'all** (yôl) ▸ *pron. Regional* You (plural).
you'd (yōōd) ▸ **1.** You had. **2.** You would.
you'll (yōōl, yŏŏl; yəl *when unstressed*) ▸ **1.** You will. **2.** You shall.
young (yŭng) ▸ *adj.* **-er, -est. 1.** Being in an early period of life or development. **2.** Newly begun or formed: *The evening is young.* **3.** Of or suggestive of youth or early life. **4.** Vigorous or fresh; youthful. **5.** Lacking experience; immature. ▸ *n.* **1.** Young persons collectively: *programs for the young.* **2.** Offspring; brood. **—young′ish** *adj.*
young·ling (yŭng′lĭng) ▸ *n.* A young person, animal, or plant.
young·ster (yŭng′stər) ▸ *n.* A young person.
your (yŏŏr, yôr; yər *when unstressed*) ▸ *adj.* The possessive form of **you.** Used as a modifier before a noun: *your boots; your reward.*
you're (yŏŏr; yər *when unstressed*) ▸ You are.
yours (yŏŏrz, yôrz) ▸ *pron. (takes sing. or pl. v.)* The one or ones belonging to you: *If I can't find my bike, I'll take yours.*
your·self (yŏŏr-sĕlf′, yôr-, yər-) ▸ *pron., pl.* **-selves** (-sĕlvz′). That one or those ones identical with you. Used: **a.** Reflexively: *Did you buy yourselves a gift?* **b.** For emphasis: *Do it yourself.*
youth (yōōth) ▸ *n., pl.* **youths** (yōōths, yōōthz). **1.** The condition or quality of being young. **2.** An early period of development or existence, esp. the time of life before adulthood. **3a.** A young person, esp. a young man. **b.** Young people collectively.
youth·ful (yōōth′fəl) ▸ *adj.* **1.** Possessing youth; young. **2.** Characteristic of youth; fresh. **3.** In an early stage; new. **—youth′ful·ly** *adv.* **—youth′ful·ness** *n.*
you've (yōōv) ▸ You have.
yowl (youl) ▸ *v.* To utter a long, loud, mournful cry; wail. **—yowl** *n.*
yo-yo (yō′yō′) ▸ *n., pl.* **-yos.** A toy consisting of a flattened spool wound with string that is spun down from and reeled up to the hand.
yr. ▸ *abbr.* **1.** year **2.** your
yt·ter·bi·um (ĭ-tûr′bē-əm) ▸ *n. Symbol* **Yb** A soft, bright, silvery rare-earth element used as an x-ray source in some laser materials, and in some special alloys. At. no. 70.
yt·tri·um (ĭt′rē-əm) ▸ *n. Symbol* **Y** A silvery metallic element used to increase the strength of magnesium and aluminum alloys. At. no. 39.
yu·an (yōō-än′) ▸ *n., pl.* **yu·an** or **yu·ans.** See **currency** table in Appendix.
Yu·ca·tán (yōō′kə-tăn′, -tän′) ▸ A peninsula mostly in SE Mexico between the Caribbean Sea and the Gulf of Mexico.
yuc·ca (yŭk′ə) ▸ *n.* Any of a genus of evergreen plants native to North America, having often tall stems and a terminal cluster of white flowers.
yuck (yŭk) ▸ *interj. Slang* Used to express rejection or strong disgust. **—yuck′y** *adj.*
Yu·go·sla·vi·a (yōō′gō-slä′vē-ə) ▸ A former country of SE Europe (1918–91) on the Balkan Peninsula, comprising the republics of Serbia, Montenegro, Croatia, Slovenia, Macedonia, and Bosnia and Herzegovina. **—Yu′go·sla′vi·an** *adj. & n.*
Yuk·on River (yōō′kŏn) ▸ A river flowing about 3,218 km (2,000 mi) from S Yukon Terr., Canada, through AK to the Bering Sea.
Yukon Territory ▸ A territory of NW Canada E of AK. Cap. Whitehorse.
Yule (yōōl) ▸ *n.* Christmas.
yule log ▸ *n.* A large log traditionally burned in a fireplace at Christmas.
Yule·tide (yōōl′tīd′) ▸ *n.* The Christmas season.
yum·my (yŭm′ē) ▸ *adj.* **-mi·er, -mi·est.** *Slang* Delightful; delicious.
Yu·pik (yōō′pĭk) ▸ *n., pl.* **-pik** or **-piks. 1.** A member of a group of Eskimoan peoples of W Alaska and extreme NE Russia. **2.** The languages of the Yupik.
yup·pie (yŭp′ē) ▸ *n. Informal* A young, affluent, usu. city-dwelling professional.
yurt (yûrt) ▸ *n.* A circular, domed, portable tent used by the nomadic Mongols of central Asia.
YWCA ▸ *abbr.* Young Women's Christian Association
YWHA ▸ *abbr.* Young Women's Hebrew Association

THESAURUS

yoke *n.* —*See* BOND (2), COUPLE, SLAVERY.
yoke *v.* —*See* COMBINE (1).
yoke with *v.* —*See* IMPOSE ON.
yokel *n.* —*See* CLODHOPPER.
yore *n.* —*See* PAST.
young *adj.* Being in an early period of growth or development ▸ fresh, green, immature, infant, juvenile, puerile, youthful. [*Compare* CHILDISH.]
young *n.* **1.** Young people collectively ▸ younger generation, youth. *Informal:* kids, young'uns. **2.** The offspring, as of an animal or bird, for example, that are the result of one breeding season ▸ brood, litter, spawn. [*Compare* PROGENY.]
youngster *n.* —*See* CHILD (1).
youth *n.* **1.** The time of life between childhood and maturity ▸ adolescence, greenness, juvenescence, juvenility, puberty, pubescence, salad days, youthfulness. *Informal:* spring, springtime. [*Compare* CHILDHOOD.] **2.** Young people collectively ▸ young. *Informal:* kids. —*See also* TEENAGER.
youthful *adj.* —*See* YOUNG.
youthfulness *n.* —*See* YOUTH (1).
yowl *v.* —*See* BAWL, CRY, HOWL.
yowl *n.* —*See* HOWL.
yucky *adj.* —*See* UNPALATABLE, UNPLEASANT.
yuk *v.* —*See* LAUGH.
yuk *n.* —*See* LAUGH.
yummy *adj.* —*See* DELICIOUS.
yup *adv.* —*See* YES.

Z

z or **Z** (zē) ► *n., pl.* **z's** or **Z's** also **zs** or **Zs**. The 26th letter of the English alphabet.

Z ► The symbol for **impedance**.

Za·ire (zī′îr, zä-îr′) ► See **Congo** 1. **—Za·ir′e·an, Za·ir′i·an** *adj. & n.*

Zam·be·zi (zăm-bē′zē) ► A river, about 2,735 km (1,700 mi), of central and S Africa rising in NW Zambia and flowing to the Mozambique Channel.

Zam·bi·a (zăm′bē-ə) ► A country of S-central Africa. **—Zam′bi·an** *adj. & n.*

za·ny (zā′nē) ► *n., pl.* **-nies**. **1.** A clown; buffoon. **2.** A comical person given to extravagant or outlandish behavior. ► *adj.* **-ni·er, -ni·est**. **1.** Ludicrously comical; clownish. **2.** Comical because of incongruity or strangeness; bizarre. **—za′ni·ly** *adv.* **—za′ni·ness** *n.*

Zan·zi·bar (zăn′zə-bär′) ► **1.** A region of E Africa, comprising **Zanzibar Island** and several adjacent islands off the NE coast of Tanzania. **2.** A city of Tanzania on the W coast of Zanzibar I.

zap (zăp) ► *v.* **zapped, zap·ping.** *Slang* **1.** To destroy or kill with or as if with a burst of gunfire, flame, or electric current. **2.** To expose to radiation. **—zap′per** *n.*

z-ax·is (zē′ăk′sĭs) ► *n., pl.* **z-ax·es** (-ăk′sēz). One of three axes in a three-dimensional Cartesian coordinate system.

za·zen (zä′zĕn′) ► *n.* Meditation as practiced in Zen Buddhism.

zeal (zēl) ► *n.* Enthusiastic devotion to a cause, ideal, or goal.

zeal·ot (zĕl′ət) ► *n.* One who is zealous, esp. one who is fanatically devoted to a cause. **—zeal′ot·ry** *n.*

zeal·ous (zĕl′əs) ► *adj.* Filled with or motivated by zeal; fervent. **—zeal′ous·ly** *adv.* **—zeal′ous·ness** *n.*

ze·bra (zē′brə) ► *n.* A swift, wild, horselike African mammal having distinctive overall markings of alternating white and black or brown stripes.

ze·bu (zē′bo͞o, -byo͞o) ► *n.* A domesticated ox of Asia and E Africa, having a prominent hump and a large dewlap.

Zech·a·ri·ah (zĕk′ə-rī′ə) ► *n.* **1.** A Hebrew prophet of the 6th cent. B.C. **2.** See **Bible** table in Appendix.

zed (zĕd) ► *n. Chiefly Brit.* The letter *z.*

Zeit·geist (tsīt′gīst′, zīt′-) ► *n.* The taste and outlook characteristic of a period or generation.

Zen (zĕn) ► *n.* A school of Buddhism practiced esp. in the Far East asserting that enlightenment can be attained through meditation and self-contemplation rather than through faith and devotion.

Zen Buddhism ► *n.* Zen.

Zend-A·ves·ta (zĕn′də-vĕs′tə) ► *n.* The sacred writings of the Zoroastrian religion.

ze·nith (zē′nĭth) ► *n.* **1.** The point on the celestial sphere that is directly above the observer. **2.** The upper region of the sky. **3.** The highest point above the observer's horizon attained by a celestial body. **4.** The point of culmination; acme.

Zeph·a·ni·ah (zĕf′ə-nī′ə) ► *n.* **1.** A Hebrew prophet of the 7th cent. B.C. **2.** See **Bible** table in Appendix.

zeph·yr (zĕf′ər) ► *n.* **1a.** The west wind. **b.** A gentle breeze. **2.** Any of various soft light fabrics, yarns, or garments.

zep·pe·lin also **Zep·pe·lin** (zĕp′ə-lĭn) ► *n.* A rigid airship having a long cylindrical body supported by internal gas cells.

ze·ro (zîr′ō, zē′rō) ► *n., pl.* **-ros** or **-roes**. **1.** The numerical symbol 0; cipher. **2.** *Math.* **a.** The identity element for addition. **b.** A cardinal number indicating the absence of any or all units under consideration. **c.** An ordinal number indicating an initial point or origin. **3.** The temperature indicated by the numeral 0 on a thermometer. **4.** *Informal* One having no influence or importance. **5.** The lowest point. ► *adj.* **1.** Of or being zero. **2a.** Having no measurable or otherwise determinable value. **b.** *Informal* Absent, inoperative, or irrelevant. ► *v.* **-roed, -ro·ing**. To adjust (an instrument or device) to zero value. ***—phrasal verb:* zero in** **1.** To aim or concentrate firepower on an exact target location. **2.** To converge intently; close in: *zero in on the cause.*

zero gravity ► *n.* The condition of apparent weightlessness occurring when the centrifugal force on a body exactly counterbalances the gravitational attraction on it.

zero hour ► *n.* The scheduled time for the start of an action, esp. a military operation.

zero population growth ► *n.* The limiting of population increase to the number needed to replace the existing population.

ze·ro-sum (zîr′ō-sŭm′, zē′rō-) ► *adj.* Of or being a situation in which a gain on one side necessarily entails an equal loss on another.

zest (zĕst) ► *n.* **1a.** Flavor or interest; piquancy. **b.** The outermost part of the rind of an orange, lemon, or other citrus fruit, used as flavoring. **2.** Spirited enjoyment; gusto. **—zest′ful** *adj.* **—zest′ful·ly** *adv.*

ze·ta (zā′tə, zē′-) ► *n.* The 6th letter of the Greek alphabet.

Zeus (zo͞os) ► *n. Gk. Myth.* The principal god of the Greek pantheon, ruler of the heavens and father of other gods and mortal heroes.

zig·gu·rat (zĭg′ə-răt′) ► *n.* A temple tower of the ancient Assyrians and Babylonians, having the form of a terraced pyramid.

zig·zag (zĭg′zăg′) ► *n.* **1a.** A line or course that proceeds by sharp turns in alternating directions. **b.** One of a series of such sharp turns. **2.** Something, such as a design, marked by zigzags. ► *adj.* Moving in or having a zigzag. ► *adv.* In a zigzag manner or pattern. ► *v.* **-zagged, -zag·ging**. To move in or form a zigzag.

zilch (zĭlch) ► *n. Slang* Zero; nothing.

zil·lion (zĭl′yən) ► *n. Informal* An extremely large indefinite number.

Zim·bab·we (zĭm-bäb′wē, -wā). Formerly **Rhodesia** ► A country of S Africa. **—Zim·bab′we·an** *adj. & n.*

zinc (zĭngk) ► *n. Symbol* **Zn** A bluish-white, lustrous metallic element used to form many alloys, including brass, and in galvanizing iron and other metals. At. no.

THESAURUS

zaftig *adj.* —*See* FAT (1), SHAPELY.

zaniness *n.* —*See* FOOLISHNESS, HUMOR.

zany *adj.* —*See* FOOLISH, FUNNY (1).

zany *n.* —*See* JOKER.

zap *v.* —*See* KILL[1], MURDER.

zeal *n.* —*See* DEVOTION, ENTHUSIASM (1), PASSION.

zealot *n.* —*See* DEVOTEE, EXTREMIST, FAN[2].

zealous *adj.* —*See* ENTHUSIASTIC, EXTREME (2), PIOUS.

zealousness *n.* —*See* ENTHUSIASM (1).

zenith *n.* —*See* CLIMAX.

zephyr *n.* —*See* BREEZE (1), WIND[1].

zero *n.* —*See* NONENTITY, NOTHING.

zero in *v.* —*See* AIM (1), CONCENTRATE.

zero hour *n.* —*See* CRISIS.

zest *n.* Spirited enjoyment ► gusto, relish. [*Compare* ENTHUSIASM.] —*See also* FLAVOR (1), SKIN (3).

zest *v.* To impart flavor to ► flavor, season, spice (up).

zesty *adj.* —*See* SPICY.

zigzag *v.* —*See* SWERVE.

zigzag *adj.* —*See* INDIRECT (1).

zilch *n.* —*See* NONENTITY, NOTHING.

zillion *n.* —*See* HEAP (2).

30. ▸ *v.* **zinced, zinc·ing** or **zincked, zinck·ing.** To coat or treat with zinc; galvanize.

zinc oxide ▸ *n.* An amorphous white or yellowish powder, ZnO, used as a pigment and in pharmaceuticals and cosmetics.

zine or **'zine** (zēn) ▸ *n.* **1.** An inexpensive, self-published, underground publication. **2.** An e-zine.

zing (zĭng) ▸ *n.* **1.** A brief high-pitched humming or buzzing sound. **2.** Liveliness; zip. ▸ *v.* **1.** To make a zing. **2.** To move swiftly. **3.** *Informal* To attack verbally. **—zing′y** *adj.*

zing·er (zĭng′ər) ▸ *n.* *Informal* A witty, often caustic remark.

zin·ni·a (zĭn′ē-ə) ▸ *n.* A widely cultivated plant with showy, variously colored flower heads.

Zi·on (zī′ən) also **Si·on** (sī′ən) ▸ *n.* **1a.** The historic land of Israel as a symbol of the Jewish people. **b.** The Jewish people; Israel. **2.** A place or religious community regarded as devoted to God. **3.** A utopia.

Zi·on·ism (zī′ə-nĭz′əm) ▸ *n.* A Jewish movement that arose in the late 19th cent., orig. seeking to reestablish a Jewish homeland in Palestine and now concerned with the support and development of the state of Israel. **—Zi′on·ist** *adj. & n.*

zip (zĭp) ▸ *n.* **1.** A brief, sharp, hissing sound. **2.** Energy; vim. **3.** *Slang* Nothing; nil; zero. ▸ *v.* **zipped, zip·ping. 1.** To move or act with speed or energy. **2.** To fasten or unfasten with a zipper.

Zip Code ▸ A trademark used for a system designed to expedite the sorting and delivery of mail by assigning a series of numbers to each delivery area in the US.

zip·per (zĭp′ər) ▸ *n.* A fastening device consisting of parallel rows of metal, plastic, or nylon teeth on adjacent edges of an opening that are interlocked by a sliding tab.

zip·py (zĭp′ē) ▸ *adj.* **-pi·er, -pi·est.** Full of energy; lively.

zir·con (zûr′kŏn′) ▸ *n.* A brown to colorless mineral, $ZrSiO_4$, that is heated, cut, and polished to form a brilliant blue-white gem.

zir·co·ni·um (zûr-kō′nē-əm) ▸ *n.* *Symbol* **Zr** A lustrous, grayish-white, strong, ductile metallic element used chiefly in ceramic and refractory compounds and as an alloying agent. At. no. 40.

zit (zĭt) ▸ *n.* *Slang* A pimple.

zith·er (zĭth′ər, zĭ*th*′-) ▸ *n.* A musical instrument composed of a flat sound box set with strings of graded length, played with the fingertips or a plectrum. **—zith′er·ist** *n.*

zi·ti (zē′tē) ▸ *n.* Pasta in medium-sized, often ridged tubes.

zlo·ty (zlô′tē) ▸ *n., pl.* **zlo·ty** or **zlo·tys.** See **currency** table in Appendix.

Zn ▸ The symbol for the element **zinc.**

zo·di·ac (zō′dē-ăk′) ▸ *n.* **1a.** A band of the celestial sphere extending about 8° to either side of the ecliptic that represents the path of the principal planets, the moon, and the sun. **b.** In astrology, this band divided into 12 equal parts called signs, bearing the name of a constellation for which it was orig. named. **2.** A diagram or figure representing the zodiac. **—zo·di′a·cal** (-dī′ə-kəl) *adj.*

-zoic ▸ *suff.* **1.** Relating to a specified manner of animal existence: *protozoic.* **2.** Of a specified geologic era: *Archeozoic.*

zom·bie (zŏm′bē) ▸ *n.* **1.** A voodoo snake god. **2a.** A supernatural power or spell that according to voodoo belief can enter into and reanimate a corpse. **b.** A corpse revived in this way. **3.** One who looks or behaves like an automaton.

zon·al (zō′nəl) ▸ *adj.* **1.** Relating to a zone. **2.** Divided into zones. **—zon′al·ly** *adv.*

zone (zōn) ▸ *n.* **1.** An area or region distinguished from adjacent parts by a distinctive feature or characteristic. **2.** Any of the five regions of the surface of the earth that are loosely divided according to prevailing climate and latitude, including the Torrid Zone, the North and South Temperate Zones, and the North and South Frigid Zones. **3.** A section of an area or territory used for a specific purpose: *a residential zone.* ▸ *v.* **zoned, zon·ing. 1.** To divide into zones. **2.** To designate or mark off into zones.

zonk (zôngk, zŏngk) ▸ *v.* *Slang* To intoxicate or become intoxicated with drugs or alcohol.

zoo (zo͞o) ▸ *n., pl.* **zoos. 1.** A park or institution in which living animals are kept and exhibited to the public. **2.** *Slang* A place or situation marked by confusion or disorder.

zoo– or **zo–** ▸ *pref.* **1.** Animal: *zoology.* **2.** Motile: *zoospore.*

zo·o·ge·og·ra·phy (zō′ə-jē-ŏg′rə-fē) ▸ *n.* The biological study of geographic distribution of animals. **—zo′o·ge·og′ra·pher** *n.*

zoological garden ▸ *n.* See **zoo** 1.

zo·ol·o·gy (zō-ŏl′ə-jē, zo͞o-) ▸ *n.* **1.** The branch of biology that deals with animals and animal life. **2.** The animal life of a particular area or period. **3.** The characteristics of a particular animal group or category. **—zo′o·log′i·cal** (-ə-lŏj′ĭ-kəl), **zo′o·log′ic** *adj.* **—zo·ol′o·gist** *n.*

zoom (zo͞om) ▸ *v.* **1.** To make or move with a continuous low-pitched buzzing or humming sound. **2.** To climb suddenly and sharply, as an airplane. **3.** To move about rapidly; swoop. **4.** To simulate movement away from or toward a subject using a zoom lens. **—zoom** *n.*

zoom lens ▸ *n.* A camera lens whose focal length can be rapidly changed, allowing rapid change in the size of an image.

-zoon ▸ *suff.* Animal; independently moving organic unit: *spermatozoon.*

zo·o·plank·ton (zō′ə-plăngk′tən) ▸ *n.* Plankton that consists of animals.

zo·o·spore (zō′ə-spôr′) ▸ *n.* A motile, flagellated asexual spore.

Zo·ro·as·ter (zôr′ō-ăs′tər) (6th cent. B.C.) ▸ Persian prophet who founded Zoroastrianism.

Zo·ro·as·tri·an·ism (zôr′ō-ăs′trē-ə-nĭz′əm) ▸ *n.* The religious system founded in Persia by Zoroaster, teaching the worship of Ormazd in the context of a universal struggle between the forces of light and of darkness. **—Zo′ro·as′tri·an** *adj. & n.*

zounds (zoundz) ▸ *interj.* Used to express anger, surprise, or indignation.

zoy·sia (zoi′shə, -sē-ə) ▸ *n.* Any of several creeping grasses widely cultivated for lawns.

Zr ▸ The symbol for the element **zirconium.**

zuc·chi·ni (zo͞o-kē′nē) ▸ *n., pl.* **-ni** or **-nis.** A variety of squash having an elongated shape and a smooth, dark green rind.

Zu·lu (zo͞o′lo͞o) ▸ *n., pl.* **-lu** or **-lus. 1.** A member of a people of SE Africa. **2.** The Bantu language of the Zulu. **—Zu′lu** *adj.*

Zu·ni (zo͞o′nē) also **Zu·ñi** (-nyē, -nē) ▸ *n., pl.* **-ni** or **-nis** also **-ñi** or **-ñis. 1.** A member of a Pueblo people of W New Mexico. **2.** The language of the Zuni.

Zu·rich (zo͝or′ĭk) ▸ A city of NE Switzerland at the N tip of the **Lake of Zurich.**

zwie·back (swē′băk′, swī′-, zwē′-, zwī′-) ▸ *n.* A usu. sweetened bread baked first as a loaf and later sliced and toasted.

zy·de·co (zī′dĭ-kō′) ▸ *n.* Popular music of S Louisiana played by small groups featuring the guitar, the accordion, and a washboard.

zy·go·sis (zī-gō′sĭs, zĭ-) ▸ *n., pl.* **-ses** (-sēz). The union of gametes to form a zygote; conjugation.

zy·gote (zī′gōt′) ▸ *n.* **1.** The cell formed by the union of two gametes, esp. a fertilized ovum before cleavage. **2.** The organism that develops from a zygote. **—zy·got′ic** (-gŏt′ĭk) *adj.*

zy·mur·gy (zī′mûr′jē) ▸ *n.* The branch of chemistry that deals with fermentation processes, as in brewing.

THESAURUS

zinger *n.* —*See* JOKE (1).
zip *n.* —*See* ENERGY, SPIRIT (1).
zip *v.* —*See* BREEZE, RUSH.
zippy *adj.* —*See* ENERGETIC.
zodiac *n.* —*See* CIRCLE (1).
zone *n.* —*See* AREA (2), TERRITORY.
zonk *v.* —*See* DAZE (1).
zonked *adj.* —*See* DRUGGED, DRUNK.
zoom *v.* —*See* RUSH.

APPENDIX

BOOKS OF THE BIBLE

Books of the Hebrew Scriptures appear as listed in the translation by the Jewish Publication Society of America. Books of the Christian Bible appear as listed in the Jerusalem Bible, a 1966 translation of the 1956 French Roman Catholic version. The Old Testament books shown in italic are considered apocryphal in many Christian churches, but they are accepted as canonical in the Roman Catholic Church, the Eastern Orthodox Church, and the Armenian and the Ethiopian Oriental Orthodox Church. The Christian Old Testament parallels the Hebrew Scriptures with the exception of these books.

Hebrew Scriptures

The Torah

Genesis
Exodus
Leviticus
Numbers
Deuteronomy

The Prophets

Joshua
Judges
I Samuel
II Samuel
I Kings
II Kings
Isaiah
Jeremiah
Ezekiel
Hosea
Joel
Amos
Obadiah
Jonah
Micah
Nahum
Habakkuk
Zephaniah
Haggai
Zechariah
Malachi

The Writings

Psalms
Proverbs
Job
Song of Songs
Ruth
Lamentations
Ecclesiastes
Esther
Daniel
Ezra
Nehemiah
I Chronicles
II Chronicles

Christian Bible

Old Testament

Genesis
Exodus
Leviticus
Numbers
Deuteronomy
Joshua
Judges
Ruth
I Samuel
II Samuel
I Kings
II Kings
I Chronicles
II Chronicles
Ezra
Nehemiah
Tobit
Judith
Esther
I Maccabees
II Maccabees
Job
Psalms
Proverbs
Ecclesiastes
Song of Songs
(Song of Solomon)
Wisdom of Solomon
Ecclesiasticus
Isaiah
Jeremiah
Lamentations
Baruch
Ezekiel
Daniel
Hosea
Joel
Amos
Obadiah
Jonah
Micah
Nahum
Habakkuk
Zephaniah
Haggai
Zechariah
Malachi

New Testament

Matthew
Mark
Luke
John
Acts of the Apostles
Romans
I Corinthians
II Corinthians
Galatians
Ephesians
Philippians
Colossians
I Thessalonians
II Thessalonians
I Timothy
II Timothy
Titus
Philemon
Hebrews
James
I Peter
II Peter
I John
II John
III John
Jude
Revelation

THREE PRINCIPAL CALENDARS

The Gregorian calendar is now in use as the civil calendar throughout most of the world. The Jewish calendar is the official calendar of the Jewish religious community. The Islamic calendar is the official calendar in many Muslim countries. Each calendar listed below begins with the first month of the year and includes the number of days each month contains. Many months have a variable number of days, as described below.

Gregorian

The Gregorian calendar, introduced in 1582 by Pope Gregory XIII, is a corrected form of the Julian calendar. It is based on a solar year of 365 days. Every fourth year is a leap year of 366 days except for centenary years not divisible by 400.

Months	Number of Days
January	31
February	28 or 29
March	31
April	30
May	31
June	30
July	31
August	31
September	30
October	31
November	30
December	31

Jewish

The Jewish calendar is based on both the solar and lunar cycles. The lunar year of 354 days is adjusted to the solar year with the intercalary month Adar Sheni in leap years. This ensures that the major religious festivals fall in their proper season.

Months	Number of Days
Tishri (Sep–Oct)	30
Heshvan (Oct–Nov)	29 or 30
Kislev (Nov–Dec)	29 or 30
Tevet (Dec–Jan)	30
Shevat (Jan–Feb)	30
Adar (Feb–Mar)	29 or 30
Adar Sheni (leap year only)	29
Nisan (Mar–Apr)	30
Iyar (Apr–May)	29
Sivan (May–Jun)	30
Tammuz (Jun–Jul)	29
Av (Jul–Aug)	30
Elul (Aug–Sep)	29

Islamic

The Islamic calendar is based on the lunar year and consists of 354 or 355 days. The number of days in each month varies with the lunar cycle. The beginning of the year retrogresses through the solar year, completing a full cycle every 32.5 years.

Months	Number of Days
Muharram	29 or 30
Safar	29 or 30
Rabi I	29 or 30
Rabi II	29 or 30
Jumada I	29 or 30
Jumada II	29 or 30
Rajab	29 or 30
Sha'ban	29 or 30
Ramadan	29 or 30
Shawwal	29 or 30
Dhu'l-Qa'dah	29 or 30
Dhu'l-Hijjah	29 or 30

CURRENCY

Unit	Country
afghani	Afghanistan
ariary	Madagascar
baht	Thailand
balboa	Panama
birr	Ethiopia
bolivar	Venezuela
boliviano	Bolivia
cedi	Ghana
colon	Costa Rica
	El Salvador
cordoba	Nicaragua
dalasi	Gambia
denar	Macedonia
dinar	Algeria
	Bahrain
	Iraq
	Jordan
	Kuwait
	Libya
	Serbia
	Sudan
	Tunisia
dirham	Morocco
	United Arab Emirates
dobra	São Tomé and Príncipe
dollar	Antigua and Barbuda
	Australia
	Bahamas
	Barbados
	Belize
	Brunei
	Canada
	Dominica
	East Timor
	Ecuador
	Fiji
	Grenada
	Guyana
	Hong Kong
	Jamaica
	Kiribati
	Liberia
	Marshall Islands
	Micronesia
	Namibia
	Nauru
	New Zealand
	Palau
	Saint Kitts and Nevis
	Saint Lucia
	Saint Vincent and the Grenadines
	Singapore
	Solomon Islands
	Suriname
	Trinidad and Tobago
	Tuvalu
	United States
	Zimbabwe
dong	Vietnam
dram	Armenia
escudo	Cape Verde
euro	Andorra
	Austria
	Belgium
	Cyprus
	Finland
	France
	Germany
	Greece
	Ireland
	Italy
	Kosovo
	Luxembourg
	Malta
	Monaco
	Montenegro
	Portugal
	San Marino
	Slovakia
	Slovenia
	Spain
	Vatican City
forint	Hungary
franc	Benin
	Burkina Faso
	Burundi
	Cameroon
	Central African Republic
	Chad
	Comoros
	Congo (Rep. of)
	Congo (Dem. Rep. of)
	Côte d'Ivoire
	Djibouti
	Equatorial Guinea
	Gabon
	Guinea
	Guinea-Bissau
	Liechtenstein

CURRENCY (continued)

Unit	Country	Unit	Country
	Mali		Mexico
	Niger		Uruguay
	Rwanda	**piso**	Philippines
	Senegal	**pound**	Egypt
	Switzerland		Lebanon
	Togo		Syria
gourde	Haiti		United Kingdom
guarani	Paraguay	**pula**	Botswana
hryvnia	Ukraine	**quetzal**	Guatemala
kina	Papua New Guinea	**rand**	South Africa
kip	Laos	**real**	Brazil
koruna	Czech Republic	**rial**	Iran
krona	Iceland		Oman
	Sweden		Yemen
krone	Denmark	**riel**	Cambodia
	Norway	**ringgit**	Malaysia
kroon	Estonia	**riyal**	Qatar
kuna	Croatia		Saudi Arabia
kwacha	Malawi	**rubel**	Belarus
	Zambia	**ruble**	Russia
kwanza	Angola	**rufiyaa**	Maldives
kyat	Myanmar	**rupee**	India
lari	Georgia		Mauritius
lats	Latvia		Nepal
lek	Albania		Pakistan
lempira	Honduras		Seychelles
leone	Sierra Leone		Sri Lanka
leu	Moldova	**rupiah**	Indonesia
	Romania	**sheqel**	Israel
lev	Bulgaria	**shilin**	Somalia
lilangeni	Swaziland	**shilling**	Kenya
lira	Turkey		Tanzania
litas	Lithuania		Uganda
loti	Lesotho	**sol**	Peru
manat	Azerbaijan	**som**	Kyrgyzstan
	Turkmenistan		Uzbekistan
marka	Bosnia and Herzegovina	**somoni**	Tajikistan
metical	Mozambique	**taka**	Bangladesh
naira	Nigeria	**tala**	Samoa
nakfa	Eritrea	**tenge**	Kazakhstan
ngultrum	Bhutan	**tugrik**	Mongolia
ouguiya	Mauritania	**vatu**	Vanuatu
pa'anga	Tonga	**won**	North Korea
pataca	Macao		South Korea
peso	Argentina	**yen**	Japan
	Chile	**yuan**	China
	Colombia		Taiwan
	Cuba	**zloty**	Poland
	Dominican Republic		

MEASUREMENT

Conversion between Metric and U.S. Customary Units

From Metric to U.S. Customary

WHEN YOU KNOW	MULTIPLY BY	TO FIND
millimeters	0.04	inches
centimeters	0.39	inches
meters	3.28	feet
	1.09	yards
kilometers	0.62	miles
milliliters	0.03	fluid ounces
liters	1.06	quarts
	0.26	gallons
cubic meters	35.31	cubic feet
grams	0.035	ounces
kilograms	2.20	pounds
metric tons (1,000 kg)	1.10	short tons
square centimeters	0.155	square inches
square meters	1.20	square yards
square kilometers	0.39	square miles
hectares	2.47	acres

From U.S. Customary to Metric

WHEN YOU KNOW	MULTIPLY BY	TO FIND
inches	2.54	centimeters
feet	30.48	centimeters
yards	0.91	meters
miles	1.61	kilometers
fluid ounces	29.57	milliliters
cups	0.24	liters
pints	0.47	liters
quarts	0.95	liters
gallons	3.79	liters
cubic feet	0.028	cubic meters
ounces	28.35	grams
pounds	0.45	kilograms
short tons (2,000 lbs)	0.91	metric tons
square inches	6.45	square centimeters
square feet	0.09	square meters
square yards	0.84	square meters
square miles	2.59	square kilometers
acres	0.40	hectares

Temperature Conversion between Celsius and Fahrenheit

$$°C = (°F - 32) \div 1.8$$

$$°F = (°C \times 1.8) + 32$$

MEASUREMENT (continued)

U.S. Customary System		
UNIT	RELATION TO OTHER U.S. CUSTOMARY UNITS	METRIC EQUIVALENT
Length		
inch	$^{1}/_{12}$ foot	2.54 centimeters
foot	12 inches or $^{1}/_{3}$ yard	0.305 meter
yard	36 inches or 3 feet	0.91 meter
rod	$16^{1}/_{2}$ feet or $5^{1}/_{2}$ yards	5.03 meters
furlong	220 yards or $^{1}/_{8}$ mile	0.20 kilometer
mile (statute)	5,280 feet or 1,760 yards	1.61 kilometers
mile (nautical)	6,076 feet or 2,025 yards	1.852 kilometers
Volume or Capacity (Liquid Measure)		
ounce	$^{1}/_{16}$ pint	29.574 milliliters
gill	4 ounces	0.12 liter
cup	8 ounces	0.24 liter
pint	16 ounces	0.47 liter
quart	2 pints or $^{1}/_{4}$ gallon	0.95 liter
gallon	128 ounces or 8 pints	3.79 liters
oil barrel	42 gallons	158.99 liters
Volume or Capacity (Dry Measure)		
cup	$^{1}/_{2}$ pint	0.275 liter
pint	2 cups or $^{1}/_{2}$ quart	0.55 liter
quart	4 cups or 2 pints	1.10 liters
peck	8 quarts or $^{1}/_{4}$ bushel	8.81 liters
bushel	4 pecks	35.239 liters
Weight		
grain	$^{1}/_{7000}$ pound	64.799 milligrams
dram	$^{1}/_{16}$ ounce	1.772 grams
ounce	16 drams	28.350 grams
pound	16 ounces	453.6 grams
ton (short)	2,000 pounds	907.18 kilograms
ton (long)	2,240 pounds	1,016.0 kilograms
Geographic Area		
acre	43,560 square feet or 4,840 square yards	4,047 square meters